THE EUROPA
WORLD
YEAR BOOK
2015

THE EUROPA WORLD YEAR BOOK 2015

VOLUME 2

ERITREA–NICARAGUA

Routledge
Taylor & Francis Group

LONDON AND NEW YORK

56th edition published 2015
by Routledge
2 Park Square, Milton Park, Abingdon, Oxon, OX14 4RN

and by Routledge
711 Third Avenue, New York, NY 10017

Routledge is an imprint of the Taylor & Francis Group, an Informa business

First published 1926

ISBN: 978-1-85743-751-5 (The Set)
        978-1-85743-772-0 (Vol. 2)
ISSN: 0956-2273

Senior Editor: Juliet Love

Senior Editor, Statistics: Philip McIntyre

Senior Editor, Directory: Iain Frame

Regional Editors: Imogen Gladman, Cathy Hartley, Dominic Heaney,
Neil Higgins, Christopher Matthews, Jackie West

International Organizations Editor: Helen Canton

Contributing Editors: Catriona Holman, Katharine Murison, Jillian O'Brien

Editorial Assistant: Eleanor Simmons

Statistics Researchers: Varun Wadhawan *(Team Manager)*, Mohd Khalid Ansari *(Senior Research
and Training Associate)*, Meghal Arora, Swati Gambhir, Nirbachita Sarkar, Swati Sejwal

Directory Editorial Researchers: Arijit Khasnobis *(Team Manager)*, C. Sandhya *(Deputy Team Leader)*,
Shubha Banerjee, Anveshi Gupta, Birendra Pratap Nayak *(Senior Editorial Researchers)*,
Sajleen Bedi, Bhawna Chauhan, Swati Chopra, Sneha Malik, Rituparna Sengupta,
Surabhi Srivastava, Atul Udaipuria

Contributors: Christopher Bell, Rebecca Bomford, Vera Browne, Katie Dawson,
Lucy Dean, Driss Fatih, Kirstie Hughes, Catriona Marcham

Editorial Director: Paul Kelly

Typeset in New Century Schoolbook
by Data Standards Limited, Frome, Somers

FOREWORD

THE EUROPA WORLD YEAR BOOK was first published in 1926. From 1960 it appeared in annual two-volume editions, and it has become established as an authoritative reference work, providing a wealth of detailed information on the political, economic and commercial institutions of the world. For this edition the work has been expanded to a three-volume set.

Volume 1 contains a comprehensive listing of more than 2,000 international organizations, commissions and specialized bodies, and the first part of the alphabetical survey of countries of the world, from Afghanistan to Equatorial Guinea. Volume 2 contains countries from Eritrea to Nicaragua, and Volume 3 countries from Niger to Zimbabwe. An Index of Territories covered in all three volumes is to be found at the end of Volume 3.

The International Organizations section gives extensive coverage to the United Nations and its related agencies and bodies. There are also detailed articles concerning other major international and regional organizations; entries for many affiliated organizations appear within these articles. In addition, the section includes briefer details of some 1,300 other international organizations. A comprehensive Index of International Organizations is included at the end of Volume 1.

Each country is covered by an individual chapter, containing: an introductory survey including contemporary political history, economic affairs, constitution and government, regional and international co-operation, and public holidays; a statistical survey presenting the latest available figures on demographics, labour force, health and welfare, agriculture, forestry, fishing, mining, industry, currency and exchange rates, government finance, international reserves and the monetary sector, cost of living, national accounts, balance of payments, external trade, railways, roads, shipping, civil aviation, tourism, media and telecommunications, and education; and a directory section listing names, addresses and other useful facts about organizations in the fields of government, election commissions, political parties, diplomatic representation, judiciary, religions, the media, telecommunications, banking, insurance, trade and industry, development organizations, chambers of commerce, industrial and trade associations, utilities, trade unions, transport, tourism, defence, and education.

The entire content of the print edition of THE EUROPA WORLD YEAR BOOK is available online at www.europaworld.com. This prestigious resource incorporates sophisticated search and browse functions as well as specially commissioned visual and statistical content. An ongoing programme of updates of key areas of information ensures currency of content, and enhances the richness of the coverage for which THE EUROPA WORLD YEAR BOOK is renowned.

Readers are referred to the nine titles in the Europa Regional Surveys of the World series: AFRICA SOUTH OF THE SAHARA, CENTRAL AND SOUTH-EASTERN EUROPE, EASTERN EUROPE, RUSSIA AND CENTRAL ASIA, THE FAR EAST AND AUSTRALASIA, THE MIDDLE EAST AND NORTH AFRICA, SOUTH AMERICA, CENTRAL AMERICA AND THE CARIBBEAN, SOUTH ASIA, THE USA AND CANADA, and WESTERN EUROPE, available both in print and online, offer comprehensive analysis at regional, subregional and country level. More detailed coverage of international organizations is to be found in THE EUROPA DIRECTORY OF INTERNATIONAL ORGANIZATIONS.

The content of THE EUROPA WORLD YEAR BOOK is extensively revised and updated by a variety of methods, including direct contact with organizations covered. Many other sources are used, such as national statistical offices, government departments and diplomatic missions. The editors thank the innumerable individuals and organizations worldwide whose generous co-operation in providing current information for this edition is invaluable in presenting the most accurate and up-to-date material available.

May 2015

ACKNOWLEDGEMENTS

The editors gratefully acknowledge particular indebtedness for permission to reproduce material from the following sources: the United Nations' statistical databases and *Demographic Yearbook*, *Statistical Yearbook* and *Monthly Bulletin of Statistics*; the United Nations Educational, Scientific and Cultural Organization's Institute for Statistics database; the *Human Development Report* of the United Nations Development Programme; the Food and Agriculture Organization of the United Nations' statistical database; the statistical databases of the World Health Organization; the statistical databases of the UNCTAD/WTO International Trade Centre; the International Labour Office's statistical database; the World Bank's statistical databases, especially the World Development Indicators database, and the *World Development Report*; the International Monetary Fund's statistical database, *International Financial Statistics* and *Government Finance Statistics Yearbook*; the World Tourism Organization's *Compendium* and *Yearbook of Tourism Statistics*; the US Geological Survey; the International Telecommunication Union; the International Road Federation's *World Road Statistics*; Lloyd's List; and *The Military Balance 2015*, a publication of the International Institute for Strategic Studies, Arundel House, 13–15 Arundel Street, London WC2R 3DX. Statistics Canada information is used with the permission of Statistics Canada. Users are forbidden to copy this material and/or redisseminate the data, in an original or modified form, for commercial purposes, without the expressed permission of Statistics Canada. Information on the availability of the wide range of data from Statistics Canada can be obtained from Statistics Canada's Regional Offices, its website at www.statcan.ca, and its toll-free access number 1-800-263-1136.

HEALTH AND WELFARE STATISTICS: SOURCES AND DEFINITIONS

Total fertility rate Source: WHO Statistical Information System (part of the Global Health Observatory). The number of children that would be born per woman, assuming no female mortality at child-bearing ages and the age-specific fertility rates of a specified country and reference period.

Under-5 mortality rate Source: WHO Statistical Information System. Defined by WHO as the probability of a child born in a specific year or period dying before reaching the age of five, if subject to the age-specific mortality rates of that year or period.

HIV/AIDS Source: UNAIDS. Estimated percentage of adults aged 15 to 49 years living with HIV/AIDS. < indicates 'fewer than'.

Health expenditure Source: WHO Statistical Information System.
US $ per head (PPP)
International dollar estimates, derived by dividing local currency units by an estimate of their purchasing-power parity (PPP) compared with the US dollar. PPPs are the rates of currency conversion that equalize the purchasing power of different currencies by eliminating the differences in price levels between countries.
% of GDP
GDP levels for OECD countries follow the most recent UN System of National Accounts. For non-OECD countries a value was estimated by utilizing existing UN, IMF and World Bank data.
Public expenditure
Government health-related outlays plus expenditure by social schemes compulsorily affiliated with a sizeable share of the population, and extrabudgetary funds allocated to health services. Figures include grants or loans provided by international agencies, other national authorities, and sometimes commercial banks.

Access to water and sanitation Source: WHO/UNICEF Joint Monitoring Programme on Water Supply and Sanitation (JMP) (Progress on Drinking Water and Sanitation, 2014 Update). Defined in terms of the percentage of the population using improved facilities in terms of the type of technology and levels of service afforded. For water, this includes house connections, public standpipes, boreholes with handpumps, protected dug wells, protected spring and rainwater collection; allowance is also made for other locally defined technologies. Sanitation is defined to include connection to a sewer or septic tank system, pour-flush latrine, simple pit or ventilated improved pit latrine, again with allowance for acceptable local technologies. Access to water and sanitation does not imply that the level of service or quality of water is 'adequate' or 'safe'.

Carbon dioxide emissions Source: World Bank, World Development Indicators database, citing the Carbon Dioxide Information Analysis Center (sponsored by the US Department of Energy). Emissions comprise those resulting from the burning of fossil fuels (including those produced during consumption of solid, liquid and gas fuels and from gas flaring) and from the manufacture of cement.

Human Development Index (HDI) Source: UNDP, *Human Development Report* (2014). A summary of human development measured by three basic dimensions: prospects for a long and healthy life, measured by life expectancy at birth; access to knowledge, measured by a combination of mean years of schooling for adults and expected years of schooling for children; and standard of living, measured by GNI per head (PPP US $). The index value obtained lies between zero and one. A value above 0.800 indicates very high human development, between 0.700 and 0.799 high human development, between 0.550 and 0.699 medium human development and below 0.550 low human development. A centralized data source for all three dimensions was not available for all countries. In some cases other data sources were used to calculate a substitute value; however, this was excluded from the ranking. Other countries, including non-UNDP members, were excluded from the HDI altogether. In total, 187 countries were ranked for 2013.

CONTENTS

CONTENTS

An Index of Territories is to be found at the end of Volume 3.

ABBREVIATIONS

AB — Aktiebolag (Joint-Stock Company); Alberta
Acad. — Academician; Academy
ACP — African, Caribbean and Pacific (countries)
ACT — Australian Capital Territory
AD — anno Domini
ADB — African Development Bank; Asian Development Bank
ADC — aide-de-camp
ADIZ — air defence identification zone
Adm. — Admiral
admin. — administration
AEC — African Economic Community; African Economic Conference
AfDB — African Development Bank
AG — Aktiengesellschaft (Joint-Stock Company)
AGOA — Africa Growth and Opportunity Act
AH — anno Hegirae
a.i. — ad interim
AID — (US) Agency for International Development
AIDS — acquired immunodeficiency syndrome
AK — Alaska
Al. — Aleja (Alley, Avenue)
AL — Alabama
ALADI — Asociación Latinoamericana de Integración
Alt. — Alternate
AM — amplitude modulation
a.m. — ante meridiem (before noon)
amalg. — amalgamated
Apdo — Apartado (Post Box)
APEC — Asia-Pacific Economic Cooperation
approx. — approximately
Apt — Apartment
AR — Arkansas
ARV — advanced retroviral
AŞ — Anonim Şirketi (Joint-Stock Company)
A/S — Aktieselskab (Joint-Stock Company)
ASEAN — Association of Southeast Asian Nations
asscn — association
assoc. — associate
ASSR — Autonomous Soviet Socialist Republic
asst — assistant
AU — African Union
Aug. — August
auth. — authorized
av., Ave — Avenija, Avenue
Av., Avda — Avenida (Avenue)
Avv. — Avvocato (Lawyer)
AZ — Arizona

b.b. — bez broja (without number)
BC — British Columbia
BC — before Christ
Bd — Board
Bd, Bld, Blv., Blvd — Boulevard
b/d — barrels per day
BFPO — British Forces' Post Office
Bhd — Berhad (Public Limited Company)
Bldg — Building
blk — block
Blvr — Bulevar
BP — Boîte postale (Post Box)
br.(s) — branch(es)
Brig. — Brigadier

BSE — bovine spongiform encephalopathy
BSEC — (Organization of the) Black Sea Economic Cooperation
bte — boîte (box)
Bul. — Bulvar (boulevard)
bulv. — bulvarīs (boulevard)

C — Centigrade
c. — circa; cuadra(s) (block(s))
CA — California
CACM — Central American Common Market
Cad. — Caddesi (Street)
CAP — Common Agricultural Policy
cap. — capital
Capt. — Captain
CAR — Central African Republic
CARICOM — Caribbean Community and Common Market
CBSS — Council of Baltic Sea States
CCL — Caribbean Congress of Labour
CDMA — Code Division Multiple Access
Cdre — Commodore
CEMAC — Communauté Economique et Monétaire de l'Afrique Centrale
Cen. — Central
CEO — Chief Executive Officer
CET — common external tariff
CFA — Communauté Financière Africaine; Coopération Financière en Afrique centrale
CFE — Treaty on Conventional Armed Forces in Europe
CFP — Common Fisheries Policy; Communauté française du Pacifique; Comptoirs français du Pacifique
Chair. — Chairman/person/woman
Chih. — Chihuahua
CI — Channel Islands
Cia — Companhia
Cía — Compañía
Cie — Compagnie
c.i.f. — cost, insurance and freight
C-in-C — Commander-in-Chief
circ. — circulation
CIS — Commonwealth of Independent States
CJD — Creutzfeldt-Jakob disease
cm — centimetre(s)
cnr — corner
CO — Colorado
Co — Company; County
c/o — care of
Coah. — Coahuila
Col — Colonel
Col. — Colima; Colonia
COMESA — Common Market for Eastern and Southern Africa
Comm. — Commission; Commendatore
Commdr — Commander
Commdt — Commandant
Commr — Commissioner
Cond. — Condiminio
Conf — Confederation
confs — conferences
Cont. — Contador (Accountant)
COO — Chief Operating Officer
COP — Conference of (the) Parties
Corp. — Corporate
Corpn — Corporation
CP — Case Postale, Caixa Postal, Casella Postale (Post Box); Communist Party

C por A — Compañía por Acciones (Joint Stock Company)
CPOB — Central Post Office Box
CPSU — Communist Party of the Soviet Union
Cres. — Crescent
CSCE — Conference on Security and Cooperation in Europe
CSTAL — Confederación Sindical de los Trabajadores de América Latina
CT — Connecticut
CTCA — Confederación de Trabajadores Centro-americanos
Cttee — Committee
cu — cubic
cwt — hundredweight

DC — District of Columbia; Distrito Capital; Distrito Central
d.d. — delniška družba, dioničko društvo (joint stock company)
DE — Delaware; Departamento Estatal
Dec. — December
Del. — Delegación
Dem. — Democrat; Democratic
Dep. — Deputy
dep. — deposits
Dept — Department
devt — development
DF — Distrito Federal
Dgo — Durango
Diag. — Diagonal
Dir — Director
Div. — Division(al)
DM — Deutsche Mark
DMZ — demilitarized zone
DNA — deoxyribonucleic acid
DN — Distrito Nacional
Doc. — Docent
Dott. — Dottore/essa
DPRK — Democratic People's Republic of Korea
Dr — Doctor
Dr. — Drive
Dra — Doctora
Dr Hab — Doktor Habilitowany (Assistant Professor)
DRC — Democratic Republic of the Congo
DR-CAFTA — Dominican Republic-Central American Free Trade Agreement
Drs — Doctorandus
DU — depleted uranium
dwt — dead weight tons

E — East; Eastern
EAC — East African Community
EBRD — European Bank for Reconstruction and Development
EC — European Community
ECA — (United Nations) Economic Commission for Africa
ECE — (United Nations) Economic Commission for Europe
ECF — Extended Credit Facility
ECLAC — (United Nations) Economic Commission for Latin America and the Caribbean
ECO — Economic Cooperation Organization
Econ. — Economics; Economist
ECOSOC — (United Nations) Economic and Social Council

ix

ECOWAS	Economic Community of West African States	Gto	Guanajuato	IUU	illegal, unreported and unregulated
ECU	European Currency Unit	GWh	gigawatt hour(s)		
Edif.	Edificio (Building)				
edn	edition	ha	hectares	Jal.	Jalisco
EEA	European Economic Area	HD	high-definition	Jan.	January
EEU	Eurasian Economic Union	HDI	Human Development Index	Jnr	Junior
EFTA	European Free Trade Association	HDTV	high-definition television	Jr	Jonkheer (Esquire); Junior
e.g.	exempli gratia (for example)	HE	His/Her Eminence; His/Her Excellency	Jt	Joint
EIB	European Investment Bank	hf	hlutafelag (Limited Company)		
EMS	European Monetary System	HI	Hawaii	Kav.	Kaveling (Plot)
EMU	Economic and Monetary Union	HIPC	heavily indebted poor country	kg	kilogram(s)
eMv	electron megavolt	HIV	human immunodeficiency virus	KG	Kommandit Gesellschaft (Limited Partnership)
Eng.	Engineer; Engineering	hl	hectolitre(s)		
EP	Empresa Pública	HLTF	High Level Task Force	kHz	kilohertz
ERM	Exchange Rate Mechanism	HM	His/Her Majesty	KK	Kaien Kaisha (Limited Company)
ESACA	Emisora de Capital Abierto Sociedad Anónima	Hon.	Honorary, Honourable	km	kilometre(s)
		HPAI	highly pathogenic avian influenza	kom.	komnata (room)
Esc.	Escuela; Escudos; Escritorio			kor.	korpus (block)
ESCAP	(United Nations) Economic and Social Commission for Asia and the Pacific	HQ	Headquarters	k'och.	k'ochasi (street)
		HRH	His/Her Royal Highness	KS	Kansas
		HS	Harmonized System	küç	küçasi (street)
ESCWA	(United Nations) Economic and Social Commission for Western Asia	HSH	His/Her Serene Highness	kv.	kvartal (apartment block); kvartira (apartment)
		Hwy	Highway		
				kW	kilowatt(s)
esq.	esquina (corner)			kWh	kilowatt hour(s)
est.	established; estimate; estimated	IA	Iowa	KY	Kentucky
etc.	et cetera	IBRD	International Bank for Reconstruction and Development		
EU	European Union			LA	Louisiana
eV	eingetragener Verein			lauk	laukums (square)
EVD	Ebola Virus Disease	ICC	International Chamber of Commerce; International Criminal Court	lb	pound(s)
excl.	excluding			LDCs	Least Developed Countries
exec.	executive			Lic.	Licenciado
Ext.	Extension	ICRC	International Committee of the Red Cross	Licda	Licenciada
				LLC	Limited Liability Company
F	Fahrenheit	ICT	information and communication technology	LNG	liquefied natural gas
f.	founded			LPG	liquefied petroleum gas
FAO	Food and Agriculture Organization	ICTR	International Criminal Tribunal for Rwanda	Lt, Lieut	Lieutenant
				Ltd	Limited
f.a.s.	free alongside ship	ICTY	International Criminal Tribunal for the former Yugoslavia		
FDI	foreign direct investment				
Feb.	February	ID	Idaho	m	metre(s)
Fed.	Federal; Federation	IDA	International Development Association	m.	million
feds	federations			MA	Massachusetts
FL	Florida	IDB	Inter-American Development Bank	Maj.	Major
FM	frequency modulation			Man.	Manager; managing
fmr(ly)	former(ly)	IDPs	internally displaced persons	MB	Manitoba
f.o.b.	free on board	i.e.	id est (that is to say)	mbH	mit beschränkter Haftung (with limited liability)
Fr	Father	IFC	International Finance Corporation		
Fr.	Franc			MD	Maryland
Fri.	Friday	IGAD	Intergovernmental Authority on Development	MDG	Millennium Development Goal
FRY	Federal Republic of Yugoslavia			MDRI	multilateral debt relief initiative
ft	foot (feet)	IHL	International Humanitarian Law	ME	Maine
FTA	free trade agreement/area	IL	Illinois	Me	Maître
FYRM	former Yugoslav republic of Macedonia	ILO	International Labour Organization/Office	mem.(s)	member(s)
		IMF	International Monetary Fund	MEP	Member of the European Parliament
		IML	International Migration Law		
g	gram(s)	in (ins)	inch (inches)	Mercosul	Mercado Comum do Sul (Southern Common Market)
g.	gatve (street)	IN	Indiana		
GA	Georgia	Inc, Incorp.		Mercosur	Mercado Común del Sur (Southern Common Market)
GATT	General Agreement on Tariffs and Trade	Incd	Incorporated		
		incl.	including	MERS	Middle East respiratory syndrome coronavirus
GCC	Gulf Cooperation Council	Ind.	Independent		
Gdns	Gardens	INF	Intermediate-Range Nuclear Forces	Méx.	México
GDP	gross domestic product			MFN	most favoured nation
GEF	Gobal Environment Facility	Ing.	Engineer	mfrs	manufacturers
Gen.	General	Insp.	Inspector	Mgr	Monseigneur; Monsignor
GeV	giga electron volts	Int.	International	MHz	megahertz
GM	genetically modified	Inzå.	Engineer	MI	Michigan
GmbH	Gesellschaft mit beschränkter Haftung (Limited Liability Company)	IP	intellectual property	MIA	missing in action
		IPU	Inter-Parliamentary Union	Mich.	Michoacán
		Ir	Engineer	MIGA	Multilateral Investment Guarantee Agency
GMO(s)	genetically modified organism(s)	IRF	International Road Federation		
GMT	Greenwich Mean Time	irreg.	irregular	Mil.	Military
GNI	gross national income	Is	Islands	Mlle	Mademoiselle
GNP	gross national product	ISIC	International Standard Industrial Classification	mm	millimetre(s)
Gov.	Governor			Mme	Madame
Govt	Government	IT	information technology	MN	Minnesota
GPOB	General Post Office Box	ITU	International Telecommunication Union	mnt.	mante (road)
Gro	Guerrero			MO	Missouri
grt	gross registered tons	ITUC	International Trade Union Confederation	Mon.	Monday
GSM	Global System for Mobile Communications			Mor.	Morelos
		Iur.	Lawyer	MOU	Memorandum of Understanding

movt	movement	Parl.	Parliament(ary)	SAARC	South Asian Association for Regional Cooperation
MP	Member of Parliament	per.	pereulok (lane, alley)		
MS	Mississippi	PE	Prince Edward Island	SACN	South American Community of Nations
MSS	Manuscripts	Perm. Rep.	Permanent Representative		
MT	Montana	PF	Postfach (Post Box)	SADC	Southern African Development Community
MW	megawatt(s); medium wave	PICTs	Pacific Island countries and territories		
MWh	megawatt hour(s)			SA de CV	Sociedad Anónima de Capital Variable (Variable Capital Company)
		PK	Posta Kutusu (Post Box)		
		Pl.	Plac, Plads (square)		
N	North; Northern	pl.	platz; place; ploshchad (square)	SAECA	Sociedad Anónima Emisora de Capital Abierto
n.a.	not available	PLC	Public Limited Company		
nab.	naberezhnaya (embankment, quai)	PLO	Palestine Liberation Organization	SAR	Special Administrative Region
				SARL	Sociedade Anônima de Responsabilidade Limitada (Joint-Stock Company of Limited Liability)
NAFTA	North American Free Trade Agreement	p.m.	post meridiem (after noon)		
		PMB	Private Mail Bag		
nám.	náměstí (square)	PNA	Palestinian National Authority		
Nat.	National	POB	Post Office Box	SARS	Severe Acute Respiratory Syndrome
NATO	North Atlantic Treaty Organization	pp.	pages		
		PPP	purchasing-power parity	Sat.	Saturday
Nay.	Nayarit	PQ	Québec	SC	South Carolina
NB	New Brunswick	PR	Puerto Rico	SD	South Dakota
NC	North Carolina	pr.	prospekt, prospekti (avenue)	Sdn Bhd	Sendirian Berhad (Private Limited Company)
NCD	National Capital District	Pres.	President		
NCO	non-commissioned officer	PRGF	Poverty Reduction and Growth Facility	SDR(s)	Special Drawing Right(s)
ND	North Dakota			SE	South-East
NE	Nebraska; North-East	Prin.	Principal	Sec.	Secretary
NEPAD	New Partnership for Africa's Development	Prof.	Professor	Secr.	Secretariat
		Propr	Proprietor	Sen.	Senior; Senator
NGO	non-governmental organization	Prov.	Province; Provincial; Provinciale (Dutch)	Sept.	September
NH	New Hampshire			SER	Sua Eccellenza Reverendissima (His Eminence)
NJ	New Jersey	prov.	provulok (lane)		
NL	Newfoundland and Labrador, Nuevo León	PRSP	Poverty Reduction Strategy Paper	SFRY	Socialist Federal Republic of Yugoslavia
NM	New Mexico	PSI	Policy Support Instrument, Poverty Strategies Initiative	SGP	Stability and Growth Pact
NMP	net material product			Sin.	Sinaloa
no	numéro, número (number)	pst.	puistotie (avenue)	SIS	Small(er) Island States
no.	number	PT	Perseroan Terbatas (Limited Company)	SITC	Standard International Trade Classification
Nov.	November				
NPT	Non-Proliferation Treaty	Pte	Private; Puente (Bridge)	SJ	Society of Jesus
nr	near	Pty	Proprietary	SK	Saskatchewan
nrt	net registered tons	p.u.	paid up	Skt	Sankt (Saint)
NS	Nova Scotia	publ.	publication; published	SLP	San Luis Potosí
NSW	New South Wales	Publr	Publisher	SMEs	small and medium-sized enterprises
NT	Northwest Territories	Pue.	Puebla		
NU	Nunavut Territory	Pvt	Private	s/n	sin número (without number)
NV	Naamloze Vennootschap (Limited Company); Nevada			Soc.	Society
				Sok.	Sokak (Street)
NW	North-West	QC	Québec	Son.	Sonora
NY	New York	QIP	Quick Impact Project	Şos.	Şosea (Road)
NZ	New Zealand	Qld	Queensland	SP	São Paulo
		Qro	Querétaro	SpA	Società per Azioni (Joint-Stock Company)
		Q. Roo	Quintana Roo		
		q.v.	quod vide (to which refer)	Sq.	Square
				sq	square (in measurements)
OAPEC	Organization of Arab Petroleum Exporting Countries			Sr	Senior; Señor
OAS	Organization of American States	Rag.	Ragioniere (Accountant)	Sra	Señora
OAU	Organization of African Unity	Rd	Road	Srl	Società a Responsabilità Limitata (Limited Company)
Oax.	Oaxaca	R(s)	rand; rupee(s)		
Oct.	October			SRSG	Special Representative of the UN Secretary-General
OECD	Organisation for Economic Co-operation and Development	REC	regional economic communities		
		reg., regd	register; registered	SSR	Soviet Socialist Republic
OECS	Organisation of Eastern Caribbean States	reorg.	reorganized	St	Saint, Sint; Street
		Rep.	Republic; Republican; Representative	Sta	Santa
Of.	Oficina (Office)			Ste	Sainte
OH	Ohio	Repub.	Republic	STI(s)	sexually transmitted infection(s)
OIC	Organization of Islamic Cooperation	res	reserve(s)	Str., str.	Strasse, strada, stradă, strasse (street)
OK	Oklahoma	retd	retired		
ON	Ontario	Rev.	Reverend	str-la	stradelă (street)
OPEC	Organization of the Petroleum Exporting Countries	RI	Rhode Island	subs.	subscribed; subscriptions
		RJ	Rio de Janeiro	Sun.	Sunday
opp.	opposite	Rm	Room	Supt	Superintendent
OR	Oregon	RN	Royal Navy	SUV	sports utility vehicle
ORB	OPEC Reference Basket	ro-ro	roll-on roll-off	sv.	Saint
Org.	Organization	RP	Recette principale	SW	South-West
ORIT	Organización Regional Interamericana de Trabajadores	Rp.(s)	rupiah(s)		
		Rpto	Reparto (Estate)		
OSCE	Organization for Security and Co-operation in Europe	RSFSR	Russian Soviet Federative Socialist Republic	Tab.	Tabasco
				Tamps	Tamaulipas
		Rt	Right	TAŞ	Turkiye Anonim Şirketi (Turkish Joint-Stock Company)
p.	page			Tas	Tasmania
p.a.	per annum	S	South; Southern; San	TD	Teachta Dàla (Member of Parliament)
PA	Palestinian Authority; Pennsylvania	SA	Société Anonyme, Sociedad Anónima (Limited Company); South Australia		
				tech., techn.	technical
				tel.	telephone

TEU	20-ft equivalent unit	UNESCO	United Nations Educational, Scientific and Cultural Organization	Ven.	Venerable
Thur.	Thursday			Ver.	Veracruz
TN	Tennessee			VHF	Very High Frequency
tř	třída (avenue)	UNHCHR	UN High Commissioner for Human Rights	VI	(US) Virgin Islands
Treas.	Treasurer			Vic	Victoria
Tue.	Tuesday	UNHCR	United Nations High Commissioner for Refugees	Vn	Veien (Street)
TV	television			vol.(s)	volume(s)
TWh	terawatt hour(s)	UNICEF	United Nations Children's Fund	VT	Vermont
TX	Texas	Univ.	University	vul.	vulitsa, vulytsa (street)
		UNODC	United Nations Office on Drugs and Crime		
u.	utca (street)	UNRWA	United Nations Relief and Works Agency for Palestine Refugees in the Near East	W	West; Western
u/a	unit of account			WA	Washington (State); Western Australia
UAE	United Arab Emirates	UNWTO	World Tourism Organization	Wed.	Wednesday
UEE	Unidade Económica Estatal	Urb.	Urbanización (District)	WEU	Western European Union
UEMOA	Union Economique et Monétaire Ouest-Africaine	US	United States	WFP	World Food Programme
		USA	United States of America	WFTU	World Federation of Trade Unions
UK	United Kingdom	USAID	United States Agency for International Development	WHO	World Health Organization
ul.	ulica, ulitsa (street)			WI	Wisconsin
UM	ouguiya	USSR	Union of Soviet Socialist Republics	WSSD	World Summit on Sustainable Development
UN	United Nations	UT	Utah		
UNAIDS	United Nations Joint Programme on HIV/AIDS			WTO	World Trade Organization
				WV	West Virginia
UNCTAD	United Nations Conference on Trade and Development	VA	Virginia	WY	Wyoming
		VAT	value-added tax		
UNDP	United Nations Development Programme	VEB	Volkseigener Betrieb (Public Company)	yr	year
UNEP	United Nations Environment Programme	v-CJD	new variant Creutzfeldt-Jakob disease	YT	Yukon Territory
				Yuc.	Yucatán

INTERNATIONAL TELEPHONE CODES

To make international calls to telephone and fax numbers listed in *The Europa World Year Book*, dial the international access code of the country from which you are calling, followed by the appropriate country code for the organization you wish to call (listed below), followed by the area code (if applicable) and telephone or fax number listed in the entry.

	Country code	+ or − GMT*		Country code	+ or − GMT*
Abkhazia	7	+4	Djibouti	253	+3
Afghanistan	93	+4½	Dominica	1 767	−4
Åland Islands	358	+2	Dominican Republic	1 809	−4
Albania	355	+1	Ecuador	593	−5
Algeria	213	+1	Egypt	20	+2
American Samoa	1 684	−11	El Salvador	503	−6
Andorra	376	+1	Equatorial Guinea	240	+1
Angola	244	+1	Eritrea	291	+3
Anguilla	1 264	−4	Estonia	372	+2
Antigua and Barbuda	1 268	−4	Ethiopia	251	+3
Argentina	54	−3	Falkland Islands	500	−4
Armenia	374	+4	Faroe Islands	298	0
Aruba	297	−4	Fiji	679	+12
Ascension Island	247	0	Finland	358	+2
Australia	61	+8 to +10	France	33	+1
Austria	43	+1	French Guiana	594	−3
Azerbaijan	994	+5	French Polynesia	689	−9 to −10
Bahamas	1 242	−5	Gabon	241	+1
Bahrain	973	+3	Gambia	220	0
Bangladesh	880	+6	Georgia	995	+4
Barbados	1 246	−4	Germany	49	+1
Belarus	375	+2	Ghana	233	0
Belgium	32	+1	Gibraltar	350	+1
Belize	501	−6	Greece	30	+2
Benin	229	+1	Greenland	299	−1 to −4
Bermuda	1 441	−4	Grenada	1 473	−4
Bhutan	975	+6	Guadeloupe	590	−4
Bolivia	591	−4	Guam	1 671	+10
Bonaire	599	−4	Guatemala	502	−6
Bosnia and Herzegovina	387	+1	Guernsey	44	0
Botswana	267	+2	Guinea	224	0
Brazil	55	−3 to −4	Guinea-Bissau	245	0
British Indian Ocean Territory			Guyana	592	−4
(Diego Garcia)	246	+5	Haiti	509	−5
British Virgin Islands	1 284	−4	Honduras	504	−6
Brunei	673	+8	Hong Kong	852	+8
Bulgaria	359	+2	Hungary	36	+1
Burkina Faso	226	0	Iceland	354	0
Burundi	257	+2	India	91	+5½
Cabo Verde	238	−1	Indonesia	62	+7 to +9
Cambodia	855	+7	Iran	98	+3½
Cameroon	237	+1	Iraq	964	+3
Canada	1	−3 to −8	Ireland	353	0
Cayman Islands	1 345	−5	Isle of Man	44	0
Central African Republic	236	+1	Israel	972	+2
Ceuta	34	+1	Italy	39	+1
Chad	235	+1	Jamaica	1 876	−5
Chile	56	−4	Japan	81	+9
China, People's Republic	86	+8	Jersey	44	0
Christmas Island	61	+7	Jordan	962	+2
Cocos (Keeling) Islands	61	+6½	Kazakhstan	7	+6
Colombia	57	−5	Kenya	254	+3
Comoros	269	+3	Kiribati	686	+12 to +13
Congo, Democratic Republic	243	+1	Korea, Democratic People's Republic		
Congo, Republic	242	+1	(North Korea)	850	+9
Cook Islands	682	−10	Korea, Republic (South Korea)	82	+9
Costa Rica	506	−6	Kosovo	381†	+3
Côte d'Ivoire	225	0	Kuwait	965	+3
Croatia	385	+1	Kyrgyzstan	996	+5
Cuba	53	−5	Laos	856	+7
Curaçao	599	−4	Latvia	371	+2
Cyprus	357	+2	Lebanon	961	+2
Czech Republic	420	+1	Lesotho	266	+2
Denmark	45	+1	Liberia	231	0

xiii

	Country code	+ or – GMT*		Country code	+ or – GMT*
Libya	218	+1	Senegal	221	0
Liechtenstein	423	+1	Serbia	381	+1
Lithuania	370	+2	Seychelles	248	+4
Luxembourg	352	+1	Sierra Leone	232	0
Macao	853	+8	Singapore	65	+8
Macedonia, former Yugoslav republic	389	+1	Sint Eustatius	1721	–4
Madagascar	261	+3	Sint Maarten	1721	–4
Malawi	265	+2	Slovakia	421	+1
Malaysia	60	+8	Slovenia	386	+1
Maldives	960	+5	Solomon Islands	677	+11
Mali	223	0	Somalia	252	+3
Malta	356	+1	South Africa	27	+2
Marshall Islands	692	+12	South Ossetia	7	+4
Martinique	596	–4	South Sudan	211	+2
Mauritania	222	0	Spain	34	+1
Mauritius	230	+4	Sri Lanka	94	+5½
Mayotte	262	+3	Sudan	249	+2
Melilla	34	+1	Suriname	597	–3
Mexico	52	–6 to –7	Svalbard	47	+1
Micronesia, Federated States	691	+10 to +11	Swaziland	268	+2
Moldova	373	+2	Sweden	46	+1
Monaco	377	+1	Switzerland	41	+1
Mongolia	976	+7 to +9	Syria	963	+2
Montenegro	382	+1	Taiwan	886	+8
Montserrat	1 664	–4	Tajikistan	992	+5
Morocco	212	0	Tanzania	255	+3
Mozambique	258	+2	Thailand	66	+7
Myanmar	95	+6½	Timor-Leste	670	+9
Nagornyi Karabakh	374	+4	Togo	228	0
Namibia	264	+2	Tokelau	690	+15
Nauru	674	+12	Tonga	676	+13
Nepal	977	+5¾	Transnistria	373	+2
Netherlands	31	+1	Trinidad and Tobago	1 868	–4
New Caledonia	687	+11	Tristan da Cunha	290	0
New Zealand	64	+12	Tunisia	216	+1
Nicaragua	505	–6	Turkey	90	+2
Niger	227	+1	'Turkish Republic of Northern Cyprus'	90 392	+2
Nigeria	234	+1	Turkmenistan	993	+5
Niue	683	–11	Turks and Caicos Islands	1 649	–5
Norfolk Island	672	+11½	Tuvalu	688	+12
Northern Mariana Islands	1 670	+10	Uganda	256	+3
Norway	47	+1	Ukraine‡	380	+2
Oman	968	+4	United Arab Emirates	971	+4
Pakistan	92	+5	United Kingdom	44	0
Palau	680	+9	United States of America	1	–5 to –10
Palestinian Territories	970 or 972	+2	United States Virgin Islands	1 340	–4
Panama	507	–5	Uruguay	598	–3
Papua New Guinea	675	+10	Uzbekistan	998	+5
Paraguay	595	–4	Vanuatu	678	+11
Peru	51	–5	Vatican City	39	+1
Philippines	63	+8	Venezuela	58	–4½
Pitcairn Islands	872	–8	Viet Nam	84	+7
Poland	48	+1	Wallis and Futuna Islands	681	+12
Portugal	351	0	Yemen	967	+3
Puerto Rico	1 787	–4	Zambia	260	+2
Qatar	974	+3	Zimbabwe	263	+2
Réunion	262	+4			
Romania	40	+2			
Russian Federation	7	+3 to +12			
Rwanda	250	+2			
Saba	599	–4			
Saint-Barthélemy	590	–4			
Saint Christopher and Nevis	1 869	–4			
Saint Helena	290	0			
Saint Lucia	1 758	–4			
Saint-Martin	590	–4			
Saint Pierre and Miquelon	508	–3			
Saint Vincent and the Grenadines	1 784	–4			
Samoa	685	+13			
San Marino	378	+1			
São Tomé and Príncipe	239	0			
Saudi Arabia	966	+3			

* The times listed compare the standard (winter) times in the various countries. Some countries adopt Summer (Daylight Saving) Time—i.e. +1 hour—for part of the year.

† Mobile telephone numbers for Kosovo use either the country code for Monaco (377) or the country code for Slovenia (386).

‡ The Republic of Crimea and the city of Sevastopol were placed in the time zone GMT+4 following their annexation by Russia in 2014.

Note: Telephone and fax numbers using the Inmarsat ocean region code 870 are listed in full. No country or area code is required, but it is necessary to precede the number with the international access code of the country from which the call is made.

ERITREA

Introductory Survey

LOCATION, CLIMATE, LANGUAGE, RELIGION, FLAG, CAPITAL

The State of Eritrea, which has a coastline on the Red Sea extending for almost 1,000 km, is bounded to the north-west by Sudan, to the south and west by Ethiopia, and to the south-east by Djibouti. Its territory includes the Dahlak Islands, a low-lying coralline archipelago off shore from Massawa. Rainfall is less than 500 mm per year in lowland areas, increasing to 1,000 mm in the highlands. The temperature gradient is similarly steep: annual average temperatures range from 17°C (63°F) in the highlands to 30°C (86°F) in Massawa. The Danakil depression in the south-east, which is more than 130 m below sea-level in places, experiences some of the highest temperatures recorded, frequently exceeding 50°C (122°F). The major language groups in Eritrea are Afar, Bilien, Hedareb, Kunama, Nara, Rashaida, Saho, Tigre and Tigrinya (spoken by about one-half of the population). English is increasingly becoming the language of business and education. Arabic is also widely spoken. The population is fairly evenly divided between Tigrinya-speaking Christians (mainly Orthodox), the traditional inhabitants of the highlands, and the Muslim communities of the western lowlands, northern highlands and east coast; there are also systems of traditional belief adhered to by a small number of the population. The national flag (proportions 1 by 2) consists of a red triangle with its base corresponding to the hoist and its apex at the centre of the fly, in which is situated, towards the hoist, an upright gold olive branch with six clusters of three leaves each, framed by a wreath of two gold olive branches; the remainder of the field is green at the top and light blue at the base. The capital is Asmara.

CONTEMPORARY POLITICAL HISTORY

Historical Context

The Treaty of Ucciali, which was signed in 1889 between Italy and Ethiopia, gave the Italian Government control over what is today the State of Eritrea. Italian exploitation of the colony continued until the defeat of the Axis powers by the Allied forces in East Africa during the Second World War. The Eritrean national identity, which was established during the Italian colonial period, was further subjugated under British administration during 1941–52. As the Allied powers and the UN discussed the future of the former Italian colony, Ethiopian territorial claims helped to foment a more militant nationalism among the Eritrean population. In 1952 a federation was formed between Eritrea and Ethiopia; however, the absence of adequate provisions for the creation of federal structures allowed Ethiopia to reduce Eritrea's status to that of an Ethiopian province by 1962.

Resistance to the Ethiopian annexation was first organized in the late 1950s, and in 1961 the Eritrean Liberation Front (ELF) launched an armed struggle. In the mid-1970s a reformist group broke away from the ELF and formed the Popular Liberation Forces (renamed the Eritrean People's Liberation Front, EPLF, in 1977), and the military confrontation with the Ethiopian Government began in earnest. A major consequence of the split between the two Eritrean groups was the civil war of 1972–74. After two phases of desertion from the ELF to the EPLF, in 1977–78 and in 1985 (following a second civil war), the ELF was left without a coherent military apparatus.

Following the 1974 revolution in Ethiopia and the assumption of power by Mengistu Haile Mariam in 1977, thousands of new recruits joined the EPLF, and the armed struggle transformed into full-scale warfare. The numerically and materially superior Ethiopian forces achieved significant victories over the EPLF, which was forced to retreat to its stronghold in the north of Eritrea. The EPLF launched counter-attacks throughout the late 1980s and slowly drove back the Ethiopian forces on all fronts. In May 1991 units of the EPLF entered Asmara, after the Ethiopian troops had fled the capital, and immediately established an interim administration.

Following the liberation of Asmara by the EPLF, and of Addis Ababa, Ethiopia, by the Ethiopian People's Revolutionary Democratic Front (EPRDF), a conference was convened in London, United Kingdom, in August 1991. Both the USA and the Ethiopian delegation accepted the EPLF administration as the legitimate provisional Government of Eritrea, and the EPLF agreed to hold a referendum on independence in 1993. The provisional Government, which was to administer Eritrea during the two years prior to the referendum, drew most of its members from the EPLF. The Government struggled to rehabilitate and develop Eritrea's war-torn economy and infrastructure, and to feed a population largely dependent on food aid. The agricultural sector had been severely disrupted by the war, and urban economic activity was almost non-existent.

At the UN-supervised referendum held in April 1993, 99.8% of Eritreans who voted endorsed national independence. The anniversary of the liberation of Asmara, 24 May, was proclaimed Independence Day, and on 28 May Eritrea formally attained international recognition. In June Eritrea was admitted to the Organization of African Unity (OAU, now the African Union—AU, see p. 188). Following Eritrea's accession to independence, a four-year transitional period was declared, during which preparations were to proceed for establishing a constitutional and pluralist political system. At the apex of the transitional Government were three state institutions: the Consultative Council (the executive authority formed from the ministers, provincial administrators and heads of government authorities and commissions); the National Assembly (the legislative authority formed from the Central Committee of the EPLF, together with 30 members from the Provincial Assemblies and 30 individuals selected by the Central Committee); and the judiciary. One of the National Assembly's first acts was the election as Head of State of Issaias Afewerki, the Secretary-General of the EPLF, by a margin of 99 votes to five.

Domestic Political Affairs

In February 1994 the EPLF transformed itself into a political party, the People's Front for Democracy and Justice (PFDJ). An 18-member Executive Committee and a 75-member Central Committee were elected; President Afewerki was elected Chairman of the latter. In March the National Assembly adopted a series of resolutions whereby the former executive body, the Consultative Council, was formally superseded by a State Council. Other measures adopted included the creation of a 50-member Constitutional Commission and the establishment of a committee charged with the reorganization of the country's administrative divisions. It was decided that the National Assembly would henceforth comprise the 75 members of the PFDJ Central Committee and 75 directly elected members. However, no mechanism was announced for their election. All but eight of the 50 members of the Constitutional Commission were government appointees, and there was no provision for any opposition participation in the interim system.

A draft constitution was discussed at international conventions held by the Constitutional Commission in July 1994 and January 1995. In May the National Assembly approved proposals to create six administrative regions to replace the 10 regional divisions that had been in place since colonial rule. In November the Assembly approved new names for the regions and finalized details of their exact boundaries and sub-divisions. Although the new Constitution came into force in 1997, President Afewerki failed actually to implement it.

In 2001 the failure of the National Assembly to ratify in time legislation on the electoral system and on political pluralism further delayed Eritrea's first post-independence elections, which were to have taken place in December, having been indefinitely postponed in 1998 (following the outbreak of hostilities with Ethiopia, see below). During 2001 President Afewerki assumed an increasingly authoritarian position. In February he dismissed the Minister of Local Government, Mahmoud Ahmed Sherifo, and dissolved the electoral commission, which Sherifo had been appointed to head. In June Afewerki replaced the Ministers of Trade and Industry and of Maritime Resources. They were among a group of 15 senior PFDJ officials, including 11 former government ministers, who, in May, had signed a letter publicly accusing Afewerki of working in an 'illegal and unconstitutional manner'. In August the Chief Justice of the Supreme Court was dismissed after he openly expressed his disapproval of Afewerki's continued interference in court operations. In mid-September six of the G15, as the signatories of the letter criticizing Afewerki had become known, were arrested, and the Government announced the 'temporary suspension' of the independent press. A few days later a further five members of the G15 were detained.

In late January 2002 the National Assembly finally ratified the electoral law, but failed to set an election date. Meanwhile, dissident members of the ruling PFDJ, including several members of the G15, announced the formation, in exile, of a new political party, the Eritrean People's Liberation Front—Democratic Party (EPLF—DP).

During 2004 several parties took steps to form a viable opposition movement to the PFDJ. In February, following talks in Germany, the EPLF—DP announced that it would reconstitute as the Eritrean Democratic Party (EDP), under the continued leadership of Mesfin Hagos. In May numerous former members of the ELF and the PFDJ combined to establish the Eritrean Popular Movement (EPM). In August two new coalitions were formed; the first united the EPM and four smaller parties under the umbrella of the Eritrean National Alliance (ENA), while the second brought the EDP, the ELF and the Eritrean Liberation Front—Revolutionary Council together. In 2004 the ENA was reorganized as the Eritrean Democratic Alliance (EDA) and in January 2005 Hiruy Tedla Bairu was elected leader of the coalition. In January 2008 the then 11 opposition parties comprising the EDA met in Addis Ababa to consolidate the alliance after divisions had emerged in the previous year. Two additional parties were admitted to the coalition: the Eritrean Islamic Congress and the Eritrean People's Movement (EPM).

Despite the continued failure of the Government to announce a date for legislative elections, in 2009 political parties began to consolidate into opposition blocs in preparation for an eventual poll. In May 2009 four opposition parties (the ELF, Islah, al-Khalas and the Eritrean Federal Democratic Movement) joined forces as the Eritrean Solidarity Front. Later that month the merger of the Eritrean People's Party (EPP) and the Democratic Movement of Gash-Setit was announced, retaining the name of the former until, in December, the EPP merged with the EDP and the EPM, to form the Eritrean People's Democratic Party (EPDP). Meanwhile, in June the Red Sea Afar Democratic Organization (RSADO) and the Democratic Movement for the Liberation of Eritrean Kunama (DMLEK) signed an agreement establishing the Democratic Front of Eritrean Nationalities, while confirming their intention to continue to work under the umbrella of the EDA. Nevertheless, Afewerki repeatedly stated his reluctance to implement a democratic framework.

In August 2010 the EDA's 11 member organizations, together with other groups and civil society representatives, held a National Conference for Democratic Change in Addis Ababa during which plans were reportedly discussed to overthrow the Eritrean Government. The EDA claimed to have staged co-ordinated military attacks against government troops inside Eritrea in February, April and May, but the Eritrean Government refused to confirm such reports of attacks on its forces. Another National Conference for Democratic Change was convened in Ethiopia, in Hawassa, in November 2011.

Recent developments: army mutiny and dissent

At some point in 2012 (it being not evident from reports exactly when) Berhane Abrehe, who had been Minister of Finance since 2001, was removed from the post following a dispute over opacity in the distribution of mining revenues from the Bisha copper mine; he was succeeded by Berhane Habtemariam, a former manager of the Eritrean National Mining Corporation (ENAMCO). In October 2012 it was reported that two senior members of the armed forces had fled to Saudi Arabia and requested asylum; this was followed in November by the defection of Minister of Information Ali Abdu, formerly a close associate of President Afewerki, who was rumoured to have sought asylum in Canada. In early 2013 reports emerged that some 200 dissident members of the armed forces had briefly seized the Ministry of Information building on 21 January, and had forced the Director-General of the state radio and television agency to broadcast an appeal for the release of all political prisoners, and for the immediate implementation of the 1997 Constitution. Troops loyal to President Afewerki had rapidly regained control of the building. On 1 February the Ministry of Information issued a decree, which was strongly criticized by the international non-governmental organization Reporters without Borders, prohibiting the broadcasts of Qatar-based television news network Al Jazeera; transmissions on Al Jazeera's English-language channels were blocked by the authorities. The ban was apparently imposed in response to the network's reports of the insurrection, and of subsequent demonstrations by Eritrean exiles outside Eritrean diplomatic missions in Cairo, Egypt, and a number of Western European capitals in support of the soldiers and in opposition to the Government. The Eritrean authorities were also accused by Reporters without Borders of responsibility for a series of transmission- and cyber-attacks on an independent radio station, Radio Erena, which had been established by Eritrean journalists in Paris, France, in 2009.

In May 2014, in a speech made to mark Eritrea's 23rd Independence Day celebrations, President Afewerki announced that a process was to be initiated to draft a new constitution, in place of the 1997 charter that had not been implemented. In June 2014 four Eritrean Roman Catholic bishops published an open letter on an opposition internet site in which they drew attention to the 'tens of thousands' of Eritreans who had fled into neighbouring states from Eritrea's authoritarian society, as well as from indefinite conscription into the armed forces. The bishops expressed concern over the fragmenting effect, and consequent 'spiritual damage' and desolation caused by the forced loosening of family units through conscription and detention. Also in June the UN Human Rights Council established a one-year Commission of Inquiry (CoI) to investigate alleged violations of human rights in Eritrea, as detailed in reports of its Special Rapporteur on the country (who had been appointed in June 2012); the Government rejected the allegations and announced that it would not co-operate with the CoI. In mid-July 2014 the leadership of opposition armed factions, including the military wings of the ELF, DMLEK and RSADO, reportedly attended a gathering in Tekele, Ethiopia, that was convened by senior Ethiopian military commanders to discuss means of removing President Afewerki. In early August it was reported that the military wing of the RSADO had determined to initiate an armed rebellion against the Afewerki regime.

Internally Displaced Persons and Refugees

According to estimates by the Internal Displacement Monitoring Centre (IDMC), in 2006 there remained some 40,000–45,000 internally displaced persons (IDPs) in Eritrea. In an effort to promote 'self-sufficiency', in September 2005 the Eritrean Government imposed severe restrictions on the distribution of food aid, and reduced from 1.3m. to 72,000 the number of people entitled to receive free food. The move was widely criticized, especially by the UN, and prompted fears of acute food shortages among the one-third of the population who were estimated to be dependent on humanitarian assistance. Government resettlement programmes were also implemented to reduce the number of IDPs, and by the end of 2010 UN agencies found that the former IDPs had returned to their communities of origin or had been resettled. However, other sources indicated that small displaced communities remained in urban areas, including Asmara and Massawa. According to figures published by the UN High Commissioner for Refugees (UNHCR), in 2014 there were around 3,100 refugees—nearly all from Somalia—in Eritrea who had been resident in the country for around 20 years. Significant flight from Eritrea's oppressive regime and prolonged military conscription has been recorded in recent years, with many Eritreans seeking shelter in Sudan and Ethiopia: according to UNHCR estimates, there was a combined total of around 216,000 Eritrean refugees residing in those countries at October 2014. Furthermore, over the last few years many Eritreans have sought asylum in Europe (around 37,000 in the first 10 months of 2014, according to UNHCR), while many have also lost their lives when endeavouring to cross the Mediterranean Sea to Europe in crowded, unseaworthy vessels. Eritreans attempting to reach asylum in Europe are believed frequently to use the services of human traffickers based in eastern Sudan.

Foreign Affairs

Relations with Sudan

Relations between the transitional Government and Sudan, which had supported the EPLF during the war, deteriorated in December 1993, following an incursion by members of an Islamist group, the Eritrean Islamic Jihad (EIJ), into Eritrea from Sudan, during which all the members of the group, and an Eritrean army commander, were killed. In response, President

Afewerki stressed the links between the EIJ and the Sudanese National Islamic Front, led by Dr Hassan al-Turabi, implying that the latter had prior knowledge of the incursion. However, following a swift denial by the Sudanese Government that it would interfere in the affairs of neighbouring states, Afewerki reaffirmed his support for the Sudanese authorities and his commitment to improving bilateral relations.

Relations between Eritrea and Sudan worsened in November 1994, when the Eritrean authorities accused Sudan of training 400 terrorists since August. In response, Sudan accused Eritrea of training some 3,000 Sudanese rebels in camps within Eritrea. In December Eritrea severed diplomatic relations with Sudan. Further destabilization was provoked in early 1995 by attacks and infiltration in Gash-Barka Province by the EIJ. The Eritrean authorities subsequently claimed to have identified six training camps on the Sudanese side of the border and also alleged that large numbers of Eritrean refugees in Sudan had been arrested by Sudanese security forces. The Sudanese Government protested strongly against Eritrea's growing support for the Sudanese opposition grouping, the National Democratic Alliance (NDA), which held a number of conferences in Asmara in the mid-1990s.

In early 1999 Sudan took steps to resolve its differences with Ethiopia, thus increasing the tension between Eritrea and Sudan. In April, however, Sudan indicated its willingness also to improve relations with Eritrea, and in May a reconciliatory agreement was signed in Qatar, which, *inter alia*, restored diplomatic relations between the two countries. Following the renewed outbreak of hostilities between Eritrea and Ethiopia in May (see below), some 94,000 Eritreans crossed the border into Sudan. After the cessation of fighting in June, UNHCR assisted the repatriation of Eritrean refugees, and by January 2002 some 36,500 Eritreans had returned home. In January 2003 refugee status was withdrawn from more than 320,000 Eritreans in Sudan, although UNHCR maintained that its repatriation programme would continue until all those registered had been returned home.

In July 2001 Eritrea and Sudan signed an agreement on border security, which aimed to eradicate smuggling and illegal infiltration, as well as ensure the safe passage of people and goods across the common border. In December 2003 Sudanese President Lt-Gen. Omar Hassan Ahmad al-Bashir accused Eritrea of arming and training rebels in the Darfur region of Sudan and maintained that Eritrea was a destabilizing force in the region. Eritrea refuted the allegations. Relations improved in 2006, following two separate rounds of peace talks in Asmara between the Sudanese Government and the rebel coalition Eastern Front during June–July. Meanwhile, in mid-June President Afewerki met al-Bashir in Khartoum, Sudan, and later that month the two countries agreed to restore diplomatic relations to ambassadorial level. However, in September al-Bashir accused Eritrea of interference in the Darfur region and urged Eritrea to expel the leaders of the National Redemption Front, which had launched attacks on Sudanese Government forces in Darfur, from Eritrean territory. Nevertheless, al-Bashir and the Eastern Front leadership returned to Asmara in mid-October to sign a peace agreement. In early November the common border between Eritrea and Sudan was officially re-opened. In June 2008 the Sudanese authorities banned all activity of Eritrean opposition groups that had been operating from Sudan, demonstrating a marked improvement in relations between the two countries. Al-Bashir visited Asmara in March 2009 and reiterated his commitment to the June 2008 agreement. In March 2010 security talks were held in Tripoli, Libya, between delegations from Eritrea, Libya and Sudan. Bilateral agreements on trade and economic co-operation were signed in July and the Sudanese and Eritrean Governments continued to display commitment to their agreement to suspend their backing of opposition groups. During President al-Bashir's two visits to Asmara in 2013, the two sides reached agreement on a number of joint infrastructure projects, including the construction of a coastal road and proposals for a 340-km electricity transmission line. In addition, Sudan subsequently committed to deport undocumented foreign nationals to support the Eritrean authorities' efforts to deter emigration and, ostensibly, people trafficking. (According to UNHCR figures, there was a total of more than 118,000 Eritrean refugees in Sudan at December 2013.) Moreover, Presidents Afewerki and al-Bashir adopted a joint position in supporting President Salva Kiir Mayardit of South Sudan following the outbreak of violent unrest in that country in December 2013. In that month a report presented to the European Parliament alleged the complicity of Eritrean and Sudanese security personnel in the abduction of Eritrean, Ethiopian and Sudanese citizens with a view to extorting money from their families in return for their release; the report stated that the practice had affected as many as 30,000 Eritreans since 2007; the Eritrean Government rejected the accusation that its officials might be involved in such activities. It was, however, reported in May 2014 that 30 military commanders had been arrested by the Eritrean security forces, in response to intelligence received from an unspecified nearby country relating to human trafficking. Visiting Khartoum in that month, President Afewerki and al-Bashir were reported to have discussed means of strengthening the economic and security ties of their respective countries.

Conflict with Ethiopia

In September 1993 the first meeting of the Ethiopian-Eritrean joint ministerial commission was held in Asmara, during which agreement was reached on measures to allow the free movement of nationals between each country, and on co-operation regarding foreign affairs and economic policy. Meetings held between President Afewerki and the Ethiopian President, Meles Zenawi, in December underlined the good relations prevailing between the two Governments.

However, relations deteriorated in late 1997 following Eritrea's adoption of a new currency (the nakfa) to replace the Ethiopian birr and the subsequent disruption of cross-border trade. In May 1998 fighting erupted between Eritrean and Ethiopian troops in the border region after both countries accused the other of having invaded their territory. Hostilities escalated in June around Badme, Zalambessa and Assab, resulting in numerous casualties for both sides. Eritrea and Ethiopia agreed to an aerial ceasefire later that month, following US and Italian mediation. In November President Afewerki and Meles (now Prime Minister of Ethiopia) were present at different sessions of a special meeting of the OAU mediation committee in Ouagadougou, Burkina Faso, which was also attended by the Heads of State of that country, Zimbabwe and Djibouti. The committee's peace proposals were accepted by Ethiopia, but rejected by Eritrea, and in February 1999 the aerial ceasefire was broken and fighting resumed in the border region. In July both sides finally confirmed their commitment to the OAU's Framework Agreement. Afewerki announced that Eritrean troops would be withdrawn from all territory captured from Ethiopia since 6 May 1998. Under the agreement, Ethiopia was also required to withdraw from all Eritrean territory captured since 6 February 1999. After requesting clarification of technical arrangements to end the war, Ethiopia informed the OAU in September that it had rejected the peace agreement, owing to inconsistencies contained therein. Eritrea accused Ethiopia of deliberately stalling proceedings, while secretly preparing for a fresh offensive.

By late May 2000 Ethiopian forces had seized Zalambessa and Eritrean troops were withdrawn from the disputed areas, although Afewerki maintained that this was merely a 'gesture of goodwill' designed to revive the peace talks, which resumed in Algiers, Algeria, on 29 May. Two days later Meles stated that the war was over and that his troops had withdrawn from most of the territory it had captured from Eritrea. Following negotiations in early June both sides expressed their readiness, in principle, to accept the OAU's ceasefire agreement, and on 18 June the Ethiopian and Eritrean Ministers of Foreign Affairs signed an agreement, which provided for an immediate ceasefire and the deployment of a UN peacekeeping force in a 25-km temporary security zone (TSZ) inside Eritrea until the issue of the demarcation of the border had been settled. In September the UN Security Council approved the deployment of the UN Mission in Ethiopia and Eritrea (UNMEE), a peacekeeping force with an initial strength of 4,200. On 12 December Eritrea and Ethiopia signed an agreement in Algiers, which formally ended the conflict between the two countries. The agreement provided for a permanent cessation of all hostilities, the immediate return of all prisoners of war, the demarcation of the common border by an independent commission, and the establishment of a Claims Commission to assess the issues of compensation and reparations. Furthermore, both countries pledged to co-operate with an independent investigation, which aimed to determine the origins of the conflict.

By late January 2001 the UNMEE force had been fully deployed and on 18 April, after all troops had been withdrawn from the border area, UNMEE declared the establishment of the TSZ, marking the formal separation of the Eritrean and Ethiopian forces. In late June UNMEE presented the final map of the

TSZ to Eritrea and Ethiopia; the Ethiopian Government immediately expressed dissatisfaction with the document, and at a meeting of the Military Co-ordination Commission in August both countries voiced objections to the existing boundaries of the TSZ. UNMEE's mandate was extended for a further six months in September (and at six-monthly intervals thereafter until May 2006). In December Eritrea and Ethiopia began presenting their cases for border demarcation to a five-member Boundary Commission at the International Court of Justice (see p. 25) in The Hague, Netherlands. In April 2002 the Commission issued a Decision on Delimitation of the Border between Eritrea and Ethiopia, after which a process of demarcating the border with pillars on the ground was to be undertaken. In July the Commission promulgated a set of Demarcation Directions (these were subsequently revised). The April 2002 Decision did not, however, clarify on which side of the boundary line the disputed, Ethiopian-held town of Badme lay, and, in the absence of any settlement, both countries immediately claimed to have been awarded Badme. In March 2003 the Boundary Commission rejected objections to the April 2002 ruling that had been raised in a January 2003 memorandum submitted by Ethiopia, and ruled categorically that Eritrea had territorial rights over Badme. Meanwhile, the UN Security Council stated that Ethiopia had committed itself under the 2000 Algiers agreement to accept the Boundary Commission's decision as 'final and binding' and urged it to accept and implement the ruling. Ethiopia subsequently agreed to allow demarcation to take place in the eastern sector of the border region, while refusing to accept the ruling in other areas and expressing grave concerns about the competency of the Boundary Commission. In October 2003, in view of continuing disagreements and obstacles to progress, it was announced that border demarcation had been delayed indefinitely.

In May 2004 the local Special Representative of the UN Secretary-General dismissed accusations raised by Eritrean officials of serious malpractice on the part of UNMEE military personnel; UNMEE, meanwhile, repeatedly requested the Eritrean authorities to withdraw restrictions imposed upon the free movement of its peacekeeping troops. In November of that year Ethiopia, while not relinquishing its hold on Badme, declared that it had, in principle, accepted the Boundary Commission's ruling and was prepared to re-enter into talks with Eritrea regarding the demarcation of the border. Eritrea rejected the integrity of the announcement. Relations deteriorated further in early 2005 as the UN Security Council and the European Union (EU, see p. 271) expressed concern over troop redeployments on both sides of the border. In March the Security Council appealed to both countries to reduce troop numbers to December 2004 levels. In October 2005 Ethiopia reaffirmed its acceptance of the Boundary Commission's ruling, and signalled its willingness to recommence talks with Eritrea. It had still not, however, withdrawn from Badme. Later in October 2005 Eritrea imposed restrictions upon the movements of UN vehicles, including a ban upon all UNMEE helicopter flights on its side of the border. In late November the UN Security Council unanimously adopted Resolution 1640, which demanded an end to all restrictions on UNMEE activities and the full implementation of the Boundary Commission's ruling, while also evoking the possibility of sanctions against Eritrea and Ethiopia, should the two countries not comply. In December Eritrea requested that all UNMEE peacekeepers and staff from Canada, Russia, the USA and EU member states leave the country. Some 180 UN staff were consequently moved into Ethiopia at that time, along with peacekeeping troops.

On 31 May 2006 the UN Security Council adopted Resolution 1681, which extended UNMEE's mandate for four months, while reducing its size to 2,300 military personnel. The Security Council demanded that Eritrea lift all restrictions placed upon UNMEE activities; however, the request was subsequently rejected by the Eritrean authorities. In late September UNMEE's mandate was extended until 31 January 2007. In mid-October 2006 UN officials urged Eritrea to withdraw 1,500 of its troops and 14 armoured vehicles from the TSZ; the Eritrean Government claimed that the soldiers were harvesting crops from state-run farms in the area. In mid-November both countries declined to attend a meeting of the Boundary Commission in The Hague to discuss border demarcation and subsequently rejected its recommendations. Following the meeting, the Boundary Commission issued a statement, which expressed frustration at both countries' refusal to co-operate with the Commission and insisted that, should no mutual agreement

between Eritrea and Ethiopia be in place by November 2007 regarding demarcation, and should no efforts have been made to commence emplacing the border pillars, the boundary would automatically stand as designated by boundary points described by the Commission in an annex to the April 2002 ruling. On 31 January 2007 the UN Security Council approved Resolution 1741, which extended UNMEE's mandate by six months, while further reducing the size of the mission, to 1,700 military personnel. UNMEE's mandate was subsequently further extended until the end of July 2008.

Concerns that conflict could resume were heightened in September 2007 when both Eritrea and Ethiopia deployed troops to the border region. In a letter to his Eritrean counterpart, the Ethiopian Minister of Foreign Affairs, Seyoum Mesfin, stated that the Ethiopian Government considered Eritrea to be in material breach of the Algiers agreement as its troops had occupied the TSZ and had restricted the movement of the UNMEE force. Both parties again insisted that they were committed to a peaceful resolution of the border dispute; however, neither side complied with the Boundary Commission's request of November 2006 physically to start demarcating the border by the end of November 2007. In early December, prior to announcing its own dissolution, the Commission stated that the boundary markings that it had determined in November 2006 represented the official border between the two countries.

As a result of persistent restrictions imposed by Eritrea on freedom of movement and the delivery of fuel supplies, in early February 2008 UNMEE began preparations to withdraw its peacekeepers from that country and to relocate them across the border into Ethiopia. Eritrea continued to restrict UNMEE operations and Ethiopia also placed constraints on UN peacekeeping units that had withdrawn from Eritrea. On 30 July the UN Security Council voted to adopt Resolution 1827, terminating the mission's mandate. In August 2009 the Claims Commission awarded Ethiopia a total of US $174m. in compensation for war damages, while Eritrea received $164m., resulting in a net payment to Ethiopia of $10m. Eritrea, stated that it would honour the ruling; however, Ethiopia declared that the compensation awarded was insufficient.

During 2010 Ethiopia continued to accuse Eritrea of sponsoring its opposition movements, most notably the Ogaden National Liberation Front and the Oromo Liberation Front. In March 2011, following a visit to New York, USA, during which, it was reported, he urged the international community to take action to prevent Eritrea from destabilizing the Horn of Africa region, Ethiopian Deputy Prime Minister and Minister of Foreign Affairs Hailemariam Desalegn announced a change of policy towards Eritrea from a defensive to a more belligerent stance. This new approach appeared to be confirmed the following month by Prime Minister Meles' offer of determined support to Eritrean opposition groups and his reiteration of claims that Eritrea was a conduit for foreign financing of terrorist groups in the region and had assisted in a foiled terrorist attack against the AU summit in Addis Ababa in January. The exiled Eritrean opposition in Ethiopia praised this active policy to bring about regime change. However, despite the fact that reports of the planned attack were also corroborated by the UN Monitoring Group on Somalia and Eritrea, the Eritrean ambassador to the AU denounced all the accusations as part of a campaign of disinformation by the Ethiopian authorities.

In March 2012 Ethiopian troops, for the first time since the end of the 1998–2000 border conflict, made an incursion into southeastern Eritrea, attacking military camps at Ramid, Gelahbe and Gimbi, on the grounds that rebel groups based there had staged a series of raids in Ethiopian territory. The Ethiopian Government further accused the Eritrean authorities of involvement in an attack on Ethiopia's north-eastern Afar region in January 2012 in which five Western tourists were killed. It was reported that Eritrea had rejected at least two offers by Ethiopia to enter into peace talks during 2013. President al-Bashir of Sudan allegedly attempted to mediate indirect contacts between Eritrea and Ethiopia towards the end of that year. In July 2014 senior Ethiopian military commanders reportedly convened a meeting of the leadership of Eritrean armed opposition factions to discuss possible means of overturning the regime of President Afewerki.

According to UNHCR figures, in December 2014 the number of Eritrean refugees in Ethiopia totalled more than 106,000. At early 2015 the border dispute between the two countries remained at an impasse. The disputed town of Badme continued to be under Ethiopian control.

Relations with Djibouti

Relations with neighbouring Djibouti have also been problematic, mainly due to territorial disputes. In April 1996 tensions mounted when Eritrea was accused of attacking positions in the disputed region of Ras Doumeira, on the border between the two countries. Later that month Djibouti formally rejected a map submitted by Eritrean officials, claiming it included territory belonging to Djibouti. In 1998 diplomatic relations were suspended following Afewerki's accusation that Djibouti was lending support to Ethiopia in the Ethiopia–Eritrea border dispute, although relations were restored in March 2000. Tensions resurfaced, in April 2008, after it was reported that Eritrean forces had mobilized near Ras Doumeira and crossed into Djiboutian territory, although Afewerki strongly denied the allegations. Djibouti responded by increasing troop numbers in the region and recalled all police and soldiers demobilized in the previous five years. Despite diplomatic attempts to settle the dispute, including appeals for restraint from the AU, hostilities broke out in June and numerous casualties were reported on both sides. The fighting drew strong international condemnation: the UN launched an investigation but Eritrea refused to co-operate, denying any wrongdoing, and President Ismaïl Omar Guelleh of Djibouti demanded joint demilitarization in the border region, appealing to the UN Security Council for mediation. Eritrea refused to comply with a request made by the UN Security Council in January 2009 ordering Eritrea to withdraw its forces from the area, and issued a strongly worded statement to the Security Council in May denying any involvement in the destabilization of either Djibouti or Somalia. In October the Djibouti Minister of Foreign Affairs and Co-operation accused Eritrea of arming and training militias to carry out acts of sabotage in Djibouti, and of fomenting chaos in the region. Following increasing pressure for the imposition of sanctions from numerous East African governments, in December the UN Security Council placed an arms embargo on Eritrea, imposed travel restrictions on political and military leaders and also froze the overseas funds and financial assets of those individuals. In March 2010 the EU imposed similar sanctions. In June Afewerki and Guelleh signed an agreement to end the border dispute between Eritrea and Djibouti, entrusting responsibility for establishing a method of resolving the demarcation issue and normalizing relations to a commission of Qatari advisers.

Relations with other countries

In August 2011 Afewerki agreed to hold talks with Ugandan President Yoweri Kaguta Museveni, whose country provides the majority of troops to the AU peacekeeping mission in Somalia. The meeting was viewed by analysts as a conciliatory move on the part of Afewerki, who was becoming increasingly isolated in the region and had continued to be accused of supporting extremist groups in Somalia (notably the militant Islamist group al-Shabaab). However, Eritrea's application to rejoin the Intergovernmental Authority on Development (IGAD) (from which it had suspended itself in 2007) was postponed by IGAD's Council of Ministers later that month, who instead demanded the imposition of further UN sanctions against Eritrea. In November 2011 the Kenyan Minister of Foreign Affairs announced a review of diplomatic ties with Eritrea in the wake of a report that arms had been flown to the Somali town of Baidoa from Eritrea. Afewerki denied the allegations and appealed for an independent investigation to be carried out.

CONSTITUTION AND GOVERNMENT

On 23 May 1997 the Eritrean Constitution was adopted, authorizing 'conditional' political pluralism and instituting a presidential regime, with a President elected for a maximum of two five-year terms. The President, as Head of State, would appoint a Prime Minister and judges of the Supreme Court; his or her mandate could be revoked should two-thirds of the members of the National Assembly so demand. A Transitional National Assembly (consisting of the 75 members of the PFDJ Central Committee, 60 members of the Constituent Assembly and 15 representatives of Eritreans residing abroad) was empowered to act as the legislature until the holding of elections to a new National Assembly. At early 2015 these had yet to take place.

REGIONAL AND INTERNATIONAL CO-OPERATION

Eritrea is a member of the African Union (AU, see p. 188); from 2003 until January 2011, however, it withdrew from active participation in AU activities in protest at the Ethiopia-based organization's perceived reluctance to condemn alleged viola-

tions by that country of the 2000 Algiers agreement ending the Eritrea–Ethiopia conflict. Eritrea is also a member of the Common Market for Eastern and Southern Africa (see p. 232) and of the Intergovernmental Authority on Development (IGAD, see p. 331), although the country unilaterally announced its suspension from IGAD in 2007. In July 2011 Eritrea requested that it be permitted formally to reactivate its membership of IGAD.

Eritrea became a member of the UN in 1993. Also in 1993 Eritrea was admitted to the group of African, Caribbean and Pacific (ACP) countries party to the Lomé Convention; in September 2001 Eritrea ratified the Cotonou Agreement (see p. 321), the successor of the Lomé Convention.

ECONOMIC AFFAIRS

In 2013, according to estimates by the World Bank, Eritrea's gross national income (GNI), measured at average 2011–13 prices, was US $3,121m., equivalent to $490 per head (or $1,180 per head on an international purchasing-power parity basis). During 2004–13, it was estimated, the population increased at an average annual rate of 3.5%. Gross domestic product (GDP) per head decreased, in real terms, by an average of 1.7% per year during 2004–13, while overall GDP increased at an average annual rate of 1.8% in 2004–13; growth in 2013 was 1.3%.

By far the most important sector of the economy is agriculture, which sustains around 80% of the population. In 2012, according to the African Development Bank (AfDB), agriculture (including forestry and fishing) accounted for an estimated 17.0% of GDP; the sector engaged an estimated 72.0% of the labour force at mid-2015, according to FAO. Most sedentary agriculture is practised in the highlands, where rainfall is sufficient to cultivate the main crops: sorghum, barley, wheat, maize, millet and chick-peas. As a result of serious environmental degradation (caused directly and indirectly by the war of independence), water scarcity and unreliable rainfall, projects have been undertaken to build water reservoirs and small dams, while badly eroded hillsides have been terraced and new trees planted in order to prevent further soil erosion. Fishing activity is on a very small scale—the total catch amounted to just 4,152 metric tons in 2012—although, according to the UN, sustainable yields of as much as 80,000 tons per year may be possible. In real terms, according to the World Bank, the GDP of the agricultural sector increased at an average annual rate of 1.8% in 2004–09; according to the AfDB, agricultural GDP decreased by 2.9% in 2011, but expanded by 6.8% in 2012.

In 2012 industrial production (comprising mining, manufacturing, construction and utilities) accounted for an estimated 23.2% of GDP, according to the AfDB. Some 5.0% of the labour force were employed in the industrial sector in 1990. According to the World Bank, industrial GDP decreased, in real terms, at an average annual rate of 2.9% in 2004–09; the GDP of the sector grew by 1.4% in 2008, but declined by 0.2% in 2009. In August 2011 the launch of production at a new cement factory, in the Gedem region near the Eritrean port city of Massawa, which was supported by funding from the People's Republic of China and was considered the national strategic project by the Government, made a notable contribution to strong economic growth in that year.

Eritrea's mineral resources are believed to be of significant potential value, although in 2012 mining and quarrying accounted for only 1.7% of GDP, according to the AfDB. Of particular importance, in view of Eritrea's acute energy shortage, is the possibility of the existence of large reserves of petroleum and natural gas beneath the Red Sea. New legislation on mining, adopted in 1995, declared all mineral resources to be state assets, but recognized an extensive role for private investors in their exploitation. In 2008 the Government assigned two offshore blocks for hydrocarbon exploration and development to a Chinese joint-venture company, Defba Oil Share Co, and in 2010 assigned another block to Canada's Centric Energy Corpn (now Africa Oil Corpn). The Government amended the Mining Law in 2011 setting its share in each of the country's mining ventures to a non-participatory 10%, and increasing its option to buy into projects from the existing maximum of 20% to 30%. Other mineral resources include potash, zinc, magnesium, copper, nickel, iron ore, chromite, marble and gold. A joint venture between the Eritrean National Mining Corpn and South Boulder Mines Ltd of Australia is currently developing the world's first open-pit potash mine, at Colluli, which is due to go into production by 2016. According to the AfDB, the mining sector's GDP increased by 14.8% in 2011 and further by 3.5% in 2012.

The manufacturing sector provided an estimated 5.9% of GDP in 2012, according to the AfDB. Until mid-1997 imported petroleum was processed at the Assab refinery, the entire output of petroleum products of which was delivered to Ethiopia. In 1997 the Eritrean authorities announced that they would shut down the refinery (owing to high costs) and import refined petroleum for the immediate future. According to the World Bank, the GDP of the manufacturing sector declined, in real terms, at an average annual rate of 11.6% in 2004–09; manufacturing GDP increased by 11.0% in 2011 and further by 4.1% in 2012, according to the AfDB.

According to the AfDB, the construction sector provided 15.5% of GDP in 2012; construction GDP increased by 14.8% in 2011 and further by 3.4% in 2012.

Most electric energy is provided by four thermal power stations, which are largely dependent on imported fuel. Imports of fuel and energy comprised an estimated 0.8% of the total cost of imports in 2003. However, electricity is provided to only around 10% of the population, the remainder relying on fuel wood and animal products. Capacity at the Hirgigo thermal power plant near Massawa was increased from 88 MW to 132 MW in 2014; the Chinese-funded increase in output was expected to help to rectify power-supply problems in the capital, as well as to supply mining operations. In early 2015 it was announced that two Chinese companies had signed a contract to supply the power plant with two new gasoline-fuelled generators (with a joint capacity of 47.5 MW), which, once in operation, would help further to expand Eritrea's electricity network.

According to the AfDB, the services sector contributed 59.9% of GDP in 2012. The dominant services are trade, public administration and transport. According to the World Bank, the GDP of the services sector increased, in real terms, at an average annual rate of 0.1% in 2004–09; the GDP of the sector remained constant in 2008, but expanded by 4.2% in 2009.

In 2012, according to the AfDB, Eritrea recorded a visible merchandise trade deficit of 2,240m. nakfa, while there was a surplus of 1,021m. nakfa on the current account of the balance of payments. In 2003 the principal sources of non-petroleum imports were the USA (accounting for an estimated 15.9% of the total), the United Arab Emirates, Italy and Saudi Arabia. Exports in that year were mostly to Sudan (which took 19.7% of the total, compared with 83.8% in 2002), Italy, Netherlands and India. Eritrea's principal exports in 2003 were food and live animals, crude materials, basic manufactures, and miscellaneous manufactured articles. The main non-petroleum imports in that year were food and live animals, machinery and transport equipment, and basic manufactures.

In 2009 it was estimated by the AfDB that Eritrea's budget deficit reached 4,585m. nakfa. Eritrea's general government gross debt was 38,872m. nakfa in 2009, equivalent to 135.0% of GDP. Eritrea's external debt at the end of 2012 totalled US $994m., of which $952m. was public and publicly guaranteed debt. According to the AfDB, the annual rate of inflation averaged 20.1% in 2004–13. Consumer prices increased by an estimated average of 12.3% in both 2012 and 2013. In 2003 unemployment and underemployment were estimated to affect as many as 50% of the labour force.

Since independence the Eritrean Government has experienced severe difficulties: vast expenditure on the war with Ethiopia, coupled with the failure of successive harvests, increased Eritrea's already considerable reliance on donations from aid organizations, and the need to resettle the huge numbers of people displaced during the war placed a further strain on government finances. The economy remains, to a considerable extent, dependent on remittances from abroad, particularly given its limited holdings of foreign exchange reserves; some of these funds are raised as part of an illicit tax system imposed on the diaspora, even extending to human trafficking activities. The UN Somalia and Eritrea Monitoring Group has recommended sanctions on such taxes in countries with large populations of Eritrean migrants. In October 2014 the Monitoring Group alleged that 'complex financial structures' may have been established to enable the Eritrean Government to use revenue from the expanding mining sector to fund the ruling People's Front for Democracy and Justice and possibly also military activities. Since 2008 the Government has allowed some controlled reforms, including the establishment of a free-trade zone in Massawa and the implementation of an automated customs data management system, as well as the pursuit of a privatization programme. The authorities have also invested in infrastructure, including upgrading the ports of Massawa and Assab and the national railway. However, no IMF financial stability assessments have yet taken place and aid inflow has dwindled. As in various other African countries, Eritrea has been able to draw instead on financing from China and a number of Gulf states. The persistence of hostile relations with two of its neighbouring countries ensures that Eritrea remains an unfavourable investment environment for many other investors; this situation also serves to legitimize the continued diversion of labour and resources to the military. Nevertheless, in recent years economic hopes have centred on the development of large mineral deposits around Bisha and Asmara, as well as on strengthening interdependence with Sudan. Eritrea's first operational mine, at Bisha, entered into production in 2011. The mine produced solely low-cost gold-silver doré until mid-2013, when it expanded operations to produce mainly copper concentrate; the deposit was also expected to yield zinc from 2015. The Asmara mining project (involving deposits of copper, gold and zinc), undertaken by the Canadian Sunridge Gold Corpn, was scheduled to commence production in 2015, and to be fully operational in 2018, giving the economy further positive prospects. Construction of another gold mine, at Koka, as part of the Zara Gold Project, was forecast to be completed in 2015. In 2013 the Government permitted an easing of the restrictions on foreign currency in a bid to counter the country's shortage of foreign exchange. A five-year National Development Plan, which was presented by President Issaias Afewerki in June 2011, focused on expanding the agricultural sector, and measures to develop new and existing infrastructure facilities. The Plan also emphasized the need to promote tourism as a source of revenue. To this end, the first phase of development (with Qatari funding) on one of the Dahlak Islands, near Massawa, was completed in 2012; in the long term, the Dahlak project was to provide an international airport, luxury resorts, connecting roads and an industrial port, as well as other basic infrastructure. Eritrea's economy recorded high growth of 7.0% in 2012. However, in view of a decline in economic activity in most sectors other than mining, the GDP growth rate shrank significantly—to only 1.3%—in 2013, and was forecast at 1.9% in 2014.

PUBLIC HOLIDAYS

2016: 1 January (New Year's Day), 7 January (Coptic Christmas), 20 January (Coptic Epiphany), 8 March (Women's Day), 29 April (Coptic Good Friday), 1 May (Workers' Day), 24 May (Independence Day), 20 June (Martyrs' Day), 6 July* (Id al-Fitr, end of Ramadan), 1 September (anniversary of the start of the armed struggle), 11 September (Coptic New Year's Day), 12 September* (Id al-Adha/Arafat), 28 September (Feast of the True Cross), 11 December* (Mouloud, Birth of the Prophet), 25 December (Christmas).

* These holidays are dependent on the Islamic lunar calendar and may vary by one or two days from the dates given.

Statistical Survey

Source (unless otherwise stated): Ministry of Trade and Industry, POB 1844, Asmara; tel. (1) 126155; fax (1) 120586.

Area and Population

AREA, POPULATION AND DENSITY*

Area (sq km)	121,144†
Population (census results)	
9 May 1984	
Males	1,374,452
Females	1,373,852
Total	2,748,304
Population (UN estimates at mid-year)‡	
2013	6,333,139
2014	6,536,172
2015	6,737,634
Density (per sq km) at mid-2015	55.6

* Including the Assab district.
† 46,774 sq miles.
‡ Source: UN, *World Population Prospects: The 2012 Revision.*

POPULATION BY AGE AND SEX
(UN estimates at mid-2015)

	Males	Females	Total
0–14 years	1,480,804	1,418,518	2,899,322
15–64 years	1,822,806	1,858,871	3,681,677
65 years and over	61,779	94,856	156,635
Total	3,365,389	3,372,245	6,737,634

Source: UN, *World Population Prospects: The 2012 Revision.*

PRINCIPAL TOWNS
(estimated population at January 2013)

Asmara (capital) .	712,882	Keren	84,512
Assab	104,075	Mitsiwa (Massawa) .	54,715

BIRTHS AND DEATHS
(averages per year, UN estimates)

	2000–05	2005–10	2010–15
Birth rate (per 1,000)	40.1	39.4	37.0
Death rate (per 1,000)	8.9	8.0	6.8

Source: UN, *World Population Prospects: The 2012 Revision.*

Life expectancy (years at birth): 62.2 (males 59.9; females 64.6) in 2012 (Source: World Bank, World Development Indicators database).

ECONOMICALLY ACTIVE POPULATION
('000, FAO estimates at mid-year)

	2013	2014	2015
Agriculture, etc.	1,853	1,910	1,968
Total labour force (incl. others) .	2,550	2,641	2,735

Source: FAO.

Health and Welfare

KEY INDICATORS

Total fertility rate (children per woman, 2012)	4.8
Under-5 mortality rate (per 1,000 live births, 2012) . . .	52
HIV/AIDS (% of persons aged 15–49, 2013)	0.6
Hospital beds (per 1,000 head, 2011)	0.7
Physicians (per 1,000 head, 2004)	0.05
Health expenditure (2011): US $ per head (PPP)	15
Health expenditure (2011): % of GDP	2.7
Health expenditure (2011): public (% of total)	50.5
Access to water (% of persons, 2008)	61
Access to sanitation (% of persons, 2008)	14
Total carbon dioxide emissions ('000 metric tons, 2010) . .	513.4
Carbon dioxide emissions per head (metric tons, 2010) . .	0.1
Human Development Index (2013): ranking	182
Human Development Index (2013): value	0.381

For sources and definitions, see explanatory note on p. vi.

Agriculture

PRINCIPAL CROPS
('000 metric tons, FAO estimates unless otherwise indicated)

	2011	2012	2013
Wheat	28.8	33.0	30.0*
Barley	65.3	70.0	65.0*
Maize	20.0	22.0	20.0*
Millet	19.7	20.0	20.0
Sorghum	75.0	80.0	80.0
Potatoes	0.1	0.2	0.2
Broad beans, horse beans, dry .	0.1	0.1	0.1
Peas, dry	2.0	2.0	2.1
Chick-peas	7.2	7.2	7.2
Lentils	0.5	0.5	0.6
Vetches	2.3	2.3	2.4
Groundnuts, with shell . . .	1.7	1.8	1.8
Sesame seed	0.2	0.2	0.2

* Unofficial figure.

Aggregate production ('000 metric tons, may include official, semi-official or estimated data): Total cereals 258.1 in 2011, 275.0 in 2012, 265.0 in 2013; Total roots and tubers 64.1 in 2011, 62.2 in 2012, 63.2 in 2013; Total vegetables (incl. melons), 52.5 in 2011, 55.0 in 2012, 48.6 in 2013.

Source: FAO.

LIVESTOCK
('000 head, year ending September, FAO estimates)

	2011	2012	2013
Cattle	2,065	2,070	2,080
Sheep	2,281	2,285	2,300
Goats	1,760	1,770	1,800
Camels	350	360	370
Chickens	1,300	1,350	1,400

Source: FAO.

LIVESTOCK PRODUCTS
('000 metric tons, FAO estimates)

	2011	2012	2013
Cattle meat	23.8	24.0	24.0
Sheep meat	6.4	6.5	6.5
Goat meat	6.0	6.0	6.1
Chicken meat	1.7	1.7	1.7
Camels' milk	23.5	23.8	23.8
Cows' milk	106.5	108.0	109.0
Goats' milk	9.2	9.2	9.2
Sheep's milk	5.7	5.8	5.8
Hen eggs	2.2	2.3	2.3
Wool, greasy	1.2	1.2	1.2

Source: FAO.

Fishing

(metric tons, live weight of capture)

	2010	2011	2012
Requiem sharks	307	281	90
Sea catfishes	128	106	118
Threadfin breams	165	159	741
Lizardfishes	801	675	2,395
Snappers and jobfishes	58	51	22
Narrow-barred Spanish mackerel	414	480	94
Tuna-like fishes	423	301	123
Barracudas	69	65	81
Carangids	109	100	83
Queenfishes	176	65	55
Penaeus shrimps	323	119	112
Total catch (incl. others)	3,286	2,639	4,152

Source: FAO.

Mining

('000 metric tons unless otherwise indicated)

	2010	2011	2012
Gold (kilograms)	50.0	11,800.0	9,700.0
Marble ('000 sq m)*	36.0	36.0	36.0
Limestone*	3.0	3.0	3.0
Salt*	27.0	27.0	28.0
Granite*	25.0	25.0	25.0

* Estimates.

Source: US Geological Survey.

Industry

SELECTED PRODUCTS
('000 metric tons unless otherwise indicated, estimates)

	2010	2011	2012
Cement	45.0	190.0	260.0
Basalt	50.0	50.0	n.a.
Gravel	80.0	80.0	80.0
Coral	58.0	58.0	58.0
Electric energy (million kWh)	311	337	n.a.

Sources: US Geological Survey; UN Industrial Commodity Statistics Database.

Finance

CURRENCY AND EXCHANGE RATES
Monetary Units
100 cents = 1 nakfa.

Sterling, Dollar and Euro Equivalents (31 December 2014)
£1 sterling = 23.997 nakfa;
US $1 = 15.375 nakfa;
€1 = 18.667 nakfa;
1,000 nakfa = £41.67 = $65.04 = €53.57.

Note: Following its secession from Ethiopia in May 1993, Eritrea retained the Ethiopian currency, the birr. An exchange rate of US $1 = 5.000 birr was introduced in October 1992 and remained in force until April 1994, when it was adjusted to $1 = 5.130 birr. Further adjustments were made subsequently. In November 1997 the Government introduced a separate national currency, the nakfa, replacing (and initially at par with) the Ethiopian birr. The exchange rate in relation to the US dollar was initially set at the prevailing unified rate, but from 1 May 1998 a mechanism to provide a market-related exchange rate was established.

Average Exchange Rate (nakfa per US $)
2012	15.3750
2013	15.3750
2014	15.375

BUDGET
(million nakfa)

Revenue*	2007	2008†	2009‡
Tax revenue	2,405	2,459	2,374
Direct taxes	1,512	1,719	1,580
Indirect domestic taxes	487	395	435
Import duties and taxes	406	345	360
Non-tax revenue	1,888	1,393	1,401
Total	4,293	3,853	3,775

Expenditure§	2007	2008†	2009‡
Current expenditure	5,900	6,905	6,824
Wages, salaries and allowances	2,234	2,275	2,430
Materials and services	2,316	2,531	2,398
Subsidies and transfers	706	1,311	931
Interest	644	788	1,065
Domestic	571	648	853
External	73	140	212
Capital expenditure	2,224	2,331	2,134
Central treasury	1,012	704	681
Externally financed	1,203	1,627	1,453
Total	8,124	9,236	8,958

* Excluding grants received (million nakfa): 628 in 2007; 604 in 2008 (estimate); 737 in 2009 (projected).
† Estimates.
‡ Projections.
§ Excluding net lending (million nakfa): −95 in 2007; 608 in 2008 (estimate); 139 in 2009 (projected).

Source: African Development Bank, *Interim Country Strategy Paper for Eritrea* (2009–11).

INTERNATIONAL RESERVES
(US $ million at 31 December)

	1999	2000	2001
Gold (national valuation)	19.7	10.4	10.5
Reserve position in IMF	0.0	0.0	0.0
Foreign exchange	34.2	25.5	39.7
Total	53.9	35.9	50.3

Foreign exchange: 84.3 in 2009; 108.6 in 2010; 109.3 in 2011.

IMF special drawing rights: 5.5 in 2011; 5.5 in 2012; 5.7 in 2013.

Source: IMF, *International Financial Statistics*.

MONEY SUPPLY
(million nakfa at 31 December)

	2009	2010	2011
Currency outside depository corporations	6,637	8,155	9,959
Transferable deposits	10,655	11,554	12,398
Other deposits	17,397	20,388	23,635
Broad money	34,689	40,097	45,992

Source: IMF, *International Financial Statistics*.

COST OF LIVING
(Consumer Price Index; base: 2005 = 100)

	2011	2012	2013
All items	256.3	287.7	323.0

Source: African Development Bank.

NATIONAL ACCOUNTS
(million nakfa at current prices)

Expenditure on the Gross Domestic Product

	2010	2011	2012
Private final consumption expenditure	27,790	31,169	35,626
Government final consumption expenditure	7,773	8,451	9,127
Gross capital formation . . .	3,027	4,009	4,533
Total domestic expenditure .	38,590	43,629	49,286
Exports of goods and services . .	1,559	5,764	9,286
Less Imports of goods and services	7,599	9,283	10,786
GDP in purchasers' values .	32,549	40,109	47,785

Gross Domestic Product by Economic Activity

	2010	2011	2012
Agriculture, forestry and fishing .	5,985	6,590	7,796
Mining and quarrying	541	704	807
Manufacturing	1,897	2,386	2,750
Construction	4,824	6,275	7,191
Wholesale and retail trade . .	5,880	7,402	8,979
Transport and communications .	3,766	4,741	5,751
Public administration and defence	8,498	10,698	12,980
Sub-total	31,391	38,795	46,253
Indirect taxes (net)	1,158	1,314	1,532
GDP in purchasers' values .	32,549	40,109	47,785

Source: African Development Bank.

BALANCE OF PAYMENTS
(US $ million)

	2000	2001*	2002†
Exports of goods f.o.b.	36.7	19.9	51.8
Imports of goods c.i.f.	−470.3	−536.7	−533.4
Trade balance	−433.5	−516.7	−481.7
Exports of services	60.7	127.5	132.6
Imports of services	−28.3	−33.4	−30.3
Balance on goods and services	−401.1	−422.6	−379.4
Other income (net)	−1.4	−4.6	−6.1
Balance on goods, services and income	−402.5	−427.2	−385.5
Private unrequited transfers (net)	195.7	175.0	205.6
Official unrequited transfers (net)	102.4	120.8	80.3

—*continued*	2000	2001*	2002†
Current balance	−104.5	−131.4	−99.6
Capital account (net)	—	7.3	3.6
Financial account	98.7	94.8	64.6
Short-term capital (net) . .	−14.7	18.7	15.9
Net errors and omissions . . .	−9.5	36.5	−7.6
Overall balance	−15.2	7.2	−39.0

* Preliminary figures.
† Estimates.

Source: IMF, *Eritrea: Selected Issues and Statistical Appendix* (June 2003).

2012 (Nakfa million): Trade balance −2,240; Services (net) 431; Income (net) −622; Current transfers (net) 3,451; *Current account* 1,021 (Source: African Development Bank).

External Trade

PRINCIPAL COMMODITIES
(distribution by SITC, US $ '000)

Imports c.i.f. (excl. petroleum)	2001	2002	2003
Food and live animals	110.9	153.0	175.2
Animal and vegetable oils, fats and waxes	13.6	7.4	19.3
Chemicals and related products .	45.5	36.4	26.2
Basic manufactures	101.5	115.6	63.3
Machinery and transport equipment	107.4	155.9	97.2
Miscellaneous manufactured articles	34.0	46.9	40.7
Total (incl. others)	422.9	537.9	432.8

Exports f.o.b.	2001	2002	2003
Food and live animals	8.8	37.7	2.4
Crude materials (inedible) except fuels	3.0	6.0	2.1
Chemicals and related products .	0.7	0.6	0.1
Basic manufactures	5.6	4.8	1.1
Miscellaneous manufactured articles	0.5	1.5	0.7
Total (incl. others)	19.0	51.8	6.6

Source: UN, *International Trade Statistics Yearbook*.

2011 (US $ '000): Total imports 849; total exports 457 (Source: African Development Bank).

PRINCIPAL TRADING PARTNERS
(US $ million)

Imports c.i.f.	2001	2002	2003
Belgium	11.9	13.7	8.6
Germany	11.8	16.4	6.7
Italy	79.0	70.4	50.1
Netherlands	13.9	17.4	10.4
Saudi Arabia	70.0	70.0	45.4
United Arab Emirates . . .	64.6	90.7	52.9
United Kingdom	9.6	10.0	11.7
USA	20.4	38.5	68.9
Total (incl. others)	422.9	537.9	432.8

Exports f.o.b.	2001	2002	2003
Djibouti	—	0.8	—
Germany	0.7	0.5	0.1
India	3.2	0.5	0.5
Italy	2.1	1.8	0.8
Netherlands	0.4	0.3	0.7
Saudi Arabia	0.3	0.1	—
Sudan	9.7	43.4	1.3
Total (incl. others)	19.0	51.8	6.6

Source: UN, *International Trade Statistics Yearbook*.

Transport

ROAD TRAFFIC
(motor vehicles in use at 31 December)

	2007
Passenger cars	31,033
Buses and coaches	1,825
Vans and lorries	22,514
Motorcycles and mopeds	3,042

Source: IRF, *World Road Statistics*.

SHIPPING

Flag Registered Fleet
(at 31 December)

	2012	2013	2014
Number of vessels	17	17	17
Total displacement ('000 grt) . .	14	14	14

Source: Lloyd's List Intelligence (www.lloydslistintelligence.com).

Tourism

ARRIVALS BY COUNTRY OF ORIGIN

	2009	2010	2011
Germany	775	880	1,004
India	718	730	577
Italy	1,944	1,754	1,694
Japan	151	60	78
Kenya	234	247	343
Sudan	5,866	6,220	19,653
United Kingdom	843	703	968
USA	511	738	831
Total (incl. others)	79,334	83,947	107,090

Tourism receipts (US $ million, excl. passenger transport): 26 in 2009.

Source: World Tourism Organization.

Communications Media

	2011	2012	2013
Telephones ('000 main lines in use)	58.0	60.1	61.9
Mobile cellular telephones ('000 subscribers)	241.9	305.3	354.8
Internet subscribers ('000) . .	7.3	n.a.	n.a.
Broadband subscribers . . .	141	125	146

Source: International Telecommunication Union.

Education

(2011/12 unless otherwise indicated)

	Institutions*	Teachers	Pupils
Pre-primary	95	1,296	45,973
Primary	695	8,166	334,245
Secondary: General	44	6,721	265,600
Secondary: Teacher-training . .	2	47*	922*
Secondary: Vocational	n.a.	289	2,520
University and equivalent level† .	n.a.	634	10,198

* 2001/02 figure(s).
† 2009/10 figures.

Sources: UNESCO Institute for Statistics; Ministry of Education, Asmara.

Pupil-teacher ratio (primary education, UNESCO estimate): 40.9 in 2011/12 (Source: UNESCO Institute for Statistics).

Adult literacy rate (UNESCO estimates): 70.5% (males 80.1%; females 61.3%) in 2012 (Source: UNESCO Institute for Statistics).

Directory

The Government

HEAD OF STATE

President: ISSAIAS AFEWERKI (assumed power May 1991; elected President by the National Assembly 8 June 1993).

CABINET
(April 2015)

The Government is formed by the People's Front for Democracy and Justice.

President: ISSAIAS AFEWERKI.

Minister of Defence: Gen. SEBHAT EPHREM.

Minister of Justice: FAWZIA HASHIM.

Minister of Foreign Affairs: OSMAN SALIH MUHAMMAD.

Minister of Information: (vacant).

Minister of Finance: BERHANE ABREHE.

Minister of Trade and Industry: ESTIFANOS HABTE.

Minister of Agriculture: AREFAINE BERHE.

Minister of Labour and Human Welfare: SALMA HASSEN.

Minister of Marine Resources: TEWOLDE KELATI.

Minister of Public Works: ABRAHA ASFAHA.

Minister of Energy and Mines: AHMED HAJJ ALI.

Minister of Education: SEMERE RUSOM.

Minister of Health: AMINA NURHUSSEIN.

Minister of Transport and Communications and of Local Government: WOLDEMIKAEL ABRAHA.

Minister of Tourism: ASKALU MENKERIOS.

Minister of Land, Water and the Environment: TESFAI GHEBRESELASSIE SEBHATU.

MINISTRIES

Office of the President: POB 257, Asmara; tel. (1) 122132; fax (1) 125123.

Ministry of Agriculture: POB 1048, Asmara; tel. (1) 181499; fax (1) 181415.

Ministry of Defence: POB 629, Asmara; tel. (1) 165952; fax (1) 124990.

Ministry of Education: POB 5610, Asmara; tel. (1) 113044; fax (1) 113866; internet www.erimoe.gov.er.

Ministry of Energy and Mines: POB 5285, Asmara; tel. (1) 116872; fax (1) 127652; internet www.moem.gov.er.

Ministry of Finance: POB 896, Asmara; tel. (1) 118131; fax (1) 127947.

Ministry of Foreign Affairs: POB 190, Asmara; tel. (1) 127838; fax (1) 123788; e-mail tesfai@wg.eol.

Ministry of Health: POB 212, Asmara; tel. (1) 117549; fax (1) 112899.

Ministry of Information: POB 872, Asmara; tel. (1) 120478; fax (1) 126747; internet www.shabait.com.

Ministry of Justice: POB 241, Asmara; tel. (1) 127739; fax (1) 126422.

Ministry of Labour and Human Welfare: POB 5252, Asmara; tel. (1) 181846; fax (1) 181760; e-mail mlhw@eol.com.er.

Ministry of Land, Water and the Environment: POB 976, Asmara; tel. (1) 118021; fax (1) 123285.

Ministry of Local Government: POB 225, Asmara; tel. (1) 114254; fax (1) 120014.

Ministry of Marine Resources: POB 923, Asmara; tel. (1) 120400; fax (1) 122185; e-mail mofisha@eol.com.er; f. 1994.

Ministry of Public Works: POB 841, Asmara; tel. (1) 120302; fax (1) 120661.

Ministry of Tourism: POB 1010, Warsay Ave, Dembe Sembel (Green Building), Asmara; tel. (1) 154100; fax (1) 154081; e-mail eritreantourism@tse.com.er.

Ministry of Trade and Industry: POB 1844, Asmara; tel. (1) 120080; fax (1) 120586; e-mail berhanem69@yahoo.co.uk.

Ministry of Transport and Communications: POB 1840, Asmara; tel. (1) 114222; fax (1) 127048; e-mail motc.rez@eol.com.er.

Provincial Administrators

There are six administrative regions in Eritrea, each with regional, subregional and village administrations.

Anseba Province: ALI MAHMUD.

Debub Province: EFREM GEBREKRISTOS.

Debubawi Keyih Bahri Province: GERGIS GIRMAI.

Gash-Barka Province: KAHSAI GHEBREHIWOT.

Maakel Province: Maj.-Gen. RAMADAN OSMAN AWLIYAI.

Semenawi Keyih Bahri Province: TSIGEREDA WOLDEGERGISH.

Legislature

NATIONAL ASSEMBLY

The National Assembly comprises the 75 members of the Central Committee of the People's Front for Democracy and Justice (PFDJ) and 75 directly elected members. In May 1997, following the adoption of the Constitution, the Constituent Assembly empowered a Transitional National Assembly (comprising the 75 members of the PFDJ, 60 members of the former Constituent Assembly and 15 representatives of Eritreans residing abroad) to act as the legislature until elections were held for a new National Assembly. As at February 2015, no such elections had taken place. In his role as Head of the Government and Commander-in-Chief of the Army, the President nominates individuals to head the various government departments. These nominations are ratified by the legislative body.

Chairman of the Transitional National Assembly: ISSAIAS AFEWERKI.

Election Commission

Election Commission: Asmara; f. 2002; five mems appointed by the President; Commissioner RAMADAN MOHAMMED NUR.

Political Organizations

Afar Federal Alliance: e-mail afa_f@hotmail.com; f. 2003.

Democratic Movement for the Liberation of Eritrean Kunama: Postfach 620 124, 50694, Köln, Germany; e-mail kcs@baden-kunama.com; internet www.baden-kunama.com; based in Germany; represents the Kunama minority ethnic group.

Eritrean Democratic Alliance (EDA): internet www.erit-alliance.com; f. 1999 as the Alliance of Eritrean National Forces, became Eritrean National Alliance in 2002, adopted present name in 2004; broad alliance of 13 parties opposed to PFDJ regime; Chair. BERHANE YEMANE 'HANJEMA'; Sec.-Gen. HUSAYN KHALIFA.

Eritrean Democratic Party (EDP): e-mail info@selfi-democracy.com; internet www.selfi-democracy.com; f. 2001 as the Eritrean People's Liberation Front—Democratic Party (EPLF—DP); breakaway group from the PFDJ; name changed to above in 2004; Chair. MESFIN HAGOS.

Eritrean Islamic Jihad (EIJ): radical opposition group; in Aug. 1993 split into a military wing and a political wing.

Eritrean Islamic Party for Justice and Development (EIPJD) (Al-Hizb Al-Islami Al-Eritree Liladalah Wetenmiya): internet www.alkhalas.org; f. 1988 as Eritrean Islamic Jihad Movement; changed name to al-Khalas in 1998; political wing of EIJ; Leader KHALIL MUHAMMAD AMER.

Eritrean Liberation Front (ELF): f. 1958; commenced armed struggle against Ethiopia in 1961; subsequently split into numerous factions (see below); mainly Muslim support; opposes the PFDJ; principal factions:

Eritrean Liberation Front—Central Command (ELF—CC): f. 1982; Chair. ABDALLAH IDRISS.

Eritrean Liberation Front—National Council (ELF—NC): Leader Dr BEYENE KIDANE.

Eritrean Liberation Front—Revolutionary Council (ELF—RC): Chair. AHMED WOLDEYESUS AMMAR.

Eritrean People's Democratic Front (EPDF): internet www.democrasia.org; f. 2004 by merger of People's Democratic Front for the Liberation of Eritrea and a faction of ERDF; Leader TEWOLDE GEBRESELASSIE.

Eritrean Popular Movement (EPM): f. 2004; Leader ABDALLAH ADEM.

Eritrean Revolutionary Democratic Front (ERDF): e-mail webmaster@eritreana.com; internet www.eritreana.com; f. 1997 following merger of Democratic Movement for the Liberation of Eritrea and a faction of People's Democratic Front for the Liberation of Eritrea; Leader BERHANE YEMANE 'HANJEMA'.

Gash Setit Organization: Leader ISMAIL NADA.

People's Front for Democracy and Justice (PFDJ): POB 1081, Asmara; tel. (1) 121399; fax (1) 120848; e-mail webmaster@shaebia.org; internet www.shaebia.org; f. 1970 as the Eritrean Popular Liberation Forces, following a split in the Eritrean Liberation Front; renamed the Eritrean People's Liberation Front in 1977; adopted present name in Feb. 1994; Christian and Muslim support; in May 1991 took control of Eritrea and formed provisional Govt; formed transitional Govt in May 1993; Chair. ISSAIAS AFEWERKI; Sec.-Gen. ALAMIN MOHAMED SAID.

Red Sea Afar Democratic Organization: Afar opposition group; Sec.-Gen. IBRAHIM HAROUN.

Diplomatic Representation

EMBASSIES IN ERITREA

China, People's Republic: 16 Ogaden St, POB 204, Asmara; tel. and fax (1) 185271; fax (1) 189361; e-mail chinaemb_er@mfa.gov.cn; internet er.china-embassy.org/chn; Ambassador QIU XUEJUN.

Djibouti: POB 5589, Asmara; tel. (1) 354961; fax (1) 351831; Ambassador AHMAD ISSA (recalled in June 2008).

Egypt: 5 Marsa Fatma St, POB 5570, Asmara; tel. and fax (1) 124935; fax (1) 123294; e-mail amb.egy.asmara@gmail.com; Ambassador MAHMOUD NAYEL.

France: 25 Nakfa St, POB 209, Asmara; tel. (1) 125196; fax (1) 123288; e-mail cad.asmara@diplomatie.gouv.fr; internet www.ambafrance-er.org; Ambassador STÉPHANE GRUENBERG.

Germany: SABA Building, 8th Floor, Warsay St, POB 4974, Asmara; tel. (1) 186670; fax (1) 186900; e-mail info@asmara.diplo.de; internet www.asmara.diplo.de; Ambassador ANDREAS ZIMMER.

Iran: Asmara; Ambassador REZA AMERI.

Israel: 32 Abo St, POB 5600, Asmara; tel. (1) 188521; fax (1) 188550; e-mail info@asmara.mfa.gov.il; Ambassador ELIE ANTEBI.

Italy: 11 171–1 St, POB 220, Asmara; tel. (1) 120160; fax (1) 121115; e-mail ambasciata.asmara@esteri.it; internet www.ambasmara.esteri.it; Ambassador MARCELLO FONDI.

Libya: 9 Shelalo St, POB 2153, Asmara; tel. (1) 127514; fax (1) 127989; Chargé d'affaires a. i. Dr AL-HASAN ALI.

Russian Federation: 21 Zobel St, POB 5667, Asmara; tel. (1) 127162; fax (1) 127164; e-mail rusemb@eol.com.er; Ambassador IGOR NIKOLAVIC CHUBAROV.

Saudi Arabia: 748 Ras Demaira St, Asmara; tel. (1) 154318; fax (1) 154321; e-mail eremb@mofa.gov.sa; Ambassador NASSER ALI AL-HOTI.

South Africa: 51–53 Hitseito St 245, Tiravalo, POB 11447, Asmara; tel. (1) 152521; fax (1) 153072; e-mail saemb_asma@yahoo.com; Ambassador MAHOMED IQBAL DAWOOD JHAZBHAY.

Sudan: 246 Hitseito St, Asmara; tel. (1) 202072; fax (1) 200760; e-mail sudanemb@eol.com.er; Ambassador SALAH MOHAMED AL-HASSAN.

United Kingdom: 66–68 Mariam Ghimbi St, POB 5584, Asmara; tel. (1) 120145; fax (1) 120104; e-mail asmara.enquiries@fco.gov.uk; internet www.ukineritrea.fco.gov.uk; Ambassador DAVID WARD.

USA: 179 Alu St, POB 211, Asmara; tel. (1) 120004; fax (1) 127584; e-mail usembassyasmara@state.gov; internet eritrea.usembassy.gov; Chargé d'affaires LOUIS MAZEL.

Yemen: POB 5566, Asmara; tel. (1) 114434; fax (1) 117921; Ambassador Dr ABDELKADIR MOHAMMED HADI.

Judicial System

The judicial system operates on the basis of transitional laws, which incorporate pre-independence laws of the Eritrean People's Liberation Front, revised Ethiopian laws, customary laws and post-independence enacted laws. The independence of the judiciary in the discharge of its functions is unequivocally stated in Decree No. 37, which defines the powers and duties of the Government. It is subject only to the law and to no other authority. The court structure is composed of first instance sub-zonal courts, appellate and first instance zonal courts, appellate and first instance high courts, a panel of high court judges, presided over by the President of the High Court, and a Supreme Court presided over by the Chief Justice, as a court of last resort. The judges of the Supreme Court are appointed by the President of the State, subject to confirmation by the National Assembly.

Supreme Court: Asmara.

High Court: POB 241, Asmara; tel. (1) 127739; fax (1) 201828; e-mail prshict@eol.com.er; Pres. MENKERIOS BERAKI.

Attorney-General: ALEMSEGED HABTESELLASIE.

Religion

Eritrea is almost equally divided between Muslims and Christians. Most Christians are adherents of the Orthodox Church, although there are Protestant and Roman Catholic communities. A small number of the population follow traditional beliefs.

CHRISTIANITY

The Eritrean Orthodox Church

In September 1993 the separation of the Eritrean Orthodox Church from the Ethiopian Orthodox Church was agreed by the respective church leaderships. The Eritrean Orthodox Church announced that it was to create a diocese of each of the country's then 10 provinces. The first five bishops of the Eritrean Orthodox Church were consecrated in Cairo, Egypt, in September 1994. In May 1998 Eritrea's first Patriarch (Abune) was consecrated in Alexandria, Egypt. In January 2006 Eritrea's third Patriarch, Abune Antonios I (who had been under house arrest since August 2005), was deposed by the Holy Synod.

Patriarch (Abune): DIOSKOROS.

The Roman Catholic Church

An estimated 3% of the total population are Roman Catholics.

Bishop of Asmara: Archbishop ABBA MENGHISTEAB TESFAMARIAM, 19 Gonder St, POB 244, Asmara; tel. (1) 120206; fax (1) 126519; e-mail kimehret@gemel.com.er.

Bishop of Barentu: Rt Rev. THOMAS OSMAN, POB 9, Barentu; tel. and fax (1) 127283.

Bishop of Keren: Rt Rev. KIDANE YEBIO, POB 460, Keren; tel. (1) 401907; fax (1) 401604; e-mail cek@tse.com.er.

The Anglican Communion

Within the Episcopal Church in Jerusalem and the Middle East, Eritrea lies within the jurisdiction of the Bishop in Egypt.

Leader: ASFAHA MAHARY.

ISLAM

Eritrea's main Muslim communities are concentrated in the western lowlands, the northern highlands and the eastern coastal region.

Leader: Sheikh AL-AMIN OSMAN AL-AMIN.

The Press

There is no independent press in Eritrea.

Chamber News: POB 856, Asmara; tel. (1) 120045; fax (1) 120138; monthly; Tigrinya, Arabic and English; publ. by Asmara Chamber of Commerce.

Eritrea Alhaditha: Asmara; tel. (1) 117099; e-mail alhadisa@zena.gov.er; Arabic; publ. by the Ministry of Information; Editor-in-Chief MOHAMMEDNUR YAHYA.

Eritrea Haddas: POB 247, Asmara; tel. (1) 201820; e-mail tigreit@zena.gov.er; Tigrinya; govt publ; Editor-in-Chief MOHAMMED IDRIS MOHAMMED.

Eritrea Profile: POB 247, Asmara; tel. (1) 114114; fax (1) 127749; e-mail profile@zena.gov.er; internet www.shabait.com; f. 1994; twice-weekly; English; publ. by the Ministry of Information; Man. Dir AZZAZI ZEREMARIAM; Editor AMANUEL MESFUN (acting).

Haddas Ertra (New Eritrea): Asmara; tel. (1) 116266; fax (1) 127749; e-mail hadas@zena.gov.er; internet www.shabait.com/haddas-ertra; f. 1991; six times a week; Tigrinya; govt publ; Editor SAMSOM HAILE; circ. 49,200.

Newsletter: POB 856, Asmara; tel. (1) 121589; fax (1) 120138; e-mail encc@aol.com.er; monthly; Tigrinya, Arabic and English; publ. by Eritrean National Chamber of Commerce; Editor MOHAMMED-SFAF HAMMED.

Broadcasting and Communications

TELECOMMUNICATIONS

Eritrea Telecommunication Services Corpn (EriTel): 11 Semaetat St, POB 234, Asmara; tel. (1) 124655; fax (1) 120938; e-mail eritel@tse.com.er; internet www.eritel.com.er; f. 1991; public enterprise; operates fixed-line and mobile cellular networks and internet services; Gen. Man. TESFASELASSIE BERHANE.

TFanus: 46 Daniel Comboni Street, POB 724, Asmara; tel. (1) 202590; fax (1) 126457; e-mail support@tfanus.com.er; internet www.tfanus.com.er; f. 1996; internet service provider.

Regulatory Authority

Ministry of Transport and Communications (Communications Department): POB 4918, Asmara; tel. (1) 115847; fax (1) 126966; e-mail motc.rez@eol.com.er; Dir-Gen. MEKONNEN FISSEHAZION.

BROADCASTING

Radio

Voice of the Broad Masses of Eritrea (Dimtsi Hafash): POB 242, Asmara; tel. (1) 120426; fax (1) 126747; govt-controlled; programmes in Arabic, Tigrinya, Tigre, Saho, Oromo, Amharic, Afar, Bilien, Nara, Hedareb and Kunama; Dir-Gen. GHIRMAY BERHE; Technical Dir BERHANE GEREZGIHER.

Voice of Liberty: Asmara; e-mail VoL@selfi-democracy.com; internet selfi-democracy.com; radio programme of the EDP; broadcasts for one hour twice a week.

Television

ERI-TV: Asmara; tel. (1) 116033; e-mail aslmelashe@yahoo.com; internet www.eri.tv; f. 1992; govt station providing educational, tech., entertainment and information services through three channels; broadcasting began in 1993; programming in Arabic, English, Tigre and Tigrinya; broadcasts for eight hours daily; Dir-Gen. ASMELASH ABRAHA.

Finance

(cap. = capital; res = reserves; dep. = deposits; m. = million; brs = branches; amounts in nakfa)

In November 1997 Eritrea adopted the nakfa as its unit of currency, replacing the Ethiopian birr, which had been Eritrea's monetary unit since independence.

BANKING

Central Bank

Bank of Eritrea: 21 Nakfa St 175, POB 849, Asmara; tel. (1) 123033; fax (1) 122091; e-mail kibreabw@boe.gov.er; f. 1993; bank of issue; Gov. KIBREAB WELDEMARIAM (acting).

Other Banks

Commercial Bank of Eritrea: 208 Liberty Ave, POB 219, Asmara; tel. (1) 121844; fax (1) 124887; e-mail gm.cber@gemel.com.er; f. 1991; cap. 658.0m., res 457.4m., dep. 21,965.8m. (Dec. 2009); Chair. BERHANE ABREHE; Gen. Man. YEMANE TESFAY; 15 brs.

Eritrean Development and Investment Bank: 29 Bedho St, POB 1266, Asmara; tel. (1) 126777; fax (1) 201976; f. 1996; cap. 45m., total assets 194.2m. (Dec. 2003); provides medium- to long-term credit; Chair. HABTEAB TESFATSION; Gen. Man. Dr GOITOM WOLDEMARIAM; 4 brs.

Housing and Commerce Bank of Eritrea: POB 235, Bahti Meskerem Sq., Asmara; tel. (1) 120350; fax (1) 202209; e-mail hcbgm@hcbe.com.er; internet erhcb.com; f. 1994; cap. 293m. (Dec. 2006); finances residential and commercial construction projects and commercial loans; Chair. HAGOS GHEBREHIWET; Gen. Man. BERHANE GHEBREHIWET; 10 brs.

INSURANCE

National Insurance Corporation of Eritrea Share Co (NICE): NICE Bldg, 171 Bidho Ave, POB 881, Asmara; tel. (1) 123000; fax (1) 123240; e-mail nice@nice-eritrea.com; internet www.nice-eritrea.com; f. 1992; partially privatized in 2004 and 2013; 60% govt-owned; general and life; Chair. GHIRMAI GHEBREMESKEL; Gen. Man. ZERU WOLDEMICHAEL.

Trade and Industry

DEVELOPMENT ORGANIZATION

Eritrea Free Zones Authority: Asmara; f. 2001; CEO ARAIA TSEGGAI.

CHAMBER OF COMMERCE

Eritrean National Chamber of Commerce: POB 856, Asmara; tel. (1) 121589; fax (1) 120138; e-mail encc@gemel.com.er.

TRADE ASSOCIATION

Red Sea Trading Corporation: 29/31 Ras Alula St, POB 332, Asmara; tel. (1) 127846; fax (1) 124353; f. 1983; import and export services; operated by the PFDJ; Gen. Man. NEGASH AFWORKI.

UTILITIES

Electricity

Eritrean Electricity Corporation (EEC): POB 911, Asmara; fax (1) 121468; e-mail eeahrg@eol.com.er; Gen. Man. ABRAHAM WOLDEMICHAEL.

Water

Dept of Water Resources: POB 1488, Asmara; tel. (1) 119636; fax (1) 124625; e-mail wrdmlwe@eol.com.er; f. 1992; Dir-Gen. MEBRAHTU EYASSU.

MAJOR COMPANIES

Exploration activities have identified reserves of base and precious metals. About 20 mining companies were involved in mineral exploration in different areas in the early 2010s.

Assab Salt Works: Assab; salt.

Bisha Mining Co.: 1 Mariam Gimby, POB 4276, Asmara; tel. (1) 124941; internet www.bishamining.com; gold and silver; Gen. Man. KEVIN MOXHAM.

Gedem Cement Factory: Massawa; cement.

Margran PLC: POB 1105, Bahti Meskerem; tel. (1) 125004; fax (1) 122395; e-mail margran@eol.com.er; granite.

TRADE UNION

National Confederation of Eritrean Workers (NCEW): POB 1188, Asmara; tel. (1) 116513; fax (1) 126606; e-mail ncew@tse.com.er; f. 1979; Gen.-Sec. TEKESTE BAIRE; Dep. Gen.-Sec. TZEGGAI MOGOS.

Transport

Eritrea's transport infrastructure was severely damaged during the three decades of war prior to independence. International creditors have since provided loans for the repair and reconstruction of the road network and for the improvement of port facilities.

RAILWAYS

The 306-km railway connection between Agordat, Asmara and the port of Massawa was severely damaged during the war of independence and ceased operations in 1975. However, in 1999 an 81-km section of the Asmara–Massawa line (between Massawa and Embatkala) became operational, and in 2001 a further 18-km section, connecting Embatkala and Ghinda, was added. In 2003 the reconstruction of the entire Asmara–Massawa line was completed. In 2007 work started on the reconstruction of the 124-km railway line west of Asmara to Akordat and Bisha, with the aim of eventually constructing a new international link from Bisha to Kassala, Sudan.

Eritrean Railway: POB 6081, Asmara; tel. (1) 123365; fax (1) 201785; Co-ordinator, Railways Rehabilitation Project AMANUEL GEBRESELLASIE.

ROADS

Eritrea has a long road network for its land base, totalling 18,540 km. Roads that are paved require considerable repair, as do many of the bridges across seasonal water courses destroyed in the war. The programme to rehabilitate the road between Asmara and the port of Massawa was completed in 2000.

SHIPPING

Eritrea has two major seaports: Massawa, which sustained heavy war damage in 1990, and Assab, which has principally served Addis Ababa, in Ethiopia. Under an accord signed between the Ethiopian and Eritrean Governments in 1993, the two countries agreed to share the facilities of both ports. Since independence, activity in Massawa has increased substantially; however, activity at Assab declined following the outbreak of hostilities with Ethiopia in May 1998. At 31 December 2014 Eritrea's flag registered fleet numbered 17 vessels, with a total displacement of 14,009 grt.

Dept of Maritime Transport: POB 679, Asmara; tel. (1) 189156; fax (1) 186541; e-mail maritime@motc-gov.er; Dir-Gen. GHEBREMEDHIN HABTE KIDANE.

BC Marine Services: 189 Warsay St, POB 5638, Asmara; tel. (1) 202672; fax (1) 127477; e-mail info@bc-marine.com; internet www.bc-marine.com; f. 2000; services include marine consultancy, marine survey and ship management; brs in Assab and Massawa; Dir Capt. NAOD GEBREAMLAK HAILE.

Eritrean Shipping Lines: 80 Semaetat Ave, POB 1110, Asmara; tel. (1) 120359; fax (1) 120331; e-mail ersl@eol.com.er; f. 1992; provides shipping services in Red Sea and Persian (Arabian) Gulf areas and owns and operates four cargo ships; Gen. Man. TEWELDE TEKESTE.

Maritime Ship Agency Services Corpn (MSASC): POB 99, Massawa; tel. (1) 552729; fax (1) 552438; e-mail mssegm@tse.com.er; f. 1991 as Maritime Ship Services Enterprise; est. as a corpn 2006; state-owned; shipping agents; Gen. Man. ABDURAHMAN AHMED (acting).

CIVIL AVIATION

There are three international airports: at Asmara, Assab and Massawa. There are also eight domestic airports.

Civil Aviation Department: POB 252, Asmara; tel. (1) 124335; fax (1) 124334; e-mail motc.rez@eol.com.er; handles freight and passenger traffic for eight scheduled carriers which use Asmara airport; Dir-Gen. PAULOS KAHSAY.

Eritrean Airlines: 89 Harnet Ave, POB 222, Asmara; tel. (1) 125500; fax (1) 125465; e-mail customer-rel@eritreanairlines.com.er; internet www.flyeritrea.com; CEO KUBROM DAFLA.

Nasair Eritrea: POB 11915, Asmara; tel. (1) 200700; fax (1) 117622; e-mail nasreddin@nasaireritrea.com; internet www.nasaireritrea.com; f. 2006; CEO NASREDDIN IBRAHIM.

Tourism

The Ministry of Tourism is overseeing the development of this sector, although its advance since independence has been inhibited by the country's war-damaged transport infrastructure, and by subsequent conflicts with Ethiopia and other regional tensions. Eritrea possesses many areas of scenic and scientific interest, including the Dahlak Islands (a coralline archipelago rich in marine life), off shore from Massawa, and the massive escarpment rising up from the coastal plain and supporting a unique ecosystem. In 2011 107,090 tourists visited Eritrea, representing an increase of 27.5% on the previous year. Tourism receipts in 2009 amounted to US $26m. Since May 2006 it has been necessary for foreign nationals to obtain a permit 10 days in advance in order to travel outside of the capital.

Eritrean Tourism Service Corpn: Asmara; operates govt-owned hotels.

Defence

As assessed at November 2014, Eritrea's active armed forces included an army of about 200,000, a navy of 1,400 and an air force of some 350; reserve forces numbered around 120,000. Between 1995 and 2002 national service was compulsory for all Eritreans between 18 and 40 years of age (with certain exceptions), for an 18-month period, including six months of military training. In 2002, however, with the introduction of the Warsai-Yika'alo Development Campaign, the authorities effectively institutionalized conscription that lasted for an indefinite term.

Defence Expenditure: Budgeted at US $78m. in 2013.

Chief of Staff of the Eritrean Defence Forces: Maj.-Gen.
PHILIPOS WOLDEYOHANNES.

Education

Education is provided free of charge in government schools and at the
seven government colleges of higher education. There are also some
fee-paying private schools. Education is officially compulsory for
children between seven and 13 years of age. Primary education
begins at the age of seven and lasts for five years. Secondary
education, beginning at 12 years of age, lasts for as much as six
years, comprising a first cycle of two years and a second of four years.
According to UNESCO estimates, in 2012 primary enrolment
included 33% of children in the relevant age-group (boys 35%; girls
31%), while the comparable ratio for secondary enrolment was 26%
(boys 28%; girls 23%). Total government expenditure on education
and training in 2006 was estimated at the equivalent of 2.0% of GDP.
In 2004/05 there were some 5,500 students enrolled on Bachelors
degree courses at the University of Asmara; however, the University
of Asmara was officially closed in September 2006. Higher education
was henceforth to be provided by newly established colleges of higher
education, each associated with a relevant government ministry. In
2012 there were seven such colleges, providing education in the fields
of technology, health sciences, medicine and dental medicine, marine
sciences and technology, business and economics, arts and social
sciences, and agriculture. In 2009/10 there were 10,198 tertiary-level
students in Eritrea.

ESTONIA

Introductory Survey

LOCATION, CLIMATE, LANGUAGE, RELIGION, FLAG, CAPITAL

The Republic of Estonia is situated in north-eastern Europe. The country is bordered to the south by Latvia, and to the east by Russia. Estonia's northern coastline is on the Gulf of Finland, and its territory includes more than 1,520 islands, mainly off its western coastline in the Gulf of Rīga and the Baltic Sea. The largest of the islands are Saaremaa and Hiiumaa, in the Gulf of Rīga. The climate is influenced by Estonia's position between the Eurasian land mass and the Baltic Sea and the North Atlantic Ocean. The mean January temperature in Tallinn is −0.6°C (30.9°F); in July the mean temperature is 17.1°C (62.8°F). Average annual precipitation is 568 mm. The official language is Estonian, which is a member of the Baltic-Finnic group of the Finno-Ugric languages. Many of the Russian residents, who comprise around one-quarter of the total population, do not speak Estonian. Most of the population profess Christianity. By tradition, Estonians belong to the Evangelical Lutheran Church. Smaller Protestant sects and the Eastern Orthodox Church are also represented. The national flag (proportions 7 by 11) consists of three equal horizontal stripes, of blue, black and white. The capital is Tallinn.

CONTEMPORARY POLITICAL HISTORY

Historical Context

The Russian annexation of Estonia, formerly under Swedish rule, was formalized in 1721. In the late 19th century, as the powers of the dominant Baltic German nobility declined, Estonians experienced a national cultural revival, which culminated in political demands for autonomy during the 1905 Russian Revolution, and for full independence after the beginning of the First World War. In March 1917 the Provisional Government in Petrograd (St Petersburg), which had taken power after the abdication of Tsar Nicholas II, approved autonomy for Estonia. A Maapäev (Provisional Council) was elected as the country's representative body. However, in October the Bolsheviks staged a coup in Tallinn. As German forces advanced towards Estonia in early 1918, the Bolshevik troops were forced to leave. Major political parties united to form the Estonian Salvation Committee, and on 24 February an independent Republic of Estonia was proclaimed. A Provisional Government, headed by Konstantin Päts, was formed, but Germany refused to recognize Estonia's independence, and its troops occupied Estonia. Following Germany's capitulation in November, a Provisional Government assumed power. After a period of armed conflict, Estonia and Soviet Russia signed the Treaty of Tartu on 2 February 1920, under the terms of which the Soviet Government recognized Estonia's independence and renounced any rights to its territory. The major Western powers recognized Estonian independence in January 1921.

Independence lasted until 1940. During most of this time the country had a liberal democratic political system, in which the Riigikogu (State Assembly) was dominant. However, the economic depression of the 1930s caused public dissatisfaction. In March 1934 Prime Minister Päts seized power in a bloodless coup. The State Assembly and political parties were disbanded, but in 1938 a new Constitution was adopted, providing for a presidential system of government, with a bicameral legislature. In April 1938 Päts was elected President.

In August 1939 the USSR and Germany signed a non-aggression treaty (the Nazi-Soviet or Molotov-Ribbentrop Pact). The 'Secret Protocols' to the treaty provided for the occupation of Estonia (along with various other territories) by the USSR. In September Estonia was forced to sign an agreement permitting the USSR to base troops there. In June 1940 the Government resigned, and the Soviet authorities appointed a new administration. In July elections were held, in which only candidates approved by the Soviet authorities were permitted to participate. On 21 July the new legislature proclaimed an Estonian Soviet Socialist Republic, and on 6 August the Republic was formally incorporated into the USSR. Soviet rule in Estonia lasted less than one year, during which mass deportations of

Estonians, the expropriation of property and severe restrictions on cultural life ensued.

German forces entered Estonia in July 1941 and remained in occupation until September 1944. Thereafter, Soviet troops occupied the whole of the country, and the process of 'sovietization', including industrialization and the collectivization of agriculture, was resumed. Structural change in the economy was accompanied by increased political repression, and deportations of Estonians continued until the death of the Soviet leader Stalin (Iosif Dzhugashvili) in 1953. The most overt form of opposition to Soviet rule was provided by the 'forest brethren' (metsavennad) guerrilla movement, which conducted armed operations against Soviet personnel and institutions until the mid-1950s.

During the late 1970s and the 1980s the questions of 'russification' and environmental degradation became subjects of intense debate in Estonia. The policy of glasnost (openness), introduced by the Soviet leader, Mikhail Gorbachev, in 1986, allowed such discussion to spread beyond dissident groups. In August 1987 a demonstration attended by some 2,000 people commemorated the anniversary of the signing of the Nazi-Soviet Pact, and a pressure group demanding its publication was subsequently formed. In 1988 the Pact was duly published, and the group was reconstituted as the Eesti Rahvusliku Sõltumatuse Partei (ERSP—Estonian National Independence Party), which sought the restoration of Estonian independence. Another opposition association, the Eestimaa Rahvarinne (Rahvarinne—Popular Front of Estonia), which included many members of the ruling Eestimaa Kommunistlik Partei (EKP—Communist Party of Estonia), and which advocated the transformation of the USSR into a confederal system, held its first congress in October. On 16 November the Estonian Supreme Soviet (Supreme Council—legislature) adopted a declaration of sovereignty, which included the right to annul all-Union (USSR) legislation. The Presidium of the USSR Supreme Soviet ruled the declaration unconstitutional, but the Estonian Supreme Soviet affirmed its decision in December.

The adoption of Estonian as the state language was accepted by the Supreme Soviet in January 1989, and the tricolour of independent Estonia was reinstated as the official flag. Meanwhile, the ERSP refused to nominate candidates for elections to the all-Union Congress of People's Deputies in March, instead announcing plans for the registration by citizens' committees of all citizens of the 1918–40 Republic of Estonia and their descendants. Voters on an electoral register, thus compiled, would elect an Eesti Kongress (Estonian Congress) as the legal successor to the pre-1940 Estonian legislature. Rahvarinne, however, participated in the elections to the Congress of People's Deputies and won 27 of the 36 contested seats. Five seats were won by the Interliikumine/Interdvizheniye (Intermovement), a political group composed predominantly of ethnic Russians opposed to the growing influence of Estonian pro-independence movements. In October 1989 delegates at the second congress of Rahvarinne voted to adopt the restoration of Estonian independence as official policy. In November the Estonian Supreme Soviet voted to annul the 1940 decision to enter the USSR, declaring that the decision had been reached under coercion from Soviet armed forces.

On 2 February 1990 a mass rally was held to commemorate the anniversary of the 1920 Treaty of Tartu. Deputies attending the rally later met to approve a declaration urging the USSR Supreme Soviet to begin negotiations on restoring Estonia's independence. On 22 February the Estonian Supreme Soviet approved the declaration, and one day later voted to abolish the constitutional guarantee of power enjoyed by the EKP, thereby permitting largely free elections to take place to the Estonian Supreme Soviet in March. Rahvarinne won 43 of the 105 seats, 35 were won by pro-independence groups, and 27 by members allied to the Interliikumine/Interdvizheniye. Candidates belonging to the EKP, which was represented in all these groups, won 55 seats. At the first session of the new legislature, Arnold Rüütel, previously Chairman of the Presidium of the Supreme Soviet, was elected to the new post of Chairman of the Supreme Soviet, in which was vested those state powers that had been the preserve of the First Secretary of the EKP. On 30 March the Supreme Soviet adopted a declaration that proclaimed the beginning of a transitional period towards independence. In late February and early March 1990 some 580,000 people (excluding those who had migrated to Estonia after the Soviet occupation of 1940 and their descendants) took part in elections to the rival parliament to the Supreme Soviet, the Estonian Congress. The Congress convened on 11–12 March 1990 and declared itself the constitutional representative of the Estonian people. The participants adopted resolutions demanding the restoration of Estonian independence and the withdrawal of Soviet troops from Estonia.

Domestic Political Affairs

In April 1990 the Supreme Soviet elected Edgar Savisaar, a leader of Rahvarinne, Prime Minister, and on 8 May it voted to restore the first five articles of the 1938 Constitution, which described Estonia's independent status. The formal name of the Republic of Estonia, was also restored, as were the pre-1940 state emblems, flag and anthem. Although the Soviet authorities did not impose formal economic sanctions on Estonia (as they did with Lithuania), relations were severely strained. In May Gorbachev (recently appointed as the first President of the USSR) annulled Estonia's declaration of independence, declaring that it violated the USSR Constitution. He also refused requests for negotiations on the status of the Republic prior to the rescission of the declaration of independence.

When troops of the USSR's Ministry of the Interior attempted military intervention in the other Baltic republics (Latvia and Lithuania) in January 1991, the Estonian leadership anticipated similar confrontation. Barricades and makeshift defences were erected, but no military action was taken. Events in Latvia and Lithuania intensified popular distrust of Estonian involvement in a renewed union, and Estonia refused to participate in a referendum on the future of the USSR, which took place in nine of the republics in March. Instead, on 3 March the Estonian authorities conducted a poll on independence. According to the official results, 82.9% of the registered electorate took part, of whom 77.8% voted in favour of Estonian independence.

When the conservative communist 'State Committee for the State of Emergency' announced that it had seized power in the USSR on 19 August 1991, Estonia, together with the other Baltic republics, expected military intervention to overthrow the pro-independence Governments. Gen. Fedor Kuzmin, the Soviet commander of the Baltic military district, informed Rüütel that he was taking full control of Estonia. Military vehicles entered Tallinn on 20 August, and troops occupied the city's television station. The Estonian Supreme Council adopted a resolution declaring the full and immediate independence of Estonia. After it became evident, on 22 August 1991, that the Soviet coup had collapsed, the Government began to take measures against those who had supported it, while the Interliiku-mine/Interdvizheniye, the Kommunisticheskaya Partiya Sovetskogo Soyuza (Communist Party of the Soviet Union) and other pro-Soviet movements were banned in Estonia.

Consolidation of statehood

As the Estonian Government moved to assert its authority over former Soviet institutions, other countries recognized Estonian independence, including, on 6 September 1991, the USSR. Later in the month Estonia, together with the other Baltic states, was admitted to the UN, as well as to the Conference on Security and Co-operation in Europe (CSCE—later the Organization for Security and Co-operation in Europe—OSCE, see p. 385). During the remainder of 1991 Estonia established diplomatic relations with most major states and was offered membership of leading international organizations. Meanwhile, a Constitutional Assembly, comprising equal numbers of delegates from the Estonian Congress and the Supreme Council, was established. In January 1992, following a series of disputes with the Supreme Council, Savisaar resigned as Prime Minister and was replaced by the erstwhile Minister of Transport, Tiit Vähi. The Supreme Council approved a new Council of Ministers at the end of the month.

Some 91% of the electorate approved the draft Constitution in a referendum held in June 1992. Under the recently adopted Citizenship Law, only citizens of pre-1940 Estonia and their descendants, or those who had successfully applied for citizenship, were entitled to vote. This ruling drew strong criticism from Russian leaders, who were concerned that the rights of Estonia's large Russian minority were being violated. The new Constitution, which entered into force in July 1992, provided for a

parliamentary system of government, with a strong presidency. Elections to the new legislature, the State Assembly, were to be held in September, concurrently with a direct presidential election, although subsequent presidents were to be elected by the State Assembly.

Legislative and presidential elections were duly held on 20 September 1992, with the participation of some 67% of the electorate. The country's Russian and other ethnic minorities, who represented 42% of the total population at that time, were again barred from voting (with the exception of those whose applications for citizenship had been granted). The elections to the 101-seat State Assembly were contested by some 40 parties and movements, largely grouped into eight coalitions. The nationalist Isamaa (Pro Patria) alliance emerged with the largest number of seats (29). The Kindel Kodu (KK—Secure Home) alliance, comprising former communists, obtained 17 seats. The Rahvarinne-led centrist alliance won 15 seats. The Mõõdukad (Moderates) electoral alliance obtained 12 seats, and the ERSP won 10 seats. None of the four candidates in the presidential election won an overall majority of the votes. The State Assembly was thus required to choose from the two most successful candidates: Rüütel, now a leading member of KK, and Lennart Meri, a former Minister of Foreign Affairs, who was supported by Isamaa. In early October the State Assembly elected Meri as Estonia's President. A new coalition Government, comprising members of Isamaa, Mõõdukad and the ERSP and headed by Mart Laar, the leader of Isamaa, was announced in October. Laar indicated that the principal objectives of his administration would be to negotiate the withdrawal of all Russian troops remaining in Estonia, and to accelerate a programme of privatization. In November four of the five constituent parties of the Isamaa alliance united to form the Rahvuslik Koonderakond Isamaa (RKI—National Pro Patria Party), under Laar's leadership.

In November 1993 Laar survived a vote of no confidence in the State Assembly. Also in November, Rahvarinne was disbanded. In May–June 1994 four ministers resigned. Defections from the Isamaa faction within the State Assembly resulted in Laar's supporters retaining control of only 19 seats in the legislature by September. Following the revelation that Laar had contravened an agreement with the IMF, the State Assembly endorsed a vote of no confidence in the Prime Minister. In October Andres Tarand, hitherto Minister of the Environment, was appointed to replace Laar. A new Council of Ministers, including representatives of the RKI, Mõõdukad, the ERSP and liberal and right-wing parties, was announced in November.

The results of the legislative elections, held on 5 March 1995, reflected widespread popular dissatisfaction with the parties of the governing coalition. The largest number of seats in the State Assembly (41 of 101) was won by an alliance of the centrist Eesti Koonderakond (Estonian Coalition Party, led by Vähi) and the Eesti Maarahva Erakond (EME—Estonian Rural Union, in which Rüütel was a prominent figure). A coalition of the newly established Eesti Reformierakond (ER—Estonian Reform Party, led by Siim Kallas, the President of the Bank of Estonia) and liberal groups obtained 19 seats, followed by Savisaar's Eesti Keskerakond (EK—Estonian Centre Party, with 16). The RKI (in coalition with the ERSP) won only eight seats, while the Mõõdukad alliance obtained six seats. The Nash Dom—Estoniya/Meie Kodu on Eestimaa (Our Home is Estonia) alliance, representing the Russian-speaking minority, won six seats. Almost 70% of the registered electorate participated.

Vähi was confirmed as Prime Minister by the legislature in April 1995, and the new Government—a coalition of the Eesti Koonderakond, the EME and the EK—was appointed later in the month. However, the Government survived only until early October, when it was revealed that Savisaar, the Minister of the Interior, had made clandestine recordings of conversations with other politicians concerning the formation of a new coalition government. After the EK refused to accept the dismissal by Vähi of Savisaar, Vähi and the remaining members of the Council of Ministers tendered their resignations. President Meri reappointed Vähi as Prime Minister, and a coalition Government, comprising members of the Eesti Koonderakond, the EME and the ER, was formed in late October. In December the RKI and the ERSP merged to form the Isamaaliit (Pro Patria Union).

A presidential election was held in the State Assembly on 26 August 1996, contested by the incumbent, Meri, and Rüütel. Following two further inconclusive rounds of voting, a larger electoral college, comprising the 101 legislative deputies and 273 representatives of local government, was convened on 20 September. As none of the five candidates contesting the election secured an overall majority, a further round of voting was held to choose between the leading candidates, Meri and Rüütel. Meri won the election, with 52% of the votes cast, and in October he was sworn in for a second presidential term.

In October 1996, following local government elections, the ER gained control of Tallinn city government. In November the Eesti Koonderakond concluded a co-operation agreement with the EK. Disagreements among the coalition partners led to the collapse of the city leadership, and Savisaar was appointed as Chairman of the city government, replacing the recently elected ER candidate. The ER threatened to leave the Government unless the co-operation agreement with the EK was cancelled, and in November six ministers, including Kallas (hitherto the Minister for Foreign Affairs), resigned, causing the collapse of the ruling coalition. A minority Government, comprising the Eesti Koonderakond, the EME and independent members, was appointed in December. In early 1997 a series of allegations of abuse of office was made against Vähi. Although a legislative motion of no confidence, presented by the leaders of four opposition parties, was defeated by a narrow margin, Vähi tendered his resignation in February. Mart Siimann, the leader of the Eesti Koonderakond parliamentary faction, was appointed Prime Minister. In March a new minority Government, again comprising the Eesti Koonderakond, the EME and independent members, was appointed. In September Vähi announced his resignation from the Eesti Koonderakond and his retirement from political life; Siimann became the new party Chairman.

The 1999 legislative elections

At legislative elections held on 7 March 1999, the EK won 28 of the 101 seats; the ER and Isamaaliit each secured 18 seats, Mõõdukad (in alliance with the Eesti Rahvaerakond—People's Party) 17, the EME seven and the Eestimaa Ühendatud Rahvapartei (United People's Party of Estonia) six. Just 57.4% of the electorate participated in the polls. Although the EK obtained the largest number of seats, it was unable to assemble a majority. A centre-right coalition Government was thus formed by the ER, Isamaaliit and Mõõdukad; Laar, now leader of Isamaaliit, was appointed Prime Minister.

In May 1999 it was announced that some 300,000 non-citizens permanently resident in Estonia (principally ethnic Russians) were to be allowed to participate in local elections to be held in October. At the elections, the governing ER-Isamaaliit-Mõõdukad alliance obtained control of 13 of Estonia's 15 county governments, and, in alliance with representatives of the Russian population, of Tallinn City Council, where Jüri Mõis was appointed Mayor, after resigning as Minister of the Interior. In November Mõõdukad and the Eesti Rahvaerakond merged to form the Rahvaerakond Mõõdukad (RM—Moderate People's Party). In June 2000 a new party, the Eestimaa Rahvaliit (Estonian People's Union), was formed by the merger of the EME and two smaller parties. Mõis resigned in May 2001, after being threatened with a fifth confidence vote. A member of Isamaaliit, Tõnis Palts, was elected as his successor.

Inconclusive rounds of voting in the presidential election took place in the State Assembly on 27–28 August 2001. The first round of the election was contested by Tarand of the RM and Peeter Kreitzberg of the opposition EK. Tarand was replaced as the candidate of the ruling coalition by Peeter Tulviste of Isamaaliit in the second and third rounds of voting, but neither candidate emerged as the victor. An electoral college, composed of the 101 parliamentary deputies and 266 representatives of local government, was therefore convened on 21 September. Toomas Savi, of the governing ER, and Rüütel, now the Honorary Chairman of Eestimaa Rahvaliit, emerged as the candidates with the greatest number of votes and progressed to a second round. Rüütel eventually emerged as the victor in the 'run-off' election, in which he secured 186 votes. He was sworn in as President on 8 October.

In December 2001 the ER announced that it was to leave the Tallinn city Government. It subsequently signed a coalition agreement with the EK, in what was widely regarded as an attempt to distance itself from the increasingly unpopular national Government, of which it remained a part. Palts was forced to resign as Mayor, when a censure motion, brought by members of the EK, was approved by a significant majority. His Isamaaliit left the city Government, and Savisaar was elected as Mayor of Tallinn in mid-December. These developments prompted Prime Minister Laar's Government to resign on 8 January 2002. In mid-January the EK and the ER signed an agreement on the formation of an interim, coalition government, despite their contrasting political ideals; eight ministers were to be appointed from the EK and six from the ER. The parties of the coalition held fewer than one-half of the seats in the State Assembly and, therefore, required the support of Eestimaa Rahvaliit. On 22 January Kallas of the ER was approved as Prime Minister.

Following a ruling by the Supreme Court prohibiting the formation of electoral blocs, in July 2002 the State Assembly voted to permit their existence until 2005, in order to avoid a delay in holding the forthcoming local elections. The elections duly took place in October 2002. Parties represented in the national Government won the majority of the votes cast. In November Savisaar was re-elected as Mayor of Tallinn. Meanwhile, in response to their parties' poor performance, in late October Toomas Hendrik Ilves, a former Minister of Foreign Affairs, resigned as Chairman of the RM, and Laar resigned the chairmanship of Isamaaliit.

Eleven parties participated in the parliamentary elections held on 2 March 2003, in which the EK received 25.4% of the votes cast and 28 seats in the 101-member State Assembly. The conservative Res Publica party (founded in 2001) obtained 24.6% and 28 seats, and the ER took 17.7% and 19 seats; Eestimaa Rahvaliit, Isamaaliit and the RM also secured representation in the State Assembly. The level of participation by the electorate was 58.2%. Although the EK secured the largest number of votes cast, Res Publica, the ER and Eestimaa Rahvaliit reached agreement on the formation of an administration. After Savisaar declined the President's offer to form a government, Juhan Parts, the leader of Res Publica, was nominated as Prime Minister, and the new coalition Government was approved on 9 April. In September the Minister of Finance, Palts, resigned, after an investigation was initiated into allegations of tax evasion. In February 2004 the RM changed its name to the Sotsiaaldemokraatlik Erakond (SDE—Estonian Social Democratic Party).

Accession to the European Union

Following Estonia's accession to the European Union (EU, see p. 271) in May 2004 (see *Regional relations*), in the following month the country took part in its first elections to the European Parliament. In October Savisaar resigned as Mayor of Tallinn, following a vote of no confidence in the City Council. He was replaced by Palts. In November Margus Hanson resigned as Minister of Defence, following the theft from his home of classified documents. (After his immunity from prosecution was removed, in November 2005 he was fined for negligence.) Also in November 2004 Andrus Ansip, the new Minister of the Economy and Communications, was elected Chairman of the ER, replacing Kallas, who had been appointed as the country's representative to the European Commission. In December the EK apparently sought to increase its support among the ethnic Russian population of Estonia, controversially signing a co-operation agreement with the de facto ruling party of Russia, Yedinaya Rossiya (United Russia). As a consequence, EK members who supported closer co-operation and integration with the EU left the party; by the end of January 2005 the party's faction in the State Assembly had diminished from 28 to 19 members.

The Minister of Foreign Affairs, Kristiina Ojuland, was dismissed in February 2005, after a security audit revealed the disappearance of 91 classified documents. On 21 March the State Assembly adopted a motion of no confidence in Minister of Justice Ken-Marti Vaher. Three days later Parts announced the resignation of his Government. On 31 March the EK, the ER and Eestimaa Rahvaliit agreed to form a coalition. Ansip was nominated to lead a new Government, which was sworn into office on 13 April. Municipal elections took place on 16 October (in which, for the first time, voting was permitted online). The EK won 25.5% of the votes cast nationwide, followed by the ER, Eestimaa Rahvaliit and Isamaaliit; Res Publica won just 8.5% of the ballot, compared with 15.2% in 2002. In the elections to the mayoralty of Tallinn, the EK won some 41% of the votes cast; in November Juri Ratas of the party was elected Mayor, succeeding the party's Chairman, Savisaar, who chose to retain his post as Minister of Economic Affairs and Communications.

In August 2006 the EK and Eestimaa Rahvaliit signed an agreement pledging their support for the candidacy of Rüütel in the forthcoming presidential election, scheduled to take place in the State Assembly later that month. However, the two parties subsequently announced that they were to boycott the ballot after Rüütel announced that he would seek re-election only if the vote was decided by the electoral college system. In the initial ballot, held on 28 August, former Speaker of the legislature Ene Ergma, the sole candidate, attracted 65 votes, narrowly failing to secure the required two-thirds' majority (68 votes). Two further rounds of voting proved similarly inconclusive, with Ergma's sole competitor, Ilves, securing 64 votes in each round. Responsibility for electing the President thus passed to the electoral college, which duly convened on 23 September and voted for Ilves over Rüütel by a margin of 174 to 162; Ilves was inaugurated on 9 October. Also in October Isamaaliit and Res Publica formally merged to form the Isamaa ja Res Publica Liit (IRL—Union of Pro Patria and Res Publica), which was co-chaired by Tõnis Lukas, hitherto Chairman of Isamaaliit, and Taavi Veskimägi, hitherto Chairman of Res Publica.

Legislative elections were held on 4 March 2007, with the participation of 61.9% of the electorate. Estonia was the first country to introduce internet voting at a national legislative election, although only a small proportion of the electorate chose to vote online. The ER was the most successful party, winning 31 seats and 27.8% of the votes cast, narrowly followed by the EK, with 29 seats and 26.1% of the votes. The IRL secured 19 seats and 17.9% of the votes, the SDE 10 seats and 10.6% of the votes. The Erakond Eestimaa Rohelised (Estonian Greens) and Eestimaa Rahvaliit each obtained six seats and 7.1% of the votes. As in 2003, the EK, despite its strong performance in the polls, was excluded from the new Government. In late March 2007 the ER, the IRL and the SDE announced that they had agreed to form a centre-right coalition commanding 60 of the 101 seats in the State Assembly. A new Government, again under the premiership of Ansip, was installed on 4 April. Urmas Paet of the ER was retained as Minister of Foreign Affairs; Jüri Pihl of the SDE was awarded the interior portfolio, while Jaak Aaviksoo of the IRL became Minister of Defence. On 5 April Savisaar was elected as Mayor of Tallinn, replacing Ratas, who had been elected as a Vice-Speaker of the State Assembly.

Following divisions within the ruling coalition parties, in February 2009 the Government secured the approval of the State Assembly for a supplementary budget further curtailing expenditure for the year; the adoption of austerity measures, which included a 10% reduction in public sector salaries, was linked to a vote of confidence in Ansip's administration. Also in February, the head of the security department at the Estonian Ministry of Defence during 2000–06, Herman Simm, pleaded guilty to treason and was sentenced to 12 and a half years' imprisonment for having reportedly passed classified military documents to the Russian Foreign Intelligence Service.

Ansip dismissed the three SDE ministers from the governing coalition in May 2009, after disagreements over unemployment benefits and further proposals aimed at improving the country's fiscal position. Following the failure of talks to bring Eestimaa Rahvaliit into the ruling coalition to replace the SDE, the ER and the IRL continued in office as a minority administration. In early June Jürgen Ligi of the ER and Marko Pomerants of the IRL were appointed Minister of Finance and Minister of the Interior, respectively.

At elections to the European Parliament held on 7 June 2009, the EK obtained two of the country's six seats, winning 26.1% of the votes cast. An independent candidate, Indrek Tarand, secured a seat, having received 25.8% of the votes cast, while the ER, the IRL and the SDE also each took one seat. The elections were notable for the poor performance of the SDE, which had been the most successful party in the 2004 European polls, when it had won three seats. The voter turnout, at 43.9%, was markedly higher than in 2004 (26.8%). The EK was also victorious in municipal elections conducted on 18 October 2009, securing 31.2% of the votes cast nationwide. The ER won 16.8% of the votes and the IRL obtained 14.1%. In Tallinn, the EK won 53.3% of the votes cast in elections the City Council, with Savisaar re-elected as Mayor. From mid-December 2010 Savisaar, as both Mayor of Tallinn and Chairman of the EK, became the focus of a political scandal, after he was accused of receiving illegal donations for his party, notably from the President of Russian Railways, Vladimir Yakunin, a close ally of the Russian premier (and former, and subsequent, President), Vladimir Putin.

Ansip's final term as Prime Minister

At elections to the State Assembly on 6 March 2011, the ER received 28.6% of the votes cast and 33 seats. The EK secured 23.3% of the votes and 26 seats, while the IRL won 20.5% of the votes and 23 seats, and the SDE 17.1% of the votes and 19 seats. The rate of participation was 63.5% of the electorate. Following an agreement between the ER and the IRL to continue their governing coalition, on 5 April Ansip subsequently appointed a new Government, in which several of the senior positions

remained unchanged, while Laar was appointed Minister of Defence.

In August 2011 a member of the Eestimaa Ühendatud Vasakpartei (Estonian United Left Party), which sought to represent the interests of the Russian minority, attempted to take hostage staff members in the offices of the Ministry of Defence in Tallinn. The gunman opened fire inside the building before he was shot and killed by police. In December it emerged that two elected officials of the IRL—a parliamentary deputy and a member of Tallinn City Council—had engaged in the illicit sale of Estonian residence permits to entrepreneurs from Russia and other countries of the Commonwealth of Independent States. The two officials were expelled from the party, while two IRL ministers—Vaher (Minister of the Interior) and Parts (Minister of Economic Affairs and Communications)—who were also allegedly implicated in the case, were to be subject to a vote of confidence from the party's ruling council. (The retention of both ministers was endorsed later in the month.)

In January 2012 Urmas Reinsalu was elected leader of the IRL, replacing Laar. In February Laar was hospitalized, after suffering a stroke, and in May Reinsalu also assumed responsibility for his ministerial defence portfolio. Meanwhile, in March the Eestimaa Rahvaliit renamed itself the Eesti Konservatiivseks Rahvaerakonnaks (EKRE—Estonian Conservative People's Party).

In March 2012 some 16,000 teachers participated in three days of strike action in support of an increase in salaries. The action followed a year of rapid economic growth (the fastest in the EU), while Estonia was for the second year running the only euro area country to record a budgetary surplus, following public sector pay freezes. In October doctors and nurses across Estonia began strike action over poor working conditions and salaries, arguing that many healthcare staff had already left the country as a result. The strike ended later in the month, after wage increases had been agreed by the Government.

In December 2012 Kristen Michal of the ER resigned as Minister of Justice; in the previous year his alleged involvement in an apparent scheme of illicit party funding had resulted in a criminal investigation being opened against him, although the charges were subsequently dropped. He was succeeded by the erstwhile Minister of Social Affairs, Hanno Pevkur, who was, in turn, replaced by Taavi Rõivas, also of the ER. Public outrage over the party financing allegations resulted in the establishment, at the initiative of President Ilves, of a People's Assembly (Rahvakogu) website, through which citizens could make suggestions regarding the electoral system, political parties and the role of civil society. In April 2013 Ilves presented 16 of the People's Assembly's legislative proposals to the State Assembly for consideration, including a proposed reduction of the threshold required for parties to obtain representation in legislative elections from 5% to 3% of the votes cast, and for reducing the minimum membership required of registered political parties from 1,000 to 200. Among numerous other proposals presented by the People's Assembly that Ilves did not present for legislative consideration was one providing for direct popular election of the country's President.

On 4 March 2014 Ansip tendered his resignation as Prime Minister, in order that his ER could provide a continuity of leadership before and after the legislative elections due to be held one year later. On 14 March Ilves nominated Rõivas, as Prime Minister. After Rõivas negotiated a new coalition between the ER and the SDE, the State Assembly voted in favour of his appointment on 24 March, and a new Council of Ministers assumed office two days later.

In elections to the European Parliament, which were conducted on 25 May 2014, the ER secured 24.3% of the votes cast and two seats, while the EK obtained 22.4% of the votes and one seat, the IRL 13.9% and one seat, the SDE 13.6% and one seat, and an independent candidate 13.2% and one seat. The rate of participation by the electorate was 36.4%.

Recent developments: the 2015 legislative elections

On 3 November 2014 Paet, the long-serving Minister of Foreign Affairs, resigned, in order to assume office as a Member of the European Parliament. He was succeeded later in the month by Keit Pentus-Rosimannus of ER, the erstwhile Minister of the Environment, who was in turn replaced by Mati Raidma. Meanwhile, also on 3 November Ligi resigned as Minister of Finance, in response to a public outcry to online criticism he had made of the Minister of Education and Research, Jevgeni Ossinovski, including comments that appeared critical of his Russian-

Estonian ethnic origins. On the same day Ligi was succeeded by Maris Lauri.

Campaigning for the March 2015 legislative elections was dominated by responses to Russia's annexation of the Crimean peninsula, ostensibly 'to protect its Russian-speaking population', in March 2014 and the subsequent conflict in the Donetsk and Luhansk oblasts (regions) of eastern Ukraine, with the presence of a predominately Russian-speaking population in certain areas of Estonia bordering Russia being a particular cause of concern: the governing coalition had urged decisive reprisals by the West, while EK leader Savisaar (who had established the party's 2004 co-operation agreement with Yedinaya Rossiya), favoured closer relations with Russia and refused to criticize its actions. The elections to the State Assembly took place on 1 March 2015, with public electronic voting again organized beforehand; some 33.0% of the electorate cast votes online during 19–25 February, compared with 27.4% in the 2011 elections. The ER, although demonstrating a slight loss in support, was again the largest party in the State Assembly, with 27.7% of the votes cast and 30 seats, ahead of the EK, which secured 24.8% and 27 seats. The SDE received 15.2% of the votes and 15 seats, the IRL 13.7% and 14 seats, the newly established, centre-right Eesti Vabaerakond (Estonian Free Democratic Party) 8.7% and eight seats, and the EKRE 8.1% and seven seats. An overall participation rate of 64.2% of the electorate was recorded. Rõivas subsequently began negotiations on the formation of a new coalition Government. In March it was announced that Savisaar had been hospitalized with a critical bacterial infection. Later in the month the formation of a coalition comprising the ER, the SRE and the IRL was announced, and on 9 April the State Assembly approved the formation of a new Government, again headed by Rõivas, and comprising seven representatives of ER and four of each of the other two coalition partners. Several of the principal posts in the outgoing administration were unchanged, including Pentus-Rosimannus as Minister of Foreign Affairs, Sven Mikser of SDE as Minister of Defence, and Pevkur as Minister of the Interior.

Foreign Affairs

Regional relations

Estonia pursues close relations with its Baltic neighbours, Latvia and Lithuania. In late 1991 the three states established a consultative interparliamentary body, the Baltic Assembly, with the aim of developing political and economic co-operation. The Baltic Assembly has maintained close links with the Nordic Council, and Estonia is also a member of the Council of the Baltic Sea States (see p. 249), established in March 1992. In January 2007 the Baltic states agreed to establish a joint Baltic battalion (under Lithuanian command), which would participate in the North Atlantic Treaty Organization (NATO, see p. 367) Response Force from January 2010 (a joint Baltic battalion had previously operated in 1994–2003); another such battalion, under Estonian command, was planned to operate within the NATO Response Force by 2016. Meanwhile, meeting in Vilnius, Lithuania, in 2009, the three Baltic Prime Ministers signed a declaration on the implementation of joint energy infrastructure projects, and the three countries established a common Nordic-Baltic energy market, which became fully functional in June 2013. Moreover, in February 2014, the combined region entered into a single energy trading market encompassing 15 countries, with the completion in that month, of the 650 MW Estlink II undersea interconnector cable between Estonia and Finland being a particularly important development, while the installation of a third electrical cable connecting Estonia and Latvia was projected for 2020. Meanwhile, despite a joint commitment between Estonia, Lithuania, Latvia and Poland to construct a 1,300-MW nuclear power plant at Visaginas in Lithuania, development subsequently stalled. The construction of a fast inter-Baltic passenger railway, Rail Baltica, with EU funding, necessitating the conversion of existing railway lines from the broader Russian gauge, to standard European dimensions, was scheduled for completion in 2024. In January 2015 the Estonian Ministry of Foreign Affairs summoned the Finnish ambassador in Tallinn to protest at criticism voiced by the Finnish Minister of Foreign Affairs of Estonia's efforts to combat Russian propaganda (amid the continuing conflict in eastern Ukraine—see below), in relation to a joint initiative by the Estonian, Lithuanian, Danish and British foreign ministers to submit proposals to the EU for a common action plan. In this context, it was announced in February 2015 that a new Russian-language television channel established by supporters of the Russian

and Belarusian opposition-in-exile, aru.tv, had commenced operations in Tallinn.

Since the restoration of Estonian independence in 1991, the republic's relations with Russia have been strained by a number of questions, most notably the presence of former Soviet troops and the rights of the large Russian minority in Estonia (equivalent to 25.3% of the population at January 2014, according to official estimates). At the dissolution of the USSR in 1991, several thousand former Soviet troops remained stationed (under Russian command) on Estonian territory. Their withdrawal commenced in 1992, but the Russian leadership increasingly linked the progress of the troop withdrawals with the question of the citizenship, and other rights, of the Russian-speaking minority in Estonia. In July 1994 a bilateral agreement was reached, awarding civil and social guarantees to all Russian military pensioners in Estonia. The withdrawal of former Soviet troops was completed in August.

Under the Citizenship Law of 1992 non-ethnic Estonians who settled in the republic after its annexation by the USSR in 1940, and their descendants, were obliged to apply for naturalization. Many of the requirements for naturalization—including an examination in the Estonian language—were criticized by the Russian Government. A new citizenship law, adopted in January 1995, gave non-citizens until July to apply for residence and work permits, by which time almost 330,000 people (more than 80% of the total number of non-citizens) had submitted applications. The deadline was extended until November 1996, while by October of that year some 110,000 people resident in Estonia had taken Russian citizenship. In December 1998 the State Assembly approved legislation requiring elected officials to demonstrate sufficient command of Estonian to participate in the basic bureaucratic procedures of office. The legislation became effective in May 1999, and on 1 July a further amendment to the Language Law, pertaining to those employed in the services sector, came into force. In April 2000, following a statement by the OSCE High Commissioner on National Minorities that the language legislation contradicted international standards on freedom of expression, the law was amended, to make knowledge of Estonian compulsory only where it was deemed necessary for the sake of public interest. In November 2001 the requirement that electoral candidates be able to speak Estonian was abolished, although legislation adopted in the same month made Estonian the official language of parliament.

A further cause of tension in Estonian–Russian relations concerned Estonia's demand for the return of some 2,000 sq km (770 sq miles) of territory that had been ceded to Russia in 1944. In June 1994 Russian President Boris Yeltsin ordered the unilateral demarcation of Russia's border with Estonia according to the post-1944 boundary. During 1995 Estonia abandoned its demand for the return of the disputed territories. Instead, Estonia appealed only for minor amendments to be made to the existing line of demarcation; more importantly, it insisted that Russia recognize the 1920 Treaty of Tartu (in which Russia recognized Estonia's independence) as the basis of future relations between the two countries. However, the Russian Government maintained that the Treaty had lost its legal force, having been superseded by the declaration on bilateral relations signed by Russia and Estonia in 1991. In September 2000, as part of the country's preparations for EU membership, Estonia decreed that from 2001 a full visa regime would come into effect for Russian citizens. Further tensions arose in December 2003, when the State Assembly approved legislation preventing Russian military pensioners from obtaining permanent residency in Estonia.

President Rüütel refused an invitation from Russian President Vladimir Putin to attend celebrations in Moscow, the Russian capital, on 9 May 2005, commemorating the 60th anniversary of the end of the Second World War in Europe, on the grounds that, for Estonia, it marked the beginning of almost 50 years of Soviet occupation. However, on 18 May the Ministers of Foreign Affairs of Estonia and Russia signed a border agreement. The treaty was ratified by the State Assembly two days later, but the addition of a preamble making reference to the Soviet occupation of Estonia prompted Russia to revoke the agreement and demand renewed negotiations.

The approval, in February 2007, of legislation by the State Assembly providing for the relocation of a Soviet war monument in Tallinn, together with draft legislation proposing a ban on politically motivated public displays of Soviet and Nazi symbols in Estonia, provoked intense indignation from the Russian Government. When the monument was dismantled, in April, pending its relocation, several days of rioting ensued in Tallinn, as a result of which at least one person was killed and several hundred injured; at least 800 people were arrested. The Russian state-sponsored youth organization, Nashi (Our Own), blockaded the Estonian embassy. In May Russia's state railway monopoly announced the suspension of deliveries of petroleum products to Estonia, purportedly on the grounds that it planned to carry out maintenance of the rail link to Estonia. The Estonian Minister of Foreign Affairs also claimed that elements in the Russian administration were responsible for a series of 'cyberattacks' against the internet sites of Estonian government ministries, agencies and companies. (In March 2009 an activist with Nashi claimed that he and other members of the organization had organized these attacks.) Along with its fellow Baltic states, Estonia adopted a stance supportive of Georgia during that country's conflict with Russia in August 2008.

As Russia's relations with the USA and the EU began to improve in 2010, the tension with Estonia also gradually began to ease. President Ilves made a strongly symbolic gesture by attending Russia's Victory Day parade (commemorating the end of the Second World War) in the capital Moscow on 9 May—the first occasion an Estonian President had done so. In 2012 the foreign affairs committees of the Estonian State Assembly and the Russian State Duma resumed contact for the first time in several years. The first visit of an Estonian Prime Minister to Russia in over a decade took place in April 2013, and in June Kirill (Gundyayev), the Patriarch of Moscow and all Rus, visited Estonia.

Meanwhile, in September 2012 Russian Minister of Foreign Affairs Sergei Lavrov expressed his country's wish to resume border treaty negotiations. In the following month all factions in the State Assembly agreed to reopen border talks. On 18 February 2014 Estonian Minister of Foreign Affairs Urmas Paet and Lavrov met in Moscow, when a revised border agreement between Russia and Estonia was finally signed; before it could enter into effect, the treaty was to be ratified by the legislature of both countries. In addition, Lavrov was invited to visit Estonia, in what would constitute the first visit by a Russian Minister of Foreign Affairs to the country. However, Russia's annexation of the Crimean peninsula in March and the reported involvement of Russian military personnel in the subsequent conflict in parts of eastern Ukraine (see the chapter on Ukraine) prompted heightened concerns in the Baltic states; the Estonian Government appealed to the international community to respond decisively to Russia's annexation of Crimea, which was considered to be in breach of international law. Meanwhile, the State Assembly suspended ratification of the border treaty until the Russian legislature also initiated its ratification process. The Estonian Government announced that it was to reinforce its troop presence and monitoring on the border with Russia, after an Estonian security service officer, Eston Kohver, was detained by Russian troops in September. (The Estonian authorities claimed that Kohver had been abducted from Estonian territory, while Russia claimed that he had crossed the border.) In early 2015 the Estonian Government continued to express support for the imposition of more stringent sanctions against Russia.

In 2012 the Estonian Government denied permission to Nord Stream—a consortium including Gazprom of Russia and Wintershall AG of Germany—to conduct studies in the Baltic Sea (including within Estonian territorial waters) for the eventual construction of a possible two further natural gas pipelines to run between Russia and Germany. (The second of the two existing pipelines was inaugurated in October.) Estonian Minister of Defence Reinsalu had argued that the pipelines could pose further strategic and security threats, despite assurances that Nord Stream's request was not motivated by Russian intentions to use the pipelines to influence Estonia's politics.

An important focus of Estonia's foreign policy was the attainment of full membership of the EU. In July 1995 Estonia became an associate member, and in October 2002 the European Commission named 10 countries, including Estonia, as ready to join the EU in 2004. A national referendum was held on 14 September 2003, in which voters were asked whether they supported Estonia's proposed accession to the EU and the adoption of legislation amending the country's Constitution; 66.8% of the votes cast by 64.1% of the electorate were in favour of Estonia's accession, which duly took effect on 1 May 2004. Meanwhile, in December 2007 Estonia, together with eight other nations, implemented the EU's Schengen Agreement, enabling its citizens to travel to and from other signatory states without border controls. The EU Treaty of Lisbon was ratified by the State

Assembly in June 2008. Meanwhile, in June 2004 Estonia was one of three new EU member states (alongside Lithuania and Slovenia) to be admitted to the exchange rate mechanism (ERM II) as a precursor to adopting the common European currency, the euro; the Estonian Government subsequently announced that it intended to adopt the euro by January 2007. However, in April 2006 the Government acknowledged that it would not be in a position to meet this deadline. In March 2009 the Government approved a new deadline of January 2011 for euro adoption. As a result of the Government's successful fiscal programme, the European Commission announced in May 2010 that Estonia had met the necessary economic criteria to adopt the euro; on 13 July EU ministers of finance endorsed Estonia's membership of the eurozone. Estonia thus formally adopted the common European currency on 1 January 2011, becoming the first Baltic state to do so. Estonia voted to join the European Financial Stability Facility (EFSF) at the end of September. The treaty establishing the European Stability Mechanism (ESM—supporting the provision of financial assistance to eurozone members that found themselves in financial difficulty), which the Government signed in February 2012, was ratified by the State Assembly on 30 August, after the Supreme Court ruled in favour of its constitutionality following a legal challenge.

Other external relations

Estonia joined NATO's 'Partnership for Peace' programme of military co-operation in March 1994. In November 2002, at a NATO summit meeting held in Prague, Czech Republic, Estonia was one of seven countries to be invited formally to accede to the Alliance, and became a full member on 29 March 2004. In November 2006 US President George W. Bush became the first US Head of State to visit Estonia, accompanied by US Secretary of State Condoleezza Rice; speaking at a joint press conference, Bush thanked President Ilves for the Estonian Government's support in the US-led 'war on terror'. In June 2007 President Ilves made an official visit to the USA, during which President Bush endorsed the Estonian Government's proposal for the establishment of a NATO 'cyber-defence' research centre in Tallinn, with US participation. In May 2008 the NATO Co-operative Cyber Defence Centre of Excellence was established in Tallinn. In November Estonia joined the USA's programme for visa-free travel.

In February 2012 NATO extended its Baltic air-policing mission (initiated in 2004) over Lithuania, Latvia and Estonia until 2018. Following the Russian annexation of Crimea in March 2014, NATO member states for the first time deployed fighter aircraft at the newly opened Ämari airbase in Estonia as part of its Baltic air-policing mission. In April the USA stationed 150 troops in Estonia (and in the other Baltic states) to begin land forces training. US President Barack Obama visited Tallinn in September, when he issued assurances regarding regional security. In February 2015 NATO announced plans to establish an expanded rapid reaction force, under which new NATO command centres were to be installed in Estonia and five other Eastern European states. US and NATO forces participated in Estonia's Independence Day military parade on 24 February, held in the eastern border town of Narva, while Russian armed forces at the same time conducted exercises in the region bordering Estonia and Latvia.

CONSTITUTION AND GOVERNMENT

A new Constitution, based on that of 1938, was adopted by a referendum held on 28 June 1992 and took effect on 3 July. Legislative authority resides with the Riigikogu (State Assembly), which has 101 members, elected by universal adult suffrage for a four-year term. The State Assembly elects the President (Head of State) for a term of five years. The President is also Supreme Commander of Estonia's armed forces. Executive power is held by the Council of Ministers, which is headed by the Prime Minister, who is nominated by the President. Judicial power is exercised by the Supreme Court, district courts and rural and city, as well as administrative, courts. For administrative purposes, Estonia is divided into 15 counties (*maakonds*), which in turn are subdivided into cities, rural municipalities and towns.

REGIONAL AND INTERNATIONAL CO-OPERATION

Estonia is a member of the Council of the Baltic Sea States (see p. 249), of the Baltic Council (see p. 459), of the Council of Europe (see p. 250), and of the Organization for Security and Co-operation in Europe (see p. 385). In 2004 it acceded to the European Union (see p. 271).

Estonia joined the UN in 1991, and was admitted to the World Trade Organization (see p. 431) in 1999 and to the Organisation for Economic Co-operation and Development (see p. 377) in 2010. The country is a member of the North Atlantic Treaty Organization (NATO, see p. 367) and hosts the NATO Cooperative Cyber Defence Centre of Excellence, which was established in 2008.

ECONOMIC AFFAIRS

In 2013, according to World Bank estimates, Estonia's gross national income (GNI), measured at average 2011–13 prices, was US $23,005m., equivalent to $17,370 per head (or $24,230 per head on an international purchasing-power parity basis). During 2004–13, according to World Bank estimates, the population declined at an average annual rate of 0.3%, while gross domestic product (GDP) per head increased, in real terms, by an average of 2.8% per year. Overall GDP increased, in real terms, at an average annual rate of 2.5% during 2004–13. According to chain-linked methodologies, real GDP increased by 4.7% in 2012 and by only 1.6% in 2013.

Agriculture (including hunting, forestry and fishing) contributed 3.6% of GDP and engaged 4.3% of the employed labour force in 2013. Animal husbandry is the main activity in the agricultural sector. Some 27.4% of Estonia's land is cultivable. The principal crops are barley, wheat, rapeseed, potatoes and fruit and vegetables. Forestry products are also important. During 2004–13, according to World Bank estimates, agricultural GDP grew, in real terms, at an average annual rate of 2.7%. According to chain-linked methodologies, the GDP of the sector increased by 16.6% in 2012, but decreased by 3.9% in 2013.

Industry (including mining and quarrying, manufacturing, construction, and power) contributed 28.9% of GDP and engaged 30.2% of the employed labour force in 2013. During 2004–13, according to World Bank estimates, industrial GDP increased, in real terms, at an average annual rate of 3.6%; industrial GDP increased by 1.4% in 2013.

Mining and quarrying contributed 1.3% of GDP and engaged 0.8% of the employed labour force in 2013. Estonia's principal mineral resource is oil shale, and there are also deposits of peat, phosphorite ore, limestone and granite. There are total estimated reserves of oil shale of some 4,000m. metric tons. Extraction of oil shale was 20.5m. tons in 2013, compared with some 31m. tons in 1980. Phosphorite ore is processed to produce phosphates for use in agriculture, but development of the industry has been accompanied by increasing environmental problems. In 2000–07 the GDP of the mining and quarrying sector increased, in real terms, at an average annual rate of 6.3%. According to chain-linked methodologies, the GDP of the mining and quarrying sector decreased by 9.5% in 2012, but increased by 1.1% in 2013.

The manufacturing sector accounted for 15.9% of GDP and engaged 18.7% of the employed labour force in 2013. The sector is based on products of food- and beverage-processing (especially dairy products), textiles and clothing, fertilizers and other chemical products, and wood and timber products (particularly furniture). According to World Bank estimates, in 2004–13 the GDP of the manufacturing sector increased, in real terms, at an average annual rate of 4.3%. Real manufacturing GDP increased by 3.1% in 2012 and by 1.6% in 2013, according to chain-linked methodologies.

The construction sector contributed 7.5% of GDP and engaged 9.1% of the employed labour force in 2013. According to chain-linked methodologies, sectoral GDP increased by 7.5% in 2012, but decreased by 3.9% in 2013.

The country relies on oil shale for over 90% of its energy requirements, meaning that it is self-sufficient in terms of electricity generation and is a net exporter of electrical energy. Estlink, an under-sea electrical cable connecting the electricity networks of Estonia and Finland, became operational in January 2007 and has provided an additional source of revenue through the export of excess power; a second under-sea cable between Estonia and Finland, Estlink II, entered into operation in early 2014. Nevertheless, Estonia is dependent on Russian gas for its other energy needs, such as heating, and on Russian oil, for both domestic use and export. In 2011 the Government announced that Estonia would participate jointly (taking a 20% share) with the Governments of Lithuania, Latvia and Poland in the construction of a 1,300-MW nuclear power plant at Visaginas, Lithuania; however, development plans for the plant still had not been finalised in early 2014. In 2013 imports of mineral fuels accounted for 12.1% of total imports.

The services sector accounted for 67.5% of GDP and engaged 65.5% of the employed population in 2013. According to World Bank estimates, during 2004–13 the GDP of the services sector increased, in real terms, by an annual average rate of 2.0%; the GDP of the sector increased by 4.2% in 2012 and by 1.6% in 2013.

In 2013 Estonia recorded a visible merchandise trade deficit of US $1,279.5m., while there was a deficit of $245.0m. on the current account of the balance of payments. After 1991 trade with the West, particularly the Nordic countries, increased considerably. In 2013 Finland was Estonia's principal source of imports, accounting for 15.1% of the total. Other important sources of imports were Germany, Sweden, Latvia, Lithuania, Poland and Russia. In that year Sweden was the principal export trading partner, accounting for 16.8% of exports. Finland, Russia, Latvia and Lithuania were other important purchasers of exports. In 2012 the principal exports were machinery, mechanical and electrical appliances, mineral products, wood, articles of wood, base metals and articles of base metal, miscellaneous manufactured articles, vehicles and related transport equipment, and chemical products. The principal imports in that year were machinery, mechanical and electrical appliances, mineral products, vehicles, chemical products, base metals and articles of base metal, prepared foodstuffs and beverages, and plastics, rubber and articles thereof.

Official forecasts provided for a budgetary deficit of €62.2m. in 2014. Estonia's general government gross debt was €1,845m. euros in 2013, equivalent to 9.9% of GDP. According to ILO, during 2004–13 the annual rate of inflation averaged 4.4%. Consumer prices increased by 2.8% in 2013. Some 8.6% of the labour force were officially registered as unemployed in 2013.

Estonia was admitted to the Organisation for Economic Co-operation and Development in December 2010 and adopted the euro as the national currency in 2011, following efforts to maintain the fiscal deficit at less than 3% of GDP. Accession to the eurozone made trade with other European Union (EU, see p. 271) countries (which between them typically purchase around three-quarters of Estonian exports) more attractive and helped to encourage foreign investment. By 2010 positive growth following the global financial crisis had resumed, and the IMF assessed that exports, which had come to substantially exceed the levels recorded before the economic crisis of 2008–09, had been the main driver of the recovery. Domestic investment also played a significant role, and Estonia has become a leader in the information and communications technology sector within the Union, as demonstrated by the basing of the new EU Agency for Large-Scale Information Technology Systems in Tallinn in 2012. Estonia has had the lowest rate of national debt as a percentage of GDP in the EU since its admission in 2004. However, Estonia's recovery growth rate (hitherto one of the highest in the EU) declined substantially in 2013, and a contraction was recorded in the first quarter of 2014, attributed to a slowing in manufacturing production. Significant growth in labour costs since 2011, resulting from shortages in the labour market, was considered to have weakened export competitiveness. The conflict in eastern Ukraine that commenced in 2014, and the ensuing deterioration in Russia's relations with Estonia and other EU states, adversely affected Estonia's export revenue; sanctions were imposed against Russia, which in August introduced a retaliatory ban on the import of foodstuffs from EU states. However, according to official figures, at November Estonian exports had only declined by 1.2% year-on-year, and overall GDP growth of 1.9% was estimated for 2014, with an increase in government tax revenue in that year. At legislative elections in March 2015 the liberal ruling coalition led by Prime Minister Taavi Rõivas was returned to government; Rõivas had issued pledges to increase foreign and business investment, and to reduce labour taxation.

PUBLIC HOLIDAYS

2016: 1 January (New Year's Day), 24 February (Independence Day), 25 March (Good Friday), 1 May (Spring Day), 15 May (Whit Sunday), 23 June (Victory Day, anniversary of the Battle of Võnnu in 1919), 24 June (Midsummer Day, Jaanipäev), 20 August (Restoration of Independence Day), 25–26 December (Christmas—Gregorian Calendar).

Statistical Survey

Source (unless otherwise stated): Statistical Office of Estonia (Statiskaamet), Tatari 51, Tallinn 10134; tel. 625-9300; e-mail stat@stat.ee; internet www.stat.ee.

Area and Population

AREA, POPULATION AND DENSITY

Area (sq km)	45,227*
Population (census results)†	
31 March 2000	1,370,052
31 December 2011	
Males	600,526
Females	693,929
Total	1,294,455
Population (official estimates at 1 January)	
2012	1,325,217
2013	1,320,174
2014	1,315,819
Density (per sq km) at 1 January 2014	29.1

* 17,462 sq miles.
† Figures refer to permanent inhabitants.

POPULATION BY AGE AND SEX
(official estimates at 1 January 2014)

	Males	Females	Total
0–14 years	106,916	101,112	208,028
15–64 years	426,978	439,030	866,008
65 years and over	81,025	160,758	241,783
Total	614,919	700,900	1,315,819

POPULATION BY ETHNIC GROUP
(official estimates at 1 January 2014)

	Number	% of total population
Estonian	909,307	69.1
Russian	332,816	25.3
Ukrainian	22,994	1.7
Belorussian	12,575	1.0
Other	38,127	2.9
Total	1,315,819	100.0

POPULATION BY COUNTY
(official estimates at 1 January 2014)

County	Area (sq km)*	Population	Density (per sq km)	County town (with population)
Harju . . .	4,333	572,103	132.0	Tallinn (411,063)
Hiiu	1,023	8,589	8.4	Kärdla (3,017)
Ida-Viru . .	3,364	149,483	44.4	Jõhvi (10,525)
Järva . . .	2,460	30,425	12.4	Paide (8,162)
Jõgeva . . .	2,604	31,145	12.0	Jõgeva (5,457)
Lääne . . .	2,383	24,323	10.2	Haapsalu (10,316)
Lääne-Viru .	3,628	59,583	16.4	Rakvere (15,400)
Pärnu . . .	4,807	82,829	17.2	Pärnu (40,005)
Põlva . . .	2,165	27,641	12.8	Põlva (5,661)
Rapla . . .	2,980	34,676	11.6	Rapla (5,054)
Saare . . .	2,922	31,756	10.9	Kuressaare (13,152)
Tartu . . .	2,993	152,188	50.8	Tartu (98,449)
Valga . . .	2,044	30,176	14.8	Valga (12,437)
Viljandi . .	3,423	47,476	13.9	Viljandi (17,602)
Võru . . .	2,305	33,426	14.5	Võru (12,571)
Total . . .	43,432	1,315,819	30.3	

* Excluding that part of Lake Peipsi that belongs to Estonia, and the area of Lake Võrtsjärv.

PRINCIPAL TOWNS
(official population estimates at 1 January 2014)

Tallinn (capital) .	411,063	Pärnu	40,005
Tartu	98,449	Kohtla-Järve . .	37,198
Narva	59,049		

BIRTHS, MARRIAGES AND DEATHS*

	Registered live births		Registered marriages		Registered deaths	
	Number	Rate (per 1,000)	Number	Rate (per 1,000)	Number	Rate (per 1,000)
2006	14,877	11.1	6,954	5.2	17,316	12.9
2007	15,775	11.8	7,022	5.2	17,409	13.0
2008	16,028	12.0	6,127	4.6	16,675	12.5
2009	15,763	11.8	5,362	4.0	16,081	12.1
2010	15,825	11.9	5,066	3.8	15,790	11.9
2011	14,679	11.1	5,499	4.1	15,244	11.5
2012	14,056	10.6	5,888	4.5	15,450	11.7
2013	13,531	10.3	5,630	4.3	15,244	11.6

* Revised figures, based on the results of the 1989 and 2000 population censuses.

Life expectancy (years at birth, official estimates): 77.3 (males 72.7; females 81.3) in 2013.

ECONOMICALLY ACTIVE POPULATION
(annual averages, '000 persons aged 15–74 years)

	2011	2012	2013
Agriculture, hunting, forestry and fishing	26.6	27.6	26.5
Mining and quarrying	5.8	4.9	4.8
Manufacturing	119.1	115.5	116.4
Electricity, gas and water supply .	11.8	12.5	10.1
Construction	58.9	58.2	56.6
Wholesale and retail trade . .	81.1	79.1	81.1
Hotels and restaurants . . .	18.4	18.8	23.4
Transport, storage and communications	65.0	69.5	66.6
Financial intermediation . . .	10.3	10.9	10.2
Real estate, renting and business activities	51.2	55.2	60.6
Public administration and defence; compulsory social security . .	39.3	40.1	43.0
Education	56.5	61.8	56.1
Health and social work . . .	34.6	34.5	36.4
Other services	24.7	26.3	29.5
Total employed	603.2	614.9	621.3
Unemployed	84.8	68.5	58.7
Total labour force	688.0	683.4	680.0

Health and Welfare

KEY INDICATORS

Total fertility rate (children per woman, 2012)	1.6
Under-5 mortality rate (per 1,000 live births, 2012) . . .	4
HIV/AIDS (% of persons aged 15–49, 2013)	1.3
Physicians (per 1,000 head, 2012)	3.3
Hospital beds (per 1,000 head, 2012)	5.6
Health expenditure (2011): US $ per head (PPP)	1,294
Health expenditure (2011): % of GDP	5.8
Health expenditure (2011): public (% of total)	80.5
Access to water (% of persons, 2012)	99
Access to sanitation (% of persons, 2012)	95
Total carbon dioxide emissions ('000 metric tons, 2010) . .	18,338.7
Carbon dioxide emissions per head (metric tons, 2010) . .	13.7
Human Development Index (2013): ranking	33
Human Development Index (2013): value	0.840

For sources and definitions, see explanatory note on p. vi.

Agriculture

PRINCIPAL CROPS
('000 metric tons)

	2011	2012	2013
Wheat	360.4	485.0	406.3
Barley	294.4	340.5	439.0
Rye	30.9	57.3	21.9
Oats	62.8	78.4	85.3
Triticale (wheat-rye hybrid) . .	13.6	24.8	8.8
Potatoes	164.7	138.9	127.7
Peas, dry	15.4	12.9	30.8
Rapeseed	144.2	157.8	174.0
Cabbages and other brassicas .	20.6	16.8	25.8
Cucumbers and gherkins . . .	11.1	9.8	9.3
Tomatoes	6.4	4.8	5.3
Carrots and turnips	24.5	17.1	21.1
Apples	2.7	1.9	4.4

Aggregate production ('000 metric tons, may include official, semi-official or estimated data): Total cereals 771.1 in 2011, 990.9 in 2012, 973.1 in 2013; Total roots and tubers 165.2 in 2011, 139.1 in 2012, 128.0 in 2013; Total vegetables (incl. melons) 88.3 in 2011, 66.2 in 2012, 79.0 in 2013; Total fruits (excl. melons) 5.8 in 2011, 5.1 in 2012, 7.6 in 2013.

Source: FAO.

LIVESTOCK
('000 head, year ending September)

	2011	2012	2013
Cattle	238	246	261
Pigs	366	375	359
Sheep	84	77	82
Chickens*	2,006	2,139	2,103

* Unofficial figures.

Source: FAO.

LIVESTOCK PRODUCTS
('000 metric tons unless otherwise indicated)

	2011	2012	2013
Cattle meat	12.2	12.3	11.5
Pig meat	50.2	48.8	49.5
Chicken meat	17.5	16.5	18.1
Cows' milk	692.4	720.7	771.6
Hen eggs	11.4	11.1	11.8
Honey (metric tons)	694	957	979
Butter	6.5	4.0	3.1
Cheese	40.6	42.6	42.9

Source: FAO.

Forestry

ROUNDWOOD REMOVALS
('000 cubic metres, excl. bark)

	2011	2012	2013*
Sawlogs, veneer logs and logs for sleepers	3,330	3,330	3,465
Pulpwood	1,845	1,980	2,007
Other industrial wood	54	54	54
Fuel wood	1,881	1,926	1,962
Total	7,110	7,290	7,488

* FAO estimates.

Source: FAO.

SAWNWOOD PRODUCTION
('000 cubic metres, incl. railway sleepers)

	2011	2012	2013*
Coniferous (softwood)	1,369	1,369	1,400
Broadleaved (hardwood) . . .	134	122	140
Total	1,503	1,491	1,540

* FAO estimates.

Source: FAO.

Fishing

('000 metric tons, live weight)

	2010	2011	2012
Capture	95.4	80.7	67.2
Atlantic herring	28.9	25.3	22.0
European sprat	47.9	35.0	27.7
Northern prawn	9.0	9.9	7.6
Aquaculture	0.6	0.4	0.4
Total catch	96.0	81.0	67.5

Source: FAO.

Mining

('000 metric tons)

	2011	2012	2013
Oil shale	18,700	18,800	20,500
Peat	927	671	1,064

Industry

SELECTED PRODUCTS
('000 metric tons unless otherwise indicated)

	2011	2012	2013
Distilled spirits ('000 hl) . . .	169.2	182.0	157.7
Wine ('000 hl)	73.3	96.3	106.6
Beer ('000 hl)	1,358.8	1,460.0	1,472.7
Soft drinks ('000 hl) . . .	315.2	483.7	432.6
Woven cotton fabric ('000 sq m) .	476	67	48
Carpets ('000 sq m) . . .	3,065	3,276	3,129
Footwear ('000 pairs) . . .	1,553	952	954
Plywood ('000 cubic m) . .	42.5	46.0	46.8
Particle board ('000 cubic m) . .	206.9	157.1	178.3
Fibreboard (million sq m) . . .	8.1	7.8	7.5
Chemical wood pulp . . .	70.6	74.4	72.8
Paper	67.6	72.1	70.5
Nitrogenous fertilizers* . . .	0.1	4.1	53.5
Building bricks (million) . . .	31.7	40.2	44.3
Cement	451.0	481.5	456.7
Electric energy (million kWh) .	12,892	11,966	13,274

* In terms of nitrogen (N).

Finance

CURRENCY AND EXCHANGE RATES

Monetary Units
100 cents = 1 euro (€).

Sterling, Dollar and Euro Equivalents (31 December 2014)
£1 sterling = 1.286 euros;
US $1 = 0.824 euros;
€10 = £7.78 = $12.14.

Average Exchange Rate (euros per US $)
2012   0.7783
2013   0.7532
2014   0.7537

Note: The kroon was included in the second European exchange rate mechanism (ERM II) from June 2004, with a central parity of 1 euro = 15.6466 kroons. On 1 January 2011 the euro was introduced to circulate alongside the kroon until 14 January, after which period the euro was formally adopted as the sole official currency of Estonia.

STATE BUDGET
(€ million, budget forecasts)

Revenue	2013	2014
Tax revenue	5,109.3	5,457.5
Personal income tax	299.0	331.1
Corporate income tax	320.8	316.0
Social tax	2,065.0	2,245.7
Value added tax	1,575.0	1,672.9
Excise duties	795.6	836.9
Other taxes	53.9	54.9
Non tax revenue	1,488.3	1,365.8
Sales of goods and services	164.4	130.3
Subsidies	1,027.0	902.9
Other revenue	296.8	332.6
Transfers of revenues	1,051.7	1,175.0
Total	7,649.2	7,998.3

Expenditure by function	2013	2014
General public services	1,403.2	1,372.9
Defence	337.1	358.1
Public order and safety	379.2	421.5
Economic affairs	906.8	976.8
Environment protection	317.9	320.2
Housing and community amenities	10.0	—
Health	948.2	1,017.9
Recreation, culture and religion	180.0	206.9
Education	734.2	760.6
Social protection	2,482.6	2,667.1
Statistical discrepancy	−15.4	−41.4
Total	7,683.8	8,060.5

Source: Ministry of Finance, Tallinn.

INTERNATIONAL RESERVES
(US $ million at 31 December)

	2011	2012	2013
Gold (Eurosystem valuation) . .	12.60	13.31	9.61
IMF special drawing rights . .	95.23	95.33	95.53
Reserve position in IMF . . .	0.01	12.58	20.30
Foreign exchange	99.63	179.44	188.94
Total	207.47	300.66	314.38

Source: IMF, *International Financial Statistics*.

MONEY SUPPLY
(incl. shares, depository corporations, national residency criteria, € million at 31 December)

	2011	2012	2013
Currency issued	2,173	2,180	2,287
Demand deposits	5,028	6,039	6,955
Other deposits	3,926	3,511	3,248
Securities other than shares . .	19	4	1
Shares and other equity . . .	2,657	2,931	3,139
Other items (net)	462	456	234
Total	14,265	15,121	15,864

Source: IMF, *International Financial Statistics*.

COST OF LIVING
(Consumer Price Index; base: 2000 = 100)

	2011	2012	2013
Food (incl. beverages) . . .	168.1	174.6	181.7
All items (incl. others) . . .	158.1	164.3	168.9

Source: ILO.

NATIONAL ACCOUNTS
(€ million at current prices)

Expenditure on the Gross Domestic Product

	2011	2012	2013
Final consumption expenditure . .	11,381.9	12,305.0	13,227.4
Households	8,053.5	8,759.2	9,373.1
Non-profit institutions serving households	233.6	254.5	273.7
General government	3,094.7	3,291.3	3,580.6
Gross capital formation	4,744.5	5,054.7	5,029.8
Gross fixed capital formation . .	4,226.9	4,762.6	5,119.1
Changes in inventories . .			
Acquisitions, less disposals, of valuables	517.6	292.1	−89.3
Total domestic expenditure . .	16,126.3	17,359.7	18,257.2
Exports of goods and services . .	14,423.9	15,589.8	16,132.2
Less Imports of goods and services	13,469.3	15,413.8	15,861.5
Statistical discrepancy	−677.2	101.0	210.9
GDP in market prices . . .	16,403.8	17,636.7	18,738.8

Gross Domestic Product by Economic Activity

	2011	2012	2013
Agriculture, forestry and fishing .	566.4	626.5	589.5
Mining and quarrying . . .	188.7	190.1	217.0
Manufacturing	2,369.3	2,482.8	2,601.2
Electricity, gas and water supply .	629.0	633.7	697.9
Construction	1,004.2	1,147.6	1,232.3
Wholesale and retail trade; repair of motor vehicles, motorcycles and personal and household goods	1,737.0	1,913.1	2,085.6
Hotels and restaurants . . .	232.1	265.0	285.7
Transport, storage and communications	1,970.6	2,125.2	2,250.8
Financial intermediation . . .	576.5	565.5	543.4
Real estate, renting and business activities	2,628.2	2,835.8	3,054.5
Public administration and defence; compulsory social security	990.2	1,031.6	1,109.4
Education	654.2	675.1	731.4
Health and social work . . .	497.6	529.1	612.3
Other community, social and personal service activities .	312.8	360.9	393.2
Gross value added in basic prices	14,356.7	15,382.0	16,404.2
Taxes on products . . . . *Less* Subsidies on products . .	2,047.1	2,254.7	2,334.6
GDP in market prices . . .	16,403.8	17,636.7	18,738.8

BALANCE OF PAYMENTS
(US $ million)

	2011	2012	2013
Exports of goods	14,596.1	14,479.5	15,251.8
Imports of goods	−15,340.5	−15,680.9	−16,531.3
Balance on goods	−744.4	−1,201.4	−1,279.5
Exports of services	5,810.6	5,663.3	6,151.0
Imports of services	−3,677.0	−3,906.7	−4,384.1
Balance on goods and services	1,389.1	555.3	487.3
Primary income received . . .	1,214.1	994.9	1,226.8
Primary income paid	−2,545.8	−2,260.9	−2,154.7
Balance on goods, services and primary income	57.4	−710.6	−440.6
Secondary income received . .	847.0	789.1	748.3
Secondary income paid . . .	−493.8	−483.2	−552.7
Current balance	410.6	−404.8	−245.0
Capital account (net)	928.8	776.9	668.5
Direct investment assets . .	1,311.1	−1,091.2	−409.4
Direct investment liabilities . .	521.0	1,648.5	1,005.4
Portfolio investment assets . .	1,411.4	−337.5	−929.4
Portfolio investment liabilities .	167.7	214.7	223.9
Financial derivatives and employee stock options (net)	−54.6	87.9	92.4
Other investment assets . .	−3,039.4	−2,146.4	−182.0
Other investment liabilities . .	−1,740.0	1,335.4	−502.5
Net errors and omissions . .	100.5	7.5	290.1
Reserves and related items .	17.1	90.8	12.0

Source: IMF, *International Financial Statistics*.

External Trade

PRINCIPAL COMMODITIES
(distribution by HS, € million)

Imports c.i.f.	2011	2012	2013
Prepared foodstuffs; beverages, spirits and vinegar; tobacco and manufactured substitutes .	707.9	779.7	838.9
Mineral products	2,276.3	2,138.0	1,711.2
Mineral fuels, mineral oils and products of their distillation; bituminous substances, etc. .	2,231.2	2,081.3	1,665.0
Petroleum oils and oils obtained from bituminous minerals, other than crude	1,854.0	1,630.3	1,186.1
Products of chemical or allied industries	963.9	1,150.3	1,075.2
Plastics, rubber and articles thereof	612.1	676.0	699.8
Plastics and articles thereof . .	487.4	527.4	551.2
Textiles and textile articles .	536.1	571.4	604.1
Base metals and articles of base metal	1,111.3	1,160.8	1,072.5
Iron and steel	484.3	484.6	390.2
Machinery and mechanical appliances; electrical equipment; sound and television apparatus . . .	3,505.4	4,017.0	3,833.2
Boilers, machinery and mechanical appliances; parts thereof . .	1,209.5	1,474.4	1,428.6
Electrical machinery equipment and parts; sound and television apparatus parts and accessories	2,295.9	2,542.6	2,404.6
Telephone sets (incl. telephones for cellular networks and other wireless networks) . . .	838.7	778.2	788.9
Vehicles, aircraft, vessels and associated transport equipment	1,032.0	1,299.7	1,446.9
Vehicles other than railway or tramway rolling-stock, and parts and accessories	884.5	1,001.8	1,094.9
Motor cars and other motor vehicles mainly designed for personal transport . . .	443.7	490.9	531.8
Total (incl. others)	12,726.8	14,096.5	13,806.2

Exports f.o.b.	2011	2012	2013
Live animals and animal products	388.7	426.6	474.0
Prepared foodstuffs; beverages, spirits and vinegar; tobacco and manufactured substitutes .	409.9	507.7	520.3
Mineral products	2,061.6	1,874.4	1,288.0
Mineral fuels, mineral oils and products of their distillation .	2,018.9	1,828.2	1,235.6
Petroleum oils and oils obtained from bituminous minerals, other than crude	1,671.3	1,474.4	822.9
Products of chemical or allied industries	564.8	645.2	703.0
Plastics, rubber and articles thereof	349.5	382.2	394.5
Wood and articles thereof; wood charcoal; cork and articles thereof	925.3	922.4	1,054.9
Wood and articles thereof; wood charcoal	923.8	921.3	1,054.2
Pulp of wood or of other fibrous cellulosic material; waste and scrap of paper or paperboard	314.4	316.0	311.1
Textiles and textile articles .	349.7	361.8	422.6

Exports f.o.b.—*continued*	2011	2012	2013
Base metals and articles of base metal	1,032.6	1,023.5	886.1
Iron and steel	428.3	399.2	272.9
Machinery and mechanical appliances; electrical equipment; sound and television apparatus . . .	3,291.5	3,579.4	3,464.6
Boilers, machinery and mechanical appliances; parts thereof . .	874.6	1,089.4	962.6
Electrical machinery equipment and parts; sound and television apparatus parts and accessories	2,416.8	2,490.0	2,502.0
Telephone sets (incl. telephones for cellular networks and other wireless networks) . . .	1,301.6	1,319.0	1,391.6
Vehicles, aircraft, vessels and associated transport equipment	591.4	612.7	813.3
Vehicles other than railway or tramway rolling-stock, and parts and accessories . . .	503.6	514.8	542.1
Miscellaneous manufactured articles	787.3	827.0	870.2
Furniture; bedding, mattresses, cushions, etc.; lamps and lighting fittings; prefabricated buildings .	702.9	739.9	781.5
Total (incl. others)	12,003.4	12,521.1	12,291.1

PRINCIPAL TRADING PARTNERS
(€ million)

Imports c.i.f.	2011	2012	2013
Belarus	147.2	210.9	87.2
Belgium	234.7	279.8	260.7
China, People's Republic . . .	455.7	480.5	458.9
Czech Republic	161.2	184.0	176.7
Denmark	200.0	221.3	238.0
Finland	1,604.5	2,105.7	2,082.3
France	210.1	255.8	276.9
Germany	1,304.3	1,438.9	1,455.8
Hungary	156.7	163.6	175.7
Italy	277.6	337.7	344.5
Latvia	1,137.8	1,272.	1,301.8
Lithuania	1,041.0	1,159.	1,224.3
Netherlands	465.2	527.5	456.9
Norway	141.9	182.5	100.3
Poland	852.2	882.0	1,086.0
Russia	1,264.6	1,003.7	787.3
Sweden	1,331.1	1,440.8	1,395.3
Ukraine	108.4	197.0	87.3
United Kingdom	438.7	560.2	578.0
USA	141.1	116.9	139.7
Total (incl. others)	12,726.8	14,096.5	13,806.2

Exports f.o.b.	2011	2012	2013
Belgium	144.2	230.9	275.0
China, People's Republic . . .	203.1	101.2	99.0
Denmark	308.1	297.4	283.4
Finland	1,807.8	1,817.7	1,986.0
France	315.5	168.4	198.0
Germany	550.1	562.5	563.8
Italy	193.3	179.3	146.5
Latvia	954.1	1,103.4	1,274.7
Lithuania	553.1	657.6	717.9
Netherlands	319.4	306.3	281.9
Nigeria	391.4	177.0	23.4
Norway	360.8	419.7	447.4
Poland	182.2	176.5	207.8
Russia	1,312.3	1,511.5	1,403.6
Spain	163.5	137.6	108.1
Sweden	1,875.2	1,997.6	2,061.3
Turkey	148.2	160.7	161.5
United Kingdom	241.2	262.3	294.6
USA	749.8	584.0	358.3
Total (incl. others)	12,003.4	12,521.1	12,291.1

Transport

RAILWAYS
(traffic)

	2011	2012	2013
Passengers carried ('000) . . .	4,736	4,416	4,215
Passenger-kilometres (million) . .	241.3	235.8	224.9
Freight carried ('000 metric tons) .	48,262	44,684	43,689
Freight ton-kilometres (million) .	6,260.6	5,126.4	4,721.6

ROAD TRAFFIC
('000 motor vehicles in use at 31 December)

	2011	2012	2013
Passenger cars	574.0	602.1	628.5
Buses and coaches	4.2	4.3	4.5
Lorries and vans	84.3	88.0	92.2
Motorcycles and mopeds . . .	23.2	35.2	38.7
Trailers	69.9	75.2	80.0

SHIPPING
Flag Registered Fleet
(at 31 December)

	2012	2013	2014
Number of vessels	147	146	146
Total displacement ('000 grt) . .	326.0	334.3	368.2

Source: Lloyd's List Intelligence (www.lloydslistintelligence.com).

International Seaborne Freight Traffic
('000 metric tons)

	2011	2012	2013
Goods loaded	35,110	31,488	31,743
Goods unloaded	13,153	11,853	11,128

CIVIL AVIATION
(traffic on scheduled services)

	2011	2012	2013
Passengers carried ('000) . . .	791.1	1,020.3	761.3
Passenger-km (million) . . .	1,051.5	1,143.5	1,122.1
Freight carried ('000 metric tons) .	n.a.	0.8	2.4
Total ton-km ('000)	n.a.	625.1	1,482.3

Tourism

FOREIGN TOURIST ARRIVALS BY COUNTRY OF ORIGIN*

	2011	2012	2013
Finland	840,714	829,225	894,504
Germany	103,559	111,251	101,596
Latvia	85,229	100,638	105,480
Lithuania	47,003	47,397	52,201
Norway	51,510	48,479	36,918
Russia	203,204	266,192	304,644
Sweden	86,287	78,412	74,313
United Kingdom and Ireland . .	69,912	54,305	43,109
Total (incl. others)	1,807,919	1,873,519	1,940,130

* Figures refer to arrivals at registered accommodation establishments.

Tourism receipts (US $ million, excl. passenger transport, unless otherwise indicated): 1,255 in 2011; 1,221 in 2012; 1,390 in 2013 (Source: World Tourism Organization).

Communications Media

	2011	2012	2013
Telephones ('000 main lines in use)	471.9	448.2	426.5
Mobile cellular telephones ('000 subscribers)	1,863.1	2,070.5	2,055.2
Internet subscribers ('000) . .	348.9	343.9	n.a.
Broadband subscribers ('000) . .	317.3	328.7	341.6
Book production: titles	3,716	3,971	3,887
Book production: copies (million) .	4.4	4.6	4.8
Daily newspapers: titles . . .	13	13	13
Other periodicals: titles . . .	1,159	1,149	1,130
Other periodicals: average annual circulation (million copies) . .	25.3	28.2	26.9

Source: partly International Telecommunication Union.

Education

(2012/13 unless otherwise indicated)

	Institutions	Teachers	Students
Pre-primary	652	6,754*	68,700
Basic	300	n.a.	112,900
General secondary	198	12,259†	94,935‡
Special	42	n.a.	3,400
Vocational and professional . .	47	729	25,699
Universities, etc.	26	6,842‖	64,806§

* 2007/08.
† 2001/02.
‡ 2006/07.
‖ 2005/06.
§ Including students enrolled in evening and correspondence courses.

Pupil-teacher ratio (primary education, UNESCO estimate): 11.5 in 2011/12 (Source: UNESCO Institute for Statistics).

Adult literacy rate (UNESCO estimates): 99.9% (males 99.8%; females 99.9%) in 2011 (Source: UNESCO Institute for Statistics).

Directory

The Government

HEAD OF STATE

President: TOOMAS HENDRIK ILVES (elected by vote of the Riigikogu 23 September 2006; inaugurated 9 October 2006; re-elected 29 August 2011; inaugurated 10 October 2011).

COUNCIL OF MINISTERS
(April 2015)

A coalition Government, comprising members of the Eesti Reformierakond (ER), Sotsiaaldemokraatlik Erakond (SDE) and the Isamaa ja Res Publica Liit (IRL).

Prime Minister: TAAVI RÕIVAS (ER).

Minister of Culture: INDREK SAAR (SDE).

Minister of Defence: SVEN MIKSER (SDE).

Minister of Economic Affairs and Infrastructure: KRISTEN MICHAL (ER).

Minister of Education and Research: JÜRGEN LIGI (ER).

Minister of Entrepreneurship: URVE PALO (SDE).

Minister of the Environment: MARKO POMERANTS (IRL).

Minister of Finance: SVEN SESTER (IRL).

Minister of Foreign Affairs: KEIT PENTUS-ROSIMANNUS (ER).

Minister of Health and Labour: RANNAR VASSILJEV (SDE).

Minister of the Interior: HANNO PEVKUR (ER).

Minister of Justice: URMAS REINSALU (IRL).

Minister for Public Administration: ARTO AAS (ER).

Minister of Rural Affairs: URMAS KRUUSE (ER).

Minister of Social Protection: MARGUS TSAHKNA (IRL).

MINISTRIES

Office of the President: A. Weizenbergi 39, Tallinn 15050; tel. 631-6202; fax 631-6250; e-mail vpinfo@vpk.ee; internet www.president.ee.

Office of the Prime Minister: Stenbocki maja, Rahukohtu 3, Tallinn 15161; tel. 693-5555; fax 693-5554; e-mail riigikantselei@riigikantselei.ee; internet www.valitsus.ee.

Ministry of Culture: Suur Karja 23, Tallinn 15076; tel. 628-2250; fax 628-2200; e-mail min@kul.ee; internet www.kul.ee.

Ministry of Defence: Sakala 1, Tallinn 15094; tel. 717-0022; fax 717-0001; e-mail info@kaitseministeerium.ee; internet www.kaitseministeerium.ee.

Ministry of Economic Affairs and Communication: Harju 11, Tallinn 15072; tel. 625-6342; fax 631-3660; e-mail info@mkm.ee; internet www.mkm.ee.

Ministry of Education and Research: Munga 18, Tartu 50088; tel. 735-0222; fax 730-1080; e-mail hm@hm.ee; internet www.hm.ee.

Ministry of the Environment: Narva mnt. 7A, Tallinn 15172; tel. 626-2802; fax 626-2801; e-mail keskkonnaministeerium@envir.ee; internet www.envir.ee.

Ministry of Finance: Suur-Ameerika 1, Tallinn 15006; tel. 611-3558; fax 611-3664; e-mail info@fin.ee; internet www.fin.ee.

Ministry of Foreign Affairs: Islandi Väljak 1, Tallinn 15049; tel. 637-7000; fax 637-7099; e-mail vminfo@vm.ee; internet www.vm.ee.

Ministry of the Interior: Pikk 61, Tallinn 15065; tel. 612-5008; e-mail info@siseministeerium.ee; internet www.siseministeerium.ee; note: the Office of the Minister of Regional Affairs forms part of the Ministry of the Interior.

Ministry of Justice: Tõnismägi 5A, Tallinn 15191; tel. 620-8100; fax 620-8109; e-mail info@just.ee; internet www.just.ee.

Ministry of Rural Affairs: Lai 39/41, Tallinn 15056; tel. 625-6101; fax 625-6200; e-mail pm@agri.ee; internet www.agri.ee.

Ministry of Social Protection: Gonsiori 29, Tallinn 15027; tel. 626-9301; fax 699-2209; e-mail info@sm.ee; internet www.sm.ee.

President

On 29 August 2011 a presidential election was conducted in the 101-member Riigikogu (State Assembly). TOOMAS HENDRIK ILVES, the incumbent, was elected to a second term of office, securing 73 votes, more than the requisite two-thirds' majority (68 votes). The only other candidate, INDREK TARAND, received 25 votes. ILVES assumed office on 10 October.

Legislature

State Assembly
(Riigikogu)

Lossi plats 1A, Tallinn 15165; tel. 631-6331; fax 631-6334; e-mail riigikogu@riigikogu.ee; internet www.riigikogu.ee.

Speaker: EIKI NESTOR.

General Election, 1 March 2015

Parties	Votes	%	Seats
Eesti Reformierakond . . .	158,970	27.7	30
Eesti Keskerakond . . .	142,458	24.8	27
Sotsiaaldemokraatlik Erakond .	87,189	15.2	15
Isamaa ja Res Publica Liit . .	78,699	13.7	14
Eesti Vabaerakond . . .	49,882	8.7	8
Eesti Konservatiivseks Rahvaerakonnaks . . .	46,772	8.1	7
Other parties . . .	9,293	1.6	—
Individual candidates . . .	887	0.2	—
Total	**574,150**	**100.00**	**101**

Election Commission

Estonian National Electoral Committee (Vabariigi Valimiskomisjon): Lossi plats 1A, Tallinn 15165; tel. 631-6540; fax 631-6541; e-mail info@vvk.ee; internet www.vvk.ee; Chair. AARO MÕTTUS.

Political Organizations

Eesti Keskerakond (EK) (Estonian Centre Party): Toom-Rüütli 3/5, Tallinn 10130; tel. 627-3460; fax 627-3461; e-mail keskerakond@keskerakond.ee; internet www.keskerakond.ee; f. 1991; absorbed the Estonian Green Party in 1998 and the Estonian Pensioners' Party in 2005; Chair. KADRI SIMSON (acting); Sec.-Gen. PRIIT TOOBAL; 14,000 mems.

Eesti Konservatiivseks Rahvaerakonnaks (EKRE) (Estonian Conservative People's Party): Pärnu mnt. 30–5, Tallinn 10141; tel. 616-1790; fax 616-1791; e-mail erl@erl.ee; f. 2000 as Eestimaa Rahvaliit (Estonian People's Union); present name adopted March 2012; right-wing; Chair. MARGO MILJAND; 10,000 mems (2009).

Eesti Kristlikud Demokraadid (EKD) (Estonian Christian Democrats): Jaama 2, 3rd Floor, Tallinn 11621; tel. 659-2357; fax 626-1431; e-mail ekd@erakond.eu; internet www.ekd.ee; f. 1998; fmrly Estonian Christian People's Party; present name adopted 2006; Chair. PEETER VÕSU.

Eesti Reformierakond (ER) (Estonian Reform Party): Tõnismagi 9, Tallinn 10119; tel. 680-8080; fax 680-8081; e-mail info@reform.ee; internet www.reform.ee; f. 1994; liberal; Chair. TAAVI RÕIVAS; 11,151 mems (2012).

Eesti Vabaerakond (EVA) (Estonian Free Democratic Party): Kopli 25-609, Tallinn 10421; tel. 505-6540; e-mail info@vabaerakond.ee; internet www.vabaerakond.ee; f. 2014; centre-right; Chair. ANDRES HERKEL.

Eestimaa Ühendatud Vasakpartei (Estonian United Left Party): Estonia pst. 7, Tallinn 10143; tel. 645-5335; fax 645-5336; e-mail info@vasak.ee; internet vasakpartei.ee; f. 2008 by merger of Konstitutsioonierakond (Constitution Party–representing the Russian-speaking minority in Estonia) and Eesti Vasakpartei (Estonian Left Party); extreme left-wing; Co-Chair. SERGEI JÜRGENS, HEINO RÜÜTEL; 2,500 mems (2008).

Erakond Eestimaa Rohelised (Estonian Greens): Haabersti kandekeskus, POB 4740, Tallinn 13503; tel. 502-6816; e-mail info@erakond.ee; internet roheline.erakond.ee; f. 2006; Chair. ALEKSANDER LAANE.

Isamaa ja Res Publica Liit (IRL) (Union of Pro Patria and Res Publica): Paldiski mnt. 13, Tallinn 10137; tel. 624-0400; e-mail info@irl.ee; internet www.irl.ee; f. 2006 by merger of Isamaaliit (f. 1995) and Ühendus vabariigi eest Res Publica (f. 2001); conservative, centre-right; Chair. URMAS REINSALU; 9,900 mems (2012).

Rahva Ühtsuse Erakond (RÜE) (People's Unity Party): Harju; tel. 559-39731; e-mail info@rue.ee; internet rue.ee; f. 2014; Chair. KRISTIINA OJULAND; 548 mems.

Sotsiaaldemokraatlik Erakond (SDE) (Estonian Social Democratic Party): Toompuiestee 16, Tallinn 10137; tel. 611-6040; fax 611-6050; e-mail kantselei@sotsdem.ee; internet www.sotsdem.ee; fmrly Rahvaerakond Mõõdukad (Moderate Peoples' Party); Chair. SVEN MIKSER; Sec.-Gen. INDREK SAAR; 6,243 mems (2014).

Diplomatic Representation

EMBASSIES IN ESTONIA

Austria: Vambola 6, Tallinn 10114; tel. 627-8740; fax 631-4365; e-mail tallinn-ob@bmeia.gv.at; internet www.bmeia.gv.at/botschaft/tallinn; Ambassador RENATE KOBLER.

Azerbaijan: Pirita tee 20T, Tallinn 10127; tel. 640-5050; fax 640-5051; e-mail tallinn@mission.mfa.gov.az; internet www.azembassy.ee; Ambassador TOFIQ ZÜLFÜQAROV.

Belarus: Magdaleena 3B, Tallinn 11312; tel. 651-5500; fax 655-8001; e-mail estonia@mfa.gov.by; internet estonia.mfa.gov.by; Ambassador ANATOLIY A. STEPUS.

Brazil: A. Lauteri 5, 4th Floor, Tallinn 10114; tel. 633-7070; fax 633-7871; e-mail brasemb.talin@itamaraty.gov.br; internet talin.itamaraty.gov.br; Ambassador VERGNIAUD ELYSEU FILHO.

China, People's Republic: Narva mnt. 98, Tallinn 15009; tel. 601-5830; fax 601-5833; e-mail chinaemb@online.ee; internet www.chinaembassy.ee; Ambassador QU ZHE.

Czech Republic: Lahe 4, Tallinn 10150; tel. 627-4400; fax 631-4716; e-mail tallinn@embassy.mzv.cz; internet www.mzv.cz/tallinn; Ambassador RICHARD KADLČÁK.

Denmark: Wismari 5, Tallinn 15047; tel. 630-6400; fax 630-6421; e-mail tllamb@um.dk; internet estland.um.dk; Ambassador SØREN KELSTRUP.

Finland: Kohtu 4, Tallinn 15180; tel. 610-3200; fax 610-3281; e-mail sanomat.tal@formin.fi; internet www.finland.ee; Ambassador KIRSTI NARINEN.

France: Toom-Kuninga 20, Tallinn 15185; tel. 616-1600; fax 616-1608; e-mail info@ambafrance-ee.org; internet www.ambafrance-ee.org; Ambassador MICHEL RAINERI.

Georgia: Viru väljak 2, Tallinn 10111; tel. 698-8590; fax 641-3000; e-mail tallinn.emb@mfa.gov.ge; internet www.estonia.mfa.gov.ge; Ambassador TEA AKHVLEDIANI.

Germany: Toom-Kuninga 11, Tallinn 15048; tel. 627-5300; fax 627-5304; e-mail info@tallinn.diplo.de; internet www.tallinn.diplo.de; Ambassador CHRISTIAN MATTHIAS SCHLAGA.

Greece: Pärnu mnt. 12, 2nd Floor, Tallinn 10148; tel. 640-3560; fax 640-3561; e-mail gremb.tal@mfa.gr; internet www.mfa.gr/tallinn; Ambassador KONSTANTINOS KATSAMBIS.

Ireland: Vene 2, 2nd Floor, Tallinn 10123; tel. 681-1888; fax 681-1889; e-mail tallinnembassy@dfa.ie; internet www.embassyofireland.ee; Ambassador FRANK FLOOD.

Italy: Vene 2, 3rd Floor, Tallinn 15075; tel. 627-6160; fax 631-1370; e-mail ambasciata.tallinn@esteri.it; internet www.ambtallinn.esteri.it; Ambassador MARCO CLEMENTE.

Japan: Harju 6, Tallinn 15069; tel. 631-0531; fax 631-0533; e-mail info@ti.mofa.go.jp; internet www.ee.emb-japan.go.jp; Ambassador TETSURO KAI.

Latvia: Tõnismägi 10, Tallinn 10119; tel. 627-7850; fax 627-7855; e-mail embassy.estonia@mfa.gov.lv; Ambassador JURIS BONE.

Lithuania: Uus 15, Tallinn 15070; tel. 616-4991; fax 641-2013; e-mail amb.ee@urm.lt; internet ee.mfa.lt; Ambassador NEILAS TANKEVIČIUS.

Macedonia, former Yugoslav republic: Suurtüki 4 A/13, Tallinn 10133; tel. and fax 644-0479; e-mail talin@mfa.gov.mk; Ambassador SAŠO VELJANOVSKI.

Moldova: Tatari 20/9–10, Tallinn 10116; tel. 642-0203; fax 642-0204; e-mail tallinn@mfa.md; internet www.estonia.mfa.md; Ambassador VICTOR GUZUN.

Netherlands: Rahukohtu 4-I, Tallinn 10130; tel. 680-5500; fax 680-5501; e-mail info@netherlandsembassy.ee; internet www.netherlandsembassy.ee; Ambassador JOS SCHELLAARS.

Norway: Harju 6, Tallinn 15054; tel. 627-1000; fax 627-1001; e-mail emb.tallinn@mfa.no; internet www.norra.ee; Ambassador DAGFINN SØRLI.

Poland: Suur-Karja 1, Tallinn 10140; tel. 627-8201; fax 644-5221; e-mail eetalamb@msz.gov.pl; internet www.tallinn.polemb.net; Ambassador ROBERT FILIPCZAK.

Russian Federation: Pikk 19, Tallinn 10133; tel. 646-4175; fax 646-4178; e-mail vensaat@online.ee; internet www.rusemb.ee; Ambassador YURII N. MERZLYAKOV.

Spain: Liivalaia 13–15, 6th Floor, Tallinn 10118; tel. 667-6651; fax 631-3767; e-mail emb.tallinn@mae.es; internet www.exteriores.gob.es/embajadas/tallin; Ambassador FERNANDO GARCÍA CASAS.

Sweden: Pikk 28, Tallinn 15055; tel. 640-5600; fax 640-5695; e-mail ambassaden.tallinn@gov.se; internet www.sweden.ee; Ambassador ANDERS LJUNGGREN.

Turkey: Narva mnt. 30, Tallinn 10152; tel. 627-2880; fax 627-2885; e-mail embassy.tallinn@mfa.gov.tr; internet tallinn.emb.mfa.gov.tr; Ambassador AHMET ÜLKER.

Ukraine: Lahe 6, Tallinn 15170; tel. 601-5815; fax 601-5816; e-mail embassyofukraine@gmail.com; internet www.mfa.gov.ua/estonia; Ambassador VIKTOR V. KRYSHANIVSKY.

United Kingdom: Wismari 6, Tallinn 10136; tel. 667-4700; fax 667-4755; e-mail infotallinn@fco.gov.uk; internet www.ukinestonia.fco.gov.uk; Ambassador CHRISTOPHER B. HOLTBY.

USA: Kentmanni 20, Tallinn 15099; tel. 668-8100; fax 668-8265; e-mail usasaatkond@state.gov; internet estonia.usembassy.gov; Ambassador JEFFREY D. LEVINE.

Judicial System

Supreme Court (Riigikohus): Lossi 17, Tartu 50093; tel. 730-9002; fax 730-9003; e-mail info@riigikohus.ee; internet www.nc.ee; Chief Justice and Chairman of the Constitutional Review Chamber PRIIT PIKAMÄE; Chairman of the Civil Chamber VILLU KÕVE; Chairman of the Criminal Chamber HANNES KIRIS; Chairman of the Administrative Law Chamber IVO PILVING.

Office of the Chancellor of Justice (Õiguskantsleri Kantselei): Kohtu 8, Tallinn 15193; tel. 693-8404; fax 693-8401; e-mail info@

oiguskantsler.ee; internet www.oiguskantsler.ee; f. 1993; reviews general application of legislative and executive powers and of local governments for conformity with the Constitution, supervises activities of state agencies in guaranteeing constitutional rights and freedoms; Chancellor of Justice INDREK TEDER.

Public Prosecutor's Office (Riigiprokuratuur): Wismari 7, Tallinn 15188; tel. 613-9400; fax 613-9402; e-mail info@prokuratuur.ee; internet www.prokuratuur.ee; State Prosecutor-Gen. LAVLY PERLING.

Religion

CHRISTIANITY

Protestant Churches

Estonian Conference of Seventh-day Adventists (Seitsmenda Päeva Adventistide Kogudus Eesti Liit): Lille 18, Tartu 51010; tel. and fax 734-3211; e-mail info@advent.ee; internet www.advent.ee; f. 1917; Pres. IVO KÄSK.

Estonian Evangelical Lutheran Church (Eesti Evangeelne Luterlik Kirik): Kiriku plats 3, Tallinn 10130; tel. 627-7350; fax 627-7352; e-mail konsistoorium@eelk.ee; internet www.eelk.ee; 172,000 mems; Archbishop Most Rev. ANDRES PÕDER.

Union of Free Evangelical Christian and Baptist Churches of Estonia (Eesti Evangeeliumi Kristlaste ja Baptistide Koguduste Liit): Koskla 18, Tallinn 10615; tel. 670-0698; fax 650-6008; e-mail liit@ekklesia.ee; internet www.ekklesia.ee; f. 1884; Pres. MEEGO REMMEL.

United Methodist Church in Estonia (Eesti Metodisti Kirik): EMK Kirikuvalitsus, Narva mnt. 51, Tallinn 10152; tel. 668-8497; fax 668-8498; e-mail keskus@metodistikirik.ee; internet www .metodistikirik.ee; f. 1907; forms part of the Northern European Area of the United Methodist Church; Superintendent TAAVI HOLLMAN.

The Eastern Orthodox Church

Since February 1996 the Estonian Apostolic Orthodox Church has been under the jurisdiction of the Ecumenical Patriarchate of Constantinople (based in İstanbul, Turkey), as it had been between 1923 and 1940. The Estonian Orthodox Church of the Moscow Patriarchate was officially registered in April 2002.

Estonian Apostolic Orthodox Church (Eesti Apostlik Õigeusu Kirik): Wismari 32, Tallinn 10136; tel. and fax 660-0780; e-mail eoc@ eoc.ee; internet www.eoc.ee; Metropolitan of Tallinn and All Estonia STEPHANOS; 64 congregations.

Estonian Orthodox Church (Moscow Patriarchate) (Moskva Patriarhaadi Eesti Õigeusu Kirik/Estonskaya Pravoslavnaya Tserkov Moskovskogo Patriarkhata): Pikk 64/4, Tallinn 10133; tel. 641-1301; fax 641-1302; e-mail mpeok@orthodox.ee; internet www .orthodox.ee; Metropolitan of Tallinn and All Estonia KORNELIUS (YAKOBS); 32 congregations.

The Roman Catholic Church

In the late 2000s there were an estimated 6,000 Roman Catholic adherents (of both the Latin and Byzantine rites) in Estonia.

Office of the Apostolic Administrator: Jaan Poska 47A, Tallinn 10150; tel. 601-3079; fax 601-3190; e-mail admapost@online.ee; internet katoliku.ee; Apostolic Administrator Most Rev. PHILIPPE JEAN-CHARLES JOURDAN (Titular Bishop of Pertusa).

ISLAM

Estonian Islamic Congregation: Sütiste 52–76, Tallinn 13420; tel. 652-2403; f. 1928; Chair. of Bd TIMUR SEIFULLEN.

JUDAISM

In the early 2000s there were an estimated 3,000 Jews resident in Estonia, principally in Tallinn.

Jewish Community of Estonia (Eesti Juudi Kogukond/Yevreiskaya Obshchina Estonii): Karu 16, Tallinn; POB 3576, Tallinn 10120; tel. 643-8566; fax 699-0568; e-mail community@jewish.ee; internet www.jewish.ee; Chair. ALLA JAKOBSON.

The Press

In 2013 there were 13 officially registered daily newspapers; in 2010 some 118 non-daily newspapers were published in Estonia. In 2013 some 1,130 periodicals were published.

PRINCIPAL NEWSPAPERS

In Estonian except where otherwise stated.

Äripäev (Business Daily): Pärnu mnt. 105, Tallinn 19094; tel. 667-0111; fax 667-0165; e-mail aripaev@aripaev.ee; internet www .aripaev.ee; f. 1989; five days a week; business and finance; Editor-in-Chief MEELIS MANDEL; circ. 10,500 (2015).

Baltic Business News (BBN): Tallinn; tel. 667-0016; e-mail bbn@ aripaev.ee; internet www.bbn.ee; daily; English; online; business and politics; affiliated with *Äripäev*; Editor TOOMAS HÕBEMÄGI.

Eesti Päevaleht (Estonian Daily): Narva mnt. 13, Tallinn 10151; tel. 680-4400; fax 680-4401; e-mail mail@epl.ee; internet epl.delfi.ee; f. 1905; 6 a week; 50% owned by Ekspress Grupp; Editor-in-Chief URMO SOONVALD; circ. 20,300 (2015).

Postimees (Postman): Maakri 23A, Tallinn 10145; tel. 666-2202; fax 666-2201; e-mail online@postimees.ee; internet www.postimees.ee; f. 1857; 6 a week; Editor-in-Chief MERIT KOPLI; circ. 49,300 (2015).

SL Õhtuleht (Evening Gazette): Narva mnt. 13, POB 106, Tallinn 10151; tel. 614-4000; fax 614-4001; e-mail leht@ohtuleht.ee; internet www.ohtuleht.ee; f. 2000; 6 a week; 50% owned by Ekspress Grupp; popular; Editor-in-Chief VÄINO KOORBERG; circ. 49,300 (2015).

Vesti dnya (News of the Day): Peterburi tee 53, Tallinn 11415; tel. 602-6865; fax 602-6867; e-mail vesti@vesti.ee; internet www.vesti .ee; five days a week; in Russian; also *Vesti nedeli* (News of the Week), Fridays; Chief Editor ALEKSANDR CHAPLYGIN; circ. 8,300 (2008).

PRINCIPAL PERIODICALS

Akadeemia: Ülikooli 21, Tartu 51007; tel. 742-3050; e-mail akadeemia@akad.ee; internet www.akad.ee; f. 1989; monthly; journal of the Union of Writers; Editor-in-Chief TOOMAS KIHO; circ. 2,090.

Delovoye Vedomosti (Business Gazette): Pärnu mnt. 105, Tallinn 19094; tel. 667-0080; fax 667-0465; e-mail delo@mbp.ee; internet www.dv.ee; weekly; Russian; affiliated with business daily *Äripäev* (q.v.); Editor-in-Chief OKSANA KABRITS; circ. 3,800 (June 2013).

Den za Dnem (Day to Day): Maakri 23A, Tallinn 10145; tel. 666-2511; fax 666-2395; e-mail tellimus@dzd.ee; internet www.dzd.ee; f. 1993; owned by Eesti Meedia (Schibsted Group); weekly; Russian; Editor-in-Chief YEVGENIYA GARANZHA; circ. 15,900 (June 2013).

Eesti Arst (Estonian Physician): Pepleri 32, Tartu 51010; tel. 742-7825; fax 742-7825; e-mail eestiarst@eestiarst.ee; internet www .eestiarst.ee; f. 1922; monthly; Editor-in-Chief ANDRES SOOSAAR; circ. 4,000.

Eesti Ekspress (Estonian Express): Narva mnt. 11E, Tallinn 10151; tel. 669-8080; fax 669-8154; e-mail ekspress@ekspress.ee; internet www.ekspress.ee; f. 1923; published regularly till 1940; resumed publication in 1990; weekly; owned by Ekspress Grupp; Publr HANS H. LUIK; Editor-in-Chief JANEK LUTS; circ. 29,800 (June 2013).

Eesti Kirik (Estonian Church): Ülikooli 1, Tartu 51003; tel. 733-7790; fax 733-7792; e-mail ek@eelk.ee; internet www.eestikirik.ee; f. 1923; weekly; organ of the Estonian Evangelical Lutheran Church; Editor-in-Chief SIRJE SEMM; circ. 2,100 (June 2013).

Eesti Loodus (Estonian Nature): Baeri maja, Veski 4, Tartu 51005; tel. 742-1143; e-mail toimetus@el.loodus.ee; internet www .loodusajakiri.ee/eesti_loodus; f. 1933; monthly; popular science; illustrated; Editor-in-Chief TOOMAS KUKK; circ. 5,200.

Eesti Naine (Estonian Woman): Niine 11, Tallinn 10414; tel. 666-2638; fax 666-2557; e-mail info@naistemaailm.ee; internet www .naistemaailm.ee; f. 1924; monthly; Editor AITA KIVI; circ. 24,000.

Hea Laps (Good Kid): Harju 1, Tallinn 10146; tel. 631-4428; e-mail toimetus@healaps.ee; internet www.healaps.ee; f. 1994; monthly; for children; Editor-in-Chief LEELO TUNGAL.

Horisont (Horizon): Endla 3, Tallinn 10122; tel. 610-4105; fax 610-4109; e-mail horisont@horisont.ee; internet www.horisont.ee; f. 1967; 6 a year; popular science; Editor-in-Chief KÄRT JÄNES-KAPP; circ. 3,000.

Keel ja Kirjandus (Language and Literature): Roosikrantsi 6, Tallinn 10119; tel. 644-9228; e-mail kk@eki.ee; internet kjk.eki.ee; f. 1958; monthly; publ. by Academy of Sciences and Union of Writers; Editor-in-Chief JOEL SANG; circ. 900.

Kodukiri (Your Home): Maakri 23A, Tallinn 10145; tel. 666-2633; fax 666-2557; e-mail malle.pajula@kirjastus.ee; internet www .naistemaailm.ee; f. 1992; monthly; Editor-in-Chief MALLE PAJULA; circ. 50,000.

Komsomolskaya Pravda—Baltiya (Young Communist League Truth—Baltics): Lembitu tn. 8-2, Tallinn 10114; tel. 668-8900; fax 668-8902; e-mail info@kompravda.eu; internet www.kompravda.eu; f. 2007; weekly; in Russian; 'Northern European' edition of Komsomolskaya Pravda (Russia); Editor-in-Chief V. N. SUNGORKIN; circ. 10,000 (June 2013).

Maaleht (Country News): Narva mnt. 11E, Tallinn 10151; tel. 661-3300; fax 661-3344; e-mail ml@maaleht.ee; internet www.maaleht .ee; f. 1987; weekly; politics, culture, agriculture and country life; Editor-in-Chief AIVAR VIIDIK; circ. 42,700 (June 2013).

Oil Shale: Ehitajate tee 5, Tallinn 19086; tel. 501-1827; fax 620-3011; e-mail meelika@kirj.ee; internet www.kirj.ee/oilshale; f. 1984; quarterly; geology, chemistry, mining, oil shale industry, power engineering; Editor-in-Chief ANTO RAUKAS; circ. 200.

Sirp (Sickle): Voorimehe 9, Tallinn 10146; tel. 682-9070; fax 682-9071; e-mail sirp@sirp.ee; internet www.sirp.ee; f. 1940; weekly; the arts; Editor-in-Chief KAAREL TARAND; circ. 4,900 (2008).

Teater, Muusika, Kino (Theatre, Music, Cinema): Voorimehe 9, Tallinn 10146; tel. 683-3132; e-mail pille@temuki.ee; internet www.temuki.ee; f. 1982; monthly; Editor-in-Chief MADIS KOLK; circ. 1,500.

Vikerkaar (Rainbow): Voorimehe 9, Tallinn 10146; tel. 683-3140; fax 683-3101; e-mail vikerkaar@vikerkaar.ee; internet www.vikerkaar.ee; f. 1986; monthly; fiction, poetry, critical works; Editor-in-Chief MÄRT VÄLJATAGA; circ. 1,500.

NEWS AGENCY

BNS (Baltic News Service): Toompuiestee 35, Tallinn 15043; tel. 610-8800; fax 610-8811; e-mail bns@bns.ee; internet www.bns.ee; f. 1991; daily news bulletins in English, Estonian, Latvian, Lithuanian and Russian; Editor-in-Chief ARTŪRAS RAČAS.

PRESS ORGANIZATIONS

Estonian Newspaper Association (Eesti Ajalehtede Liit): Pärnu mnt. 67A, Tallinn 10134; tel. 646-1005; fax 631-1210; e-mail eall@eall.ee; internet www.eall.ee; f. 1990; 40 mem. newspapers; Man. Dir MART RAUDSAAR.

Estonian Press Council (Avaliku Sõna Nõukogu): Äriklienditeenindus, POB 1228, Tallinn 11402; tel. and fax 5300-5847; e-mail asn@asn.org.ee; internet www.asn.org.ee; f. 1991; nongovernmental org.; Chair. Prof. EPP LAUK.

Union of Estonian Journalists (Eesti Ajakirjanike Liit): Gonsiori 21, Tallinn 10147; tel. 646-3699; e-mail eal@eal.ee; internet www.eal.ee; f. 1919; Dir PEETER ERNITS.

Publishers

Eesti Raamat (Estonian Book): Laki 26, Tallinn 12915; tel. and fax 658-7889; e-mail rein.poder.001@mail.ee; internet www.eestiraamat.ee; f. 1940; fiction for children and adults; Dir ANNE-ASTRI KASK.

Estonian Academy Publishers (EAP): Kohtu 6, Tallinn 10130; tel. 645-4504; fax 646-6026; e-mail niine@kirj.ee; internet www.kirj.ee; f. 1994; publishes nine academic journals incl. *Proceedings of the Estonian Academy of Sciences, Linguistica Uralica,* etc.; Dir ÜLO NIINE.

Ilmamaa: Vanemuise 19, Tartu 51014; tel. 742-7290; fax 742-7320; e-mail ilmamaa@ilmamaa.ee; internet www.ilmamaa.ee; f. 1993; general fiction, philosophy, cultural history; Dir MART JAGOMÄGI.

Ilo Publishing House: Tammsaare tee 47, Tallinn 11316; tel. 667-7855; fax 680-2230; e-mail ilo@ilo.ee; f. 1990; dictionaries, reference books, textbooks, history, management, psychology, law and children's books; Dir SIRJE-MAI PIHLAK.

Koolibri: POB 1793, Tallinn 11615; tel. 651-5300; fax 651-5301; e-mail koolibri@koolibri.ee; internet www.koolibri.ee; f. 1991; textbooks, dictionaries, children's books; Man. Dir KALLE KALJURAND.

Kunst (Fine Art): Lai 34, Tallinn 10133; POB 105, Tallinn 10502; tel. 641-1766; fax 641-1762; e-mail kunst.myyk@mail.ee; f. 1957; fine arts, fiction, tourism, history, biographies; Dir SIRJE HELME.

Logos: Narma mnt. 51, Tallinn 10152; tel. and fax 668-8499; e-mail logos@logos.ee; internet www.logos.ee; f. 1991; Christian; Chair. TIINA NÕLVAK.

Monokkel: POB 311, Tallinn 10503; tel. 501-6307; fax 656-9176; e-mail monokkel@hot.ee; internet www.hot.ee/monokkel; f. 1988; history, fiction; Dir ANTS ÕÖBIK.

Olion: Laki 26, Tallinn 12915; tel. 655-0175; fax 655-0173; e-mail kirjastus@olion.ee; internet www.olion.ee; f. 1989; politics, reference, history, biographies, children's books; Dir HÜLLE UNT.

Tartu Ülikool Kirjastus—University of Tartu Press: W. Struve 1, Tartu 50091; tel. 737-5961; fax 737-5944; e-mail tyk@ut.ee; internet www.tyk.ee; f. 1632; academic books and journals, textbooks, etc.; Man. Dir ÜLLE ERGMA.

Tiritamm: Endla 3, Tallinn 10122; tel. and fax 656-3570; e-mail tiritamm@tiritamm.ee; internet www.tiritamm.ee; f. 1991; children's books; Dir SIRJE SAIMRE.

Valgus: Tõnismägi 3A, Tallinn 10119; tel. 617-7010; fax 617-7016; e-mail info@kirjastusvalgus.ee; internet www.kirjastusvalgus.ee; f. 1965; scientific literature, resource materials and textbooks; Editor-in-Chief MADLI VALLIKIVI-PÄTS.

Varrak: Pärnu mnt. 67A, Tallinn 10134; tel. 616-1038; fax 616-1030; e-mail varrak@varrak.ee; internet www.varrak.ee; f. 1991; history,

philosophy and sociology, literary fiction, science fiction, popular fiction and children's literature; Man. Dir PRIIT MAIDE.

PUBLISHERS' ASSOCIATION

Estonian Publishers' Association (Eesti Kirjastuste Liit): Roosikrantsi 6/207, Tallinn 10119; tel. 644-9866; fax 617-7550; e-mail kirjastusteliit@eki.ee; internet www.estbook.com; f. 1991; Chair. MART JAGOMÄGI; 29 mems (Jan. 2013).

Broadcasting and Communications

TELECOMMUNICATIONS

In 2013 there were 426,500 main telephone lines in use in Estonia, and 2.1m. subscriptions to mobile cellular telecommunications services.

Eesti Telekom AS (Estonian Telecom Ltd): Valge 16, Tallinn 19095; tel. 611-1470; fax 631-1224; e-mail mailbox@telekom.ee; internet www.telekom.ee; f. 1992; privatized in 1999; subsidiaries include Eesti Mobiltelefon AS (EMT) and Elion Enterprises; CEO VALDO KALM.

Elisa Eesti: Sõpruse pst. 145, Tallinn 13417; tel. 681-1963; fax 681-1961; e-mail ariklient@elisa.ee; internet www.elisa.ee; mobile cellular telecommunications and internet service provider; Exec. Dir SAMI SEPPÄNEN.

EMT: Valge 16, Tallinn 19095; tel. 639-7130; fax 639-7132; e-mail info@emt.ee; internet www.emt.ee; f. 1991; wholly owned subsidiary of Eesti Telekom; mobile telecommunications and internet service provider; CEO VALDO KALM.

Tele2 Eesti: Jõe 2A, Tallinn 10151; tel. 686-6866; fax 686-6877; e-mail tele2@tele2.ee; internet www.tele2.ee; f. 1997; as AS Ritabell; present name adopted in 2001; mobile cellular telecommunications and internet service provider.

BROADCASTING

Supervisory Authority

Broadcasting Council: Gonsiori 21, Tallinn 15029; tel. 611-4305; fax 611-4457; e-mail rhn@er.ee; internet www.rhn.ee; mems appointed by Riigikogu (State Assembly); Chair. of Television AINAR RUUSSAAR; Chair. of Radio MARGUS ALLIKMAA.

Radio

The public broadcaster, Eesti Rahvusringhääling, was formed in 2007 by the merger of the public television and radio broadcasters. In 2005 there were additionally 28 private radio broadcasters operating in Estonia.

Eesti Rahvusringhääling (ERR) (Estonian Public Broadcasting): Gonsiori 27, Tallinn 15029; tel. 628-4100; fax 628-4155; e-mail err@err.ee; internet www.err.ee; f. 2007; radio broadcasts comprise five domestic channels (three in Estonian, one in Russian and one in English, French and German) and an external service in English; television broadcasts comprise one channel with programmes in Estonian and Russian; Chair. and Dir-Gen. AGU UUDELEPP.

Raadio Elmar: Õpetaja 9A, Tartu 51003; tel. 742-7520; e-mail elmar@elmar.ee; internet www.elmar.ee; one of six radio stations owned by Trio Grupp.

Raadio Kuku: Veerenni 58A, Tallinn 11314; tel. 630-7031; fax 630-7004; e-mail kuku@kuku.ee; internet www.kuku.ee; Editor-in-Chief HINDREK RIIKOJA.

Raadio Sky Plus: Pärnu mnt. 139F, Tallinn 11317; tel. 678-8777; e-mail info@skyplus.fm; internet www.skyplus.fm; owned by Sky Media.

Raadio Uuno: Veerenni 58A, Tallinn 11314; tel. 630-7080; e-mail uuno@uuno.ee; internet www.uuno.ee; f. 1994; Programme Man. ANDRES PANKSEPP.

Tartu Pereraadio (Tartu Family Radio): Annemõisa 8, Tartu 50708; tel. and fax 748-8458; e-mail pereraadio@pereraadio.ee; internet www.pereraadio.ee; f. 1994; Christian; Chief Exec. PAAVO PIHLAK.

Television

There are three national commercial television stations and one public broadcaster in Estonia. In addition, five cable television licences have been issued.

Eesti Rahvusringhääling (ERR) (Estonian Public Broadcasting): Gonsiori 27, Tallinn 15029; tel. 628-4100; fax 628-4155; e-mail err@err.ee; internet www.err.ee; f. 2007; radio broadcasts comprise five domestic channels (three in Estonian, one in Russian and one in English, French and German) and an external service in English; television broadcasts comprise one channel with programmes in Estonian and Russian; Chair. and Dir-Gen. AGU UUDELEPP.

Kanal 2 (Channel 2): Maakri 23A, Tallinn 10145; tel. 666-2450; fax 666-2451; e-mail info@kanal2.ee; internet www.kanal2.ee; f. 1993; commercial; Chief Exec. URMAS ORU.

TV3: Peterburgi tee 81, Tallinn 11415; tel. 622-0200; fax 622-0201; e-mail tv3@tv3.ee; internet www.tv3.ee; f. 1996; owned by Modern Times Group (Sweden); CEO PRIIT LEITO.

Broadcasting Association

Association of Estonian Broadcasters (AEB) (Eesti Ringhäälingute Liit): Ülemiste tee 3A, Tallinn 11415; tel. and fax 633-3235; e-mail erl@online.ee; internet www.ringhliit.ee; f. 1992; 19 mems; Man. Dir URMAS LOIT.

Finance

(cap. = capital; res = reserves; dep. = deposits; m. = million; brs = branches; amounts in euros unless otherwise specified)

BANKING

Supervisory Authority

Finantsinspektsioon: Sakala 4, Tallinn 15030; tel. 668-0500; fax 668-0501; e-mail info@fi.ee; internet www.fi.ee; f. 2002; joining the functions of banking and insurance supervisory authority and securities inspectorate; Chair. of Supervisory Bd JÜRGEN LIGI; Chair. of Management Bd KILVAR KESSLER.

Central Bank

Bank of Estonia (Eesti Pank): Estonia pst. 13, Tallinn 15095; tel. 668-0719; fax 668-0836; e-mail info@eestipank.ee; internet www .eestipank.info; f. 1919; closed 1940; re-established 1990; bank of issue; cap. 600.0m. kroons, res 4,253.5m. kroons, dep. 27,027.5m. kroons (Dec. 2009); Gov. ARDO HANSSON.

Commercial Banks

Estonian Credit Bank (Eesti Krediidipank): Narva mnt. 4, Tallinn 15014; tel. 669-0900; fax 661-6037; e-mail info@krediidipank.ee; internet www.krediidipank.ee; f. 1992; cap. 25.0.m., res 1.9m., dep. 256.4m. (Dec. 2012); Pres. PAVEL GORBATSEVICH; Chair. of Bd ANDRUS KLUGE; 11 brs.

SEB Pank (SEB Bank): Tornimäe 2, Tallinn 15010; tel. 665-5100; fax 665-5103; e-mail info@seb.ee; internet www.seb.ee; f. 1992; 100% owned by Scandinaviska Enskilda Banken (SEB—Sweden); cap. 42.5m., res 106.6m., dep. 3,358.9m. (Dec. 2012); Chair. of Bd RIHO UNT; 90 brs.

Swedbank AS: Liivalaia 8, Tallinn 15040; tel. 631-0310; fax 631-0410; e-mail info@swedbank.ee; internet www.swedbank.ee; f. 1991; 100% owned by Swedbank (Sweden); fmrly AS Hansapank; present name adopted 2009; cap. 85m., res 75m., dep. 6,315m. (Dec. 2012); Chair. of Council MICHAEL WOLF; Chair. of Bd HÅKAN BERG; 50 brs.

Tallinn Business Bank (Tallinna Äripank): Vana-Viru 7, Tallinn 15097; tel. 668-8000; fax 668-8001; e-mail info@tbb.ee; internet www .tbb.ee; f. 1991; cap. 14.7m., res 0.6m., dep. 106.0m. (Dec. 2012); Chair. of Bd VALERI HARITONOV.

Banking Association

Estonian Banking Association (Eesti Pangaliit): Ahtri 12, Tallinn 10151; tel. 611-6567; fax 611-6568; e-mail pangaliit@pangaliit .ee; internet www.pangaliit.ee; f. 1992; Chair. of Bd PRIIT PERENS.

STOCK EXCHANGE

Tallinn Stock Exchange (Tallinna Börs): Tartu mnt. 2, Tallinn 10145; tel. 640-8800; fax 640-8801; e-mail tallinn@nasdaqomx.com; f. 1995; 62% owned by the NASDAQ OMX Group (USA); Chair. of Man. Bd ANDRUS ALBER.

INSURANCE

In 2013 there were five insurance organizations providing life insurance and nine providing non-life insurance in Estonia.

Estonian Insurance Association (Eesti Kindlustusseltside Liit): Mustamäe tee 46, Tallinn 10621; tel. 667-1800; e-mail info@eksl.ee; internet www.eksl.ee; f. 1993; Chair. of Bd MART JESSE; 17 mem. cos.

Insurance Companies

Compensa Life Vienna Insurance Group SE: Roosikrantsi 11, Tallinn 10119; tel. 610-3000; fax 610-3010; e-mail info@compensalife .ee; internet www.compensalife.eu/ee; f. 1993; Chair. OLGA REZNIK; 20 brs.

ERGO: Tammsaare 47, Tallinn 11316; tel. 610-6500; fax 610-6501; e-mail info@ergo.ee; internet www3.ergo.ee; f. 1990; provides non-

life insurance (as ERGO Kindlustuse) and life insurance (ERGO Elukindlustus); Chair. of Supervisory Bd THOMAS HANS SCHIRMER.

If P&C Insurance: Lõõtsa 8A, Tallinn 11415; tel. 669-6684; fax 667-1101; e-mail info@if.ee; internet www.if.ee; f. 1991 as Eesti Kindlustus; subsidiary of Sampo Group; renamed AS Eesti Kindlustus 1996, AS Sampo Eesti Varakindlustus 1999, AS If Kindlustus 2002, and as above 2009; non-life; Chair. TORBJÖRN MAGNUSSON; Chief Exec. TIMO VUORINEN.

Mandatum Life Insurance Baltic SE: Viru väljak 2, Tallinn 10111; tel. 681-2300; fax 681-2399; e-mail info@mandatumlife.ee; internet www.mandatumlife.ee; f. 1997 as Sampo Life; present name adopted 2010; Chair. TIMO LAITINEN; CEO IMRE MADISON.

SEB Elu- ja Pensionikindlustus (SEB Life Insurance & Pensions Estonia): Tornimäe 2, Tallinn 15010; tel. 665-5100; fax 665-5103; e-mail info@seb.ee; internet www.seb.ee; f. 1998; fmrly Ühispanga Elukindlustuse; wholly owned by SEB Eesti; life insurance, pensions; Chair. of Management Bd RIHO UNT.

Seesam Insurance AS: Vambola 6, Tallinn 10114; tel. 628-1800; fax 628-1802; e-mail seesam@seesam.ee; internet www.seesam.ee; f. 1991; owned by the OP-Pohjola Group; non-life; Chair. of Management Bd TOOMAS ABNER; Chair. of Supervisory Bd JOUKO PÖLÖNEN.

Swedbank Insurance: Liivalaia 12, Tallinn 15039; tel. 888-2100; fax 888-2221; e-mail info@swedbank.ee; internet www.swedbank.ee; wholly owned by Swedbank AS (Sweden); life and non-life; Chair. PRIIT PERENS.

Trade and Industry

GOVERNMENT AGENCIES

Enterprise Estonia (Ettevõtluse Arendamise Sihtasutus): Lasnamäe 2, Tallinn 11412; tel. 627-9700; fax 627-9701; e-mail eas@eas.ee; internet www.eas.ee; f. 2000; Chair. ÜLARI ALAMETS.

Estonian Competition Authority (Kohkurentsiamet): Auna 6, Tallinn 10317; tel. 667-2400; fax 667-2401; e-mail info@ konkurentsiamet.ee; internet www.konkurentsiamet.ee; f. 2008; supervises competition, with specific powers in the sectors of fuel and energy, and electronic and postal communications; Dir-Gen. MÄRT OTS.

Estonian Investment Agency (EIA): Lasnamäe 2, Tallinn 11412; tel. 627-9700; fax 627-9701; e-mail invest@eas.ee; internet www .investinestonia.com; Dir KRISTI TIIVAS.

Estonian Regional and Local Development Agency (Eesti Regionaalse ja Kohaliku Arengu Sihtasutus—ERKAS): Ahtri 8, 3rd Floor, Tallinn 10151; tel. 694-3431; fax 694-3425; e-mail erkas@erkas.ee; internet www.erkas.ee; f. 2002; Chair. JÜRI ROOS.

Estonian Technical Surveillance Authority (Tehnilise Järelevalve Amet): Sõle 23A, 10614 Tallinn; tel. 667-2011; fax 667-2001; e-mail info@tja.ee; internet www.tja.ee; f. 2008; co-ordinates management of the use of radio frequencies (incl. broadcasting), manages numbering plan for telecommunications services, various responsibilities in the field of communications, incl. railways; Dir-Gen. RAIGO UUKKIVI.

CHAMBERS OF COMMERCE

Estonian Chamber of Agriculture and Commerce (Eesti Põllumajandus-Kaubanduskoda—EPKK): Vilmsi 53G, Tallinn 10147; tel. 600-9349; fax 600-9350; e-mail info@epkk.ee; internet www.epkk .ee; f. 1996; Chair. of Bd AAVO MÖLDER.

Estonian Chamber of Commerce and Industry (ECCI) (Eesti Kaubandus-Tööstuskoda): Toom-Kooli 17, Tallinn 10130; tel. 604-0060; fax 604-0061; e-mail koda@koda.ee; internet www.koda.ee; f. 1925; brs in Tartu, Jõhvi, Pärnu and Kuressaare; Pres. TOOMAS LUMAN.

INDUSTRIAL AND TRADE ASSOCIATIONS

Asscn of Construction Material Producers of Estonia (Eesti Ehitusmaterjalide Tootjate Liit—EETL): Pärnu mnt. 141, Tallinn 11314; tel. 648-1918; fax 648-9062; e-mail eetl@hot.ee; internet www .hot.ee/eetl; Man. Dir ENNO RABANE.

Asscn of Estonian Food Industry (Eesti Toiduainetööstuse Liit): Saku 15/105, Tallinn 11314; tel. 648-4978; fax 631-2718; e-mail info@ toiduliit.ee; internet www.toiduliit.ee; f. 1993; Dir SIRJE POTISEPP.

Central Union of Estonian Farmers (Eestimaa Põllumeeste Keskliit): J. Vilmsi 53G, Tallinn 10147; tel. and fax 600-8616; e-mail info@eptk.ee; internet www.eptk.ee; f. 1990; Chair. of Bd ÜLLAS HUNT.

Estonian Asscn of Fisheries (Eesti Kalaliit): Peterburi tee 2F, Tallinn 11415; tel. 622-1300; fax 622-1302; e-mail kalaliit@online.ee;

internet www.kalaliit.ee; f. 1995; 28 mems; Chair. TOOMAS KÕUHKNA; Man. Dir VALDUR NOORMÄGI.

Estonian Asscn of Information Technology and Telecommunication Companies (Eesti Infotehnoloogia ja Telekommunikatsiooni Liit): Lõõtsa 6, Tallinn 11415; tel. 617-7145; fax 617-7146; e-mail info@itl.ee; internet www.itl.ee; f. 2000; 36 mems; Pres. TAAVI KOTKA; Chair. URMAS KÕLLI.

Estonian Asscn of Small and Medium-sized Enterprises (EVEA) (Eesti Väike-Ja Keskmiste Ettevõtjate Assotsiatsioon): Liivalaia 9, Tallinn 10118; tel. 641-0920; fax 641-0916; e-mail evea@evea.ee; internet www.evea.ee; f. 1988; Pres. MARINA KAAS; CEO KERSTI KRAAS.

Estonian Forest Industries Asscn (Eesti Metsatööstuse Liit—EMTL): Viljandi mnt. 18A, Tallinn 11216; tel. 656-7643; fax 656-7644; e-mail info@emtl.ee; internet www.emtl.ee; f. 1996; Man. Dir OTT OTSMANN.

Estonian Meat Asscn (Eesti Lihaliit): Lai 39/41, Tallinn 10133; tel. 641-1179; fax 641-1035; e-mail lihaliit@hot.ee; f. 1989; Chair. of Bd AIGAR PINDMAA; Man. Dir PEETER GRIGORJEV.

Estonian Oil Asscn (Eesti Õliühing): Kiriku 6, Tallinn 10130; tel. 664-1247; fax 641-8471; e-mail toomas@oilunion.ee; internet www.oilunion.ee; f. 1993; Chair. RAIVO VARE; 12 mem. orgs.

Estonian Trade Council (Eesti Väliskaubanduse Liit): Tammsaare tee 47, Tallinn 11316; tel. 684-1252; fax 659-7017; e-mail icc@icc-estonia.ee; internet www.icc-estonia.ee; f. 1991; 110 mems; non-profit org.; promotes export trade; Chair. of Bd TIIT TAMMEMÄGI.

Federation of the Estonian Chemical Industry (Eesti Keemiatööstuse Liit): Peterburi tee 46, Tallinn 11415; tel. and fax 613-9775; e-mail info@keemia.ee; internet www.keemia.ee; f. 1991; Man. Dir HALLAR MEYBAUM.

Federation of the Estonian Engineering Industry (Eesti Masinatööstuse Liit—EML): Mäealuse 4, Tallinn 12618; tel. 651-5578; e-mail emliit@emliit.ee; internet www.emliit.ee; f. 1991; represents over 50 metalworking, machine-building, electrotechnics and electronics enterprises; Chair. of Bd TÕNU LELUMEES.

Union of Estonian Automobile Enterprises (Eesti Autoettevõtete Liit): Akadeemia tee 20, Tallinn 12611; tel. 641-2511; fax 641-2523; e-mail al@autoettevoteliit.ee; internet www.autoettevoteteliit.ee; f. 1990; Chair. REIN SIIM; 77 mem. cos.

EMPLOYERS' ORGANIZATION

Estonian Employers' Confederation (Eesti Tööandjate Kesliit): Kiriku 6, Tallinn 10130; tel. 699-9301; fax 699-9310; e-mail ettk@ettk.ee; internet ettk.tooandjad.ee; f. 1991 as Confederation of Estonian Industry; Chair. of Bd MEELIS VIRKEBAU; Pres. ENN VESKIMÄGI; 24 brs.

UTILITIES

Electricity

Under terms agreed with the European Union, Estonia was permitted to postpone the liberalization of its electricity market until 2013, in order to allow the requisite investment to be made in the oil shale power plants that generate most of the country's electricity supply.

Operations of the Estlink submarine cable, connecting the electricity networks of Estonia and Finland, commenced in January 2007.

Eesti Energia (Estonian Energy Co): Laki 24, Tallinn 12915; tel. 715-2222; fax 715-2200; e-mail info@energia.ee; internet www.energia.ee; f. 1939; producer, transmitter and distributor of thermal and electric energy; manufacture of electric motors; electrical engineering; Chair. HANDO SUTTER; 7,000 employees.

Gas

Eesti Gaas (Estonian Gas Co): Liivalaia 9, Tallinn 10118; tel. 630-3003; fax 631-3884; e-mail info@gaas.ee; internet www.gaas.ee; f. 1993; purchases and distributes natural gas; constructs pipelines; calibrates gas meters; Chair. TIIT KULLERKUPP; 255 employees.

Water

Tallinna Vesi (Tallinn Water Co): Ädala 10, Tallinn 10614; tel. 626-2200; fax 626-2300; e-mail tvesi@tvesi.ee; internet www.tallinnavesi.ee; f. 1997; supply and treatment of water; collection and treatment of waste water; 35.30% owned by United Utilities Tallinna (a subsidiary of United Utilities International, United Kingdom), 34.70% by Tallinn City Govt; CEO IAN PLENDERLEITH; 302 employees (April 2011).

TRADE UNIONS

Asscn of Estonian Energy Workers' Trade Unions (Eesti Energeetikatöötajate Ametiühingute Liit—EEAÜL): Gonsiori 3A,

Tallinn 10117; tel. 715-5527; fax 715-5528; e-mail sander.vaikma@energia.ee; internet www.energeetik.ee; Chair. SANDER VAIKMA.

Confederation of Estonian Employee Unions (Teenistujate Ametiliitude Keskorganisatsioon—TALO): Endla 3, Tallinn 15189; tel. 641-9800; fax 641-9805; e-mail talo@talo.ee; internet www.talo.ee; f. 1992; comprises nine mem. unions from the broadcasting, cultural, customs, education, engineering, journalism, radiology and scientific sectors; Chair. AGO TUULING.

Estonian Trade Union Confederation (Eesti Ametiühingute Keskliit—EAKL): Pärnu mnt. 41A, Tallinn 10119; tel. 641-2800; fax 641-2801; e-mail eakl@eakl.ee; internet www.eakl.ee; f. 1990; 20 professional mem. orgs; Chair. PEEP PERERSON; estimated 40,000 individual mems (2008).

Transport

RAILWAYS

In 2009 there were 792 km of railway track in use, of which 132 km were electrified.

Edelaraudtee: Kaare 25, Türi 72212; tel. 385-7123; fax 385-7121; e-mail info@edel.ee; internet www.edel.ee; f. 1997; owned by GB Railways (United Kingdom); operates freight services; former passenger inter-city services transferred to Elron (q.v.) in 2014; Dir KALVI PUKKA.

Eesti Raudtee (Estonian Railways): Toompuiestee 35, Tallinn 15073; tel. 615-8610; fax 615-8710; e-mail raudtee@evr.ee; internet www.evr.ee; f. 1918; privatized in 2001; renationalization completed in 2007; rail infrastructure operator and freight carrier; Chair. of Management Bd AHTI ASMANN; Chair of Supervisory Bd TAAVI MADIBERK; 860 employees (2012).

Elron: Vabaduse pst. 176, Tallinn 10917; tel. 673-7400; e-mail info@elron.ee; internet elron.ee; f. 1998 as Elektriraudtee; present name adopted October 2013; state-owned; suburban passenger services in and around Tallinn, and from 2014 commenced operating inter-city diesel passenger services fmrly operated by Edelaraudtee; Chair. TOIVO PROMM.

GoRail: Toompuiestee 37, Tallinn 10133; tel. 631-0043; fax 615-6720; e-mail info@gorail.ee; internet www.gorail.ee; f. 1998; owned by AS Go Group; operate direct, express, passenger rail services between Tallinn and St Petersburg and Moscow, both in Russia; CEO ALAR PINSEL.

ROADS

In 2012 Estonia had a total road network of 58,768 km, of which 4,011 km were main roads and 12,458 km regional roads.

Estonian Road Administration (Maanteeamet): Pärnu mnt. 463A, Tallinn 10916; tel. 611-9300; fax 611-9360; e-mail info@mnt.ee; internet www.mnt.ee; f. 1990; state-owned; Dir-Gen. AIVO ADAMSON.

INLAND WATERWAYS

In 2012 there were 335 km of navigable inland waterways.

SHIPPING

Tallinn is the main port for freight transportation. There are regular passenger services between Tallinn and Helsinki, Finland. At December 2014 the flag registered fleet comprised 146 vessels, totalling 368,248 grt.

Estonian Maritime Administration (EMA) (Veeteede Amet): Valge 4, Tallinn 11413; tel. 620-5500; fax 620-5506; e-mail eva@vta.ee; internet www.vta.ee; f. 1990; state-owned; administers and implements state maritime safety policies, ship-control, pilot, lighthouse and hydrography services; Gen. Dir ANDRUS MAIDE; 375 employees.

Principal Shipping Companies

Eesti Merelaevandus (ESCO) (Estonian Shipping Co): Sadama 4, Tallinn 15096; tel. 640-9500; fax 640-9595; e-mail online@eml.ee; internet www.eml.ee; f. 1940; owned by Tschudi Shipping Co (Norway); liner services, ship-chartering and cargo-shipping; Chair of Supervisory Bd JON EDVARD SUNDNES; Man. Dir SOEREN ANDERSEN; 500 employees.

Saaremaa Laevakompanii (Saaremaa Shipping Co): Kohtu 1, Kuressaare 93819; tel. 452-4442; fax 452-4355; e-mail info@tuulelaevad.ee; internet www.tuulelaevad.ee; f. 1992; passenger and cargo services between mainland Estonia and Saaremaa, Hiiumaa and Vormsi islands; Dir-Gen. TÕNIS RIHVK.

Tallink Grupp: Sadama 5/7, Tallinn 10111; tel. 640-9800; fax 640-9810; e-mail info@tallink.ee; internet www.tallink.ee; f. 1989 as a joint-venture Estonian-Finnish co; in 1996–2002 known as Hansatee Grupp, reverted to previous name in 2002; passenger and cargo transport; operates high-speed ferries between Tallinn and Helsinki, Finland; also operates routes to St Petersburg, Russia, and Stockholm, Sweden; Chair. of Management Bd ENN PANT.

Shipowners' Association

Estonian Shipowners' Association (Eesti Laevaomanike Liit): Kopli 101, Tallinn 11712; tel. and fax 613-5528; e-mail reederid@hot .ee; Pres. Capt. TOIVO NINNAS.

Port Authorities

Port of Sillamäe (Sillamäe Sadam—Silport): Suur-Karja 5, Tallinn 10140; tel. 640-5271; fax 640-5279; e-mail silport@silport.ee; internet www.silport.ee; operations commenced Oct. 2005; deep sea port; navigable year-round; railway facilities; free trade zone; four terminals; privately owned; Chair. VITALY IVANOV.

Port of Tallinn (Tallinna Sadam): Sadama 25, Tallinn 15051; tel. 631-8555; fax 631-8166; e-mail ts@ts.ee; internet www.ts.ee; f. 1991; the Port of Tallinn consists of five constituent harbours: Old City, Muuga, Paljassaare, Paldiski South and Saaremaa; Chair. of Bd AIN KALJURAND; Harbour Master Y. KIKAS; 367 employees (2015).

CIVIL AVIATION

There is an international airport at Tallinn.

Civil Aviation Administration (Lennuamat): Rävala pst. 8, Tallinn 10143; tel. 610-3500; fax 610-3501; e-mail ecaa@ecaa.ee; internet www.ecaa.ee; f. 1990; Dir-Gen. KRISTJAN TELVE (acting).

Avies: Sepise 1, Tallinn 11101; tel. 630-1370; fax 630-1371; e-mail info@avies.ee; internet www.flyavies.ee; f. 1991; domestic passenger services between Tallinn and Saaremaa and Hiiumaa islands, international scheduled and charter passenger and cargo services; Man. Dir VLADIMIR PISARKOV.

Estonian Air: Lennujaama 13, Tallinn 11101; tel. 640-1160; fax 650-8748; e-mail info@estonian-air.ee; internet www.estonian-air .com; f. 1991; 49% owned by Scandinavian Airlines (Denmark/Norway/Sweden), 34% state-owned; passenger and cargo flights to destinations across Europe; CEO JAN PALMÉR.

Tourism

Estonia has a wide range of attractions for tourists, including the historic towns of Tallinn and Tartu, extensive nature reserves and coastal resorts. In 2013 there were 1,940,130 foreign visitors to Estonia (as measured by arrivals at registered accommodation establishments), while receipts from tourism (excluding passenger transport) totalled US $1,390m.

Estonian Tourist Board (Turismiarenduskeskus): Lasnamäe 2, Tallinn 11412; tel. 627-9770; fax 627-9701; e-mail tourism@eas.ee; internet www.visitestonia.com; f. 1990; Dir TARMO MUTSO.

Defence

As assessed at November 2014, Estonia's total armed forces numbered 5,750, comprising an army of 5,300 (including conscripts), a navy of 200, and an air force of 250. There was also a reserve militia of 30,000. The duration of military service is eight months, or 11 months for officers and some specialists. In 1994 Estonia joined the 'Partnership for Peace' programme of military co-operation of the North Atlantic Treaty Organization (NATO), and became a full member of the Organization in March 2004.

Defence Expenditure: Budgeted at €402m. in 2015.

Commander of the Defence Forces: Lt-Gen. RIHO TERRAS.

Chief of the General Staff: Cdre IGOR SCHVEDE.

Commander of the Army: Col ARTUR TIGANIK.

Commander of the Navy: Capt. STEN SEPPER.

Commander of the Air Force: Col JAAK TARIEN.

Education

Compulsory education begins at the age of seven and lasts for nine years. Students may then attend either general secondary school or vocational school. In 2012/13 there were 26 higher education institutions, at which 64,806 students were enrolled (including those undertaking evening and correspondence courses). In 2007/08 some 20% of students at primary and secondary schools received tuition in a language other than Estonian (mainly Russian). In 2009/10 enrolment at pre-primary schools included 88% of children in the corresponding age-group. In the same year enrolment in primary education included 95% of children in the relevant age-group, while secondary education enrolment included 94% of children in the relevant age-group. In 2006 enrolment in tertiary education was equivalent to 65% of those in the relevant age-group (males 49%; females 82%). Forecast government expenditure on education amounted to €760.6m. in 2014 (9.4% of total expenditure in that year).

ETHIOPIA

Introductory Survey

LOCATION, CLIMATE, LANGUAGE, RELIGION, FLAG, CAPITAL

The Federal Democratic Republic of Ethiopia is a landlocked country in eastern Africa; it has a long frontier with Somalia near the Horn of Africa. South Sudan and Sudan lie to the west, Eritrea to the north, Djibouti to the north-east and Kenya to the south. The climate is mainly temperate because of the high plateau terrain, with an annual average temperature of 13°C (55°F), abundant rainfall in some years and low humidity. The lower country and valley gorges are very hot and subject to recurrent drought. The official language is Amharic, but many other local languages are also spoken. English is widely used in official and commercial circles. The Ethiopian Orthodox (Tewahido) Church, an ancient Christian sect, has a wide following in the north and on the southern plateau. In much of the south and east the inhabitants include Muslims and followers of animist beliefs. The national flag (proportions 1 by 2) has three equal horizontal stripes, of green, yellow and red, superimposed in the centre of which is a blue disk bearing a yellow pentagram, resembling a star, with single yellow rays extending outwards from the inner angles of the star. The capital is Addis Ababa.

CONTEMPORARY POLITICAL HISTORY

Historical Context

In September 1974 Emperor Haile Selassie was deposed by the armed forces and his imperial regime was replaced by the Provisional Military Administrative Council (PMAC), known popularly as the Dergue (Committee), led by Brig.-Gen. Teferi Benti. In December Ethiopia was declared a socialist state; however, a radical programme of social and economic reforms led to widespread unrest, and in February 1977 Lt-Col Mengistu Haile Mariam executed Teferi and his closest associates, and replaced him as Chairman of the PMAC and as Head of State.

During 1977–78, in an attempt to end opposition to the regime, the Government imprisoned or killed thousands of its opponents. Political power was consolidated in a Commission for Organizing the Party of the Working People of Ethiopia (COPWE), largely dominated by military personnel. In September 1984, at the COPWE's third congress, the Workers' Party of Ethiopia (WPE) was formally inaugurated. Mengistu was unanimously elected Secretary-General of the party, which modelled itself on the Communist Party of the Soviet Union. In February 1987, at a referendum, some 81% of the electorate endorsed a new Constitution and in June national elections were held to an 835-seat legislature, the National Shengo (Assembly). In September, at the inaugural meeting of the new legislature, the PMAC was abolished, and the People's Democratic Republic of Ethiopia was declared. The National Shengo unanimously elected Mengistu as President of the Republic, and a 24-member Council of State was also elected, to act as the Shengo's permanent organ.

Numerous groups, encouraged by the confusion resulting from the 1974 revolution, launched armed insurgencies against the Government. Of these, the most effective were based in the Ogaden, Eritrea and Tigrai regions. Somalia laid claim to the Ogaden, which is populated mainly by ethnic Somalis. Somali troops supported incursions by forces of the Western Somali Liberation Front, and in 1977 the Somalis made major advances in the Ogaden. In 1978, however, they were forced to retreat, and by the end of 1980 Ethiopian forces had gained control of virtually the whole of the Ogaden region.

The former Italian colony of Eritrea was merged with Ethiopia, in a federal arrangement, in September 1952, and annexed to Ethiopia as a province in November 1962. A secessionist movement, the Eritrean Liberation Front (ELF), was founded in Egypt in 1958. The ELF eventually split into several rival factions, the largest of which was the Eritrean People's Liberation Front (EPLF). In 1978 government troops re-established control in much of Eritrea, and the EPLF retreated to the northern town of Nakfa. In 1982 an offensive by government troops failed to capture Nakfa, and in 1984 the EPLF made several successful counter-attacks. In mid-1986 government forces abandoned the north-east coast to the rebels.

An insurgent movement also emerged in Tigrai province in the late 1970s. The Tigrai People's Liberation Front (TPLF) was armed and trained by the EPLF, but relations between the two groups deteriorated sharply in the mid-1980s. The TPLF was weakened by conflict with other anti-Government groups, and in 1985 and 1986 government forces had considerable success against the Front.

In September 1987 the newly elected National Shengo announced that five areas, including Eritrea and Tigrai, were to become 'autonomous regions' under the new Constitution. Eritrea was granted a considerable degree of self-government, but both the EPLF and the TPLF rejected the proposals. In March 1988 EPLF forces captured the town of Afabet, after which the TPLF seized all the garrisons in north-western and north-eastern Tigrai. In early 1989, following major defeats in north-western Tigrai, government forces abandoned virtually the whole region to the TPLF.

Following the capture of Massawa port by the EPLF in February 1990 (presenting a direct threat to the continued survival of the Ethiopian army in Eritrea), President Mengistu was obliged to make a number of concessions. In March Ethiopian socialism was virtually abandoned, when the WPE was renamed the Ethiopian Democratic Unity Party, and membership was opened to non-Marxists. Mengistu began introducing elements of a market economy and dismantling many of the economic structures that had been established after the 1974 revolution.

By late April 1991, troops of the Ethiopian People's Revolutionary Democratic Front (EPRDF)—an alliance of the TPLF and the Ethiopian People's Democratic Movement (EPDM)—had captured Ambo, a town 130 km west of Addis Ababa, while EPLF forces were 50 km north of Assab (Eritrea), Ethiopia's then principal port. On 21 May, faced with the prospect of the imminent defeat of his army, Mengistu fled the country. On 28 May, following the failure of negotiations in the United Kingdom, and with the public support of the USA, units of the EPRDF entered Addis Ababa. They encountered little resistance, and the EPRDF established an interim Government. Meanwhile, the EPLF had gained control of the Eritrean capital, Asmara, and announced the establishment of a provisional Government to administer Eritrea, pending a referendum on the issue of independence.

In July 1991 a national conference, convened by the EPRDF with participation by selected political parties, adopted amendments to a national charter (presented by the EPRDF), and elected an 87-member Council of Representatives, which was to govern for a transitional period of two years, after which free national elections were to be held. The national charter provided guarantees for freedom of association and expression, and for self-determination for Ethiopia's various ethnic groups. The EPLF was not officially represented at the conference, but came to an agreement with the EPRDF, whereby the EPRDF accepted the formation of the EPLF's provisional Government of Eritrea and the determination by referendum of the future of the region. In late July the Council of Representatives established a commission to draft a new constitution and elected Meles Zenawi, the leader of the EPRDF (and of the TPLF), as Chairman of the Council, a position that made him President of the transitional Government and Head of State; in August it appointed a Council of Ministers. Following a referendum in April 1993 Eritrean independence was proclaimed on 24 May.

Domestic Political Affairs

Elections to a Constituent Assembly were conducted in Ethiopia in June 1994, in which the EPRDF won 484 of the 547 seats. The Constituent Assembly ratified a new Constitution in December, which provided for the establishment of a federal government and the division of the country into nine states and two chartered cities. A new legislature, the Federal Parliamentary Assembly, was to be established, comprising two chambers: the House of People's Representatives (consisting of no more than 550 directly elected members) and the House of the Federation (composed of 117 deputies, elected by the new state assemblies). The EPRDF and its allies won an overwhelming victory in elections to the House of People's Representatives and state assemblies in May

1995. Most opposition parties boycotted the poll, although international observers accepted that the elections were conducted in a largely free and fair manner.

On 22 August 1995 the country's new Constitution and designation as the Federal Democratic Republic of Ethiopia were formally instituted, and Dr Negasso Gidada, the EPRDF nominee, and a member of the Oromo People's Democratic Organization (OPDO, which was in alliance with the EPRDF), was elected President of the Federal Republic. Meles was elected from among the members of the House of People's Representatives as Prime Minister.

The trial of 69 former government officials, including ex-President Mengistu, opened in Addis Ababa in December 1994. The defendants, 23 of whom were being tried *in absentia* (including Mengistu, who was in exile in Zimbabwe), were accused of crimes against humanity and of genocide, perpetrated during 1974–91. In February 1997 the office of the Special Prosecutor announced that an additional 5,198 people would be indicted for war crimes and genocide, of whom nearly 3,000 would be tried *in absentia*. In April the Ethiopian High Court found 37 people (13 *in absentia*) guilty of crimes against humanity and genocide; they were sentenced to up to 20 years' 'rigorous' imprisonment. In December 2006 Mengistu, along with 71 others, was found guilty of genocide, and in January 2007 he was sentenced *in absentia* to life imprisonment. In May 2008 the life sentence was overturned by the Federal Supreme Court and Mengistu was sentenced to death, along with a number of his former political associates.

Legislative elections were held on 14 May 2000: the OPDO won the largest number of seats in the House of People's Representatives, taking 178 of the 546 available. The OPDO's major partners in the EPRDF, the Amhara National Democratic Movement (ANDM—as the EPDM had been renamed in 1994) and the TPLF, gained 134 and 38 seats, respectively, securing the coalition a majority in the lower chamber. In October the new legislature was sworn in, and Meles was re-elected as Prime Minister.

In late June 2001 President Gidada was dismissed from the executive committee of the OPDO, after it was alleged that he had refused to accept the party's programme of reform and was providing support to dissidents opposed to Meles. Gidada, in turn, accused the Government of embarking on a campaign of propaganda against him. Gidada was also expelled from the EPRDF; however, he remained insistent that he would complete his presidential term, which was scheduled to end in October. By September Meles had succeeded in re-establishing control over the TPLF, and therefore the EPRDF, following his re-election as Chairman of the party. On 8 October 2001 Lt Girma Wolde Giorgis was elected by the legislature to replace Gidada as President. Later that month Prime Minister Meles effected a major reorganization of the Council of Ministers. In 2003 a number of new political parties and coalition organizations were formed, the most significant of which were the United Ethiopian Democratic Party, which was created by the merger of the Ethiopian Democratic Unity Party and the Ethiopian Democratic Party, and the United Ethiopian Democratic Forces (UEDF), under the leadership of Dr Beyene Petros.

From December 2003 clashes between the Anuak and Nuer communities over disputed land in the Gambela region of the country escalated. The increase in violence was precipitated by the killing of eight officials from the office of the UN High Commissioner for Refugees and the Federal Agency for Refugee and Returnee Affairs, reportedly committed by the Anuak, who had been angered by the proposed construction on their land of a camp to house Nuer refugees. The Anuak community was the target of a number of revenge attacks, which resulted in the death of some 100 people (although opposition sources indicated that the actual casualty figures were much higher), and it was alleged that the Government had actively encouraged reprisals against the Anuak community. By mid-2004 the situation had calmed significantly and about 8,000 of some 15,000 Anuak who had fled in January had returned to Gambela.

The 2005 legislative elections

Legislative elections were held on 15 May 2005, although voting in the Somali regional state was postponed until 21 August. Provisional results for the House of People's Representatives, published by the National Electoral Board of Ethiopia (NEBE) in late May, awarded the EPRDF 302 seats, the Coalition for Unity and Democracy (CUD) 122 and the UEDF 57; the rate of voter participation was recorded at more than 90%. The results in some 300 constituencies were, however, disputed by both the EPRDF and opposition parties amid allegations of electoral fraud, while concerns over voting irregularities were also raised by observers from the European Union (EU, see p. 271). The NEBE agreed to undertake investigations in 143 of the contested constituencies and in June the EU brokered an agreement between the EPRDF and the CUD and the UEDF, according to which both sides pledged to accept the findings of the NEBE's investigations. The NEBE announced the official results of the legislative elections in early September, including results from the Somali regional state and from 31 constituencies where voting had been reheld, according to which the EPRDF took 327 seats, the CUD 109 seats and the UEDF 52 seats. A number of smaller parties secured the remaining seats. Despite agreeing to accept the NEBE's decision, the CUD renewed its allegations of electoral fraud and in early October some 100 CUD deputies boycotted the opening of the House of People's Representatives.

In November 2005 there were further violent clashes in Addis Ababa between police and demonstrators protesting against alleged voting irregularities in the legislative elections. It was reported that some 46 people were killed and around 150 people were injured during the confrontations. A number of senior members of the CUD were among some 130 people arrested later in November and subsequently charged with treason and attempted genocide. In June 2007 38 of the defendants were found guilty of violating the Constitution and 30 of those convicted were sentenced to life imprisonment, with the remainder handed lesser terms; however, in July all 38 were pardoned and freed from prison.

Meanwhile, in January 2006 the British Government announced that it was to suspend indefinitely its direct budgetary support to Ethiopia, owing to concerns over the political situation in the country. In May a new opposition coalition, the Alliance for Freedom and Democracy (AFD), was formed by the CUD and four rebel factions: the Ethiopian People's Patriotic Front; the Ogaden National Liberation Front (ONLF); the Oromo Liberation Front (OLF) and the Sidama Liberation Front. In August Meles announced that thousands of troops had been deployed against ONLF rebels, who were allegedly receiving support from Eritrea and Somali Islamists, in the Ogaden region. In October it emerged that an official inquiry into the violent dispersal of demonstrations after the May 2005 elections had been suppressed by the Government; 193 protesters were reported to have been killed by Ethiopian security forces. Renewed violence in November 2009 resulted in the deaths of a number of Ethiopian troops as ONLF rebels launched an offensive in the Ogaden region. In January 2010 the Ethiopian Government announced that it had detained some 100 OLF rebels following clashes near Moyale in which the OLF claimed to have killed at least three Ethiopian soldiers. Meanwhile, in June 2007 the CUD was renamed the Unity for Democracy and Justice Party (UDJ/Andinet) under the leadership of Birtukan Mideksa, hitherto Vice-President of the CUD.

In April 2009 the Ethiopian Government arrested 40 suspected members of a new opposition party, the Movement for Justice, Freedom and Democracy (Ginbot 7), which had adopted a platform sanctioning any means to effect political change. After being found guilty of plotting to overthrow the Government, in December five of the defendants were sentenced to death, while terms of life imprisonment were imposed on 33 others.

The 2010 general election

In October 2009 eight opposition organizations formed the Ethiopia Federal Democratic Unity Forum (FORUM) chaired by Dr Merara Gudina, leader of the Oromo People's Congress (OPC). Tensions increased in the period leading up to the May 2010 legislative elections, with the FORUM and the US-based international non-governmental organization Human Rights Watch (HRW) accusing the Government of orchestrating a campaign to suppress opposition activity. The Government denied accusations of involvement in the violent deaths of three FORUM activists during March–May, and countered by blaming the opposition for the murder of one of its candidates in May. According to official sources, in the same month two people were also killed in a grenade attack at a meeting organized by the pro-Government OPDO. Meanwhile, in March Meles admitted that radio programming transmitted by the Voice of America (VOA), a worldwide broadcasting operation funded by the US Government, was being blocked within Ethiopia. Meles accused VOA of transmitting 'destabilizing propaganda' and likened its content to 1990s Rwandan broadcasts encouraging genocide, prompting condemnation by the US Administration.

The general election was held peacefully on 23 May 2010 and resulted in an emphatic victory for the EPRDF, which won 499 of the 547 seats contested. Pro-Government parties secured an additional 46 seats, while the FORUM (which had been weakened by internal divisions) only managed to gain control of a single seat; an independent candidate won the remaining seat. The rate of participation by the electorate was recorded at 93.4%. EU monitors announced that the election had not met international standards and criticized the Government's monopolization of state resources during campaigning, a stance reiterated by US officials, although African Union (AU, see p. 188) observers defended the results. The EPRDF claimed that the outcome reflected voter satisfaction with the Government's economic policies. Opposition leaders denounced the results, citing electoral irregularities and accusing the authorities of fraud. An appeal by Merara for the election to be held afresh was rejected by the NEBE and the Supreme Court in June.

Meles was unanimously re-elected as Prime Minister by the House of People's Representatives on 4 October 2010, and he appointed 10 new members to the Council of Ministers on the following day. Most notable among the changes was the appointment of Hailemariam Desalegn as Deputy Prime Minister and Minister of Foreign Affairs. Birtukan Mideksa, a prominent opposition leader who had been sentenced to life imprisonment for treason after the post-election unrest in 2005, was pardoned and released from gaol shortly afterwards. (Birtukan had been freed in 2007 but was rearrested the following year.) Her release was viewed by some commentators as an attempt by the Government to appease its international partners in the wake of the election controversy.

Following their overwhelming defeat in the legislative elections, a number of opposition parties underwent a process of restructuring. The remaining members of the FORUM announced in July 2010 that they had disbanded their loose coalition and formed a six-party front, committing themselves to a permanent alliance and a common policy platform. A new opposition grouping, the Alliance for Liberty, Equality and Justice in Ethiopia, was founded in August by Ginbot 7, the Afar People's Party and the Ethiopian Movement for Unity and Justice.

ONLF rebels attacked a military base in Malqaqa in May 2010 and claimed that they had gained control of the town, although the Government denied this and stated that the attack had been repelled. The leader of the United Western Somali Liberation Front, an Ogaden-based Islamist group, signed a peace deal with the Government in July, agreeing to disarm in exchange for an amnesty for its members. A similar peace agreement was signed by a faction of the ONLF, led by Salahdin Abdurahman Maow, in October. Both groups announced that they intended to regroup as political parties.

In March 2011 it was announced that nearly 250 members of the FORUM, principally of the Oromo Federalist Democratic Movement (OFDM), had been arrested in an apparent attempt to pre-empt anti-Government protests akin to those of the 'Arab Spring' in the Middle East and North Africa. In the same month it was reported that Meles had replaced some 150 officials belonging to the OPDO, after ordering their arrest on charges of corruption. In June Moga Firisa of the OFDM was elected as the new Chairman of the FORUM. In September five people, including opposition leader Andualem Arage and journalist Eskinder Nega, were arrested on the grounds that they were supporters of Ginbot 7 and involved in organizing acts of terrorism in the country; the detention earlier that month, on similar charges, of political activist Debebe Eshetu was also denounced by opposition groups. In August 2012 the OPC and the OFDM merged to form a new party, the Oromo Federal Congress (OFC), led by former OPC leader Gudina. In September two Swedish reporters, who, in December 2011, had been sentenced to 11 years' imprisonment for entering Ethiopia illegally and supporting terrorism (after entering the Ogaden region, in co-operation with the ONLF, in order to investigate human rights there), were released from prison in Addis Ababa, under an amnesty for 1,950 prisoners.

Recent developments: new Prime Minister

On 20 August 2012 Meles died in a hospital in Belgium; on the following day Hailemariam was appointed acting Prime Minister. On 15 September Hailemariam was elected to succeed Meles as Chairman of the EPRDF, and on 21 September the House of People's Representatives approved his nomination as premier in the country's first peaceful and constitutional transition of power. Also in September, Abay Weldu, the governor of Tigrai

state, was elected as the new Chairman of the TPLF. In November the legislature approved a government reorganization effected by Hailemariam: the Minister of Communication and Information Technology, Debretsion Gebremikael, was also appointed Deputy Prime Minister, Co-ordinator of Finance and the Economy, while senior EPRDF official Muktar Kedir became Deputy Prime Minister, Co-ordinator of Good Governance and Minister of the Civil Service; Dr Tewedros Adhanom, hitherto Minister of Health, received the foreign affairs portfolio.

In December 2012 the Ethiopian High Federal Court sentenced two opposition leaders, Olbana Lelisa and Bekele Gerba, to 13 and eight years' imprisonment, respectively, for having links with the OLF; a further seven defendants received prison terms of between three and 12 years for rebel activities. In the same month charges of terrorism were upheld against 29 Muslims who had been arrested in July for planning protests (as part of an ongoing campaign) against government interference in the religious affairs of the Muslim community; their trial commenced in early 2013. In separate proceedings in January, nine Ethiopians and one Kenyan national were convicted (six *in absentia*) of planning terrorist attacks in the country in collaboration with Somali Islamist group al-Shabaab (see *Regional relations*), and were sentenced to prison terms of between three and 20 years.

On 2 June 2013 the holding of a peaceful demonstration, organized by the new Semayawi (Blue) Party, was permitted in Addis Ababa for the first time since 2005. The protesters appealed for the release of political prisoners, journalists and the organizers of Muslim protests staged in 2012. However, the authorities subsequently discouraged further such gatherings by Semayawi and UDJ/Andinet.

In July 2013 Prime Minister Hailemariam carried out an extensive cabinet reorganization, including 10 new appointments; the post of justice minister, which was assigned to Getachew Ambaye, had been vacant since May, when Berhan Hailu had been dismissed from office. Following the expiry of President Wolde Giorgis' term in office, on 7 October both houses of the legislature unanimously elected former ambassador Dr Mulatu Teshome Wirtu as his replacement. In April 2014, following the election of Muktar Kedir, one of Ethiopia's three deputy Prime Ministers, to the regional presidency of Oromia regional state, Hailemariam appointed Woizero Aster Mamo, a female senior OPDO member as his replacement; she was also appointed as Co-ordinator of Good Governance and Minister of the Civil Service.

In February 2014 a senior UDJ/Andinet official was found guilty of contempt of court, having published an article in which he alleged a pro-Government bias to the national judicial system. At this time, in advance of the next general election, scheduled for 2015, the Ethiopian authorities appeared to be severely restricting the free expression of public opinion. The human rights organization Amnesty International reported in late April 2014 that 20 Semayawi members had been detained while planning an anti-Government demonstration. The so-called 'Zone 9' grouping of independent bloggers and activists announced in that month that they would resume their activities, following a voluntary six-month withdrawal from the public media, attributed to a sharp rise in state surveillance and harassment; shortly after the reactivation of Zone 9, Amnesty International reported that a number of journalists and internet bloggers who were critical of, or neutral towards, the Ethiopian regime had been arrested. In early May it was reported that nearly 50 deaths, and a high number of injuries, had resulted from clashes between the national security forces and protesters participating in student-dominated demonstrations, which had started in late April at university towns in Oromia in protest at the publication of the 'Addis Ababa and Oromia Special Zone Integrated Development Master Plan', an official blueprint for the expansion of the capital city, which contained an unpopular proposal for the eviction of Oromo farmers from their land, and which, it was also feared by opponents, would impact negatively on surrounding areas. In June, following months of negotiations on their proposed amalgamation, two of the main opposition parties, UDJ/Andinet and the All Ethiopia Unity Party (AEUP), requested permission from the NEBE to merge. In early July HRW reported that Andargachew Tsige, a senior Ginbot 7 leader, had been deported from Yemen to Ethiopia; Tsige had been handed two death sentences at trials in 2009 and 2012 in Ethiopia at which he had not been present. Shortly afterwards four other opposition leaders were detained by the authorities. A total of 10 people associated with

Zone 9 were indicted on terrorism charges in mid-July 2014 (one *in absentia*). In August the Ethiopian authorities charged six news outlets with offences including defamation and 'instigating enmity'; it was reported that, as a consequence, four implicated journalists immediately fled the country. In mid-October a leading independent media figure, Temesgen Demedsalegn, was arrested, while three journalists were convicted in that month *in absentia* of having published articles that might incite unrest. Nearly 80 members of Semayawi, including the party's president, Yilkal Getnet, were arrested in early December while attempting to stage a demonstration in Addis Ababa; following several days' detention, they were released on bail.

In October 2014 nine alleged Islamist terrorists were charged with planning to establish an Islamic state in the Oromo city of Jimma. Also in October some 13 Muslim university students, who had been arrested in October 2013 while protesting against a government directive that prohibited religious face coverings and imposed a code of religious ethics at universities, were convicted on terrorism-related charges.

Foreign Affairs

Regional relations

Relations with Somalia have been problematic since the Ogaden War of 1977–78. However, in April 1988 Ethiopia and Somalia agreed to re-establish diplomatic relations, to withdraw troops from their common border and to exchange prisoners of war. In January 2001 relations between the countries deteriorated, after the Somali Prime Minister accused Ethiopia of continuing to assist the Somali-based Rahawin Resistance Army, which had taken control of a number of towns in south-west Somalia, and of involvement in an assassination attempt on the Speaker of Somalia's transitional legislature. Relations between Somalia and Ethiopia were further strained by Meles' claim that a number of members of al-Ittihad al-Islam (Islamic Union Party—which sought independence for Ethiopia's Ogaden province) were represented in the Somali Transitional National Government (TNG). Relations between Ethiopia and Somalia improved in early 2005 and Ethiopia signalled its support for the new Somali President, Col Abdullahi Yussuf Ahmed, following his election in January. In 2006, however, repeated accusations of incursions by Ethiopian troops in support of the TNG in Baidoa, Somalia, (where it had been relocated) caused relations to deteriorate once more. In October Meles admitted the presence of military trainers in Baidoa and described his country as being 'technically at war' with its neighbour and prepared for conflict. In December the Somali Supreme Islamic Courts Council (SSICC, as the Union of Islamic Courts had been restyled) issued a deadline for Ethiopian troops to leave Somalia within one week or face a major attack; the following week, amid reports of heavy fighting between Ethiopian troops and Islamist militias near Baidoa, the SSICC urged all Somalis to join the 'war' against Ethiopia. At the end of the month Meles admitted for the first time to active military involvement by his country in Somalia, claiming that his troops were defending Ethiopia's sovereignty against what he termed terrorists and anti-Ethiopian elements. Ethiopia was supported in its actions by the AU, which conceded that the presence of Islamist militias so close to its borders might be perceived as a threat. In June 2007 Meles pledged to withdraw Ethiopian forces from Somalia upon the arrival of an AU peace-keeping force, the AU Mission in Somalia (AMISOM); however, Ethiopian forces remained in Somalia during 2008, owing to the slower-than-anticipated full deployment of AMISOM. It was eventually announced, in January 2009, that Ethiopian troops had left Somalia. However, reports emerged during 2009 and thereafter of Ethiopian troops crossing into that country to pursue insurgents belonging to the Somali Islamist group al-Shabaab. In November 2011 the Ethiopian Government officially denied reports that its forces were participating in a large-scale military operation against al-Shabaab in Somalia. By early 2013, however, it was apparent that Ethiopian troops were continuing to support Somali government forces and AMISOM in efforts to regain control of south-central regions of Somalia from al-Shabaab. In July the Ethiopian Government announced that it had begun to pull its troops out of Baidoa, citing the return of relative stability to the former rebel stronghold; it denied, however, that a complete withdrawal of Ethiopian troops from Somalia was being planned. Two Somali suicide bombers planning to target an association football match in Addis Ababa accidentally blew themselves up in mid-October 2013 before they could carry out the action, which was perceived to be a revenge attack for the continuing presence of Ethiopian troops in Somalia. In February 2014 the 4,400 Ethiopian troops who remained in Somalia officially joined AMISOM, thereby coming under international mandate and command. In June the Ethiopian security forces detained 25 people who were allegedly associated with al-Shabaab and who were accused of plotting attacks in the country.

Following the military coup in Sudan in April 1985, full diplomatic relations were restored between Ethiopia and Sudan. Relations between the two countries were strained in the late 1980s, however, by the influx into Ethiopia of thousands of Sudanese refugees, fleeing from famine and civil war in southern Sudan. The vast majority of an estimated 380,000 refugees were reported to have returned to Sudan by early 1991, as a result of the civil war in Ethiopia. The change of government in Ethiopia in May 1991 led to a considerable improvement in relations, and in October the two countries signed an agreement on friendship and co-operation. Relations deteriorated sharply in 1995, following apparent Sudanese complicity in the attempted assassination of President Muhammad Hosni Mubarak of Egypt in Addis Ababa in June, but steadily improved after 1998, following Ethiopia's conflict with Eritrea; Eritrea had been supporting Sudanese opposition movements since 1994. A protocol concerning Ethiopian access to Port Sudan was signed between the two countries in March 2000 and ratified by the Ethiopian legislature in July 2003. In November 2004 Ethiopia and Sudan finalized an agreement on the demarcation of their common border, and requested financial assistance from international organizations in order to demarcate the border on the ground. In May 2008 it was announced that an agreement would soon be concluded. Despite Meles' insistence that no citizens would be displaced, in the following month there were reports that Ethiopians living in the border regions had been forced from their homes by Sudanese troops; there were also concerns that the demarcation would transfer holy and historic areas of Ethiopia to Sudan. By November 2009 preparations had been finalized in Ethiopia for the deployment of a 200-strong air force unit to Darfur in western Sudan (where civil conflict had broken out in 2003), in addition to the 1,600 ground troops already stationed in the region as part of the AU-UN peacekeeping mission, UNAMID. The Ethiopian Government has been keen to maintain good relations with Sudan, owing to its dependence on Sudanese petroleum and fears of closer Sudan-Eritrea ties. Following South Sudan's secession from Sudan in 2011, Ethiopia agreed to deploy more than 4,200 peacekeeping forces, with the backing of the UN Security Council, in the contested border region of Abyei. From early 2014 Ethiopia hosted mediation efforts by the Intergovernmental Authority on Development (IGAD, see p. 331) aimed at securing a settlement to an outbreak of violent conflict that had erupted in South Sudan in December 2013. The deployment of a regional IGAD (see p. 331) peacekeeping mission to South Sudan, under Ethiopian command, was endorsed in May 2014 by the UN Security Council. In August Ethiopia and Sudan agreed to establish a joint defence force tasked with enhancing security along their common border.

Relations with Djibouti, which varied a little in the 2000s in relation to each country's stance on the situation in Somalia, have settled into a pragmatic focus on consolidating shared infrastructure to support Ethiopia's dependence on Djibouti port. Electricity exports from Ethiopia to Djibouti commenced in June 2011 and a memorandum of understanding was signed in February 2012 to construct a new road and oil pipeline from South Sudan linking Ethiopia to Djibouti. In April 2014 Ethiopia and Djibouti determined to strengthen military co-operation, to counter regional terrorist threats.

Ethiopia and the newly independent Eritrea signed a treaty of co-operation during a visit by the Eritrean President, Issaias Afewerki, to Addis Ababa in July 1993. A further agreement, signed in late 1994, provided for the free movement of goods between the two countries without payment of customs dues. In late 1997, however, relations with Eritrea deteriorated, following that country's adoption of a new currency (to replace the Ethiopian birr) and the subsequent disruption of cross-border trade. Fighting between Ethiopian and Eritrean troops erupted in May 1998, with both countries accusing the other of having invaded their territory. Proposals by the UN Security Council and the Organization of African Unity (OAU), now the AU, to resolve the conflict were rejected by Eritrea, necessitating the convening of a special meeting of an OAU mediation committee in Ouagadougou, Burkina Faso, in November. Ethiopia welcomed the committee's proposals, which stressed the need to demilitarize and demarcate the disputed region, but Eritrea rejected the plans. Further mediation attempts to impose a ceasefire also failed.

In mid-May 2000 Ethiopian troops launched a major offensive near the disputed towns of Badme and Zalambessa, repelling Eritrean forces. Despite demands from the UN, hostilities continued, and on 18 May the UN Security Council unanimously approved the imposition of a 12-month arms embargo on Ethiopia and Eritrea. Shortly afterwards Zalambessa fell to the Ethiopian forces, and on 25 May the Eritrean Government announced the withdrawal of its troops from all disputed areas. On 31 May Prime Minister Meles stated that Ethiopia had no territorial claims over Eritrea and that the war between the two countries was over; nevertheless, sporadic fighting continued to take place. In early June both sides expressed their willingness, in principle, to accept the OAU's peace proposals and on 18 June the Ethiopian and Eritrean Ministers of Foreign Affairs signed an agreement, which provided for an immediate ceasefire and the establishment of a 25-km temporary security zone (TSZ) on the Eritrean side of the common border until the issue of the final demarcation of the border had been settled. In mid-September the UN Security Council approved the deployment of a UN Mission in Ethiopia and Eritrea (UNMEE).

In December 2000 Ethiopia and Eritrea signed an agreement in Algiers, Algeria, which formally brought an end to the conflict. The agreement provided for a permanent cessation of all hostilities, the return of all prisoners of war, the demarcation of the common border by an independent commission, and the establishment of a Claims Commission to assess the issues of compensation and reparations. By late January 2001 the UNMEE force had arrived in the region and Ethiopian troops commenced their withdrawal from the territory they had captured from Eritrea. In March UNMEE's mandate was extended until September (and at six-monthly or four-monthly intervals thereafter) and on 18 April, after all forces had been withdrawn from the border area, the TSZ was declared to be in force. In mid-May the arms embargo imposed on the two countries by the UN in May 2000 was lifted.

In December 2001 Ethiopia and Eritrea began presenting their respective cases for border demarcation to the five-member Boundary Commission at the International Court of Justice (see p. 25) in The Hague, Netherlands. The Commission delivered its findings in April 2002; however, it did not identify on which side of the boundary line the Ethiopian-held town of Badme lay, stating that delineation had been delayed, as extensive demining was required prior to the emplacement of boundary markers. In the absence of any decision, both Ethiopia and Eritrea immediately claimed to have been awarded Badme. In early March 2003 the Boundary Commission reported to the UN Security Council that requests by Ethiopia for changes to the border ruling, in order to 'take better account of human and physical geography', threatened to undermine the peace process as a whole. Later in March the Boundary Commission categorically ruled Badme to be Eritrean territory, thus rejecting Ethiopia's territorial claim over the town. Meles subsequently vowed to continue to contest the ruling, and, in a letter to the UN Security Council in October, he requested the establishment of a new body to resolve the crisis. However, the Security Council stated that Ethiopia had, under the 2000 Algiers accord, committed itself to accept the Boundary Commission's decision as 'final and binding' and urged it to accept and implement the border ruling. With no resolution to the ongoing impasse in sight, in late October the Boundary Commission announced that the demarcation of the border had been delayed indefinitely.

In November 2004 Meles announced a five-point plan aimed at resolving the disputed border issue and declared that Ethiopia had, in principle, accepted the Boundary Commission's ruling; this was dismissed by the Eritrean authorities, however, as an attempt further to stall the process. (Ethiopia continued to occupy Badme, and remained in control of the town at early 2015.) Ethiopia and Eritrea continued to increase troop numbers in the border area in 2005, raising fears of a return to conflict. However, Ethiopia sought to reassure the international community that troop movements and the construction of trenches on its side of the TSZ were for defensive purposes only. In November the UN Security Council adopted Resolution 1640, which demanded full acceptance by Ethiopia of the Boundary Commission's ruling regarding border demarcation, that Eritrea lift persistent restrictions on UNMEE operations, and that troop numbers on both sides of the border be reduced with immediate effect.

In November 2006 both Ethiopia and Eritrea failed to attend a meeting of the Boundary Commission in The Hague and rejected its proposals; the Commission, in response, issued a statement informing them that in the event of no agreement having been reached by November 2007, and no efforts having been initiated with regard to the emplacement of border pillars, then the boundary would automatically stand as designated by boundary points described by the Commission in an annex to the statement. By late 2007 neither side had complied with the Commission's request of November 2006. In early December 2007, prior to announcing its own dissolution, the Commission stated that the boundary that it had determined in November 2006 represented the official border between the two countries.

Eritrean-imposed restrictions on the movements of UN peace-keeping personnel and the delivery of fuel led the UN to relocate its peacekeepers in Eritrea to Ethiopia from mid-February 2008. Subsequently, Eritrea continued to impede UN operations, eventually forcing UNMEE to abandon its mandate in the region. On 30 July the UN Security Council adopted Resolution 1827, terminating the mission; the last troops were withdrawn in October. In August 2009 the Claims Commission awarded Ethiopia a total of US $174m. in compensation for war damages, while Eritrea received $164m., resulting in a net payment to Ethiopia of $10m.

In March 2012 Ethiopian troops, for the first time since the end of the 1998–2000 border conflict, launched an incursion into south-eastern Eritrea, on the grounds that rebel groups based there had staged a series of raids in Ethiopian territory; at least 50 alleged members of the Afar Revolutionary Democratic Unity Front were killed during this operation. Ethiopia was reported to have offered to enter into peace talks with Eritrea on two occasions in 2013; Eritrea, however, did not respond positively to these propositions. It was reported in mid-July 2014 that Gen. Samora Muhammad Yunis, the Chief of Staff of the Ethiopian National Defence Force, together with other senior Ethiopian military commanders, convened a meeting of the leadership of Eritrean armed opposition factions, in Mekele, Ethiopia, to discuss means of removing the regime of President Afewerki of Eritrea. In October it was estimated that Ethiopia was hosting more than 104,000 refugees from Eritrea, and that more than 3,500 Eritreans had fled from that country's repressive regime into northern Ethiopia during September–October.

Ethiopia participates in the Eastern African Standby Force (EASF), initiated in 2004 under AU auspices, and envisaged, once fully deployed, as a constituent part of the AU's planned Africa Standby Force. In September 2014 an EASF logistics centre was inaugurated in Addis Ababa.

Other external relations

In 1984 some 13,000 Falashas, a Jewish group in Ethiopia, reached Sudan, from where they were flown to Israel in a secret airlift. In May 1991 Israel evacuated a further 14,000 Falashas from Addis Ababa; some 10,000 Falashmura (Ethiopian Christians whose forefathers had converted from Judaism) were subsequently granted Israeli citizenship on humanitarian grounds. In March 1999 Israel pledged to examine the possibility of bringing the estimated 19,000 Jews remaining in Ethiopia to Israel, and in April 2000 the Israeli Minister of the Interior visited Ethiopia to investigate the claims of some 26,000 Ethiopians who maintained that they belonged to the Falashmura community and were thus eligible to settle in Israel under Israeli law. In February 2003 the Israeli Government ruled that the Falashmura had been forced to convert to Christianity to avoid religious persecution and that they had the right to settle in Israel. In January 2004 Ethiopia and Israel agreed to allow the Falashmura to be flown to Israel; some 17,000 Falashmura and a further 3,000 Falashas arrived in Israel by May 2008. Israel resumed the transportation of Falashmura in January 2010, following a suspension of the airlift process in August 2008. The Israeli Government announced in November 2010 that the remaining Falashmura in Ethiopia, some 8,000 people, would be granted the right to immigrate to Israel. In August 2013 the Israeli Government completed what was reported to be the final airlift of Ethiopian Jews to Israel.

In recent years the People's Republic of China has developed closer ties with Ethiopia and has made significant economic investment in the country. However, in April 2007 members of the ONLF killed more than 70 people, including nine Chinese oil workers, in an attack on a petroleum installation in the Somali region; seven Chinese citizens were kidnapped, although they were later released unharmed.

In November 2012 Ethiopia was elected to the UN Human Rights Council, despite protests by human rights groups, which cited continued violations by the Ethiopian authorities, including a series of arrests of Muslim protesters earlier that year (see *Domestic Political Affairs*).

CONSTITUTION AND GOVERNMENT

Under the provisions of the Constitution, adopted in December 1994, the country became a federation, consisting of nine states and two chartered cities, the capital, Addis Ababa, and Dire Dawa. The states have their own parliamentary assemblies, which also elect representatives to the House of the Federation, the upper chamber of the Federal Parliamentary Assembly. The lower chamber, the House of People's Representatives, consists of no more than 550 directly elected deputies, who each serve terms of five years. The Federal Parliamentary Assembly elects a President as Head of State with a six-year term of office. However, the President fulfils mainly ceremonial functions, executive power being the preserve of the Prime Minister. The Prime Minister, who is elected by the House of People's Representatives, appoints the Council of Ministers (subject to approval by the legislature), and acts as Commander-in-Chief of the armed forces. Unless otherwise provided in the Constitution, the term of office of the Prime Minister is the duration of the mandate of the House of People's Representatives.

REGIONAL AND INTERNATIONAL CO-OPERATION

Ethiopia is a member of the African Union (see p. 188), and the headquarters of that organization are based in Addis Ababa. In January 2013 the Ethiopian Prime Minister, Hailemariam Desalegn, was elected to the organization's annually rotating chairmanship. Ethiopia is also a member of the Common Market for Eastern and Southern Africa (see p. 232) and of the Intergovernmental Authority on Development (see p. 331). In July 2001 Ethiopia ratified the Cotonou Agreement (see p. 321), the successor of the Lomé Convention of the EU.

Ethiopia was one of the 51 founding member states of the UN, established in 1945. Ethiopia submitted a request for accession to the World Trade Organization (see p. 431) in January 2003, which at early 2015 was still being processed. In July 2010 Ethiopia, an exporting member of the International Coffee Organization, ratified the 2007 International Coffee Agreement.

ECONOMIC AFFAIRS

In 2013, according to estimates by the World Bank, Ethiopia's gross national income (GNI), measured at average 2011–13 prices, was US $43,836m., equivalent to $470 per head (or $1,350 per head on an international purchasing-power parity basis). During 2004–13, it was estimated, the population increased at an average annual rate of 2.7%, while gross domestic product (GDP) per head grew, in real terms, by an average of 7.8% per year. Overall GDP increased, in real terms, at an average annual rate of 10.7% during 2004–13; it rose by 10.4% in 2013.

Agriculture (including forestry and fishing) contributed an estimated 45.5% of GDP in 2013, according to the African Development Bank (AfDB). The sector employed 74.6% of the labour force at mid-2015, according to FAO estimates, reflecting the fact that Ethiopia has the lowest level of urbanization among African countries. The principal cash crop is coffee (which accounted for 23.4% of export earnings in 2013). The principal subsistence crops are cereals (maize, sorghum, wheat and barley) and sugar cane. According to the World Bank, during 2004–12 agricultural GDP increased at an average annual rate of 8.3%. According to the AfDB, sectoral growth of 7.1% was recorded in 2013.

Industry (including mining, manufacturing, construction and power) employed 6.6% of the labour force at March 2005, and provided an estimated 11.1% of GDP in 2013, according to the AfDB. During 2004–12, according to the World Bank, industrial GDP increased by an average of 11.5% per year. Sectoral growth was 17.1% in 2012.

According to the AfDB, mining contributed only an estimated 1.3% of GDP in 2013, and employed less than 0.3% of the labour force at March 2005. Ethiopia has deposits of copper and potash. Gold, tantalite, soda ash, kaolin, dimension stones, precious metals and gemstones, salt, and industrial and construction materials are mined. In April 2000 a US company discovered large petroleum and natural gas deposits in the west of the country, and in June 2003 the Ethiopian Government granted a one-year exploration licence to Petronas of Malaysia. The licence

was renewed in early 2004 to allow exploration over a larger area. However, Petronas ceased operations in Ethiopia in 2010 and at early 2015, despite continuing exploration projects being undertaken by local and foreign hydrocarbons companies, no commercial production of petroleum or gas had yet commenced. During 2002/03–2006/07 mining GDP increased by an estimated average of 3.9% per year; growth in 2006/07 was an estimated 6.0%. According to the AfDB, the sector's GDP increased by 6.8% in 2013.

Manufacturing employed only 4.9% of the labour force at March 2005, and contributed an estimated 3.9% of GDP in 2013, according to the AfDB. During 2004–12, according to the World Bank, manufacturing GDP increased at an average annual rate of 10.2%. According to the AfDB, sectoral growth was 10.8% in 2013.

Construction employed only 1.4% of the labour force in March 2005, and contributed an estimated 4.9% of GDP in 2013, according to the AfDB. The GDP of the sector increased by 30.9% in 2013.

In years of normal rainfall, energy is derived principally from Ethiopia's massive hydroelectric power resources. In 2011 99.0% of Ethiopia's electricity was produced by hydroelectric power schemes. Moreover, the Government launched an ambitious 25-year plan in 2013 to transform the country into a renewable energy hub and a significant regional power supplier. The largest wind farm in sub-Saharan Africa, located in Tigrai province, commenced operations in October 2013. The wind farm, which comprised 84 turbines and had a capacity of 120 MW, was expected to produce about 400m. kWh per year. As part of its energy plans, the Government also signed an agreement with an Icelandic company in 2013 to construct a 1,000-MW geothermal power plant in the volcanically active Rift Valley. Imports of mineral fuels accounted for 11.5% of the cost of total imports in 2013. By that year Ethiopia's electricity generating capacity had reached some 2,200 MW.

Services, which consisted mainly of wholesale and retail trade, public administration and defence, and transport and communications, employed 13.1% of the labour force at March 2005, and contributed an estimated 43.5% of GDP in 2013, according to the AfDB. The combined GDP of the service sectors increased, in real terms, at an average rate of 14.2% per year during 2004–12, according to the World Bank. The sector grew by 10.9% in 2012.

According to IMF figures, in 2012 Ethiopia recorded a visible merchandise trade deficit of US $7,289.3m., and there was a deficit of $2,985.3m. on the current account of the balance of payments. In 2013 the principal source of imports (providing 27.0% of the total) was the People's Republic of China; other major suppliers were India and Saudi Arabia. The principal markets for exports in that year were Somalia (taking 12.3% of the total), China, Germany, the Netherlands and Saudi Arabia. The principal exports in 2013 were vegetables and vegetable products, coffee, edible vegetables and roots and tubers, live animals and cut flowers. The principal imports in that year were boilers and machinery, chemicals and related products, iron and steel, base metals and articles thereof, mineral fuels, oils and distillation products, and motor vehicles.

In the fiscal year 2014/15 Ethiopia's budgetary deficit was projected to reach 35,091m. birr. Ethiopia's general government gross debt was 186,371m. birr. in 2013, equivalent to 21.9% of GDP. Ethiopia is the principal African recipient of concessionary funding, and one of the largest recipients of European Union (EU) aid. In 2012 Ethiopia's total external debt was US $10,462m., of which $9,941m. was public and publicly guaranteed debt. In that year the cost of servicing long-term public and publicly guaranteed debt and repayments to the IMF was equivalent to 7.2% of the value of exports of goods, services and income (excluding workers' remittances). The annual rate of inflation averaged 30.3% in 2007/08–2011/12, according to official estimates. According to the IMF, consumer prices increased by 8.1% in 2013. In March 2005, according to the International Labour Organization, 1,653,700 people were registered as unemployed, representing 5.0% of the total labour force.

Ethiopia remains one of the poorest countries in the world, and its economy continues to suffer from the effects of recurrent drought, which severely disrupts agricultural production. The Ethiopian economy is also heavily dependent on assistance and grants from abroad, while regional instability and higher cargo transportation costs resulting from the country's landlocked position present further obstacles to development. However, in recent years considerable investment in the country's infrastructure has been made, with some 20.2% of budgetary expenditure being allocated to public sector projects in 2013. The third phase of the AfDB-funded Mombasa–Nairobi–Addis Ababa Road Corridor Project, under way in 2012–17, as part of the Trans-Africa Highway network, was expected significantly to increase trade between Ethiopia and Kenya. In addition, in September 2010 construction began, with Chinese financing, of a 5,000-km railway system, which was to include the modernization of the 781-km line between Addis Ababa and Djibouti port (the closest seaport). Meanwhile, the construction (again with Chinese funding) of a Light Rail Transit network in Addis Ababa—the country's first mass transit system—was completed in January 2015 and was scheduled to commence operating later that year. Despite its shortcomings, from 2004 the economy maintained consistent and broad-based growth, largely as a result of the expansion of the services and agricultural sectors, while domestic demand was fuelled by private consumption and public investment. The Government devised a Growth and Transformation Plan (GTP) for 2010–15, emphasizing the development of public sector agriculture, industry and infrastructure, while simultaneously attracting greater investment from China and India and encouraging more remittances from Ethiopians working abroad. Projects initiated under the GTP included the construction of the Grand Ethiopian Renaissance Dam, which, with a planned capacity of 6,000 MW, would be the largest hydroelectric power plant in Africa. However, the project, which was scheduled to be completed in mid-2017, proved controversial owing to concerns expressed by Egypt over water-sharing. Although there were reports in early 2014 that the Ethiopian authorities had raised only a small proportion of its share of the funds (Ethiopia's contribution was to total US $3,000m., while the remaining $1,800m. was to be provided by Chinese banks), the Government claimed in October that construction work was progressing as scheduled and that the dam was around 40% complete. It was envisaged that, dependent on rainfall patterns, two of the dam's planned 16 turbines would become operational in September 2015. Following a dramatic rise in inflation to around 40% at mid-2011, the implementation of stringent government monetary policy coupled with a deceleration in global food and fuel prices reduced the rate to about 5.6% by October 2014. Meanwhile, economic expansion was sustained, with the IMF estimating buoyant GDP growth of about 8.2% in 2013/14 and 8.5% in 2014/15.

PUBLIC HOLIDAYS

2016: 7 January* (Christmas), 20 January* (Epiphany), 2 March (Battle of Adowa), 29 April* (Good Friday), 1 May (May Day), 2 May* (Easter Monday), 5 May (Patriots' Victory Day), 28 May (Downfall of the Dergue), 6 July† (Id al-Fitr, end of Ramadan), 11 September (New Year's Day), 12 September† (Id al-Adha/Arafat), 28 September* (Feast of the True Cross), 11 December† (Mouloud, Birth of the Prophet).

* Coptic holidays.

† These holidays are dependent on the Islamic lunar calendar and may vary by one or two days from the dates given.

Note: Ethiopia uses its own solar calendar; the Ethiopian year 2007 began on 11 September 2014.

Statistical Survey

Source (unless otherwise stated): Central Statistical Authority, POB 1143, Addis Ababa; tel. (11) 553010; fax (11) 550334; internet www.csa.gov.et.

Area and Population

AREA, POPULATION AND DENSITY

Area (sq km)	1,133,380*
Population (census results)	
11 October 1994	53,477,265
28 May 2007	
Males	37,217,130
Females	36,533,802
Total	73,750,932
Population (official estimates at July)	
2011	82,101,998
2012	84,320,987
2013	86,613,986
Density (per sq km) at July 2013	76.4

* 437,600 sq miles.

POPULATION BY AGE AND SEX
(UN estimates at mid-2015)

	Males	Females	Total
0–14 years	20,734,682	20,259,362	40,994,044
15–64 years	27,146,528	27,354,324	54,500,852
65 years and over	1,612,436	1,834,770	3,447,206
Total	**49,493,646**	**49,448,456**	**98,942,102**

Source: UN, *World Population Prospects: The 2012 Revision*.

ADMINISTRATIVE DIVISIONS
(official population estimates at July 2013)

	Population		
	Males	Females	Total
Regional States			
1 Tigrai	2,489,994	2,571,997	5,061,991
2 Afar	917,999	732,000	1,649,999
3 Amhara	9,633,991	9,578,003	19,211,994
4 Oromia	16,227,993	15,992,008	32,220,001
5 Somali	2,957,999	2,360,001	5,318,000
6 Benishangul-Gumuz	522,997	504,997	1,027,994
7 Southern Nations, Nationalities			
and Peoples	8,903,996	8,983,009	17,887,005
8 Gambela	212,003	194,001	406,004
9 Harari	108,000	107,000	215,000
Chartered Cities			
1 Dire Dawa	198,000	197,000	395,000
2 Addis Ababa	1,479,000	1,624,999	3,103,999
Total*	**43,715,971**	**42,898,015**	**86,613,986**

* Including 116,999 (males 63,999, females 53,000) persons, detailed as 'special enumeration', not allocated to administrative divisions.

Note: Totals may not be equal to the sum of components, owing to rounding of some data.

PRINCIPAL TOWNS
(official population estimates at July 2013)

Addis Ababa				
(capital) . . .	3,103,673	Awasa	225,686
Mekele	286,624	Bahir Dar . . .	198,909
Nazret	282,974	Jimma	155,434
Dire Dawa . . .	269,134	Dessie	153,691
Gondar	264,964	Jijiga	152,674

Mid-2014 (incl. suburbs, UN estimate): Addis Ababa 3,168,040 (Source: UN, *World Urbanization Prospects: The 2014 Revision*).

BIRTHS AND DEATHS
(annual averages, UN estimates)

	2000–05	2005–10	2010–15
Birth rate (per 1,000)	41.3	36.4	33.3
Death rate (per 1,000)	12.5	9.5	7.7

Source: UN, *World Population Prospects: The 2012 Revision.*

Life expectancy (years at birth): 63.0 (males 61.4; females 64.6) in 2012 (Source: World Bank, World Development Indicators database).

ECONOMICALLY ACTIVE POPULATION
('000 persons aged 10 years and over, March 2005)*

	Males	Females	Total
Agriculture, hunting, forestry and fishing	14,209.4	10,998.8	25,208.2
Mining and quarrying . . .	51.4	30.6	82.1
Manufacturing	444.0	1,085.3	1,529.4
Electricity, gas and water . . .	25.2	7.7	32.9
Construction	349.9	95.7	445.6
Wholesale and retail trade; repair of motor vehicles, motorcycles and personal and household goods	652.2	984.9	1,637.1
Hotels and restaurants . .	96.8	672.3	769.1
Transport, storage and communications	132.0	14.5	146.4
Financial intermediation . .	21.6	16.3	37.9
Real estate, renting and business services	36.1	16.2	52.3
Public administration and defence; compulsory social security . .	242.0	125.9	367.9
Education	178.2	104.5	282.7
Social work	45.6	32.5	78.1
Community, social and personal services	303.5	135.2	438.7
Households with employed persons	23.1	225.5	248.6
Extraterritorial organizations and bodies	42.7	25.1	67.9
Sub-total	16,853.7	14,571.0	31,424.9
Not classifiable by economic activity	6.5	3.8	10.3
Total employed	16,860.3	14,574.8	31,435.1
Unemployed	427.9	1,225.8	1,653.7
Total labour force	17,288.2	15,800.6	33,088.8

* Excluding armed forces.

2013 (labour force survey, '000 persons aged 10 years and over, April–June): Agriculture, hunting, forestry and fishing 30,817.1; Mining, quarrying, electricity, gas and water supply 407.0; Manufacturing 1,902.2; Construction 824.8; Trade, transport, hotels and restaurants, business and administrative services 3,619.3; Public administration, community, social and other services activities 4,833.6; *Total employed* 42,403.9; Unemployed 1,981.2; *Total labour force* 44,385.1 (males 23,516.3, females 20,868.8).

Source: ILO.

Mid-2015 (FAO estimates in '000): Agriculture, etc. 37,957; Total labour force 50,906 (Source: FAO).

Health and Welfare

KEY INDICATORS

Total fertility rate (children per woman, 2012)	4.6
Under-5 mortality rate (per 1,000 live births, 2012) . . .	68
HIV/AIDS (% of persons aged 15–49, 2013)	1.2
Physicians (per 1,000 head, 2009)	0.03
Hospital beds (per 1,000 head, 2011)	6.3
Health expenditure (2011): US $ per head (PPP)	43
Health expenditure (2011): % of GDP	4.1
Health expenditure (2011): public (% of total)	50.0
Access to water (% of persons, 2012)	52
Access to sanitation (% of persons, 2012)	24
Total carbon dioxide emissions ('000 metric tons, 2010) . .	6,494.3
Carbon dioxide emissions per head (metric tons, 2010) . .	0.1
Human Development Index (2013): ranking	173
Human Development Index (2013): value	0.435

For sources and definitions, see explanatory note on p. vi.

Agriculture

PRINCIPAL CROPS
('000 metric tons)

	2011	2012	2013
Wheat	2,916	3,435	4,039
Barley	1,585	1,782	1,933
Maize	6,069	6,158	6,674
Oats	49	44	60
Millet (Dagusa)	652	742	870
Sorghum	3,951	3,604	4,338
Potatoes	475	863	776
Sweet potatoes	390	1,185	1,355
Yams	315	111.7	119
Sugar cane*	2,500	2,700	2,750
Beans, dry	388	463	193
Broad beans, horse beans, dry .	715	944	149
Peas, dry	263	327	404
Chick peas	400	410	249
Lentils	128	152	130
Vetches	306	326	128
Groundnuts, with shell . . .	103	124	103
Castor beans†	8	11	13
Rapeseed	75	73	36
Safflower seed	9	13	7
Sesame seed	245	181	187
Linseed	113	122	105
Cabbages and other brassicas .	367	394	395*
Tomatoes	82	56	55*
Onions and shallots, green* . .	33	34	35
Onions, dry	328	219	220
Garlic	124	223	170*
Bananas	291	303	300*
Oranges	49	36	36*
Mangoes, mangosteens and guavas	73	70	69*
Avocados	73	26	27*
Papayas	43	39	29*
Coffee, green	377	276	27*

* FAO estimate(s).
† Unofficial figures.

Aggregate production ('000 metric tons, may include official, semi-official or estimated data): Total cereals 18,810 in 2011, 19,651 in 2012, 22,707 in 2013; Total roots and tubers 6,275 in 2011, 8,366 in 2012, 8,522 in 2013; Total vegetables (incl. melons) 1,787 in 2011, 1,930 in 2012, 1,889 in 2013; Total fruits (excl. melons) 729 in 2011, 672 in 2012-13.

Source: FAO.

LIVESTOCK
('000 head, year ending September)

	2011	2012	2013*
Cattle	52,129	53,990	54,000
Sheep	24,221	25,489	26,500
Goats	22,613	24,061	25,000
Asses	6,438	6,748	7,000
Mules	369	350	345
Horses	1,962	1,907	2,000
Camels	979	916	925
Pigs*	32	32	33
Poultry	44,893	50,377	51,000

* FAO estimates.
Source: FAO.

LIVESTOCK PRODUCTS
('000 metric tons)

	2011	2012	2013
Cattle meat	410.0*	338.2	340.1*
Sheep meat*	85.0	86.0	87.0
Goat meat*	68.0	71.5	74.0
Pig meat*	1.8	1.9	1.9
Chicken meat*	53.9	60.5	61.8
Game meat*	85.0	85.0	85.0
Cows' milk	3,329.9	3,805.0	4,000.0
Goats' milk*	55.0	57.5	59.0
Sheep's milk*	56.3	57.5	58.8
Hen eggs*	39.6	40.0	41.0
Honey	39.9	45.9	45.0
Wool, greasy*	8.0	8.0	8.0

* FAO estimate(s).

Source: FAO.

Forestry

ROUNDWOOD REMOVALS
('000 cubic metres, excl. bark, FAO estimates)

	2011	2012	2013
Sawlogs, veneer logs and logs for sleepers	11	11	11
Pulpwood	7	7	7
Other industrial wood	2,917	2,917	2,917
Fuel wood	102,609	103,966	105,346
Total	105,544	106,901	108,281

Source: FAO.

SAWNWOOD PRODUCTION
('000 cubic metres, incl. railway sleepers)

	2001	2002	2003
Coniferous (softwood)	25*	1	1
Broadleaved (hardwood)	35*	13	17
Total	60	14	18

* FAO estimate.

2004–13: Figures assumed to be unchanged from 2003 (FAO estimates).

Source: FAO.

Fishing

(metric tons, live weight of capture)

	2010	2011	2012
Common carp	182	929	1,181
Other cyprinids	1,971	1,900	—
Tilapias	12,110	16,279	18,985
North African catfish	2,050	3,279	5,225
Nile perch	1,017	844	744
Total catch (incl. others)	18,058	24,041	28,952

Source: FAO.

Mining

('000 metric tons unless otherwise indicated, year ending 7 July)

	2009/10	2010/11	2011/12
Gold (kilograms)	6,773	10,891	12,311
Limestone	2,300	2,600*	2,900*
Gypsum and anhydrite	41	46*	52*
Pumice	128	254	290*
Sandstone	2,000	2,300	2,600*

* Estimate.

Source: US Geological Survey.

Industry

SELECTED PRODUCTS
('000 metric tons unless otherwise indicated, year ending 7 July)

	2000/01	2001/02	2002/03
Wheat flour	165	143	137
Macaroni and pasta	26	23	30*
Raw sugar	251	248*	295*
Wine ('000 hectolitres)	25	27*	32*
Beer ('000 hectolitres)	1,605	1,812*	2,123*
Mineral waters ('000 hectolitres)	395	395*	433*
Soft drinks ('000 hectolitres)	677	995	845*
Cigarettes (million)	1,904	1,511*	1,511*
Cotton yarn	5.7	7.7*	5.5*
Woven cotton fabrics ('000 sq m)	45,000	45,000*	41,000*
Nylon fabrics ('000 sq m)	1,300	1,000*	1,400*
Footwear (including rubber, '000 pairs)	n.a.	6,677	7,138
Soap	14.8	19.2*	11.6*
Tyres ('000)*	209	198	191
Clay building bricks ('000)*	20	22	21
Quicklime*	11	8	11
Cement*	819	919	890

* Year ending 31 December of later year.

Source: UN, *Industrial Commodity Statistics Yearbook*.

Raw sugar ('000 metric tons): 325.0 in 2004; 345.0 in 2005; 360.0 in 2006; 340.0 in 2007; 340 in 2008; 320 in 2009–10; 350 in 2010–11 (Source: UN Industrial Commodity Statistics Database).

Cement (hydraulic, '000 metric tons, year ending 7 July): 1,659 in 2008; 1,688 in 2009; 1,639 in 2010; 2,300 in 2011 (estimate); 3,500 in 2012 (estimate) (Source: US Geological Survey).

Beer of millet ('000 metric tons): 445.8 in 2011; 457.9 in 2012; 522.4 in 2013 (Source: FAO).

Beer of barley ('000 metric tons, estimates): 350.9 in 2010; 356.6 in 2011; 815.7 in 2012 (Source: FAO).

Finance

CURRENCY AND EXCHANGE RATES

Monetary Units
100 cents = 1 birr.

Sterling, Dollar and Euro Equivalents (30 August 2013)
£1 sterling = 20.306 birr;
US $1 = 18.770 birr;
€1 = 18.066 birr;
100 birr = £4.92 = $5.33 = €5.54.

Average Exchange Rate (birr per US $)
2010	14.410
2011	16.899
2012	17.705

GENERAL BUDGET
(million birr, year ending 7 July)

Revenue	2012/13	2013/14*	2014/15†
Taxation	107,010	129,325	157,171
Taxes on income and profits .	36,393	42,456	50,401
Domestic indirect taxes . .	32,440	37,845	44,928
Import duties	38,177	49,024	61,842
Other revenue	17,067	11,212	13,841
Total‡	124,077	140,536	171,012

Expenditure	2012/13	2013/14*	2014/15†
Current expenditure	62,782	73,529	87,557
Defence spending	6,493	7,500	8,000
Poverty-reduction expenditure§	31,481	36,725	43,599
Interest and charges . . .	2,931	3,782	5,660
Domestic	1,792	2,129	3,437
External	1,139	1,653	2,223
Other current expenditure . .	21,877	25,522	30,298
Capital expenditure	91,183	109,902	135,817
Central treasury	68,552	87,079	111,571
External assistance (grants) .	9,699	11,786	12,496
External loans	12,933	11,037	11,749
Total	153,965	183,431	223,374

* Estimates.
† Projections.
‡ Excluding grants received from abroad (million birr): 13,115 in 2012/13; 15,808 in 2013/14 (estimate); 17,271 in 2014/15 (projection).
§ Includes total spending on health, education, agriculture, roads and food security.

Source: IMF, *The Federal Democratic Republic of Ethiopia: Staff Report for the 2013 Article IV Consultation* (October 2013).

INTERNATIONAL RESERVES
(US $ million at 31 December, excluding gold)

	2007	2008	2009
IMF special drawing rights . .	0.1	—	27.4
Reserve position in IMF . . .	11.6	11.5	11.8
Foreign exchange	1,278.1	859.0	1,741.7
Total	1,289.8	870.5	1,780.9

2010: IMF special drawing rights 150.0; Reserve position in IMF 11.6.

2011: IMF special drawing rights 149.3; Reserve position in IMF 11.5.

2012: IMF special drawing rights 149.4; Reserve position in IMF 11.5.

2013: IMF special drawing rights 149.7; Reserve position in IMF 11.5.

Source: IMF, *International Financial Statistics*.

MONEY SUPPLY
(million birr at 31 December)

	2006	2007	2008
Currency outside banks . . .	11,606.4	14,445.8	17,432.9
Demand deposits at commercial banks	20,207.0	24,175.9	31,391.6
Total money (incl. others) . .	32,056.2	38,903.5	49,105.8

Source: IMF, *International Financial Statistics*.

COST OF LIVING
(Consumer Price Index, year ending 7 July; base: December 2006 = 100)

	2009/10	2010/11	2011/12
Food (incl. non-alcoholic beverages)	187.2	216.6	307.0
Clothing and footwear	188.5	242.2	323.4
Housing, water, electricity, gas and other fuels	159.1	191.1	219.4
All items (incl. others) . . .	177.9	210.2	281.0

All items (Consumer Price Index; base: 2010 = 100): 133.2 in 2011; 163.6 in 2012; 176.8 in 2013 (Source: IMF, *International Financial Statistics*).

NATIONAL ACCOUNTS
(million birr at current prices)

Expenditure on the Gross Domestic Product

	2011	2012*	2013†
Government final consumption expenditure	43,682	52,915	62,146
Private final consumption expenditure	397,595	574,867	639,772
Gross fixed capital formation .	140,904	244,320	281,263
Total domestic expenditure .	582,181	872,102	983,181
Exports of goods and services .	85,955	102,887	107,904
Less Imports of goods and services	162,490	236,384	238,345
GDP in purchasers' values .	505,646	738,605	852,740

Gross Domestic Product by Economic Activity

	2011	2012*	2013†
Agriculture, hunting, forestry and fishing	212,470	331,297	358,085
Mining and quarrying	6,810	9,301	10,307
Manufacturing	18,968	25,562	30,381
Electricity and water	4,902	6,286	7,539
Construction	19,100	30,041	38,836
Trade, hotels and restaurants .	87,937	126,423	147,236
Finance, insurance and real estate	55,992	70,581	82,241
Transport and communications .	19,891	29,715	41,077
Public administration and defence	17,447	21,837	26,954
Education	10,049	11,975	14,840
Health and social work . . .	3,711	4,652	5,786
Other services	12,157	17,918	24,021
Sub-total	469,434	685,588	787,303
Indirect taxes (net)	39,431	56,882	70,654
Less Imputed bank service charge	3,219	3,864	5,217
GDP in purchasers' values .	505,646	738,605	852,740

* Preliminary figures.
† Provisional figures.

Source: African Development Bank.

BALANCE OF PAYMENTS
(US $ million)

	2010	2011	2012
Exports of goods	2,479.5	3,029.0	3,258.0
Imports of goods	−7,364.5	−8,328.9	−10,547.3
Balance on goods	−4,885.0	−5,299.8	−7,289.3
Exports of services	2,164.7	2,785.8	2,735.9
Imports of services	−2,546.3	−3,321.8	−3,582.6
Balance on goods and services	−5,266.6	−5,835.8	−8,136.0
Primary income received . . .	8.1	8.8	8.7
Primary income paid	−71.7	−85.6	−105.5
Balance on goods, services and primary income	−5,330.1	−5,912.7	−8,232.9
Secondary income received . .	4,987.9	5,172.9	5,326.8
Secondary income paid . . .	−83.2	−43.3	−79.3
Current balance	−425.4	−783.1	−2,985.3
Direct investment liabilities . .	288.3	626.5	278.6
Other investment assets . . .	1,084.6	171.3	−142.7
Other investment liabilities . .	995.6	1,072.1	530.8
Net errors and omissions . . .	−2,929.9	−1,795.8	2,648.6
Reserves and related items .	−986.8	−708.9	330.0

Source: IMF, *International Financial Statistics*.

External Trade

PRINCIPAL COMMODITIES
(distribution by HS, US $ million)

Imports c.i.f.	2011	2012	2013
Vegetables and vegetable products	606.3	505.3	674.6
Cereals	471.4	416.7	589.3
Wheat and meslin	402.6	333.0	464.2
Animal, vegetable fats and oils, cleavage products, etc.	391.7	417.0	391.6
Palm oil and its fraction	330.9	372.9	358.3
Prepared foodstuffs; beverages, spirits, vinegar; tobacco and articles thereof	298.1	286.0	377.5
Mineral products	1,715.3	2,529.5	1,268.4
Mineral fuels, oils, distillation products, etc.	1,632.0	2,480.5	1,257.2
Refined petroleum oils	1,484.3	2,361.5	1,108.3
Chemicals and related products	830.7	1,187.9	1,335.6
Fertilizers	340.8	613.7	307.5
Mixtures of nitrogen, phosphorous and potassium fertilizers	250.2	438.0	195.3
Pharmaceutical products	120.7	174.8	526.1
Medicament mixtures, put in dosage	110.5	153.3	396.2
Plastics, rubber, and articles thereof	445.2	573.3	653.3
Plastics and articles thereof	283.9	361.9	398.8
Textiles and textile articles	361.7	472.1	476.6
Iron and steel, other base metals and articles of base metal	830.1	1,351.5	1,303.7
Iron and steel	453.2	722.0	643.0
Articles of iron and steel	210.8	412.9	436.0
Machinery and mechanical appliances; electrical equipment; parts thereof	1,776.6	2,606.2	2,431.1
Boilers, machinery, etc.	1,150.3	1,637.9	1,634.5
Self-propelled bulldozer, angledozer, grader, excavator, etc.	195.4	432.6	372.0
Electrical and electronic equipment	626.3	968.4	796.5
Vehicles, aircraft, vessels and associated transport equipment	1,003.6	1,283.3	1,230.6
Vehicles other than railway, tramway	893.8	1,238.6	1,198.9
Trucks, motor vehicles for the transport of goods	357.6	530.1	545.6
Total (incl. others)	8,896.3	11,912.9	10,955.4

Exports f.o.b.	2011	2012	2013
Live animals and animal products	273.3	262.3	259.6
Live animals	190.4	181.9	180.8
Live bovine animals	137.8	96.0	112.8
Vegetables and vegetable products	1,906.4	2,152.3	1,899.4
Live trees, plants, bulbs, roots, cut flowers, etc.	191.4	188.5	187.6
Cut flowers and flower buds for bouquets, fresh or dried	168.9	165.6	165.1
Edible vegetables and roots and tubers	416.7	488.5	540.1
Vegetables, fresh or chilled	238.1	247.8	279.1
Dried vegetables, shelled	139.3	199.3	216.8
Coffee, tea, mate and spices	887.1	923.2	636.3
Coffee	846.9	891.1	606.3
Oil seed, oleagic fruits, grain, seed, fruit, etc.	368.7	494.9	512.5
Oil seeds	363.8	459.2	477.5
Raw hides and skins, leather, furskins, etc., and articles thereof	123.4	88.6	104.3
Raw hides, skins (except furskins) and leather	122.7	85.6	101.1
Textiles and textile articles	73.7	71.2	89.0
Pearls, precious or semi-precious stones, precious metals, and articles thereof	132.5	184.8	166.1
Gold	124.6	174.8	154.5
Total (incl. others)	2,614.9	2,891.3	2,591.0

Source: Trade Map-Trade Competitiveness Map, International Trade Centre, www.intracen.org/marketanalysis.

PRINCIPAL TRADING PARTNERS
(US $ million)

Imports c.i.f.	2011	2012	2013
Brazil	81.5	139.8	99.3
China, People's Republic	1,718.1	2,572.4	2,953.0
Egypt	82.9	99.2	116.9
France (incl. Monaco)	142.9	217.8	147.4
Germany	189.6	200.4	236.7
India	749.3	994.3	1,224.7
Indonesia	188.4	348.6	360.3
Italy	386.7	578.0	459.2
Japan	443.4	497.4	517.5
Jordan	129.2	36.5	52.0
Korea, Republic	134.9	199.5	172.5
Kuwait	222.1	735.0	335.9
Malaysia	274.1	174.5	169.2
Morocco	30.5	178.8	1.1
Netherlands	81.8	105.3	209.1
Pakistan	108.9	40.0	54.4
Russia	270.9	131.9	11.5
Saudi Arabia	896.8	1,674.7	928.6
South Africa	93.1	123.5	134.0
Spain	91.7	130.8	108.7
Sudan	145.6	69.5	10.4
Thailand	131.5	160.2	177.1
Turkey	359.7	513.6	481.6
Ukraine	140.8	333.3	214.1
United Arab Emirates	482.5	275.2	345.0
United Kingdom	109.8	97.9	114.4
USA	489.0	420.5	515.2
Total (incl. others)	8,896.3	11,912.9	10,955.4

Exports f.o.b.	2011	2012	2013
Belgium	69.5	76.3	54.3
China, People's Republic	283.4	320.9	308.3
Djibouti	75.6	107.2	75.1
Egypt	46.1	44.3	50.7
France (incl. Monaco)	50.2	52.6	28.2
Germany	318.8	312.7	177.1
Hong kong	21.5	33.1	38.7
India	33.8	44.5	35.5
Israel	67.2	70.9	93.7
Italy	111.2	80.0	61.5

Exports f.o.b.—*continued*	2011	2012	2013
Japan	35.9	75.4	77.0
Jordan	26.6	36.8	27.9
Netherlands	181.2	173.7	168.9
Pakistan	13.4	45.9	49.3
Saudi Arabia	167.3	191.4	165.4
Somalia	243.3	259.8	319.8
Sudan	178.4	162.7	96.6
Sweden	39.0	27.2	14.2
Switzerland-Liechtenstein	129.4	177.0	155.4
Turkey	45.2	50.6	77.2
United Arab Emirates	82.5	79.9	75.6
United Kingdom	67.5	48.3	48.4
USA	98.0	116.1	121.3
Viet Nam	3.4	34.9	20.1
Yemen	20.7	23.8	31.8
Total (incl. others)	2,614.9	2,891.3	2,591.0

Source: Trade Map-Trade Competitiveness Map, International Trade Centre, www.intracen.org/marketanalysis.

Transport

RAILWAYS

(traffic on the Addis Ababa–Djibouti line, year ending 7 July)*

	2008/09	2009/10
Passengers carried ('000)	55	35
Passenger-km (million)	14	5
Freight carried ('000 tons)	20	2
Freight (million net ton-km)	7	1

* Including traffic on the section of the line that runs through the Republic of Djibouti; data pertaining to freight include service traffic.

ROAD TRAFFIC

(motor vehicles in use, year ending 7 July)

	2001	2002	2003
Passenger cars	59,737	67,614	71,311
Buses and coaches	11,387	18,067	20,713
Lorries and vans	43,375	34,102	51,690
Motorcycles and mopeds	2,198	2,575	1,268
Road tractors	1,275	1,396	—
Total	117,972	123,754	144,982

2007: Passenger cars 70,834; Buses and coaches 17,098; Lorries and vans 148,997; Motorcycles and mopeds 7,328.

Source: IRF, *World Road Statistics*.

SHIPPING

Flag Registered Fleet
(at 31 December)

	2012	2013	2014
Number of vessels	9	17	17
Displacement (grt)	139,017	313,105	313,105

Source: Lloyd's List Intelligence (www.lloydslistintelligence.com).

CIVIL AVIATION

(traffic on scheduled services)

	2011	2012
Kilometres flown (million)	100	119
Passengers carried ('000)	3,347	4,441
Passenger-km (million)	11,652	15,330
Total ton-km (million)	1,864	2,382

Source: UN, *Statistical Yearbook*.

2011/12 (traffic at Addis Ababa international airport, year ending 7 July): Aircraft movements 51,318; Passengers carried ('000) 5,183; Freight carried ('000 metric tons) 154,138; Mail carried ('000 metric tons) 530.

Tourism

TOURIST ARRIVALS BY COUNTRY OF ORIGIN

	2011	2012	2013
Canada	12,889	15,007	16,800
China, People's Republic	20,197	35,383	31,688
Djibouti	5,962	8,944	10,359
France	16,517	20,970	20,290
Germany	24,780	29,917	29,286
India	19,667	19,211	21,789
Italy	19,164	22,621	24,213
Kenya	19,904	20,279	23,521
Netherlands	9,052	10,613	12,496
Nigeria	16,437	16,701	18,945
Saudi Arabia	18,891	18,435	19,495
Somalia	1,842	2,388	6,218
South Africa	13,433	11,470	14,512
Sudan	17,922	16,814	20,313
United Arab Emirates	8,255	9,368	13,211
United Kingdom	28,945	31,605	36,980
USA	81,044	99,641	108,089
Total (incl. others)*	523,438	596,341	681,249

* Including Ethiopian nationals residing abroad.

Receipts from tourism (US $ million, excl. passenger transport): 770 in 2011; 607 in 2012; 416 in 2013 (provisional).

Source: World Tourism Organization.

Communications Media

	2011	2012	2013
Telephones ('000 main lines in use)	829.0	797.5	761.4
Mobile cellular telephones ('000 subscribers)	14,126.7	20,523.9	25,646.9
Broadband subscribers	4,592	6,772	238,067

Source: International Telecommunication Union.

Education

(2012/13)

	Institutions	Teachers	Students
Pre-primary	3,688	12,639	2,013,214
Primary	30,534	335,109	17,430,294
Secondary: grades 9–12	1,912	65,116	1,900,022
Secondary: teacher training	34	2,044	175,142
Secondary: technical and vocational	437	12,779	237,877
Higher education	99	23,905	585,152
Government	34	21,899	502,466
Non-government	65	2,006	82,686

Source: Ministry of Education, Addis Ababa.

Pupil-teacher ratio (primary education, UNESCO estimate): 53.7 in 2011/12 (Source: UNESCO Institute for Statistics).

Adult literacy rate (UNESCO estimates): 35.9% (males 50.0%; females 22.8%) in 2008 (Source: UNESCO Institute for Statistics).

Directory

The Government

HEAD OF STATE

President: Dr MULATU TESHOME WIRTU (took office 7 October 2013).

COUNCIL OF MINISTERS
(April 2015)

The Government is formed by members of the Amhara National Democratic Movement (ANDM), the South Ethiopian People's Democratic Movement (SEPDM), the Oromo People's Democratic Organization (OPDO), the Tigrai People's Liberation Front (TPLF) and the Somali People's Democratic Party (SPDP).

Prime Minister: HAILEMARIAM DESALEGN (SEPDM).

Deputy Prime Minister, Co-ordinator of Good Governance and Minister of the Civil Service: WOIZERO ASTER MAMO (OPDO).

Deputy Prime Minister, Co-ordinator of Finance and the Economy and Minister of Communication and Information Technology: DEBRETSION GEBREMIKAEL (TPLF).

Deputy Prime Minister: DEMEKE MEKONNEN (ANDM).

Minister of Foreign Affairs: Dr TEWEDROS ADHANOM (TPLF).

Minister of Defence: SIRAJ FERGESA (SEPDM).

Minister of Federal Affairs: Dr SHIFERAW TEKELEMARIAM (SEPDM).

Minister of Justice: GETACHEW AMBAYE (ANDM).

Minister of Finance and Economic Development: SUFYAN AHMED (OPDO).

Minister of Agriculture: TEFERA DERIBEW (ANDM).

Minister of Industry: AHMED ABETEW (ANDM).

Minister of Trade: KEBEDE CHANE (ANDM).

Minister of Science and Technology: DEMITU HAMBESSA (OPDO).

Minister of Transport: WORKNEH GEBEYEHU (OPDO).

Minister of Urban Development, Housing and Construction: MEKURIA HAILE (SEPDM).

Minister of Water and Energy: ALEMAYEHU TEGENU (OPDO).

Minister of Mines: TOLLOSA SHAGI (ANDM).

Minister of Health: Dr KESETEBERHAN ADMASU (SEPDM).

Minister of Labour and Social Affairs: ABDULFETAH ABDULAHI HASSEN (SPDP).

Minister of Culture and Tourism: AMIN ABDULKADIR (ANDM).

Minister of Women, Youth and Children's Affairs: ZENEBU TADESSE (ANDM).

Minister of Education: SHIFERAW SHIGUTE (SEPDM).

Minister of Environment Protection and Forestry: BELETE TAFESE (TPLF).

Ministers and Policy Study and Research Advisers to the Prime Minister: BEREKET SIMON (ANDM), KUMA DEMEKSA (OPDO).

Minister, Head of the Government Communication Office: REDWAN HUSSEIN (SEPDM).

Minister, Government Chief Whip: ROMAN GEBRESILASIE (TPLF).

Minister, Director-General of the Ethiopian Revenues and Customs Authority: BEKIR SHALE (OPDO).

MINISTRIES

Office of the President: POB 1031, Addis Ababa; tel. (11) 1551000; fax (11) 1552030.

Office of the Prime Minister: POB 1013, Addis Ababa; tel. (11) 1552044; fax (11) 1552020; internet www.ethiopia.gov.et.

Office for Government Communication Affairs: POB 1364/530, Addis Ababa; tel. (11) 5537355; fax (11) 5522060; e-mail shekemal@yahoo.com; internet www.gcao.gov.et.

Ministry of Agriculture: POB 62347, Addis Ababa; tel. (11) 5538134; fax (11) 5530776; internet www.moa.gov.et.

Ministry of the Civil Service: Kirkos Woreda, 1/19 Bbole Rd, Addis Ababa; tel. (11) 5549666; fax (11) 5535561; e-mail mocis@ethionet.et; internet www.mocis.gov.et.

Ministry of Communication and Information Technology: Alta Bldg, 6th Floor, Mexico Sq., POB 1028, Addis Ababa; tel. (11) 5500191; fax (11) 5515894; internet www.mcit.gov.et.

Ministry of Culture and Tourism: POB 2183, Addis Ababa; tel. (11) 5512310; fax (11) 5512889; e-mail info@tourismethiopia.org; internet www.tourismethiopia.org.

Ministry of Defence: POB 1373, Addis Ababa; tel. (11) 5511777; fax (11) 5516053; internet www.fdredefenceforce.gov.et.

Ministry of Education: POB 1367, Addis Ababa; tel. (11) 1553133; fax (11) 1550877; internet www.moe.gov.et.

Ministry of Environment Protection and Forestry: Yeka, Addis Ababa; internet www.epa.gov.et.

Ministry of Federal Affairs: POB 5608, Addis Ababa; tel. (11) 5510000; fax (11) 5511200; e-mail mofa1@ethionet.et; internet www.mofa.gov.et.

Ministry of Finance and Economic Development: POB 1037, Addis Ababa; tel. (11) 1552400; fax (11) 1551355; e-mail infopr@mofed.gov.et; internet www.mofed.gov.et.

Ministry of Foreign Affairs: POB 393, Addis Ababa; tel. (11) 5517345; fax (11) 5514300; e-mail mfa.addis@telecom.net.et; internet www.mfa.gov.et.

Ministry of Health: POB 1234, Addis Ababa; tel. (11) 5517011; fax (11) 5519366; e-mail moh@telecom.net.et; internet www.moh.gov.et.

Ministry of Industry: Addis Ababa; tel. (11) 534942; fax (11) 5534932; internet www.moi.gov.et.

Ministry of Justice: POB 1370, Addis Ababa; tel. (11) 5541868; fax (11) 517775; e-mail mojmo@ethionet.et; internet www.moj.gov.et.

Ministry of Labour and Social Affairs: POB 2056, Addis Ababa; tel. (11) 5517080; fax (11) 5518396; e-mail molsa.comp@ethionet.et; internet www.molsa.gov.et.

Ministry of Mines: POB 486, Addis Ababa; internet www.mom.gov.et; tel. (11) 5153689; fax (11) 5517874.

Ministry of Science and Technology: POB 2490, Addis Ababa; tel. (11) 4661867; e-mail most@ethionet.et; internet www.most.gov.et.

Ministry of Trade: POB 704, Addis Ababa; tel. (11) 5518025; fax (11) 5515411; e-mail henok_fekadu@yahoo.com; internet www.mot.gov.et.

Ministry of Transport: Addis Ababa; tel. (11) 5516166; fax (11) 5515665; e-mail nigusmen@yahoo.com; internet www.motr.gov.et.

Ministry of Urban Development, Housing and Construction: opp. National Bank of Ethiopia, POB 24134/1000, Addis Ababa; tel. (11) 5531688; fax (11) 5541268; e-mail mekuria.2000@gmail.com; internet www.mwud.gov.et.

Ministry of Water and Energy: Haile G/Silassie Rd, POB 5744 and 5673, Addis Ababa; tel. (11) 6611111; fax (11) 6610710; e-mail info@mowr.gov.et; internet www.mowr.gov.et.

Ministry of Women, Youth and Children's Affairs: POB 1364, Addis Ababa; tel. (11) 5517020.

Regional Governments

Ethiopia comprises nine regional governments and two chartered cities (Addis Ababa and Dire Dawa), all of which are vested with the authority for self-administration. The executive bodies are respectively headed by Presidents (regional states) and Chairmen (Addis Ababa and Dire Dawa).

PRESIDENTS
(April 2015)

Tigrai: ABAY WOLDU.

Afar: ISMAIL ALI SERRO.

Amhara: GEDU ANDARGATCHEW.

Oromia: MUKTAR KEDIR.

Somali: ABDI MOHAMED OMAR.

Benishangul-Gumuz: AHMED NASIR AHMED.

Southern Nations, Nationalities and Peoples: DESSIE DALKE.

Gambela: UMED UBONG.

Harari: MURAD ABDULHADIN.

CHAIRMEN
(April 2015)

Dire Dawa: ASAD ZIAD.

Addis Ababa: DIRIBA KUMA.

Legislature

FEDERAL PARLIAMENTARY ASSEMBLY

The legislature comprises an upper house, the House of the Federation (Yefedereshn Mekir Bet), with 108 seats (members are selected by state assemblies and are drawn one each from 22 minority nationalities and one from each professional sector of the remaining nationalities, and serve for a period of five years), and a lower house, the House of People's Representatives (Yehizbtewekayoch Mekir Bet), of no more than 550 directly elected members, who are also elected for a five-year term.

House of the Federation

House of the Federation: Addis Ababa; tel. (11) 1242309; fax (11) 1242304; internet www.hofethiopia.gov.et.

Speaker: KASSA TEKLEBERHAN.

Deputy Speaker: MOHAMMED SIREE.

House of People's Representatives

House of People's Representatives: POB 80001, Addis Ababa; tel. (11) 1241000; fax (11) 1241004; internet www.hopr.gov.et.

Speaker: ABADULA GEMEDA.

Deputy Speaker: SHITAYE MINALE.

General Election, 23 May 2010

Party	Seats
Ethiopian People's Revolutionary Democratic Front (EPRDF)	499
Somali People's Democratic Party (SPDP)	24
Benishangul Gumuz People's Democratic Party (BGPDP)	9
Afar National Democratic Party (ANDP)	8
Gambela People's Unity Democratic Movement (GPUDM)	3
Amhara National Democratic Movement (ANDM)	1
Ethiopia Federal Democratic Unity Forum (FORUM/Medrek)	1
Harari National League (HNL)	1
Independent	1
Total	547

Election Commission

National Electoral Board of Ethiopia (NEB): POB 40812, Addis Ababa; tel. (11) 5153416; e-mail info@electionethiopia.org; internet www.electionethiopia.org; f. 1993; independent board of seven politically non-affiliated mems appointed, on the Prime Minister's recommendation, by the House of People's Representatives; Chair. Dr MERGA BEKANA.

Political Organizations

A total of 79 political parties contested the 2010 legislative elections.

Afar National Democratic Party (ANDP): f. 1999; Leader ISMAIL ALI SERRO.

All Ethiopian Unity Party (AEUP): planned to merge with UDJ/Andinet prior to the 2015 general election; Chair. ABEBAW MEHARI.

Benishangul Gumuz People's Democratic Party (BGPDP): f. 2009; Chair. HABTAMU HIKA.

Ethiopia Federal Democratic Unity Forum (FORUM/Medrek): f. 2009; the Ethiopia Democratic Union Movement (EDUM) and the Somali Democratic Alliance Forces (SDAF) withdrew from the coalition in March 2010; Chair. Prof. MERERA GUDINA.

Ethiopian Social Democratic Party (ESDP): f. 1993 as the Council of Alternative Forces for Peace and Democracy in Ethiopia; opposes the EPRDF; Chair. Dr BEYENE PETROS.

Oromo Federalist Democratic Movement (OFDM): formed part of the Oromo Federalist Congress (OFC) for the 2010 elections; reportedly merged with the OPC in Feb. 2013 to form Oromo Federal Congress; Chair. BULCHA DEMEKSA; Sec.-Gen. BEKELE JIRATA.

Oromo People's Congress (OPC): Addis Ababa; e-mail oromopeoplescongress@yahoo.com; internet www.oromopeoplescongress.org; f. 2007 by fmr mems of the ONC; formed part of the Oromo Federalist Congress (OFC) for the 2010 elections; reportedly merged with OFDM in Feb. 2013 to form Oromo Federal Congress; Chair. Prof. MERERA GUDINA.

Southern Ethiopia People's Democratic Union (SEPDU): f. 1994; Chair. TILAHUN EADESHAW.

Union of Tigrians For Democracy and Sovereignty (ARENA): f. 2007; Chair. GEBRU ASTRAT.

Unity for Democracy and Justice Party (UDJ/Andinet): f. 2008; planned merger with All Ethiopian Unity Party prior to the 2015 general election; Chair. TIGISTU AWELU.

Ethiopian Justice and Democratic Forces Front (EJDFF): f. 2008; Chair. GIRMAY HADERA.

Ethiopian Democratic Union (EDU): f. 2004; Chair. Dr KEBEDE HAILEMARIAM.

Ethiopian National Unity Party (ENUP): f. 2005; Chair. ZERIHUN GEBREGZIABER.

Oromia Liberation National Party (OLNP): Chair. Dr FARIS ISAYAS.

Unity of Southern Ethiopian Democratic Forces (USEDF): f. 2005; comprises Wolaita People's Democratic Front (WPDF), Gamo Democratic Union (GDU) and Gomogofa People's Democratic Union (GPDU); Chair. TEKLE BORENA.

Ethiopian National Democratic Party (ENDP): f. 1994 by merger of five pro-Govt orgs with mems in the Council of Representatives; comprises: the Ethiopian Democratic Organization, the Ethiopian Democratic Organization Coalition (EDC), the Gurage People's Democratic Front (GPDF), the Kembata People's Congress (KPC), and the Wolaita People's Democratic Front (WPDF); Chair. FEKADU GEDAMU; Gen. Sec. ZEMENE MOLLA.

Ethiopian People's Revolutionary Democratic Front (EPRDF): Addis Ababa; internet www.eprdf.org.et; f. 1989 by the TPLF as an alliance of insurgent groups seeking regional autonomy and engaged in armed struggle against the EDUP Govt; Chair. HAILEMARIAM DESALEGN; Vice-Chair. DEMEKE MEKONNEN.

Amhara National Democratic Movement (ANDM): based in Tigrai; represents interests of the Amhara people; fmrly the Ethiopian People's Democratic Movement (EPDM); adopted present name in 1994; Chair. ADDISO LEGGESE.

Oromo People's Democratic Organization (OPDO): f. 1990 by the TPLF to promote its cause in Oromo areas; based among the Oromo people in the Shoa region; Leader MUKTAR KEDIR.

South Ethiopian People's Democratic Movement (SEPDM): f. 1992; Chair. HAILEMARIAM DESALEGN.

Tigrai People's Liberation Front (TPLF): f. 1975; the dominant org. within the EPRDF; Chair. ABAY WOLDU; Vice-Chair. DEBRETSION GEBREMIKAEL.

Gambela People's Unity Democratic Movement (GPUDM): f. 2008; Chair. OMOD OBANG ALUM.

Harari National League (HNL): f. 1994; Chair. YASIN HUSEIN.

Movement for Justice, Freedom and Democracy (Ginbot 7): 8647 Richmond Highway, Alexandria, VA 22309, USA; e-mail org@ginbot7.org; internet www.ginbot7.org; f. 2008; Leader BERHANU NEGA.

Ogaden National Liberation Front (ONLF): e-mail foreign@onlf.org; internet www.onlf.org; f. 1984; seeks self-determination for the Ogaden region; Chair. MOHAMED OMAR OSMAN.

Oromo Liberation Front (OLF): POB 73247, Washington, DC 20056, USA; tel. (202) 462-5477; fax (202) 332-7011; e-mail info@oromoliberationfront.org; internet www.oromoliberationfront.org; f. 1973; seeks self-determination for the Oromo people; participated in the Ethiopian transitional Govt until June 1992; Chair. DAWUD IBSA AYANA; Vice-Chair. ABDULFATTAH A. MOUSSA BIYYO.

Semayawi Party (Blue Party): e-mail info@semayawiparty.org; internet www.semayawiparty.org; f. 2012; Pres. Eng. YILKAL GETNET.

Sidama Liberation Front (SLF): e-mail info@sidamaliberation-front.org; internet www.sidamaliberation-front.org; campaigns for self-determination for Sidama people.

Somali People's Democratic Party (SPDP): St Jijiga Somali Regional 365; internet www.spdp.org.et; f. 1998 by merger of Ogaden National Liberation Front (ONLF) and the Ethiopian Somali Democratic League (ESDL—an alliance comprising the Somali Democratic Union Party, the Issa and Gurgura Liberation Front, the Gurgura Independence Front, the Eastern Gabooye Democratic Organization, the Eastern Ethiopian Somali League, the Horyal Democratic Front, the Social Alliance Democratic Organization, the Somali Abo Democratic Union, the Shekhash People's Democratic Movement, the Ethiopian Somalis' Democratic Movement and the Per Barreh Party); Chair. ABDIFETAH SHECK ABDULAHI; Sec.-Gen. AHMED ARAB ADEN.

Unity of Ethiopians for Democratic Change (UEDC): f. 2007 as replacement for the Alliance for Freedom and Democracy; coalition of political parties and rebel groups opposed to the Govt.

Benishangul People's Liberation Movement (BPLM): f. 1995; rebel group operating in western Ethiopia.

Ethiopian People's Front for Justice and Equality (EPFJE): armed anti-Govt group operating in southern Ethiopia; f. as Southern Ethiopian People's Front for Justice and Equality.

Ethiopian People's Patriotic Front: CP 182, 1211 Geneva 13, Switzerland; tel. 223406025; e-mail info@eppf.net; internet www .eppf.net; armed anti-Govt group operating mainly in north-western Ethiopia; Leader Prof. ALEBACHEW TEGEGNE.

Tigrai People's Democratic Movement (TPDM): f. 1979; rebel group operating in northern Tigrai region of Ethiopia.

Diplomatic Representation

EMBASSIES IN ETHIOPIA

Algeria: Woreda 23, Kebele 13, House No. 1819, POB 5740, Addis Ababa; tel. (11) 3719666; fax (11) 3719669; Ambassador ABDEL NACEUR BELAID.

Angola: Woreda 18, Kebele 26, House No. 6, POB 2962, Addis Ababa; tel. (11) 5510085; fax (11) 5514922; Ambassador ARCANJO MARIA DO NASCIMENTO.

Australia: Apt 383/384, Hilton Hotel, Menelik II Ave, POB 3715, Addis Ababa; tel. (11) 5523320; fax (11) 5523344; e-mail addisababa .info@dfat.gov.au; internet ethiopia.embassy.gov.au; Ambassador MARK SAWERS.

Austria: POB 1219, Addis Ababa; tel. (11) 3712144; fax (11) 3712140; e-mail addis-abeba-ob@bmeia.gv.at; internet www.bmeia.gv.at/botschaft/addis-abeba.html; Ambassador Dr ANDREAS MELÁN.

Belarus: Addis Ababa; e-mail ethiopia@mfa.gov.by; internet ethiopia.mfa.gov.by/en; Ambassador DMITRY KUPTEL.

Belgium: Comoros St, Kebele 8, POB 1239, Addis Ababa; tel. (11) 6611813; fax (11) 6613646; e-mail addisababa@diplobel.fed.be; internet www.diplomatie.be/addisababa; Ambassador HUGUES CHANTRY.

Benin: Nifas Silk Sub-City, Kebele 04, House No. 990, POB 200084, Addis Ababa; tel. (11) 3722605; fax (11) 3722793; e-mail ambaben_addis@yahoo.fr; Ambassador NAIM AKIBOU.

Botswana: POB 22282, Addis Ababa; tel. (11) 715422; fax (11) 714099; Ambassador MMAMOSADINYANA P. J. MOLEFE.

Brazil: Bole Sub-City, Kebele 2, House No. 2830, POB 2458, Addis Ababa; tel. (11) 6620401; fax (11) 6620412; e-mail embradisadm@ethionet.et; Ambassador IZABEL CRISTINA DE AZEVEDO.

Bulgaria: Bole Kifle Ketema, Kebele 06, Haile Gabreselassie Rd, POB 987, Addis Ababa; tel. (11) 6610032; fax (11) 6613373; e-mail bulemba@ethionet.et; internet www.mfa.bg/embassies/ethiopia; Chargé d'affaires a.i. DRAGOVEST GORANOV.

Burkina Faso: Kebele 19, House No. 281, POB 19685, Addis Ababa; tel. (11) 6615863; fax (11) 6625857; e-mail ambfet@telecom.net.et; Ambassador MINATA SAMATÉ.

Burundi: Kirkos Cub-City, Kebele 03, House No. 047, POB 3641, Addis Ababa; tel. (11) 4651300; fax (11) 4650299; e-mail burundi .emb@ethionet.et; Ambassador ALAIN-AIME NYAMITWE.

Cameroon: Bole Rd, Woreda 18, Kebele 26, House No. 168, POB 1026, Addis Ababa; tel. (11) 5504488; fax (11) 5518434; Ambassador JACQUES-ALFRED NDOUMBÉ EBOULÉ.

Canada: Nefas Silk Lafto Kifle Ketema 3, Kebele 4, House No. 122, POB 1130, Addis Ababa; tel. (11) 3713022; fax (11) 3713033; e-mail addis@international.gc.ca; internet www.canadainternational.gc .ca/ethiopia-ethiopie/index.aspx; Ambassador DAVID USHER.

Cabo Verde: Bole Rd, Higher 17, Kebele 19, House No. 107, POB 200093, Addis Ababa; tel. (11) 6610665; fax (11) 5516655; e-mail embcv@telecom.net.et; Chargé d'affaires a.i. CUSTODIA LIMA.

Chad: Bole Rd, Woreda 17, Kebele 20, House No. 2583, POB 5119, Addis Ababa; tel. (11) 6613819; fax (11) 6612050; e-mail amtchad@ethionet.et; Ambassador AHMAT AWAD SAKINE.

China, People's Republic: Jimma Rd, Woreda 24, Kebele 13, House No. 792, POB 5643, Addis Ababa; tel. (11) 3711960; fax (11) 3712457; e-mail chinaemb_et@mfa.gov.cn; internet et .china-embassy.org; Ambassador LA YIFAN.

Congo, Democratic Republic: Makanisa Rd, Woreda 23, Kebele 13, House No. 1779, POB 2723, Addis Ababa; tel. (11) 3710111; fax (11) 3713485; Ambassador GÉRARD MAPANGO KEMISHANGA.

Congo, Republic: Woreda 3, Kebele 51, House No. 378, POB 5639, Addis Ababa; tel. (11) 5514188; fax (11) 5514331; Ambassador PIERRE-JUSTE MOUNZIKA-NTSIKA.

Côte d'Ivoire: Woreda 23, Kebele 13, House No. 1308, POB 3668, Addis Ababa; tel. (11) 3711213; fax (11) 3712178; Ambassador EUGÈNE ALLOU-ALLOU.

Cuba: Woreda 17, Kebele 19, House No. 197, POB 5623, Addis Ababa; tel. (11) 620459; fax (11) 620460; e-mail embacuba@ethiopia .cubaminrex.cu; Ambassador JUAN MANUEL RODRÍGUEZ VÁZQUEZ.

Czech Republic: Kebele 15, House No. 289, POB 3108, Addis Ababa; tel. (11) 5516132; fax (11) 5513471; e-mail addisabeba@

embassy.mzv.cz; internet www.mzv.cz/addisababa; Ambassador KAREL HEJČ.

Denmark: Bole Kifle Ketema, Kebele 3, House No. 'New', POB 12955, Addis Ababa; tel. (11) 6174949; fax (11) 6187057; e-mail addamb@um.dk; internet www.etiopien.um.dk; Ambassador STEPHAN SCHÖNEMANN.

Djibouti: Bole Sub-City, Kebele 03, House No. 003, POB 1022, Addis Ababa; tel. (11) 6613200; fax (11) 6612786; Ambassador MOHAMMED IDRISS FARAH.

Egypt: Gullele Sub-City, Kebele 02, Madgascar St, POB 1611, Addis Ababa; tel. (11) 1226422; fax (11) 1226432; e-mail embassy .addisababa@mfa.gov.eg; Ambassador MOHAMED FATHI AHMED EDREES.

Equatorial Guinea: Bole Rd, Woreda 17, Kebele 23, House No. 162, POB 246, Addis Ababa; tel. (11) 6626278; Ambassador Dr RUBÉN MAYE NSUE MANGUE.

Finland: Mauritania St, Kebele 12, House No. 1431, POB 1017, Addis Ababa; tel. (11) 3205920; fax (11) 3205923; e-mail sanomat .add@formin.fi; internet www.finland.org.et; Ambassador SIRPA MAENPAA.

France: Kabana, POB 1464, Addis Ababa; tel. (11) 1236022; fax (11) 1236029; e-mail scacamb@ethionet.et; internet www.ambafrance-et .org; Ambassador BRIGITTE COLLET.

Gabon: Woreda 17, Kebele 18, House No. 1026, POB 1256, Addis Ababa; tel. (11) 6611075; fax (11) 6613700; Ambassador ANDRÉ WILLIAM ANGUILE.

The Gambia: Kebele 3, House No. 79, POB 60083, Addis Ababa; tel. (11) 6624647; fax (11) 6627895; e-mail gambiaembassy.addis@gmail .com; Ambassador MOMODOU SAJO JALLOW.

Georgia: Kirkos Sub city, House No. 717, Kebele 02/03, POB 21093/1000, Addis Ababa; tel. (11) 4671805; fax (11) 4671999; e-mail addisababa.emb@mfa.gov.ge; internet ethiopia.mfa.gov.ge; Ambassador VAKHTANG JAOSHVILI.

Germany: Yeka Kifle Ketema (Khebena), Woreda 03, POB 660, Addis Ababa; tel. (11) 1235139; fax (11) 1235152; e-mail info@addis-abeba.diplo.de; internet www.addis-abeba.diplo.de; Ambassador JOACHIM SCHMIDT.

Ghana: Jimma Rd, Woreda 24, Kebele 13, House No. 108, POB 3173, Addis Ababa; tel. (11) 3711402; fax (11) 3712511; e-mail ghmfa24@ethionet.et; Ambassador ALBERT EKOW YANKEY.

Greece: off Debre Zeit Rd, POB 1168, Addis Ababa; tel. (11) 4654911; fax (11) 4654883; internet www.telecom.net.et/~greekemb; Ambassador NIKOLAOS PROTONOTARIOS.

Guinea: Debre Zeit Rd, Woreda 18, Kebele 14, House No. 58, POB 1190, Addis Ababa; tel. 912200181 (mobile); internet guineaaddisembassy@gmail.com; Ambassador SIDIBÉ FATOUMATA KABA.

Holy See: Makanissa Rd, POB 588, Addis Ababa (Apostolic Nunciature); tel. (11) 3712100; fax (11) 3711499; e-mail na.ethiopia@diplomat.va; Apostolic Nuncio Most Rev. LUIGI BIANCO (Titular Archbishop of Falerone).

India: Arada District, Kebele 13/14, House No. 224, POB 528, Addis Ababa; tel. (11) 1235544; fax (11) 1235547; e-mail amb.addisababa@mea.gov.in; internet www.indembassyeth.in; Ambassador SANJAY VERMA.

Indonesia: Mekanisa Rd, Higher 23, Kebele 13, House No. 1816, POB 1004, Addis Ababa; tel. (11) 3712104; fax (11) 3710873; e-mail kbriadis@ethionet.et; internet www.indonesia-addis.org.et; Ambassador RAMLI SA'UD.

Iran: 317–318 Jimma Rd, POB 1144, Addis Ababa; tel. (11) 3710037; fax (11) 3712299; internet www.iranembassy-addis.net; Ambassador MOHAMMED ALI BAHRAINI.

Ireland: Kazanchis, Guinea Conakry St, POB 9585, Addis Ababa; tel. (11) 5180500; fax (11) 5523032; e-mail addisababaembassy@dfa .ie; internet www.embassyofireland.org.et; Ambassador AIDAN O'HARA.

Israel: Woreda 16, Kebele 22, House No. 283, POB 1266, Addis Ababa; tel. (11) 6460999; fax (11) 64619619; e-mail embassy@addisababa.mfa.gov.il; internet addisababa.mfa.gov.il; Ambassador BELAYNESH ZEVADIA.

Italy: Villa Italia, POB 1105, Addis Ababa; tel. (11) 1235717; fax (11) 1235689; e-mail ambasciata.addisabeba@esteri.it; internet www .ambaddisabeba.esteri.it; Ambassador RENZO MARIO ROSSO.

Japan: Woreda 18, Kebele 7, House No. 653, POB 5650, Addis Ababa; tel. (11) 5511088; fax (11) 5511350; e-mail japan-embassy@telecom.net.et; internet www.et.emb-japan.go.jp; Ambassador KAZUHIRO SUZUKI.

Kazakhstan: Addis Ababa; Ambassador YERLIK ALI.

Kenya: Woreda 16, Kebele 1, POB 3301, Addis Ababa; tel. (11) 610033; fax (11) 611433; internet kenyaembassyaddis.org; Ambassador MONICA KATHINA JUMA.

Korea, Democratic People's Republic: Woreda 20, Kebele 40, House No. 892, POB 2378, Addis Ababa; tel. (11) 6182828; Ambassador KIM HYOK CHOL.

Korea, Republic: Jimma Rd, Old Airport Area, POB 2047, Addis Ababa; tel. (11) 3728111; fax 3728115; e-mail skorea.emb@ethionet .et; internet eth.mofat.go.kr; Ambassador KIM MOON-HWAN.

Kuwait: Woreda 17, Kebele 20, House No. 128, POB 19898, Addis Ababa; tel. (11) 6615411; fax (11) 6612621; Ambassador RASHED FALEH AL-HAJERY.

Lesotho: Bole Sub-City, Kebele 03, House No. 2118, Addis Ababa; tel. (11) 6614368; fax (11) 6612837; internet lesothoaddis.org; Ambassador NYOLOSI MPHALE.

Liberia: Roosevelt St, Woreda 21, Kebele 4, House No. 237, POB 3116, Addis Ababa; tel. (11) 5513655; e-mail liberianembassyethiopia@yahoo.com; Ambassador VIVIENNE TITI WREH.

Libya: Ras Tessema Sefer, Woreda 3, Kebele 53, House No. 585, POB 5728, Addis Ababa; tel. (11) 5511077; fax (11) 5511383; e-mail libyanembassy@ethionet.et; Chargé d'affaires a.i. MOHAMED B. S. ENWIES.

Madagascar: Woreda 17, Kebele 19, House No. 629, POB 60004, Addis Ababa; tel. (11) 612555; fax (11) 610127; e-mail emb.mad@ ethionet.et; Ambassador LUDOVICH RICHARD SETILAHY.

Malawi: Bole Rd, Woreda 23, Kebele 13, House No. 1021, POB 2316, Addis Ababa; tel. (11) 3711280; fax (11) 3719742; e-mail malemb@ telecom.net.et; Ambassador CHIMANGO CHIRWA.

Mali: Kebele 03, House No. 418, POB 4561, Addis Ababa; tel. (11) 168990; fax (11) 162838; e-mail ambamaliaddis@yahoo.com; Ambassador BOUBACAR GOURO DIALL.

Mauritania: Lidete Kifle Ketema, Kebele 2, House No. 431A, POB 200015, Addis Ababa; tel. (11) 3729165; fax (11) 3729166; Ambassador HAMADY OULD MEIMOU.

Mauritius: Kebele 03, House No. 750, POB 200222, Kifle Ketema, Addis Ababa; tel. (11) 6615997; fax (11) 6614704; e-mail addisemb@ mail.gov.mu; internet www.addisababa.mail.gov.mu; Ambassador MAHENDR DOSIEAH.

Mexico: Shola Axion (Jacros Compound), Bole Sub-City, Kebele 14, House No. 050, POB 21021, Addis Ababa; tel. (11) 6479555; fax (11) 6479333; e-mail embetiopia@sre.gob.mx; internet embamex.sre.gob .mx/etiopia; Ambassador JUAN ALFREDO MIRANDA ORTIZ.

Morocco: 210 Bole Rd, POB 60033, Addis Ababa; tel. (11) 5508440; fax (11) 5511828; e-mail morocco.emb@ethionet.et; Ambassador ABDELJEBBAR BRAHIME.

Mozambique: Woreda 17, Kebele 23, House No. 2116, POB 5671, Addis Ababa; tel. (11) 3729199; fax (11) 3729197; Ambassador MANUEL JOSÉ GONÇALVES.

Namibia: Bole Sub-City, Kebele 19, House No. 575, POB 1443, Addis Ababa; tel. (11) 6611966; fax (11) 6612677; e-mail nam.emb@ethionet .et; Ambassador KAKENA S. K. NANGULA.

Netherlands: Old Airport Zone, Kifle Ketema, Lideta, Kebele 02/03, POB 1241, Addis Ababa; tel. (11) 3711100; fax (11) 3711577; e-mail add@minbuza.nl; internet ethiopia.nlembassy.org; Ambassador ALIDA PETRONELLA REMMELZWAAL.

Niger: Woreda 9, Kebele 23, POB 5791, Addis Ababa; tel. (11) 4651305; fax (11) 4651296; e-mail ambnigeraddis@yahoo.fr; Ambassador DIALLO AMINA DJIBO.

Nigeria: Gulele KK, Kebele 06, House No. 001, POB 1019, Addis Ababa; tel. (11) 1550644; fax (11) 1552307; e-mail addis_nigeria@ yahoo.com; Ambassador BULUS ZOM LOLO.

Norway: POB 8383, Addis Ababa; tel. (11) 3710799; fax (11) 3711255; e-mail emb.addisabeba@mfa.no; internet www.norway .org.et; Ambassador ODD INGE KVALHEIM.

Pakistan: Bole Kifle Ketema, Kebele 03, House No. 2038, POB 19795, Addis Ababa; tel. (11) 6188392; fax (11) 6188394; e-mail parepadisababa@mofa.gov.pk; internet www.mofa.gov.pk/ethiopia; Ambassador IMRAN YAWAR.

Poland: House No. 583, Dej Belay Zeleke Rd, Guelele Sub-City, Kebele 08, POB 27207/1000, Addis Ababa; tel. (11) 1574189; fax (11) 1574222; e-mail addisabeba.amb.sekretariat@msz.gov.pl; internet www.addisababa.msz.gov.pl; Ambassador JACEK JANKOWSKI.

Portugal: Sheraton Addis, Taitu St, POB 6002, Addis Ababa; tel. (11) 171717; fax (11) 173403; e-mail embportadis@hotmail.com; Ambassador Dr ANTÓNIO LUÍS PEIXOTO COTRIM.

Qatar: Mekanissa St, House No. 0646, Addis Ababa; tel. (11) 8966244; fax (11) 3722623; e-mail addisababa@mofa.gov.qa; Ambassador ABDULAZIZ SULTAN JASSIM AL-RUMEIHI.

Romania: Houses No. 9–10, Bole Kifle Ketema, Kebele 03, POB 2478, Addis Ababa; tel. (11) 6610156; fax (11) 6611191; e-mail roembaddis@ethionet.et; Ambassador GABRIEL CONSTANTINE.

Russian Federation: POB 1500, Addis Ababa; tel. (11) 6612060; fax (11) 6613795; e-mail ethiopia@mid.ru; internet www.ethiopia.mid .ru; Ambassador VSEVOLOD TKACHENKO.

Rwanda: POB 5618, Addis Ababa; tel. (11) 6610300; fax (11) 6610411; e-mail ambaddis@minaffet.gov.rw; internet www .ethiopia.embassy.gov.rw; High Commissioner JOSEPH NSENGIMANA.

Saudi Arabia: Kirkos Sub-City, Kebele 4, House No. 179B, POB 1104, Addis Ababa; tel. (11) 4425643; fax (11) 4425646; e-mail etemb@mofa.gov.sa; internet embassies.mofa.gov.sa/sites/ethiopia; Ambassador ABDULBAQI BIN AHMAD AJLAN.

Senegal: Africa Ave, POB 2581, Addis Ababa; tel. (11) 6611376; fax (11) 6610020; e-mail ambassene-addis@ethionet.et; Ambassador MOMAR GUÈYE.

Serbia: Woreda 15, Kebele 26, House No. 923, POB 1341, Addis Ababa; tel. (11) 5517804; fax (11) 5514192; e-mail serbembaddis@ ethionet.et; internet www.addisababa.mfa.gov.rs; Ambassador DRAGAN MRAOVIĆ.

Sierra Leone: Kefle Ketema-Nefas Silk Lafto, Woreda 04, House No. 591, POB 5619, Addis Ababa; tel. (11) 3710033; fax (11) 3711911; e-mail salonembadd@yahoo.co.uk; Ambassador OSMAN KAMARA.

Slovakia: Kebele 2, Woreda 7, Yeka Sub-City, POB 6627, Addis Ababa; tel. (11) 6450849; fax (11) 6474656; e-mail slovakiaembassy@ ethionet.et; internet www.mzv.sk/addisabeba; Ambassador JOZEF CIBULA.

Somalia: Bole Kifle Ketema, Kebele 20, House No. 588, POB 1643, Addis Ababa; tel. (11) 6180673; fax (11) 6180680; internet www .ethiopia.somaligov.net; Ambassador AHMED ABDISALAM ADAN.

South Africa: Alexander Pushkin St, Higher 23, Kebele 10, House No. 1885, Old Airport Area, POB 1091, Addis Ababa; tel. (11) 3713034; fax (11) 3711330; e-mail sa.embassy.addis@telecom.net .et; Ambassador NDUMISO NDIMA NTSHINGA.

South Sudan: Bole Olympia, POB 3140/1250, Addis Ababa; tel. (11) 5522636; e-mail embassysouthsudan@yahoo.com; Ambassador ARAP DENG KUOL.

Spain: Botswana St, POB 2312, Addis Ababa; tel. (11) 1222544; fax (11) 1222542; e-mail emb.addisabeba@maec.es; Ambassador MIGUEL ÁNGEL FERNÁNDEZ-PALACIOS MARTÍNEZ.

Sudan: Kirkos, Kebele, POB 1110, Addis Ababa; tel. (11) 5516477; fax (11) 5519989; e-mail sudan.embassy@telecom.net.et; Ambassador Gen. ABDELRAHMAN SIRELKHATIM.

Swaziland: Bole Kifle Ketema, Kebele 13, House No. 1185, POB 416, Addis Ababa; tel. (11) 6263703; fax (11) 6262152; e-mail swaziaddis@ ethionet.et; Ambassador PROMISE MSIBI.

Sweden: Lideta KK, Kebele 07/14, House No. 891, POB 1142, Addis Ababa; tel. (11) 5180000; fax (11) 5180030; e-mail ambassaden .addis-abeba@foreign.ministry.se; internet www.swedenabroad.se/ addisabeba; Ambassador JAN SADEK.

Switzerland: Jimma Rd, Old Airport Area, POB 1106, Addis Ababa; tel. (11) 3711107; fax (11) 3712177; e-mail add.vertretung@eda .admin.ch; Ambassador ANDREA SEMADENI.

Tanzania: POB 1077, Addis Ababa; tel. (11) 5511063; fax (11) 5517358; e-mail tz@ethionet.et; Ambassador Prof. JORAM MUKAMA BISWARO.

Togo: Nifas Silk Lafto KK, Kebele 13, House No. 2234, POB 25523, Addis Ababa; tel. (11) 3206515; fax (11) 3729722; e-mail togo.emb@ ethionet.et; Ambassador EKPAO NOLAKI.

Tunisia: Wereda 17, Kebele 19, Bole Rd, POB 100069, Addis Ababa; tel. (11) 6612063; fax (11) 6614568; Ambassador SAHBI KHALFALLAH.

Turkey: POB 1506, Addis Ababa; tel. (11) 6612321; fax (11) 6611688; e-mail turk.emb@ethionet.et; Ambassador OSMAN YAVUZALP.

Uganda: Kirkos Kifle Ketema, Kebele 35, House No. 31, POB 5644, Addis Ababa; tel. (11) 5513088; fax (11) 5514355; e-mail uganda .emb@ethionet.et; Ambassador MULL KATENDE.

Ukraine: Woreda 17, Kebele 3, House No. 2116, Bole Area, POB 2358, Addis Ababa; tel. (11) 6611698; fax (11) 6621288; e-mail emb_et@mfa.gov.ua; Chargé d'affaires MYKHAILO KIRICHENKO.

United Arab Emirates: Nifas Silk Lafto, Kebele 13, House No. 1826, POB 22055, Addis Ababa; tel. (11) 3203680; fax (11) 3203684; e-mail addis.ababa@mofa.gov.ae; Ambassador Dr YOUSEF EISA HASSAN AL-SABRI.

United Kingdom: POB 858, Addis Ababa; tel. (11) 6612354; fax (11) 6610588; e-mail britishembassy.addisababa@fco.gov.uk; internet www.ukinethiopia.gov.uk; Ambassador GREGORY DOREY.

USA: Entoto St, POB 1014, Addis Ababa; tel. (11) 5174000; fax (11) 5174001; e-mail pasaddis@state.gov; internet addisababa .usembassy.gov; Ambassador PATRICIA MARIE HASLACH.

Venezuela: Bole Kifle Ketema, Kebele 21, House No. 314–16, POB 1909, Addis Ababa; tel. (11) 6460601; fax (11) 5154162; Ambassador LUIS MARIANO JOUBERTT MATA.

Yemen: Old Airport Rd, Kebele 12, POB 664, Addis Ababa; tel. (11) 3712204; fax (11) 3711724; e-mail yemaa@ethionet.et; Ambassador DIRHIM ABDO NOMAN.

Zambia: Nifas Silk Kifle Ketema, Kebele 04, POB 1909, Addis Ababa; tel. (11) 3711302; fax (11) 3711566; e-mail zam.emb@ethionet.et; Ambassador SUSAN SIKANETA.

Zimbabwe: POB 5624, Addis Ababa; tel. (11) 6613877; fax (11) 6613476; e-mail zimbabwe.embassy@telecom.net.et; Ambassador Dr ALBERT RANGANAI CHIMBINDI.

Judicial System

The 1994 Constitution stipulates the establishment of an independent judiciary in Ethiopia. Judicial powers are vested in the courts, both at federal and regional state level. The supreme federal judicial authority is the Federal Supreme Court. This court has the highest and final power of jurisdiction over federal matters. The regional states of the Federal Democratic Republic of Ethiopia can establish Supreme, High and First-Instance Courts. The Supreme Courts of the regional states have the highest and the final power of jurisdiction over state matters. They also exercise the jurisdiction of the Federal High Court. According to the Constitution, courts of any level are free from any interference or influence from government bodies, government officials or any other source. In addition, judges exercise their duties independently and are directed solely by the law.

Federal Supreme Court: POB 6166, Addis Ababa; tel. (11) 1553400; fax (11) 1550278; e-mail webadmin@federalsupremecourt.gov.et; f. 1995; comprises civil, criminal and military sections; its jurisdiction extends to the supervision of all judicial proceedings throughout the country; the Supreme Court is also empowered to review cases upon which final rulings have been made by the courts (including the Supreme Court) where judicial errors have occurred; Pres. TEGNE GETANEH.

Federal High Court: POB 3483, Addis Ababa; tel. (11) 2751911; fax (11) 2755399; e-mail fedhc@telecom.net.et; hears appeals from the state courts; has original jurisdiction; Pres. WUBESHET SHIFERAW.

Awraja Courts: regional courts composed of three judges, criminal and civil.

Warada Courts: subregional; one judge sits alone with very limited jurisdiction, criminal only.

Religion

About 45% of the population are Muslims and about 40% belong to the Ethiopian Orthodox (Tewahido) Church. There are also significant Evangelical Protestant and Roman Catholic communities. The Pentecostal Church and the Society of International Missionaries carry out mission work in Ethiopia. There are also Hindu and Sikh religious institutions. It has been estimated that 5%–15% of the population follow animist rites and beliefs.

CHRISTIANITY

Ethiopian Orthodox (Tewahido) Church

The Ethiopian Orthodox (Tewahido) Church is one of the five oriental orthodox churches. It was founded in AD 328, and in 1989 had more than 22m. members, 20,000 parishes and 290,000 clergy. The Supreme Body is the Holy Synod and the National Council, under the chairmanship of the Patriarch (Abune). The Church comprises 25 archdioceses and dioceses (including those in Jerusalem, Sudan, Djibouti and the Western Hemisphere). There are 32 Archbishops and Bishops. The Church administers 1,139 schools and 12 relief and rehabilitation centres throughout Ethiopia.

Patriarchate Head Office: POB 1283, Addis Ababa; tel. (11) 1116507; internet webmaster@ethiopianorthodox.org; internet www.ethiopianorthodox.org; Patriarch (Abune) Archbishop MATIAS; Gen. Sec. L. M. DEMTSE GEBRE MEDHIN.

The Roman Catholic Church

At 31 December 2006 there were in Ethiopia an estimated 68,138 adherents of the Alexandrian-Ethiopian Rite and 513,286 adherents of the Latin Rite.

Bishops' Conference: Ethiopian and Eritrean Episcopal Conference, POB 2454, Addis Ababa; tel. (11) 1550300; fax (11) 1553113; e-mail ecs@ethionet.et; internet www.ecs.org.et; f. 1966; Pres. Most Rev. BERHANEYESUS DEMEREW SOURAPHIEL (Metropolitan Archbishop of Addis Ababa).

Alexandrian-Ethiopian Rite

Adherents are served by one archdiocese (Addis Ababa) and two dioceses (Adigrat and Emdeber).

Archbishop of Addis Ababa: Cardinal BERHANEYESUS DEMEREW SOURAPHIEL, Catholic Archbishop's House, POB 21903, Addis Ababa; tel. (11) 1111667; fax (11) 1551348; e-mail ecs@telecom.net.et.

Latin Rite

Adherents are served by the eight Apostolic Vicariates of Awasa, Gambela, Harar, Hosanna, Jimma-Bonga, Meki, Nekemte and Soddo.

Other Christian Churches

The Anglican Communion: Within the Episcopal Church in Jerusalem and the Middle East, the Bishop in Egypt has jurisdiction over seven African countries, including Ethiopia.

Armenian Orthodox Church: St George's Armenian Church, POB 116, Addis Ababa; f. 1923; Deacon VARTKES NALBANDIAN.

Ethiopian Evangelical Church (Mekane Yesus): POB 2087, Jomo Kenyatta Rd, Addis Ababa; tel. (11) 5533293; fax (11) 5534148; e-mail eecmyco@eecmy.org; internet www.eecmy.org; Pres. Rev. Dr WAKSEYOUM IDOSA; f. 1959; affiliated to Lutheran World Fed., All Africa Confed. of Churches and World Council of Churches; c. 5.57m. mems (2010).

Greek Orthodox Church: POB 571, Addis Ababa; tel. and fax (11) 1226459; Metropolitan of Axum Most Rev. PETROS YIAKOUMELOS.

Seventh-day Adventist Church: POB 145, Addis Ababa; tel. (11) 5511319; e-mail info@ecd.adventist.org; internet www.ecd.adventist.org; f. 1907; Pres. ALEMU HAILE; 130,000 mems.

ISLAM

Leader: Haji MOHAMMED AHMAD.

JUDAISM

A phased emigration to Israel of about 27,000 Falashas (Ethiopian Jews) took place during 1984–91. In February 2003 the Israeli Government ruled that the Falashmura (Ethiopian Christians whose forefathers had converted from Judaism) had been forced to convert to Christianity to avoid religious persecution and that they had the right to settle in Israel. In January 2004 Ethiopia and Israel agreed to allow the Falashmura to be flown to Israel; some 17,000 Falashmura and a further 3,000 Falashas had arrived in Israel by May 2008. However, a further 8,700 Falashmura remained in a transit camp in Gondar and the Israeli Government halted the transfer process in June. Israel resumed the transportation of Falashmura in January 2010, and in November the Israeli Government announced that the remaining Falashmura in Ethiopia—some 8,000 people—would be granted the right to emigrate to Israel. The final group (comprising some 450 Falashmura) was repatriated in August 2013, thereby concluding the programme.

The Press

DAILIES

Addis Zemen: POB 30145, Addis Ababa; internet www.ethpress.gov.et/addiszemen; f. 1941; Amharic; circ. 40,000.

The Daily Monitor: POB 22588, Addis Ababa; tel. (11) 1560788; e-mail themonitor@telecom.net.et; f. 1993; English; Editor-in-Chief NAMRUD BERHANE TSAHAY; circ. 6,000.

Ethiopian Herald: POB 30701, Addis Ababa; tel. (11) 6625466; fax (11) 6612261; e-mail info@ethpress.gov.et; internet www.ethpress.gov.et/herald; f. 1943; English; Editor-in-Chief TSEGIE GEBRE-AMLAK; circ. 37,000.

PERIODICALS

Abyotawit Ethiopia: POB 2549, Addis Ababa; fortnightly; Amharic.

Addis Fortune: Tegene Bldg, 7th Floor, House No. 542, Ginbot Haya Ave, Kebele 03, POB 259, Addis Ababa; tel. (11) 4163020; fax (11) 4163039; internet www.addisfortune.com; weekly; English; Man. Editor TAMRAT G. GIORGIS.

Addis Tribune: Tambek International, POB 2395, Addis Ababa; tel. (11) 6615228; fax (11) 6615227; e-mail tambek@telecom.net.et; internet www.addistribune.com; f. 1992; weekly; English; Editor-in-Chief YOHANNES RUPHAEL; circ. 6,000.

Al-Alem: POB 30232, Addis Ababa; tel. (11) 6625936; fax (11) 6625777; f. 1941; publ. by the Ethiopian Press Agency; weekly; Arabic; Editor-in-Chief EYOB GIDEY; circ. 2,500.

Birritu: National Bank of Ethiopia, POB 5550, Addis Ababa; tel. (11) 5530040; fax (11) 5514588; e-mail mulget17@yahoo.com; internet www.nbe.gov.et; f. 1982; quarterly; Amharic and English; banking, insurance and macroeconomic news; owned by National Bank of

Ethiopia; circ. 2,500; Editor-in-Chief DEREJE ASEGEDEW; Dep. Editors-in-Chief MULUGETA AYALEW, BEKALU AYALEW.

Capital: POB 95, Addis Ababa; tel. (11) 5531759; fax (11) 5533323; e-mail syscom@telecom.net.et; internet www.capitalethiopia.com; f. 1998; weekly; Sunday; business and economics; Editor-in-Chief BEHAILU DESALEGN.

Ethiopian Reporter: Woreda 19, Kebele 56, House No. 221, POB 7023, Addis Ababa; tel. and fax (11) 4421517; e-mail mcc@telecom .net.et; internet www.ethiopianreporter.com; weekly; English and Amharic; Editor-in-Chief ASRAT SEYOUM.

Maebel: Addis Ababa; weekly; Amharic; Editor-in-Chief ABERA WOGI.

Menelik: Editor-in-Chief ZELALEM GEBRE.

Negarit Gazeta: POB 1031, Addis Ababa; irreg.; Amharic and English; official gazette.

Nigdina Limat: POB 2458, Addis Ababa; tel. (11) 5513882; fax (11) 5511479; e-mail aachamber1@telecom.net.et; monthly; Amharic; publ. by the Addis Ababa (Ethiopia) Chamber of Commerce; circ. 6,000.

Press Digest: POB 12719, Addis Ababa; tel. (11) 5504200; fax (11) 5513523; e-mail phoenix.universal@telecom.net.et; f. 1993; weekly.

Satenaw: e-mail admin@satenaw.com; internet satenaw.com; Chief Editor HENOK ALEMAYEHU; Man. Editor ALYOU TEBEJE.

Tobia Magazine: POB 22373, Addis Ababa; tel. (11) 1556177; fax (11) 1552654; monthly; Amharic; Man. GOSHU MOGES; circ. 30,000.

Tobia Newspaper: POB 22373, Addis Ababa; tel. (11) 1556177; fax (11) 1552654; e-mail akpac@telecom.net.et; weekly; Amharic; Man. GOSHU MOGES; circ. 25,000.

Tomar: Benishangul; weekly; Amharic; Editor-in-Chief BEFEKADU MOREDA.

Yezareitu Ethiopia (Ethiopia Today): POB 30232, Addis Ababa; weekly; Amharic and English; Editor-in-Chief IMIRU WORKU; circ. 30,000.

NEWS AGENCY

Ethiopian News Agency (ENA): Patriot St, POB 530, Addis Ababa; tel. (11) 1550011; fax (11) 1551609; e-mail feedback@ena .gov.et; internet www.ena.gov.et; f. 1942; Chair. NETSANET ASFAW.

PRESS ASSOCIATIONS

Ethiopian Free Press Journalists' Association (EFJA): POB 31317, Addis Ababa; tel. and fax (11) 1555021; e-mail efja@telecom .net.et; f. 1993; granted legal recognition in 2000; activities suspended in late 2003; Pres. KIFLE MULAT.

Ethiopian Journalists' Association: POB 30288, Addis Ababa; tel. (11) 1117852; fax (11) 5513365; Pres. KEFALE MAMMO.

Ethiopian National Journalists Union: Addis Ababa; e-mail info@enju.org; internet www.enju.org; f. 2003; Pres. ANTENEH ABRAHAM; Vice-Pres. ESHETU GELETU.

Publishers

Addis Ababa University Press: POB 1176, Addis Ababa; tel. (11) 1119148; fax (11) 1550655; f. 1968; educational and reference works in English, general books in English and Amharic; Editor MESSELECH HABTE.

Berhanena Selam Printing Enterprise: POB 980, Addis Ababa; tel. (11) 1553233; fax (11) 1553939; f. 1921; fmrly Govt Printing Press; publishes and prints newspapers, periodicals, books, security prints and other miscellaneous commercial prints; Gen. Man. MULUWORK G. HIWOT.

Educational Materials Production and Distribution Enterprise (EMPDE): POB 5549, Addis Ababa; tel. (11) 6463555; fax (11) 6461295; f. 1999; textbook publishers.

Ethiopia Book Centre: POB 1024, Addis Ababa; tel. (11) 1123336; f. 1977; privately owned; publr, importer, wholesaler and retailer of educational books.

Mega Publishing: POB 423, Addis Ababa; tel. (11) 1571714; fax (11) 1571715; general publishers.

Broadcasting and Communications

TELECOMMUNICATIONS

Ethiopian Telecommunication Agency (ETA): Bekelobet, Tegene Bldg, Kirkos District, Kebele 02/03, House No. 542, POB 9991, Addis Ababa; tel. (11) 4668282; fax (11) 4655763; e-mail tele .agency@ethionet.et; internet www.eta.gov.et; aims to promote the

devt of high quality, efficient, reliable and affordable telecommunication services in Ethiopia.

Ethio Telecom (ETC): POB 1047, Addis Ababa; tel. (11) 6632597; fax (11) 6632674; e-mail etcweb@ethionet.et; internet www.ethionet .et; f. 1894; under the management of France Telecom since December 2010; Chair. DEBRE TSION GEBRE MICHAEL; CEO ANDUALEM ADMASSIE.

BROADCASTING
Radio

Afro FM: Addis Ababa; tel. (11) 1552200; e-mail hasiet@afro105fm .com; internet www.afro105fm.com; f. 2009; broadcasts in English and other foreign languages.

Radio Ethiopia: POB 654, Addis Ababa; tel. (11) 1551011; internet www.angelfire.com/biz/radioethiopia; f. 1941; Amharic, English, French, Arabic, Afar, Oromifa, Tigre, Tigrinya and Somali; Gen. Man. KASA MILOKO.

Radio Fana: POB 30702, Addis Ababa; internet www.radiofana .com; f. 1994; Amharic; operated by the EPRDF; Gen. Man. WOLDU YEMESSEL.

Radio Voice of One Free Ethiopia: broadcasts twice a week; Amharic; opposes current Govts of Ethiopia and Eritrea.

Voice of the Revolution of Tigrai: POB 450, Mekele; tel. (34) 4410545; fax (34) 4405485; e-mail vort@telecom.net.et; f. 1985; Tigrinya and Afargna; broadcasts 57 hours per week; supports Tigrai People's Liberation Front.

There are also 16 community radio stations in Ethiopia.

Television

Ethiopian Radio and Television Agency (ERTA): POB 5544, Addis Ababa; tel. (11) 5155326; fax (11) 5512685; e-mail gd1@erat .gov.et; internet www.erta.gov.et; f. 1964; semi-autonomous station; accepts commercial advertising; programmes transmitted from Addis Ababa to 26 regional stations; Chair. BEREKET SIMON; Dir-Gen. ZERAY ASSGEDOM.

Regulatory Authority

Ethiopia Broadcasting Authority (EBA): Haile-Alem Bldg, nr Urael Church, Haile Gebreslase Rd, Kazanchiz, POB 43142, Addis Ababa; tel. (11) 5538759; fax (11) 5536750; internet www.eba.gov.et; Dir-Gen. DESTA TESFAW.

Finance

(cap. = capital; res = reserves; dep. = deposits; m. = million; br(s). = branch(es); amounts in birr)

BANKING
Central Bank

In early 2013 there were 19 banks and 19 microfinance institutions in Ethiopia.

National Bank of Ethiopia: Sudan Ave, POB 5550, Addis Ababa; tel. (11) 5517438; fax (11) 5514588; e-mail nbe.gov@ethionet.et; internet www.nbe.gov.et; f. 1964; bank of issue; cap. 500.0m., res 1,814.8m., dep. 35,781.3m. (June 2009); Chair. NEWAYE-KIRSTOS GEBREAB; Gov. TEKLEWOLD ATNAFU; 1 br.

Other Banks

Abay Bank SC: Jomo Kenyatta St, City-Kirkos Kebele-17/18, POB 5887, Addis Ababa; tel. (11) 5158782; fax (11) 5528882; internet www .abaybank.com.et; f. 2010; cap. 288.5m., res 21.4m., dep. 1,475.9m. (June 2013); Chair. TADESSE KASSA KETEMA.

Addis International Bank SC (AdIB): Zequla Complex, Haile G/ Selliassie St, POB 2455, Addis Ababa; tel. (11) 5549800; fax (11) 5540530; e-mail info@addisbanksc.com; internet www.addisbanksc .com; f. 2011; cap. 147.1m., res 9.8m., dep. 211.4m. (June 2013); Chair. HAILE MELEKOT TEKLE GIORGIS; Pres. HAILU ALEMU; 5 brs.

Awash International Bank SC: Africa Ave, Bole Rd, POB 12638, Addis Ababa; tel. (11) 6614482; fax (11) 6639159; e-mail info@ awashbank.com; internet www.awash-international-bank.com; f. 1994; cap. 540.0m., res 750.0m., dep. 5,700m. (Dec. 2009); Chair. GURMU GURMU; Pres. TSEHAY SHIFERAW; 64 brs.

Bank of Abyssinia SC: Red Cross Bldg, Ras Desta Damtew Ave, POB 12947, Addis Ababa; tel. (11) 5514130; fax (11) 5510409; e-mail info@bankofabyssinia.com; internet www.bankofabyssinia.com; f. 1905; closed 1935 and reopened 1996; commercial banking services; cap. 577.0m., res 332.4m., dep. 8,656.8m., total assets 10,160.1m. (June 2013); Chair. MAHARI ALEMAYEHU; Pres. ADDISU HABBA; 61 brs.

Bunna International Bank SC: Kebele 17 Daber, Bldg, Arada Kifle Ketema, Addis Ababa; tel. (11) 1580825; fax (11) 1580832;

internet www.bunnabanksc.com; f. 2009; cap. 307.6m., res 27.7m., dep. 1,626.0m. (June 2013); Chair. MARSHAL FIKREMARKOS; Pres. ESHETU FANTAYE; 21 brs.

Commercial Bank of Ethiopia: Gambia St, POB 255, Addis Ababa; tel. (11) 5511271; fax (11) 5514522; e-mail cbe_cc@ combanketh.com; internet www.combanketh.com; f. 1943; reorg. 1996; state-owned; cap. 8,082.4m., res 1,023.0m., dep. 159,496.6m. (June 2013); Chair. BEREKET SEMON; Pres. BEKALU ZELEKE; 331 brs.

Construction and Business Bank: Higher 21, Kebele 04, POB 3480, Addis Ababa; tel. (11) 5512300; fax (11) 5515103; e-mail cbbsics@ethionet.et; internet www.cbb.com.et; f. 1975 as Housing and Savings Bank; provides credit for construction projects and a range of commercial banking services; state-owned; cap. 79.0, res 100.7m., dep. 3,517.0m. (June 2012); Chair. SHIFERAW SHIGUTE; Pres. HAILEYESUS BEKELE; 20 brs.

Dashen Bank: Beklobet, Garad Bldg, Debre Zeit Rd, POB 12752, Addis Ababa; tel. (11) 4671803; fax (11) 4653037; e-mail dashen .bank@ethionet.et; internet www.dashenbanksc.com; f. 1995; cap. 737.2m., res 767.5m., dep. 16,616.6m. (June 2013); Pres. BERHANU W. SELASSIE; Chair. TEKLU HAILE; 140 brs.

Debub Global Bank SC: Mujib Tower, Woreda 04, Kirkos Sub-City, POB 100743, Addis Ababa; tel. (11) 5581258; e-mail info@ debubglobalbank.com; internet www.debubglobalbank.com; f. 2012; Pres. ADDISU HABBA; 20 brs.

Development Bank of Ethiopia: Zosip Broz Tito St, POB 1900, Addis Ababa; tel. (11) 5511188; fax (11) 5511606; e-mail dbe@ ethionet.et; internet www.dbe.com.et; f. 1909; provides devt finance for industry and agriculture, technical advice and assistance in project evaluation; state-owned; cap. and res 418.8m., total assets 3,163.2m. (June 2002); Chair. MELAKU FANTA; Pres. ESAYAS BAHRE; 32 brs.

Lion International Bank SC (LIB): Lex Plaza Bldg, Haile G/ Selassie Ave, Addis Ababa; tel. (11) 6626000; fax (11) 6625999; e-mail lionbank@ethionet.et; internet www.anbesabank.com; f. 2006; cap. 374.9m., res 67.5m., dep. 2,170.0m. (June 2013); Chair. BERHANU G. MEDHIN; Pres. NEGUSU GEBREGZIABHER; 24 brs.

Enat Bank: Kirkos Sub-city, Woreda 8, POB 18401, Addis Ababa; tel. (11) 5504948; fax (11) 5151338; e-mail info@enatbanksc.com; internet www.enatbanksc.com; f. 2012; Chair. MEAZA ASHENAFI; Pres. FASIKA KEBEDE TEMESELEW.

NIB International Bank SC: Africa Avenue, Dembel City Centre, 6th Floor, POB 2439, Addis Ababa; tel. (11) 5503304; fax (11) 5527213; e-mail nibbank@ethionet.et; internet www.nibbank-et .com; f. 1999; cap. 999.3m., res 386.0m., dep. 7,008.5m. (June 2013); Chair. TAFESSE BOGALE; Pres. KIBRU FONDJA; 45 brs.

Oromia International Bank SC: POB 27530, Addis Ababa; tel. (11) 5572113; fax (11) 5572110; e-mail oib@orointbank.com; internet www.orointbank.com; f. 2008; cap. 374.5m., res 29.8m., dep. 2,117.2m. (June 2012); Chair. ABERA TOLA; Pres. ABIE SANO; 30 brs.

United Bank SC: Beklobet, Mekwor Plaza Bldg, Debe Zeit Rd, Kirkos District, Kebele 06, POB 19963, Addis Ababa; tel. (11) 4655222; fax (11) 4655243; e-mail hibretbank@ethionet.et; internet www.unitedbank.com.et; f. 1998; commercial banking services; cap. 600.0m., res 351.1m., dep. 8,327.2m. (June 2013); Chair. GETACHEW AYELE; Pres. BERHANU GETANEH; 72brs.

Wegagen Bank: Dembel Bldg, 6th–7th Floor, Africa Ave, POB 1018, Addis Ababa; tel. (11) 5523800; fax (11) 5523521; e-mail wegagen@ ethionet.et; internet www.wegagenbanksc.com; f. 1997; commercial banking services; cap. 1,090.8m., res 484.4m., dep. 7,909.0m. (June 2013); Chair. SEBHAT NEGGA; Pres. and CEO ARAYA GEBRE EGIZHABER; 49 brs.

Zemen Bank: Josef Tito St, POB 1212, Addis Ababa; tel. (11) 5501111; fax (11) 5539042; e-mail customerservice@zemenbank .com; internet www.zemenbank.com; f. 2008; cap. 343.8m., res 79.4m., dep. 2,504.9m. (June 2013); Chair. Dr BERHANE GHEBRAY; Pres. and CEO TSEGAY TETEMKE.

Bankers' Association

Ethiopian Bankers' Association: POB 23850, Addis Ababa; tel. and fax (11) 5533874; e-mail ethbankers@ethionet.et; internet ethiopianbankers.com; f. 2001; Pres. ADDISU HABBA; Sec.-Gen. DEREJE DEGEFU.

INSURANCE

In 2013 there were 16 insurance companies operating in Ethiopia.

Africa Insurance Co: Bole Sub-City, Worda 02, House 3170, POB 12941, Addis Ababa; tel. (11) 6637716; fax (11) 6638253; e-mail africains@ethionet.et; internet www.africainsurancesc.com; f. 1994; Man. Dir and CEO KIROS JIRANIE.

Awash Insurance Co: Awash Tower, Sengatera, Ras Abebe Aregay St, POB 12637, Addis Ababa; tel. (11) 5570001; fax (11) 5570208;

e-mail aic@ethionet.et; internet www.awashinsurance.com; f. 1994; cap. 111m.; Chair. KANAA DABA; Gen. Man. TSEGAYE KEMSI; 34 brs.

Berhan Insurance SC: Yeshitam Bldg, POB 9266, Addis Ababa; tel. (11) 4674431; fax (11) 4668701; internet berhaninsurance.com; f. 2010; general insurance; Chair. MAAZA KITAW; Man. Dir ADDISU DEMISSIE.

Ethiopian Insurance Corpn: POB 2545, Addis Ababa; tel. (11) 5512400; fax (11) 5517499; e-mail eic.md@ethionet.et; internet www .eic.com.et; f. 1976; life, property and legal liabilities insurance cover; Man. Dir YEWONDWOSEN ETEFA.

Global Insurance Co SC: Gobena Aba Tigu St, Somale Tera, POB 180112, Addis Ababa; tel. (11) 1567400; fax (11) 1566200; e-mail globalinsu@ethionet.et; internet www.globalinsurancesc.com; f. 1997; cap. 64.1m. (paid); Chair. AHMED A. SHERIEF; CEO YAHYA MOHAMMED AFFAN; 12 brs; 100 employees.

National Insurance Co of Ethiopia: ZEFCO Bldg, Debre Zeit Rd, Kirkos Sub-City, K05/06/07, House No. 894, POB 12645, Addis Ababa; tel. (11) 4661129; fax (11) 4650660; e-mail info@ niceinsurance-et.com; internet www.niceinsurance-et.com; Chair. ALEMAYEHU HAILE; Man. Dir and CEO HABTEMATIAM SHUMGIZAW.

Nile Insurance Co: POB 12836, Addis Ababa; tel. (11) 5537709; fax (11) 5514592; e-mail nileinsu@mail.telecom.net.et; f. 1995; Gen. Man. DAWIT G. AMANUEL.

Nyala Insurance SC: Mickey Leland St, POB 12753, Addis Ababa; tel. (11) 6626667; fax (11) 6626706; internet www.nyalainsurance .com; Chair. MARDOUF S. BAZAHAM; CEO YARED MOLA.

Oromia Insurance Co SC (OIC): Biftu Bldg, 6th Floor, Ras Desta St, POB 10090, Addis Ababa; tel. (11) 8962093; fax (11) 5572122; e-mail oromiainsurance@ethionet.et; internet www .oromiainsurancecompany.com.et; f. 2009; Chair. ELIAS GENETI; CEO TESFAYE DESTA.

United Insurance Co SC: Alpaulo Bldg, Debrezeit Rd, Kirkos Sub-City, Woreda 06, POB 1156, Addis Ababa; tel. (11) 5515656; fax (11) 5513258; e-mail united.insurance@telecom.net.et; internet www .unitedinsurancesc.com; Chair. ZAFU EYESUS; Man. Dir MESERET BEZABEH.

Trade and Industry

GOVERNMENT AGENCIES

Ethiopian Investment Agency: POB 2313, Addis Ababa; tel. (11) 5510033; fax (11) 5514396; e-mail ethiopian.invest@ethionet.et; internet www.ethioinvest.org; f. 1992; Dir-Gen. FITSUM AREGA.

Ethiopian Revenues and Customs Authority: Addis Ababa; tel. (11) 6629857; fax (11) 6629859; internet www.erca.gov.et; f. 2008; established through merger of the Ministry of Revenues, the Ethiopian Customs Authority and the Federal Inland Revenues; Dir-Gen. BEKER SHALE.

Privatization and Public Enterprises Supervising Agency: POB 11835, Addis Ababa; tel. (11) 5530343; fax (11) 5513955; e-mail epa.etio@ethionet.et; internet www.ppesa.gov.et; Dir-Gen. BEYENE GEBREMESKEL.

DEVELOPMENT ORGANIZATIONS

Entrepreneurship Development Center: Addis Ababa; f. 2013 by the Ministry of Urban Development, Housing and Construction in partnership with the United Nations Development Programme; CEO ETALEM ENGEDA.

Ethiopian Institute of Agricultural Research (EIAR): POB 2003, Addis Ababa; tel. (11) 6462633; fax (11) 6461294; internet www .eiar.gov.et; f. 1966; Dir-Gen. Dr SOLOMON ASSEFA.

CHAMBERS OF COMMERCE

Ethiopian Chamber of Commerce and Sectorial Associations: Mexico Sq., POB 517, Addis Ababa; tel. (11) 5514005; fax (11) 5517699; e-mail ethchamb@ethionet.et; internet www .ethiopianchamber.com; f. 1947; regional chambers in 11 localities; Pres. MULU SOLOMON; Sec.-Gen. GASHAW DEBEBE.

Addis Ababa Chamber of Commerce: POB 2458, Addis Ababa; tel. (11) 5513882; fax (11) 5511479; e-mail getachew@addischamber .com; internet www.addischamber.com; Pres. AYALEW ZEGEYE; Sec.-Gen. GETACHEW REGASSA.

INDUSTRIAL AND TRADE ASSOCIATIONS

Arsi Agricultural Development Enterprise: POB 115, Assela; tel. (22) 3311261; fax (22) 3311208; e-mail arsiagri@ethionet.et; internet www.arsiagri-enterprise.gov.et; f. 1980; privatization pending; CEO ASSEFA HAGOS.

Bale Agricultural Development Enterprise: Robe; tel. 0911608014 (mobile); e-mail baleagri@ethionet.et; cereals, pulses and oilseeds; Man. DEBEBE GOBEZE.

Coffee Plantation Development Enterprise (CPDE): Deber Zeit Rd, POB 4363, Addis Ababa; tel. (11) 4670688; fax (11) 4168788; f. 1993; Dir-Gen. EPHREM MERSIHE HAZEN.

Ethiopia Commodity Exchange (ECX): Al-Sam Tower 2, 3rd Floor, Lideta, POB 17341, Addis Ababa; tel. (11) 5547001; fax (11) 5547010; internet www.ecx.com.et; f. 2008; trading of agricultural produce; Chair. ADDISU LEGESS; CEO ERMIAS ESHATU.

Ethiopia Peasants' Association (EPA): f. 1978, as All-Ethiopia Peasants' Asscn, to promote improved agricultural techniques, home industries, education, public health and self-reliance; renamed as above in 1986; comprises 30,000 peasant asscns with c. 7m. mems; Chair. (vacant).

Ethiopian Association of Basic Metal and Engineering Industries: Bole Sub-City, House Number 0377, Addis Ababa; tel. and fax (11) 6293429; e-mail eabmei@ethionet.et; internet www.eabmei.org; Pres. ASEGED MAMMO; Gen. Man. SOLOMON MULUGETA.

Ethiopian Cement Corpn: POB 5782, Addis Ababa; tel. (11) 1552222; fax (11) 1551572; Gen. Man. REDI GEMAL.

Ethiopian Chemical Corpn: POB 5747, Addis Ababa; tel. (11) 6184305; Gen. Man. ASNAKE SAHLU.

Ethiopian Coffee Export Enterprise: POB 2591, Addis Ababa; tel. (11) 5515330; fax (11) 5510762; f. 1977; Chair. SUFIAN AHMED; Gen. Man. DERGA GURMESSA.

Ethiopian Food Corpn: POB 2345, Addis Ababa; tel. (11) 5518522; fax (11) 5513173; f. 1975; produces and distributes food items, incl. edible oil, ghee substitute, pasta, bread, maize, wheat flour, etc.; Gen. Man. BEKELE HAILE.

Ethiopian Fruit and Vegetable Marketing Enterprise: POB 2374, Addis Ababa; tel. (11) 5519192; fax (11) 5516483; f. 1980; sole wholesale domestic distributor and exporter of fresh and processed fruit and vegetables, and floricultural products; Gen. Man. KAKNU PEWONDE.

Ethiopian Grain Trade Enterprise: POB 3321, Addis Ababa; tel. (11) 4652436; fax (11) 4652792; e-mail egte@ethionet.et; internet www.egtemis.com; Gen. Man. BERHANE HAILU.

Ethiopian Horticulture Producer Exporters Association (EHPEA): NB Bldg, 6th Floor, Mickililand Rd, POB 22241, Addis Ababa; tel. (11) 6636750; fax (11) 6636753; e-mail ehpea@ethionet.et; internet www.ehpea.org.et; f. 2002; 96 mems; Pres. ZELALEM MESELE.

Ethiopian Import and Export Corpn (ETIMEX): Addis Ababa; tel. (11) 5511112; fax (11) 5515411; f. 1975; state trading corpn; import of building materials, foodstuffs, stationery and office equipment, textiles, clothing, chemicals, general merchandise, capital goods; Gen. Man. ASCHENAKI G. HIWOT.

Ethiopian Petroleum Enterprise: POB 3375, Addis Ababa; tel. and fax (11) 5512938; f. 1976; Gen. Man. YIGZAW MEKONNEN.

Ethiopian Pulses, Oilseeds and Spices Processors Exporters' Association: POB 5719, Addis Ababa; tel. (11) 1550597; fax (11) 1553299; f. 1975; Gen. Man. ABDOURUHMAN MOHAMMED.

Ethiopian Sugar Corpn: POB 20034, Addis Ababa; tel. (11) 5526653; fax (11) 5150927; e-mail info@etsugar.gov.et; internet www.etsugar.gov.et; f. 2010 to replace Ethiopian Sugar Development Agency; Dir-Gen. ABAY TSEHAYE.

Green Star Food Co LLC: POB 5579, Addis Ababa; tel. (11) 5526588; fax (11) 5526599; e-mail greenstar@telecom.net.et; f. 1984; fmrly the Ethiopian Livestock and Meat Corpn; production and marketing of canned and frozen foods; Gen. Man. DAWIT BEKELE.

Metals and Engineering Corpn (METEC): POB 21431, 1000 Addis Ababa; tel. (11) 5541572; fax (11) 1521141; internet www.metec.gov.et; comprises 15 semi-autonomous cos; Man. Dir Brig.-Gen. KINFE DAGNEW.

Natural Gum Processing and Marketing Enterprise: POB 62322, Addis Ababa; tel. (11) 5527082; fax (11) 5518110; e-mail natgum@ethionet.et; internet www.naturalgum.ebigchina.com; f. 1976; state-owned; Gen. Man. TEKLEHAIMANOT NIGATU BEYENE.

Pharmaceuticals Fund and Supply Agency (PFSA): POB 976, Addis Ababa; tel. (11) 2763266; fax (11) 2751770; e-mail pfsa@ethionet.et; Dir-Gen. MESKELLE LERA.

UTILITIES

Electricity

Ethiopian Electric Power Corpn (EEPCo): De Gaulle Sq., POB 1233, Addis Ababa; tel. (11) 1559567; fax (11) 1571860; e-mail eepcocommunication@yahoo.com; internet www.eepco.gov.et; Chair. DEBRETSION G/MICHAEL; Gen. Man. MIHRET DEBEBE.

Water

Addis Ababa Water and Sewerage Authority: POB 1505; Addis Ababa; tel. (11) 6623902; fax (11) 6623924; e-mail aawsa.ha@ethionet.et; f. 1971; Gen. Man. ASEGID GETACHEW.

TRADE UNIONS

Confederation of Ethiopian Trade Unions (CETU): POB 3653, Addis Ababa; tel. (11) 5155473; fax (11) 5514532; e-mail cetu@telecom.net.et; f. 1975; comprises 9 industrial unions and 22 regional unions with a total membership of 320,000 (1987); Pres. KASSAHUN FOLLO; Sec.-Gen. MESFIN SILESHI.

Transport

RAILWAYS

Railway construction is a central component of Ethiopia's current five-year plan (2010–15) to boost economic growth. In 2010 construction of a 5,000-km railway network to link Addis Ababa with various parts of the country was started. Phase one of the five-year project included the construction of a new 2,000-km line to the border with Djibouti. Under phase two, work commenced in late 2011 on a 34.3-km light railway network in Addis Ababa; the construction of the network was completed in January 2015 and it was scheduled to commence operating in the latter half of that year. In 2012 agreement was reached with Turkey's Yapi Merkezi and China Communications Construction Company regarding the construction of 715-km of track connecting Ethiopia to the port of Tadjoura in northern Djibouti.

Chemin de Fer Djibouti-Ethiopien (CDE): POB 1051, Addis Ababa; tel. (11) 5517250; fax (11) 5513997; f. 1909; adopted present name in 1981; jtly owned by Govts of Ethiopia and Djibouti; 781 km of track (660 km in Ethiopia), linking Addis Ababa with Djibouti; Pres. ISMAIL IBRAHIM HOUMED.

Ethiopian Railways Corporation (ERC): POB 27558/1000, Addis Ababa; tel. (11) 6189060; fax (11) 6189065; internet www.erc.gov.et; f. 2007; CEO Dr GETACHEW BETRE.

ROADS

In 2007 the total road network comprised an estimated 44,359 km of primary, secondary and feeder roads, of which 13.7% were paved, the remainder being gravel roads. In addition, there are some 30,000 km of unclassified tracks and trails. A highway links Addis Ababa with Nairobi in Kenya, forming part of the Trans-East Africa Highway. During 2003–07 work was carried out on the second phase of the Road Sector Development Programme, which upgraded 80% and 63% of paved and gravel roads, respectively, to an acceptable condition.

Comet Transport SC: POB 2402, Addis Ababa; tel. (11) 4423962; fax (11) 4426024; e-mail cometrans@ethionet.et; f. 1994; Gen. Man. MEHRETAB TEKLU.

Ethiopian Road Transport Authority: POB 2504, Addis Ababa; tel. (11) 5510244; fax (11) 5510715; e-mail kasahun_khmariam@yahoo.com; internet www.rta.gov.et; enforces road transport regulations, promotes road safety, registers vehicles and issues driving licences; Gen. Man. KASAHUN H. MARIAM.

Ethiopian Roads Authority: POB 1770, Addis Ababa; tel. (11) 5517170; fax (11) 5514866; e-mail era2@ethionet.et; internet www.era.gov.et; f. 1951; construction and maintenance of roads, bridges and airports; Dir-Gen. ZAID WOLDE GEBREAL.

Public Transport Corpn: POB 5780, Addis Ababa; tel. (11) 5153117; fax (11) 5510720; f. 1977; urban bus services in Addis Ababa and Jimma, and services between towns; Man. Dir AHMED NURU.

Sky Bus Transport System SC: Addis Ababa; tel. (11) 4673331; fax (11) 4162843; e-mail info@skybusethiopia.com; internet www.skybusethiopia.com; f. 2007; intercity coach service to 8 destinations within Ethiopia; Chief Exec. SOLOMON GAREDEW BEKELE.

SHIPPING

The formerly Ethiopian-controlled ports of Massawa and Assab now lie within the boundaries of the State of Eritrea. Although an agreement exists between the two Governments allowing Ethiopian access to the two ports, which can handle more than 1m. metric tons of merchandise annually, in mid-1998 Ethiopia ceased using the ports, owing to the outbreak of hostilities. Ethiopia's maritime trade currently passes through Djibouti (in the Republic of Djibouti), and also through the Kenyan port of Mombasa. An agreement was also signed in July 2003 to allow Ethiopia to use Port Sudan (in Sudan). At 31 December 2014 Ethiopia's flag registered fleet numbered 17 vessels, with a total displacement of 313,105 grt.

Ethiopian Shipping and Logistics Services Enterprise (ESLSE): Kirkos District, Kebele 15 (La Gare), POB 2572, Addis Ababa; tel. (11) 5518280; fax (11) 5519525; e-mail esl@ethionet.et; internet www.ethiopianshippinglines.com.et; f. 2011 following merger of the Ethiopian Shipping Lines Corpn, the Maritime and Transit Services Enterprise and the Dry Port Services Enterprise; serves Red Sea, Europe, Mediterranean, Gulf and Far East with its own fleet and chartered vessels; CEO AHMED TUSSA.

Maritime Affairs Authority: Tadesse Tefera Bldg, 5th Floor, opp. Hotel d'Afrique, POB 1861, Addis Ababa; tel. (11) 5503638; fax (11) 5503960; e-mail maritime@ethionet.et; internet www.maritime.gov.et; f. 2007; regulates maritime transport services; Dir-Gen. MEKONNEN ABERA.

CIVIL AVIATION

Ethiopia has two international airports (at Addis Ababa and Dire Dawa) and around 40 smaller airports and airfields. Bole International Airport in the capital handles 95% of the country's international air traffic and 85% of domestic flights.

Ethiopian Airlines: Bole International Airport, POB 1755, Addis Ababa; tel. (11) 5178165; fax (11) 6611474; e-mail publicrelations@ethiopianairlines.com; internet www.ethiopianairlines.com; f. 1945; operates regular services to 18 domestic destinations and 82 international destinations; CEO TEWOLDE GEBREMARIAM.

Ethiopian Civil Aviation Authority (ECAA): POB 978, Addis Ababa; tel. (11) 6650200; fax (11) 6650281; e-mail civilaviation@ethionet.et; internet www.ecaa.gov.et; regulatory authority; provides air navigational facilities; Dir-Gen. Col WOSENYELEH HUNEGNAW.

Tourism

Ethiopia's tourist attractions include early Christian monuments and churches, the ancient capitals of Gondar and Axum, the Blue Nile (or Tississat) Falls and the National Parks of the Simien and Bale Mountains. Tourist arrivals in 2013 totalled 681,249. In 2013 receipts from tourism (excluding passenger transport) amounted to an estimated US $416m.

Ministry of Culture and Tourism: POB 2183, Addis Ababa; tel. (11) 5512310; fax (11) 5512889; e-mail info@tourismethiopia.org; internet www.tourismethiopia.org.

Defence

As assessed at November 2014, Ethiopia's active armed forces numbered an estimated 138,000, including an air force of some 3,000. A total of 12,170 soldiers were stationed abroad, of whom 98 were observers.

Defence Expenditure: Budgeted at 8,000m. birr for the fiscal year 2014/15.

Chief of Staff of the Ethiopian National Defence Forces: Gen. SAMORA MUHAMMAD YUNIS.

Commander of the Ethiopian Air Force: Gen. MEHARI TEKELE.

Education

Education in Ethiopia is available free of charge, and, after a rapid growth in the number of schools, it became compulsory between the ages of seven and 13 years. Since 1976 most primary and secondary schools have been controlled by local peasant associations and urban dwellers' associations. Primary education begins at seven years of age and lasts for eight years. Secondary education, beginning at 15 years of age, lasts for a further four years, comprising two cycles of two years, the second of which provides preparatory education for entry to the tertiary level. According to UNESCO estimates, in 2009/10 total enrolment at primary schools included 81% of children in the appropriate age-group (84% of boys; 79% of girls), while secondary enrolment was equivalent to 36% of children in the appropriate age-group (39% of boys; 32% of girls). According to the Ministry of Education, in 2012/13 there were 99 institutions of higher education in Ethiopia, including universities in Addis Ababa, Bahir Dar, Alemanya, Jimma, Awassa and Makele. A total of 585,152 students were enrolled in higher education in 2012/13. In 2010 public spending on education represented 24.4% of total government expenditure.

FIJI

Introductory Survey

LOCATION, CLIMATE, LANGUAGE, RELIGION, FLAG, CAPITAL

The Republic of Fiji comprises more than 300 islands, of which around 100 are inhabited, situated about 1,930 km (1,200 miles) south of the equator in the Pacific Ocean. The four main islands are Viti Levu (where some 70% of the country's population lives), Vanua Levu, Taveuni and Kadavu. The climate is tropical, with temperatures ranging from 16°C to 32°C (60°F–90°F). Rainfall is heavy on the windward side. Fijian and Hindi are the principal languages, but English is also widely spoken. According to the 2007 census, about 64% of the population were Christians (mainly Methodists), 28% Hindus and 6% Muslims. The national flag (proportions 1 by 2) is light blue, with the United Kingdom flag as a canton in the upper hoist. In the fly is the main part of Fiji's national coat of arms: a white field quartered by a red upright cross, the quarters containing sugar canes, a coconut palm, a stem of bananas and a dove bearing an olive branch; in chief is a red panel with a yellow crowned lion holding a white cocoa pod. (Plans to redesign the flag were announced in February 2015.) The capital is Suva, on Viti Levu.

CONTEMPORARY POLITICAL HISTORY

Historical Context

The first Europeans to settle on the islands were sandalwood traders, missionaries and shipwrecked sailors, and in October 1874 Fiji was proclaimed a British possession. In September 1966 the British Government introduced a new Constitution for Fiji. It provided for a ministerial form of government, an almost wholly elected Legislative Council and universal adult suffrage. Rather than using a common roll of voters, the Constitution introduced an electoral system that combined communal (Fijian and Indian) rolls with cross-voting. In September 1967 the Executive Council became the Council of Ministers, with Ratu Kamisese Mara, leader of the multiracial (but predominantly Fijian) Alliance Party (AP), as Fiji's first Chief Minister. Following a constitutional conference in April–May 1970, Fiji achieved independence, within the Commonwealth, on 10 October 1970. The Legislative Council was renamed the House of Representatives, and a second parliamentary chamber, the nominated Senate, was established. The British-appointed Governor became the first Governor-General of Fiji, while Ratu Sir Kamisese Mara (as he had become in 1969) took office as Prime Minister.

However, Fiji was troubled by racial tensions. Although the descendants of indentured Indian workers who were brought to Fiji in the late 19th century had grown to outnumber the native inhabitants, they were discriminated against in political representation and land ownership rights (see Land Ownership Issues for subsequent developments). A new electoral system was adopted in 1970 to ensure a racial balance in the legislature.

Domestic Political Affairs

At the legislative elections held in March 1972 the AP secured 33 of the 52 seats in the House of Representatives, while the National Federation Party (NFP), traditionally supported by the Indian population, took 19 seats. At elections in March–April 1977 the NFP won 26 seats, but was unable to form a government, subsequently splitting into two factions. The AP governed in an interim capacity until the holding of further elections in September, when it was returned with its largest-ever majority. While the two main parties professed multiracial ideologies, the Fijian Nationalist Party campaigned in support of its 'Fiji for the Fijians' programme.

In 1980 Ratu Sir Kamisese Mara's suggestion that a government of national unity be formed was overshadowed by renewed disagreement between the AP and the NFP over land ownership. Fijians owned 83% of the land and strongly defended their traditional rights, while the Indian population pressed for greater security of land tenure. The AP retained power at the legislative elections held in July 1982, but its majority was reduced from 20 seats to four.

A new party, the Fiji Labour Party (FLP), was inaugurated in July 1985. Sponsored by the Fiji Trades Union Congress (FTUC), and under the presidency of Dr Timoci Bavadra, the FLP hoped to work through farmers' organizations to win votes among rural electorates, which traditionally supported the NFP. During 1985–86 disagreements between the Government and the FTUC over economic policies led to labour unrest and the withdrawal, in June 1986, of government recognition of the FTUC as the unions' representative organization.

At legislative elections in April 1987 an alliance of the FLP and NFP won 28 seats (19 of which were secured by ethnic Indian candidates) in the House of Representatives, thereby defeating the ruling AP, which took only 24 seats. The new Government, led by Bavadra, was the first in Fijian history to contain a majority of ministers of Indian, rather than Melanesian, origin, although Bavadra himself was of Melanesian descent.

The coups of 1987 and subsequent events

On 14 May 1987 the Government was overthrown by a military coup, led by Lt-Col (later Maj.-Gen.) Sitiveni Rabuka. The Governor-General, Ratu Sir Penaia Ganilau, declared a state of emergency and appointed a 19-member advisory council, including Bavadra and Rabuka. Bavadra refused to participate in the council, denouncing it as unconstitutional and biased in its composition.

Widespread racial violence ensued, and there were several public demands for Bavadra's reinstatement as Prime Minister. In July 1987 the Great Council of Fijian Chiefs, comprising the country's 70 hereditary Melanesian leaders, approved plans for constitutional reform. In September negotiations began, on the initiative of Ganilau, between delegations led by the two former Prime Ministers, Bavadra and Mara, and it was subsequently announced that the two factions had agreed to establish an interim bipartisan Government.

On 25 September 1987, however, Rabuka staged a second coup and announced his intention to declare Fiji a republic. Despite Ganilau's refusal to recognize the seizure of power, Rabuka revoked the Constitution on 1 October and proclaimed himself head of state, thus deposing Queen Elizabeth II. Ganilau conceded defeat and resigned as Governor-General. At a meeting in Canada, Commonwealth heads of government formally declared that Fiji's membership of the Commonwealth had lapsed. Rabuka installed an interim Cabinet comprising mainly ethnic Fijians. Several cases of violations of human rights by the Fijian army were reported, as the regime assumed powers of detention without trial and suspended all political activity. In December Rabuka resigned as head of state. Although he had previously refused to accept the post, Ganilau became the first President of the Fijian Republic. Mara was reappointed Prime Minister, and Rabuka became Minister for Home Affairs. The new interim Cabinet included 11 members of Rabuka's outgoing administration, but no former minister of Bavadra's deposed Government.

In February 1988 Rotuma (the only Polynesian island in the country), which lies 386 km (240 miles) to the north-west of Vanua Levu, declared itself politically independent of Fiji, the newly acquired republican status of which it refused to recognize. Fijian troops were dispatched to the island and swiftly quelled the dissent.

A new draft Constitution, approved by the interim Government in September 1988, was rejected by a multiracial constitutional committee, which disputed the specific reservation of the principal offices of state for ethnic Fijians. In September 1989 the committee published a revised draft, which was again denounced by Bavadra and the FLP-NFP alliance. In November Bavadra died and was replaced as leader of the FLP-NFP alliance by his widow, Adi Kuini Bavadra.

In January 1990 Rabuka resigned from the Cabinet and returned to his military duties. Mara agreed to remain as Prime Minister until the restoration of constitutional government. In June the Great Council of Chiefs approved the draft Constitution, while also stating its intention to form a new party, the Soqosoqo ni Vakavulewa ni Taukei (SVT) or Fijian Political Party, to advocate the cause of ethnic Fijians. The new Constitution was finally promulgated on 25 July by President Ganilau. The charter was immediately condemned by the FLP-NFP alliance. Angered by the fact that a legislative majority was guaranteed to ethnic Fijians (who were allocated 37 of the 70 elective seats, compared with 27 Indian seats), and that the Great Council of Chiefs was to nominate ethnic Fijians to 24 of the 34 seats in the Senate and to appoint the President of the Republic, the opposition organized anti-Constitution demonstrations. In May 1991 the Commonwealth stated that Fiji would not be readmitted until it changed its racially biased Constitution. In July Rabuka resigned as Commander of the Armed Forces in order to rejoin the Cabinet as Deputy Prime Minister and Minister for Home Affairs, although later that year he relinquished these posts and assumed the leadership of the SVT.

Disagreements between the Government and the FTUC re-emerged in 1991. In May the Government announced a series of reforms to the labour laws, including the abolition of the minimum wage, restrictions on strike action and derecognition of unions that did not represent at least two-thirds of the workforce. However, in late 1992 the Government officially recognized the FTUC as the sole representative of workers in Fiji.

At the legislative elections of May 1992 the SVT secured 30 of the 37 seats reserved for ethnic Fijians, while the NFP won 14 and the FLP 13 of the seats reserved for Indian representatives. The FLP agreed to participate in Parliament and to support Rabuka in his bid for the premiership, in return for a guarantee from the SVT of a full review of the Constitution and of trade union and land laws. Rabuka was, therefore, appointed Prime Minister and formed a coalition Government (comprising 14 SVT ministers and five others).

In December 1992 Rabuka formally invited the opposition leaders, Jai Ram Reddy of the NFP and Mahendra Chaudhry of the FLP, to establish a government of national unity. The initiative was largely welcomed, but Indian politicians expressed reluctance to participate in a government in which political control remained fundamentally vested with ethnic Fijians; conversely, nationalist extremists of the Taukei Solidarity Movement accused Rabuka of conceding too much political power to Fijian Indians. Following the appointment of a new Cabinet in June 1993, all 13 of the FLP legislators began an indefinite parliamentary boycott, in protest against Rabuka's failure to implement the reforms that he had agreed to introduce in return for their support for his election to the premiership in June 1992.

In December 1993 President Ganilau died. He was replaced by Ratu Sir Kamisese Mara, who took office on 18 January 1994 (and was re-elected on 18 January 1999).

At the legislative elections held in February 1994 the SVT won 31 of the 37 seats reserved for ethnic Fijians, while the Fijian Association Party (FAP, established in January by former members of the SVT) secured five. Of the 27 seats reserved for ethnic Indian representatives, 20 were won by the NFP. The SVT subsequently formed a governing coalition with the General Voters' Party (GVP, which represented the interests of the General Electors—i.e. the minority Chinese and European communities and people from elsewhere in the Pacific region resident in Fiji) and an independent member, under the premiership of Rabuka, who announced the formation of a new Cabinet composed entirely of ethnic Fijians. In response to international concern regarding the continued existence of Fiji's racially biased Constitution, Rabuka announced in June the establishment of a Constitutional Review Commission.

The issue of independence for the island of Rotuma was revived in September 1995 with the return of the King of Rotuma from exile. King Gagaj Sa Lagfatmaro, who had fled to New Zealand after receiving death threats during the military coups of 1987, appeared before the Constitutional Review Commission to petition for the island's independence within the Commonwealth, reiterating his view that Rotuma remained a British colony rather than a part of Fiji.

Racial tension intensified in October 1995, following the publication of the SVT's submission to the Constitutional Review Commission. In its report, the party detailed plans to abandon the present multiracial form of government, recommending instead the adoption of an electoral system based on racial representation, in which each ethnic group would select its own representatives. The expression of numerous extreme anti-Indian sentiments in the document was widely condemned as offensive.

Two of the four GVP members of the House of Representatives withdrew their support for the Government in early 1996, prompting an (unsuccessful) attempt by Rabuka to seek alternative coalition partners from among the opposition. The SVT was defeated in virtually every municipality at local elections in September.

Existing divisions within the Government were further exacerbated by the presentation to the House of Representatives, in September 1996, of the Constitutional Review Commission's report. The report included recommendations to enlarge the House of Representatives to 75 seats, with 25 seats reserved on a racial basis (12 for ethnic Fijians, 10 for Fijian Indians, two for General Electors and one for Rotuma Islanders), and also proposed that the size of the Senate should be reduced from 34 to 32 members (and the number of nominated ethnic Fijian senators be reduced from 24 to 15). In addition, it was proposed that the Prime Minister should be a Fijian of any race, while the President should continue to be an indigenous Fijian. The parliamentary committee reviewing the report—which was endorsed by both Rabuka and Mara—agreed on the majority of its recommendations, but proposed that the House of Representatives be enlarged to only 71 seats, with 46 seats reserved on a racial basis (23 for ethnic Fijians, 19 for Indians, three for General Electors and one for Rotuma Islanders) and 25 seats open to all races. A modified Constitution Amendment Bill was subsequently approved by both the House of Representatives and the Senate in July 1997. Rabuka was anxious to reassure nationalist Fijians that their interests would be protected under the amended Constitution and that indigenous Fijians would continue to play a pre-eminent role in government.

Fiji was readmitted to the Commonwealth in October 1997. Rabuka was granted an audience with Queen Elizabeth II in London, UK, at which he formally apologized for the military coups of 1987. The new Constitution took effect on 27 July 1998.

In late 1998 Adi Kuini Vuikaba Speed (widow of former Prime Minister Bavadra) replaced Ratu Alifereti Finau Mara as leader of the FAP. Meanwhile, the GVP and the General Electors' Association merged to form the United General Party (UGP), and Rabuka was re-elected leader of the SVT. A new party, the Veitokani ni Lewenivanua Vakarisito (VLV, Christian Democratic Alliance), founded by several senior church and military leaders and former members of the nationalist Taukei Solidarity Movement, was widely criticized for its extremist stance.

At the legislative elections of May 1999, the first to be held under the new Constitution, Rabuka's coalition Government was defeated by the FLP, led by Mahendra Chaudhry, who became Fiji's first ethnic Indian Prime Minister. Chaudhry's broadly based Government (a coalition of the FLP, FAP, VLV and the Party of National Unity—PANU) initially seemed threatened by the reluctance of FAP members to serve under an Indian Prime Minister. The members were persuaded to remain in the coalition in the interests of national unity, after the intervention of President Mara. Political stability was further marred by demands for Chaudhry's resignation by the Fijian Nationalist Vanua Takolavo Party (NVTLP), and by a number of arson attacks, allegedly linked to the SVT. Following the SVT's decisive election defeat, Rabuka resigned as party leader. Rabuka was later appointed the first independent Chairman of the newly autonomous Great Council of Chiefs. The NVTLP was widely suspected to have been responsible for three bomb explosions in Suva in August. In the same month a parliamentary vote of no confidence against Prime Minister Chaudhry was overwhelmingly defeated. In the latter half of 1999 there were persistent demands by various nationalist groups (including the SVT) that Chaudhry be replaced by a leader of indigenous Fijian descent, and a number of anti-Government demonstrations were organized.

The Government's decision to disband the Fiji Intelligence Services from December 1999 was criticized by the opposition as 'foolish' and racially motivated. Plans to amend a number of laws that did not comply with the terms of the new Constitution and proposals to adjust the distribution of power between the President and the Prime Minister, along with reports that the Government was planning to withdraw state funds previously provided to assist indigenous Fijian business interests, prompted further criticism from the opposition, and in February 2000 a faction of the FAP announced its withdrawal from the governing coalition. Furthermore, it was announced in April that the extremist nationalist Taukei movement (which had been inactive for several years) had been revived with the sole intention of deposing the Prime Minister. The movement's campaign attracted considerable public support, culminating in a march through Suva by some 5,000 people in early May.

The coup of 2000 and its repercussions

On 19 May 2000 a group of armed men, led by businessman George Speight, invaded the parliament building and ousted the Government, taking hostage Chaudhry and 30 other members of the governing coalition. President Mara condemned the coup and declared a state of emergency as Speight's supporters rampaged through the streets of Suva, looting and setting fire to Indian businesses. Speight declared that he had reclaimed Fiji for indigenous Fijians and had abrogated the Constitution. Moreover, he threatened to kill the hostages if the military intervened. Convening at Mara's invitation, the Great Council of Chiefs proposed the replacement of Chaudhry's Government with an interim administration, an amnesty for Speight and the rebels, and the amendment of the Constitution. Speight rejected the proposals, demanding that Mara also be removed from office. At the end of May Mara resigned and the Commander of the Armed Forces, Voreqe (Frank) Bainimarama, announced the imposition of martial law and a curfew to restore stability to the country.

Negotiations between the newly installed Military Executive Council and the Great Council of Chiefs continued throughout June 2000. Following the release of the four female captives from the parliament building, the Military Executive Council demanded the release of all hostages. The Military Executive Council appointed an interim administration of 19 indigenous Fijians led by Laisenia Qarase, which was sworn in on 4 July. Speight announced that he would not recognize the interim authority, and most of Fiji's mainstream political parties similarly denounced it. By mid-July Chaudhry and the remaining hostages had been released by the rebels. In accordance with Speight's wishes, Ratu Josefa Iloilovatu Uluivuda (or Josefa Iloilo), hitherto the First Vice-President, was then installed as President.

Incidents of civil unrest continued, as Speight sought to manipulate existing grievances, particularly disputes over land ownership, in order to mobilize greater support. At the end of July 2000, however, Speight was finally arrested, along with dozens of his supporters, for breaking the terms of his amnesty by refusing to relinquish weapons. In early August more than 300 rebels appeared in court, charged with a variety of firearms and public order offences. On 11 August Speight and 14 of his supporters were formally charged with treason. Meanwhile, a police investigation into a commercial deal involving the Fijian mahogany trade began; Speight had been chairman of both Fiji Pine Corporation and Fiji Hardwood Corporation before being dismissed in 1999. Chaudhry subsequently stated his belief that the coup had been motivated by commercial vested interests.

In early November 2000 about 40 soldiers staged an unsuccessful mutiny at army headquarters in Suva. Troops loyal to Bainimarama retook the barracks following an eight-hour assault in which five rebels and four loyal soldiers were killed. It was later revealed that a number of the rebel soldiers had been involved in the coup in May. The Chairman of the Great Council of Chiefs, Rabuka, denied allegations of his involvement in the mutiny.

Later in November 2000 the High Court ruled that the existing Constitution was still valid and that the elected Parliament, ousted in the coup, remained Fiji's legitimate governing authority. In response, Qarase lodged an appeal against the ruling and declared that the interim authority, of which he was leader, would continue as the country's national government until new elections could be organized and a new constitution drafted within 18 months.

In February 2001 an international panel of judges at the Court of Appeal began the hearing against the November 2000 ruling, which found the abrogation of the 1997 Constitution to be illegal. In its final judgment the court ruled that the 1997 Constitution remained the supreme law of Fiji, that the interim civilian government could not prove that it had the support of a majority of Fijian people and was therefore illegal, and that, following Mara's resignation, the office of President remained vacant. The ruling was apparently accepted by Qarase's interim authority, which announced that it would organize elections as soon as possible. However, in March 2001 Iloilo informed Chaudhry by letter that he had been dismissed as Prime Minister, claiming that by advising Iloilo to dissolve the legislature in preparation for elections he had accepted that he no longer had the mandate of Parliament. Chaudhry rejected the decision as unconstitutional and unlawful. Ratu Tevita Momoedonu, a minister in Qarase's Government, was appointed Prime Minister. However, Iloilo dismissed Momoedonu, on the advice of the Great Council

of Chiefs, and reinstated Qarase as head of the interim authority. It was subsequently announced that legislative elections would be held in August–September 2001.

There followed a period of factionalism and fragmentation among Fiji's political parties. Speight had already been appointed President of the new Matanitu Vanua (MV—Conservative Alliance Party), despite having been charged with treason for his part in the 2000 coup. In May 2001 Qarase formed the Soqosoqo Duavata ni Lewenivanua (SDL—Fiji United Party), a new contender for the indigenous Melanesian vote, thus rivalling the established SVT. Tupeni Baba, former Deputy Prime Minister in Chaudhry's Government, left the FLP and founded the New Labour United Party (NLUP). Qarase's SDL was victorious in the elections, but failed to obtain an overall majority, securing 31 of the 71 seats in the House of Representatives (rising to 32 following a by-election in late September). The FLP won 27 seats, the MV six and the NLUP two.

Refusing to allow the FLP any representation in his new Cabinet (which included two members of the MV), Qarase was accused of contravening a provision of the Constitution whereby a party winning more than 10% of the seats in the House of Representatives was entitled to a ministerial post. Qarase claimed that Chaudhry had not accepted that the Government should be based fundamentally on nationalist Fijian principles. In October 2001 Chaudhry refused to accept the position of Leader of the Opposition, a role that consequently fell to Prem Singh of the NFP. In December Parliament approved the Social Justice Bill, a programme of affirmative action favouring Fijians and Rotumans in education, land rights and business-funding policies.

Prime Minister Qarase defended himself against demands for his resignation in January 2002 following allegations that he had contravened the Electoral Act by pledging government funds to pro-indigenous Fijian businesses during the 2001 election campaign. In February 2002, furthermore, an appeal court ruled that the Prime Minister had violated the Constitution by failing to incorporate any member of the FLP in his Cabinet. Qarase had previously declared that he would resign if the legal challenge against him proved successful. Although in June Qarase and Chaudhry co-operated briefly in addressing the long-standing issue of the expiry of land leases, in August the FLP abandoned a second round of discussions on this matter and announced that it would boycott most of the proceedings in the current parliamentary session. In September the High Court ruled that Prem Singh was not entitled to retain his parliamentary seat (the validity of certain votes cast at the 2001 election having been questioned). The disputed seat was therefore allocated to the FLP. The Supreme Court finally delivered its ruling on the issue of the inclusion of the FLP in the Cabinet in July 2003, finding in favour of Chaudhry and declaring that, in order to uphold the Constitution, Qarase should form a new cabinet that included eight members of the FLP. Qarase responded by proposing to retain the incumbent 22-member Cabinet and to add 14 FLP members. Both the opposition and the SVT leader, Rabuka, criticized the proposal, which would entail more than one-half of all legislators serving as government ministers. Chaudhry also claimed that the positions offered to his party were too junior. However, Qarase remained intransigent, and at the end of August he formally nominated a Cabinet that included 14 FLP members (although Chaudhry was not among those named).

Meanwhile, the trial of Speight and his accomplices on charges of treason opened in May 2001. (Speight was refused bail to enable him to occupy the seat that he won in the legislative elections later in the year.) All the accused pleaded guilty to their involvement in the coup of May 2000, and at the conclusion of the trial in February 2002 Speight received the death sentence. However, within hours of the verdict President Iloilo signed a decree commuting the sentence to life imprisonment. Prison sentences of between 18 months and three years were imposed on 10 of Speight's accomplices, the charges of treason having been replaced by lesser charges of abduction. Between July 2002 and July 2004 a total of 86 people were arrested on charges relating to the coup, with the majority being found guilty of mutiny. In May 2004 the Great Council of Chiefs issued an historic public apology to all Indian Fijians for injustices committed against them during the coups of 1987 and 2000. Also in May, Speight made a further court appearance on charges of hostage-taking during the 2000 coup. Chaudhry and another member of Parliament were claiming US $3.6m. in compensation for the 56 days that they had been held hostage by Speight and his accomplices. In August 2004 Vice-President Ratu Jope Seniloli was found guilty of treason and sentenced to four years' imprisonment. In November, however, he was unexpectedly released from prison on medical grounds, which were widely disputed. Upon his release, Seniloli resigned as Vice-President at the insistence of the military. In December the Great Council of Chiefs approved President Iloilo's nomination of Ratu Joni Madraiwiwi as the country's new Vice-President. In November 2004 Paramount Chief Ratu Inoke Takiveikata was sentenced to life imprisonment after being found guilty on several charges relating to the mutiny. (In June 2007, following questions about the impartiality of the presiding judge, a retrial of Takiveikata was ordered; however, in November 2007 he was again arrested, on separate charges of conspiracy to assassinate Bainimarama—see *The coup of 2006 and abrogation of the Constitution*.)

In May 2005 the Government announced plans for a Reconciliation, Tolerance and Unity Bill, which would allow the review of convictions relating to involvement in the 2000 coup and the pardoning of prisoners. However, the proposals provoked considerable opposition, particularly from the FLP and from Hindu organizations. In the same month the Minister for Transport, Simione Kaitani, appeared in court on coup-related charges.

The reappointment in March 2006, by the Great Council of Chiefs, of Iloilo as President and Madraiwiwi as Vice-President was welcomed by Chaudhry and by the military as contributing to national stability. Although 25 political parties contested the legislative elections in May, only three of these won seats in the House of Representatives. The ruling SDL, which had joined forces with a number of smaller, conservative-leaning parties, secured 36 seats, while the FLP won 31 and the United People's Party (UPP—formerly the UGP—representing General Electors) two. The two successful independent candidates agreed to support the SDL.

Following his reappointment as Prime Minister in May 2006, Qarase offered seven of the 17 cabinet positions to the FLP, as required by the Constitution, although he restated his opposition to multi-party coalition government and expressed his hope that Chaudhry would not accept the proposal. Chaudhry, in turn, argued that his party was entitled to more posts and disputed the portfolios offered. The FLP was subsequently assigned nine positions in a 24-member Cabinet, although Chaudhry himself declined to accept a ministerial role.

The coup of 2006 and abrogation of the Constitution

Tensions between the Government and the military were exacerbated by repeated accusations made throughout 2006 by the Commander of the Armed Forces, Cdre Bainimarama, of racism and corruption within Qarase's administration. In February Bainimarama issued a statement declaring that he would prevent the enactment of the Reconciliation, Tolerance and Unity Bill, and in October he demanded the resignation of the Government if it failed to reject the bill within three weeks. At the end of that month, while Bainimarama was abroad visiting peacekeeping troops, the Government made an attempt to replace him. However, the Government's chosen replacement declined to accept the role, expressing support for Bainimarama. On 30 November Bainimarama issued a further ultimatum, giving Qarase 24 hours to comply with a list of demands. These demands included the removal of all government members who had supported or benefited from the 2000 coup and the suspension of three controversial pieces of legislation condemned by Bainimarama as furthering the racist agenda of the Government: the Reconciliation, Tolerance and Unity Bill, providing amnesties for those convicted of involvement in the 2000 coup; the Qoliqoli Bill, giving ethnic Fijians control of fishing rights and development of the coast; and the Indigenous Claims Tribunal Bill. In a public address on Fijian television, Qarase agreed to suspend the bills.

On 5 December 2006 soldiers took up positions outside the Prime Minister's official residence, seized strategic installations and erected road blocks around Suva. Following a meeting with Bainimarama, President Iloilo authorized the dissolution of Parliament and the establishment of an interim administration. Bainimarama declared that he had assumed executive control of the country, appointing Dr Jona Senilagakali as interim Prime Minister and urging all cabinet ministers to resign within a month. A state of emergency was subsequently declared. The suspension of Fiji's participation in meetings of the Commonwealth was announced on 9 December. Despite widespread international condemnation, there was considerable support for the coup within Fiji. Organizations representing Indian Fijians expressed support for Bainimarama, as did the Fiji

Human Rights Commission, which had questioned the legitimacy of Qarase's Government.

On 4 January 2007 Bainimarama restored executive power to President Iloilo, and on the following day, upon the resignation of Senilagakali, Bainimarama was sworn in as interim Prime Minister. Bainimarama's appointment was swiftly approved by the Great Council of Chiefs. An interim Government was then sworn in; notable appointments included that of Chaudhry as Minister for Finance, National Planning, Public Enterprise and the Sugar Industry, and Ratu Epeli Nailatikau as Minister for Foreign Affairs and External Trade. In mid-January, amid reports of intimidation on the part of the military in the aftermath of the coup, President Iloilo issued a decree granting immunity to Bainimarama, Senilagakali and members of the military and police force in the event of disciplinary action or prosecution. In February Bainimarama announced plans to hold elections in 2010, following an assessment of electoral procedures and the completion of a census. These proposals appeared to have been revised in April 2007, when it was reported that the Fijian Government had agreed to the holding of legislative elections within two years, during discussions with the European Union (EU, see p. 271) on the issue of the release of development aid, suspended as a result of the coup.

In April 2007 the Great Council of Chiefs rejected Nailatikau as a nominee for the post of Vice-President. The Council was suspended, and the Government announced a review of its procedures. Although its suspension was apparently rescinded in August, it was later reported that the official composition of the Council had been reduced from 55 to 52 members (following the dismissal of several chiefs, including the Chairman). Meanwhile, at the end of May Bainimarama declared an end to the state of emergency. In November some 16 arrests were made after plans for an apparent counter-coup, allegedly to include the assassination of Bainimarama, were reportedly uncovered. Several alleged conspirators, including a former senator, an intelligence official and Paramount Chief Ratu Inoke Takiveikata, who had previously been charged with mutiny, were indicted on charges such as treason and inciting mutiny.

A reorganization of the interim Cabinet was announced in January 2008, in which Bainimarama relinquished the home affairs and immigration portfolios, but assumed responsibility for others, including provincial development and indigenous and multi-ethnic affairs. Ratu Epeli Ganilau became Minister for Defence, National Security and Immigration. Bainimarama took charge of the 'People's Charter for Change, Peace and Progress', a directive proposed in September 2007 and expected to result in amendments to the Constitution. The draft Charter, which was released in August 2008 and was undergoing a consultation process, advocated the forging of a 'common national identity', the introduction of an Anti-discrimination Act, and a programme of reform in areas including governance and reconciliation. In anticipation of the forthcoming elections, Chaudhry resigned from the interim Cabinet, along with two other members of the FLP, in mid-August. However, shortly afterwards, Bainimarama announced that the election schedule was dependent upon the implementation of electoral reform and would therefore be subject to further delays. Following Chaudhry's departure, Bainimarama assumed personal responsibility for the finance and national planning portfolio. In a further reorganization announced in September, Bainimarama took control of the foreign affairs portfolio, transferring Nailatikau to the Ministry for Provincial Development and Indigenous and Multi-ethnic Affairs.

Meanwhile, in February 2008 it emerged that Bainimarama had assumed the role of Chairman of the Great Council of Chiefs. At the end of that month it was announced that the National Security Council, which had been dissolved in 1999, and the Fiji Intelligence Services were to be reconstituted. Also in February 2008, Qarase was charged with corruption and abuse of office by the Fiji Independent Commission Against Corruption; the allegations against the former premier pertained to his tenure as director of Fijian Holdings Ltd in 1999–2000. In March 2008 Qarase himself challenged the legality of the December 2006 coup and installation of an interim Government, but his case was dismissed by the High Court in October 2008.

In April 2009 the Court of Appeal overruled the High Court's decision, declaring that the Government installed by Bainimarama following the 2006 coup was illegal. However, the court rejected Qarase's appeal to be reinstated to the premiership, instead ordering President Iloilo to dissolve Parliament and to appoint an interim Prime Minister. Bainimarama resigned in response to the ruling. President Iloilo annulled the 1997 Constitution, reappointed himself as head of state and dismissed the entire judiciary; he then reappointed Bainimarama as Prime Minister and reinstated the Government, with modifications to some ministerial portfolios. The position of Vice-President was restored, Nailatikau being appointed to the post. President Iloilo also announced that elections would be held no later than 2014. Meanwhile, the building of the Reserve Bank of Fiji was occupied by the military, and the central bank's Governor was removed from office and reportedly detained.

Once returned to power, Bainimarama enacted a Public Emergency Decree, outlawing gatherings of more than 100 people and imposing strict censorship laws. A number of international journalists were expelled from the country, and the Australian Broadcasting Corporation's radio transmitters were shut down. Over the following weeks Bainimarama reinstated the Chief Magistrate, the Chief Justice and judges of the High Court and reopened the Magistrates' Court. The actions of President Iloilo and Prime Minister Bainimarama provoked widespread international condemnation, with the UN, Australia and New Zealand offering to mediate in political dialogue to restore democracy. Bainimarama's refusal to set a date for democratic elections before 2014 resulted in Fiji's suspension from the Pacific Islands Forum (see p. 413) in May 2009 and the country's full suspension from the Commonwealth in September.

In July 2009 Bainimarama announced plans for a new Constitution, to be enacted in 2013; the proposed Constitution, it was reported, would amend current land tenure arrangements under which indigenous Fijians owned 90% of land, and would lower the minimum voting age from 21 to 18 years. In late July 2009 President Iloilo, who was 88 years old and reportedly in ill health, announced his retirement, with effect from the beginning of August. (Iloilo died in February 2011.) Vice-President Nailatikau assumed the role in an acting capacity until October, when his position as President, for a term of three years, was confirmed. Bainimarama announced that the newly recreated post of Vice-President would not be filled.

Increasing suppression of dissent

In February 2010 Bainimarama reportedly stated that he would relinquish his role as Prime Minister in advance of the proposed 2014 elections; however, he planned to continue as Commander of the Armed Forces. In March 2010 the interim Prime Minister announced that all politicians who had served since 1987 were to be banned from contesting the 2014 elections. Although the objective was apparently to change the political culture of Fiji, the decision was criticized by observers, who viewed the action as an attempt to influence the composition of the next Government.

In late February 2010 the High Court returned a verdict of guilty in the trial of eight men, including Paramount Chief Ratu Inoke Takiveikata, charged with conspiring to assassinate Bainimarama in 2007; the men were sentenced to terms of imprisonment ranging from three to seven years. In September 2010 the retrial of Takiveikata on charges of inciting the 2000 mutiny began (his original conviction having been declared invalid by the Court of Appeal in 2007—see *The coup of 2000 and its repercussions*); he was convicted in March 2011 and sentenced to life imprisonment.

Meanwhile, in early 2010 the human rights organization Amnesty International reiterated its concerns regarding the situation in Fiji, drawing attention to the continued use of intimidation and discrimination in the suppression of freedom of expression and to the constraints placed on the independence of the judiciary. In April, furthermore, proposals for the permanent imposition of stringent restrictions on the media provoked widespread criticism. The Media Industry Development Decree, which was to replace the emergency regulations implemented 12 months previously, would permit the authorities to enter news premises and seize any documentation, materials or equipment. The draft decree provided for hefty fines on media outlets found to have breached the regulations, while individual journalists, editors and publishers risked prison sentences in addition to substantial fines. Restrictions were also imposed on foreign ownership of the media. The decree was enacted in June, whereupon it was announced that within three months all media organizations should have at least 90% Fijian ownership or risk closure. It was feared that the country's principal daily newspaper, the Australian-owned *Fiji Times*, would therefore be forced to close. In September, however, ownership of the newspaper was sold to a Suva-based company.

The interim Deputy Prime Minister and Minister for Defence, National Security and Immigration, Ratu Epeli Ganilau,

resigned from his post in November 2010, after disagreeing with a decision to deport an executive of the US-owned company Fiji Water (see *Foreign Affairs*).

In early March 2011, despite a renewed appeal by Amnesty International that the Government respect the right to protest, plans for an anti-Government demonstration were cancelled owing to the presence of large numbers of security personnel at the proposed venue for the rally. Amnesty International claimed that over the previous fortnight at least 10 politicians, trade unionists, critics of the Government and others had been arbitrarily arrested and subjected to severe physical assaults and other mistreatment by the Fiji military.

In May 2011 former army Chief of Staff Lt-Col Ratu Tevita Mara, son of the late former Prime Minister Ratu Sir Kamisese Mara, and former Commander of the Land Force Brig.-Gen. Pita Driti were charged with sedition and inciting mutiny after allegedly plotting to overthrow Bainimarama. Both men refuted the claims against them, insisting that the charges had been fabricated by the regime. Lt-Col Mara fled to Tonga a few days later, precipitating a diplomatic dispute between the Fijian and Tongan Governments (see *Foreign Affairs*).

In June 2011 it was announced that a dedicated Ministry of Sugar was to be established in Lautoka, on the west coast of Viti Levu, as part of government efforts to reform and revitalize the industry. Bainimarama was to retain responsibility for the portfolio, while Manasa Vaniqi was appointed to the newly created role of Permanent Secretary for Sugar.

In October 2011 Daniel Urai Manufolau, the President of the FTUC, was arrested on his return to Fiji from Australia, where he had met with a number of officials, including Prime Minister Julia Gillard, to discuss his concerns about the Bainimarama regime; he was subsequently charged with inciting political violence, having allegedly plotted to overthrow the interim Government. Urai, who staunchly denied the charges against him as a politically motivated fabrication, was released on bail in November. Also in November the interim Government implemented the Essential National Industries Employment Decree, which prohibited trade unions from operating in selected industries, including the national airline, four major banks, broadcasting and telecommunications, and utilities.

In September 2011 Bainimarama offered assurances that a new constitution would be drafted between September 2012 and September 2013, and pledged that the charter would establish a fully representative government based on an electoral system guaranteeing equal suffrage. The interim Prime Minister also announced that preparatory work was to commence in January 2012 on compiling an electronic register of voters for the legislative elections scheduled to take place in 2014.

In July 2012 former Prime Minister Qarase was found guilty of abuse of office and discharge of duty—charges first brought against him in 2008 (see *The coup of 2006 and abrogation of the Constitution*)—and was sentenced to one year in prison in August; he was released in April 2013, having served eight months of his sentence.

The Public Order Act and new Constitution

The Public Emergency Decree in place since 2009 was rescinded in January 2012, in a development that was widely welcomed both within Fiji and further afield. However, hopes that the announcement might constitute an important development towards the restoration of democracy and augur an improvement in basic freedoms and human rights were dashed shortly afterwards, when the details of a new Public Order Act that had been introduced in place of the emergency regulations were revealed. The highly controversial new legislation stipulated, *inter alia*, that actions taken by the Prime Minister or senior police officers could not be legally challenged; afforded the police new, wideranging powers, including the right to use force to disperse gatherings deemed to constitute a threat to public safety; and imposed tighter controls on individuals suspected of breaking the law, as well as on the staging of meetings and other public gatherings. Widely regarded as being more repressive than the emergency decree that it replaced, the Public Order Act provoked expressions of concern and disappointment from prominent figures within Fiji and the international community.

In early March 2012 Bainimarama outlined plans for the preparation of the new constitution: following a civic education programme and public consultations, a five-member Constitutional Commission would submit a draft charter for consideration by a Constituent Assembly, comprising representatives of civil society groups, faith-based organizations, national institutions, political parties and the Government. Bainimarama announced in mid-March that President Nailatikau had approved a decree formally abolishing the Great Council of Chiefs (established by the British in 1876 as the Native Council) on the grounds that it had become highly politicized and 'perpetuated élitism'. The FLP criticized the move, asserting that the dissolution of the Council was a matter for indigenous Fijians to decide, while others accused the interim Government of seeking to curb potential dissent prior to negotiations on the new constitution. On 12 November Nailatikau was reappointed to serve a further three-year presidential term under an executive decree issued by the interim Government. Also in November Kenyan constitutional expert Prof. Yash Ghai, the Chairman of the Constitutional Commission, which had been established in April and sworn in by the Chief Justice in July, claimed that the body had suffered harassment at the hands of the Government. The following month a draft constitution was submitted to President Nailatikau; however, the Constituent Assembly, which was to review the document in January–February 2013, had not yet been established and no public consultations had taken place (as originally planned) prior to the submission of the draft. Furthermore, Prof. Ghai alleged that the day after the draft constitution had been presented to Nailatikau the police confiscated all 600 printed copies of the document that were due to be distributed to the public, claiming that their production was illegal; the Constitutional Commission subsequently published the draft charter on the internet.

In January 2013 Bainimarama announced that the draft constitution was to be amended by the Office of the Attorney-General prior to being submitted to the Constituent Assembly. In the same month the Government approved a decree requiring all 17 existing political parties to re-register by 14 February to contest the next legislative elections. An increase in the membership threshold from 180 members to 5,000 to qualify for registration as a political party was regarded as a significant bar to both existing and new parties, notably prompting the dissolution of the UPP in late January, while the SDL was renamed the Social Democratic Liberal Party (SODELPA) to conform with another new stipulation, that political parties have English rather than Fijian names. A further condition of registration was a ban on membership for civil servants, the armed forces and trade union officials. In mid-March the interim Prime Minister declared that the revised draft constitution had been completed, but that the formation of the Constituent Assembly had been delayed owing to difficulties in the registration of political parties (which were to be represented in the Assembly). On 21 March Bainimarama announced that the plan to form a Constituent Assembly had been abandoned. Instead, the draft constitution produced by the Office of the Attorney-General was released immediately for public consultation. In early May Registrar Mohammed Saneem announced that three political parties had been successful in applying for re-registration—the NFP, the FLP and SODELPA. In addition, at the end of the month a new party, the People's Democratic Party (PDP), which was supported by the FTUC and headed by former cabinet minister Adi Sivia Qoro, was officially registered. In June an appeals court confirmed that Qarase was disqualified from leading SODELPA as a result of his former conviction.

The final version of the new Constitution, which stipulated that the next parliamentary elections be held by 30 September 2014, was published on 23 August 2013. The charter provided for a unicameral Parliament, composed of 50 members elected by proportional representation for a four-year term, and a President appointed by Parliament for a three-year term (renewable only once). It also granted immunity from criminal prosecution to all those who since the 2006 coup had either held office as President, Prime Minister or government minister or who had served in the military forces, the police, the corrections service, the judiciary or the public service. Also on 23 August Bainimarama announced his intention to establish a new political party to contest the 2014 legislative elections. Having been approved by President Nailatikau, the new Constitution entered into force on 6 September 2013. The charter was criticized by the international non-governmental organization Human Rights Watch for the restrictions that it placed on basic human rights, including freedom of expression, workers' rights, and freedom of assembly and association. It also attracted widespread opprobrium for its provision of full and irrevocable immunity to those who had been involved in the 2006 coup.

Recent developments: the 2014 legislative elections and restitution of democratic governance

In January 2014 Attorney-General Aiyaz Sayed-Khaiyum announced the composition of a seven-member Electoral Commission, which was to oversee the forthcoming legislative elections. Bainimarama stood down as Commander of the Armed Forces in early March in order, as a civilian, to be able to contest the elections. He was promoted to the rank of Rear Admiral on his retirement in recognition of his distinguished service. Later in March the Government announced that the elections were to be held on 17 September. At the end of March the interim Prime Minister launched a new political party, FijiFirst; despite objections raised by the opposition to the validity of its application registration, the party was officially recognized on 30 May and was to have Bainimarama as its leader and the Minister for Women, Social Welfare and Poverty Alleviation, Dr Jiko Luveni, as its President. Meanwhile, the opposition suffered a setback in April when Chaudhry was found guilty by the High Court in Suva of breaching the Exchange Control Act, thereby rendering him ineligible to contest the elections. On the day before the elections were held the Government announced the appointment of Viniana Namosimalua to the new, non-partisan post of Secretary-General to Parliament (as specified in the 2013 Constitution). Together with her deputy, Mary Qiliaso, Namosimalua was to be responsible, for parliamentary procedural and clerical administration.

In the legislative elections, which were held as scheduled on 17 September 2014, marking the restoration of democracy to Fiji after almost eight years, FijiFirst won an outright majority of 32 of the 50 seats in Parliament (with 59.2% of the vote), SODELPA secured 15 seats (28.2%) and the NFP three (5.5%); both the PDP and FLP failed to gain representation. Turnout was 84%. Despite allegations made by the opposition of systematic electoral malpractice, which were promptly rejected as unfounded by the Electoral Commission, the Multinational Observer Group claimed that the poll was credible. Bainimarama was sworn in as Prime Minister on 22 September. On the following day the leader of SODELPA, Ro Teimumu Kepa, was officially selected as the parliamentary leader of the opposition, and on 24 September the new Cabinet was sworn in; the Prime Minister assumed responsibility for the portfolios covering iTaukei affairs and sugar, Ratu Inoke Kubuabola remained as Minister for Foreign Affairs, while Attorney-General Sayed-Khaiyum was placed in charge of justice, finance, public enterprises, public service and communications. On the same day Bainimarama confirmed the appointment of Dr Luveni as Fiji's first female Speaker of Parliament.

A Fijian government delegation, led by Attorney-General Sayed-Khaiyum, visited the UN headquarters in Geneva, Switzerland, in October 2014 to discuss the findings of the second universal periodic review of Fiji's human rights situation by the UN Human Rights Council (UNHRC). Despite the recent progress made by Fiji in the field of democratization and Sayed-Khaiyum's assertion that the majority of the recommendations made by the UNHRC following Fiji's first such review (in 2009) had been implemented, the UN none the less demanded, *inter alia*, that the Constitution be reviewed by a special commission in order genuinely to reflect the will of the people, that the 2010 Media Industry Development Decree be repealed and that Fijians be allowed freely to express themselves without fear of arbitrary arrest. Presenting the Government's response to the UNHRC's demands in March 2015, Sayed-Khaiyum notably refused to repeal the media decree and claimed that the establishment of a special commission on the Constitution would violate the charter's own provisions on constitutional change. Recommendations accepted included the ratification of the UN Convention against Torture and Other Cruel, Inhuman or Degrading Treatment or Punishment and the creation of a legislative framework to address violence against women.

In February 2015 Prime Minister Bainimarama announced that a competition would be held to design a new flag for introduction by the 45th anniversary of Fiji's independence in October, emphasizing the need to remove colonial symbols. Opposition leaders criticized the plans as undemocratic, asserting that any change should be initiated in Parliament and approved by national referendum.

Land Ownership Issues

In September 1995 the Government transferred all state land (comprising some 10% of Fiji's total land area), hitherto administered by the Government Lands Department, to be administered by the iTaukei Land Trust Board (TLTB, which was founded in 1940 as the Native Land Trust Board) in order to allow the allocation of land to indigenous Fijians on the basis of native custom. However, concern among Fijian Indians increased following reports in early 1996 that many would not be able to renew their land leases (most of which were due to expire between 1997 and 2024) under the 1976 Agricultural Landlord and Tenant Act (ALTA). The reports were strongly denied by the Government, despite statements by several Fijian land-owning clans that Indians' leases would not be renewed. Moreover, a recently formed sugar cane growers' association solely for ethnic Fijians, the Taukei Cane Growers' Association, announced its intention to campaign for ethnic Fijian control of the sugar industry, largely by refusing to renew land leases to ethnic Indians (who held some 85% of sugar farm leases). By the end of 2000 almost 2,000 land leases had expired, leaving many tenant farmers and their families homeless. Some 70 farmers, who had expressed a wish not to be resettled, received rehabilitation grants of $F28,000 in December 2000, although the authorities were criticized for their apparent slowness in processing the applications. In January 2001 the Government proposed that the administration of native land leases be transferred from the ALTA to the Native Land Trust Act (NLTA), prompting fears of increased bias in favour of ethnic Fijian landowners and further instability in the sugar industry. A further 1,500 leases expired during 2001.

A dispute between tribal landowners and the Government over compensation payments for land flooded by the Monosavu hydroelectric power station led to violence in July 1998. Landowners, who had been demanding compensation since the plant's construction in 1983, seized control of the station and carried out a series of arson attacks. The dispute finally ended in October 2005 when landowners were paid a total of $A40m. in compensation for the use of their land by the Fiji Electricity Authority.

Meanwhile, the issue of the expiry of land leases continued to threaten Fiji's vital sugar industry. A committee, comprising members of both the SDL and FLP, was established to try to negotiate land leases that would satisfy both Indian Fijian tenants and their predominantly ethnic Fijian landowners. Most of the 30-year leases drawn up under the ALTA were expiring, and both tenants and the FLP were opposed to its replacement by the NLTA, which they saw as disproportionately favouring landowners. Two parliamentary bills had been approved by the Senate in April 2002, reducing the land under state control to around 1% of the total and increasing the amount under the TLTB to over 90%. In August, however, the FLP withdrew from a second session of discussions on the issue of land leases. During 2003 more than 1,100 tenants on Vanua Levu were evicted following the expiry of their land leases. By late 2005 more than 3,500 farmers had received a total of $F26m. in assistance under the ALTA. In May 2009 the Fiji Independent Commission Against Corruption began an investigation into the TLTB's lease renewal procedures. In July 2010 the Government approved a new land reform programme; under the Land Use Decree, the ALTA was to be revoked and all leases of native land would thenceforth come under the legal framework of the NLTA. In addition, the tenure of indigenous land was to be extended from 30 years to up to 99 years.

Foreign Affairs

Relations between Fiji and India deteriorated as a result of the coup of May 1987, following which many ethnic Indians emigrated. In November 1989 the Fijian Government expelled the Indian high commissioner for allegedly interfering in Fiji's internal affairs, and the status of the Indian high commission was downgraded to that of a consulate. Following the adoption of significant constitutional reforms in 1997, diplomatic relations between Fiji and India improved considerably, and in October the Indian Government invited Fiji to open a high commission in New Delhi. In February 1999 India removed its trade embargo against Fiji (which had been in force for 10 years), and in May India reopened its high commission in Suva.

However, Fiji's relations with the international community suffered a major reversal following the coup of May 2000. In June Fiji was partially suspended from the Commonwealth (having been readmitted in October 1997 following its expulsion as a result of the coups of 1987) and a delegation from the organization visited the islands to demand the reinstatement of the 1997 Constitution. Australia, New Zealand and the Commonwealth withheld formal recognition of Qarase's Government when Parliament opened in October 2001, but in December the Commonwealth Ministerial Action Group recommended that Fiji be readmitted to meetings of the Commonwealth. In November 2002 Qarase's Government confirmed its intention to reopen the Fijian high commission in India, claiming that it was needed to cater for the new business and diplomatic links being fostered by the administration. (The mission was reopened in April 2004.) Sanctions imposed by the EU remained in place until early 2002. In late 2003 the EU announced the resumption of development aid to Fiji (in abeyance since 2000). The EU suspended non-humanitarian aid after the coup of December 2006, which, once again, provoked widespread condemnation from the international community. Australia and New Zealand imposed a number of diplomatic sanctions against Fiji, placed travel restrictions on key military and government officials, and reduced aid, whereas India adopted the policy of engaging with the interim Government rather than isolating it. Fiji was once again partially suspended from the Commonwealth, in December 2006, and, as a result of the Government's lack of progress in restoring democracy, fully suspended in September 2009, a decision that entailed the severance of all Commonwealth aid. In December 2010, nevertheless, the EU concluded an Interim Economic Partnership Agreement with Fiji. Following the successful holding of legislative elections in September 2014, Fiji was reinstated as a full member of the Commonwealth later that month and there was a full resumption of EU aid (notably to the sugar industry).

In 1975 Fiji was the first Pacific island state to establish diplomatic relations with the People's Republic of China. In April 2006 Premier Wen Jiabao of China made an official visit to Fiji in order to promote greater co-operation between the two countries. China's financial support to Fiji, in the form of aid and infrastructure development, was reported to have increased substantially between 2006 and 2009, and China was one of the few nations to maintain such support following the abrogation of Fiji's Constitution in April 2009. Relations between Fiji and China continued to strengthen, with both countries pledging further to bolster bilateral dialogue and co-operation in a wide range of fields, including political and economic engagement. In July–August 2010 Bainimarama visited China, declaring his preference for close relations with that country, rather than with Australia and New Zealand. In September President Nailatikau paid an official visit to China, and in November Bainimarama returned there, at the head of a trade mission. In September 2012, during a visit to Fiji by a high-ranking Chinese delegation, the two countries signed further economic agreements, including a US $114m. loan from China towards road construction in Fiji. Ties between Fiji and China were further strengthened in November 2014 when Xi Jinping became the first Chinese President to make an official visit to Fiji; during his visit, Xi addressed a summit attended by the leaders of Fiji and seven other Pacific island states. The high-profile visit by the Chinese head of state followed that of Indian Prime Minister Narendra Modi earlier in the month.

In March 2007 the Pacific Islands Forum Foreign Ministers convened to consider the conclusions of an 'eminent persons' group', which had travelled to Fiji to assess the situation following the coup of December 2006. In addition to its criticism of alleged breaches of human rights, the group had decided that a swift return to democracy was desirable; as a consequence, the Pacific Islands Forum stressed the need for a revised timetable for elections. In August 2008 the interim Prime Minister asserted that the existing schedule for elections in March 2009 was not attainable in view of the need for electoral reforms; Bainimarama subsequently failed to attend a summit meeting of Pacific Islands Forum leaders. Following President Iloilo's abrogation of the Constitution in April 2009 (see *Domestic Political Affairs*), the Pacific Islands Forum set Bainimarama a deadline of 1 May to announce a date for the holding of democratic elections later that year; failure to comply led to Fiji's indefinite suspension from the Forum. In February 2011 the Pacific Islands Forum Foreign Ministers met in Vanuatu, to discuss the situation in Fiji: the Fijian Minister for Foreign Affairs attended the meeting, which concluded that there had not been enough progress towards the restoration of democracy in Fiji for the contact group to recommend that the Forum change its policy on Fiji's membership. In August 2012, despite acknowledging that some advances had been made in the democratic process in Fiji, the Forum again decided to uphold the country's suspension from the organization. Claiming that the Pacific Islands Forum failed adequately to address the needs of the island peoples, Bainimarama established an alternative body (notably excluding Australia and New Zealand), the Pacific Islands Development Forum, which held its inaugural summit meeting in Nadi, Fiji, in August 2013. The meeting, which focused on the environment and sustainable economic development, was attended by the political heads of 14 Pacific island states. In recognition of the restitution of democratic governance to Fiji in September 2014, in the following month the Pacific Islands Forum leaders unanimously voted to lift Fiji's suspension from the regional group. However, the new Fijian Government stated that it did not intend to return to the Forum until some institutional changes were implemented therein; it was widely understood that one of these conditions was that Australia and New Zealand should relinquish their membership of the body.

Fiji's formerly amicable relations with Australia and New Zealand were strained following the coup of December 2006, with the latter two countries being among the harshest critics of Bainimarama's regime (particularly following the abrogation of the Constitution in April 2009). Between 2007 and 2010 a series of reciprocal diplomatic expulsions took place, usually precipitated by Fijian accusations of Australian or New Zealand interference in the country's internal affairs. Following talks held in Sydney, Australia, in July 2012 between the Fijian Minister for Foreign Affairs, Ratu Inoke Kubuabola, and his Australian and New Zealand counterparts, during which the Fijian minister reported on the progress being made towards the holding of democratic elections in 2014 and the drawing up of a new constitution, Australia and New Zealand agreed to restore full diplomatic relations with Fiji (including the exchange of high commissioners) and to be more flexible with travel sanctions. Australia and New Zealand welcomed the successful conduct of legislative elections in September 2014, and commenced the further normalization of relations with Fiji, including the lifting of remaining sanctions and the re-establishment of military ties. In January 2015 a flight by a New Zealand air force aircraft patrolling Fiji's exclusive economic zone marked the formal resumption of bilateral defence links.

In July 2010 a regional organization, the Melanesian Spearhead Group, cancelled a planned meeting at which Bainimarama had been due to assume the rotating chairmanship of the Group: the previous chairman, Edward Natapei, the Prime Minister of Vanuatu, stated that allowing Bainimarama to take the chair would not be in accordance with the organization's democratic ideals. In December, after Natapei had been replaced as Prime Minister of Vanuatu, Bainimarama was permitted to assume the chair of the Melanesian Spearhead Group; the Group's annual summit meeting was convened in Suva in April 2011. In January of that year Fiji held discussions with Kiribati aimed at improving the two countries' economic co-operation, in accordance with an agreement signed in September 2010. A similar agreement had been signed with Tuvalu earlier in 2010. In September 2014, in order to ensure food security for the country, the authorities of Kiribati completed their purchase of a 23-sq-km plot of land on the Fijian island of Vanua Levu, which could also potentially be settled by I-Kiribati in the event that rising sea levels forced them to leave their homeland.

In November 2005 Fiji lodged a complaint with the International Seabed Authority concerning Tonga's sovereignty claims over the uninhabited Teleki (Minerva) Reefs. (Tonga's sovereignty proclamation was made by the Tongan King in June 1972 and was recognized by the South Pacific Forum in September.) Fiji submitted its complaint to UN officials for mediation in February 2011, claiming that the reefs (which lie within the Fijian exclusive economic zone) cannot be recognized by the UN's Convention on the Law of the Sea since they do not represent permanent terrestrial islands. In June the navies of the two countries came close to direct confrontation when the Fijian military dismantled Tonga's navigational equipment on the reefs. Bilateral tensions were also exacerbated by claims made by Bainimarama in May that the Tongan navy had breached Fiji's sovereignty by assisting former army Chief of Staff Lt-Col Tevita Mara to flee from Fiji, where he had been charged with sedition and mutiny (see *Domestic Political Affairs*). Later in May the Tongan Government rejected a Fijian request for Lt-Col Mara's extradition. It was reported in June that Lt-Col Mara had initiated a campaign in Australia to oust the Bainimarama regime. An extradition request subsequently submitted to the Australian Government by Fiji was rejected in July.

Meanwhile, in March 2009 the US ambassador's exhortations to the interim Government to restore democratic rule led to Bainimarama accusing the diplomat of interfering in Fiji's domestic affairs. Although the US authorities continued to refuse officially to recognize Bainimarama's administration, in November 2010 the Fiji Government welcomed a decision by the USA to choose Fiji to host the office of the expanded US aid programme in the Pacific. Relations between Fiji and the USA improved considerably in the latter half of 2014 following the successful holding of legislative elections, and in December representatives of the two countries' respective armed forces met in Suva to discuss military re-engagement.

In May 2013 Fiji hosted a summit meeting of the Group of 77 (G-77) developing countries, which was chaired by interim Prime Minister Bainimarama.

CONSTITUTION AND GOVERNMENT

A new Constitution entered into force on 6 September 2013. Executive power is vested in the President, who is appointed by Parliament for a term of three years (renewable only once). The President is guided by the Cabinet, which conducts the government of the Republic of Fiji and is headed by the Prime Minister. A unicameral Parliament, comprising 50 members elected by proportional representation for a four-year term, exercises legislative power.

REGIONAL AND INTERNATIONAL CO-OPERATION

Fiji is a member of the Asian Development Bank (ADB, see p. 206), the Pacific Community (see p. 410) and the Colombo Plan (see p. 445). The country was suspended from the Pacific Islands Forum (see p. 413) in 2009; Fiji hosted the inaugural summit meeting of a new regional organization, the Pacific Islands Development Forum (see p. 449), in August 2013. Following the restoration of democratic governance in Fiji in September 2014, the country's suspension from the Pacific Islands Forum was lifted in October. Fiji was a signatory of the South Pacific Regional Trade and Economic Co-operation Agreement (SPARTECA), which expired at the end of 2014, and of the Lomé Conventions and successor Cotonou Agreement, see p. 321 with the European Union (EU). Fiji participates in the Melanesian Spearhead Group, which among other benefits provides for free trade among member countries (the others being Papua New Guinea, Solomon Islands and Vanuatu). The country is also a member of the UN's Economic and Social Commission for Asia and the Pacific (ESCAP, see p. 30).

Fiji became a member of the UN in 1970 and joined the World Trade Organization (WTO, see p. 431) in 1996. Fiji is also a member of the International Sugar Organization (see p. 443) and was admitted to the Non-aligned Movement (see p. 462) in May 2011. Fiji was readmitted to the Commonwealth in September 2014, following its partial suspension in 2006 and full suspension in 2009.

ECONOMIC AFFAIRS

In 2013, according to estimates by the World Bank, Fiji's gross national income (GNI), measured at average 2011–13 prices, was US $3,905m., equivalent to $4,430 per head (or $7,610 on an international purchasing-power parity basis). During 2004–13, it was estimated, the population increased at an average annual rate of 0.8%, while gross domestic product (GDP) per head increased, in real terms, by an average of 0.1% per year. Overall GDP rose at an average annual rate of 0.9% over the same period. According to the Asian Development Bank (ADB), GDP increased by 4.6% in 2013 and by 4.2% in 2014.

In 2013 agriculture (including forestry and fishing) contributed a provisional 12.5% of GDP. According to figures from the ADB, at mid-2008 the sector engaged 1.3% of those in paid employment (excluding subsistence workers). The principal cash crop is sugar cane. According to FAO estimates, production of sugar cane increased by 3.5% in 2013. In 2013 sugar and molasses together accounted for an estimated 16.1% of domestic export earnings (excluding re-exports), compared with 40.0% in 1994. Other significant export crops are coconuts and ginger, while the most important subsistence crop is paddy rice, production of which was estimated at 5,000 metric tons in 2013. Since the mid-2000s honey production has become an increasingly significant activity. The most important livestock products are beef and poultry meat. Fiji has significant timber reserves. Lumber accounted for 6.1% of domestic exports in 2013, earning an estimated $F59.1m. Fishing is an important activity, and in 2013 fish earned an estimated $F84.4m. in export revenue (8.6% of domestic export receipts). The entire agricultural sector was disrupted by unusually severe flooding in January 2009, which resulted in major losses of crops and livestock; further severe flooding was experienced in northern and western Fiji in early 2012. Meanwhile, losses also resulted from the impact of cyclones in December 2009, March 2010 and December 2012. According to the World Bank, during 2004–12 growth in agricultural GDP was negligible. The GDP of the agricultural sector increased by 2.6% in 2013, according to official figures.

Industry (including mining, manufacturing, construction and utilities) engaged 30.3% of the employed population at mid-2008. In 2013 the sector provided a provisional 21.2% of GDP. According to the World Bank, the GDP of the industrial sector was estimated to have decreased at an average rate of 0.4% per year during 2004–12. Industrial GDP increased by 5.1% in 2013, according to the official figures.

Mining contributed a provisional 1.1% of GDP in 2013. The sector engaged only 1.0% of the employed population in 2004. Gold-mining operations resumed in October 2007. Gold production decreased from 1,653 kg in 2012 to 1,240 kg in 2013. Silver and copper are also mined. Operations at the country's first bauxite mine, in Nawailevu, commenced in November 2011. According to official figures, during 2008–13 the mining sector's GDP expanded at an average rate of 17.6% per year; mining GDP decreased by 7.9% in 2013.

Manufacturing contributed a provisional 14.7% of GDP in 2013, and engaged 13.6% of paid employees in 2004. The most important branch of the sector is food-processing, in particular sugar, molasses and coconut oil. The bottling of mineral water for export became increasingly important from the early 2000s, and by 2013 exports of mineral water contributed an estimated 16.1% of domestic export earnings. The loss of preferential access to the US market for Fijian garments at the beginning of 2005 substantially reduced export receipts from this source. The contribution of garments to domestic export earnings decreased from 23.8% of total revenue in 2004 to an estimated 10.9% in 2013. According to figures from the World Bank, manufacturing GDP decreased at an estimated average annual rate of 1.6% during 2004–12. According to official figures, sectoral GDP increased by 3.2% in 2013.

Construction contributed a provisional 3.2% of GDP in 2013, and engaged 5.4% of paid employees in 2004. According to official figures, the sector's GDP increased at an estimated average annual rate of 4.5% during 2008–13; construction GDP increased by 18.1% in 2013.

Energy is derived principally from hydroelectric power. Imports of mineral fuels represented an estimated 23.4% of the total cost of imports in 2013. A new wind farm was opened in 2007, as part of a plan for the country to become completely reliant on renewable energy sources.

The services sector engaged 68.4% of the employed population at mid-2008, and contributed a provisional 66.4% of GDP in 2013. Although intermittently affected by political unrest, tourism is a major source of foreign exchange. Visitor arrivals (excluding cruise-ship passengers) reached a record 692,630 in 2014. Australia and New Zealand are the most important sources of visitors. According to figures from the World Bank, during 2004–12 the GDP of the services sector rose at an average annual rate of 1.3%. Sectoral GDP expanded by 4.9% in 2013, according to official figures.

Fiji consistently records a visible merchandise trade deficit; it amounted to US $1,332.2m. in 2013, when the country also recorded a deficit, of US $560.8m., on the current account of the balance of payments. The principal source of imports in 2013 was Singapore (21.0%). Other important suppliers were Australia, New Zealand and the People's Republic of China. The principal market for exports in 2013 was Australia (13.6%). Other important markets included the USA, New Zealand and the UK. The principal imports in 2013 were machinery and transport equipment, followed by mineral fuels, food products, manufactured goods, miscellaneous manufactured articles and chemicals. Fiji's principal domestic exports were sugar, garments, fish, gold and lumber. Fiji also re-exports mineral fuels (including bunkers for ships and aircraft).

The overall budget deficit was estimated by the ADB at $F204.6m. in 2013, equivalent to 3.0% of GDP. In 2014/15 official development assistance from Australia was budgeted at $A61.9m. Aid from New Zealand in 2014/15 was projected at $NZ12.0m. Fiji's general government gross debt was $F3.819m.

in 2013, equivalent to 51.4% of GDP. Fiji's outstanding external debt totalled an estimated US $618m. at the end of 2014. In that year the cost of debt-servicing was equivalent to 1.7% of the revenue from exports of goods and services. The average annual rate of inflation, according to ILO figures, was 4.6% in 2004–13. According to the ADB, consumer prices rose by 0.5% in 2014. An estimated 8.6% of the total labour force were unemployed at mid-2008, according to the ADB. From the late 1980s remittances from Fijians working overseas assumed increasing importance, although in 2007–08 a substantial reduction in this source of income was recorded, partly owing to the decrease in the number of Fijian security personnel employed in the Middle East. Remittances from Fijian personnel serving in the British Army have become a significant source of income. The total value of remittances from overseas workers was US $383.2m. in 2014.

The impact on Fiji's economy of the removal of the elected Government in the military coup of December 2006 was subsequently compounded by the sharp deterioration in global economic conditions in 2008/09 and by the political instability of 2009. In April of that year the Fiji dollar was devalued by 20%. Following severe flooding in January and March–April 2012, which destroyed large areas of export crops (mainly sugar cane) and caused some $F30.6m. worth of damage, Fiji was hit by another natural disaster, in December, when the most powerful cyclone to strike the country in 20 years, Cyclone Evan, resulted in damage costing around $F75m. Despite the adverse impact on the economy of the flooding and Cyclone Evan, particularly on agriculture and tourism, overall GDP growth was 1.8% in 2012. The rate of growth accelerated to 4.6% in 2013 and remained robust in 2014, at 4.2%, partly as a result of increased public expenditure on infrastructure and higher levels of consumption and investment demand. Owing to a considerable increase in public expenditure—including the allocation of $F11m. to the Fiji Electoral Commission to help preparations for the 2014 legislative elections—and the negative impact of Cyclone Evan, according to the ADB, the budget deficit in 2013 reached the equivalent of 3.0% of GDP, compared with 1.6% in 2012. Despite being expansionary in terms of the level of spending, the 2014 budget resulted in a decrease in the fiscal deficit to 2.0% of GDP, largely owing to an increase in revenue from taxation and the privatization of state assets. The budget for 2015 involved a continuation of high levels of expenditure (ostensibly funded by further asset sales) coupled with a general adherence to prudent economic policies—including an increase in compulsory pension contributions. The budget deficit was forecast to expand to around 2.5% of GDP in 2015. The installation of a democratically elected Government in September 2014 following the successful conduct of the general election was expected to lead to renewed business confidence (both domestic and international) and to improve Fiji's access to concessional development finance. While welcoming the progress made, in November the IMF highlighted the following as being among the main policy challenges facing the Government: to reduce unemployment; to accelerate the pace of structural reform in order to increase the economy's resilience to shocks; further to alleviate poverty; to create a better business environment (including greater financial inclusion, upgrading infrastructure and streamlining state regulations); to make land use more efficient; to boost energy supplies; and to improve the monitoring of the financial sector with a view to mitigating the potential risks associated with rapid credit expansion. The ADB, which was to provide Fiji with up to $F350m. in development funding under the new country partnership strategy, covering 2014–18, forecast that GDP growth would moderate slightly in 2015, to 4.0%.

PUBLIC HOLIDAYS

2016: 1 January (New Year's Day), 25–28 March (Easter), 10 October (Fiji Day), 30 October (Deepavali), 11 December* (Birth of the Prophet Muhammad), 25–26 December (Christmas).

* This Islamic holiday is dependent on the lunar calendar and may vary by one or two days from the date given.

Statistical Survey

Sources (unless otherwise stated): Bureau of Statistics, POB 2221, Government Bldgs, Suva; tel. 3315144; fax 3303656; internet www.statsfiji
.gov.fj; Reserve Bank of Fiji, POB 1220, Suva; tel. 3313611; fax 3301688; e-mail info@rbf.gov.fj; internet www.reservebank.gov.fj.

AREA AND POPULATION

Area (incl. the Rotuma group): 18,376 sq km (7,095 sq miles). Land area of 18,333 sq km (7,078 sq miles) consists mainly of the islands of Viti Levu (10,429 sq km—4,027 sq miles) and Vanua Levu (5,556 sq km—2,145 sq miles).

Population: 775,077 at census of 25 August 1996; 837,271 (males 427,176, females 410,095) at census of 16 September 2007; *Mid-2015* (Secretariat of the Pacific Community estimate): 867,013 (Source: Pacific Regional Information System).

Density (at mid-2015): 47.2 per sq km.

Population by Age and Sex (Secretariat of the Pacific Community estimates at mid-2015): *0–14 years:* 241,874 (males 124,958, females 116,916); *15–64 years:* 579,134 (males 296,331, females 282,803); *65 years and over:* 46,005 (males 20,610, females 25,395); *Total* 867,013 (males 441,899, females 425,114). Source: Pacific Regional Information System.

Principal Towns (population at 2007 census): Suva (capital) 74,481; Lautoka 43,473; Nadi 11,685; Lami 10,752; Labasa 7,706; Ba 6,826.

Population by Ethnic Group (2007 census): Fijians 475,739; Indians 313,798; Rotuman 10,771; Chinese 4,704; European 2,953; Others 29,306; *Total* 837,271. Note: Classification of ethnicity reflects national census methodology.

Births, Marriages and Deaths (registrations, 2009 unless otherwise indicated): Live births 18,854 (birth rate 21.4 per 1,000); Marriages 7,443 in 2005 (marriage rate 8.8 per 1,000); Deaths 3,921 (death rate 4.8 per 1,000). *2011:* Live births 20,425 (birth rate 22.7 per 1,000). Source: partly UN, *Population and Vital Statistics Report*.

Life Expectancy (years at birth): 69.7 (males 66.8; females 72.8) in 2012. Source: World Bank, World Development Indicators database.

Economically Active Population (paid employment, persons aged 15 years and over, 2004): Agriculture, hunting, forestry and fishing 89,523; Mining and quarrying 3,222; Manufacturing 43,088; Electricity, gas and water 2,508; Construction 16,950; Trade, restaurants and hotels 66,043; Transport, storage and communications 22,551; Financing, insurance, real estate and business services 10,220; Community, social and personal services 61,936; *Total employed* 316,041. *Mid-2008* (paid employment, '000 persons, unless otherwise indicated): Agriculture 1.7; Industry 39.5; Services 89.1; Total employed 130.3; Unemployed 28.3; Total labour force (incl. subsistence workers) 329.8. Source: partly Asian Development Bank.

HEALTH AND WELFARE

Key Indicators

Total Fertility Rate (children per woman, 2012): 2.6.

Under-5 Mortality Rate (per 1,000 live births, 2012): 22.

HIV/AIDS (% of persons aged 15–49, 2013): 0.1.

Physicians (per 1,000 head, 2009): 0.4.

Hospital Beds (per 1,000 head, 2009): 2.1.

Health Expenditure (2012): US $ per head (PPP): 181.

Health Expenditure (2012): % of GDP: 3.8.

Health Expenditure (2012): public (% of total): 65.3.

Access to Water (% of persons, 2012): 96.

Access to Sanitation (% of persons, 2012): 87.

Total Carbon Dioxide Emissions ('000 metric tons, 2010): 1,290.8.

Carbon Dioxide Emissions Per Head (metric tons, 2010): 1.5.

Human Development Index (2013): ranking: 88.

Human Development Index (2013): value: 0.724.

For sources and definitions, see explanatory note on p. vi.

AGRICULTURE, ETC.

Principal Crops ('000 metric tons, 2013, FAO estimates): Sugar cane 1,600; Coconuts 225.0; Rice, paddy 5.0 Cassava 94.0; Sweet potatoes 9.0; Yams 5.6; Taro 80.0; Aubergines (Eggplants) 3.8; Bananas 3.5; Pineapples 2.0; Ginger 2.5.

Livestock ('000 head, year ending 2013, FAO estimates): Cattle 312; Pigs 147; Sheep 6; Goats 251; Horses 47; Chickens 4,900; Ducks 100; Turkeys 75.

Livestock Products (metric tons, 2013, FAO estimates): Poultry meat 16,882; Cattle meat 7,600; Goat meat 209; Pig meat 4,050; Hen eggs 6,000; Cows' milk 61,400; Honey 335.

Forestry ('000 cu m, 2013, FAO estimates): *Roundwood Removals* (excl. bark): Sawlogs and veneer logs 233; Pulpwood 206; Other industrial wood 6; Fuel wood 37; Total 482. *Sawnwood Production* (incl. sleepers): 90.

Fishing ('000 metric tons, live weight, 2012): Capture 45.0 (FAO estimate) (Albacore 10.2; Yellowfin tuna 3.2; Other marine fishes 20.1 (FAO estimate); Crustaceans 0.2 (FAO estimate); Molluscs 2.4); Aquaculture 0.2 (FAO estimate); *Total catch* 45.2 (FAO estimate).

Source: FAO.

MINING

Production (kg, 2013): Gold 1,240; Silver 225 (Source: US Geological Survey).

INDUSTRY

Production (metric tons, 2012, unless otherwise indicated): Sugar 155,000; Molasses 67,000; Coconut oil 4,765 (2011); Flour 98,471 (2011); Soap 2,765; Cement 150,000; Paint ('000 litres) 4,162; Beer ('000 litres) 32,000; Soft drinks ('000 litres) 184,947; Cigarettes 457 (2011); Matches ('000 gross boxes) 106; Electric energy (million kWh) 869; Ice cream ('000 litres) 2,643; Toilet paper ('000 rolls) 18,197.

FINANCE

Currency and Exchange Rates: 100 cents = 1 Fiji dollar ($F). *Sterling, US Dollar and Euro Equivalents* (31 December 2014): £1 sterling = $F3.102; US $1 = $F1.988; €1 = $F2.413; $F100 = £32.23 = US $50.31 = €41.44. *Average Exchange Rate* ($F per US $): 1.7899 in 2012; 1.8414 in 2013; 1.8873 in 2014.

General Budget ($F million, 2012): *Revenue:* Current revenue 1,846.0 (Taxes 1,682.6, Non-taxes 163.4); Capital revenue 36.4; Grants 18.0; Total 1,900.4. *Expenditure:* General public services 247.9; Defence 100.1; Education 214.9; Health 130.3; Social security and welfare 6.1; Housing and community amenities 13.0; Economic services 124.7 (Agriculture 24.0; Industry 28.0; Transport, communications and other services 72.7); Total (incl. others) 2,018.3 (Current 1,463.9, Capital 553.3, Net lending 1.0). *2013* Current revenue 2,011.3 (Taxes 1,825.6, Non-taxes 185.7); Capital revenue 21.9; Grants 19.4; Total revenue 2,052.5. Current expenditure 1,546.6, Capital expenditure 709.5, Net lending 1.0 Total expenditure 2,257.1. Source: Asian Development Bank.

International Reserves (US $ million at 31 December 2013): Gold (valued at market-related prices) 1.00; IMF special drawing rights 78.67; Reserve position in IMF 25.47; Foreign exchange 836.73; *Total* 941.86. Source: IMF, *International Financial Statistics*.

Money Supply ($F million at 31 December 2013): Currency outside depository corporations 441.6; Transferable deposits 3,068.0; Other deposits 2,094.2; Securities other than shares 119.2; *Broad money* 5,723.0. Source: IMF, *International Financial Statistics*.

Cost of Living (Consumer Price Index; base: 2008 = 100): All items 116.4 in 2011; 119.4 in 2012; 123.5 in 2013.

Gross Domestic Product ($F million at at constant 2008 prices): 4,932.8 in 2011; 5,023.1 in 2012; 5,255.6 in 2013 (provisional).

Expenditure on the Gross Domestic Product ($F million at current prices, 2011, preliminary): Government final consumption expenditure 908.1; Private final consumption expenditure 4,492.0; Increase in stocks 206.0; Gross fixed capital formation 1,324.0; *Total domestic expenditure* 6,930.1; Exports of goods and services 3,994.0; *Less* Imports of goods and services 4,193.0; *GDP in purchasers' values* 6,731.0. Source: Asian Development Bank.

Gross Domestic Product by Economic Activity ($F million at current prices, 2013, provisional): Agriculture, forestry and fishing 749.4; Mining and quarrying 65.3; Manufacturing 883.2; Electricity, gas and water 128.7; Construction 195.1; Wholesale and retail trade, hotels and restaurants 1,174.1; Transport and communications 801.7; Finance, real estate, etc. 1,181.9; Public administration and defence 338.5; Education 261.6; Health and social work 100.8; Other community, social and personal service activities 133.6; *Sub-total*

6,014.0; Indirect taxes, less subsidies 1,414.0; *GDP in purchasers' values* 7,428.0.

Balance of Payments (US \$ million, 2013): Exports of goods f.o.b. 1,047.5; Imports of goods f.o.b. –2,379.7; *Balance on goods* –1,332.2; Exports of services 1,223.7; Imports of services –564.3; *Balance on goods and services* –672.9; Primary income received 62.1; Primary income paid –155.6; *Balance on goods, services and income* –766.4; Current transfers received 279.3; Current transfers paid –73.8; *Current balance* –560.8; Capital account (net) 4.8; Direct investment assets –4.7; Direct investment liabilities 158.2; Other investment assets –77.5; Other investment liabilities 257.8; Net errors and omissions 296.3; *Reserves and related items* 74.1 (Source: IMF, *International Financial Statistics*).

EXTERNAL TRADE

Principal Commodities (\$F million, 2013, provisional): *Imports c.i.f.* Food products 747.7; Mineral fuels 1,219.9; Chemicals 337.9; Manufactured goods 560.0; Machinery and transport equipment 1,824.2; Miscellaneous manufactured articles 359.2; Total (incl. others) 5,206.5. *Exports f.o.b.:* Fish 84.4; Sugar 142.1; Garments 106.7; Lumber 59.1; Gold 82.0; Total (incl. others) 976.5 (excl. re-exports 1,068.4).

Principal Trading Partners (\$F million, 2013, provisional): *Imports c.i.f.:* Australia 706.6; China, People's Republic 518.8; Hong Kong 94.3; India 89.6; Japan 126.6; New Zealand 634.5; Singapore 1,094.8; Taiwan 62.9; United Kingdom 60.0; USA 235.7; Total (incl. others) 5,206.5. *Exports (incl. re-exports):* Australia 277.8; China, People's Republic 53.3; Hong Kong 29.2; Japan 57.5; New Zealand 109.2; Taiwan 24.0; United Kingdom 108.2; USA 264.3; Total (incl. others) 2,044.9.

TRANSPORT

Road Traffic (motor vehicles registered at 31 December 2012, provisional): Private cars 92,717; Goods vehicles 46,687; Buses 2,461; Taxis 6,556; Rental vehicles 8,036; Motorcycles 5,165; Tractors 6,157; Total (incl. others) 176,598.

Shipping: *Flag Registered Fleet* (at 31 December 2014): Vessels 35; Total displacement (grt) 32,661. Source: Lloyd's List Intelligence (www.lloydslistintelligence.com).

Civil Aviation (traffic on scheduled services, 2011): Kilometres flown 21 million; Passengers carried 1,276,205; Passenger-km 3,895 million; Total ton-km 404.0 million. Source: UN, *Statistical Year-*

book. Passengers carried ('000): 1,225 in 2012; 1,206 in 2013 (Source: World Bank, World Development Indicators database).

TOURISM

Foreign Visitors by Country of Residence (excluding cruise-ship passengers, 2013, provisional): Australia 340,151; Canada 13,052; New Zealand 108,239; Pacific Islands 39,450; United Kingdom 17,209; USA 55,385; Total (incl. others) 657,706.

Tourism Receipts (\$F million): 1,287.0 in 2011; 1,303.0 in 2012; 1,318.0 in 2013 (provisional).

COMMUNICATIONS MEDIA

Telephones (2013): 74,989 main lines in use.

Mobile Cellular Telephones (2013): 891,004 subscribers.

Internet Subscribers (2011): 39,900.

Broadband Subscribers (at 31 December 2013): 10,535.

Source: International Telecommunication Union.

EDUCATION
(at 30 June 2013 unless otherwise indicated)

Pre-Primary: 451 schools (2003); 264 teachers (2002); 7,076 pupils (2002).

Primary: 729 schools; 5,378 teachers; 135,526 pupils. Source: Ministry of Education, National Heritage, Culture and Arts, Suva.

General Secondary: 177 schools; 4,650 teachers; 67,631 pupils. Source: Ministry of Education, National Heritage, Culture and Arts, Suva.

Vocational and Special: 23 institutions; 302 teachers; 2,387 students (2009).

Teacher Training (2009): 4 institutions; 88 teachers; 633 students.

Medical (1989): 2 institutions; 493 students.

University (2004): 1 institution; 289 teachers; 16,444 students.

Pupil-teacher Ratio (primary education, UNESCO estimate): 28.0 in 2011/12.

Adult Literacy Rate (UN estimate, 1995–99): 92.9% (males 94.5%; females 91.4%). Source: UN Development Programme, *Human Development Report*.

Directory

The Government
HEAD OF STATE

President: Ratu EPELI NAILATIKAU (appointed Acting President 30 July 2009; inaugurated as President 5 Nov. 2009; reappointed 12 Nov. 2012).

CABINET
(April 2015)

Prime Minister and Minister for iTaukei Affairs and the Sugar Industry: Rear Adm. (retd) VOREQE (FRANK) BAINIMARAMA.

Attorney-General and Minister for Finance, Public Enterprises, Public Service and Communications: AIYAZ SAYED-KHAIYUM.

Minister for Industry, Trade and Tourism: FAIYAZ KOYA.

Minister for Infrastructure and Transport: PIO TIKODUADUA.

Minister for Local Government, Housing and Environment: PRAVEEN KUMAR BALA.

Minister for Lands and Mineral Resources: MERESEINI VUNIWAQA.

Minister for Fisheries and Forests: OSEA NAIQAMU.

Minister for Agriculture, Rural and Maritime Development, and National Disaster Management: INIA SERUIRATU.

Minister for Foreign Affairs: Ratu INOKE KUBUABOLA.

Minister for Immigration, National Security and Defence: TIMOCI LESI NATUVA.

Minister for Health and Medical Services: JONE USAMATE.

Minister for Education, Heritage, Arts and National Archives: Dr MAHENDRA REDDY.

Minister for Employment, Productivity and Industrial Relations: Brig.-Gen. JIOJI KONUSI KONROTE.

Minister for Youth and Sports: LAISENIA TUITUBOU.

Minister for Women, Children and Poverty Alleviation: ROSY SOFIA AKBAR.

MINISTRIES

Office of the President: Government House, Berkley Cres., Government Bldgs, POB 2513, Suva; tel. 3314244; fax 3301645.

Office of the Prime Minister: Government Bldgs, POB 2353, Suva; tel. 3211201; fax 3306034; e-mail pmsoffice@connect.com.fj; internet www.pmoffice.gov.fj.

Office of the Attorney-General: Government Bldgs, Victoria Parade, POB 2213, Suva; tel. 3309866; fax 3305421; internet www.ag.gov.fj.

Ministry of Agriculture, Rural and Maritime Development, and National Disaster Management: Hugh Robinson Complex, Grantham Rd, Raiwaqa, Suva; tel. 3384233; fax 3385234; e-mail agrihelp@govnet.gov.fj; internet www.agriculture.gov.fj.

Ministry of Education, Heritage, Arts (and National Archives): Marela House, Thurston St, PMB, Suva; tel. 3314477; fax 3314757; internet www.education.gov.fj.

Ministry of Employment, Productivity and Industrial Relations: Government Bldgs, POB 2216, Suva; tel. 3303500; fax 3304701; e-mail vilimone.baledrokadroka@govnet.gov.fj; internet www.labour.gov.fj.

Ministry of Finance, Public Enterprises, Public Service, and Communications: Government Bldgs, POB 2212, Suva; tel. 3307011; fax 3300834; e-mail psfinance@govnet.gov.fj.

Ministry of Fisheries and Forests: Government Bldgs, POB 2218, Suva; tel. 3301611; fax 3318693; internet www.fisheries.gov.fj.

Ministry of Foreign Affairs: Government Bldgs, POB 2220, Suva; tel. 3309645; fax 3317580; e-mail info@foreignaffairs.gov.fj; internet www.foreignaffairs.gov.fj.

Ministry of Health and Medical Services: Government Bldgs, POB 2223, Suva; tel. 3306177; fax 3306163; e-mail info@health.gov.fj; internet www.health.gov.fj.

Ministry of Immigration, National Security and Defence: Government Bldgs, POB 2349, Suva; tel. 3211401; fax 3300346; e-mail infohomaff@govnet.gov.fj.

Ministry of Industry, Trade and Tourism: Government Bldgs, POB 2118, Suva; tel. 3305411; fax 3310816; internet www.mit.gov.fj.

Ministry of Infrastructure and Transport: Neptune House, Walu Bay, Suva; tel. 3316876; fax 3307839; e-mail svatucawaqa@govnet.gov.fj.

Ministry of iTaukei Affairs: Government Bldgs, POB 2100, Suva; tel. 3100909; fax 3312530; e-mail tvolau@govnet.gov.fj; internet www.fijianaffairs.gov.fj.

Ministry of Lands and Mineral Resources: Government Bldgs, POB 2222, Suva; tel. 3313555; fax 3302730; e-mail lis@lands.gov.fj; internet www.lands.gov.fj.

Ministry of Local Government, Housing and Environment: Government Bldgs, POB 2131, Suva; tel. 3304364; fax 3303515; e-mail msovaki@govnet.gov.fj.

Ministry of Rural and Maritime Development and National Disaster Management: Government Bldgs, POB 2219, Suva; tel. 3313400; fax 3313035; internet www.ruraldev.gov.fj.

Ministry of Sugar: Sugar House, Marine Dr., Walu St, Lautoka.

Ministry of Women, Children and Poverty Alleviation: POB 14068, Suva; tel. 3312681; fax 3312357; internet www.welfare-women.gov.fj.

Ministry of Youth and Sports: Government Bldgs, POB 2448, Suva; tel. 3315960; fax 3305348; e-mail info@youth.gov.fj; internet www.youth.gov.fj.

Legislature

Speaker: Dr JIKO LUVENI.

Deputy Speaker: RUVENI NADALO.

General Election, 17 September 2014

Party	Votes	% of votes	Seats
FijiFirst	293,714	59.20	32
Social Democratic Liberal Party (SODELPA)	139,857	28.20	15
National Federation Party (NFP)	27,066	5.50	3
People's Democratic Party (PDP)	15,864	3.20	—
Fiji Labour Party (FLP)	11,670	2.40	—
One Fiji Party (OFP)	5,839	1.20	—
Fiji United Freedom Party (FUFP)	1072	0.20	—
Independents	1,282	0.20	—
Total	496,364	100.00	50

Election Commission

Fiji Electoral Commission: 59–63 Upper High St, Toorak, Suva; tel. 3316225; fax 3302436; internet www.electionsfiji.org; Chair. CHEN BUNN YOUNG; Supervisor of Elections MOHAMMED SANEEM.

Political Organizations

Existing political organizations were required to reregister to contest the general election in 2014; the membership threshold required to achieve registration was notably increased from 180 members to 5,000.

FijiFirst: 96 Brown St, POB 555, Suva; internet fijifirst.com; f. 2014; Leader Cdre FRANK (VOREQE) BAINIMARAMA; Pres. Dr JIKO LUVENI; Gen. Sec. AIYAZ SAYED-KHAIYUM.

Fiji Labour Party (FLP): Government Bldgs, POB 2162, Suva; tel. 3373317; fax 3373173; e-mail flp@connect.com.fj; internet www.flp.org.fj; f. 1985; Pres. LAVENIA PADARATH; Sec.-Gen. MAHENDRA PAL CHAUDHRY.

Fiji United Freedom Party (FUFP): 25 Danesh Karsanji, Rifle Range, Vutawaqa; tel. 7889999; e-mail fijiunitedfreedomparty@gmail.com; f. 2014; Leader JAGATH KARUNARATNE.

National Federation Party (NFP): 124 Princes Rd, Tamavua, POB 4399, Samabula; tel. 3305811; fax 3305317; f. 1960; est. by merger of the multiracial (but mainly Indian) Fed. Party and Nat. Democratic Party; Pres. TUPOU DRAUNIDALO; Leader BIMAN PRASAD; Gen. Sec. KAMAL IYER.

One Fiji Party (OFP): Govt Bldg, POB 2428, Suva; tel. 9061364; e-mail media@onefiji.org.fj; internet www.onefiji.org.fj; f. 2014; Leader SITIVENI SUVAKI KALOU.

People's Democratic Party (PDP): 103 Gordon St, POB 16076, Suva; internet www.pdpfiji.com; f. 2013; backed by the Fiji Trades Union Congress; Pres. LYNDA TABUYA; Gen. Sec. AMAN RAVINDRA SINGH.

Social Democratic Liberal Party (SODELPA): 66 McGregor St, POB 17889, Suva; tel. 3301544; e-mail info@sodelpa.org; internet www.sodelpa.org; f. 2013 from fmr Soqosoqo Duavata ni Lewenivanua (Fiji United Party, f. 2001); Leader RO TEIMUMU KEPA; Gen. Sec. PIO TABAIWALU.

The Fiji Democracy and Freedom Movement (Pres. USAIA WAQATAIREWA) was established in Australia in 2009. Based in New Zealand, the Coalition for Democracy in Fiji was formed in 1987. Supporters of secession are concentrated in Rotuma.

Diplomatic Representation

EMBASSIES AND HIGH COMMISSIONS IN FIJI

Australia: 37 Princes Rd, POB 214, Suva; tel. 3382211; fax 3382065; e-mail public-affairs-suva@dfat.gov.au; internet www.fiji.embassy.gov.au; High Commissioner MARGARET EILEEN TWOMEY.

China, People's Republic: 183 Queen Elizabeth Dr., PMB, Nasese, Suva; tel. 3300215; fax 3300950; e-mail chinaemb_fj@mfa.gov.cn; internet fj.china-embassy.org/chn; Ambassador ZHANG PING.

France: Dominion House, 7th Floor, Thomson St, Suva; tel. 3310526; fax 3323901; e-mail presse@ambafrance-fj.org; internet www.ambafrance-fj.org; Ambassador MICHEL DJOKOVIC.

India: LICI Bldg, Butt St, POB 471, Suva; tel. 3301125; fax 3301032; e-mail admn.suva@mea.gov.in; internet www.indianhighcommissionfiji.org; High Commissioner ANUMULA GITESH SARMA.

Indonesia: Ra Marama Bldg, 6th Floor, 91 Gordon St, POB 878, Suva; tel. 3316697; fax 3316696; e-mail kbrisuva@connect.com; internet www.kemlu.go.id/suva; Ambassador GARY RACHMAN MAKMUN JUSUF.

Japan: Dominion House, 2nd Floor, POB 13045, Suva; tel. 3304633; fax 3302984; e-mail eojfiji@connect.com.fj; internet www.fj.emb-japan.go.jp; Ambassador TAKUJI HANATANI.

Kiribati: 36 MacGregor Rd, POB 17937, Suva; tel. 3302512; fax 3315335; e-mail kiribatihighcom@connect.com.fj; High Commissioner RETETA RIMMON.

Korea, Republic: Vanua House, 8th Floor, PMB, Suva; tel. 3300977; fax 3308059; e-mail korembfj@mofat.go.kr; internet fji.mofat.go.kr; Ambassador KIM SEONG-IN.

Malaysia: Pacific House, 5th Floor, POB 356, Suva; tel. 3312166; fax 3303350; e-mail malsuva@kln.gov.my; internet www.kln.gov.my/web/fji_suva; High Commissioner EDI IRWAN MAHMUD.

Marshall Islands: Government Bldgs, 41 Borron Rd, POB 2038, Suva; tel. 3387899; fax 3387115; e-mail rmisuva@gmail.com; Ambassador FREDERICK MULLER.

Micronesia, Federated States: 37 Loftus St, POB 15493, Suva; tel. 3304566; fax 3300842; e-mail fsmsuva@sopacsun.sopac.org.fj; Ambassador GERSON JACKSON.

Nauru: Ratu Sukuna House, 7th Floor, MacArthur St, POB 2420, Suva; tel. 3313566; fax 3312032; e-mail naurulands@connect.com.fj; High Commissioner JARDEN KEPHAS.

New Zealand: Reserve Bank of Fiji Bldg, 10th Floor, Pratt St, POB 1378, Suva; tel. 3311422; fax 3300842; e-mail nzhc@unwired.com.fj; internet www.nzembassy.com/fiji; High Commissioner MARK RAMSDEN.

Papua New Guinea: 18 Rakua St, off Nailuva Rd, Government Bldgs, POB 2447, Suva; tel. 3304244; fax 3300178; e-mail kundufj@is.com.fj; High Commissioner HERA KEVAU.

Solomon Islands: 34 Reki St, Government Bldgs, POB 2647, Suva; tel. 3100355; fax 3100356; e-mail solohicom@gmail.com; High Commissioner JOHN PATTESON OTI.

South Africa: Kimberly St, Suva; tel. 3311087; fax 3311086; e-mail freestate@connect.com.fj; Chargé d'affaires ABBEY MATOTO PINDELO.

Tuvalu: 16 Gorrie St, POB 14449, Suva; tel. 3301355; fax 3308479; e-mail s.laloniu@yahoo.com; High Commissioner PAULSON PANAPA.

United Kingdom: Victoria House, 47 Gladstone Rd, POB 1355, Suva; tel. 3229100; fax 3229132; e-mail publicdiplomacysuva@fco .gov.uk; internet ukinfiji.fco.gov.uk; High Commissioner RODERICK DRUMMOND.

USA: 158 Princess Rd, Tamavua, Suva; tel. 3314466; fax 3308685; e-mail usembsuva@gmail.com; internet suva.usembassy.gov; Ambassador JUDITH BETH CEFKIN.

Vanuatu: 17 Mariko St, PMB 19249, Suva; High Commissioner NIKENIKE VUROBARAVU.

Judicial System

Justice is administered by the Supreme Court, the Fiji Court of Appeal, the High Court and the Magistrates' Courts. The Supreme Court of Fiji is the superior court of record, presided over by the Chief Justice.

Supreme Court: Suva; tel. 3211881; fax 3300674; e-mail enquiries@ judicial.gov.fj; internet www.judiciary.gov.fj; Chief Justice ANTHONY GATES.

Court of Appeal: Victoria Parade, Suva; tel. 3211307; fax 3316284; Pres. WILLIAM CALANCHINI.

High Court: Suva; Chief Registrar IRANI WAKISHTA ARACHCHI.

Magistrates' Courts: there are 15 Magistrates' Courts, which allow for 22 sitting resident magistrates; Chief Magistrate USAIA RATUVILI.

Office of the Attorney-General: Government Bldgs, POB 2213, Suva; tel. 3309866; fax 3305421; internet www.ag.gov.fj; Attorney-General AIYAZ SAYED-KHAIYUM (Minister for Justice); Solicitor-General SHARVADA SHARAMA.

Religion

CHRISTIANITY

Most ethnic Fijians are Christians. Methodists are the largest Christian group, followed by Roman Catholics. At the census of 2007 about 64.4% of the population were Christian (mainly Methodists, who comprised 34.6% of the total population).

Fiji Council of Churches: Government Bldgs, POB 2300, Suva; tel. and fax 3313798; e-mail fijichurches@connect.com.fj; f. 1964; nine mem. churches; Pres. Rev. APIMELEKI QILIHO; Gen. Sec. Rev. ISIRELI LEDUA KACIMAIWAI.

The Anglican Communion

In April 1990 Polynesia, formerly a missionary diocese of the Church of the Province of New Zealand, became a full and integral diocese. The diocese of Polynesia is based in Fiji but also includes Wallis and Futuna, Tuvalu, Kiribati, French Polynesia, Cook Islands, Tonga, Samoa and Tokelau. There were an estimated 6,319 adherents in 2007.

Bishop of Polynesia: Archbishop Dr WINSTON HALAPUA, Bishop's Office, 8 Desvoeux Rd, POB 35, Suva; tel. 3304716; fax 3302687; e-mail episcopus@connect.com.fj.

The Roman Catholic Church

Fiji comprises a single archdiocese. At 31 December 2007 there were an estimated 97,692 adherents in the country.

Bishops' Conference: Episcopal Conference of the Pacific Secretariat (CEPAC), 14 Williamson Rd, POB 289, Suva; tel. 3300340; fax 3303143; e-mail cepac@connect.com.fj; f. 1968; 17 mems; Pres. Most Rev. ANTHONY SABLAN APURON (Archbishop of Agaña, Guam); Sec.-Gen. Fr ROGER McCARRICK.

Archbishop of Suva: Fr PETER LOY CHONG, Archdiocesan Office, Nicolas House, 35 Pratt St, POB 109, Suva; tel. 3301955; fax 3301565.

Other Christian Churches

Methodist Church in Fiji & Rotuma (Lotu Wesele e Viti): Epworth Arcade, Nina St, POB 357, Suva; tel. 3311477; fax 3303771; e-mail methodistchhq@connect.com.fj; f. 1835; autonomous since 1964; 212,831 mems (2007); Pres. Rev. TEVITA NAWADRA BANIVANUA; Gen. Sec. EPINERI VAKADEWAVOSA.

Other denominations active in the country include the Assembly of God (with c. 7,000 mems), the Baptist Mission, the Congregational Christian Church and the Presbyterian Church.

HINDUISM

Most of the Indian community are Hindus. According to the census of 2007, 27.9% of the population were Hindus.

ISLAM

In 2007 some 6.3% of the population were Muslim. There are several Islamic organizations.

Fiji Muslim League: Samabula, POB 3990, Suva; tel. 3384566; fax 3370204; e-mail fijimuslim@connect.com.fj; f. 1926; Nat. Pres. HAFIZUD DEAN KHAN; Gen. Sec. MOHAMMAD TAABISH AKBAR; 26 brs and 3 subsidiary orgs.

SIKHISM

There were an estimated 2,540 Sikhs in Fiji in 2007.

Sikh Association of Fiji: Suva; Pres. MEJA SINGH.

BAHÁ'Í FAITH

National Spiritual Assembly: National Office, POB 639, Suva; tel. 3387574; fax 3387772; e-mail nsafiji@connect.com.fj; mems resident in 490 localities; national headquarters for consultancy and co-ordination.

The Press

NEWSPAPERS AND PERIODICALS

Coconut Telegraph: POB 249, Savusavu, Vanua Levu; f. 1975; monthly; serves rural communities; Editor LEMA LOW.

Fiji Calling: POB 12095, Suva; tel. 3305916; fax 3301930; publ. by Associated Media Ltd; every 6 months; English; Publr YASHWANT GAUNDER.

Fiji Cane Grower: POB 12095, Suva; tel. 3305916; fax 3305256.

Fiji Daily Post: 19 Ackland St, Viria East Industrial Subdivision, Vatuwaqa, Suva; tel. 3275176; fax 3275179; e-mail info@fijidailypost .com; internet www.fijidailypost.com; f. 1987 as *Fiji Post*; daily from 1989; English; 100% govt-owned since Sept. 2003; Chair. MALAKAI NAIYAGA; Editor-in-Chief ROBERT WOLFGRAMM.

Fiji Magic: POB 12095, Suva; tel. 3305916; fax 3302852; e-mail fijimagic@fijilive.com; internet www.fijilive.com/fijimagic; publ. by Associated Media Ltd; monthly; English; Publr YASHWANT GAUNDER; circ. 15,000.

Fiji Republic Gazette: Printing Dept, POB 98, Suva; tel. 3385999; fax 3370203; f. 1874; weekly; English.

Fiji Sun: 12 Amra St, Walubay, Suva; tel. 3307555; fax 3311455; e-mail peterl@fijisun.com.fj; internet www.fijisun.com.fj; re-est. 1999; daily; Publr and CEO PETER LOMAS; Editor EPINERI VULA.

Fiji Times: 177 Victoria Parade, Suva; tel. 3304209; fax 3301521; e-mail timesnews@fijitimes.com.fj; internet www.fijitimes.com; f. 1869; fmrly owned by News Ltd (Australia); acquired by Motibhai Group in Sept. 2010 following introduction of legislation limiting foreign ownership of media organizations; daily; English; Publr HANK ARTS; Editor-in-Chief FRED WESLEY; circ. 34,000.

Fiji Trade Review: The Rubine Group, POB 12511, Suva; tel. 3313944; monthly; English; Publr GEORGE RUBINE; Editor MABEL HOWARD.

Islands Business: 46 Gordon St, POB 12718, Suva; tel. 3303108; fax 3301423; e-mail editor@ibi.com.fj; internet www.islandsbusiness .com; regional monthly news and business magazine featuring the Fiji Islands Business supplement; English; Group Editor-in-Chief SAMISONI PARETI; circ. 3,500.

Na Tui: Government Bldgs, 422 Fletcher Rd, POB 2071, Suva; f. 1988; weekly; Fijian; Publr TANIELA BOLEA; Editor SAMISONI BOLATAGICI; circ. 7,000.

Nai Lalakai: 20 Gordon St, POB 1167, Suva; tel. 3304111; fax 3301521; e-mail fijitimes@is.com.fj; f. 1962; publ. by Fiji Times Ltd; weekly; Fijian; Editor SAMISONI KAKAIVALU; circ. 18,000.

Pacific Business: POB 12095, Suva; tel. 3305916; fax 3301930; publ. by Associated Media Ltd; monthly; English; Publr YASHWANT GAUNDER.

Pacific Telecom: POB 12095, Suva; tel. 3300591; fax 3302852; e-mail review@is.com.fj; publ. by Associated Media Ltd; monthly; English; Publr YASHWANT GAUNDER.

PACNEWS: Level 2, Damodar Centre, Gordon St, Suva; tel. 3315732; fax 3317055; e-mail pacnews1@connect.com.fj; internet www.pina.com.fj; daily news service for the Pacific region; Pres. MOSES STEVENS; Editor MAKERETA KOMAI.

Pactrainer: PMB, Suva; tel. 3303623; fax 3303943; e-mail pina@is .com.fj; monthly; newsletter of Pacific Journalism Development Centre; Editor PETER LOMAS.

The Review: POB 12095, Suva; tel. 3305916; fax 3301930; e-mail review@is.com.fj; publ. by Associated Media Ltd; monthly; English.

Sartaj: John Beater Enterprises Ltd, Raiwaqa, POB 5141, Suva; f. 1988; weekly; Hindi; Editor S. DASO; circ. 15,000.

Shanti Dut: 20 Gordon St, POB 1167, Suva; f. 1935; publ. by Fiji Times Ltd; weekly; Hindi; Editor NILAM KUMAR; circ. 12,000.

Top Shot: Suva; f. 1995; golf magazine; monthly.

The Weekender: 2 Denison Rd, POB 15652, Suva; tel. 3315477; fax 3305346; publ. by Media Resources Ltd; weekly; English; Publr JOSEFATA NATA.

REGULATORY AUTHORITY

Media Industry Development Authority (MIDA): Quarters 8, Lady Davila Road, Suva; tel. 3315477; e-mail info@mida.org.fj; internet www.mida.org.fj; Dir MATAI AKAUOLA; Chair. ASHWIN RAJ.

Publishers

Fiji Times Ltd: POB 1167, Suva; tel. 3304111; fax 3301521; e-mail timesnews@fijitimes.com.fj; f. 1869; Propr Motibhai Group; largest newspaper publr; also publrs of books and magazines; Gen. Man. HANK ARTS.

University of the South Pacific: Laucala Campus, Suva; tel. 3231000; fax 3231551; e-mail webmaster@usp.ac.fj; internet www.usp.ac.fj; f. 1986; education, natural history, regional interests; Pres. Prof. RAJESH CHANDRA.

GOVERNMENT PUBLISHING HOUSE

Printing and Stationery Department: POB 98, Suva; tel. 3385999; fax 3370203.

Broadcasting and Communications

TELECOMMUNICATIONS

Digicel Fiji: Ground Floor, Kadavu House, Victoria Parade, POB 13811, Suva; tel. 3310200; fax 3310201; e-mail customercarefiji@digicelgroup.com; internet www.digicelfiji.com; f. 2008; CEO DARREN MCLEAN.

Fiji International Telecommunications Ltd (FINTEL): 151 Rifle Range Rd, Vatuwaqa Communication Centre, Vatuwaqa, POB 59, Suva; tel. 3312933; fax 3305689; e-mail inquiries@fintelfiji.com; internet www.fintel.com.fj; f. 1976; 51% govt-owned; 49% owned by Amalgamated Telecoms Holding (ATH); Chair. AJITH KODAGODA; CEO GEORGE SAMISONI.

KIDANET: 158 Victoria Parade, POB 51, Suva; tel. 3315749; fax 3310332; e-mail info@kidanet.com.fj; internet www.kidanet.com.fj; internet service provider; CEO JONE WESELE.

Telecom Fiji Ltd (TFL): Ganilau House, Edward St, PMB, Suva; tel. 3304019; fax 3305595; e-mail contact@tfl.com.fj; internet www.tfl.com.fj; provides internet services through its subsidiary Connect Fiji Ltd; owned by Amalgamated Telecom Holdings; Chair. TOM RICKETTS; CEO MOTHILAL DE SILVA.

Vodafone Fiji Ltd: 168 Princes Rd, Tamavua, Suva; tel. 3312000; fax 3312007; e-mail aslam.khan@vodafone.com; internet www.vodafone.com.fj; 51% owned by Amalgamated Telecom Holdings Ltd, 49% by Vodafone International Holdings BV; GSM operator; CEO ASLAM KHAN.

BROADCASTING

Media Industry Development Authority (MIDA): Quarters 8, Lady Davila Road, Suva; tel. 3315477; e-mail info@mida.org.fj; internet www.mida.org.fj; Dir MATAI AKAUOLA; Chair. ASHWIN RAJ.

Radio

Fiji Broadcasting Corporation Ltd—FBCL (Radio Fiji): 69 Gladstone Rd, POB 334, Suva; tel. 3314333; fax 3220990; internet www.fbc.com.fj; f. 1954; statutory body; jointly funded by govt grant and advertising revenue; Radio Fiji 1 broadcasts nationally on AM in English and Fijian; Radio Fiji 2 broadcasts nationally on AM in English and Hindi; Gold FM broadcasts nationally on AM and FM in English; Mirchi FM and 2Day FM broadcast, mainly musical programmes, in Hindi and English, respectively; Bula FM broadcasts musical programmes in Fijian; CEO RIYAZ SAYED-KHAIYUM.

Communications Fiji Ltd: 231 Waimanu Rd, PMB, Suva; tel. 3314766; fax 3303748; e-mail info@fm96.com.fj; internet www.cfl.com.fj; f. 1985; operates 5 commercial stations; FM 96, f. 1985, broadcasts 24 hours per day, on FM, in English; Navtarang, f. 1989, broadcasts 24 hours per day, on FM, in Hindi; Viti FM, f. 1996, broadcasts 24 hours per day, on FM, in Fijian; Legend FM, f. 2002, and Radio Sargam, f. 2004, broadcast musical programmes; Man. Dir WILLIAM PARKINSON; Gen. Man. IAN JACKSON.

Radio Light/Radio Naya Jiwan/Nai Talai: Government Bldgs, 15 Tower St, POB 2525, Suva; tel. and fax 3319956; e-mail radiolight@connect.com.fj; internet www.radiolight.org; f. 1990; owned by Evangelical Bible Mission Trust Board; non-profit organization; broadcasts in English (Radio Light FM 104, FM 104.2), Hindi (Radio Naya Jiwan FM 94.6) and Fijian (Nai Talai); Gen. Man. DOUGLAS ROSE.

Radio Pasifik: The University of the South Pacific, Suva; tel. 3232797; fax 3312591; e-mail blumel_d@usp.ac.fj; f. 1996; educational, operated by CFDL Multimedia Unit; broadcasts in English, Fijian, French, Bislama, Tongan, Hindi and other Pacific island languages.

Television

FBC TV—Fiji Broadcasting Corporation: 69 Gladstone Road, Suva; tel. 3314333; fax 3220990; e-mail infocenter@fbc.com.fj; internet www.tv.fbc.com.fj; f. 2011; owned by Fiji Broadcasting Corporation Limited; English language channel, covers local and international news.

Fiji Television Ltd: 20 Gorrie St, Government Bldgs, POB 2442, Suva; tel. 3305100; fax 3304630; e-mail info@fijitv.com.fj; internet www.fijione.tv; f. 1994; operates 2 services, Fiji 1, a free channel, and Sky Fiji, a 25-channel subscription service; Chair. IOANE NAIVELI; Group CEO GEOFFREY SMITH.

Film and Television Unit (FTU): c/o Department of Information, Government Bldgs, Suva; video library; production unit established by Govt and Hanns Seidel Foundation (Germany); a weekly news magazine and local documentary programmes.

MAI TV: Carpentrer St, Garden City, Arcade 2, Raiwai, Suva; tel. 3275051; fax 3275052; e-mail feedback@tv.com.fj; internet www.tv.com.fj; f. 2006; Owner JUSTIN SMITH.

Sky Fiji: Suva; Fiji Television Limited; a 17-channel subscription service.

Finance

BANKING
(cap. = capital; res = reserves; dep. = deposits; m. = million; brs = branches; amounts in Fiji dollars)

Central Bank

Reserve Bank of Fiji: Pratt St, PMB, Suva; tel. 3313611; fax 3302094; e-mail info@rbf.gov.fj; internet www.rbf.gov.fj; f. 1984; replaced Central Monetary Authority of Fiji (f. 1973); bank of issue; administers Insurance Act, Banking Act and Exchange Control Act; cap. 2.0m., res 39.1m. (Dec. 2011); Gov. BARRY WHITESIDE.

Commercial Bank

Bank South Pacific: cnr of Renwick Rd and Pratt St, PMB, Suva; tel. 3314400; fax 3318393; internet www.bsp.com.fj; f. 1974; est. as National Bank of Fiji; 51% acquired from Fiji Govt by Colonial Ltd in 1999 and renamed Colonial National Bank; above name adopted after acquisition of the Colonial Group by BSP in 2009; cap. 15.0m., res 3.8m., dep. 605.1m. (Dec. 2010); Country Man. KEVIN MCCARTHY; 15 brs; 45 agencies.

Development Bank

Fiji Development Bank: 360 Victoria Parade, GPOB 104, Suva; tel. 3314866; fax 3314886; e-mail info@fdb.com.fj; internet www.fdb.com.fj; f. 1967; finances devt of natural resources, agriculture, transport, and other industries and enterprises; statutory body; applied for a commercial banking licence in Nov. 2004; cap. 56.1m., res 11.1m. (June 2010); Chair. ROBERT GORDON LYON; CEO DEVE TOGANIVALU; 9 brs.

Merchant Banks

Merchant Finance and Investment Company Ltd: Level 1, Ra Marama, 91 Gordon St, Suva; tel. 3314955; fax 3300026; e-mail info@mfl.com.fj; internet www.mfl.com.fj; f. 1986; fmrly Merchant Bank of Fiji Ltd; owned by Fijian Holdings Ltd (80%), South Pacific Trustees (20%); Gen. Man NAPOLIONI BATIMALA; 3 brs.

STOCK EXCHANGE

South Pacific Stock Exchange: Level 2, Plaza One, Provident Plaza, 33 Ellery St, POB 11689, Suva; tel. 3304130; fax 3304145; e-mail info@spse.com.fj; internet www.spse.com.fj; f. 1979; fmrly Suva Stock Exchange; name changed as above in 2000; Chair. Dr NUR BANO ALI; CEO JINITA PRASAD.

INSURANCE

Colonial Fiji Life Ltd: cnr of Renwick Rd and Pratt St, PMB, Suva; tel. 3314400; fax 3318393; internet www.colonial.com.fj; life and health; fmrly Blue Shield (Pacific) Ltd; owned by BSP Group, Australia; Man. Dir Ratu MALAKAI NAIYAG.

Dominion Insurance Ltd: 231 Waimanu Rd, POB 14468, Suva; tel. 3311055; fax 3303475; e-mail enquiries@dominioninsurance.com.fj; internet www.dominioninsurance.com.fj; general insurance; Chair. PHILIP TOLLEY; CEO PETER SKINNER.

FijiCare Insurance Ltd: 9th Floor, 343–359 FNPF Place, Victoria Parade, Suva; tel. 3302717; fax 3302119; e-mail fijicare@connect.com.fj; internet www.fijicare.com.fj; life and health; Chair. PHILIPP THOMAS; Man. Dir PETER MCPHERSON.

New India Assurance Co Ltd: 2nd Floor, Harifam Centre, GPOB 71, Suva; tel. 3313488; fax 3302679; e-mail newindiasuva@connect.com.fj; internet www.niafiji.com; Chief Man. VENUKUMAR KRISHNA-MURTHY.

QBE Insurance (Fiji) Ltd: Queensland Insurance Center, 18 Victoria Parade, GPOB 101, Suva; tel. 3315455; fax 3300285; e-mail info.fiji@qbe.com; internet www.qbepacific.com/Insurance.html; owned by Australian interests; fmrly known as Queensland Insurance (Fiji) Ltd, name changed as above 2004; Gen. Man. MATTHEW KEARNS.

SUN Insurance: Ground Floor, Kaunikuila House, Laucala Bay Rd, Suva; tel. 3313822; fax 3313882; e-mail info@suninsurance.com.fj; internet www.suninsurance.com.fj; f. 1999; general; Chair. PADAM RAJ LALA; CEO LOLESH K. SHARMA.

Tower Insurance Fiji Ltd: Tower House, Thomson St, GPOB 950, Suva; tel. 3315955; fax 3301376; e-mail info@towerinsurance.com.fj; internet www.towerinsurance.com.fj; owned by New Zealand interests; Gen. Man. PAUL ABSELL.

Trade and Industry

GOVERNMENT AGENCIES

Fiji Islands Trade and Investment Bureau: Civic House, 6th Floor, Victoria Parade, POB 2303, Suva; tel. 3301783; e-mail info@ftib.org.fj; internet www.ftib.org.fj; f. 1980; restyled 1988, to promote and stimulate foreign and local economic devt investment; Chair. ADRIAN SOFIELD; CEO JITOKO TIKOLEVU.

Training and Productivity Authority of Fiji (TPAF): Beaumont Rd, POB 6890, Nasinu; tel. 3392000; fax 3340184; e-mail info@tpaf.ac.fj; internet www.tpaf.ac.fj; fmrly Fiji National Training Council; present name assumed in 2002; Dir-Gen. JONE USAMATE.

DEVELOPMENT ORGANIZATIONS

Fiji Development Company Ltd: FNPF Place, 350 Victoria Parade, POB 161, Suva; tel. 3304611; fax 3304171; e-mail hfc@is.com.fj; f. 1960; subsidiary of the Commonwealth Development Corpn; Man. F. KHAN.

Fijian Development Fund Board: POB 122, Suva; tel. 3312601; fax 3302585; f. 1951; funds derived from payments from sales of copra by indigenous Fijians; funds used only for Fijian devt schemes; CEO VINCENT TOVATA.

Land Development Authority: POB 5442, Raiwaqa; tel. 3383155; fax 3387157; e-mail rsingh010@govnet.gov.fj; internet www.agriculture.org.fj; f. 1961; co-ordinates devt plans for land and marine resources; Chair. RITESHNI LATA SINGH.

CHAMBERS OF COMMERCE

Ba Chamber of Commerce: POB 99, Ba; tel. 6670134; fax 6670132; Pres. DINESH PATEL.

Fiji Chamber of Commerce and Industry: POB 14803, Suva; tel. 314040; fax 302641; Pres. PETER MASEY.

Labasa Chamber of Commerce: POB 992, Labasa; tel. 8811467; fax 8813009; Pres. ASHOK KARAN.

Lautoka Chamber of Commerce and Industry: POB 366, Lautoka; tel. 6661834; fax 6662379; e-mail vaghco@connect.com.fj; Pres. NATWARLAL VAGH.

Levuka Chamber of Commerce: POB 85, Levuka; tel. 3440248; fax 3440252; Pres. ISHRAR ALI.

Nadi Chamber of Commerce and Industry: POB 2735, Nadi; tel. 6700240; fax 6702406; e-mail rraju@connect.com.fj; internet www.nadichamber.com; f. 1947; Pres. RAM RAJU.

Nausori Chamber of Commerce: POB 228, Nausori; tel. 3478235; fax 3400134; Pres. MOTI LAL.

Sigatoka Chamber of Commerce: POB 882, Sigatoka; tel. 6500064; fax 6520006; Pres. TOM WAQA.

Suva Chamber of Commerce and Industry: 8 Dominion House, POB 337, Suva; tel. 3314044; fax 3302188; e-mail scci@unwired.com.fj; internet www.suvachamber.org; f. 1902; Pres. Dr NUR BANO ALI; 150 mems.

Tavua-Vatukoula Chamber of Commerce: POB 698, Tavua; tel. and fax 6680390; Pres. SOHAN SINGH.

INDUSTRIAL AND TRADE ASSOCIATIONS

Fiji Kava Council: POB 17724, Suva; tel. 3386576; fax 3371844; Chair. Ratu JOSATEKI NAWALOWALO.

Fiji Sawmillers' Association: Yalalevu; e-mail jayd@islandchill.com; Pres. JAY DAYAL.

Fiji Sugar Corporation Ltd: 3rd Floor, Western House, cnr of Bila and Vidilo St, PMB, Lautoka; tel. 6662655; fax 6664685; nationalized 1974; buyer of sugar cane and raw sugar mfrs; Exec. Chair. ABDUL KHAN.

Mining and Quarrying Council: 42 Gorrie St, Suva; tel. 33313188; fax 3302183; e-mail employer@is.com.fj; Chief Exec. K. A. J. ROBERTS.

National Trading Corporation Ltd: POB 13673, Suva; tel. 3315211; fax 3315584; f. 1992; govt-owned body; develops markets for agricultural and marine produce locally and overseas; processes and markets fresh fruit, vegetables and ginger products; CEO APIAMA CEGUMALINA.

Native Lands Trust Board: GPOB 116, Suva; tel. 3312733; fax 3312014; e-mail info@nltb.com.fj; internet www.nltb.com.fj; manages holdings of ethnic Fijian landowners; Gen. Man. ALIPATE QETAKI.

Sustainable Forest Industries LTD (SFI): POB 1119, Nabua, Suva; tel. 3384999; fax 3370029; e-mail info@fijimahogany.com; internet www.fijimahogany.com; Man. Dir CHRISTOPHER DONLON.

EMPLOYERS' ORGANIZATIONS

Fiji Commerce and Employers Federation (FCEF): 42 Gorrie St, GPOB 575, Suva; tel. 3313188; fax 3302183; e-mail employer@fcef.com.fj; internet www.fcef.com.fj; f. 1960; represents 525 major employers with approx. 80,000 employees; fmrly Fiji Employers' Fed; Pres. HOWARD POLITINI; CEO NESBITT HAZELMAN.

Fiji Manufacturers' Association: POB 1308, Suva; tel. and fax 3318811; e-mail fma@connect.com.fj; internet fijimanufacturers.org; f. 1971; CEO DESMOND WHITESIDE; 68 mems.

Local Inter-Island Shipowners' Association: POB 152, Suva; fax 3303389; e-mail consortship@connect.com.fj; Pres. DURGA PRASAD; Sec. LEO B. SMITH.

Textile, Clothing and Footwear Council: POB 10015, Nabua; tel. 3384777; fax 3370446; Pres. KALPESH SOLANKI.

UTILITIES

Electricity

Fiji Electricity Authority (FEA): PMB, Suva; tel. 3313333; fax 3311882; e-mail ceo@fea.com.fj; internet www.fea.com.fj; f. 1966; govt-owned; responsible for the generation, transmission and distribution of electricity throughout Fiji; CEO HASMUKH PATEL.

Water

Water Authority of Fiji: Kings Rd, 4 Miles, Nasinu, Suva; tel. 3346777; e-mail contact@waf.com.fj; internet www.waterauthority.com.fj; Chair. P. L. MUNASINGHE; CEO OPETAIA RAVAI.

TRADE UNIONS

Fiji Trades Union Congress (FTUC): 32 Des Voeux Rd, POB 1418, Suva; tel. 3315377; fax 3300306; e-mail ftucl@connect.com.fj; internet ftuc.org; f. 1952; affiliated to ITUC; 35 affiliated unions; 33,000 mems; Pres. DANIEL URAI MANUFOLAU; Gen. Sec. RAJESHWAR SINGH (acting).

Transport

RAILWAYS

Fiji Sugar Corporation Railway: Rarawai Mill, POB 155, Ba; tel. 6674044; fax 6670505; internet www.fsc.com.fj; for use in cane-harvesting season, May–Dec.; 595 km of permanent track and 225 km of temporary track (gauge of 600 mm), serving cane-growing areas at Ba, Lautoka and Penang on Viti Levu and Labasa on Vanua Levu; Exec. Chair. ABDUL KHAN.

ROADS

At the end of 2010 there were some 3,440 km of roads in Fiji, of which 49.2% were paved. A 500-km highway circles the main island of Viti Levu.

Land Transport Authority of Fiji: Lot 1, Daniva Rd, Valelevu, Nasinu; tel. 3392166; fax 3390026; e-mail infor@lta.com.fj; internet www.ltafiji.com; f. 1998; responsible for public transport services, vehicle registration, traffic management and road safety; Chair. GREG LAWLOR; CEO NAISA TUINACEVA.

SHIPPING

The principal ports of call are Suva, Lautoka, Levuka, Malau and Wairiki. On 31 December 2014 the flag registered fleet comprised 35 vessels, with a total displacement of 32,661 grt.

Maritime Safety Authority of Fiji (MSAF): POB 3259, Nadi; tel. 6750241; fax 6750242; e-mail jbilitaki@msaf.com.fj; internet www .msaf.com.fj; regulatory body for maritime sector; fmrly known as Fiji Islands Maritime Safety Administration (FIMSA); Chair. NIGEL SKEGGS; CEO JOHN TUNIDAU (acting).

Fiji Ports Corporation Ltd: POB 780, Suva; tel. 3312700; fax 3300064; e-mail fpcl@connect.com.fj; internet www.fijiports.com.fj; f. 2005; management and devt of Fiji's ports; CEO VAJIRA PIYASENA; Gen. Man. EMINONI KURUSIGA.

> **Ports Terminals Ltd:** POB 780, Suva; f. 1998; subsidiary of Fiji Ports Corporation Ltd; stevedoring, pilotage and cargo handling at Suva and Lautoka ports; Gen. Man. EMINONI KURUSIGA.

Consort Shipping Line Ltd: Lot 4, Matua St, Suva; tel. 3313344; fax 3303389; e-mail consortshipping@connect.com.fj; internet www .consortshipping.com.fj; f. 1986; est. following merger of Interport Shipping and Wong's Shipping Co; CEO HECTOR SMITH; Man. Dir JUSTIN SMIT.

Fiji Maritime Services Ltd: c/o Fiji Ports Workers and Seafarers Union, 36 Edinburgh Drive, Suva; f. 1989 by PAF and the Ports Workers' Union; services between Lautoka and Vanua Levu ports.

Pacific Agencies (Fiji) Ltd: Lot 1 Foster Rd Walubay Suva; tel. 3315444; fax 3301127; e-mail info@pacshipfiji.com.fj; internet www .pacificagenciesfiji.com; f. 2000 after merger of Burns Philp and Forum Shipping; shipping agents, customs agents and international forwarding agents, crew handling; Gen. Man. CRAIG WILLIAM STRONG.

Transcargo Express Fiji Ltd: POB 936, Suva; tel. 3313266; fax 3303389; e-mail consortship@connect.com.fj; f. 1974; Man. Dir LEO B. SMITH.

CIVIL AVIATION

There is an international airport at Nadi (about 210 km from Suva), a smaller international airport at Nausori (Suva) and numerous other airfields. Nadi is an important transit airport in the Pacific.

Airports Fiji Ltd: Nadi International Airport, Nadi; tel. 6725777; fax 6725161; e-mail info@afl.com.fj; internet www.airportsfiji.com; f. 1999; owns and operates 15 public airports in Fiji, incl. 2 international airports, Nadi International Airport and Nausori Airport; Chair. ADRIAN SOFIELD; CEO TONY GOLLIN.

Fiji Airways: Air Pacific Centre, Nadi International Airport, POB 9266, Nadi; tel. 6720777; fax 6720512; e-mail service@airpacific.com .fj; internet www.fijiairways.com; f. 1951; est. as Air Pacific Ltd, name changed in 2012; domestic and international services from Nausori Airport (serving Suva) to Nadi, and international services to Tonga, Solomon Islands, Cook Islands, Vanuatu, Samoa, Kiribati, Tuvalu, Hawaii, Japan, Hong Kong, Australia, New Zealand and the USA; 51% govt-owned, 46% owned by Qantas (Australia); Chair. NALIN PATEL; CEO and Man. Dir STEFAN PICHLER.

Pacific Sun: Nadi International Airport, POB 9270, Nadi; tel. 6723555; fax 6723611; e-mail enquiries@pacificsun.com.fj; internet www.pacificsun.com.fj; f. 1980; wholly owned subsidiary of Air Pacific Ltd; acquired Sun Air 2007; scheduled flights to domestic and regional destinations; Gen. Man. SHAENAZ VOSS.

Tourism

Scenery, climate, fishing and diving attract visitors to Fiji, where tourism is an important industry. However, the sector has been intermittently affected by political unrest. The number of visitor arrivals totalled 692,630 in 2014. Most visitors are from Australia, New Zealand, the USA and the United Kingdom. Receipts from tourism totalled a provisional $F1,318m. in 2013.

Fiji Islands Hotels and Tourism Association (FIHTA): 42 Gorrie St, GPOB 13560, Suva; tel. 3302980; fax 3300331; e-mail info@fihta.com.fj; internet www.fihta.com.fj; fmrly Fiji Hotel Association; name changed as above in 2005; 90 active mems, over 300 assoc. mems; Pres. DIXON SEETO; Exec. Officer MICHAEL WONG.

Tourism Fiji: Nadi International Airport, POB 9217, Nadi; tel. 6722433; fax 6720141; e-mail marketing@tourismfiji.com.fj; internet www.fijime.com; Chair. ELIZABETH POWELL (acting); CEO RICK HAMILTON.

Defence

As assessed at November 2014, Fiji's total armed forces numbered 3,500 (3,200 in the army and 300 in the navy). Reserves numbered approximately 6,000. The country's membership of the Commonwealth has entitled Fijians to work in the British armed forces. In November 2014 a total of 192 Fijian soldiers were serving in Iraq under the auspices of the UN Assistance Mission for Iraq (UNAMI). The country's defence budget for 2015 was an estimated $F86m.

Commander-in-Chief: President of the Republic.

Commander of the Armed Forces: Brig. MOSESE TIKOITOGA.

Commander of the Land Force: Lt-Col JONE KALOUNIWAI.

Commander of the Navy: JOHN FOX.

Chief of Staff, Strategic Headquarters: Capt. VILIAME NAUPOTO.

Education

Education in Fiji is compulsory and free at primary level. Primary education begins at six years of age and lasts for eight years. Secondary education, beginning at the age of 14, lasts for a further three years. State subsidies are available for secondary and tertiary education in cases of hardship. In June 2013 there were 729 primary schools (with a total enrolment of 135,526 pupils) and 177 general secondary schools (with an enrolment of 67,631 pupils). There were 23 vocational and technical institutions. In 2009 Fiji had four teacher-training colleges (with 633 students). According to UNESCO estimates, in 2012 enrolment at primary schools included 96.6% of children in the relevant age-group, while enrolment at secondary schools included 83.0% of children in the relevant age-group. The University of the South Pacific is based in Fiji. In 2004 university students (both on campus and at extension centres) totalled 16,444. The University of Fiji, a privately owned institution, was established in that year. In January 2010 six government colleges merged to form the Fiji National University. The budget for 2012 allocated $F214.9m. to education.

FINLAND

Introductory Survey

LOCATION, CLIMATE, LANGUAGE, RELIGION, FLAG, CAPITAL

The Republic of Finland lies in northern Europe, bordered to the far north by Norway and to the north-west by Sweden. The Russian Federation adjoins the whole of the eastern frontier. Finland's western and southern shores are washed by the Baltic Sea. The climate varies sharply, with warm summers and cold winters. The mean annual temperature is 5°C (41°F) in Helsinki and −0.4°C (31°F) in the far north. There are two official languages: Finnish and Swedish. According to official data, at March 2014 89.3% of the population spoke Finnish as their native tongue, 5.3% spoke Swedish and 5.4% had another language as their first language. There is a small Sámi (Lapp) population in the north. The majority of the inhabitants profess Christianity; about 75% belong to the Evangelical Lutheran Church. The national flag (proportions 11 by 18) displays an azure blue cross (the upright to the left of centre) on a white background. The state flag has, at the centre of the cross, the national coat of arms (a yellow-edged red shield containing a golden lion and nine white roses). The capital is Helsinki.

CONTEMPORARY POLITICAL HISTORY

Historical Context

Finland formed part of the Kingdom of Sweden until 1809, when it became an autonomous Grand Duchy under the Russian Empire. During the Russian Revolution of 1917 the territory proclaimed its independence. Following a brief civil war, a democratic Constitution was adopted in 1919. The Soviet regime that came to power in Russia attempted to regain control of Finland, but acknowledged the country's independence in 1920.

Demands by the USSR for military bases in Finland and for the cession of part of the Karelian isthmus, in south-eastern Finland, were rejected by the Finnish Government in November 1939. Consequently, the USSR attacked Finland, and the two countries fought the Winter War, which lasted 15 weeks before Finnish forces were defeated. Following its surrender, Finland ceded an area of 41,880 sq km (16,170 sq miles) to the USSR in March 1940. In the hope of recovering the lost territory, Finland joined Nazi Germany in attacking the USSR in 1941. However, a separate armistice between Finland and the USSR was concluded in 1944.

In accordance with a peace treaty signed in February 1947, Finland agreed to the transfer of about 12% of its pre-war territory (including the Karelian isthmus and the Petsamo area on the Arctic coast) to the USSR, and to the payment of reparations, which totalled about US $570m. when completed in 1952. Meanwhile, in April 1948 Finland and the USSR signed the Finno-Soviet Treaty of Friendship, Co-operation and Mutual Assistance (the YYA Treaty), which was extended for 20-year periods in 1955, 1970 and again in 1983. A major requirement of the treaty was that Finland repel any attack made on the USSR by Germany, or its allies, through Finnish territory. (The treaty was replaced by a non-military agreement in 1992.)

Domestic Political Affairs

Since independence in 1917, the politics of Finland have been characterized by coalition governments (including numerous minority coalitions) and the development of consensus between parties. The Social Democratic Party (SDP) and the Centre Party have traditionally been the dominant participants in government. The conservative opposition gained significant support at a general election in March 1979, following several years of economic crises. However, a new centre-left coalition Government, comprising the Centre Party, the SDP, the Swedish People's Party (SPP) and the Finnish People's Democratic League (an electoral alliance that included the communists), was established in May by former Prime Minister Dr Mauno Koivisto, a Social Democrat.

Dr Urho Kekkonen, who had been President since 1956, resigned in October 1981. Koivisto was elected President in January 1982. He was succeeded as head of the coalition by former Prime Minister Kalevi Sorsa, another Social Democrat.

The coalition was re-formed in December, without the Finnish People's Democratic League, which had refused to support austerity measures.

At the general election of March 1983, the SDP won 57 of the 200 seats in the Parliament (Eduskunta), compared with 52 in the 1979 election. In May Sorsa formed another centre-left coalition, comprising the SDP, the SPP, the Centre Party and the Finnish Rural Party.

The rise of conservative politics: 1987–1994

At a general election held in March 1987, the combined non-socialist parties gained a majority in the Eduskunta for the first time since the election of 1945. Although the SDP remained the largest single party, with 56 seats, the system of modified proportional representation enabled the conservative opposition National Coalition Party (NCP) to gain an additional nine seats, winning a total of 53, while increasing its share of the votes cast by only 1%. President Koivisto eventually invited Harri Holkeri, a former Chairman of the NCP, to establish a coalition Government comprising the NCP, the SDP, the SPP and the Finnish Rural Party, thus avoiding a polarization of the political parties within the Eduskunta. Holkeri became the first conservative Prime Minister since 1946.

In February 1988 Koivisto retained office after the first presidential election by direct popular vote. He did not win the required absolute majority, however, and an electoral college was convened. Koivisto was re-elected after an endorsement by Holkeri, who had also contested the presidency and who had received the third highest number of direct votes (behind Paavo Väyrynen, the leader of the Centre Party).

At a general election held in March 1991, the Centre Party won 55 seats, the SDP 48 seats and the NCP 40. In April a coalition Government, comprising the Centre Party, the NCP, the SPP and the Finnish Christian Union, took office. The new coalition constituted the country's first wholly non-socialist Government for 25 years. The Chairman of the Centre Party, Esko Aho, was appointed Prime Minister. In the first stage of a presidential election, which took place in January 1994, the two most successful candidates were Martti Ahtisaari (the SDP candidate and a senior UN official) and Elisabeth Rehn (the SPP candidate and Minister of Defence), both of whom were supporters of Finland's application for membership of the European Union (EU, see p. 271), as the European Community had been restyled in late 1993. In accordance with constitutional changes adopted since the previous election (stipulating that, if no candidate gained more than 50% of the votes cast, the electorate should choose between the two candidates with the most votes), a second stage of the election was held in February 1994. Ahtisaari secured victory, with 53.9% of the votes cast, and took office in March.

The return of the SDP

At a general election held in March 1995, the SDP won 63 seats in the Eduskunta, the Centre Party 44, the NCP 39 and the Left Alliance (formed in 1990 by a merger of the communist parties and the Finnish People's Democratic League) 22. A new coalition Government was formed in April, comprising the SDP, the NCP, the SPP, the Left Alliance and the Green League. Paavo Lipponen, the leader of the SDP, replaced Aho as Prime Minister. Sauli Niinistö, the Chairman of the NCP, became Deputy Prime Minister.

Following a general election held in March 1999, the SDP remained the largest party in the Eduskunta, with 51 seats. The Centre Party won 48 seats and the NCP 46. In April the five parties of the outgoing Government agreed to form a new coalition. Lipponen remained Prime Minister, while Niinistö was reappointed as Minister of Finance.

A presidential election was held in January and February 2000. The first round of the ballot was won by Tarja Halonen (the SDP candidate and Minister of Foreign Affairs), who received 40.0% of the votes cast; the second largest share of the vote (34.4%) was obtained by Aho. Having won a second round of voting on 6 February (with 51.6% of the votes cast), Halonen took office as the first female President of Finland on 1 March.

A new Constitution entered into force on 1 March 2000, under the provisions of which the executive power of the President was significantly reduced while the real authority of the Eduskunta was increased, with the power of decision-making being divided more equally between the Eduskunta, the Cabinet (Valtioneuvosto) and the President. In addition, the President was to co-operate more closely with the Cabinet on issues of foreign policy.

Aho took leave from domestic politics for one year from August 2000, during which time Anneli Jäätteenmäki, a former Minister of Justice, replaced Aho as Chairman of the Centre Party. Popular support for Jäätteenmäki's leadership prompted Aho's resignation in mid-2002 and the election of Jäätteenmäki as Chairperson.

The construction of Finland's fifth nuclear reactor was approved by the Cabinet in January 2002 and by the Eduskunta in May, prompting the resignation of the Green League from the coalition Government.

The 2003 and 2007 general elections

At the general election of March 2003 which attracted a turnout of 69.7%, the Centre Party gained the largest representation in the Eduskunta, winning 55 seats, while the SDP won 53. The NCP suffered a significant reverse, with the loss of six seats (from 46 to 40 seats). In April the Centre Party formed a coalition Government with the SDP and the SPP, with Jäätteenmäki as Finland's first female Prime Minister.

However, Jäätteenmäki resigned the premiership on 18 June 2003, following allegations that she had improperly used classified foreign ministry information to discredit the outgoing Prime Minister, Lipponen, and secure victory for the Centre Party in the general election. One of the documents, which were leaked by a presidential aide, Martti Manninen, recorded exchanges between Lipponen and the US President, George W. Bush, in December 2002, and was reportedly used by Jäätteenmäki to portray Lipponen as being overly supportive of US policy regarding Iraq; the majority of Finns were opposed to the US-led military action launched in Iraq in March 2003 to remove the regime of Saddam Hussain. The Deputy Chairman of the Centre Party, Matti Vanhanen, who had been assigned the post of Minister of Defence in the new Government, replaced Jäätteenmäki as Prime Minister. Jäätteenmäki also stood down as Chairperson of the Centre Party; Vanhanen was elected to replace her in October. In March 2004 Jäätteenmäki was acquitted of inciting or assisting Manninen to divulge official secrets, but Manninen was found guilty of violating official secrecy.

Lipponen resigned as leader of the SDP in June 2005; Eero Heinäluoma, hitherto General Secretary of the party, was elected to succeed him. In September Heinäluoma entered the Cabinet as Deputy Prime Minister and Minister of Finance.

A presidential election was held in January 2006. Nine candidates contested the first round of voting, at which the incumbent, Halonen, received the largest share of the votes cast, with 46.3%, followed by Niinistö, representing the NCP, who secured 24.1%, and Prime Minister Vanhanen, the Centre Party candidate, with 18.6%. Halonen narrowly defeated Niinistö in a second round of voting, in which 77.2% of the electorate participated, receiving 51.8% of the votes cast.

At the general election held in March 2007, the Centre Party retained by a slim margin its position as the largest party in the Eduskunta, securing 51 seats. The largest gains were made by the NCP, which won 50 seats. By contrast, the SDP suffered a significant loss, taking only 45 seats. The election was characterized by the lowest turnout since 1939, at just 67.9%. In April 2007 the Centre Party, the NCP, the SPP and the Green League formed a new, centre-right coalition, with Vanhanen remaining as Prime Minister. Jyrki Katainen of the NCP was appointed as Deputy Prime Minister and Minister of Finance.

Jutta Urpilainen was elected SDP Chairperson in June 2008, succeeding Heinäluoma. At municipal elections held in October the NCP overtook the SDP to become the largest party, winning 23.5% of the votes cast, compared with 21.2% for the SDP and 20.1% for the Centre Party. The nationalist True Finns increased its share of the vote to 5.4%.

Election campaign funding controversies

The admission in May 2008 by the Chairman of the Centre Party's parliamentary group, Timo Kalli, that he had failed to disclose election campaign donations, owing to a lack of penalties in place for such a violation, prompted a series of similar revelations by other members of the Eduskunta, including several ministers. At the same time, it emerged that a significant pro-

portion of candidates in the 2007 election, principally from the Centre Party and including Prime Minister Vanhanen, had received contributions from a regional development association funded by business executives. The head of development of the Centre Party, Lasse Kontiola, subsequently admitted that he had helped to establish the organization without the knowledge of senior party members. New rules covering party financing were agreed by all the principal parties prior to the local elections in October 2008.

The issue of irregularities in election campaign funding arose again in mid-2009, when the Prime Minister was accused by the opposition SDP of lying in 2008 about a campaign funding meeting, and by a current affairs television programme of having accepted a bribe in the 1990s linked to Nuorisosäätiö (Youth Foundation)—a housing organization with connections to the Centre Party—which had made a large donation to his 2006 election campaign. Vanhanen vehemently denied the accusations and resisted calls for his resignation. Further revelations of funding irregularities subsequently emerged, principally regarding the Centre Party, but also involving other parties.

In December 2009 Vanhanen unexpectedly announced that he would not stand for re-election as Chairman of the Centre Party at the party conference in June 2010, citing health reasons. In June party members elected Mari Kiviniemi, the Minister of Public Administration and Local Government, to succeed Vanhanen. One week later, as expected, Vanhanen resigned as Prime Minister, and on 22 June Kiviniemi was sworn in as Prime Minister at the head of a renewed Cabinet.

The issue of Vanhanen's campaign funding caused renewed controversy in September 2010 when the Chancellor of Justice, Jaakko Jonkka, concluded an investigation into the former Prime Minister's connection with Nuorisosäätiö. Jonkka stated that he believed that Vanhanen had acted unlawfully when, as premier, he had authorized a grant from the state-administered Raha-automaattiyhdistys (RAY—Finland's Slot Machine Association) to the housing charity, despite the latter's contribution to his campaign fund. In February 2011 the Eduskunta's constitutional law committee decided that Vanhanen was guilty of dereliction of duty by not declaring his conflict of interest, but concluded that the charge was not serious enough to warrant Vanhanen's trial by the High Court of Impeachment.

None the less, several people were tried during 2012 in connection with the political funding irregularities that emerged in 2008. In April 2012 Ilkka Kanerva, who was Minister of Foreign Affairs in 2007–08, and three businessmen were convicted of charges including accepting and offering bribes in a case linked to the Nova Group. Kanerva received a suspended prison sentence of one year and three months, while the businessmen were given terms of imprisonment. Antti Kaikkonen, a Centre Party deputy and Chairman of Nuorisosäätiö in 2003–09, was sentenced to a five-month suspended prison term in January 2013, having been found guilty of abusing his position by raising funds for Centre Party election candidates. At the same time Jukka Vihriälä, a former Centre Party deputy and Chairman of RAY in 1991–2009, received an 18-month suspended prison sentence for aggravated bribe-taking, while a former attorney for Nuorisosäätiö received a one-year suspended sentence for aggravated bribery.

The 2011 general election and 2012 presidential election

The general election held on 17 April 2011 was characterized by a massive increase in support for the True Finns, which took 19.1% of the votes cast and won 39 seats in the Eduskunta (34 more than at the 2007 election), thus becoming the third largest party. The NCP narrowly emerged as the largest grouping in the legislature for the first time in its history, with 20.4% of the vote and 44 seats (a loss of six); the SDP came second with 42 seats. While all of the parliamentary parties apart from the True Finns suffered losses, the greatest decline in support was for the Centre Party, which took 35 seats (a loss of 16) and fell from first to fourth place. The participation rate, at 70.4%, was the highest since 1995. The True Finns, while maintaining its traditional anti-immigration stance, had focused its campaign on opposition to financial support for debt-stricken countries in the eurozone; the party had benefited from growing popular resentment that Finland, whose public finances were among the soundest in the EU, was being expected to rescue countries perceived as imprudent. The Chairman of the NCP, Jyrki Katainen, began negotiations to form a government in early May. In mid-May the True Finns withdrew from these talks, refusing to comply with

Katainen's demand that prospective coalition partners support EU policy, notably regarding financial assistance for eurozone countries at risk of default.

In June 2011 Katainen announced the formation of a coalition comprising the NCP, the SDP, the Left Alliance, the Green League, the SPP and the Christian Democrats. The broad-based coalition held a comfortable majority in the Eduskunta, leaving just the True Finns and the Centre Party in opposition. The Eduskunta subsequently formally elected Katainen as Prime Minister and a new Cabinet was appointed, with the NCP and the SDP being allocated 12 of the 19 ministerial portfolios. Jutta Urpilainen, the Chairperson of the SDP, became Deputy Prime Minister and Minister of Finance, while her party colleague, Erkki Tuomioja, returned to the post of Minister of Foreign Affairs (which he had previously held in 2000–07). At the behest of the SDP, the Government was to insist that any future EU financial assistance for heavily indebted members of the eurozone be subject to strict conditions (see *Regional relations*). A motion of no confidence in the Government, tabled by the Finns Party (the new English name adopted by the True Finns in August, although not a direct translation of its name in Finnish) in protest against the response to the sovereign debt crisis in the eurozone, was defeated in December by 116 votes to 73.

In October 2011 the Eduskunta adopted various constitutional amendments, including the stipulation that the Prime Minister, rather than the President, would formally represent Finland within the EU, the explicit recognition of Finland's membership of the EU, and provision for citizens to propose new laws to parliament if they could collect the signatures of at least 50,000 supporters within a period of six months. The revisions took effect in March 2012.

A presidential election was held on 22 January and 5 February 2012. The incumbent Halonen was ineligible for re-election, having served the maximum two terms permitted by the Constitution. At the first round of voting, contested by eight candidates, Niinistö, who had been narrowly defeated in the 2006 poll and had served as Speaker of the Eduskunta during the 2007–11 legislative term, received the largest share of the votes cast, with 37.0%, followed by Pekka Haavisto, the Green candidate, who secured 18.8%, Paavo Väyrynen, representing the Centre Party, with 17.5%, and Timo Soini, the Chairman of the Finns Party, with 9.4%. Niinistö comfortably defeated Haavisto in the second round of voting, at which a turnout of 66.0% was recorded, with 62.6% of the votes cast. He took office on 1 March 2012, becoming the first President from the NCP since 1956.

Recent developments: a new Prime Minister and legislative elections

At a party congress in June 2012, the Centre Party chose as its new Chairman businessman Juha Sipilä, a relative political novice who had only been elected to the Eduskunta at the 2011 poll, with Väyrynen coming only third of the four candidates. The SPP also held a leadership election at a party congress in June 2012: Carl Haglund, a member of the European Parliament, defeated the Minister of Justice, Anna-Maja Henriksson, to succeed Stefan Wallin as SPP Chairman. Haglund also replaced Wallin as Minister of Defence in July.

The governing coalition parties consolidated their position at municipal elections held on 28 October 2012, together securing 66.4% of the votes cast nationwide. The NCP and the SDP remained the two strongest parties, with 21.9% and 19.6% of the vote, respectively, followed by the opposition Centre Party (18.7%) and the Finns Party (12.3%). Although the share of the vote won by the Finns Party represented a substantial improvement on that recorded at the 2008 municipal polls (5.4%), it was markedly lower than the 19.1% achieved by the party in the general election, prompting speculation that the Government's firm stance on the provision of emergency EU funding to struggling eurozone members had, to some extent, contained the rise in support for the Finns Party.

Ongoing plans for municipal reform were inevitably a major focus of discussion during the local election campaign. Following a series of voluntary mergers of municipalities in recent years (in response to the offer of financial incentives by the state), the Government claimed that, in view of increasing rural–urban migration and the ageing population, further consolidation was required in order to ensure the viability of the provision of public services. Earlier in October 2012 a motion of no confidence in the Government on the issue—the third to be tabled on the issue within a year—was defeated in the Eduskunta by a margin of 95 votes to 62. The Government's proposals, which entailed a significant reduction in the number of municipalities and the possibility of a number of mandatory mergers, were opposed by the Centre Party and the Finns Party. In November government ministers reached agreement on draft legislation on municipal reform, and a restructuring scheme was agreed in August 2013. Ten further municipalities merged during 2013, but the scheme appeared to have stalled in 2014, ahead of the general election scheduled to be held in April 2015.

Jan Vapaavuori of the NCP, who had served as Minister of Housing in 2007–11, was appointed as Minister of Economic Affairs in November 2012, replacing his party colleague, Jyri Häkämies, who was to assume the post of Director-General of Elinkeinoelämän Keskusliitto (Confederation of Finnish Industries).

A parliamentary motion of no confidence in the Government was defeated in February 2013 by 103 votes to 67. The motion had been filed by the Finns Party in protest against the Government's economic policies, notably the rejection of a request for a €50m. loan from a shipyard in Turku that had been seeking (and subsequently failed) to secure a contract to build a new cruise liner. The SDP continued to lose electoral support and in May effected a reorganization of its cabinet ministers. Economic concerns continued to dominate the Government's agenda and affect its popularity, with intra-cabinet disagreements in early 2014 over planned austerity measures. The Left Alliance withdrew from the coalition in March in protest at the Government's proposed reductions in social welfare expenditure. In the same month the Government survived another vote of no confidence on the issue of municipal structural reforms.

In April 2014 Prime Minister Katainen announced his intention to resign as Chairman of the NCP (and thus also as premier) at the party conference in June in order to focus on his bid to be elected to a senior position in the European Commission. He was replaced by the incumbent Minister of European Affairs and Foreign Trade, Alexander Stubb, who defeated Minister of Social Affairs and Health Paula Risikko in the second round of voting in the party leadership contest (Jan Vapaavuori, the Minister of Economic Affairs, having been beaten in the first round). Of the six NCP ministers in the new five-party Government appointed by Prime Minister Stubb in late June, only Vapaavuori retained his post. The coalition was reduced to four member parties in late September, following the withdrawal of the Green League in protest at the Government's plans to permit the construction of a new nuclear power plant in the north of the country by a Finnish-Russian consortium. Meanwhile, at an SDP conference held in May, the trade union leader Antti Rinne narrowly defeated the incumbent Urpilainen in a party leadership contest. Rinne, who advocated the assumption of a more left-wing stance by the SDP to counter the continuing popularity of the Finns Party, subsequently replaced Urpilainen as Minister of Finance.

Following the implementation in 2012 of the constitutional amendment allowing for the presentation of citizens' initiatives in the Eduskunta, one such initiative, proposing the amendment of the Marriage Act to enable same-sex couples to marry and have the right externally to adopt children, was submitted to parliament in December 2013 with nearly 167,000 signatures. In December 2014, despite an earlier recommendation from the parliamentary Legal Affairs Committee that the initiative be rejected, the Eduskunta approved the initiative. The President subsequently indicated his intention to endorse the initiative, but, owing to legislative considerations, the new marriage act was not expected to take effect until March 2017.

At the general election held on 19 April, the Centre Party increased its representation by 14 seats to hold 49 seats in the Eduskunta, thus becoming the largest party in the legislature. Its Chairman, Sipilä, was expected to begin discussions on the formation of a new coalition government. The Finns Party took second place with 38 seats, ahead of the NCP, which secured 37. The NCP's main coalition partner, the SDP, reduced its representation by eight seats, to 34 seats, while the Green League increased its representation to 15 seats.

Foreign Affairs

Regional relations

Finland has traditionally maintained a neutral stance in foreign affairs. It joined the UN and the Nordic Council (see p. 462) in 1955, but became a full member of the European Free Trade Association (EFTA) only in 1986, although a free trade agreement between Finland and the European Community (EC) took effect in 1974. In 1989 Finland joined the Council of Europe. In 1991, following the collapse of the USSR, Finland unilaterally abrogated the 1948 Finno-Soviet Treaty of Friendship, Co-operation and Mutual Assistance, which had bound Finland to a military defence alliance with the USSR and prevented the country from joining any international organization (including the EC) whose members posed a military threat to the USSR. In 1992 the Finnish Government formally applied to join the EC. Following a referendum in which 56.9% of votes cast were in favour of membership, Finland left EFTA and joined the European Union (EU, see p. 271), as the EC had been restyled, in 1995.

Finland consolidated its commitment to European integration, joining the Economic and Monetary Union (EMU), which commenced on 1 January 1999, and the Schengen Agreement on the freedom of movement in 1996. Finland regards its role in the EU as one of advocacy for the so-called 'Northern Dimension'—the Nordic and Baltic countries and Russia. In 2008 the Eduskunta ratified the Treaty of Lisbon, which was designed to reform the institutions of the EU to improve decision-making following its enlargement. The treaty entered into effect across the EU on 1 December 2009. Finland has also participated in the EU drive to strengthen regional infrastructure links, jointly establishing two underwater cable connections with Estonia as part of a wider EU plan to integrate regional power markets; Estlink I became operational in 2006 and Estlink II in 2014.

Although the coalition Government that took office in Finland in June 2011 did not include the Eurosceptic True Finns/the Finns Party, which had made large gains at the April general election, the new administration insisted that it would impose strict conditions on its support for future emergency financial assistance from the EU's European Financial Stability Facility (EFSF) to debt-stricken members of the eurozone, including the provision of collateral to Finland by recipient countries. In August the Governments of Finland and Greece, which was seeking a second financial rescue package in addition to assistance agreed in May 2010, reached a provisional agreement under which Greece would place a sum of money equal to Finland's contribution to its emergency funding plan into a Finnish escrow account as collateral. However, this bilateral accord prompted several other eurozone members to demand similar arrangements, leading to a delay in the implementation of a second bailout for Greece. The dispute was resolved in October, when eurozone ministers responsible for finance concluded a new, more complex, collateral agreement; notably, any country requesting collateral would itself have to fulfil certain conditions in exchange, including the payment of its share of the capital of the European Stability Mechanism (ESM, a permanent rescue fund that was expected to come into force in July 2012) at the time of its establishment rather than over a five-year period. Although this new arrangement was available in principle to all countries contributing to the rescue plan for Greece, only Finland opted to pursue it. The Greek and Finnish Governments duly signed a new agreement on collateral in February 2012, following which the Eduskunta approved Finland's participation in a further EFSF funding plan for Greece. In June the Eduskunta approved the ratification of the treaty establishing the ESM, which entered into force in September. The Finnish Government concluded a collateral agreement with Spain in July, in return for its support for emergency EU funding to recapitalize the Spanish banking sector; as with the rescue plan for Greece, Finland was the only country to seek collateral. In November, with the constituent parties of the coalition Government deeply divided over the issue, Finland opted not to join a group of 11 other EU member states undertaking preparatory work on the proposed introduction of a financial transactions tax. In December Finland became the 12th eurozone member to ratify an intergovernmental treaty on new, stricter fiscal arrangements (the so-called fiscal compact), which had been signed by 25 of the 27 EU member states in March, thus triggering its entry into force on 1 January 2013.

Meanwhile, at a meeting of EU ministers of internal affairs in September 2011 and again in March 2013, Finland, together with the Netherlands and Germany, vetoed the admission of Bulgaria and Romania to the EU's Schengen area (which would allow the removal of border controls between these states and existing members of the area), owing to concerns regarding corruption and organized crime.

The pursuance of friendly relations with the USSR, and latterly Russia, has generally been regarded as a priority in Finnish foreign affairs. In October 1989 Mikhail Gorbachev became the first Soviet head of state to visit Finland since 1975, and recognized Finland's neutral status. The Finno-Soviet Treaty of Friendship was replaced in 1992 by a 10-year bilateral

agreement which involved no military commitment. The agreement was to be automatically renewed for five-year periods unless annulled by either signatory. The new treaty also included undertakings by Finland and Russia not to use force against each other and to respect the inviolability of their common border and each other's territorial integrity. Finnish foreign policy towards Russia in the late 2000s included advocacy for a closer strategic relationship between the EU and Russia. In February 2010 Finland gave its final approval for the construction of a Russian-owned gas pipeline, Nord Stream, under the Baltic Sea, amid concerns from countries bordering the sea over the pipeline's potential environmental impact. The pipeline, which would carry gas directly from Russia to Germany, thus bypassing Russia's neighbours, commenced operations in September 2011. In December 2014, despite EU demands that member states curtail new energy deals with Russia in response to Russia's ongoing intervention in Ukraine and the Crimea peninsula, the Eduskunta approved plans for a Finnish consortium to construct a new nuclear plant in northern Finland in a joint venture with the Russian state-owned energy company Rosatom.

Other external relations

Although Finland did not become a member of the North Atlantic Treaty Organization (NATO, see p. 367), owing to its policy of military neutrality, it did join NATO's Partnership for Peace framework in 1994 and participates in certain NATO-led operations. Finland contributed troops to the peacekeeping Stabilization Force (SFOR) in Bosnia and Herzegovina from 1996 to 2004, the Kosovo Force (KFOR) operation responsible for establishing and maintaining security in Kosovo from 1999, and the International Security Assistance Force (ISAF) in Afghanistan from 2002. Meanwhile, in January 1997 Finland began participation in two of the then 13 EU 'battlegroups', to be deployed in rotation in crisis areas. Finland also contributed troops to an EU Force (EUFOR) mission in Bosnia and Herzegovina (which replaced SFOR in 2004) and to the UN Mission in the Central African Republic and Chad (MINURCAT) until the end of its mandate in December 2010. The debate surrounding membership of NATO came to the fore again following Russian action, first in Georgia in 2008 and subsequently in Ukraine and the Crimea peninsula in 2014. Despite support for an application for full NATO membership from senior figures of the NCP, including Prime Minister Stubb, in late 2014 the majority of the public remained opposed to such a measure. During a NATO summit meeting held in Newport, United Kingdom, in September 2014 the Finnish Chief of Defence and his Swedish counterpart signed a host nation support agreement that would permit assistance from NATO troops in the two Nordic countries in emergency situations. The agreement further strengthened ties between NATO and the two signatory nations by enabling joint training exercises and military co-operation.

Relations between Finland and the USA are cordial. US policy before the dissolution of the USSR was to support Finnish neutrality and, thereafter, was to engage actively in trade and economic relations. Following the terrorist attacks of 11 September 2001 in the USA, Finland did not participate in the US-led retaliatory military action against the Taliban regime in Afghanistan. Finnish military personnel did, however, take part in the subsequent peacekeeping operation in Afghanistan. Finland was opposed to military action against the regime of Saddam Hussein in Iraq in early 2003 without a UN Security Council resolution, but indicated that it would be prepared to take part in military action under UN auspices and in possible humanitarian and peacekeeping operations. In the event, Finland pledged US $5.1m. for reconstruction in Iraq, but did not dispatch any troops.

CONSTITUTION AND GOVERNMENT

The Constitution of Finland entered into force on 1 March 2000, amending the Constitution of July 1919. Finland has a republican Constitution, under the provisions of which executive power is divided between the Eduskunta (Parliament), the Valtioneuvosto (Cabinet) and the President. The unicameral Eduskunta has 200 members, elected by universal adult suffrage for four years on the basis of proportional representation. The President is elected for six years by direct popular vote. Legislative power is exercised by the Eduskunta. The Eduskunta elects the Prime Minister, who is then appointed by the President. The other government ministers are appointed by the President on the basis of nominations by the Prime Minister. At February 2013, following many municipal mergers, Finland was divided into 320 municipalities, which are guaranteed self-government and are entitled to levy taxes. The Åland Islands are guaranteed self-government. In their native region the Sámi have linguistic and cultural autonomy.

REGIONAL AND INTERNATIONAL CO-OPERATION

Finland joined the European Union (EU, see p. 271) in 1995, and participated in the introduction of the single European currency, the euro, in January 1999. Finland is a member of the Nordic Council (see p. 462), the Arctic Council, the Council of Europe (see p. 250), the Council of the Baltic Sea States (see p. 249) and the Organization for Security and Co-operation in Europe (OSCE, see p. 385).

Finland joined the UN in 1955. As a contracting party to the General Agreement on Tariffs and Trade, Finland joined the World Trade Organization (WTO, see p. 431) on its establishment in 1995. Finland is a member of the Organisation for Economic Co-operation and Development (OECD, see p. 377) and participates in the Partnership for Peace framework of the North Atlantic Treaty Organization (NATO, see p. 367).

ECONOMIC AFFAIRS

In 2013, according to estimates by the World Bank, Finland's gross national income (GNI), measured at average 2011–13 prices, was US $256,254m., equivalent to $47,110 per head (or $38,480 per head on an international purchasing-power parity basis). During 2004–13, it was estimated, the population increased at an average annual rate of 0.4%, while gross domestic product (GDP) per head increased, in real terms, by an average of 0.4% per year. Overall GDP increased, in real terms, at an average annual rate of 0.8% in 2004–13; GDP declined by 1.4% in 2013.

Agriculture (including hunting, forestry and fishing) contributed an estimated 3.1% of GDP in 2013 and, together with mining and quarrying, employed 4.4% of the working population in that year. Forestry is the most important branch of the sector. Animal husbandry is the predominant form of farming. The major crops are barley, oats, wheat and potatoes. During 2004–13 agricultural GDP increased, in real terms, by an average of 1.9% per year; agricultural GDP decreased by 6.2% in 2012, but increased by 0.2% in 2013.

Industry (including mining, manufacturing, construction and power) provided 30.6% of GDP in 2013. The sector, excluding mining, employed 22.6% of the working population in 2013. Industrial GDP decreased, in real terms, by an average of 0.6% per year during 2004–13; industrial GDP decreased by 7.6% in 2012 and by 2.1% in 2013.

Mining and quarrying contributed 0.5% of GDP in 2013 and employed 0.2% of the working population in 2008. Gold is the major mineral export, and zinc ore, copper ore and lead ore are also mined in small quantities. The GDP of the mining sector increased, in real terms, at an average rate of 5.3% per year during 2004–13; mining GDP increased by 1.2% in 2013.

Manufacturing provided 19.2% of GDP in 2013 and together with utilities employed 15.4% of the working population in that year. The most important branches of manufacturing measured by value of output in 2006 were electrical and optical equipment, including the electronics industry (particularly mobile telephones), pulp, paper and paper products, metal products, chemical products and non-electrical machinery and equipment. The GDP of the manufacturing sector decreased, in real terms, at an average rate of 1.3% per year during 2004–13; the sector's GDP decreased by 11.6% in 2012 and by 1.9% in 2013.

Construction provided 7.5% of GDP and employed 7.2% of the working population in 2013. Construction GDP increased, in real terms, by an average of 0.4% per year during 2004–13; the sector's GDP decreased by 2.3% in 2013.

Of total energy generated in 2012, 32.7% was derived from nuclear energy, 23.9% from hydroelectric power, 10.5% from coal and 9.4% from natural gas. In late 2012 there were four nuclear reactors in operation. Construction of a 1,600-MW fifth nuclear reactor, in Olkiluoto in south-west Finland, was subject to delays and it was not expected to commence commercial production before 2018, several years later than originally planned and hugely over budget. Despite these difficulties, the construction of a further reactor at Olkiluoto, as well as a new nuclear plant in northern Finland, Hanhikivi 1, were under consideration in 2014 and 2015 (see *Regional relations*). Meanwhile, the construction of a liquefied natural gas terminal in Tornio was expected to begin in early 2015. Imports of mineral fuels comprised 22.8% of the total cost of imports in 2013.

Services provided 66.3% of GDP and engaged 73.0% of the employed labour force in 2013. In real terms, the combined GDP of the services sector increased at an average rate of 0.9% per year during 2004–13; the sector's GDP increased by 0.6% in 2012, but decreased by 1.2% in 2013.

In 2013 Finland recorded a visible merchandise trade surplus of US $4,799m., but there was a deficit of $2,466m. on the current account of the balance of payments. In 2013 the principal source of imports was Russia (providing 18.0% of total imports); other major sources were Germany, Sweden, the People's Republic of China and the Netherlands. Sweden was the principal market for exports in the same year (accounting for 11.6% of total exports); other major purchasers were Germany, Russia, the USA, the Netherlands and the United Kingdom. The European Union (EU, see p. 271) accounted for 55.3% of exports and 56.7% of imports in 2013. The principal exports in 2012 were basic manufactures (mainly paper and paperboard), machinery and transport equipment (mainly electronic products, notably mobile telephones), chemicals and related products, mineral fuels and lubricants, chemicals and related products, crude materials, and miscellaneous manufactured articles. The principal imports were machinery and transport equipment, mineral fuels and lubricants, chemicals and related products, basic manufactures, miscellaneous manufactured articles, crude materials, and food and live animals.

In 2013, according to official figures, there was a general government deficit of €1,996m., equivalent to 1.0% of GDP. Finland's general government gross debt was €110,158m. in 2013, equivalent to 54.7% of GDP. According to the International Labour Organization, the average annual rate of inflation was 2.0% during 2004–13. Consumer prices increased by 1.5% in 2013. The average rate of unemployment was 8.2% in 2013.

Finland's economy depends chiefly on exports, notably metal products, paper and pulp, and high-technology products. However, trade was severely affected by the global economic downturn that began in late 2008, with exports and GDP decreasing by 21.3% and 8.5%, respectively, in 2009. The general government balance moved into deficit in 2009 for the first time in 10 years. By mid-2010 strong growth in the world economy, particularly in Finland's principal trading partners (Russia, Germany and Sweden), had brought about a recovery in the country's exports and GDP, which increased by 7.5% and 3.3%, respectively, in 2010. However, GDP growth decelerated to 2.8% in 2011 and declined by 0.2% in 2012. GDP showed a continued contraction in 2013, of 1.4%, partly as a result of weak investment and decreases in private consumption and external demand. Export competitiveness was also undermined by rising labour costs, unemployment and difficulties in key industrial sectors, as exemplified by the downsizing and redundancies at Nokia Corporation, hitherto a significant tax contributor and employer. Although the Government that took office in June 2011 aimed to balance the budget by 2015 through the implementation of rigorous austerity measures, the general government balance recorded annual deficits in 2011–13 (equivalent to 1.0% of GDP in 2013). Moreover, the high costs associated with the demographic pressures of an ageing population, in conjunction with generous welfare benefits, were expected to put further pressure on public finances in the medium term. In early 2014 the Organisation for Economic Co-operation and Development reiterated that Finland should take determined action to implement structural reforms to revive economic growth, restore competitiveness and preserve high standards of living. Meanwhile, in January 2014 the IMF added Finland to the countries required to undergo mandatory assessment of the stability of their financial sectors, although the country was not scheduled for assessment in that year. Among a number of recommendations made by the IMF in May were that Finland strengthen its macroprudential framework to help ward off underlying financial vulnerability to external shocks and promote stability, and that participation in the labour force be increased by raising the age of retirement and reforming the pension system. The general outlook for the Finnish economy in the short term was a slow and fragile recovery (very much limited by the continuing recession in Russia); at mid-2014 the Ministry of Finance projected that GDP would show marginal positive growth, of 0.2%, over that year as a whole. However, the general government gross debt (which as recently as 2008 had stood at only 33.8% of GDP) was forecast to increase in 2014 to above the EU-prescribed debt ceiling of 60% of GDP. Nevertheless, the European Commission stated that it would exempt Finland from potential sanctions for breaching the limit, since the situation had arisen partly from the country's contributions to financial bailouts to other ailing EU member states. In October 2014 the poor state of Finland's economy was underlined by the rating agency Standard & Poor's downgrading the country's credit rating from AAA to AA+.

PUBLIC HOLIDAYS

2016: 1 January (New Year's Day), 6 January (Epiphany), 25 March (Good Friday), 28 March (Easter Monday), 1 May (May Day), 5 May (Ascension Day), 15 May (Whit Sunday), 24–25 June (Midsummer), 5 November (All Saints' Day), 6 December (Independence Day), 24–26 December (Christmas).

Statistical Survey

Source (unless otherwise stated): Statistics Finland, PL 2B, 00022 Helsinki; tel. (29) 5512220; e-mail info@stat.fi; internet www.stat.fi.

Note: Figures in this survey include data for the autonomous Åland Islands, unless otherwise stated.

Area and Population

AREA, POPULATION AND DENSITY

Area (sq km)	
Land	303,893
Inland water	34,539
Total	338,432*
Population (census results)†	
31 December 2000	5,181,115
31 December 2010	
Males	2,638,416
Females	2,736,860
Total	5,375,276
Population (at 31 December)	
2011	5,401,267
2012	5,426,674
2013	5,451,270
Density (per sq km) at 31 December 2013	17.9‡

* 130,669 sq miles; including Åland Islands (1,552 sq km—599 sq miles).
† From 2010 Finland abandoned data collection and enumeration through traditional census methodologies in favour of an annual register based system of population reporting.
‡ Land area only.

POPULATION BY AGE AND SEX
(population at 31 December 2013)

	Males	Females	Total
0–14 years	457,579	437,442	895,021
15–64 years	1,771,139	1,728,563	3,499,702
65 years and over	451,646	604,901	1,056,547
Total	2,680,364	2,770,906	5,451,270

REGIONS
(population at 31 December 2013)

	Land area (sq km)*	Population	Density (per sq km)*
Ahvenanmaa (Åland)	1,552	28,666	18.5
Etelä-Karjala (Södra Karelen) .	5,613	132,252	23.6
Etelä-Pohjanmaa (Södra Österbotten)	13,444	193,977	14.4
Etelä-Savo (Södra Savolax) . .	13,977	152,518	10.9
Kainuu (Kajanaland) . . .	21,501	79,975	3.7
Kanta-Häme (Egentliga Tavastland)	5,200	175,481	33.7
Keski-Pohjanmaa (Mellersta Österbotten)	5,019	68,677	13.7
Keski-Suomi (Mellersta Finland).	16,704	275,320	16.5
Kymenlaakso (Kymmenedalen) .	5,148	180,845	35.1
Lappi (Lappland)	92,662	182,514	2.0

—continued	Land area (sq km)*	Population	Density (per sq km)*
Päijät-Häme (Päijänne-Tavastland)	5,125	202,424	39.5
Pirkanmaa (Birkaland) . . .	12,446	500,166	40.2
Pohjanmaa (Österbotten) . .	7,750	180,384	23.3
Pohjois-Karjala (Norra Karelen) .	17,763	165,445	9.3
Pohjois-Pohjanmaa (Norra Österbotten)	35,507	403,287	11.4
Pohjois-Savo (Norra Savolax) .	16,768	248,430	14.8
Satakunta	7,957	224,556	28.2
Uusimaa (Nyland)† . . .	9,096	1,585,473	174.3
Varsinais-Suomi (Egentliga Finland)	10,661	470,880	44.2
Total	303,893	5,451,270	17.9

* According to regional divisions at 1 January 2012; excluding inland waters, totalling 34,539 sq km.
† Including the former Itä-Uusimaa (Östra Nyland) region, which was consolidated with Uusimaa from 1 January 2011.

PRINCIPAL TOWNS
(population at 31 December 2013)*

Helsinki (Helsingfors) (capital) . .	612,664	Lahti	103,364
Espoo (Esbo) . .	260,753	Kouvola	86,926
Tampere (Tammerfors) .	220,446	Pori (Björneborg) .	83,497
Vantaa (Vanda) .	208,098	Joensuu . . .	74,471
Oulu (Uleåborg) .	193,798	Lappeenranta (Villmanstrand) .	72,658
Turku (Åbo) . .	182,072	Hämeenlinna . .	67,806
Jyväskylä . . .	134,658	Vaasa	66,321
Kuopio	106,342	Rovaniemi . . .	61,215

* According to regional divisions at 1 January 2012.

BIRTHS, MARRIAGES AND DEATHS

	Registered live births*		Registered marriages†		Registered deaths*	
	Number	Rate (per 1,000)	Number	Rate (per 1,000)	Number	Rate (per 1,000)
2006 . .	58,840	11.2	28,236	5.4	48,065	9.1
2007 . .	58,729	11.1	29,497	5.6	49,077	9.3
2008 . .	59,530	11.2	31,014	5.8	49,094	9.2
2009 . .	60,430	11.3	29,836	5.6	49,883	9.3
2010 . .	60,980	11.3	29,952	5.6	50,887	9.5
2011 . .	59,961	11.1	28,408	5.3	50,585	9.4
2012 . .	59,493	11.0	28,878	5.3	51,707	9.6
2013 . .	58,134	10.7	25,119	4.6	51,472	9.5

* Including Finnish nationals temporarily outside the country.
† Data relate only to marriages in which the bride was domiciled in Finland.

Life expectancy (years at birth): 80.6 (males 77.7; females 83.7) in 2012 (Source: World Bank, World Development Indicators database).

ECONOMICALLY ACTIVE POPULATION
('000 persons aged 15 to 74 years)

	2011	2012	2013
Agriculture, forestry and fishing; mining and quarrying . . .	110	109	107
Manufacturing; electricity, gas and water	384	382	377
Construction	176	175	176
Wholesale and retail trade; repair of motor vehicles, and household goods	303	300	296
Hotels and restaurants . .	83	86	86
Transport, storage and communications	246	245	242
Financial intermediation; insurance and real estate activities	328	336	331
Public administration and defence; compulsory social security . .	116	113	111
Education	179	175	175
Health and social work . . .	396	409	399
Other community, social and personal service activities . .	141	142	144
Sub-total	**2,462**	**2,472**	**2,444**
Not classifiable by economic activity	11	11	13
Total employed	**2,474**	**2,483**	**2,457**
Unemployed	209	207	219
Total labour force . . .	**2,682**	**2,690**	**2,676**

Health and Welfare

KEY INDICATORS

Total fertility rate (children per woman, 2012)	1.9
Under-5 mortality rate (per 1,000 live births, 2012)	3
HIV/AIDS (% of persons aged 15–49, 2011)	0.1
Physicians (per 1,000 head, 2009)	2.9
Hospital beds (per 1,000 head, 2009)	6.2
Health expenditure (2011): US $ per head (PPP) . . .	3,382
Health expenditure (2011): % of GDP	9.0
Health expenditure (2011): public (% of total)	75.4
Total carbon dioxide emissions ('000 metric tons, 2010) . .	61,844.0
Carbon dioxide emissions per head (metric tons, 2010) . .	11.5
Human Development Index (2013): ranking	24
Human Development Index (2013): value	0.879

For sources and definitions, see explanatory note on p. vi.

Agriculture

PRINCIPAL CROPS
('000 metric tons; farms with arable land of 1 ha or more)

	2011	2012	2013
Wheat	974.8	887.1	887.8
Barley	1,514.3	1,581.1	1,904.2
Rye	78.4	64.1	25.7
Oats	1,043.1	1,073.1	1,196.8
Mixed grain	57.2	53.2	66.7
Potatoes	673.3	489.6	621.7
Rapeseed	115.1	73.2	80.3
Sugar beet	675.7	410.0	480.4
Cucumbers and gherkins . .	47.8	43.1	46.7
Carrots and turnips . . .	72.8	55.8	71.4

Aggregate production ('000 metric tons, may include official, semi-official or estimated data): Total cereals 3,670 in 2011, 3,661 in 2012, 4,084 in 2013; Total roots and tubers 673 in 2011, 490 in 2012, 621 in 2013; Total vegetables (incl. melons) 277 in 2011, 247 in 2012, 272 in 2013; Total fruits (excl. melons) 21 in 2011-13.

Source: FAO.

LIVESTOCK
('000 head at 1 May; farms with arable land of 1 ha or more)

	2011	2012	2013
Horses	76	74	75
Cattle	914	912	912
Sheep	129	130	136
Pigs*	1,335	1,290	130
Poultry	5,729	6,333	7,135

* Including piggeries of dairies.

Source: FAO.

LIVESTOCK PRODUCTS
('000 metric tons)

	2011	2012	2013
Cattle meat	83.5	81.1	81.2
Pig meat	201.9	192.9	194.6
Chicken meat	93.6	99.3	103.7
Cows' milk*	2,300.7	2,296.7	2,327.8
Hen eggs	62.8	62.2	66.9

* Millions of litres.

Source: FAO.

Forestry

ROUNDWOOD REMOVALS
('000 cubic metres, excl. bark)

	2011	2012	2013
Sawlogs, veneer logs and logs for sleepers	19,641.6	19,322.3	21,431.4
Pulpwood	25,884.6	25,291.9	27,900.0
Fuel wood	5,240.6	7,695.4	7,660.2
Total	**50,766.8**	**52,309.5**	**56,991.6**

Source: FAO.

SAWNWOOD PRODUCTION
('000 cu m, incl. railway sleepers)

	2011	2012	2013
Coniferous (softwood) . . .	9,700	9,400	10,400
Broadleaved (hardwood) . . .	50	40	40
Total	**9,750**	**9,440**	**10,440**

Source: FAO.

Fishing

('000 metric tons, live weight)

	2010	2011	2012
Capture	156.1	153.7	166.9
Roaches	4.1	4.3	4.5
Northern pike	8.2	8.2	8.2
European perch	8.9	9.1	9.2
Vendace	4.6	4.6	4.6
Atlantic herring	92.8	98.0	117.5
European sprat	24.6	15.8	9.0
Aquaculture	11.8	11.3	12.7
Rainbow trout	11.0	9.9	11.3
Total catch	**167.8**	**165.0**	**179.6**

Note: Figures exclude aquatic mammals, recorded by number rather than by weight. The catch of grey seals was: 349 in 2010; 290 in 2011; 177 in 2012.

Source: FAO.

Mining

('000 metric tons unless otherwise indicated)

	2010	2011	2012
Copper ore*	14.7	16.0	n.a.
Nickel ore*	41.4	49.8	46.3
Zinc ore*	55.6	64.1	51.5
Chromium ore‡	598	693	425
Cobalt (metric tons)§	9,413	10,441	10,547
Mercury (metric tons)	9	—	—
Silver (metric tons)§	64.8	69.3	128.2
Gold (kg)§	7,628	8,461	10,814
Platinum (kg)§	718	836	830†
Phosphate rock (incl. apatite, metric tons)‖	817	870	870†
Peat: for fuel	7,533	6,847	6,800†
Peat: for horticulture	867	674	670†

* Figures refer to the metal content of ores.
† Estimated production.
‡ Figures refer to chromium oxide content.
§ Figures refer to production of metal and (for cobalt) powder and salts.
‖ Figures refer to gross weight. The phosphorus oxide content (in metric tons) was: 289 in 2010; 307 in 2011; 300 in 2012 (estimate).

Source: US Geological Survey.

Industry

SELECTED PRODUCTS
('000 metric tons unless otherwise indicated)

	2002	2003	2004*
Cellulose	7,503	7,446	7,852
Newsprint	1,190	1,238	1,217
Other paper, boards and cardboards	11,362	12,113	13,218
Plywoods and veneers ('000 cu m)	1,135	1,168	1,388
Cement	1,198	1,493	1,270
Pig iron and ferro-alloys . . .	2,829	3,091	3,037
Electricity (net, million kWh) .	71,618	80,377	82,171
Sugar	161	202	193
Rolled steel products (metric tons)	3,975	4,090	4,157
Cigarettes (million)	4,130	3,946	n.a.

* Preliminary data.

2010: Cement 1,215,000 metric tons (estimate) (Source: US Geological Survey); Electricity (net) 77,203m. kWh.

2011: Cement 1,387,000 metric tons (Source: US Geological Survey); Electricity (net) 70,390m. kWh.

2012: Cement 1,300,000 metric tons (estimate) (Source: US Geological Survey); Electricity (net) 67,687m. kWh.

2013: Electricity (net) 68,329m. kWh.

Finance

CURRENCY AND EXCHANGE RATES

Monetary Units
100 cent = 1 euro (€).

Sterling and Dollar Equivalents (31 December 2014)
£1 sterling = 1.286 euros;
US $1 = 0.824 euros;
€10 = £7.78 = $12.14.

Average Exchange Rate (euros per US $)
2012   0.7783
2013   0.7532
2014   0.7537

Note: The national currency was formerly the markka (Finnmark). From the introduction of the euro, with Finnish participation, on 1 January 1999, a fixed exchange rate of €1 = 5.94573 markkaa was in operation. Euro notes and coins were introduced on 1 January 2002. The euro and local currency circulated alongside each other until 28 February, after which the euro became the sole legal tender.

BUDGET
(€ million)

Revenue	2013	2014*	2015†
Taxes and other levies . . .	38,740	39,793	40,043
Taxes on income and property .	12,062	12,125	12,069
Taxes on turnover	17,298	17,880	17,850
Excise duties	6,573	6,918	7,163
Other taxes	2,656	2,715	2,853
Other levies	151	155	109
Miscellaneous revenues . . .	5,137	4,745	5,997
Sub-total	43,877	44,538	46,040
Interest on investments and profits received	2,030	1,995	2,783
Loans receivable	6,684	7,531	4,882
Total	52,591	54,064	53,705

Expenditure	2013	2014*	2015†
President of the Republic . . .	36	38	19
Parliament	171	158	164
Council of State	199	90	91
Ministry of Foreign Affairs . .	1,339	1,296	1,224
Ministry of Justice	884	900	901
Ministry of the Interior . . .	1,355	1,266	1,219
Ministry of Defence	2,852	2,750	2,687
Ministry of Finance	16,991	17,013	16,950
Ministry of Education and Culture	6,605	6,584	6,769
Ministry of Agriculture and Forestry	2,641	2,659	2,661
Ministry of Transport and Communications	3,182	2,970	2,854
Ministry of Employment and the Economy	3,799	3,376	3,439
Ministry of Social Affairs and Health	12,498	12,880	12,756
Ministry of the Environment . .	299	271	204
Public debt	1,737	1,814	1,766
Total	54,587	54,064	53,705

* Preliminary, excluding supplementary budget.
† Budget proposals.

INTERNATIONAL RESERVES
(US $ million at 31 December)

	2011	2012	2013
Gold (Eurosystem valuation) . .	2,487.7	2,629.1	1,898.4
IMF special drawing rights . .	1,717.6	1,729.4	1,733.5
Reserve position in IMF . . .	831.9	1,026.6	949.9
Foreign exchange	5,307.6	5,697.2	6,685.9
Total	10,344.8	11,082.3	11,267.7

Source: IMF, *International Financial Statistics*.

MONEY SUPPLY
(incl. shares, depository corporations, national residency criteria, € million at 31 December)

	2011	2012	2013
Currency issued	15,184	15,598	16,328
Bank of Finland	11,688	12,350	12,806
Demand deposits	74,084	80,986	89,648
Other deposits	47,182	42,685	37,025
Securities other than shares . .	80,206	87,680	88,780
Money market fund shares . .	9,062	3,168	3,391
Shares and other equity . . .	33,151	32,680	34,279
Other items (net)	7,191	7,501	5,075
Total	266,060	270,297	274,526

Source: IMF, *International Financial Statistics*.

COST OF LIVING
(Consumer Price Index; base: 2010 = 100)

	2011	2012	2013
Food and non-alcoholic beverages .	106.3	111.8	117.7
Clothing and footwear	101.2	103.9	102.6
Housing, water, electricity, gas and other fuels	106.3	108.1	108.5
All items (incl. others) . . .	103.4	106.3	107.9

NATIONAL ACCOUNTS
(€ million at current prices)
National Income and Product

	2011	2012	2013
Compensation of employees .	78,580	81,283	81,697
Employers' social contributions .	18,248	19,005	19,200
Operating surplus	39,585	35,708	35,666
Domestic factor incomes .	136,413	135,996	136,563
Consumption of fixed capital .	36,581	38,266	38,867
Gross domestic product at factor cost	172,994	174,262	175,430
Indirect taxes, less subsidies .	23,875	24,807	25,911
GDP in purchasers' values .	196,869	199,069	201,341
Factor income received from abroad . . . . } *Less* Factor income paid abroad	851	991	607
Gross national product . .	197,720	200,060	201,948
Less Consumption of fixed capital	36,581	38,266	38,867
National income in market prices	161,139	161,794	163,081
Other current transfers from abroad . . . . } *Less* Other current transfers from abroad	−2,099	−1,944	−2,735
National disposable income .	159,040	159,850	160,346

Expenditure on the Gross Domestic Product

	2011	2012	2013
Government final consumption expenditure	46,491	48,683	50,217
Private final consumption expenditure	105,771	109,026	111,046
Changes in inventories . . .	2,434	328	335
Acquisitions, less disposals, of valuables	69	69	69
Gross fixed capital formation .	43,779	44,305	42,647
Total domestic expenditure .	198,544	202,411	204,314
Exports of goods and services . .	77,093	78,881	76,866
Less Imports of goods and services	78,768	81,764	78,812
Statistical discrepancy	—	−459	−1,027
GDP in purchasers' values .	196,869	199,069	201,341
GDP at constant 2010 prices .	191,910	189,119	186,831

Gross Domestic Product by Economic Activity

	2011	2012	2013
Agriculture, hunting, forestry and fishing	4,649	4,533	4,634
Mining and quarrying; manufacturing; electricity, gas and water	37,530	34,482	34,542
Construction	10,905	11,336	11,221
Wholesale and retail trade; hotels and restaurants; transportation and storage	28,260	28,975	28,976
Information and communication .	8,593	8,864	8,973
Financial intermediation and insurance	4,565	4,635	4,324
Real estate activities	19,414	20,079	20,893
Business, administrative and support service activities . .	13,914	14,464	14,651
Public administration; defence; education; health and social work	812	852	874
Other community, social and personal services	19,512	20,229	20,389
Sub-total	148,154	148,449	149,477
Taxes, less subsidies, on products .	26,415	27,376	28,254
Statistical discrepancy	22,300	23,244	23,610
GDP in purchasers' values .	196,869	199,069	201,341

BALANCE OF PAYMENTS
(US $ million)

	2011	2012	2013
Exports of goods	82,756	76,438	78,559
Imports of goods	−79,265	−72,841	−73,759
Balance on goods	3,491	3,597	4,799
Exports of services	26,193	25,784	26,068
Imports of services	−28,955	−30,420	−29,837
Balance on goods and services	730	−1,039	1,030
Primary income received . . .	18,672	17,279	18,339
Primary income paid	−18,897	−17,641	−19,031
Balance on goods, services and primary income . . .	504	−1,401	338
Secondary income received . .	2,950	3,132	2,628
Secondary income paid . . .	−5,143	−4,855	−5,433
Current balance	−1,689	−3,124	−2,466
Capital account (net)	264	265	282
Direct investment assets . . .	3,552	−8,378	263
Direct investment liabilities . .	−6,008	4,937	−5,297
Portfolio investment assets . .	−6,233	−20,365	−10,666
Portfolio investment liabilities .	17,118	32,368	13,697
Financial derivatives and employee stock options (net)	1,660	1,382	2,814
Other investment assets . . .	−116,025	−2,327	37,161
Other investment liabilities . .	117,861	15,175	−38,024
Net errors and omissions . .	−10,066	−19,293	3,286
Reserves and related items .	435	640	1,051

Source: IMF, *International Financial Statistics*.

External Trade

PRINCIPAL COMMODITIES
(€ million)

Imports c.i.f.	2011	2012	2013
Food and live animals	3,248	3,467	3,611
Beverages and tobacco	546	496	574
Crude materials (inedible) except fuels	5,203	4,844	4,387
Mineral fuels, lubricants, etc.	13,137	12,997	13,343
Animal and vegetable oils and fats	240	301	349
Chemicals and related products .	6,643	6,980	6,849
Basic manufactures	7,127	6,658	6,296
Machinery and transport equipment	16,793	16,118	15,405
Miscellaneous manufactured articles	5,615	5,658	5,573
Total (incl. others)	60,535	59,517	58,407

Exports f.o.b.	2011	2012	2013
Food and live animals	1,368	1,367	1,377
Beverages and tobacco	152	160	170
Crude materials (inedible) except fuels	4,059	4,273	4,803
Mineral fuels, lubricants, etc. .	5,481	6,202	6,847
Animal and vegetable oils and fats	36	50	25
Chemicals and related products .	6,350	6,350	6,273
Basic manufactures	18,055	16,843	16,396
Machinery and transport equipment	16,654	16,612	15,115
Miscellaneous manufactured articles	3,225	3,399	3,520
Total (incl. others)	56,855	56,878	56,048

PRINCIPAL TRADING PARTNERS
(€ million)*

Imports c.i.f.	2011	2012	2013
Belgium	1,268	1,259	1,228
Brazil	839	811	651
China, People's Republic . . .	4,398	4,602	3,679
Czech Republic	706	611	621
Denmark	1,342	1,390	1,805
Estonia	1,554	1,547	1,688
France	1,980	1,820	1,924
Germany	7,528	7,335	7,355
India	673	350	500
Italy	1,583	1,592	1,537
Japan	930	740	671
Korea, Republic	601	871	461
Netherlands	3,151	3,370	3,374
Norway	1,950	2,166	1,196
Poland	1,184	1,192	1,329
Russia	11,319	10,583	10,521
Spain	801	752	882
Sweden	6,029	6,369	6,693
Switzerland	647	673	686
United Kingdom	1,777	1,760	1,859
USA	2,226	1,995	1,962
Total (incl. others)	60,535	59,517	58,407

Exports f.o.b.	2011	2012	2013
Austria	354	350	306
Belgium	1,584	1,731	1,922
Brazil	544	727	241
Canada	902	596	739
China, People's Republic . . .	2,667	2,607	2,766
Denmark	1,163	1,031	1,035
Estonia	1,339	1,710	1,748
France	1,762	1,692	1,827
Germany	5,625	5,253	5,419
India	625	483	481
Italy	1,347	1,341	1,312
Japan	975	1,068	994
Korea, Republic	568	694	843
Netherlands	3,852	3,557	3,457

Exports f.o.b.—*continued*	2011	2012	2013
Norway	1,596	1,804	1,651
Poland	1,576	1,409	1,362
Russia	5,337	5,688	5,359
Spain	988	829	792
Sweden	6,739	6,291	6,489
Switzerland	733	841	733
Turkey	790	699	690
United Kingdom	2,913	2,889	2,916
USA	2,919	3,605	3,561
Total (incl. others) . . .	56,855	56,878	56,048

* Imports by country of production; exports by country of consumption.

Transport

RAILWAYS
(traffic)

	2011	2012	2013
Passengers ('000 journeys) . .	68,376	69,300	69,300
Passenger-km (million) . . .	3,882	4,035	4,053
Freight carried ('000 metric tons)	34,827	n.a.	n.a.
Freight ton-km (million) . . .	9,395	9,275	9,470

ROAD TRAFFIC
(registered motor vehicles at 31 December)

	2011	2012	2013
Passenger cars	2,978,729	3,057,484	3,127,399
Lorries and vans	488,939	508,011	526,098
Motorcycles	236,661	244,968	251,525
Tractors	383,951	391,335	399,507
Snowmobiles*	125,937	130,581	135,473

* Excluding Åland Islands.

SHIPPING

Flag Registered Fleet
(at 31 December)

	2012	2013	2014
Number of vessels	290	292	297
Total displacement ('000 grt) . .	1,488.6	1,464.7	1,508.4

Source: Lloyd's List Intelligence (www.lloydslistintelligence.com).

International Seaborne Freight Traffic

	2011	2012	2013
Goods ('000 metric tons):			
loaded	44,208	44,520	47,028
unloaded	54,168	48,708	49,296

2010: Number of vessels entered 25,373.

Source: partly UN, *Monthly Bulletin of Statistics*.

CANAL TRAFFIC

	2008	2009	2010
Vessels in transit	34,255	42,199	47,778
Goods carried ('000 metric tons) .	2,116	1,083	1,660

CIVIL AVIATION
(traffic on scheduled services)

	2010	2011
Kilometres flown (million)	148	172
Passengers carried ('000)	8,436	9,235
Passenger-km (million)	17,786	20,386
Total ton-km (million)	2,352	2,568

Source: UN, *Statistical Yearbook*.

Passengers carried ('000): 10,732 in 2012; 10,697 in 2013 (Source: World Bank, World Development Indicators database).

Tourism

FOREIGN TOURIST ARRIVALS
(overnight stays at accommodation establishments)

Country of residence	2011	2012	2013
Estonia	228,187	235 482	187,295
France	213,588	217,886	214,248
Germany	541,031	534,239	501,650
Italy	156,509	130,847	115,681
Japan	146,433	176,919	205,988
Netherlands	164,593	164,918	158,668
Norway	173,254	182,639	174,147
Russia	1,286,598	1,506,900	1,620,419
Spain	130,046	96,820	96,876
Sweden	552,129	537,002	531,375
Switzerland	118,009	132,900	128,771
United Kingdom	389,037	405,541	454,604
USA	201,854	198,725	187,245
Total (incl. others)	5,507,468	5,802,959	5,860,447

Tourism receipts (US $ million, excl. passenger transport): 3,823 in 2011; 3,874 in 2012; 4,039 in 2013 (Source: World Tourism Organization).

Communications Media

	2010	2011	2012
Newspapers:			
number	194	188	183
total circulation ('000 copies)	2,886	2,745	2,547
Other periodicals: number	3,056	2,933	2,814
Book production: titles	12,017	11,404	11,513
Telephones ('000 main lines in use)*	1,250	1,080	890
Mobile cellular telephones ('000 subscribers)*	8,390	8,940	9,320
Broadband subscribers ('000)*	1,572.7	1,588.7	1,642.8

* Source: International Telecommunication Union.

2009: Internet users ('000 aged 15 years and over) 4,393.1 (Source: International Telecommunication Union).

2013: Telephones ('000 main lines in use) 752; Mobile cellular telephones ('000 subscribers) 9,318; Broadband subscribers ('000) 1,676.5.

Education

(2013 unless otherwise indicated)

	Institutions*	Teachers†	Students
Comprehensive schools‡	2,952	44,313	540,477
Senior secondary schools	395	7,295	105,898
Vocational and professional institutions	275	14,058	276,471§
Polytechnics	31	6,034	138,880
Universities	20	7,755	167,179

* 2010 figures.
† 2003 figures.
‡ Comprising six-year primary stage and three-year lower secondary stage.
§ 2012 figure.

Pupil-teacher ratio (primary education, UNESCO estimate): 13.6 in 2011/12 (Source: UNESCO Institute for Statistics).

Directory

The Government

HEAD OF STATE

President: SAULI NIINISTÖ (took office 1 March 2012).

CABINET
(Valtioneuvosto)
(April 2015)

A coalition comprising the National Coalition Party (NCP), the Social Democratic Party (SDP), the Swedish People's Party (SPP) and the Christian Democrats (CD). Following legislative elections held in April 2015, the Government of Alexander Stubb submitted its resignation on 28 April; it continued in a caretaker capacity while negotiations on the formation of a new coalition were ongoing.

Prime Minister: ALEXANDER STUBB (NCP).

Minister of Finance: ANTTI RINNE (SDP).

Minister of Foreign Affairs: ERKKI TUOMIOJA (SDP).

Minister of European Affairs and Foreign Trade: LENITA TOIVAKKA (NCP).

Minister of Justice: ANNA-MAJA HENRIKSSON (SPP).

Minister of International Development: SIRPA PAATERO (SDP).

Minister of the Interior: PÄIVI RÄSÄNEN (CD).

Minister of Defence: CARL HAGLUND (SPP).

Minister of Education and Communications: KRISTA KIURU (SDP).

Minister of Agriculture and Forestry: PETTERI ORPO (NCP).

Minister of Transport and Local Government: PAULA RISIKKO (NCP).

Minister of Economic Affairs: JAN VAPAAVUORI (NCP).

Minister of Labour: LAURI IHALAINEN (SDP).

Minister of Social Affairs and Health: LAURA RÄTY (NCP).

Minister of Health and Social Services: SUSANNA HUOVINEN (SDP).

Minister of the Environment: SANNI GRAHN-LAASONEN (NCP).

Minister of Culture and Housing: PIA VIITANEN (SDP).

MINISTRIES

Office of the President: Mariankatu 2, 00170 Helsinki; tel. (9) 661133; fax (9) 638247; e-mail presidentti@tpk.fi; internet www.presidentti.fi.

Prime Minister's Office: Snellmaninkatu 1A, Helsinki; POB 23, 00023 Government; tel. (9) 16001; fax (9) 16022165; e-mail info@vnk.fi; internet www.vnk.fi.

Ministry of Agriculture and Forestry: Hallituskatu 3A, Helsinki; POB 30, 00023 Government; tel. (9) 16001; fax (9) 16054202; e-mail kirjaamo.mmm@mmm.fi; internet www.mmm.fi.

Ministry of Defence: Eteläinen Makasiinikatu 8, POB 31, 00131 Helsinki; tel. (9) 16001; fax (9) 653254; e-mail tiedotus@defmin.fi; internet www.defmin.fi.

Ministry of Education and Culture: Meritullinkatu 10, Helsinki; POB 29, 00023 Government; tel. (2953) 30004; fax (9) 1359335; e-mail kirjaamo@minedu.fi; internet www.minedu.fi.

Ministry of Employment and the Economy: Aleksanterinkatu 4, 00170 Helsinki; POB 32, 00023 Government; tel. (10) 606000; fax (9) 16062166; e-mail kirjaamo@tem.fi; internet www.tem.fi.

Ministry of the Environment: Kasarmikatu 25, Helsinki; POB 35, 00023 Government; tel. (2952) 50000; fax (9) 16039320; e-mail kirjaamo.ym@ymparisto.fi; internet www.ym.fi.

Ministry of Finance: Snellmaninkatu 1A, Helsinki; POB 28, 00023 Government; tel. (295) 16001; fax (9) 16033123; e-mail valtiovarainministerio@vm.fi; internet www.vm.fi.

Ministry of Foreign Affairs: Merikasarmi, Laivastokatu 22, POB 176, 00023 Helsinki; tel. (9) 5350000; fax (9) 629840; e-mail kirjaamo .um@formin.fi; internet formin.finland.fi.

Ministry of the Interior: Kirkkokatu 12, Helsinki; POB 26, 00023 Government; tel. (295) 480171; fax (9) 16044635; e-mail kirjaamo@ intermin.fi; internet www.intermin.fi.

Ministry of Justice: Eteläesplanadi 10, Helsinki; POB 25, 00023 Government; tel. (9) 16003; fax (9) 16067730; e-mail oikeusministerio@om.fi; internet www.oikeusministerio.fi.

Ministry of Social Affairs and Health: Meritullinkatu 8, 00170 Helsinki; POB 33, 00023 Government; tel. (295) 16001; fax (9) 6980709; e-mail kirjaamo@stm.fi; internet www.stm.fi.

Ministry of Transport and Communications: Eteläesplanadi 16, Helsinki; POB 31, 00023 Government; tel. (9) 16001; fax (9) 16028596; e-mail info@lvm.fi; internet www.lvm.fi.

President and Legislature

PRESIDENT

Presidential Election, 22 January and 5 February 2012

	First round votes (%)	Second round votes (%)
Sauli Niinistö (NCP)	37.0	62.6
Pekka Haavisto (Green) . . .	18.8	37.4
Paavo Väyrynen (Centre) . .	17.5	—
Timo Soini (Finns Party) . .	9.4	—
Paavo Lipponen (SDP) . . .	6.7	—
Paavo Arhinmäki (Left Alliance)	5.5	—
Eva Biaudet (SPP)	2.7	—
Sari Essayah (CD)	2.5	—
Total	**100.0**	**100.0**

PARLIAMENT

Suomen Eduskunta

Mannerheimintie 30, 00102 Helsinki; tel. (9) 4321; fax (9) 4322274; e-mail parliament@parliament.fi; internet www.eduskunta.fi.

Speaker: JUHA SIPILÄ (Finnish Centre Party, acting).

Secretary-General: SEPPO TIITINEN.

General Election, 19 April 2015

Party	Votes	% of votes	Seats
Suomen Keskusta (Finnish Centre Party)	626,218	21.10	49
Perussuomalaiset (Finns Party)	524,054	17.65	38
Kansallinen Kokoomus (National Coalition Party) .	540,212	18.20	37
Suomen Sosialidemokraattinen Puolue (Finnish Social Democratic Party) . .	490,102	16.51	34
Vihreä Liitto (Green League) .	253,102	8.53	15
Vasemmistoliitto (Left Alliance)	211,702	7.13	12
Svenska Folkpartiet (Swedish People's Party)	144,802	4.88	9
Suomen Kristillisdemokraatit (Finnish Christian Democrats)	105,134	3.54	5
Others	73,133	2.46	1*
Total	**2,968,459**	**100.00**	**200**

* Including a representative of the Åland Islands.

Election Commission

Unit for Democracy, Language Affairs and Fundamental Rights: POB 25, 00023 Government; internet www .oikeusministerio.fi/fi/index/ministerio/organisaatio/demokratia -kieli-japerusoikeusasioidenyksikko.html; dept of the Ministry of Justice; Dir JOHANNA SUURPÄÄ.

Political Organizations

In March 2015 there were 16 registered political parties in Finland.

Itsenäisyyspuolue (IP) (Independence Party): Nikinsaarentie 31, 62900 Alajärvi; tel. (40) 565366; fax (06) 5574728; e-mail info@ipu.fi; internet ipu.fi; promotes national independence and social equality; Chair. ANTTI PESONEN.

Kansallinen Kokoomus (National Coalition Party—NCP): Kansakoulukuja 3A, 2nd Floor, 00100 Helsinki; tel. (20) 7488488; fax (20) 7488505; e-mail info@kokoomus.fi; internet www.kokoomus.fi; f. 1918; moderate conservative political ideology; Chair. ALEXANDER STUBB; Party Sec. MINNA ARVE; Chair., Parliamentary Group ARTO SATONEN; 40,000 mems.

Kommunistinen Työväenpuolue—Rauhan ja Sosialismin Puolesta (Communist Workers' Party): Tikkuraitti 11A, POB 93, 01301 Vantaa; tel. (9) 8571022; fax (9) 8573097; e-mail ktp@ktpkom .fi; internet www.ktpkom.fi; f. 1988; Sec.-Gen. RAUNO LINTUNEN.

Köyhien Asialla (For The Poor): Elsankuja 2B 9, 02230 Espoo; tel. (50) 5291171; e-mail info@koyhienasialla.fi; internet www .koyhienasialla.fi; f. 2002; Chair. TERTTU SAVOLA.

Muutos 2011 (M11) (Change 2011): POB 5, 37801 Akaa; e-mail muutostiedote@muutos2011.fi; internet www.muutos2011.fi; f. 2010; Chair. JARI LEINO; Sec. MARJUKKA KAAKKOLA; 403 mems.

Perussuomalaiset (Finns Party): Yrjönkatu 8–10B 25, 00120 Helsinki; tel. (9) 0207430800; fax (9) 0207430801; e-mail puoluetoimisto@perussuomalaiset.fi; internet www .perussuomalaiset.fi; f. 1995 by mems of defunct Suomen Maaseudun Puolue (Finnish Rural Party); changed the English version of its name from True Finns to The Finns in 2011, although not a direct translation; Swedish name, Sannfinländarna; Chair. TIMO SOINI; Sec.-Gen. RIIKKA SLUNGA-POUTSALO.

Piraattipuolue (Pirate Party of Finland): Franzéninkatu 5E 1, 00500 Helsinki; tel. (9) 453102344; e-mail info@piraattipuolue.fi; internet piraattipuolue.fi; f. 2009; campaigns for freedom of speech and reform of copyright and intellectual property laws; Chair. TAPANI KARVINEN.

Sinivalkoinen Rintama (Blue and White Front r.p.): c/o Olavi Mäenpää, Turunmaankatu 2A1, 20740 Turku; tel. (50) 5590119; e-mail olavi.maenpaa@turku.fi; f. 2009; fmrly Vapauspuolue-Suomen tulevaisuus (Liberty Party-Future of Finland); name changed 2013; Chair. OLAVI MÄENPÄÄ.

Suomen Keskusta (Finnish Centre Party): Apollonkatu 11A, 00100 Helsinki; tel. (10) 2897000; fax (10) 2897240; e-mail puoluetoimisto@ keskusta.fi; internet www.keskusta.fi; f. 1906; radical centre party founded to promote the interests of the rural population, now reformist movement favouring individual enterprise, equality and decentralization; Chair. JUHA SIPILÄ; Party Sec. TIMO LAANINEN; Chair., Parliamentary Group KIMMO TIILIKAINEN; over 200,000 mems.

Suomen Kommunistinen Puolue (SKP) (Communist Party of Finland): Hitsaajankatu 9A, 6th Floor, 00810 Helsinki; tel. (9) 77438150; fax (9) 77438160; e-mail skp@skp.fi; internet www.skp .fi; f. 1918; incorporated into Vasemmistoliitto (Left Alliance) in 1990; refounded 1997 following disputes in the latter party; Chair. JUHA-PEKKA VÄISÄNEN; Sec.-Gen. HEIKKI KETOHARJU; 3,000 mems.

Suomen Kristillisdemokraatit (Finnish Christian Democrats—CD): Karjalankatu 2C, 7th Floor, 00520 Helsinki; tel. (9) 34882200; fax (9) 34882228; e-mail kd@kd.fi; internet www.kd.fi; f. 1958 as Suomen Kristillinen Liitto (Finnish Christian Union); present name adopted 2001; Chair. PÄIVI RÄSÄNEN; Sec.-Gen. ASMO MAANSELKÄ; Chair., Parliamentary Group PETER ÖSTMAN; 12,000 mems.

Suomen Sosialidemokraattinen Puolue (Finnish Social Democratic Party—SDP): Saariniemenkatu 6, 00530 Helsinki; tel. (9) 478988; fax (9) 712752; e-mail palaute@sdp.fi; internet www.sdp.fi; f. 1899; constitutional socialist programme; mainly supported by the urban working and middle classes; Chair. ANTTI RINNE; Gen. Sec. REIJO PAANANEN; Chair., Parliamentary Group JOUNI BACKMAN; 50,000 mems.

Suomen Työväenpuolue (Finnish Workers' Party): POB 780, 00101 Helsinki; tel. (40) 7641163; e-mail tyovaenpuolue@suomi24 .fi; f. 1999; Chair. JUHANI TANSKI; Sec.-Gen. HEIKKI MÄNNIKKÖ.

Svenska Folkpartiet (Swedish People's Party—SPP): Simonkatu 8A, 00100 Helsinki; POB 430, 00101 Helsinki; tel. (9) 693070; fax (9) 6931968; e-mail info@sfp.fi; internet www.sfp.fi; f. 1906; liberal party representing the interests of the Swedish-speaking minority; Chair. CARL HAGLUND; Sec.-Gen. JOHAN JOHANSSON; 37,000 mems.

Vasemmistoliitto (Vas) (Left Alliance): Lintulahdenkatu 10, 3rd Floor, 00500 Helsinki; tel. (9) 7737700; e-mail vas@vasemmistoliitto .fi; internet www.vasemmisto.fi; f. 1990 by merger of the Finnish People's Democratic League (f. 1944), the Communist Party of Finland (f. 1918), the Democratic League of Finnish Women, and left-wing groups; Chair. PAAVO ARHINMÄKI; Sec.-Gen. MARKO VARAJÄRVI; Chair., Parliamentary Group ANNIKA LAPINTIE; c. 9,500 mems.

Vihreä Liitto (Green League): Fredrikinkatu 33A, 3rd Floor, 00120 Helsinki; tel. (9) 58604160; fax (9) 58604161; e-mail vihreat@vihreat

.fi; internet www.vihreat.fi; f. 1987; Chair. and Leader VILLE NIINISTÖ; c. 4,400 mems.

Diplomatic Representation

EMBASSIES IN FINLAND

Argentina: Bulevardi 5A 11, 00120 Helsinki; tel. (9) 42428700; fax (9) 42428701; e-mail embajada_efinl@mrecic.gov.ar; Ambassador ROBERTO DANIEL PIERINI.

Austria: Unioninkatu 22, 00130 Helsinki; tel. (9) 6818600; fax (9) 665084; e-mail helsinki-ob@bmeia.gv.at; internet www.bmeia.gv.at/botschaft/helsinki.html; Ambassador Dr ELISABETH KEHRER.

Belarus: Unioninkatu 18, 00130 Helsinki; tel. (9) 42472056; fax (9) 42472057; e-mail finland@mfa.gov.by; internet www.finland.new .mfa.gov.by; Ambassador ALEXANDER P. OSTROVSKY.

Belgium: Kalliolinnantie 5, 00140 Helsinki; tel. (9) 170412; fax (9) 628842; e-mail helsinki@diplobel.fed.be; internet www.diplomatie .be/helsinki; Ambassador IVO GOEMANS.

Brazil: Itäinen puistotie 4B 1, 00140 Helsinki; tel. (9) 6841500; fax (9) 650084; e-mail brasemb@brazil.fi; internet www.brazil.fi; Ambassador NORTON DE ANDRADE MELLO RAPESTA.

Bulgaria: Kuusisaarentie 2B, 00340 Helsinki; tel. (9) 4584055; fax (9) 4584550; e-mail embassy.helsinki@mfa.bg; internet www.mfa.bg/embassies/finland; Ambassador LYUBOMIR T. TODOROV.

Canada: Pohjoisesplanadi 25B, POB 779, 00101 Helsinki; tel. (9) 228530; fax (9) 22853385; e-mail hsnki@international.gc.ca; internet www.canadainternational.gc.ca/finland-finlande; Ambassador ANDRÉE N. COOLIGAN.

Chile: Erottajankatu 11, 2nd Floor, 00130 Helsinki; tel. (9) 6126780; fax (9) 61267825; e-mail info@embachile.fi; internet www.embachile .fi; Ambassador EDUARDO PABLO TAPIA RIEPEL.

China, People's Republic: Vanha Kelkkamäki 11, 00570 Helsinki; tel. (9) 22890110; fax (9) 22890168; e-mail chinaemb_fi@mfa.gov.cn; internet fi.chineseembassy.org; Ambassador YU QINGTAI.

Croatia: Kruunuvuorenkatu 5, 4th Floor, 00160 Helsinki; tel. (9) 6850170; fax (9) 6222221; e-mail croemb.helsinki@mvpei.hr; Ambassador KREŠIMIR KOPCIC.

Cuba: Frederikinkatu 61, 3rd Floor, 00100 Helsinki; tel. (9) 6802022; fax (9) 643163; e-mail embahelsinki@cuba.fi; internet www.cubadiplomatica.cu/finlandia; Ambassador ENRIQUE ORTA GONZÁLEZ.

Cyprus: Bulevardi 5A 19, 00120 Helsinki; tel. (9) 6962820; fax (9) 677428; e-mail mail@cyprusembassy.fi; internet www .cyprusembassy.fi; Ambassador EVANGELOS SAVVA.

Czech Republic: Armfeltintie 14, 00150 Helsinki; tel. (9) 6120880; fax (9) 630655; e-mail helsinki@embassy.mzv.cz; internet www.mfa .cz/hclsinki; Ambassador MARTIN TOMČO.

Denmark: Mannerheimintie 8, 6th Floor, POB 1042, 00100 Helsinki; tel. (9) 6841050; fax (9) 6985156; e-mail helamb@um.dk; internet www.ambhelsingfors.um.dk; Ambassador JETTE NORDAM.

Egypt: Kasarmikatu 44, 3rd Floor, 00130 Helsinki; tel. (9) 4777470; fax (9) 47774721; e-mail secretaryofembassy@hotmail.com; Ambassador MAHMOUD GAMIL AHMED ELDIEB.

Estonia: Itäinen puistotie 10, 00140 Helsinki; tel. (9) 6220260; fax (9) 62202610; e-mail embassy.helsinki@mfa.ee; internet www .estemb.fi; Ambassador MARGUS LAIDRE.

France: Itäinen puistotie 13, 00140 Helsinki; tel. (9) 618780; fax (9) 61878342; e-mail ambassade.france@welho.com; Ambassador SERGE MOSTURA.

Germany: Krogiuksentie 4B, 00340 Helsinki; POB 5, 00331 Helsinki; tel. (9) 458580; fax (9) 45858258; e-mail info@helsinki.diplo.de; internet www.helsinki.diplo.de; Ambassador DOROTHEE JANETZKE-WENZEL.

Greece: Maneesikatu 2A 4, 00170 Helsinki; tel. (9) 6229790; fax (9) 2781200; e-mail gremb.hel@mfa.gr; internet www.mfa.gr/helsinki; Ambassador DIMITRIOS KARABALIS.

Hungary: Kuusisaarenkuja 6, 00340 Helsinki; tel. (9) 43660700; fax (9) 43660701; e-mail mission.hel@kum.hu; internet www.mfa.gov .hu/emb/helsinki; Ambassador KRISTÓF FORRAI.

Iceland: Pohjoisesplanadi 27C, 2nd Floor, 00100 Helsinki; tel. (9) 6122460; fax (9) 61224620; e-mail emb.helsinki@mfa.is; internet www.iceland.org/fi; Ambassador KRISTÍN ARNADOTTIR.

India: Kulosaarentie 32, 00570 Helsinki; tel. (9) 2289910; fax (9) 6221208; e-mail amb.helsinki@mea.gov.in; internet www .indianembassy.fi; Ambassador ASHOK KUMAR SHARMA.

Indonesia: Kuusisaarentie 3, 00340 Helsinki; tel. (9) 4470370; fax (9) 4582882; e-mail info@indonesian-embassy.fi; internet www .indonesian-embassy.fi; Ambassador ELIAS GINTING.

Iran: Kulosaarentie 9, 00570 Helsinki; tel. (9) 6869240; fax (9) 68692410; e-mail embassy@iran.fi; Chargé d'affaires a.i. ALI AKBAR NAZARI MARAND.

Iraq: Lars Sonckintie 2, 00570 Helsinki; tel. (9) 68188727; fax (9) 6848977; e-mail info@iraqiembassy.fi; internet www.iraqiembassy .fi; Ambassador SAAD ABDULWAHAB JAWAD KINDEEL.

Ireland: Erottajankatu 7A, 00130 Helsinki; POB 33, 00131 Helsinki; tel. (9) 6824240; fax (9) 646022; e-mail helsinkiembassy@dfa.ie; internet www.embassyofireland.fi; Ambassador DÓNAL DENHAM.

Israel: Yrjönkatu 36A, 00100 Helsinki; tel. (9) 6812020; fax (9) 1356959; e-mail info@helsinki.mfa.gov.il; internet helsinki.mfa.gov .il; Ambassador DAN ASHBEL.

Italy: Itäinen puistotie 4A, 00140 Helsinki; tel. (9) 6811280; fax (9) 6987829; e-mail ambasciata.helsinki@esteri.it; internet www .ambhelsinki.esteri.it; Ambassador GIORGIO VISETTI.

Japan: Unioninkatu 20–22, 00130 Helsinki; tel. (9) 6860200; fax (9) 633012; e-mail inquiry@hk.mofa.go.jp; internet www.fi.emb-japan .go.jp; Ambassador KENJI SHINODA.

Korea, Republic: Erottajankatu 7A, 00130 Helsinki; tel. (9) 2515000; fax (9) 25150055; e-mail korembfi@mofat.go.kr; internet fin.mofat.go.kr; Ambassador DONGHEE CHANG.

Latvia: Armfeltintie 10, 00150 Helsinki; tel. (9) 47647244; fax (9) 47647288; e-mail embassy.finland@mfa.gov.lv; internet www.mfa .gov.lv/fi/helsinki; Ambassador UGIS BAMBE.

Lithuania: Pohjoisranta 15A, 00170 Helsinki; tel. (9) 6844880; fax (9) 68448820; e-mail info@lithuania.fi; internet fi.mfa.lt; Ambassador ARŪNAS JIEVALTAS.

Malaysia: Aleksanterinkatu 17, 00100 Helsinki; tel. (10) 3202030; fax (10) 3202041; e-mail malhsinki@kln.gov.my; internet www.kln .gov.my/perwakilan/helsinki; Ambassador Datin SERI BLANCHE OLBERY.

Mexico: Simonkatu 12A 12, 7th Floor, 00100 Helsinki; tel. (9) 5860430; fax (9) 6949411; e-mail mexican.embassy@welho.com; Ambassador NORMA PENSADO MORENO.

Morocco: Unioninkatu 15A, 00130 Helsinki; tel. (9) 6122480; fax (9) 635160; e-mail embassy.of.morocco@co.inet.fi; Ambassador MOHAMMED ARIAD.

Netherlands: Erottajankatu 19B, 00130 Helsinki; tel. (9) 228920; fax (9) 22892228; e-mail hel@minbuza.nl; internet finland .nlambassade.org; Ambassador HENK SWARTTOUW.

Norway: Rehbinderintie 17, 00150 Helsinki; POB 116, 00151 Helsinki; tel. (9) 6860180; fax (9) 68601811; e-mail emb.helsinki@ mfa.no; internet www.norja.fi; Ambassador JØRG WILLY BRONEBAKK.

Peru: Lönnrotinkatu 7B 11, 00120 Helsinki; tel. (9) 7599400; fax (9) 75994040; e-mail secretary@embassyofperu.fi; internet www .peruembassy.fi; Chargé d'affaires a.i. PAUL PAREDES PORTELLA.

Poland: Armas Lindgrenintie 21, 00570 Helsinki; tel. (9) 618280; fax (9) 6847477; e-mail helsinki.amb.info@msz.gov.pl; internet www .helsinki.polemb.net; Ambassador JANUSZ NIESYTO.

Portugal: Unioninkatu 22, 00130 Helsinki; tel. (9) 6824370; fax (9) 663550; e-mail emb.port@portugal.fi; Ambassador MARIA DE FÁTIMA DE PINA PERESTRELLO.

Romania: Stenbäckinkatu 24, 00250 Helsinki; tel. (9) 2413624; fax (9) 2413272; e-mail romania@romania.fi; internet helsinki.mae.ro; Ambassador MARIAN CĂTĂLIN AVRAMESCU.

Russian Federation: Tehtaankatu 1B, 00140 Helsinki; tel. (9) 661876; fax (9) 661006; e-mail rusembassy@co.inet.fi; internet www.rusembassy.fi; Ambassador ALEKSANDR Y. RUMYANTSEV.

Saudi Arabia: Stenbäckinkatu 26, 00250 Helsinki; tel. (9) 4778870; fax (9) 4543060; e-mail secretary@saudiembassy.fi; internet embassies.mofa.gov.sa; Ambassador NAIF AL ABOUD.

Serbia: Kulosaarentie 36, 00570 Helsinki; tel. (9) 6848522; fax (9) 6848783; e-mail info.ambascghki@kolumbus.fi; internet www .helsinki.mfa.rs; Ambassador SLAVKO KRULJEVIĆ.

Slovakia: Vähäniityntie 5, 00570 Helsinki; tel. (9) 68117810; fax (9) 68117820; e-mail emb.helsinki@mzv.sk; internet www.mzv.sk/helsinki; Ambassador TIBOR KRÁLIK.

South Africa: Pohjoinen Makasiinikatu 4, 00160 Helsinki; tel. (9) 68603100; fax (9) 68603160; e-mail saembfin@dirco.gov.za; internet www.southafricanembassy.fi; Ambassador SELLO MOLOTO.

Spain: Kalliolinnantie 6, 00140 Helsinki; tel. (9) 6877080; fax (9) 170923; e-mail emb.helsinki@maec.es; internet www.maec.es/embajadas/helsinki/es/home; Ambassador MARÍA JESÚS FIGA LÓPEZ-PALOP.

Sweden: Pohjoisesplanadi 7B, 00170 Helsinki; POB 329, 00171 Helsinki; tel. (9) 6877660; fax (9) 655285; e-mail ambassaden .helsingfors@foreign.ministry.se; internet www.sverige.fi; Ambassador ANDERS LIDÉN.

Switzerland: Kalliolinnantie 16A 2a, 00140 Helsinki; tel. (9) 6229500; fax (9) 62295050; e-mail hel.vertretung@eda.admin.ch; internet www.eda.admin.ch/helsinki; Ambassador MAURICE DARIER.

Thailand: Bulevardi 12, 2nd Floor, 00120 Helsinki; tel. (9) 6122640; fax (9) 61226466; e-mail chancery@thaiembassy.fi; internet www.thaiembassy.org; Ambassador RACHANANT THANANANT.

Tunisia: Liisankatu 14B 31, 00170 Helsinki; tel. (9) 68039614; fax (9) 68039610; e-mail at.helsinki@kolumbus.fi; Chargé d'affaires a.i. ROMDHANE EL FAYEDH.

Turkey: Puistokatu 1B A 3, 00140 Helsinki; tel. (9) 61226100; fax (9) 61226150; e-mail embassy.helsinki@mfa.gov.tr; internet helsinki.be.mfa.gov.tr; Ambassador ADNAN BASAGA.

Ukraine: Vähäniityntie 9, 00570 Helsinki; tel. (9) 2289000; fax (9) 2289001; e-mail embassy@ukraine.fi; internet www.ukraine.fi; Ambassador ANDRII OLEFIROV.

United Kingdom: Itäinen puistotie 17, 00140 Helsinki; tel. (9) 22865100; fax (9) 22865284; e-mail info.helsinki@fco.gov.uk; internet www.gov.uk/government/world/finland; Ambassador SARAH PRICE.

USA: Itäinen puistotie 14B, 00140 Helsinki; tel. (9) 616250; fax (9) 61625800; e-mail arc@usembassy.fi; internet finland.usembassy.gov; Ambassador BRUCE J. ORECK.

Venezuela: Bulevardi 1A 62, POB 285, 00100 Helsinki; tel. (9) 6860440; fax (9) 640971; e-mail embavenefin@embavene.fi; internet www.embavene.fi; Chargé d'affaires a.i. ZULAY PRIETO DE RODRIGUEZ.

Viet Nam: Kulosaarentie 12, 00570 Helsinki; tel. (9) 6229900; fax (9) 62299022; e-mail vietnamfinland@gmail.com; internet www.vietnamembassy-finland.org; Ambassador VAN KHOA BUI.

Judicial System

The administration of justice is independent of the Government and judges can be removed only by judicial sentence. The compulsory retirement age for judges is 67.

SUPREME COURT

Korkein oikeus/Högsta domstolen: Pohjoisesplanadi 3, POB 301, 00171 Helsinki; tel. (9) 95640000; fax (9) 95640154; e-mail korkein.oikeus@oikeus.fi; internet korkeinoikeus.fi; consists of a President and at least 15 Justices appointed by the President of the Republic; it is the final court of appeal in civil and criminal cases, and supervises judges and executive authorities; President PAULIINE KOSKELO.

SUPREME ADMINISTRATIVE COURT

Korkein hallinto-oikeus/Högsta förvaltningsdomstolen: Fabianinkatu 15, POB 180, 00131 Helsinki; tel. (10) 3640200; fax (10) 3640382; e-mail korkein.hallinto-oikeus@oikeus.fi; internet www.kho.fi; consists of a President and 20 Justices appointed by the President of the Republic; it is the highest tribunal for appeals in administrative cases; President PEKKA VIHERVUORI.

COURTS OF APPEAL

There are Courts of Appeal at Turku, Vaasa, Kuopio, Helsinki, Kouvola, and Rovaniemi, consisting of a President and an appropriate number of members.

ADMINISTRATIVE COURTS

There are eight Administrative Courts, which hear the appeals of private individuals and corporate bodies against the authorities in tax cases, municipal cases, construction cases, social welfare and health care cases and other administrative cases. In certain of these, the appeal must be preceded by a complaint to a separate lower appellate body. The state and municipal authorities also have a right of appeal in certain cases.

DISTRICT COURTS

Courts of first instance for almost all suits. Appeals lie to the Court of Appeal, and then to the Supreme Court. The composition of the District Court is determined by the type of case to be heard. Civil cases and 'ordinary' criminal cases can be considered by one judge. Other criminal cases and family law cases are heard by a judge and a panel of three lay judges (jurors). Other civil cases are heard by three legally qualified judges. There are 27 District Courts.

SPECIAL COURTS

In addition there are a number of special courts with more restricted jurisdictions. These are the High Court of Impeachment; the Insurance Court; the Labour Court; and the Market Court. There is no constitutional court in Finland, but the Constitutional Committee of Parliament has been entrusted with the process of verifying the compatibility of new legislation with the Constitution.

CHANCELLOR OF JUSTICE

The Chancellor of Justice (Oikeuskansleri) is responsible for ensuring that authorities and officials comply with the law. He is the chief public prosecutor, and acts as counsel for the Government.

Office of the Chancellor of Justice: Snellmaninkatu 1, Helsinki; POB 20, 00023 Government; tel. (9) 16001; fax (9) 16023975; e-mail kirjaamo@okv.fi; internet www.okv.fi; Chancellor of Justice JAAKKO JONKKA.

PARLIAMENTARY OMBUDSMAN

The Eduskunnan Oikeusasiamies is the Finnish Ombudsman appointed by the Eduskunta to supervise the observance of the law.

Office of the Parliamentary Ombudsman: Arkadiankatu 3, 00102 Helsinki; tel. (9) 4321; fax (9) 4322268; e-mail oikeusasiamies@eduskunta.fi; internet www.oikeusasiamies.fi; f. 1919; Parliamentary Ombudsman PETRI JÄÄSKELÄINEN.

In addition to the Chancellor of Justice and the Parliamentary Ombudsman, there are also specialized authorities that have similar duties in more limited fields. These include the Consumer Ombudsman, the Ombudsman for Equality, the Data Protection Ombudsman, the Ombudsman for Aliens and the Bankruptcy Ombudsman.

Religion

In 2013 75.3% of the population were members of the Evangelical Lutheran Church and around 1.1% belonged to the Orthodox Church. Some 22.1% of the population professed no religious affiliation.

CHRISTIANITY

Suomen ekumeeninen neuvosto/Ekumeniska rådet i Finland (Finnish Ecumenical Council): Katajanokankatu 7A, POB 185, 00161 Helsinki; tel. (9) 1802369; fax (9) 174313; e-mail heikki.huttunen@ekumenia.fi; internet www.ekumenia.fi; f. 1917; 11 mem. churches; Pres. Rt Rev. TEEMU SIPPO; Gen. Sec. Rev. HEIKKI HUTTUNEN.

National Churches

Suomen evankelis-luterilainen kirkko (Evangelical Lutheran Church of Finland): Department for International Relations, Eteläranta 8, POB 210, 00131 Helsinki; tel. (9) 18021; fax (9) 1802350; e-mail kirkkohallitus@evl.fi; internet www.evl.fi; 4.1m. mems (2014); Leader Archbishop Dr KARI MÄKINEN.

Suomen Ortodoksinen Kirkko (Orthodox Church of Finland): Karjalankatu 1, 70110 Kuopio; tel. (206) 100210; fax (206) 100211; e-mail kirkollishallitus@ort.fi; internet www.ort.fi; 60,000 mems; Leader Archbishop LEO of Karelia and All Finland.

The Roman Catholic Church

Finland comprises the single diocese of Helsinki, directly responsible to the Holy See. There were 11,994 adherents in the country (0.2% of the population) in 2013. The Bishop participates in the Scandinavian Episcopal Conference (based in Sweden).

Bishop of Helsinki: Rt Rev. TEEMU SIPPO, Rehbinderintie 21, 00150 Helsinki; tel. (9) 6877460; fax (9) 639820; e-mail curia@catholic.fi; internet www.katolinen.net.

Other Churches

Finlands svenska baptistsamfund (Finland Swedish Baptist Union): Rådhusgatan 44, 65100 Vasa; POB 54, 65101 Vasa; tel. (6) 3464500; fax (6) 3464510; e-mail fsb@baptist.fi; internet www.baptist.fi; f. 1856; publishes *Missionsstandaret* (12 a year); Gen. Sec. PETER SJÖBLOM; 1,300 mems.

Finlands svenska metodistkyrka (United Methodist Church in Finland—Swedish-speaking): Apollogatan 5, 00100 Helsinki; tel. (9) 449874; fax (9) 406098; e-mail kyrkostyrelsen@metodistkyrkan.fi; internet www.metodistkyrkan.fi; f. 1881; District Superintendent Rev. MAYVOR WÄRN-RANCKEN; 1,000 mems.

Jehovan Todistajat (Jehovah's Witnesses): Puutarhatie 60, 01300 Vantaa; POB 68, 01301 Vantaa; tel. (9) 825885; fax (9) 82588285; internet www.watchtower.org; 19,094 mems.

Myöhempien Aikojen Pyhien Jeesuksen Kristuksen Kirkko (The Church of Jesus Christ of Latter-day Saints—Mormon): Neitsytpolku 3A4, 00140 Helsinki; tel. (9) 6962750; fax (9) 69627510; e-mail 2015803@ldschurch.org; internet www.mormonit.fi; 4,866 mems; Mission Pres. WAYNE T. WATSON.

Suomen Adventtikirkko (Seventh-day Adventist Church in Finland): Ketarantie 4E, 33680 Tampere; POB 94, 33101 Tampere; tel. (3) 3611111; fax (3) 3600454; e-mail mervi.tukiainen@

adventtikirkko.fi; internet www.adventtikirkko.fi; f. 1894; 5,469 mems; Pres. KALERVO AROMÄKI; Sec. ANNE VRCELJ.

Suomen Baptistikirkko (Finnish Baptist Union): Kissanmaan-katu 19, 33530 Tampere; tel. (44) 3881112; e-mail jari .portaankorva@baptisti.fi; internet www.baptisti.fi; Dir JARI POR-TAANKORVA; 950 mems.

Suomen Metodistikirkko (United Methodist Church—Finnish-speaking): Punavuorenkatu 2B 17, 00120 Helsinki; tel. (44) 2592783; e-mail suomen@metodistikirkko.fi; internet www.metodistikirkko .fi; District Superintendent Rev. PASI RUNONEN; 849 mems.

Suomen Vapaakirkko (Evangelical Free Church of Finland): Lukiokatu 15, POB 198, 13101 Hämeenlinna; tel. (10) 3288000; fax (10) 3288001; e-mail svk@svk.fi; internet www.svk.fi; f. 1923; Pres. Rev. HANNU VUORINEN; 15,500 mems.

The Anglican Church and the Salvation Army are also active in the country.

BAHÁ'Í FAITH

Suomen Bahá'í-yhteisö (Bahá'í Community of Finland): POB 423, 00101 Helsinki; tel. (9) 790875; fax (9) 790058; e-mail info@bahai .fitiedotus@bahai.fi; internet www.bahai.fi; f. 1953; 700 mems.

JUDAISM

Helsingin Juutalainen Seurakunta (Jewish Community of Helsinki): Synagogue and Community Centre, Malminkatu 26, 00100 Helsinki; tel. (9) 5860310; fax (9) 58603130; e-mail srk@jchelsinki.fi; internet www.jchelsinki.fi; Pres. YARON NADBORNIK; Exec. Dir DAN KANTOR; 1,200 mems.

ISLAM

In 2013 there were 11,125 members of Islamic congregations. There are around 20 registered mosques or religious communities.

Suomen Islamilainen Yhdyskunta (Islamic Society of Finland): Lonnrotinkatu 22A 5, POB 87, 00101 Helsinki; tel. (9) 2782551; fax (9) 6121156; e-mail yhdyskunta@rabita.fi; internet www.rabita.fi; f. 1987; Imam ANAS HAJJAR.

The Press

In 2013 there were 183 newspapers in Finland; the total circulation for all types of newspaper was some 2.4m. A number of dailies are printed in Swedish. The most popular daily papers are *Helsingin Sanomat*, *Ilta-Sanomat*, *Aamulehti* and *Iltalehti*.

PRINCIPAL DAILIES
(average net circulation figures, for the year 2010, unless otherwise indicated)

Helsinki

Helsingin Sanomat: Töölönlahdenkatu 2, POB 18, 00089 Sanomat; tel. (9) 1221; fax (9) 1222366; e-mail janne.virkkunen@sanomat.fi; internet www.hs.fi; f. 1889; independent; Publr and Senior Editor-in-Chief MIKAEL PENTIKÄINEN; circ. 374,503 (weekdays), 447,682 (weekend).

Hufvudstadsbladet: Mannerheimvägen 18, POB 217, 00101 Helsinki; tel. (9) 12531; fax (9) 642930; e-mail nyheter@hbl.fi; internet www.hbl.fi; f. 1864; Swedish-language; independent; Editor-in-Chief JENS BERG; circ. 47,702 (weekdays), 50,030 (weekend).

Iltalehti: Aleksanterinkatu 9, POB 372, 00100 Helsinki; tel. (10) 665100; fax (9) 177313; e-mail il.toimitus@iltalehti.fi; internet www .iltalehti.fi; f. 1981; afternoon; independent; Man. Dir KARI KIVELÄ; Editor-in-Chief PANU POKKINEN; circ. 107,052 (weekdays), 136,245 (weekend).

Ilta-Sanomat: Töölönlahdenkatu 2, POB 45, 00089 Sanomat; tel. (9) 1221; fax (9) 1223419; e-mail uutiset@sanoma.fi; internet www .iltasanomat.fi; f. 1932; afternoon; 6 a week; independent; Publr and Editor-in-Chief TAPIO SADEOJA; circ. 150,351 (weekdays), 189,524 (weekend).

Kauppalehti (Finnish Business Daily): Eteläesplanadi 20, POB 189, 00101 Helsinki; tel. (10) 665101; fax (10) 6652423; internet www .kauppalehti.fi; f. 1898; weekdays; Man. Dir JUHA-PETRI LOIMOVUORI; Editor-in-Chief HANNU LEINONEN; circ. 70,118.

Uutispäivä Demari: Haapaniemenkatu 7–9B, 17th and 18th Floors, 00530 Helsinki; POB 338, 00531 Helsinki; tel. (9) 701041; fax (9) 7010567; e-mail toimitus@demari.fi; internet www.demari.fi; f. 1895; chief organ of the Social Democratic Party; Man. Dir HEIKKI NYKANEN; Editor-in-Chief JUHA PELTONEN; circ. 14,119.

Hämeenlinna

Hämeen Sanomat: Vanajantie 7, POB 530, 13111 Hämeenlinna; tel. (3) 61511; fax (3) 6151492; e-mail toimitus@hameensanomat.fi;
internet www.hameensanomat.fi; f. 1879; independent; Man. Dir PAULI UUSI-KILPONEN; Editor-in-Chief PAULI UUSI-KILPONEN; circ. 28,296.

Joensuu

Karjalainen: Kosti Aaltosentie 9, 80140, Joensuu; POB 99, 80141 Joensuu; tel. (13) 2551; fax (13) 2552363; e-mail toimitus@ karjalainen.fi; internet www.karjalainen.fi; f. 1874; independent; Man. Dir RAIMO PUUSTINEN; Editor PASI KOIVUMAA; circ. 45,584.

Jyväskylä

Sanomalehti Keskisuomalainen Oy: Aholaidantie 3, POB 159, 40101 Jyväskylä; tel. (14) 622000; fax (14) 622272; internet www .ksml.fi; f. 1871; Editor-in-Chief PEKKA MERVOLA; circ. 73,559.

Kemi

Pohjolan Sanomat: Sairaalakatu 2, 94100 Kemi; tel. (10) 6656555; fax (10) 6656322; e-mail ps.toimitus@pohjolansanomat.fi; internet www.pohjolansanomat.fi; f. 1915; Man. Dir MARTTI NIKKANEN; Editor-in-Chief HEIKKI LÄÄKKÖLÄ; circ. 20,070 (weekdays), 20,221 (Sat.).

Kokkola

Keskipohjanmaa: Eteläväylä, POB 45, 67101 Kokkola; tel. (20) 7504400; fax (20) 7504488; e-mail toimitus@kpk.fi; internet www .keskipohjanmaa.net; f. 1917; independent; Man. Dir EINO LAUKKA; Editor-in-Chief LASSI JAAKKOLA; circ. 25,479.

Kotka

Kymen Sanomat: Tornatorintie 3, 48100 Kotka; POB 27, 48101 Kotka; tel. (5) 210015; fax (5) 21005206; e-mail uutiset@ kymensanomat.fi; internet www.kymensanomat.fi; f. 1902; independent; Man. Dir JARMO KOSKINEN; Editor PEKKA LAKKA; circ. 23,208.

Kouvola

Kouvolan Sanomat: Lehtikaari 1, POB 40, 45101 Kouvola; tel. (5) 280014; fax (5) 28004706; e-mail toimitus@kouvolansanomat.fi; internet www.kouvolansanomat.fi; f. 1909; independent; Man. Dir JUHA OKSANEN; Editor-in-Chief PEKKA LAKKA; circ. 27,273 (weekdays), 27,610 (Sat.).

Kuopio

Savon Sanomat: Vuorikatu 21, POB 68, 70101 Kuopio; tel. (17) 303111; fax (17) 303375; e-mail lukijansanomat@iwn.fi; internet www.savonsanomat.fi; f. 1907; independent; Man. Dir HEIKKI AURASMAA; Editor-in-Chief JARI TOURUNEN; circ. 61,546.

Lahti

Etelä-Suomen Sanomat: Ilmarisentie 7, POB 80, 15101 Lahti; tel. (3) 75751; fax (3) 7575466; e-mail heikki.hakala@ess.fi; internet www.ess.fi; f. 1914; independent; Man. Dir JUKKA OTTELA; Editor-in-Chief HEIKKI HAKALA; circ. 58,400.

Lappeenranta

Etelä-Saimaa: Lauritsalantie 1, POB 3, 53501 Lappeenranta; tel. (5) 538813; fax (5) 53883206; e-mail lukijat@esaimaa.fi; internet www.esaimaa.fi; f. 1885; independent; Editor PEKKA LAKKA; circ. 30,288 (weekdays), 30,816 (Sat.).

Mikkeli

Länsi-Savo: Teollisuuskatu 2–6, 50130 Mikkeli; POB 6, 50101 Mikkeli; tel. (15) 3501; fax (15) 3503337; e-mail asiakaspalvelu@ lansi-savo.fi; internet www.lansi-savo.fi; independent; Man. Dir JUKKA TIKKA; Editor-in-Chief TAPIO HONKAMAA; circ. 25,018.

Oulu

Kaleva: Lekatie 1, 90140 Oulu; POB 170, 90401 Oulu; tel. (8) 5377111; fax (8) 5377206; e-mail kaleva@kaleva.fi; internet www .kaleva.fi; f. 1899; independent; Man. Dir TAISTO RISKI; Editor-in-Chief MARKKU MANTILA; circ. 78,216 (weekdays), 80,324 (weekend).

Pori

Satakunnan Kansa: Pohjoisranta 11E, POB 58, 28100 Pori; tel. (10) 665132; fax (10) 6658330; e-mail sk.toimitus@satakunnankansa.fi; internet www.satakunnankansa.fi; f. 1873; independent; Editor-in-Chief PETRI HAKALA; circ. 49,989.

Rovaniemi

Lapin Kansa: Veitikantie 2–8, 96100 Rovaniemi; tel. (10) 665022; fax (10) 6657720; e-mail lktoimitus@lapinkansa.fi; internet www.lapinkansa.fi; f. 1928; independent; Man. Dir JUHA RUOTSALAINEN; Editor-in-Chief ANTTI KOKKONEN; circ. 32,691 (weekdays), 32,887 (Sat.).

Salo

Salon Seudun Sanomat: Örninkatu 14, POB 117, 24101 Salo; tel. (2) 77021; fax (2) 7702200; e-mail jarmo.vahasilta@sss.fi; internet www.sss.fi; independent; Man. Dir KIRSTI KIRJONEN; Editor-in-Chief JUKKA HOLMBERG; circ. 21,828.

Savonlinna

Itä-Savo: Olavinkatu 60, POB 101, 57101 Savonlinna; tel. (15) 3503400; fax (15) 3503444; e-mail asiakaspalvelu@ita-savo.fi; internet www.ita-savo.fi; Man. Dir JUHA PELKONEN; Editor-in-Chief TUOMO YLI-HUTTALA; circ. 16,674.

Seinäjoki

Ilkka: Koulukatu 10, 60100 Seinäjoki; POB 60, 60101 Seinäjoki; tel. (6) 2477830; fax (6) 4186500; e-mail ilkka.toimitus@ilkka.fi; internet www.ilkka.fi; f. 1906; independent; Man. Dir MATTI KORKIATUPA; Editor-in-Chief MATTI KALLIOKOSKI; circ. 53,768.

Tampere

Aamulehti: Itäinenkatu 11, 33210 Tampere; tel. (10) 665111; fax (10) 6653140; e-mail matti.apunen@aamulehti.fi; internet www.aamulehti.fi; f. 1881; Editor JOUKO JOKINEN; circ. 131,539.

Turku

Turun Sanomat: Länsikaari 15, POB 95, 20101 Turku; tel. (2) 2693297; fax (2) 2693274; e-mail ts.toimitus@ts-group.fi; internet www.turunsanomat.fi; f. 1904; independent; Man. Dir MIKKO KETONEN; Editors-in-Chief KARI VAINIO, RIITTA MONTO; circ. 107,119.

Tuusula

Keski-Uusimaa: Klaavolantie 5, POB 52, 04301 Tuusula; tel. (9) 273000; fax (9) 27300205; e-mail toimitus@keskiuusimaa.fi; internet www.keskiuusimaa.fi; independent; Man. Dir JORMA HÄMÄLÄINEN; Editor-in-Chief PENTTI KIISKI; circ. 20,444.

Vaasa

Pohjalainen: Hietasaarenkatu 19, 65100 Vaasa; POB 37, 65101 Vaasa; tel. (6) 3249111; fax (6) 3249355; e-mail toimitus@pohjalainen.fi; internet www.pohjalainen.fi; f. 1903; independent; Man. Dir MATTI KORKIATUPA; Editor KALLE HEISKANEN; circ. 25,517.

Vasabladet: Hietasaarenkatu 20, POB 52, 65101 Vaasa; tel. (6) 3260211; fax (6) 3129003; e-mail nyheter@vasabladet.fi; internet www.vasabladet.fi; f. 1856; Swedish-language; liberal independent; Man. Dir JENS LILLSUNDE; Editor-in-Chief CAMILLA BERGGREN; circ. 21,529.

PRINCIPAL PERIODICALS

(average net circulation figures, for the year 2012, unless otherwise indicated)

7 päivää: Pursimiehenkatu 29–31A, 00150 Helsinki; POB 124, 00151 Helsinki; tel. (9) 86217000; fax (9) 86217230; e-mail asiakaspalvelu@seiskalive.fi; internet www.seiska.fi; f. 1992; weekly; publ. by Aller Media AS; television and radio; Editor-in-Chief EEVA-HELENA JOKITAIPALE; circ. 170,867.

Ahjo: Hakaniemenranta 1, POB 107, 00531 Helsinki; tel. (20) 774001; fax (20) 7741240; e-mail ahjo@metalliliitto.fi; internet www.ahjo.fi; 16 a year; for metal industry employees; Editor-in-Chief KIRSI TÖRMÄNEN-PETMAN; circ. 155,000 (2014).

Aku Ankka (Donald Duck): Lapinmäentie 1, 00350 Helsinki; POB 100, 00040 Helsinki; tel. (9) 1201; fax (9) 1205569; e-mail asiakaspalvelu@sanomamagazines.fi; internet www.akuankka.fi; f. 1951; weekly; children's; Editor-in-Chief JUKKA HEISKANEN; circ. 282,794.

Apu: Risto Rytintie 33, 00081 A-lehdet, Helsinki; tel. (9) 75961; fax (9) 75983101; e-mail marja.aarnipuro@apu.fi; internet www.apu.fi; f. 1933; weekly; family journal; Editor-in-Chief MARJA AARNIPURO; circ. 149,050.

Avotakka: Risto Rytintie 33, 00081 A-lehdet, Helsinki; tel. (9) 75961; fax (9) 75983110; e-mail johanna.falck@a-lehdet.fi; internet www.avotakka.fi; f. 1967; monthly; interior decoration; Editor-in-Chief JOHANNA FALCK; circ. 82,245.

Diabetes: Kirjoniementie 15, 33680 Tampere; tel. (3) 2860111; fax (3) 2860422; e-mail diabetesliitto@diabetes.fi; internet www.diabetes.fi; f. 1949; 9 a year; health; publ. by Finnish Diabetes Asscn; Editor-in-Chief TARJA SAMPO; circ. 61,607.

Eeva: Risto Rytintie 33, 00081 A-lehdet, Helsinki; tel. (9) 75961; fax (9) 786858; e-mail riitta.nykanen@a-lehdet.fi; internet www.eeva.fi; f. 1934; monthly; women's; Editor-in-Chief RIITTA NYKÄNEN; circ. 98,5436.

Erä: Maistraatinportti 1, 00015 Helsinki; tel. (9) 15661; fax (9) 145650; e-mail sepp.suuronen@kuvalehdet.fi; internet www.eralehti.fi; 13 a year; fishing and outdoor leisure; Editor JARI KAALIKOSKI; circ. 41,710.

ET-lehti: Lapinmäentie 1, 00350 Helsinki; POB 100, 00040 Sanoma Magazines; tel. (9) 1201; fax (9) 1205428; e-mail et-lehti@sanomamagazines.fi; internet www.et-lehti.fi; monthly; over-50s magazine; Editor-in-Chief RIITTA KORHONEN; circ. 226,853.

Gloria: Lapinmäentie 1, 00350 Helsinki; POB 100, 00040 Sanoma Magazines; tel. (9) 1201; fax (9) 1205427; e-mail gloria@sanomamagazines.fi; internet www.gloria.fi; monthly; women's; Editor-in-Chief MINNA JUTI; circ. 46,277.

Hevosurheilu: Tulkinkuja 3, 02650 Espoo; tel. (20) 7605300; fax (20) 7605390; e-mail hevosurheilu@hevosurheilu.fi; internet www.hevosurheilu.fi; independent; horse-racing; Editor-in-Chief JUSSI LÄHDE; circ. 23,588.

Hymy: Maistraatinportti 1, 00015 Kuvalehdet, Helsinki; tel. (9) 156665; fax (9) 1566511; e-mail esko.tulusto@kuvalehdet.fi; internet www.hymy.fi; monthly; family journal; Editor KARI KALLONEN; circ. 73,788.

Hyvä Terveys: Lapinmäentie 1, 00350 Helsinki; POB 100, 00040 Sanoma Magazines; tel. (9) 1201; fax (9) 1205456; e-mail hyva.terveys@sanomamagazines.fi; internet www.hyvaterveys.fi; 15 a year; health; Editor-in-Chief TAINA RISTO; circ. 127,385.

IT-Invalidityö: Mannerheimintie 107, 00280 Helsinki; tel. (9) 613191; fax (9) 1461443; e-mail fpd@invalidiliitto.fi; internet www.invalidiliitto.fi/portal/fi; 10 a year; for disabled people; Editor-in-Chief SINIKKA RANTALA; circ. 29,340.

Kaksplus: Maistraatinportti 1, 00015 Otavamedia; tel. (9) 1566591; e-mail kaksplus@otavamedia.fi; internet kaksplus.fi; f. 1969; monthly; for families with young children; Editor-in-Chief EMMA KOIVULA; circ. 17,794.

Kansan Uutiset: Vilhonvuorenkatu 11C 7, 00500 Helsinki; POB 64, 00501 Helsinki; tel. (9) 759601; fax (9) 75960319; e-mail ku@kansanuutiset.fi; internet www.kansanuutiset.fi; f. 1957; organ of the Left Alliance; Editor-in-Chief JOUKO JOENTAUSTA.

Katso: Pursimiehenkatu 29–31A, 00150 Helsinki; POB 124, 00151 Helsinki; tel. (9) 86217000; fax (9) 86217177; e-mail katso@katso.fi; internet www.katso.fi; f. 1960; 49 issues a year; TV, radio, film and video; Editor-in-Chief KIRSI LINDH-MANSIKKA; circ. 26,460.

Kauneus ja terveys: Risto Rytintie 33, 00081 A-lehdet, Helsinki; tel. (9) 75961; fax (9) 75983106; e-mail asiakaspalvelu@a-lehdet.fi; internet www.kauneusjaterveys.fi; 16 a year; health and beauty; Editor TITTA KIURU; circ. 72,764.

Kirkko ja kaupunki: Kasarmikatu 23, 15A, 00130 Helsinki; tel. (9) 0207542255; fax (9) 0207542343; e-mail toimitus@kirkkojakaupunki.fi; internet www.kirkkojakaupunki.fi; weekly; church and community; Editor-in-Chief SEPPO SIMOLA; circ. 203,279 (2011).

Kodin Kuvalehti: Lapinmäentie 1, 00350 Helsinki; POB 100, 00040 Helsinki; tel. (9) 1201; fax (9) 1205468; e-mail kodin.kuvalehti@sanomamagazines.fi; internet www.kodinkuvalehti.fi; fortnightly; family magazine; Editor-in-Chief MINNA MCGILL; circ. 158,375.

Kotilääkäri: Maistraatinportti 1, 00015 Otavamedia, Helsinki; tel. (9) 15661; e-mail kotilaakari@otavamedia.fi; internet www.kotilaakari.fi; f. 1889; monthly; health, well-being and beauty; Editor-in-Chief MARJATTA LEINO; circ. 28,841.

Kotiliesi: Maistraatinportti 1, 00015 Otavamedia, Helsinki; tel. (9) 15661; e-mail kotiliesi@otavamedia.fi; internet www.kotiliesi.fi; f. 1922; 27 a year; women's; Editor-in-Chief LEENI PELTONEN; circ. 105,588.

Kotivinkki: Risto Rytintie 33, 00081 A-lehdet, Helsinki; tel. (9) 75961; e-mail outi.gylden@a-lehdet.fi; internet www.kotivinkki.fi; 23 a year; women's; Editor-in-Chief OUTI GYLDÉN; circ. 90,734.

Maaseudun Tulevaisuus (The Rural Future): Simonkatu 6, POB 440, 00100 Helsinki; tel. (9) 204132100; e-mail ilmoitus@maaseuduntulevaisuus.fi; internet www.maaseuduntulevaisuus.fi; f. 1916; independent; Man. Dir HEIKKI LAURINEN; Editor-in-Chief LAURI KONTRO; circ. 81,774.

Me Naiset: Lapinmäentie 1, 00350 Helsinki; POB 100, 00040 Helsinki; tel. (9) 1201; fax (9) 1205414; e-mail menaiset@sanomamagazines.fi; internet www.menaiset.fi; f. 1952; weekly; women's; Editor JOHANNA LAHTI; circ. 138,594.

Metsälehti: Pohjoinen Rautatiekatu 21B, 00100 Helsinki; tel. (9) 31549800; fax (9) 31549879; e-mail eliisa.kallioniemi@metsalehti.fi; internet www.metsakustannus.fi; f. 1933; fortnightly; forestry;

FINLAND   *Directory*

owned by the Forestry Development Centre Tapio; Editor-in-Chief
ELIISA KALLIONIEMI; circ. 34,403.

MikroBitti: Lapinmäentie 1, 00350 Helsinki; POB 100, 00040
Sanoma Magazine; tel. (9) 1201; fax (9) 1205456; e-mail otto@
mikrobitti.fi; internet www.mbnet.fi; f. 1984; monthly; Editor-in-
Chief PASI ANDREJEFF; circ. 58,957.

MikroPC: Annankatu 34–36B, 00100 Helsinki; POB 920, 00101
Helsinki; tel. (20) 44240; e-mail asiakaspalvelu@talentum.com;
internet mikropc.net; 12 a year; computers; Editor-in-Chief MIKKO
TORIKKA; circ. 12,285 (2011).

Partio: Töölönkatu 55, 00250 Helsinki; tel. (9) 88651100; fax (9)
88651199; e-mail info@partio.fi; internet www.partio.fi; 4 a year; the
Scout movement; Editor MINNA HELLE; circ. 39,256.

Pellervo: Simonkatu 6, POB 77, 00101 Helsinki; tel. (9) 4767501; fax
(9) 6948845; e-mail toimisto@pellervo.fi; internet www.pellervo.fi;
f. 1899; monthly; agricultural and co-operative, home and country
life journal; organ of the Confederation of Finnish Co-operatives;
Editor-in-Chief TEEMU PAKARINEN; circ. 31,961 (2011).

PerusSuomalainen: Mannerheimintie 40B 56, 00100 Helsinki; tel.
(20) 7430800; fax (20) 7430801; e-mail peruss@perussuomalaiset.fi;
internet www.perussuomalaiset.fi; f. 1996; 12 a year; organ of the
Perussuomalaiset/Sannfinländarna (PS—Finns Party); Editor
MATIAS TURKKILA; circ. 100,000 (2011).

Pirkka: POB 410, 00811 Helsinki; tel. (9) 42427330; internet www
.pirkka.fi; 10 a year; Swedish; Editor-in-Chief MINNA JÄRVENPÄÄ;
circ. 1,720,139.

Reserviläinen: Döbelninkatu 2, 00260 Helsinki; tel. (9) 40562016;
fax (9) 499875; e-mail toimitus@reservilainen.fi; internet www
.reservilainen.fi; 8 a year; military; Editor MIRVA BROLA; circ. 69,000
(2011).

Sähköviesti/Elbladet: Fredrikinkatu 51–53B, POB 100, 00101
Helsinki; tel. (9) 530520; fax (9) 53052900; e-mail pekka
.tiusanen@energia.fi; internet www.energiaviesti.fi; f. 1939; quarterly; publ. by Finnish Energy Industries; Editor-in-Chief PEKKA
TIUSANEN; circ. 601,387 (2011).

Seura: Maistraatinportti 1, 00015 Kuvalehdet; tel. (9) 15661; fax (9)
145650; e-mail seura@kuvalehdet.fi; internet www.seura.fi; f. 1934;
49 a year; family journal; Editor-in-Chief SAIJA HAKONIEMI; circ.
143,485.

STTK—lehti: Mikonkatu 8A, 6th Floor, 00100 Helsinki; POB 421,
00101 Helsinki; tel. (9) 131521; fax (9) 652367; e-mail marja-liisa
.rajakangas@sttk.fi; internet www.sttk.fi; 8 a year; organ of STTK
(Finnish Confed. of Professionals); Editor-in-Chief MARJA-LIISA
RAJAKANGAS; circ. 30,000 (2011).

Suomen Kuvalehti: Maistraatinportti 1, 00240 Helsinki; tel. (9)
15661; fax (9) 1566212; e-mail suomen.kuvalehti@kuvalehdet.fi;
internet www.suomenkuvalehti.fi; f. 1916; 49 a year; illustrated
news; Editor-in-Chief TAPANI RUOKANEN; circ. 86,786.

Suuri Käsityö: Lapinmäentie 1, 00350 Helsinki; POB 100, 00040
Helsinki; tel. (9) 1201; fax (9) 1205352; e-mail suuri.kasityolehti@
sanomamagazines.fi; internet www.suurikasityo.fi; f. 1974;
monthly; needlework, knitting and dress-making magazine; Editor-in-Chief HEIDI LAAKSONEN; circ. 60,185.

Talouselämä: Annankatu 34–36B, 00100 Helsinki; POB 920, 00101
Helsinki; tel. (9) 204424390; fax (9) 204424108; e-mail te@talentum
.fi; internet www.talouselama.fi; f. 1938; 46 a year; economy,
business; Man. Dir AARNE AKTAN; Editor-in-Chief REIJO RUOKANEN;
circ. 80,868.

Taloustaito: Kalevankatu 4, 00100 Helsinki; tel. (9) 618871; fax (9)
604435; e-mail antti.marttinen@veronmaksajat.fi; internet www
.taloustaito.fi; economics and taxation; Editor-in-Chief ANTI MART-
TINEN; circ. 242,250.

Tekniikan Maailma: Maistraatinportti 1, 00240 Helsinki; tel. (9)
15661; fax (9) 1566511; e-mail tekniikan.maailma@kuvalehdet.fi;
internet www.tekniikanmaailma.fi; f. 1953; 23 a year; motoring,
technology, aviation, photography; Editor-in-Chief VELIMATTI HON-
KANEN; circ. 120,298.

Tekniikka & Talous: Annankatu 34–36B, 00100 Helsinki; POB
920, 00101 Helsinki; tel. (20) 4424100; fax (20) 4424101; e-mail
tilpal@talentum.fi; internet www.tekniikkatalous.fi; Editor-in-Chief
TERHO PUUSTINEN; circ. 60,018.

Tiede: Lapinmäentie 1, 00350 Helsinki; POB 100, 00040 Sanoma
Magazines; tel. (9) 1201; e-mail tiede@sanomamagazines.fi; internet
www.tiede.fi; f. 1980; popular science; Editor-in-Chief JUKKA RUUKKI;
circ. 60,951.

Tieteen Kuvalehti: Siltasaarenkatu 18–20A, 00530 Helsinki; tel.
(20) 7608590; internet tieku.fi; f. 1986; 18 a year; science, nature,
technology; publ. by Bonnier Publications Int; Editor JENS HENNE-
BERG; circ. 36,785.

Trendi: Risto Rytintie 33, 00081 A-lehdet, Helsinki; tel. (9) 75961;
e-mail jenni.lieto@a-lehdet.fi; internet www.trendi.fi; 12 a year;
women's lifestyle; Editor-in-Chief JENNI LIETO; circ. 44,395.

Tuulilasi: Risto Rytintie 33, 00081 A-lehdet, Helsinki; tel. (9) 75961;
fax (9) 75983103; e-mail tuulilasi@a-lehdet.fi; internet www
.tuulilasi.fi; f. 1963; 16 a year; motoring; Editor-in-Chief LAURI
LARMELA; circ. 68,748.

Työ Terveys Turvallisuus: Topeliuksenkatu 41A, 00250 Helsinki;
tel. (30) 4741; fax (30) 4742478; e-mail info-ttt@ttl.fi; internet www
.ttl.fi; f. 1971; 6 a year; occupational safety and health; Editor-in-
Chief HARRI VAINIO; circ. 55,928.

Valitut Palat: Pitäjänmäentie 14, 00380 Helsinki; POB 106, 00381
Helsinki; tel. (9) 503441; fax (9) 5034499; e-mail asiakaspalvelu@
valitutpalat.fi; internet www.valitutpalat.fi; monthly; Finnish Reader's Digest; Editor-in-Chief ILKKA VIRTANEN; circ. 157,979.

Veikkaaja: Töölönlahdenkatu 2, POB 45, 00089 Helsinki; tel. (9)
1221; fax (9) 1223419; e-mail tilaajapalvelu@urheilusanomat.fi;
internet www.veikkaaja.fi; 51 a year; sports; Editor-in-Chief TAPIO
SADEOJA; circ. 40,017.

Voi hyvin: Risto Rytintie 33, 00081 A-lehdet, Helsinki; tel. (9)
75961; fax (9) 75983109; e-mail voihyvin@a-lehdet.fi; internet
www.voihyvin.fi; f. 1986; 10 a year; health, well-being; Editor-in-
Chief KRISTA LAUNONEN; circ. 43,378.

Yhteishyvä: Fleminginkatu 34, 00510 Helsinki; tel. (9) 1882621; fax
(9) 1882626; e-mail kirsi.ervola@sok.fi; internet www.yhteishyva.fi;
f. 1905; monthly; free to members of co-operative group; Editor-in-
Chief KIRSI ERVOLA; circ. 1,815,893.

NEWS AGENCY

Oy Suomen Tietotoimisto—Lehtikuva (STT—Lehtikuva):
Malminkatu 16A, 00100 Helsinki; POB 550, 00101 Helsinki; tel.
(9) 695811; fax (9) 69581335; e-mail toimitus@stt.fi; internet www.stt
.fi; f. 1887; 8 regional bureaux; independent national agency
distributing domestic and international news in Finnish and
Swedish; formed by the merger of Suomen Tietotoimisto and
Lehtikuva; CEO and Editor-in-Chief MIKA PETTERSSON.

PRESS ASSOCIATIONS

Aikakauslehtien Liitto (Finnish Periodical Publishers' Association): Lönnrotinkatu 11A, POB 267, 00121 Helsinki; tel (9)
22877280; fax (9) 603478; e-mail toimisto@aikakauslehdet.fi;
internet www.aikakauslehdet.fi; f. 1946; aims to further the interests of publishers of magazines and periodicals, to encourage co-
operation between publishers, and to improve standards; Chair.
RAILI MÄKINEN.

Sanomalehtien Liitto—Tidningarnas Förbund (Finnish Newspapers Association): Eteläranta 10, 00130 Helsinki; tel. (9)
22877300; e-mail info@sanomalehdet.fi; internet www
.sanomalehdet.fi; f. 1908; represents newspapers' interests; Exec.
Dir JUKKA HOLMBERG; 182 mem. newspapers.

Suomen Journalistiliitto—Finlands Journalistförbund r.y.
(Union of Journalists): Siltasaarenkatu 16, 00530 Helsinki; tel. (9)
6122330; fax (9) 605396; e-mail info@journalistiliitto.fi; internet
www.journalistiliitto.fi; f. 1921; 15,000 mems; Pres. ARTO NIEMINEN.

Publishers

Alfamer/Karisto Oy: Kaisaniemenkatu 13, 00100 Helsinki; tel. (9)
7742810; fax (9) 77428111; e-mail alfamer@alfamer.fi; internet www
.alfamer.fi; motor sports, militaria; Man. Dir EIJA SAHLBERG.

Oy Amanita Ltd: Salkolantie 25, 31470 Somerniemi; tel. (2)
7489500; fax (2) 7489510; e-mail info@amanita.fi; internet www
.amanita.fi; f. 1982; non-fiction; Man. Dir LAURI LINNILÄ.

Art House Oy: Bulevardi 19C, 00120 Helsinki; tel. (9) 6940752; fax
(9) 6933762; e-mail myynti@arthouse.fi; internet www.arthouse.fi;
f. 1975; Finnish and foreign fiction, non-fiction, popular science,
horror, fantasy, science fiction, detective fiction; Publr PAAVO
HAAVIKKO.

Atena Kustannus Oy: Asemakatu 6, POB 436, 40101 Jyväskylä;
tel. (10) 4214200; e-mail atena@atena.fi; internet www.atena.fi;
f. 1986; cultural history, popular science, current affairs, biography;
Pres. PEKKA MÄKELÄ.

Basam Books Oy: Hämeentie 155A 6, POB 42, 00561 Helsinki; tel.
and fax (9) 75793839; e-mail info@basambooks.fi; internet www
.basambooks.fi; f. 1993; independent; literary fiction, poetry, non-
fiction; Publr BATU SAMALETDIN.

Gummerus Kustannus Oy: Lapinlahdenkatu 1C, POB 749, 00100
Helsinki; tel. (10) 6836200; fax (9) 58430200; e-mail info@gummerus
.fi; internet www.gummerus.fi; f. 1872; fiction, non-fiction, reference,
dictionaries, languages; independent; Man. Dirs JUHANI PEKKALA,
LIISA SUVIKUMPU.

Hogrefe Psykologien Kustannus Oy: Kaisaniemenkatu 10,
00100 Helsinki; tel. (9) 6126060; fax (9) 6123005; e-mail myynti@

psykologienkustannus.fi; internet www.psykologienkustannus.fi; f. 1965; literature on psychology; Man. Dir ALEKSI LEVO.

Karisto Oy: Paroistentie 2, POB 102, 13101 Hämeenlinna; tel. (3) 63151; fax (3) 6161565; e-mail kustannusliike@karisto.fi; internet www.karisto.fi; f. 1900; non-fiction and fiction, printing; Man. Dir MIKA KOTILAINEN.

Kirjapaja: Itälahdenkatu 27A, 00210 Helsinki; tel. (9) 6877450; fax (9) 68774545; e-mail mira.pitkanen@kirjapaja.fi; internet www.kirjapaja.fi; f. 1942; Christian literature, general fiction, non-fiction, reference, juvenile; Vice-Pres. ANNE-MARIA LANTTA.

Kustannus-Mäkelä Oy: POB 14, 03601 Karkkila; tel. (9) 2257995; fax (9) 2257660; e-mail makela@kustannusmakela.fi; internet www.kustannusmakela.fi; f. 1971; juvenile, fiction; Man. Dir ORVO MÄKELÄ.

Oy Like Kustannus Ltd: POB 37, 00521 Helsinki; tel. (9) 6229970; fax (9) 1351372; e-mail like@like.fi; internet www.like.fi; f. 1987; film literature, fiction, non-fiction, comics; Man. Dir PÄIVI PAAPPANEN.

Maahenki Oy: Eerikinkatu 28, 00180 Helsinki; tel. (9) 7512020; fax (9) 75120211; e-mail maahenki@msl.fi; internet www.maahenki.fi; art, nature; Man. Dir ULLA SARVIALA.

Otava Publishing Co Ltd: Uudenmaankatu 10, 00120 Helsinki; tel. (9) 19961; fax (9) 1996560; e-mail pasi.vainio@otava.fi; internet www.otava.fi; f. 1890; part of Otava-United Magazines Group Ltd; non-fiction, fiction, children's and textbooks; Man. Dir PASI VAINIO.

Schildts & Söderströms: Bulevarden 7, POB 870, 00120 Helsinki; tel. (9) 6841860; fax (9) 68418610; e-mail info@sets.fi; internet www.sets.fi; f. 2012 following the merger of Schildts Förlags Ab (f. 1913) and Söderströms Förlag (f. 1891); subjects mainly in Swedish; Man. Dir BARBRO TEIR.

Suomalaisen Kirjallisuuden Seura, SKS (Finnish Literature Society): Mariankatu 7A, 4th Floor, 00170 Helsinki; tel. (20) 1131231; fax (9) 13123220; e-mail sks@finlit.fi; internet www.finlit.fi/books; f. 1834; Finnish language and literature, linguistics, folklore, cultural studies and history; Publishing Dir TERO NORKOLA.

Tammi Publishers: Korkeavuorenkatu 37, POB 410, 00101 Helsinki; tel. (10) 5060300; fax (10) 5060399; e-mail tammi@tammi.fi; internet www.tammi.fi; f. 1943; fiction, general, non-fiction, children's, juvenile, textbooks, educational materials, audio books; owned by Bonnier AB; Pres. JACOB DALBORG.

Weilin & Göös Oy: Bulevardi 12, 00120 Helsinki; tel. (9) 43771; fax (9) 4377270; e-mail asiakaspalvelu@wg.fi; internet www.wg.fi; f. 1872; non-fiction, encyclopedias; Dir JAANA KORPI.

Werner Söderström Corpn (WSOY): POB 222, 00121 Helsinki; Korkeavuorenkatu 37, POB 314, 00101 Helsinki; tel. (10) 5060200; internet www.wsoy.fi; f. 1878; fiction and non-fiction, science, juvenile, textbooks, reference, comics, the printing industry; Pres. JACOB DAHLBORG.

PUBLISHERS' ASSOCIATION

Suomen Kustannusyhdistys (Finnish Book Publishers' Association): Lönnrotinkatu 11A, POB 177, 00121 Helsinki; tel. (9) 22877252; fax (9) 6121226; e-mail sirkku.palomaki@kustantajat.fi; internet www.kustantajat.fi; f. 1858; Pres. PASI VAINIO; Dir SAKARI LAIHO; 100 mems.

Broadcasting and Communications

REGULATORY AUTHORITY

Finnish Communications Regulatory Authority (FICORA): Itämerenkatu 3A, POB 313, 00181 Helsinki; tel. (295) 390275; fax (295) 390270; internet www.viestintavirasto.fi; f. 1988; affiliated to Ministry of Transport and Communications; CEO ASTA SIHVONEN-PUNKKA.

TELECOMMUNICATIONS

DNA Ltd: Läkkisepäntie 21, POB 10, 00620 Helsinki; tel. (44) 144044; internet www.dna.fi; f. 2007; offers mobile communications services through DNA Finland Ltd and fixed-network broadband and television services through DNA Services Ltd; Chair. LEINO JARMO; CEO JUKKA LEINONEN.

Elisa Corpn: Ratavartijankatu 5, Helsinki; POB 1, 00061 Elisa; tel. (10) 26000; fax (10) 26060; internet www.elisa.com; f. 1882; as Helsingin Telefooni; Chair. RAIMO LIND; CEO VELI-MATTI MATTILA.

Finnet International Ltd: Sinebrychoffgat. 11, POB 949, 00101 Helsinki; tel. (9) 315315; fax (9) 605531; e-mail fl@finnet.fi; internet www.finnet.fi; f. 1921; Chair. AIMO SUIKKANEN.

Telecon Ltd: POB 55, 02231 Espoo; tel. (40) 9526900; e-mail info@telecon.fi; internet www.telecon.fi; f. 1980; Man. Dir JOUKO JOKINEN.

TeliaSonera Finland Oyj: Teollisuuskatu 15, Helsinki; POB 220, 00051 Sonera; tel. (20) 401; fax (20) 4069100; internet www.teliasonera.fi; f. 2002 by merger of Telia AB (Sweden) and Sonera Ltd; Chair. MARIE EHRLING; Pres. and CEO JOHAN DENNELIND; 190.6m. subscribers worldwide (2013).

BROADCASTING

Radio

The first commercial radio stations were introduced in 1985. The economic recession of the early 1990s led to the collapse of many commercial stations. However, the industry began to recover in the late 1990s, and the first national commercial radio station, Radio Nova, was launched in May 1997. In 1999 RAB Finland was established to promote and develop the Finnish private radio industry by providing information services. By 2008 the number of commercial radio stations reached 57.

In May 1999 the first part of the national Digital Audio Broadcast (DAB) network was launched by Yleisradio (YLE—Finnish Broadcasting Company). The Finnish DAB transmitter network was closed down in 2005; YLE continued its digital transmissions through the Digital Video Broadcasting (DVB) television network.

Yleisradio Oy (YLE) (Finnish Broadcasting Company): YLE Centre, Radiokatu 5, 00024 Helsinki; tel. (9) 14801; fax (9) 14803216; e-mail fbc@yle.fi; internet www.yle.fi; f. 1926; 99.9% state-owned, with management appointed by the Administrative Council; Chair. KARI NEILIMO; Dir-Gen. LAURI KIVINEN.

  YLE Radio 1 (Radio Ylen Ykkönen): POB 6, 00024 Helsinki; 24-hour arts and culture in Finnish; Dir HEIKKI PELTONEN.

  YLE R2 (YleX): POB 17, 00024 Helsinki; tel. (9) 14801; fax (9) 1482650; e-mail tomi.saarinen@yle.fi; internet ylex.fi; f. 2003; 24-hour popular culture for young people in Finnish; Dir JYRI KATAJA-RAHKO.

  YLE R3 (Radio Suomi): 24-hour news, current affairs, sport, regional programmes in Finnish; Dir MARJA KESKITALO.

  YLE R4 (Radio Extrem): Swedish-language channel for young people.

  YLE R5 (Radio Vega): POB 62, 00024 Rundradion; tel. (9) 14801; e-mail mika.kosunen@yle.fi; internet www.yle.fi/vega; news, current affairs, art, culture and regional programmes in Swedish; Dir MIKA KOSUNEN.

  YLE Radio Finland: POB 78, 00024 Yleisradio; tel. (9) 14804320; fax (9) 14801169; e-mail rfinland@yle.fi; internet www.yle.fi/rfinland; broadcasts in Finnish, Swedish, English, German, French, Russian and Classical Latin.

  YLE Sámi Radio: POB 38, 99871 Inari; tel. (16) 6757500; fax (16) 6757501; e-mail sami.radio@yle.fi; Sámi-language network covering northern Lapland.

Digita Oy: Jämsänkatu 2, 00520 Helsinki; POB 135, 00521 Helsinki; tel. (20) 411711; fax (20) 4117234; e-mail info@digita.fi; internet www.digita.fi; f. 1999; operates the radio and television broadcasting network covering the whole of Finland; 36 main broadcasting stations and 151 substations; Chair. ARNE WESSBERG; Man. Dir JUHA-PEKKA WECKSTRÖM.

Groove FM: Pursimiehenkatu 29–31C, 00150 Helsinki; tel. (20) 7768360; e-mail juha.kakkuri@groovefm.fi; internet www.groovefm.fi; Station Dir JUHA KAKKURI.

Iskelmä: Tallberginkatu 1C, 00180 Helsinki; tel. (20) 7474000; e-mail erkka.jaakkola@sbs.fi; internet www.iskelma.fi; Media Dir JUHA OURILA.

NRJ: Kiviaidankatu 2I, 00210 Helsinki; tel. (9) 681900; fax (9) 68190102; e-mail marko.lintussari@nrj.fi; internet www.nrj.fi; Man. Dir ANTTI PAKKALA.

RadioMedia: Mikonkatu 15A, 00100 Helsinki; tel. (9) 22877340; fax (9) 648221; e-mail info@radiomedia.fi; internet www.radiomedia.fi; f. 1999; promotes Finnish private radio industry by providing extensive information services free of charge; Chair. LEENA PUNTILA; Man. Dir STEFAN MÖLLER.

Radio Nova: Ilmalankatu 2C, POB 123, 00241 Helsinki; tel. (9) 88488700; fax (9) 88488720; e-mail radionova-toimitus@mtv.fi; internet www.radionova.fi; largest commercial radio station; 74% owned by Alma Media; Marketing Dir PÄIVI NURMESNIEMI.

Radio SuomiPOP: Pursimiehenkatu 29–31C, 00150 Helsinki; tel. (20) 7768360; e-mail studio@radiosuomipop.fi; internet www.radiosuomipop.fi; Station Dir JUHA KAKKURI.

The Voice: Tallberginkatu 1C, 00180 Helsinki; tel. (20) 7474000; e-mail toimitus@voice.fi; internet www.voice.fi; Commercial Dir OUTI REKOLA.

Television

Digital Video Broadcasting (DVB) began in Finland in 2001. Analogue transmission networks were closed down from 1 September 2007.

Yleisradio Oy (YLE): operates 5 national channels: TV 1, TV 2, YLE FST (in Swedish), TV Finland (digital satellite channel broadcast in Nordic countries and elsewhere in Europe) and YLE Teema (a specialized channel for culture, education and science)

YLE TV 1: POB 97, 00024 Yleisradio; tel. (9) 14801; fax (9) 14803424; internet www.yle.fi/tv1; f. 1957; programmes in Finnish; Channel Controller PENTTI VÄLIAHDET.

YLE TV2: POB 196, 33101 Tampere; tel. (3) 3456111; fax (3) 3456892; e-mail ilkka.saari@yle.fi; internet www.yle.fi/tv2; f. 1964; programmes in Finnish and Swedish; Channel Controller RIKU SAARANLUOMA.

Canal Digital Finland Oy: POB 866, 33101 Tampere; tel. (20) 7699000; fax (20) 7699006; e-mail asiakaspalvelu@canaldigital.fi; internet www.canaldigital.fi; f. 1998; subsidiary of Telenor ASA (Norway).

MTV Finland: Ilmalankatu 2C, Helsinki; tel. (10) 300100; e-mail palaute@mtv3.fi; internet www.mtv3.fi; f. 1957; independent nationwide commercial television company comprising 9 channels: MTV3 and Subtv, as well as 7 subscription channels (MTV3 MAX, MTV3 Fakta, MTV Ava, MTV3 Sarja, MTV3 Scifi, Sub Juniori and Sub Leffa); became part of Alma Media Corpn in 1998; acquired by Bonnier (Sweden) in 2005; Pres. and CEO HEIKKI ROTKO.

Nelonen Media (Sanoma Entertainment Finland Oy): Töölönlahdenkatu 2, POB 95, 00089 Helsinki; tel. (9) 45451; fax (9) 4545400; e-mail hans.edin@nelonen.fi; internet www.nelonenmedia.fi; f. 1997; fmrly Oy Ruutunelonen Ab; independent commercial television co; part of Sanoma Group; Pres. KARI LAAKSO.

Finance

The Bank of Finland is the country's central bank and the centre of Finland's monetary and banking system. It functions 'under guarantee and supervision of the Eduskunta (Parliament) and the Bank supervisors delegated by the Eduskunta'.

At the end of 2011 there were a total of 313 banks operating in Finland.

BANKING

(cap. = capital; res = reserves; dep. = deposits; m. = million; brs = branches; amounts in euros)

Supervisory Authority

Financial Supervisory Authority (FIN-FSA): Snellmaninkatu 6, POB 103, 00101 Helsinki; tel. (10) 8315339; fax (10) 8315328; e-mail finanssivalvonta@finanssivalvonta.fi; internet www.finanssivalvonta.fi; f. 2009 to replace the Financial Supervision Authority and the Insurance Supervisory Authority; maintains confidence in the financial markets by supervising the markets and the bodies working within them; Chair. PENTTI HAKKARAINEN; Dir-Gen. ANNELI TUOMINEN.

Central Bank

Suomen Pankki/Finlands Bank (Bank of Finland): Snellmaninaukio, POB 160, 00101 Helsinki; tel. (10) 8311; fax (9) 174872; e-mail info@bof.fi; internet www.bof.fi; f. 1811; Bank of Issue under the guarantee and supervision of the Eduskunta; cap. 841m., res 1,334m., dep. 14,402m. (Dec. 2010); Gov. ERKKI LIIKANEN; 4 brs.

Commercial Banks

Danske Bank PLC: Hiililaiturinkuja 2, Helsinki; POB 1568, 00075 Sampo; tel. (10) 5460000; fax (10) 5462533; internet www.danskebank.fi; f. 1886 as Postisäästöpankki; name changed as above 2012; owned by Danske Bank (Denmark); cap. 106m., res 271.2m., dep. 19,592.8m. (Dec. 2012); CEO RISTO TORNIVAARA; 63 brs.

Nordea Bank Finland PLC (Nordea Pankki Suomi Oyj): Aleksanterinkatu 36B, 00100 Helsinki; tel. (9) 1651; fax (9) 16554500; internet www.nordea.fi; f. 1995; cap. 2,319m., res 3,474m., dep. 156,939m. (Dec. 2013); Group CEO CHRISTIAN CLAUSEN; 416 brs.

Co-operative Banks

Pohjola Bank PLC: Teollisuuskatu 1B, 00510 Helsinki; POB 308, 00013 Helsinki; tel. (10) 252011; fax (10) 2522002; internet www.pohjola.fi; f. 1902 as Osuuspankkien Keskuspankki Oyj; current name adopted 2008; cap. 428m., res 1,257m., dep. 21,746m. (Dec. 2013); part of OP–Pohjola Group Central Co-operative; Chair. REIJO KARHINEN; Pres. and CEO ERKKI MIKAEL SILVENNOINEN; 677 brs.

POP Bank: Hevosenkenkä 3, 02600 Espoo; tel. (9) 6811700; fax (9) 68117070; internet www.poppankki.fi; f. 1997; group comprising co-operative banks; Pres. HEIKKI SUUTALA; 111 brs.

Savings Bank

Aktia Bank Plc (Aktia Savings Bank PLC): Mannerheimintie 14, POB 207, 00100 Helsinki; tel. (10) 2475000; fax (10) 2476356; e-mail aktia@aktia.fi; internet www.aktia.fi; f. 1852 as Helsingfors Sparbank; current name adopted 2008; cap. 163m., res 136.4m., dep. 5,102.4m. (Dec. 2012); Chair. DAG WALLGREN; Man. Dir JUSSI LAITINEN; approx. 55 brs.

Mortgage Banks

OP-Asuntoluottopankki (OP Mortgage Bank): POB 308, 00101 Helsinki; tel. (9) 4041; fax (9) 4042620; e-mail iloniemi@pohjola.com; f. 2000; part of OP–Pohjola Group Central Co-operative; Man. Dir LAURI ILONIEMI.

Investment Bank

Nordiska Investeringsbanken (Nordic Investment Bank): Fabianinkatu 34, POB 249, 00171 Helsinki; tel. (10) 618001; fax (10) 6180723; e-mail info@nib.int; internet www.nib.int; f. 1975; owned by Govts of Denmark, Estonia, Finland, Iceland, Latvia, Lithuania, Norway and Sweden; all member countries are represented on the Bd of Dirs by their ministers responsible for finance and the economy; cap. 418.6m., res 2,195.1m., dep. 4,193m. (Dec. 2013); Pres. and CEO HENRIK NORMANN.

Banking Associations

Finanssialan Keskusliitto r.y. (Federation of Finnish Financial Services): Bulevardi 28, 00120 Helsinki; tel. (20) 7934200; fax (20) 7934202; e-mail fk@fkl.fi; internet www.fkl.fi; f. 2007 by merger of the Finnish Bankers' Association, the Federation of Finnish Insurance Companies, the Employers' Association of Finnish Financial Institutions and the Finnish Finance Houses' Association; Chair. REIJO KARHINEN; Man. Dir PIIA-NOORA KAUPPI.

Säästöpankkiliitto (Finnish Savings Banks Association): Linnoitustie 9, POB 68, 02601 Espoo; tel. (9) 548051; fax (20) 6029108; e-mail pasi.kamari@saastopankki.fi; internet www.saastopankki.fi; f. 1906; 25 mems; Chair. JUSSI HAKALA; CEO PASI KÄMÄRI; 190 brs.

Suomen Hypoteekkiyhdistys (Mortgage Society of Finland): Yrjönkatu 9A, 2nd Floor, 00101 Helsinki; POB 509, 00101 Helsinki; tel. (9) 228361; fax (9) 647443; e-mail hypo@hypo.fi; internet www.hypo.fi; f. 1860; Pres. ARI PAUNA.

STOCK EXCHANGE

NASDAQ Helsinki: Fabianinkatu 14, POB 361, 00131 Helsinki; tel. (9) 616671; fax (9) 61667368; e-mail nordicexchange.helsinki@nasdaqomx.com; internet www.nasdaqomx.com; f. 1912 as Helsingin Pörssi; merged with OMX AB (Sweden) in 2003; became part of OMX Nordic Exchange with Copenhagen (Denmark), Reykjavík (Iceland) and Stockholm (Sweden) exchanges in 2006; acquired by NASDAQ Stock Market, Inc (USA) in 2008; Group CEO ROBERT GREIFELD.

INSURANCE

In January 2011 there were 63 insurance companies operating in Finland, 24 of which were branches of foreign insurance companies.

A-Vakuutus Oy (A-Vakuutus Mutual Insurance Co): Lapinmäentie 1, 00350 Helsinki; tel. (10) 253000; fax (10) 2532908; e-mail a-vakuutus@a-vakuutus.fi; internet www.a-vakuutus.fi; non-life; Man. Dir JOUKO PÖLÖNEN.

Eurooppalainen Insurance Co Ltd: Lapinmäentie 1, 00013 Pohjola; tel. (10) 253000; internet www.eurooppalainen.fi; f. 1922; non-life; part of Pohjola Bank plc; Man. Dir MIKAEL SILVENNOINEN.

Garantia Insurance Co Ltd: Salomonkatu 17A, 9th Floor, POB 600, 00101 Helsinki; tel. (20) 7479800; fax (20) 7479801; e-mail garantia@garantia.fi; internet www.garantia.fi; f. 1993; non-life; Man. Dir MIKAEL ENGLUND.

If Vahinkovakuutusyhtiö Oy (If P & C Insurance Ltd): Niittyportti 4, 02200 Espoo; tel. 10191515; fax 105144028; internet www.if.fi; f. 1999; subsidiary of Sampo plc; Chair. KARI STADIGH; Pres. and CEO TORBJÖRN MAGNUSSON.

Keskinäinen Eläkevakuutusyhtiö Ilmarinen (Ilmarinen Mutual Pension Insurance Co): Porkkalankatu 1, 00018 Ilmarinen; tel. (10) 28411; fax (10) 2843445; e-mail info@ilmarinen.fi; internet www.ilmarinen.fi; f. 1961; statutory employment pensions; Man. Dir HARRI SAILAS.

Keskinäinen Henkivakuutusosakeyhtiö Suomi (Suomi Mutual Life Assurance Co): Aleksanterinkatu 15B, 00100 Helsinki; POB 1068, 00101 Helsinki; tel. (10) 2530066; fax (10) 2527806; e-mail hvpalvelukeskus@suomi-yhtio.fi; internet www.suomi-yhtio.fi; f. 1890; life insurance; Pres. and CEO JARI SOKKA.

Keskinäinen työeläkevakuutusyhtiö Varma (Varma Mutual Pension Insurance Co): Salmisaarenranta 11, POB 1, 00098 Varma; tel. (10) 2440; fax (10) 2444752; e-mail info@varma.fi; internet www.varma.fi; f. 1998; fmrly Varma-Sampo; CEO RISTO MURTO.

Keskinäinen Vakuutusyhtiö Fennia (Fennia Mutual Insurance Co): Televisiokatu 1, 00017 Helsinki; tel. (10) 5031; fax (10) 5037680; e-mail info@fennia.fi; internet www.fennia.fi; f. 1882; non-life; Man. Dir ANTTI KULJUKKA.

Keskinäinen Vakuutusyhtiö Kaleva (Kaleva Mutual Insurance Co): Bulevardi 56, 00100 Helsinki; POB 347, 00101 Helsinki; tel. (10) 515225; internet www.kalevavakuutus.fi; f. 1874; Man. Dir MATTI RANTANEN.

LähiTapiola Keskinäinen Eläkevakuutusyhtiö (LähiTapiola Mutual Pension Insurance Co): Revontulentie 7, POB 9, 02010 Tapiola; tel. (9) 4531; fax (20) 6051084; internet www.lahitapiola.fi; Chair. and Pres. ERKKI MOISANDER; Man. Dir SATU HUBER.

LähiTapiola Keskinäinen Henkivakuutusyhtiö (LähiTapiola Mutual Life Insurance Co): 02010 Tapiola; tel. (9) 4531; fax (9) 4532146; internet www.lahitapiola.fi; Chair. and Pres. ERKKI MOISANDER; Man. Dir MINNA KOHMO.

LähiTapiola Keskinäinen Vakuutusyhtiö (LähiTapiola General Mutual Insurance Co): 02010 Tapiola; tel. (9) 4531; fax (9) 4532146; internet www.lahitapiola.fi; non-life; Chair. and Pres. ERKKI MOISANDER; Man. Dir JUKKA KINNUNEN.

LähiTapiola Vakuutus Keskinäinen Yhtiö (Local Insurance Mutual Co): Revontulenkuja 1, POB 50, 02601 Espoo; tel. (20) 5222111; fax (20) 5222332; e-mail myynti@lahivakuutus.fi; internet www.lahivakuutus.fi; f. 1917; non-life; name changed as above following merger with Tapiola Group in 2012; Chair. and Pres. ERKKI MOISANDER.

Mandatum Life Insurance Co ltd: Bulevardi 56, 00120 Helsinki; tel. (10) 515225; e-mail asiakaspalvelu@mandatumlife.fi; internet www.mandatumlife.fi; f. 1997; subsidiary of Sampo plc; Chair. KARI STADIGH; CEO PETRI NIEMISVIRTA.

Nordea Life Assurance Finland: Aleksis Kiven Katu 9, 00020 Helsinki; tel. (9) 16527601; fax (9) 16527666; internet www.nordea.fi/selekta; Man. Dir PEKKA LUUKKANEN.

Palonvara Mutual Insurance Co: Oksasenkatu 1, 53100 Lappeenranta; tel. (20) 5222004; fax (20) 5223100; e-mail palvelu@palonvara.fi; internet www.palonvara.fi; f. 1912; non-life; Man. Dir JUKKA HERTTI.

Pohjantähti Keskinäinen Vakuutusyhtiö (Pohjantähti Mutual Insurance Co): Keinusaarentie 2, POB 164, 13101 Hämeenlinna; tel. (20) 7634000; fax (3) 5899890; internet www.pohjantahti.fi; f. 1895; non-life; Pres. and CEO EERO YLÄ-SOININMÄKI.

Vahinkovakuutusosakeyhtiö Pohjola (Pohjola Non-Life Insurance Co Ltd): Lapinmäentie 1, 00013 Pohjola; tel. (10) 253000; internet www.pohjola.fi; f. 1891; non-life; Chair. REIJO KARHINEN; Pres. MIKAEL SILVENNOINEN.

Veritas Eläkevakuutus (Veritas Pension Insurance Co Ltd): Olavintie 2, POB 133, 20101 Turku; tel. (10) 55010; fax (10) 5501690; e-mail veritas@veritas.fi; internet www.veritas.fi; f. 1905; Pres. PETER BOSTRÖM; Man. Dir JAN-ERIK STENMAN.

Insurance Associations

Federation of Accident Insurance Institutions: Bulevardi 28, POB 275, 00121 Helsinki; tel. (40) 4504208; internet www.tvl.fi; f. 1920; publishes *Tapaturmavakuutuslehti* quarterly (circ. 3,300); Man. Dir JUSSI KAUMA.

Finnish Motor Insurers' Centre: Bulevardi 28, 00120 Helsinki; tel. (40) 4504750; fax (40) 4504696; internet www.lvk.fi; f. 1938; Man. Dir ULLA NIKU-KOSKINEN.

Finnish Pension Alliance TELA: Lastenkodinkuja 1, 00180 Helsinki; tel. (10) 6806700; fax (10) 6806706; e-mail tela@tela.fi; internet www.tela.fi; f. 1964; Pres. and CEO HARRI SAILAS.

Nordic Nuclear Insurers: Kalevankatu 18A, 00100 Helsinki; tel. (9) 6803410; fax (9) 68034115; internet www.atompool.com; f. 2002; Man. Dir EERO HOLMA.

Trade and Industry

GOVERNMENT AGENCIES

Finpro: Porkkalankatu 1, 00180 Helsinki; POB 358, 00181 Helsinki; tel. (20) 46951; fax (20) 4695200; e-mail info@finpro.fi; internet www.finpro.fi; f. 1919 as Finnish Export Association; Chair. HARRI KERMINEN; Pres. and CEO KARI HÄYRINEN.

Invest in Finland: Porkkalankatu 1, 00180 Helsinki; tel. (20) 4695555; fax (20) 4695201; e-mail info@investinfinland.fi; internet www.investinfinland.fi; promoting foreign investments to Finland; merged with Finpro in 2011; Exec. Vice-Pres. VILLE AITTOMÄKI.

CHAMBERS OF COMMERCE

Helsingin Seudun Kauppakamari (Helsinki Region Chamber of Commerce): Kalevankatu 12, 00100 Helsinki; tel. (9) 228601; fax (9) 22860228; e-mail kauppakamari@helsinki.chamber.fi; internet www.helsinki.chamber.fi; f. 1917; Chair. JUKKA HIENONEN; Man. Dir HEIKKI J. PERÄLÄ; 6,500 mems.

Keskuskauppakamari (Finland Chamber of Commerce): Aleksanterinkatu 17, POB 1000, 00101 Helsinki; tel. (9) 42426200; fax (9) 650303; e-mail keskuskauppakamari@chamber.fi; internet www.keskuskauppakamari.fi; f. 1918; CEO RISTO E. J. PENTTILÄ; 18,000 mems; represents 19 regional chambers of commerce.

INDUSTRIAL AND TRADE ASSOCIATIONS

Betoniteollisuus r.y. (Finnish Concrete Industry Asscn): Unioninkatu 14, POB 11, 00131 Helsinki; tel. (9) 12991; fax (9) 1299291; e-mail jussi.mattila@rakennusteollisuus.fi; internet www.betoni.com; f. 1929; Chair. and CEO JUSSI MATTILA; 48 mems.

Centralförbundet för lant- och skogsbruksproducenter (Central Union of Agricultural Producers and Forest Owners): Simonkatu 6, POB 510, 00100 Helsinki; tel. (20) 4131; fax (20) 4132409; e-mail michael.hornborg@mtk.fi; internet www.mtk.fi; f. 1917; Pres. JUHA MARTTILA; Sec.-Gen. ANTTI SAHI; 152,500 mems.

Kalatalouden Keskusliitto (Federation of Finnish Fisheries Associations): Malmin kauppatie 26, 00700 Helsinki; tel. (9) 6844590; fax (9) 68445959; e-mail kalastus@ahven.net; internet www.ahven.net; f. 1891; Dir MARKKU MYLLYLÄ; 616,000 mems.

Metsäteollisuus r.y. (Finnish Forest Industries' Federation): Snellmaninkatu 13, 00170 Helsinki; POB 336, 00171 Helsinki; tel. (9) 13261; fax (9) 1324445; e-mail forest@forestindustries.fi; internet www.forestindustries.fi; f. 1918; Chair. JUSSI PESONEN; mems: 120 cos in the forestry industry and sales or trade asscns.

Sähköenergialiitto r.y. (Finnish Electricity Association): c/o Oy Turku Energia, POB 105, 20101 Turku; tel. 447422706 (mobile); e-mail sener.energia@gmail.com; internet www.sener.fi; f. 1926; research on electricity networks and electrical applications; Man. JARKKO LEHTONEN; 74 mems.

Suomalaisen Työn Liitto (Association for Finnish Work): Mikonkatu 17A, 00100 Helsinki; POB 429, 00101 Helsinki; tel. (9) 6692430; fax (9) 69624333; e-mail stl@avainlippu.fi; internet www.avainlippu.fi; f. 1912; public relations for Finnish products and for Finnish work; Chair. of Council TAPIO PAJUHARJU; Chair., Exec. Bd ANNE BERNER; CEO TERO LAUSALA; c. 2,500 mems.

Suomen Kaupan Liitto (Federation of Finnish Commerce): Eteläranta 10, POB 340, 00130 Helsinki; tel. (9) 172850; fax (9) 664616; e-mail kauppa@kauppa.fi; internet www.kauppa.fi; f. 2005 by merger of the Federation of Finnish Commerce and Trade and the Commercial Employers' Association; Chair. MAARIT TOIVANEN-KOIVISTO; 24 mem. asscns with more than 7,000 firms.

Svenska lantbruksproducenternas centralförbund (SLC) (Central Union of Swedish-speaking Agricultural Producers): Fredriksgatan 61A 34, 00100 Helsinki; tel. (9) 5860460; fax (9) 6941358; e-mail holger.falck@slc.fi; internet www.slc.fi; f. 1945; Chair. HOLGER FALCK; 12,000 mems (approx.).

Teknisen Kaupan (Association of Finnish Technical Traders): Sarkiniementie 3, 4th Floor, 00210 Helsinki; tel. (9) 6824130; fax (9) 68241310; e-mail tekninen.kauppa@tekninen.fi; internet www.tekninen.fi; f. 1918; organization of the main importers dealing in steel and metals, machines and equipment, heavy chemicals and raw materials; Chair. AKI OJANEN; Man. Dir MARKKU UITTO; 400 mems.

EMPLOYERS' ORGANIZATIONS

Elinkeinoelämän Keskusliitto (EK) (Confederation of Finnish Industries): Eteläranta 10, 00130 Helsinki; POB 30, 00131 Helsinki; tel. (9) 42020; fax (9) 42022299; e-mail ek@ek.fi; internet www.ek.fi; f. 1907; aims to promote co-operation between cos and mem. organizations and to protect the interests of mems in employment issues; 27 asscns consisting of about 16,000 enterprises with 980,000 employees; Chair. MATTI ALAHUHTA; Dir-Gen. JYRI HÄKÄMIES.

Autoliikenteen Työnantajaliitto r.y. (Employers' Federation of Road Transport): Nuijamiestentie 7, 00400 Helsinki; tel. (9) 47899480; fax (9) 5883995; e-mail mari.vasarainen@alt.fi; internet www.alt.fi; f. 1945; Chair. ANTTI NORRLIN; c. 1,000 mems.

Elintarviketeollisuusliitto r.y. (Finnish Food and Drink Industries' Federation): Pasilankatu 2, POB 115, 00240 Helsinki; tel. (9) 148871; fax (9) 14887201; e-mail info@etl.fi; internet www.etl.fi; Chair. JUHA GRÖHN; Dir-Gen. HEIKKI JUUTINEN.

Kemianteollisuus (KT) r.y. (Chemical Industry Federation): Eteläranta 10, POB 4, 00131 Helsinki; tel. (9) 172841; fax (9) 630225; internet www.chemind.fi; Dir-Gen. TIMO LEPPÄ; 13 mem asscns.

Kenkä- ja Nahkateollisuus r.y. (Association of Finnish Shoe and Leather Industries): Eteläranta 10, 00130 Helsinki; tel. (9) 172841; fax (9) 179588; e-mail olavi.viljanmaa@jalas.com; Chair. OLAVI VILJANMAA.

Kumiteollisuus r.y. (Rubber Manufacturers' Association of Finland): Eteläranta 10, 7th Floor, 00130 Helsinki; POB 4, 00131 Helsinki; tel. (9) 172841; fax (9) 630225; e-mail sami.nikander@kemianteollisuus.fi; internet www.kumiteollisuus.fi; f. 1961; Chair. ARI LEHTORANTA; Man. Dir SAMI NIKANDER; 16 mems.

Lääketeollisuus r.y. (Pharma Industry Finland—PIF): Porkkalankatu 1, 00180 Helsinki; POB 206, 00181 Helsinki; tel. (9) 61504900; fax (9) 61504941; e-mail pif@pif.fi; internet www.pif.fi; Chair. and CEO JUSSI MERIKALLIO.

Muoviteollisuus r.y. (Finnish Plastics Industries Federation): Eteläranta 10, POB 4, 00131 Helsinki; tel. (9) 172841; fax (9) 171164; e-mail vesa.karha@plastics.fi; internet www.plastics.fi; Chair. and CEO VESA KÄRHÄ.

Palvelualojen Työnantajat (Service Sector Employers—PALTA): Eteläranta 10, 6th Floor, POB 62, 00131 Helsinki; tel. (20) 5955000; fax (20) 5955001; e-mail info@palta.fi; internet www.palta.fi; f. 2011 following the merger of Tieto- ja tekniikka-alojen työnantajaliitto (TIKLI) with three other service sector orgs; Chair. RÖNKKÖ TUOMO; 1,700 mems.

Rakennusteollisuus RT r.y. (Confederation of Finnish Construction Industries): Unioninkatu 14, POB 381, 00131 Helsinki; tel. (9) 12991; fax (9) 628264; e-mail rt@rakennusteollisuus.fi; internet www.rakennusteollisuus.fi; f. 2001; Chair. LAURI KIVEKÄS; Dir-Gen. TARMO PIPATTI; 2,700 mem. cos.

Satamaoperaattorit r.y. (Finnish Port Operators' Asscn): Köydenpunojankatu 8, 00180 Helsinki; tel. (9) 6859530; fax (9) 68595353; e-mail juha.mutru@satamaoperaattorit.fi; internet www.satamaoperaattorit.fi; f. 1906; fmrly Suomen Lastauttajain Liitto (SLL) r.y.; Chair. MATTI ESKO; Man. Dir JUHA MUTRU.

Suunnittelu- ja konsultointiyritykset (SKOL) r.y. (Finnish Association of Consulting Firms—SKOL): Eteläranta 10, POB 10, 00131 Helsinki; tel. (9) 19231; fax (9) 624462; e-mail skolry@teknologiateollisuus.fi; internet www.skolry.fi; f. 1951; Man. Dir MATTI MANNONEN; 195 mems.

Teknokemian Yhdistys r.y. (Finnish Cosmetic, Toiletry and Detergent Association): Eteläranta 10, 00130 Helsinki; POB 311, 00131 Helsinki; tel. (9) 172841; e-mail info@teknokemia.fi; internet www.teknokemia.fi; Dir-Gen. SARI KARJOMAA; 52 mems.

Teknologiateollisuus r.y. (Technology Industries of Finland): Eteläranta 10, POB 10, 00131 Helsinki; tel. (9) 19231; fax (9) 624462; e-mail martti.maenpaa@teknologiateollisuus.fi; internet www.teknologiateollisuus.fi; f. 1903 as Metalliteollisuuden Keskusliitto r.y.; Chair. JARI PAASIKIVI.

Viestinnän Keskusliitto (Federation of the Finnish Media Industry): Lönnrotinkatu 11A, POB 291, 00121 Helsinki; tel. (9) 22877200; fax (9) 603527; e-mail hakan.gabrielsson@vkl.fi; internet www.vkl.fi; Man. Dir VALTTERI NIIRANEN.

Yleinen Teollisuusliitto r.y. (General Industry Association): Eteläranta 10, 7th Floor, POB 325, 00130 Helsinki; tel. (9) 6220410; fax (9) 176135; internet www.ytl.fi; Chair. JUHA LAURIO; Man. Dir PEKKA TSUPARI.

Kultaseppien Työnantajaliitto r.y. (Employers' Association of Goldsmiths): Eteläranta 10, 00130 Helsinki; tel. (9) 172841; fax (9) 630225; Chair. ILKKA RUOHOLA.

Suomen Kiinteistöliitto r.y. (Finnish Real Estate Federation): Annankatu 24, 3rd Floor, 00100 Helsinki; tel. (9) 16676761; fax (9) 16676400; e-mail info@kiinteistoliitto.fi; internet www.kiinteistoliitto.fi; f. 1907; Pres. MATTI INHA; Man. Dir HARRI HILTUNEN; 23 mem asscns.

Suomen Varustamot r.y. (Finnish Shipowners' Association): see under Shipping.

Tupakkateollisuusliitto r.y. (Finnish Tobacco Industries' Federation): Eteläranta 10, 00130 Helsinki; tel. (45) 3186650; e-mail paavo.heiskanen@ytl.fi; Chair. FARID HAMADI.

UTILITIES

Electricity

Fortum Oyj: Keilaniementie 1, 02150 Espoo; POB 1, 00048 Fortum; tel. (10) 4511; fax (10) 4524777; e-mail asiakapavelu@fortum.com; internet www.fortum.fi; f. 1998 following merger of the Imatran Voima Group and the Neste Group; 50.76% state-owned; generation, distribution and sale of electricity and heat, as well as the operation and maintenance of power plants; listed on the Helsinki exchange in Dec. 1998; Chair. SARI BALDAUF; Pres. and CEO TAPIO KUULA.

Kemijoki Oy: Valtakatu 11, POB 8131, 96101 Rovaniemi; tel. (20) 7034400; fax (16) 7402380; e-mail info@kemijoki.fi; internet www.kemijoki.fi; f. 1954; electric power; 50.1% state-owned; Chair. of Supervisory Bd MATTI RUOTSALA; Pres. and CEO TUOMAS TIMONEN; 266 employees.

Pohjolan Voima Oy (PVO): Töölönkatu 4, POB 40, 00101 Helsinki; tel. (10) 4785000; fax (9) 69306335; e-mail info@pvo.fi; internet www.pohjolanvoima.fi; Chair. TAPIO KORPEINEN; Pres. and CEO LAURI VIRKKUNEN.

Regional electricity providers operate, of which the largest is Helsingin Energia.

Helsingin Energia (Helsinki Energy): Kampinkuja 2, 00090 Helen; tel. (9) 6171; fax (9) 6172360; e-mail helsingin.energia@helen.fi; internet www.helen.fi; f. 1909; municipal undertaking; generates and distributes electrical power and district heating; distributes natural gas; Man. Dir PEKKA MANNINEN.

Gas

Gasum Oy: Miestentie 1, POB 21, 02151 Espoo; tel. (20) 4471; fax (20) 4478619; e-mail minna.ojala@gasum.fi; internet www.gasum.fi; f. 1994; imports and sells natural gas, owns and operates natural gas transmission system; operates 6 subsidiaries, Gasum Energiapalvelut Oy, Gasum Paikallisjakelu Oy, Gasum Eesti AG, Gasum Tekniikka Oy, Helsingin Kaupunkikaasu Oy and Kaasupörssi Oy; 25% owned by OAO Gazprom (Russia) and 75% state-owned; Pres. and CEO JOHANNA LAMMINEN.

Water

Helsingin seudun ympäristöpalvelut (Helsinki Region Environmental Services Authority): Opastinsilta 6D–E, POB 100, 00520 Helsinki; tel. (9) 15611; fax (9) 15612011; e-mail hsy@hsy.fi; internet www.hsy.fi; responsible for water supply and sewerage of the greater Helsinki area; Man. Dir RAIMO INKINEN.

CO-OPERATIVES

Pellervo (Confederation of Finnish Co-operatives): Simonkatu 6, POB 77, 00101 Helsinki; tel. (9) 4767501; fax (9) 6948845; e-mail toimisto@pellervo.fi; internet www.pellervo.fi; f. 1899; central organization of co-operatives; Pres. MARTTI ASUNTA; Man. Dir SAMI KARHU; 258 mem. societies (incl. 11 central co-operative societies).

Munakunta (Co-operative Egg Producers' Association): Piispanristintie 8, POB 6, 20761 Piispanristi; tel. (2) 214420; fax (2) 2144222; e-mail info@munakunta.fi; internet www.munakunta.fi; f. 1922; Man. Dir JAN LÄHDE; 500 mems.

Valio Ltd (Finnish Co-operative Dairies' Association): Meijeritie 6, 00370 Helsinki; POB 10, 00039 Valio; tel. (10) 381121; fax (9) 5625068; e-mail pekka.laaksonen@valio.fi; internet www.valio.fi; f. 1905; production and marketing of dairy products; Pres. and CEO PEKKA LAAKSONEN.

TRADE UNIONS

Akava (Confederation of Unions for Professional and Managerial Staff): Maistraatinportti 2, 00240 Helsinki; tel. (20) 7489400; fax (9) 142595; internet www.akava.fi; f. 1950; 30 affiliates, incl. asscns of doctors, engineers, social workers and teachers; Pres. STURE FJÄDER; total membership 552,800.

Suomen Ammattiliittojen Keskusjärjestö (SAK) r.y. (Central Organization of Finnish Trade Unions): Hakaniemenranta 1A, 00530 Helsinki; POB 157, 00531 Helsinki; tel. (20) 774000; fax (20) 7740225; e-mail sak@sak.fi; internet www.sak.fi; f. 1907; 20 affiliated unions comprising over 1m. mems; Pres. LAURI LYLY; Sec. KIRSI SAINIO.

STTK (Finnish Confederation of Professionals): Mikonkatu 8A, 6th Floor, POB 421, 00101 Helsinki; tel. (9) 131521; fax (9) 652367; e-mail sttk@sttk.fi; internet www.sttk.fi; f. 1946; Pres. MIKKO PALOLA; 17 affiliated unions; 608,000 mems.

Transport

ADMINISTRATIVE BODIES

Liikennevirasto (Finnish Transport Agency): Opastinsilta 12A, POB 33, 00521 Helsinki; tel. (20) 637373; fax (20) 6373700; e-mail viestinta@liikennevirasto.fi; internet www.fta.fi; f. 2010 by merger of waterways section of Finnish Maritime Administration, Finnish Rail Administration and Finnish Road Administration; attached to the Ministry of Transport and Communications; responsible for maintenance and development of transport infrastructure; Dir-Gen. ANTTI VEHVILÄINEN.

TraFi (Transport Safety Agency): Kumpulantie 9, POB 320, 00101 Helsinki; tel. (29) 5345000; fax (20) 5345095; e-mail kirjaamo@trafi.fi; internet www.trafi.fi; f. 2010 by merger of 4 sectoral bodies; attached to Ministry of Transport and Communications; responsible for safety and supervision of maritime, rail and road traffic and civil aviation; Dir-Gen. KARI WIHLMAN.

RAILWAYS

Finland had 5,944 km of wide-gauge (1,524 mm Russian gauge) railways in 2012, providing internal services and connections with Sweden and Russia. The state rail network is owned by the Finnish Transport Agency which oversees the maintenance and development of the country's rail network (see Administrative Bodies), while VR Group operates train services on the network. A high-speed rail link between Helsinki and St Petersburg, Russia became operational in December 2010. An underground railway service has been provided by Helsinki City Transport since 1982. In 2010 it was proposed to build a 312-km cross-border railway line linking Finland's main railway hub of Kolari to Skibotn in Norway. An 18-km railway route connecting the Helsinki-Vantaa airport and the adjacent Aviapolis business and commercial district to the Helsinki commuter rail network was under construction in 2012. The line, known as the Ring Rail Line Kehärata, was expected to open in 2015.

Karhula-Sunila Railway: Ratakatu 8, 48600 Karhula; tel. (5) 298221; fax (5) 298225; f. 1937; goods transport; privately owned; operates 6 km of railway (1,524 mm gauge); Man. PERTTI HONKALA.

VR Group: Vilhonkatu 13, POB 488, 00101 Helsinki; tel. (307) 10; fax (307) 21700; e-mail contactcenter@vr.fi; internet www.vr.fi; began operating 1862; joint-stock co since 1995; operates 5,784 km of railways; Pres. and CEO MIKAEL ARO; Chief Financial Officer OUTI HENRIKSSON.

ROADS

Finland had 78,161 km of highways in 2010, of which 13,329 km were main roads (including 779 km of motorway). Some 65% of the road network was paved in that year. In 2010 €823m. was spent on road infrastructure, including private roads.

Destia: Heidehofintie 2, POB 206, 01301 Helsinki; tel. (20) 44411; fax (20) 4442297; e-mail destia@destia.fi; internet www.destia.fi; f. 2008 to assume activities of fmr Tieliikelaitos (Finnish Road Enterprise); state-owned enterprise; provides transport infrastructure and transport environment services; Pres. and CEO HANNU LEINONEN.

INLAND WATERWAYS

Finland has a total of 19,500 km (approx.) of public, charted fairways. Lakes cover 33,672 sq km. The inland waterway system comprises 7,842 km of buoyed-out channels, 40 open canals and 37 lock canals. Merchant shipping routes include about 4,000 km. The total length of canals is 116 km. The most economically significant canal is the Saimaa Canal, which is 43 km long and connects Lake Saima to the Gulf of Finland. In 2006 cargo vessel traffic on inland waterways (including on the Saimaa Canal) amounted to 2.4m. metric tons, timber floating amounted to 0.9m. tons and passenger traffic to 479,709 passengers. The Finnish Transport Agency (see Administrative Bodies) is responsible for maintaining the inland waterways.

SHIPPING

The chief port of export is Kotka. Reclamation of land was carried out to build a second container port in Kotka. It opened in 2001 and has the capacity to handle 500,000 20-ft equivalent units (TEUs) of cargo per year. The main port of import is Helsinki, which has three specialized harbours. The West Harbour handles most of the container traffic, the North Harbour cargo ferry traffic and the South Harbour passenger traffic. Other important international ports are Turku (Åbo), Rauma and Hamina. The Transport Safety Agency (see Administrative Bodies) is responsible for maritime administration. At 31 December 2014 the flag registered fleet numbered 297 registered vessels, with a combined displacement of 1.5m. grt, of which 56 were general cargo and 35 were passenger ships.

Port Authority Association

Suomen Satamaliitto (Finnish Port Association): Toinen Linja 14, 00530 Helsinki; tel. (9) 7711; fax (9) 7530474; e-mail info@satamaliitto.fi; internet www.finnports.com; f. 1923; 31 mems; Exec. Dir ANNALEENA MÄKILÄ.

Port Authorities

HaminaKotka: Merituulentie 424, POB 196, 48310 Kotka; tel. (20) 7908800; fax (20) 7908891; e-mail marketing@haminakotka.fi; internet www.haminakotka.fi; Man. Dir KIMMO NASKI.

Helsinki: Port of Helsinki, Olympiaranta 3, POB 800, 00099 Helsinki; tel. (9) 3101621; fax (9) 31033802; e-mail port.helsinki@hel.fi; internet www.portofhelsinki.fi; Man. Dir KIMMO MÄKI.

Rauma: Port of Rauma, Hakunintie 19, 26100 Rauma; tel. (2) 8344712; fax (2) 8226369; e-mail harbour.office@portofrauma.com;

internet www.portofrauma.com; Port Dir HANNU ASUMALAHTI; Harbour Master and Port Security Officer TANJA ROBERTS.

Turku: Turku Port Authority, Linnankatu 90, 20100 Turku; tel. (2) 2674111; fax (2) 2674125; e-mail turkport@port.turku.fi; internet www.port.turku.fi; Man. Dir CHRISTIAN RAMBERG; Harbour Master KARI RIUTTA.

Shipowners' Association

Suomen Varustamot r.y. (Finnish Shipowners' Association): Hämeentie 19, 00500 Helsinki; tel. (10) 8410500; e-mail info@shipowners.fi; internet www.shipowners.fi; f. 1932 as Suomen Varustamoyhdistys r.y; adopted current name in June 2008 following a merger with the Cargo Ship Association and the Åland Shipowners' Association; 27 mems; Man. Dir OLOF WIDÉN.

Principal Companies

ESL Shipping Oy: Lintulahdenkuja 10, POB 91, 00500 Helsinki; tel. (9) 5211; fax (9) 5219999; e-mail operations@eslshipping.fi; internet www.eslshipping.fi; worldwide tramp services; subsidiary of Aspo Oyj; Pres. MARKUS KARJALAINEN.

Finnlines PLC: Porkkalainkatu 20A, POB 197, 00180 Helsinki; tel. (10) 34350; fax (10) 3435200; e-mail info.fi@finnlines.com; internet www.finnlines.com; f. 1949; liner and contract services between Finland and other European countries; overland and inland services combined with direct sea links; Pres. and CEO UWE BAKOSCH; 85 cargo ferries.

Alfons Håkans Oy Ab: Linnankatu 36C, 20100 Turku; tel. (2) 515500; fax (2) 2515873; e-mail office.turku@alfonshakans.fi; internet www.alfonshakans.fi; Man. Dir and Chair. STEFAN HÅKANS; 32 tugs and 4 barges.

Rettig Oy Ab Bore: Bulevardi 46, POB 115, 00121 Helsinki; tel. (9) 61883300; fax (9) 61883398; e-mail info@bore.eu; internet www.bore.eu; f. 1897; acquired Bror Husell Chartering Ab in 2005 and Rederi Ab Engship in 2006; Man. Dir THOMAS FRANCK; 17 cargo ships, 3 car carriers and 1 bulk vessel.

RG Line Oy Ab: Satamaterminaali, 65170 Vaasa; tel. (20) 7716810; fax (20) 7716820; e-mail info@rgline.com; internet www.rgline.com; operates ferry services across the Gulf of Bothnia from Vaasa to Umeå, Sweden.

Tallink Silja Oy: Keilaranta 9, POB 43, 02151 Espoo; tel. (9) 18041; fax (9) 1804402; internet www.tallinksilja.com; f. 2006 by merger of Tallink Finland Oy and Silja Oy; part of the AS Tallink Group; passenger and cargo services in the Baltic; CEO ENN PANT; 19 vessels.

CIVIL AVIATION

An international airport is situated at Helsinki-Vantaa, 19 km from Helsinki. International and domestic services also operate to and from airports at Ivalo, Joensuu, Jyväskylä, Kajaani, Kemi-Tornio, Kokkola-Pietarsaari (formerly Kruunupyy), Kuopio, Lappeenranta, Mariehamn, Oulu, Pori, Rovaniemi, Savonlinna, Tampere-Pirkkala, Turku, Vaasa and Varkaus. Domestic services are available at airports at Enontekiö, Kittilä, Kuusamo and Mikkeli. The Transport Safety Agency (see Administrative Bodies) is the regulatory authority for civil aviation.

Finavia Corporation: Lentäjäntie 3, POB 50, 01531 Vantaa; tel. (20) 708000; fax (20) 7082099; e-mail info@finavia.fi; internet www.finavia.fi; state-owned commercial enterprise; provides air navigation services and maintains state-owned airports; Pres. and CEO KARI SAVOLAINEN.

Principal Airlines

Blue1: POB 168, 01531 Vantaa; tel. (20) 5856000; fax (20) 5856001; e-mail blue1@blue1.com; internet www.blue1.com; f. 1988 as Air Botnia; name changed in 2004; domestic and international services; member of SAS Group since 1998 and of Star Alliance since 2004; Pres. and CEO STEFAN WENTJÄRVI.

Finnair Oyj: Tietotie 11A, POB 15, 01053 Vantaa; tel. (9) 81881; fax (9) 8184979; e-mail maria.mroue@finnair.fi; internet www.finnair.com; f. 1923; 55.8% state-owned; 12 domestic services, 39 European services and 12 international services (to Asia and North America); Pres. and CEO PEKKA VAURAMO.

Tourism

Europe's largest inland water system, vast forests, wildlife, magnificent scenery and the possibility of holiday seclusion are Finland's main attractions. Most visitors come from Sweden, Germany, Russia, the UK, the Netherlands and Norway. Overnight stays by foreign tourists at registered accommodation establishments totalled some

5.9m. in 2013, compared with 4.9m. in 2009. Receipts from tourism (excluding passenger traffic) amounted to US $4,039m. in 2013.

Matkailun edistämiskeskus (Finnish Tourist Board): Töölönkatu 11, POB 625, 00101 Helsinki; tel. (29) 5058000; fax (29) 5058999; e-mail mek@mek.fi; internet www.mek.fi; f. 1973; Dir-Gen. JAAKKO LEHTONEN.

Defence

As assessed at November 2014, the armed forces of Finland numbered 22,200 comprising an army of 16,000 (including 11,000 conscripts), a navy of 3,500 (including 1,900 conscripts) and an air force of 2,700 (including 750 conscripts). There were also some 354,000 reserves and a 2,800-strong border guard (under the Ministry of the Interior). In November 2004 the European Union (EU) defence ministers agreed to create a number of 'battlegroups' (each comprising about 1,500 men), which could be deployed at short notice to carry out peacekeeping activities at crisis points around the world. The EU battlegroups, two of which were to be ready for deployment at any one time, following a rotational schedule, reached full operational capacity from 1 January 2007. In November 2012 Denmark, Finland, Iceland, Sweden and Norway agreed to the joint operation of military transport aircraft. In 2013 Finnish troops contributed to operations in countries including Afghanistan and Lebanon.

Defence Expenditure: Budget estimated at €2,687m. for 2015.

Chief of Defence: Gen. JARMO LINDBERG.

Education

The Ministry of Education and Culture is the central body responsible for providing education. Tuition is free and the core curriculum is the same for all students. All children are entitled to receive one year of voluntary pre-primary education, usually at the age of six years. Compulsory schooling is provided in comprehensive schools and lasts for nine years, divided into a six-year lower stage, beginning at the age of seven, and a three-year upper stage (or lower secondary stage), beginning at the age of 13. Some comprehensive schools offer a voluntary 10th year in which additional basic education is provided. After comprehensive school, pupils may continue their studies, either at a general upper secondary school or a vocational upper secondary school. The upper secondary school curriculum is designed for three years but may be completed in two or four years. Courses leading to basic vocational qualifications take three years to complete. The matriculation examination taken at the end of three years of general upper secondary school gives eligibility for higher education, as do a Finnish polytechnic degree, a post-secondary level vocational qualification or a three-year vocational diploma. In 2011/12 enrolment at pre-primary level included 69% of children in the relevant age-group. Enrolment at primary schools in that year included 98% of those in the relevant age-group, while the comparable rate for secondary enrolment was 93%. Higher education is provided by 20 universities and 31 polytechnics. In 2005 enrolment at tertiary level was equivalent to 92% of those in the relevant age-group. Of total proposed budgetary expenditure by the central Government for 2015, €6,769m. (equivalent to 12.6% of total proposed expenditure) was allocated to the Ministry of Education and Culture.

FINNISH EXTERNAL TERRITORY
THE ÅLAND ISLANDS

Introductory Survey

LOCATION, LANGUAGE, RELIGION, FLAG, CAPITAL

The Åland Islands are a group of more than 6,700 islands (of which some 60 are inhabited) in the Gulf of Bothnia, between Finland and Sweden. Swedish is the official language, spoken by 88.7% of the inhabitants in 2013; of the remaining population, 4.8% were Finnish-speaking. The majority profess Christianity: in 2013 79.7% were adherents of the Evangelical Lutheran Church of Finland. The flag displays a red cross, bordered with yellow, on a blue background, the upright of the cross being to the left of centre. The capital is Mariehamn, which is situated on Åland, the largest island in the group.

CONTEMPORARY POLITICAL HISTORY

For geographical and economic reasons, the Åland Islands were traditionally associated closely with Sweden. In 1809, when Sweden was forced to cede Finland to Russia, the islands were incorporated into the Finnish Grand Duchy. However, following Finland's declaration of independence from the Russian Empire in 1917, the Ålanders demanded the right to self-determination and sought to be reunited with Sweden, with support from the Swedish Government. In 1920 Finland granted the islands autonomy but refused to acknowledge their secession, and in 1921 the Åland question was referred to the League of Nations. In June the League granted Finland sovereignty over the islands, while directing that certain conditions pertaining to national identity be included in the autonomy legislation offered by Finland and that the islands should be a neutral and non-fortified region. Elections were held in accordance with the new legislation, and the new Landsting (provincial parliament) held its first plenary session in June 1922. The revised Autonomy Act of 1951 provided for independent rights of legislation in internal affairs and for autonomous control over the islands' economy. This Act could not be amended or repealed by the Finnish legislature without the consent of the Landsting.

In 1988 constitutional reform introduced the principle of a majority parliamentary government, to be formed by the Lantrådskandidat, the member of the Landsting nominated to conduct negotiations between the parties. These negotiations may yield two alternative outcomes: either the nominee will submit a proposal to create a new government—Landskapsregeringen (Executive Council), consisting of five to seven members and headed by a Lantråd (Chairman)—or the nominee will fail to reach agreement on a new government (in which case renewed negotiations will ensue). The first formal parliamentary government and opposition were duly established. The governing coalition consisted of the three largest parties that had been elected to the Landsting in October 1987 (the Centre Party, the Liberals and the Moderates), which together held 22 seats in the 30-member legislature.

At a general election held in October 1991 the Centre Party increased its representation in the Landsting to 10, while the Liberal Party won seven seats, and the Moderates and Social Democrats won six and four seats, respectively. The Centre and Moderate parties formed a new coalition Government, in which the Liberal Party was replaced by the Social Democratic Party.

A revised Autonomy Act, providing Åland with a greater degree of autonomous control, took effect on 1 January 1993. The rules regarding legislative authority were modernized, and the right of the Åland legislature (henceforth known as the Lagting) to enact laws was extended. Åland was given greater discretion with respect to its budget, and the revised Act also introduced changes in matters such as right of domicile, land-ownership regulations and administrative authority. The Autonomy Act contains a provision that, in any treaty which Finland may conclude with a foreign state and to which Åland is a party, the Lagting must consent to the statute implementing the treaty in order for the provision to enter into force in Åland. A referendum on the issue of Åland's proposed accession to membership of the European Union (EU, see p. 271) in 1995 was held in November 1994, immediately after similar referendums in Finland and Sweden had both shown a majority in favour of membership. Despite low participation in the referendum, 73.7% of the votes cast supported membership and Åland duly joined the EU, together with Finland and Sweden, on 1 January 1995. Under the terms of the treaty of accession, Åland was accorded special exemption from tax union with the EU in order to stimulate the ferry and tourism industries. (In 1998 two of Europe's largest ferry operators, Silja and Viking—both Finnish, re-routed their major services via Åland in order to continue to conduct duty-free sales, which were later abolished within the rest of the EU.)

At the general election of October 1995 the Centre Party secured nine seats and the Liberal Party won eight, while the Moderates and Social Democrats maintained the representation that they had achieved in the previous parliament. The new coalition Government comprised members of the Centre and Moderate Parties and one independent.

At a general election held in October 1999 the Centre Party and the Liberal Party each won nine seats. The Moderate Party secured only four seats, while the Social Democrats maintained their level of representation. The Obunden Samling (Non-aligned Coalition) won four seats. A coalition Government was formed comprising the Centre Party, the Moderate Party and the Independents. In March 2001, following a motion of no confidence in the Lagting, the Chairman of the Government, Roger Nordlund of the Centre Party, dissolved the coalition and formed a new administration comprising members of the Centre Party and the Liberal Party.

A general election was held in October 2003, at which the Centre Party and the Liberal Party each won seven seats. The two parties formed a new Government in coalition with the Social Democrats (who had won six seats) and the Moderate Party (with four seats), under Nordlund.

In August 2004 the Finnish Government agreed new, more stringent regulations securing the islands' demilitarized status, following reports that this had been violated by troop movements over the past two decades.

In January 2005, following a motion of no confidence in the Lagting, the governing coalition was dissolved and Nordlund formed a new administration comprising members of the Centre Party, the Social Democrats and the Moderate Party.

In May 2006 the European Court of Justice (ECJ) ruled that Finland was in breach of EU regulations on tobacco products by allowing the continued sale of snus (Swedish oral tobacco) in the Åland Islands. (The sale of oral tobacco was prohibited in the EU in 1992, but Sweden was granted an exemption from the ban when it joined the Union in 1995.) Trade in snus, particularly on ferries registered in the Åland Islands, had been worth several million euros annually. As Finland had no powers to legislate in health matters in the islands, the matter was referred to the Lagting, which in January 2007 adopted legislation aimed at complying with the Court's judgment; however, this was deemed insufficient by the European Commission, as it prohibited only snus (rather than oral tobacco in general) from entering the market, and did not apply to the sale of snus on vessels registered in the Åland Islands once they had left Finnish territorial waters. In October the European Commission once again referred the case to the ECJ. Consequently, the Lagting adopted further legislation, which was enacted in January 2008, introducing an outright ban on snus sales on Åland-registered ships, including in Swedish territorial waters; as a result, the European Commission withdrew its case against Finland later in 2008.

The opposition Liberal Party became the largest party in the Lagting following a general election held in October 2007, at which it won 10 seats. The Centre Party won eight seats, while the Independents took four. The representation of the Moderate Party and the Social Democrats declined to three seats each. A turnout of 67.8% was recorded. The Liberal Party and the Centre Party subsequently formed a coalition Government, under Viveka Eriksson, the Liberal leader.

In September 2008 Finland ratified the Lisbon Treaty, which aimed to improve decision-making in the enlarged EU. However, the Åland Islands, which under the amended Act of Autonomy were also required to ratify the treaty, demanded concessions from the Finnish Government prior to ratification. The Åland Government's demands included a seat in the European Parliament, the right to appear before the ECJ (where Åland had been represented by Finland in the case regarding snus sales), participation in the meetings of the Council of the EU and shared control over the principle of subsidiarity (that the EU should only act when an objective can be better achieved at the supranational level). By November 2009 no formal concessions had been granted by the Finnish Government; none the less, on 25 November the Lagting voted to ratify the treaty, six days before it was scheduled to enter into effect across the EU. Earlier in November the Lagting's legal affairs committee had recommended that the legislature approve the treaty, but urged the Åland Government to continue to seek greater participation for the islands in EU affairs.

At a general election held on 16 October 2011, the incumbent coalition partners, the Liberal Party and the Centre Party, lost their majority, their respective representation declining to six and seven seats. The Social Democrats increased their number of seats, to six, while the Moderates and the Independents each secured four seats and the separatist Åland's Future three. A turnout of 66.6% was recorded. Later that month a new coalition Government, comprising the Social Democrats, the Centre Party, the Independents and the Moderates, was formed under Camilla Gunell of the Social Democrats.

GOVERNMENT

The Åland Islands are governed according to the Autonomy Act, which was introduced in 1920, revised in 1951 and further revised with effect from January 1993. The islands' demilitarized status and autonomy are guaranteed by international treaties. The legislative body is the Lagting, comprising 30 members, elected every four years on a basis of proportional representation. All Ålanders over the age of 18 years, possessing Åland regional citizenship, have the right to vote and to seek election. A Landskapsregeringen (Executive Council), consisting of five to seven members, is elected by the Lagting, and the Lantråd, its Chairman, is the highest-ranking politician in Åland after the Talman (Speaker) of the Lagting. The President has the right to veto Lagting decisions only when the Lagting exceeds its legislative competence, or when there is a threat to the security of the country. The Governor of Åland represents the Government of Finland and is appointed by the Finnish President (with the agreement of the Speaker of the Åland legislature). The Åland Islands elect one representative to the Finnish Parliament, the Eduskunta. There are 16 municipalities in the Åland Islands.

REGIONAL CO-OPERATION

The Åland Islands joined the European Union (EU, see p. 271) in 1995, together with Finland, following a referendum in November 1994. The islands have had their own representation in the Nordic Council since 1970.

ECONOMIC AFFAIRS

In 2011 the gross domestic product (GDP) of the Åland Islands, measured at current prices, was €1,140.4m. In 2012 4.2% of the working population were employed in agriculture (including hunting, forestry and fishing), which contributed 2.3% of GDP in 2011. Forests covered 60% of the islands in 2013, and only 9.0% of the total land area was arable. The principal crops are potatoes, onions, wheat, barley and oats, and apples. Dairy farming and sheep rearing are also important.

Industry (including mining, manufacturing, construction and power) provided 14.3% of GDP in 2011 and employed 15.3% of the working population in 2012. Manufacturing contributed 6.7% of GDP in 2011 and engaged 6.9% of the working population in 2012.

Since 1960 the economy of the islands has expanded and diversified. Fishing has declined as a source of income, and shipping (particularly the operation of ferry services between Finland and Sweden), trade and tourism have become the dominant economic sectors. In 2011 services accounted for 83.3% of GDP and engaged 80.5% of the employed labour force in 2012. The transport sector, including shipping, employed 11.9% in 2011, and, together with storage and communications, contributed 27.6% of GDP in 2011. The political autonomy of the islands and their strategic location between Sweden and Finland have contributed to expanding banking and trade sectors; financial services engaged 3.1% of the employed labour force in 2012, while trade and hotels employed 14.1%. Tourist arrivals totalled 415,839 in 2013.

The Finnish state collects taxes, duties and fees from the Åland Islands, which receives 0.45% of total Finnish government income in return. If the taxes raised in the Åland Islands exceed 0.5% of corresponding Finnish tax revenues, the islands receive the excess amount in the form of a tax redemption. Consumer prices increased at an average annual rate of 2.0% in 2004–13; prices rose by 2.3% in 2012 and by 1.1% in 2013. The unemployment rate stood at 3.9% in 2013. Finland participated in Economic and Monetary Union (EMU), introducing the single European currency, the euro, in January 1999. The Finnish currency, the markka, was used by the islands until the end of 2001. Euro notes and coins were introduced on 1 January 2002, and, as in Finland as a whole, the euro became the sole legal tender from 1 March 2002. As part of a €6,250,000 operational programme for 2007–13 focusing on competitiveness in local enterprises and the generation of employment, the EU assessed the main challenges to the Åland Islands to stem from their ageing population, lack of higher education opportunities, overdependence on the marine and shipping sector and structural problems relating to the decline of agricultural jobs, as well as regional development disparities between the main city of Mariehamn and the rest of the archipelago. Under the EU's operational programme for 2014–20 the islands were to receive €4,995,500 (financed by the European Regional Development Fund and the European Social Fund). The islands' location between southern Finland and the Stockholm region of Sweden provides a strategic advantage, but also makes the region sensitive to economic fluctuations in these neighbouring markets.

Statistical Survey

Source: Statistics Åland, POB 1187, 22111 Mariehamn; tel. (18) 25490; fax (18) 19495; e-mail info@asub.ax; internet www.asub.ax.

AREA AND POPULATION

Area: 13,324 sq km (5,144 sq miles), of which 1,553 sq km (600 sq miles) is land and 11,772 sq km (4,545 sq miles) is water.

Population (official figures at 31 December 2013): 28,666 (males 14,302, females 14,364).

Density (land area only, 31 December 2013): 18.5 per sq km.

Population by Age and Sex (official figures at 31 December 2013): *0–14 years:* 4,658 (males 2,428, females 2,230); *15–64 years:* 18,303 (males 9,194, females 9,109); *65 years and over:* 5,705 (males 2,680, females 3,025); *Total:* 28,666 (males 14,302, females 14,364).

Principal Towns (official figures at 31 December 2013): Mariehamn (capital) 11,393; Godby 918; Storby 517; Prästgården 439; Ödkarby 358; Söderby 358.

Births, Marriages and Deaths (2013): Registered live births 287 (birth rate 10.0 per 1,000); Marriages 118 (marriage rate 4.1 per 1,000); Deaths 269 (death rate 9.4 per 1,000).

Life Expectancy (years at birth, 2008–12): 81.5 (males 79.7; females 83.2).

Immigration and Emigration (2013): Immigrants 861 (Finland 324; Sweden 381); Emigrants 714 (Finland 277; Sweden 358).

Economically Active Population (2012): Agriculture, fishing and aquaculture 577; Mining and quarrying 16; Manufacturing 944; Electricity, gas, steam and air conditioning supply 85; Water supply, sewerage, waste management and remediation activities 100; Construction 959; Wholesale and retail trade, and repair of motor vehicles 1,347; Transportation and storage 1,641; Accommodation and food services 587; Information and communication 531; Finance and insurance activities 432; Real estate 77; Professional, scientific and technical activities 500; Administrative and support services 346; Public administration and defence 1,035; Education 1,058; Health and social work 2,673; Arts, entertainment and recreation 375; Other service activities 454; *Sub-total* 13,737; Activities not classified 194; *Total employed* 13,931; Unemployed 546; *Total labour force* 14,477. *2013* (preliminary): Total employed 13,910; Unemployed 583; Total labour force 14,493.

HEALTH AND WELFARE

Physicians (2003): 59.

Hospital Beds (2013): 102.

AGRICULTURE, ETC.

Agricultural Production (metric tons, 2013, unless otherwise indicated): Milk ('000 litres) 15,375; Beef 525; Pork 7; Mutton 86; Poultry 1,497 (2002); Eggs 311; Wheat 3,752; Rye 266; Triticale (wheat-rye hybrid) 81 (2003); Barley and oats 3,269; Peas 22; Turnip rape 40 (2006); Sugar beet 163; Potatoes 17,007; Onions 6,160; Cucumbers 101; Leeks 150; Chinese cabbage and lettuce 1,424; Apples 3,033; Strawberries ('000 litres) 16; Tomatoes 209; Parsley ('000 bunches) 33; Dill ('000 bunches) 16; Celery 15; Carrots 116.

Livestock (2013 unless otherwise indicated): Cattle 8,232; Pigs 294 (2009); Hens 15,887; Sheep 13,126; Horses 179.

Forestry Production (cu m, roundwood, 2013): Logs 71,821; Pulp 149,889.

Fishing (metric tons, live weight, 2013): Capture 4,333 (Baltic herring and sprat 3,769; Cod 332; Whitefish 58; Perch 84; Pike-perch 9; Pike 13); Aquaculture 4,821; *Total catch* 9,154.

INDUSTRY

Selected Indicators (2013): Electric energy 61m. kWh (incl. 58m. kWh from wind power); Dwellings completed 159.

FINANCE

Currency: Finnish currency was used until the end of 2001. Euro notes and coins were introduced on 1 January 2002, and the euro became the sole legal tender from 1 March. For details of exchange rates, see Finland.

Budget (€ '000, 2013): Revenue 321,027; Expenditure 360,615.

Cost of Living (Consumer Price Index; base: 2010 = 100): All items 103.6 in 2011; 106.0 in 2012; 107.3 in 2013.

Gross Domestic Product (€ million at constant 2011 prices): 1,197.4 in 2009; 1,214.7 in 2010; 1,140.4 in 2011.

Expenditure on the Gross Domestic Product (€ million at current prices, 2011): Wages and salaries 502; Employers' contribution to social security 118; Operating surplus 225; Fixed capital depreciation 205; *Total domestic expenditure* 1,050; Indirect taxes 138; *Less* Subsidies 48; *GDP in market prices* 1,140.

Gross Domestic Product by Economic Activity (€ million at current prices, 2011): Agriculture, hunting, forestry and fishing 24.7; Mining and quarrying 0.9; Manufacturing 60.3; Construction 68.4; Energy supply and water 20.7; Trade, restaurants and hotels 84.4; Transport, storage and communications 289.7; Financing, insurance, real estate and business services 196.1; Government services 234.2; Other community, social and personal services 54.4; Non-profit institutions 17.3; *GDP at factor cost* 1,051.2; Indirect taxes 137.7; *Less* Subsidies 48.4; *GDP in purchasers' values* 1,140.4.

EXTERNAL TRADE

2013 (€ '000): *Imports:* Total 247,606 (Live animals and products thereof 45,225; Vegetable products 9,101; Edible preparations, beverages, liquors and tobacco 31,321; Mineral products 10,540; Articles of plastics and rubber 14,316; Pulp and paper 29,349; Textiles and textile articles 8,314; Machinery, equipment and appliances 46,649; Miscellaneous manufactured articles 12,741); *Exports:* Total 118,457 (Live animals and products thereof 5,922; Products of the chemicals or allied industries 7,201; Articles of plastics and rubber 22,969; Wood and cork and products thereof 8,039; Textiles and textile articles 894; Base metals and articles of base metals 4,579; Vehicles, ships and transport equipment 40,846; Optical appliances 3,902). Note: Figures exclude trade with mainland Finland.

TRANSPORT

Road Traffic (registered motor vehicles, 31 December 2013): Private motor cars 21,565; Vans 4,278; Lorries 754; Buses 51; Motorcycles 1,643; Tractors 3,831.

Shipping: *Flag Registered Fleet* (2014): Vessels 27; Total displacement 216,827 grt (Source: Lloyd's List Intelligence—www.lloyds listintelligence.com). *Traffic:* 7,901 vessels entered (2013); 2,017,235 passenger arrivals (incl. ferry services, 2013).

Civil Aviation (traffic, Mariehamn airport, 2013): Passengers 52,492; Freight 496 metric tons; Post 15 metric tons.

TOURISM

Tourist Arrivals (2013): 415,839 (163,329 from Finland; 198,736 from Sweden).

EDUCATION

Primary and Secondary Schools (2013): Institutions 23 (Comprehensive schools 23, of which 9 also offer upper-stage education); Pupils 2,856 (Comprehensive schools 1,867, Upper-stage schools 989).

Pupils Enrolled in Post-Comprehensive Education (2013): General programme 478 (males 199, females 279); Vocational 707 (males 410, females 297); Other 47 (males 14, females 33); Åland University of Applied Sciences 511 (males 329, females 182).

Directory

Government and Legislature

The legislative body is the Lagting, comprising 30 members, elected every four years on a basis of proportional representation. All Ålanders over the age of 18 years, possessing Åland regional citizenship, have the right to vote and to seek election. The Landskapsregeringen (Executive Council), consisting of five to seven members, is elected by the Lagting, and the Lantråd, its Chairman, is the highest-ranking politician in Åland after the Talman (Speaker) of the Lagting. The Finnish President has the right to veto Lagting decisions only when the Lagting exceeds its legislative competence, or when there is a threat to the security of the country. The Governor of Åland represents the Government of Finland and is appointed by the Finnish President (with the agreement of the Speaker of the Åland legislature).

Governor: PETER LINDBÄCK.

EXECUTIVE COUNCIL
(Landskapsregeringen)

Självstyrelsegården, POB 1060, 22111 Mariehamn; tel. (18) 25000; fax (18) 19155; e-mail marina.sundstrom@regeringen.ax; internet www.regeringen.ax.

The governing coalition comprises members of the Social Democrats, the Centre Party and the Moderates. Its composition in April 2015 was as follows:

Chairman (Lantråd): CAMILLA GUNELL (Social Democrats).

Deputy Chairman (Vicelantråd) and Minister of Finance: ROGER NORDLUND (Centre Party).

Minister for Infrastructure: VERONICA THÖRNROOS (Centre Party).

Minister for Social and Environmental Affairs: CARINA AALTO-NEN (Social Democrats).

Minister for Enterprise: FREDRIK KARLSTRÖM (Moderates).

Minister for Education and Culture: JOHAN EHN (Moderates).

Minister for Administrative Affairs: WILLE VALVE (Moderates).

PARLIAMENT
(Lagting)

Självstyrelsegården, POB 69, 22101 Mariehamn; tel. (18) 25000; fax (18) 13302; e-mail susanne.eriksson@regeringen.ax; internet www.lagtinget.ax.

Speaker (Talman): BRITT LUNDBERG (Centre Party).

Election, 16 October 2011

	Votes	% of votes	Seats
Åländsk Center (Centre Party)	3,068	23.65	7
Liberalerna på Åland (Liberal Party)	2,630	20.27	6
Ålands Socialdemokrater (Social Democrats) . . .	2,404	18.53	6
Moderaterna Åland (Moderates of Åland)	1,810	13.95	4
Obunden Samling (Independents)	1,639	12.63	4
Ålands Framtid (Åland's Future)	1,286	9.91	3
Valmansf. för Henrik Appelqvist	138	1.06	—
Total	12,975	100.00	30

Political Organizations

Unless otherwise indicated, the address of each of the following organizations is: Ålands Lagting, 6th Floor, POB 69, 22101 Mariehamn; tel. (18) 25000; fax (18) 13302.

Åländsk Center (Centre Party): tel. (18) 25360; fax (18) 16630; e-mail centern@lagtinget.ax; internet www.centern.ax; f. 1976; Chair. HARRY JANSSON.

Ålands Framtid (Åland's Future): tel. (18) 25366; e-mail info@alandsframtid.ax; internet www.alandsframtid.ax; f. 2003; separatist; Leader AXEL JONSSON.

Ålands Socialdemokrater (Social Democrats): Ekonomiegatan 1, POB 69, 22101 Mariehamn; tel. (18) 25461; e-mail socialdemokraterna@lagtinget.ax; internet www.socialdemokraterna.ax; Chair. CAMILLA GUNELL; Sec. HELENA FLÖJT-JOSEFSSON.

Liberalerna på Åland (Liberal Party): tel. (18) 25362; fax (18) 16075; e-mail liberalerna@lagtinget.ax; internet www.liberalerna.ax; Chair. KATRIN SJÖGREN.

Moderaterna Åland (Moderates of Åland): tel. (18) 25357; e-mail moderat@lagtinget.ax; internet www.moderaterna.ax; Chair. JOHAN EHN.

Obunden Samling (Independents): tel. (18) 25368; fax (18) 16370; e-mail danne.sundman@lagtinget.ax; internet www.obs.ax; f. 1987; Chair. HENRIETTA HELLSTRÖM.

Religion

The majority of the islands' population is Christian. In 2013 79.7% of inhabitants were adherents of the Evangelical Lutheran Church of Finland. In 2006 there were small numbers of Jehovah's Witnesses (49), Roman Catholics (39), Greek Orthodox Christians (24) and Adventists (12); 58 people practised other religions.

The Press

Ålandstidningen: Strandgatan 16, POB 50, 22101 Mariehamn; tel. (18) 26026; fax (18) 15755; e-mail niklas.lampi@alandstidningen.ax; internet www.tidningen.ax; f. 1891; 6 a week; Man. Dir DAN-JOHAN DAHLBLOM; Editor-in-Chief NIKLAS LAMPI; circ. 10,355 (2007).

Nya Åland: Uppgårdsvägen 6, POB 21, 22100 Mariehamn; tel. (18) 23444; fax (18) 23450; e-mail redaktion@nyan.ax; internet www

.nyan.ax; f. 1981; 5 a week; Man. Dir STEFAN NORRGRANN; Editor-in-Chief JONAS BLADH; circ. 7,256 (2005).

Broadcasting and Communications

TELECOMMUNICATIONS

Sonera: Karlbergsvägen 12, POB 51, 22101 Mariehamn; tel. (18) 57000; fax (18) 57109; e-mail info@amt.ax; internet www.sonera.ax; subsidiary of TeliaSonera (Sweden).

Ålands Telefonandelslag: Hantverkargränd 1, 22150 Jomala; tel. (18) 41053; fax (18) 41299; e-mail jomala@altel.ax; internet www.altel.ax; f. 1910.

Ålands Telekommunikation Ab (ÅLCOM): Servicegatan 12, POB 233, 22101 Mariehamn; tel. (18) 23500; fax (18) 17643; e-mail info@alcom.ax; internet www.alcom.ax; mobile telecommunications and internet service provider; jtly owned by Ålands Telefonandelslag and Mariehamns Telefon Ab; Chair. ANDERS JOHNSSON; CEO DANIEL DAHLÉN.

Mariehamns Telefon Ab: Ålandsvägen 52, POB 1228, 22111 Mariehamn; tel. (18) 27044; fax (18) 15900; e-mail anders@mtel.ax; internet www.mtel.ax; f. 1892; Dir ANDERS JOHNSSON.

RADIO AND TELEVISION

Ålands Radio och TV Ab: Ålandsvägen 24, POB 140, 22101 Mariehamn; tel. (18) 26060; fax (18) 26520; e-mail info@radiotv.ax; internet www.radiotv.ax; f. 1996; broadcasts radio programmes in Swedish, 115.5 hours a week; operates 3 analogue and 5 digital television channels; Man. Dir PIA ROTHBERG-OLOFSSON; Editor-in-Chief ASTRID OLHAGEN.

Steel FM: Strandgränd 2, 22100 Mariehamn; tel. (18) 16200; fax (18) 22079; e-mail mail@steelfm.net; internet www.steelfm.net; commercial radio broadcaster; Dir FREDRIK KARLSTRÖM.

TV Åland: Elverksgatan 1, 22100 Mariehamn; tel. (18) 14035; fax (18) 14037; e-mail redaktion@tv.ax; internet www.tv.ax; f. 1984; television producer and broadcaster; broadcasts by cable to 75% of islands; CEO PIA ROTHENBERG OLOFSSON.

Finance

BANKS

(cap. = capital; res = reserves; dep. = deposits; m. = million; amounts in euros; brs = branches)

Ålandsbanken Abp (Bank of Åland): Nygatan 2, POB 3, 22100 Mariehamn; tel. (204) 29011; fax (204) 29228; e-mail aland@alandsbanken.fi; internet www.alandsbanken.fi; f. 1919 as Ålands Aktiebank; name changed to Bank of Åland Ltd 1980, changed as above in 1998; merged with Ålands Hypoteksbank Ab in November 1995; cap. 29.1m., res 85.2m., dep. 2,690.1m. (Dec. 2012); Chair. KAJ-GUSTAF BERGH; Man. Dir PETER WIKLÖF; 16 brs.

Andelsbanken för Åland: Köpmansgatan 2, POB 34, 22101 Mariehamn; tel. (18) 6330; e-mail andelsbanken.for.aland@op.fi; co-operative; mem. of OP–Pohjola Group; Man. Dir HÅKAN CLEMES.

Nordea Bank Finland PLC and Pohjola Bank PLC are also represented.

INSURANCE

Alandia Group: Ålandsvägen 31, POB 121, 22101 Mariehamn; tel. (18) 29000; fax (18) 13290; e-mail mhamn@alandia.com; internet www.alandia.com; f. 1938; life, non-life and marine; comprises 3 subsidiaries; Man. Dir LEIF NORDLUND.

Ålands Ömsesidiga Försäkringsbolag (Åland Mutual Insurance Co): Köpmansgatan 6, POB 64, 22101 Mariehamn; tel. (18) 27600; fax (18) 27610; e-mail info@omsen.ax; internet www.omsen.ax; f. 1866; life and non-life; Chair. STURE CARLSON; Man. Dir GÖRAN LINDHOLM.

Trade and Industry

TRADE ASSOCIATIONS

Ålands Näringsliv (Invest in Åland): Nygatan 6, 22100 Mariehamn; tel. (18) 29029; fax (18) 21129; e-mail info@naringsliv.ax; internet www.naringsliv.ax; f. 2011 by the merger of Åland Chamber of Commerce, the Åland Employers' Confederation and Åland Businesmen's Asscn; Chair. PETER WIKLÖF; Man. Dir ANDERS EKSTRÖM.

Företagarna på Åland (Fed. of Åland Business Owners): Skarpansvägen 17, 22100 Mariehamn; tel. (18) 23277; fax (457) 5267141; e-mail ombudsman@foretagare.ax; internet www.foretagare.ax; f. 1957; c. 250 mem. cos; Chair. DICK JANSSON.

EMPLOYERS' ORGANIZATIONS

Ålands Fiskodlarförening (Åland Fish Farmers' Asscn): Tingsvägen 3, 22710 Föglö; tel. (18) 17834; e-mail info@fiskodlarna.ax; internet www.fiskodlarna.aland.fi; Chair. PIA LINDBERG.

Ålands Producentförbund (Åland Agricultural Producers' Asscn): Ålands Landsbygdscentrum, Jomalagårdsväg 17, 22150 Jomala; tel. (18) 329840; fax (18) 329801; e-mail birgitta.eriksson@landsbygd.aland.fi; f. 1946; Chair. JOMALA TAGE ERIKSSON; Man. Dir HENRY LINDSTRÖM.

UTILITIES

Electricity

Ålands Elandelslag: Godbyvägen 193, 22100 Mariehamn; tel. (18) 39250; fax (18) 31562; e-mail info@el.ax; internet www.el.ax; f. 1957; distribution; Man. Dir FOLKE ENGBLOM.

Ålands Vindenergi Andelslag: Hamngatan 8, 22100 Mariehamn; tel. (18) 526300; fax (18) 12090; e-mail postmaster@allwinds.ax; internet www.alandsvindenergi.ax; there are 21 wind power farms on the Åland islands, 8 of which it owns; owns 20% of shares in Leovind Ab, which owns 6 turbines; Chair. ANNETTE LARSON; Man. Dir HENRIK LINDQVIST.

Kraftnät Åland: Elverksgatan 10, POB 71, 22101 Mariehamn; tel. (18) 5395; fax (18) 539250; e-mail info@kraftnat.ax; internet www.kraftnat.ax; f. 1996; production, transmission; fully owned by Åland government; Man. Dir JAN KAHLROTH.

Water

Ålands Vatten Ab: Vattenverksvägen 34, 22150 Jomala; tel. (18) 32860; fax (18) 31471; e-mail alandsvatten@vatten.ax; internet www.vatten.ax; f. 1970; supplies water to 70% of population; Man. Dir CHRISTIAN NORDAS.

VA-verket: Torggatan 17, POB 5, 22101 Mariehamn; tel. (18) 5310; fax (18) 531206; e-mail info@mariehamn.ax; internet www.mariehamn.ax; Dir JOUNI HUHTALA.

TRADE UNIONS

FFC Ålands Lokalorganisation: Ålandsvägen 55, POB 108, 22101 Mariehamn; tel. (18) 19920; fax (18) 19912; internet www.facket.ax; Ombudsman HENRIK LAGERBERG; Gen. Sec. CHRISTINA HENRIKSSON.

Tjänstemannaorganisationerna på Åland, TCÅ r.f. (Union of Salaried Employees in Åland): Norragatan 1B5, 22100 Mariehamn; tel. (18) 16210; e-mail fackct@tca.ax; Chair. YVONNE ASPHOLM; Dir MARIE-SUSANNE STENWALL.

Transport

The islands are linked to the Swedish and Finnish mainlands by ferry services and by air services from Mariehamn airport. There are no railways, but local bus services are available, along with inter-island ferries.

Ålandstrafiken: Strandgatan 25, 22100 Mariehamn; tel. (18) 525100; fax (18) 17815; e-mail info@alandstrafiken.ax; internet www.alandstrafiken.ax; operates buses on the islands and ferry services between the islands.

ROADS

In 2008 there was a road network of 918.6 km, of which 757.6 km were paved. There is also a bicycle route network, covering some 61.2 km in 2008.

SHIPPING

Ferry services operate from the Åland Islands to Sweden, the Finnish mainland and Estonia.

Principal Companies

Lundqvist Rederierna: Norra Esplanadgatan 9B, 22100 Mariehamn; tel. (18) 26050; fax (18) 26428; e-mail info@lundqvist.aland.fi; internet www.lundqvist.aland.fi; f. 1927; tanker services; Man. Dir BEN LUNDQVIST; total tonnage c. 820,000 dwt.

Rederi Ab Lillgaard: Köpmangatan 9, POB 136, 22101 Mariehamn; tel. (18) 13120; fax (18) 17220; e-mail info@lillgaard.aland.fi; internet www.lillgaard.aland.fi; f. 1966; operates services from the Åland Islands to the Finnish mainland and Sweden; Man. Dir ANDERS NORDLUND.

Rederiaktiebolaget Eckerö: Torggatan 2B, POB 175, 22101 Mariehamn; tel. (18) 28050; fax (18) 23223; e-mail info@eckeroshipping.com; internet www.eckeroshipping.com; f. 1961; fleet of 10 ships; operates Eckerö Line, Eckerö Linjen, Eckerö Shipping (fmrly Birka Cargo Ab Ltd) and Birka Cruises; ferry routes between the Åland

Islands and Sweden, and between Finland and Estonia, and freight routes between Finland and Sweden; Man. Dir JARI SORVETTULA.

Rederiaktiebolaget Gustaf Erikson: Norra Esplanadgatan 4B, 22100 Mariehamn; tel. (18) 27070; fax (18) 12670; e-mail info@geson .aland.fi; internet www.geson.ax; f. 1913; manages dry cargo and refrigerated vessels; Man. Dir GUN ERIKSON-HJERLING.

Viking Line Abp: Norragatan 4, POB 166, 22101 Mariehamn; tel. (18) 27000; fax (18) 16944; e-mail nn@vikingline.fi; internet www .vikingline.fi; f. 1963; operates cruise and ferry services between Finland and Sweden and throughout the Baltic Sea; 7 car/passenger vessels; total tonnage 212,474 grt; Chair. BEN LUNDQVIST; Man. Dir and Chief Exec. MIKAEL BACKMAN.

CIVIL AVIATION

The islands' airport is at Mariehamn. In 2013 the airport handled 52,492 passengers, 496 metric tons of freight and 15 tons of post. It is served by Finnair and AirÅland Ab.

AirÅland Ab: Mariehamns Airport, Flygfältsvägen 67, 22120 Mariehamn; tel. (18) 17110; fax (18) 23730; e-mail info@airaland.com; internet www.airaland.com; f. 2005; routes from Mariehamn to Helsinki and Stockholm; the Swedish company NextJet operates all AirÅland Ab flights; CEO CARIN HOLMQVIST.

Tourism

The Åland archipelago has numerous bays, inlets, islands and open stretches of water, and is an area of great natural beauty. Cycling, canoeing, kayaking and hiking attract tourists to the islands. Major tourist attractions include the Maritime Museum, the museum ship Pommern and the Maritime Quarter. Most visitors are from the Nordic countries, particularly from mainland Finland and Sweden. In 2013 tourist arrivals totalled 415,839 (including 163,329 from Finland and 198,736 from Sweden).

Ålands Turist Förbund (Åland Tourism Board): Storagatan 8, 22100 Mariehamn; tel. (18) 24000; fax (18) 24265; e-mail info@ visitaland.com; internet www.visitaland.com; f. 1989; CEO LOTTA BERNER-SJÖLUND.

Ålands Turist och Konferens Ab: Hotell Arkipelag, Strandgatan 35, 22100 Mariehamn; tel. (18) 15349; fax (18) 21077; e-mail info@ turist-konferens.aland.fi; internet www.turist-konferens.aland.fi; Man. Dir HENRIK NORDSTRÖM.

Defence

By law, the archipelago is demilitarized. For general details, see Finland.

Education

The education system is similar to that of Finland, except that Swedish is the language of instruction and Finnish an optional subject. There is one university: Åland University of Applied Sciences. In 2012 a total of 1,278 people were undertaking post-secondary general or vocational education in the Åland Islands. In 2013 there were 511 students at the Åland University of Applied Sciences.

FRANCE

Introductory Survey

LOCATION, CLIMATE, LANGUAGE, RELIGION, FLAG, CAPITAL

The French Republic is situated in Western Europe. It is bounded to the north by the English Channel (la Manche), to the east by Belgium, Luxembourg, Germany, Switzerland and Italy, to the south by the Mediterranean Sea, Andorra, Monaco, and Spain, and to the west by the Atlantic Ocean. The Mediterranean island of Corsica is part of metropolitan France, while 12 overseas possessions (French Guiana, Guadeloupe, Martinique, Réunion, French Polynesia, Mayotte, Saint-Barthélemy, Saint-Martin, Saint Pierre and Miquelon, the Wallis and Futuna Islands, the French Southern and Antarctic Territories, and New Caledonia) also form an integral part of the Republic. The climate is temperate throughout most of the country, but in the south it is of the Mediterranean type, with warm summers and mild winters. The principal language is French; additionally, small minorities speak Alsatian, Basque, Breton, Corsican and Provençal, among other regional languages and dialects. A majority of French citizens profess Christianity, and about 74% of the population are adherents of the Roman Catholic Church. Other Christian denominations are represented, and there are also Muslim and Jewish communities. The national flag (proportions 2 by 3) has three equal vertical stripes, of blue, white and red. The capital is Paris.

CONTEMPORARY POLITICAL HISTORY

Historical Context

In September 1939, following Nazi Germany's invasion of Poland, France and the United Kingdom declared war on Germany, thus entering the Second World War. In June 1940 France was forced to sign an armistice, following a swift invasion and occupation of French territory by German forces. After the liberation of France from German occupation in 1944, a provisional government took office under Gen. Charles de Gaulle, leader of the Free French forces during the wartime resistance. The war in Europe ended in May 1945, when German forces surrendered at Reims. In 1946, following a referendum, the Fourth Republic was established and de Gaulle announced his intention to retire from public life.

France had 26 different governments from 1946 until the Fourth Republic came to an end in 1958 with an insurrection in Algeria (then an overseas department) and the threat of civil war. In May 1958 the President, René Coty, invited Gen. de Gaulle to form a government. In June the Assemblée Nationale (National Assembly) invested de Gaulle as Prime Minister, with the power to rule by decree for six months. A new Constitution, approved by referendum in September, was promulgated in October; thus the Fifth Republic came into being, with de Gaulle taking office as President in January 1959. The new system provided for a strong presidency, the authority of which would be strengthened by national referendums and a stable executive.

The early years of the Fifth Republic were overshadowed by the Algerian crisis. De Gaulle granted Algeria independence in 1962, withdrew troops and repatriated French settlers. In May 1968 students and workers joined in a revolt against the Government's authoritarian education and information policies, low wage rates and lack of social reform. For a time the Republic appeared threatened, but the student movement collapsed and the general strike was settled by the provision of large wage rises. In April 1969 President de Gaulle resigned following his defeat in a referendum on regional reform.

Domestic Political Affairs

Georges Pompidou, who had been Prime Minister from 1962–68, was elected President in June 1969. The Gaullist government coalition was returned at a general election in March 1973. Pompidou died in April 1974. In the presidential election held in May, Valéry Giscard d'Estaing, formerly leader of the centre-right Républicains Indépendants (RI), narrowly defeated François Mitterrand, the First Secretary of the Parti Socialiste (PS). A coalition Government was formed from members of the RI, the Gaullist Union des Démocrates pour la République (UDR) and the centrist parties. In August 1976 Jacques Chirac resigned as Prime Minister and subsequently transformed the UDR into a new party, the Rassemblement pour la République (RPR). In February 1978 the governing non-Gaullist parties formed the Union pour la Démocratie Française (UDF) to compete against RPR candidates in the legislative elections held in March, when the incumbent coalition retained a working majority.

In the April/May 1981 presidential election Mitterrand defeated Giscard d'Estaing. At elections for a new National Assembly, held in June, the PS and associated groups, principally the Mouvement des Radicaux de Gauche (MRG), won an overall majority of seats, following which four members of the Parti Communiste Français (PCF) were appointed to the Council of Ministers. The new Government introduced a programme of social and labour reforms, including the nationalization of several major industrial enterprises and financial institutions.

Legislative elections took place in March 1986, using for the first time a system of proportional representation based on party lists. Although the PS remained the largest single party in the National Assembly, the centre-right parties, led by an RPR-UDF alliance, commanded a majority of seats. The PCF suffered a severe decline in support, while the far-right Front National (FN) won legislative representation for the first time. A period of political 'cohabitation' ensued when President Mitterrand invited the RPR leader, Chirac, to form a new Council of Ministers.

In April 1986 Chirac introduced legislation allowing his Government to legislate by decree on economic and social issues and on the proposed reversion to a voting system comprising single-member constituencies for legislative elections. However, Mitterrand insisted on exercising his right, as President, to withhold approval of decrees that reversed the previous Government's social reforms. Accordingly, in July Chirac resorted to the 'guillotine' procedure (setting a time limit for consideration of legislative proposals) to gain parliamentary consent for legislation providing for the privatization of 65 state-owned companies, which, since it had been approved by the predominantly right-wing Sénat (Senate) and the Constitutional Council, the President was legally bound to approve.

Mitterrand was re-elected as President in May 1988, defeating Chirac. A general election took place in June, with a reintroduced single-seat majority voting system, at which an alliance of the PS and the MRG secured the largest number of seats. Michel Rocard of the PS, who had been appointed as Prime Minister following the presidential election, resumed that role. Rocard resigned in May 1991 and was succeeded by Edith Cresson, France's first female Prime Minister. However, after the poor performance of the PS in regional elections in March 1992, Cresson was replaced in April by Pierre Bérégovoy. In June the National Assembly approved constitutional changes allowing the ratification of the Treaty on European Union (the Maastricht Treaty), subject to approval by referendum. In the referendum, held in September, 51.1% of voters supported ratification.

At elections to the National Assembly held in March 1993, the RPR won 247 of the 577 seats, the UDF 213 and the PS 54. Chirac had indicated that he was not available for the post of Prime Minister as he intended to concentrate on his candidacy in the 1995 presidential election. Another RPR member, Édouard Balladur, was therefore appointed premier.

In the first round of voting in the presidential election in April 1995, Lionel Jospin, the PS candidate, obtained 23% of the votes, while Chirac and Balladur, both representing the RPR, took 21% and 19%, respectively. Jean-Marie Le Pen, the leader of the FN, won 15%. In the second round, in May, Chirac defeated Jospin, taking 53% of the votes. Chirac appointed Alain Juppé (Minister of Foreign Affairs in the previous Government) as Prime Minister at the head of an RPR/UDF coalition.

At legislative elections held in May–June 1997, the PS secured 241 seats, the RPR 134 and the UDF 108. The unexpected victory of the PS, which began a further period of 'cohabitation', was widely attributed to public dissatisfaction with Juppé's administration and the imposition of economic austerity measures necessitated under the terms of Economic and Monetary Union

(EMU) within the European Union (EU, see p. 271). Jospin became Prime Minister at the head of a 'plural left' coalition.

In March 1999 a Paris public prosecutor upheld a ruling of the Constitutional Council that the President of the Republic should enjoy immunity from prosecution for all crimes, other than high treason, for the duration of his presidential term. This decision followed the disclosure of documentation purporting to show that Chirac had been aware of the existence of at least 300 fictitious employees, reputedly including RPR members or supporters, on the payroll of the Paris city council during his tenure as Mayor in 1977–95. In September 2000 a transcript of a videotape made by Jean-Claude Méry, a former RPR official who had been imprisoned on charges of embezzlement in the mid-1990s, was published posthumously in the French press. In the recording Méry stated that Chirac had personally ordered him to arrange for municipal funds to be diverted to political parties. In December Michel Roussin, who had been Chirac's principal private secretary from 1989–93, was arrested, while the former unofficial treasurer for the RPR was questioned. Their testimony included details of the systematic levying of an illegal commission on public works contracts awarded by the city council.

In April 2001 the investigating judge in the case, Eric Halphen, announced the existence of evidence implicating Chirac in the alleged illegal use of funds in the Paris city council, but stated that the doctrine of presidential immunity prevented Chirac from being brought to trial. New revelations concerning Chirac's purported involvement in financial malpractice emerged in June: the President was alleged to have spent up to 3.1m. francs of state 'secret funds'—issued annually by the Office of the Prime Minister for the security services, to pay bonuses to staff, and as a contingency fund—on luxury holidays for himself and his family in 1992–95, although suspicions were voiced that these trips might have been financed by the alleged illicit commission payments made by building firms to the Paris city council. Chirac declared himself innocent of all charges made against him, and confirmed that he would not participate in any court case. In September 2001 the Appeal Court dismissed Halphen as the leading investigator into the case regarding the use of illicit funds in the Paris city council; Halphen was ruled to have exceeded his powers by calling the President as a witness, and by introducing certain items of evidence, including Méry's videotape. Although the case could be tried again, this decision effectively ruled out any development in the case so long as Chirac remained President. In October the Court of Cassation confirmed the Constitutional Council's directive that an incumbent President could not be prosecuted, additionally ruling that a head of state could not undergo formal investigation while in power, even for offences allegedly committed prior to taking office.

Meanwhile, the tensions caused by the prolonged period of 'cohabitation' from 1997 prompted moves towards constitutional change. In June 2000 the National Assembly approved a reduction in the presidential term from seven to five years, in order to bring it into line with the life of a parliament. Amid concerns that the Senate might not support the bill by the two-thirds' majority required, Chirac called a referendum. Held in September, the referendum attracted only a 30.6% turnout; 73.2% of voters were in favour of the change, which would take effect from the 2002 presidential election. In May 2001 the Constitutional Council approved a proposal, aimed at preventing a further period of 'cohabitation', to hold the presidential election in advance of the parliamentary elections due in May 2002.

The 2002 presidential election

Prior to the first round of the presidential election, which was held in April 2002, Chirac and Jospin had been widely expected to progress to a second round. However, partly as a result of the wide choice of candidates (16), a relatively low turnout, and a campaign focus on issues related to 'insecurity' and law and order, Jospin polled only 16.2% of the votes, while Chirac won 19.9% and Le Pen 16.9%. The splintering of the governmental 'plural left' coalition proved detrimental for Jospin and the PS, as four of the coalition partners presented individual candidates for the presidency, together securing 16.3% of votes cast. The qualification of Le Pen for the second-round poll precipitated widespread demonstrations, and the majority of the defeated candidates rallied around Chirac as the preferred candidate. In the second round, in May, Chirac's victory, with 82.2% of the vote, was widely interpreted as a resounding defeat for the far right. Chirac appointed Jean-Pierre Raffarin, of Démocratie Libérale (DL), as Prime Minister. Raffarin appointed an interim Government, including Nicolas Sarkozy as Minister of the Inter-

ior, Interior Security and Local Freedoms, and Dominique de Villepin as Minister of Foreign Affairs. Chirac was subsequently instrumental in the organization of a new centre-right electoral alliance, which was initially titled the Union pour la Majorité Présidentielle.

At the legislative elections in June 2002 the Union pour la Majorité Présidentielle, which incorporated the greater part of the RPR and DL, and significant elements of the UDF, secured 355 of the 577 seats in the National Assembly, while a further 43 representatives of other parties of the centre-right and right were elected, thus ensuring a clear working majority for the pro-presidential grouping. Of the 176 seats awarded to parties of the broad left, the PS was the most successful, with 140 deputies. The new Government was largely unchanged from the interim administration and cited law and order, a programme of decentralization, and further privatizations among its priorities. In November the Union pour la Majorité Présidentielle formally constituted itself as the Union pour un Mouvement Populaire (UMP), absorbing the RPR and DL, in addition to factions of the UDF and the Rassemblement pour la France; Juppé was elected as President of the new party.

Further concerns about the extent of corruption in public life were raised during the trial in late 2003 of Juppé and 26 other defendants on charges that the Paris city council and private companies had illegally paid staff of the RPR during Juppé's tenure as Secretary-General of the party (in 1988–95) and as Deputy Mayor of Paris (1983–95). In January 2004 Juppé was found guilty and given an 18 months' suspended prison sentence; 13 business executives also received suspended terms of imprisonment. In addition, Juppé was banned from holding public office for a period of 10 years, but was permitted to remain in office as Mayor of Bordeaux, and as a parliamentary deputy, pending an appeal. Although the constitutional immunity from prosecution and investigation of the President of the Republic prevented any inquiry into Chirac's conduct, the judges ruled that Juppé had been directly subordinate to Chirac in the latter's capacity as President of the RPR. (Moreover, Chirac was the Mayor of Paris for the entire duration of Juppé's service as the Deputy Mayor.) In December the appeal court upheld Juppé's conviction, but reduced the length of the ban on holding public office from 10 years to one; Juppé subsequently resigned his mayorship, having relinquished the UMP presidency in July.

Meanwhile, in March 2003 the two houses of Parliament, meeting in congress, approved several constitutional changes relating to the proposed decentralization programme, which provided for the eventual possibility of territorial units receiving varying degrees of autonomy and powers, for the institution of deliberative assemblies and for the holding of local referendums in such territories. Moreover, the amendments permitted the introduction of legislation pertaining to decentralization on a temporary, or experimental, basis. Notably, the first article of the Constitution was amended to assert that the organization of the Republic was decentralized.

A major topic of political debate in 2003 and early 2004 concerned the wearing of the Islamic headscarf by female Muslim pupils at state schools. Although a 1989 ruling of the Council of State declared that the wearing of religious symbols in state schools did not violate the principle of the secularity of the state, formalized in 1905, so long as they were deemed to be of a 'non-ostentatious' nature, the ruling had subsequently been used to exclude a number of Muslim students from educational establishments. Legislation explicitly forbidding the wearing of conspicuous religious symbols, including the Muslim headscarf/veil, Jewish skullcaps and large Christian crosses, in state-operated primary and secondary schools came into effect in September 2004.

Widespread public discontent with the Government was reflected in the outcome of regional and cantonal elections held in March 2004, as a result of which the parties of the centre-right lost control of 13 regions to parties of the left and centre-left, which thereby controlled all of the regions of metropolitan France excluding Alsace and Corsica. Raffarin tendered his resignation as Prime Minister on 30 March, but was immediately reappointed to that position by President Chirac. Sarkozy was appointed as Minister of State, Minister of the Economy, Finance and Industry in a new Government formed the following day, and was replaced as Minister of the Interior, Internal Security and Local Freedoms by de Villepin. In November Sarkozy was elected President of the UMP. At the insistence of Chirac that the head of the ruling party should not be permitted simultaneously to hold ministerial office, Sarkozy resigned from the Government.

De Villepin appointed Prime Minister

In May 2005 a national referendum took place on the ratification of the Treaty establishing a Constitution for Europe. Following an intense campaign, during which Chirac and leading members of the UMP and the PS demonstrated their support for the EU constitutional treaty, 54.9% of those voting rejected its ratification. Raffarin subsequently resigned as Prime Minister. He was succeeded by de Villepin, and Sarkozy returned to government office as Minister of State, Minister of the Interior and Land Management (while continuing to head the UMP).

In October 2005 violence broke out in Clichy-sous-Bois, a suburb of Paris largely populated by immigrant communities and suffering from high unemployment and poor social housing, following the deaths of two youths (both of whom were of African extraction) who had allegedly been fleeing a police identity check. The rioting subsequently spread to several suburbs to the north-east of the capital. By early November some 300 towns and cities across France were experiencing unrest, mainly led by young males of African origin, while some 9,500 riot police had been deployed in an attempt to curb the violence. When the violence claimed a fatality, de Villepin announced a series of enhanced security measures and a programme aimed at improving education, employment and housing in deprived suburban areas. None the less, rioting continued, and on 8 November de Villepin imposed a state of emergency. Adopting an uncompromising stance, Sarkozy announced that all convicted rioters who were not of French nationality would be deported, including those holding residence permits. By mid-November, although the violence had subsided, nearly 300 schools and public buildings had been burned down and 4,770 people had been arrested. In December the Prime Minister launched a national campaign against discrimination, with measures including the imposition of fines on businesses found to have practised discrimination and incentives for companies to locate in deprived areas and to employ young people. The state of emergency was lifted in January 2006.

In April 2006, following a series of mass demonstrations and strike action in Paris and other cities, the Government abandoned plans for a new employment contract that would have allowed small companies to dismiss workers aged under 26 years more easily during their first two years of employment. De Villepin's popularity suffered a further reverse in May in the wake of the disclosure of an apparent attempt by the Prime Minister to discredit his political rivals (including Sarkozy) in an investigation into secret offshore accounts with the Luxembourg bank Clearstream.

At a PS congress in November 2006, Ségolène Royal, a regional councillor, was elected as the party's presidential candidate. In January 2007 the UMP elected Sarkozy unopposed as the party's candidate for the presidency, in accordance with a change to the party's statutes allowing members to select the presidential candidate; he resigned from the Government in March. The first round of the presidential election, held on 22 April, was contested by 12 candidates and attracted a high turnout of 83.8% of the electorate. Sarkozy and Royal progressed to the second round of voting, winning 31.2% and 25.9% of the valid votes cast, respectively. The UDF candidate, François Bayrou, won 18.6% of the vote, while Le Pen's support declined to only 10.4%. At the second round of the election, held on 6 May, Sarkozy was elected as President, securing 53.1% of the vote.

The Sarkozy presidency

Sarkozy formally acceded to the presidency on 16 May 2007. The new Council of Ministers included prominent figures from across the political divide—François Fillon, a close adviser of the President and former Minister of National Education, Higher Education and Research, was appointed Prime Minister; Bernard Kouchner, a member of Royal's presidential campaign team and former minister under Jospin, was appointed Minister of Foreign and European Affairs; and Juppé returned to government office as Minister of State, Minister of Ecology and Sustainable Development.

At elections to the National Assembly, held in June 2007, the UMP remained the largest party in the lower house, albeit with a reduced majority, winning 313 of 577 seats. Despite losing the presidential election and suffering the subsequent defection of Kouchner, the PS secured 186 seats. Prior to the elections the UDF was restyled the Mouvement Démocrate (MoDem) by its leader, Bayrou, while former members of the UDF allied to the President established a new party, the Nouveau Centre. In the event, the Nouveau Centre won 22 seats, while MoDem took just three. Following the elections Sarkozy reappointed Fillon as Prime Minister and effected a government reorganization. The erstwhile Minister of the Economy, Finance and Employment, Jean-Louis Borloo, assumed the post vacated by Juppé, who failed to win re-election to the National Assembly, and Borloo was, in turn, replaced by Christine Lagarde (hitherto Minister of Agriculture and Fisheries).

Investigations into allegations of wrongdoing on the part of members of the previous administration continued. In November 2007 Chirac (having lost his right to immunity from prosecution following the end of his presidency) was placed under formal investigation regarding misuse of public funds in relation to the alleged existence of fictitious city council employees during his tenure as Mayor of Paris. Furthermore, in December 2009 Chirac was placed under formal investigation regarding his alleged involvement in the payment of wages to RPR supporters under false pretences during his mayoralty. Chirac's trial in both cases, on charges of embezzlement and breach of trust, commenced in March 2011. In December Chirac was convicted of the charges against him and received a two-year suspended prison sentence; although he continued to plead his innocence, the former President announced that he lacked the strength to appeal against the verdict. Meanwhile, in July 2007 de Villepin was placed under formal investigation regarding the Clearstream affair. In late 2008 it was announced that de Villepin was to stand trial for complicity in false accusation and using forgeries, among other charges, in relation to this case. De Villepin claimed that the charges were politically motivated, owing to his rivalry with Sarkozy. The trial of de Villepin and four other defendants commenced in September 2009. In January 2010 de Villepin was cleared of the charges against him, but three of the other defendants were convicted for their roles in the affair. De Villepin established a new political movement, République Solidaire, in June, and relinquished his membership of the UMP in February 2011.

In October 2007 new legislation increasing restrictions on immigration was approved by Parliament. The legislation included provisions for the evaluation of individual immigrants' knowledge of French language and culture, and the compilation of population statistics based on ethnicity. Opposition to the legislation, however, focused on the provision for voluntary DNA testing of immigrants from non-EU countries who were suspected of falsely claiming to have a relative resident in France. This measure prompted the PS to refer the proposed bill to the Constitutional Council. In November the Constitutional Council endorsed the provision on DNA testing, but declared the compilation of population statistics by ethnicity to be unconstitutional.

In February 2008 the FN leader, Le Pen, was convicted of conspiring to justify war crimes and denying crimes against humanity, following comments he had made regarding the occupation of France by German forces in 1940–44 in an interview in a far-right periodical in 2005. He received a three-month suspended prison sentence and a fine of €10,000.

In July 2008 significant constitutional changes were narrowly approved by the National Assembly and the Senate. Parliament was awarded new powers to oversee certain presidential appointments and to set its own agenda for one-half of its sessions (formerly, the entire agenda was decided by the Prime Minister and the Council of Ministers). The use of motions of confidence to force legislation through the National Assembly was restricted, Parliament had to be notified of any deployment of troops within three days, and parliamentary approval was required for military action extending beyond four months. The President was limited to two terms of office and curbs were imposed on the President's emergency powers. However, the President was now permitted to address Parliament in a joint session, a right that had been denied to the holder of that office since 1875.

In January 2009 large numbers of public and private sector workers took part in a one-day nationwide strike organized by trade unions in protest at a government economic stimulus plan, which the unions criticized for its perceived failure to offer adequate protection for workers and wages. The strike, which represented the most serious challenge to Sarkozy's authority since his election to the presidency, resulted in widespread disruption. Rejecting concessions, including new welfare measures and tax reductions for the low-paid, as inadequate, union and opposition leaders called a further one-day nationwide strike in March, which attracted even greater support than the previous day of action.

Debate on national identity

In June 2009 Sarkozy exercised his newly acquired right under the recent constitutional amendments to outline government policy for the forthcoming year before a joint session of Parliament, an event viewed by many commentators as a manifestation of the President's increasing assumption of political and executive control at the expense of the Prime Minister. Sarkozy provoked controversy during his speech by expressing support for a proposed parliamentary inquiry on the wearing of all-enveloping female Islamic dress. His declaration that the *burqa* was 'not welcome' in France helped to revive political debate on Islamic clothing, some five years after the wearing of conspicuous religious symbols had been outlawed in state schools. In November Eric Besson, the Minister of Immigration, Integration, National Identity and Shared Development, announced the launch of a debate on French national identity, which would include public consultations organized by local authorities, with the aim of addressing tensions in community relations exemplified by the controversy over full-face veils. In February 2010 Fillon announced a series of government proposals arising from the debate: these included measures to strengthen the teaching of 'republican values' in schools and a requirement that candidates for French citizenship sign a charter of rights and responsibilities. New legislation, which outlawed the covering of the face in public and prescribed penalties of one year's imprisonment and a sizeable fine for anyone forcing a woman to wear a full-face veil, was approved by Parliament in the latter half of the year and entered into force in April 2011. In September the Government announced a ban with immediate effect on praying outdoors in Paris, prompting criticism from some Muslim groups, which accused the Government of bowing to pressure from the FN by thereby outlawing the Muslim practice of holding prayer meetings in the street when mosques were overcrowded.

The Government suffered a heavy defeat at regional elections held over two rounds in March 2010. The PS, led by Martine Aubry, who had narrowly defeated Royal in a party leadership contest in November 2008, achieved its best result for 30 years. In the second round of voting, the PS in alliance with Europe Ecologie (an electoral coalition led by Les Verts—the Greens) and other parties of the left, won 54.1% of the vote, emerging with control of all but one of metropolitan France's 22 regions (having added the Territorial Collectivity of Corsica to the 20 regions hitherto controlled by the left). The UMP and its right-wing allies won 35.4% of the vote, while the FN performed strongly, securing 9.4%; many commentators believed that the recent debate on national identity and Islamic dress contributed to the FN's resurgence by encouraging anti-immigrant sentiment. Sarkozy's standing had been damaged by his attempts to introduce a number of unpopular reforms, notably a planned rise in the retirement age.

Pension reforms and the deportation of Roma

In June 2010 Eric Woerth, the Minister of Labour, Solidarity and the Civil Service, announced details of the Government's plans for reform of the state pension system as part of concerted efforts to reduce the burgeoning budget deficit. Notably, the proposals envisaged raising the minimum retirement age from 60 to 62 years by 2018 and the qualifying age for a full pension from 65 to 67 years. Trade unions organized a one-day strike and rallies later that month in protest against the planned reforms. In July the reputations of both the President and Woerth were tarnished by accusations that they had accepted allegedly illegal donations to the UMP and to Sarkozy's 2007 presidential election campaign from Liliane Bettencourt, the principal shareholder of the L'Oréal cosmetics business, whose financial affairs were under police investigation. Sarkozy and Woerth strongly rejected the allegations, but, on the President's advice, Woerth resigned as treasurer of the UMP; he left the Government in a cabinet reorganization in November. As Parliament debated the pension legislation, several days of action, involving nationwide strikes and demonstrations, were organized in September and October, attended by up to 1.2m. people according to official figures (or 3.5m. according to the unions) and causing severe disruption across the public sector. None the less, the legislation secured parliamentary approval in October, following some minor concessions by the Government, and was promulgated in November. (In November 2011 the Government brought forward the increase in the minimum retirement age from 2018 to 2017.)

A government decision in July 2010 to expel illegal Roma migrants was condemned by opposition parties, human rights groups and the EU. The policy was introduced in response to an attack on a police station in central France by a group of Roma, following an incident in which a young traveller who had driven through a checkpoint without stopping had been shot dead by a gendarme. President Sarkozy ordered the dismantlement of 300 unauthorized Roma camps within three months and the immediate return of Roma who had committed public order offences or were living in France illegally to their countries of origin, mainly Romania and Bulgaria (citizens of which required work or residency permits if they wished to remain in France longer than three months). The President also pledged to withdraw French citizenship from foreign-born persons convicted of serious offences. As the deportation of Roma continued, in September the European Commission threatened to initiate legal proceedings against France unless the French Government demonstrated that it would incorporate a directive on the free movement of EU citizens within the Union into French law. The Government subsequently provided the assurances demanded by the Commission, promising to include the necessary measures in a new immigration bill recently presented to Parliament. In accordance with earlier pledges, this proposed legislation required candidates for French citizenship to sign a charter of rights and responsibilities and, most controversially, provided for the removal of citizenship from anyone who had acquired it within the previous 10 years if they were sentenced to at least five years' imprisonment by a French or foreign court. The immigration bill was approved by the National Assembly in October, despite opposition from some UMP deputies, but was rejected by the Senate in February 2011. A revised version of the bill, which did not include the provision relating to the removal of citizenship, was adopted by Parliament in May. Meanwhile, in February it was announced that more than 3,700 Roma had been returned to their countries of origin since July 2010, and that 70% of unauthorized Roma camps had been dismantled.

Towards the 2012 elections

Sarkozy effected a government reorganization in November 2010, retaining Fillon as Prime Minister and appointing Juppé as Minister of State, Minister of Defence and Veterans. Notable departures included those of Woerth and of Kouchner, who had publicly expressed reservations about the expulsion of Roma; Minister of State Michèle Alliot-Marie replaced Kouchner as Minister of Foreign and European Affairs. Another reorganization in February 2011 was occasioned by the resignation of Alliot-Marie, who had sustained criticism for her close links to the regime of the recently deposed Tunisian President, Zine al-Abidine Ben Ali (see *Other external relations*). She was replaced as Minister of Foreign and European Affairs by Juppé, whose defence portfolio was assumed by Gérard Longuet. The appointment of Christine Lagarde as managing director of the IMF necessitated a further cabinet reorganization in June. Among the changes, François Baroin, hitherto Minister of the Budget, Public Finances, the Civil Service and State Reform, and Government Spokesman, succeeded Lagarde as Minister of the Economy, Finance and Industry.

Jean-Marie Le Pen retired as President of the FN in January 2011; his daughter, Marine Le Pen, was elected as his successor, subsequently declaring her intention to contest the presidency in 2012. Also in January, the PS confirmed that it would hold a primary election in October, in which any registered French voter who supported left-wing values could take part, to select the party's candidate for the state presidency. Royal had earlier announced, in November 2010, her intention to seek the PS presidential nomination; François Hollande, Aubry's predecessor as First Secretary of the party, declared his candidacy in March 2011, followed by Aubry herself in June.

Meanwhile, the PS and the FN both performed strongly in local elections in March 2011, with the UMP barely surpassing the FN in terms of its share of the vote in the first round. At indirect partial elections to the Senate held on 25 September, the centre-right parties, dominated by the UMP, lost their majority in the upper chamber for the first time since the establishment of the Fifth Republic in 1958.

Hollande was selected as the presidential candidate of the PS at the party's primary election, defeating Aubry with 56.6% of the votes cast in a second round held on 16 October 2011, in which almost 2.9m. people voted. Six candidates had contested the first round, at which Hollande had won 39.2% of the vote and Aubry 30.4%; Arnaud Montebourg, who advocated far-ranging political and constitutional reforms, was notably placed third, with 17.2%

of the vote, while Royal secured only 6.9%. With a solid lead in opinion polls, Hollande presented his election manifesto in January 2012, pledging to create thousands of new jobs, and to increase taxes on the banking sector and high earners. The decision by the credit rating agency Standard & Poor's to downgrade France's long-term sovereign debt rating to AA+ that month represented a significant reverse for Sarkozy's Government, which had emphasized the importance of retaining the country's AAA rating when announcing austerity measures in November 2011. Sarkozy did not confirm his intention to seek re-election until February 2012, when he defended his economic policies, including raising the retirement age and reducing the number of state employees, insisting that France's economic position would have deteriorated further without such action. In March, in an apparent attempt to court right-wing voters, the President proposed lowering the number of immigrants to France from 180,000 to 100,000 per year.

During the run-up to the presidential election the Government's campaign against religious extremism was heightened in the wake of the murder of seven people (including three Jewish children) in the Toulouse area by an Islamist gunman in March 2012. A series of raids and arrests of suspected Islamist militants was carried out at a number of locations throughout France; 13 of the detainees were subsequently charged with terrorism offences. In addition, the Government proposed new anti-terrorism legislation aimed at preventing the recruitment and training of potential terrorists. Following France's military intervention in Mali in January 2013 (see *Other external relations*), the Government warned of possible Islamist retaliatory attacks in France and increased its domestic terrorism threat level accordingly.

Recent developments: The Hollande presidency

The first round of the presidential election was held on 22 April 2012 and was contested by 10 candidates. Hollande narrowly defeated Sarkozy, with 28.6% of the valid votes cast against the latter's 27.2%. Marine Le Pen came third with 17.9% of the vote (a record share for an FN presidential candidate), her pledge to give French citizens priority over foreigners for jobs, housing and social welfare proving popular amid rising unemployment. At the second round, held on 6 May, Hollande again defeated Sarkozy, winning 51.6% of the votes against his opponent's 48.4%. On 15 May Hollande was sworn in as the first Socialist French President for 17 years and on the following day he appointed Jean-Marc Ayrault, the long-standing leader of the PS in the National Assembly, as the new Prime Minister. Other significant appointments included Hollande's chief campaign manager, Pierre Moscovici, as Minister of the Economy and Finance, and former Prime Minister Laurent Fabius as Minister of Foreign Affairs.

At the legislative elections held on 10 and 17 June 2012, the PS secured 280 seats—compared with 186 in 2007—and, with the support of its left-wing allies, commanded a very narrow overall majority in the lower house (as well as controlling a majority in the Senate). The UMP's tally of seats decreased from an absolute majority of 313 to 194, while the FN, reflecting its strong performance in the presidential election, obtained seats in the legislature (albeit only two) for the first time since 1997. Despite the apparent strength of the left-wing at both national and local/regional level, the new administration's popularity soon began to founder as it was forced to adopt a number of harsh measures to address the numerous problems caused by the ailing economy (notably the high levels of public debt and rising unemployment). The increasing marginalization and discontent felt by many of the country's unemployed youth was vividly illustrated by the riots that erupted in the northern city of Amiens in mid-August. Sixteen police officers were injured in clashes with the rioters (many of whom were from immigrant backgrounds) and police forces throughout France were placed on high alert.

The new Government's controversial plans to legalize same-sex marriage and to introduce legislation to allow gay couples to adopt children provoked a series of public protests and counter-protests throughout France attended by tens of thousands of people. Despite the scale of the opposition, supported by the Catholic Church and the conservative opposition, the proposed bill was approved by Parliament in April 2013 and promulgated in May.

Meanwhile, following his failure to retain the presidency and the UMP's subsequent defeat in the legislative elections, Sarkozy withdrew from front-line politics (although it was widely rumoured that he intended to stand for re-election in the 2017 presidential election). In July 2012 the former President's home

and offices in Paris were searched by the police as part of an investigation into allegations of the illicit funding of Sarkozy's 2007 presidential election campaign by the heiress Liliane Bettencourt (in the wake of his loss of office, Sarkozy no longer enjoyed presidential immunity). Sarkozy was placed under formal investigation over the claims in March 2013 and in the following month French prosecutors launched an investigation into allegations that he had also received illegal campaign funds from the former Libyan leader Col Muammar al-Qaddafi. In October the case against Sarkozy regarding Bettencourt was dropped.

The UMP was severely weakened in the latter half of 2012 as a result of an acrimonious leadership struggle between former Prime Minister Fillon and the more right-wing Jean-François Copé, who had held the position of Secretary-General of the party since 2010. The UMP was thrown into turmoil in November 2012 when both candidates claimed victory in the vote to elect the new leader of the party amid mutual accusations of electoral fraud. Although the final official result awarded a narrow victory to Copé (by just 98 votes), Fillon demanded a recount on the grounds that 1,300 votes from three overseas territories had been omitted. Fillon claimed that, if these votes were included in the final tally, he would win the leadership contest by 26 votes. Ultimately, however, following a fresh ballot count by an internal party commission, Copé was confirmed as the new leader of the UMP, with an increased majority, at the end of November. Fillon, who refused to recognize the legality of the recount, established a breakaway faction of the UMP, the Rassemblement-UMP (R-UMP), composed of more than 70 parliamentary deputies, and demanded another leadership vote within three months. A compromise was reached between Copé and Fillon in December when they agreed to hold a new leadership contest (under the auspices of an independent body) before October 2013; the R-UMP was dissolved in January of that year.

In March 2013 Jérôme Cahuzac, Minister-delegate to the Minister of Economy and Finance, in charge of the Budget, resigned following allegations of tax avoidance. This represented a highly embarrassing scandal for Hollande, since it took place against a background of growing government demands that the public make ever greater sacrifices in an attempt to revive the economy and since the President had sought to distance his administration from the financial scandals and perceived lack of integrity of the Sarkozy presidency. Cahuzac, who was charged with tax fraud, was officially excluded from the PS in early April and all ministers were required to publish full details of their personal wealth on an official website by the middle of that month. Also in April, in a further bid for greater transparency within government and in an attempt to regain public trust, Hollande drafted legislation to appoint a special prosecutor charged with handling cases of fraud and corruption and to create a central agency to combat such misdeeds among the ranks of officialdom. Despite these attempts at re-establishing his credibility, the President's popularity ratings continued to plummet as the economy showed no signs of any real recovery and unemployment reached record levels. Hollande's administration suffered a further setback in July when the Minister of Ecology, Sustainable Development and Energy, Delphine Batho, was dismissed for publicly criticizing planned cuts in government expenditure. As support for the PS declined, the popularity of the FN, under the 'modernizing' leadership of Marine Le Pen, appeared to be strengthening—as indicated by its victory over the UMP in a regional by-election in October, and an increased share of votes in municipal elections held in late March 2014, when the FN won control of 11 towns. Following the heavy losses suffered by the PS (mainly to the advantage of the UMP and a centrist electoral alliance, L'Alternative, comprising MoDem and the Union des Démocrates et Indépendants—UDI) in the municipal elections, at which the party lost control of some 150 towns and cities, on 31 March President Hollande appointed Manuel Valls, hitherto Minister of the Interior, to replace Ayrault—who had resigned earlier that day—as Prime Minister. On 2 April a new Council of Ministers took office, in which Europe Ecologie Les Verts (as the Greens had been restyled in November 2010 following their merger with Europe Ecologie), which had previously run two ministries, refused to participate. Among the most notable ministerial changes was the transfer of responsibility for the finance portfolio from Moscovici to the more experienced Michel Sapin (who had held the same post in 1992–93) and the appointment of Royal as Minister of Ecology, Sustainable Development and Energy. The growing popularity of the FN was vividly illustrated by the party's success in the elections to the European Parliament in May 2014 when it secured 25% of the vote (24 seats), against 21% (20 seats) for the UMP and a mere 14% (13 seats) for the PS.

Following public criticism of the Government's continuing adherence to certain policies of economic austerity (as advocated by Germany) by left-leaning Minister of Economy, Industrial Recovery and Digital Economy Arnaud Montebourg, who was supported by Minister of National Education, Higher Education and Research Benoît Hamon and Minister of Culture and Communication Aurélie Filippetti, on 25 August 2014 Valls tendered the resignation of the entire Council of Ministers in a bid to avert a political crisis. Hollande accepted the resignation and immediately requested that Valls form a new Government. Aside from the replacement of the three dissident ministers by Hollande loyalists, the new cabinet, which was announced on 26 August, remained little changed from the former administration.

Meanwhile, Sarkozy's prospects for a possible return to politics appeared somewhat jeopardized in July 2014 when he was taken into temporary police custody for questioning and placed under formal investigation regarding allegations of corruption and influence-peddling in the Bettencourt case. None the less, there was a reversal in the former President's political fortunes in late November when he was re-elected to head the UMP (Copé having stood down in May following the party's poor performance in the European elections), by a comfortable margin of 64.5% of the vote; his closest rival, former Minister of Agriculture, Food and Forestry Bruno Le Maire, received 29.2%, while the third candidate, Hervé Mariton, won a mere 6.3%. Sarkozy's victory in the party leadership contest was widely viewed as a first step towards a bid to regain the presidency in 2017.

As part of the Government's attempts to streamline bureaucracy and reduce public expenditure, in mid-December 2014 the National Assembly approved legislation to reduce the number of regions in metropolitan France from 22 to 13 through a series of mergers; the new regions would officially come into existence from 1 January 2016. The unpopularity of the Government's proposed economic policies even within the ranks of its own PS deputies was evidenced in mid-February 2015, when concerns grew within the cabinet that it might not garner a majority in the National Assembly for the adoption of a wide-ranging package of economic reforms aimed at deregulating sectors of the economy (the so-called 'loi Macron', named after the Minister of Economy, Industry and Digital Economy, Emmanuel Macron). Proposed measures included extending Sunday trading, the deregulation of certain law professions and changes to legislation governing worker representation in small companies. Instead of risking defeat in the Assembly, on 17 February the Government made use of Article 49.3 of the Constitution in order to push through the legislation without a vote. (The clause allows the Government, in certain circumstances, to bypass the National Assembly). A motion of censure, called by the UMP and the UDI, was rejected by the National Assembly two days later.

Meanwhile, the threat posed by an apparent growth in support for Islamist militancy in France was vividly illustrated by several violent incidents that took place in Paris in January 2015. The first, on 7 January, involved an attack by two gunmen on the offices of the satirical weekly newspaper *Charlie Hebdo* in which 12 people (including several well-known French cartoonists and a police officer) were killed. It appeared that the newspaper had been targeted as a result of its past publication of controversial cartoons depicting the Prophet Muhammad. The perpetrators, two French-born, Muslim brothers of Algerian descent—Saïd and Chérif Kouachi—who claimed to be members of the Yemeni branch of the militant Islamist al-Qa'ida organization (commonly known as al-Qa'ida in the Arabian Peninsula), fled the capital but were shot dead in a gunfight with police officers in a small town some 30 km to the north-east of Paris two days later. Meanwhile, on 8 January, in an apparently related incident, another gunman, Amedy Coulibaly, carried out the fatal shooting of a female police officer in a suburb to the south of Paris. On the following day, the same assailant, a French-born Muslim of Malian descent, who was an associate of the Kouachi brothers and who claimed allegiance to the militant group Islamic State in Iraq and the Levant (see *Other external relations*), killed four people—all of whom were Jewish—in a kosher supermarket in east Paris and took 15 other customers hostage. A few hours later Coulibaly was killed in a shoot-out with police when they ended the siege by storming the shop.

In the immediate wake of the attacks the French authorities raised the country's national security alert system to its highest level and deployed more than 10,000 troops across the country to protect public spaces and potentially vulnerable sites such as synagogues and schools. Numerous large-scale, popular demonstrations and vigils were held throughout France (and around the world) to denounce terrorism, support freedom of expression and express solidarity with the victims. The largest of these demonstrations was the mass rally held in central Paris on 11 January 2015, which was attended by 1.5m.–2m. people, including President Hollande (whose popularity rating increased in the aftermath of the attacks), some 40 other heads of state and government, and many political and religious leaders. Later in the month the French Government announced that over the following three years around 2,680 new security-related jobs (focusing on counter-terrorism intelligence) were to be created and that some of the recent cuts in defence expenditure were to be reversed. Of particular concern to the authorities was the reported rise in the number of French citizens travelling to Syria and Iraq to join the jihadist groups fighting in those countries and the potential dangers that they posed to their homeland on their return to France.

Corsica

Demands for the independence of Corsica increased markedly during the 1960s and 1970s, with particular discontent being expressed at the resettlement on the island of French citizens displaced from Algeria following its independence in 1962. In 1972 the status of Corsica was upgraded to that of a region, administered by a centrally appointed préfet (prefect). (It had hitherto formed an administrative department within the region of Provence-Alpes-Côte d'Azur.) The assassination of two gendarmes at Aléria, in eastern Corsica, in August 1975, marked a significant escalation in the campaign for Corsican independence; from 1976 the clandestine Fronte di Liberazione Naziunale Corsu (FLNC) was regarded as the leading pro-independence organization. Also in 1976, Corsica was subdivided into two departments, Corse-du-Sud and Haute-Corse. Demands for greater autonomy or independence persisted, with intermittent bombing campaigns conducted by separatists both in Corsica and in continental France. As a result of the enactment of a decentralization law in 1982, in the text of which Corsica was referred to as a Collectivité Territoriale (Territorial Collectivity), the Corsican regional council was replaced by a directly elected 61-seat assembly with augmented executive and consultative powers. In April 1991 the National Assembly adopted legislation granting greater autonomy to Corsica and officially conferring on it the nomenclature and full status of a Territorial Collectivity; a seven-member Conseil Exécutif (Executive Council, the membership of which was subsequently increased to nine) was to be formed, chosen from a 51-member Assemblée de Corse (Corsican Assembly), which would be elected by universal suffrage in March 1992.

In February 1998, in the most serious act of violence committed by separatist militants to date, the Prefect of Corsica, Claude Erignac, was assassinated. The killing was condemned by the FLNC and the primary suspect in the case, Yvan Colonna, was convicted of murder in December 2007 and sentenced to life imprisonment. Meanwhile, peace negotiations involving the Government and representatives of Corsica commenced in Paris in December 1999. Four Corsican militant groups called an unconditional ceasefire, and pledged to disarm should their aims, including the recognition of the Corsican people as a nation, and the granting of official status to the Corsican language on the island, be achieved. The peace process resulted in agreement on a number of proposals known as the Matignon accords, which were approved by the Corsican Assembly in July 2000. Under the proposals, subject to the maintenance of peace on Corsica and the approval of the National Assembly, a referendum would be held on eventual revisions to the Constitution in 2004, prior to the introduction of a single political and administrative body for the island with formal, but limited, legislative powers, replacing the two existing administrative departments. The proposals also provided for instruction in the Corsican language to take place in all primary schools. Although most militant groups maintained a ceasefire following the signature of the accords, increasing concern was expressed at the prevalence of organized crime in Corsica, while sporadic, low-level attacks by militants continued. In May 2001 the National Assembly approved a more moderate version of the bill to amend the status of Corsica, with a view to presenting a text that would be acceptable to the Constitutional Council; consequently, Corsican language instruction at primary schools was to be optional, rather than compulsory, and the French Parliament would be required to pass enabling legislation before local bills approved by the Corsican Assembly could take effect. By September the process envisaged by the accords appeared to be stalling; the moderate nationalist leader Jean-Guy Talamoni, who had been involved in negotiating the accords, announced that the moderate separatist Corsica Nazione had decided to withdraw from the provisions of the accords. Nevertheless, the final bill on greater autonomy, which had been subject to further amendments, had received the approval of both the National Assembly and the Senate by December. In January 2002 the Constitutional Council ruled that the section of the bill that permitted the Corsican Assembly to amend national legislation on the island was illegitimate, although the section that permitted the optional use of Corsican language in primary schools was approved.

In April 2002, following the defeat of Lionel Jospin in the first round of the presidential election and a statement by Jacques Chirac to the effect that Corsican aspirations for greater autonomy were insignificant, nationalists on the island announced their withdrawal from the Matignon process. In May the FLNC-Union des Combatants (FLNC-UDC—as the main faction of the organization was now known) announced that it was to resume its separatist campaign, while stating its preference for a negotiated settlement. In June the new centre-right Government unexpectedly announced that it was to seek several constitutional amendments that would permit the eventual decentralization of a number of powers, and that Corsica could be expected to be affected by these measures. In July Nicolas Sarkozy, the Minister of the Interior, visited Corsica, where he announced efforts to relaunch a dialogue with nationalists. However, amid scepticism regarding the Government's intentions, the number of small-scale bomb attacks on the island increased sharply in 2002, to reach the highest annual total recorded (in excess of 220) since 1997. In February 2003 the Corsican Assembly voted in favour of a proposal, supported by Sarkozy, whereby the two administrative departments in Corsica were to be replaced by a single collectivity, subject to approval by a referendum in Corsica. Following the endorsement in March by the National Assembly of constitutional changes that permitted local referendums, it was announced that such a plebiscite was to be held in July. Although several separatist groups, including the FLNC-UDC, Corsica Nazione, and the political wing of the FLNC-UDC, Indipendenza, announced their support for the proposal, other more radical groups expressed concern that plans to devolve to the new collectivity limited legislative and additional tax-raising powers that had been included in the Matignon accords had not been revived. At the referendum, which was held on 6 July and attracted a relatively high turnout of 60.5%, the proposal was narrowly defeated, with 51.0% of the votes against the restructuring.

Following the defeat of the Government's proposal in the referendum, there was an escalation of violence by Corsican separatist groups, both in Corsica and in mainland France. In October 2003 Sarkozy announced that measures to combat widespread violence, terrorism and organized crime on Corsica would now be a government priority. However, the incidence of bombings and other attacks intensified in 2004, despite the FLNC-UDC's announcement of an unconditional ceasefire in November 2003. Many of these attacks, the majority of which were claimed by the Clandestini Corsi group, were on North African Muslims. In March 2005 the FLNC-UDC ended its ceasefire to coincide with the start of the trial in Paris of its alleged leader, Charles Pieri, who was accused of extortion, misappropriation of funds, financing terrorism and associating with criminals for a terrorist enterprise. Pieri, who had been imprisoned since December 2003, was convicted and sentenced to a 10-year custodial sentence; he was released in December 2009.

Militant activity in Corsica continued throughout 2006, with the FLNC-UDC claiming responsibility for a series of attacks. In May 2007 14 members of a militant separatist organization, FLNC des Anonymes, were convicted by a court in Paris of perpetrating a succession of bombings in Corsica during 2001–02 and received sentences of between one and 12 years' imprisonment. In December 2007 militants carried out a number of bombings on the island, following the conviction of Colonna for the assassination of Erignac, and the arrest of 13 members of Corsica Nazione suspected of involvement in bomb attacks carried out in 2006–07.

The political situation in Corsica remained tense in 2008. In January around 500 protesters occupied the Corsican Assembly in Ajaccio after a demonstration led by nationalist groups and trade unions. During the occupation, offices within the assembly building were set on fire. Five people were arrested in connection with the arson attack and placed under judicial investigation. The initial judicial hearing at a court in Ajaccio was marked by violent clashes between separatist protesters and police in the regional capital and in Bastia. Four of the defendants were acquitted later in 2008; all four were members of U Rinnovu, a nationalist movement founded in 1998. Meanwhile, in May 2008 a hitherto unrecognized organization, FLNC 1976, claimed responsibility for a recent spate of attacks in Corsica, including the destruction of public buildings, police stations and holiday homes. The newly established movement sought to reunite the factions of the FLNC—the FLNC-UDC and the FLNC du 22 Octobre (founded in October 2002). In February 2009 Corsica Nazione, U Rinnovu and two other nationalist movements merged to form a new pro-independence political party, Corsica Libera, led by Talamoni.

In January 2010 the FLNC-UDC claimed responsibility for 14 recent bomb attacks and renewed its threats against the authorities, in protest at a controversial 20-year development plan supported by the mainland French Government and the Corsican executive. The plan, which envisaged sanctioning development on previously protected land, also attracted criticism from environmental groups and moderate pro-independence parties. At the regional elections in March a left-wing grouping led by Paul Giacobbi of the Parti Radical de Gauche won 24 of the 51 seats in the Corsican Assembly, following 26 years of political dominance by the right; Giacobbi was elected President of the Executive Council.

In response to the murder of a prominent Corsican lawyer in October 2012 and the fatal shooting of the President of the Chamber of Commerce and Industry of South Corsica the following month, the French Government pledged to restore order on the island by rigorously tackling the escalating organized crime (particularly money laundering and racketeering).

In June 2014 it was reported that the FLNC had announced that it was to begin demilitarization and that it would end its clandestine activities.

In December 2014 the Corsican Assembly approved a change in status for Corsica to a Collectivité Territoriale Unique (Single Territorial Collectivity), whereby the regional and departmental councils were to be merged. The change was approved by the National Assembly in February 2015 and was scheduled to take place on 1 January 2018.

Developments in the Overseas Territories

In November 1998, following a lengthy campaign for the independence of the Pacific overseas territory of New Caledonia by indigenous Melanesian (Kanak) separatists, a referendum on self-determination was held in the territory. At the referendum a gradual transfer of powers to local institutions was approved, and the Republican Constitution was amended accordingly. Further enabling legislation was approved by Parliament in February 1999, and certain powers were transferred to local institutions in subsequent years. Notably, the constitutional amendments approved in March 2003 that sought to permit other communities eventually to gain increased autonomy were not to apply to New Caledonia.

Proposals to restructure the administration of France's Caribbean overseas territories, Guadeloupe and Martinique, were rejected in referendums held in July 2003. However, in concurrent referendums held in Saint-Barthélemy and Saint-Martin in December, the electorate voted in favour of seceding from Guadeloupe to assume the status of Collectivités d'Outre-Mer (Overseas Collectivities). The administrative process was completed in February 2007, when it was approved by the Constitutional Council.

In January 2004 the National Assembly approved an organic law and an ordinary law, the combined effect of which was to grant the status of Overseas Collectivity to French Polynesia; this legislation was endorsed, with minor amendments, in February, by the Constitutional Council and came into effect the following month. At a referendum held in the Overseas Collectivity of Mayotte in March 2009, the electorate voted overwhelmingly in favour of becoming an Overseas Department with the same political status as Metropolitan Departments. The result was welcomed by the French Government, but the African Union—AU (see p. 188) and the Government of the Comoros, which claims sovereignty over Mayotte, rejected the referendum. Despite these objections, Mayotte's change of status took effect at the end of March 2011, with Mayotte accorded the status of Single Territorial Collectivity, in which departmental and regional structures are merged. In response to an official request made by the authorities of Mayotte in October, the EU recognized Mayotte as a Région Ultrapériphérique (Outermost Region) of France from 1 January 2014, thereby allowing the territory to draw upon EU funds to aid its economic development.

Following referendums held in French Guiana and Martinique in 2010, from January 2016 the two territories were to have the status of Single Territorial Collectivity, in which departmental and regional structures are merged.

Foreign Affairs
Regional relations

France was a founder member of the European Community, which became the European Union (EU, see p. 271) in 1992 under the Treaty on European Union (the Maastricht Treaty). The French Government was an enthusiastic proponent of efforts to strengthen integration within the EU, most notably the Treaty establishing a Constitution for Europe. Following the rejection of the constitutional treaty at referendums in France and the Netherlands in 2005, in December 2007 a new treaty was signed in Lisbon, Portugal, by the heads of state or of government of the then 27 EU member countries. The so-called Lisbon Treaty was ratified by the French Parliament in February 2008, and entered into force across the EU in December 2009.

In May 1992 France and Germany announced that they would establish a joint defence force, the Eurocorps, which would be based on the Franco-German Brigade (established in 1987) and would provide the foundation for the formation of a European army under the aegis of Western European Union. In January 1993 an agreement was signed between NATO and the French and German Governments, establishing formal links between the Eurocorps and NATO's military structure (although the former was to remain an independent entity). Between 1993 and 1996 Belgium, Spain and Luxembourg also agreed to participate in the Eurocorps, which became operational in November 1995. In 2010 Poland was accepted as the sixth 'framework' nation, with effect from 1 January 2016. The force maintains its headquarters in Strasbourg and currently has the capability of calling on some 60,000 troops (12,000 from France) from the five existing framework nations; the troops are pledged for deployment, when requested, in EU, UN, Organization for Security and Co-operation in Europe (OSCE) or NATO rapid response peacekeeping missions. Eurocorps troops were deployed in Bosnia and Herzegovina and in Kosovo in 2000 and in Afghanistan in 2004–05 and again in 2012. In February 2014 it was announced that troops from the Franco-German Brigade—an integral part of the Eurocorps—were to be dispatched to support the UN peacekeeping mission in Mali. To meet the need to improve Europe's rapid response capabilities, from early 2007 a series of EU 'battlegroups' (each consisting of 1,500–2,500 troops) became operational for deployment—on a rotation basis—to crisis areas. In March 2009 President Nicolas Sarkozy won a vote of confidence in the National Assembly over his decision to bring France back into NATO's integrated military command structure, despite criticism from opponents that such a move would weaken French independence from the USA. Sarkozy insisted that the country would benefit from being able to take part in strategic decision-making and emphasized the fact that France would retain its independent nuclear capability and autonomy in defence decisions. In July 2011 the so-called 'Weimar Triangle' grouping, comprising France, Germany and Poland, agreed to create a 1,700-strong Weimar Combat Group, which was to be fully operational as an EU battlegroup from 2013.

Relations deteriorated between France and Germany following the election of Sarkozy as President in May 2007. The German Government expressed its opposition to several of Sarkozy's foreign affairs initiatives, notably the negotiation of accords on nuclear energy with Libya and French plans to form a so-called Mediterranean Union, comprising the seven EU member states in the Mediterranean region (Cyprus, France, Greece, Italy, Malta, Portugal and Spain) and certain littoral Middle Eastern and North African states. Germany feared that such an organization would undermine the ongoing Euro-Mediterranean Partnership (the Barcelona Process—a framework launched in 1995 for co-operation between all EU member states and 10 other Mediterranean states). However, in March 2008 Sarkozy and the German Chancellor, Angela Merkel, announced that an agreement had been reached, under which all EU member states would be involved in the formation of the new union, which was restyled the Union for the Mediterranean (UfM) and inaugurated in July. The UfM also included the 10 Mediterranean partners in the Barcelona Process, including Turkey, which agreed in March to participate, following reassurances from France that the new grouping would not, as originally envisaged under Sarkozy's plans for a Mediterranean Union, function as an alternative to Turkey's membership of the EU.

Tensions arose between Sarkozy and Merkel in May 2010, at an emergency summit of leaders of eurozone member states in Brussels, over the proposed establishment of the European Financial Stability Facility (EFSF), a temporary fund to support member countries suffering severe financial difficulties with the aim of preserving the stability of the currency. Sarkozy reportedly threatened to withdraw France from economic and monetary union if Germany did not support the €440,000m. fund, before agreement on its creation was finally reached. Relations between the two leaders subsequently improved, however, and they jointly advocated the establishment of a permanent crisis mechanism, the European Stability Mechanism (ESM), on which EU heads of government reached agreement in October. At bilateral talks in December, Sarkozy and Merkel affirmed their commitment to the single currency and also welcomed the stationing of a battalion of German troops in the French town of Illkirch-Graffenstaden, near Strasbourg, the first time German troops had been based in France since the Second World War. In December 2011, prior to a summit meeting of EU heads of state and of government, Sarkozy and Merkel jointly proposed a series of measures aimed at strengthening economic and fiscal policy co-ordination and surveillance within the eurozone, including a commitment to balanced budgets and automatically triggered sanctions for any country recording a fiscal deficit exceeding 3% of gross domestic product. Amid mounting concern regarding the sovereign debt crisis in the eurozone, the majority of EU member states agreed, in principle, to the proposals at the summit meeting, with the exception of the United Kingdom, which vetoed their incorporation into an existing treaty owing to its opposition to a tax on financial transactions. In March 2012 the heads of state and of government of 25 of the then 27 EU member states signed the so-called 'fiscal compact' (the Treaty on Stability, Co-ordination and Governance in the Economic and Monetary Union), with the Czech Republic joining the UK in withholding its assent; the compact came into force on 1 January 2013 (having been ratified by more than the 12 eurozone member countries required for the compact to take effect).

Despite having openly supported Sarkozy in the 2012 presidential election, Chancellor Merkel pledged to work with the new French President, François Hollande, in attempting to resolve the eurozone economic crisis. However, the two leaders held rather different opinions as to the optimum mode of approach: Hollande stressed that he wished to focus on stimulating new growth through fresh expenditure and job creation, while Merkel insisted that emphasis should continue to be placed on fiscal austerity and debt reduction (as laid out in the fiscal compact). In the latter half of the year, however, Hollande was criticized for apparently abandoning his electoral promise to seek a renegotiation of the fiscal compact.

A dispute with Italy arose in April 2011 after the Italian Government granted temporary residence permits to some 20,000 recent immigrants (mostly Tunisians fleeing the civil unrest in their home country), thereby allowing them to travel freely within the EU. Large numbers of Tunisian migrants tried to cross the border into France in the preceding weeks, many of whom were returned by the French authorities. Italy contended that this denial of entry was in breach of the EU's Schengen Agreement on internal borders. (The European Commission later stated that France had acted within its rights in turning back the migrants.) In September the French, German and Spanish ministers responsible for home affairs rejected as inadequate the European Commission's proposals to extend the existing safeguard mechanism to Schengen area procedures, which allowed extraordinary national border controls to be imposed for a limited time in response to exceptional circumstances (involving terrorist, safety or security threats); the ministers objected to a five-day limit on the restoration of border controls, after which time the authorization of the Commission would be required. Despite the opposition of the Commission and the European Parliament, in June 2012 the home affairs ministers of the EU member states drew up a draft proposal to introduce an emergency mechanism whereby internal border controls could be unilaterally reimposed for up to two years by an individual state if another member state did not reliably control its border. Also included in the proposed amendments to the Schengen Agreement was a significant expansion of the grounds on which the closure of intra-European borders could be justified. These proposals were prompted by the notable increase in uncontrolled refugee movements in southern Europe as a result of the 'Arab Spring' and the ongoing economic crisis. The European Parliament approved a compromise package of amendments to the Schengen Agreement in June 2013, but stressed that the reimposition of border controls should be used only as a last resort.

Other external relations

France has been active in promoting the establishment of regional peacekeeping forces in Africa. In the early 1990s French troops were dispatched to Rwanda to train government forces and to supply military equipment, following the outbreak of armed conflict between the Government and the opposition Front Patriotique Rwandais. In April 1994 French troops re-entered Rwanda to establish a 'safe humanitarian zone' for refugees fleeing the civil war. Evidence emerged in early 1998 that appeared to support allegations that France had sold arms to Rwanda during the massacres in 1994 (after the imposition of a UN embargo on the delivery of military equipment to any party in the conflict). The Rwandan Government rejected the findings of a commission of inquiry, subsequently established to investigate the affair, which effectively exonerated France. Bilateral relations further deteriorated following the decision in November 2006 by a French magistrate to issue arrest warrants for nine senior Rwandan military and government officials on suspicion of involvement in the killing in 1994 of the former Rwandan President, Juvénal Habyarimana. The magistrate also alleged that the incumbent Rwandan President, Paul Kagame, had ordered the missile attack in which Habyarimana was killed (which had been the catalyst for the massacres); however, under French law, as a head of state, Kagame was immune from prosecution. The Rwandan Government, which denied the allegations, subsequently severed relations with France. Despite a further deterioration in relations occasioned by the publication by the Rwandan Government in August 2008 of a report alleging the involvement of several senior French military and political figures (among them, Mitterrand and de Villepin) in the 1994 massacres, full diplomatic relations were restored in November 2009. In February 2010 Sarkozy became the first French President to visit Rwanda since 1984; during his visit he admitted that France and the international community had made 'mistakes' in their failure to prevent the massacres, but did not issue a formal apology. In March 2010 Agathe Habyarimana, the widow of the former President, who was the subject of an extradition request by Rwandan prosecutors for her alleged role in the genocide, was arrested at her home near Paris; however, in September 2011 a Parisian court rejected the request for her extradition. Also in September 2011, Kagame visited France in an attempt to strengthen bilateral relations, holding talks with Sarkozy. Meanwhile, in December 2010 a French judge, Marc Trévidic, placed six senior Rwandan military officials—including the Minister of Defence and the Chief of Defence Staff—under judicial investigation in connection with the killing of Juvénal Habyarimana after questioning them in Burundi for several days (with the agreement of the Rwandan authorities); the warrants for their arrest that were issued in 2006 were subsequently revoked. In January 2012 Trévidic announced that a team of technical experts charged with re-examining the attack in which Habyarimana was killed had concluded that the evidence indicated that the missiles involved could not have been fired from a base occupied by forces loyal to Kagame; however, by the end of 2014 the investigation under Trévidic appeared to have reached no clear conclusion. In a significant development in the quest for justice, in February 2014 the trial opened in Paris of a former Rwanda army and intelligence chief, Pascal Simbikangwa, on charges of complicity in the 1994 genocide; Simbikangwa had been arrested by the French authorities in 2008 while living under an alias on the island of Mayotte. Simbikangwa was found guilty in March 2014 and sentenced to 25 years' imprisonment.

From late 2002 more than 3,000 French troops were dispatched to Côte d'Ivoire to assist the 550 French troops already based there (Opération Licorne), initially to protect French citizens resident in the country from civil unrest and subsequently to co-operate with the UN Operation in Côte d'Ivoire (UNOCI, see p. 92) in monitoring a ceasefire between Ivorian government troops and rebel forces in the north of the country. Following the recommencement of military operations by Ivorian government forces against the rebel-controlled north, nine French troops were killed during an air strike in November 2004.

The French military, acting on the direct orders of President Jacques Chirac, responded by disabling the Ivorian air force on the ground. France's perceived intervention in the conflict provoked riots in the principal city, Abidjan, and elsewhere in the country, and numerous attacks were carried out against French civilians and targets. French troops, which had been boosted by further reinforcements, entered Abidjan to secure the international airport and protect French and other foreign citizens, airlifting an estimated 9,000 people out of the city. (The French Government subsequently admitted that its troops had killed some 20 Ivorian civilians during clashes with rioters; the Ivorian authorities claimed the number was significantly higher.) In December 2010 the French Government advised the 15,000 French nationals in Côte d'Ivoire to leave the country temporarily, amid security concerns following a disputed presidential election in the previous month. In April 2011 French troops stationed in the country (which now numbered some 1,600) assisted forces loyal to Alassane Ouattara, the winner of the presidential election, to oust outgoing President Laurent Gbagbo, who had refused to cede office. President Nicolas Sarkozy attended Ouattara's formal inauguration as Ivorian President in May. Sarkozy and Ouattara signed a joint security agreement in January 2012, during a state visit by the Ivorian President to France. In May 2014 the French Minister of Defence visited Côte d'Ivoire, where he announced that the number of French troops deployed to the country was to be increased from 500 to 800, with effect from 1 January 2015, at which time Opération Licorne was to be restructured as a logistical hub and advance operational military presence for a new French mechanism mandated to combat terrorism in the Sahel region. Legislation governing future defence co-operation between Côte d'Ivoire and France was approved by President Ouattara in July 2014.

In January 2013 some 4,000 French troops were dispatched to Mali, in response to a request by the Malian interim President, Dioncounda Traoré, to help the government troops launch a counter-offensive against Islamist forces that had seized control of much of northern Mali and were advancing south towards the capital, Bamako. By the end of the month the air strikes conducted by the French military (which were unanimously backed by the UN Security Council) had proved effective and most of the major towns that had been captured by the jihadists (including Tombouctou and Gao) had been retaken. In early February President Hollande visited Tombouctou, where he pledged that French troops would remain in Mali as long as required and would not leave until they had handed over operations to the UN-supported, African-led International Support Mission to Mali (AFISMA), which was under the command of the Economic Community of West African States (ECOWAS, see p. 258). A phased withdrawal of French troops from Mali commenced in April, although the French Government announced that some 1,000 troops would remain in the country indefinitely to counter the ongoing threat from Islamist militants. Responsibility for security in Mali was transferred to a new UN peacekeeping force—the UN Multidimensional Integrated Stabilization Mission in Mali (MINUSMA)—in July.

Following an escalation in communal violence in the Central African Republic (CAR), in November 2013 the French Government pledged to dispatch additional troops to assist the AU peacekeeping force operating there in a bid to restore order; around 400 French troops were already stationed in the country's capital, Bangui. The first French reinforcements arrived in the CAR in early December; by February 2014, amid escalating violence, a total of about 2,000 French troops were stationed in the country. At the request of the CAR Government, the French troops were expected to remain in the country until after elections scheduled to be held in mid-2015. Meanwhile, following the passage of a UN resolution in early December 2013, the AU peacekeeping mission transferred responsibility for operations to the newly established African-led International Support Mission to the Central African Republic (Mission Internationale de Soutien à la Centrafrique—MISCA).

France's relations with the USA have frequently been characterized by a desire to establish French independence of action, particularly with regard to military concerns and international relations. In the aftermath of the terrorist attacks in the USA attributed to the militant Islamist al-Qa'ida organization, on 11 September 2001, France offered full military and logistical support to the US authorities in their campaign against al-Qa'ida. However, France criticized several aspects of the foreign policy of the Administration of US President George W. Bush.

Although France supported UN Security Council Resolution 1441 (presented by the USA and the UK) in November 2002, which demanded the expedited admittance of UN weapons inspectors to Iraq, it opposed any UN Security Council resolution authorizing any automatic resort to force against Iraq, and was a prominent opponent of the US-led military action that commenced in March 2003. However, following the conclusion of large-scale hostilities in Iraq, France gave full support to UN Security Council Resolution 1483, approved in May, which recognized the Coalition Provisional Authority as the legal occupying power in Iraq.

The election of Sarkozy as President in May 2007 precipitated a significant improvement in relations between France and the USA. Following US pleas for members of NATO to increase the deployment of forces in Afghanistan, by mid-2010 Sarkozy had increased France's contribution to the International Security Force (ISAF) in that country to 4,000 troops (the fifth largest contingent after the USA, the UK, Germany and Italy). A phased withdrawal of French troops from Afghanistan commenced in October 2011, as part of NATO's plan to end its combat mission there by the end of 2014. Following the killing of four French soldiers by a member of the Afghan National Army in January 2012, President Sarkozy announced that France would complete its withdrawal of combat troops from Afghanistan by the end of 2013, a year ahead of the NATO deadline. However, in fulfilment of one of his electoral pledges, the new French President, François Hollande, brought the completion date of the withdrawal forward to the end of 2012 (while promising to increase non-military aid to Afghanistan). In early 2013 around 1,500 non-combat, logistical French troops remained in Afghanistan, some 500 of whom were involved in the training of the Afghan military; this final group of French military personnel left Afghanistan at the end of 2014. In February 2014 Hollande undertook a state visit to the USA, during which he held discussions with US President Barack Obama on a number of issues including Iran, the global economic recovery and measures to combat climate change.

One of the priorities of French foreign policy under the presidency of Sarkozy was to secure an increased role for France in the Middle East. In early 2012 France was a strong proponent of enforcing stricter sanctions against Iran, amid ongoing concerns regarding its nuclear enrichment programme; in July the EU imposed an embargo on Iranian petroleum exports and a freeze on the assets of the Iranian central bank in the EU. However, following a landmark interim agreement on the Iranian nuclear programme reached between Iran and the so-called P5+1 (the five permanent members of the UN Security Council—including France—and Germany) in Geneva in November 2013, the EU eased some of its sanctions against Iran in January 2014. However, despite the conduct of further negotiations throughout the year, by early 2015 no comprehensive agreement had yet been reached between Iran and the P5+1.

During a visit to the Persian (Arabian) Gulf area in January 2008, Sarkozy signed an agreement with the United Arab Emirates (UAE), under which France was to assist the development of a programme to produce nuclear energy in that country. A permanent French military base in Abu Dhabi was officially inaugurated by Sarkozy in May 2009.

Initiatives by President Sarkozy to establish closer relations with Libya provoked widespread criticism. In July 2007 Sarkozy travelled to Libya for an official state visit, during which he signed an agreement on defence co-operation and a memorandum of understanding on the development of civil nuclear technology in Libya. During a state visit to France in December by the Libyan leader, Col Muammar al-Qaddafi, several bilateral agreements were signed, including, most controversially, contracts for the sale of military equipment to Libya and a further agreement on nuclear energy.

The French Government was criticized for its slow response to large-scale pro-democracy demonstrations in Tunisia that eventually led to the flight from that country of its President, Zine al-Abidine Ben Ali, in January 2011. Criticism was particularly focused on the Minister of State, Minister of Foreign and European Affairs, Michèle Alliot-Marie, who had responded to the anti-Government demonstrations by offering French assistance in training the regime's internal security forces; Alliot-Marie resigned in February. During a visit to Tunis by President Hollande in July 2013, the French leader pledged €500m. to support Tunisia's democratic transition. In contrast to its initial response to the situation in Tunisia, France was swift to show its support for the popular movement against Qaddafi's regime in Libya that emerged in mid-February 2011. As the situation in Libya descended into civil war, on 10 March France became the first country to recognize the National Transitional Council, based in the rebel-held city of Benghazi, as the legitimate representative of the Libyan people. Later in March France led international efforts to secure a UN Security Council resolution authorizing an air exclusion zone over Libya. Following the adoption on 17 March of Resolution 1973, which permitted UN member states to take 'all necessary measures' (short of military occupation) to protect civilians in Libya, French and British air and naval forces played a particularly prominent role in the international coalition against Qaddafi's forces, which came under NATO command at the end of March. France also supplied arms to rebel forces, despite concerns that this could be regarded as a breach of Resolution 1973. After Qaddafi and his forces had been ejected from the Libyan capital, Tripoli, in August, Sarkozy, together with British Prime Minister David Cameron, visited the city in September. The NATO operation in Libya ended in October, following the capture by opposition forces of the last remaining government-controlled city and the death of Qaddafi at the hands of the rebels.

In April 2011 Sarkozy was one of several foreign leaders to urge the Syrian authorities to halt the violent suppression of anti-Government protests that had commenced in mid-March. In August, by which time it was estimated that more than 2,000 people had been killed since the uprising began, Sarkozy called for the Syrian President, Bashar al-Assad, to relinquish office. France was also a strong advocate of exerting greater international pressure on Assad's administration to end the violence in Syria, supporting two draft UN Security Council resolutions condemning government repression in that country in October 2011 and February 2012; however, the resolutions were vetoed by both the People's Republic of China and Russia. In March 2013, by which time some 70,000 people had been killed in the Syrian conflict, President Hollande urged the EU to lift its full arms embargo on Syria so that it could supply arms to the rebel forces in their struggle against Assad's regime; most parts of the embargo were lifted in June. In August 2014 Hollande publicly confirmed in an interview with the French daily newspaper *Le Monde* that France had directly supplied the Syrian rebels with arms earlier in the year.

In response to a resurgence in sectarian violence in Iraq, largely led by the militant group the Islamic State in Iraq (which from 2013 was widely referred to as the Islamic State in Iraq and the Levant—ISIL—following the group's involvement with extremist Sunni groups in Syria seeking to topple the regime of President Assad, and subsequently renamed Islamic State), in November 2013 France offered to provide the beleaguered country with arms, training and intelligence co-operation. The considerable territorial gains made by ISIL military operations in Iraq and Syria during the first half of 2014 and the growing incidence of atrocities allegedly committed by members of the group (including the widely broadcast beheadings of US and British aid workers and journalists) prompted the USA to launch air strikes against the militants in these two countries in August. In the following month France became the first country directly to support this US action when President Hollande authorized air strikes by the French air force on ISIL targets in Iraq (although not in Syria). In apparent retaliation for the French military intervention in Iraq, an extremist militant group in Algeria with reported links to ISIL abducted and subsequently beheaded a French tourist at the end of September. It was reported in February 2015 that a French aircraft carrier, *Charles de Gaulle*, was being deployed in the Persian (Arabian) Gulf as part of US-led operations against ISIL in Iraq.

France's relations with Turkey were severely strained in 2011 by the introduction to the French Parliament of draft legislation outlawing the denial of killings deemed by French law to constitute genocide, including the massacre of Armenians under the Ottoman Empire during the First World War, which Parliament had voted to recognize as genocide in 2001. President Sarkozy, who supported the proposed law, insisted that it applied to all acts of genocide and was not aimed at any state in particular. Following the bill's approval by the National Assembly in December 2011, the Turkish Prime Minister recalled the Turkish ambassador to France (which is home to an estimated 500,000 ethnic Armenians) and suspended bilateral political and military co-operation. The legislation was approved by the Senate in January 2012, but was invalidated the following month when the Constitutional Council ruled that it was unconstitutional on the grounds that it infringed on freedom of expression.

CONSTITUTION AND GOVERNMENT

The Constitution of the Fifth Republic was promulgated in 1958 following its approval at a referendum. Under its terms, legislative power is held by the bicameral Parlement (Parliament), comprising a Sénat (Senate) and an Assemblée Nationale (National Assembly). Members of the Senate are elected by an electoral college (326 senators represent departments in Metropolitan France and the Overseas Departments, 10 represent Overseas Territories and 12 represent French nationals abroad). A law approved by Parliament in July 2003 introduced a number of reforms to senatorial elections; henceforth, senators were to be elected for a term of six years, with one-half of the seats renewable every three years (compared with a term of nine years and one-third of the seats renewable every three years previously). With effect from 2011, the number of senators was increased to 348, and the minimum age for eligible candidates to the Senate was reduced from 35 to 30 years. (The first stage of reform, whereby the number of senators increased from 321 to 331, took place at the partial senatorial elections held in September 2004; this number was subsequently increased to 343 at the partial senatorial elections held in September 2008.) The National Assembly has 577 members, with 555 for metropolitan France and 22 for the overseas possessions. Members of the National Assembly are elected by universal adult suffrage, under a single-member constituency system of direct election, using a second ballot if the first ballot failed to produce an absolute majority for any one candidate. The term of the National Assembly is five years, subject to dissolution. Executive power is held by the President. Since 1962 the President has been directly elected by popular vote (using two ballots if necessary). A constitutional amendment passed in October 2000 shortened the term of office from seven to five years, and a further amendment enacted in July 2008 limited the President to a maximum of two consecutive terms in office. The President appoints a Council of Ministers, headed by the Prime Minister, which administers the country and is responsible to Parliament.

Metropolitan France comprises 22 administrative regions containing 96 departments. In December 2014 the National Assembly approved legislation to reduce the number of metropolitan regions to 13 through a series of mergers, with effect from 1 January 2016. Under the decentralization law of March 1982, administrative and financial power in metropolitan France was transferred from the préfets, who became Commissaires de la République, to locally elected Conseils Généraux (which were renamed Conseils Départementaux—departmental assemblies—with effect from March 2015) and Conseils Régionaux (regional assemblies). Corsica has its own directly elected legislative assembly, the Assemblée de Corse. The 12 overseas possessions comprise five Régions et Départements d'Outre Mer (Overseas Regions and Departments—French Guiana, Guadeloupe, Martinique, Mayotte and Réunion); five Collectivités d'Outre Mer (Overseas Collectivities—French Polynesia, Saint-Barthélemy, Saint-Martin, Saint Pierre and Miquelon and the Wallis and Futuna Islands); and two other territories (the French Southern and Antarctic Territories, and New Caledonia—which has a unique status as a *sui generis* Collectivity); all of which are integral parts of the French Republic.

REGIONAL AND INTERNATIONAL CO-OPERATION

France was a founder member of the European Community, now the European Union (EU, see p. 271), and uses the single currency, the euro. France is also a member of the Council of Europe (see p. 250), which is based in Strasbourg, and the Organization for Security and Co-operation in Europe (OSCE, see p. 385). France is the host nation for the European Space Agency (see p. 269).

France was a founder member of the UN in 1945, and is a permanent member of the Security Council. As a contracting party to the General Agreement on Tariffs and Trade, France joined the World Trade Organization (WTO, see p. 431) on its establishment in 1995. France participates in the Group of Seven major industrialized nations (G7, see p. 460) and the Group of 20 major industrialized and systemically important emerging market nations (G20, see p. 451). France is also a member of the North Atlantic Treaty Organization (NATO, see p. 367) and the Organisation for Economic Co-operation and Development (OECD, see p. 377), which has its headquarters in Paris. It presides over the Franc Zone (see p. 326).

ECONOMIC AFFAIRS

In 2013, according to estimates by the World Bank, France's gross national income (GNI), measured at average 2011–13 prices, was US $2,789,619m., equivalent to $42,250 per head (or $37,580 on an international purchasing-power parity basis). During 2004–13, it was estimated, the population grew by an average of 0.6% per year, while gross domestic product (GDP) per head increased, in real terms, by an average of 0.2% per year. Overall GDP increased, in real terms, at an average rate of 0.8% per year in 2004–13; real GDP rose by 0.3% in 2013, measured both at constant prices and according to chain-linking methodologies.

In 2013 agriculture (including forestry and fishing) contributed 1.7% of GDP and engaged 3.1% of the economically active population. The principal crops are wheat, sugar beet, maize and barley. Livestock, dairy products and wine are also important. According to World Bank figures, agricultural GDP decreased, in real terms, by an average of 0.5% per year in 2004–13. According to chain-linking methodologies, the sector's GDP declined by 8.2% in 2012 and by 1.4% in 2013.

Industry (including mining, manufacturing, construction and power) provided 19.8% of GDP and employed 20.2% of the working population in 2013. Industrial GDP decreased, in real terms, by an average of 0.6% per year during 2004–13, according to World Bank figures.

In 2013 mining and quarrying, along with utilities, contributed 2.5% of GDP and employed 0.1% of the working population. Petroleum and natural gas are extracted and metallic minerals, including iron ore, copper and zinc, are mined. The production of coal, an industry which used to dominate the sector, came to an end in 2004 with the closure of France's last operating coal mine. According to chain-linking methodologies, the mining and quarrying sector declined by 2.1% in 2013.

Manufacturing provided 11.3% of GDP and employed 11.9% of the working population in 2013. Manufacturing GDP decreased, in real terms, at an average annual rate of 1.5% in 2003–09, according to World Bank figures. Overall sectoral GDP declined by 0.8% in 2013.

In 2013 the construction sector provided 6.0% of GDP and employed 6.6% of the working population. According to chain-linking methodologies, sectoral GDP declined by 2.1% in 2013.

France has only limited fossil fuel resources and in the early 2000s was the world's largest producer of nuclear power per head of population. In 2012 nuclear power provided 76.6% of total electricity production and hydroelectric power 10.2%. In that year France had 58 nuclear power stations, many of which would need to be replaced in around 2020. Construction work on a new nuclear reactor, the European Pressurized Reactor (EPR), began at Flamanville in Normandy in 2007 and the much delayed reactor was scheduled to be operational in 2017. Construction of a second EPR, at Penly in Normandy, which was due to begin in 2012, was shelved indefinitely. The Government introduced legislation in mid-2014, which in early 2015 was due to be debated in the Senate, to cap at current levels (63.2 GW) installed nuclear capacity, to reduce the share of nuclear power in the generation of energy in France from 75% to 50% by 2025 and to increase the share of renewable energy to 32% of final energy consumption by 2030. Imports of energy products comprised 17.1% of the value of total merchandise imports in 2013; in the early 2000s the major sources of petroleum imported to France were Saudi Arabia and Norway.

Services accounted for 78.5% of GDP and employed 76.7% of the working population in 2013. France is consistently the country with the largest number of tourist visitors in the world; there were an estimated 84.7m. tourist arrivals in 2013 and tourism receipts in that year totalled US $56,557m., according to figures by the World Tourism Organization. The GDP of the services sector increased, in real terms, at an average rate of 1.2% per year in 2004–13, according to World Bank figures. According to chain-linking methodologies, GDP for market services rose by 0.4% in 2013, while GDP for non-market services rose by 1.2% in that year.

In 2013 France recorded a visible merchandise trade deficit of US $56,450m., and there was a deficit of $32,220m. on the current account of the balance of payments. In 2013 the principal source of imports (providing 17.1% of the total) was Germany; other major sources were the People's Republic of China, Belgium, Italy, the USA and Spain. Germany was also the principal market for exports in that year (accounting for 16.4% of the total); other major trading partners were Belgium, Italy, the United Kingdom, Spain and the USA. The European Union (EU) as a whole provided 57.3% of imports in 2012 and took 59.2% of exports. The principal exports in 2013 were machinery and mechanical appliances, and electrical equipment, vehicles, aircraft, vessels and associated transport equipment, chemicals and related products, aircraft and spacecraft, iron and steel, prepared foodstuffs, beverages, spirits, vinegar, tobacco, and articles thereof, pharmaceutical products, and plastics and rubber articles. The principal imports in that year were machinery and mechanical appliances, and electrical equipment, mineral products, vehicles, aircraft, vessels and associated transport equipment, chemicals and related products, and iron and steel, other base metals and articles of base metal.

The general government deficit for 2013 was €89,500m., equivalent to 4.2% of GDP. France's general government gross debt was €1,939,700m. in 2013, equivalent to 91.8% of GDP. The average annual rate of inflation in 2004–13 was 1.6%. Consumer prices increased by 0.9% in 2013, according to official figures. The rate of unemployment averaged 9.8% in 2013.

The French economy, which is currently the second largest in Europe after Germany, was less severely affected than most advanced economies by the global financial crisis and downturn that began in late 2008, partly owing to the country's high levels of government spending and generous social security provisions, which helped to maintain consumer demand. GDP contracted by 2.7% in 2009 (compared with 4.3% in the eurozone as a whole), before returning to positive growth, of 1.5% in 2010 and 2.0% in 2011. However, the unemployment rate remained high in 2011, particularly among youth. Moreover, stimulus measures introduced to counter the economic crisis had exacerbated the fiscal deficit, which amounted to 7.1% of GDP in 2010. Following the introduction of austerity measures by the Government of Nicolas Sarkozy, the deficit decreased to 5.2% of GDP in 2011; this was, nevertheless, still considerably higher than the EU-mandated limit of 3%. The new Socialist Government of François Hollande, which came to power in mid-2012, vowed to focus on growth rather than austerity and favoured tax increases (particularly for those on high incomes) rather than expenditure cuts. In 2012 government gross debt rose to more than 90% of GDP and the fiscal deficit remained above 3% of GDP (at 4.9%). Furthermore, unemployment continued to grow (exceeding 3m. in September 2012, for the first time since 1999), partly as a result of a downturn in the manufacturing sector. According to official figures, overall GDP remained constant in 2012 and increased by only 0.3% in 2013. In November 2012, in an apparent shift in policy direction, the Government announced that it planned to implement some cuts in public spending in order to provide funds for the country's ailing corporate sector (in an attempt to make it more competitive). In 2013 government gross debt increased to 91.8% of GDP and was forecast to rise to a record 94.3%, according to IMF projections, in 2014. However, the fiscal deficit narrowed further in 2013, to 4.2% of GDP; in May the European Commission agreed to defer to 2015 the deadline for France to reach or go below the 3% threshold. Unemployment continued to rise in 2013, reaching more than 3.3m. in December. With the French economy showing little sign of any real recovery, in November the credit rating agency Standard & Poor's downgraded the country's credit rating from AA+ to AA. Hollande's imposition of a controversial 75% rate of tax on annual incomes exceeding €1m. was in force for two years (2013–14); the revenue from the tax proved relatively meagre and critics claimed that it had damaged the country's business reputation and competitiveness. In general, the economy remained weak throughout 2014, with unemployment reaching a record high of 3.49m. in November. In that month the OECD forecast that, despite stronger external demand, continuing resilience in private consumption and some improvements in investment and profitability, GDP would expand by only 0.4% over the year as a whole. The Government announced a Stability Programme in April which aimed further to reduce the fiscal deficit largely through further cuts in public spending, while at the same time encouraging investment through regulatory and labour market reform and reductions in corporate taxes. However, in the event, the fiscal deficit increased to an estimated 4.4% of GDP in 2014 (against a target of 3.8%). The deficit for 2015 was forecast to decrease to 4.1% of GDP in 2015 and to 2.7% in 2017. Further economic reforms aimed at deregulating sections of the economy were forced through the National Assembly in February 2015 (see *Domestic Political Affairs*). In that month the European Commission agreed to defer France's deadline to reach or go below the 3% threshold for a further two years, to 2017. In late 2014 the IMF predicted that in 2015 the UK would overtake France as the second largest economy in Europe.

PUBLIC HOLIDAYS

2016: 1 January (New Year's Day), 28 March (Easter Monday), 1 May (Labour Day), 5 May (Ascension Day), 8 May (Liberation Day), 16 May (Whit Monday), 14 July (National Day, Fall of the Bastille), 15 August (Assumption), 1 November (All Saints' Day), 11 November (Armistice Day), 25 December (Christmas Day).

Statistical Survey

Source (unless otherwise stated): Institut national de la statistique et des études économiques, 18 blvd Adolphe Pinard, 75675 Paris Cedex 14; tel. 1-41-17-50-50; internet www.insee.fr.

Note: Unless otherwise indicated, figures in this survey refer to metropolitan France, excluding the Overseas Possessions.

Area and Population

AREA, POPULATION AND DENSITY

Area (sq km)	543,965*
Population (census results)†	
8 March 1999	58,518,395
1 January 2011‡	63,070,344
Population (official estimates at 1 January)§	
2012	63,409,191
2013	63,659,608
2014	63,928,608
Density (per sq km) at 1 January 2014	117.5

* 210,026 sq miles.

† Excluding professional soldiers and military personnel outside the country with no personal residence in France.

‡ New annual census methodology. Data refer to median figures based on the collection of raw data over a five-year period (2009–13).

§ Provisional figures.

POPULATION BY AGE AND SEX
(official estimates at 1 January 2014, provisional)

	Males	Females	Total
0–14 years	6,011,617	5,739,756	11,751,373
15–64 years	20,066,243	20,492,031	40,558,274
65 years and over	4,913,422	6,705,539	11,618,961
Total	**30,991,282**	**32,937,326**	**63,928,608**

POPULATION BY NATIONALITY

(numbers resident in France at 1999 census, revised figures)

Country of citizenship	Population	%
France	55,257,502	94.42
Portugal	553,663	0.95
Morocco	504,096	0.86
Algeria	477,482	0.82
Turkey	208,049	0.36
Italy	201,670	0.34
Spain	161,762	0.28
Tunisia	154,356	0.26
Germany	78,381	0.31
Belgium	66,666	0.11
Yugoslavia*	50,543	0.09
Poland	33,758	0.06
Others	772,760	1.32
Total	58,520,688	100.00

* The successor states of the former Socialist Federal Republic of Yugoslavia, comprising Bosnia and Herzegovina, Croatia, the former Yugoslav republic of Macedonia, Slovenia and the Federal Republic of Yugoslavia (now Montenegro and Serbia).

REGIONS

(official population estimates at 1 January 2013, provisional)

	Area (sq km)	Population	Density (per sq km)	Principal city
Alsace	8,280.2	1,861,020	224.8	Strasbourg
Aquitaine	41,308.4	3,303,392	80.0	Bordeaux
Auvergne	26,012.9	1,355,630	52.1	Clermont-Ferrand
Basse-Normandie	17,589.3	1,479,242	84.1	Caen
Bourgogne (Burgundy)	31,582.0	1,643,931	52.1	Dijon
Bretagne (Brittany)	27,207.9	3,259,659	119.8	Rennes
Centre	39,150.9	2,572,931	65.7	Orléans
Champagne–Ardenne	25,605.8	1,333,497	52.1	Châlons-en-Champagne
Corse (Corsica)	8,679.8	322,120	37.1	Ajaccio
Franche-Comté	16,202.3	1,177,906	72.7	Besançon
Haute-Normandie	12,317.4	1,848,102	150.0	Rouen
Ile-de-France	12,012.3	11,978,363	997.2	Paris
Languedoc-Roussillon	27,375.8	2,727,286	99.6	Montpellier
Limousin	16,942.3	741,047	43.7	Limoges
Lorraine	23,547.4	2,350,657	99.8	Nancy
Midi-Pyrénées	45,347.9	2,946,507	65.0	Toulouse
Nord-Pas-de-Calais	12,414.1	4,052,156	326.4	Lille
Pays de la Loire	32,081.8	3,658,351	114.0	Nantes
Picardie (Picardy)	19,399.5	1,924,737	99.2	Amiens
Poitou-Charentes	25,809.5	1,792,159	69.4	Poitiers
Provence-Alpes-Côte d'Azur	31,399.6	4,937,445	157.2	Marseille
Rhône-Alpes	43,698.2	6,393,470	146.3	Lyon
Total	543,965.4	63,659,608	117.0	—

PRINCIPAL TOWNS*

(incl. suburbs, estimated population at 1 January 2007)

Paris (capital)	10,197,678	Metz	322,459
Marseille–Aix-en-Provence	1,433,462	Montpellier	320,760
Lyon	1,422,331	Tours	307,146
Lille	1,014,586	Saint-Etienne	283,996
Nice	946,630	Rennes	281,734
Toulouse	858,233	Avignon	275,613
Bordeaux	809,224	Orléans	268,470
Nantes	569,961	Clermont-Ferrand	261,239
Toulon	546,801	Béthune	258,967
Douai-Lens	512,029	Mulhouse	239,859
Strasbourg	440,704	Dijon	237,925
Grenoble	427,739	Le Havre	235,818
Rouen	389,876	Angers	226,809
Valenciennes	355,709	Reims	211,966
Nancy	330,232	Brest	205,195

* Data refer to contiguous urban agglomerations (unités urbaines).

Mid-2014 ('000, incl. suburbs, UN estimate): Paris 10,764 (Source: UN, *World Urbanization Prospects: The 2014 Revision*).

BIRTHS, MARRIAGES AND DEATHS*

	Registered live births		Registered marriages		Registered deaths	
	Number	Rate (per 1,000)	Number	Rate (per 1,000)	Number	Rate (per 1,000)
2006	796,896	13.0	267,260	4.4	516,416	8.4
2007	785,985	12.7	267,194	4.3	521,016	8.4
2008	796,044	12.8	258,739	4.2	532,131	8.6
2009	793,420	12.7	245,151	3.9	538,116	8.6
2010	802,224	12.7	245,334	3.9	540,469	8.6
2011†	792,996	12.5	231,100	3.7	534,795	8.5
2012†	790,290	12.4	239,840	3.8	559,227	8.8
2013†	780,000	12.2	225,000	3.5	561,000	8.8

* Including data for national armed forces outside the country.
† Provisional figures.

Life expectancy (years at birth): 82.6 (males 79.2; females 86.1) in 2012 (Source: World Bank, World Development Indicators database).

ECONOMICALLY ACTIVE POPULATION

(labour force survey, annual averages, '000 persons aged 15 years and over)

	2011	2012	2013
Agriculture, forestry and fishing	750.0	750.4	783.1
Mining and quarrying	23.4	27.5	26.9
Manufacturing	3,201.3	3,130.9	3,034.3
Electricity, gas and water supply	368.4	379.5	404.3
Construction	1,795.8	1,769.4	1,693.2
Wholesale and retail trade; repair of motor vehicles, motorcycles and personal and household goods	3,197.9	3,214.2	3,201.5
Hotels and restaurants	975.9	966.6	941.1
Transport, storage and communications	2,044.6	2,040.0	2,051.8
Financial intermediation	859.6	840.5	842.2
Real estate, renting and business activities (incl. scientific and technical)	3,108.0	3,116.8	3,196.7
Public administration and defence; compulsory social security	2,508.8	2,440.1	2,350.6
Education	1,729.6	1,845.9	1,848.8
Health and social work	3,398.9	3,462.6	3,609.2
Other community, social and personal service activities	1,096.5	1,060.1	870.3
Households with employed persons	598.1	585.0	694.3
Extraterritorial organizations and bodies	28.7	22.8	23.3
Sub-total	25,685.9	25,652.3	25,571.6
Not classifiable by economic activity	92.1	102.0	192.0
Total employed	25,778.0	25,754.3	25,763.5
Unemployed	2,612.1	2,811.2	2,813.1
Total labour force	28,390.1	28,565.5	28,576.6
Males	14,837.9	14,926.6	14,909.0
Females	13,552.2	13,638.9	13,667.7

Note: Totals may not be equal to the sum of components, owing to rounding.

Health and Welfare

KEY INDICATORS

Total fertility rate (children per woman, 2012)	2.0
Under-5 mortality rate (per 1,000 live births, 2012)	4
HIV/AIDS (% of persons aged 15–49, 2011)	0.4
Physicians (per 1,000 head, 2012)	3.2
Hospital beds (per 1,000 head, 2009)	6.9
Health expenditure (2011): US $ per head (PPP)	4,128
Health expenditure (2011): % of GDP	11.6
Health expenditure (2011): public (% of total)	76.8
Total carbon dioxide emissions ('000 metric tons, 2010)	361,272.8
Carbon dioxide emissions per head (metric tons, 2010)	5.6
Human Development Index (2013): ranking	20
Human Development Index (2013): value	0.884

For sources and definitions, see explanatory note on p. vi.

Agriculture

PRINCIPAL CROPS
('000 metric tons)

	2011	2012	2013
Wheat	35,994.0	40,300.8	38,613.9
Rice, paddy	128.3	123.2	82.0
Barley	8,775.0	11,347.0	10,315.9
Maize	15,913.3	15,614.1	15,053.0
Rye	124.4	160.3	143.1
Oats	318.5	400.8	432.3
Sorghum (excl. sorghum for forage and silage)	281.6	239.2	278.8
Buckwheat	91.4	105.0	154.8
Triticale (wheat-rye hybrid)	1,987.3	2,300.5	2,032.0
Potatoes	7,440.2	6,340.8	6,975.0
Sugar beet	38,106.1	33,688.4	33,613.8
Broad beans, horse beans, dry	344.8	273.5	245.5
Peas, dry	670.1	561.5	498.9
Soybeans (soya beans)	122.5	103.9	110.3
Sunflower seed	1,880.7	1,573.0	1,582.4
Rapeseed	5,369.0	5,463.1	4,370.1
Linseed	30.5	23.7	16.1
Cabbages and other brassicas	113.1	108.9	97.1
Artichokes	50.6	41.5	36.4
Lettuce and chicory	314.0	325.6	306.9
Spinach	110.5	99.1	118.7
Tomatoes	597.5	588.7	593.2
Cauliflowers and broccoli	364.6	336.9	337.8
Pumpkins, squash and gourds	123.5	109.0	95.5
Cucumbers and gherkins	134.9	134.1	130.2
Onions and shallots, green	60.7	60.2	63.8
Onions, dry	150.0	132.7	207.7
Beans, green	37.0*	70.7	67.9*
Peas, green	258.5	241.2	229.0
String beans	340.3	334.4	304.5
Carrots and turnips	624.5	542.9	565.3
Maize, green	414.6	366.2	349.8
Mushrooms and truffles	115.7	116.6	104.6
Chicory roots	100.9	116.7	88.3
Cantaloupes and other melons	276.7	293.7	264.9
Apples	1,857.3	1,384.9	1,737.5
Pears	170.8	124.2	148.9
Apricots	155.1	189.7	133.6
Sweet cherries	48.1	30.4	39.3
Peaches and nectarines	301.8	275.3	233.8
Plums and sloes	175.6	199.0	171.0
Strawberries	52.5	55.4	55.8
Grapes	6,641.0	5,384.6	5,518.4
Kiwi fruit	73.5	65.3	56.0
Tobacco, unmanufactured	14.0	12.4	9.7

* FAO estimate.

Aggregate production ('000 metric tons, may include official, semi-official or estimated data): Total cereals 63,953.9 in 2011, 70,981.6 in 2012, 67,518.3 in 2013; Total roots and tubers 7,440.2 in 2011, 6,340.8 in 2012, 6,975.0 in 2013; Total vegetables (incl. melons) 5,494.5 in 2011, 5,283.5 in 2012, 5,235.3 in 2013; Total fruits (excl. melons) 9,573.1 in 2011, 7,800.6 in 2012, 8,183.1 in 2013.

Source: FAO.

LIVESTOCK
('000 head, year ending 30 September)

	2011	2012	2013
Cattle	19,085.6	19,005.6	19,095.8
Pigs	13,975.5	13,759.9	13,487.6
Sheep	7,618	7,462	7,234
Goats	1,381	1,308	1,291
Horses	425	414	408
Asses*	15	15	15
Mules	33	31	31
Chickens	161,284	164,984	167,635
Ducks	26,789	26,297	26,162
Turkeys	23,743	22,452	19,967

* FAO estimates.

Source: FAO.

LIVESTOCK PRODUCTS
('000 metric tons)

	2011	2012	2013
Cattle meat	1,566.5	1,496.9	1,400.4
Sheep meat	115.0	113.4	110.9
Pig meat	2,217.4	2,161.7	2,120.9
Chicken meat	1,086.7	1,094.0	1,120.3
Duck meat	290.9	279.8	276.9
Turkey meat	398.0	387.1	340.3
Cows' milk	24,361.1	23,998.4	23,714.4
Sheep's milk	273.6	271.2	259.1
Goats' milk	655.3	613.7	580.7
Honey	13.8	11.8	11.4
Hen eggs	865.9	853.6*	944.0*
Wool, greasy†	14	14	14

* Unofficial figure.
† FAO estimates.

Source: FAO.

Forestry

ROUNDWOOD REMOVALS
('000 cubic metres, excluding bark)

	2011*	2012	2013
Sawlogs, veneer logs and logs for sleepers	18,035	15,657	15,922
Pulpwood	9,844	8,742	7,880
Other industrial wood	508	546	649
Fuel wood	26,653	26,550†	27,220†
Total	55,041	51,495†	51,671†

* FAO estimates.
† Unofficial figure.

Source: FAO.

SAWNWOOD PRODUCTION
('000 cubic metres, including railway sleepers)

	2011*	2012	2013
Coniferous (softwood)	7,213	6,750	6,544
Broadleaved (hardwood)	1,462	1,318	1,357
Total	8,675	8,068	7,901

* FAO estimates.

Source: FAO.

Fishing

('000 metric tons, live weight)

	2010	2011	2012
Capture*	426.0	448.2	425.7
Saithe (Pollock)	3.3	13.9	12.9
Atlantic herring	4.4	12.9	24.4
European pilchard (Sardine)	26.2	24.1	20.4
Skipjack tuna	35.6	30.9	23.5
Yellowfin tuna	43.4	43.8	42.2
Atlantic mackerel	13.7	16.2	20.9
Blue whiting (Poutassou)	7.9	4.4	0.7
Monkfishes (Angler)	17.3	19.8	20.6
Aquaculture*	224.4	206.9	204.9
Rainbow trout	32.0*	29.5	29.5*
Pacific cupped oyster	95.0*	83.5	82.0*
Blue mussel	61.8	61.0	61.0*
Total catch*	650.4	655.1	630.6

* FAO estimate(s).

Note: Figures exclude aquatic plants ('000 metric tons, all capture): 22.6 in 2010; 44.0 in 2011; 13.9 in 2012. Figures also exclude coral (metric tons): 9.3 in 2010; 10.3 in 2011; 10.3 in 2012 and sponges (metric tons, FAO estimates): 0.2 in 2010–12.

Source: FAO.

Mining

('000 metric tons unless otherwise indicated)

	2010	2011	2012
Crude petroleum ('000 barrels) .	6,606	6,508	5,949
Natural gas (marketed production, million cu m)	1,245	1,132	1,100
Gold (kg)*†	1,500	—	—
Kaolin and kaolinitic clay‡ . .	315	315	315
Salt*	5,867	5,430	5,457
Gypsum and anhydrite (crude) .	3,440	4,231	3,685
Mica*	20	20	20
Talc (crude)*	420	420	420

* Estimates.
† Figures refer to the metal content of ores and concentrates.
‡ Figures refer to marketable production.

Source: US Geological Survey.

Industry

SELECTED PRODUCTS
('000 metric tons unless otherwise indicated)

	2010	2011	2012
Wine*	4,532	5,107	5,286
Chemical wood pulp*	1,073	1,103	1,058
Newsprint*	984	942	878
Liquefied petroleum gas ('000 barrels)†	24,346	24,300	24,300‡
Motor gasoline (petrol—'000 barrels)†	115,596	115,000	115,000†
Jet fuels and kerosene ('000 barrels)†	35,113	35,100	35,000‡
Distillate fuel oil ('000 barrels)† .	224,950	224,900	220,000‡
Residual fuel oil ('000 barrels)†	59,313	59,300	59,000‡
Coke-oven coke	3,151	2,958	n.a.
Pig iron†	10,137	9,698	9,532
Crude steel†	15,414	15,780	15,609
Aluminium (unwrought— primary)†	356	334	349
Lead (unwrought)†	82.0‡	53.9	75.0‡
Zinc (incl. slab and secondary)† .	163.0	164.0	161.0
Electric energy (incl. Monaco, million kWh)	569,156	561,960	n.a.

* Source: FAO.
† Source: US Geological Survey.
‡ Estimate.

2013 ('000 metric tons): Chemical wood pulp 2,181; Newsprint 934.

Source (unless otherwise indicated): UN Industrial Commodities Statistics Database.

Finance

CURRENCY AND EXCHANGE RATES

Monetary Units
100 cent = 1 euro (€).

Sterling and Dollar Equivalents (31 December 2014)
£1 sterling = 1.286 euros;
US $1 = 0.824 euros;
€10 = £7.78 = $12.14.

Average Exchange Rate (euros per US $)
2012   0.7783
2013   0.7532
2014   0.7537

Note: The national currency was formerly the French franc. From the introduction of the euro, with French participation, on 1 January 1999, a fixed exchange rate of €1 = 6.5596 French francs was in operation. Euro notes and coins were introduced on 1 January 2002. The euro and local currency circulated alongside each other until 17 February, after which the euro became the sole legal tender.

GOVERNMENT FINANCE
(general government transactions, € '000 million)

Revenue	2011	2012	2013
Taxes	552.9	580.0	600.8
Taxes on income and inheritance	238.2	256.5	269.5
Taxes on capital	10.3	9.6	10.5
Taxes on production and imports	310.7	319.2	328.2
Social contributions . . .	376.2	387.1	398.9
Other revenue	117.5	116.6	119.0
Total	**1,046.6**	**1,083.7**	**1,118.7**

Expenditure	2011	2012	2013
Compensation of employees . .	263.6	268.6	273.3
Use of goods and services . .	104.2	107.0	110.6
Interest	53.6	53.3	47.7
Subsidies	34.7	36.5	36.4
Grants	394.3	408.2	420.2
Other social benefits . . .	118.5	121.6	125.2
Other expenses	99.2	105.0	105.9
Net acquisition of non-financial assets	83.3	85.2	88.9
Total	**1,151.5**	**1,185.4**	**1,208.2**

INTERNATIONAL RESERVES
(US $ million at 31 December)

	2011	2012	2013
Gold*	123,285	130,291	94,077
IMF special drawing rights .	14,675	14,586	14,145
Reserve position in IMF . . .	7,789	8,474	7,960
Foreign exchange	26,147	30,350	27,414
Other reserve assets	—	821	1,329
Total	**171,896**	**184,522**	**144,925**

* Valued at market-related prices.

Source: IMF, *International Financial Statistics*.

MONEY SUPPLY
(incl. shares, depository corporations, national residency criteria, € million at 31 December)

	2011	2012	2013
Currency issued	168,950	173,530	181,735
Banque de France	91,628	98,826	104,982
Demand deposits	527,854	543,348	569,353
Other deposits	1,234,267	1,276,583	1,303,684
Securities other than shares . .	1,241,945	1,213,706	1,139,602
Money market fund shares . .	348,332	363,743	316,414
Shares and other equity . .	610,750	635,188	596,032
Other items (net)	−644,879	−682,323	−567,606
Total	**3,487,219**	**3,523,775**	**3,539,214**

Source: IMF, *International Financial Statistics*.

COST OF LIVING
(Consumer Price Index; base: 1998 = 100)

	2011	2012	2013
Food (incl. non-alcoholic beverages)	127.7	131.4	132.9
Clothing	103.3	105.9	106.6
Housing, water, gas, electricity, etc.	141.3	146.1	149.8
All items (incl. others) . . .	123.7	126.1	127.2

NATIONAL ACCOUNTS
(€ '000 million at current prices)
Expenditure on the Gross Domestic Product

	2011	2012	2013
Final consumption expenditure	1,634.1	1,657.4	1,679.8
Households	1,106.9	1,117.5	1,126.4
Non-profit institutions serving households	41.0	42.1	43.4
General government	486.1	497.8	509.9
Gross capital formation	478.0	474.8	465.2
Gross fixed capital formation	461.6	469.8	466.9
Changes in inventories	15.7	4.3	−2.4
Acquisitions, less disposals, of valuables	0.7	0.7	0.7
Total domestic expenditure	2,112.0	2,132.2	2,145.0
Exports of goods and services	572.6	587.3	597.8
Less Imports of goods and services	625.3	628.5	629.1
GDP in market prices	2,059.3	2,091.1	2,113.7

Gross Domestic Product by Economic Activity

	2011	2012	2013
Agriculture, forestry and fishing	34.0	34.8	32.1
Industry (incl. energy)	254.1	260.0	262.1
Food products, beverages and tobacco	41.3	43.3	44.3
Mining, energy and water supply	43.7	45.4	47.0
Automobile, electronic and intermediate goods industries	167.2	167.9	168.3
Coke and refined petroleum	1.9	3.4	2.5
Construction	112.7	114.8	113.9
Mainly market services	1,031.8	1,041.9	1,052.7
Trade, transport, hotels and restaurants	328.8	333.5	337.2
Information and communications	94.2	93.1	88.7
Financial activities	79.0	79.2	84.3
Real estate and renting activities	235.8	239.2	242.5
Business services	239.1	240.2	242.3
Other services	55.0	56.7	57.6
Mainly non-market services	416.9	426.9	436.1
Public administration and defence; compulsory social security	150.6	154.2	156.4
Education, health and social work	266.3	272.7	279.7
Gross value added at basic prices	1,849.5	1,878.4	1,896.9
Taxes, less subsidies, on products	209.8	212.7	216.8
GDP in market prices	2,059.3	2,091.1	2,113.7

BALANCE OF PAYMENTS
(US $ '000 million)*

	2011	2012	2013
Exports of goods	592.92	560.47	580.84
Imports of goods	−686.44	−630.77	−637.30
Balance on goods	−93.52	−70.30	−56.45
Exports of services	222.84	236.17	254.96
Imports of services	−191.92	−204.52	−230.72
Balance on goods and services	−62.60	−38.65	−32.22
Primary income received	217.62	209.83	205.34
Primary income paid	−155.26	−157.60	−153.32
Balance on goods, services and primary income	−0.24	13.58	19.81
Secondary income received	33.57	14.63	16.18
Secondary income paid	−82.54	−69.50	−76.22
Current balance	−49.22	−41.29	−40.23

—*continued*	2011	2012	2013
Capital account (net)	0.01	0.71	2.40
Direct investment assets	−62.92	−48.84	0.38
Direct investment liabilities	40.83	30.89	6.48
Portfolio investment assets	228.85	2.25	−86.89
Portfolio investment liabilities	89.20	34.00	180.90
Financial derivatives and employee stock options liabilities	19.56	18.46	22.36
Other investment assets	−118.63	56.12	8.23
Other investment liabilities	−128.12	−60.86	−114.28
Net errors and omissions	−27.94	14.06	18.63
Reserves and related items	−8.38	5.49	−2.01

* Figures refer to transactions of metropolitan France, French Guiana, Guadeloupe, Martinique, Mayotte, Monaco and Réunion with the rest of the world.

Source: IMF, *International Financial Statistics.*

External Trade

PRINCIPAL COMMODITIES
(distribution by HS, US $ million)

Imports*	2011	2012	2013
Prepared foodstuffs; beverages, spirits, vinegar; tobacco and articles thereof	26,746.6	25,821.2	27,477.9
Mineral products	119,332.7	118,901.6	114,033.2
Mineral fuels, oils, distillation products, etc.	114,781.2	114,935.8	110,115.0
Crude petroleum oils	52,125.9	47,566.4	45,627.9
Petroleum oils, not crude	32,993.4	37,159.8	34,791.5
Petroleum gases	23,755.7	24,258.3	24,762.2
Chemicals and related products	81,293.1	79,284.1	78,277.7
Organic chemicals	19,999.4	20,526.3	18,989.9
Pharmaceutical products	26,486.0	26,379.6	26,056.2
Medicament mixtures put in dosage	19,654.6	19,340.6	18,298.5
Plastics, rubber, and articles thereof	35,219.1	32,332.4	33,103.0
Plastics and articles thereof	25,834.7	24,084.4	24,895.6
Textiles and textile articles	31,366.2	28,121.8	29,437.4
Iron and steel, other base metals and articles of base metal	52,707.9	45,056.0	44,470.4
Machinery and mechanical appliances; electrical equipment; parts thereof	137,393.0	127,140.9	129,911.8
Boilers, machinery, etc.	77,464.0	72,693.3	74,490.9
Electrical and electronic equipment	59,929.0	54,447.6	55,420.9
Vehicles, aircraft, vessels and associated transport equipment	93,885.7	89,242.4	90,364.8
Vehicles other than railway, tramway	64,219.1	55,168.0	58,829.7
Cars (incl. station wagons)	35,698.9	30,297.5	31,336.2
Aircraft, spacecraft, and parts thereof	27,269.8	31,148.7	29,541.9
Optical, medical apparatus, etc.; clocks and watches; musical instruments; parts thereof	22,194.7	21,851.6	22,713.9
Total (incl. others)	700,851.6	663,268.6	668,658.1

Exports	2011	2012	2013
Live animals and animal products	17,343.9	16,430.8	17,081.0
Vegetables and vegetable products	20,640.6	18,307.0	21,131.5
Prepared foodstuffs; beverages, spirits, vinegar; tobacco and articles thereof	37,489.6	37,434.4	38,864.5
Beverages, spirits and vinegar	17,621.9	17,881.2	18,377.4
Mineral products	28,117.3	26,452.1	23,779.8
Mineral fuels, oils, distillation products, etc.	26,552.3	24,952.2	22,210.6
Chemicals and related products	92,548.5	90,961.2	93,756.1
Pharmaceutical products	32,911.1	34,745.9	37,004.9
Medicament mixtures put in dosage	26,428.1	27,282.3	27,811.5
Plastics, rubber and articles thereof	31,967.9	29,683.9	30,434.5
Plastics and articles thereof	22,367.0	20,895.0	22,127.8
Iron and steel, other base metals and articles of base metal	46,640.6	41,023.9	40,107.2
Iron and steel	19,329.2	17,064.8	15,925.6
Machinery and mechanical appliances; electrical equipment; parts thereof	113,978.6	108,707.0	109,867.1
Boilers, machinery, etc.	66,389.1	64,238.1	65,153.3
Electrical and electronic equipment	47,589.6	44,468.8	44,713.8
Vehicles, aircraft, vessels and associated transport equipment	105,219.4	104,535.2	106,510.9
Vehicles other than railway, tramway	53,103.3	46,806.8	46,394.1
Cars (incl. station wagons)	23,163.1	20,176.9	18,658.1
Parts and access of motor vehicles	18,816.9	16,416.5	17,238.7
Aircraft, spacecraft, and parts thereof	49,813.5	54,507.0	56,452.2
Aircraft, (helicopter, aeroplanes) and spacecraft (satellites)	43,346.6	47,278.9	48,630.3
Optical, medical apparatus, etc.; clocks and watches; musical instruments; parts thereof	20,665.8	19,727.4	20,629.5
Optical, photo, technical, medical apparatus	18,462.8	17,317.0	17,984.6
Total (incl. others)	581,541.9	556,575.7	566,879.0

* Including re-imports.

Source: Trade Map-Trade Competitiveness Map, International Trade Centre, www.intracen.org/marketanalysis.

PRINCIPAL TRADING PARTNERS
(US $ million)

Imports*	2011	2012	2013
Austria	6,460.8	6,634.5	7,112.5
Belgium	54,401.7	50,091.9	52,359.6
China, People's Republic	56,189.4	53,037.0	53,843.1
Czech Republic	8,130.8	7,141.4	7,386.3
France	8,204.3	6,306.2	6,523.2
Germany	118,607.8	114,581.6	114,204.5
Ireland	9,001.0	8,956.1	8,859.4
Italy	50,752.1	47,128.6	47,686.1
Japan	12,995.9	11,757.4	10,658.2
Kazakhstan	7,170.2	6,749.3	7,076.5
Netherlands	30,107.8	28,818.7	28,878.9
Norway	9,451.8	7,187.1	7,063.3
Poland	10,684.6	10,156.3	10,575.7

Imports*—continued	2011	2012	2013
Portugal	6,623.5	6,222.1	6,711.4
Russia	19,348.5	15,366.4	14,062.7
Saudi Arabia	6,340.5	7,085.7	8,065.8
Spain	41,946.5	39,666.5	40,691.7
Sweden	8,369.0	7,449.2	7,746.8
Switzerland	16,081.5	15,563.1	16,927.1
Turkey	8,173.1	7,288.8	7,956.6
United Kingdom	30,586.2	29,304.4	27,539.3
USA	39,589.9	42,364.1	43,411.3
Total (incl. others)	700,851.6	663,268.6	668,658.1

Exports	2011	2012	2013
Algeria	8,004.7	8,178.2	7,849.2
Belgium	41,857.9	40,758.3	43,594.7
Brazil	5,551.1	5,951.1	6,302.6
China, People's Republic	18,716.1	19,387.8	19,590.0
Germany	96,159.8	91,548.5	93,187.1
Hong Kong	6,107.9	7,678.4	6,396.1
Italy	47,480.2	41,070.3	40,270.7
Japan	9,065.2	9,491.7	9,038.4
Korea, Republic	5,823.2	4,725.1	5,635.8
Morocco	5,965.0	5,179.2	5,125.0
Netherlands	24,888.3	23,573.7	23,262.9
Poland	9,229.1	8,506.1	8,920.9
Russia	10,352.9	11,726.3	10,208.8
Singapore	7,146.3	7,539.6	7,196.4
Spain	42,281.3	37,564.9	38,346.1
Sweden	7,792.7	6,514.8	6,170.6
Switzerland	18,229.4	17,649.7	17,372.5
Turkey	9,320.1	8,875.0	8,324.4
United Kingdom	38,470.7	37,531.4	39,115.1
USA	32,468.2	34,113.8	35,789.8
Total (incl. others)	581,541.9	556,575.7	566,879.0

* Including re-imports.

Source: Trade Map-Trade Competitiveness Map, International Trade Centre, www.intracen.org/marketanalysis.

Transport

RAILWAYS
(traffic)

	2011	2012	2013
Total passenger journeys ('000)	1,112,020	1,134,270	1,144,180
Passenger-km (million)	82,750	82,620	81,990
Freight carried ('000 metric tons)	71,860	63,310	60,620
Freight ton-km (million)	26,840	24,440	23,150

Source: Société Nationale des Chemins de fer Français, Paris.

ROAD TRAFFIC
('000 motor vehicles in use at 31 December)

	2009	2010	2012*
Passenger cars	31,050	31,300	31,033
Lorries and vans	6,300	6,359	6,451
Buses and coaches	85	86	87
Motorcycles and mopeds	3,532	3,000	n.a.

* Data for 2011 were not available.

Source: IRF, *World Road Statistics*.

INLAND WATERWAYS

	2012	2013
Freight carried ('000 metric tons)	58,452	58,199
Freight ton-km (million)	7,830	7,912

Source: Voies navigables de France.

SHIPPING

Flag Registered Fleet
(all registers, at 31 December)

	2012	2013	2014
Number of vessels	1,016	1,022	1,038
Total displacement ('000 grt) . .	6,377.9	5,816.8	5,867.9

Source: Lloyd's List Intelligence (www.lloydslistintelligence.com).

Seaborne Freight Traffic
('000 metric tons)

	2010	2012	2013
Goods loaded	99,864	96,924	99,888
Goods unloaded	199,308	193,212	190,404

Note: Data for 2011 were not available.

Source: UN, *Monthly Bulletin of Statistics.*

CIVIL AVIATION

(revenue traffic on scheduled services)*

	2011	2012	2013
Passengers carried ('000) . . .	69,754	72,352	75,108
Passenger-km (million) . . .	136,357	140,791	148,142
Total ton-km (million) . . .	4,228	4,246	4,275

* Including data for airlines based in French overseas possessions.

Source: Direction Générale de l'Aviation Civile.

Tourism

FOREIGN TOURIST ARRIVALS BY COUNTRY OF ORIGIN
('000, estimates)

	2011	2012	2013
Belgium and Luxembourg . . .	10,769	11,127	10,462
China, People's Republic . . .	1,130	1,394	1,720
Germany	11,622	12,232	13,036
Italy	8,068	8,057	7,815
Netherlands	6,493	6,350	6,547
Spain	5,434	6,047	5,317
Switzerland (incl. Liechtenstein) .	5,661	6,073	6,474
United Kingdom and Ireland . .	12,833	12,713	13,158
USA	3,352	3,020	3,102
Total (incl. others)	81,550	83,050	84,726

Receipts from tourism (US $ million, excl. passenger transport): 55,116 in 2011; 53,408 in 2012; 56,557 in 2013.

Source: World Tourism Organization.

Communications Media

	2011	2012	2013
Telephones ('000 main lines in use)	40,370	39,674	39,079
Mobile cellular telephones ('000 subscribers)	59,816	62,260	63,324
Broadband subscribers ('000) . .	22,749	23,975	24,940

Internet subscribers ('000): 21,800 in 2010.

Source: International Telecommunication Union.

Education

(public and private, metropolitan France, French Guiana, Guadeloupe, Martinique and Réunion, 2013/14 unless otherwise indicated)

	Institutions	Teachers*	Students ('000)
Pre-primary	15,343		2,580.9
Primary		364,315	4,132.6
Integration and adaptation schooling	37,237		47.2
Secondary:			
Lower	7,057	237,277	3,237.6
Upper—Professional . .	1,583	250,367	670.3
Upper—General/Technical .	2,642		1,470.6
Higher	4,564	87,724	2,429.9

* 2004/05.

Source: Ministry of National Education, Higher Education and Research, Paris.

Directory

The Government

HEAD OF STATE

President: FRANÇOIS HOLLANDE (took office 15 May 2012).

COUNCIL OF MINISTERS
(April 2015)

Prime Minister: MANUEL VALLS.

Minister of Foreign Affairs and International Development: LAURENT FABIUS.

Minister of Ecology, Sustainable Development and Energy: SÉGOLÈNE ROYAL.

Minister of National Education, Higher Education and Research: NAJAT VALLAUD-BELKACEM.

Keeper of the Seals, Minister of Justice: CHRISTIANE TAUBIRA.

Minister of Finance and Public Accounts: MICHEL SAPIN.

Minister of Defence: JEAN-YVES LE DRIAN.

Minister of Social Affairs, Health and Women's Rights: MARISOL TOURAINE.

Minister of Labour, Employment, Vocational Training and Social Dialogue: FRANÇOIS REBSAMEN.

Minister of the Interior: BERNARD CAZENEUVE.

Minister of Agriculture, Food and Forestry, Government Spokesperson: STÉPHANE LE FOLL.

Minister of Economy, Industry and Digital Economy: EMMANUEL MACRON.

Minister of Housing, Territorial Equality and Rural Policy: SYLVIA PINEL.

Minister of Decentralization and Public Service: MARYLISE LEBRANCHU.

Minister of Culture and Communication: FLEUR PELLERIN.

Minister of Cities, Youth and Sports: PATRICK KANNER.

Minister of Overseas Territories: GEORGE PAU-LANGEVIN.

Secretary of State to the Prime Minister, for Relations with Parliament: JEAN-MARIE LE GUEN.

Secretary of State to the Prime Minister, in charge of State Reform and Simplification: THIERRY MANDON.

Secretary of State to the Minister of Foreign Affairs and International Development, in charge of European Affairs: HARLEM DÉSIR.

Secretary of State to the Minister of Foreign Affairs and International Development, in charge of Development and Francophonie: ANNICK GIRARDIN.

Secretary of State to the Minister of Foreign Affairs and International Development, in charge of Foreign Trade, Tourism Development and French Nationals Abroad: MATTHIAS FEKL.

Secretary of State to the Minister of Ecology, Sustainable Development and Energy, in charge of Transport, Maritime Economy and Fisheries: ALAIN VIDALIES.

Secretary of State to the Minister of Finance and Public Accounts, in charge of the Budget: CHRISTIAN ECKERT.

Secretary of State to the Minister of Defence, in charge of Veterans and Memory: JEAN-MARC TODESCHINI.

Secretary of State to the Minister of Social Affairs and Health, in charge of the Elderly, Family and Autonomy: LAURENCE ROSSIGNOL.

Secretary of State to the Minister of Social Affairs and Health, in charge of Disabled People and Combating Exclusion: SÉGOLÈNE NEUVILLE.

Secretary of State to the Minister of Social Affairs, Health and Women's Right, in charge of Women's Rights: PASCALE BOISTARD.

Secretary of State to the Minister of Economy, Industrial Recovery and Digital Economy, in charge of Trade, Crafts, Social Economy, Solidarity and Consumer Affairs: CAROLE DELGA.

Secretary of State to the Minister of Economy, Industrial Recovery and Digital Economy, in charge of Digital Economy: AXELLE LEMAIRE.

Secretary of State to the Minister of Decentralization and Public Service, in charge of Territorial Reform: ANDRÉ VALLINI.

Secretary of State to the Minister of Cities, Youth and Sports, in charge of City Affairs: MYRIAM EL KHOMRI.

Secretary of State to the Minister of Cities, Youth and Sports, in charge of Sports: THIERRY BRAILLARD.

MINISTRIES

Office of the President: Palais de l'Elysée, 55–57 rue du Faubourg Saint Honoré, 75008 Paris; tel. 1-42-92-81-00; fax 1-47-42-24-65; internet www.elysee.fr.

Office of the Prime Minister: Hôtel de Matignon, 57 rue de Varenne, 75007 Paris; tel. 1-42-75-80-00; fax 1-42-75-78-31; e-mail premier-ministre@premier-ministre.gouv.fr; internet www.gouvernement.fr.

Ministry of Agriculture, Food and Forestry: 78 rue de Varenne, 75349 Paris Cedex 07; tel. 1-49-55-49-55; fax 1-49-55-40-39; e-mail infodoc@agriculture.gouv.fr; internet agriculture.gouv.fr.

Ministry of Cities, Youth and Sports: 110 rue de Grenelle, 75357 Paris Cedex 07; tel. 1-40-45-90-00; internet www.sports.gouv.fr.

Ministry of Culture and Communication: 3 rue de Valois, 75001 Paris; tel. 1-40-15-80-00; fax 1-40-15-85-30; internet www.culturecommunication.gouv.fr.

Ministry of Decentralization and Public Service: 80 rue de Lille, 75007 Paris; tel. 1-40-04-04-04; internet www.fonction-publique.gouv.fr.

Ministry of Defence: 14 rue Saint Dominique, 75007 Paris; tel. 1-80-50-14-00; fax 1-47-05-40-91; e-mail sdbc.courrier-ministre.fct@intradef.gouv.fr; internet www.defense.gouv.fr.

Ministry of Ecology, Sustainable Development and Energy: 92055 La Défense Cedex; tel. 1-40-81-21-22; internet www.developpement-durable.gouv.fr.

Ministry of the Economy and Finance: 139 rue de Bercy, 75572 Paris Cedex 12; tel. 1-40-04-04-04; internet www.economie.gouv.fr.

Ministry of Foreign Affairs and International Development: 37 quai d'Orsay, 75351 Paris Cedex 07; tel. 1-43-17-53-53; fax 1-43-17-52-03; internet www.diplomatie.gouv.fr.

Ministry of Housing, Territorial Equality and Rural Policy: 92055 La Défense Cedex; tel. 01-40-81-21-22; internet www.territoires.gouv.fr.

Ministry of the Interior: place Beauvau, 75008 Paris; tel. 1-49-27-49-27; fax 1-43-59-89-50; e-mail sirp@interieur.gouv.fr; internet www.interieur.gouv.fr.

Ministry of Justice: 13 place Vendôme, 75042 Paris Cedex 01, tel. 1-44-77-60-60; fax 1-44-77-60-02; e-mail cyberjustice@justice.gouv.fr; internet www.justice.gouv.fr.

Ministry of Labour, Employment, Vocational Training and Social Dialogue: 101 rue de Grenelle, 75700 Paris; tel. 1-40-56-60-00; fax 1-44-38-20-20; internet travail-solidarite.gouv.fr.

Ministry of National Education, Higher Education and Research: 1 rue Descartes, 75231 Paris Cedex 05; tel. 1-55-55-90-01; e-mail sup-info@education.gouv.fr; internet www.enseignementsup-recherche.gouv.fr.

Ministry of Overseas Territories: 27 rue Oudinot, 75007 Paris; tel. 1-53-69-20-00; internet www.outre-mer.gouv.fr.

Ministry of Social Affairs and Health: 14 ave Duquesne, 75007 Paris; tel. 1-40-56-60-00; internet www.social-sante.gouv.fr.

Ministry of Cities, Youth and Sports: 110 rue de Grenelle, 75357 Paris Cedex 07; tel. 1-40-45-90-00; internet www.sports.gouv.fr.

President and Legislature

PRESIDENT

Presidential Election, First Ballot, 22 April 2012

Candidates	Votes	% of votes
François Hollande (Parti Socialiste)	10,272,705	28.63
Nicolas Sarkozy (Union pour un Mouvement Populaire)	9,753,629	27.18
Marine Le Pen (Front National)	6,421,426	17.90
Jean-Luc Mélenchon (Front de Gauche)*	3,984,822	11.10
François Bayrou (Mouvement Démocrate)	3,275,122	9.13
Eva Joly (Europe Ecologie Les Verts)	828,345	2.31
Nicolas Dupont-Aignan (Debout la République)	643,907	1.79
Philippe Poutou (Nouveau Parti Anticapitaliste)	411,160	1.15
Nathalie Arthaud (Lutte Ouvrière)	202,548	0.56
Jacques Cheminade (Solidarité et Progrès)	89,545	0.25
Total	35,883,209	100.00

* A coalition of left-wing parties, including the Parti de Gauche and the Parti Communiste.

Presidential Election, Second Ballot, 6 May 2012

Candidate	Votes	% of votes
François Hollande (Parti Socialiste)	18,000,668	51.64
Nicolas Sarkozy (Union pour un Mouvement Populaire)	16,860,685	48.36
Total	34,861,353	100.00

PARLIAMENT
(Parlement)

National Assembly
(Assemblée Nationale)

126 rue de l'Université, 75355 Paris Cedex 07; tel. 1-40-63-60-00; fax 1-45-55-75-23; e-mail infos@assemblee-nationale.fr; internet www.assemblee-nationale.fr.

President: CLAUDE BARTOLONE (PS).

General Election, 10 June and 17 June 2012

Party	% of votes cast in first ballot	% of votes cast in second ballot*	Seats
Parti Socialiste (PS)	29.35	40.91	280
Union pour un Mouvement Populaire (UMP)	27.12	37.95	194
Various left-wing candidates	3.40	1.82	22
Europe Ecologie Les Verts	5.46	3.60	17
Various right-wing candidates	3.51	3.08	15
Parti Radical de Gauche (PRG)	1.65	2.34	12
Le Nouveau Centre	2.20	2.47	12
Front de Gauche†	6.91	1.08	10
Parti Radical	1.24	1.35	6
Front National (FN)	13.60	3.66	2
Alliance Centriste (AC)	0.60	0.54	2
Le Centre pour la France (CEN)‡	1.77	0.49	2
Regionalist candidates	0.56	0.59	2
Various far-right candidates	0.19	0.13	1
Various far-left candidates	0.98	—	—
Various ecologist candidates	0.96	—	—
Others	0.52	—	—
Total	100.00	100.00	577

* Held where no candidate had won the requisite overall majority in the first ballot, between candidates who had received at least 12.5% of the votes in that round. The total number of valid votes cast was 25,952,859 in the first round, and 23,029,183 in the second round.
† Alliance of Parti Communiste Français and Parti de Gauche.
‡ Alliance led by Mouvement Démocrate (MoDem).

Senate
(Sénat)

15 rue de Vaugirard, 75291 Paris Cedex 06; tel. 1-42-34-20-00; fax 1-42-34-26-77; e-mail communication@senat.fr; internet www.senat.fr.

President: GÉRARD LARCHER (UMP).

Senators are elected for a term of six years, with one-half of the seats renewable every three years; seats are allocated through a combination of majority voting and proportional representation. The minimum age for eligible candidates to the Senate is 30 years.

A partial election to the Senate took place on 25 September 2011, when the number of senators was increased to 348. A partial election was held on 28 September 2014. The strength of the parties at 15 April 2015 was as follows:

Grouping	Seats
Groupe Union pour un Mouvement Populaire . . .	144
Groupe Socialiste et Apparentés	110
Groupe Union des Démocrates et Indépendants . .	41
Groupe Communiste Républicain et Citoyen . . .	19
Groupe du Rassemblement Démocratique et Social Européen	13
Groupe Ecologiste	10
Non-attached	9
Total	**348***

* Including two vacant seats. The election of two French Polynesian Senators in September 2014 was annulled by the French Constitutional Court in February 2015 on the grounds that a march by supporters of a political party to the polling station on the day of the election constituted an attempt to exert undue pressure on voters; a new election was scheduled to be held on 3 May.

Territorial Collectivity of Corsica

In 1992 Corsica officially assumed the status of a Collectivité Territoriale (Territorial Collectivity), in accordance with legislation approved by Parliament in the previous year, thereby gaining a degree of political and administrative autonomy. The island of Corsica is generally considered as one of the 22 régions of metropolitan France.

The 51-member Assemblée de Corse (Corsican Assembly) was constituted following elections held in March 1992. Members of the Assembly are elected by universal suffrage for a term of six years, according to a system of proportional representation. Three additional seats are allocated to the list receiving the largest number of votes. The nine-member Conseil Exécutif (Executive Council) is elected by the Assembly from among the members of the largest parliamentary group.

President of the Executive Council: PAUL GIACOBBI (PRG—L'Alternance).

Members: PAUL MARIE BARTOLI, EMMANUELLE DE GENTILI, PIERRE GHIONGA, MARIA GUIDICELLI, JEAN-LOUIS LUCIANI, MARIE-THÉRÈSE OLIVESI, VANINA PIERI, JEAN ZUCCARELLI.

President of the Corsican Assembly: DOMINIQUE BUCCHINI (PCF—L'Alternance).

Corsican Assembly (Assemblée de Corse): 22 cours Grandval, 20187 Ajaccio Cedex 1; tel. 4-95-51-64-64; fax 4-95-51-67-75; e-mail contact@corse.fr; internet www.corse.fr; f. 1982.

Election, 14 and 21 March 2010

	Seats
L'Alternance*	24
Rassembler pour la Corse†	12
Femu a Corsica‡	11
Corsica Libera	4
Total	**51**

* Electoral list comprising the Parti Radical de Gauche (PRG), the Parti Communiste Français (PCF), the Parti de Gauche (PG), the Parti Socialiste (PS) and allies.
† Electoral list comprising the Union pour un Mouvement Populaire (UMP) and allies.
‡ Moderate nationalist electoral list.

Political Organizations

Alliance Centriste (AC): 31 rue de Tournon, 75006 Paris; tel. 1-46-33-77-60; fax 1-46-33-77-91; internet www.alliancecentriste.fr;

f. 2009; centrist; part of the Union des Démocrates et Indépendants; Pres. JEAN ARTHUIS; Sec.-Gen. THIERRY BENOIT.

Les Alternatifs: 40 rue de Malte, 75011 Paris; tel. 1-43-57-44-80; fax 1-43-57-64-50; e-mail contact@alternatifs.org; internet www.alternatifs.org; f. 1997; socialist, ecologist, feminist; Spokesperson JEAN-JACQUES BOISLAROUSSIE.

Centre National des Indépendants et Paysans (CNIP): 6 rue Quentin Bauchart, 75008 Paris; tel. 1-47-23-47-00; fax 1-47-23-47-03; e-mail contact@cni.asso.fr; internet www.cni.asso.fr; f. 1949; right-wing; works with the Union pour un Mouvement Populaire; Pres. GILLES BOURDOULEIX; Sec.-Gen. BRUNO NORTH.

Chasse Pêche Nature Traditions (CPNT): 245 blvd de la Paix, BP 87546, 64075 Pau Cedex; tel. 5-59-14-71-71; fax 5-59-14-71-72; internet www.cpnt.fr; f. 1989 as Chasse-Pêche-Traditions; emphasizes defence of rural traditions and the sovereignty of the state within Europe; Pres. FRÉDÉRIC NIHOUS; Sec.-Gen. ERICK MAROLLEAU.

Corsica Libera: 1 rue Miot, BP 304, 20297 Bastia Cedex; tel. 4-95-31-66-96; fax 4-95-31-78-91; e-mail corsicalibera@corsicalibera.com; internet www.corsicalibera.com; f. 2009 by merger of 4 Corsican separatist parties, incl. Corsica Nazione (f. 1992); Pres. ERIC SIMONI; Leader JEAN-GUY TALAMONI.

Debout la République (DLR): 17 rue des Rossignols, BP 18, 91330 Yerres; tel. 1-69-49-17-37; e-mail courrier@debout-la-republique.fr; internet www.debout-la-republique.fr; f. 2008; Gaullist, republican; Pres. NICOLAS DUPONT-AIGNAN; Sec.-Gen. JEAN-PIERRE ANTONI.

Europe Ecologie Les Verts: 247 rue du Faubourg Saint-Martin, 75010 Paris; tel. 1-53-19-53-19; fax 1-53-19-03-93; e-mail verts@lesverts.fr; internet www.lesverts.fr; f. 1984; ecologist; fmrly called Les Verts; name changed to above following merger with Europe Ecologie in Nov. 2010; Nat. Sec. EMMANUELLE COSSE.

Force Européenne Démocrate: 176 ave Jean Jaurès, 93000 Bobigny; internet www.forceeuropeennedemocrate.fr; f. 2012; centrist; part of the Union des Démocrates et Indépendants; Pres. JEAN-CHRISTOPHE LAGARDE.

Front National (FN): 76–78 rue des Suisses, 92000 Nanterre; tel. 1-41-20-20-00; fax 1-41-12-10-86; e-mail contact@frontnational.com; internet www.frontnational.com; f. 1972; extreme right-wing nationalist; Pres. MARINE LE PEN; Sec.-Gen. STEEVE BRIOIS.

Génération Ecologie: 35 ave du Pont Juvenal, 34000 Montepellier; tel. and fax 9-52-47-48-40; e-mail gen.ecologie@gmail.com; internet www.generationecologie.org; f. 1991; ecologist; Pres. YVES PIETRASANTA; Sec.-Gen. FRÉDÉRIC BŒUF-SALOR.

La Gauche Moderne: 7 rue Boutard, 92200 Neuilly-sur-Seine; e-mail contact.lagauchemoderne@gmail.com; internet www.lagauchemoderne.org; f. 2007; moderate, left-wing; part of the Union des Démocrates et Indépendants; Pres. JEAN-MARIE BOCKEL; Sec.-Gen. CHRISTIAN DEBÈVE.

Lutte Ouvrière (LO): BP 233, 75865 Paris Cedex 18; tel. 1-48-10-86-20; fax 1-48-10-86-26; e-mail contact@lutte-ouvriere.org; internet www.lutte-ouvriere.org; f. 1968; Trotskyist; Spokesperson NATHALIE ARTHAUD.

Mouvement Démocrate (MoDem): 133 bis rue de l'Université, 75007 Paris; tel. 1-53-59-20-00; fax 1-53-59-20-59; internet www.mouvementdemocrate.fr; f. 1978 as the Union pour la Démocratie Française (UDF) to unite for electoral purposes non-Gaullist 'majority' candidates; reconstituted as a unified party in 1998; reconstituted in November 2007 to oppose the UMP; elements of the UDF allied to fmr President, Nicolas Sarkozy, left the party and formed the Nouveau Centre in May 2007; contested the 2012 legislative elections as the main part of the Le Centre pour la France (CEN) coalition; formed L'Alternative (The Alternative) coalition with the Union des Démocrates et Indépendants in 2013; Pres. FRANÇOIS BAYROU; Sec.-Gen. MARC FESNEAU.

Mouvement Ecologiste Indépendant (MEI): 26 ter rue Nicolaï, 75012 Paris; tel. 3-84-47-48-80; e-mail jacques.lancon@orange.fr; internet m-e-i.fr; f. 1994; ecologist; 1,000 mems; Pres. ANTOINE WAECHTER; Nat. Sec. JACQUES MAUHOURAT.

Mouvement National Républicain (MNR): BP 10008, 93161 Noisy-le-Grand Cedex; tel. 9-51-45-84-93; fax 9-51-45-84-93; e-mail presse@m-n-r.fr; internet www.m-n-r.fr; f. 1999 by breakaway faction of FN; extreme right-wing nationalist; Sec.-Gen. HUBERT SAVON.

Mouvement pour la France (MPF): 33 ave de Ségur, 75007 Paris; e-mail contact@pourlafrance.fr; internet www.pourlafrance.fr; f. 1994; far-right, nationalist; Pres. PHILIPPE DE VILLIERS; Sec.-Gen. PATRICK LOUIS.

Mouvement Républicain et Citoyen (MRC): 3 ave de Corbéra, 75012 Paris; tel. 1-55-78-05-40; fax 1-44-83-83-10; e-mail contact@mrc-france.org; internet www.mrc-france.org; f. 2002 as Pôle Républicain on the basis of the Mouvement des Citoyens; present name adopted 2003; socialist; sceptical of increased European integration or devolution of powers from the nation state; Pres. JEAN-LUC LAURENT.

Le Nouveau Centre: 84 rue de Grenelle, 75007 Paris; tel. 1-44-39-28-00; fax 1-44-39-28-09; e-mail contact@nouveaucentre.fr; internet www.nouveaucentre.fr; f. 2007 by mems of the UDF allied to the then President, Nicolas Sarkozy, and his UMP party; part of the Union des Démocrates et Indépendants; Pres. HERVÉ MORIN; Sec.-Gen. PHILIPPE VIGIER; Parliamentary Leader FRANÇOIS SAUVADET.

Nouveau Parti Anticapitaliste (NPA): 2 rue Richard Lenoir, 93100 Montreuil; tel. 1-48-70-42-30; fax 1-48-59-39-59; e-mail ecrire@npa2009.org; internet www.npa2009.org; f. Feb. 2009 to replace the dissolved Ligue Communiste Révolutionnaire; socialist, democratic, ecologist; seeks to break with traditional hierarchical party structures; Principal Speaker CHRISTINE POUPIN; 9,123 mems.

Parti Communiste Français (PCF): 2 place du Colonel Fabien, 75019 Paris; tel. 1-40-40-12-12; fax 1-40-40-13-56; e-mail pcf@pcf.fr; internet www.pcf.fr; advocates independent foreign policy; formed the Front de Gauche with the Parti de Gauche in 2008; Nat. Sec. PIERRE LAURENT.

Parti de Gauche (PG): 63 ave de la République, 75011 Paris; e-mail contact@lepartidegauche.fr; internet www.lepartidegauche.fr; f. 2008 by fmr mems of PS and MARS-Gauche Républicaine; left-wing, republican; formed the Front de Gauche with the Parti Communiste Français in 2008; Co-Pres MARTINE BILLARD, JEAN-LUC MÉLENCHON.

Parti Radical: 1 place de Valois, 75001 Paris; tel. 1-42-61-02-02; fax 1-42-61-02-04; e-mail contact@laurenthenart.com; internet www.partiradical.net; f. 1901; fmrly affiliated to the UMP; part of the Union des Démocrates et Indépendants; Pres. LAURENT HÉNART; Sec.-Gen. NATHALIE DELATTRE.

Parti Radical de Gauche (PRG): 13 rue Duroc, 75007 Paris; tel. 1-45-66-67-68; fax 1-45-66-47-93; e-mail prg@prg.com.fr; internet www.planeteradicale.org; f. 1972 as the Mouvement des Radicaux de Gauche; left-wing; Pres. JEAN-MICHEL BAYLET; Sec.-Gen. GUILLAUME LACROIX.

Parti Socialiste (PS): 10 rue de Solférino, 75333 Paris Cedex 07; tel. 1-45-56-77-00; fax 1-47-05-15-78; e-mail interps@parti-socialiste.fr; internet www.parti-socialiste.fr; f. 1971; First Sec. JEAN-CHRISTOPHE CAMBADÉLIS.

Rassemblement pour l'Indépendance et la Souveraineté de la France (RIF): BP 10014, 75362 Paris Cedex 08; tel. and fax 1-46-44-94 16; e-mail secretariat.rif@tele2.fr; f. 2003; nationalist, opposed to the transfer of powers from nation states to the European Union; Pres. ALAIN BOURNAZEL; Sec.-Gen. ROBERT CHARPENTIER.

République Solidaire: 91 bis rue du Cherche-Midi, 75006 Paris; tel. 1-84-16-10-47; internet www.republiquesolidaire.fr; f. 2010; republican; Pres. JEAN-PIERRE GRAND; Sec.-Gen. MARC BERNIER.

Solidarité et Progrès (S&P): BP 27, 92114 Clichy Cedex; tel. 1-76-69-14-50; fax 1-47-39-05-80; internet www.solidariteetprogres.org; f. 1996; associated with the LaRouche movement; Pres. JACQUES CHEMINADE.

Union des Démocrates et Indépendants (UDI): 22 bis rue des Volontaires, 75015 Paris; tel. 1-53-71-20-17; e-mail contact@parti-udi.fr; internet www.parti-udi.fr; f. 2012; centrist; comprises several ind. parties, incl. Alliance Centriste, Force Européenne Démocrate, La Gauche Moderne, Nouveau Centre, Parti Radical, Parti Libéral Démocrate; formed L'Alternative (The Alternative) coalition with the Mouvement Démocrate in 2013; Pres. JEAN-CHRISTOPHE LAGARDE.

Union pour un Mouvement Populaire (UMP): 238 rue de Vaugirard, 75015 Paris; tel. 1-40-76-60-00; e-mail webmaster@u-m-p.org; internet www.u-m-p.org; f. 2002; founded as Union pour la Majorité Présidentielle by mems of the fmr Rassemblement pour la République and Démocratie Liberale parties, in conjunction with elements of the UDF, now MoDem (q.v.); centre-right grouping formed to ensure that President Jacques Chirac had a majority grouping in the National Assembly; 317,771 mems. (Jan. 2007); Pres. NICOLAS SARKOZY; Sec.-Gen. LUC CHATEL.

Diplomatic Representation

EMBASSIES IN FRANCE

Afghanistan: 32 ave Raphaël, 75016 Paris; tel. 1-45-25-05-29; fax 1-42-24-47-14; e-mail contact@ambafghanistan-fr.com; internet www.ambafghanistan-fr.com; Ambassador Dr ASSAD OMER.

Albania: 57 ave Marceau, 75116 Paris; tel. 1-47-23-31-00; fax 1-47-23-59-85; e-mail embassy.paris@mfa.gov.al; internet www.ambasadat.gov.al/france; Ambassador DRITAN TOLA.

Algeria: 50 rue de Lisbonne, 75008 Paris; tel. 1-53-93-20-20; fax 1-53-93-20-69; e-mail chancellerie@amb-algerie.fr; internet www.amb-algerie.fr; Ambassador AMAR BENDJAMA.

Andorra: 1 place d'Andorre, 75016 Paris; tel. 1-40-06-03-30; fax 1-40-06-03-64; e-mail ambaixada_franca@govern.ad; internet www.mae.ad/ca/ambaixades-andorra/ambaixada-andorra-franca; Ambassador MARIA UBACH FONT.

Angola: 19 ave Foch, 75116 Paris; tel. 1-45-01-58-20; fax 1-45-00-33-71; e-mail sg@emb-ang.fr; internet www.ambassadeangolafrance.org; Ambassador MIGUEL DA COSTA.

Argentina: 6 rue Cimarosa, 75116 Paris; tel. 1-44-05-27-00; fax 1-45-53-46-33; e-mail efran@mrecic.gov.ar; internet www.efran.mrecic.gov.ar; Ambassador MARIA DEL CARMEN SQUEFF.

Armenia: 9 rue Viète, 75017 Paris; tel. 1-42-12-98-00; fax 1-42-12-98-03; e-mail ambarmen@wanadoo.fr; internet www.france.mfa.am; Ambassador VIGUEN TCHITETCHIAN.

Australia: 4 rue Jean Rey, 75724 Paris; tel. 1-40-59-33-00; fax 1-40-59-33-10; e-mail info.paris@dfat.gov.au; internet www.france.embassy.gov.au; Ambassador STEPHEN BRADY.

Austria: 6 rue Fabert, 75007 Paris; tel. 1-40-63-30-63; fax 1-45-55-63-65; e-mail paris-ob@bmeia.gv.at; internet www.amb-autriche.fr; Ambassador Dr URSULA PLASSNIK.

Azerbaijan: 78 ave d'Iéna, 75016 Paris; tel. 1-44-18-60-20; fax 1-44-18-60-25; e-mail paris@mission.mfa.gov.az; internet www.azambassade.fr; Ambassador ELCHIN AMIRBAYOV.

Bahrain: 3 bis place des Etats-Unis, 75116 Paris; tel. 1-47-23-48-68; fax 1-47-20-55-75; e-mail ambassade@ambahrein-france.com; internet www.mofa.gov.bh/paris; Ambassador Dr NASSER AL-BELOOSHI.

Bangladesh: 109 ave Henry Martin, 75016 Paris; tel. 1-46-51-90-33; fax 1-46-51-90-35; e-mail bangembpar@yahoo.com; internet bangladoot-paris.org; Ambassador M. SHAHIDUL ISLAM.

Belarus: 38 blvd Suchet, 75016 Paris; tel. 1-44-14-69-79; fax 1-44-14-69-70; e-mail france@mfa.gov.by; internet france.mfa.gov.by; Ambassador PAVEL LATUSHKA.

Belgium: 9 rue de Tilsitt, 75840 Paris Cedex 17; tel. 1-44-09-39-39; fax 1-47-54-07-64; e-mail paris@diplobel.fed.be; internet www.diplomatic.be/paris; Ambassador PATRICK VERCAUTEREN DRUBBEL.

Benin: 87 ave Victor Hugo, 75116 Paris; tel. 1-45-00-98-82; fax 1-45-01-82-02; e-mail contact@ambassade-benin.fr; internet www.ambassade-benin.fr; Ambassador JULES-ARMAND ANIAMBOSSOU.

Bolivia: 12 ave du Président Kennedy, 75016 Paris; tel. 1-42-24-93-44; fax 1-45-25-86-23; e-mail embolivia.paris@wanadoo.fr; Ambassador JEAN-PAUL GUEVARA ÁVILA.

Bosnia and Herzegovina: 174 rue de Courcelles, 75017 Paris; tel. 1-42-67-34-22; fax 1-40-53-85-22; e-mail amb.pariz@mvp.gov.ba; internet www.amb-bosnie-herzegovine.fr; Ambassador NINA SAJIĆ.

Brazil: 34 cours Albert 1er, 75008 Paris; tel. 1-45-61-63-00; fax 1-42-89-03-45; e-mail ambassade@bresil.org; internet www.bresil.org; Ambassador JOSÉ MAURICIO BUSTANI.

Brunei: 7 rue de Presbourg, 75116 Paris; tel. 1-53-64-67-60; fax 1-53-64-67-83; e-mail ambassade.brunei@wanadoo.fr; Ambassador Dato' Paduka ZAINIDI Haji SIDUP.

Bulgaria: 1 ave Rapp, 75007 Paris; tel. 1-45-51-85-90; fax 1-45-51-18-68; e-mail bulgamb@wanadoo.fr; internet www.amb-bulgarie.fr; Ambassador ANGUEL TCHOLAKOV.

Burkina Faso: 159 blvd Haussmann, 75008 Paris; tel. 1-43-59-90-63; fax 1-42-56-50-07; e-mail contact@ambaburkina-fr.org; internet ambaburkina-fr.org; Ambassador ERIC Y. TIARÉ.

Burundi: 10–12 rue de l'Orme, 75019 Paris; tel. 1-45-20-60-61; fax 1-45-20-02-54; e-mail ambabu.paris@wanadoo.fr; Ambassador DIEU-DONNÉ NDABARUSHIMANA.

Cabo Verde: 3 rue de Rigny, 75008 Paris; tel. 1-42-12-73-50; fax 1-40-53-04-36; e-mail ambassade-cap-vert2@wanadoo.fr; internet www.ambassadecapvert.fr; Ambassador MARIA FÁTIMA DA VEIGA.

Cambodia: 4 rue Adolphe Yvon, 75116 Paris; tel. 1-45-03-47-20; fax 1-45-03-47-40; e-mail arc@ambcambodgeparis.info; internet www.ambcambodgeparis.info; Ambassador NARANG NOUTH.

Cameroon: 73 rue d'Auteuil, 75116 Paris; tel. 1-47-43-98-33; fax 1-46-51-24-52; Ambassador LEJEUNE MBELLA MBELLA.

Canada: 35 ave Montaigne, 75008 Paris; tel. 1-44-43-29-00; fax 1-44-43-29-99; e-mail paris_webmaster@international.gc.ca; internet www.canadainternational.gc.ca/france; Ambassador LAWRENCE CANNON.

Central African Republic: 30 rue des Perchamps, 75116 Paris; tel. 1-45-25-39-74; fax 1-55-74-40-25; e-mail accueil@amb-rcaparis.org; internet www.amb-rcaparis.org; Ambassador EMMANUEL BONGO PASSI.

Chad: 65 rue des Belles Feuilles, 75116 Paris; tel. 1-45-53-36-75; fax 1-45-53-16-09; e-mail ambassadedutchadparis@wanadoo.fr; internet ambatchad-paris.org; Ambassador HISSÈNE BRAHIM TAHA.

Chile: 2 ave de la Motte-Picquet, 75007 Paris; tel. 1-44-18-59-60; fax 1-44-18-59-61; e-mail echile.francia@minrel.gov.cl; internet chileabroad.gov.cl/francia; Ambassador PATRICIO HALES DIB.

China, People's Republic: 11 ave George V, 75008 Paris; tel. 1-49-52-19-50; fax 1-47-20-24-22; e-mail chinaemb_fr@mfa.gov.cn; internet www.amb-chine.fr; Ambassador ZHAI JUN.

Colombia: 22 rue de l'Elysée, 75008 Paris; tel. 1-42-65-46-08; fax 1-42-66-18-60; e-mail eparis@cancilleria.gov.co; internet www.embcolfrancia.com; Ambassador FEDERICO RENJIFO.

Comoros: 20 rue Marbeau, 75116 Paris; tel. 1-40-67-90-54; fax 1-40-67-72-96; Ambassador AHMED BOURHANE.

Congo, Democratic Republic: 32 cours Albert 1er, 75008 Paris; tel. 1-42-25-57-50; fax 1-45-62-16-52; e-mail contact@ambardcparis.com; internet www.ambardcparis.com; Ambassador CHRISTIAN ILEKA ATOKI.

Congo, Republic: 37 bis rue Paul Valéry, 75116 Paris; tel. 1-45-00-60-57; fax 1-40-67-17-33; e-mail ambacongo_france@yahoo.fr; Ambassador HENRI LOPES.

Costa Rica: 4, Square Rapp, 4ème étage, 75007 Paris; tel. 1-45-78-96-96; fax 1-45-78-99-66; e-mail embcr@wanadoo.fr; internet www.ambassade-costarica.org; Ambassador CARLOS BONILLA SANDOVAL.

Côte d'Ivoire: 102 ave Raymond Poincaré, 75116 Paris; tel. 1-53-64-62-62; fax 1-45-00-47-97; e-mail rciparis@ambassadecotedivoire.fr; internet france.diplomatie.gouv.ci; Ambassador CHARLES PROVIDENCE GOMIS.

Croatia: 7 sq. Thiers, 75116 Paris; tel. 1-53-70-02-80; fax 1-53-70-02-90; e-mail vrh.pariz@mvep.hr; internet fr.mvp.hr; Ambassador IVO GOLDSTEIN.

Cuba: 16 rue de Presles, 75015 Paris; tel. 1-45-67-55-35; fax 1-45-66-80-92; e-mail embacu@ambacuba.fr; internet www.cubadiplomatica.cu/francia; Ambassador HÉCTOR IGARZA.

Cyprus: 23 rue Galilée, 75116 Paris; tel. 1-47-20-86-28; fax 1-40-70-13-44; e-mail ambrechypre@wanadoo.fr; internet www.mfa.gov.cy; Ambassador MARIOS LYSSIOTIS.

Czech Republic: 15 ave Charles Floquet, 75007 Paris; tel. 1-40-65-13-00; fax 1-40-65-13-13; e-mail paris@embassy.mzv.cz; internet www.mzv.cz/paris; Ambassador MARIE CHATARDOVÁ.

Denmark: 77 ave Marceau, 75116 Paris; tel. 1-44-31-21-21; fax 1-44-31-21-88; e-mail paramb@um.dk; internet www.ambparis.um.dk; Ambassador ANNA DORTE RIGGELSEN.

Djibouti: 26 rue Emile Ménier, 75116 Paris; tel. 1-47-27-49-22; fax 1-45-53-50-53; e-mail ambassadeur@ambdjibouti.org; Ambassador AYEID MOUSSEID YAHYA.

Dominican Republic: 45 rue de Courcelles, 75008 Paris; tel. 1-53-63-95-95; fax 1-45-63-35-63; e-mail embajadom@wanadoo.fr; internet www.embajadadominicana.fr; Ambassador ROSA MARGARITA HERNANDEZ.

Ecuador: 34 ave de Messine, 75008 Paris; tel. 1-45-61-10-21; fax 1-42-56-06-64; e-mail eecufrancia@mmrree.gob.ec; internet francia.embajada.gob.ec; Ambassador CARLOS JÁTIVA NARANJO.

Egypt: 56 ave d'Iéna, 75116 Paris; tel. 1-53-67-88-30; fax 1-47-23-06-43; e-mail paris_emb@mfa.gov.eg; Ambassador IHAB BADAWI.

El Salvador: 12 rue Galilée, 75116 Paris; tel. 1-47-20-42-02; fax 1-40-70-01-95; e-mail embparis@wanadoo.fr; Ambassador FRANCISCO GALINDO-VELEZ.

Equatorial Guinea: 29 blvd de Courcelles, 75008 Paris; tel. 1-45-61-98-20; fax 1-45-61-98-25; e-mail embarege_paris@hotmail.com; Ambassador MIGUEL OYONO NDONG MIFUMU.

Eritrea: 1 rue de Staël, 75015 Paris; tel. 1-43-06-15-56; fax 1-43-06-07-51; Ambassador HANA SIMON.

Estonia: 17 rue de la Baume, 75008 Paris; tel. 1-56-62-22-00; fax 1-49-52-05-65; e-mail estonie@mfa.ee; internet www.est-emb.fr; Ambassador SVEN JÜRGENSON.

Ethiopia: 35 ave Charles Floquet, 75007 Paris; tel. 1-47-83-83-95; fax 1-43-06-52-14; e-mail embeth@free.fr; Ambassador NEGA TSEGAYE TESSEMA.

Finland: 1 place de Finlande, 75007 Paris; tel. 1-44-18-19-20; fax 1-45-51-3-23; e-mail sanomat.par@formin.fi; internet www.amb-finlande.fr; Ambassador RISTO PIIPPONEN.

Gabon: 41 rue de la Bienfaisance, 75008 Paris; tel. 1-42-99-68-68; fax 1-72-81-05-89; e-mail cab.ambassadegabonfrance@yahoo.fr; internet www.affaires-etrangeres.gouv.ga/ambassade/france; Ambassador GERMAIN NGOYO MOUSSAVOU.

The Gambia: 117 rue St Lazare, 75008 Paris; tel. 1-73-18-00-60; fax 1-53-04-05-99; e-mail ambgambia_france117@hotmail.com; Ambassador OUSMAN BADJIE.

Georgia: 104 ave Raymond Poincaré, 75116 Paris; tel. 1-45-02-16-16; fax 1-45-02-16-01; e-mail ambassade.georgie@mfa.gov.ge; internet www.france.mfa.gov.ge; Ambassador ECATERINE SIRADZE-DELAUNAY.

Germany: 13–15 ave Franklin D. Roosevelt, 75008 Paris; tel. 1-53-83-45-00; fax 1-53-83-45-02; e-mail ambassade@amb-allemagne.fr; internet www.paris.diplo.de; Ambassador SUSANNE MARIANNE WASUM-RAINER.

Ghana: 8 Villa Saïd, 75116 Paris; tel. 1-45-00-09-50; fax 1-45-00-81-95; e-mail ambghanaparis@yahoo.fr; Ambassador JOHANNA ODONKOR SVANIKIER.

Greece: 17 rue Auguste Vacquerie, 75116 Paris; tel. 1-47-23-72-28; fax 1-47-23-73-85; e-mail gremb.par@mfa.gr; internet www.amb-grece.fr; Ambassador THÉODORE M. PASSAS.

Guatemala: 2 rue Villebois-Mareuil, 75017 Paris; tel. 1-42-27-78-63; fax 1-47-54-02-06; Ambassador MARCO TULIO CHICAS SOSA.

Guinea: 51 rue de la Faisanderie, 75116 Paris; tel. 1-47-04-81-48; fax 1-47-04-57-65; e-mail accueil@ambaguinee-paris.org; Ambassador AMARA CAMARA.

Guinea-Bissau: 94 rue Saint Lazare, 75009 Paris; tel. 1-48-74-36-39; fax 1-48-78-36-39; e-mail ambaguineebxo@wanadoo.fr; Ambassador (vacant).

Haiti: 10 rue Théodule Ribot, BP 275, 75017 Paris; tel. 1-47-63-47-78; fax 1-42-27-02-05; e-mail ambhaitiparis@orange.fr; Chargé d'affaires a.i. FRITZNER GASPARD.

Holy See: 10 ave du Président Wilson, 75116 Paris (Apostolic Nunciature); tel. 1-53-23-01-50; fax 1-47-23-65-44; e-mail noncapfr@wanadoo.fr; Apostolic Nuncio Most Rev. LUIGI VENTURA.

Honduras: 8 rue Crevaux, 75116 Paris; tel. 1-47-55-86-45; fax 1-47-55-86-48; e-mail ambassade.honduras@yahoo.com; Ambassador MAX VELÁSQUEZ DÍAZ.

Hungary: 5 bis sq. de l'ave Foch, 75116 Paris; tel. 1-45-00-94-97; fax 1-56-36-02-68; e-mail mission.par@mfa.gov.hu; internet www.mfa.gov.hu/emb/paris; Ambassador GEORGE KAROLYI.

Iceland: 52 ave Victor Hugo, 75116 Paris; tel. 1-44-17-32-85; fax 1-40-67-99-96; e-mail paris@mfa.is; internet www.iceland.is/fr; Ambassador BERGLIND ASGEIRSDÓTTIR.

India: 15 rue Alfred Dehodencq, 75016 Paris; tel. 1-40-50-70-70; fax 1-40-50-09-96; e-mail pic.2@wanadoo.fr; internet www.amb-inde.fr; Ambassador ARUN K. SINGH.

Indonesia: 47–49 rue Cortambert, 75116 Paris; tel. 1-45-03-07-60; fax 1-45-04-50-32; e-mail komparis@online.fr; internet www.amb-indonesie.fr; Ambassador REZLAN ISHAR JENIE.

Iran: 4 ave d'Iéna, 75116 Paris; tel. 1-40-69-79-00; fax 1-40-70-01-57; e-mail cabinet@amb-iran.fr; internet www.amb-iran.fr; Ambassador ALI AHANI.

Iraq: 53 rue de la Faisanderie, 75016 Paris; tel. 1-45-53-33-70; fax 1-45-53-33-80; e-mail paremb@iraqmfamail.com; internet www.amb-iraq.fr; Ambassador FARID MUSTAFA KAMIL YASSEIN.

Ireland: 12 ave Foch, 75116 Paris; tel. 1-44-17-67-00; fax 1-44-17-67-50; e-mail paris@dfa.ie; internet www.embassyofireland.fr; Ambassador GERALDINE BYRNE-NASON.

Israel: 3 rue Rabelais, 75008 Paris; tel. 1-40-76-55-00; fax 1-40-76-55-55; e-mail information@paris.mfa.gov.il; internet embassies.gov.il/paris; Ambassador YOSSI GAL.

Italy: 51 rue de Varenne, 75343 Paris Cedex 07; tel. 1-49-54-03-00; fax 1-45-54-04-10; e-mail ambasciata.parigi@esteri.it; internet www.ambparigi.esteri.it; Ambassador GIANDOMENICO MAGLIANO.

Japan: 7 ave Hoche, 75008 Paris; tel. 1-48-88-62-00; fax 1-42-27-50-81; e-mail info-fr@ps.mofa.go.jp; internet www.fr.emb-japan.go.jp; Ambassador YOICHI SUZUKI.

Jordan: 80 blvd Maurice Barrès, 92200 Neuilly-sur-Seine; tel. 1-55-62-00-00; fax 1-55-62-00-06; e-mail amjo.paris@wanadoo.fr; Ambassador MAKRAM MUSTAFA QUEISI.

Kazakhstan: 59 rue Pierre Charron, 75008 Paris; tel. 1-45-61-52-00; fax 1-45-61-52-01; e-mail info@amb-kazakhstan.fr; internet www.amb-kazakhstan.fr; Ambassador NURLAN DANENOV.

Kenya: 3 rue Freycinet, 75016 Paris; tel. 1-56-62-25-25; fax 1-47-20-44-41; e-mail info@ambassade-kenya.fr; internet www.kenyaembassyparis.org; Ambassador SALMA AHMED.

Korea, Republic: 125 rue de Grenelle, 75007 Paris; tel. 1-47-53-01-01; fax 1-47-53-00-41; e-mail koremb-fr@mofat.go.kr; internet fra.mofat.go.kr; Ambassador LEE HYE-MIN.

Kuwait: 2 rue de Lübeck, 75016 Paris; tel. 1-47-23-54-25; fax 1-47-20-33-59; Ambassador ALI SULAIMAN al-SAEID.

Laos: 74 ave Raymond Poincaré, 75116 Paris; tel. 1-45-53-02-98; fax 1-47-57-27-89; e-mail contact@ambalaos-france.com; internet www.ambalaos-france.com; Ambassador OUAN PHOMMACHACK.

Latvia: 6 villa Saïd, 75116 Paris; tel. 1-53-64-58-10; fax 1-53-64-58-19; e-mail embassy.france@mfa.gov.lv; internet www.am.gov.lv/paris; Ambassador SANITA PAVLUTA-DESLANDES.

Lebanon: 3 villa Copernic, 75116 Paris; tel. 1-40-67-75-75; fax 1-40-67-16-42; e-mail na@ambliban.fr; internet www.ambassadeliban.fr; Ambassador BOUTROS ASSAKER.

Liberia: 12 place du Général Catroux, 75017 Paris; tel. 1-47-63-58-55; fax 1-42-12-76-14; e-mail libem.paris@wanadoo.fr; Ambassador Dr C. WILLIAM ALLEN.

Libya: 6–8 rue Chasseloup-Laubat, 75015 Paris; tel. 1-47-04-71-60; fax 1-47-55-96-25; Ambassador ALSHIABANI MANSOUR ABUHAMOUD.

Lithuania: 22 blvd de Courcelles, 75017 Paris; tel. 1-40-54-50-50; fax 1-40-54-50-75; e-mail amb.fr@urm.lt; internet fr.mfa.lt; Ambassador DALIUS ČEKUOLIS.

Luxembourg: 33 ave Rapp, 75007 Paris; tel. 1-45-55-13-37; fax 1-45-51-72-29; e-mail paris.amb@mae.etat.lu; internet paris.mae.lu; Ambassador PAUL DÜHR.

Macedonia, former Yugoslav republic: 5 rue de la Faisanderie, 75116 Paris; tel. 1-45-77-10-50; fax 1-45-77-14-84; e-mail paris@mfa.gov.mk; internet www.missions.gov.mk/paris; Ambassador AGRON BUDZAKU.

Madagascar: 4 ave Raphaël, 75016 Paris; tel. 1-45-04-62-11; fax 1-45-03-58-70; e-mail accueil@ambassade-madagascar.fr; Chargé d'affaires a.i. VÉRONIQUE RESAKA.

Malaysia: 2 bis rue Bénouville, 75116 Paris; tel. 1-45-53-11-85; fax 1-47-27-34-60; e-mail malparis@kln.gov.my; internet www.kln.gov.my/web/fra_paris; Ambassador TAN SRI ISMAIL OMAR.

Mali: 89 rue du Cherche-Midi, BP 175, 75263 Paris Cedex 06; tel. 1-45-48-58-43; fax 1-45-48-55-34; e-mail ambamali.paris@wanadoo.fr; Ambassador BOUBACAR SIDIKI TOURE.

Malta: 23 rue d'Artois, 75008 Paris; tel. 1-56-59-75-90; fax 1-45-62-00-36; e-mail maltaembassy.paris@gov.mt; internet www.mfa.gov.mt/france; Ambassador VINCENT CAMILLERI.

Mauritania: 5 rue de Montévidéo, 75116 Paris; tel. 1-45-04-88-54; fax 1-40-72-82-96; e-mail ambassade.mauritanie@wanadoo.fr; Ambassador ABDOULAYE IDRISSA WAGNE.

Mauritius: 127 rue de Tocqueville, 75017 Paris; tel. 1-42-27-30-19; fax 1-40-53-02-91; e-mail paris@amb-maurice.fr; Ambassador MARIE JOSEPH JACQUES CHASTEAU DE BALYON.

Mexico: 9 rue de Longchamp, 75116 Paris; tel. 1-53-70-27-70; fax 1-47-55-65-29; e-mail embfrancia@sre.gob.mx; internet www.sre.gob.mx/francia; Ambassador AGUSTÍN GARCÍA-LÓPEZ.

Moldova: 22 rue Berlioz, 75116 Paris; tel. 1-40-67-11-20; fax 1-40-67-11-23; e-mail ambassade.moldavie@wanadoo.fr; internet www.franta.mfa.md; Ambassador OLEG SEREBRIAN.

Monaco: 22 blvd Suchet, 75016 Paris; tel. 1-45-04-74-54; fax 1-45-04-45-16; e-mail ambassade.en.france@gouv.mc; Ambassador SOPHIE THÉVENOUX.

Mongolia: 5 ave Robert Schuman, 92100 Boulogne-Billancourt; tel. 1-46-05-28-12; fax 1-46-05-30-16; e-mail info@ambassadedemongolie.fr; internet www.ambassademongolie.fr; Ambassador MUNDAGBAATAR BATSAIKHAN.

Montenegro: 216 blvd Saint-Germain, 75007 Paris; tel. 1-53-63-80-30; fax 1-42-22-83-90; e-mail ambasadacg@orange.fr; Ambassador IRENA RADOVIC.

Morocco: 5 rue Le Tasse, 75016 Paris; tel. 1-45-20-69-35; fax 1-45-20-22-58; e-mail info@amb-maroc.fr; internet www.amb-maroc.fr; Ambassador CHAKIB BENMOUSSA.

Mozambique: 82 rue Laugier, 75017 Paris; tel. 1-47-64-91-32; fax 1-44-15-90-13; e-mail embamocparis@wanadoo.fr; Ambassador ALEXANDRE DA CONCEIÇÃO ZANDAMELA.

Myanmar: 60 rue de Courcelles, 75008 Paris; tel. 1-56-88-15-90; fax 1-45-62-13-30; e-mail me-paris@wanadoo.fr; internet myanmarembassy-france.org; Ambassador HAN THU.

Namibia: 80 ave Foch, 75016 Paris; tel. 1-44-17-32-65; fax 1-44-17-32-73; e-mail info@embassyofnamibia.fr; internet www.embassyofnamibia.fr; Ambassador FRIEDA NANGULA ITHETE.

Nepal: 45 bis rue des Acacias, 75017 Paris; tel. 1-46-22-48-67; fax 1-42-27-08-65; e-mail nepalinparis@noos.fr; Ambassador MOHAN KRISHNA SHRESTHA.

Netherlands: 7–9 rue Eblé, 75007 Paris; tel. 1-40-62-33-00; fax 1-40-62-34-56; e-mail ambassade@amb-pays-bas.fr; internet www.amb-pays-bas.fr; Ambassador ED KRONENBURG.

New Zealand: 103 rue de Grenelle, 75007 Paris; tel. 1-45-01-43-43; fax 1-45-01-43-44; e-mail embassy.nz.fr@gmail.com; internet www.nzembassy.com/france; Ambassador ROSEMARY BANKS.

Niger: 154 rue de Longchamp, 75116 Paris; tel. 1-45-04-80-60; fax 1-45-04-79-73; e-mail ambassadeniger@wanadoo.fr; Ambassador ABDERAHAMANE MAYAKI ASSANE.

Nigeria: 173 ave Victor Hugo, 75116 Paris; tel. 1-47-04-68-65; fax 1-47-04-47-54; e-mail embassy@nigeriafrance.com; internet www.nigeriafrance.com; Ambassador HAKEEM O. SULAIMAN.

Norway: 28 rue Bayard, 5e étage, 75008 Paris; tel. 1-53-67-04-00; fax 1-53-67-04-40; e-mail emb.paris@mfa.no; internet www.norvege.no; Ambassador ROLF EINAR FIFE.

Oman: 50 ave d'Iéna, 75116 Paris; tel. 1-47-23-01-63; fax 1-47-23-77-10; e-mail paris@mofa.gov.om; internet www.ambassadeoman.com; Ambassador Sheikh HUMAID BIN ALI BIN SULTAN AL-MAANI.

Pakistan: 18 rue Lord Byron, 75008 Paris; tel. 1-45-62-23-32; fax 1-45-62-89-15; e-mail pakemb_paris@yahoo.com; internet www.pakembparis.com; Ambassador GHALIB IQBAL.

Panama: 145 ave de Suffren, 75015 Paris; tel. 1-45-66-42-44; fax 1-45-67-99-43; e-mail panaemba.francia@wanadoo.fr; internet ambassadedupanama.fr; Ambassador HENRY J. FAARUP.

Paraguay: 1 rue St Dominique, 75007 Paris; tel. 1-42-22-85-05; fax 1-42-22-83-57; e-mail paraguay.ambassade@wanadoo.fr; Ambassador EMILIO GIMÉNEZ FRANCO.

Peru: 50 ave Kléber, 75116 Paris; tel. 1-53-70-42-00; fax 1-47-04-32-55; e-mail perou.ambassade@amb-perou.fr; Ambassador CRISTINA VELITA DE LABOUREIX.

Philippines: 4 Hameau de Boulainvilliers/45 rue du Ranelagh, 75016 Paris; tel. 1-44-14-57-00; fax 1-46-47-56-00; e-mail ambaphilparis@wanadoo.fr; internet www.parispe.dfa.gov.ph; Ambassador THERESA P. LAZARO.

Poland: 1 rue de Talleyrand, 75343 Paris Cedex 07; tel. 1-43-17-34-05; fax 1-43-17-35-07; e-mail paris.amb.info@msz.gov.pl; internet www.paryz.msz.gov.pl; Ambassador ANDRZEJ BYRT.

Portugal: 3 rue de Noisiel, 75116 Paris; tel. 1-47-27-35-29; fax 1-44-05-94-02; e-mail mailto@embaixada-portugal-fr.org; internet www.embaixada-portugal-fr.org; Ambassador JOSÉ FILIPE MORAES CABRAL.

Qatar: 1 rue de Tilsitt, 75008 Paris; tel. 1-45-51-90-71; fax 1-45-51-77-07; e-mail paris@mofa.gov.qa; internet www.qatarambassade.com; Ambassador MESHAL BIN HAMAD MOHAMED JABR AL-THANI.

Romania: 5 rue de l'Exposition, 75007 Paris; tel. 1-47-05-10-46; fax 1-45-56-97-47; e-mail secretariat@amb-roumanie.fr; internet paris.mae.ro; Ambassador BOGDAN MAZURU.

Russian Federation: 40–50 blvd Lannes, 75116 Paris; tel. 1-45-04-05-50; fax 1-45-04-17-65; e-mail ambrus@wanadoo.fr; internet www.france.mid.ru; Ambassador ALEKSANDRE ORLOV.

Rwanda: 12 rue Jadin, 75017 Paris; tel. 1-71-19-91-91; fax 1-71-19-99-95; e-mail ambarwanda.paris@gmail.com; Ambassador JACQUES KABALE NYANGEZI.

San Marino: 22 rue d'Artois, 75008 Paris; tel. and fax 1-47-23-04-75; e-mail saint-marin@wanadoo.fr; Ambassador GIANPIERO SAMORI.

Saudi Arabia: 5 ave Hoche, 75008 Paris; tel. 1-56-79-40-00; fax 1-56-79-40-01; e-mail amb.arabiesaoudite@gmail.com; Ambassador Dr MUHAMMAD BIN ISMAIL AL AL-SHEIKH.

Senegal: 14 ave Robert Schuman, 75007 Paris; tel. 1-47-05-39-45; fax 1-45-56-04-30; e-mail repsen@wanadoo.fr; internet www.ambasseneparis.com; Ambassador PAUL BADJI.

Serbia: 5 rue Léonard de Vinci, 75116 Paris; tel. 1-40-72-24-24; fax 1-40-72-24-11; e-mail ambasadapariz@wanadoo.fr; internet www.paris.mfa.gov.rs; Ambassador RAJKO RISTIĆ.

Seychelles: 51 ave Mozart, 75016 Paris; tel. 1-42-30-57-47; fax 1-42-30-57-40; e-mail ambsey@aol.com; Ambassador BERNARD SHAMLAYE.

Singapore: 16 rue Murillo, 75008 Paris; tel. 1-56-79-68-00; fax 1-56-79-68-29; e-mail singemb_par@sgmfa.gov.sg; internet www.mfa.gov.sg/paris; Ambassador TAN YORK CHOR.

Slovakia: 125 rue du Ranelagh, 75016 Paris; tel. 1-77-93-73-33; fax 1-42-88-76-53; e-mail emb.paris@mzv.sk; internet www.mzv.sk/paris; Ambassador MAREK EŠTOK.

Slovenia: 28 rue Bois-le-Vent, 75016 Paris; tel. 1-44-96-50-71; fax 1-45-24-67-05; e-mail vpa@gov.si; internet paris.embassy.si; Ambassador VERONIKA STABEJ.

Somalia: 26 rue Dumont d'Urville, 75116 Paris; tel. 1-39-52-73-08; e-mail webmaster@somaligov.net; internet www.france.somaligov.net; Ambassador ALI SAID FAQI.

South Africa: 59 quai d'Orsay, 75343 Paris Cedex 07; tel. 1-53-59-23-23; fax 1-53-59-23-68; e-mail info@afriquesud.net; internet www.afriquesud.net; Ambassador RAPULANE SIDNEY MOLEKANE.

Spain: 22 ave Marceau, 75008 Paris Cedex 08; tel. 1-44-43-18-00; fax 1-47-23-59-55; e-mail emb.paris@mae.es; internet www.exteriores.gob.es/embajadas/paris; Ambassador RAMÓN DE MIGUEL.

Sri Lanka: 16 rue Spontini, 75016 Paris; tel. 1-55-73-31-31; fax 1-55-73-18-49; e-mail sl.france@wanadoo.fr; internet www.srilankaembassy.fr; Chargé d'affaires a.i. SHOBINI GUNASEKERA.

Sudan: 11 rue Alfred Dehodencq, 75016 Paris; tel. 1-42-25-55-71; fax 1-54-63-66-73; e-mail ambassade-du-soudan@wanadoo.fr; Ambassador NASRELDIN AHMED WALI.

Suriname: 94 rue du Ranelagh, 75016 Paris; tel. 1-45-25-93-00; fax 1-56-43-76-96; e-mail amb.frankrijk@foreignaffairs.gov.sr; internet www.ambassadesurinamefr.org; Ambassador HARVEY H. NAARENDORP.

Sweden: 17 rue Barbet-de-Jouy, 75007 Paris; tel. 1-44-18-88-00; fax 1-44-18-88-77; e-mail info@amb-suede.fr; internet www.sweden abroad.com/paris; Ambassador VERONIKA WAND-DANIELSSON.

Switzerland: 142 rue de Grenelle, 75007 Paris; tel. 1-49-55-67-00; fax 1-49-55-67-67; e-mail par.vertretung@eda.admin.ch; internet www.eda.admin.ch/paris; Ambassador BERNARDINO REGAZZONI.

Syria: 20 rue Vaneau, 75007 Paris; tel. 1-40-62-61-00; fax 1-47-05-92-73; e-mail info@ambassadesyrie.fr; internet www.ambassadesyrie.fr; Ambassador MOUNZIR MAKHOUS.

Tajikistan: 14 ave d'Eylau, 75016 Paris; tel. 1-70-92-93-42; e-mail info@tajembfrance.fr; internet www.tajembfrance.fr; Ambassador HOMIDJON T. NAZAROV.

Tanzania: 7 rue Léonard de Vinci, 75116 Paris; tel. 1-53-70-63-66; fax 1-47-55-05-46; e-mail ambtanzanie@wanadoo.fr; internet tanzaniaembassy.fr; Ambassador BEGUM KARIM TAJ.

Thailand: 8 rue Greuze, 75116 Paris; tel. 1-56-26-50-50; fax 1-56-26-04-45; e-mail thaipar@wanadoo.fr; internet www.thaiembassy.fr; Ambassador APICHART CHINWANNO.

Togo: 8 rue Alfred Roll, 75017 Paris; tel. 1-43-80-12-13; fax 1-43-80-06-05; e-mail france@ambassadetogo.org; internet france .ambassadetogo.org; Ambassador CALIXTE BATOSSIE MADJOULBA.

Tunisia: 25 rue Barbet-de-Jouy, 75007 Paris; tel. 1-45-55-95-98; fax 1-45-56-02-64; e-mail atn.paris@wanadoo.fr; internet ambassade-tunisie.fr; Ambassador MOHAMED ALI CHIHI.

Turkey: 16 ave de Lamballe, 75016 Paris; tel. 1-53-92-71-11; fax 1-45-20-41-91; e-mail ambassade.paris@mfa.gov.tr; internet paris .emb.mfa.gov.tr; Ambassador HAKKI AKIL.

Turkmenistan: 13 rue Picot, 75116 Paris; tel. 1-47-55-05-36; fax 1-47-55-05-68; e-mail turkmenamb@free.fr; Ambassador TCHARY G. NIYAZOV.

Uganda: 13 ave Raymond Poincaré, 75116 Paris; tel. 1-56-90-12-20; fax 1-45-05-21-22; e-mail uganda.embassy@club-internet.fr; Ambassador NISHIMA JAYANT MADHVANI.

Ukraine: 21 ave de Saxe, 75007 Paris; tel. 1-43-06-07-37; fax 1-43-06-02-94; e-mail ambassadeukraine.fr@gmail.com; internet www .mfa.gov.ua/france; Ambassador OLEG V. SHAMSHUR.

United Arab Emirates: 2 blvd de la Tour Maubourg, 75007 Paris; tel. 1-44-34-02-00; fax 1-47-55-61-04; e-mail ambassade.emirats@ wanadoo.fr; Ambassador MUHAMMAD ABDULLAH AL-MEER RAEESI.

United Kingdom: 35 rue du Faubourg St Honoré, 75383 Paris Cedex 08; tel. 1-44-51-31-00; fax 1-44-51-31-09; e-mail public.paris@ fco.gov.uk; internet ukinfrance.fco.gov.uk; Ambassador Sir PETER RICKETTS.

USA: 2 ave Gabriel, 75382 Paris Cedex 08; tel. 1-43-12-22-22; fax 1-42-66-97-83; internet france.usembassy.gov; Ambassador JANE HARTLEY.

Uruguay: 15 rue Le Sueur, 75116 Paris; tel. 1-45-00-81-37; fax 1-45-01-25-17; e-mail urufrancia@mrree.gub.uy; Ambassador Dr OMAR GONZÁLEZ MESA.

Uzbekistan: 22 rue d'Aguesseau, 75008 Paris; tel. 1-53-30-03-53; fax 1-53-30-03-54; e-mail contact@ouzbekistan.fr; internet www .ouzbekistan.fr; Ambassador RAVSHAN USMANOV.

Venezuela: 11 rue Copernic, 75116 Paris; tel. 1-45-53-29-98; fax 1-47-55-64-56; e-mail info@amb-venezuela.fr; internet www .embavenez-paris.fr; Ambassador HÉCTOR MICHEL MUJICA RICARDO.

Viet Nam: 61 rue de Miromesnil, 75008 Paris; tel. 1-44-14-64-00; e-mail vnparis.fr@gmail.com; internet ambassade-vietnam.com; Ambassador DUONG CHI DUNG.

Yemen: 25 rue Georges Bizet, 75116 Paris; tel. 1-53-23-87-87; fax 1-47-23-69-41; e-mail ambyemenparis@easynet.fr; Ambassador KHALED ISMAIL AL-AKWA'A.

Zambia: 18 ave de Tourville, 75007 Paris; tel. 1-56-88-12-70; fax 1-56-88-03-50; e-mail zambiansparis@wanadoo.fr; Chargé d'affaires PHILOMENA KACHESA.

Zimbabwe: 10 rue Jacques Bingen, 75017 Paris; tel. 1-56-88-16-00; fax 1-56-88-16-09; e-mail zimparisweb@wanadoo.fr; internet www .zimparis.gov.zw; Ambassador RUDO MABEL CHITIGA.

Judicial System

The judiciary is independent of the Government. Judges of the Cour de Cassation (Court of Cassation) and the First President of the Cour d'Appel (Court of Appeal) are appointed by the executive from nominations of the High Council of the Judiciary.

Subordinate cases are heard by Tribunaux d'Instance and more serious cases by Tribunaux de Grande Instance. Parallel to these Tribunals are the Tribunaux de Commerce, for commercial cases, composed of judges elected by traders and manufacturers among themselves. These do not exist in every district. Where there is no Tribunal de Commerce, commercial disputes are judged by Tribunaux de Grande Instance.

The Conseils des Prud'hommes (Boards of Arbitration) consist of an equal number of workers or employees and employers ruling on the differences that arise over Contracts of Work.

The Tribunaux Correctionnels (Correctional Courts) for criminal cases correspond to the Tribunaux de Grande Instance for civil cases. They pronounce on all graver offences (délits), including those involving imprisonment. Offences committed by juveniles of under 18 years go before specialized tribunals.

From all these Tribunals appeal lies to the Cour d'Appel (Court of Appeal).

The Cours d'Assises (Courts of Assize) have no regular sittings, but are called when necessary to try every important case, such as murder. They are presided over by judges who are members of the Courts of Appeal, and are composed of elected judges (jury). Their decision is final, except where shown to be wrong in law, and then recourse is to the Court of Cassation. The Court of Cassation is not a supreme court of appeal but a higher authority for the proper application of the law. Its duty is to see that judgments are not contrary either to the letter or the spirit of the law; any judgment annulled by the Court involves the trying of the case anew by a court of the same category as that which made the original decision.

A programme of extensive reforms in the judicial system, which aimed to reduce political control of the judiciary and to increase citizens' rights, was introduced in stages between 1997 and 2001. A notable innovation introduced by these reforms was the introduction of the convention that a person accused of a crime is presumed innocent unless otherwise proven.

In 2011 reforms to reduce the number of judicial districts from 1,190 to 862 were completed.

Cour de Cassation (Court of Cassation): 5 quai de l'Horloge, 75055 Paris Cedex 01; tel. 1-44-32-95-95; fax 1-44-32-78-29; e-mail webmstre@courdecassation.fr; internet www.courdecassation.fr; seven First Attorneys-General, 29 Attorneys-General, 88 Counsellors and 65 Junior Counsellors; First Pres. BERTRAND LOUVEL; Attorney-General JEAN-CLAUDE MARIN.

Cour d'Appel de Paris (Paris Court of Appeal): 34 quai des Orfèvres, 75055 Paris Cedex 01; tel. 1-44-32-52-52; internet www .ca-paris.justice.fr; there are 61 Presidents of Chambers, 124 Counsellors, 22 Attorneys-General and 36 Deputies; First Pres. JACQUES DEGRANDI; Solicitor-Gen. FRANÇOIS FALLETTI.

Tribunal de Grande Instance de Paris: 4 blvd du Palais, 75055 Paris RP; tel. 1-44-32-51-51; fax 1-43-29-12-55; internet www .ca-paris.justice.fr; Pres. CHANTAL ARENS; Solicitor of the Republic of Paris FRANÇOIS MOLINS.

Tribunal de Commerce de Paris: 1 quai de Corse, 75181 Paris Cedex 04; tel. 1-44-32-83-83; fax 1-40-46-07-28; e-mail sandrine .carret@greffe-tc-paris.fr; internet www.greffe-tc-paris.fr; Pres. FRANK GENTIN.

Tribunal des Conflits: Conseil d'Etat, 1 place du Palais Royal, 75100 Paris Cedex 01; tel. 1-40-20-80-87; internet www .tribunal-conflits.fr; decides whether cases shall be submitted to the ordinary or administrative courts; Pres. THE KEEPER OF THE SEALS, MINISTER OF JUSTICE; Vice-Pres. JEAN-LOUIS GALLET.

Cour des Comptes (Audit Court): 13 rue Cambon, 75001 Paris Cedex 01; tel. 1-42-98-95-00; fax 1-42-60-01-59; e-mail courdescomptes@ccomptes.fr; internet www.ccomptes.fr; an administrative tribunal competent to judge the correctness of public accounts. It is the arbiter of common law of all public accounts laid before it. The judgments of the Court may be annulled by the Conseil d'Etat (Council of State); First Pres. DIDIER MIGAUD; Solicitor-Gen. GILLES JOHANET.

Chambres Régionales et Territoriales des Comptes: In 1983 jurisdiction over the accounts of local administrations (régions, départements and communes) and public institutions (hospitals, council housing, etc.) was transferred from the Cour des Comptes (Audit Court) to local Chambres Régionales. Chambres Territoriales were subsequently created in New Caledonia (in 1988), French Polynesia (in 1990), and Mayotte, Saint-Barthélemy, Saint-Martin and Saint Pierre and Miquelon (in 2007). The 32 courts (26 Chambres Régionales and six Chambres Territoriales) are autonomous, but under the jurisdiction of the state. Appeals may be brought before the Audit Court.

Conseil d'Etat (Council of State): 1 place du Palais-Royal, 75100 Paris 01 SP; tel. 1-40-20-80-00; fax 1-40-20-80-08; e-mail chantal .leveque@conseil-etat.fr; internet www.conseil-etat.fr; the Council of State is the consultative organ of the Government and the supreme administrative court. It gives opinions to the Government in the legislative and administrative domain (interior, finance, public works and social sections) and has three functions in administrative jurisdiction: to judge in the first and last resort such cases as appeals against excess of power laid against official decrees or individuals; to judge appeals against judgments made by Tribunaux Administratifs, Cours Administratives d'Appel and resolutions of courts of litigation;

and to annul decisions made by various specialized administrative authorities that adjudicate without appeal, such as the Cour des Comptes (Audit Court); Pres. THE PRIME MINISTER; Vice-Pres. JEAN-MARC SAUVÉ; Gen. Sec. FRANÇOISE SENERS.

Tribunaux Administratifs (Administrative Tribunals): Certain cases arising between civil servants (when on duty) and the Government, or between any citizen and the Government are judged by special administrative courts. The Administrative Tribunals, of which there are 31 in metropolitan France 11 nine in the overseas possessions, are situated in the capital of each area.

Conseil Constitutionnel (Constitutional Council): 2 rue de Montpensier, 75001 Paris; tel. 1-40-15-30-00; fax 1-40-20-93-27; e-mail informatique@conseil-constitutionnel.fr; internet www.conseil -constitutionnel.fr; Pres. JEAN-LOUIS DEBRÉ.

Religion

CHRISTIANITY

Conseil d'Eglises Chrétiennes en France: 58 ave de Breteuil, 75007 Paris; tel. 1-72-36-69-60; fax 1-73-72-96-67; e-mail anne.jan@ cef.fr; f. 1987; ecumenical organization comprising representatives from all Christian denominations to express opinions on social issues; 21 mems; Pres. Pastor CLAUDE BATY, Cardinal ANDRÉ VINGT-TROIS, Most Rev. EMMANUEL (ADAMAKIS); Secs Pastor JANE STRANZ, Fr FRANCK LEMAÎTRE.

The Roman Catholic Church

For ecclesiastical purposes, France comprises nine Apostolic Regions, together forming 24 archdioceses (of which one, Strasbourg, is directly responsible to the Holy See), 72 dioceses (including one, Metz, directly responsible to the Holy See) and one Territorial Prelature. The Archbishop of Paris is also the Ordinary for Catholics of Oriental Rites. At 31 December 2006 an estimated 74.4% of the population were adherents of the Roman Catholic Church.

Bishops' Conference: Conférence des Evêques de France, 58 ave de Breteuil, 75007 Paris; tel. 1-72-36-68-00; fax 1-73-72-97-22; e-mail cef@cef.fr; internet www.eglise.catholique.fr; Pres. Most Rev. GEORGES PAUL PONTIER (Archbishop of Marseille); Sec.-Gen. Fr OLIVIER RIBADEAU DUMAS.

Archbishop of Lyon and Primate of Gaul: Cardinal PHILIPPE BARBARIN, 6 ave Adolphe Max, 69321 Lyon Cedex 05; tel. 4-78-81-48-15; fax 4-78-81-47-70; e-mail petre@lyon.catholique.fr; internet lyon .catholique.fr.

Archbishop of Albi: Most Rev. JEAN MARIE HENRI LEGREZ.

Archbishop of Auch: Most Rev. MAURICE GARDÈS.

Archbishop of Avignon: Most Rev. JEAN-PIERRE MARIE CATTENOZ.

Archbishop of Besançon: Most Rev. JEAN-LUC MARIE MAURICE LOUIS BOUILLERET.

Archbishop of Bordeaux: Cardinal JEAN-PIERRE BERNARD RICARD.

Archbishop of Bourges: Most Rev. ARMAND MAILLARD.

Archbishop of Cambrai: Most Rev. FRANÇOIS GARNIER.

Archbishop of Chambéry: Most Rev. PHILIPPE BALLOT.

Archbishop of Clermont: Most Rev. HIPPOLYTE SIMON.

Archbishop of Dijon: Most Rev. ROLAND MINNERATH.

Archbishop of Marseille: Most Rev. GEORGES PAUL PONTIER.

Archbishop of Montpellier: Most Rev. PIERRE-MARIE CARRÉ.

Archbishop of Paris: Cardinal ANDRÉ ARMAND VINGT-TROIS.

Archbishop of Poitiers: Most Rev. PASCAL JEAN MARCEL WINTZER.

Archbishop of Reims: Most Rev. THIERRY JORDAN.

Archbishop of Rennes: Most Rev. PIERRE D'ORNELLAS.

Archbishop of Rouen: Most Rev. JEAN-CHARLES DESCUBES.

Archbishop of Sens-Auxerre: Most Rev. HERVÉ JEAN ROBERT GIRAUD.

Archbishop of Strasbourg: Most Rev. JEAN-PIERRE GRALLET.

Archbishop of Toulouse: Most Rev. ROBERT JEAN-LOUIS LE GALL.

Archbishop of Tours: Most Rev. BERNARD-NICOLAS JEAN-MARIE AUBERTIN.

Protestant Churches

There are some 950,000 Protestants in France.

Eglise Méthodiste: 3 rue Paul Verlaine, 30100 Alès; tel. 4-66-86-20-72; e-mail ales@ales.umc-europe.org; internet ales.umc-europe.org; Pres. JEAN PIERRE OZIL; the total Methodist community was estimated at 1,000 mems in 2001.

Fédération Protestante de France: 47 rue de Clichy, 75311 Paris; tel. 1-44-53-47-12; fax 1-42-81-40-01; e-mail fpf@protestants.org; internet www.protestants.org; f. 1905; Pres. Pastor FRANÇOIS CLAVAIROLY; Gen. Sec. Pastor GEORGES MICHEL.

The Federation includes:

Armée du Salut (Foundation and Congregation): 60 rue des Frères Flavien, 75976 Paris Cedex 20; tel. 1-43-62-25-00; fax 1-43-62-25-57; e-mail info@armeedusalut.fr; internet www .armeedusalut.fr; f. 1881; Pres. Col MASSIMO PAONE.

Communauté Protestante Evangélique de Vannes: 18 blvd Edouard Herriot, 56000 Vannes; tel. and fax 2-97-47-16-75; e-mail communauteprotestante.vannes@wanadoo.fr; Pres. of the Council of the Church MARK PLUNIER.

Eglise Protestante de la Confession d'Augsbourg d'Alsace et de Lorraine (EPCAAL): 1 quai St Thomas, BP 80022, 67081 Strasbourg Cedex; tel. 3-8825-90-00; fax 3-88-25-90-99; e-mail contact@uepal.fr; internet www.uepal.fr; 250,000 mems; mem. of Union des Eglises Protestantes d'Alsace et de Lorraine; Pres. CHRISTIAN ALBECKER.

Eglise Protestante Evangélique de Rochefort: 30 Quéreux de la Laiterie, 17300 Rochefort; tel. 5-46-87-21-44; internet eper.fr.

Eglise Protestante Réformée d'Alsace et de Lorraine (EPRAL): 1 quai St Thomas, BP 80022, 67081 Strasbourg Cedex; tel. 3-88-25-90-00; fax 3-88-25-90-99; e-mail contact@uepal.fr; mem. of Union des Eglises Protestantes d'Alsace et de Lorraine; 33,000 mems; Pres. Pastor CHRISTIAN KRIEGER.

Eglise Protestante Unie de France: 47 rue de Clichy, 75311 Paris Cedex 09; tel. 1-48-74-90-92; e-mail communication@ eglise-protestante-unie.fr; internet www.eglise-protestante-unie .fr; f. 2012; formed by merger of Eglise Evangélique Luthérienne (f. 1872) and Eglise Réformée de France; Pres. Pastor LAURENT SCHLUMBERGER.

Fédération des Eglises Evangéliques Baptistes de France: 47 rue de Clichy, 75311 Paris Cedex 09; tel. 1-53-20-15-40; fax 1-53-20-15-41; e-mail secretariat@feebf.com; internet www.feebf.com; 6,000 mems; f. 1910; Pres. JEAN DUPUPET.

Mission Populaire Evangélique de France: 47 rue de Clichy, 75009 Paris Cedex 09; tel. 1-48-74-98-58; fax 1-48-78-52-37; e-mail mpef@free.fr; internet www.missionpopulaire.org; 4,000 mems, f. 1871; Pres. Pastor BERTRAND VERGNIOL.

Union des Eglises Evangéliques Libres de France: 12 rue Claude-Perrault, 31500 Toulouse; tel. 5-61-26-06-18; fax 5-61-99-02-82; e-mail pierre.lacoste@protestants.org; internet www.ueel .org; 2,500 mems; Pres. Pastor PIERRE LACOSTE; Sec. RAYMOND CHAMARD.

Union Nationale des Eglises Protestantes Réformées Evangéliques de France: 74 rue Henri Revoil, 30900 Nîmes; tel. 4-66-23-95-05; e-mail uneprefcompta@orange.fr; internet www.unepref .com; f. 1938; 3,500 mems; Pres. JEAN-RAYMOND STAUFFACHER; Sec. MONIQUE BRUGUIÈRE.

Scots Kirk Paris (Church of Scotland): 17 rue Bayard, 75008 Paris; tel. and fax 1-48-78-47-94; e-mail scotskirk@wanadoo.fr; internet www.scotskirkparis.com; Minister Rev. JIM COWIE.

The Orthodox Church

There are about 200,000 Orthodox believers in France, of whom 100,000 are Russian Orthodox and 50,000 Greek Orthodox. There are 85 parishes and eight monasteries.

Administration of Russian Orthodox Churches in Western Europe (Jurisdiction of the Ecumenical Patriarchate): Cathédrale St Alexandre-Nevski, 12 rue Daru, 75008 Paris; tel. and fax 1-46-22-38-91; e-mail administration.diocesaine@exarchat.eu; internet www.exarchat.eu; Pres. Most Rev. JOB (Archbishop of Russian Orthodox Churches in Western Europe and Exarch of the Ecumenical Patriarch).

Assembly of the Orthodox Churches of France (Greek Orthodox Church): Cathédrale St Stéphane, 7 rue Georges Bizet, 75116 Paris; tel. 1-47-20-82-35; fax 1-47-20-83-15; e-mail eglise.orthodoxe .grecque@wanadoo.fr; f. 1997; Metropolitan of France Most Rev. EMMANUEL (ADAMAKIS).

Russian Orthodox Church (Moscow Patriarchate): 26 rue Péclet, 75015 Paris; tel. 1-48-28-99-90; fax 1-48-28-74-54; e-mail presse@egliserusse.eu; internet www.egliserusse.eu; the diocese of Chersonesus covers France, Portugal, Spain and Switzerland; Bishop of Chersonesus NESTOR SIROTENKO.

The Anglican Communion

Within the Church of England, France forms part of the diocese of Gibraltar in Europe. The Bishop is resident in London (UK).

Archdeacon of France: Ven. IAN FREDERICK NAYLOR, 3 bis rue Pasteur, 64000 Pau; tel. 5-59-30-91-84; e-mail if.naylor@orange.fr.

Other Christian Denominations

Société Religieuse des Amis (Quakers, Assemblée de France)/ Centre Quaker International: 114 rue de Vaugirard, 75006 Paris; tel. 1-45-48-74-23; e-mail assembleedefrance@gmail.com; internet quaker.chez-alice.fr; f. 1920; 10 meetings nationwide; Clerk SYLVETTE THOMPSON.

ISLAM

In numerical terms, Islam is the second most important religion in France; in 2006 there were about 5m. adherents, of whom some 35% resided in the Ile-de-France region.

Conseil Français du Culte Musulman (CFCM): 270 rue Lecourbe, 75015 Paris; tel. 1-45-58-05-73; fax 1-45-58-24-06; internet www.lecfcm.fr; f. 2003 to represent Islamic interests to the public authorities; Pres. DALIL BOUBAKEUR; Sec.-Gen. T. SEBTI.

Fédération Nationale des Musulmans de France (FNMF): 33 rue Polonceau, 75018 Paris; e-mail fnmf1@aol.com; f. 1985; 20 asscns; Pres. MOHAMED BECHARI.

Institut Musulman de la Grande Mosquée de Paris: 2 bis place du Puits de l'Ermite, 75005 Paris; tel. 1-45-35-97-33; fax 1-45-35-16-23; e-mail rectorat@mosquee-de-paris.net; internet www .mosqueedeparis.net; f. 1926; cultural, diplomatic, social, judicial and religious sections; research and information and commercial annexes; Rector Dr DALIL BOUBAKEUR.

JUDAISM

There are about 650,000 Jews in France.

Conseil Représentatif des Institutions Juives de France (CRIF): 39 rue Broca, 75005 Paris; tel. 1-42-17-11-11; fax 1-42-17-11-50; e-mail infocrif@crif.org; internet www.crif.org; 63 asscns; Pres. ROGER CUKIERMAN.

Consistoire Central—Union des Communautés Juives de France: 19 rue Saint Georges, 75009 Paris; tel. 1-49-70-88-00; fax 1-42-81-03-66; e-mail administration@consistoirecentral.fr; internet www.consistoiredefrance.fr; f. 1808; 230 asscns; Chief Rabbi of France HAÏM KORSIA; Pres. JOËL MERGUI; Dir-Gen. FRÉDÉRIC ATTALI.

Consistoire Israélite de Paris: 17 rue Saint Georges, 75009 Paris; tel. 1-40-82-26-26; e-mail contact@consistoire.org; internet www .consistoire.org; f. 1808; 40,000 mems; Pres. JOËL MERGUI; Chief Rabbi of Paris MICHEL GUGENHEIM; Chief Rabbi of the Consistoire Israélite de Paris ALAIN GOLDMANN.

Fonds Social Juif Unifié (FSJU): Espace Rachi, 39 rue Broca, 75005 Paris; tel. 1-42-17-10-10; fax 1-42-17-10-82; e-mail contact@ fsju.org; internet www.fsju.org; f. 1950; unites the principal orgs supporting Jewish cultural, educational and social activity in France, and seeks to establish closer links between French Jewry and Israel; Pres. ARIEL GOLDMANN.

BAHÁ'Í FAITH

Centre National Bahá'í: 45 rue Pergolèse, 75116 Paris; tel. 1-45-00-90-26; e-mail info@bahai.fr; internet www.bahai-fr.org.

The Press

Most major daily newspapers are owned by individual publishers or by the powerful groups that have developed round either a company or a single personality. The major groups are as follows:

Amaury Group: 25 ave Michelet, 93408 Saint Ouen Cedex; tel. 1-40-10-30-30; fax 1-40-11-15-26; owns *Le Parisien, Aujourd'hui en France*, the sports daily *L'Equipe*, the bi-weekly magazine *France Football*, the weekly *L'Equipe Magazine* and the monthly *Vélo Magazine*; Pres. MARIANNE SIPROUDHIS; Man. Dir MARIE-ODILE AMAURY.

Bayard Presse: 18 rue Barbès, 92128 Montrouge Cedex; tel. 1-74-31-60-60; e-mail communication@bayard-presse.com; internet www .bayardpresse.fr; f. 1873; Roman Catholic press group; owns 143 publs worldwide, incl. the national daily *La Croix*, the magazines *Pèlerin, Panorama, Notre Temps* and several specialized religious publications; Pres. GEORGES SANEROT.

Lagardère Active: 121 ave de Malakoff, 75216 Paris Cedex 16; tel. 1-40-69-16-00; fax 1-40-69-18-54; e-mail contactpresse@hfp.fr; internet www.lagardere.com; f. 2006 by merger of Hachette Filipacchi Médias (f. 1999) and Lagardère Active; controls magazines in France incl. *Paris-Match, Pariscope, Jeune et Jolie, Photo, France-Dimanche, Elle, Télé 7 Jours*; owns 220 magazines worldwide; CEO DENIS OLIVENNES.

Mondadori France: 8 rue François Ory, 92543 Montrouge Cedex; tel. 1-41-33-50-01; e-mail contact@mondadori.fr; internet www .mondadori.fr; fmrly Editions Mondiales, and subsequently Emap France; present name adopted 2006; owned by Arnoldo Mondadori Editore, SpA (Italy); controls more than 40 magazines in France, incl.

Nous Deux, FHM, Science et Vie, Télé-Star, Top Santé, Télépoche, Auto Plus and also specialized magazines; Man. Dir ERNESTO MAURI.

DAILY NEWSPAPERS (PARIS)

La Croix: 18 rue Barbès, 92128 Montrouge Cedex; tel. 1-74-31-60-60; fax 1-74-31-60-69; e-mail lecteurs.lacroix@bayard-presse.com; internet www.la-croix.com; f. 1883; Roman Catholic; Editor JEAN-BAPTISTE DE FOMBELLE; Dir DOMINIQUE QUINIO; circ. in France 98,918 (2012).

Les Echos: 16 rue du Quatre Septembre, 75112 Paris Cedex 02; tel. 1-49-53-65-65; fax 1-45-61-48-92; e-mail redassist@lesechos.fr; internet www.lesechos.fr; f. 1908; acquired by Groupe LVMH in 2007; economic and financial; Editor-in-Chief HENRI GIBIER; circ. in France 119,613 (2012).

L'Equipe: 4 rue Rouget-de-l'Isle, 92130 Issy-les-Moulineaux Cedex; tel. 1-40-93-20-20; fax 1-40-93-20-08; e-mail courrierdeslecteurs@ lequipe.presse.fr; internet www.lequipe.fr; f. 1946; sport; owned by Groupe Amaury; Chair. LOUIS GILLET; Editorial Dir FABRICE JOUHAUD; circ. in France 279,615 (2011).

Le Figaro: 14 blvd Haussmann, 75009 Paris; tel. 1-42-21-62-00; fax 1-42-21-64-05; internet www.lefigaro.fr; f. 1828; owned by Groupe Dassault; morning; news and literary; magazine on Sat.; 3 weekly supplements; Pres. SERGE DASSAULT; Dir-Gen. OLIVIER COSTA DE BEAUREGARD; Editorial Dir FRANZ-OLIVIER GIESBERT; circ. in France 329,367 (2011).

France-Soir: 13 rue Camille Desmoulins, 92130 Issy-les-Moulineaux; tel. 1-56-21-00-00; internet www.francesoir.fr; f. 1941 as *Défense de la France*; present title adopted 1944; Editor RÉMY DESSARTS; circ. in France 23,934 (2008).

L'Humanité: 32 rue Jean Jaurès, 93528 Saint-Denis Cedex; tel. 1-49-22-72-72; fax 1-49-22-74-00; internet www.humanite.presse.fr; f. 1904; communist; morning; Pres. PATRICK LE HYARIC; Editorial Dir PATRICK APEL-MULLER; circ. 49,061 (2008).

International Herald Tribune: 6 bis rue des Graviers, 92521 Neuilly-sur-Seine Cedex; tel. 1-41-43-93-00; fax 1-41-43-93-38; e-mail iht@iht.com; internet www.iht.com; f. 1887; present name adopted 1966; owned by The New York Times Co (USA); English language; Publr STEPHEN DUNBAR-JOHNSON; Man. Editor ALISON SMALE; worldwide circ. 240,322 (2008).

Le Journal Officiel de la République Française: 26 rue Desaix, 75727 Paris Cedex 15; tel. 1-40-58-75-00; fax 1-45-79-17-84; e-mail info@journal-officiel.gouv.fr; internet www.legifrance.gouv.fr; f. 1870; official journal of the Govt; publishes laws, decrees, parliamentary proceedings and economic bulletins; Dir XAVIER PATIER.

Libération: 11 rue Béranger, 75154 Paris Cedex 03; tel. 1-42-76-17-89; fax 1-42-72-94-93; internet www.liberation.com; f. 1973; 37.8% owned by Edouard de Rothschild; Pres. FRANÇOIS MOULIAS; Editorial Dir LAURENT JOFFRIN; circ. in France 119,165 (2011).

Metro: 35 rue Greneta, 75002 Paris; tel. 1-55-34-45-00; fax 1-55-34-45-03; e-mail courrier@publications-metro.fr; internet www .metrofrance.com; f. 2002; distributed free of charge in Paris, Marseille, Lyon, Toulouse, Lille, Bordeaux, Nice, Nantes, Rennes, Strasbourg and Cannes; Propr Metro International (Sweden); Dir-Gen. SOPHIE SACHNINE; Editor CHRISTOPHE JOLY; circ. 490,382 (2011).

Le Monde: 80 blvd Auguste Blanqui, 75707 Paris Cedex 13; tel. 1-42-17-20-00; fax 1-42-17-21-21; e-mail lemonde@lemonde.fr; internet www.lemonde.fr; f. 1944; independent; Chair., Supervisory Bd PIERRE BERGÉ; Dir of Publication LOUIS DREYFUS; Editorial Dir GILLES VAN KOTE (acting); circ. in France 292,062 (2011).

Paris-Turf: Société des Editions France Libre, Bâtiment 270, 45 ave Victor Hugo, BP 60279 Aubervilliers, 93534 La Plaine Saint-Denis Cedex; e-mail info@paris-turf.com; internet www.paris-turf.com; horse racing; Editorial Dir FRANÇOIS HALLOPÉ; circ. 55,894 (2011).

Le Parisien: 25 ave Michelet, 93405 Saint-Ouen Cedex; tel. 1-40-10-30-30; fax 1-40-10-35-16; e-mail courriers@leparisien.com; internet www.leparisien.fr; f. 1944; morning; sold in Paris and surrounding areas; Dir-Gen. JEAN HORNAIN; Editorial Dir STÉPHANE ALBOUY; circ. in France (incl. *Aujourd'hui en France*) 454,298 (2011).

Le Quotidien du Médecin: 21 rue Camille Desmoulins, 92789 Issy-les-Moulineaux Cedex; tel. 1-73-28-13-11; fax 1-73-28-13-10; e-mail redaction@quotimed.com; internet www.quotimed.com; medical journal; Pres. and Dir-Gen. Dr GÉRARD KOUCHNER; Editorial Dir RICHARD LISCIA; circ. 179,949 (Dec. 2011).

La Tribune: 26 rue d'Oradour-sur-Glane, 75725 Paris Cedex 15; tel. 1-44-82-16-16; fax 1-44-82-17-92; e-mail directiondelaredaction@ latribune.fr; internet www.latribune.fr; economic and financial; Pres., Dir of Publication VALÉRIE DECAMP; Editorial Dir JACQUES ROSSELIN; circ. in France 77,122 (2008).

20 Minutes: 50–52 blvd Hausmann, 75427 Paris Cedex 09; tel. 1-53-26-65-65; fax 1-53-26-65-68; e-mail redac-chef@20minutes.fr; internet www.20minutes.fr; f. 2002; distributed free of charge;

Propr Schibsted (Norway); Pres. PIERRE-JEAN BOZO; circ. (2008) 475,287 (Paris), 782,091 (total France).

SUNDAY NEWSPAPERS (PARIS)

Le Journal du Dimanche: 121 ave de Malakoff, 75216 Paris Cedex 16; tel. 1-40-69-16-00; fax 1-40-69-18-54; internet www.lejdd.fr; owned by Groupe Lagardère; Editorial Dir DENIS OLIVENNES; circ. 257,257 (2011).

Le Parisien Dimanche: 25 ave Michelet, 93405 Saint Ouen Cedex; tel. 1-40-10-30-30; fax 1-40-10-35-16; e-mail infoat@leparisien.fr; internet www.leparisien.fr; circ. 199,204 (2011).

PRINCIPAL PROVINCIAL DAILY NEWSPAPERS

Amiens

Le Courrier Picard: 29 rue de la République, BP 1021, 80010 Amiens Cedex 01; tel. 3-22-82-60-00; fax 3-22-82-60-11; e-mail courrier@courrier-picard.fr; internet www.courrier-picard.fr; f. 1944; Chair./Man. MICHEL COLLET; Editor-in-Chief DIDIER LOUIS; circ. 58,239 (2011).

Angers

Le Courrier de l'Ouest: 4 blvd Albert Blanchoin, BP 10728, 49007 Angers Cedex 01; tel. 2-41-68-86-88; fax 2-41-44-31-43; e-mail redac .angers@courrier-ouest.com; internet www.courrierdelouest.fr; f. 1944; acquired in 2005 by Ouest-France group; Pres. and Man. Dir MATTHIEU FUCHS; Editor-in-Chief PATRICE GULLIER; circ. 99,253 (2008).

Angoulême

La Charente Libre: 16903 Angoulême Cedex 09; tel. 5-45-94-16-00; fax 5-45-94-16-19; e-mail charente@charentelibre.fr; internet www .charentelibre.com; Publishing Dir JEAN-PIERRE BARJOU; Editorial Dir JACQUES GUYON; Editor-in-Chief JEAN-LOUIS HERVOIS; circ. 34,929 (2011).

Auxerre

L'Yonne Républicaine: 8–12 ave Jean Moulin, 89000 Auxerre; tel. 3-86-49-52-00; fax 3-86-46-52-35; e-mail direction@ lyonne-republicaine.fr; internet www.lyonne-republicaine.fr; f. 1944; Pres. and Dir-Gen. JEAN-PIERRE CAILLARD; Editor-in-Chief DIDIER LAGEDAMON; circ. 36,134 (2008).

Bordeaux

Sud-Ouest: 23 quai de Queyries, 33094 Bordeaux Cedex; tel. 5-35-31-31-31; fax 5-56-00-32-17; e-mail contact@sudouest.com; internet www.sudouest.com; f. 1944; independent; Pres. and Dir of Publication BRUNO FRANCESCHI; Editor-in-Chief PATRICK VENRIES; circ. 288,524 (2011).

Bourges

Le Berry Républicain: 1–3 place Berry, 18023 Bourges Cedex; tel. 2-48-27-63-63; fax 2-48-48-17-19; e-mail redaction.berry@ centrefrance.com; internet www.leberry.fr; Editor-in-Chief BERNARD STEPHAN; circ. 34,915 (weekdays), 11,350 (Sun.) (2011).

Chalon-sur-Saône

Le Journal de Saône-et-Loire: 9 rue des Tonneliers, BP 134, 71100 Chalon-sur-Saône; tel. 3-85-44-68-68; fax 3-85-93-02-96; e-mail infos@lejsl.com; internet www.lejsl.com; f. 1826; Editor-in-Chief MICHEL MEKKI; circ. 58,831 (2008).

Chartres

L'Echo Républicain: 21 rue Vincent Chevard, 28000 Chartres; tel. 2-37-88-88-88; fax 2-37-91-17-42; internet www.lechorepublicain.fr; f. 1929; Pres. and Dir-Gen. RICHARD METZGER; Editor-in-Chief HUGUES DE LESTAPIS; circ. 31,575 (2011).

Clermont-Ferrand

La Montagne: 245 rue du Clos Four, 63056 Clermont-Ferrand Cedex 2; tel. 4-73-17-17-17; fax 4-73-17-18-19; e-mail lamontagne@ centrefrance.com; internet www.lamontagne.fr; f. 1919; independent; Pres. and Dir-Gen. JEAN-PIERRE CAILLARD; Editors-in-Chief PHILIPPE ROUSSEAU, PHILIPPE VAZEILLE; circ. 183,982 (2011).

Dijon

Le Bien Public-Les Dépêches: 7 blvd du Chanoîne Kir, BP 550, 21015 Dijon Cedex; tel. 3-80-42-42-42; fax 3-80-42-44-35; e-mail bienpublic@lebienpublic.fr; internet www.bienpublic.com; f. 1850 as *Le Bien Public*; merged with *Les Dépêches* in 2001; Pres. JEAN

VIANSSON PONTÉ; Editor-in-Chief JEAN-LOUIS PIERRE; circ. 43,378 (2011).

Epinal

Vosges Matin: 40 quai des Bons Enfants, 88000 Epinal Cedex; tel. 3-29-82-98-00; fax 3-29-82-99-29; e-mail vomredacweb@vosgesmatin .fr; internet www.vosgesmatin.fr; f. 1945; Editor-in-Chief GÉRARD NOËL; circ. 26,232 (2008).

Grenoble

Le Dauphiné Libéré: Isles des Cordées, 38913 Veurey-Voroize Cedex; tel. 4-76-88-71-00; fax 4-76-88-70-96; e-mail redaction@ ledauphine.com; internet www.ledauphine.com; f. 1945; Pres., Dir-Gen. and Editor-in-Chief HENRI-PIERRE GUILBERT; circ. 227,187 (2011).

Lille

La Voix du Nord: 8 place du Général de Gaulle, BP 549, 59023 Lille Cedex; tel. 3-20-78-40-40; fax 3-20-78-42-44; e-mail contact@ lavoixdunord.fr; internet www.lavoixdunord.fr; f. 1944; Dir-Gen. JACQUES HARDOIN; Editor-in-Chief JEAN-MICHEL BRETONNIER; circ. 259,912 (2011).

Limoges

L'Echo du Centre: 29 rue Claude-Henri Gorceix, 87022 Limoges Cedex 09; tel. 5-55-04-49-99; fax 5-55-04-49-78; internet www.l-echo .info; f. 1943; 5 edns; communist; Dir of Publication GUY DUMIGNARD; Editor-in-Chief BERNARD CUNY.

Le Populaire du Centre: 15 rue du Général-Catroux, BP 541, 87011 Limoges Cedex 1; tel. 5-55-58-59-00; fax 5-55-58-59-77; e-mail lepopulaire@centrefrance.com; internet www.lepopulaire.fr; f. 1905; Chair. and Dir of Publication ALAIN VÉDRINE; Editor-in-Chief OLIVIER BONNICHON; circ. 40,884 (2011).

Lyon

Le Progrès: 4 rue Montrochet, 69002 Lyon; tel. 4-72-22-23-23; fax 4-78-90-52-40; internet www.leprogres.fr; f. 1859; Dir of Publication PIERRE FANNEAU; circ. 202,794 (2011).

Tribune de Lyon: 9 rue de l'Arbre sec, 69001 Lyon; tel. 4-72-69-15-15; fax 4-72-44-92-04; e-mail fsapy@tribunedelyon.fr; internet www .tribunedelyon.fr; f. 2005; daily; Dir of Publication FRANÇOIS SAPY; circ. 2,543 (2010).

Le Mans

Le Maine Libre: 28–30 place de l'Eperon, BP 299, 72013 Le Mans Cedex 2; tel. 2-43-83-72-50; fax 2-43-28-28-19; e-mail redaction@ maine-libre.com; internet www.lemainelibre.fr; acquired in 2005 by the Ouest-France group; Pres. and Dir-Gen. MATTHIEU FUCHS; Editor-in-Chief JÉRÔME GLAIZE; circ. 44,973 (2011).

Marseille

La Marseillaise: 19 cours d'Estienne d'Orves, BP 1862, 13001 Marseille Cedex 01; tel. 4-91-57-75-00; fax 4-91-57-75-25; internet www.journal-lamarseillaise.com; f. 1944; communist; Man. Dir PAUL BIAGGINI; Editor-in-Chief ROLLAND MARTINEZ.

MarseillePlus: 248 ave Roger-Salengro, 13015 Marseille; tel. 4-91-84-00-00; fax 4-91-84-80-07; e-mail redaction@marseilleplus.com; internet www.marseilleplus.com; f. 2002; Mon.–Fri. mornings; distributed free of charge; Editorial Dir GUILHEM RICAVY; circ. 60,718 (2011).

La Provence: 248 ave Roger-Salengro, 13015 Marseille; tel. 4-91-84-45-45; fax 4-91-84-49-95; e-mail contact@laprovence.com; internet www.laprovence.com; f. 1996 by merger of *Le Provençal* with *Le Méridional*; Dir of Publication STÉPHANE DUHAMEL; Editorial Dir HEDI DAHMANI; circ. 130,388 (2011).

Metz

Le Républicain Lorrain: 3 ave des Deux Fontaines, 57140 Woippy; tel. 3-87-34-17-89; fax 3-87-34-17-90; e-mail pm.pernet@ republicain-lorrain.fr; internet www.republicain-lorrain.fr; f. 1919; independent; Dir-Gen. and Dir of Publication PIERRE WICKER; Editor-in-Chief JACQUES VIRON; circ. 123,592 (2011).

Montpellier

Midi Libre: Mas de Grille, 34923 Montpellier Cedex 09; tel. 4-67-07-67-07; fax 4-67-07-68-13; internet www.midilibre.com; f. 1944; Pres. and Dir of Publication ALAIN PLOMBAT; Editorial Dir PHILIPPE PALAT; circ. 140,375 (2011).

Direct Montpellier Plus: Les portes d'Antigone, Bldg A, 43 place Vauban, 2nd Floor, 340000 Montpellier; internet www

.direct-montpellier-plus.com; f. 2005 by *Midi Libre*; daily; distributed free of charge; Editorial Dir ALAIN PLOMBAT.

Morlaix

Le Télégramme: 7 voie d'accès au Port, BP 243, 29672 Morlaix; tel. 2-98-62-11-33; fax 2-98-63-45-45; e-mail telegramme@ bretagne-online.com; internet www.letelegramme.com; f. 1944; fmrly *Le Télégramme de Brest et de l'Ouest*; Pres. and Man. Dir EDOUARD COUDURIER; Editor-in-Chief MARCEL QUIVIGER; circ. 204,785 (2011).

Mulhouse

L'Alsace: 18 rue de Thann, 68945 Mulhouse Cedex 09; tel. 3-89-32-70-00; fax 3-89-32-11-26; e-mail redaction@alsapresse.com; internet www.alsapresse.com; f. 1944; Chair. JACQUES ROMANN; Editor-in-Chief FRANCIS LAFFON; circ. 97,244 (2008).

Nancy

L'Est Républicain: rue Théophraste-Renaudot, Nancy Houdemont, 54185 Heillecourt Cedex; tel. 3-83-59-80-26; fax 3-83-59-80-13; e-mail secretariat.general@estrepublicain.fr; internet www.estrepublicain.fr; f. 1889; Dir of Publication PIERRE WICKER; Editor-in-Chief RÉMI GODEAU; circ. 149,172 (2011).

Nantes

Presse Océan: 15 rue Deshoulières, BP 22418, 44024 Nantes Cedex 01; tel. 2-40-44-24-00; fax 2-40-44-24-40; e-mail redac.locale.nantes@ presse-ocean.com; internet www.presseocean.fr; f. 1944; acquired in 2005 by the Ouest-France group; Dir of Publication MATTHIEU FUCHS; Editor-in-Chief DOMINIQUE LUNEAU; circ. 32,684 (2011).

Nevers

Le Journal du Centre: 3 rue du Chemin de Fer, BP 106, 58001 Nevers; tel. 3-86-71-45-27; fax 3-86-71-45-20; e-mail redaction.jdc@ centrefrance.com; internet www.lejdc.fr; f. 1943; Dir of Publication JEAN-PIERRE CAILLARD; Editor-in-Chief JEAN-YVES VIF; circ. 27,940 (2011).

Nice

Nice-Matin: 214 blvd du Mercantour, 06290 Nice Cedex 03; tel. 4-93-18-28-38; fax 4-93-83-93-97; internet www.nicematin.fr; f. 1945; Dir of Publication ROBERT NAMIAS; Pres. and Group Editorial Dir ROBERT NAMIAS; Editorial Man. Dir DENIS CARREAUX; circ. 101,882 (2011).

Orléans

La République du Centre: rue de la Halte, 45770 Saran; tel. 2-38-78-79-80; fax 2-38-78-79-79; e-mail dleger@larep.com; internet www.larep.com; f. 1944; Dir of Publication JEAN-PIERRE CAILLARD; Editor-in-Chief CHRISTINE BROUDIC; circ. 39,905 (2011).

Perpignan

L'Indépendant: 'Le Mas de la Garrigue', 2 ave Alfred Sauvy, 66605 Rivesaltes Cedex; tel. 4-68-64-88-88; fax 4-68-64-88-38; internet www.lindependant.com; f. 1846; daily; also *Indépendant-Dimanche* (Sun.); Pres. OLIVIER GEROLAMI; Editorial Dir JOSÉ LOZANO; circ. 60,119 (2011).

Reims

L'Union: 5 rue de Talleyrand, 51083 Reims Cedex; tel. 3-26-50-50-50; fax 3-26-50-51-69; e-mail dirgen@journal-lunion.fr; internet www.lunion.presse.fr; f. 1944; Chair. JACQUES TILLIER; Editor-in-Chief SÉBASTIEN LACROIX; circ. 106,381 (2008).

Rennes

Ouest-France: 10 rue du Breil, 35051 Rennes Cedex 09; tel. 2-99-32-60-00; fax 2-99-32-60-25; internet www.ouest-france.fr; f. 1944; publ. by non-profit-making Association pour le Soutien des Principes de la Démocratie Humaniste; 40 local edns (weekdays), 9 edns (Sun.); the largest circulation of any daily newspaper in France; Chair. and Man. Dir FRANÇOIS RÉGIS HUTIN; Editor-in-Chief JEAN-LUC EVIN; circ. Mon.–Fri. 748,223; Sun. 359,174 (2011).

Roubaix

Nord-Eclair: 42 rue du Général Sarrail, 59100 Roubaix Cedex 1; tel. 3-20-25-02-50; fax 3-20-25-62-98; e-mail contact@nordeclair.fr; internet www.nordeclair.fr; f. 1944; Pres. JACQUES HARDOIN; Dir-Gen. and Editorial Dir JEAN-RENÉ LORE; circ. 24,267 (2011).

Rouen

Paris-Normandie: 33 rue des Grosses Pierres, BP 40047, 76250 Deville-lès-Rouen; tel. 2-35-14-56-56; fax 2-35-14-56-15; e-mail redaction.web@paris-normandie.fr; internet www.paris-normandie .com; f. 1944; Pres. and Dir-Gen. PHILIPPE HERSANT; Editor-in-Chief SOPHIE BLOCH; circ. 52,606 (2011).

Strasbourg

Les Dernières Nouvelles d'Alsace: 17–21 rue de la Nuée Bleue, BP 406/R1, 67077 Strasbourg Cedex; tel. 3-88-21-55-00; fax 3-88-21-56-41; e-mail dnasug@sdv.fr; internet www.dna.fr; f. 1877; non-party; Dir-Gen. FRANCIS HIRN; Editor-in-Chief DOMINIQUE JUNG; circ. 168,238 (2011).

Toulon

Var Matin: place Besagne, Zac Besagne, bâtiment A, 83000 Toulon; tel. 4-94-93-31-00; e-mail toulonloc@nicematin.fr; internet www .varmatin.com; f. 1975; Editorial Man. Dir DENIS CARREAUX; Editor PATRICE MAGGIO; circ. 70,209 (2011).

Toulouse

La Dépêche du Midi: ave Jean Baylet, 31095 Toulouse Cedex; tel. 5-62-11-33-00; fax 5-61-44-74-74; internet www.ladepeche.com; f. 1870; Dir of Publication BRUNO PACHENT; Editor-in-Chief JEAN-CLAUDE SOULERY; circ. 177,863 (2011).

Tours

La Nouvelle République du Centre-Ouest: 232 ave de Grammont, 37048 Tours Cedex 1; tel. 2-47-31-70-00; fax 2-47-31-70-70; e-mail nr.redactionenchef@nrco.fr; internet www .lanouvellerepublique.fr; f. 1944; non-party; Pres. OLIVIER SAINT-CRICQ; Editor-in-Chief BRUNO BÉCARD; circ. 183,482 (2011).

Troyes

L'Est-Eclair: 71 ave du Maréchal Leclerc, 10120 St André les Vergers; tel. 3-25-71-75-75; fax 3-25-79-58-54; e-mail redaction@ lest-eclair.fr; internet www.lest-eclair.fr; f. 1945; Pres. and Dir of Publication JACQUES TILLIER; Editor-in-Chief PATRICK PLANCHE-NAULT; circ. 25,852 (2011).

SELECTED PERIODICALS
(average net circulation figures for 2012, unless otherwise stated)

Current Affairs and Politics

Annales—Histoire, Sciences sociales: 190–198 ave de France, 75013 Paris; tel. 1-49-54-24-75; fax 1-49-54-26-88; e-mail annales@ ehess.fr; internet www.editions.ehess.fr/revues/annales -histoire-sciences-sociales; f. 1929; 4 a year; Editorial Dir ETIENNE ANHEIM.

Armées d'Aujourd'hui: Délégation à l'Information et à la Communication de la Défense, 14 rue Saint-Dominique, 75700 Paris; tel. 1-56-77-23-03; fax 1-56-77-23-04; e-mail journalistes@dicod.defense .gouv.fr; monthly; military and technical; produced by the Délégation à l'Information et à la Communication de la Défense; Editor-in-Chief Lt Col PHILIPPE DUPAS; circ. 100,000 (2008).

Le Canard Enchaîné: 173 rue Saint Honoré, 75051 Paris Cedex 01; tel. 1-42-60-31-36; fax 1-42-27-97-87; e-mail redaction@ lecanardenchaine.fr; internet lecanardenchaine.fr; f. 1915; weekly; satirical; Dir MICHEL GAILLARD; Editors-in-Chief LOUIS-MARIE HOREAU, ERIK EMPTAZ; circ. 537,000 (2010).

Charlie Hebdo: 26 rue Serpollet, 75020 Paris; tel. 1-76-21-53-00; fax 1-76-21-53-01; e-mail redaction@charliehebdo.fr; internet www .charliehebdo.fr; f. 1992 (as revival of 1969–81 publication); left-wing, satirical; Editor and Dir of Publication (vacant); Editor-in-Chief GÉRARD BIARD.

Commentaire: 116 rue du Bac, 75007 Paris; tel. 1-45-49-37-82; fax 1-45-44-32-18; e-mail infos@commentaire.fr; internet www .commentaire.fr; f. 1978; quarterly; Dir JEAN-CLAUDE CASANOVA.

Courrier International: 6–8 rue Jean-Antoine de Baïf, 75212 Paris Cedex 13; tel. 1-46-46-16-00; fax 1-46-46-16-01; e-mail communication@courrierinternational.com; internet www .courrierinternational.com; f. 1990; weekly; current affairs and political; Editorial Dir ERIC CHOL; circ. 199,422.

L'Express: 29 rue de Châteaudun, 75308 Paris Cedex 09; tel. 1-75-55-10-00; fax 1-75-55-12-05; internet www.lexpress.fr; f. 1953; weekly, Thur.; Editorial Dir CHRISTOPHE BARBIER; circ. 521,989.

L'Humanité Dimanche (HD): 5 rue Pleyel, Immeuble Calliope, 93528 Saint-Denis Cedex; tel. 1-49-22-72-72; fax 1-49-22-73-37; internet www.humanite.presse.fr; f. 2006 to replace *L'Humanité Hebdo*; current affairs; weekly (Sun.); Editor PATRICK APEL-MULLER.

Marianne: 32 rue René Boulanger, 75484 Paris Cedex 10; tel. 1-53-72-29-00; fax 1-53-72-29-72; internet www.marianne.net; f. 1997;

weekly, Sat.; current affairs; Dir MAURICE SZAFRAN; Editorial Dir ERIC CONAN; circ. 246,715.

Le Monde Diplomatique: 1–3 ave Stephen Pichon, 75013 Paris Cedex; tel. 1-53-94-96-01; fax 1-53-94-96-26; e-mail secretariat@ monde-diplomatique.fr; internet www.monde-diplomatique.fr; f. 1954; monthly; international affairs; Pres. and Dir of Publication SERGE HALIMI; circ. 144,000.

L'Obs: 12 place de la Bourse, 75002 Paris; tel. 1-44-88-34-34; e-mail mcroissandeau@nouvelobs.com; internet tempsreel.nouvelobs.com; f. 1964; fmrly *Le Nouvel Observateur*; weekly, Thur.; left-wing political and literary; Dir of Publication MATTHIEU CROISSANDREAU; circ. 526,732.

Paris-Match: 149 rue Anatole France, 92534 Levallois-Perret Cedex; tel. 1-41-34-60-00; fax 1-41-34-79-59; e-mail parismatch@ hfp.fr; internet www.parismatch.com; f. 1949; weekly, Thur.; magazine of French and world affairs; Editorial Dir OLIVIER ROYANT; Editor-in-Chief GILLES MARTIN-CHAUFFIER; circ. 670,913.

Passages: 10 rue Clément, 75006 Paris; tel. 1-43-25-23-57; fax 1-43-25-62-59; e-mail passages4@wanadoo.fr; internet www .passages-adapes.fr; f. 1987; quarterly; multidisciplinary discussions of geostrategic issues, seeking to present major contemporary events in an ethical and historical perspective; Dir EMILE H. MALET.

Le Peuple: 263 rue de Paris, Case 432, 93514 Montreuil Cedex; tel. 1-48-18-83-05; fax 1-48-59-28-31; e-mail lepeuplecgt@free.fr; internet www.lepeuple-cgt.com; f. 1921; fortnightly; official organ of the Confédération Générale du Travail (trade union confederation); Dir DANIEL PRADA; Editor-in-Chief FRANÇOISE DUCHESNE.

Le Point: 74 ave du Maine, 75014 Paris; tel. 1-44-10-10-10; fax 1-44-10-12-19; e-mail support@lepoint.fr; internet www.lepoint.fr; f. 1972; weekly, Thur.; politics and current affairs; Pres. and Dir-Gen. CYRILLE DUVAL; Editor-in-Chief JÉRÔME BÉGLÉ; circ. 432,813.

Politique Internationale: 11 rue du Bois de Boulogne, 75116 Paris; tel. 1-45-00-15-26; fax 1-45-00-16-87; internet www .politiqueinternationale.com; f. 1978; quarterly; Dir-Gen. PATRICK WAJSMAN; Editor-in-Chief ANNE LE FUR.

Regards: 5 villa des Pyrénées, 75020 Paris; e-mail remi.douat@ regards.fr; internet www.regards.fr; monthly; communist; politics, current affairs, culture; Dir of Publication CLÉMENTINE AUTAIN; Editor-in-Chief CATHERINE TRICOT.

Revue Défense Nationale: Ecole Militaire, 1 place Joffre, BP 8607, 75325 Paris Cedex 07; tel. 1-44-42-31-90; fax 1-44-42-31-89; e-mail contact@defnat.com; internet www.defnat.com; f. 1939; monthly; publ. by Cttee for Study of National Defence; strategic debate, military, economic, political and scientific problems; Dir Adm. ALAIN COLDEFY; Editor-in-Chief JEAN DUFOURCQ.

Revue des Deux Mondes: 97 rue de Lille, 75007 Paris; tel. 1-47-53-61-94; fax 1-47-53-61-99; e-mail presse@revuedesdeuxmondes.fr; internet www.revuedesdeuxmondes.fr; f. 1829; monthly; current affairs; Pres. MARC LADREIT DE LACHARRIÈRE; Editor-in-Chief VALÉRIE TORANIAN.

Rivarol: 82 blvd Masséna, 75013 Paris; tel. 1-53-34-97-97; fax 1-53-34-97-98; e-mail contact@rivarol.com; internet www.rivarol.com; f. 1951; weekly; conservative; political, literary and satirical; Dir FABRICE JÉRÔME BOURBON.

Technikart: Passage du Cheval-Blanc, 2 rue de la Roquette, 75011 Paris; tel. 1-43-14-33-44; fax 1-43-14-33-40; e-mail rturcat@ technikart.com; internet www.technikart.com; monthly; cultural review; Editor-in-Chief RAPHAËL TURCAT; circ. 38,500 (2008).

La Vie: 80 blvd Auguste-Blanqui, 75013 Paris; tel. 1-48-88-46-00; fax 1-48-88-46-01; e-mail courrier@lavie.fr; internet www.lavie.fr; f. 1945; acquired by Le Monde SA in 2000; weekly; general, Christian; Dir of Publication BÉATRICE GARRETTE; circ. 116,215.

VSD: 13 rue Henri Barbusse, 92624 Gennevilliers Cedex; tel. 1-73-05-45-45; fax 1-56-99-51-28; e-mail lecteurs@vsd.fr; internet www .vsd.fr; f. 1977; weekly, Wed.; current affairs, leisure; Dir of Publication ROLF HEINZ; Editor-in-Chief PHILIPPE BOURBEILLON; circ. 137,098.

The Arts

L'Architecture d'Aujourd'hui: 19 rue Martel, 75010 Paris; tel. 1-58-05-17-49; fax 1-58-05-16-98; e-mail redaction@ larchitecturedaujourdhui.fr; internet www.larchitecture daujourdhui.fr; f. 1930; relaunched in 2009; 6 a year; Dir of Publication ANTOINE VERNHOLES.

Beaux Arts Magazine: 3 carrefour de Weiden, 92130 Issy-les-Moulineaux; tel. 1-41-08-38-00; e-mail beauxarts@dipinfo.fr; internet www.beauxartsmagazine.com; f. 1983; monthly; review of art, architecture, cinema, design; Dir of Publication THIERRY TAITTINGER; Editor-in-Chief FABRICE BOUSTEAU; circ. 61,246.

Critique: 7 rue Bernard Palissy, 75006 Paris; tel. 1-44-39-39-20; fax 1-44-39-39-23; e-mail critique@wanadoo.fr; f. 1946; 9 a year; publ. by Les Éditions de Minuit; general review of French and foreign literature, philosophy, art, social sciences and history; Dir PHILIPPE ROGER.

Diapason: 8 rue François Ory, 92543 Montrouge Cedex; tel. 1-41-33-50-01; internet www.diapasonmag.fr; f. 1956; monthly; classical music; Editor-in-Chief EMMANUEL DUPUY; circ. 37,016.

Esprit: 212 rue Saint Martin, 75003 Paris; tel. 1-48-04-92-90; fax 1-48-04-50-53; e-mail redaction@esprit.presse.fr; internet www.esprit .presse.fr; f. 1932; 10 a year; philosophy, history, sociology; Dir OLIVIER MONGIN; Editor-in-Chief MARC-OLIVIER PADIS.

Les Inrockuptibles: 24 rue Saint Sabin, 75011 Paris; tel. 1-42-44-16-16; fax 1-42-44-16-00; e-mail christian.fevret@inrocks.com; internet www.lesinrocks.com; f. 1986; weekly, Tue.; music, cinema, literature and television; Editorial Dir BERNARD ZEKRI; circ. 60,318.

Lire: 29 rue de Châteaudun, 75308 Paris Cedex 09; tel. 1-75-55-10-00; fax 1-75-55-17-04; e-mail redaction@lire.fr; internet www.lire.fr; f. 1975; monthly; literary review; Editorial Dir FRANÇOIS BUSNEL; circ. 67,110.

Livres-Hebdo: 35 rue Grégoire-de-Tours, 75006 Paris; tel. 1-44-41-28-00; fax 1-43-29-77-85; internet www.livreshebdo.fr; f. 1979; weekly; book publishing; Editor-in-Chief CHRISTINE FERRAND; circ. 163,320.

Le Magazine Littéraire: 717 route des Boulangers, 78926 Yvelines Cedex 9; tel. 1-55-56-71-25; e-mail courrier@magazine-litteraire .com; internet www.magazine-litteraire.com; f. 1966; monthly; literature; Editorial Dir JOSEPH MACÉ-SCARON; circ. 31,712.

Le Matricule des Anges: BP 20225, 34004 Montpellier Cedex 1; tel. and fax 4-67-92-29-33; e-mail lmda@lmda.net; internet www.lmda .net; f. 1992; monthly; literary criticism; Dir of Publication THIERRY GUICHARD.

La Quinzaine Littéraire: 135 rue Saint-Martin, 75194 Paris Cedex 04; tel. 1-48-87-48-58; fax 1-48-87-13-01; e-mail nadeau.maurice@ orange.fr; internet www.quinzaine-litteraire.net; f. 1966; fortnightly; Dir MAURICE NADEAU; Editor-in-Chief ERIC PHALIPPOU.

Rock & Folk: 12 rue Mozart, 92587 Clichy Cedex; tel. 1-41-40-32-32; internet www.rocknfolk.com; f. 1966; monthly; music; publ. by Éditions Larivière; Editor-in-Chief PHILIPPE MANŒUVRE; circ. 36,399.

Les Temps Modernes: 26 rue de Condé, 75006 Paris; tel. 1-43-29-08-47; fax 1-40-51-83-38; e-mail les.temps.modernes@free.fr; f. 1945 by J.-P. Sartre; 6 a year; literary review; publ. by Gallimard; Dir CLAUDE LANZMANN.

Economic and Financial

Capital: 13 rue Henri Barbusse, 92624 Gennevilliers Cedex; tel. 1-73-05-48-53; fax 1-47-92-65-90; e-mail capital@prismamedia.com; internet www.capital.fr; f. 1991; monthly; business, finance; Editor-in-Chief FRANÇOIS GENTHIAL; circ. 305,379.

Challenges: 33 rue Vivienne, 75002 Paris; tel. 1-44-88-34-34; e-mail pf@challenges.fr; internet www.challenges.fr; weekly; economics and politics; Editor-in-Chief VINCENT BEAUFILS; circ. 231,209.

L'Expansion: 29 rue de Châteaudun, 75308 Paris Cedex 09; tel. 1-75-55-10-00; internet www.lexpansion.com; f. 1967; monthly; economics and business; Editorial Dir CHRISTINE KERDELLANT; circ. 142,630.

Mieux Vivre Votre Argent: 29 rue de Châteaudun, 75308 Paris Cedex 09; tel. 1-75-55-10-00; fax 1-75-55-11-40; e-mail jpviallon@ mieuxvivre.fr; internet www.votreargent.fr; monthly; f. 1918; investment, economics; Dir of Publication RIK DE NOLF; Editor-in-Chief JEAN-FRANÇOIS FILLIATRE; circ. 221,876.

Le Monde-Initiatives: 1–3 ave Stephen Pichon, 75013 Paris; tel. 1-53-94-96-26; fax 1-53-94-96-01; e-mail initiatives@lemonde.fr; f. 2002; monthly; circ. 50,000 (2002).

Le Nouvel Economiste: 38 bis rue du Fer à Moulin, 75005 Paris; tel. 1-75-44-41-00; e-mail patrick.arnoux@nouveleconomiste.fr; internet www.nouveleconomiste.fr; f. 1976; weekly, Fri.; Pres. and Editorial Dir HENRI J. NIJDAM; circ. 16,929.

L'Usine Nouvelle: Antony Parc II–10, place du Général de Gaulle, 92160 Antony Cedex; tel. 1-77-92-92-92; fax 1-56-79-42-34; internet www.usinenouvelle.com; f. 1945; weekly, Thur; technical and industrial journal; Editorial Dir LAURENT GUEZ; Editor-in-Chief THIBAUT DE JAEGHER; circ. 48,094.

Valeurs Actuelles: 1 rue Lulli, 75002 Paris; tel. 1-40-54-11-00; fax 1-40-54-12-85; internet www.valeursactuelles.com; f. 1966; weekly; politics, economics, international affairs; Dir-Gen. YVES DE KERDREL; circ. 88,241.

History and Geography

Annales de Géographie: 21 rue de Montparnasse, 75006 Paris; tel. 1-44-39-54-47; fax 1-40-46-49-93; e-mail infos@armand-colin.com; f. 1891; every 2 months.

Cahiers de Civilisation Médiévale: 24 rue de la Chaine, 86022 Poitiers Cedex 9; tel. 5-49-45-45-63; fax 5-49-45-45-73; e-mail martin

.aurell@univ-poitiers.fr; internet cescm.labo.univ-poitiers.fr/poles-editoriaux/cahiers-de-civilisation-medievale; f. 1958; Centre d'Etudes Supérieures de Civilisation Médiévale; quarterly; medieval studies, concentrating on the 10th–12th centuries; Dir MARTIN AURELL; circ. 1,000 (2013).

GEO: 413 rue Henri Barbusse, 92624 Gennevilliers Cedex; tel. 1-73-05-45-45; internet www.geomagazine.fr; f. 1979; monthly; architecture, culture, people, photo-journalism, travel; Editor-in-Chief ERIC MEYER; circ. 249,248.

La Géographie: 184 blvd Saint Germain, 75006 Paris; tel. 1-45-48-54-62; fax 1-42-22-40-93; e-mail socgeo@socgeo.org; internet www.socgeo.org; f. 1821; quarterly of the Société de Géographie; Chair. Prof. JEAN-ROBERT PITTE; Editor-in-Chief GILLES FUMEY.

L'Histoire: 74 ave du Maine, 75014 Paris; tel. 1-44-10-10-10; fax 1-44-10-54-47; e-mail courrier@histoire.presse.fr; internet www.histoire.presse.fr; f. 1978; monthly; Dir-Gen. PHILIPPE CLERGET; Editor-in-Chief VALÉRIE HANNIN; circ. 55,915.

Historia: 74 ave du Maine, 75014 Paris; tel. 1-44-10-10-10; fax 1-44-10-54-30; e-mail pczete@tallandier.fr; internet www.historia.fr; f. 1909; monthly; Editor-in-Chief PIERRE BARON; circ. 75,464.

National Geographic France: 13 rue Henri Barbusse, 92230 Gennevilliers; tel. 1-73-05-45-45; e-mail publication@nationalgeographic.fr; internet www.nationalgeographic.fr; f. 1999; monthly; geography, people, science, travel; Dir MARTIN TRAUTMANN; Editor-in-Chief JEAN-PIERRE VRIGNAUD; circ. 92,647.

Revue d'Histoire Diplomatique: 13 rue Soufflot, 75005 Paris; tel. 1-43-54-05-97; fax 1-46-34-07-60; e-mail librairie@pedone.info; internet www.pedone.info; f. 1837; quarterly; Editors BÉNÉDICTE PEDONE-RIBOT, MARC PEDONE.

Revue Historique: 56 rue Jacob, 75006 Paris; tel. 1-58-71-71-35; e-mail revuehistorique@puf.com; f. 1876; quarterly; Dirs CLAUDE GAUVARD, JEAN-FRANÇOIS SIRINELLI.

Revue de Synthèse: Centre International de Synthèse, 45 rue d'Ulm, 75005 Paris; tel. 1-44-32-26-54; fax 1-44-32-26-56; e-mail revuedesynthese@ens.fr; internet www.revue-de-synthese.eu; f. 1900; 4 a year; history, philosophy, social sciences; Editor-in-Chief ERIC BRIAN.

Home, Fashion and General

Art & Décoration: 149 rue Anatole France, 92534 Levallois-Perret Cedex; tel. 1-41-34-67-38; e-mail artdeco@lagardere-active.com; internet www.maison-deco.com/magazine-art-decoration; f. 1897; 9 a year; Dir of Publication CONSTANCE BENQUÉ; Editor-in-Chief CLÉMENCE BLANCHARD; circ. 303,003.

Be: 149 rue Anatole France, 92534 Levallois-Perret Cedex; tel. 1-41-34-60-00; e-mail anne.bianchi@lagardere-active.com; internet www.be.com; f. 2010; monthly; women's magazine; publ. by Lagardère Active; Editor-in-Chief ANNE BIANCHI; circ. 151,424.

Closer: 8 rue François Ory, 92543 Montrouge Cedex; tel. 1-46-48-48-14; internet www.closermag.fr; f. 2005; weekly; publ. by Mondadori France; celebrity news, TV, radio, films; Editor-in-Chief LAURENCE PIEAU; circ. 393,009.

Cosmopolitan: 10 blvd des Frères Voisin, 92792 Issy-les-Moulineaux Cedex 9; tel. 1-41-46-88-88; fax 1-41-48-84-93; e-mail cosmopub@gmc.tm.fr; internet www.cosmopolitan.fr; f. 1973; monthly; Editor-in-Chief SYLVIE OVERNOY; circ. 420,152.

Elle: 149 rue Anatole France, 92300 Levallois-Perret; tel. 1-41-34-60-00; fax 1-41-34-67-97; e-mail ellemagazine@hfp.fr; internet www.elle.fr; f. 1945; monthly; Dirs-Gen. ARNAUD LAGARDÈRE, ARJIL COMMANDITÉE-ARCO; Editor-in-Chief VALÉRIE TORANIAN; circ. 409,162.

Femme Actuelle: 13 rue Henri Barbusse, 92624 Gennevilliers; tel. 1-73-05-45-45; e-mail lectrices@femmeactuelle.fr; internet www.femmeactuelle.fr; f. 1984; weekly, Mon.; Editor-in-Chief ISABELLE CATÉLAN; circ. 843,416.

Ici-Paris: 149 rue Anatole France, 92534 Levallois-Perret; tel. 1-41-34-60-00; fax 1-41-34-89-34; f. 1945; weekly; celebrity gossip, news; publ. by Lagadère Active; Editors-in-Chief GIANNI LORENZON, JOËL LAFFAY; circ. 331,720.

Le Journal de la Maison: 149–151 rue Anatole France, 92534 Levallois-Perret Cedex; tel. 1-41-34-60-00; internet www.maison-deco.com/magazine-le-journal-de-la-maison; monthly; home; Editor-in-Chief ANNE GASTINEAU; circ. 178,625.

Marie-Claire: 10 blvd des Frères Voisin, 92792 Issy-les-Moulineaux Cedex 9; tel. 1-41-46-88-88; fax 1-41-46-86-86; e-mail mcredac@gmc.tm.fr; internet www.marieclaire.fr; f. 1954; monthly; Editor-in-Chief CHRISTINE LEIRITZ; circ. 494,382.

Marie-France: 10 blvd des Frères Voisin, 92792 Issy-Les-Moulineaux; tel. 1-41-46-83-77; e-mail contact@mariefrance.fr; f. 1944; monthly; Dir of Publication PASCAL CHEVALIER; circ. 186,353.

Maxi: 30–32 rue de Chabrol, 75010 Paris; tel. 1-40-22-75-00; fax 1-48-24-08-40; e-mail courrier@maxi.presse.fr; internet www.maxi-mag.fr; f. 1986; weekly; 100% subsidiary of Bauer Media Group; Editor-in-Chief KATHARINA HORBATSCH; circ. 429,897.

Modes et Travaux: 8 rue François Ory, 92543 Montrouge Cedex; tel. 1-46-48-48-48; fax 1-46-48-19-00; e-mail redaction.modesettravaux@mondadori.fr; internet www.modesettravaux.fr; f. 1919; monthly; publ. by Mondadori France; Editor PATRICIA WAGNER; circ. 461,919.

Notre Temps: 18 rue Barbès, 92128 Montrouge; tel. 1-74-31-60-60; fax 1-74-31-60-90; e-mail redaction@notretemps.com; internet www.notretemps.com; f. 1968; monthly; for retired people; Editor-in-Chief CAROLE RENUCCI; circ. 880,960.

Nous Deux: 8 rue François Ory, 92543 Montrouge Cedex; tel. 1-46-48-43-40; fax 1-46-48-43-20; e-mail contact@mondadori.fr; f. 1947; weekly; Editor MARION MINUIT; circ. 296,405.

Parents: 149–151 rue Anatole France, 92534 Levallois-Perret Cedex; tel. 1-41-34-60-00; fax 1-41-34-70-79; e-mail redaction-infobebes@lagardere-active.com; internet www.parents.fr; f. 1969; monthly; magazine for parents; Editorial Dir CATHERINE LELIÈVRE; circ. 272,729.

Pleine Vie: 8 rue François Ory, 92543 Montrouge Cedex; tel. 1-41-33-10-31; e-mail jeanne.thiriet@mondadori.fr; internet www.pleinevie.fr; f. 1997; monthly; intended for women aged 50 and over; Editor JEANNE THIRIET; circ. 730,000.

Point de Vue: 23 rue du Châteaudun, 75308 Paris Cedex 09; tel. 1-75-55-10-00; e-mail info@pointdevue.fr; internet www.pointdevue.fr; f. 1945; weekly, Mon.; general illustrated; publ. by Roularta Media; Editorial Dir COLOMBE PRINGLE; circ. 239,240.

Prima: 13 rue Henri Barbusse, 92624 Gennevilliers Cedex; tel. 1-73-05-45-45; internet www.prima.fr; f. 1982; monthly; intended for women of 40 years and over; also *Prima Maison* and *Prima Cuisine Gourmande*; Editor-in-Chief GWENDOLINE MICHAELIS; circ. 396,548.

Psychologies Magazine: 149–151 rue Anatole France, 92534 Levallois–Perret Cedex; tel. 1-41-34-60-00; e-mail laurence.r@psychologies.com; internet www.psychologies.com; monthly; Dir-Gen. ARNAUD DE SAINT SIMON; Editor-in-Chief ISABELLE MAURY; circ. 353,496.

Public: 149 rue Anatole France, 92534 Levallois-Perret Cedex; tel. 1-41-34-60-00; fax 1-41-34-90-98; internet www.public.fr; f. 2003; weekly, Mon.; celebrity news, TV, radio, films; Editorial Dir NICOLAS PIGASSE; Editor-in-Chief ANAÏS JOUVANCY; circ. 339,848.

Questions de Femmes: 117 rue de la Tour, 75116 Paris; tel. 1-45-03-80-00; e-mail fazire@groupe-ayache.com; internet www.questionsdefemmes.com; f. 1996; monthly; Editor-in-Chief FABIENNE AZIRE; circ. 85,557.

Santé Magazine: 22 rue Letellier, 75015 Paris; tel. 1-43-23-45-72; e-mail direction@santemagazine.fr; internet www.santemagazine.fr; f. 1976; monthly; health; Editor-in-Chief ALINE PERRAUDIN; circ. 349,841.

Top Santé: 8 rue François Ory, 92543 Montrouge Cedex; tel. 1-46-48-43-66; internet www.topsante.com; f. 1990; monthly; health; Editor SOPHIE DELAUGÈRE; circ. 404,385.

Vivre Plus: 18 rue Barbès, 92128 Montrouge; tel. 1-74-31-60-60; fax 1-74-31-60-69; internet www.vivreplus.fr; f. 2004 as *Côté Femme*; restyled as above 2006; monthly; aimed at women aged 40 years and above; Editor-in-Chief ODILE AMBLARD.

Vogue Paris: 26 rue Cambacérès, 75008 Paris; tel. 1-53-43-60-00; fax 1-53-43-61-61; e-mail info@condenast.fr; internet www.vogue.fr; monthly; Editor-in-Chief EMMANUELLE ALT; Publr DELPHINE ROYANT; circ. 160,050.

Voici: 13 rue Henri Barbusse, 92624 Gennevilliers Cedex; tel. 1-73-05-45-45; e-mail voici@prisma-presse.com; internet www.voici.fr; f. 1987; weekly, Mon.; celebrity news, TV, radio, films; Editor-in-Chief MARION ALOMBERT; circ. 426,238.

Leisure Interests and Sport

Cahiers du Cinéma: 65 rue Montmartre, 75002 Paris; tel. 1-53-44-75-75; fax 1-43-43-95-04; e-mail sdelorme@cahiersducinema.com; internet www.cahiersducinema.com; f. 1951; monthly; film reviews; Dir of Publication JÉRÔME CUZOL; Editor-in-Chief STÉPHANE DELORME; circ. 21,900.

Le Chasseur Français: 8 rue François Ory, 92543 Montrouge Cedex; tel. 1-41-33-50-01; f. 1885; monthly; hunting, shooting, fishing; Dir of Publication ERNESTO MAURI; Editor-in-Chief ANTOINE BERTON; circ. 308,533.

France-Football: 4 cours de l'Ile Seguin, BP 10302, 92102 Boulogne-Billancourt Cedex; tel. 1-40-93-20-20; fax 1-40-93-20-17; internet www.francefootball.fr; f. 1947; weekly; owned by Amaury Group; Editorial Dir DENIS CHAUMIER; circ. 101,240.

Le Journal de Mickey: 10 rue Thierry Le Luron, 92592 Levallois-Perret; tel. 1-41-34-88-73; fax 1-41-34-93-90; e-mail journaldemickey@lagardere-active.com; internet www

.journaldemickey.com; f. 1934; weekly; cartoon magazine; publ. by Disney Hachette Presse; circ. 135,322.

Pariscope: 149–151 rue Anatole France, 92534 Levallois-Perret Cedex; tel. 1-41-34-60-60; fax 1-41-34-78-30; f. 1965; listings and reviews of events in Paris and Ile-de-France; weekly; Dir of Publication THOMAS KOUCK; Editorial Dir NATHALIE PESICIC; circ. 50,057.

Photo: 21 ave Gaston Monmousseau, 93240 Stains; tel. 1-48-22-11-66; e-mail photo@photo.fr; internet www.photo.fr; f. 1967; monthly; specialist photography magazine; Editorial Dir ERIC COLMET-DAÂGE; circ. 26,380.

Positif: 38 rue Milton, 75009 Paris; tel. 1-43-26-17-80; fax 1-43-26-29-77; e-mail posed@wanadoo.fr; internet www.revue-positif.net; f. 1952; monthly; film reviews; publ. by Editions Scope; Editor-in-Chief MICHEL CIMENT.

Première: 149 rue Anatole France, 92534 Levallois-Perret Cedex; tel. 1-41-34-60-00; fax 1-41-34-89-92; internet www.premiere.fr; monthly; film reviews; Dir of Publication THOMAS KOUCK; Editor-in-Chief MATHIEU CARRATIER; circ. 139,078.

Télé 7 Jours: 149 rue Anatole France, 92534 Levallois-Perret Cedex; tel. 1-41-34-60-00; fax 1-41-34-79-70; e-mail claire.leost@ lagardere-active.com; internet www.tele7.fr; weekly; television; Dir of Publication CLAIRE LEOST; Editorial Dir THIERRY MOREAU; circ. 1,357,506.

Télé Poche: 8 rue François Ory, 92543 Montrouge Cedex; tel. 1-41-33-50-00; fax 1-41-33-57-48; e-mail pierreyves.simon@emapfrance .com; internet www.telepoche.fr; f. 1966; weekly; publ. by Mondadori France; television; Editor-in-Chief ERIC PAVON; circ. 493,606.

Télérama: 8 rue Jean-Antoine de Baïf, Paris 75212 Cedex 13; tel. 1-55-30-55-30; fax 1-47-64-02-04; internet www.telerama.fr; f. 1972; weekly, Wed.; radio, TV, film, literature and music; Editorial Dir FABIENNE PASCAUD; circ. 621,417.

Télé Star: 8 rue François Ory, 92543 Montrouge Cedex; tel. 1-41-33-53-50; e-mail lecteurs.telestar@mondadori.fr; internet www.telestar .fr; f. 1976; weekly; television; Editorial Dir ERIC PAVON; circ. 1,093,507.

Télé Z: 10 ave de Messine, 75008 Paris; tel. 1-53-83-93-40; internet www.telez.fr; weekly; television; Editor-in-Chief LUCIE DUKAT; circ. 1,400,083.

Vélo Magazine: cours de l'Ile Seguin, BP 10302, 92102 Boulogne-Billancourt Cedex; tel. 1-40-93-20-20; fax 1-40-93-20-09; e-mail redac@velomagazine.fr; internet www.velomagazine.fr; monthly; cycling; Editor-in-Chief GILLES COMTE; circ. 49,539.

Voiles et Voiliers: 21 rue du Faubourg Saint-Antoine, 75550 Paris Cedex 11; tel. 1-44-87-87-87; fax 1-44-87-87-09; e-mail accueil@ voilesetvoiliers.com; internet www.voilesetvoiliers.com; monthly; sailing and nautical sports; Dir of Publication FRANÇOIS RÉGIS HUTIN; circ. 51,025.

Religion and Philosophy

Actualité Juive: 14 rue Raymonde Salez, 93260 Les Lilas; tel. 1-43-60-20-20; fax 1-43-60-20-21; e-mail a-j-presse@actuj.com; internet www.actuj.com; weekly; Dir LYDIA BENATTAR; circ. 17,000 (2004).

Etudes: 14 rue d'Assas, 75006 Paris; tel. 1-44-39-48-48; fax 1-44-39-48-17; e-mail etudes@free.fr; internet www.revue-etudes.com; f. 1856; monthly; general interest; Editor-in-Chief FRANÇOIS EUVÉ.

France Catholique: 60 rue de Fontenay, 92350 Le Plessis-Robinson; tel. 1-46-30-79-01; fax 1-46-30-04-64; e-mail france-catholique@wanadoo.fr; internet www.france-catholique.fr; weekly; Dir FRÉDÉRIC AIMARD; Editor-in-Chief GÉRARD LECLERC; circ. 16,000 (2004).

Le Monde des Religions: 80 blvd Auguste-Blanqui, 75707 Paris Cedex 13; tel. 1-48-88-46-00; fax 1-42-27-04-19; e-mail contact@ lemondedesreligions.fr; internet www.lemondedesreligions.fr; f. 2003 to replace *Actualité des Religions*; 6 a year; Editorial Dir VIRGINIE LAROUSSE; circ. 43,306.

Pèlerin: 18 rue Barbès, 92128 Montrouge; tel. 1-74-31-60-60; fax 1-74-31-60-21; e-mail pelerin@bayard-presse.com; internet www .pelerin.info; f. 1873; weekly; Dir GEORGES SANEROT; Editor-in-Chief ANTOINE D'ABBUNDO; circ. 211,091.

Philosophie Magazine: 10 rue Ballu, 75009 Paris; tel. 1-43-80-46-10; internet www.philomag.com; f. 2006; monthly; Dir FABRICE GERSCHEL; Editor CÉDRIC ENJALBERT; circ. 53,489.

Prier: 80 blvd Auguste-Blanqui, 75707 Paris Cedex 13; tel. 1-48-88-46-00; fax 1-42-27-29-03; e-mail contacts-prier@mp.com.fr; internet www.prier.presse.fr; f. 1978; monthly; review of modern prayer and contemplation; Editor XAVIER ACCART.

Réforme: 53–55 ave du Maine, 75014 Paris; tel. 1-43-20-32-67; fax 1-43-21-42-86; e-mail reforme@reforme.net; internet www.reforme .net; f. 1945; weekly; considers current affairs from a Protestant Christian perspective; Dir ANTOINE NOUIS; Editor-in-Chief NATHALIE DE SENNVILLE-LEENHARDT; circ. 6,000 (2003).

Revue des Sciences Philosophiques et Théologiques: Le Saulchoir, 45 rue de la Glacière, 75013 Paris; tel. 1-42-17-45-60; internet rspt.fr; f. 1907; quarterly; Dir GILLES BERCEVILLE.

Silence: Ecologie, Alternatives, Non-violence: 9 rue Dumenge, 69317 Lyon Cedex 04; tel. 4-78-39-55-33; fax 4-78-28-85-12; internet www.revuesilence.net; f. 1982; monthly.

Témoignage Chrétien: 3–5 rue de Metz, 75010 Paris; tel. 1-44-83-82-82; fax 1-44-83-82-88; e-mail contacttc@temoignagechretien.fr; internet www.temoignagechretien.fr; f. 1941; weekly; Christianity and politics; Editor-in-Chief CHRISTINE PEDOTTI.

La Voix Protestante: 14 rue de Trévise, 75009 Paris; tel. 1-47-70-23-53; fax 1-48-01-09-13; e-mail contact@lavoixprotestante.org; internet www.eglise-protestante-unie.fr/region-parisienne -reformee-r8; monthly review of Protestant churches in Paris; Dir FREDERIC GENTY.

Science and Technology

Air et Cosmos: 1 bis ave de la République, 75011 Paris; tel. 1-49-29-30-00; fax 1-49-29-32-01; e-mail air-cosmos@air-cosmos.com; internet www.aerospacemedia.com; f. 1963; weekly; aerospace; Dir-Gen. and Editorial Dir ROBERT MONTEUX; Editor-in-Chief GUILLAUME LECOMPTE-BOINET; circ. 20,290.

Annales de Chimie—Science des Matériaux: Lavoisier SAS, 14 rue de Provigny, 94236 Cachan Cedex; tel. 1-47-40-67-00; fax 1-47-40-67-02; e-mail acsm@lavoisier.fr; internet acsm.revuesonline.com; f. 1789; 6 a year; chemistry and material science.

L'argus: 11–13 rue des Petits Hotels, 75010 Paris; tel. 1-53-29-11-00; internet www.largus.fr; f. 1927; motoring weekly; Editorial Dir DIDIER LAURENT; circ. 29,946.

Astérisque: Société Mathématique de France, Institut Henri Poincaré, 11 rue Pierre et Marie Curie, 75231 Paris Cedex 05; tel. 1-44-27-67-99; fax 1-40-46-90-96; e-mail revues@smf.ens.fr; internet smf .emath.fr/publications/asterisque; f. 1973; 6–8 a year; mathematics, Editor-in-Chief ERIC VASSEROT; Sec. NATHALIE CHRISTIAËN.

L'Astronomie: 3 rue Beethoven, 75016 Paris; tel. 1-42-24-13-74; fax 1-42-30-75-47; e-mail redac.saf@wanadoo.fr; internet www .saf-lastronomie.com; f. 1887; monthly; publ. by Société Astronomique de France; Editor-in-Chief MARIE-CLAUDE PASKOFF.

Auto-Moto: 149 rue Anatole France, 92534 Levallois-Perret Cedex; tel. 1-41-34-60-00; fax 1-41-34-95-26; e-mail redaction@autonews.fr; internet www.autonews.fr; monthly; cars; Dir BRUNO LESOUËF; Editor-in-Chief CHRISTOPHE BOULAIN; circ. 241,075.

Auto Plus: 8 rue François Ory, 92543 Montrouge Cedex; tel. 1-41-33-51-16; fax 1-41-33-57-06; e-mail olivier.bernis@mondadori.fr; internet www.autoplus.fr; fortnightly; cars; Editor-in-Chief OLIVIER BERNIS; circ. 305,359.

Biochimie: Centre Universitaire des Saints Pères, 45 rue des Saints Pères, 75270 Paris Cedex 06; tel. 1-42-86-33-77; fax 1-42-86-33-73; e-mail redaction.biochemie@ibpc.fr; internet www.elsevier.com/ locate/biochi; f. 1914; monthly; biochemistry; Editor-in-Chief RICHARD BUCKINGHAM.

Electronique Pratique: 3 blvd Ney, 75018 Paris; tel. 1-44-65-80-80; fax 1-44-65-80-90; e-mail publicite@electroniquepratique.com; internet www.electroniquepratique.com; monthly; electronics; Editorial Dir PATRICK VERCHER.

Industries et Technologies: Antony Parc II–10, place du Général de Gaulle, 92160 Antony Cedex; tel. 1-77-92-92-92; fax 1-77-92-98-51; e-mail p.wagner@industries-technologies.com; internet www .industries-technologies.com; f. 1958 as *Industries et Techniques*; present name adopted 2002; monthly; Editor-in-Chief MURIEL DE VERICOURT.

Ingénieurs de l'Automobile: Editions VB, 7 rue Jean Mermoz, 78000 Versailles; tel. 1-39-20-88-05; fax 1-39-20-88-06; e-mail vblcda@lcda.fr; internet www.lcda.fr/site/ingenieurs_de _l_automobile-gb.php; f. 1927; 6 a year; technical automobile review, in French and English; Editor-in-Chief ERIC BIGOURDAN; circ. 9,000 (2012).

Matériaux et Techniques: EDP Sciences, 17 ave du Hoggar, Parc d'Activités de Courtaboeuf, BP 112, 91944 Les Ulis Cedex A; tel. 1-69-18-75-75; fax 1-69-28-84-91; e-mail contact@edpsciences.org; internet www.mattech-journal.org; f. 1913; 7 a year; review of engineering research and progress on industrial materials; publ. by EDP Sciences; Editors-in-Chief RENÉ GRAS, VINCENT VERNEY.

Le Monde Informatique: 40 blvd Henri Sellier, 92150 Suresnes; tel. 1-41-97-02-02; fax 1-41-97-02-01; e-mail redac_weblmi@ it-news-info.com; internet www.lemondeinformatique.fr; f. 1981; weekly; information science; Editor-in-Chief SERGE LEBLAL; circ. 29,236 (2006).

Le Moniteur des Travaux Publics et du Bâtiment: 17 rue d'Uzès, 75108 Paris Cedex 02; tel. 1-40-13-30-30; fax 1-40-13-50-21; e-mail contact.groupemoniteur@groupemoniteur.fr; internet www.lemoniteur.fr; f. 1903; weekly; construction; Dir-Gen. OLIVIER DE LA CHAISE; Dir of Publication GUILLAUME PROT; circ. 48,257.

Psychologie Française: 71 ave Edouard-Vaillant, 92774 Boulogne Cedex; tel. 1-55-20-58-32; fax 1-55-20-58-34; e-mail a.dore@elsevier .com; f. 1956; quarterly; review of the Société Française de Psychologie, publ. by Elsevier France; Editor ALINE CHEVALIER.

La Recherche: 74 ave du Maine, 75014 Paris; tel. 1-40-10-10-10; fax 1-40-10-54-30; e-mail courrier@larecherche.fr; internet www .larecherche.fr; monthly; science; Dir of Publication PHILIPPE CLERGET; Editor-in-Chief ALINE RICHARD; circ. 38,422.

Science et Vie: 8 rue François Ory, 92543 Montrouge Cedex; tel. 1-41-33-50-01; fax 1-46-48-48-67; e-mail svmens@mondadori.fr; internet www.science-et-vie.com; f. 1913; monthly; Dir of Publication CARMINE PERNA; Editorial Dir MATTHIEU VILLIERS; circ. 338,218.

Sciences et Avenir: 12 place de la Bourse, 75002 Paris; tel. 1-44-88-34-34; e-mail redaction@sciences-et-avenir.com; internet sciencesetavenirmensuel.nouvelobs.com; monthly; Dir of Publication LAURENT JOFFRIN; circ. 270,576.

NEWS AGENCIES

Agence France-Presse (AFP): 13 place de la Bourse, 75002 Paris; tel. 1-40-41-46-46; fax 1-40-41-46-32; e-mail contact@afp.com; internet www.afp.fr; f. 1944; 24-hour service of world political, financial, entertainment, science and technology, sporting news, and photographs; 200 bureaux, and 2,260 correspondents worldwide; Pres. and Dir-Gen. EMMANUEL HOOG; Editor-in-Chief MARIELLE EUDES.

Agence Parisienne de Presse: 16 rue Saint Fiacre, 75002 Paris; tel. 1-42-36-51-02; fax 1-42-36-04-62; f. 1949; Man. Dir MICHEL BURTON.

Infomédia SAS: 58 rue de Châteaudun, 75009 Paris; tel. 1-48-01-87-34; e-mail redaction@infomedia-sas.com; internet www .infomedia-sas.com; f. 1988; economic and financial news; Pres. JEAN-DAMIEN CHÂTELAIN.

PRESS ASSOCIATIONS

Comité de Liaison de la Presse: 13 rue Lafayette, 75009 Paris; tel. 1-44-06-42-57; e-mail comite-liaison-presse@orange.fr; liaison organization for press, radio and cinema.

Fédération Française des Agences de Presse (FFAP): 24 rue du Faubourg Poissonnière, 75010 Paris; tel. 1-42-47-01-00; e-mail contact@ffap.fr; internet www.ffap.fr; comprises 5 syndicates (news, photographs, television, general information and multimedia) with a total membership of 109 agencies; Pres. and Dir of Publication KATHLEEN GROSSET.

Fédération Nationale de la Presse Française (FNPF): 13 rue La Fayette, 75009 Paris; tel. 1-53-20-90-50; fax 1-44-90-43-72; f. 1944; mems: Syndicat de la Presse Quotidienne Nationale, Syndicat Professionnel de la Presse Magazine et d'Opinion, Syndicat de la Presse Quotidienne Départementale, Fédération de la Presse Périodique Régionale, Fédération Nationale de la Presse d'Information Spécialisée.

Fédération Nationale de la Presse d'Information Spécialisée: 17 rue Castagnary, 75015 Paris; tel. 1-44-90-43-60; fax 1-44-90-43-72; e-mail contact@fnps.fr; internet www.fnps.fr; comprises Syndicat National de la Presse Agricole et Rurale, Syndicat de la Presse et de l'Edition des Professions de Santé, Syndicat de la Presse Culturelle et Scientifique, Syndicat de la Presse Economique, Juridique et Politique, Syndicat de la Presse Professionnelle, Syndicat de la Presse Magazine et Spécialisée and Syndicat de la Presse Sociale, representing some 1,350 specialized or professional publications; Pres. CHRISTIAN BRUNEAU.

Fédération de la Presse Périodique Régionale: 72 rue d'Hauteville, 75010 Paris; tel. 1-45-23-98-00; fax 1-45-23-98-01; e-mail sphr@ sphr.fr; internet www.sphr.fr; f. 1970; present name adopted 1992; mems: Syndicat de la Presse Hebdomadaire Régionale, Syndicat National des Publications Régionales, Syndicat de la Presse Judiciaire de Province, Syndicat National de la Presse Judiciaire; represents 250 regional periodical publications; Pres. ERIC LEJEUNE; Sec.-Gen. WILLIAMS CAPTIER.

Syndicat de la Presse Quotidienne Régionale: 17 place des Etats-Unis, 75116 Paris; tel. 1-40-73-80-20; fax 1-47-20-48-94; internet www.spqr.fr; f. 1986; regional dailies; Pres. JEAN VIANSSON PONTÉ; Sec.-Gen. JACQUES HARDOIN.

PRESS INSTITUTE

Institut Français de Presse: 83 bis rue Notre Dame des Champs, 75006 Paris; tel. 1-53-63-53-20; e-mail ifp@u-paris2.fr; internet ifp .u-paris2.fr; f. 1937; university training programme in mass communication and journalism; maintains research and documentation centre; open to research workers, students, journalists; Dir NATHALIE SONNAC.

Publishers

Actes Sud: Le Méjan, place Nina-Berberova, BP 90038, 13633 Arles; tel. 4-90-49-86-91; fax 4-90-96-95-25; e-mail contact@actes-sud.fr; internet www.actes-sud.fr; f. 1978; French and translated literature, music, theatre, studies of Arabic and Islamic civilizations; Pres. FRANÇOISE NYSSEN; Editorial Dir BERTRAND PY.

Editions Albin Michel: 22 rue Huyghens, 75014 Paris Cedex 14; tel. 1-42-79-10-00; fax 1-43-27-21-58; e-mail virginie.caminade@ albin-michel.fr; internet www.albin-michel.fr; f. 1901; general, fiction, history, classics; Pres. FRANCIS ESMÉNARD; Man. Dir RICHARD DUCOUSSET.

Armand Colin Editeur: 21 rue du Montparnasse, 75006 Paris Cedex 06; tel. 1-44-39-54-47; fax 1-40-46-49-93; e-mail infos@ armand-colin.com; internet www.armand-colin.com; f. 1870; imprint of Hachette Livre; literature, history, human and social sciences, university textbooks; Dir-Gen. PHILIPPE CLÉMENÇOT.

Assouline: 26 place Vendome, 75001 Paris; tel. 1-42-60-76 09; fax 1-42-60-33-85; e-mail production@assouline.com; internet www .assouline.com; f. 1994; art, fashion, design, lifestyle; Dir PROSPER ASSOULINE.

Editions de l'Atelier: 51-55 rue Hoche, 94200 Ivry-sur-Seine; tel. 1-45-15-20-20; fax 1-45-15-20-22; e-mail contact@editionsatelier.com; internet www.editionsatelier.com; f. 1929; religious, educational, political and social, including labour movement; Dir-Gen. BERNARD STÉPHAN.

Groupe Bayard: 18 rue Barbès, 92128 Montrouge Cedex; tel. 1-74-31-60-60; fax 1-74-31-61-61; e-mail communication@bayardpresse .com; internet www.groupebayard.com; f. 1870; children's books, religion, human sciences; Pres. GEORGES SANEROT; Man. Dir HUBERT CHICOU.

Beauchesne Editeur: 7 Cité du Cardinal Lemoine, 75005 Paris; tel. 1-53-10-08-18; fax 1-53-10-85-19; e-mail contact@ editions-beauchesne.com; internet www.editions-beauchesne.com; f. 1850; scripture, religion and theology, philosophy, religious history, politics, encyclopaedias; Man. Dir JEAN-ETIENNE MITTELMANN.

Editions Belfond: 12 ave d'Italie, 75627 Paris Cedex 13; tel. 1-44-16-05-00; fax 1-44-16-05-06; e-mail belfond@placedesediteurs.com; internet www.belfond.fr; f. 1963; fiction, poetry, documents, history, arts; Chair. JÉRÔME TALAMON; Editorial Dir JULIETTE JOSTE.

Berger-Levrault: 104 ave du Président Kennedy, 75016 Paris; tel. 1-40-64-42-32; fax 1-40-64-42-30; e-mail ble@berger-levrault.fr; internet www.berger-levrault.fr; f. 1676; fine arts, health, social and economic sciences, law; Pres. and Dir-Gen. ALAIN SOURISSEAU; Man. Dir PIERRE-MARIE LEHUCHER.

Bordas: 31 ave Pierre de Coubertin, 75013 Paris; tel. 1-72-36-40-00; fax 1-72-36-40-10; e-mail cjacqueson@bordas.tm.fr; internet www .editions-bordas.com; f. 1946; imprint of Editis (q.v.); encyclopaedias, dictionaries, history, geography, arts, children's and educational; Pres. OLIVIER QUERENET DE BREVILLE; Dir of Publication CATHERINE LUCET.

Buchet-Chastel: 7 rue des Canettes, 75006 Paris; tel. 1-44-32-05-60; fax 1-44-32-05-61; e-mail informations@libella.fr; internet www .buchetchastel.fr; f. 1929; literature, music, crafts, religion, practical guides; part of the Libella publishing group; Chair. VERA MICHALSKI.

Editions Calmann-Lévy: 31 rue de Fleurus, 75006 Paris; tel. 1-49-54-36-00; e-mail editions@calmann-levy.com; internet www .editions-calmann-levy.com; f. 1836; French and foreign literature, history, social sciences, economics, sport, leisure; Dir-Gen. FLORENCE SULTAN.

Editions Casterman: 87 quai Panhard et Levassor, 75647 Paris Cedex 13; tel. 1-55-28-12-00; fax 1-55-28-12-60; e-mail info@ casterman.com; internet www.casterman.com; f. 1780; juvenile, comics, fiction, education, leisure, art; since 1999 subsidiary of Flammarion; Editorial Dir BENOÎT MOUCHARD.

Editions du Cerf: 24 rue des Tanneries, 75013 Paris; tel. 1-80-05-36-36; fax 1-80-05-36-10; internet www.editionsducerf.fr; f. 1929; religion, history, philosophy; Chair. MICHEL BON; Man. Dir JEAN-FRANÇOIS COLOSIMO.

Editions Champ Vallon: rue Gérin, 01420 Seyssel; tel. and fax 4-50-56-15-51; e-mail info@champ-vallon.com; internet www .champ-vallon.com; f. 1980; social sciences, literary history, literary criticism; Dirs MYRIAM MONTEIRO-BRAZ, PATRICK BEAUNE.

Editions Chiron: 1155 rue de Fontenay, 94300 Vincennes; tel. 1-30-48-74-50; fax 1-34-98-02-44; e-mail info@editionschiron.com; internet www.editionschiron.com; f. 1907; sport, education, fitness, health, dance, games; Dir THIERRY HEUNINCK.

Editions Dalloz: 31–35 rue Froidevaux, 75685 Paris Cedex 14; tel. 1-40-64-54-54; fax 1-40-64-54-97; e-mail ventes@dalloz.fr; internet www.dalloz.fr; f. 1824; law, philosophy, political science, business and economics; imprint of Hachette Livre; Pres. and Dir-Gen. SYLVIE FAYE.

Dargaud: 15–27 rue Moussorgski, 75895 Paris Cedex 18; tel. 1-53-26-32-32; fax 1-53-26-32-00; e-mail contact@dargaud.fr; internet www.dargaud.fr; f. 1943; juvenile, cartoons, comics, video, graphic novels; Dir-Gen. JEAN-CHRISTOPHE DELPIERRE.

Editions de Boccard: 11 rue de Médicis, 75006 Paris; tel. 1-43-26-00-37; fax 1-43-54-85-83; e-mail info@deboccard.com; internet www.deboccard.com; f. 1866; history, archaeology, religion, orientalism, medievalism; Dir ISABELLE MALAISE.

La Découverte: 9 bis rue Abel Hovelacque, 75013 Paris; tel. 1-44-08-84-01; fax 1-44-08-84-39; e-mail ladecouverte@editionsladecouverte.com; internet www.editionsladecouverte.fr; f. 1959; imprint of Editis (q.v.); economic, social and political science, literature, history; Man. Dir FRANÇOIS GÈZE.

Editions Denoël: 33 rue Saint-André des Arts, 75006 Paris; tel. 1-44-39-73-73; fax 1-44-39-73-90; e-mail denoel@denoel.fr; internet www.denoel.fr; f. 1930; imprint of Editions Gallimard; general literature, science fiction, crime, history; Dir-Gen. BÉATRICE DUVAL.

La Documentation Française: 29 quai Voltaire, 75344 Paris Cedex 07; tel. 1-40-15-70-00; fax 1-40-15-72-30; e-mail depcom@ladocumentationfrancaise.fr; internet www.ladocumentationfrancaise.fr; f. 1945; govt publs; politics, law, economics, culture, science; Dir of Publication XAVIER PATIER.

Dunod: 5 rue Laromiguière, 75005 Paris Cedex; tel. 1-40-46-35-00; fax 1-40-46-49-95; e-mail infos@dunod.com; internet www.dunod.com; f. 1800; science, computer science, electronics, economics, accountancy, management, psychology and humanities; imprint of Hachette Livre; Dir-Gen. NATHALIE DE BAUDRY D'ASSON.

Edilarge Editions Ouest-France: 13 rue du Breil, 35063 Rennes Cedex; tel. 2-99-32-58-27; fax 2-99-32-58-30; e-mail editorial@edilarge.fr; internet www.edilarge.fr; history, guides; subsidiary of Ouest-France group; fmrly Editions Ouest-France; Chair. FRANÇOIS-XAVIER HUTIN; Dir-Gen. SERVANE BIGUAIS.

Edisud: Les Joncades Basses 13210 Saint-Rémy-de-Provence; tel. 4-90-90-21-10; fax 4-42-21-56-20; e-mail info@edisud.com; internet www.edisud.com; f. 1971; health, wellness; Dir CHARLY-YVES CHAUDOREILLE.

Editis: 30 pl. d'Italie, 75702 Paris Cedex 13; tel. 1-53-53-30-00; fax 1-72-36-47-10; e-mail benoit.liva@vupublishing.net; internet www.editis.com; f. 1835 as Havas; renamed Vivendi Universal Publishing 2001, then VUP-Investima 10 in 2003; present name adopted Oct. 2003; wholly owned subsidiary of Grupo Planeta since May 2008; education, literature, reference; imprints include Bordas, La Découverte, Editions First, Fleuve Noir, Editions Nathan, Editions Robert Laffont, Le Robert; Dir of Publishing ALAIN KOUCK.

Editions Eyrolles: 61 blvd Saint Germain, 75240 Paris Cedex 05; tel. 1-44-41-11-11; fax 1-44-41-11-44; e-mail editeurs@editions-eyrolles.com; internet www.editions-eyrolles.com; f. 1918; science, computing, technology, electronics, management, law; Pres. and Dir-Gen. SERGE EYROLLES.

Fayard: 13 rue du Montparnasse, 75006 Paris; tel. 1-45-49-82-00; fax 1-45-49-82-54; e-mail rights@editions-fayard.fr; internet www.editions-fayard.fr; f. 1857; literature, biography, history, religion, essays, music; CEO SOPHIE DE CLOSETS.

Editions des Femmes Antoinette Fouque: 35 rue Jacob, 75006 Paris; tel. 1-42-22-60-74; fax 1-42-22-62-73; e-mail contact@desfemmes.fr; internet www.desfemmes.fr; f. 1973; mainly women authors; fiction, essays, art, history, politics, psychoanalysis, talking books; Dir ANTOINETTE FOUQUE.

Editions First: 12 ave d'Italie, 75013 Paris; tel. 1-45-49-60-00; fax 1-45-49-60-01; e-mail firstinfo@efirst.com; internet www.efirst.com; f. 1992; imprint of Editis (q.v.); general non-fiction; Pres. VINCENT BARBARE.

Editions Flammarion: 87 quai Panhard et Levassor, 75647 Paris Cedex 13; tel. 1-40-51-31-00; fax 1-43-29-21-48; internet editions.flammarion.com; f. 1876; general literature, art, human sciences, sport, children's books, medicine; subsidiary of Flammarion Group; Pres. and Dir-Gen. TERESA CREMISI.

Editions Fleurus: 15–27 rue Moussorgski, 75018 Paris; tel. 1-53-26-33-35; fax 1-53-26-33-36; e-mail fleuruseditions@fleuruseditions.com; internet www.editionsfleurus.com; f. 1944; arts, education, leisure, religion; also Mame, Mango, Rustica, Tardy, Critérium, Desclée, Droguet et Ardant; Chair. VINCENT MONTAGNE; Man. Dir HILAIRE DE LAAGE.

Fleuve Noir: 12 ave d'Italie, 75627 Paris Cedex 13; tel. 1-44-16-05-00; fax 1-44-16-05-07; e-mail deborah.druba@universpoche.com; internet www.fleuvenoir.fr; f. 1949; imprint of Editis (q.v.); general fiction, crime, thrillers, fantasy and science fiction; Pres. and Dir-Gen. MARIE-CHRISTINE CONCHON; Editorial Dir DEBORAH DRUBA.

Editions Foucher: 11 rue Paul Bert, 92247 Malakoff Cedex; tel. 1-41-23-65-65; e-mail cfages@editions-foucher.fr; internet www.editions-foucher.fr; f. 1936; science, economics, law, medicine textbooks; Dir of Publication OLIVIER JAOUI.

Editions Gallimard: 5 rue Gaston-Gallimard, 75328 Paris Cedex 07; tel. 1-49-54-42-00; fax 1-45-44-94-03; e-mail pub@gallimard.fr; internet www.gallimard.fr; f. 1911; general fiction, literature, history, poetry, children's, philosophy; Dir ANTOINE GALLIMARD; Editorial Dir TERESA CREMISI.

Editions Grasset et Fasquelle: 61 rue des Saints Pères, 75006 Paris; tel. 1-44-39-22-00; fax 1-42-22-64-18; e-mail dfanelli@grasset.fr; internet www.grasset.fr; f. 1907; contemporary literature, criticism, general fiction and children's books; Pres. OLIVIER NORA.

Librairie Gründ: 60 rue Mazarine, 75006 Paris; tel. 1-44-16-09-00; fax 1-45-49-60-01; e-mail grund@grund.fr; internet www.grund.fr; f. 1880; art, natural history, children's books, guides; Chair. ALAIN GRÜND.

Hachette Livre: 43 quai de Grenelle, 75905 Paris Cedex 15; tel. and fax 1-43-92-30-00; internet www.hachette.com; f. 1826; group comprises over 40 publishing houses in France and abroad, particularly in the UK and Spain; Pres. and Dir-Gen. ARNAUD NOURRY.

L'Harmattan Edition: 7 rue de l'Ecole Polytechnique, 75005 Paris; tel. 1-40-46-79-20; fax 1-43-25-82-03; e-mail harmat@worldnet.fr; internet www.editions-harmattan.fr; f. 1975; politics, human sciences, developing countries; Dir DENIS PRYEN.

Editions Hatier: 8 rue d'Assas, 75278 Paris Cedex 06; tel. 1-49-54-49-54; fax 1-40-49-00-45; e-mail informationspedagogiques@editions-hatier.fr; internet www.editions-hatier.fr; f. 1880; children's books, fiction, history, science, nature guides; Chair. BERNARD FOULON; Dir-Gen. CÉLIA ROSENTRAUB.

Hermann: 6 rue Labrouste, 75015 Paris; tel. 1-45-57-45-40; fax 1-40-60-12-93; e-mail hermann.sa@wanadoo.fr; internet www.editions-hermann.fr; f. 1876; sciences and art, humanities; Editorial Dir ARTHUR COHEN.

J'ai Lu: 87 quai Panhard et Levassor, 75647 Paris Cedex 13; tel. 1-40-51-31-00; fax 1-43-29-21-48; e-mail ajasmin@jailu.com; internet www.jailu.com; f. 1958; fiction, paperbacks; subsidiary of Flammarion Group; Chair. CHARLES-HENRI FLAMMARION; Man. Dir BERTRAND LOBRY.

Editions Julliard: 24 ave Marceau, 75008 Paris; tel. 1-53-67-14-00; fax 1-53-67-14-14; internet www.julliard.fr; f. 1942; general literature, biography, essays; imprint of Editions Robert Laffont/Editis; Dirs BETTY MIALET, BERNARD BARRAULT.

Editions du JurisClasseur: 141 rue de Javel, 75747 Paris Cedex 15; tel. 1-45-58-93-76; fax 1-45-58-94-00; e-mail editorial@juris-classeur.com; internet www.juris-classeur.com; mem. of Groupe Lexis-Nexis (ReedElsevier); imprints include Litec and Légisoft; law, economics, taxation; Dir of Publication PHILIPPE CARILLON.

Karthala Editions: 22–24 blvd Arago, 75013 Paris; tel. 1-43-31-15-59; fax 1-45-35-27-05; e-mail karthala@orange.fr; internet www.karthala.com; f. 1980; politics, history, geography, anthropology, religious studies, Christianity, Islam, the Arabic-speaking world; Exec. Dir XAVIER AUDRAIN; Dir of Publication ROBERT AGENEAU.

Editions Jeanne Laffitte: 25 Cours d'Estienne d'Orves, BP 1903, 13225 Marseille Cedex 01; tel. 4-91-59-80-43; fax 4-91-54-25-64; e-mail editions@jeanne-laffitte.com; internet www.jeanne-laffitte.com; f. 1978; art, geography, culture, medicine, history; Chair. and Man. Dir JEANNE LAFFITTE.

Editions Robert Laffont: 24 ave Marceau, 75381 Paris Cedex 08; tel. 1-53-67-14-00; fax 1-53-67-14-14; e-mail gmessina@robert-laffont.fr; internet www.laffont.fr; f. 1941; imprint of Editis (q.v.); Pres. and Dir-Gen. ALAIN KOUCK.

Larousse: 21 rue du Montparnasse, 75006 Paris Cedex 06; tel. 1-44-39-44-00; fax 1-44-39-43-43; e-mail livres-larousse@larousse.fr; internet www.larousse.com; f. 1852; general, specializing in dictionaries, illustrated books on scientific subjects, encyclopaedias, classics; imprint of Hachette Livre (q.v.); Dir of Publication ISABELLE JEUGE-MAYNART.

Editions J.-C. Lattès: 17 rue Jacob, 75006 Paris; tel. 1-44-41-74-00; fax 1-43-25-30-47; e-mail mpageix@editions-jclattes.fr; internet www.editions-jclattes.fr; f. 1968; imprint of Hachette Livre (q.v.); general fiction and non-fiction, biography; Man. Dir ISABELLE LAFFONT.

Letouzey et Ané: 87 blvd Raspail, 75006 Paris; tel. 1-45-48-80-14; fax 1-45-49-03-43; e-mail letouzey@free.fr; internet www.letouzey.com; f. 1885; theology, religion, archaeology, history, ecclesiastical encyclopaedias and dictionaries, biography; Man. Dir FLORENCE LETOUZEY.

Le Livre de Poche: 31 rue de Fleurus, 75006 Paris Cedex 06; tel. 1-49-54-37-00; fax 1-49-54-37-01; internet www.livredepoche.com; f. 1953; general literature, dictionaries, encyclopaedias; Man. Editor LAURA BEHN.

Editions Magnard: 5 allée de la 2ème Division Blindée, 75015 Paris; fax 1-42-79-46-80; e-mail contact@magnard.fr; internet www .magnard.fr; f. 1933; children's and educational books; subsidiary of Editions Albin Michel; Dir of Publication GUILLAUME DERVIEUX.

Elsevier Masson: 62 rue Camille Desmoulins, 92442 Issy les Moulineaux Cedex; tel. 1-71-16-55-99; internet www .elsevier-masson.fr; f. 2005; medicine and science, books and periodicals; publrs for various academies and societies; subsidiary of Elsevier; Pres. DANIEL RODRIGUEZ.

Mercure de France: 26 rue de Condé, 75006 Paris; tel. 1-55-42-61-90; e-mail mercure@mercure.fr; internet www.mercuredefrance.fr; f. 1893; general fiction, history, biography, sociology; Pres. and Man. Dir ISABELLE GALLIMARD.

Editions de Minuit: 7 rue Bernard Palissy, 75006 Paris; tel. 1-44-39-39-20; fax 1-44-39-39-23; e-mail contact@leseditionsdeminuit.fr; internet www.leseditionsdeminuit.fr; f. 1945; general literature; Man. Dir IRÈNE LINDON.

Editions Nathan: 25 ave Pierre de Coubertin, 75211 Paris Cedex 13; tel. 1-45-87-50-00; fax 1-47-07-57-57; e-mail frubert@nathan.fr; internet www.nathan.fr; f. 1881; educational books for all levels; Man. Dir CATHERINE LUCET.

Editions Payot & Rivages: 106 blvd Saint Germain, 75006 Paris; tel. 1-44-41-39-90; fax 1-44-41-39-69; e-mail editions@payotrivages .com; internet www.payot-rivages.fr; f. 1917; literature, human sciences, philosophy; Pres. FRANÇOISE NYSSEN; Dir-Gen. BENOÎTE MOUROT.

Editions Picard: 82 rue Bonaparte, 75006 Paris; tel. 1-43-26-97-78; fax 1-43-26-42-64; e-mail livres@librairie-picard.com; internet www .editions-picard.com; f. 1869; archaeology, architecture, history of art, history, pre-history, auxiliary sciences, linguistics, musicological works, antiquarian books; Chair. and Man. Dir CHANTAL PASINI-PICARD.

Editions Plon: 12 ave d'Italie, 75013 Paris; tel. 1-44-16-09-00; fax 1-44-41-30-53; e-mail stephane.billerey@editions-plon.com; internet www.plon.fr; f. 1852; imprint of Editis (q.v.); fiction, history, anthropology, human sciences, biography; Pres. and Dir-Gen. VINCENT BARBARE.

Editions P.O.L.: 33 rue Saint André des Arts, 75006 Paris; tel. 1-43-54-21-20; fax 1-43-54-11-31; e-mail pol@pol-editeur.fr; internet www .pol-editeur.fr; literature; arts; Dir-Gen. PAUL OTCHAKOVSKI-LAURENS.

Presses de la Cité: 12 ave d'Italie, 75625 Paris Cedex 13; tel. 1-44-16-05-00; e-mail pressesdelacite@placedesediteurs.com; internet www.pressesdelacite.com; f. 1944; subsidiary of Editis (q.v.); fiction and factual literature for general audience; Dir JEAN ARCACHE.

Presses de Sciences Po: 117 blvd Saint-Germain, 75006 Paris; tel. 1-45-49-83-64; fax 1-45-49-83-34; e-mail info.presses@sciences-po.fr; internet www.pressesdesciencespo.fr; f. 1975; history, politics, linguistics, economics, sociology, health, sustainable development; Dir MARIE-GENEVIÈVE VANDESANDE.

Presses Universitaires de France: 6 ave Reille, 75014 Paris Cedex 14; tel. 1-58-10-31-00; fax 1-58-10-31-82; e-mail info-ventes@puf.com; internet www.puf.com; f. 1921; philosophy, psychology, psychoanalysis, psychiatry, education, sociology, theology, history, geography, economics, law, linguistics, literature, science; Editorial Dir MONIQUE LABRUNE.

Presses Universitaires de Grenoble: 5 place Robert-Schuman, BP 1549, 38025 Grenoble Cedex 1; tel. 4-76-29-43-09; fax 4-76-44-64-31; e-mail editorial@pug.fr; internet www.pug.fr; f. 1972; psychology, law, economics, management, history, statistics, literature, medicine, science, politics; Man. Dir SYLVIE BIGOT.

Presses Universitaires de Nancy—Editions Universitaires de Lorraine: 42–44 ave de la Libération, BP 3347, 54014 Nancy Cedex; tel. 3-54-50-46-90; fax 3-54-50-46-94; e-mail edulor-edition@ univ-lorraine.fr; internet www.univ-lorraine.fr/content/ presses-universitaires-de-nancy-editions-universitaires-de-lorraine; f. 1976; literature, history, law, social sciences, politics; Dir FERRI BRIQUET.

Editions Privat: 10 rue des Arts, BP 38028, 31080 Toulouse Cedex 06; tel. 5-61-33-77-00; fax 5-34-31-64-44; e-mail info@editions-privat .com; internet www.editions-privat.com; f. 1839; regional, national and international history, heritage, health; Pres. OLIVIER LAMARQUE.

Editions du Seuil: 25 blvd Romain Rolland, 75993 Paris Cedex 14; tel. 1-40-46-50-50; fax 1-40-46-43-00; e-mail contact@seuil.com; internet www.seuil.com; f. 1935; acquired by La Martinière in 2003; modern literature, fiction, illustrated books, non-fiction; Pres. and Dir-Gen. OLIVIER BÉTOURNÉ.

Editions du Signe: 1 rue Alfred Kastler, BP 10094, Eckbolsheim, 67038 Strasbourg Cedex 02; tel. 3-88-78-91-91; fax 3-88-78-91-99; e-mail info@editionsdusigne.fr; internet www.editionsdusigne.fr; f. 1987; Christianity; Chair. and Man. Dir CHRISTIAN RIEHL.

Editions Stock: 31 rue de Fleurus, 75006 Paris Cedex 06; tel. 1-49-54-36-55; fax 1-49-54-36-62; e-mail hamalric@editions-stock.fr; internet www.editions-stock.fr; f. 1708; literature, translations, biography, human sciences, guides; Dir of Publication MANUEL CARCASSONNE; Man. Editor MARIE-CHARLOTTE BROSSIER.

Succès du Livre: 60 rue St André des Arts, 75006 Paris; tel. 1-44-41-65-00; fax 1-44-41-65-36; internet www.succesdulivre.com; f. 1987; fiction, biography; Pres. ALEXANDRE FALCO.

Editions de la Table Ronde: 3326 rue de Condé, 75006 Paris; tel. 1-40-46-70-70; fax 1-40-46-71-01; e-mail editionslatableronde@ editionslatableronde.fr; internet www.editionslatableronde.fr; f. 1944; fiction, essays, religion, travel, theatre, youth; Dir-Gen. ALICE DÉON.

Editions Tallandier: 2 rue Rotrou, 75006 Paris; tel. 1-40-46-43-88; fax 1-40-46-43-98; e-mail info@tallandier.com; internet www .tallandier.com; f. 1865; history, reference; Dir XAVIER DE BARTILLAT.

Editions Tawhid: 6 impasse Victor Hugo, 69003 Lyon 3; tel. 4-72-74-19-39; fax 4-78-24-01-56; e-mail info@edition-tawhid.com; internet www.islam-france.com; Islamic interest; Man. Dir YAMIN MAKRI.

Editions Vigot: 23–27 rue de l'Ecole de Médecine, 75006 Paris; tel. 1-43-29-54-50; fax 1-46-34-56-12; e-mail ventelibraires@vigot.fr; internet www.vigot.fr; f. 1890; medicine, pharmacology, nature, veterinary science, sport, fitness, tourism, cookery; Chair. CHRISTIAN VIGOT; Man. Dir DANIEL VIGOT.

Librairie Philosophique J. Vrin: 6 place de la Sorbonne, 75005 Paris; tel. 1-43-54-03-47; fax 1-43-54-48-18; e-mail contact@vrin.fr; internet www.vrin.fr; f. 1911; university textbooks, philosophy, education, science, law, religion; Dir of Publication DENIS ARNAUD.

Librairie Vuibert: 5 allée de la 2ème Division Blindée, 75015 Paris; tel. 1-42-79-44-00; fax 1-42-79-46-80; e-mail valerie.devillers@ vuibert.fr; internet www.vuibert.com; f. 1877; school and university textbooks, psychology, law; subsidiary of Editions Albin Michel; Dir of Publication GUILLAUME DERVIEUX.

XO Editions: 33 ave du Maine, BP 142, 75755 Paris Cedex 15; tel. 1-56-80-26-80; fax 1-56-80-26-72; e-mail edito@xoeditions.com; internet www.xoeditions.com; f. 2000; general fiction, biography, current affairs, politics; Dir BERNARD FIXOT.

PUBLISHERS' AND BOOKSELLERS' ASSOCIATIONS

Cercle de la Librairie (Syndicat des Industries et Commerces du Livre): 35 rue Grégoire de Tours, 75006 Paris Cedex; tel. 1-44-41-28-00; fax 1-44-41-28-19; e-mail p.fouché@electre.com; internet www .cercledelalibrairie.org; f. 1847; a syndicate of the book trade, grouping the principal asscns of publrs, booksellers and printers; Chair. DENIS MOLLAT; Man. Dir PHILIPPE BEAUVILLARD.

Chambre Syndicale de l'Edition Musicale: 74 rue de la Fédération, 75015 Paris; tel. 1-48-74-09-29; e-mail csdem@csdem.org; internet www.csdem.org; f. 1925; music publrs' asscn; Pres. NELLY QUEROL.

Fédération Française Syndicale de la Librairie: 24 place de la République, 14100 Lisieux; tel. 2-31-62-16-87; fax 2-31-63-97-37; f. 1892; booksellers' asscn; Chair. COLETTE HEDOUX.

Syndicat National de l'Edition: 115 blvd Saint-Germain, 75006 Paris; tel. 1-44-41-40-50; fax 1-44-41-40-77; internet www.sne.fr; f. 1892; publrs' asscn; 670 mems; Chair. VINCENT MONTAGNE.

Syndicat National de la Librairie Ancienne et Moderne: 4 rue Gît-le-Cœur, 75006 Paris; tel. 1-43-29-46-38; fax 1-43-25-41-63; e-mail slam-livre@wanadoo.fr; internet www.slam-livre.fr; f. 1914; booksellers' asscn; 250 mems; Pres. ANNE LAMORT.

Broadcasting and Communications

TELECOMMUNICATIONS

Alcatel-Lucent: 148/152 route de la Reine, 92100 Boulogne-Billancourt; tel. 1-55-14-10-10; e-mail execoffice@alcatel-lucent .com; internet www.alcatel-lucent.com; f. 2006 by merger of Alcatel (f. 1898) and Lucent (USA, f. 1996); telecommunications and business systems, broadband access, terrestrial and submarine optical networks; Chair. PHILIPPE CAMUS; CEO MICHEL COMBES.

Bouygues Télécom: 37–39 rue Boissière, 75116 Paris; tel. 1-44-20-10-00; internet www.bouygtel.com; f. 1994; mobile cellular telecommunications; Pres. and Dir-Gen. OLIVIER ROUSSAT.

Groupe Iliad (Free): 8 rue de la Ville l'Evêque, 75008 Paris; tel. (1) 73-50-20-00; fax (1) 73-50-20-01; e-mail presse@iliad.fr; internet www.iliad.fr; f. 1991; provides fixed-line telecommunications, broadband internet and television through subsidiaries Free, One.Tel and Iliad Télécom; subsidiary Free Mobile awarded licence to operate mobile cellular telecommunications in 2009; Pres. CYRIL POIDATZ; Dir-Gen. MAXIME LOMBARDINI.

Numericable: 10 rue Albert Einstein, 77420 Champs-sur-Marne; tel. 1-55-92-46-00; fax 1-55-92-46-90; e-mail communication@ ncnumericable.com; internet www.numericable.fr; f. 2006 by merger of NC Numéricâble (f. 1997) and Noos (f. 1986); fixed-line operator, consumer internet access, cable television; Pres. and Dir-Gen. ERIC DENOYER.

Orange: 78 rue Olivier de Serres, Paris 75015; tel. 1-44-44-22-22; fax 1-44-44-80-34; e-mail infos.groupe@orange.com; internet www .orange.com; 33.1% state-owned, following privatization in 2004; fmrly France Télécom; name changed to present 2013; Chair. and CEO STÉPHANE RICHARD.

SFR: 1 place Carpeaux, Tour Séquoia, 92915 Paris La Défense Cedex; tel. 8-05-77-66-66; internet www.sfr.fr; f. 1993; mobile cellular telecommunications; 100% owned by Vivendi SA; merged with Neuf Cegetel in 2008; 15m. subscribers (March 2010); Pres. and Dir-Gen. JEAN-YVES CHARLIER.

REGULATORY AUTHORITIES

Agence Nationale des Fréquences (ANFR): 78 ave du Général de Gaulle, BP 400, 94704 Maisons-Alfort Cedex; tel. 1-45-18-72-73; fax 1-45-18-72-00; e-mail rtte@anfr.fr; internet www.anfr.fr; Pres. ARNAUD MIQUEL; Dir-Gen. GILLES BRÉGANT.

Autorité de Régulation des Communications Electroniques et des Postes (ARCEP): 7 sq. Max Hymans, 75730 Paris Cedex 15; tel. 1-40-47-70-00; fax 1-40-47-71-98; e-mail courrier@arcep.fr; internet www.arcep.fr; f. 2005; fmrly Autorité de Régulation des Télécommunications; Chair. JEAN-LUDOVIC SILICANI; Dir-Gen. PHILIPPE DISTLER.

BROADCASTING

Conseil Supérieur de l'Audiovisuel (CSA): Tour Mirabeau, 39–43 quai André Citroën, 75739 Paris Cedex 15; tel. 1-40-58-38-00; fax 1-45-79-00-06; internet www.csa.fr; f. 1989 as replacement for the Commission Nationale de la Communication et des Libertés; supervises all French broadcasting; awards licences to private radio (including digital radio) and television stations, allocates frequencies, has a co-decisional power to appoint chairs of public broadcasting companies, monitors programme standards; consists of 9 mems, appointed for 6 years: 3 nominated by the Pres. of the Republic; 3 by the Pres. of the National Assembly; and 3 by the Pres. of the Senate; Pres. OLIVIER SCHRAMECK; Gen. Man. FRÉDÉRIC LENICA.

Institut National de l'Audiovisuel: 4 ave de l'Europe, 94360 Bry-sur-Marne Cedex; tel. 1-49-83-26-74; fax 1-49-83-23-89; e-mail assistance@ina.fr; internet www.ina.fr; f. 1975; research and professional training in the field of broadcasting; radio and TV archives, TV production; Publ. *Les Nouveaux Dossiers de l'Audiovisuel*; (6 a year); Pres. and Dir-Gen. (vacant).

Télédiffusion de France (TDF): 106 ave Marx Dormoy, 92120 Montrouge; tel. 1-55-95-10-00; e-mail e-tdf@tdf.fr; internet www.tdf .fr; f. 1975; partly privatized 1987; restructured in 2007; comprises 3 sections: TDF France, TDF Multimedia and TDF International; responsible for broadcasting programmes produced by the production companies, for the organization and maintenance of the networks, for study and research into radio and television equipment; broadcasts digital terrestrial television; Dir-Gen. OLIVIER HUART.

Radio

State-controlled Radio

Public radio services are provided by three entities: Radio France for the domestic audience; Réseau Outre-Mer 1ère for the French overseas departments and territories; and Radio France Internationale for foreign countries (and those of foreign origin in France).

Société Nationale de Radiodiffusion (Radio France): 116 ave du Président Kennedy, 75786 Paris Cedex 16; tel. 1-56-40-22-22; fax 1-56-40-35-87; internet www.radio-france.fr; f. 1975; planning and production of radio programmes; provides 7 national services, 44 local stations and 2 European services; Pres. and Dir-Gen. MATHIEU GALLET.

> **France Bleu:** Maison de Radio France, 75220 Paris Cedex 16; tel. 1-56-40-22-22; e-mail brigitte.tauzin@radiofrance.com; internet www.francebleu.com; f. 1980, restructured 2000; network of domestic services; Dir CLAUDE ESCLATINE.

> **France Culture:** tel. 1-56-40-27-91; e-mail caroline.cesbron@ radiofrance.com; internet franceculture.com; domestic, nationwide service; Dir OLIVIER POIVRE D'ARVOR.

> **France-Info:** tel. 1-56-40-20-43; e-mail romain.beignon@ radiofrance.com; internet www.france-info.com; domestic, nationwide service; continuous news and information; f. 1987; Dir LAURENT GUIMIER.

> **France Inter:** tel. 1-56-40-37-57; e-mail emmanuel.perreau@ radiofrance.com; internet www.franceinter.com; domestic, nation-

wide service; general programmes, for entertainment and information; Dir LAURENCE BLOCH.

> **France Musique:** tel. 1-56-40-36-12; e-mail christophe.sillieres@ radiofrance.com; internet www.francemusique.fr; domestic, nationwide service; Dir MARIE-PIERRE DE SURVILLE.

> **Le Mouv':** tel. 5-62-30-70-16; internet www.lemouv.com; domestic, nationwide service; music and general interest for people aged 18–35; f. 1997; Dir BRUNO LAFORESTRIE.

> **Réseau FIP:** tel. 1-56-40-16-15; internet www.fipradio.fr; f. 1971; comprises 10 local stations; continuous music; Dir ANNE SÉRODE.

Radio France Internationale (RFI): 116 ave du Président Kennedy, BP 9516, 75786 Paris Cedex 16; tel. 1-56-40-12-12; fax 1-56-40-47-59; internet www.rfi.fr; f. 1975; broadcasts on MW and FM transmitters, mainly to Africa, Eastern Europe, North America, the Caribbean, South-East Asia and the Middle East, in French; also broadcasts in 12 other languages: Arabic, Cambodian, English, Farsi, Hausa, Mandarin, Spanish, Portuguese, Romanian, Russian, Swahili, Vietnamese; Pres. MARIE-CHRISTINE SARAGOSSE.

Réseau Outre-Mer 1ère: 35–37 rue Danton, 92240 Malakoff; tel. 1-55-22-71-00; internet www.la1ere.fr; f. 1983; fmrly FR3 DOM-TOM, subsequently Résau France Outre-mer until 2010; controls broadcasting in the French overseas territories; local stations providing terrestrial, satellite and cable channels and radio networks; Dir MICHEL KOPS.

Independent Radio

BFM: 12 rue d'Oradour sur Glane, 75015 Paris; tel. 1-71-19-11-81; fax 1-71-19-11-80; e-mail stemplet@radiobfm.com; internet www .radiobfm.com; f. 1992; broadcasts on cable and 14 FM frequencies; politics, economics; Pres. ALAIN WEILL; Dir-Gen. HERVÉ BÉROUD.

Chérie FM: 22 rue Boileau, 75203 Paris Cedex 16; tel. 1-40-71-40-00; e-mail vgrandclaude@nrj.fr; internet www.cheriefm.fr; broadcasts popular music and entertainment programming on FM nationwide; mem. of Groupe NRJ; Dir MAXIME AYEL.

Europe 1: 26 bis rue François, 75008 Paris; tel. 1-53-35-72-60; e-mail courrier@europe1.fr; internet www.europe1.fr; owned by Groupe Lagardère, which also owns Europe 2 (for younger listeners) and RFM; broadcasting on long wave and 99 FM frequencies; Pres. DENIS OLIVENNES.

Nostalgie: 22 rue Boileau, 75203 Paris Cedex 16; tel. 1-40-71-40-00; e-mail sbosc@nrj.fr; internet www.nostalgie.fr; mem. of Groupe NRJ; broadcasts popular music and entertainment programming on FM nationwide; Dir MAXIME AYEL.

NRJ: 22 rue Boileau, 75203 Paris Cedex 16; tel. 1-40-71-40-00; e-mail vgrandclaude@nrj.fr; internet www.nrj.fr; broadcasts contemporary popular music and entertainment programming on FM nationwide; Pres. and Dir-Gen. JEAN-PAUL BAUDECROUX.

Radio Classique: 12 bis place Henri Bergson, 75382 Paris Cedex 08; tel. 1-40-08-50-00; fax 1-40-08-50-80; internet www.radioclassique .fr; f. 1983; classical music; Pres. FRANCIS MOREL.

Radio Monte-Carlo (RMC): 12 rue d'Oradour sur Glane, 75740 Paris Cedex 15; tel. 1-71-19-11-91; fax 1-71-19-11-90; internet www .rmcinfo.fr; broadcasting on long wave and 148 FM frequencies; information, talk and sports programmes; Dir ALAIN WEILL.

RTL: 22 rue Bayard, 75008 Paris; tel. 1-40-70-44-00; fax 1-40-70-42-72; e-mail contact@rtl.fr; internet www.rtl.fr; broadcasting on long wave and 150 FM frequencies; CEO CHRISTOPHER BALDELLI.

Skyrock: 37 bis rue Grenéta, 75002 Paris; tel. 1-44-88-82-00; fax 1-44-88-89-57; internet www.skyrock.com; f. 1986; contemporary rap and hip-hop music; Pres. PIERRE BELLANGER; Dir-Gen. FRANK CHENEAU.

Television

In November 2011 France completed the transfer from analogue to digital television.

State-controlled Television

France Télévisions: 7 esplanade Henri-de-France, 75907 Paris; tel. 1-56-22-60-00; fax 1-56-22-60-21; internet www .francetelevisions.fr; f. 1992; supervisory authority for the nat. public television networks (France 2, France 3, France 4 and France 5); Pres. RÉMY PFLIMLIN; Sec.-Gen. CHRISTIAN VION.

> **France 2:** 7 esplanade Henri-de-France, 75907 Paris Cedex 15, tel. 1-56-22-42-42; fax 1-56-22-55-87; e-mail contact@france2.fr; internet www.france2.fr; f. 1975; general programmes for a nationwide audience; Dir-Gen. THIERRY THUILLIER.

> **France 3 (F3):** 7 esplanade Henri-de-France, 75907 Paris Cedex 15; tel. 1-56-22-30-30; internet www.france3.fr; f. 1975 as France Régions 3 (FR3); general programmes for a nationwide audience (with a larger proportion of cultural and educational programmes than France 2), and regional programmes transmitted from 13 regional stations; Dir-Gen. FRANÇOIS GUILBEAU.

France 4: 7 esplanade Henri-de-France, 75907 Paris Cedex 15; tel. 1-56-22-68-68; fax 1-56-22-68-69; e-mail yann.renoard@francetv.fr; internet www.france4.fr; f. 2005; 100% owned by France Télévisions; digital TV station; creative and cultural programming; Dir-Gen. EMMANUELLE GUILBART.

France 5: 10–12 rue Horace Vernet, 92785 Issy-les-Moulineaux Cedex; tel. 1-56-22-91-91; e-mail telespectateurs@france5.fr; internet www.france5.fr; f. 1994 as La Cinquième; present name adopted 2002; educational programmes and documentaries; Dir-Gen. BRUNO PATINO.

France 24: 5 rue des Nations Unies, 92445 Issy-les-Moulineaux; tel. 1-73-01-24-24; fax 1-73-01-24-56; e-mail webdesk@france24.com; internet www.france24.com; f. 2006; jointly owned by TF1 and France Télévisions; cable, satellite and internet broadcasts; 24-hour news broadcasts in Arabic, English and French; aims to present international news from a French perspective; CEO MARIE-CHRISTINE SARAGOSSE.

ARTE France: 4 quai du Chanoine Winterer, 67000 Strasbourg; tel. 3-88-14-22-22; fax 3-88-14-22-00; internet www.arte.tv; f. 1992 to replace La Sept; arts, cultural programmes, in French and German; Pres. VÉRONIQUE CAYLA; Dir-Gen. ANNE DURUPTY.

TV5 Monde: 131 ave de Wagram, 75017 Paris; tel. 1-44-18-55-55; internet www.tv5.org; f. 1984; broadcasts French-language programmes via satellite and cable to 203 countries worldwide; 49% owned by Audiovisuel Extérieur de la France, 12.58% by France Télévisions and 3.29% by ARTE France; Dir-Gen. YVES BIGOT.

Television programmes for France's overseas departments and territories are provided by Réseau Outre-Mer 1ère (see under Radio).

Independent Television

Canal Plus: 1 place du Spectacle, 92863 Issy-Les-Moulineaux Cedex 9; tel. 1-71-35-35-35; fax 1-44-25-12-34; internet www.canalplus.fr; f. 1984; owned by Vivendi; coded programmes financed by audience subscription; uncoded programmes financed by advertising sold by Canal Plus; specializes in drama (including films) and sport; launched a 'pay-per-view' service for sports events in 1996; produces 21 theme channels in 6 countries; Pres. and Dir-Gen. BERTRAND MÉHEUT.

demain!: 1 rue Patry, 92220 Bagneux; tel. 1-45-36-89-00; fax 1-45-36-89-01; e-mail contact@demain.fr; internet www.demain.fr; f. 1997; information about employment for job-seekers; Dir-Gen. ALAIN BELAIS.

D8: 1 place du Spectacle, 92863 Issy-Les-Moulineaux Cedex 9; tel. 1-71-35-35-35; internet www.d8.tv; f. 2005 as Direct 8; renamed as present 2012; free-to-air digital television channel; owned by Groupe Canal Plus; Pres. BERTRAND MÉHEUT; Dir of Programmes XAVIER GANDON.

Gulli: 4 rue de Presbourg, 75116 Paris; tel. 1-40-69-16-00; fax 1-40-69-18-54; e-mail tachaine@gullitv.fr; internet www.gullitv.fr; f. 2005; free-to-air digital television channel for children; Dir-Gen. ANTOINE VILLENEUVE.

i>TELE: 1 place du Spectacle, 92863 Issy-Les-Moulineaux Cedex 9; tel. 1-71-35-55-55; e-mail communication.itele@canal-plus.com; internet www.itele.fr; f. 1999; free-to-air digital television channel; 24-hr news broadcasts; part of Groupe Canal Plus; Dir-Gen. CÉCILIA RAGUENEAU.

LCI (La Chaîne Info): 1 quai du Point du Jour, 92656 Boulogne-Billancourt Cedex; tel. 1-41-41-12-34; e-mail ccomfi@tf1.fr; internet lci.tf1.fr; f. 1994; news, information; part of Groupe TF1; Pres. NONCE PAOLINI; Dir-Gen. ERIC REVEL.

M6: 89 ave Charles de Gaulle, 92575 Neuilly-sur-Seine Cedex; tel. 1-41-92-66-66; fax 1-41-92-66-10; e-mail pholl@m6.fr; internet www.m6.fr; f. 1986 as TV6; re-formed as M6 1987; 48.43% owned by RTL Group; subsidiaries include W9 (a free-to-air digital television channel); specializes in drama, music and magazines; Chair., Man. Bd NICOLAS DE TAVERNOST.

NT1: 1 quai du Point du Jour, 92656 Boulogne-Billancourt Cedex; tel. 1-49-22-20-01; fax 1-49-22-20-71; e-mail contact@nt1.fr; internet www.nt1.tv; free-to-air digital television channel; owned by AB Groupe; Pres. CLAUDE BERDA.

Télévision Française 1 (TF1): 1 quai du Point du Jour, 92656 Boulogne-Billancourt Cedex; tel. 1-41-41-12-34; fax 1-41-41-28-40; internet www.tf1.fr; f. 1975 as a state-owned channel, privatized 1987; 43.1% owned by Bouygues SA; general programmes; Pres. and Dir-Gen. NONCE PAOLINI.

Finance

(cap. = capital; res = reserves; dep. = deposits; m. = million; br.(s) = branch(es); amounts in euros)

BANKING

Central Bank

Banque de France: 39 rue Croix des Petits Champs, BP 140-01, 75001 Paris; tel. 1-42-92-42-92; fax 1-42-92-45-00; e-mail infos@banque-france.fr; internet www.banque-france.fr; f. 1800; nationalized 1946; became independent 1994; acts as banker to the Treasury, issues bank notes, controls credit and money supply and administers France's gold and currency assets; in 1993 the National Assembly approved legislation to make the Banque de France an independent central bank, with a General Council to supervise activities and appoint the principal officials, and a 9-mem. monetary policy committee, independent of govt control, to be in charge of French monetary policy; a mem. of the European System of Central Banks since June 1998; cap. and res 25,870m., dep. 118,397m., total assets 506,050m. (Dec. 2009); Gov. CHRISTIAN NOYER; 96 brs.

Financing Institution

Société de Financement de l'Economie Française (SFEF): Paris; f. Oct. 2008 to assist the banking sector in the financial crisis; 66% owned by a group of 7 banks, 34% state-owned; provider of govt-guaranteed loans to banks; Chair. FRANÇOISE MALRIEU; Dir-Gen. HENRY RAYMOND.

State Savings Bank

Caisse des Dépôts et Consignations: 56 rue de Lille, 75356 Paris Cedex 07; tel. 1-58-50-00-00; fax 1-58-50-02-46; internet www.caissedesdepots.fr; f. 1816; manages state savings system, holds widespread investments in industrial cos; res 4,284m., dep. 93,910m., total assets 286,648m. (Dec. 2012); Dir-Gen. JEAN-PIERRE JOUYET; 1 br.

Commercial Banks

Allianz Banque: Tour Neptune, 20 place de Seine, La Défense, 92400 Courbevoie; tel. 1-53-24-48-48; fax 1-53-24-48-41; e-mail serviceclient@banqueagf.fr; internet www.allianzbanque.fr; f. 2000; affiliated to Group Allianz; Pres. PASCAL THÉBÉ; Dir-Gen. FABIEN WATHLÉ.

Arkea Banque Enterprises et Institutionnels: allée Louis Lichou, 29480 Le Relecq-Kerhuon Cedex; tel. 2-99-29-92-00; fax 2-98-43-83-03; e-mail banque-ei@arkea.com; internet www.arkea-banque-ei.com; f. 1985; present name adopted 2000; subsidiary of Crédit Mutuel Arkéa; cap. 530m., res 54.2m., dep. 5,058.2m. (Dec. 2012); Chair. MARCEL GARNIER; Pres., Executive Bd GÉRARD BAYOL.

Banque BIA: 67 ave Franklin D. Roosevelt, 75008 Paris; tel. 1-53-76-62-62; fax 1-42-89-09-59; e-mail contact@bia-paris.fr; internet www.bia-paris.fr; f. 1975 as Banque Intercontinentale Arabe; present name adopted 2006; 50% owned by Banque Extérieure d'Algérie, 50% by Libyan Arab Foreign Bank; cap. 158.1m., res 1.8m., dep. 1,142.4m. (Dec. 2012); Chair. MUHAMMAD LOUKAL.

Banque CIC Est: 31 rue Jean Wenger-Valentin, 67958 Strasbourg Cedex 9; tel. 3-88-37-61-23; fax 3-88-37-61-81; internet www.cic.fr; f. 2008 from merger of CIC Banque SNVB and CIC Banque CIAL; 100% owned by Crédit Industriel et Commercial; cap. 225.0m., res 886.3m., dep. 44,740m. (Dec. 2009); Chair. and Dir-Gen. NICOLAS THÉRY; Gen. Mans LUC DYMARSKI, PIERRE JACHEZ.

Banque CIC Sud Ouest: 42 cours du Chapeau Rouge, 33000 Bordeaux; tel. 5-56-00-59-50; fax 5-57-85-55-74; internet www.cic.fr/sb; f. 1880 as Société Bordelaise de Crédit Industriel et Commercial et de Dépôts; present name adopted in 2010; 100% owned by Crédit Industriel et Commercial; cap. 155.3m., res 86.3m., dep. 9,239.3m. (Dec. 2012); Chair. and Dir-Gen. PASCALE RIBAULT; 265 brs.

Banque CIO-BRO: BP 84001, 2 ave Jean-Claude Bonduelle, 44040 Nantes Cedex 1; tel. 0-83-97-89-37; fax 2-40-12-93-80; e-mail cio-international@cio.cic.fr; internet www.cic.fr/cio-bro; f. 2006 by merger of Crédit Industriel de l'Ouest (f. 1957) and Banque Régionale de l'Ouest (f. 1913); 100% owned by Crédit Industriel et Commercial; Chair. MICHEL MICHENKO; Man. Dir JEAN-PIERRE BICHON.

Banque Degroof France SA: 1 rond-point des Champs-Élysées, 75008 Paris; tel. 1-45-61-55-55; fax 1-45-61-96-25; internet www.degroof.fr; f. 2011; 100% owned by Banque Degroof SA (Belgium); Chair. REGNIER HAEGELSTEEN; Man. Dir LIONEL GIOT.

Banque Espírito Santo et de la Vénétie: 45 ave Georges Mandel, 75116 Paris; tel. 1-44-34-48-00; fax 1-44-34-48-48; e-mail besv@besv.fr; internet www.besv.fr; f. 1945; present name adopted 1998; absorbed Via Banque in 2002; 42% owned by Espírito Santo Financial Group SA (Luxembourg); cap. 75.1m., res 77.8m., dep. 476.6m. (Dec. 2012); Pres. PHILLIPE GUIRAL; 1 br.

Banque Européenne du Crédit Mutuel (BECM): 34 rue du Wacken, 67000 Strasbourg Cedex 9; tel. 3-88-14-74-74; fax 3-88-14-75-10; e-mail becm@becm.fr; internet www.creditmutuel.fr/becm/fr; f. 1992 as Banque de l'Economie—Crédit Mutuel; name changed as above in June 2012; cap. 378.3m., res 1,546.7m., total assets 8,320.4m. (Dec. 2006); Chief Exec. RENÉ DANGEL; 27 brs.

Banque Fédérative du Crédit Mutuel: 34 rue du Wacken, 67000 Strasbourg; tel. 3-88-14-88-14; fax 3-88-14-67-00; internet www.bfcm.creditmutuel.fr; f. 1895; cap. 1,327m., res 10,455m., dep. 145,830m. (Dec. 2012); Pres. and Chair. ETIENNE PFLIMLIN; Dir-Gen. MICHEL LUCAS; 16 brs.

Banque Nationale de Paris Intercontinentale: 12 rue Chauchat, 75009 Paris; tel. 1-40-14-22-11; fax 1-40-14-69-34; internet www.bnpgroup.com; f. 1940; present name adopted 1972; 100% owned by BNP Paribas; cap. 30.5m., res 5.0m., dep. 8.9m. (Dec. 2008); Chair. and Dir-Gen. BAUDOUIN PROT.

Banque Neuflize OBC: 3 ave Hoche, 75008 Paris; tel. 1-56-21-70-00; fax 1-56-21-84-60; internet www.neuflizeobc.fr; f. 1966 as De Neuflize, Schlumberger, Mallet & Cie; acquired clients of fmr Banque OBC—Odier Bungener Courvoisier and adopted present name 2006; 100% owned by ABN AMRO France; private banking; cap. 383.5m., res 168.2m., dep. 6,410.7m. (Dec. 2012); Chair., Supervisory Bd JEROEN RIJPKEMA; Pres. and Chair., Management Bd PHILLIPE VAYSSETTES; 12 brs.

Banque Palatine: 42 rue d'Anjou, 75382 Paris Cedex 08; tel. 1-55-27-94-94; e-mail contact@palatine.fr; internet www.palatine.fr; f. 1971; fmrly Banque Sanpaolo; present name adopted 2005; 100% owned by Caisse Nationale des Caisses d'Epargne; cap. 538.8m., res 234.8m., dep. 9,834m. (Dec. 2012); Chair., Supervisory Bd PIERRE-YVES DRÉAN; Chair., Management Bd JEAN-YVES FOREL; 60 brs.

BNP Paribas: 16 blvd des Italiens, 75009 Paris; tel. 1-40-14-45-46; fax 1-40-14-69-40; internet www.bnpparibas.com; f. 2000 by merger of Banque Nationale de Paris and Paribas; cap. 26,812m., res 1,935m., dep. 741,689m. (Dec. 2013); Pres. JEAN LEMIERRE; CEO JEAN-LAURENT BONNAFÉ.

Cetelem: 14 bis blvd de l'Hôpital, 75221 Paris Cedex 05; tel. 1-55-43-55-43; fax 1-55-43-55-30; e-mail frederic.tardy@cetelem.fr; internet www.cetelem.fr; f. 1953; owned by BNP Paribas; cap. 848.8m., res 1,423.3m., dep. 32,906.8m. (Dec. 2006); Chair. and CEO FRANÇOIS VILLEROY DE GALHAU.

CIC Nord Ouest: 33 ave le Corbusier, BP 567, 59800 Lille; tel. 3-20-12-64-64; fax 3-20-12-64-05; e-mail brouchbr@cmcic.fr; internet www.cic.fr; f. 2006 by merger of Banque Scalbert-Dupont (f. 1977) and Crédit Industriel de Normandie (f. 1932); 100% owned by Crédit Industriel et Commercial; cap. 230m., res 92m., dep. 16,906m. (Dec. 2012); Chair. and Dir-Gen. STELLI PRÉMAOR.

Compagnie Financière Edmond de Rothschild Banque: 47 rue du Faubourg St Honoré, 75401 Paris Cedex 08; tel. 1-40-17-25-25; fax 1-40-17-24-02; e-mail info@lcfr.fr; internet www.lcf-rothschild.fr; f. 1971; present name adopted 1986; cap. 83.1m., res 209.2m., dep. 1,586.4m. (Dec. 2012); Chair., Supervisory Bd BENJAMIN DE ROTHSCHILD; Dir-Gen. MARC LÉVY.

Crédit Agricole Corporate and Investment Bank (Calyon): 9 quai Paul Doumer, 92920 Paris La Défense Cedex; tel. 1-41-89-00-00; fax 1-41-89-36-33; internet www.ca-cib.com; f. 1975 as Banque Indosuez, subsequently Crédit Agricole Indosuez and Calyon Corporate and Investment Bank; present name adopted 2010; 100% owned by Crédit Agricole; merchant and offshore banking; cap. 7,255m., res 8,265m., dep. 185,161m. (Dec. 2012); Pres. and CEO JEAN-PAUL CHIFFLET; 15 brs in France, 44 outside France.

Crédit Foncier de France: 19 rue des Capucines, 75001 Paris Cedex 01; tel. 1-42-44-80-00; fax 1-42-44-86-99; e-mail cbuying-france@creditfoncier.fr; internet www.creditfoncier.fr; f. 1852; 100% owned by Caisses d'Epargne et de Prévoyance; mortgage banking; cap. 1,731m., res 1,848m., dep. 44,365m. (Dec. 2012); Chair., Bd of Dirs FRANÇOIS DROUIN; Chief Exec. BRUNO DELETRÉ; 162 brs.

Crédit Industriel et Commercial (CIC): 6 ave de Provence, 75009 Paris Cedex 09; tel. 1-45-96-96-96; fax 1-45-96-96-66; internet www.cic.fr; f. 1990 by merger; present name adopted 1999; 70.81% owned by Banque Fédérative du Crédit Mutuel; cap. 608m., res 9,056m., dep. 109,327m. (Dec. 2012); Chair. and Dir-Gen. MICHEL LUCAS; Gen. Man. ALAIN FRADIN.

Crédit du Nord: 59 blvd Haussmann, 75008 Paris; tel. 1-40-22-40-22; fax 1-20-57-74-05; internet www.credit-du-nord.fr; f. 1974 by merger; name changed as above in 1976; 80% owned by Société Générale; cap. 890.3m., res 228.5m., dep. 34,786.5m. (Dec. 2012); Chair. JEAN-FRANÇOIS SAMMARCELLI; 675 brs.

HSBC France: 103 ave des Champs-Elysées, 75419 Paris Cedex 08; tel. 1-40-70-70-40; fax 1-40-70-70-09; e-mail contact@hsbc.fr; internet www.hsbc.fr; 100% owned by HSBC Bank PLC (UK); f. 2005 by merger of CCF (fmrly Crédit Commercial de France) with 3 other banks; cap. 337.0m., res 237m., dep. 64,081m. (Dec. 2012); CEO JEAN BEUNARDEAU; 223 brs in France.

HSBC Private Bank France: 103 ave des Champs-Elysées, 75008 Paris Cedex 08; tel. 1-49-52-20-00; fax 1-49-52-20-99; internet www.hsbcprivatebankfrance.com; f. 2003 by merger; 100% owned by HSBC Holdings plc; cap. 43m., res 138.5m., dep. 869m. (Dec. 2009); Chief Exec. EDWARD ARCHER.

LCL—Le Crédit Lyonnais: 19 blvd des Italiens, 75002 Paris; tel. 1-42-95-70-00; fax 1-42-68-37-19; internet www.lcl.com; f. 1863 as Crédit Lyonnais; present name adopted 2005; privatized 1999; acquired by Crédit Agricole in June 2003; cap. 1,848m., res 2,328m., dep. 86,139m. (Dec. 2012); Gen. Dir YVES NANQUETTE; Chief Exec. LAURENT PAILLASSOT; 2,064 brs.

Lyonnaise de Banque: 8 rue de la République, 69001 Lyon; tel. 4-78-92-02-12; fax 4-78-92-03-00; e-mail ddi@lb.cicomore.fr; internet www.cic.fr/lb; f. 1865 as Société Lyonnaise de Dépôts et de Crédit Industriel; name changed as above in 1988; 100% owned by Crédit Industriel et Commercial; cap. 260.8m., res 145.5m., dep. 13,324.5m. (Dec. 2012); Chair. and Chief Exec. RÉMY WEBER; 368 brs.

Natixis: 45 rue Saint Dominique, 75007 Paris Cedex 02; tel. 1-58-32-30-00; internet www.natixis.com; f. 1999 as Natexis Banques Populaires; present name adopted 2006; 71.54% owned by BPCE (France); cap. 4,938m., res 5,410m., dep. 254,930m. (Dec. 2012); Chair. FRANÇOIS PEROL; CEO LAURENT MIGNON.

Société Générale: Tour Société Générale, 17 cours Valmy, 92972 Paris La Défense; tel. 1-42-14-20-00; fax 1-53-43-87-69; internet www.socgen.com; f. 1864; name changed as above in 1983; cap. 975m., res 25,602m., dep. 592,219m. (Dec. 2012); Chair. LORENZO BINI SMAGHY; CEO FRÉDÉRIC OUDÉA; 2,000 brs in France.

Société Marseillaise de Crédit (SMC): 75 rue Paradis, 13006 Marseille; tel. 4-91-13-33-00; fax 4-91-13-33-16; e-mail infos@smc.fr; internet www.smc.fr; f. 1865; owned by Crédit du Nord (France); cap. 24.5m., res 278.2m., dep. 5,800.3m. (Dec. 2012); Chair. and Chief Exec. EMMANUEL BARTHELEMY; Gen. Man. and Pres. OLIVIER DELAPORTE; 174 brs.

Union de Banques Arabes et Françaises (UBAF): 190 ave Charles de Gaulle, 92523 Neuilly-sur-Seine Cedex; tel. 1-46-40-61-01; fax 1-47-38-13-88; e-mail ubaf.paris@ubaf.fr; internet www.ubaf.fr; f. 1970; 47.01% owned by Crédit Agricole CIB, 52.99% by Arab banks and institutions; cap. 250.7m., res 36.6m., dep. 1,339.4m. (Dec. 2012); Chair., Management Bd FAROUK EL-OKDAH; CEO AYMERIC DE REYNIÈS.

VTB Bank (France) SA (BCEN—Eurobank): 79–81 blvd Haussmann, 75382 Paris Cedex 08; tel. 1-40-06-43-21; fax 1-40-06-48-48; internet www.vtb.fr; f. 1921 as Comptoir Parisien de Banque et de Change; changed name to Banque Commerciale pour l'Europe du Nord in 1972; present name adopted 2006; 87.04% owned by VTB Bank (Austria); cap. 185.3m., res 57.4m., dep. 524.8m. (Dec. 2012); Chair., Supervisory Council MIKHAIL YAKUNIN; Chair., Executive Bd RICHARD VORNBERG.

Co-operative and Savings Banks

BPCE: 50 ave Pierre Mendès, Paris Cedex 13; tel. 1-58-40-41-42; internet www.bpce.fr; f. 2009 by merger of Banque Fédérale des Banques Populaires (BFBP) with Caisse Nationale des Caisses d'Epargne (CNCE); controls and co-ordinates 20 co-operative Banques Populaires (including those listed below) and 17 Caisses d'Epargne; cap. 17,502m., res 10,042m., dep. 582,334m. (Dec. 2012); Chair. FRANÇOIS PÉROL.

Banque Populaire d'Alsace: 4 quai Kléber, 67000 Strasbourg; tel. 3-88-62-77-11; fax 3-88-62-70-35; e-mail contact@alsace.banquepopulaire.fr; internet www.alsace.banquepopulaire.fr; f. 2003 by merger of Banque Populaire de la Région Economique de Strasbourg and Banque Populaire du Haut Rhin; cap. 402.6m., res 525.9m., dep. 4,860.2m. (Dec. 2012); Pres. THIERRY CAHN; Dir-Gen. CHRISTINE JACGLIN; 96 brs.

Banque Populaire Aquitaine Centre Atlantique: 10 quai des Queyries, 33072 Bordeaux Cedex; tel. 5-49-08-65-20; e-mail contact@bpaca.banquepopulaire.fr; internet www.bpaca.banquepopulaire.fr; formed by merger of Banque Populaire du Sud-Ouest and Banque Populaire Centre-Atlantique; cap. 523.1m., res 771.9m., dep. 8,059.4m. (Dec. 2012); Chair. JACQUES RAYNAUD; Gen. Man. DOMINIQUE GARNIER.

Banque Populaire Bourgogne Franche-Comté: 14 blvd de la Trémouille, BP 20810, 21008 Dijon Cedex; tel. 8-20-33-75-00; fax 8-20-20-36-20; internet www.bpbfc.banquepopulaire.fr; f. 2002 by merger of Banque Populaire de Bourgogne and Banque Populaire de Franche-Comté, du Mâconnais et de l'Ain; cap. 530.9m., res 379.8m., dep. 7,126.5m. (Dec. 2012); Pres. MICHAEL GRASS; Dir-Gen. BRUNO DUCHESNE; 151 brs.

Banque Populaire Côte d'Azur (BPCA): BP 241, 457 promenade des Anglais, 06024 Nice; tel. 4-93-21-52-00; fax 4-93-21-54-45; e-mail contact@cotedazur.banquepopulaire.fr; internet www

.cotedazur.banquepopulaire.fr; f. 1986; present name adopted 2002; cap. 197m., res 323.3m., dep. 2,940.7m. (Dec. 2012); Pres. BERNARD FLEURY; Gen. Man. JEAN-FRANÇOIS COMAS; 100 brs.

Banque Populaire Loire et Lyonnais: 141 rue Garibaldi, BP 3152, 69003 Lyon; tel. 4-89-95-55-55; fax 4-78-71-03-99; e-mail contact@bp2l.banquepopulaire.fr; internet www.loirelyonnais .banquepopulaire.fr; f. 2000 by merger of Banque Populaire de Lyon and Banque Populaire de la Loire; cap. 425.4m., res 334.2m., dep. 5,024.9m. (Dec. 2012); Chair. JEAN BRUNET-LECOMTE; Gen. Man. JEAN-PIERRE LEVAYER.

Banque Populaire du Massif Central: BP 53, 18 blvd Jean Moulin, 63002 Clermont-Ferrand; tel. 4-73-23-46-23; fax 4-73-23-47-99; internet www.massifcentral.banquepopulaire.fr; f. 1920; cap. 196m., res 373.1m., dep. 3,463.4m. (Dec. 2012); Pres. DOMINIQUE MARTINIE; Gen. Man. CATHERINE HALBERSTADT.

Banque Populaire Rives de Paris: 76–78 ave de France, 75024 Paris Cedex 13; tel. 1-40-92-61-00; fax 1-46-57-61-53; internet www.rivesparis.banquepopulaire.fr; f. 2004 by merger of BICS-Banque Populaire and Banque Populaire Nord de Paris; cap. 705.7m., res 1,253.2m., dep. 13,528.7m. (Dec. 2012); Chair. MARC JARDIN; Gen. Man. YVES GEVIN.

BRED Banque Populaire: 18 quai de la Rapée, 75604 Paris Cedex 12; tel. 1-48-98-60-00; fax 1-40-04-71-57; e-mail webmaster@bred.fr; internet www.bred.fr; f. 1919; present name adopted 1994; cap. 520.3m., res 453.9m., dep. 19,318.7m. (Dec. 2012); Chair. STEVE GENTILI; Gen. Man. OLIVIER KLEIN; 339 brs (including 70 in the French Overseas Departments).

Crédit Coopératif: BP 211, Parc de la Défense, 33 rue des Trois Fontanot, 92002 Nanterre; tel. 1-47-24-85-00; fax 1-47-24-89-25; e-mail din@coopanet.com; internet www.credit-cooperatif.coop; f. 1893; present name adopted 2001; joined the Banque Fédérale des Banques Populaires group in 2002; merged with Caisse Centrale de Crédit Coopératif in 2003; cap. 780m., res 504.2m., dep. 9,698.9m. (Dec. 2012); Pres. JEAN-LOUIS BANCEL.

Caisse Centrale du Crédit Mutuel: 88–90 rue Cardinet, 75847 Paris Cedex 17; tel. 1-44-01-10-10; fax 1-44-01-12-30; internet www .creditmutuel.com; f. 1963; central org. of 10 autonomous banks (Caisses Fédérales); cap. 126.9m., res 294m., dep. 5,205.6m. (Dec. 2012); Chair. BERNARD FLOURIOT; Gen. Man. ALAIN FRADIN.

Crédit Agricole: 91–93 blvd Pasteur, 75015 Paris; tel. 1-43-23-52-02; fax 1-43-23-20-28; internet www.credit-agricole.fr; f. 1920; central institution for co-operative banking group comprising 39 Caisses Regionales and a central bank (CNCA); emphasis on agribusiness; cap. 7,494m., res 38,704m., dep. 701,916m. (Dec. 2012); Pres. and CEO JEAN-PAUL CHIFFLET; 9,130 brs.

Crédit Mutuel Arkéa: 1 rue Louis Lichou, 29480 Le Relecq-Kerhoun; tel. 2-98-00-22-22; fax 2-98-00-27-24; internet www .arkea.com; f. 2002; co-operative and mutual savings bank; cap. 2,018.9m., res 2,461.5m., dep. 30,824.2m. (Dec. 2012); Chair. JEAN-PIERRE DENIS; Gen. Man. RONAN LE MOAL.

Supervisory Body

Association Française des Etablissements de Crédit et des Entreprises d'Investissement (AFECEI): 36 rue Taitbout, 75009 Paris; tel. 1-48-01-88-88; fax 1-48-24-13-31; e-mail atassi@afecei.asso .fr; internet www.afecei.asso.fr; f. 1984; advises the Govt on monetary and credit policy and supervises the banking system; 14 mems; Pres. JEAN-PAUL CHIFFLET; Dir-Gen. ARIANE OBOLENSKY.

Banking Association

Fédération Bancaire Française: 18 rue La Fayette, 75009 Paris Cedex 09; tel. 1-48-00-52-52; fax 1-42-46-76-40; e-mail fbf@fbf.fr; internet www.fbf.fr; f. 2001; 390 mems; Pres. FRANÇOIS PÉROL; Dir-Gen. MARIE-ANNE BARBAT-LAYANI.

STOCK EXCHANGE

Euronext Paris: 39 rue Cambon, 75039 Paris Cedex 01; tel. 1-49-27-10-00; fax 1-49-27-11-71; e-mail info@euronext.com; internet www .euronext.fr; formed in 2000 by merger of Amsterdam, Paris and Brussels exchanges, and joined in 2002 by the Lisbon stock exchange and the London futures exchange LIFFE; merged with the New York Stock Exchange in 2007 to form NYSE Euronext; Chair. JAN-MICHIEL HESSELS.

Stock Exchange Associations

Autorité des Marchés Financiers (AMF): 17 place de la Bourse, 75082 Paris Cedex 2; tel. 1-53-45-60-00; fax 1-53-45-61-00; e-mail centrededoc@amf-france.org; internet www.amf-france.org; f. 2003 by merger of Commission des Opérations de Bourse and Conseil des Marchés Financiers; 350 mems (2007); Pres. GÉRARD RAMEIX; Sec.-Gen. BENOÎT DE JUVIGNY.

Fédération des Investisseurs Individuels et des Clubs d'Investissement (F2iC): 39 rue Cambon, 75001 Paris; tel. 1-42-60-12-47; fax 1-42-60-10-14; e-mail info@f2ic.fr; internet www.f2ic.fr; f. 1968; fmrly Fédération Française des Clubs d'Investissement (FFCI); represents shareholders and investment clubs in matters concerning public and political institutions; Pres. CHARLES-HENRI D'AUVIGNY; Sec.-Gen. ALDO SICURANI.

INSURANCE

AG2R La Mondiale: 32 ave Emile Zola, Mons en Baroeul, 59370 Lille Cedex 9; tel. 3-20-67-37-00; internet www.ag2rlamondiale.fr; f. 1905; renamed as above in 2010 following merger of La Mondiale and AG2R; life insurance; Dir-Gen. ANDRÉ RENAUDIN.

Allianz (AGF): 87 rue de Richelieu, 75002 Paris; tel. 1-44-86-20-00; fax 1-44-86-42-42; e-mail ecrire@allianz.fr; internet www.allianz.fr; f. 1968 by merger; affiliated to Allianz (Germany); name changed as above 2009; insurance and reinsurance; Pres. and Dir-Gen. JACQUES RICHIER.

Assurances du Crédit Mutuel IARD, SA: BP 373 R 10, 34 rue du Wacken, 67010 Strasbourg Cedex; tel. 3-88-14-90-90; fax 3-88-14-90-00; internet www.creditmutuel.fr; Pres. MICHEL LUCAS; Dir ALAIN FRADIN.

Aviva: 580 ave de l'Europe, 92270 Bois Colombes Cedex; tel. 1-76-62-50-00; e-mail veronique_eriaud@aviva.fr; internet www.aviva.fr; f. 1998 as CGU France by merger to incorporate fmr Abeille Assurances; present name adopted 2002; affiliated to CGNU Group (UK); CEO NICOLAS SCHIMEL.

AXA Assurances IARD: 313 Terrasses de l'Arche, 92727 Nanterre Cedex; tel. 1-47-74-10-01; fax 1-47-74-10-01; internet www.axa.fr; CEO NICOLAS MOREAU; Chair., Management Bd HENRI DE CASTRIES.

Caisse Centrale des Assurances Mutuelles Agricoles: 8–10 rue d'Astorg, 75008 Paris; tel. 1-44-56-77-77; fax 1-44-56-79-46; e-mail relations.exterieures@groupama.com; internet www.groupama .com; affiliated to Groupama; CEO THIERRY MARTEL.

Caisse Nationale de Prévoyance-Assurances (CNP): 4 place Raoul Dautry, 75716 Paris Cedex 15; tel. 1-42-18-88-88; fax 1-42-34-70-14; internet www.cnp.fr; f. 1945; general insurance; Pres EDMOND ALPHANDÉRY; CEO GILLES BENOIST.

Cardif: 8 rue du Port, 92728 Nanterre Cedex; tel. 1-41-42-83-00; internet www.cardif.fr; general insurance; Dir-Gen. ERIC LOMBARD.

GAN Assurances: 8–10 rue d'Astorg, 75383 Paris Cedex 08; tel. 1-70-94-20-00; fax 1-42-47-67-66; e-mail gan.rimbault.philippe@ wanadoo.fr; internet www.ganassurances.fr; f. 1820, fire; f. 1830, life; f. 1865, accident; affiliated to Groupama; Pres. JEAN-FRANÇOIS LEMOUX; Dir ERIC GELPE.

Garantie Mutuelle des Fonctionnaires: 76 rue de Prony, 75857 Paris Cedex 17; tel. 1-47-54-10-10; fax 1-47-54-18-97; e-mail webgmf@gmf.fr; internet www.gmf.fr; f. 1934; Pres. and CEO THIERRY DEREZ; Man. Dir PATRICE FORGET.

Generali France: 11 blvd Haussmann, 75311 Paris Cedex 09; tel. 1-58-38-74-00; fax 1-58-38-74-01; e-mail dep-agence-web-interne@ generali.fr; internet www.generali-patrimoine.fr; f. 1832; subsidiary of Generali (Italy); Pres. and CEO CLAUDE TENDIL.

Groupama SA: 8–10 rue d'Astorg, 75008 Paris; tel. 1-49-31-31-311-44-56-77-77; e-mail relations.exterieures@groupama.com; internet www.groupama.com; life insurance; CEO THIERRY MARTEL.

Mutuelles du Mans Assurances (MMA): 14 blvd Alexandre Oyon, 72030 Le Mans Cedex 09; tel. 2-43-41-72-72; fax 2-43-41-72-26; internet www.mma.fr; f. 1828; life and general insurance; comprises 3 companies: MMA-IARD, DAS and MMA-VIE; Pres. and Dir-Gen. JEAN-CLAUDE SEYS; Dir-Gen. JACQUES LENORMAND.

Predica: 50 rue de la Procession, 75724 Paris Cedex 15; tel. 1-43-23-03-33; fax 1-43-23-03-47; e-mail communication-pole-assurances@ ca-predica.fr; internet www.ca-predica.fr; affiliated to Crédit Agricole; general insurance; Pres. PIERRE DERAJINSKI; Dir-Gen. JÉRÔME GRIVET.

Suravenir: BP 103, 232 rue Général Paulet, 29802 Brest Cedex 09; tel. 2-98-34-65-00; fax 2-98-34-65-11; internet www.suravenir.fr; f. 1984; subsidiary of Crédit Mutuel Arkéa; general insurance; Pres., Supervisory Bd JEAN-PIERRE CORLAY; Pres., Management Bd BERNARD LE BRAS.

UAF Patrimoine: 50–56 rue de la Procession, 75015 Paris; tel. 1-43-23-60-13; e-mail brigitte.le-morvan@ca-predica.fr; internet www .uafpatrimoine.fr; life insurance; part of Predica; Dir ERIC MORVAN.

Insurance Associations

Chambre Syndicale des Courtiers d'Assurances (CSCA): 91 rue Saint Lazare, 75009 Paris; tel. 1-48-74-19-12; fax 1-42-82-91-10; e-mail csca@csca.fr; internet www.csca.fr; f. 2006; formed by merger of the Fédération Française des Courtiers d'Assurances and the Syndicat Français des Assureurs Conseils; c. 1,000 mems; Chair. DOMINIQUE SIZES.

Syndicat Français des Assureurs-Conseils: 14 rue de la Grange Batelière, 75009 Paris; tel. 1-55-33-51-51; fax 1-48-00-93-01; e-mail sfac@sfac-assurance.fr; internet www.sfac-assurance.fr; Pres. ALAIN MORICHON.

Fédération des Agents Généraux d'Assurances (AGEA): 30 rue Olivier Noyer, 75014 Paris; tel. 1-70-98-48-00; e-mail regis.devaux@agea.fr; internet www.agea.fr; Pres. HERVÉ DE VEYRAC.

Fédération Française des Sociétés d'Assurances (FFSA): 26 blvd Haussmann, 75311 Paris; tel. 1-42-47-90-00; fax 1-42-47-93-11; internet www.ffsa.fr; f. 1937; Pres. BERNARD SPITZ; Sec.-Gen. GILLES WOLKOWITSCH.

Trade and Industry

GOVERNMENT AGENCIES

Business France: 77 blvd Saint-Jacques, 75680 Paris Cedex 14; tel. 1-40-73-32-70; fax 1-40-74-73-29; e-mail info@businessfrance.fr; internet www.businessfrance.fr; f. 2015 by the merger of Agence Française pour les Investissements Internationaux (f. 2001) and UBIFRANCE—l'Agence Française pour le Développement International des Entreprises (f. 2004); promotes and assists foreign investment in France; CEO. MURIEL PÉNICAUD; Man. Dir CAROLINE LEBOUCHER.

Conseil du Commerce de France: 40 blvd Malesherbes, 75008 Paris; tel. 1-40-15-03-03; fax 1-40-15-97-22; e-mail conseilducommerce@cdcf.com; internet www.cdcf.com; Pres. GÉRARD ATLAN; Sec.-Gen. FANNY FAVOREL-PIGE.

DEVELOPMENT ORGANIZATIONS

Agence pour la Création d'Entreprises (APCE): 14 rue Delambre, 75682 Paris Cedex 14; tel. 1-42-18-58-58; fax 1-42-18-58-00; e-mail info@apce.com; internet www.apce.com; Pres. DOMINIQUE RESTINO; Dir-Gen. ALAIN BELAIS.

Groupe IDI: 18 ave Matignon, 75008 Paris; tel. 1-55-27-80-00; fax 1-40-17-04-44; e-mail idi@idi.fr; internet www.idi.fr; f. 1970 as Institut de Développement Industriel; provides venture capital, takes equity shares in small and medium-sized businesses; Chair. LUCE GENDRY.

CHAMBERS OF COMMERCE

There are Chambers of Commerce in all the larger towns for all the more important commodities produced or manufactured.

Assemblée des Chambres Françaises de Commerce et d'Industrie: 46–48 ave de la Grande Armée, 75858 Paris Cedex 17; tel. 1-40-69-37-00; fax 1-47-20-61-28; e-mail contactsweb@acfci.cci.fr; internet www.acfci.cci.fr; f. 1964; unites 154 local and 21 regional Chambers of Commerce and Industry; Pres. ANDRÉ MARCON.

> **Chambre de Commerce et d'Industrie de Paris Ile-de-France:** 27 ave de Friedland, 75382 Paris Cedex 08; tel. 1-55-65-75-26; fax 1-55-65-75-97; e-mail cpdp@ccip.fr; internet www.ccip.fr; f. 1803; Pres. PIERRE-ANTOINE GAILLY; Dir-Gen. ETIENNE GUYOT; 307,000 mems in Paris and surrounding regions (Hauts de Seine, Seine-Saint-Denis and Val de Marne).

INDUSTRIAL AND TRADE ASSOCIATIONS

Armateurs de France: 47 rue de Monceau, 75008 Paris; tel. 1-53-89-52-52; fax 1-53-89-52-53; e-mail info@armateursdefrance.org; internet www.armateursdefrance.org; fmrly Comité Central des Armateurs de France; shipping; Pres. RAYMOND VIDIL; Delegate-Gen. ERIC BANEL; 47 mems.

Assemblée Permanente des Chambres d'Agriculture (APCA): 9 ave George V, 75008 Paris; tel. 1-53-57-10-10; fax 1-53-57-10-05; e-mail accueil@apca.chambagri.fr; internet www.chambres-agriculture.fr; f. 1929; agriculture; Pres. GREY VASSEUR.

Association Nationale des Industries Alimentaires (ANIA): 21 rue Leblanc, 75015 Paris; tel. 1-53-83-86-00; fax 1-53-83-92-37; e-mail infos@ania.net; internet www.ania.net; f. 1971; food produce; Dir-Gen. CATHERINE CHAPALAIN; 22 nat. feds and 23 regional asscns.

Ateliers d'Art de France: 6 rue Jadin, 75017 Paris; tel. 1-44-01-08-30; fax 1-44-01-08-35; e-mail info@ateliersdart.com; internet www.ateliersdart.com; f. 1868; craft and design trades; Chair. SERGE NICOLE; Sec.-Gen. VALÉRIE FORMÉ; 5,400 mems.

Comité des Constructeurs Français d'Automobiles: 2 rue de Presbourg, 75008 Paris; tel. 1-49-52-51-00; fax 1-49-52-51-88; e-mail ccfa@ccfa.fr; internet www.ccfa.fr; f. 1909; motor manufacturing; Chair. PATRICK BLAIN; 5 mems.

Comité National des Pêches Maritimes et des Elevages Marins (CNPMEM): 134 ave de Malakoff, 75116 Paris; tel. 1-72-71-18-00; fax 1-72-71-18-50; e-mail cnpmem@comite-peches.fr; internet www.comite-peches.fr; marine fisheries; Pres. GÉRARD ROMITI; Dir-Gen. HUBERT CARRÉ; 136 mems.

Comité Professionnel du Pétrole (CPDP): 212 ave Paul Doumer, 92508 Rueil-Malmaison Cedex; tel. 1-47-16-94-60; fax 1-47-08-10-57; e-mail contact@cpdp.org; internet www.cpdp.org; f. 1950; petroleum industry; Dir-Gen. JEAN-LUC DELILLE; 51 mems.

Commissariat à l'Energie Atomique (CEA) (Atomic Energy Commission): Bâtiment le ponant D, 25 rue Leblanc, 75015 Paris; tel. 1-64-50-10-00; fax 1-40-56-29-70; e-mail dcom@aramis.cea.fr; internet www.cea.fr; f. 1945; promotes the uses of nuclear energy in science, industry and national defence; involved in research on nuclear materials; reactor devt; fundamental research; innovation and transfer of technologies; military applications; bio-technologies; robotics; electronics; new materials; radiological protection and nuclear safety; Gen. Administrator and High Commissioner BERNARD BIGOT.

Confédération des Industries Céramiques de France (CICF): 2 bis rue Michelet, 92130 Issy-Les-Moulineaux; tel. 1-57-75-90-10; fax 1-57-75-06-64; e-mail cicf@ceramique.org; internet www.ceramique.org; f. 1937; ceramic industry; Chair. PIERRE DE LAFARGE; Sec.-Gen. DELPHINE PALOUX-HUSSON; 85 mems, 5 affiliates.

Les Entreprises du Médicament (LEEM): 88 rue de la Faisanderie, 75782 Paris Cedex 16; tel. 1-45-03-88-88; fax 1-45-04-47-71; e-mail dcre@leem.org; internet www.leem.org; fmrly Syndicat National de l'Industrie Pharmaceutique; pharmaceuticals; Chair. PATRICK ERRARD; 270 mem. cos.

FEBEA (France) (Fédération des Enterprises de la Beauté): 137 rue de l'Université, 75007 Paris; tel. 1-56-69-67-89; fax 1-56-69-67-90; e-mail febea@febea.fr; internet www.febea.fr; makers of perfume, cosmetics and toiletries; Pres. ALAIN GRANGÉ CABANE; 300 mems.

Fédération des Chambres Syndicales de l'Industrie du Verre: 114 rue la Boétie, 75008 Paris; tel. 1-42-65-60-02; fax 1-42-66-23-88; e-mail contact@fedeverre.fr; internet www.fedeverre.fr; f. 1938; glass industry; Pres. JACQUES BORDAT.

Fédération des Chambres Syndicales des Minerais, Minéraux Industriels et Métaux non-Ferreux (FEDEM): 17 rue de l'Amiral Hamelin, 75783 Paris Cedex 16; tel. 1-40-76-44-50; fax 1-45-63-61-54; e-mail contact@fedem.fr; internet www.fedem.fr; f. 1945; minerals and non-ferrous metals; Chair. CATHERINE TISSOT-COLLE; Delegate-Gen. CLAIRE DE LANGERON; 16 affiliated syndicates.

Fédération des Exportateurs de Vins et Spiritueux de France: 7 rue de Madrid, 75008 Paris; tel. 1-45-22-75-73; fax 1-45-22-94-16; e-mail contact@fevs.com; internet www.fevs.com; f. 1922 as Commission d'Exportation des Vins de France; exporters of wines and spirits; Pres. CLAUDE DE JOUVENCEL; 450 mems.

Fédération Française de l'Acier (FFA): 6 rue André Campra, Immeuble Le Cézanne, 93212 La Plaine Saint-Denis Cedex; tel. 1-71-92-20-00; fax 1-71-92-25-00; e-mail svp.clients@ffa.fr; internet www.ffa.fr; f. 1945; steel-making; Pres. PHILIPPE DARMAYAN.

Fédération Française du Bâtiment (FFB): 33 ave Kléber, 75784 Paris Cedex 16; tel. 1-40-69-51-00; fax 1-45-53-58-77; e-mail ffbbox@ffb.fr; internet www.ffbatiment.fr; f. 1906; building trade; Pres. DIDIER RIDORET; 57,000 mems.

Fédération Française des Industries Lainière et Cotonnière (FFILC): 37–39 rue de Neuilly, BP 121, 92582 Clichy Cedex; tel. 1-47-56-31-48; fax 1-47-37-06-20; e-mail uitcotonlaine@textile.fr; internet www.textile.fr; f. 1902; manufacturing of wool, cotton and associated textiles; mem. of Union des Industries Textiles (UIT); Pres. BENOÎT HACOT; Delegate-Gen. HUBERT DU POTET; 350 mems.

Fédération Française du Négoce de l'Ameublement et de l'Equipement de la Maison (FNAEM): 59 rue Saint Lazare, 75009 Paris; tel. 1-42-85-87-55; fax 1-42-80-68-84; internet www.fnaem.fr; furnishing.

Fédération Française de la Tannerie-Mégisserie (FFTM): 122 rue de Provence, 78087 Paris; tel. 1-45-22-96-45; fax 1-42-93-37-44; e-mail fftm@leatherfrance.com; internet www.leatherfrance.com; f. 1885; leather industry; Pres. BERTRAND SAUVE; 60 mems.

Fédération Forge Fonderie: 45 rue Louis Blanc, 92038 Paris La Défense Cedex; tel. 1-43-34-76-30; fax 1-43-34-76-31; e-mail contact@fondeursdefrance.org; internet www.forgefonderie.org; f. 2013 from the merger of Association Française de Forge and Les Fondeurs de France; metal casting; Dir-Gen. JEAN-LUC BRILLANCEAU; 300 mems.

Fédération des Industries Electriques, Electroniques et de Communication (FIEEC): 17 rue de l'Amiral Hamelin, 75783 Paris Cedex 16; tel. 1-45-05-70-57; fax 1-45-05-72-02; e-mail comm@fieec.fr; internet www.fieec.fr; f. 1925; electrical and electronics industries; Delegate-Gen. ERIC JOURDE; 26 professional mems and 5 associate mems.

Fédération des Industries Mécaniques (FIM): 39–41 rue Louis Blanc, 92400 Courbevoie; tel. 1-47-17-60-00; fax 1-47-17-64-37; e-mail webmaster@fim.fimeca.com; internet www.fim.net; f. 1840; mechanical and metal-working; Pres. JÉRÔME FRANTZ; Dir-Gen. MICHEL ATHIMON.

Fédération des Industries Nautiques: 200 Port de Javel Haut, 75015 Paris; tel. 1-44-37-04-00; fax 1-45-77-21-88; e-mail info@fin.fr;

internet www.fin.fr; f. 1964; nautical industries; Pres. YVES LYON-CAEN; Vice-Pres JEAN-PIERRE GOUDANT, COLETTE CERTOUX; 600 mems.

Fédération Nationale du Bois (FNB): 6 rue François 1er, 75008 Paris; tel. 1-56-69-52-00; fax 1-56-69-52-09; e-mail infos@fnbois.com; internet www.fnbois.com; f. 1884; timber and wood products; Chair. LAURENT DENORMANDIE; 1,850 mems.

Fédération Nationale de l'Industrie Laitière (FNIL): 42 rue de Châteaudun, 75314 Paris Cedex 09; tel. 1-49-70-71-11; fax 1-42-80-63-94; e-mail fnil@atla.asso.fr; internet www.maison-du-lait.com; f. 1971; dairy products; Pres. OLIVIER PICOT.

Fédération du Négoce de Bois et des Matériaux (FNBM): 215 bis blvd St Germain, 75007 Paris; tel. 1-45-48-28-44; fax 1-45-48-42-89; e-mail contact@fnbm.fr; internet www.fnbm.fr; timber trade; Delegate-Gen. LAURENT MARTIN SAINT LÉON; 1,100 mems.

Groupe Intersyndical de l'Industrie Nucléaire (GIIN): 39–41 rue Louis Blanc, 92400 Courbevoie; tel. 1-47-17-62-78; fax 1-43-34-76-25; e-mail contact@giin.fr; internet www.giin.fr; f. 1959; aims to promote the interests of the French nuclear industry; 200 mem. firms.

Groupement des Industries de Construction et d'Activités Navales: 60 rue de Monceau, 75008 Paris; tel. 1-56-59-15-15; fax 1-45-63-59-37; e-mail contact@gican.asso.fr; internet www.gican.asso.fr; f. 1992; owned by the French marine industry; Chair. PATRICK BOISSIER; Delegate-Gen. HUGUES D'ARGENTRÉ; 160 mems.

Groupement des Industries Françaises Aéronautiques et Spatiales (GIFAS): 8 rue Galilée, 75116 Paris; tel. 1-44-43-17-00; fax 1-40-70-91-41; e-mail infogifas@gifas.asso.fr; internet www.gifas.asso.fr; f. 1910; aerospace industry; Pres. MARWAN LAHOUD; Dir-Gen. Gen. PIERRE BOURLOT; 300 mems.

Syndicat Général des Cuirs et Peaux: 18 blvd Montmartre, 75009 Paris; tel. 1-45-08-08-54; fax 1-40-39-97-31; e-mail cuirsetpeaux@wanadoo.fr; internet www.sgcp.net; f. 1977; present name adopted 1996; untreated leather and hides; Chair. DENIS GEISSMANN; Sec.-Gen. FRANCIS AMIET; 25 mems.

Union de la Bijouterie Horlogerie (UBH): 109 rue du Faubourg Saint Honoré, 75008 Paris; tel. 1-44-70-77-97; fax 1-44-70-77-96; e-mail contact@u-b-h.com; internet u-b-h.com; f. 2013 by the merger of the Syndicat Saint Eloi and Fédération Nationale des Chambres Syndicales des Horlogers, Bijoutiers, Joailliers et Orfèvres; jewellery, watch- and clock-making; Pres. GUY SUBRA; 900 mems.

Union des Armateurs à la Pêche de France: 59 rue des Mathurins, 75008 Paris; tel. 1-42-66-32-60; fax 1-47-42-91-12; e-mail uapf@uapf.org; f. 1945; fishing vessels; Chair. JEAN-YVES LABBÉ; Delegate-Gen. MARC GHIGLIA.

Union des Fabricants de Porcelaine de Limoges: 7 bis rue du Général Cérez, 87000 Limoges; tel. 5-55-77-29-18; fax 5-55-77-36-81; e-mail ufpl@porcelainelimoges.org; porcelain manufacturing; Chair. ALAIN MOULY.

Union des Industries Chimiques (UIC): Le Diamant A, 14 rue de la République, 92800 Paris La Défense Cedex 10; tel. 1-46-53-11-00; fax 1-46-96-00-59; e-mail uicgeneral@uic.fr; internet www.uic.fr; f. 1860; chemical industry; Pres. PHILIPPE GŒBEL; Dir-Gen. JEAN PELIN; 24 affiliated unions.

Union des Industries Métallurgiques et Minières (UIMM): 56 ave de Wagram, 75017 Paris; tel. 1-40-54-20-20; fax 1-47-66-22-74; e-mail uimm@uimm.fr; internet www.uimm.fr; metallurgy and mining; Chair. FRÉDÉRIC SAINT-GEOURS; 76 regional asscns.

Union Inter-secteurs Papiers Cartons pour le Dialogue et l'Ingenierie Sociale (UNIDIS): 23–25 rue d'Aumale, 75009 Paris; tel. 1-53-89-25-27; fax 1-53-89-25-26; e-mail arnaud.couvreur@unidis.fr; internet www.unidis.fr; f. 1864 as Union des Industries Papetières pour les Affaires Sociales; name changed to present 2012; paper, cardboard and cellulose; Chair. LAURENT AUDOUIN; Delegate-Gen. ARNAUD COUVREUR; 8 mem asscns.

Union des Industries Textiles (UIT): 37–39 rue de Neuilly, BP 121, 92582 Clichy Cedex; tel. 1-47-56-31-00; fax 1-47-30-25-28; e-mail uit@textile.fr; internet www.textile.fr; f. 1900; textiles; Chair. YVES DUBIEF; 570 mem. cos (2012).

Union des Métiers et des Industries de l'Hôtellerie (UMIH): 22 rue d'Anjou, 75008 Paris; tel. 1-44-94-19-94; fax 1-47-42-15-20; e-mail fnih@imagenet.fr; internet www.umih.fr; hospitality; Chair. ROLAND HÉGUY.

Union Nationale de l'Imprimerie et de la Communication (UNIC): 68 blvd Saint Marcel, 75005 Paris; tel. 1-44-08-64-46; fax 1-43-36-09-51; e-mail unic@com-unic.fr; internet www.com-unic.fr; f. 2008 by merger of Fédération de l'Imprimerie et de la Communication Graphique and Syndicat National des Industries de la Communication Graphique et de l'Imprimerie Françaises; printing, communication and design; Pres. JACQUES CHIRAT; 1,300 mems.

Union Professionnelle Artisanale (UPA): 53 rue Ampère, 75017 Paris; tel. 1-47-63-31-31; fax 1-47-63-31-10; e-mail upa@upa.fr;

internet www.upa.fr; f. 1975; unites crafts and other manual workers in 3 trade bodies and more than 100 regional orgs; Chair. JEAN-PIERRE CROUZET.

EMPLOYERS' ORGANIZATIONS

Association Française des Entreprises Privées (AFEP): 11 ave Delcassé, 75008 Paris; tel. 1-43-59-65-35; e-mail c.alfonsomartin@afep.com; internet www.afep.com; f. 1982; Chair. PIERRE PRINGUET; 107 mem. cos.

Centre des Jeunes Dirigeants d'Entreprise (CJD): 19 ave Georges V, 75008 Paris; tel. 1-53-23-92-50; fax 1-53-23-92-30; e-mail cjd@cjd.net; internet www.cjd.net; f. 1938; asscn for young entrepreneurs (under 45 years of age); Pres. RICHARD THIRIET; 4,500 mems.

Confédération Générale des Petites et Moyennes Entreprises (CGPME): 10 terrasse Bellini, 92806 Puteaux Cedex; tel. 1-47-62-73-73; fax 1-47-73-08-86; e-mail bbrisson@cgpme.fr; internet www.cgpme.fr; small and medium-sized cos; Chair. JEAN-FRANÇOIS ROUBAUD.

Les Entrepreneurs et Dirigeants Chrétiens (Les EDC): 24 rue Hamelin, 75116 Paris; tel. 1-45-53-09-01; fax 1-47-27-43-32; e-mail lesedc@lesedc.org; internet www.lesedc.org; fmrly Centre Français du Patronat Chrétien; asscn of Christian employers; Nat. Pres. LAURENT BATAILLE.

Entreprise et Progrès: 41 blvd Malesherbes, 75008 Paris; tel. 1-45-74-52-62; fax 1-45-74-52-63; e-mail benedicte.debeaufort@entrepriseprogres.com; internet entrepriseprogres.com; f. 1970; represents 110 enterprises; Pres. DENIS TERRIEN; Sec.-Gen. BÉNÉDICTE DE BEAUFORT.

Entreprises de Taille Humaine Indépendantes et de Croissance (ETHIC): 48 blvd de la Tour-Maubourg, 75007 Paris; tel. 1-53-85-90-85; fax 1-53-85-90-80; e-mail btorjman@ethic.fr; internet www.ethic.fr; f. 1976; represents small enterprises and promotes ethical values in business; Pres. SOPHIE DE MENTHON.

Mouvement des Entreprises de France (MEDEF): 55 ave Bosquet, 75007 Paris Cedex 07; tel. 1-53-59-19-19; fax 1-45-51-20-44; internet www.medef.fr; f. 1998 to replace Conseil National du Patronat Français; employers' asscn grouping 700,000 cos from all sectors of activity in 85 professional feds and 152 regional orgs; Pres. PIERRE GATTAZ; Dir-Gen. MICHEL GUILBAUD.

UTILITIES
Electricity

EDF: 22–30 ave de Wagram, 75382 Paris Cedex 8; tel. and fax 1-40-42-46-37; e-mail masteredf@edfgdf.fr; internet www.edf.fr; established under the Electricity and Gas Industry Nationalization Act of 1946 as Electricité de France; responsible for generating and supplying electricity for distribution to consumers in metropolitan France; 15% of the company was sold to the private sector in November 2005; Chair. and CEO JEAN-BERNARD LÉVY.

Gas

GDF SUEZ: 1 place Samuel de Champlain, Faubourg de l'Arche, 92930 Paris la Défense; tel. 1-44-22-45-31; e-mail actionnaires@gdfsuez.com; internet www.gdfsuez.com; est. as Gaz de France under the Electricity and Gas Industry Nationalization Act of 1946; responsible for distribution of gas in metropolitan France; partially privatized in 2005; present name adopted in July 2008 following merger with Suez; merged with International Power (UK) in 2011; Chair. and CEO GÉRARD MESTRALLET.

Water

Lyonnaise des Eaux: 16 place de l'Iris, 92040 Paris la Défense Cedex; tel. 1-58-81-40-00; e-mail sophie.le.scaon@lyonnaise-des-eaux.fr; internet www.lyonnaise-des-eaux.fr; f. 1858; fmrly Suez-Lyonnaise des Eaux; present name adopted 2001; CEO PHILIPPE MAILLARD.

Veolia Eau (Veolia Water): 52 rue d'Anjou, 75384 Paris Cedex 8; tel. 1-49-24-49-24; fax 1-49-24-69-59; e-mail webmaster@veoliawater.com; internet www.veoliawater.com; f. 1853 as the Compagnie Générale des Eaux; subsidiary of Veolia Environnement; provides drinking water and manages waste water; Chair. and CEO ANTOINE FRÉROT.

TRADE UNIONS

There are three major trade union organizations: the Confédération Française Démocratique du Travail (CFDT), the Confédération Générale du Travail (CGT) and Force Ouvrière (FO).

Confédération Française Démocratique du Travail (CFDT): 4 blvd de la Villette, 75955 Paris Cedex 19; tel. 1-42-03-80-00; fax 1-53-72-85-67; e-mail international@cfdt.fr; internet www.cfdt.fr; f. 1919 as Confédération Française des Travailleurs Chrétiens (CFTC);

present title and constitution adopted 1964; moderate; co-ordinates 1,100 trade unions, 96 departmental and overseas unions, 3 confederal unions and 15 affiliated professional federations, all of which are autonomous. There are also 22 regional orgs; affiliated to European Trade Union Confederation and to ITUC; Sec.-Gen. LAURENT BERGER; 868,601 mems.

Confédération Générale du Travail (CGT) (Labour): 263 rue de Paris, 93516 Montreuil Cedex; tel. 1-55-82-80-00; fax 1-49-88-18-57; e-mail info@cgt.fr; internet www.cgt.fr; f. 1895; National Congress is held every 3 years; Sec.-Gen. THIERRY LEPAON; 700,000 mems.

Force Ouvrière (FO): 141 ave du Maine, 75680 Paris Cedex 14; tel. 1-40-52-84-55; fax 1-40-52-84-71; e-mail olt@force-ouvriere-hebdo.fr; internet www.force-ouvriere.fr; f. 1948 by breakaway from the more left-wing CGT; mem. of ITUC and of the European Trade Union Confederation; Sec.-Gen. JEAN-CLAUDE MAILLY; c. 1m. mems.

Other federations:

Confédération Française de l'Encadrement (CFE—CGC): 59 rue du Rocher, 75008 Paris; tel. 1-55-30-12-12; fax 1-55-30-13-13; e-mail presse@cfecgc.fr; internet www.cfecgc.fr; f. 1944; organizes managerial staff, professional staff and technicians; co-ordinates unions in every industry and sector; Nat. Pres. CAROLE COUVERT; Sec.-Gen. MAIRE-FRANÇOISE LEFLON; 160,000 mems (2006).

Confédération Française des Travailleurs Chrétiens (CFTC): 128 ave Jean Jaurès, 93697 Pantin Cedex; tel. 1-73-30-49-00; fax 1-73-30-49-28; e-mail eurint@cftc.fr; internet www.cftc.fr; f. 1919; present form in 1964 after majority CFTC became CFDT; mem. European Trade Union Confederation, World Confederation of Labour; Chair. PHILIPPE LOUIS; Sec.-Gen. PASCALE COTON; 142,000 mems.

Fédération Nationale des Syndicats Autonomes de l'Enseignement Supérieur et de la Recherche: 6–8 rue Gaston Lauriau, 93513 Montreuil Cedex; tel. 1-46-59-01-01; fax 1-46-59-01-23; e-mail accueil@supautonome.com; internet supautonome .com; f. 1948; higher education and research; Pres. JEAN-LOUIS CHARLET; Sec.-Gen. MICHEL GAY.

Fédération Nationale des Syndicats d'Exploitants Agricoles (FNSEA) (National Federation of Farmers' Unions): 11 rue de la Baume, 75008 Paris; tel. 1-53-83-47-47; fax 1-53-83-48-48; e-mail fnsea@fnsea.fr; internet www.fnsea.fr; f. 1946; comprises 92 departmental feds and 32,000 local unions; Pres XAVIER BEULIN; 600,000 mems.

Fédération Syndicale Unitaire (FSU): 104 rue Romain Rolland, 93260 Les Lilas; tel. 1-41-63-27-30; fax 1-41-63-15-48; e-mail fsu .nationale@fsu.fr; internet www.fsu.fr; f. 1993; fed. of civil service and education workers' unions; Sec.-Gen. BERNADETTE GROISON; 163,000 mems.

UNSA Education: 87 bis ave Georges Gosnat, 94853 Ivry-sur-Seine Cedex; tel. 1-56-20-29-50; fax 1-56-20-29-89; e-mail national@ unsa-education.org; internet www.unsa-education.org; f. 1948; federation of teachers' unions; comprises 22 mem. unions; fmrly Fédération de l'Education Nationale; Sec.-Gen. LAURENT ESCURE.

Transport

RAILWAYS

Most of the French railways are controlled by the Société Nationale des Chemins de fer Français (SNCF), established in 1937, while the Réseau Ferré de France (RFF, f. 1997, and from January 2015 reintegrated into SNCF as SNCF Réseau) manages track and infrastructure. The SNCF is divided into 22 régions (areas). In 2011 the RFF operated 30,884 km of track, of which 16,321 km were electrified. A high-speed service (train à grande vitesse—TGV) operates between Paris and various other destinations: Lyon (TGV Sud-Est), extending to Marseille or Nîmes (TGV Méditerranée), Bordeaux or Nantes (TGV Atlantique), Lille (TGV Nord Europe) and Strasbourg and destinations in Germany, Luxembourg and Switzerland (TGV Est Européen). The Rhine–Rhône high-speed line opened in 2011, linking central and eastern France with Germany and Switzerland. A high-speed line to Barcelona began direct services in late 2013. Further high-speed lines, between Nîmes and Montpellier and Brittany and the Loire Valley, were expected to be completed by 2017. The Parisian transport system is controlled by a separate authority, the Régie Autonome des Transports Parisiens (RATP). A number of small railways in the provinces are run by independent organizations.

Société Nationale des Chemins de fer Français (SNCF): 34 rue du Commandant Mouchotte, 75014 Paris; tel. 1-53-25-32-30; fax 1-53-25-61-08; e-mail webcom@sncf.fr; internet www.sncf.fr; f. 1937; from Jan. 2015 comprised SNCF, SNCF Réseau (infrastructure

operations) and SNCF Mobilités (transport services); Pres. GUILLAUME PÉPY.

SNCF Réseau: 92 ave de France, 75648 Paris Cedex 13; tel. 1-53-94-30-00; fax 1-53-94-38-00; internet www.rff.fr; f. 1997 as Réseau Ferré de France to assume ownership and financial control of national rail infrastructure; state-owned; reintegrated into SNCF in Jan. 2015; Pres. and Dir-Gen. JACQUES RAPOPORT; Asst Gen. Dir ALAIN QUINET.

Channel Tunnel (Le Tunnel sous la Manche)

Groupe Eurotunnel: BP 69, 62904 Coquelles Cedex; tel. 3-21-00-65-43; internet www.eurotunnel.fr; Anglo-French consortium contracted to design, finance and construct the Channel Tunnel under a concession granted for a period up to 2052 (later extended to 2086); receives finance exclusively from the private sector, including international commercial banks; the Channel Tunnel was formally opened in May 1994; operates a series of road vehicle 'shuttle' trains and passenger and freight trains through the Channel Tunnel; Chair. and Chief Exec. JACQUES GOUNON.

ROADS

At 31 December 2012 there were 11,491 km of motorways (autoroutes), 8,894 km of highways, 377,965 km of secondary roads and 664,343 km of other roads.

Fédération Nationale des Transports Routiers (FNTR): 6 rue Ampère, 75017 Paris; tel. 1-44-29-04-29; fax 1-44-29-04-01; e-mail contact@fntr.fr; internet www.fntr.fr; f. 1933; road transport; Chair. JEAN-CHRISTOPHE PIC; 12,500 mem. cos.

METROPOLITAN TRANSPORT

Régie Autonome des Transports Parisiens (RATP): 54 quai de la Rapée, 75599 Paris Cedex 12; tel. 1-58-78-20-20; internet www .ratp.fr; f. 1949; state-owned; operates the Paris underground (comprising 16 lines totalling 200 km, and 381 stations), Réseau Express Régional (RER) suburban railways (totalling 115 km in 2007), 3 suburban tramlines, and 345 bus routes; Chair. and CEO PIERRE MONGIN.

Five provincial cities also have underground railway systems: Marseille, Lyon, Lille, Rennes and Toulouse. Tram networks have been constructed in several provincial cities since the 1980s.

INLAND WATERWAYS

In 2011 there were 5,019 km of navigable waterways.

Voies navigables de France: 175 rue Ludovic Boutleux, BP 30820, 62408 Béthune Cedex; tel. 3-21-63-24-24; fax 3-21-63-24-42; e-mail direction-generale@vnf.fr; internet www.vnf.fr; f. 1991; management and development of France's inland waterways; responsible for 3,800 km of navigable canals and 2,900 km of navigable rivers; Pres. ALAIN GEST; Dir-Gen. MARC PAPINUTTI.

SHIPPING

Seven of the major ports, Marseille, Le Havre, Dunkerque, Nantes Saint-Nazaire, Rouen, Bordeaux and La Rochelle, are operated by autonomous authorities (Grands Ports Maritimes), although the state retains supervisory powers. At 31 December 2014 the flag registered fleet numbered 1,038 vessels, with a combined displacement of 5.9m. grt., of which 52 were general cargo ships and 265 were fishing vessels.

Conseil Supérieur de la Marine Marchande (CSMM): 244 blvd St Germain, 75007 Paris; tel. 1-44-49-81-84; fax 1-44-49-80-81; e-mail jean-marie.berthet@developpement-durable.gouv.fr; internet www.csmm.equipement.gouv.fr; f. 1896; merged with the Conseil National des Communautés Portuaires (f. 1987) in 2002; govt consultative and co-ordinating body for maritime transport, ports and port authorities; 39 mems, including 12 trade union mems; Pres. MICHEL QUIMBERT; Sec.-Gen. JEAN-MARIE BERTHET.

Grand Port Maritime de Bordeaux: 182 quai de Bacalan, CS 41320, 33082 Bordeaux Cedex; tel. 5-56-90-58-00; fax 5-56-90-58-77; e-mail postoffice@bordeaux-port.fr; internet www.bordeaux-port.fr; Dir-Gen. CHRISTOPHE MASSON.

Grand Port Maritime de Dunkerque: 2505 route de l'Ecluse Trystram, BP 46534, 59386 Dunkerque Cedex 01; tel. 3-28-28-78-78; fax 3-28-28-78-77; internet www.dunkerque-port.fr; CEO CHRISTINE CABAU WOEHREL.

Grand Port Maritime du Havre: Terre-Plein de la Barre, BP 1413, 76067 Le Havre Cedex; tel. 2-32-74-74-00; fax 2-32-74-74-29; e-mail internetpah@havre-port.fr; internet www.havre-port.fr; f. 2008; Exec. Dir HERVÉ MARTEL.

Grand Port Maritime de La Rochelle: BP 70394, 17001 La Rochelle Cedex 1; tel. (5) 46-00-53-60; fax (5) 46-43-12-54; internet www.larochelle.port.fr; Dir-Gen. MICHEL PUYRAZAT.

Grand Port Maritime de Marseille: 23 pl. de la Joliette, BP 81965, 13226 Marseille Cedex 02; tel. 4-91-39-40-00; fax 4-91-39-57-00;

e-mail gpmm@marseille-port.fr; internet www.marseille-port.fr; Dir-Gen. CHRISTINE CABAU WOEHREL.

Grand Port Maritime de Nantes Saint-Nazaire: 18 quai Ernest Renaud, BP 18609, 44186 Nantes Cedex 4; tel. 2-40-44-20-20; fax 2-40-44-21-81; internet www.nantes.port.fr; f. 1966; Dir-Gen. JEAN-PIERRE CHALUS.

Grand Port Maritime de Rouen: 34 blvd de Boisguilbert, BP 4075, 76022 Rouen Cedex 03; tel. 2-35-52-54-56; fax 2-35-52-54-13; e-mail dg@rouen.port.fr; internet www.rouen.port.fr; Dir-Gen. PHILIPPE DEISS.

Port de Calais: 54 rue du quai de la Loire, CS 90283, 62105 Calais Cedex; tel. 3-21-46-29-00; fax 3-21-46-29-99; e-mail developpement.portuaire@calais-port.fr; internet www.calais-port.com; Pres. JEAN-MARC PUISSESSEAU.

Principal Shipping Companies

Note: Not all the vessels belonging to the companies listed below are registered under the French flag.

Brittany Ferries: Port du Bloscon, BP 72, 29680 Roscoff Cedex; tel. 2-98-29-28-13; fax 2-98-29-27-00; e-mail service.client@brittany-ferries.fr; internet www.brittany-ferries.fr; f. 1972 as Bretagne-Angleterre-Irlande (BAI); transport between France, Ireland, Spain and the UK; Chair. JEAN-MARC ROUÉ; Man. Dir MARTINE JOURDREN.

Compagnie Maritime Marfret: 13 quai de la Joliette, 13002 Marseille; tel. 4-91-56-91-00; fax 4-91-56-91-01; e-mail bvidil@marfret.fr; internet www.marfret.fr; f. 1951 as Marseille-Fret; name changed to present in 1987; freight services to the Mediterranean, South America, the Caribbean, Canada and northern Europe; Chair RAYMOND VIDIL; Dir-Gen. BERNARD VIDIL.

Corsica Ferries: 5 bis rue Chanoîne Leschi, BP 275, 20296 Bastia; tel. 4-95-32-95-95; fax 4-95-32-14-71; e-mail infos@corsicaferries.com; internet www.corsica-ferries.fr; f. 1968; affiliated to Groupe Lota Maritime; passenger and freight ferry services between Corsica, Sardinia, mainland France, and mainland Italy; Pres. PASCAL LOTA; CEO PIERRE MATTEI.

Esso France: 2 rue des Martinets, 92569 Rueil-Malmaison Cedex; tel. 1-47-10-60-00; fax 1-47-10-60-03; internet www.esso.com/europe-french/fr_homepage.asp; f. 1952; merged with Mobil Oil Française in 2003; Chair. and Man. Dir PATRICK HEINZLE.

Groupe CMA—CGM: 4 quai d'Arenc, 13235 Marseille Cedex 02; tel. 4-88-91-90-00; fax 4-88-91-90-95; internet www.cma-cgm.com; f. 1996 by merger of Compagnie Générale Maritime and Compagnie Maritime d'Affrètement; freight services to USA, Canada, the Caribbean, Central and South America, the Mediterranean, the Middle East, the Far East, India, Australia, New Zealand, Indonesia, East Africa, and other Pacific and Indian Ocean areas; 25 ships owned; Chair. and CEO JACQUES R. SAADÉ; displacement 1,900,000 grt (2001).

Louis Dreyfus Armateurs (LDA): 28 quai Gallieni, 92158 Suresnes Cedex; tel. 1-70-38-60-00; fax 1-70-79-15-02; e-mail gehannep@lda.fr; internet www.lda.fr; gas and bulk carriers; Pres. PHILIPPE LOUIS-DREYFUS; CEO PIERRE GEHANNE.

Maersk Tankers France SAS: 35 ter ave André Morizet, 92100 Boulogne Billancourt; tel. 1-46-99-60-15; fax 1-72-70-34-90; e-mail managementmtpar@maersk.com; internet www.maersktankers.com; subsidiary of A.P. Møller-Mærsk AS (Denmark); fmrly Broström Tankers, SAS; name changed to present in June 2010; oil product and chemical coastal tankers and tramping; CEO HANNE B. SØRENSEN.

Société d'Armement et de Transport (Socatra): 9 allées de Tourny, 33000 Bordeaux; tel. 5-56-00-00-56; fax 5-40-16-02-31; e-mail management@socatra.com; internet www.socatra.com; f. 1977; Chair. F. BOZZONI; Man. Dir M. DUBOURG.

Société Nationale Maritime Corse-Méditerranée (SNCM): 61 blvd des Dames, BP 61963, 13226 Marseille Cedex 02; tel. 4-91-56-32-00; fax 4-91-56-36-36; e-mail info@sncm.fr; internet www.sncm.fr; passenger and roll-on/roll-off ferry services between France and Corsica, Sardinia, North Africa; 25% state-owned, managed by Veolia Transport (owners of a 28% share) from 2006; Chair. GÉRARD COUTURIER; displacement 141,454 grt.

Société Services et Transports: route du Hoc Gonfreville-L'Orcher, 76700 Harfleur; tel. 2-35-24-72-00; fax 2-35-53-36-25; petroleum and gas transport, passenger transport; Chair. YVES ROUSIER; Man. Dir JACQUES CHARVET; displacement 118,274 grt.

CIVIL AVIATION

The principal international airports are at Orly and Roissy-Charles de Gaulle (Paris), Bordeaux, Lille, Lyon, Marseille, Nice, Strasbourg and Toulouse.

Aéroports de Paris: 291 blvd de Raspail, 75675 Paris Cedex 14; tel. 1-43-35-70-00; fax 1-43-35-72-00; e-mail webmaster@adp.fr; internet www.adp.fr; f. 1945; majority state-controlled authority in charge of Paris airports at Orly and Roissy-Charles de Gaulle, 11 other airports for light aircraft, including Le Bourget, and a heliport at Issy-les-Moulineaux; Chair. and CEO AUGUSTIN DE ROMANET; Man. Dir FRANÇOIS RUBICHON.

Airlines

Air France–KLM: 45 rue de Paris, 95747 Roissy Cedex; tel. 1-41-56-78-00; fax 1-41-56-70-29; internet www.airfranceklm.com; f. 2004 by the merger of Air France (France) and KLM (Netherlands); Chair. and CEO ALEXANDRE DE JUNIAC.

Air France: 45 rue de Paris, 95747 Roissy Cedex; tel. 1-41-56-78-00; fax 1-41-56-70-29; internet www.airfrance.fr; f. 1933; 18.6% state-owned; merged with KLM (Netherlands) in 2004; internal, international, European and intercontinental services; 240 destinations in 105 countries worldwide; Chair. and CEO FRÉDÉRIC GAGEY.

Brit Air: Aéroport, CS 27925-29679 Morlaix; tel. 2-98-63-63-63; fax 2-98-62-77-66; internet www.britair.com; f. 1973; domestic and European flights; wholly owned by Air France; Pres. and Dir-Gen. MARC LAMIDEY.

Corsairfly: 2 ave Charles Lindbergh, 94636 Rungis Cedex; tel. 1-49-79-49-59; tel. www.corsairfly.com; f. 1981; scheduled flights between metropolitan France and Italy, Madagascar, Morocco, Kenya, and the French overseas possessions, and chartered flights to other medium- and long-range destinations; owned by TUI AG Group (Germany); Pres. PIERRE CHESNEAU; Man. Dir HERVÉ PIERRET.

Hex'Air: La Relhiade, 43320 Chaspuzac; tel. 4-71-08-62-28; fax 4-71-08-04-10; e-mail contact@hexair.com; internet www.hexair.com; f. 1991; domestic services; Pres. and Dir-Gen. ALEXANDRE ROUCHON.

Régional—Compagnie Aérienne Européenne: Aéroport Nantes Atlantique, 44345 Bouguenais Cedex; tel. 2-40-13-53-00; fax 2-40-13-53-08; e-mail contact@regional.com; internet www.regional.com; f. 2001 by merger of Flandre Air, Proteus and Regional Airlines; operates European and domestic flights; subsidiary of Air France; Pres. and Dir-Gen. JEAN-YVES GROSSE.

XL Airways France: BP 13760, 95727 Roissy Cedex; tel. 9-69-32-09-12; e-mail relationsclientele@xlairways.fr; internet www.xlairways.fr; f. 1995 as Star Airlines; acquired by XL Leisure Group (UK) in 2006; charter and scheduled flights between France and Corsica, Cuba, the Dominican Republic, Egypt, Italy, the Maldives, Mexico, Morocco, Senegal and Tunisia; Dir-Gen. LAURENT MAGNIN.

Airline Associations

Fédération Nationale de l'Aviation Marchande (FNAM): 28 rue de Châteaudun, 75009 Paris; tel. 1-45-26-23-24; fax 1-45-26-23-95; e-mail info@fnam.fr; internet www.fnam.fr; f. 1990; Pres. LIONEL GUÉRIN; Delegate-Gen. GUY TARDIEU.

Chambre Syndicale du Transport Aérien (CSTA): 28 rue de Châteaudun, 75009 Paris; tel. 1-45-26-23-24; fax 1-45-26-23-95; e-mail info@fnam.fr; f. 1947; represents French airlines at national level; Pres. LIONEL GUÉRIN.

Tourism

France is the world's most popular tourist destination. Paris is famous for its boulevards, historic buildings, theatres, art treasures, fashion houses, restaurants and night clubs. The Mediterranean and Atlantic coasts and the French Alps are the most popular tourist resorts. Among other attractions are the many ancient towns, the châteaux of the Loire, the fishing villages of Brittany and Normandy, and spas and places of pilgrimage, such as Vichy and Lourdes. The theme park, Disneyland Resort Paris, also attracts large numbers of tourists. There were some 84.7m. tourist arrivals in 2013; tourism receipts totalled US $56,557m. in that year. Most visitors are from the UK and Ireland, Germany, Belgium and Luxembourg, and Italy.

Atout France: 79–81 rue de Clichy, 75009 Paris; tel. 1-42-96-70-00; e-mail editorial@atout-france.fr; internet www.atout-france.fr; f. 2009 following merger of Maison de la France and ODIT France; Pres. FRANÇOIS HUWART; Dir-Gen. CHRISTIAN MANTEI.

Direction Générale de la Compétitivité, de l'Industrie et des Services (DGCIS): 67 rue Barbès, 94200 Ivry-sur-Seine; internet www.dgcis.gouv.fr; f. 2009; Dir PASCAL FAURE.

There are Regional Tourism Committees in the 22 metropolitan regions. There are more than 3,600 Offices de Tourisme and Syndicats d'Initiative (tourist offices operated by the local authorities) throughout France.

Defence

French military policy is decided by the Supreme Defence Council. Military service was compulsory until November 2001, when legislation to create fully professional armed forces took effect. As assessed at November 2014, the total active armed forces numbered 215,000, comprising an army of 115,000, a navy of 36,750, an air force of 45,500, and other staff numbering 17,750. In addition, there was a paramilitary gendarmerie of 103,400. Reserves stood at 27,650 (army 15,400; navy 4,850; air force 4,350; other staff 3,050); there were also 40,000 paramilitary reserves. In November 2011 civilian forces stood at 70,976 (army 20,600; navy 7,091; air force 7,517; paramilitary gendarmerie 1,925; other staff 35,768). France is a member of the North Atlantic Treaty Organization (NATO) and possesses its own nuclear weapons. France withdrew from the integrated military command of NATO in 1966, but re-entered it in April 2009. In November 2004 the European Union (EU) ministers responsible for defence agreed to create a number of 'battlegroups' (each comprising about 1,500 troops), which could be deployed at short notice to crisis areas around the world. The EU battlegroups, two of which were to be ready for deployment at any one time, following a rotational schedule, reached full operational capacity from 1 January 2007.

Defence Expenditure: Budgeted at €39,200m. in 2014.

Chief of Staff of the Armed Forces: Gen. PIERRE DE VILLIERS.

Chief of Staff of the Ground Forces: Gen. JEAN-PIERRE BOSSER.

Chief of Staff of the Navy: Adm. BERNARD ROGEL.

Chief of Staff of the Air Forces: Gen. DENIS MERCIER.

Director-General of the National Gendarmerie: DENIS FAVIER.

Education

Responsibility for education in France rests with the Ministry of National Education, Youth and Community Life, which defines the curriculum to be followed in schools. Administrative control of the education system, from primary to higher levels, is delegated to 30 educational districts (académies). Education is compulsory and free for children aged six to 16 years. In 2012/13 enrolment at primary level included 98% of children in the relevant age-group, while enrolment at secondary level included 97% of children in the relevant age-group. Primary education begins at six years of age and lasts for five years. At the age of 11 all pupils enter the first cycle of secondary education (enseignement secondaire), with a four-year general course at a collège. At the age of 15 pupils may enter the second cycle at a lycée d'enseignement général et technologique, choosing a course leading to the general or technological baccalauréat examination after three years. Alongside these lycées, vocational education is provided in the lycées professionnels, where pupils prepare for the professional baccalauréat over three years or a vocational qualification (certificat d'aptitude professionnelle—CAP) over two years. In 2013 16.8% of pupils attended private schools in France (including écoles élémentaires, collèges and lycées), most of which are administered by the Roman Catholic Church.

The minimum qualification for entry to university is the baccalauréat and anyone possessing that qualification is entitled to receive a university education. There are three levels of university education. The first degree, the licence, is obtained after three years of study. The master recherche and master professionnel are obtained after five years of study; the master recherche is required for progress to the doctorat, while the master professionnel provides vocational education. The doctorat requires eight years' study and the submission of a thesis. Universities are complemented by the prestigious grandes écoles, entry to which is by competitive examination; these institutions have traditionally supplied France's administrative élite. In 2012/13 there were 80 universities under the Ministries of Education (including universities in the French Overseas Regions and Departments); in 2013/14 there was a total of 4,564 higher education institutions.

Total expenditure on education (including state, overseas territory, business and household expenditure, including education, higher education and vocational training) was estimated at €144,800m. in 2013.

FRENCH OVERSEAS POSSESSIONS

Ministry of Overseas Territories: 27 rue Oudinot, 75007 Paris, France; tel. 1-53-69-20-00; internet www.outre-mer.gouv.fr.
Minister of Overseas Territories: GEORGE PAU-LANGEVIN.
The national flag of France, proportions two by three, with three equal vertical stripes, of blue, white and red, is used in the Overseas Possessions.

French Overseas Regions and Departments

As amended in March 2003, the Constitution defines French Guiana, Guadeloupe, Martinique and Réunion as being Régions d'Outre-mer (Overseas Regions) and Départements d'Outre-mer (Overseas Departments) within the French Republic. National legislation is fully applicable, although, other than in the areas of justice, the police, the armed forces and public freedoms, some provision is made for local adaptation within the framework of the law. Following referendums held in French Guiana and Martinique in 2010, from January 2016 the two territories were to be accorded the status of Collectivité Territoriale Unique (Single Territorial Collectivity), in which departmental and regional structures are merged. At a referendum held in the Collectivité d'Outre-mer (Overseas Collectivity) of Mayotte in 2009, the electorate voted in favour of becoming an Overseas Department of France. The change took effect at the end of March 2011, with Mayotte immediately being accorded the status of Single Territorial Collectivity.

FRENCH GUIANA

Introductory Survey

LOCATION, CLIMATE, LANGUAGE, RELIGION, CAPITAL

French Guiana (Guyane) lies on the north coast of South America, with Suriname to the west and Brazil to the south and east. The climate is humid, with a season of heavy rains from April to July and another short rainy season in December and January. Average temperature at sealevel is 27°C (85°F), with little seasonal variation. French is the official language, but a Creole patois is also spoken. The majority of the population belongs to the Roman Catholic Church, although other Christian churches are represented. The capital is Cayenne.

CONTEMPORARY POLITICAL HISTORY

Historical Context

French occupation commenced in the early 17th century. After brief periods of Dutch, English and Portuguese rule, the territory was finally confirmed as French in 1817. The colony steadily declined, after a short period of prosperity in the 1850s as a result of the discovery of gold in the basin of the Approuague river. French Guiana, including the notorious Devil's Island, was used as a penal colony and as a place of exile for convicts and political prisoners before the practice was halted in 1937. The colony became a Department of France in 1946.

Domestic Political Affairs

French Guiana's reputation as an area of political and economic stagnation was dispelled by the growth of pro-independence sentiments, and the use of violence by a small minority, compounded by tensions between the Guyanais and large numbers of immigrant workers. In 1974 French Guiana was granted regional status, as part of France's governmental reorganization, thus acquiring greater economic autonomy. In that year, none the less, demonstrations against unemployment, the worsening economic situation and French government policy with regard to the Department led to the detention of leading trade unionists and pro-independence politicians. Further industrial and political unrest in the late 1970s prompted the Parti Socialiste Guyanais (PSG), then the strongest political organization, to demand greater autonomy for the Department. In 1980 there were several bomb attacks against 'colonialist' targets by an extremist group, Fo nou Libéré la Guyane. Reforms introduced by the French Socialist Government in 1982–83 devolved some power over local affairs to the new Conseil Régional (Regional Council). In the 1983 election to the Regional Council the left-wing parties gained a majority of votes, but not of seats, and the balance of power was held by the separatist Union des Travailleurs Guyanais (UTG), the political wing of which became the Parti National Populaire Guyanais (PNPG) in 1985. At the election to the Conseil Général (General Council) held in 1985, the PSG and left-wing independents secured a majority of seats.

The PSG increased its strength on the Regional Council following an election in 1986, and Georges Othily of the PSG was re-elected President of the Council. Left-wing parties again won a majority of seats at the election to the General Council in 1988. In September 1989 Othily was elected to take French Guiana's seat in the French Sénat (Senate). Othily had been expelled from the PSG for having worked too closely with the opposition parties. However, he attracted support from those who regarded the party's domination of French Guiana as corrupt. In December Othily formed his own party, the Forces Démocratiques Guyanaises (FDG), which included other dissident members of the PSG.

The PSG dominated in elections to both the General Council and the Regional Council in 1992: party leader Elie Castor retained the presidency of the former while PSG Secretary-General Antoine Karam was elected as President of the Regional Council. In a referendum in September, 67% of voters in French Guiana approved ratification of the Treaty on European Union (see p. 271), although a high abstention rate was recorded.

At the 1993 elections to the Assemblée Nationale (National Assembly) Léon Bertrand of the Gaullist Rassemblement pour la République (RPR) was re-elected, along with Christiane Taubira-Delannon, the founder of the independent left-wing Walwari movement. The PSG's representation in the General Council fell following the 1994 cantonal elections; none the less, one of its members, Stéphan Phinéra-Horth, was subsequently elected President of the Council.

A boycott of classes by secondary school pupils, who were demanding improved conditions of study, escalated in late 1996 into a crisis that was regarded as exemplifying wider social tensions between the Department and metropolitan France. The refusal of the Prefect, Pierre Dartout, to receive schools' representatives prompted protests in Cayenne, which swiftly degenerated into rioting and looting. The central Government dispatched anti-riot police to assist the local security forces. However, the conviction of several people implicated in the rioting provoked further protests and clashes with security forces, and a one-day general strike in Cayenne, organized by the UTG, was widely observed. The extent of the security forces' actions in suppressing the demonstrations was criticized, as was the approach of the Department's administrators. An agreement on educational reform was subsequently reached.

In April 1997 violent incidents followed the arrest of five pro-independence activists suspected of setting fire to the home of the public prosecutor during the disturbances of the previous year. Five others, including leading members of the UTG and the PNPG, were subsequently detained in connection with the arson incident. The transfer of all 10 detainees to Martinique prompted further violent protests in Cayenne: police reinforcements were dispatched by the central Government to help suppress the violence.

In 1997 Léon Bertrand and Christiane Taubira-Delannon were both re-elected to the National Assembly. Elections to the Regional and General Councils were held in 1998. The PSG lost seats on both bodies. Karam was re-elected to the presidency of the Regional Council. André Lecante, an independent left-wing councillor, was elected as President of the General Council. In September Georges Othily was re-elected to the Senate.

Demands for further autonomy

In January 1999 representatives of 10 separatist organizations from French Guiana, Guadeloupe and Martinique, including the Mouvement de la Décolonisation et d'Emancipation Sociale (MDES) and the PNPG, signed a joint declaration denouncing 'French colonialism', in which they stated their intention to campaign for the reinstatement of the three Caribbean Overseas Departments on a UN list of territories to be decolonized. In December the Presidents of the Regional Councils of French Guiana, Guadeloupe and Martinique signed a joint declaration in Basse-Terre, Guadeloupe, affirming their intention to propose, to the President and the Government, a legislative amendment aimed at creating a new status of overseas region. However, the Secretary of State for Overseas Departments and Territories, Jean-Jack Queyranne, in early 2000 dismissed the declaration as unconstitutional and exceeding the mandate of politicians responsible. In March, during a visit to the Department by Queyranne, rioting broke out following his refusal to meet a delegation of separatist organizations. Later that month the Regional Council overwhelmingly rejected reforms proposed by Queyranne, which included the creation of a Congress in French Guiana, as well as the extension of the Departments' powers in areas such as regional co-operation. Nevertheless, the proposals were approved by the National Assembly in November, and ratified by the Constitutional Council in the following month.

In November 2000 several people were injured following riots in Cayenne. The riots followed a pro-autonomy march, organized by the UTG. Protesters claimed they had been excluded from talks on French Guiana's status. Nevertheless, discussions were held in December in Paris attended by Queyranne's successor, Christian Paul, various senior politicians from French Guiana and representatives from the PSG, the RPR, Walwari, and the FDG. In 2001 it was agreed that a document detailing proposals for increased autonomy for French Guiana was to be presented to the French Government for approval. These proposals included: the division of the territory into four districts; the creation of a Collectivité Territoriale (Territorial Collectivity), governed by an Assembly elected for a five-year term; and the establishment of an independent executive council. There was also a request that the territory be given control over legislative and administrative affairs, as well as legislative authority on matters concerning French Guiana alone. In November the French Government announced itself to be in favour of the suggested constitutional developments; in March 2003 a constitutional amendment conferred the status of Région d'Outre-mer (Overseas Region) on French Guiana (in addition to it being an Overseas Department).

Left-wing independent Joseph Ho-Ten-You was elected President of the General Council in 2001. At legislative polls in 2002, Taubira-Delannon was re-elected to the National Assembly.

In 2002 the gendarmerie and the national police began a series of operations in the south of the Department aimed at stopping the illegal gold trade. As well as causing extensive environmental damage, unlicensed gold-mining operations were a chief cause of illegal immigration, and a focus for other criminal activities, such as drugs-smuggling and gun-running.

In elections to the Regional Council in March 2004 the PSG won a majority of seats; Karam was re-elected President of the Council. In May 2005 a national referendum was held on ratification of the European Union constitutional treaty: in the Department 60.1% of participating voters were in favour of adopting the treaty; however, voter turnout was just 23.1%. The treaty was ultimately rejected by a majority of voters in metropolitan France.

At the first round of the national presidential election in April 2007, the Union pour un Mouvement Populaire (UMP) candidate, Nicolas Sarkozy, won 41% of the votes cast in the Department, ahead of Ségolène Royal of the PS, who attracted 33%. At the second round in May, Sarkozy secured the presidency, winning 53% of the votes cast in the Department. Meanwhile, at elections to the National Assembly, held in June, Taubira-Delannon, representing Walwari, and Chantal Berthelot of the PSG secured the Department's two seats. Following municipal elections in March 2008, Alain Tien-Long replaced Pierre Désert as President of the General Council. Georges Patient and Jean-Etienne Antoinette were elected as the Department's senate representatives in September.

Efforts to halt illegal gold-mining were intensified in 2008. In February, during a visit to French Guiana, President Sarkozy announced a four-month deployment of gendarmes and military personnel in Operation Harpie, which aimed to disrupt unlicensed mining activities and combat illegal immigration, especially from Brazil. As part of his visit, Sarkozy met Brazilian President Lula da Silva and agreed to increase border co-operation between the two countries. Operation Harpie was expanded and renewed for a further six months in 2009 and became a permanent mission from March 2010. According to official data, there were 771 unauthorized mining sites in French Guiana in 2013, up from 392 in 2011. A visit to the region by French President François Hollande in December 2013 apparently prompted the Brazilian legislature to approve a 2008 co-operation agreement with France concerning the prevention of illegal mining activity in the border region.

Regional and national elections

At elections to the Regional Council held on 14 and 21 March 2010, the UMP list secured 21 of the 31 council seats, with 56.1% of the ballot. The left-wing list, led by Walwari and the MDES, obtained the remaining 10 seats and won 43.9% of the votes cast. Rodolphe Alexandre was elected as President of the Regional Council. The rate of participation by the electorate was 50.5%. Municipal elections were conducted on 20 and 27 March 2011, following which Alain Tien-Long was re-elected as President of the General Council. In April Denis Labbé was appointed as Prefect, replacing Daniel Férey.

The first round of the French presidential election was conducted on 21 April 2012 (one day earlier than in mainland France): François Hollande, representing the PS, attracted 42.6% of the territory's votes, compared with 27.2% for Sarkozy. A second round run-off election was held two weeks later, at which Hollande secured 62.1% of the ballot, defeating Sarkozy, who attracted 38.0%. Hollande also triumphed nationally and was sworn in as President in mid-May. Christiane Taubira-Delannon of French Guiana was notably appointed as Keeper of the Seals, Minister of Justice in Hollande's new cabinet. In legislative elections, which took place in June, Berthelot was re-elected to the National Assembly, while the territory's remaining mandate was won by Gabriel Serville of the PSG. Eric Spitz replaced Labbé as Prefect in June 2013.

Economic unrest

The French Minister of Overseas Territories, Victorin Lurel, visited French Guiana in September 2012 to hold discussions with the local authorities regarding the high cost of living in the territory. A bill to address the problem of inflated prices in French Guiana and other French Overseas Possessions, drafted by Lurel, was approved by Parliament in November. The legislation provided for the imposition of price controls on a range of staple goods and the introduction of measures to encourage competition. In December 2013 the French Government extended the price controls to cover petrol purchases in the French Overseas Regions and Departments. However, on multiple occasions between mid-2013 and early 2014 owners of petrol stations in French Guiana and other French Overseas Departments, fearing that the move would disrupt their business model and undermine profit margins, closed their establishments in a co-ordinated act of protest. The closures ended in February 2014 after a compromise was agreed with the French authorities.

Candidates representing left-wing lists comfortably won the most council seats in municipal polls conducted on 23 and 30 March 2014. Elections to the European Parliament took place in French Guiana on 25 May. The Europe-Ecologie-Les Verts list secured 40.9% of the local ballot, compared with 15.0% for the UMP and 14.2% for the far-right Front National list. Turnout was only 10.0%, however. Patient retained his senate seat in elections held on 28 September, while Karam gained control of the territory's other seat in the upper chamber; both men were affiliated with the Socialist senate group.

Recent developments: institutional reform

President Sarkozy, during a visit to the region in June 2009, proposed a series of referendums on the issue of increased autonomy for the French Overseas Regions in the Caribbean. French Guiana's plebiscite was duly held on 10 January 2010. The electorate, fearful of losing economic support from mainland France and unwilling to confer greater power upon the local political élite, voted overwhelmingly to reject any increase in autonomy, with 69.8% voting against the proposal. The rate of participation by the electorate was 48.2%. A further referendum on institutional reform was held on 24 January, and 57.5% of participants voted in favour of French Guiana becoming a Collectivité Territoriale Unique (Single Territorial Collectivity), replacing the existing two-tier departmental and regional administrative structure. (French Guiana would remain an Overseas Department and an Overseas Region.) Only 27.4% of the electorate took part in the plebiscite. The authorities hoped that the merger of the departmental and regional levels of government would increase efficiency and reduce operating costs. In mid-2011 the National Assembly approved legislation to facilitate this transition, and in January 2015 a further law was approved granting Single Territorial Collectivity status on French Guiana (and Martinique) from 1 January 2016. Polls were scheduled for December 2015 to elect the 51 members of a new, consolidated legislative body, which would replace the Regional Council and the General Council.

CONSTITUTION AND GOVERNMENT

France is represented in French Guiana by an appointed Prefect. There are two councils with local powers: the General Council, with 19 members, and the Regional Council, with 31 members. Both are elected by universal adult suffrage for a period of six years. Both Councils were scheduled to be replaced by a single, 51-member body from January 2016. French Guiana elects two representatives each to the National Assembly and the Senate in Paris. French Guiana is also represented at the European Parliament.

REGIONAL AND INTERNATIONAL CO-OPERATION

In January 2015 a delegation led by Regional Council President Rodolphe Alexandre began discussions with representatives of the Caribbean Community and Common Market (CARICOM, see p. 222) on associate membership of the regional grouping.

ECONOMIC AFFAIRS

In 2012, according to official estimates, French Guiana's gross domestic product (GDP), measured at current prices, was €3,806m., equivalent to €15,416 per head; growth in 2012 was 4.0%. Between 1999 and 2007 GDP increased, in real terms, at an average rate of 4.3% per year. Between the censuses of 2006 and 2012 the population increased at an average annual rate of 2.5%.

Agriculture (including fishing) engaged an estimated 0.6% of the economically active population in 2012. In 2003 the sector contributed 4.6% of GDP. In 2012 agricultural products accounted for some 3.8% of total export earnings, at €11.2m. The dominant activities are fisheries and forestry, although the contribution of the latter to export earnings has declined in recent years. In 2012 shrimp production was recorded at 742 metric tons. The aquaculture industry faced competition from shrimp producers in Latin America and Asia and rising fuel prices. The principal crops for local consumption are cassava, vegetables and rice, and sugar cane is grown for making rum; rum production in 2013 was 1,359 hl, a decrease on the 2,626 hl, produced in 2012. Livestock rearing was also largely for subsistence. In 2013 Guianese abattoirs produced an estimated 1,241 tons of meat, mostly pork, poultry and beef. Rice, pineapples and citrus fruit are cultivated for export. According to UN estimates, agricultural GDP decreased at an average annual rate of 0.8% in 1990–98; in 1998 agricultural GDP increased by an estimated 0.3%.

Industry, including construction and agrarian and food industries, contributed an estimated 20.3% to GDP in 2003, while in 2012 it engaged 16.0% of the employed labour force. The mining sector is dominated by the extraction of gold, which involves small-scale alluvial operations as well as larger local and multinational mining concerns. The first new concession in 70 years was awarded to Cambior in 2004 for a 25-year period. The US Geological Survey estimated gold production in 2012 at a 1,300 kg. Gold exports in 2013 were put at €67.5m. Crushed rock for the construction industry is the only other mineral extracted in significant quantities. Deposits of bauxite, columbo-tantalite and kaolin are also present. There is little manufacturing activity, except for the processing of fisheries products (mainly shrimp-freezing) and the distillation of rum. The manufacturing sector engaged 5.5% of the employed labour force in 2012. In 1990–98 industrial GDP (excluding construction) increased at an average annual rate of 7.8%. The construction sector engaged 7.5% of the employed labour force in 2012. It expanded at an average of 2.0% per year in 1990–98.

French Guiana's Petit-Saut 116-MW hydroelectric dam, on the Sinnamary river, provided most of the territory's electrical energy requirements. Imports of fuels and combustibles accounted for 15.0% of total imports in 2013.

The services sector engaged an estimated 83.5% of the employed labour force in 2012 and, according to official sources, contributed 75.2% of GDP in 2003. The European Space Agency's satellite-launching centre at Kourou has provided a considerable stimulus to the economy, most notably the construction sector (which engaged an estimated 7.5% of the employed labour force in 2012). The space centre was estimated to contribute approximately one-quarter of French Guiana's GDP and approximately one-half of its tax revenues. In 2014 there were 11 rocket launches. The tourism sector expanded in the last two decades of the 20th century, although its potential is limited by the lack of infrastructure away from the coast. In 2009 some 83,000 visitor arrivals were recorded, while receipts from tourism totalled US $49m. in 2007. In 2003 it was estimated that tourism contributed 3% of GDP.

French Guiana recorded a merchandise trade deficit of some €1,296.4m in 2013. In that year the principal source of imports was metropolitan France (which supplied 42.9% of total imports); the Department's other major suppliers were Trinidad and Tobago, the People's Republic of China and the USA. Trinidad and Tobago was the principal market for exports in that year (40.7%); other important purchasers were France and the countries of the European Union. The principal imports in 2013 were capital industry products, chemicals, petroleum products, products of agriculture and food industries, consumer industry products, and metals and metal products; the principal exports were capital industry products, mineral products, and products of agriculture and food industries.

According to preliminary figures, the 2014 regional budget was balanced at €163.0m. The departmental budget for that year put revenue at €367.0m., while expenditure was €415.8m. The annual rate of inflation averaged 1.8% in 2004–13; the average rate of inflation in 2013 was 1.4%. Unemployment in mid-2013 was esti-

mated at 21.3% of the total labour force. However, there is a shortage of skilled labour, offset partly by immigration.

Economic development in French Guiana has been hindered by the Department's location, poor infrastructure and unskilled labour force, although there is considerable potential for further growth in the fishing, forestry, mining and tourism sectors. A particular concern was the continuing high rate of unemployment. French Guiana's geographical characteristics—large parts of the territory are accessible only by river—have resulted in difficulties in regulating key areas of the economy, such as gold-mining and forestry. Owing to a recovery in gold exports and strong internal demand, GDP expanded by 4.0% in 2010. Increased activity in the construction and space sectors supported economic growth of 4.5% in 2011. Rising gold exports and buoyant levels of investment and domestic consumption also contributed to this recovery, while the tourism industry registered modest growth. A significant offshore petroleum discovery was announced in that year, potentially containing up to 700m. barrels of oil, although further exploratory drilling in 2012–13 yielded disappointing results. In spite of a deceleration in domestic demand, GDP rose by 4.8% in 2012, again primarily driven by increased gold shipments and robust growth in the construction and space sectors. However, gold and timber exports both decreased sharply during 2013, while activity in the construction and space industries also declined. Although there was an increase in household consumption, and agricultural and tourism indicators were generally positive, it seemed likely that GDP growth had slowed during that year.

PUBLIC HOLIDAYS

2016: 1 January (New Year's Day), 8–9 February (Lenten Carnival), 10 February (Ash Wednesday), 28 March (Easter Monday), 1 May (Labour Day), 5 May (Ascension Day), 8 May (Liberation Day), 16 May (Whit Monday), 10 June (Abolition of Slavery), 14 July (National Day, Fall of the Bastille), 15 August (Assumption), 1 November (All Saints' Day), 11 November (Armistice Day), 25 December (Christmas Day).

Statistical Survey

Sources (unless otherwise indicated): Institut National de la Statistique et des Etudes Economiques (INSEE), Service Régional de Guyane, ave Pasteur, BP 6017, 97306 Cayenne Cédex; tel. 5-94-29-73-00; fax 5-94-29-73-01; internet www.insee.fr/fr/regions/guyane; Chambre de Commerce et d'Industrie de la Guyane (CCIG), Hôtel Consulaire, pl. de l'Esplanade, BP 49, 97321 Cayenne Cédex; tel. 5-94-29-96-00; fax 5-94-29-96-34; internet www.guyane.cci.fr.

AREA AND POPULATION

Area: 83,534 sq km (32,253 sq miles).

Population: 157,213 at census of 8 March 1999; 237,549 at census of 1 January 2011. Note: According to new census methodology, data in 2011 refer to median figures based on the collection of raw data over a five-year period (2009–13). *2013* (official estimate at 1 January): 250,109. *Mid-2015* (UN estimate): 261,729 (Source: UN, *World Population Prospects: The 2012 Revision*.

Density (at mid-2015): 3.1 per sq km.

Population by Age and Sex (UN estimates at mid-2015): *0–14 years:* 82,499 (males 42,056, females 40,443); *15–64 years:* 165,793 (males 82,223, females 83,570); *65 years and over:* 13,437 (males 6,555, females 6,882); *Total* 261,729 (males 130,834, females 130,895) (Source: UN, *World Population Prospects: The 2012 Revision*).

Principal Towns (official population estimates at 1 January 2012): Cayenne (capital) 55,198; Saint-Laurent-du-Maroni 40,597; Matoury 29,712; Kourou 25,490; Rémire-Montjoly 20,689.

Births, Marriages and Deaths (2012): Registered live births 6,609 (birth rate 26.8 per 1,000); Registered marriages 650 (marriage rate 2.6 per 1,000); Registered deaths 789 (death rate 3.2 per 1,000). *2013:* Registered live births 6,474.

Life Expectancy (years at birth): 77.4 (males 74.1; females 81.1) in 2014. Source: Pan American Health Organization.

Employment (persons aged 15 years and over, provisional estimates at 31 December 2012): Agriculture, forestry and fishing 298; Mining, electricity, gas and water supply 1,445; Manufacturing 2,639; Construction 3,858; Wholesale and retail trade; repair of motor vehicles, motorcycles, etc. 4,633; Transport 2,421; Hotels and restaurants 1,668; Information and communication 625; Financial intermediation 564; Real estate, renting and business activities 4,644; Public administration and defence; education, health and social work 24,439; Other community, social and personal service activities 2,108; *Total employed* 49,342. Note: Data exclude 2,864 persons employed without salary.

HEALTH AND WELFARE

Key Indicators

Total Fertility Rate (children per woman, 2014): 3.0.

Under-5 Mortality Rate (per 1,000 live births, 2011): 15.0.

Physicians (per 1,000 head, c. 2010): 1.8.

Hospital Beds (per 1,000 head, 2012): 2.6.

Access to Water (% of persons, 2012): 90.

Access to Sanitation (% of persons, 2012): 90.

Source: mostly Pan American Health Organization.

For other sources and definitions, see explanatory note on p. vi.

AGRICULTURE, ETC.

Principal Crops ('000 metric tons, 2013): Rice, paddy 2.0; Cassava 24.4; Sugar cane 9.7; Cabbages and other brassicas 5.0 (FAO estimates); Tomatoes 4.4; Cucumbers and gherkins 1.6 (FAO estimates); Beans, green 0.9 (FAO estimates); Bananas 6.9 (FAO estimates); Plantains 2.4. *Aggregate Production* ('000 metric tons, may include official, semi-official or estimated data): Total vegetables (incl. melons) 20.5; Total fruits (excl. melons) 20.9.

Livestock ('000 head, 2013, FAO estimates): Cattle 14.5; Pigs 8.9; Sheep 1.4.

Livestock Products (metric tons, 2013): Cattle meat 355; Pig meat 416; Chicken meat 470 (FAO estimates); Cows' milk 550; Hen eggs 550 (FAO estimates).

Forestry ('000 cubic metres, 2013, FAO estimates): *Roundwood Removals* (excl. bark): Sawlogs, veneer logs and logs for sleepers 74.9; Other industrial wood 9.0; Fuel wood 131.1; Total 215.0. *Sawnwood Production* (incl. railway sleepers): Total 31.5.

Fishing (metric tons, live weight, 2012, FAO estimates): Capture 3,700 (Marine fishes 2,958; Shrimps 742); Aquaculture 35; *Total catch* 3,735.

Source: FAO.

MINING

Production ('000 metric tons unless otherwise indicated, 2012, estimates): Cement 62,000; Gold (metal content of ore, kilograms) 1,300; Sand 500. Source: US Geological Survey.

INDUSTRY

Production (2013): Rum 1,359 hl; Electric energy 875 million kWh (Source: l'Institut d'Emission des Départements d'Outre-mer, *Rapport Annuel 2013*).

FINANCE

Currency and Exchange Rates: 100 cent = 1 euro (€). *Sterling and Dollar Equivalents* (31 December 2014): £1 sterling = €1.286; US $1 = €0.824; €10 = £7.78 = $12.14. *Average Exchange Rate* (euros per US dollar): 0.778 in 2012; 0.753 in 2013; 0.754 in 2014. Note: The national currency was formerly the French franc. From the introduction of the euro, with French participation, on 1 January 1999, a fixed exchange rate of €1 = 6.55957 French francs was in operation. Euro notes and coins were introduced on 1 January 2002. The euro and French currency circulated alongside each other until 17 February, after which the euro became the sole legal tender. Some of the figures in this Survey are still in terms of francs.

Budgets (excl. debt rescheduling, € million, 2014, preliminary): *Regional Government:* Current revenue 113.5 (Taxes 73.1, Grants 40.4); Capital revenue 49.5; Total 163.0. Current expenditure 96.3; Capital expenditure 66.7; Total 163.0. *Departmental Government:* Revenue 367.0 (Current revenue 328.9, Capital revenue 38.1); Expenditure 415.8 (Current expenditure 345.3, Capital expenditure 70.5). Source: Département des Etudes et des Statistiques Locales.

Cost of Living (Consumer Price Index; base: 2000 = 100): All items 121.6 in 2011; 123.4 in 2012; 125.2 in 2013. Source: ILO.

Expenditure on the Gross Domestic Product (€ million at current prices, 2012, estimates): Total final consumption expenditure 3,675 (General government and non-profit institutions serving households 1,862, Households 1,813); Gross capital formation 1,143; *Total domestic expenditure* 4,818; Exports of goods and services 1,239; *Less* Imports of goods and services 3,637; Statistical discrepancy 1,386; *GDP in purchasers' values* 3,806. Source: Institut d'Emission des Départements d'Outre-mer, *Guyane: Rapport Annuel 2013*.

Gross Domestic Product by Economic Activity (€ million at current prices, 2003): Agriculture, hunting, forestry and fishing 95; Food industries 39; Manufacturing 180; Energy 40; Construction 163; Services 1,564 (Restaurants and hotels 42, Transport –85, Commerce 223, Other market services 560; Non-market services 824); *Sub-total* 2,081; Financial intermediation services indirectly measured –42; Import duties, less subsidies 169; *GDP in purchasers' values* 2,207.

EXTERNAL TRADE

Principal Commodities (€ million, 2013): *Imports c.i.f.:* Agriculture, forestry and fishing 16.4; Products of agriculture and food industries 214.7; Consumer industry products 167.2 (Pharmaceuticals 57.6); Capital industry products 515.8 (Industrial and agricultural machinery 177.2; Transport equipment 188.1); Mineral products, rubber and plastic 66.2; Chemicals 241.0; Metal and metal products 102.2; Petroleum products 238.9; Total (incl. others) 1,589.0. *Exports f.o.b.:* Agriculture, forestry and fishing 0.6; Products of agriculture and food industries 11.2; Consumer industry products 0.9; Capital industry products 185.0 (Electronic goods and computer equipment 24.1; Industrial and agricultural machinery 80.0; Transport equipment 70.9); Mineral products, rubber and plastic 67.5; Metals and products thereof 7.5; Petroleum products 4.4; Total (incl. others) 292.6 (Source: Institut d'Emission des Départements d'Outre-mer, *Guyane: Rapport Annuel 2013*).

Principal Trading Partners (€ million, 2008): *Imports c.i.f.:* France (metropolitan) 485.4; Germany 31.9; Italy 17.6; Martinique 38.4; Netherlands 21.2; Spain 17.0; Trinidad and Tobago 51.4; Total (incl. others) 1,065.0. *Exports f.o.b.:* France (metropolitan) 37.3; Germany 11.4; Guadeloupe 7.7; Italy 9.5; Martinique 8.3; Spain 2.5; Switzerland 15.0; Total (incl. others) 96.3. *2011* (€ million): Total imports 1,333.1; Total exports 154.4 (Source: Institut d'Emission des Départements d'Outre-mer, *Guyane: Rapport Annuel 2011*). *2012* (€ million): Total imports 1,486.5; Total exports 223.4 (Source: Institut d'Emission des Départements d'Outre-mer, *Guyane: Rapport Annuel 2012*). *2013* (€ million): Total imports 1,589.0; Total exports 292.6 (Source: Institut d'Emission des Départements d'Outre-mer, *Guyane: Rapport Annuel 2013*).

TRANSPORT

Road Traffic ('000 motor vehicles in use, 2001): Passenger cars 32.9; Commercial vehicles 11.9 (Source: UN, *Statistical Yearbook*). *2002:* 50,000 motor vehicles in use. *1 January 2010:* ('000 commercial motor vehicles in use): Buses 0.4; Vans and trucks 17.3.

Shipping: *Flag Registered Fleet* (at 31 December 2014): Vessels registered 2; Total displacement: 3,881 grt. Source: Lloyd's List Intelligence (www.lloydslistintelligence.com).

International Seaborne Shipping (traffic, 2013): Goods carried 656,282 metric tons in 2012; 653,941 metric tons in 2013. Source: Institut d'Emission des Départements d'Outre-mer, *Guyane: Rapport Annuel 2013*.

Civil Aviation (2013): Aircraft movements 10,415; Freight carried (incl. post) 5,843 metric tons; Passengers carried 436,991. Source: Institut d'Emission des Départements d'Outre-mer, *Guyane: Rapport Annuel 2013*.

TOURISM

Tourist Arrivals by Country (2007): France 62,016; Guadeloupe 14,362; Martinique 22,739; Total (incl. others) 108,801. *2009:* 83,000 tourist arrivals.

Receipts from Tourism (US $ million, incl. passenger transport): 49 in 2007.

Source: World Tourism Organization.

COMMUNICATIONS MEDIA

Telephones ('000 main lines in use): 45.5 in 2010.

Mobile Cellular Telephones ('000 subscribers): 217.7 in 2009.

Internet Users ('000): 58.0 in 2009.

Broadband Subscribers ('000): 30.2 in 2009.

Source: International Telecommunication Union.

EDUCATION

Pre-primary (2013/14): 43 institutions; 15,277 students (14,377 state, 900 private).

Primary (2013/14): 121 institutions (113 state, 8 private); 27,951 students (26,027 state, 1,924 private).

Specialized Pre-primary and Primary (2013/14): 443 students (443 state only).

Secondary (2013/14): 47 institutions (42 state, 5 private); 32,966 students (30,581 state, 2,385 private).

Higher (2012/13): 3,434 students.

Teachers (2008/09 unless otherwise indicated): *Primary:* 2,243 teachers (2,121 state, 122 private); *Secondary:* 2,433 teachers (2,285 state, 148 private); *Higher* (2004/05): 63 teachers. Source: Ministère de l'Education Nationale, *Repères et références statistiques. 2012/13* (state schools): 2,377 in primary; 2,571 in secondary.

Adult Literacy Rate: 83.0% (males 83.6%, females 82.3%) in 1998. Source: Pan American Health Organization.

Directory

The Government

(April 2015)

HEAD OF STATE

President: FRANÇOIS HOLLANDE.

Prefect: ERIC SPITZ, Préfecture, 1 rue Fiedmont, BP 7008, 97307 Cayenne Cédex; tel. 5-94-39-45-00; fax 5-94-30-02-77; e-mail courrier@guyane.pref.gouv.fr; internet www.guyane.pref.gouv.fr.

DEPARTMENTAL ADMINISTRATION

President of the General Council: ALAIN TIEN-LIONG, Hôtel du Département, pl. Léopold Héder, BP 5021, 97397 Cayenne Cédex; tel. 5-94-29-55-89; fax 5-94-29-55-25; e-mail atienliong@cg973.fr; internet www.cg973.fr.

President of the Regional Council: RODOLPHE ALEXANDRE (UMP), Cité Administrative Régionale, 4179 route de Montabo, Carrefour de Suzini, BP 7025, 97307 Cayenne Cédex; tel. 5-94-29-20-20; fax 5-94-31-95-22; e-mail cabcrg@cr-guyane.fr; internet www.cr-guyane.fr.

Elections, Regional Council, 14 and 21 March 2010

	Seats
Guyane 73*	21
Deux Ans: Un Marathon pour Bâtir†	10
Total	31

* Electoral list comprising the Union pour un Mouvement Populaire (UMP) and allies.
† Electoral list comprising various left-wing parties led by Walwari and the Mouvement de Décolinisation et d'Emancipation Sociale (MDES).

REPRESENTATIVES TO THE FRENCH PARLIAMENT

Deputies to the French National Assembly: GABRIEL SERVILLE (Gauche Démocrate et Républicaine), CHANTAL BERTHELOT (Socialiste, Républicain et Citoyen).

Representatives to the French Senate: GEORGES PATIENT (Groupe Socialiste), JEAN-ETIENNE ANTOINETTE (Groupe Socialiste).

GOVERNMENT OFFICE

Economic, Social and Environmental Regional Committee: 66 ave du Général de Gaulle, 97300 Cayenne; tel. 5-94-28-96-01; fax 5-94-30-73-65; e-mail info@ceser-guyane.fr; internet www.ceser-guyane.fr; Pres. ARIANE FLEURIVAL.

Political Organizations

Forces Démocratiques de Guyane (FDG): 41 rue du 14 Juillet, BP 403, 97300 Cayenne; tel. 5-94-28-96-79; fax 5-94-30-80-66; e-mail g.othily@senat.fr; f. 1989 by a split in the PSG; Sec.-Gen. GIL HORTH.

Mouvement de Décolonisation et d'Emancipation Sociale (MDES): 21 rue Maissin, 97300 Cayenne; tel. 5-94-30-55-97; fax 5-94-30-97-73; e-mail mdes.parti@wanadoo.org; f. 1991; pro-independence; Sec.-Gen. MAURICE PINDARD.

Parti Progressiste Guyanais (PPG): 1994 Route de Montabo, 97300 Cayenne; e-mail jmj_taubira@yahoo.fr; internet www.partiprogressisteguyanais.fr; f. 2013; Sec.-Gen. JEAN-MARIE TAUBIRA.

Parti Socialiste (PS): 7 rue de l'Adjudant Pindard, 97300 Cayenne Cédex; tel. 5-94-37-81-33; fax 5-94-37-81-56; e-mail fede973.partisocialiste@wanadoo.fr; internet guyane.parti-socialiste.fr; departmental br. of the metropolitan party; Leader LÉON JEAN BAPTISTE EDOUARD.

Parti Socialiste Guyanais (PSG): 1 Cité Césaire, BP 46, 97300 Cayenne; tel. 5-94-28-11-44; fax 5-94-28-46-92; e-mail partisocialisteguyanais@orange.fr; f. 1956; left-wing; Sec.-Gen. MARIE JOSÉ LALSIE.

Union pour un Mouvement Populaire (UMP): 42 rue du Docteur Barrat, 97300 Cayenne; tel. 5-94-28-80-74; fax 5-94-28-80-75; internet www.u-m-p.org; f. 2002 as Union pour la Majorité Presidentielle by mems of the fmr Rassemblement pour la République and Union pour la Démocratie Française; centre-right; departmental br. of the metropolitan party; Sec.-Gen. LUC CHATEL.

Les Verts Guyane: 64 rue Madame Payé, 97300 Cayenne; tel. 5-94-40-97-27; e-mail tamanoir.guyane@wanadoo.fr; internet guyane.lesverts.fr; ecologist; departmental br. of the metropolitan party; Regional Sec. JOSÉ GAILLOU.

Walwari: 35 rue Schoelcher, BP 803, 97300 Cayenne Cédex; tel. 5-94-30-31-00; fax 5-94-31-84-95; e-mail info@walwari.org; internet www.walwari.org; f. 1993; left-wing; Leader CHRISTIANE TAUBIRA-DELANNON; Sec.-Gen. JOËL PIED.

Judicial System

Court of Appeal: 1 rue Louis Blanc, 97300 Cayenne; tel. 5-94-27-48-48; fax 5-94-27-48-72; Pres. PIERRE GOUZENNE.

There is also a Tribunal de Grande Instance and a Tribunal d'Instance.

Religion

CHRISTIANITY

The Roman Catholic Church

French Guiana comprises the single diocese of Cayenne, suffragan to the archdiocese of Fort-de-France, Martinique. Some 80% of the population are Roman Catholics. French Guiana participates in the Antilles Episcopal Conference, currently based in Port of Spain, Trinidad and Tobago.

Bishop of Cayenne: Rt Rev. EMMANUEL M. P. L. LAFONT, Evêché, 24 rue Madame Payé, BP 378, 97328 Cayenne Cédex; tel. 5-94-28-98-48; fax 5-94-30-20-33; e-mail emmanuel.lafont@wanadoo.fr; internet www.guyane.catholique.fr.

The Anglican Communion

Within the Church in the Province of the West Indies, French Guiana forms part of the diocese of Guyana. The Bishop is resident in Georgetown, Guyana. There were fewer than 100 adherents in 2000.

Other Churches

In 2000 there were an estimated 7,000 Protestants and 7,200 adherents professing other forms of Christianity.

Assembly of God: 1051 route de Raban, 97300 Cayenne; tel. 5-94-35-23-04; fax 5-94-35-23-05; e-mail jacques.rhino@wanadoo.fr; internet www.addguyane.fr; Pres. JACQUES RHINO; c. 500 mems.

Church of Jesus Christ of Latter-day Saints (Mormons): Route de la Rocade, 97305 Cayenne; 362 mems.

Seventh-day Adventist Church: Mission Adventiste de la Guyane, 39 rue Schoëlcher, BP 169, 97324 Cayenne Cédex; tel. 5-94-25-64-26; fax 5-94-37-93-02; e-mail adventiste.mission@wanadoo.fr; f. 1949; Pres. and Chair. ALAIN LIBER; Sec.-Treas. DANIEL CARBIN; 2,299 mems.

The Jehovah's Witnesses are also represented.

The Press

France-Guyane: 17 rue Lallouette, BP 428, 97329 Cayenne; tel. 5-94-29-70-00; fax 5-94-29-70-02; e-mail infos@franceguyane.fr; internet www.franceguyane.fr; daily; Publishing Dir DENIS BERRIAT; Editor-in-Chief JÉRÔME RIGOLAGE; circ. 9,000.

Le Marron—Petit Journal de Kourou: BP 53, 97372 Kourou; tel. 5-94-32-49-54; fax 5-94-32-10-70; e-mail pjk@blada.com; internet www.blada.com; f. 2001; Dir ODILE FARJAT.

Ròt Kozé: 11 rue Maissin, 97300 Cayenne; tel. 5-94-30-55-97; fax 5-94-30-97-73; e-mail redacteur@rotkoze.com; internet www.rotkoze.com; f. 1990; left-wing organ of the MDES party; monthly; Dir MAURICE PINDARD.

La Semaine Guyanaise: 6 ave Louis Pasteur, 97300 Cayenne; tel. 5-94-31-09-83; fax 5-94-31-95-20; e-mail semaineguyanaise@nplus.gf; internet www.semaineguyanaise.com; weekly (Thur.); Dir ALAIN CHAUMET; Editor-in-Chief JÉRÔME VALLETTE.

Publishers

Editions Anne C.: 8 Lot Mapaou, route de Baduel, BP 212, 97325 Cayenne; tel. and fax 5-94-35-20-10; e-mail canne@nplus.gf; internet www.redris.pagesperso-orange.fr/HTML/Livres.htm; f. 1998; French-Creole children's and youth literature.

Ibis Rouge Editions: chemin de la Levée, BP 267, 97357 Matoury Cédex; tel. 5-94-35-95-66; fax 5-94-35-95-68; e-mail jlm@ibisrouge.fr; internet www.ibisrouge.fr; f. 1995; general literature, French-Creole, and academic; Publr JEAN-LOUIS MALHERBE; agencies in Guadeloupe and Martinique.

PUBLISHERS' ASSOCIATION

Promolivres Guyane: BP 96, 97394 Rémire-Montjoly Cédex; tel. 5-94-29-55-56; fax 5-94-38-52-82; e-mail promolivreguyane@wanadoo.fr; f. 1996; asscn mems incl. editors, booksellers, journalists and librarians; promotes French Guianese literature; Pres. TCHISSÉKA LOBELT.

Broadcasting and Communications

TELECOMMUNICATIONS

Caribsat Guyane: 2 blvd de la République, 97300 Cayenne; tel. 5-94-29-74-06; e-mail guyane@caribsat.fr; internet www.caribsat.fr; satellite broadband provider.

Digicel Antilles Françaises et Guyane: see Martinique—Telecommunications; Dir-Gen. FRANCK ROGIER.

France Telecom: 76 ave Voltaire, BP 8080, 97300 Cayenne; tel. 5-94-39-91-15; fax 5-94-39-91-00; e-mail eline.miranda@francetelecom.com.

Orange Caraïbe: see Guadeloupe—Telecommunications.

Outremer Telecom: 112 ave du Général de Gaulle, 97300 Cayenne; tel. 5-94-28-71-15; fax 5-94-23-93-59; e-mail communication@outremer-telecom.fr; internet www.outremer-telecom.fr; f. 1998; mobile telecommunications provider; Group CEO JEAN-MICHEL HEGESIPPE.

ONLY: 112 ave du Général de Gaulle, 97300 Cayenne; tel. 5-94-28-71-15; fax 5-94-23-93-59; e-mail contact@outremer-telecom.fr; internet www.only.fr; f. 2004 as Outremer Telecom Guyane; subsidiary of Outremer Telecom, France; present name adopted following merger of Volubis, ONLY and OOL in 2006; mobile and fixed telecommunications provider

BROADCASTING

Guyane 1ère (Outre-mer Première): France Télévisions, blvd du Docteur Lama, 97354 Rémire-Montjoly; tel. 5-94-25-67-00; fax 5-94-30-26-49; internet guyane.la1ere.fr; acquired by Groupe France Télévisions in 2004; fmrly Société Nationale de Radio-Télévision Française d'Outre-mer, name changed to Réseau France Outre-mer (RFO) in 1998; present name adopted in 2010; radio and TV; Regional Dir FRED AYANGMA.

Radio

KFM Guyane: 6 rue François Arago, 97300 Cayenne; tel. 5-94-31-30-38; fax 5-94-37-84-20; internet www.kfmguyane.skyrock.com; f. 1993 as Radio Kikiwi; present name adopted 2003.

Métis FM: Cayenne; internet www.metis.fm; popular music station.

Mig FM Guyane: 100 ave du Général de Gaulle, 97300 Cayenne; tel. 5-94-30-77-67; fax 5-94-31-86-81; f. 1995; Creole.

NRJ Guyane: 2 blvd de la République, 97300 Cayenne; tel. 5-94-39-54-88; fax 5-94-39-54-79; e-mail wladimir@nrjguyane.com; internet www.nrjguyane.com; f. 2006; commercial station; Man MARC HO-A-CHUCK.

Ouest FM Guyane: Cayenne; tel. 5-94-38-29-19; e-mail contact@ouestfm.net; internet www.ouestfm.net; commercial music station.

Radio Joie de Vivre: 39 rue Schoëlcher, 97324 Cayenne Cédex; BP 169, 97300 Cayenne; tel. 5-94-31-29-00; fax 5-94-29-47-26; f. 1993; operated by the Seventh-day Adventist church; Gen. Man. ESAÏE AUGUSTE.

Radio Littoméga (RLM): 24 blvd Malouet, BP 108, 97320 Saint-Laurent-du-Maroni; tel. 5-94-34-22-09; e-mail centre.cl@wanadoo.fr; internet www.rlm100.com; f. 1994; Dir ARIELLE BERTRAND.

Radio Saint-Gabriel: Salle Paul VI, Cité Mirza, 97300 Cayenne; tel. 5-94-31-17-11; fax 5-94-28-17-51; e-mail radiosaintgabriel@wanadoo.fr; f. 2001; Roman Catholic; Man. HENRI-CLAUDE ASSÉLOS.

Radio UDL (Union de la Défense des Libertés): 7 rue Félix Eboué, BP 5, 97393 Saint-Laurent-du-Maroni; tel. 5-94-34-27-90; fax 5-94-34-04-78; e-mail radio.udl@wanadoo.fr; internet www.udlradio.com; f. 1982; Man. JEAN GONTRAND.

Radio Voix dans le Désert: 5 chemin du Château, 97300 Cayenne; tel. 5-94-31-73-95; fax 5-73-76-88-00; e-mail president@rvld.fr; internet www.rvld.fr; f. 1993; operated by the Assembly of God church; Pres. EDDY LAUTRIC.

Television

Antenne Créole Guyane: 31 ave Louis Pasteur, 97300 Cayenne; tel. 5-94-28-82-88; fax 5-94-29-13-08; e-mail acg@acg.gf; internet www.acg.gf; f. 1994; sole local private TV station; gen. interest with focus on music and sports; produces 30% of own programmes; received by 95% of the population, accounting for 25% of viewers (2003); Pres. MARC HO-A-CHUCK; Gen. Man. WLADIMIR MANGACHOFF.

Canal+ Guyane: 14 Lotissement Marengo, Z. I. de Collery, 97300 Cayenne; tel. 8-10-50-15-02; fax 5-94-30-53-35; internet www.canalplus-caraibes.com/guyane; f. 1996; subsidiary of Groupe Canal+, France; satellite TV station; Dir OLEG BACCOVICH.

Finance

(cap. = capital; res = reserves; dep. = deposits; m. = million; brs = branches)

BANKING

Central Bank

Institut d'Emission des Départements d'Outre-mer (IEDOM): 8 rue Christophe Colomb, BP 6016, 97306 Cayenne Cédex; tel. 5-94-29-36-50; fax 5-94-30-02-76; e-mail direction@iedom-guyane.fr; internet www.iedom.fr; f. 1959; Dir FABRICE DUFRESNE.

Commercial Banks

Banque Française Commerciale Antilles-Guyane (BFC Antilles-Guyane): 8 pl. des Palmistes, BP 111, 97345 Cayenne; tel. 5-94-29-11-11; fax 5-94-30-13-12; e-mail service-client@bfc-ag.com; internet www.bfc-ag.com; f. 1985; Pres. CHRISTIAN DUVILLET.

BNP Paribas Guyane SA: 2 pl. Victor Schoëlcher, BP 35, 97300 Cayenne; tel. 5-94-39-63-00; fax 5-94-30-23-08; e-mail bnpg@bnpparibas.com; internet www.bnpparibas.com; f. 1964 following purchase of BNP Guyane (f. 1855); name changed 2000; 94% owned by BNP Paribas SA, 3% by BNP Paribas Martinique and 3% by BNP Paribas Guadeloupe; Dir and CEO YVES LELEU; Gen. Sec. GILLES TROY; 2 brs.

Crédit Agricole: see Martinique—Finance.

Development Bank

Société Financière pour le Développement Economique de la Guyane (SOFIDEG): PK 3, 700 route de Baduel, BP 860, 97339 Cayenne Cédex; tel. 5-94-29-94-29; fax 5-94-30-60-44; e-mail sofideg@nplus.gf; f. 1982; bought from the Agence Française de Développement (AFD—q.v.) by BRED-BP in 2003; Dir FRANÇOIS CHEVILLOTTE.

Insurance

Allianz IARD: 34 rue Léopold Heder, BP 462, 97300 Cayenne Cédex; tel. 5-94-30-27-66; fax 5-94-30-69-09; e-mail agfguyana@wanadoo.fr; internet www.allianz.fr; life and short-term insurance; Dir (Latin America) Dr HELGA JUNG.

Groupama Antilles Guyane: see Martinique—Insurance.

Trade and Industry

GOVERNMENT AGENCIES

Direction de l'Agriculture et de la Forêt (DAF): Parc Rebard, BP 5002, 97305 Cayenne Cédex; tel. 5-94-29-63-74; fax 5-94-29-63-63; e-mail daf.guyane@agriculture.gouv.fr; internet daf.guyane.agriculture.gouv.fr; Dir FRANÇOIS CAZOTTES.

Direction Régionale et Départementale des Affaires Maritimes (DRAM): 2 bis, rue Mentel, BP 6008, 97300 Cayenne Cédex; tel. 5-94-29-36-15; fax 5-94-29-36-16; e-mail Dram-Guyane@developpement-durable.gouv.fr; responsible for shipping, fishing and other maritime issues at nat. and community level; Dir STÉPHANE GATTO.

Direction Régionale de l'Industrie, de la Recherche et de l'Environnement (DRIRE): Pointe Buzaré, BP 7001, 97307 Cayenne Cédex; tel. 5-94-29-75-30; fax 5-94-29-07-34; e-mail drire-antilles-guyane@industrie.gouv.fr; internet www.ggm.drire.gouv.fr; active in industry, business services, transport, public works, tourism and distribution; Regional Dir JOEL DURANTON.

DEVELOPMENT ORGANIZATIONS

Agence de l'Environnement et de la Maîtrise de l'Energie (ADEME): 28 ave Léopold Heder, 97300 Cayenne Cédex; tel. 5-94-

31-73-60; fax 5-94-30-76-69; e-mail ademe.guyane@ademe.fr; internet www.ademe-guyane.fr; Dir SUZANNE PONS.

Agence Française de Développement (AFD): Lotissement les Héliconias, route de Baduel, BP 1122, 97345 Cayenne Cédex; tel. 5-94-29-90-90; fax 5-94-30-63-32; e-mail afdcayenne@afd.fr; internet www.afd-guyane.org; fmrly Caisse Française de Développement; Dir ROBERT SATGE.

Agence Régionale de Développement Économique de la Guyane (ARD): 1 pl. Schoëlcher, BP 325, 97325 Cayenne Cédex; tel. 5-94-25-66-66; fax 5-94-25-43-19; e-mail ard .guyane-developpement@wanadoo.fr; f. 2009 to replace Agence pour la Création et le Développement des Entreprises en Guyane; Pres. CAROL OSTORERO; Dir PASCAL VELINORE.

Fédération des Organisations Amérindiennes de Guyane (FOAG): Centre des Cultures, rue Capt. Charles Claude, 97319 Awala Yalirnapo; tel. 6-94-42-27-76; fax 5-94-33-50-06; e-mail foag@ nplus.gf; f. 1993; civil liberties org. representing the rights of the indigenous peoples of French Guiana; Pres. Chief JEAN AUBÉRIC CHARLES.

CHAMBERS OF COMMERCE

Chambre d'Agriculture: 8 ave du Général de Gaulle, BP 544, 97333 Cayenne Cédex; tel. 5-94-29-61-95; fax 5-94-31-00-01; e-mail chambre.agriculture.973@wanadoo.fr; internet www .chambres-agriculture.fr; Pres. CHRISTIAN EPAILLY; Dir THIERRY BASSO.

Chambre de Commerce et d'Industrie de la Guyane (CCIG): Hôtel Consulaire, pl. de l'Esplanade, BP 49, 97321 Cayenne Cédex; tel. 5-94-29-96-00; fax 5-94-29-96-34; e-mail contact@guyane.cci.fr; internet www.guyane.cci.fr; Pres. JEAN-PAUL LE PELLETIER.

Chambre de Métiers: 41 Lotissement, Artisanal Zone Galmot, 97300 Cayenne Cédex; tel. 5-94-25-24-70; fax 5-94-30-54-22; e-mail m.toulemonde@cm-guyane.fr; internet www.cm-guyane.fr; Pres. HARRY CONTOUT; Sec.-Gen. FRANCELINE MATHIAS-DANIEL.

Jeune Chambre Economique de Cayenne: 1 Cité A. Horth, route de Montabo, BP 1094, Cayenne; tel. 5-94-31-62-99; fax 5-94-31-76-13; internet www.jcicayenne.com; f. 1960; Pres. YÂSIMÍN VAUTOR; Gen. Sec. ANGÉLIQUE BOURGEOIS.

EMPLOYERS' ORGANIZATIONS

Groupement Régional des Agriculteurs de Guyane (GRAGE): PK 15 route nationale 1, Domaine de Soula, 97355 Macouria; tel. 5-94-38-71-26; e-mail 973@confederationpaysanne.fr; internet www .grage.gf; affiliated to the Confédération Paysanne; Pres. SYLVIE HORTH.

MEDEF Guyane: 27A Résidence Gustave Stanislas, Source de Baduel, BP 820, 97338 Cayenne Cédex; tel. 5-94-31-17-71; fax 5-94-30-32-13; e-mail updg@nplus.gf; internet medefguyane.fr; f. 2005; fmrly Union des Entreprises de Guyane; Pres. ALAIN CHAUMET.

Ordre des Pharmaciens du Département Guyane: 7 ave du Général de Gaulle, 97300 Cayenne; tel. 5-94-32-17-62; fax 5-94-32-17-66; e-mail delegation_guyane@ordre.pharmacien.fr; internet www.ordre.pharmacien.fr; Pres. ALINE ABAUL-BALUSTRE.

Syndicat des Transformateurs du Bois de Guyane (STBG): Menuisserie Cabassou, PK 4.5, route de Cabassou, 97354 Remire-Montjoly; tel. 5-94-31-34-49; fax 5-94-35-10-51; f. 2002; represents artisans using wood; Pres. YVES ELISE; Sec. FRANÇOIS AUGER.

UTILITIES
Electricity

EDF Guyane: blvd Jubelin, BP 6002, 97306 Cayenne; tel. 5-94-39-64-00; fax 5-94-30-10-81; internet guyane.edf.com; electricity producer; Dir JEAN-PHILIPPE BLAVA.

Water

Société Guyanaise des Eaux: 2738 route de Montabo, BP 5027, 97306 Cayenne Cédex; tel. 5-94-25-59-26; fax 5-94-30-59-60; internet www.suez-environnement.fr; f. 1978; CEO JEAN-LOUIS CHAUSSADE; Gen. Man. RODOLPHE LELIEVRE.

TRADE UNIONS

Centrale Démocratique des Travailleurs Guyanais (CDTG): 99–100 Cité Césaire, BP 383, 97328 Cayenne Cédex; tel. 5-94-31-02-32; fax 5-94-31-81-05; e-mail sg.cdtg@wanadoo.fr; internet cdtg-guyane.com; affiliated to the Confédération Française Démocratique du Travail; Sec.-Gen. GÉRARD FAUBERT.

Fédération Syndicale Unitaire Guyane (FSU): Mont Lucas, Bâtiment G, No C37, 97300 Cayenne; tel. 5-94-30-05-69; fax 5-94-38-36-58; e-mail fsu973@fsu.fr; f. 1993; departmental br. of the Fédération Syndicale Unitaire; represents public sector employees

in teaching, research and training, agriculture, justice, youth, sports and culture; Sec. ALAIN BRAVO.

Union Départementale Confédération Française des Travailleurs Chrétiens Guyane (UD CFTC): 19 lot Gibelin 1, BP 763, 97351 Matoury Cédex; tel. 5-94-35-63-14; fax 5-94-90-59-05; e-mail lydie.leneveu@wanadoo.fr; Sec. LYDIE LENEVEU.

Transport

RAILWAYS

There are no railways in French Guiana.

ROADS

In 2004 there were 1,300 km (808 miles) of roads in French Guiana, of which 397 km were main roads. Much of the network is concentrated along the coast.

SHIPPING

Grand Port Maritime de Guyane at Dégrad-des-Cannes, on the estuary of the river Mahury, is the principal port, handling the majority of maritime traffic. There are other ports at Le Larivot, Saint-Laurent-du-Maroni and Kourou. Saint-Laurent is used primarily for the export of timber, and Le Larivot for fishing vessels. There are river ports on the Oiapoque and on the Approuague. There is a ferry service across the Maroni river between Saint-Laurent and Albina, Suriname. The rivers provide the best means of access to the interior, although numerous rapids prevent navigation by large vessels. A bridge across the Oyapock river, linking the cities of Oiapoque in Brazil and Saint-Georges de l'Oyapock in French Guiana, was completed in 2011. In December 2014 French Guiana's flag registered fleet comprised two vessels, with an aggregate displacement of some 3,881 grt.

Compagnie Maritime Marfret: Immeuble Face Scierie Patoz, Z. I. Degrad-des-Cannes, 97354 Rémire-Montjoly; tel. 5-94-31-04-04; fax 5-94-35-18-44; e-mail jccelse@marfret.fr; internet www .marfret.fr; Gen. Man. JEAN-CHRISTIAN CELSE-L'HOSTE.

Grand Port Maritime de Guyane: Z. I. de Dégrad-des-Cannes, Rémire-Montjoly, 97354 Cayenne Cédex; tel. 5-94-35-44-90; f. 1974 as Port International Dégrad-des-Cannes; under management of Chambre de Commerce et de l'Industrie de la Guyane 1988–2012; publicly owned since 2013.

SOMARIG (Société Maritime et Industrielle de la Guyane): Z. I. de Dégrad-des-Cannes, Rémire-Montjoly, BP 81, 97354 Cayenne Cédex; tel. 5-94-35-42-00; fax 5-94-35-53-44; e-mail cay.genmbox@ cma-cgm.com; internet www.cma-cgm.com; f. 1960; owned by Groupe CMA—GGM (France); Man. Dir HERVÉ ROUCHON.

CIVIL AVIATION

Rochambeau International Airport, situated 17.5 km (11 miles) from Cayenne, is equipped to handle the largest jet aircraft. There are also airports at Maripasoula, Saul and Saint Georges. Access to remote inland areas is frequently by helicopter.

Air Guyane: Aéroport de Rochambeau, 97300 Matoury; tel. 5-94-29-36-30; fax 5-94-30-54-37; e-mail reservations@airguyane.com; internet www.airguyane.com; f. 1980; 46% owned by Guyane Aéro Invest, 20% owned by Sodetraguy; operates domestic services; Pres. CHRISTIAN MARCHAND.

Tourism

The main attractions are the natural beauty of the tropical scenery and the Amerindian villages of the interior. In 2005 there were 27 hotels with 1,184 rooms. Receipts from tourism in 2007 were US $49m. while in 2009 tourist arrivals totalled an estimated 83,000.

Comité du Tourisme de la Guyane: 12 rue Lallouette, BP 801, 97338 Cayenne Cédex; tel. 5-94-29-65-00; fax 5-94-29-65-01; e-mail ctginfo@tourisme-guyane.com; internet www.tourisme-guyane .com; Pres. SYLVIE DESERT; Dir-Gen. ERIC MADELEINE.

Délégation Régionale au Tourisme, au Commerce et à l'Artisanat pour la Guyane: 9 rue Louis Blanc, BP 7008, 97300 Cayenne Cédex; tel. 5-94-28-92-90; fax 5-94-31-01-04; e-mail 973.pole3e@ dieccte.gouv.fr; Delegate DIDIER BIRONNEAU (acting).

L'Ensemble Culturel Régional (ENCRE): 82 ave du Général de Gaulle, BP 6007, 97306 Cayenne Cédex; tel. 5-94-28-94-00; fax 5-94-28-94-04; e-mail encre.crg@wanadoo.fr; f. 2004 by merger of Ecole Nationale de Musique et de Danse and Office Culturel de la Région Guyane; fmrly Asscn Régionale de Développement Culturel; Pres. ANTOINE KARAM.

Fédération des Offices du Tourisme et Syndicat d'Initiative de la Guyane (FOTSIG): 12 rue Lallouette, BP 702, 97301 Cayenne; tel. 5-94-30-96-29; fax 5-94-31-23-41; e-mail frguyane@fnotsi .net; Pres. JULIETTE GOUSSET.

Defence

As assessed at November 2014, France maintained a military force of 2,150 in French Guiana, including a gendarmerie. The headquarters is in Cayenne.

Education

Education is modelled on the French system and is compulsory and free for children between six and 16 years of age. Primary education begins at six years of age and lasts for five years. Secondary education, beginning at 11 years of age, lasts for up to seven years, comprising a first cycle of four years and a second of three years.

In 2013/14 there were 43 pre-primary schools, 121 primary schools and 47 secondary schools. In the same period there were 43,228 students in pre-primary and primary education, while in secondary education there were 32,966 students, of whom some 93% were educated in the state sector. Higher education in law, administration, French language and literature and teacher training is provided by a branch of the Université des Antilles et de la Guyane in Cayenne, although in 2013 French Guiana withdrew from participation in this regional university; a new Université de la Guyane was to be established. There is also a technical institute at Kourou and an agricultural college. In 2012/13 some 3,434 students were enrolled in higher education in French Guiana.

GUADELOUPE

Introductory Survey

LOCATION, CLIMATE, LANGUAGE, RELIGION, CAPITAL

Guadeloupe is the most northerly of the Windward Islands group in the West Indies. Dominica lies to the south, and Antigua and Montserrat to the north-west. Guadeloupe is formed by two large islands, Grande-Terre and Basse-Terre, separated by a narrow sea channel (but linked by a bridge), with a smaller island, Marie-Galante, to the south-east, and another, La Désirade, to the east. The climate is tropical, with an average temperature of 26°C (79°F), and a more humid and wet season between June and November. French is the official language, but a Creole patois is widely spoken. The majority of the population profess Christianity, and belong to the Roman Catholic Church. The capital is the town of Basse-Terre; the other main town and the principal commercial centre is Pointe-à-Pitre, on Grande-Terre.

CONTEMPORARY POLITICAL HISTORY

Historical Context

Guadeloupe was first occupied by the French in 1635, and has remained French territory, apart from a number of brief occupations by the British in the 18th and early 19th centuries. It gained departmental status in 1946.

Domestic Political Affairs

The deterioration of the economy provoked industrial and political unrest during the 1960s and 1970s, including outbreaks of serious rioting in 1967. Pro-independence parties (which had rarely won more than 5% of the total vote at elections in Guadeloupe) resorted, in some cases, to violence as a means of expressing their opposition to the economic and political dominance of white, pro-French landowners and government officials. In 1980 and 1981 there was a series of bomb attacks on hotels, government offices and other targets by a group called the Groupe de Libération Armée, and in 1983 and 1984 there were further bombings by a group styling itself the Alliance Révolutionnaire Caraïbe (ARC). Further sporadic acts of violence continued in 1985–88.

In 1974 Guadeloupe was granted the status of a Region, and an indirectly elected Conseil Régional (Regional Council) was formed. In direct elections to a new Regional Council in 1983 the centre-right coalition succeeded in gaining a majority of the seats and control of the administration. In 1984 Lucette Michaux-Chevry, the President of the Conseil Général (General Council), formed a new conservative centre party, Le Parti de la Guadeloupe, which remained in alliance with the right-wing Rassemblement pour la République (RPR). However, at the election for the General Council held in 1985, the left-wing combination of the Parti Socialiste (PS) and the Parti Communiste Guadeloupéen (PCG) gained a majority of seats on the enlarged Council, and the PS leader, Dominique Larifla, was elected its President. In July demonstrations and a general strike, organized by pro-separatist activists in order to obtain the release of a leading member of the Mouvement Populaire pour une Guadeloupe Indépendante, quickly intensified into civil disorder and rioting in the main commercial centre, Pointe-à-Pitre.

In elections to the Regional Council in 1986, the two left-wing parties together won a majority of seats. Félix Proto of the PS assumed the presidency of the Council. The left-wing parties also won a majority of seats at the election to the General Council in the same year, and Larifla was re-elected President of the Council.

In April 1989 the separatist Union Populaire pour la Libération de la Guadeloupe (UPLG) organized protests in Port Louis to demand the release of 'political prisoners', which led to violent clashes with the police. A number of activists of the now disbanded ARC staged a hunger strike while awaiting trial in Paris, accused in connection with politically motivated offences. Anti-Government demonstrations took place in the following month. In June the Assemblée Nationale (National Assembly) approved legislation granting an amnesty for crimes that had taken place before July 1988, and that were intended to undermine the authority of the French Republic in the Overseas Departments. The agreement of those seeking greater independence in Guadeloupe to work within the democratic framework had gained parliamentary support for the amnesty. In March 1990 the UPLG declared that it would henceforth participate in elections, and would seek associated status (rather than full independence) for Guadeloupe.

In March 1992 concurrent elections were held to the General Council and the Regional Council. Larifla was re-elected as President of the former, despite his refusal to contest as part of the local official PS list of candidates. In the election to the Regional Council the official PS list (headed by Frédéric Jalton) secured nine seats and the dissident PS members seven. Former members of the PCG, who had formed a new organization, the Parti Progressiste Démocratique Guadeloupéen (PPDG), won five seats. The RPR, the centre-right Union pour la Démocratie Française (UDF) and other right-wing candidates formed an electoral alliance, Objectif Guadeloupe, to contest the elections, together securing 15 of the 41 seats in the Regional Council. Jalton's refusal to reach an agreement with the dissident PS members prompted Larifla's list to support the presidential candidacy of Michaux-Chevry. Thus, despite an overall left-wing majority in the Regional Council, the right-wing Michaux-Chevry was elected as President. In December, however, the French Council of State declared the election to the Regional Council invalid, owing to the failure of Larifla's list to pay a registration deposit. Other heads of lists were subsequently found to have submitted incomplete documents to the election commission. Fresh elections took place in January 1994, at which Objectif Guadeloupe took 22 seats, while the PS and dissident PS retained a total of only 10 seats.

In a referendum in September 1992 some 68% of voters in Guadeloupe endorsed ratification of the Treaty on European Union (see p. 271).

The persistence of divisions between the socialists was evident at the 1993 election to the National Assembly. Michaux-Chevry was re-elected, as were Eric Moutoussamy (for the PPDG) and Jalton. Larifla, meanwhile, was defeated by Edouard Chammougon, a candidate of the independent right. The left retained control of the General Council following cantonal elections in 1994. Larifla was subsequently re-elected President of the Council.

Michaux-Chevry and Larifla were elected to the French Sénat (Senate) in September 1995; Philippe Chaulet of the RPR was subsequently elected to take Michaux-Chevry's seat in the National Assembly.

The RPR performed strongly in the election to the Regional Council in March 1998; Michaux-Chevry was re-elected President of the Council. The composition of the General Council remained largely unchanged following concurrent cantonal elections, although the RPR doubled its representation; Marcellin Lubeth, of the PPDG, was elected to the presidency, defeating Larifla.

Social and industrial unrest intensified in Guadeloupe in October 1999, prior to a two-day visit by Prime Minister Lionel Jospin. Demonstrations escalated into rioting in Pointe-à-Pitre, following the sentencing of Armand Toto—a leading member of the Union Générale des Travailleurs de la Guadeloupe (UGTG)—to four months' imprisonment for assaulting two policemen and threatening to kill another while occupying the premises of a motor vehicle company in support of a dismissed worker. Moreover, banana producers demonstrated around the port of Basse-Terre, demanding aid for the restructuring of their businesses as compensation for a significant decline in banana prices on the European market. Jospin announced an emergency plan for the banana sector.

Demands for further autonomy

In December 1999 the Presidents of the Regional Councils of French Guiana, Guadeloupe and Martinique signed a joint declaration in Basse-Terre, affirming their intention to propose a legislative amendment aimed at creating a new status of overseas region. The declaration, however, was dismissed by the Secretary of State for Overseas Departments and Territories, Jean-Jack Queyranne, in February 2000 as unconstitutional. Amended proposals regarding the institutional evolution of Guadeloupe were approved by the National Assembly in November, and in December they were ratified by the Constitutional Council.

Jacques Gillot of Guadeloupe Unie, Socialisme et Réalité (GUSR) secured the presidency of the General Council in the wake of the March 2001 municipal elections.

Following a meeting of members of the Regional Council and the General Council in June 2001, a series of administrative restructuring proposals was agreed upon. These included: the division of the territory into four districts; the creation of a Collectivité Territoriale (Territorial Collectivity), governed by a 41-member Assembly elected for a five-year term; and the establishment of an independent executive council. Furthermore, the proposals included a request that the territory be given control over legislative and administrative affairs, as well as legislative authority on matters concerning Guadeloupe alone. In March 2003 the French parliament approved constitutional changes that, *inter alia*, allowed for local referendums to be held on proposals for greater decentralization in overseas possessions. Under the changes, the Department of Guadeloupe was also designated an Région d'Outre-mer (Overseas Region). In the referendum, held in December, some 73% of participating voters rejected legislative reforms that envisaged the replacement of the General Council and the Regional Council with a single assembly, owing to fears that restructuring would lead to autonomy for the Department and the consequent loss of central government funding. However, at the referendums concurrently held in the dependencies of Saint-Barthélemy and Saint-Martin, a clear majority of voters in each commune (95.5% and 76.2%, respectively) were in favour of seceding from Guadeloupe to form separate Collectivités d'Outre-mer (Overseas Collectivities—q.v.). The reorganization was subsequently approved by the Senate on 6 February 2007 and by the National Assembly the following day. On 21 February Saint-Barthélemy and the French part of Saint-Martin were formally designated Overseas Collectivities. Following elections to their respective Conseils Territoriaux (Territorial Councils), held in July 2007, the two Overseas Collectivities acceded to administrative independence. Each Overseas Collectivity was to elect one representative to the Senate (in 2008) and one deputy to the National Assembly (in 2012); in the interim, they were to continue to be represented by Guadeloupean parliamentarians.

In June 2002 all four incumbent deputies were defeated in an election to the National Assembly; they were replaced by Gabrielle Louis-Carabin and Joël Beaugendre, both representing the Union pour la Majorité Présidentielle (UMP), a right-wing alliance that included the Objectif Guadeloupe, Eric Jalton, also of a right-wing coalition, and Victorin Lurel of the PS. The RPR subsequently merged into the successor party to the UMP, Union pour un Mouvement Populaire (also known as the UMP).

At an election to the Regional Council in March 2004 the Guadeloupe pour Tous list, a coalition comprising the PS, the PPDG, the GUSR and other left-wing candidates, won a resounding victory. Lurel subsequently became President of the Regional Council.

In May 2005 a national referendum was held on ratification of the European Union constitutional treaty: some 58.6% of participating voters in the Department were in favour of adopting the treaty. The treaty was ultimately rejected by a majority of voters in metropolitan France.

Nicolas Sarkozy of the UMP won 43% of the votes cast in Guadeloupe in the first round of the 2007 national presidential election, ahead of PS candidate Ségolène Royal, who attracted 38%. Sarkozy emerged victorious in the second round, winning 49% of the vote in the Department. At elections to the National Assembly, held on 10 and 17 June, Gabrielle Louis-Carabin of the UMP, Lurel of the PS and Eric Jalton of the PCG were re-elected, while Jeanny Marc-Matthiasin of the GUSR was also successful. At municipal elections held in March 2008 the PS and GUSR retained control of the General Council, and Gillot was subsequently re-elected as its President.

Internal unrest

From January 2009 the island suffered overwhelming disruption as a result of a general strike organized by Lyannaj Kont Pwofitasyon (LKP—League against Profiteering), an alliance of 47 trade unions, political parties and other associations, over the rising cost of living. Violent protests continued throughout February, and military police from metropolitan France were deployed in order to restore order.

The 44-day strike ended in March and businesses began to reopen after a deal was agreed between the unions, the local authorities and employers' representatives, involving widespread measures to improve living standards. However, a further LKP-led demonstration, attended by over 1,000 protesters, was organized to coincide with the visit of President Sarkozy to the archipelago in June. During his visit Sarkozy proposed a referendum on the issue of increased autonomy for Guadeloupe. Although the Guadeloupean authorities rejected the proposal (unlike French Guiana and Martinique), they were given 18 months in which to hold consultations and to propose a formula for the reform of territorial institutions. Legislation was adopted by the French National Assembly in November 2010 that decreed the implementation of institutional reform in all the Overseas Departments and Regions (as well as in metropolitan France) by 2014 (although this was later delayed). Further legislation in July 2011 approved a reduction in the number of members of the territory's Regional and General Councils.

Local and national elections

In an election to the Regional Council held in March 2010, the PS-led list, Tous pour la Guadeloupe, secured an overwhelming victory in the first round of voting, with 56.5% of the ballot, gaining 31 of the 41 council seats. The UMP alliance, Ensemble pour la Guadeloupe, and the left-wing Région Autrement obtained four seats each, with 14.0% and 12.4% of the votes cast, respectively, while the Pou Gwadloup an nou ay list took the remaining two seats with 7.0% of the ballot. Lurel was re-elected as President of the Regional Council. The rate of participation by the electorate was 49.8%. Left-wing candidates performed strongly in the municipal polls conducted on 20 and 27 March 2011, and Gillot was subsequently re-elected as President of the General Council. Gillot was also re-elected to the Senate on 25 September, while Felix Desplan of the PS and Jacques Cornano, a left-wing independent, secured the territory's other two senate seats. Meanwhile, in August Amaury de Saint-Quentin was appointed as Prefect.

The first round of the French presidential election was conducted on 21 April 2012 (one day earlier than in mainland France): François Hollande, representing the PS, attracted 57.0% of the territory's votes, compared with 23.4% for Sarkozy. A run-off election was held two weeks later, at which Hollande secured 71.9% of the ballot in the region, defeating Sarkozy, who attracted 28.1%. Hollande also triumphed nationally and was sworn in as President in mid-May. Lurel was notably appointed as Minister of Overseas Territories in Hollande's new cabinet. In legislative elections, which took place in June, Lurel, Jalton and Louis-Carabin were re-elected to the National Assembly, while the territory's remaining mandate was won by Ary Chalus, an independent left-wing candidate. Since Lurel had accepted a position in the Council of Ministers, he was replaced in the legislature by his alternate, Hélène Vainqueur-Christophe of the PS, and in August he was succeeded as President of the Regional Council by Josette Borel-Lincertin (also a member of the PS). Marcelle Pierrot became the islands' new Prefect in January 2013.

Economic unrest

Lurel returned to Guadeloupe in September 2012 to hold discussions with business and labour organizations regarding the high cost of living in the territory. Proposed legislation to address the problem of inflated prices (and consequent social unrest) in Guadeloupe and other French Overseas Possessions, drafted by Lurel, was approved by the French Parliament in November. Most notably, the legislation provided for the imposition of price controls on a range of staple goods and the introduction of measures to encourage competition. In December 2013 the French Government extended the price controls to cover petrol purchases in the French Overseas Regions and Departments. However, on multiple occasions between mid-2013 and early 2014, owners of petrol stations in Guadeloupe, French Guiana, Martinique, Mayotte and Réunion, fearing that the move would disrupt their business model and undermine profit margins, closed their establishments in a co-ordinated act of protest. The closures ended in February 2014 after a compromise was agreed with the French authorities.

Recent developments: 2014 and 2015 elections

Candidates representing left-wing lists comfortably won the most council seats in municipal polls conducted on 23 and 30 March 2014. Turnout in the respective rounds was 61.4% and 67.4%. Lurel returned to Guadeloupe in April after losing his place in the Council of Ministers. Borel-Lincertin resigned as President of the Regional Council later that month, and on 2 May Lurel was elected Council President. Shortly thereafter, he also reassumed his former duties as a deputy in the National Assembly, replacing Vainqueur-Christophe. Elections to the European Parliament took place in Guadeloupe on 25 May. The UMP secured 28.2% of the local ballot, compared with 23.7% for the left-wing Choisir Notre Europe. However, the rate of participation by the electorate was just 9.3%. Pierrot was succeeded as Prefect by Jacques Billant in December. Departmental elections were held on 22 and 29 March 2015. Following these elections, the

General Council was renamed the Departmental Council (according to national legislation adopted in May 2013). The PS won a majority (20) of the 42 seats on the new Departmental Council, followed by various parties of the left, with 18 seats. Elections to the Regional Council were scheduled to be held in December.

Preliminary structural reform proposals were approved by the National Assembly in July 2014 and by the Senate in October. It was envisaged that, *inter alia*, many of the powers of the General Council (known as a Departmental Council from March 2015) would be transferred to the Regional Council (and the municipal councils), potentially leading to the eventual dissolution of the former. Proponents argued that these measures would increase administrative efficiency and reduce costs.

CONSTITUTION AND GOVERNMENT

France is represented in Guadeloupe by an appointed prefect. There are two councils with local powers: the 42-member Conseil Départemental (Departmental Council) and the 41-member Conseil Régional (Regional Council). Both are elected by universal adult suffrage for a period of up to six years. Guadeloupe elects four deputies to the National Assembly in Paris, and sends three indirectly elected representatives to the Senate. The Department is also represented at the European Parliament.

REGIONAL AND INTERNATIONAL CO-OPERATION

Guadeloupe (along with Martinique) was formally admitted to the Association of Caribbean States (see p. 444) as an associate member in April 2014. The territory was also seeking the same status within the Organisation of Eastern Caribbean States (OECS, see p. 463) and the Caribbean Community and Common Market (CARICOM, see p. 222).

ECONOMIC AFFAIRS

In 2012, according to official estimates, Guadeloupe's gross domestic product (GDP), measured at current prices, was €8,033m., equivalent to €19,593 per head. During 1993–2008 GDP increased, in real terms, at an average annual rate of 3.1%. Between the censuses of 2000 and 2011, according to provisional figures, the population increased at an average annual rate of 0.3%. GDP grew by 2.1% in 2012.

Agriculture, hunting, forestry and fishing contributed an estimated 2.8% of GDP in 2010 and engaged an estimated 1.5% of the employed population in 2012. In 2013, according to provisional official figures, agricultural produce (including that related to agrarian production and food industries) accounted for 37.7% of exports. The principal crops are bananas, sugar cane, cassava and potatoes. Fishing, mostly at an artisanal level, fulfils about two-thirds of domestic requirements, and there is some shrimp farming. According to UN estimates, agricultural GDP decreased at an average annual rate of 0.3% in 1990–98; the sector increased by 4.1% in 1998.

The industrial sector (including mining, manufacturing, construction, power and food industries) contributed an estimated 12.5% of GDP in 2010 and engaged an estimated 12.4% of the employed population in 2012. Construction contributed 7.7% of GDP in 2010 and engaged an estimated 5.4% of the working population in 2012. The main manufacturing activity is food processing, particularly sugar production, rum distillation, and flour-milling. The sugar industry declined in recent years, owing to deteriorating equipment and a reduction in the area planted with sugar cane (from 20,000 ha in 1980 to an estimated 10,650 ha in 2013). Sugar production totalled 39,275 metric tons in 2013, compared to 46,731 tons in 2012. Industrial GDP (excluding construction) increased at an average annual rate of 5.2% in 1990–98. Construction expanded at an average rate of 2.2% per year in the same period.

Of some 700,000 tons of petroleum imported annually, about one-third is used for the production of electricity. Efforts are currently being concentrated on the use of renewable energy resources—notably solar, geothermal and wind power—for energy production; there is also thought to be considerable potential for the use of bagasse (a by-product of sugar cane) as a means of generating energy. The 64 MW power plant at Le Moule produces some 400m. kWh of electricity annually—almost one-third of Guadeloupe's requirements—using a mixture of coal (75%) and bagasse (25%). Imports of fuels and combustibles accounted for a provisional 20.0% of total expenditure on imports in 2013. In that year Guadeloupe's total electricity production was 1,728m. kWh.

The services sector engaged an estimated 86.1% of the employed population in 2012 and provided an estimated 84.7% of GDP in 2010. Tourism is the Department's principal source of income, and there is significant potential for the further development of the sector, particularly eco-tourism. In 2013 tourist arrivals totalled some 487,416 and receipts from tourism amounted to US $671m. Almost three-quarters of arrivals (73.9%) came from metropolitan France in 2013.

In 2013 Guadeloupe recorded a merchandise trade deficit of some €2,482.9m., according to provisional figures. In that year the value of exports was €264.5m., about one-10th of the total value of imports,

which were worth €2,747.4m. The principal source of imports was metropolitan France (52.1% in 2008), which was also the principal market for exports (38.5%). The USA, Germany, and Trinidad and Tobago are also important trading partners. According to provisional official figures, the principal exports in 2013 were agricultural, fishing and food products, petroleum products, transport equipment, and mechanical and electrical equipment. The principal imports were petroleum products, mechanical and electrical equipment, agricultural, fishing and food products, transport equipment, and pharmaceutical products.

Guadeloupe's departmental budget was balanced at a preliminary €691.1m in 2014. The regional budget was also balanced at a preliminary €352.2m. in 2014. The annual rate of inflation averaged 1.9% in 2004–13. In 2013 the annual inflation rate was 0.9%. Some 22.9% of the labour force was unemployed in 2012.

Guadeloupe's location, small domestic market, and inflated labour and service costs have restricted economic growth. The banana sector was adversely affected by the end of the EU's quota system from 2006 and the gradual elimination of tariffs on non-European bananas from 2010. After contracting in 2009, the economy returned to growth in 2010, supported by higher levels of investment, domestic consumption and tourism activity. However, agricultural performance was undermined by unfavourable weather conditions, while ash from a volcanic eruption on the neighbouring island of Montserrat also caused significant damage to crops. In spite of strong export growth, an upturn in tourist spending and robust levels of domestic consumption, overall economic expansion slowed to 1.8% in 2011, owing mainly to a sharp deceleration in investment inflows. GDP growth improved in 2012 as the economy expanded by 2.1%. Nevertheless, the construction industry continued to struggle, while a slowdown in domestic demand and the high unemployment rate were further concerns. The tourism sector performed strongly in 2013 and trade levels rose during the year, but construction indicators remained negative, while household consumption decreased. Agricultural performance was variable, with a marked decline in sugar output, but an upturn in banana shipments. According to provisional data, GDP grew by 0.7% in 2013.

PUBLIC HOLIDAYS

2016: 1 January (New Year's Day), 8–9 February (Lenten Carnival), 10 February (Ash Wednesday), 25–28 March (Easter), 1 May (Labour Day), 5 May (Ascension Day), 8 May (Victory Day), 16 May (Whit Monday), 10 June (Abolition of Slavery), 14 July (National Day), 15 August (Assumption), 1 November (All Saints' Day), 11 November (Armistice Day), 25 December (Christmas Day).

Statistical Survey

Sources (unless otherwise indicated): Institut National de la Statistique et des Etudes Economiques (INSEE), Service Régional de la Guadeloupe, ave Paul Lacavé, BP 96, 97102 Basse-Terre; tel. 5-90-99-02-50; internet www.insee.fr/fr/regions/guadeloupe; Service de Presse et d'Information, Ministère des Départements et Territoires d'Outre-mer, 27 rue Oudinot, 75700 Paris 07 SP, France; tel. 1-53-69-20-00; fax 1-43-06-60-30; internet www.outre-mer.gouv.fr.

AREA AND POPULATION

(Note: In July 2007 Saint-Barthélemy and Saint-Martin seceded from Guadeloupe to become Overseas Collectivities.)

Area: 1,630 sq km (629.3 sq miles), comprising continental Guadeloupe 1,438 sq km (Basse-Terre à l'Ouest 848 sq km, Grande-Terre à l'Est 590 sq km) and dependencies 194 sq km (La Désirade 22 sq km, Iles des Saintes 14 sq km, Marie-Galante 158 sq km).

Population: 422,496 at census of 8 March 1999; 404,635 at census of 1 January 2011. Note: According to new census methodology, data in 2011 refer to median figures based on the collection of raw data over a five-year period (2009–13). *2013* (official estimate at 1 January): 405,739. *Mid-2015* (UN estimate): 470,168 (Source: UN, *World Population Prospects: The 2012 Revision*).

Density (at mid-2015): 288.4 per sq km.

Population by Age and Sex (UN estimates at mid-2015): *0–14 years:* 98,362 (males 50,162, females 48,200); *15–64 years:* 305,426 (males 142,877, females 162,549); *65 years and over:* 66,380 (males 28,215, females 38,165); *Total* 470,168 (males 221,254, females 248,914). Source: UN, *World Population Prospects: The 2012 Revision.*

Principal Towns (official population estimates at 1 January 2012): Les Abymes 58,606; Baie-Mahault 29,976; Le Gosier 26,613; Sainte-Anne 24,712; Petit Bourg 23,782; Le Moule 22,689; Sainte-Rose 20,379; Capesterre-Belle-Eau 19,407; Basse-Terre (capital) 11,534.

Births, Marriages and Deaths (2012): Registered live births 5,233 (birth rate 12,9 per 1,000); Registered marriages 1,291 (marriage rate 3.2 per 1,000); Registered deaths 2,873 (death rate 7.1 per 1,000).

Life Expectancy (years at birth): 81.2 (males 77.8, females 84.3) in 2014. Source: Pan American Health Organization.

Employment (persons aged 15 years and over, provisional estimates at 31 December 2012): Agriculture, forestry and fishing 1,740; Mining and water supply 2,041; Manufacturing 6,156; Construction 6,295; Wholesale and retail trade; repair of motor vehicles, motorcycles, etc. 14,852; Transport, storage and communication 7,617; Hotels and restaurants 4,698; Financial intermediation 3,274; Real estate, renting and business activities 11,509; Public administration, health and social work 51,593; Other community, social and personal service activities 7,605; *Total employed* 117,380. Note: Data exclude 6,189 persons employed without salary.

HEALTH AND WELFARE

Key Indicators

Total Fertility Rate (children per woman, 2014): 2.1.

Under-5 Mortality Rate (per 1,000 live births, 2011): 7.6.

Physicians (per 1,000 head, c. 2010): 2.6.

Hospital Beds (per 1,000 head, 2012): 5.5.

Access to Water (% of persons, 2012): 99.

Access to Sanitation (% of persons, 2012): 97.

Source: mainly Pan American Health Organization.

For other sources and definitions, see explanatory note on p. vi.

AGRICULTURE, ETC.

Principal Crops ('000 metric tons, 2013, FAO estimates): Sweet potatoes 1.8; Sugar cane 720.0; Cabbages and other brassicas 2.5; Lettuce and chicory 3.8; Tomatoes 5.0; Cucumbers and gherkins 5.5; Bananas 60.1; Plantains 8.2. *Aggregate Production* ('000 metric tons, may include official, semi-official or estimated data): Total roots and tubers 15.2; Total vegetables (incl. melons) 53.8; Total fruits (excl. melons) 86.1.

Livestock ('000 head, year ending September 2013, FAO estimates): Cattle 75.0; Chickens 300.

Livestock Products ('000 metric tons, 2013, FAO estimates): Cattle meat 3.0; Pig meat 1.5; Chicken meat 1.4; Hen eggs 2.0.

Forestry ('000 cu m, 2013, FAO estimates): *Roundwood Removals* (excl. bark): Sawlogs, veneer logs and logs for sleepers 0.3; Fuel wood 15.0; Total 15.3. *Sawnwood Production* (incl. railway sleepers): Total 1.0.

Fishing (metric tons, live weight, 2012, FAO estimates): Capture 11,100 (Common dolphinfish 780; Other mackerel-like fishes 1,750; Marine fishes 8,180; Stromboid conchs 225); Aquaculture 12; *Total catch* 11,112.

Source: FAO.

MINING

Production ('000 metric tons, 2010, estimates): Cement 230; Pumice 210; Salt 49. Source: US Geological Survey.

INDUSTRY

Production (2013): Sugar 39,275 metric tons; Rum 73,938 hl; Electric energy 1,728 million kWh. Source: Institut d'Emission des Départements d'Outre-mer, *Guadeloupe: Rapport Annuel 2013*.

FINANCE

Currency and Exchange Rates: The French franc was used until the end of February 2002. Euro notes and coins were introduced on 1 January 2002, and the euro became the sole legal tender from 18 February. Some of the figures in this Survey are still in terms of francs. For details of exchange rates, see French Guiana.

Budget (excl. debt rescheduling, € million, 2014, preliminary): *Regional Government:* Current revenue 270.6 (Taxes 187.6, Other current revenue 83.0); Capital revenues 81.6; Total 352.2. Current expenditure 211.8; Capital expenditure 140.4; Total 352.2. *Departmental Government:* Revenue 691.1 (Current revenue 633.9, Capital revenue 57.1); Expenditure 691.1 (Current expenditure 607.7, Capital expenditure 83.4). Source: Département des Etudes et des Statistiques Locales.

Money Supply (million French francs at 31 December 1996): Currency outside banks 1,148; Demand deposits at banks 6,187; Total money 7,335.

Cost of Living (Consumer Price Index; base: 2000 = 100): All items 125.1 in 2011; 127.5 in 2012; 128.6 in 2013. Source: ILO.

Expenditure on the Gross Domestic Product (€ million at current prices, 2012, estimates): Total final consumption expenditure 8,467 (General government and non-profit institutions serving households 3,572, Households 4,895); Gross fixed capital formation 1,419; *Total domestic expenditure* 9,886; Exports of goods and services 808; *Less* Imports of goods and services 2,686; Statistical discrepancy 25; *GDP in purchasers' values* 8,033. Source: Institut d'Emission des Départements d'Outre-mer, *Guadeloupe: Rapport Annuel 2013*.

Gross Domestic Product by Economic Activity (€ million at current prices, 2006): Agriculture, hunting, forestry and fishing 197; Food industries 87; Other manufacturing 265; Energy 37; Construction 713; Services 6,094 (Restaurants and hotels 253, Transport 249, Commerce 948, Other market services 2,269, Non-market services 2,375); *Sub-total* 7,393; Financial intermediation services indirectly measured (FISIM) –325; Import duties, less subsidies 690; *GDP in purchasers' values* 7,758.

EXTERNAL TRADE

Principal Commodities (€ million, 2013, provisional): *Imports c.i.f.:* Products of agriculture, fishing and food industries 463.6; Textiles, clothing, leather and footwear 123.4; Chemicals 126.7; Pharmaceutical products 154.4; Mineral products, rubber and plastic 141.5; Metal and metal products 164.0; Mechanical and electrical equipment 513.8; Transport equipment 237.3; Petroleum products 551.6; Miscellaneous manufactured goods 124.7; Total (incl. others) 2,747.4. *Exports f.o.b.:* Products of agriculture, fishing and food industries 99.7; Petroleum products 48.2; Chemicals 9.4; Mechanical and electrical equipment 25.8; Transport equipment 29.8; Metals and metallic products 9.4; Total (incl. others) 264.5. (Source: Institut d'Emission des Départements d'Outre-mer, *Guadeloupe: Rapport Annuel 2013*).

Principal Trading Partners (€ million, 2008): *Imports c.i.f.:* Aruba 98; China, People's Republic 87; France (metropolitan) 1,355; Germany 110; Italy 65; Martinique 210; Spain 40; USA 146; Total (incl. others) 2,601. *Exports f.o.b.:* France (metropolitan) 79; French Guiana 40; Germany 3; Martinique 44; Poland 5; Portugal 4; USA 4; Total (incl. others) 205. *2011* (€ million): Total imports 2,642.4; Total exports 234.8 (Source: Institut d'Emission des Départements d'Outre-mer, *Guadeloupe: Rapport Annuel 2011*). *2012* (€ million, provisional): Total imports 2,662.9; Total exports 216.1 (Source: Institut d'Emission des Départements d'Outre-mer, *Guadeloupe: Rapport Annuel 2012*). *2013* (€ million, provisional): Total imports 2,747.4; Total exports 264.5 (Source: Institut d'Emission des Départements d'Outre-mer, *Guadeloupe: Rapport Annuel 2013*).

TRANSPORT

Road Traffic ('000 motor vehicles in use, 2002): Passenger cars 117.7; Commercial vehicles 31.4 (Source: UN, *Statistical Yearbook*). *1 January 2010* ('000 commercial motor vehicles in use): Buses 0.8; Vans and trucks 39.6.

Shipping: *Flag Registered Fleet* (at 31 December 2014): Vessels 12; Total displacement 3,940 grt (Source: Lloyd's List Intelligence—www.lloydslistintelligence.com). *International Seaborne Traffic* (2010 unless otherwise indicated): Freight vessels entered 1,257 (1995); Freight vessels departed 1,253 (1995); Gross freight handled 3,156,160 metric tons; Containers handled 150,534 TEUs; Passengers carried 924,446 (2004).

Civil Aviation (2013): Aircraft movements 26,786; Freight carried (incl. post) 13,998 metric tons; Passengers carried 2,033,763. Source: Institut d'Emission des Départements d'Outre-mer, *Guadeloupe: Rapport Annuel 2013*.

TOURISM

Tourist Arrivals by Country (2013): Dominica 6,389; France 360,000; Germany 2,744; Guyana 23,963; Haiti 12,680; Italy 2,787; Switzerland 4,817; USA 14,128; Total (incl. others) 487,416.

Receipts from Tourism (US $ million, excl. passenger transport): 583 in 2011; n.a. in 2012; 671 in 2013.

Source: World Tourism Organization.

COMMUNICATIONS MEDIA

Telephones ('000 main lines in use): 255.7 in 2010.

Mobile Cellular Telephones ('000 subscribers): 314.7 in 2004.

Internet Users ('000): 109.0 in 2009.

Source: International Telecommunication Union.

EDUCATION

Pre-primary (2013/14): 131 institutions; 19,306 students (17,136 state, 2,170 private).

Primary (2013/14): 206 institutions; 35,278 students (31,207 state, 4,071 private).

Specialized Pre-primary and Primary (2013/14): 536 students (518 state, 18 private).

Secondary (2013/14): 94 institutions; 49,491 students (44,303 state, 5,188 private).

Higher (2012/13): 9,125 students.

Teachers (2007/08 unless otherwise indicated): *Primary:* 3,382 (3,139 state, 243 private); *Secondary:* 4,675 (4,223 state, 452 private); *Higher* (2004/05): 203 (Source: Ministère de l'Education Nationale, *Repères et références statistiques.*) *2012/13* (state schools): 2,931 in primary; 4,078 in secondary; 458 in higher.

Adult Literacy Rate: 90.1 (males 89.7; females 90.5) in 1998. Source: Pan American Health Organization.

Directory

The Government

(April 2015)

HEAD OF STATE

President: FRANÇOIS HOLLANDE.

Prefect: JACQUES BILLANT, Préfecture, Palais d'Orléans, rue Lardenoy, 97109 Basse-Terre Cédex; tel. 5-90-99-39-00; fax 5-90-81-58-32; e-mail webmestre@guadeloupe.pref.gouv.fr; internet www.guadeloupe.pref.gouv.fr.

DEPARTMENTAL ADMINISTRATION

President of the Departmental Council: Dr JOSETTE BOREL-LINGERTINE (PS), Hôtel du Département, blvd Félix Eboué, 97109 Basse-Terre; tel. 5-90-99-77-77; fax 5-90-99-76-00; e-mail info@cg971.fr; internet www.cg971.fr.

President of the Regional Council: VICTORIN LUREL (PS), 1 rue Paul Lacavé, Petit-Paris, 97109 Basse-Terre; tel. 5-90-80-40-40; fax 5-90-81-34-19; internet www.cr-guadeloupe.fr.

Elections, Departmental Council, 22 and 29 March 2015

	Seats
Parti Socialiste	20
Divers Gauche	18
Union pour un Mouvement Populaire	2
Divers Droit	2
Total	**42**

Elections, Regional Council, 14 and 21 March 2010

	Seats
Tous pour la Guadeloupe*	31
Ensemble pour la Guadeloupe†	4
Région Autrement‡	4
Pou Gwadloup an nou ay	2
Total	**41**

*Comprising the Parti Socialiste (PS) and other left-wing candidates.
†Comprising the Union pour un Mouvement Populaire (UMP) and other right-wing candidates.
‡Comprising smaller left-wing parties and dissident socialists.

REPRESENTATIVES TO THE FRENCH PARLIAMENT

Deputies to the French National Assembly: ERIC JALTON (Socialiste, Républicain et Citoyen), GABRIELLE LOUIS CARABIN (Socialiste, Républicain et Citoyen), ARY CHALUS (Radical, Républicain, Démocrate et Progressiste), VICTORIN LUREL (Socialiste, Républicain et Citoyen).

Representatives to the French Senate: JACQUES CORNANO (Groupe Socialiste), FÉLIX DESPLAN (Groupe Socialiste), JACQUES GILLOT (Groupe Socialiste).

GOVERNMENT OFFICES

Culture, Education and Environment Committee: 16 rue Peynier, 97100 Basse-Terre; tel. 5-90-41-05-15; fax 5-90-41-05-23; e-mail cr-cesr-guadeloupe@wanadoo.fr; internet www.cr-guadeloupe.fr; Pres. JEAN-JACQUES JÉRÉMIE.

European Affairs and Co-operation Committee: 16 rue Peynier, 97100 Basse-Terre; tel. 5-90-41-05-15; fax 5-90-41-05-23; e-mail cr-cesr-guadeloupe@wanadoo.fr; internet www.cr-guadeloupe.fr.

Regional Economic and Social Committee: 16 rue Peynier, 97100 Basse-Terre; tel. 5-90-41-05-15; fax 5-90-41-05-23; e-mail cr-cesr-guadeloupe@wanadoo.fr; internet www.cr-guadeloupe.fr.

Political Organizations

Combat Ouvrier: BP 213, 97156 Pointe-à-Pitre Cédex; tel. 5-90-26-23-58; e-mail menendez@wanadoo.fr; internet www.combat-ouvrier.net; Trotskyist; associated with national party Lutte Ouvrière; mem. of the Internationalist Communist Union; Leader JEAN-MARIE NOMERTIN.

Guadeloupe Unie, Socialisme et Réalité (GUSR): Pointe-à-Pitre; e-mail gusr@ais.gp; internet perso.mediaserv.net/gusr; 'dissident' faction of the Parti Socialiste; Pres. GUY LOSBAR.

Konvwa pou Liberasyon Nasyon Gwadloup (KLNG): Pointe-à-Pitre; f. 1997; pro-independence; Leader LUC REINETTE.

Parti Communiste Guadeloupéen (PCG): 119 rue Vatable, 97110 Pointe-à-Pitre; tel. 5-90-88-23-07; f. 1944; Sec.-Gen. FÉLIX FLÉMIN.

Parti Socialiste (PS): 8 Résidence Légitimus, blvd Légitimus, 97110 Pointe-à-Pitre; tel. and fax 5-90-21-65-72; fax 5-90-83-20-51; e-mail fede971@parti-socialiste.fr; internet www.parti-socialiste.fr; Regional Sec. MAX MATHIASIN.

Union pour un Mouvement Populaire (UMP): Les Portes de Saint Martin Bellevue, 97150 Saint Martin; tel. and fax 5-90-87-50-01; fax 5-90-87-75-72; e-mail ump-sxm@laposte.net; internet www.u-m-p.org; f. 2002; centre-right; local br. of the metropolitan party; Pres., Departmental Cttee LAURENT BERNIER.

Les Verts Guadeloupe: 5 rue François Arago, 97110 Pointe-à-Pitre; tel. 5-90-35-41-90; fax 5-90-25-02-62; internet guadeloupe.lesverts.fr; ecologist; departmental br. of the metropolitan party; Regional spokespersons HARRY DURIMEL, JOCELYNE HATCHI.

Judicial System

Court of Appeal: Palais de Justice, 4 blvd Félix Eboué, 97100 Basse-Terre; tel. 5-90-80-63-36; fax 5-90-80-63-19; e-mail ca-basse-terre@justice.fr; First Pres. BERTRAND DAROLLE; Procurator-Gen. CATHE-RINE CHAMPRENAULT.

There are two Tribunaux de Grande Instance and four Tribunaux d'Instance.

Religion

The majority of the population belong to the Roman Catholic Church.

CHRISTIANITY

The Roman Catholic Church

Guadeloupe comprises the single diocese of Basse-Terre, suffragan to the archdiocese of Fort-de-France, Martinique. Some 76% of the population are Roman Catholics. The Bishop participates in the Antilles Episcopal Conference, based in Port of Spain, Trinidad and Tobago.

Bishop of Basse-Terre: Mgr JEAN-YVES RIOCREUX, Evêché, pl. Saint-Françoise, BP 369, 97100 Basse-Terre Cédex; tel. 5-90-81-36-69; fax 5-90-81-98-23; e-mail eveche@catholique-guadeloupe.info; internet www.catholique-guadeloupe.info.

OTHER CHURCHES

Seventh-day Adventist Church: Eglise Adventiste de la Guadeloupe, BP 5, 97181 Les Abymes Cédex; tel. 5-90-82-79-76; fax 5-90-83-44-24; e-mail adventiste.federation@wanadoo.fr; internet www.adventiste-gp.org; f. 1931; Pres. ALAIN ANGERVILLE; Sec. JACQUES BIBRAC; 12,007 mems (2011).

Other denominations active in Guadeloupe include the Baptist Church and Jehovah's Witnesses.

The Press

Destination Guadeloupe: Pointe-à-Pitre; tel. 4-66-77-62-37; e-mail virginie@destination-guadeloupe.com; internet www

.destination-guadeloupe.com; tourism; quarterly; Dir VIRGINIE LARNAC.

France Antilles: ZAC Moudong Sud, 97122 Baie-Mahault; tel. 5-90-90-25-25; fax 5-90-91-78-31; e-mail f.breland@media-antilles.fr; internet www.guadeloupe.franceantilles.fr; f. 1964; subsidiary of Groupe France Antilles; daily; Dir ALEXANDRE THEVENET; circ. 50,000.

Match: 35 rue Peynier, 97110 Pointe-à-Pitre; tel. 5-90-82-18-68; fax 5-90-82-01-87; f. 1943; fortnightly; Dir (vacant); circ. 6,000.

Nouvelles Etincelles: 119 rue Vatable, 97110 Pointe-à-Pitre; tel. 5-90-91-00-85; fax 5-90-91-06-53; e-mail nouvelles-etincelles@wanadoo.fr; internet nouvellesetincelles.com; f. 1944 as *l'Etincelle*, organ of the Parti Communiste Guadeloupéen (q.v.); present name adopted 2005; weekly; Dir CHRISTIAN CÉLESTE; circ. 5,000.

Publishers

Editions Exbrayat: 12 Allée des Marguerites, Les Jardins d'Arnouville, 97170 Petit-Bourg; tel. 5-90-26-32-33; fax 5-90-26-32-66; e-mail andre.exbrayat@exbrayat.com; internet commerce.ciel.com/exbrayat; Dir PAQUITA EXBRAYAT-SANCHEZ.

Editions Jasor: 46 rue Schoëlcher, 97110 Pointe-à-Pitre; tel. 5-90-91-18-48; fax 5-90-21-07-01; e-mail editionsjasor@wanadoo.fr; f. 1989; French-Creole culture, biography and language, and youth fiction; Dir RÉGINE JASOR.

PLB Editions: route de Mathurin, 97190 Gosier; tel. 5-90-89-91-17; fax 5-90-89-91-05; e-mail plbeditions@wanadoo.fr; internet www.plbeditions.com; f. 1997; regional natural history and French-Creole youth fiction; Dirs CHANTAL MATTET, THIERRY PETIT LE BRUN.

Broadcasting and Communications

TELECOMMUNICATIONS

Acticom Sat: 31 bis rue Beaurenon, Grand–Bourg de Marie–Galante, 97122 Baie-Mahault; tel. 5-90-28-17-01; e-mail contact@caribsat.fr; internet www.caribsat.fr; part of Caribsat; satellite broadband provider; Man. MARYSE COPPET.

Digicel Antilles Françaises et Guyane: see Martinique—Telecommunications; Dir-Gen. (Guadeloupe) VINCENT VIENNET.

Orange Caraïbe: BP 2203, 97196 Jarry Cédex; tel. 5-90-38-45-55; fax 8-10-50-05-59; e-mail webmaster@orange.gp; internet www.orangecaraibe.com; f. 1996; subsidiary of Orange France; fixed lines, mobile telecommunications and internet services provider; network coverage incl. Martinique and French Guiana; Dir-Gen. JEAN-PHILIPPE GAY.

Outremer Telecom: SCI, Brand, voie Verte, Z. I. de Jarry, 97122 Baie-Mahault; e-mail communication@outremer-telecom.fr; internet www.outremer-telecom.fr; f. 1998; mobile telecommunications provider; Group CEO JEAN-MICHEL HEGESIPPE.

ONLY: SCI, Brand, voie Verte, Z. I. de Jarry, 97122 Baie-Mahault; e-mail communication@outremer-telecom.fr; internet www.outremer-telecom.fr; f. 1998 as Outremer Telecom Guadeloupe; present name adopted following merger of Volubis, ONLY and OOL in 2006; subsidiary of Outremer Telecom, France; fixed and mobile telecommunications provider.

BROADCASTING

Guadeloupe 1ère (Outre-mer Première): Morne Bernard Destrellan, BP 180, 97122 Baie-Mahault; tel. 5-90-60-96-96; fax 5-90-60-96-82; e-mail rfo@rfo.fr; internet guadeloupe.la1ere.fr; f. 1964; acquired by Groupe France Télévisions in 2004; fmrly Société Nationale de Radio-Télévision Française d'Outre-mer; name changed as Réseau France Outre-mer (RFO) in 1998; present name adopted in 2010; radio and TV; Regional Dir ROGER CESSY.

Radio

Kilti FM: Immeuble 573 rue de la Chapelle, Z. I. de Jarry, 97122 Baie-Mahault; tel. 5-90-32-52-61; fax 5-90-25-66-03; e-mail kiltifm@wanadoo.fr; f. 2006; French and Creole; Man. ORTEZ SONGO.

NRJ Guadeloupe: 2 blvd de la Marne, 97200 Fort-de-France; tel. 5-96-63-63-63; fax 5-96-73-73-15; e-mail webmaster@nrjantilles.com; internet www.nrjantilles.com.

Ouest FM: Immeuble Vivies, rue Thomas Edyson, Z. I. Jarry, 97122 Baie-Mahault; tel. 5-94-38-29-19; fax 5-90-26-02-97; e-mail contact@ouestfm.com; internet www.ouestfm.net; f. 2008; commercial radio station; French.

Radio Caraïbes International (RCI Guadeloupe): Carrefour Grand Camp, BP 40, 97151 Pointe-à-Pitre Cédex; tel. 5-90-83-96-96; fax 5-90-83-96-97; internet gp.rci.fm; f. 1962; Man. THIERRY FUNDÉRÉ.

Radio Contact: 40 bis, rue Lamartine, 97110 Pointe-à-Pitre; tel. 5-90-82-25-41; fax 5-96-91-56-77; internet www.radio-contact.net; operated by l'Asscn Citoyenne de Sauvegarde et de Défense des Intérêts des Guadeloupéens.

Radio Inter S'Cool (RIS): Lycée Ducharmoy, 97120 Saint-Claude; tel. and fax 5-90-80-38-40; e-mail ris.amme@wanadoo.fr; internet www.radiointerscool.net; educational and school-focused programmes; French and Creole; Pres. NICOLE CYPRIEN.

Radyo Tanbou: 153 résidence Espace, 97110 Pointe-à-Pitre; tel. 5-90-21-66-45; fax 5-90-21-66-48; e-mail kontak@radyotanbou.com; internet www.radyotanbou.com; French and Creole; operated by the l'Asscn pour le Développement de l'Information et de la Culture Guadeloupéenne.

RHT Guadeloupe (Radio Haute Tension): route de Petit Marquisat, Routhiers, 97130 Capesterre Belle Eau; tel. 5-90-25-73-96; e-mail contact@rhtguadeloupe.fr; internet www.rhtguadeloupe.fr; f. 1986; Dir RUDDY CORNELIE.

Zouk Radio: Immeuble Général Bricolage, Petit Pérou, 97139 Les Abymes; tel. 5-90-89-25-80; fax 5-90-89-26-22; internet www.zoukradio.fr; commercial music station; French and Creole.

Television

Antilles Télévision (ATV): see Martinique—Television.

Archipel 4: Immeuble Debs-Montauban, 97190 Gosier; tel. 5-93-21-05-20; f. 2002; Chair. JEAN-CLAUDE THOMASEAU.

Canal Plus Antilles: Immeuble Canal Media, Moudong Centre Jarry, 97122 Baie-Mahault; tel. 5-90-38-09-00; fax 5-90-38-09-04; e-mail mrichol@canalantilles.gp; internet www.canalantilles.com; f. 1993; subsidiary of Groupe Canal Plus, France; satellite TV station; Pres. JEAN-NOËL TRONC.

Canal 10: Immeuble CCL, blvd de Houelbourg, Z.I. de Jarry, BP 2271, 97122 Baie-Mahault; tel. 5-90-26-73-03; fax 5-90-26-61-25; e-mail contact@canal10-tv.com; internet www.canal10-tv.com; f. 1990; focus on social, economic and cultural issues in Guadeloupe; produces 100% of its programmes; Dir MICHEL RODRIGUEZ.

La Une Guadeloupe (L'A1): 20 rue Henri Becquerel, Z. I. de Jarry, 97122 Baie-Mahault; tel. 5-90-38-06-06; fax 5-90-38-06-07; f. 1998; fmrly TCI; gen. interest; purchases majority of programmes from TF1, France; Pres. JOSÉ GADDARKHAN.

Finance

(cap. = capital; res = reserves; dep. = deposits; m. = million; brs = branches; amounts in euros unless otherwise indicated)

BANKING

Central Bank

Institut d'Emission des Départements d'Outre-mer (IEDOM): Parc d'activité la Providence, ZAC de Dothémare, BP 196, 97139 Les Abymes; tel. 5-90-93-74-00; fax 5-90-93-74-25; e-mail iedom-pap-etudes@iedom-guadeloupe.fr; internet www.iedom.fr; f. 1959; Dir CHARLES APANON.

Commercial Banks

Banque des Antilles Françaises: Parc d'Activités de la Jaille, BP 46, Bâtiments 5 et 6, 97122 Baie-Mahault; tel. 5-90-60-42-00; fax 5-90-60-99-33; internet www.bdaf.fr; f. 1967 by merger of Banque de la Martinique and Banque de la Guadeloupe; subsidiary of Financière Océor, France; cap. 83.7m., res 7.7m., dep. 1,244.4m. (Dec. 2010); Pres. and Chair. PHILIPPE GARSUAULT; Gen. Man. DIDIER LOING; 19 brs.

Banque Française Commerciale Antilles-Guyane (BFC Antilles-Guyane): Immeuble BFC, Grand Camp-La Rocade, 97139 Pointe-à-Pitre; tel. 5-90-21-56-52; fax 5-90-21-56-62; e-mail f.aujoulat@bfc-ag.com; internet www.bfc-ag.com; f. 1976 as br. of Banque Française Commerciale, SA, separated 1984; cap. 51.1m., res 6.1m., dep. 661.6m. (Dec. 2012); Chair. CHRISTIAN DUVILLET; Dir-Gen. ALAIN STASSINET.

BNP Paribas Guadeloupe: pl. de la Rénovation, BP 161, 97155 Pointe-à-Pitre; tel. 5-90-90-58-58; fax 5-90-90-04-07; e-mail dg@bnp.gp; internet guadeloupe.bnpparibas.net; f. 1941; subsidiary of BNP Paribas, France; Gen. Man. DANIEL DELANIS; Gen. Sec. FRANÇOIS PASETTI; 12 brs.

BRED Banque Populaire (BRED-BP): Immeuble Simcar, blvd Marquisat de Houelbourg, Z. I. de Jarry, 97122 Baie-Mahault; tel. 5-90-82-65-46; internet www.bred.banquepopulaire.fr; cap. 242m. (Oct. 2005); Group Chair. STÈVE GENTILI.

Crédit Agricole de la Guadeloupe: Petit Pérou, 97176 Abymes Cédex; tel. 5-90-90-65-65; fax 5-90-90-65-89; e-mail catelnet@ca-guadeloupe.fr; internet www.ca-guadeloupe.fr; total assets 1,228.1m. (Dec. 2003); f. 1984; Pres. CHRISTIAN FLÉREAU; Gen. Man. ROGER WUNSCHEL; 30 brs.

Crédit Maritime de la Guadeloupe: 36 rue Achille René-Bois-neuf, BP 292, 97175 Pointe-à-Pitre; tel. 5-90-21-08-40; fax 5-90-83-46-37; e-mail pointe-a-pitre-agence-cmm@creditmaritime.com; internet www.creditmaritime-outremer.com; Dir GÉRARD CADIC; 4 agencies.

Société Générale de Banque aux Antilles (SGBA): 30 rue Frébault, BP 55, 97152 Pointe-à-Pitre; tel. 5-90-25-49-77; fax 5-90-25-49-78; e-mail sgba@wanadoo.fr; internet www.sgba.fr; f. 1979; cap. 32.6m., res –15.3m., dep. 360.5m. (Dec. 2009); Chair. ALEXANDRE MAYMAT; Man. Dir PHILIPPE RICHARD; 5 brs in Guadeloupe, 3 brs in Martinique.

Development Bank

Société de Crédit pour le Développement de Guadeloupe (SODEGA): Carrefour Raizet Baimbridge, BP 54, 97152 Pointe-à-Pitre; tel. 5-90-82-65-00; fax 5-90-90-17-91; e-mail credit@sodega.fr; internet www.sodega.fr; f. 1970; bought from the Agence Française de Développement (q.v.) by BRED Banque Populaire (q.v.) in 2003.

INSURANCE

Allianz Vie France: Le Patio de Grand Camp, BP 212, 97156 Pointe-à-Pitre Cédex; tel. 5-90-21-38-88; fax 5-90-82-78-25; e-mail agf.guavie@wanadoo.fr; internet www.allianz.fr; life insurance.

GAN Guadeloupe: 59–61 rue Achille René Boisneuf, BP 152, 97171 Pointe-à-Pitre Cédex; tel. 5-90-89-32-00; fax 5-90-04-43; internet www.groupama.es; subsidiary of Groupama, France; Dir-Gen. ALEXANDRE PASCAL; Man. GILLES CANO.

Mutuelle d'Assurance de Guadeloupe (MAG): Immeuble Capma & Capmi, blvd Légitimus, (face à Air France), 97110 Pointe-à-Pitre Cédex; tel. 5-90-82-22-71; fax 5-90-91-19-40; internet www.monceauassurances.com; fmrly Capma & Capmi; Chair. and Dir Gen. GILLES DUPIN.

Optimum Assurances: 3 bis rue Henri Bequerel, Jarry, 97122 Baie-Mahault; tel. 5-90-26-96-47; fax 5-90-26-81-27; internet www.assurances-guadeloupe.info; Dir-Gen. URBALD REINE.

WAB Assurances: Immeuble Stratégie, Moudong Sud, 97122 Baie-Mahault Cédex, tel. 5-90-32-66-66; fax 5-90-32 66 74; e-mail philippe.bech@wab-assu.com; internet www.wabassu.fr; f. 2005; Dir-Gen. PHILIPPE BECH.

Trade and Industry

GOVERNMENT AGENCIES

Direction de l'Alimentation, de l'Agriculture et de la Forêt (DAAF): Jardin Botanique, 97100 Basse-Terre; tel. 5-90-99-09-09; fax 5-90-99-09-10; e-mail daaf971@agriculture.gouv.fr; internet daaf971@agriculture.gouv.fr; Dir VINCENT FAUCHER.

Direction Régionale des Affaires Maritimes (DRAM): 20 rue Henri Becquerel, BP 2466, 97085 Jarry; tel. 5-90-41-95-50; fax 5-90-90-07-33; e-mail Dram-Guadeloupe@developpement-durable.gouv.fr; responsible for shipping, fishing and other maritime issues at national and community level; Dir FRÉDÉRIC BLUA.

Direction Régionale du Commerce Extérieur Antilles-Guyane (DRCE): see Martinique—Trade and Industry.

Direction Régionale de l'Industrie, de la Recherche et de l'Environnement (DRIRE): 552 rue de la Chapelle, Z. I. de Jarry, 97122 Baie-Mahault; tel. 5-90-38-03-47; fax 5-90-38-03-50; e-mail pierre.juan@industrie.gouv.fr; internet www.ggm.drire.gouv.fr; active in industry, business services, transport, public works, tourism and distribution; Departmental Co-ordinator MICHEL MASSON.

DEVELOPMENT ORGANIZATIONS

Agence de l'Environnement et de la Maîtrise de l'Energie (ADEME): Immeuble Café Center, rue Ferdinand Forest, Z. I. de Jarry, 97122 Baie-Mahault; tel. 5-90-26-78-05; fax 5-90-26-87-15; e-mail ademe.guadeloupe@ademe.fr; internet www.ademe.fr; developing energy and waste management; Man. CLAUDE COROSINE.

Agence Française de Développement (AFD): Parc d'activités de la Jaille, Bâtiment 7, BP 110, 97122 Baie-Mahault; tel. 5-90-89-65-65; fax 5-90-83-03-73; e-mail afdpointeaPitre@afd.fr; internet www.afd-guadeloupe.org; fmrly Caisse Française de Développement; Man. BERTRAND BOISSELET.

CHAMBERS OF COMMERCE

Chambre d'Agriculture de la Guadeloupe: Espace régional Agricole, Convenance BP 35, 97122 Baie-Mahault; tel. 5-90-25-17-17; fax 5-90-26-07-22; e-mail cda_direction@guadeloupe.chambagri.fr; Pres. ERIC NELSON; Dir JOËL PEDURAND.

Chambre de Commerce et d'Industrie de Région des Iles de Guadeloupe: Hôtel Consulaire, rue Félix Eboué, 97110 Pointe-à-Pitre Cédex; tel. 5-90-93-76-00; fax 5-90-90-21-87; e-mail contact@pointe-a-pitre.cci.fr; internet www.pointe-a-pitre.cci.fr; f. 1832; Pres. COLETTE KOURY; Sec. HENRI NAGAPIN; 34 full mems and 17 assoc. mems.

Chambre de Métiers et de l'Artisanat de la Guadeloupe (CMA): route Choisy, BP 61, 97120 Saint-Claude; tel. 5-90-80-23-33; fax 5-90-80-08-93; e-mail sgstc@cmguadeloupe.org; internet www.cmguadeloupe.org; Pres. JOËL LOBEAU; 11,630 mems (2005).

EMPLOYERS' ORGANIZATIONS

Association des Moyennes et Petites Industries (AMPI): rue Pierre et Marie Curie, Z.I. de Jarry, BP 2325, 97187 Jarry Cédex; tel. 5-90-26-38-27; fax 5-90-95-52-57; e-mail mpi.guadeloupe@wanadoo.fr; internet www.industrieguadeloupe.com; f. 1974; Pres. FRANK DESALMA; Gen. Sec CHRISTOPHE WACHTER; 117 mem. cos.

Interprofession Guadeloupéenne pour la Canne à Sucre (IGUACANNE): Espace Régional Agricole de Convenance, 97122 Baie-Mahault; f. 2005; represents sugar cane growers, sugar producers and professional bodies; Pres. ATHANASE COQUIN.

Ordre des Pharmaciens du Département Guadeloupe: Immeuble Capital 16, 1°, ZAC de Houelbourg, SUD 2, 97122 Baie-Mahault; tel. 5-90-21-66-05; fax 5-90-21-66-07; e-mail delegation_guadeloupe@ordre.pharmacien.fr; Pres. MAGGY CHEVRY-NOL.

Syndicat des Producteurs-Exportateurs de Sucre et de Rhum de la Guadeloupe et Dépendances: Z. I. de Jarry, 97122 Baie-Mahault; BP 2015, 97191 Pointe-à-Pitre; tel. 5-90-23-53-15; fax 5-90-23-52-34; f. 1937; Pres. M. VIGNERON; 4 mems.

Union des Entreprises-Mouvement des Entreprises de France (UDE-MEDEF): Immeuble SCI BTB, voie Principale de Jarry, 97122 Baie-Mahault; tel. 5-90-26-83-58; fax 5-90-26-83-67; e-mail ude.medef@medef-guadcloupe.com; Pres. WILLY ANGÈLE.

UTILITIES

Electricity

EDF Guadeloupe: BP 85, 97153 Pointe-à-Pitre; tel. 5-90-82-40-34; fax 5-90-83-30-02; e-mail marie-therese.fournier@edfgdf.fr; internet guadeloupe.edf.fr; electricity producer; Dir YVAN DELMAS; Man. MAX BORDELAIS.

Water

Veolia Water—Compagnie Générale des Eaux Guadeloupe: 18 ZAC de Houelbourg III, Voie verte de Jarry, 97122 Baie-Mahault; tel. 5-90-89-76-76; fax 5-90-91-39-10; e-mail mail-elise@gde-guadeloupe.com; internet www.generaledeseaux.gp; fmrly SOGEA; Dir (Americas) AUGUSTE LAURENT.

TRADE UNIONS

Confédération Générale du Travail de la Guadeloupe (CGTG): 4 Cité Artisanale de Bergevin, BP 779, 97110 Pointe-à-Pitre Cédex; tel. 5-90-82-34-61; fax 5-90-91-04-00; f. 1961; Sec.-Gen. JEAN-MARIE NOMERTIN; 5,000 mems.

Fédération Syndicale Unitaire Guadeloupe (FSU Guadeloupe): BP 82, 97005 Pointe-à-Pitre Cédex; tel. 5-90-23-13-66; fax 5-90-23-19-83; e-mail fsu971@fsu.fr; internet sd971.fsu.fr; f. 1993; departmental br. of the Fédération Syndicale Unitaire; represents public sector employees in teaching, research and training, and also agriculture, justice, youth and sports, and culture; Sec.-Gen. EDDY SÉGUR.

Union Générale des Travailleurs de la Guadeloupe (UGTG): rue Paul Lacavé, 97110 Pointe-à-Pitre; tel. 5-90-83-10-07; fax 5-90-89-08-70; e-mail ugtg@ugtg.org; internet www.ugtg.org; f. 1973; confederation of pro-independence trade unions incl. Union des Agents de la Sécurité Sociale (UNASS), l'Union des Employés du Commerce (UEC), Union des Travailleurs de l'Etat et du Département (UTED), l'Union des Travailleurs des Collectivités (UTC), l'Union des Travailleurs de l'Hôtellerie, du Tourisme et de la Restauration (UTHTR), l'Union des Travailleurs des Produits Pétroliers (UTPP), l'Union des Travailleurs de la Santé (UTS), and l'Union des Travailleurs des Télécommunications (UTT); Gen. Sec. ELIE DOMOTA; 4,000 mems.

Transport

RAILWAYS

There are no railways in Guadeloupe.

ROADS

There were 2,069 km (1,286 miles) of roads in Guadeloupe, of which 323 km were Routes Nationales.

SHIPPING

The Guadeloupe Port Caraïbes (formerly Port Autonome de la Guadeloupe) comprises five sites. The two principal seaports are at Pointe-à-Pitre, which offers both cargo-handling and passenger facilities, and the container terminal at Jarry (Baie-Mahault); the smaller port of Basse-Terre caters to freight and inter-island passenger traffic. There is also a sugar terminal at Folle-Anse (Saint-Louis) and a marina at Bas-du-Fort with 1,000 berths for pleasure craft. In December 2014 Guadeloupe's flag registered fleet comprised 12 vessels, with an aggregate displacement of some 3,940 grt.

Agence Petrelluzzi Transit et Maritime: 17 rue de la Chapelle, 97122 Baie-Mahault; tel. 5-90-38-12-12; fax 5-90-26-69-26; e-mail info@transitpetrelluzzi.com; internet transitpetrelluzzi.com; f. 1896; Dir PATRICK PETRELLUZZI.

Compagnie Générale Maritime Antilles-Guyane: Route du WTC, Zone Portuaire, BP 92, 97122 Baie-Mahault; tel. 5-90-25-57-00; fax 5-90-25-57-81; e-mail ptp.mbellemare@cma-cgm.com; internet www.cma-cgm.com; subsidiary of CMA-CGM, France; shipping agents, stevedoring; Gen. Man. MARLÈNE BELLEMARE.

Guadeloupe Port Caraïbes: Quai Ferdinand de Lesseps, BP 485, 97165 Pointe-à-Pitre Cédex; tel. 5-90-68-61-70; fax 5-90-68-61-71; e-mail contact@port-guadeloupe.com; internet guadeloupe-portcaraibes.com; port authority; fmrly Port Autonome de la Guadeloupe; became a Grand Port Maritime, a publicly owned entity administered by a supervisory board, following adoption of legislation in 2013; Dir-Gen. LAURENT MARTENS.

Compagnie Générale Portuaire: Marina Bas-du-Fort, 97110 Pointe-à-Pitre; tel. 5-90-93-66-20; fax 5-90-90-81-53; e-mail marina@marina-pap.com; internet www.marina-pap.com; port authority; Man. PHILIPPE CHEVALLIER; Harbour Master TONY BRESLAU; 1,000 berths for non-commercial traffic.

Société Guadeloupéenne de Consignation et Manutention (SGCM): 8 rue de la Chapelle, BP 2360, 97001 Jarry Cédex; tel. 5-90-38-05-55; fax 5-90-26-95-39; e-mail gerard.petrelluzzi@sgcm.fr; f. 1994; shipping agents, stevedoring; also operates Navimar Cruises inter-island tour co; Gen. Man. GERARD PETRELLUZZI; 17 berths.

Transcaraïbes S.A.: BP 2453, 97085 Pointe-à-Pitre; tel. 5-90-26-63-27; fax 5-90-26-67-49; e-mail transcaraibes.gpe@wanadoo.fr; f. 1976; shipping agents, stevedoring; office in Martinique; Gen. Man. ERIK URGIN.

CIVIL AVIATION

Raizet International Airport is situated 3 km (2 miles) from Pointe-à-Pitre and is equipped to handle jet-engined aircraft. There are smaller airports on the islands of Marie-Galante, La Désirade and Saint-Barthélémy. The island is served by a number of regional airlines, including LIAT (see Antigua and Barbuda). In 2013 American Airlines began a direct service from Miami, FL, USA, to Pointe-à-Pitre.

Air Antilles Express: Aeroport Pôle Caraibes, Point-à-Pitre; tel. 5-90-21-14-47; e-mail ar@media-caraibes.com; internet www.airantilles.com; f. 2002; subsidiary of Compagnie Aerienne Inter Regionale Express, France; serves Guadeloupe, Martinique, St-Barthélemy, St-Martin, St Maarten and the Dominican Republic; seasonal flights to San Juan, La Romana, Antigua and St Lucia; Dir CHRISTIAN MARCHAND.

Air Caraïbes (CAT): Aéroport International Guadeloupe, Pôle Caraïbes, 97139 Abymes; tel. 5-90-82-47-41; fax 5-90-82-47-49; e-mail drh@aircaraibes.com; internet www.aircaraibes.com; f. 2000 following merger of Air St Martin, Air St Barts, Air Guadeloupe and Air Martinique; owned by Groupe Dubreuil; operates daily inter-island, regional and international services within the Caribbean, and flights to Brazil, French Guiana and Paris; CEO SERGE TSYGALNITZKY; 16 aircraft; 800,000 passengers (2006).

Air Caraïbes Atlantique: Aéroport, 97232 Le Lamentin; f. 2003; subsidiary of Air Caraïbes; services between Pointe-à-Pitre, Fort-de-France (Martinique) and Paris; Pres. FRANÇOIS HERSEN.

Tourism

Guadeloupe is a popular tourist destination, especially for visitors from metropolitan France (who account for some 89% of tourists) and the USA. The main attractions are the beaches, the mountainous scenery and the unspoilt beauty of the island dependencies. In 2013 some 487,416 tourists visited Guadeloupe. Receipts from tourism totalled US $671m. in the same year.

Comité du Tourisme: 5 sq. de la Banque, BP 555, 97166 Pointe-à-Pitre Cédex; tel. 5-90-82-09-30; fax 5-90-83-89-22; e-mail info@lesilesdeguadeloupe.com; internet www.lesilesdeguadeloupe.com; Pres. JOSETTE BOREL-LINCERTIN; Dir THIERRY GARGAR.

Délégation Régionale au Tourisme, au Commerce et l'Artisanat: 5 rue Victor Hugues, 97100 Basse-Terre; tel. 5-90-81-10-44; fax 5-90-81-94-82; e-mail drtourisme.guadeloupe@wanadoo.fr; Dir CHRISTIAN FOURCRIER.

Syndicat d'Initiative de Pointe-à-Pitre: Centre Commercial de la Marina, 97110 Pointe-à-Pitre; tel. 5-90-90-70-02; fax 5-90-90-74-70; e-mail syndicatinitiativedepap@wanadoo.fr; internet www.sivap.gp; Pres. DENYS FORTUNE; Man. NADIA DEGLAS.

Defence

As assessed at November 2014, France maintained a military force of about 1,200 in Fort-de-France (Martinique).

Education

The education system is similar to that of metropolitan France (see the chapter on French Guiana). In 2013/14 there were 131 pre-primary and 206 primary schools. Secondary education was provided at 94 institutions in that year. In 2013/14 there were 19,306 students in pre-primary and 35,278 in primary education (a further 536 pupils attended specialized pre-primary and primary schools), while in secondary education there were 49,491 students, of whom some 90% attended state schools. A branch of the Université des Antilles et de la Guyane, at Pointe-à-Pitre, has faculties of law and economics, sciences, medicine, teacher training, sports science and humanities. In addition, there are colleges of agriculture, fisheries, hotel management, nursing, midwifery and childcare. In 2012/13 there was a total of 9,125 students in higher education.

MARTINIQUE

Introductory Survey

LOCATION, CLIMATE, LANGUAGE, RELIGION, CAPITAL

Martinique is one of the Windward Islands in the West Indies, with Dominica to the north and Saint Lucia to the south. The island is dominated by the volcanic peak of Mont Pelée. The climate is tropical, but tempered by easterly and north-easterly breezes. The more humid and wet season runs from July to November, and the average temperature is 26°C (79°F). French is the official language, but a Creole patois is widely spoken. The majority of the population professes Christianity and belongs to the Roman Catholic Church. The capital is Fort-de-France.

CONTEMPORARY POLITICAL HISTORY

Historical Context

Martinique has been a French possession since 1635. The prosperity of the island was based on the sugar industry, which was devastated by the volcanic eruption of Mont Pelée in 1902. Martinique became a Department of France in 1946, when the Governor was replaced by a Prefect, and an elected Conseil Général (General Council) was created.

During the 1950s there was a growth of nationalist feeling, as expressed by Aimé Césaire's Parti Progressiste Martiniquais (PPM) and the Parti Communiste Martiniquais (PCM). However, economic power remained concentrated in the hands of the *békés* (descendants of white colonial settlers), who owned most of the agricultural land and controlled the lucrative import-export market. This provided little incentive for innovation or self-sufficiency, and fostered resentment against lingering colonial attitudes.

Domestic Political Affairs

In 1974 Martinique, together with Guadeloupe and French Guiana, was given regional status as part of France's governmental reorganization. An indirectly elected Conseil Régional (Regional Council) was created, with some control over the local economy. In 1982 and 1983 the socialist Government of President François Mitterrand made further concessions towards autonomy by giving the local councils greater control over taxation, local police and the economy. At the first direct elections to the new Regional Council, held in February 1983, left-wing parties (the PPM, the PCM and the Fédération Socialiste de la Martinique—FSM) won a majority of seats. This success, and the election of Césaire as President of the Regional Council, strengthened his influence against the pro-independence elements in his own party. (Full independence for Martinique attracted support from only a small minority of the population; the majority sought reforms that would bring greater autonomy, while retaining French control.) At an election to the enlarged General Council in 1985, the left-wing parties increased their representation, but the centre-right coalition of the Union pour la Démocratie Française (UDF) and the Rassemblement pour la République (RPR) maintained their control of the administration.

At the general election to the Assemblée Nationale (National Assembly) in 1986, Césaire and a member of the FSM were elected from a unified list of left-wing candidates, while the RPR and the UDF (which had also presented a joint list) each won one seat. In the concurrent election to the Regional Council the left-wing parties (including the PPM, the FSM and the PCM) won a narrow majority of seats. Césaire retained the presidency of the Council until 1988, when he relinquished the post to Camille Darsières (the Secretary-General of the PPM). Indirect elections were also held in 1986 for Martinique's two seats in the Sénat (Senate). The left-wing parties again united, and Martinique acquired a left-wing senator for the first time since 1958, a PPM member, while the other successful candidate belonged to the UDF.

Left-wing candidates secured all four seats at elections to the National Assembly in 1988 and the parties of the left also achieved a majority at General Council elections. Emile Maurice of the RPR was, none the less, elected President of the Council for a seventh term.

In 1990 the results of the 1986 election to the Regional Council were annulled because of a technicality, and another election was held. Pro-independence candidates secured nine seats. The PPM-FSM-PCM coalition lost its absolute majority on the Regional Council; Camille Darsières was, however, re-elected to the presidency of the Regional Council. At an election to the General Council in 1992, left-wing parties secured a narrow majority. Claude Lise, a PPM deputy to the National Assembly, was elected President. In concurrent elections to the Regional Council the RPR and the UDF, contesting the election as the Union pour la France (UPF), won the most seats. Emile Capgras of the PCM was elected President of the Regional Council.

In September 1992 some 72% of voters in Martinique approved ratification of the Treaty on European Union (see p. 271), although the abstention rate was high.

In the 1993 elections to the National Assembly André Lesueur and Pierre Petit of the RPR were elected, as was a third right-wing candidate, Anicet Turinay of the UPF. In September 1995 Lise was elected to the Senate, while the incumbent PPM representative, Rodolphe Désiré, was returned to office.

At elections to the National Assembly in 1997, Turinay and Petit, representing the RPR, were re-elected, together with Camille Darsières of the PPM and Alfred Marie-Jeanne of the Mouvement Indépendantiste Martiniquais (MIM). At elections to the Regional Council in the following year, the left retained its majority. Marie-Jeanne was elected President of the Regional Council. In a concurrent election to the General Council the left again increased its majority; Lise was re-elected to the presidency of the General Council.

A two-month strike by workers in the banana sector, which had severely disrupted economic activity around the port of Fort-de-France, was ended in January 1999, when a pay agreement was reached. However, in October, prior to a two-day visit to Martinique by Prime Minister Lionel Jospin, banana producers occupied the headquarters of the French naval forces for several days, demanding the disbursement of exceptional aid to compensate for a dramatic decline in prices on the European market. The Prime Minister announced an emergency plan for the banana sector and agreed, in principle, to a proposal for greater autonomy for the local authorities in conducting relations with neighbouring countries and territories.

In December 1999 the Presidents of the Regional Councils of French Guiana, Guadeloupe and Martinique signed a joint declaration in Basse-Terre, Guadeloupe, affirming their intention to propose, to the Government, a legislative amendment aimed at creating a new status of overseas region, despite an earlier statement to the contrary by Jospin. Modified proposals regarding the institutional future and socio-economic development of the Departments were approved by the National Assembly and were ratified by the Constitutional Council in December. Following a meeting of members of both Councils in June 2001, a series of proposals on greater autonomy was agreed upon. These included: the division of the territory into four districts; the creation of a Collectivité Territoriale (Territorial Collectivity), governed by a 41-member Assembly elected for a five-year term; and the establishment of an independent executive

council. Furthermore, the proposals included a request that the territory be given control over legislative and administrative affairs, as well as legislative authority on matters concerning Martinique alone. In March 2003 the French parliament approved constitutional changes that, *inter alia*, allowed for local referendums to be held on proposals for greater decentralization in overseas possessions. The status of Région d'Outre-mer (Overseas Region) was also conferred on Martinique (in addition to it being an Overseas Department). In the referendum, held on 7 December, some 51% of participating voters rejected legislative reforms that envisaged the replacement of the General Council and the Regional Council with a single assembly.

In an election to the General Council in March 2001, Lise was re-elected President. At elections to the National Assembly in June 2002, Marie-Jeanne was re-elected, while Turinay lost his seat to Louis-Joseph Manscour of the PS, and Darsières lost his to Pierre-Jean Samot of the left-wing Bâtir le Pays Martinique (BPM); Alfred Almont, representing the right-wing alliance of the Union pour la Majorité Présidentielle (UMP) and the RPR, secured the remaining seat. The RPR subsequently merged into the successor party to the UMP, the Union pour un Mouvement Populaire (also known as the UMP). In 2003 Samot resigned his seat after breaking campaign funding rules. A by-election was won by Philippe Edmond-Mariette, also of BPM.

At an election to the Regional Council in March 2004 the Patriotes Martiniquais, a pro-independence alliance, comprising the MIM, the Conseil National des Comités Populaires and the Alliance pour le Pays Martinique (which was absorbed by the two larger groupings after the first round of voting), won an overwhelming majority, obtaining 28 of the 41 council seats.

In May 2005 a national referendum was held on ratification of the European Union constitutional treaty: 69% of voters in the Department were in favour of adopting the treaty, although turnout was low. The treaty was ultimately rejected by a majority of voters in metropolitan France. In December more than 1,000 protesters took part in demonstrations in Fort-de-France against a law, approved in the previous February, that proposed changing the school syllabus to reflect the 'positive' role of French colonialism. In January 2006 the relevant article of law was removed in accordance with a ruling by the Constitutional Council that it lay outside the competence of the legislature.

In the first round of the 2007 national presidential election Ségolène Royal of the PS won 49% of the votes cast on the island, ahead of Nicolas Sarkozy, the UMP candidate, who attracted 34%. Royal won 61% of the second round vote in the Department, however, nationally, Sarkozy emerged victorious. At elections to the National Assembly in June, Marie-Jeanne, Manscour and Almont were all re-elected, while Serge Letchimy of the PPM was also successful. Following elections to the General Council in March 2008, Lise was again re-elected as the Council's President.

A general strike began in early February 2009 in protest against the increasingly high cost of living, following similar unrest in Guadeloupe. Riot police were sent from metropolitan France in an effort to control the demonstrations, and violent confrontations between police and protesters ensued. The strike, which had caused significant economic disruption, ended on 11 March.

Regional and national elections

In elections to the Regional Council on 14 and 21 March 2010, the PPM won a decisive victory, with 48.4% of the ballot, gaining 26 of the Council's 41 seats. The MIM secured 12 seats and the UMP-led list obtained the remaining three, with 41.0% and 10.6% of the votes cast, respectively. Letchimy was duly elected as President of the Regional Council. The rate of participation by the electorate was 55.1%. Left-wing candidates performed strongly in the municipal polls conducted on 20 and 27 March 2011, following which the BPM's Josette Manin (representing a PPM-led coalition) was elected as Martinique's first female President of the General Council. Also in that month, Laurent Prévost was appointed as Prefect. In September Serge Larcher of the PPM was re-elected to the Senate, while another left-wing candidate, Maurice Antiste, won control of the island's second Senate seat.

The first round of the French presidential election was conducted on 21 April 2012 (one day earlier than in mainland France): François Hollande, representing the PS, attracted 52.0% of the territory's votes, compared with 26.3% for Sarkozy. A second round run-off election was held two weeks later, at which Hollande secured 68.4% of the ballot, defeating Sarkozy, who attracted 31.6%. Hollande also triumphed nationally and was sworn in as President in mid-May. In legislative elections, which took place in June, Marie-Jeanne and Letchimy were re-elected to the National Assembly, while the island's two remaining mandates were won by Jean-Philippe Nilor (of the MIM) and Bruno Nestor Azerot (an independent left-wing candidate).

The French Minister of Overseas Territories, Victorin Lurel, visited Martinique in September 2012 to hold discussions with the local authorities regarding the high cost of living on the island. A bill to address the problem of inflated prices (and consequent social unrest) in Martinique and other French Overseas Possessions, drafted by Lurel, was approved by the French Parliament in November. Most notably, the legislation provided for the imposition of price controls on a range of staple goods and the introduction of measures to encourage competition. In December 2013 the French Government extended the price controls to cover petrol purchases in the French Overseas Regions and Departments. However, on multiple occasions between mid-2013 and early 2014, owners of petrol stations in Martinique, French Guiana, Guadeloupe, Mayotte and Réunion, fearing that the move would disrupt their business model and undermine profit margins, closed their establishments in a co-ordinated act of protest. The closures ended in February 2014 after a compromise was agreed with the French authorities.

Candidates representing left-wing lists comfortably won the most council seats in municipal polls conducted on 23 and 30 March 2014. Elections to the European Parliament took place in Martinique on 25 May. The left-wing Union pour les Outremer secured 27.5% of the local ballot, while Choisir Notre Europe, another left-wing grouping, garnered 20.7% and the UMP 16.5%. Turnout was only 11.4%, however.

Recent developments: institutional reform

A referendum on the issue of increased autonomy for the island was held on 10 January 2010. The electorate, fearful of losing economic support from mainland France and unwilling to confer greater power upon the local political élite, voted overwhelmingly to reject any increase in autonomy, with 78.9% voting against the proposal. The rate of participation by the electorate was 55.4%. Nevertheless, a further vote, this time on institutional reform, was held on 24 January, in which 68.3% of participants voted in favour of changing the status of Martinique to a Collectivité Territoriale Unique (Single Territorial Collectivity), replacing the existing two-tier departmental and regional administrative structure (Martinique would remain an Overseas Department and an Overseas Region.). Only 35.8% of the electorate took part in the plebiscite. The authorities hoped that the merger of the departmental and regional levels of government would increase efficiency and reduce operating costs. In mid-2011 the National Assembly approved legislation to facilitate this transition and in January 2015 a further law was approved granting Single Territorial Collectivity status on Martinique (and French Guiana) from 1 January 2016. Polls were scheduled for December 2015 to elect the 51 members of a new, consolidated legislative body, which would replace the Regional Council and the General Council. In turn, the new assembly would then elect a nine-member executive council. These arrangements were endorsed by the Constitutional Council in April 2013.

CONSTITUTION AND GOVERNMENT

France is represented in Martinique by an appointed Prefect. There are two councils with local powers: the 45-member Conseil Général (General Council) and the 41-member Conseil Régional (Regional Council). Both are elected by universal adult suffrage for a period of up to six years. Both Councils were scheduled to be replaced by a single, 51-member body from January 2016. Martinique elects four deputies to the National Assembly in Paris, and sends two indirectly elected representatives to the Senate. The Department is also represented at the European Parliament.

REGIONAL AND INTERNATIONAL CO-OPERATION

Martinique became an associate member of the Association of Caribbean States (see p. 444) in April 2014 and of the Organisation of Eastern Caribbean States (OECS, see p. 463) in February 2015. The territory was also seeking the same status within the Caribbean Community and Common Market (CARICOM, see p. 222).

ECONOMIC AFFAIRS

In 2012, according to official estimates, Martinique's gross domestic product (GDP), measured at current prices, was estimated at €8,352m., equivalent to €21,527 per head. During 2000–10 GDP increased, in real terms, at an average rate of 4.0% per year; growth in 2010 was 4.6%. According to provisional figures, in 2002–11 the population increased at an average annual rate of 0.1%.

Agriculture, hunting, forestry and fishing contributed 2.8% of GDP in 2009, and according to provisional figures engaged an estimated 3.6% of the active labour force in 2012. The principal cash crops are bananas, sugar cane (primarily for the production of rum), limes, melons and pineapples. The cultivation of cut flowers is also of some significance. Roots and tubers and vegetables are grown for local consumption. Agricultural production increased at an average rate of 1.3% per year during 1990–98; the sector declined by 0.2% in 1999.

According to provisional figures, the industrial sector (including construction and public works) engaged 12.1% of the employed population in 2012 and contributed 13.5% of GDP in 2009. The most important manufacturing activities are petroleum refining (exports of fuels and combustibles accounted for 46.8% of the value of total exports in 2013) and the production of agricultural products

(20.1% of exports in 2013), the production of rum being of particular significance. Other areas of activity include metals, cement, chemicals, plastics, wood, printing and textiles.

In 2012 construction engaged a preliminary 5.2% of the employed labour force and in 2009 the sector contributed 5.5% to GDP.

Energy is derived principally from mineral fuels. In 2013 imports of fuels and combustibles (including crude petroleum destined for the island's refinery) accounted for 16.9% of the value of total imports.

The services sector engaged a provisional 84.3% of the employed population in 2012 and provided 83.7% of GDP in 2009. Tourism is a major activity on the island and one of the most important sources of foreign exchange: in 2013 some 489,705 visitor arrivals were recorded, while earnings from the tourism industry totalled an estimated US $484m. in 2013; the vast majority of visitors were from metropolitan France (78.8% in 2012).

In 2013 Martinique's merchandise trade deficit totalled €2,257.4m. In that year Martinique's export earnings were worth only approximately 14.5% of the total value of imports. Metropolitan France was the principal source of imports (54.9% in 2008); Guadeloupe was the principal market for exports (57.2%) in that year. French Guiana, member countries of the European Union (EU, see p. 271) and the USA were also significant trading partners. The principal exports in 2013 were fuels and combustibles, agricultural products and products of food industries. The principal imports in that year included fuels and combustibles, food industry products, mechanical, electrical and electronic equipment, natural hydrocarbons, transport equipment and pharmaceutical products.

In 2014 the regional budget was balanced at €397.0m., and the departmental budget was also balanced at €677.3m., according to preliminary figures. The annual rate of inflation averaged 1.8% in 2004–13; consumer prices increased by 1.3% in 2013. Some 22.8% of the labour force was unemployed in 2013.

Martinique's economic development has created a society that combines a relatively high standard of living with a weak economic base in agricultural and industrial production. The linking of wage levels to those of metropolitan France, despite the island's lower level of productivity, has increased labour costs and restricted development. Martinique's economy was badly affected by the global financial crisis of 2008–09, although it recovered strongly in 2010, with GDP expanding by 5.2%. However, economic growth slowed to just 1.4% in 2011, owing to lower agricultural productivity, a decline in exports and a deceleration in domestic consumption. The cruise ship sector suffered a slowdown in that year, although the broader tourism industry continued to recover, while the inauguration of several large-scale construction projects ensured that investment levels remained steady. In spite of an increase in exports and cruise ship arrivals during 2012, the economy registered growth of only 1.3% in that year as a result of lower domestic demand, a fall in stop-over tourists and a downturn in construction activity. According to provisional data, GDP contracted by 0.5% in 2013. Tourism indicators were positive in that year, although trade levels declined, household consumption was subdued and the construction industry remained depressed. Moreover, the unemployment rate (22.8% in 2013) was still very high, while sporadic outbreaks of industrial unrest were a further source of concern.

PUBLIC HOLIDAYS

2016: 1 January (New Year's Day), 8–9 February (Lenten Carnival), 10 February (Ash Wednesday), 25–28 March (Easter), 1 May (Labour Day), 5 May (Ascension Day), 8 May (Victory Day), 16 May (Whit Monday), 10 June (Abolition of Slavery), 14 July (National Day), 15 August (Assumption), 1 November (All Saints' Day), 11 November (Armistice Day), 25 December (Christmas Day).

Statistical Survey

Sources (unless otherwise indicated): Institut National de la Statistique et des Etudes Economiques (INSEE), Service Régional de Martinique, Centre Administratif Delgrès, blvd de la Pointe des Sables, Hauts de Dillon, BP 641, 97262 Fort-de-France Cédex; tel. 5-96-60-73-73; fax 5-96-60-73-50; e-mail antilles-guyane@insee.fr; internet www.insee.fr/fr/regions/martinique; Ministère des Départements et Territoires d'Outre-mer, 27 rue Oudinot, 75700 Paris 07 SP; tel. 1-53-69-20-00; fax 1-43-06-60-30; internet www.outre-mer.gouv.fr.

AREA AND POPULATION

Area: 1,100 sq km (424.7 sq miles).

Population: 381,427 at census of 8 March 1999; 392,291 at census of 1 January 2011. Note: According to new census methodology, data in 2011 refer to median figures based on the collection of raw data over a five-year period (2009–13). *2013* (official estimate at 1 January): 386,486. *Mid-2015* (UN estimate): 405,688 (Source: UN, *World Population Prospects: The 2012 Revision*).

Density (at mid-2015): 368.8 per sq km.

Population by Age and Sex (UN estimates at mid-2015): *0–14 years:* 72,508 (36,174 males, 36,334 females); *15–64 years:* 263,646 (120,489 males, 143,157 females); *65 years and over:* 69,534 (29,833 males, 39,701 females); *Total:* 405,688 (186,496 males, 219,192 females).

Principal Towns (official population estimates at 1 January 2012): Fort-de-France (capital) 85,667; Le Lamentin 39,700; Le Robert 23,715; Schoelcher 20,103.

Births, Marriages and Deaths (2012): Registered births 4,458 (birth rate 11.5 per 1,000); Registered marriages 1,145 (marriage rate 3.0 per 1,000); Registered deaths 2,818 (death rate 7.3 per 1000).

Life Expectancy (years at birth): 81.6 (males 78.2; females 84.8) in 2014. Source: Pan American Health Organization.

Employment (persons aged 15 years and over at 31 December 2012, provisional): Agriculture, hunting, forestry and fishing 4,507; Mining, quarrying and utilities 2,319; Manufacturing 6,225; Construction 6,494; Trade 14,320; Hotels and restaurants 5,164; Transportation and storage 5,804; Communication 2,164; Finance and insurance 3,579; Real estate activities 835; Professional services 12,809; Public administration, education, health and other social services 50,715; Other services 9,579; *Total* 124,514. Note: Figures for employment exclude 6,757 persons employed without salary.

HEALTH AND WELFARE

Key Indicators

Total Fertility Rate (children per woman, 2014): 1.8.

Under-5 Mortality Rate (per 1,000 live births, 2011): 8.5.

Physicians (per 1,000 head, 2010): 26.2.

Hospital Beds (per 1,000 head, 2012): 4.1.

Source: mainly Pan American Health Organization.

For definitions and other sources, see explanatory note on p. vi.

AGRICULTURE, ETC.

Principal Crops ('000 metric tons, 2013, FAO estimates): Yams 1.4; Sugar cane 177.9; Lettuce and chicory 7.7, Tomatoes 6.1; Cucumbers and gherkins 6.5; Bananas 272.9; Plantains 14.7; Pineapples 2.0. *Aggregate Production* ('000 metric tons, may include official, semi-official or estimated data): Total vegetables (incl. melons) 34.8; Total fruits (excl. melons) 291.3.

Livestock ('000 head, year ending September 2013, FAO estimates): Cattle 18; Sheep 12; Pigs 12; Goats 6.

Livestock Products ('000 metric tons, 2013, FAO estimates): Cattle meat 1.0; Pig meat 1.1; Chicken meat 1.6; Cows' milk 3.0; Hen eggs 2.7.

Forestry ('000 cubic metres, 2013, FAO estimates): *Roundwood Removals* (excl. bark): Sawlogs, veneer logs and logs for sleepers 2.4; Fuel wood 10.0; Total 12.4. *Sawnwood Production* (incl. railway sleepers): 1.0.

Fishing (metric tons, live weight, 2012, FAO estimates): Capture 7,900 (Clupeoids 4,650; Common dolphinfish 147; Other marine fishes 1,800; Caribbean spiny lobster 180; Clams, etc. 715); Aquaculture 24; *Total catch* 7,924.

Source: FAO.

MINING

Production ('000 metric tons, 2010, estimates): Cement 221; Pumice 130; Salt 200. Source: US Geological Survey.

INDUSTRY

Production ('000 metric tons, 2011): Motor spirit (petrol) 147 (estimate); Kerosene 123, Gas-diesel (distillate fuel) oils 209; Residual fuel oils 410; Liquefied petroleum gas 21 (estimate); Electric energy (million kWh) 1,734 (estimate) (Source: UN Industrial Commodity Statistics Database). *2013:* Raw sugar 2,188 metric tons; Rum (hl) 81,100. (Source: Institut d'Emission des Départements d'Outre-mer, *Martinique: Rapport Annuel 2013*).

FINANCE

Currency and Exchange Rates: The French franc was used until the end of 2001. Euro notes and coins were introduced on 1 January 2002, and the euro became the sole legal tender from 18 February.

Some of the figures in this Survey are still in terms of francs. For details of exchange rates, see French Guiana.

Budget (excl. debt rescheduling, € million, 2014, preliminary): *Regional Government:* Current revenue 247.7 (Taxes 173.5, Other current revenue 74.2); Capital revenues 149.3; Total 397.0. Current expenditure 196.2; Capital expenditure 200.8; Total 397.0. *Departmental Government:* Revenue 677.3 (Current revenue 619.6, Capital revenue 57.6); Expenditure 677.3 (Current expenditure 574.3, Capital expenditure 102.9). Source: Département des Etudes et des Statistiques Locales.

Cost of Living (Consumer Price Index; base: 2000 = 100): All items 124.5 in 2011; 126.3 in 2012; 127.9 in 2013. Source: ILO.

Gross Domestic Product (€ million at current prices, estimates): 8,128 in 2010; 8,291 in 2011; 8,352 in 2012. Source: Institut d'Emission des Départements d'Outre-mer, *Martinique: Rapport Annuel 2013*.

Expenditure on the Gross Domestic Product (€ million at current prices, 2012, estimates): Total final consumption expenditure 8,904 (General government and non-profit institutions serving households 3,701, Households 5,203); Changes in stocks –140; Gross fixed capital formation 1,507; *Total domestic expenditure* 10,271; Exports of goods and services 1,066; *Less* Imports of goods and services 2,985; *GDP in purchasers' values* 8,352. Source: Institut d'Emission des Départements d'Outre-mer, *Martinique: Rapport Annuel 2013*.

Gross Domestic Product by Economic Activity (€ million at current prices, 2006): Agriculture 160; Food industries 122; Other manufacturing 282; Energy 164; Construction 453; Services 6,088 (Restaurants and hotels 232, Transport 222, Commerce 852, Other market services 2,387, Non-market services 2,395); *Sub-total* 7,269; *Less* Financial intermediation services indirectly measured 298; Taxes, less subsidies 667; *GDP in purchasers' values* 7,638.

EXTERNAL TRADE

Principal Commodities (€ million, 2013): *Imports c.i.f.:* Agriculture, forestry and fishing 52.6; Natural hydrocarbons, etc. 309.7; Products of food industries 401.2; Textiles, clothing, leather and footwear 103.3; Petroleum products 446.8; Chemicals 120.9; Pharmaceutical products 142.2; Rubber, plastic and mineral products 132.7; Metal and metal products 107.9; Mechanical, electronics and electrical equipment 358.4; Transport equipment 257.7; Miscellaneous manufactured products 111.5; Total (incl. others) 2,641.1. *Exports f.o.b.:* Agriculture, forestry and fishing 77.1; Products of food industries 57.1; Petroleum products 179.7; Metal and metal products 9.9, Mechanical, electronics and electrical equipment 9.2; Transport equipment 20.4; Total (incl. others) 383.7. (Source: Institut d'Emission des Départements d'Outre-mer, *Martinique: Rapport Annuel 2013*).

Principal Trading Partners (€ million, 2008): *Imports c.i.f.:* Aruba 78; France (metropolitan) 1,519; Germany 72; Guadeloupe 44; Italy 45; Japan 36; Netherlands 54; Spain 26; United Kingdom 326; USA 199; Total (incl. others) 2,766. *Exports f.o.b.:* Antigua 4; France (metropolitan) 90; French Guiana 38; Guadeloupe 210; Netherlands Antilles 3; USA 9; Total (incl. others) 367. *2011* (€ million): Total imports 2,709.4; Total exports 308.3. *2012* (€ million): Total imports 2,764.8; Total exports 406.8. *2013* (€ million): Total imports 2,641.0; Total exports 383.7. (Source: Institut d'Emission des Départements d'Outre-mer, *Martinique: Rapport Annuel 2013*).

TRANSPORT

Road Traffic ('000 commercial motor vehicles in use, 1 January 2010): Buses 1.2; Vans and tractors 34.3.

Shipping: *Flag Registered Fleet* (at 31 December, 2014): Vessels 3; Total displacement 510 grt (Source: Lloyd's List Intelligence— www.lloydslistintelligence.com). *International Seaborne Traffic* (2011): Goods loaded 856,000 metric tons (petroleum products 359,000 metric tons); Goods unloaded 2,026,000 metric tons (petroleum products 923,000 metric tons).

Civil Aviation (2013 unless otherwise indicated): Freight (incl. 2,667 metric tons of post) carried 13,914 metric tons (2009); Passengers carried 1,623,870. Source: partly Institut d'Emission des Départements d'Outre-mer, *Martinique: Rapport Annuel 2013*.

TOURISM

Tourist Arrivals by Country (excl. same-day visitors and cruise ship arrivals, 2003): France (metropolitan) 357,726; Guadeloupe 40,668; French Guiana 10,619; Total (incl. others) 453,159. *2012* (excl. same-day visitors and cruise ship arrivals): Total 487,769 (Canada 9,154; France 384,526; French Guiana 13,626; Guadeloupe 45,556;). (Source: World Tourism Organization). *Total Arrivals* (excl. same-day visitors and cruise ship arrivals): 498,578 in 2011; 478,359 in 2012; 489,705 in 2013. (Source: partly Institut d'Emission des Départements d'Outre-mer, *Martinique: Rapport Annuel 2013*).

Receipts from Tourism (US $ million, excl. passenger transport): 516 in 2011; 462 in 2012; 484 in 2013. Source: World Tourism Organization.

COMMUNICATIONS MEDIA

Telephones ('000 main lines in use): 172.0 in 2010.

Mobile Cellular Telephones ('000 subscribers): 295.4 in 2004.

Internet Users ('000): 170.0 in 2009.

Broadband Subscribers: 6,000 in 2010.

Source: International Telecommunication Union.

EDUCATION

Pre-primary (2013/14): 74 institutions; 15,420 students (14,366 state, 1,054 private).

Primary (2013/14): 178 institutions; 25,467 students (23,189 state, 2,278 private).

Specialized Pre-primary and Primary (2013/14): 347 students (347 state only).

Secondary (2013/14): 80 institutions; 38,615 students (34,843 state, 3,772 private).

Higher (2012/13): 7,829 students.

Teachers (2004/05): *Primary:* 3,031 (2,787 state, 244 private); *Secondary:* 4,553 (4,177 state, 376 private); *Higher:* 186. Source: Ministère de l'Education Nationale, *Repères et références statistiques—édition 2005*. *2012/13* (state schools): 2,650 in primary; 3,510 in secondary.

Institutions (2003/04): 258 primary schools; 41 lower secondary schools; 22 state upper secondary schools; 24 private institutions. Source: Préfecture de Martinique, *Livret d'accueil des services de l'Etat en Martinique*. *2012/13:* 72 pre-primary schools; 180 elementary and special schools; 80 secondary schools.

Adult Literacy Rate: 98.0% (males 97.6%, females 98.3%) in 2005. Source: Pan American Health Organization.

Directory

The Government

(April 2015)

HEAD OF STATE

President: FRANÇOIS HOLLANDE.

Prefect: FABRICE RIGOULET-ROZE, Préfecture, 82 rue Victor Sévère, BP 647–648, 97262 Fort-de-France Cédex; tel. 5-96-39-36-00; fax 5-96-71-40-29; e-mail contact.prefecture@martinique.pref.gouv.fr; internet www.martinique.pref.gouv.fr.

DEPARTMENTAL ADMINISTRATION

President of the General Council: JOSETTE MANIN (PPM), Conseil général de la Martinique, blvd Chevalier Sainte-Marthe, 97200 Fort-de-France Cédex; tel. 5-96-55-26-00; fax 5-96-73-59-32; internet www.cg972.fr.

President of the Regional Council: SERGE LETCHIMY, Hôtel de la Région, ave Gaston Deferre, BP 601, 97200 Fort-de-France Cédex; tel. 5-96-59-63-00; fax 5-96-72-68-10; e-mail service .communication@cr-martinique.fr; internet www.cr-martinique.fr.

Elections, Regional Council, 14 and 21 March 2010

	Seats
Parti Progressiste Martiniquais (PPM)	26
Mouvement Indépendantiste Martiniquais (MIM) . .	12
Rassembler la Martinique*	3
Total	41

* Electoral list comprising the Union pour un Mouvement Populaire (UMP) and allies.

REPRESENTATIVES TO THE FRENCH PARLIAMENT

Deputies to the French National Assembly: ALFRED MARIE-JEANNE (Gauche, Démocrate et Républicaine), BRUNO NESTOR AZEROT (Gauche, Démocrate et Républicaine), SERGE LETCHIMY (Socialiste, Républicain et Citoyen), JEAN-PHILIPPE NILOR (Gauche, Démocrate et Républicaine).

Representatives to the French Senate: SERGE LARCHER (Groupe Socialiste), MAURICE ANTISTE (Groupe Socialiste).

GOVERNMENT OFFICES

Culture, Education and Environment Committee: Hôtel de la Région, ave Gaston Deferre, Plateau Roy Cluny, BP 601, 97200 Fort-de-France; tel. 5-96-59-64-43; fax 5-96-59-63-21; e-mail ccee@cr-martinique.fr; internet www.cr-martinique.fr.

Economic, Social and Environmental Regional Committee: Hôtel de la Région, ave Gaston Deferre, Plateau Roy Cluny, BP 601, 97200 Fort-de-France; tel. 5-96-59-63-00; fax 5-96-59-64-31; e-mail cesr-s@region-martinique.com; internet www.cr-martinique.fr.

European Affairs and Co-operation Committee: Hôtel de la Région, ave Gaston Deferre, Plateau Roy Cluny, BP 601, 97200 Fort-de-France; Dir JEAN YVES LACASCADE.

Political Organizations

Bâtir le Pays Martinique: Fort-de-France; f. 1998; left-wing; split from the Parti Communiste Martiniquais; Leader PIERRE-JEAN SAMOT; Nat. Sec. DAVID ZOBDA.

Combat Ouvrier: BP 821, 97258 Fort-de-France Cédex; e-mail l .maugee972@orange.fr; internet www.combat-ouvrier.net; Trotskyist; mem. of the Communist Internationalist Union; Leader GHISLAINE JOACHIM-ARNAUD.

Conseil National des Comités Populaires (CNCP): 8 rue Pierre et Marie Curie, Terres Sainville, 97200 Fort-de-France; tel. 5-96-63-75-23; e-mail cncp@netcaraibes.com; internet www.m-apal.com; f. 1983; pro-independence party affiliated to the Union Général des Travailleurs de Martinique; Pres. JOSETTE MASSOLIN; Spokesperson ROBERT SAÉ.

Fédération Socialiste de la Martinique (FSM): 52 rue du Capitaine Pierre-Rose, 97200 Fort-de-France; tel. 5-96-60-14-88; fax 5-96-63-81-06; e-mail federation.socialiste-martinique@ wanadoo.fr; internet martinique.parti-socialiste.fr; local br. of the Parti Socialiste (PS); Fed. Sec. LOUIS JOSEPH MANSCOUR; Spokesperson FRÉDÉRIC BUVAL.

Forces Martiniquaises de Progrès (FMP): 12 rue Ernest Deproge, 97200 Fort-de-France; tel. 5-96-57-74-10; fax 5-96-63-36-19; e-mail miguel.laventure@fmp-regionales.org; internet www .jrdmedias.com/laventure/index.html; f. 1998 to replace the local br. of the Union pour la Démocratie Française; Pres. MIGUEL LAVENTURE.

Mouvement des Démocrates et Écologistes pour une Martinique Souveraine (MODEMAS): Fort-de-France; f. 1992; left-wing, pro-independence; Pres. GARCIN MALSA.

Mouvement Indépendantiste Martiniquais (MIM): Fort-de-France; internet www.mim-matinik.org; f. 1978; pro-independence party; First Sec. ALFRED MARIE-JEANNE.

Mouvement Populaire Franciscain: angle des rues Couturier et Holo, 97240 Le François; tel. 5-96-54-20-40; e-mail direction@ pont-abel.fr; left-wing; Leader MAURICE ANTISTE.

Osons Oser: Fort-de-France; f. 1998; right-wing; affiliated with the metropolitan Union pour un Mouvement Populaire (UMP); Pres. PIERRE PETIT.

Parti Communiste Martiniquais (PCM): angle des rues A. Aliker et E. Zola, Terres-Sainville, 97200 Fort-de-France; tel. 5-96-71-86-83; fax 5-96-63-13-20; e-mail ed.justice@wanadoo.fr; internet journal-justice-martinique.com; f. 1957; Sec.-Gen. GEORGES ERICHOT.

Parti Progressiste Martiniquais (PPM): Ancien Réservoir de Trénelle, 97200 Fort-de-France; tel. 5-96-71-88-01; fax 5-96-72-68-56; e-mail contact@ppm-martinique.fr; internet www .ppm-martinique.fr; f. 1958; left-wing; Leader SERGE LETCHIMY; Sec.-Gen. DIDIER LAGUERRE.

Parti Régionaliste Martiniquais: Fort-de-France; f. 2010 by fmr mems of UMP (q.v.); right-wing; Pres. CHANTAL MAIGNAN; Sec.-Gen. CHRISTIAN RAPHA.

Rassemblement Démocratique pour la Martinique (RDM): Résidence Pichevin 2, Bâtiment Hildevert, Les Hauts du Port, 97200 Fort-de-France; tel. 5-96-71-89-97; internet rfdm.e-monsite.com; f. 2006; Sec.-Gen. CLAUDE LISE.

Union pour un Mouvement Populaire (UMP): angle des rues de la République et Vincent Allègre, 97212 Saint Joseph; tel. 5-96-57-96-68; fax 5-96-57-32-68; internet www.u-m-p.org; centre-right; local br. of the metropolitan party; Pres., Departmental Cttee MARC SEFIL.

Les Verts Martinique: Lotissement Donatien, 54 rue Madinina, Cluny, 97200 Fort-de-France; tel. and fax 5-96-71-58-21; e-mail louisleonce@wanadoo.fr; ecologist; departmental br. of the metropolitan party; Leader LOUIS-LÉONCE LECURIEUX-LAFFERONNAY.

Judicial System

Court of Appeal: ave St John Perse, Morne Tartenson, BP 634, 97262 Fort-de-France Cédex; tel. 5-96-70-62-62; fax 5-96-63-52-13; e-mail ca-fort-de-france@justice.fr; highest court of appeal for Martinique and French Guiana; First Pres. Bruno Steinmann; Procurator-Gen. Bernard Rabatel.

There are two Tribunaux de Grande Instance, at Fort-de-France and Cayenne (French Guiana), and three Tribunaux d'Instance (two in Fort-de-France and one in Cayenne).

Religion

The majority of the population belong to the Roman Catholic Church.

CHRISTIANITY

The Roman Catholic Church

Some 80% of the population are Roman Catholics. Martinique comprises the single archdiocese of Fort-de-France. The Archbishop participates in the Antilles Episcopal Conference, based in Port of Spain, Trinidad and Tobago.

Archbishop of Fort-de-France and Saint-Pierre: Most Rev. David Macaire, Archevêché, 5–7 rue du Révérend Père Pinchon, BP 586, 97207 Fort-de-France Cédex; tel. 5-96-63-70-70; fax 5-96-63-75-21; e-mail archeveche-martinique@wanadoo.fr; internet martinique.catholique.fr.

Other Churches

Among the denominations active in Martinique are the Assembly of God, the Evangelical Church of the Nazarene and the Seventh-day Adventist Church.

The Press

Antilla: Le Lamentin, BP 46, 97281 Fort-de-France, Cédex 1; tel. 5-96-75-48-68; fax 5-96-75-58-46, e-mail antilla@orango.fr; internet www.antilla-blog.com; f. 1981; weekly; politics and economics; Publ. Dir Alfred Fortune; Editor-in-Chief Tony Delsham.

France Antilles: pl. François Mitterrand, 97207 Fort-de-France; tel. 5-96-59-08-83; fax 5-96-60-29-96; e-mail redaction.fa@media-antilles.fr; internet www.martinique.franceantilles.fr, f. 1964; subsidiary of Groupe France Antilles; daily; Editor Paul-Henri Coste; circ. 30,000 (Martinique edn).

Journal Asé Pléré Annou Lité (Journal APAL): 8 rue Pierre et Marie Curie, Terres Sainville, 97200 Fort-de-France; tel. 5-96-63-75-23; fax 5-96-70-30-82; e-mail journ.apal@orange.fr; internet www.m-apal.com; f. 1983; monthly; organ of the Conseil Nat. des Comités Populaires (q.v.) and the Union Général des Travailleurs de Martinique (q.v.); Dir Robert Saé.

Journal Combat Ouvriére: 1111 Rés Matéliane, L'Aiguille, 97128 Goyave; e-mail l.maugee972@orange.fr; internet www.combat-ouvrier.net; f. 1970; fortnightly; communist; Publ. Dir Philippe Anais; circ. 14,000.

Justice: angle rue André Aliker et E. Zola, 97200 Fort-de-France; tel. 5-96-71-86-83; fax 5-96-63-13-20; e-mail ed.justice@wanadoo.fr; internet journal-justice-martinique.com; f. 1920; weekly; organ of the Parti Communiste Martinique (q.v.); Dir Fernand Papaya; circ. 8,000.

Le NAIF-Magazine: Résidence K, Pointe des Nègres, route Phare, 97200 Fort-de-France; tel. 5-96-61-62-55; fax 5-96-61-85-76; e-mail docedouard@yahoo.fr; internet www.lenaif.net; weekly; publ. by CIC; Owner Camille Chauvet.

Le Progressiste: c/o Parti Progressiste Martiniquais, Ancien Réservoir de Trénelle, 97200 Fort-de-France; tel. 5-96-71-88-01; e-mail d.compere@ool.fr; internet www.ppm-martinique.fr; weekly; organ of the PPM; Publ. Dir Daniel Compere; circ. 13,000.

TV Magazine: pl. François Mitterand, 97232 Lamentin; tel. 5-96-42-51-28; fax 5-96-42-98-94; e-mail tv.mag@media-antilles.fr; f. 1989; weekly; Editor-in-Chief Lucienne Chénard.

Publishers

Editions Exbrayat: 5 rue des Oisillons, route de Balata, 97234 Fort-de-France; tel. 5-96-64-60-58; fax 5-96-64-70-42; e-mail editions.exbrayat@exbrayat.com; internet commerce.ciel.com/exbrayat; regional art, history, natural history, culinaria, maps and general fiction; 2 brs in Guadeloupe; Commercial Dir Paquita Exbrayat-Sanchez; Sec. Herminie Marie-Claire.

Editions Lafontaine: Bâtiment 12, Maniba, 97222 Case Pilote; tel. and fax 5-96-78-87-98; e-mail info@editions-lafontaine.com; internet www.editions-lafontaine.com; f. 1994; Creole, French and English literature, general fiction, culture, history, youth and educational; Dir Jeannine 'Jala' Lafontaine.

Broadcasting and Communications

TELECOMMUNICATIONS

Caribsat Martinique: Fort-de-France; tel. 5-96-64-74-61; e-mail martinique@caribsat.fr; internet www.caribsat.fr; satellite internet provider.

Digicel Antilles Françaises Guyane: Oasis, Quartier Bois Rouge, 97224 Ducos; tel. 8-10-63-56-35; fax 5-96-42-09-01; e-mail contact@digicelgroup.fr; internet www.digicel.fr; f. 2000 as Bouygues Telecom Caraïbe; acquired from Bouygues Telecom, France, in 2006; mobile cellular telephone operator; network coverage incl. Guadeloupe and French Guiana; CEO (French Caribbean) Yann Kerebel; Dir-Gen. (Martinique) Sébastien Aubé.

Orange Caraïbe: see Guadeloupe—Telecommunications.

Outremer Telecom: Z. I. la Jambette, BP 280, 97285 Lamentin Cédex 2; e-mail communication@outremer-telecom.fr; internet www.outremer-telecom.fr; f. 1998; mobile telecommunications provider; CEO Jean-Michel Hegesippe.

ONLY: Z. I. la Jambette, BP 280, 97285 Lamentin Cédex 2; e-mail communication@outremer-telecom.fr; internet www.outremer-telecom.fr; f. 1998 as Outremer Telecom Martinique; present name adopted following merger of Volubis, ONLY and OOL in 2006; telecommunications provider; subsidiary of Outremer Telecom, France; Head of Operations (French West Indies and French Guiana) Frédéric Hayot.

BROADCASTING

Atlantic FM Martinique: Lorrain; tel. 5-96-71-33-38; e-mail radio.atlanticfm@yahoo.fr; internet www.atlanticfm.fr.

Martinique 1ère (Outre-mer Première): La Clairière, BP 662, 97263 Fort-de-France Cédex; tel. 5-96-59-52-00; fax 5-96-59-52-26; internet martinique.la1ere.fr; acquired by Groupe France Télévisions in 2004; fmrly Société Nationale de Radio-Télévision Française d'Outre-mer; name changed to Réseau France Outre-mer (RFO) in 1998; present name adopted in 2010; radio and TV; Regional Dir Stéphanie Gaumont.

Radio

Radio Asé Pléré Annou Lité (Radio APAL) (Radio Pèp-la): 8 rue Pierre et Marie Curie, Terres Sainville, 97200 Fort-de-France; tel. 5-96-63-75-23; fax 5-96-70-30-82; e-mail radio.apal@orange.fr; internet www.m-apal.com; f. 1989; affiliated to the Conseil Nat. des Comités Populaires (q.v.) and the Union Général des Travailleurs de Martinique (q.v.); French and Creole; Dir Michel Ne'Dan; Station Man. Jean-Claude Louis-Sydney.

Radio Banlieue Relax (RBR): 107 ave Léona Gabriel, Cité Dillon, 97200 Fort-de-France; tel. 5-96-60-00-90; fax 5-96-73-06-53; e-mail radio.br@orange.fr; internet www.rbrfm.com; f. 1981; regional social and cultural programmes; Pres. Frantz Cléoron; Dir Jocelyn Herté.

Radio Canal Antilles (RCA): plateau Fofo, 97233 Schoelcher; e-mail radiocanalantilles@orange.fr; tel. 5-96-61-74-19; fax 5-96-61-23-58; internet membres.multimania.fr/canalantilles; f. 1980; fmrly Radio 105; regional social and cultural programmes; Radio France Internationale relay; Pres. Serge Pognon.

Radio Caraïbes International (RCI Martinique): 2 blvd de la Marne, 97200 Fort-de-France Cédex; tel. 5-96-63-98-70; fax 5-96-63-26-59; internet www.rcimartinique.fm; commercial radio station; Dir José Anelka; Station Man. Vincent Chrétien; Editor-in-Chief Jean-Philippe Ludon.

Radio Evangile Martinique (REM): 54 Route des Religieuses, 97200 Fort-de-France; tel. 5-96-70-68-48; fax 5-96-70-17-51; e-mail rem@evgi.net; internet rem.evgi.net; f. 1993; Pres. Raymond Sormain; Dir Lucien Coique.

Other radio stations include: Chérie FM (formerly Campêche FM); Difé Radio; Fun Radio (formerly Maxxi FM); Radio 22; Radio Actif Martinique; Radio Alizés; Radio Archipel; Radio Espérance; Radio Espoir; Radio Inter Tropicale; Radio Solidarité Rurale—La Voix des Mornes; and West Indies Radio.

Television

Antilles Télévision (ATV): 28 ave des Arawacks, Chateauboeuf, 97200 Fort-de-France; tel. 5-96-75-44-44; fax 5-96-75-55-65; e-mail contact@atvweb.fr; internet www.antillestelevision.fr; f. 1993; general interest; accounts for 22% of viewers; also broadcasts to French Guiana and Guadeloupe; Chair. Fabrice Jean-Jean; Dir-Gen. Daniel Robin; Editor-in-Chief Karl Sivatte.

Canal Plus Antilles: see Guadeloupe—Television.

Kanal Martinique Télévision (KMT) (Kanal Matinik Télévision): voie 7, Rénéville, 97200 Fort-de-France; tel. 5-96-63-64-85; e-mail webmaster@kmttelevision.com; internet kmttelevision.com; f. 2004; operated by l'Asscn pour le Développement des Techniques Modernes de Communication; Pres. ROLAND LAOUCHEZ.

Finance

(cap. = capital; res = reserves; dep. = deposits; m. = million; brs = branches; amounts in euros)

BANKING

Central Bank

Institut d'Emission des Départements d'Outre-mer (IEDOM): 1 blvd du Général de Gaulle, BP 512, 97206 Fort-de-France Cédex; tel. 5-96-59-44-00; fax 5-96-59-44-04; e-mail agence@iedom-martinique.fr; internet www.iedom.fr; Dir VICTOR-ROBERT NUGENT.

Commercial Banks

Banque des Antilles Françaises: see Guadeloupe—Finance.

BNP Paribas Martinique: 72 ave des Caraïbes, BP 588, 97200 Fort-de-France; tel. 5-96-59-46-00; fax 5-96-63-71-42; e-mail bnpm@bnp.mq; internet www.bnpparibas.mq; f. 1941; subsidiary of BNP Paribas, France; 12 brs; Chair. BAUDOUIN PROT.

BRED Banque Populaire: Z. I. la Jambette, 97232 Le Lamentin; tel. 5-96-63-77-63; e-mail courrier-direct@bred.fr; internet www .bred.banquepopulaire.fr; cap. 242m. (Oct. 2005); Regional Man. BRUNO DUVAL; brs in Martinique and French Guiana.

Crédit Agricole: rue Case Nègre, pl. d'Armes, BP 370, 97232 Le Lamentin Cédex 2; tel. 8-20-39-93-10; fax 5-96-51-37-12; internet www.ca-martinique.fr; f. 1950; total assets 1,263m. (Dec. 2004); Pres. XAVIER DELIN; Dir JEAN-MARIE CARLI; 30 brs in Martinique and French Guiana.

Société Générale de Banque aux Antilles (SGBA): see Guadeloupe—Finance.

INSURANCE

AGF Allianz Vie France: ZAC de l'Etang Z'Abricots, Bâtiment C, 97200 Fort-de-France; tel. 5-96-50-55-61; fax 5-96-50-55-71; e-mail marvie1@agfmar.com; internet www.allianz.fr; life insurance; subsidiary of Allianz Group.

Assurance Outre-mer: Hauts Dillon Delgres, Fort-de-France; tel. 5-96-73-09-70; fax 5-96-70-09-25; e-mail contact@assurance-outremer.fr; internet www.assurance-outremer.com; Dir-Gen. THIERRY COAT.

DPA Assurance: 126 route des Religieuses 97200 Fort de France; tel. 5-96-63-84-49; fax 5-96-63-09-52; e-mail dp.a@wanadoo.fr; internet www.dpa-assurances.com.

Groupama Antilles Guyane: 10 Lotissement Bardinet Dillon, BP 559, 97242 Fort-de-France Cédex; tel. 5-96-75-33-33; fax 5-96-75-06-78; internet www.groupama.fr; f. 1978; Group CEO THIERRY MARTEL; Dir-Gen. DIDIER COURIER; 6 brs in Martinique, 7 brs in Guadeloupe, 3 brs in French Guiana.

Groupement Français d'Assurances Caraïbes (GFA Caraïbes): 46–48 rue Ernest Desproges, 97205 Fort-de-France; tel. 5-96-59-04-04; fax 5-96-72-49-94; e-mail contact@gfa-caraibes.fr; internet www.gfacaraibes.fr; subsidiary of Gruppo Generali, Italy; Chair. JEAN-CLAUDE WULLENS; Man. Dir STÉPHANE COUDOUR.

Trade and Industry

GOVERNMENT AGENCIES

Direction Régionale du Commerce Extérieur Antilles-Guyane (DRCE): Bureaux 406 et 408, BP 647, 97262 Fort-de-France Cédex; tel. 5-96-39-49-90; fax 5-96-60-08-14; e-mail drceantilles@missioneco.org; internet www.tresor.economie.gouv .fr/region/antilles-guyane; Regional Dir MICHEL ROUSSELLIER; Regional Asst (Martinique) XAVIER BUCHOUX.

Direction Régionale de l'Industrie, de la Recherche et de l'Environnement (DRIRE): see French Guiana—Trade and Industry.

Direction de la Santé et du Développement Social (DSDS): Centre d'Affaires AGORA, l'Etang Z'abricots, Pointe des Grives, BP 658, 97263 Fort-de-France Cédex; tel. 5-96-39-42-43; fax 5-96-60-60-12; e-mail josiane.pinville@sante.gouv.fr; internet www.martinique .sante.gouv.fr; Dir CHRISTIAN URSULET.

DEVELOPMENT ORGANIZATIONS

Agence Française de Développement (AFD): 1 blvd du Général de Gaulle, BP 804, 97244 Fort-de-France Cédex; tel. 5-96-59-44-73;

fax 5-96-59-44-88; e-mail afdfortdefrance@groupe-afd.org; internet www.afd.fr; fmrly Caisse Française de Développement; Man. ERIC BORDES.

Secrétariat Général pour les Affaires Régionales (SGAR)—Bureau de la Coopération Régionale: Préfecture, 97262 Fort-de-France; tel. 5-96-39-49-78; fax 5-96-39-49-59; e-mail jean-charles .barrus@martinique.pref.gouv.fr; successor to the Direction de l'Action Economique Régionale (DAER); research, documentation, and technical and administrative advice on investment in industry and commerce; Chief JEAN-CHARLES BARRUS.

CHAMBERS OF COMMERCE

Chambre d'Agriculture: pl. d'Armes, BP 312, 97286 Le Lamentin Cédex 2; tel. 5-96-51-75-75; fax 5-96-51-93-42; e-mail ca972@martinique.chambagri.fr; internet www.martinique.chambagri.fr; Pres. LOUIS-DANIEL BERTOME; Dir NICAISE MONROSE.

Chambre de Commerce et d'Industrie de la Martinique: 50 rue Ernest Desproge, BP 478, 97200 Fort-de-France Cédex; tel. 5-96-55-28-00; fax 5-96-60-66-68; e-mail dic@martinique.cci.fr; internet www .martinique.cci.fr; f. 1907; Pres. MANUEL BAUDOUIN; Dir-Gen. FRANTZ SABIN.

Chambre des Métiers et de l'Artesanat de la Martinique: 2 rue du Temple, Morne Tartenson, BP 1194, 97200 Fort-de-France; tel. 5-96-71-32-22; fax 5-96-70-47-30; e-mail cmm972@wanadoo.fr; internet www.cma-martinique.com; f. 1970; Pres. HERVÉ LAUREOTE; Sec.-Gen. HERVÉ ETILÉ; 8,000 mems.

INDUSTRIAL ORGANIZATION

Association Martiniquaise pour la Promotion de l'Industrie (AMPI): Centre d'Affaires de la Martinique, Bâtiment Pierre, 1er étage, Californie, BP 1042, 97232 Le Lamentin; tel. 5-96-50-74-00; fax 5-96-50-74-37; e-mail industrie@ampi.mq; internet www .industriemartinique.com; f. 1972 as Asscn des Moyennes et Petites Industries; 119 mem. cos; Pres. PIERRE MARIE-JOSEPH; Sec.-Gen. RICHARD CRESTOR.

EMPLOYERS' ORGANIZATIONS

Banalliance: Centre d'Affaires le Baobab, rue Léon Gontran Damas, 97232 Le Lamentin; tel. 5-96-57-42-42; fax 5-96-57-35-18; f. 1996; banana growers' alliance; Pres. DANIEL DISER; Dir-Gen. SANDRA ALEXIA; 220 mems.

Banamart: Quartier Bois Rouge, 97224 Ducos; tel. 5-96-42-43-44; fax 5-96-51-47-70; internet www.banamart.com; f. 2005 by merger of SICABAM and GIPAM; represents banana producers; Pres. NICOLAS MARRAUD DES GROTTES; Dir-Gen. PIERRE MONTEUX.

IMALFLHOR (Interprofession Martiniquaise des Fruits, Legumes et Produits Horticoles): Immeuble La Chapelle, Route du stade, Place d'Armes; tel. 5-96-59-70-56; fax 5-96-51-06-63; e-mail contact .imaflhor@gmail.com; internet sites.google.com/site/imaflhor/home; f. 2010; supports and develops agricultural production; Chair. FRANÇOIS DE MEILLAC.

Ordre des Médecins de la Martinique: 80 rue de la République, 97200 Fort-de-France; tel. 5-96-63-27-01; fax 5-96-60-58-00; e-mail martinique@972.medecin.fr; Pres. HELENON RAYMOND; Sec.-Gen. ELANA EMILE.

Ordre des Pharmaciens de la Martinique: Apt G-01, Immeuble Gaëlle, Résidence Studiotel-Grand Village, BP 587, 97233 Schoelcher; tel. 5-96-52-23-67; fax 5-96-52-20-92; e-mail delegation_martinique@ordre.pharmacien.fr; internet www.ordre .pharmacien.fr; Pres. JEAN BIGON.

UTILITIES

Electricity

EDF Martinique (Electricité de France Martinique): Pointe des Carrières, BP 573, 97242 Fort-de-France Cédex 01; tel. 5-96-59-20-00; fax 5-96-60-29-76; e-mail edf-services-martinique@edfgdf.fr; internet www.edf.fr/martinique; f. 1975; electricity supplier; successor to Société de Production et de Distribution d'Electricité de la Martinique (SPDEM); Chair. and CEO HENRI PROGLIO; 174,753 customers (2006).

Water

Veolia Water-Société Martiniquaise des Eaux (SME): pl. d'Armes, BP 213, 97284 Le Lamentin Cédex 02; tel. 5-96-51-80-51; fax 5-96-51-80-55; e-mail sme@sme.mq; internet www.smeaux.fr; f. 1977 as Société Martiniquaise des Eaux; Dir-Gen. JEAN-PIERRE PIERRE.

TRADE UNIONS

Confédération Générale du Travail de la Martinique (CGTM): Maison des Syndicats, blvd Général de Gaulle, 97200 Fort-de-

France; tel. 5-96-70-25-89; fax 5-96-63-80-10; e-mail contact@cgt-martinique.fr; internet www.cgt-martinique.fr; f. 1961; affiliated to World Fed. of Trade Unions; Sec.-Gen. GHISLAINE JOACHIM-ARNAUD.

Fédération Syndicale Unitaire Martinique (FSU): route des Réligieuses, Bâtiment B, Cité Bon Air, 97200 Fort-de-France; tel. 5-96-63-63-27; fax 5-96-71-89-43; e-mail fsu@fsu-martinique.fr; internet www.fsu-martinique.fr; f. 1993; departmental br. of the Fédération Syndicale Unitaire; represents public sector employees in teaching, research and training, and also agriculture, justice, youth and sports, and culture; Sec.-Gen. BERNADETTE GROISON.

Union Générale des Travailleurs de Martinique (UGTM): 8 rue Pierre et Marie Curie, Terres Sainville, 97200 Fort-de-France; tel. 5-96-63-75-23; fax 5-96-70-30-82; e-mail ugtm.centrale@wanadoo.fr; f. 1999; Pres. LÉON BERTIDE; Sec.-Gen. PATRICK DORÉ.

UNSA Education Martinique (UE): Maison des Syndicats, Salles 4–5, Jardin Desclieux, 97200 Fort-de-France; tel. 5-96-72-64-74; fax 5-96-70-16-80; e-mail unsa-education972@orange.fr; internet www.unsa-education.org; 22-mem. fed; Sec.-Gen. MIREILLE JACQUES.

Transport

RAILWAYS

There are no railways in Martinique.

ROADS

There were 2,077 km (1,291 miles) of roads in 1998, of which 261 km were motorways and first-class roads.

SHIPPING

CMA-CGM CGM Antilles-Guyane: ZIP de la Pointe des Grives, BP 574, 97242 Fort-de-France Cédex; tel. 5-96-55-32-00; fax 5-96-63-08-87; e-mail fdf.jgourdin@cma-cgm.com; internet www.cma-cgm.com; subsidiary of CMA-CGM, France; also represents other passenger and freight lines; Pres. RODOLPHE SAADÉ; Man. Dir JACQUES GOURDIN.

Direction Régionale des Affaires Maritimes (DRAM): Centre de Sécurité des Navires, Fort-de-France Cédex; tel. 5-96-60-42-44; fax 5-96-63-67-30; e-mail affaires.maritimes.martinique@wanadoo.fr; Dir LUC NOSLIER.

Grand Port Maritime de la Martinique: quai de l'Hydro Base, BP 782, 97244 Fort-de-France Cédex; tel. 5-96-59-00-00; fax 5-96-71-35-73; e-mail contact@martinique.port.fr; internet www.martinique.port.fr; f. 1953 under management of Chambre de Commerce et de l'Industrie de la Martinique; present name adopted 2013 when port became publicly owned; Dir JEAN-RÉMY VILLAGEOIS.

CIVIL AVIATION

Aimé Césaire International Airport is located at Le Lamentin, 12 km from Fort-de-France and is equipped to handle jet-engined aircraft. Three scheduled airlines operate flights to Paris: Air France, Corsair and Air Caraïbes. Regional services are provided primarily by Air Caraïbes to Guadeloupe, St-Martin, St-Barthélemy, St Lucia and Guyana. Air France also provides a regular service to French Guiana. The regional airline LIAT (based in Antigua and Barbuda) provides scheduled services to all islands of the Eastern Caribbean. In 2013 American Airlines began a direct service from Miami, FL, USA, to Fort-de-France. Seaborne Airlines also launched a weekly service from San Juan to Martinique in that year.

Direction des Services Aéroportuaires: BP 279, 97285 Le Lamentin; tel. 5-96-42-16-00; fax 5-96-42-18-77; e-mail aeroport@martinique.cci.fr; internet www.martinique.aeroport.fr; Dir FRANTZ THODIARD.

Air Caraïbes: see Guadeloupe—Transport.

Tourism

Martinique's tourist attractions are its beaches and coastal scenery, its mountainous interior, and the historic towns of Fort-de-France and Saint-Pierre. In 2013 the number of tourists who stayed on the island totalled 489,705. Receipts from tourism were €484m. in 2013.

Comité Martiniquais du Tourisme: Immeuble Beaupré, Pointe de Jaham, 97233 Schoelcher; tel. 5-96-61-61-77; fax 5-96-61-22-72; e-mail infos.cmt@martiniquetourisme.com; internet www.martiniquetourisme.com; Pres. KARINE ROY-CAMILLE.

Délégation Régionale au Tourisme: 41 rue Gabriel Périé, 97200 Fort-de-France; tel. 5-96-71-42-68; fax 5-96-73-00-96; e-mail drtmartinique.ndl@wanadoo.fr; Delegate VALÉRIE LEOTURE.

Fédération Martiniquaise des Offices de Tourisme et Syndicats d'Initiative (FMOTSI): Maison du Tourisme Vert, 9 blvd du Général de Gaulle, BP 491, 97207 Fort-de-France Cédex; tel. 5-96-63-18-54; fax 5-96-70-17-61; e-mail contact@fmotsi.net; internet www.fmotsi.net; f. 1984; Pres. JOSÉ REINETTE; Sec.-Gen. JEAN-MARC LUSBEC.

Defence

As assessed at November 2014, France maintained a military force of about 1,200. There was also a naval base, headquartered in Fort-de-France, and a gendarmerie.

Education

The educational system is similar to that of metropolitan France (see chapter on French Guiana). In 2013/14 there were 74 pre-primary schools, 178 primary schools and 80 secondary schools. In 2013/14 there were 40,887 pupils in pre-primary and primary education, while in secondary education there were 38,615 students, of whom some 90% attended state schools. Higher education is provided by a branch of the Université des Antilles et de la Guyane. In 2012/13 there were 7,829 students enrolled in higher education on the island.

MAYOTTE

Introductory Survey

LOCATION, CLIMATE, LANGUAGE, RELIGION, CAPITAL

Mayotte forms part of the Comoros archipelago, which lies between the island of Madagascar and the east coast of the African mainland. The territory comprises a main island, Mayotte (Mahoré), and a number of smaller islands. The climate is tropical, with temperatures averaging between 24°C and 27°C (75°F to 81°F) throughout the year. The official language is French, but Shimaore (Maorese) and Shibushi are also spoken. Islam is the main religion. The capital is Dzaoudzi, which is connected to the island of Pamandzi by a causeway.

CONTEMPORARY POLITICAL HISTORY

Historical Context

Since the Comoros unilaterally declared independence in July 1975, Mayotte has been administered separately by France. The independent Comoran state claims sovereignty of Mayotte, and officially represents it in international organizations, including the UN. In December 1976 France introduced the special status of Collectivité Territoriale (Territorial Collectivity) for the island. Following a coup in the Comoros in May 1978, Mayotte rejected the new Government's proposal that it should rejoin the other islands under a federal system, and reaffirmed its intention of remaining linked to France. In December 1979 the Assemblée Nationale (National Assembly) approved legislation that extended Mayotte's special status for another five years, during which the islanders were to be consulted. In October 1984, however, the National Assembly further prolonged Mayotte's status, and the referendum on the island's future was postponed indefinitely.

Domestic Political Affairs

Relations between the main political party on Mayotte, the Mouvement Populaire Mahorais (MPM), and the French Government rapidly deteriorated after the Franco-African summit in November 1987, when the French Prime Minister, Jacques Chirac, expressed reservations concerning the elevation of Mayotte to the status of a Département d'Outre-mer (Overseas Department), despite his announcement, in early 1986, that he shared the MPM's aim to upgrade Mayotte's status. In the second round of the French presidential election, which took place in May 1988, François Mitterrand, the incumbent President and the candidate of the Parti Socialiste (PS), received 50.3% of the votes cast on Mayotte, defeating Chirac, the candidate of the Rassemblement pour la République (RPR). At elections to the French National Assembly, which took place in June, Henry Jean-Baptiste was re-elected as Mayotte's representative to that body. (Later that month, he joined the newly formed centrist group in the National Assembly, the Union du Centre.) In elections to the Conseil Général (General Council) of Mayotte in September and October, the MPM retained the majority of seats.

In 1989–90 concern about the number of Comoran immigrants seeking employment on the island resulted in an increase in racial tension. A paramilitary organization, known as Caiman, was subsequently formed in support of the expulsion of illegal immigrants, but was refused legal recognition by the authorities. In June 1992 growing resentment resulted in further attacks against Comoran immigrants resident in Mayotte. In September representatives of the MPM met the French Prime Minister, Pierre Bérégovoy, to request the reintroduction of entry visas to restrict immigration from the Comoros. Later that month the MPM organized a boycott of Mayotte's participation in the French referendum on the Treaty on European Union (see p. 271), in support of the provision of entry visas.

At elections to the National Assembly, which took place in March 1993, Jean-Baptiste was returned, securing 53.4% of the votes cast, while the Secretary-General of the RPR, Mansour Kamardine, received 44.3% of the votes.

Elections to the General Council (which was enlarged from 17 to 19 members) took place in March 1994: the MPM retained 12 seats, while the RPR secured four seats, and independent candidates three seats. During an official visit to Mayotte in November, the French Prime Minister, Edouard Balladur, announced the reintroduction of entry visas as a requirement for Comoran nationals, and the adoption of a number of security measures, in an effort to reduce illegal immigration to the island.

In elections to the French Sénat (Senate) in September 1995, the incumbent MPM representative, Marcel Henry, was returned by a large majority; Mayotte's representation in the Senate was later increased to two seats. In October the French Government pledged that a referendum on the future status of the island would be conducted by 1999. In October 1996 it was confirmed that two commissions, one based in Paris and the other in Mayotte, were preparing a consultation document and that the resulting referendum would take place before the end of the decade.

Partial elections to fill nine seats in the General Council were held in March 1997; the MPM secured three seats (losing two that it had previously held), the RPR won three seats, the local PS one seat, and independent right-wing candidates two seats. In elections to the National Assembly Jean-Baptiste, representing the alliance of the Union pour la Démocratie Française (UDF) and the Force Démocrate, defeated Kamardine, securing 51.7% of the votes cast in the second round of voting, which took place in June.

In April 1998 one of the commissions charged with examining the future status of Mayotte submitted its report, which concluded that the present status of Territorial Collectivity was no longer appropriate, but did not advocate an alternative. In May the MPM declared its support for an adapted form of departmental administration. In May 1999 Jean-Baptiste introduced draft legislation to the National Assembly, which proposed the holding of a referendum regarding the island's future before the end of the year. In August, following negotiations with the French Government, Mayotte members of the RPR and the PS and Younoussa Bamana, the leader of the MPM, signed a draft document providing for the transformation of Mayotte into a Collectivité Départementale (Departmental Collectivity), if approved at a referendum. However, both Henry and Jean-Baptiste rejected the document. The two politicians subsequently announced their departure from the MPM and formed a new political party, the Mouvement Départementaliste Mahorais (MDM), while reiterating their demands that Mayotte be granted full overseas departmental status.

Mayotte becomes a Departmental Collectivity

Following the approval of Mayotte's proposed new status by the General Council and the municipal councils, an accord to this effect was signed by political representatives of France and Mayotte on 27 January 2000. On 2 July a referendum was held, in which the population of Mayotte voted overwhelmingly in favour of the January accord, granting Mayotte the status of Departmental Collectivity for a period of 10 years.

At elections to the General Council, held in March 2001, no party established a majority. The MPM experienced significant losses, with only four of its candidates being elected, while the RPR won five seats, the Mouvement des Citoyens (MDC) two, the MDM one, the PS one, and various right-wing independent candidates six seats. Bamana was re-elected as President of the General Council. The French parliament approved Mayotte's status as a Departmental Collectivity in July.

In the first round of the French presidential election, which was held on 21 April 2002, Chirac received the highest number of votes on Mayotte, winning 43.0% of the valid votes cast; the second round, held on 5 May, was also won resoundingly by Chirac, who secured 88.3% of the votes cast on the island, defeating the candidate of the extreme right-wing Front National, Jean-Marie Le Pen. At elections to the National Assembly, held in June, Kamardine, representing the recently formed Union pour la Majorité Présidentielle (UMP, which

incorporated the RPR, the Démocratie Libérale and significant elements of the UDF), defeated the MDM-UDF candidate, Siadi Vita. In November the UMP was renamed the Union pour un Mouvement Populaire (retaining the same acronym).

At elections to the General Council in March 2004, the UMP won eight seats in alliance with the MPM, which secured one seat, while the MDM and the MDC, also in alliance, obtained five and two seats, respectively; independent candidates were elected to the remaining three seats. With the election of Saïd Omar Oili, an independent, as President of the General Council on 2 April, executive power was transferred from the Prefect to the Council. In May a national referendum on ratification of the European Union (EU) constitutional treaty was held: 86.5% of Mayotte's electorate voted in favour of adopting the treaty; however, it was ultimately rejected by a majority of French voters.

In November 2005 a French parliamentary commission was convened to report on the state of illegal immigration in Mayotte. The commission's first report, which was published in February 2006, found that there were between 45,000 and 60,000 illegal immigrants living in Mayotte, of whom 90% were Comoran. (According to the census of 2002 the official French population numbered 160,265.) The number of births on the island had risen by more than 50% over a 10-year period, reaching 7,676 in 2004, of which some two-thirds were to women lacking official documentation. The report proposed closer co-operation with the Comoran authorities. Recommendations to stem the flow of immigrants included the introduction of biometric identity cards in Mayotte and the Comoros, and an increase in the number of border police.

Nicolas Sarkozy of the UMP secured 30.5% of the votes cast on Mayotte in the first round of the French presidential election, held on 22 April 2007. However, in the second round, which took place on 6 May, Ségolène Royal of the PS won 60.0% of the votes cast, although Sarkozy was elected to the presidency. At elections to the National Assembly, held on 10 and 17 June, Kamardine was defeated by Abdoulatifou Aly, who was affiliated to the Mouvement Démocrate (MoDem), which had been formed following the presidential election by François Bayrou, the leader of the UDF, to oppose Sarkozy's UMP.

Meanwhile, in February 2007 Vincent Bouvier was appointed Prefect and remained in the post until July 2008, when Denis Robin assumed the position. Also in February 2007 new legislation approved by the French National Assembly introduced statutory and institutional measures granting Mayotte many of the powers afforded to territories with full overseas departmental status, with the exception of certain fiscal, financial and social welfare powers. This followed a constitutional amendment in 2003 whereby Mayotte acquired the status of Collectivité d'Outre-mer (Overseas Collectivity) and expedited the process towards becoming an Overseas Department. The 2007 legislation provided a framework for measures to be implemented to facilitate the transfer of full fiscal control to Mayotte by January 2014.

Elections for 10 of the 19 seats in the General Council took place over two rounds held on 9 and 16 March 2008. The UMP, the MDM and the Nouvel Élan pour Mayotte (founded in 2007 by Omar Oili) all secured two seats, the PS won one seat and three seats were taken by independent candidates. On 20 March 2008 Ahamed Attoumani Douchina was elected to replace Omar Oili as President of the Council.

Mayotte becomes an Overseas Department

In April 2008 the General Council adopted a resolution providing for the transfer of Mayotte's status from that of Overseas Collectivity to an Overseas Department. At a referendum, held on 29 March 2009, 95.2% of voters approved of Mayotte attaining the status of an Overseas Department within the French Republic (despite the recognition of the island by the African Union and the Comoran Government as an inseparable part of the Comoran state). In October 2010 the French Senate endorsed the departmentalization of Mayotte and the following month the National Assembly approved the appropriate legislation.

Meanwhile, in August 2009 Hubert Derache replaced Robin as Prefect. In December protests on Pamandzi against the rise in the cost of living resulted in some 15 people being injured during clashes with the security forces. In January 2010 President Sarkozy made a brief visit to Mayotte during which he discussed the issue of immigration with local officials.

On 31 March 2011 Mayotte officially became the 101st Department of France and the fifth Overseas Department. On 3 April Daniel Zaïdani was elected President of the General Council and in July Thomas Degos replaced Derache as Prefect. In October the authorities of Mayotte made an official request to the EU to consider Mayotte as a Région Ultrapériphérique (RUP—Outermost Region) of France. Recognition as an RUP would allow Mayotte to draw upon EU funds to aid its economic development.

Persistent unrest on the island caused by the continued high cost of living led to a 44-day general strike in October and early November 2011, followed by a further two days' shutdown in December. The French Prime Minister, François Fillon, dispatched Robin to attempt to mediate an agreement between trade unions, employers and the Government to end the strike action. In late December an agreement was signed, imposing until March 2012 a reduction in the price of 11 staple goods; in addition, families with modest incomes were to receive food tokens.

The 2012 elections

The first round of the French presidential election was conducted on 22 April 2012: Sarkozy attracted 48.7% of Mayotte's votes, compared with 36.6% for François Hollande of the PS. A second round election was held two weeks later, at which Sarkozy secured 51.0% of the ballot, defeating Hollande, who obtained 49.1%. Nevertheless, Hollande triumphed nationally and was sworn in as President in mid-May. In the French legislative elections held on 10 and 17 June, Mayotte's representation in the National Assembly was increased to two seats; the seats were won by Ibrahim Aboubacar, representing the PS, and Boinali Saïd, an independent left-wing candidate. In July the EU approved Mayotte's petition to be recognized as an RUP; this new status came into effect on 1 January 2014.

The French Minister of Overseas Territories, Victorin Lurel, visited Mayotte in July 2012 to hold discussions with the local authorities regarding the high cost of living on the island. A bill to address the problem of inflated prices (and consequent social unrest) in the French Overseas Possessions was promulgated by President Hollande in November.

In January 2013 Jacques Witkowski was appointed to replace Degos as Prefect. In response to a further series of public sector strikes, Lurel, during a visit to Mayotte in October, signed a decree approving price indexation for public officials of up to 5%, with retroactive effect from 1 January; nevertheless, industrial unrest continued. In November Lurel announced a further decree, which was to enter into force on 1 January 2014, to regulate fuel prices in the Overseas Departments, thereby reducing the profits of oil companies. The new legislation was met with opposition by French oil and gas company Total, and in early 2014 petrol service stations owned by Total were temporarily closed on Mayotte in protest against its introduction. Following discussions between the French Government, oil companies and petrol station owners, an additional decree was adopted in February to facilitate the implementation of the new fuel price regulations. Government officials asserted that the concerns of the private sector had been taken into consideration during the drafting process.

Meanwhile, in June 2013 it was announced that Witkowski would request the French Government to dissolve Mayotte's police Groupement d'Intervention Régional (GIR—Regional Intervention Force), after five of its members were taken into custody in connection with a drugs-trafficking network on the island. A former head of the GIR, Gérard Gautier, was arrested in France in November and subsequently extradited to Mayotte, where he was charged with involvement in drugs-trafficking operations.

In June 2013 Zaïdani was formally accused of embezzling public funds after completing a number of allegedly unlawful transactions. Zaïdani, who denied any wrongdoing, appeared in court in November 2014, and legal proceedings were ongoing in early 2015.

Recent developments: the 2014 elections

Candidates representing left-wing lists narrowly won the most council seats in municipal polls conducted on 23 and 30 March 2014. Elections to the European Parliament took place in Mayotte on 25 May. The UMP secured 34.6% of the local ballot, compared with 31.9% for the left-wing Union pour les Outremer and 13.6% for Choisir Notre Europe, another left-wing organization. Turnout was just 33.4%. Witkowski was succeeded as Prefect by Seymour Morsy in September.

The French Minister of the Interior, Bernard Cazeneuve, visited Mayotte in June 2014 for discussions with island officials on new measures to combat illegal immigration. According to the Minister, annual deportations from Mayotte averaged around 16,000. President Hollande travelled to Mayotte in August; talks with local leaders focused on economic development and the ongoing immigration crisis, which, he argued, could be resolved only through regional co-operation.

Departmental elections were held on 22 and 29 March 2015, at which, according to national legislation adopted in May 2013, the General Council was renamed the Conseil Départemental (Departmental Council) and was expanded to comprise 26 members. Of these, 10 were representatives of the UMP, eight represented a grouping of right-wing parties, four were from the Union Démocrates et Indépendents and four represented a grouping of left-wing parties.

(For further details of the recent history of the island, see the Comoros.)

CONSTITUTION AND GOVERNMENT

The Constitution of the Fifth Republic of France, adopted by referendum on 28 September 1958 and promulgated on 6 October 1958 applies on Mayotte. The French Government is represented in Mayotte by an appointed Prefect. There is a Conseil Départemental (Departmental Council), with 26 members, elected by universal adult suffrage over two rounds for a term of six years; the members of the Council elect a President who acts as head of government. Mayotte elects two deputies to the Assemblée Nationale (National Assembly) and two representatives to the Sénat (Senate). Mayotte is also represented at the European Parliament. Mayotte became an Overseas Department in March 2011 and received the status of Région Ultrapériphérique (Outermost Region) on 1 January 2014.

ECONOMIC AFFAIRS

Mayotte's gross domestic product (GDP) per head in 2009 was €6,575, according to official figures. Total GDP in that year amounted to €1,396m. Between the censuses of 2007 and 2012 the population of Mayotte increased at an average annual rate of 2.7%.

The economy is based mainly on agriculture. In 2007 some 8.5% of the employed labour force were engaged in this sector. The principal export crops are ylang ylang (an ingredient of perfume) and vanilla. Mayotte imports large quantities of foodstuffs, which comprised 25.5% of the value of total imports in 2012. In 2003 it was estimated that some 44% of the population was dependent on *gratte* (subsistence) farming. Cassava, maize and pigeon peas are cultivated for domestic consumption; while rice is widely eaten there is little domestic production. More than 90% of farms grow bananas, often mixed with coconuts (grown for their milk and oil, both of which are used in cooking); together banana and coconut plantations occupy some 45% of agricultural land (approximately 20,000 ha in total, some 55% of the surface area of Mayotte). Mangoes are also widespread, and around one-third of mango trees grow wild. Livestock-rearing (of cattle, goats—for meat—and chickens) and fishing are also important activities. Aquaculture was first introduced in 1998 and in 2005 there were five producers catering mainly to the export market.

Industry (which is dominated by the construction sector) engaged 12.7% of the employed population in 2007. There are no mineral resources on the island. Imports of petroleum products comprised 18.7% of the value of total imports in 2012 and base metals and metal products comprised 6.9%. Mayotte also imports considerable quantities of capital goods (15.1% of the value of total imports) and transport equipment (7.4%).

Services engaged 78.8% of the employed population in 2007. The annual number of tourist arrivals (excluding cruise-ship passengers) totalled 52,400 in 2013; receipts from tourism in 2006 amounted to €16.3m.

In 2013 Mayotte recorded a trade deficit of €461.0m. The principal export in 2012 was fish; exports of ylang ylang were also significant. The principal imports in that year were foodstuffs, petroleum products, capital goods, transport equipment, base metals and metal products, and plastic materials and rubber. The main source of imports in 2012 was France (52.8%); the People's Republic of China was another major supplier. France was also the principal market for exports (taking 38.0% of exports in that year); the other significant purchasers were the Comoros and Réunion.

In 2013 Mayotte's total budgetary revenue was €360.3m., while total expenditure was €316.4m. The annual rate of inflation recorded by Mayotte averaged 2.1% in 2006–14; consumer prices increased by 0.9% in the year to December 2014. Some 19.5% of the labour force was unemployed in 2014.

Mayotte suffers from a persistently high trade deficit, owing to its reliance on imports, and is largely dependent on French aid. As Mayotte's labour force has continued to increase (mostly owing to a high birth rate and the continued arrival of immigrants, many of them entering the territory illegally—see *Domestic Political Affairs*, above), the high unemployment rate (36.3% at mid-2012) has caused particular concern. From late 2011 public sector strikes disrupted trade and deterred visitors; despite measures undertaken by the French Government to address social discontent by reducing inequalities with mainland France, including a decree approving price indexation for public officials in October 2013, industrial unrest persisted. Nevertheless, after the European Union (EU) officially granted Mayotte the status of a Région Ultrapériphérique (Outermost Region) of France on 1 January 2014, the island was expected to benefit from increased development funding. In December 2013 the EU had approved a grant of €60m. for 2014–20 towards the development of the island's agricultural sector. Economic activity increased during 2013, with tourist arrivals, investment and household consumption all rising in that year. However, Mayotte's short-term economic prospects remained hampered by the small size of the private sector, an uncompetitive agricultural industry and undeveloped tourism infrastructure.

PUBLIC HOLIDAYS

The principal holidays of metropolitan France are observed.

Statistical Survey

Source (unless otherwise stated): Institut National de la Statistique et des Études Économiques (INSEE) de Mayotte; Z.I. Kawéni, BP 1362, 97600 Mamoudzou; tel. 269-61-36-35; fax 269-61-39-56; e-mail antenne-mayotte@insee.fr; internet www.insee.fr/fr/regions/mayotte/default.asp.

AREA AND POPULATION

Area: 374 sq km (144 sq miles).

Population: 186,452 at census of 31 July 2007; 212,645 at census of 21 August 2012. *Mid-2015* (UN estimate): 233,993 (Source: UN, *World Population Prospects: The 2012 Revision*).

Density (at mid-2015): 625.6 per sq km.

Population by Age and Sex (UN estimates at mid-2015): *0–14 years:* 102,339 (males 52,172, females 50,167); *15–64 years:* 125,788 (males 61,657, females 64,131); *65 years and over:* 5,866 (males 3,090, females 2,776); *Total* 233,993 (males 116,919, females 117,074) (Source: UN, *World Population Prospects: The 2012 Revision*).

Population by Country of Origin (2002, before adjustment for double counting): Mayotte 103,705; France 6,323; Comoros 45,057; Madagascar-Mauritius-Seychelles 4,601; Total (incl. others) 160,301.

Principal Towns (population of communes at 2012 census): Mamoudzou 57,281; Koungou 26,488; Dzaoudzi (capital) 14,311; Dembeni 10,923; Tsingoni 10,454; Sada 10,195; Bandraboua 10,132.

Births and Deaths (2007): Registered live births 7,658 (birth rate 41.1 per 1,000); Registered deaths 587 (death rate 3.1 per 1,000). *2012:* Birth rate 30.5 per 1,000; Death rate 4.6 per 1,000.

Life expectancy (years at birth): 77.6 (males 74.0; females 81.3) in 2010 (Source: World Bank, World Development Indicators database).

Economically Active Population (persons aged 14 years and over, census of 31 July 2007): Agriculture and fishing 3,204; Construction 3,024; Other industry 1,805; Wholesale and retail trade 3,154; Hotels and restaurants 609; Transport, telecommunications and real estate 5,043; Public administration 6,535; Education, health and social care 7,247; Other services 7,289; *Total employed* 37,910 (males 24,157, females 13,753); Unemployed 13,614 (males 5,922, females 7,692); *Total labour force* 51,524 (males 30,079, females 21,445). *2014* (labour force survey April–June, persons aged 15 years and over): Total employed 43,300; Unemployed 10,500; Total labour force 53,800.

HEALTH AND WELFARE

Key Indicators

Total Fertility Rate (children per woman, 2004): 4.5.

Physicians (per 1,000 head, 1997): 0.4.

Hospital Beds (per 1,000 head, 2007): 1.5.

For definitions see explanatory note on p. vi.

AGRICULTURE, ETC.

Livestock (2003): Cattle 17,235; Goats 22,811; Chickens 80,565.

Fishing (metric tons, live weight, 2012): Capture (FAO estimate) 31,826 (Skipjack tuna 7,245; Yellowfin tuna 19,727); Aquaculture 85 (FAO estimate); *Total catch* 31,911 (FAO estimate). Source: FAO.

INDUSTRY

Electric Energy (million kWh): 285 in 2013 (Source: Institut d'Emission des Départements d'Outre-mer, *Rapport Annuel 2013*).

FINANCE

Currency and Exchange Rates: 100 cent = 1 euro. *Sterling and Dollar Equivalents* (31 December 2014): £1 sterling = €1.286; US $1 = €0.824; €10 = £7.78 = US $12.14. *Average Exchange Rate* (euros per US dollar): 0.7782 in 2012; 0.7532 in 2013; 0.7537 in 2014. The French franc was used until the end of February 2002. Euro notes and coins were introduced on 1 January 2002, and the euro became the sole legal tender from 18 February.

Budget of the Collectivity (€ million, 2013): Total revenue 360.3; Total expenditure 316.4 (Source: Institut d'Emission des Départements d'Outre-mer, *Rapport Annuel 2013*).

French State Expenditure (€ million, 2013): Direct expenditure 437.53; Indirect expenditure 100.42; *Total expenditure* 537.95 (Source: Institut d'Emission des Départements d'Outre-mer, *Rapport Annuel 2013*).

Cost of Living (Consumer Price Index; base: December 2006 = 100): 115.7 in 2012; 117.1 in 2013; 118.2 in 2014.

Expenditure on the Gross Domestic Product (€ million, 2009, INSEE estimates): Government final consumption expenditure 726; Private final consumption expenditure 799; Gross fixed capital formation 372; *Total domestic expenditure* 1,897; Exports of goods and services 31; *Less* Imports of goods and services 532; *GDP in purchasers' values* 1,396.

EXTERNAL TRADE

Principal Commodities (€ million, 2012): *Imports c.i.f.:* Foodstuffs 101.1; Petroleum products 74.3; Chemical products 18.5; Pharmaceutical products 17.3; Textiles 11.2; Plastic materials and rubber 24.5; Base metals and metal products 27.3; Capital goods 60.1; Transport equipment 29.5; Total (incl. others) 397.1. *Exports f.o.b.:* Agricultural products 0.5; Foodstuffs 0.2; Base metals and metal products 0.8; Machinery and appliances 0.3; Transport equipment 0.9; Total (incl. others) 5.3. *2013:* Total imports 465.9; Total exports 4.9.

Principal Trading Partners (€ million, 2012): *Imports:* China, People's Republic 34.1; France (Metropolitan) 209.5; Germany 15.7; Thailand 12.4; Total (incl. others) 397.1. *Exports* (incl. re-exports): Total 5.3. Note: The principal markets for exports are France (Metropolitan—some 38% of exports in 2012), Comoros and Réunion. *2013:* Total imports 465.9; Total exports 4.9.

Source: Institut d'Emission des Départements d'Outre-mer, *Rapport Annuel 2013*.

TRANSPORT

Road Traffic (2008): Motor vehicles in use 7,781.

Shipping (2013 unless otherwise indicated): *Maritime Traffic:* Vessel movements 530 (2005); Goods unloaded 308,429 metric tons; Goods loaded 41,535 metric tons; Passengers 31,962 (arrivals 8,556, departures 23,406).

Civil Aviation (2013): Passengers carried 325,670; Freight carried 1,378 metric tons; Post carried 758 metric tons (Source: Institut d'Emission des Départements d'Outre-mer, *Rapport Annuel 2013*).

TOURISM

Foreign Tourist Arrivals (excl. cruise ship passengers): 48,200 in 2011; 45,800 in 2012; 52,400 in 2013.

Foreign Tourist Arrivals by Country of Residence (2013): France (metropolitan) 27,500; Réunion 21,000; Total (incl. others) 52,400.

Tourism Receipts (€ million): 13.7 in 2004; 14.5 in 2005; 16.3 in 2006.

COMMUNICATIONS MEDIA

Telephones ('000 main lines in use, 2013): 10.0.

Mobile Cellular Telephones ('000 subscribers, 2008): 48.1.

Internet Users ('000, 2000): 1.8.

Source: International Telecommunication Union.

EDUCATION

Pre-primary (2013/14 unless otherwise indicated): 71 schools (2012/13); 17,842 pupils.

Primary (2013/14 unless otherwise indicated): 135 schools (including special schools—2012/13); 34,690 pupils.

General Secondary (2013/14 unless otherwise indicated): 19 schools (2009); 21,579 pupils.

Vocational and Technical (2013/14 unless otherwise indicated): 9 institutions (2009); 11,656 students.

Students Studying in France or Réunion (2009): Secondary 1,452; Higher 2,253; *Total* 3,705.

Teaching Staff (2013, state schools): Primary 2,673; Secondary 2,168; Higher 16.

Directory

The Government
(April 2015)

HEAD OF STATE

President: FRANÇOIS HOLLANDE.

Prefect: SEYMOUR MORSY.

DEPARTMENTAL ADMINISTRATION

President of the Departmental Council: IBRAHIM RAMDANI, 108 rue de l'Hôpital, BP 101, 97600 Mamoudzou; tel. 269-61-12-33; fax 269-61-10-18; internet www.cg976.fr.

Election, Departmental Council, 22 and 29 March 2015

Party	Seats
Union pour un Mouvement Populaire	10
Divers Droite	8
Divers Gauche	4
Union Démocrates et Indépendants	4
Total	**26**

REPRESENTATIVES TO THE FRENCH PARLIAMENT

Deputies to the French National Assembly: BOINALI SAÏD (Divers Gauche), IBRAHIM ABOUBACAR (PS).

Representatives to the French Senate: THANI MOHAMED SOILIHI (Divers Gauche), ABDOURAHAMANE SOILIHI (UMP).

GOVERNMENT DEPARTMENTS

Office of the Prefect: BP 676, Kawéni, 97600 Mamoudzou; tel. 269-63-50-00; fax 269-60-18-89; e-mail communication@mayotte.pref .gouv.fr; internet www.mayotte.pref.gouv.fr.

Department of Business, Competition, Consumption, Labour and Employment: BP 174, 97600 Mamoudzou; tel. 269-61-16-57; fax 269-61-03-37; e-mail dd-976.sct@dieccte.gouv.fr; internet www .mayotte.dieccte.gouv.fr.

Department of the Environment, Planning and Housing: BP 109, 97600 Mamoudzou; tel. 269-61-12-54; fax 269-61-07-11; e-mail de-mayotte@equipement.gouv.fr.

Department of Food, Agriculture and Forestry: BP 103, 97600 Mamoudzou; tel. 269-61-12-13; fax 269-61-10-31; e-mail daaf976@ agriculture.gouv.fr; internet daf.mayotte.agriculture.gouv.fr.

Department of Youth, Sports and Social Cohesion: BP 104, 97600 Mamoudzou; tel. 269-61-60-50; fax 269-61-82-10; e-mail drjscs976@drjscs.gouv.fr.

Political Organizations

Fédération du Front National (FN): route nationale 1, M'tsahara, 97630 M'tzamboro; BP 1331, 97600 Mamoudzou Cédex; tel. and fax 269-60-50-24; Regional Sec. ALI-MANSOIB SOIHIBOU.

Fédération de Mayotte de l'Union pour un Mouvement Populaire (UMP): route nationale, Immeuble 'Jardin Créole', 97600 Mamoudzou; tel. 269-61-64-64; fax 269-60-87-89; e-mail alisouf@ ump976.org; centre-right; local branch of the metropolitan party; Departmental Pres. ASSANI HAMISSI; Departmental Sec. ALI SOUF.

Fédération du Mouvement National Républicain (MNR) de Mayotte: 15 rue des Réfugiers, 97615 Pamandzi; tel. and fax 269-60-33-21; Departmental Sec. ABDOU MIHIDJAY.

Mouvement des Citoyens (MDC): Chirongui; Leader ALI HALIFA.

Mouvement Départementaliste Mahorais (MDM): 97610 Dzaoudzi; f. 2001 by fmr mems of the MPM; Pres. ADRIEN GIRAUD; Sec.-Gen. MOHAMED ALI BEN ALI.

Mouvement de la Gauche Ecologiste de Mayotte: 6 ave Mamanne, Quartier Artisanal, Localité de Pamandzi, 97600 Pamandzi; tel. and fax 269-61-09-70; internet mayotte.lesverts.fr; fmrly Les Verts Mayotte; affiliated to Mouvement de la Gauche Réunionnaise; Gen. Sec. AHAMADA SALIME.

Mouvement Populaire Mahorais (MPM): route de Vahibé, Passamainti, 97600 Mamoudzou; Leader YOUNOUSSA BAMANA.

Parti Socialiste (PS): BP 314, 97600 Mamoudzou; local branch of the metropolitan party; Fed. Sec. IBRAHIM ABUBACAR.

Judicial System

Palais de Justice: Immeuble Espace, BP 106 (Kawéni), 97600 Mamoudzou; tel. 269-61-11-15; fax 269-61-19-63.

Tribunal de Grande Instance: 16 rue de l'hôpital, BP 106, 97600 Mamoudzou; tel. 269-61-11-15; fax 269-61-19-63; Pres. JEAN-BAPTISTE FLORI.

Tribunal d'Instance: Mamoudzou; Pres. ALAIN CHATEAUNEUF.

Procureur de la République: PHILIPPE FAISANDIER.

Religion

Muslims comprise about 98% of the population. Most of the remainder are Christians, mainly Roman Catholics.

CHRISTIANITY

The Roman Catholic Church

Mayotte is within the jurisdiction of the Apostolic Administrator of the Comoros.

Office of the Apostolic Administrator: 7 rue de l'Hôpital, BP 1012, 97600 Mamoudzou; tel. and fax 269-61-11-53; fax 269-61-48-25.

The Press

Albalad: Immeuble Mega, 97600 Kawéni, Mamoudzou; tel. 269-60-66-15; e-mail halda.halidi@awicompany.fr; internet www .albaladmayotte.com; f. 2010; owned by Al Waseet International; daily; French; Dir of Publication PASCAL ABLA; Editor-in-Chief HALDA HALIDI; circ. 1,000.

Flash Infos Mayotte: Société Mahoraise de Presse, 7 rue Salamani Cavani/M'Tsapéré, BP 60, 97600 Mamoudzou; tel. 269-61-20-04; fax 269-60-35-90; e-mail flash-infos@wanadoo.fr; internet www .mayottehebdo.com; f. 1999; owned by Somapresse; daily e-mail bulletin; Dir LAURENT CANAVATE.

Horizon Austral: Société Mahoraise de Presse, 7 rue Salamani Cavani/M'Tsapéré, BP 60, 97600 Mamoudzou; tel. 269-61-20-04; fax 269-60-35-90; e-mail contact@mayottehebdo.com; internet www .mayottehebdo.com; f. 2007; owned by Somapresse; Dir of Publication LAURENT CANAVATE.

Le Mahorais: 11 centre commercial, Lukida, 97600 Mamoudzou; tel. 269-61-66-75; fax 269-61-66-72; internet www.lemahorais.com; weekly; French; Publ. Dir SAMUEL BOSCHER; Editor-in-Chief LUCIE TOUZÉ.

Mayotte Hebdo: Société Mahoraise de Presse, 7 rue Salamani Cavani/M'Tsapéré, BP 60, 97600 Mamoudzou; tel. 269-61-20-04; fax 269-60-35-90; e-mail contact@mayottehebdo.com; internet www.mayottehebdo.com; f. 2000; weekly; French; incl. the economic supplement *Mayotte Eco* and cultural supplement *Tounda* (weekly); owned by Somapresse; Dir LAURENT CANAVATE; circ. 2,300.

Mayotte Magazine: BP 268, Z.I. Kawéni, 97600 Mamoudzou; tel. 06-39-09-03-29; e-mail contact@mayottemagazine.com; internet www.mayottemagazine.fr; f. 2007; 4 a year; Dir STÉPHANIE LÉGERON.

Zan'Goma: Impasse du Jardin Fleuri, Cavani, 97600 Mamoudzou; f. 2005; monthly; French; Publ. Dir MONCEF MOUHOUDHOIRE.

Broadcasting and Communications

TELECOMMUNICATIONS

Mayotte Télécom Mobile: 27, pl. Mariaźe, 97600 Mamoudzou; mobile cellular telephone operator; local operation of Société Réunionnaise du Radiotéléphone based in Réunion.

RADIO AND TELEVISION

Mayotte 1ère: BP 103, 97610 Dzaoudzi; tel. 269-60-10-17; fax 269-60-18-52; e-mail annick.henry@rfo.fr; internet mayotte.la1ere.fr; f. 1977; acquired by Groupe France Télévisions in 2004; fmrly Réseau France Outre-mer, name changed as above in 2010; radio broadcasts in French and more than 70% in Mahorian; television transmissions began in 1986; a satellite service was launched in 2000; Dir-Gen. GENEVIÈVE GIARD; Regional Dir GERALD PRUFER.

Finance
(brs = branches)

BANKS

Issuing Authority

Institut d'Emission des Départements d'Outre-mer: ave de la Préfecture, BP 500, 97600 Mamoudzou; tel. 269-61-05-05; fax 269-61-

05-02; internet agence@iedom-mayotte.fr; internet www.iedom.fr; Dir Yves Mayet.

Commercial Banks

Banque Française Commerciale Océan Indien: route de l'Agriculture, BP 222, 97600 Mamoudzou; tel. 269-61-10-91; fax 269-61-17-40; e-mail pleclerc@bfcoi.com; internet www.bfcoi.com; f. 1976; jtly owned by Société Générale and Mauritius Commercial Bank Ltd; Pres. Gérald Lacaze; brs at Dzaoudzi and Sada.

Banque de la Réunion: 30 pl. Mariage, 97600 Mamoudzou; tel. 269-61-20-30; fax 269-61-20-28; internet www.banquedelareunion.fr; owned by Groupe Banque Populaire et Caisse d'Epargne (France); 2 brs.

BRED Banque Populaire: Centre d'Affaires Mayotte, pl. Mariage, Z.I. 3, 97600 Mamoudzou; tel. 269-64-80-86; fax 269-60-51-10; internet www.bred.fr; owned by Groupe Banque Populaire et Caisse d'Epargne (France).

INSURANCE

AGF: pl. Mariage, BP 184, 97600 Mamoudzou; tel. 269-61-44-33; fax 269-61-14-89; e-mail jl.henry@wanadoo.fr; Gen. Man. Jean-Luc Henry.

Groupama: BP 665, Z.I. Nel, Lot 7, 97600 Mamoudzou; tel. 269-62-59-92; fax 269-60-76-08.

Prudence Créole: Centre Commercial et Médical de l'Ylang, BP 480, 97600 Mamoudzou; tel. 269-61-11-10; fax 269-61-11-21; e-mail prudencecreolemayotte@wanadoo.fr; 87% owned by Groupe Générali; 2 brs.

Trade and Industry

DEVELOPMENT ORGANIZATION

Agence Française de Développement (AFD): Résidence Sarah, pl. du Marché, BP 610, Kawéni, 97600 Mamoudzou; tel. 269-64-35-00; fax 269-62-66-53; e-mail afdmamoudzou@groupe-afd.org; internet www.afd.fr; Dir Patrick Salles.

EMPLOYERS' ORGANIZATIONS

Mouvement des Entreprises de France Mayotte (MEDEF): Z.I. Kawéni, Immeuble GMOI, BP 570, 97600 Mamoudzou; tel. 269-61-44-22; fax 269-61-46-10; e-mail contact@medef-mayotte.com; internet www.medef-mayotte.com; Pres. Laurent Havet; Sec.-Gen. Vincent Schublin.

Ordre National des Médecins: BP 675 Kawéni, 97600 Mamoudzou; tel. 269-61-02-47; fax 269-61-36-61.

UTILITIES

Electricity

Electricité de Mayotte (EDM): BP 333, Z.I. Kawéni, 97600 Kawéni; tel. 269-62-96-80; internet www.electricitedemayotte.com; f. 1997; subsidiary of SAUR; Dir-Gen. Augusto Soares dos Reis.

Water

Syndicat Intercommunal de l'Eau et de l'Assainissement de Mayotte (SIEAM): BP 289, 97600 Mamoudzou; tel. 269-62-11-11; fax 269-61-55-00; e-mail sieam@sieam.fr; internet www.sieam.fr; Pres. Maoulida Soula.

TRADE UNIONS

Confédération Inter-Syndicale de Mayotte (CISMA-CFDT): 18 rue Mahabou, BP 1038, 97600 Mamoudzou; tel. 269-61-12-38; fax 269-61-36-16; f. 1993; Gen. Sec. Saïd Boinali.

Fédération Départementale des Syndicats d'Exploitants Agricoles de Mayotte (FDSEAM): 150 rue Mbalamanga-Mtsapéré, 97600 Mamoudzou; tel. and fax 269-61-34-83; e-mail fdsea.mayotte@wanadoo.fr; f. 1982; Pres. Laïna Mogné-Mali; Dir Ali Bacar.

Union Départementale Force Ouvrière de Mayotte (FO): Z.I. de Kaweni, Rond Point El-Farouk, BP 1109, 97600 Mamoudzou; tel. 269-61-18-39; fax 269-61-22-45; Sec.-Gen. Hamidou Madi MColo.

Transport

ROADS

In 2011 the road network totalled approximately 230 km, of which 90 km were main roads.

SHIPPING

Coastal shipping is provided by locally owned small craft. There is a deep-water port at Longoni. Construction of a second quay at Longoni was one of the stated aims of the 2008–14 development contract between Mayotte and the French Government; in December 2008 the Agence Française de Développement approved the allocation of a €10m. loan towards the extension of Longoni port.

Service des Affaires Maritimes: BP 37, 97615 Pamandzi; tel. 269-60-31-38; fax 269-60-31-39; e-mail c.mait.sam-mayotte@developpment-durable.gouv.fr; Head of Service Olivier Bisson.

Service des Transports Maritimes (STM): BP 186, 97600 Dzaoudzi; tel. 269-64-39-72; fax 269-60-80-25; e-mail denys.cormy@cg976.fr; internet www.mayotte-stm.com; Dir Denys Cormy; 8 vessels.

CIVIL AVIATION

There is an airport at Dzaoudzi, serving daily commercial flights to the Comoros; four-times weekly flights to Réunion; twice-weekly services to Madagascar; twice-weekly direct flights to Paris, France; and weekly services to Kenya and Mozambique. In 2004 plans were approved for the construction of a new runway to allow the commencement of direct flights to Paris, France; the runway was scheduled to be completed by 2015. Plans for a new terminal at the airport in Dzaoudzi were announced in late 2010 as a result of which the number of visitors passing through the airport each year was expected to increase to 615,000 by 2025; the new terminal became operational in 2014.

Air Austral: pl. Mariage, BP 1429, 97600 Mamoudzou; tel. 269-60-90-90; fax 269-61-61-94; e-mail mayotte@air-austral.com; internet www.air-austral.com; Pres. Gérard Ethève.

Tourism

Tropical scenery provides the main tourist attraction. Excluding cruise ship passengers, Mayotte received 52,400 visitors in 2013; tourism receipts totalled €16.3m. in 2006.

Comité Départemental du Tourisme de Mayotte (CDTM): rue Amiral Lacaze 5, 97400 Saint-Denis, Réunion; tel. 269-61-09-09; fax 269-61-03-46; e-mail mayottetourisme.lareunion@orange.fr; internet www.mayotte-tourisme.com; Dir George Mecs.

RÉUNION

Introductory Survey

LOCATION, CLIMATE, LANGUAGE, RELIGION, CAPITAL

Réunion is an island in the Indian Ocean, lying about 800 km (500 miles) east of Madagascar. The climate varies greatly according to altitude: at sea level it is tropical, with average temperatures between 20°C (68°F) and 28°C (82°F), but in the uplands it is much cooler, with average temperatures between 8°C (46°F) and 19°C (66°F). Rainfall is abundant, averaging 4,714 mm annually in the uplands, and 686 mm at sea level. The population is of mixed origin, including people of European, African, Indian and Chinese descent. The official language is French. A large majority of the population are Christians belonging to the Roman Catholic Church. The capital is Saint-Denis.

CONTEMPORARY POLITICAL HISTORY

Historical Context

Réunion was first occupied by France in 1642, and was ruled as a colony until 1946, when it received full departmental status. In 1974 it became an Département d'Outre-mer (Overseas Department) with the status of a region.

In 1978 the Organization of African Unity (OAU, now the African Union, see p. 188) adopted a report recommending measures to hasten the independence of the island, and condemned its occupation by a 'colonial power'. However, while the left-wing political parties on the island advocated increased autonomy (amounting to virtual self-government), there was little popular support for complete independence.

Domestic Political Affairs

In June 1992 a delegation from the Conseil Régional (Regional Council) met French President François Mitterrand to submit proposals for economic reforms, in accordance with the aim of establishing parity between Réunion and metropolitan France. In July, however, the French Government announced increases in social security benefits that were substantially less than had been expected, resulting in widespread discontent on the island. In September the Parti Communiste Réunionnais (PCR), which in alliance with the Free-DOM list of independent candidates controlled 26 of the 45 seats in the Regional Council, demanded that the electorate refuse to participate in the forthcoming French referendum on ratification of the Treaty on European Union (see p. 271), in protest at the alleged failure of the French Government to recognize the requirements of the Overseas Departments. At the referendum, which took place later that month, the ratification of the treaty was approved by the voters of Réunion, although only 26.3% of the registered electorate voted.

Elections to the French National Assembly were held in March 1993; two incumbent right-wing deputies retained their seats, while the PCR, the Parti Socialiste (PS) and the Rassemblement pour la République (RPR) each secured one of the remaining seats. At elections to the 47-seat Conseil Général (General Council), which took place in March 1994, the PCR retained 12 seats, while the number of PS deputies increased to 12. The number of seats held by the RPR and the Union pour la Démocratie Française (UDF) declined to five and 11, respectively. The PCR and PS subsequently established a coalition. In April a member of the PS, Christophe Payet, was elected President of the General Council; the right-wing parties (which had held the presidency of the General Council for more than 40 years) boycotted the poll. The PS and PCR agreed to control the administration of the General Council jointly.

In the second round of the French presidential election, which took place in May 1995, the socialist candidate, Lionel Jospin, secured 56% of the votes cast on Réunion, while Jacques Chirac, the official candidate of the RPR, won 44% of the votes (although Chirac obtained the highest number of votes overall).

Equality with metropolitan France

With effect from the beginning of 1996 the social security systems of the Overseas Departments were aligned with those of metropolitan France. Paul Vergès, joint candidate of the PCR and the PS, was elected to the French Sénat (Senate) in April. In the by-election to replace Vergès, which took place in September, Claude Hoarau, the PCR candidate, was elected as a deputy to the National Assembly. A new majority alliance between Free-DOM, the RPR and the UDF was subsequently formed in the Regional Council, with the re-election of its 19-member permanent commission in October.

Four left-wing candidates were successful in elections to the National Assembly held in May and June 1997. Claude Hoarau (PCR) retained his seat and was joined by Huguette Bello and Elie Hoarau, also both from the PCR, and Michel Tamaya (PS), while André Thien Ah Koon, representing the RPR-UDF coalition, was re-elected.

In February 1998 the PCR (led by Vergès), the PS and several right-wing mayors presented a joint list of candidates, known as the Rassemblement, to contest forthcoming elections. In the elections to the Regional Council, which took place on 15 March, the Rassemblement secured 19 seats, while the UDF obtained nine seats and the RPR eight, with various left-wing candidates representing Free-DOM winning five. Vergès was elected President of the Regional Council on 23 March, with the support of the deputies belonging to the Rassemblement and Free-DOM groups. In concurrent elections to an expanded 49-member General Council, right-wing candidates (including those on the Rassemblement's list) secured 27 seats, while left-wing candidates obtained 22 seats, with the PCR and the PS each winning 10 seats. At the end of the month Jean-Luc Poudroux, of the UDF, was elected President of the General Council.

At municipal elections, held in March 2001, the left-wing parties experienced significant losses. Notably, the PS mayor of Saint-Denis, Michel Tamaya, was defeated by the RPR candidate, René-Paul Victoria. At elections to the General Council, held concurrently, the right-wing parties also made substantial gains, obtaining 38 of the 49 seats; the UDF retained its majority, and Poudroux was re-elected as President. In July Elie Hoarau was obliged to resign from the National Assembly, following his conviction on charges of electoral fraud, for which he received a one-year prison sentence.

In the first round of the French presidential election, which was held on 21 April 2002, Jospin secured 39.0% of the valid votes cast in the Department (although he was eliminated nationally), followed by Chirac, who received 37.1%. In the second round, on 5 May, Chirac overwhelmingly defeated the candidate of the extreme right-wing

Front National (FN), Jean-Marie Le Pen, with 91.9% of the vote. At elections to the National Assembly in June, Thien Ah Koon, allied to the new Union pour la Majorité Présidentielle (UMP, which had recently been formed by the merger of the RPR, the Démocratie Libérale and elements of the UDF), and Bello were re-elected. Tamaya lost his seat to Victoria of the UMP, Claude Hourau lost to Bertho Audifax of the UMP, while Elie Hourau, who was declared ineligible to stand for re-election, was replaced by Christophe Payet of the PS. (In November the UMP was renamed the Union pour un Mouvement Populaire.)

In elections to the Regional Council, which took place on 21 and 28 March 2004, the Alliance, a joint list of candidates led by the PCR, secured 27 seats. The UMP won 11 seats, and an alliance of the PS and Les Verts Réunion obtained seven seats. Following concurrent elections to the General Council, to renew 25 of the 49 seats, right-wing candidates held 30 seats, while left-wing candidates held 19. On 1 April Nassimah Dindar of the UMP was elected to succeed Poudroux as President of the General Council. Paul Vergès was re-elected as President of the Regional Council on the following day. In February 2005 Gélite Hoarau replaced Vergès as the PCR's representative to the Senate.

In May 2005 a national referendum on ratification of the proposed constitutional treaty of the European Union (EU) was held: 59.9% of Réunion's electorate joined with a majority of French voters in rejecting the treaty.

Presidential and local elections

In the first round of the French presidential election, held on 22 April 2007, Ségolène Royal of the PS secured 46.2% of the votes cast in Réunion, while Nicolas Sarkozy of the UMP received 25.1%. Sarkozy was elected to the presidency in the second round of voting on 6 May; however, voting on Réunion again favoured Royal, who received 63.6% of the island vote. At legislative elections in June, Victoria and Bello both retained their seats in the National Assembly, but Audifax lost his seat to Jean-Claude Fruteau of the PS. Didier Robert of the UMP defeated Paul Vergès, while Patrick Lebreton of the PS was also elected. In March 2008 Dindar was re-elected to the presidency of the General Council.

In January 2009 workers in Guadeloupe, a French overseas territory in the Caribbean, commenced industrial action in protest against rising fuel and food prices. The unrest rapidly spread to other Departments, including Réunion, where unemployment and living costs had increased significantly. In March protests staged in Saint-Denis to demand price reductions and a wage increase for low-paid workers degenerated into violence; police responded by firing tear gas to disperse the crowds.

In January 2010 President Sarkozy visited Réunion for the first time since his election to the presidency. Also in that month Michel Lalande replaced Pierre-Henry Maccioni as Prefect. Elections to the Regional Council took place on 14 and 21 March 2010 at which the La Réunion en Confiance alliance led by Robert won 27 seats. The Liste de l'Alliance, headed by Vergès' PCR, took 12 seats, while the PS-led Pour une Réunion plus Juste avec l'Union des Socialistes alliance secured six seats. On 26 March Robert was elected to succeed Vergès as President of the Regional Council.

In early 2012 further social unrest erupted, initially directed at the high cost of fuel prices with transporters blocking fuel outlets; subsequently protests at the generally high cost of living spread across the island and security forces were brought in from France to quell the violence. Some 233 arrests were made and nine police officers were injured, according to the Prefecture. Following negotiations between local politicians, civil society representatives, transporters and petrol companies, an agreement was reached to lower prices of fuel and electricity for households on modest income and to freeze prices for 60 staple products.

The 2012 elections

The first round of the French presidential election was conducted on 22 April 2012: François Hollande, representing the PS, attracted 53.3% of the island's votes, compared with 18.0% for Sarkozy. A second round election was held two weeks later, at which Hollande secured 71.5% of the ballot, comprehensively defeating Sarkozy, who won only 28.5%. Hollande also triumphed nationally and was sworn in as President in mid-May. In the legislative elections, which took place on 10 and 17 June, Réunion's representation in the National Assembly was increased from five to seven seats. The PS secured five of the seats, with the two remaining mandates won, respectively, by an independent left-wing candidate and a representative of Le Centre pour la France (a coalition led by the Mouvement Démocrate). Jean-Luc Marx was inaugurated as the island's new Prefect on 27 August, replacing Lalande.

The French Minister of Overseas Territories, Victorin Lurel, visited Réunion in July 2012 to hold discussions with the local authorities regarding the high cost of living on the island. A bill to address the issue of inflated prices (and consequent social unrest) in Réunion and other French Overseas Possessions, drafted by Lurel, was promulgated by President Hollande in November.

In November 2013 the French Minister of Labour, Employment, Vocational Training and Social Dialogue, Michel Sapin, visited Réunion, where he announced further measures to address the continued high rate of unemployment and to promote vocational training. In the same month Lurel announced a decree, which entered into force on 1 January 2014, to regulate fuel prices in the Overseas Departments; an additional decree was adopted in February to facilitate the implementation of the new fuel price regulations. Meanwhile, the French Government declared a state of natural disaster on Réunion in early January, following a severe cyclone in which one person was killed, and Lurel made a further visit to the island. The damage to Réunion's agricultural industry was estimated at €50m.

Candidates representing right-wing lists won the most council seats in municipal polls conducted on 23 and 30 March 2014. Elections to the European Parliament took place in Réunion on 25 May. The Union pour les Outremer, a left-wing grouping, secured 23.3% of the local ballot, while the UMP garnered 22.2%, the left-wing Choisir Notre Europe 15.5% and the far-right FN list 13.0%. Turnout was only 20.4%, however. Marx was succeeded as Prefect by Dominique Sorain in September.

Recent developments: structural reforms

Preliminary structural reform proposals were approved by the French National Assembly in July 2014. It was envisaged that, *inter alia*, many of the powers of the General Council would be transferred to the Regional Council (and the municipal councils), potentially leading to the eventual dissolution of the former. Although Dindar declared her opposition to the proposals, proponents argued that they would increase administrative efficiency and reduce costs.

President Hollande visited Réunion in August 2014. Talks with local leaders focused on the island's economic development, particularly the plight of the sugar industry, which faced an uncertain future owing to the end of government subsidies from 2017 (in accordance with a ruling by the World Trade Organization). Hollande announced that an additional €38m. of financial assistance would be made available to bolster the sugar sector.

Departmental elections were held on 22 and 29 March 2015, at which, according to national legislation adopted in May 2013, the General Council was renamed the Conseil Départemental (Departmental Council) and was expanded to comprise 50 members. Of these, most notably, 12 represented a grouping of left-wing parties, 10 were representatives of the UMP, eight were from the Union de la Droite, six were from the PS, and both the Union Démocrates et Indépendants and the Parti Communiste Français secured four representatives.

CONSTITUTION AND GOVERNMENT

The Constitution of the Fifth Republic of France, adopted by referendum on 28 September 1958 and promulgated on 6 October 1958 applies on Réunion. France is represented in Réunion by an appointed Prefect. There are two councils with local powers: the 50-member Conseil Départmental (Departmental Council) and the 45-member Conseil Régional (Regional Council). Both are elected for up to six years by direct universal suffrage. Réunion has seven directly elected deputies in the French Assemblée Nationale (National Assembly) and four indirectly elected representatives in the Sénat (Senate). The Department is also represented at the European Parliament.

REGIONAL AND INTERNATIONAL CO-OPERATION

Réunion is represented by France in the Indian Ocean Commission (IOC, see p. 447) which it joined in 1986. Réunion was given the right to host ministerial meetings of the IOC, but would not be allowed to occupy the presidency, owing to its status as a non-sovereign state. As an integral part of France, Réunion belongs to the European Union (see p. 271).

ECONOMIC AFFAIRS

Réunion's gross national income (GNI) in 1995 was estimated at 29,200m. French francs, equivalent to about 44,300 francs per head. Between the censuses of 1999 and 2008, Réunion's population increased at an average annual rate of 1.6%. In 2012, according to official figures, Réunion's gross domestic product (GDP), measured at current prices, was €16,080m.; in that year GDP per head totalled €19,477. GDP increased, in real terms, at an average annual rate of 5.6% in 2000–10; it declined by 0.7% in 2012.

Agriculture (including hunting, forestry and fishing) contributed 1.3% of GDP in 2007, and engaged an estimated 1.2% of the salaried working population in 2013. The principal cash crops are sugar cane (sugar accounted for 37.9% of export earnings in 2007), maize, tobacco, vanilla, and geraniums and vetiver root, which are cultivated for the production of essential oils. Other major crops are tomatoes, cauliflowers, potatoes, cabbages, and lettuce and chicory. Fishing and livestock production are also important to the economy. According to the UN, agricultural GDP increased at an average annual rate of 3.9% during 1990–2000; growth in 2001 was 3.1%.

Industry (including mining, manufacturing, construction and power) contributed 16.6% of GDP in 2007, and employed an estimated 12.5% of the working salaried population in 2013. The principal branch of manufacturing is food-processing, particularly the production of sugar and rum. Other significant sectors include the fabrication of construction materials, mechanics, printing, metalwork, textiles and garments, and electronics. According to the UN, industrial GDP (excluding construction) increased at an average annual rate of 4.3% during 1990–99; growth in 2001 was 3.7%.

There are no mineral resources on the island. Energy is derived principally from thermal and hydroelectric power. Power plants at Bois-Rouge and Le Gol produce around 45% of the island's total energy requirements; almost one-third of the electricity generated is produced using bagasse, a by-product of sugar cane. Imports of petroleum fuel comprised 12.8% of the value of total imports in 2013.

Services (including transport, communications, trade and finance) contributed 82.0% of GDP in 2007, and employed an estimated 86.2% of the salaried working population in 2013. The public sector accounts for more than two-thirds of employment in the services sector. Tourism is also significant; in 2013 some 416,000 tourists visited Réunion. According to the World Tourism Organisation, tourism revenue totalled €315m. in 2012.

Réunion's economy is overwhelmingly dependent on imports and as a result the island recorded a merchandise trade deficit of € 4,162.5m. in 2013. The principal sources of imports in 2010 were France (54.2%), Singapore and the People's Republic of China. The principal market for exports in 2010, were France (31.6%), Mayotte, Spain, Madagascar and Hong Kong. The principal exports in 2013 were other industrial products, prepared foodstuffs, industrial products, industrial and household waste, transport equipment, and electrical and electronic equipment and components. The principal imports in 2013 were prepared foodstuffs, electrical and electronic equipment and components, refined petroleum products, transport equipment, pharmaceutical products, metal products, miscellaneous manufactured products, textiles and footwear, plastic products, and chemicals and perfumes.

In 2009 the budget balanced at €750m. The departmental budget for that year amounted to €1,415.0m.; some 62.5% of revenue was to be provided by the State. The annual rate of inflation averaged 1.6% in 2004–13; consumer prices increased by 1.4% in 2014. According to ILO, an estimated 28.5% of the labour force were unemployed in 2012.

Réunion has a relatively developed economy, but is dependent on financial aid from France. The economy has traditionally been based on agriculture and is, therefore, vulnerable to poor climatic conditions. From the 1990s the production of sugar cane (the principal agricultural activity) was adversely affected by increasing urbanization, which resulted in a decline in agricultural land. Economic progress has been largely sustained by tourism and domestic consumption. In October 2013 the French Government announced measures to address the continued high rate of unemployment, including the provision of an additional 5,000 subsidized contracts, although local officials were urged to implement the existing 20,000 subsidized contracts. Réunion's Action Plan for growth in 2014–20, submitted to the European Commission in mid-2013, cited a focus on youth and employment as its main priority; the Plan also emphasized the need to improve the island's accessibility, with the rehabilitation of transport links and establishment of information technology infrastructure, in order to expand external trade, and to strengthen growth in the tourism sector towards a long-term objective of 1m. tourist arrivals by 2020. According to the French Institut National de la Statistique et des Etudes Economiques, the economy expanded by just 0.7% in 2013 (the same low rate of growth as in the previous year). The agricultural and construction sectors contracted, visitor numbers declined, trade decreased, and investment levels remained very low.

PUBLIC HOLIDAYS

The principal holidays of metropolitan France are observed.

Statistical Survey

Source (unless otherwise indicated): Institut National de la Statistique et des Etudes Economiques, Service Régional de la Réunion, 15 rue de l'Ecole, 97490 Sainte-Clotilde; tel. 262-48-81-00; fax 262-41-09-81; internet www.insee.fr/fr/insee_regions/reunion.

AREA AND POPULATION

Area: 2,507 sq km (968 sq miles).

Population: 706,180 (males 347,076, females 359,104) at census of 8 March 1999; 828,581 at census of 1 January 2011. Note: According to new census methodology, data in 2011 refer to median figures based on the collection of raw data over a five-year period (2009–13). *Mid-2015* (UN estimate): 895,099 (Source: UN, *World Population Prospects: The 2012 Revision*).

Density (at mid-2015): 357.0 per sq km.

Population by Age and Sex (UN estimates at mid-2015): *0–14 years:* 220,992 (males 112,022, females 108,970); *15–64 years:* 593,611 (males 291,935, females 301,676); *65 years and over:* 80,496 (males 34.919, females 45,577); *Total* 895,099 (males 438,876, females 456,223) (Source: UN, *World Population Prospects: The 2012 Revision*).

Principal Localities (population at 1 January 2011): Saint-Denis (capital) 145,347; Saint-Paul 103,916; Saint-Pierre 80,356; Le Tampon 74,998; Saint-André 55,090; Saint-Louis 52,523.

Births, Marriages and Deaths (2013): Registered live births 14,002 (birth rate 16.6 per 1,000); Registered marriages 2,791 (marriage rate 3.6 per 1,000); Registered deaths 4,258 (death rate 5.1 per 1,000).

Life Expectancy (years at birth, 2013): Males 77.0; females 83.5.

Employment (persons aged 15 years and over, provisional estimates at 31 December 2013): Agriculture, forestry and fishing 2,900; Mining and utilities 3,420; Manufacturing 13,054; Construction 12,996; Wholesale and retail trade; repair of motor vehicles, motorcycles, etc. 31,264; Transport 11,305; Hotels and restaurants 6,924; Information and communication 3,865; Financial activities and real estate 7,247; Private services 22,428; Public administration and defence; education, health and social work 98,244; Other community, social and personal service activities 21,359; *Total employed* 235,006. Note: Data exclude 20,992 persons employed without salary.

HEALTH AND WELFARE

Key Indicators

Total Fertility Rate (children per woman, 2013): 2.4.

Physicians (per 1,000 head, 2012): 2.8.

Hospital Beds (per 1,000 head, 2000): 3.7.

For definitions, see explanatory note on p. vi.

AGRICULTURE, ETC.

Principal Crops ('000 metric tons, 2013, FAO estimates): Maize 16.2; Potatoes 6.0; Sugar cane 1,900.0; Cabbages and other brassicas 3.2; Lettuce and chicory 3.2; Tomatoes 8.8; Cauliflowers and broccoli 6.3; Pumpkins, squash and gourds 0.9; Eggplants (Aubergines) 0.9; Onions and shallots, green 4.8; Beans, green 3.8; Carrots and turnips 2.3; Bananas 7.6; Tangerines, mandarins, clementines and satsumas 4.0; Mangoes, mangosteens and guavas 2.8; Pineapples 22.7. *Aggregate Production* ('000 metric tons, may include official, semi-official or estimated data): Total vegetables (incl. melons) 48.0; Total fruits (excl. melons) 71.7.

Livestock ('000 head, 2013, FAO estimates): Cattle 30.0; Pigs 68.5; Sheep 1.0; Goats 40.0; Chickens 15,500.

Livestock Products ('000 metric tons, 2013, FAO estimates): Cattle meat 1.6; Pig meat 15.0; Chicken meat 17.2; Rabbit meat 1.9; Cow's milk 33.0; Hen eggs 7.0.

Forestry ('000 cu m, 1991): *Roundwood Removals:* Sawlogs, veneer logs and logs for sleepers 4.2; Other industrial wood 0.9 (FAO estimate); Fuel wood 31.0 (FAO estimate); Total 36.1. *Sawnwood Production:* 2.2. *1992–2013:* Annual production assumed to be unchanged from 1991 (FAO estimates).

Fishing (metric tons, live weight, 2012, FAO estimates): Capture 2,693 (Albacore 333; Yellowfin tuna 465; Bigeye tuna 389; Swordfish 1,092; Common dolphinfish 91); Aquaculture 115 (FAO estimate); *Total catch* (incl. others) 2,808 (FAO estimate).

Source: FAO.

INDUSTRY

Selected Products (metric tons, 2013, unless otherwise indicated): Sugar 197,800; Oil of geranium 2 (2007); Oil of vetiver root 0.4 (2002); Rum (hl) 97,500; Electric energy (million kWh) 2,813 (Source: partly Institut d'Emission des Départements d'Outre-mer, *Rapport Annuel 2013*).

FINANCE

Currency and Exchange Rates: The French franc was used until the end of February 2002. Euro notes and coins were introduced on 1 January 2002, and the euro became the sole legal tender from 18 February. Some of the figures in this Survey are still in terms of francs. For details of exchange rates, see Mayotte.

Budgets (€ million, 2012): *Departmental Budget:* Current revenue 1,354.2 (Tax revenue 856.2, Grants 470.3, Other 27.7); Capital revenue 114.0; Total revenue 1,468.2. Current expenditure 1,256.5 (Wages 207.6, Other goods and services 42.0, Interest payments 12.0, Other 994.9); Capital expenditure 234.9; Total expenditure 1,491.4. *Regional Budget:* Revenue 753.4 (Current 509.2, Capital 244.2); Expenditure 814.6 (Current 372.0, Capital 442.6) (Source: partly Institut d'Emission des Départements d'Outre-mer, *Rapport Annuel 2013*).

Cost of Living (Consumer Price Index; base: 2000 = 100): All items 124.7 in 2012; 126.4 in 2013; 126.7 in 2014. Source: ILO.

Expenditure on the Gross Domestic Product (€ million at current prices, 2012, provisional): Private final consumption expenditure 9,730; Government final consumption expenditure 6,250; Gross capital formation 3,510; *Total domestic expenditure* 19,490; Exports of goods 310; *Less* Imports of goods 4,650; Tourist expenditure 310; Statistical discrepancy 620; *GDP in market prices* 16,080.

Gross Domestic Product by Economic Activity (€ million at current prices, 2007): Agriculture, forestry and fishing 177; Mining, manufacturing, electricity, gas and water 917; Construction 1,274; Wholesale and retail trade 1,182; Transport and communications 820; Finance and insurance 704; Public administration 1,521; Education, health and social work 3,128; Other services (incl. hotels and restaurants) 3,472; *Sub-total* 13,196; *Less* Financial intermediation services indirectly measured 462; *Gross value-added at basic prices* 12,734; Taxes on products, *less* subsidies on products 1,235; *GDP in market prices* 13,969.

EXTERNAL TRADE

Principal Commodities (€ million, 2013): *Imports:* Animals and animal products 109.1; Prepared foodstuffs 783.1; Refined petroleum products 568.9; Electrical and electronic equipment and components 723.0; Transport equipment 521.6; Other industrial products 1,645.5 (Textiles and footwear 259.9; Pharmaceutical products 267.1; Miscellaneous manufactured products 278.8); Total (incl. others) 4,458.3. *Exports:* Prepared foodstuffs 191.1; Refined petroleum products 0.9; Industrial and household waste 22.2, Electrical and electronic equipment and components 21.1; Transport equipment 22.2; Other industrial products 31.5; Total (incl. others) 296.1 (Source: Source: Institut d'Emission des Départements d'Outre-mer, *Rapport Annuel 2013*).

Principal Trading Partners (€ million, 2010): *Imports:* Belgium 52.1; China, People's Republic 287.5; France 2,312.8; Germany 200.6; Italy 89.8; Singapore 389.8; South Africa 100.0; Spain 62.0; Total (incl. others) 4,265.2. *Exports f.o.b.:* France 88.9; Hong Kong 13.4; Italy 6.7; Japan 10.5; Madagascar 15.1; Mauritius 7.4; Mayotte 26.5; Spain 18.0; USA 8.4; Total (incl. others) 281.5.

TRANSPORT

Road Traffic (1 January 2005): Motor vehicles in use 338,500.

Shipping: *Flag Registered Fleet* (at 31 December 2014): Vessels 14; Total displacement 10,649 grt (Source: Lloyd's List Intelligence—www.lloydslistintelligence.com). *Traffic* (2013 unless otherwise indicated): Passengers carried 33,904; Vessels entered 709 (2007); Freight unloaded 3,391,900 metric tons; Freight loaded 625,100 metric tons; Containers unloaded 111,952 TEUs (2007); Containers loaded 112,921 TEUs (2007).

Civil Aviation (2013): Passenger arrivals 1,030,000; Passenger departures 1,032,000; Freight unloaded 17,510 metric tons; Freight loaded 7,146 metric tons (Source: Institut d'Emission des Départements d'Outre-mer, *Rapport Annuel 2013*).

TOURISM

Tourist Arrivals: 471,300 in 2011; 446,500 in 2012; 416,000 in 2013 (Source: Institut d'Emission des Départements d'Outre-mer, *Rapport Annuel 2013*).

Arrivals by Country of Residence (2013): France (metropolitan) 337,300; Other EU 21,700; Total (incl. others) 416,000 (Source: Institut d'Emission des Départements d'Outre-mer, *La Réunion: Rapport Annuel 2013*).

Tourism Receipts (US $ million, excl. passenger transport): 296 in 2010; 344 in 2011; 315 in 2012 (Source: World Tourism Organization).

COMMUNICATIONS MEDIA

Telephones ('000 main lines in use, 2010): 480.9.

Mobile Cellular Telephones ('000 subscribers, 2008): 579.2.

Internet Users ('000, 2009): 300.

Broadband Subscribers ('000, 2009): 185.

Source: International Telecommunication Union.

EDUCATION

Pre-primary and Primary (2013/14): Schools 523 (pre-primary 157, primary 366); public sector pupils 108,691 (pre-primary 40,361, primary 68,330); private pupils 9,305 (pre-primary 3,305, primary 6,000).

Secondary (2013/14): Schools 130 (119 public sector, 11 private); pupils 101,015 (public sector 93,571, private 7,444).

University (2012/13): Institutions 3; students 12,204.

Other Higher (2011/12): Students 5,879.

Teaching Staff (2012/13, state schools): Pre-primary and primary 6,162; Secondary 8,414; University 421.

Directory

The Government

(April 2015)

HEAD OF STATE

President: FRANÇOIS HOLLANDE.

Prefect: DOMINIQUE SORAIN, Préfecture, pl. du Barachois, 97405 Saint-Denis Cedex; tel. 262-40-77-77; fax 262-41-73-74; e-mail courrier@reunion.pref.gouv.fr; internet www.reunion.pref.gouv.fr.

DEPARTMENTAL ADMINISTRATION

President of the Departmental Council: NASSIMAH DINDAR (UMP), Hôtel du Département, 2 rue de la Source, 97488 Saint-Denis Cedex; tel. 262-90-30-30; fax 262-90-39-99; internet www.cg974.fr.

President of the Regional Council: DIDIER ROBERT (UMP), Hôtel de Région Pierre Lagourgue, ave René Cassin, Moufia, BP 7190, 97719 Saint-Denis Cedex 9; tel. 262-48-70-00; fax 262-48-70-71; e-mail region.reunion@cr-reunion.fr; internet www.regionreunion.com.

Election, Departmental Council, 22 and 29 March 2015

Party	Seats
Divers Droite	12
Union pour un Mouvement Populaire	10
Union de la Droite	8
Parti Socialiste	6
Parti Communiste Français	4
Union Démocrates et Indépendants	4
Divers	2
Divers Gauche	2
Mouvement Démocrate	2
Total	50

Election, Regional Council, 14 and 21 March 2010

Party	Seats
La Réunion en Confiance	27
Liste de l'Alliance	12
Pour une Réunion Plus Juste avec l'Union des Socialistes	6
Total	45

REPRESENTATIVES TO THE FRENCH PARLIAMENT

Deputies to the French National Assembly: ERICKA BAREIGTS (PS), HUGUETTE BELLO (Divers Gauche), JEAN-JACQUES VLODY (PS), PATRICK LEBRETON (PS), JEAN-CLAUDE FRUTEAU (PS), MONIQUE ORPHÉ (PS), THIERRY ROBERT (Le Centre pour la France/MoDem).

Representatives to the French Senate: DIDIER ROBERT (UMP), MICHEL FONTAINE (UMP), PAUL VERGÈS (PCR), MICHEL VERGOZ (PS).

GOVERNMENT OFFICES

Department of Business, Competition, Consumption, Labour and Employment: 112 rue de la République, 97488, Saint-Denis Cedex; tel. 262-94-07-07; fax 262-94-08-30; e-mail dd-974.direction@direccte.gouv.fr.

Department of the Environment, Planning and Housing: 2 rue Juliette Dodu, 97706 Saint-Denis Cedex; tel. 262-40-26-26; fax 262-40-27-27; e-mail deal-reunion@developpement-durable.gouv.fr; internet www.reunion.developpement-durable.gouv.fr.

Department of Food, Agriculture and Forestry: blvd de la Providence, 97489 Saint-Denis Cédex; tel. 262-30-89-89; fax 262-30-89-99; e-mail daaf974@agriculture.gouv.fr; internet www.daaf974.agriculture.gouv.fr.

Department of Youth, Sports and Social Cohesion: 14 allée des Saphirs, 97487 Saint-Denis Cedex; tel. 262-20-96-40; fax 262-20-96-41; internet www.reunion.drjscs.gouv.fr.

Political Organizations

Mouvement Démocrate (MoDem): Saint-Denis; internet www.mouvementdemocrate.fr; f. 2007; fmrly Union pour la Démocratie Française (UDF); centrist.

Mouvement pour l'Indépendance de la Réunion (MIR): f. 1981 to succeed the fmr Mouvement pour la Libération de la Réunion; grouping of parties favouring autonomy; Leader ANSELME PAYET.

Parti Communiste Réunionnais (PCR): Saint-Denis; f. 1959; Pres. PAUL VERGÈS; Sec.-Gen. ELIE HOARAU.

> **Mouvement pour l'Egalité, la Démocratie, le Développement et la Nature:** affiliated to the PCR; advocates political unity; Leader RENÉ PAYET.

Parti Socialiste (PS)—Fédération de la Réunion (PS): 190 route des Deux Canons Immeuble, Futura, 97490 Saint-Clotilde; tel. 262-29-32-06; fax 262-28-53-03; e-mail psreunion@wanadoo.fr; internet www.parti-socialiste.fr; left-wing; Sec. ANNETTE GILBERT.

Union pour un Mouvement Populaire (UMP)—Fédération de la Réunion: 6 bis blvd Vauban, BP 11, 97461 Saint-Denis Cedex; tel. 262-20-21-18; fax 262-41-73-55; f. 2002; centre-right; local branch of the metropolitan party; Departmental Sec. DIDIER ROBERT.

Les Verts Réunion: Apt 30, Res ARIAL, 132 rue Général de Gaulle, 97400 Saint-Denis; tel. 262-55-73-52; fax 262-25-03-03; e-mail sr-verts-reunion@laposte.net; internet lesverts.fr; ecologist; Regional Sec. JEAN ERPELDINGER.

Judicial System

Court of Appeal: Palais de Justice, 166 rue Juliette Dodu, 97488 Saint-Denis; tel. 262-40-58-58; fax 262-20-16-37; Pres. DOMINIQUE FERRIÈRE.

Religion

A substantial majority of the population are adherents of the Roman Catholic Church. There is a small Muslim community.

CHRISTIANITY

The Roman Catholic Church

Réunion comprises a single diocese, directly responsible to the Holy See. The number of adherents is equivalent to around 80% of the population.

Bishop of Saint-Denis de la Réunion: Mgr GILBERT GUILLAUME MARIE-JEAN AUBRY, Evêché, 36 rue de Paris, BP 55, 97461 Saint-Denis Cedex; tel. 262-94-85-70; fax 262-94-85-73; e-mail eveche.lareunion@wanadoo.fr; internet www.diocese-reunion.org.

The Press

DAILIES

Journal de l'Ile de la Réunion: Centre d'affaires Cadjee, 62 blvd du Chaudron, BP 40019, 97491 Sainte-Clotilde Cedex; tel. 262-48-66-00; fax 262-48-66-50; internet www.clicanoo.re; f. 1951; CEO and Dir of Publication JEAN-BAPTISTE MARIOTTI; Editor-in-Chief YVES MONT-ROUGE; circ. 35,000.

Quotidien de la Réunion et de l'Océan Indien: BP 303, 97712 Saint-Denis Cedex 9; tel. 262-92-15-10; fax 262-28-25-28; e-mail laredaction@lequotidien.re; internet www.lequotidien.re; f. 1976; Dir MAXIMIN CHANE KI CHUNE; circ. 38,900.

Témoignages: 6 rue du Général Emile Rolland, BP 1016, 97828 Le Port Cedex; tel. 262-55-21-21; e-mail temoignages@wanadoo.fr; internet www.temoignages.re; f. 1944; affiliated to the Parti Communiste Réunionnais; daily; Dir JEAN-MAX HOARAU; Editor-in-Chief ALAIN ILAN CHOJNOW; circ. 6,000.

PERIODICALS

Al-Islam: Centre Islamique de la Réunion, BP 437, 97459 Saint-Pierre Cedex; tel. 262-25-45-43; fax 262-35-58-23; e-mail centre-islamique-reunion@wanadoo.fr; internet www.islam-reunion.fr; f. 1975; 4 a year; Dir ISSAC GANGAT.

L'Eco Austral: Technopole de la Réunion 2, rue Emile Hugot, BP 10003, 97801 Saint-Denis Cedex 9; tel. 262-41-51-41; fax 262-41-31-14; internet www.ecoaustral.com; f. 1993; monthly; regional economic issues; Editor ALAIN FOULON; circ. 50,000.

L'Economie de la Réunion: c/o INSEE, Parc Technologique, 10 rue Demarne, BP 13, 97408 Saint-Denis Messag Cedex 9; tel. 262-48-89-00; fax 262-48-89-89; e-mail bureau-de-presse@insee.fr; internet www.insee.fr/reunion; 4 a year; Dir of Publication VALERIE ROUX; Editor-in-Chief CLAIRE GRANGE.

Lutte Ouvrière—Ile de la Réunion: BP 184, 97470 Saint-Benoît; fax 262-48-00-98; e-mail contact@lutte-ouvriere-ile-de-la-reunion.org; internet www.lutte-ouvriere.org/en-regions/la-reunion; monthly; Communist; digital.

Le Mémento Industriel et Commercial Réunionnais: 80 rue Pasteur, BP 397, 97468 Saint-Denis; tel. 262-21-94-12; fax 262-41-10-85; e-mail memento@memento.fr; internet www.memento.fr; f. 1970; monthly; Editor-in-Chief GEORGES-GUILLAUME LOUAPRE-POTTIER; circ. 20,000.

La Réunion Agricole: Chambre d'Agriculture, 24 rue de la Source, BP 134, 97463 Saint-Denis Cedex; tel. 262-94-25-94; fax 262-21-06-17; e-mail herve.cailleaux@reunion.chambagri.fr; internet www.reunion.chambagri.fr; f. 2007; monthly; Dir JEAN-BERNARD GON-THIER; Chief Editor HERVÉ CAILLEAUX; circ. 8,000.

Leader Réunion: 14 rue de la Guadeloupe, ZA Foucherolles, 97490 Sainte-Clotilde; tel. 262-92-10-60; Dir of Publication CAROLE MANOTE.

Visu: 97712 Saint-Denis Cedex 9; tel. 262-90-20-60; fax 262-90-20-61; weekly; Editor-in-Chief PHILIPPE PEYRE; circ. 53,000.

NEWS AGENCY

Imaz Press Réunion: 12 rue Victor MacAuliffe, 97400 Saint-Denis; tel. 262-20-05-65; fax 262-20-05-49; e-mail ipr@ipreunion.com; internet www.ipreunion.com; f. 2000; photojournalism and news agency; Dir RICHARD BOUHET.

Broadcasting and Communications

TELECOMMUNICATIONS

Orange Réunion: 35 blvd du Chaudron, BP 7431, 97743 Saint-Denis Cedex 9; tel. 262-20-02-00; fax 262-20-67-79; internet reunion.orange.fr; f. 2000; subsidiary of Orange France; mobile cellular telephone operator.

Outremer Telecom Réunion: 12 et 14 rue Henri Cornu, Technopole de la Réunion, BP 150, 97801 Saint-Denis, Cedex 9; tel. 262-20-023-00; fax 262-97-53-99; internet www.outremer-telecom.fr; telecommunications provider.

Société Réunionnaise du Radiotéléphone (SRR): 21 rue Pierre Aubert, 97490 Sainte-Clotide; BP 17, 97408 Saint-Denis, Messag Cedex 9; tel. 262-48-19-70; fax 262-48-19-80; internet www.srr.fr; f. 1995; subsidiary of SFR Cegetel, France; mobile cellular telephone operator; CEO JEAN-PIERRE HAGGAÏ; 431,719 subscribers in Réunion, 46,341 in Mayotte (as Mayotte Télécom Mobile) in 2003.

BROADCASTING

Réunion 1ère: 1 rue Jean Chatel, 97716 Saint-Denis Cedex; tel. 262-40-67-67; fax 262-21-64-84; internet reunion.la1ere.fr; acquired by Groupe France Télévisions in 2004; fmrly Réseau France Outre-mer, present name adopted in 2010; radio and television relay services in French; broadcasts two television channels (Télé-Réunion and Tempo) and three radio channels (Radio-Réunion, France-Inter and France-Culture); Dir-Gen. GENEVIÈVE GIARD; Regional Dir ROBERT MOY.

Radio

In 2005 there were 46 licensed private radio stations. These included:

Antenne Réunion Radio: Saint-Denis; e-mail direction@antennereunion.fr; internet www.antennereunion.fr; f. 2011.

Cherie FM Réunion: 3 rue de Kerveguen, 97400 Sainte-Clotilde; tel. 262-97-32-00; fax 262-97-32-32; Editor-in-Chief LEA BERTHAULT.

NRJ Réunion: 3 rue de Kerveguen, 97490 Sainte-Clotilde; tel. 262-97-32-00; fax 262-97-51-10; e-mail c.duboc@h2r.re; commercial radio station; Station Man. SYLVAIN PEGUILLAN.

Radio Festival: 3 rue de Kerveguen, 97490 Sainte-Clotilde; tel. 262-97-32-00; fax 262-97-32-32; e-mail redaction@radiofestival.fr; internet www.radiofestival.re; f. 1995; commercial radio station; Pres. MARIO LECHAT; Editor-in-Chief JEAN-PIERRE GERMAIN.

Radio Free-DOM: 131 rue Jules Auber, BP 666, 97400 Saint-Denis Cedex; tel. 262-41-51-51; fax 262-21-68-64; e-mail freedom@freedom.fr; internet www.freedom.fr; f. 1981; commercial radio station; Dir Dr CAMILLE SUDRE.

Television

Antenne Réunion: rue Emile Hugot, BP 80001, 97801 Saint-Denis Cedex 9; tel. 262-48-28-28; fax 262-48-28-26; e-mail direction@antennereunion.fr; internet www.antennereunion.fr; f. 1991; broadcasts 10 hours daily; Pres. CHRISTOPHE DUCASSE; Dir-Gen. PHILIPPE ROUSSEL.

Canal Réunion: 6 rue René Demarne, Technopole de la Réunion, 97490 Sainte-Clotilde; tel. 262-97-98-99; fax 262-97-98-90; e-mail contact@canalreunion.net; internet www.canalreunion.com; subscription television channel; broadcasts a minimum of 19 hours daily; Chair. JEAN-NOEL TRONC; Dir JEAN-BERNARD MOURIER.

TV-4: 8 chemin Fontbrune, 97400 Saint-Denis; tel. 262-52-73-73; broadcasts 19 hours daily.

Other privately owned television services include TVB, TVE, RTV, Télé-Réunion and TV-Run.

Finance

(cap. = capital; res = reserves; dep. = deposits; m. = million; brs = branches)

BANKING

Central Bank

Institut d'Emission des Départements d'Outre-mer: 4 rue de la Compagnie des Indes, 97487 Saint-Denis Cedex; tel. 262-90-71-00; fax 262-21-41-32; e-mail agence@iedom-reunion.fr; internet www.iedom.fr/reunion; Dir THIERRY BELTRAND.

Commercial Banks

Banque Française Commerciale Océan Indien (BFCOI): 60 rue Alexis de Villeneuve, BP 323, 97466 Saint-Denis Cedex; tel. 262-40-55-55, fax 262-25-21-47; e-mail webmaster@bfcoi.com; internet www.bfcoi.com; f. 1976; cap. €16.7m., res €65.9m., dep. €1,302.4m. (Dec. 2008); Pres. PIERRE GUY-NOEL; Gen. Man. ROGER MUNOZ; 8 brs.

Banque Nationale de Paris Intercontinentale: 67 rue Juliette Dodu, BP 113, 97463 Saint-Denis; tel. 262-40-30-02; fax 262-41-39-09; e-mail contactreunion@bnpparibas.com; internet www.bnpgroup.com; f. 1927; 100% owned by BNP Paribas; Chair. MICHEL PEBEREAU; Man. Dir DANIEL DEGUIN; 16 brs.

Banque de la Réunion (BR), SA: 27 rue Jean Chatel, 97711 Saint-Denis Cedex; tel. 262-40-01-23; fax 262-40-00-61; internet www.banquedelareunion.fr; f. 1853; owned by Groupe Banque Populaire et Caisse d'Epargne (France); cap. €65.4m., res €112.0m., dep. €2,010.8m. (Dec. 2008); Pres. PHILIPPE GARSUAULT; Gen. Man. BERNARD FRÉMONT; 20 brs.

BRED-Banque Populaire: 33 rue Victor MacAuliffe, 97461 Saint-Denis; tel. 262-90-15-60; fax 262-90-15-99; Dir SÉBASTIEN NAHON.

Crédit Agricole de la Réunion: Parc Jean de Cambiaire, Cité des Lauriers, BP 84, 97462 Saint-Denis Cedex; tel. 262-40-81-81; fax 262-40-81-40; internet www.ca-reunion.fr; f. 1949; total assets €2,564m. (Dec. 2004); Chair. CHRISTIAN DE LA GIRODAY; Gen. Man. CHRISTIAN VALETTE.

Development Bank

Société Financière pour le Développement Economique de la Réunion (SOFIDER): 3 rue Labourdonnais, BP 867, 97477 Saint-Denis Cedex; tel. 262-40-32-32; fax 262-40-32-00; internet www.sofider.re; part of the Agence Française de Développement; Dir-Gen. SANDRA BOINON.

Trade and Industry

GOVERNMENT AGENCIES

Agence de Gestion des Initiatives Locales en Matière Européenne (AGILE)—Cellule Europe Réunion: 3 rue Felix Guyon, 97400 Saint-Denis; tel. 262-90-10-80; fax 262-21-90-72; e-mail celleurope@agile-reunion.org; internet www.agile-reunion.org; responsible for local application of EU structural funds; Dir SERGE JOSEPH.

Agence Régionale de Santé Océan Indien (ARS-OI): 2 bis ave Georges Brassens, CS 60050, 97408 Saint-Denis Messag Cedex 9; tel. 262-97-90-00; e-mail ars-oi-delegation-reunion@ars.sante.fr; internet www.ars.ocean-indien.sante.fr; f. 2010; responsible for implementation of health policies in Réunion and Mayotte; Dir-Gen. CHANTAL DE SINGLY.

Conseil Economique Social et Environnemental Régional (CESER): 10 rue du Béarn, BP 17191, 97804 Saint-Denis Messag Cedex 9; tel. 262-97-96-30; fax 262-97-96-31; e-mail ceser-reunion@ceser-reunion.fr; internet www.ceser-reunion.fr; f. 1984; Pres. JEAN-RAYMOND MONDON.

Direction Régionale du Commerce Extérieur (DRCE): 3 rue Serge Ycard, 97490 Sainte-Clotilde; tel. 262-92-24-70; fax 262-92-24-76; e-mail reunion@missioneco.org; internet www.missioneco.org/reunion; Dir PHILIPPE GENIER.

DEVELOPMENT ORGANIZATIONS

Agence de Développement de la Réunion (AD): rue Serge Ycard, BP 33, 97490 Sainte-Clotilde Cedex; tel. 262-92-24-92; fax 262-92-24-88; e-mail info@adreunion.com; internet www.adreunion.com; Chair. JISMY SOUPRAYENMESTRY.

Agence Française de Développement (AFD): 44 rue Jean Cocteau, BP 2013, 97488 Saint-Denis Cedex; tel. 262-90-00-90; fax 262-21-74-58; e-mail afdstdenis@re.groupe-afd.org; internet www.afd.fr; Dir MARC DUBERNET.

Association pour le Développement Industriel de la Réunion: 8 rue Philibert, BP 327, 97466 Saint-Denis Cedex; tel. 262-94-43-00; fax 262-94-43-09; e-mail adir@adir.info; internet www.adir.info; f. 1975; Pres. MAURICE CERISOLA; Sec.-Gen. FRANÇOISE DELMONT DE PALMAS; 190 mems.

Chambre d'Agriculture de la Réunion: 24 rue de la Source, BP 134, 97463 Saint-Denis Cedex; tel. 262-94-25-94; fax 262-21-06-17; e-mail president@reunion.chambagri.fr; internet www.reunion.chambagri.fr; Pres. JEAN-YVES MINATCHY; Gen. Man. JEAN-FRANÇOIS APAYA.

Jeune Chambre Economique de Saint-Denis de la Réunion: 25 rue de Paris, BP 1151, 97483 Saint-Denis; internet saintdenis.jcer.fr; f. 1963; Chair. SYLVIE CRESPO; 30 mems.

CHAMBERS OF COMMERCE

Chambre de Commerce et d'Industrie de la Réunion (CCIR): 5 bis rue de Paris, BP 120, 97463 Saint-Denis Cedex; tel. 262-94-20-00; fax 262-94-22-90; e-mail sg.dir@reunion.cci.fr; internet www.reunion.cci.fr; f. 1830; Pres. ERIC MAGAMOOTOO; Dir MOHAMED AHMED.

Chambre de Métiers et de l'Artisanat: 42 rue Jean Cocteau, BP 261, 97465 Saint-Denis Cedex; tel. 262-21-04-35; fax 262-21-68-33; e-mail cdm@cm-reunion.fr; internet www.cm-reunion.fr; f. 1968; Pres. BERNARD PICARDO; Sec. BENJAMINE DE OLIVEIRA; 14 mem. orgs.

EMPLOYERS' ASSOCIATIONS

Conseil de l'Ordre des Pharmaciens: 1 bis rue Sainte Anne, Immeuble le Concorde, Appt. 26, 1er étage, 97400 Saint-Denis; tel. 262-41-85-51; fax 262-21-94-86; e-mail delegation_reunion@ordre.pharmacien.fr; Pres. CHRISTIANE VAN DE WALLE.

Fédération Régionale des Coopératives Agricoles de la Réunion (FRCA): 8 bis, route de la Z.I. No. 2, 97410 Saint-Pierre; tel. 262-96-24-40; fax 262-96-24-41; internet www.frca-reunion.coop; f. 1979; Pres. JEAN-FLORE BARRET; Sec.-Gen. RITO FERRERE; 27 mem. orgs.

Coopérative Agricole des Huiles Essentielles de Bourbon (CAHEB): 83 rue de Kerveguen, 97430 Le Tampon; BP 43, 97831 Le Tampon; tel. 262-27-02-27; fax 262-27-35-54; e-mail caheb@geranium-bourbon.com; f. 1963; represents producers of essential oils; Pres. MARIE ROSE SEVERIN; Sec.-Gen. LAURENT JANCI.

Société Coopérative Agricole Fruits de la Réunion: 18 Bellevue Pâturage, 97450 Saint-Louis; fax 262-91-41-04; f. 2002; Pres. CHRISTIAN BARRET.

Union Réunionnaise des Coopératives Agricoles (URCOOPA): Z. I. Cambaie, BP 90, 97862 Saint-Paul Cedex; tel. 262-45-37-10; fax 262-45-37-05; e-mail urcoopa@urcoopa.fr; internet www.urcoopa.fr; f. 1982; represents farmers; comprises Coop Avirons (f. 1967), Société Coopérative Agricole Nord-Est (CANE), SICA Lait (f. 1961), and CPPR; Pres. ARY MONDON; Dir-Gen. OLIVIER RONIN.

Mouvement des Entreprises de France Réunion (MEDEF): 14 rampes Ozoux, BP 354, 97467 Saint-Denis; tel. 262-20-01-30; fax 262-41-68-56; e-mail medef.reunion@wanadoo.fr; Pres. FRANÇOIS CAILLÉ.

Ordre National de Médecins: 3 résidence Laura, 4 rue Milius, 97400 Saint-Denis; tel. 262-20-11-58; fax 262-21-08-02; e-mail reunion@974.medecin.fr; internet www.odmreunion.net; Pres. Dr YVAN TCHENG.

Syndicat des Pharmaciens de la Réunion: 1 ave Marcel Hoarau, 97490 Sainte-Clotilde; tel. 262-28-53-60; fax 262-28-79-67; e-mail synd974@resopharma.fr; Pres. FRÉDE SAUTRON.

Syndicat des Producteurs de Rhum de la Réunion: chemin Frédéline, BP 354, 97453 Saint-Pierre Cedex; tel. 262-25-84-27; fax 262-35-60-92; Chair. OLIVIER THIEBLIN.

Syndicat du Sucre de la Réunion: BP 50109, 40 route Gabriel Macé, 97492 Sainte-Clotilde, Cedex; tel. 262-47-76-76; fax 262-21-87-35; internet www.sucre.re; f. 1908; Pres. PHILIPPE LABRO.

TRADE UNIONS

CFE-CGC de la Réunion: 1 Rampes Ozoux, Résidence de la Rivière, Appt 2A, BP 873, 97477 Saint-Denis Cedex; tel. 262-90-11-95; fax 262-90-11-99; e-mail union@cfecgccreunion.com; internet www.cfecgcreunion.com; departmental br. of the Confédération Française de l'Encadrement-Confédération Générale des Cadres; represents engineers, teaching, managerial and professional staff and technicians; Pres. ALAIN IGLICKI; Sec.-Gen. DANIEL THIAW-WING-KAI.

Fédération Départementale des Syndicats d'Exploitants Agricoles de la Réunion (FDSEA): 105 rue Amiral Lacaze, Terre Sainte, 97410 Saint-Pierre; tel. 262-96-33-53; fax 262-96-33-90; e-mail fdsea-reunion@wanadoo.fr; affiliated to the Fédération Nationale des Syndicats d'Exploitants; Sec.-Gen. JEAN-BERNARD HOARAU.

Fédération Syndicale Unitaire Réunion (FSU): 4 rue de la Cure, BP 279, 97494 Sainte-Clotilde Cedex; tel. 262-86-29-46; fax 262-22-35-28; e-mail fsu974@fsu.fr; internet sd974.fsu.fr; f. 1993; departmental br. of the Fédération Syndicale Unitaire; represents public sector employees in sectors incl. teaching, research, and training, and also agriculture, justice, youth and sports, and culture; Sec. CHRISTIAN PICARD.

Union Départementale Confédération Française Démocratique du Travail (UD CFDT): Résidence Pointe des Jardins, 1 rue de l'Atillerie, 97400 Saint-Denis; tel. 262-41-22-85; fax 262-41-26-85; e-mail usctr@wanadoo.fr.

Union Départementale Force Ouvrière de la Réunion (FO): 81 rue Labourdonnais, BP 853, 97477 Saint-Denis Cedex; tel. 262-21-31-35; fax 262-41-33-23; e-mail eric.marguerite@laposte.net; Sec.-Gen. ERIC MARGUERITE.

Union Régionale UNSA-Education: BP 169, 97464 Saint-Denis Cedex; tel. 262-20-02-25; fax 262-21-58-65; e-mail urreunio@unsa.org; represents teaching staff; Sec.-Gen. ERIC CHAVRIACOUTY.

Transport

ROADS

A route nationale circles the island, generally following the coast and linking the main towns. Another route nationale crosses the island from south-west to north-east linking Saint-Pierre and Saint-Benoît.

Société d'Economie Mixte des Transports, Tourisme, Equipements et Loisirs (SEMITTEL): 24 chemin Benoite-Boulard, 97410 Saint-Pierre; tel. 262-55-40-60; fax 262-55-49-56; e-mail contact@semittel.re; f. 1984; bus service operator; Pres. MARRIE PERIANAYAGOM.

Société des Transports Départementaux de la Réunion (SOTRADER): 2 allée Bonnier, 97400 Saint-Denis; tel. 262-94-89-40; fax 262-94-89-50; f. 1995; bus service operator; Dir-Gen. FRÉDÉRIC DELOUYE.

SHIPPING

In 1986 work was completed on the expansion of the Port de la Pointe des Galets, which was divided into the former port in the west and a new port in the east (the port Ouest and the port Est), known together as Port-Réunion. In 2009 some 3.3m. metric tons of freight were unloaded and 594,700 tons loaded at the two ports. In 2012 legislation was adopted in France which transformed Port-Réunion into the Grand Port Maritime de La Réunion, a publicly-owned entity administered by a supervisory board.

Port Authority (Concession Portuaire): rue Evariste de Parny, BP 18, 97821 Le Port Cedex; tel. 262-42-90-00; fax 262-42-47-90; internet www.reunion.port.fr; Dir BRUNO DAVIDSEN.

CMA CGM Réunion: 85 rue Jules Verne, Z.I. No. 2, BP 2007, 97822 Le Port Cedex; tel. 262-55-10-10; fax 262-43-23-04; e-mail lar.genmbox@cma-cgm.com; internet www.cmacgm.com; f. 1996 by merger of Cie Générale Maritime and Cie Maritime d'Affrètement; shipping agents; Man. Dir JÉRÔME DELHOUME.

Mediterranean Shipping Co France (Réunion), S.A. (MSC): 1 bis, Gustave Eiffel, Z.A.C. 2000, BP 221, 97825 Le Port Cedex; tel. 262-42-78-00; fax 262-42-78-10; e-mail msclareunion@mscfr.mscgva.ch; internet www.mscreunion.com.

Réunion Ships Agency (RSA): 17 rue R. Hoareau, BP 10186, 97825 Le Port Cedex; tel. 262-43-33-33; fax 262-42-03-10; e-mail rsa@indoceanic.com; internet www.indoceanic.com; f. 1975; subsidiary of Indoceanic Services; Man. Dir HAROLD JOSÉ THOMSON.

Société d'Acconage et de Manutention de la Réunionnaise (SAMR): 3 ave Théodore Drouhet, Z.A.C. 2000, BP 40, 97821 Le Port Cedex; tel. 262-55-17-55; fax 262-55-17-62; stevedoring; Pres. DOMINIQUE LAFONT; Man. MICHEL ANTONELLI.

Société de Manutention et de Consignation Maritime (SOMACOM): 3 rue Gustave Eiffel, Zac 2000, BP 97420, Le Port; tel. 262-42-

60-00; fax 262-42-60-10; stevedoring and shipping agents; Gen. Man. DANIEL RIGAT.

Société Réunionnaise de Services Maritimes (SRSM): 3 ave Théodore Drouhet, Z.A.C. 2000, BP 2006, 97822 Le Port Cedex; tel. 262-55-17-55; fax 262-55-17-62; e-mail n.hoarau@dri-reunion.com; freight only; Man. MICHEL ANTONELLI.

CIVIL AVIATION

Réunion's international airport, Roland Garros-Gillot, is situated 8 km from Saint-Denis. The Pierrefonds airfield, 5 km from Saint-Pierre, commenced operating as an international airport in 1998 following its development at an estimated cost of nearly 50m. French francs. Air France, Corsair and Air Austral operate international services. In 2009 Roland Garros-Gillot handled some 1.75m. passengers, while Pierrefonds airport handled 126,651 passengers.

Air Austral: 4 rue de Nice, 97400 Saint-Denis; tel. 262-90-90-91; fax 262-29-28-95; e-mail reservation@air-austral.com; internet www .airaustral.com; f. 1975; subsidiary of Air France; CEO MARIE-JOSEPH MALÉ.

Tourism

Réunion's attractions include spectacular scenery and a pleasant climate. In January 2010 the island had around 2,090 hotel rooms. In 2013 some 416,000 tourists visited Réunion. According to the World Tourism Organisation, receipts from tourism (excluding passenger transport) totalled US $315m. in 2012.

Délégation Régionale au Commerce, à l'Artisanat et au Tourisme: Préfecture de la Réunion, 97400 Saint-Denis; tel. 262-40-77-58; fax 262-50-77-15; Dir PHILIPPE JEAN LEGLISE.

L'Île de la Réunion Tourisme (IRT): pl. du 20 décembre 1848, BP 615, 97472 Saint-Denis Cedex; tel. 262-21-00-41; fax 262-21-00-21; e-mail ctr@la-reunion-tourisme.com; internet www.reunion.fr; fmrly Comité du Tourisme de la Réunion; name changed as above in 2009; Pres. JACQUELINE FARREYROL.

Office du Tourisme Intercommunal du Nord: 2 pl. Etienne Regnault, 97400 Saint-Denis; tel. 262-41-83-00; fax 262-21-37-76; e-mail info@ot-nordreunion.com; Pres. FRÉDÉRIC FOUCQUE; Dir CATHERINE GLAVNIK.

Defence

Réunion is the headquarters of French military forces in the Indian Ocean and French Southern and Antarctic Territories. As assessed at November 2013, there were 1,900 French troops stationed on Réunion and Mayotte, including a gendarmerie.

Education

Education is modelled on the French system, and is compulsory for 10 years between the ages of six and 16 years. Primary education begins at six years of age and lasts for five years. Secondary education, which begins at 11 years of age, lasts for up to seven years, comprising a first cycle of four years and a second of three years. In the academic year 2013/14 there were 43,666 pupils enrolled at pre-primary schools and 74,330 at primary schools. In 2012/13 there were 101,015 pupils enrolled at secondary schools. There is a university, with several faculties, providing higher education in law, economics, politics, and French language and literature, and a teacher-training college. In 2012/13 some 12,204 students were enrolled at the university.

French Overseas Collectivities

As amended in March 2003, the Constitution defines French Polynesia, Saint Pierre and Miquelon, and the Wallis and Futuna Islands as having the status of Collectivités d'Outre-mer (Overseas Collectivities) within the French Republic. Under an organic law of February 2007, Saint-Barthélemy and Saint-Martin were, additionally, each accorded the status of Overseas Collectivity. The territories within this category have a greater degree of independence than do the Overseas Departments and Territories, with the particular status of each being defined by an individual organic law. Local assemblies may establish internal legislation. An organic law of February 2004 accords to French Polynesia the unique designation of Pays d'Outre-mer (Overseas Country), while it retains the legal status of an Overseas Collectivity. Mayotte, which was previously an Overseas Collectivity became an Overseas Department of France in 2011.

FRENCH POLYNESIA

Introductory Survey

LOCATION, CLIMATE, LANGUAGE, RELIGION, FLAG, CAPITAL

French Polynesia comprises several scattered groups of islands in the South Pacific Ocean, lying about two-thirds of the way between the Panama Canal and New Zealand. Its nearest neighbours are the Cook Islands, to the west, and the Line Islands (part of Kiribati), to the north-west. French Polynesia consists of the following island groups: the Windward Islands (Iles du Vent—including the islands of Tahiti and Moorea) and the Leeward Islands (Iles Sous le Vent—located about 160 km north-west of Tahiti) which, together, constitute the Society Archipelago; the Tuamotu Archipelago, which comprises some 80 atolls scattered east of the Society Archipelago in a line stretching north-west to south-east for about 1,500 km; the Gambier Islands, located 1,600 km south-east of Tahiti; the Austral Islands, lying 640 km south of Tahiti; and the Marquesas Islands, which lie 1,450 km north-east of Tahiti. There are 35 islands and 83 atolls in all, of which 76 are populated. The average monthly temperature throughout the year varies between 20°C (68°F) and 29°C (84°F), and most rainfall occurs between November and April, the average annual precipitation being 1,625 mm (64 in). The official languages are French and Tahitian. Seven Polynesian languages and their dialects are spoken by the indigenous population. The principal religion is Christianity; about 54% of the population is Protestant and some 38% Roman Catholic. The official flag is the French tricolour. Subordinate to this, the French Polynesian flag (proportions 2 by 3), comprises three horizontal stripes, of red, white (half the depth) and red, with, in the centre, the arms of French Polynesia, consisting of a representation in red of a native canoe, bearing a platform supporting five stylized persons, on a circular background (five wavy horizontal dark blue bands, surmounted by 10 golden sunrays). The capital is Papeete, on the island of Tahiti.

CONTEMPORARY POLITICAL HISTORY

Historical Context

Tahiti, the largest of the Society Islands, and the other island groups were annexed by France in the late 19th century. The islands were governed from France under a decree of 1885 until 1946, when French Polynesia became an Overseas Territory (Territoire d'Outre-Mer), administered by a Governor in Papeete. A Territorial Assembly and a Council of Government were established to advise the Governor.

Between May 1975 and May 1982 a majority in the Territorial Assembly sought independence for French Polynesia. Following pressure by Francis Sanford, leader of the largest autonomist party in the Assembly, a new Constitution for the territory was negotiated with the French Government and approved by a newly elected Assembly in 1977. Under the provisions of the new statute, France retained responsibility for foreign affairs, defence, monetary matters and justice, but the powers of the territorial Council of Government were increased, especially in the field of commerce. The French Governor was replaced by a High Commissioner, who was to preside over the Council of Government and was head of the administration, but had no vote. The Council's elected Vice-President, responsible for domestic affairs, was granted greater powers. An Economic, Social and Cultural Council, responsible for all development matters, was also created, and French Polynesia's economic zone was extended to 200 nautical miles (370 km) from the islands' coastline.

Domestic Political Affairs

Following elections to the Territorial Assembly in May 1982, the Gaullist Tahoera'a Huiraatira (People's Rally), led by Gaston Flosse, which secured 13 of the 30 seats, formed successive ruling coalitions, first with the Ai'a Api (New Land) party and in September with the Te Pupu Here Ai'a Te Nuna'a Ia Ora (Patriotic Party for an Autonomous Polity). Seeking self-government, especially in economic matters, elected representatives of the Assembly held discussions with the French Government in Paris in 1983, and in September 1984 a new statute was approved by the French Assemblée Nationale (National Assembly). This allowed the territorial Government greater powers, mainly in the sphere of commerce and development; the Council of Government was replaced by a Council of Ministers, whose President was to be elected from among the members of the Territorial Assembly. Flosse became the first President of the Council of Ministers.

At elections held in March 1986 the Tahoera'a Huiraatira gained the first outright majority to be achieved in the territory, winning 24 of the 41 seats in the Territorial Assembly. Leaders of opposition parties expressed dissatisfaction with the election result, claiming that the Tahoera'a Huiraatira victory had been secured only as a result of the disproportionate allocation of seats to one of the five constituencies. The constituency at the centre of the dispute comprised the Mangareva and Tuamotu islands, where the two French army bases at Hao and Mururoa constituted a powerful body of support for Flosse and the Tahoera'a Huiraatira. At concurrent elections for French Polynesia's two seats in the National Assembly in Paris, Flosse and Alexandre Léontieff, the candidates of the Rassemblement pour la République (RPR—to which the Tahoera'a Huiraatira was affiliated, latterly the Union pour un Mouvement Populaire), were elected. Later in March the French Prime Minister, Jacques Chirac, appointed Flosse as Secretary of State for South Pacific Affairs in the French Council of Ministers. Flosse ceded his seat in the National Assembly to Edouard Fritch.

In April 1986 Flosse was re-elected President of the Council of Ministers. However, he was severely criticized by leaders of the opposition for his allegedly inefficient and extravagant use of public funds, and was accused of corrupt electoral practice. Flosse resigned as President in February 1987, and was replaced by Jacques Teuira.

In December 1987, amid growing discontent over his policies, Teuira and the entire Council of Ministers resigned and were replaced by a coalition of opposition parties and the Te Tiaraama party (a breakaway faction of the Tahoera'a Huiraatira) under the presidency of Alexandre Léontieff. Amendments to the Polynesian Constitution, which were approved by the French legislature and enacted by July 1990, augmented the powers of the President of the Council of Ministers and increased the competence of the Territorial Assembly.

At territorial elections in March 1991 the Tahoera'a Huiraatira won 18 of the 41 seats. Flosse then formed a coalition with the Ai'a Api to secure a majority of 23 seats in the Territorial Assembly. Emile Vernaudon, leader of the Ai'a Api, was elected President of the Assembly and Flosse was elected President of the Council of Ministers. In September Flosse announced the end of the coalition between his party and the Ai'a Api, accusing Vernaudon of disloyalty, and signed a new alliance with the Te Pupu Here Ai'a Te Nuna'a Ia Ora, led by Jean Juventin.

In April 1992 Flosse was found guilty of fraud (relating to an illegal sale of government land to a member of his family) and there were widespread demands for his resignation. In November Juventin and Léontieff were charged with 'passive' corruption, relating to the construction of a golf course by a Japanese company. In the following month the French Court of Appeal upheld the judgment against Flosse, who received a six-month suspended prison sentence. More than 3,000 people demonstrated in January 1993, demanding the resignation of Flosse and Juventin. In September 1994 Flosse succeeded in having the conviction rescinded, on a procedural issue, in a second court of appeal. In October 1997, however, Léontieff was found guilty of accepting substantial bribes in order to facilitate a business venture and was sentenced to three years' imprisonment (one-half of which was to be suspended). In May 1998 Léontieff was sentenced to a further three years' imprisonment (two of which were to be suspended) for corruption.

When the French authorities resumed nuclear testing in September 1995 (see *Nuclear Testing and Relations with Metropolitan France*), peaceful protests in Tahiti rapidly developed into full-scale riots, as several thousand demonstrators rampaged through Papeete, demanding an end to French rule.

In November 1995 the Territorial Assembly adopted a draft statute of autonomy, which proposed the extension of the territory's powers to areas such as fishing, mining and shipping rights, international transport and communications, broadcasting and the offshore economic zone. However, France would retain full responsibility for defence, justice and security in the islands. Advocates of independence for French Polynesia criticized the statute for promising only relatively superficial changes. The statute was approved by the French National Assembly in December and entered into force in April 1996.

At territorial elections in May 1996 the Tahoera'a Huiraatira achieved an outright majority, securing 22 of the 41 seats, although the principal pro-independence party, Tavini Huiraatira/Front de Libération de la Polynésie (FLP), won 10 seats, making considerable gains throughout the territory (largely owing to increased popular hostility towards France since the resumption of nuclear-weapons tests at Mururoa Atoll—see *Nuclear Testing and Relations with Metropolitan France*). Flosse defeated the pro-independence leader, Oscar Temaru, to remain as President of the Council of Ministers, and Justin Arapari was elected President of the Territorial Assembly. Allegations of voting irregularities led to the annulment of the results in 11 constituencies; following by-elections in May 1998, the Tahoera'a Huiraatira increased its representation by one seat.

At elections for French Polynesia's two seats in the French National Assembly in May 1997 Michel Buillard and Emile Vernaudon, both supporters of the RPR, were elected. Flosse was re-elected as the territory's representative to the French Sénat (Senate) in September 1998.

In 1999 a constitutional amendment designating French Polynesia as an Overseas Country (Pays d'Outre-Mer) and creating a new Polynesian citizenship was approved by the French legislature. Although France was to retain control over areas such as foreign affairs, defence, justice and electoral laws, French Polynesia would have the power to negotiate with other Pacific countries and sign its own international treaties. The constitutional amendment was presented to a joint session of the French Senate and National Assembly for final ratification in January 2000, although no decision on the matter was taken.

In November 1999 Flosse was found guilty of accepting more than 2.7m. French francs in bribes from the owner of an illegal casino, allegedly to help fund his party. Flosse was sentenced to a two-year suspended prison term, a large fine and a one-year ban on seeking office. Flosse's refusal to resign as President of the Council of Ministers prompted demonstrations in Tahiti. However, in May 2001 the High Court reversed the ruling against Flosse, and in November 2002 the Court of Appeal in Paris announced that he should be pardoned.

At elections in May 2001, the Tahoera'a Huiraatira secured 28 of the 49 seats in the newly enlarged Territorial Assembly, and a fifth successive term in office. The pro-independence Tavini Huiraatira took 13 seats. Flosse was subsequently re-elected President of the Council of Ministers. In June 2002 elections for the territory's two seats in the National Assembly were won by Tahoera'a Huiraatira candidates Michel Buillard and Béatrice Vernaudon. In May 2003 it was announced that French Polynesia was to be allocated one additional seat in the French Senate.

In July 2003 the Territorial Assembly followed the French legislature in ratifying the constitutional amendment that would allow French Polynesia to be designated as an Overseas Country of France. The final text of the autonomy statute was approved by the National Assembly in January 2004, and a decree of formal designation was signed by President Jacques Chirac in March. French Polynesia was thus granted greater authority over matters such as labour law, civil aviation and regional relations, with France retaining control of law and order, defence and money supply.

At elections to the further enlarged Assembly in May 2004, the Tahoera'a Huiraatira won 28 of the 57 seats. An opposition coalition, the Union pour la Démocratie (UPD), comprising Tavini Huiraatira and various minor parties, secured 27 seats and the remaining two seats were taken by opposition parties favouring autonomy. The Tahoera'a Huiraatira thus lost its overall majority in the Assembly for the first time in 20 years. Antony Géros of Tavini Huiraatira was elected President of the Assembly and Oscar Temaru, leader of Tavini Huiraatira, was elected President of the Council of Ministers.

In September 2004 disagreement over the appropriation bill brought the legislative process to a halt. Three members of the Assembly resigned from the UPD coalition, two of them to sit as independents, with the third joining the opposition Tahoera'a Huiraatira. In October separate motions of no confidence were filed against the Government by the Tahoera'a Huiraatira and the newly

formed Te' Avei'a (Te Ara) party, which included six former members of the ruling UPD coalition. Oscar Temaru's appeals to the French Government to dissolve the Assembly and to hold new elections were supported by 22,000 people in the largest demonstration ever witnessed in French Polynesia. The French Minister for Overseas Territories, Brigitte Girardin, refused to accept the demands. The motions of no confidence were endorsed by 29 of the 57 legislators (the members of the UPD refusing to vote), and 23 Tahoera'a Huiraatira and six Te' Avei'a members subsequently elected Gaston Flosse as President of the Council of Ministers. However, the UPD members boycotted the vote and refused to recognize Flosse's authority. Temaru and his ministers refused to vacate the presidential building, forcing Flosse's newly appointed Council of Ministers to operate in adjacent buildings.

Oscar Temaru's removal and Gaston Flosse's election as President of the Council of Ministers were both upheld by the French Conseil d'Etat (Council of State). Under the new autonomy statute, the Assembly could vote to dissolve itself if it received a petition from 10% of the electorate, roughly equivalent to 15,000 people; by 19 November 2004 the UPD claimed to have collected 42,890 signatures, representing some 28% of the electorate. Both Temaru and Flosse sent delegations to Paris, to make representations to the French Government, led respectively by Nicole Bouteau (leader of the No Oe e Te Nunaa party) and Edouard Fritch. Following an investigation, the French Council of State declared the election results in the Windward Islands null and void, thus requiring the holding of by-elections within three months. The 37 legislators affected automatically lost their seats, among them Flosse, Temaru and the President of the Assembly, Antony Géros, who was replaced by Hiro Tefaarere. In late November leading representatives from all parties, including Flosse, Temaru, Bouteau, Philip Schyle (of the Fe'tia Api party) and Jacky Briant (of the Heuira-Greens party), were summoned to Paris for discussions. Despite an initial agreement in principle to hold fresh legislative elections, the talks soon failed. In mid-December the Council of State validated Flosse's appointment as President.

By-elections were held in the Windward Islands constituency in February 2005. The parties of Bouteau and Schyle stood on a joint platform (the Alliance pour une Démocratie Nouvelle—ADN), offering a 'third way'. The Tahoera'a Huiraatira won 10 of the 37 seats, and the seven party UPD coalition won 25. The ADN took the constituency's remaining two seats. Overall, therefore, the Tahoera'a Huiraatira and the UPD now held 27 seats each in the Assembly. The ADN held three seats, but refused to co-operate with either of the main groupings, as a result of which neither was able to form a majority. Temaru introduced a motion of no confidence against Flosse, which was endorsed by 30 of the 57 members. Temaru was subsequently elected President of the Council of Ministers by 29 votes to 26 and Antony Géros was returned as President of the Assembly.

In July 2005 the former minister and Secretary-General of the Tahoera'a Huiraatira, Jean-Christophe Bouissou, left the party to form the Rautahi Party. He was joined by two other former ministers, leaving the Tahoera'a Huiraatira with 23 seats in the Assembly and the UPD 29 seats. In November the Government presented an economic reform programme that included a proposed increase in the minimum wage, to be financed through a 'solidarity' tax on personal income. However, a series of public protests culminating in a four-day general strike led the Temaru Government to seek alternative sources of revenue, principally by increasing the duty on alcohol and tobacco. In December two Tahoera'a Huiraatira members of the Assembly left the party to sit as independents, thereby reducing the group's representation to 21 seats.

In February 2006 Temaru signed a new agreement with French High Commissioner Anne Boquet, on behalf of the French Government, regarding the proportion of the economic development grant (dotation générale de développement économique—DGDE—see *Economic Affairs*) that could be used towards the Government's operating costs: the proportion would be reduced gradually from 50% in 2005 to 20% from 2008. Meanwhile, in January 2006 the Minister for Post and Telecommunications and Sports, Emile Vernaudon, was convicted of having used public property for personal benefit while serving as Mayor of Mahina (a district of Papeete) between 1992 and 1999; he received a one-year suspended prison sentence and substantial fine. In April 2006 Antony Géros was replaced as President of the Assembly by Philip Schyle, of the Fe'tia Api party.

In June 2006 a criminal court in Tahiti found former President Gaston Flosse guilty of corruption in relation to his son's purchase of a hotel. Flosse was given a three-month suspended prison sentence, but was allowed to remain as a member of the Territorial Assembly and representative to the Senate in Paris. In December, following reports of dissent within the ruling coalition, the Assembly approved a motion of no confidence in the Government, resulting in Temaru's removal from office. He was replaced by Gaston Tong Sang, a member of the Tahoera'a Huiraatira party and Mayor of Bora Bora, who received the support of 31 of the 57 members of the legislature.

In February 2007 hundreds of opposition supporters took to the streets of Papeete to demand fresh elections. In March Emile

Vernaudon was convicted of corruption and therefore barred from public office. He was given a suspended 18-month prison sentence (in December he was arrested on further charges). In April Edouard Fritch was narrowly elected President of the Assembly. At the second round of a French presidential election held in May, 51.9% of French Polynesian voters chose the candidate of the Union pour un Mouvement Populaire (UMP), Nicolas Sarkozy, over the candidate of the Parti Socialiste, Ségolène Royal—a slightly narrower margin than in metropolitan France. In June, at French legislative elections, the two Tahoera'a Huiraatira candidates were elected as deputies to the National Assembly: Buillard, an incumbent deputy, defeated Temaru to regain one of the seats, while Bruno Sandras was newly elected to the second seat.

French Polynesia continued to experience political instability during 2007. Gaston Tong Sang's Government survived two motions of no confidence in January and June, but suffered a serious setback in July with the withdrawal of the Tahoera'a Huiraatira, Tong Sang's own party, from the majority grouping in the Assembly. The decision signalled a major shift in local politics, which had perhaps been foreshadowed by mounting criticism of Tong Sang by the Tahoera'a Huiraatira leader, Gaston Flosse. Five members of the Tahoera'a Huiraatira resigned from the Council of Ministers and Tong Sang was removed from office in August by a successful no-confidence motion. Temaru was subsequently elected President, defeating Fritch in a second round of voting. In September Temaru announced the formation of a 'pact' between the two major political parties, thus ensuring a clear majority in the Assembly. Temaru attended discussions in France with President Sarkozy in October on proposals for reform, including the introduction of two election rounds and the setting of a maximum of 15 appointees to the Council of Ministers. The reforms were approved by the French Senate in November. Meanwhile, Tong Sang announced the creation of the O Porinetia To Tatou Ai'a (Polynesia, Our Homeland) party.

At legislative elections in January and February 2008, the To Tatou Ai'a coalition, of which Tong Sang's O Porinetia To Tatou Ai'a was a leading member, won a total of 27 seats, while Temaru's political alliance, the Union pour la Démocratie (UPLD), secured 20 and the Tahoera'a Huiraatira only 10. Edouard Fritch of the Tahoera'a Huiraatira was elected President of the Assembly. Gaston Flosse unexpectedly declared his candidacy for the subsequent presidential election and, with the support of UPLD members, was able to defeat Tong Sang after Temaru, the third candidate, withdrew from the contest. A new parliamentary alliance between the Tahoera'a Huiraatira and the UPLD had been established: the Union pour le Développement, la Stabilité et la Paix (Union for Development, Stability and Peace—UDSP). Temaru was elected President of the Assembly in late February, following Fritch's resignation from the post.

Increasing political instability

The installation of a new Government did not bring the expected political stability. In April 2008 the establishment of Te Mana o Te May Motu (The Power of the Islands), a new parliamentary grouping reported to be allied with To Tatou Ai'a, was announced. In the same month a no-confidence motion submitted by Tong Sang resulted in Flosse's removal from office; two members of Flosse's coalition group had reportedly defected to Te Mana o Te May Motu. Tong Sang was elected President. In August a former minister and Assembly President, Hiro Tefaarere, established a new political party, À rohi (Let's Act), expressing frustration with the prevailing political situation, and its dominance by the pro- and anti-independence movements. Gaston Flosse was re-elected as a representative to the French Senate in September, while Richard Tuheiava, a member of the UPLD, secured the newly created second senatorial seat. Flosse resigned from the UMP, and was subsequently charged with misuse of public funds (see below). In December the Government lost its majority in the Assembly when one member of the coalition withdrew. In February 2009 Tong Sang resigned as President, prompted by an impending motion of no confidence. Within days, Oscar Temaru was elected as President. Edouard Fritch was subsequently elected to replace Temaru as President of the Assembly.

In February 2009 Gaston Flosse was found guilty of misappropriating some 2.4m. francs CFP of public funds in 2004, receiving a suspended one-year prison sentence, a fine of 2m. francs CFP, and a one-year ban from public office. Flosse appealed against the conviction, and in November 2011, once again, his suspension from public office was overturned. In a further prosecution, in May 2010, Flosse was convicted of obstructing an investigation into a former intelligence unit that had operated during his presidency, by destroying the records of its activities, and in October the French Polynesian Court of Appeal upheld his conviction (as did the Court of Cassation in France in September 2011).

Meanwhile, in April 2009 Philip Schyle, of Tong Sang's To Tatou Ai'a coalition, replaced Fritch as President of the Assembly, following a parliamentary vote. President Temaru presented a new Council of Ministers, incorporating several supporters of Tong Sang in the coalition Government. In October six members of the Assembly representing the outer islands withdrew from the coalition Government, claiming that their views had been disregarded, and consequently Temaru's support in the Assembly was seriously reduced. Temaru was ousted by a parliamentary vote of no confidence and replaced by Tong Sang, who became President for the third time since 2006.

In January 2010 President Sarkozy referred to the political situation in French Polynesia as a 'comedy', and announced that he would initiate further reforms in order to provide greater political stability. During an official visit to France (which included discussions of the nuclear compensation issue—see *Nuclear Testing and Relations with Metropolitan France*) in that month, Tong Sang submitted a proposal that the French Polynesian President be directly chosen by the local electorate, rather than elected by the members of the French Polynesian Assembly, with the objective of increasing political stability.

In February 2010 thousands of islanders were forced to evacuate their homes when the most severe cyclone for decades struck French Polynesia. The Tuamotu Archipelago was the worst affected area with hundreds of houses seriously damaged or completely destroyed by Cyclone Oli. The cost of repairs to housing and infrastructure was unofficially estimated to be 2,000m. francs CFP.

In April 2010 Oscar Temaru was elected President of the Assembly following Philip Schyle's unexpected resignation, indicating that the coalition between Flosse's Tahoera'a Huiraatira and Tong Sang's To Tatou Ai'a had been seriously undermined. Sarkozy refused Tong Sang's request to call early elections, claiming that electoral reform was a prerequisite of fresh elections. In discussions on electoral reform in late 2010 the French Government suggested that any motion of no confidence (the instrument that had frequently been used to defeat recent administrations) should require the support of at least 60% of members of the Assembly. It also suggested that the Society Archipelago adopt an electoral system separate from that of the other islands, and that the number of seats in the Assembly be reduced. Members of all the principal political groupings criticized the proposals.

In January 2011 Emile Vernaudon was found guilty of misusing funds amounting to 114m. francs CFP belonging to the Office des Postes et Télécommunications (OPT—the state-owned post and telecommunications company) during 2005–06. Vernaudon was sentenced to five years in prison and barred from holding public office for five years. Furthermore, 11 other officials were convicted of similar offences in connection with the OPT, including Gaston Flosse, who, in January 2013, was sentenced to five years' imprisonment for his role in the affair. In June 2014 Flosse's conviction was overturned on appeal. A retrial was expected to take place in April 2015.

President Tong Sang's refusal in February 2011 to accept a proposed budget, approved by the Assembly, led him to publish budget proposals of his own and to dismiss Vice-President Edouard Fritch and five cabinet ministers for failing to support his version. A motion to annul Tong Sang's budget was approved by 44 of the 57 members of the Assembly, and at the beginning of April he was removed from office following his defeat in a parliamentary motion of no confidence. Oscar Temaru, leader of the pro-independence Tavini Huiraatira, thus returned to the position of President. Jacqui Drollet was elected President of the Assembly.

In the largest trial in French Polynesian history, 87 people appeared in court in April 2011 in connection with payments made to individuals during the presidency of Gaston Flosse in 1990s. In what became known as the 'phantom jobs case', it was alleged that Flosse had secured the support of numerous politicians, journalists, trade unionists and clergymen by paying them a salary for jobs that did not exist. In October Flosse was found guilty of making corrupt payments and was sentenced to four years' imprisonment. A total of 56 people were convicted in the case. In February 2013 the Court of Appeal amended Flosse's sentence to a four-year suspended prison term and a fine of €125,000. He was additionally to be deprived of his civic rights for a three-year period. However, he subsequently lodged an appeal with the Court of Cassation in Paris, thus allowing him to contest the territorial elections due in April and May. (For further developments, see *Recent developments: Gaston Flosse's presidency and dismissal from office*.)

Meanwhile, the deteriorating economic situation in French Polynesia continued to cause concern, and in April 2011 more than 3,000 people demonstrated outside the parliament buildings to protest against a perceived lack of action by politicians to address issues such as rising unemployment. In May the French Government agreed to provide a loan of €41.9m. to ease the economic crisis. In the following month the Territorial Assembly approved an economic reform plan that envisaged a number of controversial measures, including salary reductions of up to 50% for public sector workers and the closure of the news agency Agence Tahitienne de Presse.

Further electoral reforms and the 2013 elections

In August 2011 President Sarkozy promulgated legislation amending the islands' electoral system. The reforms, which were aimed at increasing political stability, included a new system of proportional representation (whereby the winning list in the second round of polling would receive one-third of the 57 seats in the Assembly, with the remainder distributed according to the lists' relative strength); a reduction in the number of members of the Council of Ministers from up to 15 to between seven and 10; and a requirement of 60% of votes, rather than a simple majority, for a motion of no confidence to succeed. In addition, the President of the Council of Ministers of French Polynesia would be limited to serving a maximum of two consecutive terms. Contrary to earlier proposals, the number of seats in the Assembly was maintained at 57. However, having hitherto comprised six electoral constituencies, the islands would henceforth constitute one, albeit composed of eight sections: three for the Windward Islands (Iles du Vent—Society Islands) and one each for the Leeward Islands (Iles Sous le Vent—Society Islands), the Gambier Islands-East Tuamotu Archipelago, the West Tuamotu Archipelago, the Austral Islands and the Marquesas Islands.

In September 2011 Oscar Temaru caused controversy and risked jeopardizing relations with France when he lobbied leaders at a Pacific Islands Forum (see p. 413) meeting to support French Polynesia's bid to be reinscribed on the UN's list of Non-Self-Governing Territories. (Former French President Charles de Gaulle had removed French Polynesia from the list in 1946.) A draft resolution to re-inscribe the territory was lodged with the UN General Assembly's secretariat in early 2013. The campaign for reinscription received a significant boost with a public declaration of support by the Maohi Protestant Church—the dominant Christian denomination in French Polynesia. In a statement the Church argued that reinscription would be an effective way to protect the islands' heritage and to hold the French Government accountable for its actions at the nuclear test sites of Mururoa and Fangataufa.

At the French presidential election of 2012, Sarkozy secured the largest share of the vote in French Polynesia in the second round, in May, winning 53.3%, but was defeated nationwide by François Hollande of the Parti Socialiste. At elections to the French National Assembly in June, the Tahoera'a Huiraatira secured all three of French Polynesia's seats (the territory having been allocated an additional seat), with Edouard Fritch, Jonas Tahuaitu and Jean-Paul Tuaiva elected as deputies.

In January 2013 a new political grouping, the A Ti'a Porinetia (Rally of Polynesians), incorporating members of the To Tatou Ai'a and a number of smaller organizations, was launched under the leadership of former economy minister Teva Rohfritsch. The new electoral rules required party lists to secure a minimum of 12.5% of the votes to proceed to a second round, which appeared to encourage the formation of larger groupings.

Following the first round of elections to the Assembly, on 21 April 2013, three parties were eligible to contest the second round on 5 May: Flosse's Tahoera'a Huiraatira, Temaru's UPLD and Rohfritsch's A Ti'a Porinetia. In the event, the Tahoera'a Huiraatira won a decisive victory, securing 19 seats, with the additional 19 seats allocated to the leading party under the new electoral system bringing its total to 38, while the UPLD took 11 seats and A Ti'a Porinetia eight. Temaru attributed his party's loss to the effects of the severe economic crisis. Later in the month the Assembly elected Flosse to his fifth term of office as President.

Recent developments: Gaston Flosse's presidency and dismissal from office

Despite attempts by Gaston Flosse to withdraw the resolution from the agenda, on 17 May 2013, the day that Flosse took office as President, the UN General Assembly voted to reinscribe French Polynesia on its list of Non-Self-Governing Territories. In the following month Flosse wrote to President Hollande requesting that the French Government organize a referendum on self-determination in the territory and stating that he would not recognize any future referendum organized under the auspices of the UN. By early 2015 the French authorities had not formally responded to the request and were not co-operating with requests for information from the UN Special Committee on Decolonization.

Meanwhile, Flosse's reputation as a controversial figure continued to affect his new administration. In mid-2013 three former members of the disbanded Groupement d'Intervention de la Polynésie (GIP)—a militia-like unit created by Flosse in the late 1990s, initially to assist with emergency relief efforts, but which subsequently became associated with alleged political operations against Flosse's opponents—were charged in connection with the death of a journalist in December 1997. Jean-Pascal Couraud, editor-in-chief of *Les Nouvelles* newspaper and a staunch critic of Flosse, was alleged to have been drowned following interrogation by the GIP members. Their trial, on charges of kidnapping, was expected to begin by 2016.

In April 2014 the French Senate lifted the parliamentary immunity of Flosse with regard to corruption charges, brought against him in February, of abusing public funds by arranging for a free water supply to a neighbourhood containing his residence. His son-in-law Edouard Fritch had also been charged with the same offence. Despite the charges, Fritch won the mayoral election in Pirae in March and

thus had to relinquish his seat in the French National Assembly because of the limit on the number of mandates a French politician can hold. In June Maina Sage, representing the Tahoera'a Huiraatira, was elected to the seat in the French National Assembly vacated by Fritch.

In July 2014 the Court of Cassation in Paris upheld Flosse's conviction on corruption charges in the 'phantom jobs case' of 2011 (see *Increasing political instability*), but the French Government intervened to stop the sentence being enacted while President Hollande considered the possibility of a pardon. On 6 September, however, following the rejection of his appeal against conviction by the Court of Appeal in Tahiti, and in the absence of a presidential pardon from Hollande, Flosse finally resigned as President of French Polynesia. Edouard Fritch was subsequently confirmed as Flosse's successor. Fritch was replaced as President of the Territorial Assembly by Marcel Tuihani, who received 38 votes in the legislature, compared with 11 votes for the opposition candidate, Antony Géros. Flosse's conviction also led to his expulsion from the French Senate, where he had the distinction of being the only member not to have attended a single sitting of the chamber during the previous year. At elections to the Senate in late September, two candidates of the Tahoera'a Huiraatira, Iriti Teura and Vincent Dubois (Flosse's son-in-law), were successful. Meanwhile, Flosse remained defiant, announcing his intention to stand for election in 2018 (once he again became eligible to hold public office) and symbolically returning the Légion d'honneur he had been awarded by the French Government, in protest against Hollande's refusal to grant him a pardon. Flosse's subsequent employment as an adviser to the Tahoera'a Huiraatira suggested that he was likely to remain influential in French Polynesian politics.

In November 2014 Fritch took part in talks on climate change in Nouméa, New Caledonia, between Pacific island leaders and President Hollande, the French Minister of Foreign Affairs and International Development, Laurent Fabius, and Hollande's Special Envoy for the Protection of the Planet, Nicolas Hulot. Regional leaders had requested the discussions in the hope of persuading France to represent their concerns as fully as possible at the forthcoming UN climate change conference, scheduled to take place in Paris in December 2015.

Meanwhile, ongoing concerns about the difficult economic situation in the territory prompted Fritch to appeal to French Prime Minister Manuel Valls for additional financial assistance during a meeting in Paris in October 2014. In proposals for the 2015 budget Fritch had declined to increase taxation levels, stating that he wanted to implement a more inclusive budget for all French Polynesians.

The election of Iriti Teura and Vincent Dubois to the Senate in September 2014 was annulled by the French Constitutional Court in February 2015 on the grounds that a march by some 400 supporters of the Tahoera'a Huiraatira to the polling station on the day of the election constituted an attempt to exert undue pressure on voters; a new election was scheduled to be held on 3 May.

Nuclear Testing and Relations with Metropolitan France

France's use of French Polynesia for nuclear testing was highly controversial. In July 1962 the French Government transferred its nuclear-testing facilities to Mururoa and Fangataufa Atolls, in the Tuamotu Archipelago, establishing the Centre d'Expérimentation du Pacifique (CEP). The first nuclear device was tested at Fangataufa four years later in July 1966. In July 1985 the *Rainbow Warrior*, the flagship of the anti-nuclear environmentalist group Greenpeace, which was to have led a protest flotilla to Mururoa, was sunk in Auckland Harbour, New Zealand, in an explosion that killed one crew member. Two agents of the French secret service, the Direction Générale de Sécurité Extérieure (DGSE), were subsequently convicted of manslaughter and imprisoned in New Zealand. According to official reports, between 1966 and 1974 France conducted 46 atmospheric tests in the territory; 147 underground tests were carried out between 1975 and 1991. In April 1992 the French Government announced that nuclear tests would be suspended until the end of the year. In January 1993 French Polynesia accepted assistance worth 7,000m. francs CFP in compensation for lost revenue and in aid for development projects.

Shortly after his election in May 1995, President Jacques Chirac announced that France would resume nuclear testing. The decision provoked almost universal outrage in the international community, and was condemned for its apparent disregard for regional opinion, as well as for undermining the considerable progress made towards a worldwide ban on nuclear testing. Scientists also expressed concern at the announcement; some believed that further explosions at Mururoa might lead to the collapse of the atoll, which had already been weakened considerably. Large-scale demonstrations and protest marches throughout the region were accompanied by boycotts of French products and the suspension of several trade and defence co-operation agreements. Opposition to the French Government intensified in July 1995, when French commandos violently seized *Rainbow Warrior II*, the flagship of Greenpeace, and its crew, which had been protesting peacefully near the test site. In defiance of international opinion, the first test was carried out in September, and a further five took place until January 1996. Work to dismantle facilities at the test site was completed in July 1998. Some 1,800 French military personnel were present at the CEP site in 1998.

In early 1999 a study by the Commission de Recherche et d'Information Indépendantes sur la Radioactivité (CRIIRAD), a French non-governmental organization, reported that there was serious radioactive leakage into underground water, lagoons and the ocean at Mururoa and Fangataufa Atolls, and a French government official admitted that fractures had been found in the coral cone at the Mururoa and Fangataufa nuclear testing sites. During President Chirac's visit to Papeete in July 2003 some 200 members of an association of those formerly employed at Mururoa and Fangataufa—Moruroa e Tatou—staged a demonstration to demand that France recognize the connection between nuclear testing and the subsequent health problems of those involved. The Nuclear Veterans' Association continued to seek compensation from the French Government: according to the group around 30% of some 15,000 former nuclear workers were either suffering—or had died—from cancers or related diseases.

In May 2005 CRIIRAD published declassified secret reports from 1966 on nuclear testing in the Gambier Islands, which suggested that the French military had deliberately suppressed information about the extent of contamination from radioactive fallout. A French Polynesian commission of inquiry subsequently reported that, contrary to the information given to the public, each of the 46 atmospheric tests between 1966 and 1974 had caused radioactive fallout on the islands around the test sites.

In January 2009 France agreed to finance the rehabilitation of its former military base on Hao Atoll. The 'clean-up' operation, which was expected to take seven years, was projected to cost the equivalent of US $80m. In March the French Government announced the establishment of an independent commission to examine individual compensation claims from civilian and military workers affected by the nuclear tests. Legislation approved in December provided for compensation payments for 18 formally recognized illnesses, including leukaemia and thyroid cancer. Prior to the adoption of the legislation, an estimated 2,000 demonstrators attended a peaceful march in Papeete, claiming that the scope of the new law was inadequate. In October 2013 the organization Moruroa e Tatou wrote an open letter to the French President, François Hollande, criticizing his Government's reluctance to accept its obligations to the test victims and his failure to carry out promised amendments to the compensation law. By late 2014, according to Moruroa e Tatou, of almost 900 compensation claims lodged with the French authorities, only 12 had been successful.

In February 2010 French Polynesia concluded a new agreement with France, under which the DGDE, which had been introduced to offset the loss of revenue resulting from the closure of the nuclear testing facilities, would be replaced at the end of the year by three new financial instruments, as part of an arrangement that would continue to take into consideration the economic legacy of the nuclear testing programme. However, the annual sum provided would remain unchanged, at some 18,000m. francs CFP (nearly €151m.). About 60% of this funding was to be disbursed by the French Polynesian Government, while more than 30% was to be allocated to approved infrastructure projects.

In March 2011, amid increasing fears for the stability of Mururoa Atoll, the local Government urged the French President to dispatch experts to the area to assess the risks to the population if the atoll were to collapse and release radiation, and possibly trigger a tsunami. The French authorities claimed that ongoing monitoring of the atoll would provide sufficient warning of a potential collapse. Further declassified documents, released in mid-2013, provided evidence that the entire territory had been affected by radioactive fallout, and that Tahiti had been exposed to levels of plutonium some 500 times higher than the maximum accepted safe level of the material, contrary to official public information communicated subsequent to the tests.

In November 2014 the Territorial Assembly approved a resolution demanding compensation for environmental damage caused by the nuclear testing programme of some US $930m. from metropolitan France (in addition to $132m. for the continued occupation of Fangataufa and Mururoa Atolls) and appealed for international experts, rather than the French Government, to oversee the process. The resolution, which was approved by 36 of the 57 legislators, was not supported by President Fritch, and divisions within the ruling Tahoera'a Huiraatira over the issue were described as unprecedented.

CONSTITUTION AND GOVERNMENT

French Polynesia was designated as an Overseas Country (Pays d'Outre-Mer) within the French Republic in 2004. Its status is that of an Overseas Collectivity (Collectivité d'Outre-Mer). The French Government is represented in French Polynesia by its High Commissioner, and controls various important spheres of government, including defence, foreign diplomacy and justice. A local Assembly, with 57 members, is elected for a five-year term by universal adult suffrage. The Assembly may elect a President of an executive body, the Council of Ministers, who in turn submits a list of between seven and 10 members of the Assembly to serve as ministers (decreased from 15 in legislation promulgated by the French President in August 2011), for approval by the Assembly.

In addition, French Polynesia elects three deputies to the French Assemblée Nationale (National Assembly) in Paris and two representatives to the French Sénat (Senate), all chosen on the basis of universal adult suffrage. French Polynesia is also represented at the European Parliament.

REGIONAL AND INTERNATIONAL CO-OPERATION

French Polynesia forms part of the Franc Zone (see p. 326), and is an associate member of the UN's Economic and Social Commission for Asia and the Pacific (ESCAP, see p. 30). Although France is also a member of the organization, French Polynesia has membership in its own right of the Pacific Community (see p. 410), which is based in New Caledonia and provides technical advice, training and assistance in economic, cultural and social development to the region. In October 2006 French Polynesia became an associate member of the Pacific Islands Forum (see p. 413). In November 2011 leaders from French Polynesia, American Samoa, the Cook Islands, Niue, Samoa, Tokelau, Tonga and Tuvalu formed the Polynesian Leaders' Group. The group was to hold annual summit meetings with the aim of sharing knowledge in the areas of the economy, education and the environment, and of promoting Polynesian culture, tradition and languages.

ECONOMIC AFFAIRS

In 2000, according to World Bank estimates, French Polynesia's gross national income (GNI), measured at average 1998–2000 prices, was US $3,795m., equivalent to $16,150 per head (or $24,680 per head on an international purchasing-power parity basis). During 2004–13, it was estimated, the population rose at an average annual rate of 1.1%. According to the UN's Economic and Social Commission for Asia and the Pacific (ESCAP), gross domestic product (GDP) per head increased at an average annual rate of 0.7% in 2001–11. Overall GDP rose at an average annual rate of 1.9% in 2001–11. According to UN estimates, real GDP increased by 2.4% in 2012.

According to UN estimates, agriculture, forestry and fishing contributed only 3.1% of GDP in 2012. The sector engaged 9.2% of the employed labour force at the 2007 census, and 2.9% of salaried workers at the end of 2013. Coconuts are the principal cash crop, and in 2013, according to FAO, the estimated harvest was 85,000 metric tons. The quantity of copra exported decreased from 6,195.5 tons in 2013 to 4,986.3 tons in 2014; however, the value of copra exports increased from 421.0m. francs CFP to 486.9m. francs CFP over the same period. Monoï oil is produced by macerating tiaré flowers in coconut oil, and in 2014 296.0 tons of the commodity (representing an increase of 21.6% over the previous year) were exported. Vegetables, fruit (including pineapples, citrus fruit and noni fruit), vanilla and coffee are also cultivated. In 2014 vanilla exports reached 17.7 tons and provided revenue of 367.5m. francs CFP. Most commercial fishing, principally for tuna, is conducted, under licence, by Japanese and Korean fleets. The total fish catch in 2012was 14,153 tons. In addition, production by the aquaculture sector, mainly shrimps, reached 81 tons. Another important activity is the production of cultured black pearls. The quantity of exports of cultured pearls totalled 14.3 tons in 2014, providing earnings of 8,621.5m. francs CFP. According to UN figures, the GDP of the agricultural sector contracted at an average annual rate of 1.3% in 2004–12. Agricultural GDP was estimated to have increased by 3.1% in 2012.

According to UN estimates, industry (comprising mining, manufacturing, construction and utilities) provided 12.1% of GDP in 2012. In 2007 17.3% of the employed labour force were engaged in the industrial sector. The sector engaged 14.8% of salaried workers at the end of 2013. According to the UN, industrial GDP increased at an average annual rate of 0.4% in 2004–12. The GDP of the industrial sector was estimated to have expanded by 2.1% in 2012. There is a small manufacturing sector, which is heavily dependent on agriculture. Coconut oil and copra are produced, as are beer, dairy products and vanilla essence.

According to UN estimates, mining, manufacturing and utilities provided 7.3% of GDP in 2012 (with manufacturing alone accounting for 5.2%). Mining and manufacturing engaged 6.4% of the employed labour force in 2007, and utilities a further 0.6%. Mining, manufacturing and utilities engaged 0.2%, 5.9% and 1.7% of salaried workers, respectively, at the end of 2013. The sectoral GDP decreased at an average annual rate of 0.1% in 2004–12, according to figures from the UN. The GDP of the sector was estimated to have expanded by 1.9% in 2012. Deposits of cobalt were discovered during the 1980s, and in early 2014 the Government granted a licence to an Australian company to explore the viability of reviving phosphate mining on Makatea Atoll.

Construction is an important industrial activity, contributing 4.8% of GDP in 2012. The sector engaged 10.3% of the employed labour force in 2007, and 6.9% of salaried workers at the end of 2013. According to the UN, the GDP of the construction sector increased at an average annual rate of 1.3% in 2004–12. The GDP of the sector was estimated to have expanded by 2.5% in 2012.

Hydrocarbon fuels are the main source of energy in French Polynesia, with the Papeete thermal power station providing about three-quarters of the total electricity produced. Mineral fuels accounted for 17.4% of the total value of merchandise imports in 2013. Hydroelectric power dams, with the capacity to generate more than one-third of the electricity requirements of Tahiti's population, have been constructed. Solar energy is also increasingly important, especially on the less-populated islands. Electricity production on Tahiti reached 515m. kWh in 2013.

The services sector provided 84.8% of GDP in 2012. Services engaged 73.4% of the employed labour force in 2007, and 82.4% of salaried workers at the end of 2013. The GDP of the services sector expanded at an average annual rate of 2.2% in 2004–12, according to UN estimates. The sector's GDP was estimated to have increased by 2.4% in 2012. Tourism is a major source of revenue. In 2013 164,393 tourists visited French Polynesia, compared with 168,978 in the previous year. In 2013 37.0% of visitor arrivals were from the USA, 20.0% from France and 8.0% from Japan. Receipts from tourism in 2012 totalled an estimated US $438m.

In 2012, according to the Institut d'Émission d'Outre-Mer (IEOM—the French overseas reserve bank), French Polynesia recorded a visible merchandise trade deficit of 145,798m. francs CFP. On the current account of the balance of payments there was a surplus of 23,698m. francs CFP. In 2013 the principal sources of imports were France (which provided 24.1% of total imports), the Republic of Korea, the People's Republic of China, the USA, New Zealand and Singapore. The principal markets for exports in that year were Japan (accounting for 29.3% of the total), Hong Kong, the USA and France. The principal imports included mineral products; machinery and mechanical appliances, electrical equipment, and sound and television apparatus; prepared foodstuffs, beverages, spirits and vinegar, and tobacco and manufactured substitutes; vehicles, aircraft, vessels and associated transport equipment; live animals and animal products; and products of chemical or allied industries. The principal exports were cultured pearls, precious and semi-precious stones and related items; live animals and animal products; and prepared foodstuffs, beverages, spirits and vinegar, and tobacco and manufactured substitutes.

In the 2013 budget, current revenue totalled 105,174m. francs CFP, while spending amounted to 118,833m. francs CFP, of which current expenditure accounted for 95,962m. and capital spending 22,871m. In 2003 an economic development grant (DGDE) from metropolitan France, amounting to some 18,000m. francs CFP (almost €151m.) annually and to be paid in perpetuity, was introduced to offset the loss of revenue resulting from the closure of the nuclear testing facilities. The DGDE was replaced by three new financial instruments at the end of 2010, but the annual sum provided remained unchanged. About 60% of the funding was to be disbursed by the French Polynesian Government, while about 30% was to be allocated to approved infrastructure projects. In 2012 state expenditure by France in French Polynesia totalled 173,800m. francs CFP.

The annual rate of inflation averaged 2.4% during 2005–13. Consumer prices rose by 1.4% in 2013. A high unemployment rate (21.8% of the labour force in 2012) has been exacerbated by the predominance of young people in the population.

The financial crisis in the islands resulted in a marked contraction in the economy in 2009 and weak growth in the following years. During this period investor confidence remained weak, and international credit monitoring agencies continued to cite political instability as a major factor in the successive downgrading of their ratings for French Polynesia. In late 2012, following a series of discussions in Paris, the French Government agreed to release €34m. of €50m. in financial assistance that had been withheld by the previous administration. The Government elected in mid-2013 announced plans to raise some US $100m. by increasing taxes on higher earners, as well as on sales of alcohol and tobacco, and in its budget for 2014 proposed reducing the public sector by some 300 employees, in an attempt to tackle the estimated $300m. of public debt. Attracting foreign investment was a principal strategy of the new administration's economic policy. In mid-2014 an agreement was reached with a Hawaiian company to provide some $3,000m. to finance the construction of a major resort complex on Tahiti. The 52-ha development was to include five hotels, a casino, conference centre, aquatic park and shopping centre. The Government claimed that the project would create significant employment and revive the territory's flagging tourism industry. The unemployment rate stood at some 30% in mid-2014, having doubled since 2007, and was estimated to be as high as 50% for young people. However, opposition leader Oscar Temaru and local churches were strongly opposed to the development, particularly as its proponents proposed the introduction of special labour laws, allowing workers at the site to be paid at a level well below the minimum wage. During late 2013 and 2014 the Government sought Chinese investment to support plans to construct a new port in the south of Tahiti and to rebuild the island's international airport. Another potential source of revenue emerged in early 2014, following the granting to an Australian company of a licence to investigate the possibility of resuming phosphate mining on Makatea Atoll in the Tuamotu Archipelago, which had been heavily mined from the late 1800s until 1966. Plans for a major aquaculture project to be established on Makemo Atoll, with $1,700m. of Chinese finance, were also agreed in early 2014, although the likelihood of their implementation remained uncertain in early 2015.

PUBLIC HOLIDAYS

2016: 1 January (New Year's Day), 5 March (Arrival of the Gospel), 25 March (Good Friday), 28 March (Easter Monday), 1 May (Labour Day), 5 May (Ascension Day), 8 May (Victory Day), 16 May (Whit Monday), 29 June (Internal Autonomy Day), 14 July (Fall of the Bastille), 15 August (Assumption), 1 November (All Saints' Day), 11 November (Armistice Day), 25 December (Christmas Day).

Statistical Survey

Source (unless otherwise indicated): Institut Statistique de la Polynésie Française, Immeuble Uupa, 1er étage, rue Edouard Ahne, BP 395, 98713 Papeete; tel. 473434; fax 427252; e-mail ispf@ispf.pf; internet www.ispf.pf.

AREA AND POPULATION

Area: Total 4,167 sq km (1,609 sq miles); Land area 3,521 sq km (1,359 sq miles).

Population: 259,596 at census of 20 August 2007; 268,207 at census of 22 August 2012. *By Island Group* (2012 census): Society Archipelago 235,295 (Windward Islands 200,714, Leeward Islands 34,581); Marquesas Archipelago 9,261; Austral Islands 6,820; Tuamotu-Gambier Islands 16,831; Total 268,207. *2014* (official estimate at 1 January): 270,500.

Density (land area only, at 1 January 2015): 76.8 per sq km.

Population by Age and Sex (UN estimates at mid-2015): *0–14 years:* 62,607 (males 31,966, females 30,641); *15–64 years:* 198,808 (males 101,891, females 96,917); *65 years and over:* 21,349 (males 10,439, females 10,910); *Total* 282,764 (males 144,296, females 138,468) (Source: UN, *World Population Prospects: The 2012 Revision*).

Principal Towns (population at 2012 census): Faa'a 29,719; Papeete (capital) 25,763; Punaauía 27,622; Moorea-Maiao 17,234; Pirae 14,094; Mahina 14,368; Paea 12,513; Taiarapu-Est 12,202; Papara 11,081. *2014* (incl. suburbs, UN estimate at mid-year): Papeete (capital) 132,917 (Source: UN *World Population Prospects: The 2014 Revision*).

Births, Marriages and Deaths (2013): Registered live births 4,200 (birth rate 15.5 per 1,000); Marriages 1,474 (marriage rate 5.5 per 1,000); Registered deaths 1,434 (death rate 5.3 per 1,000).

Life Expectancy (years at birth, 2012): 76.1 (males 73.9; females 78.5) (Source: World Bank, World Development Indicators database).

Economically Active Population (persons aged 14 years and over, 2007 census, excluding persons in military service): Agriculture, hunting, forestry and fishing 8,809; Mining and manufacturing 6,081; Electricity, gas and water 585; Construction 9,825; Trade, restaurants and hotels 21,064; Transport, storage and communications 7,049; Financial services 1,666; Real estate, housing and services to business 4,391; Other private services 5,326; Education, health and social welfare 15,115; Public administration 15,347; *Total employed* 95,258 (males 56,674, females 38,584); Unemployed 12,668 (males 7,006, females 5,662); *Total labour force* 107,926 (males 63,680, females 44,246). *2013* (salaried workers at 31 December): Agriculture, hunting, forestry and fishing 1,762; Mining and quarrying 133; Manufacturing 3,615; Electricity, gas and water 1,024; Construction 4,235; Trade, restaurants and hotels 15,814; Transport, storage and communications 6,677; Financial services 1,637; Real estate, housing and services to business 5,150; Public administration 13,214; Education 467; Health and social welfare 3,665; Other community, social and personal services 2,173; Persons employed in private households 1,470; Total 61,036.

HEALTH AND WELFARE
Key Indicators

Total Fertility Rate (children per woman, 2013): 2.0.

Physicians (per 1,000 head, 2012): 1.9.

Total Carbon Dioxide Emissions ('000 metric tons, 2010): 883.7.

Carbon Dioxide Emissions Per Head (metric tons, 2010): 3.3.

For definitions, see explanatory note on p. vi.

AGRICULTURE, ETC.

Principal Crops (metric tons, 2013, FAO estimates): Cassava 4,000; Other roots and tubers 6,000; Sugar cane 3,500; Vegetables and melons 6,450; Pineapples 4,300; Coconuts 82,000; Vanilla 60; Coffee, green 22.

Livestock (year ending September 2013, FAO estimates): Cattle 7,400; Horses 2,200; Pigs 30,000; Goats 16,800; Sheep 440; Chickens 305,000; Ducks 30,000.

Livestock Products (metric tons, 2013, FAO estimates): Cattle meat 130; Pig meat 1,600; Goat meat 75; Chicken meat 630; Cows' milk 1,250; Hen eggs 2,900; Other poultry eggs 88; Honey 50.

Fishing (metric tons, live weight, 2012): Capture 14,153 (Skipjack tuna 1,266; Albacore 3,868; Yellowfin tuna 1,480; Bigeye tuna 664; Blue marlin 523; Wahoo 310; Common dolphinfish 539; Other marine fishes 4,259); Aquaculture 81; *Total catch* 14,234. Note: Figures exclude pearl oyster shells: 2,574.

Source: FAO.

INDUSTRY

Selected Products (metric tons, 2013, unless otherwise indicated): Copra 10,629; Coconut oil 6,879 (2010); Oilcake 6,099; Electric energy (Tahiti only) 515m. kWh. Source: partly Institut d'Emission d'Outre-Mer.

FINANCE

Currency and Exchange Rates: 100 centimes = 1 franc de la Communauté française du Pacifique (franc CFP or Pacific franc). *Sterling, Dollar and Euro Equivalents* (31 December 2014): £1 sterling = 153.408 francs CFP; US $1 = 98.288 francs CFP; €1 = 119.332 francs CFP; 1,000 francs CFP = £6.52 = $10.17 = €8.38. *Average Exchange Rate* (francs CFP per US $): 92.88 in 2012; 89.88 in 2013; 89.94 in 2014. Note: Until 31 December 1998 the value of the franc CFP was fixed at 5.5 French centimes (1 French franc = 18.1818 francs CFP). Since the introduction of the euro, on 1 January 1999, an official exchange rate of 1,000 francs CFP = €8.38 (€1 = 119.332 francs CFP) has been in operation. Accordingly, the value of the franc CFP has been adjusted to 5.4969 French centimes (1 French franc = 18.1920 francs CFP), representing a 'devaluation' of 0.056%.

Territorial Budget (million francs CFP, 2012): Current revenue 123,217 (Direct taxes 24,154; Indirect taxes 57,148); Expenditure 147,891 (Current 113,350, Capital 34,541).

French State Expenditure (million francs CFP): 175,558 (incl. military budget 21,005) in 2009; 178,995 in 2010; 172,482 in 2011.

Money Supply (million francs CFP at 31 December 2013): Currency in circulation 14,399; Demand deposits 156,490; *Total money* 170,889. Source: Institut d'Emission d'Outre-Mer.

Cost of Living (Consumer Price Index; base: 2005 = 100): All items 118.2 in 2011; 119.6 in 2012; 121.3 in 2013. Source: UN, *Monthly Bulletin of Statistics*.

Gross Domestic Product (million francs CFP at constant 2005 prices): 601,108.6 in 2010; 614,245.2 in 2011; 628,655.6 in 2012. Source: UN Statistics Division, National Accounts Main Aggregates Database.

Expenditure on the Gross Domestic Product (million francs CFP at current prices, 2012): Government final consumption expenditure 211,561.9; Private final consumption expenditure 412,827.6; Increase in stocks 1,871.8; Gross fixed capital formation 147,977.8; *Total domestic expenditure* 774,239.1; Exports of goods and services 135,020.7; *Less* Imports of goods and services 245,706.9; *GDP in purchasers' values* 663,552.9. Source: UN National Accounts Main Aggregates Database.

Gross Domestic Product by Economic Activity (million francs CFP at current prices, 2012): Agriculture, hunting, forestry and fishing 18,303.6; Mining, electricity, gas and water 12,654.9; Manufacturing 30,893.8; Construction 28,480.2; Trade, restaurants and hotels 96,193.6; Transport, storage and communications 61,165.7; Other activities 348,747.2; *Sub-total* 596,438.9; Net of indirect taxes 67,113.9 (obtained as a residual); *GDP in purchasers' values*

663,552.9. Source: UN National Accounts Main Aggregates Database.

Balance of Payments (million francs CFP, 2012): Exports of goods 12,502; Imports of goods –158,300; *Trade balance* –145,798; Exports of services 105,218; Imports of services –48,033; *Balance on goods and services* –88,613; Other income (net) 58,485; *Balance on goods, services and income* –30,128; Current transfers (net) 53,825; *Current balance* 23,698; Capital account (net) –57; Direct investment (net) 9,952; Portfolio investment (net) 1,990; Other investment (net) –15,661; *Overall balance* 19,922. Source: Institut d'Emission d'Outre-Mer.

EXTERNAL TRADE

Principal Commodities (million francs CFP, 2013, excl. military transactions): *Imports c.i.f.:* Live animals and animal products 14,225.9 (Meat and edible meat offal 8,729.6); Vegetable products 5,531.3; Prepared foodstuffs; beverages, spirits and vinegar; tobacco and manufactured substitutes 18,686.7 (Preparations of cereals, flour, starch or milk 4,506.4); Mineral products 29,526.3 (Mineral fuels, mineral oils and products of their distillation; bituminous substances; mineral waxes 28,135.4); Products of chemical or allied industries 13,821.7 (Pharmaceutical products 7,406.0); Plastics, rubber and articles thereof 5,835.8; Base metals and articles thereof 7,943.1; Machinery and mechanical appliances; electrical equipment; sound and television apparatus 25,284.5 (Boilers, machinery, mechanical appliances and parts 14,213.2; Electrical machinery, equipment, etc. 11,071.3); Vehicles, aircraft, vessels and associated transport equipment 16,350.1 (Road vehicles, parts and accessories 9,177.5); Miscellaneous manufactured articles 5,608.5; Total (incl. others) 161,522.5. *Exports f.o.b.:* Live animals and animal products 1,483.6 (Fish and crustaceans, molluscs and other aquatic invertebrates 1,099.5); Animal or vegetable fats and oils, and products thereof 434.8; Prepared foodstuffs; beverages, spirits and vinegars; tobacco and manufactured substitutes 713.1 (Preparations of vegetables, fruit, nuts or other parts of plants 523.4); Natural or cultured pearls, precious or semi-precious stones, precious metals and articles thereof; imitation jewellery; coin 8,565.1; Total (incl. others) 13,593.0.

Principal Trading Partners (million francs CFP, 2013, excl. military transactions): *Imports:* Australia 4,721.5; Belgium 2,803.8; China, People's Republic 15,969.3; France 38,964.1; Germany 5,163.2 Italy 3,860.5; Japan 2,517.5; Korea, Republic of 17,732.9; Netherlands 1,738.3; New Zealand 13,041.0; Singapore 11,327.7; Spain 2,213.0; Thailand 4,140.1; United Kingdom 1,677.0; USA 15,588.4; Total (incl. others) 161,522.5. *Exports:* China, People's Republic 211.6; France 1,900.1; Hong Kong 3,735.9; Japan 3,989.4; New Caledonia 229.6; New Zealand 147.2; USA 1,981.6; Total (incl. others) 13,593.0.

TRANSPORT

Road Traffic (2009): Four-wheeled vehicles 15,909; Two-wheeled vehicles 2,432; *Total* 18,341.

Shipping (2013, unless otherwise indicated): *International Traffic:* Passengers carried 27,852 (2003); Freight handled 901,457 (loaded 43,582, unloaded 857,875) metric tons. *Domestic Traffic:* Passengers carried 1,611,818; Total freight handled 413,219 metric tons. Source: Institut d'Emission d'Outre-Mer.

Civil Aviation (2013 unless otherwise indicated): *International Traffic:* Passengers carried 520,756 (2012); Freight handled 9,314 metric tons. *Domestic Traffic:* Passengers carried 628,049 (2012); Freight handled 2,100 metric tons.

TOURISM

Visitors: 162,776 in 2011; 168,978 in 2012; 164,393 in 2013.

Tourist Arrivals by Country of Residence (2013): Australia 9,167; Canada 7,206; France 32,946; Germany 3,477; Italy 8,103; Japan 13,175; New Caledonia 3,826; New Zealand 6,477; USA 60,862; Total (incl. others) 164,393. Source: Institut d'Emission d'Outre-Mer.

Tourism Receipts (US $ million, excl. passenger transport): 406 in 2010; 460 in 2011; 438 in 2012. Source: World Tourism Organization.

COMMUNICATIONS MEDIA

Telephones (2013): 55,000 main lines in use.

Mobile Cellular Telephones (subscribers, 2013): 236,900.

Broadband Subscribers (2013): 44,900.

Source: International Telecommunication Union.

EDUCATION

Pre-primary (2008/09, unless otherwise indicated): 40 schools (2006/07); 408 teachers (1996/97); 14,306 pupils.

Primary (incl. special schools and young adolescents' centres, 2013/14, unless otherwise indicated): 231 schools (incl. pre-primary, 2010/11); 2,811 teachers (1996/97); 37,343 pupils.

Secondary (2013/14 unless otherwise indicated): 51 schools (first and second cycles, 2008/09); 2,035 teachers (general secondary only, 1998/99); 31,837 pupils.

Tertiary (2006/07, unless otherwise indicated): 50 teachers (1999); 681 students.

Source: partly Institut d'Emission d'Outre-Mer.

Directory

The Government

High Commissioner: LIONEL BEFFRE.

Secretary-General: GILLES CANTAL.

COUNCIL OF MINISTERS
(April 2015)

The Government is formed by Tahoera'a Huiraatira.

President with responsibility for Community Life, Administrative Modernization, Digital Economy, International and European Affairs, and Territorial Equality: EDOUARD FRITCH.

Vice-President and Minister of the Economy, Finance and the Budget, Public Service, and Energy: NUIHAU LAUREY.

Minister for Economic Recovery, International Transport, Tourism, Trade, Enterprise and Industry, and Government Spokesman: JEAN-CHRISTOPHE BOUISSOU.

Minister for Development of the Primary Sector: FRÉDÉRIC RIVETA.

Minister for Labour, Social Dialogue, Employment, Professional Training, Research, and Rights of Women: PRISCILLE TEA FROGIER.

Minister for Housing, Urban Development, City Policy, Property, and Business Domain: TEARII ALPHA.

Minister for Education, and Higher Education: NICOLE FAREATA SANQUER.

Minister for Youth and Sports, with responsibility for Relations with French Polynesia's Institutions, and the Economic, Social and Cultural Council: RENÉ TEMEHARO.

Minister for Health and Solidarity: PATRICK HOWELL.

Minister for Infrastructure, Spatial Planning, Urban Development, and Land and Sea Transport: ALBERT SOLIA.

Minister for Language Promotion, Culture, Communication, and Environment: HEREMOANA MAAMAATUAIAHUTAPU.

GOVERNMENT OFFICES

Office of the High Commissioner of the Republic: ave Pouvana'a a Oopa, Nouveau Bâtiment, BP 115, 98713 Papeete; tel. 468700; fax 468769; e-mail courrier@polynesie-francaise.pref.gouv.fr; internet www.polynesie-francaise.pref.gouv.fr.

Office of the President: Quartier Broche, ave Pouvana'a a Oopa, BP 2551, 98713 Papeete; tel. 472000; fax 472210; internet www.presidence.pf.

Ministry of Development of the Primary Sector: Bâtiment de l'Ancien Gouvernement, ave Pouvana'a a Oopa, Papeete; tel. 504455; internet web.presidence.pf.

Ministry of Economic Recovery, International Transport, Tourism, Trade, Enterprise and Industry: Bâtiment du GIE Tahiti Tourisme, quai des Paquebots, front de mer, Papeete; tel. 508860; internet web.presidence.pf.

Ministry of Economy, Finance and the Budget, Public Service, and Energy: Bâtiment de la Culture, face au CESC, 1er étage, Papeete; tel. 803000; internet web.presidence.pf.

Ministry of Education, and Higher Education: route de l'Hippodrome, près de l'école Tuterai Tane, Pirae; tel. 544900; internet web.presidence.pf.

Ministry of Housing, Urban Development, City Policy, Property, and Business Domain: Immeuble Tefenua, 5ème étage, rue Dumont d'Urville, BP 2551, 98713 Papeete; tel. 549575; fax 454343; internet web.presidence.pf.

Ministry of Infrastructure, Spatial Planning, Urban Development, and Land and Sea Transport: Bâtiment Administratif A2, 5ème étage, Papeete; tel. 468019; internet web.presidence.pf.

Ministry of Labour, Social Dialogue, Employment, Professional Training, Research, and Rights of Women: Présidence de la Polynésie Française, quartier Broche, ave Pouvana'a a Oopa; tel. 472280; internet www.equipement.gov.pf.

Ministry of Youth and Sports: 24, ave du Petit-Thouars, face au parking Tarahoi, Papeete; tel. 472500; internet web.presidence.pf.

Ministry of Language Promotion, Culture, Communication, and Environment: Papeete; tel. 548780; internet web.presidence.pf.

Ministry of Health and Solidarity: Papeete; tel. 460092; internet web.presidence.pf.

Legislature

ASSEMBLY

Elections to the Assembly took place over two rounds, in accordance with the modified electoral process, on 21 April and 5 May 2013.

President: MARCEL TUIHANI.

Assembly: Assemblée de la Polynésie Française, rue du Docteur Cassiau, BP 28, 98713 Papeete; tel. 416300; fax 416372; e-mail administratif@assemblee.pf; internet www.assemblee.pf.

Election (second round), 5 May 2013

Party	Seats
Tahoera'a Huiraatira*	38
Union pour la Démocratie (UPLD)†	11
A Ti'a Porinetia	8
Total	57

* The Tahoera'a Huiraatira's total includes the 19 seats allocated to the winning list in the second round under the new electoral system.

† Coalition led by Tavini Huiraatira.

PARLIAMENT

Deputies to the French National Assembly: JONAS TAHUAITU (DVD), JEAN-PAUL TUAIVA (DVD), MAINA SAGE (Tahoera'a Huiraatira).

Representatives to the French Senate: Iriti Teura and Vincent Dubois, both of the Tahoera'a Huiraatira, were elected to the French Senate in September 2014, but their election was annulled by the French Constitutional Court in February 2015; a new election was scheduled to be held on 3 May.

Political Organizations

A Ti'a Porinetia (Rally of Polynesians): POB 4110, 98713 Papeete; tel. and fax 823636; e-mail contact@atiaporinetia.org; internet www.atiaporinetia.org; f. 2013; coalition of parties fmrly belonging to the To Tatou Ai'a coalition and a number of smaller groups; Pres. TEVA ROHFRITSCH.

Fe'tia Api (New Star): c/o Assemblée de la Polynésie Française, rue du Docteur Cassiau, BP 28, 98713 Papeete; tel. 416131; fax 416136; f. 1996; part of Alliance pour une Démocratie Nouvelle coalition; pro-autonomy; Leader PHILIP SCHYLE.

Heiura-Les Verts Polynésiens: BP 44, Bora Bora; tel. and fax 677174; e-mail heiura@heiura-lesverts.pf; ecologist; Leader JACKY BRYANT.

Ia Mana Te Nunaa (Power to the People): BP 140 114, Arue, Tahiti 98701; tel. 426699; e-mail iamanatenunaa@mail.pf; internet www.iamanatenunaa.com; f. 1976; advocates 'socialist independence'; Pres. JACQUI DROLLET.

No Oe E Te Nunaa (This Country is Yours): Immeuble Fara, rue Nansouty, BP 40205, Fare Tony, 98713 Papeete; tel. 423718; e-mail contact@noetn.com; internet www.noetn.com; favours autonomy; part of Alliance pour une Démocratie Nouvelle coalition; Leader NICOLE MOEA BOUTEAU; Sec.-Gen. ROSALIE TIRIANA ZAVAN.

O Porinetia To Tatou Ai'a (Polynesia, Our Homeland): BP 4061, 98713 Papeete; tel. and fax 584848; e-mail contact@oporinetia.pf; internet www.oporinetia.pf; f. 2007; est. by fmr mems of Tahoera'a Huiraatira; leading mem. of A Ti'a Porinetia (fmrly To Tatou Ai'a) coalition; Pres. GASTON TONG SANG.

Taatiraa No Te Hau: POB 42217, Papeete; tel. 437494; fax 422546; e-mail info@taatiraanotehau.com; internet www.taatiraanotehau.com; f. 1977; Pres. CHARLES FONG LOI.

Tahoera'a Huiraatira (People's Rally): rue du Commandant Destremeau, BP 471, Papeete; tel. 429898; fax 450004; e-mail tahitinui@

tahoeraa.pf; internet tahoeraahuiraatira.pf; f. 1977; fmrly l'Union Tahitienne; supports links with France, with internal autonomy; affiliated to the metropolitan Union pour un Mouvement Populaire (UMP); Pres. EDOUARD FRITCH; Sec.-Gen. BRUNO SANDRAS.

Tapura Amui No Te Faatereraa Manahune-Tuhaa Pae: c/o Assemblée de la Polynésie Française, rue du Docteur Cassiau, BP 28, 98713 Papeete; represents the Austral Islands; Leader CHANTAL FLORES.

Tavini Huiraatira No Te Ao Ma'ohi/Front de Libération de la Polynésie (Polynesian People's Servant): rue des Remparts, Papeete; tel. 424902; fax 434209; e-mail contact@tavinihuiraatira .com; internet www.tavinihuiraatira.com; f. 1977; leading mem. of Union pour la Démocratie (Union for Democracy—UPLD) coalition; independence movement; anti-nuclear; Leader OSCAR TEMARU; Sec.-Gen. LÉON TEFAU.

Te' Avei'a (Te Ara): BP 11 362, 98709 Mahina, Tahiti; tel. and fax 851385; e-mail mail@teaveia.pf; internet www.teaveia.pf; f. 2004; est. by fmr mems of Fe'tia Api and Tavini Huiraatira; Pres. ANTONIO PEREZ.

Te Henua Enana Kotoa: Nuku Hiva, BP 56 Taiohae; tel. and fax 920422; Leader LOUIS TAATA.

Te Niu Hau Manahune (Principle of Democracy): Rangiroa; f. 2007; Pres. TEINA MARAEURA; Vice-Pres BENOÎT KAUTAI, TEMAURI FOSTER.

Te Pupu Here Ai'a Te Nuna'a Ia Ora (Patriotic Party for an Autonomous Polity): BP 3195, Papeete; tel. 420766; f. 1965; advocates autonomy.

Judicial System

Audit Office: Chambre Territoriale des Comptes, rue Edouard Ahnne, BP 331, 98713 Papeete; tel. 509710; fax 509719; e-mail ctcpf@pf.ccomptes.fr; Pres. JEAN LACHKAR; Clerk of the Court MARIE-HÉLÈNE ANDRIOT.

Court of Administrative Law: ave Pouvana'a a Oopa, BP 4522, 98713 Papeete; tel. 509025; fax 451724; e-mail greffe.ta-papeete@ juradm.fr; internet polynesie-francaise.tribunal-administratif.fr; Pres. JEAN-YVES TALLEC; Clerk of the Court DONA GERMAIN.

Court of Appeal: Cour d'Appel de Papeete, 42 ave Pouvana'a a Oopa, BP 101, 98713 Papeete; tel. 415500; fax 424416; e-mail sec.pp .ca-papeete@justice.fr; internet www.ca-papeete.justice.fr; Pres. OLIVIER AIMOT; Attorney-Gen. SERGE SAMUEL; Clerk of the Court RENE ARLANDA.

Court of the First Instance: Tribunal de Première Instance de Papeete, ave Bruat, BP 4633, 78718 Papeete; tel. 415500; fax 454012; e-mail sec.pr.tpi-papeete@justice.fr; internet www.ca-papeete .justice.fr; Pres. Sir FRANCIS JULLEMIER MILLASSEAU; Procurator JOSÉ THOREL; Clerk of the Court KARL LEQUEUX.

Religion

About 54% of the population are Protestants and 38% are Roman Catholics.

CHRISTIANITY

Protestant Church

Maohi Protestant Church: BP 113, Papeete; tel. 460600; fax 419357; e-mail eepf@mail.pf; f. 1884; autonomous since 1963; fmrly l'Eglise Evangélique en Polynésie Française (Etaretia Evaneria I Porinetia Farani); Pres. of Council Rev. TAAROANUI MARAEA; c. 95,000 mems.

The Roman Catholic Church

French Polynesia comprises the archdiocese of Papeete and the suffragan diocese of Taiohae o Tefenuaenata (based in Nuku Hiva, Marquesas Is). At 31 December 2007 there were an estimated 101,090 adherents in French Polynesia. The Archbishop and the Bishop participate in the Episcopal Conference of the Pacific, based in Fiji.

Archbishop of Papeete: (vacant), Archevêché, BP 94, Vallée de la Mission, 98713 Papeete; tel. 420251; fax 424032; e-mail catholic@ mail.pf.

Other Churches

Other denominations active in French Polynesia include the Assemblies of God, Church of Jesus Christ of Latter-day Saints (Mormon), Sanito and Seventh-day Adventist missions. At mid-2000 there were an estimated 30,000 adherents to other forms of Christianity.

The Press

La Dépêche de Tahiti: ave George Clémenceau, BP 50, 98713 Papeete; tel. 475283; fax 475260; e-mail journal@ladepeche.pf; internet www.ladepeche.pf; f. 1964; acquired by Groupe France Antilles in 1988; daily; French; Man. Dir ALEXANDRE THÉVENET; Editor LARA DUPUY; circ. 20,500.

Fenua'Orama: BP 629, 98713 Papeete; tel. 475293; fax 475297; e-mail fenuaorama@hersantmedia.pf; publ. by Groupe France Antilles; monthly; women's lifestyle; Editor-in-Chief DANIEL PARDON; circ. 13,700.

L'Hebdo Maohi: Papeete; tel. and fax 4581827; e-mail journal@ hebdo.pf; internet www.hebdo.pf; weekly; Man. and Publ. Dir TERII PAQUIER; circ. 3,000.

Journal Officiel de la Polynésie Française: c/o Imprimerie Officielle, 43 rue des Poilus Tahitiens, BP 117, 98713 Papeete; tel. 500580; fax 425261; e-mail imprimerie.officielle@imprimerie.gov.pf; f. 2004 as *Compte Rendu Intégral des Débats de l'Assemblée de la Polynésie Française*; bi-weekly; publ. by the Imprimerie Officielle; circ. 100.

Le Semeur Tahitien: BP 94, 98713 Papeete; tel. 502351; fax 424032; e-mail catholic@mail.pf; f. 1909; 22 a year; French; publ. by the Roman Catholic Church; Editor ROSA TAUHIRO.

Tahiti Beach Press: BP 887, 98713 Papeete; tel. 426850; fax 423356; e-mail tahitibeachpres@mail.pf; internet www .tahitibeachpress.com; f. 1980; monthly; English; Publr G. WARTI; circ. 10,000.

Tahiti Pacifique Magazine: BP 368, Maharepa, Moorea; tel. 562894; fax 563007; e-mail tahitipm@mail.pf; internet tahiti-pacifique.com; monthly; French; Dir and Editor ALEX W. DU PREL; circ. 6,500.

Ve'a Katorika: BP 94, 98713 Papeete; tel. 502351; fax 424032; e-mail archeveche@catholic.pf; internet www.diocesedepapeete .com; f. 1909; monthly; publ. by the Roman Catholic Church; Administrator MICHEL COPPENRATH.

Ve'a Porotetani: BP 113, Papeete; tel. 460623; fax 419357; e-mail eepf@mail.pf; f. 1921; monthly; French and Tahitian; publ. by the Maohi Protestant Church; Dir TAARII MARAEA; Editor-in-Chief EVA RAAPOTO; circ. 5,000.

Other publications include *Le To'ere*, weekly; *Conso + Info Plus*, *Tahiti Business* and *Ve'a Ora Magazine*, monthly; and *Dixit* and *Fenua Economie*, annually.

NEWS AGENCY

Agence France-Presse (AFP): BP 629, Papeete; tel. 508100; fax 508109; Group Chair. and CEO EMMANUEL HOOG; Group Man. Dir RÉMI TOMASZEWSKI.

Publishers

Editions Haere Pō: BP 1958, Papeete 98713; tel. and fax 480401; e-mail anapat@mail.pf; internet www.haerepo.org; f. 1981; travel, history, linguistics, literature, culture, anthropology, religion, land tenure and local interest.

Au Vent des Iles: BP 5670, 98716 Pirae; tel. 509595; fax 509597; e-mail mail@auventdesiles.pf; internet www.auventdesiles.pf; f. 1992; South Pacific interest, fiction and trade; Gen. Man. CHRISTIAN ROBERT.

GOVERNMENT PRINTER

Imprimerie Officielle: 43 rue des Poilus Tahitiens, BP 117, 98713 Papeete; tel. 500580; fax 425261; e-mail imprimerie.officielle@ imprimerie.gov.pf; f. 1843; printers, publrs; Dir CLAUDINO LAURENT.

Broadcasting and Communications

TELECOMMUNICATIONS

Office des Postes et Télécommunications (OPT): Hôtel des Postes, 8 rue de la Reine Pomare IV, 98714 Papeete; tel. 414242; fax 436767; e-mail contact@opt.pf; internet www.opt.pf; state-owned telecommunications co; subsidiaries incl. Tahiti Nui Telecom (international voice services), Tikiphone (mobile network), Mana (internet service), Tahiti Nui Satellite (satellite broadcaster), ISS (software and network solutions); Chair. FRANÇOIS VOIRIN; Dir-Gen. BENJAMIN TEIHOTU (acting).

Tahiti Nui Telecommunications (TNT): BP 11843, 98709 Mahina; tel. 415400; fax 437553; e-mail admin.tnt@ tahitinui-telecom.com; internet www.tahitinui-telecom.com; f. 2001; owned by OPT; provides international telephone services; Chair. JEAN-CLAUDE TERIIEROOITERAI.

Tikiphone SAS (Vini): POB 440, 98713 Papeete; tel. 481313; fax 482300; internet www.tikiphone.pf; f. 1994; subsidiary of OPT; operates Vini, French Polynesia's first mobile telephone network; more than 208,000 subscribers; Gen. Man. YANNICK TERIIEROOI-TERAI.

Regulatory Authority

Agence de Réglementation du Numérique: Immeuble Toriki, rue Dumont d'Urville, Quartier Orovini, BP 5019, 98716 Pirae; tel. 544535; fax 532801; e-mail direction@arn.gov.pf; internet www.arn.pf; fmrly Services des Postes et Télécommunications; name changed as above 2011; Dir TAMATOA POMMIER.

BROADCASTING

Radio

RFO Polynésie: Centre Pamatai, Faa'a, BP 60125, 98702 Papeete; tel. 861616; fax 861611; e-mail rfopfr@mail.pf; internet polynesie.la1ere.fr; f. 1934; public service radio and television station operated by Réseau France Outre-Mer (RFO), Paris; daily programmes in French and Tahitian; Dir-Gen. GENEVIÈVE GIARD; Regional Dir MICHEL KOPS.

Private Stations

NRJ Tahiti: BP 50, 98718 Papeete; tel. and fax 421042; fax 464346; internet www.nrj.pf; affiliated to NRJ France; French; entertainment; broadcasts 14 hrs daily; Station Man. NADINE RICHARDSON.

Radio Maohi: Maison des Jeunes, Pirae; tel. 819797; fax 825493; e-mail tereo@mail.pf; French and Tahitian; owned by the political party Tahoera'a Huiraatira.

Radio One: Fare Ute, BP 3601, 98713 Papeete; tel. 434100; fax 422421; e-mail contact@radio1.pf; internet www.radio1.pf; French; relays Europe 1 news bulletins from Paris; CEO SONIA ALINE.

Radio (Te Reo O) Tefana (La Voix de Tefana): BP 6295, 98702 Faa'a; tel. 819797; fax 825493; e-mail tereo@mail.pf; f. 1987; French and Tahitian; affiliated to the Tavini Huiraatira party; Pres. VITO MAAMAATUAIAHUTAPU; Dir and Station Man. TERIIMATEATA MANA; Editor-in-Chief MICAËL TAPUTU.

Radio Te Vevo O Te Tiaturiraa: 51 rue Dumont d'Urville, BP 1817, 98713 Papeete; tel. 412341; fax 412322; e-mail contacts@mail.pf; religious; affiliated with the Assemblies of God church; Treas. THIERRY ALBERT.

Other radio stations include Pacific FM, Radio Fara, Radio la Voix de l'Espérance (LVDL), Radio Ma'ohi-RTL, Radio Maria No Te Hau, Radio Paofai, Radio Te Vevo No Papara, Star FM and Tiare FM.

Television

RFO Polynésie: see Radio.

TNS (Tahiti Nui Satellite): 8 rue de la Reine Pomare IV, 98714 Papeete; tel. 414370; fax 432707; e-mail tns@opt.pf; internet www.tns.pf; f. 2000; 100% owned by the Office des Postes et Télécommunications; news and entertainment; relays 25 television channels and 6 radio channels, in French, Tahitian and English, incl. TNTV; also relays ABC Asia Pacific Television, Australia, and Canal Plus, France; Man. VETEA TROUCHE-BONNO; over 10,000 subscribers.

TNTV (Tahiti Nui Television): Quartier Mission, BP 348, 98713 Papeete; tel. 473636; fax 532721; e-mail tntv@tntv.pf; internet www.tntv.pf; f. 2000; broadcasts in French and Tahitian 19 hours daily; Chair. MEDERIC BERNARDINO; Dir-Gen. PHILIPPE ROUSSEL.

Finance

(cap. = capital; res = reserves; dep. = deposits; m. = million; brs = branches; amounts in francs CFP)

BANKING

Commercial Banks

Banque de Polynésie SA: 355 blvd Pomare, BP 530, 98713 Papeete; tel. 466666; fax 466664; e-mail bdp@sg-bdp.pf; internet www.sg-bdp.pf; f. 1973; 80% owned by Société Générale, France; cap. 1,380m., res 3,352m., dep. 136,408.2m. (Dec. 2011); Chair. JEAN-LOUIS MATTEI; Gen. Man. OLIVIER RAUCH; 25 brs.

Banque de Tahiti SA: 38 rue François Cardella, BP 1602, 98713 Papeete; tel. 417000; fax 423376; e-mail contact@bt.pf; internet www.banque-tahiti.pf; f. 1969; owned by Financière Océor (95.4%); merged with Banque Paribas de Polynésie in 1998; cap. 1,814.8m., res 5,271.2m., dep. 180,703.7m. (Dec. 2008); Chair. PHILIPPE GARSUAULT; Dir-Gen. PATRICE TEPELIAN; 18 brs.

Banque SOCREDO—Société de Crédit et de Développement de l'Océanie: 115 rue Dumont d'Urville, BP 130, 98713 Papeete; tel. 415123; fax 433661; e-mail socres@bank-socredo.pf; internet www.socredo.pf; f. 1959; public body; in partnership with French cos BNP Paribas, Cardif Assurance and Crédit Agricole, which provide technical assistance; cap. 22,000m., res 8,950.7m., dep. 160,838.6m. (Dec. 2011); Chair. CLAUDE PERIOU; Gen. Man. JAMES ESTALL; 26 brs.

Insurance

AGF Vie & AGF IART Polynésie Française: Immeuble Sienne, rue Dumont d'Urville, BP 4452, 98713 Papeete; tel. 549100; fax 549101; e-mail gestion-vie@agf.pf; internet www.allianz.fr; life and general non-life insurance.

GAN Pacifique: 9 ave Bruat, BP 339, 98713 Papeete; tel. 503150; fax 431918; subsidiary of Groupama, France; general non-life insurance; Chair. JEAN-FRANÇOIS LEMOUX; CEO PASCAL ALEXANDRE.

Poe-ma Insurances: Marina Fare Ute, BP 4652, 98713 Papeete; tel. 502650; fax 450097; e-mail info@poema.pf; internet www.poema.pf; f. 1991; general non-life insurance; Man. Dir VINCENT GEORGE.

Trade and Industry

GOVERNMENT AGENCIES

Direction Générale des Affaires Economiques (DGAE): Fare Ute, Bâtiment des Affaires Economiques, BP 82, 98713 Papeete; tel. 509797; fax 434477; e-mail dgae@economie.gov.pf; internet www.dgae.gov.pf; Man. Dir HERVÉ DUQUESNAY.

Etablissement Public des Grands Travaux (EGT): 51 rue du Commandant Destremeau, BP 9030, Motu Uta, 98715 Papeete; tel. 508100; fax 508102; e-mail contact@egt.pf; internet www.egt.pf; responsible for public works; Pres. JONAS TAHUAITU; Dir ERIC NOBLE-DEMAY.

Service de l'Artisanat Traditionnel (ART): Immeuble Lejeune, 1er étage, 82 rue du Général de Gaulle, BP 4451, 98713 Papeete; tel. 545400; fax 532321; e-mail secretariat@artisanat.gov.pf; f. 1984; Dir LAETITIA GALENON.

Service de l'Emploi, de la Formation et de la Insertion Professionnelles (SEFI): Immeuble Papineau, rue Tepano Jaussen, 2ème étage, BP 540, 98713 Papeete; tel. 461212; fax 450280; internet www.sefi.pf; Dir PAUL NATIER.

Service du Commerce Extérieur: 53 rue Nansouty, Immeuble Teissier au 1er étage, BP 20727, 98713 Papeete; tel. 506464; fax 436420; e-mail commerceexterieur@economie.gov.pf; internet www.tahiti-export.pf; Dir WILLIAM VANIZETTE.

Service du Développement de l'Industrie et des Métiers (SDIM): BP 9055, Motu Uta, 98715 Papeete; tel. 502880; fax 412645; e-mail infos@sdim.pf; internet www.sdim.pf; f. 1988; industry and small business devt administration; Dir DENIS GRELLIER.

Société de Financement du Développement de la Polynésie Française (SOFIDEP): Centre Paofai, Bâtiment BC, 1er étage, blvd Pomare, BP 345, 98713 Papeete; tel. 509330; fax 509333; e-mail sem.sofidep@mail.pf; Dir PIERRE FONTAINE.

DEVELOPMENT ORGANIZATIONS

Agence Française de Développement (AFD): Immeuble Hokule'a, 2 rue Cook Paofai, BP 578, 98713 Papeete; tel. 544600; fax 544601; e-mail afdpapeete@pf.groupe-afd.org; internet www.afd.fr; public body; devt finance institute; Dir FRANÇOIS GIOVALUCCHI.

Moruroa e Tatou (Moruroa et Nous): 403 blvd Pomare, BP 5456, 98716 Pirae, Papeete; tel. 460666; e-mail moruroaetatou@mail.pf; internet www.moruroaetatou.com; f. 2001; represents fmr employees of the Centre d'Expérimentation du Pacifique (CEP) and their families; Pres. ROLAND POUIRA OLDHAM; c. 4,500 mems.

SODEP (Société pour le Développement et l'Expansion du Pacifique): BP 4441, Papeete; tel. 429449; f. 1961; est. by a consortium of banks and private interests; regional devt and finance co.

CHAMBERS OF COMMERCE

Chambre d'Agriculture et de la Pêche Lagonaire: route de l'Hippodrome, BP 5383, Pirae; tel. 425393; fax 438754; e-mail courrier@vanille.pf; f. 1886; Pres. HENRI TAURAA; Sec.-Gen. JACQUES ROOMATAAROA; 10 mems.

Chambre de Commerce, d'Industrie, des Services et des Métiers de Polynésie Française (CCISM): 41 rue du Docteur Cassiau, BP 118, 98713 Papeete; tel. 472700; fax 540701; e-mail info@cci.pf; internet www.ccism.pf; f. 1880; Pres. GILLES YAU; Gen. Man. ABNER GILLOUX; 34 mems.

Jeune Chambre Economique de Tahiti: BP 20669, Papeete; tel. 810114; fax 702703; e-mail contact@jcitahiti.com; internet www.jcitahiti.com; Pres. THIERRY LEOU.

EMPLOYERS' ORGANIZATIONS

Confédération Générale des Petites et Moyennes Entreprises de Polynésie Française Te Rima Rohi (CGPME): BP 1733, 98713 Papeete; tel. 426333; fax 835608; e-mail courrier@cgpme.pf; internet www.cgpme.pf; Pres. CHRISTOPHE PLÉE; c. 1,000 mems.

Affiliated organizations include:

Chambre Syndicale des Fleuristes de Polynésie Française: tel. 800505; fax 573649; e-mail tahitifleurs@mail.pf; f. 2007; Pres. ALAIN MENARD.

Syndicat des Gérants de Stations Services (SGSS): tel. 455479; fax 427314; Pres. CHRISTIAN BASTIEN.

Syndicat des Restaurants, Bars et Snacks Bars de Polynésie Française (SRBSBPF): Le Mandarin, BP 302, 98713 Papeete; tel. 503350; fax 421632; e-mail charl.beaumont@mail.pf; Pres. CHARLES BEAUMONT.

Syndicat Polynésien des Entreprises et Prestataires de Service (SPEPS): tel. 584629; fax 545641; e-mail rdp@mail.pf; Pres. SÉBASTIEN BOUZARD.

Union Polynésienne de l'Hôtellerie (UPHO): 76 rue Wallis, BP 1733 Motu Uta, Papeete; tel. 426333; fax 429553; e-mail chris.beaumont@mail.pf; Pres. CHRISTOPHE BEAUMONT.

Union Polynésienne des Professions Libérales (UPPL): BP 4554, Papeete; e-mail gibeaux.tahiti@mail.pf; Pres. CHARLIE GIBEAUX.

MEDEF Polynésie Française (MEDEF PF): Immeuble Farnham, rue Clappier, BP 972, 98713 Papeete; tel. 541040; fax 423237; e-mail medef@medef.pf; internet www.medef.pf; f. 1983; fmrly Conseil des Employeurs; affiliated to Mouvement des Entreprises de France (MEDEF); comprises 15 professional and interprofessional orgs, representing 500 cos; Pres. LUC TAPETA-SERVONNAT; Sec.-Gen. JEAN-CLAUDE LECUELLE.

Affiliated organizations include:

Association des Transporteurs Aériens Locaux de Polynésie Française (ATAL): BP 314, 98713 Papeete; tel. 864004; fax 864009; Pres. MARCEL GALENON.

Association Tahitienne des Professionnels de l'Audiovisuel (ATPA): Papeete; internet www.atpa.tv; f. 2004; 17 mems.

Chambre Syndicale des Commissionnaires en Douane, Agents de Fret et Déménageurs de Polynésie Française: BP 972, 98713 Papeete; tel. 541044; fax 423237; e-mail cscdafd@medef.pf; Pres. TITAINA SANNE-BOURNE.

Comité de Polynésie de l'Association Française des Banques: c/o Banque de Tahiti, BP 1602, 98713 Papeete; tel. 417030; fax 423376; e-mail ptepelian@bt.pf; Pres. PATRICE TEPELIAN.

Fédération Générale du Commerce: BP 1607, 98713 Papeete; tel. 541042; fax 422359; e-mail fgc@mail.pf; internet www.fgc.pf; Pres. JACQUES BILLON-TYRARD; Sec. PATRICIA LO MONACO.

Professionnels du Conseil et de la Formation (PCF): Immeuble Farnham, 1er étage, rue Clappier, Papeete; tel. 541040; fax 423237; e-mail mcdc@mail.pf; f. 2004; established as Organisation Professionnelle du Conseil, de l'Intérim et de la Formation; name changed as above 2012; represents workers in consultancy, training, audit and research, communication and expertise; 10 mem. cos; Pres. FANNY GOSSE; Sec. LAURENT DEVEMY.

Syndicat des Agences Maritimes au Long Cours: BP 274, 98713 Papeete; tel. 428972; fax 432184; e-mail amitahiti@amitahiti.pf; Pres. MAEVA SIU.

Syndicat des Employeurs du Secteur de l'Assurance (SESA): BP 358, 98713 Papeete; tel. 506262; fax 506263; Pres. ALAIN LEBRIS.

Syndicat des Industriels de Polynésie Française (SIPOF): Immeuble Farnham, BP 3521, 98713 Papeete; tel. 541040; fax 423237; e-mail sipof@medef.pf; internet www.sipof.pf; f. 1974; represents workers in industry, engineering, manufacturing and printing; 2,222 mems in 61 cos; Co-Pres FRANCIS GUEBEL, YOANN LAMISSE; Sec. SÉBASTIEN MOLLARD.

Syndicat Professionnel des Concessionnaires Automobiles: BP 916, 98713 Papeete; tel. 454545; fax 431260; Pres. PAUL YEO CHICHONG.

Union des Industriels de la Manutention Portuaire (UNIM): BP 570, 98713 Papeete; tel. 545700; fax 426262; Pres. JULES CHANGUES.

Groupement Interprofessionnel du Monoï de Tahiti (GIMT): BP 14 165, Arue, Tahiti; tel. 414851; fax 431849; internet www.monoidetahiti.pf; f. 1992; asscn of monoï manufacturers.

UTILITIES

Electricity

Electricité de Tahiti (EDT): route de Puurai, BP 8021, Faa'a-Puurai; tel. 867777; fax 834439; e-mail ressourceshumaines@edt.pf; internet www.edt.pf; subsidiary of Groupe Suez, France; Pres. HERVÉ DUBOST-MARTIN; Gen. Man. DOMINIQUE BAYEN; c. 103,920 customers (2012).

Water

Polynésienne des Eaux: BP 20795, 98713 Papeete; tel. 505800; fax 421548; e-mail contact@polynesienne-des-eaux.pf.

TRADE UNIONS

Under French Polynesian legislation, to be officially recognized, trade unions must receive the vote of at least 5% of the workforce at professional elections.

Chambre Syndicale des Métiers du Génie Civil et des Travaux Publics (CSMGCTP): BP 51120, 98716 Pirae; tel. 502100; fax 436922; Pres. DANIEL PALACZ.

Confédération des Syndicats des Travailleurs de Polynésie/Force Ouvrière (CSTP/FO): Immeuble Farnham, 1er étage, BP 1201, 98713 Papeete; tel. 426049; fax 450635; e-mail pfrebault@cstp-fo.pf; Pres. COCO TERAIEFA CHANG; Sec.-Gen. PATRICK GALENON.

Confédération des Syndicats Indépendants de la Polynésie Française (CSIP): Immeuble Allegret, 1er étage, ave du Prince Hinoï, BP 468, 98713 Papeete; tel. 532274; fax 532275; Sec.-Gen. CYRIL LE GAYIC.

Confédération Syndicale A Tia I Mua (CFDT): Fare Ia Ora, Mamao, BP 4523, Papeete; tel. 544010; fax 450245; e-mail atiaimua@ifrance.com; affiliated to the Confédération Française Démocratique du Travail; Gen. Sec. JEAN-MARIE YAN TU.

Conseil Fédéral des Syndicats Libres de Polynésie O Oe To Oe Rima: Immeuble Brown, 1er étage, BP 52866, 98716 Pirae; tel. 483445; fax 483445; Gen. Sec. RONALD TEROROTUA.

Union Fédérale des Syndicats Autonomes/Confédération OTAHI (OTAHI UFSA): ancien Immeuble SETIL, 1er étage, ave du Prince Hinoi, BP 148, 98713 Papeete; tel. 450654; fax 451327; Sec.-Gen. LUCIE TIFFENAT.

Transport

ROADS

French Polynesia has 792 km of roads, of which about one-third are bitumen-surfaced and two-thirds stone-surfaced.

Direction des Transports Terrestres: 93 ave Pomare V, Fariipiti, BP 4586, 98713 Papeete; tel. 502060; fax 436021; e-mail dtt@transport.gov.pf; internet www.transports-terrestres.pf; f. 1988; Dir ROLAND TSU.

SHIPPING

The principal port is at Papeete, on Tahiti.

Port Authority: Port Autonome de Papeete, BP 9164, Motu Uta, 98715 Papeete; tel. 474800; fax 421950; e-mail portppt@portppt.pf; internet www.portdepapeete.pf; Harbour Master MARCEL PELLETIER; Port Dir PATRICK BORDET.

Agence Maritime Internationale de Tahiti: BP 274, 98713 Papeete; tel. 428972; fax 432184; e-mail amitahiti@amitahiti.pf; f. 1978; services from Asia, the USA, Australia, New Zealand and Europe; Gen. Mans JEAN SIU, MAEVA SIU.

CMA CGM Papeete: 2 rue Wallis, BP 96, Papeete; tel. 545252; fax 436806; e-mail ppt.genmbox@cma-cgm.com; internet www.cma-cgm.com; fmrly CGM Tour du Monde SA; shipowners and agents; international freight services; Group Chair. and CEO JACQUES R. SAADÉ; Dir RODOLPHE SAADÉ.

Compagnie Polynésienne de Transport Maritime: BP 220, 98713 Papeete; tel. 426242; fax 434889; e-mail aranui@mail.pf; internet www.aranui.com; shipping co; Dir JULES WONG; Gen. Man. PHILIPPE WONG.

EURL Transport Maritime des Tuamotu Ouest: BP 1816, 98713 Papeete; tel. 422553; fax 422557; inter-island passenger service; Dir SIMÉON RICHMOND.

SA Compagnie Française Maritime de Tahiti: Immeuble Importex, No. 45, Fare Ute, POB 368, 98713 Papeete; tel. 426393; fax 420617; e-mail taporo@mail.pf; Pres. and Man. MORTON GARBUTT.

SARL Société de Transport Insulaire Maritime (STIM): BP 635, 98713 Papeete; tel. 549954; fax 452444; Dir ROLAND PAQUIER.

Société de Navigation des Australes: BP 1890, Papeete; tel. 509609; fax 420609; e-mail snathp@mail.pf; inter-island passenger service; Dir HERVÉ DANTON.

CIVIL AVIATION

There is one international airport, Faa'a airport, 6 km from Papeete, on Tahiti, and there are numerous smaller airports and aerodromes throughout French Polynesia. Since October 2004 the Government has commissioned studies into the possible siting of a new international airport on Tubai in the Austral Islands, or in the Marquesas at either Nuku Hiva or Hiva Oa. International services are operated by Air France, Air Tahiti Nui, Air New Zealand, LAN-Chile, Hawaiian Airlines (USA) and Air Calédonie International.

Service d'Etat de l'Aviation Civile: BP 6404, 98702, Faa'a, Papeete; tel. 861000; fax 861009; e-mail webmaster@seac.pf; internet www.seac.pf; Dir PATRICK MOUYSSET.

Aéroport de Tahiti (ADT): BP 60161, 98702, Faa'a Centre; tel. 866060; fax 837391; e-mail secretariat@tahiti-aeroport.pf; internet www.tahiti-aeroport.pf; f. 2010; 50% govt-owned; management and devt of airports at Faa'a, Bora Bora, Raiatea and Rangiroa; Dir-Gen. FRÉDÉRIC MOR.

Air Moorea: BP 6019, 98702 Faa'a; tel. 864262; fax 864269; e-mail direction@airmoorea.pf; internet www.airmoorea.pf; f. 1968; operates internal services between Tahiti and Moorea Island and domestic charter flights; Pres. MARCEL GALENON; CEO FREDDY CHANSEAU.

Air Tahiti: BP 314, 98713 Papeete; tel. 864012; fax 864069; e-mail direction.generale@airtahiti.pf; internet www.airtahiti.aero; f. 1953; Air Polynésie 1970–87; operates domestic services to 46 islands; Chair. CHRISTIAN VERNAUDON; CEO MARCEL GALENON.

Air Tahiti Nui: Immeuble Dexter, Pont de l'Est, BP 1673, 98713 Papeete; tel. 460303; fax 460290; e-mail fly@airtahitinui.pf; internet www.airtahitinui.com; f. 1996; commenced operations 1998; scheduled services to the USA, France, Japan, New Zealand and Australia; CEO ETIENNE HOWAN.

Tourism

Tourism is an important and developed industry in French Polynesia, particularly on Tahiti. Tourist arrivals increased from 162,776 in 2011 to 168,978 in 2012, but fell to 164,393 in 2013. Most visitors are from the USA, France and Japan. In 2012 earnings from tourism totalled an estimated US \$438m.

GIE Tahiti Tourisme: Fare Manihini, blvd Pomare, BP 65, 98713 Papeete; tel. 504030; fax 436619; e-mail hvaxelaire@tahiti-tourisme.pf; internet www.tahiti-tourisme.pf; f. 1966 as autonomous public body; transformed into private corpn in 1993; relaunched Dec. 2005 following merger between GIE Tahiti Tourisme and Tahiti Manava Visitors' Bureau; Chair. HIRIA OTTINO; CEO ANNE-SOPHIE LESUR.

Service du Tourisme (SDT): Paofai Bldg (Entry D), blvd Pomare, Papeete; tel. 476200; fax 476202; e-mail service.tourisme@tourisme.gov.pf; govt dept; manages Special Fund for Tourist Development; Dir BRUNO JORDAN.

Defence

As assessed at November 2014, France maintained a combined force of 950 army and navy personnel in French Polynesia. France began testing nuclear weapons at Mururoa and Fangataufa Atolls, in the Tuamotu Archipelago, in 1966. The military presence has been largely connected with the Centre d'Expérimentation du Pacifique (CEP) and the Commission d'Energie Atomique (CEA). An indefinite suspension of tests was announced in mid-1993. In June 1995, however, the French Government announced its decision to resume nuclear testing at Mururoa Atoll. The final test was conducted in January 1996. The defence budget for 2006 was 24,000m. francs CFP.

Commander of the French Armed Forces in French Polynesia, of the Pacific Maritime Area and of the Centre d'Expérimentation du Pacifique: Rear-Adm. ANNE CULLERE.

Education

Education is compulsory for eight years between six and 14 years of age. It is free of charge for day pupils in government schools. Primary education, lasting six years, is financed by the territorial budget, while secondary and technical education are supported by state funds. A total of 14,306 children were enrolled in kindergarten in 2008/09. In 2013/14 37,343 pupils attended primary school. Secondary education is provided by public lycées, public high schools and private or church schools. A total of 31,837 pupils attended secondary school in 2013/14. The French Polynesian Government assumed responsibility for secondary education in 1988. Technical and professional education includes eight technical institutions, a tourism training programme, preparation for entrance to the metropolitan Grandes Ecoles, a National Conservatory for Arts and Crafts and training centres for those in the construction industry, health services, traditional handicrafts, primary school teaching and social work. The French University of the Pacific was established in French Polynesia in 1987. In 1999 it was divided into two separate branches, of which the University of French Polynesia is now based in Papeete. In 2012 a total of 3,051 students were enrolled at the Papeete branch. In 2004 French state spending on education, higher education and research amounted to 50,500m. francs CFP.

SAINT-BARTHÉLEMY

Saint-Barthélemy is one of the Leeward Islands in the Lesser Antilles. The volcanic island lies in the Caribbean Sea, 230 km north-west of Guadeloupe and 20 km south-east of Saint-Martin. Saint-Barthélemy occupies only 21 sq km, but has green-clad volcanic hillsides, as well as white beaches and surrounding reefs and islets. The climate is tropical, moderated by the sea, with an annual average temperature of 27.5°C (81°F) and a more humid and wet season between May and November. The island normally receives about 1,100 mm (43 ins) of rain annually. According to official estimates, at 1 January 2011 Saint-Barthélemy had a permanent population of 9,035 predominantly white inhabitants of Breton, Norman and Poitevin descent. There are fewer descendants of the Swedish inhabitants, who ruled Saint-Barthélemy for almost one century (until a referendum in 1878). French is the official language, but English and two Creole patois are widely spoken. A Norman dialect of French is also still sometimes in use. The majority of the population professes Christianity and belongs to the Roman Catholic Church. The principal town is Gustavia, its main port, in the south-west.

On 7 December 2003 the Guadeloupean dependency of Saint-Barthélemy participated in a department-wide referendum on Guadeloupe's future constitutional relationship with France. Although the proposal to streamline administrative and political processes was defeated, an overwhelming majority of those participating in Saint-Barthélemy, 95.5%, voted in favour of secession from Guadeloupe to form a separate Collectivité d'Outre-mer (Overseas Collectivity). The reorganization was subsequently approved by the French Sénat (Senate) on 6 February 2007 and by the Assemblée Nationale (National Assembly) the following day. On 21 February the island was formally designated an Overseas Collectivity.

Legislative elections to form a 19-member legislative assembly, the Conseil Territorial (Territorial Council), were held in July 2007. At the first round of elections the Saint-Barth d'abord/Union pour un Mouvement Populaire (UMP) list, headed by Bruno Magras, won a clear majority of 72.2% of the total votes cast, thereby obviating the need for a second round. The election was also contested by three

other groupings: the Tous unis pour St-Barthélemy list, lead by Karine Miot-Richard, the Action Equilibre et Transparence list headed by Maxime Desouches—each of which secured 9.9% of the ballot—and Benoît Chauvin's Ensemble pour St-Barthélemy, which attracted the remaining 7.9% of the votes cast. Some 70.6% of the electorate participated in the election. The Saint-Barth d'abord/UMP list obtained 16 of the 19 legislative seats, while the three other contenders were allocated one seat each. On 15 July Magras assumed the presidency of the Territorial Council and Saint-Barthélemy was officially installed as an Overseas Collectivity.

At an election held on 21 September 2008 Michel Magras of the UMP was elected as the territory's representative in the French Senate. In December 2011 Philippe Chopin replaced Jacques Simonnet as Prefect-Delegate. In elections to the Territorial Council on 18 March 2012, Magras's party, Saint-Barth d'abord, won 73.8% of the ballot and retained its 16 seats. The list led by Tous pour Saint Barth increased its representation to two seats while the remaining seat was secured by Saint Barth en Mouvement.

On 1 January 2012 Saint-Barthélemy became an Overseas Territory under European Union law, rather than an Outermost Region (unlike the other French Caribbean territories).

The first round of the French presidential election was conducted on 21 April 2012 (one day earlier than in mainland France). Nicolas Sarkozy, representing the UMP, attracted 43.6% of the votes in Saint-Barthélemy and Saint-Martin, compared with 26.8% for François Hollande of the Parti socialiste. A second round run-off election was held two weeks later, at which Sarkozy secured 59.4% of the ballot, defeating Hollande, who won 40.6%. Nevertheless, Hollande triumphed nationally and was sworn in as President in mid-May. In an election to the National Assembly in June Daniel Gibbes of the UMP was chosen to represent the territory (and Saint-Martin).

Legislation to address the problem of inflated prices in Saint-Barthélemy and other French Overseas Possessions was approved by the French Parliament in November 2012. Most notably, the legislation provided for the imposition of price controls on a range of staple goods and the introduction of measures to encourage competition.

Elections to the European Parliament took place in Saint-Barthél-emy on 25 May 2014. The UMP secured 43.5% of the local ballot, while the far-right Front National list garnered 31.7%. Turnout was only 14.9%, however. An election to Saint-Barthélemy's seat in the French Senate was held on 28 September. The incumbent, Michel Magras, was re-elected for a further term.

Prefect-Delegate: PHILIPPE CHOPIN.

Territorial Council

Hôtel de la Collectivité, BP 133, Gustavia; e-mail contact@comstbarth.fr; internet www.comstbarth.fr.

President: BRUNO MAGRAS (Saint-Barth d'abord/UMP).

Election, Territorial Council, 18 March 2012

	Seats
Saint-Barth d'abord	16
Tous pour Saint Barth	2
Saint Barth en Mouvement	1
Total	**19**

Deputy to the French National Assembly: DANIEL GIBBES (UMP).

Representative to the French Senate: MICHEL MAGRAS (UMP).

SAINT-MARTIN

The Collectivité d'Outre-mer (French Overseas Collectivity) of Saint-Martin forms the northern half of the island of Saint Martin (the remainder, Sint Maarten, being part of the Kingdom of the Nether-lands). The small volcanic island lies among the Leeward group of the Lesser Antilles in the Caribbean Sea, 8 km south of the British Overseas Territory of Anguilla and 265 km north-west of the French Overseas Department of Guadeloupe, of which Saint-Martin was formerly a dependency. The 10.2-km border between the French and the Dutch territories of the island is the only land frontier in the Lesser Antilles. Saint-Martin occupies about 60% of the island (51 sq km or 20 sq miles). The climate is tropical and moderated by the sea. Saint-Martin normally receives about 1,000 mm (43 ins) of rain annually. According to official estimates, at 1 January 2011 Saint-Martin had a population of 36,286. French is the official language, but a Creole patois is widely spoken, as well as English, Dutch and Spanish. The majority of the population professes Christianity and belongs to the Roman Catholic Church. The principal town is Marigot, in the south-west of the territory, on the north coast of the island, between the sea and the Simpson Bay Lagoon.

On 7 December 2003 the Guadeloupean dependency of Saint-Martin participated in a department-wide referendum on Guade-loupe's future constitutional relationship with France. Although the proposal to streamline administrative and political processes was defeated, a majority of those participating in Saint-Martin, 76.2%, elected to secede from Guadeloupe to form a separate Overseas Collectivity. The reorganization was subsequently approved by the French Sénat (Senate) on 6 February 2007 and by the Assemblée Nationale (National Assembly) the following day. On 21 February the territory of Saint-Martin was formally designated an Overseas Collectivity.

Legislative elections to form a 23-member legislative assembly to be known as the Conseil Territorial (Territorial Council) were held in July 2007. At the first round ballot, held on 1 July, the Union pour le Progrès/Union pour un Mouvement Populaire (UPP/UMP) list, headed by Louis-Constant Fleming, won 40.4% of the total votes cast, while the Rassemblement, responsabilité et réussite (RRR) list, led by Alain Richardson, secured 31.9%, and Jean-Luc Hamlet's Réussir Saint-Martin obtained 10.9%. As no list emerged with an absolute majority, a further round of voting was contested by the three parties that had secured more than 10% of the vote. At this second round, held on 8 July, the UPP/UMP list won 49.0% of the vote and obtained 16 of the 23 legislative seats, the RRR received 42.2% of the vote (six seats), and Réussir Saint-Martin 8.9% (one seat). Voter participation was slightly higher, at 50.8%. Fleming assumed the presidency of the Territorial Council on 15 July, and Saint-Martin was officially installed as an Overseas Collectivity. However, in July 2008 Fleming was forced to resign the presidency after the French Council of State disqualified him from his seat on the Territorial Council for one year, owing to irregularities in his financial accounts for the 2007 election campaign. In August the Territorial Council elected Frantz Gumbs as its new President; however, in April 2009 the Council of State annulled the election of Gumbs due to voting irregularities. First Vice-President Daniel Gibbes was installed as interim President pending a re-run of the election, which was to be held within 30 days. On 5 May Gumbs was re-elected as President with 16 votes, defeating Alain Richardson, who received six votes, and Marthe Ogoundélé, who gained one vote.

Meanwhile, at an election held on 21 September 2008 Fleming, representing the UMP, was elected as Saint-Martin's representative to the French Senate. In December 2011 Philippe Chopin replaced Jacques Simonnet as Prefect-Delegate. First round elections to the 16-member Territorial Council took place on 18 March 2012. The RRR won the largest percentage of valid votes (34.1%, or 3,077 votes),

just ahead of the list headed by Daniel Gibbes (Team Daniel Gibbes 2012), which secured 32.0% (2,889 votes). The UPP attracted 13.3% of the ballot. The RRR consolidated its success at a second round of voting, held on 25 March; the party secured 56.9% of the ballot (5,451 votes), compared to Team Daniel Gibbes 2012, which attracted 43.1% (4,134 votes). Alain Richardson was sworn in as President of the Territorial Council on 1 April. However, Gibbes was chosen to represent the territory (and Saint-Barthélemy) in elections to the National Assembly in June.

The first round of the French presidential election was conducted on 21 April 2012 (one day earlier than in mainland France). Nicolas Sarkozy of the UMP attracted 43.6% of the votes in Saint-Martin and Saint-Barthélemy, compared with 26.8% for François Hollande of the Parti socialiste. A second round run-off election was held two weeks later, at which Sarkozy secured 59.4% of the ballot, defeating Hollande, who won 40.6%. Nevertheless, Hollande triumphed nationally and was sworn in as President in mid-May.

Legislation to address the problem of inflated prices in Saint-Martin and other French Overseas Possessions was approved by the French Parliament in November 2012. Most notably, the bill pro-vided for the imposition of price controls on a range of staple goods and the introduction of measures to encourage competition.

The Council of State ordered Richardson to relinquish the presi-dency of the Territorial Council in April 2013 after it was determined that he had breached campaign finance regulations. Aline Hanson was installed as his replacement later that month. In December Fleming resigned as the territory's senator. An election to determine his successor was not held until 28 September 2014; the left-wing candidate Guillaume Arnell was elected to represent Saint-Martin in the French Senate. Meanwhile, elections to the European Parlia-ment took place in Saint-Martin on 25 May. The UMP secured 37.8% of the local ballot, while the far-right Front National list garnered 16.9% and the left-wing Choisir Notre Europe 15.2%. Turnout was only 10.7%, however.

Prefect-Delegate: PHILIPPE CHOPIN.

Territorial Council

rue de l'Hôtel de la Collectivité, BP 374, Marigot; tel. 5-90-87-50-04; fax 5-90-87-88-53; internet www.com-saint-martin.fr.

President: ALINE HANSON.

Election, Territorial Council, 18 and 25 March 2012

	% of first round votes	% of second round votes
Rassemblement, responsabilité et réussite (RRR)	34.1	56.9
Team Daniel Gibbes 2012	32.0	43.1
Union pour le Progrès (UPP)	13.3	—
Saint Martin pour Tous	9.4	—
Movement for the Advancement of the People (MAP)	7.4	—
Génération Solidaire	3.7	—
Total	**100.0**	**100.0**

Deputy to the French National Assembly: DANIEL GIBBES (UMP).

Representative to the French Senate: GUILLAUME JACQUES ARNELL (DVG).

SAINT PIERRE AND MIQUELON

Introductory Survey

LOCATION, CLIMATE, LANGUAGE, RELIGION, CAPITAL

The territory of Saint Pierre and Miquelon (Iles Saint-Pierre-et-Miquelon) consists of a number of small islands which lie about 25 km (16 miles) from the southern coast of Newfoundland and Labrador, Canada, in the North Atlantic Ocean. The principal islands are Saint Pierre, Miquelon (Grande Miquelon) and Langlade (Petite Miquelon)—the last two being linked by an isthmus of sand. Winters are cold, with temperatures falling to −20°C (−4°F), and summers are mild, with temperatures averaging between 10° and 20°C (50° and 68°F). The islands are particularly affected by fog in June and July. The language is French, and the majority of the population profess Christianity and belong to the Roman Catholic Church. The capital is Saint-Pierre, on the island of Saint Pierre.

CONTEMPORARY POLITICAL HISTORY

Historical Context

The islands of Saint Pierre and Miquelon are the remnants of the once extensive French possessions in North America. They were confirmed as French territory in 1815.

Domestic Political Affairs

Saint Pierre and Miquelon gained departmental status in 1976. The departmentalization proved unpopular with many of the islanders, since it incorporated the territory's economy into that of the European Community (EC, now European Union, see p. 271—EU), and was regarded as failing to take into account the islands' isolation and dependence on Canada for supplies and transport links. In 1982 socialist and other left-wing candidates, campaigning for a change in the islands' status, were elected unopposed to all seats in the territory's General Council (Conseil général). Saint Pierre and Miquelon was excluded from the Mitterrand administration's decentralization reforms, undertaken in 1982.

In 1976 Canada imposed an economic interest zone extending to 200 nautical miles (370 km) around its shores. Fearing the loss of traditional fishing areas and thus the loss of the livelihood of the fishermen of Saint Pierre, the French Government claimed a similar zone around the islands. Hopes of discovering valuable reserves of petroleum and natural gas in the area heightened the tension between France and Canada.

In December 1984 legislation was approved giving the islands the status of a Territorial Collectivity (Collectivité territoriale) with effect from 11 June 1985. This was intended to allow Saint Pierre and Miquelon to receive the investment and development aid suitable for its position, while allaying Canada's fears of EC exploitation of its offshore waters. France continued to claim a 200-mile fishing and economic zone around Saint Pierre and Miquelon, while Canada wanted the islands to have only a 12-mile zone. The dispute was submitted to international arbitration. Discussions began in March 1987, and negotiations to determine quotas for France's catch of Atlantic cod over the period 1988–91 were to take place simultaneously. In the mean time, Canada and France agreed on an interim fishing accord, which would allow France to increase its cod quota. The discussions collapsed in October 1987, however, and French trawlers were prohibited from fishing in Canadian waters. In February 1988 Albert Pen and Gérard Grignon, Saint Pierre's elected representatives to the French legislature, together with two members of the Saint Pierre administration and 17 sailors, were arrested for fishing in Canadian waters. This episode, and the arrest of a Canadian trawler captain in May for fishing in Saint Pierre's waters, led to an unsuccessful resumption of negotiations in September. An agreement was reached on fishing rights in March 1989, whereby France's annual quotas for Atlantic cod and other species were determined for the period until the end of 1991. At the same time the Governments agreed upon the composition of an international arbitration tribunal which would delineate the disputed maritime boundaries and exclusive economic zones.

The international arbitration tribunal's ruling, issued in June 1992, was generally deemed to be favourable to Canada. France was allocated an exclusive economic zone around the territory totalling 2,537 square nautical miles (8,700 sq km), compared with its demand for more than 13,000 square nautical miles. The French authorities claimed that the sea area granted would be insufficient to sustain the islands' fishing community. Talks on new fishing quotas for the area off Newfoundland (known as Newfoundland and Labrador from 2001) failed, and, in the absence of a new agreement, industrial fishing in the area was effectively halted until November 1994, when the Governments of the two countries signed an accord specifying new quotas for a period of at least 10 years. In the following month deputies in the French National Assembly (Assemblée nationale) expressed concern that the terms of the agreement would be detrimental to Saint Pierre and Miquelon's interests, although the Government asserted that the accord recognized the islanders' historic fishing rights in Canadian waters.

In September 1992 some 64% of voters approved ratification of the Treaty on European Union (see p. 271), although only a small percentage of the electorate participated in the referendum.

A number of government proposals regarding the socio-economic and institutional development of the Overseas Departments, certain provisions of which were also to be applied to Saint Pierre and Miquelon, were definitively approved by the French National Assembly in November 2000. Measures included provisions for improving and supporting the economic development of the islands, as well as the introduction of proportional representation in elections to the General Council. In the June 2002 general election Gérard Grignon, representing an alliance of the Union pour la Majorité Présidentielle and the Union pour la Démocratie Française (UDF), was re-elected to the National Assembly, with 69% of the second round votes.

In March 2003, as part of a wider constitutional reform, the islands were given the status of an Overseas Collectivity (Collectivité d'outre-mer). At elections to the Senate in September 2004 the mayor of Miquelon, Denis Detcheverry, narrowly defeated the mayor of Saint Pierre, Karine Claireaux. In May 2005 a national referendum was held on ratification of the EU constitutional treaty: 62.7% of the local electorate voted in favour of adopting the treaty; however, voter turnout was only 37.1%. The treaty was ultimately rejected by a majority of voters in metropolitan France. At elections to the General Council in March 2006 Archipel Demain won 13 of Saint Pierre's 15 seats; the left-wing Cap sur l'Avenir (CSA) took the remaining two seats. Archipel Demain also won three of the four available seats allocated to Miquelon; SPM Ensemble took the remaining seat. Stéphane Artano of Archipel Demain was elected President of the General Council.

Further provisions of the 2003 constitutional reform were effected in February 2007, following the approval by the French Parliament of an organic law that amended the statutes and institutions of French Overseas Possessions. The legislation redesignated the General Council as a Territorial Council (Conseil territorial) and granted local government wider fiscal powers and greater control over the operation of the exclusive economic zone. In the second round of the elections to the National Assembly in June, Grignon was narrowly defeated by Annick Girardin, representing the Parti Radical de Gauche in association with CSA. In 2011 Artano remained as President of the Territorial Council despite having been convicted, in November 2009, of misappropriation of public funds and fined €7,500 by the territory's Higher Court of Appeal. Artano had approved expense claims deemed excessive from his predecessor, Marc Plantegenest. Plantegenest was fined €60,000 and given a four-month suspended prison sentence. Both men appealed the convictions, but in November 2010 the original decision was upheld.

In September 2011 the mayor of Saint Pierre, Karine Claireaux, representing the Parti Socialiste (PS), was elected to the French Senate. Claireaux secured a majority in the first round of voting, defeating Grignon, who was representing the Union pour un Mouvement Populaire (UMP), and Detcheverry, the outgoing senator. In November Patrice Latron succeeded Jean-Régis Borius as Prefect of the territory. The elections to the Territorial Council in March 2012 were contested by Archipel Demain and the left-wing, CSA-led Ensemble pour l'Avenir electoral list: Archipel Demain secured 15 seats; CSA candidates won the remaining four seats. Artano was re-elected as President of the Council. In the first round of the French presidential election, held on 22 April, François Hollande of the PS won 33.8% of the votes cast on the islands, ahead of the incumbent, Nicolas Sarkozy of the UMP, who received 18.6%. Hollande, who secured 65.3% of the islands' votes in the second round, on 6 May, was elected President nationally. Annick Girardin was re-elected to the National Assembly at the first round of elections, held on 10 June.

In mid-2012 a strategic action plan (2012–14), published under the auspices of the Office of the Prefect, established a new framework for French state support for the islands. The document identified five strategic priorities that were to guide French central policy on the territory: economic diversification; sustainable development of the fisheries, ports and agriculture; enhanced social cohesion; increased regional trade and integration (especially with regard to Canada); and greater efficiency in public services. The French Minister of Overseas Territories, Victorin Lurel, completed a visit to the islands in February 2013, during which he reiterated the central Government's support for efforts to diversify the economy of Saint Pierre and Miquelon, in particular through the promotion of aquaculture and the development of port and tourism infrastructure.

In June 2013 the governments of Canada and France reached agreement on an Enhanced Co-operation Agenda, aiming to boost bilateral trade and economic co-operation. As part of the initiative, regional co-operation between Saint Pierre and Miquelon and the

Atlantic provinces of Canada was to be developed. However, in the context of growing international competition for control of the potentially enormous energy resources in the North Atlantic and Arctic regions, the long-standing Canadian–French dispute over coastal limits was rekindled in 2013. In July, during a meeting with St Pierre and Miquelon's representatives to the French Parliament, President Hollande pledged to 'defend the interests of the archipelago' and confirmed France's intention to submit a claim with the UN for the extension of the continental shelf of Saint-Pierre and Miquelon. In December Canada lodged a submission with the UN Commission on the Limits of the Continental Shelf (CLCS) providing information (albeit incomplete) in support of a substantial expansion of the limits of its continental shelf in the Atlantic Ocean, which, if accepted, would permit Canada to expand its territorial waters beyond 200 nautical miles. In April 2014 the French Government submitted its own claim with the CLCS for the extension of the continental shelf of Saint Pierre and Miquelon beyond 200 nautical miles; Canada filed formal objections to the French claim in September.

At municipal elections in March 2014, Karine Claireaux was re-elected as mayor of Saint Pierre; representatives of Claireaux's Ensemble pour Construire electoral list became the largest group in the Saint Pierre municipal council, with 22 members, ahead of the CSA list (seven members) led by Yannick Cambray. In Miquelon-Langlade, 15 members were elected to the municipal council on a non-party basis. In a development that appeared to indicate the growing importance of the territorial issue for the French authorities, in April Annick Girardin became the first elected representative from Saint Pierre and Miquelon to serve in the French Government. Girardin was appointed Secretary of State to the Minister of Foreign Affairs and International Development, with responsibility for Development and the Francophonie, following a cabinet reorganization effected by newly elected French Prime Minister Manuel Valls. In accordance with French laws restricting the holding of dual mandates, Girardin's seat in the National Assembly was to be transferred to her deputy for the duration of her tenure in the Council of Ministers. However, Girardin's deputy immediately resigned owing to ill health, triggering a by-election in late June, which Girardin won in the first round with almost 60% of the votes. Girardin was thus re-elected to the French National Assembly; her seat was assigned to her new deputy, Stéphane Claireaux, in July. In a further boost to the profile of St Pierre and Miquelon's elected representatives, in November Karine Claireaux was appointed President of the Office of the French National Council of the Sea and Coasts (Conseil national de la mer et des littoraux). In September Jean-Christophe Bouvier replaced Patrice Latron as Prefect of the territory.

Meanwhile, in early 2014 President of the Council Artano called for a debate on the possible institutional evolution of Saint Pierre and Miquelon to a 'collectivité unique' (single collectivity), in order to streamline administrative and political processes by replacing the existing structure (consisting of two municipalities and the Territorial Council) with a single administrative unit. This topic was discussed in March during visits to the Islands by the French Minister-delegate for Decentralization, Anne-Marie Escoffier, and the Minister of Overseas Territories, Victorin Lurel.

In December 2014 President Hollande paid an official visit to the islands (the first such visit by a French head of state since 1999). The visit was ostensibly arranged in order for the President to participate in a ceremony commemorating the islands' role in supporting the Free French forces of Gen. Charles de Gaulle during the Second World War; however, France's ongoing claim to an extended continental shelf in the region was also considered a likely motivating factor for the visit. Hollande held talks with the local authorities concerning the economic challenges confronting the territory, particularly in light of the fact that several publicly funded infrastructure projects, vital as a source of employment, were nearing completion. Detailed proposals for the construction of privately operated container port, which would potentially serve as a major transshipment hub in the region, were also presented to the President.

CONSTITUTION AND GOVERNMENT

Since 2003 St Pierre and Miquelon has had the status of an Overseas Collectivity (Collectivité d'outre-mer). The French Government is represented in the territory by an appointed Prefect. There is a Territorial Council (Conseil territorial, known as the General Council—Conseil général—until February 2007), with 19 members (15 for Saint Pierre and four for Miquelon), elected by adult universal suffrage for a period of six years. The Council holds powers that are broadly similar to those exercised by the regional and departmental assemblies in mainland France. The President of the Council is the head of the local government. Saint Pierre and Miquelon elects one deputy to the National Assembly (Assemblée nationale) and one representative to the Senate (Sénat) in Paris. In addition, there are two municipal councils, each headed by a mayor, responsible for local services in St Pierre (29 members) and Miquelon-Langlade (15 members).

ECONOMIC AFFAIRS

In 2008 the GDP of Saint Pierre and Miquelon was estimated at €172m. in current prices, equivalent to €28,327 per head. GDP per head increased by an estimated average of 1.6% per year during 2004–08.

In 2008 the primary sector accounted for less than 1% of GDP, and employed less than 2% of the economically active population in 2010. The soil and climatic conditions of Saint Pierre and Miquelon do not favour agricultural production, which is mainly confined to small-holdings, except for market-gardening and the production of eggs and chickens.

The principal economic activity of the islands is traditionally fishing and related industries. However, the sector has been severely affected by disputes with Canada regarding territorial waters and fishing quotas, and a five-year moratorium, from 1992, led to the near-collapse of the important cod fishery. By 2005 the fishing fleet had been reduced to some 26 vessels, of which only 15 were considered to be active. New arrangements have been to the detriment of Saint Pierre and Miquelon, although there is some optimism regarding the potential for the exploitation of shellfish, notably mussels and scallops. The total fish catch increased from 747 metric tons in 1996 to 6,485 tons in 2000. However, thereafter the trend has been one of steady decline: the industrial fishing catch decreased from more than 2,000 tons in 2001 to 1,114 tons in 2013. By 2013 the total fish catch had fallen to 2,573 tons, some 57% of which came from traditional or small-scale fishing.

Fish-processing—producing frozen and salted fish, and fish meal for fodder—provided the basis for industrial activity, employing around 100 people in 2006. Much of the fish processed was imported. Electricity is generated by two thermal power stations, with a combined capacity of 26.2 MW, and a wind power station (on Miquelon) with a capacity of 0.6 MW. In 2011 the French state-owned energy company EDF confirmed plans to construct a new 20 MW thermal power plant in St Pierre; the plant was scheduled to replace the existing facilities by 2015. The islands' energy needs are almost entirely dependent on imports of petroleum products from the USA and Canada. Although wind power contributed just 2.0% of total energy generated in 2012, it is expected to be an increasingly significant component in the islands' future energy strategy.

The construction sector provided 8.0% of GDP in 2008, and employed 6.5% of the working population in 2010. Services accounted for some 84% of GDP in 2008, and employed almost 86% of the working population in 2010.

The resolution of a boundary dispute between the Canadian provinces of Nova Scotia and Newfoundland and Labrador in 2002 accorded the islands about 500 sq miles of waters over the Gulf of Saint Lawrence basin, believed to contain substantial reserves of petroleum and gas. In May 2005, following four years of negotiations, the Governments of France and Canada signed an agreement on the exploration and exploitation of 'transboundary' hydrocarbon fields. Two Canadian oil companies were given exclusive licences to explore the area until April 2006. In 2009 ConocoPhillips Canada and Bardoil Energy SPM, a locally registered company, filed applications for two exploration licences within the French exclusive economic zone. However, in 2010 it was reported that ConocoPhillips had withdrawn its application.

The replenishment of ships' (mainly trawlers') supplies was formerly an important economic activity, but has now also been adversely affected by the downturn in the industrial fishing sector. Efforts were made to promote tourism, and the opening of the Saint Pierre–Montréal air route in 1987 led to an increase in air traffic in the 1990s. In 1999 the completion of a new airport capable of accommodating larger aircraft further improved transport links. Tourist arrivals in 2013, at 11,676, were some 32% lower than figures for 2012 (17,210). This steep decline was attributed in large part to a marked reduction in the number of visits by cruise ships to the archipelago in 2013. Growth in the sector has largely stagnated in recent years; tourism accounted for only about 2% of wealth creation in 2013, while occupying some 8% of companies in the territory.

In 2013 Saint Pierre and Miquelon recorded a merchandise trade deficit of €91.4m. Most trade is with Canada and France, and with other countries of the EU (see p. 271). The only significant exports are wastes and scraps of iron, which provided 55.0% of the total value of exports in 2013, and fresh, frozen and prepared fish products (42.8%). The principal imports are manufactured products, mineral fuels and food and beverages. Items such as clothing and other consumer goods are generally imported from France.

The annual rate of inflation averaged 6.0% in 1997–2005; consumer prices increased by 1.6% in 2013. The rate of unemployment in 2013 was estimated at 7.1%.

Given the decline of Saint Pierre and Miquelon's fishing industry, the development of port services and aquaculture, and the expansion of tourism (particularly from Canada and the USA) are regarded as the principal means of maintaining economic progress. Hydrocarbon exploration has also been identified as a potential future source of revenue, if not from direct exploitation of resources within Saint

Pierre and Miquelon's own territory, then by providing services to companies operating in Canadian waters. In April 2014 the French authorities submitted a claim before the UN Commission on the Limits of the Continental Shelf to thousands of square miles of sea bed around Saint Pierre and Miquelon, thought to be rich with petroleum deposits. The claim was issued in response to ongoing Canadian efforts to map the Atlantic sea bed off its eastern coast, in support of a substantial expansion of its continental shelf in the Atlantic Ocean (see *Domestic Political Affairs*). It is expected that Canada will take all measures to contest the claim. Greater economic co-operation with Canada's Atlantic provinces has been identified as a requisite for long-term growth and stability in Saint Pierre and Miquelon, although this was likely to be dependent on a satisfactory resolution of the French–Canadian territorial dispute. The economy is dominated by public services and consumer spending, while construction (mainly public works) has also become an important economic activity. The islands remain highly dependent on budgetary assistance from the French central Government, and face potential problems in the future due to their ageing population, with increasing numbers of young people leaving the islands to study and work in mainland France and Canada. In 2011 the islands' largest fish-processing company and a major local employer, SPM Seafoods International, was placed in receivership. The development contributed to the ongoing decline in the fish catch. However, as a part of plans to support and develop the fishing industry, in 2014 the local authorities approved financing of some €0.6m. for the purchase of freezer facilities by the Société des nouvelles pêcheries de Miquelon (SNPM). Moreover, in late 2014 plans for the construction of a container port, which would capitalize on the islands' proximity to major North American shipping routes and potentially serve as a major transshipment hub in the region, were being developed by a private consortium.

PUBLIC HOLIDAYS

2016: 1 January (New Year's Day), 28 March (Easter Monday), 1 May (Labour Day), 5 May (Ascension Day), 8 May (Liberation Day), 16 May (Whit Monday), 14 July (National Day, Fall of the Bastille), 15 August (Assumption), 1 November (All Saints' Day), 11 November (Armistice Day), 25 December (Christmas Day).

Statistical Survey

Source: Préfecture, pl. du Lieutenant-Colonel Pigeaud, BP 4200, 97500 Saint-Pierre; tel. 41-10-10; fax 41-47-38.

AREA AND POPULATION

Area: 242 sq km (93.4 sq miles): Saint Pierre 26 sq km, Miquelon-Langlade 216 sq km.

Population: 6,125 at census of March 2006; 6,080 (Saint Pierre 5,456, Miquelon Langlade 624) at census of 1 January 2011. Note: According to new census methodology, data in 2011 refer to median figures based on the collection of raw data over a five-year period (2009–13). *2015* (estimate at 1 January): 6,299 (Saint Pierre 5,662, Miquelon Langlade 637).

Density (at 1 January 2015): 26.0 per sq km.

Births, Marriages and Deaths (1997): Live births 92; Marriages 36; Deaths 51. *2013:* Live births 59; Deaths 39.

Economically Active Population (1999): Fish and fish-processing 76; Other manufacturing 194; Construction 261; Transport 150; Trade 418; Financial services 79; Real estate services 7; Business services 383; Education 490; Government employees 732; *Total employed* 2,790; Unemployed 408; *Total labour force* 3,198. *2006 Census* (preliminary): Total employed 2,876; Registered unemployed 318; Total labour force 3,194 (males 1,751, females 1,443). *2010:* Total employed 2,921 (Agriculture 55, Construction 190, Other industry 170, Administration, teaching, health and welfare 1,360, Trade, transport and other services 1,146). *Unemployment* (at 31 December 2013): 199 (males 99, females 100).

AGRICULTURE

Principal Crops (metric tons unless otherwise indicated, 2013 unless otherwise indicated): Lettuce ('000 units) 10.9; Potatoes 8.2 (2011); Tomatoes 6 (FAO estimate); Strawberries 1 (FAO estimate) (Source: partly FAO).

Livestock ('000 head, 2013, FAO estimates): Sheep 0.3; Chickens 40; Ducks 1 (Source: FAO).

FISHING

Total Catch (all capture, metric tons, live weight, 2012): Atlantic cod 733; Yellowtail flounder 321; Queen crab 327; Total (incl. others) 3,261.

Source: FAO.

FINANCE

Currency and Exchange Rates: French currency was used until the end of 2001. Euro notes and coins were introduced on 1 January 2002, and the euro became the sole legal tender from 18 February. Some of the figures in this Survey are still in terms of French francs. For details of exchange rates, see French Guiana.

Expenditure by Metropolitan France (million francs, 1997): 280.

Budget (€ 'million, 2013): *Revenue:* Current 33.5 (Direct taxes 13.9; Indirect taxes 11.0; Grants and subsidies 5.4); Capital 9.7; Total 43.2. *Expenditure:* Current 30.2; Capital 9.8; Total 40.0. Source: Institut d'Emission des Départements d'Outre-mer.

Money Supply (million francs at 31 December 1997): Currency outside banks 281; Demand deposits at banks 897; Total money 1,178.

Cost of Living (Consumer Price Index; base: December previous year = 100): 103.1 in 2011; 102.8 in 2012; 101.2 in 2013.

Expenditure on the Gross Domestic Product (€ million at current prices, 2007): Government final consumption expenditure 82.7; Private final consumption expenditure 110.4; Gross fixed capital formation 40.2; Change in stocks −1.2; *Total domestic expenditure* 232.1; Exports of goods and services 8.3; *Less* Imports of goods and services 79.2; *GDP in purchasers' values* 161.1. Source: Institut d'Emission des Départements d'Outre-mer.

Gross Domestic Product by Economic Activity (€ million, 2008): Agriculture, forestry and fishing 1.1; Construction 12.5; Other industry 4.6; Trade 14.6; Hotels and restaurants 3.2; Information and communication 3.7; Transport and storage 3.7; Scientific and technical professional services 4.1; Financial services 8.0; Public administration 77.6; Other services (incl. private households) 23.9; *Sub-total* 157.0; Taxes, less subsidies, on products and imports 15.0; *GDP in purchasers' values* 172.0. Source: Institut d'Emission des Départements d'Outre-mer.

EXTERNAL TRADE

Principal Commodities (€ million, 2013): *Imports:* 93.4 (Food and beverages 16.2, Mineral fuels 20.2, Other—largely raw materials 56.9); *Exports:* 2.0 (Fresh or frozen fish 0.4, Other fish preparations 0.3, Crustaceans, fresh refrigerated 0.1, Molluscs, fresh frozen 0.1, Ferrous waste and scrap 1.1) (Source: Institut d'Emission des Départements d'Outre-mer).

Note: Most trade is with Canada, France (imports), other countries of the European Union (exports) and the USA.

TRANSPORT

Road Traffic (2013): 6,753 motor vehicles in use.

Shipping (2007): Ships entered 867 (Source: Service des Douanes). *Flag Registered Fleet* (at 31 December 2014): Vessels 3; Total displacement 638 grt (Source: Lloyd's List Intelligence—www.lloydslistintelligence.com).

Civil Aviation (2013): Passengers carried 34,366; Freight carried 88.0 metric tons (Source: Service de l'Aviation Civile de Saint Pierre et Miquelon).

TOURISM

Tourist Arrivals: 11,450 in 2011; 17,210 in 2012; 11,676 in 2013.

Tourist Arrivals by Country of Residence (2013): France 1,743; Other (mostly Canada and USA) 9,933; *Total* 11,676.

Source: Institut d'Emission des Départements d'Outre-mer.

COMMUNICATIONS MEDIA

Radio Receivers (estimate, '000 in use): 5.0 in 1997.

Television Receivers (estimate, '000 in use): 3.5 in 1997.

EDUCATION

Primary (2002 unless otherwise indicated): 8 institutions; 73 teachers; 674 students (2011).

Secondary (2002 unless otherwise indicated): 2 institutions; 56 teachers; 364 students (2011).

Technical (2002 unless otherwise indicated): 1 institution; 25 teachers; 139 students (2011).

Source: Service de l'Education Nationale de Saint Pierre et Miquelon.

Note: At the time of the 2006 census, 211 students of higher education were studying outside of Saint Pierre and Miquelon.

Directory

The Government

(April 2015)

HEAD OF STATE

President: FRANÇOIS HOLLANDE.

Prefect: JEAN-CHRISTOPHE BOUVIER, pl. du Lieutenant-Colonel Pigeaud, BP 4200, 97500 Saint-Pierre; tel. 41-10-10; fax 41-47-38; e-mail courrier@saint-pierre-et-miquelon.pref.gouv.fr; internet www.saint-pierre-et-miquelon.pref.gouv.fr.

TERRITORIAL COUNCIL

Conseil Territorial: 2 pl. de Monseigneur François Maurer, BP 4208, 97500 Saint-Pierre; tel. 41-01-02; fax 41-22-97; e-mail accueil@ct975.fr; internet www.cg975.fr; the Conseil territorial (fmrly the Conseil général) has 19 mems: Saint Pierre 15, Miquelon four. Following the last election to the Conseil territorial, held in March 2012, the composition of the Conseil by party was as follows: Archipel Demain 15, Cap sur l'Avenir 4.

President: STÉPHANE ARTANO.

Economic, Social and Cultural Committee: rue Bordas, BP 4313, 97500 Saint-Pierre; tel. 41-45-50; fax 41-42-45; e-mail comite.ec.soc.spm@cheznoo.net; advisory body; 20 appointed members; Pres. XAVIER LANDRY.

GOVERNMENT OFFICES

Directorate of Land, Food and the Sea: blvd Constant Colmay, BP 4217, 97500 Saint-Pierre; tel. 41-12-00; fax 41-39-50; e-mail dtam-975@equipement-agriculture.gouv.fr; internet www.saint-pierre-et-miquelon.developpement-durable.gouv.fr; Dir JEAN-FRANÇOIS PLAUT.

Directorate of Social Cohesion, Labour, Employment and Population: 8 rue des Petits Pêcheurs, BP 4212, 97500 Saint-Pierre; tel. 41-19-60; fax 41-19-61; e-mail stefp.975.administration@travail.gouv.fr; Dir ALAIN FRANCES.

Directorate of Tax Services: 27 blvd Constant Colmay, BP 4236, 97500 Saint-Pierre; tel. 41-10-80; fax 41-32-51; e-mail dsf.saint-pierre-et-miquelon@dgfip.finances.gouv.fr; internet services-fiscaux.spmnet.com; Dir PASCALE BOYER.

National Education Service: place du Général de Gaulle, BP 4239, 97500 Saint-Pierre; tel. 41-04-60; fax 41-26-04; e-mail ia@ac-spm.fr; internet www.ac-spm.fr; Man. RÉGINE VIGIER.

Territorial Health Administration: blvd Port en Bessin, BP 4333, 97500 Saint-Pierre; tel. 41-16-90; fax 41-16-91; e-mail dd975-direction@sante.gouv.fr; Man. RAYMOND DELVIN.

REPRESENTATIVES TO THE FRENCH PARLIAMENT

Deputy to the French National Assembly: STÉPHANE CLAIREAUX (acting) (PRG-SPM); Annick Girardin has been the elected Deputy to the French National Assembly for St Pierre and Miquelon since 2007; her seat was transferred to Claireaux, her substitute, in July 2014, following her appointment to the French Council of Ministers.

Representative to the French Senate: KARINE CLAIREAUX (PS).

Political Organizations

Archipel Demain: 7 rue des Français Libres, BP 1179, 97500 Saint-Pierre; tel. 41-42-19; fax 41-48-06; e-mail contact@archipeldemain.fr; internet www.archipeldemain.fr; f. 1985; Pres. GÉRARD GRIGNON; Sec.-Gen. BERNARD BRIAND; incl. Archipel Demain Miquelon (Leader CÉLINE GASPARD).

Cap sur l'Avenir (CSA): 7 rue René Autin, BP 4477, 97500 Saint-Pierre; tel. 41-99-98; fax 41-99-97; e-mail agirardin@assemblee-nationale.fr; internet capsurlavenir975.unblog.fr; f. 2000; left-wing and green coalition; associated with the PRG-SPM; Pres. ANNICK GIRARDIN.

Ensemble pour Construire: BP 305, 97500 Saint-Pierre; e-mail ensemblepourconstruire@cheznoo.net; internet www.ensemblepourconstruire.com; affiliated with the metropolitan Parti Socialiste; supported the Ensemble pour l'Avenir electoral list during the 2012 elections to the Conseil territorial; Pres. KARINE CLAIREAUX.

Parti Radical de Gauche SPM (PRG-SPM): 7 rue René Autin, BP 4477, 97500 Saint-Pierre; tel. 41-99-08; fax 41-99-97; internet www.planeteradicale.org/-St-Pierre-et-Miquelon; local br. of the metropolitan party; associated with CSA; Pres. YANNICK CAMBRAY; Sec. TATIANA VIGNEAU.

SPM Ensemble: c/o Mairie de Miquelon, 2 rue du Baron de l'espérance, Miquelon, 97500 Saint-Pierre; internet spmensemble.oldiblog.com; f. 2006; left-wing, independent; advocates parity between the islands of Saint-Pierre and Miquelon; STÉPHANE COSTE.

Union pour un Mouvement Populaire (UMP): 15 rue Ange Gautier, BP 113, 97500 Saint-Pierre; tel. 41-35-73; fax 41-29-97; e-mail francoiszimmermann@ump975.org; internet www.ump975.net; centre-right; local br. of the metropolitan party; Pres., Departmental Cttee FRANÇOIS ZIMMERMANN.

Judicial System

Tribunal Supérieur d'Appel: 14 rue Emile Sasco, BP 4215, 97500 Saint-Pierre; tel. 41-03-20; fax 41-03-23; e-mail francois.billon@justice.fr; Presiding Magistrate JEAN-YVES GOUEFFON; Procurator HERVÉ LEROY.

Tribunal de Première Instance: 4 rue Borda, BP 4215, 97500 Saint-Pierre; tel. 41-03-20; fax 41-41-03-22; Presiding Magistrate VÉRONIQUE VEILLARD.

Religion

Almost all of the inhabitants are adherents of the Roman Catholic Church.

CHRISTIANITY

The Roman Catholic Church

The islands form the Apostolic Vicariate of the Iles Saint-Pierre et Miquelon. At 31 December 2006 there were an estimated 6,076 adherents.

Vicar Apostolic: MARIE PIERRE FRANÇOIS AUGUSTE GASCHY (Titular Bishop of Usinaza), Vicariat Apostolique, BP 4245, 97500 Saint-Pierre; tel. 41-02-40; fax 41-47-09; e-mail mission-catho.spm@wanadoo.fr.

Other Churches

Eglise Evangélique de Saint-Pierre et Miquelon: 5 bis rue Paul Lebailly, BP 4325, 97500 Saint-Pierre; tel. 41-92-39; fax 41-59-75; e-mail pasteurspm@cheznoo.net; internet www.cheznoo.net/eglise_evangelique.spm; f. 1995; affiliated to the Fédération Nationale des Assemblées de Dieu de France and Commission des Eglises Evangéliques d'Expression Française à l'Extérieure; Pastor FRANCIS NOVERT.

The Press

L'Echo des Caps Hebdo: rue Georges Daguerre, BP 4213, 97500 Saint-Pierre; tel. 41-10-90; fax 41-49-33; e-mail echohebd@cheznoo.net; internet www.mairie-stpierre.fr/fr/32-l-echo-des-caps.html; f. 1982; weekly; Dir KARINE CLAIREAUX; Editor-in-Chief JEAN-LOUIS MAHÉ; circ. 3,300.

Recueil des Actes Administratifs: 15 place du Général de Gaulle, BP 4233, 97500 Saint-Pierre; tel. 41-09-50; fax 41-09-54; e-mail imprimeriepref@cheznoo.net; f. 1866; monthly; Dir DANIEL KOELSCH.

Le Vent de la Liberté: 1 rue Amiral Muselier, BP 1179, 97500 Saint-Pierre; tel. 41-42-19; fax 41-48-06; e-mail archipel@cheznoo.net; f. 1986; monthly; Dir GÉRARD GRIGNON; circ. 550.

Broadcasting and Communications

TELECOMMUNICATIONS

Globaltel: Galerie Albert Briand, 18 rue Albert Briand, Saint-Pierre; tel. 40-00-00; e-mail contact@globaltel-spm.com; internet www.globaltel-spm.com; f. 2007; awarded a licence to provide mobile telephone services in 2012; services commenced in 2014; CEO CHRISTOPHE BOUTIN.

SPM Telecom: 6 pl. du Général de Gaulle, BP 4253, 97500 Saint Pierre; tel. 41-00-15; fax 41-00-19; e-mail accueil@spmtelecom.com; internet www.spmtelecom.com; Dir XAVIER BOWRING.

RADIO AND TELEVISION

Réseau Outre-mer 1ère: BP 4227, 97500 Saint-Pierre; tel. 41-11-11; fax 41-11-80; internet saintpierremiquelon.la1ere.fr; acquired by Groupe France Télévisions in 2004; fmrly Société Nationale de

Radio-Télévision Française d'Outre-mer, became Réseau France Outre-mer (RFO) in 1998, present name adopted in 2010; broadcasts 24 hours of radio programmes daily on three stations and 195 hours of television programmes weekly on two channels, Télé St Pierre et Miquelon and Tempo; Gen. Man. YVES GARNIER; Regional Dir MOZARIO GABBANI.

Radio Atlantique: 1er étage du Centre Culturel et Sportif, BP 1282, 97500 Saint-Pierre; tel. 41-24-93; fax 41-56-33; e-mail contact@radioatlantique.com; internet www.cheznoo.net/radioatlantique; f. 1982; private; broadcasts 24 hours of radio programmes daily; Pres. ANDRÉ URTIZBÉRÉA; Sec. MYLÈNE BOUROULT.

Finance

(cap. = capital, res = reserves, dep. = deposits; m. = million; brs = branches; amounts in euros)

BANKING

Central Bank

Institut d'Emission des Départements d'Outre-mer (IEDOM): 22 pl. du Général de Gaulle, BP 4202, 97500 Saint-Pierre; tel. 41-06-00; fax 41-25-98; e-mail agence@iedom-spm.fr; internet www.iedom.fr; f. 1978; Dir YANN CARON.

Commercial Bank

Banque de Saint-Pierre et Miquelon (BDSPM): 2 rue Jacques Cartier, BP 4223, 97500 Saint-Pierre; tel. 41-07-00; fax 41-07-42; internet www.bdspm.fr; f. 1889; name changed as above in 2009, following merger with Crédit Saint Pierrais; subsidiary of Groupe BPCE, France; cap. 15.5m., res 0.2m., dep. 113.2m. (Dec. 2010); Pres. PHILIPPE GARSUAULT; Dir-Gen. PIERRE BALSAN; 2 brs.

In addition, two metropolitan banks—la Banque Postale and la Caisse d'épargne Ile-de-France—have branches in St Pierre and Miquelon.

Co-operative Bank

Coopérative immobilière des îles Saint-Pierre-et-Miquelon (CISPM): 29 rue du Maréchal de Lattre de Tassigny, BP 1025, 97500 Saint-Pierre; tel. 41-03-40; fax 41-44-77; e-mail cispm@cheznoo.net; internet www.cispm.unblog.fr; f. 1950; Dir SABINE ROS.

INSURANCE

Cabinet Paturel Assurances, Allianz: 29 bis rue Boursaint, BP 4288, 97500 Saint-Pierre; tel. 41-04-40; fax 41-51-65; e-mail npaturel@allianz-spm.fr; internet www.allianz-spm.fr; Dir NATHALIE PATUREL.

Mutuelle des Iles: 52 rue Maréchal Foch, BP 1112, 97500 Saint-Pierre; tel. 41-28-69; fax 41-51-13; e-mail mispm@cheznoo.net.

Trade and Industry

DEVELOPMENT AGENCIES

Agence Française de Développement (AFD): 22 place du Général de Gaulle, BP 4202, 97500 Saint-Pierre; tel. 41-06-00; fax 41-25-98; e-mail ledom-spm@iedom-spm.fr; internet saintpierreetmiquelon.afd.fr; fmrly Caisse Française de Développement; Man. BRUNO CLAVREUL.

Société de Développement et de Promotion de l'Archipel (SODEPAR): Palais Royal, rue Borda, BP 4365, 97500 Saint-Pierre; tel. 41-15-15; fax 41-15-16; e-mail sodepar.spm@sodepar.com; internet www.sodepar.com; f. 1989; economic devt agency; Chair. STÉPHANE ARTANO; Dir FRANÇOISE LETOURNEL.

CHAMBER OF COMMERCE

Chambre d'Agriculture, de Commerce, d'Industrie, de Métiers et de l'Artisanat (CACIMA): 4 rue Constant-Colmay, BP 4207, 97500 Saint-Pierre; tel. 41-45-12; fax 41-32-09; e-mail cacim@ccimspm.org; internet www.cacimaspm.fr; Pres. XAVIER BOWRING; Sec. ROMUALD DERRIBLE.

TRADE UNIONS

Syndicat des Armateurs à la Pêche Côtière: BP 937, 97500 Saint-Pierre; tel. 41-30-13; fax 41-73-89; e-mail kenavo@cheznoo.net; Pres. JEAN BEAUPERTUIS.

Syndicat CFDT (Union Interprofessionnelle SPM): 15 rue du Docteur Dunan, BP 4352, 97500 Saint-Pierre; tel. 41-23-20; fax 41-27-99; e-mail cfdt.spm@cheznoo.net; internet www.cfdtspm.com; affiliated to the Confédération Française Démocratique du Travail; Sec.-Gen. VÉRONIQUE PERRIN.

Union Départementale Force Ouvrière: 15 rue du Docteur Dunan, BP 4241, 97500 Saint-Pierre; tel. 41-25-22; fax 41-46-55; e-mail udfospm975@cheznoo.net; affiliated to the Confédération Générale du Travail-Force Ouvrière; Sec.-Gen. ALAIN TANGUY.

Union Intersyndicale CGT de Saint-Pierre et Miquelon: rue du 11 Novembre, 97500 Saint-Pierre; tel. 41-41-86; fax 41-30-21; e-mail cgtsp@cheznoo.net; affiliated to the Confédération Générale du Travail; Sec.-Gen. RONALD MANET.

UNSA-Education: rue du Docteur Dunan, 97500 Saint-Pierre; tel. 41-38-05; fax 41-34-08; e-mail 975@se-unsa.org; represents teaching staff; Sec.-Gen. ANDRÉ URTIZBEREA.

Transport

SHIPPING

Packet boats and container services operate between Saint-Pierre and Halifax, Nova Scotia (Canada), Boston, MA (USA), and France. There is a ferry service between Saint-Pierre, Miquelon and Newfoundland and Labrador. The seaport at Saint-Pierre has three jetties and 1,200 metres of quays.

Alliance Europe Le Havre: 1 rue Abbé Pierre Gervain, 97500 Saint-Pierre; tel. 20-53-53; fax 20-53-86; e-mail corinne.spm@alliance-europe.fr; internet alliance-europe.fr; f. 2004 as successor to Compagnie Maritime des Transports Frigorifiques (f. 1980); operates weekly container and ro-ro shipping services between Saint Pierre and Miquelon and ports in northern Europe; also operates air freight service; Gen. Man. JEAN-MARC ROUX.

Régie de Transports Maritimes: pl. du Général de Gaulle, BP 4468, 97500 Saint-Pierre; tel. 41-08-75; fax 41-98-95; e-mail rtm@cg975.fr; internet www.cg975.fr; govt-operated; operates inter-island passenger ferry services and services between Saint-Pierre and Newfoundland, Canada; Dir CAROLINE CECCHETTI.

CIVIL AVIATION

There is an airport on Saint Pierre, served by airlines linking the territory with five destinations in Canada.

Service de l'Aviation Civile de Saint-Pierre et Miquelon: Aérodrome Saint-Pierre Pointe Blanche, BP 4265, 97500 Saint-Pierre; tel. 41-18-00; fax 41-18-18; e-mail sacspm@aviation-civile.gouv.fr; internet www.cheznoo.net/sacspm; Dir LUC COLLET.

Air Saint-Pierre: 18 rue Albert Briand, Saint-Pierre, BP 4225, 97500 Saint-Pierre; tel. 41-00-00; fax 41-00-02; e-mail contact@airsaintpierre.com; internet www.airsaintpierre.com; f. 1964; connects the territory directly with Newfoundland and Labrador, Nova Scotia and Québec, Canada; Pres. BENOIT OLANO; Man. THIERRY BRIAND.

Tourism

There were an estimated 11,676 tourist arrivals in 2013, a decrease of 32.2% compared with figures for the previous year (17,210). (Major fluctuations in visitor arrivals are largely attributable to changes in the number of cruise ships calling at the territory.) In 2013 some 63% of foreign visitors came from Canada, followed by visitors from France (15%) and the USA (10%). In 2010 there were 18 establishments offering tourist accommodation.

Comité Régional du Tourisme: pl. du Général de Gaulle, BP 4274, 97500 Saint-Pierre; tel. 41-02-00; fax 41-33-55; e-mail info@tourismespm.com; internet www.st-pierre-et-miquelon.info; f. 1989; fmrly Service Loisirs Accueil; Pres. FRANÇOIS RIVOLLET; Dir PIERRE-YVES CASTAING.

Defence

France is responsible for the islands' defence.

Education

The education system is modelled on the French system, and education is compulsory for children aged between six and 16 years. In 2014 there were 11 schools at primary and secondary levels (six of which were public and five were private). In 2011 there were 1,177 students at all levels of the education system. At the time of the 2006 census, 211 students of higher education were studying outside Saint Pierre and Miquelon. Agreements with universities in New Brunswick, Newfoundland and Labrador and Nova Scotia allow students from Saint Pierre and Miquelon to enjoy the same rights as Canadian students.

THE WALLIS AND FUTUNA ISLANDS

Introductory Survey

LOCATION, CLIMATE, LANGUAGE, RELIGION, CAPITAL

Wallis and Futuna comprises two groups of islands: the Wallis Islands, including Wallis Island (also known as Uvea) and some 20 islets (*motu*) on the surrounding reef, and the Futuna (or Hoorn) Islands to the south-west, comprising the two small islands of Futuna and Alofi. The islands are located north-east of Fiji and west of Samoa. Temperatures are generally between about 23°C (73°F) and 30°C (86°F), and there is a cyclone season between December and March. French and the indigenous Polynesian languages Wallisian (Uvean) and Futunian are spoken throughout the islands. Nearly all of the population is nominally Roman Catholic. The capital is Mata'Utu, on Wallis Island.

CONTEMPORARY POLITICAL HISTORY

Historical Context

French protectorate status was formalized for Wallis and for the two kingdoms of Futuna in the 19th century. The islands were subsequently treated as a dependency of New Caledonia. During the Second World War (1939–45), Wallis was used as an air force base by the USA. In 1959 the traditional Kings and chiefs requested integration into the French Republic. The islands formally became a Territoire d'Outre-Mer (Overseas Territory) in July 1961, following a referendum in December 1959, in which 94.4% of the electorate requested this status (almost all the opposition was in Futuna, which itself recorded dissent from only 22.2% of the voters; Wallis was unanimous in its acceptance).

Although there was no movement in Wallis and Futuna seeking secession of the territory from France (in contrast with the situation in the other French Pacific Territories, French Polynesia and New Caledonia), the two Kings whose kingdoms share the island of Futuna requested in November 1983, through the Territorial Assembly, that the island groups of Wallis and Futuna become separate Overseas Territories of France, arguing that the administration and affairs of the territory had become excessively concentrated on the island of Wallis.

Domestic Political Affairs

At elections to the 20-member Territorial Assembly in March 1982, the Rassemblement pour la République (RPR) and its allies won 11 seats, while the remaining nine were secured by candidates belonging to, or associated with, the Union pour la Démocratie Française (UDF). Later that year one member of the Lua Kae Tahi, a group affiliated to the metropolitan UDF, defected to the RPR group. In November 1983, however, three of the 12 RPR members joined the Lua Kae Tahi, forming a new majority. In the subsequent election for President of the Territorial Assembly, this 11-strong bloc of UDF-associated members supported the ultimately successful candidate, Falakiko Gata, even though he had been elected to the Territorial Assembly in 1982 as a member of the RPR.

In April 1985 Falakiko Gata formed a new political party, the Union Populaire Locale (UPL), which was committed to giving priority to local, rather than metropolitan, issues.

In 1987 a dispute broke out between two families both laying claim to the throne of Sigave, the northern kingdom on the island of Futuna. The conflict arose following the deposition of the former King, Sagato Keletaona, and his succession by Sosefo Vanaï. The intervention of the island's administrative authorities, who attempted to ratify Vanaï's accession to the throne, was condemned by the Keletaona family as an interference in the normal course of local custom, according to which such disputes are traditionally settled by a fight between the protagonists.

At elections to the Territorial Assembly in March 1987, the UDF (together with affiliated parties) and the RPR each won seven seats. However, by forming an alliance with the UPL, the RPR maintained its majority, and Falakiko Gata was subsequently re-elected President. At elections to the French Assemblée Nationale (National Assembly) in June 1988, Benjamin Brial was re-elected deputy. However, the result was challenged by an unsuccessful candidate, Kamilo Gata, and, following an investigation by the French Constitutional Council, was declared invalid, owing to electoral irregularities. At a rescheduled poll in January 1989, Kamilo Gata was elected, with 57.4% of the total votes.

Statistical information, gathered in 1990, showed that the emigration rate of Wallis and Futuna islanders had risen to over 50%. In October of that year 13,705 people (of whom 97% were Wallisians and Futunians) lived in the territory, while 14,186 were resident in New Caledonia. At the 1996 census the number of Wallisians and Futunians resident in New Caledonia had increased to 17,563. According to the results, a proportion of the islanders had chosen to emigrate to other French Overseas Possessions or to metropolitan France, mainly owing to the lack of employment opportunities in the islands.

At elections to the Territorial Assembly in March 1992, the newly founded Taumu'a Lelei (Bright Future) secured 11 seats, while the RPR won nine. The new Assembly was remarkable for being the first since 1964 in which the RPR did not hold a majority. At elections to the French National Assembly in March 1993, Kamilo Gata was re-elected deputy, obtaining 52.4% of the total votes cast to defeat Clovis Logologofolau. In June 1994 the Union Locale Force Ouvrière organized a general strike in protest at the increasing cost of living in the territory and the allegedly inadequate education system. It was reported that demonstrations continued for several days, during which the Territorial Assembly building was damaged in an arson attack.

In October 1994 it was reported that the King of Sigave (or Keletaona), Lafaele Malau, had been deposed by a unanimous decision of the kingdom's chiefs. The action followed the appointment of two customary leaders to represent the Futunian community in New Caledonia, which had led to unrest among the inhabitants of Sigave.

At elections to the Territorial Assembly in December 1994, the RPR secured 10 seats, while a coalition group, Union Populaire pour Wallis et Futuna (UPWF), won seven, and independent candidates three. Mikaele Tauhavili was subsequently elected President of the Assembly.

Elections to the Territorial Assembly took place in March 1997. A participation rate of 87.2% was recorded at the poll, in which RPR candidates secured 14 seats and left-wing candidates (including independents and members of various political groupings) won six seats. Victor Brial, a representative of the RPR, was elected President. At the second round of elections to the French National Assembly, in June, Brial defeated Kamilo Gata, obtaining 51.3% of the votes cast. Allegations of irregularities during the March elections were investigated and upheld for 11 seats. As a result, new elections were organized for those seats in September 1998, following which the RPR's representation in the Assembly was reduced from 14 to 11 seats, while left-wing and independent members increased their share of seats from six to nine. In that month Fr Robert Laufoaulu was elected to the French Sénat (Senate), defeating Kamilo Gata in a vote by the Territorial Assembly. Laufoaulu, a priest and director of Catholic education in the islands, stood as a left-wing candidate, but was nominated by RPR members elected with the support of right-wing politicians.

In January 2001 Patalione Kanimoa of the RPR was elected as President of the Territorial Assembly by the majority of the RPR (eight votes) and of the UPWF (four votes). Soane Muni Uhila, the previous incumbent, then formed a new party, La Voix des Peuples Wallisiens et Futuniens, along with five other RPR dissidents. The new majority RPR-UPWF grouping elected Albert Likuvalu (of the UPWF) president of the permanent commission.

In June 2001 senior officials from Wallis and Futuna and New Caledonia agreed on a project to redefine their bilateral relationship under the Nouméa Accord (see New Caledonia) on greater autonomy, signed in 1998. The Accord gave the New Caledonian authorities the power to control immigration from Wallis and Futuna; following decades of migration, the population of Wallis and Futuna was 15,000, while the number of migrants and descendants from the islands in New Caledonia had risen to 20,000. In exchange for controlling immigration, New Caledonia stated that it would make a financial contribution to economic development in Wallis and Futuna. The Nouméa Accord also envisaged a separate arrangement allowing for open access to New Caledonia for residents of Wallis and Futuna. Furthermore, in January 2002 a delegation from Wallis and Futuna met French President Jacques Chirac in Paris to discuss the situation of members of their community living in New Caledonia. An accord was finally signed in December 2003, having been delayed by ongoing ethnic tensions in New Caledonia. Under the agreement, Wallis and Futuna and New Caledonia were henceforth to deliver separate public services. Concerns had been raised by the former's increasing debt (estimated to total 2,500m. francs CFP) to the Government of New Caledonia, particularly the New Caledonian hospital. It was therefore hoped that Wallis and Futuna would become more self-sufficient in the areas of health and secondary education and that the islanders would be encouraged to remain on Wallis and Futuna, while those already settled in New Caledonia would become more integrated.

Meanwhile, at elections in March 2002 for the Territorial Assembly, the RPR won 12 of the 20 seats, while socialist candidates, or affiliated independents, won eight. Some 83% of the electorate participated in the poll. The election campaign was the first to give parties coverage on television and radio, provided by the national broadcasting company. The territory's only newspaper, *Te-Fenua Fo'ou*, ceased publication in April, following a dispute over the King of Wallis's alleged support for an electoral candidate,

Make Pilioko. The newspaper contested that Pilioko, a former member of the Territorial Assembly, was unfit for office, having been convicted in 1999 of misuse of public funds. The publisher and editor of *Te-Fenua Fo'ou*, respectively Michel Boudineau and Laurent Gourlez (both of whom were French), were summoned before the King and ordered not to publish any further articles on the matter. However, the newspaper asserted its right to freedom of expression and, in defiance of the King, printed and distributed its next edition from New Caledonia. The police subsequently removed computers and other equipment from the newspaper's office in Mata'Utu. Boudineau filed a complaint with the French authorities for theft and obstruction of press freedom but, none the less, was forced to close the publication.

At elections to the French National Assembly in June 2002, Victor Brial, representing a coalition of the Union pour la Majorité Présidentielle (subsequently Union pour un Mouvement Populaire— UMP) and the RPR, was re-elected as the Wallis and Futuna deputy, winning 50.4% of the votes cast in the first round. (The RPR was fully absorbed into the UMP structure that year.) However, in December the French Constitutional Council ruled that the result was invalid as certain ballot papers had been improperly marked; Brial (now representing the UMP) subsequently won the by-election in March 2003. Meanwhile, in November 2002 Soane Patita Maituka was enthroned as King of Alo (known as the Tu'i Agaifo) following the deposition of Sagato Alofi in the previous month. In December the French Senate approved a bill providing for a constitutional amendment that would allow Wallis and Futuna (along with French Polynesia) to be designated as a Pays d'Outre-Mer (Overseas Country); both houses of the French legislature in Paris ratified the amendments to the Constitution in March 2003. Wallis and Futuna was given the status of a Collectivité d'Outre-Mer (Overseas Collectivity).

In October 2003 Pasilio Keletaona was deposed as King of Sigave by members of his own clan. He was succeeded in March 2004 by Visesio Moeliku.

In February 2005 Albert Likuvalu, representing the newly formed Alliance grouping, a coalition of UDF members and left-wing independents, was elected President of the Territorial Assembly by 11 votes to nine, replacing Patalione Kanimoa of the UMP grouping. The Alliance comprised three members of the UDF and two left-wing ministers, including Likuvalu himself; they were supported by the UPWF grouping.

In January 2005 the local court found the King of Wallis Island's grandson, Tomasi Tuugahala, guilty of unintentional homicide while driving under the influence of alcohol. Tuugahala took refuge in the King's palace and refused to surrender himself to the police. The King of Wallis (or Lavelua), Tomasi Kulimoetoke, and his chiefs claimed that the matter had been settled in accordance with traditional custom, but the incident brought them into confrontation with the French authorities and with pro-reform groups in Wallis and Futuna who wished to depose the Lavelua. In May the King's Prime Minister, Kapeliele Faupala, criticized the Chief Administrator of the islands, Xavier de Fürst, for interfering in traditional affairs and urged him to leave the territory. Later in the month Tuugahala gave himself up to the authorities and was flown to New Caledonia to begin an 18-month prison sentence. However, in June de Fürst suspended allowances and salaries to the Lavelua and his Council of Ministers, while officially recognizing an alternative council composed of members of rival royal families from Futuna, headed by Clovis Logologofolau.

In August 2005 the King of Wallis reiterated a pledge of allegiance to France but maintained that the crisis was the result of de Fürst's interference. In September the alternative council of ministers announced its intention to install Chief Sosefo Mautamakia as King of Wallis, prompting protests by supporters of the incumbent Lavelua, who mounted blockades and occupied the international airport. Meanwhile, in the New Caledonian capital of Nouméa, a group of some 500 supporters marched to the French High Commission to present a petition demanding the intervention of France. The Secretary-General of the French High Commission in New Caledonia, Louis Lefranc, was dispatched to undertake negotiations; he reaffirmed France's recognition of Tomasi Kulimoetoke as Lavelua and overruled de Fürst's earlier decisions. As a result of negotiations among the royal clans themselves, no attempt was made to install a new King.

In March 2006 the two Kings of Futuna, accompanied by ministers of the kingdoms and members of the local assembly, travelled to France to meet President Jacques Chirac, Prime Minister Dominique de Villepin and other senior government officials. The delegation emphasized the need for improved transport links between Futuna and Wallis, citing disruption caused on Futuna by recent severe weather conditions and the temporary cessation of flights between the two islands because of a faulty aircraft. In August Xavier de Fürst was replaced by Richard Didier as Chief Administrator.

In January 2007 a delegation from Wallis visited Futuna, amid reported tensions between the islands, to present a Memorandum of Understanding encompassing the three kingdoms, the details of which were not immediately publicized. At the legislative elections in April 2007 three new members were elected to the Territorial Assembly, with many votes, as usual, cast according to clan loyalties. Pesamino Taputai was elected as the Assembly's President and used his inaugural speech to urge the islands' leaders to resolve the issues that continued to impede good relations between Wallis and Futuna.

In the second round of the French presidential election, in May 2007, Wallis and Futuna showed similar levels of support for both candidates: Nicolas Sarkozy of the UMP, who secured a majority overall, received 50.2% of the votes cast locally, while the Parti Socialiste (PS) candidate, Ségolène Royal, received 49.8%. Elections to the French National Assembly were held in the following month, with the incumbent UMP deputy, Victor Brial, defeated in the second round by the PS-affiliated candidate, Albert Likuvalu. In December the islands' former deputy to the National Assembly, Victor Brial, was elected President of the Territorial Assembly, with 13 out of 20 votes, including those of members affiliated with the UMP and the Mouvement Démocrate (MoDem—formerly known as the UDF), while his only opponent, Siliako Lauhéa, received six.

In May 2007 the King of Wallis, Lavelua Tomasi Kulimoetoke, died after 48 years in office. Following his death, the subject of his successor was declared taboo for six months. In July 2008 the Council of Ministers of Wallis announced its decision to nominate Kapiliele Faupala, who had presided over the local Council of Ministers since 2004, to succeed him. Despite some vocal opposition by certain other royal clans on Wallis to Faupala's nomination, his coronation took place later that month at a ceremony in Mata'Utu. Meanwhile, it had emerged in August 2007 that Soane Patita Maituka, the King of Alo, was in hospital in New Caledonia with a serious illness. In February 2008, following criticism of the style of leadership of the Tu'i Agaifo and the reaching of a unanimous decision by the four chiefly clans of Alo, the King was removed from office. Petelo Vikena, a former public servant, was subsequently chosen to replace him, and his coronation took place in November 2008. However, the choice of Vikena was not supported by some chiefly clans, which criticized the unilateral appointment by the chiefly council and the lack of consensus.

In July 2008 the French Government appointed Philippe Paolantoni as the new Chief Administrator of Wallis and Futuna, to succeed Richard Didier. In the French senatorial elections of September Fr Robert Laufoaulu was re-elected to represent Wallis and Futuna for a second six-year term.

In January 2010, amid reports of acts of vandalism against royal property, Petelo Vikena abdicated as King of Alo. Meanwhile, the King of Sigave, Visesio Moeliku, was reported to have relinquished his position several months previously. The kingdom of Futuna was thus placed in an unusual situation, being required to function without either of its two Kings. In July Polikalepo Kolivai was crowned King of Sigave, although two rival clans refused to recognize his accession.

In March 2010 a cyclone was reported to have destroyed 90% of traditional houses on Futuna, as well as most of the island's crops and many public amenities. French military aircraft based in New Caledonia, followed by a warship, brought emergency supplies of food and other necessities, and in June the French Minister in charge of the Overseas Possessions, Marie-Luce Penchard, undertook to provide financial and technical assistance for rebuilding Futuna's infrastructure. From April 2010 the supply of electricity and water on Wallis was intermittently disrupted when employees of the utility company Electricité et Eau de Wallis et Futuna (EEWF, a subsidiary of the French Groupe Suez) staged a strike, reportedly in support of an executive who had been dismissed for misconduct. In July the King of Wallis announced that the contract with EEWF had been terminated (although such an action was not legally within his powers), and the company's offices were taken over by a small group of employees, who stated that they were establishing a new company with the support of the King. Hundreds of people participated in protests, urging the restoration of power and water supplies. Later that month the new Chief Administrator, Michel Jeanjean, authorized the police to intervene to allow access to the power plant, after which normal supplies were resumed.

The Australian Parliamentary Secretary for Pacific Island Affairs, Richard Marles, became the first member of the Australian Parliament to visit Wallis and Futuna in July 2011, when, together with Marie-Luce Penchard, he joined celebrations marking the 50th anniversary of the islands' status as a French Overseas Territory. Ongoing concern about the rising cost of living culminated in demonstrations throughout the islands attended by some 1,500 people in November 2011. Protesters demanding lower fuel prices and air fares marched to the government buildings in Mata'Utu. The demonstrations coincided with widespread strike action by public sector employees demanding the same system of pay indexation as their French state counterparts.

Recent developments

At elections to the Territorial Assembly in March 2012, the incumbent President of the Territorial Assembly, Pesamino Taputai, and his two predecessors, Siliaki Lauhéa and Victor Brial, all failed to secure re-election to the legislature. Vetelino Nau of the UPWF was elected as President of the Territorial Assembly, receiving 11 out of 20 votes, including those of six unaffiliated members. Sosefo Suve of Taumu'a Lelei was elected to replace Nau in November.

At the French presidential election of 2012 the successful PS candidate, François Hollande, received 56.1% of the votes cast in Wallis and Futuna in the second round of voting in May, in contrast to the other French Pacific Territories, which returned majorities for the incumbent Nicolas Sarkozy. The territory also distinguished itself by registering the highest voter participation rate of any part of the Republic, at some 82% of the electorate. In the closely contested second round of the French legislative elections, in June, the UMP's candidate, David Vergé, defeated his closest rival, Mikaele Kulimoetoke, by just 42 votes. A number of Vergé's opponents filed a challenge against the result, and in January 2013 the French Constitutional Council annulled his election, citing irregularities in his campaign accounts. An election to select a new deputy took place in March, concurrently with polls to fill four seats in the Territorial Assembly, which had become vacant in December 2012, after the French Conseil d'Etat (Council of State) annulled the election of the four members representing the constituency of Alo. Napoli Polutele, an independent who was supported by the UMP, was elected to the French National Assembly with 37.5% of the votes cast, defeating Kulimoetoke, who received 32.3% and Lauriane Vergé (the wife of David Vergé), who secured 30.2%. Polutele's decision in June to join the Socialist group in the French National Assembly led to persistent criticism by members of the UMP in Wallis and Futuna, who had supported Polutele and funded his electoral campaign.

In December 2012 Cyclone Evan caused substantial damage to property and roads on Wallis, including the destruction of 300 homes. Supplies were dispatched from New Caledonia in the aftermath of the storm, and, in a significant demonstration of French solidarity with the territory, the Minister of Overseas Territories, Victorin Lurel, made an official visit to the island to assess the damage. Some US $400,000 in emergency assistance was subsequently made available for rehabilitation works.

Michel Aubouin replaced Michel Jeanjean as Chief Administrator at the end of March 2013. Nivaleta Iloai became the first female President of the Territorial Assembly upon her election to the position on 1 April.

Following four years of negotiations between the chiefly clans of Alo to select a successor to Petelo Vikena (who had abdicated the throne in January 2010), in January 2014 Petelo Sea was nominated to be the new King of Alo; his enthronement took place later that month.

The trial of 20 people accused of defrauding the French Government began in Wallis and Futuna in April 2014. The allegations involved the misappropriation in 2007–08 of more than US $27m. through the abuse of a taxation law intended to stimulate investment in the territory. The case was brought following an investigation into a dramatic increase in the number of companies involved in public works in the islands and also following the discovery that large investments had been made in apparently non-existent hotel projects. In August 16 of the accused were found guilty, including a police officer from New Caledonia and his French partner, who each received a five-year prison sentence and a fine of $670,000, and a former Secretary of the Territorial Assembly. An appeal against the convictions of 10 of the defendants was lodged in the Court of Appeal in New Caledonia in January 2015. In March the prison sentences of the police officer and his partner were reduced to three years (with one year suspended) and their fines reduced to $470,000.

In July 2014 some 350 people marched and mounted barricades in front of the Territorial Assembly, in support of a strike by public sector workers involved in a dispute over the status of public officials in the territory. After 18 days of industrial action, an agreement was reached establishing a commission to revise documentation defining the role of public servants.

Fr Robert Laufoaulu was re-elected to the French Senate for a third six-year term in September 2014.

Kapiliele Faupala, the King of Wallis, was removed from power in September 2014 by traditional chiefs who had reportedly accused him of excessive political interference, notably regarding the dismissal of two local Prime Ministers earlier in the year. A further vacancy arose in the following month, when the King of Sigave, Polikalepo Kolivai, reportedly abdicated. Successors to both Kings had yet to be selected at early 2015.

Discussions between the recently elected President of the Territorial Assembly, Mikaele Kulimoetoke, and the French Prime Minister, Manuel Valls, in December 2014 led to a significant agreement, under which the French Government would settle Wallis and Futuna's debt of some US $24m. with the hospital in New Caledonia where its residents receive health care. Valls also pledged to support legislation (approved by the French National Assembly in October) that would reduce electricity prices on Wallis and Futuna to the same level as those in mainland France. (Energy prices were some five times higher in the territory than in metropolitan France, although islanders' average earnings were around three times lower than those of their mainland French counterparts.)

CONSTITUTION AND GOVERNMENT

The Collectivité d'Outre-Mer (Overseas Collectivity) of Wallis and Futuna is administered by a representative of the French Government, the Chief Administrator, who is assisted by the Territorial Assembly. The Assembly has 20 members and is elected for a five-year term. The three traditional kingdoms, one on Wallis and two sharing Futuna, have equal rights, although the Kings' powers are limited. In addition, Wallis and Futuna elects one deputy to the French Assemblée Nationale (National Assembly) in Paris and one representative to the French Sénat (Senate). The islands may also be represented at the European Parliament.

REGIONAL AND INTERNATIONAL CO-OPERATION

Wallis and Futuna forms part of the Franc Zone (see p. 326). Although France is also a member of the organization, Wallis and Futuna has membership in its own right of the Pacific Community (see p. 410), which is based in New Caledonia and provides technical advice, training and assistance in economic, cultural and social development to the region. Wallis and Futuna was granted observer status at the Pacific Islands Forum (see p. 413) in 2006 and submitted an application for associate membership in 2008.

ECONOMIC AFFAIRS

In 1995 it was estimated that Wallis and Futuna's gross domestic product (GDP) was US $28.7m., equivalent to some $2,000 per head. Most monetary income in the islands is derived from government employment and from remittances sent home by islanders employed in New Caledonia and metropolitan France.

Agricultural activity is of a subsistence nature. Yams, taro, bananas, cassava and other food crops are also cultivated. Tobacco is grown for local consumption. Pigs, goats and chickens are reared on the islands. Apiculture was revived in 1996, and in 2000 honey production was sufficient to meet the demands of the local market. Fishing activity in the exclusive economic zone of Wallis and Futuna increased during the 1990s; the total catch was estimated at 850 metric tons in 2012, compared with 70 tons in 1991.

Mineral fuels are the main source of electrical energy, although it is hoped that hydroelectric power can be further developed, especially on Futuna. There is a 4,000-kW thermal power station on Wallis, and a 2,600-kW thermal power station on Futuna. The hydroelectric power station on the Vainifao river, on Futuna, provides around 10% of the production needed. Total electricity output in 2013 amounted to 18.8m. kWh.

There were 291 businesses operating in Wallis and Futuna in 2000, of which 24 were in the industrial and artisanal sector, 68 in construction and 199 in the service and commercial sectors; 47 of those businesses were located on Futuna. A new commercial centre opened in Wallis in 2002. The tourism sector is very limited. In 2008 Wallis had four hotels and Futuna two establishments. In November 2005 the French Government agreed to provide some €8m. towards expanding the domestic airport at Vele, on Futuna, to receive international traffic. Foreign visitor arrivals, mainly from New Caledonia and France, totalled 2,456 in 2006.

In 2013 the value of the islands' imports totalled 5,293m. francs CFP. In that year the major imports were prepared foodstuffs, followed by pharmaceutical and cosmetic products, transport equipment, mechanical equipment, household equipment, and chemicals, rubber and plastic products. Exports of Trochus shells provided revenue of 11.6m. francs CFP in 2006. However, total exports declined to 1.0m. francs CFP in 2009. Traditional food products, mother of pearl (from the Trochus shell) and handicrafts are the only significant export commodities. Exports of copra from Wallis ceased in 1950, and from Futuna in the early 1970s. The principal sources of imports in 2007 were France, which supplied 27.8% of the total, Singapore and Australia. In 2004 most of the islands' exports were purchased by Italy. In August 2001 the frequency of supplies to Wallis and Futuna was significantly improved when the Sofrana shipping company, based in Auckland, began operating a new route linking New Zealand, Tonga and the Samoas to Wallis and Futuna.

There was a deficit of 380m. francs CFP on the territorial budget in 2012. French aid to Wallis and Futuna increased from a total of 7,048m. francs CFP in 1999 to 12,064.2m. francs CFP in 2008. In December 2002 France proposed a broad 15-year sustainable development strategy for Wallis and Futuna.

The annual rate of inflation in 2008–13 averaged 2.9%. The annual rate of inflation at June 2013 was 2.1%. The high level of unemployment has remained a major economic and social issue; 12.8% of the total labour force was classified as unemployed and seeking work at the time of the 2008 census. More than 50% of those in formal employment are engaged in the public sector.

Wallis and Futuna is heavily dependent upon metropolitan France and on remittances from islanders working overseas, particularly in New Caledonia. Of the estimated 20% of the population in salaried employment, some 70% work in the public sector. France agreed to provide US $50m. in 2007–11 for infrastructural development, health, education and vocational training. Funding from the

European Union (EU, see p. 271) of €16.5m. for the period 2008–13 was to focus on renewable energy, improved management of the islands' natural resources and sustainable development; EU funding for 2014–20 increased to €19.6m. The islands suffer from problems associated with an ageing population, as a large proportion of younger people seek employment opportunities overseas. The territory is also vulnerable to the effects of severe climatic events, such as cyclones and tidal surges, which are expected to increase in frequency with changing weather patterns. Exploratory investigations during 2013 revealed the presence of cobalt deposits in the seabed near the islands, the future exploitation of which presented a potential alternative source of revenue for Wallis and Futuna. Proposed legislation to reduce electricity costs in the islands, which was approved by the French National Assembly in October 2014 and endorsed by the French Prime Minister in December (see *Recent developments*), was expected to have a beneficial effect on the territory's economy. Moreover, a planned new cathedral to be built on the southern tip of Wallis island to house the relics of St Pierre Chanel, patron saint of Oceania, had the potential to create a significant new pilgrimage site, attracting many more visitors to the territory.

PUBLIC HOLIDAYS

2016: 1 January (New Year's Day), 28 March (Easter Monday), 28 April (Saint Pierre-Chanel Day), 1 May (Labour Day), 5 May (Ascension Day), 8 May (Victory Day), 16 May (Whit Monday), 29 June (Saints Peter and Paul Day), 14 July (Fall of the Bastille), 29 July (Territory Day), 15 August (Assumption), 1 November (All Saints' Day), 11 November (Armistice Day), 25 December (Christmas Day).

Statistical Survey

Source (unless otherwise indicated): Service Territorial de la Statistique et des Études Économiques, Immeuble Pukavila, RT1, BP 638, Mata'Utu, Falaleu, 98600 Wallis; tel. 722403; fax 722487; e-mail stats@wallis.co.nc; internet www.spc.int/prism/Country/WF/WFindex.html.

AREA AND POPULATION

Area (sq km): 142. *By Island:* Uvea (Wallis Island) 78; Futuna Island 46; Alofi Island 18. The collectivity also includes a group of uninhabited volcanic and coralline islets (18 sq km).

Population: 13,445 (males 6,669, females 6,776) at census of 21 July 2008; 12,197 at census of 22 July 2013: Wallis Island—Uvea 8,584; Futuna Island 3,613 (Alo 2,156, Sigave 1,457).

Density (at 2013 census): 85.9 per sq km.

Population by Age and Sex (at 2008 census): *0–14 years:* 4,081 (2,181 males, 1,900 females); *15–64 years:* 8,387 (4,047 males, 4,340 females); *65 years and over:* 977 (441 males, 536 females); *Total:* 13,445 (6,669 males, 6,776 females).

Principal Villages (population at 2013 census): Mata'Utu (capital) 1,075; Utufua 615; Liku 589; Falaleu 586; Alele 551; Ono 537; Taoa 531.

Births, Marriages and Deaths (2009 unless otherwise indicated): Registered live births 230 (birth rate 17.2 per 1,000); Registered marriages 53 (marriage rate 3.9 per 1,000, 2008); Registered deaths 90 (death rate 6.7 per 1,000, 2008). *2012* Registered live births 176 (birth rate 14.2 per 1,000); Registered deaths 78 (death rate 6.3 per 1,000).

Life Expectancy (years at birth): 74.3 (males 73.1; females 75.5) in 2003.

Economically Active Population (2008 census): Total employed 3,373 (males 1,867, females 1,506); Unemployed persons seeking work 496 (males 296, females 200); Total labour force 3,869 (males 2,163, females 1,706). *2012:* Total employed 2,062.

HEALTH AND WELFARE

Key Indicators

Total Fertility Rate (children per woman, census of 2008): 2.0.

Under-5 Mortality Rate (per 1,000 live births, average of 2005–2008): 5.2.

Physicians (per 1,000 head, 2003): 0.7.

Access to Sanitation (% of persons, census of July 2003): 80.9.

Access to Water (% of persons, census of July 2003): 68.5.

For definitions, see explanatory note on p. vi.

AGRICULTURE, ETC.

Principal Crops ('000 metric tons, 2013, FAO estimates): Cassava 2.0; Taro (coco yam) 1.5; Yams 0.5; Other roots and tubers 1.1; Coconuts 3.3; Vegetables and melons 0.8; Bananas 7.0. *Aggregate Production* ('000 metric tons, may include official, semi-official or estimated data): Total fruits (excl. melons) 12.0; Total roots and tubers 5.1.

Livestock ('000 head, year ending September 2013, FAO estimates): Pigs 25; Goats 7; Chickens 65.

Livestock Products (metric tons, 2013, FAO estimates): Pig meat 315; Goat meat 15; Chicken meat 48; Cows' milk 48; Hen eggs 50; Honey 10.

Fishing (metric tons, live weight, 2012, FAO estimates): Total catch 850 (Marine fishes 803). Figures exclude Trochus shells (metric tons) 30.

Source: FAO.

INDUSTRY

Selected Products (metric tons, 2013, unless otherwise indicated): Coconut oil 164 (2012, FAO estimate); Copra 252.5 (2006, FAO estimate); Electric energy 18.8m. kWh (Wallis Island 15.6; Futuna Island 3.3). Sources: FAO; Institut d'Emission d'Outre-Mer.

FINANCE

Currency and Exchange Rates: see French Polynesia.

Territorial Budget (million francs CFP, 2012): *Revenue:* Current 2,864; Capital 187; Total 3,051. *Expenditure:* Current 2,994; Capital 437; Total 3,431.

Money Supply (million francs CFP at 31 December 2013): Currency in circulation 2,158; Demand deposits 3,872; *Total money* 6,029. Source: Institut d'Emission d'Outre-Mer.

Cost of Living (Consumer Price Index; base: June 2008 = 100): All items 107.8 in 2011; 113.2 in 2012; 115.6 in 2013.

EXTERNAL TRADE

Principal Commodities (million francs CFP): *Imports c.i.f.* (2013): Prepared foodstuff 1,640; Pharmaceutical and cosmetic products 391; Household equipment 301; Transport equipment 455; Mechanical equipment 321; Electrical and electronic equipment 423; Chemicals, rubber and plastic products 311; Metals and metal products 162; Fuels 1,104; Total (incl. others) 5,923. *Exports f.o.b.* (2001): Preparations of molluscs and other aquatic invertebrates 0.3; Coral and shells 5.5; Braids and mats of vegetable material 0.9; Total 5.6. *2009:* Total exports 1.0. Source: mainly Institut d'Emission d'Outre-Mer.

Principal Trading Partners: *Imports c.i.f.* ('000 million francs CFP, 2007): Australia 0.7; Fiji 0.3; France (incl. Monaco) 1.5; New Caledonia 0.3; New Zealand 0.5; Singapore 0.8; Total (incl. others) 5.4. *Exports f.o.b.* (million francs CFP, 2004): Italy 4.6; Total 4.6. Source: mainly Institut d'Emission d'Outre-Mer.

TRANSPORT

Road Traffic (vehicles in use, 2001): Scooters 1,093; Cars 1,293. Source: Ministère de l'Agriculture, de l'Alimentation, de la Pêche et des Affaires Rurales, *Recensement agricole du territoire 2001*.

Shipping: *Flag Registered Fleet* (at 31 December 2014): Vessels registered 3; Total displacement: 32,880 grt. Source: Lloyd's List Intelligence (www.lloydslistintelligence.com).

Civil Aviation (2013): *Domestic Traffic:* Aircraft movements 1,404; Passenger movements 13,017; Freight handled 21.5 metric tons; Mail handled 11.9 metric tons. *International Traffic:* Aircraft movements 353; Passenger movements 32,816; Freight handled 155.9 metric tons; Mail handled 71.1 metric tons. Source: Institut d'Emission d'Outre-Mer.

TOURISM

Foreign Visitors (2006): *Total Arrivals:* 2,456. *Overnight Stays in Hotel Establishments:* 607.

Foreign Visitor Arrivals by Nationality (2006): Australia 37; Fiji 45; France 674; French Polynesia 62; New Caledonia 1,310; Total (incl. others) 2,456.

COMMUNICATIONS MEDIA

Telephones (2012): 3,130 main lines installed.

Internet Users (2009): 1,300.

Broadband Subscribers (2012): 1,177.

Source: International Telecommunication Union.

EDUCATION

Pre-primary (2005): 3 institutions; 260 pupils.

Primary (2013, unless otherwise indicated): 18 institutions (2008); 1,867 pupils (incl. pre-primary). Source: Institut d'Emission d'Outre-Mer.

Secondary (2012, unless otherwise indicated): 7 institutions (2 vocational) (2006); 1,929 students. Source: Institut d'Emission d'Outre-Mer.

Higher (students, 2005/06): 14 in New Caledonia; 60 in metropolitan France; 6 in French Polynesia. Source: Institut d'Emission d'Outre-Mer.

Teachers (2003): Pre-primary and primary 168; Secondary 209.

Adult Literacy Rate (census of July 2003): 78.8% (males 78.2%; females 79.3%).

Directory

The Government
(April 2015)

Chief Administrator (Administrateur Supérieur): MICHEL AUBOUIN.

COUNCIL OF THE TERRITORY

The Council is chaired by the Chief Administrator and comprises the members by right (the Kings of Wallis, Sigave and Alo) and three appointed members.

GOVERNMENT OFFICES

Government Headquarters: Bureau de l'Administrateur Supérieur, BP 16, Mata'Utu, Havelu, Hahake, 98600 Uvea, Wallis Islands; tel. 722727; fax 722300; e-mail webmestre@wallis-et-futuna.pref.gouv.fr; internet www.wallis-et-futuna.pref.gouv.fr.

Department of Catholic Schools: Direction Diocésaine de l'Enseignement Catholique, BP 80, Mata'Utu, 98600 Uvea, Wallis Islands; tel. 722766; fax 722815; e-mail decwf.wallis@wallis.co.nc; responsible for pre-primary and primary education since 1969.

Department of Cultural Affairs: BP 131, Mata'Utu, Aka'aka, 98600 Uvea, Wallis Islands; tel. 722563; fax 722667; e-mail culture.wf@mail.wf.

Department of the Environment: BP 294, Mata'Utu, Havelu, Hahake, 98600 Uvea, Wallis Islands; tel. 720597; fax 720351; e-mail senv@mail.wf.

Department of Justice: BP 12, Mata'Utu, Havelu, Hahake, 98600 Uvea, Wallis Islands; tel. 722715; fax 722531; e-mail tpi@wallis.co.nc.

Department of Labour and Social Affairs Inspection (SITAS): BP 385, Mata'Utu, Hahake, 98600 Uvea, Wallis Islands; tel. 722288; fax 722384; e-mail sitas.wf@mail.wf.

Department of Public Works and Rural Engineering: BP 13, Mata'Utu, Kafika, Hahake, 98600 Uvea, Wallis Islands; tel. 722626; fax 722115; e-mail tpwallis@mail.wf.

Department of Rural Affairs and Fisheries: BP 19, Mata'Utu, Aka'aka, 98600 Uvea, Wallis Islands; tel. 722606; fax 720404; e-mail ecoru@mail.wf; internet www.wallis-et-futuna.pref.gouv.fr.

Department of Youth and Sports: BP 51, Mata'Utu, Kafika, Hahake, 98600 Uvea, Wallis Islands; tel. 722188; fax 722322; e-mail mjs-986@jeunesse-sports.gouv.fr; internet www.bafa-bafd.jeunes.gouv.fr.

Health Agency: Agence de Santé, BP 4G, 98600 Uvea, Wallis Islands; tel. 720700; fax 722399; e-mail sante@adswf.org; internet www.adswf.org; operates 2 hospitals at Sia on Uvea and Kaleveleve on Futuna, respectively.

Legislature

TERRITORIAL ASSEMBLY

The Territorial Assembly has 20 members and is elected for a five-year term. Within the Assembly, ministers may form political groupings of five members or more. These groupings are not necessarily formed along party lines, and alliances may be made in support of a common cause. The most recent general election took place on 25 March 2012.

President: MIKAELE KULIMOETOKE (Divers gauche).

Territorial Assembly: Assemblée Territoriale, BP 31, Mata'Utu, Havelu, Hahake, 98600 Uvea, Wallis Islands; tel. 722004; fax 721807; e-mail cab-pres.at@wallis.co.nc.

PARLIAMENT

Deputy to the French National Assembly: NAPOLI POLUTELE (Ind.).

Representative to the French Senate: Fr ROBERT LAUFOAULU (UMP).

The Kingdoms

WALLIS
(Capital: Mata'Utu on Uvea)

Lavelua, King of Wallis: (vacant).

Council of Ministers (Aliki Fau): The Council is composed of six ministers who assist the King:

Kivalu: the Prime Minister and King's spokesman at official meetings.

Mahe: the second Prime Minister and King's counsel.

Kulitea: responsible for cultural and customary matters.

Uluimonoa: responsible for the sea.

Fotuatamai: responsible for health and hygiene.

Mukoifenua: responsible for land and agriculture.

In addition, the Puliuvea is responsible for the King's security and the maintenance of public order.

The Kingdom of Wallis is divided into three administrative districts (Hihifo, Hahake, Mua), and its traditional hierarchy includes three district chiefs (Faipule), 20 village chiefs (Pule) and numerous hamlet chiefs (Lagiaki).

SIGAVE
(Capital: Leava on Futuna)

Keletaona, King of Sigave: (vacant).

Council of Ministers: six ministers, chaired by the King.

The Kingdom of Sigave is located in the north of the island of Futuna; there are five village chiefs.

ALO
(Capital: Ono on Futuna)

Tu'i Agaifo, King of Alo: PETELO SEA.

Council of Ministers: five ministers, chaired by the King.

The Kingdom of Alo comprises the southern part of the island of Futuna and the entire island of Alofi. There are nine village chiefs.

Political Organizations

Alliance: c/o Assemblée Territoriale; f. 2005; coalition of UDF mems and left-wing independents; Pres. APITONE MUNIKIHAAFATA.

Mouvement Démocrate (MoDem): c/o Assemblée Territoriale; fmrly known as Union pour la Démocratie Française; name changed as above in 2007; centrist; based on Uvean (Wallisian) support.

Taumu'a Lelei (Bright Future): c/o Assemblée Territoriale; f. 1992; Leader SOANE MUNI UHILA.

Union pour un Mouvement Populaire (UMP): c/o Assemblée Territoriale; f. 2002; est. as Union pour la Majorité Présidentielle; includes fmr mems of Rassemblement pour la République; centre-right; local br. of the metropolitan party; Territorial Leader ROBERT LAUFOAULU; Territorial Sec. VICTOR BRIAL.

Union pour Wallis et Futuna (UPWF): c/o Assemblée Territoriale; f. 1994; est. as Union Populaire pour Wallis et Futuna; affiliated to Parti Socialiste of France since 1998; Leader SILIAKO LAUHÉA.

Judicial System

The Statute provided for two parallel judicial systems: customary law, which applied to the indigenous population; and French state law. The competencies of the respective systems are not always clearly defined, which has been a cause of tensions between the indigenous monarchy and the French authorities. On Uvea, under customary law there are separate courts for civil matters (Fono Puleaga) and village matters (Fono Fenua). Disputes over land are dealt with by the Council of the Territory, presided over by the King. A similar system exists on Futuna. Judgments may be referred to a Chambre d'Annulation at the Court of Appeal at Nouméa, New Caledonia.

Court of the First Instance: Tribunal de Première Instance, BP 12, Havelu, Mata'Utu, Hahake, 98600 Uvea, Wallis Islands; tel. 722715; fax 722531; e-mail pr.tpi@wallis.co.nc; f. 1983; Pres. FRANCIS ALARY.

Religion

Almost all of the inhabitants profess Christianity and are adherents of the Roman Catholic Church.

CHRISTIANITY

The Roman Catholic Church

The Territory comprises a single diocese, suffragan to the archdiocese of Nouméa (New Caledonia). The diocese estimated that there were 14,400 adherents at 31 December 2007. The Bishop participates in the Catholic Bishops' Conference of the Pacific, currently based in Fiji.

Bishop of Wallis and Futuna: GHISLAIN MARIE RAOUL SUZANNE DE RASILLY, Evêché Lano, BP G6, Mata'Utu, 98600 Uvea, Wallis Islands; tel. 722932; fax 722783; e-mail eveche.wallis@wallis.co.nc.

The Press

'Uvea Mo Futuna: Tuku'atu Ha'afuasia, Uvea, Wallis Islands; e-mail filihau@uvea-mo-futuna.com; f. 2002; daily; electronic; Editor FILIHAU ASI TALATINI.

The Territory's only newspaper, *Te-Fenua Fo'ou*, was forced to close in April 2002, following a dispute with the King of Wallis. *Fenua Magazine* was launched by a group of local business people in September 2002 but closed in September 2003 owing to a lack of advertising revenue. There is currently no printed press in Wallis and Futuna.

Broadcasting and Communications

TELECOMMUNICATIONS

Orange Wallis & Futuna (Orange WF): Télécommunications Extérieures de Wallis et Futuna, BP 54, Mata'Utu, 98600 Uvea, Wallis Islands; tel. 722436; fax 722255; e-mail orangewf@mail.wf; owned by FCR–SA Orange Group; Man. JACQUES PAMBRUN.

Service des Postes et Télécommunications: BP 00, Mata'Utu, 98600 Uvea, Hahake, Wallis Islands; tel. 720809; fax 722662; e-mail actel.spt@mail.wf; internet www.spt.wf; Dir MANUELE TAOFIFENUA.

BROADCASTING

Radio and Television

France Télévisions Pôle Wallis et Futuna: BP 102, Pointe Matala, Mata'Utu, 98600 Uvea, Wallis Islands; tel. 722020; fax 722346; e-mail rfo.wallis@wallis.co.nc; internet www.wallisfutuna.la1ere.fr; f. 1979; acquired by Groupe France Télévisions in 2004; fmrly Radiodiffusion Française d'Outre-Mer, present name adopted in 1998; transmitters at Mata'Utu (Uvea) and Alo (Futuna); programmes broadcast 24 hours daily in Uvean (Wallisian), Futunian and French; a television service on Uvea, transmitting for 12 hours daily in French, began operations in 1986; a television service on Futuna was inaugurated in 1994; satellite television began operations in 2000; Regional Dir JEAN-JACQUES AGOSTINI; Station Man. LOUIS AUGUSTE; Editor-in-Chief RENÉ LATASTE.

Finance

BANKING

Bank of Issue

Institut d'Emission d'Outre-Mer: BP G5, Mata'Utu, 98600 Uvea, Wallis Islands; tel. 722505; fax 722003; e-mail direction@ieomwf.fr; internet www.ieom.fr/wallis-et-futuna; f. 1998; Dir GUY DELAMAIRE.

Other Banks

Agence Française de Développement: Route territoriale n°1, Aka'aka, Hahake, BP 976, Wallis Islands; tel. 720107; fax 722551; e-mail afdmatautu@afd.fr; internet wallisetfutuna.afd.fr; fmrly Caisse Française de Développement; devt bank; Man. JEAN-YVES CLAVEL.

Banque de Wallis et Futuna: BP 59, Mata'Utu, 98600 Uvea, Wallis Islands; tel. 722124; fax 722156; e-mail bertrand.creuze@bnpparibas .com; internet www.bnpparibas.com/en/bnp-paribas-wallis-futuna; f. 1991; 51% owned by BNP Paribas (New Caledonia); CEO BERTRAND CREUZE.

Paierie de Wallis et Futuna: BP 29, Mata'Utu, 98600 Uvea, Wallis Islands; tel. 721250; fax 722120; Man. LOUIS WAESELYNCK.

Insurance

GAN Assurances: BP 52, Mata'Utu, Hahake, 98600 Uvea, Wallis Islands; subsidiary of GAN Assurances, France; general non-life insurance.

Poe-ma Insurances: Matala'a, Utufua, Mua, BP 728, Vaitupu, 98600 Uvea, Wallis Islands; tel. 450096; fax 450097; e-mail poema@ mail.pf.

Trade and Industry

UTILITIES

Electricité et Eau de Wallis et Futuna (EEWF): BP 28, Mata'Utu, 98600 Uvea, Wallis Islands; tel. 721500; fax 721196; e-mail eewf@wallis.co.nc; 32.4% owned by the territory and 66.6% owned by Electricité et Eau de Calédonie (Groupe Suez, France); production and distribution of electricity on Wallis and Futuna; production and distribution of potable water on Wallis since 1986; Dir JEAN-MARC PETIT.

TRADE UNIONS

Union Interprofessionnelle CFDT Wallis et Futuna (UI CFDT): BP 178, Mata'Utu, 98600 Uvea, Wallis Islands; tel. 721880; Sec.-Gen. KALOLO HANISI.

Union Territoriale Force Ouvrière: BP 325, Mata'Utu, 98600 Uvea, Wallis Islands; tel. 721732; fax 721732; Sec.-Gen. CHRISTIAN VAAMEI.

Transport

ROADS

Uvea has a few kilometres of road, one route circling the island, and there is also a partially surfaced road circling the island of Futuna; the only fully surfaced roads are in Mata'Utu.

SHIPPING

There are two wharves on Uvea for bulk goods, at Mata'Utu, and liquid fuels, at Halalo, respectively. There is one wharf at Leava on Futuna. Wallis and Futuna is served by two container ships: the *Southern Moana*, operated jointly by Moana Services of New Caledonia and Pacific Direct Line of New Zealand between Auckland (New Zealand), Nouméa (New Caledonia) and the islands; and the *Sofrana Bligh*, operated by SOFRANA between Auckland and the islands. Plans to expand the harbour facilities at Mata'Utu and to make improvements to the fishing port of Halalo have been subject to delay.

Société Française Navigation (SOFRANA): BP 24, Mata'Utu, 98600 Uvea, Wallis Islands; tel. 720511; fax 720568; f. 1986; subsidiary of Sofrana Unilines, New Zealand; 1 vessel.

CIVIL AVIATION

There is an international airport in Hihifo district on Uvea, about 5 km from Mata'Utu. Air Calédonie International (Aircalin—New Caledonia) is the only airline to serve Wallis and Futuna. The company operates five flights a week from Wallis to Futuna, one flight a week from Wallis to Tahiti (French Polynesia) and two flights a week from Wallis to Nouméa (New Caledonia). The airport on Futuna is at Pointe Vele, in the south-east, in the Kingdom of Alo.

Service d'Etat de l'Aviation Civile de Wallis et Futuna: BP 01, Mata'Utu, Malae, Hihifo, 98600 Uvea, Wallis Islands; tel. 721201; fax 722954; e-mail seac-wf.encadrement@mail.wf; Dir VALERIE PUCCI.

Tourism

Tourism remains undeveloped. There are four small hotels on Uvea, Wallis Islands. In 2006 foreign visitors to the islands totalled 2,456. In 2008 Wallis had four hotels and Futuna two establishments. The 2013 Pacific Mini Games were held on Wallis and Futuna in September that year.

Defence

Defence is the responsibility of France. The French naval command for the Pacific area is based in French Polynesia.

Education

Education is compulsory for children aged between six and 16 years. Primary education lasts for five years. Each village has a primary school run by the state. The main medium of instruction in village schools is French. In 2008 there were 18 primary schools and seven secondary schools (including two vocational schools) in Wallis and Futuna. Primary and pre-primary pupils totalled 1,867 in 2013 and secondary students numbered 1,929 in 2012. In 2005/06 a total of 80 students were attending various universities overseas. A two-year post-secondary programme was established in the islands in 1990.

Other French Overseas Territories

The other French territories are the French Southern and Antarctic Territories, and New Caledonia. The latter has a unique status as a Collectivité *sui generis* within the framework of the French Republic.

Powers are devolved to New Caledonia under the terms of the 1998 Nouméa Accord.

THE FRENCH SOUTHERN AND ANTARCTIC TERRITORIES

Introduction

The Terres australes et antarctiques françaises (French Southern and Antarctic Territories) are administered under a special statute. The territory comprises Adélie Land, a narrow segment of the mainland of Antarctica together with a number of offshore islets, three groups of sub-Antarctic islands (the Kerguelen and Crozet Archipelagos, and Saint-Paul and Amsterdam Islands) in the southern Indian Ocean, and the Iles Eparses, in the Indian Ocean, comprising Bassas da India, Juan da Nova, Europa and Les Glorieuses, which are also claimed by Madagascar, and Tromelin, also claimed by Madagascar and Mauritius.

Under the terms of legislation approved by the French Government in 1955, the French Southern and Antarctic Territories were placed under the authority of a chief administrator, responsible to the government member for the overseas possessions. The Prefect and Chief Administrator is assisted by a Consultative Council, which meets at least twice annually. The Council is composed of seven members who are appointed for five years by the government member for the overseas possessions (from among members of the Office of Scientific Research and from those who have participated in scientific missions in the sub-Antarctic islands and Adélie Land). Under the terms of a decree promulgated in 1997, administration of the French Southern and Antarctic Territories was formally transferred from Paris to Saint-Pierre, Réunion, in April 2000. The Iles Eparses, administrative control of which was transferred from the Prefect of Réunion to the Prefect and Chief Administrator of the French Southern and Antarctic Territories in January 2005, became an integral part of the French Southern and Antarctic Territories under an organic law promulgated in February 2007.

From 1987 certain categories of vessels were allowed to register under the flag of the Kerguelen Archipelago, provided that 25% of their crew (including the captain and at least two officers) were French. These specifications were amended to 35% of the crew and at least four officers in April 1990. Under new legislation enacted in May 2005 this 'Kerguelen Register' was replaced with a new French International Register, whereby, *inter alia*, the captain, one officer and at least 25% of the crew would be required to be nationals of a European Union (EU) member state, or of a country in the European Economic Area. In 2013 21 vessels were registered to the French Southern Territories, of which seven were fishing vessels.

A permanent French base was established in 1950 at Martin de Viviès, on Amsterdam Island, followed by a second at Port-aux-Français, in the Kerguelen Archipelago, in 1951. The first permanent French base on the mainland was built in 1952 at Port Martin. Having been destroyed by fire, it was replaced in 1956 by a new permanent base at Dumont d'Urville. A fourth base was opened in 1964 at Alfred Faure on Ile de la Possession, in the Crozet Archipelago. In 1992 the French Government created a Public Interest Group, the Institut Français pour la Recherche et la Technologie Polaires (IFRTP—renamed the Institut Polaire Français Paul Emile Victor—IPEV—in 2002), to assume responsibility for the organization of scientific and research programmes in the French Southern and Antarctic Territories. Under an agreement between the IFRTP and Italy's Programma Nazionale di Ricerche in Antartide in 1993, work began on a joint project, Concordia, with a permanent base to be established at Dome C. Concordia was officially opened for winter operation in 2005. France is a signatory to the Antarctic Treaty (see p. 457).

Fishing for crayfish, Patagonian toothfish and tuna in the territories' Exclusive Economic Zones is strictly regulated by quotas (see Statistical Survey). During 2013 65 vessels were licensed to fish in the Iles Eparses zone, and eight in the Southern territories. Following the implementation of a new satellite surveillance system in February 2004, illegal fishing incursions were believed to have been reduced by some 90% by November 2005. An agreement to increase co-operation between France and Australia in combating illegal fishing in the southern Antarctic was signed in 2007 and was ratified by Australia in 2011 (it had previously been ratified by the French Government).

Limited numbers of tourists have since 1994 been permitted to visit Crozet, Kerguelen and Amsterdam: about 60 tourists travel to the territories each year aboard the supply and oceanographic vessel *Marion Dufresne II*. In 2006 Crozet, Kerguelen, Amsterdam and Saint Paul were designated as nature and marine reserves.

Statistical Survey

Area (sq km): Kerguelen Archipelago 7,215, Crozet Archipelago 340, Amsterdam Island 58, Saint-Paul Island 8, Adélie Land (Antarctica) 432,000, Iles Eparses 39 (Bassas da India 1, Europa 28, Juan de Nova 4, Les Glorieuses 5, Tromelin 1).

Population (the population, comprising members of scientific missions, fluctuates according to season, being higher in the summer, but the average is around 225; the figures given are approximate): Kerguelen Archipelago, Port-aux-Français 80; Amsterdam Island at Martin de Viviès 30; Adélie Land at Base Dumont d'Urville 27; the Crozet Archipelago at Alfred Faure (on Ile de la Possession) 35; Saint-Paul Island is uninhabited; Total population (April 2000): 172. *2003/04:* Adélie Land at Base Concordia 41 (joint French-Italian team).

Fishing (catch quotas in metric tons): *2013/14:* Crayfish (spiny lobsters) in Amsterdam and Saint-Paul: 385. *2014/15:* Patagonian toothfish (caught by French and foreign fleets) in the Kerguelen and Crozet Archipelagos: 6,000.

Currency: French currency was used until the end of 2001. Euro notes and coins were introduced on 1 January 2002, and the euro became the sole legal tender from 18 February. For details of exchange rates, see French Guiana.

Budget: Around €26m. in domestic revenues per year (revenues derived from duties levied on the catch of 46 licensed fishing vessels was estimated at €5.6m. in 2012), supplemented with subsidies from the French overseas ministry and grants from the French environment ministry.

External Trade: Exports consist mainly of crayfish and other fish to France and Réunion. The Territories also derive revenue from the sale of postage stamps and other philatelic items.

Directory

Government: rue Gabriel Dejean, 97410 Saint Pierre, Réunion; tel. 262-96-78-78; fax 262-96-78-06; e-mail amandine.george@taaf.fr; internet www.taaf.fr; Prefect, Chief Administrator CÉCILE POZZO DI BORGOT.

Consultative Council: Pres. JEAN-PIERRE CHARPENTIER.

Publications: The central administration in Réunion produces two quarterly publications relating to the French Southern and Antarctic Territories: the legal bulletin *Journal officiel des Terres australes et antarctiques françaises* and a newsletter, *Terres Extrêmes*.

Institut Polaire Français Paul Emile Victor (IPEV): Technopôle de Brest-Iroise, BP 75, 29280 Plouzané, France; tel. 2-98-05-65-00; fax 2-98-05-65-55; e-mail communication-ipev@ipev.fr; internet www.institut-polaire.fr; f. 1992 as Institut Français pour la Recherche et la Technologie Polaires, name changed 2002; Dir YVES FRENOT; 5 permanent bases.

Research Stations: There are meteorological stations and geophysical research stations on Kerguelen, Amsterdam, Adélie Land and Crozet. Research in marine microbiology is conducted from the

Crozet and Kerguelen Archipelagos, and studies of atmospheric pollution are carried out on Amsterdam Island. Additionally, a joint French-Italian research station, Concordia, operates at Dome C. The French atomic energy authority, the Commissariat à l'Energie Atomique, also maintains a presence on Crozet, Kerguelen and Adélie Land.

Transport: An oceanographic and supply vessel, the *Marion Dufresne II*, operated by the French Government, provides regular links between Réunion and the sub-Antarctic islands. A polar research vessel, *Astrolabe*, operated by P&O Maritime Services, France and operating from Hobart, Tasmania, calls five times a year at the Antarctic mainland.

NEW CALEDONIA

Introductory Survey

LOCATION, CLIMATE, LANGUAGE, RELIGION, CAPITAL

New Caledonia comprises one large island and several smaller ones, lying in the South Pacific Ocean, about 1,500 km (930 miles) east of Queensland, Australia. The main island, New Caledonia (Grande Terre), is long and narrow, and has a total area of 16,372 sq km. Rugged mountains divide the west of the island from the east, and there is little flat land. The nearby Loyalty Islands, which are administratively part of New Caledonia, are 1,981 sq km in area, and a third group of islands, the uninhabited Chesterfield Islands, lies about 400 km north-west of the main island. The islands are surrounded by the world's largest continuous coral barrier reef, encompassing some 40,000 sq km. The climate is generally mild, with an annual average temperature of about 24°C (75°F) and a rainy season between December and March. The average rainfall in the east of the main island is about 2,000 mm (80 in) per year, and in the west about 1,000 mm (40 in). French is the official language and the mother tongue of the Caldoches (French settlers). The indigenous Kanaks (Melanesians) also speak Melanesian languages: 29 languages were taken into account at the census of 1996, when it was recorded that 38% of the total indigenous Kanak population spoke a Melanesian language. Other immigrants speak Polynesian and Asian languages. New Caledonians almost all profess Christianity, the majority of whom are Roman Catholics. There is a substantial Protestant minority. The capital is Nouméa, on the main island.

CONTEMPORARY POLITICAL HISTORY

Historical Context

New Caledonia became a French possession in the 19th century, when the island was annexed as a dependency of Tahiti. A separate administration was subsequently established, and a Conseil Général (General Council) was elected to defend local interests. France took possession of Melanesian land and began mining nickel and copper. This displacement of the indigenous Kanak population provoked a number of rebellions. New Caledonia became a Territoire d'Outre-Mer (Overseas Territory) of the French Republic in 1946. In 1956 the first Territorial Assembly, with 30 members, was elected by universal adult suffrage, although the French Governor effectively retained control of the functions of government. New Caledonian demands for a measure of self-government were answered in 1976 by a new statute, which gave the Council of Government, elected from the Territorial Assembly, responsibility for certain internal affairs. The post of Governor was replaced by that of French High Commissioner to the territory. In 1978 the Kanak-supported, pro-independence parties obtained a majority of the posts in the Council of Government. In early 1979, however, the French Government dismissed the Council, following its failure to support a proposal for a 10-year 'contract' between France and New Caledonia on the grounds that the plan did not acknowledge the possibility of New Caledonian independence. The territory was then placed under the direct authority of the High Commissioner.

Domestic Political Affairs

A general election was held in July 1979, but new electoral legislation, which affected mainly the pro-independence parties, ensured that minor parties failed to gain representation in the Assembly. Two parties loyal to France—Rassemblement pour la Calédonie dans la République (RPCR) and Fédération pour une Nouvelle Société Calédonienne (FNSC)—together won 22 of the 36 seats.

Political tension increased in September 1981, following the assassination of Pierre Declercq, the Secretary General of the pro-independence Union Calédonienne (UC). In December the French Government proposed reforms that included equal access for all New Caledonians to positions of authority, land reforms and the fostering of Kanak cultural institutions. To assist in effecting these changes, the French Government announced that it would rule by decree for at least one year. In 1982 the FNSC joined with the opposition Front Indépendantiste (FI) to form a government that was more in favour of the proposed reforms.

In November 1983 the French Government proposed a five-year period of increased autonomy from July 1984 and a referendum in 1989 to determine New Caledonia's future. The statute was rejected by the Territorial Assembly in April 1984, but approved none the less by the French Assemblée Nationale (National Assembly) in September. Under the provisions of the statute, the Territorial Council of Ministers was given responsibility for many internal matters of government, its President henceforth being an elected member instead of the French High Commissioner; a second legislative chamber, with the right to be consulted on development planning and budgetary issues, was created at the same time. All of the main parties seeking independence (except the Libération Kanak Socialiste—LKS—party, which left the FI) boycotted elections for the new, enlarged Territorial Assembly in November 1984. Only 50.1% of the electorate participated in the polls, at which the anti-independence RPCR won 34 of the 42 seats. Following the dissolution of the FI, a new pro-independence movement, the Front de Libération Nationale Kanak et Socialiste (FLNKS), was formed. On 1 December the FLNKS Congress established a 'provisional' Government, headed by Jean-Marie Tjibaou. Amid escalating violence, three settlers were murdered that month by pro-independence activists and 10 Kanaks were killed by *métis* (mixed race) settlers.

In January 1985 Edgard Pisani, the new High Commissioner, announced a plan under which the territory might become independent 'in association with' France on 1 January 1986, subject to the result of a referendum in July 1985. Kanak groups opposed the plan, insisting that the indigenous population be allowed to determine its own fate. At the same time, the majority of the population, which supported the RPCR, demonstrated against the plan and in favour of remaining within the French Republic. A resurgence of violence followed the announcement of Pisani's plan, and a state of emergency was declared after two incidents in which a leading member of the FLNKS was killed by security forces and the son of a French settler was killed by Kanak activists.

In April 1985 the French Prime Minister, Laurent Fabius, proposed the deferral of the referendum on independence until an unspecified date not later than the end of 1987 and the division of the territory into four regions, each to be governed by its own elected autonomous council, which would have extensive powers in the spheres of planning and development, education, health and social services, land rights, transport and housing. The elected members of all four councils together would serve as regional representatives in a Territorial Congress (to replace the Territorial Assembly). The 'Fabius plan' was generally well received by the FLNKS, but condemned by the RPCR, and the proposals were rejected by the predominantly anti-independence Territorial Assembly in May. Nevertheless, the necessary legislation was approved by the French National Assembly in July, and the Fabius plan entered into force. Elections were held in September: as expected, only in the region around Nouméa, where the bulk of the population was non-Kanak, was an anti-independence majority recorded. However, the pro-independence Melanesians, despite their majorities in the three non-urban regions, would be in a minority in the Territorial Congress.

The FLNKS boycotted elections to the French National Assembly in March 1986, in which only about 50% of the electorate in New Caledonia participated. In May the French Council of Ministers approved a draft law providing for a referendum to be held in New Caledonia within 12 months, at which voters would choose between independence and a further extension of regional autonomy. In December, despite strong French diplomatic opposition, the UN General Assembly voted to re-inscribe New Caledonia on the UN list of non-self-governing territories, thereby affirming the population's right to self-determination. The FLNKS boycotted the referendum on 13 September 1987, at which 98.3% of the votes cast were in favour of New Caledonia's continuation as part of the French Republic. At 59%, the turnout was higher than expected, although 90% of the electorate abstained in constituencies inhabited by a majority of Kanaks.

In October 1987 seven pro-French loyalists were acquitted of murdering 10 Kanak separatists in 1984. Jean-Marie Tjibaou, who reacted to the ruling by declaring that his supporters would have to abandon their stance of pacifism, and his deputy, Yeiwéné Yeiwéné, were indicted for 'incitement to violence'. In April 1988 four gendarmes were killed, and 27 held hostage in a cave on the island of Uvéa (the neighbouring Wallis Island), by supporters of the FLNKS. Although 12 of the hostages were subsequently released, six members of a French anti-terrorist squad were captured. French security forces laid siege to the cave, and made an assault upon it in May, leaving 19 Kanaks and two gendarmes dead. Following the siege, it was alleged that three Kanaks had been executed or left to die, after being arrested.

At elections to the French National Assembly in June 1988, both New Caledonian seats were retained by the RPCR. At negotiations in Paris, Jacques Lafleur (leader of the RPCR) and Jean-Marie Tjibaou agreed to transfer the administration of the territory to Paris for 12 months. Under the provisions of the agreement (known as the Matignon Accord), the territory was to be divided into three administrative provinces prior to a territorial plebiscite on independence to be held in 1998. Only people resident in the territory in 1988, and their direct descendants, would be allowed to vote in the plebiscite. The agreement also provided for a programme of economic development, training in public administration for Kanaks and institutional reforms. The Matignon Accord was presented to the French electorate in a referendum, held on 6 November 1988, and approved by 80% of those voting (although an abstention rate of 63% of the electorate was recorded). The programme was approved by a 57% majority in New Caledonia, where the rate of abstention was 37%. In November, under the terms of the agreement, 51 separatists were released from prison, including 26 Kanaks implicated in the incident on Uvéa.

In May 1989 Tjibaou and Yeiwéné were murdered by separatist extremists, alleged to be associated with the Front Uni de Libération Kanak (FULK), which had hitherto formed part of the FLNKS but opposed the Matignon Accord. Elections to the three Provincial Assemblies were nevertheless held, as scheduled, in June: the FLNKS won a majority of seats in the North Province and the Loyalty Islands Province, while the RPCR obtained a majority in the South Province. The RPCR also emerged as the dominant party in the Territorial Congress, with 27 of the 54 seats; the FLNKS secured 19 seats.

The year of direct rule by France ended on 14 July 1989, when the Territorial Congress and Provincial Assemblies assumed the administrative functions allocated to them in the Matignon Accord. In November the French National Assembly approved an amnesty (as stipulated in the Matignon Accord) for all who had been involved in politically motivated violence in New Caledonia before August 1988. In April 1991 the LKS announced its intention to withdraw from the Matignon Accord, accusing the French Government, as well as several Kanak political leaders, of seeking to undermine Kanak culture and tradition. At elections for the New Caledonian representative to the French Sénat (Senate) in September 1992, the RPCR's candidate, Simon Loueckhote, narrowly defeated Roch Wamytan, the Vice-President of the FLNKS.

At provincial elections in July 1995, the RPCR retained an overall majority in the Territorial Congress, while the FLNKS remained the second largest party. Considerable gains were made by a newly formed party led by Nouméa businessman Didier Leroux, Une Nouvelle-Calédonie pour Tous (UNCT). However, a political crisis subsequently arose as a result of the UNCT's decision to align itself with the FLNKS, leaving the RPCR with a minority of official positions in the congressional committees. Lafleur would not accept a situation in which the UNCT appeared to be the dominant party in the chamber, and Pierre Frogier, the RPCR President of the Congress, refused to convene a congressional sitting under such circumstances. The deadlock was broken when the FLNKS proposed the allocation of congressional positions on a proportional basis.

Elections to the French National Assembly in May–June 1997 were boycotted by the FLNKS and LKS. Lafleur and Frogier, both RPCR candidates, were elected to represent New Caledonia. Intensive negotiations involving the RPCR, the FLNKS and the French Government took place in late 1995 and early 1996. France's refusal to grant final approval for a nickel smelter project in the North Province until the achievement of consensus in the discussions on autonomy resulted in the virtual cessation of negotiations during the remainder of 1996.

In February 1997 the French Minister for Overseas Territories, Jean-Jacques de Peretti, visited New Caledonia in a failed attempt to achieve an exchange agreement on nickel between the Société Minière du Sud Pacifique (SMSP), controlled by the North Province, and a subsidiary of the French mining conglomerate Eramet, Société Le Nickel (SLN). However, at the end of the month, in a reversal of policy, the French Government announced its decision not to compensate SLN for any losses incurred. During March large-scale demonstrations were held by the UC and the pro-independence trade union, the Union Syndicale des Travailleurs Kanak et des Exploités (USTKE), in support of SMSP's acquisition of the smelter. Meanwhile, another trade union, the Union des Syndicats des Ouvriers et Employés de Nouvelle Caledonie (USOENC, which represented a high proportion of SLN employees), organized a protest rally against the unequal exchange of mining sites. Frustrated at

SLN's seemingly intransigent position during the negotiations, the FLNKS organized protests and blockades at all the company's major mining installations and restricted shipments of ore around New Caledonia, forcing the closure of four mines. In January 1998 Roch Wamytan (now President of the FLNKS) urged the French Prime Minister, Lionel Jospin, to settle the dispute in order that official negotiations on the political future of New Caledonia, in preparation for the referendum, might begin. The position of the FLNKS had been somewhat undermined by the decision, in the previous month, of a breakaway group of pro-independence politicians—including prominent members of the UC, the Parti de Libération Kanak (PALIKA), and the LKS—to begin negotiations with the RPCR concerning the dispute. These moderate supporters of independence formed the Fédération des Comités de Coordination des Indépendantistes (FCCI) in 1998.

In February 1998, in response to the demands of Kanak political leaders, the French Government, Eramet, SMSP and others signed the Bercy Accord, whereby Eramet was to relinquish control of its site at Koniambo, located in the North Province, in exchange for the Poum mine, operated by SMSP, in the South Province. (The Bercy Accord was the foundation for the 'rebalancing' of New Caledonia's economy under the Nouméa Accord—see below—by creating wealth beyond the South Province.) In April SMSP formed a joint venture with the Canadian mining company Falconbridge to develop the Koniambo nickel deposits. If construction of a nickel smelter had not begun by the end of 2005, control of the nickel deposits was to revert from SMSP to SLN. Meanwhile, the French Government agreed to pay compensation of some 1,000m. French francs to Eramet for the reduction in the company's reserves. An agreement was concluded in February 1999 to enable the transfer of 30% of SLN's share capital (and 8% of Eramet's capital) to a newly created company representing local interests, the Société Territoriale Calédonienne de Participation Industrielle (STCPI), to be owned by the development companies of the three New Caledonian provinces. In July 2000, following two years of negotiations, New Caledonia's political leaders signed an agreement on the formation of the STCPI, the new company to be owned equally by PROMOSUD (representing the South Province) and NORDIL (combining the interests of the North Province and the Loyalty Islands). In September shares in SLN and Eramet were transferred to the STCPI, reducing Eramet's interest in SLN from 90% to 60%.

The Nouméa Accord

Tripartite negotiations on the constitutional future of New Caledonia resumed in February 1998 between representatives of the French Government, the FLNKS and the RPCR. In April 5 May the three sides signed the Nouméa Accord, which postponed the referendum on independence for a period of 15–20 years but provided for a gradual transfer of powers to local institutions, with the exception of defence, foreign policy, law and order, justice and monetary affairs, which were to remain the responsibility of the French Government until after the referendum. The document also acknowledged the negative impact of many aspects of French colonization on New Caledonia and emphasized the need for greater recognition of the importance of the Kanak cultural identity in the political development of the islands.

In July 1998 the French legislature adopted the proposed changes regarding the administration of New Caledonia, which were to be incorporated in an annex to the French Constitution. The Nouméa Accord, which designated New Caledonia as a Pays d'Outre-Mer (Overseas Country) of France, was presented to the electorate in a referendum on 8 November, when it was decisively approved, with 71.9% of votes cast in favour of the agreement. The North Province registered the strongest vote in favour of the agreement (95.5%), while the South Province recorded the most moderate level of approval (62.9%). Draft legislation regarding the definitive adoption of the accord was approved by the French National Assembly in December and by the Senate in February 1999. However, in March the French Constitutional Council declared its intention to allow any French person who had resided in New Caledonia for 10 years or more to vote in provincial elections. This decision was criticized by Roch Wamytan, leader of the FLNKS, as well as by French legislators, who claimed that it breached the Nouméa Accord, whereby only those residing in New Caledonia in 1998 would be permitted to vote in provincial elections. Pro-independence groups threatened to boycott the elections (to be held in May). In response, the French Government announced that the Accord would be honoured, claiming that the Constitutional Council had breached the Nouméa Accord, and stating that this contravention would be rectified. In June the French Council of Ministers announced that it had drafted legislation restricting eligibility for voting in provincial elections and in any future referendums on sovereignty to those who had been eligible to vote in the November 1998 referendum on the Nouméa Accord and to their children upon reaching the age of majority. This decision was condemned by the right-wing Front National, and by Lafleur, leader of the RPCR.

At the general election held on 9 May 1999, no party gained an absolute majority. However, the RPCR won 24 of the 54 seats in the

Congress and formed a coalition with the recently established FCCI and, on an informal level, with the Front National, thus creating an anti-independence block of 31 seats in the chamber. The pro-independence FLNKS won 18 seats. Simon Loueckhote was re-elected President of the Congress. On 28 May the Congress elected Jean Lèques as the first President of the Government (Council of Ministers) of New Caledonia, under the increased autonomy terms of the Nouméa Accord. The new Government was elected on the basis of proportional representation and replaced the French High Commissioner as New Caledonia's executive authority. Following claims of irregularities, fresh elections were held in the Loyalty Islands Province in June 2000, but the results did not alter the composition of the Congress.

Municipal elections confirmed the predominance of the RPCR in the south in March 2001, when it won 39 of the 49 seats in Nouméa. However, overall, the RPCR controlled only 14 of the 33 municipalities in New Caledonia, while pro-independence parties held 19. Jean Lèques resigned as President and was replaced by fellow RPCR politician Frogier in April. Déwé Gorodey of the FLNKS was elected Vice-President. The election to the two most senior posts took place after the Congress had elected an 11-member Government consisting of seven RPCR-FCCI coalition members, three from the FLNKS and one from the UC. In October the French Conseil d'Etat (State Council) ruled that the 11th seat in the New Caledonian Government had been incorrectly allocated to the FLNKS. As a result, FCCI leader Raphaël Mapou replaced Aukusitino Manuohalalo of the FLNKS as Minister for Social Security and Health. Roch Wamytan was replaced as President of the UC by his deputy, Pascal Naouna. In November Wamytan lost the presidency of the FLNKS, following a leadership struggle between its two main factions, the UC and PALIKA. The political bureau of the FLNKS was to lead the party until its internal disputes were settled.

Prior to the French legislative elections of June 2002, the RPCR became affiliated to the metropolitan Union pour la Majorité Presidentielle—latterly Union pour un Mouvement Populaire—to form Le Rassemblement-UMP. The UC and PALIKA could not agree upon their choice of President for the FLNKS. The UC therefore refused to take part in the elections and urged its supporters to abstain from the poll, thereby depriving the President of PALIKA, Paul Néaoutyine, of any chance of re-election to the National Assembly in Paris. Lafleur, now representing Le Rassemblement-UMP, was thus re-elected as a deputy, as was Frogier, also for Le Rassemblement UMP.

In November 2002 the sole UC member of the Government, Gerald Cortot, resigned, prompting the dissolution of the Government, as stipulated in the Nouméa Accord. The Congress appointed a new administration, with Frogier reappointed as President; the incoming Government contained seven members of the Rassemblement-UMP-FCCI coalition, two from the FLNKS and one from the UC.

At the legislative elections in May 2004, Le Rassemblement-UMP lost its majority in the South Province, where it won only 16 of the 40 seats, and thus in the Congress of New Caledonia, occupying only 16 of the 54 seats. The recently formed, anti-independence Avenir Ensemble secured 19 seats in the South Province and proceeded to take 16 seats in the Congress. Each Provincial Assembly in turn elected its President: Philippe Gomès of Avenir Ensemble became President of the South Province, replacing Lafleur; Néaoutyine of the Union Nationale pour l'Indépendance (UNI) was re-elected in the North Province; and Néko Hnépeune, also of the UNI-FLNKS alliance, was elected President in the Loyalty Islands. The incoming Congress elected Harold Martin of Avenir Ensemble as its President and began the process of appointing a new Government. In early June Marie-Noëlle Thémereau of Avenir Ensemble and Gorodey of the UNI-FLNKS were respectively nominated President and Vice-President. However, the Government disintegrated within hours, following the resignation of the three Rassemblement-UMP ministers, who claimed that their party was entitled to four posts under power-sharing terms set out in the Nouméa Accord. The Congress granted Le Rassemblement-UMP the seats, but with the result that the decision of the Council of Ministers on its leadership reached a stalemate. In late June a new vote returned Thémereau and Gorodey to their elected posts.

In October 2004 an operating licence was granted to Canadian mining company Inco for the development of a proposed nickel-cobalt plant at Goro in the South Province. Concerns about the disposal of industrial waste into the sea had been raised in a public inquiry in the previous August, and in February 2005 protesters from a Kanak environmental organization, Réébhù Nùù, blockaded the Goro site. In December Goro was again blockaded, this time by protesters from another Kanak organization, the Conseil Autochtone pour la Gestion des Ressources Naturelles en Kanaky Nouvelle-Calédonie (CAU-GERN). CAUGERN received the support of USTKE and the local Customary Senate in raising concerns relating to the socio-economic and political impact of nickel-mining activities, as well as with regard to the environmental repercussions.

Control of the Koniambo mine was transferred to the Canadian company Falconbridge and SMSP in December 2005. Falconbridge was acquired by a Swiss-based company, Xstrata PLC, in August 2006. (Under the terms of a 2007 agreement, Xstrata Nickel had a 49% stake and SMSP a 51% stake in the Koniambo joint venture. Xstrata merged with another Swiss-based company, Glencore, in May 2013, the new company becoming known solely as Glencore a year later.) Meanwhile, Inco became a wholly owned subsidiary of the Brazilian enterprise, Companhia Vale do Rio Doce (commonly known as Vale from November 2007). In April 2006 the development of the Goro Nickel mine again became a major issue when members of Réébhù Nùù blockaded access routes to the site and caused damage to equipment estimated at US $10m. Construction work at the nickel plant was halted. The FLNKS assumed the role of mediator on behalf of Réébhù Nùù, Goro Nickel, the New Caledonian Government and community leaders, while USTKE announced its support for the Réébhù Nùù campaign. Following reassurances about the security of the site, Goro Nickel announced that it would restart construction work. However, opposition to the project persisted. In June a New Caledonian court ruled that the possible environmental consequences of the scheme had not been comprehensively investigated, and cancelled its licence to operate; however, the company's construction licence remained intact. In July Réébhù Nùù, joined by CAUGERN, warned of further action if Goro Nickel failed to halt construction by a deadline of 24 September. On 25 September the CSTNC began a general strike to demand the expulsion of several hundred Filipino employees of Goro Nickel and the resignations of local government officials. In November Réébhù Nùù succeeded in gaining an injunction from a French court on Goro Nickel's construction of a waste facility. This ruling was rescinded in February 2007. Mounting costs, continuing local opposition and technical problems further delayed the project. (Goro Nickel was renamed Vale Nouvelle-Calédonie in 2010.)

In April 2006 Lafleur founded a new political party with Simon Loueckhote, the Rassemblement pour la Calédonie (RPC). In early 2007 the French legislature approved a constitutional amendment that limited voting rights to those who had been resident in New Caledonia prior to 1998. Due to enter into force in 2009, the legislation did not cover the French presidential and legislative elections of 2007. Nicolas Sarkozy of the UMP defeated Ségolène Royal of the Parti Socialiste in the second round of the presidential election, in May, garnering 62.9% of the votes in New Caledonia. Sarkozy's margin of victory was significantly smaller within metropolitan France. At elections to the National Assembly in June, the Rassemblement-UMP candidates, incumbent deputy Frogier and Gaël Yanno, were elected in a second round.

As had been widely anticipated, Thémereau of Avenir Ensemble resigned as President in July 2007. Frogier was elected President of the Congress of New Caledonia in late July, following reports that Avenir Ensemble and Le Rassemblement UMP had signed an agreement, a so-called 'majority accord', into which the President of the RPC, Loueckhote, had also entered. The Congress elected a new Council of Ministers in August, meeting an FLNKS demand for four of the 11 cabinet positions. Martin was subsequently elected President and Gorodey returned to the position of Vice-President.

In October 2007 the French High Commissioner in New Caledonia, Michel Mathieu, resigned amid reports of a disagreement with the French Minister-Delegate for the Overseas Possessions, Christian Estrosi, who had signalled a new approach to the issue of strike action in New Caledonia. Yves Dassonville replaced Mathieu in November.

The elections of 2009 and beyond

In March 2009, as required by the Nouméa Accord, the New Caledonian Congress unanimously approved new legislation governing the operations of the nickel industry. Legislative elections were held in the territory's three provinces on 10 May, whereupon each Provincial Assembly elected its President. Pierre Frogier of Le Rassemblement-UMP replaced Philippe Gomès as President of the South Province. Paul Néaoutyine, leader of the UNI, was re-elected in the North Province. In the Loyalty Islands Néko Hnépeune, also of the UNI-FLNKS, was re-elected as President. Members of anti-independence parties occupied 31 of the 54 seats in the New Caledonian Congress (of which Le Rassemblement-UMP took 13). Calédonie Ensemble, established in 2008 by former members of Avenir Ensemble and led by Gomès, was allocated 10 seats. The pro-independence groups made some gains and took 23 seats, eight of which were occupied by the UC and eight by the UNI.

At its inaugural session, the Congress chose Gomès as the territory's President. Disagreements delayed the election of the Vice-President until mid-June 2009, when Pierre Ngaihoni of the UC was appointed to the position. Martin replaced Frogier as President of the Congress. In October, following the confirmation of irregularities relating mainly to the extensive use of proxy votes, the results of the Loyalty Islands were declared invalid by the State Council in France. At new polls, on 6 December, the UC-FLNKS alliance retained six seats in the Provincial Assembly, while the Parti Travailliste increased its representation from two to four seats, the LKS won two seats and two seats were taken by another pro-independence grouping.

The gradual process of transferring powers from metropolitan France continued, as stipulated in the Nouméa Accord (with the exception of certain areas such as defence and foreign policy, which were to remain the responsibility of the French Government until after the referendum on independence that was to take place between 2014 and 2018). With responsibility for primary education, post and telecommunications, training in public administration, labour, external trade and mining having already been granted to the New Caledonian authorities, the policing and security of domestic maritime transport became the responsibility of New Caledonia in two stages, in January and July 2011, followed by secondary and private primary education in January 2012 (although the French Government was to continue to pay the salaries of teaching staff), and by the policing and security of internal air transport in January 2013. In accordance with legislation adopted by the Congress in December 2011, the transfer of responsibility for civil and commercial law and for civil security were effected in July 2013 and January 2014, respectively.

A meeting on the further implementation of the Nouméa Accord took place in Paris in June 2010. It was resolved at a subsequent meeting that a committee of experts would be established to study the options for the future political status of New Caledonia. At the same time the French Government undertook to provide 45,000m. francs CFP in development assistance for New Caledonia during the period 2011–15. In July 2010 the French Prime Minister, François Fillon, paid a visit to New Caledonia, during which the 'Kanak' flag (which had formed a symbol of the pro-independence movement over the past 20 years) was, with the approval of the Congress, officially raised for the first time, concurrently with the French national flag. However, the display of two flags was regarded by some as symbolizing disunity, and President Gomès, among others, argued that a new single flag should be designed to represent New Caledonia following decolonization. A new French High Commissioner, Albert Dupuy, replaced Dassonville in October 2010.

In February 2011 members of the pro-independence UC withdrew from the Council of Ministers, on the grounds that Gomès was opposed to the use of two flags. As this resignation automatically resulted in the removal from office of the entire Government, Gomès protested that the flag dispute was a ploy to remove him from office. He accused Le Rassemblement-UMP of allying itself with the UC to this end. In early March the Congress elected a Government. However, the new administration collapsed within minutes after one of the incoming ministers of Calédonie Ensemble submitted his resignation. Martin of Avenir Ensemble, who had replaced Gomès of Calédonie Ensemble as President, continued in office in an interim capacity, with Guy Tuyienon of the UC as his Vice-President. A fortnight later another Government was appointed, only to disintegrate immediately when Calédonie Ensemble withdrew. In April a further attempt to establish a government was unsuccessful.

In May 2011, following negotiations in Paris between political leaders from New Caledonia and members of the French Government, the French Prime Minister François Fillon announced that the Congress would elect a new collegial government on 10 June, rather than proceed with an early general election as initially requested by Gomès. At the election to the Government in June, Martin was re-elected as President and Tuyienon as Vice-President. Despite initial threats to withdraw once again, Calédonie Ensemble agreed to remain in the collegial Government. Meanwhile, the French Senate approved changes to the electoral law of New Caledonia that were designed to promote greater political stability. Henceforth, an incoming government was be given a grace period of 18 months, thus permitting the exercise of a definite mandate. In July the French Prime Minister hosted further talks in Paris between the signatories to the Nouméa Accord. In August Nicolas Sarkozy made his first presidential visit to the Pacific islands. During his visit he endorsed the Government's recent decision to use the indigenous 'Kanak' flag alongside the French tricolour in all official settings.

At elections to the French Senate in September 2011, New Caledonia contested two seats, having been allocated an additional seat. Pierre Frogier and Hilarion Vendégou, both representing the UMP group, were successful, ending Frogier's long-standing mandate as a deputy of the French National Assembly. At the French presidential election of 2012, Sarkozy secured the largest share of the vote in New Caledonia in the second round in May, winning 63.0%, but was defeated nationwide by François Hollande of the Parti Socialiste. Pro-independence groups had urged voters to support Hollande. Elections to the National Assembly were conducted in June. Philippe Gomès and Sonia Lagarde, both representing Calédonie Ensemble, were narrowly elected as New Caledonia's deputies in a second round of voting.

Meanwhile, Calédonie Ensemble also secured the presidency of the Congress in August 2012, when Gérard Poadja defeated the incumbent, Roch Wamytan, the FLNKS-UC candidate, in a third round of voting. Senator Frogier resigned as President of the South Province in September in order to devote himself to revitalizing Le Rassemblement-UMP, following its poor performance in the legislative elections in June. Cynthia Ligeard, also of Le Rassemblement-

UMP and hitherto Vice-President of the province, was elected as his successor.

The 10th round of talks between the signatories to the Nouméa Accord was hosted by French Prime Minister Ayrault in Paris in December 2012. As regards the ongoing process of transferring responsibility for certain areas to New Caledonia, the Prime Minister announced the establishment of an inter-ministerial structure charged with assisting the New Caledonian authorities to exercise their new powers. The signatories welcomed the recent decision of the Congress to create a commission to consider the contentious issue of designing a new single flag (pending which the 'Kanak' flag and the French national flag would continue to be displayed together), and decided that a 'conference of Presidents', involving those of the Provincial Assemblies, the local Council of Ministers and the Congress, should be formed to consider changes to the division of fiscal resources between the three provinces, the current system being unfavourable to the South Province.

Jean-Jaques Brot took office as the French High Commissioner in New Caledonia in February 2013, following the retirement of the incumbent Dupuy. French Prime Minister Jean-Marc Ayrault visited New Caledonia in July, underlining France's commitment to the final phase of the Nouméa Accord, providing for the organization of a self-determination referendum between 2014 and 2018. In August Wamytan of the FLNKS-UC reassumed the presidency of the Congress following his victory (in three rounds of voting) over two anti-independence candidates, the incumbent Poadja, of Calédonie Ensemble, and Loueckhote of the RPC.

Recent developments: 2014 elections

In February 2014, in the run-up to the legislative elections scheduled to be held in May, Wamytan claimed that there were major discrepancies in the two electoral rolls of New Caledonia (the Special Roll for those eligible to vote and the Annex Table for those not eligible). The congressional President asserted that, in contravention of the Nouméa Accord, around 6,700 of those registered on the Special Roll had taken up residency in New Caledonia after 1998, and that furthermore some 2,000 young indigenous Kanak voters who should have been listed on the Special Roll were instead on the Annex Table, which had allowed them to vote only in elections to the French Parliament. Conversely, a number of anti-independence politicians claimed that some 4,000 Kanaks had wrongly been included on the Special Roll. The French Government sent a group of senior magistrates to New Caledonia to investigate the various allegations. However, following an examination of the rolls, no voters were removed, prompting the FLNKS to initiate legal challenges demanding that those who had failed to take up residency by 1998 be struck off the Special Roll. The outcome of these challenges differed across New Caledonia, although the majority were reportedly rejected.

Municipal polls were conducted in March 2014. Sonia Largarde of Calédonie Ensemble notably secured the mayoralty of Nouméa, defeating Gaël Yanno, in a second round of voting, as she had done in the 2012 elections to the French National Assembly. (Yanno and his supporters had split from Le Rassemblement-UMP in March 2013 and formed a new party, the Mouvement Populaire Calédonien—MPC). Overall, however, the anti-independence parties controlled only 13 of the 33 municipalities.

Concerns over the environmental impact of the nickel industry were renewed in 2014. Operations at the nickel plant at Goro were temporarily suspended in May that year, after a major spillage of effluent contaminated a river. The incident prompted demonstrations by Kanaks demanding the permanent closure of the plant. Damage caused by the protesters was estimated at more than US $34m. A spillage of liquid nickel at the Koniambo plant in December also led to several weeks of closure there.

Anti-independence parties retained a majority in the New Caledonian Congress as a result of the legislative elections held in the territory's three provinces on 11 May 2014, occupying 29 of the 54 seats, while pro-independence parties increased their total representation to 25 seats. Calédonie Ensemble replaced Le Rassemblement-UMP as the largest anti-independence party, securing 15 seats to the latter's five. Following the elections, the three principal anti-independence movements—Calédonie Ensemble, the Front pour l'Unité (FUP, an alliance dominated by Le Rassemblement-UMP and Avenir Ensemble, the latter of which held two congressional seats) and the Union pour la Calédonie dans la France (UCF, comprising the MPC, the RPC and the Mouvement Républicain Calédonien—MPC), jointly holding six seats)—signed a power-sharing agreement covering the South Province, the Congress and the Government. In accordance with this accord, Philippe Michel, of Calédonie Ensemble, was elected as President of the South Province on 16 May, succeeding Cynthia Ligeard, of Le Rassemblement-UMP. (Paul Néaoutyine and Néko Hnépeune were respectively re-elected in the North Province and the Loyalty Islands.) On 23 May Yanno was elected as President of the new Congress, which, in turn, chose Ligeard as the territory's President on 5 June. The territorial vice-presidency remained vacant owing to disagreements among the pro-independence parties entitled to select a nominee for the post.

Ligeard identified economic and social reform as a priority for her 11-member Government, emphasizing a desire to improve air access to the territory and to increase tourist arrivals.

In August 2014 Michel cancelled a Memorandum of Understanding signed in April with Eramet and Vale on the exploration of nickel deposits in the South Province, alleging that the agreement, concluded under Ligeard's presidency of the province, was illegal. The Assembly of the South Province approved the establishment of a special commission of inquiry into the agreement in September.

Meanwhile, Jean-Jaques Brot resigned as the French High Commissioner in New Caledonia in July 2014, during an official visit to Nouméa by the Minister of Overseas Territories, George Pau-Langevin, prompting speculation regarding disagreements over the French Government's plans for New Caledonia. His sudden resignation followed an address to the Congress by Pau-Langevin, in which she announced that two senior envoys would be dispatched to New Caledonia to advise on the decolonization process. Vincent Bouvier replaced Brot in August. Consultations involving political party leaders and the French Government's two envoys were held at the French High Commission in September in an attempt to find some consensus ahead of the 12th round of talks between the signatories to the Nouméa Accord, due to be hosted by the French Prime Minister, Manuel Valls, in Paris in October. However, Le Rassemblement-UMP refused to participate, with senator Pierre Frogier doubting the impartiality of the two French officials, both of whom had been involved in drafting the Nouméa Accord. One of the principal areas of disagreement was the composition of the electoral rolls to be used in the self-determination referendum to be held by 2018. This issue prompted the UC to boycott the Paris talks in October, while Frogier also departed early from the discussions, which Valls none the less deemed to have achieved progress.

President Hollande visited New Caledonia in November 2014, insisting that the self-determination referendum envisaged in the Nouméa Accord would take place by 2018 (amid demands from some politicians for the negotiation of a new accord and the deferral of the planned plebiscite) and reaffirming the French state's impartiality on the issue. Thousands of people staged a march in Nouméa in support of remaining a part of France during Hollande's visit, which was the first to the territory by a French President.

The Government collapsed on 16 December 2014 when Calédonie Ensemble's three ministers resigned from the Government, accusing their coalition partners in the FUP of violating the power-sharing agreement reached following the May elections by refusing to vote in favour of fiscal reforms (see *Economic Affairs*), which were nevertheless adopted by the Congress with the support of the pro-independence UNI. On 31 December the Congress elected the same Government, which then failed to elect a new President, with neither Ligeard nor Philippe Germain, the nominee of Calédonie Ensemble, garnering sufficient support. A further attempt to elect a new President, on 21 January 2015, was also unsuccessful. The five pro-independence ministers abstained from both votes. Ligeard remained in office in a caretaker capacity. Bouvier convened a meeting of the government ministers on 17 February aimed at resolving the impasse, but they failed to reach agreement on a new President and no vote took place. On 1 April eight of the 11 ministers convened at a meeting called by the French High Commission. Three pro-independence government ministers supported the anti-independence Calédonie Ensemble's candidate in order to break the deadlock: Germain was elected President by six of the eight members present. At that meeting Jean-Louis d'Angleberme of the pro-independence UC was selected as the new Vice-President.

Regional Affairs

During a visit to Nouméa in September 2008, the French Minister of Defence, Hervé Morin, stated that the number of French military personnel stationed in New Caledonia was to be reduced by 10%–15%, partly owing to the islands' proximity to the regional power of Australia. New Caledonia was to be designated as a regional hub for marine defence. Closer co-operation with the armed forces of both Australia and New Zealand was envisaged following visits to Nouméa by senior delegations from these two countries in April 2009. A new defence co-operation agreement between France and Australia entered into force in July 2009. In November 2010 the first annual bilateral consultation between New Caledonia and Australia took place.

In February 2010 a bilateral co-operation agreement with Vanuatu, first signed in June 2006, was renewed for a period of five years. The accord provided for greater collaboration in the areas of education, health, culture, trade, law and order, and good governance. In June 2010 a mission of the Melanesian Spearhead Group (MSG), led by the Prime Minister of Vanuatu, Edward Natapei, visited New Caledonia and expressed concern at the slow progress being made in implementing the Nouméa Accord, and in particular at the persistent economic and social imbalance between the provinces of New Caledonia. The pro-independence FLNKS, which is a member of the MSG, hosted a summit meeting of the Group in Nouméa in June 2013. In May 2014 the Vanuatu Government protested to France over the establishment of a 1.3m.-sq km marine reserve covering New Caledonia's entire exclusive economic zone, the Natural Park of the Coral Sea, as it contained the uninhabited Matthew and Hunter Islands, which are claimed by both France and Vanuatu.

CONSTITUTION AND GOVERNMENT

New Caledonia was designated as a Pays d'Outre-Mer (Overseas Country) in 1999. Its status of Collectivité (Collectivity) *sui generis*, conferred following a constitutional revision of 2003, is unique within the French Republic in that the local assembly is permitted to pass its own laws and a local citizenship may be bestowed upon permanent residents. The French Government is represented in New Caledonia by its High Commissioner, and controls a number of important spheres, including external relations and defence. In July 1989 administrative reforms were introduced, as stipulated in the Matignon Accord (which had been approved by national referendum in November 1988). New Caledonia was divided into three Provinces (North, South and Loyalty Islands), each governed by an assembly, which is elected on a proportional basis. The members of the three Provincial Assemblies together form the Congress. Members are subject to re-election every five years. The responsibilities of the Congress include New Caledonia's budget and fiscal affairs, infrastructure and primary education, while the responsibilities of the Provincial Assemblies include local economic development, land reform and cultural affairs. The Government of New Caledonia is elected by the Congress, and comprises between seven and 11 members. Under the terms of the Nouméa Accord (which was approved by a referendum in November 1998), the Government replaces the French High Commissioner as New Caledonia's executive authority. A gradual transfer of power from metropolitan France to local institutions was to be effected over a period of between 15 and 20 years under the terms of the Nouméa Accord.

In addition, New Caledonia elects two deputies to the French National Assembly in Paris and two representatives to the French Senate on the basis of universal adult suffrage; one Economic and Social Councillor is also nominated. New Caledonia may also be represented at the European Parliament.

REGIONAL AND INTERNATIONAL CO-OPERATION

New Caledonia forms part of the Franc Zone (see p. 326). It is an associate member of the UN's Economic and Social Commission for Asia and the Pacific (ESCAP, see p. 30) and a member, in its own right, of the Pacific Community (see p. 410). New Caledonia became an associate member of the Pacific Islands Forum (see p. 413) in 2006 and seeks full membership of the Forum. The Front de Libération Nationale Kanak Socialiste (FLNKS) was admitted to the Melanesian Spearhead Group in 1990.

ECONOMIC AFFAIRS

In 2000, according to World Bank estimates, New Caledonia's gross national income (GNI) at average 1998–2000 prices totalled US $2,989,6m., equivalent to $14,060 per head (or $22,210 per head on an international purchasing-power parity basis). During 2004–13, it was estimated, the population rose by an average of 1.5% per year. According to the UN Economic and Social Commission for Asia and the Pacific (ESCAP), gross domestic product (GDP) per head increased, in real terms, at an average annual rate of 2.0% in 2002–12. According to UN estimates, overall GDP increased at an average annual rate of 3.1% in 2004–13; GDP expanded by 2.4% in 2013.

According to UN estimates, in 2013 the agricultural sector (including forestry and fishing) accounted for just 1.4% of GDP. In 2013 1.8% of the employed labour force were engaged in the sector, according to official sources. Maize, yams, sweet potatoes and coconuts have traditionally been the principal crops, and pumpkins (squash) became an important export crop for the Japanese market from the 1990s. Livestock consists mainly of cattle, pigs and poultry. The main fisheries products are albacore, tuna and prawns (most of which are exported to Japan). The aquaculture industry has expanded steadily, with production of blue shrimp reaching 1,643 metric tons in 2012, in comparison with 691 tons in 1994. In 2013 exports of marine products were worth 2,053m. francs CFP, thus accounting for 1.8% of total exports. According to UN estimates, the GDP of the agricultural sector decreased at an average rate of 0.7% per year in 2004–13; agricultural GDP rose by 1.6% in 2013.

According to the UN, industry (comprising mining, manufacturing, construction and utilities) provided an estimated 25.0% of GDP in 2013. The industrial sector employed 23.8% of the working population in 2013, according to official sources. According to UN estimates, the GDP of the industrial sector expanded at an average rate of 2.1% per year in 2004–13; industrial GDP increased by 3.8% in 2013.

Although mining employed only 1.8% of New Caledonia's working population in 2013, according to official sources, it constitutes the most important industrial activity. In 2013, according to the UN, mining (including utilities) contributed an estimated 1.4% of GDP. New Caledonia is a major producer of ferro-nickel and is believed to possess about one-quarter of the world's known nickel reserves. New Caledonia is one of the world's largest producers of nickel. Output of nickel ore totalled 11.1m wet tons in 2013. In that year the export revenue from nickel ore, ferro-nickel and nickel matte amounted to a total of 83,616m. francs CFP, accounting for 75.0% of total export revenue. The nickel plant at Goro, one of the largest such construction projects in the world, had been expected to reach full annual production capacity of some 60,000 metric tons of nickel and at least 4,300 tons of cobalt in 2014, but this was not achieved. The similarly controversial Koniambo facility, with a projected annual production capacity of 60,000 tons, entered into operation in April 2013 and was officially inaugurated in November 2014. In 1999 a joint French and Australian research mission made an offshore discovery of what was believed to be the world's largest gas deposit, measuring an estimated 18,000 sq km. It was hoped that this might indicate the presence of considerable petroleum reserves. According to UN estimates, the GDP of the mining sector (including utilities) remained constant in 2004–13; sectoral GDP increased by 0.7% in 2012, but decreased by 2.4% in 2013.

The manufacturing sector, which engaged 10.9% of the employed labour force in 2013, according to official sources, consists mainly of small and medium-sized enterprises, most of which are situated around the capital, Nouméa, producing building materials, furniture, salted fish, fruit juices and perishable foods. According to the UN, manufacturing activities accounted for an estimated 12.8% of GDP in 2013.

According to the UN, the construction sector provided an estimated 10.9% of GDP in 2013. The sector engaged 9.3% of the employed labour force in 2013, according to official sources. According to UN estimates, the GDP of the construction sector expanded at an average annual rate of 5.3% in 2004–13; sectoral GDP increased by 0.8% in 2013.

Electrical energy is provided mainly by thermal power stations (77.7% in 2013), by hydroelectric plants and, more recently, by wind power. Mineral products accounted for 27.6% of total imports in 2013. As part of the Government's plans to reduce imports of diesel fuel, six 5-MW wind farms have been established at two different sites, with a combined total of more than 100 hurricane-proof turbines producing electricity for about 50,000 people. Plans for the nickel plant at Koniambo envisaged the construction of a 390-MW power station. In 2013 production of electric energy reached an estimated 2,300m. kWh.

According to the UN, service industries contributed an estimated 73.6% of GDP in 2013. The services sector engaged 74.4% of the employed labour force in 2013, according to official sources. According to UN estimates, the GDP of the services sector increased at an average annual rate of 3.4% in 2004–13, rising by 1.5% in 2013. Although service industries, notably tourism, continue to make the largest contribution to the New Caledonian economy, the tourism sector has failed to witness an expansion similar to that experienced in many other Pacific islands, and tourist arrivals have been intermittently affected by political unrest. The majority of tourists come from France, Australia and Japan. The number of visitor arrivals by air decreased slightly from 112,204 in 2012 to 107,753 in 2013. Over the same period the number of visiting cruise-ship passengers rose from 277,941 to 385,523. Receipts from tourism amounted to €133.3m. in 2010.

In 2012 New Caledonia's merchandise trade deficit was 161,764m. francs CFP, and there was a deficit of 175,396m. francs CFP on the current account of the balance of payments in that year. The principal imports in 2013 were mineral products, machinery and electrical equipment, food products, beverages and tobacco, transport equipment, chemical products, and base metals and articles. The principal exports in that year remained nickel products, prawns and fish. France was the main supplier of imports in 2013, accounting for 23.4% of the total. Other important suppliers of imports were Singapore and Australia. The principal markets for New Caledonia's exports in 2013 were France, representing 15.5% of the total, Japan, Australia, the Republic of Korea, the People's Republic of China and Taiwan.

The 2012 territorial budget projected expenditure of 207,934m. francs CFP. Over the period 2011–15 France was to provide development assistance of 45,000m. francs CFP for New Caledonia. The annual rate of inflation in Nouméa averaged 1.9% in 2004–13. Consumer prices rose by 0.2% in 2014. In 2012 the total of those registered as unemployed averaged 6,229, equivalent to 6.6% of the total labour force.

The economy of New Caledonia has been dominated by the nickel industry. The Koniambo mining project, which became operational in April 2013, had been expected to achieve production capacity of 60,000 metric tons of nickel metal per year by the end of 2014 (equivalent to 5% of global production), but this target was extended to 2015, with output of only 12,600 tons recorded in 2014, partly owing to power shortages. The Goro plant had been scheduled to generate a similar output by 2014, but production in 2012–14 was substantially lower than expected, owing to significant technical problems that halted production for several months. A nickel stabi-

lization fund was established: with an initial allocation of 1,500m. francs CFP, the fund was intended to counter substantial fluctuations in average international nickel prices, which rose by nearly 40% in 2010, on average, and by a more modest 5% in 2011, but declined by 23.4% in 2012 and by 14.3% in 2013, with world supply exceeding demand. However, a ban on exports of unprocessed ores implemented by Indonesia in January 2014 improved the outlook for the nickel market: prices rose by some 13% in 2014 and were expected to increase further in 2015–16 when a deficit in supply was anticipated. The fall in revenue from nickel exports in 2012–13 contributed to a deceleration in the rate of growth of GDP from 3.3% in 2011 to 2.9% in 2012 and to 2.4% in 2013, according to UN figures. The number of tourist arrivals declined to its lowest level for 15 years in 2009, largely as a result of the global economic downturn. Nevertheless, a continued decrease in arrivals by air in 2010 was offset by an increase in cruise-ship visitors. There was a further strong expansion in cruise-ship visitors in 2011, while the holding of the Pacific Games in New Caledonia contributed to a 13.8% increase in arrivals by air. Following more modest rises in 2012, arrivals by air declined by 4.0% in 2013, while cruise-ship visitors increased by 38.7%. In November 2012 legislation adopted by the French legislature aimed at addressing the high cost of living in its overseas territories included provisions on curbing bank fees in New Caledonia, which were of particular concern; overall, prices in New Caledonia were some 34% higher on average than in metropolitan France, while food prices were up to 90% higher. Nevertheless, large-scale protests against high consumer prices in 2013 included a 12-day general strike in May. To end the strike, the authorities agreed to lower or freeze prices of most goods until the end of 2014. Reforms aimed at restoring fiscal sustainability, reducing inequality and boosting economic growth were agreed in August 2014 at a conference of political parties, employers' representatives and trade unions. The measures, which included the introduction of a consumption tax from 2016, were largely adopted in December.

PUBLIC HOLIDAYS

2016: 1 January (New Year's Day), 28 March (Easter Monday), 1 May (Labour Day), 5 May (Ascension Day), 8 May (Liberation Day), 16 May (Whit Monday), 14 July (Fall of the Bastille), 15 August (Assumption), 24 September (Anniversary of possession by France), 1 November (All Saints' Day), 11 November (Armistice Day), 25 December (Christmas Day).

Statistical Survey

Source (unless otherwise stated): Institut de la Statistique et des Etudes Economiques, BP 823, 98845 Nouméa; tel. 275481; fax 288148; internet www.isee.nc.

AREA AND POPULATION

Area (sq km): New Caledonia island (Grande Terre) 16,372; Loyalty Islands 1,981 (Lifou 1,207, Maré 642, Ouvéa 132); Isle of Pines 152; Belep Archipelago 70; Total 18,575 (7,172 sq miles).

Population: 245,580 at census of 27 July 2009; 268,767 at census of 26 August 2014. *Population by Province* (2014 census): Loyalty Islands 18,297; North Province 50,487; South Province 199,983. *2015* (UN estimate at mid-year): 263,147 (Source: UN, *World Population Prospects: The 2012 Revision*). Note: UN estimate not adjusted to take account of results of 2014 census.

Density (mid-2015): 14.2 per sq km.

Population by Age and Sex (UN estimates at mid-2015): *0–14 years:* 58,499 (males 30,038, females 28,461); *15–64 years:* 177,891 (males 89,858, females 88,033); *65 years and over:* 26,757 (males 12,843, females 13,914); *Total* 263,147 (males 132,739, females 130,408) (Source: UN, *World Population Prospects: The 2012 Revision*).

Population by Ethnic Group (2009 census): Indigenous Kanaks (Melanesians) 99,078; French and other Europeans 71,721; Wallisians and Futunians (Polynesian) 21,262; Tahitians (Polynesian) 4,985; Indonesians 3,985; Others 44,549. Note: Classification of ethnicity reflects national census methodology.

Principal Towns (population of communes at 2014 census): Nouméa (capital) 99,926; Dumbéa 31,812; Le Mont-Dore 27,155; Païta 20,616.

Births, Marriages and Deaths (2012): Registered live births 4,445 (birth rate 17.0 per 1,000); Registered marriages 964 (marriage rate 3.7 per 1,000); Registered deaths 1,322 (death rate 4.1 per 1,000).

Life Expectancy (years at birth, 2012): 77.1 (males 74.0; females 80.4).

Economically Active Population (salaried workers, annual averages, 2012): Agriculture, hunting, forestry and fishing 1,586; Mining and quarrying 1,615; Manufacturing 9,555; Electricity, gas and water 1,475; Construction 7,989; Trade, and repairs of vehicles and domestic goods 10,133; Hotels and restaurants 4,911; Transport and communications 5,139; Financing activities 2,161; Real estate and business services 7,881; Public administration 829; Education 2,739; Health and welfare 2,435; Other private sector services 5,015; Non-market services 24,508; *Total employed* 87,972; Unemployed 6,229; *Total labour force* 94,201. *2013:* Agriculture, hunting, forestry and fishing 1,658; Mining and quarrying 1,638; Manufacturing 9,848; Electricity, gas and water 1,512; Construction 8,403; Trade, and repairs of vehicles and domestic goods 10,229; Hotels and restaurants 4,606; Transport and communications 5,122; Financing activities 2,210; Real estate and business services 8,262; Public administration 846; Education 2,806; Health and welfare 2,621; Other private sector services 5,104; Non-market services 25,233; Total employed 90,096.

HEALTH AND WELFARE

Key Indicators

Total Fertility Rate (children per woman, 2007): 2.2.

Physicians (per 1,000 head, 2008): 2.2.

Hospital Beds (per 1,000 head, 2003): 3.7.

Total Carbon Dioxide Emissions ('000 metric tons, 2010): 3,920.0.

Carbon Dioxide Emissions Per Head (metric tons, 2010): 15.7.

For definitions, see explanatory note on p. vi.

AGRICULTURE, ETC.

Principal Crops ('000 metric tons, 2013, FAO estimates): Maize 3.5; Potatoes 1.6; Sweet potatoes 1.7; Cassava 1.5; Yams 6.0; Coconuts 19.0; Vegetables (incl. melons) 8.4; Bananas 1.0.

Livestock ('000 head, year ending September 2013, FAO estimates): Horses 12.0; Cattle 92.0; Pigs 37.5; Sheep 2.4; Goats 8.2; Poultry 500.

Livestock Products (metric tons, 2013): Cattle meat 3,294; Pig meat 2,670; Chicken meat 832; Cows' milk 320 (FAO estimate); Hen eggs 2,015 (Unofficial figure).

Forestry ('000 cu m, 2013, FAO estimates): *Roundwood Removals:* Sawlogs and veneer logs 12.7; Fuel wood 12.2; Other industrial wood 2.0; Total 26.9. *Sawnwood Production:* 3.3 (all broadleaved). Sawnwood production assumed to be unchanged from 1994.

Fishing (metric tons, live weight, 2012): Capture 3,580 (Albacore 1,715; Yellowfin tuna 573; Other marine fishes 267; Sea cucumbers 309); Aquaculture 1,663* (Blue shrimp 1,643); *Total catch* 5,243* (excl. trochus shells 175).

* FAO estimate.

Source: FAO.

MINING

Production (2013): Nickel ore (metal content, '000 metric tons) 69.2; Nickel ore ('000 wet tons) 11,123.

INDUSTRY

Production (2013 unless otherwise indicated, provisional): Ferronickel 40,459 metric tons (nickel content); Nickel matte 13,279 metric tons (nickel content); Electric energy 2,300 million kWh; Cement 123,668 metric tons (2012, Source: US Geological Survey).

FINANCE

Currency and Exchange Rates: see French Polynesia.

French Government Expenditure ('000 million francs CFP, incl. military expenditure): 155.8 in 2011; 156.4 in 2012; 155.8 in 2013.

Territorial Budget (million francs CFP): *Revenue:* 173,975 in 2010; 183,921 in 2011; 217,506 in 2012. *Expenditure:* 167,717 in 2010; 178,400 in 2011; 207,934 in 2012.

Money Supply (million francs CFP at 31 December 2013): Currency in circulation 16,069; Demand deposits 273,632; *Total money* 289,701. Source: Institut d'Emission d'Outre-Mer.

Cost of Living (Consumer Price Index for Nouméa; base: December 2010 = 100): All items 103.5 in 2012; 104.8 in 2013; 105.0 in 2014.

Gross Domestic Product (US $ million at constant 2005 prices): 7,572.5 in 2011; 7,736.5 in 2012; 7,922.7 in 2013. Source: UN Statistics Division, National Accounts Main Aggregates Database.

Expenditure on the Gross Domestic Product (million francs CFP at current prices, 2013): Government final consumption expenditure 217,800; Private final consumption expenditure 556,373; Gross capital formation 350,416; *Total domestic expenditure* 1,124,589; Exports of goods and services 175,391; *Less* Imports of goods and services 424,980; *GDP in purchasers' values* 874,999. Source: UN Statistics Division, National Accounts Main Aggregates Database.

Gross Domestic Product by Economic Activity (million francs CFP at current prices, 2013): Agriculture, hunting, forestry and fishing 11,136; Mining and utilities 11,074; Manufacturing 101,893; Construction 86,779; Retail trade, and hotel and restaurants 105,704; Transport, storage and communication 60,467; Other services 420,356; *Gross value added in basic prices* 797,409; Taxes and subsidies on products (net) 77,590 (figure obtained as residual); *GDP in market prices* 874,999. Source: UN Statistics Division, National Accounts Main Aggregates Database.

Balance of Payments (million francs CFP, 2012): Exports of goods 122,579; Imports of goods –284,343; *Trade balance* –161,764; Exports of services 50,970; Imports of services –127,607; *Balance on goods and services* –238,401; Other income received 54,432; Other income paid –51,359; *Balance on goods, services and income* –235,328; Current transfers received 86,699; Current transfers paid –26,768; *Current balance* –175,396; Capital account (net) 645; Direct investment (net) 221,892; Portfolio investment (net) 7,677; Other investment (net) –36,025; *Overall balance* 18,792. Source: Institut d'Emission d'Outre-Mer.

EXTERNAL TRADE

Principal Commodities (million francs CFP, 2013, provisional): *Imports:* Food products, beverages and tobacco 40,084; Mineral products 80,171; Chemical products 22,008; Plastic and rubber articles 11,409; Paper and paper articles 4,645; Textiles and textile articles 6,755; Base metals and articles thereof 15,883; Machinery and mechanical appliances, and electrical equipment 46,410; Transport equipment 30,255; Total (incl. others) 290,908. *Exports:* Nickel ore 17,498; Ferro-nickel 51,039; Nickel matte 15,079; Marine products 2,053 (Prawns 1,302); Total (incl. others) 111,506.

Principal Trading Partners (million francs CFP, 2013, provisional): *Imports:* Australia 25,768; France 68,095; Japan 5,721; New Zealand 12,165; Singapore 56,719; USA 12,696; Total (incl. others) 290,908. *Exports:* Australia 14,625; China, People's Republic 11,231; France 17,266; Japan 16,199; Korea, Republic 12,681; South Africa 2,709; Taiwan 9,718; USA 5,674; Total (incl. others) 111,506.

TRANSPORT

Shipping (2013 unless otherwise indicated): *Domestic Traffic* ('000 metric tons): Freight unloaded 3,245; Freight loaded 93. *International Traffic:* ('000 metric tons, 2010): Freight unloaded 109,006; Freight loaded 496,113. *Flag Registered Fleet* (at 31 December 2014): Vessels 1; Total displacement 821 grt (Source: Lloyd's List Intelligence—www.lloydslistintelligence.com).

Civil Aviation (La Tontouta international airport, Nouméa, 2013 unless otherwise indicated): *Aircraft Movements:* Aircraft arriving 1,834; Aircraft departing 1,833. *Passenger Traffic:* Passengers arriving 237,848; Passengers departing 238,814. *Freight Traffic:* Freight unloaded 4,013 metric tons; Freight loaded 940 metric tons. *Mail* (2012): Mail arriving 807 metric tons; Mail departing 189 metric tons (Source: Department of Civil Aviation).

TOURISM

Foreign Arrivals: *Arrivals by Air:* 111,875 in 2011; 112,204 in 2012; 107,753 in 2013. *Cruise-ship Passenger Arrivals:* 235,684 in 2011; 277,941 in 2012; 385,523 in 2013.

Tourist Arrivals by Country of Residence (arrivals by air, 2013): Australia 15,722; France 39,183; Japan 15,674; New Zealand 6,334; Total (incl. others) 107,753 (Source: Institut d'Emission d'Outre-Mer).

Tourism Receipts (€ million): 137.8 in 2008; 133.8 in 2009; 133.3 in 2010.

COMMUNICATIONS MEDIA

Telephones (2013): 85,000 main lines in use.

Mobile Cellular Telephones (2013): 240,500 subscribers.

Broadband Subscribers (2013): 53,600.

Source: International Telecommunication Union.

EDUCATION

Pre-primary (2013 unless otherwise indicated): 83 schools (2004); 12,710 pupils.

Primary (2013): 267 schools (incl. pre-primary); 1,939 teachers (incl. pre-primary); 22,437 pupils (incl. special education).

Secondary (2013): 73 schools; 2,773 teachers (incl. higher); 33,314 pupils.

Higher (2005): 4 institutions; 111 teaching staff.

Adult Literacy Rate (1989): Males 94.0%; Females 92.1%.

Directory

The Government

(April 2015)

STATE GOVERNMENT

High Commissioner: VINCENT BOUVIER.

Secretary-General: THIERRY SUQUET.

LOCAL GOVERNMENT

Secretary-General: ALAIN SWETSCHKIN.

COUNCIL OF MINISTERS

President, responsible for Economy, Commercial Law, Taxation, Customs, External Trade, Judicial Protection of Children and Youth, and Civil Security: PHILIPPE GERMAIN.

Vice-President, responsible for Labour, Employment, Social Dialogue, Vocational Training, Relations with the Economic, Social and Environmental Council: JEAN-LOUIS D'ANGLEBERMES.

Minister for Culture, Women Affairs and Citizenship: DÉWÉ GORODEY.

Minister for the Budget, Housing, the Digital Economy, Audio-Visual Communications, Monetary and Credit Affairs, and Relations with the Congress, Government Spokesperson: THIERRY CORNAILLE.

Minister for Infrastructure, Domestic and International Air Travel, Terrestrial and Maritime Transport and the Development Plan for New Caledonia (NC 2025): GILBERT TYUIENON.

Minister for Public Service and Road Safety: CYNTHIA LIGEARD.

Minister for Education, Higher Education, Research and Civic Service: ANDRÉ-JEAN LEOPOLD.

Minister for Land Development, Traditional Affairs, Ecology, Sustainable Development, Management and Conservation of Natural Resources (Biological and Non-Biological) in the Special Economic Zone, Monitoring Priority Development Areas (ZODEP) and Relations with the Customary Senate and the Custom Councils: ANTHONY LECREN.

Minister for Health, Youth and Sports: VALENTINE EURISOUKE.

Minister for Civil Law, Insurance Law, Town Planning Law, Transfer of Skills, Simplification and Modernization of Administration, Francophonie Affairs, Construction of Médipôle de Koutio, Relations with the Provinces and Communes: BERNARD DELADRIERE.

Minister for Social Protection, Solidarity and Disability, Agriculture, Animal Husbandry, Fisheries and Family Policy: SONIA BACKES.

GOVERNMENT OFFICES

Office of the High Commissioner: Haut-commissariat de la République en Nouvelle-Calédonie, 1 ave du Maréchal Foch, BP C5, 98844 Nouméa Cedex; tel. 266300; fax 272828; e-mail haussariat@nouvelle-caledonie.gouv.fr; internet www .nouvelle-caledonie.gouv.fr.

Secretariat-General of the High Commissioner: 9 bis rue de la République, BP C5, 98844 Nouméa Cedex; tel. 246711; fax 246740; internet www.nouvelle-caledonie.gouv.fr.

New Caledonian Government: Présidence du Gouvernement, 8 route des Artifices, Artillerie, BP M2, 98849 Nouméa Cedex; tel. 246565; fax 246580; e-mail presidence@gouv.nc; internet www.gouv .nc.

Office of the Secretary-General of the Government of New Caledonia: 8 route des Artifices, BP M2, 98849 Nouméa Cedex; tel. 246532; fax 246620; e-mail alain.swetschkin@gouv.nc; internet www .gouv.nc.

GOVERNMENT DEPARTMENTS

Department of the Budget and Financial Affairs (DBAF): 18 ave Paul Doumer, BP M2, 98849 Nouméa Cedex; tel. 256082; fax 283133; e-mail dbaf@gouv.nc.

Department of Civil Aviation: 179 rue Gervolino, BP H01, 98849 Nouméa Cedex; tel. 265200; fax 265202; e-mail dac-nc@ aviation-civile.gouv.fr; internet www.dac.nc.

Department of Computer Technology (DTSI): 127 rue Arnold Daly, Magenta Ouemo, BP 15101, 98804 Nouméa Cedex; tel. 275888; fax 281919; e-mail dtsi@gouv.nc.

Department of Cultural, Women and Citizenship: 21 rue de Georges Clémenceau, BP T5, 98852 Nouméa Cedex; tel. 269760; fax 269767; e-mail dccfc@gouv.nc; internet www.gouv.nc/dccfc.

Department of Economic Affairs (DAE): 7 rue du Général Galliéni, BP 2672, 98846 Nouméa Cedex; tel. 232250; fax 232251; e-mail dae@gouv.nc; internet www.dae.gouv.nc.

Department of Education (DENC): Immeuble Foch, 19 ave du Maréchal Foch, BP 8244, 98807 Nouméa Cedex; tel. 239600; fax 272921; e-mail denc@gouv.nc; internet www.denc.gouv.nc.

Department of Fiscal Affairs (DSF): Hôtel des Impôts, 13 rue de la Somme, BP D2, 98848 Nouméa Cedex; tel. 257500; fax 251166; e-mail dsf@gouv.nc; internet www.dsf.gouv.nc.

Department of Health and Social Services (DASS): 5 rue Général Galliéni, BP N4, 98851 Nouméa Cedex; tel. 243700; fax 243733; e-mail dass@gouv.nc; internet www.dass.gouv.nc.

Department of Human Resources and Civil Service (DRHFP): 18 ave Paul Doumer, BP M2, 98849 Nouméa Cedex; tel. 256112; fax 274700; e-mail drhfpnc@gouv.nc; internet www.drhfpnc.gouv.nc.

Department of Industry, Mines and Energy (DIMENC): 1 ter rue Edouard Unger, 1ère étage, Vallée du Tir, BP 465, 98845 Nouméa Cedex; tel. 270230; fax 272345; e-mail dimenc@gouv.nc; internet www.dimenc.gouv.nc.

Department of Infrastructure, Topography and Land Transport (DITTT): 1 bis rue Edouard Unger, 1ère étage, Vallée du Tir, BP A2, 98848 Nouméa Cedex; tel. 280300; fax 281760; e-mail dittt@ gouv.nc; internet www.dittt.gouv.nc.

Department of Labour and Employment (DTE): 12 rue de Verdun, BP 141, 98845 Nouméa Cedex; tel. 275572; fax 270494; e-mail dtenc@gouv.nc; internet www.dtnc.gouv.nc.

Department of Veterinary, Food and Rural Affairs (DAVAR): 209 rue Auguste Bénébig, Haut Magenta, BP 256, 98845 Nouméa Cedex; tel. 255100; fax 255129; e-mail davar@gouv.nc; internet www .davar.gouv.nc.

Department of Vocational Training (DFPC): 19 ave du Maréchal Foch, BP 110, 98845 Nouméa Cedex; tel. 246622; fax 281661; e-mail dfpc@gouv.nc; internet www.dfpc.gouv.nc.

Department of Youth and Sports (DJS): 23 rue Jean Jaurès, BP 810, 98845 Nouméa Cedex; tel. 252384; fax 254585; e-mail djs@gouv .nc; internet www.djs.gouv.nc.

Legislature

PROVINCIAL ASSEMBLIES

Members of the Provincial Assemblies are elected on a proportional basis for a five-year term. Each Provincial Assembly elects its President. A number of the members of the Provincial Assemblies sit together to make up the Congress of New Caledonia. The Assembly of the North Province has 22 members (including 15 sitting for the Congress), the Loyalty Islands 14 members (including seven for the Congress) and the South Province has 40 members (including 32 for the Congress).

North Province: BP 41, 98860 Koné; tel. 417100; fax 472475; e-mail presidence@province-nord.nc; internet www.province-nord.nc; Pres. PAUL NÉAOUTYINE (UNI).

South Province: Hôtel de la Province Sud, route des Artifices, Port Moselle, BP L1, 98849 Nouméa Cedex; tel. 258000; fax 274900; e-mail cabinet@province-sud.nc; internet www.province-sud.nc; Pres. PHILIPPE MICHEL (Calédonie Ensemble).

Loyalty Islands Province: BP 50, Wé, 98820 Lifou; tel. 455100; fax 451440; e-mail presidence@loyalty.nc; internet www.province-iles .nc; Pres. NÉKO HNÉPEUNE (UC-FLNKS).

Election, 11 May 2014 (official results by province)

Party	North	South	Loyalty Islands
L'Avenir en Partage. Ensemble, vers un Avenir Éclairé et Apaisé	—	16	—
Union Calédonienne-Front de Libération Nationale Kanak Socialiste (UC-FLNKS) . .	9	—	6
Union pour la Calédonie dans la France	—	8	—
Union Nationale pour l'Indépendance (UNI) . .	9	—	—
Front pour l'Unité . . .	—	9	—
Construisons notre Nation Arc en Ciel	—	7	—
Parti Travailliste	—	—	2
Dynamique Autochtone . .	—	—	2
Une Province Pour Tous . .	3	—	—
Union pour Construire les Loyauté	—	—	2
Palika Iles	—	—	2
Entente Provinciale Nord . .	1	—	—
Total	**22**	**40**	**14**

CONGRESS

A proportion of the members of the three Provincial Assemblies sit together, in Nouméa, as the Congress of New Caledonia. There are 54 members (32 from the South Province, 15 from the North Province and seven from the Loyalty Islands Province) of a total of 76 sitting in the Provincial Assemblies.

President: GAËL YANNO, Congrès de la Nouvelle-Calédonie, 1 blvd Vauban, BP P3, 98851 Nouméa Cedex; tel. 273129; fax 270219; e-mail courrier@congres.nc; internet www.congres.nc.

Election, 11 May 2014 (official results for New Caledonia as a whole)

Party	Votes	%	Seats
L'Avenir en Partage. Ensemble, vers un Avenir Éclairé et Apaisé	24,863	23.61	13
Union Calédonienne-Front de Libération Nationale Kanak Socialiste (UC-FLNKS) . .	13,602	12.92	9
Front pour l'Unité	13,649	12.97	7
Union pour la Calédonie dans la France	12,539	11.91	6
Construisons Notre Nation Arc en Ciel	12,289	11.67	6
Union Nationale pour l'Indépendance	8,876	8.43	6
Une Province pour Tous . .	2,561	2.43	2
Parti Travailliste	3,678	3.49	1
Entente Provinciale Nord . .	2,191	2.08	1
Palika Iles	2,053	1.95	1
Dynamique Autochtone . .	1,566	1.49	1
Union pour Construire les Loyauté	1,564	1.49	1
Front National	2,706	2.57	—
Convergence Pays	2,190	2.08	—
L'Autre Voix	939	0.89	—
Total	**105,266**	**100.00**	**54**

PARLIAMENT

Deputies to the French National Assembly: PHILIPPE GOMÈS (Divers droite-Calédonie Ensemble—DVD-CE), SONIA LAGARDE (DVD-CE).

Representatives to the French Senate: (elected in September 2011) PIERRE FROGIER (UMP), HILARION VENDÉGOU (UMP).

Political Organizations

L'Avenir Ensemble (AE): 2 bis blvd Vauban, 98800 Nouméa; tel. 281179; fax 281011; e-mail avenirensemble@lagoon.nc; internet www.avenirensemble.nc; f. 2004; combined list incl. fmr mems of Rassemblement pour la Calédonie dans la République and Alliance pour la Calédonie; anti-independence party; supports unification of all ethnic groups; Leader HAROLD MARTIN.

Calédonie Ensemble (CE): 40 rue de la République, 98807 Nouméa; tel. 248824; fax 288906; internet www.caledonie-ensemble .com; f. 2008; anti-independence party est. by fmr mems of L'Avenir Ensemble; contested the 2014 elections as two lists: L'Avenir en Partage. Ensemble, vers un Avenir Eclairé et Apaisé (in the South Province) and Une Province pour Tous (in the North Province); Leader PHILIPPE GOMÈS.

Construisons Notre Nation Arc en Ciel: internet construisonsnotrenationarcenciel.com; list of pro-independence candidates that contested the 2014 elections; Leader ROCH WAMYTAN.

Convergence Pays: Nouméa; tel. 816333; e-mail contact@convergence-pays.nc; internet www.convergence-pays.nc; f. 2012; Leader STÉPHANE HENOCQUE.

Entente Provinciale Nord: electoral list that contested the 2014 elections in the North Province; allied to the Front pour l'Unité; Leader FRANCIS EURIBOA.

Fédération des Comités de Coordination des Indépendantistes (FCCI): 42 ter rue de Verdun, Nouméa; internet www.fcci-nc .org; f. 1998; est. by breakaway group of FLNKS; includes Front du Développement des Iles Loyauté and Front Uni de Libération Kanak; Leaders RAPHAËL MAPOU, FRANÇOIS BURCK.

Front Calédonien (FC): extreme right-wing; Leader M. SARRAN.

Front de Libération Nationale Kanak et Socialiste (FLNKS): 9 rue Austerlitz, Immeuble SAM3, 98800 Nouméa Cedex; tel. 265880; fax 265887; f. 1984; est. following dissolution of Front Indépendantiste; pro-independence; Spokesman VICTOR TUTUGORO; a grouping of the following parties:

Parti de Libération Kanak (PALIKA): f. 1975; Leader PAUL NÉAOUTYINE.

Rassemblement Démocratique Océanien (RDO): Nouméa; f. 1994; est. by breakaway faction of Union Océanienne (f. 1989); supports Kanak sovereignty; Chair. ALOISIO SAKO.

Union Calédonienne (UC): 4 rue de la Gazelle, Aérodrome de Magenta, Nouméa; tel. 272599; fax 276257; internet unioncaledonienne.com; f. 1952; pro-independence; left FLNKS coalition prior to elections of 2004 but subsequently returned; 11,000 mems; Pres. DANIEL GOA; Sec. Gen. GÉRARD REIGNIER.

Union Progressiste Mélanésienne (UPM): f. 1974; est. as Union Progressiste Multiraciale; Pres. VICTOR TUTUGORO; Sec.-Gen. RENÉ POROU.

Front pour l'Unité (FPU): electoral alliance formed to contest the 2014 elections; including members of Le Rassemblement-UMP and L'Avenir Ensemble; Leader CYNTHIA LIGEARD.

Front National (FN): 12 bis rue du Général Mangin, 98800 Nouméa; tel. 258068; fax 258064; e-mail george@province-sud.nc; internet www.frontnational.com; right-wing; Leader GUY GEORGE.

Génération Calédonienne: f. 1995; youth-based; aims to combat corruption in public life; Pres. JEAN-RAYMOND POSTIC.

Le Groupe MUR: BP 1211, 98845 Nouméa Cedex; tel. and fax 419385; coalition of Mouvement des Citoyens Calédoniens, Union Océanienne (f. 1989) and Rassemblement des Océaniens dans la Calédonie; Jt Pres TINO MANUOHALALO (MCC), MICHEL HEMA (UO), MIKAELE TUIFUA (ROC).

Libération Kanak Socialiste (LKS): Maré, Loyalty Islands; moderate, pro-independence; Leader NIDOÏSH NAISSELINE.

Le Mouvement de la Diversité (LMD): 98802 Nouméa; tel. 997700; fax 240620; f. 2009; allied to L'Avenir Ensemble; Pres. SIMON LOUECKHOTE.

Parti Travailliste: Nouméa; f. 2007; pro-independence; Pres. LOUIS KOTRA UREGEI.

Le Rassemblement-UMP: 13 rue de Sébastopol, BP 306, 98845 Nouméa; tel. 282620; fax 284033; e-mail contact@rassemblement.nc; internet www.rassemblement.nc; f. 1976; est. as Rassemblement pour la Calédonie dans la République; affiliated to the metropolitan Union pour un Mouvement Populaire; in favour of retaining the status quo in New Caledonia; Leader PIERRE FROGIER; Sec.-Gen. THIERRY SANTA.

Rassemblement pour la Calédonie (RPC): 5 rue Lamartine, Orphanage, 98800 Nouméa; internet rpc1.e-monsite.com; f. 2006; Pres. ISABELLE LAFLEUR.

Union Calédonienne Renouveau (UC Renouveau): Hôtel de la province des îles Loyauté, BP 50, Wé Lifou; tel. 455100; fax 451440; Leader JACQUES LALIE.

Union Nationale pour l'Indépendance (UNI): c/o Le Congrès de la Nouvelle Calédonie, Nouméa ; electoral coalition comprising all the constituents of the FLNKS except the UC; Leader PAUL NÉAOUTYINE.

Union pour la Calédonie dans la France: Nouméa; internet ucf .nc; Head SONIA BACKES.

A union of the following parties:

Mouvement Populaire Calédonien (MPC): Nouméa; internet m-p-c.nc; f. 2013; est. following a split in Le Rassemblement—UMP; Pres. GAËL YANNO.

Mouvement Républicain Calédonien: e-mail mouvementrepublicaincaledonien@gmail.com; internet www .mouvement-republicain-caledonien.com; Pres. PHILIPPE BLAISE.

Rassemblement pour la Calédonie: 5 rue Lamartine, Orphelinat; tel. 286800; e-mail pc@mls.nc; internet www.rpc1.e-monsite .com; Pres. ISABELLE LAFLEUR.

Other political organizations and lists that contested the elections of May 2014 included: Dynamique Autochtone, L'Autre Voix and Union pour Construire les Loyauté.

Judicial System

Court of Administrative Law: 85 ave du Général de Gaulle, Immeuble Carcopino 3000, 4ème étage, BP 63, 98851 Nouméa Cedex; tel. 250630; fax 250631; e-mail greffe.ta-noumea@juradm.fr; internet www.ta-noumea.juradm.fr; f. 1984; Pres. RÉGIS FRAISSE.

Court of Appeal: Palais de Justice, BP F4, 98848 Nouméa; tel. 279350; fax 269185; e-mail pp.ca-noumea@justice.fr; internet www .ca-noumea.justice.fr; First Pres. THIERRY DRACK; Procurator-Gen. ANNIE BRUNET-FUSTER.

Court of the First Instance: 2 blvd Extérieur, BP F4, 98848 Nouméa; tel. 279372; fax 276531; e-mail p.tpi-noumea@justice.fr; Pres. JEAN PRADAL; Procurator of the Republic CLAIRE LANET; there are 2 subsidiary courts, with resident magistrates, at Koné (North Province) and Wé (Loyalty Islands Province).

Customary Senate of New Caledonia: Sénat Coutumier, 68 ave J. Cook, BP 1059, Nouville; tel. 242000; fax 249320; e-mail senat-coutumier@gouv.nc; f. 1990; consulted by Local Assembly and French Govt on matters affecting land, Kanak tradition and identity; composed of 16 elected mems (2 from the regional council of each of the 8 custom areas) for a 5-year period; Pres. PAUL VAKIÉ.

Religion

The majority of the population is Christian, with Roman Catholics comprising about 55% of the total in 2002. About 3% of the inhabitants, mainly Indonesians, are Muslims.

CHRISTIANITY

The Roman Catholic Church

The Territory comprises a single archdiocese, with an estimated 131,000 adherents in December 2007. The Archbishop participates in the Catholic Bishops' Conference of the Pacific, based in Fiji.

Archbishop of Nouméa: Most Rev. MICHEL-MARIE-BERNARD CAL-VET, Archevêché, 4 rue Mgr-Fraysse, BP 3, 98845 Nouméa; tel. 265353; fax 265352; e-mail archeveche@ddec.nc; internet www .ddec.nc/diocese.

The Anglican Communion

Within the Church of the Province of Melanesia, New Caledonia forms part of the diocese of Vanuatu. The Archbishop of the Province is the Bishop of Central Melanesia (resident in Honiara, Solomon Islands). At mid-2000 there were an estimated 160 adherents.

Protestant Churches

At mid-2000 there were an estimated 30,000 adherents.

Eglise Evangélique en Nouvelle-Calédonie et aux Iles Loyauté: BP 277, Nouméa; f. 1960; Pres. Rev. SAILALI PASSA; Gen. Sec. Rev. TELL KASARHEROU.

Other churches active in the Territory include the Assembly of God, the Free Evangelical Church, the New Apostolic Church, the Pentecostal Evangelical Church, the Presbyterian Church and the Tahitian Evangelical Church. At mid-2000 there were an estimated 15,500 adherents professing other forms of Christianity.

The Press

L'Avenir Calédonien: 10 rue Gambetta, Nouméa; organ of the Union Calédonienne; Dir GABRIEL PAÏTA.

La Calédonie Agricole: BP 111, 98845 Nouméa Cedex; tel. 243160; fax 284587; internet www.chambres-agriculture.fr; quarterly; official publ. of the Chambre d'Agriculture; Pres. GÉRARD PASCO; Man. YANNICK COUETE; Chief Editors PIERRE ARDORINO, SOPHIE GOLFIER; circ. 4,000.

Le Chien Bleu: BP 16018, Nouméa; tel. 288505; fax 261819; e-mail courrier@lechienbleu.nc; internet www.lechienbleu.nc; monthly; satirical; Man. Editor ETIENNE DUTAILLY.

Eglise de Nouvelle-Calédonie: BP 3, 98845 Nouméa; fax 265352; f. 1976; monthly; official publ. of the Roman Catholic Church; circ. 450.

Les Infos: 42 route de l'Anse-Vata, BP 8134, 98807 Nouméa; tel. 251808; fax 251882; e-mail lesinfos@lagoon.nc; weekly; Editor-in-Chief THIERRY SQUILLARIO.

Journal Officiel de la Nouvelle-Calédonie: Imprimerie Administrative, BP M2, 98849, Nouméa Cedex; tel. 239423; fax 256021; e-mail webmestre.juridoc@gouv.nc; internet www.juridoc.gouv.nc; f. 1853; est. as *Bulletin Officiel de la Nouvelle-Calédonie*; present name adopted in 1988; only the paper version is official; twice a week; publ. by Govt of New Caledonia; record of state legislative devts in New Caledonia.

Mwà Véé: Centre Tjibaou, BP 378, 98845 Nouméa; tel. 414555; fax 414556; e-mail adck@adck.nc; f. 1993; quarterly; French; publ. by l'Agence de Développement de la Culture Kanak; Kanak history, culture and heritage; Publr EMMANUEL KASARHE'ROU; Editor GÉRARD DEL RIO.

Les Nouvelles Calédoniennes: 41–43 rue de Sébastopol, BP G5, 98848 Nouméa; tel. 272584; fax 281627; e-mail xserre@canl.nc; internet www.lnc.nc; f. 1971; daily; Publr FRÉDÉRIC AURAND; Gen. Man. FRANÇOIS LEVASSOR; Editor-in-Chief XAVIER SERRE; circ. 20,000.

Tazar: Immeuble Gallieni II, 12 rue de Verdun, 98800 Nouméa; tel. 282277; fax 283443; monthly; publ. by Mission d'Insertion des Jeunes de la Province Sud; youth.

Télé 7 Jours: Route de Vélodrome, BP 2080, 98846 Nouméa Cedex; tel. 284598; weekly.

NEWS AGENCY

Agence France-Presse (AFP): 15 rue Docteur Guégan, 98800 Nouméa; tel. 263033; fax 278699; Correspondent FRANCK MADOEUF.

Publishers

Editions d'Art Calédoniennes: 3 rue Guynemer, BP 1626, Nouméa; tel. 277633; fax 281526; art, reprints, travel.

Editions du Santal: 5 bis rue Emile-Trianon, 98846 Nouméa; tel. and fax 262533; history, art, travel, birth and wedding cards; Dir PAUL-JEAN STAHL.

Grain de Sable: BP 577, 98845 Nouméa; tel. and fax 273057; e-mail graindesable@canl.nc; internet www.pacific-bookin.com; literature, travel; Publr LAURENCE VIALLARD.

Ile de Lumière: BP 8401, Nouméa Sud; tel. 289858; history, politics.

Savannah Editeur SNP: Yacht Marianne, BP 3086, 98846 Nouméa; tel. 784711; e-mail savannahmarc@hotmail.com; f. 1994; est. as Savannah Edns; present name adopted in 2006; sports, travel, leisure; Publr JOËL MARC.

Société d'Etudes Historiques de la Nouvelle-Calédonie: BP 63, 98845 Nouméa; tel. 767155; e-mail seh-nc@lagoon.nc; f. 1969; Pres. VALET GABRIEL.

Broadcasting and Communications

TELECOMMUNICATIONS

Citius: Immeuble Administratif, 1 rue du Contre Amiral Joseph Bouzet, Route de Nouville, 98800 Nouméa; tel. 266687; fax 266668; e-mail infoweb@citius.nc; internet www.citius.nc; f. 2008; Man. PASCAL BOUTTIER.

Offices des Postes et Télécommunications (OPT): Le Waruna, 2 rue Monchovet, Port Plaisance, 98841 Nouméa Cedex; tel. 268217; fax 262927; e-mail direction@opt.nc; internet www.opt.nc; provides postal and fixed-line tel. services, and operates Mobilis mobile cellular tel. network (f. 2003); Pres. THIERRY CORNAILLE.

BROADCASTING

Radio

Nouvelle-Calédonie 1ère: Nouvelle-Calédonie 1ère, 1 rue Maréchal Leclerc, Mont Coffyn, BP G3, 98848 Nouméa Cedex; tel. 239999; fax 239975; e-mail comrfonc@francetv.fr; internet nouvellecaledonie .la1ere.fr; f. 1942; fmrly Radiodiffusion Française d'Outre-mer (RFO); French; relays Radio Australia's French service; Dir-Gen. MICHEL KOPS; Regional Dir WALLES KOTRA.

NRJ Nouvelle-Calédonie: 41–43 rue Sébastopol, BP G5, 98848 Nouméa; tel. 263434; fax 279447; e-mail nrj@nrj.nc; internet www .nrj.nc; f. 1984; Dir RICARDO GREMY.

Radio Djiido (Kanal K): Résidence La Caravelle, 3 rue Sainte Cécile, Vallée du Tir, BP 10459, 98805 Nouméa Cedex; tel. 778768; fax 272187; e-mail radiodjiido@radiodjiido.nc; internet www.radiodjiido.nc; f. 1985; pro-independence community station; broadcasts in French; socio-cultural programmes; 60% local news,

30% regional, 10% international; Station Man. THIERRY KAMÉR-ÉMOIN; Editor-in-Chief CÉDRICK WAKAHUGNEME.

Radio Océane: 1 ave d'Auteuil, Lotissement FSH, Koutio, 98835 Dumbéa; tel. 410095; fax 410099; e-mail oceane.fm@lagoon.nc; Dir YANN DUVAL.

Radio Rythme Bleu: 8 ave Foch, BP 578, 98845 Nouméa Cedex; tel. 254646; fax 284928; e-mail rrb@lagoon.nc; internet www.rrb.nc; f. 1984; music and local, nat. and int. news; Pres. JEAN-YVES PELTIER; Dir ELIZABETH NOUAR.

Television

RFO-Télé Nouvelle-Calédonie: Réseau France Outre-mer (RFO), 1 rue Maréchal Leclerc, Mont Coffyn, BP G3, 98848 Nouméa Cedex; tel. 239999; fax 239975; internet www.rfo.fr; f. 1965; part of the France Télévisions group, France; 3 channels; Gen. Man. BERNARD JOYEUX; Editor-in-Chief GONZAGUE DE LA BOURDONNAYE.

Canal+ Calédonie: 30 rue de la Somme, BP 1797, 98845 Nouméa; tel. 265343; fax 265338; e-mail abonnement@canal-caledonie.com; internet www.canalcaledonie.com; subsidiary of Canal Plus, France; subscription service; broadcasts 24 hours daily; CEO SERGE LAMAGNÈRE.

Canal Outre-mer (Canal+): Nouméa; f. 1995; cable service.

NCTV: Immeuble Koné-La Grange, rue de la Caférie, 98860 Koné; tel. 475880; internet www.nctv.nc; f. 2013; first indigenous television station; Head JEAN PIERRE DJAIWE.

Finance

(cap. = capital; res = reserves; dep. = deposits; m. = million; brs = branches; amounts in francs CFP unless otherwise stated)

BANKING

Agence Française de Développement: 1 rue Barleux, BP J1, 98849 Nouméa Cedex; tel. 242600; fax 282413; e-mail afdnoumea@afd.fr; internet nc.afd.fr; Gen. Man. JEAN-MICHEL SEVERINO; Pres. LAURENCE TUBIANA.

Banque Calédonienne d'Investissement (BCI): 54 ave de la Victoire, BP K5, 98849 Nouméa; tel. 256565; fax 274035; e-mail bci@bci.nc; internet www.bci.nc; f. 1988; cap. 7,500m.; Chair. DIDIER LEROUX; Dir-Gen. JEAN-PIERRE GIANOTTI.

Banque de Nouvelle-Calédonie: 10 ave Foch, BP L3, 98849 Nouméa Cedex; tel. 257402; fax 275619; e-mail contact@bnc.nc; internet www.bnc.nc; f. 1974; adopted present name in 2002; 95.8% owned by Financière Océor, France; cap. 7,999m., dep. 96,878m. (Dec. 2009); Pres. PHILIPPE GARSUAULT; Gen. Man. OLIVIER GUEDSON; 7 brs.

BNP Paribas Nouvelle-Calédonie (France): 37 ave Henri Lafleur, BP K3, 98849 Nouméa Cedex; tel. 258400; fax 258469; e-mail bnp.nc@bnpparibas.com; internet www.bnpparibas.nc; f. 1969 as Banque Nationale de Paris; present name adopted in 2001; cap. €28.0m. (Dec. 2011); CEO PATRICK SOULAGES; 10 brs.

Société Générale Calédonienne de Banque: 44 rue de l'Alma, Siège et Agence Principale, BP G2, 98848 Nouméa Cedex; tel. 256300; fax 256322; e-mail svp.sgcb@sgcb.nc; internet www.sgcb.com; f. 1981; cap. 1,068.3m., res 8,900m., dep. 135,024.3m. (Dec. 2010); Gen. Man. JEAN-PIERRE DUFOUR; Chair. JEAN-LOUIS MATTEI; 21 brs.

INSURANCE

AGF Vie & AGF IART Nouvelle-Calédonie: 99 ave du Générale de Gaulle, BP 152, 98845 Nouméa; tel. 283838; fax 281628; e-mail agfvienc@agfvie.nc; life and general non-life insurance.

GAN Pacifique: 30 route de la Baie des Dames, Immeuble Le Centre-Ducos, BP 7953, 98800 Nouméa Cedex; tel. 243070; fax 278884; e-mail ganoumea@canl.nc; subsidiary of GAN Assurances, France; general non-life insurance; Chair. JEAN-FRANÇOIS LEMOUX; Dir-Gen. PATRICK REYNAUD.

Poe-ma Insurances: 3 rue Sébastopol, BP 8069, 98807 Nouméa; tel. 274263; fax 274267; e-mail info@poema.nc; Bureau Man. FRÉDÉRIC DUCOS.

Trade and Industry

DEVELOPMENT ORGANIZATIONS

Agence de Développement de la Culture Kanak (ADCK): Centre Culturel Tjibaou, rue des Accords de Matignon, BP 378, 98845 Nouméa Cedex; tel. 414555; fax 414546; e-mail adck@adck.nc; internet www.adck.nc; Pres. MARIE-CLAUDE TJIBAOU; Dir EMMANUEL KASARHEROU.

Agence de Développement Economique de la Nouvelle-Calédonie (ADECAL): 15 rue Guynemer, BP 2384, 98846 Nouméa Cedex; tel. 249077; fax 249087; e-mail adecal@offratel.nc; internet www.adecal.nc; f. 1995; promotes investment within New Caledonia; Gen. Man. JEAN-MICHEL ARLIE.

Agence de Développement Rural et d'Aménagement Foncier (ADRAF): 1 rue de la Somme, BP 4228, 98847 Nouméa Cedex; tel. 258600; fax 258604; e-mail adraf@adraf.nc; internet www.adraf.nc; f. 1986, reorg. 1989; acquisition and redistribution of land; Chair. MICHEL MATHIEU; Dir-Gen. JULES HMALOKO.

Conseil Economique et Social: 30 route Baie des Dames, Immeuble Le Centre, Ducos, BP 4766, 98847 Nouméa Cedex; tel. 278517; fax 278509; e-mail ces@gouv.nc; internet www.ces.gouv.nc; represents trade unions and other orgs involved in economic, social and cultural life; Pres. YVES TISSANDIER; Sec.-Gen. FRANÇOIS-PAUL BUFNOIR.

Institut Calédonien de Participation (ICAP): 1 rue Barleux, BP J1, 98849 Nouméa; tel. 276218; fax 282280; e-mail icap@icap.nc; internet www.icap.nc; f. 1989; est. to finance devt projects and encourage the Kanak population to participate in the market economy; Pres. PAUL NÉAOUTYINE; Man. YVES GOYETCHE.

Institut pour le Développement des Compétences en Nouvelle-Calédonie: 1 rue de la Somme, BP 497, 98845 Nouméa Cedex; tel. 281082; fax 272079; e-mail idc.nc@idcnc.nc; internet www.idcnc.nc; f. 2006; Dir PHILIPPE MARTIN.

Société de Développement et d'Investissement des Iles Loyauté (SODIL SA): 12 rue du Général Mangin, Immeuble Richelieu, BP 2217, 98846 Nouméa Cedex; tel. 276663; fax 276709; e-mail sodil@lagoon.nc; f. 1991; financing, promotion and sustainable devt of industry, tourism and artisanal cos; priority areas are transport, food-processing, aquaculture, and regional and int. tourism; Pres. HNAEJË HAMU; Man. SAMUEL HNEPEUNE.

Société d'Equipement de Nouvelle-Calédonie (SECAL): 28 rue du Général Mangin, BP 2517, 98846 Nouméa Cedex; tel. 232666; fax 232676; e-mail contact@secal.nc; internet www.secal.nc; f. 1971; urban management and devt, public sector construction and civil engineering; Pres. SIMONE MIGNARD.

Société de Financement et de Développement de la Province Sud (PROMOSUD): BP 295, 98845 Nouméa Cedex; tel. 241972; fax 271326; e-mail info@promosud.nc; internet www.promosud.nc; f. 1991; financing, promotion and economic devt of cos in priority sectors, incl. tourism, fishing and aquaculture, and processing industries; Pres. PIERRE BRETEGNIER; Man. THIERRY PAYEN.

Société de Financement et d'Investissement de la Province Nord (SOFINOR): 85 ave du Général de Gaulle, BP 66, 98800 Nouméa; tel. 281353; fax 281567; e-mail dirgen@smsp.nc; internet www.sofinor.nc; f. 1990; economic devt, management and financing; priority areas include mining and metal production, aquaculture and fishing, tourism, transport, real estate and engineering; Pres. GUIGUI DOUNEHOTE; Man. LOUIS MAPOU.

CHAMBERS OF COMMERCE

Chambre d'Agriculture: 3 rue A. Desmazures, BP 111, 98845 Nouméa Cedex; tel. 243160; fax 284587; e-mail direction@canc.nc; f. 1909; Pres. GÉRARD PASCO; Dir YANNICK COUETTE; 33 mems.

Chambre de Commerce et d'Industrie: 15 rue de Verdun, BP M3, 98849 Nouméa Cedex; tel. 243100; fax 243131; e-mail cci@cci.nc; internet www.cci.nc; f. 1879; Pres. ANDRÉ DESPLAT; Gen. Man. MICHEL MERZEAU; 12,000 mems.

Chambre de Métiers et de l'Artisanat: 10 ave James Cook, BP 4186, 98846 Nouméa Cedex; tel. 282337; fax 282729; e-mail cma@cma.nc; internet www.cma.nc; Pres. JEAN-CLAUDE MERLET; Sec.-Gen. PAUL SANCHEZ.

EMPLOYERS' ORGANIZATION

MEDEF de Nouvelle-Calédonie (Fédération Patronale des Chefs d'Entreprise en Nouvelle-Calédonie): 6 rue Jean Jaurès, 98800 Nouméa Cedex; tel. 273525; fax 274037; e-mail medefnc@medef.nc; internet www.medef.nc; f. 1936; represents leading cos of New Caledonia in defence of professional interests, co-ordination, documentation and research in socio-economic fields; affiliated to Mouvement des Entreprises de France; Pres. JEAN-FRANÇOIS BOUILLAGUET.

UTILITIES

Electricity

Electricité et Eau de Nouvelle-Calédonie (EEC): 15 rue Jean Chalier, PK 4, 98800 Nouméa Cedex; tel. 463636; fax 463510; e-mail clientele@eec.nc; internet www.eec.nc; f. 1929; est. as UNLECO; present name adopted in 1984; subsidiary of GDF SUEZ, France; producers and distributors of electricity; Pres. and Dir-Gen. FRANÇOIS GUICHARD; Gen. Man. YVES MORAULT.

Société Néo-Calédonienne d'Energie (ENERCAL): 87 ave du Général de Gaulle, BP C1, 98848 Nouméa Cedex; tel. 250250; fax 250253; e-mail dg@enercal.nc; internet www.enercal.nc; f. 1955; 16%

owned by EDEV, France; production and distribution of electricity; Chair. PHILIPPE GOMES; CEO JEAN-MICHEL DEVÉZA.

Water

Société Calédonienne des Eaux (CDE): 13 rue Edmond Harbulot, PK 6, BP 812, 98845 Nouméa Cedex; tel. 413737; fax 433796; e-mail clientele@cde.nc; water distribution; Gen. Man. ALAIN CARBONEL.

TRADE UNIONS

Confédération Générale des Travailleurs de Nouvelle-Calédonie (COGETRA): Vallée du Tir.

Confédération Générale du Travail-Force Ouvrière de Nouvelle-Calédonie (CGT-FO NC): 13 rue Jules Ferry, BP R2, 98851 Nouméa Cedex; tel. 274950; fax 278202; e-mail cgtfonc@lagoon.nc; f. 1984; Sec.-Gen. JACQUES BERNALEAU.

Confédération Syndicale des Travailleurs de Nouvelle-Calédonie (CSTNC): 49 rue Auer Ducos, 98800 Nouméa; tel. and fax 269648; e-mail cst-nc@laposte.net; Sec.-Gen. SYLVAIN NÉA.

Union Territoriale de la Confédération Française de l'Encadrement-Confédération Générale des Cadres (UT-CFE-CGC): Centre Commercial La Belle Vie, 224 rue Jacques Ikékawé, PK 6, BP 30536, 98895 Nouméa Cedex; tel. 410300; fax 410310; e-mail utcfecgc@utcfecgc.nc; internet www.utcfecgc.nc; f. 1996; territorial br. of the Confédération Française de l'Encadrement-Confédération Générale des Cadres; Pres. CHRISTOPHE COULSON; Sec.-Gen. JEAN MARIE ARMAND.

Transport

ROADS

In 2006 there was a total of 5,622 km of roads in New Caledonia.

Société Anonyme des Voies Express à Péage (SAVEXPRESS): 15 rue de Verdun, BP M3, 98849 Nouméa Cedex; tel. 411930; fax 412899; e-mail savexpress@savexpress.nc; f. 1979; highway management and devt; Chair. CYNTHIA LIGEARD; Man. MAXIME CHASSOT.

SHIPPING

Most traffic is through the port of Nouméa. Passenger and cargo services, linking Nouméa to other towns and islands, are regular and frequent. There is also a harbour for yachts and pleasure craft at Nouméa.

Port Autonome de la Nouvelle-Calédonie: 34 ave James Cook, BP 14, 98845 Nouméa Cedex; tel. 255000; fax 275490; e-mail noumeaportnc@canl.nc; Port Man. PHILIPPE LAFLEUR; Harbour Master JEAN LEDEN.

Moana Services: 2 bis rue Berthelot, BP 2099, 98846 Nouméa; tel. 273898; fax 259315; e-mail moana@canl.nc; internet www.moana.nc; f. 2000; shipping and logistics agency; representatives for Moana Shipping (Wallis), Maersk Line (Denmark) and PFL Cargo (New Zealand); Gen. Man. LUCIEN BOURGADE.

SEM de la Baie de la Moselle (SODEMO): 6 rue de la Frégate-Nivôse, BP 2960, 98846 Nouméa; tel. 277197; fax 277129; e-mail contact@sodemo.nc; internet www.sodemo.nc; f. 1987; operates Port Moselle for pleasure craft and boatyard; Pres. JEAN WASMAN; Man. FRANÇOIS LE BRUN.

Sofrana NC: 14 ave James Cook, BP 1602, 98845 Nouméa; tel. 275191; fax 272611; e-mail info@sofrana.nc; internet www.sofrana.nc; f. 1968; subsidiary of Sofrana Holding; shipping agents and stevedores; barge operators; Chair. JEAN-BAPTISTE LEROUX; Gen. Man. FRANÇOIS BURNOUF.

CIVIL AVIATION

There is an international airport, La Tontouta, 47 km from Nouméa, and an internal network, centred on Magenta airport, which provides air services linking Nouméa to other towns and islands. A major expansion of the airport at La Tontouta was effected in 2008–12. Air Calédonie International (Aircalin) operates flights to various Asia-Pacific destinations. Other airlines providing services to the island include Air New Zealand, Air Vanuatu and Qantas.

Air Calédonie: Aérodrome, 100 rue Roger Gervolino, BP 212, 98845 Nouméa Cedex; tel. 250302; fax 281340; e-mail direction@ air-caledonie.nc; internet www.air-caledonie.nc; f. 1954; services throughout mainland New Caledonia and its islands; operates 4 aircraft; Pres. NIDOÏSH NAISSELINE; CEO WILLIAM IHAGE.

Air Calédonie International (Aircalin): 47 rue de Sébastopol, BP 3736, 98846 Nouméa Cedex; tel. 265500; fax 265561; internet www .aircalin.com; f. 1983; 27% owned by Agence pour la Desserte Aérienne de la Nouvelle-Calédonie (NC Air Transport Agency), 72% by Caisse Nationale des Caisses d'Epargne et de Prévoyance, 1% by others; services to Sydney and Brisbane (Australia), Auckland (New Zealand), Nadi (Fiji), Papeete (French Polynesia), Wallis and Futuna Islands, Port Vila (Vanuatu), Osaka and Tokyo (Japan) and Seoul (Republic of Korea); Chair. and Dir BERNARD DELADRIÈRE; Pres. and CEO JEAN-MICHEL MASSON.

Cofely Airport Pacific: La Tontouta International Airport, BP 5, 98840 La Tontouta; tel. 352600; fax 352601; e-mail clotilde.david@ cofely-airport-pacific.nc; f. 1995; fmrly Tontouta Air Service; renamed as above 2011; owned by Endel Group; operates Tontouta airport and freight management services; Gen. Man. ELVIR PEROCEVIC.

Tourism

The number of visitors arriving by air in New Caledonia decreased from 112,204 in 2012 to 107,753 in 2013; in the latter year 36.4% came from France, 14.6% from Australia and 14.5% from Japan. The number of visiting cruise-ship passengers rose from 277,941 in 2012 to 385,523 in 2013. A total of 2,643 hotel rooms were available in 2004. In 2010 receipts from tourism amounted to €133.3m. New Caledonia hosted the Pacific Games in 2011.

GIE Nouvelle-Calédonie Tourisme Point Sud: Galerie Nouméa Centre, 20 rue Anatole France, BP 688, 98845 Nouméa Cedex; tel. 242080; fax 242070; e-mail info@nctps.com; internet www .nouvellecaledonietourisme-sud.com; f. 2001; Dir-Gen. JEAN-MICHEL FOUTREIN.

GIE Nouvelle-Calédonie Tourisme Province Nord: Centre Commercial Le Village, 35 ave du Maréchal Foch, BP 115, 98845 Nouméa Cedex; tel. 277805; fax 274887; e-mail info@ tourismeprovincenord.nc; internet www.tourismeprovincenord.nc; f. 2003; Dir JACQUELINE RIAHI.

Defence

As assessed at November 2014, France maintained a 1,450-strong force, including army and navy personnel, as well as a gendarmerie, in New Caledonia. The French naval command for the Pacific area is based in French Polynesia.

Commander of the French Armed Forces in New Caledonia: Brig.-Gen. JEAN-FRANÇOIS PARLANTI.

Education

Education is compulsory for 10 years between six and 16 years of age. Schools are operated by both the state and churches, under the supervision of three Departments of Education: the Provincial department responsible for primary level education, the New Caledonian department responsible for primary level inspection, and the state department responsible for secondary level education. Primary education begins at six years of age, and lasts for five years; secondary education, beginning at 11 years of age, comprises a first cycle of four years and a second, three-year cycle. Overall, in 2006 73.7% of pre-primary and primary pupils, and 67.6% of secondary pupils, were enrolled at public institutions. In 2013 there were 12,710 pupils enrolled in pre-primary education, 22,437 in primary education (including special education) and 33,314 in secondary education. Four institutions provide higher education. Students may also attend universities in France. In 1987 the French University of the Pacific (based in French Polynesia) was established, with a centre in Nouméa, and divided into two universities in 1999. Several other vocational tertiary education centres exist in New Caledonia, including a teacher-training college and two agricultural colleges. In 2003 total public expenditure on education was 66,914m. francs CFP, of which some 42,362m. francs CFP was provided by the French state.

GABON

Introductory Survey

LOCATION, CLIMATE, LANGUAGE, RELIGION, FLAG, CAPITAL

The Gabonese Republic is an equatorial country on the west coast of Africa, with Equatorial Guinea and Cameroon to the north and the Republic of the Congo to the south and east. The climate is tropical, with an average annual temperature of 26°C (79°F) and an average annual rainfall of 2,490 mm (98 ins). The official language is French, but Fang (in the north) and Bantu dialects (in the south) are also widely spoken. About 60% of the population are Christians, mainly Roman Catholics. Most of the remainder follow animist beliefs. The national flag (proportions 3 by 4) has three equal horizontal stripes, of green, yellow and blue. The capital is Libreville.

CONTEMPORARY POLITICAL HISTORY

Historical Context

Formerly a province of French Equatorial Africa, Gabon was granted internal autonomy in November 1958, and proceeded to full independence on 17 August 1960. Léon M'Ba, the new Republic's President, established Gabon as a one-party state. Following his death in November 1967, M'Ba was succeeded by the Vice-President, Albert-Bernard (later Omar) Bongo, who organized a new ruling party, the Parti Démocratique Gabonais (PDG). Gabon enjoyed political stability and rapid economic growth in the 1970s, underpinned by substantial foreign investment in the development and exploitation of its petroleum reserves. However, the social and economic problems that accompanied the subsequent decline in world petroleum prices led to the emergence in 1981 of the opposition Mouvement de Redressement National (MORENA), which demanded the restoration of a multi-party system and formed a government-in-exile in Paris, France.

Domestic Political Affairs

In May 1989 the Chairman of MORENA, Fr Paul M'Ba Abessole, visited Gabon and, after a meeting with Bongo, announced that he and many of his supporters would return to Gabon. In January 1990 representatives of MORENA announced that M'Ba Abessole had been dismissed from the leadership of the movement. M'Ba Abessole subsequently formed a breakaway faction, known as MORENA des Bûcherons (renamed Rassemblement National des Bûcherons—RNB—in 1991 to avoid confusion with the rival MORENA—Originels).

A number of arrests took place in October 1989, following an alleged conspiracy to overthrow the Government reportedly initiated by Pierre Mamboundou, the leader of the Union du Peuple Gabonais (UPG, an opposition movement based in Paris). In early 1990 Bongo announced that extensive political reforms, including a multi-party system, were to be introduced at the end of a five-year transitional period. In March–April a national conference, attended by representatives of more than 70 political organizations, rejected these proposals and demanded the immediate establishment of a multi-party system and the formation of a new government, which would hold office only until legislative elections could take place. Bongo acceded to the decisions of the conference, and in late April Casimir Oyé Mba, the Governor of the Banque des Etats de l'Afrique Centrale, was appointed Prime Minister of a transitional administration, which included several opposition members. In May constitutional changes were approved that would facilitate the transition to a multi-party political system. Future elections to the presidency would be contested by more than one candidate, and the tenure of office would be reduced to five years, renewable only once.

Legislative elections were scheduled for 16 and 23 September 1990. The first round of the elections was disrupted by violent protests by voters who claimed that the PDG was engaging in electoral fraud. Following further allegations of widespread electoral malpractices, results in 32 constituencies were declared invalid, although the election of 58 candidates (of whom 36 were members of the PDG) was confirmed. The interim Government subsequently conceded that electoral irregularities had taken place, and further voting was postponed until 21 and 28 October.

At the elections the PDG won an overall majority in the 120-member Assemblée Nationale (National Assembly), with 62 seats, while opposition candidates secured 55 seats.

In November 1990 a Government of National Unity, under Oyé Mba, was formed. Sixteen posts were allocated to members of the PDG, while the remaining eight portfolios were distributed among members of five opposition parties. A new draft Constitution, which was promulgated on 22 December, endorsed reforms that had been included in the transitional Constitution, introduced in May. Further measures included the proposed establishment of an upper house, the Sénat (Senate). A Constitutional Council was to replace the administrative chamber of the Supreme Court, and a National Communications Council was to be created.

The final composition of the National Assembly was determined in March 1991, when elections took place in five constituencies, where the results had been annulled, owing to alleged malpractice. Following the completion of the elections, the PDG held a total of 66 seats in the National Assembly, while various opposition groups held 54 seats. The two most prominent opposition movements, the Parti Gabonais du Progrès (PGP) and the RNB, held 19 and 17 seats, respectively.

In May 1991 six opposition parties formed an alliance, the Coordination de l'Opposition Démocratique (COD), in protest against the delay in the implementation of the new Constitution. The COD also demanded the appointment of a new Prime Minister, the abolition of certain institutions under the terms of the Constitution, and the liberalization of the state-controlled media. Following a general strike, organized by the COD, Bongo announced the resignation of the Council of Ministers, and declared that he was prepared to implement fully the new Constitution. He also claimed that, in accordance with the Constitution, several institutions, including the High Court of Justice, had been dissolved, and that a Constitutional Court and a National Communications Council had been established. However, opposition parties within the COD refused to be represented in a new Government of National Unity, of which Oyé Mba was appointed as Prime Minister. In June Oyé Mba appointed a new coalition Government, in which 14 members of the previous Council of Ministers retained their portfolios. Members of MORENA—Originels, the Union Socialiste Gabonaise (USG) and the Association pour le Socialisme au Gabon were also represented in the Government.

Bongo re-elected

At the first contested presidential election, held on 5 December 1993, Bongo was re-elected as President, winning 51.2% of the votes cast, while M'Ba Abessole secured 26.5% of the votes. (There were 11 further candidates.) Despite reports by international observers that the elections had been conducted fairly, the official announcement of the results prompted rioting by opposition supporters, and, alleging electoral malpractice, the opposition appealed to the Constitutional Court to annul the outcome. Claiming victory, M'Ba Abessole formed a Haut Conseil de la République, later redesignated as the Haut Conseil de la Résistance (HCR), which included the majority of opposition presidential candidates, and a parallel government.

The Constitutional Court ruled against the appeal by the opposition and endorsed the election results, and on 22 January 1994 Bongo was officially inaugurated as President. In February a general strike, called in support of demands for salary increases to compensate for a devaluation of the CFA franc in January, degenerated into violence. Strike action was suspended after four days, following negotiations between the Government and trade unions; nine people had been killed during that period, according to official figures (although the opposition claimed that a total of 38 had died). A national curfew and state of alert were imposed from January until early April.

In March 1994 the National Assembly approved a constitutional amendment that provided for the establishment of a Senate (which the opposition had resisted). In August the opposition parties announced that they were prepared to participate in a coalition government, on condition that it was installed as a transitional organ pending legislative elections. In September negotiations between the Government and opposition took place in Paris, under the auspices of the Organization of African Unity (OAU, now the African Union—AU, see p. 188), in order to resolve remaining differences concerning the results of the presidential election and the proposed formation of a government of national unity.

At the end of September 1994 an agreement was reached whereby a transitional coalition government was to be installed, with local government elections scheduled to take place after a period of one year, followed by legislative elections six months later; the electoral code was to be revised and an independent electoral commission established, in an effort to ensure that the elections be conducted fairly. In early October Oyé Mba resigned from office and dissolved the Council of Ministers. Shortly afterwards Bongo appointed Dr Paulin Obame-Nguema of the PDG as Prime Minister. Obame-Nguema subsequently formed a 27-member Council of Ministers, which included six opposition members. The composition of the new Government was, however, immediately criticized by the opposition, on the grounds that it was entitled to one-third of ministerial portfolios in proportion to the number of opposition deputies in the National Assembly; the HCR announced that the opposition would boycott the new administration, which, it claimed, was in violation of the Paris accord. Four opposition members consequently refused to accept the portfolios allocated to them, although two of these finally agreed to join the Government. (The portfolios that remained vacant were later assigned to a further two opposition members.)

At a national referendum held on 24 July 1995 the constitutional provisions adopted under the terms of the Paris accord were approved by 96.5% of votes cast, with 63% of the electorate participating. In May 1996 Bongo agreed to establish a Commission Nationale Electorale (National Election Commission—CNE) to formulate an electoral timetable, in consultation with all the official parties. Access to state-controlled media and election funding was to be equitably divided. On 20 May the National Assembly's mandate expired, and Obame-Nguema's Government resigned at the beginning of June, in accordance with the Paris accord. Bongo, however, rejected the resignation on the grounds that the Government should, before leaving office, organize the elections and finalize pending agreements with the IMF and the World Bank.

Having been rescheduled on several occasions, the first round of voting in legislative elections eventually took place on 15 December 1996, with the PDG obtaining 47 of the 55 seats that were decided at that time. The PDG secured a substantial majority (84) of the seats decided in the second round, which was held on 29 December, while the RNB obtained seven, the PGP six and independent candidates four, with a further 14 seats shared by the Cercle des Libéraux Réformateurs (CLR), the UPG, the USG and others. Polling was unable to proceed for the five remaining seats, and results in a number of other constituencies were later annulled, owing to irregularities. (Following by-elections held in August 1997, during which five people were reportedly killed in violent incidents in north-east Gabon, the PDG held 88 seats, the PGP nine and the RNB five.) Obame-Nguema was reappointed Prime Minister on 27 January, and a new Council of Ministers, dominated by members of the PDG, was announced on the following day. The PGP, the main opposition party represented in the National Assembly, had refused to participate in the new Government.

Elections to the new Senate took place on 26 January and 9 February 1997 (with the senators elected by members of municipal councils and departmental assemblies). The PDG won 53 of the Senate's 91 seats, while the RNB secured 20 seats, the PGP four, the Alliance Démocratique et Républicaine (ADERE) three, the CLR one, and the Rassemblement pour la Démocratie et le Progrès (RDP) one, with independent candidates obtaining nine seats. The results for a number of seats were annulled, however, and in subsequent by-elections, held later that year, the PDG increased its representation to 58 seats, while the RNB held 20 seats and the PGP four.

Constitutional amendments

In April 1997 a congress of deputies and senators adopted constitutional amendments which extended the presidential term to seven years and provided for the creation of the post of Vice-President (who was not to have any power of succession). In late May Didjob Divungui-di-N'Dingue of the ADERE was appointed to the new post.

In September 1998 opposition parties withdrew their members from the CNE in protest against alleged irregularities in the voter registration process for the forthcoming presidential poll. At the election, which was held on 6 December, Bongo was re-elected with 66.6% of votes cast, while Mamboundou received 16.5% of the votes and M'Ba Abessolé secured 13.4%. The reported rate of participation was 53.8%. Opposition parties rejected the results, again alleging electoral malpractice, and called for fresh elections to be held. None the less, Bongo was inaugurated as President on 21 January 1999, and a new 42-member Council of Ministers, headed by Jean-François Ntoutoume Emane, was subsequently appointed.

Elections to the National Assembly took place on 9 and 23 December 2001. Three opposition parties accused the Government of falsely inflating voter registration lists and boycotted the elections, while others called for the first round to be annulled, as a result of reputed irregularities and high abstention rates. In the event, the elections were postponed in three districts until 6 January 2002, owing to violent incidents, and voting was repeated on 20 January in a further two constituencies where candidates had received the same number of votes and in a third district where violence had marred the initial ballot. An outbreak of Ebola Virus Disease (EVD) resulted in the indefinite postponement of voting in the north-eastern district of Zadie. The PDG won 86 seats in the Assembly, which were supplemented by 19 seats secured by independents with links to the PDG and other parties affiliated to the ruling party. Opposition parties obtained a total of 14 seats (the Rassemblement pour le Gabon—RPG—as the RNB had been restyled, eight, the Parti Social-Démocrate—PSD—two and the UPG one). A new, enlarged 39-member Council of Ministers, which included four opposition representatives, was appointed in late January. Ntoutoume Emane was reappointed as Prime Minister, while M'Ba Abessolé was named Minister of State for Human Rights and Missions.

During March and April 2002 the Constitutional Court annulled the results of voting in the December 2001 elections to the National Assembly in 12 constituencies owing to irregularities. On 26 May and 9 June by-elections took place in these 12 constituencies and in Zadie; the PDG won 10 of the 13 seats contested, increasing its representation to 88 seats. Elections to the Senate took place on 9 February 2003; the PDG won more than 60 of the upper chamber's 91 seats, followed by the RPG, which secured eight seats.

In July 2003 the National Assembly voted to revoke the Constitution's limit on the number of terms of office for which the President was eligible to seek re-election. Opposition politicians claimed that Bongo thus intended to become 'President-for-Life' by means of continuous fraud in future presidential elections. In September, in response to a series of strikes and protests, the Government and representatives of labour groups announced the signing of a so-called 'social truce', which included commitments to lower the prices of essential items and reduce the extent of political patronage over the following three years. However, renewed protests over reductions in state expenditure were staged in early 2004.

In September 2004 President Bongo Ondimba (who had added his father's name to his own in November 2003) carried out a minor cabinet reorganization, in which several leading opposition figures were awarded ministerial portfolios. It was widely believed that the inclusion of opposition leaders in the Government was intended to reduce the number of candidates opposing Bongo Ondimba and the PDG in the upcoming presidential and legislative elections. In October 2005 disquiet arose among opposition groups, following the decision of the CNE to exclude nine presidential candidates, two of whom subsequently appealed successfully against their exclusion, from contesting the election.

At the presidential election held on 27 November 2005 Bongo Ondimba was re-elected, winning 79.2% of votes cast. Mamboundou, the candidate of the UPG, secured 13.6%, while Zacharie Myboto, a former government minister representing the Union Gabonaise pour la Démocratie et le Développement (UGDD), received 6.6%. The rate of voter participation was recorded at 63.5%. Mamboundou and Myboto disputed the validity of the results, alleging electoral malpractice, and each claimed victory for himself. However, international election observers declared the elections to have been largely free and transparent. The ensuing unrest caused by supporters of the defeated candidates was broadly quelled following the deployment of security forces throughout the country in January 2006. On 20 January President Bongo Ondimba appointed Jean Eyéghé Ndong of the PDG as Prime Minister, who later that month formed an expanded Council of Ministers composed overwhelmingly of PDG members.

The PDG consolidates power

Legislative elections took place on 17 December 2006, although voting in seven constituencies was postponed until 24 December for logistical reasons. The PDG retained control of the National Assembly, winning 82 of the 120 seats, while parties allied to the PDG secured a further 17 seats; the opposition won 17 seats (the UPG secured the largest number of opposition seats with eight) and independents won four. Electoral observers endorsed the results, but the opposition complained that it had not been given adequate access to state media during the election campaign. In late January 2007 Ndong, who had been reappointed to the premiership, announced a largely unchanged 50-member Council of Ministers, which was again dominated by members of the PDG. Results in 20 constituencies were subsequently annulled owing to allegations of procedural irregularities and fraud. By-elections were held on 10 June at which the PDG won 11 of the 20 seats available. Parties allied to the PDG won six seats, while the opposition took two; the remaining seat was secured by an independent candidate.

In December 2007 President Bongo Ondimba appointed a new Government, retaining Ndong as Prime Minister; further governmental reorganizations were effected in February 2008 and January 2009. At elections to the Senate held on 18 January 2009 the ruling PDG retained its majority, winning 75 of the 102 seats in the upper house.

Ali Bongo Ondimba assumes the presidency

On 8 June 2009 the death was announced of President Bongo Ondimba. It was reported that he had died of a heart attack while receiving medical treatment in Spain; he had 'temporarily' withdrawn from public duties the previous month following the death of his wife in March. Under the terms of the Constitution, interim power was transferred to Rose Francine Rogombé, the President of the Senate, who was charged with responsibility for organizing a presidential election within 45 days. Despite requests by the political opposition for a delay to the timetable to allow an extensive revision of the electoral register, the Constitutional Court declared that the ballot would take place on 30 August. The PDG's selection of Ali Bongo Ondimba, the son of the former President and Minister of National Defence, as its presidential candidate resulted in serious divisions within the party and in mid-June Prime Minister Ndong announced the resignation of his Government and his intention to contest the election as an independent candidate. Interim President Rogombé named Paul Biyoghé Mba as Ndong's successor and the outgoing Government was reappointed virtually unchanged.

At the presidential election, which was held as scheduled on 30 August 2009, Bongo Ondimba was initially reported to have secured 41.7% of the valid votes cast, the independent candidate André Mba Obame (the Minister of the Interior) 25.9% of the votes, and Mamboundou, again representing the UPG, 25.2%. Violent protests ensued, most notably in Libreville and Port-Gentil, resulting in the deaths of at least three people, and French business interests and diplomatic offices in Gabon were attacked. It was subsequently announced that a recount of the votes would take place; finally on 12 October the Constitutional Court announced that Bongo Ondimba had secured 41.8% of the valid votes cast, while the share of votes attributed to Mamboundou and Mba Obame was amended to 25.6% and 25.3%, respectively, thus reversing their placings in the election. Bongo Ondimba was sworn in as President on 16 October 2009 and a new Government, reduced in size from 44 to 30 members, was appointed the following day. Biyoghé Mba retained the premiership. No opposition party members were accorded ministerial positions.

In February 2010 three political movements representing the Fang ethnic group (the UGDD, the Mouvement Africain de Développement and the Rassemblement National des Républicains) united under the leadership of Mba Obame to form the Union Nationale. However, in January 2011 the Ministry of the Interior announced the dissolution of the Union Nationale and accused Mba Obame of treason after he declared himself the victor of the 2009 presidential election and appointed a 19-member parallel government. Rallies held in support of Mba Obame degenerated into violent clashes between demonstrators and the security forces. Mba Obame and his associates fled to the Libreville premises of the UN Development Programme, refusing to leave until late February 2011 due to safety concerns.

The operations of numerous media outlets that had provided coverage of Mba Obame and other opposition figures were suspended by the government-controlled Conseil National de la Communication throughout 2011 and early 2012. Meanwhile, in January 2011 President Bongo Ondimba effected a reorganization of the Council of Ministers, appointing 10 new ministers, including Pacôme Rufin Ondzounga as Minister of National Defence. In March three military officials were sentenced to prison terms of up to seven years, after being found guilty of planning to stage a coup against President Bongo Ondimba in 2009.

Legislative elections were conducted on 17 December 2011. According to the official results, the ruling PDG secured an overwhelming victory, winning 114 seats in the National Assembly. Of the remaining six seats, the RPG secured three, while the CLR, the PSD and the Union pour la Nouvelle République each obtained a single seat. AU observers endorsed the results, although they reported some 'shortcomings'. The rate of participation by the electorate was only 34.3%. Numerous opposition parties had urged a boycott, arguing that the elections would lack transparency since biometric voting cards had not been issued. In February 2012 the Constitutional Court annulled the results in six PDG-controlled constituencies because of voting irregularities. By-elections in those constituencies were conducted in May, when the PDG again won all six seats.

Biyoghé Mba resigned as Prime Minister in February 2012; Raymond Ndong Sima, hitherto the minister responsible for agriculture, was appointed as his successor. Ndong Sima announced a new Government later that month. Notably, Emmanuel Issozet Ngondet was named as the new Minister of Foreign Affairs, International Co-operation and Francophone Affairs.

Mba Obame, who had been receiving medical treatment abroad since mid-2011, returned to Gabon on 11 August 2012. An unsanctioned demonstration was held in Libreville on 15 August in support of his demands for a national reconciliation conference and fresh legislative elections. Violent confrontations ensued between Mba Obame's supporters and the security forces, resulting in approximately 60 arrests and the death of one demonstrator. On the following day the premises of TV+, a television station owned by Mba Obame, came under attack by heavily armed assailants, who destroyed the station's broadcasting equipment. (The TV+ building was attacked again in early September.) In September 33 of the detained protesters received one-year prison terms for their involvement in the unrest. Also in that month 20 opposition parties, including Mba Obame's Union Nationale (still officially dissolved), established a coalition, the Union des Forces de Changement. This new opposition grouping signed an accord appealing for a national conference to be convened to discuss 'democratic political change' within the country. (Mba Obame subsequently left the country again to seek medical treatment.)

Recent developments: new Government

Local elections were conducted on 14 December 2013; later that month the CNE announced provisional results according to which the PDG had won 1,517 of the 2,404 municipal seats and secured control of the majority of departmental assemblies overall. Subsequently, a PDG candidate, Rose Christiane Ossouka Raponda, previously the Minister of the Budget, was elected Mayor of Libreville (replacing former premier Ntoutoume Emane). Meanwhile, on 24 January 2014 President Bongo Ondimba appointed Daniel Ona Ondo (hitherto First Vice-President of the National Assembly) as Prime Minister, in place of Ndong Sima. A new Government was formed at the end of January; among the newly appointed members, the Minister of the Interior, Public Security, Immigration and Decentralization Guy Bertrand Mapangou and Minister of National Defence Ernest Mpouho were regarded as particularly close associates of Bongo Ondimba. In mid-April the Minister of Forests, the Environment and the Protection of Natural Resources and his deputy were detained for several hours, reportedly by Ministry employees who were protesting over their pay and working conditions; they were eventually freed by police. At the beginning of September it was reported that the Minister of National Education and Technical Education, Leon Nzouba, had resigned his post, having been widely criticized over his indecisive handling of a dispute concerning 900 secondary school students who had challenged the grading methodology of recent public examinations. This represented the first resignation from the Cabinet for nearly two decades. A rising level of popular discontent was reported in 2014 with respect to the poor national infrastructure, frequent power cuts and shortages of potable water.

Foreign Affairs

Regional relations

In March 2003 relations with Equatorial Guinea became tense, following Gabon's occupation of the uninhabited island of Mbagne (Mbañé, Mbanie), situated in Corisco Bay, north of Libreville. Both countries claimed sovereignty over the island. Equatorial Guinea rejected Bongo's proposal for joint exploitation of any petroleum reserves found in the vicinity of the island, despite an official visit to Libreville in May by the Equato-Guinean President, Gen. (Theodoro) Obiang Nguema Mbasogo. Attempts to reach a negotiated settlement failed in December, although the two countries agreed to the appointment of a UN mediator in the dispute in January 2004 and in July a provisional agreement was reached to explore jointly for petroleum in the disputed territories. However, in late 2006 negotiations were suspended indefinitely. In February 2011 Obiang Nguema and Ali Bongo Ondimba, attending a meeting hosted by UN Secretary-General Ban Ki-Moon in New York, USA, confirmed that they would seek the intervention of the International Court of Justice in settling the dispute. (At December 2014 the they had not yet submitted a request to the Court.)

Gabon is a member of the Communauté Economique et Monétaire de l'Afrique Centrale (CEMAC, see p. 327), which was officially established in 1999. The Gabonese Government contributed troops to regional peacekeeping operations, including a contingent in the Central African Republic (CAR) that was created by CEMAC in late 2002, and a successor Communauté Economique des Etats de l'Afrique Centrale (CEEAC, see p. 445) mission from 2008. The full implementation of an agreement concluded in June 2013 to abolish, from January 2014, visa requirements between CEMAC member states was postponed, owing to reservations expressed by the Government of Equatorial Guinea in November 2013 concerning a possible influx of migrants. (Prior to the mid-2013 agreement Gabon had long opposed subregional freedom of movement on similar grounds.) In March 2011 the UN Regional Office for Central Africa (UNOCA, see p. 101) was inaugurated in Libreville, with a mandate focused on subregional peace consolidation and conflict prevention.

Gabon contributed 500 troops to the African-led International Support Mission to the CAR (MISCA), which was authorized in December 2013 by the UN Security Council, and has also contributed troops to the UN Multidimensional Integrated Stabilization Mission in the CAR (MINUSCA), which was authorized by the Council in April 2014 and assumed authority from MISCA in September.

In August 2014 Gabon suspended air and sea links with Guinea, Liberia and Sierra Leone, as a precautionary measure in view of the ongoing intensive outbreak in those countries of EVD.

Gabon is a signatory of a code of conduct concerning the repression of acts of piracy in the Gulf of Guinea, that was adopted in June 2013 under the auspices of the UN and regional organizations including CEEAC (see p. 445) and the Gulf of Guinea Commission (see p. 461).

Other external relations

President Omar Bongo Ondimba pursued a policy of close co-operation with France in the fields of economic and foreign affairs. Relations became strained in March 1997, however, when allegations that Bongo had been a beneficiary in an international fraud emerged during a French judicial investigation into the affairs of the petroleum company Elf Aquitaine (now part of Total). In October 1999 a further judicial investigation into the affairs of Elf Aquitaine, carried out by Swiss authorities, revealed that André Tarallo (a senior Elf Aquitaine executive) had used bank accounts in that country secretly to transfer large sums of money to several African heads of state, among them Bongo. Bongo denied personally receiving direct payments from Elf and maintained that such 'bonus' payments were made only to the Gabonese Government. However, a report released in November, following a separate investigation by the US Congress into money-laundering and corruption among political figures, alleged further improper financial dealing between Bongo and Elf. In March 2003 the trial commenced in Paris of 37 defendants accused of permitting the embezzlement of the equivalent of some €300m. of funds from Elf Aquitaine. In November Tarallo was sentenced to four years' imprisonment and fined €2m., while 29 others also received prison terms. Tarallo was released on the grounds of ill-health in January 2004; however, his sentence was increased to seven years'

imprisonment, following appeals by the prosecution in March 2005. Following the election to the French presidency of Nicolas Sarkozy (who had pledged to implement stricter immigration policies) in May 2007, further tensions ensued between France and Gabon. In early 2008 two Gabonese students were deported, although a visit to Gabon by a delegation of French officials in April signalled an improvement in relations. Nevertheless, in February 2009 the French authorities announced that they had frozen a number of Bongo Ondimba's bank accounts, following a ruling by a court in Bordeaux, France, in October 2008 that he return a payment of some €450,000 made to him in order to secure the release of a French businessman who had been imprisoned in Libreville in 1996.

In November 2009, on his first visit abroad since acceding to the presidency, Ali Bongo Ondimba met President Sarkozy in Paris and in February 2010 Sarkozy made a reciprocal visit to Gabon. A visit to Gabon by French Prime Minister François Fillon in July 2011 was censured by opposition groups critical of France's support of President Bongo Ondimba. Nevertheless, Fillon announced that the French garrison in Gabon would be upgraded to the status of France's main military base in the region. Reports emerged in September alleging that former French President Jacques Chirac and other prominent French politicians had received clandestine payments totalling US $20m. from the leaders of several ex-French colonies in Africa, including Omar Bongo Ondimba, in exchange for French support for their respective regimes. Despite denials by the French and Gabonese authorities, in November a former government official in Omar Bongo Ondimba's administration corroborated these allegations. President Ali Bongo Ondimba met the new French President, François Hollande, in Paris in July 2012, amid further criticism from Gabonese opposition groups, which accused Hollande of reneging on electoral pledges to end the 'Françafrique' policy perceived to maintain France's influence in Africa while upholding corrupt regimes. During a further official visit to Paris undertaken in early September 2014, following the extension in April of an invitation by the French administration, Ali Bongo Ondimba met President Hollande, as well as a number of French government ministers. Bongo Ondimba invited French companies to invest in Gabon. A contingent of around 900 French troops was stationed in Gabon in 2014.

Following a visit to Gabon in February 2004 by the Chinese President, Hu Jintao, agreements were signed providing for greater economic co-operation between the two countries; most notably, the French oil corporation Total concluded an agreement to export Gabonese oil to the People's Republic of China. Relations were further strengthened following Omar Bongo Ondimba's visit to China in September, during which he secured some US $5m. in aid from the Jintao administration. However, in early 2013 the Gabonese Government withdrew exploitation rights of onshore oil assets from Addax Petroleum of China, owing to alleged breaches of contract; following a legal dispute at an international tribunal, in January 2014 Addax Petroleum paid US $400m. to continue exploitation in the country.

CONSTITUTION AND GOVERNMENT

The Constitution of March 1991 provides for a multi-party system, and vests executive power in the President, who is directly elected by universal suffrage for a period of seven years. The President appoints the Prime Minister, who is Head of Government and who (in consultation with the President) appoints the Council of Ministers. Legislative power is vested in the Assemblée Nationale, comprising 120 members, who are elected by direct universal suffrage for a term of five years, and the 102-member Sénat (Senate), which is elected by members of municipal councils and departmental assemblies for a term of six years. The independence of the judiciary is guaranteed by the Constitution. Gabon is divided into nine provinces, each under an appointed governor, and 37 prefectures.

REGIONAL AND INTERNATIONAL CO-OPERATION

Gabon is a member of the African Union (see p. 188), the Central African organs of the Franc Zone (see p. 326), the Communauté Economique des Etats de l'Afrique Centrale (CEEAC, see p. 445), and of the Gulf of Guinea Commission (see p. 461).

Gabon became a member of the UN in 1960. As a contracting party to the General Agreement on Tariffs and Trade, Gabon joined the World Trade Organization (see p. 431) on its establishment in 1995.

ECONOMIC AFFAIRS

In 2013, according to estimates by the World Bank, Gabon's gross national income (GNI), measured at average 2011–13 prices, was US $17,807m., equivalent to $10,650 per head (or $17,220 per head on an international purchasing-power parity basis). During 2004–13, it was estimated, the population increased at an average annual rate of 2.4%, while gross domestic product (GDP) per head increased, in real terms, by an average of 1.2% per year. Overall GDP increased, in real terms, at an average annual rate of 3.6% in 2004–13. GDP increased by 5.9% in 2013.

Agriculture (including forestry and fishing) contributed a provisional 3.3% of GDP in 2013, according to the African Development Bank (AfDB). About 23.3% of the labour force was estimated to be employed in the agricultural sector in mid-2015, according to FAO estimates. Cocoa, coffee, oil palm and rubber are cultivated for export. Gabon has yet to achieve self-sufficiency in staple crops: imports of food, live animals and prepared foodstuffs accounted for 15.0% of the value of total imports in 2010. The principal subsistence crops are plantains, cassava and yams. The exploitation of Gabon's forests (which cover about 85% of the land area) is a principal economic activity. In 2010 wood and wood products accounted for an estimated 3.0% of total exports. Although Gabon's territorial waters contain important fishing resources, their commercial exploitation is minimal. According to World Bank estimates, agricultural GDP increased at an average annual rate of 1.9% in 2004–12. According to the AfDB, the sector grew by 3.8% in 2013.

Industry (including mining, manufacturing, construction and power) contributed a provisional 59.0% of GDP in 2013, according to the AfDB. About 14.1% of the working population were employed in the sector in 1991. According to World Bank estimates, industrial GDP increased at an average annual rate of 2.0% in 2004–12; industrial GDP expanded by 7.3% in 2011.

Mining accounted for a provisional 46.2% of GDP in 2013 (with the majority of that contributed by the petroleum sector alone), according to the AfDB. In 2010 sales of petroleum and petroleum products provided an estimated 87.1% of export revenue. Production of crude petroleum was estimated at 237,000 barrels per day (b/d) in 2013, down from some 364,000 b/d in 1997. However, recent explorations have doubled oil reserves compared with 1996 levels. At the end of 2013 Gabon had proven petroleum reserves of 2,000m. barrels, sufficient to sustain production at current levels for some 23 years. Proven natural gas reserves totalled 1,000,000m. cu ft at the end of 2013. Gabon is among the world's foremost producers and exporters of manganese (which contributed an estimated 2.4% of export earnings in 2010). In 2012 3,637 metric tons of manganese was mined. Major reserves of iron ore remain undeveloped, and there are also substantial niobium (columbium) reserves at Mabounie. Small amounts of gold are extracted, and the existence of many mineral deposits, including talc, barytes, phosphates, rare earths, titanium and cadmium, has also been confirmed. In 1996–2002, according to the IMF, mining GDP declined at an estimated average annual rate of 6.5%. According to the AfDB, the mining sector declined by 1.5% in 2013.

According to the AfDB, the manufacturing sector contributed a provisional 6.5% of GDP in 2013. The principal activities are the refining of petroleum and the processing of other minerals, the preparation of timber and other agro-industrial processes. The chemicals industry is also significant. According to World Bank estimates, manufacturing GDP increased at an average annual rate of 3.2% in 2004–12; it increased by 6.1% in 2012. According to the AfDB the sector grew by 8.0% in 2013.

The construction sector contributed a provisional 5.5% of GDP in 2013, according to AfDB figures. The sector declined by 2.4% in 2012, but grew by 15.5% in 2013.

In 2011 some 45.7% of electrical energy was provided by hydroelectric power, with the remainder provided by natural gas (33.0%) and petroleum (20.7%). Imports of mineral products comprised an estimated 12.2% of the total value of merchandise imports in 2010. Construction began of a new hydroelectric dam in Mitzic in December 2010 by French company Bouygues SA; the project was expected to cost US $108m. with a projected capacity of 40 MW.

Services engaged 18.8% of the economically active population in 1991 and, according to the AfDB, provided a provisional 37.6% of GDP in 2013. According to World Bank estimates, the GDP of the services sector increased at an average annual rate of 4.7% in 2004–12; services GDP increased by 6.7% in 2012.

According to IMF estimates, in 2011 Gabon recorded a merchandise trade surplus of 7,084,000m. francs CFA, and there was a surplus of 2,655,000m. francs CFA on the current account of the balance of payments. In 2010 the principal source of imports was France (30.7% of the total); other major sources were Belgium, the USA and the People's Republic of China. The principal market for exports in that year was the USA (58.3%); the Netherlands, Malaysia and China were also important purchasers. The principal exports in 2010 were mineral fuels and lubricants and wood and wood products. The principal imports in that year were machinery, mechanical and electrical equipment and parts thereof, mineral products, base metals and their articles, vehicles and associated transport equipment, chemicals and related products, live animals and animal products, and prepared foodstuffs.

In 2012 there was an estimated budgetary deficit of 38,000m. francs CFA. Gabon's general government gross debt was 1,532,090m. francs CFA in 2011, equivalent to 17.3% of GDP. Gabon's external debt totalled US $2,879m. at the end of 2011, of which $2,464m. was public and publicly guaranteed debt. In 2005 the cost of servicing long-term public and publicly guaranteed debt and repayments to the IMF was equivalent to 3.4% of the value of exports of goods, services and income (excluding workers' remittances). According to the ILO, in 2004–13 the average annual rate of inflation was 2.2%. Consumer prices increased by 0.5% in 2013. The Government estimated about 20% of the labour force to be unemployed in 1996.

Gabon's potential for economic growth is based on its considerable mineral and forestry resources. Petroleum provides the country's principal source of income; however, reserves in existing fields are in decline. Following his accession to the presidency, in October 2009 Ali Bongo Ondimba announced the adoption of an extensive public investment programme (totalling US $12,000m. over seven years), which was intended to transform Gabon into an emerging economy by 2025. The export of unprocessed timber was banned in January 2010 to encourage the creation of a domestic processing industry. As part of government efforts to stimulate growth and economic diversification, Special Economic Zones were established near Libreville (in 2011) and Port-Gentil (in 2012), while the Central African Stock Exchange, serving the member states of the Communauté Economique et Monétaire de l'Afrique Centrale (see p. 327), has been operational in the capital, Libreville, since 2008. Loans totalling US $439m. were secured from the AfDB in late 2011 to fund various infrastructural development projects. By 2014 the Government's public investment programme had proved successful in mobilizing revenue from non-oil sectors, particularly mining (the construction of new manganese plants having stimulated production and exports of the mineral), wood-processing and construction. The services, agro-industry, fisheries and tourism sectors are also a focus of expansion. Higher public expenditure resulted, however, in the overall budget balance moving into deficit from 2012, with rising deficits projected by the IMF in the medium term. In November 2014 the IMF reported that GDP growth had slowed in that year, to a projected 5.1%, owing in part to a significant reduction in public expenditure made in response to the weakening fiscal position. As a means of ensuring future fiscal sustainability the IMF recommended progressive reductions in fuel subsidies, greater control over public salaries, and prioritizing investment towards the most economically beneficial infrastructure projects. The IMF expressed support for ongoing efforts to develop the business environment and human capital. The country's continuing high rate of unemployment (estimated at 20% overall) and widespread poverty have been noted by IMF reports. The new Government that was formed in January 2014 was instructed by President Bongo Ondimba to focus on social objectives, and the IMF report published in November recommended that carefully targeted social expenditure should be maintained. Visiting France in September Bongo Ondimba invited French companies to invest in Gabon and actively to participate in the diversification of the country's economy.

PUBLIC HOLIDAYS

2016: 1 January (New Year's Day), 28 March (Easter Monday), 17 April (Women's Day), 1 May (Labour Day), 5 May (Ascension Day), 16 May (Whit Monday), 6 July* (Id al-Fitr, end of Ramadan), 15 August (Assumption), 17 August (Anniversary of Independence), 12 September* (Id al-Adha, Feast of the Sacrifice), 1 November (All Saints' Day), 25 December (Christmas).

*These holidays are dependent on the Islamic lunar calendar and may vary by one or two days from the dates given.

Statistical Survey

Source (unless otherwise stated): Direction Générale de la Statistique et des Etudes Economiques, BP 2119, Libreville; tel. 01-72-13-69; fax 01-72-04-57; e-mail plan@dgsee.yahoo.fr; internet www.stat-gabon.org.

Area and Population

AREA, POPULATION AND DENSITY

Area (sq km)	267,667*
Population (census results)	
31 July 1993	
Males	501,784
Females	513,192
Total	1,014,976
1 December 2003	1,269,000†
Population (UN estimates at mid-year)‡	
2013	1,671,715
2014	1,711,295
2015	1,751,199
Density (per sq km) at mid-2015	6.5

* 103,347 sq miles.
† Provisional (Source: UN, *Population and Vital Statistics Report*).
‡ Source: UN, *World Population Prospects: The 2012 Revision*.

POPULATION BY AGE AND SEX
(UN estimates at mid-2015)

	Males	Females	Total
0–14 years	338,585	332,014	670,599
15–64 years	502,622	489,602	992,224
65 years and over	39,609	48,767	88,376
Total	880,816	870,383	1,751,199

Source: UN, *World Population Prospects: The 2012 Revision*.

REGIONS
(1993 census)

Region	Area (sq km)	Population	Density (per sq km)	Chief town
Estuaire . .	20,740	463,187	22.3	Libreville
Haut-Ogooué .	36,547	104,301	2.9	Franceville
Moyen-Ogooué .	18,535	42,316	2.3	Lambaréné
N'Gounié . .	37,750	77,781	2.1	Mouila
Nyanga . .	21,285	39,430	1.9	Tchibanga
Ogooué-Ivindo .	46,075	48,862	1.1	Makokou
Ogooué-Lolo .	25,380	43,915	1.7	Koulamoutou
Ogooué-Maritime .	22,890	97,913	4.3	Port-Gentil
Woleu-N'Tem .	38,465	97,271	2.5	Oyem
Total . . .	267,667	1,014,976	3.8	

PRINCIPAL TOWNS
(population at 1993 census)

Libreville (capital) .	419,596	Mouila	16,307
Port-Gentil . . .	79,225	Lambaréné . . .	15,033
Franceville . . .	31,183	Tchibanga . . .	14,054
Oyem	22,404	Koulamoutou . .	11,773
Moanda . . .	21,882	Makokou . . .	9,849

Mid-2014 (incl. suburbs, UN estimate): Libreville (capital) 694,633 (Source: UN, *World Urbanization Prospects: The 2014 Revision*).

BIRTHS AND DEATHS
(annual averages, UN estimates)

	2000–05	2005–10	2010–15
Birth rate (per 1,000) . .	33.4	32.9	32.1
Death rate (per 1,000) . . .	11.2	10.2	9.2

Source: UN, *World Population Prospects: The 2012 Revision*.

Life expectancy (years at birth): 63.1 (males 62.1; females 64.1) in 2012 (Source: World Bank, World Development Indicators database).

ECONOMICALLY ACTIVE POPULATION
(FAO estimates, '000 persons at mid-year)

	2013	2014	2015
Agriculture, etc.	196	198	200
Total labour force (incl. others) .	807	831	857

Source: FAO.

2005 (persons aged 15 years and over): Total employed 639,180; Unemployed 115,499; Total labour force 664,117.

Health and Welfare

KEY INDICATORS

Total fertility rate (children per woman, 2012)	4.1
Under-5 mortality rate (per 1,000 live births, 2012) . . .	62
HIV/AIDS (% of persons aged 15–49, 2013)	3.9
Physicians (per 1,000 head, 2004)	0.3
Hospital beds (per 1,000 head, 2010)	6.3
Health expenditure (2011): US $ per head (PPP)	516
Health expenditure (2011): % of GDP	3.4
Health expenditure (2011): public (% of total)	52.9
Access to water (% of persons, 2012)	92
Access to sanitation (% of persons, 2012)	41
Total carbon dioxide emissions ('000 metric tons, 2010) . .	2,574.2
Carbon dioxide emissions per head (metric tons, 2010) . .	1.7
Human Development Index (2013): ranking	112
Human Development Index (2013): value	0.674

For sources and definitions, see explanatory note on p. vi.

Agriculture

PRINCIPAL CROPS
('000 metric tons, FAO estimates)

	2011	2012	2013
Maize	44	44	45
Cassava (Manioc)	255	300	315
Taro (Cocoyam)	60	63	65
Yams	195	200	210
Sugar cane	265	260	280
Groundnuts, with shell . . .	23	24	24
Oil palm fruit	20	20	21
Bananas	17	17	17
Plantains	295	285	272
Natural rubber	21	21	21

Aggregate production ('000 metric tons, may include official, semi-official or estimated data): Total cereals 45 in 2011, 46 in 2012, 47 in 2013; Total roots and tubers 514 in 2011, 567 in 2012, 594 in 2013; Total vegetables (incl. melons) 50 in 2011, 51 in 2012, 48 in 2013; Total fruits (excl. melons) 333 in 2011, 325 in 2012, 311 in 2013.

Source: FAO.

LIVESTOCK
('000 head, year ending September, FAO estimates)

	2011	2012	2013
Cattle	38	38	38
Pigs	215	218	225
Sheep	198	200	210
Goats	96	100	110
Chickens	3,100	3,100	3,200

Source: FAO.

LIVESTOCK PRODUCTS
('000 metric tons, FAO estimates)

	2011	2012	2013
Cattle meat	1.1	1.2	1.2
Pig meat	3.2	3.2	3.4
Chicken meat	3.8	3.8	3.9
Rabbit meat	1.9	1.9	1.9
Game meat	25.5	26.2	26.2
Cows' milk	2.4	2.5	2.5
Hen eggs	2.4	2.5	2.5

Source: FAO.

Forestry

ROUNDWOOD REMOVALS
('000 cubic metres)

	2005	2006	2007
Sawlogs, veneer logs and logs for sleepers	3,200	3,500	3,400
Fuel wood*	1,070	1,070	1,070
Total*	4,270	4,570	4,470

* FAO estimates.

2008–13: Production assumed to be unchanged from 2007 (FAO estimates).

Source: FAO.

SAWNWOOD PRODUCTION
('000 cubic metres, incl. railway sleepers, unofficial figures)

	2009	2010	2011
Total	250	338	500

2012–13: Production assumed to be unchanged from 2011 (FAO estimates).

Source: FAO.

Fishing

('000 metric tons, live weight)

	2008	2009*	2010*
Capture	42.5*	32.0	32.0
Tilapias	4.7*	4.4	4.4
Other freshwater fishes	5.0*	5.0	5.0
Barracudas	0.4	0.3	0.3
Bobo croakers	1.4	1.0	1.0
West African croakers	1.1	0.8	0.8
Lesser African threadfin	0.8	5.0	5.0
Bonga shad	8.3	5.6	5.6
Penaeus shrimp	0.1	—	—
Aquaculture	0.1	0.1	0.2
Total catch	42.6*	32.1	32.2

* FAO estimate(s).

2011–12: Figures assumed to be unchanged from 2010 (FAO estimates).

Source: FAO.

Mining

	2010	2011	2012
Crude petroleum ('000 barrels)	92,126	91,615	88,330
Diamonds (carats)*	500	500	n.a.
Manganese ore ('000 metric tons): gross weight†	3,201	4,070	3,637
Manganese ore ('000 metric tons): metal content‡	1,416	1,858	1,650
Gold (kg)*†§	—	—	666

* Estimated production.
† Figures refer to the metal content of ore.
‡ Figures refer to the weight of chemical-grade pellets.
§ Excluding production smuggled out of the country (estimated at more than 400 kg annually).

Source: US Geological Survey.

Industry

PETROLEUM PRODUCTS
('000 metric tons)

	2009	2010	2011
Motor spirit (petrol)	90	96	96
Kerosene	27	29	29
Distillate fuel oils	278	298	297
Residual fuel oils and asphalt	392	420	418

Source: mostly UN Industrial Commodity Statistics Database.

SELECTED OTHER PRODUCTS
(metric tons unless otherwise indicated)

	2007	2008	2009
Flour	55,917	60,137	61,877
Refined palm oil	3,612	4,100	6,546
Timber production ('000 cu m)	287.4	244.6	190.4
Veneer sheets ('000 cu m)	264.6	263.0	264.1
Raw sugar	25,935	25,808	26,239
Beer ('000 hl)	1,000.0	1,068.1	1,126.2
Wine ('000 hl)	n.a.	43.3	38.3
Soft drinks ('000 hl)	800.4	848.7	917.4
Hydraulic cement	228,601	230,000*	250,000*
Electric energy (million kWh)	1,737	1,838	1,864

* Estimate.

Electric energy (million kWh): 1,853 in 2010; 1,769 in 2011.

Hydraulic cement (metric tons, estimates): 200,000 in 2010; 200,000 in 2011; 220,000 in 2012.

Sources: partly US Geological Survey; UN Industrial Commodity Statistics database.

Finance

CURRENCY AND EXCHANGE RATES

Monetary Units
100 centimes = 1 franc de la Coopération Financière en Afrique Centrale (CFA).

Sterling, Dollar and Euro Equivalents (31 December 2014)
£1 sterling = 843.273 francs CFA;
US $1 = 540.283 francs CFA;
€1 = 655.957 francs CFA;
10,000 francs CFA = £11.56 = $18.51 = €15.24.

Average Exchange Rate (francs CFA per US $)
2011   471.87
2012   510.53
2013   494.04

Note: An exchange rate of 1 French franc = 50 francs CFA, established in 1948, remained in force until January 1994, when the CFA franc was devalued by 50%, with the exchange rate adjusted to 1 French franc = 100 francs CFA. This relationship to French currency remained in effect with the introduction of the euro on 1 January 1999. From that date, accordingly, a fixed exchange rate of €1 = 655.957 francs CFA has been in operation.

BUDGET
('000 million francs CFA)

Revenue	2011	2012*	2013†
Taxes	1,309	1,140	1,280
Taxes on income, profits and			
capital gains	686	444	560
Individual	200	72	71
Corporations and other			
enterprises	486	372	489
Taxes on goods and services	198	253	261
Taxes on international trade and			
transactions	375	390	398
Other taxes	51	53	61
Other revenue	1,160	1,406	1,267
Non-oil tax revenue . . .	1,082	1,230	1,201
Other non-oil revenue . .	78	176	66
Total	2,469	2,546	2,547

Expenditure‡	2011	2012*	2013†
Current expenditure	1,172	1,466	1,530
Wages and salaries . . .	450	529	551
Goods and services . . .	299	333	360
Interest payments . . .	79	88	147
Capital expenditure	1,000	1,044	1,217
Domestically financed			
investment	750	796	848
Externally financed investment	250	248	369
Total	2,172	2,510	2,747

* Estimates.
† Projections.
‡ Excluding net lending ('000 million francs CFA): 19 in 2011; 74 in 2012 (estimate); 40 in 2013 (projection).
Source: IMF, *Gabon: 2012 Article IV Consultation* (March 2013).

INTERNATIONAL RESERVES
(US $ million at 31 December)

	2010	2011	2012
Gold*	9.64	19.62	21.61
IMF special drawing rights . .	204.53	203.89	204.11
Reserve position in IMF . . .	0.83	0.93	1.02
Foreign exchange	1,530.53	1,952.49	2,146.44
Total	1,745.53	2,176.93	2,373.18

* Valued at market-related prices.
2013: IMF special drawing rights 204.52; Reserve position in IMF 1.06.
Source: IMF, *International Financial Statistics*.

MONEY SUPPLY
('000 million francs CFA at 31 December)

	2011	2012	2013
Currency outside depository			
corporations	351.22	357.85	411.99
Transferable deposits . . .	885.35	863.95	1,020.14
Other deposits	540.01	731.99	734.55
Total money	1,776.59	1,953.79	2,166.69

Source: IMF, *International Financial Statistics*.

COST OF LIVING
(Consumer Price Index; base: 2000 = 100)

	2007	2008	2009
Clothing	109.8	109.5	107.2
Rent, water, electricity, gas and			
other fuels	113.1	123.4	128.5
All items (incl. others) . . .	112.7	118.5	120.8

All items: 124.1 in 2011; 127.4 in 2012; 128.1 in 2013.
Food (base: 2007 = 100): 121.4 in 2011, n.a. in 2012, 127.7 in 2013.
Source: ILO.

NATIONAL ACCOUNTS
('000 million francs CFA at current prices)
Expenditure on the Gross Domestic Product

	2011	2012	2013*
Government final consumption			
expenditure	1,161	1,308	1,483
Private final consumption			
expenditure	2,659	2,962	3,173
Gross fixed capital formation .	1,724	1,780	2,183
Changes in inventories . . .	10	—	—
Total domestic expenditure .	5,554	6,050	6,839
Exports of goods and services .	5,639	5,630	5,132
Less Imports of goods and services	2,326	2,616	3,052
GDP at purchasers' values .	8,866	9,064	8,920

Gross Domestic Product by Economic Activity

	2011	2012	2013*
Agriculture, livestock, hunting,			
forestry and fishing	251	270	280
Mining and quarrying	4,685	4,509	3,864
Manufacturing	463	497	541
Electricity, gas and water . .	64	70	75
Construction	360	388	456
Trade, restaurants and hotels .	356	403	456
Finance, insurance and real estate	927	984	1,101
Transport and communications .	399	437	477
Public administration and defence	678	778	882
Education	128	147	166
Health and social work . . .	55	60	66
GDP at factor cost	8,368	8,542	8,365
Indirect taxes	499	523	555
GDP at purchasers' values .	8,866	9,064	8,920

* Provisional figures.
Note: Deduction for imputed bank service charge assumed to be distributed at origin.
Source: African Development Bank.

BALANCE OF PAYMENTS
('000 million francs CFA)

	2010	2011*	2012†
Exports of goods f.o.b.	7,464	10,463	9,927
Petroleum	6,512	9,382	8,760
Imports of goods f.o.b.	−2,718	−3,378	−3,502
Trade balance	4,747	7,084	6,425
Services and other income (net) .	−3,221	−4,116	−3,839
Balance on goods, services and			
income	1,525	2,969	2,586
Current transfers (net) . . .	−237	−313	−301
Current balance	1,289	2,655	2,285
Direct investment (net) . . .	499	696	696
Other investment assets and			
liabilities (net)	−1,098	−1,829	−2,294
Errors and omissions	−1,012	−1,011	−575
Overall balance	−321	511	112

* Estimates.
† Projections.
Source: IMF, *Gabon: 2012 Article IV Consultation* (March 2013).

External Trade

PRINCIPAL COMMODITIES
(distribution by SITC, US $ million)

Imports	2007	2008	2009
Food and live animals . . .	308.8	359.3	352.9
Meat and meat preparations . .	98.8	117.8	104.6
Cereal and cereal preparations .	89.6	105.0	111.1
Beverages and tobacco . . .	49.8	54.4	54.1
Mineral fuels, lubricants, etc. .	103.1	121.2	182.2
Petroleum, petroleum products and related materials	90.4	117.7	168.3
Chemicals and related products	192.8	332.7	243.7
Medicinal and pharmaceutical products	67.7	178.3	73.7
Basic manufactures	432.2	425.1	562.9
Iron and steel	190.3	150.3	217.5
Machinery and transport equipment	796.5	996.5	884.5
General industrial machinery and equipment	179.3	304.9	224.5
Electrical machinery, apparatus and appliances	93.4	109.0	119.6
Road vehicles	199.7	226.5	187.6
Miscellaneous manufactured articles	171.4	195.5	170.7
Total (incl. others)	2,110.2	2,563.1	2,500.9

Exports	2007	2008	2009
Crude materials (inedible), except fuels	754.3	744.1	637.9
Cork and wood	499.8	477.2	447.4
Metalliferous ore and metal scrap .	226.4	211.3	161.5
Manganese ores and concentrates	223.0	206.9	157.5
Mineral fuels, lubricants, etc. .	5,256.7	8,530.2	4,452.7
Basic manufactures	170.2	170.3	121.6
Cork and wood manufactures .	164.8	156.4	111.0
Veneers, plywood, particle board and other wood	164.8	156.4	111.0
Total (incl. others)	6,302.0	9,565.9	5,356.0

Source: UN, *International Trade Statistics Yearbook*.

2010 ('000 million francs CFA): *Imports:* Live animals and animal products 82.1 (Meat and edible offal 55.3); Vegetable products 59.1; Prepared foodstuffs 79.8; Mineral products 179.4 (Petroleum and petroleum products 156.1); Chemical products 115.6; Plastics and articles 53.2; Base metals and articles of base metal 164.4 (Iron or steel 103.3); Machinery, mechanical and electrical equipment and parts thereof 424.9 (Mechanical equipment 323.7; Electrical equipment 101.1); Vehicles and associated transport equipment 155.4 (Road vehicles 102.9); Total imports (incl. others) 1,475.4. *Exports:* Petroleum 3,715.8; Manganese ores and concentrates 103.2; Wood and wood products 128.6; Total exports (incl. others) 4,262.1.

PRINCIPAL TRADING PARTNERS
(US $ million)

Imports c.i.f.	2007	2008	2009
Belgium	276.9	352.1	392.6
Brazil	43.7	58.9	45.3
Cameroon	65.4	60.3	52.1
China, People's Republic .	82.7	101.0	122.2
Congo, Republic	15.3	56.4	19.5
France (incl. Monaco) . . .	760.0	907.8	823.7
Germany	50.2	44.0	37.0
Greece	32.4	6.2	0.1
India	22.2	20.7	31.7
Italy	57.2	56.6	128.8
Japan	56.3	52.5	52.6

Imports c.i.f.—*continued*	2007	2008	2009
Netherlands	67.5	87.6	103.3
South Africa	44.8	42.1	44.8
Spain	58.2	48.0	46.0
Sweden	30.1	13.2	6.5
Thailand	43.6	72.7	42.5
Togo	11.0	29.8	3.5
United Arab Emirates . . .	25.7	27.3	28.7
United Kingdom	33.7	64.1	72.1
USA	126.0	190.7	178.4
Total (incl. others)	2,110.2	2,563.1	2,500.9

Exports f.o.b.	2007	2008	2009
Bermuda	0.0	124.3	0.0
China, People's Republic . . .	599.7	1,260.0	427.9
Congo, Republic	17.3	29.2	82.4
France (incl. Monaco) . . .	711.7	574.3	244.9
India	57.6	613.1	43.3
Italy	75.4	266.7	36.2
Japan	349.0	66.1	5.4
Korea, Republic	8.2	2.1	86.1
Malaysia	155.1	133.0	215.3
Netherlands	31.3	346.9	159.3
South Africa	20.3	26.3	60.1
Spain	95.3	314.8	282.1
Thailand	198.4	0.3	1.1
Trinidad and Tobago . . .	22.1	163.2	0.0
United Kingdom	97.2	2.0	112.4
USA	3,366.6	4,966.2	3,160.4
Total (incl. others)	6,302.0	9,565.9	5,356.0

Source: UN, *International Trade Statistics Yearbook*.

2010 ('000 million francs CFA): *Imports:* Belgium 199.2; Benin 31.8; Cameroon 24.1; China, People's Republic 103.7; France 452.3; Germany 23.4; Italy 39.0; Japan 27.1; Netherlands 60.0; South Africa 24.0; Spain 25.1; Thailand 28.9; United Kingdom 56.9; USA 159.7, Total (incl. others) 1,475.4. *Exports:* Australia 96.5; China, People's Republic 218.2; France 161.9; India 86.7; Indonesia 61.8; Malaysia 219.9; Netherlands 236.1; Spain 130.3; Switzerland 80.6; Trinidad and Tobago 186.5; USA 2,485.2; Total (incl. others) 4,262.1.

Transport

RAILWAYS
(traffic)

	2007	2008	2009
Passengers carried ('000) . . .	215.3	220.2	211.9
Freight carried ('000 metric tons) .	4,382	n.a.	2,878

ROAD TRAFFIC
(estimates, motor vehicles in use)

	1994	1995	1996
Passenger cars	22,310	24,000	24,750
Lorries and vans	14,850	15,840	16,490

Source: IRF, *World Road Statistics*.

SHIPPING

Flag Registered Fleet
(at 31 December)

	2012	2013	2014
Number of vessels	57	59	59
Total displacement ('000 grt) . .	170.3	170.6	171.6

Source: Lloyd's List Intelligence (www.lloydslistintelligence.com).

International Seaborne Freight Traffic
(million metric tons, Port-Gentil and Owendo)

	2007	2008	2009
Goods loaded	5,593	5,270	3,977
Goods unloaded	1,488	1,611	1,579

CIVIL AVIATION
(traffic on scheduled services)

	2007	2008	2009
Kilometres flown (million) . .	10	10	10
Passengers carried ('000) . .	535	546	525
Passenger-kilometres (million) .	947	966	931
Total ton-kilometres (million) .	161	157	148

Source: UN, *Statistical Yearbook*.

Passengers carried: 226,388 in 2010; 112,651 in 2011; 8,298 in 2012 (Source: World Bank, World Development Indicators database).

Tourism

	2011	2012	2013
Tourist arrivals ('000)	881	934	n.a.
Tourism receipts (US $ million) .	83	88	91

Source: African Development Bank.

Communications Media

	2011	2012	2013
Telephones ('000 main lines in use)	22.5	22.6	19.3
Mobile cellular telephones ('000 subscribers)	2,370.2	2,930.0	3,590.0
Broadband subscribers ('000) . .	4.5	5.0	8.9

Internet subscribers: 22,200 in 2010.

Source: International Telecommunication Union.

Education

(2010/11 unless otherwise indicated, estimates)

	Institutions	Teachers	Pupils		
			Males	Females	Total
Pre-primary .	9*	517†	22,416	22,809	45,225
Primary . .	1,175*	12,961	162,708	155,238	317,946
Secondary:					
General . .	88‡	5,062	70,623	75,457	146,080
Technical and vocational .	11‡	394†	5,025§	2,562§	7,587§
Tertiary . . .	2*	585§	6,414‖	3,662‖	10,076‖

* 1991/92 figure.
† 2000/01 figure.
‡ 1996 figure.
§ 1998/99 figure.
‖ 2002/03 figure.

Source: UNESCO Institute for Statistics.

Pupil-teacher ratio (primary education, UNESCO estimate): 24.5 in 2010/11 (Source: UNESCO Institute for Statistics).

Adult literacy rate (UNESCO estimates): 82.3% (males 84.9%; females 79.9%) in 2012 (Source: UNESCO Institute for Statistics).

Directory

Note: The telephone numbers listed in this Directory are those used when dialling from within Gabon. In order successfully to dial from abroad, it is necessary to omit the initial 0.

The Government

HEAD OF STATE

President: ALI BONGO ONDIMBA (inaugurated 16 October 2009).

COUNCIL OF MINISTERS
(April 2015)

The Government is formed by members of the Parti Démocratique Gabonais.

Prime Minister and Head of Government: Prof. DANIEL ONA ONDO.

Minister of Foreign Affairs, the Francophonie and Regional Integration: EMMANUEL ISSOZET NGONDET.

Minister of Justice, Keeper of the Seals: SÉRAPHIN MOUNDOUNGA.

Minister of Communication, Relations with the Constitutional Institutions, Government Spokesperson: DENISE MEKAM'NE.

Minister of Youth and Sport: BLAISE LOUEMBÉ.

Minister of Agriculture, Stockbreeding, Fisheries and Food Security: LUC OYOUBI.

Minister of the Interior, Public Security and Decentralization: GUY BERTRAND MAPANGOU.

Minister of Mines, Industry and Tourism: CHRISTOPHE AKAGHA MBA.

Minister of Trade, Small and Medium-sized Enterprises, Handicrafts and the Development of Services: GABRIEL TCHANGO.

Minister of Transport: PAULETTE MENGUÉ M'OWONO.

Minister of Infrastructure, Housing and Territorial Management: MAGLOIRE NGAMBIA.

Minister of Forests, the Environment and the Protection of Natural Resources: NOËL NELSON MESSONE.

Minister of Higher Education and Scientific Research: PACÔME MOUBELET BOUBEYA.

Minister of National Education and Technical and Professional Training: IDA ASSENOUET RÉTÉNO N'DIAYE.

Minister of the Digital Economy and Posts: PASTOR NGOUA NEME.

Minister of National Defence: ERNEST MPOUHO.

Minister of the Economy, the Promotion of Investments and Planning: RÉGIS IMMONGAULT TATAGANI.

Minister of Petroleum and Hydrocarbons: ETIENNE NGOUBOU.

Minister of Energy and Water Resources: DÉSIRÉ GUEDON.

Minister of the Budget and Public Accounts: CHRISTIAN MAGNAGNA.

Minister of Labour, Employment and Professional Training: SIMON NTOUTOUME EMANE.

Minister of Health and Social Security: JEAN-PIERRE OYIBA.

Minister of Human Rights, Equal Opportunities and Gabonese Nationals Abroad: ALEXANDRE TAPOYO.

Minister of Culture, the Arts and Civic Education: RUFIN MOUSSAVOU.

Minister of the Civil Service and Administrative Reform: JEAN MARIE OGANDAGA.

Minister-delegate in charge of Technical and Professional Training: CALIXTE NSIE.

Minister-delegate to the Minister of Foreign Affairs, the Francophonie and Regional Integration: DIEUDONNÉ NZENGUÉ.

Minister-delegate in charge of Housing: SERGE ENAME NSOLET.

Minister-delegate in charge of Social Security: MARIE FRANÇOISE DIKOUMBA.

Minister-delegate to the Minister of the Budget and Public Accounts: MARCELLIN AGAYA.

Minister-delegate to the Minister of Labour, Employment and Professional Training: PHILIPPE MVÉ NKOGHÉ.

Minister-delegate to the Minister of the Interior, Public Security and Decentralization: GUY MAXIENT MAMIAKA.

Minister-delegate to the Minister of the Economy, the Promotion of Investments and Planning: MARIE JULIE BILOGHE.

Minister-delegate in charge of Health: YUSSUF SIDIBE NZENGUE AKASSA.

Minister-delegate in charge of the Forest Economy: BASILE MBOUMBA.

MINISTRIES

Office of the President: BP 546, Libreville; tel. 01-72-76-00; fax 01-76-26-29.

Office of the Prime Minister: Immeuble du 2 Décembre, ave Jean Paul II, BP 95, Libreville; tel. 01-77-56-24; fax 01-77-20-04; internet www.primature.gouv.ga.

Ministry of Agriculture, Stockbreeding, Fisheries and Food Security: Immeuble de l'Ancienne Primature, ave Cornut Gentille, BP 551, Libreville; tel. 01-74-00-43; fax 01-77-37-44; internet www .agriculture.gouv.ga.

Ministry of the Budget and Public Accounts: ave Félix Eboue, Immeuble Principal, BP 165, Libreville; tel. 01-79-50 14; fax 01-79-57-37; e-mail budgetgab@hotmail.fr; internet www.budget.gouv.ga.

Ministry of the Civil Service and Administrative Reform: BP 496, Libreville; tel. 01-76-06-72; internet fonction-publique.gouv.ga.

Ministry of Communication and Relations with the Constitutional Institutions: Libreville.

Ministry of Culture, the Arts and Civic Education: blvd de l'Indépendance, Libreville; tel. 01-72-94-09; fax 01-77-33-93; e-mail dgculturegabon@yahoo.com; internet www.culture.gouv.ga.

Ministry of the Digital Economy, Communication and Posts: blvd de l'Indépendance, BP 2280, Libreville; tel. 01-76-34-35; fax 01-76 01-09; internet www.economie-numerique.gouv.ga.

Ministry of the Economy, the Promotion of Investments and Planning: Immeuble Arambo, BP 747, Libreville; tel. 01-79-55-27; fax 01-72-18-18; internet www.economie.gouv.ga.

Ministry of Energy and Water Resources: Libreville; tel. 04-10-18-18; e-mail conscom.energie.ga@gmail.com; internet www.energie .gouv.ga.

Ministry of Foreign Affairs, the Francophonie and Regional Integration: blvd du Bord de Mer, BP 2245, Libreville; tel. 01-74-23-71; fax 01-74-23-74; e-mail mae@diplomatie.gouv.ga; internet www .affaires-etrangeres.gouv.ga.

Ministry of Forests, the Environment and the Protection of Natural Resources: blvd Triomphal Omar Bongo Ondimba, BP 199, Libreville; tel. 01-76-13-81; internet www.eaux-forets.gouv.ga.

Ministry of Health and Social Security: BP 50, Libreville; tel. 01-76-35-90; internet www.sante.gouv.ga.

Ministry of Higher Education and Scientific Research: Libreville; internet www.enseignement-superieur.gouv.ga.

Ministry of Infrastructure, Housing and Territorial Management: BP 803, Libreville; tel. 01-74-71-96; fax 01-77-33-31; internet www.equipement.gouv.ga.

Ministry of Human Rights, Equal Opportunities and Gabonese Nationals Abroad: Libreville; internet www.droits-humains .gouv.ga.

Ministry of the Interior, Public Security, Immigration and Decentralization: ave de Cointet, BP 2110, Libreville; tel. 01-76-20-64; fax 01-72-13-89; internet www.interieur.gouv.ga.

Ministry of Justice: BP 547, Libreville; tel. 01-72-18-30; fax 01-72-33-84; internet www.justice.gouv.ga.

Ministry of Labour, Employment and Professional Training: Libreville; internet www.travail.gouv.ga.

Ministry of Mines, Industry and Tourism: Immeuble du 2 Décembre, 852 blvd Triomphal Bâtiment B, 3e étage, BP 874, Libreville; tel. 01-77-86-54; e-mail sg@mines.gouv.ga; internet www.mines.gouv.ga.

Ministry of National Defence: BP 13493, Libreville; tel. 01-76-35-67; fax 01-72-71-87; internet www.defense-nationale.gouv.ga.

Ministry of National Education and Technical and Professional Training: BP 6, Libreville; tel. 01-76-42-65; fax 01-76-46-41; internet www.education-nationale.gouv.ga.

Ministry of Petroleum and Hydrocarbons: BP 1172, Libreville; internet www.petrole.gouv.ga.

Ministry of Trade, Small and Medium-sized Enterprises, Handicrafts and the Development of Services: BP 4120, Libreville; tel. 01-72-49-75; internet www.pme.gouv.ga.

Ministry of Transport: BP 803, Libreville; tel. 01-74-71-96; fax 01-77-33-31.

Ministry of Youth and Sport: BP 2150, Libreville; tel. 01-74-00-19; fax 01-74-65-89; internet www.jeunesse-sports.gouv.ga.

President

Presidential Election, 30 August 2009

Candidate	Valid votes	% of valid votes
Ali Bongo Ondimba (PDG) . . .	141,952	41.73
André Mba Obame (Ind.) . . .	88,028	25.88
Pierre Mamboundou (UPG) . . .	85,797	25.22
Zacharie Myboto (UGDD) . . .	13,418	3.94
Casimir Oyé Mba (Ind.)	3,118	0.92
Pierre-Claver Maganga Moussavou (PSD)	2,576	0.76
Bruno Ben Moubamba (Ind.) . .	963	0.28
Georges Bruno Ngoussi (Ind.) . .	915	0.27
Jules Artides Bourdès Ogouliguende (CDJ)	695	0.20
Albert Ondo Ossa (Ind.)	674	0.20
Others	2,028	0.60
Total	340,178*	100.00

* The total number of votes officially attributed to candidates by the Constitutional Court amounted to 340,164. However, that body declared the total number of valid votes cast to be 340,178. Additionally, there were 17,443 spoiled ballots. Several of the defeated candidates formally protested against the results and a recount of the votes was subsequently held. On 12 October the Constitutional Court announced that Bongo Ondimba had secured 141,665 valid votes, equating to 41.79%, while the number of votes attributed to Mamboundou and Mba Obame was amended to 86,875 (25.64%) and 85,814 (25.33%), respectively, thus reversing their placings in the election. No figures for the remaining candidates or the total number of votes cast were made available.

Legislature

NATIONAL ASSEMBLY

National Assembly: Palais Léon Mba, blvd Triomphal Omar Bongo, BP 29, Libreville; tel. 01-74-90-21; fax 01-72-61-96; internet www.assemblee-nationale.ga.

President: GUY NDZOUBA NDAMA.

General Election, 17 December 2011

Party	Seats
Parti Démocratique Gabonais (PDG)	114*
Rassemblement pour le Gabon (RPG)	3
Cercle des Libéraux Réformateurs (CLR)	1
Parti Social-Démocrate (PSD)	1
Union pour la Nouvelle République (UPNR)	1
Total	120†

* One seat was won in alliance with the Parti Gabonais du Centre Indépendant (PGCI).
† The results of voting in six constituencies were subsequently annulled by the Constitutional Court owing to irregularities. On 5 May 2012 by-elections were held for the six seats, all of which were won by the PDG, leaving party representations unchanged.

SENATE

Senate: Libreville; internet www.senat.ga.

President: LUCIE MILEBOU AUBUSSON.

Election, 18 January 2009

Party	Seats
Parti Démocratique Gabonais (PDG)	75
Rassemblement pour le Gabon (RPG)	6
Parti Gabonais du Centre Indépendant (PGCI)	3
Union du Peuple Gabonais (UPG)	3
Cercle des Libéraux Réformateurs (CLR)	2
Parti Social-Démocrate (PSD)	2
Union Gabonaise pour la Démocratie et le Développement (UGDD)	2
Alliance Démocratique et Républicaine (ADERE)	1
Independents	8
Total	**102**

Following the appointment of a PDG senator as ambassador to France, a by-election was held on 5 May 2012 for the vacated seat. This was won by the PDG

Election Commission

Commission Electorale Nationale Autonome et Permanente (CENAP): Libreville; f. 2006 to replace the Commission Nationale Electorale; Pres. appointed by the Constitutional Court; Pres. RENÉ ABOGHÉ ELLA.

Political Organizations

Alliance Démocratique et Républicaine (ADERE): Pres. (vacant); Sec.-Gen. DIDJOB DIVUNGUI-DI-N'DINGUE.

Cercle des Libéraux Réformateurs (CLR): f. 1993 by breakaway faction of the PDG; Leader JEAN-BONIFACE ASSELE.

Congrès pour la Démocratie et la Justice (CDJ): tel. 01-70-00-00; e-mail contact@bourdes-gabon.com; internet www.bourdes-gabon.com; Pres. JULES BOURDÈS OGOULIGUENDE.

Mouvement d'Emancipation Socialiste du Peuple: Leader MOUANGA MBADINGA.

Parti Démocratique Gabonais (PDG): Immeuble PETROGAB, BP 268, Libreville; tel. 01-70-31-21; fax 01-70-31-46; internet www.gabon-pdg.org; f. 1968; sole legal party 1968–90; Leader ALI BONGO ONDIMBA; Sec.-Gen. FAUSTIN BOUKOUBI.

Parti Gabonais du Centre Indépendant (PGCI): allied to the PDG; Leader LUCCHERI GAHILA.

Parti Gabonais du Progrès (PGP): f. 1990; Pres. BENOÎT MOUITY NZAMBA.

Parti Social-Démocrate (PSD): f. 1991; Leader PIERRE-CLAVER MAGANGA MOUSSAVOU.

Rassemblement pour la Démocratie et le Progrès (RDP): Pres. PÉPIN MOUNGOKODJI.

Rassemblement pour le Gabon (RPG): f. 1990 as MORENA des Bûcherons; renamed Rassemblement National des Bûcherons in 1991, name changed as above in 2000; allied to the PDG; Pres. Fr PAUL M'BA ABESSOLE.

Rassemblement National des Bûcherons—Démocratique (RNB): Libreville; f. 1991; Leader PIERRE ANDRÉ KOMBILA.

Union Démocratique et Sociale (UDS): f. 1996; Leader HERVÉ OSSAMANÉ ONOUVIÉ.

Union Nationale (UN): f. 2010 through the merger of the Union Gabonaise pour la Démocratie et le Développement (UGDD), the Mouvement Africain de Développement (MAD) and the Rassemblement National des Républicains (RNR); forcibly banned by the Government in Jan. 2011; ban revoked in Jan. 2015; Leader ZACHARIE MYBOTO.

Union pour la Nouvelle République (UPNR): Immeuble Score, 657 ave du Col Parant, BP 4049, Libreville; tel. 01-77-40-13; fax 01-77-40-17; e-mail info@louisgastonmayila.com; internet www.louisgastonmayila.com; f. 2007 following the merger of the Front pour l'Unité Nationale (FUNDU) and the Rassemblement des Républicains Indépendants (RRI); Leader LOUIS-GASTON MAYILA.

Union du Peuple Gabonais (UPG): BP 6048, Awendjé, Libreville; tel. 07-14-61-61 (mobile); internet www.upg-gabon.org; f. 1989 in Paris, France; Sec.-Gen. BRUNO BEN MOUBAMBA.

Union pour le Progrès National (UPN): Leader DANIEL TENGUE NZOUNDO.

Diplomatic Representation

EMBASSIES IN GABON

Algeria: blvd du Bord de mer, BP 4008, Libreville; tel. 01-44-38-02; fax 01-73-14-03; e-mail algerie@ambassade-lbv-algerie.com; Ambassador DJIHED-EDDINE BELKAS.

Angola: BP 4884, Libreville; tel. 01-73-04-26; fax 01-73-76-24; Ambassador TOKO DIAKENGA SERÃO.

Benin: BP 3851, Akebe, Libreville; tel. 01-73-76-82; fax 01-73-77-75; e-mail ambassade.benin@inet.ga; internet www.maebenin.bj/Libreville.htm; Ambassador SYMPHORIEN CODJO ACHODÉ.

Brazil: blvd de l'Indépendance, BP 3899, Libreville; tel. 01-76-05-35; fax 01-74-03-43; e-mail emblibreville@inet.ga; internet libreville.itamaraty.gov.br; Ambassador BRUNO LUIZ DOS SANTOS COBUCCIO.

Cameroon: blvd Léon Mba, BP 14001, Libreville; tel. 01-73-28-00; Ambassador SAMUEL MVONDO AYOLO.

China, People's Republic: blvd Triomphale Omar Bongo, BP 3914, Libreville; tel. 01-74-32-07; fax 01-74-75-96; e-mail gzy@internetgabon.com; internet ga.china-embassy.org; Ambassador SUN JIWEN.

Congo, Democratic Republic: BP 2257, Libreville; tel. 01-73-11-61; fax 01-73-81-41; Ambassador KABANGI KAUMBU BULA.

Congo, Republic: BP 269, Libreville; tel. 01-73-29-06; e-mail ambacobrazzalibreville@yahoo.fr; Ambassador PIERRE NZILA.

Côte d'Ivoire: Charbonnages, BP 3861, Libreville; tel. 01-73-82-70; fax 01-73-82-87; e-mail ambacigabon@yahoo.fr; Ambassador PHILIPPE MANGOU.

Egypt: Immeuble Floria, 1 blvd de la Mer, Quartier Batterie IV, BP 4240, Libreville; tel. 01-73-25-38; fax 01-73-25-19; Ambassador HISHAM FATHY MOHAMED.

Equatorial Guinea: BP 1462, Libreville; tel. 01-73-25-23; fax 01-73-25-22; Ambassador JOSÉ ESONO BACALE.

France: 1 rue du pont Pirah, BP 2125, Libreville; tel. 01-79-70-00; fax 01-79-70-09; e-mail scac@ambafrance-ga.org; internet www.ambafrance-ga.org; Ambassador DOMINIQUE RENAUX.

Germany: blvd de l'Indépendance, Immeuble les Frangipaniers, BP 299, Libreville; tel. 01-76-01-88; fax 01-72-40-12; e-mail amb-allegmagne@inet.ga; internet www.libreville.diplo.de; Ambassador STEFAN GRAF.

Guinea: BP 4046, Libreville; tel. 01-73-85-09; fax 01-73-85-11; Ambassador MOHAMED SAMPIL.

Italy: Immeuble Personnaz et Gardin, 321 rue de la Mairie, BP 2251, Libreville; tel. 01-74-28-92; fax 01-74-80-35; e-mail ambasciata.libreville@esteri.it; internet www.amblibreville.esteri.it; Ambassador PAOLO DE NICOLO.

Japan: blvd du Bord de Mer, BP 2259, Libreville; tel. 01-73-22-97; fax 01-73-60-60; e-mail amb.japon@lv.mofa.go.jp; internet www.ga.emb-japan.go.jp; Ambassador MASAO KOBAYASHI.

Korea, Republic: BP 2620, Libreville; tel. 01-73-40-00; fax 01-73-99-05; e-mail gabon-ambcoree@mofa.go.kr; internet gab.mofa.go.kr; Ambassador CHEOLKYU CHOE.

Lebanon: BP 3341, Libreville; tel. and fax 01-73-68-77; e-mail amb.lib.gab@inet.ga; Ambassador KENJ EL HAJAL.

Mali: BP 4007, Quartier Batterie IV, Libreville; tel. 01-73-82-73; fax 01-73-82-80; e-mail ambamaga@yahoo.fr; Ambassador DADIE YACOUBA DAGNAKO.

Mauritania: BP 3917, Libreville; tel. 01-74-31-65; fax 01-74-01-62; Ambassador El Hadj THIAM.

Morocco: blvd de l'Indépendance, Immeuble CK 2, BP 3983, Libreville; tel. 01-77-41-51; fax 01-77-41-50; e-mail sifamalbv@inet.ga; Ambassador ALI BOJI.

Nigeria: ave du Président Léon-M'Ba, Quartier blvd Léon-M'Ba, BP 1191, Libreville; tel. 01-73-22-03; fax 01-73-29-14; e-mail nigeriamission@internetgabon.com; Ambassador BASSEY ARCHIBONG.

Russian Federation: BP 3963, Libreville; tel. 01-72-48-68; fax 01-72-48-70; e-mail ambrusga@mail.ru; internet www.gabon.mid.ru; Ambassador DMITRY V. KOURAKOV.

São Tomé and Príncipe: BP 489, Libreville; tel. 01-72-09-94; Ambassador URBINO JOSÉ GONHALVES BOTELÇO.

Saudi Arabia: Haut de Gue-Gue, derrière l'Hotel Intercontinental, Libreville; tel. 01-73-84-44; fax 01-73-58-37; e-mail gaemb@mofa.gov.sa; internet embassies.mofa.gov.sa/sites/gabon; Ambassador ADNAN ABDULRAHMAN ABDUL ALMANDEEL.

Senegal: Quartier Sobraga, BP 3856, Libreville; tel. 01-77-42-67; fax 01-77-42-68; e-mail ambasengab@yahoo.fr; Ambassador SAOUDATOU NDIAYE SECK.

South Africa: Immeuble les Arcades, 142 rue des Chavannes, BP 4063, Libreville; tel. 01-77-45-30; fax 01-77-45-36; e-mail libreville

.consular@foreign.gov.za; internet www.dirco.gov.za/gabon; Ambassador PEARL NOMVUME MAGAQA.

Spain: Immeuble Diamant, 2ème étage, blvd de l'Indépendance, BP 1157, Libreville; tel. 01-72-12-64; fax 01-74-88-73; e-mail ambespga@mail.mae.es; Ambassador ANTONIO ALVAREZ BARTHE.

Togo: BP 14160, Libreville; tel. 01-73-29-04; fax 01-73-32-61; Ambassador (vacant).

Ukraine: BP 23746, Libreville; tel. 01-44-51-03; e-mail emb_ga@mfa.gov.ua; Ambassador SERGIY MISHUSTIN.

USA: Avorbam, La Sablière, BP 4000, Libreville; tel. 01-45-71-00; fax 01-74-55-07; e-mail usembassylibreville@state.gov; internet libreville.usembassy.gov; Chargé d'affaires CYNTHIA AKUETTEH.

Judicial System

Justice is dispensed on behalf of the Gabonese people by the three autonomous chambers of the Supreme Court (judicial, administrative and accounting), the Constitutional Court, the Council of State, the Courts of Appeal, the Audit Court, the Provincial Courts, the High Court and the other special courts of law.

Supreme Court (Cour de Cassation): Palais de Justice, BP 1043, Libreville; tel. 01-72-17-00; fax 01-76-66-18; e-mail siege@courdecassation-gabon.org; internet www.courdecassation-gabon.org; three chambers: judicial, administrative and accounting; Pres. HONORÉ MOUNDOUNGA; Sec.-Gen. MARIE SYLVIE NGASSADJOGO.

Constitutional Court: BP 4025, Libreville; tel. 01-76-62-88; fax 01-76-10-17; internet www.cour-constitutionnelle.ga; has jurisdiction on: the control of the constitutionality of laws before promulgation; all electoral litigations; all matters concerning individual fundamental rights and public liberties; the interpretation of the Constitution; and arbitration of conflicts of jurisdiction arising among the state's institutions; Pres. MARIE MADELEINE MBORANTSUO.

Council of State: BP 547, Libreville; tel. 01-72-17-00; Pres. MARTIN AKENDENGUE.

Courts of Appeal: Libreville and Franceville.

Audit Court (Cour des Comptes): BP 752, Libreville; tel. 01-70-54-15; fax 01-70-40-81; e-mail cour_des_comptes_gabon@yahoo.fr; Pres. GILBERT NGOULAKIA.

Religion

About 60% of Gabon's population are Christians, mainly adherents of the Roman Catholic Church. About 40% are animists and fewer than 1% are Muslims.

CHRISTIANITY

The Roman Catholic Church

Gabon comprises one archdiocese, four dioceses and one apostolic vicariat. Some 50% of the population are Roman Catholics.

Bishops' Conference: Conférence Episcopale du Gabon, BP 2146, Libreville; tel. 01-72-20-73; f. 1989; Pres. Most Rev. TIMOTHÉE MODIBO-NZOCKENA (Bishop of Franceville).

Archbishop of Libreville: Most Rev. BASILE MVÉ ENGONE, Archevêché, Sainte-Marie, BP 2146, Libreville; tel. and fax 01-72-20-73; e-mail basilemve@yahoo.fr.

Protestant Churches

Christian and Missionary Alliance: BP 13021, Libreville; tel. 01-73-24-39; e-mail fdgabon@gmail.com; active in the south of the country; Dir Dr DAVID THOMPSON; 115 org. mem. churches, 11,226 baptized mems.

Eglise Evangélique du Gabon: BP 10080, Libreville; tel. 01-72-41-92; f. 1842; independent since 1961; 205,000 mems; Pres. Pastor JEAN-JACQUES NDONG EKOUAGHÉ; Sec. Rev. BASILE NGUEMA OLLOGHO. The Evangelical Church of South Gabon and the Evangelical Pentecostal Church are also active in Gabon.

The Press

La Concorde: Libreville; f. 2005; owned by TV+ group; daily; Dir FRANÇOIS ONDO EDOU; circ. 10,000.

Economie Gabon +: Immeuble BICP, BP 4562, Libreville; tel. 01-44-11-62; e-mail contact@economie-gabon.com; internet www.economie-gabon.com; quarterly; Dir of Publication PHILIPPE CHANDEZON.

Gabon Libre: BP 6439, Libreville; tel. 01-72-42-22; weekly; Dir DZIME EKANG; Editor RENÉ NZOVI.

Gabon-Matin: BP 168, Libreville; daily; publ. by Agence Gabonaise de Presse; Man. HILARION VENDANY; circ. 18,000.

Gabon Show: Libreville; f. 2004; independent; satirical; printed in Cameroon; Man. Editor FULBERT WORA; weekly; circ. 3,000.

Journal Officiel de la République Gabonaise: BP 563, Libreville; f. 1959; fortnightly; Man. EMMANUEL OBAMÉ.

Le Peuple: BP 2170, Libreville; tel. 06-03-09-94 (mobile); e-mail lepeuple@lepeuple.info; internet www.lepeuple.info; f. 2002; weekly; Dir of Publication and Editor-in-Chief AUGUSTIN MVEME OBIANG.

Le Progressiste: blvd Léon-M'Ba, BP 7000, Libreville; tel. 01-74-54-01; f. 1990; Dir BENOÎT MOUITY NZAMBA; Editor JACQUES MOURENDE-TSIOBA.

La Relance: BP 268, Libreville; tel. 01-72-93-08; weekly; publ. of the Parti Démocratique Gabonais; Pres. JACQUES ADIAHÉNOT; Dir RENÉ NDEMEZO'O OBIANG.

Le Réveil: BP 20386, Libreville; tel. and fax 01-73-17-21; weekly; Man. ALBERT YANGARI; Editor RENÉ NZOVI; circ. 8,000.

L'Union: Sonapresse, BP 3849, Libreville; tel. 01-73-58-61; fax 01-73-58-62; e-mail union.sonapresse@gmail.com; internet www.union.sonapresse.com; f. 1974; 75% state-owned; daily; official govt publ; Dir-Gen. ALBERT YANAGRI; circ. 20,000.

Zoom Hebdo: Carrefour London, BP 352, Libreville; tel. 01-76-44-54; fax 01-74-67-50; e-mail zoomhebdo@assala.net; internet www.zoomhebdo.com; Friday; f. 1991; Dir-Gen. HANS RAYMOND KWAAI-TAAL; circ. 12,000–20,000.

PRESS ASSOCIATIONS

Association de la Presse Privée Ecrite Libre (APPLE): Libreville.

Observatoire Gabonais des Médias (OGM): Libreville.

NEWS AGENCIES

Agence Gabonaise de Presse (AGP): BP 168, Libreville; tel. 01-44-35-07; fax 01-44-35-08; internet www.agpgabon.ga; f. 1960; Pres. LIN JOËL NDEMBET; Dir OLIVIER MOUKETOU.

BERP International: BP 8483, Libreville; tel. 06-06-62-91 (mobile); fax 01-74-15-54 (mobile); e-mail berp8483@hotmail.com; internet www.infosplusgabon.com/berp.php3; f. 1995; Dir ANTOINE LAWSON.

Publishers

Gabonaise d'Imprimerie (GABIMP): BP 154, Libreville; tel. 01-70-20-88; fax 01-70-31-85; e-mail gabimp@inet.ga; f. 1973; Dir CLAIRE VIAL.

Multipress Gabon: blvd Léon-M'Ba, BP 3875, Libreville; tel. 01-73-22-33; fax 01-73-63-72; e-mail secretariat@multipress-gabon.com; internet multipress-gabon.com; f. 1973; monopoly distributors of magazines and newspapers; Dir-Gen. JEAN-LUC PHALEMPIN.

Société Nationale de Presse et d'Edition (SONAPRESSE): BP 3849, Libreville; tel. and fax 01-73-58-60; e-mail unionplus@intergabon.com; internet union.sonapresse.com; f. 1975; Man. Dir ALBERT YANGARI.

Broadcasting and Communications

TELECOMMUNICATIONS

At the end of 2013 there were four providers of mobile cellular telephone services in Gabon, while Gabon Télécom was the sole provider of fixed-line services.

Airtel Gabon SA: 124 ave Bouët, Montagne Sainte, BP 9259, Libreville; tel. 07-28-01-11 (mobile); e-mail info.africa@ga.airtel.com; internet africa.airtel.com/gabon; f. 2000; fmrly Zain Gabon, present name adopted 2010; Dir-Gen. ANTOINE PAMBORO.

Gabon Télécom: Immeuble du Delta Postal, BP 20000, Libreville; tel. 01-78-70-00; fax 01-78-67-70; e-mail gabontelecom@gabontelecom.ga; internet www.gabontelecom.ga; f. 2001; provider of telecommunications, incl. satellite, internet and cellular systems; 51% owned by Maroc Telecom; Dir-Gen. ABDERRAHIM KOUMAA.

Moov Gabon: Immeuble Rénovation, blvd du Bord de Mer, BP 12470, Libreville; tel. 01-76-83-83; fax 01-76-83-88; internet www.moov.ga; f. 2000; Dir-Gen. ABDOULAYE CISSÉ.

USAN Gabon: Libreville; e-mail info@azur-gabon.com; internet www.azur-gabon.com; f. 2009; provides mobile cellular services under Azur network; Dir-Gen. GEORGE AKOURY.

Regulatory Authorities

Agence de Régulation des Communications Electroniques et des Postes (ARCEP): Quartier Haut de Gué-Gué, face Bureau de la Francophonie, BP 50000, Libreville; tel. 01-44-68-11; fax 01-44-68-06; e-mail artel@inet.ga; internet www.artel.ga; f. 2012 following merger of the Agence de Régulation des Télécommunications (f. 2001) and the Agence de Régulation des Postes (f. 2001); Pres. LIN MOMBO; Dir-Gen. SERGE ESSONGUÉ EWAMPONGO.

Agence Nationale des Infrastructures Numériques et des Fréquences: Cours Pasteur, Immeuble de la Solde, BP 798, Libreville; tel. 01-79-52-77; e-mail info@aninf.ga; internet www.aninf.ga; f. 2011; Dir-Gen. ALEX BERNARD BONGO ONDIMBA.

BROADCASTING

Conseil National de la Communication: BP 6437, Libreville; tel. 01-72-82-60; fax 01-72-82-71; e-mail infos@cnc.ga; f. 1991; Pres. JEAN FRANÇOIS NDONGOU.

Radio

The national network, 'La Voix de la Rénovation', and a provincial network broadcast for 24 hours each day in French and local languages.

Africa No. 1: BP 1, Libreville; tel. 01-74-07-34; fax 01-74-21-33; e-mail africaradio1@yahoo.fr; internet www.africa1.com; f. 1981; 35% state-controlled; int. commercial radio station; daily programmes in French and English; Pres. ELMAHJOUR AMMAR GOMAA; Sec.-Gen. LOUIS BARTHÉLEMY MAPANGOU.

Radiodiffusion-Télévision Gabonaise (RTG): BP 150, Libreville; tel. 01-73-20-25; fax 01-73-21-53; internet www.rtg1.ga; f. 1959; state-controlled; broadcasts two channels, RTG1 and RTG2; Dir-Gen. (RTG1) DAVID ELLA MINTSA; Dir-Gen. (RTG2) FLORENCE MBANI; Dir of Radio GILLES TERENCE NZOGHE.

Radio Génération Nouvelle: tel. 07-42-72-83 (mobile); e-mail contact@generation-nouvelle.org; f. 1996; Dir JEAN-BONIFACE ASSELE.

Television

Radiodiffusion-Télévision Gabonaise (RTG): see Radio.

Radio Télévision Nazareth (RTN): Okala Carrière, BP 9563, Libreville; tel. 01-76-82-58; fax 01-72-20-44; e-mail rtntv@yahoo.fr; internet www.rtngabon.info; Pres. and Dir-Gen. GEORGES BRUNO NGOUSSI.

TV+: Immeuble Dumez, blvd du Bord de mer, BP 8344, Libreville; operation suspended in Jan. 2012; Owner ANDRÉ MBA OBAME.

Finance

(cap. = capital; res = reserves; dep. = deposits; m. = million; brs = branches; amounts in francs CFA)

BANKING

In 2013 there were nine banks and three other financial institutions in Gabon.

Central Bank

Banque des Etats de l'Afrique Centrale (BEAC): BP 112, Libreville; tel. 01-76-13-52; fax 01-74-45-63; e-mail beaclbv@beac.int; internet www.beac.int; f. 1973; HQ in Yaoundé, Cameroon; bank of issue for mem. states of the Communauté Economique et Monétaire de l'Afrique Centrale (CEMAC, fmrly Union Douanière et Economique de l'Afrique Centrale), comprising Cameroon, the Central African Repub., Chad, the Repub. of the Congo, Equatorial Guinea and Gabon; cap. 88,000m., res 227,843m., dep. 4,110,966m. (Dec. 2007); Gov. LUCAS ABAGA NCHAMA; Dir in Gabon DENIS MEPOREWA; 4 brs in Gabon.

Commercial Banks

Banque Internationale pour le Commerce et l'Industrie du Gabon, SA (BICIG): ave du Colonel Parant, BP 2241, Libreville; tel. 01-76-26-13; fax 01-74-40-34; e-mail bicignet@bnpparibas.com; internet bicig-gabon.com; f. 1973; 26.30% state-owned, 46.67% owned by BNP Paribas SA; cap. 18,000.0m., res 4,577.9m., dep. 374,650.8m. (Dec. 2013); Pres. ETIENNE GUY MOUVAGHA TCHIOBA; Dir-Gen. CLAUDE AYO-IGUENDHA; 9 brs.

BGFI Bank: blvd de l'Indépendance, BP 2253, Libreville; tel. 01-74-32-40; fax 01-79-62-19; e-mail agence_libreville@bgfi.com; internet www.bgfi.com; f. 1972 as Banque Gabonaise et Française Internationale (BGFI); name changed as above in March 2000; res 194,846m., dep. 2,544,573m., total assets 3,023,037m. (Dec. 2013); Pres. and Dir-Gen. HENRI-CLAUDE OYIMA; 9 brs.

Citibank: 810 blvd Quaben, rue Kringer, BP 3940, Libreville; tel. 01-73-19-16; fax 01-73-37-86; total assets 1,000m. (Dec. 2004); Dir-Gen. JULIETTE WEISFLOG.

Ecobank Gabon: 214 ave Bouet, 9ème étage, Montagne Sainte, BP 12111, Libreville; tel. 01-76-20-71; fax 01-76-20-75; e-mail ecobankga@ecobank.com; internet www.ecobank.com; Chair. JOSEPH BERRE OWONDAULT; Dir-Gen. GAËLLE BITEGHE.

Orabank Gabon: Immeuble des Frangipaniers, blvd de l'Indépendance, BP 20333, Libreville; tel. 01-77-50-78; fax 01-72-41-97; e-mail info-ga@orabank.net; internet www.orabank.net; f. 2002; 85.47% owned by Oragroup SA (Togo); Pres. RENÉ-HILAIRE ADIAHENO; Dir-Gen. MAMOUDOU KANE; 3 brs.

Union Gabonaise de Banque, SA (UGB): ave du Colonel Parant, BP 315, Libreville; tel. 01-77-70-00; fax 01-76-46-16; e-mail ugbdio@internetgabon.com; internet www.ugb-banque.com; f. 1962; a subsidiary of Groupe Attijariwafa Bank; cap. 7,400.0m., res 6,471.8m., dep. 301,704.8m. (Dec. 2011); Dir-Gen. ABDELAZIZ YAAQOUBI; 4 brs.

Development Banks

Banque Gabonaise de Développement (BGD): rue Alfred Marche, BP 5, Libreville; tel. 01-76-24-29; fax 01-74-26-99; e-mail infos@bgd-gabon.com; internet www.bgd-gabon.com; f. 1960; 69.01% state-owned; cap. 25,200m., res 7,677m. (Dec. 2006); Dir-Gen. ROGER OWONO MBA.

Banque de l'Habitat du Gabon (BHG): BP 574, Libreville; tel. 01-76-99-75; fax 01-76-99-77; Dir-Gen. MAGLOIRE NGAMBIA.

Financial Institutions

Alios Finance Gabon (AFG): Immeuble SOGACA, BP 63, Libreville; tel. 01-76-08-46; fax 01-76-01-03; internet www.alios-finance.com; car finance; 43% owned by CFAO Gabon, 10% state-owned; cap. and res 2,828.0m., total assets 18,583.0m. (Dec. 2003); Dir-Gen. FAISSAL CHAHROUR.

BICI-Bail Gabon: Immeuble BICIG, 5ème étage, ave du Colonel Parant, BP 2241, Libreville; tel. 01-77-75-52; fax 01-77-48-15; internet www.bicig.ga/bicibail.htm; BNP Paribas-owned.

Société Financière Transafricaine (FINATRA): blvd de l'Indépendance, BP 8645, Libreville; tel. and fax 01-77-40-87; e-mail finatra@bgfi.com; internet www.bgfi.com; f. 1997; 50% owned by BGFI Bank; Dir-Gen. MARIE CÉLINE NTSAME-MEZUI.

INSURANCE

In 2010 there were eight insurance companies in Gabon, of which three provided life insurance and five provided non-life insurance.

Assinco: BP 7812, Libreville; tel. 01-72-19-25; fax 01-72-19-29; e-mail assinco@assinco-sa.com; internet assinco-sa.com; Dir EUGÉNIE DENDÉ.

Assureurs Conseils Gabonais (ACG): Immeuble Shell-Gabon, rue de la Mairie, BP 2138, Libreville; tel. 01-74-32-90; fax 01-76-04-39; e-mail acg@ascoma.com; represents foreign insurance cos; Dir MICHELLE VALETTE.

Axa Gabon: 1935 blvd de l'Indépendance, BP 4047, Libreville; tel. 01-79-80-80; fax 01-74-18-46; e-mail axa-assurances@axa-gabon.ga; internet www.axa-gabon.com; f. 1985; Dir JOËL MULLER.

Gras Savoye Gabon: ave du Colonel Parant, BP 2148, Libreville; tel. 01-74-31-53; fax 01-74-68-38; e-mail contact@ga.grassavoye.com; internet www.ga.grassavoye.com; insurance broker; Dir FERDINAND VIGNAC.

NSIA Gabon: Résidence les Frangipaniers, blvd de l'Indépendance, BP 2221–2225, Libreville; tel. 01-72-13-90; fax 01-74-17-02; e-mail nsiagabon@groupensia.com; internet www.nsiagabon.com; f. 2000 by acquisition of Assurances Mutuelles du Gabon; name changed as above in 2006; non-life insurance; owned by NSIA Participations S.A. Holding (Côte d'Ivoire); Dir-Gen. CÉSAR ÉKOMIE-AFENE.

NSIA Vie Gabon: BP 2221, Libreville; tel. 01-72-13-90; fax 01-74-17-02; e-mail nsiaviegabon@groupensia.com; Dir-Gen. FIDÈLE MBANA.

OGAR Gabon: 1881 blvd de l'Indépendance, BP 201, Libreville; tel. 01-76-15-96; fax 01-76-58-16; e-mail ogar@inet.ga; internet groupeogar.com; non-life insurance; Pres. BERNARD BARTOSZEK; also OGAR Vie for life insurance.

Saham Assurances Gabon: Immeuble Rénovation, ave du Colonel Parant, BP 6239, Libreville; tel. 01-76-06-51; fax 01-76-06-52; e-mail gabon@groupecolina.com; internet www.sahamassurance.ga; fmrly Colina Assurances Gabon; name changed as above in 2014; non-life insurance; Dir-Gen. ERARD NONYU MOUTASSIE.

Sunu Assurances Vie Gabon (UAG-Vie): ave du Colonel Parant, BP 2137, Libreville; tel. 01-74-34-34; fax 01-72-48-57; e-mail gabon.sunuvie@sunu-group.com; internet www.sunu-group.com; fmrly Union des Assurances du Gabon-Vie; present name adopted 2015; life insurance; 80.65% owned by Groupe SUNU; Pres. ALBERT ALEWINA CHAVIHOT; Dir-Gen. APOLLINAIRE EVA ESSANGONE.

Insurance Association

Fédération Gabonaise des Sociétés d'Assurances (FEGASA): BP 4005, Libreville; tel. 01-74-45-29; fax 01-77-58-23; Pres. FIDÈLE MBANA.

Trade and Industry

GOVERNMENT AGENCIES

Agence Gabonaise de Sécurité Alimentaire: Libreville; Pres. ANDRE JULES NDJAMBE; Dir-Gen. Dr SYLVAIN PATRICK ENKORO.

Centre de Développement des Entreprises (CDE): Quartier Okala, BP 13740, Libreville; tel. 01-76-87-65; fax 01-76-87-64; internet www.cdegabon.com; f. 2010 to replace the Agence pour la Promotion des Investissements Privés du Gabon (APIP); promotes private investment; Pres. ANICETTE NANDA OVIGA; Dir-Gen. ALFRED NGUIA BANDA.

Comité de Privatisation: Libreville; Sec.-Gen. FÉLIX ONKEYA.

Conseil Economique et Social du Gabon: BP 1075, Libreville; tel. 01-73-19-47; fax 01-73-19-40; e-mail ces@inet.ga; internet www.cesgabon.ga; comprises representatives from salaried workers, employers and Govt; commissions on economic, financial and social affairs, and forestry and agriculture; Pres. PAUL BIYOGHE MBA.

Fonds Gabonais d'Investissement Stratégique: Libreville; f. 2010; Pres. CLAUDE AYO INGUENDA; Dir SERGE THIERRY MICKOTO CHAVAGNE.

DEVELOPMENT ORGANIZATIONS

Agence de Collecte et Commercialisation des Produits Agricoles (ACCOPA): Libreville; Pres. CHRISTIAN MENVIE M'OBAME; Dir-Gen. CHRIS MOMBO NZASSI.

Agence Française de Développement (AFD): blvd de l'Indépendance, BP 64, Libreville; tel. 01-74-33-74; fax 01-74-51-25; e-mail afdlibreville@groupe-afd.org; internet www.afd.fr; Dir YVES PICARD.

Agence Nationale des Grands Travaux (ANGT): Immeuble du Bord de mer, 1er étage, BP 23765, Libreville; tel. 07-04-62-77 (mobile); e-mail info@angtmedia.com; internet www.angt-gabon.com; f. 2010; Dir-Gen. JIM DUTTON.

Agence Nationale de Promotion de la Petite et Moyenne Entreprise (PromoGabon): BP 2111, Libreville; tel. 06-26-79-19 (mobile); fax 01-74-89-59; internet www.promogabon.ga; f. 1964; state-controlled; promotes and assists small and medium-sized industries; Pres. SIMON BOULAMATARI; Man. Dir GEORGETTE ONGALA.

Agence de Régulation du Marché des Produits Forestiers: Libreville; Dir-Gen. PIERRE NGAVOURA.

Conservation et Utilisation Rationelle des Ecosystèmes Forestiers en Afrique Centrale (ECOFAC): Bas de Gué-Gué, BP 14533, Libreville; tel. and fax 01-73-23-43.

Fonds de Garantie pour le Logement (FGL): Libreville; f. 2011.

Groupes d'Etudes et de Recherches sur la Démocratie et le Développement Economique et Social au Gabon (GERDDES-Gabon): BP 13114, Libreville; tel. 06-25-14-38 (mobile); fax 07-38-04-20 (mobile); e-mail gerddesgabon@yahoo.fr; internet gerddes-gabon.asso-web.com; f. 1991; Pres. MARYVONNE C. NTSAME NDONG.

Institut Gabonais d'Appui au Développement (IGAD): BP 20423, Libreville; tel. and fax 01-74-52-47; e-mail igad@inet.ga; internet www.igadgabon.com; f. 1992; Dir-Gen. CHRISTIAN RENARDET.

Office National du Développement Rural (ONADER): Libreville; Pres. PAUL STEEVE FLAVIEN ONDZOUNGA; Dir BLAISE ESSIELE.

Office National de Laboratoires Agricoles: Libreville; Pres. JEAN FIRMIN KOUMAZOCK; Dir-Gen. PATRICK MBA BEKOUNG.

Office des Recherches, d'Introduction, d'Adaptation et de Multiplication du Matériel Végétal (ORIAM): Libreville; Pres. CHARLES MBA BISSIGUÉ; Dir-Gen. HENRI-GRÉGOIRE NGOUA ASSOUMÉ.

Programme Régionale de Gestion de l'Information Environnementale en Afrique Centrale (PRGIE): BP 932, Libreville; tel. 01-44-12-40; fax 01-77-42-61; e-mail urge@adie-prgie.org.

Société d'Investissement pour l'Agriculture Tropicale: BP 3928, Libreville; tel. 01-72-22-16; fax 01-72-22-17; e-mail gabon@siat-group.com; internet www.siatgabon.com; f. 2004; Pres. PIERRE VANDEBEECK; Dir-Gen. GERT VANDERSMISSEN.

CHAMBER OF COMMERCE

Chambre de Commerce, d'Agriculture, d'Industrie et des Mines du Gabon: BP 2234, Libreville; tel. 01-72-20-64; fax 01-74-12-20; f. 1935; regional offices at Port-Gentil and Franceville; Pres. JEAN BAPTISTE BIKALOU; Dir-Gen. ALAIN REMPANOT MEPIAT.

EMPLOYERS' ORGANIZATION

Confédération Patronale Gabonaise: Immeuble les Frangipaniers, blvd de l'Indépendance, BP 410, Libreville; tel. 01-76-02-43; fax 01-74-86-52; e-mail infocpg@patronatgabonais.ga; internet www.lacpg.org; f. 1959; represents industrial, mining, petroleum, public works, forestry, banking, insurance, commercial and shipping interests; Pres. HENRI-CLAUDE OYIMA; Sec.-Gen. CHRISTIANE QUINIO.

UTILITIES

In 2011 the Government announced the formation of the state-owned Société d'Electricité, de Téléphone, et d'Eau du Gabon, which was to cover the provision of basic services.

Agence de Régulation du Secteur de l'Eau Potable et de l'Energie Electrique (ARSEE): BP 1215, Libreville; tel. 01-44-28-55; e-mail contact@arsee-gabon.net; internet www.arsee-gabon.net; f. 2010; Dir-Gen. ALAIN HERTH.

Société d'Energie et d'Eau du Gabon (SEEG): BP 2187, Libreville; tel. 01-76-78-07; fax 01-76-11-34; e-mail laroche.lbv@inet.ga; internet www.seeg-gabon.com; f. 1950; 51% owned by Veolia (France); controls 35 electricity generation and distribution centres and 32 water production and distribution centres; Dir-Gen. JEAN-PAUL CAMUS.

TRADE UNIONS

Confédération Gabonaise des Syndicats Libres (CGSL): BP 8067, Libreville; tel. 06-03-97-73 (mobile); e-mail cgsl_2012@yahoo.fr; f. 1991; Sec.-Gen. JEAN CLAUDE BEKALÉ; 19,000 mems (2007).

Confédération Syndicale Gabonaise (COSYGA): BP 14017, Libreville; tel. 06-68-07-26 (mobile); fax 01-74-21-70; e-mail mintsacosyga@yahoo.fr; f. 1969 by the Govt, as a specialized organ of the PDG, to organize and educate workers, to contribute to social peace and economic devt, and to protect the rights of trade unions; Gen. Sec. MARTIN ALLINI; 14,610 mems (2007).

Organisation Nationale des Employés du Pétrole (ONEP): Libreville; Sec.-Gen. PAUL AIMÉ BAGAFOU.

Transport

RAILWAYS

The construction of the Transgabonais railway, which comprises a section running from Owendo (the port of Libreville) to Booué (340 km) and a second section from Booué to Franceville (357 km), was completed in 1986. By 1989 regular services were operating between Libreville and Franceville. Some 3.6m. metric tons of freight and 226,079 passengers were carried on the network in 2010, which in that year totalled 814 km. In 1998 the railways were transferred to private management.

Agence des Régulation des Transports Ferroviaires (ARTF): Libreville; adviser, controller and arbiter in the devt of the railways; Pres. CÉLESTIN NDOLIA-NHAUD.

Société d'Exploration du Chemin de Fer Transgabonais (SETRAG): BP 578, Libreville; tel. 01-70-24-78; fax 01-70-20-38; operates Transgabonais railway; 84% owned by COMILOG; Chair. HENRI JOBIN.

ROADS

In 2007 there were an estimated 9,170 km of roads, including 2,793 km of main roads and 6,377 km of secondary roads; about 11.9% of the road network was paved.

Action Rapide Transit (ART): BP 9391, Libreville; tel. 01-73-79-40; fax 01-73-79-51; e-mail contactlbv@artgabon.com; internet artgabon.com; f. 1993; freight; Dir-Gen. PHILIPPE BERGON.

AGS Frasers: BP 9161, Libreville; tel. 01-70-23-16; fax 01-70-41-56; e-mail direction-gabon@ags-demenagement.com; internet www.agsfrasers.com; Man. BERNARD DURET.

APRETRAC: BP 4542, Libreville; tel. 01-72-84-93; fax 01-74-40-45; e-mail apretrac@assala.net; Dir CHRISTOPHE DISSOU.

Fonds Routier (FR): Galerie des Jardins d'Ambre, BP 16201, Libreville; tel. 01-76-93-90; fax 01-76-93-96; e-mail info@fer-gabon.org; internet www.frgabon.org; f. 1993; Pres. RAPHAËL MAMIAKA; Dir-Gen. LANDRY PATRICK OYAYA.

GETMA Gabon: BP 7510, Libreville; tel. 01-70-28-14; fax 01-70-40-20; Dir BERTRAND ROSE.

Trans form: BP 7538, Libreville; tel. 01-70-43-95; fax 01-70-21-91; e-mail transformgab@yahoo.fr; f. 1995; Dir JEAN-PIERRE POULAIN.

INLAND WATERWAYS

The principal river is the Ogooué, navigable from Port-Gentil to Ndjolé (310 km) and serving the towns of Lambaréné, Ndjolé and Sindara.

Compagnie de Navigation Intérieure (CNI): BP 3982, Libreville; tel. 01-72-39-28; fax 01-74-04-11; f. 1978; responsible for inland waterway transport; agencies at Port-Gentil, Mayumba and Lambaréné; Dir-Gen. FRANÇOIS OYABI.

SHIPPING

The principal deep-water ports are Port-Gentil, which handles mainly petroleum exports, Owendo, 15 km from Libreville, which services mainly barge traffic, and Mayumba. The main ports for timber are at Owendo, Mayumba and Nyanga, and there is a fishing port at Libreville. At 31 December 2014 Gabon's flag registered fleet numbered 59 vessels and had a total displacement of 171,596 grt.

Compagnie de Manutention et de Chalandage d'Owendo (COMACO): BP 2131, Libreville; tel. 01-70-26-35; f. 1974; Pres. GEORGES RAWIRI; Dir in Libreville M. RAYMOND.

Compagnie Nationale de Navigation Intérieure et Internationale: Libreville.

Conseil Gabonais des Chargeurs (CGC): Libreville; internet www.cgcworld.com; f. 1971; Pres. LUCCHERIE NGAYILA; Dir-Gen. LILIANE NADÈGE NGARI.

Office des Ports et Rades du Gabon (OPRAG): Owendo, BP 1051, Libreville; tel. 01-70-00-48; fax 01-70-37-35; e-mail info@ports-gabon.com; internet ports-gabon.com; f. 1974; 25-year management concession acquired in April 2004 by the Spanish PIP group; national port authority; Pres. ALI BONGO ONDIMBA; Dir-Gen. RIGOBERT IKAMBOUAYAT NDÉKA.

SAGA Gabon: Zone OPRAG, BP 518, Port-Gentil; tel. 01-55-58-19; fax 01-55-21-71; e-mail sagalbv@internetgabon.com; internet www.saga.fr; Chair. G. COGNON; Man. Dir DANIEL FERNÁNDEZ.

SDV Gabon: Zone Portuaire d'Owendo, BP 77, Libreville; tel. 01-70-26-36; fax 01-70-23-34; e-mail shipping.lbv@ga.dti.bollore.com; internet www.sdv.com; freight by land, sea and air.

Société Nationale d'Acconage et de Transit (SNAT): BP 3897, Libreville; tel. 01-70-04-04; fax 01-70-13-11; e-mail snat.direction@ga.dti.bollore.com; freight transport and stevedoring; Dir-Gen. MARC GÉRARD.

CIVIL AVIATION

There are international airports at Libreville, Port-Gentil and Franceville, and 65 other public and 50 private airfields, linked mostly with the forestry and petroleum industries.

Agence Nationale de l'Aviation Civile (ANAC): BP 2212, Libreville; tel. 01-44-54-00; fax 01-44-54-01; e-mail anac@anac-gabon.com; internet www.anacgabon.org; f. 2008; Pres. EMMANUEL NZÉ-BÉKALÉ; Dir-Gen. DOMINIQUE OYINAMONO.

Nouvelle Air Affaires Gabon: BP 3962, Libreville; tel. 01-73-25-13; fax 01-73-49-98; e-mail online@sn2ag.com; internet www.sn2ag.com; f. 1975; domestic passenger chartered and scheduled flights, and medical evacuation; Chair. HERMINE BONGO ONDIMBA.

Société de Gestion de l'Aéroport de Libreville (ADL): BP 363, Libreville; tel. 01-73-62-44; fax 01-73-61-28; e-mail dg@adlgabon.com; internet www.adlgabon.com; f. 1988; 26.5% state-owned; management of airport at Libreville; Pres. CHANTAL LIDJI BADINGA; Dir-Gen. JEAN-MARC SANSOVINI.

Tourism

Tourist arrivals were estimated at 934,000 in 2012, and receipts from tourism totalled US $91m. in 2013. The tourism sector is being extensively developed, with new hotels and associated projects and the promotion of national parks.

Centre Gabonais de Promotion Touristique (GABONTOUR): 622 ave du Colonel Parant, BP 2085, Libreville; tel. 01-72-85-04; fax 01-72-85-03; e-mail accueil@gabontour.ga; internet www.gabontour.ga; f. 1988; Dir-Gen. ALBERT ENGONGA BIKORO.

Office National Gabonais du Tourisme: BP 161, Libreville; tel. 01-72-21-82.

Defence

As assessed at November 2014, the army consisted of 3,200 men, the air force of 1,000 men and the navy of an estimated 500 men. Paramilitary forces (gendarmerie) numbered 2,000. Military service is voluntary. France maintains a detachment of 450 troops in Gabon.

Defence Expenditure: Budgeted at an estimated 87,600m. francs CFA for 2014.

Chief of Staff of the Armed Forces: Gen. AUGUSTE ROGER BIBAYE ITANDAS.

Chief of Staff of the Army: ROCK ONGANGA.

Chief of Staff of the Navy: YVES KEBA MALEKOU.

Education

Education is officially compulsory and free of charge for 10 years between six and 16 years of age. According to UNESCO estimates, in 2000/01 80% of children in the relevant age-group (81% of boys; 80% of girls) attended primary schools, while in 2001/02 enrolment at secondary schools was equivalent to 53% of children in the relevant age-group. Primary and secondary education is provided by the State and mission schools. Primary education begins at the age of six and lasts for five years. Secondary education, beginning at 12 years of age, lasts for up to seven years, comprising a first cycle of four years and a second of three years. The Université Omar Bongo is based at Libreville and the Université des Sciences et des Techniques de Masuku at Franceville. Many students go to France for university and technical training. In 2000 spending on education represented 3.8% of total budgetary expenditure.

THE GAMBIA

Introductory Survey

LOCATION, CLIMATE, LANGUAGE, RELIGION, FLAG, CAPITAL

The Republic of The Gambia is a narrow territory around the River Gambia on the west coast of Africa. Apart from a short coastline on the Atlantic Ocean, the country is a semi-enclave in Senegal. The climate is tropical, with a rainy season from July to September. Away from the river swamps most of the terrain is covered by savannah bush. Average temperatures in Banjul range from 23°C (73°F) in January to 27°C (81°F) in July, while temperatures inland can exceed 40°C (104°F). English is the official language, while the principal vernacular languages are Mandinka, Fula and Wolof. About 85% of the inhabitants are Muslims; most of the remainder are Christians, and there are a small number of animists. The national flag (proportions 2 by 3) has red, blue and green horizontal stripes, with two narrow white stripes bordering the central blue band. The capital is Banjul.

CONTEMPORARY POLITICAL HISTORY

Historical Context

Formerly administered with Sierra Leone, The Gambia became a separate British colony in 1888. A universal adult franchise was established in 1960. Following legislative elections in May 1962, the leader of the People's Progressive Party (PPP), Dr (later Sir) Dawda Kairaba Jawara, became Premier. Full internal self-government followed in October 1963. On 18 February 1965 The Gambia became an independent country within the Commonwealth, with Jawara as Prime Minister. The country became a republic on 24 April 1970, whereupon Jawara took office as President. He was re-elected in 1972 and again in 1977.

The first direct presidential election was held in May 1982. Jawara, who was opposed by the leader of the National Convention Party (NCP), Sheriff Mustapha Dibba, was re-elected, with 72% of the votes cast. In the concurrent legislative elections the PPP won 27 of the 35 elective seats in the House of Representatives. At legislative elections in March 1987 the PPP took 31 of the 36 directly elected seats in the House of Representatives. In the presidential election Jawara was re-elected with 59% of the votes cast; Dibba received 27% of the votes. Rumours of corruption and the abuse of power at ministerial level persisted throughout the decade.

Plans were announced in August 1981 for a confederation of The Gambia and Senegal, to be called Senegambia. The confederal agreement came into effect in February 1982; a Confederal Council of Ministers, headed by President Abdou Diouf of Senegal (with President Jawara as his deputy), held its inaugural meeting in January 1983, as did a 60-member Confederal Assembly. However, the confederation was dissolved in September, and a period of tension between the two countries followed: Senegal accused The Gambia of harbouring rebels of the Mouvement des Forces Démocratiques de la Casamance (MFDC), an organization seeking independence for the Casamance region—which is virtually separated from the northern segment of Senegal by the enclave of The Gambia. In January 1991 the two countries signed an agreement of friendship and co-operation.

Jawara was elected for a sixth time in April 1992, receiving 58% of the votes cast, while Dibba took 22%. In elections to the House of Representatives the PPP retained a clear majority, with 25 elected members. The NCP secured six seats, the Gambian People's Party (GPP) two and independent candidates the remaining three.

Domestic Political Affairs

On 22 July 1994 Jawara was deposed by a self-styled Armed Forces Provisional Ruling Council (AFPRC), a group of five young army officers led by Lt (later Col) Yahya Jammeh, in a bloodless coup. The AFPRC suspended the Constitution and banned all political activity. Jammeh pronounced himself Head of State and appointed a mixed civilian and military Government. Purges of the armed forces and public institutions were implemented, and in November it was announced that 10 of Jawara's former ministers would be tried on charges of corruption.

The AFPRC's timetable for a transition to civilian rule, published in October 1994, envisaged a programme of reform culminating in the inauguration of new elected institutions in December 1998. The length of the transition period prompted criticism both internationally and domestically. In November 1994 Jammeh commissioned a National Consultative Committee, which proposed a return to civilian government in 1996.

The draft of a report by a Constitutional Review Commission (established in April 1995) was published in March 1996. Opponents of the AFPRC criticized provisions of the Constitution that, they alleged, had been formulated with the specific intention of facilitating Jammeh's election to the presidency (although the Head of State had frequently asserted that he would not seek election).

A constitutional referendum took place on 8 August 1996, at which 70.4% of voters endorsed the new document. A presidential decree was issued in the following week reauthorizing party political activity. Shortly afterwards, however, a further decree (Decree 89) was promulgated, according to which all holders of executive office in the 30 years prior to July 1994 were to be prohibited from seeking public office, with the PPP, the NCP and the GPP barred from contesting the forthcoming presidential and parliamentary elections; the measure was strongly criticized by the Commonwealth Ministerial Action Group on the Harare Declaration (CMAG, see p. 236). Thus, the only parties from the Jawara era authorized to contest the elections were the People's Democratic Organization for Independence and Socialism (PDOIS) and the People's Democratic Party.

In August 1996 a political party supporting Jammeh, the Alliance for Patriotic Reorientation and Construction (APRC), was established. In early September Jammeh resigned from the army, in order to contest the presidency as a civilian, as required by the Constitution. According to official results of the presidential election held on 26 September, Jammeh secured the presidency with 55.8% of the votes cast, ahead of Ousainou Darboe, the leader of the United Democratic Party (UDP), who received 35.8%. The rate of participation by voters was again high, although observers, including CMAG, expressed doubts as to the credibility of the election results. The dissolution of the AFPRC was announced the same day. Jammeh was inaugurated as President on 18 October.

At legislative elections, which took place on 2 January 1997, the APRC won an overwhelming majority in the National Assembly, securing 33 elective seats. The UDP obtained seven elective seats, the National Reconciliation Party (NRP) two, the PDOIS one and independent candidates two. As Head of State, Jammeh was empowered by the Constitution to nominate four additional members of parliament, from whom the Speaker and Deputy Speaker would be chosen. The opening session of the National Assembly, on 16 January, denoted the full entry into force of the Constitution and thus the inauguration of the Second Republic.

In May 2001 the National Assembly and the President approved a number of constitutional amendments, which were to be submitted to a referendum. The opposition protested against the proposed changes, which included the extension of the presidential term from five to seven years, the introduction of a presidential prerogative to appoint local chiefs, and the replacement of the permanent Independent Election Commission (IEC) with an ad hoc body.

The 2001 presidential election

In July 2001 Jammeh announced the abrogation of Decree 89, although several prominent individuals who had participated in pre-1994 administrations, including Jawara, remained prohibited from seeking public office. None the less, the PPP, the NCP and the GPP were subsequently re-established. In August 2001 the UDP, the PPP and the GPP formed a coalition and announced that Darboe would be its presidential candidate.

At the presidential election, held on 18 October 2001, Jammeh was re-elected with 52.8% of the votes cast, according to official results, ahead of Darboe, who won 32.6%. Although Darboe conceded defeat, members of the opposition subsequently disputed the legitimacy of the results. None the less, international observers described the poll as being largely free and fair. In December, at his inauguration, President Jammeh granted an unconditional amnesty to Jawara, guaranteeing the former President's security should he decide to return to The Gambia.

In December 2001 the UDP-PPP-GPP coalition announced that it would boycott the upcoming legislative elections owing to concerns about the integrity of the electoral lists. The IEC declared that the APRC had thus secured 33 of the 48 elective seats in the enlarged National Assembly, in constituencies where the party was unopposed owing to the boycott. At the elections, which took place on 17 January, the APRC won 12 of the 15 contested seats, giving the party a total of 45 elective seats; the PDOIS obtained two seats, and the NRP one. An additional five members of parliament were appointed by President Jammeh, in accordance with the Constitution. Dibba, whose NCP had formed an alliance with the APRC prior to the elections, was appointed Speaker of the new National Assembly.

In May 2002 the National Assembly approved legislation that imposed stricter regulations over the print media, in accordance with which all journalists not working for the state-controlled media would be required to register with a National Media Commission (NMC). In June Jawara returned to The Gambia from exile; at the end of the month he was officially received by Jammeh and later tendered his resignation as leader of the PPP.

In June 2003 the NMC was created, despite opposition from journalists, and was given far-reaching powers, including the authority to imprison journalists for terms of up to six months. In December legislation providing for terms of imprisonment of up to three years for journalists found guilty of libel or sedition, and obliging members of the media to re-register with the state, was approved by the National Assembly, despite protests by members of the Gambian and international media. In December 2004 Deyda Hydara, the editor of the independent newspaper *The Point*, who had been severely critical of the new legislation, was murdered in Banjul. The incident precipitated a demonstration in the capital, reportedly attended by several hundred journalists, and later that month a one-week media strike was observed. (In June 2014 the Economic Community of West African States—ECOWAS—Court of Justice declared that the Gambian authorities had not conducted a comprehensive investigation into Hydara's death and criticized the Government for fomenting impunity in the country.)

The National Alliance for Democracy and Development (NADD), a coalition of five opposition parties, including the NRP, the PDOIS and the UDP, was formed in January 2005 with the aim of presenting a single candidate to contest the next presidential election. In June four deputies, among them three opposition leaders—Hamat Bah of the NRP and Sidia Jatta and Halifa Sallah of the PDOIS—were expelled from the National Assembly following their registration as members of the NADD. (According to Gambian law, deputies were not permitted to switch allegiance between political parties during the term of a parliament.) By-elections to the vacant seats were held in September at which the NADD retained three of the contested constituencies, while the APRC took the remaining seat. In November Bah and Sallah, along with another senior member of the NADD, Omar Jallow, were arrested and charged with sedition. They were released on bail in mid-December and in February 2006 all charges against them were dropped. However, in the same month a rift in the NADD became apparent, with the NRP and the UDP withdrawing and forming a new coalition.

A presidential election was held on 22 September 2006, at which Jammeh won 67.3% of the votes cast. His nearest rival was Darboe (candidate for the UDP, the NRP and the Gambia Party for Democracy and Progress) with 26.7%, while Halifa Sallah of the NADD was placed third with some 6.0%.

Jammeh's third elective term

The ruling APRC won 42 seats at legislative elections held on 25 January 2007, while the UDP took four seats, the NADD one seat and an independent candidate one seat. Sallah and Bah failed to be re-elected to the National Assembly.

Secretary of State for Health and Social Welfare Dr Tamsir Mbowe was dismissed in November 2007. Although no official reason was given, Mbowe was reported to have made controversial claims that President Jammeh had succeeded in finding a cure for HIV/AIDS.

Halifa Sallah was arrested and detained in June 2009 along with a number of other journalists and editors, reportedly

accused of being disrespectful to President Jammeh with regard to the murder of Hydara in 2004 in articles published in Sallah's newspaper *Foroyaa*. In July 2009 six journalists were imprisoned on charges of sedition; they were pardoned and released in September, although President Jammeh reiterated that those who were disrespectful towards him would be subjected to punishment.

The army Chief of Defence Staff, Gen. Lang Tombong Tamba, was dismissed in October 2009 and replaced by his hitherto deputy, Brig.-Gen. Massaneh Kinteh. A further four senior military officials were also dismissed. In February 2010 President Jammeh implemented a major reorganization of the Government, appointing four new ministers and creating a new Ministry of Economic Planning and Industrial Development; two additional reorganizations followed in March. Also in March six senior members of the security forces, most notably the Commander of the Navy, Sarjo Fofona, were removed from their posts and placed under arrest. Later that month Fofona, Tamba and Lt-Col Ndure Cham (another former Chief of Defence Staff), *inter alios*, were accused of planning a coup against the Jammeh regime during the previous year and were charged with treason. Eight of the accused, including Tamba and other high-ranking military officers, were found guilty in July and received death sentences, a decision that was condemned by the European Union (EU, see p. 271). The Court of Appeal and the Supreme Court upheld these sentences in April 2011 and October 2012, respectively, although in November 2014 they were commuted to life sentences by the latter. (In June 2010 prosecutors also accused Tamba and Fofona of taking part in a plot to overthrow the President in 2006. Both received prison sentences of 20 years on this charge in May 2011.) Critics of the regime claimed that the coup plot was a fabrication devised by Jammeh to remove potential political rivals.

Senior UDP official Femi Peters was fined and imprisoned for one year in April 2010, after being convicted of orchestrating an illegal public meeting, prompting expressions of concern from the EU, the United Kingdom and the USA. An appeal against Peters' sentence was rejected in August, although he was released in December. The President carried out another cabinet reorganization in June, most notably appointing Dr Mamadou Tangara as Minister of Foreign Affairs, International Co-operation and Gambians Abroad. Abdou Kolley, after being replaced as Minister of Finance and Economic Affairs in March, was restored to his former position in a further government reorganization in July. Additional changes were made to the Government in early 2011, following the death of the Minister of Health and Social Welfare, Dr Abu Bakarr Gaye. Fatim Badjie, who had been dismissed as Minister of Information and Communication Infrastructure in 2009, returned to the Cabinet as Gaye's replacement in February 2011, while in January Mambury Njie, hitherto the Minister of Economic Planning and Industrial Development, had assumed responsibility for the finance and economic affairs portfolio.

Jammeh retains the presidency

In March 2011 the head of the IEC announced that a presidential election would take place on 24 November, to be followed by legislative elections in early 2012 and local government elections in 2013. President Jammeh stated that his party, the APRC, would not campaign, as he was confident of being re-elected. Several opposition politicians publicly stated that the shortening of the election campaign period to 11 days placed them at a significant electoral disadvantage, given the President's permanent access to national media. A report published in July 2011 by the Observatory for the Protection of Human Rights Defenders expressed concern at the repression of journalists and civil society in The Gambia, and voiced fears that such instances could increase as the election approached.

In June 2011 the former Minister of Communications and Information Technology, Amadou Scatred Janneh, was one of four people arrested on suspicion of conspiracy to commit treason and sedition. The four were allegedly members of a civil society organization named Coalition for Change—The Gambia, which claimed to challenge dictatorship and promote basic freedoms through non-violent action. Janneh was sentenced to life imprisonment in January 2012 (his three co-accused received six-year prison terms), although he was granted a presidential pardon in September.

In October 2011 the main opposition parties announced that they had failed to agree on a single joint candidate to oppose Jammeh in the forthcoming presidential election. On 24 November Jammeh was re-elected to the office of the President for a fourth term, receiving 71.5% of votes cast. His nearest opponent, Darboe of the UDP, won 17.4% of the votes, while Hamat Bah, representing a United Front of four opposition parties—the Gambia Party for Democracy and Progress (GPDP), the NADD, the NRP, and the PDOIS—took 11.1%. The rate of voter participation was 83%. Two days prior to the polling date, ECOWAS had announced that it would not be observing the elections, stating that conditions within the country—including domination of mass media by the ruling party, a lack of neutrality in state institutions, and widespread intimidation of the opposition and electorate—were not conducive to the holding of free and fair elections. Nevertheless, the elections were observed by missions from the African Union (AU), the Commonwealth, and the Organization of Islamic Co-operation. These bodies broadly agreed that the elections had been conducted in a fair and transparent manner, although the AU mission observed in its report that the APRC had benefited from superior media access and financial resources.

In February 2012 Jammeh effected a major reorganization of his Cabinet; only eight members of the outgoing Government were retained, although Tangara and Njie were again respectively appointed to head the foreign affairs and finance ministries.

Legislative elections, which were held on 29 March 2012, were boycotted by all opposition parties with the exception of the NRP, which took one seat. The APRC was unopposed in 25 constituencies and won 43 of the 48 elective seats available. The remaining four seats were secured by independent candidates. An official voter turnout of 50% was recorded.

In April 2012 Jammeh announced that Njie had replaced Tangara as Minister of Foreign Affairs, International Co-operation and Gambians Abroad. Tangara became Minister of Fisheries, Water Resources and National Assembly Matters, while Kolley was again appointed to head the finance ministry. Later in April, in a further reorganization of the Government, Tangara was moved to head the higher education ministry, with President Jammeh assuming responsibility for Tangara's former portfolio. Ousman Sonko was reappointed as Minister of the Interior in May. Chief of Defence Staff Lt-Gen. Masanneh Kinteh, along with another high-ranking officer in the armed forces, was dismissed in July. Tangara was again given control of the foreign affairs portfolio in August, while Njie briefly assumed responsibility for higher education until his dismissal later that month. In November Susan Waffa-Ogoo became the minister responsible for foreign affairs, with Tangara resuming his former role at the higher education ministry. Also in that month Jammeh appointed new heads of the fisheries, health, lands, and information ministries. Jammeh again made changes to the composition of the Government in January and March 2013. (His frequent reorganizations of the Cabinet and the military were regarded by analysts as an effort to preclude any serious threat to his authority).

Meanwhile, in August 2012 Jammeh attracted international censure when he announced his intention to expedite the executions of all prisoners who had been sentenced to death, many of whom had been convicted of political offences such as treason. Amid allegations of due process violations, nine of the 47 detainees on death row were executed later that month (the first official enactment of capital punishment in the country since 1985); however, ostensibly due to international pressure, Jammeh suspended the remaining executions in September. The authorities closed two newspapers that had provided coverage of the executions, while a new opposition group, the National Transitional Council of The Gambia, was formed in Senegal. In November Njie, who had reportedly criticized Jammeh for authorizing the executions, was arrested, and in the following month was charged with committing an unspecified economic crime. Baba Leigh, a prominent imam who had also condemned the executions, was detained in December, and former Minister of Justice Amie Bensouda was arrested and released on bail in the same month, although no formal charges were announced. Leigh was finally released from detention in May 2013, following expressions of concern from the EU and the USA, while Njie was exonerated in July 2014.

Local government elections, which were held on 4 April 2013, were boycotted by all opposition parties, except the NRP, on the grounds that the IEC had not provided a fair electoral system. The APRC secured 104 of the 114 council seats, while independents won the remaining 10. An independent candidate, Abdoulie Bah, notably defeated the APRC incumbent to secure the mayoralty of Banjul. In May the Minister of Justice and Attorney-General, Lamin Jorbarteh, was removed from his post and arrested on several charges, including abuse of office. In July the National Assembly approved legislation that introduced new penalties for the publication of material deemed anti-Government on the internet. In August Amie Joof, who had replaced Jorbateh as Minister of Justice and Attorney-General, was dismissed; she was succeeded in the post by Mama Fatima Singhateh. In December Jorbarteh and two other former senior officials, who were accused of conspiring to remove a former Chief Justice, Joseph Wowo, were sentenced to two years' imprisonment by a Special Criminal Court in Banjul. In January 2014 the Court also sentenced Wowo to two years' imprisonment, while imposing a further one-year term on Jorbarteh, for abuse of office. In early March the Chief Justice was again replaced.

Meanwhile, at the end of September 2013 human rights activists staged protests in New York, USA, to coincide with a visit by Jammeh, who delivered a speech highly critical of perceived Western interference in The Gambia's affairs at the UN General Assembly. On 2 October Jammeh announced the decision to withdraw The Gambia from the Commonwealth, which he referred to as a 'neo-colonial institution', and later issued a statement that the Governments of the USA and the United Kingdom had waged a concerted campaign to destabilize the country. Two books authored by Jammeh, which denounced British rule of The Gambia and alleged looting of its resources, and detailed perceived ways in which the country had been disadvantaged by membership of the Commonwealth, were promoted nationwide from February 2014. Furthermore, Jammeh proclaimed in the following month that an unspecified domestic vernacular would be installed as The Gambia's official language in place of English.

Mamour Alieu Jagne received the foreign affairs portfolio following another cabinet reorganization in April 2014. Jammeh replaced the Minister of Presidential Affairs twice in July, while in August he appointed Basirou Mahoney as Minister of Justice and Attorney-General, Ousman Badjie as Minister responsible for Works, and Bala Garba-Jahumpa as Minister of Foreign Affairs. Badjie was dismissed in November and his duties were assumed by the Office of the President. In January 2015 Garba-Jahumpa was given responsibility for the works portfolio and was succeeded as Minister of Foreign Affairs by Neneh Macdouall-Gaye; Sheriff Bojang became Minister of Information and Communication Infrastructure. Later that month Jammeh named Lamin Nyabally as the new Minister of Presidential Affairs and Aboubacar Senghore as Minister of Justice and Attorney-General. However, shortly thereafter, Senghore was himself replaced by Mama Fatima Singhateh.

In August 2014, meanwhile, the National Assembly adopted controversial legislation that prescribed life sentences, under certain circumstances, for persons convicted of homosexual acts. Jammeh, who earlier that year had publicly referred to homosexuals as 'vermin', promulgated the bill in October. The approval of this discriminatory legislation, and a concomitant crackdown on homosexuals in the country, attracted condemnation from the EU, the USA, the UN High Commissioner for Human Rights and international human rights organizations. In December the EU withheld €13m. of aid owing to human rights concerns, and later that month the USA cancelled The Gambia's participation in the African Growth and Opportunity Act, which had provided Gambian exporters with preferential access to the US market. The Gambian Government remained defiant, however, and threatened to end all communication with the EU and other members of the international community that were critical of its policies.

Recent developments: attempted coup

Foreign-based anti-Government dissidents, who had reportedly entered The Gambia from Senegal, staged an abortive coup on 30 December 2014 while Jammeh was on a visit to the United Arab Emirates. The presidential compound came under attack by a small group of armed assailants under the command of Lt-Col Lamin Sanneh, a former State Guard officer who had been living in exile in the USA; however, loyalist troops successfully repulsed the offensive, killing Sanneh and three of his accomplices and detaining another. The remaining conspirators fled the country. The coup attempt was condemned by Senegal, the USA and UN Secretary-General Ban Ki-Moon. Relatives of the coup organizers were among those detained without charge by the Gambian authorities during early 2015, raising concerns about arbitrary arrests and due process violations. In January prosecutors in the USA charged three US citizens of Gambian extraction—Cherno Njie, Papa Faal and Alagie Barrow—with plotting to overthrow the Jammeh administration and install

Njie as President. Faal, appearing in a US court in late January, pleaded guilty to the coup charges, while legal proceedings against Njie and Barrow were ongoing in the USA in early 2015. In February a military trial for six soldiers accused of involvement in the failed coup commenced in Banjul, and in April all six were found guilty with three of the accused sentenced to death, while the three other defendants received terms of life imprisonment.

Foreign Affairs

Regional relations

After the 1994 coup The Gambia's traditional aid donors and trading partners suspended much co-operation. The Jammeh administration therefore sought new links: diplomatic relations with Libya, severed in 1980, were restored in November 1994, and numerous co-operation agreements ensued. Links with the Republic of China (Taiwan) were re-established in July 1995, whereupon Taiwan became one of The Gambia's major sources of funding. In November 2013, however, The Gambia terminated diplomatic relations with Taiwan, citing 'national strategic interest', and the ambassadors of both countries were withdrawn.

Despite the presence in Senegal of prominent opponents of his Government, Jammeh also sought to improve relations with that country. In June 1997 the two countries agreed to take joint measures to combat insecurity, illegal immigration, arms-trafficking and drugs-smuggling. In January 1998 the Government of Senegal welcomed an offer by Jammeh to mediate in the conflict in the southern province of Casamance: the separatist MFDC is chiefly composed of the Diola ethnic group, of which Jammeh is a member. In December 2000 the Gambian Government sent a delegation to participate in talks between the MFDC and the Senegalese Government. A dispute between the two countries arose in August 2005 when Gambian authorities increased the price of the ferry across the Gambia river at Banjul and in retaliation Senegalese lorry drivers commenced a blockade of the common border. The conflict was resolved in October, under the mediation of the Nigerian President, Olusegun Obasanjo, and an agreement was reached to build a bridge over the Gambia river. However, renewed fighting in Senegal's Casamance province from March 2006 resulted in further inflows of refugees into The Gambia, including a number of rebel leaders sought by the Senegalese authorities.

The Government severed diplomatic relations with Iran in November 2010. Although no formal explanation for this action was provided, Gambian officials intimated that it was related to the interception by Nigerian authorities, the previous month, of a consignment of illegal weapons from Iran that was allegedly en route to The Gambia. The final destination of the arms shipment was reportedly a property in The Gambia belonging to President Jammeh (although the Gambian Government dismissed this claim), and there was speculation in Senegal that the weapons would have been smuggled across the border to the MFDC to aid the separatist insurgency, raising tensions between the two West African nations. Nevertheless, bilateral relations improved following discussions in January 2011 between Tangara and high-ranking Senegalese officials (including President Abdoulaye Wade) in Senegal. In February Senegal and The Gambia agreed to establish a Boundary Management Commission to address matters relating to their common border. In August, in an official state visit to The Gambia, Wade reiterated the hope that President Jammeh would assist in enabling a peaceful resolution to the situation in Casamance, a sentiment that was echoed by the new Senegalese President, Macky Sall, in April 2012. However, relations were strained following the controversial prisoner executions that took place in The Gambia in August (see *Domestic Political Affairs*), as two Senegalese citizens were among those executed.

Other external relations

Relations with the United Kingdom were strained in 2001, following the expulsion of the British Deputy High Commissioner, Bharat Joshi, from The Gambia in August. The Gambian authorities alleged that the diplomat had interfered in the country's internal affairs, following his attendance at an opposition meeting. In September the Gambian Deputy High Commissioner in London was expelled from the United Kingdom, and further retaliatory measures were implemented against The Gambia. Relations were restored during 2002. The Gambian Government suspended political dialogue with the EU in January 2013, having rejected demands for improved governance and respect for human rights (which included the free operation of independent media, the removal of restrictions on accessing and sharing information electronically, and a moratorium on the death penalty). The Gambia's withdrawal from the Commonwealth in October was widely regarded as a response to continued criticism of the country's human rights situation.

CONSTITUTION AND GOVERNMENT

The Constitution of the Second Republic of The Gambia, which was approved in a national referendum on 8 August 1996, entered into full effect on 16 January 1997. The Constitution provides for the separation of the powers of the executive, legislative and judicial organs of state. Under its terms, the Head of State is the President of the Republic, who is directly elected by universal adult suffrage. No restriction is placed on the number of times a President may seek re-election. Legislative authority is vested in the National Assembly, elected for a five-year term and comprising 48 members elected by direct suffrage and five members nominated by the President of the Republic. The President appoints government members, who are responsible both to the Head of State and to the National Assembly. Tribalism and other forms of sectarianism in politics are forbidden. The Gambia is divided into eight local government areas.

REGIONAL AND INTERNATIONAL CO-OPERATION

The Gambia is a member of the African Union (see p. 188), of the Economic Community of West African States (ECOWAS, see p. 258), of the Community of Sahel-Saharan States—CEN-SAD (see p. 446) and of the Gambia River Basin Development Organization (OMVG, see p. 447).

The Gambia became a member of the UN in 1965, was admitted to the World Trade Organization (WTO, see p. 431) in 1996.

ECONOMIC AFFAIRS

In 2013, according to estimates by the World Bank, The Gambia's gross national income (GNI), measured at average 2011–13 prices, was US $941m., equivalent to $510 per head (or $1,620 on an international purchasing-power parity basis). During 2004–13, it was estimated, the population increased at an average annual rate of 3.2%, while gross domestic product (GDP) per head increased by 0.1%. Overall GDP increased, in real terms, at an average annual rate of 3.3% in 2004–13; GDP increased by 5.6% in 2013.

Agriculture (including forestry and fishing) contributed 23.5% of GDP in 2013, according to preliminary official figures. According to FAO, 4.3% of the labour force were estimated to be employed in the sector in mid-2015. The dominant agricultural activity has traditionally been the cultivation of groundnuts, and exports of that commodity accounted for an estimated 68.2% of domestic export earnings in 1999. However, in 2011 groundnuts accounted for just 2.0% of total exports, although production volumes had increased throughout the late 2000s. A significant proportion of the groundnut crop is frequently smuggled for sale in Senegal. Cotton, citrus fruits, mangoes, avocados and sesame seed are also cultivated for export. The principal staple crops are millet, rice, maize and sorghum, although The Gambia remains heavily dependent on imports of rice and other basic foodstuffs. Fishing makes an important contribution to the domestic food supply. According to official estimates, agricultural GDP increased at an average annual rate of 1.4% in 2004–13. Agricultural GDP increased by an estimated 9.7% in 2013.

Industry (including manufacturing, construction, mining and power) contributed 15.6% of GDP in 2013, according to preliminary official figures. About 10.3% of the labour force were employed in the sector at the time of the 1993 census. According to official estimates, industrial GDP increased at an average annual rate of 3.6% in 2004–13; growth in 2013 was 7.0%.

The Gambia has few viable mineral resources, although seismic surveys have indicated the existence of petroleum deposits off shore. Deposits of kaolin and salt are currently unexploited. In early 2008 the discovery of commercially exploitable quantities of uranium was announced. Mining contributed 3.4% of GDP in 2013, according to preliminary official figures, and the GDP of the sector grew by an estimated 12.1% in 2013.

Manufacturing contributed 5.8% of GDP in 2013, according to preliminary official figures, and employed 6.6% of the labour force in 1993. The sector is dominated by agro-industrial activities, most importantly the processing of groundnuts and fish. Beverages and construction materials are also produced for the domestic market. According to official estimates, manufacturing GDP increased at an average annual rate of 1.9% in 2004–13; growth in the sector was 2.5% in 2012, but manufacturing GDP declined by 1.1% in 2013.

According to preliminary official figures, construction contributed 5.2% of GDP in 2013, while the construction sector alone employed 3.0% of the total labour force in 1993. Construction GDP increased at an average annual rate of 1.3% in 2004–13; the sector grew by 14.5% in 2013.

The Gambia is highly reliant on imported energy. Imports of mineral fuels and lubricants comprised an estimated 23.8% of the value of total merchandise imports in 2013.

The services sector contributed 60.9% of GDP in 2013, according to preliminary official figures, and employed about 34.3% of the labour force in 1993. The tourism industry is of particular significance as a generator of foreign exchange. Tourism contributed about 16% of annual GDP in the late 2000s, and employed some 10,000 workers at that time. The Jammeh administration has expressed its intention further to exploit the country's potential as a transit point for regional trade and also as a centre for regional finance and telecommunications. According to official estimates, the GDP of the services sector increased at an average annual rate of 4.2% in 2004–13; estimated sevices growth in 2013 was 3.7%.

In 2012 The Gambia recorded an estimated visible merchandise trade deficit of US \$176.4m., while there was a deficit of \$15.8m. on the current account of the balance of payments. In 2013 the principal source of imports was Côte d'Ivoire, which supplied an estimated 22.9% of total imports; other major sources were Brazil, the People's Republic of China and Senegal. The largest market for exports in that year was Mali (an estimated 36.1% of total exports). Other major purchasers were Guinea and Senegal. The principal exports in 2013 were textile and textile articles, vegetable products, and prepared foodstuffs; beverages and spirits tobacco. The principal imports in 2013 were mineral products (largely mineral fuels and oils), vegetable products, prepared foodstuffs; beverages and spirits tobacco, vehicles, aircraft and transport equipment, machinery and mechanical appliances, and animal and vegetable fats and oils.

In 2013, according to IMF projections, the budget was balanced, with revenue equalling expenditure of 7,270m. dalasi. The Gambia's general government gross debt was 26,752m. dalasi in 2013, equivalent to 81.9% of GDP. The Gambia's total external debt was US \$513m. at the end of 2012, of which \$396m. was public and publicly guaranteed debt. In that year, the cost of servicing long-term public and publicly guaranteed debt and repayments to the IMF was equivalent to 7.1% of the value of exports of goods, services and income (excluding workers' remittances). According to ILO the average annual rate of inflation was 4.4% in 2004–13. According to the official figures, consumer prices increased by an average of 5.8% in 2013. The rate of unemployment was estimated at some 26% of the labour force in mid-1994.

Relations between The Gambia and the international financial community have often been strained, particularly owing to concerns over alleged inaccuracies in economic data provided by the Gambian authorities. Nevertheless, the IMF, which had resumed assistance in 2007, approved a US \$28m. Extended Credit Facility in May 2012 to support the Government's Programme for Accelerated Growth and Employment 2012–15. According to the IMF, real GDP contracted significantly in 2011 as a result of a devastating drought, which caused widespread crop failure during the 2011/12 growing season. By late 2012, however, the economy had staged a recovery, driven by a resurgence in crop production and a robust tourism sector, and growth had strengthened to more than 6% by 2013. A 15% valued-added tax entered into force in January 2013, as part of an effort by the Government to boost revenues and modernize the tax regime. The IMF expressed concern at the country's high budget deficit (estimated at 8.75% of GDP in 2013), which necessitated increased domestic borrowing, and its potentially unsustainable public debt (estimated at over 80% of GDP in late 2013), urging restraint in extra-budgetary expenditure and the adoption of additional adjustment measures. In spite of a marked downturn in the tourism sector (owing to concerns among Western tourists about an outbreak of the deadly Ebola Virus Disease in West Africa) and a poor harvest, the IMF estimated that real GDP growth had reached 7.4% in 2014; the Ministry of Finance and Economic Affairs, however, reported that there had been a small contraction in the economy during that year. The Government's fiscal position remained under pressure as a result of unbudgeted spending and a financial crisis at the state-run National Water and Electricity Co, with public debt consequently rising further during 2014. The IMF forecast growth of 7.0% in 2015.

PUBLIC HOLIDAYS

2016: 1 January (New Year's Day), 18 February (Independence Day), 25 March (Good Friday), 28 March (Easter Monday), 1 May (Workers' Day), 25 May (African Liberation Day), 2 July* (Laylat al-Qadr, Night of Power), 6 July* (Eid al-Fitr, end of Ramadan), 22 July (Anniversary of the Second Republic), 15 August (Assumption/St Mary's Day), 12 September* (Eid al-Kebir, Feast of the Sacrifice), 2 October* (Islamic New Year), 11 October* (Ashoura), 11 December* (Eid al-Moulid, Birth of the Prophet), 25 December (Christmas).

* These holidays are dependent on the Islamic lunar calendar and may vary by one or two days from the dates given.

Statistical Survey

Sources (unless otherwise stated): Gambia Bureau of Statistics, Kanifing Institutional Layout, PO Box 3504, Serrekunda; tel. 4377847; fax 4377848; e-mail info@gbos.gov.gm; internet www.gbos.gm; Central Statistics Department, Central Bank Building, 1/2 Ecowas Ave, Banjul; tel. 4228364; fax 4228903; e-mail director@csd.gm; internet www.gambia.gm/Statistics/statistics.html.

Area and Population

AREA, POPULATION AND DENSITY

Area (sq km)	11,295*
Population (census results)	
15 April 2003	1,360,681
8 April 2013†	
Males	930,699
Females	951,751
Total	1,882,450
Population (UN estimates at mid-year)‡	
2014	1,908,953
2015	1,970,081
Density (per sq km) at mid-2015	174.4

* 4,361 sq miles.

† Provisional.

‡ Source: UN, *World Population Prospects: The 2012 Revision*; estimates not adjusted to take account of results of 2013 census.

POPULATION BY AGE AND SEX

(UN estimates at mid-2015)

	Males	Females	Total
0–14 years	453,858	446,059	899,917
15–64 years	496,765	527,457	1,024,222
65 years and over	23,791	22,151	45,942
Total	**974,414**	**995,667**	**1,970,081**

Note: Estimates not adjusted to take account of results of 2013 census.

Source: UN, *World Population Prospects: The 2012 Revision*.

ADMINISTRATIVE DIVISIONS
(population at 2013 census, provisional)

Banjul	31,301	Kerewan		221,054
Basse	239,916	Kuntaur		99,108
Brikama	699,704	Mansakonko		82,361
Georgetown	126,910	**Total**		1,882,450
Kanifing	382,096			

PRINCIPAL TOWNS
(population at 1993 census)

Serrekunda	151,450	Lamin		10,668
Brikama	42,480	Gunjur		9,983
Banjul (capital)	42,407	Basse		9,265
Bakau	38,062	Soma		7,925
Farafenni	21,142	Bansang		5,405
Sukuta	16,667			

Mid-2014 (incl. suburbs, UN estimate): Banjul 489,490 (Source: UN, *World Urbanization Prospects: The 2014 Revision*).

BIRTHS AND DEATHS
(annual averages, UN estimates)

	2000–05	2005–10	2010–15
Birth rate (per 1,000)	44.8	43.6	42.9
Death rate (per 1,000)	11.6	10.5	9.8

Source: UN, *World Population Prospects: The 2012 Revision*.

Life expectancy (years at birth): 58.6 (males 57.3; females 59.9) in 2012 (Source: World Bank, World Development Indicators database).

ECONOMICALLY ACTIVE POPULATION
('000, FAO estimates at mid-year)

	2013	2014	2015
Agriculture, etc.	649	677	694
Total labour force (incl. others)	865	899	934

Source: FAO.

Health and Welfare

KEY INDICATORS

Total fertility rate (children per woman, 2012)	5.8
Under-5 mortality rate (per 1,000 live births, 2012)	73
HIV/AIDS (% of persons aged 15–49, 2013)	1.2
Physicians (per 1,000 head, 2008)	0.1
Hospital beds (per 1,000 head, 2011)	1.1
Health expenditure (2011): US $ per head (PPP)	87
Health expenditure (2011): % of GDP	4.7
Health expenditure (2011): public (% of total)	62.3
Access to water (% of persons, 2012)	90
Access to sanitation (% of persons, 2012)	60
Total carbon dioxide emissions ('000 metric tons, 2010)	473.0
Carbon dioxide emissions per head (metric tons, 2010)	0.3
Human Development Index (2013): ranking	172
Human Development Index (2013): value	0.441

For sources and definitions, see explanatory note on p. vi.

Agriculture

PRINCIPAL CROPS
('000 metric tons)

	2011	2012	2013
Rice, paddy	51.1	54.2	56.0*
Maize	23.6	30.1	30.0*
Millet	87.2	116.1	119.0*
Sorghum	20.6	23.1	25.0†
Cassava (Manioc)†	9.7	10.5	11.5
Groundnuts, with shell	83.9	119.6	88.0
Oil palm fruit†	35.0	35.0	35.0
Guavas, mangoes and mangosteens†	1.3	1.3	n.a.

* Unofficial figure.
† FAO estimate(s).

Aggregate production ('000 metric tons, may include official, semi-official or estimated data): Total cereals 183.2 in 2011, 224.3 in 2012, 230.7 in 2013; Total pulses 2.2 in 2011, 2.5 in 2012, 2.6 in 2013; Total vegetables (incl. melons) 12.0 in 2011, 12.5 in 2012, n.a. in 2013; Total fruits (excl. melons) 8.8 in 2011, 9.0 in 2012, n.a. in 2013.

Source: FAO.

LIVESTOCK
('000 head, year ending September)

	2011	2012	2013
Cattle	398	373	380
Goats	304	312	320
Sheep	180*	112	150
Pigs	15*	6	7
Asses	56	58*	60*
Horses	28*	19	20
Chickens	1,000*	1,274	1,300*

* FAO estimate.

Source: FAO.

LIVESTOCK PRODUCTS
('000 metric tons, FAO estimates)

	2010	2011	2012
Cattle meat	4.1	3.8	3.8
Goat meat	0.9	0.8	0.8
Sheep meat	0.7	0.5	0.3
Chicken meat	1.2	1.3	1.5
Game meat	1.2	1.3	1.3
Cows' milk	9.3	9.4	9.5
Hen eggs	0.9	0.9	1.0

Source: FAO.

Forestry

ROUNDWOOD REMOVALS
('000 cubic metres, excluding bark, FAO estimates)

	2011	2012	2013
Sawlogs, veneer logs and logs for sleepers*	106	106	106
Other industrial wood†	7	7	7
Fuel wood	703	712	721
Total	816	825	834

* Assumed to be unchanged since 1994.
† Assumed to be unchanged since 1993.

Source: FAO.

Fishing

('000 metric tons, live weight of capture)

	2010	2011*	2012
Tilapias	1.2	1.1	1.0
Sea catfishes	3.8	3.3	2.9
Bonga shad	12.6	12.7	12.7
Sardinellas	7.6	5.4	3.2
Sharks, rays, skates . . .	0.5	0.4	0.3
Total catch (incl. others) . . .	46.6*	41.5	36.1

* FAO estimate(s).

Source: FAO.

Mining

	2009	2010	2011
Laterites ('000 metric tons) . .	103	226	1,035
Silica sand ('000 metric tons) . .	1,062	1,121	n.a.

2007 (metric tons): Clay 6,713; Zircon 355.

Source: US Geological Survey.

Industry

SELECTED PRODUCTS
('000 metric tons unless otherwise stated)

	2010	2011	2012
Beer of barley*	3.4	3.0	3.0
Palm oil—unrefined*	3.0	3.0	3.2
Groundnut oil†	20.0	12.0	12.0
Electric energy (million kWh)† .	245.2	255.7	n.a.

* FAO estimates.
† Unofficial figures.
‡ Source: UN Industrial Commodity Statistics Database.

Beer of millet ('000 metric tons, FAO estimates): 50.4 in 2003, 55.4 in 2004–05.

Source: mainly FAO.

Finance

CURRENCY AND EXCHANGE RATES

Monetary Units
100 butut = 1 dalasi (D).

Sterling, Dollar and Euro Equivalents (30 April 2014)
£1 sterling = 67.0653 dalasi;
US $1 = 39.8700 dalasi;
€1 = 55.2200 dalasi;
1,000 dalasi = £14.91 = $25.08 = €18.11.

Average Exchange Rate (dalasi per US $)
2011   29.462
2012   32.077
2013   35.958

BUDGET
(million dalasi)

Revenue*	2011	2012†	2013‡
Tax revenue	3,780	4,221	5,001
Direct taxes	1,225	1,520	1,629
Domestic taxes on goods and services	1,683	1,833	2,049
Taxes on international trade .	830	856	1,310
Other taxes	42	12	13
Non-tax revenue	484	565	610
Total	4,264	4,786	5,611

Expenditure§	2011	2012†	2013‡
Current expenditure . . .	4,579	5,068	5,882
Wages and salaries . . .	1,693	1,804	1,875
Other goods and services . .	1,273	1,540	2,320
Interest payments . . .	967	1,079	1,160
Internal	785	877	940
External	183	202	220
Subsidies	646	645	527
Capital expenditure	2,292	3,607	2,267
Gambia Local Fund	307	299	409
Foreign financed	1,985	3,308	1,857
Total	6,871	8,675	8,149

* Excluding grants received (million dalasi): 1,355 in 2011; 2,611 in 2012 (preliminary); 1,659 in 2013 (projection).
† Preliminary figures.
‡ Projections.
§ Excluding lending minus repayments (million dalasi): −1,252 in 2011; −1,278 in 2012 (preliminary); −878 in 2013 (projection).

Source: IMF, *The Gambia: Staff Report for the 2013 Article IV Consultation; Informational Annex; Press Release on the Executive Board Discussion; and Statement by the Executive Director for The Gambia* (September 2013).

INTERNATIONAL RESERVES
(US $ million at 31 December)

	2011	2012	2013
IMF special drawing rights . .	37.73	37.45	35.98
Reserve position in IMF . . .	2.37	2.37	2.37
Foreign exchange	183.15	196.42	172.20
Total	223.24	236.24	210.55

Source: IMF, *International Financial Statistics*.

MONEY SUPPLY
(million dalasi at 31 December)

	2011	2012	2013
Currency outside depository corporations	2,376.33	2,818.59	3,255.17
Transferable deposits	4,251.17	4,524.47	6,128.48
Other deposits	7,913.64	8,254.87	8,493.36
Broad money	14,281.91	15,597.92	17,877.00

Source: IMF, *International Financial Statistics*.

COST OF LIVING
(Consumer Price Index; base: 2004 = 100)

	2011	2012	2013
Food and non-alcoholic beverages .	143.5	150.7	160.9
Housing, fuel and utilities . .	129.6	141.2	157.5
Clothing, textiles and footwear .	114.5	117.0	120.4
All items (incl. others) . . .	133.4	139.0	147.0

NATIONAL ACCOUNTS
(million dalasi at current prices)
Expenditure on the Gross Domestic Product

	2010	2011	2012
Government final consumption expenditure	2,676	2,694	2,201
Private final consumption expenditure	23,032	20,798	24,514
Gross capital formation . . .	4,903	6,755	6,848
Total domestic expenditure .	30,611	30,247	33,563
Exports of goods and services . .	1,185	2,790	3,794
Less Imports of goods and services	6,890	8,636	10,451
Non-factor services (net) . . .	1,585	2,240	2,415
Statistical discrepancy . . .	172	—	—
GDP in purchasers' values .	26,663	26,641	29,322
GDP at constant 2004 prices .	21,633	20,697	21,958

2013 (preliminary figures): Government final consumption expenditure 2,395; Private final consumption expenditure 27,130; Gross capital formation 6,849; *Total domestic expenditure* 36,374; Exports of goods and services 6,328; *Less* Imports of goods and services 10,273; *GDP in purchasers' values* 32,430 (Source: African Development Bank).

Gross Domestic Product by Economic Activity

	2011	2012	2013*
Agriculture, hunting, forestry and fishing	5,942	6,523	7,164
Mining and quarrying	792	897	1,049
Manufacturing	1,460	1,671	1,756
Electricity, gas and water . .	331	335	376
Construction	1,131	1,330	1,592
Wholesale and retail trade . .	6,458	7,014	7,410
Hotels and restaurants . . .	696	762	915
Finance and insurance . . .	2,795	3,038	3,280
Transport and communications .	3,464	3,997	4,618
Real estate, renting and business activities	873	898	947
Public administration and defence	565	608	652
Education	297	321	333
Health and social work . . .	293	295	316
Other services	108	114	120
Sub-total	25,205	27,803	30,528
Less Financial intermediation services indirectly measured .	1,058	1,126	1,217
GDP at factor cost	24,147	26,677	29,311
Indirect taxes, *less* subsidies . .	2,494	2,645	3,118
GDP in purchasers' values .	26,641	29,322	32,430

* Preliminary figures.

BALANCE OF PAYMENTS
(US $ million, year ending 30 June)

	2010	2011	2012
Exports of goods	139.92	162.14	182.46
Imports of goods	−245.76	−295.60	−358.84
Balance on goods	−105.84	−133.46	−176.38
Exports of services	130.64	143.73	151.46
Imports of services	−73.17	−68.41	−80.27
Balance on goods and services	−48.37	−58.14	−105.19
Primary income received . . .	14.35	13.05	9.83
Primary income paid	−22.40	−28.79	−28.47
Balance on goods, services and primary income . . .	−56.42	−73.88	−123.82
Secondary income received . .	212.75	181.59	163.10
Secondary income paid . . .	−135.28	−60.37	−54.68
Current balance	21.05	47.34	−15.40
Capital account (net)	—	4.15	—
Direct investment liabilities . .	37.37	36.18	33.52
Other investment assets . . .	20.30	−0.32	24.92
Other investment liabilities . .	−82.24	−34.85	−82.47
Net errors and omissions . . .	−89.75	−101.86	−25.34
Reserves and related items .	−93.27	−49.36	−64.77

Source: IMF, *International Financial Statistics*.

External Trade

PRINCIPAL COMMODITIES
(distribution by HS, US $ million)

Imports c.i.f.	2011	2012	2013
Vegetable products	55.0	66.3	64.7
Cereals	35.9	44.2	36.9
Rice	35.9	44.2	31.7
Milling products; malt, starches, insulin; wheat gluten . . .	11.8	15.4	21.9
Wheat or meslin flour . . .	11.2	14.1	18.7
Animal, vegetable fats and oils	17.2	18.9	17.5
Fixed vegetable fats, oils and their fractions	16.7	18.0	16.6
Prepared foodstuffs; beverages and spirits; tobacco, etc. .	30.9	32.3	41.8
Sugars and sugar confectionery .	15.4	17.1	27.5
Cane or beet sugar and chemically pure sucrose, in solid form	14.7	16.6	27.2
Mineral products	87.7	117.4	95.3
Salt, sulphur, earth, stone, plaster, lime and cement	11.9	14.6	12.1
Cements, portland, aluminous, slag, and similar hydraulic materials	11.0	12.9	10.3
Mineral fuels, oils, etc.	75.8	102.8	83.2
Petroleum oils, not crude . .	75.6	102.5	82.4
Chemicals and related products	20.3	19.8	14.8
Pharmaceutical products . . .	10.4	8.9	6.8
Textiles and textile articles .	16.1	12.9	16.4
Iron and steel, and base metals	15.2	10.3	6.3
Machinery and mechanical appliances	36.0	32.0	24.2
Machinery, boilers, etc. . . .	12.3	15.1	12.2
Electrical and electronic equipment	23.7	17.0	12.0
Vehicles, aircraft and transport equipment . . .	23.8	28.5	34.6
Vehicles other than railway, tramway	23.2	27.9	34.4
Cars (incl. station wagons) . .	16.8	20.5	22.2
Total (incl. others)	340.7	380.0	350.2

Exports f.o.b.	2011	2012	2013
Live animals and animal products	7.1	7.1	4.3
Fish, crustaceans, molluscs and preparations thereof	2.9	1.1	1.6
Dairy products	4.1	6.0	2.7
Milk and cream, concentrated or sweetened	1.6	5.1	2.5
Vegetable products	8.7	8.8	11.5
Edible fruit, nuts, peel of citrus fruit, melons	2.2	3.0	5.4
Brazil nuts, cashew nuts and coconuts	2.1	3.0	5.3
Coffee, tea, maté and spices . .	3.1	2.8	1.9
Oil seed, oleagic fruits, grain, seed, fruit, etc.	1.9	1.6	3.3
Animal, vegetable fats and oils, cleavage products, etc. . .	3.6	5.1	2.1
Prepared foodstuffs; beverages and spirits; tobacco, etc. .	12.1	11.3	6.5
Sugars and sugar confectionery .	3.5	2.1	3.4
Cane or beet sugar and chemically pure sucrose, in solid form	3.0	1.8	3.3
Meat, fish and seafood food preparations	3.8	3.2	0.7
Mineral products	1.6	6.3	2.3
Mineral fuels, oils, etc.	0.7	6.3	2.3
Petroleum oils, not crude . .	0.7	6.3	2.3
Plastics and plastic articles .	4.3	1.3	0.7
Plastics and articles thereof . .	4.1	1.2	0.7

Exports f.o.b.—*continued*	2011	2012	2013
Plastic packing goods or closures, stoppers, lids, caps, etc. . .	3.9	1.0	0.3
Raw hides and skins, leather, furskins, and articles thereof	2.2	8.1	0.9
Wood and articles of wood, wood charcoal	2.1	8.1	0.6
Veneer sheets, sheets for plywood and wood sawn lengthwise	0.5	5.7	0.4
Textiles and textile articles .	46.8	63.6	69.0
Man made filaments . . .	41.4	58.3	67.3
Woven fabrics of synthetic filament yarn	41.3	58.3	67.3
Other made textile articles, sets, worn clothing, etc. . . .	5.2	5.2	1.3
Worn clothing and articles . .	5.2	5.1	1.3
Vehicles, aircraft, vessels and associated transport equipment	1.3	2.1	4.7
Vehicles other than railway, tramway	1.2	2.1	4.7
Total (incl. others)	94.9	118.8	106.2

Source: Trade Map-Trade Competitiveness Map, International Trade Centre, www.intracen.org/marketanalysis.

PRINCIPAL TRADING PARTNERS
(US $ million)

Imports c.i.f.	2011	2012	2013
Belgium	15.0	16.8	17.0
Brazil	39.6	26.2	38.4
China, People's Republic . . .	28.7	32.5	24.2
Côte d'Ivoire	72.5	101.2	80.3
Denmark	4.3	2.7	2.0
France (incl. Monaco) . . .	8.1	7.9	12.7
Germany	11.2	10.1	9.2
India	9.5	13.1	14.6
Indonesia	3.9	14.2	10.9
Italy	2.7	4.4	3.5
Japan	3.8	13.8	0.9
Malaysia	12.3	5.4	5.5
Netherlands	12.2	9.6	7.9
Pakistan	2.5	4.7	7.9
Senegal	15.9	22.8	20.4
Singapore	8.1	2.2	1.4
South Africa	4.2	4.2	1.8
Spain	3.6	4.6	6.9
Switzerland	1.5	5.9	4.8
Turkey	13.2	17.0	16.3
United Arab Emirates . . .	7.3	5.9	13.8
United Kingdom	15.8	13.8	14.4
USA	5.8	6.2	9.0
Uruguay	0.7	6.0	0.7
Viet Nam	3.6	2.7	5.9
Total (incl. others)	340.7	380.0	350.2

Exports f.o.b.	2011	2012	2013
China, People's Republic . . .	3.0	8.0	0.7
France (incl. Monaco) . . .	1.5	0.0	0.1
Guinea	22.0	34.0	34.3
Guinea-Bissau	10.8	10.3	3.1
India	2.4	2.9	4.6
Mali	15.9	37.2	38.4
Senegal	33.4	17.7	18.3
United Kingdom	2.2	4.4	1.1
Viet Nam	0.0	0.2	2.7
Total (incl. others)	94.9	118.8	106.2

Source: Trade Map-Trade Competitiveness Map, International Trade Centre, www.intracen.org/marketanalysis.

Transport

ROAD TRAFFIC
(motor vehicles in use)

	2010
Passenger cars	9,107
Buses	1,389
Lorries and vans	2,601*

* Figure for 2007.

Source: IRF, *World Road Statistics*.

SHIPPING

Flag Registered Fleet
(at 31 December)

	2011	2012	2013
Number of vessels	9	8	8
Total displacement (grt) . . .	33,372	29,396	29,396

Source: Lloyd's List Intelligence (www.lloydslistintelligence.com).

International Seaborne Freight Traffic
(at Banjula sea port, '000 metric tons)

	2010	2011	2012
Goods loaded	281.4	450.6	352.8
Goods unloaded	1,266.8	1,405.9	1,401.7

Tourism

FOREIGN VISITORS BY COUNTRY OF ORIGIN*

	2010	2011	2012
Belgium	1,983	2,234	5,322
Denmark	2,627	1,316	1,660
Germany	2,290	3,020	5,350
Netherlands	8,870	12,906	18,699
Norway	1,370	1,253	1,540
Spain	3,878	4,963	3,570
Sweden	6,493	6,387	8,057
United Kingdom	40,250	46,982	58,029
USA	1,263	2,036	3,149
Total (incl. others)	91,099	106,393	157,323

* Air charter tourist arrivals.

2013: Total tourist arrivals 171,000.

Receipts from tourism (US $ million, excl. passenger transport): 74 in 2010; 83 in 2011; 88 in 2012.

Source: World Tourism Organization.

Communications Media

	2011	2012	2013
Telephones ('000 main lines in use)	50.4	64.2	64.2
Mobile cellular telephones ('000 subscribers)	1,401.2	1,526.2	1,848.9
Broadband subscribers . . .	400	500	438

Sources: International Telecommunication Union.

Education

(2006/07)

	Institutions	Teachers	Students Males	Students Females	Students Total
Primary . . .	491	4,428	108,540	111,883	220,423
Junior secondary	186	2,385	34,432	32,047	66,479
Senior secondary	66	845	19,024	14,697	33,721

Source: Department of State for Education, Banjul.

2011/12 (UNESCO estimates): *Pupils:* Pre-primary 64,677 (2009/10); Primary 244,033; Secondary 124,397 (2009/10) (Source: UNESCO Institute for Statistics).

Pupil-teacher ratio (primary education, UNESCO estimate): 33.9 in 2011/12 (Source: UNESCO Institute for Statistics).

Adult literacy rate (UNESCO estimates): 52.0% (males 61.4%; females 43.1%) in 2012 (Source: UNESCO Institute for Statistics).

Directory

The Government

HEAD OF STATE

President: Col (retd) Alhaji YAHYA A. J. J. JAMMEH (proclaimed Head of State 26 July 1994; elected President 26 September 1996, re-elected 18 October 2001, 22 September 2006 and 24 November 2011).

Vice-President: Dr ISATOU NJIE-SAIDY.

THE CABINET
(April 2015)

President and Minister of Defence, Commander-In-Chief of the Armed Forces: Col (retd) Alhaji YAHYA A. J. J. JAMMEH.

Vice-President and Minister of Women's Affairs: Dr ISATOU NJIE-SAIDY.

Minister of Presidential Affairs, Minister of Fisheries, Secretary-General of the Government and Head of the Civil Service: LAMIN NYABALLY.

Minister of Foreign Affairs: NENEH MACDOUALL-GAYE.

Minister of Finance and Economic Affairs: ABDOU KOLLEY.

Minister of Tourism and Culture: BENJAMIN A. ROBERTS.

Minister of Higher Education, Research, Science and Technology: Dr ABOUBACAR SENGHORE.

Minister of Basic and Secondary Education: FATOU LAMIN FAYE.

Minister of Health and Social Welfare: OMAR SEY.

Minister of Trade, Industry, Regional Integration and Employment: ABDOU JOBE.

Minister of the Environment, Climate Change, Water Resources, Parks and Wildlife: PA OUSMAN JARJU.

Minister of Petroleum: SIRA WALLY NDOW-NJIE.

Minister of Energy: Dr EDWARD SAJA SANNEH.

Minister of Lands and Regional Government: MOMODOU AKI BAYO.

Minister of Justice and Attorney-General: MAMA FATIMA SINGHATEH.

Minister of Information and Communication Infrastructure: SHERIFF BOJANG.

Minister of the Interior: OUSMAN SONKO.

Minister of Youth and Sports: ALIEU K. JAMMEH.

Minister of Transport, Works and Infrastructure: BALA GARBA-JAHUMPA.

MINISTRIES

Office of the President: PMB, State House, Banjul; tel. 4223811; e-mail info@statehouse.gm; internet www.statehouse.gm.

Office of the Vice-President: State House, Banjul; tel. 4227605; fax 4224401; e-mail info@ovp.gov.gm; internet www.ovp.gov.gm.

Ministry of Agriculture: The Quadrangle, Banjul; tel. 4228270; fax 4229325; e-mail info@moa.gov.gm; internet www.moa.gov.gm.

Ministry of Basic and Secondary Education: Willy Thorpe Bldg, Banjul; tel. 4228232; fax 4224180; e-mail info@mobse.gov.gm; internet www.mobse.gov.gm.

Ministry of Energy: Futurelec Bldg, Bertil Harding Highway, Kotu, Banjul; tel. 8905105; fax 4466560; e-mail info@moe.gov.gm; internet www.moe.gov.gm.

Ministry of the Environment, Climate Change, Water Resources, Parks and Wildlife: Kairaba Ave, Serekunda; tel. 4399447; fax 4399518; e-mail info@mofen.gov.gm; internet www.mofen.gov.gm.

Ministry of Finance and Economic Affairs: The Quadrangle, POB 9686, Banjul; tel. 4227221; fax 4227954; e-mail info@mof.gov.gm; internet www.mof.gov.gm.

Ministry of Fisheries: Marina Parade, Banjul; tel. 4227773; fax 4225009; e-mail info@mofwrnam.gov.gm; internet www.mofwrnam.gov.gm.

Ministry of Foreign Affairs: 4 Marina Parade, Banjul; tel. 4223577; fax 4227917; e-mail info@mofa.gov.gm; internet www.mofa.gov.gm.

Ministry of Health and Social Welfare: The Quadrangle, Banjul; tel. 4228624; fax 4229325; e-mail info@moh.gov.gm; internet www.moh.gov.gm.

Ministry of Higher Education, Research, Science and Technology: Bertil Harding Highway, Kotu, Banjul; tel. 4466752; fax 4465408; e-mail info@moherst.gov.gm; internet www.moherst.gov.gm.

Ministry of Information and Communication Infrastructure: GRTS Bldg, MDI Rd, Kanifing, Banjul; tel. 4378028; fax 4378029; e-mail info@moici.gov.gm; internet www.moici.gov.gm.

Ministry of the Interior: 5 J. R. Forster St, Banjul; tel. 4223277; fax 4201320; e-mail info@moi.gov.gm; internet www.moi.gov.gm.

Ministry of Justice and Attorney-General's Chambers: Marina Parade, Banjul; tel. 4225352; fax 4229908; e-mail info@moj.gov.gm; internet www.moj.gov.gm.

Ministry of Lands and Regional Government: Banjul; internet www.molgl.gov.gm.

Ministry of Tourism and Culture: New Administrative Bldg, The Quadrangle, Banjul; tel. 4229844; fax 4227753; e-mail info@motc.gov.gm; internet www.motc.gov.gm.

Ministry of Trade, Industry, Regional Integration and Employment: Central Bank Bldg, Independence Dr., Banjul; tel. 4228868; fax 4227756; e-mail info@motie.gov.gm; internet www.motie.gov.gm.

Ministry of Transport, Works and Infrastructure: MDI Rd, Kanifing, Banjul; tel. 4375761; fax 4375765; e-mail info@mowci.gov.gm; internet www.mowci.gov.gm.

Ministry of Youth and Sports: The Quadrangle, Banjul; tel. 4225264; fax 4225267; e-mail info@moys.gov.gm; internet www.moys.gov.gm.

President

Presidential Election, 24 November 2011

Candidate	Valid votes	% of valid votes
Yahya A. J. J. Jammeh (APRC) . . .	470,550	71.54
Ousainou N. Darboe (UDP)	114,177	17.36
Hamat Bah (Independent)	73,060	11.11
Total*	657,787	100.00

*In addition, there were 264 invalid votes.

Legislature

National Assembly: Parliament Buildings, Independence Dr., Banjul; tel. 4227241; fax 4225123; e-mail assemblyclerk@yahoo .com; internet www.nationalassembly.gm.

Speaker: ABDOULIE BOJANG.

General Election, 29 March 2012*

Party	Votes	% of votes	Seats
Alliance for Patriotic Reorientation and Construction (APRC) . . .	80,289	51.82	43
National Reconciliation Party (NRP)	14,606	9.43	1
Independents	60,055	38.76	4
Total	154,950	100.00	48†

*The election was boycotted by six of the seven main opposition parties, including the United Democratic Party and the National Alliance for Democracy and Development.
† The President of the Republic is empowered by the Constitution to nominate five additional members of parliament. The total number of members of parliament is thus 53.

Election Commission

Independent Electoral Commission (IEC): Election House, Bertil Harding Highway, Kanifing East Layout, POB 793 Banjul; tel. 4373804; fax 4373803; e-mail info@iec.gm; internet www.iec.gm; f. 1997; Chair. Alhaji MUSTAPHA CARAYOL.

Political Organizations

Alliance for Patriotic Reorientation and Construction (APRC): Sankung Sillah Bldg, Kairaba Ave, Banjul; tel. 9745687; f. 1996; governing party; Chair. President YAHYA A. J. J. JAMMEH.

Gambia Moral Congress (GMC): 78 Bertil Harding Highway, Kotu, Banjul; e-mail info@Gambia-Congress.org; internet www .gambia-congress.org; f. 2008; Exec. Chair. MAI N. K. FATTY.

The Gambia Party for Democracy and Progress (GPDP): POB 4014, Kombo St Mary, Serrekunda; tel. 9955226; f. 2004; Sec.-Gen. HENRY GOMEZ.

National Alliance for Democracy and Development (NADD): 30 Papa Sarr St, Churchill, Serrekunda; f. Jan. 2005 to contest 2006 elections; Co-ordinator HALIFA SALLAH; comprises parties listed below:

> **People's Democratic Organization for Independence and Socialism (PDOIS):** POB 2306, 1 Sambou St, Churchill, Serrekunda; tel. and fax 4393177; e-mail foroyaa@qanet.gm; f. 1986; socialist; Leaders HALIFA SALLAH, SAM SARR, SIDIA JATTA.

> **People's Progressive Party (PPP):** c/o Omar Jallow, Ninth St East, Fajara M Section, Banjul; tel. and fax 4392674; f. 1959; fmr ruling party in 1962–94; centrist; Chair. OMAR JALLOW.

National Convention Party (NCP): 38 Sayerr Jobe Ave, Banjul; tel. 6408128 (mobile); f. 1977; left-wing; Leader EBRIMA JANKO SANYANG.

National Democratic Action Movement (NDAM): 1 Box Bar Rd, Nema, Brikama Town, Western Division, Banjul; tel. 7788882; e-mail ndam_gambia@hotmail.com; f. 2002; reformist; Leader and Sec.-Gen. LAMIN WAA JUWARA.

National Reconciliation Party (NRP): 69 Daniel Goddard St, Banjul; tel. 4201371; fax 4201732; f. 1996; formed an alliance with the UDP in 2006; Leader HAMAT N. K. BAH.

United Democratic Party (UDP): 1 Rene Blain St, Banjul; tel. 4221730; fax 4224601; e-mail info@udpgambia.com; f. 1996; formed an alliance with the NRP in 2006 and with the GMC in 2011; reformist; Sec.-Gen. and Leader OUSAINOU N. DARBOE; Nat. Pres. DEMBO BOJANG.

Diplomatic Representation

EMBASSIES IN THE GAMBIA

Cuba: C/801, POB 4627, Banjul; tel. and fax 4495382; e-mail embacuba@ganet.gm; Ambassador LAZARO HERRERA MARTINEZ.

Guinea-Bissau: 78 Atlantic Rd, Fajara (Bakau), Banjul; tel. 4226862; Ambassador FRANCISCA MARIA MONTEIRA SILVA VAZ TURPIN.

Libya: Independence Dr., Banjul; tel. 4223213; fax 4223214; Ambassador Dr ALI MUHAMMAD DUKALY.

Nigeria: 52 Garba Jalumpa Ave, Bakau, POB 630, Banjul; tel. 4495803; fax 4496456; e-mail nighcgambia@yahoo.com; Ambassador ESTHER JOHN AUDU.

Qatar: Banjul; tel. 4410889; fax 4410700; e-mail banjul@mofa.gov .qa; Ambassador MUHAMMAD NASSER ESSA AL-KAABI.

Senegal: 159 Kairaba Ave, POB 385, Banjul; tel. 4373752; fax 4373750; Ambassador BABACAR DIAGNE.

Sierra Leone: 67 Daniel Goddard St, Banjul; tel. 4228206; fax 4229819; e-mail mfodayyumkella@yahoo.co.uk; Ambassador SOULAY DARAMY.

Turkey: 29 Kaira Ave, 4th St, Brufut Gardens, Banjul; e-mail embassy.banjul@mfa.gov.tr; Ambassador ENGIN SONER.

United Kingdom: 48 Atlantic Rd, Fajara, POB 507, Banjul; tel. 4495133; e-mail UKinTheGambia@fco.gov.uk; internet ukingambia .fco.gov.uk/en; Ambassador COLIN CRORKIN.

USA: The White House, Kairaba Ave, Fajara, PMB 19, Banjul; tel. 4392856; fax 4392475; e-mail consularbanjul@state.gov; internet banjul.usembassy.gov; Chargé d'affaires a.i. GEORGE STAPLES.

Venezuela: Banjul; Ambassador EDUARDO MEDINA RUBIO.

Judicial System

The judicial system of The Gambia is based on English Common Law and legislative enactments of the Republic's parliament, which include an Islamic Law Recognition Ordinance whereby an Islamic Court exercises jurisdiction in certain cases between, or exclusively affecting, Muslims.

The Constitution of the Second Republic guarantees the independence of the judiciary. The Supreme Court is defined as the final court of appeal. Provision is made for a special criminal court to hear and determine all cases relating to theft and misappropriation of public funds.

Supreme Court of The Gambia: Law Courts, Independence Dr., Banjul; tel. 4227383; fax 4228380; consists of the Chief Justice and up to six other judges; Chief Justice ELI NAWAZ CHOWHAN.

Court of Appeal: Banjul; Pres. ESTHER AWO OTA.

High Court: Banjul; consists of the Chief Justice and up to seven other judges.

The **Banjul Magistrates Court**, the **Kanifing Magistrates Court** and the **Divisional Courts** are courts of summary jurisdiction presided over by a magistrate or in his absence by two or more lay justices of the peace. There are resident magistrates in all divisions. The magistrates have limited civil and criminal jurisdiction, and appeal from these courts lies with the Supreme Court. **Islamic Courts** have jurisdiction in matters between, or exclusively affecting, Muslim Gambians and relating to civil status, marriage, succession, donations, testaments and guardianship. The Courts administer Islamic *Shari'a* law. A cadi, or a cadi and two assessors, preside over and constitute an Islamic Court. Assessors of the Islamic Courts are Justices of the Peace of Islamic faith. **District Tribunals** have appellate jurisdiction in cases involving customs and traditions. Each court consists of three district tribunal members, one of whom is selected as president, and other court members from the area over which it has jurisdiction.

Attorney-General: MAMA FATIMA SINGHATEH.

Solicitor-General: LAMIN K. MBOGE.

Religion

More than 90% of the population are Muslims. The remainder are mainly Christians, and there are small numbers of animists, mostly of the Diola and Karoninka ethnic groups.

ISLAM

Banjul Central Mosque: King Fahd Bin Abdul Aziz Mosque, Box Bar Rd, POB 562, Banjul; tel. 4228094; Imam Ratib Alhaji CHERNO KAH.

The Gambia Supreme Islamic Council: MDI Rd, Kanifing South, POB 804, Banjul; tel. 4484740; fax 4371977; f. 1962; Pres. Alhaji MOMODOU LAMIN TOURAY.

CHRISTIANITY

The Gambia Christian Council: MDI Rd, Kanifing, POB 27, Banjul; tel. 4392092; f. 1966; seven mems (churches and other Christian bodies); Chair. Rt Rev. ROBERT P. ELLISON (Roman Catholic Bishop of Banjul); Sec.-Gen. Rev. PRISCILLA JOHNSON.

The Anglican Communion

The diocese of The Gambia, which includes Senegal and Cabo Verde, forms part of the Church of the Province of West Africa (CPWA). In September 2012 the CPWA was subdivided into two internal provinces: the Internal Province of Ghana, comprising the 10 dioceses in Ghana, and the Internal Province of West Africa, comprising the remaining five dioceses. The Primate and Metropolitan of the Province of West Africa and the Archbishop of the Internal Province of West Africa is the Bishop of The Gambia. There are about 1,500 adherents in The Gambia.

Primate and Metropolitan of the Province of West Africa, Archbishop of the Internal Province of West Africa and Bishop of The Gambia: Rt Rev. Dr SOLOMON TILEWA JOHNSON, Bishopscourt, POB 51, Banjul; tel. 4228405; fax 4229495; e-mail anglican@qanet.gm.

The Roman Catholic Church

The Gambia comprises a single diocese (Banjul), directly responsible to the Holy See. Some 3% of the population are Roman Catholics. The diocese administers a development organization (Caritas, The Gambia), and runs a number of schools and training centres. The Gambia participates in the Inter-territorial Catholic Bishops' Conference of The Gambia and Sierra Leone (based in Freetown, Sierra Leone).

Bishop of Banjul: Rt Rev. ROBERT PATRICK ELLISON, Bishop's House, POB 165, Banjul; tel. 4391957; fax 4390998; e-mail rpel202@yahoo.co.uk.

Protestant Churches

Abiding Word Ministries (AWM): 156 Mosque Rd, PMB 207, Serrekunda Post Office, Serrekunda; tel. 7640126; fax 4374069; e-mail info@awmgambia.com; internet www.awmgambia.com; f. 1988; Senior Pastor Rev. FRANCIS FORBES.

Evangelical Lutheran Church in The Gambia: POB 5275, Brikama West Coast Region; tel. 9083755; fax 7043336; e-mail leadership@elctg.org; internet www.elctg.org.

Methodist Church: 1 Macoumba Jallow St, POB 288, Banjul; tel. 4227506; fax 4228510; f. 1821; Chair. and Gen. Supt Rev. WILLIAM PETER STEPHENS.

BAHÁ'Í FAITH

National Spiritual Assembly: POB 2532, Serrekunda; tel. 4229015; e-mail nsagambia@gamtel.gm; internet bci.org/bahaigambia.

The Press

All independent publications are required to register annually with the Government and to pay a registration fee.

The Daily News: 65 Kombo Sillah Dr., Churchill's Town, POB 2849, Serrekunda; tel. 8905629; e-mail dailynews34@yahoo.com; internet dailynews.gm; f. 2009; 3 a week; Dir MADI M. K. CEESAY; Editor-in-Chief SAIKOU JAMMEH.

The Daily Observer: Gacem Rd, Kanifing Industrial Area, Bakau, POB 131, Banjul; tel. 4399801; fax 4496878; e-mail webmaster@observer.gm; internet www.observer.gm; f. 1992; daily; pro-Govt; Dep. Editor-in-Chief ALHAGIE JOBE; circ. 5,000.

Foroyaa (Freedom): 1 Sambou St, Churchill's Town, POB 2306, Serrekunda; tel. and fax 4393177; e-mail online@foroyaa.gm; internet www.foroyaa.gm; f. 1987; daily; publ. by the PDOIS; Editors HALIFA SALLAH, SAM SARR, SIDIA JATTA.

The Gambia Daily: Dept of Information, 14 Daniel Goddard St, Banjul; tel. 4225060; fax 4227230; e-mail gamna@gamtel.gm; f. 1994; govt organ; Dir of Information EBRUMA COLE; circ. 500.

The Point: 2 Garba Jahumpa Rd, Fajara, POB 66, Bakau, New Town, Banjul; tel. 4497441; fax 4497442; e-mail thepoint13@yahoo

.com; internet www.thepoint.gm; f. 1991; 3 a week; Man. Dir PAP SAINE; Editor-in-Chief OSMAN KARGBO; circ. 3,000.

The Standard: Sait Matty Rd, POB 4566, Bakau; tel. 7643558; fax 4496481; e-mail info@standard.gm; internet www.standard.gm; f. 2010; daily; Man. Dir LAMIN FATTY; Editor SAINEY DARBOE.

NEWS AGENCY

The Gambia News Agency (GAMNA): Dept of Information, 14 Daniel Goddard St, Banjul; tel. 4225060; fax 4227230; e-mail gamna@gamtel.gm; Dir EBRIMA COLE.

PRESS ASSOCIATION

The Gambia Press Union (GPU): 78 Mosque Rd, Serrekunda, POB 1440, Banjul; tel. and fax 4377020; e-mail gpu@qanet.gm; internet www.gambiapressunion.org; f. 1978; affiliated to West African Journalists' Association; Pres. EMIL TOURAY; Sec.-Gen. GIBAIRU JANNEH.

Publishers

National Printing and Stationery Corpn: Sankung Sillah St, Kanifing; tel. 4374403; fax 4395759; f. 1998; state-owned.

Baroueli: 73 Mosque Rd, Serrekunda, POB 976, Banjul; tel. 4392480; e-mail baroueli@qanet.gm; f. 1986; educational.

Observer Company: Bakau New Town Rd, Kanifing, PMB 131, Banjul; tel. 4496087; fax 4496878; e-mail webmaster@observer.gm; internet www.observer.gm; f. 1995; indigenous languages and non-fiction.

Sunrise Publishers: POB 955, Banjul; tel. 4393538; e-mail sunrise@qanet.gm; internet www.sunrisepublishers.net; f. 1985; regional history, politics and culture; Man. PATIENCE SONKO-GODWIN.

Broadcasting and Communications

TELECOMMUNICATIONS

In 2013 the Gambia telecommunications sector comprised four mobile cellular telephone operators and one fixed-line operator. A fifth mobile licence was issued to Nigeria-owned Globacom in 2010.

Africell (Gambia): 43 Kairaba Ave, POB 2140, Banjul; tel. 4376022; fax 4376066; e-mail mmakkaoui@africell.gm; internet www.africell.gm; f. 2001; provider of mobile cellular telecommunications; CEO ALIEU BADARA MBYE.

Comium Gambia: 27 Kairaba Ave, Pipeline, KSMD, Banjul; tel. 6601601; fax 6601602; e-mail info@comium.gm; internet www.comium.gm; f. 2007; operates mobile cellular telephone network under the Nakam brand; Man. Dir AMER ATWI.

The Gambia Telecommunications Co Ltd (GAMTEL): Gamtel House, 3 Nelson Mandela St, POB 387, Banjul; tel. 4229999; fax 4228004; e-mail gen-info@gamtel.gm; internet www.gamtel.gm; f. 1984; state-owned; Man. Dir BABOUCARR SANYANG.

Gamcel: 59 Mamadi Maniyang Highway, Kanifing; tel. 4398169; fax 4372932; internet www.gamcel.gm; f. 2000; wholly owned subsidiary of GAMTEL providing mobile cellular telephone services.

QCell Gambia: QCell House, Kairaba Ave, Serrekunda; tel. 3333111; fax 4376311; e-mail support@qcell.gm; internet www.qcell.gm; f. 2008; mobile cellular services; CEO MUHAMMED JAH.

BROADCASTING

Radio

The Gambia Radio and Television Services (GRTS): GRTV Headquarters, MDI Rd, Kanifing, POB 158, Banjul; tel. 4373913; fax 4374242; e-mail bora@gamtel.gm; internet www.grts.gm; f. 1962; state-funded, non-commercial broadcaster; radio broadcasts in English, Mandinka, Wolof, Fula, Diola, Serer and Serahuli; Dir-Gen. LAMIN MANGA.

Capital FM 100.4: 2 Kairaba Ave; tel. 7979359; e-mail saul@capitalfm.gm.

Farafenni Community Radio: Farafenni; tel. 9931964; Gen. Man. SAINEY DIBBA.

Brikama Community Radio Station: Brikama; tel. 4483000; fax 4484100; e-mail brikamacommunityradio@yahoo.co.uk; f. 1998; FM broadcaster; Admin. Man. BAKARY K. TOURAY.

Kora FM: 10 Kanifing, Banjul; internet 4399756; e-mail info@korafm.gm; internet korafm.gm; independent commercial broadcaster.

Paradise FM: Banjul; internet www.paradisefm.gm; operates from 3 stations: 105.7 Mhz in Kololi, 105.5 Mhz in Farafenni and 105.8 Mhz in Basse.

Radio 1 FM: 44 Kairaba Ave, POB 2700, Serrekunda; tel. 4396076; fax 4394911; e-mail george.radio1@qanet.gm; f. 1990; private station broadcasting FM music programmes to the Greater Banjul area; Dir GEORGE CHRISTENSEN.

Teranga FM: Sinchu Alhagie Village, Kombo North, West Coast Region; f. 2009; Man. ISMAILA SISAY.

West Coast Radio: Manjai Kunda, POB 2687, Serrekunda; tel. 4460911; fax 4461193; e-mail info@westcoast.gm; internet www .westcoast.gm; FM broadcaster; Man. Dir PETER GOMEZ.

Unique FM: Garba Jahumpa Rd, Bakau; tel. 7555777; internet www.uniquefm.gm; f. 2007; Man. LAMIN MANGA.

The Gambia also receives broadcasts from Radio Democracy for Africa (f. 1998), a division of the Voice of America, and the British Broadcasting Corpn.

Television

The Gambia Radio and Television Services (GRTS): see Radio; television broadcasts commenced 1995.

There is also a private satellite channel, Premium TV.

Finance

(cap. = capital; res = reserves; dep. = deposits; m. = million; br(s). = branch(es); amounts in dalasi)

BANKING

At the end of 2013 there were 13 banks operating in the country, of which one was an Islamic bank and 12 were conventional commercial banks.

Central Bank

Central Bank of The Gambia: 1–2 ECOWAS Ave, Banjul; tel. 4228103; fax 4226969; e-mail info@cbg.gm; internet www.cbg.gm; f. 1971; bank of issue; monetary authority; cap. 81.0m., res 4.3m., dep. 1,702.7m. (Dec. 2009); Gov. AMADOU COLLEY.

Other Banks

Access Bank (Gambia) Ltd: 47 Kairaba Ave, Fajara, POB 3177, Serrekunda; tel. 4396679; fax 4396640; e-mail jammehm@ accessbankgambia.com; internet www.accessbankplc.com/gm; f. 2007; Man. Dir OLEKA OJIOGO.

Arab-Gambian Islamic Bank: 7 ECOWAS Ave, POB 1415, Banjul; tel. 4222222; fax 4223770; e-mail info@agib.gm; internet www.agib .gm; f. 1996; 21.1% owned by The Gambia National Insurance Co Ltd, 20.0% owned by Islamic Development Bank (Saudi Arabia); Chair. ADAM NURU; Man. Dir SALISU SIRAJO; 1 br.

Banque Sahelo-Saherienne pour l'Investissement et Commerce Gambie Ltd: 52 Kairaba Ave, PMB 204, KMC; tel. 4498078; fax 4498080; e-mail bsic@bsicgambia.gm; internet www .bsicgambia.gm; f. 2008; Gen. Man. YOUSEF SGHAYER AHMED TURKMAN.

Ecobank Gambia Ltd: 42 Kairaba Ave, POB 3466, Serrekunda; tel. 4399030; fax 4399034; e-mail egacustomercare@ecobank.com; internet www.ecobank.com; cap. 456.3m., res 11.8m., dep. 2,478.7m. (Dec. 2013); Man. Dir MAREME MBAYE NDIAYE.

First International Bank Ltd: 2 Kairaba Ave, Serrekunda; tel. and fax 4396580; e-mail info@fibgm.com; internet www.fibankgm .com; f. 1999; 61.9% owned by Slok Ltd (Nigeria); cap. 150.7m., res 7.8m., dep. 570.3m. (Dec. 2010); Chair. EDRISSA JOBE; Man. Dir YASSIN BAYO; 8 brs.

Guaranty Trust Bank (Gambia): 56 Kairaba Ave, Fajara, POB 1958, Banjul; tel. 4376371; fax 4376398; e-mail corpaffgm@gtbank .com; internet gtbankgambia.com; f. 2002; subsidiary of Guaranty Trust Bank PLC (Nigeria); Chair. AMADOU SAMBA; Man. Dir OLUFEMI OMOTOSO.

International Commercial Bank (Gambia) Ltd: GIPFZA House, Ground Floor, 48 Kairaba Ave, Serrekunda, KMC, POB 1600, Banjul; tel. 4377878; fax 4377880; e-mail icbank@icbank-gambia .com; internet www.icbank-gambia.com; f. 2005; CEO LALIT MOHAN TEWARI; 3 brs.

Keystone Bank Gambia: 11A Liberation Ave, POB 211, Banjul; tel. 4227944; fax 4229312; e-mail mgcisse@ibc.gm; internet gambia .bankphb.com; f. 1968; fmrly International Bank for Commerce (Gambia) Ltd, subsequently Bank PHB, name changed as above 2013; cap. 60m., res 59.9m., dep. 434.6m. (Dec. 2006); Man. Dir CHUKS CHIBUNDU; 2 brs.

Skye Bank Gambia: 70 Kairaba Ave, Fajara, KSMD; tel. 4414370; e-mail info@skyebankgm.com; internet www.skyebankgm.com; subsidiary of Skye Bank PLC (Nigeria); Man. Dir MOHAMED GILLEN.

Standard Chartered Bank (Gambia) Ltd: 8/10 ECOWAS Ave, POB 259, Banjul; tel. 4202929; fax 4202692; e-mail Humphrey .Mukwereza@gm.standardchartered.com; internet www .standardchartered.com/gm; f. 1894; 75% owned by Standard Chartered Holdings BV, The Netherlands; cap. 200m., res 36.6m., dep. 3,349.7m. (Dec. 2013); Chair. MOMODOU B. A. SENGHORE; CEO HUMPHREY MUKWEREZA; 5 brs.

Trust Bank Ltd (TBL): 3–4 ECOWAS Ave, POB 1018, Banjul; tel. 4225777; fax 4225781; e-mail info@trustbank.gm; internet www .tblgambia.com; f. 1997; fmrly Meridien BIAO Bank Gambia Ltd; 22.12% owned by Data Bank, 36.97% by Social Security and Housing Finance Corpn; cap. 200.0m., res 109.7m., dep. 4,085.9m. (Dec. 2013); Chair. KEN OFORI ATTA; Man. Dir PA MACOUMBA NJIE; 17 brs.

Zenith Bank (Gambia) Ltd: 49 Kairaba Ave, Fajara, POB 2823, Serrekunda; tel. 4399471; e-mail enquiry@zenithbank.gm; internet www.zenithbank.gm; f. 2008; subsidiary of Zenith Bank PLC; Man. Dir EMEKA ANYAEGBUNA.

INSURANCE

At the end of 2013 there were 13 insurance companies operating in the country, of which 10 provided non-life insurance, two life insurance and one both non-life and life insurance.

Capital Express Assurance (Gambia) Ltd: 22 Anglesea St, POB 268, Banjul; tel. 4227480; fax 4229219; e-mail capinsur@gamtel.gm; f. 1985; subsidiary of Capital Express Assurance Limited (Nigeria); CEO KUNLE ADEGBOYE.

The Gambia National Insurance Co Ltd (GNIC): 19 Kairaba Ave, Fajara, KSMD, POB 750, Banjul; tel. 4395725; fax 4395716; e-mail info@gnic.gm; internet www.gnic.gm; f. 1974; privately owned; Chair. MATARR O. DRAMMEH; Man. Dir FYE K. CEESAY; 3 brs.

Global Security Insurance Co Ltd: 73A Independence Dr., POB 1400, Banjul; tel. 4223716; fax 4223715; e-mail global@gamtel.gm; f. 1996; Man. Dir EBOU L. BITTAYE.

Great Alliance Insurance Co: 10 Nelson Mandela St, POB 1160, Banjul; tel. 4227839; fax 4229444; f. 1989; Pres. BAI MATARR DRAMMEH; Man. Dir DEBORAH H. FORSTER.

IGI Gamstar Insurance Co Ltd: 79 Daniel Goddard St, POB 1276, Banjul; tel. 4228610; fax 4229755; e-mail gamstarinsurance@ hotmail.com; f. 1991; Man. Dir FRANK UCHE.

International Insurance Co. Ltd: Duwa Jabbi Bldg, 5 OAU Blvd, POB 1254, Banjul; tel. 4202761; fax 4202763; e-mail iic@gamtel.gm; Man. Dir SENOR THOMAS-SOWE.

Londongate (Gambia) Insurance Co: 1–3 Liberation Ave, POB 602, Banjul; tel. 4201740; fax 4201742; e-mail izadi@londongate.gm; internet www.londongate.co.uk/gambia_profile.htm; f. 1999; owned by Boule & Co Ltd; Man. Dir ISHA JANNEH.

New Vision Insurance Co Ltd: 3–4 ECOWAS Ave, POB 239, Banjul; tel. 4223045; fax 4223040; Dir BIRAN BAH.

Prime Insurance Co Ltd: 10C Nelson Mandela St, POB 277, Banjul; tel. 4222476; fax 4222475; e-mail info@primeinsurance .gm; internet www.primeinsurance.gm; f. 1997; Gen. Man. DAWDA SARGE.

Sunshine Insurance Company Ltd: 7/8 Nelson Mandela St, Banjul; tel. 4202645; fax 4202648; e-mail sunshine.insurance@ qanet.gm; Man. Dir ALMAMY B. JOBARTEH.

Takaful Gambia Ltd: 71 Dobson St, Banjul, POB 12, Banjul; tel. 4229820; fax 4229823; e-mail info@takaful.gm; internet www .takafulinsurance.gm; Man. Dir MAMODOU M. JOOF.

Insurance Association

Insurance Association of The Gambia (IAG): IAG Secretariat, 10C Nelson Mandela St, POB 277, Banjul; tel. 4229952; fax 4201637; e-mail info@iag.gm; internet www.iag.gm; f. 1987; Pres. DAWDA SARGE; Sec.-Gen. HENRY M. JAWO.

Trade and Industry

GOVERNMENT AGENCIES

The Gambia Investment and Export Promotion Agency (GIEPA): GIEPA House, 48A Kairaba Ave, Serrekunda, KMC, POB 757, Banjul; tel. 4377377; fax 4377379; e-mail info.info@giepa .gm; internet www.giepa.gm; f. 2001; fmrly The Gambia Investment Promotion and Free Zones Agency (f. 2001), the implementing agency of the Gateway Project, funded by the World Bank and the Gambian Government, responsible for fostering local and foreign direct investment; name changed as above in 2010; Chair. FATOU SINYAN MERGAN; CEO FATOU M. JALLOW.

Indigenous Business Advisory Services (IBAS): POB 2502, Bakau; tel. 4496098; e-mail payibas@gamtel.gm; Man. Dir Manga Sanyang.

DEVELOPMENT AGENCY

The Gambia Rural Development Agency (GARDA): Soma Village, Jarra West, PMB 452, Serrekunda; tel. 4496676; fax 4390095; f. 1990; Exec. Dir Kebba Bah.

CHAMBER OF COMMERCE

The Gambia Chamber of Commerce and Industry (GCCI): Kerr Jula, Bertil Harding Highway, Bijilo, POB 3382, Serrekunda; tel. 4463452; e-mail info@gcci.gm; internet www.gcci.gm; f. 1967; Pres. Muhammad Jagana; CEO Alieu Secka.

INDUSTRIAL AND TRADE ASSOCIATION

The Gambia Cotton Growers Association: Banjul; Pres. Alpha Bah; Sec.-Gen. Omar Sumpo Ceesay.

UTILITIES

Public Utilities Regulatory Authority (PURA): 94 Kairaba Ave, POB 4230, Bakau; tel. 4399601; fax 4399905; e-mail info@pura.gm; internet www.pura.gm; f. 2001; monitors and enforces standards of performance by public utilities; Chair. (vacant); Dir-Gen. Ansumana Sanneh (acting).

National Water and Electricity Co Ltd (NAWEC): 53 Mamady Manjang Highway, Kanifing, POB 609, Banjul; tel. 4376607; fax 4375990; e-mail nawecmd@qanet.gm; internet www.nawec.gm; f. 1996; in 1999 control was transferred to the Bassau Development Corpn, Côte d'Ivoire, under a 15-year contract; electricity and water supply, sewerage services; Chair. Mustapha Colley; Man. Dir Ebrima Sanyang.

TRADE UNIONS

The Gambia National Trades Union Congress (GNTUC): Trade Union House, 31 OAU Blvd, POB 698, Banjul; Pres. Mustapha Wada; Sec.-Gen. Ebrima Garba Cham.

The Gambia Workers' Confederation: Trade Union House, 72 OAU Blvd, POB 698, Banjul; tel. and fax 4222754; e-mail gambiawc@hotmail.com; f. 1958 as The Gambia Workers' Union; present name adopted in 1985; Sec.-Gen. Pa Momodou Faal; 52,000 mems (2007).

Transport

Gambia Public Transport Service Co: Factory St, Kanifing Housing Estate, POB 801, Kanifing; tel. 4392230; fax 4392454; f. 2013 to replace The Gambia Public Transport Corpn; operates road transport and ferry services; Man. Dir Bakary Huma.

RAILWAYS

There are no railways in The Gambia.

ROADS

In 2004 there were an estimated 3,742 km of roads in The Gambia, of which 1,652 km were main roads, and 1,300 km were secondary roads. In that year only 19.3% of the road network was paved. Some roads are impassable in the rainy season. The expansion and upgrading of the road network is planned, as part of the Jammeh administration's programme to improve The Gambia's transport infrastructure. Among intended schemes is the construction of a motorway along the coast, with the aid of a loan of US $8.5m. from Kuwait.

SHIPPING

The River Gambia is well suited to navigation. A weekly river service is maintained between Banjul and Basse, 390 km above Banjul, and a ferry connects Banjul with Barra. Small ocean-going vessels can reach Kaur, 190 km above Banjul, throughout the year. The Gambia's flag registered fleet consisted of eight vessels, totalling 29,396 grt, at 31 December 2014.

The Gambia Ports Authority: 34 Liberation Ave, POB 617, Banjul; tel. 4227266; fax 4227268; e-mail info@gamport.gm; internet www.gamports.com; f. 1972; Man. Dir Mohammed Lamin Gibba.

The Gambia Shipping Agency Ltd: 1A Cotton St, POB 257, Banjul; tel. 4227518; fax 4227929; e-mail thomas.nielsen@bollore.com; f. 1984; shipping agents and forwarders; Gen. Man. Thomas Nielsen; 30 employees.

Interstate Shipping Co (Gambia) Ltd: 43 Buckle St, POB 220, Banjul; tel. 4229388; fax 4229347; e-mail interstate@gamtel.gm; transport and storage; Man. Dir B. F. Sagnia.

Maersk Gambia Ltd: 80 OAU Blvd, POB 1399, Banjul; tel. 4224450; fax 4224025; e-mail gamsalimp@maersk.com; f. 1993; owned by Maersk Line.

CIVIL AVIATION

Banjul International Airport is situated at Yundum, 27 km from the capital.

The Gambia Civil Aviation Authority (GCAA): Banjul International Airport, Yundum; tel. 4472831; fax 4472190; e-mail dggcaa@qanet.gm; internet www.gcaa.aero/portal; f. 1991; Chair. Salifu Mboge; Dir-Gen. Abdoulie Jammeh.

Gambia Bird Airlines Ltd: Gambia Bird House, 38 Kairaba Ave, Kanifing; tel. 4392733; fax 4392702; e-mail info@gambiabird.com; internet www.gambiabird.com; f. 2009; CEO Thomas Wazinski.

The Gambia International Airlines: PMB 353, Banjul; tel. 4472770; fax 4223700; internet www.gia.gm; f. 1996; state-owned; sole handling agent at Banjul, sales agent; Chair. Muhammed M. O. Kah; Man. Dir Bakary Nyassi.

Tourism

Tourists are attracted by The Gambia's beaches and also by its abundant birdlife. A major expansion of tourism facilities was carried out in the early 1990s. Although there was a dramatic decline in tourist arrivals in the mid-1990s (owing to the political instability), the tourism sector recovered well. An annual 'Roots Festival' was inaugurated in 1996, with the aim of attracting African-American visitors to The Gambia. In 2013 some 171,000 tourists visited The Gambia, while earnings from tourism totalled US $88m. in 2012.

The Gambia Hotel Association: c/o Golden Beach Hotel, Coastal Rd, POB 2345, Bijilo; tel. 7725379; fax 4463722; e-mail info@gambiahotels.gm; internet www.gambiahotels.gm; Chair. Marc Van Maldegem.

The Gambia Tourism Board: Kololi, POB 4085, Bakau; tel. 4462491; fax 4462487; e-mail info@gtboard.gm; internet www.visitthegambia.gm; f. 2001 as The Gambia Tourist Authority; name changed as above in 2011; Chair. Bakary K. Jammeh.

Defence

As assessed at November 2014, the Gambian National Army comprised 800 men (including a marine unit of about 70 and the National Guards) in active service. The Armed Forces comprise the Army, the Navy and the National Guards. Military service has been mainly voluntary; however, the Constitution of the Second Republic, which entered into full effect in January 1997, makes provision for conscription.

Defence Expenditure: Estimated at D189m. in 2013.

Chief of Defence Staff: Maj.-Gen. Ousman Badjie.

Commander of the Gambian National Army: Brig.-Gen. Serign Modou Njie.

Commander of the Navy: Commodore Madani Senghore.

Education

Primary education, beginning at seven years of age, is free but not compulsory and lasts for nine years. It is divided into two cycles of six and three years. Secondary education, from 16 years of age, lasts for a further three years. According to UNESCO estimates, in 2012 total enrolment at primary schools included 71% of children in the relevant age-group (boys 69%; girls 73%), while secondary enrolment in 2010 was equivalent to 57% of the appropriate age-group (boys 59%; girls 56%). The Jammeh administration has, since 1994, embarked on an ambitious project to improve educational facilities and levels of attendance and attainment. A particular aim has been to improve access to schools for pupils in rural areas. Post-secondary education is available in teacher-training, agriculture, health and technical subjects. The University of The Gambia, at Banjul, was officially opened in 2000. Some 2,842 students were enrolled at the university in 2009/10. In 2010 spending on education represented 22.8% of total budgetary expenditure.

GEORGIA

Introductory Survey

LOCATION, CLIMATE, LANGUAGE, RELIGION, FLAG, CAPITAL

Georgia is situated in the west and central South Caucasus, on the southern foothills of the Greater Caucasus mountain range. There is a frontier with Turkey to the south-west and a western coastline on the Black Sea. The northern frontier with Russia follows the axis of the Greater Caucasus. Armenia lies to the south, and Azerbaijan to the south-east. Two territories within Georgia remained outside the control of the central Government: Abkhazia, in the north-west, and South Ossetia, in the north. The Black Sea coast and the Rioni plains have a warm, humid, subtropical climate, with annual rainfall of more than 2,000 mm and average temperatures of 6°C (42°F) in January and 23°C (73°F) in July. Eastern Georgia has a more continental climate, with cold winters and hot, dry summers. The official language is Georgian, a member of the South Caucasian (Kartavelian) language group, which is written in the Georgian script. Most of the population are adherents of Christianity; the principal denomination is the Georgian Orthodox Church. Islam is professed by Ajars, Azeris, Kurds and some others. The national flag (proportions 100 by 147) consists of a white field, with a centred red cross and a smaller red cross in each quarter. The capital is Tbilisi.

CONTEMPORARY POLITICAL HISTORY

Historical Context

A powerful kingdom in medieval times, Georgia was annexed by the Russian Empire from the 19th century. An independent Georgian state was established on 26 May 1918, ruled by a Menshevik Socialist Government. Although it received recognition from the Bolshevik Government of Soviet Russia in May 1920, Bolshevik troops invaded Georgia and proclaimed a Georgian Soviet Socialist Republic (SSR) on 25 February 1921. In December 1922 it was absorbed into the Transcaucasian Soviet Federative Socialist Republic (TSFSR), which, on 22 December, became a founder member of the USSR. In 1936 the TSFSR was disbanded and Georgia reverted to the status of an SSR.

During the 1930s Georgians suffered persecution under the Soviet leader, Stalin (Iosif V. Dzhugashvili), himself a Georgian. Most members of the Georgian leadership were dismissed after Stalin's death in 1953, and demonstrations in support of Stalin in the Georgian capital, Tbilisi, in 1956 were violently dispersed. In 1972 the First Secretary of the Sakartvelos Komunisturi Partia (SKP—Communist Party of Georgia), Eduard Shevardnadze, attempted to remove officials who had been accused of corruption. Shevardnadze remained leader of the SKP until 1985, when he became Minister of Foreign Affairs of the USSR.

The increased freedom of expression that followed the election of Mikhail Gorbachev as Soviet leader in 1985 allowed the formation of 'unofficial groups', which organized demonstrations in November 1988 against russification in Georgia. In February 1989 Abkhazians renewed a campaign for secession from Georgia (see Abkhazia). On the night of 8–9 April Soviet security forces attacked demonstrators who were advocating Georgian independence in the Georgian capital, Tbilisi, killing 16 people. Despite the resignation of state and party officials, anti-Soviet sentiment increased sharply. In November the Georgian Supreme Soviet (Supreme Council—legislature), which was dominated by SKP members, declared the supremacy of Georgian laws over all-Union (USSR) laws; in February 1990 it declared Georgia 'an annexed and occupied country', and in March abolished the SKP's monopoly on power. Legislation permitting full multi-party elections was adopted in August.

In the elections to the Supreme Soviet, held on 28 October and 11 November 1990, the pro-independence Mrgvali Magida-Tavisupali Sakartvelo (Round Table-Free Georgia) coalition, founded earlier in the year and led by Zviad Gamsakhurdia, a former dissident, won 155 seats in the 250-seat chamber, and 64% of the votes cast, while the SKP won 64 seats. All associations involved in the election campaign had declared support for Georgia's independence. The elections were boycotted by many non-ethnic Georgians. The new Supreme Soviet convened on 14 November and elected Gamsakhurdia as its Chairman. It renamed the territory the Republic of Georgia and adopted the flag of the 1918–21 state. Tengiz Sigua was appointed Chairman of the Council of Ministers. The new Supreme Soviet declared illegal the conscription of Georgians into the Soviet armed forces. Many young men were reported to have joined nationalist paramilitary groups or the National Guard (a de facto republican army), which the Supreme Soviet established in January 1991.

The Georgian authorities boycotted the all-Union referendum on the future of the USSR, held in March 1991, but voting took place in Abkhazia and in the former autonomous oblast of South Ossetia (which had been abolished in December 1990). It was reported that in both territories there was overwhelming support for the preservation of the USSR. At a referendum conducted by the Government on 31 March 1991, 93% of those participating voted for Georgian independence. On 9 April the Georgian Supreme Council approved a decree formally restoring the independence of Georgia, which thus became the first republic to secede from the USSR. Gamsakhurdia won direct elections to the new post of executive President, held in May, receiving 86.5% of the votes cast. Voting did not take place in Abkhazia or South Ossetia.

Domestic Political Affairs

Gamsakhurdia was strongly criticized, after he initially refrained from publicly condemning the attempted coup by conservative communists in Moscow, the Russian and Soviet capital, in August 1991 (the SKP was subsequently disbanded). After the coup collapsed, Tengiz Kitovani, the former leader of the National Guard (who had been dismissed by Gamsakhurdia in August), announced that his followers were no longer subordinate to the President. Sigua resigned as Chairman of the Council of Ministers in mid-August, joining Kitovani in opposition to Gamsakhurdia. In September opposition parties organized a series of demonstrations to demand Gamsakhurdia's resignation. Several people were killed in clashes. Gamsakhurdia ordered the arrest of prominent opposition leaders, imposing a state of emergency in Tbilisi.

In December 1991 armed conflict broke out in Tbilisi, as the opposition, led by Kitovani and by Jaba Ioseliani, the leader of the paramilitary Mkhedrioni (Horsemen), attempted to oust the President. More than 100 people were killed. On 2 January 1992 the opposition declared Gamsakhurdia deposed and formed a Military Council, which appointed Sigua as acting Chairman of the Council of Ministers. Gamsakhurdia and some of his supporters ('Zviadists') fled Georgia four days later. The office of President was abolished, and the functions of Head of State were, instead, to be exercised by the Chairman of the Supreme Council. Sigua subsequently formed a new Government.

The return of Eduard Shevardnadze

In March 1992 Shevardnadze returned to Georgia, and a 50-member State Council, comprising 50 members, drawn from all the major political organizations, and including Sigua, Ioseliani and Kitovani, led by Shevardnadze, was formed. By April government troops had re-established control in the rebellious areas. In July, however, Zviadists took a deputy premier hostage in western Georgia. This was followed by the kidnapping of the Minister of Internal Affairs and several other officials. In response, the State Council dispatched more than 3,000 National Guardsmen to Abkhazia, where the hostages were believed to be held, prompting armed resistance by Abkhazian militia. By August several of the hostages had been released, although unrest in Abkhazia continued.

An estimated 75% of the electorate participated in elections to the Supreme Council held on 11 October 1992. The centrist Mshvidoba (Peace) bloc won 29 seats, more than any other grouping, in the 235-member legislature. Shevardnadze was the sole candidate at the concurrent direct election of the legislature's Chairman (and the Head of State), winning more than 95% of the votes cast. The new Supreme Council convened in November.

Opposition towards Shevardnadze from within his own administration prompted the dismissal, in May 1993, of Kitovani as Minister of Defence. In August the Council of Ministers tendered its resignation. In September Shevardnadze appointed a new Council of Ministers, headed by Otar Patsatsia, a former SKP official. By late September Shevardnadze's position was made more precarious by a Zviadist resurgence in western Georgia. As the rebel forces advanced eastwards, Shevardnadze persuaded the Supreme Council to agree to Georgia's membership of the Commonwealth of Independent States (CIS, see p. 241), established in December 1991 by 11 former Soviet republics. In October 1993 Russian troops were dispatched to Georgia, and by November the Zviadists had been entirely routed from the country. In January 1994 it was reported that Gamsakhurdia had committed suicide.

Following the restoration of a degree of stability, Shevardnadze created his own party, the Sakartvelos Mokalaketa Kavshiri (SMK—Citizens' Union of Georgia). In August 1995 the Supreme Council adopted a new Constitution, which provided for a strong executive presidency. The post of Prime Minister was to be abolished and the most senior position in the Government to be the Minister of State. The territorial status of Abkhazia and Ajara was not defined, while the incorporation of the former South Ossetian territories into various other regions was confirmed. The official signing of the Constitution was postponed until 17 October following an assassination attempt against Shevardnadze. After Igor Giorgadze, the Minister of State Security, was subsequently named by state prosecutors as the chief instigator of the plot, he fled abroad.

A presidential election was held on 5 November 1995, in which Shevardnadze won almost 75% of the votes cast. Elections to the new 235-member unicameral Sakartvelos Parlamenti (Georgian Parliament) were held concurrently, under a mixed electoral system. Following a further two rounds of voting, the SMK had secured a total of 107 seats. Parliament convened in late November, electing as its Chairman Zurab Zhvania, the General Secretary of the SMK. In December Shevardnadze formed a new Government, headed by Minister of State Nikoloz Lekishvili.

In May 1996 Ioseliani was convicted of complicity in the August 1995 assassination attempt on Shevardnadze and imprisoned. In June 1996 supporters of Gamsakhurdia received lengthy prison sentences for their roles in the civil conflict of 1993. In September 1996 Kitovani was convicted on charges of establishing an illegal armed formation and was sentenced to eight years' imprisonment. (He was released in May 1999.)

In February 1998 Shevardnadze survived a further attempt on his life. In March Guram Absandze, a former Minister of Finance, was arrested in Moscow and returned to Georgia to stand trial on charges of organizing the assassination attempt. He was sentenced to 17 years' imprisonment in 2001, but was pardoned in April 2002. Further arrests were made in May 1999, in connection with a further plot to overthrow Shevardnadze. All of those arrested were reported to have links with Giorgadze; one of the accused died in detention, and 10 others were sentenced to terms of imprisonment in November 2001.

Meanwhile, in August 1998 the hitherto ambassador to Russia, Vazha Lortkipanidze, was appointed Minister of State. In October Zviadists staged an armed insurrection in western Georgia. Following the escape of the captured rebel leaders, the Minister of State Security resigned. In July 1999 Parliament approved a constitutional amendment, increasing from 5% to 7% the quorum for parliamentary representation in those seats elected by proportional representation. Legislative elections, in which 68% of the electorate participated, were held on 31 October and 14 November. The SMK obtained a total of 130 seats. The Sakartvelos Aghordzinebis Kavshiri (Union for the Revival of Georgia) bloc, led by Aslan Abashidze (the leader of the Autonomous Republic of Ajara), and the Mretsveloba Gadaarchens Sakartvelos (MGS—Industry Will Save Georgia) bloc secured 58 seats and 15 seats, respectively.

Shevardnadze secured 79.8% of the votes cast in the presidential election of 9 April 2000. Electoral violations, but no major infringements, were reported by the Organization for Security and Co-operation in Europe (OSCE, see p. 385). On 11 May Parliament endorsed the appointment of Giorgi Arsenishvili as Minister of State.

In September 2001 the Minister of Justice, Mikheil Saakashvili, resigned. Shortly afterwards, he founded a new political party, the Natsionaluri Modzraoba (NM—National Movement). In the same month Shevardnadze resigned as Chairman of the SMK. In October public discontent culminated in large-scale protests in Tbilisi, after security officials raided Rustavi 2, an independent television station that had been critical of the

Government. Zhvania urged the Minister of State Security and the Minister of Internal Affairs to resign, to avert further protests. However, the latter refused to comply with this request, and popular protests intensified. On 1 November Shevardnadze dismissed the Government. The Prosecutor-General subsequently resigned, as did Zhvania, who was replaced as parliamentary Chairman by Nino Burjanadze. Later in the month a new Government was formed, with Avtandil Jorbenadze as Minister of State. Zhvania founded a new political party, the Gaertianebuli Demokratebi (GD—United Democrats), in June 2002. At municipal elections, held in that month, the SMK suffered a serious reverse, and the breakaway Axali Konservatiuli Partia (AKP—New Conservative Party) won the largest number of seats nationwide. Jorbenadze was subsequently elected as Chairman of the SMK.

The 'rose revolution' and the Saakashvili presidency

The preliminary results of legislative elections held on 2 November 2003 indicated that the pro-Shevardnadze Akhali Sakartvelostvis (AS—For a New Georgia) bloc had obtained the majority of the votes cast. However, international monitors from the Council of Europe and the OSCE noted electoral irregularities, and there were widespread allegations of falsification. On 4 November a large protest was staged in Tbilisi against the conduct of the elections; Saakashvili (who claimed that his NM had attracted the most support) led demands for Shevardnadze's resignation. On 20 November the Central Electoral Commission (CEC) announced the final results of the elections (five members of the Commission refused to endorse the results). The AS bloc received 57 legislative seats (including 38 of the 150 seats allocated by proportional representation), followed by Abashidze's renamed Demokratiuli Aghordzinebis Pavshiri (DAP—Democratic Union of Revival), with 39 seats (33 on a proportional basis), and the NM, with 36 seats (32 on a proportional basis). The Sakartvelos Leiboristuli Partia (SLP—Georgian Labour Party) obtained 21 seats, the Burjanadze-Demokratebi (Burjanadze-Democrats—B-D) bloc, formed by Zhvania and Burjanadze, 16, the Axali Memarjveneebi (AM—New Rights) bloc 15 and the MGS bloc two; 16 independents were elected. A concurrent referendum approved an eventual reduction in the number of parliamentary deputies to a maximum of 150. The NM and the B-D bloc reiterated claims that the results were invalid, while Western governments also criticized the conduct of the elections. On 22 November some 30,000 demonstrators, led by Saakashvili, proceeded to the parliament building, precipitating what became known as the 'rose revolution'. Troops attached to the Ministry of Internal Affairs failed to prevent protesters from besieging the main parliamentary chamber. Shevardnadze, having been evacuated from the building, declared a nationwide state of emergency. On 23 November, following mediation by the Russian Minister of Foreign Affairs, Shevardnadze agreed to tender his resignation, in return for guarantees of immunity from prosecution. Burjanadze assumed the presidency in an interim capacity, and the state of emergency was lifted. Jorbenadze and several other ministers resigned on 25 November, when the Supreme Court annulled the results of the legislative elections for the 150 mandates allocated by proportional representation. On 27 November Zhvania was approved as Minister of State, and new government appointments were made.

In the presidential election, held on 4 January 2004, Saakashvili obtained 96.3% of the votes cast, with an electoral turnout of 88.0%. Saakashvili was inaugurated as President on 25 January. In early February Parliament adopted several constitutional amendments proposed by Saakashvili, providing, *inter alia*, for the reintroduction of the post of Prime Minister. On 17 February Parliament approved a new Government, headed by Zhvania as Prime Minister, comprising predominantly young, Western-educated ministers. In March Saakashvili announced the appointment of Salomé Zurabishvili, hitherto the French ambassador to Georgia, as Minister of Foreign Affairs.

Elections to fill the 150 proportional seats in Parliament were held on 28 March 2004. A coalition of the NM and the GD won 67.3% of the votes cast and 135 seats (giving them a total of 152 seats in Parliament). Although international observers commended the conduct of the elections, some violations were reported. The Memarjvene Opozicia (Rightist Opposition) alliance of MGS and the AKP was the only other grouping to secure seats on a party-list basis, with 7.5% of the votes and 15 seats, giving them 23 seats overall. Abashidze, whose DAP obtained 6.0% of the proportional votes, claimed that the results had been falsified. In April 2004 Parliament re-elected Burjanadze as

Chairman. As part of a ministerial reorganization in June, Irakli Okruashvili became Minister of Internal Affairs, while Kakha Bendukidze, a prominent industrialist, was appointed Minister of the Economy. In the same month the Sakartvelos Respublikuri Partia (SRP—Republican Party of Georgia) announced that it would no longer co-operate with the NM-GD bloc. In November the NM and the GD merged to form the Ertiani Natsionaluri Modzraoba (ENM—United National Movement), headed by Saakashvili. In December Okruashvili was appointed Minister of Defence; the Ministry of State Security was merged with the Ministry of Internal Affairs, and Bendukidze became State Minister, responsible for Economic Reform.

On 3 February 2005 Prime Minister Zhvania was discovered dead, apparently from poisoning attributed to a domestic gas leak. On 17 February Parliament approved a reorganized Government, headed by the hitherto Minister of Finance, Zurab Noghaideli. On 23 February Parliament endorsed the constitutional amendments providing for a reduction in the number of parliamentary deputies, with effect from the 2008 legislative elections. In July 2005 Parliament approved legislation providing for the election of the mayor of Tbilisi by the Tbilisi City Council, rather than directly by the electorate. The dismissal of Zurabishvili as Minister of Foreign Affairs on 19 October prompted protest rallies.

In March 2006 a protest against the reportedly routine use of violence by police officers was staged outside the parliament building in Tbilisi. Four officers belonging to the interior ministry's special police force received custodial sentences in July on charges of killing a bank employee, Sandro Girgvliani. On 21 July Giorgi Khaindrava was dismissed as State Minister, responsible for Conflict Resolution, following his outspoken criticism of the response of the Minister of Internal Affairs, Vano Merabishvili, to Girgvliani's killing. In September some 29 people were arrested on suspicion of plotting a coup, 13 of whom were subsequently charged. At municipal elections on 5 October, the ENM secured a decisive victory, attracting 66.5% of the total votes cast. On 10 November Okruashvili was dismissed as Minister of Defence, after he made controversial comments regarding South Ossetia; he was replaced by Davit Kezerashvili.

In January 2007 Saakashvili signed into law numerous constitutional amendments, as a result of which the President would no longer dismiss or appoint judges. Additionally, presidential and legislative elections were henceforth to be conducted simultaneously. In September Parliament approved a government reorganization. Later in the month Okruashvili, who had established a new opposition party, the Modzraoba Ertiani Sakartvelostvis (MES—Movement for a United Georgia), publicly accused Saakashvili of corruption and of conspiring to kill a prominent Georgian businessman resident in the United Kingdom, Arkadi (Badri) Patarkatsishvili, who owned several media organizations in Georgia. Okruashvili was subsequently arrested on charges of financial malpractice, prompting a rally to demand his release and the holding of early legislative elections. In October Okruashvili withdrew the accusations of criminal behaviour he had made against Saakashvili, and also confessed to criminal charges against him; he was released on bail. In November he stated that he had been forced to retract the accusations while in detention, and left Georgia. Later that month he was detained in Germany in response to a request of the Georgian authorities, but was subsequently transferred to France, where he was released on bail in January 2008. In March a Georgian court found Okruashvili guilty of embezzlement, and sentenced him *in absentia* to 11 years' imprisonment. In April it was announced that France had granted Okruashvili political asylum.

Meanwhile, in October 2007 an opposition alliance presented a joint manifesto, demanding early legislative elections, electoral reform, and the release of political prisoners. In November Patarkatsishvili declared that he would fund organized opposition protests. In early November the opposition led a campaign of rallies outside the parliamentary building demanding Saakashvili's resignation. On 7 November special forces violently dispersed opposition supporters; later that day the Government declared a national state of emergency, under which broadcasts of the Imedi television channel (partially owned by Patarkatsishvili) were suspended. On the following day Saakashvili announced that a presidential election would be held on 5 January 2008, to be followed by a referendum on early legislative elections. The authorities announced that two opposition leaders had been charged with conspiring to overthrow the Government with Russian support, and that Patarkatsishvili was suspected

of complicity. On 16 November the state of emergency was ended by parliamentary decree; on the same day Saakashvili dismissed Noghaideli and nominated Vladimer Gurgenidze, hitherto the Chairman of the (privately owned) Bank of Georgia, to the premiership. Parliament subsequently approved a reorganized Government. On 25 November Saakashvili resigned the presidency, in order to campaign for the forthcoming election; Burjanadze replaced him in an interim capacity. In early December Imedi resumed broadcasts.

President Saakashvili re-elected

An alliance of nine opposition parties nominated Levan Gachechiladze, a non-partisan parliamentary deputy, as its presidential candidate. In December 2007 Patarkatsishvili announced his withdrawal from the poll and returned to the United Kingdom, claiming that the Georgian authorities planned his assassination. At the presidential election, held on 5 January 2008, Saakashvili was re-elected with 53.5% of votes cast; Gachechiladze secured 25.7%. At the concurrent referendum on the scheduling of early legislative elections, some 79.9% of votes cast were in favour of the proposal. The CEC officially recognized the election results on 13 January and Saakashvili was inaugurated on 20 January. Parliament approved a reorganized administration in late January (opposition deputies boycotted the session). In February the death of Patarkatsishvili at his British residence prompted speculation that he had been assassinated, but medical investigations concluded that he had died from natural causes. In March Parliament adopted further constitutional amendments, reducing the number of legislative deputies from 235 to 150, of whom 75 were to be elected by proportional representation and 75 in single-member constituencies.

In early May 2008 Saakashvili appointed Ekaterine Tkeshelashvili (Prosecutor-General since January) Minister of Foreign Affairs, replacing Davit Bakradze, who had resigned to head the ENM list of candidates in the forthcoming early parliamentary elections. In the elections, held on 21 May, the ENM secured 59.2% of votes cast on a party-list basis and 119 seats overall in the legislative elections, while the Gaertianebuli Opozicia (Joint Opposition) alliance, comprising eight parties, among them MES, Sakartvelos Gza (Georgia's Way—led by Zurabishvili), the Sakartvelos Konservatiuli Partia (Conservative Party of Georgia) and AM, as well as four individual deputies, won 17.7% of votes and 17 seats. Although an international observer mission issued a generally positive assessment of the elections, the Joint Opposition accused the authorities of extensive electoral malpractice, and announced a boycott of the new Parliament. Bakradze was elected parliamentary Chairman in June.

On 9 August 2008, two days after military conflict with Russia broke out in South Ossetia (q.v.), and which subsequently spread to other regions of Georgia, Parliament approved a presidential decree declaring a state of war with Russia, and martial law within Georgia. In October, in the aftermath of the conflict, Saakashvili dismissed Gurgenidze as Prime Minister. Grigol Mgaloblishvili, hitherto Ambassador to Turkey, was nominated to replace him. Parliament approved the appointment of Mgaloblishvili and four new ministers on 1 November. An opposition demonstration was staged in early November to demand Saakashvili's resignation, after political leaders accused him of responsibility for Georgia's defeat in the military conflict with Russia. Meanwhile, several former prominent supporters of Saakashvili expressed increasing dissatisfaction with his leadership. In November Burjanadze established a new opposition party, the Demokratiuli Modzraoba-Ertiani Sakartvelo (DM-ES—Democratic Movement-United Georgia), and in early December Noghaideli also announced the creation of a political association, the Modzraoba Samartliani Sakartvelostvis (MSS—Movement for a Fair Georgia). In December Saakashvili reorganized the Government; Vasil (Davit) Sikharulidze, hitherto Ambassador to the USA, became Minister of Defence, and Grigol Vashadze was appointed Minister of Foreign Affairs. Shortly beforehand, it was announced that Irakli Alasania, the Permanent Representative of Georgia to the UN, had submitted his resignation; after returning to Georgia, he criticized the Government and demanded that Saakashvili step down. Burjanadze also demanded that an early presidential election be conducted. On 30 January 2009 Mgaloblishvili tendered his resignation as Prime Minister on grounds of ill health. On the same day Saakashvili nominated First Deputy Prime Minister and Minister of Finance Nika Gilauri as his successor.

In early 2009, following disagreements within the main opposition, Alasania established a new opposition grouping, the

Aliansi Sakartvelostvis (Alliance for Georgia), comprising the SRP and the AM. In March the Ministry of Internal Affairs announced that its forces had arrested 10 suspects, of whom nine were members of the DM-ES, on charges of the illegal purchase of armaments; Burjanadze dismissed broadcast video evidence as part of a campaign by the authorities against her party. In April demonstrations demanding that Saakashvili resign commenced in Tbilisi and other cities; these protests, which were attended by as many as 50,000 people, continued daily until July.

Meanwhile, on 5 May 2009, the authorities announced that they had acted to forestall an army mutiny at a military base east of Tbilisi. In July a commission empowered to draft a new Constitution was convened, although representatives of the main opposition declined invitations to participate. Also in May Alasania established a new opposition party, Chveni Sakartvelo—Davisuphali Demokratebi (ChS-DD—Our Georgia-Free Democrats). In August Saakashvili transferred Sikharulidze to the position of foreign affairs adviser to the President; he was succeeded as Minister of Defence by Bachana Akhalaia. This appointment was criticized by numerous human rights groups and opposition figures, on the grounds that Akhalaia had been responsible for the maltreatment of prisoners when he had headed Georgia's penitential department.

In December 2009 Noghaideli signed a co-operation agreement on behalf of the MSS with Boris Gryzlov, the Chairman of the Supreme Council of the ruling party of Russia, Yedinaya Rossiya (United Russia). In March 2010 Burjanadze also visited Russia, meeting Russian premier Vladimir Putin and Minister of Foreign Affairs Sergei Lavrov. Also in March the Imedi television channel broadcast a fabricated news bulletin purporting to show an ongoing Russian invasion of Georgia, and announcing that Saakashvili had been assassinated and that several prominent opposition figures, among them Burjanadze and Noghaideli, had expressed support for the invasion. The Georgian National Communications Commission ordered Imedi to apologize for the broadcast, which had provoked mass panic domestically.

The ENM secured a decisive victory in nationwide local elections on 30 May 2010, receiving more than 65% of votes cast. In the first direct mayoral election in Tbilisi, the incumbent, Giorgi Ugulava of the ENM, retained the office with about 55% of the votes, defeating Alasania. OSCE and Council of Europe observers issued a report stating that the conduct of the elections had demonstrated progress towards meeting democratic commitments but noted incidences of malpractice.

On 15 October 2010 Parliament approved a new Constitution, providing for the transfer of many executive powers from the President to the Prime Minister and the Government, with effect from after the next presidential election, scheduled for October 2013. Meanwhile, in October 2010 several prominent opposition leaders, including Gachechiladze and Okruashvili, established a new political movement, the Qartuli Partia (QP—Georgian Party). In November Tkeshelashvili was appointed Deputy Prime Minister, State Minister, responsible for Reintegration. Later that month one person was killed in a bomb attack near the SLP offices inTbilisi (following similar explosions near the US embassy in September, and near the city's principal railway station in October). In November Zurabishvili resigned as leader of Sakartvelos Gza. In January 2011 members of the MSS voted to remove Noghaideli from the chairmanship of the party, replacing him with Sergo Javkhidzre. On 28 June a court in Tbilisi convicted 15 people (three *in absentia*) of acts of terrorism in connection with the bomb attacks in Tbilisi in late 2010.

The 2012 legislative elections and defeat of the ENM

On 21 May 2011 several days of anti-Government protests, led by Burjanadze, began in Tbilisi and Batumi. On 26 May (Independence Day) police forces violently dispersed the crowd of demonstrators, resulting in the death of at least four people. More than 100 protesters were arrested. (A number of policemen were subsequently dismissed for excessive use of force.) At the end of May Parliament approved controversial new legislation prohibiting the public display of Nazi and Soviet symbols, and placing restrictions on former Soviet officials from holding office. In June Gachechiladze and other senior members of the QP announced their resignation from the party, effectively leaving it without leadership in the country. Later in June Okruashvili (who remained in France) was charged *in absentia* with forming an armed group, in connection with an alleged conspiracy to organize a Russian-supported insurrection in Georgia. In July a constitutional amendment was approved, providing for the relocation of Parliament from Tbilisi to Kutaisi after the 2012

elections. In July 2011 large demonstrations, led by Georgian Orthodox Church priests, were staged in Tbilisi in protest at the introduction of legislation extending new rights to minority religious groups. In September a Tbilisi court imposed terms of imprisonment on 15 opposition members who had been charged with supporting Okruashvili's alleged conspiracy.

In December 2011 a wealthy businessman, Bidzina Ivanishvili, who had announced his intention to oppose Saakashvili in the next presidential election, formed a movement known as Qartuli Ocneba (QO—Georgian Dream). Later in the month Parliament adopted legislation that imposed restrictions on financing political parties. Meanwhile, Ivanishvili's Georgian citizenship was abrogated by a presidential order, on the grounds that he had contravened regulations by obtaining French, as well as Georgian and Russian citizenship, and in January 2012 he appointed his wife, Ekaterina Khvedelidze, to head QO. In February Ivanishvili formally established QO as a coalition incorporating his own party, which became known as Qartuli Ocneba-Demokratiuli Sakartvelo (QO-DS—Georgian Dream-Democratic Georgia), and other main opposition groups, including ChS-DD and the SRP. Although Ivanishvili subsequently announced his willingness to rescind his French citizenship, in April the authorities rejected his request that his Georgian citizenship be reinstated. The founding congress of QO as a political party was held later in the month. On 22 May Parliament adopted constitutional amendments permitting citizens of European Union (EU, see p. 271) member states to seek election in Georgia. Although this measure permitted Ivanishvili to stand as a candidate, he dismissed the measure as 'absurd'. Later in the month supporters of Ivanishvili staged a large anti-Government protest in central Tbilisi. Smaller similar demonstrations in took place in other towns. In early June Tbilisi City Court fined Ivanishvili some US $90.9m., after he was found guilty of violating party funding rules. (On appeal, the fine was reduced by around one-half.) Earlier in the year Ivanishvili had been fined $1.7m. for making illegal donations to political parties.

On 29 June 2012 Parliament adopted amendments to the electoral code, notably obligating providers of cable television to transmit channels broadcasting news programming for a period of 60 days prior to the holding of national elections (thereby increasing public access to a number of opposition television channels). Parliament approved Saakashvili's appointment of Merabishvili as Prime Minister on 4 July. Most of the members of the outgoing Government remained in office, while Merabishvili was succeeded in his former position of Minister of Internal Affairs by the hitherto Minister of Defence, Akhalaia, whose former portfolio was allocated to the hitherto Minister of Education and Science, Dimitri Shashkin. On 1 August Saakashvili announced that elections to Parliament would be held on 1 October. Ivanishvili subsequently accused Saakashvili of misusing his authority to impose measures against opposition leaders. Meanwhile, in May, Parliament had relocated from Tbilisi to a newly constructed building in Kutaisi.

In September 2012 the broadcast of a video documenting torture and abuse in a prison in Tbilisi prompted outrage and large demonstrations in the capital. Khatuna Kalmakhelidze resigned as Minister of Prisons and Probation. Akhalaia subsequently also resigned as Minister of Internal Affairs.

In elections to Parliament, conducted on 1 October 2012, Ivanishvili's QO-DS coalition was the most successful grouping, obtaining 55.0% of the votes cast to those seats allocated on the basis of proportional representation, and 85 of the 150 electoral seats overall. The ENM was the only other party to obtain representation, with 40.3% of the votes cast and 65 seats. Shortly after preliminary figures showed that the ENM had been defeated, Saakashvili announced that he accepted the election results, and that he would endorse the appointment of ministerial nominees proposed by Ivanishvili (as Prime Minister-designate). Later in the month Saakashvili announced the restoration of Ivanishvili's Georgian citizenship. On 25 October Parliament approved the appointment of a Government led by Ivanishvili. The new administration included two Deputy Prime Ministers: former international footballer Kakha Kaladze, who also became Minister of Energy and Natural Resources; and ChS-DD leader Alasania, who concurrently held the defence portfolio.

In November 2012 a number of senior members of Saakashvili's administration, including Akhalaia, were arrrested. Together with the hitherto Chief of Joint Staff of the Armed Forces and a former army commander, they were subsequently charged with abuse of power. The ENM criticized the detentions as having been politically motivated. In the same month Okruashvili was arrested upon his return from France. In January 2013 he was acquitted of the corruption charges for which he had received the 11-year prison sentence, and released on bail (with other charges pending against him, including those relating to the formation of an armed group). On 12 January Parliament enacted an amnesty providing for the release of some 3,000 people in detention and the reduction of sentences for others, having overturned a veto of the legislation by President Saakashvili. The struggle between the ruling coalition and the President was also reflected in a demand by the new Minister of Foreign Affairs later in January that Saakashvili replace all the country's principal ambassadors. Meanwhile, divisions emerged within the QO-DS coalition, on 21 January Alasania was dismissed as deputy premier, while remaining Minister of Defence. Following an attempt by Ivanishvili to postpone Saakashvili's annual address to Parliament, the President decided to make the speech at the National Library on the scheduled day, 8 February; however, proceedings were disrupted by anti-Government protesters, including released prisoners, some of whom assaulted ENM deputies. Saakashvili, who accused QO-DS of orchestrating the protests, finally conducted the address at the presidential palace. On the same day Ivanishvili appointed the Minister of Education and Science, Giorgi Margvelashvili, additionally to the post of Deputy Prime Minister.

Continuing antagonism between Ivanishvili and Saakashvili focused on constitutional amendments proposed by QO-DS, which notably removed the President's power to dismiss or appoint a government without parliamentary approval. The ENM subsequently agreed to support the constitutional amendments, which were adopted by Parliament on 25 March and signed into effect by Saakashvili two days later.

Riots, in which at least 17 of people were injured, broke out in central Tbilisi in May 2013, after several thousand protesters, whose leaders included Georgian Orthodox Church priests, attempted to disrupt a small demonstration by homosexual activists. Both Ivanishvili and Patriarch Ilia II of the Georgian Orthodox Church (who had demanded that the demonstration be prohibited) condemned the violence. Later in May the Secretary-General of the ENM and former Prime Minister, Merabishvili, and the Governor of Kakheti Mtkare (region) a former minister and incumbent regional Governor, Zurab Tchiaberashvili, were arrested on corruption charges, including the misuse of public funds to finance the ENM's 2012 election campaign. Rallies were subsequently staged nationwide in support of Merabishvili.

On 26 July 2013 Giorgi Kvirikashvili, the hitherto Minister of Economic and Sustainable Development was appointed additionally as First Deputy Prime Minister; Margvelashvili had resigned from his government position, after being selected as the candidate of QO-DS in the presidential election scheduled for 27 October. Bakradze was subsequently confirmed as the presidential candidate of the ENM. In August Akhalaia was acquitted on charges of having exceeded his powers, although he remained in detention, pending trial on further charges. Akhalaia was sentenced to three years' and nine months' imprisonment in October, having been convicted of using excessive force to suppress a prison uprising in 2006.

Recent Developments: The Margvelashvili presidency

On 27 October 2013 Margvelashvili was decisively elected President, obtaining 62.1% of the votes cast in an election contested by 23 candidates. Bakradze was placed second, with 21.7%, and Burjanadze was third, with 10.2%. On 17 November Margvelashvili was inaugurated as President; on the same day the Constitutional reforms adopted in 2010, principally comprising a reduction in the powers of the President, officially entered into effect. (In early October Parliament had approved a further constitutional amendment, proposed by QO-DS, which reduced some powers vested in the Prime Minister.) Meanwhile, Ivanishvili confirmed that he was to resign as Prime Minister. Parliament confirmed the appointment of the hitherto Minister of Internal Affairs, Irakli Garibashvili, as Prime Minister on 20 November. Garibashvili also succeeded Ivanishvili as the Chairman of QO-DS on 24 November. A senior police official, Aleksandre Tchikaidze, received the internal affairs portfolio.

In December 2013 disagreements between parliamentary deputies on the occasion of the adoption of the 2014 state budget escalated into a violent altercation. Later that month a court in Tbilisi ordered the removal from office of Ugulava as the city mayor, pending his trial on charges of misappropriating public funds. At the end of the month the Government appointed a constitutional review commission, which was to revise the Constitution by September 2014, and also indicated its intention to reverse the recent relocation of Parliament to Kutaisi. A new Prosecutor-General, Giorgi Badashvili, was appointed in January 2014, following the resignation of his recently appointed predecessor, Otar Partskhaladze, after he was revealed to have had a criminal conviction in Germany. In February Merabishvili was sentenced to five years' imprisonment on charges including abuse of office and bribing voters, while Tchiaberashvili received a fine. In the same month the trial *in absentia* of Davit Kezerashvili, the Minister of Defence under President Saakashvili, began; Kezerashvili had been detained in France after various criminal charges had been brought against him by the Georgian Government, but a French court had refused a request for his extradition on the grounds that the case was politically motivated. In March the Office of the Prosecutor-General summoned Saakashvili (who had taken up a position at a lecturer at a university in the USA) for questioning in connection with 10 cases under investigation. Elguja Khokrishvili was appointed Minister of Regional Development and Infrastructure in mid-April, replacing Davit Narmania, who had resigned to contest direct elections, scheduled for May, as the QO-DS candidate to the post of mayor of Tbilisi. On 28 July criminal charges were filed by the Georgian prosecutor's office against Saakashvili, who was accused of abuse of power during the 2007 demonstrations and in connection with the police raid against Imedi TV in 2007–08. Saakashvili, who remained in exile, denounced the action of the Georgian authorities as being politically motivated.

Local elections were held across Georgia on 15 June 2014. QO-DS was the most successful party overall, securing some 51% of votes cast nationwide while the ENM received 22%, and Narmania, was elected as mayor of Tbilisi. On 27 July Parliament approved a governmental reorganization.

On 4 November 2014 Prime Minister Garibashvili dismissed Alasania as Minister of Defence, after the latter claimed that the arrest of a number of his ministry officials on corruption charges had been politically motivated and reflected opposition within the ruling coalition to the country's Euro-Atlantic direction. Alasania's ChS-DD party consequently withdrew from the Government, depriving it of 10 seats and its majority in Parliament. The resignation of the State Minister for European and Euro-Atlantic Integration, Alex Petriashvili, who was a member of ChS-DD, the Minister of Foreign Affairs, Maia Panjikidze (Alasania's sister-in-law), and several deputy ministers was announced on the following day. Mindia Janelidze, hitherto a security adviser to Garibashvili, replaced Alasania, while the Prime Minister denied strenuously (also in response to concerns expressed by the US Administration) that any change in the country's foreign policy orientation was planned. In mid-November former Minister of Foreign Affairs Bakradze was appointed to succeed Petriashvili. The ENM organized an opposition rally, which was attended by some 30,000, in Tbilisi on 15 November, in protest at the policies of Garibashvili's Government, including its failure to take action against the strengthening of Russian control over Abkhazia and South Ossetia.

On 23 January 2015 Tchikaidze tendered his resignation as Minister of Internal Affairs, in response to the death in suspicious circumstances, three days earlier, of Yuri Vazagashvili, who had campaigned for the opening of a full investigation (which he accused Tchikaidze of impeding) into the shooting dead by police officers of his son and another man in 2006; Yuri Vazagashvili was killed following the detonation of an explosive device placed upon his son's grave. Three days later, Tchikaidze's deputy, Vakhtang Gomelauri, was appointed to succeed him. In early February five former police officials and six serving members of a special unit attached to the Ministry of Internal Affairs, including a former deputy minister, were arrested and charged with murder in connection with the operation, and a further police officer was subsequently charged with the murder of Vazagashvili.

Ajara

The Autonomous Republic of Ajara, in south-west Georgia, proved to be the least troubled of the country's three autonomous territories (for information on the other two territories, which claim secession from Georgia, see the separate introductory surveys on Abkhazia and South Ossetia). Despite being of ethnic Georgian origin, the Adjars retained a sense of separate identity, owing to their adherence to Islam. In April 1991 there were prolonged demonstrations against proposals to abolish Ajaran autonomy. Elections to the Supreme Council (legislature) of

Ajara were held in September 1996, and Aslan Abashidze, Chairman of the Supreme Council since 1991, was re-elected to that position. Abashidze established an autocratic administration in the territory, and withheld certain tax and other payments (most notably those owing from customs dues arising at Adjara's border with Turkey) owed to the national authorities, and in many regards the territory, although formally secessionist, was effectively independent of the authorities in Tbilisi for much of the 1990s and early 2000s.

In November 2001 Abashidze contested unopposed a direct election to the new post of Head of the Republic, which replaced that of Chairman of the Ajaran Supreme Council, following the approval of amendments to the region's Constitution in July. n early December Ajara's new bicameral legislature (composed of the Council of the Republic and the Senate) held its inaugural session.

After President Shevardnadze resigned on 23 November 2003, Abashidze declared a state of emergency in Ajara. In March 2004, after the new President, Mikheil Saakashvili, was prevented from entering Ajara, he issued an ultimatum, demanding that Abashidze recognize the authority of the central Government. Economic sanctions were imposed on Ajara, and Abashidze declared a renewed state of emergency and a curfew. Following Russian mediation, Abashidze agreed to allow the organization of the national parliamentary elections in Ajara. The state of emergency was suspended, and legislative elections duly proceeded on 28 March.

Tensions escalated further on 2 May 2004, when Abashidze ordered the destruction of bridges linking Ajara with neighbouring regions of Georgia, following military manoeuvres by government troops close to the boundary. Saakashvili immediately threatened to dismiss Abashidze, unless the Ajaran leader agreed to comply with the 'Georgian constitutional framework' within 10 days. Large public demonstrations against Abashidze ensued. Following discussions with Igor Ivanov, the Chairman of the Security Council of the Russian Federation, on 5 May Abashidze resigned and departed for Russia. Saakashvili imposed presidential rule on Ajara, and on 6 May Parliament voted to approve the President's authority to dismiss the legislature and the Government of Ajara, and to schedule new elections there, thereby substantially reducing the territory's autonomy. The Ajaran Supreme Council also voted to abolish the post of Head of the Republic, scheduled new parliamentary elections, and dissolved itself. Levan Varshalomidze was appointed as the head of an interim council to rule the region. On 20 June elections to the new unicameral legislature, the Supreme Council, took place. The pro-presidential Saakashvili-Bamarjvebuli Achara (Saakashvili-Victorious Ajara) party received 75% of the votes cast and 28 of the 30 seats in the Council. On 1 July Parliament approved legislation granting the President of Georgia the authority to dismiss the Ajaran Government, dissolve the Ajaran parliament and annul its legislation. Mikheil Makharadze was elected Chairman of the newly elected Supreme Council; Varshalomidze was the sole candidate for Chairman of the Government. Abashidze's personal assets were confiscated by the authorities, and in December a warrant was issued for his arrest on charges of abuse of office, terrorist offences, and embezzlement. The relocation of the Constitutional Court of Georgia from Tbilisi to Abashidze's former residence in Batumi took effect in September 2006. In January 2007 the Batumi city court convicted Abashidze *in absentia* of abuse of office and the embezzlement of state funds, and sentenced him to 15 years' imprisonment.

On 30 July 2008 the Supreme Council adopted amendments to Adjara's electoral code, prior to forthcoming legislative elections, scheduled for 4 October: the Council was to be reduced from 30 to 18 deputies; the minimum requisite share of the votes cast for parties to obtain representation from party list was reduced from 7% to 5%; and the composition of the local Central Election Commission (CEC) was reformed to include opposition representatives. In September, following the conflict in South Ossetia and other parts of Georgia, the CEC rescheduled the elections to the Supreme Council for 3 November. A number of opposition parties consequently declared a boycott of the poll, and a voter turnout of only 44.9% was recorded. Saakashvili's ENM secured about 78.8% of votes cast, while the Kristianul-Demokratiuli Modzraoba (Christian Democratic Movement—established by a former associate of Abashidze, Giorgi Targamadze) was the only other party to gain representation, with 14.7% of votes.

In March 2009 the head of the republican branch of the DM-ES, Zurab Avaliani, was detained, along with nine others, pending trial on charges of illegal arms-smuggling and plotting politically motivated violence. (Avaliani was subsequently sentenced to 18 months' imprisonment on charges of illegal possession of firearms.) In April 2010 Varshalomidze openly criticized the centralization of powers in Georgia and demanded the restoration of greater autonomy to Ajara. In May the head of the Ministry of Internal Affairs emergency situations service in Ajara was killed in an explosion near Batumi; in early 2011, following the arrest of two suspects, the Georgian authorities claimed that the killing had been ordered by Russian military intelligence agents based in Abkhazia.

In May 2012 several amendments to Ajara's Constitution were approved, including an increase in the number of deputies in the Supreme Council, with effect from the elections due to be held in October, from 18 to 21. At the elections, held concurrently with those to the Georgian Parliament on 1 October, the QO-DS coalition of Bidzina Ivanishvili was the most successful group in Ajara, obtaining 57.6% of the votes cast to those seats elected on the basis of party lists; the ENM was the only other party to obtain representation, with 37.4% of the vote. On 28 October Avtandil Beridze became Chairman of the Supreme Council. Ivanishvili's nomination of Archil Khabadze, hitherto director of Cartu Bank's Batumi branch office, as Chairman of the Government was approved by the Supreme Council on 30 October, and a new Government headed by him was subsequently formed. Meanwhile, Ivanishvili's new Georgian Government issued pledges to increase the autonomous powers of Ajara.

In March 2014 a vote of no confidence in Beridze (who had been criticized by the Georgian authorities for his intention of purchasing a luxury car from public funds) was defeated in the Supreme Council. In September, after Khabadze dismissed several senior officials, seven members of the QO-DS faction in the Supreme Council announced their intention of proposing a further motion of no confidence to support his impeachment, on grounds of poor management, corruption and violating budgetary legislation. However, members of the QO-DS faction were subsequently reprimanded by the national party for making statements that had not been agreed with the party leadership in Tbilisi. When Alasania's ChS-DD withdrew from the ruling coalition at national level in November two party members of the Supreme Council left the QO-DS faction. In early February 2015 the chair of the human rights committee in the Supreme Council also resigned from the QO-DS, which consequently lost its parliamentary majority. Later that month two members of the QO-DS faction supported the ENM in a vote to remove the Deputy Chairman of the Supreme Council and another QO-DS official.

Foreign Affairs

Regional relations

Georgia was one of only four republics of those that had constituted the USSR not to seek membership of the CIS at its formation in December 1991. However, as civil and separatist conflicts threatened to destroy Georgia, Shevardnadze was forced to reverse policy, and in late 1993 the republic was admitted to that body. Relations with Russia were strained by developments in Abkhazia from 1992, although in February 1994 Georgia and Russia signed a 10-year treaty of friendship and co-operation, which provided, *inter alia*, for the establishment of Russian military bases in Georgia. In May 1999 Georgia failed to renew its adherence to the CIS Collective Security Treaty. (In March 2006 Georgia and Russia signed an agreement providing for Russia's withdrawal from the military bases that it maintained at Akhalkalaki and Batumi and from its Tbilisi headquarters; the withdrawal of Russian forces from the military bases was completed ahead of schedule, in November 2007.)

The lifting of customs and travel restrictions on the Russian–Abkhazian border in September 1999 angered Georgia, and further tension occurred later in the year, owing to the renewed conflict in Russia's Chechen Republic (Chechnya), which neighbours Georgia. Georgia denied allegations that it was harbouring Chechen soldiers and selling arms to Chechen separatists. During 2000 there were violent disturbances and kidnappings in the Pankisi Gorge, close to the Chechen border. Russia's decision to implement a full visa regime for Georgian citizens entering its territory from January 2001 caused further antagonism, particularly since citizens of Abkhazia and South Ossetia were to be exempt from the requirement. In January 2002 Georgian security forces launched a campaign to restore order to Pankisi. Later that month the Georgian Deputy Minister of State Security was shot dead in the Pankisi Gorge, and in

February four police officers were held hostage for three days there. In May a US-led military-training programme commenced in Georgia, to equip the armed forces for operations in Pankisi, where international Islamist militants were reported to have established bases. In August Georgia accused Russia of perpetrating an act of aggression, when the aerial bombardment of Pankisi by unmarked aircraft led to at least one death; Russia denied responsibility. In October President Shevardnadze and his Russian counterpart, Vladimir Putin, reached an agreement, according to which the two countries were to resume joint patrols of their common border.

Relations with Russia deteriorated after the accession to power in Georgia of President Saakashvili. The decision of the Georgian Parliament, in February 2006, to request the replacement of Russian peacekeepers in South Ossetia with international forces aggravated tensions further. In March Russia banned the import of wine from Georgia, ostensibly owing to suspected contamination with pesticides. In October President Saakashvili announced that four Russian military officers, who had been detained in September on suspicion of espionage, had been transferred to the authority of the OSCE, which arranged for their return to Russia. In response to the detention of the officers, Russia withdrew its ambassador from Georgia, suspended all transport and postal links between the two countries, and expelled several hundred ethnic Georgians (whom the Russian authorities described as illegal immigrants) from Russia. (Russia's ambassador returned to Tbilisi in January 2007.) Georgia expelled three Russian embassy staff in November 2007, on the grounds that they were engaged in subversive activities against the Government, prompting Russia to expel three Georgian diplomats in retaliation.

In July 2008 Russia acknowledged that four Russian aircraft had entered airspace over South Ossetia, claiming that the mission was intended to deter Georgia from flying military reconnaissance drones over the region. On 7–8 August Georgian troops launched an attack against Tskhinvali and other locations in South Ossetia; shortly afterwards, Russian troops entered the territory, and rapidly obtaining control over the region. In a statement subsequently shown to be greatly exaggerated, Russian President Dmitrii Medvedev accused Georgia of perpetrating 'genocide', claiming that up to 2,000 people had been killed as a result of the Georgian attack. Russian aircraft commenced bombardment of Georgian targets, including the town of Gori, the port of Poti and the military base at Senaki. On 9 August Parliament approved a presidential decree declaring a state of war with Russia, and martial law within Georgia. On 12 August Russian President Dmitrii Medvedev ordered an end to Russia's military operations. Georgia and Russia agreed to a peace plan, mediated by French President Nicolas Sarkozy on behalf of the EU, providing for an immediate ceasefire and the withdrawal of Russian troops to pre-conflict positions. However, Russia failed to implement fully the withdrawal of troops as stipulated. On 14 August Parliament voted unanimously in favour of Georgia's withdrawal from the CIS (to take full effect from the following year). On 26 August Medvedev endorsed legislation by which Russia officially recognized South Ossetia and Abkhazia as independent, sovereign states. Georgia, the USA and EU condemned the decision, and only a small number of states subsequently extended recognition. On 29 August Georgia formally suspended diplomatic relations with Russia.

Following an EU-mediated peace agreement, reached on 8 September 2008, Russia announced that 3,800 of its troops were to remain in each of South Ossetia and Abkhazia, although all remaining forces would be withdrawn from all other Georgian territories within 10 days of the deployment of EU monitors. On 17 September Russia signed friendship, economic and military co-operation treaties with South Ossetia and Abkhazia. Following the deployment of the European Union Monitoring Mission in Georgia (EUMM) on 1 October, the withdrawal of the remaining Russian troops from areas adjacent to the two secessionist territories was verified by the deadline of 10 October. However, Georgia claimed that Russia was in violation of the ceasefire agreement, on the grounds that it retained troops in areas previously held by Georgian forces, and that the number of troops in South Ossetia and Abkhazia exceeded the pre-conflict levels. Meanwhile, on 9 October the Council of CIS Foreign Ministers officially suspended Georgia's membership. (Full withdrawal from the organization was finalized in August 2009.) In November discussions between Russian, US and Georgian representatives, also attended by South Ossetian and Abkhazian officials, were reconvened in Geneva, Switzerland,

under the aegis of the UN, the EU and the OSCE (and subsequently continued to be held at intervals). At the end of December the mandate of the OSCE mission in Georgia (deployed in South Ossetia since 1992) expired, owing to Russia's refusal to approve a further extension.

A report by Human Rights Watch, issued in January 2009, cited 'indiscriminate and disproportionate attacks' by both Russia and Georgia; following investigations by both Governments, Russia (despite earlier claims) had only been able to attribute 162 fatalities to Georgian forces. An independent report supported by the EU into the conflict, which was published in September, concluded that Georgia had instigated the conflict, and that its initial attack upon Tshkhinvali was not warranted by international law, while Russia's military response was described as disproportionate, and its recognition of South Ossetia and Abkhazia as independent states a violation of international law.

In March 2009 Russia confirmed that military bases were to be established in Abkhazia and South Ossetia. On 30 April President Medvedev signed border treaties with Abkhazia and South Ossetia, under which Russia was to guard the state borders of Abkhazia prior to the establishment of Abkhazian border forces. The EU expressed 'deep concern' at both agreements, which it stated violated the terms of the peace agreement. The mandate of UNOMIG expired on 15 June, after its extension had been vetoed by Russia.

The only road crossing between Russia and those regions of Georgia controlled by the Georgian authorities, at Verkhnyi Lars—Kazbegi, closed since 2006, reopened in March 2010. In October the Russian Ministry of Foreign Affairs denounced as an attempt to destabilize the region a decision by the Georgian authorities to abolish visa requirements for the residents of Russia's seven North Caucasus republics. In November Georgia announced the arrest of 13 people suspected of being members of a Russian espionage network, including four Russian citizens, and in December a further six people were detained in connection with a series of explosions in Tbilisi. In June 2011 a Russian military officer who had been based in Abkhazia, Yevgenii Borisov, was sentenced to 30 years' imprisonment *in absentia* for organizing the bomb attacks; Borisov's deputy received a life sentence *in absentia* and a further four defendants were sentenced to terms of 30 years (one *in absentia*), while lesser sentences were imposed on the remaining eight.

Following an appeal brought by Georgia against Russia, which accused Russian forces of ethnically motivated abuses in both South Ossetia and Abkhazia during the 2008 conflict, in April 2011 the International Court of Justice dismissed the case, on the grounds that Georgia had made no attempt to resolve the dispute with Russia beforehand. In November, after lengthy discussions between Georgian and Russian representatives in Bern, Switzerland, it was announced that the negotiators had finally reached an agreement that would allow Russia to join the World Trade Organization (WTO, see p. 431); trade between Russia and Abkhazia and South Ossetia was to be controlled by Swiss monitors. A presidential decree, announced by Saakashvili in February 2012 in a perceived gesture of reconciliation, permitted Russian citizens (in common with those of numerous Western countries) to remain in Georgia for 90 days without a visa.

A new Government headed by Bidzina Ivanishvili, who had pledged to improve bilateral relations with Russia, was installed following elections in October 2012; nevertheless, it was subsequently confirmed that Georgia would not restore diplomatic relations until Russia ended its presence in South Ossetia and Abkhazia. On 1 November Ivanishvili appointed Zurab Abashidze, the Georgian ambassador to Russia in 2000–04, to the new post of the Prime Minister's Special Representative for Relations with Russia. In December 2012 the first direct discussions between Georgian and Russian officials since the 2008 conflict were conducted in Geneva, when a plan for a partial normalization in bilateral relations was agreed.

Although the longstanding ban by Russia on Georgian wine imports was ended, Georgia's relations with Russia remained tense. Measures unilaterally implemented by the Russian military in May 2013 to amend the South Ossetian administrative border with Georgia, slightly expanding the area under separatist control, and the subsequent erection of fencing along the new border, were met with strong protests from the Georgian Government and international community. In January 2014 Parliament adopted a resolution expressing 'extreme concern' over developments in Ukraine (where the Government's withdrawal from the signature of an EU Association Agreement had precipitated an escalating political crisis), and emphasizing that Georgia's decision to sign an Agreement with the EU was irreversible. Meanwhile, President Margvelashvili protested that the Russian authorities' unilateral extension of its border zone with Abkhazia 11 km further into the separatist territory, purportedly to maintain security during the organization of the Sochi Winter Olympics in February (in Russian territories that immediately neighboured Abkhazia), constituted a violation of Georgian sovereignty. Russia's de facto military seizure of the Crimean peninsula from Ukraine at the end of February and formal annexation of the territory in March, which was followed by conflict in the Donetsk and Luhansk oblasts (regions) of eastern Ukraine (see Ukraine), prompted considerable concern in Georgia. On 7 March, shortly after a further resolution adopted by Parliament condemned Russia's intervention in Crimea, Russian military aircraft entered Georgia's airspace in contravention of the 2008 peace agreement. Bilateral discussions on the normalization of relations were suspended, and later in March the Georgian Government denounced the annexation as a substantial threat to regional stability. Former President Saakashvili subsequently established links with the new Ukrainian leadership and several members of his previous administrations joined the Government, including, most notably, Sandro (Oleksandr) Kvitashvili, a former Georgian Minister of Health and Rector of Tbilisi State University, who was appointed as Minister of Health in the Ukrainian Government in December 2014. The Georgian Ministry of Foreign Affairs summoned the Ukrainian ambassador in February 2015, after Saakashvili was appointed as an adviser to President Petro Poroshenko; nevertheless, Ukraine refused to extradite Saakashvili and the former Georgian Minister of Justice and Prosecutor-General Zurab Adeishvili, both of whom had been charged with a number of offences by the Georgian authorities.

Meanwhile, in late 2014 Russian state oil company Rosneft acquired 49% of the Georgian-registered company Petrocas Energy Group, which operated a significant oil terminal at the port of Poti and a network of gas stations. A comprehensive 'Agreement on Alliance and Strategic Partnership', which was signed between Russia and Abkhazia in November, envisaged the creation of a combined group of armed forces and of a joint law enforcement centre, and joint protection at Abkhazia's border with Georgia, together with freedom of movement across its border with Russia; the Georgian Government denounced the accord (which was ratified by the Russian legislature in January 2015) as a further move towards the annexation of the territory. The Georgian authorities further criticized the signature of a border agreement between Russia and South Ossetia in February (which followed repeated actions by the Russian military to amend South Ossetia's administrative border with Georgia). An accord providing for even deeper integration than the agreement with Abkhazia, the 'Treaty on Alliance and Integration', was signed between Russia and South Ossetia in March. Meanwhile, the Russian Government denounced as 'provocative' plans, confirmed in early 2015, to establish a joint Georgia-NATO training centre in the country.

Other external relations

Relations with the USA became increasingly cordial in the mid-2000s. Following his inauguration as President, in February 2004 Saakashvili visited Washington, DC, USA, where he attended talks with US President George W. Bush. In May 2005 President Bush made a state visit to Georgia, during which he endorsed the Government's efforts to bring about reform. In July 2006 Saakashvili again visited Washington, DC, on which occasion President Bush affirmed his support for Georgian aspirations to North Atlantic Treaty Organization (NATO, see p. 367) membership. In September 2008, following the military conflict with Russia (see *Regional relations*), US Vice-President Dick Cheney announced that the USA would pledge US $1,000m. in reconstruction aid to Georgia. In January 2009 Georgia and the USA signed a bilateral charter on strategic partnership in areas that included defence, trade and energy. Although the new Administration of President Barack Obama, which came to power in that month, sought to achieve a rapprochement with Russia, in July Vice-President Joe Biden visited Tbilisi and reaffirmed US support for the Saakashvili administration. In August 2011 the US Senate adopted a resolution condemning the continuing presence of Russian troops in Abkhazia and South Ossetia. Following discussions with Obama in Washington, DC, in January 2012, Saakashvili announced plans for significantly increased defence co-operation between Georgia and the USA. Amid an escalating political crisis in Ukraine, in February 2014

Prime Minister Garibashvili visited Washington, DC, to meet Obama and other US officials, who pledged assistance for Georgia's EU integration process.

In November 2002 Georgia formally applied for membership of NATO. In October 2004 NATO approved a two-year Individual Partnership Action Plan with Georgia. At a NATO summit meeting, held in Romania in April 2008, the Alliance failed to extend offers of a Membership Action Plan (MAP) to Georgia. Following a summit meeting in Lisbon, Portugal, in November 2010, NATO issued a final declaration reiterating support for Georgia's eventual full membership of the Alliance. In December 2011 the Georgian Government welcomed a statement by NATO that officially named Georgia (among others) as an 'aspirant' state. During a visit to Georgia in January 2015, the NATO Deputy Secretary-General confirmed that plans were to proceed for the establishment of a joint Georgia-NATO training centre in the country by the end of the year.

In 1996 Georgia signed an agreement on partnership and co-operation with the EU, and in 1999 it joined the Council of Europe. In March 2005 the European Commission recommended strengthening relations with Georgia under its European Neighbourhood Policy, in which Georgia had been included in June 2004. In December 2008 the European Commission presented an Eastern Partnership programme, offering further economic integration, and enhanced trade and visa arrangements, for Georgia, Armenia, Azerbaijan, Ukraine, Moldova and Belarus. In July 2010 the EU began negotiations with Georgia on the establishment of an Association Agreement, which was to entail the creation of a free trade area. At an EU summit meeting in Vilnius, Lithuania, on 28–29 November 2013, President Margvelashvili initialled the Association Agreement, which included free trade area provisions, and also signed a framework agreement for Georgian participation in EU-led crisis management operations. Amid escalating conflict in eastern Ukraine, EU officials brought forward the planned signature of the Agreement to mid-2014. Georgia and the EU signed the Association Agreement on 27 June, and it was ratified by the European Parliament on 18 December. The Georgian Government, citing the obligations undertaken under the Association Agreement and a continuing visa liberalization dialogue with the EU, adopted more restrictive regulations (which hitherto had been extremely liberal) on the procedures for issuing visas and residency permits, which entered into effect on 1 September.

CONSTITUTION AND GOVERNMENT

The Constitution was introduced in August 1995, and was subsequently revised on numerous occasions, most notably in 2010, when (with effect from 2013) numerous presidential powers were transferred to the Prime Minister and the Government. The President of Georgia is Head of State, and also Commander-in-Chief of the Armed Forces. The President is directly elected for a five-year term (and may not hold office for more than two consecutive terms). The Government is the supreme body of the executive branch, which exercises domestic and foreign policy of the State and is accountable before Parliament. The Government is headed by the Prime Minister. The supreme representative body is the unicameral Sakartvelos Parlamenti (Georgian Parliament), which is directly elected for four years. Of the 150 parliamentary deputies, 77 are elected on the basis of proportional representation and 73 by majority vote in single-member constituencies. Judicial power is exercised by the Supreme Court, the members of which are elected by Georgian Parliament, on the recommendation of the President, and by general courts. Georgia contains two nominally autonomous territories: the Autonomous Republic of Ajara; and Abkhazia. The status of Abkhazia and South Ossetia were both disputed; following conflict in August 2008, both territories became entirely under the control of their respective separatist authorities, with Russian military support. Those parts of the country under central government control are divided into nine mkharebi (regions—singular mkhare) headed by trustees (governors) appointed by the President, and the city of Tbilisi, headed by a mayor. A second tier of local government comprises seven cities of special status and 60 districts (raions), and a third tier comprises a total of 966 villages and settlements.

REGIONAL AND INTERNATIONAL CO-OPERATION

Georgia is a member of the Organization of the Black Sea Economic Co-operation (see p. 399), the Council of Europe (see p. 250) and the Organization for Democracy and Economic Development (GUAM, see p. 463).

Georgia joined the UN in 1992 and became a full member of the World Trade Organization (WTO, see p. 431) in 2000.

ECONOMIC AFFAIRS

In 2013, according to estimates by the World Bank, Georgia's gross national income (GNI), measured at average 2011–13 prices, was US $15,976m., equivalent to $3,570 per head (or $7,040 per head on an international purchasing-power parity basis). During 2004–13, it was estimated, the population increased by an average of 0.4% per year, while gross domestic product (GDP) per head increased, in real terms, at an average annual rate of 5.7%. According to official estimates, overall GDP increased, in real terms, by an average of 5.9% annually during 2004–13; it grew by 3.3% in 2013.

Agriculture contributed 9.3% of GDP in 2013 and engaged 53.4% of the total employed labour force in 2007. Georgia's climate allows the cultivation of subtropical crops, such as tea and oranges. Other fruits (including wine grapes), flowers, tobacco, grain and hazelnuts are also cultivated. The mountain pastures are used for sheep and goat-farming. In 2002 private farms accounted for 94% of the agricultural crop harvest. During 2004–13, according to official figures, agricultural GDP increased, in real terms, by an average of 0.2% per year. Real GDP of the sector decreased by 3.7% in 2012, but increased by 11.3% in 2013.

Industry contributed 23.7% of GDP in 2013 and engaged 10.4% of the total employed labour force in 2007. According to official figures, industrial GDP increased, in real terms, at an average annual rate of 7.1% in 2004–13. Real industrial GDP increased by 12.6% in 2012 and by a further 1.6% in 2013.

Mining and quarrying accounted for just 0.9% of GDP in 2013, and the sector engaged 0.3% of the total employed labour force in 2007. The principal minerals extracted are manganese ore, petroleum and coal. There are also deposits of copper, gold, silver and natural gas. During 2004–13, according to the official figures, mining GDP increased, in real terms, by an average of 6.5% per year; real GDP of the sector increased by 2.8% in 2013.

The manufacturing sector (including household processing) contributed 10.4% of GDP in 2013; the sector engaged 4.9% of the total employed labour force in 2007. During 2004–13, according to official figures, manufacturing GDP increased, in real terms, by an average of 9.8% per year; real GDP of the sector increased by 8.6% in 2013.

The construction sector contributed 6.6% of GDP in 2013, and engaged 4.2% of the employed labour force in 2007. According to official figures, during 2004–13 construction GDP increased, in real terms, by an average of 3.9% per year; the sector's GDP increased, in real terms, by 18.2% in 2012, but decreased by 10.5% in 2013.

Hydroelectric power provided 77.4% of the country's electricity in 2011. However, Georgia's largest hydroelectric power station was located in the secessionist region of Abkhazia, and the IMF estimated that more than one-third of the power it produced was consumed without payment. Imports of mineral fuels and lubricants comprised 17.1% of total imports in 2013. After 1999 Georgia was involved in a number of regional development projects to deliver both petroleum and gas through international pipelines. Georgia also hoped to develop its own energy resources. New gas-turbine electricity generators commenced operations in 2006, and the reconstruction of several hydroelectric power plants was proposed, as part of measures intended to make Georgia self-sufficient in electricity.

The services sector contributed 67.0% of GDP in 2013 and engaged 36.2% of the employed labour force in 2007. Trade and transport and communications are the sector's most significant areas of activity, with telecommunications and hotels and restaurants demonstrating the greatest growth in the early 2000s. During 2004–13, according to official figures, the GDP of the services sector increased, in real terms, at an average annual rate of 7.2%; the sector's GDP increased, in real terms by 3.8% in 2013.

In 2013 Georgia recorded a visible merchandise trade deficit of US $3,506.2m., and there was a deficit of $1,002.0m. on the current account of the balance of payments. In 2013 Turkey was the principal source of imports (accounting for 17.1% of the total); other major sources were Azerbaijan, Ukraine, Russia, the People's Republic of China and Germany. The principal market for exports in that year was Azerbaijan (accounting for 24.4% of the total); other important purchasers were Armenia, Ukraine, Russia, Turkey and Bulgaria. The principal imports in 2013 were mineral products (especially petroleum and petroleum oils), machinery and electrical equipment, vehicles, vessels, aircraft and other transport equipment, chemicals and related products, prepared foodstuffs, beverages, spirits and tobacco, and base metals. The principal exports in that year were vehicles, vessels, aircraft and other transport equipment, base metals and articles thereof, prepared foodstuffs, beverages, spirits and tobacco, vegetable products, chemicals, and mineral products.

In 2013 there was a budgetary deficit of 262.2m. lari (equivalent to 1.0% of GDP). Georgia's general government gross debt was 8,640m. lari in 2013, equivalent to 32.2% of GDP. At the end of 2012 Georgia's total external debt was US $13,426m., of which $4,876m. was public and publicly guaranteed debt; in that year, the cost of servicing long-term public and publicly guaranteed debt and repayments to the IMF was equivalent to 23.3% of the value of exports of goods, services and income (excluding workers' remittances). The annual rate of inflation averaged 5.2% during 2004–13; consumer prices decreased by 0.5% in 2013, but increased by 3.1% in 2014. In 2013 the average rate of unemployment was 14.6%.

In 1992 Georgia became a member of the IMF and the World Bank, and also joined the European Bank for Reconstruction and Development (EBRD, see p. 266).

The administrations of President Mikheil Saakashvili (2004–13) introduced wide-ranging reforms and anti-corruption measures, and foreign direct investment increased substantially. A Russian embargo on the import of various Georgian foodstuffs and beverages, implemented in 2005, forced the country to seek new markets. A priority was the promotion of Georgia as a regional trade and logistic centre, and free industrial zones were established at the port of Poti and in Kutaisi. In December 2011 the European Union (EU, see p. 271) declared that Georgia had made satisfactory progress in implementing reforms, and that negotiations would begin on the establishment of a free trade area under the Eastern Partnership framework. Eurobond issues by the Government, the Bank of Georgia, Georgian Railways and Georgian Oil and Gas Corporation were undertaken in 2011–12. Following the establishment of a new Government in Georgia in late 2012, it was announced that Russia had agreed to resume imports of Georgian wine, and some normalization in trade links subsequently took place. Amid the escalating crisis in eastern Ukraine from early 2014, the signature of an EU Association Agreement, which included free trade area provisions, was brought forward to June, and the US Administration also pledged additional financial assistance. The IMF approved a three-year stand-by arrangement (SBA) of US $154m. and an immediate disbursement of $62m. for Georgia in July. Meanwhile, the Government's decision to restrict the private ownership of land with a ban on its sale to foreign nationals had contributed to a significant fall in investment from the levels recorded under the administration of Saakashvili. The IMF, in its first review of SBA-supported performance in January 2015, predicted that Georgia would benefit from a low international price of petroleum and the entry into force of the free trade area with the EU in September 2014. GDP growth strengthened to 4.7% in 2014 (according to official preliminary figures). However, in early 2015 Georgia's economy registered increased adverse effects from an economic crisis in Russia, including a sharp decline in exports and remittances, and depreciation of the national currency, and the Government lowered the growth target for that year from 5% to 2%.

PUBLIC HOLIDAYS

2016: 1–2 January (New Year), 7 January (Christmas), 19 January (Theophany), 3 March (Mothers' Day), 8 March (International Women's Day), 21 March (Nowruz, Spring Holiday), 9 April (Restoration of Independence Day), 29 April–2 May (Easter and Commemoration of the Deceased), 9 May (Victory Day), 12 May (St Andrew's Day), 26 May (Independence Day), 28 August (Assumption), 14 October (Mtskhetoba), 23 November (St George's Day).

Statistical Survey

Source (unless otherwise indicated): National Statistics Office of Georgia, 0180 Tbilisi, Tsotne Dadiani 30; tel. (32) 36-72-10; fax (32) 36-72-13; e-mail info@ geostat.ge; internet www.geostat.ge.

Area and Population

AREA, POPULATION AND DENSITY

Area (sq km)	69,700*
Population (census results)†	
12 January 1989	5,400,841
17 January 2002‡	
Males	2,061,753
Females	2,309,782
Total	4,371,535
Population (official estimates at 1 January)§	
2012	4,497,600
2013	4,483,800
2014	4,490,500
Density (per sq km) at 1 January 2014‖	64.4

* 26,911 sq miles, including a significant amount of territory outside Georgian government control.
† Population is *de jure*. The de facto total at the 2002 census was 4,355,700.
‡ Those territories of the former Autonomous Oblast (region) of South Ossetia that remained outside Georgian government control, as well as those of the separatist 'Republic of Abkhazia', were not included in the census of 2002; it was estimated that around 230,000 people lived in these territories at that time. An Abkhazian census, conducted in that territory in February 2011, reported a population of 240,705.
§ Excluding the population of those territories outside Georgian government control.
‖ Area figure includes, whereas population figure excludes, territories outside Georgian government control, therefore actual density can be assumed to be significantly lower.

POPULATION BY AGE AND SEX
('000, official estimates at 1 January 2014)

	Males	Females	Total
0–14 years	404.9	364.5	769.4
15–64 years	1,499.0	1,595.0	3,094.0
65 years and over	237.5	389.6	627.1
Total	2,141.4	2,349.1	4,490.5

POPULATION BY ETHNIC GROUP
(2002 census result, excl. areas outside Georgian government control)

	Number ('000)	% of total population
Georgian	3,661.2	83.8
Azeri	284.8	6.5
Armenian	248.9	5.7
Russian	67.7	1.5
Ossetian	38.0	0.9
Kurdish	20.8	0.5
Others	50.1	1.1
Total (incl. others)	4,371.5	100.0

Note: Classification of ethnicity reflects national census methodology.

ADMINISTRATIVE DIVISIONS
('000, official population estimates at 1 January 2014*)

Territory	Population	Principal city
Autonomous Republic		
Ajara	396.6	Batumi (161.2)
Mkharebi (Regions)		
Guria	138.8	Ozurgeti (77.7)
Imereti	703.3	Kutaisi (197.0)
Kakheti	405.0	Telavi (70.9)
Kvemo Kartli	513.1	Rustavi (122.9)
Mtskheta-Mtianeti	108.8	Mtskheta (57.4)
Racha-Lechkumi and Kvemo-Svaneti	45.9	Ambrolauri (13.6)
Samegrelo-Zemo Svaneti . . .	476.3	Zugdidi (177.0)
Samstkhe-Javakheti . . .	213.7	Akhaltsikhe (48.5)
Shida Kartli†	313.8	Gori (145.8)
Capital City		
Tbilisi	1,175.2	—
Total	4,490.5	—

* These figures exclude the population of the 'Republic of Abkhazia', which declared an enumerated population of 240,705 at February 2011.
† Most of the territories of South Ossetia are included in Shida Kartli Mkhare.

PRINCIPAL TOWNS
(estimates at 1 January 2014)

Tbilisi (capital) . .	1,175,200	Gori*		145,800
Kutaisi . . .	197,000	Marneuli* . . .		130,600
Zugdidi* . . .	177,000	Rustavi . . .		122,900
Batumi . . .	161,200	Gardabani* . . .		100,100

* Figure refers to the population of the municipality.

BIRTHS, MARRIAGES AND DEATHS

	Registered live births		Registered marriages		Registered deaths	
	Number	Rate (per 1,000)	Number	Rate (per 1,000)	Number	Rate (per 1,000)
2006 . .	47,795	10.9	21,845	5.0	42,255	9.6
2007 . .	49,287	11.2	24,891	5.7	41,178	9.4
2008 . .	56,565	12.9	31,414	7.2	43,011	9.8
2009 . .	63,377	14.4	31,752	7.2	46,625	10.6
2010 . .	62,585	14.1	34,675	7.8	47,864	10.7
2011 . .	58,014	12.9	30,863	6.9	49,818	11.1
2012 . .	57,031	12.7	30,412	6.8	49,348	11.0
2013 . .	57,878	12.9	34,693	7.7	48,553	10.8

Life expectancy (years at birth, official estimates): 75.2 (males 70.8; females 79.4) in 2013.

ECONOMICALLY ACTIVE POPULATION
(annual averages, '000 persons aged 15 years and over)*

	2005	2006	2007
Agriculture, hunting and forestry	947.8	966.4	910.5
Mining and quarrying	5.8	3.4	4.7
Manufacturing	89.8	81.5	82.7
Electricity, gas and water supply	23.4	18.4	18.2
Construction	43.1	54.8	71.2
Wholesale and retail trade; repair of motor vehicles and personal and household goods . . .	188.2	168.1	168.8
Hotels and restaurants . . .	16.3	16.9	18.0
Transport, storage and communications	69.3	77.8	71.7
Financial intermediation . . .	13.3	14.3	17.3
Real estate, renting and business activities	25.9	26.9	34.7
Public administration and defence; compulsory social security . .	81.8	78.5	64.3

—continued	2005	2006	2007
Education	130.9	132.2	124.2
Health and social work . . .	58.0	52.2	59.9
Other community, social and personal service activities . .	38.2	41.9	43.9
Private households with employed persons	9.2	11.7	11.1
Extraterritorial organizations and bodies	3.3	2.3	2.9
Sub-total	1,744.3	1,747.3	1,704.3
Activities not adequately defined .	0.3	—	—
Total employed	1,744.6	1,747.3	1,704.3
Unemployed	279.3	274.5	261.0
Total labour force	2,023.9	2,021.8	1,965.3
Males	1,074.4	1,085.9	1,031.8
Females	949.5	935.9	933.5

* Figures exclude employment in the informal sector, estimated to total about 750,000 persons at the end of 1997, and those employed in the armed forces.

Source: mainly ILO.

2013 ('000 persons aged 15 years and over): Total employed 1,712.1; Unemployed 291.8; Total labour force 2,003.9.

Health and Welfare

KEY INDICATORS

Total fertility rate (children per woman, 2012)	1.8
Under-5 mortality rate (per 1,000 live births, 2012) . . .	20
HIV/AIDS (% of persons aged 15–49, 2013)	0.3
Physicians (per 1,000 head, 2012)	4.2
Hospital beds (per 1,000 head, 2009)	3.1
Health expenditure (2011): US $ per head (PPP)	526
Health expenditure (2011): % of GDP	9.4
Health expenditure (2011): public (% of total)	18.1
Access to water (% of persons, 2012)	99
Access to sanitation (% of persons, 2012)	93
Total carbon dioxide emissions ('000 metric tons, 2010) .	6,241.2
Carbon dioxide emissions per head (metric tons, 2010) . .	1.4
Human Development Index (2013): ranking	79
Human Development Index (2013): value	0.744

For sources and definitions, see explanatory note on p. vi.

Agriculture

PRINCIPAL CROPS
('000 metric tons)

	2011	2012	2013
Wheat	96.8	80.7	81.0
Barley	30.3	20.7	35.0
Maize	269.6	267.0	363.9
Potatoes	273.9	249.7	296.6
Sunflower seed*	8.0	9.0	10.0
Cabbages and other brassicas .	35.2	34.5	26.0
Tomatoes	61.6	63.9	75.0
Cucumbers and gherkins . . .	25.5	38.7	31.5
Onions, dry	14.6	17.8	17.0
Watermelons	42.8	36.7	66.4
Oranges	0.6	3.5	1.4
Apples	64.3	45.0	68.6
Pears	17.6	16.1	17.0

—continued	2011	2012	2013
Sour (Morello) cherries . . .	2.7	5.1	5.6
Peaches and nectarines . . .	19.1	7.1	23.7
Plums and sloes	7.2	10.7	8.7
Grapes	159.6	144.0	222.8
Hazelnuts (with shell)	31.1	24.7	39.7
Tea	2.9	2.6	3.3
Tobacco, unmanufactured . . .	0.1	0.1	0.1

* Unofficial figures.

Aggregate production ('000 metric tons, may include official, semi-official or estimated data): Total cereals 404.7 in 2011, 376.4 in 2012, 487.9 in 2013; Total treenuts 38.1 in 2011, 30.8 in 2012, 52.1 in 2013; Total roots and tubers 273.9 in 2011, 249.7 in 2012, 296.6 in 2013; Total vegetables (incl. melons) 228.6 in 2011, 235.2 in 2012, 271.2 in 2013; Total fruits (excl. melons) 365.2 in 2011, 348.9 in 2012, 499.1 in 2013.

Source: FAO.

LIVESTOCK
('000 head at 1 January)

	2011	2012	2013
Horses*	40.0	40.0	40.0
Cattle	1,049.4	1,087.6	1,128.8
Buffaloes	17.8†	18.0†	18.0*
Pigs	110.1	105.1	204.3
Sheep	596.8	576.8	688.2
Goats	57.1	53.6	54.4
Chickens†	6,050	5,900	5,759
Turkeys†	471	460	400

* FAO estimate(s).
† Unofficial figure(s).

Source: FAO.

LIVESTOCK PRODUCTS
('000 metric tons)

	2011	2012	2013
Cattle meat	21.3	16.2	20.2
Sheep meat	4.0	2.5	2.8
Pig meat	11.6	11.8	14.9
Chicken meat	12.0	11.7	10.1
Cows' milk*	587.5	594.6	608.3
Hen eggs*	26.8	26.3	27.5

* Unofficial figures.

Source: FAO.

Forestry

ROUNDWOOD REMOVALS
('000 cu m, excl. bark)

	2011	2012	2013
Sawlogs, veneer logs and logs for sleepers	105.0*	96.4†	131.2†
Fuel wood	733.0*	324.0	495.0
Total	838.0	420.3	626.2

* FAO estimate.
† Unofficial figure.

Source: FAO.

SAWNWOOD PRODUCTION
('000 cu m, incl. railway sleepers)

	2011*	2012†	2013†
Coniferous (softwood)	30.0	19.5	12.3
Broadleaved (hardwood) . . .	40.0	58.5	36.8
Total	70.0	78.0	49.0

* FAO estimates.
† Unofficial figures.

Source: FAO.

Fishing

(metric tons, live weight)

	2010	2011	2012
Capture*	46,049	26,547	12,070
Mullets	11	1	—
European anchovy	40,819	25,919	11,007
Sea snails*	500	500	500
Aquaculture*	470	650	650
Total catch*	46,519	27,197	12,720

* FAO estimates.

Source: FAO.

Mining

('000 metric tons unless otherwise indicated)

	2010	2011*	2012*
Coal	240.6	250.0	240.0
Crude petroleum	51.1	50.0	50.0
Natural gas (million cu m)	7.9	7.9	8.0
Manganese ore*	400.0	400.0	380.0
Cement*	856.9	860.0	870.0

* Estimated production.

Source: US Geological Survey.

Industry*

SELECTED PRODUCTS*

('000 metric tons unless otherwise indicated)

	2009	2010	2011
Wine ('000 hl)	152.2	259.0	304.3
Beer ('000 hl)	685	828	787
Vodka and liqueurs ('000 hl)	125	139	166
Soft drinks ('000 hl)	1,247	1,541	1,374
Mineral water ('000 hl)	1,046	1,429	1,549
Cigarettes (million)	5,218	5,002	4,429
Residual fuel oils	5	—	—
Building bricks (million)	6.4	6.4	11.1
Electric energy (million kWh)	8,165	9,992	10,747

* Data for those areas of South Ossetia outside central government control and for the separatist 'Republic of Abkhazia' are not included.

2007: Refined sugar 133.9.

Source: mainly UN Industrial Commodity Statistics Database.

Wine ('000 metric tons, unofficial figures): 103.4 in 2010; 110.8 in 2011; 112.7 in 2012 (Source: FAO).

Finance

CURRENCY AND EXCHANGE RATES

Monetary Units
100 tetri = 1 lari.

Sterling, Dollar and Euro Equivalents (31 December 2014)
£1 sterling = 2.909 lari;
US $1 = 1.864 lari;
€1 = 2.263 lari;
100 lari = £34.38 = $53.66 = €41.46.

Average Exchange Rate (lari per US $)
2012   1.651
2013   1.663
2014   1.766

BUDGET
(million lari)*

Revenue†	2011	2012	2013
Tax revenue	6,134.8	6,671.0	6,659.3
Taxes on income	1,551.1	1,764.8	1,934.2
Taxes on profits	832.3	851.0	806.5
Value-added tax	2,784.4	3,040.3	2,847.8
Excise	615.0	659.6	722.3
Customs duties	93.3	90.1	89.4
Other taxes	258.7	265.2	259.1
Other current revenue	515.4	618.2	535.9
Capital revenue	449.2	329.9	167.2
Total	7,099.4	7,619.1	7,362.4

Expenditure‡	2011	2012	2013
Wages and salaries	1,136.2	1,202.6	1,395.1
Use of goods and services	1,211.0	1,297.8	1,010.9
Interest	288.0	253.5	237.5
Subsidies	426.0	514.1	547.6
Social benefits	1,655.5	1,857.6	2,294.9
Grants	13.0	16.7	14.8
Other current expenditure	1,056.9	1,353.4	1,222.3
Capital expenditure	1,675.3	1,498.5	1,140.6
Total	7,461.9	7,994.2	7,863.7

* Figures represent a consolidation of the state budget (covering the central Government and local administrations) and extra-budgetary funds.
† Excluding grants received (million lari): 223.5 in 2011; 270.8 in 2012; 239.1 in 2013.
‡ Including net lending.

INTERNATIONAL RESERVES
(excl. gold, US $ million at 31 December)

	2011	2012	2013
IMF special drawing rights	223.27	221.29	221.90
Reserve position in the IMF	0.01	0.02	0.02
Foreign exchange	2,594.91	2,651.65	2,601.47
Total	2,818.19	2,872.95	2,823.38

Source: IMF, *International Financial Statistics*.

MONEY SUPPLY
(million lari at 31 December)

	2011	2012	2013
Currency outside depository corporations	1,438.99	1,550.03	1,899.63
Transferable deposits	2,629.58	2,711.79	3,678.83
Other deposits	3,029.20	3,641.92	4,258.16
Broad money	7,097.78	7,903.74	9,836.62

Source: IMF, *International Financial Statistics*.

COST OF LIVING
(Consumer Price Index for five cities*; base: December 2003 = 100)

	2011	2012	2013
Food and non-alcoholic beverages	171.5	198.3	196.9
Clothing and footwear	85.0	80.2	77.4
Housing, utilities and other fuels	207.6	158.3	171.3
All items (incl. others)	170.4	168.8	167.9

* Tbilisi, Kutaisi, Batumi, Gori and Telavi.

All items (Consumer Price Index; base: 2005= 100): 153.7 in 2012; 152.9 in 2013; 157.6 in 2014.

NATIONAL ACCOUNTS
(million lari at current prices)

National Income and Product

	2011	2012	2013
Compensation of employees . .	7,755.2	8,823.8	8,069.0
Net operating surplus	5,979.1	5,825.2	7,212.8
Net mixed income	4,321.5	4,794.1	4,984.8
Domestic primary incomes	18,055.8	19,443.1	20,266.6
Consumption of fixed capital . .	2,660.8	2,797.0	2,809.5
Gross domestic product (GDP) at factor cost	20,716.6	22,240.1	23,076.1
Taxes on production and imports .	3,751.5	4,055.2	3,918.4
Less Subsidies	124.1	128.0	147.2
GDP in market prices . . .	24,344.0	26,167.3	26,847.3
Primary incomes received from abroad	1,273.7	1,778.8	1,535.4
Less Primary incomes paid abroad	1,986.0	2,020.5	2,042.1
Gross national income (GNI) .	23,631.7	25,925.6	26,340.7
Less Consumption of fixed capital .	2,660.8	2,797.0	2,809.5
Net national income	20,970.9	23,128.6	23,531.2
Current transfers from abroad .	2,431.5	2,504.7	2,636.1
Less Current transfers paid abroad	217.6	178.9	198.1
Net disposable income . . .	23,184.8	25,454.4	25,969.2

Expenditure on the Gross Domestic Product

	2011	2012	2013
Government final consumption expenditure	4,430.5	4,632.5	4,478.7
Private final consumption expenditure	18,017.8	18,875.4	19,054.0
Increase in stocks	893.7	1,078.6	760.2
Gross fixed capital formation . .	5,474.3	6,496.8	5,892.7
Total domestic expenditure .	28,816.3	31,083.3	30,185.6
Exports of goods and services . .	8,822.9	9,983.0	11,997.9
Less Imports of goods and services	13,334.2	15,124.3	15,475.2
Statistical discrepancy	39.0	225.3	139.1
GDP in market prices . . .	24,344.0	26,167.3	26,847.4
GDP at constant 2003 prices .	13,687.5	14,533.6	15,123.7

Gross Domestic Product by Economic Activity

	2011	2012	2013
Agriculture, forestry and fishing	1,854.9	1,933.3	2,195.0
Mining and quarrying	208.8	230.8	210.3
Manufacturing	2,085.6	2,288.5	2,468.5
Electricity, gas and water supply .	634.8	637.0	699.8
Processing of products by households	655.8	601.0	658.4
Construction	1,407.9	1,756.9	1,568.2
Wholesale and retail trade; repair of motor vehicles, motorcycles and personal and household goods	3,552.7	3,769.5	4,026.8
Hotels and restaurants . . .	466.3	510.6	526.2
Transport, storage and communications	2,212.0	2,395.5	2,451.2
Financial intermediation . . .	536.1	633.5	706.1
Real estate, renting and business activities*	1,804.6	1,963.0	2,143.5
Public administration and defence; compulsory social security . .	2,443.0	2,526.3	2,365.4
Education	1,050.0	1,092.3	1,202.5

—continued	2011	2012	2013
Health and social services . . .	1,275.5	1,362.2	1,338.5
Other community, social and personal services	1,021.7	1,066.2	1,069.6
Private households with employed persons	25.2	29.3	29.6
Sub-total	21,234.9	22,795.9	23,659.6
Less Financial intermediation services indirectly measured .	259.5	290.8	324.7
Gross value added in basic prices	20,975.4	22,505.3	23,335.0
Taxes on products	3,492.7	3,790.0	3,659.5
Less Subsidies on products . .	124.1	128.0	147.2
GDP in market prices . . .	24,344.0	26,167.3	26,847.4

* Including imputed rent of owner-occupied dwellings.

BALANCE OF PAYMENTS
(US $ million)

	2011	2012	2013
Exports of goods	3,223.0	3,459.1	4,190.8
Imports of goods	−6,722.6	−7,685.2	−7,697.0
Balance on goods	−3,499.6	−4,226.1	−3,506.2
Exports of services	2,018.9	2,562.0	2,983.8
Imports of services	−1,265.2	−1,447.4	−1,561.4
Balance on goods and services	−2,745.9	−3,111.5	−2,083.8
Primary income received . . .	758.0	1,077.5	922.1
Primary income paid	−1,181.0	−1,224.3	−1,227.0
Balance on goods, services and primary income	−3,168.8	−3,258.3	−2,388.7
Secondary income received . .	1,339.0	1,454.1	1,505.7
Secondary income paid . . .	−129.9	−108.3	−119.0
Current balance	−1,959.7	−1,912.5	−1,002.0
Capital account (net)	127.1	125.6	123.3
Direct investment assets . . .	−182.7	−216.9	−120.3
Direct investment liabilities . .	861.3	425.9	725.9
Portfolio investment assets . .	—	−33.1	6.0
Portfolio investment liabilities .	108.5	881.5	−42.4
Financial derivatives and employee stock options assets . . .	12.1	10.7	5.1
Financial derivatives and employee stock options liabilities . .	−7.0	−5.2	−7.5
Other investment assets . . .	205.2	−349.2	−170.9
Other investment liabilities . .	1,002.8	935.5	576.8
Net errors and omissions . . .	14.9	−24.6	−13.3
Reserves and related items .	182.5	−162.4	80.6

Source: IMF, *International Financial Statistics*.

External Trade

PRINCIPAL COMMODITIES
(distribution by HS, US $ million)

Imports	2011	2012	2013
Vegetable products	363.3	414.6	375.5
Cereals	206.4	257.7	219.1
Wheat and meslin . . .	184.2	240.0	184.3
Prepared foodstuffs; beverages, spirits and vinegar and tobacco . . .	543.7	552.0	594.1
Mineral products	1,369.0	1,473.1	1,641.2
Mineral fuels, oils, distillation products, etc.	1,206.7	1,351.0	1,348.4
Petroleum and petroleum oils .	911.0	951.0	954.4
Petroleum gases	236.6	318.0	316.7
Chemicals and related products	510.0	582.5	671.6
Pharmaceutical products . . .	228.4	264.2	317.7

Imports—*continued*	2011	2012	2013
Medicaments	201.4	232.5	280.7
Plastics, rubber and articles thereof	294.9	346.9	344.1
Textiles and textile articles	285.7	228.3	235.8
Base metals and articles thereof	594.1	655.0	558.8
Machinery and electrical equipment	1,220.3	1,380.5	1,239.7
Vehicles, vessels, aircraft and other transport equipment	783.7	997.8	1,019.9
Vehicles other than railway, tramway	705.0	920.1	914.9
Motor cars	510.5	662.8	710.5
Miscellaneous manufactured articles	220.8	259.4	256.9
Total (incl. others)	7,057.8	7,901.8	7,885.2

Exports	2011	2012	2013
Vegetable products	165.9	178.6	285.4
Edible fruit, nuts, peel of citrus fruit, melons	140.0	97.7	194.0
Fresh or dried nuts	130.1	83.7	166.7
Prepared foodstuffs; beverages, spirits and vinegar and tobacco	216.9	266.5	404.7
Beverages, spirits and vinegar	192.2	233.1	356.3
Undenatured ethyl alcohol, spirits, liqueurs and other spirituous beverages	67.9	80.0	99.9
Mineral products	189.2	142.2	270.2
Ores, slag and ash	95.8	57.4	164.3
Copper ores and concentrates	85.1	53.5	161.6
Mineral fuels, oils, distillation products, etc.	72.5	50.3	71.0
Chemicals and related products	228.5	261.1	258.7
Fertilizers	144.1	137.3	130.7
Nitrogenous minerals or chemical fertilizers	144.1	137.2	130.6
Natural or cultured pearls, precious or semi-precious stones	118.6	96.8	90.0
Pearls, precious stones, metals, coins, etc.	118.6	96.8	90.0
Unwrought, semi-manufactured or powdered gold	109.9	88.0	73.3
Base metals and articles thereof	527.2	454.9	461.2
Iron and steel	439.9	372.6	363.3
Ferro alloys	254.9	260.5	229.9
Ferrous waste and scrap	116.8	43.9	6.8
Vehicles, vessels, aircraft and other transport equipment	546.5	667.7	807.7
Vehicles other than railway, tramway	489.0	637.3	768.5
Motor cars	450.3	587.3	703.9
Total (incl. others)	2,189.1	2,375.4	2,908.5

PRINCIPAL TRADING PARTNERS
(US $ million)

Imports c.i.f.	2011	2012	2013
Austria	78.0	82.7	61.4
Azerbaijan	610.8	633.5	651.6
Brazil	110.2	120.1	99.4
Bulgaria	255.6	271.5	200.0
China, People's Republic	524.8	566.0	563.7
Czech Republic	91.9	82.9	75.9
France	97.3	106.1	164.4
Germany	480.6	541.9	449.2
Greece	61.9	50.9	59.5
Iran	64.8	99.4	129.2
Italy	184.8	271.0	220.6
Japan	174.1	312.6	319.9

Imports c.i.f.—*continued*	2011	2012	2013
Kazakhstan	70.6	131.8	55.3
Netherlands	133.2	142.7	124.2
Poland	63.1	85.8	88.8
Romania	188.3	259.0	322.9
Russia	389.7	473.8	587.8
Spain	82.2	88.3	89.3
Turkey	1,272.4	1,392.9	1,346.0
Turkmenistan	55.5	30.7	48.0
Ukraine	705.6	597.1	602.4
United Arab Emirates	226.4	161.7	184.5
United Kingdom	88.5	115.1	91.4
USA	245.8	213.2	253.8
Total (incl. others)	7,057.8	7,901.6	7,885.2

Exports f.o.b.	2011	2012	2013
Armenia	223.0	261.0	315.4
Azerbaijan	425.9	626.9	709.9
Belarus	28.3	33.5	40.5
Belgium	33.6	60.4	61.5
Bulgaria	93.7	69.7	150.8
Canada	114.8	104.6	81.4
China, People's Republic	28.9	25.6	33.9
Germany	49.1	38.6	73.0
Italy	75.5	53.3	81.5
Kazakhstan	156.9	62.3	103.6
Mexico	28.6	7.3	3.0
Netherlands	17.7	11.8	22.5
Russia	36.6	45.8	190.7
Spain	23.7	15.9	66.9
Turkey	227.6	142.8	182.9
Ukraine	141.2	167.0	192.8
United Arab Emirates	40.0	38.9	69.7
USA	143.5	226.2	136.4
Total (incl. others)	2,189.1	2,375.4	2,908.5

Transport

RAILWAYS
(traffic)

	2011	2012	2013
Passengers carried (million)	3.3	3.1	3.0
Passenger-km (million)	641.4	625.4	584.8
Freight ('000 tons)	20,123.4	20,076.0	18,185.0
Freight net ton-km (million)	6,054.8	5,976.6	5,525.9

ROAD TRAFFIC
('000 motor vehicles in use)

	2012	2013	2014
Passenger cars	620.9	672.7	672.7
Buses	49.2	51.2	51.9
Lorries and vans	73.0	78.5	83.9
Total (incl. others)	762.2	831.6	906.7

SHIPPING
Flag Registered Fleet
(at 31 December)

	2012	2013	2014
Number of vessels	196	173	172
Total displacement ('000 grt)	185.7	136.3	184.7

Source: Lloyd's List Intelligence (www.lloydslistintelligence.com).

CIVIL AVIATION
(traffic on scheduled services)

	2011	2012	2013
Passengers carried ('000)* . . .	200	200	200
Passenger-km (million)	413.5	360.1	396.0
Freight ('000 metric tons) . . .	1.2	0.4	0.4
Total ton-km (million)	1.5	0.5	0.4

* Figures are rounded.

Tourism

FOREIGN VISITOR ARRIVALS

Country of residence	2011	2012	2013
Armenia	699,382	921,929	1,291,838
Azerbaijan	714,418	931,933	1,075,857
Iran	60,191	89,697	85,598
Russia	278,458	513,930	767,396
Turkey	738,085	1,533,236	1,597,438
Ukraine	58,966	76,610	126,797
Total (incl. others)	2,822,363	4,428,221	5,392,303

Tourism receipts (US $ million, excl. passenger transport): 955 in 2011; 1,411 in 2012; 1,720 in 2013 (provisional).

Source: World Tourism Organization.

Communications Media

	2011	2012	2013
Telephones ('000 main lines in use)	1,340.4	1,275.9	1,201.2
Mobile cellular telephones ('000 subscribers)	4,430.3	4,698.6	4,993.1
Broadband subscribers ('000)	324.6	392.4	444.6
Newspapers: titles	284	301	311
Newspapers: circulation ('000) .	100	100	100

Source: International Telecommunication Union.

Education

(2008/09 unless otherwise indicated)

	Institutions	Students*
Pre-primary schools†	1,197	77,922
General education: schools (primary)‡§ . }	2,320	553,016
General education: schools (secondary)§ . }		
General education: evening schools† .	14	100
State secondary professional schools .	30	2,177
Private secondary professional schools .	4	434
State higher schools (incl. universities) .	38§	80,009‖
Private higher schools (incl. universities)	47§	29,524‖

* Some figures are rounded.
† Data for 2005/06.
‡ Including primary schools covering part of the secondary syllabus.
§ Data for 2013/14.
‖ 2012/13.

Teachers (2007/08, unless otherwise indicated): Pre-primary 7,783 (2004/05); Total in general day schools 67,152 (59,689 in public schools, 7,463 in private schools—2012/13); Total in secondary professional schools 873 (803 public, 70 private—2008/09); Total full- and part-time professors in institutes of higher education 11,424 in 2008 (7,142 in public institutions, 4,282 in non-state institutions).

Pupil-teacher ratio (primary education, UNESCO estimate): 6.3 in 2011/12 (Source: UNESCO Institute for Statistics).

Adult literacy rate (UNESCO estimates): 99.7% (males 99.8%; females 99.7%) in 2012 (Source: UNESCO Institute for Statistics).

Directory

The Government

HEAD OF STATE

President: GIORGI MARGVELASHVILI (elected 27 October 2013; inaugurated 17 November 2013).

GOVERNMENT
(April 2015)

The Government principally comprises members of Qartuli Ocneba-Demokratiuli Sakartvelo, and also includes representatives of the Erovnuli Phorumi and the Sakartvelos Respublikuri Partia, and independents.

Prime Minister: IRAKLI GARIBASHVILI.

First Deputy Prime Minister, Minister of Economic and Sustainable Development: GIORGI KVIRIKASHVILI.

Deputy Prime Minister, Minister of Energy: KAKHA KALADZE.

State Minister, responsible for Reconciliation and Civic Equality: PAATA ZAKAREISHVILI.

State Minister, responsible for Diaspora Affairs: GELA DUMBADZE.

Minister of European and Euro-Atlantic Integration: DAVID BAKRADZE.

Minister of Education and Science: TAMAR SANIKIDZE.

Minister of Regional Development and Infrastructure: DAVIT SHAVLIASHVILI.

Minister of Finance: NODAR KHADURI.

Minister of Sport and Youth Affairs: LEVAN KIPIANI.

Minister of Environmental Protection and Natural Resources: ELGUJA KHOKRISHVILI.

Minister of Defence: MINDIA JANELIDZE.

Minister of Justice: THEA TSULUKIANI.

Minister of Culture and the Protection of Monuments: MIKHEIL GIORGADZE.

Minister of Internally Displaced Persons from the Occupied Territories, Accommodation, and Refugees: SOZAR SUBARI.

Minister of Foreign Affairs: TAMAR BERUCHASHVILI.

Minister of Agriculture: OTAR DANELIA.

Minister of Internal Affairs: VAKHTANG GOMELAURI.

Minister of Labour, Health and Social Affairs: DAVID SERGEENKO.

Minister of Prisons and Probation: GIORGI MGEBRISHVILI.

MINISTRIES

Office of the President: 0103 Tbilisi, M. Abdushelishvili 1; tel. (32) 228-27-36; fax (32) 228-27-14; e-mail secretariat@admin.gov.ge; internet www.president.gov.ge.

Chancellery of the Government: 0134 Tbilisi, P. Ingorovka 7; tel. (32) 299-09-00; fax (32) 292-10-69; internet www.government.gov.ge.

Office of the State Minister, responsible for Diaspora Affairs: 0134 Tbilisi, P. Ingorovka 7; tel. (32) 293-17-42; fax (32) 293-17-05; e-mail info@diaspora.gov.ge; internet www.diaspora.gov.ge.

Office of the State Minister, responsible for Reconciliation and Civic Equality: 0134 Tbilisi, P. Ingorovka 7; tel. (32) 298-92-56;

fax (32) 292-16-50; e-mail press@smr.gov.ge; internet www.smr.gov
.ge.

Ministry of Agriculture: 0159 Tbilisi, Gelovani 6; tel. (32) 237-66-89; fax (32) 237-80-13; e-mail infomoa@moa.gov.ge; internet moa.gov
.ge.

Ministry of Culture and the Protection of Monuments: 0105 Tbilisi, Sanapiro 4; tel. (32) 293-22-55; fax (32) 299-99-66; e-mail pr@culture.gov.ge; internet www.mcs.gov.ge.

Ministry of Defence: 0112 Tbilisi, Gen. Kvinitadze 20; tel. and fax (32) 272-35-35; e-mail pr@mod.gov.ge; internet www.mod.gov.ge.

Ministry of Economic and Sustainable Development: 0108 Tbilisi, Chanturia 12; tel. (32) 299-11-11; fax (32) 292-15-34; e-mail ministry@economy.ge; internet www.economy.ge.

Ministry of Education and Science: 0102 Tbilisi, D. Uznadze 52; tel. (32) 220-02-20; fax (32) 243-88-12; e-mail pr@mes.gov.ge; internet www.mes.gov.ge.

Ministry of Energy: 0105 Tbilisi, Sanapiro 2; tel. (32) 235-78-04; fax (32) 235-78-28; e-mail mail@energy.gov.ge; internet www.energy
.gov.ge.

Ministry of Environmental Protection and Natural Resources: 0114 Tbilisi, G. Gulua 6; tel. (32) 272-72-34; e-mail pr@moe.gov.ge; internet www.moe.gov.ge.

Ministry of European and Euro-Atlantic Integration: 0134 Tbilisi, P. Ingorovka 7; tel. and fax (32) 293-28-67; e-mail office@eu-nato.gov.ge; internet www.eu-nato.gov.ge.

Ministry of Finance: 0114 Tbilisi, V. Gorgasali 16; tel. (32) 226-14-44; fax (32) 245-74-55; e-mail minister@mof.ge; internet www.mof
.ge.

Ministry of Foreign Affairs: 0108 Tbilisi, Sh. Chitadze 4; tel. (32) 294-50-00; fax (32) 294-50-01; e-mail inform@mfa.gov.ge; internet www.mfa.gov.ge.

Ministry of Labour, Health and Social Affairs: 0119 Tbilisi, A. Tsereteli 144; tel. (32) 251-00-12; fax (32) 251-00-19; e-mail info@moh
.gov.ge; internet www.moh.gov.ge.

Ministry of Internal Affairs: 0190 Tbilisi, Kakheti 38; tel. (32) 241-84-44; fax (32) 241-10-17; e-mail monitoringi@mia.gov.ge; internet www.police.ge.

Ministry of Internally Displaced Persons from the Occupied Territories, Accommodation, and Refugees: 0177 Tbilisi, Tamarashvili 15 A; tel. (32) 231-15-98; fax (32) 231-15-96; e-mail info@mra.gov.ge; internet www.mra.gov.ge.

Ministry of Justice: 0146 Tbilisi, Gorgasali 24A; tel. (32) 240-52-02; fax (32) 275-82-37; e-mail press-center@justice.gov.ge; internet www
.justice.gov.ge.

Ministry of Labour, Health and Social Affairs: 0119 Tbilisi, A. Tsereteli 144; tel. (32) 251-00-12; fax (32) 251-00-19; e-mail info@moh
.gov.ge; internet www.moh.gov.ge.

Ministry of Prisons and Probation: 0177 Tbilisi, Al. Qazbegi 42; tel. (32) 231-27-34; fax (32) 231-19-01; e-mail info@mcla.gov.ge; internet www.mcla.gov.ge.

Ministry of Regional Development and Infrastructure: 0177 Tbilisi, Al. Qazbegi 12; tel. (32) 251-07-12; e-mail press@mrdi.gov.ge; internet www.mrdi.gov.ge.

Ministry of Sport and Youth Affairs: 0162 Tbilisi, Cholokashvili 9; tel. (32) 223-54-33; fax (32) 229-20-49; e-mail sport@msy.gov.ge; internet msy.gov.ge.

President

Presidential Election, 27 October 2013

Candidates				Votes	%
Giorgi Margvelashvili (QO-DS)		. .	.	1,012,569	62.12
Davit Bakradze (ENM)	.	. . .		354,103	21.72
Nino Burjanadze (DM-ES)	.	. . .		166,061	10.19
Others	.	. . . . .		97,255	5.97
Total	. .	. . . .		1,629,988	100.00

Legislature

Georgian Parliament
(Sakartvelos Parlamenti)

Kutaisi, Abashidze 26; tel. (32) 228-90-06; fax (32) 299-93-86; e-mail contact@parliament.ge; internet www.parliament.ge.

Chairman: DAVIT USUPASHVILI.

General Election, 1 October 2012

Parties and blocs	%*	A†	B†	Total
			Seats	
Bidzina Ivanishvili-Qartuli Ocneba (Bidzina Ivanishvili-Georgian Dream)‡	54.97	44	41	85
Ertiani Natsionaluri Modzraoba .	40.34	33	32	65
Others	4.70	—	—	—
Total	100.00	77	73	150

* Percentage refers to the share of the vote cast for seats awarded on the basis of party lists.
† Of the 150 seats in the Sakartvelos Parlamenti, 77 (A) are awarded according to proportional representation on the basis of party lists, and 73 (B) are elected in single-mandate constituencies.
‡ An electoral alliance of Qartuli Ocneba-Demokratiuli Sakartvelo, the Sakartvelos Konservatiuli Partia, Mretsveloba Gadaarchens Sakartvelos, the Erovnuli Phorumi, Chveni Sakartvelo-Davisuphali Demokratebi and the Sakartvelos Respublikuri Partia.

Election Commission

Central Electoral Commission of Georgia (CEC): 0108 Tbilisi, Aghmashenebeli 13-km; tel. (32) 251-00-51; e-mail correspondence@cec.gov.ge; internet www.cec.gov.ge; Chair. TAMAR ZHVANIA.

Political Organizations

The following were among the most prominent parties registered in early 2015:

Axali Memarjveneebi—Axlebi (AM) (New Rights): 0179 Tbilisi, I. Abashidze 18; tel. (32) 272-35-58; fax (32) 222-23-47; e-mail info@nrp
.ge; internet www.nrp.ge; f. 2001; Chair. PIKRIA CHIKHRADZE.

Chveni Sakartvelo-Davisuphali Demokratebi (ChS—DD) (Our Georgia-Free Democrats): 0194 Tbilisi, E. Cherkezishvili 4; tel. (32) 210-48-83; f. 2009; right-of-centre; opposed to administration of Pres. Saakashvili; contested 2012 legislative elections in coalition led by Qartuli Ocneba-Demokratiuli Sakartvelo (q.v.); Leader IRAKLI ALASANIA.

Demokratiuli Modzraoba-Ertiani Sakartvelo (DM—ES) (Democratic Movement-United Georgia): 0160 Tbilisi, Abuladze 8; tel. (32) 255-03-77; e-mail mail@democrats.ge; internet www
.democrats.ge; f. 2008; supports closer relations with Russia; Chair. NINO BURJANADZE; 35,000 mems (2012).

Erovnuli Phorumi (National Forum): 0160 Tbilisi, Lvovi 82; tel. (32) 37-80-88; fax (32) 99-65-77; internet forumi.ge; f. 2006; contested 2012 legislative elections in coalition led by Qartuli Ocneba-Demokratiuli Sakartvelo (q.v.); Chair. KAKHABER SHARTAVA.

Ertiani Natsionaluri Modzraoba (ENM) (United National Movement): 0118 Tbilisi, Kakheti 45A; tel. (32) 292-30-84; fax (32) 292-30-91; e-mail info@unm.ge; internet www.unm.ge; f. 2004; liberal conservative; Chair. MIKHEIL SAAKASHVILI; Sec.-Gen. IVANE MERABISHVILI.

Kristianul-Demokratiuli Modzraoba (KDM) (Christian Democratic Movement): 0162 Tbilisi, Tsagareli 59; tel. (32) 214-10-33; fax (32) 214-10-38; e-mail info@cdm.ge; internet www.cdm.ge; f. 2008; Chair. GIORGI TARGAMADZE.

Mretsveloba Gadaarchens Sakartvelos (MGS) (Industry Will Save Georgia): 0105 Tbilisi, Marjvena Sanapiro 7; tel. (32) 294-09-81; f. 1999; Leader GIORGI TOPHADZE.

Qartuli Ocneba-Demokratiuli Sakartvelo (QO-DS) (Georgian Dream-Democratic Georgia): 0105 Tbilisi, Erekle II Moedani 3; tel. (32) 219-77-11; internet www.gd.ge; f. 2012 by prominent businessman Bidzina Ivanishvili; Chair. MANANA KOBAKHIDZE.

Sakartvelos Demokratiuli Partia (Democratic Party of Georgia): c/o Sakartvelos Parlamenti, 0118 Tbilisi, Rustaveli 8; f. 2008; right-of-centre; Chair. GIA TORTLADZE.

Sakartvelos Evropeli Demokratebi (European Democrats of Georgia): Tbilisi, Kvinitadze 4; tel. (32) 230-78-71; e-mail europeandemocrats@gmail.com; internet www.ged.ge; f. 2011; Chair. PAATA DAVITAIA.

Sakartvelos Konservatiuli Partia (SKP) (Conservative Party of Georgia): 0179 Tbilisi, Krtsanisis II shesakhvevi 15-17; tel. (32) 225-27-90; fax (32) 222-61-23; e-mail office@conservatives.ge; internet www.conservatives.ge; f. 2001; contested 2012 legislative elections in coalition led by Qartuli Ocneba-Demokratiuli Sakartvelo (q.v.); Chair. ZVIAD DZIDZIGURI (acting); 12,000 mems.

Sakartvelos Leiboristuli Partia (SLP) (Georgian Labour Party): 0112 Tbilisi, Javakhishvili 88; tel. (32) 291-16-17; fax (32) 294-29-22; e-mail georgianlabourparty@gmail.com; internet www.labour.ge; f. 1996; Chair. SHALVA NATELASHVILI.

Sakartvelos Respublikuri Partia (SRP) (Republican Party of Georgia): 0108 Tbilisi, Phanaskerteli 20/81; tel. (32) 292-00-58; fax (32) 292-06-34; e-mail respublikelebi@gmail.com; internet www .republicans.ge; f. 1995; politically, economically and socially liberal; contested 2012 legislative elections in coalition led by Qartuli Ocneba-Demokratiuli Sakartvelo (q.v.); Chair. KHATUNA SAMNIDZE.

Diplomatic Representation

EMBASSIES IN GEORGIA

Armenia: 0102 Tbilisi, Tetelashvili 4; tel. (32) 295-94-43; fax (32) 296-42-87; e-mail armgeorgiaembassy@mfa.am; Ambassador HOVHANNES MANUKIAN.

Azerbaijan: Tbilisi, Kipshidzse 2/1; tel. (32) 224-22-20; fax (32) 224-22-33; e-mail tbilisi@mission.mfa.gov.az; internet www.azembassy .ge; Ambassador AZER TOFIG HUSEYN.

Brazil: Tbilisi, Chanturia 6/2; tel. (32) 293-24-19; fax (32) 293-24-16; e-mail brasemb.tbilisi@itamaraty.gov.br; Ambassador CARLOS ALBERTO LOPES ASFORA.

Bulgaria: 0102 Tbilisi, V. Gorgasali 15; tel. (32) 291-01-94; fax (32) 291-02-70; e-mail embassy.tbilisi@mfa.bg; internet www.mfa.bg/ embassies/georgia; Ambassador PLAMEN BONCHEV.

China, People's Republic: 0179 Tbilisi, Barnov 52, POB 224; tel. (32) 225-90-00; fax (32) 225-09-96; e-mail chinaemb_ge@mfa.gov.cn; Ambassador YUE BI.

Czech Republic: 0162 Tbilisi, Chavchavadze 37/6; tel. (32) 291-69-40; fax (32) 291-67-44; e-mail tbilisi@embassy.mzv.cz; internet www .mzv.cz/tbilisi; Ambassador TOMÁŠ PERNICKÝ.

Estonia: 0171 Tbilisi, Saburtalo, Likhauri 4; tel. (32) 236-51-22; fax (32) 236-51-38; e-mail tbilisisaatkond@mfa.ee; internet www.tbilisi .vm.ee; Ambassador PRIIT TURK.

France: 0114 Tbilisi, Krtsanisi 49; tel. (32) 272-14-90; fax (32) 272-13-55; e-mail ambafrance@access.sanet.ge; internet www .ambafrance-ge.org; Ambassador RENAUD SALINS.

Germany: 0103 Tbilisi, Telavi 20, Sheraton Metekhi Palace Hotel; tel. (32) 244-73-00; fax (32) 244-73-64; e-mail info@tiflis.diplo.de; internet www.tiflis.diplo.de; Ambassador Dr ORTWIN HENNIG.

Greece: 0179 Tbilisi, T. Tabidze 37D; tel. (32) 291-49-70; fax (32) 291-49-80; e-mail grcmb.tbi@mfa.gr; internet www.greekembassy.ge; Ambassador ELEFTHERIOS PROIOS.

Holy See: 0108 Tbilisi, Jgenti 40, Nutsubidze Plateau; tel. (32) 253-76-01; fax (32) 253-67-04; e-mail nuntius@vatican.ge; Apostolic Nuncio MAREK SOLCZYŃSKI (Titular Archbishop of Caesarea in Mauretania).

Hungary: 0160 Tbilisi, Lvovi 83; tel. (32) 239-90-08; fax (32) 239-90-04; e-mail mission.tbs@mfa.gov.hu; internet www.mfa.gov.hu/ kulkepviselet/ge/hu; Ambassador SÁNDOR SZABÓ.

Iran: 0160 Tbilisi, Chavchavadze 80; tel. (32) 291-36-56; fax (32) 291-36-28; e-mail embassy@iran.ge; Ambassador ABBAS TALEBIFAR.

Iraq: 0160 Tbilisi, Lvovi 77; tel. (32) 223-45-01; fax (32) 229-45-03; e-mail iraqiageoemb@yahoo.com; Ambassador BAKIR AHMAD AZIZ ALJAF.

Israel: 0102 Tbilisi, D. Agmashenebeli 61; tel. (32) 255-65-00; fax (32) 255-65-33; e-mail press@tbilisi.mfa.gov.il; internet tbilisi.mfa .gov.il; Ambassador YUVAL FUCHS.

Italy: 0108 Tbilisi, Chitadze 3A; tel. (32) 299-64-18; fax (32) 299-64-15; e-mail embassy.tbilisi@esteri.it; internet www.ambtbilisi.esteri .it; Ambassador FEDERICA FAVI.

Japan: Tbilisi, Krtsanisi 7D; tel. (32) 275-21-11; fax (32) 275-21-12; e-mail protocol@tb.mofa.go.jp; internet www.ge.emb-japan.go.jp; Ambassador TOSHIO KAITANI.

Kazakhstan: 0179 Tbilisi, Shatberashvili 23; tel. (32) 299-76-84; fax (32) 229-24-89; e-mail tbilisi@mfa.kz; Ambassador ERMUHAMED ERTYSBAEV.

Latvia: 0144 Tbilisi, Akhmeta 16; tel. (32) 224-48-58; fax (32) 238-14-06; e-mail embassy.georgia@mfa.gov.lv; internet www.mfa.gov.lv/ georgia; Ambassador ELITA GAVELE.

Lithuania: 0162 Tbilisi, T. Abuladze 25; tel. (32) 291-29-33; fax (32) 222-17-93; e-mail amb.ge@urm.lt; internet ge.mfa.lt; Ambassador JONAS PASLAUSKAS.

Netherlands: 0103 Tbilisi, Telavi 20, Sheraton Metekhi Palace Hotel; tel. (32) 227-62-00; fax (32) 227-62-32; e-mail tbi@minbuza.nl; internet www.dutchembassy.ge; Ambassador HANS PETER PAUL MARIA HORBACH.

Poland: 0108 Tbilisi, Zubalashvili 19; tel. (32) 292-03-98; fax (32) 292-03-97; e-mail tbilisi.amb.sekretariat@msz.gov.pl; internet www .tbilisi.msz.gov.pl; Ambassador ANDRZEJ CIESZKOWSKI.

Romania: Tbilisi, Lvov Kushitashvili 7; tel. (32) 238-53-10; fax (32) 238-52-10; e-mail ambasada@caucasus.net; internet tbilisi.mae.ro; Ambassador DUMITRU BADEA.

Sweden: 0162 Tbilisi, Kipshidze 15; tel. (32) 255-03-20; fax (32) 222-48-90; e-mail ambassaden.tbilisi@gov.se; Ambassador MARTINA QUICK.

Switzerland: 0114 Tbilisi, Krtsanisi 11; tel. (32) 275-30-01; fax (32) 275-30-06; e-mail tif.vertretung@eda.admin.ch; internet www.eda .admin.ch/tbilisi; Ambassador Dr GUENTHER BAECHLER.

Turkey: 0162 Tbilisi, Chavchavadze 35; tel. (32) 225-20-72; fax (32) 222-06-66; e-mail tiblisbe@dsl.ge; internet tbilisi.emb.mfa.gov.tr; Ambassador LEVENT GÜMRÜKÇÜ.

Turkmenistan: Tbilisi; Ambassador DOVLETMURAD MURATOV.

Ukraine: 0162 Tbilisi, Chavchavadze 76; tel. (32) 231-11-61; fax (32) 231-11-81; e-mail emb_ge@mfa.gov.ua; internet www.mfa.gov.ua/ georgia; Ambassador VASYL H. TSYBENKO.

United Kingdom: 0114 Tbilisi, Krtsanisi 51; tel. (32) 227-47-47; fax (32) 227-47-92; e-mail british.embassy.tbilisi@fco.gov.uk; internet www.gov.uk/government/world/georgia; Ambassador ALEXANDRA HALL.

USA: 0131 Tbilisi, Balanchivadze 11; tel. (32) 227-70-00; fax (32) 253-23-10; e-mail tbilisivisa@state.gov; internet georgia.usembassy.gov; Ambassador RICHARD NORLAND.

Judicial System

Constitutional Court: 6010 Ajara, Batumi, M. Abashidze 16-18; tel. (422) 27-00-99; fax (422) 27-01-44; e-mail const@constcourt.ge; internet www.constcourt.ge; f. 1996; consists of 9 members; Pres. GIORGI PAPUASHVILI.

Supreme Court: 0110 Tbilisi, Zubalashvili 32; tel. (32) 299-01-64; fax (32) 299 70 01; e-mail info@supremecourt.ge; internet www .supremecourt.ge; Chair. KONSTANTIN KUBLASHVILI.

High Council of Justice: 0144 Tbilisi, Bochorma 12; tel. (32) 227-31-00; fax (32) 227-31-01; e-mail council@hcoj.gov.ge; internet www .hcoj.gov.ge; f. 1997; 15-member council that co-ordinates the appointment of judges and their activities; Chair. KONSTANTIN KUBLASHVILI (Chair. of the Supreme Court); Exec. Sec. LEVAN MURUSIDZE.

Prosecutor-General: GIORGI BADASHVILI, 0114 Tbilisi, Gorgasali 24; tel. (32) 240-52-22; e-mail presscenter@pog.gov.ge; internet pog .gov.ge.

Religion

CHRISTIANITY

The Orthodox Church

The Georgian Orthodox Church is divided into 27 dioceses.

Georgian Patriarchate: 0105 Tbilisi, Erekle II Moedani 1; tel. (32) 299-03-78; fax (32) 298-71-14; e-mail info@patriachate.ge; internet www.patriarchate.ge; Catholicos-Patriarch of All Georgia ILIA II.

The Roman Catholic Church

The Apostolic Administrator of Latin Rite Catholics of the Caucasus (Armenia and Georgia) is resident in Tbilisi.

Apostolic Administrator of Latin Rite Catholics of the Caucasus: Most Rev. GIUSEPPE PASOTTO (Titular Bishop of Musti), 0105 Tbilisi, G. Abesadze 6; tel. and fax (32) 99-60-50; e-mail ammapost@ geo.net.ge.

The Armenian Apostolic Church

Primate of the Armenian Apostolic Church in Georgia: Rt Rev. Bishop VAZGEN MIRZAKHANIAN, 0105 Tbilisi, Krasilnaya 5, St Gevork Church; tel. (32) 272-17-50.

ISLAM

The principal Islamic communities in Georgia are those among the Adjars and Abkhaz (who are Sunni Muslims) and Azeris (who are Shi'ite). There is only one mosque in Tbilisi, which is shared by Sunni and Shi'ite communities. A new Muslim Affairs Department was established in 2011, to assume the jurisdiction over Georgia hitherto held by the Spiritual Board of Muslims of the Caucasus, based in Azerbaijan.

Muslim Affairs Department of Georgia: 0105 Tbilisi, Botankuri 32; f. 2011; non-governmental organization; Chair. Mufti JAMAL BAGSHADZE.

JUDAISM

A large part of the country's long-established Jewish population emigrated, particularly to Israel, after the collapse of the USSR. In 2009 there were an estimated 30,000 Jews in Georgia, with the largest communities in Tbilisi and Kutaisi.

The Press

PRINCIPAL NEWSPAPERS

In Georgian, except where otherwise stated.

Asaval-Dasavali: 0160 Tbilisi, Abladzis 39; tel. (32) 215-25-25; e-mail mail@asavali.ge; internet www.asavali.ge; weekly; Editor-in-Chief LASHA NADAREISHVILI.

Droni (The Times): 0108 Tbilisi, Kostava 14; tel. (32) 299-56-54; e-mail newspdroni@usa.net; internet www.droni.ge; 2 a week; Editor-in-Chief GIORGI CHOCHISHVILI.

Georgia Today: 0105 Tbilisi, Nato Vachnadze 9; tel. (32) 292-08-30; fax (32) 292-08-82; e-mail info@georgiatoday.ge; internet www .georgiatoday.ge; f. 2000; weekly; in English; Gen. Man. GEORGE SHARASHIDZE.

Georgian Times: 0107 Tbilisi, Kikodze 12; tel. (32) 293-44-05; fax (32) 293-49-63; e-mail editor@geotimes.ge; internet www.geotimes .ge; f. 1993; weekly, Mondays; in English, Georgian and Russian; Editors DALI BZHALAVA, NANA GAGUA.

The Messenger: 0108 Tbilisi, Belinski 43; tel. (32) 293-91-69; fax (32) 293-62-32; e-mail messenger@messenger.com.ge; internet www .messenger.com.ge; f. 1919, revived 1990 and 1993; daily; in English; Editor-in-Chief ZAZA GACHECHILADZE.

Resonance (Rezonansi): 0160 Tbilisi, Gotua 3; tel. (32) 237-79-69; fax (32) 238-79-69; e-mail resonancenewspaper@yahoo.com; internet www.resonancedaily.com; f. 1990; daily; Editor-in-Chief ZURAB MATCHARADZE; circ. 7,000.

PRINCIPAL PERIODICALS

Dila (The Morning): 0196 Tbilisi, Kostava 14; tel. (32) 293-41-30; e-mail dila1904@yahoo.com; internet www.dila.ge; f. 1904; present name adopted 1947; every two weeks; illustrated; for 5- to 12-year-olds; Editor-in-Chief DODO TSIVTSIVADZE; circ. 4,500.

Liberali: Tbilisi; internet www.liberali.ge; f. 2009; weekly; current affairs, politics; Editor-in-Chief SHORENA SHAVERDASHVILI; circ. 5,000 (2010).

Metsniereba da Tekhnologiebi (Science and Technologies): 0108 Tbilisi, Rustaveli 52, Georgian Academy of Sciences; e-mail tech@gw .acnet.ge; f. 1949; monthly; journal of the Georgian Academy of Sciences; English, Georgian and Russian; Editor VLADIMER CHAV-CHANIDZE.

Sakartvelos Metsnierebata Erovnuli Akademiis Moambe/ Bulletin of Georgian National Academy of Sciences: 0108 Tbilisi, Rustaveli 52; tel. (32) 299-75-93; fax (32) 299-88-91; e-mail bulletin@science.org.ge; internet www.science.org.ge/bulletin; f. 1940; 3 a year; in Georgian and English; Editor-in-Chief GEORGI KVESITADZE.

Tabula: Tbilisi; tel. (32) 242-03-00; fax (32) 291-61-21; e-mail info@ tabula.ge; internet www.tabula.ge; f. 2010; politics and current affairs; supports administration of Pres. Saakashvili (2004–13) and free market economics; Chief Editor TAMAR CHERGOLEISHVILI.

NEWS AGENCIES

Civil.ge: 0171 Tbilisi, Dolidze 2; tel. (32) 233-25-16; e-mail civilgeorgia@una.ge; internet www.civil.ge; f. 2001; in Georgian, English and Russian; independent; Editor-in-Chief GIORGI SEPASH-VILI.

Inter-Press: 0160 Tbilisi, Iosebidze 49; tel. (32) 238-78-00; fax (32) 245-07-80; e-mail interpress@ipn.ge; internet www.interpressnews .ge; f. 2000; in Georgian, Russian and English.

Prime News Agency (PNA): 0105 Tbilisi, Leselidze 28; tel. (32) 292-32-63; fax (32) 292-32-65; e-mail info@primenewsonline.com; f. 1997; news on Armenia, Azerbaijan and Georgia; Gen. Man. DEMNA CHAGELISHVILI.

Sarke Information Agency: 0102 Tbilisi, D. Agmashenebeli 54; tel. (32) 295-06-59; fax (32) 295-08-37; e-mail info@sarke.com; internet www.sarke.com; f. 1992; professional agency for economic and business news in Georgia; privately owned; Dir VALERIAN KHUKHUNASHVILI; Editor-in-Chief VICTORIA GUJELASHVILI.

JOURNALISTS' ASSOCIATIONS

Independent Association of Georgian Journalists: 0105 Tbilisi, Lermontov 10; tel. (599) 207-70-52; fax (32) 293-44-05; e-mail pochkhua@geotimes.ge; internet www.iagj.org.ge; f. 2000; Pres. ZVIAD POCHKHUA.

Journalists' Federation of Georgia: 0105 Tbilisi, Erekle II Moedani 6; tel. (32) 298-24-46; e-mail foraf@geotvr.ge.

Publishers

Ganatleba (Education): 0164 Tbilisi, Chubinashvili 50; tel. (32) 295-50-97; f. 1957; educational, literature; Dir L. KHUNDADZE.

Meridian Publishing Co (Sh. P. Kh. Gamomtsemloba 'Meridiani'): Tbilisi, A. Kazbegi 45; tel. (32) 239-15-22; fax (32) 295-56-35; e-mail info@meridianpub.com; f. 1994; academic and schools; Editor-in-Chief GIORGI GIGINEISHVILI.

Metsniereba (Sciences): 0160 Tbilisi, Gamrekeli 19; tel. and fax (32) 237-22-97; e-mail publicat@gw.acnet.ge; f. 1941; owned by Georgian Academy of Sciences; Dir DAVID KOLOTAURI; Editor CISANA KARTOZIA.

Nakaduli (Stream): 0194 Tbilisi, Pekini 28; tel. (32) 238-46-52; e-mail ngvineria@yahoo.com; f. 1938; books for children and youth.

Sakartvelo (Georgia): 0102 Tbilisi, Marjanishvili 5; tel. (32) 295-42-01; f. 1921; fmrly *Sabchota Sakartvelo* (Soviet Georgia); political, scientific and fiction; Dir JANSUL GVINJILIA.

Tbilisi State University Publishing House: 0128 Tbilisi, Chav-chavadze 14; tel. (32) 225-14-32; e-mail publishing@tsu.ge; f. 1933; scientific and educational literature; Dir TAMAR EBRALIDZE.

Broadcasting and Communications

TELECOMMUNICATIONS

In 2013 there were 1.2m. fixed telephone lines and 5.0m. subscriptions to mobile telephone services in the country.

Georgian National Communications Commission (Sakartvelos Komunikatsiebis Erovnuli Komisia): 0144 Tbilisi, Ketevan Tsamebuli Ave/Bochorma 50/18; tel. (32) 292-16-67; fax (32) 292-16-25; e-mail post@gncc.ge; internet www.gncc.ge; f. 2000; Chair. VAKH-TANG ABASHIDZE.

Geocell (Geoseli): 0160 Tbilisi, Gotua 3, POB 48; tel. (32) 277-01-77; fax (32) 277-01-01; e-mail social@geocell.ge; internet www.geocell .com.ge; f. 1996; mobile cellular communications.

Magti: 0186 Tbilisi, Politkovskaya 5; tel. (32) 217-17-17; fax (32) 217-11-71; e-mail office@magtigsm.ge; internet www.magticom.ge; f. 1997; mobile cellular communications; launched 3G mobile services July 2006; Gen. Dir LARS P. REICHELT.

Maximali: 0108 Tbilisi, Aghmashenebeli 147; tel. (32) 242-99-99; fax (32) 242-92-92; e-mail office@vtel.ge; internet www.maximali.ge; f. 2008; wireless internet service provider; covers six major cities including Tbilisi, Batumi, Rustavi and Poti, and 20 rural areas; owned by VTEL Georgia; Exec. Dir TEIMURAZ GOGOBERIDZE.

Silknet: 0112 Tbilisi, Tsinamdzgvrishvili 95; tel. (32) 210-00-00; fax (32) 210-00-01; internet www.silknet.com; fmrly United Telecommunications Co of Georgia, operating under the brand names Vaneks and Elektrosvyaz Ajarii, present name adopted March 2010; owned by Bank TuranAlem (Kazakhstan); mobile telecommunications and internet service provider; CEO LEVAN BUCHUKURI.

Telecom Georgia (Sakartvelos Telekomi): 0108 Tbilisi, Rustaveli 31; tel. (32) 244-18-00; fax (32) 244-18-29; f. 1994; provides international telecommunications services; 100% owned by Metromedia International Group Inc (USA); Gen. Dir OTAR ZUMBURIDZE.

BROADCASTING

Television

Georgian Public Broadcasting (SSM) (Sakartvelos Sazogadoebrivi Mautsqebeli): 0171 Tbilisi, Kostava 68; tel. (32) 240-93-77; e-mail info@gpb.ge; internet www.gpb.ge; f. 2005; comprises two television channels: Public TV (f. 1956) and Second Channel (f. 1971), and two radio stations: Public Radio (f. 1925) and Radio Two (f. 1995); Gen. Dir GIORGI BARATASHVILI.

Imedi TV: 0159 Tbilisi, Lubliana 5; tel. (32) 246-31-59; fax (32) 246-30-41; e-mail contact@imedi.ge; internet www.imedi.ge; f. 2001; Dir-Gen. GIORGI ARVELADZE.

Mze TV (Sun TV): 0171 Tbilisi, Kostava 75B; tel. (32) 233-55-98; e-mail reklama@mze.ge; internet www.mze.ge; f. 2003; Dir ZAZA TANANASHVILI.

Rustavi 2: 0177 Tbilisi, Vazha-Pshavela 45; tel. (32) 220-11-11; fax (32) 253-69-11; e-mail tv@rustavi2.com; internet www.rustavi2.com; f. 1994; independent; Gen. Dir GIORGI GEGESHIDZE.

Radio

Georgian Public Broadcasting (SSM): see Television.

Radio Imedi: 0159 Tbilisi, Lubliana 5; tel. (32) 292-11-88; fax (32) 292-11-99; e-mail news4@radioimedi.ge; internet www.radio-imedi .ge; f. 2001; national broadcasting, 24 hours; news; Dir IRAKLI KHETERELI.

Radio Sakartvelo (Radio Georgia): 0159 Tbilisi, Marshal Gelovani 2; tel. (32) 238-30-30; fax (32) 233-60-60; e-mail contact@fortuna.ge; internet www.fortuna.ge; f. 1999; owns and operates 4 stations, incl. Radio Fortuna and Radio Fortuna Plus; popular and classical music; Gen. Dir TAMAR CHIGOGIDZE.

Finance

(cap. = capital; res = reserves; dep. = deposits; m. = million; brs = branches; amounts in lari, unless otherwise indicated)

BANKING

Central Bank

National Bank of Georgia: 0105 Tbilisi, Leonidze 3–5; tel. (32) 240-64-06; fax (32) 244-25-77; e-mail info@nbg.gov.ge; internet www.nbg .gov.ge; f. 1991; cap. 15.0m., res 108.8m., dep. 2,750.9m. (Dec. 2009); Pres. and Chair. of Bd GIORGI KADAGIDZE.

Other Banks

In 2012 some 23 commercial banks were in operation in Georgia.

Bank of Georgia (Sakartvelos Banki): 0160 Tbilisi, Gagarin 29A; tel. (32) 244-44-44; fax (32) 244-42-47; e-mail ir@bog.ge; internet www.bankofgeorgia.ge; f. 1991; present name adopted 1994; cap. 37.0m., res 641.0m., dep. 2,814.2m. (Dec. 2012); 77.5% owned by BNY (Nominees) Ltd (United Kingdom); CEO IRAKLI GILAURI; 164 brs.

Bank Republic: 0179 Tbilisi, Gr. Abashidze 2; tel. (32) 292-55-55; fax (32) 292-55-44; e-mail info@republic.ge; internet www.republic .ge; f. 1991; 93.64% owned by Société Générale (France); cap. 76.0m., res 55.0m., dep. 490.3m. (Dec. 2012); Chair. of Bd LASHA PAPASHVILI; CEO CHRISTIAN CARMAGNOLLE.

Cartu Bank: 0162 Tbilisi, Chavchavadze 39A; tel. (32) 292-55-92; fax (32) 291-22-79; e-mail info@cartubank.ge; internet www.cartubank .ge; f. 1996; cap. 93.1m., res 25.0m., dep. 67.0m. (Dec. 2012); Dir-Gen. NODAR JAVAKHISHVILI; 5 brs.

Kor Standard Bank (KSB): 0103 Tbilisi, Tsereteli 3; tel. (32) 250-00-00; fax (32) 250-77-07; e-mail info@ksb.ge; internet www.ksb.ge; f. 2008 by merger; development bank; Gen. Dir THEA LORTKIPANIDZE.

Liberty Bank: 0162 Tbilisi, Chavchavadze 74; tel. (32) 255-55-00; fax (32) 291-22-69; e-mail info@libertybank.ge; internet www .libertybank.ge; f. 2002; fmrly People's Bank of Georgia; name changed as above after 91.2% stake acquired by Liberty Investments Holding in 2009; cap. 53.3m., res 64.2m., dep. 725.0m. (Dec. 2012); CEO LADO GURGENIDZE.

PrivatBank: 0119 Tbilisi, Tsereteli 114; tel. (32) 255-55-55; fax (32) 235-50-80; e-mail pbankgeorgia@privatbank.ge; internet www .privatbank.ge; f. 1992; present name adopted 2010; cap. 93m., res 16m., dep. 240m. (Dec. 2012); Chair. of Bd ALEKSANDRE CHOCHIA.

ProCredit Bank, Georgia: 0160 Tbilisi, Kazbegi 21; tel. (32) 220-22-22; fax (32) 220-22-23; e-mail info@procreditbank.ge; internet www.procreditbank.ge; f. 1999; present name adopted 2003; owned by ProCredit Holding (Germany); Gen. Dir ASMUS ROTNE; 55 brs (Dec. 2013).

TBC Bank: 0102 Tbilisi, Marjanishvili 7; tel. (32) 227-27-27; fax (32) 277-27-74; e-mail info@tbcbank.com.ge; internet www.tbcbank.com .ge; f. 1992; owned by international financial institutions; cap. 16.5m., res 295.5m., dep. 2,939.0m. (Dec. 2012); Pres. of Bd of Dirs VAKHTANG BUTSKHRIKIDZE; 13 brs.

VTB Georgia (VneshTorgBank Georgia): 0114 Tbilisi, Chanturia 14; tel. (32) 250-55-05; fax (32) 293-32-91; e-mail info@vtb.ge; internet www.vtb.com.ge; f. 1995 as United Georgian Bank; name changed as above 2006; 96.3% owned by VTB OJSC (Russia); cap. 148.0m., res 1.0m., dep. 294.2m. (Dec. 2012); Dir-Gen. ARCHIL KONTSELIDZE; 19 brs.

STOCK EXCHANGE

Georgian Stock Exchange (Sakartvelos Saphondo Birsha): 0162 Tbilisi, Chavchavadze 74A; tel. (32) 222-07-18; fax (32) 225-18-76; e-mail info@gse.ge; internet www.gse.ge; f. 1999; Chair. of Supervisory Bd GEORGE LOLADZE; Gen. Dir VAKHTANG SVANADZE.

INSURANCE

Insurance State Supervision Service of Georgia (Sakartvelos Dazghvevis Sakhelmtsipho Zedamkhedvelobis Samsakhuri): 0164 Tbilisi, G. Chitaia 21; tel. (32) 295-64-89; fax (32) 295-71-42; e-mail isssg@inbox.ge; f. 1997; provides state regulation of insurance activity; Dir ARCHIL TSERTSVADZE.

Aldagi BCI Insurance Co (Aldagi Bisiai Sadazghvevo kompania): 0179 Tbilisi, Qazgegis 3-5, Melikishvili 10; tel. (32) 244-48-08; fax (32) 229-49-05; e-mail aldagi@aldagi.com.ge; internet www.bci.ge; formed by merger of Aldagi Insurance Co and British-Caucasian Insurance Co.

Alpha Insurance Co: 0160 Tbilisi, Al. Qazbegi 16A; tel. (32) 264-06-40; e-mail insurance@alpha.ge; internet www.alpha.ge; f. 2009; subsidiary of Aversi Pharma; Gen. Dir MAKA SOLOGHASHVILI.

Archimedes Global Georgia: 0177 Tbilisi, Otar Chkheidzis 10; tel. (32) 245-11-45; e-mail info@archimedes.ge; internet www .archimedes.ge; f. 2007; medical; owned by Archimedes Global (Israel); Dir TEA AKHALADZE.

GPI (Georgian Pension and Insurance) Holding Co (Jipiai Holdingi): 0171 Tbilisi, Kostava 67; tel. (32) 250-51-11; fax (32) 236-52-22; e-mail info@gpih.ge; internet www.gpih.ge; f. 2001; majority share owned by Vienna Insurance Group—VIG (Austria); merged with VIG-owned IRAO Insurance Co in 2011, retaining separate brands; Gen. Dir PAATA LOMADZE.

IC Group Insurance Co: 0162 Tbilisi, Mosashvili 24; tel. (32) 220-88-88; fax (32) 291-24-27; e-mail icgroup@icgroup.ge; internet www .icgroup.ge; f. 2005; acquired People's Insurance Co in 2009.

Unison Insurance Co: 0160 Tbilisi, Budapeshti 15; tel. (32) 299-19-91; fax (32) 295-22-40; e-mail unison@unison.ge; internet www .unison.ge; f. 2011; Gen. Dir VASIL AKHRAKHADZE.

Trade and Industry

GOVERNMENT AGENCY

National Investment Agency: Invest In Georgia: 0108 Tbilisi, Chanturia 12; tel. (32) 243-34-33; fax (32) 298-27-55; e-mail enquiry@ investingeorgia.org; internet www.investingeorgia.org; f. 2002 to promote foreign direct investment; Dir KETI BOCHORISHVILI.

CHAMBER OF COMMERCE

Georgian Chamber of Commerce and Industry (GCCI) (Sakartvelos Savachro-Samoetsvelo Palata): 0114 Tbilisi, Berdznis 29; tel. (32) 272-07-10; fax (32) 72-31-81; e-mail info@gcci.ge; internet www.gcci.ge; f. 1960; brs in Sukhumi and Batumi; Pres. KAKHA BAINDURASHVILI.

EMPLOYERS' ORGANIZATION

Georgian Employers' Association (GEA): 0177 Tbilisi, Gazapkhuli 14; tel. (32) 221-02-54; fax (32) 223-21-71; e-mail employer@ employer.ge; internet www.employer.ge; f. 2000; Dir ELGUJA MELADZE.

UTILITIES

Regulatory Authority

Georgian National Energy and Water Supply Regulation Commission (GNERC) (Sakartvelos Energetikisa da Tsqalmomagebis Maregulirebeli Erovnuli Komisia): 0194 Tbilisi, Mitskevich 19; tel. (32) 242-01-80; fax (32) 242-01-60; e-mail mail@gnerc.org; internet www.gnerc.org; f. 1997; Chair. IRINA MILORAVA.

Electricity

Electricity System Commercial Operator (ESCO) (Elektroenergetikuli Sistamis Komertsiuli Operatori): 0114 Tbilisi, Tskneti, Baratashvili 2; tel. (32) 241-04-20; fax (32) 260-19-15; e-mail office@ esco.ge; internet www.esco.ge; f. 2006; trades electricity and reserve capacity in order to maintain the balance of supply and demand; Gen. Dir VAKHTANG AMBOKADZE.

Georgian State Electrosystem (GSE) (Sakartvelos Sakhelmtsipho Elektrosistema—SSE): 0105 Tbilisi, Baratashvilis 2; tel. (32) 251-02-02; fax (32) 298-37-04; e-mail info@gse.com.ge; internet www .gse.com.ge; f. 2002 by merger; operator of electricity transmission grid; Chair. of Managing Bd SULKHAN ZUMBURIDZE.

Gas

Georgian Oil and Gas Corpn (GOGC) (Sakartvelos Navtobisa da Gazis Korporatsia) (SNGK): 0152 Tbilisi, Kakhetis Gzatketsili 21; tel. (32) 224-40-40; fax (32) 224-40-41; e-mail public@gogc.ge; internet www.gogc.ge; f. 2006; state-owned; exclusive operator, owner, user, disposer and manager of natural and liquid gas imports and transit in Georgia; Gen. Dir DAVID TVALABEISHVILI.

Water

Tbilisi Water Utility (Tbilisis Tskali): 0179 Tbilisi, M. Kostava 1st Alley 33; tel. (32) 248-71-10; scheduled for privatization; fmrly Tbiltskalkanali; water supply and sewerage system; Dir GIORGI GELBAKIANI.

TRADE UNION CONFEDERATION

Georgian Trade Union Confederation (GTUC) (Sakartvelos Prophesiuli Kavshirebis Gaertianeba): 0100 Tbilisi, Vazha Phshavelas 43; tel. and fax (32) 238-29-95; e-mail gtua@geo.net.ge; internet www.gtuc.ge; f. 1995; Chair. IRAKLI PETRIASHVILI; 25 mem. unions.

Transport

RAILWAYS

In 2010 Georgia's rail network totalled approximately 1,566 km, of which 1,486 km were electrified. In December 2004 the construction of a railway between Kars, Turkey, and Azerbaijan via Akhalkalaki, Georgia, was agreed; the project was scheduled for completion in 2015.

In 2015 the Tbilisi Metro comprised two lines with 22 stations, totalling 26.4 km in length. A short extension was under construction.

Georgian Railways (Sakartvelos Rkinigza): 0112 Tbilisi, Tamar Mepis 15; tel. (32) 219-95-73; fax (32) 219-95-72; e-mail sag@railway.ge; internet www.railway.ge; f. 1872; Chair. and Dir-Gen. MAMUKA BAKHTADZE.

Tbilisi Metro: 0112 Tbilisi, Vagzlis Moedani 2; tel. (32) 235-77-77; fax (32) 293-41-41; e-mail info@metro.ge; internet www.ttc.com.ge; f. 1966; operated by Tbilisi Transport Co; Gen. Dir ZURAB KIKALISHVILI.

ROADS

In 2012 the total length of roads in use was an estimated 18,869 km (including 1,528 km of main roads and 5,307 km of secondary roads).

SHIPPING

There are international shipping services to and from Black Sea and Mediterranean ports. The main ports are at Batumi (in the Autonomous Republic of Ajara, q.v.) and Poti. At 31 December 2014 the Georgian flag registered fleet comprised 172 vessels, with a combined displacement of 184,692 grt.

Poti Sea Port (Photis Sazghvao Navsadguri): 4401 Samegrelo-Zemo Svaneti Mkhare, Poti, D. Agmashenebeli 52; tel. (393) 22-06-60; fax (393) 22-06-88; e-mail contact@potiseaport.com; f. 1858; commercial port; Gen. Dir JOSEPH CROWLEY.

CIVIL AVIATION

Georgia's primary airport is Tbilisi International Airport, Lochini. There are three other airports in operation, in Batumi, Kutaisi and Senaki.

Civil Aviation Authority: 0160 Tbilisi, Al. Qazbegi 12; tel. (32) 236-30-29; fax (32) 294-75-09; f. 2002; Dir GIORGI MZHAVANADZE.

Georgian Airways (Jorjian Airveisi): 0108 Tbilisi, Rustaveli 12; tel. (32) 299-97-30; fax (32) 299-96-60; e-mail info@georgian-airways.com; internet www.georgian-airways.com; f. 1993; fmrly Airzena,

renamed as above in 2004; privately owned; flights to destinations in Europe and the Middle East; CEO IASE ZAUTASHVILI.

Tourism

Georgia's numerous sites of interest to tourists include the historic buildings of Tbilisi and the ancient Georgian capital of Mtskheta, the cave cities at Uplistsikhe and Vardzia, and the mountain landscapes of Svaneti and vineyards of Kazbegi. According to the World Tourism Organization, there were 5.4m. tourist arrivals in 2013, when receipts from tourism (including passenger transport) totalled a provisional US $1,720m.

Georgian National Tourism Administration: 0105 Tbilisi, Sanapiro 4; tel. (32) 243-69-99; fax (32) 243-60-87; e-mail info@gnta.ge; internet www.gnta.ge; forms part of the Ministry of Economic and Sustainable Development; Chair. GIORGI SIGUA.

Defence

Compulsory military service lasts for 18 months. As assessed at November 2014, total armed forces numbered some 20,650: an army of 17,750, an air force of 1,300 and a National Guard of 1,600. There were paramilitary forces of 11,700, comprising a border guard of 5,400 and 6,300 troops controlled by the Ministry of Internal Affairs, including a combined navy and coastguard.

In March 1994 Georgia joined the 'Partnership for Peace' programme of military co-operation of the North Atlantic Treaty Organization (NATO).

The European Union Monitoring Mission in Georgia (EUMM), established in October 2008 following conflict in South Ossetia, comprising some 340 personnel, including 200 monitors contributed by 22 countries. As assessed at November 2014, there were 7,000 Russian troops within the internationally recognized boundaries of Georgia.

Defence Expenditure: Budgeted at 750m. lari in 2015.

Chief of the General Staff: Maj.-Gen. VAKHTANG KAPANADZE.

Commander of the Land Forces: Col IVERI SUBELIANI (acting).

Commander of the Air Forces: Col GOCHA SHINGAZRDILOV.

Education

Education is compulsory for nine years, between the ages of six and 14. Secondary education, beginning at the age of 10, lasts for a maximum of seven years, comprising a compulsory cycle of five years and an optional second cycle of two years. In 2007/08 pre-primary enrolment was equivalent to 58% of children in the relevant age-group. In 2011/12 primary enrolment included 98% of the relevant age-group; the ratio for secondary enrolment was 79% of the relevant age-group in 2007/08.

There were 38 state and 47 independent institutions of higher education in 2013/14. In 2012/13 there were 109,533 students enrolled at institutions of higher education (including universities). In 2008 state expenditure on education amounted to 553.8m. lari (8.0% of total consolidated state budgetary expenditure).

GEORGIAN SECESSIONIST TERRITORIES

Two regions within the constitutional boundaries of Georgia—Abkhazia and South Ossetia—have declared independence from the Georgian state, and in practice exist separately from Georgia. In neither case has the independence of the proclaimed republics been widely recognized, with Russia being the principal supporter of the ensuing secessionist polities.

ABKHAZIA

Introductory Survey

STATUS

The self-styled 'Republic of Abkhazia', located in the north-west of Georgia, and neighbouring Russia to the north and the Black Sea to the west, declared its independence from Georgia in July 1992, precipitating military conflict. The conflict continued until 1994, following which Abkhazia enjoyed a de facto independence from Georgia, although the formal status of the territory remained unresolved, and ensuing peace talks were inconclusive. There was renewed conflict in 2008, with Russia intervening to support the Abkhazian separatists, and later that year Russia formally announced that it recognized the statehood of the 'Republic of Abkhazia'. A small number of other countries subsequently extended recognition to the separatist authorities.

LOCATION, CLIMATE, LANGUAGE, RELIGION, FLAG, CAPITAL

Abkhazia is situated in the north-west of Georgia, and covers an area of 8,665 sq km. Russia lies to the north, across the River Psou, while the remainder of Georgia lies to the east, across the River Ingur (Enguri). The south-western boundary is with the Black Sea. The climate is mild and mostly subtropical. Average temperatures in the principal city, Sukhumi, range from 7°C (44°F) in January to 23°C (73°F) in July, although the climate in the mountainous regions is substantially cooler. Precipitation averages around 1,390 mm per year in the lowlands, but in the highlands may exceed 3,000 mm. The population principally speak Abkhaz, a language of the North-western Caucasian family that is usually written in a form of the Cyrillic script, although Russian is also in general use. Although most Abkhaz outside Abkhazia are Muslims, a survey undertaken in the territory in 2003 found that a small majority of the population of the territory were adherents of Orthodox Christianity, with around one-sixth of the population adhering to Islam. The separatist authorities use a flag (proportions 1 by 2) with seven horizontal stripes, alternately green and white. A red canton contains a white hand surmounted by an arch of seven white stars. The principal city and capital of the self-proclaimed 'Republic' is Sukhumi (Sukhum, known as Aqwa in Abkhaz).

CONTEMPORARY POLITICAL HISTORY

Historical Context

Formerly a colony of the Eastern Roman or 'Byzantine' Empire, Abkhazia was an important power in the ninth and 10th centuries, but it was later dominated by Georgian, Turkish and Russian rulers. For much of the Soviet period it formed a nominally Autonomous Republic (ASSR) within the Georgian Soviet Socialist Republic (SSR). However, following the Bolshevik occupation of 1921, it was initially granted the status of an SSR, before the Soviet leader, Stalin (Iosif Dzhugashvili), absorbed it into Georgia in 1931 (which, itself, constituted part of the Transcaucasian Soviet Federative Socialist Republic until 1936). Tens of thousands of ethnic Georgians were subsequently resettled in Abkhazia. A movement for secession from Georgia was revived in 1989, by which time the predominantly Muslim Abkhaz comprised only 17.8% of the area's population, and Georgians constituted the largest ethnic group (45.7%). The Georgian Government repeatedly rejected Abkhazian secessionist demands, which were also fiercely resisted by the local Georgian population. In 1989 the total population was 537,000, of which 17.8% were Abkhazians, and 45.7% ethnic Georgians.

In August 1990 the Abkhazian Supreme Soviet voted to declare independence from Georgia. This declaration was pronounced invalid by the Georgian Supreme Soviet. Later in the month Georgian deputies in the Abkhazian legislature succeeded in reversing the declaration of independence, and inter-ethnic unrest (which had erupted in 1989) continued. Following the overthrow of Zviad Gamsakhurdia as President of Georgia in January 1992, there was renewed unrest in Abkhazia, as large numbers of ethnic Georgians demonstrated in support of Gamsakhurdia. In July the Abkhazian legislature declared the sovereignty of the 'Republic of Abkhazia'.

Domestic Political Affairs

A period of armed conflict began in August 1992, when the Georgian Government dispatched some 3,000 members of the National Guard to the republic, in order to release senior officials who had been taken hostage by supporters of Gamsakhurdia and who were being held in Abkhazia. The Chairman of the Abkhazian legislature and leader of the independence campaign, Vladislav Ardzinba, retreated north with his forces, while Russian paratroopers were dispatched to the region to protect Russian (former Soviet) military bases, amid reports that Russia was supplying military assistance to the separatists. In October separatist forces regained control of northern Abkhazia; hostilities intensified further in the first half of 1993. A provisional peace agreement was signed in July by Georgian and Abkhazian leaders. The ceasefire held until September, when, after intense fighting, Abkhazian forces recaptured Sukhumi, the republic's capital, on 30 September. Almost all Georgian forces were expelled from Abkhazia, and the Georgian Head of State, Eduard Shevardnadze, was forced to flee Sukhumi by air, under heavy bombardment, after the leader of the pro-Shevardnadze administration in Abkhazia, Zhiuli Shartava, was assassinated. Several hundred people were believed to have been killed during the fighting, and more than 200,000 people (mostly ethnic Georgians) fled Abkhazia. In December Georgian and Abkhazian officials signed an eight-point Memorandum of Understanding at UN-sponsored talks in Geneva, Switzerland. A small number of UN military personnel, part of the UN Observer Mission in Georgia (UNOMIG), were subsequently dispatched to Sukhumi in a peacekeeping capacity.

Peace talks were conducted throughout 1994, with the fundamental disagreement between the Georgian and Abkhazian delegations concerning the future status of Abkhazia: Ardzinba demanded full independence, while the Georgian Government insisted on the preservation of Georgia's territorial integrity. A full ceasefire was declared in May, in accordance with which 2,500 Commonwealth of Independent States (CIS)—mainly Russian—peacekeepers were deployed in June, joining an augmented UN observer force. Nevertheless, hostilities continued.

In November 1994 the Abkhazian legislature adopted a new Constitution, declaring the 'Republic of Abkhazia' to be a sovereign state. Ardzinba was elected as President. The Georgian Government condemned this declaration of sovereignty, and the peace negotiations were suspended. Protests were also expressed by the USA, Russia and the UN Security Council, all of which reaffirmed their recognition of Georgia's territorial integrity. Peace talks were resumed in 1995. In January 1996, at a summit meeting of CIS leaders in Moscow, Russia, it was agreed to implement Shevardnadze's request for economic sanctions to be imposed against Abkhazia until it consented to rejoin Georgia.

On 23 November 1996 elections to the secessionist Abkhazian 'legislature', the National Assembly, were held. In March 1997 the Abkhazian faction in the Sakartvelos Parlamenti (Georgian Parliament) staged a hunger strike, demanding the withdrawal of the CIS peacekeeping forces from Abkhazia. However, the peacekeepers' mandate was repeatedly extended. The mandate of UNOMIG, which expired on 31 July, was subsequently granted successive six-monthly extensions. Russian proposals for a settlement of the conflict, which provided for substantial autonomy for Abkhazia within Georgia, were welcomed by Shevardnadze, but rejected by Ardzinba. In August, for the first time since 1992, Ardzinba visited Tbilisi, together with the Russian Minister of Foreign Affairs, Yevgenii Primakov, where they met Shevardnadze. In November 1997 it was agreed to establish a joint Co-ordinating Council, in which representatives of the parties to the conflict, as well as Russian, UN and European Union (EU, see p. 271) delegates, were to participate.

In May 1998 Abkhazian troops attempted to enter the neutral zone between Abkhazia and the remainder of Georgia, resulting in tens of thousands of ethnic Georgian refugees fleeing the region. Negotiations resumed in June. In January 1999 Ardzinba agreed to Georgia's principal demand for the repatriation to Gali of some 35,000 ethnic Georgians who had been forced to flee. On 3 October Ardzinba, the sole candidate, was re-elected President, in an internationally unrecognized poll. In a referendum held concurrently, 97% of the votes cast were reported to have upheld Abkhazian independence. In July 2000 a UN-sponsored protocol on stabilization measures was signed by Abkhazia and Georgia, although violent incidents continued.

In March 2001, at a summit meeting held in Yalta, Crimea, Ukraine, under UN auspices, Abkhazia and Georgia signed an accord renouncing the use of force. Hostilities resumed in October, when a UN helicopter was shot down over the Kodori Gorge, killing all nine passengers. The operations of UNOMIG were suspended, and violence in the region intensified. The Abkhazian authorities blamed Georgia for subsequent aerial attacks on villages in the Kodori Gorge. The Georgian Government, in turn, attributing responsibility for the attacks to Russia, dispatched troops to the region in October, in what the UN deemed a violation of the 1994 ceasefire agreement.

In October 2001 Parliament voted to request the immediate withdrawal of the CIS peacekeeping forces from Abkhazia; however, Shevardnadze argued against their removal, as no substitute force was forthcoming. UNOMIG resumed its activities in February 2002, following the extension of its mandate. At a CIS summit meeting held in March Shevardnadze and the Russian President, Vladimir Putin, agreed to amend the mandate of the CIS peacekeeping forces, to satisfy Georgian demands, among them the inclusion of forces from countries other than Russia. Abkhazian legislative elections, held on 2 March, were again deemed to be illegal by the Georgian Government. Following a protocol signed by the Georgian and Abkhazian authorities in April, the Georgian troops were withdrawn from the Kodori Gorge. In July the UN Security Council adopted Resolution 1427, which urged the resumption of negotiations on Abkhazia's status within Georgia.

In January 2003 the Georgian National Security Council ruled that the country would not approve a renewal of the CIS peacekeepers' mandate (which had recently expired) unless a number of conditions were met. In February the National Security Council finally removed all objections to the renewal of the peacekeepers' mandate, and in early March, following talks in Sochi, Russia, Shevardnadze and Russian President Vladimir Putin agreed to expedite the repatriation of displaced persons to Abkhazia, and to extend indefinitely the mandate of the CIS peacekeeping forces, until either Georgia or Abkhazia demanded their withdrawal.

The Presidency of Sergei Bagapsh

An internationally unrecognized presidential election took place on 3 October 2004, in which former Prime Minister of Abkhazia, Raul Khajimba, the candidate endorsed by Ardzinba and supported by Russia, was initially declared the winner. However, Khajimba's rival Sergei Bagapsh was ultimately judged to have received the most votes, by a narrow margin. Khajimba disputed this result, demanding the annulment of the ballot. An agreement was reached on 6 December, under the mediation of Russian officials, according to which the two candidates were to participate jointly in a new election. Bagapsh was to contest the presidency, with Khajimba as his Vice-President, and with the powers of the latter role to be augmented by an amendment to the separatist territory's 'constitution'. In the repeated election on 12 January 2005, Bagapsh was elected President with some 90% of the votes cast. Following his inauguration in February, Bagapsh nominated Aleksandr Ankvab, a close ally, as Prime Minister.

In October 2005 Parliament adopted a resolution establishing a deadline of 15 June 2006 for the Russian peacekeeping forces in the region to demonstrate compliance with their mandate. In February 2006 negotiations took place in Geneva, under the aegis of the UN, between representatives of the Georgian and Abkhazian authorities. In May the UN-sponsored Co-ordinating Council convened in Tbilisi to oversee talks between the two sides. In July Georgian forces launched an operation to disarm an armed militia group, Monadire (Hunter), in the upper Kodori Gorge, capture its leader, Emzar Kvitsiani, and 'restore constitutional order' to the region. On 27 July President Saakashvili announced that Georgian forces had, for the first time in 13 years, regained full control of the Kodori Gorge and surrounding regions; on the following day Saakashvili ordered the Abkhazian parliament-in-exile to relocate to Chkhalta, in the newly captured region, which was officially designated Upper Abkhazia. In an address at a session of the UN General Assembly in September Saakashvili stated that Georgia would acquiesce to an agreement on the non-resumption of hostilities and the safe return of refugees only if Russian peacekeeping troops in Abkhazia were replaced by a multinational police force. In October the UN Security Council adopted a resolution that urged Georgia to refrain from 'provocative' actions in Abkhazia.

On 4 and 18 March 2007 some 108 candidates contested the (unrecognized) elections for Abkhazia's 35-member legislature. In mid-March three military helicopters conducted a series of aerial bombings in the Georgian-controlled Kodori Gorge. Both the Russian and separatist Abkhazian authorities denied any involvement in the attacks, although reports stated that the helicopters had entered the territory from Russian airspace. Following the announcement in July that Russia was to host the 2014 Winter Olympic Games in Sochi, near the border with Abkhazia, reports that Russian enterprises intended to import materials for the construction of sports facilities from Abkhazia (with considerable potential benefit to the local economy) prompted strong protests from Georgia. The widespread practice of granting Russian passports to residents of Abkhazia (and of South Ossetia) was a significant source of tension between Georgia and Russia from the mid-2000s, which intensified in early 2008; in March Russia announced its unilateral withdrawal from the CIS sanctions against the separatist Abkhazian regime imposed in 1996. Also in March 2008 the separatist Abkhazian authorities rejected a new proposal for a resolution of the status of the territory (granting it extensive autonomous powers within Georgia) presented by President Saakashvili.

In May 2008 Russia (which in April had announced that it was to establish closer relations with the separatist territories) dispatched 400 troops to Abkhazia, with the stated intention of repairing a railway line; Georgia formally protested against the measure. In June a bomb exploded in Sukhumi, prompting the Abkhazian authorities, which claimed that Georgian special forces had perpetrated this and other attacks with the aim of destabilizing the region, to close the border between Abkhazia and the remainder of Georgia. On 9 August, following the onset of hostilities in and around South Ossetia, the Abkhazian separatist forces commenced military action to expel Georgian troops from the Kodori Gorge. Two days later, Russia announced that some 9,000 Russian troops had been dispatched to Abkhazia; on 12 August Abkhazian forces, with Russian support, were reported to have regained control of the Kodori Gorge. Later in August a mass demonstration was staged in Abkhazia to urge Russia to recognize the region's independence. An EU-mediated peace agreement was reached on 8 September; Russia announced its intention of maintaining 3,800 troops in each of Abkhazia and South Ossetia. Following Russia's formal recognition, on 26 August, of Abkhazia and South Ossetia as independent states, on 24 September the Abkhazian People's Assembly ratified a friendship and co-operation treaty (signed by the leaders of the two separatist Republics and the Russian President on 17 September) committing Russia to military support. Bagapsh confirmed that two Russian military bases would be established in Abkhazia, and announced that the security of the border between Abkhazia and the remainder of Georgia would be strengthened. Meanwhile, on 6 September Nicaragua formally recognized the independence of both Abkhazia and South Ossetia, becoming the second state to do so. On 9 October the Council of CIS Foreign Ministers, officially confirming the suspension of Georgia's membership of the organization, also announced the suspension of the activities of the CIS peacekeeping forces in Abkhazia. Meanwhile, the Abkhazian (and South Ossetian) authorities refused an EU Monitoring Mission (EUMM) in Georgia, established under the September peace agreement, access to their territories.

In January 2009 the United Abkhazia movement, which was founded in 2004, and was closely associated with Bagapsh, was formally reconstituted as a political party. In March 2009 the Russian Government signed an agreement providing for the extension of some 2,360m. roubles in financial aid to Abkhazia. In the same month an agreement allowing a Russian military base to remain in the territory for 49 years was signed. On 30 April Russian President Dmitrii Medvedev signed border treaties with Abkhazia (and South Ossetia), which provided for Russia to guard the state borders of Abkhazia prior to the establishment of Abkhazian border forces. Meanwhile, separatist officials had given residents a deadline of 20 March, by which time they would be required to renounce their Georgian citizenship and receive Abkhazian (or Russian) passports.

A joint statement, issued in May 2009, by the opposition Forum of National Unity of Abkhazia (FNUA) and a war veterans' union strongly criticized Bagapsh after he granted various economic concessions, including the transfer of control, for a period of 10 years, over Abkhazia's airport and railways, to Russia. In late May the authorities signed a five-year agreement giving Rosneft, the Russian state-owned oil company, the right to prospect for petroleum and natural gas off Abkhazia's Black Sea coast. At the end of the month Khajimba resigned as Vice-President, following a number of disagreements with Bagapsh (the position remained vacant until February 2010).

On 12 August 2009 Putin, as Russian premier, visited Abkhazia to reaffirm Russian support for the separatist regime, announcing that Russia would finance the reinforcement of Abkhazia's borders and further Russian military operations within the territory, in addition to providing budgetary aid. On the same day two explosions in Sukhumi and Gagra killed two people and injured three. The

Abkhazian authorities blamed Georgian security services for the blasts. At the end of the month the Russian Army's Chief of the General Staff, Gen. Nikolai Makarov, stated that troop levels had been reduced to 1,700 in both Abkhazia and South Ossetia. In September Venezuela became the third state to recognize the independence of both Abkhazia and South Ossetia. (An Abkhazian embassy opened in the Venezuelan capital, Caracas, in July 2010, and Bagapsh subsequently made an official visit to the country.)

In the (internationally unrecognized) presidential election held on 12 December 2009, contested by five candidates, Bagapsh was overwhelmingly elected to a further term of office, receiving, according to official figures, 61.2% of the votes cast; his nearest rival was Khajimba, with 15.3%. The official rate of participation was 73.5%. On 12 February 2010 Bagapsh was inaugurated to a new presidential term, and Ankvab was appointed Vice-President; one day later he was replaced as Prime Minister by Sergei Shamba, hitherto Minister of Foreign Affairs. Khajimba was elected Chairman of the FNUA in May.

On 17 February 2010 Abkhazia signed an agreement with Russia allowing the construction of a land base at Gudauta, which would accommodate up to 3,000 Russian land troops for at least 49 years. In August, shortly after a visit to Abkhazia by President Medvedev, Russia announced that it had deployed anti-aircraft missiles in the territory; the EU expressed concern, stating that the deployment would be in contravention of the ceasefire agreement. On 7 September the UN General Assembly adopted a non-binding resolution (following similar resolutions in 2008 and 2009) reiterating the right of return of all displaced persons and refugees to breakaway Abkhazia and South Ossetia; in the same month Shamba stated that unless Georgia officially recognized Abkhazia's independence it would be impossible for ethnic Georgian refugees to return to the region. In a concession to demands by the Abkhaz and South Ossetian delegations in the ongoing negotiations in Geneva, President Saakashvili, addressing the European Parliament in November 2010, declared that Georgia would 'never use military force to restore its territorial integrity'; although the Presidents of Abkhazia and South Ossetia issued similar pledges, Russia welcomed the announcement without making a reciprocal affirmation.

The search for international recognition

On 29 May 2011 Bagapsh died, following a lung operation. In the ensuing election to the Abkhazian presidency, held on 26 August, Ankvab, who had been acting President since Bagapsh's death, was elected President, obtaining 54.9% of the votes cast in a poll contested by three candidates (including Shamba) and in which 71.9% of the electorate participated. On 26 September Ankvab was inaugurated as President, with Mikhail Logua serving as Vice-President. One day later Ankvab appointed Leonid Lakerbaya as Prime Minister, and a new Government was appointed during October.

Abkhazia has made only limited progress towards obtaining international recognition for the secessionist administration. In May 2011 the Pacific island state of Vanuatu announced that it had become the fifth state to recognize Abkhazian statehood (after Russia, Nicaragua, Venezuela and Nauru, while failing to extend such recognition to South Ossetia). Following the inauguration of a new Prime Minister in Vanuatu in June, recognition was rescinded, but it was reinstated in the following month. (However, in March 2013 the Vanuatu authorities announced that they had not extended formal recognition to Abkhazia, and instead announced the intention of entering into diplomatic relations with Georgia.) Tuvalu also recognized the statehood of Abkhazia in September, although in March 2014 it withdrew this recognition, instead establishing diplomatic relations with Georgia. Meanwhile, the Abkhazian authorities and Russia strongly opposed the Georgian Government's introduction in July of 'neutral' identity documents, which allowed residents of Abkhazia and South Ossetia to travel abroad without accepting Georgian citizenship.

On 22 February 2012 an assassination attempt against Ankvab was staged by unidentified assailants, who attacked the presidential convoy near Sukhumi, killing two of his bodyguards. The first round of elections to the Abkhazian secessionist legislature were held on 10 March, with a second round in 20 of the single-mandate constituencies on 24 March. It was announced by the region's electoral commission that independent candidates nominated by civic 'initiative groups' had secured 26 of the 35 seats, while the opposition FNUA had received four seats and United Abkhazia, which supported Ankvab, three seats. (Polls were to be repeated in two constituencies at a later date, owing, respectively, to insufficient voter turnout and electoral irregularities in the first round.) The opening session of the new National Assembly took place on 3 April, when a deputy of long standing, Valerii Bganba, was elected Speaker. Meanwhile, on 16 March, Medvedev announced the creation of a new post, of Representative of the Russian President to Abkhazia (similar posts were also created later that month for South Ossetia and the Moldovan secessionist territory of Transnistria). Aleksandr Tkachev, who had been recently appointed to a fourth term as the Governor of the neighbouring Krasnodar Krai (province) of Russia,

was appointed additionally to that role. By mid-April six suspects (of whom two were subsequently released) had been detained in the investigation into the assassination attempt against Ankvab. However, two of the suspects, including former Minister of Internal Affairs, Almasbei Kchach, were found dead during April, with both deaths being officially attributed to suicide.

In April 2012 the Abkhazian foreign ministry announced its withdrawal from meetings of the joint Incident Prevention and Response Mechanism (IPRM—undertaken between international security monitors and local security officials in the areas of tension since early 2009), accusing the head of the EUMM, Andrzej Tyszkiewicz, of bias and disrespect of Abkhazia's sovereignty, and demanding that he leave the region. Following postponement of IPRM meetings, the Abkhazian authorities declared that they were prepared to continue participation, on the condition that the EUMM would no longer be represented by Tyszkiewicz. In May 2012 the Russian Government announced that its security forces had discovered large caches of armaments in Abkhazia, and accused the Georgian authorities of supporting the terrorist activities of Chechen rebels. In June the Abkhazian authorities appealed to the UN, the USA and the Organization for Security and Co-operation in Europe (OSCE) to pressure the Georgian authorities to end what they termed as acts of terrorism in the border Gali district, claiming that they were responsible for the kidnapping of a number of civilians in the region. Georgia welcomed an OSCE resolution, adopted in June, which acknowledged Georgia's territorial integrity and referred to Abkhazia and South Ossetia as 'occupied territories'. Georgian Prime Minister Bidzina Ivanishvili, whose party coalition was elected to government in October, proposed the restoration of the railway link between Georgia and Russia via Abkhazia, while Ankvab indicated that he was willing to negotiate on the issue.

In February 2013 anti-Government protests, organized by Khajimba's FNEA in response to an increase in electricity costs and bread prices, were attended by around 1,500 people in Sukhumi. At further demonstrations in early March, Khajimba demanded that Lakerbaya's administration resign. In early April Giorgi Baramia resigned as Chairman of the Government of the Autonomous Republic of Abkhazia, based in Tbilisi and recognized by the Georgian authorities. Later in the month President Saakashvili refused to confirm in post his acting successor, Vakhtang Kolbaya, on the grounds that Kolbaya, an associate of the former Chairman of the Georgian legislature, Nino Burjanadze (who had become increasingly closely linked with the ruling authorities in Russia), was purportedly connected to the 'occupying forces'. (Consequently, Kolbaya remained formally acting Chairman.) Meanwhile, the FNEA criticized the issuing of Abkhazian passports to ethnic Georgians residents in the Gali district of eastern Abkhazia, on the grounds that the correct procedures for granting passports to non-ethnic Abkhaz were not being followed. In mid-June, a party congress of United Abkhazia announced the withdrawal of its support for President Ankvab, and that the party was, henceforth, to constitute part of the opposition. Although this decision was not without controversy (and resulted in the resignation of a proportion of the party's members), in the following month United Abkhazia was one of several political parties and groups, also including the FNEA, to form an opposition Co-ordination Council. In August Ankvab met Putin (who had returned to the Russian presidency in 2012) on two occasions, in Sochi, and in Abkhazia, in what appeared to be a demonstration of continued Russian support for his administration. On 9 September the First Secretary at the Russian Embassy in Sukhumi, Dmitrii Vishernev, was assassinated outside his home in the city; the killing was condemned by a joint statement of the members of the Abkhazian National Assembly as constituting not simply a crime, but also a determined attempt to undermine the territory's relations with Russia. It was announced that Ankvab would personally supervise the investigation into Vishernev's killing. In late September Putin appointed his close ally, Vladislav Surkov, as a presidential aide with special responsibilities for Russian socio-economic relations with Abkhazia and South Ossetia. Meanwhile, the participation of members of Russian Don Cossack organizations in commemorative parades held in Sukhumi on 30 September, to mark the 20th anniversary of Abkhazia's de facto independence, precipitated controversy, chiefly as a result of some of the imagery carried by members of these organizations, including references to the extreme Russian nationalist Black Hundreds organizations of pre-Soviet Russia.

On 10 July 2013 a Co-ordination Council of opposition parties was formed in Abkhazia; notably it included the United Abkhazia party, which, until the previous month, had supported the separatist President, Ankvab. In September 2013 the First Secretary at the Russian Embassy in Sukhumi, Dmitrii Vishernev, was assassinated outside his home in the city; a statement issued by the Abkhazian National Assembly condemned the killing, describing it as an attempt to undermine the territory's relations with Russia. It was announced that Ankvab would personally supervise the investigation into Vishernev's killing. In November a National Assembly deputy was charged with ordering the abduction and murder of Russian businessman Sergey Klemantovich and a female companion. In late December Logua announced his resignation as Vice-President, on the grounds of ill health. No replacement was appointed, and in early February 2014 Ankvab submitted draft constitutional legislation to the National Assembly providing for the abolition of the post of Vice-President.

Meanwhile, in January 2014 the Russian authorities unilaterally extended their border zone 11 km further into Abkhazia, purportedly to support increased security during the organization of the Sochi Winter Olympics in February (which were held in territories adjacent to Abkhazia), prompting strenuous protests from the new Georgian President, Giorgi Margvelashvili. Abkhazia also temporarily relaxed visa restrictions for foreign nationals seeking to enter the republic from Russia in an attempt to benefit economically from the event; however, the Georgian Government again protested that the decision constituted a violation of Georgian law and that such tourists would be liable for criminal prosecution. In the event, the intensified security measures imposed by Russia on the region, including the border zone, prior to the Games amid concerns of terrorist attacks, effectively suspended most cross-border traffic. Russia's annexation of the Crimean peninsula of Ukraine in February–March exacerbated tensions with the Georgian authorities; Ankhab declared recognition of the results of a referendum conducted in Crimea on 16 March (widely considered illegal by the international community), at which its population voted overwhelmingly in support of the territory joining Russia as a federal subject. In April the Abkhazian Minister of Foreign Affairs, Vyacheslav Chirikba, and his South Ossetian counterpart met Russian Minister of Foreign Affairs Sergei Lavrov in Moscow, where a trilateral co-operation plan between their respective ministries for 2014–15 was signed.

Ousting of Ankhab and early presidential election

In May 2014 a political confrontation developed in Abkhazia, following intensifying anti-Government demonstrations organized by the opposition Co-ordination Council, which was led by Khajimba's FNUA. President Ankvab declared that he was prepared to enter into a dialogue with the opposition, but rejected demands by the Co-ordination Council for the resignation of the Cabinet of Ministers and the Prosecutor-General, and the formation of a government of national unity. In addition to complaining at the alleged corruption and misappropriation of Russian aid funds by the Ankhab administration, the opposition protested that the authorities had granted Abkhaz citizenship to ethnic Georgians in eastern districts, and also sought closer links with Russia, including membership of its Customs Union (which became the Eurasian Economic Union in 2015). The Russian Government dispatched Surkov to mediate in the conflict, while declaring it to be an internal affair of Abkhazia. On 27 May several thousand supporters, led by the opposition groups, seized control of the presidential offices and the public television channel in Sukumi, forcing Ankhab to flee to a Russian base in Gugauta, north of the capital. The opposition on 29 May established a 21-member Provisional National Council, which adopted executive powers. The National Assembly declared Ankvab unable to exercise his presidential powers, appointed the Speaker, Valerii Bganba, as acting President, and scheduled an early presidential election for 24 August. Although Ankvab denounced the opposition action as a coup, he formally tendered his resignation on 1 June. His ally, Prime Minister Lakerbaya, resigned one day later. The incumbent Government officially remained in office in an interim capacity, with the hitherto First Deputy Prime Minister and Minister of Finance and the Economy Vladimir Delba becoming acting Prime Minister.

Bganba subsequently dismissed two deputy premiers (who were considered to be allies of Ankvab) and the heads of Gali, Tkvarcheli and Ochamchire districts, and on 5 June 2014 the National Assembly voted in favour of removing the Prosecutor-General. On 13 June Bganba ordered the Ministry of the Interior to refer to the Central Election Commission a list of ethnic Georgians in the eastern districts whose Abkhaz passports were judged to have been illegally issued, who would then be removed from the voters' list. Following a report by the Prosecutor-General's Office, initiated by opposition pressure, in April, Khajimba announced that 25,000–26,000 of these passport holders would be excluded from voting in the forthcoming presidential poll.

By July 2014 four candidates had successfully registered to contest the election (after dismissed deputy premier Beslan Eshba had been disqualified for failing an Abkhaz language test): Khajimba; the head of the security service, Aslan Bjania; Minister of Defence Mirab Kishmaria; and a former Minister of the Interior, Leonid Dzapshba. The candidates all signed a 15-point Social-Political Agreement on priorities for the next President, which included the preservation of the region's sovereign status, the suppression of corruption, and the drafting of social and economic development programmes and of a military doctrine. During the election campaign Khajimba's supporters temporarily occupied the state television and radio building with the stated intention of preventing a broadcast by Bjania's followers. In the same month a bomb attack was staged against

the Chairman of the Central Election Commission (who was unharmed).

On 24 August 2014 Khajimba, who (as in the December 2009 presidential poll) enjoyed open Russian support, was narrowly elected to the presidency with 50.6% votes cast; the second-placed candidate, Bjania, took 35.9%. Besla Butba, the incumbent acting Deputy Prime Minister and a former presidential candidate, was subsequently designated as the new premier. The Government of Georgia and the international community again denounced the election as illegitimate. Shortly after his election, Khajimba, meeting President Putin near Moscow, agreed to sign a new comprehensive co-operation treaty with Russia. Khajimba was inaugurated on 25 September, and a new Government, headed by the Chairman of the Party for the Economic Development of Abkhazia, Beslan Butba, was formed in mid-October. It was reported in November that Butba had been attacked and slightly injured in Sukhumi by assailants who were subsequently identified as being employees of the territory's customs department.

Recent developments: treaty with Russia

In October 2014 a draft bilateral 'Agreement on Alliance and Integration' proposed by Russia prompted controversy in Abkhazia and strenuous protests from the Georgian Government: it envisaged the creation of a combined group of armed forces, and of a joint law enforcement centre, the harmonization of legislation, and joint protection at Abkhazia's border with Georgia, together with freedom of movement across its border with Russia. In exchange for Abkhazia's acceptance of the agreement, Russia would make substantial financial investments, and increase social benefits for those of the population with Russian citizenship. Moreover, it was reported in October that the Russian authorities favoured the construction of a highway connecting Abkhazia to the North Caucasus. Later that month the Abkhazian authorities presented an amended version of the agreement: amongst other changes, the phrasing 'mutually agreed foreign policy' in the Russian draft became 'co-ordinated foreign policy', while a provision to facilitate procedures for Russians to obtain Abkhazian citizenship was removed. Despite continued objections in Abkhazia, notably a statement by the Public Chamber of Abkhazia that the accord could have future consequences for Abkhazia's sovereignty, the revised text, which was renamed the 'Agreement on Alliance and Strategic Partnership', was signed by Khajimba and Putin in Sochi on 24 November. On that day parallel demonstrations by supporters and opponents of the treaty were staged in Sukhumi, and its signature was denounced by Georgia as a further illegal move towards Abkhazia's annexation. Putin announced afterwards that Russia would allocate some 5,000m. roubles to Abkhazia for the implementation of the treaty's objectives in 2015, in addition to about 4,000m. roubles in investment for 2015–17. Also in November Butba signed a preliminary agreement with a Russian company on the reconstruction of the airport near Sukhumi.

In February 2015, when a border agreement was signed between Russia and South Ossetia, it was reported that signature of a similar accord between Abkhazia and Russia had been delayed by disagreement over territory around the border village of Aibga. During a visit to Sukhumi in that month, Russian presidential aide Vladislav Surkov declared that the border between Abkhazia and Russia should ultimately be abolished under the Alliance and Strategic Partnership treaty. Abkhazia's Minister of Foreign Affairs, Vyacheslav Chirikba, and his Russian counterpart, Sergei Lavrov, meeting in Moscow in March, signed a memorandum on carrying out co-ordinated foreign policy in accordance with the treaty. Lavrov also stated that the Russian Government was prepared to negotiate on the restoration of a railway link between Georgia and Russia via Abkhazia, while emphasizing that the Abkhazian and Georgian authorities would be responsible for agreeing terms for the initiative.

On 16 March 2014 Butba announced his resignation as Prime Minister, expressing frustration that many of the prime ministerial powers were being exercised by the presidential administration. On 20 March he was succeeded as Artur Mikvabia, a close associate of Khajimba and member of the National Assembly. A new, reorganized Government, in which several of the incumbent ministers were retained, was appointed on 10 April.

PUBLIC HOLIDAYS

2016: 1–2 January (New Year), 7 January (Christmas), 14 January (Azhurnyhua, Creation of the World and Renewal), 8 March (International Women's Day), 9 May (Victory Day), 12 September* (Kurbannykhua, Feast of the Sacrifice), 30 September (Liberation Day), 26 November (Constitution Day).

* This holiday is dependent on the Islamic lunar calendar and may vary by one or two days from the date given.

Directory

The Government of the 'Republic of Abkhazia'

PRESIDENT AND VICE-PRESIDENT

President: RAUL KHAJIMBA (elected 14 August 2014, inaugurated 25 September).

CABINET OF MINISTERS
(April 2015)

Prime Minister: ARTUR MIKVABIA.

First Deputy Prime Minister: SHAMIL ADZYNBA.

Deputy Prime Minister: DMITRII SERIKOV.

Minister of Foreign Affairs: VYACHESLAV CHIRIKBA.

Minister of Justice: MARINA PILIA.

Minister of Internal Affairs: RAUL LOLUA.

Minister of Defence: Gen. MIRAB KISHMARIA.

Minister of Emergency Situations: LEV KVITSINIA.

Minister of Taxes and Duties: RAUF TSIMTSBA.

Minister of Resorts and Tourism: AVTANDUL GARTSKIA.

Minister of Health: ANDZOR GOOV.

Minister of the Economy: ADGUR ARDZINBA.

Minister of Labour, Employment and Social Provision: SUREN KERSELYAN.

Minister of Finance: AMRA KVARANDZIA.

Minister of Agriculture: TIMUR ESHBA.

Minister of Education and Science: ADGURA KAKOBA.

Minister of Culture and the Protection of Historic-Cultural Heritage: ELVIRA AREALIA.

Note: The Chairmen of the State Customs Committee, and of the State Committees for Ecology and the Protection of Nature, the Management of State Property and Privatization, of Standards and Consumer and Technical Supervision, of Repatriation, of Physical Culture and Sport, and of Youth Affairs, are also members of the Cabinet of Ministers.

MINISTRIES

Office of the President: 384900 Sukhumi, nab. Makhajirov 32; tel. (840) 222-46-22; fax (840) 222-71-17; e-mail sukhum-krma@yandex.ru; internet www.abkhaziagov.org.

Office of the Cabinet of Ministers: 384900 Sukhumi, ul. nab. Makhajirov 32; tel. (840) 226-46-21; e-mail info@govabk.org.

Ministry of Agriculture: 384900 Sukhumi, ul. Lakoba 21; tel. (840) 226-19-05.

Ministry of Culture and the Protection of Historic-Cultural Heritage: 384900 Sukhumi, ul. Lakoba 21; tel. (840) 229-75-44; fax (840) 229-75-42; e-mail mc_ra@mail.ru; internet mkra.org.

Ministry of Defence: 384900 Sukhumi, Abjuiskoye shosse 57; tel. (840) 226-57-86.

Ministry of the Economy: 384900 Sukhumi, ul. Lakoba 21; tel. (840) 226-45-81.

Ministry of Education and Science: 384900 Sukhumi, ul. Zvanba 9; tel. (840) 226-46-51; e-mail minobr-ra@yandex.ru.

Ministry of Emergency Situations: 384900 Sukhumi.

Ministry of Finance: 384900 Sukhumi, ul. Lakoba 21; tel. (840) 226-30-05; e-mail minfinra@yandex.ru.

Ministry of Foreign Affairs: 384900 Sukhumi, ul. Lakoba 21; tel. (840) 226-70-69; fax (840) 226-34-45; e-mail info@mfaapsny.org; internet www.mfaapsny.org.

Ministry of Health: 384900 Sukhumi, ul. Zvanba 20; tel. and fax (840) 226-10-77; e-mail mz_apsny@rambler.ru.

Ministry of Internal Affairs: 384900 Sukhumi, ul. Akademika Marra 35; tel. (840) 229-72-73; e-mail minfinra@yandex.ru; internet mvdra.org.

Ministry of Justice: 384900 Sukhumi, ul. Lakoba 21; tel. (840) 226-67-66.

Ministry of Labour, Employment and Social Provision: 384900 Sukhumi, ul. Zvanba 9; tel. and fax (840) 226-97-13; e-mail mintruda@mail.ru.

Ministry of Resorts and Tourism: 384900 Sukhumi.

Ministry of Taxes and Duties: 384900 Sukhumi.

THE AUTONOMOUS REPUBLIC OF ABKHAZIA

Note: A nominal officially recognized Government of the territory, listed below, and a legislature, the Supreme Council, continued to be based in Tbilisi.

Chairman of the Government: VAKHTANG KOLBAYA.

Minister of Education and Culture: DMITRII JAIANI.

Minister of Finance and the Economy: MURMAN PARPALIA.

Minister of Health and Social Welfare: KETEVAN BAKARADZE.

Minister of Regional Management Affairs: KONSTANTIN KUCHU-KHIDZE.

Note: the Chairmen of the Departments for: Internally Displaced Persons' Affairs; Justice; and Agriculture, Environmental Protection and Natural Resources are also members of the Government of the Autonomous Republic of Abkhazia.

Representative Office of the Government of the Autonomous Republic of Abkhazia: 0186 Tbilisi, Kazbegi 42; tel. (32) 237-61-44; fax (32) 37-46-22; e-mail info@abkhazia.gov.ge; internet www.abkhazia.gov.ge.

President

Presidential Election, 24 August 2014

Candidates	Votes	%
Raul Khajimba	50,586	50.60
Aslan Bjania	35,869	35.88
Mirab Kishmaria	6,390	6.39
Leonid Dzapshba	3,397	3.40
Against all candidates	1,870	1.87
Total*	99,966	100.00

* Including 1,854 invalid votes (1.85% of the total).

Legislature

The National Assembly of the 'Republic of Abkhazia'
384900 Sukhumi, ul. Zvanba 1; tel. (840) 226-65-39; e-mail mail@parlamentra.org; internet www.parlamentra.org.

Speaker: VALERII BGANBA.

General Election, 10 March and 24 March 2012*

Parties and blocs	Seats
Independents	27
Forum of National Unity of Abkhazia	4
United Abkhazia	3
Communist Party of Abkhazia	1
Total	35

* Including the result of repeat elections held in one constituency on 6 May, and in another constituency on 20 May and 3 June.

Election Commission

Central Election Commission: Sukhumi; Chair. BATAL TABAGUA.

Political Organizations

The following are among the principal political parties to operate in Abkhazia.

Communist Party of Abkhazia (Apkhazetis Komunisturi Partiya): 384900 Sukhumi; f. 1921; reconstituted 1991; Pres. LEV SHAMBA.

Forum of National Unity of Abkhazia (FNEA) (Apkhazetis Erovnuli Ertianobis Phorumi): 384900 Sukhumi; f. 2005 as social organization, constituted as political party in 2008; mem. of opposition Co-ordination Council, established Jul. 2013; Chair. RAUL KHAJIMBA.

Party for the Economic Development of Abkhazia (Partiya ERA) (Apkhazetis Ekonomikuri Ganvitarebis Partiya): 384900 Sukhumi, ul. Lakoba 34; tel. (8402) 26-04-44; e-mail info@era-abkhazia.org; internet www.era-abkhazia.org; f. 2007; economically reformist, supportive of business interests, mem. of opposition Co-ordination Council, established Jul. 2013; Chair. BESLAN BUTBA.

People's Party of Abkhazia (Kiaraz): 384900 Sukhumi, ul. Guliya 6; tel. (840) 226-19-57; fax (840) 226-17-77; internet www.kiaraz.org; f. 1992; democratic centralist; mem. of opposition Co-ordination Council, established Jul. 2013; Chair. YAKUB LAKOBA.

Republican Party of Abkhazia (Respublikuri Partiya Apkhazetis): 384900 Sukhumi; Chair. IVLIAN KHAINDRAVA.

Social Democratic Party of Abkhazia (Sotsialur Demokratiuli Partiis Apkhazetis): 384900 Sukhumi; f. 2004; Chair. GENNADY ALAMIYA.

United Abkhazia (Ertiani Apkhazetis): 384900 Sukhumi; f. 2004 as a socio-political movement, constituted as political party 2009; formerly supportive of administration of Pres. Ankvab, but joined opposition Co-ordination Council, established Jul. 2013; Chair. DAUR TARBA.

Diplomatic Representation

EMBASSY IN ABKHAZIA

At April 2015 the 'Republic of Abkhazia' was officially recognized by the four UN member states of Nauru, Nicaragua, Russia and Venezuela. Three other unrecognized secessionist territories in the post-Soviet space—Nagornyi Karabakh, South Ossetia and Transnistria—also stated their recognition of Abkhazia's statehood. By 2015 only Russia and the unrecognized 'Republic of South Ossetia' maintained embassies in Abkhazia.

Russian Federation: 384900 Sukhumi, ul. Lakoba 103; tel. (840) 226-91-04; fax (840) 226-36-93; e-mail rusembsukhum@mail.ru; internet www.abkhazia.mid.ru; Ambassador SEMEN V. GRIGORIYEV.

The Press

In 2012, besides the newspaper *Respublika Abkhaziya* and the news agency Apsnypress, both of which were owned by the secessionist authorities, there were several private newspapers. Their circulation ranged from 1,000 to 5,000.

PRINCIPAL NEWSPAPERS

Chegemskaya Pravda (The Chegem Truth): 384900 Sukhumi, ul. Jonua 6; f. 2004; in Russian; weekly; Editor-in-Chief INAL KHASHIG; circ. 1,100 (2011).

Ekho Abkhazii (Echo of Abkhazia): 384900 Sukhumi, ul. Adigalar 34; f. 2001; weekly; in Russian; Editor VITALI SHARIA.

Novyi Den (New Day): 384900 Sukhumi; weekly; pro-opposition; Editor SERGEI ARUTINOV.

Nuzhnaya Gazeta (The Essential Newspaper): 384900 Sukhumi; tel. (940) 921-78-75; e-mail izika@mail.ru; internet www.abh-ng.ru; f. 1997; weekly; Russian; Editor-in-Chief IZIDA CHANIA; circ. 3,000 (2011).

Respublika Abkhaziya (The Republic of Abkhazia): 384900 Sukhumi; tel. (840) 226-89-89; internet www.gazeta-ra.info; owned by the authorities of the 'Republic of Abkhazia'; Russian; 3 a week; Chief Editor V. CHAMAGUA; weekly circ. 3,130 (2012).

NEWS AGENCY

Apsnypress: 384900 Sukhumi, Zvanba 9; tel. (840) 226-41-37; e-mail apsnypress@mail.ru; internet www.apsnypress.info; f. 1995; owned by the authorities of the 'Republic of Abkhazia'; Dir MANANA GURGULIA.

Finance

(cap. = capital; res = reserves; dep. = deposits; m. = million)

BANKING

Central Bank

National Bank of the 'Republic of Abkhazia': 384900 Sukhumi, ul. Leona 14; tel. (840) 229-76-23; fax (840) 229-76-22; e-mail info@a.nb-ra.org; internet www.nb-ra.org; f. 1991; cap. US $370.0m.; Chair. BESLAN BARATELIA.

Trade and Industry

CHAMBER OF COMMERCE

Chamber of Commerce and Industry: Sukhumi, Konfederatov 37; tel. (840) 226-33-87; e-mail info@tppra.org; internet www.tppra.org; f. 2002; Pres. GENNADY L. GAGULIA.

SOUTH OSSETIA

Introductory Survey

STATUS

The self-styled 'Republic of South Ossetia' declared its independence from the Georgian Soviet Socialist Republic in September 1990. In response, the Georgian authorities formally abolished the nominally autonomous status of the territory, and violent conflict broke out. This continued until 1992, following which many areas that had been included in the former South Ossetian Autonomous Oblast enjoyed a de facto independence from Georgia, although the formal status of the territory remained unresolved. There was renewed conflict in 2008, when Russia intervened to support the South Ossetian separatists, who succeeded in obtaining control of those sections of territory in the region that had remained under Georgian control. Later that year Russia formally announced that it recognized the statehood of the 'Republic of South Ossetia'. A small number of other countries subsequently extended recognition to the separatist authorities.

LOCATION, CLIMATE, LANGUAGE, RELIGION, FLAG, CAPITAL

South Ossetia is situated in the north of Georgia, and covers an area of 3,900 sq km. It borders Russia (principally the Republic of North Osetiya—Alaniya) to the north, the boundary comprising part of the Great Caucasus Range, while the remainder of Georgia lies to the west, south and east. The climate of South Ossetia is milder than that of the North Caucasus, although snowfall can occur in the highlands at any time of year. Average temperatures in Tshkhinvali range from 5°C (41°F) in January to 20°C (68°F) in July. Precipitation in southern lowland regions averages 350 mm–600 mm per year, but amounts to 1,000 mm–1,800 mm in the highlands. The population speak Ossetian, an Indo-European language of the Persian group commonly written in the Cyrillic script, while Russian and Georgian are also in use. Most Ossetians are adherents of Orthodox Christianity. The separatist authorities use a flag (proportions 1 by 2) with three equal horizontal stripes, of white, red and yellow. The principal city and capital of the self-proclaimed 'Republic' is Tshkhinvali.

CONTEMPORARY POLITICAL HISTORY

Historical Context

Ossetia (Osetiya), the original inhabitants of which are an Orthodox Christian East Iranian people, was divided into two territories under the Soviet leader Stalin (Iosif Dzhugashvili, 1924–53), with North Osetiya (later North Osetiya—Alaniya) falling under Russian jurisdiction as a nominally Autonomous Republic and South Ossetia assuming the lesser status of an Autonomous Oblast (region) within Georgia. At the census of 1979 ethnic Ossetians comprised 66% of the oblast's population. The long-standing Georgian animosity towards the Ossetians was exacerbated by the Ossetians' traditional pro-Russian stance. Tensions intensified in 1989, when Ossetian demands for greater autonomy and eventual reunification with North Osetiya (and thus integration into Russia) led to violent clashes between local Georgians and Ossetians. Troops of the Soviet Ministry of Internal Affairs were dispatched to South Ossetia in January 1990, but in September the South Ossetian Supreme Soviet (legislature) proclaimed South Ossetia's independence from Georgia (as the 'South Ossetian Soviet Democratic Republic') and its state sovereignty within the USSR. This decision was declared unconstitutional by the Georgian Supreme Soviet, which in December revoked the region's nominally autonomous status. Following renewed violence, the Georgian legislature declared a state of emergency in Tskhinvali, the principal city in South Ossetia.

Domestic Political Affairs

In January 1991 Soviet President Mikhail Gorbachev annulled both South Ossetia's declaration of independence and the Georgian Supreme Soviet's decision of December 1990. Violence continued throughout 1991, with the resulting displacement of many thousands of refugees. In December the South Ossetian Supreme Soviet declared a state of emergency and a general mobilization, in response to the Georgian Government's dispatch of troops to the region. In the same month the South Ossetian legislature adopted a second declaration of the region's independence, as well as a resolution in favour of its integration into Russia. The resolutions were endorsed at a referendum held in the region in January 1992. Hostilities continued, compounded by the intervention of Georgian government troops.

In June 1992 negotiations between Georgian leader Eduard Shevardnadze and President Boris Yeltsin of Russia led to an agreement to secure a resolution to the conflict (in which more than 400 Georgians and 1,000 Ossetians had been killed since 1989). Joint Peacekeeping Forces (JPKF), comprising Georgian, Ossetian and Russian troops, were deployed in July 1992, and the return of refugees began. An Organization for Security and Co-operation in Europe (OSCE) mission to Georgia was established in December. However, some parts of South Ossetia remained effectively a seceded territory; on 23 December 1993 the separatist authorities introduced a new 'Constitution', which referred to the 'Republic of South Ossetia'. (The region was characterized by the existence of areas controlled either by supporters of the central Government in Tbilisi, or of the separatist 'Republic', a state of affairs that continued until 2008.) In July 1995 representatives from Georgia, Russia, North Osetiya and South Ossetia reopened talks on a political settlement, under the aegis of the OSCE. Following a series of meetings between President Shevardnadze and Ludvig Chibirov, the Chairman of the South Ossetian legislature, to negotiate South Ossetia's political status, in September 1996 the separatist legislature approved an amendment to its Constitution to allow the introduction of a presidential system of government; Chibirov was elected 'President' on 10 November.

Quadripartite negotiations were held throughout 1997. Talks held in Moscow in March confirmed the principle of Georgia's territorial integrity, while allowing a measure of self-determination for South Ossetia. In September Shevardnadze and Chibirov signed an agreement on the return of refugees to South Ossetia. Legislative elections took place in the separatist-controlled regions of South Ossetia in May 1999; the local Communist Party (CP) secured about 39% of the votes cast. In April 2001 a referendum was held in South Ossetia, at which 69% of those who participated voted in favour of adopting amendments to the 1993 Constitution, including the designation of both Georgian and Russian as official languages, in addition to Ossetian.

Eduard Kokoyev (Kokoiti) elected President

In a presidential election held in November–December 2001 a Russian-based businessman, Eduard Kokoyev (Kokoiti), emerged as the victor, after a second round of voting, securing 55% of the votes cast. Kokoyev was inaugurated on 18 December. Kokoyev subsequently consolidated his power in the territory, and his Unity Party won a majority of seats in legislative elections held on 23 May 2004.

Proposals for the granting to South Ossetia of broad autonomy, presented by the Georgian Government of President Mikheil Saakashvili in 2004–05, were consistently rejected by the separatist leadership. In early 2006 the Sakartvelos Parlamenti (Georgian Parliament) adopted a resolution, urging the Government to replace Russian peacekeepers deployed in South Ossetia as part of the JPKF with an international force, following concern that Russian troops had been providing armaments to separatists. Amid rising tensions, in July Oleg Alborov, secretary of South Ossetia's 'National Security Council', was killed when a bomb exploded outside his residence in Tskhinvali. South Ossetian officials alleged that the attack had been staged at the orders of Georgia. In August South Ossetian officials began issuing Russian passports to residents of the territory, provoking outrage from Georgia; it was reported in 2007 that most of the citizens in those regions under separatist control had been issued with Russian passports.

On 12 November 2006 a presidential election was held in those areas of South Ossetia controlled by the separatist authorities. Kokoyev was overwhelmingly elected to a second term in office, reportedly attracting 98.1% of the votes cast. The poll coincided with a referendum on whether South Ossetia should preserve its de facto independent status. Results released by the 'South Ossetian Central Election Commission' indicated that 99% of those who voted had cast their ballots in favour of independence; voter turnout was reported to be 95.2% of the registered electorate. Concurrently, what was termed an 'alternative election' for a regional President was held in the Georgian-controlled South Ossetian territories; this poll was won by Dmitry Sanakoyev, a former rebel leader. A referendum held in these territories also overwhelmingly expressed approval for the commencement of negotiations with the central authorities in Tbilisi on the establishment of a federal Georgian state, of which South Ossetia would form a unit. Although these polls were not officially recognized, nationally or internationally, Sanakoyev adopted the title 'President of South Ossetia' and announced the formation of an alternative 'Government', based in the village of Kurta, in December. On 10 May 2007 Sanakoyev became head of the new Provisional Administration of South Ossetia, officially established under a resolution by the Georgian Parliament on 8 May.

Renewed military conflict

From early 2008 peacekeeping officials reported an increasing number of ceasefire violations in South Ossetia. In July the Russian authorities acknowledged that four Russian aircraft had entered airspace over the region. The South Ossetian separatist authorities reported that six people were killed in a Georgian bombardment of Tskhinvali on 1 August, although Georgia claimed that South Ossetian forces had initiated the hostilities. Following further exchanges of fire and shelling, on 3 August the separatist South Ossetian authorities began to evacuate children to Russia.

On 7–8 August 2008 Georgian troops commenced a concerted offensive, including an aerial bombardment, against Tskhinvali; the Georgian Government announced that its troops had entered the city and had secured control of most of South Ossetia, stating that its purpose was to 'restore constitutional order'. In response, Russia deployed large numbers of troops into South Ossetia, purportedly to protect the security of Russian citizens resident there. After an intensive counter-offensive, the Russian military (supported by volunteer militias, particularly from Chechnya) rapidly claimed to have gained control of Tskhinvali and repulsed the Georgian troops; the separatists also gained control of neighbouring regions hitherto under Georgian control. Looting, retaliatory attacks against ethnic Georgians and burning of Georgian villages were subsequently reported by human rights organizations. In a statement subsequently shown to be greatly exaggerated, the Russian President, Dmitrii Medvedev, accused Georgia of perpetrating 'genocide' against the ethnic Ossetian population, and alleged that up to 2,000 people had been killed as a result of the Georgian attack on Tskhinvali. Russian aircraft commenced bombardment of Georgian targets, including the port of Poti and the military base at Senaki. On 26 August Russia recognized South Ossetia and Abkhazia as independent, sovereign states. Georgia, the USA and the European Union (EU) condemned the decision.

Following an EU-mediated peace agreement, reached on 8 September 2008, the deployment of an EU Monitoring Mission (EUMM) commenced in Georgia on 1 October (although the authorities of South Ossetia and Abkhazia refused monitors access to their territories); the Russian Government had announced that 3,800 Russian troops were to remain in each of South Ossetia and Abkhazia. On 17 September Russia signed friendship, economic and military co-operation treaties with the leaders of South Ossetia and Abkhazia. On 3 October a car bomb at a Russian military base near Tskhinvali killed nine troops; Kokoyev attributed the attack to Georgian special forces. On 22 October Aslanbek Bulantsev, previously the head of the Russian Federal Security Service (FSB) directorate's financial department in Vladikavkaz, North Osetiya—Alaniya, was appointed Chairman of the Government (prime minister), replacing Yurii Morozov. A report by US-based Human Rights Watch, issued in January 2009, concluded that South Ossetian forces had perpetrated numerous abuses against ethnic Georgians in the territory, including abductions and killings. In March the Russian Government signed an agreement providing for the extension of some 2,800m. roubles in financial aid to South Ossetia; the territory was also to receive 8,500m. roubles in post-conflict reconstruction aid. On 29 March a Georgian policeman died and six others were injured in an explosion while patrolling the borders of South Ossetia; 11 other police officers had been killed in the region since the imposition of the official ceasefire.

In April 2009 the electoral commission refused to register the opposition People's Party, led by Roland Kelekhsayev, to contest legislative elections in the following month; a few days previously it had permitted a newly established group, which the opposition claimed comprised allies of Kokoyev, to register as the People's Party of the Republic of South Ossetia (PP). It also rejected the candidacy of Vyacheslav Gobozov, the Chairman of the opposition Fatherland Republican Party of South Ossetia (Fatherland). In the elections, held on 31 May, three parties, all of which were perceived as broadly supportive of Kokoyev, won seats in the legislature. Kokoyev's Unity South Ossetian Republican Political Party (Unity) received 46.3% of the votes cast and secured 17 seats; the PP won 22.6% of the votes cast and nine seats, while the CP obtained 22.2% of the vote and eight seats.

Following a series of reported disputes over the control of reconstruction funding, Kokoyev dismissed Bulantsev as Chairman of the Government on 3 August 2009. Vadim Brovtsev, the head of a firm producing construction materials in Chelyabinsk, Russia, was appointed to the post the following day. The anniversary of the declaration of independence—which was formally recognized only at that time by Russia and Nicaragua (although Venezuela and Nauru extended recognition later in the year)—was marked by the renewed affirmation of support from the Russian leadership. An official ceremony, staged in Tskhinvali in August, marked the inauguration of a gas pipeline, financed by the Russian state-controlled corporation, Gazprom, linking South Ossetia with North Osetiya—Alaniya, enabling the region to receive gas directly from Russia. In September Russia and South Ossetia signed a defence agreement permitting Russia to maintain military bases in the territory for a period of at least 49 years.

The publication of an independent fact-finding report in September 2009, supported by the EU, was a cause of contention in both Georgia and Russia. The report concluded that Georgia had instigated the conflict, and that its initial attack upon Tshkhinvali was not warranted by international law, while Russia's military response was described as disproportionate, and its recognition of South Ossetia and Abkhazia as independent states as in violation of international law.

In April 2010 Brovtsev attracted increasing government and media pressure, owing to allegations of official involvement by the separatist authorities in the embezzlement of Russian funds allocated for reconstruction. During the ongoing negotiations in Geneva, Switzerland, President Saakashvili, addressing the European Parliament in November, declared that Georgia would 'never use military force to restore its territorial integrity'; although the Presidents of Abkhazia and South Ossetia issued similar pledges, Russia made no reciprocal affirmation. In January 2011 Russian and South Ossetian troops conducted joint military exercises in the territory.

The 2011 and 2012 presidential elections

On 15 June 2011 the Supreme Court of South Ossetia ruled against proposals to hold a constitutional referendum, providing for the abolition of restrictions on the number of terms a president was permitted to serve, deciding that the legislature was permitted to authorize such a measure. On 5 October the South Ossetian legislature voted to remove Stanislav Kochiyev as its Chairman, in protest against his persistent opposition to the proposed constitutional changes. The presidential election, which was conducted on 13 and 27 November, appeared to have been won in the second round by the former Minister of Education, Alla Jioyeva, who defeated the Russian-supported candidate, Anatolii Bibilov, receiving around 59% of the votes cast. (Also on 13 November a referendum was held, at which 83.5% of votes cast, with a voter turnout of about 65%, were in favour of making Ossetian and Russian the territory's official languages.) On 29 November the Supreme Court upheld a challenge to the election result by Bibilov and ordered that a new poll be conducted, in which Jioyeva was to be barred from participating owing to alleged irregularities in her campaign. Popular protests ensued and the arrest of a number of local activists was reported. Jioyeva denounced the planned repeated poll as illegitimate and announced her intention to stage her own 'inauguration' ceremony on 10 February 2012. On 9 February, however, she was hospitalized, during a raid on her offices by security forces. In the first round of the repeated election, held on 25 February and contested by four candidates, the head of the region's security service, Leonid Tibilov was placed first, with 42.5% of the votes cast, according to preliminary figures, and his nearest challenger was a special envoy for human rights issues, David Sanakoyev, with 24.6%. (Bibilov did not contest the election.) At the 'run-off' poll, held on 8 April, Tibilov was elected to the presidency, with 54.1% of the votes cast. Sanakoyev officially recognized the legitimacy of the election results, while urging that alleged incidents of irregularities be investigated. Tibilov was inaugurated as President on 19 April. On 25 April Tibilov signed a decree dismissing Brovtsev as acting premier, and appointed Rostik Khugayev, a businessman from Samara, Russia, as his successor. Tibilov announced that an investigation was to be opened into alleged widespread corruption and embezzlement (in particular, of funding supplied by Russia for post-war reconstruction) by the outgoing administration, and announced that he intended to form a 'government of national unity'. At the end of May Sanakoyev was appointed as Minister of Foreign Affairs, replacing the long-standing incumbent, Murat Jioyev, who became Tibilov's special envoy for post-conflict resolution issues. Alla Jioyeva was appointed as a Deputy Chairman of the Government, while Bibilov became Minister of Civil Defence, Emergency Situations and Clean-up Operations.

Meanwhile, on 26 March 2012 Medvedev announced the creation of a new post, of Representative of the Russian President to South Ossetia (similar posts were also created in the same month for Abkhazia and the Moldovan secessionist territory of Transnistria). Taimuraz Mamsurov, the head of the neighbouring Republic (within the Russian Federation) of North Osetiya—Alaniya, was appointed additionally to that role. The Georgian authorities welcomed an OSCE resolution, adopted in June, that acknowledged Georgia's territorial integrity and referred to Abkhazia and South Ossetia as 'occupied territories'. (At that time the statehood of the 'Republic of South Ossetia' was still only recognized by five countries—Russia, Nicaragua, Venezuela, Nauru and Tuvalu—and of these Tuvalu subsequently, in March 2014, withdrew recognition.)

In August 2012 the Georgian Government condemned an official visit by President Medvedev to Tskhinvali as in contravention of the Law On Occupied Territories of Georgia, adopted in October 2008, which imposed restrictions on entry to the regions. In September 2012 an unsuccessful attempt was made to kill South Ossetia's Deputy Minister of Defence with an explosive device; later that month the South Ossetian authorities announced that their troops had arrested an official of the Georgian Ministry of Internal Affairs, following an attack on a border security post. In January 2013 Tibilov declared that the new Georgian Government headed by Bidzina Ivanishvili, which was installed in October 2012, had failed to resolve human rights issues in accordance with pre-election pledges: in particular, that the Law On Occupied Territories remained in force,

and that South Ossetian citizens who had been convicted in Georgia remained in detention, despite the Georgian legislature's approval, in December 2012, of an amnesty for a large number of political prisoners. In the same month the South Ossetian Ministry of Justice registered three new political parties, among them one led by Sanakoyev, New Ossetia, and another led by Bibilov, United Ossetia.

As concerns about corruption (and, in particular, the associated failure to rehouse permanently some of those displaced by the 2008 conflict) in South Ossetia continued, the Prosecutor-General appointed by Tibilov, former Chairman of the Government Merab Chigoyev (a member of the CP) opened numerous criminal investigations into cases of corruption; by mid-2013 international arrest warrants had been requested against three former government officials. Meanwhile, Russia reduced the level of assistance funding allocated to South Ossetia, having conducted its own enquiry into the embezzlement of funding in the territory.

Tibilov met Russian President Vladimir Putin in Sochi for discussions in May 2013. A decision, implemented by the Russian military in that month, to unilaterally amend the South Ossetian administrative border with the remainder of Georgia, resulting in a slight expansion of the areas of the territory under separatist control, provoked considerable controversy, and also led to a number of arrests of Georgians deemed to have illicitly crossed the border. The subsequent construction of barbed wire fencing along the new de facto border (which resumed in early 2014) prompted further vehement protests from the Georgian Government and expressions of concern from the international community.

Meanwhile, controversy surrounded the future status of South Ossetia: while both Medvedev and Putin had described the recognition of South Ossetia as an independent state as irreversible, discussion continued on possible unification with North Osetiya, or on the eventual admission of South Ossetia to the Russian-led Customs Union (which became the Eurasian Economic Union in 2015). In September 2013 Putin appointed a close ally, Vladislav Surkov, as a presidential aide with special responsibilities for Russian socio-economic relations with Abkhazia and South Ossetia. The South Ossetian authorities signed wide-ranging co-operation agreements with North Osetiya and another Russian territory in the North Caucasus, the Karachai-Cherkess Republic, in November. Under a decree issued in January 2014, the Russian Government was to provide financial aid of some 1,000m. roubles annually to South Ossetia during 2014–16. In early January Bibilov's United Ossetia (UO) demanded that Tibilov schedule concurrently with forthcoming legislative elections a referendum on South Ossetia's proposed unification with North Osetiya within the Russian Federation. On 20 January Tibilov dismissed Khugayev's Government, citing delays in post-war reconstruction, and increasing social and economic problems, and also acknowledging the previous misappropriation of Russian funds. Domenti Kulumbegov, First Deputy Chairman of the Government since June 2013, and who had also served as deputy premier under Kokoiti, was appointed acting Chairman, and the outgoing Cabinet of Ministers remained in office in an interim capacity.

Russia's annexation of the Crimean peninsula of Ukraine in February–March 2014 exacerbated tensions with the Georgian authorities; the South Ossetian Ministry of Foreign Affairs expressed recognition of the results of a referendum conducted in Crimea on 16 March (widely considered illegal by the international community), at which its population voted overwhelmingly in support of the territory joining Russia as a federal subject. On 2 April Tibilov formally appointed Kulumbegov as Chairman of the Government, after Parliament had endorsed his nomination. Later in the month several of the incumbent ministers were formally confirmed in their existing positions, while other members of the outgoing administration further continued to remain in office in an acting capacity, pending the formation of a new Government. Meanwhile, in March Tibilov scheduled South Ossetian legislative elections for 8 June. In April Alla Jioyeva was replaced as Deputy Chairman of the Government by Erik Pukhayev. Also in April the respective Ministers of Foreign Affairs of South Ossetia and Abkhazia met the Russian Minister of Foreign Affairs, Sergei Lavrov, in Moscow, where a trilateral co-operation plan between their ministries for 2014–15 was signed.

Recent developments: closer relations with Russia

The elections on 8 June 2014, which were contested by eight political parties, resulted in a dramatic change in the composition of Parliament. UO won an overwhelming majority with 43.0% of votes cast and 20 seats, while newly-emerged organizations, the People's Unity Socialist Party and Front took, respectively, 13.2% and six seats, and 7.5% and four seats; in contrast, Unity and the CP failed to retain any parliamentary representation, and the Narodnaya Partiya obtained only 9.1% and four seats. In view of Bibilov's declared objective that South Ossetia unite with North Osetiya—Alaniya within the Russian Federation, concerns were voiced internationally that the election results (in conjunction with a political takeover in Abkhazia) would increase the potential for Russia to annex the regions. Later in

June South Ossetia formally recognized the independence of the self-proclaimed 'People's Republics' of Donetsk and Luhansk that had been established by separatist forces in eastern Ukraine. Demands led by Bibilov subsequently increased for the organization of a referendum, similar to that held in Crimea, on South Ossetia joining the Russian Federation.

In November 2014, when a comprehensive defence and security agreement was signed between Russia and Abkhazia, the authorities of South Ossetia announced that a similar treaty, providing for even deeper integration, was being prepared for the territory. It was subsequently reported that signature of the treaty had been delayed by the aspirations of Bibilov and his supporters for full accession to the Russian Federation. In January 2015 seven South Ossetian opposition parties complained at the process and demanded that the draft treaty be published. However, on 18 February Lavrov and Sanakoyev signed a border agreement between their respective states, prompting further protests from the Georgian Government. Amid Georgia's orientation towards the North Atlantic Treaty Organization (NATO), in February local media outlets also circulated Russian statements that certain border regions of Georgia should be reunified with South Ossetia. On 6 March President Putin endorsed the draft treaty, under which the armed forces, security agencies and customs services of South Ossetia would be merged with those of Russia, and (as in Abkhazia) a joint information co-ordinating centre of law enforcement agencies would be established. The Russian authorities were in exchange to finance a gradual rise in the salaries of South Ossetian state employees to the level in the North Caucasus, and to increase the pensions of those holding Russian passports from 2016. On 13 March Parliament voted in support of a motion of no confidence in Sanakoyev as Minister of Foreign Affairs; his removal from office was to depend upon the decision of President Tibilov, or upon a second legislative vote of no confidence within a period of two months. The motion had been presented by UO deputies, led by Bibilov, who expressed discontent that Sanakoyev had made public a revised draft of the treaty with Russia in January, as well as the fact that, several years after Venezuela and Nicaragua had formally recognized South Ossetian statehood, no ambassadors had been appointed to represent South Ossetia to those countries. After a postponement, the 'Treaty on Alliance and Integration' was signed by Tibilov and Putin on 18 March, and was ratified by Parliament on 3 April. Meanwhile, Tibilov had failed to effect Sanakoyev's removal and a vote on a second motion of no confidence on 15 April had been prevented by the absence of minority deputies, while the dispute had also caused antagonism between Bibilov and judicial institutions.

PUBLIC HOLIDAYS

2016: 1–2 January (New Year), 7 January (Christmas), 8 March (International Women's Day), 29 April–2 May (Easter), 1 May (Labour Day), 9 May (Victory Day), 26 August (Independence Day), 21 September (Madymyram (Nativity of the Blessed Virgin Mary).

Directory

The Government of the 'Republic of South Ossetia'

HEAD OF STATE

President: LEONID TIBILOV (elected 8 April 2012, inaugurated 19 April).

CABINET OF MINISTERS
(April 2015)

Chairman: DOMENTI KULUMBEGOV.

Head of the Presidential Administration: BORIS CHOCHIYEV.

Head of the Government Apparatus: OLEG GAGLOYEV.

Deputy Chairman: ALAN TEKHOV.

Deputy Chairman: ERIK PUKHAYEV.

Minister of Agriculture: MAIRBEG GUCHMAZOV.

Minister of Foreign Affairs: DAVID SANAKOYEV.

Minister of Defence: VALERII YAKHNOVETS.

Minister of Internal Affairs: AKHSAR LAVOYEV.

Minister of Civil Defence, Emergency Situations and Clean-up Operations: SERGEI SANAKOYEV.

Minister of Justice: ALAN JIOYEV.

Minister of Finance: AZA KHABALOVA.

Minister of Economic Development: VILYAM DZAGOYEV.

Minister of Education and Science: MARINA CHIBIROVA.

Minister of Health and Social Development: GRIGORII KULIJANOV.

Minister of Culture: MADINA OSTAYEVA.

Minister of Construction, Architecture, and Housing and Community Services: EDUARD DZAGOYEV.

MINISTRIES

Office of the Presidency and Government: 100001 Tskhinvali, Govt House, ul. Stalina 18; tel. and fax (9974) 45-25-52; e-mail ospress@mail.ru; internet presidentruo.org.

Ministry of Agriculture: 100001 Tskhinvali, ul. Khetgurova 1; tel. (1) 45-00-01; fax (44) 45–47–63.

Ministry of Construction, Architecture, and Housing and Community Services: 100001 Tskhinvali, ul. Khetgurova 1; tel. (9974) 45-00-01; fax (44) 45-47-63.

Ministry of Civil Defence, Emergency Situations and Clean-up Operations: 100001 Tskhinvali, ul. Khetgurova 1; tel. (9974) 45-00-01; fax (44) 45-47-63.

Ministry of Culture: 100001 Tskhinvali, ul. Stalina 12; tel. (9974) 45-34-81.

Ministry of Defence: 100001 Tskhinvali, ul. Khetgurova 1; tel. (9974) 45-00-01; fax (44) 45-47-63.

Ministry of Economic Development: 100001 Tskhinvali, ul. Khetgurova 1; tel. (9974) 45-00-01; fax (44) 45-47-63.

Ministry of Education and Science: 100001 Tskhinvali, ul. Khetgurova 1; tel. (9974) 45-00-01; fax (44) 45-47-63.

Ministry of Finance: 100001 Tskhinvali, ul. Stalina 18, 4th Floor; tel. (9974) 45-26-52; e-mail ospress@yandex.ru.

Ministry of Foreign Affairs: 100001 Tskhinvali, ul. Stalina 18, 4th Floor; tel. and fax (9974) 45-22-43; e-mail mfa-rso@mail.ru; internet mfa-rso.su.

Ministry of Health and Social Development: 100001 Tskhinvali, ul. Khetgurova 1; tel. (9974) 45-00-01; fax (44) 45-47-63.

Ministry of Internal Affairs: 100001 Tskhinvali, ul. Khetgurova 1; tel. (9974) 45-00-01; fax (44) 45-47-63.

Ministry of Justice: 100001 Tskhinvali, ul. Khetgurova 1; tel. (9974) 45-00-01; fax (44) 45-47-63.

President

Presidential Election, First Round, 25 March 2012, preliminary results

Candidates	%
Leonid Tibilov	42.48
David Sanakoyev	24.58
Dmitrii Medoyev	23.79
Stanislav Kochiyev	5.26
Against all candidates	0.80
Total*	100.00

* Including invalid votes (3.09% of the total).

Second Round, 8 April 2012, final results

Candidates	Votes	%
Leonid Tibilov	15,786	54.12
David Sanakoyev	12,439	42.65
Against all candidates	279	0.96
Total*	29,166	100.00

* Including 662 invalid votes (2.27% of the total).

Legislature

Parliament of the Republic of South Ossetia
100001 Tskhinvali, ul. Oktyabrskaya 74; tel. (9974) 45-18-37; e-mail parlament.iatz@yandex.ru; internet www.parliamentrso.org.

Chairman: ANATOLII BIBILOV.

General Election, 8 June 2014

Parties and blocs	Votes	%	Seats
United Ossetia	9,083	42.99	20
People's Unity Socialist Party	2,790	13.20	6
People's Party of the Republic of South Ossetia	1,915	9.06	4
Front	1,574	7.45	4
New Ossetia	1,267	6.00	—
Unity South Ossetian Republican Political Party	1,219	5.77	—
Communist Party of the Republic of South Ossetia	890	4.21	—
Motherland	802	3.80	—
Fatherland Republican Socialist Party of South Ossetia	658	3.11	—
Total*	21,072	100.00	34

* Including 874 invalid votes (equivalent to 4.14% of the total).

Election Commission

Central Electoral Commission: Tskhinvali; internet www.cik.ruo.su; Chair. BELLA PLIYEVA.

Political Organizations

In mid-2014 the following political parties were among those registered in South Ossetia.

Communist Party of the Republic of South Ossetia (CP) (Kommunisticheskaya Partiya Respubliki Yuzhnoi Osetii): c/o 100001 Tskhinvali, Parliament Bldg; internet kpruo.ru; f. 1993; supports the unification of South Ossetia and North Osetiya—Alaniya; First Sec. VALERII KAZIYEV.

Fatherland Republican Socialist Party of South Ossetia (Fydybasta): Tshkinvali; supports the devt of an inclusive democratic state; Leader STANISLAV GOBOZOV.

Front (Nykhas): Tskhinvali; f. 2013; Chair. RUSLAN GAGLOYEV.

A Just Ossetia (Spravedlivaya Osetiya/Raestag Ir): 100001 Tskhinvali; f. 2009; Chair. KOSTA KOSHTE.

Motherland (Rodina): Tshkinvali; f. 2012; Chair. DOMBAY GASSIYEV.

New Ossetia (Novaya Osetiya/Nauag Iryston): Tskhinvali; f. 2012; Chair. DAVID SANAKOYEV.

Ossetia-Liberty Square (Iriston-Saribary Fazuat): 100001 Tshkinvali; f. 2012; Chair. ALLA JIOYEVA.

People's Party of the Republic of South Ossetia (Narodnaya Partiya Respubliki Yuzhnoi Osetii): 100001 Tskhinvali, ul. Geroev 3; e-mail npruo@km.ru; supports an independent, democratic and socially liberal South Ossetia; Chair. KAZIMIR PLIYEV.

People's Unity Socialist Party (Sotsialisticheskaya Partiya 'Yedinstvo Naroda'): Tskhinvali; f. 2013; Chair. VLADIMIR KELEKHSAEV.

United Ossetia (Yedinaya Osetiya): Tskhinvali; f. 2012; supports continued self-determination of South Ossetia, whether as an independent state, in union with North Osetiya—Alaniya as part of the Russian Federation, as a member state of a proposed Eurasian Union, or in some other manner; Chair. ANATOLII BIBILOV.

Unity South Ossetian Republican Political Party (Yedinstvo): c/o 100001 Tskhinvali, Parliamentary Bldg; f. 2003; supports a strong state with an executive presidency, and the integration of South Ossetia with North Osetiya—Alaniya and a strengthening of links with the Russian Federation; Chair. ZURAB KOKOYEV.

Diplomatic Representation

EMBASSY IN SOUTH OSSETIA

At April 2015 the 'Republic of South Ossetia' was officially recognized by the four UN member states of Nauru, Nicaragua, Russia and Venezuela. Three other unrecognized secessionist territories in the post-Soviet space—Abkhazia, Nagornyi Karabakh and Transnistria—also stated their recognition of South Ossetia's statehood. By 2015 only Russia maintained an embassy in South Ossetia.

Russia: 100001 Tskhinvali, ul. Ostrovskogo 17; tel. (997) 4453960; fax (997) 4456863; e-mail rusembrso@yandex.ru; Ambassador ELBRUS K. KARGIYEV.

The Press

SELECTED PUBLICATIONS

XXI vek (The 21st Century): Tskhinvali; published sporadically; Editor TIMUR TSKHOVREBOV.

Khurzaerin (Sunrise): Tskhinvali; e-mail mail@xurzarin.ru; internet www.xurzarin.ru; f. 1924; fmrly *Soveton Iryston (Soviet Ossetia)*; 5 a week; social, political and economic affairs; in Ossetian; circ. 1,700 (2012).

Yuzhnaya Osetiya (South Ossetia): 383570 Tskhinvali, ul. Moskovskaya 7; tel. (9974) 45-26-42; e-mail southosetiya@yandex.ru; internet www.ugo-osetia.ru; f. 1983; owned by the Government and parliament of the 'Republic of South Ossetia'; in Russian; social and political affairs; publishes official documents of the 'Republic of South Ossetia'; 3 a week; Editor LUDVIG CHIBIROV.

NEWS AGENCIES

OSinform Information Agency (OSinform Informatsionnoye Agentstvo): Tskhinvali; tel. (929) 808-00-11; e-mail info@osinform.ru; internet www.osinform.ru; f. 2006; Dir LIRA TSKHOVREBOVA.

RES—Republic Information Agency (Informatsionnoye agenstvo 'RES'): 100001 Tskhinvali, ul. Stalina 16; tel. and fax (9997) 45-50-52; internet www.cominf.org; f. 1992; subsidiary of the State Committee of the 'Republic of South Ossetia' for Information, Communications and Mass Media; Dir ALLA JIOYEVA.

Finance

BANKING

Central Bank

National Bank of South Ossetia: Tskhinvali, ul. Stalina 20; tel. (34) 45-24-33; Chair. FELIX ZASSEYEV.

Trade and Industry

CHAMBER OF COMMERCE

Chamber of Commerce and Industry of the 'Republic of South Ossetia' (CCIRSO): 100001 Tskhinvali, ul. Kommunarov 124; tel. (9744) 45-18-59; e-mail tppuo@yandex.ru; internet www.ccirso.com; f. 2002; Chair. ROIN KOZAYEV.

GERMANY

Introductory Survey

LOCATION, CLIMATE, LANGUAGE, RELIGION, FLAG, CAPITAL

The Federal Republic of Germany, which was formally established in October 1990 upon the unification of the Federal Republic of Germany (FRG, West Germany) and the German Democratic Republic (GDR, East Germany), lies in the heart of Europe. It is bordered by nine countries: Denmark to the north, the Netherlands, Belgium, Luxembourg and France to the west, Switzerland and Austria to the south, and the Czech Republic and Poland to the east. The climate is temperate, with an annual average temperature of 9°C (48°F), although there are considerable variations between the North German lowlands and the Bavarian Alps. The language is German. There is a small Sorbian-speaking minority (numbering about 100,000 people). About 30% of the population are Roman Catholics and a further 29% are members of the Evangelical Lutheran (Protestant) church. The national flag (proportions 3 by 5) consists of three equal horizontal stripes, of black, red and gold. The capital is Berlin.

CONTEMPORARY POLITICAL HISTORY

Historical Context

Following the defeat of the Nazi regime and the ending of the Second World War in 1945, Germany was divided, according to the Berlin Agreement, into US, Soviet, British and French occupation zones. Berlin was similarly divided. The former German territories east of the Oder and Neisse rivers, with the city of Danzig (now Gdańsk), became part of Poland, while the northern part of East Prussia, around Königsberg (now Kaliningrad), was transferred to the USSR. After the failure of negotiations to establish a unified German administration, the US, French and British zones were integrated economically in 1948. In May 1949 a provisional Constitution, the Grundgesetz (Basic Law), came into effect in the three zones (except in Saarland), and federal elections were held in August. On 21 September 1949 a new German state, the Federal Republic of Germany (FRG), was established in the three western zones. The FRG was governed from Bonn in North Rhine-Westphalia (Nordrhein-Westfalen). (Saarland was not incorporated into the FRG until 1957.) In October 1949 Soviet-occupied Eastern Germany declared itself the German Democratic Republic (GDR), with the Soviet zone of Berlin as its capital. This left the remainder of Berlin (West Berlin) as an effective enclave of the FRG within the territory of the GDR, although it remained formally under British, French and US occupation.

The FRG and the GDR developed divergent political and economic systems. The leaders of the GDR created a socialist state, based on the Soviet model. As early as 1945 large agricultural estates in eastern Germany were nationalized, followed in 1946 by major industrial concerns. Exclusive political control was exercised by the Sozialistische Einheitspartei Deutschlands (SED—Socialist Unity Party of Germany), which had been formed in April 1946 by the merger of the Communist Party of Germany and the branch of the Sozialdemokratische Partei Deutschlands (SPD—Social Democratic Party of Germany) in the Soviet zone. Other political parties in eastern Germany were under the strict control of the SED; no independent political activity was permitted.

The transfer, as war reparations, of foodstuffs, livestock and industrial equipment to the USSR from eastern Germany had a devastating effect on the area's economy in the immediate post-war period. In June 1953 increasing political repression and severe food shortages led to uprisings and strikes, which were suppressed by Soviet troops. The continued failure of the GDR to match the remarkable economic recovery of the FRG prompted a growing number of refugees to cross from the GDR to the FRG (between 1949 and 1961 an estimated 2.5m. GDR citizens moved permanently to the FRG). Emigration was accelerated by the enforced collectivization of many farms in 1960, and in August 1961 the GDR authorities constructed a guarded wall between East and West Berlin (the Berlin Wall).

Domestic Political Affairs

In May 1971 Walter Ulbricht was succeeded as First Secretary (later restyled General Secretary) of the SED by Erich Honecker. Ulbricht remained Chairman of the Council of State (Head of State), a post that he had held since 1960, until his death in August 1973. He was succeeded in this office by Willi Stoph, but in October 1976 Stoph returned to his previous post as Chairman of the Council of Ministers, and Honecker became Chairman of the Council of State. Under Honecker, despite some liberalization of relations with the FRG, there was little relaxation of repressive domestic policies. Honecker strongly opposed the political and economic reforms that began in the USSR and some other Eastern European countries in the mid-1980s.

The 1949 elections in the FRG resulted in victory for the conservative Christlich-Demokratische Union Deutschlands (CDU—Christian Democratic Union of Germany), together with its sister party in Bavaria, the Christlich-Soziale Union (CSU—Christian Social Union). The SPD was the largest opposition party. Dr Konrad Adenauer, the leader of the CDU, was elected Federal Chancellor by the Bundestag (Federal Assembly); Theodor Heuss became the first President of the Republic, the constitutional head of state (a largely ceremonial position). Under Adenauer's chancellorship (which lasted until 1963) and the direction of Dr Ludwig Erhard, his Minister of Economics (and successor as Chancellor), the FRG rebuilt itself rapidly to become one of the most affluent and economically dynamic states in Europe, as well as an important strategic ally of other Western European states and the USA. The Paris Agreement of 1954 gave full sovereign status to the FRG from 5 May 1955, and also granted it membership of the North Atlantic Treaty Organization (NATO, see p. 367).

The CDU/CSU held power in coalition with the SPD from 1966 to 1969, under the chancellorship of Dr Kurt Kiesinger, but lost support at the 1969 general election. The SPD formed a coalition Government with the Freie Demokratische Partei (FDP—Free Democratic Party), under the chancellorship of Willy Brandt, the SPD leader. Following elections in November 1972, the SPD became, for the first time, the largest party in the Bundestag. In May 1974, however, Brandt resigned as Chancellor after the discovery that his personal assistant had been a clandestine agent of the GDR. He was succeeded by Helmut Schmidt, also of the SPD. The SPD-FDP coalition retained a majority in the Bundestag at the elections of 1976 and 1980. In September 1982 the coalition collapsed when the two parties failed to agree on budgetary measures. In October the FDP formed a Government with the CDU/CSU, under the chancellorship of the CDU leader, Dr Helmut Kohl. This new partnership was consolidated by the results of the general election of March 1983, when the CDU/CSU substantially increased its share of the vote. The CDU/CSU-FDP coalition retained office after the general election of January 1987.

During 1949–69 the FRG, under the CDU/CSU, remained largely isolated from Eastern Europe, owing to the FRG Government's refusal to recognize the GDR as an independent state or to maintain diplomatic relations with any other states that recognized the GDR. When Brandt became Chancellor in 1969, he adopted a more conciliatory approach to relations with Eastern Europe and, in particular, towards the GDR, a policy which came to be known as Ostpolitik. In 1970 formal discussions were conducted between representatives of the GDR and the FRG for the first time, and there was a significant increase in diplomatic contacts between the FRG and the other countries of Eastern Europe. In that year treaties were signed with the USSR and Poland, in which the FRG formally renounced claims to the eastern territories of the Third Reich and recognized the 'Oder–Neisse line' as the border between Germany (actually the GDR) and Poland. Further negotiations between the GDR and the FRG, following a quadripartite agreement on West Berlin in September 1971, clarified access rights to West Berlin and also allowed West Berliners to visit the GDR. In December 1972 the two German states signed a Basic Treaty, agreeing to develop normal, neighbourly relations with each other, to settle all differences without resort to force, and to respect each other's independence. The treaty permitted both the FRG and the GDR to join the UN in September 1973, and allowed many western countries to establish diplomatic relations with the GDR, although both German states continued to deny each other formal diplomatic recognition.

In December 1981 the first official meeting for 11 years took place between the two countries' leaders, when Chancellor Schmidt travelled to the GDR for discussions with Honecker. Inter-German relations deteriorated following the deployment, in late 1983, of US nuclear missiles in the FRG, and the subsequent siting of additional Soviet missiles in the GDR. Nevertheless, official contacts were maintained, and Honecker made his first visit to the FRG in September 1987.

The fall of the Berlin Wall

Relations between the two German states were dramatically affected by political upheavals that occurred in the GDR in late 1989 and 1990. In the latter half of 1989 many thousands of disaffected GDR citizens emigrated illegally to the FRG, via Czechoslovakia, Poland and Hungary. The exodus was accelerated by the Hungarian Government's decision, in September 1989, to permit citizens of the GDR to leave Hungary without exit visas. Meanwhile, there was a growth in popular dissent within the GDR, led by Neues Forum (New Forum), an independent citizens' action group which had been established to encourage discussion of democratic reforms, justice and environmental issues.

In early October 1989, following official celebrations to commemorate the 40th anniversary of the foundation of the GDR, anti-Government demonstrations erupted in East Berlin and other large towns. In mid-October, as the political situation became more unsettled, Honecker resigned as General Secretary of the SED, Chairman of the Council of State and Chairman of the National Defence Council, citing reasons of ill health. He was replaced in all these posts by Egon Krenz, a senior member of the SED Politburo. Krenz immediately initiated a dialogue with Neues Forum (which was legalized in November) and with church leaders. There was also a liberalization of the media, and an amnesty was announced for all persons who had been detained during the recent demonstrations and for those imprisoned for attempting to leave the country illegally. However, large demonstrations, to demand further reforms, continued in many towns throughout the GDR.

On 7 November 1989, in a further attempt to placate the demonstrators, the entire membership of the GDR Council of Ministers resigned. On the following day the SED Politburo also resigned and was replaced. On 9 November restrictions on foreign travel for GDR citizens were ended, and all border crossings to the FRG were opened. During the weekend of 10–11 November an estimated 2m. GDR citizens crossed into West Berlin, and the GDR authorities began to dismantle sections of the Berlin Wall. Dr Hans Modrow, a leading member of the SED who was regarded as an advocate of greater reforms, was appointed Chairman of a new Council of Ministers. The new Government pledged to introduce comprehensive political and economic reforms and to hold free elections in 1990.

In early December 1989 the Volkskammer (the GDR's legislature) voted to remove provisions in the Constitution that protected the SED's status as the single ruling party. However, the mass demonstrations continued, prompted by revelations of corruption and personal enrichment by the former leadership and of abuses of power by the State Security Service (Staatssicherheitsdienst, known colloquially as the Stasi, which was subsequently disbanded). A special commission was established to investigate such charges, and former senior officials, including Honecker and Stoph, were expelled from the SED and placed under house arrest, pending legal proceedings. As the political situation became increasingly unstable, the SED Politburo and Central Committee, including Krenz, resigned, and both bodies, together with the post of General Secretary, were abolished. Shortly afterwards, Krenz also resigned as Chairman of the Council of State; he was replaced by Dr Manfred Gerlach, the Chairman of the Liberal-Demokratische Partei Deutschlands (LDPD—Liberal Democratic Party of Germany). Dr Gregor Gysi, a prominent defence lawyer who was sympathetic to the opposition, was elected to the new post of Chairman of the SED (restyled the Partei des Demokratischen Sozialismus—PDS, Party of Democratic Socialism, in February 1990).

In December 1989 and January 1990 all-party talks took place in the GDR, resulting in the formation, in February, of a new administration, designated the Government of National Responsibility (still led by Modrow), to remain in office until elections

were held. The GDR's first free legislative elections took place on 18 March 1990, with the participation of 93% of those eligible to vote. The East German CDU obtained 40.8% of the total votes cast, while the newly re-established East German SPD and the PDS secured 21.8% and 16.4%, respectively. In April a coalition Government was formed, headed by Lothar de Maizière, leader of the Eastern CDU. Five parties were represented in the new Government: the CDU, the SPD, the Liga der Freien Demokraten (League of Free Democrats) and two smaller parties. The PDS was not invited to join the coalition.

The reunification of Germany

As a result of the changes within the GDR and the subsequent free contact between Germans of east and west, the reunification of the two German states became a realistic possibility. In November 1989 Chancellor Kohl proposed a plan for the eventual unification of the two countries by means of an interim confederal arrangement. In December Kohl made his first visit to the GDR, where he held discussions with the East German leadership. The two sides agreed to develop contacts at all levels and to establish joint economic, cultural and environmental commissions. The GDR Government initially insisted that the GDR remain a sovereign, independent state. However, in February 1990, in response to growing popular support among GDR citizens for unification, Modrow publicly advocated the establishment of a united Germany. Shortly afterwards, Kohl and Modrow met in Bonn, where they agreed to establish a joint commission to achieve full economic and monetary union between the GDR and the FRG. The new coalition Government of the GDR, formed in April, pledged its determination to achieve German unification in the near future. In May the legislatures of the GDR and the FRG approved the Treaty Between the FRG and the GDR Establishing a Monetary, Economic and Social Union, which came into effect on 1 July. Later in July the Volkskammer approved the re-establishment on GDR territory of the five Länder (states)—Brandenburg, Mecklenburg-Western Pomerania (Mecklenburg-Vorpommern), Saxony (Sachsen), Saxony-Anhalt (Sachsen-Anhalt) and Thuringia (Thüringen)—which had been abolished by the GDR Government in 1952. On 31 August 1990 the Treaty Between the FRG and the GDR on the Establishment of German Unity was signed in East Berlin by representatives of the two Governments. The treaty stipulated, *inter alia*, that the newly restored Länder would accede to the FRG on 3 October, and that the 23 boroughs of East and West Berlin would jointly form the Land (state) of Berlin.

Owing to the complex international status of the FRG and the GDR and the two countries' membership of opposing military alliances (respectively, NATO and the Warsaw Pact), the process of German unification also included negotiations with other countries. In February 1990 representatives of 23 NATO and Warsaw Pact countries agreed to establish the so-called 'two-plus-four' talks (the FRG and the GDR, plus the four countries that had occupied Germany after the Second World War—France, the USSR, the United Kingdom and the USA) to discuss the external aspects of German unification. In June both German legislatures approved a resolution recognizing the inviolability of Poland's post-1945 borders, stressing that the eastern border of a future united Germany would remain along the Oder–Neisse line. In July, at bilateral talks in the USSR with Chancellor Kohl, the Soviet leader, Mikhail Gorbachev, agreed that a united Germany would be free to join whichever military alliance it wished, thus permitting Germany to remain a full member of NATO. The USSR also pledged to withdraw its armed forces (estimated at 370,000 in 1990) from GDR territory within four years, and it was agreed that a united Germany would reduce the strength of its armed forces to 370,000 within the same period. This agreement ensured a successful result to the 'two-plus-four' talks, which were concluded in September in the Soviet capital, Moscow, where the Treaty on the Final Settlement with Respect to Germany was signed. In late September the GDR withdrew from the Warsaw Pact.

On 1 October 1990 representatives of the four countries that had occupied Germany after the Second World War met in New York, USA, to sign a document in which Germany's full sovereignty was recognized. Finally, on 3 October, the two German states were formally unified. On the following day, at a session of the Bundestag (which had been expanded to permit the representation of former deputies of the GDR Volkskammer), five prominent politicians from the former GDR were sworn in as Ministers without Portfolio in the Federal Government. The

Federal President, Richard von Weizsäcker, became the first President of the reunified nation.

Prior to unification, the CDU, the SPD and the FDP of the GDR had merged with their respective counterparts in the FRG to form three single parties. At state elections in the newly acceded Länder, held in mid-October 1990, the CDU won control of four Land legislatures, while the SPD gained a majority only in Brandenburg. This surge of support for Chancellor Kohl and the CDU was confirmed by the results of elections to the Bundestag in early December (the first all-German elections since 1933), at which the CDU and CSU secured a total of 319 seats in the 662-member Bundestag. Kohl was formally re-elected to the post of Federal Chancellor in January 1991, immediately after the formation of the new Federal Government. This comprised 20 members, but included only three politicians from the former GDR. The FDP's representation was increased from four to five ministers, reflecting the party's increased representation in the legislature. In June the Bundestag voted in favour of Berlin as the future seat of the legislature and of government; the transfer of most organs of government from Bonn to Berlin took place in 1999.

Events following reunification: 1991–98

One of the most serious problems confronting the Government following unification was that of escalating unemployment in eastern Germany, as a result of the introduction of market-orientated reforms intended to integrate the economic system of the former GDR with that of the rest of the country. A substantial increase in the crime rate in eastern Germany was also recorded. A further disturbing issue, particularly in the eastern Länder, was the resurgence of extreme right-wing and neo-Nazi groups. Moreover, there were also fears of a resurgence of political violence, following a series of terrorist acts culminating in the assassination, in April 1991, of Detlev Rohwedder, the executive head of the Treuhandanstalt (the trustee agency that had been established in March 1990 to supervise the privatization of state-owned enterprises in the former GDR). Responsibility for this and other attacks was claimed by the Rote Armee Fraktion (Red Army Faction), an extreme left-wing terrorist organization that had been active in the FRG during the 1970s. (The Red Army Faction eventually disbanded in 1998.)

Investigations into the abuse of power by the former GDR administration, conducted during the early 1990s, prompted the dismissal or resignation from government posts of several former SED politicians. In January 1991 the authorities temporarily suspended efforts to arrest Honecker on charges of manslaughter (for complicity in the deaths of people who had been killed while attempting to escape from the GDR), owing to the severe ill health of the former GDR leader. In March it was announced that Honecker had been transferred, without the permission of the German authorities, to the USSR, and in December he took refuge in the Chilean embassy in Moscow. In January 1992 some 2m. Stasi files were opened to public scrutiny. In February Erich Mielke, the former head of the Stasi, was brought to trial on charges of murder, and in September Markus Wolf, the former head of East Germany's intelligence service, was charged with espionage, treason and corruption; both were subsequently found guilty and each was sentenced to six years' imprisonment. Meanwhile, Honecker returned to Germany from Russia in July. He was brought to trial in November, together with five other defendants (among them Mielke and Stoph), on charges of manslaughter and embezzlement. In April 1993, however, the charges against Honecker were suspended. (The former East German leader, who was terminally ill, had been allowed to leave for Chile in January of that year; he died in May 1994.) Stoph was also released on grounds of ill health.

In May 1994 Roman Herzog, the candidate of the CDU (previously the President of the Federal Constitutional Court) was elected Federal President by the Bundesversammlung (Federal Convention, a body comprising the members of the Bundestag and delegates chosen by the regional legislatures); he took office in July. The CDU/CSU-FDP coalition was re-elected at a general election held in October; its majority in the Bundestag was, however, sharply reduced, from 134 to 10 seats. In November the ruling coalition negotiated a new political programme; shortly afterwards Kohl was formally re-elected as the Federal Chancellor.

In May 1995 the Federal Constitutional Court ruled that alleged former East German spies should not be prosecuted by federal courts regarding crimes that were committed against the Federal Republic on behalf of the former GDR prior to unification; consequently, in October the 1992 conviction of Markus Wolf was overturned. In November 1996 the Constitutional Court ruled that the legal principles of the FRG regarding human rights could be retroactively applied to actions carried out within the former GDR. Thus, in May 1997 Wolf was convicted on charges of abduction, coercion and assault, receiving a suspended sentence of two years' imprisonment. In August Egon Krenz and two other former senior SED members, Günther Schabowski and Günther Kleiber, were found guilty of the manslaughter and attempted manslaughter of people who had sought to flee the former GDR; all three were sentenced to terms of imprisonment. (Schabowski and Kleiber were pardoned in September 2000; Krenz was released from prison on probation in December 2003.)

The activities of extreme right-wing organizations increased significantly in 1997, with suggestions that some sections of the armed forces were being infiltrated by neo-Nazi interests. In April 1998 the extreme right-wing and openly xenophobic Deutsche Volksunion (DVU—German People's Union) won unprecedented support (12.9% of the votes cast) at an election to the Land parliament for the economically depressed region of Saxony-Anhalt in eastern Germany.

Tensions within the CDU/CSU-FDP coalition became apparent in 1997, mainly concerning the desirability and means of meeting the 'convergence criteria' for participation in European Economic and Monetary Union (EMU) by 1999. Record levels of unemployment continued to cause concern, as well as an unexpectedly large deficit on the 1997 budget. In April 1998, despite evidence of widespread opposition to the new single European currency, the Bundestag voted in favour of Germany's participation in EMU.

The SPD-led coalition: 1998–2005

At the general election held in September 1998 the CDU/CSU-FDP coalition was defeated by the SPD, which won 298 of the 669 seats in the Bundestag. Following the election, Kohl resigned as Chairman of the CDU; he was replaced by the party's parliamentary leader, Dr Wolfgang Schäuble. Meanwhile, the SPD and Bündnis 90/Die Grünen (Alliance 90/The Greens, which held 47 seats) negotiated a coalition pact. In October Gerhard Schröder of the SPD, formerly the Minister-President of Lower Saxony (Niedersachsen), was elected Federal Chancellor by a large majority of Bundestag members. The new Federal Government included three ministers representing Bündnis 90/Die Grünen, the most prominent of whom was the new Federal Vice-Chancellor and Minister of Foreign Affairs, Joschka Fischer. Oskar Lafontaine, the Chairman of the SPD, was appointed Minister of Finance.

Lafontaine resigned abruptly in March 1999 from the Government, the Bundestag and the SPD chairmanship, citing a lack of support for his economic policies and management from within both the business community and the governing coalition. Hans Eichel of the SPD was appointed as the new Minister of Finance. In the following month Schröder was elected to the post of Chairman of the SPD. In May Johannes Rau, the candidate of the SPD (hitherto Minister-President of North Rhine-Westphalia) was elected Federal President, taking office in July.

During November 1999 the opposition CDU became embroiled in a scandal concerning the discovery of a system of secret bank accounts, which had been used to deposit undisclosed illegal donations to the party throughout the 1990s. (In accordance with the Basic Law, all substantial funding of political parties must be declared.) The former Chancellor, Kohl, admitted knowledge of some secret party funding, but repeatedly refused to name any sources; in January 2000 Kohl was forced to resign from his honorary chairmanship of the CDU after he became the subject of a criminal investigation. In February Schäuble resigned as Chairman of the CDU, accepting responsibility for mishandling the funding scandal.

The CDU's Secretary-General, Angela Merkel, was elected Chairman at the party congress in April 2000. Merkel, who had secured significant support as a result of her determination to expose the CDU's financial irregularities, was considered more liberal than her predecessors. In May the state prosecutor concluded that there were sufficient grounds for the criminal prosecution of Kohl on charges of fraud and bribery (although, as an incumbent member of the legislature, Kohl was immune from prosecution). In his testimony in June to the parliamentary committee Kohl admitted accepting illegal secret contributions to party funds, but denied allegations that such donations had influenced government policy decisions. In February 2001 Kohl agreed to pay a fine of DM 300,000 in exchange for the abandonment of the criminal investigation into his acceptance of illegal contributions; this arrangement subsequently gained judicial approval. The parliamentary inquiry continued, however, as did Kohl's refusal to name the illegal contributors to his party. Kohl did not seek re-election in the Bundestag elections of 2002.

In December 1999 the Government agreed to pay a substantial sum in compensation to people who had worked as forced labourers for German companies or been deprived of their assets under the Nazi regime; it was hoped that this would forestall a growing number of lawsuits taken out against German industrial interests and banks by survivors of the Holocaust. Chancellor Schröder announced that the Government would provide one-half of the proposed DM 10,000m. fund; the remainder was to be raised by Germany's largest banks and companies. Payments began in May 2001.

In June 2000, following negotiations between the Government and the nuclear industry, Schröder announced that an agreement had been concluded which aimed to decommission the country's 19 nuclear power plants (which accounted for almost one-third of power requirements) without compensation by 2021. Although a significant number of members of Bündnis 90/Die Grünen had favoured an immediate cessation of nuclear power generation, in September 2001 the Federal Government adopted a bill regulating the phasing out of nuclear power, which was subsequently approved by the Bundestag (see *Challenges for the CDU and the FDP*).

In September 2001, following attacks on New York and Washington, DC, USA by suspected Islamist extremists, the Government abolished the so-called 'religious privilege', thus removing legal protection for, and allowing the banning of, any religious organization suspected of promoting terrorism. In December police raided the premises of 20 militant Islamist groups throughout Germany, some of which were suspected of having links with the al-Qa'ida organization of the Saudi-born militant Islamist Osama bin Laden (which was widely believed to have organized the attacks in the USA in September). Evidence subsequently emerged that at least three of the presumed perpetrators of the US atrocities had recently lived in Hamburg and other German cities. Plans to introduce more liberal immigration laws were abandoned, and further legislation was introduced to increase national security, including the extension of existing anti-terrorism legislation, which had hitherto only covered terrorist acts in Germany, to apply, in addition, to such acts committed in other countries. Measures to block funding channels for militant activists allowed the police access to bank account details of alleged terrorists. Further steps to control money-laundering were introduced, including the foundation of a centralized Financial Intelligence Unit.

At the general election held on 22 September 2002 the SPD-Bündnis 90/Die Grünen coalition was re-elected with a reduced majority. The SPD's position was severely weakened and the Government's popularity suffered as a result of financial austerity measures adopted in an attempt to ward off economic recession. At two Land elections in February 2003 the SPD suffered emphatic defeats by the CDU, which thus strengthened the CDU's majority in the Bundesrat to such an extent that it was able to block government legislation.

In August 2003 the Federal Government approved the 12 bills that comprised Schröder's Agenda 2010 package of economic reforms, the main aims of which were to reduce the rate of unemployment and to revive Germany's stagnant economy. The proposals were, however, deeply unpopular among the general public, trade unions (which had long been traditional allies of the SPD) and many SPD members. Bills to reform health provision and labour regulations were adopted by the Bundestag in September, as were welfare and tax reforms in October. The CDU used its majority in the Bundesrat to force amendments to tax reductions, fearing that they would lead to an increase in public debt.

At the SPD conference held in November 2003, Schröder was re-elected Chairman of the party; however, many SPD members felt that the Agenda 2010 reforms were a betrayal of the party's core values, and during 2003 the party lost some 5% of its membership. In December the various bills comprising Agenda 2010, including the amended tax reductions, were finally adopted by both legislative bodies. Bitterness and divisions remained within the SPD, and in February 2004 Schröder announced his resignation as SPD Chairman; he was, however, to remain in his post as Chancellor. The SPD subsequently elected Franz Müntefering as its new leader.

In May 2004 the Bundesversammlung elected Dr Horst Köhler (hitherto the Managing Director of the International Monetary Fund—IMF), the joint candidate of the CDU and the FDP, as the new Federal President; he was inaugurated on 1 July. (Köhler was elected Federal President for a second term in May 2009.)

In July 2004 the Bundesrat adopted legislation on the reform (and ultimately a reduction) of unemployment and social welfare benefits. Opposition, manifested in street protests, was strong throughout Germany, but particularly so in the Länder of the former GDR, where long-term unemployment was endemic. None the less, the legislation on welfare reform took effect in January 2005. Declining support for the SPD was demonstrated in Land elections in 2004-05, reflecting not only the widespread anger at the reforms, but also the long-standing frustration of many east Germans at the failure to achieve economic integration of the east since reunification.

Following the SPD's defeat in North Rhine-Westphalia in May 2005, Schröder announced his intention to call an early general election, ostensibly because the CDU's increased majority in the Bundesrat rendered his Government unviable. As the Basic Law does not technically allow early elections, Schröder called and deliberately lost a vote of confidence in his administration in July, thereby enabling President Köhler to dissolve the Bundestag. Two legal challenges against this process were dismissed by the Federal Constitutional Court in August, and the election was confirmed for 18 September.

As the rift between Schröder and the left wing of the SPD deepened, Lafontaine, the former Chairman and Minister of Finance, left the party and, in July 2005, established a new party with the PDS and other defectors from the SPD, known as Linkspartei.PDS (Die Linke—Left Party.PDS). Die Linke formed an electoral alliance with another left-wing grouping, Wahlalternative Arbeit und soziale Gerechtigkeit (WASG—Electoral Alternative Jobs and Social Justice). Its manifesto included the repeal of social reforms, an increase in the minimum wage and the imposition of higher taxes on the rich. The party swiftly gained considerable support, particularly in the east. (In June 2007 the two parties completed a formal merger, as Die Linke, under the joint leadership of Lafontaine and Prof. Lothar Bisky.)

The 'grand coalition': 2005–09

At the election to the Bundestag, held on 18 September 2005, the CDU/CSU won a total of 225 of the 614 seats (later increased to 226 following a delayed ballot in one constituency), while the SPD secured 222. Owing to the strong performance of Die Linke, which won 54 seats, neither the CDU/CSU nor the SPD could form a majority government with their preferred coalition partners (respectively the FDP, with 61 seats, and Bündnis 90/Die Grünen, with 51 seats). Neither party was willing to form a coalition with Die Linke. Following three weeks of negotiations among the parties, Merkel was designated Chancellor on 10 October at the head of a 'grand coalition' of the CDU/CSU and SPD. The coalition agreement focused on a programme of job creation, economic reform and reform of the federal system. Müntefering was designated Vice-Chancellor and Minister of Labour and Social Affairs, and the SPD retained control of a total of eight of the 14 ministries. Merkel was formally elected as Federal Chancellor by the Bundestag on 22 November, becoming both the first woman and the first former citizen of the GDR to lead the country.

Amendments to 25 articles of the Basic Law were approved by the Bundestag in June 2006 and by the Bundesrat in July. The amendments were intended to simplify relations between the two legislative houses, as well as between the Federal and Land Governments, and to define their respective responsibilities more clearly; they were also intended to expedite the legislative process, since the amendments substantially reduced the number of bills needing approval from the Bundesrat. Conversely, the Land Governments represented in the Bundesrat gained increased authority over services, including schools and prisons. In July the coalition partners reached an agreement on the reform of health care provision, which was intended to reduce rising costs and to limit reliance on employers' contributions to finance health insurance schemes: the proposals were formally approved by the Bundestag in February 2007, and implementation of the reforms was completed on 1 January 2009. In July 2006, meanwhile, anti-terrorism legislation, adopted following the 11 September 2001 attacks in the USA, was renewed for a five-year period by the Government. Under the renewed legislation, the Bundesnachrichtendienst (BND—the federal intelligence service) was given greater powers, including access to information regarding passengers on international flights.

At an SPD conference in October 2007, party members voted to approve a policy programme that appeared to move the party toward the left. Prior to the conference, some senior members of the party, including Müntefering, had criticized proposals to relax some of the measures included in the Schröder Government's Agenda 2010 programme. In November 2007 Müntefering announced his resignation from the Government, citing personal reasons. Olaf Scholz was appointed to replace him as Minister of Labour and Social Affairs, while the Minister of Foreign Affairs, Frank-Walter Steinmeier, assumed the additional role of Vice-Chancellor. In September 2008 continuing internal disagreements within the SPD culminated in the resignation of Kurt Beck as party Chairman. Müntefering was confirmed as his successor by a special party conference in October. Steinmeier had earlier been selected as the party's candidate for the chancellorship at the next federal election.

In June 2008 the Government approved a draft bill to provide extensive new powers for the Bundeskriminalamt (BKA—Federal Criminal Police Office) to combat terrorism, allowing the BKA to search computers via the internet, monitor telephone conversations and put an individual's home under surveillance, even if he or she was not suspected of a crime. Despite criticism from the opposition and from human rights groups, the legislation was passed by the Bundestag in November, and was approved by the Bundesrat in December, following the inclusion of several amendments, notably that prior permission by the judiciary would always be required for remote searches of computers.

During 2008 and 2009 the Government sought to mitigate the effects of worldwide recession on the German economy. In October 2008 it announced that it would guarantee private bank deposits, in order to maintain confidence in the banking system, and over the following three months it announced new spending totalling some €80,000m., to stimulate the economy. Disagreements between the SPD and the CDU intensified in early 2009, leading to the postponement of policy initiatives, including environmental measures and labour market reforms.

Merkel retains power at the 2009 election

At the general election in September 2009 the CDU/CSU together won 239 of the 622 seats in the Bundestag, while the SPD sustained a severe loss of support, securing 146 seats (compared with 222 in 2005). The FDP increased its representation, winning 93 seats, while Die Linke and Bündnis 90/Die Grünen also increased their representation (to 76 and 68 seats, respectively). Negotiations on forming a coalition proceeded swiftly between the CDU/CSU and the FDP. Following the conclusion of an agreement on policy, which included a commitment to the tax reductions demanded by the FDP, the new Government was sworn in on 28 October: it included the FDP Chairman, Guido Westerwelle, as Vice-Chancellor and Minister of Foreign Affairs, while Rainer Brüderle of the FDP became Minister of Economics and Technology. FDP members were also allocated the ministries in charge of justice, health and development. Wolfgang Schäuble, previously the Minister of the Interior, became Minister of Finance, and the defence portfolio was given to Karl Theodor zu Guttenberg of the CSU, previously the Minister of Economics and Technology. After the election Müntefering resigned from the chairmanship of the SPD and was replaced by Sigmar Gabriel, a former Minister of the Environment.

In November 2009 the Chief of Staff of the Bundeswehr (armed forces), Gen. Wolfgang Schneiderhan, together with an official in the Federal Ministry of Defence, resigned in response to a controversy over an air attack by US forces in Afghanistan in September, which had been requested by a German commander in the area (see *Foreign Affairs*). It was alleged by a national newspaper, *Bild*, that the Ministry of Defence had withheld information on the number of civilians killed in the attack. The Minister of Labour and Social Affairs, Franz Josef Jung, who had been Minister of Defence at the time of the attack, also resigned. (He was replaced by Ursula von der Leyen, who had hitherto held responsibility for family affairs.) A parliamentary inquiry into the events began in December, and the affair reinforced widespread public disquiet over Germany's military involvement in Afghanistan, which had been presented by the Government as a mission to assist reconstruction rather than as participation in the conflict there. In December the Government gained parliamentary approval for measures intended to accelerate economic recovery, which included tax reductions (for individuals and businesses) that had been favoured by the FDP. Critics of the plan expected it to add to an already unprecedented level of public debt.

In January 2010 Lafontaine announced his retirement as joint Chairman of Die Linke and as a member of the Bundestag, owing to ill health. At a party conference in May Klaus Ernst and Gesine Lötzsch were elected to succeed him and Bisky, who had also retired as joint Chairman of the party. In February the Federal Constitutional Court ruled that the controversial reform of unemployment and social welfare benefits introduced by the Schröder Government in 2004 was unconstitutional, on the grounds that it failed to guarantee a 'dignified minimum' income for the recipients of benefits. The Court ordered the Government to implement a new system of welfare benefits by January 2011, requiring a significant increase in government expenditure.

Challenges for the CDU and the FDP

In early May 2010 the legislature approved loans to Greece amounting to €22,400m. over a three-year period, as part of the emergency assistance approved earlier in that month by the ministers responsible for finance of countries participating in the single European currency, the euro (see *Regional relations*). The unpopularity of this measure within Germany at a time of domestic economic austerity was believed to have led to a decline in support for the CDU at a regional election in North Rhine-Westphalia in May: the SPD also lost support, and Bündnis 90/Die Grünen and Die Linke made considerable gains. (In July the SPD and Bündnis 90/Die Grünen formed a minority government in North Rhine-Westphalia, reliant on the support of Die Linke.) As a result of the CDU's defeat in North Rhine-Westphalia, the Federal Government lost its majority in the Bundesrat. Later in May the Minister-President of Hesse, Roland Koch, a senior conservative member of the CDU, resigned from his post in what was perceived as a withdrawal of support for Merkel's leadership.

On 31 May 2010 President Köhler unexpectedly announced his resignation, following criticism of comments he had made about Germany's military involvement in Afghanistan, which were interpreted by some as implying that Germany's commercial interests justified military deployment abroad. At the election of a new Federal President on 30 June, Christian Wulff of the CDU (hitherto Minister-President of Lower Saxony) was the successful candidate, defeating Joachim Gauck, a pastor and respected former East German dissident: however, since as many as three rounds of voting in the Bundesversammlung had been necessary to ensure a sufficient majority in his support, the election was regarded as a humiliating rebuke for the Government. Meanwhile, earlier in June there were widespread protests following the Government's announcement of a four-year programme of economic austerity measures, with the aim of reducing the budgetary deficit.

In September 2010 the Government announced a delay in the planned closure of Germany's 17 remaining nuclear power stations: the operations of the most recently built nuclear plants were to continue for a further 14 years beyond 2021 (the deadline originally decided by the SPD-led Government in 2000), while older plants were to continue in use for eight years after 2021. In November 2010 the Minister of Defence, zu Guttenberg, announced that, controversially, conscription to the armed forces was to be suspended with effect from July 2011, and was to be replaced by voluntary military or community service.

In November 2010, as Germany made a rapid recovery from recession, with unemployment decreasing, Merkel was re-elected unopposed to the leadership of the CDU. In March 2011 zu Guttenberg resigned from his ministerial post, after being accused of using unattributed material in the doctoral thesis that he had submitted in 2006: he denied the allegations, but the University of Bayreuth revoked his doctorate. He was replaced as Minister of Defence by Thomas de Maizière, hitherto Minister of the Interior.

Following a severe earthquake in Japan in March 2011, which seriously damaged the Fukushima nuclear power station, large demonstrations opposing nuclear power took place in four German cities. The Government ordered safety reviews to be undertaken at all the country's nuclear power stations, and in May it announced the permanent closure of the seven oldest reactors (an eighth was already off-line), and the closure of the remainder by 2022. Critics of the revised policy expressed the fear that there would be an increase in emissions of carbon dioxide from coal- and gas-fired power stations, despite a proposed acceleration in the development of renewable sources of energy.

At regional elections held in March 2011 Bündnis 90/Die Grünen, which opposed nuclear power, attracted greatly increased support. In Saxony-Anhalt the CDU formed a coalition with the SPD, as before; Bündnis 90/Die Grünen almost doubled their share of the votes, but the FDP's share declined below 5%, and the party lost its representation in the Land legislature, since parties failing to obtain at least 5% of the vote cannot be allocated seats in Bundestag or Landtag elections. In Baden-Württemberg, controlled by the CDU since the 1950s, Bündnis 90/Die Grünen received almost one-quarter of the votes, and was able to form a coalition with the SPD, led as Minister-President by Winfried Kretschmann, the first member of Bündnis 90/Die Grünen to hold that office in any of the Länder. On the same day, at an election in Rhineland-Palatinate, the share of the votes won by Bündnis 90/Die Grünen more than tripled, and here too the party formed a coalition with the SPD; although the CDU had slightly increased its share of the votes, the FDP again lost its representation in the Land legislature. In April Guido Westerwelle resigned as national Chairman of the FDP and as Federal Vice-Chancellor, but retained his post as Minister of Foreign Affairs. In May Philipp Rösler, hitherto the Minister of Health, replaced Westerwelle as Chairman of the FDP and Vice-Chancellor, also assuming the post of Minister of Economics and Technology.

Further Land elections in 2011 continued to reveal a decline in the popularity of the CDU and, particularly, of its federal coalition partner, the FDP, whose advocacy of tax reductions and relatively sceptical attitude towards the European Union (EU) had failed to attract support; the share of the votes won by Bündnis 90/Die Grünen, on the other hand, consistently increased. In Bremen, in May, the governing coalition of the SPD and Bündnis 90/Die Grünen was returned to power: the FDP again lost all its seats. In September, in Mecklenburg-Western Pomerania, the ruling 'grand coalition' of the SPD and the CDU was re-elected, while the FDP yet again lost its representation, and Bündnis 90/Die Grünen entered the legislature and was thus represented in all 16 Land legislatures for the first time. Also in September, at an election in Berlin, the CDU increased its support slightly, but the FDP again failed to attract enough votes to stay in the city's legislature. Bündnis 90/Die Grünen increased its support, and the Piratenpartei Deutschland (Pirate Party Germany, originally formed in 2006 to campaign for, among other things, freedom of information) unexpectedly entered the city legislature. In November 2011 the SPD formed a 'grand coalition' in Berlin with the CDU.

In late September 2011 a vote took place in the federal legislature on the proposed enhancement of the European Financial Stability Facility (EFSF) so as to assist Greece and other members of the eurozone that were experiencing severe economic difficulties. Despite dissent within the ruling coalition parties, and public resentment at the high cost of supporting other EU members, the Government won the vote, which had been regarded as a test of confidence in Chancellor Merkel's European policy (see *Regional relations*).

In November 2011 the existence of a violent neo-Nazi group, the Nationalsozialistischer Untergrund (NSU—National Socialist Underground), based in Zwickau, was revealed only after the suicide of two of its members: the group was believed to have been responsible for 10 murders, mostly of people of Turkish origin, since 2000, and for two bomb attacks and a number of bank robberies. Suspected accomplices who were subsequently arrested included a former official of the extremist right-wing Nationaldemokratische Partei Deutschlands (NPD—National Democratic Party of Germany). In November 2012 Beate Zschäpe, a member of the Zwickau group, was charged with complicity in the 10 murders. In December 2011, meanwhile, federal and state ministers responsible for internal affairs agreed to make a new attempt to ban the NPD, which, although unsuccessful in federal elections, currently had representation in two Land legislatures (Mecklenburg-Western Pomerania and Saxony); a previous attempt to ban the party had been rejected by the Constitutional Court in 2003. In January 2012 ministers approved the establishment of a national register of right-wing extremists. In December ministers for internal affairs from all 16 Länder again unanimously urged a ban on the NPD on the grounds that the party encouraged xenophobia, disregarded human rights and was anti-democratic, and in December 2013 the ministers submitted a formal request to the Constitutional Court for such a ban.

In February 2012 President Wulff resigned, after prosecutors had asked the Bundestag to remove his presidential immunity from prosecution, in order to allow possible legal proceedings against him for improper conduct: Wulff had received a low-interest home loan from the wife of a businessman in 2008, and subsequently denied (in the legislature of Lower Saxony, where he was then Minister-President) having financial dealings with the businessman, and in December 2011 he had allegedly attempted to prevent *Bild* from reporting the story. On resigning Wulff denied that he had done anything illegal, but acknowledged that he had lost public trust. (Wulff was subsequently acquitted by the Lower Saxony Land court in February 2014 of taking bribes.) Joachim Gauck, the unsuccessful candidate in the 2010 presidential election, was nominated for the post of Federal President by the SPD and Bündnis 90/Die Grünen, with the support of Merkel: Gauck was elected by the Bundesversammlung in March 2012.

An early regional election was held in Saarland in March 2012, following the breakdown of the 'experimental' governing coalition there comprising the CDU, the FDP and Bündnis 90/Die Grünen: support for the CDU increased slightly, but the FDP lost its representation. Support for the SPD increased, and the Piratenpartei won four seats. The CDU and the SPD formed a coalition administration in Saarland with effect from May. In Schleswig-Holstein the governing CDU-FDP coalition was defeated at elections in May; Die Linke lost its representation, and the Piratenpartei entered the legislature. A new governing coalition was formed in June 2012 by the SPD, Bündnis 90/Die Grünen and the Südschleswigscher Wählerverband, a small party representing the Danish-speaking minority. In North Rhine-Westphalia, meanwhile, the May election (which took place after the minority SPD-Bündnis 90/Die Grünen administration lost a vote on the budget in March) revealed an increase in support for the SPD, while the CDU, whose electoral campaign had emphasized the importance of regional debt reduction, lost votes. The incumbent coalition, therefore, continued in office in North Rhine-Westphalia, this time with a secure majority. Once again the Piratenpartei won seats (thus achieving a place in four regional legislatures to date), but Die Linke lost its representation. At both the May Land elections the FDP performed better than in recent months, retaining its representation (albeit reduced) in Schleswig-Holstein and increasing its support in North Rhine-Westphalia. Later in May Norbert Röttgen, until the recent Land election the chairman of the CDU in North Rhine-Westphalia, and widely blamed for the party's defeat, was dismissed from his post as Federal Minister of the Environment, Nature Conservation and Nuclear Safety; his ministerial post was assumed by Peter Altmaier, also of the CDU.

In September 2012 Peer Steinbrück, who had been Federal Minister of Finance in 2005–09, was selected as the SPD's candidate for the post of Chancellor, should his party be successful in the federal election to be held in the following year. In December 2012 the CDU re-elected Merkel as party chairwoman and as its candidate for Chancellor. In January 2013 an election in Lower Saxony resulted in a defeat for the CDU-FDP administration: although it remained the largest party, the CDU lost support, while the SPD, Bündnis 90/Die Grünen and the FDP all increased their share of the votes. Neither Die Linke nor the Piratenpartei received sufficient votes to keep their representation in the Land legislature. The SPD and Bündnis 90/Die Grünen formed a coalition administration for Lower Saxony, with a one-seat majority. This result gave SPD-led Länder a majority in the Bundesrat.

In March 2013 the German authorities banned three Islamist groups on the grounds that they were anti-democratic, and in June police raids were made on a suspected Islamist militant network in Baden-Württemberg, Bavaria and Saxony. Meanwhile, the trial of the neo-Nazi Zschäpe and four alleged accomplices began in May.

Recent developments: a new 'grand coalition'

In April 2013 a new political party, Alternative für Deutschland (AfD), held its inaugural conference: the party's principal objective was the dismantling of the single European currency, which it claimed had failed to solve the problems of the EU's poorer member states. The AfD principally attracted support from former CDU/CSU voters who objected to the Government's decisions to give financial support to failing European economies (see *Regional relations*). With two regional elections and the federal election all due in September, the CDU/CSU continued to campaign on the basis of its success in maintaining Germany's economic stability, while the SPD proposed the introduction of a statutory minimum wage and higher taxes for the most wealthy. At the Bavarian election, held on 15 September (one week before the federal election), the CSU regained the absolute majority which it had lost in 2009, while the FDP, with which it had been governing in coalition, received less than 5% of the votes and was therefore excluded from the regional legislature. One week later, in Hesse, the CDU won the Landtag vote, precipitating lengthy discussions on the composition of an administration; a coalition was announced in late December between the CDU and Bündnis 90/Die Grünen.

At the federal election on 23 September 2013 the CDU/CSU narrowly failed to achieve an absolute majority, securing a combined total of 311 seats, while the SPD won 193, Die Linke 64 and Bündnis 90/Die Grünen 63. The FDP received slightly less than 5% of 'second' (party) votes (4.8%) and therefore lost its entire representation in the Bundestag (where it had previously held 93 seats). Philipp Rösler immediately announced his resignation as FDP Chairman; he was replaced in December by Christian Lindner. The AfD received 4.7% of 'second' votes and thus likewise failed to gain any seats, but its performance was perceived as relatively successful for such a recently formed party. In October the SPD began formal negotiations on entering a 'grand coalition' with the CDU/CSU, as had existed twice before (in 1966–69 and 2005–09). Discussions continued until late November 2013. The SPD succeeded in securing the introduction of a statutory minimum wage (which subsequently passed into law in 2014), as well as a reduction of the retirement age and an increase in public spending, but the party's demand for increased taxation for higher earners was not met. On 17 December the Bundestag confirmed Merkel as Chancellor at the head of a CDU/CSU-SPD coalition Government. The new administration included six SPD ministers, including Sigmar Gabriel, the party's Chairman, as Vice-Chancellor and Minister of Economic Affairs and Energy, Frank-Walter Steinmeier (SPD) as Minister of Foreign Affairs (the post he had held under the 2005–09 'grand coalition'), and Thomas de Maizière (CDU) as Minister of the Interior, while Wolfgang Schäuble (CDU) retained the post of Minister of Finance. In February 2014 Hans-Peter Friedrich (CSU), the Federal Minister of Food and Agriculture, resigned following allegations that he had breached confidentiality during a secret inquiry. He was replaced by Christian Schmidt of the CSU.

In February 2014 the Federal Constitutional Court voted to remove the requirement for political parties to achieve at least 3% of the vote in European parliamentary elections in order to gain representation in the EU legislature. The growing strength of the Eurosceptic movement in Germany, as elsewhere in the EU, was demonstrated when the AfD won representation in the European Parliament in May, gaining seven seats—an equal number to that secured by Die Linke. The FDP retained just three seats and the removal of the 3% threshold benefited seven smaller parties (including the Piratenpartei and the NPD) which each gained one seat. In July the Bundestag passed legislation establishing a minimum wage of €8.50 per hour, which came into effect for most sectors on 1 January 2015 and subsequently to be reviewed on an annual basis. In August and September 2014 parliamentary elections were held in the Länder of Saxony, Brandenburg and Thuringia. The AfD continued to build support, entering the legislature in each Land for the first time. Following the Saxony vote on 31 August, the CDU under Minister-President Stanislaw Tillich entered into a new 'grand coalition' with the SPD, since the FDP, the CDU's former coalition partner, had lost its representation in the Landtag, as had the NPD. In Brandenburg the SPD won 30 seats in the election on 14 September and continued to govern in coalition with Die Linke. Meanwhile, in Thuringia, following a vote also held on 14 September, the incumbent CDU–SPD coalition was replaced in December by a coalition of Die Linke, the SPD and Bündnis 90/Die Grünen, under Minister-President Bodo Ramelow of Die Linke. The FDP again lost all its seats, leaving it with a presence in just six out of 16 Land legislatures.

In January 2015 the weekly demonstrations of a Dresden-based group known as Pegida (Patriotic Europeans against the Islamization of the West, formed in October 2014 as a populist anti-immigration movement) began to draw increasing media attention in the aftermath of an attack by Islamist gunmen on the offices of a satirical newspaper, *Charlie Hebdo* in Paris, France. Pegida's marches, together with those of its offshoots in other German cities (notably in Leipzig) and in other European countries initially attracted increasing numbers (with up to 25,000 marchers in Dresden), but also attracted much larger counter-demonstrations. Pegida's support base appeared to be fragmenting by March 2015. In her New Year's address, Merkel

had warned demonstrators against becoming associated with extremism and prejudice through their participation in the Pegida rallies. The management of immigration procedures remained high on the German political agenda in early 2015. Data published by the Organization for Economic Co-operation and Development (OECD) showed that immigration in 2013 was at its highest level since 1993; in 2013 Germany was the largest recipient of asylum seekers in the EU, and was also the leading destination for workers moving between nations within the EU. Proposals presented to the Bundestag by the SPD in March 2015 for a points system, to control immigration and ensure coverage of skills gaps, initially met with little enthusiasm from the CDU/CSU, which had hitherto given focus to limiting migrants' access to benefits.

Meanwhile, legislative elections took place in Hamburg on 15 February 2015. The SPD retained power with 58 seats, but lost its overall majority; the SPD was to enter into a coalition with Bündnis 90/Die Grünen, which secured 15 seats. Die Linke achieved 11 seats, while the FDP overturned expectations to win nine seats. The AfD narrowly exceeded the 5% threshold to secure eight seats—its first representation in a western Land parliament and a reflection of renewed public uncertainty over the situation in the eurozone following the election of an anti-austerity government in Greece. The CDU, with 20 seats, achieved its worst ever result in the city.

Foreign Affairs

Regional relations

The orientation of Germany's foreign policy after unification broadly followed that of the FRG. The united Germany remained committed to a leading role in the European Community (EC—now EU), of which the FRG was a founding member, and NATO, while placing greater emphasis on defence co-operation with France. Germany was also strongly committed to close relations with Eastern Europe, in particular with the USSR and, subsequently, its successor states.

In December 1992 the Bundestag ratified the Treaty on European Union (the Maastricht Treaty). At the same time the lower house approved an amendment to the Basic Law (negotiated in May 1992 with the Länder), whereby the state assemblies would be accorded greater involvement in the determination of German policy within the EC. The Bundesrat ratified the Maastricht Treaty later in December. In April 1998 the Bundestag approved Germany's participation in Economic and Monetary Union (EMU), which took effect in January 1999. Following the eventual approval of the draft EU constitutional treaty on 18 June 2004 by the Heads of State and of Government of the member countries, German legislative ratification, which required a two-thirds' majority in both houses, was secured in May 2005. However, following the subsequent rejection of the proposed constitution at public referendums in France and the Netherlands, the process of ratification in other member countries halted. In June 2007 a preliminary agreement was reached for a reform treaty to replace the defunct constitutional treaty. The reform treaty was signed by EU leaders in Lisbon, Portugal, in December 2007, and was ratified by the Bundestag in May 2008. In June 2009 the Federal Constitutional Court rejected a legal challenge by members of the federal legislature (mostly belonging to Die Linke) who claimed that the so-called Treaty of Lisbon was incompatible with German law: the Court ruled, however, that new domestic legislation must be adopted to ensure greater participation by the Bundestag in EU decisions affecting Germany. The Treaty of Lisbon entered into effect across the EU in December 2009. In May 2010 the German Government, with other countries participating in the common European currency, the euro, undertook to provide assistance for the severely indebted Greek economy. Merkel argued that the Treaty of Lisbon should be amended to provide a permanent mechanism for helping member states to avoid insolvency and to ensure financial stability within the eurozone, and the European Stability Mechanism (ESM—see below) was formally inaugurated as the replacement of the European Financial Stability Facility (EFSF) in October 2012.

During 2011 the German Government undertook a leading role in maintaining the stability of the eurozone, by providing assistance for heavily indebted member states (although this was widely unpopular among German tax-payers), and by urging the adoption of more rigorous rules and closer EU integration to prevent future sovereign debt crises. In May the Bundestag approved Germany's contribution to an assistance programme for Portugal. In September the Bundestag voted in favour of enhancing the EFSF by increasing Germany's guarantee commitments. Merkel repeatedly urged the adoption of measures for closer fiscal and economic integration and enforceable budgetary discipline in the EU, but at a meeting of EU heads of state and government in December proposals for a 'fiscal compact' to be incorporated in amendments to the Treaty of Lisbon were defeated when the United Kingdom imposed its veto, after safeguards for British financial services were not forthcoming. The compact was to be adopted, instead, by a separate intergovernmental treaty (the Treaty on Stability, Co-ordination and Governance in the Economic and Monetary Union), according to which members would agree to adopt binding legislation on balancing their budgets; failure to adhere to this would incur penalties imposed by the European Court of Justice. At a further summit meeting in January 2012 it was announced that all EU members except the Czech Republic and the UK had agreed to support the pact (which was formally concluded in March, subject to ratification by member states, and which entered into force on 1 January 2013). In February 2012 EU ministers of finance agreed upon a second assistance programme for Greece, with the aim of reducing Greece's debt to 120% of gross domestic product by 2020. The programme, involving loans of more than €130,000m. and (as demanded by Germany) reductions in the value of bonds held by private creditors, was conditional upon stringent reductions in public spending, under external supervision, and aroused considerable resentment of Germany in Greece. The assistance was approved by the Bundestag in February. In June the Bundestag voted to ratify both the establishment of the ESM and the fiscal compact: objections were immediately submitted to the Constitutional Court by members of Die Linke and other opponents, who argued that the measures were unconstitutional and would therefore require a national referendum. The Court overruled the objections in September, but stated that the German legislature must approve any increase in Germany's contribution to the ESM.

During 2012 the German Government maintained its insistence on the imposition of austerity measures on indebted countries in the eurozone, despite disagreement with, among others, the newly elected French Government. Merkel expressed firm opposition to proposals for the introduction of 'eurobonds' (debt jointly guaranteed by all eurozone member governments, in order to reduce the cost of borrowing for the most indebted states), arguing that this would remove incentives for reform, and would violate EU treaties and the German constitution. At a meeting of EU heads of government in June, however, Merkel agreed to compromise on proposals that she had previously rejected, allowing the ESM to provide support for banks directly (instead of through governments), and permitting the ESM to buy government bonds in order to reduce a country's borrowing costs. Despite Greece's difficulties in reducing its debt levels, Merkel continued to affirm that the stability of the eurozone depended on retaining Greek membership.

In January 2015 negotiations began on the terms of the Greek bailout (which was due to expire at the end of February) following the election of a radical anti-austerity government in Greece, led by the Coalition of the Radical Left (SYRIZA), which had pledged to achieve the write-off of one-half of Greece's outstanding debt. Merkel remained strongly opposed to any reduction in austerity measures by the new Greek Government. A four-month extension to the bailout deal was agreed by eurozone ministers in late February, following the presentation of an interim package of reforms by Greece. (These were, however, challenged by the heads of the IMF and ECB, who stated that further progress on sales tax, pension and labour market reforms was needed.)

While close relations with France remained a priority following Merkel's election as Chancellor in November 2005, she expressed the belief that Germany had worked too exclusively with France in the past and announced her intention to strengthen relations with smaller EU states and the USA. Following the election in May 2007 of Nicolas Sarkozy as French President, the two leaders differed over agreements signed by Sarkozy during late 2007 for the sale of nuclear technology to countries in the Middle East, and French proposals for a grouping to link the seven EU member states in the Mediterranean region and Middle Eastern and African littoral countries; however, in March 2008, following negotiations between French and German representatives, Merkel and Sarkozy announced an agreement on the formation of the Union for the Mediterranean, which incorporated all EU member states, the European Commission and 15 Mediterranean countries. In February 2011 the German and French Governments initiated what later became

known as the Euro-Plus Pact, an agreement among EU members to work towards raising the age at which workers qualified for pensions, abolishing wage indexation, harmonizing corporate taxes, and creating legally binding limits on budget deficits. During 2011, as the two governments co-operated in seeking a solution to the eurozone debt crisis, the French Government disagreed with Germany's insistence on the involvement of private investors in reducing Greece's debt (since several French banks held large amounts of Greek debt), but supported the fiscal compact on budgetary discipline. Following his election in May 2012 the socialist President of France, François Hollande, urged the adoption of measures to stimulate economic growth within the eurozone, rather than the austerity programmes favoured by the German Government; he initially refused to support the EU's fiscal pact, but agreed to do so after the adoption in June of an additional plan to stimulate growth. Hollande argued in favour of the introduction of 'eurobonds', which Merkel opposed.

In the course of the negotiations on EU enlargement during the 1990s, Germany strongly supported Poland's accession (which took place in May 2004), citing the need for reconciliation with its eastern neighbour. In August 2004 Chancellor Schröder attended a ceremony in Warsaw to mark the 60th anniversary of the failed uprising there, during which he acknowledged the 'immeasurable suffering' inflicted by Nazi troops on Poland. The Polish Government, as well those of Estonia, Latvia, Lithuania and Ukraine, opposed the construction of a pipeline to transport natural gas to Germany from Russia, fearing that it could be used to divert energy away from those countries for political reasons. The establishment in November 2007 of a new, centre-right, largely pro-EU Government in Poland under Prime Minister Donald Tusk led to the formation of close political links between the two countries, boosted by a significant increase in German investment in the Polish economy.

In October 2005 preliminary negotiations for the possible accession of Turkey to the EU began. In February 2008, during a visit to Germany, the Turkish Prime Minister, Reçep Tayyip Erdoğan, urged the sizable Turkish population within Germany to retain their ethnic identity, and provoked an angry reaction from several German politicians, who expressed fears that such remarks could undermine efforts to integrate people of Turkish origin into German society. Merkel's Government continued to express concern over democratic standards in Turkey, and over the Turkish refusal to recognize Cyprus, and favoured offering Turkey a 'privileged partnership' with the EU, rather than full membership.

In the early 21st century Russia was the source of around one-third of Germany's natural gas requirements, and the security of this supply (about 80% of which arrived via Ukraine) was of major concern to the German Government. In September 2005 the two Governments concluded an agreement on the construction of a pipeline directly linking Russia and Germany under the Baltic Sea. The 'Nord Stream' pipeline (actually twin pipelines) was intended to transport a combined total of up to 55,000m. cu m of Russian natural gas per year to Western Europe. Transport of gas began in November 2011; both pipelines were fully operational by October 2012. In November 2010 Merkel expressed support for Russia's application to join the World Trade Organization (see p. 431) and for the eventual establishment of a free trade area between Russia and the EU. Following Vladimir Putin's re-election as President in May 2012, the two leaders exchanged visits, but Merkel criticized the Russian Government's treatment of its political opponents, and in November the Bundestag approved a motion deploring deteriorating standards of human rights in Russia. The German Government also criticized Russia's continuing support for the administration of President Bashar al-Assad in Syria during the anti-government unrest that began in 2011 (see *Other external relations*), urging Russia not to provide the Syrian authorities with advanced weaponry. In March 2014 Merkel expressed to President Putin her view that Russia's intervention in the Crimea region of Ukraine (culminating in its annexation of the Crimea peninsula) was a breach of international law. In August Germany supported EU sanctions against Russia following the crash of a Malaysia Airlines passenger airliner over eastern Ukraine (widely believed to have been shot down by Russian-supported separatist fighters). In February 2015, following the collapse of the Minsk I ceasefire agreement of September 2014 and the intensification of fighting in the Donbas region of eastern Ukraine (and amid reports that the US Senate Armed Services Committee was preparing legislation to allow the USA to arm Ukrainian forces), Merkel and French President Hollande met with Ukrainian

President Petro Poroshenko and President Putin to discuss fresh proposals for a diplomatic solution to the conflict. Immediately thereafter, Merkel travelled to Washington, DC, USA for talks on the Ukraine crisis with US President Barack Obama and to Ottawa for discussions with Canadian Prime Minister Stephen Harper. On 12 February, following the quadripartite meeting of France, Germany, Ukraine and Russia, held in Minsk, a cease-fire agreement (Minsk II) was concluded which, *inter alia*, provided for an immediate ceasefire and the withdrawal of heavy weapons from the conflict zone.

Other external relations

Following the Iraqi invasion and annexation of Kuwait in August 1990, the German Government expressed support for the deployment of US-led allied forces in the region of the Persian (Arabian) Gulf, and contributed substantial amounts of financial and technical aid to the effort to liberate Kuwait, although there were mass demonstrations against the allied action in many parts of Germany. Germany did not contribute troops to the allied force, in accordance with a provision in the Basic Law that was widely interpreted as prohibiting intervention outside the area of NATO operations. In July 1992, however, the Government announced that it was to send a naval destroyer and reconnaissance aircraft to the Adriatic Sea to participate in the UN force monitoring the observance of UN sanctions on the Federal Republic of Yugoslavia (FRY). This deployment was subsequently approved by the Bundestag. In April 1993 the Constitutional Court ruled that German forces could join the UN operation to enforce an air exclusion zone over Bosnia and Herzegovina. Germany dispatched troops to assist the UN relief effort in Somalia in mid-1993. In May 1994 the Constitutional Court declared the participation of German military units in collective international defence and security operations, with the approval of the Bundestag in each instance, to be compatible with the Basic Law. In early 1999 Germany participated in the NATO military offensive against the FRY, despite misgivings from left-wing elements within the ruling SPD-Bündnis 90/Die Grünen coalition. From 2004 onwards Germany participated in the EU peacekeeping operation in Bosnia and Herzegovina.

In the aftermath of the terrorist attacks in the USA on 11 September 2001, Chancellor Schröder pledged 'unlimited solidarity' with the US Administration, and announced plans to send 3,900 troops to take part in the US-led military action in Afghanistan, although these plans were strongly opposed by the majority of members of the junior partner in the governing coalition, Bündnis 90/Die Grünen. In November Schröder narrowly won a parliamentary vote on the troop deployment, which was linked to a vote of confidence in his Government. In November 2002 the Bundestag voted to extend the deployment of troops in Afghanistan by a further year, and the mandate was thereafter renewed annually, with the size of the German contingent participating in the International Security Assistance Force (ISAF) increasing to almost 5,000 by 2011, mostly stationed in the northern province of Kunduz. In September 2009 an estimated 100 Afghan civilians were killed in an air attack by US forces: the attack had been requested by a local German commander. The incident led to the resignation in November of the Chief of Staff of the Bundeswehr. Although the mandate for maintaining German forces in Afghanistan was again renewed by the Bundestag in December, the events reinforced domestic opposition to their deployment in that country. From mid-2010 the German Government increased to 200 the number of German police officers involved in training and developing the Afghan police force. The number of German troops participating in ISAF was reduced in 2012, and in October 2013 the Kunduz base was formally handed over to Afghan security forces. The ISAF mission officially ended as planned in December 2014. Germany undertook to continue investing up to €430m. annually in Afghanistan in 2014–16, primarily for developing the rule of law and combating corruption. In March 2013 a German court began hearing a lawsuit brought by the families of the civilians killed in the 2009 air attack, demanding compensation, but the case was dismissed in December 2013.

Germany opposed US plans for the reconstruction of Iraq following the removal of Saddam Hussein in March–April 2003 and advocated instead greater UN involvement and the swifter transfer of governing powers to Iraqis. In September, however, Chancellor Schröder offered to provide resources for the training of Iraqi police, security staff and military personnel (while continuing to refuse to send German peacekeeping troops to Iraq). The continuing 'war on terror' precipitated further tensions in late 2005, following reports that the USA's Central

Intelligence Agency (CIA) had routed over 400 flights through German airports, allegedly with the knowledge of the Minister of the Interior, as part of its programme of 'extraordinary rendition', whereby, it was alleged, suspected Islamist militants were secretly transferred to third countries, some of which were suspected of practising torture, for interrogation. Germany's relations with the USA improved after Merkel took office, and the importance of bilateral co-operation was emphasized during her first official visit to the USA in January 2006, which was returned by the US President, George W. Bush, in July. In November 2009 Merkel visited the USA for discussions with President Barack Obama, during which she requested that US nuclear weapons should no longer be stationed in Germany. While the USA is Germany's principal trading partner outside the EU, it has frequently voiced concern over Germany's consistently large export surplus, urging that Germany should stimulate domestic demand for the benefit of other exporters. In October 2013 Merkel described as 'completely unacceptable' revelations that the US intelligence services had monitored her mobile telephone conversations; further outrage was caused by reports that equipment in the US and British embassies in Germany had been used to intercept government communications.

From 2006 Germany participated, with the permanent members of the UN Security Council, in discussions on Iran's nuclear programme (the so-called P5 + 1 talks), with the aim of dissuading Iran from developing nuclear weapons; in November 2013 participants reached agreement on a reduction of economic sanctions against Iran in return for an undertaking to delay nuclear development over a six-month period. In February 2014 the P5 +1 group began negotiations with Iran on a longer-term agreement; the talks were ongoing in early 2015.

After a popular movement began in February 2011 against Col Muammar al-Qaddafi's regime in Libya, which by March had descended into civil war, Chancellor Merkel was criticized for abstaining from a vote on a UN Security Council resolution, proposed by the UK, France and Lebanon, authorizing an air exclusion zone over Libya. Germany was the only Western nation to abstain from the vote, which none the less resulted in the adoption of a resolution that permitted UN member states to take 'all necessary measures' (short of military occupation) to protect civilians in Libya. During 2011 and 2012 the German Government repeatedly demanded an end to violence against civilians by the Syrian Government, urged the Syrian President to resign, and supported economic sanctions against Syria. As the situation in Syria deteriorated during 2013 the German Government refused to support proposals for providing weapons to anti-government forces in Syria, or for military intervention in that country, although it approved the provision of humanitarian aid.

The People's Republic of China is one of Germany's principal trading partners. From 2002 China became Germany's second largest export market outside Europe (after the USA), and by 2010 China had become Germany's principal supplier of imports. Merkel made an official visit to China in July 2010, when the two Governments announced that intergovernmental consultations would take place annually, and in June 2011 the Chinese Premier, Wen Jiabao, visited Germany; during his visit, a number of agreements on economic and other co-operation were concluded. While visiting China in August 2012 (her second visit there in that year) Merkel urged China to assist the eurozone by continuing to increase its investments in European sovereign bonds and companies. During a visit by the new Chinese Premier, Li Keqiang, in May 2013, Merkel assured him that Germany would expedite negotiations between the EU and China on the pricing of the latter's exports, particularly in view of accusations that China was unfairly subsidizing exports of solar panels and telephone equipment. The new Chinese President, Xi Jinping, paid an official visit to Germany in March 2014; Merkel made a three-day visit to China in August for trade talks.

CONSTITUTION AND GOVERNMENT

The Grundgesetz (Basic Law), which came into force in the British, French and US Zones of Occupation in Germany (excluding Saarland) on 23 May 1949, became the Constitution of the entire German nation with the accession of the five newly re-established eastern Länder (states) and East Berlin to the Federal Republic on 3 October 1990.

Germany is a federal republic with a bicameral legislature. The country's main legislative organ, is the Bundestag (Federal

Assembly), with 631 deputies, who are elected for four years by universal adult suffrage (using a mixed system of proportional representation and direct voting). The upper chamber is the Bundesrat (Federal Council), which consists of 69 members representing the 16 Länder. Each Land has between three and six seats, depending on the size of its population. The term of office of Bundesrat members varies in accordance with Land election dates.

Executive authority rests with the Bundesregierung (Federal Government), led by the Bundeskanzler (Federal Chancellor), who is elected by an absolute majority of the Bundestag and appoints the other Ministers. The Bundespräsident (Federal President) is elected by a Bundesversammlung (Federal Convention), which meets only for this purpose and consists of the Bundestag and an equal number of members elected by Land parliaments. The President is a constitutional head of state with little influence on government.

Germany is composed of 16 Länder (states). Each Land has its own constitution, legislature and government, with the right to enact laws except on matters that are the exclusive right of the Federal Government, such as defence, foreign affairs and finance. Education, police, culture and environmental protection are in the control of the Länder. Local responsibility for the execution of Federal and Land laws is undertaken by the Gemeinden (communities).

REGIONAL AND INTERNATIONAL CO-OPERATION

Germany was a founding member of the European Community, now European Union (EU, see p. 271) and participated in the introduction of the single European currency, the euro, in January 1999. It is also a member of the Council of Europe (see p. 250), of the Organization for Security and Co-operation in Europe (OSCE, see p. 385), and of the Council of the Baltic Sea States.

Germany joined the UN in 1973; it was elected as a non-permanent member of the Security Council for the period 2011–12. As a contracting party to the General Agreement on Tariffs and Trade, Germany joined the World Trade Organization (WTO, see p. 431) on its establishment in 1995. Germany is a member of the Organisation for Economic Co-operation and Development (OECD, see p. 377) and the North Atlantic Treaty Organization (NATO, see p. 367). It participates in the Group of Seven major industrialized nations (G7, see p. 460) and the Group of 20 major industrialized and systemically important emerging market nations (G20, see p. 451).

ECONOMIC AFFAIRS

In 2013, according to estimates by the World Bank, Germany's gross national income (GNI), measured at average 2011–13 prices, was US $3,716,838m., equivalent to $46,100 per head (or $44,540 per head on an international purchasing-power parity basis). During 2004–13 Germany's population registered a decrease of 0.3%, while gross domestic product (GDP) per head grew, in real terms, by an average of 1.6% annually. According to the World Bank, overall GDP expanded, in real terms, at an average annual rate of 1.3% in 2004–13; GDP increased by 0.4% in 2013.

Agriculture (including hunting, forestry and fishing) engaged 1.5% of the employed labour force and provided 0.9% of Germany's GDP in 2013. The principal crops are sugar beet, wheat, barley and potatoes. Wine production is also important in western Germany. According to the World Bank, agricultural GDP decreased, in real terms, at an average annual rate of 1.7% in 2004–13; it increased by 1.6% in 2012, but decreased by 1.0% in 2013.

Industry (including mining, power, manufacturing and construction) engaged 24.7% of the employed labour force and contributed 30.7% of GDP in 2013. According to the World Bank, industrial GDP increased at an average annual rate of 1.3% in 2004–13; it declined by 0.7% in 2012, and in 2013 remained almost constant with a negligible growth rate.

The mining sector (together with energy, gas and water supply) engaged 1.3% of the employed labour force and contributed 3.9% of GDP in 2013. The principal mining activities are the extraction of lignite (low-grade brown coal), hard coal and salts. According to the UN, GDP of mining along with utilities decreased, in real terms, at an average annual rate of 0.8% in 2003–12; it decreased by 15.0% in 2011, but increased by 1.3 in 2012.

The manufacturing sector employed 17.6% of the employed labour force and provided 22.2% of GDP in 2013. Measured by value of output, the principal branches of manufacturing in 2004 were motor vehicles and parts (accounting for 20.1% of the total), non-electric machinery (11.4%), chemical products (9.7%) and food products (9.0%). According to World Bank figures, real manufacturing GDP increased at an average annual rate of 1.9% in 2004–13; it declined by 0.7% in 2012, but increased by 0.2% in 2013.

The construction sector employed 5.7% of the employed labour force and provided 4.6% of GDP in 2013. According to the UN, the GDP of the sector declined by an average annual rate of 0.4% during 2003–12; construction GDP increased by 4.6% in 2011, but declined by 2.4% in 2012.

Of the total energy produced in 2012, coal accounted for 46.9%, nuclear power for 16.3%, natural gas for 11.5% and hydroelectric power for 3.5%. In 2010, in a reversal of a decision in 2000 to end the use of nuclear power by 2021, the Government announced plans to delay the closure of its 17 nuclear power plants. In March 2011, following radiation leaks from a nuclear plant in Japan that had been damaged in an earthquake, this decision was suspended and seven nuclear reactors were shut down. (An eighth was already off-line.) In August 2011 revisions to the Atomic Energy Act entered into force, whereby nuclear power use for commercial electricity generation was to be phased out by 2022. In 2013 imports of mineral fuels accounted for an estimated 14.9% of Germany's total imports.

Services engaged 73.8% of the employed labour force and contributed 68.4% of GDP in 2013. According to World Bank, the GDP of the services sector increased, in real terms, at an average annual rate of 1.5% in 2004–13. Financial services, real estate, renting and business activities accounted for 25.9% of GDP in 2013. Trade, transport and communications accounted for 20.2% of GDP in 2013. According to the World Bank, real GDP of this sector grew at an average annual rate of 1.5% in 2004–13. Overall services GDP grew by 0.7% in 2013.

In 2013 Germany recorded a visible merchandise trade surplus of US $279,470m., and there was a surplus of $256,030m. on the current account of the balance of payments. Germany was the world's largest exporter of goods in the years 2004–08, although exports from the People's Republic of China exceeded those from Germany in 2009 by over $20,000m. Germany conducted more than one-half of its total trade with other countries of the European Union (EU, see p. 271) in 2008. The principal source of imports in 2013 was the Netherlands (providing 9.9% of total imports) followed by the People's Republic of China, France, the USA and Italy. France was the principal export trading partner, purchasing 9.1% of exports in 2013; the other major purchasers of exports were the USA, the United Kingdom, the Netherlands, China and Austria. The principal imports in 2013 were machinery and transport equipment, mineral fuels and lubricants, manufactured goods chiefly classified by material, and chemicals and related products, miscellaneous manufactured articles, and food and live animals. The principal exports were machinery and transport equipment, chemicals and related products, and manufactured goods chiefly classified by material, miscellaneous manufactured articles, and medical and pharmaceutical products.

The general government deficit for 2012 was €37,000m., equivalent to 0.1% of GDP. In 2013 general government gross debt was €2,147,030m., equivalent to 78.4% of GDP. Annual inflation averaged 1.3% during 2004–13. Consumer prices fell by 1.9% in 2013. The unemployment rate was 6.5% in 2013.

Germany is the largest economy in Europe, although the area comprising the former German Democratic Republic (East Germany) remains less prosperous than the former Federal Republic of Germany (West Germany). The German economy entered recession in 2008; as a major exporter (particularly of machinery and vehicles), the country was vulnerable to the global decline in demand, which was exacerbated by the rise in the value of the euro, and industrial output declined sharply. Germany's GDP declined by 5.1% in 2009, the largest contraction in the country's post-war history. Measures were adopted in 2008–09 to stimulate the economy, to support the banking sector and to subsidize companies to retain employment while reducing working hours (which kept unemployment low), with the result that public sector borrowing increased substantially. The budget deficit rose to equal 3.2% of GDP in 2009 (thus exceeding the 3% upper limit stipulated by the EU's Stability and Growth Pact). In 2010, however, GDP increased by 4.0%, reflecting rapid growth in exports to emerging markets (and to China in particular). Austerity measures, announced in June 2010, together with an increase in tax revenues reduced the budget deficit to 0.8% of

GDP in 2011, and a surplus equivalent to 0.1% of GDP was recorded in 2012, followed by a balanced budget in 2013. GDP growth was maintained in 2011, at 3.3%, slowing to 0.7% in 2012, when there was a decline in exports to other eurozone members, although this was offset by strong growth in exports to countries outside the EU. Unemployment averaged just 5.2% in 2013 (compared with an average of around 12% in the eurozone as a whole). Germany's GDP increased by 0.4% in 2013, with export levels still affected by the economic problems of other members of the eurozone; although modest, growth was sustained by domestic demand, as employment levels remained high and relatively generous wage increases stimulated consumer spending. Low interest rates also served to stimulate consumption and support housing construction. Under the 'grand coalition' which took office in December 2013, there has been greater emphasis on regulation (to support social partnership), while balancing the budget has remained a priority. A statutory minimum wage of €8.50 per hour was introduced at the beginning of 2014. Employment continued to rise during the year, although there persisted significant disparities between some of the Eastern and Western Länder in terms of their standard of living; a report published in February 2015 identified Bremen, Berlin and Mecklenburg-Western Pomerania as the Länder most affected by poverty, and Baden-Württemburg and Bavaria as the least affected. Sharp reductions in energy costs caused by falling world oil prices led to deflation of 0.5% in consumer prices in January 2015 compared with January 2014. While overall the German economy remained among the strongest in the EU, the Deutsche Bundesbank (the central bank) reduced its GDP growth forecasts to 1.4% in 2014 and 1.0% in 2015, following a slowdown in output and exports in mid-2014, attributed to the economic climate in the wider eurozone and to the impact of sanctions against Russia.

PUBLIC HOLIDAYS

2016: 1 January (New Year's Day), 6 January (Epiphany)*, 25 March (Good Friday), 28 March (Easter Monday), 1 May (Labour Day), 5 May (Ascension Day), 16 May (Whit Monday), 26 May (Corpus Christi)*, 15 August (Assumption)*, 3 October (Day of Unity), 31 October (Reformation Day)*, 1 November (All Saints' Day)*, 16 November (Day of Prayer and Repentance)*, 25–26 December (Christmas), 31 December (New Year's Eve).

* Religious holidays observed in certain Länder only.

Statistical Survey

Source (unless otherwise indicated): Statistisches Bundesamt, Gustav-Stresemann-Ring 11, 65189 Wiesbaden; tel. (611) 752405; fax (611) 753330; e-mail poststelle@destatis.de; internet www.destatis.de.

Area and Population

AREA, POPULATION AND DENSITY

Area (sq km)*	357,124
Population (census results)	
9 May 2011†	
Males	39,153,540
Females	41,066,140
Total	80,219,695
Population (official estimates at 31 December)	
2011	80,327,900
2012	80,523,746
2013	80,767,463
Density (per sq km) at 31 December 2013	226.2

* 137,886 sq miles.

† Figures are rounded according to differing methodologies, as a result the total may not be equal to the sum of components.

POPULATION BY AGE AND SEX
(official estimates at 31 December 2013)

	Males	Females	Total
0–14 years	5,444,613	5,162,216	10,606,829
15–64 years	26,869,943	26,466,454	53,336,397
65 years and over	7,242,523	9,581,714	16,824,237
Total	39,557,079	41,210,384	80,767,463

LÄNDER
(official population estimates at 31 December 2013)

	Area (sq km)	Population	Density (per sq km)	Capital
Baden-Württemberg .	35,751	10,631,278	297.4	Stuttgart
Bayern (Bavaria) . .	70,550	12,604,244	178.7	München
Berlin	892	3,421,829	3,836.1	Berlin
Brandenburg . . .	29,482	2,449,193	83.1	Potsdam
Bremen	404	657,391	1,627.2	Bremen
Hamburg	755	1,746,342	2,313.0	Hamburg
Hessen (Hesse) . . .	21,115	6,045,425	286.3	Wiesbaden
Mecklenburg-Vorpommern (Mecklenburg-Western Pomerania) .	23,189	1,596,505	68.8	Schwerin
Niedersachsen (Lower Saxony)	47,635	7,790,559	163.5	Hannover
Nordrhein-Westfalen (North Rhine-Westphalia) . . .	34,088	17,571,856	515.5	Düsseldorf
Rheinland-Pfalz (Rhineland-Palatinate) . . .	19,854	3,994,366	201.2	Mainz
Saarland	2,569	990,718	385.6	Saarbrücken
Sachsen (Saxony) . .	18,420	4,046,385	219.7	Dresden
Sachsen-Anhalt (Saxony-Anhalt) . .	20,449	2,244,577	109.8	Magdeburg
Schleswig-Holstein .	15,799	2,815,955	178.2	Kiel
Thüringen (Thuringia) .	16,172	2,160,840	133.6	Erfurt
Total	357,124	80,767,463	226.2	—

PRINCIPAL TOWNS
(official population estimates at 31 December 2013 unless otherwise indicated)

Berlin (capital) . .	3,421,829	Karlsruhe . . .	299,103
Hamburg	1,746,342	Mannheim . . .	296,690
München (Munich) .	1,407,836	Augsburg . . .	276,542
Köln (Cologne) . . .	1,034,175	Wiesbaden . . .	273,871
Frankfurt am Main .	701,350	Gelsenkirchen . .	257,850
Stuttgart	604,297	Mönchengladbach .	255,430
Düsseldorf	598,686	Braunschweig (Brunswick) . .	247,227
Dortmund	575,944	Chemnitz . . .	242,022
Essen	569,884	Kiel . . .	241,533
Bremen	548,547	Aachen (Aix-la-Chapelle)† . .	240,086

Leipzig	531,562	Halle an der Saale*	231,565
Dresden	530,754	Magdeburg	231,021
Hannover (Hanover)†	514,137	Krefeld	222,058
		Freiburg im	
Nürnberg (Nuremberg)	498,876	Breisgau	220,286
Duisburg	486,855	Lübeck	212,958
Bochum	361,734	Oberhausen	209,097
Wuppertal	343,488	Erfurt	204,880
Bielefeld	328,864	Mainz	204,268
Bonn	311,287	Rostock	203,431
Münster	299,708		

* Including Halle-Neustadt.
† Population estimates at 31 December 2012.

BIRTHS, MARRIAGES AND DEATHS

	Registered live births		Registered marriages		Registered deaths	
	Number	Rate (per 1,000)	Number	Rate (per 1,000)	Number	Rate (per 1,000)
2006	672,724	8.2	373,681	4.5	821,627	10.0
2007	684,862	8.3	368,922	4.5	827,155	10.1
2008	682,514	8.3	377,055	4.6	844,439	10.3
2009	665,126	8.1	378,439	4.6	854,544	10.4
2010	677,947	8.3	382,047	4.7	858,768	10.5
2011	662,685	8.1	377,816	4.6	852,328	10.4
2012	673,544	8.4	387,423	4.8	869,582	10.8
2013	682,069	8.4	373,655	4.7	893,825	11.1

Life expectancy (years at birth): 80.9 (males 78.6; females 83.3) in 2012 (Source: World Bank, World Development Indicators database).

IMMIGRATION AND EMIGRATION
('000 persons)

	2011	2012	2013*
Immigrant arrivals	958.3	1,080.9	1,226.5
Emigrant departures	679.0	712.0	789.2

* Preliminary figures.

ECONOMICALLY ACTIVE POPULATION
('000 persons aged 15 years and over, annual averages, preliminary)

	2011	2012	2013
Agriculture, forestry and fishing	669	666	646
Industry	7,850	7,991	8,008
Manufacturing	7,279	7,422	7,440
Construction	2,376	2,410	2,430
Trade, transport, accommodation and food services	9,620	9,717	9,789
Information and communication	1,177	1,198	1,204
Financial and insurance activities	1,201	1,198	1,198
Real estate, renting and business activities	5,826	5,906	5,968
Public services, education, health and other services	12,851	12,947	13,038
Total employed	41,570	42,033	42,281
Unemployed	2,976	2,897	2,950
Total labour force	44,546	44,930	45,231

Health and Welfare

KEY INDICATORS

Total fertility rate (children per woman, 2012)	1.4
Under-five mortality rate (per 1,000 live births, 2012)	4
HIV/AIDS (% of persons aged 15–49, 2011)	0.1
Physicians (per 1,000 head, 2011)	3.8
Hospital beds (per 1,000 head, 2009)	8.2
Health expenditure (2011): US $ per head (PPP)	4,996
Health expenditure (2011): % of GDP	11.3
Health expenditure (2011): public (% of total)	76.5
Total carbon dioxide emissions ('000 metric tons, 2010)	745,383.8
Carbon dioxide emissions per head (metric tons, 2010)	9.1
Human Development Index (2013): ranking	6
Human Development Index (2013): value	0.911

For sources and definitions, see explanatory note on p. vi.

Agriculture

PRINCIPAL CROPS
('000 metric tons)

	2011	2012	2013
Wheat	22,783	22,409	25,019
Barley	8,734	10,391	10,344
Maize	5,184	5,515	4,387
Rye	2,521	3,878	4,689
Oats	627	757	628
Triticale (wheat-rye hybrid)	2,004	2,295	2,609
Potatoes	11,800	10,666	9,670
Sugar beet	29,578	27,687	22,829
Broad beans, dry	61	61	60
Sunflower seed	53	63	46
Rapeseed	3,870	4,821	5,784
Cabbages and other brassicas	829	803	704
Cauliflowers and broccoli	144	177	154
Cucumbers and gherkins	250	244	223
Onions, dry	506	485	406
Beans, green	39	45	50
Carrots and turnips	534	593	584
Grapes*	1,250	1,226	1,140
Apples	898	972	804
Pears	47	34	40
Cherries	37	23	24
Plums and sloes	59	36	49
Strawberries	154	156	150
Currants	10	11	13

* Unofficial figures.

Aggregate production ('000 metric tons, may include official, semi-official or estimated data): Total cereals 41,920 in 2011, 45,397 in 2012, 47,757 in 2013; Total roots and tubers 11,800 in 2011, 10,666 in 2012, 9,670 in 2013; Total vegetables (incl. melons) 3,594 in 2011, 3,821 in 2012, 3,416 in 2013; Total fruits (excl. melons) 2,572 in 2011, 2,567 in 2012, 2,334 in 2013.

Source: FAO.

LIVESTOCK
('000 head at December)

	2011	2012	2013
Horses*	545.0	500.0	530.0
Cattle	12,562.6	12,477.4	12,587.0
Pigs	26,758.1	28,131.7	27,690.1
Sheep	2,088.5	1,657.8	1,641.0
Goats	160	162	165*
Chickens	118,640†	121,040†	122,000*
Geese and guinea fowls	272†	268*	270*
Ducks	2,930†	3,000*	3,000*
Turkeys	11,196†	12,000*	12,100*

* FAO estimate(s).
† Unofficial figure.

Source: FAO.

LIVESTOCK PRODUCTS
('000 metric tons)

	2011	2012	2013
Cattle meat	1,170.4	1,146.3	1,106.4
Sheep meat	39.9	36.5	34.7*
Pig meat	5,616.1	5,474.0	5,494.2
Chicken meat	895.9	903.3	950.9*
Cows' milk	30,323.5	30,506.9	31,122.0
Goats' milk	25.6	26.0	20.8
Hen eggs	782.3	832.0	892.8*
Honey	25.8	15.7	15.7†
Wool, greasy†	13.0	13.5	13.5

* Unofficial figure.
† FAO estimate(s).

Source: FAO.

Forestry

ROUNDWOOD REMOVALS
('000 cubic metres, excluding bark)

	2011	2012	2013
Sawlogs, veneer logs and logs for sleepers	29,016	26,632	26,841
Pulpwood	13,249	13,211	12,296
Other industrial wood	3,093	3,020	2,915
Fuel wood	10,783	9,476	11,155
Total	56,141	52,338	53,207

Source: FAO.

SAWNWOOD PRODUCTION
('000 cubic metres, including railway sleepers)

	2011	2012	2013
Coniferous (softwood)	21,633	20,076	20,428
Broadleaved (hardwood)	996	1,005	1,050
Total	22,628	21,081	21,478

Source: FAO.

Fishing

('000 metric tons, live weight)

	2010	2011	2012
Capture	243.1	233.9	207.5
Freshwater fishes	12.0	13.0	6.2
Atlantic cod	19.5	16.4	18.9
Saithe (Pollock)	13.0	11.6	9.4
Blue whiting (Poutassou)	9.1	0.3	6.2
Atlantic herring	37.0	37.0	51.2
European sprat	21.1	14.7	11.7
Atlantic horse mackerel	21.4	24.6	22.6
Atlantic mackerel	18.9	24.1	18.9
Common shrimp	18.4	17.0	16.4
Aquaculture	40.7	39.1	26.3
Common carp	9.6	5.1	5.5
Rainbow trout	20.0	9.3	9.4
Blue mussel	4.9	20.8	6.9
Total catch	283.8	273.0	233.8

Note: Figures exclude aquatic mammals, recorded by number rather than by weight. The number of harbour porpoises caught was: 4 in 2010, 5 in 2011, n.a. in 2012.

Source: FAO.

Mining

('000 metric tons unless otherwise indicated)

	2010	2011	2012
Coal, lignite	169,403	176,502	185,432
Coal, anthracite and bituminous	12,900	12,059	10,770
Crude petroleum ('000 42-gallon barrels)	18,400	19,600	19,200
Natural gas, marketable (million cu m)	12,571	11,799	10,660

Source: US Geological Survey.

Industry

SELECTED PRODUCTS
('000 metric tons unless otherwise indicated)

	2011	2012	2013
Margarine	409	395	387
Flour	5,408	5,531	5,724
Refined sugar	4,234	4,184	3,422
Beer ('000 hl)	87,084	86,083	83,838
Cigarettes (million)	220,060	206,175	181,791
Newsprint	2,459	2,211	2,138
Motor spirit (petrol)	21,016	20,578	19,851
Diesel oil*	30,426	30,638	29,755
Cement	33,532	31,925	30,927
Sulphuric acid	1,761	2,071	1,899
Nitrogenous fertilizers	1,345	1,330	1,353
Artificial resins and plastics	17,471	16,682	16,940
Synthetic rubber	1,077	1,033	1,149
Soap	350	155	n.a.
Aluminium (unwrought):			
primary	317	282	271
secondary	851	822	809
Passenger cars and minibuses ('000)	6,589	6,199	6,324
Bicycles ('000)	1,327	1,195	987
Footwear ('000 pairs)†	22,471	18,547	n.a.
Electricity (million kWh)	512,718	511,330	n.a.

* Including light heating oil.
† Excluding rubber and plastic footwear.

2010 ('000 metric tons unless otherwise indicated): Cotton yarn (pure and mixed) 21; Woven cotton fabrics ('000 sq m) 159,785; Refined lead (unwrought) 326.

Finance

CURRENCY AND EXCHANGE RATES

Monetary Units
100 cent = 1 euro (€).

Sterling and Dollar Equivalents (31 December 2014)
£1 sterling = 1.286 euros;
US $1 = 0.824 euros;
€10 = £7.78 = $12.14.

Average Exchange Rate (euros per US $)
2012   0.7783
2013   0.7532
2014   0.7537

Note: The national currency was formerly the Deutsche Mark (DM). From the introduction of the euro, with German participation, on 1 January 1999, a fixed exchange rate of €1 = DM 1.95583 was in operation. Euro notes and coins were introduced on 1 January 2002. The euro and local currency circulated alongside each other until 28 February, after which the euro became the sole legal tender.

GOVERNMENT FINANCE
(general government transactions, non-cash basis, € '000 million)

Summary of Balances

	2010	2011	2012
Revenue	1,089.8	1,157.2	1,193.8
Less Expense	1,201.5	1,181.0	1,197.5
Net operating balance	−111.7	−23.8	−3.8
Less Net acquisition of non-financial assets	−7.4	−2.3	−6.1
Net lending/borrowing	−104.3	−21.5	2.3

Revenue

	2010	2011	2012
Taxes	554.3	597.1	622.0
Taxes on income, profits and capital gains	265.5	290.5	310.5
Taxes on goods and services	269.1	285.0	288.5
Social contributions	421.2	437.0	448.9
Grants	5.7	5.0	5.1
Other revenue	108.6	118.2	117.8
Total	1,089.8	1,157.2	1,193.8

Expense/Outlays

Expense by economic type	2010	2011	2012
Compensation of employees	195.7	199.5	203.8
Use of goods and services	121.8	126.6	131.0
Consumption of fixed capital	43.2	44.5	46.0
Interest	63.5	65.7	63.8
Subsidies	28.8	27.2	24.6
Grants	25.9	27.0	28.1
Social benefits	633.2	633.2	643.4
Other expense	89.5	57.4	56.8
Total	1,201.5	1,181.0	1,197.5

Outlays by functions of government*	2010	2011	2012
General public services	156.0	162.0	162.8
Defence	26.2	27.6	28.2
Public order and safety	40.4	41.1	41.7
Economic affairs	118.0	91.1	91.3
Environmental protection	16.0	16.3	15.6
Housing and community amenities	14.9	13.7	12.2
Health	179.1	182.8	187.0
Recreation, culture and religion	20.0	20.8	20.8
Education	110.6	113.7	115.6
Social protection	512.9	509.5	516.3
Total	1,194.1	1,178.7	1,191.5

* Including net acquisition of non-financial assets.

Source: IMF, *Government Finance Statistics Yearbook*.

Public Finance (cash basis, core and extra budgets, adjusted figures, €'000 million): *Revenue:* 1,163.4 in 2012; 1,194.8 in 2013. *Expenditure:* 1,174.4 in 2012; 1,204.2 in 2013.

INTERNATIONAL RESERVES
(US $ million at 31 December)

	2011	2012	2013
Gold (Eurosystem valuation)	171,926	181,434	130,843
IMF special drawing rights	18,265	17,908	17,678
Reserve position in IMF	10,580	11,549	10,962
Foreign exchange	38,083	37,964	38,725
Total	238,854	248,855	198,208

Source: IMF, *International Financial Statistics*.

MONEY SUPPLY
(incl. shares, depository corporations, national residency criteria, € '000 million at 31 December)

	2011	2012	2013
Currency issued	229.2	235.6	246.0
Deutsche Bundesbank	399.7	435.9	470.2
Demand deposits	1,148.2	1,311.4	1,409.2
Other deposits	1,865.9	1,770.5	1,628.6
Securities other than shares	1,419.0	1,303.8	1,180.3
Money market fund shares	6.2	7.3	4.1
Shares and other equity	521.0	557.2	534.7
Other items (net)	−385.0	−360.8	−337.0
Total	4,804.4	4,824.9	4,665.9

Source: IMF, *International Financial Statistics*.

COST OF LIVING
(Consumer Price Index; base: 2010 = 100)

	2011	2012	2013
Food (incl. non-alcoholic beverages)	102.8	106.3	110.4
Clothes and shoes	101.2	103.3	104.4
Housing, energy and fuel	103.1	105.4	107.5
All items (incl. others)	102.1	104.1	105.7

NATIONAL ACCOUNTS
(€ million at current prices, rounded to nearest €10m.)

National Income and Product

	2011	2012	2013
Compensation of employees	1,338,665	1,389,676	1,428,316
Net operating surplus/mixed income	688,669	665,672	671,623
Domestic primary incomes	2,027,334	2,055,348	2,099,939
Consumption of fixed capital	474,229	490,756	502,089
Gross domestic product (GDP) at factor cost	2,501,563	2,546,104	2,602,028
Net taxes on production and imports*	197,537	203,796	207,452
GDP in market prices	2,699,100	2,749,900	2,809,480
Balance of primary income from abroad	69,448	72,308	72,382
Gross national income (GNI)	2,768,548	2,822,208	2,881,862
Less Consumption of fixed capital	474,229	490,756	502,089
Net national income	2,294,319	2,331,452	2,379,773
Current transfers from abroad	50,270	51,475	52,563
Less Current transfers paid abroad	83,472	87,041	94,121
Net national disposable income	2,261,117	2,295,886	2,338,215

* Data obtained as residuals.

Expenditure on the Gross Domestic Product

	2011	2012	2013
Government final consumption expenditure	505,722	521,290	541,208
Private final consumption expenditure	1,506,803	1,539,477	1,571,511
Increase in stocks	11,857	−23,852	−22,315
Gross fixed capital formation	544,271	551,239	555,826
Total domestic expenditure	2,568,653	2,588,154	2,646,230
Exports of goods and services	1,209,385	1,262,872	1,280,127
Less Imports of goods and services	1,078,938	1,101,126	1,116,877
GDP in purchasers' values	2,699,100	2,749,900	2,809,480

Gross Domestic Product by Economic Activity

	2011	2012	2013
Agriculture, hunting, forestry and fishing	19,529	21,581	21,657
Mining and quarrying* Electricity, gas and water supply*	79,511	87,203	97,880
Manufacturing	551,314	558,745	561,285
Construction	107,437	111,984	116,493
Wholesale and retail trade; repair of motor vehicles, motorcycles and personal and household goods; and transport and accommodation	390,439	389,987	393,363
Information and communication	111,945	117,214	117,975
Financial intermediation and insurance	100,518	102,426	103,167
Real estate, renting and business activities†	536,075	537,931	551,640
Public administration and defence; compulsory social security Education Health and social work Other community, social and personal service activities, incl. hotels and restaurants Private households with employed persons	527,315	543,128	562,152
Gross value added in basic prices	2,424,083	2,470,199	2,525,612
Taxes, less subsidies, on products*	275,017	279,701	283,868
GDP in market prices	2,699,100	2,749,900	2,809,480

* Data obtained as residuals.
† Including deduction for financial intermediation services indirectly measured.

BALANCE OF PAYMENTS
(US $ '000 million)

	2011	2012	2013
Exports of goods	1,432.76	1,380.30	1,440.13
Imports of goods	−1,205.73	−1,127.11	−1,160.66
Balance on goods	227.03	253.19	279.47
Exports of services	247.96	240.60	261.01
Imports of services	−295.18	−287.67	−324.53
Balance on goods and services	179.80	206.12	215.95
Primary income received	304.20	277.63	276.80
Primary income paid	−208.80	−181.54	−179.11
Balance on goods, services and primary income	275.18	302.20	313.64
Secondary income received	68.99	64.33	68.64
Secondary income paid	−117.04	−114.24	−126.25
Current balance	227.13	252.29	256.03
Capital account (net)	2.31	1.63	2.65
Direct investment assets	−108.97	−115.98	−80.94
Direct investment liabilities	88.99	50.58	51.27
Portfolio investment assets	−29.49	−141.58	−186.66
Portfolio investment liabilities	72.07	58.15	−32.10
Financial derivatives and employee stock options (net)	−37.13	−32.79	−24.15
Other investment assets	−194.62	−212.42	244.14
Other investment liabilities	−10.69	121.54	−297.28
Net errors and omissions	−5.69	20.27	68.20
Reserves and related items	3.92	1.70	1.16

Source: IMF, *International Financial Statistics*.

OVERSEAS DEVELOPMENT AID
(€ million)

	2010	2011	2012
Bilateral	6,082	6,256	6,678
Multilateral	3,722	3,880	3,389
Total	9,804	10,136	10,067

External Trade

PRINCIPAL COMMODITIES
(distribution by SITC, € million)

Imports c.i.f.	2011	2012	2013
Food and live animals	52,639	54,190	55,540
Crude materials (inedible) except fuels	38,095	36,428	34,516
Mineral fuels, lubricants, etc.	121,686	135,294	133,393
Petroleum, petroleum products, etc.	78,844	87,866	86,424
Gas, natural and manufactured	33,985	39,605	40,327
Chemicals and related products	114,160	113,755	112,286
Organic chemicals	23,276	24,553	23,980
Medicinal and pharmaceutical products	37,027	35,973	35,247
Basic manufactures	124,255	116,620	113,339
Machinery and transport equipment	303,480	300,255	294,741
Power-generating machinery and equipment	28,552	28,406	27,773
General industrial machinery, equipment and parts	33,774	34,591	35,161
Office machines and automatic data-processing equipment	27,762	26,809	25,333
Telecommunications and sound equipment	26,486	29,362	28,255
Other electrical machinery, apparatus and appliances	66,422	62,024	60,925
Road vehicles (incl. air-cushion vehicles) and parts	71,174	72,674	71,141
Other transport equipment	28,411	26,228	27,161
Miscellaneous manufactured articles	101,072	101,684	103,609
Articles of apparel and clothing accessories (excl. footwear)	28,179	26,649	27,630
Total (incl. others)	902,523	905,925	898,164

Exports f.o.b.	2011	2012	2013
Food and live animals	45,878	48,735	51,535
Chemicals and related products	162,980	170,950	172,716
Medical and pharmaceutical products	50,818	56,031	56,975
Basic manufactures	145,602	142,635	139,170
Machinery and transport equipment	510,453	528,945	523,654
Power-generating machinery and equipment	39,785	42,197	40,981
Machinery specialized for particular industries	48,844	47,884	46,834
General industrial machinery and equipment	75,920	78,522	79,422
Office machines and automatic data-processing equipment	19,877	19,002	18,010
Telecommunications and sound equipment	17,342	18,691	18,178
Electrical machinery, apparatus and appliances	81,094	80,040	80,949
Road vehicles (incl. air-cushion vehicles) and parts	177,938	183,026	182,085
Other transport equipment	34,756	43,318	41,660
Miscellaneous manufactured articles	108,940	109,795	111,442
Total (incl. others)	1,061,225	1,095,766	1,093,115

PRINCIPAL TRADING PARTNERS
(€ million)

Imports c.i.f.	2011	2012	2013
Austria	37,028.4	36,419.4	36,792.5
Belgium	38,327.7	37,763.0	38,994.6
Brazil	11,259.9	10,614.7	8,885.3
China, People's Republic	79,528.2	78,529.3	74,544.4
Czech Republic	32,684.2	32,493.0	33,010.3
Denmark	12,178.1	11,346.2	11,580.6
France	65,948.3	64,035.5	64,018.3
Hungary	18,207.9	18,466.5	19,491.2
Ireland	12,334.0	10,093.2	8,780.7
Italy	47,843.5	47,957.2	46,929.9
Japan	23,595.1	21,910.3	19,491.6
Korea, Republic	9,622.7	8,457.0	8,048.3
Netherlands	81,804.3	85,737.9	88,679.6
Norway	20,634.0	26,273.1	22,115.0
Poland	32,305.4	33,027.3	36,013.0
Russia	40,886.2	42,765.1	41,234.5
Slovakia	10,726.1	12,015.1	12,252.9
Spain	22,490.7	23,206.5	23,639.5
Sweden	14,115.4	13,774.0	13,907.7
Switzerland-Liechtenstein	37,422.9	38,206.7	38,321.5
Turkey	11,790.5	12,071.1	12,298.5
United Kingdom	44,740.7	42,820.1	42,513.2
USA	48,531.5	51,070.5	48,581.9
Total (incl. others)	902,522.8	905,925.4	898,164.0

Exports f.o.b.	2011	2012	2013
Austria	57,670.9	56,591.2	56,276.5
Belgium	46,976.3	43,822.2	42,437.9
Brazil	11,163.1	11,727.5	11,287.2
China, People's Republic	64,863.1	66,746.1	66,911.6
Czech Republic	30,824.5	31,288.7	31,073.4
Denmark	14,769.3	14,893.9	15,843.7
France	101,444.3	102,910.7	99,979.9
Hungary	15,774.5	16,207.2	17,504.4
India	10,855.6	10,421.0	9,146.5
Italy	62,043.6	55,528.7	53,247.3
Japan	15,115.4	17,137.8	17,075.9
Korea, Republic	11,698.2	13,399.0	14,447.3
Netherlands	69,422.8	70,380.8	70,970.3
Poland	43,502.7	41,823.2	42,472.6
Russia	34,458.8	38,103.3	35,801.6
Spain	34,811.1	31,047.5	31,348.8
Sweden	22,034.3	21,092.1	20,700.4
Switzerland-Liechtenstein	48,446.7	49,472.5	46,924.1
Turkey	20,118.3	20,100.0	21,372.0
United Kingdom	65,569.7	73,282.5	75,488.5
USA	73,775.6	86,971.4	89,347.8
Total (incl. others)	1,061,225.3	1,095,766.4	1,093,114.6

Transport

FEDERAL RAILWAYS
(traffic)

	2011	2012	2013
Passengers (million)	2,474	2,571	2,581
Freight carried ('000 tons)	374,737	366,140	373,738
Freight net ton-km (million)	113,317	110,065	112,613

ROAD TRAFFIC
('000 licensed vehicles at 1 January)

	2012	2013	2014
Passenger cars	42,927.6	43,431.1	43,851.2
Lorries	2,528.7	2,578.6	2,629.2
Buses	76.0	76.0	76.8
Motorcycles	3,908.1	3,983.0	4,055.0
Trailers	6,213.9	6,358.6	6,500.4

SHIPPING
Inland Waterways

	2011	2012	2013
Freight ton-km (million)	55,027	58,488	60,070

Flag Registered Fleet
(at 31 December)

	2012	2013	2014
Number of vessels	1,211	1,195	1,165
Total displacement ('000 grt)	14,246.5	12,731.9	11,718.3

Source: Lloyd's List Intelligence (www.lloydslistintelligence.com).

International Seaborne Traffic
(incl. transshipments, '000 metric tons)

	2011	2012	2013
Freight unloaded	177,085	175,559	171,421
Freight loaded	112,480	115,977	119,194

CIVIL AVIATION
(traffic on scheduled services)

	2010	2011
Kilometres flown (million)	1,331	1,418
Passengers carried ('000)	101,852	112,016
Passenger-km (million)	201,537	220,036
Total ton-km (million)	27,767	29,925

Source: UN, *Statistical Yearbook*.

Passengers carried ('000): 105,978 in 2012; 105,016 in 2013 (Source: World Bank, World Development Indicators database).

Tourism

FOREIGN TOURIST ARRIVALS
('000)*

Country of residence	2011	2012	2013
Austria	1,494.7	1,567.5	1,631.4
Belgium and Luxembourg	1,412.6	1,470.2	1,064.6
Denmark	1,242.8	1,356.7	1,133.3
France	1,462.1	1,535.1	1,384.1
Italy	1,538.4	1,581.0	1,443.2
Japan	642.5	734.5	692.6
Netherlands	4,035.8	4,169.4	1,939.3
Poland	684.2	737.3	405.8
Spain	889.5	889.7	585.4
Sweden	846.6	897.0	160.9
Switzerland	2,301.5	2,489.6	2,594.0
United Kingdom	2,054.8	2,162.5	2,294.1
USA	2,163.8	2,314.0	2,200.7
Total (incl. others)	28,099.8	30,410.5	31,545.1

* Figures refer to arrivals at all accommodation types.

Tourism receipts (€ million, excl. passenger transport): 38,902 in 2011; 38,068 in 2012; 41,217 in 2013 (Source: World Tourism Organization).

Communications Media

	2011	2012	2013
Telephones ('000 main lines in use)	51,400	50,100	48,700
Mobile cellular telephones ('000 subscribers)	90,900	92,400	98,470
Broadband subscribers ('000) . .	27,186	27,907	28,603

Source: International Telecommunication Union.

Education

(2013/14 unless otherwise indicated)

	Institutes	Teachers*	Students
Pre-primary	1,329	2,548	27,696
Primary	15,749	193,474	2,708,400
Secondary (and other orientation stage) . . .	4,248	48,894	651,309
Alternative format schools	1,782	38,258	453,930
Intermediate	2,399	66,675	1,015,160
Grammar	3,124	179,348	2,329,990
Integrated comprehensive	1,452	54,762	753,231
Free Waldorf schools . .	214	6,728	81,996
Special	3,191	71,270	343,343
Vocational	8,833	122,883	2,530,586
Higher:			
non-university institutions	317	} 233,259† {	992,163‡
universities	106		1,706,262‡

* 2012/13.

† 2013, full-time academic and creative arts staff.

‡ 2014/15, preliminary.

Note: Figures exclude evening schools, adult education and schools for nurses, midwives, etc. Data for teachers include full-time and part-time teaching staff unless otherwise indicated.

Pupil-teacher ratio (primary education, UNESCO estimate): 11.7 in 2011/12 (Source: UNESCO Institute for Statistics).

Directory

The Government

HEAD OF STATE

Federal President: JOACHIM GAUCK (assumed office 18 March 2012).

THE FEDERAL GOVERNMENT
(April 2015)

A coalition of the Christlich-Demokratische Union Deutschlands/Christlich-Soziale Union (CDU/CSU) and the Sozialdemokratische Partei Deutschlands (SPD).

Federal Chancellor: ANGELA MERKEL (CDU).

Federal Vice-Chancellor and Federal Minister of Economic Affairs and Energy: SIGMAR GABRIEL (SPD).

Federal Minister of Foreign Affairs: FRANK-WALTER STEINMEIER (SPD).

Federal Minister of the Interior: THOMAS DE MAIZIÈRE (CDU).

Federal Minister of Justice and Consumer Protection: HEIKO MAAS (SPD).

Federal Minister of Finance: WOLFGANG SCHÄUBLE (CDU).

Federal Minister of Labour and Social Affairs: ANDREA NAHLES (SPD).

Federal Minister of Food and Agriculture: CHRISTIAN SCHMIDT (CSU).

Federal Minister of Defence: URSULA VON DER LEYEN (CDU).

Federal Minister of Family Affairs, Senior Citizens, Women and Youth: MANUELA SCHWESIG (SPD).

Federal Minister of Health: HERRMANN GRÖHE (CDU).

Federal Minister of Transport and Digital Infrastructure: ALEXANDER DOBRINDT (CSU).

Federal Minister of the Environment, Nature Conservation, Building and Nuclear Safety: BARBARA HENDRICKS (SPD).

Federal Minister of Education and Research: JOHANNA WANKA (CDU).

Federal Minister of Economic Co-operation and Development: GERD MÜLLER (CSU).

Head of the Federal Chancellery and Federal Minister for Special Tasks: PETER ALTMAIER (CDU).

MINISTRIES

Office of the Federal President: 11010 Berlin; Bundespräsidial-amt, Spreeweg 1, 10557 Berlin; tel. (30) 20000; fax (30) 20001999; e-mail bundespraesidialamt@bpra.bund.de; internet www.bundespraesident.de.

Federal Chancellery: Bundeskanzler-Amt, Willy-Brandt Str. 1, 10557 Berlin; tel. (30) 40000; fax (30) 40002357; e-mail internetpost@bpa.bund.de; internet www.bundeskanzlerin.de.

Press and Information Office of the Federal Government: Dorotheenstr. 84, 10117 Berlin; 11044 Berlin; tel. (30) 182720; fax (30) 18102720; e-mail internetpost@bundesregierung.de; internet www.bundesregierung.de.

Federal Ministry of Defence: Stauffenbergstr. 18, 10785 Berlin; tel. (30) 1824000; fax (30) 18245357; e-mail poststelle@bmvg.bund.de; internet www.bmvg.de.

Federal Ministry of Economic Co-operation and Development: Dahlmannstr. 4, 53113 Bonn; Postfach 120322, 53045 Bonn; tel. (228) 995350; fax (228) 995353500; e-mail info@bmz.bund.de; internet www.bmz.de.

Federal Ministry of Economic Affairs and Energy: 11019 Berlin; Scharnhorststr. 34–37, 10115 Berlin; tel. (30) 186150; fax (30) 186157010; e-mail info@bmwi.bund.de; internet www.bmwi.de.

Federal Ministry of Education and Research: Heinemannstr. 2, 53175 Bonn; tel. (228) 99570; fax (228) 995783601; e-mail information@bmbf.bund.de; internet www.bmbf.de.

Federal Ministry of the Environment, Nature Conservation, Building and Nuclear Safety: Stresemannstr. 128–130, 10117 Berlin; tel. (30) 183050; fax (30) 183054375; e-mail service@bmu.bund.de; internet www.bmu.de.

Federal Ministry of Family Affairs, Senior Citizens, Women and Youth: Glinkastr. 24, 10117 Berlin; tel. (30) 185550; fax (30) 185551145; e-mail poststelle@bmfsfj.bund.de; internet www.bmfsfj.de.

Federal Ministry of Finance: 11016 Berlin; Wilhelmstr. 97, 10117 Berlin; tel. (30) 186820; fax (30) 186824248; e-mail poststelle@bmf.bund.de; internet www.bundesfinanzministerium.de.

Federal Ministry of Food and Agriculture: 11055 Berlin; Wilhelmstr. 54, 10117 Berlin; tel. (30) 185290; fax (30) 185294262; e-mail poststelle@bmelv.bund.de; internet www.bmelv.de.

Federal Ministry of Foreign Affairs: 11013 Berlin; Werderscher Markt 1, 10117 Berlin; tel. (30) 18170; fax (30) 18173402; e-mail poststelle@auswaertiges-amt.de; internet www.auswaertiges-amt.de.

Federal Ministry of Health: 53107 Bonn; Rochusstr. 1, 53123 Bonn; tel. (228) 994410; fax (228) 994411921; e-mail info@bmg.bund.de; internet www.bmg.bund.de.

Federal Ministry of the Interior: Alt-Moabit 101D, 10559 Berlin; tel. (30) 186810; fax (30) 186812926; e-mail poststelle@bmi.bund.de; internet www.bmi.bund.de.

Federal Ministry of Justice and Consumer Protection: Mohrenstr. 37, 10117 Berlin; tel. (30) 185800; fax (30) 185809525; e-mail poststelle@bmj.bund.de; internet www.bmj.de.

Federal Ministry of Labour and Social Affairs: Wilhelmstr. 49, 10117 Berlin; tel. (30) 185270; fax (30) 185271830; e-mail info@bmas .bund.de; internet www.bmas.de.

Federal Ministry of Transport and Digital Infrastructure: Invalidenstr. 44, 10115 Berlin; tel. (30) 183000; fax (30) 183001920; e-mail buergerinfo@bmvbs.bund.de; internet www.bmvbs.de.

Legislature

Federal Assembly
(Bundestag)

Pl. der Republik 1, 11011 Berlin; tel. (30) 2270; fax (30) 22736979; e-mail mail@bundestag.de; internet www.bundestag.de.

President: Prof. Dr NORBERT LAMMERT (CDU).

Vice-Presidents: PETER HINTZE (CDU/CSU), Dr JOHANNES SINGHAMMER (CDU/CSU), EDELGARD BULMAHN (SPD), ULLA SCHMIDT (SPD), PETRA PAU (Die Linke), CLAUDIA ROTH (Bündnis 90/Die Grünen).

General Election, 22 September 2013

Parties and Groups	Votes*	% of votes*	Seats
Christlich-Demokratische Union Deutschlands/Christlich-Soziale Union (CDU/CSU)†	18,165,446	41.54	311
Sozialdemokratische Partei Deutschlands (SPD)	11,252,215	25.73	193
Die Linke	3,755,699	8.59	64
Bündnis 90/Die Grünen	3,694,057	8.45	63
Freie Demokratische Partei (FDP) .	2,083,533	4.76	—
Alternative für Deutschland (AfD) .	2,056,985	4.70	—
Others	2,718,921	6.22	—
Total	**43,726,856**	**100.00**	**631**

*Figures refer to valid second votes (i.e. for state party lists). The total number of valid first votes (for individual candidates) was 44,309,925. In addition, there were 684,883 invalid first votes and 583,069 invalid second votes.

† Of which the CDU received 14,921,877 votes (34.13%—255 seats) and the CSU received 3,243,569 votes (7.42%—56 seats).

Federal Council
(Bundesrat)

Niederkirchnerstr. 1–4, 10117 Berlin; tel. (18) 91000; fax (30) 189100400; e-mail bundesrat@bundesrat.de; internet www .bundesrat.de.

The Bundesrat has 69 members. Each Land (state) has three, four, five or six votes, depending on the size of its population, and may send as many members to the sessions as it has votes. The head of government of each Land is automatically a member of the Bundesrat. Members of the Federal Government attend the sessions, which are held every two to three weeks.

President: VOLKER BOUFFIER (CDU) (1 Nov. 2014–31 Oct. 2015).

Länder	Seats
Nordrhein-Westfalen (North Rhine-Westphalia) .	6
Bayern (Bavaria)	6
Baden-Württemberg	6
Niedersachsen (Lower Saxony)	6
Hessen (Hesse)	5
Sachsen (Saxony)	4
Rheinland-Pfalz (Rhineland-Palatinate)	4
Berlin	4
Schleswig-Holstein	4
Brandenburg	4
Sachsen-Anhalt (Saxony-Anhalt)	4
Thüringen (Thuringia)	4
Hamburg	3
Mecklenburg-Vorpommern (Mecklenburg-Western Pomerania)	3
Saarland	3
Bremen	3
Total	**69**

The Land Governments

The 16 Länder of Germany are autonomous but not sovereign states, enjoying a high degree of self-government and extensive legislative powers. Thirteen of the Länder have a Landesregierung (Government) and a Landtag (Assembly). The equivalent of the Landesregierung in Berlin, Bremen and Hamburg is the Senat (Senate). The equivalent of the Landtag is the Abgeordnetenhaus (House of Representatives) in Berlin and the Bürgerschaft (City Council) in Bremen and Hamburg.

BADEN-WÜRTTEMBERG

The Constitution was adopted by the Assembly in Stuttgart on 11 November 1953 and came into force on 19 November. The Minister-President, who is elected by the Assembly, appoints and dismisses Ministers. The Government is currently formed by a coalition of Bündnis 90/Die Grünen and the SPD.

Minister-President: WINFRIED KRETSCHMANN (Bündnis 90/Die Grünen).

Landtag von Baden-Württemberg

Haus des Landtags, Konrad-Adenauer-Str. 3, 70173 Stuttgart; tel. (711) 20630; fax (711) 2063299; e-mail post@landtag-bw.de; internet www.landtag-bw.de.

President of Assembly: WILFRIED KLENK (CDU).

Election, 27 March 2011

Party	Seats
Christlich-Demokratische Union Deutschlands (CDU)	60
Bündnis 90/Die Grünen	36
Sozialdemokratische Partei Deutschlands (SPD) .	35
Freie Demokratische Partei (FDP)	7
Total	**138**

The Land is divided into four administrative districts: Stuttgart, Karlsruhe, Tübingen and Freiburg.

BAYERN (BAVARIA)

The Constitution of Bavaria provides for a unicameral Assembly and a Constitutional Court. Provision is also made for referendums. The Minister-President, who is elected by the Assembly for five years, appoints the Ministers and Secretaries of State with the consent of the Assembly.

Minister-President: HORST SEEHOFER (CSU).

Bayerischer Landtag

Landtagsamt, Maximilaneum, 81627 München; tel. (89) 41260; fax (89) 41261392; e-mail landtag@bayern.landtag.de; internet www .bayern.landtag.de.

President of Assembly: BARBARA STAMM (CSU).

Election, 15 September 2013

Party	Seats
Christlich-Soziale Union (CSU)	101
Sozialdemokratische Partei Deutschlands (SPD) .	42
Freie Wähler	19
Bündnis 90/Die Grünen	18
Total	**180**

Bayern is divided into seven districts: Mittelfranken, Oberfranken, Unterfranken, Schwaben, Niederbayern, Oberpfalz and Oberbayern.

BERLIN

The Abgeordnetenhaus (House of Representatives) is the legislative body. The executive agency is the Senate, which is composed of the Regierender Bürgermeister (Governing Mayor) and up to 10 Senators, from among whom the deputy mayor is elected. The Governing Mayor and the senators are elected by a majority of the House of Representatives. The Senate is responsible to the House of Representatives and dependent on its confidence.

Regierender Bürgermeister: MICHAEL MÜLLER (SPD).

Abgeordnetenhaus von Berlin
(House of Representatives)

Niederkirchnerstr. 5, 10117 Berlin; tel. (30) 23250; e-mail verwaltung@parlament-berlin.de; internet www.parlament-berlin .de.

President of House of Representatives: RALF WIELAND (SPD).

Election, 18 September 2011

Party	Seats
Sozialdemokratische Partei Deutschlands (SPD) .	48
Christlich-Demokratische Union Deutschlands (CDU)	39
Bündnis 90/Die Grünen	30
Die Linke	20
Piratenpartei Deutschland	15
Total	152

BRANDENBURG

The Constitution of Brandenburg was adopted on 14 June 1992 and came into force on 20 August. It was amended on 7 April 1999. The Assembly elects the Minister-President, who appoints Ministers. The Government is currently formed of a coalition of the SPD and Die Linke.

Minister-President: Dr DIETMAR WOIDKE (SPD).

Landtag Brandenburg

Postfach 601064, 14410 Potsdam; Am Havelblick 8, 14473 Potsdam; tel. (331) 9660; fax (331) 9661210; e-mail poststelle@landtag .brandenburg.de; internet www.landtag.brandenburg.de.

President of Assembly: BRITTA STARK (SPD).

Election, 14 September 2014

Party	Seats
Sozialdemokratische Partei Deutschlands (SPD) .	30
Christlich-Demokratische Union Deutschlands (CDU)	21
Die Linke	17
Alternative für Deutschland (AfD)	11
Bündnis 90/Die Grünen	6
Brandenburger Vereinigte Bürgerbewegungen/Freie Wähler (BVB/Freie Wähler)	3
Total	88

BREMEN

The Constitution of the Free Hanseatic City of Bremen was approved by referendum on 12 October 1947. The main constitutional organs are the Bürgerschaft (City Council), the Senate and the Constitutional Court. The Senate is the executive organ elected by the Council for the duration of its own tenure of office. The Senate elects from its own ranks two Bürgermeister (Mayors), one of whom becomes President of the Senate. Decisions of the Council are subject to the delaying veto of the Senate. The Government is currently formed from a coalition of the SPD and Bündnis 90/Die Grünen.

First Bürgermeister and President of the Senate: JENS BÖHRNSEN (SPD).

Bremische Bürgerschaft (Bremen City Council)

Am Markt 20, 28195 Bremen; tel. (421) 3614555; fax (421) 36112492; e-mail geschaeftsstelle@buergerschaft.bremen.de; internet www .bremische-buergerschaft.de.

President of the City Council: CHRISTIAN WEBER (SPD).

Election, 22 May 2011

Party	Seats
Sozialdemokratische Partei Deutschlands (SPD) .	36
Bündnis 90/Die Grünen	21
Christlich-Demokratische Union Deutschlands (CDU)	20
Die Linke	5
Bürger in Wut (BIW)	1
Total	83

HAMBURG

The Constitution of the Free and Hanseatic City of Hamburg was adopted in June 1952. The Bürgerschaft (City Council) elects the President of the Senate (government), who appoints and dismisses members of the Senate. The Senate is currently composed of members of the SPD.

President of Senate and First Bürgermeister: OLAF SCHOLZ (SPD).

Bürgerschaft der Freien und Hansestadt Hamburg (Hamburg City Council)

Rathaus, Rathausmarkt 1, 20095 Hamburg; tel. (40) 428312408; fax (40) 428312558; e-mail oeffentlichkeitsservice@bk.hamburg.de; internet www.hamburgische-buergerschaft.de.

President: CAROLA VEIT (SPD).

Election, 15 February 2015

Party	Seats
Sozialdemokratische Partei Deutschlands (SPD) .	58
Christlich-Demokratische Union Deutschlands (CDU)	20
Bündnis 90/Die Grünen	15
Die Linke	11
Freie Demokratische Partei (FDP)	9
Alternative für Deutschland (AfD)	8
Total	121

HESSEN (HESSE)

The Constitution of this Land dates from 1 December 1946. The Minister-President is elected by the Assembly, and appoints and dismisses Ministers with its consent. The Assembly can force the resignation of the Government by a vote of no confidence. The Government is currently formed by a coalition of the CDU and the FDP.

Minister-President: VOLKER BOUFFIER (CDU).

Hessischer Landtag

Schlosspl. 1–3, 65183 Wiesbaden; tel. (611) 3500; fax (611) 350434; e-mail oeffentlichkeit@ltg.hessen.de; internet www .hessischer-landtag.de.

President of Assembly: NORBERT KARTMANN (CDU).

Election, 22 September 2013

Party	Seats
Christlich-Demokratische Union Deutschlands (CDU)	47
Sozialdemokratische Partei Deutschlands (SPD) .	37
Bündnis 90/Die Grünen	14
Die Linke	6
Freie Demokratische Partei (FDP)	6
Total	110

Hessen is divided into three governmental districts: Kassel, Giessen and Darmstadt.

MECKLENBURG-VORPOMMERN (MECKLENBURG-WESTERN POMERANIA)

The Constitution was adopted by the Assembly on 14 May 1993. The Assembly elects the Minister-President, who appoints and dismisses Ministers. The Government is currently formed by a coalition of the SPD and the CDU.

Minister-President: Dr ERWIN SELLERING (SPD).

Landtag Mecklenburg-Vorpommern

Schloss, Lennéstr. 1, 19053 Schwerin; tel. (385) 5250; fax (385) 5252141; e-mail poststelle@landtag-mv.de; internet www .landtag-mv.de.

President of Assembly: SYLVIA BRETSCHNEIDER (SPD).

Election, 4 September 2011

Party	Seats
Sozialdemokratische Partei Deutschlands (SPD) .	27
Christlich-Demokratische Union Deutschlands (CDU)	18
Die Linke	14
Bündnis 90/Die Grünen	7
Nationaldemokratische Partei Deutschlands (NPD) .	5
Total	71

NIEDERSACHSEN (LOWER SAXONY)

The Constitution was adopted by the Assembly on 19 May 1993 and came into force on 1 June. The Minister-President is elected by the Assembly, with whose consent he/she appoints and dismisses Ministers. The Government is currently formed of a coalition of the SPD and Bündnis 90/Die Grünen.

Minister-President: STEPHAN WEIL (SPD).

Landtag Niedersachsen

Hinrich-Wilhelm-Kopf-Pl. 1, 30159 Hannover; tel. (511) 30300; fax (511) 30302806; e-mail poststelle@lt.niedersachsen.de; internet www.landtag-niedersachsen.de.

President of Assembly: BERND BUSEMANN (CDU).

Election, 20 January 2013

Party	Seats
Christlich-Demokratische Union Deutschlands (CDU)	54
Sozialdemokratische Partei Deutschlands (SPD)	49
Bündnis 90/Die Grünen	20
Freie Demokratische Partei (FDP)	14
Total	137

NORDRHEIN-WESTFALEN (NORTH RHINE-WESTPHALIA)

The present Constitution was adopted by the Assembly on 6 June 1950, and was endorsed by the electorate in the elections held on 18 June. The Government is presided over by the Minister-President, who appoints Ministers. After an early election which was held on 13 May 2012 the SPD and Bündnis 90/Die Grünen formed a Government.

Minister-President: HANNELORE KRAFT (SPD).

Landtag von Nordrhein-Westfalen

Postfach 101143, 40002 Düsseldorf; Pl. des Landtags 1, 40221 Düsseldorf; tel. (211) 8840; fax (211) 8842258; e-mail email@landtag.nrw.de; internet www.landtag.nrw.de.

President of Assembly: CARINA GÖDECKE (SPD).

Election, 13 May 2012

Party	Seats
Sozialdemokratische Partei Deutschlands (SPD)	99
Christlich-Demokratische Union Deutschlands (CDU)	67
Bündnis 90/Die Grünen	29
Freie Demokratische Partei (FDP)	22
Piratenpartei Deutschland	20
Total	237

The Land is divided into five governmental districts: Düsseldorf, Münster, Arnsberg, Detmold and Köln.

RHEINLAND-PFALZ (RHINELAND-PALATINATE)

The three chief agencies of the Constitution of this Land are the Assembly, the Government and the Constitutional Court. The Minister-President is elected by the Assembly, with whose consent he or she appoints and dismisses Ministers. Following the election of 27 March 2011, the SPD formed a coalition with Bündnis 90/Die Grünen.

Minister-President: MALU DREYER (SPD).

Landtag Rheinland-Pfalz

Postfach 3040, 55020 Mainz; Deutschhauspl. 12, 55116 Mainz; tel. (6131) 2080; fax (6131) 2082447; e-mail poststelle@landtag.rlp.de; internet www.landtag.rlp.de.

President of Assembly: JOACHIM MERTES (SPD).

Election, 27 March 2011

Party	Seats
Sozialdemokratische Partei Deutschlands (SPD)	42
Christlich-Demokratische Union Deutschlands (CDU)	41
Bündnis 90/Die Grünen	18
Total	101

SAARLAND

Under the Constitution, which came into force on 1 January 1957, Saarland was politically integrated into the FRG as a Land. It was economically integrated into the FRG in July 1959. The Minister-President is elected by the Assembly. Following an early election on 25 March 2012, the CDU formed a coalition with the SPD.

Minister-President: ANNEGRET KRAMP-KARRENBAUER (CDU).

Landtag des Saarlandes

Postfach 101833, 66018 Saarbrücken; Franz-Josef-Röder Str. 7, 66119 Saarbrücken; tel. (681) 50020; fax (681) 5002546; e-mail r.riemann@landtag-saar.de; internet www.landtag-saar.de.

President of the Assembly: HANS LEY (CDU).

Election, 25 March 2012

Party	Seats
Christlich-Demokratische Union Deutschlands (CDU)	19
Sozialdemokratische Partei Deutschlands (SPD)	17
Die Linke	9
Piratenpartei Deutschland	4
Bündnis 90/Die Grünen	2
Total	51

SACHSEN (SAXONY)

The Constitution of Sachsen was adopted on 26 May 1992 and came into force on 6 June. The Assembly elects the Minister-President and can force the resignation of the Government by a vote of no confidence, if a majority of parliamentarians can agree on a replacement candidate. The Government is currently formed from a coalition of the CDU and FDP.

Minister-President: STANISLAW TILLICH (CDU).

Sächsischer Landtag

Postfach 120705, 01008 Dresden; Bernhard-von-Lindenau Pl. 1, 01067 Dresden; tel. (351) 49350; fax (351) 4935900; e-mail info@slt.sachsen.de; internet www.landtag.sachsen.de.

President of Assembly: Dr MATTHIAS RÖSSLER (CDU).

Election, 31 August 2014

Party	Seats
Christlich-Demokratische Union Deutschlands (CDU)	59
Die Linke	27
Sozialdemokratische Partei Deutschlands (SPD)	18
Alternative für Deutschland (AfD)	14
Bündnis 90/Die Grünen	8
Total	126

Sachsen is divided into three districts: Chemnitz, Dresden and Leipzig.

SACHSEN-ANHALT (SAXONY-ANHALT)

The Constitution of Sachsen-Anhalt was adopted on 16 July 1992. The Assembly elects the Minister-President, who appoints and dismisses Ministers. The Government is formed by a coalition of the CDU and SPD.

Minister-President: Dr REINER HASELOFF (CDU).

Landtag von Sachsen-Anhalt

Dompl. 6–9, 39104 Magdeburg; tel. (391) 5600; fax (391) 5601123; e-mail kontakt@lt.sachsen-anhalt.de; internet www.landtag.sachsen-anhalt.de.

President of Assembly: DETLEF GÜRTH (CDU).

Election, 20 March 2011

Party	Seats
Christlich-Demokratische Union Deutschlands (CDU)	41
Die Linke	29
Sozialdemokratische Partei Deutschlands (SPD)	26
Bündnis 90/Die Grünen	9
Total	105

SCHLESWIG-HOLSTEIN

The Provisional Constitution was adopted by the Assembly on 13 December 1949. The Assembly elects the Minister-President, who appoints and dismisses Ministers. The Government is currently formed by a coalition of the SPD, Bündnis 90/Die Grünen and the SSW.

Minister-President: TORSTEN ALBIG (SPD).

Landtag Schleswig-Holstein

Düsternbrooker Weg 70, 24105 Kiel; tel. (431) 9880; fax (431) 9881119; e-mail annette.wiese-krukowska@landtag.ltsh.de; internet www.landtag.ltsh.de.

President of Assembly: KLAUS SCHLIE (CDU).

Election, 6 May 2012

Party	Seats
Christlich-Demokratische Union Deutschlands (CDU)	22
Sozialdemokratische Partei Deutschlands (SPD) .	22
Bündnis 90/Die Grünen	10
Freie Demokratische Partei (FDP)	6
Piratenpartei Deutschland	6
Südschleswigscher Wählerverband (SSW) . . .	3
Total	**69**

THÜRINGEN (THURINGIA)

The Constitution of Thüringen was adopted on 25 October 1993. The Assembly elects the Minister-President and can force the resignation of the Government by a vote of no confidence, if a majority of parliamentarians agree on a replacement candidate. The Government is currently formed of a coalition of Die Linke, the SPD and Bündnis 90/Die Grünen.

Minister-President: BODO RAMELOW (Die Linke).

Thüringer Landtag

Jürgen-Fuchs Str. 1, 99096 Erfurt; tel. (361) 3772006; fax (361) 3772004; e-mail pressestelle@landtag.thueringen.de; internet www.thueringen.de/tlt.

President of Assembly: CHRISTIAN CARIUS (CDU).

Election, 14 September 2014

Party	Seats
Christlich-Demokratische Union Deutschlands (CDU)	34
Die Linke	28
Sozialdemokratische Partei Deutschlands (SPD) .	12
Alternative für Deutschland (AfD)	11
Bündnis 90/Die Grünen	6
Total	**91**

Election Commission

Bundeswahlleiter (Federal Returning Officer): Statistisches Bundesamt, 65180 Wiesbaden; tel. (611) 754863; fax (611) 724000; e-mail bundeswahlleiter@destatis.de; internet www.bundeswahlleiter.de; Federal Returning Officer RODERICH EGELER (Pres., Federal Office of Statistics); Deputy Federal Returning Officer DIETER SARREITHER.

Political Organizations

Alternative für Deutschland (AfD) (Alternative for Germany): Frankfurter Landstr. 153–155, 61231 Bad Nauheim; e-mail geschaeftsstelle@alternativefuer.de; internet www.alternativefuer.de; f. 2013; anti-euro; Spokespersons Dr KONRAD ADAM, Prof. Dr BERND LUCKE, Dr FRAUKE PETRY.

Bündnis 90/Die Grünen (Alliance 90/The Greens): Pl. vor dem Neuen Tor 1, 10115 Berlin; tel. (30) 284420; fax (30) 28442210; e-mail info@gruene.de; internet www.gruene.de; f. 1993; merger of Bündnis 90 (f. 1990 as an electoral political assen of citizens' movements of the former GDR) and Die Grünen (f. 1980, largely composed of the membership of the Grüne Aktion Zukunft, the Grüne Liste, Umweltschutz and the Aktionsgemeinschaft Unabhängiger Deutscher, also including groups of widely varying political views); essentially left-wing party programme includes ecological issues, democratization of society at all levels, social justice, comprehensive disarmament; Co-Chair. SIMONE PETER, CEM ÖZDEMIR.

Bürger in Wut (BIW) (Citizens in Rage): Torstr. 195, 10115 Berlin; tel. (30) 208664660; fax (30) 208664661; e-mail info@buerger-in-wut.de; internet www.buerger-in-wut.de; f. 2004; supports free democracy; Chair. JAN TIMKE.

Christlich-Demokratische Union Deutschlands/Christlich-Soziale Union (CDU/CSU) (Christian Democratic and Christian Social Union): Pl. der Republik 1, 11011 Berlin; tel. (30) 22755550; fax (30) 22756061; e-mail fraktion@cducsu.de; internet www.cducsu.de; alliance of the CDU and its sister party in Bavaria, the CSU; forms a single group in the Bundestag; Parliamentary Leader VOLKER KAUDER.

CDU: Klingelhöferstr. 8, 10785 Berlin; tel. (30) 220700; fax (30) 22070111; e-mail info@cdu.de; internet www.cdu.de; f. 1945; became a federal party in 1950; advocates united action between Catholics and Protestants for rebuilding German life on a Christian-Democratic basis, while guaranteeing private property

and the freedom of the individual, and for a 'free and equal Germany in a free, politically united and socially just Europe'; other objectives are to guarantee close ties with allies within NATO and the EU; c. 520,000 mems; Chair. Dr ANGELA MERKEL; Sec.-Gen. Dr PETER TAUBER.

CSU: Franz Josef Strauss-Haus, Nymphenburger Str. 64, 80335 München; tel. (89) 12430; fax (89) 1243299; e-mail landesleitung@csu-bayern.de; internet www.csu.de; f. 1945; Christian Social party, aiming for a free market economy 'in the service of man's economic and intellectual freedom'; also combines national consciousness with support for a united Europe; 181,000 mems; Chair. HORST SEEHOFER; Sec.-Gen. ANDREAS SCHEUER.

Deutsche Kommunistische Partei (DKP) (German Communist Party): Hoffnungstr. 18, 45127 Essen; tel. (201) 1778890; fax (201) 17788929; e-mail pv@dkp-online.de; internet www.dkp.de; Chair. PATRIK KÖBELE.

Freie Demokratische Partei (FDP) (Free Democratic Party): Reinhardtstr. 14, 10117 Berlin; tel. (30) 28495820; fax (30) 28495822; e-mail fdp-point@fdp.de; internet www.fdp-bundespartei.de; f. 1948; represents democratic liberalism and makes the individual the focal point of the state and its laws and economy; in Aug. 1990 incorporated the 3 liberal parties of the former GDR—the Association of Free Democrats, the German Forum Party and the FDP; publishes *Elde*; c. 70,000 mems; Chair. CHRISTIAN LINDNER; Parliamentary Leader RAINER BRÜDERLE; Sec.-Gen. NICOLA BEER.

Freie Wähler (FW) (Independent Voters): Mühlenstr. 1, 27777 Ganderkesee; tel. (4222) 2094925; fax (4222) 2094923; e-mail info@freiewaehler.eu; internet www.freiewaehler.eu; f. 1946; non-ideological, centrist; regional orgs in all 16 Länder; Chair. HUBERT AIWANGER; c. 280,000 mems.

Die Linke (Left Party): Karl-Liebknecht-Haus, Kleine Alexanderstr. 28, 10178 Berlin; tel. (30) 24009397; fax (30) 24009310; e-mail bundesgeschaeftsstelle@die-linke.de; internet www.die-linke.de; successor to the Sozialistische Einheitspartei Deutschlands (SED—Socialist Unity Party, f. 1946 as a result of the unification of the Social Democratic Party and the Communist Party in Eastern Germany), which had been the dominant political force in the GDR until late 1989; renamed Partei des Demokratischen Sozialismus 1990; restyled Linkspartei.PDS 2005; adopted present name 2007 following merger with Wahlalternative Arbeit und soziale Gerechtigkeit (WASG—Electoral Alternative Jobs and Social Justice); has renounced Stalinism, opposes fascism, right-wing extremism and xenophobia, advocates a socially and ecologically sustainable market economy with public, collective and private ownership of the means of production, opposes terrorism, supports international disarmament and peaceful solutions to international conflicts; Co-Chair. KATJA KIPPING, BERND RIEXINGER; Parliamentary Leader GREGOR GYSI; Sec.-Gen. MATTHIAS HÖHN.

Nationaldemokratische Partei Deutschlands (NPD) (National Democratic Party of Germany): Seelenbinderstr. 42, 12555 Berlin; Postfach 840157, 12531 Berlin; tel. (30) 650110; fax (30) 65011140; e-mail parteizentrale@npd.de; internet www.npd.de; f. 1964; right-wing; 7,000 mems; youth organization Junge Nationaldemokraten (JN), 6,000 mems; Chair. FRANK FRANZ.

Neues Forum (New Forum): Winsstr. 60, 10405 Berlin; tel. (30) 2479404; fax (30) 24725605; e-mail info@neuesforum.de; internet www.neuesforum.de; f. 1989 as a citizens' action group; played prominent role in democratic movement in former GDR; campaigns for peace, social justice and protection of the environment; Leaders SABINE SCHAAF, REINHARD SCHULT, KLAUS TONNDORF.

Piratenpartei Deutschland (Pirate Party of Germany): Pflugstr. 9A, 10115 Berlin; tel. (30) 27572040; fax (30) 609897517; e-mail bgs_anfragen@piratenpartei.de; internet www.piratenpartei.de; f. 2006; advocates freedom of information, environmental protection, transparency of government; Chair. STEFAN KÖRNER.

Die Republikaner (REP) (Republican Party): Postfach 870210, 13162 Berlin; tel. (8233) 7950871; fax (8233) 7951138; e-mail bgst@rep.de; internet www.rep.de; f. 1983; conservative right-wing; publishes *Neue Republik*; c. 15,000 mems; Chair. JOHANN GÄRTNER.

Sozialdemokratische Partei Deutschlands (SPD) (Social Democratic Party of Germany): Willy-Brandt-Haus, Wilhelmstr. 141, 10963 Berlin; tel. (30) 25991500; fax (30) 25991507; e-mail parteivorstand@spd.de; internet www.spd.de; f. 1863; maintains that a vital democracy can be built only on the basis of social justice; advocates for the economy as much competition as possible, as much planning as necessary to protect the individual from uncontrolled economic interests; favours a positive attitude to national defence, while supporting controlled disarmament; rejects any political ties with communism; 548,491 mems (July 2007); Chair. SIGMAR GABRIEL; Parliamentary Leader THOMAS OPPERMANN; Sec.-Gen. YASMIN FAHIMI.

Südschleswigscher Wählerverband (SSW) (South Schleswig Voters' Committee): Schiffbrücke 42, 24939 Flensburg; tel. (461)

14408310; fax (461) 14408313; e-mail info@ssw.de; internet www
.ssw.de; f. 1948; represents the Danish minority in Schleswig-
Holstein and Friesian community in northern Germany; Chair.
FLEMMING MEYER; Gen. Sec. MARTIN LORENZEN.

There are also numerous other small parties, none of which is
represented in the Bundestag, covering all shades of the political
spectrum and various regional interests.

Diplomatic Representation

EMBASSIES IN GERMANY

Afghanistan: Taunusstr. 3, Ecke Kronbergerstr. 5, 14193 Berlin;
tel. (30) 20673518; fax (30) 20673525; e-mail info@
botschaft-afghanistan.de; internet www.botschaft-afghanistan.de;
Ambassador HAMID SIDIG.

Albania: Friedrichstr. 231, 10969 Berlin; tel. (30) 2593040; fax (30)
25931890; e-mail embassy.berlin@mfa.gov.al; internet www
.ambasadat.gov.al/germany; Ambassador ARTUR KUKO.

Algeria: Görschstr. 45, 13187 Berlin; tel. (30) 437370; fax (30)
48098716; e-mail info@algerische-botschaft.de; internet www
.algerische-botschaft.de; Ambassador EDDINE AOUAM.

Angola: Wallstr. 58, 10179 Berlin; tel. (30) 24089755; fax (30)
24089712; e-mail botschaft@botschaftangola.de; internet www
.botschaftangola.de; Ambassador ALBERT CORREIA NETO.

Argentina: Kleiststr. 23–26, 4th Floor, 10787 Berlin; tel. (30)
2266890; fax (30) 2291400; e-mail info_ealem@mrecic.gov.ar;
Ambassador DANIEL ADÁN DZIEWEZO POLSKI.

Armenia: Nussbaumallee 4, 14050 Berlin; tel. (30) 40509110; fax
(30) 40509125; e-mail armgermanyembassy@mfa.am; internet www
.germany.mfa.am; Chargé d'affaires a.i. ASHOT SMBATYAN.

Australia: Wallstr. 76–79, 10179 Berlin; tel. (30) 8800880; fax (30)
880088210; e-mail info.berlin@dfat.gov.au; internet www.germany
.embassy.gov.au; Ambassador DAVID RITCHIE.

Austria: Stauffenbergstr. 1, 10785 Berlin; tel. (30) 202870; fax (30)
2290569; e-mail berlin-ob@bmeia.gv.at; internet www
.oesterreichische-botschaft.de; Ambassador NIKOLAUS MARSCHIK.

Azerbaijan: Hubertusallee 43, 14193 Berlin; tel. (30) 2191613; fax
(30) 21916152; e-mail berlin@mission.mfa.gov.az; internet www
.azembassy.de; Ambassador PARVIZ SHAHBAZOV.

Bahrain: Klingelhöferstr. 7, 10785 Berlin; tel. (30) 86877777; fax
(30) 86877788; e-mail berlin.mission@mofa.gov.bh; internet www
.mofa.gov.bh; Ambassador IBRAHIM MAHMOUD AHMED ABDULLAH.

Bangladesh: Dovestr. 1, 5th Floor, 10587 Berlin; tel. (30) 39897531;
fax (30) 39897510; e-mail info@bangladeshembassy.de; internet
www.bangladeshembassy.de; Ambassador MUHAMMAD ALI SORCAR.

Belarus: Am Treptower Park 32, 12435 Berlin; tel. (30) 5363590; fax
(30) 53635923; e-mail germany@mfa.gov.by; internet www.germany
.mfa.gov.by; Ambassador ANDREI GIRO.

Belgium: Jägerstr. 52–53, 10117 Berlin; tel. (30) 206420; fax (30)
20642200; e-mail berlin@diplobel.fed.be; internet www.diplomatie
.be/berlin; Ambassador GHISLAIN D'HOOP.

Benin: Englerallee 23, 14195 Berlin; tel. (30) 236314710; fax (30)
236314740; e-mail diplo@ambassade-benin.de; internet www
.ambassade-benin.de; Ambassador ISIDORE BIO.

Bolivia: Wichmannstr. 6, 10787 Berlin; tel. (30) 2639150; fax (30)
26391515; e-mail berlin@embajada-bolivia.de; internet www.bolivia
.de; Ambassador ELIZABETH SALGUERO CARRILLO.

Bosnia and Herzegovina: Ibsenstr. 14, 10439 Berlin; tel. (30)
81471233; fax (30) 81471231; e-mail mail@botschaftbh.de; internet
www.botschaftbh.de; Ambassador EDIN DILBEROVIĆ.

Botswana: Lennestr. 5, 10785 Berlin; tel. (30) 887195010; fax (30)
887195012; Ambassador TSWELOPELE CORNELIA MOREMI.

Brazil: Wallstr. 57, 10179 Berlin; tel. (30) 726280; fax (30) 72628320;
e-mail brasemb.berlim@itamaraty.gov.br; internet berlim
.itamaratay.gov.br/de; Ambassador MARIA LUIZA RIBEIRO VIOTTI.

Brunei: Kronenstr. 55–58, 10117 Berlin; tel. (30) 20607600; fax (30)
20607666; e-mail berlin@brunei-embassy.de; Chargé d'affaires a.i.
CHEE LEONG bin CHAN.

Bulgaria: Mauerstr. 11, 10117 Berlin; tel. (30) 2010922; fax (30)
2086838; e-mail embassy.berlin@mfa.bg; internet www.mfa.bg/
embassies/germany; Ambassador RADI DRAGNEV NAIDENOV.

Burkina Faso: Karolingerpl. 10–11, 14052 Berlin; tel. (30)
30105990; fax (30) 301059920; e-mail embassy_burkina_faso@
t-online.de; internet www.ambassade-bf.org; Ambassador (vacant).

Burundi: Berliner Str. 36, 10715 Berlin; tel. (30) 2345670; fax (30)
23456720; e-mail info@burundi-embassy-berlin.com; internet www
.burundiembassy-germany.de; Ambassador EDOUARD BIZIMANA.

Cabo Verde: Stavanger Str. 16, 10439 Berlin; tel. (30) 20450955; fax
(30) 20450966; e-mail info@embassy-capeverde.de; internet www
.embassy-capeverde.de; Ambassador MARIA CRISTINA RODRIGUES DE
ALMEIDA PEREIRA.

Cambodia: Benjamin-Vogelsdorff-Str. 2, 13187 Berlin; tel. (30)
48637901; fax (30) 48637973; e-mail rec-berlin@t-online.de;
internet www.kambodscha-botschaft.de; Ambassador THAI CHUN.

Cameroon: Ulmenallee 32, 14050 Berlin; tel. (30) 89068090; fax (30)
890680929; e-mail berlin@ambacam.de; internet www.ambacam.de;
Ambassador JEAN-MARC MPAY.

Canada: Leipziger Pl. 17, 10117 Berlin; tel. (30) 203120; fax (30)
20312590; e-mail brlin@international.gc.ca; internet www
.canadainternational.gc.ca/germany-allemagne; Ambassador MARIE
GERVAIS-VIDRICAIRE.

Chad: Lepsiusstr. 114, 12165 Berlin; tel. (30) 31991620; fax (30)
319916220; e-mail contact@ambatchadberlin.de; internet www
.ambatchadberlin.de; Chargé d'affaires a.i. SOLALTA NGARMBATINAN.

Chile: Mohrenstr. 42, 10117 Berlin; tel. (30) 7262035; fax (30)
726203603; e-mail comunicaciones@echilealemania.de; internet
www.embajadaconsuladoschile.de; Ambassador MARIANO FERNÁN-
DEZ AMUNÁTEGUI.

China, People's Republic: Märkisches Ufer 54, 10179 Berlin; tel.
(30) 275880; fax (30) 27588221; internet www.china-botschaft.de;
Ambassador SHI MINGDE.

Colombia: Taubenstr. 23, 10117 Berlin; tel. (30) 2639610; fax (30)
26396125; e-mail info@botschaft-kolumbien.de; internet www
.botschaft-kolumbien.de; Ambassador JUAN MAYR MALDONADO.

Congo, Democratic Republic: Ulmenallee 42A, 14050 Berlin; tel.
(30) 30111298; fax (30) 30111297; e-mail ambardc_berlin@yahoo.de;
Ambassador KAMANGA CLEMENTINE SHAKEMBO.

Congo, Republic: Wallstr. 69, 10179 Berlin; tel. (30) 49400753; fax
(30) 48479897; e-mail botschaftkongobzv@hotmail.de; Ambassador
JACQUES YVON NDOLOU.

Costa Rica: Dessauer Str. 28–29, 10963 Berlin; tel. (30) 26398990;
fax (30) 26557210; e-mail emb@botschaft-costarica.de; internet www
.botschaft-costarica.de; Ambassador JOSÉ JOAQUÍN CHAVERRI
SIEVERT.

Côte d'Ivoire: Schinkelstr. 10, 14193 Berlin; tel. (30) 8906960; fax
(30) 890696206; e-mail contact@ambaci.de; internet www.ambaci
.de; Ambassador HOUADJA LÉON ADOM KACOU.

Croatia: Ahornstr. 4, 10787 Berlin; tel. (30) 21915514; fax (30)
23628965; e-mail berlin@mvpei.hr; internet de.mfa.hr; Ambassador
Dr RANKO VILOVIĆ.

Cuba: Stavangerstr. 20, 10439 Berlin; tel. (30) 44717319; fax (30)
9164553; e-mail embacuba-berlin@t-online.de; internet www
.cubadiplomatica.cu/alemania; Ambassador RENÉ JUAN MUJICA
CANTELAR.

Cyprus: Kurfürstendamm 182, 10707 Berlin; tel. (30) 3086830; fax
(30) 27591454; e-mail info@botschaft-zypern.de; internet www.mfa
.gov.cy/mfa/embassies/berlinembassy.nsf; Ambassador MINAS A.
HADJIMICHAEL.

Czech Republic: Wilhelmstr. 44, 10117 Berlin; tel. (30) 226380; fax
(30) 2294033; e-mail berlin@embassy.mzv.cz; internet www.mzv.cz/
berlin; Ambassador TOMÁŠ JAN PODIVÍNSKÝ.

Denmark: Rauchstr. 1, 10787 Berlin; tel. (30) 50502000; fax (30)
50502050; e-mail beramb@um.dk; internet tyskland.um.dk; Ambassador PER POULSEN-HANSEN.

Dominican Republic: Dessauer Str. 28–29, 10963 Berlin; tel. (30)
25757760; fax (30) 25757761; e-mail info@embajadadominicana.de;
Ambassador GABRIEL RAFAEL CALVENTI.

Ecuador: Joachimstaler Str. 10–12, 10719 Berlin; tel. (30) 8009695;
fax (30) 800969699; e-mail alemania@embassy-ecuador.org; internet
www.ecuadorembassy.de; Ambassador JORGE ENRIQUE JURADO
MOSQUERA.

Egypt: Stauffenbergstr. 6–7, 10785 Berlin; tel. (30) 4775470; fax (30)
4771049; e-mail embassy@egyptian-embassy.de; internet www
.egyptian-embassy.de; Ambassador MUHAMMAD ABD AL-HAMID IBRA-
HIM HIGAZY.

El Salvador: Joachim-Karnatz-Allee 47, 10557 Berlin; tel. (30)
2064660; fax (30) 20646629; e-mail embasalvarfa@googlemail.com;
internet www.botschaft-elsalvador.de; Ambassador JOSÉ ATILIO
BENÍTEZ PARADA.

Equatorial Guinea: Rohlfsstr. 17–19, 14195 Berlin; tel. (30)
88663877; fax (30) 88663879; e-mail botschaft@guinea-ecuatorial
.de; internet www.botschaft-aequatorialguinea.de; Ambassador
(vacant).

Eritrea: Stavangerstr. 18, 10439 Berlin; tel. (30) 4467460; fax (30)
44674621; e-mail embassyeritrea@t-online.de; internet www
.botschaft-eritrea.de; Ambassador PETROS TSEGGAI ASGHEDOM.

Estonia: Hildebrandstr. 5, 10785 Berlin; tel. (30) 25460602; fax (30)
25460601; e-mail embassy.berlin@mfa.ee; internet www.estemb.de;
Ambassador Dr KAJA TAEL.

Directory

Ethiopia: Boothstr. 20A, 12207 Berlin; tel. (30) 772060; fax (30) 7720626; e-mail emb.ethiopia@t-online.de; internet www .aethiopien-botschaft.de; Chargé d'affaires a.i. ATSEDE KIDANU ABRHA.

Finland: Rauchstr. 1, 10787 Berlin; tel. (30) 505030; fax (30) 50503333; e-mail sanomat.ber@formin.fi; internet www.finnland .de; Ambassador PÄIVI LUOSTARINEN.

France: Pariser Pl. 5, 10117 Berlin; tel. (30) 590039000; fax (30) 590039110; e-mail kanzlei@botschaft-frankreich.de; internet www .ambafrance-de.org; Ambassador PHILIPPE ETIENNE.

Gabon: Hohensteiner Str. 16, 14197 Berlin; tel. (30) 89733440; fax (30) 89733444; e-mail botschaft@botschaft-gabun.de; internet www .botschaft-gabun.de; Ambassador JEAN-CLAUDE BOUYOBART.

Georgia: Rauchstr. 11, 10787 Berlin; tel. (30) 4849070; fax (30) 48490720; e-mail berlin.emb@mfa.gov.ge; internet germany.mfa.gov .ge; Ambassador LADO CHANTURIA.

Ghana: Stavanger Str. 17 and 19, 10439 Berlin; tel. (30) 5471490; fax (30) 44674063; e-mail chancery@ghanaemberlin.de; internet www .ghanaemberlin.de; Ambassador AKUA SENA DANSUA.

Greece: Jägerstr. 54–55, 10117 Berlin; tel. (30) 206260; fax (30) 20626444; e-mail info@griechische-botschaft.de; internet www.mfa .gr/germany; Ambassador PANOS KALOGEROPOULOS.

Guatemala: Joachim-Karnatz-Allee 47, 10557 Berlin; tel. (30) 2064363; fax (30) 20643659; e-mail sekretariat@ botschaft-guatemala.de; internet www.botschaft-guatemala.de; Ambassador CARLOS HUMBERTO JIMÉNEZ LICONA.

Guinea: Jägerstr. 67–69, 10117 Berlin; tel. (30) 20074330; fax (30) 200743333; e-mail berlin@ambaguinee.de; Ambassador FATOUMATA BALDE.

Haiti: Uhlandstr. 14, 10623 Berlin; tel. (30) 88555134; fax (30) 88624279; e-mail amb.allemagne@diplomatie.ht; Chargé d'affaires a.i. PATRICK SAINT HILAIRE.

Holy See: Lilienthalstr. 3A, 10965 Berlin; Postfach 610218, 10923 Berlin; tel. (30) 616240; fax (30) 61624300; e-mail apostolische@ nuntiatur.de; internet www.nuntiatur.de; Apostolic Nuncio Most Rev. NIKOLA ETEROVIC (Titular Archbishop of Cibale).

Honduras: Cuxhavenerstr. 14, 10555 Berlin; tel. (30) 39749711; fax (30) 39749712; e-mail informacion.embahonduras.de@gmail.com; internet www.embajadahonduras.de; Ambassador RAMON CUSTODIO ESPINOZA.

Hungary: Unter den Linden 76, 10117 Berlin; tel. (30) 203100; fax (30) 2291314; e-mail infober@kum.hu; internet www.mfa.gov.hu/ kulkepviselet/de; Ambassador Dr JÓZSEF CZUKOR.

Iceland: Rauchstr. 1, 10787 Berlin; tel. (30) 50504000; fax (30) 50504300; e-mail infoberlin@mfa.is; internet www.botschaft-island .de; Ambassador GUNNAR SNORRI GUNNARSSON.

India: Tiergartenstr. 17, 10785 Berlin; tel. (30) 257950; fax (30) 25795102; e-mail infowing@indianembassy.de; internet www .indianembassy.de; Ambassador VIJAY KESHAV GOKHALE.

Indonesia: Lehrter Str. 16–17, 10557 Berlin; tel. (30) 478070; fax (30) 44737142; internet www.botschaft-indonesien.de; Ambassador FAUZI BOWO.

Iran: Podbielskiallee 65–67, 14195 Berlin; tel. (30) 843530; fax (30) 84353534; e-mail info@iranbotschaft.de; internet berlin.mfa.gov.ir; Ambassador ALI MAJEDI.

Iraq: Pacelliallee 19–21, 14195 Berlin; tel. (30) 81488100; fax (30) 81488222; e-mail info@iraqiembassy-berlin.de; internet www .iraqiembassy-berlin.de; Ambassador Dr HUSSAIN M. F. ALKHATEEB.

Ireland: Jägerstr. 51, 10117 Berlin; tel. (30) 220720; fax (30) 22072299; e-mail berlin@dfa.ie; internet www.embassyofireland .de; Ambassador MICHAEL COLLINS.

Israel: Auguste-Viktoria-Str. 74–76, 14193 Berlin; tel. (30) 89045500; fax (30) 89045309; e-mail botschaft@israel.de; internet www.israel.de; Ambassador YAKOV HADAS-HANDELSMAN.

Italy: Hiroshimastr. 1, 10785 Berlin; tel. (30) 254400; fax (30) 25440169; e-mail segreteria.berlino@esteri.it; internet www .ambberlino.esteri.it; Ambassador PIETRO BENASSI.

Jamaica: Schmargendorfer Str. 32, 12159 Berlin; tel. (30) 85994511; fax (30) 85994540; e-mail jamador.de; internet www.jamador .de; Ambassador MARGARET JOBSON.

Japan: Hiroshimastr. 6, 10785 Berlin; tel. (30) 210940; fax (30) 21094222; e-mail info@botschaft-japan.de; internet www.de .emb-japan.go.jp; Ambassador TAKESHI NAKANE.

Jordan: Heerstr. 201, 13595 Berlin; tel. (30) 3699600; fax (30) 36996011; e-mail jordan@jordanembassy.de; internet www .jordanembassy.de; Ambassador MAZEN IZZEDDIN AL-TAL.

Kazakhstan: Nordendstr. 14–17, 13156 Berlin; tel. (30) 47007111; fax (30) 47007125; e-mail info@botschaft-kaz.de; internet www .botschaft-kasachstan.de; Ambassador BOLAT NUSSUPOV.

Kenya: Markgrafenstr. 63, 10969 Berlin; tel. (30) 2592660; fax (30) 25926650; e-mail office@embassy-of-kenya.de; internet www .kenyaembassyberlin.de; Ambassador JOSEPH KIPNG'ETICH MAGUTT.

Korea, Democratic People's Republic: Glinkastr. 5–7, 10117 Berlin; tel. (30) 20625990; fax (30) 22651929; e-mail info@ dprkorea-emb.de; Ambassador RI SI-HONG.

Korea, Republic: Stülerstr. 8–10, 10787 Berlin; tel. (30) 260650; fax (30) 2606551; e-mail koremb-ge@mofat.go.kr; internet www .koreaemb.de; Ambassador LEE KYUNG-SOO.

Kosovo: Wallstr. 65, 10179 Berlin; tel. (30) 240476913; fax (30) 240476929; e-mail embassy.germany@ks-gov.net; Ambassador SKENDER XHAKALIU.

Kuwait: Griegstr. 5–7, 14193 Berlin; tel. (30) 8973000; fax (30) 89730010; e-mail info@kuwait-botschaft.de; internet www .kuwait-botschaft.de; Ambassador MONTHER AL-EISSA.

Kyrgyzstan: Otto-Suhr-Allee 146, 10585 Berlin; tel. (30) 34781338; fax (30) 34781362; e-mail info@botschaft-kirgisien.de; internet www .botschaft-kirgisien.de; Ambassador Dr BOLOT OTUNBAEV.

Laos: Bismarckallee 2A, 14193 Berlin; tel. (30) 89060647; fax (30) 89060648; e-mail info@laos-botschaft.de; Ambassador SITHONG CHITNHOTHINH.

Latvia: Reinerzstr. 40–41, 14193 Berlin; tel. (30) 82600222; fax (30) 82600233; e-mail embassy.germany@mfa.gov.lv; internet www.mfa .gov.lv/berlin; Ambassador ELITA KUZMA.

Lebanon: Berliner Str. 127, 13187 Berlin; tel. (30) 47498610; fax (30) 47487858; e-mail lubnan@t-online.de; internet www .libanesische-botschaft.info; Ambassador Dr MUSTAPHA ADIB.

Lesotho: Kurfürstenstr. 84, 10787 Berlin; tel. (30) 2575720; fax (30) 25757222; e-mail info@lesothoembassy.de; internet www .lesothoembassy.de; Ambassador LINEO LYDIA NTOANE.

Liberia: Kurfürstenstr. 84, 10787 Berlin; tel. (30) 26391194; fax (30) 26394893; e-mail info@liberiaembassygermany.de; internet www .liberiaembassygermany.de; Ambassador ETHEL DAVIES.

Libya: Podbielskiallee 42, 14195 Berlin; tel. (30) 2005960; fax (30) 20059699; e-mail info@libysche-botschaft.de; internet www .libyschebotschaft.de; Ambassador SENNUSSI ABDULKADER KWIDEER.

Liechtenstein: Mohrenstr. 42, 10117 Berlin; tel. (30) 52000630; fax (30) 52000631; e-mail vertretung@ber.llv.li; Ambassador Prince STEFAN OF LIECHTENSTEIN.

Lithuania: Charitéstr. 9, 10117 Berlin; tel. (30) 89068010; fax (30) 89068115; e-mail info-botschaft@mfa.lt; internet de.mfa.lt; Ambassador DEIVIDAS MATULIONIS.

Luxembourg: Klingelhöferstr. 7, 10785 Berlin; tel. (30) 2639570; fax (30) 26395727; e-mail berlin.amb@mae.etat.lu; internet berlin .mae.lu; Ambassador GEORGES JOSEPH NICOLAS SANTER.

Macedonia, former Yugoslav republic: Hubertusallee 5, 14193 Berlin; tel. (30) 8906950; fax (30) 89541194; e-mail makedonische .botschaft@t-online.de; internet www.missions.gov.mk/berlin; Chargé d'affaires a.i. DRAGAN PETKOVSKI.

Madagascar: Seepromenade 92, Postfach 100168, 14612 Falkensee (Brandenburg); tel. (3322) 23140; fax (3322) 231429; e-mail info@ botschaft-madagaskar.de; internet www.botschaft-madagaskar.de; Chargé d'affaires a.i. RADAFIARISOA LÉA RAHOLINIRINA.

Malawi: Westfälische Str. 86, 10709 Berlin; tel. (30) 8431540; fax (30) 84315430; e-mail malawiberlin@aol.com; internet www .malawiembassy.de; Chargé d'affaires a.i. OLIVER M. C. KUMBAMBE.

Malaysia: Klingelhöferstr. 6, 10785 Berlin; tel. (30) 88574900; fax (30) 88574950; e-mail mwberlin@malemb.de; internet www.malemb .de; Chargé d'affaires a.i. Datuk MOHD SHUHADA BIN OTHMAN.

Mali: Kurfürstendamm 72, 10709 Berlin; tel. (30) 3199883; fax (30) 31998848; e-mail ambmali@01019freenet.de; internet www .ambassade-repmali-berlin.de; Ambassador HAWA BA KEÏTA.

Malta: Klingelhöferstr. 7, 10785 Berlin; tel. (30) 2639110; fax (30) 26391123; e-mail maltaembassy.berlin@gov.mt; Ambassador ALBERT FRIGGIERI.

Mauritania: Kommandantenstr. 80, 10117 Berlin; tel. (30) 2065883; fax (30) 20674750; e-mail ambarim.berlin@gmx.de; Ambassador MOHAMED MAHMOUD BRAHIM KHLIL.

Mauritius: Kurfürstenstr. 84, 10787 Berlin; tel. (30) 2639360; fax (30) 26558323; e-mail berlin@mauritius-embassy.de; internet mfa .govmu.org/portal/sites/mfamission/berlin/index.htm; Chargé d'affaires a.i. GAJJALUXMI MOOTOOSAMY.

Mexico: Klingelhöferstr. 3, 10785 Berlin; tel. (30) 2693230; fax (30) 269323700; e-mail mail@mexale.de; internet embamex.sre.gob.mx/ alemania; Ambassador PATRICIA ESPINOSA CANTELLANO.

Moldova: Gotlandstr. 16, 10439 Berlin; tel. (30) 44652970; fax (30) 44652972; e-mail office@botschaft-moldau.de; internet www .germania.mfa.md; Ambassador AURELIU CIOCOI.

Monaco: Klingelhöferstr. 7, 10785 Berlin; tel. (30) 2639033; fax (30) 2690344; e-mail berlin@ambassade-monaco.de; Ambassador CLAUDE JOËL GIORDAN.

Mongolia: Dietzgenstr. 31, 13156 Berlin; tel. (30) 4748060; fax (30) 47480616; e-mail berlin@mfa.gov.mn; internet www.botschaft-mongolei.de; Ambassador BOLOR TSOLMON.

Montenegro: Charlottenstr. 35–36, 10117 Berlin; tel. (30) 51651070; fax (30) 516510712; e-mail germany@mfa.gov.me; Ambassador VERA JOLIČIČ-KULIŠ.

Morocco: Niederwallstr. 39, 10117 Berlin; tel. (30) 2061240; fax (30) 20612420; e-mail kontakt@botschaft-marokko.de; internet www.maec.gov.ma/berlin; Ambassador Dr OMAR ZNIBER.

Mozambique: Stromstr. 47, 10551 Berlin; tel. (30) 39876500; fax (30) 39876503; e-mail info@embassy-of-mozambique.de; Ambassador AMADEU PAULO SAMUEL DA CONCEIÇÃO.

Myanmar: Thielallee 19, 14195 Berlin; tel. (30) 2061570; fax (30) 20615720; e-mail info@botschaft-myanmar.de; internet www.botschaft-myanmar.de; Chargé d'affaires a.i. AYE KO KO.

Namibia: Reichsstr. 17, 14052 Berlin; tel. (30) 2540950; fax (30) 25409555; e-mail namibiaberlin@aol.com; internet www.namibia-botschaft.de; Chargé d'affaires a.i. SITWALA MAPENZI.

Nepal: Guerickestr. 27, 2nd Floor, 10587 Berlin; tel. (30) 34359920; fax (30) 34359906; e-mail berlin@nepalembassy.de; internet www.nepalembassy-germany.com; Chargé d'affaires a.i. PRAKASH MANI PAUDEL.

Netherlands: Klosterstr. 50, 10179 Berlin; tel. (30) 209560; fax (30) 20956441; e-mail bln@minbuza.nl; internet deutschland.nlbotschaft.org; Ambassador MONICA THEODORA VAN DAALEN.

New Zealand: Friedrichstr. 60, 10117 Berlin; tel. (30) 206210; fax (30) 20621114; e-mail nzember@infoem.org; internet www.nzembassy.com/germany; Ambassador PETER RODNEY HARRIS.

Nicaragua: Joachim-Karnatz-Allee 45, 10557 Berlin; tel. (30) 2064380; fax (30) 22487891; e-mail embajada.berlin@embanic.de; Ambassador KARLA LUZETTE BETETA BRENES.

Niger: Machnowerstr. 24, 14165 Berlin; tel. (30) 80589660; fax (30) 80589662; e-mail ambaniger@t-online.de; internet www.ambassade-niger.de; Ambassador AMINATOU GAOH.

Nigeria: Neue Jakobstr. 4, 10179 Berlin; tel. (30) 212300; fax (30) 21230212; e-mail info@nigeriaembassygermany.org; internet www.nigeriaembassygermany.org; Chargé d'affaires a.i. KENNETH OGORO OKEH.

Norway: Rauchstr. 1, 10787 Berlin; tel. (30) 505058600; fax (30) 505058601; e-mail emb.berlin@mfa.no; internet www.norwegen.no; Ambassador ELISABETH WALAAS.

Oman: Clayallee 82, 14195 Berlin; tel. (30) 8100510; fax (30) 81005199; Ambassador Dr KHALID SULAIMAN ABD AL-RAHMAN BA OMAR.

Pakistan: Schaperstr. 29, 10719 Berlin; tel. (30) 212440; fax (30) 21244210; e-mail mail@pakemb.de; internet www.pakemb.de; Ambassador SYED HASAN JAVED.

Panama: Wichmannstr. 6, 10787 Berlin; tel. (30) 22605811; fax (30) 22605812; e-mail info@botschaft-panama.de; internet www.botschaft-panama.de; Chargé d'affaires a.i. LERYS AMALEKS LOBO DE HOLZHAENGER.

Paraguay: Hardenbergstr. 12, 10623 Berlin; tel. (30) 3199860; fax (30) 31998617; e-mail embapar@embapar.de; internet www.embapar.de; Ambassador FERNANDO DANIEL OJEDA CÁCERES.

Peru: Mohrenstr. 42, 10117 Berlin; tel. (30) 2064103; fax (30) 20641077; e-mail info@embaperu.de; internet www.botschaft-peru.de; Ambassador JOSÉ ANTONIO MEIER ESPINOSA.

Philippines: Uhlandstr. 97, 10715 Berlin; tel. (30) 8649500; fax (30) 8732551; e-mail info@philippine-embassy.de; internet www.philippine-embassy.de; Ambassador MELITA SANTA MARIA-THOMECZEK.

Poland: Lassenstr. 19–21, 14193 Berlin; tel. (30) 223130; fax (30) 2213155; e-mail berlin.amb.sekretariat@msz.gov.pl; internet berlin.msz.gov.pl; Ambassador Dr JERZY MARGAŃSKI.

Portugal: Zimmerstr. 56, 10117 Berlin; tel. (30) 590063500; fax (30) 590063600; e-mail mail@botschaftportugal.de; internet www.botschaftportugal.de; Ambassador LUÍS DE ALMEIDA SAMPAIO.

Qatar: Hagenstr. 56, 14193 Berlin; tel. (30) 862060; fax (30) 86206150; internet www.katar-botschaft.de; Ambassador ABD AL-RAHMAN MUHAMMAD AL-KHULAIFI.

Romania: Dorotheenstr. 62–66, 10117 Berlin; tel. (30) 21239202; fax (30) 21239399; e-mail office@rumaenische-botschaft.de; internet berlin.mae.ro; Chargé d'affaires a.i. ADRIANA STĂNESCU.

Russian Federation: Unter den Linden 63–65, 10117 Berlin; tel. (30) 2291110; fax (30) 2299397; e-mail info@russische-botschaft.de; internet www.russische-botschaft.de; Ambassador VLADIMIR M. GRININ.

Rwanda: Jägerstr. 67–69, 10117 Berlin; tel. (30) 20916590; fax (30) 209165959; e-mail info@rwanda-botschaft.de; internet www.rwanda-botschaft.de; Ambassador CHRISTINE NKULIKIYINKA.

Saudi Arabia: Tiergartenstr. 33–34, 10785 Berlin; tel. (30) 8892500; fax (30) 88925179; Ambassador Prof. Dr OSSAMA ABD AL-MAJID ALI SHOBOKSHI.

Senegal: Dessauer Str. 28–29, 10963 Berlin; tel. (30) 8562190; fax (30) 85621921; internet www.botschaft-senegal.de; Ambassador ABDOUL AZIZ NDIAYE.

Serbia: Taubertstr. 18, 14193 Berlin; tel. (30) 8957700; fax (30) 8252206; e-mail info@botschaft-smg.de; internet berlin.mfa.rs; Chargé d'affaires a.i. JASMINA VELIČKOVIĆ.

Sierra Leone: Herwarthstr. 4, 12207 Berlin; tel. (30) 77205850; fax (30) 772058529; e-mail embassy@slembassy-germany.org; internet www.slembassy-germany.org; Ambassador JONGOPIE SIAKA STEVENS.

Singapore: Vossstr. 17, 10117 Berlin; tel. (30) 2263430; fax (30) 22634375; e-mail singemb_ber@sgmfa.gov.sg; internet www.mfa.gov.sg/content/mfa/overseasmission/berlin.html; Ambassador JAI S. SOHAN.

Slovakia: Hildebrandstr. 25, 10785 Berlin; tel. (30) 88926200; fax (30) 88926222; e-mail emb.berlin@mzv.sk; internet www.mzv.sk/berlin; Ambassador IGOR SLOBODNÍK.

Slovenia: Hausvogteipl. 3–4, 10117 Berlin; tel. (30) 2061450; fax (30) 20614570; e-mail vbn@gov.si; internet berlin.veleposlanistvo.si; Ambassador MARTA KOS MARKO.

Somalia: Heilmanring 10, 13627 Berlin; tel. (30) 80201438; Ambassador MOHAMUD MOHAMED TIFOW.

South Africa: Tiergartenstr. 18, 10785 Berlin; tel. (30) 220730; fax (30) 22073190; e-mail berlin.info@foreign.gov.za; internet www.suedafrika.org; Ambassador MAKHENKESI ARNOLD STOFILE.

South Sudan: Leipziger Pl. 8, 10117 Berlin; tel. (30) 20644590; fax (30) 206445919; e-mail info@embassy-southsudan.de; internet www.embassy-southsudan.de; Ambassador SITONA ABDALLA OSMAN.

Spain: Lichtensteinallee 1, 10787 Berlin; tel. (30) 2540070; fax (30) 25799557; e-mail emb.berlin.inf@maec.es; internet www.maec.es/subwebs/embajadas/berlin; Ambassador JUAN PABLO GARCÍA-BERDOY Y CEREZO.

Sri Lanka: Niklasstr. 19, 14163 Berlin; tel. (30) 80909749; fax (30) 80909757; e-mail info@srilanka-botschaft.de; internet www.srilanka-botschaft.de; Ambassador KARUNATILAKA AMUNUGAMA.

Sudan: Kurfürstendamm 151, 10709 Berlin; tel. (30) 8906980; fax (30) 89409693; e-mail poststelle@sudan-embassy.de; internet www.sudan-embassy.de; Ambassador Dr BADR-ELDIN ABD-ALLA MOHAMED.

Sweden: Rauchstr. 1, 10787 Berlin; tel. (30) 505060; fax (30) 50506789; e-mail ambassaden.berlin@foreign.ministry.se; internet www.swedenabroad.com/berlin; Ambassador STAFFAN CARLSSON.

Switzerland: Otto-von-Bismarck-Allee 4A, 10557 Berlin; tel. (30) 3904000; fax (30) 3911030; e-mail ber.vertretung@eda.admin.ch; internet www.eda.admin.ch/berlin; Ambassador Dr URS CHRISTIAN TIMOTHEUS GULDIMANN.

Syria: Rauchstr. 25, 10787 Berlin; tel. (30) 501770; fax (30) 50177311; e-mail info@syrianembassy.de; internet www.syrianembassy.de; Ambassador (vacant).

Tajikistan: Perleberger Str. 43, 10559 Berlin; tel. (30) 3479300; fax (30) 34793029; e-mail info@botschaft-tadschikistan.de; Ambassador MALIKSHO NEMATOV.

Tanzania: Eschenallee 11, 14050 Berlin; tel. (30) 3030800; fax (30) 30308020; e-mail info@tanzania-gov.de; internet www.tanzania-gov.de; Ambassador PHILIP S. MARMO.

Thailand: Lepsiusstr. 64–66, 12163 Berlin; tel. (30) 794810; fax (30) 79481511; e-mail general@thaiembassy.de; internet www.thaiembassy.de; Ambassador NONGNUTH PHETCHARATANA.

Togo: Grabbeallee 43, 13156 Berlin; tel. (30) 49908968; fax (30) 49908967; e-mail bbotschafttogo@web.de; internet www.botschaft-togo.de; Ambassador KWAMI CHRISTOPHE DIKENOU.

Tunisia: Lindenallee 16, 14050 Berlin; tel. (30) 3641070; fax (30) 30820683; e-mail at.berlin@tunesien.tn; Ambassador NÉJIB M'NIF.

Turkey: Tiergartenstr. 19–21, 10785 Berlin; tel. (30) 275850; fax (30) 27590915; e-mail botschaft.berlin@mfa.gov.tr; Ambassador HÜSEYIN AVNI KARSLIOĞLU.

Turkmenistan: Langobardenallee 14, 14052 Berlin; tel. (30) 30102452; fax (30) 30102453; e-mail info@botschaft-turkmenistan.de; internet www.botschaft-turkmenistan.de; Ambassador TOYLY ATAYEV.

Uganda: Axel-Springer-Str. 54A, 10117 Berlin; tel. (30) 2060990; fax (30) 24047557; e-mail info@ugandaembassyberlin.de; internet www.ugandaembassyberlin.de; Ambassador MARCEL R. TIBALEKA.

Ukraine: Albrechtstr. 26, 10117 Berlin; tel. (30) 28887116; fax (30) 28887163; e-mail ukremb@ukrainishe-botschaft.de; internet www .mfa.gov.ua/germany; Ambassador ANDRIJ MELNYK.

United Arab Emirates: Hiroshimastr. 18–20, 10787 Berlin; tel. (30) 516516; fax (30) 51651900; internet www.uae-embassy.de; Ambassador JUMAA MUBARAK AL-JUNAIBI.

United Kingdom: Wilhelmstr. 70, 10117 Berlin; tel. (30) 204570; e-mail ukingermany@fco.gov.uk; internet www.gov.uk/government/ world/germany; Ambassador SIMON MCDONALD.

USA: Clayallee 170, 14191 Berlin; tel. (30) 83050; fax (30) 83051050; internet germany.usembassy.gov; Ambassador JOHN B. EMERSON.

Uruguay: Budapester Str. 39, 10787 Berlin; tel. (30) 2639016; fax (30) 26390170; e-mail urubrande@t-online.de; internet www .urualemania.de; Ambassador ALBERTO ANTONIO GUANI AMARILLA.

Uzbekistan: Perleberger Str. 62, 10559 Berlin; tel. (30) 3940980; fax (30) 39409862; e-mail botschaft@uzbekistan.de; internet www .uzbekistan.de; Ambassador DURBEK AMANOV.

Venezuela: Schillstr. 10, 10785 Berlin; tel. (30) 8322400; fax (30) 83224020; e-mail embavenez.berlin@botschaft-venezuela.de; internet www.botschaft-venezuela.de; Ambassador Adm. ORLANDO MANIGLIA FERREIRA.

Viet Nam: Elsenstr. 3, 12435 Berlin; tel. (30) 53630108; fax (30) 53630200; e-mail sqvnberlin@t-online.de; internet www .vietnambotschaft.org; Ambassador NGUYEN THI HOANG ANH.

Yemen: Budapester Str. 37, 10787 Berlin; tel. (30) 8973050; fax (30) 89730562; e-mail info@botschaft-jemen.de; internet www .botschaft-jemen.de; Chargé d'affaires a.i. Dr WALID ABD AL-WAHED MOHAMED AL-ETHARY BAHABIB.

Zambia: Axel-Springer-Str. 54A, 10117 Berlin; tel. (30) 2062940; fax (30) 20629419; e-mail info@zambiaembassy.de; internet www .zambiaembassy.de; Ambassador BWALYA STANLEY KASONDE CHITI.

Zimbabwe: Kommandantenstr. 80, 10117 Berlin; tel. (30) 2062263; fax (30) 20455062; Ambassador RUTH MASODZI CHIKWIRA.

Judicial System

Justice is administered in accordance with the federal structure through the courts of the Federation and the Länder, as well as the Federal Constitutional Court and the Constitutional Courts of the Länder. Judges are independent and responsible to the law. They are not removable except by the decision of a court. One-half of the judges of the Federal Constitutional Court are elected by the Bundestag and the other half by the Bundesrat. A committee for the selection of judges participates in the appointment of judges of the Superior Federal Courts.

FEDERAL CONSTITUTIONAL COURT

Bundesverfassungsgericht: Schlossbezirk 3, 76131 Karlsruhe; Postfach 1771, 76006 Karlsruhe; tel. (721) 91010; fax (721) 9101382; e-mail bverfg@bundesverfassungsgericht.de; internet www .bundesverfassungsgericht.de; Pres. Prof. Dr ANDREAS VOSSKUHLE; Vice-Pres. Prof. Dr FERDINAND KIRCHHOF.

SUPERIOR FEDERAL COURTS

Bundesarbeitsgericht (Federal Labour Court): Hugo-Preuss-Pl. 1, 99084 Erfurt; tel. (361) 26360; fax (361) 26362000; e-mail bag@ bundesarbeitsgericht.de; internet www.bundesarbeitsgericht.de; Pres. INGRID SCHMIDT; Vice-Pres. Dr RUDI MÜLLER-GLÖGE.

Bundesgerichtshof (Federal Court of Justice): Herrenstr. 45A, 76133 Karlsruhe; tel. (721) 1590; fax (721) 1592512; e-mail poststelle@bgh.bund.de; internet www.bundesgerichtshof.de; Pres. BETTINA LIMPERG; Vice-Pres. WOLFGANG SCHLICK; Federal Prosecutor-Gen. HARALD RANGE.

Bundessozialgericht (Federal Social Court): Graf-Bernadotte-Pl. 5, 34119 Kassel; tel. (561) 31071; fax (561) 3107475; e-mail bundessozialgericht@bsg.bund.de; internet www.bsg.bund.de; Pres. PETER MASUCH; Vice-Pres. Dr RUTH WETZEL-STEINWEDEL.

Bundesverwaltungsgericht (Federal Administrative Court): Simsonpl. 1, 44107 Leipzig; Postfach 100854, 04008 Leipzig; tel. (341) 20070; fax (341) 20071000; e-mail pressestelle@bverwg.bund .de; internet www.bverwg.de; Pres. Dr KLAUS RENNERT; Vice-Pres. Dr JOSEF CHRIST.

Bundesfinanzhof (Federal Financial Court): Ismaninger Str. 109, 81675 München; Postfach 860240, 81629 München; tel. (89) 92310; fax (89) 9231201; e-mail bundesfinanzhof@bfh.bund.de; internet www.bundesfinanzhof.de; Pres. Prof. Dr RUDOLF MELLINGHOFF; Vice-Pres. HERMANN-ULRICH VISKORF.

Religion
CHRISTIANITY

Arbeitsgemeinschaft Christlicher Kirchen in Deutschland (Council of Christian Churches in Germany): Ludolfusstr. 2–4, 60487 Frankfurt a.M.; Postfach 900617, 60446 Frankfurt a.M.; tel. (69) 2470270; fax (69) 24702730; e-mail info@ack-oec.de; internet www.oekumene-ack.de; 25 affiliated Churches, including the Roman Catholic Church and the Orthodox Church in Germany; Pres. Bishop Dr KARL-HEINZ WIESEMANN.

The Roman Catholic Church

Germany comprises seven archdioceses and 20 dioceses. In 2011 there were some 24.5m. adherents (about 30.0% of the population).

Bishops' Conference: Deutsche Bischofskonferenz, Kaiserstr. 161, 53113 Bonn; tel. (228) 103214; fax (228) 103254; e-mail pressestelle@ dbk.de; internet www.dbk.de; Pres. Cardinal Dr REINHARD MARX; Sec. Dr HANS LANGENDÖRFER.

Archbishop of Bamberg: Most Rev. LUDWIG SCHICK, Dompl. 3, 96049 Bamberg; tel. (951) 5020; fax (951) 502250.

Archbishop of Berlin: (vacant), Niederwallstr. 8–9, 10117 Berlin; Postfach 040406, 10064 Berlin; tel. (30) 326840; fax (30) 32684276; e-mail info@erzbistumberlin.de; internet www.erzbistumberlin.de.

Archbishop of Freiburg im Breisgau: Most Rev. STEPHAN BURGER, Schoferstr. 2, 79098 Freiburg i. Br.; tel. (761) 2188243; fax (761) 2188427; e-mail erzbischof@ordinariat-freiburg.de; internet www .erzbistum-freiburg.de.

Archbishop of Hamburg: Most Rev. STEFAN HESSE, Postfach 101925, 20013 Hamburg; Danzigerstr. 52A, 20099 Hamburg; tel. (40) 24877100; fax (40) 24877233; e-mail pforte@egv-erzbistum-hh .de; internet www.erzbistum-hamburg.de.

Archbishop of Köln (Cologne): Cardinal RAINER MARIA WOELKI, Marzellenstr. 32, 50668 Köln; tel. (221) 16420; fax (221) 16421700; e-mail info@erzbistum-koeln.de; internet www.erzbistum-koeln.de.

Archbishop of München (Munich) and Freising: Cardinal Dr REINHARD MARX, Rochsusstr. 5–7, 80333 München; Postfach 100551, 80079 München; tel. (89) 21370; fax (89) 21371585; e-mail pressestelle@erzbistum-muenchen.de; internet www .erzbistum-muenchen.de.

Archbishop of Paderborn: Most Rev. HANS-JOSEF BECKER, Erzbischöfliches Generalvikariat, Dompl. 3, 33098 Paderborn; tel. (5251) 1251287; fax (5251) 1251470; e-mail info@ erzbistum-paderborn.de; internet www.erzbistum-paderborn.de.

The Evangelical (Protestant) Church

In 2011 the Evangelische Kirche in Deutschland, which includes the Lutheran, Uniate and Reformed Protestant Churches, had some 23.6m. members, amounting to about 28.9% of the population.

Evangelische Kirche in Deutschland (EKD) (Evangelical Church in Germany): Herrenhäuser Str. 12, 30419 Hannover; tel. (511) 27960; fax (511) 2796707; e-mail presse@ekd.de; internet www .ekd.de; the governing bodies of the EKD are its Synod of 120 clergy and lay members, which meets at regular intervals, the Conference of member churches, and the Council, composed of 15 elected members; the EKD has an ecclesiastical secretariat of its own (the Evangelical Church Office), including a special office for foreign relations; Chair. of the Council Bishop HEINRICH BEDFORD-STROHM.

Synod of the EKD: Herrenhäuser Str. 12, 30419 Hannover; tel. (511) 2796114; fax (511) 2796707; e-mail synode@ekd.de; Pres. Dr IRMGARD SCHWAETZER.

Deutscher Evangelischer Kirchentag (German Evangelical Church Convention): Magdeburger Str. 59, 36037 Fulda; Postfach 1555, 36005 Fulda; tel. (661) 969500; fax (661) 9695090; e-mail fulda@kirchentag.de; internet www.kirchentag.de; Pres. ANDREAS BARNER; Gen. Sec. Dr ELLEN UEBERSCHÄR.

Churches and Federations within the EKD:

Reformierter Bund (Reformed Alliance): Knochenhauerstr. 42, 30159 Hannover; tel. (511) 47399374; fax (511) 47399428; e-mail info@reformierter-bund.de; internet www.reformierter-bund.de; f. 1884; unites the Reformed Territorial Churches and Congregations of Germany (with an estimated 2m. mems). The central body of the Reformed League is the 'Moderamen', the elected representation of the various Reformed Churches and Congregations; Moderator Rev. PETER BUKOWSKI; Gen. Sec. Rev. JÖRG SCHMIDT.

Union Evangelischer Kirchen in der EKD (UEK): Herrenhäuser Str. 12, 30419 Hannover; tel. (511) 2796529; fax (511) 2796717; e-mail postfach@uek-online.de; internet www.uek-online.de; f. 2003 by merger of Arnoldshainer Konferenz and Evangelische Kirche der Union; union of 13 regional churches (10 United, two Reformed and one Lutheran) with approx. 13.4m. mems; promotes unity among churches in the EKD; Chair. Bishop HEINRICH BEDFORD-STROHM (Evangelical Church in Bavaria); Vice-Chair. CHRISTIAN DRÄGERT

(Evangelical Church in the Rhineland), BRIGITTE ANDRAE (Evangelical Church in Central Germany).

Bremen Evangelical Church: Franziuseck 2–4, 28199 Bremen; tel. (421) 55970; fax (421) 5597265; e-mail kirchenkanzlei@kirche-bremen.de; internet www.kirche-bremen.de; Pres. EDDA BOSSE.

Church of Lippe: Leopoldstr. 27, 32756 Detmold; Postfach 2153, 32711 Detmold; tel. (5231) 97660; fax (5231) 976850; e-mail lka@lippische-landeskirche.de; internet www.lippische-landeskirche.de; Supt DIETMAR ARENDS.

Evangelical Church in Baden: Blumenstr. 1, 76133 Karlsruhe; tel. (721) 91750; fax (721) 9175553; e-mail info@ekiba.de; internet www.ekiba.de; Bishop Dr JOCHEN CORNELIUS-BUNDSCHUH.

Evangelical Church in Berlin-Brandenburg-schlesische Oberlausitz: Georgenkirchstr. 69, 10249 Berlin; tel. (30) 243440; fax (30) 24344500; e-mail info@ekbo.de; internet www.ekbo.de; Bishop Dr MARKUS DRÖGE.

Evangelical Church in Central Germany: Michaelisstr. 39, 99084 Erfurt; tel. (361) 518000; fax (361) 51800198; e-mail landeskirchenamt@ekmd.de; internet www.ekmd-online.de; 858,453 mems; Bishop ILSE JUNKERMANN.

Evangelical Church in Hessen and Nassau: Pauluspl. 1, 64285 Darmstadt; tel. (6151) 4050; fax (6151) 405220; e-mail info@ekhn.de; internet www.ekhn.de; Pres. Dr VOLKER JUNG.

Evangelical Church of Kurhessen-Waldeck: Wilhelmshöher Allee 330, 34131 Kassel; Postfach 410260, 34114 Kassel-Wilhelmshöhe; tel. (561) 93780; fax (561) 9378400; e-mail landeskirchenamt@ekkw.de; internet www.ekkw.de; Bishop Prof. Dr MARTIN HEIN.

Evangelical Church of the Palatinate: Dompl. 5, 67346 Speyer; tel. (6232) 6670; fax (6232) 667480; e-mail landeskirchenrat@evkirchepfalz.de; internet www.evpfalz.de; Pres. CHRISTIAN SCHAD.

Evangelical Church in the Rhineland: Hans-Böckler-Str. 7, 40476 Düsseldorf; Postfach 300339, 40403 Düsseldorf; tel. (211) 45620; fax (211) 4562444; e-mail lka@ekir.de; internet www.ekir.de; Pres. MANFRED REKOWSKI.

Evangelical Church of Westphalia: Altstädter Kirchpl. 5, 33602 Bielefeld; tel. (521) 5940; fax (521) 594129; e-mail info@evangelisch-in-westfalen.de; internet www.ekvw.de; Pres. ANNETTE KURSCHUS.

Vereinigte Evangelisch-Lutherische Kirche Deutschlands (VELKD) (The United Evangelical-Lutheran Church of Germany): Herrenhäuserstr. 12, 30419 Hannover; Postfach 210220, 30419 Hannover; tel. (511) 27960; fax (511) 2796182; e-mail zentrale@velkd.de; internet www.velkd.de; f. 1948; unites all but 3 of the Lutheran territorial Churches within the Evangelical Church in Germany; Presiding Bishop Dr GERHARD ULRICH (Schleswig-Holstein); 9.5m. mems.

Evangelical-Lutheran Church in Bavaria: Katharina-von-Bora-Str. 11, 80333 München; tel. (89) 55950; fax (89) 5595484; e-mail landesbischof@elkb.de; internet www.bayern-evangelisch.de; Bishop Prof. Dr HEINRICH BEDFORD-STROHM; 2.5m. mems.

Evangelical-Lutheran Church in Brunswick: Dietrich-Bonhoeffer-Str. 1, 38300 Wolfenbüttel; tel. (5331) 8020; fax (5331) 802707; e-mail info@lk-bs.de; internet www.landeskirche-braunschweig.de; Bishop Prof. Dr CHRISTOPH MEYNS.

Evangelical-Lutheran Church of Hannover: Haarstr. 6, 30169 Hannover; tel. (511) 5635830; fax (511) 56358311; e-mail landesbischoefin@evlka.de; internet www.evlka.de; Bishop RALF MEISTER; 2.9m. mems.

Evangelical-Lutheran Church in Northern Germany: Königstr. 54, 22767 Hamburg; tel. (306) 201100; fax (306) 201109; e-mail info@nordkirche.de; internet www.nordkirche.de; f. 2012 by the merger of Evangelical Lutheran Church of Mecklenburg, Evangelical-Lutheran Church of North Elbe and the Pomeranian Evangelical Church; Chair. Rt Rev. GERHARD ULRICH (Schleswig and Holstein).

Evangelical-Lutheran Church of Schaumburg-Lippe: Herderstr. 27, 31665 Bückeburg; tel. (5722) 9600; fax (5722) 96010; e-mail lka@lksl.de; internet www.landeskirche-schaumburg-lippe.de; Bishop Dr KARL-HINRICH MANZKE.

Also affiliated to the EKD:

Evangelical-Lutheran Church in Oldenburg: Philosophenweg 1, 26121 Oldenburg; tel. (441) 77010; fax (441) 77012199; e-mail info@kirche-oldenburg.de; internet www.kirche-oldenburg.de; Bishop JAN JANSSEN; 446,899 mems.

Evangelical-Lutheran Church in Württemberg: Augustenstr. 124, 70197 Stuttgart; Postfach 101342, 70012 Stuttgart; tel. (711) 2227658; fax (711) 2227681; e-mail kontakt@elk-wue.de; internet www.elk-wue.de; Bishop FRANK OTFRIED JULY.

Evangelical-Lutheran Church of Saxony: Lukasstr. 6, 01069 Dresden; Postfach 120552, 01006 Dresden; tel. (351) 46920; fax (351) 4692109; e-mail kirche@evlks.de; internet www.evlks.de; 784,706 mems; Bishop JOCHEN BOHL.

Evangelical-Reformed Church: Saarstr. 6, 26789 Leer; tel. (491) 91980; fax (491) 9198251; e-mail info@reformiert.de; internet www.reformiert.de; Pres. Rev. JANN SCHMIDT.

Herrnhuter Brüdergemeine/Europäisch-Festländische Brüder-Unität (European Continental Province of the Moravian Church): Badwasen 6, 73087 Bad Boll; tel. (7164) 94210; fax (7164) 942199; f. 1457; there are 25 congregations in Germany, Denmark, Estonia, Latvia, the Netherlands, Sweden, Albania and Switzerland, with approx. 18,000 mems; Chair. FRIEDER VOLLPRECHT.

Other Protestant Churches

Arbeitsgemeinschaft Mennonitischer Gemeinden in Deutschland (Association of Mennonite Congregations in Germany): Stauferstr. 43, 85051 Ingolstadt; tel. (841) 9008216; e-mail amg.frieder.boller@mennoniten.de; internet www.mennoniten.de; f. 1886; re-organized 1990; Chair. Pastor FRIEDER BOLLER.

Bund Evangelisch-Freikirchlicher Gemeinden in Deutschland K.d.ö.R. (Union of Evangelical Free Churches—Baptists—in Germany): Johann-Gerhard-Oncken-Str. 7, 14641 Wustermark; tel. (33234) 74105; fax (33234) 74199; e-mail info@baptisten.de; internet www.baptisten.de; f. 1942; Pres. HARTMUT RIEMENSCHNEIDER; Gen. Sec. CHRISTOPH STIBA.

Bund Freier evangelischer Gemeinden (Covenant of Free Evangelical Churches in Germany): Goltenkamp 4, 58452 Witten; Postfach 4005, 58426 Witten; tel. (2302) 9370; fax (2302) 93799; e-mail info@bund.feg.de; internet www.feg.de; f. 1854; Pres. ANSGAR HÖRSTING; Administrator KLAUS KANWISCHER; 40,000 mems.

Evangelisch-altreformierte Kirche von Niedersachsen (Evangelical Reformed Church of Lower Saxony): Hauptstr. 33 49824 Laar; tel. (5947) 242; e-mail beuke1@ewetel.net; f. 1838; Sec. Rev. Dr GERRIT JAN BEUKER.

Evangelisch-methodistische Kirche (United Methodist Church): Ludolfusstr. 2–4, 60487 Frankfurt a.M.; tel. (69) 2425210; fax (69) 242521129; e-mail bischoefin@emk.de; internet www.emk.de; f. 1968; Presiding Bishop ROSEMARIE WENNER.

Freikirche der Siebenten-Tags-Adventisten (Seventh-Day Adventist Church): Senefelderstr. 15, 73760 Ostfildern; Postfach 4260, 73745 Ostfildern; tel. (711) 4481914; fax (711) 4481960; e-mail info@adventisten.de; internet www.adventisten.de; f. 1863; Pres. JOHANNES NAETHER.

Die Heilsarmee in Deutschland (Salvation Army in Germany): Salierring 23–27, 50677 Köln; tel. (221) 208190; fax (221) 20819899; e-mail info@heilsarmee.de; internet www.heilsarmee.de; f. 1886; Leader Col HORST CHARLET.

Mülheimer Verband Freikirchlich-Evangelischer Gemeinden (Pentecostal Church): Habenhauser Dorfstr. 27, 28279 Bremen; tel. (421) 8399130; fax (421) 8399136; e-mail geschaeftsstelle@muelheimer-verband.de; internet www.muelheimer-verband.de; f. 1913.

Selbständige Evangelisch-Lutherische Kirche (Independent Evangelical-Lutheran Church): Schopenhauerstr. 7, 30625 Hannover; tel. (511) 557808; fax (511) 551588; e-mail selk@selk.de; internet www.selk.de; f. 1972; Pres. Bishop HANS-JÖRG VOIGT; Exec. Sec. Rev. MICHAEL SCHAETZEL; 34,934 mems.

Other Christian Churches

Other Christian churches had 4.5m.–5m. members in 2005, of whom 1.5m.–2m. persons were members of Orthodox churches.

Alt-Katholische Kirche (Old Catholic Church): Gregor-Mendel-Str. 28, 53115 Bonn; tel. (228) 232285; fax (228) 238314; e-mail konfig@alt-katholisch.de; internet www.alt-katholisch.de; seceded from the Roman Catholic Church as a protest against the declaration of Papal infallibility in 1870; belongs to the Utrecht Union of Old Catholic Churches; in full communion with the Anglican Communion; Bishop Dr MATTHIAS RING; 25,000 mems.

Apostelamt Jesu Christi: Madlower Hauptstr. 39, 03050 Cottbus; tel. (355) 541227; e-mail kha@kirche-apostelamt-jesu-christi.eu; internet www.kirche-ajc.de.

Armenisch-Apostolische Orthodoxe Kirche in Deutschland (Armenian Apostolic Orthodox Church in Germany): Allensteiner Str. 5, 50735 Köln; tel. (221) 7126223; fax (221) 7126267; e-mail armenische_dioezese@hotmail.com; internet armenische-kirche.de; Archbishop KAREKIN BEKDJIAN.

Griechisch-Orthodoxe Metropolie von Deutschland (Greek Orthodox Metropolitanate of Germany): Dietrich-Bonhoeffer-Str. 2, 53227 Bonn; Postfach 300555, 53185 Bonn; tel. (228) 973840; fax (228) 97378424; e-mail sekretariat@orthodoxie.net; internet www.orthodoxie.net; f. 1963; Metropolitan of Germany and Exarch of Central Europe AUGOUSTINOS LABARDAKIS.

Religiöse Gesellschaft der Freunde (Quäker) (Religious Society of Friends—Quakers): Planckstr. 20, 10117 Berlin; tel. (30) 2082284; fax (30) 20458142; e-mail berlin@quaeker.org; internet www .quaeker.org; f. 1925; 260 mems.

Russische Orthodoxe Kirche—Berliner Diözese (Russian Orthodox Church): Wildensteiner Str. 10, 10318 Berlin; tel. (30) 5099611; fax (30) 5098153; e-mail red.stimme@snafu.de; Archbishop of Berlin and Germany Archbishop FEOFAN.

ISLAM

Of those who answered the non-compulsory question on religion in the 2011 census, 1.9% designated themselves as Muslim.

Zentralrat der Muslime in Deutschland eV (ZMD) (Central Council of Muslims in Germany): Sachsenring 20, 50677 Köln; tel. (221) 1394450; fax (221) 1394681; e-mail sekretariat@zentralrat.de; internet www.zentralrat.de; f. 1994; 21 mem. asscns; Pres. Dr AIMAN A. MAZYEK.

JUDAISM

The membership of Jewish synagogues in Germany numbered some 105,000 in 2012.

Zentralrat der Juden in Deutschland (Central Council of Jews in Germany): Tucholskystr. 9, Leo-Baeck-Haus, 10117 Berlin; Postfach 040207, 10061 Berlin; tel. (30) 2844560; fax (30) 28445613; e-mail info@zentralratdjuden.de; internet www.zentralratdjuden.de; Pres. JOSEF SCHUSTER; Sec.-Gen. STEPHAN J. KRAMER; 105,000 mems (2012).

Jüdische Gemeinde zu Berlin (Jewish Community in Berlin): Oranienburger Str. 28–31, 10117 Berlin; tel. (30) 880280; fax (30) 88028103; e-mail service@jg-berlin.org; internet www.jg-berlin.org; Pres. Dr GIDEON JOFFE.

The Press

A significant feature of the German press is the large number of daily newspapers published in regional centres, of which the *Westdeutsche Allgemeine Zeitung* in Essen has the largest circulation. The most important national publications are *Bild* in Hamburg and *Süddeutsche Zeitung* in Munich, followed by the *Frankfurter Allgemeine Zeitung* in Frankfurt am Main and Berlin's *Die Welt*.

Axel Springer Verlag AG: Axel-Springer-Str. 65, 10888 Berlin; and Axel-Springer-Pl. 1, 20350 Hamburg; tel. (30) 25910; fax (30) 251606; tel. (40) 34700; fax (40) 345811; internet www.asv.de; f. 1946; includes 5 major dailies *Berliner Morgenpost, Bild, BZ, Die Welt, Hamburger Abendblatt*, 3 Sunday papers *Bild am Sonntag, BZ am Sonntag, Welt am Sonntag*, and radio, television, women's and family magazines; Chair. Dr MATHIAS DÖPFNER.

Bauer Verlagsgruppe: Burchardstr. 11, 20077 Hamburg; and Charles-de-Gaulle-Str. 8, 81737 München; tel. (40) 30190; fax (40) 30191043; tel. (89) 67860; fax (89) 6374404; internet www .bauerverlag.de; f. 1875; publ. 42 magazines in Germany, incl. *Auf einen Blick, Bravo, Neue Post, Tina, tv14, tv Hören und Sehen, TV Movie*; Pres. HEINZ HEINRICH BAUER.

Gruner + Jahr AG & Co KG: Am Baumwall 11, 20459 Hamburg; tel. (40) 37030; fax (40) 37036000; e-mail unternehmens kommunikation@guj.de; internet www.guj.de; publ., among others, *Brigitte, Capital, Eltern, GEO, Schöner Wohnen* and *Stern*; Mems, Exec. Bd. JULIA JÄKEL, TORSTEN-JÖRN KLEIN, ACHIM TWARDY.

Hubert Burda Media Holding GmbH & Co KG: Arabellastr. 23, 81925 München; tel. (89) 9250-0; e-mail info@hubert-burda-media .com; internet www.burda.de; f. 1908; publs 74 magazine titles in Germany, incl. *Bild + Funk, Bunte, Burda Modemagazin, Elle, Focus, Freizeit Revue, Freundin, Meine Familie & Ich*; Chair. Dr HUBERT BURDA.

WAZ Mediengruppe: Friedrichstr. 34–38, 45128 Essen; tel. (201) 804-0; fax (201) 8041644; e-mail kontakt@waz-mediengruppe.de; internet www.waz-mediengruppe.de; f. 1976; publ. regional dailies, incl. *Westdeutsche Allgemeine Zeitung*, and magazines incl. *Frau Aktuell* and *Gong*; Man. Dirs BODO HOMBACH, CHRISTIAN NIENHAUS.

PRINCIPAL DAILIES

Aachen

Aachener Zeitung: Dresdner Str. 3, 52068 Aachen; Postfach 500110, 52085 Aachen; tel. (241) 5101310; fax (241) 5101360; e-mail redaktion@zeitungsverlag-aachen.de; internet www.az-web .de; f. 1946; Editor-in-Chief BERND MATHIEU; circ. 128,711 (Dec. 2011, with *Aachener Nachrichten*).

Augsburg

Augsburger Allgemeine: Curt-Frenzel-Str. 2, 86167 Augsburg; tel. (821) 7770; fax (821) 7772039; e-mail redaktion@ augsburger-allgemeiner.de; internet www.augsburger-allgemeine .de; Editor-in-Chief WALTER ROLLER; circ. 331,637 (March 2012, with *Allgäuer Zeitung*).

Bautzen

Serbske Nowiny: Tuchmacherstr. 27, 02625 Bautzen; tel. (3591) 577232; fax (3591) 577202; e-mail redaktion@serbske-nowiny.de; internet www.serbske-nowiny.de; f. 1842; evening; Sorbian; Editor JANEK SCHÄFER.

Berlin

Berliner Kurier: Karl-Liebknecht-Str. 29, 10178 Berlin; tel. (30) 23279; fax (30) 23275533; e-mail post@berliner-kurier.de; internet www.berliner-kurier.de; f. 1990; evening; publ. by Berliner Verlag GmbH; Editor-in-Chief HANS-PETER BUSCHHEUER; circ. 117,456 (Dec. 2011).

Berliner Morgenpost: Axel-Springer-Str. 65, 10888 Berlin; tel. (30) 25910; fax (30) 2516071; e-mail redaktion@morgenpost.de; internet www.morgenpost.de; f. 1898; publ. by Ullstein GmbH; Editor-in-Chief CARSTEN ERDMANN; circ. 126,411 (Dec. 2011).

Berliner Zeitung: Karl-Liebknecht-Str. 29, 10178 Berlin; tel. (2) 23279; fax (30) 23275533; e-mail berliner-zeitung@berliner-zeitung .de; internet www.berliner-zeitung.de; f. 1945; morning (except Sun.); publ. by Berliner Verlag GmbH; Editor BRIGITTE FEHRLE; circ. 144,229 (Dec. 2011).

B.Z.: B.Z. Ullstein GmbH, Kurfürstendamm 21–22, 10719 Berlin; tel. (30) 25910; fax (30) 259173006; e-mail redaktion@bz-berlin.de; internet www.bz-berlin.de; f. 1877; Mon.–Sat.; Editor-in-Chief PETER HUTH; circ. 161,726 (Dec. 2011, with *B.Z. am Sonntag*).

Der Tagesspiegel: Askanischer Pl. 3, 10963 Berlin; tel. (30) 290210; fax (30) 26009332; e-mail redaktion@tagesspiegel.de; internet www .tagesspiegel.de; f. 1945; Editors-in-Chief STEPHAN-ANDREAS CAS-DORFF, LORENZ MAROLDT; circ. 131,178 (Dec. 2011).

Die Welt: Axel-Springer-Str. 65, 10888 Berlin; tel. (30) 25910; fax (30) 259171606; internet www.welt.de; f. 1946; publ. by Axel Springer Verlag AG; Editor-in-Chief JAN-ERIC PETERS; circ. 263,817 (Dec. 2011, Mon.–Fri. only).

Bielefeld

Neue Westfälische: Niedernstr. 21–27, 33602 Bielefeld; Postfach 100225, 33502 Bielefeld; tel. (521) 5550; fax (521) 555348; e-mail redaktion@neue-westfaelische.de; internet www.nw-news.de; f. 1967; publ. by Zeitungsgruppe Neue Westfälische; Editor-in-Chief THOMAS SEIM; circ. 253,082 (Dec. 2011).

Braunschweig
(Brunswick)

Braunschweiger Zeitung: Hamburger Str. 277, 38114 Braunsch-weig; Postfach 8052, 38130 Braunschweig; tel. (531) 39000; fax (531) 3900610; e-mail chefredaktion@bzv.de; internet www .braunschweiger-zeitung.de; Editor-in-Chief ARMIN MAUS; circ. 157,105 (Dec. 2011).

Bremen

Weser-Kurier: Martinistr. 43, 28195 Bremen; Postfach 107801, 28078 Bremen; tel. (421) 36710; fax (421) 36711000; e-mail chefredaktion@weser-kurier.de; internet www.weser-kurier.de; f. 1945; Editor-in-Chief SILKE HELLWIG; circ. 168,424 (Dec. 2011, with *Bremer Nachrichten*).

Chemnitz

Freie Presse: Brückenstr. 15, 09111 Chemnitz; Postfach 261, 09002 Chemnitz; tel. (371) 6560; fax (371) 65617070; e-mail die .tageszeitung@freiepresse.de; internet www.freiepresse.de; f. 1963; morning; Editor TORSTEN KLEDITZSCH; circ. 277,442 (Dec. 2011, incl. regional edns).

Cottbus

Lausitzer Rundschau: Str. der Jugend 54, 03050 Cottbus; Post-fach 100279, 03002 Cottbus; tel. (355) 4810; fax (355) 481245; e-mail redaktion@lr-online.de; internet www.lr-online.de; independent; morning; Editor-in-Chief JOHANNES FISCHER; circ. 93,042 (Dec. 2011).

Darmstadt

Darmstädter Echo: Holzhofallee 25–31, 64295 Darmstadt; Post-fach 100155, 64276 Darmstadt; tel. (6151) 387373; fax (6151) 387900; e-mail chefredaktion@darmstaedter-echo.de; internet www

.echo-online.de; f. 1945; Editor-in-Chief Dr MICHAEL HORN; circ. 88,828 (Dec. 2011).

Dortmund

Westfälische Rundschau: Friedrichstr. 34–36, 45128 Essen; tel. (201) 8040; internet www.wr.de; publ. by WAZ Mediengruppe; Editor-in-Chief MALTE HINZ; circ. 210,000 (2008).

Dresden

Sächsische Zeitung: Haus der Presse, Ostra-Allee 20, 01067 Dresden; tel. (351) 48640; fax (351) 48642354; e-mail redaktion@sz-online.de; internet www.sz-online.de; f. 1946; morning; publ. by Gruner + Jahr AG; Editor-in-Chief THOMAS SCHULTZ-HOMBERG; circ. 285,000 (Dec. 2011).

Düsseldorf

Handelsblatt: Kasernenstr. 67, 40213 Düsseldorf; Postfach 102741, 40018 Düsseldorf; tel. (211) 8870; fax (211) 8872980; e-mail handelsblatt@vhb.de; internet www.handelsblatt.de; Mon.–Fri.; business and finance; publ. by Verlagsgruppe Handelsblatt GmbH; Editor-in-Chief BERND ZIESEMER; circ. 147,208 (Dec. 2011).

Rheinische Post: Zülpicherstr. 10, 40549 Düsseldorf; tel. (211) 5050; fax (211) 5051929; internet www.rp-online.de; f. 1946; Editor-in-Chief SVEN GÖSMANN; circ. 373,810 (Dec. 2011, incl. regional edns).

Westdeutsche Zeitung: Königsallee 27, 40212 Düsseldorf; tel. (211) 83820; fax (211) 83822225; e-mail westdeutsche.zeitung@wz-newsline.de; internet www.wz-newsline.de; Editor-in-Chief LOTHAR LEUSCHEN (acting); circ. 159,246 (Dec. 2011).

Erfurt

Thüringer Allgemeine: Gottstedter Landstr. 6, 99092 Erfurt; tel. (361) 2274; fax (361) 2275007; e-mail redaktion@thueringer-allgemeine.de; internet www.thueringer-allgemeine.de; f. 1946; morning; Editor-in-Chief PAUL-JOSEF RAUE; circ. 338,500 (Sept. 2011, with *Ostthüringer Zeitung* and *Thüringische Landeszeitung*).

Essen

Neue Ruhr Zeitung/Neue Rhein Zeitung: Friedrichstr. 34–38, 45128 Essen; tel. (201) 8040; fax (201) 8041070; e-mail redaktion@nrz.de; internet www.derwesten.de/nachrichten/nrz.html; f. 1946; Editor-in-Chief RÜDIGER OPPERS; circ. 180,000.

Westdeutsche Allgemeine Zeitung: Friedrichstr. 34–38, 45128 Essen; tel. (201) 8040; fax (201) 8042841; e-mail zentralredaktion@waz.de; internet www.derwesten.de/nachrichten/faz.html; f. 1948; Editor-in-Chief ULRICH REITZ; circ. 580,000.

Frankfurt am Main

Frankfurter Allgemeine Zeitung: Hellerhofstr. 2–4, 60327 Frankfurt a.M.; tel. (69) 75910; fax (69) 75912332; e-mail info@faz.net; internet www.faz.net; f. 1949; Editors WERNER D'INKA, BERTHOLD KOHLER, Dr GÜNTHER NONNENMACHER, Dr FRANK SCHIRRMACHER, HOLGER STELTZNER; circ. 380,427 (Dec. 2011).

Frankfurter Neue Presse: Frankenallee 71–81, 60327 Frankfurt a.M.; Postfach 100801, 60008 Frankfurt a.M.; tel. (69) 75010; fax (69) 75014846; e-mail fnp.redaktion@fsd.de; internet www.fnp.de; independent; Editor-in-Chief RAINER M. GEFELLER.

Frankfurter Rundschau: Karl-Gerold-Pl. 1, 60594 Frankfurt a.M.; tel. (69) 21991; fax (69) 21993720; e-mail politik@fr-online.de; internet www.fr-online.de; f. 1945; Editor-in-Chief Dr UWE VORKÖTTER; circ. 124,479 (Dec. 2011).

Freiburg im Breisgau

Badische Zeitung: Pressehaus, Basler Str. 88, 79115 Freiburg i. Br.; tel. (761) 4960; fax (761) 4965029; e-mail redaktion@badische-zeitung.de; internet www.badische-zeitung.de; f. 1946; Editor-in-Chief THOMAS HAUSER; circ. 148,061 (Dec. 2011).

Gera

Ostthüringer Zeitung: Alte Str. 3, 04626 Löbichau; tel. (3447) 525911; fax (3447) 525914; e-mail redaktion@otz.de; internet www.otz.de; morning; Editor-in-Chief JÖRG RIEBARTSCH.

Hagen

Westfalenpost: Schürmannstr. 4, 58097 Hagen; tel. (2331) 9170; fax (2331) 9174206; e-mail westfalenpost@westfalenpost.de; internet www.derwesten.de/nachrichten/wp.html; f. 1946; publ. by WAZ Mediengruppe; Editor-in-Chief STEFAN HANS KLÄSENER.

Halle an der Saale

Mitteldeutsche Zeitung: Delitzscher Str. 65, 06112 Halle (Saale); tel. (345) 5650; fax (345) 5654350; e-mail service@mz-web.de; internet www.mz-web.de; f. 1946 as *Freiheit* (organ of the ruling party in the GDR); refounded 1990 following unification; publ. by M. DuMont Schauberg Gruppe; Editors-in-Chief HANS-JÜRGEN GREYE, HARTMUT AUGUSTIN; circ. 221,404 (Dec. 2011).

Hamburg

Bild: Axel-Springer-Pl. 1, 10969 Hamburg; tel. (40) 34700; fax (40) 345811; internet www.bild.de; f. 1952; publ. by Axel Springer Verlag AG; Chief Editor KAI DIEKMANN; circ. 2,715,105 (Dec. 2011).

Hamburger Abendblatt: Axel-Springer-Pl. 1, 20350 Hamburg; tel. (40) 34700; fax (40) 34726110; internet www.abendblatt.de; publ. by Axel Springer Verlag AG; Editor-in-Chief LARS HAIDER; circ. 212,263 (Dec. 2011).

Hamburger Morgenpost: Griegstr. 75, 22763 Hamburg; tel. (40) 8090570; fax (40) 9057640; e-mail verlag@mopo.de; internet www.mopo.de; publ. by Morgenpost Verlag; Editor-in-Chief FRANK NIGGEMEIER; circ. 107,584 (Dec. 2011).

Hannover
(Hanover)

Hannoversche Allgemeine Zeitung: August-Madsack-Str. 1, 30559 Hannover; tel. (511) 5180; fax (511) 5182899; e-mail redaktion@haz.de; internet www.haz.de; Editors-in-Chief HENDRIK BRANDT, MATTHIAS KOCH; circ. 540,570 (Dec. 2011).

Heidelberg

Rhein-Neckar-Zeitung: Neugasse 2, 69117 Heidelberg; tel. (6221) 5190; fax (6221) 519217; e-mail rnz-kontakt@rnz.de; internet www.rnz.de; f. 1945; morning; Publrs JOACHIM KNORR, WINFRIED KNORR, INGE HOELTZCKE, DANIEL SCHULZE; circ. 92,754 (Dec. 2011).

Ingolstadt

Donaukurier: Stauffenbergstr. 2A, 85051 Ingolstadt; tel. (841) 96660; fax (841) 9666255; e-mail ingolstadt.redaktion@donaukurier.de; internet www.donaukurier.de; f. 1872; Editor-in-Chief GERD SCHNEIDER; circ. 88,772 (Dec. 2011).

Kassel

Hessische/Niedersächsische Allgemeine: Frankfurter Str. 168, 34121 Kassel; Postfach 101009, 34010 Kassel; tel. (561) 20300; fax (561) 2032406; e-mail info@hna.de; internet www.hna.de; f. 1959; independent; Editor-in-Chief HORST SEIDENFADEN; circ. 224,507 (Dec. 2011).

Kempten

Allgäuer Zeitung: Heisinger Str. 14, 87437 Kempten; Postfach 3155, 87440 Kempten; tel. (831) 2060; fax (831) 206123; e-mail redaktion@azv.de; internet www.all-in.de; f. 1945; Publrs GEORG FÜRST VON WALDBURG-ZEIL, GÜNTER HOLLAND, ELLINOR HOLLAND; circ. 102,874 (Dec. 2011).

Kiel

Kieler Nachrichten: Fleethörn 1–7, 24103 Kiel; Postfach 1111, 24100 Kiel; tel. (431) 9030; fax (431) 9032935; internet www.kn-online.de; publ. by Axel Springer Verlag; Editor-in-Chief JÜRGEN HEINEMANN; circ. 103,053 (Dec. 2011).

Koblenz

Rhein-Zeitung: August-Horch-Str. 28, 56070 Koblenz; tel. (261) 89200; fax (261) 892770; e-mail redaktion@rhein-zeitung.net; internet www.rhein-zeitung.de; Editor-in-Chief CHRISTIAN LINDNER; circ. 198,688 (Mon.–Fri.), 216,837 (Sat.) (2011).

Köln
(Cologne)

Express: Postfach 100410, 50450 Köln; Amsterdamer Str. 192, 50735 Köln; tel. (221) 2240; fax (211) 2242700; e-mail info@express.de; internet www.express.de; f. 1964; publ. by DuMont Schauberg Gruppe; Editor-in-Chief RUDOLF KREITZ; circ. 182,498 (Dec. 2011).

Kölner Stadt-Anzeiger: Amsterdamer Str. 192, 50735 Köln; tel. (221) 2240; fax (221) 2242524; internet www.ksta.de; f. 1876; Editor-in-Chief PETER PAULS; circ. 328,092 (Dec. 2011, with *Kölnische Rundschau*).

Kölnische Rundschau: Stolkgasse 25–45, 50667 Köln; Postfach 102145, 50461 Köln; tel. (221) 1632551; fax (221) 1632491; e-mail koeln@kr-redaktion.de; internet www.rundschau-online.de; f. 1946; Publr HELMUT HEINEN.

Konstanz

Südkurier: Max-Stromeyer-Str. 178, 78467 Konstanz; Postfach 102001, Presse- und Druckzentrum, 78420 Konstanz; tel. (7531) 9990; fax (7531) 991485; e-mail chefredaktion@suedkurier.de; internet www.suedkurier.de; f. 1945; Editor-in-Chief STEFAN LUTZ; circ. 131,191 (Dec. 2011).

Leipzig

Leipziger Volkszeitung: Petersssteinweg 19, 04107 Leipzig; tel. (341) 21810; fax (341) 21811640; e-mail post@lvz-online.de; internet www.lvz-online.de; f. 1894; morning; publ. by Verlagsgesellschaft Madsach and Axel Springer Verlag AG; Editor-in-Chief JAN EMENDÖRFER; circ. 217,014 (Dec. 2011).

Leutkirch im Allgäu

Schwäbische Zeitung: Rudolf-Roth-Str. 18, 88299 Leutkirch im Allgäu; Postfach 1145, 88291 Leutkirch im Allgäu; tel. (7561) 80100; fax (7561) 80378; e-mail redaktion@schwaebische-zeitung.de; internet www.schwaebische-zeitung.de; f. 1945; Editor-in-Chief HENDRIK GROTH; circ. 175,051 (Dec. 2011).

Lübeck

Lübecker Nachrichten: Herrenholz 10–12, 23556 Lübeck; tel. (451) 1440; fax (451) 1441022; e-mail redaktion@ln-luebeck.de; internet www.ln-online.de; f. 1945; Tue.–Sun.; publ. by Axel Springer Verlag AG; Editor-in-Chief GERALD GOETSCH; circ. 104,033 (Dec. 2011).

Ludwigshafen

Die Rheinpfalz: Amtsstr. 5–11, 67059 Ludwigshafen; Postfach 211147, 67011 Ludwigshafen; tel. (621) 590201; fax (621) 5902272; e-mail rheinpfalz@rheinpfalz.de; internet www.rheinpfalz.de; Editor-in-Chief MICHAEL GARTHE; circ. 243,572 (Dec. 2011).

Magdeburg

Volksstimme: Bahnhofstr. 17, 39104 Magdeburg; tel. (391) 59990; fax (391) 388400; e-mail chefredaktion@volksstimme.de; internet www.volksstimme.de; f. 1890; morning; 18 regional edns; publ. by Magdeburger Verlags- und Druckhaus GmbH; Editor-in-Chief ALOIS KÖSTER; circ. 193,615 (Dec. 2011, incl. regional edns).

Mainz

Allgemeine Zeitung: Erich-Dombrowski-Str. 2, 55127 Mainz; tel. (6131) 4830; fax (6131) 485868; e-mail az-mainz@vrm.de; internet www.main-rheiner.de; f. 1850; publ. by Verlagsgruppe Rhein-Main; Editor-in-Chief FRIEDRICH ROEINGH; circ. 95,494 (March 2008, incl. regional edns).

Mannheim

Mannheimer Morgen: Dudenstr. 12–26, 68167 Mannheim; Postfach 102164, 68021 Mannheim; tel. (621) 39201; fax (621) 3921376; e-mail redaktion@mamo.de; internet www.morgenweb.de; f. 1946; Editor-in-Chief DIRK LÜBKE; circ. 125,634 (Dec. 2011).

München
(Munich)

Abendzeitung: Rundfunkpl. 4, 80335 München; tel. (89) 23770; fax (89) 2377409; e-mail info@abendzeitung.de; internet www.abendzeitung.de; f. 1948; evening; Editor-in-Chief ARNO MAKOWSKY; circ. 131,399 (Dec. 2011).

Münchner Merkur: Paul-Heyse-Str. 2–4, 80336 München; tel. (89) 53060; fax (89) 5306408; internet www.merkur-online.de; Editor-in-Chief KARL SCHERMANN; circ. 268,762 (Dec. 2011).

Süddeutsche Zeitung: Hultschiner Str. 8, 81677 München; tel. (89) 21830; fax (89) 21839715; e-mail wir@sueddeutsche.de; internet www.sueddeutsche.de; f. 1945; publ. by Süddeutscher-Verlag GmbH; Editor-in-Chief KURT KISTER; circ. 427,748 (Dec. 2011).

TZ: Paul-Heyse-Str. 2–4, 80336 München; tel. (89) 53060; fax (89) 5306552; e-mail sekretariat@tz-online.de; internet www.tz-online.de; f. 1968; Editor-in-Chief RUDOLF BÖGEL; circ. 141,250 (Dec. 2011).

Münster

Westfälische Nachrichten: An der Hansalinie 1, 48163 Münster; tel. (251) 6900; fax (251) 6904570; internet www.wn.de; Editor-in-Chief Dr NORBERT TIEMANN; circ. 210,030 (June 2008, incl. regional edns).

Neubrandenburg

Nordkurier: Friedrich-Engels-Ring 29, 17033 Neubrandenburg; tel. (395) 45750; fax (395) 4575694; e-mail chefredaktion@nordkurier.de; internet www.nordkurier.de; Editor-in-Chief Dr ANDRÉ UZULIS; circ. 88,841 (Dec. 2011).

Nürnberg
(Nuremberg)

Nürnberger Nachrichten: Marienstr. 9–11, Postfach 90327, 90402 Nürnberg; tel. (911) 2160; fax (911) 2162432; e-mail info@nordbayern.de; internet www.nn-online.de; f. 1945; Editor-in-Chief HEINZ-JOACHIM HAUCK; circ. 282,469 (Dec. 2011).

Oldenburg

Nordwest-Zeitung: Peterstr. 28–34, 26121 Oldenburg; Postfach 2527, 26015 Oldenburg; tel. (441) 998801; fax (441) 99882029; internet www.nwz-online.de; publ. by Nordwest-Zeitung Verlagsgesellschaft mbH & Co KG; Editor-in-Chief ROLF SEELHEIM; circ. 123,706 (Dec. 2011).

Osnabrück

Neue Osnabrücker Zeitung: Breiter Gang 10–16 and Grosse Str. 17–19, 49074 Osnabrück; Postfach 4260, 49032 Osnabrück; tel. (541) 3100; fax (541) 310485; e-mail redaktion@neue-oz.de; internet www.neue-oz.de; f. 1967; Editor-in-Chief RALF GEISENHANSLÜKE; circ. 282,238 (Dec. 2011).

Passau

Passauer Neue Presse: Medienstr. 5, 94036 Passau; tel. (851) 8020; fax (851) 802256; e-mail info@pnp.de; internet www.pnp.de; f. 1946; Editor-in-Chief ERNST FUCHS; circ. 166,010 (Dec. 2011).

Potsdam

Märkische Allgemeine: Friedrich-Engels-Str. 24, 14473 Potsdam; Postfach 601153, 14411 Potsdam; tel. (331) 28400; fax (331) 2840310; e-mail chefredaktion@mazonline.de; internet www.maerkischeallgemeine.de; f. 1990; morning; independent; Chief Editor Dr KLAUS ROST; circ. 138,092 (Dec. 2011).

Regensburg

Mittelbayerische Zeitung: Kumpfmühler Str. 9, 93047 Regensburg; tel. (941) 207270; fax (941) 207307; e-mail mittelbayerische@mittelbayerische.de; internet www.mittelbayerische.de; f. 1945; Editor-in-Chief MANFRED SAUERER; circ. 119,375 (Dec. 2011).

Rostock

Ostsee-Zeitung: Richard-Wagner-Str. 1A, 18055 Rostock; tel. (81) 3650; fax (81) 365244; e-mail redaktion@ostsee-zeitung.de; internet www.ostsee-zeitung.de; f. 1952; publ. by Axel Springer Verlag AG; Editor-in-Chief JAN EMENDÖRFER; circ. 149,553 (Dec. 2011, incl. regional edns).

Saarbrücken

Saarbrücker Zeitung: Gutenbergstr. 11–23, 66117 Saarbrücken; tel. (681) 5020; fax (681) 502501; internet www.saarbruecker-zeitung.de; f. 1761; Editor PETER STEFAN HERBST; circ. 149,308 (Dec. 2011).

Stuttgart

Stuttgarter Nachrichten: Plieninger Str. 150, 70567 Stuttgart; Postfach 104452, 70039 Stuttgart; tel. (711) 72050; fax (711) 72057138; e-mail cvd@stn.zgs.de; internet www.stuttgarter-nachrichten.de; f. 1946; Editor-in-Chief CHRISTOPH REISINGER; circ. 190,000 (Dec. 2011, with *Stuttgarter Zeitung*).

Stuttgarter Zeitung: Plieninger Str. 150, 70567 Stuttgart; Postfach 106032, 70049 Stuttgart; tel. (711) 72050; fax (711) 72051112; e-mail redaktion@stz.zgs.de; internet www.stuttgarter-zeitung.de; f. 1945; Editor-in-Chief JOACHIM DORFS.

Trier

Trierischer Volksfreund: Hanns-Martin-Schleyer-Str. 8, 54294 Trier; Postfach 3770, 54227 Trier; tel. (651) 71990; fax (651) 7199990; e-mail redaktion@volksfreund.de; internet www.volksfreund.de; Editor-in-Chief ISABELL FUNK; circ. 92,685 (Dec. 2011).

Würzburg

Main-Post: Berner Str. 2, 97084 Würzburg; tel. (931) 60010; fax (931) 6001242; e-mail redaktion@mainpost.de; internet www.mainpost.de; f. 1883; independent; Editor-in-Chief MICHAEL REINHARD; circ. 128,325 (Dec. 2011).

SUNDAY AND WEEKLY PAPERS

Bayernkurier: Nymphenburger Str. 64, 80636 München; tel. (89) 120040; fax (89) 12004133; e-mail redaktion@bayernkurier.de; internet www.bayernkurier.de; f. 1950; weekly; organ of the CSU; Editor-in-Chief PETER HAUSMANN; circ. 63,364 (Dec. 2011).

Bild am Sonntag: Axel-Springer-Pl. 1, 20350 Hamburg; tel. (40) 34700; fax (40) 34726110; internet www.bild-am-sonntag.de; f. 1956; Sunday; publ. by Axel Springer Verlag AG; Editor-in-Chief MARION HORN; circ. 1,394,173 (Dec. 2011).

B.Z. am Sonntag: Axel-Springer-Str. 65, 10888 Berlin; tel. (30) 25910; fax (30) 259173131; e-mail redaktion@bz-berlin.de; internet www.bz-berlin.de; f. 1992; publ. by Ullstein GmbH; Editor-in-Chief PETER HUTH; circ. 88,670 (Dec. 2011).

Frankfurter Allgemeine Sonntagszeitung: Hellerhofstr. 2–4, 60327 Frankfurt a.M.; tel. (69) 75910; fax (69) 75911773; e-mail sonntagszeitung@faz.de; internet www.faz.de; Sunday; Publrs WERNER D'INKA, BERTHOLD KOHLER, GÜNTHER NONNENMACHER, JÜRGEN KAUBE, HOLGER STELTZNER; circ. 401,337 (Dec. 2011).

Sonntag Aktuell: Plieninger Str. 150, 70567 Stuttgart; Postfach 104462, 70039 Stuttgart; tel. (711) 72050; fax (711) 72057138; e-mail redaktion@soak.zgs.de; internet www.sonntag-aktuell.de; Sunday; Editor-in-Chief Dr CHRISTOPH REISINGER; circ. 593,877 (June 2014).

Welt am Sonntag: Axel-Springer-Str. 65, 10888 Berlin; tel. (30) 25910; fax (30) 259171606; e-mail leserbriefe@wams.de; internet www.welt.de; f. 1948; Sunday; publ. by Axel Springer Verlag AG; Editor-in-Chief JAN-ERIC PETERS; circ. 402,287 (Dec. 2010).

Die Zeit: Buceriusstr., Eingang Speersort 1, Pressehaus, 20095 Hamburg; tel. (40) 32800; fax (40) 327111; e-mail diezeit@zeit.de; internet www.zeit.de; f. 1946; weekly; Editor-in-Chief GIOVANNI DI LORENZO; circ. 537,129 (Dec. 2011).

SELECTED PERIODICALS

Agriculture

Bauernzeitung: Wilhelmsaue 37, 10713 Berlin; Postfach 310448, 10634 Berlin; tel. (30) 464060; fax (30) 46406319; e-mail info@bauernverlag.de; internet www.bauernzeitung.de; f. 1960; weekly; covers agricultural news in Brandenburg, Mecklenburg-Western Pomerania, Saxony, Saxony-Anhalt and Thüringen; Editor-in-Chief Dr THOMAS TANNEBERGER; circ. 23,369 (Jan.–March 2013).

Bayerisches Landwirtschaftliches Wochenblatt: Bayerstr. 57, 80335 München; Postfach 200523, 80005 München; tel. (89) 53098901; fax (89) 5328537; e-mail ulrich.graf@dlv.de; internet www.wochenblatt-dlv.de; f. 1810; weekly; organ of the Bayerischer Bauernverband; Editor-in-Chief SEPP KELLERER; circ. 102,936 (Jan.–March 2013).

dlz agrarmagazin: Postfach 400580, 80705 München; Lothstr. 29, 80797 München; tel. (89) 127051; fax (89) 12705546; e-mail dlv.muenchen@dlv.de; internet www.dlz-agrarmagazin.de; monthly; publ. by Deutscher Landwirtschaftsverlag GmbH; Editor-in-Chief DETLEF STEINERT; circ. 70,279 (Jan.–March 2013).

Eisenbahn-Landwirt: Ostring 6, 76131 Karlsruhe; Postfach 2026, 76008 Karlsruhe; tel. (721) 62830; fax (721) 628310; e-mail info@druck-verlag-sw.de; internet www.druck-verlag-sw.de; f. 1918; monthly; gardening; organ of the Hauptverband der Bahn-Landwirtschaft; publ. by Druckhaus Karlsruhe, Druck + Verlagsgesellschaft Südwest mbH; Dir ROLF HAASE; circ. 72,647 (Jan.–March 2013).

Landpost: Wollgrasweg 31, 70599 Stuttgart; tel. (711) 167790; fax (711) 4586093; e-mail info@vdaw.de; internet www.vdaw.de; f. 1945; weekly; agriculture and gardening; Editor ERICH REICH; circ. 12,597 (Jan.–March 2013).

Top Agrar: Hülsebrockstr. 2–8, 48165 Münster; Postfach 7847, 48042 Münster; tel. (2501) 801640; fax (2501) 801654; e-mail redaktion@topagrar.com; internet www.topagrar.com; monthly; focusing on key agricultural issues; Editors BERTHOLD ACHLER, HEINZ-GÜNTER TOPÜTH, Dr LUDGER SCHULZE PALS; circ. 114,744 (Jan.–March 2013).

The Arts and Literature

Art. Das Kunstmagazin: Am Baumwall 11, 20459 Hamburg; tel. (40) 37030; fax (40) 37035618; e-mail kunst@art-magazin.de; internet www.art-magazin.de; f. 1979; monthly; publ. by Gruner + Jahr AG & Co KG; Editor-in-Chief TIM SOMMER; circ. 53,336 (2010).

Cinema: Christoph-Probst-Weg 1, 20251 Hamburg; tel. (40) 41310; e-mail info@milchstrasse.de; internet www.cinema.de; monthly; film reviews, interviews; publ. by Cinema Verlag GmbH; Editor-in-Chief ARTUR JUNG; circ. 77,321 (Jan.–March 2013).

Literarische Welt: Axel-Springer-Str. 65, 10888 Berlin; tel. (30) 25910; fax (30) 259171606; e-mail literaturwelt@welt.de; internet www.welt.de/kultur/literarischewelt; f. 1971; weekly; literary supplement of *Die Welt*; Editor THOMAS SCHMID.

Musikexpress: Mehringdamm 33, 10960 Berlin; tel. (30) 881880; fax (30) 88188223; e-mail redaktion@musikexpress.de; internet www.musikexpress.de; f. 1983; monthly; popular music; publ. by Axel Springer Mediahouse Berlin GmbH; Editor-in-Chief SEVERIN MEVISSEN; circ. 53,706 (Jan.–March 2013).

Praxis Deutsch: Im Brande 17, 30926 Seelze/Velber; tel. (511) 40004150; fax (511) 40004170; e-mail redaktion.pd@friedrich-verlag.de; internet www.friedrich-verlag.de; 6 a year; German language and literature; publ. by Erhard Friedrich Verlag GmbH; Editor SONJA HEINLEIN; circ. 9,000.

Theater der Zeit: Klosterstr. 68, 10179 Berlin; tel. (30) 24722414; fax (30) 24722415; e-mail redaktion@theaterderzeit.de; internet www.theaterderzeit.de; f. 1946; 10 a year; theatre, drama, opera, children's theatre, puppet theatre, dance; Editors HARALD MÜLLER, Dr SEBASTIAN KIRSCH, DORTE LENA EILERS, GUNNAR DECKER, DÖRING MIRKA; circ. 5,000.

Theater heute: Nestorstr. 8–9, 10709 Berlin; tel. (30) 25449510; fax (30) 25449512; e-mail redaktion@theaterheute.de; internet www.theaterheute.de; f. 1960; monthly, with a yearbook in August; Editors BARBARA BURCKHARDT, EVA BEHRENDT, Dr FRANZ WILLE; circ. 15,000.

xia intelligente architektur: Fasanenweg 18, 70771 Leinfelden-Echterdingen; tel. (711) 7591286; fax (711) 7591410; e-mail ait-red@ait-online.de; internet www.xia-online.de; f. 1890; quarterly; Editor Dr FRIEDRICH H. DASSLER; circ. 16,458 (Oct. 2010).

Economics, Finance and Industry

Absatzwirtschaft: Grafenberger Allee 293, 40237 Düsseldorf; Postfach 101102, 40002 Düsseldorf; tel. (211) 8870; fax (211) 8871420; e-mail absatzwirtschaft@fachverlag.de; internet www.absatzwirtschaft.de; f. 1958; monthly; marketing; Editor-in-Chief CHRISTOPH BERDI; circ. 25,139 (Jan.–March 2013).

Börse Online: Bayerstr. 71–73, 80335 München; tel. (89) 272640; fax (89) 27264199; e-mail verlag@finanzen.net; internet www.finanzen.net; f. 1987; weekly; German and international stocks and stock-related investments; publ. by Finanzen Verlag GmbH; Editor-in-Chief JENS CASTNER; circ. 39,118 (Jan.–March 2013).

Capital: Am Baumwall 11, 20459 Hamburg; tel. (40) 37030; fax (40) 31990310; e-mail capital@capital.de; internet www.capital.de; f. 1962; monthly; business magazine; publ. by Gruner + Jahr AG & Co KG; Editor-in-Chief HORST VON BUTTLAR; circ. 163,186 (Jan.–March 2013).

Creditreform: Grafenberger Allee 293, 40237 Düsseldorf; Postfach 101102, 40002 Düsseldorf; tel. (211) 8870; fax (211) 8871410; e-mail creditreform-service@fachverlag.de; internet www.creditreform-magazin.de; f. 1879; Editor-in-Chief INGO SCHENK; circ. 129,870 (Jan.–March 2013).

H&V Journal Handelsvermittlung und Vertrieb: Springer-Verlag GmbH, Tiergartenstr. 17, 69121 Heidelberg; tel. (6221) 4870; f. 1949; monthly; Editor-in-Chief (vacant); circ. 10,132 (Jan.–March 2013).

Impulse: Hammerbrookstr. 93, 20097 Hamburg; tel. (40) 60945220; fax (40) 609452299; e-mail chefredaktion@impulse.de; internet www.impulse.de; f. 1980; monthly; business and entrepreneurship; publ. by Impulse Medien GmbH; Editor-in-Chief Dr NIKOLAUS FÖRSTER; circ. 63,606 (Jan.–March 2013).

Industrieanzeiger: Ernst-Mey-Str. 8, 70771 Leinfelden-Echterdingen; tel. (711) 7594451; fax (711) 7594398; e-mail werner.goetz@konradin.de; internet www.industrieanzeiger.de; f. 1879; 32 a year; Editor-in-Chief WERNER GÖTZ; circ. 40,028 (Jan.–March 2013).

Management International Review: University of Kiel, Westring 425, 24118 Kiel; tel. (431) 8801635; fax (431) 8803963; e-mail mir@bwl.uni-kiel.de; internet www.mir-online.de; f. 1960; 6 a year; English; publ. by Axel Springer Verlag AG; Editors Prof. Dr MICHAEL-JÖRG OESTERLE (Stuttgart), Prof. Dr JOACHIM WOLF (Kiel).

VDI Nachrichten: VDI-Pl. 1, 40468 Düsseldorf; Postfach 101054, 40001 Düsseldorf; tel. (211) 61880; fax (211) 6188306; e-mail redaktion@vdi-nachrichten.com; internet www.vdi-nachrichten.com; f. 1923; weekly, Fri.; technology and economics; Editor-in-Chief KEN FOUHY; circ. 162,718 (Jan.–March 2013).

WirtschaftsWoche: Kasernenstr. 67, 40213 Düsseldorf; tel. (211) 8870; fax (211) 8872980; e-mail roland.tichy@wiwo.de; internet www.wiwo.de; weekly; business; Editor-in-Chief ROLAND TICHY; circ. 173,251 (Jan.–March 2013).

Home, Fashion and General

Bild der Frau: Axel-Springer-Pl. 1, 20350 Hamburg; tel. (40) 34700; e-mail service@bildderfrau.de; internet www.bildderfrau.de; f. 1983; weekly; publ. by Funke Mediengruppe; Editor-in-Chief SANDRA IMMOOR; circ. 902,664 (Jan.–March 2013).

Bravo: Charles-de-Gaulle-Str. 8, 81737 München; tel. (89) 67860; e-mail post@bravo.de; internet www.bravo.de; bi-weekly; publ. by Bauer Verlagsgruppe; for young people; Editor-in-Chief NADINE NORDMANN; circ. 248,221 (Jan.–March 2013).

Brigitte: Am Baumwall 11, 20459 Hamburg; tel. (40) 37030; fax (40) 37035845; e-mail infoline@brigitte.de; internet www.brigitte.de; f. 1954; fortnightly; women's magazine; also publishes *Brigitte Balance* (2 a year; circ. 130,000, Oct. 2010) and *Brigitte Woman* (monthly; circ. 237,815, Jan.–March 2013); publ. by Gruner + Jahr AG & Co KG; Editor-in-Chief STEPHAN SCHÄFER; circ. 574,096 (Jan.–March 2013).

Bunte: Arabellastr. 23, 81925 München; tel. (89) 92500; fax (89) 92502340; e-mail bunte@burda.com; internet www.bunte.de; f. 1948; weekly; celebrity gossip; publ. by Bunte Entertainment Verlag GmbH; Editor-in-Chief PATRICIA RIEKEL; circ. 564,747 (Jan.–March 2013).

Burda Style: Arabellastr. 23, 81925 München; tel. (89) 92500; fax (89) 92502340; e-mail service@burdastyle.de; internet www.burdastyle.de; f. 1949; monthly; fashion, patterns; publ. by Hubert Burda Media Holding GmbH & Co KG; Editor-in-Chief DAGMAR BILY; circ. 134,998 (Jan.–March 2013).

Cosmopolitan: Charles-de-Gaulle-Str. 8, 81737 München; tel. (89) 67860; fax (89) 67869719; e-mail info@cosmopolitan.de; internet www.cosmopolitan.de; f. 1980; monthly; lifestyle; Editor-in-Chief KERSTIN WENG; circ. 258,572 (Jan.–March 2013).

Elle: Arabellastr. 23, 81925 München; tel. (89) 92500; fax (89) 92502340; e-mail elleonline@elle.burda.com; internet www.elle.de; monthly; fashion; also publishes *Elle Decoration* (6 a year; circ. 109,887); publ. by Hubert Burda Media Holding GmbH & Co KG; Editor-in-Chief SABINE NEDELCHEV; circ. 206,264 (Jan.–March 2013).

Eltern: Weihenstephaner Str. 7, 81673 München; tel. (89) 415200; fax (89) 4152651; e-mail redaktion@eltern.de; internet www.eltern.de; f. 1966; monthly; for parents of young children; also publishes *Eltern Family* (monthly; for parents of older children; circ. 135,440); publ. by Gruner + Jahr AG & Co KG; Editor-in-Chief MARIE-LUISE LEWICKI; circ. 264,728 (Jan.–March 2013).

Essen & Trinken: Am Baumwall 11, 20459 Hamburg; tel. (40) 37034214; fax (40) 37034212; e-mail service@essen-und-trinken.de; internet www.essen-und-trinken.de; f. 1972; monthly; food and drink; also publishes *Essen & Trinken Für Jeden Tag* (monthly; recipes; circ. 191,800); publ. by Gruner + Jahr AG & Co KG; Editors-in-Chief CLEMENS VON LUCK, ÉLISABETH HERZEL; circ. 192,789 (Jan.–March 2013).

Familie & Co: Schnewlinstr. 6, 79098 Freiburg i. Br.; tel. (761) 70578559; fax (761) 70578656; e-mail redaktion@familymedia.de; internet www.familie.de; f. 1996; monthly; publ. by Family Media GmbH & Co; also publishes *Baby & Co* (circ. 96,085); Editor-in-Chief DIRK MÜLLER; circ. 176,612 (Jan.–March 2013).

Frau aktuell: Münchener Str. 101/09, 85737 Ismaning; tel. (89) 272700; fax (89) 272708990; e-mail fa@mzv-direkt.de; internet www.frau-aktuell.de; f. 1965; weekly; publ. by Westdeutsche Zeitschriftenverlag GmbH & Co KG; circ. 177,974 (Jan.–March 2013).

Frau und Mutter: Prinz Georg Str. 44, 40477 Düsseldorf; tel. (211) 4499240; fax (211) 4499289; e-mail redaktion@kfdfum.de; internet www.frauundmutter.de; monthly; women's magazine published by the Catholic Women's Community; Editors BARBARA LECKEL, NIKOLA HOLLMAN; circ. 506,500 (Jan.–March 2013).

Frau im Spiegel: Münchener Str. 101/09, 85737 Ismaning; tel. (89) 272700; fax (89) 272708990; e-mail fis@mzv-direkt.de; internet www.frau-im-spiegel.de; f. 1947; weekly; aimed at women over 35; also publishes *Frau im Spiegel Legenden* (quarterly; focusing on a particular celebrity); Editor-in-Chief CLAUDIA CIESLARCZYK; circ. 270,292 (Jan.–March 2013).

Frau im Trend: Burda Senator Verlag GmbH, Arabellastr. 23, 81925 Munich; tel. (89) 92500; fax (89) 92502340; e-mail freizeitfreunde@burda.com; women's magazine; Editor-in-Chief THOMAS OTTO; circ. 313,771 (Jan.–March 2013).

Freizeit Revue: Hubert-Burda-Pl. 1, 77652 Offenburg; tel. (781) 8401; fax (781) 842254; e-mail freizeitfreunde@burda.com; internet www.freizeitfreunde.de; weekly; celebrities, food, health and beauty; publ. by Hubert Burda Media Holding GmbH & Co KG; Editor-in-Chief ROBERT PÖLZER; circ. 843,047 (Jan.–March 2013).

Freundin: Arabellastr. 23, 81925 München; tel. (89) 92500; fax (89) 92502340; e-mail freundin@burda.com; internet www.freundin.de; f. 1948; fortnightly; for young women; publ. by Hubert Burda Media Holding GmbH & Co KG; Editor-in-Chief NIKOLAUS ALBRECHT; circ. 406,258 (Jan.–March 2013).

Für Sie: Jahreszeitenverlag GmbH, Possmoorweg 2, 22301 Hamburg; tel. (40) 27170; e-mail redaktion@fuer-sie.de; internet www.fuer-sie.de; fortnightly; women's magazine; Editor-in-Chief SABINE FÄTH; circ. 371,234 (Jan.–March 2013).

Gala: Schaarsteinweg 14, 20459 Hamburg; tel. (40) 37030; fax (40) 37034364; e-mail redaktion@gala.de; internet www.gala.de; f. 1994;

weekly; celebrity gossip; publ. by Norddeutsche Verlagsgesellschaft mbH; Editor-in-Chief CHRISTIAN KRUG; circ. 326,050 (Jan.–March 2013).

GEO: Am Baumwall 11, 20459 Hamburg; tel. (40) 37030; fax (40) 37035648; e-mail info@geo.de; internet www.geo.de; f. 1976; monthly; reports on science, politics and religion; publ. by Gruner + Jahr AG & Co KG; also publishes *GEO Epoche* (quarterly; history; circ. 76,452), *GEO Saison* (monthly; travel; circ. 92,988), *GEO Special* (6 a year; travel; circ. 58,951), *Geolino* (monthly; general interest for children aged 8–14 years; circ. 197,200); Editor-in-Chief PETER-MATTHIAS GAEDE; circ. 289,552 (Jan.–March 2013).

Guter Rat: Superillu Verlag GmbH & Co KG, Potsdamer Str. 7, 10785 Berlin; tel. (30) 7544306610; fax (30) 7544306395; e-mail redaktion@guter-rat.de; internet www.guter-rat.de; f. 1945; monthly; consumer magazine; Editor-in-Chief ROBERT SCHNEIDER; circ. 230,623 (Jan.–March 2013).

Das Haus: Postfach 810164, 81901 München; Arabellastr. 23, 81925 München; tel. (89) 92500; fax (89) 92503055; e-mail userservice@haus.de; internet www.haus.de; 10 a year; home improvement; publ. by Hubert Burda Media Holding GmbH & Co KG; Editor-in-Chief GABY MIKETTA; circ. 1,890,456 (Oct.–Dec. 2010).

Living At Home: Am Baumwall 11, 20459 Hamburg; tel. (40) 37034267; fax (40) 37035838; e-mail info@livingathome.de; internet www.livingathome.de; f. 2000; monthly; lifestyle magazine covering furnishing, decorating, cooking, entertaining and gardening; publ. by Exclusive & Living digital GmbH; Editor-in-Chief BETTINA BILLERBECK; circ. 160,267 (Jan.–March 2013).

Meine Familie & Ich: Arabellastr. 23, 81925 München; tel. (89) 92500; fax (89) 92502340; e-mail redaktion@daskochrezept.de; internet www.daskochrezept.de; 13 a year; food and drink, health and beauty; publ. by MFI Verlag GmbH; Editor-in-Chief BIRGITT MICHA; circ. 396,290 (Jan.–March 2013).

Neue Post: Burchardstr. 11, 20067 Hamburg; tel. (40) 30194123; fax (40) 30194133; e-mail info@bauerdigital.de; internet neue-post.wunderweib.de; weekly; celebrity gossip, women's interest; publ. by Bauer Verlagsgruppe; Editor-in-Chief KATHRIN KELLERMANN; circ. 687,575 (Jan.–March 2013).

Petra: Jahreszeiten Verlag GmbH, Possmoorweg 2, 22301 Hamburg; tel. (40) 27170; fax (40) 27172056; e-mail redaktion@petra.de; internet www.petra.de; monthly; fashion and beauty; Editor-in-Chief NINA MAURISCHAT; circ. 242,149 (Jan.–March 2013).

Reader's Digest Deutschland: Verlag Das Beste GmbH, Vordernbergstr. 6, 70191 Stuttgart; Postfach 100020, 70049 Stuttgart; tel. (711) 66020; fax (711) 6602547; e-mail verlag@readersdigest.de; internet www.readersdigest.de; f. 1948; owned by Reader's Digest Asscn Inc, Pleasantville, NY (USA); magazines, general, serialized and condensed books, music and video programmes; Man. Dir WERNER NEUNZIG; circ. 583,959 (Jan.–March 2013).

Schöner Wohnen: Am Baumwall 11, 20459 Hamburg; tel. (40) 37030; fax (40) 37035677; e-mail info@schoener-wohnen.de; internet www.schoener-wohnen.de; f. 1960; monthly; homes and gardens; publ. by Gruner + Jahr AG & Co KG; Editor-in-Chief STEPHAN SCHÄFER; circ. 274,745 (Jan.–March 2013).

7 Tage: Postfach 2071, 76490 Baden-Baden; Rotweg 8, 76532 Baden-Baden; tel. (7221) 35010; fax (7221) 3501204; e-mail kontakt@klambt.de; internet www.klambt.de; f. 1843; weekly, Mon.; celebrities, women's interest; Editor-in-Chief PETER VIKTOR KULIG; circ. 105,863 (Sept. 2008).

Law

Der Betrieb: Grafenberger Allee 293 40237, Düsseldorf; Postfach 101102, 40002 Düsseldorf; tel. (211) 8870; fax (211) 8871410; e-mail m.wieczorek@fachverlag.de; internet www.der-betrieb.de; weekly; business administration, revenue law, corporate law, labour and social legislation; Editor MARKO WIECZOREK; circ. 19,453 (Jan.–March 2013).

Deutsche Richterzeitung: Geschäftsstelle des Deutschen Richterbundes, Kronenstr. 73, 10117 Berlin; tel. (30) 20612520; fax (30) 20612525; e-mail redaktion@richterzeitung.de; internet www.driz.de; f. 1909; monthly; publ. by Carl Heymanns Verlag; Chair., Editorial Bd SVEN REBEHN; circ. 11,000 (2010).

Juristenzeitung: Wilhelmstr. 18, 72074 Tübingen; Postfach 2040, 72010 Tübingen; tel. (7071) 9230; fax (7071) 51104; e-mail info@mohr.de; internet www.mohr.de; f. 1951; fortnightly; Editors MATTHIAS JESTAEDT, HERBERT ROTH, ASTRID STADLER, ERIC HILGENDORF; circ. 3,100 (2015).

Juristische Rundschau: Genthiner Str. 13, 10785 Berlin; tel. (30) 30260050; fax (30) 3026005251; e-mail info@degruyter.com; internet www.degruyter.de; f. 1925; monthly; publ. by De Gruyter Rechtswissenschaften Verlags GmbH; Editors-in-Chief Prof. Dr DIRK OLZEN, Dr GERHARD SCHÄFER.

Neue Juristische Wochenschrift: Beethovenstr. 7B, 60325 Frankfurt a.M.; Postfach 110241, 60037 Frankfurt a.M.; tel. (69)

7560910; fax (69) 75609149; e-mail redaktion@njw.de; internet www
.njw.de; f. 1947; weekly, Fri.; Editor-in-Chief TOBIAS FREUDENBERG;
circ. 33,030 (Jan.–March 2013).

**Rabels Zeitschrift für ausländisches und internationales
Privatrecht:** Mittelweg 187, 20148 Hamburg; tel. (40) 41900234;
fax (40) 41900288; e-mail rabelsz@mpipriv.de; internet www
.mpipriv.de; f. 1927; quarterly; German, English and French
contributions, English summaries; Editors JÜRGEN BASEDOW, HOL-
GER FLEISCHER, REINHARD ZIMMERMANN.

Zeitschrift für die gesamte Strafrechtswissenschaft: Lüt-
zowstr. 33, 10785 Berlin; tel. (30) 30260050; fax (30) 3026005251;
e-mail info@degruyter.com; internet www.degruyter.de; f. 1881;
quarterly; publ. by De Gruyter Rechtswissenschaften Verlags
GmbH; Editor-in-Chief Prof. Dr KRISTIAN KÜHL.

Leisure Interests and Sport

AUTO BILD: Axel-Springer-Pl. 1, 20350 Hamburg; tel. (40) 34700;
fax (40) 345660; e-mail redaktion@autobild.de; internet www
.autobild.de; f. 1986; weekly; publ. by Axel Springer Verlag AG;
Editor-in-Chief BURKHARD KNOPKE; circ. 472,496 (Jan.–March 2013).

Auto Motor und Sport: Leuschnerstr. 1, 70174 Stuttgart; tel. (711)
1821267; fax (711) 1822220; e-mail redaktion_ams@motorpresse.de;
internet www.auto-motor-und-sport.de; fortnightly; publ. by Motor
Presse Stuttgart GmbH & Co KG; Editors-in-Chief RALPH ALEX, JENS
KATEMANN; circ. 368,107 (Jan.–March 2013).

Bild + Funk: Münchener Str. 101/09, 85737 Ismaning; tel. (89)
272700; fax (89) 27270749; e-mail redaktion@bildundfunk.de;
internet www.bildundfunk.de; weekly, Fri.; publ. by Gong Verlag
GmbH & Co KG; radio and television; Editor-in-Chief CARSTEN
PFEFFERKORN; circ. 145,125 (Jan.–March 2013).

Computer Bild Spiele: Axel-Springer-Pl. 1, 20350 Hamburg; tel.
(40) 34729136; fax (40) 34726749; e-mail leserbriefe@
computerbildspiele.de; internet www.computerbildspiele.de; f. 1999;
monthly; computer gaming; publ. by Axel Springer Verlag AG;
Editor-in-Chief CHRISTIAN BIGGE; circ. 145,482 (Jan.–March 2013).

FF Magazin: Meyer & Meyer Fachverlag & Buchhandel GmbH,
Von-Coels-Str. 390, 52080 Aachen; tel. (241) 958100; fax (241)
9581010; e-mail verlag@m-m-sports.com; internet www.ff-magazin
.com; f. 2004; 10 a year; women's football; Editor-in-Chief MARTINA
VOSS; circ. 30,000.

Funk Uhr: Axel-Springer-Pl. 1, 20350 Hamburg; tel. (40) 34723824;
fax (40) 34722601; e-mail funkuhrabo@axelspringer.de; f. 1952;
weekly; television listings; publ. by Axel Springer Verlag AG; Editor-
in-Chief CHRISTIAN HELLMANN; circ. 506,316 (Jan.–March 2013).

GameStar: Lyonel-Feininger-Str. 26, 80807 München; tel. (89)
360860; fax (89) 36086118; e-mail brief@gamestar.de; internet
www.gamestar.de; f. 1996; monthly; computer gaming; publ. by IDG
Entertainment Media GmbH; Editor-in-Chief HEIKO KLINGE; circ.
87,072 (Jan.–March 2013).

Garten Flora: Wilhelmsaue 37, 10713 Berlin; tel. (30) 464060;
e-mail info@bauernverlag.de; internet www.gartenflora.de; f. 1985
as *Flora Garten*; name changed to present 2011; monthly; gardening;
publ. by Deutscher Bauernverlag GmbH; Editor-in-Chief CHRISTIAN
GEHLER; circ. 169,465 (Jan.–March 2013).

Gong: Gong Verlag GmbH & Co KG, Münchner Str. 101/09, 85737
Ismaning; Postfach 400748, 401809 München; tel. (89) 272700; fax
(89) 272707490; e-mail redaktion@gong.de; internet www.gong.de;
f. 1948; radio and TV weekly; Editor-in-Chief CARSTEN PFEFFERKORN;
circ. 266,864 (Jan.–March 2013).

Hörzu: Axel-Springer-Pl. 1, Postfach 4110, 20350 Hamburg; tel. (40)
34700; fax (40) 34729629; e-mail leserbriefe@hoerzu.de; internet
www.hoerzu.de; f. 1946; weekly; radio and television; publ. by Axel
Springer Verlag AG; Editor-in-Chief CHRISTIAN HELLMANN; circ.
1,259,142 (Oct. 2010).

Kicker-Sportmagazin: Badstr. 4–6, 90402 Nürnberg; tel. (911)
2160; fax (911) 9922420; e-mail info@kicker.de; internet www.kicker
.de; f. 1920; 2 a week; illustrated sports magazine; publ. by Olympia
Verlag GmbH; Editor-in-Chief JEAN-JULIEN BEER; circ. (Jan.–March
2013) 186,852 (Mon.), 161,206 (Thur.).

Mein schöner Garten: Hubert-Burda-Pl. 1, 77652 Offenburg; tel.
(781) 8401; fax (781) 842254; e-mail garten@burda.com; internet
www.mein-schoener-garten.de; monthly; gardening; publ. by
Hubert Burda Media GmbH & Co KG; Editor-in-Chief ANDREA
KÖGEL; circ. 408,593 (Jan.–March 2013).

Sport Bild: Axel-Springer-Str. 65, 10888 Hamburg; tel. (40) 348830;
fax (40) 34725435; e-mail sportbild@sportbild.de; internet www
.sportbild.de; f. 1988; weekly; publ. by Axel Springer Verlag AG;
Editor-in-Chief MANFRED HART; circ. 402,222 (Jan.–March 2013).

TV Digital: Axel-Springer-Pl. 1, 20350 Hamburg; tel. (40) 34700; fax
(40) 34729629; e-mail leserservice@tvdigital.de; internet www
.tvdigital.de; f. 2004; fortnightly; publ. by Axel Springer Verlag AG;

Editor-in-Chief CHRISTIAN HELLMANN; circ. 1,955,750 (Jan.–March
2013).

TV Hören und Sehen: Burchardstr. 11, 20077 Hamburg; tel. (40)
30190; fax (40) 30191991; e-mail briefe@tv-hoeren-und-sehen.de;
internet www.tvhus.de; f. 1962; weekly; television listings; publ. by
Bauer Verlagsgruppe; Editor-in-Chief UWE BOKELMANN; circ.
730,034 (Jan.–March 2013).

Medicine, Science and Technology

Angewandte Chemie: Boschstr. 12, 69469 Weinheim; Postfach
101161, 69451 Weinheim; tel. (6201) 606315; fax (6201) 606331;
e-mail angewandte@wiley-vch.de; internet www.angewandte.de;
f. 1888; applied chemistry; weekly; also publishes international
edn in English; publ. by Wiley-VCH Verlag GmbH & Co KGaA;
Editor-in-Chief PETER GÖLITZ.

Ärztliche Praxis: Gabrielenstr. 9, 80636 München; tel. (89)
89817404; fax (89) 89817400; e-mail khp@rbi.de; internet www
.aerztlichepraxis.de; weekly; publ. by Reed Business Information
GmbH; Editor-in-Chief ANDREAS BORCHERT; circ. 56,243 (Sept. 2008).

Chemie Ingenieur Technik: Boschstr. 12, 69469 Weinheim; Postfach 101161, 69451 Weinheim; tel. (6201) 606520; fax (6201) 606203;
e-mail cit@wiley.com; internet www.cit-journal.de; f. 1928; monthly;
publ. by Wiley-VCH Verlag GmbH & Co KG; Editor Dr BARBARA
BÖCK.

Der Chirurg: Tiergartenstr. 17, 69121 Heidelberg; tel. (6221) 4870;
fax (6221) 48768210; e-mail christiane.jurek@springer.com; internet
www.derchirurg.de; f. 1928; surgery; monthly; publ. by Springer
Science + Business Media Deutschland GmbH; Editor-in-Chief
HENNING DRALLE.

Computer Bild: Axel-Springer-Pl. 1, 20350 Hamburg; tel. (40)
34723933; fax (40) 34729377; e-mail redaktion@computerbild.de;
internet www.computerbild.de; f. 1996; fortnightly; publ. by Axel
Springer Verlag AG; Editor-in-Chief AXEL TELZEROW; circ. 498,908
(Jan.–March 2013).

Deutsche Apotheker Zeitung: Birkenwaldstr. 44, 70191 Stuttgart; Postfach 101061, 70009 Stuttgart; tel. (711) 25820; fax (711)
2582290; e-mail daz@deutscher-apotheker-verlag.de; internet www
.deutscher-apotheker-verlag.de; f. 1861; weekly, Thur.; Editor-in-
Chief PETER DITZEL; circ. 29,140 (Jan.–March 2013).

Deutsche Medizinische Wochenschrift: Rüdigerstr. 14, 70469
Stuttgart; Postfach 301120, 70469 Stuttgart; tel. (711) 8931232; fax
(711) 8931235; e-mail martin.middeke@thieme.de; internet www
.thieme.de/dmw; f. 1875; weekly; Editor-in-Chief Prof. Dr MARTIN
MIDDEKE; circ. 7,610 (Jan.–March 2013).

Deutsche Zahnärztliche Zeitschrift: Deutscher Ärzte-Verlag,
Dieselstr. 2, 50859 Köln; Postfach 400265, 50832 Köln; tel. (2234)
7011242; fax (2234) 701115; e-mail dey@aerzteverlag.de; internet
www.online-dzz.de; f. 1945; monthly; dental medicine; Editors Prof.
Dr WERNER GEURTSEN, Prof. Dr GUIDO HEYDECKE; circ. 18,000 (Jan.
2013).

Elektro Automation: Ernst-Mey-Str. 8, 70771 Leinfelden-
Echterdingen; tel. (711) 7594417; fax (711) 7594221; e-mail ea
.redaktion@konradin.de; internet www.ea-online.de; f. 1948;
monthly; publ. by Konradin Verlag Robert Kohlhammer GmbH;
Editor-in-Chief MICHAEL CORBAN; circ. 18,034 (Jan.–March 2013).

Erziehung und Wissenschaft: Stamm Verlag GmbH, Goldam-
merweg 16, 45134 Essen; tel. (201) 843000; fax (201) 472590; e-mail
info@stamm.de; internet www.erziehungundwissenschaft.de;
f. 1948; monthly; organ of the Gewerkschaft Erziehung und
Wissenschaft; national edn, plus 5 regional edns; Editor-in-Chief
ULF RÖDDE; circ. 260,719 (Jan.–March 2013).

Geographische Rundschau: Georg-Westermann-Allee 66, 38104
Braunschweig; tel. (531) 708385; fax (531) 708374; e-mail gr@
westermann.de; internet www.geographischerundschau.de; f. 1949;
11 a year; Man. Editor REINER JUENGST; circ. 6,000 (2013).

Handchirurgie, Mikrochirurgie, Plastische Chirurgie: Rüdigerstr. 14, 70469 Stuttgart; Postfach 301120, 70451 Stuttgart; tel.
(711) 89310; fax (711) 8931453; f. 1969; 6 a year; Editors KARL-JOSEF
PROMMERSBERGER, RICCARDO E. GIUNTA; circ. 1,600.

International Journal of Earth Sciences (Geologische
Rundschau): Geologische Vereinigung eV, Vulkanstr. 23, 56743
Mendig; tel. (02652) 989360; fax (02652) 989361; e-mail info@g-v
.de; internet www.g-v.de; f. 1910; 8 a year; English; general,
geological; publ. by Springer Science + Business Media Deutschland
GmbH; Editor-in-Chief Prof. Dr WOLF-CHRISTIAN DULLO.

International Journal of Materials Research (Zeitschrift für
Metallkunde): Max-Planck-Institut für Metallforschung, Heisen-
bergstr. 3, 70569 Stuttgart; tel. (711) 6893651; fax (711) 6893653;
e-mail ijmr@is.mpg.de; internet www.ijmr.de; monthly; publ. by Carl
Hanser Verlag; Editor-in-Chief Prof. Dr ERIC J. MITTEMEIJER.

Journal of Neurological Surgery: Georg Thieme Verlag, Rüdigerstr. 14, 70469 Stuttgart; Postfach 301120, 70469 Stuttgart; tel.

(711) 89310; fax (711) 8931298; e-mail zblneurochir@thieme.de; f. 1936; quarterly; German and English; neurosurgery, spinal surgery, traumatology; Editor Prof. Dr V. ROHDE; circ. 1,650 (2008/09).

Journal of Neurology: Springer Verlag, Tiergartenstr. 17, 69121 Heidelberg; tel. (6221) 4878434; fax (6221) 48768434; e-mail christine.lodge@springer.com; internet www.jon.springer.de; f. 1891; Editors-in-Chief Dr ROGER A. BARKER, Prof. Dr MICHAEL STRUPP, Prof. Dr MASSIMO FILIPPI.

Medizinische Klinik: Neumarkter Str. 43, 81673 München; tel. (89) 43721300; fax (89) 43721399; e-mail verlag@urban-vogel.de; internet www.urban-vogel.de; f. 1904; monthly; official organ of the Deutsche Gesellschaft für Innere Medizin; publ. by Verlag Urban & Vogel GmbH; Editor ANNA-MARIA WORSCH; circ. 20,118 (Oct. 2010).

Nachrichten aus der Chemie: Varrentrappstr. 40–42, 60486 Frankfurt a.M.; Postfach 900440, 60444 Frankfurt a.M.; tel. (69) 79170; fax (69) 7917232; e-mail gdch@gdch.de; internet www.gdch.de; f. 1953; monthly; journal of the German Chemical Society; Editor-in-Chief Dr ERNST GUGGOLZ; circ. 30,051 (Oct. 2010).

National Geographic Deutschland: Am Baumwall 11, 20459 Hamburg; tel. (40) 37035511; fax (40) 37035598; internet www.nationalgeographic.de; f. 1999; monthly; culture, history, nature, the Earth, the universe, people, animals, archaeology, paleontology, travel, research, expeditions; also publishes *NG World* (German and English; monthly; for children aged 7–13 years; circ. 91,021); Editor-in-Chief THOMAS SCHMIDT; circ. 166,844 (Jan.–March 2013).

natur: Konradin Medien GmbH, Bretonischer Ring 13, 85630 Grasbrunn; tel. (89) 45616220; fax (89) 45616300; e-mail redaktion-natur@konradin.de; internet www.natur.de; f. 1904; monthly; popular nature journal; Editor-in-Chief JAN BERNDORFF; circ. 54,276 (Jan.–March 2013).

Naturwissenschaftliche Rundschau: Birkenwaldstr. 44, 70191 Stuttgart; Postfach 101061, 70009 Stuttgart; tel. (711) 2582295; fax (711) 2582283; e-mail nr@wissenschaftliche-verlagsgesellschaft.de; internet www.naturwissenschaftliche-rundschau.de; f. 1948; publ. by Gesellschaft Deutscher Naturforscher und Ärzte; monthly; scientific; Editor Dr KLAUS REHFELD; circ. 2,500.

Planta Medica: Georg Thieme Verlag, Rüdigerstr. 14, 70469 Stuttgart; Postfach 301120, 70451 Stuttgart; tel. (711) 89310; fax (711) 8931298; e-mail plantamedica@thieme.de; internet www.thieme.de/fz/plantamedica; f. 1953; 18 a year; official organ of the Society of Medicinal Plant Research; Editor-in-Chief Prof. Dr LUC PIETERS.

P.M.: Weihenstephaner Str. 7, 81673 München; tel. (89) 415200; fax (89) 4152565; e-mail kontakt@pm-magazin.de; internet www.pm-magazin.de; f. 1978; monthly; technology, natural sciences, medicine, psychology, nature and the environment, history, philosophy, anthropology, culture, multimedia, the internet; publ. by Gruner + Jahr AG & Co KG; Editor-in-Chief HANS-HERMANN SPRADO; circ. 229,737 (Jan.–March 2013).

rfe-Electrohandler: Am Friedrichshain 22, 10407 Berlin; tel. (30) 421510; fax (30) 42151251; e-mail rfe.redaktion@hussberlin.de; internet www.rfe-eh.de; f. 1952; monthly; technology and marketing of consumer goods, electronics, digital imaging, multimedia, audio, video, broadcasting, TV; Man. Editor HORST WINKLER; circ. 15,310 (Jan.–March 2013).

Zeitschrift für Allgemeinmedizin: Dieselstr. 2, 50859 Köln; Postfach 400265, 50832 Köln; tel. (2234) 70110; fax (2234) 7011255; e-mail bluhme-rasmussen@aerzteverlag.de; internet www.online-zfa.de; f. 1924; monthly; general and family medicine; publ. by Deutscher Ärzte-Verlag; Editors Prof. Dr HEINZ-HARALD ABHOLZ, Prof. Dr MICHAEL M. KOCHEN, Dr SUSANNE RABADY, Prof. Dr WILHELM NIEBLING, Prof. Dr ANDREAS SÖNNICHSEN.

Zeitschrift für Zahnärztliche Implantologie: Deutscher Ärzte-Verlag, Dieselstr. 2, 50859 Köln; Postfach 400265, 50832 Köln; tel. (2234) 7011241; fax (2234) 70116241; e-mail schubert@aerzteverlag.de; internet www.online-zzi.de; f. 1984; quarterly; dental medicine, implantology; Editors Prof. Dr STEFAN SCHULTZE-MOSGAU, Dr PETER GEHRKE, Dr KARL-LUDWIG ACKERMANN, Prof. Dr MARTIN LORENZONI, Prof. Dr GERMÁN GÓMEZ-ROMÁN; circ. 9,400 (Dec. 2014).

Politics, History and Current Affairs

akzente: Dag-Hammarskjöld-Weg 1–5, 65760 Eschborn; tel. (6196) 790; fax (6196) 791115; e-mail akzente@giz.de; internet www.giz.de; quarterly; politics, essays, photo-journalism, int. and devt co-operation; publ. by the Deutsche Gesellschaft für Internationale Zusammenarbeit (GIZ) GmbH; Editor MIRIAM DROLLER.

Deutschland: Frankfurter Societäts-Medien GmbH, Frankenallee 71–81, 60327 Frankfurt a.M.; tel. (69) 75014352; fax (69) 75014361; e-mail deutschland@fs-medien.de; internet www.deutschland.de; 2 a month; edns in German, Arabic, Chinese, English, French, Hungarian, Japanese, Portuguese, Russian, Spanish, Turkish; Editor-in-Chief PETER HINTEREDER; circ. 378,123 (Sept. 2008).

Eulenspiegel: Gubener Str. 47, 10243 Berlin; tel. (30) 2934630; fax (30) 29346321; e-mail verlag@eulenspiegel-zeitschrift.de; internet www.eulenspiegel-zeitschrift.de; f. 1946; political, satirical and humorous monthly; Editor-in-Chief Dr MATHIAS WEDEL; circ. 100,000.

FOCUS: Arabellastr. 23, 81925 München; tel. (89) 92500; fax (89) 92502026; e-mail anzeigen@focus.de; internet www.focus.de; f. 1993; weekly; political, general; publ. by FOCUS Magazin Verlag GmbH; Editor-in-Chief JÖRG QUOOS; circ. 539,281 (Jan.–March 2013).

Gesellschaft-Wirtschaft-Politik (GWP): Sürderstr. 22A, 51375 Leverkusen; tel. (214) 4039097; fax (214) 5006147; e-mail redaktion@gwp-pb.de; internet www.budrich-journals.de; f. 1951; quarterly; economics, politics, sociology, education; publ. by Verlag Barbara Budrich; Editors Prof. Dr SIBYLLE REINHARDT, Prof. Dr BERNHARD SCHÄFERS, Prof. Dr ROLAND STURM, EDMUND BUDRICH.

Internationale Politik: Rauchstr. 17–18, 10787 Berlin; tel. (30) 25423145; fax (30) 25423167; e-mail tempel@dgap.org; internet www.internationalepolitik.de; f. 1945; 6 a year; journal of the German Council on Foreign Relations; edns in English (*IP International Edition*, quarterly) and Russian (bimonthly); Editor-in-Chief Dr SYLKE TEMPEL; circ. 5,500.

Merkur (Deutsche Zeitschrift für europäisches Denken): Mommsenstr. 27, 10629 Berlin; tel. (30) 32709414; fax (30) 32709415; e-mail merkur.zeitschrift@snafu.de; internet www.online-merkur.de; f. 1947; monthly, 12 a year; double issue in Oct./Nov; literary, political, aesthetic; Editor CHRISTIAN DEMAND; Man. Editor EKKEHARD KNÖRER; circ. 4,800.

Neue Gesellschaft/Frankfurter Hefte: c/o Friedrich-Ebert-Stiftung Berlin, Hiroshimastr. 17, 10785 Berlin; tel. (30) 269357151; fax (30) 269359238; e-mail ng-fh@fes.de; internet www.ng-fh.de; f. 1946; monthly; cultural, political; Editor-in-Chief THOMAS MEYER; circ. 6,000.

Der Spiegel: Ericusspitze 1, 20457 Hamburg; tel. (40) 30072687; fax (40) 30072247; e-mail spiegel@spiegel.de; internet www.spiegel.de; f. 1947; weekly; political, general; Editor-in-Chief KLAUS BRINKBÄUMER; circ. 894,270 (Jan.–March 2013).

Stern: Am Baumwall 11, 20459 Hamburg; tel. (40) 37030; e-mail info@stern.de; internet www.stern.de; f. 1948; weekly; news, history, lifestyle; publ. by Gruner + Jahr AG & Co KG; also publishes *Stern Fotographie* (quarterly; circ. 10,000) and *Stern Gesund Leben* (6 a year; circ. 94,297); Editor-in-Chief FRANK THOMSEN; circ. 837,619 (Jan.–March 2013).

Universitas: Happelstr. 12, 69120 Heidelberg; tel. (6221) 6739800; e-mail universitas@heidelberger-lese-zeiten-verlag.de; internet www.heidelberger-lese-zeiten-verlag.de; f. 1946; monthly; scientific, literary and philosophical; Editor DIRK KATZSCHMANN; circ. 1,500.

VdK-Zeitung: Linienstr. 131, 10115 Berlin; tel. (30) 9210580-0; fax (30) 9210580-999; e-mail kontakt@vdk.de; internet www.vdk.de; f. 1950; monthly; publ. by Sozialverband VdK Deutschland eV; also maintains office in Munich; Editors JENS KAFFENBERGER, MICHAEL PAUSDER; circ. 1,556,333 (June 2014).

vorwärts: Stresemannstr. 30, 10963 Berlin; Postfach 610322, 10925 Berlin; tel. (30) 25594100; fax (30) 25594192; e-mail verlag@vorwaerts.de; internet www.vorwaerts.de; f. 1994; affiliated to the Social Democratic Party (SPD); publ. by Berliner vorwärts Verlagsgesellschaft mbH; Editor-in-Chief KARIN NINK; circ. 405,937 (Jan.–March 2013).

Religion and Philosophy

chrismon plus rheinland: Kaiserswerther Str. 450, 40474 Düsseldorf; Postfach 302255, 40402 Düsseldorf; tel. (211) 43690150; fax (211) 43690100; e-mail redaktion@chrismon-rheinland.de; internet www.chrismon-rheinland.de; f. 2004; monthly; Protestant; Editor-in-Chief VOLKER GÖTTSCHE; circ. 16,596 (Oct. 2010).

Christ in der Gegenwart: Hermann-Herder-Str. 4, 79104 Freiburg i. Br.; tel. (761) 2717276; fax (761) 2717243; e-mail cig@herder.de; internet www.christ-in-der-gegenwart.de; f. 1948; weekly; Editor-in-Chief JOHANNES RÖSER; circ. 32,669 (Jan.–March 2013).

Christlicher Digest: Hauptstr. 108, 77652 Offenburg; tel. (781) 28948707; fax (781) 28948709; e-mail info@christlicherdigest.de; internet www.christlicherdigest.de; f. 2002 by merger of *Evangelischer Digest* (f. 1958), *Katholischer Digest* (f. 1949) and *Der Sonntagsbrief* (f. 1974); monthly, 10 a year; publ. by Verlag Christlicher Digest GmbH & Co KG; Editor FRED HEINE; circ. 40,000.

Der Dom: Karl-Schurz-Str. 26, 33100 Paderborn; tel. (5251) 153241; fax (5251) 153133; e-mail redaktion@derdom.de; internet www.derdom.org; f. 1946; weekly, Sun.; Catholic; publ. by Bonifatius GmbH, Druck-Buch-Verlag; Editor-in-Chief MATTHIAS NÜCKEL; circ. 33,500 (Dec. 2012).

Katholische Sonntagszeitung für Deutschland: Postfach 111920, 86044 Augsburg; Hafnerberg 2, 86152 Augsburg; tel. (821) 502420; fax (821) 5024241; e-mail redaktion@suv.de; internet www

.katholische-sonntagszeitung.de; f. 1885; weekly; Publr Dr JOHANNES MÜLLER; circ. 57,719 (Jan.–March 2013).

Katholisches Sonntagsblatt: Senefelderstr. 12, 73760 Ostfildern; Postfach 4280, 73745 Ostfildern; tel. (711) 4406121; fax (711) 4406170; e-mail redaktion@kathsonntagsblatt.de; internet www .kathsonntagsblatt.de; f. 1848; weekly; publ. by Schwabenverlag AG; Editor-in-Chief REINER SCHLOTTHAUER; circ. 43,942 (Jan.–March 2013).

Kirche+Leben: Cheruskerring 19, 48147 Münster; tel. (2361) 5828833; fax (2361) 5828856; e-mail info@bmv-verlag.de; internet www.kirche-und-leben.de; f. 1945; weekly; Catholic; Editor-in-Chief Dr HANS-JOSEF JOEST; circ. 81,349 (Jan.–March 2013).

Kirchenzeitung für das Erzbistum Köln: Ursulapl. 1, 50668 Köln; Postfach 102041, 50460 Köln; tel. (221) 1619131; fax (221) 1619216; e-mail redaktion@kirchenzeitung-koeln.de; internet www .kirchenzeitung-koeln.de; weekly; Editor-in-Chief ROBERT BOECKER; circ. 32,449 (Jan.–March 2013).

Philosophisches Jahrbuch: Philosophie Department Lehrstuhl III, Geschwister-Scholl-Pl. 1, 80539 München; e-mail redaktion.phj@ lrz.uni-muenchen.de; f. 1893; 2 a year; publ. by Verlag Karl Alber GmbH; Editor MARCELA GARCÍA.

PRESS ORGANIZATION

Deutscher Presserat (German Press Council): Fritschestr. 27/28, 10585 Berlin; Postfach 100549, 10565 Berlin; tel. (30) 3670070; fax (30) 36700720; e-mail info@presserat.de; internet www.presserat.de; f. 1956; self-regulatory body, composed of publishers and journalists; formulates guidelines and investigates complaints against the press; Dir LUTZ TILLMANNS.

NEWS AGENCIES

dpa (Deutsche Presse-Agentur GmbH): Mittelweg 38, 20148 Hamburg; Postfach 130282, 20102 Hamburg; tel. (40) 41130; fax (40) 411332305; e-mail info@dpa.com; internet www.dpa.de; f. 1949; supplies all the daily newspapers, broadcasting stations and more than 1,000 further subscribers throughout Germany with its international, national and regional text, photo, audio, graphics and online services; English, Spanish, Arabic and German language news is also transmitted via direct satellite and the internet to press agencies, newspapers, radio and television stations, online services and non-media clients in more than 100 countries; 1,200 employees worldwide; Dir-Gen. MICHAEL SEGBERS; Editor-in-Chief WOLFGANG BÜCHNER.

PRESS AND JOURNALISTS' ASSOCIATIONS

Bundesverband Deutscher Zeitungsverleger eV (German Newspaper Publishers' Association): Markgrafenstr. 15, 10969 Berlin; tel. (30) 7262980; fax (30) 726298299; e-mail bdzv@bdzv.de; internet www.bdzv.de; f. 1954; 11 affiliated Land asscns; Pres. HELMUT HEINEN; Dir-Gen. WOLFF DIETMAR.

Deutscher Journalisten-Verband (German Journalists' Association): Charlottenstr. 17, 10117 Berlin; tel. (30) 72627920; fax (30) 726279213; e-mail djv@djv.de; internet www.djv.de; f. 1949; 17 Land asscns; Chair. MICHAEL KONKEN; Man. Dir KAJO DÖHRING.

Verband Deutscher Zeitschriftenverleger eV (VDZ) (Association of German Magazine Publishers): Haus der Presse, Markgrafenstr. 15, 10969 Berlin; tel. (30) 7262980; fax (30) 7262898103; e-mail info@vdz.de; internet www.vdz.de; f. 1929; 5 affiliated Land asscns; Pres. Dr HUBERT BURDA; CEO STEPHAN SCHERZER.

Verein der Ausländischen Presse in Deutschland eV (VAP) (Foreign Press Association): Pressehaus 1306, Schiffbauerdamm 40, 10117 Berlin; tel. (30) 22489547; fax (30) 22489549; e-mail info@ vap-deutschland.org; internet www.vap-deutschland.org; f. 1906; c. 400 mems; Chair. PASCAL THIBAUT.

Publishers

The following is a selection of the most prominent German publishing firms:

ADAC Verlag GmbH & Co KG: Hansastr. 19, 80686 München; tel. (89) 76760; fax (89) 6762925; e-mail verlag@adac.de; internet www .adac.de; f. 1958; guidebooks, legal brochures, maps, magazines; Pres. Dr PETER MEYER.

Apollo Medien GmbH: Emil-Hoffmann-Str. 1, 50996 Köln; tel. (2236) 3999200; fax (2236) 3999229; e-mail apollo@apollo-medien.de; internet www.apollo-medien.de; f. 1981 as SYBEX Verlags- und Vertriebs-GmbH; name changed to present in 2011; computer books and software; Man. Dirs HOLGER SCHNEIDER, ANJA SCHRIEVER.

Aufbau Verlag GmbH & Co KG: Prinzenstr. 85, 10969 Berlin; tel. (30) 283940; fax (30) 28394100; e-mail info@aufbau-verlag.de;

internet aufbau-verlag.de; f. 1945; fiction, non-fiction, classical literature; Dirs RENÉ STRIEN, TOM ERBEN, MATTHIAS KOCH.

J. P. Bachem Verlag GmbH: Ursulapl. 1, 50668 Köln; tel. (221) 1619900; fax (221) 1619909; e-mail verlag@bachem.de; internet www .bachem-verlag.de; f. 1818; history, dialect, art history, architecture, sociology and walking/cycling tours of the Cologne, Ruhr and Rhine area; church and society; Dir CLAUS BACHEM.

Bauverlag BV GmbH: Avenwedderstr. 55, 33311 Gütersloh; tel. (1805) 5522533; fax (1805) 5522535; e-mail leserservice@bauverlag .de; internet www.bauverlag.de; f. 2002 following the merger of Fachzeitschriften GmbH (Gütersloh) and Bauverlag GmbH (Walluf); civil engineering, architecture, environment, energy, etc.; Dir KARL-HEINZ MÜLLER.

Verlag C. H. Beck oHg: Wilhelmstr. 9, 80801 München; Postfach 400340, 80703 München; tel. (89) 381890; fax (89) 38189398; e-mail info@beck.de; internet www.beck.de; f. 1763; law, science, theology, archaeology, philosophy, philology, history, politics, art, literature; Dirs Dr HANS DIETER BECK, Dr WOLFGANG BECK.

Bibliographisches Institut GmbH: Mecklenburgische Str. 53, 14197 Berlin; tel. (30) 897858230; fax (30) 89785978233; internet www.bi-media.de; f. 1805; encyclopaedias, dictionaries, atlases, textbooks, calendars; Chair. MARION WINKENBACH; Dirs TIMO BLÜMER, KLAUS KÄMPFE-BURGHARDT.

BLV Buchverlag GmbH & Co KG: Lothstr. 19, 80797 München; tel. (89) 1202120; fax (89) 120212120; e-mail blv.verlag@blv.de; internet www.blv.de; f. 1946; gardening, nature, sports, fitness, hunting, fishing, food and drink, health; Man. Dir ANTJE WOLF.

Breitkopf & Härtel KG: Walkmühlstr. 52, 65195 Wiesbaden; tel. (611) 450080; fax (611) 450085961; e-mail info@breitkopf.com; internet www.breitkopf.com; f. 1719; music and music books; Dir LIESELOTTE SIEVERS.

Bruckmann Verlag GmbH: Infanteriestr. 11A, 80797 München; tel. (89) 1306990; fax (89) 130699100; e-mail info@bruckmann.de; internet www.bruckmann.de; f. 1858; travel guides, illustrated travel books, video cassettes; Publishing Dir SABINE SCHULZ.

Bund-Verlag GmbH: Heddernheimer Landstr. 144, 60439 Frankfurt a.M.; Postfach, 60424 Frankfurt a.M.; tel. (69) 7950100; fax (69) 79501011; e-mail kontakt@bund-verlag.de; internet www .bund-verlag.de; f. 1947; labour and social law; Man. Dir RAINER JÖDE.

Verlag Georg D. W. Callwey GmbH & Co: Streitfeldstr. 35, 81673 München; tel. (89) 4360050; fax (89) 436005113; e-mail info@callwey .de; internet www.callwey.de; f. 1884; architecture, gardens, crafts; Man. Dirs Dr MARCELLA PRIOR-CALLWEY, DOMINIK BAUR-CALLWEY.

Carlsen Verlag GmbH: Völckersstr. 14–20, 22765 Hamburg; Postfach 500380, 22703 Hamburg; tel. (40) 398040; fax (40) 39804390; e-mail info@carlsen.de; internet www.carlsen.de; f. 1953; children's and comic books; Dirs RENATE HERRE, JOACHIM KAUFMANN.

Delius Klasing Verlag: Siekerwall 21, 33602 Bielefeld; tel. (521) 5590; fax (521) 55988114; e-mail info@delius-klasing.de; internet www.delius-klasing.de; f. 1911; yachting, motor boats, surfing, mountain biking, race biking, football, motor cars; Dir KONRAD DELIUS.

Deutsche Verlags-Anstalt (DVA): Neumarkter Str. 28, 81673 München; tel. (89) 41360; fax (89) 41363721; e-mail markus .desaga@dva.de; internet www.randomhouse.de/dva; f. 1831; general; owned by Random House Group Ltd (UK).

Deutscher Taschenbuch Verlag GmbH & Co KG (DTV): Friedrichstr. 1A, 80801 München; Postfach 750219, 80704 München; tel. (89) 381670; fax (89) 346428; e-mail verlag@dtv.de; internet www.dtv .de; f. 1961; general fiction, history, music, reference, children, natural and social sciences, medicine, textbooks; Man. Dirs WOLFGANG BALK, BERND BLÜM.

Egmont vgs Verlagsgesellschaft mbH: Gertrudenstr. 30–36, 50667 Köln; Postfach 101251, 50452 Köln; tel. (221) 208110; fax (221) 2081166; e-mail info@vgs.de; internet www.vgs.de; f. 1970; fiction, hobbies, natural sciences, culture, popular culture, cinema, television, history; Man. Dir KLAUS-THORSTEN FIRNIG.

Bildungsverlag EINS GmbH: Hansestr. 115, 51149 Köln; tel. (220) 38982101; fax (220) 38982190; e-mail sco@bildungsverlag1 .de; internet www.bildungsverlag1.de; f. 2001 by merger of Gehlen, Kieser, Stam Verlag, Wolf, Dürr+Kessler and Konkordia; educational; Dir WILMAR DIEPGROND.

Elsevier GmbH: Hackerbrücke 6, 80335 München; Postfach 201930, 80019 München; tel. (89) 55830; fax (89) 5383939; e-mail info@elsevier.de; internet www.elsevier.de; f. 1878; biological science, medical science; Dirs OLAF LODBROK, MARTIN BECK.

S. Fischer Verlag GmbH: Postfach 700355, 60553 Frankfurt a.M.; Hedderichstr. 114, 60596 Frankfurt a.M.; tel. (69) 60620; fax (69) 6062214; e-mail kontakt@fischerverlage.de; internet www

.fischerverlage.de; f. 1886; general, paperbacks; Pres. Dr JÖRG BONG; Man. Dirs MICHAEL JUSTUS, Dr UWE ROSENFELD.

Franz Cornelsen Bildungsgruppe: Mecklenburgische Str. 53, 14197 Berlin; tel. (30) 897850; fax (30) 89786299; e-mail mail@franz-cornelsen-bildungsholding.de; internet www.franz-cornelsen-bildungsholding.de; f. 1946 as Cornelsen Verlag GmbH & Co; name changed to present in 2010; school textbooks, educational software; Chair. Dr ALEXANDER BOB; Man. Dirs Dr HANS-ULRICH DANIEL, URBAN MEISTER.

Franzis Verlag GmbH: Richard-Reitzner-Allee 2, 85540 München; tel. (89) 255561000; fax (89) 255561679; e-mail info@franzis.de; internet www.franzis.de; f. 1924; Gen. Mans THOMAS KÄSBOHRER, WERNER MÜTZEL, WOLFGANG MATERNA.

GRÄFE UND UNZER Verlag GmbH: Grillparzerstr. 12, 81675 München; tel. (89) 419810; fax (89) 41981113; e-mail sarah.kirchner@graefe-und.unzer.de; internet www.graefe-und-unzer.de; f. 1990; cookery and wine, fitness, health and well-being, self-help, gardening, nature, pets; Dirs Dr CHRISTIAN KOPP, DOROTHEE SEELIGER, Dr TILL WAHNBAECK.

Walter de Gruyter GmbH: Genthiner Str. 13, 10785 Berlin; Postfach 303421, 10728 Berlin; tel. (30) 260050; fax (30) 26005251; e-mail info@degruyter.com; internet www.degruyter.com; f. 1919; humanities and theology, literary studies, linguistics, law, natural sciences, medicine, mathematics; imprints: Birkhäuser, Versita, De Gruyter Akademie, De Gruyter Mouton, De Gruyter Oldenbourg and De Gruyter Saur; Pres. ANKE BECK.

De Gruyter Saur: Rosenheimer Str. 143, 81671 München; Postfach 401649, 80716 München; tel. (89) 769020; fax (89) 76902150; e-mail info@degruyter.com; internet www.saur.de; f. 1949; library science, reference, dictionaries, encyclopaedias, books, journals, microfiches, CD-ROMs, DVDs, online databases; brs in Leipzig, Osnabrück and Zürich (Switzerland); an imprint of Walter de Gruyter GmbH & Co KG.

Carl Hanser Verlag GmbH & Co KG: Kolbergerstr. 22, 81679 München; Postfach 860420, 81631 München; tel. (89) 998300; fax (89) 984809; e-mail info@hanser.de; internet www.hanser.de; f. 1928; modern literature, plastics, technology, chemistry, science, economics, computers, children's books; Man. Dirs WOLFGANG BEISLER, STEPHAN D. JOSS, JO LENDLE.

Harenberg Kommunikation Verlags- und Mediengesellschaft mbH & Co KG: Postfach 101852, 44018 Dortmund; Königswall 21, 44137 Dortmund; tel. (231) 90560; fax (231) 9056110; e-mail post@harenberg.de; internet www.harenberg.de; f. 1973; almanacs, encyclopaedias, calendars, periodicals; Man. Dir CHRISTOPH HELLERUNG.

Haufe-Lexware GmbH & Co KG: Munzinger Str. 9, 79111 Freiburg i. Br.; tel. (761) 8980; fax (761) 8983990; e-mail info@haufe-lexware.com; internet haufe-lexware.com; f. 1934; business, law, taxation, information management, finance, social science; Man. Dirs MARTIN LAQUA, MARKUS REITHWIESNER.

Verlag Herder GmbH: Hermann-Herder-Str. 4, 79104 Freiburg i. Br.; tel. (761) 27170; fax (761) 2717520; e-mail info@herder.de; internet www.herder.de; f. 1801; Catholic literature; Publr MANUEL GREGOR HERDER.

Heyne Verlag: Neumarkter Str. 28, 81673 München; tel. (89) 41360; fax (89) 41363721; e-mail vertrieb.verlagsgruppe@randomhouse.de; internet www.heyne.de; f. 1934; fiction, biography, history, cinema, etc.; Publr ULRICH GENZLER.

Hoffmann und Campe Verlag: Harvestehuder Weg 42, 20149 Hamburg; tel. (40) 441880; fax (40) 44188202; e-mail email@hoca.de; internet www.hoffmann-und-campe.de; f. 1781; biography, fiction, history, economics, science; Man. Dir MARKUS KLOSE.

Hüthig GmbH: Im Weiher 10, 69121 Heidelberg; Postfach 102869, 69018 Heidelberg; tel. (6221) 4890; fax (6221) 489481; e-mail fachmedien@huethig.de; internet www.huethig.de; f. 1925; chemistry, chemical engineering, metallurgy, dentistry, etc.; Dir FABIAN MÜLLER.

Langenscheidt GmbH & Co KG: Mies-van-der-Rohe-Str. 1, 80807 München; tel. (89) 360960; fax (89) 36096222; e-mail presse@langenscheidt.de; internet www.langenscheidt.de; f. 1972; dictionaries, language courses, reference; Man. Dir CARSTEN KURREIK.

S. Karger GmbH: Wilhelmstr. 20A, 79098 Freiburg i. Br.; tel. (761) 452070; fax (761) 4520714; e-mail information@karger.de; internet www.karger.de; f. 1890; medicine, psychology, natural sciences; Dirs THOMAS KARGER, GABRIELLA KARGER TRAVELLA, SIBYLLE GROSS.

Verlag Kiepenheuer & Witsch GmbH & Co KG: Bahnhofsvorpl. 1, 50667 Köln; tel. (221) 376850; fax (221) 3768511; e-mail redaktion@kiwi-verlag.de; internet www.kiwi-verlag.de; f. 1947; general fiction, biography, history, sociology, politics; Man. Dir HELGE MALCHOW.

Ernst Klett Verlag GmbH: Rotebühlstr. 77, 70178 Stuttgart; Postfach 106016, 70049 Stuttgart; tel. (711) 66721333; fax (711) 6672000; e-mail pr@klett.de; internet www.klett.de; f. 1897; primary

school and secondary school textbooks, atlases, teaching aids; Publr MICHAEL KLETT.

Verlag W. Kohlhammer GmbH: Hessbrühlstr. 69, 70565 Stuttgart; tel. (711) 78630; fax (711) 78638430; e-mail kohlhammer@kohlhammer.de; internet www.kohlhammer.de; f. 1866; periodicals, general textbooks; Man. Dirs Dr JÜRGEN GUTBROD, LEOPOLD FREIHERR VON UND ZU WEILER.

Kösel-Verlag: Flüggenstr. 2, 80639 München; tel. (89) 178010; fax (89) 17801111; e-mail info@koesel.de; internet www.koesel.de; f. 1593; philosophy, religion, psychology, spirituality, family and education; Head of Publishing MARTIN SCHERER.

Kreuz Verlag GmbH: Hermann-Herder-Str. 4, 79104 Freiburg i. Br.; tel. (761) 2717440; fax (761) 2717360; e-mail service@verlagkreuz.de; internet www.kreuzverlag.de; f. 1983; theology, psychology, pedagogics; Dirs OLAF CARSTENS, MANUEL HERDER, HANS DIETER VOGT.

Verlag für Kunst und Kunsttherapie GmbH: Neckarstr. 13, 72622 Nürtingen; tel. (70) 2256343; fax (70) 2253286; e-mail info@verlag-kunst-kunsttherapie.de; internet www.verlag-kunst-kunsttherapie.de; f. 1952; art books and reproductions; Man. Dir Prof. JÜRGEN THIES.

Peter Lang GmbH—Internationaler Verlag der Wissenschaften: Eschborner Landstr. 42–50, 60489 Frankfurt a.M.; Postfach 940225, 60460 Frankfurt a.M.; tel. (69) 7807050; fax (69) 78070550; e-mail zentrale.frankfurt@peterlang.com; internet www.peterlang.de; f. 1971; theology, philosophy, pedagogics, linguistics, English, German, Romance language and literature, history, political science, law, economics, business administration; Dir Dr JÖRG MEIDENBAUER.

Langenscheidt GmbH & Co KG: Mies-van-der-Rohe-Str. 1, 80807 München; tel. (89) 360960; fax (89) 36096222; e-mail presse@langenscheidt.de; internet www.langenscheidt.de; f. 1972; dictionaries, language courses, reference. Man. Dir CARSTEN KURREIK.

Bastei Lübbe GmbH & Co KG: Schanzenstr. 6–20, 51063 Köln; tel. (221) 82000; internet www.luebbe.de; f. 1964; general fiction and non-fiction, biography, history, etc.; Publr STEFAN LÜBBE; Man. Dir THOMAS SCHIERACK.

Luchterhand-Fachverlag: Luxemburger Str. 449, 50939 Köln; tel. (2631) 8012000; fax (2631) 8012204; internet www.luchterhand-fachverlag.de; f. 1924; insurance, law, taxation, labour; imprint of Wolters Kluwer Deutschland GmbH; Man. Dir Dr ULRICH HERMANN.

Mairdumont GmbH & Co KG: Marco-Polo-Str. 1, 73760 Ostfildern; tel. (711) 45020; fax (711) 4502310; internet www.mairdumont.com; f. 1848; road maps, atlases, tourist guides; Man. Dirs Dr STEPHANIE MAIR-HUYDTS, Dr FRANK MAIR, Dr THOMAS BRINKMANN, UWE ZACHMANN.

J. B. Metzler Verlag: Werastr. 21–23, 70182 Stuttgart; Postfach 103241, 70028 Stuttgart; tel. (711) 21940; fax (711) 2194119; e-mail info@metzlerverlag.de; internet www.metzlerverlag.de; f. 1682; literature, music, linguistics, history, cultural studies, philosophy, textbooks; Dir JÖRN LAAKMANN.

Verlag Moderne Industrie AG & Co KG: Justus-von-Liebig-Str. 1, 86899 Landsberg; tel. (8191) 1250; fax (8191) 125211; e-mail info@mi-verlag.de; internet www.mi-verlag.de; f. 1952; management, investment, technical; Man. Dir FABIAN MÜLLER.

Verlagsgesellschaft Rudolf Müller GmbH & Co KG: Stolberger Str. 84, 50933 Köln; Postfach 410949, 50869 Köln; tel. (221) 54970; fax (221) 5497326; e-mail info@rudolf-mueller.de; internet www.rudolf-mueller.de; f. 1840; architecture, construction, engineering, education; Publrs Dr CHRISTOPH MÜLLER, RUDOLF M. BLESER.

MVS Medizinverlage Stuttgart GmbH & Co KG: Rüdigerstr. 14, 70469 Stuttgart; Postfach 301120, 70451 Stuttgart; tel. (711) 89310; fax (711) 8931298; e-mail kundenservice@thieme.de; internet www.thieme.de/thieme-gruppe/mvs-medizinverlage-stuttgart-17193.htm; imprints are Hippokrates, Sonntag, Enke, TRIAS, Haug Sachbuch; CEO Dr THOMAS SCHERB.

Verlag Friedrich Oetinger GmbH: Poppenbütteler Chaussee 53, 22397 Hamburg; Postfach 658220, 22374 Hamburg; tel. (40) 60790902; fax (40) 6072326; e-mail oetinger@verlagsgrupper-oetinger.de; internet www.oetinger.de; f. 1946; juvenile, illustrated books; Man. Dirs SILKE WEITENDORF, TILL WEITENDORF.

Pabel-Moewig Verlag KG: Karlsruher Str. 31, 76437 Rastatt; tel. (7222) 130; fax (7222) 13218; e-mail info@vpm.de; internet www.vpm.de; f. 1989; magazines; Gen. Man. WALTER A. FUCHS.

Piper Verlag GmbH: Georgenstr. 4, 80799 München; tel. (89) 3818010; fax (89) 338704; e-mail info@piper.de; internet www.piper.de; f. 1904; literature, philosophy, theology, psychology, natural sciences, political and social sciences, history, biographies, music; Dirs MARCEL HARTGES, HANS-JOACHIM HARTMANN.

Verlagsgruppe Random House GmbH: Neumarkter Str. 28, 81673 München; tel. (89) 41360; fax (89) 41363721; e-mail vertrieb

.verlagsgruppe@randomhouse.de; internet www.randomhouse.de; f. 1994; part of Penguin Random House (est. 2013); general, reference; Man. Dirs Dr FRANK SAMBETH, KLAUS ECK, CLAUDIA REITTER.

Ravensburger Buchverlag Otto Maier GmbH: Robert-Bosch-Str. 1, 88214 Ravensburg; tel. (751) 860; fax (751) 861311; e-mail buchverlag@ravensburger.de; internet www.ravensburger.de; f. 1883; subsidiary of Ravensburger AG; Man. Dir KARSTEN SCHMIDT.

Philipp Reclam jun. Verlag GmbH: Siemensstr. 32, 71254 Ditzingen bei Stuttgart; tel. (7156) 1630; fax (7156) 163197; e-mail info@reclam.de; internet www.reclam.de; f. 1828; literature, literary criticism, fiction, history of culture and literature, philosophy and religion, biography, fine arts, music; Dirs FRANK R. MAX, FRANZ SCHÄFER.

Rowohlt Verlag GmbH: Hamburger Str. 17, 21465 Reinbek bei Hamburg; tel. (40) 72720; fax (40) 7272319; e-mail info@rowohlt.de; internet www.rowohlt.de; f. 1908/1953; politics, science, fiction, translations of international literature; Dirs PETER KRAUS VOM CLEFF, ALEXANDER FEST.

Schattauer GmbH: Hoelderlinstr. 3, 70174 Stuttgart; tel. (711) 229870; fax (711) 2298750; e-mail info@schattauer.de; internet www.schattauer.de; f. 1949; medicine and related sciences; Man. Dirs DIETER BERGEMANN, Dr WULF BERTRAM, JAN HAAF.

Verlag Dr Otto Schmidt KG: Postfach 511026, 50946 Köln; Gustav-Heinemann-Ufer 58, 50968 Köln; tel. (221) 9373801; fax (221) 93738900; e-mail info@otto-schmidt.de; internet www.otto-schmidt.de; f. 1905; university textbooks, jurisprudence, tax law; Man. Dir Dr FELIX HEY.

Egmont Franz Schneider Verlag GmbH: Gertrudenstr. 30–36, 50667 Köln; Postfach 101251, 50452 Köln; tel. (221) 208110; fax (221) 2081166; e-mail info@schneiderbuch.de; internet www.schneiderbuch.de; f. 1913; children's books; Man. Dir KLAUS THORSTEN FIRNIG.

Springer Science+Business Media Deutschland GmbH: Heidelberger Pl. 3, 14197 Berlin; tel. (30) 827870; fax (30) 8214091; internet www.springer.com; f. 1842; wholly owned subsidiary of Springer Science+Business Media Netherlands BV; CEO DERK HAANK.

Stollfuss Medien GmbH & Co KG: Dechenstr. 3–11, 53115 Bonn; tel. (228) 7240; fax (228) 72491181; e-mail info@stollfuss.de; internet www.stollfuss.de; reference, fiscal law, economics, investment, etc.; Man. Dir WOLFGANG STOLLFUSS.

Suhrkamp Verlag GmbH & Co KG: Pappelallee 78–79, 10437 Berlin; tel. (30) 7407440; fax (30) 740744199; e-mail info@suhrkamp.de; internet www.suhrkamp.de; f. 1950; modern German and foreign literature, philosophy, poetry; Chair. ULLA UNSELD-BERKÉWICZ.

Georg Thieme Verlag: Rüdigerstr. 14, 70469 Stuttgart; Postfach 301120, 70451 Stuttgart; tel. (711) 89310; fax (711) 8931298; e-mail info@thieme.com; internet www.thieme.de; f. 1886; medicine and natural sciences; Man. Dirs Dr ALBRECHT HAUFF, Dr WOLFGANG KNÜPPE.

Thienemann Verlag GmbH: Blumenstr. 36, 70182 Stuttgart; tel. (711) 210550; fax (711) 2105539; e-mail info@thienemann.de; internet www.thienemann.de; f. 1849; picture books, children's books, juveniles; Man. Dir CHRISTIAN SCHUMACHER-GEBLER.

Verlag Eugen Ulmer GmbH & Co: Wollgrasweg 41, 70599 Stuttgart; Postfach 700561, 70574 Stuttgart; tel. (711) 45070; fax (711) 4507120; e-mail info@ulmer.de; internet www.ulmer.de; f. 1868; agriculture, horticulture, science, periodicals; Dir MATTHIAS ULMER.

Verlag Ullstein GmbH: Charlottenstr. 13, 10969 Berlin; tel. (30) 25913570; fax (30) 25913523; f. 1894; literature, art, music, theatre, modern history, biography; Pres. Dr JÜRGEN RICHTER.

Ullstein Buchverlage GmbH: Friedrichstr. 126, 10117 Berlin; tel. (30) 23456300; fax (30) 23456303; e-mail info@ullstein-buchverlage.de; internet www.ullsteinbuchverlage.de; f. 1894; general fiction, history, art, philosophy, religion, psychology; Dirs Dr SIV BUBLITZ, Dr ALEXANDER LORBEER.

Wiley-VCH Verlag GmbH & Co KGaA: Boschstr. 12, 69469 Weinheim; Postfach 101161, 69451 Weinheim; tel. (6201) 6060; fax (6201) 606328; e-mail info@wiley-vch.de; internet www.wiley-vch.de; f. 1921; natural sciences, especially chemistry, chemical engineering, civil engineering, architecture, biotechnology, materials science, life sciences, information technology and physics, scientific software, business, management, computer science, finance and accounting; Man. Dirs BIJAN GHAWAMI, Dr JON WALMSLEY.

PRINCIPAL ASSOCIATION OF BOOK PUBLISHERS AND BOOKSELLERS

Börsenverein des Deutschen Buchhandels eV (German Publishers and Booksellers Association): Braubachstr. 16, 60311 Frankfurt a.M.; tel. (69) 1306325; fax (69) 1306399; e-mail verleger-ausschuss@boev.de; internet www.boersenverein.de; f. 1825; Chair. HEINRICH RIETHMÜLLER; Man. Dir ALEXANDER SKIPIS.

Broadcasting and Communications

REGULATORY AUTHORITIES

Bundesnetzagentur für Elektrizität, Gas, Telekommunikation, Post und Eisenbahnen (Bundesnetzagentur) (Federal Network Agency for Electricity, Gas, Telecommunications, Post and Railways): Tulpenfeld 4, 53113 Bonn; Postfach 8001, 53105 Bonn; tel. (228) 140; fax (228) 148872; e-mail info@bnetza.de; internet www.bundesnetzagentur.de; f. 1997; fmrly Regulierungsbehörde für Telekommunikation und Post, renamed 2005; responsible for supervising the liberalization and deregulation of the post and telecommunications sector, as well as electricity, gas and railways; Pres. JOCHEN HOMANN.

die medienanstalten: Friedrichstr. 60, 10117 Berlin; tel. (30) 2064690-0; fax (30) 2064690-99; e-mail info@die-medienanstalten.de; internet www.die-medienanstalten.de; consortium of 14 Land commercial media authorities.

TELECOMMUNICATIONS

Deutsche Telekom AG: Postfach 2000, 53105 Bonn; Friedrich-Ebert-Allee 140, 53113 Bonn; tel. (228) 1810; fax (228) 18171915; e-mail impressum@telekom.de; internet www.telekom.de; f. 1989; partially privatized 1995 with further privatization pending; 14.8% state-owned, 16.9% owned by Kreditanstalt für Wiederaufbau, 68.3% owned by private shareholders; fmr monopoly over national telecommunications network removed 1998; Chair., Supervisory Bd Prof. Dr ULRICH LEHNER; Chair., Management Bd and CEO TIMOTHEUS HÖTTGES.

E-Plus Service GmbH & Co. KG: Edison-Allee 1, 14473 Potsdam; tel. (211) 4480; fax (331) 7003130; e-mail kundenservice@eplus.de; internet www.eplus.de; f. 1993; 13.6m. subscribers (June 2007); owned by KPN Mobile NV (Netherlands); Chair., Supervisory Bd EELCO BLOK; Chair., Management Bd and CEO THORSTEN DIRKS.

Kabel Deutschland Holding AG: Betastr. 6–8, 85774 Unterföhring; tel. (89) 96010187; fax (89) 96010888; e-mail elmar.baur@kabeldeutschland.de; internet www.kabeldeutschland.de; f. 2003; fixed-line telephone through cable, mobile services, broadband internet and cable TV services; 76.57% owned by Vodafone Group PLC (UK); Chair., Supervisory Bd JENS SCHULTE BOCKUM; CEO Dr MANUEL CUBERO.

Mobilcom debitel AG: Hollerstr. 126, 24782 Büdelsdorf; tel. (180) 5022240; e-mail info@mobilcom-debitel.de; internet www.mobilcom-debitel.de; f. 2009 following merger with mobilCom Communicationstecknik AG; mobile cellular telecommunications and internet service provider; Chair., Supervisory Bd CHRISTOPH VILANEK; Man Dirs INGO ARNOLD, RICKMANN VON PLATEN.

Telefónica O₂ Germany GmbH & Co OHG: Georg-Brauchle-Ring 23–25, 80992 München; tel. (89) 24421201; fax (89) 24421209; internet www.telefonica.de; f. 1995 as VIAG Interkom; name changed to O₂ Germany in 2002; mobile cellular telecommunications; acquired by Telefónica SA (Spain) 2006; 25.1m. subscribers (June 2014); Man. Dirs RACHEL EMPEY, MARKUS HAAS.

T-Mobile Deutschland GmbH: POB 300463, 53184 Bonn; Landgrabenweg 151, 53227 Bonn; tel. (228) 93631717; fax (228) 93631719; e-mail info@telekom.de; internet www.t-mobile.de; f. 1993; 34.3m. subscribers (June 2007); subsidiary of Deutsche Telekom AG; Chair., Management Bd GEORG PÖLZL.

Vodafone GmbH: Am Seestern 1, 40547 Düsseldorf; tel. (211) 5330; fax (211) 5332200; e-mail kontakt@vodafone.com; internet www.vodafone.de; f. 1992 as Mannesmann Mobilfunk GmbH; present name adopted 2013; 38m. subscribers (March 2010); subsidiary of Vodafone Group PLC (UK); acquired fixed-line services provider Arcor AG in 2008; CEO JENS SCHULTE-BOCKUM.

BROADCASTING

Radio

Regional public radio stations are co-ordinated by the ARD (see Public Stations). There are also numerous regional commercial radio stations.

In early 2009 Digital Audio Broadcasting (DAB) services were available to approximately 80% of the population.

Public Stations

Arbeitsgemeinschaft der öffentlich-rechtlichen Rundfunkanstalten der Bundesrepublik Deutschland (ARD) (Association of Public Law Broadcasting Organizations): Bertramstr. 8, 60320 Frankfurt a.M.; tel. (69) 15687211; fax (69) 15687100; e-mail info@ard.de; internet www.ard.de; f. 1950; Chair. PETER BOUDGOUST;

the co-ordinating body of Germany's public service radio and television orgs; each of the following orgs broadcasts radio and television channels:

Bayerischer Rundfunk (BR): Rundfunkpl. 1, 80355 München; tel. (89) 590001; fax (89) 59002375; e-mail info@br.de; internet www.bronline.de; Dir-Gen. Prof. Dr ULRICH WILHELM.

Deutsche Welle: Kurt-Schumacher-Str. 3, 53113 Bonn; tel. (228) 4290; fax (228) 4293000; e-mail info@dw.de; internet www.dw-world.de; f. 1953; German short-wave radio (DW-Radio), satellite television service (DW-TV) and online service; broadcasts daily in 30 languages for Europe and overseas; Dir-Gen. PETER LIMBOURG.

Hessischer Rundfunk (hr): Bertramstr. 8, 60320 Frankfurt a.M.; tel. (69) 1551; fax (69) 1552900; internet www.hr-online.de; Dir-Gen. Dr HELMUT REITZE.

Mitteldeutscher Rundfunk (mdr): Kanstr. 71–73, 04275 Leipzig; tel. (341) 3000; fax (341) 3006788; e-mail zuschauerservice@mdr.de; internet www.mdr.de; f. 1992; Dir-Gen. Prof. Dr KAROLA WILLE.

Norddeutscher Rundfunk (NDR): Rothenbaumchaussee 132–134, 20149 Hamburg; tel. (40) 41560; fax (40) 447602; e-mail info@ndr.de; internet www.ndr.de; f. 1956; Dir-Gen. LUTZ MARMOR.

Radio Bremen: Diepenau 10, 28195 Bremen; tel. (421) 2460; fax (421) 24641200; e-mail info@radiobremen.de; internet www.radiobremen.de; f. 1945; Dir-Gen. JAN METZGER.

Rundfunk Berlin-Brandenburg (rbb): Masurenallee 8–14, 14057 Berlin; tel. (30) 97993-0; fax (30) 97993-19; e-mail presse@rbb-online.de; internet www.rbb-online.de; f. 2003; Dir-Gen. DAGMAR REIM.

Saarländischer Rundfunk (SR): Funkhaus Halberg, 66100 Saarbrücken; tel. (681) 6020; fax (681) 6023874; e-mail info@sr-online.de; internet www.sr-online.de; f. 1952; Dir-Gen. THOMAS KLEIST.

Südwestrundfunk (SWR): Neckarstr. 230, 70150 Stuttgart; tel. (49) 9290; fax (49) 92911300; e-mail info@swr.de; internet www.swr.de; Dir-Gen. PETER BOUDGOUST.

Westdeutscher Rundfunk (WDR): Appellhofpl. 1, 50667 Köln; tel. (221) 2200; fax (221) 2204800; e-mail redaktion@wdr.de; internet www.wdr.de; Dir-Gen. TOM BUHROW.

Deutschlandradio: Raderberggürtel 40, 50968 Köln; tel. (221) 3451831; fax (221) 3451839; e-mail hoererservice@dradio.de; internet www.dradio.de; f. 1994 by merger of Deutschlandfunk, Deutschlandsender Kultur and RIAS Berlin; national public service radio broadcaster; 3 stations: Deutschlandfunk, Deutschlandradio Kultur and DRadio Wissen; jtly managed by ARD and ZDF; Dir-Gen. Dr WILLI STEUL.

Commercial Radio

Verband Privater Rundfunk und Telemedien eV (VPRT) (Asscn of Commercial Broadcasters and Audiovisual Cos): Stromstr. 1, 10555 Berlin; tel. (30) 398800; fax (30) 39880148; e-mail info@vprt.de; internet www.vprt.de; f. 1984; 140 mems (April 2011); Man. Dir Dr TOBIAS SCHMID.

Television

There are three main public service television channels. The autonomous regional broadcasting organizations combine to provide material for the First Programme, which is produced by ARD. The Second Programme (Zweites Deutsches Fernsehen—ZDF) is completely separate and is controlled by a public corporation of all the Länder. It is partly financed by advertising. The Third Programme (ARTE Deutschland) provides a cultural and educational service, with contributions from both ARD and ZDF. There are also three other public service channels (KI.KA, Phoenix and 3Sat), which are jointly managed by ARD and ZDF. Commercial television channels also operate.

Analogue broadcasting was discontinued throughout Germany in early December 2008.

Public Stations

ARD: Programmdirektion Deutsches Fernsehen: Arnulfstr. 42, 80335 München; tel. (89) 59003344; fax (89) 59003249; e-mail info@daserste.de; internet www.daserste.de; co-ordinates the regional public service television organizations (see Radio); Chair. LUTZ MARMOR; Dir of Programmes VOLKER HERRES.

ARTE Deutschland TV GmbH: Postfach 100213, 76483 Baden-Baden; tel. (7221) 9369-26; fax (7221) 9369-70; internet www.arte.tv; f. 1991; arts, cultural programmes, in French and German; Pres. Dr VÉRONIQUE CAYLA.

KI.KA—Der Kinderkanal ARD/ZDF: Gothaer Str. 36, 99094 Erfurt; tel. (361) 2181890; fax (361) 2181848; e-mail kika@kika.de;

internet www.kika.de; f. 1997; children's programming; jtly managed by ARD and ZDF; Dir Prof. Dr KAROLA WILLE.

Phoenix: Langer Grabenweg 45–47, 53175 Bonn; tel. (1802) 8217; fax (1802) 8213; e-mail info@phoenix.de; internet www.phoenix.de; f. 1997; digital channel broadcasting news and current affairs programmes; jtly managed by ARD and ZDF; Dirs of Programming MICHAELA KOLSTER, MICHAEL HIRZ.

Zweites Deutsches Fernsehen (ZDF): 55100 Mainz; tel. (6131) 700; fax (6131) 7012157; e-mail info@zdf.de; internet www.zdf.de; f. 1961 by the Land govts as a second television channel; Dir-Gen. Dr THOMAS BELLUT.

3Sat: ZDF-Str. 1, 55127 Mainz; tel. (6131) 700; fax (6131) 702157; e-mail info@zdf.de; internet www.3sat.de; f. 1984; satellite channel broadcasting cultural programmes in Germany, Austria and German-speaking areas of Switzerland; 32.5% each owned by ARD and ZDF, 25.0% owned by ÖRF (Austria) and 10.0% owned by SRG SSR idée suisse (Switzerland); Dir-Gen. Dr THOMAS BELLUT.

Commercial Television

Kabel Deutschland Holding AG: see Telecommunications.

ProSiebenSat.1 Media AG: Medienallee 7, 85774 Unterföhring; tel. (89) 950710; fax (89) 95071122; e-mail info@prosiebensat1.com; internet www.prosiebensat1.com; f. 2000 by merger of ProSieben Media AG (f. 1989) and Sat.1 (f. 1984); operates Sat.1, ProSieben, Kabel eins and sixx; Chair., Management Bd THOMAS EBELING; Chair., Supervisory Bd Dr WERNER BRANDT.

RTL Television GmbH: Picassopl. 1, 50679 Köln; tel. (49) 2214560; fax (49) 2214561690; e-mail pressezentrum@rtl.de; internet www.rtl-television.de; f. 1984; subsidiary of RTL Group (Luxembourg); CEO ANKE SCHÄFERKORDT.

Sky Deutschland AG: Medienallee 26, 85774 Unterföhring; tel. (89) 995802; fax (89) 99586239; e-mail info@sky.de; internet www.sky.de; f. 1988; fmrly called Premiere Fernsehen GmbH & Co KG; name changed to present in 2009; subscriber service offering 53 television channels; 95.8% stake owned by Sky German Holdings GmbH; CEO BRIAN SULLIVAN.

Verband Privater Rundfunk und Telemedien eV (VPRT): see under Radio; represents privately owned satellite, cable and digital television cos.

VOX Film- und Fernseh- GmbH: Picassopl. 1, 50679 Köln; tel. (221) 9534370; e-mail mail@vox.de; internet www.vox.de; f. 1991; cable, satellite and digital terrestrial channel broadcasting entertainment programmes; 99.7% owned by RTL Group (Luxembourg) and 0.3% owned by Development Company for Television Program; CEO BERND REICHART.

Association

Bundesverband Digitale Wirtschaft eV (BVDW): Berliner Allee 57, 40212 Düsseldorf; tel. (211) 6004560; fax (211) 60045633; e-mail info@bvdw.org; internet www.bvdw.org; 630 mems (July 2013); Pres. MATTHIAS EHRLICH; Man. Dir MARCO JUNK.

Finance

(cap. = capital; res = reserves; dep. = deposits; m. = million; brs = branches; amounts in euros)

The Deutsche Bundesbank, the central bank of Germany, consists of the central administration in Frankfurt am Main (considered to be the financial capital of the country), nine main regional offices (Hauptverwaltungen) and 47 smaller branches. In carrying out its functions as determined by law the Bundesbank is independent of the Federal Government, but is required to support the Government's general economic policy. As a member of the European System of Central Banks (ESCB), the Bundesbank implements the single monetary policy determined by the Governing Council of the European Central Bank (ECB).

All credit institutions other than the Bundesbank are subject to supervision through the Federal Financial Supervisory Authority (Bundesanstalt für Finanzdienstleistungsaufsicht) in Bonn. Banks outside the central banking system are divided into three groups: private commercial banks, credit institutions incorporated under public law and co-operative credit institutions. All these commercial banks are 'universal banks', conducting all kinds of customary banking business. There is no division of activities. As well as the commercial banks there are a number of specialist banks, such as private or public mortgage banks.

The group of private commercial banks includes all banks incorporated as a company limited by shares (Aktiengesellschaft—AG, Kommanditgesellschaft auf Aktien—KGaA) or as a private limited company (Gesellschaft mit beschränkter Haftung—GmbH) and those which are known as 'regional banks' because they do not usually function throughout Germany; and those banks which are established as sole proprietorships or partnerships and mostly have no branches outside their home town. The main business of all private commercial banks is short-term lending. The private bankers fulfil the most varied tasks within the banking system.

The public law credit institutions are the savings banks (Sparkassen) and the Landesbank-Girozentralen. The latter act as central banks and clearing houses on a national level for the savings banks. Laws governing the savings banks limit them to certain sectors—credits, investments and money transfers—and they concentrate on the areas of home financing, municipal investments and the trades. In 2013 there were 426 institutions in the savings bank sector in Germany.

The head institution of the co-operative system is the DZ BANK (Deutsche Zentral-Genossenschaftsbank AG). In 2013 there were 1,083 credit co-operatives and two central institutions.

In 2013 there were 1,820 banks in Germany.

SUPERVISORY BODY

Bundesanstalt für Finanzdienstleistungsaufsicht (BaFin) (Federal Financial Supervisory Authority): Postfach 1253, 53002 Bonn; Graurheindorfer Str. 108, 53117 Bonn; tel. (228) 41080; fax (228) 41081550; e-mail poststelle@bafin.de; internet www.bafin.de; f. 2002; independent public-law institution; supervises banks, financial services providers, insurance cos and securities trading; Pres. Dr ELKE KÖNIG.

BANKS

Central Banking System

Germany participates in the ESCB, which consists of the ECB and the national central banks of all European Union (EU) member states.

Deutsche Bundesbank: Postfach 100602, 60006 Frankfurt a.M.; Wilhelm-Epstein-Str. 14, 60431 Frankfurt a.M.; tel. (69) 95660; fax (69) 95663077; e-mail presse-information@bundesbank.de; internet www.bundesbank.de; f. 1957; aims, in conjunction with the other members of the ESCB, to maintain price stability in the eurozone. The Bundesbank, *inter alia*, holds and maintains foreign reserves of the Federal Republic of Germany, arranges for the execution of domestic and cross-border payments and contributes to the stability of payment and clearing systems. The Bundesbank (which has nine regional offices—Hauptverwaltungen—and 47 smaller branches) is the principal bank of the Federal Land Govts, carrying accounts for public authorities, executing payments and assisting with borrowing on the capital market. The Bundesbank has reserve positions in, and claims on, the IMF and the ECB. The Executive Board determines the Bundesbank's business policy; members of the Federal Govt may take part in the deliberations of the Board; cap. 2,500m., res 2,500m., dep. 131,673m. (Dec. 2009); Pres. Prof. Dr JENS WEIDMANN; Vice-Pres. SABINE LAUTENSCHLÄGER.

Hauptverwaltung Bayern: Ludwigstr. 13, 80539 München; tel. (89) 28895; fax (89) 28893598; e-mail pressestelle.hv-muenchen@bundesbank.de; internet www.bundesbank.de/hv/hv_muenchen.php; Pres. ALOIS MÜLLER.

Hauptverwaltung Berlin: Postfach 120163, 10591 Berlin; Leibnizstr. 10, 10625 Berlin; tel. (30) 34750; fax (30) 34751990; e-mail pressestelle.hv-berlin@bundesbank.de; internet www.bundesbank.de/hv/hv_berlin.php; Pres. CLAUS TIGGES.

Hauptverwaltung Düsseldorf: Postfach 101148, 40002 Düsseldorf; Berliner Allee 14, 40212 Düsseldorf; tel. (211) 8740; fax (211) 8742424; e-mail stab.hv-duesseldorf@bundesbank.de; internet www.bundesbank.de/hv/hv_duesseldorf.php; Pres. NORBERT MATYSIK.

Hauptverwaltung Frankfurt: Postfach 111232, 60047 Frankfurt a.M.; Taunusanlage 5, 60329 Frankfurt a.M.; tel. (69) 23880; fax (69) 23881044; e-mail pressestelle.hv-frankfurt@bundesbank.de; internet www.bundesbank.de/hv/hv_frankfurt.php; Pres. HANS-JOACHIM KOHSE.

Hauptverwaltung Hamburg: Postfach 570348, 22772 Hamburg; Willy-Brandt-Str. 73, 20459 Hamburg; tel. (40) 37070; fax (40) 37073342; e-mail pressestelle.hv-hamburg@bundesbank.de; internet www.bundesbank.de/hv/hv_hamburg.php; Pres. ADELHEID SAILER-SCHUSTER.

Hauptverwaltung Hannover: Postfach 245, 30002 Hannover; Georgspl. 5, 30159 Hannover; tel. (511) 30330; fax (511) 30332500; e-mail pressestelle.hv-hannover@bundesbank.de; internet www.bundesbank.de/hv/hv_hannover.php; Pres. STEPHAN FREIHERR VON STENGLIN.

Hauptverwaltung Leipzig: Postfach 901121, 04358 Leipzig; Str. des 18. Oktober 48, 04103 Leipzig; tel. (341) 8600; fax (341) 8602389; e-mail pressestelle.hv-leipzig@bundesbank.de; internet www.bundesbank.de/hv/hv_leipzig.php; Pres. HANS CHRISTOPH POPPE.

Hauptverwaltung Rheinland-Pfalz und Saarland: Postfach 3009, 55020 Mainz; Hegelstr. 65, 52122 Mainz; tel. (6131) 3770;

e-mail pressestelle.hv-mainz@bundesbank.de; internet www.bundesbank.de/hv/hv_mainz.php; Pres. STEFAN HARDT.

Hauptverwaltung Stuttgart: Postfach 106021, 70049 Stuttgart; Marstallstr. 3, 70173 Stuttgart; tel. (711) 9440; fax (711) 9441903; e-mail hv-stuttgart@bundesbank.de; internet www.bundesbank.de/hv/hv_stuttgart.php; Pres. BERNHARD SIBOLD.

Private Commercial Banks

In 2013 184 commercial banks were operating in Germany. The most prominent of these are listed below:

Berliner Volksbank eG: 10892 Berlin; Budapester Str. 35, 10787 Berlin; tel. (30) 30630; fax (30) 30631550; e-mail service@berliner-volksbank.de; internet www.berliner-volksbank.de; f. 1880; cap. 349.3m., res 325.3m., dep. 8,801.1m. (Dec. 2012); Chair., Management Bd Dr HOLGER HATJE; 170 brs.

BHF-Bank Aktiengesellschaft: Bockenheimer Landstr. 10, 60323 Frankfurt a.M.; tel. (69) 7180; fax (69) 7182296; e-mail corp-comm@bhf-bank.com; internet www.bhf-bank.com; f. 1970 by merger of Frankfurter Bank (f. 1854) and Berliner Handels-Gesellschaft (f. 1856); current name adopted 2005; cap. 200m., res 294.7m., dep. 5,200.7m. (Dec. 2012); Man. Dir MATTHIAS GRAF VON KROCKOW; 12 brs.

Commerzbank AG: Kaiserpl., 60311 Frankfurt a.M.; tel. (69) 13620; fax (69) 285389; e-mail info@commerzbank.com; internet www.commerzbank.de; f. 1870; acquired Dresdner Bank in Jan. 2009; 25.0% stake owned by Federal Govt; cap. 8,204m., res 9,328m., dep. 320,703m. (Dec. 2012); Chair., Supervisory Bd KLAUS-PETER MÜLLER; Chair., Management Bd MARTIN BLESSING.

Deutsche Bank AG: Theodor-Heuss-Allee 70, 60486 Frankfurt a.M.; tel. (69) 9100; fax (69) 91034225; e-mail deutsche.bank@db.com; internet www.deutsche-bank.de; f. 1870; cap. 2,380m., res 22,425m., dep. 646,262m. (Dec. 2012); Chair., Supervisory Bd PAUL ACHLEITNER; Co-Chair., Management Bd ANSHU JAIN, JÜRGEN FITSCHEN; 983 brs.

HSBC Trinkaus & Burkhardt AG: Königsallee 21–23, 40212 Düsseldorf; tel. (211) 9100; fax (211) 910616; internet www.hsbctrinkhaus.de; f. 1785; current name adopted 2006; cap. 75.4m., res 442.5m., dep. 12,947.2m. (Dec. 2012); Chair., Management Bd ANDREAS SCHMITZ; 7 brs.

Sal. Oppenheim Jr & Cie KGaA: Postfach 102743, 50467 Köln; Unter Sachsenhausen 4, 50667 Köln; tel. (221) 14501; fax (221) 1451512; e-mail info@oppenheim.de; internet www.oppenheim.de; f. 1789; name changed as above in 2010; cap. 700m., res 1,139m., dep. 5,034m. (Dec. 2012); Chair. MATTHIAS GRAF VON KROCKOW; 11 brs.

SEB AG: 60283 Frankfurt a.M.; Ulmenstr. 30, 60283 Frankfurt a.M.; tel. (69) 2580; fax (69) 2587578; e-mail info@seb.de; internet www.seb.de; f. 1958 as BfG Bank AG; adopted current name 2001; owned by Skandinaviska Enskilda Banken AB (Sweden); cap. 775.2m., res 522m., dep. 27,225.5m. (Dec. 2012); Chair., Management Bd JAN SINCLAIR; 175 brs.

Targobank AG & Co KGaA: Postfach 101818, 40009 Düsseldorf; Kasernenstr. 10, 40213 Düsseldorf; tel. (211) 89840; fax (211) 8984222; internet www.targobank.de; f. 1926 as KKB Bank KGaA; acquired by Crédit Mutuel Group (France) in 2008; present name adopted in 2010; cap. 133.1m., res 687.1m., dep. 10,675.1m. (Dec. 2012); Chair., Management Bd FRANZ JOSEF NICK; 286 brs.

UBS Deutschland AG: Landstr. 2–4, 60313 Frankfurt a.M.; tel. (69) 21790; fax (69) 21796511; internet www.ubs.com/deutschland; f. 1998 as Warburg Dillon Read AG by merger of Schweizerischer Bankverein (Deutschland) and Union Bank of Switzerland (Deutschland) AG; present name adopted 2005; cap. 176m., res 221.4m., dep. 4,709.6m. (Dec. 2012); Chair. and CEO STEPHAN ZIMMERMANN; 10 brs.

UniCredit Bank AG (HypoVereinsbank): Kardinal-Faulhaber-Str. 1, 80333 München; tel. (89) 3780; fax (89) 378113422; e-mail info@unicreditgroup.de; internet www.hypovereinsbank.de; f. 1998 by merger of Bayerische Hypotheken- und Wechsel Bank AG (f. 1835) and Bayerische Vereinsbank AG (f. 1869); 95.4% owned by UniCredito Italiano SpA; name changed as above in 2009; cap. 2,407m., res 17,606m., dep. 137,859m. (Dec. 2012); Chair., Supervisory Bd FEDERICO GHIZZONI; Chair., Bd of Management Dr THEODOR WEIMER; 618 brs.

Public-Law Credit Institutions

Together with the private banks, the banks incorporated under public law (savings banks—Sparkassen—and their central clearing houses—Landesbank-Girozentralen) play a major role within the German banking system. In 2013 there were 426 savings banks.

BayernLB: Brienner Str. 18, 80333 München; tel. (89) 217101; fax (89) 217123578; e-mail kontakt@bayernlb.de; internet www.bayernlb.de; f. 1972 as Bayerische Landesbank Girozentrale; present name adopted 2002; cap. 6,556m., res 4,735m., dep. 174,975m. (Dec. 2012); Chair., Management Bd GERD HÄUSLER.

Bremer Landesbank Kreditanstalt Oldenburg-Girozentrale (Bremer Landesbank): Domshof 26, 28195 Bremen; tel. (421) 3320; fax (421) 3322322; e-mail kontakt@bremerlandesbank.de; internet www.bremerlandesbank.de; f. 1983; 92.5% owned by Norddeutsche Landesbank and 7.5% owned by Bremen city council; cap. 245m., res 510m., dep. 22,432m. (Dec. 2012); Chair. Dr STEPHAN ANDREAS KAULVERS.

DekaBank Deutsche Girozentrale: Mainzer Landstr. 16, 60325 Frankfurt a.M.; tel. (69) 71470; fax (69) 71471376; e-mail konzerninfo@deka.de; internet www.dekabank.de; f. 1999 by merger of Deutsche Girozentrale-Deutsche Kommunalbank and Dekabank GmbH; present name adopted 2002; central institution of Sparkassen org.; issues bonds (Pfandbriefe); cap. 191.7m., res 262m., dep. 61,024.2m. (Dec. 2012); Chair., Management Bd FRANZ S. WAAS.

HSH Nordbank AG: Gerhart-Hauptmann-Pl. 50, 20095 Hamburg; tel. (40) 33330; fax (40) 333334001; e-mail info@hsh-nordbank.com; internet www.hsh-nordbank.com; f. 2003 by merger of Hamburgische Landesbank-Girozentrale and Landesbank Schleswig-Holstein Girozentrale; 12.37% owned by Hamburg city council, 10.97% by Schleswig-Holstein Land Govt; cap. 3,018m., res 504m., dep. 71,242m. (Dec. 2012); Chair. HILMAR KOPPER; CEO Dr CONSTANTIN VON OESTERREICH.

Landesbank Baden-Württemberg (LBBW): Postfach 106049, 70049 Stuttgart; Am Hauptbahnhof 2, 70173 Stuttgart; tel. (711) 1270; fax (711) 12743544; e-mail kontakt@lbbw.de; internet www.lbbw.de; f. 1999 by merger of Landesgirokasse, L-Bank Landeskreditbank Baden-Württemberg and Südwestdeutsche Landesbank Girozentrale; 19.57% owned by Land Govt of Baden-Württemberg; cap. 2,584m., res 6,547m., dep. 64,069m. (Dec. 2012); Chair., Management Bd HANS-JÖRG VETTER.

Landesbank Berlin AG: Alexanderpl. 2, 10178 Berlin; tel. (30) 869801; fax (30) 86983074; e-mail information@lbb.de; internet www.lbb.de; f. 1818; name changed as above in 2006; cap. 1,200m., res 1,015m., dep. 50,048m. (Dec. 2012); Chair., Management Bd Dr JOHANNES EVERS; 150 brs.

Landesbank Hessen-Thüringen Girozentrale (Helaba): Main Tower, Neue Mainzer Str. 52–58, 60297 Frankfurt a.M.; tel. (69) 913201; fax (69) 291517; e-mail presse@helaba.de; internet www.helaba.de; f. 1953, 8.10% owned by Hesse Land Govt, 4.05% by Thuringia Land Govt, 68.85% by Sparkassen- und Giroverband Hessen-Thüringen, 4.75% each by Rheinischer Sparkassen- und Giroverband, Sparkassenverband Westfalen-Lippe, FIDES Beta GmbH and FIDES Alpha GmbH; total assets 178,508m. (2014); Chair., Management Bd HANS-DIETER BRENNER.

Landesbank Saar (SaarLB): Ursulinenstr. 2, 66111 Saarbrücken; tel. (681) 38301; fax (681) 3831200; e-mail service@saarlb.de; internet www.saarlb.de; f. 1941; name changed as above in 2003; 49.9% owned by Bayerische Landesbank, 35.2% by Saarland Land Govt; cap. 260.6m., res 94.4m., dep. 12,284.5m. (Dec. 2012); Chair., Management Bd THOMAS-CHRISTIAN BUCHBINDER.

Norddeutsche Landesbank Girozentrale (NORD/LB): Friedrichswall 10, 30159 Hannover; tel. (511) 3610; fax (511) 3612502; e-mail info@nordlb.de; internet www.nordlb.de; f. 1970 by merger of several north German banks; cap. 1,607m., res 3,316m., dep. 89,654m. (Dec. 2012); Chair., Management Bd Dr GUNTER DUNKEL; 108 brs.

Portigon AG: Herzogstr. 15, 40217 Düsseldorf; tel. (211) 82601; fax (211) 8266119; e-mail presse@portigon.com; internet www.portigon.com; f. 2012; fmrly known as WestLB AG; cap. 499m., res –667m., dep. 12,702m. (Dec. 2012); Chair., Management Bd DIETRICH VOIGTLÄNDER; 3 brs.

Central Bank of Co-operative Banking System

DZ BANK AG (Deutsche Zentral-Genossenschaftsbank): Pl. der Republik, 60265 Frankfurt a.M.; tel. (69) 744701; fax (69) 74471685; e-mail mail@dzbank.de; internet www.dzbank.de; f. 1949; cap. 3,160m., res 1,303m., dep. 200,631m. (Dec. 2012); Chair., Management Bd WOLFGANG KIRSCH; 46 brs.

DZ BANK is a specialist wholesale bank and is the central institution in the German co-operative banking sector, which comprises local co-operative banks, three regional central banks and a number of specialist financial institutions. In 2013 there were 1,079 credit co-operatives and two central institutions.

Specialist Banks

Although Germany is considered the model country for universal banking, banks that specialize in certain types of business are also extremely important. A selection of the most prominent among these is given below:

Aareal Bank AG: Paulinenstr. 15, 65189 Wiesbaden; tel. (611) 3480; fax (611) 3482549; e-mail aareal@aareal-bank.com; internet www.aareal-bank.com; f. 1923; privatized 1989; fmrly DePfa Bank AG,

present name adopted 2002; cap. 480m., res 613m., dep. 12,954m. (Dec. 2012); Chair. Dr WOLF SCHUMACHER.

Berlin-Hannoversche Hypothekenbank AG (Berlin Hyp): Budapester Str. 1, 10787 Berlin; tel. (30) 259990; fax (30) 25999131; e-mail kommunikation@berlinhyp.de; internet www.berlinhyp.de; f. 1996 by merger; cap. 753.4m., res 75.3m., dep. 21,536.7m. (Dec. 2012); Chair., Management Bd Dr JOHANNES EVERS; Chair., Supervisory Bd JAN BETTINK.

COREALCREDIT BANK AG: Postfach 170162, 60075 Frankfurt a.M.; Grüneburgweg 58–62, 60322 Frankfurt a.M.; tel. (69) 71790; fax (69) 7179100; e-mail info@corealcredit.de; internet www.corealcredit.de; f. 1962 as Allgemeine Hypotheken Bank AG; name changed to Allgemeine HypothekenBank Rheinboden in 2001; present name adopted 2007; specializes in commercial property market; cap. 100.3m., res 1,373.4m., dep. 4,074m. (Dec. 2012); Chair., Management Bd Dr CLAUS NOLTING; 6 brs.

Deutsche Hypothekenbank AG: Georgspl. 8, 30159 Hannover; tel. (511) 30450; fax (511) 3045459; e-mail mail@deutsche-hypo.de; internet www.deutsche-hypo.de; f. 1872; subsidiary of Norddeutsche Landesbank Girozentrale; cap. 230.6m., res 681.7m., dep. 9,713.5m. (Dec. 2012); Chair., Supervisory Bd Dr GUNTER DUNKEL; Chair., Management Bd Dr THOMAS STEPHAN BÜRKLE; 6 brs.

Deutsche Pfandbriefbank AG: Von-der-Tann-Str. 2, 80539 München; tel. (89) 28800; fax (89) 288010319; e-mail info@hyporealestate.de; internet www.hyporealestate.com; f. 2001 as HVB Real Estate Bank AG; adopted current name 2009 following merger with Depfa Deutsche Pfandbriefbank AF; part of Hypo Real Estate Group (under state control since 2009); cap. 1,379m., res 5,047m., dep. 19,692m. (Dec. 2012); Chair., Supervisory Bd Dr BERND THIEMANN; Chair., Management Bd MANUELA BETTER.

Deutsche Postbank AG: Friedrich-Ebert-Allee 114–126, 53113 Bonn; tel. (228) 9200; fax (228) 92035151; e-mail presse@postbank.de; internet www.postbank.de; f. 1990; 51.98% owned by Deutsche Bank AG; cap. 547m., res 1,944m., dep. 151,231m. (Dec. 2012); Chair., Management Bd STEFAN JÜTTE; 850 brs.

Hypothekenbank Frankfurt AG: Helfmann-Park 5, 65760 Eschborn; tel. (69) 25480; fax (69) 254871204; e-mail roland.fischer@hypothekenbankfrankfurt.com; internet www.hypothekenbankfrankfurt.com; f. 2012; fmrly known as Eurohypo AG; part of Commerzbank Group; cap. 914m., res 2,333m., dep. 64,822m. (Dec. 2012); CEO and Chair., Management Bd Dr THOMAS KÖNTGEN; 16 brs.

IKB Deutsche Industriebank AG: Wilhelm-Bötzkes-Str. 1, 40474 Düsseldorf; Postfach 101118, 40002 Düsseldorf; tel. (211) 82210; fax (211) 82213959; e-mail info@ikb.de; internet www.ikb.de; f. 1949; fmrly Industriekreditbank AG; name changed as above in 1991; cap. 1,621.3m., res 563.3m., dep. 25,400.3m. (March 2012); Chair., Management Bd HANS JÖRG SCHÜTTLER; 7 brs.

KfW Bankengruppe (Kreditanstalt für Wiederaufbau): Postfach 111141, 60046 Frankfurt a.M.; Palmengartenstr. 5–9, 60325 Frankfurt a.M.; tel. (69) 74310; fax (69) 74312944; e-mail info@kfw.de; internet www.kfw.de; f. 1948; 80% owned by Federal Govt and 20% by Land Govts; cap. 3,300m., res 9,609m., dep. 441,390m. (Dec. 2012); Chair., Management Bd Dr ULRICH SCHRÖDER.

Münchener Hypothekenbank eG (MünchenerHyp): Karl-Scharnagl-Ring 10, 80539 München; tel. (89) 538780; fax (89) 5387900; e-mail serviceteam800@muenchenerhyp.de; internet www.muenchenerhyp.de; f. 1896; cap. 503.2m., res 283.8m., dep. 7,982.5m. (Dec. 2012); Chair., Supervisory Bd KONRAD IRTEL; Chair., Management Bd Dr LOUIS HAGEN; 11 brs.

Bankers' Organizations

Bankenverband—Bundesverband deutscher Banken (Asscn of German Banks): Postfach 040307, 10062 Berlin; Burgstr. 28, 10178 Berlin; tel. (30) 16630; fax (30) 16631399; e-mail bankenverband@bdb.de; internet www.bdb.de; f. 1951; Gen. Man. MICHAEL KEMMER.

Bundesverband der Deutschen Volksbanken und Raiffeisenbanken eV (BVR) (National Association of German Co-operative Banks): Schellingstr. 4, 10785 Berlin; tel. (30) 20210; fax (30) 20211900; e-mail info@bvr.de; internet www.bvr.de; f. 1972; Pres. UWE FRÖHLICH; 1,121 mems (2011).

Bundesverband Öffentlicher Banken Deutschlands eV (VÖB) (Association of German Public Sector Banks): Lennéstr. 11, 10785 Berlin; tel. (30) 81920; fax (30) 8192222; e-mail postmaster@voeb.de; internet www.voeb.de; 32 mems and 33 assoc. mems; Pres. GUNTER DUNKEL; Chair. Prof. Dr LIANE BUCHHOLZ.

Deutscher Sparkassen- und Giroverband eV (German Savings Banks Asscn): Charlottenstr. 47, 10117 Berlin; tel. (30) 202250; fax (30) 20225250; e-mail info@dsgv.de; internet www.dsgv.de; Pres. GEORG FAHRENSCHON.

STOCK EXCHANGES

Bayerische Börse AG: Karolinenplatz 6, 80333 München; tel. (89) 5490450; fax (89) 54904531; e-mail info@boerse-muenchen.de; internet www.boerse-muenchen.de; f. 1830; 77 mems; Management Bd ANDREAS SCHMIDT, JOCHEN THIEL.

Berlin: Börse Berlin AG, Fasanenstr. 85, 10623 Berlin; tel. (30) 3110910; fax (30) 31109179; e-mail kundenbetreuung@boerse-berlin.de; internet www.boerse-berlin.de; f. 1685; 109 mems; Pres. Dr JÖRG WALTER.

Düsseldorf: Börse Düsseldorf AG, Ernst-Schneider-Pl. 1, 40212 Düsseldorf; tel. (211) 13890; fax (211) 133287; e-mail kontakt@boerse-duesseldorf.de; internet www.boerse-duesseldorf.de; f. 1935; 110 mem. firms; Chair. DIRK ELBERSKIRCH.

Frankfurt am Main: Deutsche Börse AG, Börsenpl. 4, 60313 Frankfurt a.M.; tel. (69) 2110; fax (69) 21111021; internet www.exchange.de; f. 1585 as Frankfurter Wertpapierbörse; 269 mems; CEO RETO FRANCIONI; Chair., Supervisory Bd KURT F. VIERMETZ.

North Germany (Hamburg): BÖAG Börsen AG, Kleine Johannisstr. 2–4, 20457 Hamburg; tel. (40) 3613020; fax (40) 36130223; internet www.boersenag.de; f. 1999 by merger of Hanseatische Wertpapierbörse Hamburg and Niedersächsische Börse zu Hannover; 109 mems; Pres. UDO BANDOW; Chair. Dr THOMAS LEDERMANN.

North Germany (Hannover): BÖAG Börsen AG, Rathenaustr. 2, 30159 Hannover; tel. (511) 327661; fax (511) 324915; e-mail s.lueth@boersenag.de; internet www.boersenag.de; f. 1999 by merger of Hanseatische Wertpapierbörse Hamburg and Niedersächsische Börse zu Hannover; 81 mems; Chair. Prof. Dr HANS HEINRICH PETERS.

Stuttgart: Boerse-Stuttgart AG, Börsenstr. 4, 70174 Stuttgart; tel. (711) 2229850; fax (711) 222985555; e-mail info@boerse-stuttgart.de; internet www.boerse-stuttgart.de; f. 1861; 121 mems; Pres. ROLF LIMBACH; Man. Dir Dr CHRISTOPH MURA.

INSURANCE

German law specifies that property and accident insurance may not be jointly underwritten with life, sickness, legal protection or credit insurance by the same company. Insurers are therefore obliged to establish separate companies to cover the different classes of insurance. In March 2010 there were 2,217 insurance companies operating in Germany.

Aachener und Münchener Lebensversicherung AG (Aachen-Münchener): AachenMünchener-Pl. 1, 52064 Aachen; tel. (241) 4560; fax (241) 4565678; e-mail service@amv.de; internet www.amv.de; f. 1868; subsidiary of Generali Deutschland Holding AG; Chair. MICHAEL WESTKAMP.

Allianz AG: Königinstr. 28, 80802 München; tel. (89) 38000; fax (89) 38003425; e-mail info@allianz.de; internet www.allianz.de; f. 1890; Chair., Supervisory Bd Dr WERNER ZEDELIUS; Chair., Management Bd Dr MARKUS RIEß.

Allianz Lebensversicherungs-AG: 10850 Berlin; tel. (89) 100104; fax (89) 400104; e-mail lebensversicherung@allianz.de; internet www.allianz.com; f. 1922; Chair., Supervisory Bd Dr HELMUT PERLET; Chair., Management Bd MICHAEL DIEKMANN.

Allianz Private Krankenversicherungs AG: Fritz-Schäffer-Str. 9, 81737 München; tel. (89) 67850; fax (89) 67856523; e-mail service.apkv@allianz.de; internet www.allianz.de; f. 1925; Chair, Supervisory Bd Dr MAXIMILIAN ZIMMERER; Chair, Management Bd Dr BIRGIT KÖNIG.

Allianz Versicherungs AG: Königinstr. 28, 80802 München; tel. (89) 38000; fax (89) 38003425; e-mail info@allianz.de; internet www.allianz.de; f. 1985; Chair. Dr WERNER ZEDELIUS.

AXA Krankenversicherung AG: Colonia-Allee 10–20, 50167 Köln; tel. (1803) 556622; fax (221) 14832602; internet www.axa.de; f. 1962; 100% owned by AXA Konzern AG; Chair., Supervisory Bd JACQUES DE VAUCLEROY; Chair., Management Bd Dr THOMAS BUBERL.

AXA Lebensversicherung AG: Colonia-Allee 10–20, 51067 Köln; tel. (1803) 556622; fax (221) 14822750; e-mail service@axa.de; internet www.axa.de; f. 1853; Chair., Supervisory Bd JACQUES DE VAUCLEROY; Chair., Management Bd Dr THOMAS BUBERL.

AXA Versicherung AG: Colonia-Allee 10–20, 51067 Köln; tel. (221) 14819727; fax (221) 14822740; e-mail service@axa.de; internet www.axa.de; f. 1839 as Colonia Kölnischer Freuer Versicherung AG; present name adopted 2001; non-life insurance; Chair., Supervisory Bd JACQUES DE VAUCLEROY; Chair., Management Bd Dr THOMAS BUBERL.

Continentale Krankenversicherung AG: Ruhrallee 92, 44139 Dortmund; tel. (231) 9190; fax (231) 9193255; e-mail info@continentale.de; internet www.continentale.de; f. 1926; Chair., Supervisory Bd Dr HORST HOFFMANN; Chair., Management Bd HELMUT POSCH.

DBV-Winterthur Lebensversicherung AG: Frankfurter Str. 50, 65189 Wiesbaden; tel. (1803) 328100; fax (1803) 328400; e-mail info@dbv.de; internet www.dbv.de; f. 1871; Chair. BERNHARD GERTZ.

Debeka Krankenversicherungsverein AG: Ferdinand-Sauerbruch-Str. 18, 56073 Koblenz; tel. (261) 4980; fax (261) 4985555; e-mail kundenservice@debeka.de; internet www.debeka.de; f. 1905; Chair. PETER GREISLER; Gen. Man. UWE LAUE.

Deutsche Krankenversicherung AG: Aachener Str. 300, 50933 Köln; tel. (221) 57894005; fax (1805) 786000; e-mail service@dkv.com; internet www.dkv.com; f. 1927; Chair. Dr CLEMENS MUTH.

ERGO Lebensversicherung AG: Überseering 45, 22297 Hamburg; tel. (211) 4777100; fax (40) 63763302; e-mail info@ergo.de-mail.de; internet www.ergo.de; subsidiary of ERGO Versicherungsgruppe AG, part of Munich Re; f. 1899; Chair. Dr DANIEL VON BORRIES.

ERGO Versicherungsgruppe AG: Victoriaplatz 2, 40477 Düsseldorf; tel. (211) 4770; fax (211) 4771500; e-mail kontakt@ergo.de; internet www.ergo.com; f. 1997; subsidiary of Munich Re; Chair., Supervisory Bd Dr NIKOLAUS VON BOMHARD; Chair., Management Bd Dr TORSTEN OLETZKY.

Generali Versicherungen: Adenauerring 7, 81737 München; e-mail service.de@generali.com; internet www.generali.de; subsidiary of Generali Deutschland Holding AG; Chair. WINFRIED SPIES.

Gothaer Versicherungsbank Versicherungsverein AG: Arnoldipl. 1, 50969 Köln; tel. (221) 30907070; fax (221) 30907079; e-mail info@gothaer.de; internet www.gothaer.de; f. 1820; Chair., Supervisory Bd Dr WERNER GÖRG; Chair., Management Bd Dr ROLAND SCHULZ.

Haftpflicht-Unterstützungs-Kasse kraftfahrender Beamter Deutschlands AG in Coburg (HUK-COBURG): Bahnhofspl., 96450 Coburg; tel. (9561) 960; fax (9561) 963636; e-mail info@huk-coburg.de; internet www.huk.de; f. 1933; CEO Dr WOLFGANG WEILER.

HDI Versicherung AG: HDI Pl. 1, 30659 Hannover; tel. (511) 3031444; fax (511) 6451152916; e-mail sach.vertrag@hdi.de; internet www.hdi.de; f. 1903; name changed 2012.

HDI-Gerling Industrie Versicherung AG: HDI Pl. 1, 30659 Hannover; tel. (511) 6450; fax (511) 6454545; e-mail info@hdi-gerling.de; internet www.hdi-gerling.de; f. 2001; Chair. Dr CHRISTIAN HINSCH.

HDI-Gerling Lebensversicherung AG: Charles de Gaulle Platz 1, 50679 Köln; tel. (221) 1445599; fax (221) 1443833; e-mail leben.service@hdi-gerling.de; internet www.hdi-gerling.com; f. 1918; Chair. HEINZ-PETER ROß.

IDUNA Vereinigte Lebensversicherung AG für Handwerk, Handel und Gewerbe: Neue Rabenstr. 15–19, 20354 Hamburg; tel. (40) 41240; fax (40) 41242958; e-mail info@signal-iduna.de; internet www.signal-iduna.de; f. 1906; part of Signal Iduna Group; Chair., Supervisory Bd REINHOLD SCHULTE; Chair., Managing Bd ULRICH LEITERMANN.

LVM Versicherungen: Kolde-Ring 21, 48126 Münster; tel. (251) 7020; fax (251) 7021099; e-mail info@lvm.de; internet www.lvm.de; f. 1896; Chair. JOCHEN BORCHERT; Gen. Man. JOCHEN HERWIG.

R + V Versicherung-AG Reinsurance: Raiffeisenplatz 1, 65189 Wiesbaden; tel. (800) 5331112; fax (611) 5334500; e-mail ruv@ruv.de; internet www.ruv.de; f. 1935; all classes of reinsurance; Chair. Dr FRIEDRICH CASPERS.

SIGNAL Krankenversicherung AG: Joseph-Scherer-Str. 3, 44139 Dortmund; tel. (231) 1357991; fax (231) 1354638; e-mail info@signal-iduna.de; internet www.signal-iduna.de; f. 1907; part of Signal Iduna Group; Chair., Supervisory Bd REINHOLD SCHULTE; Chair., Managing Bd ULRICH LEITERMANN.

Talanx AG: Riethorst 2, 30659 Hannover; tel. (511) 37470; fax (511) 37472525; e-mail info@talanx.com; internet www.talanx.com; f. 1996; owned by HDI; Chair., Supervisory Bd WOLF-DIETER BAUMGARTL; CEO HERBERT K. HAAS.

Württembergische AG Versicherungs-Beteiligungsgesellschaft: Gutenbergstr. 30, 70176 Stuttgart; tel. (711) 6620; fax (711) 662822520; e-mail keu@wuerttembergische.de; internet www.wuerttembergische.de; f. 1828; Chair., Supervisory Bd ALEXANDER ERDLAND; Chair., Management Bd NORBERT HEINEN.

Reinsurance

DARAG Deutsche Versicherungs- und Rückversicherungs-AG: Hafenstr. 32, 22880 Wedel; tel. (41) 370160; fax (41) 37016179; e-mail info@darag.de; internet www.darag.de; f. 1958; re-formed 1990; fire and non-life, technical, cargo transport, marine hull, liability, aviation insurance and reinsurance; Chair., Supervisory Bd GÜNTHER SKRZYPEK; Chair., Management Bd ARNDT GOSSMANN.

Deutsche Rückversicherung AG: Postfach 290110, 40528 Düsseldorf; Hansaallee 177, 40549 Düsseldorf; tel. (211) 455401; fax (211) 4554199; e-mail info@deutscherueck.de; internet www.deutscherueck.de; f. 1951; Chair., Supervisory Bd Dr FRANK WALTHES; Gen. Man. Dr ARNO JUNKE.

General Reinsurance AG: Theodor-Heuss-Ring 11, 50668 Köln; tel. (221) 97380; fax (221) 9738494; e-mail askgenre@genre.com;

internet www.genre.com; f. 1846; acquired by General Re in 2009; name changed as above in 2010; Chair. FRANKLIN MONTROSS, IV.

Hamburger Internationale Rückversicherung AG: Postfach 1161, 25452 Rellingen; Halstenbeker Weg 96A, 25462 Rellingen; tel. (4101) 4710; fax (4101) 471298; f. 1965; Chair., Exec. Bd Dr WOLFGANG EILERS.

Hannover Rück SE: Postfach 610369, 30603 Hannover; Karl-Wiechert-Allee 50, 30625 Hannover; tel. (511) 56040; fax (511) 56041188; e-mail info@hannover-re.com; internet www .hannover-re.com; f. 1966; Chair., Supervisory Bd HERBERT K. HAAS; Chair., Management Bd ULRICH WALLIN.

Münchener Rückversicherungs-Gesellschaft AG (Munich RE): Königinstr. 107, 80802 München; tel. (89) 38910; fax (89) 399056; internet www.munichre.com; f. 1880; all classes of reinsurance; Chair. Dr NIKOLAUS VON BOMHARD.

Swiss Re Germany AG: Dieselstr. 11, 85774 Unterföhring bei München; tel. (89) 38440; fax (89) 38442279; e-mail info.srmuc@ swissre.com; internet www.swissre.com; Chair. Dr WALTER B. KIELHOLZ; Gen. Man. MICHEL M. LIÈS.

Principal Insurance Association

Gesamtverband der Deutschen Versicherungswirtschaft eV (German Insurance Asscn): Wilhelmstr. 43/43G, 10117 Berlin; tel. (30) 20205000; fax (30) 20206000; e-mail berlin@gdv.de; internet www.gdv.de; f. 1948; affiliating 1 mem. asscn and 470 mem. cos; Pres. Dr ALEXANDER ERDLAND; CEO Dr JÖRG VON FÜRSTENWERTH.

Trade and Industry

GOVERNMENT AGENCIES

Bundesverband Grosshandel, Aussenhandel, Dienstleistungen eV (Federation of German Wholesale, Foreign Trade and Services): Am Weidendamm 1A, 10117 Berlin; tel. (30) 59000950; fax (30) 590099519; e-mail info@bga.de; internet www.bga.de; f. 1949; wholesale, foreign trade and services sector; Man. Dir GERHARD HANDKE; 79 mem. asscns.

Finanzmarktstabilisierungsanstalt (Financial Market Stabilization Agency): Taunusanlage 6, 60329 Frankfurt a.M.; tel. (69) 23883000; fax (69) 9566509090; e-mail info@soffin.de; internet www .soffin.de; f. Oct. 2008 by Federal Govt to manage a stabilization fund; provides emergency funding for financial institutions; may grant up to €400m. to guarantee debt securities and liabilities, and up to €10m. for recapitalization; Chair., Management Cttee Dr CHRISTOPHER PLEISTER.

Germany Trade & Invest GmbH: Friedrichstr. 60, 10117 Berlin; tel. (30) 2000990; fax (30) 200099111; e-mail office@gtai.com; internet www.gtai.com; f. 2009 following merger of Bundesagentur für Aussenwirtschaft with Invest in Germany GmbH; promoted by Federal Ministry of Economics and Energy; Chair. and Co-CEO Dr BENNO BUNSE; Co-CEO Dr JÜRGEN FRIEDRICH.

Hauptverband des Deutschen Einzelhandels eV: Am Weidendamm 1A, 10117 Berlin; tel. (30) 7262500; fax (30) 72625099; e-mail hde@einzelhandel.de; internet www.einzelhandel.de; f. 1919; Chair. JOSEF SANKTJOHANSER; Exec. Dir STEFAN GENTH.

Der Mittelstandsverbund—ZGV eV: Am Weidendamm 1A, 10117 Berlin; tel. (30) 590099618; fax (30) 59099617; e-mail info@ mittelstandsverbund.de; internet www.mittelstandsverbund.de; f. 1992; Pres. WILFRIED HOLLMANN; c. 320 mems.

CHAMBERS OF COMMERCE

Deutscher Industrie- und Handelkammerstag eV (DIHK) (Association of German Chambers of Commerce and Industry): Breite Str. 29, 10178 Berlin; tel. (30) 203080; fax (30) 203081000; e-mail info@dihk.de; internet www.dihk.de; Pres. ERIC SCHWEITZER; Chief Exec. Dr MARTIN WANSLEBEN; affiliates 80 Chambers of Commerce and Industry.

There are Chambers of Industry and Commerce in all the principal towns and also 13 regional associations including:

Arbeitsgemeinschaft Hessischer Industrie- und Handelskammern: Börsenpl. 4, 60313 Frankfurt a.M.; tel. (69) 21971384; fax (69) 21971448; e-mail info@ihk-hessen.de; internet www .ihk-hessen.de; Chair. MATHIAS MÜLLER; Man. Dir MATTHIAS GRÄSSLE; 10 mems.

Arbeitsgemeinschaft Norddeutscher Industrie- und Handelskammern eV (IHK Nord): Adolphspl. 1, 20457 Hamburg; tel. (40) 36138459; fax (40) 36138553; e-mail info@ihk-nord.de; internet www.ihk-nord.de; Chair. OLAF KAHLE.

Baden-Württembergischer Industrie- und Handelskammertag: Jägerstr. 40, 70174 Stuttgart; tel. (711) 22550060; fax (711) 22550077; e-mail info@bw.ihk.de; internet www.bw.ihk.de; Pres. Dr PETER KULITZ; Man. Dir Dr MICHAEL ALPERT.

Bayerischer Industrie- und Handelskammertag eV (BIHK): Balanstr. 55–59, 81541 München; tel. (89) 51160; fax (89) 51161240; e-mail info@bihk.de; internet www.bihk.de; f. 1909; Pres. Prof. Dr EBERHARD SASSE; Chief Exec. Dr MANFRED GÖSSL; c. 950,000 mems.

IHK-Arbeitsgemeinschaft Rheinland-Pfalz: Schlossstr. 2, 56068 Koblenz; tel. (261) 1060; fax (261) 106234; e-mail service@ koblenz.ihk.de; internet www.ihk-arbeitsgemeinschaft-rlp.de; Pres. PETER ADRIAN; four mems.

IHK Industrie- und Handelskammer Erfurt: Arnstädter Str. 34, 99096 Erfurt; tel. (361) 34840; fax (361) 3485950; e-mail info@erfurt .ihk.de; internet www.erfurt.ihk.de; f. 1991; Pres. DIETER BAUHAUS.

IHK Schleswig-Holstein: Bergstr. 2, 24103 Kiel; tel. (431) 51940; fax (431) 5194234; e-mail ihk@kiel.ihk.de; internet www .ihk-schleswig-holstein.de; Chair. FRIEDERIKE C. KÜHN; Man. Dir PETER MICHAEL STEIN.

Industrie- und Handelskammer Chemnitz: Str. der Nationen 25, 09111 Chemnitz; Postfach 464, 09004 Chemnitz; tel. (371) 69000; fax (371) 6900191565; e-mail chemnitz@chemnitz.ihk.de; internet www.chemnitz.ihk24.de; Pres. FRANZ VOIGT.

Industrie- und Handelskammer Hannover: Schiffgraben 49, 30175 Hannover; tel. (511) 31070; fax (511) 3107333; e-mail info@ hannover.ihk.de; internet www.hannover.ihk.de; f. 1899; Pres. Dr HANNES REHM; Man. Dir Dr HORST SCHRAGE.

Industrie- und Handelskammer Magdeburg: Alter Markt 8, 39104 Magdeburg; tel. (391) 56930; fax (391) 5693193; e-mail kammer@magdeburg.ihk.de; internet www.magdeburg.ihk.de; f. 1825; Pres. KLAUS OLBRICHT.

Industrie- und Handelskammern in Nordrhein-Westfalen eV: Marienstr. 8, 40212 Düsseldorf; tel. (211) 367020; fax (211) 3670221; e-mail info@ihk-nrw.de; internet www.ihk-nrw.de; Pres. PAUL BAUWENS-ADENAUER; Chief Exec. Dr RALF MITTELSTÄDT; 16 mems.

Industrie- und Handelskammer Potsdam: Breite Str. 2A–C, 14467 Potsdam; tel. (331) 27860; fax (331) 2786111; e-mail info@ potsdam.ihk.de; internet www.potsdam.ihk24.de; f. 1990; public; Pres. BEATE FERNENGEL; CEO Dr MANFRED WÄSCHE; 72,000 mem. cos.

Industrie- und Handelskammer zu Schwerin: Ludwig-Bölkow-Haus, Graf-Schack-Allee 12, 19053 Schwerin; tel. (385) 51030; fax (385) 5103999; e-mail info@schwerin.ihk.de; internet www .ihkzuschwerin.de; Pres. HANS THON; Man. Dir SIEGBERT EISENACH.

INDUSTRIAL AND TRADE ASSOCIATIONS

Bundesverband der Deutschen Industrie eV (BDI) (Federation of German Industry): Breite Str. 29, 10178 Berlin; tel. (30) 20280; fax (30) 20282450; e-mail info@bdi.eu; internet www.bdi.eu; Pres. ULRICH GRILLO; Dir-Gen. Dr MARKUS KERBER; 83 mems.

BDI-Bundesverband Baustoffe -Steine und Erden eV (BBS) (Building Materials): Kochstr. 6–7, 10969 Berlin; tel. (30) 72619990; fax (30) 726199912; e-mail info@bvbaustoffe.de; internet www .baustoffindustrie.de; f. 1948; Pres. ANDREAS KERN.

BDI-Bundesverband der Deutschen Entsorgungs-, Wasser- und Rohstoffwirtschaft eV (BDE) (Waste Disposal, Water Management and Raw Material Management): Behrenstr. 29, 10117 Berlin; tel. (30) 59003350; fax (30) 590033599; e-mail info@bde-berlin .de; internet www.bde-berlin.de; f. 1961; Pres. PETER KURTH; Dir-Gen. Dr ANDREAS BRUCKSCHEN.

BDI-Bundesvereinigung der Deutschen Ernährungsindustrie eV (BVE) (Food): Claire-Waldorf-Str. 7, 10117 Berlin; tel. (30) 2007860; fax (30) 200786299; e-mail bve@bve-online.de; internet www.bve-online.de; f. 1949; Chair. Dr WOLFGANG INGOLD; Chief Exec. CHRISTOPH MINHOFF.

BDI-Bundesverband der Deutschen Gießerei-Industrie (BDG) (Foundries): Hansaallee 203, 40549 Düsseldorf; tel. (211) 68710; fax (211) 6871333; e-mail info@bdguss.de; internet www .bdguss.de; f. 1865; Pres. Dr ERWIN FLENDER; Man. Dir MAX SCHUMACHER.

BDI-Bundesverband der Deutschen Luft- und Raumfahrtindustrie eV (BDLI) (German Aerospace Industries Asscn): Friedrichstr. 60, 10117 Berlin; tel. (30) 2061400; fax (30) 20614090; e-mail kontakt@bdli.de; internet www.bdli.de; f. 1955; Pres. BERNHARD GERWERT; Man. Dir DIETMAR SCHRICK; c. 215 mems.

BDI-Bundesverband Glasindustrie eV (Glass): Am Bonneshof 5, 40474 Düsseldorf; Postfach 101753, 40008 Düsseldorf; tel. (211) 4796134; fax (211) 9513751; e-mail info@bvglas.de; internet www .bvglas.de; Chair. Prof. HANS-JOACHIM KONZ; 400 mem. asscns.

BDI-Bundesverband Keramische Industrie eV (Ceramics): Schillerstr. 17, 95100 Selb; Postfach 1624, 95090 Selb; tel. (9287) 8080; fax (9287) 70492; e-mail info@keramverbaende.de; internet www .keramverbaende.de; Pres. ROLF-MICHAEL MÜLLER.

BDI-Bundesverband Schmuck und Uhren eV (Jewellery, Timepieces and Silverware): Poststr. 1, 75172 Pforzheim; tel. (7231)

1455510; fax (7231) 1455521; e-mail info@bv-schmuck-uhren.de; internet www.bv-schmuck-uhren.de; Pres. Dr UWE STAIB; Man. Dir THILO BRÜCKNER.

BDI-Gesamtverband der deutschen Textil- und Modeindustrie eV (Textiles and Clothing): Reinhardtstr. 12–14, 10117 Berlin; tel. (30) 7262200; fax (30) 72622044; e-mail info@textil-mode.de; internet www.textil-mode.de; f. 1948; Pres. INGEBORG NEUMANN; Dir-Gen. Dr UWE MAZURA.

BDI-Mineralölwirtschaftsverband eV (German Petroleum Industry): Georgenstr. 25, 10117 Berlin; tel. (30) 20220530; fax (30) 20220555; e-mail info@mwv.de; internet www.mwv.de; f. 1946; Chair. MICHAEL SCHMIDT; Man. Dir Dr KLAUS PICARD.

BDI-Verband der Chemischen Industrie eV (VCI) (Chemical Industry): Mainzer Landstr. 55, 60329 Frankfurt a.M.; tel. (69) 25560; fax (69) 25561471; e-mail dialog@vci.de; internet www.vci.de; f. 1877; Pres. Dr MARIJN E. DEKKERS; Dir-Gen. Dr UTZ TILLMANN; 1,650 mems.

BDI-Verband Deutscher Papierfabriken eV (Paper): Adenauerallee 55, 53113 Bonn; tel. (228) 267050; fax (228) 2670562; internet www.vdp-online.de; Pres. Dr MORITZ J. WEIG; Dir-Gen. KLAUS WINDHAGEN.

BDI-Verband der Kali- und Salzindustrie eV (VKS) (Potash and Salt): Reinhardtstr. 18A, 10117 Berlin; Postfach 080651, 10006 Berlin; tel. (30) 84710690; fax (30) 847106921; e-mail info.berlin@vks-kalisalz.de; internet www.vks-kalisalz.de; f. 1905; Chair. NORBERT STEINER; Man. Dir HARTMUT BEHNSEN.

BDI-Verein der Zuckerindustrie (Sugar): Am Hofgarten 8, 53113 Bonn; tel. (228) 22850; fax (228) 2285100; e-mail wvz-vdz@zuckerverbaende.de; internet www.zuckerverbaende.de; f. 1850; Chair. AXEL AUMÜLLER; Dir-Gen. GÜNTER TISSEN.

BDI-Vereinigung Rohstoffe und Bergbau eV (Raw Materials and Mining): Am Schillertheater 4, 10625 Berlin; tel. (30) 3151820; fax (30) 31518235; e-mail info@v-r-b.de; internet www.v-rohstoffe-bergbau.de; f. 1953; Pres. Dr JOACHIM GEISLER; Gen. Man. Dr THORSTEN DIERCKS; 12 mem. asscns.

BDI-Wirtschaftsverband Erdöl- und Erdgasgewinnung eV (Oil and Gas Producers): Berliner Allee 26, 30175 Hannover; tel. (511) 121720; fax (511) 1217210; e-mail info@erdoel-erdgas.de; internet www.erdoel-erdgas.de; f. 1945; Pres. Dr GERNOT KALK-OFFEN; Gen. Man. JOSEF SCHMID.

BDI-Wirtschaftsverband Stahl- und Metallverarbeitung eV (WSM) (Steel and Metal-processing Industry): Uerdinger Str. 58–62, 40474 Düsseldorf; tel. (211) 95786822; fax (211) 95786840; e-mail info@wsm-net.de; internet www.wsm-net.de; Pres. Dr GERHARD BRÜNINGHAUS; Dir-Gen. CHRISTIAN VIETMEYER.

BDI-Wirtschaftsverband Stahlbau und Energietechnik (SET) (Steel and Energy): Sternstr. 36, 40479 Düsseldorf; Postfach 320420, 40419 Düsseldorf; tel. (211) 4987092; fax (211) 4987036; e-mail info@set-online.de; internet www.set-online.de; Chair. KLAUS DIETER RENNERT; Dir-Gen. R. MAASS.

BDI-Zentralverband Elektrotechnik- und Elektronikindustrie eV (ZVEI) (Electrical and Electronic Equipment): Lyoner Str. 9, 60528 Frankfurt a.M.; Postfach 710844, 60498 Frankfurt a.M.; tel. (69) 63020; fax (69) 6302317; e-mail zvei@zvei.org; internet www.zvei.org; f. 1918; Pres. MICHAEL ZIESEMER; CEO Dr KLAUS MITTELBACH; 1,400 mems.

Centralvereinigung Deutscher Wirtschaftsverbände für Handelsvermittlung und Vertrieb (Trade and Marketing): Am Weidendamm 1A, 10117 Berlin; tel. (30) 72625600; fax (30) 72625699; e-mail centralvereinigung@cdh.de; internet www.cdh.de; f. 1902; Pres. DIRK P. GOELDNER; c. 48,000 mems.

Deutscher Hotel- und Gaststättenverband eV (DEHOGA): Am Weidendamm 1A, 10117 Berlin; tel. (30) 7262520; fax (30) 72625242; e-mail info@dehoga.de; internet www.dehoga-bundesverband.de; f. 1949; Pres. ERNST FISCHER; CEO INGRID HARTGES.

GermanFashion Modeverband Deutschland eV: An Lyskirchen 14, Postfach 101865, 50676 Köln; tel. (221) 77440; fax (221) 7744137; e-mail info@germanfashion.net; internet www.germanfashion.net; Pres. GERD OLIVER SEIDENSTICKER.

Gesamtverband kunststoffverarbeitende Industrie eV (GKV) (Plastics): Kaiser-Friedrich-Promenade 43, 61348 Bad Homburg; tel. (6172) 926661; fax (6172) 926674; e-mail info@gkv.de; internet www.gkv.de; f. 1950; Chair. DIRK WESTERHEIDE; Man. Dir Dr OLIVER MÖLLENSTÄDT; 750 mems.

Hauptverband der Deutschen Bauindustrie eV (Building): Kurfürstenstr. 129, 10785 Berlin; tel. (30) 212860; fax (30) 21286240; e-mail info@bauindustrie.de; internet www.bauindustrie.de; f. 1948; Pres. Prof. THOMAS BAUER; Dir-Gen. MICHAEL KNIPPER; 23 mem. asscns.

Hauptverband der Deutschen Holz und Kunststoffe verarbeitenden Industrie und verwandter Inustriezweige eV (HDH) (Woodwork and Plastic): Flutgraben 2, 53604 Bad-Honnef;

tel. (2224) 93770; fax (2224) 937777; e-mail info@hdh-ev.de; internet www.hdh-ev.de; f. 1948; Pres. JOHANNES SCHWÖRER; Man. Dir DIRK-UWE KLAAS; 21 mem. asscns.

Hauptverband Papier- und Kunststoffverarbeitung eV (HPV) (Paper and Plastic): Chausseestr. 22, 10115 Berlin; tel. (30) 24781830; fax (30) 247818340; e-mail info@hpv-ev.org; internet www.hpv-ev.org; f. 1948; 10 regional groups, 20 production groups; Pres. Dr HEINRICH SPIES; Dir-Gen. STEFAN RÖSSING; 1,300 mems.

SPECTARIS—Deutscher Industrieverband für optische, medizinische und mechatronische Technologien eV (Optical, Medical and Mechatronical Technologies): Werderscher Markt 15, 10117 Berlin; tel. (30) 4140210; fax (30) 41402133; e-mail info@spectaris.de; internet www.spectaris.de; f. 1949; CEO Dr TOBIAS WEILER.

Verband der Automobilindustrie eV (Motor Cars): Behrenstr. 35, 10117 Berlin; Postfach 80462, 10004 Berlin; tel. (30) 8978420; fax (30) 897842600; e-mail info@vda.de; internet www.vda.de; Pres. MATTHIAS WISSMANN.

Verband Deutscher Maschinen- und Anlagenbau eV (VDMA) (German Engineering Federation): Lyoner Str. 18, 60528 Frankfurt a.M.; Postfach 710864, 60498 Frankfurt a.M.; tel. (69) 66030; fax (69) 66031511; e-mail vdma@vdma.org; internet www.vdma.org; f. 1892; Pres. Dr REINHOLD FESTGE; Gen. Man. Dr HANNES HESSE.

Verband für Schiffbau und Meerestechnik eV (German Shipbuilding and Ocean Industries Asscn): Steinhoeft 11, 20459 Hamburg; tel. (40) 2801520; fax (40) 28015230; e-mail info@vsm.de; internet www.vsm.de; f. 1884; Pres. HARALD FASSMER; Man. Dirs REINHARD LUEKEN, Dr RALF SÖREN MARQUARDT.

Wirtschaftsverband der Deutschen Kautschukindustrie eV (WDK) (Rubber): Zeppelinallee 69, 60487 Frankfurt a.M.; Postfach 900360, 60443 Frankfurt a.M.; tel. (69) 79360; fax (69) 7936140; e-mail info@wdk.de; internet www.wdk.de; f. 1894; Pres. RALF HOLSCHUMACHER; Man. Dir BORIS ENGELHARDT; c. 90 mems.

WirtschaftsVereinigung Metalle (Metal): Wallstr. 58–59, 10179 Berlin; tel. (30) 726207100; fax (30) 726207198; e-mail info@wvmetalle.de; internet www.wvmetalle.de; Pres. OLIVER BELL; Dir-Gen. MARTIN KNEER.

Wirtschaftsvereinigung Stahl (Steel): Sohnstr. 65, 40237 Düsseldorf; tel. (211) 67070; fax (211) 6707310; e-mail info@stahl-online.de; internet www.stahl-online.de; f. 1998; Pres. and CEO HANS-JÜRGEN KERKHOFF.

Zentralverband des Deutschen Handwerks: Mohrenstr. 20–21, 10117 Berlin; tel. (30) 206190; fax (30) 20619460; e-mail info@zdh.de; internet www.zdh.de; f. 1949; Pres. HANS PETER WOLLSEIFER; Gen. Sec. HOLGER SCHWANNECKE; 53 mem. chambers, 48 asscns.

EMPLOYERS' ORGANIZATIONS

Bundesvereinigung der Deutschen Arbeitgeberverbände (BDA) (Confederation of German Employers' Associations): Breite Str. 29, 10178 Berlin; tel. (30) 20330; fax (30) 20331055; e-mail bda@arbeitgeber.de; internet www.arbeitgeber.de; f. 1904; represents the professional and regional interests of German employers in the social policy field, affiliates 14 regional asscns and 52 branch asscns, of which some are listed under industrial asscns; Pres. INGO KRAMER; Man. Dir Dr REINHARD GÖHNER.

Affiliated associations:

Arbeitgeberverband der Cigarettenindustrie eV (Employers' Association of Cigarette Manufacturers): Kapstadtring 10, 22297 Hamburg; tel. (40) 63784840; fax (40) 63784842; e-mail md@adc-online.de; internet www.adc-online.de; f. 1950; Pres. MICHAEL WENZEL; Dir MICHAEL DREIER.

Arbeitgeberverband der Deutschen Binnenschiffahrt eV (Employers' Association of German Inland Waterway Transport): Dammstr. 15–17, 47119 Duisburg; Postfach 170428, 47184 Duisburg; tel. (203) 8000650; fax (203) 8000651; e-mail infobdb@binnenschiff.de; internet www.schulschiff-rhein.de; f. 1974; Pres. GEORG HÖTTE; Dir JÖRG RUSCHE.

Arbeitgeberverband der Deutschen Kautschukindustrie (ADK) eV (German Rubber Industry Employers' Association): Schiffgraben 36, 30175 Hannover; tel. (511) 85050; fax (511) 8505203; e-mail info@adk-verband.de; internet www.adk-ev.de; Pres. Dr SVEN VOGT; Gen. Man. Dr VOLKER SCHMIDT.

Arbeitgeberverband Deutscher Eisenbahnen eV (German Railway Employers' Association): Volksgartenstr. 54A, 50677 Köln; tel. (221) 9318450; fax (221) 93184588; e-mail info@agvde.de; internet www.agvde.de; Pres. DIETMAR SCHWEIZER; Dir Dr HANS-PETER ACKMANN.

Arbeitgeberverband des Privaten Bankgewerbes eV (Private Banking Employers' Association): Burgstr. 28, 10178 Berlin; tel. (30) 590011270; fax (30) 590011279; e-mail service@agvbanken.de; internet www.agvbanken.de; f. 1954; Pres. Dr STEPHAN LEITHNER; Dir Dr GERD BENRATH; 140 mems.

Arbeitgeberverband der Versicherungsunternehmen in Deutschland (Employers' Association of Insurance Companies): Arabellastr. 29, 81925 München; tel. (89) 9220010; fax (89) 92200150; e-mail agvvers@agv-vers.de; internet www.agv-vers.de; f. 1950; Pres. Dr JOSEF BEUTELMANN; Dir-Gen. Dr MICHAEL NIEBLER.

Bundesarbeitgeberverband Chemie eV (Federation of Employers' Associations in the Chemical Industry): Abraham-Lincoln-Str. 24, 65189 Wiesbaden; Postfach 1280, 65002 Wiesbaden; tel. (611) 778810; fax (611) 7788123; e-mail info@bavc.de; internet www.bavc.de; f. 1949; Pres. MARGRET SUCKALE; Dir-Gen. Dr KLAUS-PETER STILLER; 10 mem. asscns.

Bundesarbeitgeberverband Glas und Solar eV: Max-Joseph-Str. 5, 80333 München; Postfach 200219, 80002 München; tel. (89) 41119430; fax (89) 411194344; e-mail info@bagv.de; internet www.bagv.de; f. 2010; fmrly Arbeitgeberverband der Deutschen Glasindustrie eV; Pres. REINHARD RUNTE; CEO HARMS LEFNAER.

Deutscher Bauernverband eV (DBV) (German Farmers' Association): Claire-Waldoff-Str. 7, 10117 Berlin; tel. (30) 31904407; fax (30) 31904431; e-mail presse@bauernverband.net; internet www.bauernverband.de; f. 1948; Pres. JOACHIM RUKWIED; Sec.-Gen. Dr BERNHARD KRÜSKEN.

Gesamtmetall—Die Arbeitgeberverbände der Metall- und Elektro-Industrie eV (Federation of the Metal Trades Employers' Associations): Vossstr. 16, 10117 Berlin; Postfach 060249, 10052 Berlin; tel. (30) 551500; e-mail info@gesamtmetall.de; internet www.gesamtmetall.de; f. 1890; Pres. RAINER DULGER; 22 mem. asscns.

Vereinigung der Arbeitgeberverbände der Deutschen Papierindustrie eV (Federation of Employers' Associations of the German Paper Industry): Scheffelstr. 29, 76593 Gernsbach; Postfach 1232, 76585 Gernsbach; tel. (7224) 6401119; fax (7224) 6401463; e-mail vap@papierzentrum.org; internet www.vap-papier.de; Pres. MARTIN KRENGEL; CEO STEPHAN MEISSNER; 8 mem. asscns.

Vereinigung der Arbeitgeberverbände energie- und versorgungswirtschaftlicher Unternehmungen (VAEU) (Employers' Federation of Energy and Power Supply Enterprises): Theaterstr. 3, 30159 Hannover; tel. (511) 911090; fax (511) 9110940; e-mail agv.energie@t-online.de; internet www.vaeu.de; f. 1962; Pres. Dr BERNHARD BECK; Dir JOBST KLEINEBERG; 7 mem. asscns.

Regional employers' associations:

Arbeitgeber- und Wirtschaftsverbände Sachsen-Anhalt eV (AWSA) (Employers' and business associations of Saxony-Anhalt): Humboldtstr. 14, 39112 Magdeburg; Postfach 4152, 39106 Magdeburg; tel. (391) 6288819; fax (391) 6288810; e-mail info@aw-sa.de; internet www.wir-setzen-akzente.de; Pres. KLEMENS GUTMANN; 31 mem. asscns.

Landesvereinigung Baden-Württembergischer Arbeitgeberverbände eV (Baden-Württemberg Federation of Employers' Associations): Löffelstr. 22–24, 70597 Stuttgart; Postfach 700501, 70574 Stuttgart; tel. (711) 76820; fax (711) 7651675; e-mail info@agv-bw.de; internet www.agv-bw.de; f. 1951; Pres. Dr DIETER HUNDT; Dir PEER-MICHAEL DICK; 42 mem. asscns.

Landesvereinigung der Unternehmensverbände Nordrhein-Westfalen eV (North Rhine-Westphalia Federation of Employers' Associations): Uerdinger Str. 58–62, 40474 Düsseldorf; Postfach 300643, 40406 Düsseldorf; tel. (211) 45730; fax (211) 4573179; e-mail info@unternehmernrw.net; internet www.unternehmernrw.net; Pres. HORST-WERNER MAIER-HUNKE; Dir Dr LUITWIN MALLMANN; 129 mem. asscns.

Landesvereinigung Unternehmerverbände Rheinland-Pfalz eV (LVU) (Federation of Employers' Associations in the Rhineland Palatinate): Hindenburgstr. 32, 55118 Mainz; Postfach 2966, 55019 Mainz; tel. (6131) 55750; fax (6131) 557539; e-mail contact@lvu.de; internet www.lvu.de; f. 1963; Pres. Dr GERHARD F. BRAUN; CEO WERNER SIMON.

Die Unternehmensverbände im Lande Bremen eV (Federation of Employers' Associations in the Land of Bremen): Schiller Str. 10, 28195 Bremen; Postfach 100727, 28007 Bremen; tel. (421) 368020; fax (421) 3680249; e-mail info@uvhb.de; internet www.uvhb.de; Pres. INGO KRAMER; Dir CORNELIUS NEUMANN-REDLIN; 22 mem. asscns.

Unternehmerverbände Niedersachsen eV (UVN) (Federation of Employers' Associations in Lower Saxony): Schiffgraben 36, 30175 Hannover; tel. (511) 8505243; fax (511) 8505268; e-mail uvn@uvn-online.de; internet www.uvn-online.de; f. 1951; Pres. WERNER M. BAHLSEN; CEO Dr VOLKER MÜLLER; 70 mem. asscns.

UVNord—Vereinigung der Unternehmensverbände in Hamburg und Schleswig-Holstein eV (Federation of Employers' Associations in Hamburg and Schleswig-Holstein): Kapstadtring 10, 22297 Hamburg; fax (40) 63785151; e-mail froehlich@uvnord.de; internet www.uvnord.de; f. 2000; Pres. Prof. Dr ULI WACHHOLTZ; Dir Dr MICHAEL THOMAS FRÖHLICH; 71 mem. asscns.

vbw—Vereinigung der Bayerischen Wirtschaft eV (Federation of Employers' Associations in Bavaria): Max-Joseph-Str. 5, 80333 München; Postfach 202026, 80020 München; tel. (89) 55178100; fax (89) 55178111; e-mail info@vbw-bayern.de; internet www.vbw-bayern.de; Pres. ALFRED GAFFAL; Gen. Man. BERTRAM BROSSARDT; 100 mem. asscns.

Verband der Wirtschaft Thüringens eV (Association of Thuringian Management): Lossiusstr. 1, 99094 Erfurt; tel. (361) 67590; fax (361) 6759222; e-mail info@vwt.de; internet www.vwt.de; Pres. HARTMUT KOCH; Dir STEPHAN FAUTH; 36 mem. asscns.

Vereinigung der Unternehmensverbände in Berlin und Brandenburg eV (Federation of Employers' Associations in Berlin and Brandenburg): Am Schillertheater 2, 10625 Berlin; tel. (30) 310050; fax (30) 31005166; e-mail uvb@uvb-online.de; internet www.uvb-online.de; Pres. Dr UDO NIEHAGE; 60 mem. asscns.

Vereinigung der hessischen Unternehmerverbände eV (Hessian Federation of Enterprise Associations): Emil-von-Behring-Str. 4, 60439 Frankfurt a.M.; Postfach 500561, 60394 Frankfurt a.M.; tel. (69) 958080; fax (69) 95808126; e-mail info@vhu.de; internet www.vhu.de; f. 1947; Pres. Prof. DIETER WEIDEMANN; Man. Dir VOLKER FASBENDER; 69 mem. asscns.

Vereinigung der Saarländischen Unternehmensverbände eV (Federation of Employers' Associations in Saarland): Harthweg 15, 66119 Saarbrücken; Postfach 650433, 66143 Saarbrücken; tel. (681) 954340; fax (681) 9543474; e-mail kontakt@vsu.de; internet www.vsu.de; Pres. Dr OSWALD BUBEL; Dir Dr JOACHIM MALTER; 19 mem. asscns.

Vereinigung der Sächsischen Wirtschaft eV (VSW) (Federation of Employers' Associations in Saxony): Washingtonstr. 16/16A, 01139 Dresden; Postfach 300200, 01131 Dresden; tel. (351) 255930; fax (351) 2559378; e-mail vsw@hsw-mail.de; internet www.wirtschaftsverbaende-sachsen.de; f. 1998; Pres. BODO FINGER; Gen. Man. Dr ANDREAS WINKLER; 40 mem. asscns.

Vereinigung der Unternehmensverbände für Mecklenburg-Vorpommern eV (Federation of Employers' Associations of Mecklenburg-Western Pomerania): Graf-Schack-Allee 10, 19053 Schwerin; tel. (385) 6356100; fax (385) 6356151; e-mail info@vumv.de; internet www.vumv.de; Pres. THOMAS LAMBUSCH; Dir NICO FICKINGER; 27 mem. asscns.

UTILITIES

Regulatory Authority

Bundesnetzagentur für Elektrizität, Gas, Telekommunikation, Post und Eisenbahnen: see Broadcasting and Communications.

Electricity and Gas

Supply of electricity and gas is dominated by four companies (RWE, E.ON, Vattenfall Europe and EnBW). A large number of regional utilities, many of which are part-owned by the four major companies, supply electricity and gas to towns and municipalities in one or more of the federal Länder.

Energie Baden-Württemberg AG (EnBW): Durlacher Allee 93, 76131 Karlsruhe; tel. (49) 7216300; e-mail kontakt@enbw.com; internet www.enbw.com; production, distribution and supply of electricity and gas; CEO Dr FRANK MASTIAUX.

E.ON SE: E.ON-Pl. 1, 40479 Düsseldorf; tel. (211) 45790; fax (211) 4579501; e-mail info@eon.com; internet www.eon.com; f. 2000 by merger of VEBA AG and VIAG AG; production, distribution and supply of electricity and gas; operates in 19 countries worldwide; Chair. and CEO Dr JOHANNES TEYSSEN.

E.ON Energie AG: Brienner Str. 40, 80333 München; tel. and fax (89) 125401; e-mail info@eon-energie.com; internet www.eon-energie.com; f. 2000 by merger of Bayernwerk AG and Preussenelektra AG; production, transmission and supply of electricity; subsidiary of E.ON SE; Chair. INGO LUGE.

EWE AG: Tirpitzstr. 39, 26122 Oldenburg; tel. (441) 48050; fax (441) 48053999; e-mail info@ewe.de; internet www.ewe.de; f. 1943; supplier of electricity and natural gas; serves northern Germany; Chair. Management Bd Dr WERNER BRINKER.

GASAG Berliner Gaswerke AG: Henriette-Herz-Pl. 4, 10178 Berlin; tel. (30) 78720; fax (30) 78724794; e-mail service@gasag.de; internet www.gasag.de; f. 1992; regional gas supplier for Berlin; Man. Dir OLAF CZERNOMORIEZ.

GasVersorgung Süddeutschland GmbH (GVS): Schulze-Delitzsch-Str., 770565 Stuttgart; tel. (711) 78125; fax (711) 78121411; e-mail sunc@gvs-erdgas.de; internet www.gvs-erdgas.de; f. 1961; supplies gas to 750 towns and municipalities in Baden-Württemberg; CEO MAURO RINAUDO.

Mainova AG: Solmsstr. 38, 60623 Frankfurt a.M.; tel. (69) 21302; fax (69) 21381122; internet www.mainova.de; f. 1998 by merger of Stadtwerke Frankfurt and Maingas AG; supply of electricity, natural gas and water in Frankfurt am Main and surrounding area; 75.2% owned by Frankfurt a.M. city administration, 24.4% owned by Thüga AG; Chair. and CEO Dr CONSTANTIN H. ALSHEIMER.

MITGAS Mitteldeutsche Gasversorgung GmbH: Industriestr. 10, 06184 Halle (Saale); Postfach 300552, 06025 Halle (Saale); tel. (34605) 60; fax (34605) 61610; e-mail service@mitgas.de; internet www.mitgas.de; f. 2000; regional gas supplier with customers in Saxony, Saxony-Anhalt and Thuringia; 24.60% owned by VNG-Beteiligungs-GmbH; Man. Dirs CARL-ERNST GIESTING, Dr ANDREAS AUERBACH.

RWE Vertrieb AG: Opernpl. 1, 45128 Essen; Postfach 103061, 45030 Essen; tel. (201) 1200; internet www.rwe.de; f. 1898; production, distribution and supply of electricity, gas and water; subsidiaries in 6 European countries (Czech Republic, Hungary, the Netherlands, Poland, Slovakia, the UK) and the USA; Chair. Dr MANFRED SCHNEIDER; CEO PETER TERIUM.

swb AG: Theodor-Heuss-Allee 20, 28215 Bremen; tel. (421) 3590; fax (421) 3592499; e-mail info@swb-gruppe.de; internet www.swb-gruppe.de; f. 1854; supplies electricity, natural gas and water in Bremen and northern Germany; 100% owned by EWE AG; CEO Dr TORSTEN KÖHNE.

Vattenfall Europe AG: Chausseestr. 23, 10115 Berlin; tel. (30) 818222; fax (30) 81823950; e-mail info@vattenfall.de; internet www.vattenfall.de; f. 2002 by merger of Bewag, HEW, LAUBAG and VEAG; production, distribution and supply of electricity; Chair., Management Bd TUOMO J. HATAKKA.

WINGAS GmbH & Co KG: Friedrich-Ebert-Str. 160, 34119 Kassel; Postfach 104020, 34112 Kassel; tel. (561) 3010; fax (561) 3011702; e-mail info@wingas.de; internet www.wingas.de; f. 1993; distribution of natural gas; also supplies gas to public utilities, regional gas suppliers, industrial facilities and power plants; jt venture of Wintershall Holding AG and Gazprom (Russia); Chair. Dr GERHARD KÖNIG.

Water

Responsibility for water supply lies with the municipalities. As a result, there are over 6,000 water supply utilities in Germany. The ownership structures of those utilities are diverse. Many municipalities have formed limited or joint-stock companies with private sector partners to manage water supply, such as the supplier for the capital (Berliner Wasserbetriebe), while others have contracted private companies to provide water services.

Berliner Wasserbetriebe: Neue Jüdenstr. 1, 10179 Berlin; fax (30) 86442810; e-mail info@bwb.de; internet www.bwb.de; f. 1856; merger in 1988 of Berliner Wasserwerke and Berliner Entwässerungswerke; supplier of water and sanitation services to Berlin; subsidiary of Berlinerwasser Gruppe (50.1% owned by Berlin regional Govt, 24.95% each by RWE Vertrieb AG and Veolia Environment (France); Chair., Management Bd JÖRG SIMON.

Gelsenwasser AG: Willy-Brandt-Allee 26, 45891 Gelsenkirchen; tel. (209) 7080; fax (209) 708650; e-mail info@gelsenwasser.de; internet www.gelsenwasser.de; privately owned enterprise, supplying water and sanitation services by agreement with several municipalities in North Rhine-Westphalia and across Germany; also supplies electricity and gas; Chair., Management Bd HENNING R. DETERS.

Association

Bundesverband der Energie- und Wasserwirtschaft eV (BDEW) (German Association of Energy and Water Companies): Reinhardtstr. 32, 10117 Berlin; tel. (30) 3001990; fax (30) 3001993900; e-mail info@bdew.de; internet www.bdew.de; f. 2007; Pres. JOHANNES KEMPMANN; Chair., Management Bd HILDEGARD MÜLLER; c. 1,800 mems.

TRADE UNIONS

The main German trade union federations are the Deutscher Gewerkschaftsbund (DGB), the dbb beamtenbund und tarifunion and the Christlicher Gewerkschaftsbund Deutschlands (CGB). Following German unification in October 1990, the trade unions of the former GDR were absorbed into the member unions of the DGB.

National Federations

Christlicher Gewerkschaftsbund Deutschlands (Christian Workers' Union—CGB): Obentrautstr. 57, 10963 Berlin; Postfach 610212, 10923 Berlin; tel. (30) 21021730; fax (30) 21021740; e-mail cgb.bund@cgb.info; internet www.cgb.info; f. 1899; 14 affiliated unions; Pres. MATTHÄUS STREBL; Gen. Sec. CHRISTIAN HERTZOG; c. 280,000 mems.

dbb beamtenbund und tarifunion (Civil Servants' Federation): Friedrichstr. 169–170, 10117 Berlin; tel. (30) 408140; fax (30) 40814999; e-mail post@dbb.de; internet www.dbb.de; f. 1918; 43 affiliated unions; Pres. KLAUS DAUDERSTÄDT; c. 1.27m. mems (2014).

Deutscher Gewerkschaftsbund (DGB): Henriette-Herz-Pl. 2, 10178 Berlin; tel. (30) 240600; fax (30) 24060324; e-mail info.bvv@dgb.de; internet www.dgb.de; f. 1949; 8 affiliated unions; Pres. REINER HOFFMANN; Vice-Pres. ELKE HANNACK; 6,142,720 mems (2013).

Transport

RAILWAYS

At 2011 the length of railway lines in use in Germany was 33,576 km, of which 19,826 km were electrified. High-speed InterCity Express (ICE) trains operate between several German cities, and offer links to Austria (Vienna and Innsbruck), Belgium (Brussels and Liège), Denmark (Copenhagen and Arhus), France (Paris and Marseille), the Netherlands (Arnhem, Utrecht and Amsterdam) and Switzerland (Zürich and Interlaken); plans to offer a direct ICE service from London to Frankfurt were subject to delays and the service was not expected to operate before 2016. High-speed trains operated by Thalys link Cologne with Paris, Brussels and Amsterdam.

Regulatory Bodies

Eisenbahn-Bundesamt (EBA) (Federal Railway Authority): Heinemannstr. 6, 53175 Bonn; tel. (228) 98260; fax (228) 9826199; e-mail poststelle@eba.bund.de; internet www.eba.bund.de; supervisory and authorizing body; ensures safety of railway passengers; supervises construction; inspects and approves rolling stock and monitors safe condition of railway infrastructure and signalling; Pres. GERALD HÖRSTER.

Bundeseisenbahnvermögen (BEV) (Federal Railroad Assets): Kurt-Georg-Kiesinger-Allee 2, 53175 Bonn; tel. (228) 30770; fax (228) 3077160; e-mail bonn@bev.bund.de; internet www.bev.bund.de; Pres. MARIE-THERES NONN.

Federal Railway

Deutsche Bahn AG (German Railways): Potsdamer Pl. 2, 10785 Berlin; tel. (1805) 996633; fax (30) 29761919; e-mail medienbetreuung@bku.db.de; internet www.deutschebahn.com; f. 1994 by merger of Deutsche Bundesbahn and Deutsche Reichsbahn; state-owned; CEO and Chair., Management Bd RÜDIGER GRUBE; Chair., Supervisory Bd Dr UTZ-HELLMUTH FELCHT.

Metropolitan Railways

Berliner Verkehrsbetriebe (BVG) (Berlin Transport Authority): Anstalt des öffentlichen Rechts, Holzmarktstr. 15–17, 10179 Berlin; tel. (30) 19449; fax (30) 25649256; e-mail info@bvg.de; internet www.bvg.de; f. 1929; operates 144.9 km of underground railway; also runs tram and bus services; Chair., Management Bd Dr SIGRID EVELYN NIKUTTA.

Hamburger Hochbahn AG: Steinstr. 20, 20095 Hamburg; tel. (40) 32880; fax (40) 326406; e-mail info@hochbahn.de; internet www.hochbahn.de; f. 1911; operates 104.7 km of underground railway on 4 lines; also operates 120 bus routes; Chair., Management Bd GÜNTER ELSTE; Chair., Supervisory Bd FRANK HORCH.

Münchner Verkehrsgesellschaft mbH (MVG): Emmy-Noether-Str. 2, 80287 München; tel. (89) 21910; fax (89) 21912378; e-mail lobundtadel@mvg.swm.de; internet www.mvg-mobil.de; subsidiary of Stadtwerke München GmbH; operates underground railway (6 lines totalling 91 km), tramway (10 lines totalling 71 km), 67 bus lines (452 km); Chair., Management Bd HERBERT KÖNIG.

VAG Verkehrs-Aktiengesellschaft: 90338 Nürnberg; Südliche Fürther Str. 5, 90429 Nürnberg; tel. (911) 2830; fax (911) 2834800; e-mail service@vag.de; internet www.vag.de; wholly owned subsidiary of Städtische Werke Nürnberg GmbH; operates underground railway (3 lines totalling 31 km), tramway (5 lines totalling 34 km) and bus services (53 routes); Chair., Management Bd JOSEF HASLER; Chair., Supervisory Bd Dr MICHAEL REINDL.

Association

Verband Deutscher Verkehrsunternehmen (VDV) (Association of German Transport Undertakings): Kamekestr. 37–39, 50672 Köln; tel. (221) 579790; fax (221) 57979-8000; e-mail info@vdv.de; internet www.vdv.de; f. 1895; public transport, freight transport by rail; publishes *Der Nahverkehr* (10 a year), *Bus + Bahn* (monthly) and *Güterbahnen* (quarterly); Pres. JÜRGEN FENSKE; Exec. Dir OLIVER WOLFF.

ROADS

In 2012 there were 12,879 km of motorway, 39,604 km of highways and 178,034 km of secondary roads in a total road network of 643,517 km.

INLAND WATERWAYS

The inland waterways network in Germany centres around the Rhine, Danube and Elbe rivers. The Main–Danube Canal linking the North Sea and the Black Sea was opened in 1992. There were around 7,675 km of navigable inland waterways in 2012. Inland shipping accounts for about 12.1% of total freight traffic.

Associations

Bundesverband der Deutschen Binnenschiffahrt eV (BDB): Dammstr. 15–17, 47119 Duisburg; tel. (203) 8000650; fax (203) 8000621; e-mail infobdb@binnenschiff.de; internet www.binnenschiff.de; f. 1978; central Inland Waterway Association to further the interests of operating firms; Pres. GEORG HÖTTE; Man. Dirs JENS SCHWANEN, JÖRG RUSCHE.

Bundesverband Öffentlicher Binnenhäfen eV: Leipziger Pl. 8, 10117 Berlin; tel. (30) 39881981; fax (30) 340608553; e-mail info-boeb@binnenhafen.de; internet www.binnenhafen.de; Pres. RAINER SCHÄFER; Man. Dir BORIS KLUGE.

Bundesverband der Selbstständigen Abteilung Binnenschiffahrt eV (BDS): August-Bier-Str. 18, 53129 Bonn; tel. (228) 746337; fax (228) 746569; e-mail zentrale@bds-binnenschiffahrt.de; internet www.bds-binnenschiffahrt.de; Man. Dir ANDREA BECKSCHÄFER.

Deutsche Binnenreederei AG: Revaler Str. 100, 10245 Berlin; tel. (30) 293760; fax (30) 29376201; e-mail dbr@binnenreederei.de; internet www.binnenreederei.de; f. 1949; Dir-Gen. PIOTR CHAJDER-OWSKI.

Unternehmensverband Hafen Hamburg eV: Mattentwiete 2, 20457 Hamburg; tel. (40) 3789090; fax (40) 37890970; e-mail info@uvhh.de; internet www.uvhh.de; Pres. GUNTHER BONZ.

Verein für europäische Binnenschiffahrt und Wasserstraßen eV (VBW): Dammstr. 15–17, 47119 Duisburg; tel. (203) 8000627; fax (203) 8000628; e-mail info@vbw-ev.de; internet www.vbw-ev.de; f. 1877; represents all brs of the inland waterways; Pres. HEINZ-JOSEF JOERIS.

SHIPPING

The port of Hamburg is the largest in Germany and the third largest in Europe. Other principal ports are Bremerhaven, Rostock-Überseehafen and Wilhelmshaven. At 31 December 2014 the flag registered fleet totalled 1,165 vessels, with a combined displacement of 11.7m. grt, of which 175 were general cargo ships and 98 were fishing vessels. Some important shipping companies are:

Argo Shipping GmbH: Postfach 107529, 28075 Bremen; Am Wall 187–189, 28195 Bremen; tel. (421) 2575184; fax (421) 2575432; e-mail argoshipping@argo-adler.de; internet www.argo-adler.de; f. 1896; shipowners; Propr MAX ADLER.

Aug. Bolten, Wm. Miller's Nachfolger GmbH & Co KG: Postfach 112269; Mattentwiete 8, 20457 Hamburg; tel. (40) 36010; fax (40) 3601423; e-mail info@aug-bolten.de; internet www.aug-bolten.de; shipowner, manager and broker, port agent; Man. Dirs OLE KRAFT, MICHAEL SAY.

Bugsier- Reederei- und Bergungs-Gesellschaft mbH & Co: Johannisbollwerk 10, 20459 Hamburg; tel. (40) 311110; fax (40) 313693; e-mail info@bugsier.de; internet www.bugsier.de; salvage, towage, tugs, ocean-going heavy lift cranes, submersible pontoons, harbour tugs; Man. Dirs J. W. SCHUCHMANN, HAJO SCHUCHMANN.

Christian F. Ahrenkiel GmbH & Co KG: An der Alster 45, 20099 Hamburg; tel. (40) 248380; fax (40) 24838375; e-mail info@ahrenkiel .net; internet www.ahrenkiel.net; f. 1950; shipowners, operators and managers; Man. Dirs KLAUS G. WOLFF, OLAF STAATS.

DAL Deutsche Afrika-Linien/John T. Essberger GmbH & Co KG: Palmaille 45, 22767 Hamburg; tel. (40) 380160; fax (40) 38016629; e-mail info@rantzau.de; internet www.dal.biz; Europe and South Africa; Man. Dirs HARTMUT LÜHR, Dr E. VON RANTZAU, H. VON RANTZAU.

Deutsche Seereederei GmbH: Lange Str. 1A, 18055 Rostock; tel. (381) 4584043; fax (381) 4584001; e-mail info@deutsche-seereederei .de; internet www.deutsche-seereederei.do; shipping, tourism, real estate, industry and finance; Man. Dirs ARNO PÖKER, MICHAEL WESTENBERGER.

Ernst Russ GmbH: Alsterufer 10, 20354 Hamburg; tel. (40) 414070; fax (40) 41407111; e-mail info@ernst-russ.de; internet www .ernst-russ.de; f. 1893; worldwide.

F. Laeisz Schiffahrtsgesellschaft mbH & Co KG: Postfach 111111, 20411 Hamburg; Trostbrücke 1, 20457 Hamburg; tel. (40) 368080; fax (40) 364876; e-mail info@laeisz.de; internet www.laeisz .de; f. 1983; CEO NIKOLAUS H. SCHÜES.

Hamburg Südamerikanische Dampfschiffahrts-Gesellschaft KG: Postfach 111533, 20415 Hamburg; Willy-Brandt-Str. 59–61, 20457 Hamburg; tel. (40) 37050; fax (40) 37052400; e-mail central@ ham.hamburgsud.com; internet www.hamburgsud.com; f. 1871; worldwide services; Chair. Dr OTTMAR GAST.

Hapag-Lloyd AG: Ballindamm 25, 20095 Hamburg; tel. (40) 30010; fax (40) 336432; e-mail info.de@hlag.com; internet www.hapag-lloyd .com; f. 1970; 61.6% stake owned by Albert Ballin consortium (comprising city of Hamburg, Kühne Holding AG, Signal Iduna, HSH Nordbank, M.M. Warburg Bank and HanseMerkur); 38.4% stake owned by TUI AG; Chair. MICHAEL BEHRENDT.

John T. Essberger GmbH & Co KG: Palmaille 45, 22767 Hamburg; tel. (40) 380160; fax (40) 38016629; e-mail info@rantzau.de; internet www.essberger.biz; f. 1924; Man. Dirs Dr E. VON RANTZAU, H. VON RANTZAU, HARTMUT LÜHR.

KG Fisser & v. Doornum GmbH & Co: Bernhard-Nocht-Str. 113, 20359 Hamburg; tel. (40) 441860; fax (40) 4108050; e-mail management@fissership.com; internet www.fissership.com; f. 1879; tramping services; Man. Dirs Dr MICHAEL FISSER, SVEN HEYMANN.

Oldenburg-Portugiesische Dampfschiffs-Rhederei GmbH & Co KG (OPDR): Kajen 10, 20459 Hamburg; tel. (40) 361580; fax (40) 364431; e-mail info@opdr.de; internet www.opdr.de; f. 1882; Gibraltar, Spain, Portugal, Madeira, North Africa, Canary Islands; Man. Dirs TILL OLE BARRELET, MARK WILKINSON.

Oldendorff Carriers GmbH & Co KG: Postfach 2135, 23509 Lübeck; Willy-Brandt-Allee 6, 235544 Lübeck; tel. (451) 15000; fax (451) 73522; internet www.oldendorff.com; fmrly Egon Oldendorff; Chair. HENNING OLDENDORFF; CEO PETER TWISS.

Peter Döhle Schiffahrts-KG: Elbchaussee 370, 22609 Hamburg; tel. (40) 381080; fax (40) 38108255; e-mail pd-info@doehle.de; internet www.doehle.de; f. 1956; shipbrokers, chartering agent, shipowners; Pres. JOCHEN DÖHLE.

Rhenus Maritime Services GmbH (RMS): Krausstr. 1A, 47119 Duisburg; tel. (203) 8040; fax (203) 804330; e-mail info.rms@de .rhenus.com; internet www.rheinmaas.de; f. 1948; CEO THOMAS MAAßEN, THOMAS ULLRICH.

Sloman Neptun Schiffahrts-AG: Posttach 101469, 28014 Bremen; Langenstr. 44, 28195 Bremen; tel. (421) 17630; fax (421) 1763321; e-mail info@sloman-neptun.com; internet www.sloman-neptun.com; f. 1873; liner services from Northern Europe and Mediterranean to North Africa; gas carriers; agencies; Mans SVEN-MICHAEL EDYE, DIRK LOHMANN

Walther Möller & Co: Gr. Elbstr. 14, 22767 Hamburg; tel. (40) 3803910; fax (40) 38039199; e-mail info@wmco.de; internet www .wmco.de; f. 1941; Man. Dir LARS PETZ.

Shipping Organizations

Verband Deutscher Reeder eV (German Shipowners' Association): Burchardstr. 24, 20095 Hamburg; Esplanade 6, 20354 Hamburg; tel. (40) 350970; fax (40) 35097211; e-mail vdr@reederverband .de; internet www.reederverband.de; f. 1907; Pres. MICHAEL BEHRENDT; CEO RALF NAGEL.

Zentralverband der Deutschen Seehafenbetriebe eV (Federal Association of German Seaport Operators): Am Sandtorkai 2, 20457 Hamburg; tel. (40) 366203; fax (40) 366377; e-mail info@ zds-seehaefen.de; internet www.zds-seehaefen.de; f. 1934; Chair. KLAUS DIETER PETERS; 190 mems.

CIVIL AVIATION

There are two international airports in the Berlin region (a third, Tempelhof airport, closed in October 2008) and further international airports at Dresden, Düsseldorf, Frankfurt, Hamburg, Hannover, Köln-Bonn, Leipzig, München and Stuttgart. Construction of a major new international airport at Schönefeld, south-east of Berlin, to be known as Berlin Brandenburg Willy Brandt Airport, commenced in 2007 but was subject to lengthy delays; at early 2015 no official opening date had yet been announced.

Air Berlin GmbH & Co Luftverkehrs KG: Saatwinkler Damm 42-43, 13627 Berlin; tel. (30) 34343434; fax (30) 41021003; e-mail serviceteam@airberlin.com; internet www.airberlin.com; f. 1979; offers flights to some 25 destinations in Germany and to some 40 other countries; CEO WOLFGANG PROCK-SCHAUER.

Condor Flugdienst GmbH: Condor Pl. 1, 60549 Frankfurt a.M.; tel. (6107) 9390; fax (6107) 939440; internet www.condor.com; f. 1956; subsidiary of Thomas Cook AG; low-cost airline; Chair., Management Bd RALF TECKENTRUP; Chair., Supervisory Bd HEINER WILKENS.

Deutsche Lufthansa AG: Flughafen-Bereich West, 60546 Frankfurt a.M.; tel. (69) 6960; internet konzern.lufthansa.com; f. 1953; extensive worldwide network; Chair., Supervisory Bd WOLFGANG MAYRHUBER; Chair., Exec. Bd CARSTEN SPOHR.

Germania Fluggesellschaft: Riedemannweg 58, 13627 Berlin; tel. (30) 522808700; e-mail info@germania.aero; internet www .flygermania.de; f. 1979; operates as Germania; charter and scheduled flights.

Germanwings GmbH: Germanwings-Str. 2, 51147 Köln; tel. (900) 1919100; fax (220) 31027300; e-mail kontakt@germanwings.com; internet www.germanwings.com; f. 2002; low-cost airline, offers flights to 60 destinations within Europe; owned by Deutsche Lufthansa AG; CEO THOMAS WINKELMANN.

Lufthansa Cargo AG: Flughafen-Bereich West, Tor 25, Gebäude 451, 60546 Frankfurt a.M.; tel. (69) 6960; fax (69) 69691185; e-mail lhcargo@dlh.de; internet lufthansa-cargo.com; f. 1994; wholly owned subsidiary of Deutsche Lufthansa AG; freight-charter worldwide; Chair., Management Bd KARL ULRICH GARNADT; Chair., Supervisory Bd SIMONE MENNE.

Lufthansa CityLine GmbH: Flughafen Köln/Bonn, Waldstr. 247, 51147 Köln; tel. (2203) 5960; fax (2203) 596801; e-mail lh-cityline@ dlh.de; internet www.lufthansacityline.com; scheduled services; subsidiary of Deutsche Lufthansa AG; Man. Dirs STEPHAN KLAR, KLAUS FROESE.

TUIfly GmbH: Flughafenstr. 10, Postfach 420240, 30855 Langenhagen; tel. (511) 97270; fax (511) 9727739; internet www.tuifly.com; f. 2007 following merger of Hapag-Lloyd Flug and Hapag-Lloyd Express; charter and scheduled passenger services; Exec. Chair. MICHAEL FRENZEL.

Tourism

Germany's tourist attractions include spas, summer and winter resorts, mountains, medieval towns and castles, and above all a variety of fascinating cities. The North and Baltic Sea coasts, the Rhine Valley, the Black Forest, the mountains of Thuringia, the Erzgebirge and Bavaria are the most popular areas. The total number of foreign visitors was 31.5m. in 2013; receipts from tourism in that year totalled €41,217m.

Deutsche Zentrale für Tourismus eV (DZT) (German National Tourist Board): Beethovenstr. 69, 60325 Frankfurt a.M.; tel. (69) 97464; fax (69) 97464233; e-mail info@germany.travel; internet www .germany.travel; f. 1948; CEO PETRA HEDORFER.

Defence

Germany is a member of the North Atlantic Treaty Organization (NATO). In October 2006 the Government endorsed a review of German defence policy, which contained proposals to redefine the primary role of the Bundeswehr from border defence to intervention in international conflicts. Under the proposals, the Bundeswehr would be expanded to allow for the deployment of up to 14,000 troops in five international missions simultaneously. As assessed at November 2014, Germany's armed forces totalled some 181,550. This included an army of 63,450, a navy of 15,850, an air force of 31,400, a joint support service of 44,850, a joint medical service of 19,500 and other staff of 6,500. There was also a reserve of 45,000 (army 14,800; navy 1,800; air force 6,050; joint support service 15,650; joint medical service 6,100; and Ministry of Defence 600). In July 2011 conscription to the armed forces was suspended.

As assessed at November 2014, the USA had 40,500 troops stationed in Germany and the UK 12,300, while France maintained forces of 2,000 personnel. Canada had 226 troops stationed in Germany.

In November 2004 the European Union (EU) ministers responsible for defence agreed to create a number of 'battlegroups' (each comprising about 1,500 men), which could be deployed at short notice to crisis areas around the world. The EU battlegroups, two of which were to be ready for deployment at any one time, following a rotational schedule, reached full operational capacity from 1 January 2007.

Defence Expenditure: Budgeted at €32,400m. for 2014.

Chief of Staff of the Bundeswehr: Gen. VOLKER WIEKER.

Education

The Grundgesetz (Basic Law) assigns control of the education system to the governments of the Länder and to the Schulamt (lower-level school supervisory authorities). There is, however, quite close co-operation to ensure a large degree of conformity in the system. Enrolment at pre-primary level included 91% of children in the relevant age-group in 2009. Compulsory schooling, which is free, begins at six years of age and continues for nine years (or 10 years in some Länder). Until the age of 18 years, all young people who do not continue to attend a full-time school must attend a part-time vocational school, the Berufsschule. Primary education lasts four years (six years in Berlin and Brandenburg). In 2011/12 enrolment at primary level included 98% of children in the relevant age-group. Attendance at elementary school (Grundschule) is obligatory for all children, after which their education continues at secondary school. Secondary education, which lasts for up to nine years, is divided into lower secondary, which is compulsory, between the ages of 10 and 15/16 years, and upper secondary, which lasts from 15/16 years of age to 18/19 years. At the end of the lower secondary cycle pupils who reach the required standard receive a leaving certificate, the Hauptabschluss or Mittlerer Schulabschluss. There are four principal types of secondary school: grammar school (Gymnasium), intermediate school (Realschule), high school (Hauptschule) and comprehensive school (Gesamtschule). At upper secondary, admission to the Gymnasiale Oberstuf (which has also been established in schools other than the Gymnasium) is dependent on high achievement in the lower secondary leaving certificate, and admission to vocational education at upper secondary level is also based on achievement at lower secondary level. The Abitur (grammar school leaving certificate) is a prerequisite for entry into university education. Post-secondary non-tertiary education takes place at vocational schools (Berufsfachschule), technical colleges (Fachoberschule), at evening classes or through a dual system of vocational school and training in a work placement. Tertiary education includes universities, technical colleges (Technische Hochschule), universities of applied sciences (Fachhochschule), teacher training colleges and colleges of art and music. According to preliminary official figures, 1,706,262 students were enrolled in universities and equivalent institutions in 2014/15, and a further 992,163 were enrolled in non-university higher education.

Federal, Land and municipal expenditure on education was budgeted at some €120,600m. for 2014.

GHANA

Introductory Survey

LOCATION, CLIMATE, LANGUAGE, RELIGION, FLAG, CAPITAL

The Republic of Ghana lies on the west coast of Africa, with Côte d'Ivoire to the west and Togo to the east. It is bordered by Burkina Faso to the north. The climate is tropical, with temperatures generally between 21°C and 32°C (70°–90°F) and average annual rainfall of 2,000 mm (80 in) on the coast, decreasing inland. English is the official language, but there are 11 major national languages (each with more than 250,000 speakers) which have government-sponsored status. The most widely spoken of these are the four Akan ethnic languages, the two Mole-Dagbani ethnic languages, and Ewe and Ga. According to the 2010 census, Christians comprised an estimated 71.2% of the population, around 17.6% were Muslims and a sizeable minority followed traditional beliefs and customs. The national flag (proportions 2 by 3) has three equal horizontal stripes, of red, yellow and green, with a five-pointed black star in the centre of the yellow stripe. The capital is Accra.

CONTEMPORARY POLITICAL HISTORY

Historical Context

Ghana was formed as the result of a UN-supervised plebiscite in May 1956, when the British-administered section of Togoland, a UN Trust Territory, voted to join the Gold Coast, a British colony, in an independent state. Ghana was duly granted independence, within the Commonwealth, on 6 March 1957 and Dr Kwame Nkrumah, the Prime Minister of the former Gold Coast since 1952, became Prime Minister of the new state. Ghana became a republic on 1 July 1960, with Nkrumah as President. In 1964 the Convention People's Party, led by Nkrumah, was declared the sole authorized party.

In February 1966 Nkrumah was deposed in a military coup, the leaders of which established a governing National Liberation Council, led by Gen. Joseph Ankrah. In April 1969 Ankrah was replaced by Brig. (later Lt-Gen.) Akwasi Afrifa, and a new Constitution was introduced. Power was returned in October to an elected civilian Government, led by Dr Kofi Busia. However, in response to increasing economic and political difficulties, the army again seized power in January 1972, under the leadership of Lt-Col (later Gen.) Ignatius Acheampong. In July 1978 Acheampong was deposed by his deputy, Lt-Gen. Frederick Akuffo, who assumed power in a bloodless coup. Tensions within the army became evident in May 1979, when junior military officers staged an unsuccessful coup attempt. The alleged leader of the conspirators, Flight-Lt Jerry Rawlings, was imprisoned, but was subsequently released by other officers. On 4 June he and his associates successfully seized power, amid popular acclaim, established the Armed Forces Revolutionary Council, and introduced measures to eradicate corruption. Acheampong and Akuffo were among nine senior officers who were convicted on charges of corruption and executed.

Civilian rule was restored in September 1979; however, on 31 December 1981 Rawlings seized power for a second time, and established a governing Provisional National Defence Council (PNDC), with himself as Chairman. The PNDC's policies initially received strong support, but discontent with the regime and with the apparent ineffectiveness of its economic policies was reflected by a series of coup attempts.

Domestic Political Affairs

In July 1990, in response to pressure from Western aid donors to introduce further democratic reforms, the PNDC announced that a National Commission for Democracy (NCD) would organize a series of regional debates to consider Ghana's political and economic future. In December Rawlings announced proposals for the introduction of a constitution by the end of 1991; the PNDC was to consider recommendations presented by the NCD, and subsequently to convene a consultative body to determine constitutional reform.

In March 1991 the NCD presented a report on the democratic process, which recommended the election of an executive President for a fixed term, the establishment of a legislature and the creation of the post of Prime Minister. In May the PNDC endorsed the restoration of a multi-party system and approved the NCD's recommendations, although the formation of political associations remained prohibited. Later in May the Government announced the establishment of a 260-member Consultative Assembly, which was to present a draft constitution to the PNDC. The Government also appointed a nine-member committee of constitutional experts, who, in August, submitted a series of recommendations for constitutional reform, which included the establishment of a parliament and a council of state. It was proposed that the President, who would also be Commander-in-Chief of the Armed Forces, would be elected by universal suffrage for a four-year term of office, while the leader of the party that commanded a majority in the legislature would be appointed as Prime Minister. Later in August Rawlings announced that presidential and legislative elections were to take place in late 1992. In December 1991 the Government established an Interim National Electoral Commission (INEC), which was to be responsible for the demarcation of electoral regions and the supervision of elections and referendums. In March 1992 Rawlings announced a programme for transition to a multi-party system, which was to be completed on 7 January 1993.

At the end of March 1992 the Consultative Assembly approved the majority of the constitutional recommendations that had been submitted to the PNDC. However, the proposed creation of the post of Prime Minister was rejected by the Assembly; executive power was to be vested in the President, who would appoint a Vice-President. Opposition groups subsequently objected to a provision in the draft Constitution that members of the Government be exempt from prosecution for human rights violations allegedly committed during the PNDC's rule. At a national referendum on 28 April, however, the draft Constitution was approved by 92% of votes cast, with 43.7% of the electorate voting.

On 18 May 1992 the Government introduced legislation permitting the formation of political associations; political parties were henceforth required to apply to the INEC for legal recognition, although emergent parties were not permitted to use names or slogans associated with 21 former political organizations that remained proscribed. In June a number of political associations were established, many of which were identified with supporters of former President Nkrumah; six opposition movements, including the People's National Convention (PNC), were subsequently granted legal recognition. In the same month a coalition of pro-Government organizations, the National Democratic Congress (NDC), was formed to contest the forthcoming elections on behalf of the PNDC. However, an existing alliance of Rawlings' supporters, the Eagle Club, refused to join the NDC, and created its own political organization, the Eagle Party (later known as the EGLE—Every Ghanaian Living Everywhere—Party). In August the Government promulgated a new electoral code, which included a provision that in the event that no presidential candidate received more than 50% of votes cast the two candidates with the highest number of votes would contest a second round within 21 days. In September, in accordance with the new Constitution, Rawlings officially retired from the air force (while retaining the post of Commander-in-Chief of the Armed Forces in his capacity as Head of State) and accepted a nomination to contest the presidential election as a candidate of the NDC. The NDC, the EGLE Party and the National Convention Party (NCP) subsequently formed a pro-Government electoral coalition, the Progressive Alliance.

Rawlings was elected President on 3 November 1992, securing 58.3% of the votes cast. The four opposition parties that had presented candidates, the PNC, the New Patriotic Party (NPP), the National Independence Party (NIP) and the People's Heritage Party (PHP), claimed that there had been widespread electoral malpractice, although international observers maintained that, despite isolated irregularities, the election had been conducted fairly. Later in November these four parties withdrew from the forthcoming legislative elections (scheduled for 8 December), in protest at the Government's refusal to comply with their demands for the compilation of a new electoral register and the investigation of alleged misconduct during the presidential election. As a result, the legislative elections were postponed until late December and the nomination of new candidates permitted. In December the opposition claimed that many of its members had left Ghana, as a result of widespread intimidation by the Government. In the legislative elections, which took place on 29 December, the NDC secured 189 of the 200 seats in the Parliament, while the NCP obtained eight seats, the EGLE Party one seat and independent candidates the remaining two. According to official figures, however, only 29% of the electorate voted in the elections.

Establishment of the Fourth Republic

On 7 January 1993 Rawlings was sworn in as President of what was designated the Fourth Republic, the PNDC was dissolved and the new Parliament was inaugurated. In May a 17-member Council of Ministers was inaugurated. In December the PHP, the NIP and a faction of the PNC, all of which comprised supporters of ex-President Nkrumah, merged to form a new organization, the People's Convention Party (PCP).

Presidential and parliamentary elections were scheduled for December 1996. In May the Popular Party for Democracy and Development merged with the PCP, and in August the NPP and the PCP formed an electoral coalition, the Great Alliance; it was subsequently announced that John Kufuor, of the NPP, was to be the Great Alliance's presidential candidate. The NCP stated that it would support the NDC in the forthcoming elections, and in September the NDC nominated Rawlings as its presidential candidate. By 18 September, the official deadline for the nomination of candidates, only the Great Alliance, the Progressive Alliance (the NDC, the EGLE Party and the Democratic People's Party—DPP) and the PNC had succeeded in having their nomination papers accepted.

In the presidential election, which took place on 7 December 1996, Rawlings was re-elected, with 57.2% of the votes cast, while Kufuor secured 39.8%. In the parliamentary elections the NDC's representation was reduced to 133 seats, while the NPP won 60 seats, the PCP five and the PNC one seat. (The final seat was won by the NPP in a by-election in June 1997 following a legal dispute.) Despite opposition claims of malpractice, international observers declared that the elections had been conducted fairly, and an electoral turnout of 76.8% was reported. At the end of December the PCP announced that the Great Alliance had broken down. On 7 January 1997 Rawlings was sworn in as President.

In August 1998 the NCP and the PCP merged to form the Convention Party. An earlier attempt by the party to register as the Convention People's Party (CPP) had been rejected on the grounds that the use of the name of a proscribed party was unconstitutional. (This decision was reversed in 2000, however, when the Convention Party was permitted to adopt the name and logo of Nkrumah's former party.) In October 1998 the NPP nominated Kufuor to stand as its presidential candidate, in elections due to be held in 2000. At an NDC congress in December 1998 the position of 'Life Chairman' of the party was created for Rawlings, who confirmed that he would comply with the terms of the Constitution and not stand for a third term as President, and subsequently announced that the incumbent Vice-President, Prof. John Evans Atta Mills, was to contest the election on behalf of the NDC. In June 1999, owing to dissatisfaction within the NDC at the changes carried out at the party congress and at Rawlings' pronouncement regarding his successor, a group of party members broke away to form a new political organization, the National Reform Party (NRP). At the end of April Mills had been elected unopposed as the NDC presidential candidate.

An estimated 62% of the electorate voted in the elections, which took place on 7 December 2000. Regional observers declared the polling to have been conducted in an orderly and fair manner. In the elections to the 200-seat Parliament the NPP won 100 seats, while the NDC obtained 92 seats, the PNC three, the CPP one, and independent candidates four. The NPP thus became the largest parliamentary party for the first time, gaining an unprecedented degree of support in rural areas. In the presidential election Kufuor won 48.2% of the valid votes cast, and Mills 44.5%, thus necessitating a second round, which proceeded on 28 December; Kufuor was elected to the presidency, with 56.9% of the valid votes cast.

The Kufuor presidency

On 7 January 2001 Kufuor was inaugurated as President and subsequently appointed a new Government, which notably included one member from each of the CPP, the NRP and the PNC. Kufuor ordered the suspension of the heads of six public sector financial institutions, to facilitate an investigation into allegations of embezzlement, while in February he announced that a National Reconciliation Commission (NRC) was to be established to investigate allegations of human rights abuses and other violations committed by state representatives. The NRC was officially launched in May and commenced public hearings in January 2003, by which time some 2,800 complaints had been received, mostly relating to events that took place under military regimes.

In March 2002 the Minister of the Interior and the Minister for the Northern Region both resigned, following the deaths of some 40 people during clashes between the Mamprusi and Kusasi ethnic groups in the north of Ghana, which had been prompted by the abduction and murder of Ya-na Yakuba Andani, king of the Dagomba, in Yendi. A commission of inquiry was established, headed by traditional leaders, and a state of emergency was declared. The state of emergency ended in the majority of districts in October 2003, but remained in place in Tamale municipality and Yendi district until August 2004. Unrest, however, continued during 2005. Renewed violence broke out in mid-2009, in which three people were killed. A curfew was established in an attempt to curtail the fighting.

Meanwhile, in April 2002 the election of Dr Obed Asamoah as the new Chairman of the NDC created divisions within the party between supporters of Asamoah and Rawlings. In September a number of accusations of financial impropriety were made against Rawlings and his former associates. In November, following the arrest of three NDC deputies on charges of fraud and the reckless loss of state revenues, the NDC boycotted the Parliament in protest; this followed an earlier boycott over a controversial US $1,000m. development loan. In February 2004 Rawlings appeared before the NRC to answer questions about the murders of three high court judges and a retired military officer in 1982, and about extrajudicial military killings in 1984. In July 2004 the NRC ended its hearings, prior to the submission of its report in October, which recommended that victims of state brutality receive compensation and that state institutions, including the security services, be reformed.

Parliamentary and presidential elections were held on 7 December 2004. Kufuor, representing the NPP, was declared the winner of the presidential election after securing 52.4% of the valid votes cast, while Mills (the NDC's candidate) won 44.6%. In the elections to the enlarged Parliament the NPP won 128 of the 230 seats, with 55.6% of the vote, while the NDC took 94 seats, the PNC four and the CPP three. The new Parliament was inaugurated on 7 January 2005. On the same day Kufuor was sworn in as President, following which he reorganized the Government.

The Mills presidency

With Kufuor ineligible for re-election to the presidency, Nana Addo Dankwa Akufo-Addo, who had held the foreign affairs portfolio until July 2007, was to represent the NPP, while Mills was again selected as the candidate of the NDC. As preparations for the presidential and legislative elections began in late August 2008 violence threatened to undermine the conduct of the ballot. Conflict at a political rally, believed to be a result of continued unrest over the murder of Andani in Dagomba in 2002, left at least three people dead and many more injured. The announcement by the Electoral Commission (EC) that the electoral register could contain as many as 1m. false names further heightened tensions. Nevertheless, voting proceeded in a largely peaceful atmosphere. In the first round of the presidential election, on 7 December 2008, Akufo-Addo won 49.1% of the votes cast while Mills secured 47.9%. As no candidate had secured more than 50% of the valid votes cast, Mills and Akufo-Addo contested a second round of voting, held on 28 December, at which Mills emerged winner with some 50.2% of votes cast. He was inaugurated as President on 7 January 2009. Following legislative elections, held concurrently with the first round of the presidential election, the NDC became the largest party in the Parliament, with 113 of the 230 seats, while the NPP's representation was reduced to 109 seats; the PNC took two seats and the CPP one seat.

The Minister of Health, Dr George Sepa Yankey, and the Minister of State at the Presidency, Seidu Amadu, resigned in October 2009 following allegations that they had accepted bribes from a British construction company, which had in the previous month been ordered by a British court to pay fines of more than US $7m. for offering illegal payments to officials in Ghana in the 1990s; five other senior Ghanaian officials were also implicated in the alleged corruption. However, following a police investigation, all seven officials were exonerated in June 2011.

In January 2010 President Mills inaugurated a Constitution Review Commission (CRC), which was charged with recommending changes to the 1992 Constitution for approval at a referendum. Community and district constitutional review consultations, with the aim of soliciting public contributions to the work of the CRC, began in April. It was reported that public opinion strongly favoured restructuring of the principal state organs, and in particular a redistribution and separation of power between the presidential executive and the legislature. In December 2011 Mills received the CRC's final report, which recommended, *inter alia*, restricting the President's power of appointment, strengthening Parliament and the independence of the judiciary, and greater decentralization to local government. The report also advocated the creation of a National Development Planning Commission, the abrogation of the death penalty and, controversially, the preservation of the constitutional clauses granting former PNDC members immunity from prosecution. The Government established an Implementation Committee in October 2012 to move forward with the majority of the CRC's recommendations.

Mills' authority had been undermined throughout his presidency by the relentless, public criticism of his administration by former President Rawlings. The divisions within the NDC culminated in July 2011, when Rawlings' wife, Nana Konadu Agyeman Rawlings, stood against Mills in a primary election to select the ruling party's 2012 presidential candidate. In the event, Mills secured the NDC presidential nomination after winning 97% of the votes cast, reinforcing his control over the party. (Nana Rawlings resigned from the NDC in October 2012 and was promptly named as the presidential nominee of the recently formed National Democratic Party; however, she failed to meet the deadline for submission of the relevant paperwork and her candidature was consequently rejected by the EC.)

In accordance with a Supreme Court judgment, Mills declared in November 2011 that prisoners would be entitled to vote in the 2012 presidential and legislative elections and that special measures to facilitate this would be effected.

Recent developments: Mahama becomes President

President Mills died on 24 July 2012 after suffering a stroke. Vice-President John Dramani Mahama was duly sworn in as his successor later that day, while Kwesi Bekoe Amissah-Arthur subsequently assumed the vice-presidency. This constitutional transfer of power—still a relatively uncommon occurrence in West Africa—earned Ghana international plaudits and underlined the strength of the country's maturing democracy. In August Mahama was confirmed as the NDC's candidate in the approaching presidential poll.

Mahama secured a first round victory in the presidential election, held on 7 December 2012, winning 50.7% of the vote compared with 47.7% for Akufo-Addo of the NPP. In several constituencies, owing to technical problems with new biometric equipment, voting also took place on the following day. The rate of participation by the electorate was approximately 80%. Although international observers expressed satisfaction with the conduct of the election, the NPP denounced the results as fraudulent and submitted an appeal to the Supreme Court. NPP supporters organized protests in Accra and Kumasi, some of which turned violent. In the concurrent legislative elections, the NDC gained control of 148 parliamentary seats, while the NPP obtained 123, independent candidates three and the PNC one. (A bill had been adopted in October to increase the number of seats in Parliament from 230 to 275.) Mahama was sworn in as President on 7 January 2013; with the notable exception of former President Kufuor, the ceremony was boycotted by members of the NPP. Later that month Mahama announced his new Cabinet, which included Kwesi Ahwoi as Minister of the Interior, Seth Terpker as Minister of Finance and Economic Planning, Hannah Tetteh as Minister of Foreign Affairs and Regional Integration, and Marietta Brew Appiah-Oppong as Attorney-General and Minister of Justice. The NPP ended its boycott of parliamentary proceedings in March. After protracted consideration, the Supreme Court on 29 August rejected the NPP's legal challenge and upheld Mahama's victory.

Mahama reorganized his Cabinet in mid-2014. Among the changes announced, Mark Owen Woyongo was appointed as Minister of the Interior, Benjamin Bewa-Nyog Kunbuor became Minister of Defence, and Ekow Spio-Garbrah was given responsibility for the trade and industry portfolio. In November Mahama established a new Ministry of Power, which was tasked with addressing the country's chronic electricity supply problems. Meanwhile, in October the NPP again chose Akufo-Addo to represent the party as its candidate in the next presidential election, due in 2016. However, according to local media reports, the NPP remained deeply divided as a result of long-standing differences between the party's main factions.

In March 2015 Mahama effected further changes to the composition of the Cabinet, although the most senior portfolios remained unaltered. Collins Dauda, hitherto the Minister of Water Resources, Works and Housing, was appointed Minister of Local Government and Rural Development, while Dr Kwaku Agyeman Mensah, previously the Minister of Health, assumed Dauda's vacated role. Alex Segbefia became the new Minister of Health and Dr Mustapha Ahmed was appointed Minister of Youth and Sports.

Foreign Affairs

Ghana was, in early 2015, the fourth largest African contributing nation to UN peacekeeping operations and the eighth largest of all peacekeeping contributing nations. At January 2015 Ghana was contributing 2,993 personnel to UN peacekeeping missions worldwide. At that time, Ghana was notably deploying sizeable contingents in the Democratic Republic of the Congo (DRC), the Darfur region of Sudan, Liberia, Mali, South Sudan and Côte d'Ivoire, and outside Africa was contributing 871 troops to the UN Interim Force in Lebanon.

In October 1992 Ghana denied claims that it was implicated in subversive activity by Togolese dissidents based in Ghana, and in March 1993 the Rawlings administration further denied allegations, made by the Togolese Government, of Ghanaian complicity in an armed attack on the residence of Togo's President, Gen. Gnassingbé Eyadéma. In January 1994 relations with Togo deteriorated further, following an attempt to overthrow the Togolese Government, which the Togolese authorities claimed had been staged by armed dissidents based in Ghana. The Ghanaian chargé d'affaires in Togo was arrested, and Togolese forces killed 12 Ghanaians and attacked a customs post and several villages near the border. Ghana, however, denied any involvement in the coup attempt, and threatened to retaliate against further acts of aggression. Later that year, however, relations improved, and in November full diplomatic links were formally restored. In December Togo's border with Ghana (which had been closed in January 1994) was reopened. Following the death of Eyadéma in early 2005 and the subsequent unrest in Togo precipitated by the assumption of power by Eyadéma's son, Faure Gnassingbé, some 15,000 Togolese refugees were reported to have registered in Ghana. In May 2010 it was reported that some 3,500 refugees had fled from Ghana into northern Togo, as a result of renewed ethnic conflict and land disputes in the north of the country.

During the conflict in Liberia, which commenced in December 1989, Ghana contributed troops to the Monitoring Group (ECOMOG) of the Economic Community of West African States (ECOWAS, see p. 258). As Chairman of the ECOWAS Conference of Heads of State and Government, Rawlings mediated negotiations between the warring Liberian factions in the mid-1990s, and by mid-1997 some 17,000 Liberian refugees had arrived in Ghana. In 2003 Ghana also hosted peace negotiations concerning Liberia, and from September contributed troops to the ECOWAS Mission in Liberia (ECOMIL). In October the Ghanaian troops were transferred to a longer-term UN stabilization force, the UN Mission in Liberia (UNMIL, see p. 88). In late 2005 there were some 40,000 Liberian refugees registered in Ghana, although this number had declined to 11,585 by the end of 2010. Due to the improving security climate in Liberia, in June 2012 the Ghanaian Government revoked the refugee status that had been granted to Liberians who had fled the conflict in their country. Former refugees were required to return to Liberia or apply for residency in Ghana. Ghana was contributing 748 personnel to UNMIL at January 2015.

In June 1997 Ghana, Côte d'Ivoire, Guinea and Nigeria formed the 'committee of four', which was established by ECOWAS to monitor the situation in Sierra Leone, following the staging of a military coup; troops were dispatched to participate in a peacekeeping force. Following the reinstatement of the democratically elected Government in March, ECOMOG units remained in the country and continued to launch attacks against rebel forces, which still retained control of a number of areas. In December 2005 the Ghanaian troops participating in the UN Mission in Sierra Leone (UNAMSIL) returned to Ghana on the termination of the peacekeeping mission.

In November 2001 some 400 Ghanaian troops were dispatched to participate in peacekeeping duties in the DRC, under the auspices of the UN Mission in the Democratic Republic of the Congo (MONUC, see p. 93). Ghana continued to participate in the UN peacekeeping contingent (which had been reconstituted as the UN Organization Stabilization Mission in the Democratic Republic of the Congo—MONUSCO), contributing 487 personnel at January 2015.

After the outbreak of an armed rebellion in Côte d'Ivoire in September 2002, Ghana denied accusations by the Ivorian rebels that it had intervened in support of President Laurent Gbagbo. In October Ghana pledged to provide troops to an ECOWAS military mission in Côte d'Ivoire (ECOMICI), and the first contingent of the 266 Ghanaian soldiers to be contributed was deployed in February 2003. The Ghanaian troops were subsequently transferred to a UN Operation in Côte d'Ivoire (UNOCI, see p. 92), which was deployed from April 2004. A conference held in Accra in August led to the signing of a peace accord between rival Ivorian factions, Accra III. At January 2015 169 Ghanaian personnel were deployed in Côte d'Ivoire as part of UNOCI. Political instability and factional violence in Côte d'Ivoire following a disputed presidential election in late 2010 precipitated the inflow of large numbers of Ivorian refugees into Ghana (estimated to total 18,000 by October 2011). Alassane Ouattara, who had been sworn in as the new Ivorian President in May 2011 after months of fighting, visited Ghana in October and pressured Mills to extradite Ivorian refugees accused of committing human rights abuses during the post-election turmoil. A repatriation accord was also signed by Ghana, Côte d'Ivoire and the office of the UN High Commissioner for Refugees (UNHCR), to facilitate the voluntary return of Ivorian refugees, while former fighters were to be resettled in other countries. Côte d'Ivoire closed its border with Ghana in September 2012 as a result of an apparent cross-border raid that had targeted Ivorian troops. The authorities in Côte d'Ivoire suspected that the attack had been perpetrated by pro-Gbagbo militants sheltering in Ghana. Indeed, a UN report, leaked in the following month, alleged that a regional network of Gbagbo-aligned combatants had established its headquarters in Ghana and was orchestrating destabilizing activities in Côte d'Ivoire. The Ivorian Government reopened the border to air traffic in late September, and the land and sea frontiers were normalized in October following the implementation of additional border security measures. A number of Gbagbo loyalists were arrested in Ghana during 2012, and the Ghanaian authorities extradited Charles Blé Goude, a former member of Gbagbo's Government who was accused of committing war crimes, to Côte d'Ivoire in January 2013. Bilateral relations had improved following the death of President Mills in mid-2012, who had been perceived to favour Gbagbo. In February 2014 representatives from Ghana and Côte d'Ivoire resumed talks aimed at resolving a long-standing dispute over the maritime boundary between the two countries. In September, in an effort to reach an amicable compromise with the Ivorian authorities, Ghana commenced arbitration action at the International Tribunal for the Law of the Sea. According to UNHCR estimates, 10,943 Ivorian refugees were present in Ghana in late 2014.

Although in March 2011 the United Kingdom pledged to increase annual aid to Ghana to £100m. by 2014/15 (up from £85m. in 2010/11), British Prime Minister David Cameron caused controversy in Ghana in late 2011 by indicating that aid would be reduced to nations that failed to reform discriminatory laws against homosexuals. President Mills firmly rejected any liberalization of Ghana's conservative laws regarding homosexuality and criticized Cameron for encroaching on domestic Ghanaian affairs.

CONSTITUTION AND GOVERNMENT

Under the terms of the Constitution, which was approved by national referendum on 28 April 1992, Ghana has a multi-party political system. Executive power is vested in the President, who is the Head of State and Commander-in-Chief of the Armed Forces. The President is elected by direct universal suffrage for a maximum of two four-year terms of office. Legislative power is vested in a 275-member unicameral Parliament, which is elected by direct universal suffrage for a four-year term. The President appoints a Vice-President, and nominates a Council of Ministers, subject to approval by the Parliament. The Constitution also provides for a 25-member Council of State, principally comprising regional representatives and presidential nominees, and a 20-member National Security Council, chaired by the Vice-President, which act as advisory bodies to the President.

Ghana has 10 regions, each headed by a Regional Minister, who is assisted by a regional co-ordinating council. The regions constitute 216 districts, each with an Assembly (either Metropolitan, Municipal or District), which is headed by a Chief Executive (either Metropolitan, Municipal or District). Regional colleges, which comprise representatives selected by the Metropolitan, Municipal and District Assemblies and by regional Houses of Chiefs, elect a number of representatives to the Council of State.

REGIONAL AND INTERNATIONAL CO-OPERATION

Ghana is a member of the African Union (see p. 188) and of the Economic Community of West African States (ECOWAS, see p. 258).

Ghana became a member of the UN in 1957 and was admitted to the World Trade Organization (WTO, see p. 431) in 1995. Ghana also participates in the Group of 77 (G77, see p. 447) developing countries. Ghana is also a member of the International Cocoa Organization (ICCO, see p. 442), and of the International Coffee Organization (ICO, see p. 442). In 2004 Ghana became a full member of the Community of Sahel-Saharan States (see p. 446).

ECONOMIC AFFAIRS

In 2013, according to estimates by the World Bank, Ghana's gross national income (GNI), measured at average 2011–13 prices, was US $45,605m., equivalent to $1,760 per head (or $3,880 on an international purchasing-power parity basis). During 2004–13, it was estimated, the population increased at an average annual rate of 2.4%, while gross domestic product (GDP) per head grew, in real terms, by an average of 5.2% per year. Overall GDP increased at an average annual rate of 7.8% in 2004–13; growth in 2013 was 7.1%.

Agriculture (including forestry and fishing) contributed 19.9% of GDP in 2014, according to provisional figures. An estimated 53.1% of the economically active population was employed in the sector at mid-2015, according to FAO. The principal cash crop is cocoa beans, contributing 29.7% of total exports in 2013. Ghana is the world's second largest producer of cocoa beans after Côte d'Ivoire, and, according to FAO, 835,500 metric tons of cocoa beans were harvested in 2013. Coffee, bananas, cassava, oil palm, coconuts, limes, kola nuts and shea-nuts (karité nuts) are also produced. The development of the palm oil and cassava sectors is currently under way. Timber production is also important, with the forestry sector accounting for 2.1% of GDP in 2013, and cork and wood, and manufactures thereof, contributing 3.1% of total export earnings in that year. In 2009 Ghana signed a Voluntary Partnership Agreement on Forest Law Enhancement, Governance and Trade with the European Union (EU, see p. 271); the Agreement commits each party to trade only in verified legal timber and timber products. Fishing satisfies more than three-quarters of domestic requirements, and contributed 1.4% of GDP in 2013. During 2007–13, according to official figures, agricultural GDP increased at an average annual rate of 4.7%; growth in 2013 was 5.2%.

Industry (including mining, manufacturing, construction and power) contributed 28.4% of GDP in 2014, according to provisional figures. Industrial GDP increased at an average annual rate of 13.7% in 2007–13; growth in 2013 was 7.0%.

Mining contributed 9.1% of GDP in 2014, according to provisional figures. Gold and diamonds are the major minerals exported (in 2012 gold production reached 86,699 kg), although Ghana also exploits large reserves of bauxite and manganese ore. The Government is attempting to increase exploitation of salt, bauxite and clay. The GDP of the mining sector increased by an average of 31.5% per year in 2007–13; mining GDP grew by a massive 206.7% in 2011, mostly owing to the commencement of crude petroleum production, before decelerating to 16.4% in 2012 and further to 11.7% in 2013.

Manufacturing contributed 5.9% of GDP in 2014, according to provisional figures. The most important sectors are food processing, textiles, vehicles, cement, paper, chemicals and petroleum. Manufacturing GDP increased at an average annual rate of 4.8% in 2007–13; the sector grew by 0.6% in 2013.

The construction sector contributed 12.3% of GDP in 2014, according to provisional figures. The GDP of the sector increased at an average annual rate of 14.9% in 2007–13; growth was 8.6% in 2013.

According to figures published by the World Bank, some 67.5% of Ghana's production of electricity was from hydroelectric power in 2011, with the Akosombo and Kpong plants being the major sources, and 24.3% from natural gas. Electricity is exported to Benin and Togo. The Government is seeking to double the country's electricity generation capacity, primarily through thermal and renewable energy sources. In 2004 the World Bank agreed to finance the construction of the West African Gas Pipeline, which was to supply natural gas from Nigeria to Ghana, Benin and Togo; the first gas was delivered in 2010. Imports of petroleum comprised 4.7% of the total value of merchandise imports in 2013.

The services sector contributed 51.7% of GDP in 2014, according to provisional figures. The GDP of the services sector increased at an average annual rate of 8.7% in 2007–13; growth in 2013 was 8.8%.

In 2013, according to IMF figures, Ghana recorded a visible merchandise trade deficit of US $3,848.4m, and there was a deficit of $5,685.1m. on the current account of the balance of payments. In 2013 the principal source of imports was the People's Republic of China (providing 22.8% of the total); other major sources were Belgium and India. Iran was the principal market for exports (taking 20.4% of the total) in that year; other important purchasers were South Africa, the UAE, Switzerland-Liechtenstein, Italy and France (including Monaco). The principal exports in 2013 were gold (which accounted for 34.4% of total export earnings), cocoa and cocoa preparations, crude petroleum, and Brazil nuts, cashew nuts and coconuts. The principal imports in 2013 were machinery, mechanical appliances and electrical equipment; vehicles, aircraft, vessels and associated transport equipment; chemicals and related products; and iron and steel, other base metals and articles of base metal.

Ghana's overall budget deficit in 2013 was 7,107.5m. Ghana cedis. General government gross debt was 52,009m. Ghana cedis in 2013, equivalent to 55.6% of GDP. Ghana's total external debt amounted to US $12,436m. at the end of 2012, of which $8,606m. was public and publicly guaranteed debt. In that year the cost of debt-servicing long-term public and publicly guaranteed debt and repayments to the IMF was equivalent to 4.2% of the value of exports of goods, services and income (excluding workers' remittances). According to ILO, in 2004–13 the average annual rate of inflation was 13.5%. Consumer prices increased by 11.6% in 2013, according to official sources. In 2010 around 5.8% of the total labour force was unemployed in Ghana.

Although Ghana's economy made steady progress following the transfer to civilian rule in 1992, it remained vulnerable to unfavourable weather conditions, while continued reliance on commodity exports increased the country's exposure to the vagaries of the global market. Real GDP expanded by 15.0% in 2011. This dramatic increase in growth, one of the highest rates worldwide, was driven predominantly by petroleum production, which had commenced in December 2010. In mid-2011 Ghana achieved the World Bank per head income threshold for classification as a lower middle income country, resulting in a decrease in funding commitments from many donors and a growing reliance on non-concessional financing. Structural factors relating to economic management began to complicate the country's development from 2012. The current account deficit widened in that year, while the increasing public sector wage bill and the provision of large-scale energy subsidies strained government finances. In June 2013 the Government partially removed subsidies for petroleum products and from October implemented a regular price adjustment regime for utilities. However, the current account deficit continued to expand in that year following a deterioration in the fiscal deficit and a 28% decline in the price of gold (Ghana's most valuable export), placing additional pressure on international reserves. According to the IMF, the resultant weakening of the domestic currency and the implementation of administered price rises precipitated an increase in inflation to 11.7% in 2013, while real GDP growth slowed to 7.1% (down from 8.8% in 2012). The Government responded by freezing public sector wages and recruitment, raising taxes, and announcing new proposals to add value to the country's exports. As in other emerging markets, Ghana experienced considerable currency depreciation in the first half of 2014 as a result of adjustments to the US dollar, to which the central bank responded by imposing capital controls and raising interest rates. However, the impact of these measures was limited, and in August, with the local currency and economic indicators continuing to weaken, the administration initiated negotiations with the IMF to discuss a potential economic stabilization programme. In September the Government issued a US $1,000m. bond to bolster its finances, and in February 2015 the IMF announced that agreement had been reached on a $940m. Extended Credit Facility arrangement, with tranches to be disbursed over a three-year period. The Government, for its part, agreed to intensify its fiscal consolidation efforts. The 2015 budget incorporated a variety of austerity measures, including a new tax on oil products, an extension of the public sector recruitment freeze and the further revocation of energy subsidies. The IMF reported that economic growth slowed again in 2014, to 4.5%, while inflation rose to an estimated 17%. Although the current account deficit narrowed to approximately 9.9% of GDP, from 11.9% of GDP in 2013, this was not an indication of a recovery in exports (prices for Ghana's traditional commodities, gold and cocoa, remained low in 2014, and oil prices also declined sharply in the latter stages of the year). Instead, the smaller deficit reflected lower import volumes, as internal demand slackened owing to currency depreciation and high interest rates. A major hindrance to growth throughout 2014 was the erratic performance of the country's electricity supply network, with power outages and load-shedding occurring on a regular basis. A number of development agreements were concluded during 2014 and early 2015 in an effort to boost generating capacity, while the commencement of domestic natural gas production in November 2014 was also expected to augment the country's energy matrix. The IMF projected real GDP growth of 3.5% in 2015.

PUBLIC HOLIDAYS

2016: 1 January (New Year's Day), 6 March (Independence Day), 25–28 March (Easter), 1 May (Labour Day), 25 May (African Union Day), 1 July (Republic Day), 6 July* (Eid-al-Fitr, end of Ramadan), 12 September* (Eid-al-Adha, Feast of the Sacrifice), 21 September (Founder's Day), 2 December (National Farmers' Day), 25–26 December (Christmas).

* These holidays are dependent on the Islamic lunar calendar and may vary by one or two days from the dates given.

Statistical Survey

Source (except where otherwise stated): Ghana Statistical Service, POB GP1098, Accra; tel. (30) 2671732; fax (30) 2671731; internet www.statsghana.gov.gh.

Area and Population

AREA, POPULATION AND DENSITY

Area (sq km)	238,533*
Population (census results)	
26 March 2000	18,912,079
26 September 2010	
Males	12,024,845
Females	12,633,978
Total	24,658,823
Population (UN estimates at mid-year)†	
2013	25,904,600
2014	26,442,176
2015	26,984,328
Density (per sq km) at mid-2015	113.1

* 92,098 sq miles.
† Source: UN, *World Population Prospects: The 2012 Revision.*

POPULATION BY AGE AND SEX
(UN estimates at mid-2015)

	Males	Females	Total
0–14 years	5,240,322	5,021,912	10,262,234
15–64 years	7,749,102	8,046,277	15,795,379
65 years and over	419,032	507,683	926,715
Total	13,408,456	13,575,872	26,984,328

Source: UN, *World Population Prospects: The 2012 Revision.*

REGIONS
(population at 2010 census)

Region	Area (sq km)	Population	Density (per sq km)	Capital
Ashanti	24,389	4,780,380	196.0	Kumasi
Brong Ahafo . .	39,557	2,310,983	58.4	Sunyani
Central	9,826	2,201,863	224.1	Cape Coast
Eastern	19,323	2,633,154	136.3	Koforidua
Greater Accra . .	3,245	4,010,054	1,235.8	Accra
Northern	70,384	2,479,461	35.2	Tamale
Upper East . . .	8,842	1,046,545	118.4	Bolgatanga
Upper West . .	18,476	702,110	38.0	Wa
Volta	20,570	2,118,252	103.0	Ho
Western	23,921	2,376,021	99.3	Takoradi
Total	238,533	24,658,823	103.4	

PRINCIPAL TOWNS
(population at 2010 census)

Kumasi	2,035,064	Tema		402,637
Accra (capital) . .	1,848,614	Tamale		371,351
Sekondi-Takoradi .	559,548	Cape Coast . . .		169,894

Mid-2014 (incl. suburbs, UN estimate): Accra (capital) 2,241,690 (Source: UN, *World Urbanization Prospects: The 2014 Revision*).

BIRTHS AND DEATHS
(annual averages, UN estimates)

	2000–05	2005–10	2010–15
Birth rate (per 1,000) . . .	34.3	33.1	31.1
Death rate (per 1,000) . . .	10.5	9.6	9.1

Source: UN, *World Population Prospects: The 2012 Revision.*

Life expectancy (years at birth): 60.9 (males 60.0; females 61.9) in 2012 (Source: World Bank, World Development Indicators database).

ECONOMICALLY ACTIVE POPULATION
(persons aged 15 years and over at 2010 census)

	Males	Females	Total
Agriculture, hunting, forestry and fishing	2,303,140	2,008,595	4,311,735
Mining and quarrying	92,353	21,852	114,205
Manufacturing	449,826	670,296	1,120,122
Electricity, gas and water . . .	27,690	13,141	40,831
Construction	308,527	8,998	317,525
Trade, restaurants and hotels .	687,439	1,836,662	2,524,101
Transport, storage and communications	380,946	29,672	410,618
Financing, insurance, real estate and business services . . .	158,493	81,175	239,668
Public administration and defence	111,618	42,012	153,630
Education	228,400	177,800	406,200
Health and social services . .	54,835	69,556	124,391
Household activities . . .	33,626	44,307	77,933
Activities of extraterritorial organizations	2,015	917	2,932
Other services	217,940	311,847	529,787
Total employed	5,056,848	5,316,830	10,373,678
Unemployed	283,346	349,648	632,994
Total labour force	5,340,194	5,666,478	11,006,672

Mid-2015 (estimates in '000): Agriculture, etc. 6,793; Total labour force 12,784 (Source: FAO).

Health and Welfare

KEY INDICATORS

Total fertility rate (children per woman, 2012)	3.9
Under-5 mortality rate (per 1,000 live births, 2012) . . .	72
HIV/AIDS (% of persons aged 15–49, 2013)	1.3
Physicians (per 1,000 head, 2010)	0.1
Hospital beds (per 1,000 head, 2011)	0.9
Health expenditure (2011): US $ per head (PPP)	99
Health expenditure (2011): % of GDP	5.3
Health expenditure (2011): public (% of total)	55.9
Access to water (% of persons, 2012)	87
Access to sanitation (% of persons, 2012)	14
Total carbon dioxide emissions ('000 metric tons, 2010) . .	8,998.8
Carbon dioxide emissions per head (metric tons, 2010) . .	0.4
Human Development Index (2013): ranking	138
Human Development Index (2013): value	0.573

For sources and definitions, see explanatory note on p. vi.

Agriculture

PRINCIPAL CROPS
('000 metric tons)

	2011	2012	2013
Rice, paddy	464.0	481.1	569.5
Maize	1,684.0	1,949.9	1,764.5
Millet	183.9	179.7	155.1
Sorghum	287.1	280.0	256.7
Sweet potatoes*	130.0	135.0	135.0
Cassava (Manioc)	14,240.9	14,547.3	14,550.0
Taro (Cocoyam)	1,299.6	1,270.3	1,270.0
Yams	6,295.5	6,638.9	6,640.0
Sugar cane*	145.0	148.0	150.0
Groundnuts, with shell . .	465.1	475.1	408.8
Coconuts	344.0	345.0	366.2
Oil palm fruit*	2,004.3	2,150.0	2,100.0
Tomatoes	320.5	321.0	340.2
Chillies and peppers, green . .	95.0	110.0	102.2
Onions, dry	120.0	130.0	138.2
Beans, green*	28.0	30.0	25.0
Okra	55.0	60.0	63.9
Bananas	75.0	80.0	84.2
Plantains	3,619.8	3,556.5	3,675.3
Oranges	600.0	625.0	663.2
Lemons and limes*	45.0	46.0	47.1
Pineapples	550.0	600.0	636.5
Cocoa beans	700.0	879.3	835.5
Natural rubber	20.2	20.2	21.4

* FAO estimates.

Aggregate production ('000 metric tons, may include official, semi-official or estimated data): Total cereals 2,619 in 2011, 2,891 in 2012, 2,746 in 2013; Total roots and tubers 21,966 in 2011, 22,592 in 2012, 24,461 in 2013; Total vegetables (incl. melons) 669 in 2011, 706 in 2012, 745 in 2013; Total fruits (excl. melons) 5,098 in 2011, 5,126 in 2012, 5,334 in 2013.

Source: FAO.

LIVESTOCK
('000 head, year ending September)

	2011	2012	2013*
Horses*	2.7	2.7	2.9
Asses*	14.3	14.4	14.4
Cattle	1,498	1,543	1,550
Pigs	568	602	620
Sheep	3,887	4,019	4,000
Goats	5,137	5,435	5,500
Chickens	52,575	57,885	60,000

* FAO estimates.

Source: FAO.

LIVESTOCK PRODUCTS
('000 metric tons)

	2011	2012	2013
Cattle meat	20.6	21.2	21.9
Sheep meat	17.5	18.1	18.7
Goat meat	20.3	21.2	22.4
Pig meat	19.1	20.2	21.4
Chicken meat	41.0	46.3	51.0
Game meat*	74.3	74.3	74.3
Cows' milk*	39.0	41.0	41.0
Hen eggs*	39.8	40.0	42.0

* FAO estimates.

Source: FAO.

Forestry

ROUNDWOOD REMOVALS
('000 cubic metres, excl. bark)

	2011	2012	2013
Sawlogs, veneer logs and logs for sleepers	1,289	1,282	1,587
Fuel wood*	38,985	40,204	41,448
Total	40,274	41,486	43,035

* FAO estimates.

Source: FAO.

SAWNWOOD PRODUCTION
('000 cubic metres, incl. railway sleepers)

	2011	2012	2013
Total (all broadleaved)* . . .	515	519	511

* Unofficial figures.

Source: FAO.

Fishing

('000 metric tons, live weight)

	2010	2011	2012
Capture*	351.2	344.9	365.0
Freshwater fishes*	90.0	90.0	90.0
Bigeye grunt	13.7	8.1	13.1
Red pandora	4.8	4.3	4.3
Round sardinella	36.7	21.5	24.9
Madeiran sardinella	11.3	10.7	9.3
European anchovy	45.1	51.2	50.2
Skipjack tuna	53.8	50.4	57.7
Yellowfin tuna	12.5	10.8	9.2
Bigeye tuna	6.8	4.4	2.9
Atlantic bumper	7.5	10.9	6.9
Aquaculture*	10.2	19.0	27.5
Total catch*	361.4	363.9	392.4

* FAO estimates.

Source: FAO.

Mining

('000 metric tons unless otherwise indicated)

	2010	2011	2012
Bauxite	595	400	753
Manganese ore: gross weight .	1,529	1,729	1,244
Manganese ore: metal content .	426	484	348
Silver (kg)*	3,313	3,088	3,100
Gold (kg)†	76,332	82,993	86,699
Salt (unrefined)	85	100‡	100‡
Crude petroleum ('000 barrels) .	2,050‡	24,196	26,429
Diamonds ('000 carats) . . .	334	302	233

* Silver content of exported doré.
† Gold content of ores and concentrates, excluding smuggled or undocumented output.
‡ Estimated figure.

Source: US Geological Survey.

Industry

SELECTED PRODUCTS
('000 metric tons unless otherwise indicated)

	2010	2011	2012
Groundnut oil*	72.2	62.7	64.2
Coconut oil*	9.8	9.9	9.6
Palm oil†	120.0	122.0	122.0
Palm kernel oil†	16.0	21.0	14.1
Beer of barley*	86.4	120.0	125.0
Gasoline (petrol)	338	n.a.	n.a.
Jet fuel	117	n.a.	n.a.
Kerosene	71	n.a.	n.a.
Distillate fuel oil	292.6	n.a.	n.a.
Residual fuel oil	96.8	n.a.	n.a.
Cement	2,100‡	2,550	3,000‡
Electric energy (million kWh)	10,167	11,200	12,164

* FAO estimates.
† Unofficial figure(s).
‡ Estimate.

2012: Electric energy (million kWh) 12,927.

Sources: FAO; US Geological Survey; Energy Commission of Ghana; UN Industrial Commodity Statistics Database.

Finance

CURRENCY AND EXCHANGE RATES

Monetary Units
100 Ghana pesewas = 1 Ghana cedi.

Sterling, Dollar and Euro Equivalents (31 December 2014)
£1 sterling = 4.9947 Ghana cedis;
US $1 = 3.2001 Ghana cedis;
€1 = 3.8852 Ghana cedis;
10 Ghana cedis = £2.00 = $3.12 = €2.57.

Average Exchange Rate (Ghana cedis per US $)
2011   1.5119
2012   1.7958
2013   1.9540

Note: A new currency, the Ghana cedi, equivalent to 10,000 new cedis (the former legal tender), was introduced over a six-month period beginning in July 2007.

GENERAL BUDGET
(million Ghana cedis)

Revenue*	2011	2012	2013
Tax revenue	9,854.6	12,655.2	14,466.7
Income and property	4,036.6	5,536.2	6,301.7
Personal (PAYE)	1,360.9	2,204.4	2,367.5
Company tax	1,568.0	2,361.5	2,315.6
Domestic goods and services	606.2	730.3	694.3
Petroleum tax	438.5	544.5	525.1
International trade	1,516.0	1,990.1	2,331.0
Import duties	1,511.0	1,886.9	2,231.0
Value added tax	2,376.1	2,777.3	3,317.1
Import exceptions	634.6	778.9	842.0
National health insurance levy	550.2	714.0	806.7
Other	135.0	128.4	174.0
Non-tax revenue	1,822.0	2,853.0	4,265.4
Total	11,676.6	15,508.2	18,732.1

Expenditure	2011	2012	2013
Recurrent expenditure	9,705.0	15,973.4	21,087.4
Wages and salaries	4,534.9	6,665.5	8,115.4
Goods and services	723.9	1,321.9	938.5
Transfers	2,504.6	4,477.8	6,838.8
National Health Fund (NHF)	377.0	587.2	752.8
Reserve fund	330.5	1,072.1	797.7
Interest payments	1,611.2	2,436.2	4,397.0
Domestic (accrual)	1,307.9	1,879.7	3,788.3
External (accrual)	303.3	556.4	608.7
Capital expenditure	3,675.0	4,971.3	5,189.8
Domestic	1,962.8	2,436.7	2,533.2
External	1,712.2	2,534.6	2,656.6
Total	13,380.0	20,944.7	26,277.2

* Excluding grants received (million Ghana cedis): 1,175.0 in 2011; 1,160.3 in 2012; 437.6 in 2013.

Source: Bank of Ghana, Accra.

INTERNATIONAL RESERVES
(US $ million at 31 December)

	2011	2012	2013
Gold (national valuation)	321.7	337.2	200.1
IMF special drawing rights	430.6	398.5	366.7
Foreign exchange	5,052.8	4,969.0	4,882.6
Total	5,805.1	5,704.7	5,449.3

Source: IMF, *International Financial Statistics*.

MONEY SUPPLY
(million Ghana cedis at 31 December)

	2011	2012	2013
Currency outside depository corporations	3,767.3	4,923.0	5,500.5
Transferable deposits	8,296.7	10,892.5	13,160.4
Other deposits	6,216.1	7,051.5	8,665.3
Broad money	18,280.0	22,867.1	27,326.3

Source: IMF, *International Financial Statistics*.

COST OF LIVING
(Consumer Price Index; base: 2002 = 100)

	2010	2011	2012
Food and non-alcoholic beverages	291.8	303.6	317.4
Clothing and footwear	262.3	296.2	344.6
Housing, water, electricity and other fuels	424.7	469.7	513.0
All items (incl. others)	336.5	365.8	403.5

2013 (Consumer Price Index; base: 2012 = 100): Food and non-alcoholic beverages 107.3; Clothing and footwear 117.4; Housing, water, electricity and other fuels 119.9; *All items* (incl. others): 111.6. (Source: Bank of Ghana, Accra).

NATIONAL ACCOUNTS
(million Ghana cedis at current prices)

Expenditure on the Gross Domestic Product

	2011	2012*	2013*
Government final consumption expenditure	9,955	15,732	15,606
Private final consumption expenditure	36,757	34,628	55,329
Increase in stocks	2,405	1,355	1,303
Gross fixed capital formation	15,317	23,334	21,280
Total domestic expenditure	64,434	75,049	93,517
Exports of goods and services	26,390	36,069	39,578
Less Imports of goods and services	29,727	39,773	44,338
Statistical discrepancy	−1,280	3,614	4,705
GDP in purchasers' values	59,816	74,959	93,462
GDP in constant 2006 prices	27,891	30,343	32,507

* Preliminary figures.

Gross Domestic Product by Economic Activity

	2012	2013	2014*
Agriculture and livestock . . .	13,687	16,729	17,954
Forestry and logging	1,880	1,992	2,145
Fishing	1,102	1,249	1,544
Mining and quarrying	6,961	9,036	9,891
Manufacturing	4,263	4,849	6,445
Electricity and water	843	987	1,171
Construction	8,370	10,765	13,327
Transport, storage and communications	9,631	12,366	14,507
Wholesale and retail trade, restaurants and hotels . . .	7,577	9,996	10,799
Finance, insurance, real estate and business services	6,954	9,317	11,229
Public administration and defence	4,952	6,319	8,839
Education	3,101	3,789	4,628
Health and social work . . .	921	1,132	1,363
Other community, social and personal services	2,701	3,886	4,871
Sub-total	72,943	92,412	108,711
Indirect taxes, less subsidies . .	4,689	5,946	8,954
Less Financial intermediation services indirectly measured .	2,317	3,419	4,229
GDP at market prices . . .	75,315	94,939	113,436

* Provisional figures.

BALANCE OF PAYMENTS
(US $ million)

	2011	2012	2013
Exports of goods	12,785.4	13,552.3	13,751.9
Imports of goods	−15,842.7	−17,763.2	−17,600.3
Balance on goods	−3,057.3	−4,210.9	−3,848.4
Exports of services	1,871.1	3,259.7	2,454.0
Imports of services	−3,666.6	−4,238.4	−4,897.8
Balance on goods and services	−4,852.7	−5,189.7	−6,292.2
Primary income received . . .	55.4	55.3	284.5
Primary income paid	−1,304.0	−2,185.9	−1,636.5
Balance on goods, services and primary income	−6,101.4	−7,320.3	−7,644.2
Secondary income received . .	2,597.4	2,696.7	1,963.9
Secondary income paid . . .	—	−8.0	−4.8
Current balance	−3,503.9	−4,631.5	−5,685.1
Capital account (net)	445.1	283.4	19.6
Direct investment assets . . .	25.4	−1.1	−0.7
Direct investment liabilities . .	3,222.2	3,294.5	3,227.0
Portfolio investment assets . .	437.4	1,338.2	1,276.2
Portfolio investment liabilities .	−189.7	−216.3	−617.3
Other investment assets . . .	—	128.3	475.0
Other investment liabilities . .	763.8	−872.0	1,104.9
Net errors and omissions . . .	−673.8	−68.0	−497.8
Reserves and related items .	475.8	−744.6	−698.2

Source: IMF, *International Financial Statistics.*

External Trade

PRINCIPAL COMMODITIES
(distribution by HS, US $ million)

Imports c.i.f.	2011	2012	2013
Live animals and animal products	586.0	554.9	613.0
Fish, crustaceans, molluscs and aquatic invertebrates . . .	241.1	216.7	325.8
Vegetables and vegetable products	647.8	578.2	516.2
Cereals	546.7	470.4	442.7
Rice	390.6	347.4	344.2
Prepared foodstuffs; beverages, spirits, vinegar; tobacco and articles thereof .	652.6	606.1	690.7
Mineral products	488.3	775.0	466.9
Salt, sulphur, earth, stone, plaster, lime and cement	366.6	418.4	332.5
Chemicals and related products	1,337.2	1,393.1	1,099.1
Miscellaneous chemical products .	464.5	432.4	303.7
Insecticides, fungicides, herbicides packaged for retail sale	370.9	337.2	230.8
Plastics, rubber, and articles thereof	625.6	682.2	576.0
Plastics and articles thereof . .	419.8	438.0	395.4
Pulp of wood, paper and paperboard, and articles thereof	1,965.2	942.2	189.7
Printed books, newspapers, pictures, etc	1,797.6	775.9	11.0
Stamps; cheque forms, banknotes, bond certificates, etc.	1,758.9	730.1	—
Iron and steel, other base metals and articles of base metal	1,181.9	1,440.5	998.7
Iron and steel	400.1	419.2	324.8
Articles of iron or steel . . .	494.1	718.5	430.5
Machinery and mechanical appliances; electrical equipment; parts thereof .	3,031.2	3,306.6	2,297.6
Machinery, nuclear reactors, boilers, etc. .	1,835.4	2,093.2	1,517.5
Electrical, electronic equipment .	1,195.9	1,213.4	780.1
Vehicles, aircraft, vessels and associated transport equipment	1,935.2	2,362.1	1,414.0
Vehicles other than railway, tramway	1,910.0	2,315.1	1,375.3
Cars (incl. station wagons) . .	860.4	1,064.5	520.3
Trucks, motor vehicles for the transport of goods	628.0	796.8	519.4
Total (incl. others)	13,573.3	14,011.9	10,018.2

Exports f.o.b.	2011	2012	2013
Vegetables and vegetable products	1,134.5	3,312.2	570.8
Edible fruit, nuts, peel of citrus fruit, melons	554.3	3,138.3	444.5
Brazil nuts, cashew nuts and coconuts	512.4	3,128.0	417.8
Prepared foodstuffs; beverages, spirits, vinegar; tobacco and articles thereof .	2,442.0	2,118.0	4,729.8
Cocoa and cocoa preparations .	2,294.4	2,040.9	4,632.8
Cocoa beans, raw, roasted . .	2,071.6	1,971.7	4,555.8
Mineral products	7,499.3	4,747.0	3,337.3
Mineral fuels, oils, distillation products, etc.	7,338.1	4,560.9	3,128.7
Crude petroleum oils . . .	2,862.0	3,691.2	3,015.4
Petroleum gases	4,330.8	621.4	10.6
Wood, wood charcoal, cork, and articles thereof . . .	484.6	378.3	475.6
Wood and articles of wood, wood charcoal	482.9	377.4	474.0
Pearls, precious stones, metals, coins, etc.	4,852.8	7,111.3	5,389.6
Gold, unwrought or in semi-manufactured forms . . .	4,836.6	7,107.3	5,364.6
Total (incl. others)	18,400.6	18,761.2	15,580.2

Source: Trade Map-Trade Competitiveness Map, International Trade Centre, www.intracen.org/marketanalysis.

PRINCIPAL TRADING PARTNERS
(US $ million)

Imports c.i.f.	2011	2012	2013
Australia	160.3	212.0	165.6
Belgium	809.3	924.1	918.1
Brazil	282.5	191.2	261.8
Canada	253.0	216.1	265.4
China, People's Republic . . .	2,062.1	2,405.3	2,280.5
France (incl. Monaco)	269.2	240.8	257.9
Germany	481.0	540.5	483.9
India	578.7	592.4	608.8
Indonesia	106.1	130.7	174.5
Italy (incl. San Marino) . . .	276.2	289.4	355.2
Japan	181.5	269.3	177.9
Korea, Republic	336.9	315.8	447.9
Malaysia	117.4	122.9	101.2
Morocco	180.7	99.0	143.4
Netherlands	415.6	414.3	336.5
Nigeria	54.0	285.6	60.5
South Africa	398.1	485.8	415.3
Spain	193.9	264.4	241.8
Sweden	249.5	201.2	164.6
Thailand	335.7	243.5	264.7
Togo	138.7	142.9	184.3
United Arab Emirates	307.1	357.2	0.9
United Kingdom	2,243.9	1,403.2	—
USA	1,307.3	1,563.8	—
Viet Nam	118.2	135.0	220.2
Total (incl. others)	13,573.3	14,011.9	10,018.2

Exports f.o.b.	2011	2012	2013
Belgium	403.4	130.7	124.7
Benin	87.3	85.5	195.7
Burkina Faso	500.6	369.5	229.3
China, People's Republic . . .	257.9	628.1	457.6
Côte d'Ivoire	717.4	81.8	58.8
France (incl. Monaco)	1,722.4	1,412.4	941.6
Germany	169.7	198.0	117.7
India	722.2	1,876.7	465.8
Iran	13.9	5.3	3,183.8
Italy (incl. San Marino) . . .	1,041.5	1,229.3	1,097.5
Malaysia	139.6	272.7	116.4
Netherlands	710.7	760.5	758.4

Exports f.o.b.—*continued*	2011	2012	2013
Nigeria	197.0	249.0	141.1
South Africa	3,146.8	4,544.2	2,833.2
Spain	132.6	268.9	207.7
Switzerland-Liechtenstein . .	865.9	1,214.8	1,172.0
Togo	4,594.0	879.8	75.5
Turkey	171.2	228.3	95.6
United Arab Emirates	993.9	1,637.6	1,659.7
United Kingdom	378.7	260.8	279.4
USA	444.9	297.3	326.2
Total (incl. others)	18,400.6	18,761.2	15,580.2

Source: Trade Map-Trade Competitiveness Map, International Trade Centre, www.intracen.org/marketanalysis.

Transport

RAILWAYS
(traffic)

	2002	2003	2004
Passenger-km (million) . . .	61	86	80
Net ton-km (million)	244	242	216

Source: UN, *Statistical Yearbook*.

ROAD TRAFFIC
(motor vehicles in use at 31 December)

	2006	2007	2009*
Passenger cars	275,424	493,770	439,527
Buses and coaches	43,665	121,113	145,144
Lorries and vans	92,154	158,379	124,512
Motorcycles and mopeds . . .	100,636	149,063	203,756

* Data for 2008 were not available.

Source: IRF, *World Road Statistics*.

SHIPPING

Flag Registered Fleet
(at 31 December)

	2012	2013	2014
Number of vessels	118	125	129
Total displacement ('000 grt) . .	93.0	112.9	114.0

Source: Lloyd's List Intelligence (www.lloydslistintelligence.com).

CIVIL AVIATION
(traffic on scheduled services)

	2002	2003	2004
Kilometres flown (million) . .	12	12	5
Passengers carried ('000) . . .	256	241	96
Passenger-km (million) . . .	912	906	363
Total ton-km (million)	107	101	41

Source: UN, *Statistical Yearbook*.

Passengers carried: 491,583 in 2011; 691,272 in 2012; 815,612 in 2013 (Source: World Bank, World Development Indicators database).

Tourism

ARRIVALS BY NATIONALITY

	2004	2005	2006
Côte d'Ivoire	28,069	25,155	25,921
France	21,096	10,089	11,915
Germany	28,168	14,094	17,132
Liberia	15,310	14,472	16,938
Netherlands	14,133	13,663	14,673
Nigeria	80,131	47,983	56,278
Togo	17,472	11,888	13,859
United Kingdom	50,547	36,747	36,795
USA	38,508	50,475	62,795
Total (incl. others)*	583,819	428,533	497,129

* Includes Ghanaian nationals resident abroad: 158,917 in 2004; 159,821 in 2005; 155,826 in 2006.

Total tourist arrivals ('000): 698 in 2008; 803 in 2009; 931 in 2010.

Receipts from tourism (US $ million, excl. passenger transport): 620 in 2010; 694 in 2011; 914 in 2012.

Source: World Tourism Organization.

Communications Media

	2011	2012	2013
Telephones ('000 main lines in use)	284.7	285.0	270.4
Mobile cellular telephones ('000 subscribers)	21,165.8	25,618.4	28,026.5
Internet subscribers ('000) . .	63.0	n.a.	n.a.
Broadband subscribers ('000) . .	62.6	65.3	68.8

Source: International Telecommunication Union.

Education

(2013/14 unless otherwise indicated)

	Institutions	Teachers	Students ('000)		
			Males	Females	Total
Pre-primary . .	20,100	50,575	829.4	816.2	1,645.6
Primary . . .	20,502	136,878	2,101.8	2,015.4	4,117.2
Junior secondary	9,076	100,921	765.2	708.7	1,473.9
Senior secondary	840	38,636	398.5	352.2	750.7
Technical and vocational . .	186	3,730	29.1	12.0	41.1
Tertiary* . .	n.a.	10,013	183.9	111.4	295.3

* 2011/12 figures.

2012/13 (unless otherwise indicated): *Teacher training* 39 institutions; *Universities* 7 institutions (1998/99).

Source: UNESCO and Ministry of Education, Accra.

Pupil-teacher ratio (primary education, UNESCO estimate): 31.7 in 2012/13 (Source: UNESCO Institute for Statistics).

Adult literacy rate (UNESCO estimates): 71.5% (males 78.3%; females 65.3%) in 2010 (Source: UNESCO Institute for Statistics).

Directory

The Government

HEAD OF STATE

President and Commander-in-Chief of the Armed Forces: JOHN DRAMANI MAHAMA (took office 24 July 2012; re-elected 7 December).

Vice-President: KWESI BEKOE AMISSAH-ARTHUR.

CABINET
(April 2015)

Minister of Finance and Economic Planning: SETH TERPKER.

Minister of Foreign Affairs and Regional Integration: HANNAH SERWAA TETTEH.

Minister of Local Government and Rural Development: COLLINS DAUDA.

Minister of Food and Agriculture: FIFI FIAVI FRANKLIN KWETEY.

Minister of Education: Prof. NAANA OPOKU AGYEMANG.

Minister of the Environment, Science and Technology: MAHAMA AYARIGA.

Minister of Lands and Natural Resources: NII OSAH MILLS.

Minister of Roads and Highways: ALHAJI INUSAH FUSEINI.

Minister of Water Resources, Works and Housing: Dr KWAKU AGYEMAN-MENSAH.

Minister of Communications: Dr EDWARD OMANE BOAMAH.

Minister of Gender, Children and Social Protection: NANA OYE LITHUR.

Minister of Defence: BENJAMIN BEWA-NYOG KUNBUOR.

Minister of Justice, Attorney-General: MARIETTA BREW APPIAH-OPPONG.

Minister of Energy and Petroleum: EMMANUEL ARMAH KOFI BUAH.

Minister of Transport: DZIFA ATTIVOR.

Minister of Employment and Labour Relations: HARUNA IDDRISU.

Minister of Health: Dr ALEX SEGBEFIA.

Minister of Youth and Sports: Dr MUSTAPHA AHMED.

Minister of Chieftaincy and Traditional Affairs: Dr HENRY SEIDU DAANNAA.

Minister of the Interior: MARK OWEN WOYONGO.

Minister of Trade and Industry: EKOW SPIO-GARBRAH.

Minister of Tourism, Culture and Creative Arts: ELIZABETH OFOSU-AGYARE.

Ministry of Fisheries and Aquaculture Development: SHERRY HANNY AYITTEY.

Minister of Power: Dr KWABENA DONKOR.

Ministers of State at the Presidency: ALHASSAN AZONG, AKWASI OPPONG-FOSU, ABDUL RASHID HASSAN PELPUO, ELVIS AFRIYIE-ANKRAH, COMFORT DOYOE CUDJOE GHANSAH.

REGIONAL MINISTERS
(April 2015)

Ashanti: PETER ANARFI-MENSAH.

Brong Ahafo: ERIC OPOKU.

Central: AQUINAS QUANSAH.

Eastern: ANTWI BOASIAKO-SEKYERE.

Greater Accra: NII LARYEA AFOTEY AGBO.

Northern: Alhaji LIMUNA MOHAMMED-MUNIRU.

Upper East: JAMES ZUUGAH TIIGAH.

Upper West: Alhaji AMIN AMIDU SULEMANI.

Volta: HELEN ADLOA NTOSO.

Western: PAUL EVANS AIDOO.

MINISTRIES

Office of the President: Flagstaff House, Liberation Crescent, Accra; tel. (30) 2666997; e-mail contact@presidency.gov.gh; internet www.presidency.gov.gh.

Ministry of Communications: POB M38, Accra; tel. (30) 2666465; fax (30) 2667114; e-mail info@moc.gov.gh; internet www.moc.gov.gh.

Ministry of Culture and Chieftaincy: POB 1627, State House, Accra; tel. (30) 2685012; fax (30) 2678361; e-mail chieftancycultur@yahoo.com.

Ministry of Defence: Burma Camp, Accra; tel. (30) 2775665; fax (30) 2772241; e-mail kaddok@internetghana.com.

Ministry of Education: POB M45, Accra; tel. (30) 2683627; fax (30) 2664067; e-mail pro@moe.gov.gh; internet www.moe.gov.gh.

Ministry of Employment and Social Welfare: POB 1627, State House, Accra; tel. (30) 2684532; fax (30) 2663615.

Ministry of Energy: FREMA House, Spintex Rd, POB T40 (Stadium Post Office), Stadium, Accra; tel. (30) 2683961; fax (30) 2668262; e-mail moen@energymin.gov.gh; internet www.energymin.gov.gh.

Ministry of the Environment, Science and Technology: POB M232, Accra; tel. (30) 2660005.

Ministry of Finance and Economic Planning: POB M40, Accra; tel. (30) 2665587; fax (30) 2666079; e-mail minister2009@mofep.gov.gh; internet www.mofep.gov.gh.

Ministry of Food and Agriculture: POB M37, Accra; tel. (30) 2663036; fax (30) 2668245; e-mail info@mofa.gov.gh; internet www.mofa.gov.gh.

Ministry of Foreign Affairs and Regional Integration: Treasury Rd, POB M53, Accra; tel. (30) 2664952; fax (30) 2665363; e-mail ghmaf00@ghana.com; internet www.mfa.gov.gh.

Ministry of Health: POB M44, Accra; tel. (30) 2684208; fax (30) 2663810; e-mail info@moh-ghana.org; internet www.moh-ghana.org.

Ministry of the Interior: POB M42, Accra; tel. (30) 2684400; fax (30) 2684408; e-mail mint@mint.gov.gh; internet www.mint.gov.gh.

Ministry of Justice and Attorney-General's Department: POB M60, Accra; tel. (30) 2665051; fax (30) 2667609; e-mail info@mjag.gov.gh.

Ministry of Lands and Natural Resources: POB M212, Accra; tel. (30) 2687314; fax (30) 2666801; e-mail motgov@hotmail.com; internet www.ghana-mining.org/ghweb/en/ma.html.

Ministry of Local Government and Rural Development: POB M50, Accra; tel. (30) 2664763; fax (30) 2682003; e-mail info@mlgrdghanagov.com; internet www.mlgrdghanagov.com.

Ministry of Power: Accra.

Ministry of Roads and Highways: Accra; tel. (30) 2618668; fax (30) 2672676; internet www.mrt.gov.gh.

Ministry of Tourism: POB 4386, Accra; tel. (30) 2666314; fax (30) 2666182; e-mail humphrey.kuma@tourism.gov.gh; internet www.touringghana.com.

Ministry of Trade and Industry: POB M47, Accra; tel. (30) 2663327; fax (30) 2662428; e-mail info@moti.gov.gh; internet www.moti.gov.gh.

Ministry of Transport: POB M57, Accra; tel. (30) 2681780; fax (30) 2681781; e-mail info@mot.gov.gh; internet mot.gov.gh.

Ministry of Water Resources, Works and Housing: POB M43, Accra; tel. (30) 2665940; fax (30) 2685503; e-mail mwh@ighmail.com.

Ministry of Women's and Children's Affairs: POB M186, Accra; tel. (30) 2688187; fax (30) 2688182; e-mail info@mowacgov.com; internet www.mowacghana.net.

Ministry of Youth and Sports: POB M252, Accra; tel. (30) 2664716; fax (30) 2662794; e-mail moysgh@gmail.com; internet www.moys.gov.gh.

President

Presidential Election, 7 December 2012

Candidate	Valid votes	% of valid votes
John Dramani Mahama (NDC)	5,574,761	50.70
Nana Addo Dankwa Akufo-Addo (NPP)	5,248,898	47.74
Papa Kwesi Nduom (PPP)	64,362	0.59
Henry Herbert Lartey (GCPP)	38,223	0.35
Hassan Ayariga (PNC)	24,617	0.22
Abu Sakara Foster (CPP)	20,323	0.18
Jacob Osei Yeboah (Ind.)	15,201	0.14
Kwasi Addai Odike (UFP)	8,877	0.08
Total	**10,995,262***	**100.00**

* Excluding 251,720 spoiled papers.

Legislature

PARLIAMENT

Parliament: Parliament House, Accra; tel. (30) 2664042; fax (30) 2665957; e-mail clerk@parliament.gh; internet www.parliament.gh.

Speaker: EDWARD DOE ADJAHO.

General Election, 7 December 2012

Party	Seats
National Democratic Congress (NDC)	148
New Patriotic Party (NPP)	123
People's National Convention (PNC)	1
Independents	3
Total	**275**

COUNCIL OF STATE

The Council of State is an advisory body of the President of the Republic. It consists of a former Chief Justice, a former Chief of Defence Staff of the Armed Forces, a former Inspector-General of Police, the President of the National House of Chiefs, 10 elected members (one from each of Ghana's regions) and 11 members appointed by the President. The Chairman is elected by members from among their number.

Chairman: JOHN HENRY MARTEY NEWMAN.

Election Commission

Electoral Commission (EC): POB M214, Accra; tel. (30) 2228421; internet www.ec.gov.gh; f. 1993; appointed by the President; Chair. Dr KWADWO AFARI-GYAN.

Political Organizations

Convention People's Party (CPP): 64 Mango Tree Ave, Asylum Down, POB 104, Accra-North; tel. (30) 2227763; e-mail info@conventionpeoplesparty.org; internet conventionpeoplesparty.org; f. 1998 as Convention Party by merger of the National Convention Party (f. 1992) and the People's Convention Party (f. 1993); present name adopted in 2000; Nkrumahist; Chair. SAMIA YABA NKRUMAH; Gen. Sec. IVOR KOBINA GREENSTREET.

Democratic People's Party (DPP): 698/4 Star Ave, Kokomlemle, Accra; tel. (30) 2221671; f. 1992; Chair. THOMAS WARD-BREW; Gen. Sec. Alhaji MUHAMMAD SALISU SULAIMANA.

EGLE (Every Ghanaian Living Everywhere) Party: POB TN 16132, Teshie Nungua, Accra; tel. (30) 2713994; fax (30) 2776894; f. 1992 as the Eagle Party; Gen. Sec. KOJO IMBIAH-TISMARK.

Great Consolidated Popular Party (GCPP): Citadel House, POB 3077, Accra; tel. (30) 2311498; internet greatconsolidatedpopularparty.org; f. 1996; Nkrumahist; Chair. Dr HENRY HERBERT LARTEY; Sec.-Gen. FREDERICK DADZIE (acting).

National Democratic Congress (NDC): 641/4 Ringway Close, POB 5825, Kokomlemle, Accra-North; tel. (30) 2223195; fax (30) 2220743; e-mail info@ndc.org.gh; internet www.ndc.org.gh; f. 1992; party of fmr Pres. Jerry Rawlings; Chair. Dr KWABENA ADJEI; Gen. Sec. JOHNSON ASIEDU NKETIAH.

National Democratic Party (NDP): Accra; f. 2012 by breakaway faction of NDC; Chair. Dr NII ARMAH JOSIAH ARYEH; Gen. Sec. Dr JOSPEH MAMBOA ROCKSON.

National Reform Party (NRP): 31 Mango Tree Ave, Asylum Down, POB 19403, Accra-North; tel. (30) 2228578; fax (30) 2227820; f. 1999 by a breakaway group from the NDC; Sec.-Gen. OPOKU KYERETWIE.

New Patriotic Party (NPP): C912/2 Duade St, Kokomlemle, POB 3456, Accra-North; tel. (30) 2264288; fax (30) 2229048; e-mail info@newpatrioticparty.org; internet www.newpatrioticparty.org; f. 1992; Chair. PAUL AWENTAMI AFOKO; Gen. Sec. KWADWO OWUSU-AFRIYIE.

People's National Convention (PNC): POB AC 120, Arts Centre, Accra; tel. (30) 2226528; e-mail info@pncghana.org; internet pncghana.org; f. 1992; Nkrumahist; Chair. Alhaji AHMED RAMADAN; Gen. Sec. BERNARD MORNAH.

Progressive People's Party (PPP): Asylum Down, Accra; tel. (30) 7020483; e-mail communications@pppghana.org; internet www.pppghana.org; f. 2011; Leader PAPA KWESI NDUOM.

Reformed Patriotic Democrats (RPD): POB 13274, Kumasi; tel. 243616660 (mobile); f. 2007 by former mems of the NPP; Founding Leader KWABENA AGYEI.

United Front Party (UFP): 14 Blohum St, Kumasi; tel. (540) 379242; f. 2012; Leader Akwasi Addai Odike; Sec.-Gen. Samuel Bekoe Owusu.

United Ghana Movement (UGM): 1 North Ridge Cres., POB C2611, Cantonments, Accra; tel. (30) 2225581; fax (30) 2223506; e-mail info@ugmghana.org; f. 1996 by a breakaway group from the NPP; Chair. Wereko Brobby.

United Renaissance Party (URP): Nima Hwy, POB 104, Accra-North; tel. (30) 28914411; f. 2006; Chair. Eric Charles Kofi Wayo.

Diplomatic Representation

EMBASSIES AND HIGH COMMISSIONS IN GHANA

Algeria: 22 Josif Tito Ave, POB 2747, Cantonments, Accra; tel. (30) 2776719; fax (30) 2776828; e-mail embdzacc@africaonline.com.gh; Ambassador Larbi Katti.

Angola: 5 Agbaamo St, Airport West Residential Area, Accra; tel. (30) 2766477; fax (30) 2775791; e-mail sec@angolaembassyghana.org; internet www.angolaembassyghana.org; Ambassador Ana Maria Teles Carreira.

Australia: 2 Second Rangoon Close (cnr Josef Tito Ave), Cantonments, Accra; tel. (30) 2216400; fax (30) 2216410; e-mail Accrahc.Enquiries@dfat.gov.au; internet www.ghana.embassy.gov.au; High Commissioner Joanna Marie Adamson.

Benin: 129A North Airport Rd, Accra; tel. (30) 2774860; fax (30) 2774889; e-mail ambab.accra@yahoo.fr; Ambassador Assounan Nouhouoi.

Brazil: Millennium Heights Bldg 2A, 14 Liberation Link, Airport Commercial Area, POB CT3859, Accra; tel. (30) 2774908; fax (30) 2778566; e-mail brasemb@africaonline.com.gh; internet www.embrazil.com.gh; Ambassador Luis Irene Gala.

Bulgaria: 3 Kakramadu Rd, POB 3193, East Cantonments, Accra; tel. (30) 2772404; fax (30) 2774231; e-mail bulemb2003@yahoo.com; internet www.mfa.bg/accra; Chargé d'affaires a.i. George Mitev.

Burkina Faso: 772 Asylum Down, off Farrar Ave, POB 65, Accra; tel. (30) 2221988; fax (30) 2221936; e-mail ambafaso@ghana.com; Ambassador Sini Pierre Sanou.

Canada: 42 Independence Ave, Sankara Interchange, POB 1639, Accra; tel. (30) 2211521; fax (30) 2211523; e-mail accra@international.gc.ca; internet www.canadainternational.gc.ca/ghana; High Commissioner Christopher Thornley.

China, People's Republic: 6 Agostino Neto Rd, Airport Residential Area, POB 3356, Accra; tel. (30) 2777073; fax (30) 2774527; e-mail chinaemb_gh@mfa.gov.cn; internet gh.chineseembassy.org; Ambassador Gong Jianzhong.

Colombia: Plot 16, 1st Circular Road, Cantonments, Accra; tel. (30) 2798701; e-mail eghana@cancilleria.gov.co; Ambassador Claudia Turbay Quintero.

Côte d'Ivoire: 9 18th Lane, off Cantonments Rd, POB 3445, Christiansborg, Accra; tel. (30) 2774611; fax (30) 2773516; e-mail acigh@ambaci-ghana.org; internet www.ambaci-ghana.org; Ambassador Bernard Ehui Koutoua.

Cuba: 22A Akosombo Rd, Airport Residential Area, POB 9163 Airport, Accra; tel. (30) 2775868; fax (30) 2774998; e-mail embghana@africaonline.com.gh; Ambassador Jorge Fernando Lefebre Nicolás.

Czech Republic: C260/5, 2 Kanda High Rd, POB 5226, Accra-North; tel. (30) 2223540; fax (30) 2225337; e-mail accra@embassy.mzv.cz; internet www.mzv.cz/accra; Ambassador Margita Fuchsová.

Denmark: 67 Dr Isert Rd, North Ridge, POB CT596, Accra; tel. (30) 2253473; fax (30) 2228061; e-mail accamb@um.dk; internet www.ambaccra.um.dk; Ambassador Margit Thomsen.

Egypt: 38 Senchi St, Airport Residential Area, Accra; tel. (30) 2776854; fax (30) 2776795; e-mail boustaneaccra@hotmail.com; internet www.mfa.gov.eg/Accra_Emb; Ambassador Omar Ahmed Abdelwahab Selim.

Ethiopia: 2 Milne Close, Airport Residential Area, POB 1646, Accra; tel. (30) 2775928; fax (30) 2776827; e-mail ethioemb@ghana.com; Ambassador Cifty Abasiga Ababulgu.

France: 12th Rd, off Liberation Ave, POB 187, Accra; tel. (30) 2214550; fax (30) 2214589; e-mail info@ambafrance-gh.org; internet www.ambafrance-gh.org; Ambassador Frédéric Clavier.

Germany: 6 Ridge St, North Ridge, POB 1757, Accra; tel. (30) 2211000; fax (30) 2221347; e-mail info@accra.diplo.de; internet www.accra.diplo.de; Ambassador Rüdiger John.

Guinea: 11 Osu Badu St, Dzorwulu, POB 5497, Accra-North; tel. (30) 2777921; fax (30) 2760961; e-mail embagui@ghana.com; Ambassador Kaba Arafan Kabinet.

Holy See: 8 Drake Ave, Airport Residential Area, POB 9675, Accra; tel. (30) 2777759; fax (30) 2774019; e-mail nuncio@ghana.com; Apostolic Nuncio Most Rev. Jean-Marie Speich (Titular Archbishop of Sulci).

India: 9 Ridge Rd, Roman Ridge, POB CT 5708, Cantonments, Accra; tel. (30) 2775601; fax (30) 2772176; e-mail indiahc@ncs.com.gh; internet www.indiahc-ghana.com; High Commissioner K. Jeeva Sagar.

Iran: 3 Nme Lane, Airport Residential Area, POB 12673, Accra-North; tel. (30) 2774474; fax (30) 2777043; e-mail iranemb.acc@mfa.gov.ir; internet accra.mfa.ir; Ambassador Mohammed Suleymani.

Israel: 2 First Circular Rd, Unit 1, Josni Residence Cantonments, Accra; tel. (30) 2743838; fax (30) 2743857; e-mail amb-sec@accra.mfa.gov.il; internet embassies.gov.il/accra; Ambassador Sharon Bar-Lili.

Italy: Jawaharlal Nehru Rd, POB 140, Accra; tel. (30) 2775621; fax (30) 2777301; e-mail ambasciata.accra@esteri.it; internet www.ambaccra.esteri.it; Ambassador Luca Fratini.

Japan: Fifth Ave, POB 1637, West Cantonments, Accra; tel. (30) 2765060; fax (30) 2762553; internet www.gh.emb-japan.go.jp; Ambassador Kaoru Yoshimura.

Korea, Democratic People's Republic: 139 Nortei Ababio Loop, Ambassadorial Estate, Roman Ridge, POB 13874, Accra; tel. (30) 2777825; Ambassador Kim Pyong Gi.

Korea, Republic: 3 Abokobi Rd, POB GP13700, East Cantonments, Accra-North; tel. (30) 2776157; fax (30) 2772313; e-mail ghana@mofat.go.kr; internet gha.mofat.go.kr; Ambassador Kim Jea-Min.

Lebanon: F864/1, off Cantonments Rd, Osu, POB 562, Accra; tel. (30) 2776727; fax (30) 2764290; e-mail lebanon@its.com.gh; Ambassador Ali Hassan Halabi.

Liberia: 10 Odoi Kwao St, Airport Residential Area, POB 895, Accra; tel. (30) 2775641; fax (30) 2775987; Ambassador (vacant).

Libya: 14 Sixth St, Airport Residential Area, POB 9665, Accra; tel. (30) 2774819; fax (30) 2774953; Ambassador Dr Ali Ahmed Ghudban.

Malaysia: 18 Templesi Lane, Airport Residential Area, POB 16033, Accra; tel. (30) 2763691; fax (30) 2764910; e-mail mwaccra@africaonline.com.gh; internet www.kln.gov.my/web/gha_accra; High Commissioner Cheong Loon Lai.

Mali: 1st Bungalow, Liberia Rd, Airport Residential Area, POB 1121, Accra; tel. and fax (30) 2666942; e-mail ambamali@ighmail.com; Ambassador Aïssata Konandji Coulibaly.

Morocco: 1 Switchback Lane, PMB 117, Accra; tel. (30) 2775669; fax (30) 2785549; e-mail ambassade.maroc.ghana@gmail.com; Ambassador Nouzha Alaoui M'Hamdi.

Namibia: Accra; Ambassador Charles Bernardi Josob.

Netherlands: 89 Liberation Rd, Ako Adjei Interchange, POB CT1647, Accra; tel. (30) 2214350; fax (30) 2773655; e-mail acc@minbuza.nl; internet ghana.nlembassy.org; Ambassador Hans Docter.

Niger: E104/3 Independence Ave, POB 2685, Accra; tel. (30) 2224962; fax (30) 2229011; Ambassador Dan Nana Aicha Dan Ladi.

Nigeria: 20/21 Onyasia Cres., Roman Ridge Residential Area, Accra; tel. (30) 2776158; fax (30) 2776159; e-mail admin.hc@nigeriahighcommissionghana.org; internet www.nigeriahighcommissionghana.org; High Commissioner Ademola Oluseyi Onafowokan.

Russian Federation: Jawaharlal Nehru Rd, Switchback Lane, POB 1634, Accra; tel. (30) 2775611; fax (30) 2772699; e-mail russia@4u.com.gh; internet www.ghana.mid.ru; Ambassador Dmitry Y. Suslov.

Saudi Arabia: 10 Noi Fetreke St, Roman Ridge Ambassadorial Estate Ext., Airport Residential Area, POB 670, Accra; tel. (30) 2774311; fax (30) 2774829; e-mail ghemb@mofa.gov.sa; internet embassies.mofa.gov.sa/sites/ghana; Ambassador Hisham Mishal Al-Suwailem.

Senegal: 8F Odoi Kwao St, Airport Residential Area, PMB CT 342, Cantonments, Accra; tel. (30) 2770285; fax (30) 2770286; e-mail senegalaccra@hotmail.fr; Ambassador Chérif Oumar Diagné.

Sierra Leone: 83A Senchi St, Airport Residential Area, POB 55, Cantonments, Accra; tel. (30) 2769190; fax (30) 2769189; e-mail slhc@ighmail.com; High Commissioner Mokowa Adu-Gyamfi.

South Africa: Speed House 1, 3rd Soula St, Labone North POB 298, Accra; tel. (30) 2740450; fax (30) 2762381; e-mail sahcgh@africaonline.com.gh; High Commissioner Jeanette T. Ndlovu.

South Sudan: Accra; Chargé d'affaires a.i. Chan Choty Polino Akijnyjok.

Spain: Drake Ave Extension, Airport Residential Area, PMB KA44, Accra; tel. (30) 2774004; fax (30) 2776217; e-mail emb.accra@maec.es; internet www.spanish-embassy.com/accra.html; Ambassador Olga Cabarga Gómez.

Switzerland: Kanda Highway, North Ridge, POB 359, Accra; tel. (30) 2228125; fax (30) 2223583; e-mail acc.vertretung@eda.admin.ch; internet www.eda.admin.ch/accra; Ambassador GERHARD BRÜGGER.

Togo: Togo House, near Cantonments Circle, POB C120, Accra; tel. (30) 2777950; fax (30) 2765659; e-mail togamba@ighmail.com; Ambassador JEAN-PIERRE GBIKPI-BENISSAN.

Turkey: POB CT149, Cantonments, Accra; tel. (30) 2218180; e-mail embassy.accra@mfa.gov.tr; internet www.akra.be.mfa.gov.tr; Ambassador PENBE NESRIN BEYAZIT.

United Kingdom: Osu Link, off Gamel Abdul Nasser Ave, POB 296, Accra; tel. and fax (30) 2213250; fax (30) 2213274; e-mail high.commission.accra@fco.gov.uk; internet ukinghana.fco.gov.uk; High Commissioner JON BENJAMIN.

USA: 24 Fourth Circular Rd, POB GP 2288, Cantonments, Accra; tel. (30) 2741150; fax (30) 2741692; e-mail pressaccra@state.gov; internet ghana.usembassy.gov; Ambassador GENE A. CRETZ.

Zambia: 6 Agostino Neto Rd, Airport Residential Area, Accra; tel. (30) 2767689; e-mail info@zamhighghana.org; High Commissioner TIMOTHY MWABA WALAMBA.

Judicial System

The civil law in force in Ghana is based on the Common Law, doctrines of equity and general statutes that were in force in England in 1874, as modified by subsequent Ordinances. Ghanaian customary law is, however, the basis of most personal, domestic and contractual relationships. Criminal Law is based on the Criminal Procedure Code, 1960, derived from English Criminal Law, and since amended. The Superior Court of Judicature comprises a Supreme Court, a Court of Appeal, a High Court and a Regional Tribunal; Inferior Courts include Circuit Courts, Circuit Tribunals, Community Tribunals and such other Courts as may be designated by law. In 2001 'fast-track' court procedures were established to accelerate the delivery of justice.

Supreme Court: Accra; consists of the Chief Justice and not fewer than nine other Justices; is the final court of appeal in Ghana and has jurisdiction in matters relating to the enforcement or interpretation of the Constitution; Chief Justice GEORGINA THEODORA WOOD.

Court of Appeal: Consists of the Chief Justice and not fewer than five Judges of the Court of Appeal. It has jurisdiction to hear and determine appeals from any judgment, decree or order of the High Court.

High Court: Comprises the Chief Justice and not fewer than 12 Justices of the High Court. It exercises original jurisdiction in all matters, civil and criminal, other than those for offences involving treason. Trial by jury is practised in criminal cases in Ghana and the Criminal Procedure Code, 1960, provides that all trials on indictment shall be by a jury or with the aid of Assessors.

Circuit Courts: Exercise original jurisdiction in civil matters where the amount involved does not exceed 10 Ghana cedis. They also have jurisdiction with regard to the guardianship and custody of infants, and original jurisdiction in all criminal cases, except offences where the maximum punishment is death or the offence of treason. They have appellate jurisdiction from decisions of any District Court situated within their respective circuits.

District Courts: To each magisterial district is assigned at least one District Magistrate who has original jurisdiction to try civil suits in which the amount involved does not exceed 5 Ghana cedis. District Magistrates also have jurisdiction to deal with all criminal cases, except first-degree felonies, and commit cases of a more serious nature to either the Circuit Court or the High Court. A Grade I District Court can impose fines and sentences of imprisonment of up to two years and a Grade II District Court may impose fines and a sentence of imprisonment of up to 12 months. A District Court has no appellate jurisdiction, except in rent matters under the Rent Act.

Juvenile Courts: Jurisdiction in cases involving persons under 17 years of age, except where the juvenile is charged jointly with an adult. The Courts comprise a Chairman, who must be either the District Magistrate or a lawyer, and not fewer than two other members appointed by the Chief Justice in consultation with the Judicial Council. The Juvenile Courts can make orders as to the protection and supervision of a neglected child and can negotiate with parents to secure the good behaviour of a child.

National Public Tribunal: Considers appeals from the Regional Public Tribunals. Its decisions are final and are not subject to any further appeal. The Tribunal consists of at least three members and not more than five, one of whom acts as Chairman.

Regional Public Tribunals: Hears criminal cases relating to prices, rent or exchange control, theft, fraud, forgery, corruption or any offence which may be referred to them by the Provisional National Defence Council.

Special Military Tribunal: Hears criminal cases involving members of the armed forces. It consists of between five and seven members.

Attorney-General: MARIETTA BREW APPIAH-OPPONG.

Religion

According to the 2010 census, 71.2% of the population were Christians and 17.6% Muslims, while 5.2% followed indigenous beliefs. 5.3% of the population did not profess any religion.

CHRISTIANITY

Christian Council of Ghana: POB GP919, Accra; tel. (30) 2776678; fax (30) 2776725; e-mail info@christiancouncilofghana.org; internet www.christiancouncilofghana.org; f. 1929; advisory body comprising 16 mem. churches and 2 affiliate Christian orgs (2005); Chair. Most Rev. Prof. AMENU AMENU; Gen. Sec. Rev. Dr KWABENA OPUNI-FRIMPONG.

Ghana Pentecostal and Charismatic Council: Otenshie, East Legon, POB CT 483, Accra; tel. and fax (30) 2522226; e-mail info@gpccghana.org; internet gpccghana.org; f. 1969; Pres. Apostle Dr OPOKU ONYINAH; Gen. Sec. Apostle SAMUEL YAW ANTWI.

The Anglican Communion

Anglicans in Ghana are adherents of the Church of the Province of West Africa, comprising 15 dioceses and a missionary region, of which 10 are in Ghana. In 2012 two internal provinces were created out of the Province of West Africa, one for Ghana and the other for West Africa itself. The Archbishop of the Internal Province of West Africa is the Primate and Metropolitan of the Province of West Africa.

Archbishop of the Internal Province of Ghana and Bishop of Kumasi: Rt Rev. DANIEL YINKAH SAFO, Bishop's Office, St Cyprian's Ave, POB 144, Kumasi; tel. and fax (32) 2024117; e-mail anglicandioceseofkumasi@yahoo.com.

Bishop of Accra: Rt Rev. Dr DANIEL SYLVANUS MENSAH TORTO, Bishopscourt, POB 8, Accra; tel. (30) 2662292; fax (30) 2668822; e-mail adaccra@ghana.com.

Bishop of Cape Coast: Rt Rev. DANIEL ALLOTEY, Bishopscourt, POB A233, Adisadel Estates, Cape Coast; tel. (33) 2132502; fax (33) 2132637; e-mail danallotey@priest.com.

Bishop of Dunkwa-on-Offin: Rt Rev. EDMUND DAWSON AHMOAH, POB DW42, Dunkwa-on-Offin; tel. (24) 4464764.

Bishop of Ho: Rt Rev. MATTHIAS MEDADUES-BADOHU, Bishopslodge, POB MA 300, Ho; e-mail matthiaskwab@googlemail.com.

Bishop of Koforidua: Rt Rev. FRANCIS QUASHIE, POB 980, Koforidua; tel. (34) 2022329; fax (34) 2022060; e-mail cpwa_gh@yahoo.com; internet koforidua.org.

Bishop of Sekondi: Rt Rev. JOHN KWAMINA OTOO, POB 85, Sekondi; tel. (31) 20669125; e-mail angdiosek@yahoo.co.uk.

Bishop of Sunyani: Rt Rev. Dr FESTUS YEBOAH-ASUAMAH, Bishop's House, POB 23, Sunyani, BA; tel. (35) 2027205; fax (35) 2027203; e-mail anglicandiocesesyi@yahoo.com.

Bishop of Tamale: Rt Rev. Dr JACOB AYEEBO, POB 110, Tamale NR; tel. (37) 2022639; fax (37) 2022906; e-mail bishopea2000@yahoo.com.

Bishop of Wiawso: Rt Rev. ABRAHAM KOBINA ACKAH, POB 4, Sefwi, Wiawso; e-mail bishopackah@yahoo.com.

The Roman Catholic Church

Ghana comprises four archdioceses, 15 dioceses and one apostolic vicariate. Some 13% of the total population are Roman Catholics.

Ghana Bishops' Conference: National Catholic Secretariat, POB 9712, Airport, Accra; tel. (30) 2500491; fax (30) 2500493; e-mail dscncs@africaonline.com.gh; internet www.ghanacbc.org; f. 1960; Pres. Rt Rev. LUCAS ABADAMLOORA (Bishop of Navrongo-Bolgatanga).

Archbishop of Accra: Most Rev. GABRIEL CHARLES PALMER-BUCKLE, Chancery Office, POB 247, Accra; tel. (30) 2222728; fax (30) 2231619; e-mail cpalmerbuckle@yahoo.com; internet www.accracatholic.org.

Archbishop of Cape Coast: Most Rev. MATTHIAS KOBENA NKETSIAH, Archbishop's House, POB 112, Cape Coast; tel. (33) 2133471; fax (33) 2133473; e-mail archcape@ghanacbc.com.

Archbishop of Kumasi: Most Rev. GABRIEL JUSTICE YAW ANOKYE, POB 99, Kumasi; tel. (32) 2024012; fax (32) 2029395; e-mail cadiokum@ghana.com.

Archbishop of Tamale: Most Rev. PHILIP NAAMEH, Archbishop's House, Gumbehini Rd, POB 42, Tamale; tel. and fax (37) 2022425; e-mail tamdio2@yahoo.co.uk.

Other Christian Churches

African Methodist Episcopal Zion Church: POB MP522, Mamprobi, Accra; tel. (30) 2669200; f. 1898; Pres. Rt Rev. SETH O. LARTEY.

Christian Methodist Episcopal Church: POB AN 7639, Accra; tel. 244630267 (mobile); internet www.cmetenth.org/Ghana%20Regional%20Conference.htm; Pres. KENNETH W. CARTER; Mission Supervisor Rev. ADJEI K. LAWSON.

Church of Pentecost: POB 2194 Accra; tel. (30) 2777611; fax (30) 2774721; e-mail info@thecophq.org; internet www.thecophq.org; Chair. Apostle Dr OPOKU ONYINAH; Gen. Sec. Apostle ALFRED KODUAH; 1,503,057 mems.

Evangelical-Lutheran Church of Ghana: POB KN197, Kaneshie, Accra; tel. 244314136 (mobile); e-mail elcga@africaonline.com.gh; Pres. Rt Rev. Dr PAUL KOFI FYNN; 27,521 mems (2010).

Evangelical-Presbyterian Church of Ghana: 19 Main St, Tesano, PMB, Accra-North; tel. (30) 2220381; fax (30) 2233173; e-mail epchurch@ghana.com; f. 1847; Moderator Rev. FRANCIS AMENU; 295,000 mems.

Ghana Baptist Convention: POB AN 19909, Accra-North; tel. (30) 2242316; fax (30) 2242319; e-mail ags@gbconvention.com; internet gbconvention.com; f. 1963; Pres. Rev. Dr STEPHEN K. ASANTE; Sec. Rev. DAVID NARTEH OCANSEY; 65,000 mems.

Ghana Mennonite Church: POB 5485, Accra; fax (30) 2220589; f. 1957; Moderator Rev. EMMANUEL GALBAH-NUSETOR; Sec. JOHN ADETA; 5,000 mems.

Ghana Union Conference of Seventh-day Adventists: POB GP1016, Accra; tel. (30) 2223720; fax (30) 2227024; e-mail info@adventistgh.org; internet www.adventistgh.org; f. 1943; Pres. Pastor SAMUEL A. LARMIE; Sec. Pastor KWAME KWANIN-BOAKYE; 368,171 mems.

Methodist Church of Ghana: Wesley House, E252/2, Liberia Rd, POB 403, Accra; tel. (30) 2670355; fax (30) 2679223; e-mail mcghqs@ucomgh.com; internet www.methodistchurch-gh.org; Presiding Bishop Most Rev. Dr EMMANUEL ASANTE; 584,969 mems (2007).

Presbyterian Church of Ghana: POB 1800, Accra; tel. (30) 2662511; fax (30) 2665594; e-mail info@pcgonline.org; internet www.pcgonline.org; f. 1828; Moderator Rev. Prof. EMMANUEL MARTEY; Clerk Rev. Dr SAMUEL AYETE-NYAMPONG; 422,500 mems.

The African Methodist Episcopal Church, the Christ Reformed Church, the F'Eden Church, the Gospel Revival Church of God, the Religious Society of Friends (Quakers) and the Society of the Divine Word are also active in Ghana.

ISLAM

According to the 2010 census, Muslims had a particularly large concentration in the Northern Region, comprising some 60% of its population. The majority are Malikees.

Coalition of Muslim Organizations (COMOG): Accra; Pres. Alhaji ADAM MAHAMA (acting).

Ghana Muslims Representative Council: 31/1 Columbia Rd, POB 1180, Sekondi-Takoradi; tel. (31) 2026094.

Chief Imam: Sheikh USMAN NUHU SHARABUTU.

BAHÁ'Í FAITH

National Spiritual Assembly: POB AN 7098, Accra-North; tel. (30) 2222127; e-mail bahaighana@yahoo.com; Sec. GLADYS QUARTEY-PAPAFIO.

The Press

DAILY NEWSPAPERS

The Daily Dispatch: 1 Dade Walk, North Labone, POB C1945, Cantonments, Accra; tel. (30) 2763339; e-mail ephson@usa.net; Editor BEN EPHSON.

Daily Graphic: Graphic Communications Group Ltd, 3 Graphic Rd, POB 742, Accra; tel. (30) 2684001; fax (30) 2234754; e-mail gpack@graphic.com.gh; internet graphic.com.gh; f. 1950; state-owned; Editor RANSFORD TETTEH; circ. 100,000.

Daily Guide: POB 115, Accra; tel. (30) 2229576; fax (30) 2231459; e-mail dailyguidenews@yahoo.com; internet dailyguideghana.com; owned by Western Publications Ltd; Editor FORTUNE ALIMI.

Ghanaian Chronicle: 37 Bobo St, Tesano, PMB, Accra-North; tel. (30) 2232713; fax (30) 2232608; e-mail chronicle@africaonline.com.gh; internet thechronicle.com.gh; Editor EMMANUEL AKLI; circ. 60,000.

The Ghanaian Times: New Times Corpn, Ring Rd West, POB 2638, Accra; tel. (30) 228282; fax (30) 220733; e-mail info@ghanaiantimes.com.gh; internet www.ghanaiantimes.com.gh; f. 1958; state-owned; Editor DAVID AGBENU; circ. 45,000.

The Mail: POB CT4910, Cantonments, Accra; e-mail mike@accra-mail.com; internet www.accra-mail.com; Editor Alhaji ABDUL RAHMAN HARUNA ATTAH.

The Statesman: House No. 359/4, Faanofa Rd, Kokomlemle, Accra; tel. and fax 244217504 (mobile); fax (30) 2220043; e-mail statesman_gh@yahoo.com; internet www.thestatesmanonline.com; f. 1949; official publ. of the New Patriotic Party; Editor-in-Chief ASARE OTCHERE-DARKO; Editor KWABENA AMANKWAH.

The Telescope: Takoradi; f. 2005; Editor LOUIS HENRY DANSO.

PERIODICALS

Thrice-weekly

The Independent: Clear Type Press Bldg Complex, off Graphic Rd, POB 4031, Accra; tel. and fax (30) 2661091; f. 1989; Editor ANDREW ARTHUR.

Network Herald: 34 Crescent Rd, Labone, Accra; tel. (30) 2701184; fax (30) 2762173; e-mail support@ghana.com; internet www.networkherald.gh; f. 2001; Editor ELVIS QUARSHIE.

Bi-weekly

Ghana Palaver: Palaver Publications, POB WJ317, Wejia, Accra; tel. (30) 2850495; e-mail editor@ghana-palaver.com; internet www.ghana-palaver.com; f. 1994; Editor JOJO BRUCE QUANSAH.

The Ghanaian Lens: Accra; internet www.ghanaianlens.com; Editor KOBBY FIAGBE.

The Ghanaian Voice: Newstop Publications, POB 514, Mamprobi, Accra; tel. (30) 2324644; fax (30) 2314939; Editor CHRISTIANA ANSAH; circ. 100,000.

Weekly

Business and Financial Times: PMB CT16, Cantonments, Accra; tel. and fax (30) 2785366; fax (30) 2775449; e-mail info@thebftonline.com; internet www.thebftonline.com; f. 1989; 4 a week; Editor WILLIAM SELASSY ADJADOGO; circ. 40,000.

The Crusading Guide: Kofi Baako's Residence, North Labone Estates, POB 8523, Accra-North; tel. (30) 2770361; fax (30) 2761541; e-mail info@thenewcrusadingguideonline.com; internet thenewcrusadingguideonline.com; Editor KWEKU BAAKO, Jr.

Free Press: Tommy Thompson Books Ltd, POB 6492, Accra; tel. (30) 2225994; independent; Editor FRANK BOAHENE.

Ghana Life: Ghana Life Publications, POB 11337, Accra; tel. (30) 2229835; Editor NIKKI BOA-AMPONSEM.

Ghana Market Watch: Accra; internet www.ghanamarketwatch.com; f. 2006; financial; CEO AMOS DOTSE.

Graphic Showbiz: Graphic Communications Group Ltd, POB 742, Accra; tel. (30) 2684001; fax (30) 2684025; e-mail graphicshowbiz@gmail.com; f. 2000; state-owned; Editor NANABANYIN DADSON.

Graphic Sports: Graphic Communications Group Ltd, POB 742, Accra; tel. (30) 2228911; fax (30) 2234754; e-mail info@graphicghana.com; state-owned; Editor FELIX ABAYATEYE; circ. 60,000.

Gye Nyame Concord: Accra; e-mail gnconcord@yahoo.com; internet www.ghanaweb.com/concord.

The Heritage: POB AD676, Arts Center, Accra; tel. (30) 2236051; fax (30) 2237156; e-mail heritagenewspaper@yahoo.co.uk; Chair. STEPHEN OWUSU; Editor A. C. OHENE.

The Mirror: Graphic Communications Group Ltd, POB 742, Accra; tel. (30) 2684001; fax (30) 2234754; e-mail mirror@graphic.com.gh; internet graphic.com.gh; f. 1953; state-owned; Sat.; Editor E. N. O. PROVENCAL; circ. 90,000.

The National Democrat: Democrat Publications, POB 13605, Accra; Editor ELLIOT FELIX OHENE.

Public Agenda: Box MP2989, Accra-North; tel. (21) 2238820; e-mail pagenda@4u.com.gh; f. 1994; Editor AMOS SAFO; circ. 12,000.

The Standard: Standard Newspapers & Magazines Ltd, POB KA 9712, Accra; tel. (30) 2513537; fax (30) 2500493; e-mail snam.ncs@ghanacbc.org; Roman Catholic; Editor ISAAC FRITZ ANDOH; circ. 10,000.

The Vanguard: Accra; Editor OSBERT LARTEY.

The Weekend: Newstop Publications, POB 514, Mamprobi, Accra; tel. (30) 2324644; fax (30) 2314939; Editor EMMANUEL YARTEY; circ. 40,000.

Weekly Spectator: New Times Corpn, Ring Rd West, POB 2638, Accra; tel. (30) 2228282; fax (30) 2229398; internet spectator.newtimesonline.com/spectator; state-owned; f. 1963; Sun.; Editor ENIMIL ASHON; circ. 165,000.

Other

The African Woman Magazine: Ring Rd West, POB AN 15064, Accra; tel. and fax (30) 2241636; e-mail mail@theafricanwoman.com;

internet www.theafricanwoman.com; f. 1957; monthly; Editor NII ADUMUAH ORGLE.

AGI Newsletter: c/o Asscn of Ghana Industries, POB 8624, Accra-North; tel. (30) 2779023; e-mail agi@agighana.org; internet www.agighana.org; f. 1974; monthly; Editor CARLO HEY; circ. 1,500.

AGOO: Newstop Publications, POB 514, Mamprobi, Accra; tel. (30) 2324644; fax (30) 2314939; monthly; lifestyle magazine; Publr KOJO BONSU.

Armed Forces News: General Headquarters, Directorate of Public Relations, Burma Camp, Accra; tel. (30) 2776111; f. 1966; quarterly; Editor ADOTEY ANKRAH-HOFFMAN; circ. 4,000.

Business Watch: Sulton Bridge Co Ltd, POB C3447, Cantonments, Accra; tel. (30) 2233293; monthly.

Christian Messenger: Presbyterian Book Depot Bldg, POB 3075, Accra; tel. and fax (30) 2663124; e-mail danbentil@yahoo.com; f. 1883; English-language; fortnightly; Editor GEORGE MARTINSON; circ. 40,000.

Ghana Journal of Science: National Science and Technology Press, Council for Scientific and Industrial Research, POB M32, Accra; tel. (30) 2500253; monthly; Editor Dr A. K. AHAFIA.

Ghana Review International (GRi): POB GP14307, Accra; tel. (30) 2677437; fax (30) 2677438; e-mail accra@ghanareview.com; internet www.ghanareview.com; publishes in Accra, London and New York; CEO NANA OTUO ACHEAMPONG; circ. 100,000.

Ghana Today: Information Services Dept, POB 745, Accra; tel. (30) 2228011; fax (30) 2228089; e-mail isd@mino.gov.gh; English; political, economic, investment and cultural affairs; Dir ELVIS ADANYINA.

Ideal Woman (Obaa Sima): POB 5737, Accra; tel. (30) 2221399; f. 1971; monthly; Editor KATE ABBAM.

New Legon Observer: POB LG 490, Accra, Ghana; tel. (30) 2512503; fax (30) 2512504; e-mail newlegonobserver@ug.edu.gh; internet www.egnghana.org/publications/newLegonObserver.php; f. 2007; publ. by Ghana Society for Development Dialogue; fortnightly.

The Post: Ghana Information Services, POB 745, Accra; tel. (30) 2228011; fax (30) 2228089; e-mail isd@mino.gov.gh; f. 1980; monthly; current affairs and analysis; Dir ALPHONSE KOBLAVIE (acting); circ. 25,000.

Radio and TV Times: Ghana Broadcasting Corpn, Broadcasting House, POB 18167, Accra; tel. (30) 2508927; fax (30) 2773612; f. 1960; quarterly; Editor SAM THOMPSON; circ. 5,000.

Students World: POB M18, Accra; tel. (30) 2774248; fax (30) 2778715; e-mail afram@wwwplus.co.za; f. 1974; monthly; educational; Man. Editor ERIC OFEI; circ. 10,000.

Uneek: POB 230, Achimota, Accra; tel. (30) 2543853; fax (30) 2231355; e-mail info@uneekmagazine.com; f. 1998; monthly; leisure, culture; CEO and Editor FRANCIS ADAMS.

The Watchman: Watchman Gospel Ministry, POB GP4521, Accra; tel. (24) 3780716; e-mail watchmannewspaper@yahoo.com; f. 1986; Christian news; monthly; Pres. and CEO DIVINE P. KUMAH; Chair. Dr E. K. OPUNI; circ. 2,000.

Other newspapers include **The Catalyst, The Crystal Clear Lens, The Enquirer** and **Searchlight**. There are also internet-based news sites, including **Ghana Today**, at www.ghanatoday.com, and **ThisWeekGhana**, at www.thisweekghana.com.

NEWS AGENCY

Ghana News Agency: POB 2118, Accra; tel. (30) 2662381; fax (30) 2669841; e-mail ghnews@ghana.com; internet www.ghananewsagency.org; f. 1957; Gen. Man. Dr BERNARD OTABIL; 10 regional offices and 110 district offices.

PRESS ASSOCIATION

Ghana Journalists' Association: Press Centre, Abdul Nasser Ave, Ringway Estates, POB 4636, Accra; tel. and fax (30) 2234694; e-mail info@gjaghana.org; internet gjaghana.org; Pres. ROLAND AFFAIL MONNEY.

Publishers

Advent Press: Osu La Rd, POB 0102, Osu, Accra; tel. (30) 2777861; fax (30) 2775327; e-mail eaokpoti@ghana.com; f. 1937; publishing arm of the Ghana Union Conference of Seventh-day Adventists; Gen. Man. EMMANUEL C. TETTEH.

Adwinsa Publications (Ghana) Ltd: 17 Suncity Rd, Agbogba North Legon, POB 92, Legon, Accra; tel. and fax (24) 2366537; e-mail adwinsa@yahoo.com; internet www.adwinsa.com; f. 1977; general, educational; Man. Dir KWAKU OPPONG AMPONSAH.

Afram Publications: C 184/22 Midway Lane, Abofu-Achimota, POB M18, Accra; tel. (30) 4314103; e-mail info@aframpubghana.com; internet aframpubghana.com; f. 1973; textbooks and general; Chair. Prof. ESI SUTHERLAND ADDY; Man. Dir HARRIET TAGOE.

Africa Christian Press: POB 30, Achimota, Accra; tel. (30) 2244147; fax (30) 2220271; e-mail acpbooks@ghana.com; f. 1964; religious, fiction, theology, children's, leadership; Gen. Man. RICHARD A. B. CRABBE.

Allgoodbooks Ltd: POB AN10416, Accra-North; tel. (30) 2664294; fax (30) 2665629; e-mail allgoodbooks@hotmail.com; f. 1968; children's; Man. Dir MARY ASIRIFI.

Asempa Publishers: POB GP919, Accra; tel. 289672514 (mobile); e-mail asempa@iburstgh.com; f. 1970; religion, social issues, African music, fiction, children's; Gen. Man. SARAH O. APRONTI.

Catholic Book Centre: North Liberia Rd, POB 3285, Accra; tel. (30) 2226651; fax (30) 2237727.

Educational Press and Manufacturers Ltd: POB 9184, Airport-Accra; tel. (30) 2220395; f. 1975; textbooks, children's; Man. G. K. KODUA.

Encyclopaedia Africana Project: POB 2797, Accra; tel. (30) 2776939; fax (30) 2779228; e-mail eap@africaonline.com.gh; internet encyclopaediaafricana.org; f. 1962; reference; Dir GRACE BANSA.

Frank Publishing Ltd: POB MB414, Accra; tel. (30) 2240711; f. 1976; secondary school textbooks; Man. Dir FRANCIS K. DZOKOTO.

Ghana Publishing Co Ltd (Assembly Press): Barnes Rd, POB 124, Accra; tel. (30) 2664338; fax (30) 2664330; e-mail info@ghanapublishingcompany.com; internet www.ghanapublishingcompany.com; f. 1965; state-owned; textbooks and general fiction and non-fiction; Chair. Rev. HELENA OPOKU-SARKODIE; Man. Dir DAVID K. DZREKE.

Ghana Universities Press: POB GP4219, Accra; tel. (30) 2513401; fax (30) 2513402; f. 1962; scholarly, academic and general and textbooks; CEO Dr JOHN K. BOSOMTWE (acting).

Sam-Woode Ltd: A979/15 1st Adoley Link, Sahara-Dansoma, POB 12719, Accra-North; tel. (30) 2305287; fax (30) 2310482; e-mail samwoode@ghana.com; internet samwoode.com; f. 1984; educational and children's; Chair. KWESI SAM-WOODE; CEO RICHARD K. OGUAA.

Sedco Publishing Ltd: Sedco House, 5 Tabon St, North Ridge, POB 2051, Accra; tel. (30) 2221332; fax (30) 2220107; e-mail info@sedcopublishing.com; internet www.sedcopublishing.com; f. 1975; educational; Chair. COURAGE K. SEGBAWU; Man. Dir FRANK SEGBAWU.

Smartline (Publishing) Ltd: C3 Coastal Estates, DTD Batsonaa, Spintex Rd, Accra; tel. (30) 2810555; fax (30) 2810426; e-mail info@smartlinepublishers.com; internet smartlinepublishers.com; f. 1997; CEO ELLIOT AGYARE.

Sub-Saharan Publishers: POB 358, Legon, Accra; tel. and fax (30) 2233371; e-mail sub-saharan@ighmail.com; Man. Dir AKOSS OFORI-MENSAH.

Unimax Macmillan Ltd: 42 Ring Rd South Industrial Area, POB 10722, Accra-North; tel. (30) 2227443; fax (30) 2225215; e-mail info@unimacmillan.com; internet www.unimacmillan.com; representative of Macmillan UK; atlases, educational and children's; Man. Dir EDWARD ADDO.

Waterville Publishing House: 101 Miamona Cl., South Industrial Area, POB 195, Accra; tel. (30) 2689973; fax (30) 2689974; f. 1963; general fiction and non-fiction, textbooks, paperbacks, Africana; Man. Dir EMMANUEL AMOH.

Woeli Publishing Services: 19 ECOWAS Rd, POB NT601, Accra New Town; tel. and fax (30) 289535570; e-mail woeli@woelipublishing.com; internet www.woelipublishing.com; f. 1984; children's, fiction, academic; Dir WOELI A. DEKUTSEY.

PUBLISHERS' ASSOCIATIONS

Ghana Book Development Council: POB M430, Accra; tel. (30) 2229178; f. 1975; govt-financed agency; promotes and co-ordinates writing, production and distribution of books; Exec. Dir D. A. NIMAKO.

Ghana Book Publishers' Association (GBPA): POB LT471, Laterbiokorshie, Accra; tel. (30) 2912764; fax (30) 2810641; e-mail ghanabookpubs@yahoo.co.uk; internet www.ghanabookpublishers.org; f. 1976; Pres. ASARE KONADU YAMOAH.

Private Newspaper Publishers' Association of Ghana (PRINPAG): POB 125, Darkuman, Accra; Exec. Sec. KENTEMAN NII LARYEA SOWAH.

Broadcasting and Communications

REGULATORY AUTHORITY

National Communications Authority (NCA): 1 Rangoon Close, POB 1568, Cantonments, Accra; tel. (30) 2776621; fax (30) 2763449; e-mail info@nca.org.gh; internet www.nca.org.gh; f. 1996; regulatory body; Chair. KOFI TOTOBI QUAKYI; Dir-Gen. PAAROCK ASSUMAN VANPERCY.

TELECOMMUNICATIONS

In 2013 there were six companies operating in the telecommunications sector in Ghana. Airtel Ghana and Vodafone Ghana provided both mobile cellular and fixed-line telephone services, whereas the four other operators provided solely mobile cellular telephone services. At December 2013 there were 270,400 subscribers to fixed-line services and 28m. subscribers to mobile services.

Airtel Ghana: PMB, Accra; e-mail customercare.gh@gh.airtel.com; internet africa.airtel.com; f. 2008; name changed as above in 2010; provides both mobile cellular and fixed-line telephone services; Man. Dir PHILIP SOWAH; 10,320 fixed-line and 3.19m. mobile subscribers (Dec. 2012).

Expresso Telecoms Ghana: POB 10208, Accra; tel. 28282100 (mobile); fax 28210103 (mobile); internet www.expressotelecom.com; fmrly Kasapa Telecom Ltd; present name adopted 2010; owned by Expresso Telecom Group (UAE); Man. Dir EL AMIR AHMED EL AMIR YOUSIF; 165,863 subscribers (Dec. 2012).

Glo Mobile Ghana: 4 Adjuma Cres., South Industrial Area, Kaneshie, Accra; e-mail info@glomobileghana.com; internet www.gloworld.com/Ghana; COO GEORGE ANDAH; 1.5m. subscribers (Dec. 2012).

Millicom Ghana Ltd: Millicom Place, Barnes Rd, PMB 100, Accra; tel. 277551000 (mobile); fax 277503999 (mobile); e-mail info@tigo.com.gh; internet www.tigo.com.gh; f. 1990; mobile cellular telephone services through the network Tigo; Man. Dir CARLOS CACERES; 3.69m. subscribers (Dec. 2012).

MTN Ghana: Auto Parts Bldg, 41A Graphic Rd, South Industrial Area, POB 281, International Trade Fair Lane, Accra; tel. 244300000 (mobile); fax (30) 2231974; e-mail customercare@mtn.com.gh; internet www.mtn.com.gh; f. 1994; Ghana's largest mobile cellular telephone provider, through the network MTN (fmrly Areeba); 100% owned by MTN (South Africa); CEO SERAME TAUKOBONG; 11.73m. subscribers (Dec. 2012).

Vodafone Ghana: Telecom House, nr Kwame Nkrumah Circle, PMB 221, Accra-North; tel. (30) 2200200; fax (30) 2221002; e-mail info.gh@vodafone.com; internet www.vodafone.com.gh; f. 1995; name changed as above in 2008, following acquisition of 70% shares in Ghana Telecommunications Company (GT) by Vodafone Group PLC (United Kingdom), 30% govt-owned; operates mobile cellular, fixed-line networks and data services; Chair. KOBINA QUANSAH; CEO HARIS BROUMIDIS; 274,661 fixed-line and 5.25m. mobile subscribers (Dec. 2012).

BROADCASTING

There are internal radio broadcasts in English, Akan, Dagbani, Ewe, Ga, Hausa and Nzema, and an external service in English and French. There are three transmitting stations, with a number of relay stations. The Ghana Broadcasting Corporation operates two national networks, Radio 1 and Radio 2, which broadcast from Accra, and four regional FM stations. In October 2013 there were 28 television and 328 radio stations licensed in Ghana. The Government intended to switch off the analogue television signal and replace it with digital broadcasting throughout the country by June 2015.

Ghana Broadcasting Corpn (GBC): Broadcasting House, Ring Rd Central, Kanda, POB 1633, Accra; tel. and fax (30) 2227779; e-mail radioghana@yahoo.com; internet www.gbcghana.com; f. 1935; four digital channels launched in 2014; Dir-Gen. Maj. (retd) ALBERT B. DON-CHEBE; Chair. RICHARD KWAME ASANTE; Dir of TV (vacant); Dir of Radio YAW OWUSU ADDO.

CitiFM: 11 Tettey Loop, Adabraka, Accra; tel. (30) 2226171; fax (30) 2224043; e-mail info@citifmonline.com; internet www.citifmonline.com; f. 2004; Man. Dir SAMUEL ATTA MENSAH.

Joy FM: 355 Faanofa St, Kokomlemle, POB 17202, Accra; tel. (30) 2701199; fax (30) 2224405; e-mail info@myjoyonline.com; internet www.myjoyonline.com; f. 1995; news, information and music broadcasts; Dir KWESI TWUM.

Metro TV: POB C1609, Cantonments, Accra; tel. (30) 2765701; fax (30) 2765703; e-mail admin@metroworld.tv; internet www.metrotv.com.gh; Chair. KWADWO DABO FRIMPONG; CEO TALAL FATTAL.

Radio Ada: POB KA9482, Accra; tel. (30) 2500907; fax (30) 2516442; e-mail radioada@kalssinn.net; f. 1998; community broadcasts in Dangme; Dirs ALEX QUARMYNE, WILNA QUARMYNE.

Radio Gold FM: POB 17298, Accra; tel. (30) 3300281; fax (30) 3300284; e-mail radiogold@ucomgh.com; internet www.myradiogoldlive.com; Man. Dir BAFFOE BONNIE.

Sky Broadcasting Co Ltd: 45 Water Rd, Kanda Overpass, North Ridge, POB CT3850, Cantonments, Accra; tel. (30) 2225716; fax (30) 2221983; e-mail vayiku@yahoo.com; internet www.spirit.fm; f. 2000; Gen. Man. STEVE ESHUN.

TV3: 12th Rd, Kanda (opposite French embassy), Accra; tel. (30) 2763458; fax (30) 2763450; e-mail info@tv3.com.gh; internet www.tv3.com.gh; f. 1997; private television station; programming in English and local languages; CEO SANTOKH SINGH.

Vibe FM: Pyramid House, 3rd Floor, Ring Rd Central, Accra; internet www.vibefm.com.gh; educational; CEO MIKE COOKE.

Finance

(cap. = capital; res = reserves; dep. = deposits; m. = million; brs = branches; amounts in Ghana cedis)

BANKING

At the end of 2012 there were 26 deposit money banks (of which 15 were foreign owned), 136 rural and community banks (RCBs) and 52 non-banking financial institutions in Ghana. There was also a mini central bank for the RCBs, ARB Apex Bank Ltd, financed mainly through the Rural Financial Services Project, which is a Government of Ghana project.

Central Bank

Bank of Ghana: 1 Thorpe Rd, POB 2674, Accra; tel. (30) 2666174; fax (30) 2662996; e-mail bogsecretary@bog.gov.gh; internet www.bog.gov.gh; f. 1957; bank of issue; cap. 10.0m., res 741.1m., dep. 3,685.9m. (Dec. 2009); Gov. Dr HENRY AKPENAMAWU KOFI WAMPAH.

Commercial Banks

Bank of Africa (Ghana) Ltd: 131–3 Farrar Ave, Cantonments, POB C1541, Accra; tel. (30) 2249690; fax (30) 2249697; e-mail enquiries@boaghana.com; internet www.boaghana.com; f. 1997; fmrly Amalgamated Bank Ltd, present name adopted 2011; cap. 100.9m., res 36.7m., dep. 406.8m. (Dec. 2013); Man. Dir KOBBY ANDAH; 18 brs.

Energy Bank Ghana Ltd: 30 Independence Ave (Gnat Height), Ridge Area, Accra; tel. (30) 2234033; fax (30) 2234337; internet www.energybankghana.com; f. 2009; commenced operations in 2011; cap. 60.0m., res 4.8m., dep. 115.7m. (Dec. 2012); Chair. Dr JIMOH IBRAHIM; Man. Dir and CEO SAM AYININUOLA.

Fidelity Bank: Ridge Towers, PMB 43, Cantonments, Accra; tel. (30) 2214490; fax (30) 2678868; e-mail info@myfidelitybank.net; internet www.fidelitybank.com.gh; f. 2006; cap. 83.0m., res 64.2m., dep. 1,414.2m. (Dec. 2013); Chair. WILLIAM PANFORD BRAY; CEO and Man. Dir EDWARD EFFAH; 8 brs.

Ghana Commercial Bank Ltd: Thorpe Rd, POB 134, Accra; tel. (30) 2663964; fax (30) 2662168; e-mail gcbmail@gcb.com.gh; internet www.gcb.com.gh; f. 1953; 21.4% state-owned; cap. 100.0m., res 150.8m., dep. 2,624.9m. (Dec. 2013); Chair. Dr FRITZ AUGUSTINE GOCKEL; Man. Dir SIMON DORNOO; 158 brs.

Prudential Bank Ltd: 8 Nima Ave, Ring Rd Central, PMB GPO, Accra; tel. (30) 2781201; fax (30) 2781210; e-mail headoffice@prudentialbank.com.gh; internet www.prudentialbank.com.gh; f. 1996; cap. 62.4m., res 29.6m., dep. 692.5m. (Dec. 2013); Exec. Chair. JOHN SACKAH ADDO; Man. Dir STEPHEN SEKYERE ABANKWA; 16 brs.

uniBank (Ghana) Ltd: Royal Castle Rd, POB AN15367, Kokomlemle, Accra; tel. (30) 2233328; fax (30) 2253695; e-mail info@unibankghana.com; internet www.unibankghana.com; f. 2001; cap. 60.1m., res 30.8m., dep. 765.8m. (Dec. 2012); Chair. OPOKU-GYAMFI BOATENG; Man. Dir FELIX NYARKO-PONG.

Development Banks

Agricultural Development Bank (ADB): ADB House, 37 Independence Ave, POB 4191, Accra; tel. (30) 2770403; fax (30) 2784893; e-mail info@agricbank.com; internet www.agricbank.com; f. 1965; 51.8% state-owned, 48.2% owned by Bank of Ghana; credit facilities for farmers and commercial banking; cap. 75.0m., res 161.0m., dep. 1,061.1m. (Dec. 2013); Chair. NANA SOGLO ALLOH, IV; Man. Dir STEPHEN KPORDZIH; 50 brs.

National Investment Bank Ltd (NIB): 37 Kwame Nkrumah Ave, POB 3726, Accra; tel. (30) 2661701; fax (30) 2661730; e-mail info@nib-ghana.com; internet www.nib-ghana.com; f. 1963; 86.4% state-owned; provides long-term investment capital, jt venture promotion, consortium finance man. and commercial banking services; cap. 70.0m., res –9.6m., dep. 336.7m. (Dec. 2009); Chair. TOGBE AFEDE; Man. Dir PATRICK TEI KWAPONG; 27 brs.

Merchant Banks

CAL Bank Ltd: 23 Independence Ave, POB 14596, Accra; tel. (30) 2680068; fax (30) 2680081; e-mail info@calbank.net; internet www.calbank.net; f. 1990; cap. 100.0m., res 129.6m., dep. 833.8m. (Dec. 2013); Chair. PAAROCK VANPERCY; Man. Dir FRANK BRAKO ADU, Jr.

Ecobank Ghana Ltd (EBG): 19 Seventh Ave, Ridge West, POB 16746, Accra; tel. (30) 2681146; fax (30) 2680428; e-mail ecobankgh@ecobank.com; internet www.ecobank.com; f. 1989; 92.2% owned by Ecobank Transnational Inc (Togo, operating under the auspices of the Economic Community of West African States); merged with The Trust Bank Ltd June 2012; cap. 226.6m., res 201.3m., dep. 3,765.8m. (Dec. 2013); Chair. LIONEL VAN LARE DOSOO; Man. Dir SAMUEL ASHITEY ADJEI; 7 brs.

First Atlantic Bank Ltd: Atlantic Pl., 1 Seventh Ave, Ridge West, POB C1620, Cantonments, Accra; tel. (30) 2682203; fax (30) 2479245; e-mail info@firstatlanticbank.com.gh; internet www.firstatlanticbank.com.gh; f. 1994; cap. 60.0m., res 31.8m., dep. 347.9m. (Dec. 2013); Chair. KAREN AKIWUMI-TANOH; Man. Dir GABRIEL EDGAL; 7 brs.

Universal Merchant Bank (Ghana) Ltd: Merban House, 44 Kwame Nkrumah Ave, POB 401, Accra; tel. (30) 2666331; fax (30) 2667305; e-mail info@merchantbank.com.gh; internet www.merchantbank.com.gh; f. 1972; fmrly Merchant Bank (Ghana) Ltd; present name adopted 2014; cap. 158.8m., res 34.2m., dep. 588.2m. (Dec. 2013); Chair. NOEL ADDO; Man. Dir and CEO JOHN AWUAH; 21 brs.

Foreign Banks

Barclays Bank of Ghana Ltd (UK): Barclays House, John Evans Atta Mills High St, POB 2949, Accra; tel. (30) 2664901; fax (30) 2669254; e-mail barclays.ghana@barclays.com; internet www.barclays.com/africa/ghana/; f. 1971; 90% owned by Barclays Bank Plc; 10% owned by Govt of Ghana; cap. 115.0m., res 152.0m., dep. 1,506.0m. (Dec. 2011); Man. Dir PATIENCE AKYIANU; 62 brs.

FBN Bank Ghana Ltd: Meridian House, Ring Rd Central, PMB 16, Accra; tel. (30) 2236136; fax (30) 2238228; e-mail icb@icbank-gh.com; internet www.icbank-gh.com; f. 1996; fmrly International Commercial Bank (Ghana) Ltd, name changed as above in 2014; Chair. OBA OTUDEKO; Group CEO SEYI OYESEFO; 11 brs.

Guaranty Trust Bank (Ghana) Ltd: 25A Castle Rd, Ambassadorial Area Ridge, PMB CT416, Accra; tel. (30) 2676474; fax (30) 2662727; e-mail gh.corporateaffairs@gtbank.com; internet www.gtbghana.com; f. 2004; 70% owned by Guaranty Trust Bank Plc, 15% owned by Netherlands Development Finance Co (FMO), 15% owned by Alhaji Yusif Ibrahim; cap. 82.6m., res 78.2m., dep. 661.1m. (Dec. 2013); Man. Dir LEKAN SANUSI.

Societe Generale Ghana Ltd: Ring Rd Central, POB 13119, Accra; tel. (30) 2202001; fax (30) 2248920; internet www.societegenerale.com.gh; f. 1976 as Social Security Bank; 51.0% owned by Société Générale, France; cap. 62.3m., res 95.3m., dep. 926.1m. (Dec. 2013); Chair. KOFI AMPIM; Man. Dir GILBERT HIE; 45 brs.

Stanbic Bank Ghana: Valco Trust House, Castle Rd Ridge, POB CT2344, Cantonments, Accra; tel. (30) 2687670; fax (30) 2687669; e-mail customercare@stanbic.com.gh; internet www.stanbic.com.gh; f. 1999; subsidiary of the Standard Bank of South Africa Ltd; Chair. DENNIS W. KENNEDY; Man. Dir ANDANI ALHASSAN; 2 brs.

Standard Chartered Bank Ghana Ltd (UK): 6 John Evans Atta Mills High St, POB 768, Accra; tel. (30) 2664591; fax (30) 2667751; internet www.standardchartered.com/gh; f. 1896 as Bank of British West Africa; cap. 61.6m., res 187.2m., dep. 1,708.9m. (Dec. 2012); Chair. ISHMAEL YAMSON; Country CEO KWEKU BEDU ADDO; 23 brs.

Zenith Bank Ghana (Nigeria): Premier Towers, Liberia Rd, PMB CT393, Accra; tel. (30) 2611500; fax (30) 2660760; e-mail info@zenithbank.com.gh; internet www.zenithbank.com.gh; cap. 61.2m., res 99.5m., dep. 1,637.8m. (Dec. 2013); Chair. MARY CHINERY-HESSE; CEO DANIEL ASIEDU; 19 brs.

Banking Association

Ghana Association of Bankers (GAB): POB 41, Accra; tel. (30) 2670629; fax 2667138; e-mail info@ghanaassociationofbankers.com; internet ghanaassociationofbankers.com; f. 1980; Pres. SIMON DORNOO; CEO DANIEL ATO KWAMINA MENSAH.

STOCK EXCHANGE

Ghana Stock Exchange (GSE): Cedi House, 5th Floor, Liberia Rd, POB 1849, Accra; tel. (30) 2669908; fax (30) 2669913; e-mail info@gse.com.gh; internet www.gse.com.gh; f. 1990; 35 listed cos in early 2009; Chair. Dr SAM MENSAH; Man. Dir KOFI YAMOAH.

INSURANCE

At 1 January 2013 there were 25 non-life insurance companies, 18 life insurance companies and two reinsurance companies in Ghana.

Donewell Insurance Co Ltd: F333/1 Carl Quest St, Kuku Hill, Osu RE, POB 2136, Osu, Accra; tel. (30) 2760483; fax (30) 2760484; e-mail info@donewellinsurance.com; internet www.donewellinsurance.com; f. 1992; Chair. ESTHER LILY NKANSAH; Man. Dir FRANCISCA NYAMEKYE KARIKARI.

Enterprise Insurance Co Ltd: Enterprise House, 11 John Evans Atta Mills High St, POB GP50, Accra; tel. (30) 2666847; fax (30) 2666186; e-mail info@enterprisegroup.com.gh; internet enterprisegroup.net.gh; f. 1972; Chair. TREVOR TREFGARNE; Group CEO KELI GADZEKPO.

Ghana Life Insurance Co: House No 17, Aviation Rd, Airport Residential Area, POB 8168, Accra; e-mail info@ghanalifeinsurance.com; internet www.ghanalifeinsurance.net; f. 1980; Chair. Eng. Chief CYRIL U. O. AJAGU; Man. Dir and CEO IVAN AVEREYIREH ABUBAKAR.

Ghana Union Assurance Co Ltd: F828/1 Ring Rd East, POB 1322, Accra; tel. (30) 2780627; fax (30) 2780647; e-mail gua@ghanaunionassurance.com; internet ghanaunionassurance.com; f. 1973; insurance underwriting; Chair. Dr A. B. K ANANE; Man. Dir NANA AGYEI DUKU.

Metropolitan Insurance Co Ltd: Caledonian House, Kojo Thompson Rd, POB GP20084, Accra; tel. (30) 2220966; fax (30) 2237872; e-mail met@metinsurance.com; internet www.metinsurance.com; f. 1991; Chair. SAM E. JONAH; CEO KWAME-GAZO AGBENYADZIE.

Phoenix Life Assurance Co: Phoenix House, Kanda Highway, Accra; internet www.phoenixlifegh.com; Chair. EMMANUEL ADU-SARKODEE; Man. Dir JEMIMA KISSI.

SIC Insurance Co Ltd: 28/29 Ring Road East, Osu, POB 2363, Accra; tel. (30) 2780600; fax (30) 2662205; e-mail sicinfo@sic-gh.com; internet www.sic-gh.com; f. 1962; 60% state-owned; all classes of insurance; Chair. FELICITY ACQUAH; Man. Dir DORIS AWO NKANI.

Social Security and National Insurance Trust (SSNIT): Pension House, POB MB 149, Accra; tel. (30) 266773; fax (30) 2686373; e-mail public@ssnit.org.gh; internet www.ssnit.org.gh; f. 1972; covers over 974,666 contributors (Feb. 2012); Chair. JOSHUA ALABI; Dir-Gen. ERNEST THOMPSON.

Starlife Assurance Co Ltd: C653/3 5th Cres., Asylum Down, POB AN 5783, Accra; tel. (30) 2258946; fax (30) 2258947; e-mail info@starlifegh.com; internet www.starlife.com.gh; f. 2005; Chair. OPOKU GYAMFI BOATENG; Exec. Vice-Chair. FRANK OPPONG-YEBOAH.

Vanguard Assurance Co Ltd: 25 Independence Ave, POB 1868, Accra; tel. (30) 2666485; fax (30) 2668610; e-mail vacmails@vanguardassurance.com; internet www.vanguardassurance.com; f. 1974; foreign travel, general accident, marine, motor and life insurance; Chair. KWADWO OBUAOBISA KETEKU; CEO DANKYI CHARLES ANSONG (acting); 13 brs.

Regulatory Authority

National Insurance Commission: Insurance Pl., 67 Independence Ave, POB CT3456, Cantonments, Accra; tel. (30) 2238300; fax (30) 2237248; e-mail info@nicgh.org; internet www.nicgh.org; f. 2006; Chair. LIONEL MOBILA; Commr of Insurance LYDIA LARIBA BAWA.

Insurance Association

Ghana Insurers Association (GIA): 248/9 Kanda, Sunyani Ave, Accra; tel. (30) 2251092; e-mail info@ghanainsurers.org; Pres. KWAME-GAZO AGBENYADZIE.

Trade and Industry

GOVERNMENT AGENCIES

Divestiture Implementation Committee: F35, 5 Ring Rd East, North Labone, POB CT102, Cantonments, Accra; tel. (30) 2772049; fax (30) 2773126; e-mail info@dic.com.gh; internet www.dic.com.gh; f. 1988; Chair. SETH TERPKER; Exec. Sec. BENSON POKU-ADJEI.

Environmental Protection Agency (EPA): 91 Starlets Rd, POB M326, Accra; tel. (30) 2664697; fax (30) 2662690; e-mail epaed@africaonline.com.gh; internet www.epa.gov.gh; f. 1974; Chair. EMMANUEL F. SIISI-WILSON; Exec. Dir DANIEL S. AMLALO.

Export Development and Agricultural Investment Fund (EDAIF): Ghana Olympic Committee Bldg, 3rd Floor, Ridge, POB MB493, Accra; tel. (30) 2918968; fax (30) 2671573; e-mail info@edifghana.org; internet www.edaifgh.org; f. 2000; established as Export Development and Investment Fund; named changed as above 2012; Chair. Prof. FRANCIS DODOO; Chief Exec. Dr BARFOUR OSEI.

Forestry Commission of Ghana (FC): 4 3rd Ave Ridge, PMB 434, Accra; tel. (30) 2401210; fax (30) 2401197; e-mail info@hq.fcghana.com; internet www.fcghana.org; CEO SAMUEL AFARI-DARTEY.

Ghana Export Promotion Authority (GEPA): Republic House, Tudu Rd, POB M146, Accra; tel. (30) 2683153; fax (30) 2677256; e-mail gepa@gepaghana.org; internet www.gepaghana.com; f. 1974; Chair. KOBINA ADE COKER; CEO AGYEMAN KWADWO OWUSU.

Ghana Free Zones Board: 5th Link Rd, East Cantonments, POB M626, Accra; tel. (30) 2780535; fax (30) 2785036; e-mail info@gfzb .gov.gh; internet www.gfzb.gov.gh; f. 1995; approves establishment of cos in export-processing zones; Chair. HARUNA IDDRISU; Exec. Sec. Dr EKWOW SPIO-GARBRAH.

Ghana Heavy Equipment Ltd (GHEL): Old Warehouse under the Bridge, Airport West, POB 1524, Accra; tel. (30) 2680118; fax (30) 2660276; e-mail info@ghelgh.com; internet www.ghelgh.com; fmrly subsidiary of Ghana National Trading Corpn; organizes exports, imports and production of heavy equipment; CEO YIDANA MAHAMI.

Ghana Investment Promotion Centre (GIPC): Public Services Commission Bldg, Ministries, POB M193, Accra; tel. (30) 2665125; fax (30) 2663801; e-mail info@gipcghana.com; internet www .gipcghana.com; f. 1994; negotiates new investments, approves projects, registers foreign capital and decides extent of govt participation; Chair. Dr MICHAEL AGYEKUM ADDO; CEO MAWUENA DUMOR TREBAH.

Ghana Minerals Commission (MINCOM): 12 Switchback Rd Residential Area, POB M248, Cantonments, Accra; tel. (30) 2771318; fax (30) 2773324; e-mail mincom@mc.ghanamining.org; internet www.ghanamining.org; f. 1986 to regulate and promote Ghana's mineral industry; CEO BENJAMIN NII AYI ARYEE.

Ghana National Petroleum Authority (NPA): Centurion Bldg No. 11, 5 Circular Rd, PMB CT, Accra; tel. (30) 2766196; fax (30) 2766193; e-mail info@npa.gov.gh; internet www.npa.gov.gh; f. 2005; oversees petroleum sector; Chair. KOJO FYNN; Chief Exec. ALEX MOULD.

Ghana Standards Authority: POB MB245, Accra; tel. (30) 2500065; fax (30) 2500092; e-mail info@gsa.gov.gh; internet www .gsa.gov.gh; f. 1967; establishes and promulgates standards; promotes standardization, industrial efficiency and devt and industrial welfare, health and safety; operates certification mark scheme; 402 mems; Chair. SAMUEL ADU-YEBOAH; Exec. Dir Dr GEORGE BEN CRENTSIL.

Ghana Trade Fair Co Ltd: Trade Fair Centre, POB 111, Accra; tel. (30) 2776611; fax (30) 2772012; e-mail info@tradefair.com.gh; internet www.tradefair.com.gh; f. 1989; Chair. Capt. (retd) KOJO BUTAH; CEO Dr EBENEZER ERASMUS OKPOTI KONEY (acting).

Ghana Trade and Investment Gateway Project (GHATIG): POB M47, Accra; tel. (30) 2663439; fax (30) 2773134; e-mail gateway1@ghana.com; promotes private investment and trade, infrastructural devt of free-trade zones and export-processing zones.

GNPA Ltd: POB 15331, Accra-North; tel. (30) 2228321; fax (30) 2221049; e-mail info@gnpa-ghana.com; internet www.gnpa-ghana .com; f. 1976 as Ghana National Procurement Agency; state-owned; part of Ministry of Trade and Industry; procures and markets a wide range of goods and services locally and abroad; CEO DOUGLAS Y. KUMASI.

National Board for Small-scale Industries (NBSSI): POB M85, Accra; tel. (30) 2668641; fax (30) 2661394; e-mail nbssided@ghana .com; f. 1985; part of Ministry of Trade and Industry; promotes small and medium-scale industrial and commercial enterprises by providing credit, advisory services and training; Exec. Dir LUKMAN ABDUL-RAHIM.

DEVELOPMENT ORGANIZATIONS

Agence Française de Développement (AFD): 8th Rangoon Close, Ring Rd Central, POB 9592, Airport, Accra; tel. (30) 2778755; fax (30) 2778757; e-mail afdaccra@afd.fr; internet www .afd.fr; f. 1985; fmrly Caisse Française de Développement; Resident Man. AMÉLIE JULY.

Private Enterprise Foundation (PEF): POB CT1671, Cantonments, Accra; tel. (30) 2515603; fax (30) 2515600; e-mail info@ pefghana.org; internet www.pefghana.org; f. 1994; promotes development of private sector; Pres. ASARE AKUFFO.

Social Investment Fund: off El-Wak Stadium Rd, nr Agricultural Engineering Dept, POB 3919, Cantonments, Accra; tel. (30) 2778921; fax (30) 2778404; e-mail info@sifinghana.org; internet www .sifinghana.org; f. 1998; Chair. JACOB BENJAMIN QUARTEY-PAPAFIO; Exec. Dir JOSEPH ACHEAMPONG.

CHAMBER OF COMMERCE

Ghana Chamber of Commerce and Industry (GCCI): World Trade Centre, 1st Floor, POB 2325, Accra; tel. (30) 2662860; fax (30) 2662866; e-mail info@ghanachamber.org; internet www .ghanachamber.org; f. 1961; promotes and protects industry and commerce, organizes trade fairs; 3,500 individual mems and 10 mem. chambers; Pres. SETH ADJEI BAAH; CEO STEPHEN OTENG.

INDUSTRIAL AND TRADE ORGANIZATIONS

Federation of Associations of Ghanaian Exporters (FAGE): POB M124, Accra; tel. (30) 2766176; fax (30) 2766253; e-mail fage-ghana@gmx.net; non-governmental, not-for-profit org. for exporters of non-traditional exports; Pres. ANTHONY SIKPA; over 2,500 mems.

Forestry Commission of Ghana, Timber Industry Development Division (TIDD): 4 Third Ave, Ridge, POB MB434, Accra; tel. (30) 2221315; fax (30) 2220818; e-mail info@hq.fcghana.com; internet www.ghanatimber.org; f. 1985; promotes the development of the timber industry and the sale and export of timber; Exec. Dir Dr BEN DONKOR.

Ghana Cocoa Board (COCOBOD): Cocoa House, 41 Kwame Nkrumah Ave, POB 933, Accra; tel. (30) 2661872; fax (30) 2661681; e-mail cocobod@cocobod.gh; internet www.cocobod.gh; f. 1947; monopoly purchaser of cocoa until 1993; responsible for purchase, grading and export of cocoa, coffee and sheanuts; also encourages production and scientific research aimed at improving quality and yield of these crops; controls all exports of cocoa; subsidiaries include the Cocoa Marketing Co (Ghana) Ltd and the Cocoa Research Institute of Ghana; Chair. Dr PERCIVAL YAW KURANCHIE; CEO Dr STEPHEN K. OPUNI.

Grains and Legumes Development Board: POB 4000, Kumasi; tel. (32) 2024231; fax (32) 2024778; e-mail gldb@africaonline.com.gh; f. 1970; subsidiary of Ministry of Food and Agriculture; produces, processes and stores seeds and seedlings, and manages national seed security stocks; Chair. Dr GODFRIED ADJEI DIXON; Exec. Dir Dr ROBERT AGYEIBI ASUBOAH.

EMPLOYERS' ORGANIZATION

Ghana Employers' Association (GEA): State Enterprises Commission Bldg, POB GP2616, Accra; tel. (30) 2678455; fax (30) 2678405; e-mail gea@ghanaemployers.com; internet www .ghanaemployers.com; f. 1959; 600 mems (2006); Pres. TERENCE RONALD DARKO; First Vice-Pres. YAW ADU GYAMFI.

Affiliated Bodies

Association of Ghana Industries (AGI): Addison House, 2nd Floor, Trade Fair Centre, POB AN8624, Accra-North; tel. (30) 2779023; fax (30) 2763383; e-mail agi@agighana.org; internet www.agighana.org; f. 1957; Pres. JAMES ASARE-ADJEI; Exec. Dir SETH TWUM-AKWABOAH; c. 500 mems.

Ghana Booksellers' Association: POB 10367, Accra-North; tel. (30) 2773002; fax (30) 2773242; e-mail minerva@ghana.com; Pres. FRED J. REIMMER; Gen. Sec. ADAMS AHIMAH.

Ghana Chamber of Mines: 22 Sir Arku Korsah Rd, Airport Residential Area, POB 991, Accra; tel. (30) 2760652; fax (30) 2760653; e-mail chamber@ghanachamberofmines.org; internet www .ghanachamberofmines.org; f. 1928; Pres. DANIEL OWIREDU; CEO Dr TONI AUBYNN.

Ghana Timber Association (GTA): POB 1020, Kumasi; tel. and fax (32) 2025153; f. 1952; promotes, protects and develops timber industry; Pres. BOATENG OPOKU.

UTILITIES

Regulatory Bodies

Energy Commission (EC): Ghana Airways Ave, Airport Residential Area, Plot 40, Spintex Rd, PMB Ministries, Accra; tel. (30) 2813756; fax (30) 2813764; e-mail info@energycom.gov.gh; internet www.energycom.gov.gh; f. 2001; Chair. Dr FRANCIS DAKURAH; Exec. Sec. Dr ALFRED OFOSU AHENKORAH.

Public Utilities Regulatory Commission (PURC): 51 Liberation Rd, African Liberation Circle, POB CT3095, Cantonments, Accra; tel. (30) 2244181; fax (30) 2244188; e-mail purcsec@purc.com.gh; internet www.purc.com.gh; f. 1997; Chair. EMMANUEL KWAKU ANNAN.

Electricity

Electricity Co of Ghana (ECG): Electro-Volta House, POB 521, Accra; tel. (30) 2676727; fax (30) 2666262; e-mail ecgho@ghana.com; internet www.ecgonline.info; Chair. Dr TONY OTENG GYASI; Man. Dir WILLIAM HUTTON-MENSAH.

Ghana Grid Company Ltd (GRIDCo): POB CS 7979, Tema; tel. (30) 27011185; fax (30) 2676180; e-mail info@gridcogh.com; internet www.gridcogh.com; f. 2006; Chair. EMMANUEL APPIAH KORANG; CEO Dr THOMAS WOBIL ANSAH.

Volta River Authority (VRA): Electro-Volta House, 28th February Rd, POB MB77, Accra; tel. (30) 2664941; fax (30) 2662610; e-mail prunit@vra.com; internet www.vra.com; f. 1961; govt owned; controls the generation and distribution of electricity; Northern Electricity Department of VRA f. 1987 to distribute electricity in northern Ghana; Prof. AKILAGPA SAWYERR; CEO ISAAC KIRK KOFFI.

Water

The Volta Basin Authority (VBA) was created by Ghana, Benin, Burkina Faso, Côte d'Ivoire, Mali and Togo in 2006 to manage the resources of the Volta River basin.

Ghana Water Co Ltd (GWCL): 28th February Rd, POB MB194, Accra; tel. (30) 2666781; fax (30) 2663552; e-mail info@gwcl.com.gh; internet www.gwcl.com.gh; f. 1965 to provide, distribute and conserve water supplies for public, domestic and industrial use, and to establish, operate and control sewerage systems; jointly managed by Aqua Vitens (Netherlands) and Rand Water (South Africa); Chair. ARNOLD H. K. SESHIE; Man. Dir KWAKU GODWIN DOVLO.

CO-OPERATIVES

Department of Co-operatives: POB M150, Accra; tel. (30) 2666212; fax (30) 2772789; f. 1944; govt-supervised body, responsible for registration, auditing and supervision of co-operative socs; Registrar R. BUACHIE-APHRAM.

Ghana Co-operatives Council Ltd (GACOCO): POB 4034, Accra; tel. 244267014 (mobile); fax (30) 2672014; e-mail gacopco@yahoo.com; f. 1951; co-ordinates activities of all co-operative socs and plays advocacy role for co-operative movement; comprises 11 active nat. asscns and 2 central orgs; Sec.-Gen. ALBERT AGYEMAN PREMPEH.

The national associations and central organizations include the Ghana Co-operative Marketing Asscn Ltd, the Ghana Co-operative Credit Unions' Asscn Ltd, the Ghana Co-operative Distillers' and Retailers' Asscn Ltd, and the Ghana Co-operative Poultry Farmers' Asscn Ltd.

TRADE UNIONS

Ghana Federation of Labour: POB Trade Fair 509, Accra; tel. (30) 2252105; fax (30) 2307394; e-mail gflgh@hotmail.com; internet www.gflghana.org; f. 1999; Sec.-Gen. ABRAHAM KOOMSON; 30,200 mems.

Ghana Trades Union Congress (GTUC): Hall of Trades Unions, Liberia Rd, POB 701, Accra; tel. (30) 2662568; fax (30) 2667161; e-mail info@ghanatuc.org; internet www.ghanatuc.org; f. 1945; 17 affiliated unions; Chair. ALEX K. BONNEY; Sec.-Gen. KOFI ASAMOAH.

Transport

RAILWAYS

Ghana has a railway network of 977 km, which connects Accra, Kumasi, Awaso and Takoradi. In 2010 a concessionary loan of US $4,000m. was secured from the Export-Import Bank of China to extend the Takoradi–Kumasi railway to Paga on the border with Burkina Faso.

Ghana Railway Co Ltd (GRC): POB 251, Takoradi; f. 1901; responsible for the operation and maintenance of all railways; to be run under private concession from April 2004; 947 km of track in use in 2003; Chair Dr CLEMENT HAMMAH; Man. Dir BENJAMIN AMOFA (acting).

Ghana Railway Development Authority (GRDA): Ministry of Transport, PMB, Accra; tel. (21) 681780; fax (21) 681781; internet grda.gov.gh; f. 2005; regulatory and devt authority; Chair. PEACE JUDITH GEORGE; Man. Dir EMMANUEL OPOKU.

ROADS

In 2012 Ghana had a total road network of approximately 66,200 km, of which 41% was considered to be in 'good condition'.

Ghana Highway Authority: POB 1641, Accra; tel. (30) 2666591; fax (30) 2665571; e-mail eokonadu@highways.mrt.gov.gh; internet www.highways.gov.gh; f. 1974 to plan, develop, administer and maintain trunk roads and related facilities; Chair. JOE GIDISU (acting); Chief Dir TESCHMAKER ANTHONY ESSILFIE.

Intercity State Transport Company (STC) Coaches Ltd: POB 7384, 1 Adjuma Cres., Ring Rd West Industrial Area, Accra; tel. (30) 2221912; fax (30) 2221945; e-mail stc@ghana.com; internet beta.stcghana.com.gh; f. 1965; fmrly State Transport Co; 80% owned by the Social Security and National Insurance Trust, 20% state-owned; above name adopted in 2003; regional and international coach services; Chair. E. K. ASANTE; Man. Dir SAMUEL NUAMAH DONKOR.

SHIPPING

The two main ports are Tema (near Accra) and Takoradi, both of which are linked with Kumasi by rail. There are also important inland ports on the Volta, Ankobra and Tano rivers. At 31 December 2014 the flag registered fleet comprised 129 vessels, totalling some 114,000 grt.

Ghana Maritime Authority (GMA): E354/3 Third Ave, East Ridge, PMB 34, Ministries, Accra; tel. (30) 2662122; fax (30) 2677702; e-mail info@ghanamaritime.org; internet www.ghanamaritime.org; f. 2002; policymaking body; part of Ministry of Transport; regulates maritime industry; Dir-Gen. ISSAKA PETER AZUMA.

Ghana Ports and Harbour Authority (GPHA): POB 150, Tema; tel. (30) 3202631; fax (30) 3202812; e-mail headquarters@ghanaports.net; internet www.ghanaports.gov.gh; f. 1986; holding co for the ports of Tema and Takoradi; Dir-Gen. NESTER PERCY GALLEY.

Alpha (West Africa) Line Ltd: POB 451, Tema; operates regular cargo services to West Africa, the United Kingom, the USA, the Far East and northern Europe; shipping agents; Man. Dir AHMED EDGAR COLLINGWOOD WILLIAMS.

Liner Agencies and Trading (Ghana) Ltd: POB 214, Tema; tel. (30) 3202987; fax (30) 3202989; e-mail enquiries@liner-agencies.com; international freight services; shipping agents; Dir J. OSSEI-YAW.

Maersk Ghana Ltd: Obourwe Bldg, Torman Rd, Fishing Harbour Area, POB 8800, Community 7, Tema; tel. (30) 3218700; fax (30) 3202048; e-mail gnamkt@maersk.com; internet www.maerskline.com/ghana; f. 2001; owned by Maersk Line (Denmark); offices in Tema, Takoradi and Kumasi; Man. Dir JEFF GOSCINIAK.

Scanship (Ghana) Ltd: Mensah Utreh Rd, Commercial Warehouse Area, POB 64, Tema; tel. (30) 3202561; fax (30) 3202571; e-mail scanship.ghana@gh.dti.bollore.com; shipping agents.

Shipping Association

Ghana Shippers' Authority: Enterprise House, 5th Floor, High St, POB 1321, Accra; tel. (30) 2666915; fax (30) 2668768; e-mail info@shippers-gh.com; internet shippers.org.gh; f. 1974; fmrly Ghana Shippers' Council, present name adopted 2010; represents interests of 28,000 registered Ghanaian shippers; also provides cargo-handling and allied services; Chair. G. M. GRIFFITHS; Chief Exec. KOFI MBIAH.

CIVIL AVIATION

The main international airport is at Kotoka (Accra). There are also airports at Kumasi, Takoradi, Sunyani, Tamale, Yendi, Navrongo and Wa. The construction of a dedicated freight terminal at Kotoka Airport was completed in 1994; in 2010 45,615 metric tons of freight were handled by the airport. In 2012 2.27m. passengers passed through Kotoka Airport. Following upgrade work, Tamale Airport became the country's second international airport in 2008. Kumasi Airport has also been substantially rehabilitated in recent years and it was hoped that it would commence offering international flights by the end of 2015.

Ghana Civil Aviation Authority (GCAA): PMB, Kotoka International Airport, Accra; tel. (30) 2776171; fax (30) 2773293; e-mail info@gcaa.com.gh; f. 1986; Chair. CHRISTIAN EDEM DOVLO; Dir-Gen. KWAME MAMPHEY.

Afra Airlines Ltd: 7 Nortei St, Airport Residential Area, Accra; tel. 244932488 (mobile); e-mail lukebutler@afraairlines.com; f. 2005; CEO LUKE BUTLER.

Antrak Air: 50 Senchi St, Airport Residential Area, Accra; tel. (30) 2782814; fax (30) 2782816; e-mail info@antrakair.com; internet www.antrakair.com; f. 2003; passenger and cargo services for domestic and international routes; Chair. ASOMA BANDA.

Gemini Airlines Ltd (Aero Gem Cargo): America House, POB 7238, Accra-North; tel. (30) 2771921; fax (30) 2761939; e-mail aerogemcargo@hotmail.com; f. 1974; operates weekly cargo flight between Accra and London; Gen. Man. ENOCH ANAN-TABURY.

Tourism

Ghana's attractions include fine beaches, game reserves, traditional festivals, and old trading forts and castles. In 2010 some 931,000 tourists visited Ghana. Revenue from tourism totalled US $914m. in 2012 (excluding passenger transport).

Ghana Tourist Board: POB GP3106, Accra-North; tel. (30) 2222153; fax (30) 2244611; e-mail gtb@africaonline.com.gh; internet www.touringghana.com; f. 1968; Exec. Dir JULIUS DEBRAH.

Ghana Association of Tourist and Travel Agencies (GATTA): Swamp Grove, Asylum Down, POB 7140, Accra-North; tel. (30) 2222398; fax (30) 2231102; e-mail info@gattagh.com; internet www.gattagh.com; Pres. HILLARIUS McCASH AKPAH; Exec. Sec. TINA OSEI.

Ghana Tourist Development Co Ltd: POB 8710, Accra-North; tel. (30) 2770720; fax (30) 2770694; e-mail info@ghanatouristdevelopment.com; internet www.ghanatouristdevelopment.com; f. 1974; develops tourist infrastructure, incl. hotels, restaurants and casinos; operates duty-free shops; Man. Dir ALFRED KOMLADZEI.

Defence

As assessed at November 2014, Ghana's total armed forces numbered 15,500 (army 11,500, navy 2,000 and air force 2,000). In 2000 the Government restructured the armed forces; the army was subsequently organized into north and south commands, and the navy into western and eastern commands. In 2004 a peacekeeping training centre, which was primarily to be used by ECOWAS, was established in Accra. At November 2014 a total of 2,754 Ghanaian troops were stationed abroad, of whom 65 were observers.

Defence Expenditure: Estimated at 1,150m. cedis for 2015.

Commander-in-Chief of the Armed Forces: Pres. JOHN DRAMANI MAHAMA.

Chief of Defence Staff: Vice-Adm. MATHEW QUASHIE.

Chief of Air Staff: Air Vice-Marshall MICHAEL SAMSON-OJE.

Chief of Army Staff: Maj.-Gen. RICHARD KWAME OPOKU-ADUSEI.

Chief of Naval Staff: Rear Adm. GEOFFREY MAWULI BIEKRO.

Education

Education is officially compulsory and free of charge for eight years, between the ages of six and 14. Primary education begins at the age of six and lasts for six years, comprising two cycles of three years each. Secondary education begins at the age of 12 and lasts for a further seven years, comprising a first cycle of three years and a second of four years. Following three years of junior secondary education, pupils are examined to determine admission to senior secondary school courses, or to technical and vocational courses. In 2013, according to UNESCO, primary enrolment included 87% of children in the relevant age-group (boys 87%; girls 87%), while the comparable ratio for secondary enrolment in 2009 was estimated at 46% (boys 48%; girls 44%). Some 295,300 students were enrolled in tertiary education in 2011/12. There were seven universities in Ghana in 1998/99. In 2012/13 tertiary institutions also included 39 teacher-training colleges and 181 technical and vocational institutes. In 2012 spending on education was equivalent to 24.4% of total budgetary expenditure.

GREECE

Introductory Survey

LOCATION, CLIMATE, LANGUAGE, RELIGION, FLAG, CAPITAL

The Hellenic Republic lies in south-eastern Europe. The country consists mainly of a mountainous peninsula between the Mediterranean Sea and the Aegean Sea, bounded to the north by Albania, the former Yugoslav republic of Macedonia and Bulgaria, and to the east by Turkey. To the south, east and west of the mainland lie numerous Greek islands, of which the largest is Crete. The climate is Mediterranean, with mild winters and hot summers. The average temperature in the capital is 28°C (82°F) in July and 9°C (48°F) in January. The language is Greek, of which there are two forms—the formal language (katharevoussa), and the language commonly spoken and taught in schools (demotiki). Almost all of the inhabitants profess Christianity, and the Greek Orthodox Church, to which about 97% of the population adhere, is the established religion. The national flag (proportions 2 by 3) displays nine equal horizontal stripes of blue and white, with a white cross throughout a square canton of blue at the upper hoist. The capital is Athens (Athinai).

CONTEMPORARY POLITICAL HISTORY

Historical Context

The liberation of Greece from the German occupation (1941–44) was followed by a civil war, which lasted until 1949. The communist forces were defeated, and the constitutional monarchy re-established. King Konstantinos (Constantine) II acceded to the throne on the death of his father, King Pavlos (Paul), in 1964. A succession of weak governments and conflicts between the King and his ministers culminated in a coup, led by right-wing army officers, in April 1967. An attempted counter-coup, led by the King, failed, and he went into exile. Col Georgios Papadopoulos became Prime Minister in December 1967 and Regent in March 1972.

Following an abortive naval mutiny, Greece was declared a republic in June 1973, and Papadopoulos was appointed President. Martial law was ended, and a civilian Government was appointed. A student uprising in Athens in November was violently suppressed by the army, and Papadopoulos was overthrown by another military coup. Lt-Gen. Phaidon Ghizikis was appointed President, and a mainly civilian Government, led by Adamantios Androutsopoulos, was installed, but effective power lay with a small group of officers and the military police under Brig.-Gen. Demetrios Ioannides. Following the failure of the military junta's attempt to overthrow President Makarios of Cyprus, and the Turkish invasion of the island, the Androutsopoulos administration collapsed in July 1974. Ghizikis summoned from exile a former Prime Minister, Konstantinos Karamanlis, who was invited to form a civilian Government of National Salvation. Martial law was ended, the press was released from state control and political parties were allowed to operate freely. A general election in November resulted in victory for Karamanlis's Nea Demokratia (ND—New Democracy), which won 220 of the 300 parliamentary seats. A referendum in December rejected proposals for a return to constitutional monarchy, and in June 1975 a new republican Constitution, providing for a parliamentary democracy, was promulgated. In the same month Prof. Konstantinos Tsatsos was elected President by the Vouli (Parliament).

At legislative elections in November 1977 ND was returned to power. In May 1980 Karamanlis was elected President; Georgios Rallis subsequently assumed the leadership of ND and was appointed Prime Minister. On 1 January 1981 Greece acceded to the European Community (EC, now the European Union— EU, see p. 271). The main opposition Panellinio Socialistiko Kinima (PASOK—Panhellenic Socialist Movement) secured an absolute majority at elections to Parliament in October, and the PASOK leader, Andreas Papandreou, became Prime Minister.

In March 1985 Karamanlis resigned in protest at plans by Papandreou to reduce his executive powers, and Parliament elected Christos Sartzetakis, a judge, as President. PASOK was returned to power at legislative elections in June, winning 161 seats in the 300-member Vouli. In March 1986 Parliament

approved a series of constitutional amendments limiting the powers of the President. In November 1988 several prominent ministers, having been implicated in a financial scandal, were forced to resign. In early 1989 the Elliniki Aristera (Greek Left) party, led by Leonidas Kyrkos, formed an electoral alliance with the 'Exterior' faction of the Kommunistiko Komma Ellados (KKE—Communist Party of Greece), under the leadership of Charilaos Florakis, to create the Synaspismos tis Aristeras kai tis Proodou (Synaspismos—Coalition of the Left and Progress). At elections in June, ND won the largest proportion of the votes cast, but failed to attain an overall majority in Parliament. Synaspismos eventually agreed to form an interim administration with ND, which was headed by Tzannis Tzannetakis, an ND deputy. The coalition Government announced its intention to govern for only three months, and to implement a *katharsis* (campaign of purification) of Greek politics. The administration duly resigned in October, having initiated investigations into the alleged involvement of officials of the former socialist Government in various malpractices. (In 1991 Papandreou and three of his former ministers were tried on charges of complicity in large-scale embezzlement during their terms of office. In 1992 Papandreou was acquitted, and two of the former ministers received minor sentences; the third had died during the trial.) The President of the Supreme Court, Ioannis Grivas, was appointed Prime Minister of an interim Government comprising non-political figures, which was to oversee further legislative elections. The results of the elections, conducted in November 1989, were again inconclusive. ND, PASOK and Synaspismós subsequently formed an interim coalition. However, following a dispute over military promotions in February 1990, the Government collapsed, and the former administration was reinstated on an interim basis. Further elections, conducted in April, resolved the impasse; ND secured 150 seats in Parliament. Mitsotakis secured the support of Konstantinos Stefanopoulos, the leader (and the sole parliamentary representative) of the Komma Dimokratikis Ananeosis (Party of Democratic Renewal), thereby enabling him to form the country's first single-party Government since 1981. In May 1990 Karamanlis took office as President for a five-year term, following his election by 153 of the 300 members of Parliament. Stefanopoulos formally joined ND in June.

Domestic Political Affairs

In April 1992 the Prime Minister successfully sought a vote of confidence from Parliament, following the dismissal of the Minister of Foreign Affairs, Antonis Samaras, and Mitsotakis's assumption of the portfolio in order to address attempts by the former Yugoslav republic of Macedonia (FYRM) to achieve international recognition as the Republic of Macedonia (see below). In August Michalis Papakonstantinou was allocated the foreign affairs portfolio.

In September 1993 two ND deputies resigned, following an appeal for support by Politiki Anixi (POLAN—Political Spring), a centre-right party that had been established in July by Samaras. The consequent loss of Mitsotakis's one-seat majority in Parliament obliged him to offer the Government's resignation and schedule early legislative elections. At the elections, conducted in October, PASOK obtained 46.9% of the total votes cast and 170 of the 300 parliamentary seats, while ND received 39.3% of the votes and 111 seats, and POLAN 4.9% of the votes and 10 seats. In October Mitsotakis resigned as leader of ND.

In March 1995 Stefanopoulos was elected President by 181 of the 300 members of Parliament. From mid-1995 tensions within the governing PASOK became increasingly evident. A group of 'dissident' PASOK deputies, including Konstantinos Simitis and Theodoros Pangalos, urged the resignation of Andreas Papandreou, and the implementation of further reforms within the party. In November Papandreou was admitted to hospital, and on 15 January 1996 he submitted his resignation as Prime Minister. Three days later, Simitis was elected to the premiership by the PASOK parliamentary faction. Simitis awarded Pangalos the foreign affairs portfolio, and pro-European ministers replaced the majority of Papandreou's former associates.

Following Papandreou's death in June, Simitis was elected leader of PASOK. In early legislative elections, held on 22 September, PASOK won 162 of the 300 parliamentary seats, with 41.5% of the votes cast, while ND obtained 108 seats (38.2%). Principal ministers in the outgoing Government were retained in the new PASOK administration. In March 1997 Konstantinos (Kostas) Karamanlis (a nephew of the former President and ND party leader) was elected leader of ND.

In February 1999 it emerged that dissident Kurdish leader Abdullah Öcalan, who had been charged with terrorism by Turkey, had been given refuge at the Greek embassy in Kenya, before being detained by the Turkish authorities. The Ministers of the Interior, Public Administration and Decentralization, of Foreign Affairs, and of Public Order subsequently resigned, prompting a government reorganization. Vasiliki Papandreou was appointed Minister of the Interior, Public Administration and Decentralization, and Georgios Papandreou (the son of the late Andreas Papandreou) replaced Pangalos as Minister of Foreign Affairs.

On 9 February 2000 Stefanopoulos was re-elected President by 269 of the 300 members of Parliament. At early legislative elections on 9 April, PASOK was returned to office, winning 43.8% of the votes cast and 158 parliamentary seats, narrowly defeating ND, with 42.7% of the votes and 125 seats. On 12 April Simitis formed a new Government. Simitis reorganized the Government in October 2001, following his re-election as PASOK party leader. In January 2004 Simitis announced his resignation from the leadership of PASOK, and scheduled early legislative elections for 7 March, asserting that an administration with a new mandate was necessary to address developments on the issue of Cyprus (see below). On 8 February Georgios Papandreou was elected unopposed as the President of PASOK.

The 2004 elections: ND Government

At the legislative elections held on 7 March 2004, ND secured 45.4% of the votes cast, thereby removing PASOK, which won 40.6% of the votes, from government. A new administration, headed by Karamanlis, was installed on 10 March. Greece's hosting of the summer Olympic Games in August was widely considered to be a success for the Government (although the cost was reported to have greatly exceeded projections). However, in November the Government publicly conceded that the PASOK administration had significantly understated public debt and budgetary deficit figures for several years in order for Greece to qualify for membership of the EU's economic and monetary union (EMU) in January 2001, after evidence to that effect emerged. The statement provoked a dispute between the ruling ND and PASOK, which criticized the revision of past official figures. On 8 February 2005 Karolos Papoulias, a member of PASOK and a former Minister of Foreign Affairs, was elected unopposed as President, receiving 279 votes in the 300-member Vouli; Papoulias was inaugurated as President on 12 March.

In early February 2006 the Government revealed that mobile cellular telephones belonging to Karamanlis, to prominent government and opposition members, and to public officials had been clandestinely monitored between June 2004 and March 2005. Later in February 2006 an extensive reorganization of the Government included the appointment of Dora Bakoyannis, a member of ND, the hitherto Mayor of Athens, and the daughter of former Prime Minister Mitsotakis, as Minister of Foreign Affairs. At local government elections, which took place on 15 and 22 October, ND retained control of some 30 prefectural councils and the municipalities of Athens and Thessaloníki, and PASOK increased its representation from 19 to 22 councils. In December, following an independent inquiry, the mobile cellular telecommunications operator Vodafone Greece was ordered to pay €76m., after being held responsible for the illegal surveillance (believed to be linked to security concerns relating to the holding of the summer Olympic Games in 2004).

On 25 August 2007 Karamanlis declared a state of emergency after forest fires resulted in the deaths of some 65 people. In late August an estimated 10,000 people held a protest in Athens at the perceived inadequacy of the Government's response to the emergency; it was further alleged that poor control of forests had prompted arsonists to take action to clear land for unauthorized building. At legislative elections conducted on 16 September ND was returned to power, securing 41.8% of the votes cast and 152 seats in Parliament. PASOK, with 38.1% of the votes, won a reduced number of seats (102), followed by the KKE (with 8.2% of votes and 22 seats) and Synaspismos Rizospastikís Aristeras (SYRIZA—Coalition of the Radical Left—5.0% of votes and 14 seats); an extreme nationalist organization, Laikos Orthodoxos

Synagermos (LAOS—Popular Orthodox Rally), received 3.8% of the votes and 10 seats, obtaining parliamentary representation for the first time. The rate of participation by the electorate was some 74.1%. Karamanlis subsequently established a smaller administration.

PASOK's return to power

The international financial crisis from late 2008 exacerbated economic hardship and public discontent, and there were widespread skirmishes between police and disaffected youths. On 6 December a 15-year-old was shot and killed in Exarchia, an impoverished district of Athens. Two police officers were charged in connection with the killing, which precipitated rioting in Athens, Thessaloníki and other towns. Students occupied numerous universities and schools in Athens and Thessaloníki, benefiting from a constitutional provision that prohibited police from entering the grounds of certain educational establishments. A one-day national strike by public sector unions in protest against the Government's economic policies proceeded on 10 December, and developed into more general protests against further austerity measures planned by the Government. In early January 2009 a protest, organized mainly by students and teachers against the education reforms, police repression and the social system, was violently suppressed by police.

In January 2009 Karamanlis announced an extensive ministerial reorganization, in an effort to restore public confidence in the Government. At elections to the European Parliament on 7 June, PASOK secured 36.7% of the votes cast and eight seats, ND obtained 32.3% of the votes and eight seats, the KKE 8.4% and two seats, and LAOS 7.2% and two seats; 52.6% of the registered electorate participated in the elections. On 2 September Karamanlis requested the dissolution of Parliament, and announced that the legislative elections (due in September 2011) would be brought forward to October 2009. Parliament was officially dissolved on 9 September.

In the legislative elections held on 4 October 2009 PASOK secured victory, with 43.9% of the votes cast and 160 seats, while ND received 33.5% of the votes and 91 seats; the KKE received 7.5% and 21 seats, LAOS 5.6% and 15 seats, and SYRIZA 4.6% and 13 seats. The rate of participation was recorded at 70.9% of the registered electorate. In response to the party's defeat, Karamanlis resigned as President of ND; he was succeeded, in November, by Samaras (who had rejoined the party in 2004). The President of PASOK, Georgios Papandreou, appointed a new Government, which won a motion of confidence in Parliament on 19 October; Papandreou assumed the foreign affairs portfolio, in addition to the premiership, while former Minister of Foreign Affairs Theodoros Pangalos became a Deputy Prime Minister. In December anti-Government demonstrations on the anniversary of the killing of the student resulted in violence in central Athens and Thessaloníki; more than 150 people were arrested. Later in December the adoption of an austerity budget by Parliament prompted further public protests and days of national strike; these intensified from February 2010. A new programme of spending reductions and tax increases (opposed by ND) was adopted by Parliament on 5 March; a large trade union protest in central Athens was disrupted by members of extremist groups, resulting in violent clashes.

Meanwhile, on 3 February 2010 President Papoulias was elected, again unopposed, by Parliament for a further term of office, obtaining the support of 266 deputies. On 2 May the EU, the IMF and the European Central Bank (ECB) 'troika' reached agreement with Greece on a €110,000m. austerity programme intended to stabilize the Greek economy, which was adopted by Parliament four days later. (Three PASOK deputies who had opposed the motion were subsequently expelled from the party, thereby reducing its representation in the legislature to 157 seats.) Meanwhile, on 5 May, when a national strike was scheduled, a large-scale demonstration in Athens against the planned measures escalated into violence, and protesters attempted to occupy the parliamentary building; three people died in a fire at a bank that had been attacked.

In June 2010 trade unions organized a strike against austerity measures (which included further extensive changes to the pension system), and a large-scale demonstration took place in Athens. Nevertheless, on 8 July (when a further one-day strike was held) the pension reforms were adopted in Parliament. A subsequent strike by truck drivers from late July, in protest at government plans to issue cheaper truck licences, resulted in nationwide fuel shortages and the suspension of transport services. The strike action was suspended on 1 August, after protesters agreed to enter into dialogue with the Government.

On 7 September 2010 Prime Minister Papandreou implemented an extensive government reorganization that was intended to support efforts to combat the debt crisis. Minister of Finance Georgios Papaconstantinou was retained, while Papandreou's additional portfolio of foreign affairs was reallocated to Deputy Prime Minister Pangalos. In the same month truck drivers resumed strike action, as Parliament adopted legislation liberalizing licensing regulations in the sector. Meanwhile, a police officer was sentenced to life imprisonment for the intentional killing of the student in December 2008, while his patrol partner received a custodial term of 10 years for complicity. Local elections took place on 7 and 14 November 2010 (prior to a reorganization of administrative divisions). PASOK won 34.6% of the votes cast nationwide, narrowly defeating ND (which received 32.8% of the votes), despite registering a significant loss of support compared with the 2009 legislative elections; PASOK secured governorships in eight of the 13 regions and ND in five.

During December 2010 public transport workers staged further one-day strikes in protest at salary reductions and the planned restructuring of state-owned transport companies. Later that month the adoption of the austerity budget for 2011 precipitated further protests in Athens. Public transport strikes continued in early 2011, despite a court order ruling the action to be illegal. Nevertheless, on 16 February Parliament adopted legislation providing for the reform of the public transport system. On 23 February, when a national strike and protests were organized, Parliament approved legislation liberalizing licensing regulations in a large number of professions.

Deepening fiscal crisis and new rescue plan

On 17 June 2011 Papandreou again reorganized the Government; notably, Papaconstantinou was removed from his position as Minister of Finance and replaced by Evangelos Venizelos, hitherto the Minister of National Defence, who also became a deputy premier. At the end of June, amid a two-day national strike and violent protests outside the parliament building, Parliament approved a programme of austerity measures, prescribed by the EU and the IMF in order to mitigate the deepening financial crisis and allow the release of further emergency funds; lending was duly approved by EU Ministers of Finance in early July. On 21 July, at an emergency summit meeting, held in Brussels, Belgium, eurozone leaders agreed the terms of a new rescue plan for Greece.

At the beginning of October 2011 the Government acknowledged that it would not meet budget deficit targets agreed with the EU and the IMF, and agreed further austerity measures, which included severe retrenchment in the state sector. On 20 October, amid a further two-day national strike and a protest staged by some 100,000 people outside the parliamentary building that escalated into violent clashes, Parliament adopted the new austerity measures. At a summit meeting in Brussels on 26–27 October, eurozone leaders reached a new agreement intended to reverse the escalating sovereign debt crisis. A second emergency funding plan of €130,000m. for Greece was conditionally approved (after it had become evident that the programme agreed in July was no longer adequate to prevent a Greek debt default).

At the end of October 2011, however, Papandreou unexpectedly announced that the new rescue plan would require endorsement at a national referendum. Eurozone leaders demanded that he attend emergency discussions, and disbursement of funds was again suspended, pending adoption of the rescue plan. The proposed referendum also prompted criticism from within the Government and PASOK, with one PASOK parliamentarian resigning from the party. Convening an emergency cabinet meeting on 3 November, Papandreou agreed to abandon the planned referendum and to enter into dialogue with ND on the creation of an interim administration. On 5 November Papandreou's Government narrowly survived a vote of confidence in Parliament. Nevertheless, since ND remained unwilling to participate in a transitional government headed by Papandreou, he announced his resignation on the following day. On 10 November Lucas Papademos, a former Vice-President of the ECB, received a mandate from President Papoulias to establish a transitional coalition administration. Several prominent members of the outgoing PASOK Government remained in the cabinet, while ND representatives received principal portfolios. Early legislative elections, initially scheduled for February 2012, were later postponed until May.

A general strike in protest against the austerity measures was organized by trade unions at the beginning of December 2011,

and a protest, which resulted in clashes with police, was staged to coincide with the adoption of the 2012 budget by Parliament on 6 December 2011. In early 2012 the agreement of government party leaders to the implementation of spending reductions and labour market reforms became an urgent priority in order to permit the rescue plan to proceed, and thereby avert a default on its debt by Greece. On 10 February LAOS withdrew its four representatives from the governing coalition and a PASOK deputy minister resigned, in protest against the austerity measures. The measures were formally adopted by 199 votes to 74 in Parliament on 12 February, while violent protests, with a number of arson attacks against shops and banks, took place in central Athens. On 21 February eurozone ministers responsible for finance formally agreed the second rescue plan, with a number of additional preconditions. Amid continuing anti-austerity protests, Parliament subsequently began to adopt reforms in accordance with EU requirements, and agreement was reached on debt-restructuring. In mid-March eurozone member states and the IMF approved joint financing amounting to some €172,600m. over four years, and the first critical EU instalment was subsequently released. On 20 March Venizelos announced his resignation as Minister of Finance, following his election as PASOK leader.

Legislative elections and revised rescue plan

The legislative elections were conducted on 6 May 2012: ND obtained 108 seats, SYRIZA 52 seats and PASOK 41 seats. After attempts by the main parties to form a governing coalition were unsuccessful, new elections were scheduled, and an interim administration was installed, headed by Panagiotis Pikrammenos (hitherto the President of the supreme administrative court, the Council of State). At the legislative elections held on 17 June ND won 29.7% of the votes and 129 seats in Parliament, while SYRIZA secured 71 seats and PASOK won 33 seats. Four smaller parties also obtained representation, among them the extreme nationalist Chrysi Avgi (Golden Dawn) party, which took 18 seats. The results were widely interpreted as a public endorsement of continued Greek membership of the eurozone. On 21 June a new Government was formed under the premiership of Antonis Samaras, the President of ND, who had succeeded in reaching a coalition agreement with PASOK and the small Dimokratiki Aristera (DIMAR—Democratic Left) party. Ioannis Stournaras, an independent economist, received the post of Minister of Finance in early July. The new administration, principally comprising members of ND (PASOK and DIMAR each proposed two independent politicians) was approved by a vote of confidence in Parliament on 8 July.

In September 2012 discussions with the EU-IMF-ECB troika were suspended, pending the finalization of further austerity measures by the Government, resulting in a delay in the disbursement of a loan instalment required to avert the country's bankruptcy. Meanwhile, emergency workers staged protests outside Parliament against a planned 5%–10% reduction in wages for public sector workers, and a further general strike took place. Large anti-austerity demonstrations were organized to coincide with the visit to Athens of German Chancellor Angela Merkel on 9 October. Increasing dissension over austerity policies was reported within the ruling coalition, and essential legislation on privatization was only narrowly approved in Parliament at the end of October.

Despite further violent protests and strike action, in early November 2012 new, stringent measures, which included a two-year increase in the retirement age, were adopted in Parliament. One ND representative and six PASOK deputies were subsequently expelled from their respective parties owing to their failure to support the programme; DIMAR also opposed the measures. Parliamentary approval of a revised budget for 2013 followed in November; however, eurozone Ministers of Finance delayed a decision on the release of funds. On 27 November the troika reached agreement on the disbursement of funds and also on further concessions for the reduction of Greece's debt. In early December, in fulfilment of an additional condition, Greece succeeded in purchasing about €31,800m. of its debt from holders of sovereign bonds.

In February 2013 a former mayor of Thessaloníki and two other officials were sentenced to life imprisonment for the embezzlement of some €18m. in public funds. In early March former Minister of National Defence and prominent PASOK politician Akis Tsohatzopoulos received an eight-year term of imprisonment for failing to disclose his financial assets; three other former ministers were charged with similar offences. In early June the Government announced the closure of the state radio and television broadcasting network, ERT, in an effort to satisfy redundancy targets imposed by the troika. Transmission was halted on the same day, under an emergency ministerial decree, despite the opposition of PASOK and DIMAR, prompting public protests. Although PASOK subsequently reached consensus with ND, on 21 June DIMAR withdrew from the Government. On 24 June Samaras announced a government reorganization, in an effort to avert the necessity of scheduling new legislative elections; the new administration included 11 PASOK members, notably PASOK leader Venizelos, who was appointed Deputy Prime Minister and Minister of Foreign Affairs.

In early July 2013 disbursement of the next tranche of aid to Greece was approved, after the Government agreed to implement further large-scale public sector dismissals demanded by the troika. Later that month Parliament voted to charge former Minister of Finance Papaconstantinou (who had been expelled from PASOK in December 2012) over his failure to investigate cases of alleged tax evasion, following the unauthorized publication, by investigative journalist Kostas Vaxevanis, of a list, which had been supplied to the Government by French officials, of more than 2,000 Greeks with Swiss bank accounts.

Government measures against Chrysi Avgi

Amid reports that members of Chrysi Avgi were staging a campaign of intimidation against immigrants and committing other anti-social acts, in September 2013 an anti-fascist activist, Pavlos Fyssas, was killed by a self-declared sympathizer of Chrysi Avgi in the outskirts of Athens. Police raided Chrysi Avgi headquarters in Athens and at least 10 members of the organization were arrested in connection with the murder, which prompted nationwide protests. Minister of National Defence Dimitris Avramopoulos ordered an investigation into allegations that members of the armed forces were involved in the formation and training of a military wing by Chrysi Avgi, and two senior police officers were obliged to resign owing to suspected connections to the organization. Later in September some 19 members, including Chrysi Avgi's leader, Nikolaos Michaloliakos, and six prominent parliamentary deputies, were arrested on charges of organizing a criminal group. In October Parliament voted in favour of removing the parliamentary immunity of the six deputies, and of suspending state financing for political parties whose leaders were charged with serious crimes.

Meanwhile, in September and November 2013 public sector workers staged further nationwide strike action in protest against government plans for continued retrenchment in the civil service in compliance with the demands of the troika. The Government survived a parliamentary vote of no confidence on 11 November, which had been proposed in response to a police raid on former ERT offices earlier that month; however, a PASOK deputy was expelled from the party after supporting the motion, while in December the Government's parliamentary majority was further reduced by the expulsion from ND of a deputy who had voted against the introduction of a controversial property tax. Amid concerns that elections to the European Parliament in May 2014 would precipitate increased political instability, the Government insisted in early January that the country was emerging from recession. Greece (which had assumed the rotating presidency of the Council of the EU for a period of six months on 1 January 2014) continued negotiations with the troika on economic reform proposals for that year. Following a further delay in funding, in mid-March it was announced that agreement had been reached on the release of some €10,000m. in assistance.

At elections to the European Parliament on 25 May 2014, SYRIZA secured 26.6% of the votes cast and six of the 21 seats allocated to Greece, ND obtained 22.7% of the votes and five seats, while Chrysi Avgi won 9.4% and three seats. A recently formed left-wing alliance led by PASOK, Elia—Dimokratiki Parataki (Olive Tree—Democratic Realignment) obtained 8.0% and two seats. A party formed by television presenter Stavros Theodorakis, To Potami (The River), obtained 6.6% and two seats, the KKE won 6.1% and two seats, and the right-wing Anexartitoi Ellines (ANEL—Independent Greeks) 3.5% and one seat. The rate of participation was 58.2%.

In June 2014 it was announced that Stournaras was to become the new Governor of the Bank of Greece. He was succeeded as Minister of Finance by Gikas Hardouvelis, as part of an extensive government reorganization. Among other appointments was that of Argyris Dinopoulous of ND as Minister of the Interior. In September legislation introducing greater penalties for racially- or sexually-motivated crimes was adopted. In October the Greek state prosecutor recommended that all Chrysi Avgi parliamentary deputies be placed on trial on charges of organizing and participating in a criminal group, and weapons offences. It was subsequently announced that the trial of 72 Chrysi Avgi members, including Michaloliakos and all former deputies, would begin in April 2015. A 24-hour general strike took place in late November 2014 in protest against austerity measures.

Recent developments: early legislative elections and SYRIZA victory

With opinion polls recording a progressive increase in the popularity of anti-austerity party SYRIZA, in early December 2014 Samaras brought forward a parliamentary vote to elect a new President. Inconclusive first and second rounds of parliamentary voting took place on 17 and 23 December. On 29 December Samaras's nominated candidate, former European Commissioner Stavros Dimas, failed to secure election after a third round of voting. In accordance with the Constitution, Parliament was consequently dissolved on 31 December, and early legislative elections were scheduled for 25 January 2015. As widely predicted, SYRIZA secured victory in the elections to Parliament (although it was narrowly short of an absolute majority), with 36.3% of the votes cast and 149 seats, while ND's representation declined sharply, to 27.8% of the votes and 76 seats. Chrysi Avgi received 6.3% and 17 seats, To Potami, with 6.1% of the votes, entered Parliament, also with 17 seats; the KKE obtained 5.5% and 15 seats, ANEL 4.8% and 13 seats, and PASOK (also suffering a significant loss of support) 4.7% and 13 seats. Although initially expected to form an alliance with To Potami, the leader of SYRIZA, Alexis Tsipras, reached a coalition agreement with ANEL (which also opposed the bailout agreement), and was inaugurated as Prime Minister on 25 January. His Government, largely comprising SYRIZA members, was formed two days later. Giannis Dragasakis was appointed Deputy Prime Minister, while Yanis Varoufakis, formerly an economic adviser to premier Georgios Papandreou, became Minister of Finance. Tsipras nominated Prokopis Pavlopoulos as his candidate for President of Greece, and on 18 February Pavlopoulos was elected by Parliament, with the support of 233 votes. He was inaugurated on 13 March.

In accordance with his pre-election pledges, Tsipras entered into negotiations with the troika in an effort to secure concessionary terms for the funded bailout agreement, which was due to expire on 28 February 2015. Despite ECB warnings that continued access to funding for the country's banks depended on the completion of a final bailout review and agreement on a new programme of reforms, he also announced his intention to reverse a number of austerity measures already implemented, such as privatizations. In early February the ECB announced that it would no longer accept Greek bonds in exchange for loan-funding, thereby increasing pressure on Greece's central bank. Following continued negotiations, amid the renewed possibility of a Greek debt default or exit from the eurozone, Tsipras was obliged to abandon ambitious objectives, notably to secure a large-scale debt cancellation and a moratorium on debt payments from the troika. On 24 February the Government presented a revised programme of policy measures, which included commitments to combat tax evasion, corruption, and fuel- and tobacco-smuggling, and to implement labour reforms; housing guarantees and free medical care were to be provided for the unemployed (although other pre-election pledges, such as the creation of jobs and a large increase in the minimum wage, were to be deferred). After the reform proposals were accepted by eurozone ministers responsible for finance, Greece was granted a four-month extension of its bailout programme. However, the release of funds was dependent on EU approval of reform implementation. A new list of reforms was submitted to eurozone leaders on 1 April, but little progress was achieved in negotiations that month.

Domestic extremism

Throughout the 1990s and early 2000s numerous bomb attacks against military and commercial targets in Greece were carried out by dissident groups, in particular the extremist left-wing Epanastatiki Organosi dekaefta Noemvri (17N—November 17 Revolutionary Organization), active since 1975, and the Epanastatikos Laikos Agonas (ELA—Revolutionary People's Struggle). In June 2000 a British defence attaché, Brig. Stephen Saunders, was assassinated by the 17N group. The first arrest of a member of 17N took place in June 2002, and the police subsequently arrested the movement's leader, Alexandros Giotopoulos. Shortly afterwards the Government announced that 17N had been disbanded. By January 2003 a total of 19 suspected members of 17N had been apprehended. The trial of all 19 alleged members of 17N was concluded in December; Giotopoulos and five others were sentenced to life imprisonment, and eight defendants received lesser custodial sentences. In October five members of the ELA, including the movement's leader, were each sentenced to 25 years' imprisonment on charges relating to more than 100 bomb attacks.

Meanwhile, another extremist left-wing organization, Epanastatikos Agonas (EA—Revolutionary Struggle), which had emerged in 2003, claimed responsibility for numerous bomb attacks, including an assassination attempt against the Minister of Culture, Georgios Voulgarakis, in May 2006 and a rocket attack against the US Embassy in Athens in January 2007. Public disorder after December 2008 (see above) also gave rise to a resurgence in extremist activity. A group believed to be affiliated to the EA, the Sechta ton Epanastaton (SE—Sect of Revolutionaries), issued threats to attack police and government facilities, and in June 2009 claimed responsibility for the killing of a police officer. In September four terrorist suspects, alleged to be members of the previously unknown Synomosia Pyrinon Tis Fotias (SPF—Conspiracy of Fire Nuclei), were arrested on charges related to a bomb attack at the residence of a former Minister of Public Order in July, and against a PASOK parliamentary deputy earlier in September. In June 2010 an employee at the Ministry of Civic Protection was killed by a parcel bomb. In November the SPF claimed responsibility for the dispatch of parcel bombs to a number of embassies in Athens, as well as to foreign government headquarters and embassies abroad. Following a police operation in December, a total of 26 suspected members of the SPF were arrested in connection with the parcel bombs and other attacks in Athens. In July 2011 six members of the SPF received prison sentences of between 11 and 25 years for bomb attacks in 2009. Amid continued social unrest, in January 2013 incendiary attacks were staged against party headquarters, the residences of journalists and commercial premises, while a gun attack took place at the office of Prime Minister Antonis Samaras; the incidents were widely attributed to left-wing anarchist groups. In November such a group claimed responsibility for an attack in Athens in which two Chrysi Avgi members were shot and killed and a third was injured. In July 2014 a former leading member of the ELA was arrested in Athens, following an armed exchange.

Regional Affairs

Relations with Turkey have been characterized by long-standing disputes concerning Cyprus (q.v.) and sovereignty over the continental shelf beneath the Aegean Sea. Tensions were exacerbated by the unilateral declaration of an 'independent' Turkish Cypriot state in Cyprus in November 1983 (the 'Turkish Republic of Northern Cyprus'—TRNC'). In March 1987 a disagreement between Greece and Turkey over petroleum-prospecting rights in disputed areas of the Aegean Sea almost resulted in military conflict. In January 1988, however, the Greek and Turkish Prime Ministers, meeting in Davos, Switzerland, agreed that joint committees should be established to negotiate peaceful solutions to disputes. In early 1996, however, tensions with Turkey were exacerbated by conflicting claims of sovereignty over Imia (Kardak), a group of uninhabited islands in the Aegean Sea.

In July 1997 the Greek Prime Minister, Konstantinos Simitis, and the Turkish President, Süleyman Demirel, held direct talks, which led to an agreement, the Madrid Declaration, pledging not to use violence or the threat of violence to resolve bilateral disputes. Relations between the two countries improved, after Greece offered both financial and material assistance to Turkey in August 1999, following a severe earthquake in the north-west of that country. Turkey reciprocated Greece's provision of emergency assistance when an earthquake struck Athens in September. At an EU summit, held in Helsinki, Finland, in December, Turkey was granted official candidate status, Greece having formally lifted its veto against Turkey's membership of the EU, although conditions were attached concerning resolution of both the Cyprus issue and the dispute with Greece in the Aegean. In January 2000 the Greek Minister of Foreign Affairs, Georgios Papandreou, met Turkish government leaders for discussions in Ankara, the Turkish capital.

The issue of Cyprus continued to dominate Greece's relations with Turkey (see the chapter on Cyprus). In February 2004 agreement was reached on proposals for reunification, which would allow Cyprus's accession to the EU as a single state. The final plan for reunification, submitted for approval in both the Republic of Cyprus and the 'TRNC' at referendums on 24 April, was endorsed in the latter, but rejected in the former (with the result that only that part of Cyprus administered by the principally Greek Cypriot Republic of Cyprus joined the EU on 1 May). In May the Turkish Prime Minister, Reçep Tayyip Erdoğan, made an official visit to Greece (the first by a Turkish premier in 16 years).

Following the installation of a new Greek Government in October 2009, Erdoğan proposed the establishment of a bilateral working group at ministerial level, in an effort to resolve outstanding issues of contention. In May 2010 Erdoğan, together with 10 Turkish ministers, made an official visit to Greece, where a joint government meeting was conducted, and 21 co-operation accords were signed. In March 2011 the Turkish Minister of Foreign Affairs and his Greek counterpart, meeting in Athens for discussions, pledged continued improvement in bilateral relations.

In 1985 Greece and Albania reopened their borders, which had remained closed since 1940, and Greece formally annulled claims to North Epirus (southern Albania), where there is a sizeable Greek minority. During the early 1990s, however, bilateral relations were severely strained by concerns over the treatment of the ethnic Greek population in Albania and over the illegal immigration of several thousand Albanians to Greece. In March 1996 President Stefanopoulos signed a treaty of friendship and co-operation with Albania's President, Sali Berisha. Albania agreed to provide Greek-language education in schools serving the ethnic Greek population, and Greece declared its willingness to issue temporary work permits for seasonal workers from Albania. A new border crossing was opened between Greece and Albania in May 1999. Following the stabilization of the political situation in Albania, the influx of Albanians into Greece decreased considerably.

Attempts after 1991 by the former Yugoslav republic of Macedonia (FYRM) to achieve international recognition as an independent state were strenuously opposed by the Greek Government, which insisted that 'Macedonia' was a purely geographical term (delineating an area that included a large part of northern Greece) and expressed fears that the adoption of such a name could imply ambitions on the Greek province of Macedonia. In early 1993 the Greek administration withdrew its former objection to the use of the word 'Macedonia', and its derivatives, as part of a fuller name for the new republic. In March the Greek Government accepted a UN proposal that the title 'the former Yugoslav republic of Macedonia' should be used temporarily and agreed to hold direct talks with the FYRM to consider confidence-building measures. In September 1995 the ministers responsible for foreign affairs of Greece and the FYRM, meeting in New York, USA, under UN auspices, signed an interim accord to normalize relations between the two countries, which included recognition of the existing international border. Under the terms of the agreement, Greece was to grant access to the port facilities at Thessaloníki and to remove all obstructions to the cross-border movement of people and goods, while the FYRM was to approve a new state flag; the measures were successfully implemented by October. Negotiations were to be pursued regarding the issue of a permanent name for the FYRM. In March 1997 the Greek Minister of Foreign Affairs visited the FYRM for the first time since its independence.

Greece strongly objected to the decision by the USA, announced in November 2004, that it would henceforth recognize the FYRM by its constitutional name of 'the Republic of Macedonia'. Negotiations on the issue, mediated by the UN, continued, while the Greek Government repeatedly threatened to obstruct the FYRM's aspirations to North Atlantic Treaty Organization (NATO, see p. 367) and EU accession, if it failed to agree to a compromise resolution. In January 2007 Greece protested at a decision by the FYRM Government to rename the international airport near the FYRM's capital, Skopje, after Alexander 'the Great' (who was considered by Greece to be integral to its cultural heritage). At a NATO conference convened in Bucharest, Romania, in April 2008, Greece vetoed the FYRM's application for membership, threatening similarly to obstruct the country's application to join the EU. In November the FYRM Government submitted legal proceedings against Greece to the International Court of Justice (ICJ, see p. 25) at The Hague, Netherlands, claiming that it had violated the terms of a UN-mediated interim accord regulating relations between the two countries, which stipulated that Greece would not veto the FYRM's accession to international institutions under that provisional name. On 5 December 2011 the ICJ ruled that Greece had contravened the interim accord by vetoing the FYRM's application to join NATO in 2008 and dismissed Greece's counterclaim that the FYRM had previously breached the accord. In November 2012 (by which time the FYRM Government urgently sought a settlement owing to its EU membership aspirations) negotiations were resumed, with mediation by Matthew Nimetz, the UN Secretary-General's Personal Envoy; however, talks continued to be unproductive. Following SYRIZA's election to government in January 2015, premier Tsipras confirmed that it would maintain the strenuous stance of previous administrations in the dispute.

The new SYRIZA-led Government began to establish closer links with Russia (following a deterioration in Russia's relations with EU states resulting from its annexation of the Crimean peninsula in March 2014—see the chapter on Ukraine). In April 2015 Tsipras met Russian President Vladimir Putin in Moscow, Russia, where he reportedly expressed criticism of the sanctions imposed on Russia by the EU.

CONSTITUTION AND GOVERNMENT

Under the Constitution of June 1975, and as subsequently revised, Greece is a parliamentary republic. The unicameral Vouli (Parliament) has 300 members, directly elected by universal adult suffrage for four years. The President is Head of State and is elected by Parliament for a five-year term. The President formally appoints the leader of the party with an absolute majority of seats in Parliament, or where no such party exists, the party with a plurality of seats, as Prime Minister, and upon his recommendation, the other members of the Government. Judicial power is exercised by the Supreme Court of Civil and Penal Law, courts of first instance, and courts of justice of the peace. Greece comprises seven decentralized administrations, 13 administrative regions (perifereia) and 325 municipalities.

REGIONAL AND INTERNATIONAL CO-OPERATION

Greece is a member of the North Atlantic Treaty Organization (NATO, see p. 367), the Organisation for Economic Co-operation and Development (OECD, see p. 377) and the Organization of the Black Sea Economic Co-operation (see p. 399). Greece became a full member of the EC (now the European Union—EU, see p. 271) in 1981, having signed the Treaty of Accession in 1979.

Greece is a founding member of the UN. As a contracting party to the General Agreement on Tariffs and Trade, Greece joined the World Trade Organization (see p. 431) on its establishment in 1995.

ECONOMIC AFFAIRS

In 2013, according to estimates by the World Bank, Greece's gross national income (GNI), measured at average 2011–13 prices, was US $248,597m., equivalent to $22,530 per head (or $25,630 per head on an international purchasing-power parity basis). During 2004–13, it was estimated, the population remained constant, with a negligible average annual rate of decline, while gross domestic product (GDP) per head decreased, in real terms, at an average annual rate of 1.7%. Overall GDP decreased, in real terms, at an average annual rate of 1.8% in 2004–13. Real GDP declined by 3.9% in 2013.

Agriculture (including hunting, forestry and fishing) contributed 3.8% of GDP in 2013, according to provisional figures, and engaged 13.8% of the employed labour force in the fourth quarter of 2013. The principal cash crops are vegetable products and fruit (which, together, accounted for 3.2% of total export earnings in 2013), olives, maize and wheat. According to the World Bank, real agricultural GDP declined at an average annual rate of 2.3% during 2005–13; the GDP of the sector decreased by 0.8% in 2012, but increased by 0.1% in 2013.

Industry (including mining, manufacturing, utilities and construction) provided 13.8% of GDP in 2013, according to provisional figures, and engaged 15.5% of the employed labour force in the fourth quarter of 2013. According to the World Bank, during 2005–13 real industrial GDP declined at an average annual rate of 6.0%; the GDP of the industrial sector decreased by 6.4% in 2013.

Mining and quarrying contributed a provisional 0.4% of GDP in 2013, and engaged 0.3% of the employed labour force in the fourth quarter of 2013. Mineral fuels and lubricants, iron and steel, and aluminium and aluminium alloys are the major mineral and metal exports. At the end of 2013, proven coal reserves stood at 3,020m. metric tons. Lignite, magnesite, silver ore and marble are also mined. In addition, Greece has small reserves of uranium, natural gas and gold.

Manufacturing provided a provisional 8.5% of GDP in 2013, and engaged 9.2% of the employed labour force in the fourth quarter of 2013. According to the World Bank, the GDP of the manufacturing sector decreased, in real terms, by an average annual rate of 3.4% in 2005–13; manufacturing GDP decreased by 3.3% in 2013.

Construction provided a provisional 2.2% of GDP in 2013, and engaged 4.6% of the employed labour force in the fourth quarter of 2013. According to the UN, the GDP of the construction sector decreased, in real terms, at an average annual rate of 10.6% in 2003–12; construction GDP decreased by 15.6% in 2012.

Energy is derived principally from lignite, which accounted for 55.8% of production in 2012, followed by natural gas (20.8%) and petroleum (7.6%). Greece is exploiting an offshore petroleum deposit in the north-eastern Aegean Sea. Solar power resources are also being developed. Mineral fuels represented 37.3% of the total value of imports in 2013.

The services sector contributed 82.4% of GDP in 2013, according to provisional figures, and engaged 70.7% of the employed labour force in the fourth quarter of 2013. Tourism is an important source of foreign exchange. There were 17.9m. visitor arrivals in 2013, according to official figures, and provisional figures from the World Tourism Organization indicated that receipts from the tourist sector totalled US $15,930m. in that year (excluding passenger transport). According to the World Bank, during 2005–13 the GDP of the services sector decreased, in real terms, at an average annual rate of 1.4%; sectoral GDP declined by 3.5% in 2013.

In 2013 Greece recorded a visible merchandise trade deficit of US $22,904m., and there was a surplus of $1,409m. on the current account of the balance of payments. In 2013 the principal source of imports was Russia (14.4%), followed by Germany; other major sources were Iraq and Italy. The principal market for exports in that year was Turkey (11.7%); other major purchasers were Italy, Germany and Bulgaria. The principal exports in that year were mineral fuels and lubricants (in particular, non-crude petroleum oils). Other major exports were prepared foodstuffs, beverages, spirits, vinegar, tobacco and articles thereof, and chemicals and related products. The principal imports were mineral fuels and lubricants (mainly crude petroleum and petroleum products), chemicals and chemical products (mainly pharmaceutical products), mechanical and electrical equipment, transport equipment, and base metals and articles thereof.

According to provisional data, the budgetary deficit amounted to €18,847m. in 2013. Greece's general government gross debt was €318,741m. in 2013, equivalent to 175.1% of GDP. Greece's total external debt was estimated at €182,702m. at the end of 2004 (equivalent to 110.5% of that year's GDP). In 2004–13 the average annual rate of inflation was 2.6%; consumer prices increased by 1.5% in 2012, but decreased by 0.9% in 2013. The rate of unemployment was 27.0% in the fourth quarter of 2013.

Greece's debt and budget deficit became unsustainable owing to the international financial crisis of 2008–09, and in May 2010 the EU, the IMF and the European Central Bank (ECB) 'troika' agreed a €110,000m. rescue programme for the country. After it became evident that this funding was insufficient, a second bailout plan was negotiated. Despite social unrest (see *Domestic Political Affairs*), the required austerity measures, which included a 22% reduction in the minimum wage and extensive job losses in the public sector, were adopted by Parliament in February 2012, and eurozone countries agreed additional funding totalling €130,000m. for the new bailout plan; the first instalment of funds was disbursed later that month. In December, in fulfilment of a further condition, Greece succeeded in buying back about €31,800m. of its debt, with private sector holders of Greek sovereign bonds accepting a loss on the value of their investments. In March 2013 Piraeus Bank successfully issued a €500m. bond (the first by a Greek bank in five years). The fifth instalment of lending by the troika amounted to €9,900m. in total, and was disbursed in two tranches in July and August 2014. Following the victory of anti-austerity party SYRIZA in early legislative elections in January 2015 (see *Domestic Political Affairs*), the new Government of Alexis Tsipras demanded a renegotiation of the terms of the existing bailout, which was due to expire at the end of February. Tsipras had initially pledged to reverse some of the previous austerity measures, including privatizations, a reduction in the minimum wage and the dismissal of public sector workers. In early February the ECB announced that it would no longer accept Greek bonds in exchange for loans, thereby obliging Greece's central bank to finance the country's banks, resulting in a dramatic rise in government borrowing costs. Under increased pressure, on 24 February eurozone ministers responsible for finance approved revised policy measures presented by the Government, which included commitments to combat tax evasion, corruption, and fuel and tobacco smuggling, and to implement labour reforms. Greece was duly granted a four-month extension of its bailout programme, thereby averting an imminent Greek debt default or exit from the eurozone. However, the disbursement of further funds was subject to agreement on reform implementation, and little progress was made in negotiations with eurozone ministers responsible for finance in April.

Greece's reserves were critically depleted following a debt repayment to the IMF in April, with further repayments due throughout 2015.

PUBLIC HOLIDAYS

2016: 1 January (New Year's Day), 6 January (Theophany), 14 March (Clean Monday), 25 March (Independence Day), 29 April–2 May (Greek Orthodox Easter), 1 May (Labour Day), 20 June (Whit Monday), 15 August (Assumption of the Virgin Mary), 28 October ('Ochi' Day, anniversary of Greek defiance of Italy's 1940 ultimatum), 25–26 December (Christmas).

Statistical Survey

Source (unless otherwise stated): National Statistical Service of Greece, Odos Lykourgou 14–16, 101 66 Athens; tel. (210) 4852084; fax (210) 4852552; e-mail info@statistics.gr; internet www.statistics.gr.

Area and Population

AREA, POPULATION AND DENSITY

Area (sq km)	131,957*
Population (census results)†	
18 March 2001	10,934,097
9 May 2011	
Males	5,303,223
Females	5,513,063
Total	10,816,286
Population (official estimates at 1 January)§ . . .	
2012	11,123,034
2013	11,062,508
Density (per sq km) at 1 January 2013	83.8

* 50,949 sq miles.

† Including armed forces stationed abroad, but excluding foreign forces stationed in Greece.

§ Estimates not adjusted to take account of final results of the 2011 census.

POPULATION BY AGE AND SEX
(official estimates at 1 January 2013)

	Males	Females	Total
0–14 years	830,252	791,770	1,622,022
15–64 years	3,596,291	3,618,061	7,214,352
65 years and over	986,747	1,239,387	2,226,134
Total	**5,413,290**	**5,649,218**	**11,062,508**

Note: Estimates not adjusted to take account of the final results of the 2011 census.

ADMINISTRATIVE DIVISIONS
(resident population at 2011 census)

Regions	Area (sq km)	Population	Density (per sq km)
Attica	3,808	3,828,434	1,005.4
East Macedonia and Thrace .	14,156	608,182	43.0
Central Macedonia . . .	18,810	1,880,297	100.0
Epirus	9,203	336,856	36.6
West Macedonia	9,451	283,689	30.0
Thessaly	14,036	732,762	52.2
Central Greece	15,549	547,390	35.2
Peloponnese	15,491	577,903	37.3
West Greece	11,350	679,796	59.9
Ionian Islands	2,307	207,855	90.1
North Aegean	3,836	199,231	51.9
South Aegean	5,286	309,015	58.5
Crete	8,336	623,065	74.7
Autonomous Monastic State .			
Holy Mountain (Mount Athos)	336	1,811	5.4
Total	**131,957**	**10,816,286**	**82.0**

PRINCIPAL TOWNS
(population at 2011 census)

Athína (Athens, the capital) . . .	664,046	Larissa	162,591
Thessaloníki (Salonika) . . .	325,182	Volos	144,449
Patras (Patrai) . .	213,984	Pésterion	139,981
Iraklion	173,993	Rodos	115,490
		Níkaia-Ágios Ioánnis	
Piraeus	163,688	Réndis	112,486

BIRTHS, MARRIAGES AND DEATHS

	Registered live births		Registered marriages		Registered deaths	
	Number	Rate (per 1,000)	Number	Rate (per 1,000)	Number	Rate (per 1,000)
2006 . .	112,042	10.1	57,802	5.2	105,476	9.5
2007 . .	111,926	10.0	61,377	5.5	109,895	9.8
2008 . .	118,302	10.5	53,500	4.8	107,979	9.6
2009 . .	117,933	10.5	59,212	5.3	108,316	9.6
2010 . .	114,766	10.2	56,338	5.0	109,084	9.7
2011 . .	106,428	9.6	55,099	4.9	111,099	9.9
2012 . .	100,371	9.0	49,705	4.5	116,668	10.5
2013 . .	94,134	8.5	n.a.	n.a.	111,794	10.1

Life expectancy (years at birth): 80.6 (males 78.0; females 83.4) in 2012 (Source: World Bank, World Development Indicators database).

ECONOMICALLY ACTIVE POPULATION
(sample surveys, '000 persons aged 15 years and over, October—December*)

	2011	2012	2013
Agriculture, hunting, forestry and fishing	496.7	485.5	493.9
Mining and quarrying	12.2	10.9	9.4
Manufacturing	388.1	349.8	331.9
Electricity, gas and water supply .	52.0	50.9	55.1
Construction	227.0	187.5	160.5
Wholesale and retail trade; repair of motor vehicles, motorcycles and personal and household goods	723.4	657.0	636.1
Hotels and restaurants . . .	286.8	262.3	253.3
Transport, storage and communications	261.1	257.0	261.5
Financial intermediation . . .	116.8	103.5	108.3
Real estate, renting and business activities	295.0	288.3	272.3
Public administration and defence; compulsory social security . .	341.8	349.0	338.9

—continued	2011	2012	2013
Education	303.0	279.6	289.7
Health and social work . . .	234.3	225.0	215.1
Other community, social and personal service activities . .	129.4	118.3	112.6
Private households with employed persons	63.2	55.6	49.6
Extraterritorial organizations and bodies	2.0	1.6	1.6
Total employed	3,932.8	3,681.9	3,589.7
Unemployed	1,025.9	1,295.5	1,363.1
Total labour force	4,958.7	4,977.5	4,952.8
Males	2,847.3	2,851.7	2,840.6
Females	2,111.3	2,125.8	2,112.2

* Including members of the regular armed forces, but excluding persons on compulsory military service.

Note: Totals may not be equal to the sum of components, owing to rounding.

Health and Welfare

KEY INDICATORS

Total fertility rate (children per woman, 2012)	1.5
Under-5 mortality rate (per 1,000 live births, 2012) . . .	5
HIV/AIDS (% of persons aged 15–49, 2012)	0.2
Physicians (per 1,000 head, 2009)	6.2
Hospital beds (per 1,000 head, 2009)	4.8
Health expenditure (2011): US $ per head (PPP)	2,322
Health expenditure (2011): % of GDP	9.0
Health expenditure (2011): public (% of total)	66.1
Total carbon dioxide emissions ('000 metric tons, 2010) . .	86,717.2
Carbon dioxide emissions per head (metric tons, 2010) . .	7.7
Human Development Index (2013): ranking	29
Human Development Index (2013): value	0.853

For sources and definitions, see explanatory note on p. vi.

Agriculture

PRINCIPAL CROPS
('000 metric tons)

	2011	2012	2013
Wheat	1,702	1,569	1,586
Rice, paddy	255	216	227
Barley	328	326	353
Maize	2,166	2,010	2,185
Oats	163	119	148
Potatoes	758	579	829
Sugar beet	324	435	336
Olives	1,874	2,081	2,000*
Cabbages	180	186	188
Lettuce	130	128	132*
Tomatoes	1,170	980	1,040
Cauliflowers and broccoli . .	86	89	78
Pumpkins, squash and gourds .	77	82	83*
Cucumbers and gherkins . .	175	142	152
Aubergines (Eggplants) . .	78	73	71
Chillies and peppers, green .	131	168	206
Onions, dry	243	250	231
Beans, green	55	71	64
Watermelons	648	565	621
Cantaloupes and other melons .	127	119	110
Oranges	895	792	806
Tangerines, mandarins, clementines and satsumas . .	129	106	97†

—continued	2011	2012	2013
Lemons and limes	66	55	50
Apples	256	251	244†
Pears	62	67	65
Apricots	83	83	84
Peaches and nectarines . . .	690	760	666†
Grapes	857	978	957
Figs	9	10	9
Tobacco, unmanufactured . .	24	24	24*

* FAO estimate.
† Unofficial figure.

Aggregate production ('000 metric tons, may include official, semi-official or estimated data): Total cereals 4,658 in 2011, 4,288 in 2012, 4,552 in 2013; Total roots and tubers 762 in 2011, 583 in 2012, 834 in 2013; Total vegetables (incl. melons) 3,429 in 2011, 3,166 in 2012, 3,288 in 2013; Total fruits (excl. melons) 3,350 in 2011, 3,452 in 2012, 3,335 in 2013.

Source: FAO.

LIVESTOCK
('000 head, year ending 30 September)

	2011	2012	2013
Horses*	28	28	29
Asses*	40	43	43
Mules*	20	22	22
Cattle	681	685	679
Pigs	1,120	1,099	1,077
Sheep	9,781	9,587	9,520
Goats	4,296	4,238	4,250
Chickens*	33,000	33,500	34,000

* FAO estimates.

Source: FAO.

LIVESTOCK PRODUCTS
('000 metric tons)

	2011	2012	2013
Cattle meat	79.0*	74.9*	76.5†
Sheep meat*	89.8	87.6	77.0
Goat meat*	49.7	44.7	37.0
Pig meat*	101.0	100.9	99.8
Horse meat†	2.8	2.8	2.8
Chicken meat*	125.0	127.2	126.3
Cows' milk*	787.0	819.8	805.0
Sheep's milk	773.0*	699.5*	705.0†
Goats' milk	402.1*	347.0†	340.0†
Hen eggs†	100.0	102.0	103.0
Honey†	14.5	14.8	15.0
Wool, greasy†	7.8	7.8	7.8

* Unofficial figure(s).
† FAO estimate(s).

Source: FAO.

Forestry

ROUNDWOOD REMOVALS
('000 cubic metres, excl. bark)

	2010	2011	2012*
Sawlogs, veneer logs and logs for sleepers	258	278	756
Other industrial wood	79	61	192
Fuel wood	711	857	795
Total	1,048	1,196	1,743

* FAO estimates.

2013: Production assumed to be unchanged from 2012 (FAO estimates).

Source: FAO.

SAWNWOOD PRODUCTION
('000 cubic metres, incl. railway sleepers)

	2009	2010	2011*
Coniferous (softwood)	68	68	64
Broadleaved (hardwood) . . .	38	50	44
Total	106	118	108

* FAO estimates.

2012–13: Production assumed to be unchanged from 2011 (FAO estimates).

Source: FAO.

Fishing

('000 metric tons, live weight)

	2010	2011	2012*
Capture	71.0*	63.8*	60.0
European pilchard (sardine) .	6.5	5.8	5.5
European anchovy	12.0	8.9	8.4
Aquaculture	121.2	137.2*	137.6
European seabass	39.0	44.1*	42.5
Gilthead seabream . . .	57.2	70.9*	72.3
Mediterranean mussel . .	17.1	17.2	17.5
Total catch	192.3*	201.0*	197.6

* FAO estimate(s).

Note: Figures exclude corals and sponges (metric tons, capture only): 7.0 in 2010; 7.0 in 2011 (FAO estimate); 6.0 in 2012 (FAO estimate).

Source: FAO.

Mining

('000 metric tons unless otherwise indicated)

	2010	2011	2012
Lignite	53,600	58,400	62,335
Crude petroleum ('000 barrels) .	636	676	662
Natural gas*	11	11	n.a.
Iron ore*†	560	550	550
Bauxite	1,902	2,300*	1,816
Zinc†	20.0	39.1	41.8
Lead†	12.2*	16.6	18.1
Nickel†	13.8	14.1	14.0*
Silver (kilograms)*†	29.0	30.0	32.0
Magnesite (crude)	396	542	351
Salt (unrefined)	190*	175	192
Bentonite	1,382	1,188	1,235
Gypsum and anhydrite . . .	700	587	746
Feldspar	23	10	12*
Perlite (crude)	760*	843	876
Pozzolan	850	350	285
Pumice	400	469	386
Marble ('000 cu m)	250*	285*	320

* Estimate(s).
† Figures refer to the metal content of ores and concentrates.

Source: US Geological Survey.

Industry

SELECTED PRODUCTS
('000 metric tons unless otherwise indicated)

	2010	2011	2012
Olive oil, virgin*	341	331	350
Wine	337*	295*	295†
Beer of barley*	405	370	350
Liquefied petroleum gas ('000 barrels)	8,030	8,000†	8,000†
Naphthas ('000 barrels)† . . .	8,400	8,400	8,400
Motor spirit (petrol) ('000 barrels)	36,865	32,000†	32,000†
Jet fuels ('000 barrels) . . .	12,775	14,000†	14,000†
Distillate fuel oils ('000 barrels) .	51,468	47,000†	47,000†
Residual fuel oils ('000 barrels) .	37,814	42,000†	42,000†
Cement (hydraulic)†	11,000	11,000	11,000
Crude steel (incl. alloys) . . .	1,839	1,993	2,000†
Aluminium (primary, unwrought)	136.8	167.5	165.0

* Unofficial figure(s).
† Estimate(s).

Sources: FAO; US Geological Survey.

Electric energy (million kWh): 61,365 in 2009; 57,392 in 2010; 59,436 in 2011 (Source: UN Industrial Commodity Statistics Database).

Finance

CURRENCY AND EXCHANGE RATES

Monetary Units
100 cent = 1 euro (€).

Sterling, Dollar and Euro Equivalents (31 December 2014)
£1 sterling = 1.286 euros;
US $1 = 0.824 euros;
€10 = £7.78 = $12.14.

Average Exchange Rate (euros per US $)
2012   0.7783
2013   0.7532
2014   0.7537

Note: The national currency was formerly the drachma. Greece became a member of the euro area on 1 January 2001, after which a fixed exchange rate of €1 = 340.75 drachmae was in operation. Euro notes and coins were introduced on 1 January 2002. The euro and local currency circulated alongside each other until 28 February, after which the euro became the sole legal tender.

CENTRAL GOVERNMENT BUDGET
(€ million)*

Revenue	2012	2013†	2014‡
Ordinary budget	51,497	51,528	53,919
Tax revenue	47,178	44,613	46,849
Direct taxes	21,096	20,065	22,568
Personal income tax . .	9,968	7,978	7,399
Corporate income tax . .	1,715	1,681	4,043
Indirect taxes	26,082	24,548	24,281
Consumption taxes (fuels) .	4,464	4,228	4,334
Value-added tax . . .	14,955	13,848	13,533
Non-tax revenue	4,318	6,915	7,070
Investment budget	3,601	4,595	5,152
Total	55,098	56,122	59,071

Expenditure§	2012	2013†	2014‡
Ordinary budget	64,672	54,914	52,878
Salaries and pensions . . .	21,595	19,713	19,321
Interest payments	12,223	6,100	5,900
Investment budget	6,114	6,650	6,800
Total	70,786	61,564	59,678

* Figures refer to the budgetary transactions of the central Government, excluding the operations of social security funds and public entities (such as hospitals, educational institutions and government agencies) with individual budgets.
† Provisional figures.
‡ Budget estimates; expenditure figures exclude potential adjustments arising from the implementation of private sector investment in national debt servicing (PSI).
§ Excluding amortization payments (€ million): 23,905 in 2012; 12,755 in 2013 (provisional figure); 24,930 in 2014 (budget estimate). Also excluded is expenditure on military procurement (€ million): 410 in 2012; 650 in 2013 (provisional figure); 533 in 2014 (budget estimate).

Source: Bank of Greece, Athens.

INTERNATIONAL RESERVES
(US $ million at 31 December)*

	2011	2012	2013
Gold†	5,650.9	5,985.4	4,332.6
IMF special drawing rights . .	849.3	850.7	854.2
Reserve position in IMF . .	369.6	370.1	371.0
Foreign exchange	29.8	48.8	194.5
Total	6,899.6	7,255.0	5,752.3

* Figures exclude deposits made with the European Monetary Institute.
† Gold reserves are valued at market-related prices.

Source: IMF, *International Financial Statistics*.

MONEY SUPPLY
(incl. shares, depository corporations, national residency criteria, € '000 million at 31 December)

	2011	2012	2013
Currency issued	23.73	24.33	25.39
Bank of Greece	42.17	38.79	35.44
Demand deposits	73.97	64.38	68.05
Other deposits	104.87	102.13	101.79
Securities other than shares . .	1.57	3.17	1.46
Money market fund shares . .	0.73	0.83	0.71
Shares and other equity . . .	54.77	56.03	63.59
Other items (net)	−21.50	−28.39	−19.50
Total	238.15	222.48	241.49

Source: IMF, *International Financial Statistics*.

COST OF LIVING
(Consumer Price Index; base: 2009 = 100)

	2011	2012	2013
Food and non-alcoholic beverages .	103.2	104.7	104.7
Fuel and light	161.8	181.2	189.7
Clothing	101.1	102.4	101.7
Rent	116.4	125.6	132.6
All items (incl. others) . . .	108.2	109.8	108.8

Source: Bank of Greece.

NATIONAL ACCOUNTS
(€ million at current prices, provisional)
National Income and Product

	2011	2012	2013
Compensation of employees . .	73,466	66,371	59,306
Gross operating surplus . . .	110,750	106,205	102,202
Gross domestic product (GDP) at factor cost	184,216	172,576	161,508
Taxes on production and imports .	27,551	25,044	24,115
Less Subsidies	4,014	3,416	3,185
GDP in market prices . . .	207,752	194,204	182,438
Primary incomes received from abroad	6,253	6,639	6,244
Less Primary incomes paid abroad	11,863	5,412	6,304
Gross national income (GNI) .	202,142	195,430	182,379
Less Consumption of fixed capital .	37,426	37,027	34,469
Net national income	164,716	158,403	147,909
Current transfers from abroad .	1,683	1,943	4,244
Less Current transfers paid abroad	3,536	2,935	2,973
Net national disposable income	162,863	157,411	149,181

Expenditure on the Gross Domestic Product

	2011	2012	2013
Final consumption expenditure .	189,149	175,791	166,381
Households	140,658	130,197	125,448
Non-profit institutions serving households	4,406	4,505	4,460
General government	44,085	41,089	36,472
Gross capital formation . . .	32,833	27,121	21,466
Gross fixed capital formation .	31,997	22,744	20,452
Changes in inventories . . .	836	4,377	1,014
Total domestic expenditure .	221,964	202,912	187,847
Exports of goods and services .	52,880	54,838	55,147
Less Imports of goods and services	67,110	63,546	60,555
GDP in purchasers' values .	207,752	194,204	182,438

Gross Domestic Product by Economic Activity

	2011	2012	2013
Agriculture, forestry and fishing .	6,367	6,326	6,106
Mining and quarrying . . .	719	720	661
Manufacturing	14,205	13,953	13,622
Electricity, gas and water supply .	4,881	4,576	4,341
Construction	6,274	4,428	3,518
Wholesale and retail trade; repair of motor vehicles and household goods; transport and storage; hotels and restaurants . . .	42,511	40,593	39,198
Information and communications	6,619	5,951	6,007
Financial intermediation . . .	8,762	8,293	7,596
Real estate, renting and business activities	44,359	41,821	39,108
Public administration and defence; compulsory social security; education; health and social work	40,339	37,003	33,147
Other service activities; private households with employed persons	7,264	7,550	7,241
Gross value added in basic prices	182,302	171,216	160,544
Taxes, less subsidies, on products	25,449	22,988	21,894
GDP in market prices . . .	207,752	194,204	182,438

BALANCE OF PAYMENTS
(US $ million)

	2011	2012	2013
Exports of goods	27,954	28,088	29,678
Imports of goods	−65,838	−53,369	−52,582
Balance on goods	−37,884	−25,281	−22,904
Exports of services	40,168	35,343	37,289
Imports of services	−19,624	−16,058	−14,772
Balance on goods and services	−17,339	−5,996	−386
Primary income received	4,618	4,925	4,546
Primary income paid	−16,599	−6,973	−8,683
Balance on goods, services and primary income	−29,320	−8,044	−4,524
Secondary income received	6,116	6,628	10,201
Secondary income paid	−5,379	−4,756	−4,268
Current balance	−28,583	−6,172	1,409
Capital account (net)	3,660	3,010	4,032
Direct investment assets	−1,818	−679	698
Direct investment liabilities	1,092	1,663	2,945
Portfolio investment assets	6,846	−74,031	2,373
Portfolio investment liabilities	−33,421	−54,284	−10,036
Financial derivatives and employee stock options (net)	−985	−1,078	−857
Other investment assets	9,939	17,998	23,148
Other investment liabilities	29,924	111,921	−29,059
Net errors and omissions	36	−494	−1,108
Reserves and related items	−13,310	−2,145	−6,455

Source: IMF, *International Financial Statistics*.

External Trade

PRINCIPAL COMMODITIES
(distribution by HS, US $ million)

Imports c.i.f.	2011	2012	2013
Live animals and animal products	3,110.5	2,828.8	2,971.5
Vegetables and vegetable products	1,951.9	1,684.2	1,800.0
Prepared foodstuffs; beverages, spirits, vinegar; tobacco and articles thereof	3,241.3	2,931.2	3,088.9
Mineral products	16,912.7	23,585.3	22,944.1
Mineral fuels, oils, distillation products, etc.	16,698.6	23,477.8	22,817.6
Crude petroleum oils	10,016.1	16,522.3	16,052.2
Non-crude petroleum oils	4,301.2	4,284.4	4,371.4
Petroleum gases	1,886.3	2,105.9	1,894.3
Chemicals and related products	8,140.8	7,103.8	7,103.0
Pharmaceutical products	4,178.7	3,664.8	3,537.7
Medicaments put in dosage	3,528.8	3,109.5	2,944.7
Plastics, rubber, and articles thereof	2,414.6	2,076.3	2,386.3
Plastics and articles thereof	1,955.2	1,669.3	1,917.0
Pulp of wood, paper and paperboard, and articles thereof	1,417.2	1,141.3	1,199.9
Textiles and textile articles	2,824.5	2,260.8	2,360.5
Iron and steel, other base metals and articles of base metal	4,449.9	3,586.2	3,471.3

Imports c.i.f.—*continued*	2011	2012	2013
Machinery and mechanical appliances; electrical equipment; parts thereof	7,354.5	6,677.4	5,929.8
Machinery, boilers, etc.	3,302.7	2,597.2	2,867.4
Electrical, electronic equipment	4,051.8	4,080.3	3,062.5
Vehicles, aircraft, vessels and associated transport equipment	4,002.0	4,208.1	3,391.6
Vehicles other than railway, tramway	2,060.9	1,348.7	1,559.2
Ships, boats and floating structures	1,707.6	2,525.7	1,615.1
Cruise ship, cargo ship, barges, etc.	1,664.3	2,475.6	1,579.0
Optical, medical apparatus, etc.; clocks and watches; musical instruments; parts thereof	1,101.6	908.8	1,058.4
Miscellaneous manufactured articles	1,140.6	950.8	986.2
Total (incl. others)	60,832.2	62,341.3	61,151.1

Exports f.o.b.	2011	2012	2013
Live animals and animal products	1,350.3	1,335.2	1,368.9
Vegetables and vegetable products	1,454.2	1,571.4	1,665.7
Edible fruit, nuts, peel of citrus fruit, melons	909.2	974.7	1,103.2
Prepared foodstuffs; beverages, spirits, vinegar; tobacco and articles thereof	2,568.4	2,602.0	2,643.3
Vegetable, fruit, nut preparations	1,066.9	1,123.6	1,165.9
Mineral products	10,015.2	14,257.8	15,118.8
Mineral fuels, oils, distillation products, etc.	9,577.3	13,679.0	14,461.0
Non-crude petroleum oils	9,030.1	12,975.9	13,639.5
Chemicals and related products	2,399.0	2,355.8	2,613.3
Pharmaceutical products	1,212.7	1,230.5	1,392.0
Medicaments put in dosage	1,139.6	1,113.8	1,284.3
Plastics, rubber, and articles thereof	1,362.9	1,315.4	1,327.4
Plastics and articles thereof	1,234.9	1,170.6	1,200.3
Textiles and textile articles	1,693.9	1,687.7	1,657.3
Iron and steel, other base metals and articles of base metal	4,530.1	3,755.1	1,574.4
Iron and steel	1,179.4	817.5	634.1
Aluminium and articles thereof	1,730.0	1,539.6	1,574.4
Machinery and mechanical appliances; electrical equipment; parts thereof	2,413.3	2,381.3	2,254.3
Machinery, boilers, etc.	1,062.5	992.9	971.8
Electrical, electronic equipment	1,350.7	1,388.4	1,282.5
Total (incl. others)	31,711.1	35,179.7	36,259.5

Source: Trade Map-Trade Competitiveness Map, International Trade Centre, www.intracen.org/marketanalysis.

Total imports (incl. petroleum and value of ships, € '000 million): 48,616.8 in 2011; 49,317.5 in 2012 (provisional); 46,849.1 in 2013 (provisional).

Total exports (incl. petroleum and value of ships, € '000 million): 24,295.5 in 2011; 27,585.1 in 2012 (provisional); 27,571.4 in 2013 (provisional).

PRINCIPAL TRADING PARTNERS
(US $ million)

Imports c.i.f.	2011	2012	2013
Azerbaijan	162.5	634.8	924.3
Belgium	2,195.6	1,687.0	1,712.2
Bulgaria	1,609.0	1,669.3	1,852.5
China, People's Republic	3,591.4	2,944.6	2,914.2
Cyprus	927.9	721.3	503.8
Denmark	674.3	717.6	554.0
Egypt	908.3	571.2	766.9
France (incl. Monaco)	3,034.2	2,678.3	2,852.4
Germany	6,396.8	5,756.1	5,839.1
India	776.4	367.9	427.7
Iran	2,727.4	1,981.9	50.1
Iraq	805.0	2,269.3	4,791.9
Italy	5,569.5	4,879.9	4,678.4
Kazakhstan	1,196.5	1,636.7	1,887.3
Korea, Republic	1,459.7	2,416.5	1,343.9
Libya	440.4	2,173.3	1,530.0
Netherlands	3,289.1	2,865.6	2,821.2
Romania	660.4	613.7	684.8
Russia	5,776.1	7,731.3	8,786.0
Saudi Arabia	1,948.5	3,437.7	1,559.3
Spain	1,879.2	1,671.6	1,782.0
Switzerland-Liechtenstein	834.4	638.9	617.4
Turkey	1,604.1	1,424.7	1,472.3
United Kingdom	1,726.0	1,455.0	1,490.0
USA	1,146.6	735.2	670.0
Total (incl. others)	60,832.2	62,341.3	61,151.1

Exports f.o.b.	2011	2012	2013
Albania	592.4	537.1	456.0
Algeria	495.9	507.4	468.1
Belgium	394.4	414.6	389.3
Bulgaria	1,724.2	1,944.9	1,852.2
China, People's Republic	405.6	491.1	557.2
Cyprus	1,903.1	1,719.1	1,512.0
Egypt	482.5	444.1	788.2
France (incl. Monaco)	905.8	857.8	850.7
Germany	2,453.8	2,234.7	2,347.4
Israel	308.0	766.6	525.2
Italy	2,956.2	2,702.5	3,240.7
Lebanon	218.0	946.9	661.1
Libya	221.4	1,010.6	990.5
Macedonia, FYR	793.6	1,066.7	988.1
Netherlands	637.5	568.2	564.9
Poland	364.5	352.0	382.5
Romania	829.9	738.0	797.9
Russia	548.7	600.0	539.3
Saudi Arabia	349.4	495.6	539.3
Serbia	390.8	395.9	365.1
Singapore	817.6	698.4	279.9
Spain	639.6	691.7	763.7
Turkey	2,485.4	3,815.4	4,256.7
United Arab Emirates	632.6	599.2	498.2
United Kingdom	1,239.1	1,096.5	1,288.5
USA	1,711.6	1,325.0	1,240.7
Total (incl. others)	31,711.1	35,179.7	36,259.5

Source: Trade Map-Trade Competitiveness Map, International Trade Centre, www.intracen.org/marketanalysis.

Total imports (€ million, incl. petroleum products, provisional figures): 48,616.8 in 2011; 49,317.5 in 2012 (provisional); 46,849.1 in 2013 (provisional).

Total exports (€ million, incl. petroleum products): 24,295.5 in 2011; 27,585.1 in 2012 (provisional); 27,571.4 in 2013 (provisional).

Transport

RAILWAYS
(estimated traffic)

	2007	2008	2009
Passenger-kilometres (million)	1,954	2,003	1,413
Net ton-kilometres (million)	835	786	538

2010–11: Figures assumed to be unchanged from 2009.

Source: World Bank, World Development Indicators database.

ROAD TRAFFIC
(motor vehicles in use at 31 December)

	2011	2012	2013
Passenger cars	5,203,591	5,167,557	5,124,208
Buses and coaches	27,121	26,962	26,783
Lorries and vans	1,321,296	1,318,918	1,315,836
Motorcycles	1,534,902	1,556,435	1,568,596
Total	8,086,910	8,069,872	8,035,423

SHIPPING

Flag Registered Fleet
(at 31 December)

	2012	2013	2014
Number of vessels	1,454	1,397	1,408
Total displacement ('000 grt)	41,702.9	42,189.1	42,715.8

Source: Lloyd's List Intelligence (www.lloydslistintelligence.com).

International Seaborne Freight Traffic
('000 metric tons)

	2010	2011	2012
Goods loaded	23,813	27,450	37,782
Goods unloaded	47,732	48,769	56,487

CIVIL AVIATION
(traffic on scheduled services)

	2010	2011
Kilometres flown (million)	79	72
Passengers carried ('000)	9,931	9,180
Passenger-kilometres (million)	7,560	7,177
Total ton-kilometres (million)	761	693

Source: UN, *Statistical Yearbook*.

2013: Passengers carried ('000) 8,563 (Source: World Bank, World Development Indicators database).

Tourism

FOREIGN TOURIST ARRIVALS BY NATIONALITY
(arrivals of non-resident tourists at national borders)

Country	2011	2012	2013
Albania	411,245	469,213	504,809
Belgium	432,625	326,937	344,554
Bulgaria	686,209	599,110	691,874
Cyprus	439,757	424,827	399,008
France	1,149,388	977,376	1,152,217
Germany	2,240,481	2,108,787	2,267,546
Italy	938,232	848,073	964,314
Netherlands	560,723	478,483	580,867
Poland	450,618	254,682	385,474
Russia	738,927	874,787	1,352,901
Serbia and Montenegro	692,059	620,450	778,765
Sweden	333,906	319,756	368,834
Switzerland	361,405	299,619	346,518
Turkey	552,090	602,306	831,113
United Kingdom	1,758,093	1,920,794	1,846,333
USA	484,708	373,831	466,520
Total (incl. others)	16,427,247	15,517,622	17,919,580

Tourism receipts (US $ million, excl. passenger transport): 14,801 in 2011; 13,217 in 2012; 16,036 in 2013 (Source: World Tourism Organization).

Communications Media

	2011	2012	2013
Telephones ('000 main lines in use)	5,745.0	5,461.2	5,332.5
Mobile cellular telephones ('000 subscribers)	12,128.0	13,360.3	12,999.8
Internet subscribers ('000)	2,510.3	n.a.	n.a.
Broadband subscribers ('000)	2,462.7	2,685.4	2,910.1

Source: International Telecommunication Union.

Education

(2012/13 unless otherwise indicated)

	Institutions	Teachers	Students
Pre-primary	5,792	13,853	166,576
Primary	4,698	65,557	630,043
Secondary: General	3,145	69,992	565,842
Secondary: Technical, vocational and ecclesiastical	627	18,378	124,540
Higher: Universities	22*	11,076	168,637*
Higher: Technical, vocational and ecclesiastical	16	6,227	113,469

* Excludes Medical School of Athens.

Pupil-teacher ratio (primary education, UNESCO estimate): 10.3 in 2006/07 (Source: UNESCO Institute for Statistics).

Adult literacy rate (UNESCO estimates): 97.4% (males 98.4%; females 96.4%) in 2012 (Source: UNESCO Institute for Statistics).

Directory

The Government

HEAD OF STATE

President: PROKOPIS PAVLOPOULOS (elected by vote of the Vouli 18 February 2015, inaugurated 13 March).

GOVERNMENT
(April 2015)

A coalition of Synaspismos Rizospastikis Aristeras (SYRIZA—Coalition of the Radical Left) and Anexartitoi Ellines (ANEL—Independent Greeks).

Prime Minister and Chairman of the Government: ALEXIS TSIPRAS (SYRIZA).

Deputy Prime Minister: GIANNIS DRAGASAKIS (SYRIZA).

Minister of the Interior and Administrative Reconstruction: NIKOS VOUTSIS (SYRIZA).

Minister of the Economy, Infrastructure, Shipping and Tourism: GIORGOS STATHAKIS (SYRIZA).

Minister of Production Reconstruction, Environment and Energy: PANAGIOTIS LAFAZANIS (SYRIZA).

Minister of Finance: YANIS VAROUFAKIS (SYRIZA).

Minister of Culture, Education and Religious Affairs: ARISTIDES BALTAS (SYRIZA).

Minister of Labour: PANOS SKOURLETIS (SYRIZA).

Minister of Health and Social Security: PANAGIOTIS KOUROUMPLIS (SYRIZA).

Minister of Foreign Affairs: NIKOS KOTZIAS (SYRIZA).

Minister of National Defence: PANOS KAMMENOS (ANEL).

Minister of Justice, Transparency and Human Rights: NIKOS PARASKEVOPOULOS (Independent).

MINISTRIES

Office of the President: Odos Vassileos Georgiou 2, 100 28 Athens; tel. (210) 7283111; fax (210) 7248938; internet www.presidency.gr.

Office of the Prime Minister: Maximos Mansion, Herodou Atticou 19, 106 74 Athens; tel. (210) 3385491; fax (210) 3238129; e-mail primeminister@primeminister.gr; internet www.primeminister.gr.

Ministry of Culture, Education and Religious Affairs: Rethymnou 1, Athens; tel. (210) 8201793; fax (210) 8201779; e-mail tep.dds@culture.gr; internet www.yppo.gr/0/eindex.jsp.

Ministry of the Economy, Infrastructure, Shipping and Tourism: 101 80 Athens; e-mail public@mnec.gr; internet www.mindev.gov.gr/el/.

Ministry of Finance: Karageorgi Servias 10, 105 62 Athens; tel. (210) 3375000; fax (210) 3332608; e-mail kataggelies@sdoe.gr; internet www.minfin.gr.

Ministry of Foreign Affairs: Odos Sofias 1, 106 71 Athens; tel. (210) 3681000; fax (210) 3681717; e-mail mfa@mfa.gr; internet www.mfa.gr.

Ministry of Health and Social Security: Odos Aristotelous 17, 101 87 Athens; tel. (210) 5232821; e-mail secretary.gen@yyka.gov.gr; internet www.yyka.gov.gr.

Ministry of the Interior and Administrative Reconstruction: Odos Stadiou 27, 10183 Athens; tel. (213) 1364000; fax (213) 1364130; internet www.ypes.gr.

Ministry of Justice, Transparency and Human Rights: Odos Mesogeion 96, 115 27 Athens; tel. (210) 7767300; fax (210) 7767187; e-mail ypdipimi@otenet.gr; internet www.ministryofjustice.gr.

Ministry of Labour: Odos Pireos 40, 104 37 Athens; tel. (210) 5295248; fax (210) 5249805; e-mail info@ypakp.gr; internet www.ypakp.gr.

Ministry of National Defence: Odos Mesogeion 227–231, Holargos, 154 51 Athens; tel. (210) 6598100; fax (210) 6443832; e-mail minister@mod.mil.gr; internet www.mod.mil.gr.

Ministry of Production Reconstruction, Environment and Energy: Odos Amalia 17, 115 23 Athens; tel. (210) 1515000; fax (210) 6447608; e-mail service@dorg.minenv.gr; internet www.ypeka.gr.

Legislature

Parliament
(Vouli)

Parliament Bldg, Leoforos Vassilissis Sofias 2, 100 21 Athens; tel. (210) 3707000; fax (210) 3707814; e-mail infopar@parliament.gr; internet www.hellenicparliament.gr.

President: ZOI KONSTANTOPOULOU.

General Election, 25 January 2015

Parties	Valid votes	% of votes	Seats
Synaspismos Rizospastikís Aristeras	2,245,978	36.34	149
Nea Demokratia	1,718,694	27.81	76
Chrysi Avgi	388,387	6.28	17
To Potami	373,924	6.05	17
Kommunistiko Komma Elladas	338,188	5.47	15
Anexartitoi Ellines	293,683	4.75	13
Panellínio Socialistiko Kinima.	289,469	4.68	13
Others	532,549	8.61	—
Total	**6,180,872**	**100.00**	**300**

Election Commission

National Election Commission: 155 61 Athens; tel. (210) 6535522; fax (210) 6546886; controlled by the Ministry of the Interior and Administrative Reconstruction.

Political Organizations

Anexartitoi Ellines (ANEL) (Independent Greeks): Charokopou 2 & Leoforos Siggrou 196, Kallithea, 176 71 Athens; tel. (210) 9545000; internet www.anexartitoiellines.gr; f. 2012 by fmr mems of Nea Demokratia (q.v.); Leader PANOS KAMMENOS.

Chrysi Avgi (Golden Dawn): Diligiannis 50, 104 39 Athens; tel. (210) 7521080; e-mail info@xryshaygh.com; internet xryshaygh.com; f. 1993; extreme nationalist; Leader NIKOLAOS MICHALOLIAKOS.

Dimokratiki Aristera (DIMAR) (Democratic Left): Kriezotou 4, 106 71 Athens; tel. (210) 3820790; fax (210) 3834831; internet www.dimokratikiaristera.gr; f. 2010 by fmr mems of SYN (q.v.); Pres. FOTIS KOUVELIS.

Dimokratiko Koinoniko Kinima (DIKKI) (Democratic Social Movement): Odos Karolou 28, 104 37 Athens; tel. (210) 5234288; fax (210) 5239856; e-mail info@dikki.org; internet www.dikki.org; f. 1995; leftist; contested Oct. 2009 legislative elections as part of SYRIZA; Co-ordinator, Steering Committee PANTAGIOTIS MANTAS.

Kinima Dimokraton Sosialiston (To Kinima) (Movement of Democratic Socialists): Athens; tel. (210) 3700000; fax (210) 3811852; e-mail tokinima@tokinima.gr; internet www.tokinima.gr; f. 2015, following a split with PASOK; advocates fulfilling the terms of the existing bailout, before devising a national reform plan for approval by referendum; 252 mems; Pres. GEORGIOS A. PAPANDREOU.

Koinoniki Symfonia (KS) (Social Contract): Patision 153, 112 52 Athens; tel. (211) 0123803; fax (210) 3603558; e-mail koinonikisymfonia@gmail.com; internet www.koinonikisymfonia.gr; f. 2012 by fmr mems of PASOK (q.v.); Leader LOUKA KATSELI.

Koma Isotitas Eirinis kai Filias/Dostluk Eşitlik Bariş Partisi (Party of Freedom, Peace and Friendship): V. Plouavlu (Sulantepe) Gümülcine, 691 00 Komotini; tel. and fax (2531) 102124; e-mail deb_partisi@debpartisi.org; internet www.debpartisi.org; f. 1991; represents interests of Turkish minority in Western Thrace; Pres. MUSTAFA ALI CAVUS.

Kommunistiko Komma Elladas (KKE) (Communist Party of Greece): Leoforos Irakliou 145, Perissos, Nea Ionia, 142 31 Athens; tel. (210) 2592111; fax (210) 2592298; e-mail cpg@int.kke.gr; internet inter.kke.gr; f. 1918; banned 1947, re-emerged 1974; Gen. Sec. DIMITRIS KOUTSOUMPAS.

Laikos Orthodoxos Synagermos (LAOS) (Popular Orthodox Rally): Leofoos Kallirrois 52, 117 45 Athens; tel. (210) 3665000; fax (210) 3665209; e-mail pr@laos.gr; internet www.laos.gr; f. 2000; nationalist; Pres. GEORGIOS KARATZAFERIS.

Nea Demokratia (ND) (New Democracy): Leoforos Syngrou 340, 176 73 Kallithea, Athens; tel. (210) 9444000; fax (210) 7251491; e-mail ndpress@nd.gr; internet www.nd.gr; f. 1974; broad-based centre-right party advocating social reform in the framework of a liberal economy; supports European integration and enlargement; Pres. ANTONIS SAMARAS.

Oikologoi Prasinoi (OP) (Ecologist Greens): Plateia Eleytherias 14, 105 53 Athens; tel. (210) 3306301; fax (210) 3834390; e-mail ecogreen@otenet.gr; internet www.ecogreens-gr.org; f. 2002; mem. of European Green Party; Mems. of Executive Secretarial Committee CHRISTINA EUTHIMIATOU, KOSTAS KALOGRANIS, KOSTAS PAPAKONSTANTINOU, DIMITRA LYMPEROPOULOU, FILIPPOS GANOULIS, KOSTAS LOUKERIS.

Panellínio Arma Politon (PAP) (Panhellenic Citizens' Chariot): Anthimou Gazi 9, 105 61 Athens; tel. (210) 3226445; internet www.armapoliton.gr; f. 2011 by fmr mems of PASOK (q.v.); left-wing; Leader GIANNIS DIMARAS.

Panellínio Socialistiko Kinima (PASOK) (Panhellenic Socialist Movement): Odos Hippocrates 22, 106 80 Athens; tel. (210) 3665000; fax (210) 3665209; e-mail pasok@pasok.gr; internet www.pasok.gr; f. 1974; incorporates Democratic Defence and Panhellenic Liberation Movement resistance orgs; supports social welfare, decentralization and self-management, aims for Mediterranean socialist devt through international co-operation; Pres. EVANGELOS VENIZELOS; Sec. of the Nat. Council MICHAEL KARCHIMAKIS; 500 local orgs, 30,000 mems.

Symfonia Gia Ti Nea Ellada (SNE) (Pact for a New Greece): Valaoritou 17 & Amerika, 106 71 Athens; tel. (210) 3314540; fax (210) 3314541; e-mail info@neel.gr; internet newgreece.eu; f. 2013; socialist; Pres. ANDREAS LOVERDOS.

Synaspismós Rizospastikís Aristerás (SYRIZA) (Coalition of the Radical Left): Pl. Eleftherias 1, 105 53 Athens; tel. (210) 3378400; fax (210) 3217003; e-mail info@syriza.gr; internet www.syriza.gr; f. 2004; umbrella organization of far-left groups, including SYN, q.v. and (DIKKI, q.v.); Leader ALEXIS TSIPRAS.

Synaspismós Tis Aristerás Ton Kinimáton Kai Tis Oikologias (SYN) (Coalition of the Left of Movements and Ecology): Pl. Eleftherias 1, 105 53 Athens; tel. (210) 3378400; fax (210) 3217003; e-mail info@syn.gr; internet www.syn.gr; f. 1991; present name adopted 2003; contested legislative elections as part of SYRIZA; Pres. ALEXIS TSIPRAS.

To Potami (The River): Sevastoupoleos 22, 115 26 Athens; tel. (210) 7470100; fax (210) 7470115; e-mail info@topotami.gr; internet topotami.gr; f. 2014; Pres. STAVROS THEODORAKIS.

Diplomatic Representation

EMBASSIES IN GREECE

Albania: Odos Vekiareli 7, Filothei, 152 37 Athens; tel. (210) 6876200; fax (210) 6876223; e-mail embassy.athens@mfa.gov.al; internet www.ambasadat.gov.al/greece; Ambassador DASHNOR DERVISHI.

Algeria: Leoforos Vassileos Konstantinou 14, 116 35 Athens; tel. (210) 7564191; fax (210) 7018681; e-mail embalg@otenet.gr; Ambassador TEDJINI SALAOUANDJI.

Angola: Odos El. Venizelou 24, 152 37 Filothei-Athens; tel. (210) 6898681; fax (210) 6898683; e-mail info@angolaembassy.gr; internet www.angolanembassy.gr; Ambassador ISABEL MERCEDES DA SILVA FEIJÓ.

Argentina: 3rd Floor, Leoforos Vassilissis Sofias 59, 115 21 Athens; tel. (210) 7224753; fax (210) 7227568; e-mail egrec@mrecic.gov.ar; internet www.egrec.mrecic.gov.ar; Chargé d'affaires a.i. MÓNICA DEREGIBUS.

Armenia: Leoforos Konstantinou Paleologou 95, 152 32 Khalandri; tel. (210) 6831130; fax (210) 6831183; e-mail embassy.athens@mfa.am; Ambassador GAGIK GHALATCHIAN.

Australia: Thon Bldg, Odos Kifisias & Odos Alexandras, POB 14070, 115 23 Ambelokipi-Athens; tel. (210) 8704000; fax (210) 8704111; e-mail ae.athens@dfat.gov.au; internet www.greece.embassy.gov.au; Ambassador JOHN GRIFFIN.

Austria: Leoforos Vassilissis Sofias 4, 106 74 Athens; tel. (210) 7257270; fax (210) 7257292; e-mail athen-ob@bmeia.gv.at; internet www.bmeia.gv.at/botschaft/athen; Ambassador MELITTA SCHUBERT.

Azerbaijan: Leoforos Vassilissis Sofias 25, 106 74 Athens; tel. (210) 3632721; fax (210) 3639087; e-mail embassy@azembassy.gr; internet www.azembassy.gr; Ambassador RAHMAN MUSTAFAYEV.

Bangladesh: Odos Marathonodromon 119, Palaio Psychiko, 154 52 Athens; tel. (210) 6720250; fax (210) 6754513; e-mail mission.athens@mofa.gov.bd; internet bdembassyathens.gr; Chargé d'affaires a.i. TARIKUL ISLAM.

Belgium: Odos Sekeri 3, 106 71 Athens; tel. (210) 3617886; fax (210) 3604289; e-mail athens@diplobel.fed.be; internet www.diplomatie.be/athens; Ambassador MARC VAN DEN REECK.

Bosnia and Herzegovina: Odos Filellinon 25, 6th Floor, 105 57 Athens; tel. (210) 6410788; fax (210) 6411978; e-mail info@bhembassy.gr; internet www.bhembassy.gr; Ambassador DRAGAN BOŽANIĆ.

Brazil: Leoforos Vassilissis Sofias 23, 106 74 Athens; tel. (210) 7213039; fax (210) 7244731; e-mail brasemb.atenas@itamaraty.gov.br; Ambassador EDGARD ANTONIO CASCIANO.

Bulgaria: Odos Stratigou Kallari 33A, Palaio Psychiko, 154 52 Athens; tel. (210) 6748105; fax (210) 6748130; e-mail embassy.athens@mfa.bg; internet www.mfa.bg/embassies/greece; Ambassador EMILIYA KRALEVA.

Canada: Odos Ioannou Ghennadiou 4, 115 21 Athens; tel. (210) 7273400; fax (210) 7273480; e-mail athns@international.gc.ca; internet www.canadainternational.gc.ca/greece-grece; Ambassador ROBERT PECK.

Chile: Odos Rigillis 12, 106 74 Athens; tel. (210) 7292647; fax (210) 7252565; e-mail nvegab@minrcl.gov.cl; Chargé d'affaires a.i MARTIN DONOSO PLATE.

China, People's Republic: Odos Demokratias 10–12, Palaio Psychiko, 154 52 Athens; tel. (210) 6723282; fax (210) 6723819; e-mail chinaemb_gr@mfa.gov.cn; internet gr.chineseembassy.org; Ambassador ZOU XIAOLI.

Congo, Democratic Republic: Odos Kodrou 20, 152 31 Halandri; tel. (210) 6776123; fax (210) 6776124; e-mail ambardcathenes@yahoo.fr; Chargé d'affaires a.i. HENRI BENJAMIN NTIKALA BOOTO.

Croatia: Odos Tzavela 4, 154 51 Psychiko; tel. (210) 6777033; fax (210) 6711208; e-mail croath@mvep.hr; Ambassador IVAN VELIMIR STRAČEVIĆ.

Cuba: Odos Sofokleos 5, 152 37 Filothei; tel. (210) 6855550; fax (210) 6842807; e-mail secretaria@embacuba.gr; internet www.cubadiplomatica.cu/grecia/en/home.aspx; Ambassador OSVALDO JESÚS COBACHO MARTÍNEZ.

Cyprus: Odos Xenofontos 2A, 105 57 Athens; tel. (210) 3734800; fax (210) 7258886; e-mail athensembassy@mfa.gon.cy; internet www.mfa.gov.cy; Ambassador KYRIAKOS KENEVEZOS.

Czech Republic: Odos Georgiou Seferis 6, 154 52 Palaio Psychiko; tel. (210) 6713755; fax (210) 6710675; e-mail athens@embassy.mzv.cz; internet www.mzv.cz/athens; Ambassador HANA ŠEVČÍKOVÁ.

Denmark: Odos Mourouzi 10, 106 74 Athens; tel. (210) 7256440; fax (210) 7256473; e-mail athathen@um.dk; internet www.graekenland.um.dk; Ambassador METTE KNUDSEN.

Egypt: Leoforos Vassilissis Sofias 3, 106 71 Athens; tel. (210) 3618612; fax (210) 3603538; e-mail emb.egypt@yahoo.gr; Ambassador AHMAD FOUAD AL-BIDEWY.

Estonia: Leoforos Messoghion 2–4, Athens Tower, 23rd Floor, 115 27 Athens; tel. (210) 7475660; fax (210) 7475661; e-mail embassy.athens@mfa.ee; internet www.estemb.gr; Ambassador MARGUS RAVA.

Finland: Odos Hatziyianni Mexi 5, 115 28 Athens; tel. (210) 7255860; fax (210) 7255864; e-mail sanomat.ate@formin.fi; internet www.finland.gr; Ambassador PAULI MÄKELÄ.

France: Leoforos Vassilissis Sofias 7, 106 71 Athens; tel. (210) 3391000; fax (210) 3391009; e-mail info@ambafrance-gr.org; internet www.ambafrance-gr.org; Ambassador JEAN-LOUP KUHN-DELFORGE.

Georgia: Odos Taygetou 27 & Marathonodromou, 154 52 Palaio Psychiko, Athens; tel. (210) 6742186; fax (210) 6716722; e-mail athens.emb@mfa.gov.ge; internet greece.mfa.gov.ge; Chargé d'affaires a.i. EKATERINE LORTKIPANIDZE.

Germany: Odos Karaoli & Dimitriou 3, Kolonaki, 106 75 Athens; tel. (210) 7285111; fax (210) 7285335; e-mail info@athen.diplo.de; internet www.athen.diplo.de; Ambassador Dr PETER SCHOOF.

Holy See: POB 65075, Odos Mavili 2, 154 52 Palaio Psychiko; tel. (210) 6722728; fax (210) 6742849; e-mail nunate@ath.forthnet.gr; Apostolic Nuncio EDWARD JOSEPH ADAMS.

Hungary: Leoforos Vassileos Konstantinou 38, Pangrati, 116 35 Athens; tel. (210) 7256800; fax (210) 7256840; e-mail mission.ath@kum.hu; internet www.mfa.gov.hu/emb/athens; Ambassador ESZTER SÁNDORFI.

India: Odos Kleanthous 3, 106 74 Athens; tel. (210) 7216227; fax (210) 7211252; e-mail embassy@indianembassy.gr; internet www.indianembassy.gr; Ambassador TSEWANG TOPDEN.

Indonesia: Odos Marathonodromou 99, 154 52 Palaio Psychiko; tel. (210) 6742345; fax (210) 6756955; e-mail athena.kbri@kemlu.go.id; internet www.indonesia.gr; Ambassador BENNY BAHANADEWA.

Iran: Odos Stratigou Kalari 16, 154 52 Palaio Psychiko; tel. (210) 6471436; fax (210) 6477945; e-mail irembatn@otenet.gr; internet www.iranembassy.gr; Ambassador BEHROUZ BEHNAM.

Iraq: Odos Mazaraki 4, Palaio Psychiko, 154 52 Athens; tel. (210) 6722330; fax (210) 6717185; e-mail iraqath@otenet.gr; internet www.iraqembassy-athens.com; Ambassador BURHAN JAF.

Ireland: Leoforos Vassileos Konstantinou 7, 106 74 Athens; tel. (210) 7232771; fax (210) 7293383; e-mail athensembassy@dfa.ie; internet www.embassyofireland.gr; Ambassador NOEL NOEL KILKENNY.

Israel: Odos Marathonodromou 1, 154 52 Palaio Psychiko; tel. (210) 6705500; fax (210) 6705555; e-mail pr@athens.mfa.gov.il; internet athens.mfa.gov.il; Ambassador IRIT BEN-ABBA.

Italy: Odos Sekeri 2, 106 74 Athens; tel. (210) 3617260; fax (210) 3617330; e-mail ambasciata.atene@esteri.it; internet www.ambatene.esteri.it; Ambassador CLAUDIO GLAENTZER.

Japan: Odos Ethnikis Antistasseos 46, Halandri, 152 31 Athens; tel. (210) 6709900; fax (210) 6709980; e-mail embjapan@at.mofa.go.jp; internet www.gr.emb-japan.go.jp; Ambassador MASUO NISHIBAYASHI.

Jordan: Odos Papadiamanti 21, 154 52 Palaio Psychiko; tel. (210) 6744161; fax (210) 6740578; e-mail jor_emb1@otenet.gr; internet www.jordanembassy.gr; Ambassador FAWAZ AITAN.

Kazakhstan: Odos Imittou 122, 15 669 Papagou; tel. (210) 6515643; fax (210) 6516362; e-mail athens@kazembassy.gr; internet www.kazembassy.gr; Ambassador SERGEI NURTAYEV.

Korea, Republic: Leoforos Messoghion 2–4, Athens Tower, A-Building, 19th Floor, 115 27 Athens; tel. (210) 6984080; fax (210) 6984083; e-mail gremb@mofa.go.kr; Ambassador GIL-SOU SHIN.

Kuwait: Odos Marathonodromou 27, 154 52 Palaio Psychiko; tel. (210) 6743593; fax (210) 6775875; e-mail info@kuwaitembassy.gr; Ambassador RAED ABDULLAH AL-RIFAI.

Latvia: Odos Vassilissis Constantinou 38, 116 35 Athens; tel. (210) 7294483; fax (210) 7294479; e-mail embassy.greece@mfa.gov.lv; internet www.mfa.gov.lv/greece; Ambassador IVARS PUNDURS.

Lebanon: Odos 25 Maritou 6, 154 52 Palaio Psychiko; tel. (210) 6755873; fax (210) 6755612; e-mail officesm@lebaneseembassygreece.gr; internet www.lebaneseembassygreece.gr; Chargé d'affaires a.i. RANIA ABDALLAH.

Libya: Odos Vyronos 13, 154 52 Palaio Psychiko; tel. (210) 6472120; fax (210) 6742761; Ambassador AHMED YAGOB GZLLAL.

Lithuania: Leoforos Vassilissis Konstantinous 38, 116 35 Athens; tel. (210) 7294356; fax (210) 7294347; e-mail amb.gr@urm.lt; internet gr.mfa.lt; Ambassador ALFONSAS EIDINTAS.

Luxembourg: Leoforos Vassilissis Sofias 23A & Odos Neophytou Vamva 2, 106 74 Athens; tel. (210) 7256400; fax (210) 7256405; e-mail athenes.amb@mae.etat.lu; internet athenes.mae.lu; Ambassador CHRISTIAN MARC BIEVER.

Malta: Leoforos Vassilissis Sofias 96, 115 28 Athens; tel. (210) 7785138; fax (210) 7785242; e-mail maltaembassy.athens@gov.mt; Ambassador CHARLES STAFRACE.

Mexico: Plateia Filikis Etairias 14, 5th Floor, 106 73 Athens; tel. (210) 7294780; fax (210) 7294783; e-mail embgrecia@sre.gob.mx; internet embamex.sre.gob.mx/grecia; Ambassador RICARDO-TARCISIO NAVARRETE-MONTES DE OCA.

Moldova: Odos Georgiou Bacu 20, 115 24 Athens; tel. (210) 6990372; fax (210) 6990660; e-mail atena@mfa.md; internet www.grecia.mfa.gov.md; Ambassador Dr VALENTIN CIUMAC.

Montenegro: Odos Loukianou 5, Kolonaki, 106 75 Athens; tel. (210) 7241212; fax (210) 7241076; e-mail greece@mfa.gov.me; Ambassador PETAR POPOVIĆ.

Morocco: Odos Marathonodromou 5, 154 52 Palaio Psychiko; tel. (210) 6744209; fax (210) 6749480; e-mail sifamath@otenet.gr; Ambassador ABDELKADER AL-ANSARI.

Netherlands: Leoforos Vassileos Konstantinou 5–7, 106 74 Athens; tel. (210) 7254900; fax (210) 7254907; e-mail ath@minbuza.nl; internet www.dutchembassy.gr; Ambassador JAN VERSTEEG.

Nigeria: Odos Strait 17, 152 37 Filothei, Athens; tel. (210) 8021168; fax (210) 8024208; e-mail nigeria.athens@mfa.gov.ng; Ambassador M. AYODEJI LAWRENCE AYODELE.

Norway: Leoforos Vassilissis Sofias 23, 106 74 Athens; tel. (210) 7246173; fax (210) 7244989; e-mail emb.athens@mfa.no; internet www.norway.gr; Ambassador SJUR LARSEN.

Pakistan: Odos Loukianou 6, Kolonaki, 106 75 Athens; tel. (210) 7290122; fax (210) 7257641; e-mail parepathen@otenet.gr; internet www.mofa.gov.pk/greece; Ambassador Dr SAEED KHAN MOHMAND.

Panama: Odos Filellinon 1-3 & Akti Miaouli, 185 36 Piraeus; tel. (210) 4286441; fax (210) 4286448; e-mail embassy@panamaembassy.gr; Ambassador CRISTINA EDUVIGIS LIAKOPULOS DE PAPADIKIS.

Peru: Odos Koumbari 2, Kolonaki, 106 74 Athens; tel. (210) 7792761; fax (210) 7792905; e-mail lepruate@otenet.gr; internet www.peru.gr; Ambassador JORGE ROMÁN MOREY.

Philippines: Odos Antheon 26, 154 52 Palaio Psychiko; tel. (210) 6721883; fax (210) 6721872; e-mail athenspe@otenet.gr; internet athenspe.dfa.gov.ph; Ambassador MEYNARDO L. B. MONTEALEGRE.

Poland: Odos Chryssanthemon 22, 154 52 Palaio Psychiko; tel. (210) 6797700; fax (210) 6797711; e-mail ateny.amb.sekretariat@msz.gov.pl; internet athens.mfa.gov.pl; Chargé d'affaires a.i. SANDRA HARMOZA.

Portugal: Leoforos Vassilissis Sofias 23, 106 74 Athens; tel. (210) 7290096; fax (210) 7245122; e-mail embportg@otenet.gr; Ambassador JOAQUIM JOSÉ MARQUES.

Qatar: Leoforos Kifissias 212 & Odos Perikleous 2, 154 51 Neo Psychiko Athens; tel. (210) 7255031; fax (210) 7255024; e-mail athens@mofa.gov.qa; internet www.qatarembassy.gr; Ambassador SOLTAN SAAD AL-MORAIKHI.

Romania: Odos Emmanuel Benaki 7, 154 52 Palaio Psychiko; tel. (210) 6728875; fax (210) 6728883; e-mail secretariat@romaniaemb.gr; internet atena.mae.ro; Ambassador LUCIAN FĂTU.

Russian Federation: Odos Nikiforou Litra 28, 154 52 Palaio Psychiko; tel. (210) 6725235; fax (210) 6479708; e-mail embraf@otenet.gr; internet www.greece.mid.ru; Ambassador ANDREI M. MASLOV.

Saudi Arabia: Odos Palaiologhou & Agias Annis 2, Halandri, 152 32 Athens; tel. (210) 6716911; fax (210) 6749833; e-mail gremb@mofa.gov.sa; Ambassador ESSAM BIN EBRAHIM BAIT ALMAL.

Serbia: Leoforos Vassilissis Sofias 106, 115 27 Athens; tel. (210) 7774344; fax (210) 7796436; e-mail beograd@hol.gr; internet www.athens.mfa.gov.rs; Chargé d'affaires a.i. BRANKO LAZAREVIĆ.

Slovakia: Odos Georgiou Seferis 4, 154 52 Palaio Psychiko; tel. (210) 6771980; fax (210) 6771878; e-mail emb.athens@mzv.sk; internet www.mzv.sk/athens; Ambassador PETER MICHALKO.

Slovenia: Leoforos Kifissias 280 & Odos Dimokratias 1, 154 51 Neo Psychiko; tel. (210) 6720090; fax (210) 6775680; e-mail vat@gov.si; internet www.atene.veleposlanistvo.si; Ambassador ROBERT BASEJ.

South Africa: Leoforos Kifissias 60, 151 25 Maroussi; tel. (210) 6178020; fax (210) 6106640; e-mail athens.info@dirco.gov.za; Ambassador SOPHONIA RAPULANE MAKGETLA.

Spain: Odos D. Areopagitou 21, 117 42 Athens; tel. (210) 9213123; fax (210) 9213090; e-mail emb.atenas@maec.es; Ambassador ALFONSO LUCINI.

Sudan: Odos Mousson 6, 154 52 Palaio Psychiko, Athens; tel. (210) 6742520; fax (210) 6742521; Ambassador ABDELMONIEM AHMED EL AMIN EL-HUSEIN.

Sweden: Leoforos Vassileos Konstantinou 7, 106 74 Athens; tel. (210) 7266100; fax (210) 7266150; e-mail ambassaden.athen@foreign.ministry.se; internet www.swedenabroad.com/athen; Ambassador CHARLOTTE WRANGBERG.

Switzerland: Odos Iassiou 2, 115 21 Athens; tel. (210) 7230364; fax (210) 7249209; e-mail ath.vertretung@eda.admin.ch; internet www.eda.admin.ch/athens; Ambassador LORENZO AMBERG.

Thailand: Odos Marathonodromou 25 & Odos Kyprou, 154 52 Palaio Psychiko; tel. (210) 6710155; fax (210) 6749508; e-mail thaiath@otenet.gr; Ambassador JOOMPOL MANASCHUANG.

Tunisia: Odos Antheon 2 & Odos Marathonodromou, 154 52 Palaio Psychiko; tel. (210) 6717590; fax (210) 6713432; e-mail atathina@otenet.gr; Ambassador TAREK SAADI.

Turkey: Odos Vassileos Gheorghiou II 8, 106 74 Athens; tel. (210) 7263000; fax (210) 7229597; e-mail embassy.athens@mfa.gov.tr; internet athens.emb.mfa.gov.tr; Ambassador KERIM URAS.

Ukraine: Odos Stefanou Delta 2, 152 37 Filothei; tel. (210) 6800230; fax (210) 6854154; e-mail emb_gr@mfa.gov.ua; internet www.mfa.gov.ua/greece; Ambassador VOLODYMYR SHKUROV.

United Arab Emirates: Leoforos Kifissias 280 & Odos Agriniou 3, 152 32 Halandri; tel. (210) 6770220; fax (210) 6770274; Ambassador SULTAN MUHAMMAD MAJID AL-ALI.

United Kingdom: Odos Ploutarchou 1, 106 75 Athens; tel. (210) 7272600; fax (210) 7272723; e-mail information.athens@fco.gov.uk; internet ukingreece.fco.gov.uk; Ambassador JOHN KITTMER.

Uruguay: Odos Menandrou 1, 145 61 Kifissia; tel. (210) 3602635; fax (210) 3613549; e-mail urugrec@otenet.gr; Ambassador ADRIANA LISSIDINI DOTTI.

USA: Leoforos Vassilissis Sofias 91, 106 10 Athens; tel. (210) 7212951; fax (210) 6456282; e-mail usembassy@usembassy.gr; internet athens.usembassy.gov; Ambassador DAVID DUANE PEARCE.

Venezuela: Odos Papadiamanti 15, 154 52 Palaio Psychiko; tel. (210) 6729169; fax (210) 6727464; e-mail emvenath@hol.gr; internet www.embavenez.gr; Ambassador FREDERIC F. STEPHAN FERNÁNDEZ-COUSTOLLE.

Viet Nam: Odos Yakinthon 50, Palaio Psychiko, 154 52 Athens; tel. (210) 6128733; fax (210) 6128734; e-mail vnemb.gr@mofa.gov.vn; internet www.mofa.gov.vn/vnemb.gr; Ambassador TRAN THI HA PHUONG.

Judicial System

SUPREME ADMINISTRATIVE COURTS

Special Supreme Tribunal: Odos Patision 30, Athens; consists of 11 members: three presidents (of the Supreme Court, Council of State and Court of Audit), four judges of the Supreme Court and four judges of the Council of State; has final jurisdiction in matters of constitutionality.

Council of State

Odos Panepistimiou 47–49, 105 64 Athens; tel. (210) 2132102; fax (210) 3710097; e-mail ste@ste.gr; internet www.ste.gr.

Has appellate powers over acts of the administration and final rulings of administrative courts; has power to rule upon matters of judicial review of laws.

President: RIZOS SOTIRIOS.

Supreme Court of Civil and Penal Law

Leoforos Alexandros 121, 115 10 Athens; tel. (210) 6411506; fax (210) 6433799; internet www.areiospagos.gr.

Supreme court in the State, also having appellate powers; consists of six sections (four Civil, two Penal) and adjudicates in quorum.

President: ATHANASIOS KOUTROMANOS.

COURTS OF APPEAL

There are 12 Courts of Appeal with jurisdiction in cases of Civil and Penal Law of second degree, and, in exceptional penal cases, of first degree.

COURTS OF FIRST INSTANCE

There are 59 Courts of First Instance with jurisdiction in cases of first degree, and, in exceptional cases, of second degree. They function both as Courts of First Instance and as Criminal Courts. For serious crimes the Criminal Courts function with a jury.

In towns where Courts of First Instance sit there are also Juvenile Courts. Commercial Tribunals do not function in Greece, and all commercial cases are tried by ordinary courts of law. There are, however, Tax Courts in some towns.

OTHER COURTS

There are 360 Courts of the Justice of Peace throughout the country. There are 48 Magistrates' Courts (or simple Police Courts).

In all the above courts, except those of the Justice of Peace, there are District Attorneys. In Courts of the Justice of Peace, the duties of District Attorney are performed by the Public Prosecutor.

Religion

CHRISTIANITY

The Eastern Orthodox Church

The Greek branch of the Eastern Orthodox Church is the officially established religion of the country, to which nearly 97% of the population profess adherence.

Within the Greek state, there is also the semi-autonomous Church of Crete, which is under the spiritual jurisdiction of the Ecumenical Patriarchate of Constantinople (based in İstanbul, Turkey).

There are also four Metropolitan Sees of the Dodecanese, which are dependent on the Ecumenical Patriarchate, and, finally, the peninsula of Athos, which constitutes the region of the Holy Mountain (Mount Athos) and comprises 20 monasteries. These are dependent on the Ecumenical Patriarchate of Constantinople, but are autonomous and are safeguarded constitutionally.

The Orthodox Church of Greece: Odos Ioannou Gennadiou 14, 115 21 Athens; tel. (210) 7218381; e-mail contact@ecclesia.gr; internet www.ecclesia.gr; f. 1850.

Primate of Greece: IERONYMOS II (LIAPIS).

Archbishop of Crete: Archbishop IRENAIOS (whose See is in Heraklion).

The Roman Catholic Church

Greece comprises four archdioceses (including two, Athens and Rhodes, directly responsible to the Holy See), four dioceses, one Apostolic Vicariate and one Apostolic Exarchate for adherents of the Byzantine Rite. There is also an Ordinariate for Armenian Catholics. There are an estimated 180,637 adherents in the country, including 2,500 of the Byzantine Rite and 300 of the Armenian Rite.

Latin Rite

Bishops' Conference: G. Papandreou 15, 841 00 Syros; tel. (22) 81084783; fax (22) 8108684781; e-mail syrensis@otenet.gr; f. 1967;

Pres. Rt Rev. FRAGKISKOS PAPAMANOLIS (Bishop of Syros and Milos, and of Santorini).

Archbishop of Athens: Archbishop SEBASTIANOS ROSSOLÁTOS, Odos Homirou 9, 106 72 Athens; tel. (210) 3624311; fax (210) 3618632.

Archbishop of Corfu, Zante and Cefalonia: Most Rev. IOANNIS SPITERIS, Montzeníkhou 3, 491 00 Kérkyra; tel. (26610) 30277; fax (26610) 31675; e-mail cathepco@otenet.gr.

Archbishop of Naxos, Andros, Tinos and Mykonos: Most Rev. NIKÓLAOS PRINTESIS, 842 00 Tinos; tel. (22830) 22382; fax (22830) 24769; e-mail kamipai@cathecclesia.gr.

Archbishop of Rhodes: (vacant), Odos Ionos Dragoumi 5, 851 00 Rhodes; tel. (22410) 21845; fax (22410) 26688.

Apostolic Vicariate of Thessaloníki: Kolokotroni 19B, 564 30 Thessaloníki; tel. (2310) 654256; fax (26610)31675; e-mail cathepco@otenet.gr; Apostolic Vicar JOANNIS SPITERIS.

Byzantine Rite

Apostolic Exarchate for Greek Catholics of the Byzantine Rite: Odos Akarnon 246, 112 53 Athens; tel. (210) 8670170; fax (210) 8677039; e-mail grcathex@hol.gr; 3 parishes; 3,500 adherents (31 Dec. 2006); Apostolic Exarch Most Rev. DIMITRIOS SALACHAS (Titular Bishop of Carcabia).

Armenian Rite

Ordinariate for Catholics of the Armenian Rite in Greece: Odos René Pyo 2, 117 44 Athens; tel. (210) 9014089; fax (210) 9012109; 350 adherents (31 Dec. 2006); Ordinary (vacant); Apostolic Administrator Most Rev. HOVSEP BEZAZIAN (Titular Archbishop of Adana of the Armenian Rite).

Protestant Church

Greek Evangelical Church: Odos Markon Botsari 24, 117 41 Athens; tel. (210) 3231079; fax (210) 3316577; e-mail info@gec.gr; internet www.gec.gr; f. 1858; comprises 32 organized churches; 5,000 adherents (1996); Moderator Rev. MELETIS MELETIADIS.

ISLAM

The law provides a Chief Mufti as religious head of the Muslims; the Muslims in Greece possess a number of mosques and schools.

JUDAISM

The Jewish population of Greece, estimated in 1943 at 75,000 people, was severely reduced as a result of the Nazi German occupation. In 1994 there were about 5,000 Jews in Greece.

Central Board of the Jewish Communities of Greece: Odos Voulis 36, 105 57 Athens; tel. (210) 3244315; fax (210) 3313852; e-mail info@kis.gr; internet www.kis.gr; f. 1945; officially recognized representative body of the Jewish communities of Greece; Pres. MOSES CONSTANTINIS.

The Press

PRINCIPAL DAILY NEWSPAPERS

Morning papers are not published on Mondays, nor afternoon papers on Sundays. The afternoon papers generally enjoy a wider circulation than do the morning ones.

Adesmeftos Typos (Rizos): Thiseseos 218, Kallithea, 176 75 Athens; tel. (210) 9405888; fax (210) 9407173; e-mail info@adesmeytos.gr; internet www.adesmeytos.gr; f. 1998; afternoon; publ. by Makedonikes Publications; Dir DIMITRIS RIZOS; Editor KOSTAS SARRIKOSTAS; circ. weekdays 12,973, Sun. 11,837 (2009).

Apogevmatini (The Afternoon): Odos Phidiou 12, 106 78 Athens; tel. (210) 6430011; fax (210) 3304800; e-mail info@apogevmatini.gr; internet www.apogevmatini.gr; f. 1956; independent; Editor MIHAIL VASILIADIS; circ. 12,815 (2009).

Avgi (Dawn): Odos Ag. Konstantiou 12, 104 31 Athens; tel. (210) 5231831; fax (210) 5231822; e-mail editors@avgi.gr; internet www.avgi.gr; f. 1952; morning; independent newspaper of the left; Dir NIKOS PHILES; circ. 2,791 (2012).

Ekathimerini (The Daily): Ethnarchou Makariou & Odos Falireos 2, Neo Faliro, 185 47, Piraeus, Athens; tel. (210) 4808000; fax (210) 4808205; e-mail info@ekathimerini.com; internet www.kathimerini.gr; f. 1919; morning; conservative; Editor ALEXIS PAPAHELAS; circ. 46,086 (2009).

Eleftherotypia (Press Freedom): Odos Minou 10–16, 117 43 Athens; tel. (211) 1096400; fax (210) 9028311; e-mail elef@enet.gr; internet www.enet.gr; f. 1974; afternoon; Publr HARRIS IKONOMOPOULOS; Chief Editor VANGELIS PANAGOPOULOS; circ. daily 41,511, Sun. 148,652 (2009).

Espresso: C. Averof 26–28, 142 32 Nea Ionia; tel. (210) 2503100; e-mail espresso@espressonews.gr; internet www.espressonews.gr; f. 2000; afternoon; publ. by Daily Press; Publr ANTONIS LIMBERIS; circ. daily 17,752, Sun. 10,453 (2012).

Ethnos (Nation): Odos Benaki 152, Metamorfosi Halandriou, 152 38 Athens; tel. (210) 6061000; fax (210) 6391337; e-mail editor@ethnos.gr; internet www.ethnos.gr; f. 1981; afternoon; Dir GIORGOS CHARVALIAS; Editor THANASIS TSEKOURAS; circ. daily 24,732, Sun. 102,241 (2012).

Express: 46 Leoforos Lavrion, POB 4814, Keratea, 190 01 Attica; tel. (213) 0161700; fax (213) 0161849; e-mail info@express.gr; internet www.express.gr; f. 1963; morning; financial; publ. by Kalofolia Group SA; Publr D. G. KALOFOLIAS; Editor G. DIAMANTOPOULOS; circ. 28,000.

Filathlos: Odos Dimitros 31, 177 78 Athens; tel. (210) 3489000; fax (210) 3489015; e-mail info@filathlos.gr; internet www.filathlos.gr; f. 1982; morning; sports; Publr and Editor G. KOLOKOTRONIS; circ. 8,879.

Goal News: Odos Benaki & Ag. Nektariou, Halandriou, 152 38 Athens; tel. (210) 6061800; fax (210) 6061801; e-mail goal@pegasus.gr; internet www.sentragoal.gr; f. 2002; sport; publ. by Pegasus Publishing SA; Editor KOSTAS KOUKOULAS; circ. Tue.–Sun. 7,058, Mon. 9,911 (2013).

Imerissia (Daily): Odos Benaki & Ag. Nektariou, Metamorfosi Halandriou, 152 38 Athens; tel. (210) 6061000; fax (210) 6014636; e-mail imerissia@pegasus.gr; internet www.imerisia.gr; f. 1947; morning; financial; Dir ANTONIS DALIPIS; circ. 39,000.

Kerdos (Profit): Rizariou 16, 152 33 Athens; tel. (210) 6747881; fax (210) 6747893; e-mail mail@kerdos.gr; internet www.kerdos.gr; f. 1985; morning; financial; Editor KATERINA MPOURA; circ. 18,000.

Naftemporiki (Daily Journal): Odos Lenorman 205, 104 42 Athens; tel. (210) 5198000; fax (210) 5139905; e-mail info@naftemporiki.gr; internet www.naftemporiki.gr; f. 1924; morning; non-political journal of finance, commerce and shipping; Dir NIKOS FRANTZIS; Editor DIMITRIS PLAKOUTSIS; circ. 20,000.

Peloponnesos: Valtetsiou 1 & Maizonos, 262 23 Patras; tel. (2610) 312530; fax (2610) 312535; e-mail pelop@pelop.gr; internet www.pelop.gr; f. 1886; independent; conservative; Publr and CEO THEODOROS H. LOULOUDIS; circ. 7,000.

Protathlitis (Champions): Dimokratias 34, Melissia, 151 27 Athens; tel. (210) 8109000; fax (210) 8040149; e-mail info@championsday.gr; f. 1998; sport; circ. Tue.–Sun. 4,929, Mon. 4,995 (2013).

Rizospastis (Radical): Leoforos Heraklion 145, 142 32 Nea Ionia; tel. (210) 2592600; fax (210) 2592800; e-mail mailbox@rizospastis.gr; internet www.rizospastis.gr; f. 1974; morning; publ. by Modern Age Publishing SA; Editor STEFANOS LOUKAS; circ. 7,214 (2013).

Sport Day: Davaki 58, Kallithea, 176 72 Athens; tel. (210) 9508100; fax (210) 9508160; e-mail info@sday.gr; internet www.sday.gr; f. 2005; sport; circ. Tue.–Sun. 7,741, Mon. 9,812 (2013).

Ta Nea (News): Odos Michalakopoulou 80, 115 28 Athens; tel. (211) 3657000; fax (211) 3658301; e-mail info@tanea.gr; internet www.tanea.gr; f. 1931; liberal; afternoon; publ. by Lambrakis Press SA; Editor VAGGELIS LIALIOUTIS; circ. 28,764 (2013).

To Fos Ton Spor: Athinon 122, 104 42 Athens; tel. (210) 5154000; fax (210) 5141330; e-mail fos@otenet.gr; f. 1968; sport; Editor STRATOS MAKRIS; circ. Tue.–Sun. 10,856, Mon. 14,032 (2013).

To Vima (Tribune): Odos Michalakopoulou 80, 115 28 Athens; tel. (210) 3657000; fax (210) 3658004; e-mail tovima@dolnet.gr; internet www.tovima.gr; f. 1922; liberal; publ. by Lambrakis Press SA; Dir STAVROS R. PSYCHARIS; Editor STELIOS SOFIANOS; circ. daily 38,712, Sun. 172,368 (2009).

WEEKLY PUBLICATIONS

Aksia (Value): Papanikoli 22, 152 32 Chalandri; tel. (210) 6811642; fax (210) 6811671; e-mail info@axianews.gr; f. 1998; Publr ANTONIS PIKOULAS; Editor D. PAPAKONSTANTINOU; circ. 13,165 (2009).

Athens News: Odos Doiranis 181, Kallithea, 176 73 Athens; tel. (213) 0087150; fax (210) 9431110; e-mail athensnews@athensnews.eu; internet www.athensnews.gr; f. 1952; weekly; in English; owned by NEP Publishing Company SA; Editor IOANNA PAPADIMITROPOULOU; circ. 10,000.

Kathimerini Tis Kiriakis (Every Day on Sunday): Minoos 10–16, 117 43 Athens; tel. (210) 9296001; fax (210) 9028311; e-mail ke@enet.gr; internet www.enet.gr; f. 1919; Dir JOHN VLASTARIS; Editors ALEXANDRA DALIANI, VAGELIS SIAFAKAS; circ. 134,665 (2009).

Proto Thema (One Topic): Apostolou Pavlou 6, 15 123 Marousi; tel. (210) 6880700; fax (210) 6892778; e-mail protothemaonline@gmail.com; internet www.protothema.gr; f. 2005; Sunday; circ. 150,659 (2013).

Real News: Leoforos Kifisias 215, 151 24 Athens; tel. (211) 2008300; fax (211) 2008399; e-mail news@realnews.gr; internet www.real.gr; f. 2008; Sunday; Publr NIKOS HATZINIKOLAOU; circ. 88,719 (2013).

Sto Karfi Tou Savvatokyriakou (The Weekend Nail): Krimeas 2 & Mesogion 125, 115 26 Athens; tel. (210) 6901000; fax (210) 6915741; e-mail info@stokarfi.gr; internet digital.stokarfi.gr; f. 2004; Saturdays; left-wing; Dir KOSTAS GIANNOPOULOS; circ. 23,344 (2009).

Xrisi Efkeria (Golden Opportunity): Golden Opportunity Publ., Sakasomouli Hekataios 95 &73, 117 44 Athens; tel. (210) 9091333; fax (210) 9091420; e-mail contact@xe.gr; internet www.xe.gr; f. 1993; publ. by Golden Opportunity Publications; CEO DIMITRIS TRITARIS; circ. 41,293 (2009).

SELECTED PERIODICALS

Aktines (Rays): Odos Karytsi 14, 105 61 Athens; f. 1938; monthly; Christian publication on current affairs, science, philosophy, arts; circ. 10,000.

Asfalistikn Agora (The Insurance Market): Dionysus 126, 151 24 Maroussi; tel. (210) 6196879; fax (210) 6196943; e-mail aagora@aagora.gr; internet www.aagora.gr; f. 1977; publ. by Rouchotas D. & Co; monthly; Publr AMALIA ROUCHOTAS; Editor-in-Chief ATHANASIOS KORMA.

Computer Gia Olous (Computers for All): Capt. Dedousi 1 & Mesogion 304, Holargos, 155 62 Athens; tel. (210) 9238672; fax (210) 9216847; e-mail cpress@compupress.gr; internet www.cgomag.gr; monthly; Editor FORTIS KARATZIAS.

Deltion Diikiseos Epichiriseon Euro-Unial (Euro-Unial Business Administration Bulletin): Odos Alopekis 27-29, 106 75 Athens; tel. (210) 7235735; fax (210) 7240000; e-mail info@dde.gr; internet www.dde.gr; f. 1962; monthly; Editor IOANNIS N. PAPAMICHALAKIS; circ. 26,000 (2006).

Ebdomi (Seventh): Kanari 18, 153 51 Pallini; tel. (210) 6030655; fax (210) 9658949; e-mail scarabe@hol.gr; internet www.ebdomi.com; weekly; political-economic and cultural journal of Eastern Attica; Publr ANNA VENETSANOU.

Economiki Epitheorissi (Economic Review): Odos Vlahava 6–8, 105 51 Athens; tel. (210) 3314714; fax (210) 3252283; e-mail info@economia.gr; internet www.economia.gr; f. 1934; monthly; economy, business and politics; publ. by Group Economia-Kerkyra Publications; Dir and Publr ALEXANDRA VOVOLINI; Editors ANDREAS PETSINIS, SPYROS A. VRETOS; circ. 45,000.

Electrologos (Electrician): Odos Pileos & Leoforos Pentelis 3, Vrilissia, 152 35 Athens; tel. (210) 6800470; fax (210) 6800476; e-mail technoekdotiki@technoekdotiki.gr; internet www.electrologos.gr; f. 1991; monthly; technical; Publr VOULA MOURTA; Editor CHRISTINA SOURRA; circ. 11,500 (2009).

Elnavi (Greek Shipping Industry): Odos Aristidou 19, 185 31 Piraeus; tel. (210) 4522100; fax (210) 4282467; e-mail elnavi@elnavi.gr; internet www.elnavi.gr; f. 1974; monthly; shipping; Publr ELIAS KALAPOTHARAKOS; Dirs STEFANOS PAPANDREOU, THEANO KALAPOTHARAKOU; circ. 4,000 (2009).

Epiloghi (Selection): Kapodistrioy 2 & Demokratias 83, 154 51 Neo Psychiko; tel. (210) 6401850; fax (210) 6424850; e-mail press@allmedia.gr; internet www.epilogimag.gr; f. 1962; monthly; economics and business journal; publ. by All Media Publications; Dir CHRISTOS PAPAIOANNOU; Editor THOMI MELIDOU.

Greek Diplomatic Life: Giving Fountain 5, 106 78 Athens; tel. (210) 3806534; fax (210) 3818983; e-mail diplomat@otenet.gr; f. 1978; bi-monthly; Publr BOUTSIKOS NIKOLAOS; circ. 5,500 (2009).

Gynaika (Women): Odos Fragoklissias 7, Marousi, 151 25 Athens; tel. (210) 6199149; fax (210) 6104707; e-mail admin@e-gynaika.com; internet www.e-gynaika.gr; f. 1950; monthly; Publr CHRISTOS TERZOPOULOS; circ. 45,000.

Hot Doc: Athens; internet www.hotdoc.gr; f. 2012; politics and current affairs; every 2 weeks; Editor KOSTAS VAXEVANIS.

Idaniko Spiti (Ideal Home): Odos Benaki 5, Halandri, 152 38 Athens; tel. (210) 6061777; fax (210) 6061891; e-mail idanikospiti@pegasus.gr; internet www.idanikospiti.gr; f. 1990; monthly; interior decoration; Editor ALEXANDRA VAGENA; circ. 13,000 (2009).

Kynigos Kai Fysi (Hunter and Nature): Kallirrois 85, 117 45 Athens; tel. (210) 7755464; fax (210) 7785776; e-mail onel@onel.gr; internet www.go-outdoor.gr; publ. by Onel SA; Publr KAKAVOULIS ELEFTHERIOS.

Mastoremata (Do-it-yourself): Odos Thorikou, Viopa Kalyvion, Kalyvia, 190 10 Attica; tel. (229) 9021360; fax (229) 9021359; e-mail info@mastoremata.gr; internet www.mastoremata.gr; monthly; publ. by Stefanos Karidakis SA; Publr PROKOPIS KARIDAKIS; Editor DIMITRIS GEORGOPOULOS.

Pantheon: Odos Christou Lada 3, 102 37 Athens; fax (210) 3228797; every two weeks; Publr and Dir N. THEOFANIDES.

Ptisi & Diastima (Flight & Space): Ioannou Metaxa 80, Koropi, 194 00 Athens; tel. (210) 9792500; fax (210) 9792528; e-mail ptisi@ptisi.gr; internet www.ptisi.gr; f. 1979; monthly; Editor FAITHON KARAIOSSIFIOIS; circ. 1,467.

Radiotileorasi (Radio-TV): Odos Rhigillis 4, 106 74 Athens; tel. (210) 7407252; fax (210) 7224812; e-mail radiotileorasi@ert.gr; internet www.radiotileorasi.gr; weekly; Editor VASILEIA ZERVOU; circ. 55,000.

Stigmes (Moments): Psaromiligkon 17, Heraklion, 712 02 Crete; tel. (281) 0288333; fax (281) 0301927; e-mail spiti@stigmes.gr; internet www.stigmes.gr; 6 a year; Cretan culture; Editor NIKOS KARELLIS.

Technika Chronika (Technical Times): Odos Nikis, Syndagma, 102 48 Athens; tel. (210) 3291200; fax (210) 3221772; e-mail tee@central.tee.gr; internet www.tee.gr; f. 1932; weekly; general technical subjects; Editor IOANNIS ALAVANOS; circ. 100,000.

Tilerama: Odos Voukourestiou 18, 106 71 Athens; tel. (210) 3607160; fax (210) 3607032; f. 1977; weekly; radio and television; circ. 189,406.

To Pontiki (The Mouse): Odos Massalias 10, 106 81 Athens; fax (210) 6898226; e-mail asfalistiko@topontiki.gr; internet www.topontiki.gr; weekly; humour; Dir and Editor K. PAPAIOANNOU.

NEWS AGENCY

Athens Macedonian News Agency (ANA-MPA): Odos Tsoha 36, 115 21 Athens; tel. (210) 6400560; fax (210) 6400581; e-mail sofia@amna.gr; internet www.amna.gr; f. 1895; as Athens News Agency; name changed to above following merger with Macedonian Press Agency in 2008; correspondents in leading capitals of the world and towns throughout Greece; Gen. Man. ANTONIS SKYLLAKOS; Gen. Dir SOFIA KRITHARA.

PRESS ASSOCIATIONS

Enosis Antapokriton Xenou Tipou (Foreign Press Association of Greece): Odos Valaoritou 12, 3rd Floor, 106 71 Athens; tel. (210) 3637318; fax (210) 3605035; e-mail fpa@fpa.gr; internet www.fpa.gr; f. 1916; Pres. MARIA PETRAKIS; Gen. Sec. ELENI COLLIOPOULOU; 300 mems.

Enosis Demosiograpson Idioktiton Periodikou Tipou (Union of Journalists and Proprietors of the Periodical Press EDIPT): Leoforos Vas Sofias 25, 3rd Floor, Athens; tel. (210) 7220875; fax (210) 7215128; e-mail info@edipt.gr; internet www.edipt.gr; f. 1939; Pres. MICHAEL SAVAKIS; Gen. Sec. HELEN GKOGKONI-ABAZI; 300 mems.

Enosi Idioktiton Imerision Efimeridon Athinon (Athens Daily Newspaper Publishers' Association): Mourouzi 14, 106 74 Athens; tel. (210) 7209810; fax (210) 7246456; e-mail postmaster@eihea.gr; internet www.eihea.gr; f. 1951; Pres. STAVROS PSYCHARIS; Sec. ALEXIS ZAOUSSIS.

Enosis Syntakton Imerission Ephimeridon Athinon (Journalists' Union of Athens Daily Newspapers): Odos Akademias 20, 106 71 Athens; tel. (210) 3675400; fax (210) 3632608; e-mail info@esiea.gr; internet www.esiea.gr; f. 1914; Pres. MARIA ANTONIADES; Gen. Sec. MARILENA KATSIMI; 2,110 mems.

Enosis Syntakton Periodikou Tipou (Journalists' Union of the Periodical Press): Odos Valaoritou 9, 6th Floor, 106 71 Athens; tel. (210) 3633427; fax (210) 3638627; e-mail espit@otenet.gr; internet www.espit.gr; f. 1959; Pres. THEMIS K. BEREDIMAS; Gen. Sec. ALATAS THANASIS; 835 mems.

Publishers

Agkyra Publications: Odos Lamprou Katsoni 271, Aghi Anargyri, 135 62 Athens; tel. (210) 2693800; fax (210) 2693806; internet www.agyra.gr; f. 1890; general; Man. Dir DIMITRIOS PAPADIMITRIOU.

Akritas: Odos Chalkokondili 36, 104 32 Athens; tel. (210) 9334554; fax (210) 9404950; e-mail akritas@pkbooks.gr; internet www.akritas.net.gr; f. 1978; history, Orthodox Christianity, children's books.

Arsenides Publishers: Odos Akadimias 57, 106 79 Athens; tel. (210) 3629538; fax (210) 3633923; e-mail tarsen@otenet.gr; f. 1952; philosophy, psychology, sociology, history, biography, literature, children's books.

Ekdotike Athenon: Odos Hippokratous 13, 106 79 Athens; tel. (210) 3608911; fax (210) 3608914; e-mail info@ekdotikeathenon.gr; internet www.ekdotikeathenon.gr; f. 1962; history, archaeology, art.

Exandas Publications: Odos Didotou 57, 106 81 Athens; tel. (210) 3804885; fax (210) 3813065; e-mail info@exandasbooks.gr; internet www.exandasbooks.gr; f. 1974; fiction, literature, social sciences; Pres. MAGDA N. KOTZIA.

Govostis Publishing: Zoodohou Pigis 73, 106 81 Athens; tel. (210) 3815433; fax (210) 3816661; e-mail cotsos@govostis.gr; internet www.govostis.gr; f. 1926; arts, fiction, politics; Pres. COSTAS GOVOSTIS.

Denise Harvey: Katounia, 340 05 Limni, Evia; tel. and fax (22270) 31154; e-mail dhp@dharveypublisher.gr; internet www

.deniseharveypublisher.gr; f. 1972; books concerned with post-Byzantine Greek culture, incl. literature, theology, history, travel, music, and social anthropology (English); Man. Dir DENISE HARVEY.

Hestia-I.D. Kollaros S.A. & Co: Odos Evripidou 84, 105 53 Athens; tel. (210) 3213704; fax (210) 220821; e-mail info@hestia.gr; internet www.hestia.gr; f. 1885; literature, history, politics, psychoanalysis, philosophy, children's books, political and philosophical essays; Gen. Dir EVA-MARIA KARAITIDI.

Kastaniotis Editions: Odos Zalogou 11, 106 78 Athens; tel. (210) 3301208; fax (210) 3822530; e-mail info@kastaniotis.com; internet www.kastaniotis.com; f. 1968; fiction and non-fiction, incl. arts, social sciences and psychology, children's books; Man. Dir ATHANASIOS KASTANIOTIS.

Kritiki Publishing: Odos Patission 75, 104 34 Athens; tel. (210) 8211811; fax (210) 8211026; e-mail biblia@kritiki.gr; internet www.kritiki.gr; f. 1987; economics, politics, literature, philosophy, business management, popular science; Publr THEMIS MINOGLOU.

Livani Publishing Organization: Odos Solonos 98, 106 80 Athens; tel. (210) 3661200; fax (210) 3617791; e-mail rights@livanis.gr; internet www.livanis.gr; f. 1972; fiction, non-fiction, children's books; Publr A. A. LIVANI.

Minoas: Odos Davaki Konstantinou 34, 144 51 Metamorfosi; tel. (210) 2711222; fax (210) 2711056; e-mail info@minoas.gr; internet www.minoas.gr; f. 1952; fiction, art, history; Man. Dir IOANNIS KONSTANTAROPOULOS.

Papazissis Publishers: Nikitara 2, 106 78 Athens; tel. (210) 3822496; fax (210) 3809150; e-mail papazisi@otenet.gr; internet www.papazisi.gr; f. 1929; economics, politics, law, history, school books; Man. Dir ALEXANDROS PAPAZISSIS.

Patakis Publishers: Pan. Tsaldari 38, 104 37 Athens; tel. (210) 3650000; fax (210) 3811940; e-mail bookstore@patakis.gr; internet www.patakis.gr; f. 1974; art, reference, fiction, educational, philosophy, psychology, sociology, religion, music, children's books, audiobooks; Pres. STEFANOS PATAKIS.

PUBLISHERS' ASSOCIATIONS

Book Publishers' Association of Athens: Odos Stournari 5, 106 83 Athens; tel. (210) 3830029; fax (210) 3823222; e-mail info@seva.gr; internet www.seva.gr; f. 1945; Pres. KONSTANTINOS PAPADOPOULOS; Sec. PHAEDON KYDONIATIS.

Hellenic Federation of Publishers and Booksellers: Odos Themistokleus 73, 106 83 Athens; tel. (210) 3804760; fax (210) 3301617; e-mail secretary@poev.gr; internet www.poev.gr; f. 1961; Pres. RAGIA ANNIE; Gen. Sec. STATHATOS NICHOLAS.

Broadcasting and Communications

TELECOMMUNICATIONS

By the end of 2009 some 531 licensed service providers were operating in the telecommunications sector: voice telephony and fixed-line networks (178); voice telephony (141); fixed-line networks (87); satellite networks (34); 2G and 3G mobile technology (13); terrestrial trunk radio (TETRA—5); and wireless local area network (W-LAN—73).

Forthnet: Odos Manis, 153 51 Pallini; tel. (1) 9559258; fax (1) 9559055; e-mail info@forthnet.gr; internet www.forthnet.gr; broadband and satellite telecommunications services; internet service provider; CEO PANAYIOTIS PAPADOPOULOS.

Hellenic Telecommunications Organization (OTE) (Organismos Telepikoinonion tis Elladas): Leoforos Kifissias 99, 151 24 Maroussi, Athens; tel. (210) 6117434; fax (210) 3405129; e-mail media-office@ote.gr; internet www.ote.gr; f. 1949; 10% owned by the Government, 40% by Deutsche Telekom (Germany); mobile cellular telecommunications and internet service provider; Chief Exec. and Chair. MICHAEL TSAMAZ.

COSMOTE: Leoforos Kifissias 99, 151 24 Marousi, Athens; tel. (210) 6177777; fax (210) 6177594; e-mail mediarelations@cosmote.gr; internet www.cosmote.gr; f. 1998; 59% owned by OTE; mobile cellular telecommunications and internet service provider; Pres. and CEO MICHAEL TSAMAZ.

Otesat-Maritel: Odos Egaleo 8, 185 45 Piraeus; tel. (210) 4599500; fax (210) 4599600; e-mail otesat-maritel@otesat-maritel.com; internet www.otesat-maritel.com; OTE subsidiary; marine telecommunications; Chair. THEODOROS VENIAMIS; CEO GEORGE POLYCHRONOPOULOS.

Vodafone Greece: 1–3 Tzavella St, 152 31 Halandri; tel. (210) 6702000; fax (210) 6703200; internet www.vodafone.gr; 55% owned by Vodafone Europe Holdings (UK); mobile cellular telecommunications and internet service provider; Chair. GLAUKOS PERSIANIS.

WIND Hellas Telecommunications: Leoforos Kifissias 66, 151 25 Marousi, Athens; tel. (210) 6158000; fax (210) 5100001; e-mail crm@wind.gr; internet www.wind.com.gr; f. 1992 as Telestet; renamed as above in 2007; fixed and mobile cellular telecommunications, internet services; Chair. and CEO NASSOS ZARKALIS.

Regulatory Authority

Hellenic Telecommunications and Post Commission: Leoforos Kifissias 60, 151 25 Athens; tel. (210) 6151000; fax (210) 6105049; e-mail info@eett.gr; internet www.eett.gr; regulatory body; Chair. CONSTANTINOS LOUROPOULOS.

RADIO AND TELEVISION

In June 2011, in addition to the publicly owned four national analogue terrestrial TV stations, three national digital TV stations and one satellite TV station, there were seven main national private TV networks and approximately 150 local and regional TV stations broadcasting across the country. The closure of the state broadcaster, Elliniki Radiophonia Tileorassi (ERT), was announced by the Government in June 2013; however, former ERT employees continued to broadcast online in protest against the broadcaster's closure. Meanwhile, transitional broadcasting arrangements were made, with the official establishment of Nea Elliniki Radiofonia, Internet, Tileorasi (NERIT—New Hellenic Radio, Internet and Television) in May 2014 (www.nerit.gr). In April 2015 the Parliament approved draft legislation permitting the re-establishment of ERT.

Private Stations

Antenna TV: Leoforos Kifissias 10–12, Maroussi, 151 25 Athens; tel. (210) 6886100; fax (210) 6834349; e-mail webmaster@antenna.gr; internet www.antenna.gr; f. 1989; Chair. M. X. KYRIAKOU.

Mega Channel: Roussou 4 & Mesogeion Ave, 115 26 Athens; tel. (210) 6903000; fax (210) 6983600; e-mail ngeorgiou@megatv.com; internet www.megatv.com; f. 1989; Chair. STAVROS PSYCHARIS; Man. Dir ELIAS E. TSIGAS.

Serres TV: Nigritis 27, 621 24 Serres; tel. (2321) 51688; fax (2321) 58020; e-mail info@serrestv.gr; internet www.serrestv.gr.

Star Channel: Odos Thermopylon 87, 351 00 Lamia; tel. (22310) 46725; fax (22310) 46728; e-mail star@star-online.gr; internet www.lamiastar.gr; f. 1988; Pres. NIKE CHEIMONIDIS.

Traki TV: 30 Venizelos, 681 00 Alexandroupolis; tel. (2551) 52000; fax (2551) 37731; e-mail info@thrakinet.tv; internet www.thrakinet.tv.

TRT: Ferron 65, 383 34 Volos; tel. (2421) 28801; fax (2421) 36888; e-mail commercial@trttv.com; internet www.trttv.com; f. 1990; Pres. and CEO EVANGELOS ANTONIOU.

TV-100: Odos Aggelaki 16, 546 21 Thessaloníki; tel. (231) 265828; fax (231) 267532; e-mail depthe@fm100.gr; internet www.fm100.gr; f. 1988.

Finance

(cap. = capital; res = reserves; dep. = deposits; m. = million; brs = branches; amounts in euros)

BANKING

Following the restructuring of the banking sector, by 2013 four principal banks (the National Bank of Greece, Alpha Bank, Eurobank Ergasias SA and Piraeus Bank) held approximately 96% of deposits.

Central Bank

Bank of Greece: Leoforos E. Venizelos 21, 102 50 Athens; tel. (210) 3201111; fax (210) 3232239; e-mail sec.secretariat@bankofgreece.gr; internet www.bankofgreece.gr; f. 1927; cap. 111.2m., res 694.1m., dep. 10,266.6m. (Dec. 2009); Gov. YANNIS STOURNARAS; 17 branches and 33 agencies.

Commercial Banks

Alpha Bank: Stadiou 40, 102 52 Athens; tel. (210) 3260000; fax (210) 3265052; e-mail secretariat@alpha.gr; internet www.alpha.gr; f. 1879; present name adopted 2000; cap. 1,100.3m., res 3,025.9m., dep. 52,401.1m. (Dec. 2012); Chair. and Gen. Man. IOANNIS S. COSTOPOULOS; 713 brs.

Attica Bank: Odos Omirou 23, 106 72 Athens; tel. (210) 3669000; fax (210) 3667245; e-mail info@atticabank.gr; internet www.atticabank.gr; f. 1925; cap. 185.9m., res 324.6m., dep. 3,648.6m. (Dec. 2012); Chair. of Bd and Exec. Dir IOANNIS GAMVRILIS; 80 brs.

Black Sea Trade and Development Bank: Odos Komninon 1, 546 24 Thessaloníki; tel. (231) 290400; fax (231) 221796; e-mail info@bstdb.org; internet www.bstdb.org; f. 1997; owned by 11 member states: Greece, Russian Federation, Turkey (16.5% each); Bulgaria, Romania, Ukraine (13.5% each); Albania, Armenia, Azerbaijan,

Georgia, Moldova (2.0% each); cap. 494.4m., res 44.2m., total assets 983.6m. (Dec. 2012); Pres. ANDREY KONDAKOV.

Eurobank Ergasias SA: Odos Leoforos Amalias 20, 105 57 Athens; tel. (210) 3337688; fax (210) 3337256; e-mail info@eurobank.gr; internet www.eurobank.gr; f. 1990; present name adopted 2000; 93.6% owned by the Hellenic Financial Stability Fund (HFSF); cap. 2,545m., res 2,636m., dep. 30,407m. (Dec. 2012); Pres. EYTHYMIOS N. CHRISTODOULOU; CEO NIKOLAS NANOPOULOS; 379 brs.

Geniki Bank—General Bank of Greece: Odos Messogeion 109–111, 115 10 Athens; tel. (210) 6975200; fax (210) 6975910; e-mail intdiv@geniki.gr; internet www.geniki.gr; f. 1937; present name adopted 1998; controlling stake acquired by Société Générale (France) in 2004, and obtained by Piraeus Bank in Dec. 2012; cap. 100.3m., res 1,056.6m., dep. 2,252.6m. (Dec. 2012); Chair. TRYFON KOUTALIDIS; 80 brs.

National Bank of Greece (NBG): Odos Aeolou 86, 102 32 Athens; tel. (210) 3341000; fax (210) 4806510; e-mail contact.center@nbg.gr; internet www.nbg.gr; f. 1841; state-controlled, but operates independently of the Govt; cap. 6,309.7m., res 2,702.7m., dep. 91,585.8m. (Dec. 2012); CEO ALEXANDROS TOURKOLIAS; 540 brs.

Piraeus Bank: Odos Amerikis 4, 105 64 Athens; tel. (210) 3335000; fax (210) 3335080; e-mail investor-relations@piraeusbank.gr; internet www.piraeusbank.gr; f. 1916; cap. 1,092.9m., res 2,957.9m., dep. 68,925.8m. (Dec. 2012); Chair. MICHALIS G. SALLAS; 85 brs.

STOCK EXCHANGE

Athens Stock Exchange: Odos Sophokleous 10, 105 59 Athens; tel. (210) 3211301; fax (210) 3213938; e-mail webmaster@ase.gr; internet www.ase.gr; f. 1876; Pres. CAPRALOS SPYROS; Vice-Pres. LAZARIDIS SOKRATIS.

PRINCIPAL INSURANCE COMPANIES

In 2012 there were 69 insurance companies operating in Greece, of which 13 provided life insurance, 45 provided non-life insurance, and 11 provided both life and non-life insurance.

ATE Insurance SA: Leoforos Syngrou 173, 171 21 Kallithea, Athens; tel. (210) 9379100; fax (210) 9358924; e-mail info@agroins.com; internet www.ateinsurance.gr; f. 1980; as Agrotiki Insurance SA Hellenic General Insurance Company; name changed as above in 2005; member of Piraeus Bank Group (Greece); Pres. SPYRIDON PAPASPYROU; CEO JORDAN HADJIOSIPH.

Atlantiki Enosis/Atlantic Union: Odos Messoghion 71 & Ilidos 36, 115 26 Athens; tel. (210) 7454000; fax (210) 7794446; e-mail atlantiki@atlantiki.gr; internet www.atlanticunion.gr; f. 1970; subsidiary of La Baloise (Switzerland); Pres. STASINOPOULOS SARANDOS.

Axa Insurance: Odos Michalakopoulou 48, 115 28 Athens; tel. (210) 7268000; fax (210) 7268408; e-mail info@axa-insurance.gr; internet www.axa-insurance.gr; f. 1999; fmrly Alpha Insurance; Pres. GRANIER JEAN-LAURENT RAYMONT MARIE; Man. Dir ERIC PIERRE KLEIJNEN.

Crédit Agricole Life: Odos Mitropoleos 45, 105 56 Athens; tel. (210) 3283545; fax (210) 3283520; e-mail info@ca-life.gr; f. 2001 as Emporiki Life; as a joint venture of Emporiki Bank and insurance arm of Crédit Agricole; became a subsidiary of Crédit Agricole Assurances in 2010; name changed as above in 2011; life insurance; Chair. PANAYIOTIS VARELAS; Man. Dir RICHARD SUTTON.

Dynamis: Leoforos Syngrou 320, 176 73 Kallithea, Athens; tel. (210) 9006900; fax (210) 9237768; e-mail info@dynamis.gr; internet www.dynamis.gr; f. 1977; Pres. and CEO PAUL G. KARAKOSTAS.

ERGO General Insurance Co SA: Odos Sofias 97, 115 21 Athens; tel. (210) 3705300; fax (210) 3244134; e-mail ergo@ergohellas.gr; internet www.ergohellas.gr; f. 1972; as Victoria General Insurance Co SA; Man. Dir G. ANDONIADIS.

Ethniki Hellenic General Insurance Co SA: Leoforos Syngrou 103–105, 117 45 Athens; tel. (210) 9099111; internet www.ethniki-asfalistiki.gr; f. 1891; Pres. DEMETRIOS GEORGE DIMOPOULOS.

Groupama Phoenix: Leoforos Syngrou 213-215, N. Smirni, 171 21 Athens; tel. (210) 3295111; fax (210) 3239135; e-mail info@groupama-phoenix.com; internet www.groupama-phoenix.com; f. 1928; general.

Horizon General Insurance Co: Leoforos Amalias 26A, 105 57 Athens; tel. (210) 3227932; fax (210) 3225540; e-mail info@horizonins.gr; f. 1965; Gen. Man THEODORE ACHIS.

Imperial: Leoforos Syngrou 253, N. Smirni, 171 22 Athens; tel. (210) 9426352; fax (210) 9426202; e-mail imperial@imperial.gr; internet www.imperial.gr; f. 1971; Gen. Man. GEORGE TZANIS.

ING: Leoforos Syngrou 198, 176 71 Kallithea, Athens; tel. (210) 9506000; fax (210) 9506076; e-mail info@ing.gr; internet www.ing.gr; f. 1980; CEO LUIS MIGUEL GOMEZ ORTIZ.

Interamerican Hellenic Life Insurance Co: Odos Sygrou 124–126, 176 80 Athens; tel. (210) 9462000; fax (210) 9461008; e-mail custserv@interamerican.gr; internet www.interamerican.gr; f. 1969; 79.4% owned by Eureko (the Netherlands); subsidiary cos provide medical, property, casualty, and automobile insurance; Chair. DAVID SANDERSE.

MetLife Alico: Leoforos Kifissias 119, 151 24 Maroussi, Athens; tel. (210) 8787000; fax (210) 6123722; e-mail contact@metlifealico.gr; internet www.metlifealico.gr; f. 1964; life insurance; Group Chair. and CEO STEVEN A. KANDARIAN.

Sideris Insurance Co: Odos Lekka 3–5, 105 63 Athens; tel. (281) 0301678; fax (281) 0301679; e-mail info@sideris-insurance.gr; internet www.sideris-insurance.gr; Dir G. SIDERIS.

Syneteristiki General Insurance Co: Leoforos Syngrou 367, 175 64 Kallithea, Athens; tel. (210) 9491280; fax (210) 9403148; e-mail com@syneteristiki.gr; internet www.syneteristiki.gr; Gen. Man. DIMITRIS ZORBAS.

Insurance Association

Hellenic Association of Insurance Companies: Odos Xenophontos 10, 105 57 Athens; tel. (210) 3334100; fax (210) 3334149; e-mail info@eaee.gr; internet www.eaee.gr; f. 1907; 71 mem cos; Pres. ALEXANDROS SARRIGEORGIOU; Gen. Man. MARGARITA ANTONAKI.

Trade and Industry
CHAMBERS OF COMMERCE

Athens Chamber of Commerce and Industry: Odos Akademias 7, 106 71 Athens; tel. (210) 3604815; fax (210) 3616464; e-mail info@acci.gr; internet www.acci.gr; f. 1919; Pres. CONSTANTINOS MICHALOS; Sec.-Gen. NIKOS SOFIANOS; 70,000 mems.

Athens Chamber of Small and Medium-sized Industries: Odos Akademias 18, 106 71 Athens; tel. (210) 3680700; fax (210) 3614726; e-mail info@acsmi.gr; internet www.acsmi.gr; f. 1940; Pres. RAVANIS PAUL; Gen. Sec. LIAMETIS VASILIOS; c. 60,000 mems.

Piraeus Chamber of Commerce and Industry: Odos Loudovikou 1, Pl. Odessa, 185 31 Piraeus; tel. (210) 4177241; fax (210) 4178680; e-mail evep@pcci.gr; internet www.pcci.gr; f. 1919; Pres. VASSILIS KORKIDIS; Gen. Sec. DIMITRIOS MARKOMICHALIS.

Piraeus Chamber of Industry: Odos Karaiscou 111, 185 32 Piraeus; tel. (210) 4110443; fax (210) 4179495; e-mail info@bep.gr; internet www.bep.gr; f. 1925; Pres. ANDRIANOS MIHALARIAS; Gen. Sec. GERASIMOS MICHALAKIS.

Thessaloníki Chamber of Commerce and Industry (TCCI): Odos Tsimiski 29, 546 24 Thessaloníki; tel. (231) 0370100; fax (231) 0370166; e-mail root@ebeth.gr; internet www.ebeth.gr; f. 1918; Pres. DIMITRIOS BAKATSELOS; Sec.-Gen. KONSTANTINOS CHANTZARIDIS; 18,000 mems.

INDUSTRIAL AND TRADE ASSOCIATIONS

Federation of Industries of Northern Greece (FING): Morihovou 1, 546 25 Thessaloníki; tel. (231) 0539817; fax (231) 0541933; e-mail info@sbbe.gr; internet www.sbbe.gr; f. 1915; Pres. NIKOS PENTOZ; Gen. Sec. ATHANASIOS SAVAKIS.

Hellenic Cotton Board: Leoforos Syngrou 150, 176 71 Kallithea, Athens; tel. (210) 9225011; fax (210) 9243676; f. 1931; state org.; Pres. P. K. MYLONAS.

SEV Hellenic Federation of Enterprises: Odos Xenophontos 5, Syntagma, 105 57 Athens; tel. (211) 5006000; fax (210) 3222929; e-mail info@sev.org.gr; internet www.sev.org.gr; f. 1907; Chair. THEODORE FESSAS.

Hellenic Organization of Small and Medium Enterprises and Handicrafts (EOMMEX): Odos Xenias 16, 115 28 Athens; tel. (210) 7491100; fax (210) 7491146; e-mail interel@eommex.gr; internet www.eommex.gr; f. 1977; Pres. CHRIS PITELIS.

UTILITIES
Regulatory Authority

Regulatory Authority for Energy (RAE): Leoforos Piraeus 132, 118 54 Athens; tel. (210) 3727400; fax (210) 3255460; e-mail info@rae.gr; internet www.rae.gr; f. 2000; Chair. Dr NIKOS VASILAKOS.

Electricity

Operator of the Electricity Market SA (LAGIE): Kastoros 72, 18545 Piraeus; tel. (210) 9466700; fax (210) 9466766; e-mail info@lagie.gr; internet www.lagie.gr; electric energy transmission; Pres. and CEO ANASTASIOS GARIS.

Public Power Corpn (DEH): Odos Chalkokondili 30, 104 32 Athens; tel. (210) 5293417; fax (210) 5238445; e-mail info@dei.com.gr; internet www.dei.gr; f. 1950; 51% state-owned; generating capacity of 96 power stations: 12,843 MW (2008); generation, transmission and distribution of electricity; Chair. and CEO Prof. ARTHOUROS ZERVOS.

Gas

Public Gas Corpn (DEPA): Marinou Antipa 92, Leoforos Antipa, 141 21 Athens; tel. (210) 2701000; fax (210) 2701010; e-mail pr@depa .gr; internet www.depa.gr; f. 1988; 35% owned by Hellenic Petroleum SA, 65% state-owned; began gas imports 1997, initially for industrial use; Chair. and CEO HARRIS SACHINIS.

Water

In 1980 a law was approved, creating Municipal Enterprises for Water Supply and Sewerage (DEYA) to manage drinking water and sewerage throughout Greece. Since then some 90 DEYA have been established.

The Hellenic Union of Municipal Enterprises for Water Supply and Sewerage (EDEYA): Odos Papakyriazi 37-43, 412 22 Larissa; tel. (241) 0258261; fax (241) 0532347; e-mail info@edeya .gr; internet www.edeya.gr; f. 1989; Dir GEORGE MARINAKIS; 155 mems.

TRADE UNIONS

There are about 5,000 registered trade unions, grouped together in 82 federations and 86 workers' centres, which are affiliated to the Greek General Confederation of Labour.

Greek General Confederation of Labour (GSEE): Odos Patission 69 & Aenian 2, 104 34 Athens; tel. (210) 8202100; fax (210) 8202186; e-mail info@gsee.gr; internet www.gsee.gr; f. 1918; Pres. IOANNIS PANAGOPOULOS; Sec.-Gen. NIKOLAOS KIOUTSOUKIS; 700,000 mems.

Pan-Hellenic Federation of Seamen's Unions (PNO): Akti Miaouli 47–49, 185 36 Piraeus; tel. (210) 4292958; fax (210) 4293040; e-mail gram@pno.gr; internet www.pno.gr; f. 1920; confederation of 14 marine unions; Pres. IOANNIS CHELAS; Gen. Sec. JOHN HALAS.

Supreme Administration of Greek Civil Servants' Trade Unions (ADEDY): Odos Psylla Philellinon 2, 105 57 Athens; tel. (213) 1616900; fax (210) 3246165; e-mail adedyed@adedy.gr; internet www.adedy.gr; Pres. ANTONAKOS ANDONIS; Gen. Sec. AKRIBOS APOSTOLOS.

Transport

RAILWAYS

In 2009 there were 1,552 km of railway track in use. Construction of a 26-km electrified extension to the Athens–Piraeus line, in order to provide a three-line urban railway system for Athens, designated Metro Line 1, was completed in 2000. Metro Lines 2 and 3, each measuring some 9 km, opened prior to the holding of the Summer Olympic Games in 2004.

Attiko Metro: Leoforos Messoghion 191–93, 115 25 Athens; tel. (210) 6792399; fax (210) 6726126; e-mail info@ametro.gr; internet www.ametro.gr; f. 1991; operates lines 2 and 3 of underground railway in Athens; Chair. and CEO CHRISTOS TSITOURAS.

Organismos Sidirodromon Ellados (OSE) (Hellenic Railways Organization Ltd): Odos Karolou 1–3, 104 37 Athens; tel. (210) 5248395; fax (210) 5243290; internet www.ose.gr; f. 1971; state railways; Chair. NIKOLAOS BALTAS; Dir-Gen. A. LAZARIS.

Urban Rail Transport S.A. (STASY): Odos Athinas 67, 105 52 Athens; tel. (214) 4141499; fax (214) 3223935; e-mail kgram@stasy .gr; internet www.stasy.gr; f. 2011; state-owned; Chair. and CEO NIKOLAOS C. PAPATHANASSIS.

ROADS

In 2012 there were 116,960 km of roads in Greece. Of this total, an estimated 9,299 km were main roads, and 1,197 km were motorways. The construction of the 680-km Egnatia highway, extending from the Adriatic coast to the Turkish border, was one of the largest road projects in Europe and was completed in 2009.

INLAND WATERWAYS

There are no navigable rivers in Greece.

Corinth Canal: built 1893; over 6 km long, links the Corinthian and Saronic Gulfs; shortens the journey from the Adriatic to Piraeus by 325 km; spanned by three single-span bridges, two for road and one for rail; can be used by ships of a maximum draught of 22 ft and width of 60 ft; managed since June 2001 by Sea Containers Group (UK).

SHIPPING

At the end of 2014 the Greek flag registered fleet totalled 1,408 vessels, with a combined aggregate displacement of 42.7m. grt., of which 254 were bulk carriers, 25 fishing carriers, 21 gas tankers and 83 general cargo ships. Greece controls one of the largest merchant fleets in the world. The principal ports are Piraeus, Patras and Thessaloníki.

Union of Greek Shipowners: Akti Miaouli 85, 185 38 Piraeus; f. 1916; Pres. NICOS EFTHYMIOU.

Port Authorities

Organismos Limenos Patras (Patras Port Authority): South Patras Port, Akti Dimeon, 26110 Patras; tel. (261) 0365113; fax (261) 0365110; e-mail info@patrasport.gr; internet www.patrasport .gr; Pres. and CEO KONSTANTINOS PLATIKOSTAS.

Organismos Limenos Piraeus (OLP) (Piraeus Port Authority): Piraeus Port Authority, Akti Miaouli 10, 185 38 Piraeus; tel. (210) 4550000; fax (210) 4550280; e-mail ceo@olp.gr; internet www.olp.gr; f. 1930; 25% privatized; Pres. and Man. Dir GIORGOS ANOMERITIS.

Organismos Limenos Thessaloníki (Port of Thessaloníki): Thessaloníki Port Authority, POB 10467, 541 10 Thessaloníki; tel. (231) 0593102; fax (231) 0593281; e-mail ceooffice@thpa.gr; internet www .thpa.gr; Pres. and CEO STYLIANOS AGGELOUDIS.

Shipping Companies

The following are among the largest or most important shipping companies.

Anangel Shipping Enterprises: Akti Miaouli, POB 80004, 185 10 Piraeus; tel. (210) 4224500; fax (210) 4224819; f. 1971; subsidiary of Agelef Shipping Group (UK); Man. Dir J. PLATSIDAKIS.

Attica Holdings: Leoforos Syngrou 123–25 & Odos Torva 3, 117 45 Athens; tel. (210) 8919500; fax (210) 8919509; internet www .attica-group.com; f. 1918; subsidiary cos include Blue Star Ferries and Superfast.com; Chair. KYRIAKOS D. MAGEIRAS; CEO SPIROS PASCHALIS.

Blue Star Ferries: Leoforos Syngrou 123–25 & Odos Torva 3, 117 45 Athens; tel. (210) 8919800; fax (210) 8919829; e-mail bluestarferries@bluestarferries.com; internet www.bluestarferries .com; subsidiary of Attica Holdings (q.v.); operates passenger and cargo ferry services between the Greek mainland and islands, and between Greece and Italy.

Chandris (Hellas) Co: POB 80067, Akti Miaouli 95, 185 38 Piraeus; tel. (210) 4584000; fax (210) 4290256; e-mail chandris-hellas@ chandris-group.gr; internet www.chandris-hellas.gr; f. 1915; Man. Dirs A. C. PIPERAS, M. G. SKORDIAS.

Costamare Shipping Co: Leoforos Syngrou & Odos Zephyrou 60, 175 64 Athens; tel. (210) 9490000; fax (210) 9409051; e-mail info@ costamare.com; internet www.costamare.com; f. 1975; container-shipping; Pres. KONSTANTINOS KONSTANTAKOPOULOS.

Golden Union Shipping Co: Odos Aegales 8, 185 45 Piraeus; tel. (210) 4061000; fax (210) 4061199; e-mail infgusc@goldenunion.gr; internet www.goldenunion.gr; f. 1977; dry cargo bulk operations; Chair. and Man. Dir THEODORE VENIAMIS.

Marmaras Navigation Co: Odos Zephyrou 58B, 175 64 Palaio Faliro; tel. (210) 4589000; fax (210) 4589037; e-mail crew@ marmaras-nav.gr; internet www.marmaras-nav.gr; Dir D. DIAMANTIDES.

Minoan Lines Shipping Co: Odos 25 August 17, 712 02 Heraklion; tel. (2810) 399800; fax (2810) 330308; e-mail info@minoan.gr; internet www.minoan.gr; f. 1972; operates passenger and cargo ferry services between the Greek mainland and Crete, and between Greece and Italy; Man. Dir ANTONIS MANIADAKIS.

Naftomar Shipping and Trading Co: Leoforos C. Karamanlis 243, 166 73 Voula; tel. (210) 8914200; fax (210) 8914235; e-mail naftomar@naftomar.gr; internet www.naftomar.gr; f. 1972; specializes in the shipping of liquid petroleum gas; Man. Dir RIAD ZEIN.

Thenamaris Ships Management Co: Odos Athinas 16 & Odos Vorreou, Kavouri, 166 71 Athens; tel. (210) 8909000; fax (210) 8909653; e-mail op@thenamaris.com; internet www.thenamaris .gr; f. 1970; Dir K. MARTINOS.

Tsakos Group: Macedonia House, Leoforos Syngrou 367, POB 79141, Paleon Faliron, 175 64 Athens; tel. (210) 9480700; fax (210) 9480710; e-mail mail@tsakoshellas.gr; internet www.tsakosgroup .com; f. 1970; subsidiary cos include: Tsakos Shipping and Trading; Tsakos Energy Navigation; Tsakos Industrias Navales; Dir Capt PANAGIOTIS N. TSAKOS.

CIVIL AVIATION

There are international airports at Athens, Eleftherios Venizelos-Spata, Thessaloníki, Alexandroupolis, Corfu, Lesbos, Andravida, Rhodes, Kos and Heraklion/Crete, and 24 domestic airports (of which 13 are authorized to receive international flights).

Aegean Airlines: Leoforos Viltanioti 31, 145 64 Kifissia Athens; tel. (210) 6261700; fax (210) 6261900; internet www.aegeanair.com;

f. 1987; domestic and international services; Pres. and Chief Exec. THEODOROS VASSILAKIS.

Olympic Air: Eleftherios Venizelos Athens International Airport, Bldg 97, 190 19 Athens; tel. (210) 3550700; fax (210) 3550407; e-mail groups@olympicair.com; internet www.olympicair.com; f. 2009 in succession to state-owned Olympic Airways (f. 1957); owned by Aegean Airlines (q.v.); Chair. ANDREAS VGENOPOULOS.

Tourism

The sunny climate, the natural beauty of the country, and its history and traditions attract tourists to Greece. There are numerous islands and many sites of archaeological interest. The number of tourists visiting Greece increased from 1m. in 1968 to 17.9m. in 2013, when receipts from tourism amounted to US $16,036m. (excluding passenger transport).

Ellinikos Organismos Tourismou (EOT) (Greek National Tourist Organization): Odos Tsoha 7, 115 21 Athens; tel. (210) 8707000; e-mail info@gnto.gr; internet www.visitgreece.gr; Pres. ZIKOS KONSTANTINOS.

Defence

Greece returned to the military structure of the North Atlantic Treaty Organization (NATO) in 1980, after an absence of six years. Military service is compulsory, and lasts for up to nine months. As assessed at November 2014, the armed forces numbered 144,950 (including conscripts), with an army of 93,500, a navy of 18,450, an air force of 21,400 and 11,600 joint-service troops; in addition, there were paramilitary forces of 4,000. Reservists, which included a national guard of 33,000, totalled 216,650. The USA occupied three military bases in Greece, with a total of 380 troops stationed there at November 2012.

Defence Expenditure: Budgeted at €4,160m. in 2014.

Chief of the General Staff of the National Defence: Gen. MICHALIS KOSTARAKOS.

Chief of the General Staff of the Army: Lt-Gen. VASSILIOS TELLIDIS.

Chief of the General Staff of the Navy: Vice-Adm. EVANGELOS APOSTOLAKIS.

Chief of the General Staff of the Air Force: Lt-Gen. CHRISTOS VAITSIS.

Education

Education is available free of charge at all levels, and is officially compulsory for all children between the ages of six and 15 years. Primary education begins at the age of six and lasts for six years. Secondary education, beginning at the age of 12, is generally for six years, divided into two equal cycles. The vernacular language (demotiki) has replaced the formal version (katharevoussa) in secondary education. Pre-primary enrolment in 2009/10 included 76% of children in the relevant age-group. The comparable ratio in the same year at secondary schools was 99%. In 2003/04 the equivalent of 70% of the relevant age-group were enrolled in tertiary education (males 60%; females 79%). There were 22 universities in 2011/12 (excluding the Medical School of Athens), with a total enrolment of 168,804 students. In 2006 budgetary spending on education represented an estimated 9.9% of total expenditure, according to preliminary figures.

GRENADA

Introductory Survey

LOCATION, CLIMATE, LANGUAGE, RELIGION, FLAG, CAPITAL

Grenada, a mountainous, heavily forested island, is the most southerly of the Windward Islands, in the West Indies. The country also includes some of the small islands known as the Grenadines, which lie to the north-east of Grenada. The most important of these are the low-lying island of Carriacou and its neighbour, Petit Martinique. The climate is semi-tropical, with an average annual temperature of 28°C (82°F) in the lowlands. Annual rainfall averages about 1,500 mm (60 ins) in the coastal area and 3,800 mm to 5,100 mm (150 ins–200 ins) in mountain areas. Most of the rainfall occurs between June and December. The majority of the population speak English, although a French patois is sometimes spoken. Some 85% of Grenada's population were of African descent, while 11% were of mixed ethnic origins. Most of the population profess Christianity, and the main denominations are Roman Catholicism (some 45% of the population) and Anglicanism (about 14% of the population). The national flag (proportions 1 by 2) consists of a diagonally quartered rectangle (yellow in the upper and lower segments, green in the right and left ones) surrounded by a red border bearing six five-pointed yellow stars (three at the upper edge of the flag, and three at the lower edge). There is a red disc, containing a large five-pointed yellow star, in the centre, and a representation of a nutmeg (in yellow and red) on the green segment near the hoist. The capital is St George's.

CONTEMPORARY POLITICAL HISTORY

Historical Context

Grenada was initially colonized by the French but was captured by the British in 1762. The Treaty of Versailles recognized British control in 1783. Grenada continued as a British colony until 1958, when it joined the Federation of the West Indies, remaining a member until the dissolution of the Federation in 1962. Full internal self-government and statehood in association with the United Kingdom were achieved in March 1967. During this period, the political life of Grenada was dominated by Herbert Blaize, the leader of the Grenada National Party (GNP), and Eric Gairy, a local trade union leader, who in 1950 founded the Grenada United Labour Party (GULP), with the support of an associated trade union. Gairy became Premier after the elections of 1967 and again after those of 1972, which he contested chiefly on the issue of total independence.

Domestic Political Affairs

Grenada became independent, within the Commonwealth, on 7 February 1974, with Gairy as Prime Minister. Domestic opposition to Gairy was expressed in public unrest, and the formation by the three opposition parties—the GNP, the United People's Party and the New Jewel Movement (NJM)—of the People's Alliance, which contested the 1976 general election and reduced GULP's majority in the lower house.

The opposition regarded the rule of Sir Eric Gairy, as he became in 1977, as increasingly autocratic and corrupt, and in 1979 he was replaced in a bloodless coup by the leader of the left-wing NJM, Maurice Bishop. The new People's Revolutionary Government (PRG) suspended the Constitution and announced the imminent formation of a People's Consultative Assembly to draft a new constitution. Meanwhile, Grenada remained a monarchy, with the British Queen as Head of State, represented in Grenada by a Governor-General. During 1980–81 there was an increase in repression, against a background of mounting anti-Government violence and the PRG's fears of an invasion by US forces.

By mid-1982 relations with the USA, the United Kingdom and the more conservative members of the Caribbean Community and Common Market (CARICOM, see p. 222) were becoming increasingly strained: elections had not been arranged, restrictions against the privately owned press had been imposed, many detainees were still awaiting trial, and Grenada was aligning more closely with Cuba and the USSR. Cuba was contributing funds and construction workers for the airport at Point Salines, a project that further strengthened the US Government's conviction that Grenada was to become a centre for Soviet manoeuvres in the area.

In June 1983 Bishop sought to improve relations with the USA, and announced the appointment of a commission to draft a new constitution. The more left-wing members of the PRG denounced this attempt at conciliation as an ideological betrayal. A power struggle developed between Bishop and his deputy, Bernard Coard. In October Bishop was placed under house arrest, allegedly for his refusal to share power with Coard. The commander of the People's Revolutionary Army (PRA), Gen. Hudson Austin, subsequently announced that Bishop had been expelled from the NJM. On 19 October thousands of Bishop's supporters stormed the house, freed Bishop, and demonstrated outside the PRA headquarters. PRA forces responded by firing into the crowd. Later in the day, Bishop, three of his ministers and two trade unionists were executed by the PRA. The Government was replaced by a 16-member Revolutionary Military Council (RMC), led by Gen. Austin and supported by Coard. The remaining NJM ministers were arrested and imprisoned, and a total curfew was imposed.

Regional and international outrage at the assassination of Bishop, in addition to fears of a US military intervention, was so intense that after four days the RMC relaxed the curfew, reopened the airport and promised a swift return to civilian rule. However, the Organisation of Eastern Caribbean States (OECS, see p. 463) resolved to intervene in an attempt to restore democratic order, and asked for assistance from the USA, which readily complied. (It is unclear whether the decision to intervene preceded or followed a request for help to the OECS by the Grenadian Governor-General, Sir Paul Scoon.) On 25 October 1983 some 1,900 US military personnel invaded the island, accompanied by 300 troops from Jamaica, Barbados and member countries of the OECS. Fighting continued for some days, and the USA gradually increased its troop strength, with further reinforcements waiting offshore with a US naval task force. The RMC's forces were defeated, while Coard, Austin and others who had been involved in the coup were detained.

In November 1983 Scoon appointed a non-political interim Council to assume responsibility for the government of the country until elections could be held. Nicholas Brathwaite, a former Commonwealth official, was appointed Chairman. The 1974 Constitution was reinstated and an electoral commission was created. By mid-December the USA had withdrawn all its forces except 300 support troops, who remained until September 1985.

Several political parties that had operated clandestinely or from exile during the PRG's rule re-emerged and announced their intention to contest the elections for a new House of Representatives. Sir Eric Gairy returned to Grenada in January 1984 to lead GULP, but did not stand as a candidate himself. In May three former NJM ministers formed the Maurice Bishop Patriotic Movement (MBPM). A number of centrist parties emerged or re-emerged, including Blaize's GNP. Fears that a divided opposition would allow GULP to win a majority of legislative seats resulted in an agreement by several of these organizations, in August 1984, to form the New National Party (NNP), led by Blaize. The NNP achieved a convincing victory in the December election, and Blaize became Prime Minister.

The trial of 19 detainees (including Coard, his wife, Phyllis, and Gen. Austin), accused of murder and conspiracy against Bishop and six of his associates, opened in November 1984, although there were repeated adjournments. One of the detainees agreed to give evidence for the State in return for a pardon. Eventually, in December 1986, the jury returned verdicts on 196 charges of murder and conspiracy to murder. Fourteen of the defendants were sentenced to death, three received prison sentences of between 30 and 45 years, and one was acquitted. In 1991 the Court of Appeal upheld the original verdicts on the defendants in the Bishop murder trial, and further pleas for clemency were rejected. Preparations for the imminent hanging of the 14, however, provoked international outrage, and in

August Brathwaite announced that the death sentences were to be commuted to life imprisonment.

In 1987 breakaway members of the NNP launched a new party, the National Democratic Congress (NDC), led by George Brizan. In January 1989 Blaize was replaced as NNP leader by his cabinet colleague, Keith Mitchell, although he remained Prime Minister. In July, however, following allegations of corruption by the NDC, Blaize dismissed Mitchell and the Chairman of the NNP. Amid uncertainty as to whether the Blaize faction had formed a separate party, two more members of the Government resigned, thus reducing support for the Government to only five of the 15 members of the House of Representatives. Blaize did not officially announce the formation of a new party, the National Party, until late August, by which time he had advised the acting Governor-General to prorogue Parliament. Blaize died in December, and the Governor-General appointed Ben Jones, Blaize's former deputy, as Prime Minister. At the general election in March 1990 no party achieved an absolute majority, although the NDC achieved a working parliamentary majority. Nicholas Brathwaite became Prime Minister. Brathwaite resigned as Prime Minister in February 1995, and was succeeded by Brizan.

The NNP's political domination

The NNP secured eight of the 15 seats in the House of Representatives at the general election of June 1995, while the NDC's representation was reduced to five seats. The remaining two seats were secured by GULP. Mitchell became Prime Minister.

In November 1998 the resignation of the Minister of Foreign Affairs, Raphael Fletcher, from the Government and NNP in order to join GULP, resulted in an early general election being called. The NNP obtained all of the 15 seats in the House of Representatives in the subsequent ballot in January 1999, becoming the first political party in the country's history to secure two successive terms in government.

In October 1999 Coard, serving a term of life imprisonment with 16 others for the 1983 murder of Bishop and a number of his associates, issued a statement in which he accepted full responsibility for the crimes. In 2002 it was announced that three former soldiers gaoled in 1986 for Bishop's murder and that of seven others during the 1983 coup were to be released. Furthermore, in 2004 the Court of Appeal ruled that the 17 prisoners would be resentenced, since the life sentences imposed on them were unconstitutional. However, the day before the resentencing, the Court of Appeal of the Eastern Caribbean Supreme Court, based in Saint Lucia, overturned the ruling. This decision was confirmed in 2005; lawyers for the men appealed against the judgment to the Privy Council, based in the United Kingdom, occasioning a ruling in February 2007 for the resentencing of 13 of the prisoners (three of their original number had been released in 2006, while Phyllis Coard had secured early release in 2000 on medical grounds). In June 2007 the Supreme Court ordered the release of three of the prisoners and reduced the sentences of the remaining 10. Three further prisoners secured an early release in 2008, and in September 2009 the remaining seven, including Bernard Coard, were set free, to the disapproval of large sections of the population.

The NNP secured a third successive term in office in the general election of November 2003, although its parliamentary majority was reduced to just one seat. The NDC won the seven remaining seats in the 15-seat House of Representatives. Keith Mitchell was sworn in again as Prime Minister.

Grenada was devastated by Hurricane Ivan in September 2004, which killed 39 Grenadians and destroyed 90% of the housing stock. According to the OECS, full rehabilitation would cost at least US $814m. Widespread looting and violent crime was brought under relative control after intervention from regional (primarily Trinidadian) security forces. The island was struck by another huge storm, Hurricane Emily, in 2005. The cost of the damage was estimated at $200m. In January 2006 Mitchell announced that a 5% salary tax to help finance rebuilding efforts would be introduced.

The NDC in office

The NNP failed to secure a fourth successive term in office in a general election on 8 July 2008, with the NDC winning 11 of the 15 legislative seats and 51% of the valid votes cast. The NNP won the remaining four seats and 48% of the ballot. Turnout was high, at 80%, and observers from the Organization of American States reported positively upon the procedure of the election. Tillman Thomas, the NDC leader, was sworn in as Prime Minister and the new Cabinet duly installed: notable appointments

included Nazim Burke as Minister of Finance, Planning, Economy, Energy and Co-operatives, and Peter David as Minister of Foreign Affairs.

In October 2009 the High Court of Justice effected the liquidation of *Grenada Today*, following the newspaper's inability to pay compensation to former Prime Minister Keith Mitchell, who had successfully sued the newspaper for libel. The compensation award, at US $71,000, was generally viewed as excessive, and press freedom advocates appealed for a limit on libel damages.

Following a cabinet reorganization in November 2010, three ministers, Peter David, Glynis Roberts and Michael Church (who had been demoted as punishment for taking an unauthorized trip to Switzerland to attend a trade meeting), failed to attend the official ceremony to be sworn in to office. Their action prompted speculation about the unity of the Government and Church submitted his resignation shortly afterwards. Press reports alleged that the reorganization had led to divisions within the Cabinet, although Thomas rejected these claims.

Thomas reorganized the Cabinet again in September 2011 amid media reports of rising factionalism within the ruling party. In January 2012 Joseph Gilbert, Minister of Environment, Foreign Trade and Export Development, was dismissed after allegedly concluding an unauthorized agreement with a US firm in relation to the establishment of a casino on the island. The resignations in April of Peter David, Minister of Tourism and Civil Aviation, and Karl Hood, Minister of Foreign Affairs, both of whom expressed dissatisfaction with the Government, prompted the opposition to call for a vote of no confidence in the administration. At the vote in mid-May the motion was defeated, but Hood sought to file a further motion of no confidence in the Government in August, prompting Thomas to ask the Governor-General to prorogue Parliament in order to avoid a second vote. Increasing divisions within the ruling NDC, together with a weak economic situation, made the prospect of the Government's defeat in such a vote seem highly likely. As a result, Parliament did not convene for the remainder of 2012 and, in accordance with the Constitution (which states that the legislature must sit at least once in any six-month period), was dissolved in January 2013 in preparation for a general election. Three former cabinet members, Glynis Roberts, Peter David and Karl Hood, all of whom had been dismissed from the NDC in September 2012, formed a new political party, the National United Party, in advance of the ballot.

Recent developments: Mitchell back in office

The NNP won a resounding victory at the general election on 19 February 2013, securing all 15 seats in the House of Representatives and some 58.8% of total votes cast. Turnout was high, at an estimated 85%. On taking office as Prime Minister Keith Mitchell emphasized the need for national unity, in acknowledgement of the political instability that had characterized the previous Government. The new Cabinet included Elvin Nimrod as Deputy Prime Minister and Attorney-General and Nickolas Steele as Minister of Foreign Affairs and International Business. Mitchell took responsibility for the finance, national security, energy and home affairs portfolios, among others.

In July 2013 the NNP Government came under criticism from the International Press Institute (IPI), based in Vienna, Austria, over controversial proposed legislation, the Electronic Crimes Act, according to which (among other provisions) sending offensive electronic messages would become a criminal offence. Having commended Grenada for becoming the first Caribbean country to decriminalize libel, in 2012, the IPI perceived this new bill as a step backwards. However, the Act was signed into law in September 2013, prompting international organization Reporters Without Borders to voice its concern. In response to these criticisms, the House of Representatives abrogated the most contentious clauses within the Act in March 2014.

In August 2013 Parliament approved the Grenada Citizen by Investment Act, which would enable Grenadian passports to be bought in exchange for a certain, unspecified amount of investment in the country. Similar schemes had already been introduced in a number of other Caribbean countries, although that in Grenada contained a residency requirement.

Nazim Burke was elected as the new NDC leader in February 2014, although discord within the former ruling party was still evident. According to media reports in October, several prominent NDC members were dissatisfied with Burke's leadership and were manoeuvring to reinstall Thomas as party leader. Meanwhile, NDC dissident Peter David joined the NNP in May. Mitchell appointed David as a senator in November. In addition, in a concurrent cabinet reorganization, the Prime Minister notably named Clarice Modeste-Curwen as the new Minister of Foreign Affairs and Steele as Minister of Health and Social Security.

In July 2014 the Government announced plans to hold a referendum on a new constitution in February 2015. Issues for consideration in the plebiscite included the creation of an Electoral Commission, the replacement of the Privy Council by the Caribbean Court of Justice as the nation's final appellate court and the redesignation of the country's official title as Grenada, Carriacou and Petite Martinique. However, by April 2015 no date had been set for the plebiscite.

Foreign Affairs

Regional relations

Negotiations on the delimitation of Grenada's maritime border with Trinidad and Tobago had been in abeyance since 1993. However, a treaty demarcating the boundary was finally ratified in April 2010, allowing for the initiation of offshore petroleum and gas exploration. Discussions on finalizing an agreement on joint exploration operations took place in May 2013.

In 2005 Grenada became one of 13 Caribbean nations to sign the Petrocaribe accord, under which it was allowed to purchase petroleum from Venezuela at reduced prices. In December 2014 Grenada was admitted to the Venezuelan-led Bolivarian Alliance for the Peoples of our America-People's Trade Treaty (Alianza Bolivariana para los Pueblos de Nuestra América-Tratado de Comercio de los Pueblos—ALBA-TCP, see p. 459).

Other external relations

In 1996 Grenada signed two treaties with the USA, relating to mutual legal assistance and extradition, as part of a regional campaign to combat drugs-trafficking. An agreement on maritime security co-operation was signed by Grenada and the USA in 2011.

In 2000 Grenada restored diplomatic relations with Libya, suspended in 1983. From 1983 Grenada had maintained diplomatic relations with Taiwan instead of the People's Republic of China; however, in 2004 Taiwan recalled its ambassador to Grenada after Mitchell visited mainland China. Mitchell emphasized that the destruction caused by Hurricane Ivan had forced the Government to reconsider its international relationships and in 2005 Grenada established official ties with China; Taiwan duly severed its relations with Grenada. In 2009 the Chinese Government provided Grenada with aid and loans amounting to some US $6m. Taiwan commenced legal proceedings against Grenada during 2011 to reclaim outstanding loan repayments totalling $28m. Major airlines and cruise lines operating in Grenada were court ordered to deposit fees owed to the Taiwanese authorities into an escrow account, depriving the Grenadian Government, which launched a legal challenge against Taiwan's actions, of an important revenue source. In January 2015 Taiwan withdrew its legal case against Grenada and agreed to restructure and reschedule the country's bilateral debt burden. In April 2013 it was announced that China would provide $31.5m. for the reconstruction of a football stadium destroyed by Hurricane Ivan. In June, following talks between Mitchell and Chinese President Xi Jinping, it was announced that Grenada would receive $8.7m. in grant assistance.

CONSTITUTION AND GOVERNMENT

The Constitution of Grenada was adopted upon independence in 1974. Grenada has dominion status within the Commonwealth. The British monarch is Head of State and is represented locally by a Governor-General. The Cabinet, led by the Prime Minister, holds executive power. Parliament comprises the Senate, made up of 13 Senators appointed by the Governor-General on the advice of the Prime Minister and the Leader of the Opposition, and the 15-member House of Representatives, elected by universal adult suffrage. The Cabinet is responsible to Parliament. Judicial power is vested in the Eastern Caribbean Supreme Court, although in certain cases further appeal can be made to the Privy Council in the United Kingdom.

REGIONAL AND INTERNATIONAL CO-OPERATION

Grenada is a member of the Caribbean Community and Common Market (CARICOM, see p. 222). It is also a member of the Economic Commission for Latin America and the Caribbean (ECLAC, see p. 34), the Organization of American States (OAS, see p. 392), the Association of Caribbean States (see p. 444), and of the Community of Latin American and Caribbean States (see p. 460), which was formally inaugurated in December 2011.

Grenada is a member of the Eastern Caribbean Securities Exchange (based in Saint Christopher and Nevis), and of the Eastern Caribbean Central Bank (ECCB, see p. 451). In June 2010 Grenada was a signatory to the Revised Treaty of Basseterre, establishing an Economic Union among the member nations of the Organisation of Eastern Caribbean States (OECS, see p. 463). The Economic Union, which involved the removal of barriers to trade and the movement of labour as a step towards a single financial and economic market, came into effect in January 2011. Freedom of movement between the signatory states was granted to OECS nationals on 1 August. In December 2014 Grenada became a member of the Bolivarian Alliance for the Peoples of our America-People's Trade Treaty (Alianza Bolivariana para los Pueblos de Nuestra América-Tratado de Comercio de los Pueblos—ALBA-TCP, see p. 459).

Grenada acceded to the UN in 1974, upon independence. It joined the World Trade Organization (see p. 431) in 1996. The country is a member of the Commonwealth (see p. 234). Grenada is a signatory to the Cotonou Agreement (see p. 321), the successor arrangement to the Lomé Conventions between the African, Caribbean and Pacific (ACP) countries and the European Union.

ECONOMIC AFFAIRS

In 2013, according to estimates by the World Bank, Grenada's gross national income (GNI), measured at average 2011–13 prices, was US $790m., equivalent to $7,460 per head (or $11,120 per head on an international purchasing-power parity basis). During 2004–13 Grenada's population increased at an average rate of 0.3% per year, while gross domestic product (GDP) per head increased, in real terms, by an average of 0.6% per year. Overall GDP increased, in real terms, at an average annual rate of 1.1% in 2004–13, according to the Eastern Caribbean Central Bank (ECCB, see p. 451); real GDP decreased by 1.2% in 2012, but increased by 2.4% in 2013.

Agriculture (including hunting, forestry and fishing) contributed 5.5% of GDP in 2013. The sector engaged 19.1% of the employed labour force in mid-2015, according to FAO estimates. Grenada is one of the world's largest producers of nutmeg (although Indonesia produces some 75% of the world's total). In the first six months of 2014 exports of nutmeg and mace (the pungent red membrane around the nut) accounted for an estimated 14.7% of Grenada's total domestic export earnings. The importance of bananas to the economy has fallen in recent years; by 2012 FAO estimated output at only 3,400 metric tons. Livestock production, for domestic consumption, is important on Carriacou. There are extensive timber reserves on the island of Grenada; forestry development is strictly controlled and involves a programme of reafforestation. Exports of fish contributed an estimated 17.2% of export earnings in 2013. According to the ECCB, agricultural GDP decreased at an average annual rate of 0.5% in 2004–13; the sector increased by 8.4% in 2013.

Industry (mining, manufacturing, construction and utilities) provided 15.0% of GDP in 2013 and engaged 23.9% of the employed labour force in 1998. According to the ECCB, industrial GDP decreased by an annual average of 1.4% during 2004–13; the sector's GDP declined by 8.7% in 2012, but increased by 10.6% in 2013.

The mining and quarrying sector accounted for only 0.3% of GDP in 2013 and just 0.2% of employment in 1998. Mining GDP decreased by an annual average of 7.1% in 2004–13; the sector contracted by 14.1% in 2012, but expanded by 27.0% in 2013.

Manufacturing, which contributed 3.6% of GDP in 2013 and employed 7.7% of the working population in 1998, consists mainly of the processing of agricultural products and of cottage industries producing garments and spice-based items. Rum, soft drinks, paints and varnishes, household paper products and the tyre-retreading industries are also important. According to the ECCB, manufacturing GDP increased by an average of 0.8% per year in 2004–13; the sector's GDP declined by 2.3% in 2013.

The construction sector contributed 6.8% of GDP in 2013 and engaged 15.4% of the labour force in 1998. Construction GDP declined by an average of 3.8% per year in 2004–13, according to the ECCB; the sector's GDP declined by 18.0% in 2012, but expanded by 26.3% in 2013.

Grenada is dependent upon imports for its energy requirements, and in 2013 mineral fuels and lubricants accounted for an estimated 25.4% of the total cost of imports. Electricity generation totalled 204.0m. kWh in 2011. The Government was pursuing alternative sources of energy generation, including geothermal initiatives.

The services sector contributed 79.5% of GDP in 2013. Tourism and financial and business services were the main contributors to GDP. Receipts from tourism totalled an estimated EC $327.5m. in 2013, a decrease on the previous year. Tourist arrivals decreased in 2013, by 12.9%, although this was mainly driven by a fall in cruise ship arrivals. These totalled 197,308, compared with 242,757 in 2012. The more lucrative stop-over market, however, expanded in 2013, but only by 0.4%. The offshore financial sector is also economically significant. Financial services contributed 6.3% to the economy in 2013. According to the ECCB, the GDP of the services sector increased at an average annual rate of 1.8% in 2004–13; the sector increased by 1.4% in 2013.

In 2013 Grenada reported a deficit on merchandise trade of EC $752.7m. and there was a deficit of $597.6m. on the current account of the balance of payments. The principal source of imports was the USA, accounting for 30.9% of the total in 2008. The USA is also the principal market for exports, taking 16.4% of the total in 2008, along with Dominica. The principal export were food and live animals, accounting for 65.2% of total exports in 2013; other major exports were miscellaneous manufactured articles and machinery and transport equipment. The principal imports in that year were mineral fuels, oils and distillation products, food and live animals, machinery and transport equipment, manufactured goods, miscellaneous manufactured articles, and chemical and related products. The trade deficit is partly offset by earnings from tourism, capital receipts and remittances from the many Grenadians working abroad.

In 2013 there was an overall budgetary deficit of EC $148.0m., equivalent to 6.6% of GDP. Grenada's general government gross debt was EC $2,412m. in 2013, equivalent to 109.8% of GDP. Grenada's total external debt was US $591m. in 2012, of which US $490m. was public and publicly guaranteed debt. In 2012 the cost of servicing long-term public and publicly guaranteed debt and repayments to the IMF was equivalent to 7.7% of the value of exports of goods, services and income (excluding workers' remittances). The average annual rate of inflation was 1.8% in 2010–13; consumer prices remained constant in 2013, according to the IMF. The unemployment rate was 33.5% of the labour force in September 2013.

Grenada's economy contracted in 2009–10 as a result of the global economic downturn, prompting the Government to introduce a value-added tax in 2010 to generate additional revenues. According to the ECCB, there was negligible economic growth in 2011 and a contraction of 1.2% in 2012. The country's poor economic situation was reflected in government wage arrears and several missed debt service payments to bilateral creditors in 2012. In March 2013 the World Bank suspended disbursements to Grenada until the country made good on overdue payments amounting to some US $750,000. In an attempt to reduce the island's dependence on tourism, which is particularly vulnerable to external economic conditions, in that year the Government launched a farm labour subsidy programme that placed particular emphasis on the rehabilitation and replanting of nutmeg and cocoa. It was hoped that the scheme would provide employment for between 1,500 and 2,000 labourers. In October, following talks with IMF officials, Prime Minister Keith Mitchell announced the implementation of a three-year fiscal restructuring programme, which included debt consolidation, new tax levels and improved tax collection. The Citizenship by Investment programme (see *Domestic Political Affairs*) was also expected to strengthen the Government's financial position. In June 2014 the IMF authorized a three-year Extended Credit Facility worth $22m. to support the administration's fiscal adjustments, and further funding from other multilateral bodies was also pledged. The 2015 budget prioritized maintaining fiscal discipline, and the Government predicted GDP growth of 2.6% in 2014. The IMF's growth estimate was more modest, at 1.1%, with further growth of 1.2% forecast for 2015. The decision, in January 2015, by Taiwan to write off 50% of outstanding debt owed by Grenada was a welcome boost for the Government, and facilitated further debt-restructuring agreements with other creditor nations.

PUBLIC HOLIDAYS

2016: 1 January (New Year's Day), 7 February (Independence Day), 25 March (Good Friday), 28 March (Easter Monday), 1 May (Labour Day), 16 May (Whit Monday), 26 May (Corpus Christi), 1 August (Emancipation Holiday), 8–10 August (Carnival), 25 October (Thanksgiving Day), 25–26 December (Christmas).

Statistical Survey

AREA AND POPULATION

Area: 344.5 sq km (133.0 sq miles).

Population: 102,632 at census of 25 May 2001; 103,328 (males 52,651, females 50,677) at census of 12 May 2011 (preliminary). *Mid-2015* (UN estimate) 106,694 (Source: UN, *World Population Prospects: The 2012 Revision*).

Density (mid-2015): 309.7 per sq km.

Population by Age and Sex (UN estimates at mid-2015): *0–14 years:* 28,298 (males 14,501, females 13,797); *15–64 years:* 70,823 (males 35,910, females 34,913); *65 years and over:* 7,573 (males 3,097, females 4,476); *Total* 106,694 (males 53,508, females 53,186) (Source: UN, *World Population Prospects: The 2012 Revision*).

Parishes (population at 2011 census, preliminary): Carriacou 5,354; St Andrew 25,722; St David 12,561; St George 36,823; St John 7,802; St Mark 4,086; St Patrick 10,980; *Total* 103,328.

Principal Town (population at 2011 census, preliminary): St George's (capital) 2,982. *Mid-2014* (UN estimate, incl. suburbs): St George's 37,822 (Source: UN, *World Urbanization Prospects: The 2014 Revision*).

Births and Deaths (registrations, 2001, provisional): Live births 1,899 (birth rate 18.8 per 1,000); Deaths 727 (death rate 7.2 per 1,000); *2014*: Birth rate 16.3 per 1,000; Death rate 8.0 per 1,000 (Source: Pan American Health Organization).

Life Expectancy (years at birth): 72.6 (males 70.2; females 75.2) in 2012. Source: World Bank, World Development Indicators database.

Employment (employees only, 1998): Agriculture, hunting, forestry and fishing 4,794; Mining and quarrying 58; Manufacturing 2,579; Electricity, gas and water 505; Construction 5,163; Wholesale and retail trade 6,324; Restaurants and hotels 1,974; Transport, storage and communications 2,043; Financing, insurance and real estate 1,312; Public administration, defence and social security 1,879; Community services 3,904; Other services 2,933; *Sub-total* 33,468; Activities not adequately defined 1,321; *Total employed* 34,789 (males 20,733, females 14,056). *Mid-2015* (estimates): Agriculture, etc. 9,000; Total labour force 47,000 (Source: FAO).

HEALTH AND WELFARE

Key Indicators

Total Fertility Rate (children per woman, 2012): 2.2.

Under-5 Mortality Rate (per 1,000 live births, 2012): 14.

Physicians (per 1,000 head, 2009): 0.8.

Hospital Beds (per 1,000 head, 2009): 2.4.

Health Expenditure (2011): US $ per head (PPP): 694.

Health Expenditure (2011): % of GDP: 6.5.

Health Expenditure (2011): public (% of total): 48.3.

Access to Water (% of persons, 2012): 97.

Access to Sanitation (% of persons, 2012): 98.

Total Carbon Dioxide Emissions ('000 metric tons, 2010): 260.4.

Total Carbon Dioxide Emissions Per Head (metric tons, 2010): 2.5.

Human Development Index (2013): ranking: 79.

Human Development Index (2013): value: 0.744.

For sources and definitions, see explanatory note on p. vi.

AGRICULTURE, ETC.

Principal Crops ('000 metric tons, 2013, FAO estimates unless otherwise indicated): Sugar cane 7.2; Pigeon peas 0.8; Coconuts 6.3; Bananas 3.3; Plantains 0.3; Oranges 0.6; Grapefruit and pomelos 1.5; Apples 0.6; Plums and sloes 0.7; Mangoes, mangosteens and guavas 1.3; Avocados 1.5; Cocoa beans 0.8 (unofficial figure); Nutmeg, mace and cardamom 0.5. *Aggregate Production* ('000 metric tons, may include official, semi-official or estimated data): Roots and tubers 2.5; Vegetables (incl. melons) 4.1 Fruits (excl. melons) 14.4.

Livestock ('000 head, year ending September 2013, FAO estimates): Cattle 4.5; Pigs 3.0; Sheep 13.2; Goats 7.2; Chickens 270.

Livestock Products ('000 metric tons, 2013, FAO estimates): Chicken meat 0.7; Cows' milk 0.7; Hen eggs 1.4.

Fishing (metric tons, live weight, 2012): Red hind 120; Coney 23; Snappers and jobfishes 95; Parrotfishes 111; Blackfin tuna 160; Yellowfin tuna 829; Atlantic sailfish 178; Swordfish 24; Common dolphinfish 183; *Total catch* (incl. others) 2,258.

Source: FAO.

INDUSTRY

Production (1994 unless otherwise indicated): Rum 300,000 litres; Beer 2,400,000 litres; Wheat flour 4,000 metric tons (1996); Cigarettes 15m.; Electricity 204.0 million kWh (2011). Source: UN, *Industrial Commodity Statistics Yearbook*.

FINANCE

Currency and Exchange Rates: 100 cents = 1 Eastern Caribbean dollar (EC $). *Sterling, US Dollar and Euro Equivalents* (31 December 2014): £1 sterling = EC $4.214; US $1 = EC $2.700; €1 = EC $3.278; EC $100 = £23.73 = US $37.04 = €30.51. *Exchange Rate:* Fixed at US $1 = EC $2.70 since July 1976.

Budget (EC $ million, 2013): *Revenue:* Tax revenue 419.0 (Taxes on income and profits 66.1, Taxes on property 15.1, Taxes on domestic goods and services 212.7, Taxes on international trade and transactions 125.1); Other current revenue 18.2; Total 437.2 (excluding grants received 31.3) *Expenditure:* Current expenditure 462.1 (Personal emoluments 243.5, Goods and services 75.9, Interest payments 70.6, Transfers and subsidies 72.2); Capital expenditure and net lending 154.3; Total 616.5. Source: Eastern Caribbean Central Bank.

International Reserves (US $ million at 31 December 2013): IMF special drawing rights 15.16; Foreign exchange 135.41; *Total* 150.57. Source: IMF, *International Financial Statistics*.

Money Supply (EC $ million at 31 December 2013): Currency outside depository corporations 115.69; Transferable deposits 376.73; Other deposits 1,556.44; *Broad money* 2,048.86. Source: IMF, *International Financial Statistics*.

Cost of Living (Consumer Price Index; base: 2010 = 100): 103.0 in 2011; 105.5 in 2012; 105.5 in 2013. Source: IMF, *International Financial Statistics*.

Gross Domestic Product (EC $ million at constant 2006 prices): 1,892.04 in 2011; 1,870.19 in 2012; 1,915.50 in 2013. Source: Eastern Caribbean Central Bank.

Expenditure on the Gross Domestic Product (EC $ million at current prices, 2013): Government final consumption expenditure 379.28; Private final consumption expenditure 2,000.25; Gross capital formation 452.99; *Total domestic expenditure* 2,832.52; Exports of goods and services 566.29; *Less* Imports of goods and services 1,142.74; *GDP in purchasers' values* 2,256.07. Source: Eastern Caribbean Central Bank.

Gross Domestic Product by Economic Activity (EC $ million at current prices, 2013): Agriculture and fishing 110.01; Mining and quarrying 5.22; Manufacturing 71.51; Electricity and water 85.99; Construction 135.25; Wholesale and retail trade 157.59; Hotels and restaurants 73.73; Transport and communications 235.79; Housing, real estate and business activities 258.62; Financial services 125.18; Public administration and defence 175.31; Other services 552.53; *Sub-total* 1,986.73; *Less* Financial intermediation services indirectly measured (FISIM) 25.89; *GDP at factor cost* 1,960.83; Taxes on products, less subsidies 295.24; *GDP in market prices* 2,256.07. Source: Eastern Caribbean Central Bank.

Balance of Payments (EC $ million, 2013): Goods (net) –752.69; Services (net) 185.53; *Balance of goods and services* –567.16; Other income (net) –79.92; Current transfers (net) 49.44; *Current balance* –597.64; Capital account (net) 118.57; Direct investment 305.35; Portfolio investment 46.77; Other investments 154.62; Net errors and omissions 57.12; *Overall balance* 84.79. Source: Eastern Caribbean Central Bank.

EXTERNAL TRADE

Principal Commodities (distribution by SITC, EC $ million, 2013): *Imports c.i.f.:* Food and live animals 205.46; Mineral fuels and related materials 252.20; Chemicals and related products 68.69; Manufactured goods 138.82; Machinery and transport equipment 167.90; Miscellaneous manufactured articles 114.40; Total (incl. others) 994.78. *Exports f.o.b:* Food and live animals 66.20; Chemicals and related products 4.90; Manufactured goods 10.38; Machinery and transport equipment 7.73; Miscellaneous manufactured articles 7.90; Total (incl. others) 101.52 (re-exports 14.08). Source: Eastern Caribbean Central Bank.

Principal Trading Partners (US $ million, 2008): *Imports c.i.f.:* Barbados 6.5; Brazil 9.2; Canada 10.1; China, People's Republic 12.0; France (incl. Monaco) 3.2; Germany 5.2; Guyana 3.9; Japan 13.0; Netherlands 4.8; Trinidad and Tobago 90.3; United Kingdom 16.1; USA 112.2; Venezuela 25.5; Total (incl. others) 363.3. *Exports f.o.b.:* Antigua and Barbuda 1.0; Barbados 2.9; Belgium 1.0; Canada 0.9; Dominica 5.0; France (incl. Monaco) 0.3; Guyana 0.6; Jamaica 0.5; Japan 6.5; Netherlands 1.1; Saint Christopher and Nevis 2.6; Saint Lucia 3.4; Saint Vincent and the Grenadines 1.0; Trinidad and Tobago 0.6; USA 5.0; Total (incl. others) 30.5. Source: Trade Map-Trade Competitiveness Map, International Trade Centre, www.intracen.org/marketanalysis. *2013* (EC $ million): Total imports 994.78; Total exports 101.52 (re-exports 14.08). (Source: Eastern Caribbean Central Bank).

TRANSPORT

Road Traffic ('000 motor vehicles in use, 2001): Passenger cars 15.8; Commercial vehicles 4.2. Source: UN, *Statistical Yearbook*.

Shipping: *Flag Registered Fleet* (at 31 December 2014): 9 vessels (total displacement 1,931 grt). Source: Lloyd's List Intelligence (www.lloydslistintelligence.com).

Civil Aviation (aircraft arrivals, 1995): 11,310.

TOURISM

Visitor Arrivals: 428,596 (incl. 113,947 stop-over visitors and 309,564 cruise ship passengers) in 2011; 362,091 (incl. 112,335 stop-over visitors and 242,757 cruise ship passengers) in 2012; 315,303 (incl. 112,777 stop-over visitors and 197,308 cruise ship passengers) in 2013.

Tourism Receipts (EC $ million): 315.3 in 2011; 329.1 in 2012; 327.5 in 2013 (estimate).

Source: Eastern Caribbean Central Bank.

COMMUNICATIONS MEDIA

Telephones (2013): 28,585 main lines in use.

Mobile Cellular Telephones (2013): 133,000 subscribers.

Internet Subscribers (2010): 14,400.

Broadband Subscribers (2013): 18,000.

Source: International Telecommunication Union.

EDUCATION

Pre-primary (2009/10 unless otherwise indicated): 74 schools (1994); 246 teachers; 3,562 pupils.

Primary (2009/10 unless otherwise indicated): 57 schools (1995); 851 teachers; 13,663 pupils.

Secondary (2009/10 unless otherwise indicated): 20 schools (2002); 566 teachers; 11,500 pupils.

Higher (excl. figures for the Grenada Teachers' Training College, 1993): 66 teachers; 651 students.

Source: partly UNESCO Institute for Statistics.

Pupil-teacher Ratio (primary education, UNESCO estimate): 16.1 in 2009/10 (Source: UNESCO Institute for Statistics).

Adult Literacy Rate: 96.0% in 2003. Source: UN Development Programme, *Human Development Report*.

Directory

The Government

HEAD OF STATE

Queen: HM Queen ELIZABETH II.

Governor-General: Dame CECILE LA GRENADE (took office 7 May 2013).

THE CABINET
(April 2015)

The Government was formed by the New National Party.

Prime Minister and Minister of Finance, Energy, National Security, Public Administration, Disaster Preparedness, Home Affairs, Implementation and Information: KEITH MITCHELL.

Deputy Prime Minister, and Minister of Legal Affairs, Labour, Carriacou and Petite Martinique Affairs and Local Government: ELVIN NIMROD.

Minister of Economic Development, Planning, Trade, Co-operatives and International Business: OLIVER JOSEPH.

Minister of Communications, Works, Physical Development, Public Utilities and Information Communication Technology: GREGORY BOWEN.

Minister of Culture: BRENDA HOOD.

Minister of Tourism and Civil Aviation: YOLANDE BAIN-HORSFORD.

Minister of Agriculture, Lands, Forestry, Fisheries and the Environment: ROLAND BHOLA.

Minister of Education and Human Resource Development: ANTHONY BOATSWAIN.

Minister of Health and Social Security: NICKOLAS STEELE.

Minister of Foreign Affairs: Dr CLARICE MODESTE-CURWEN.

Minister of Youth, Sports and Religious Affairs: EMMALIN PIERRE.

Minister of Social Development, Housing and Community Development: DELMA THOMAS.

Minister in the Prime Minister's Office: Dr ALEXANDRA OTWAY-NOEL.

MINISTRIES

Office of the Governor-General: Government House, Bldg 5, Financial Complex, The Carenage, St George's; tel. 440-6639; fax 440-6688; e-mail pato@spiceisle.com.

Office of the Prime Minister: Ministerial Complex, 6th Floor, Botanical Gardens, Tanteen, St George's; tel. 440-2255; fax 440-4116; e-mail pmsec@gov.gd; internet www.gov.gd/ministries/opm .html.

Ministry of Agriculture, Lands, Forestry, Fisheries and the Environment: Ministerial Complex, 3rd Floor, Botanical Gardens, Tanteen, St George's; tel. 440-2708; fax 440-4191; e-mail agriculture@gov.gd; internet www.agriculture.gov.gd.

Ministry of Carriacou and Petit Martinique Affairs and Local Government: Beauséjour, Carriacou; tel. 443-6026; fax 443-6040; e-mail minccoupm@spiceisle.com.

Ministry of Communications, Works, Physical Development, Public Utilities and Information Communication Technology: Ministerial Complex, 4th Floor, Botanical Gardens, Tanteen, St George's; tel. 440-2271; fax 440-4122; e-mail ministryofworks@gov .gd.

Ministry of Economic Development, Planning, Trade, Energy, Co-operatives and International Business: Financial Complex, The Carenage, St George's; tel. 440-2731; fax 440-4115.

Ministry of Education and Human Resource Development: Ministry of Education Bldg, Ministerial Complex, Botanical Gardens, Tanteen, St George's; tel. 440-2737; fax 440-6650; internet www.grenadaedu.com.

Ministry of Foreign Affairs: Ministerial Complex, 4th Floor, Botanical Gardens, Tanteen, St George's; tel. 440-2640; fax 440-4184; e-mail foreignaffairs@gov.gd.

Ministry of Health and Social Security: Ministerial Complex, Southern Wing, 1st and 2nd Floors, Botanical Gardens, Tanteen, St George's; tel. 440-2649; fax 440-4127; e-mail min-healthgrenada@spiceisle.com.

Ministry of Legal Affairs and Labour: Ministerial Complex, 3rd Floor, St George's; tel. 440-2532; fax 440-4923; e-mail ministry_labourga@hotmail.com.

Ministry of National Security, Public Administration, Disaster Preparedness, Home Affairs, Implementation and Information: Ministerial Complex, 6th Floor, Botanical Gardens, Tanteen, St George's; tel. 440-2265; fax 440-4116; e-mail pmsec@gov.gd.

Ministry of Social Development, Housing and Community Development: Ministerial Complex, 2nd Floor, Botanical Gardens, Tanteen, St George's; tel. 440-2103; fax 435-5864; e-mail mofhlcd@gov.gd.

Ministry of Tourism, Civil Aviation and Culture: Ministerial Complex, 4th Floor, Botanical Gardens, Tanteen, St George's; tel. 440-0366; fax 440-0443; e-mail tourism@gov.gd; internet www .grenada.mot.gd.

Ministry of Youth, Sports and Religious Affairs: Ministerial Complex, 3rd Floor, Botanical Gardens, Tanteen, St George's; tel. 440-6917; fax 440-6924; e-mail sports@gov.gd.

Legislature

PARLIAMENT

Houses of Parliament: Office of the Houses of Parliament, Botanical Gardens, Tanteen, POB 315, St George's; tel. 440-2090; fax 440-4138; e-mail order.order@spiceisle.com.

Senate

President: CHESTER HUMPHREY.

There are 13 appointed members.

House of Representatives

Speaker: GEORGE JAMES McGUIRE.

General Election, 19 February 2013

	Votes	%	Seats
New National Party (NNP) .	32,225	58.77	15
National Democratic Congress (NDC)	22,260	40.59	—
Others*	346	0.63	—
Total valid votes	54,831	100.00	15

* Comprising the Good Old Democracy Party (GOD), the Grenada Renaissance Party (GRP), the Grenada United Patriotic Movement (GUPM), the Movement for Independent Candidates (MIC), the National United Front (NUF) and the People's United Labour Party (PULP).

Political Organizations

Good Old Democracy Party (GOD): St George's; contested the 2013 elections; Leader JUSTIN McBURNIE.

Grenada Renaissance Party (GRP): St George's; contested the 2013 elections; Leader DESMOND CUTHBERT SANDY.

Grenada United Labour Party (GULP): St George's; tel. 438-1234; e-mail gulp@spiceisle.com; f. 1950; merged with United Labour Congress in 2001; right-wing; did not contest 2013 elections; Pres. and Leader WILFRED HAYES.

Grenada United Patriotic Movement (GUPM): St George's; contested the 2013 elections.

National Democratic Congress (NDC): NDC Headquarters, Lucas St, St George's; tel. 440-3769; e-mail info@ndcgrenada.net; internet www.ndcgrenada.org; f. 1987 by fmr mems of the NNP and merger of Democratic Labour Congress and Grenada Democratic Labour Party; centrist; Leader NAZIM BURKE.

National United Front (NUF): St George's; e-mail info@nationalunitedfront.org; internet www.nationalunitedfront.org; f. 2012 by expelled mems of the NDP; Chair. SIDDIQUI SYLVESTER; Leader GLYNIS ROBERTS.

New National Party (NNP): Upper Lucas St, Mount Helicon, POB 646, St George's; tel. 440-1875; fax 440-1876; e-mail nnpadmin@spiceisle.com; internet www.nnpnews.com; f. 1984 following merger of Grenada Democratic Movt, Grenada National Party and National Democratic Party; centrist; Leader Dr KEITH MITCHELL; Dep. Leader GREGORY BOWEN.

People's United Labor Party (PULP): St George's; contested the 2013 elections; Leader WINSTON FREDERICK.

Diplomatic Representation

EMBASSIES IN GRENADA

Brazil: Mount Cinnamon Hill, Morne Rouge, POB 1226, Grand Anse, St George's; tel. 439-7162; fax 439-7165; e-mail brasemb.saintgeorges@mre.gov.br; Ambassador RICARDO ANDRE VIEIRA DINIZ.

China, People's Republic: Azar Villa, Calliste, POB 1079, St George's; tel. 439-6228; fax 439-6231; e-mail chinaemb_gd@mfa.gov.cn; internet gd.china-embassy.org; Ambassador OU BOQIAN.

Cuba: L'Anse aux Epines, St George's; tel. 444-1884; fax 444-1877; e-mail embacubagranada@caribsurf.com; internet www.cubadiplomatica.cu/granada; Ambassador MARIA CARIDAD BALAGUER LABRADA.

USA: L'Anse aux Epines, POB 54, St George's; tel. 444-1173; fax 444-4820; e-mail usembgd@caribsurf.com; Ambassador LARRY LEON PALMER (resident in Barbados).

Venezuela: Upper Lucas St, Belmont, POB 201, St George's; tel. 440-1721; fax 440-6657; e-mail vennes@caribsurf.com; Ambassador JORGE ALFONZO GUERRERO VELOZ.

Judicial System

Justice is administered by the Eastern Caribbean Supreme Court, based in Saint Lucia, composed of a High Court of Justice and a Court of Appeal. The Itinerant Court of Appeal consists of three judges and sits three times a year; it hears appeals from the High Court and the Magistrates' Court. Three judges of the High Court are resident in Grenada. The Magistrates' Court administers summary jurisdiction.

High Court Judges: PAULA GILFORD, MARGARET PRICE FINDLAY.

Registrar: LISA TELESFORD.

Office of the Attorney-General: Communal House, 414 H. A. Blaize St, St George's; tel. 440-2050; fax 435-2964; e-mail legalaffairs@spiceisle.com; Attorney-Gen. CAJETON HOOD.

Religion

CHRISTIANITY

The Roman Catholic Church

Grenada comprises the single diocese of Saint George's, suffragan to the archdiocese of Castries (Saint Lucia). The Bishop participates in the Antilles Episcopal Conference (based in Port of Spain, Trinidad and Tobago). Some 45% of the population are Roman Catholics.

Bishop of St George's in Grenada: Rev. VINCENT DARIUS, Bishop's House, Morne Jaloux, POB 375, St George's; tel. 443-5299; fax 443-5758; e-mail bishopgrenada@spiceisle.com; internet www.stgdiocese.org.

The Anglican Communion

Anglicans in Grenada are adherents of the Church in the Province of the West Indies. The country forms part of the diocese of the Windward Islands. The Bishop resides in Kingstown, Saint Vincent.

Other Christian Churches

The Presbyterian, Methodist, Plymouth Brethren, Baptist, Salvation Army, Jehovah's Witness, Pentecostal and Seventh-day Adventist faiths are also represented.

The Press

NEWSPAPERS

Barnacle: Mt Parnassus, St George's 3530; tel. 435-0981; e-mail barnacle@spiceisle.com; internet www.barnaclegrenada.com; f. 1991; business journal; every 2 weeks; Editor IAN GEORGE.

The Grenada Informer: Market Hill, POB 622, St George's; tel. 440-1530; fax 440-4119; e-mail grenada.informer@yahoo.com; internet www.thegrenadainformer.com; f. 1985; weekly.

The Grenadian Voice: Frequente Industrial Park, Bldg 1B, Maurice Bishop Hwy, POB 633, St George's; tel. 440-1498; fax 440-4117; e-mail gvoice@spiceisle.com; weekly; Man. Editor LESLIE PIERRE; circ. 3,000.

The New Today: POB 1970, St George's; tel. 435-9363; e-mail newtoday@spiceisle.com; internet thenewtoday.gd.

Media Workers Association of Grenada: Bruce St, POB 1995, St George's; e-mail secretary@mwaggrenada.org; Pres. SHERE-ANN NOEL.

Publishers

Anansi Publications: Woodlands, St George's; tel. 440-0800; e-mail aclouden@spiceisle.com; f. 1986; Man. Dir ALVIN CLOUDEN.

St George's University Publications: Office of University Publications, University Centre, St George's; tel. 444-4175; fax 444-1770; e-mail mlambert@sgu.edu; internet www.sgu.edu/university-communications; f. 2007; Dir MARGARET LAMBERT.

Broadcasting and Communications

TELECOMMUNICATIONS

Digicel Grenada Ltd: Point Salines, POB 1690, St George's; e-mail grenadacustomercare@digicelgroup.com; internet www.digicelgrenada.com; tel. 439-4463; fax 439-4464; f. 2003; owned by an Irish consortium; Chair. DENIS O'BRIEN; Man. (Grenada) PATRICIA MAHER.

Flow: Grenville St, POB 725, St George's; tel. 232-3569; internet discoverflow.co/grenada; f. 2008 following purchase of Grenada Cablevision; fmrly owned by Columbus Communications Grenada Ltd, bought by Cable & Wireless (UK) in 2015; Country Man. GAIL PURCELL.

Grenada Postal Corporation (GPC): Burns Point, St George's; tel. 440-2526; fax 440-4271; e-mail grenadapost@grenadapost.net; internet www.grenadapost.net; Chair. ADRIAN FRANCIS; Dir of Post LEO ROBERTS.

LIME: POB 119, The Carenage, St George's; tel. 440-1000; fax 440-4134; internet www.lime.com; f. 1989; fmrly Cable & Wireless Grenada Ltd; name adopted as above 2008; until 1998 known as Grenada Telecommunications Ltd (Grentel); 30% govt-owned; fixed lines, mobile telecommunications and internet services provider; CEO PHIL BENTLEY; CEO (Caribbean) MARTIN JOOS.

Regulatory Authorities

Eastern Caribbean Telecommunications Authority: Vide Boutielle, Castries, POB 1886, Saint Lucia; tel. 458-1701; fax 458-1698; e-mail ectel@ectel.int; internet www.ectel.int; f. 2000 to regulate telecommunications in Grenada, Dominica, Saint Christopher and Nevis, Saint Lucia and Saint Vincent and the Grenadines.

National Telecommunications Regulatory Commission (NTRC): Maurice Bishop Highway, Grand Anse Shopping Centre, POB 854, St George's; tel. 435-6872; fax 435-2132; e-mail gntrc@ectel.int; internet www.ntrc.gd; Chair. Dr SPENCER THOMAS; Co-ordinator JOHN GILCHRIST.

BROADCASTING

Radio

City Sound FM: River Rd, St George's; tel. 440-9616; e-mail citysound97i5@yahoo.com; internet www.citysoundfm.com; f. 1996.

Grenada Broadcasting Network (Radio): see Television.

HOTT FM: Observatory Rd, POB 535, St George's; tel. 444-5521; fax 440-4180; e-mail gbn@spiceisle.com; internet www.gbn.gd; f. 1999 as Sun FM, present name adopted 2007; contemporary music.

Klassic AM: Observatory Rd, POB 535, St George's; tel. 444-5521; fax 440-4180; e-mail gbn@spiceisle.com; internet www.klassicgrenada.com.

Harbour Light of the Windwards: 400 Harbour Light Way, Tarleton Point, Carriacou; tel. and fax 443-7628; e-mail harbourlight@spiceisle.com; internet www.harbourlightradio.org; f. 1991; owned by Aviation Radio Missionary Services; Christian radio station; Man. Dir Dr RANDY CORNELIUS.

KYAK 106 FM: Church St, Hillsborough, Carriacou; tel. 443-6262; e-mail info@kyak106.com; internet www.kyak106.com; f. 1996; Office Man. DOREEN STANISLAUS.

Sister Isle Radio: Fort Hill, Hillsborough, Carriacou; tel. 443-8141; fax 443-8142; e-mail sisterisle@gmail.com; internet www.sisterisleradio.com; f. 2005.

WeeFM: Cross St, POB 555, St George's; tel. 440-4933; e-mail weefmradio@hotmail.com; internet www.weefmgrenada.com.

Television

Television programmes from Trinidad and Tobago and Barbados can be received on the island.

Grenada Broadcasting Network (GBN): Observatory Rd, POB 535, St George's; tel. 444-5521; fax 440-4180; e-mail gbn@spiceisle .com; internet www.klassicgrenada.com; f. 1972; 60% owned by One Caribbean Media Ltd, 40% govt-owned; 2 radio stations and 1 television station, GBN TV; Chair. CRAIG REYNALD; CEO VICTOR FERNANDES.

Finance

(cap. = capital; res = reserves; dep. = deposits; brs = branches;
amounts in Eastern Caribbean dollars)

The Eastern Caribbean Central Bank, based in Saint Christopher and Nevis, is the central issuing and monetary authority for Grenada.

Eastern Caribbean Central Bank—Grenada Office: Monckton St, St George's; tel. 440-3016; fax 440-6721; e-mail eccbgnd@spiceisle .com; Country Dir LINDA FELIX-BERKLEY.

BANKING

Commercial Banks

CIBC FirstCaribbean International Bank: Church St, POB 37, St George's; tel. 440-3232; fax 440-4103; internet www.cibcfcib.com; f. 2002 as FirstCaribbean International Bank following merger of Barclays and Canadian Imperial Bank of Commerce (CIBC)'s Caribbean operations; Barclays relinquished its stake in 2006, present name adopted in 2011; CEO RIK PARKHILL; 4 brs.

Grenada Co-operative Bank Ltd: 8 Church St, POB 135, St George's; tel. 440-2111; fax 440-6600; e-mail co-opbank@caribsurf .com; internet www.grenadaco-opbank.com; f. 1932; cap. 24.8m., res 13m., dep. 568.7m. (Sept. 2013); Chair. DERICK STEELE; Man. Dir and Sec. RICHARD W. DUNCAN; brs in St Andrew's, St George's, St Patrick's and Hillsborough.

Grenada Development Bank: Melville St, POB 2300, St George's; tel. 440-2382; fax 440-6610; e-mail gdbbank@spiceisle.com; internet www.grenadadevelopmentbank.com; f. 1965; govt-owned; Chair. MICHAEL ARCHIBALD.

RBTT Bank Grenada Ltd: Grand Anse, POB 4, St George's; tel. 440-3521; fax 440-4153; e-mail RBTTLTD@caribsurf.com; internet www.rbtt.com; f. 1983 as Grenada Bank of Commerce; name changed as above 2002; 10% govt-owned; national insurance scheme 15%; public 13%; RBTT Bank Caribbean Ltd, Castries 62%; cap. 11.0m., res 11.1m., dep. 389m. (Oct. 2013); Chair. PATRICIA NARAYANSINGH; Regional CEO SURESH SOOKOO; 4 brs.

Republic Bank (Grenada) Ltd: Republic House, Maurice Bishop Hwy, Grand Anse, POB 857, St George's; tel. 444-2265; fax 444-5500; e-mail republichouse@republicgrenada.com; internet www .republicgrenada.com; f. 1979; fmrly National Commercial Bank of Grenada; name changed as above in 2006; 51% owned by Republic Bank Ltd, Port of Spain, Trinidad and Tobago; cap. 15.0m., res 19.5m., dep. 633.1m. (Sept. 2013); Chair. RONALD HARFORD; Man. Dir KEITH A. JOHNSON; 6 brs.

Scotiabank Grenada (Canada): Granby and Halifax Sts, POB 194, St George's; tel. 440-3274; fax 440-4173; e-mail bns.grenada@ scotiabank.com; internet www.scotiabank.com/gd/en; f. 1963; Country Man. ELIE BENDALY; 3 brs.

REGULATORY AUTHORITY

Grenada Authority for the Regulation of Financial Institutions (GARFIN): POB 3973, Queens Park, St George's; tel. 440-6575; fax 440-4780; e-mail garfininfo@garfin.org; internet www .garfingrenada.org; f. 1999 as Grenada International Financial Services Authority; name changed to above in 2007; regulates non-banking financial sector; Chair. TIMOTHY ANTOINE; Exec. Dir ANGUS SMITH.

STOCK EXCHANGE

Eastern Caribbean Securities Exchange: Bird Rock, Basseterre, Saint Christopher and Nevis; tel. (869) 466-7192; fax (869) 465-3798; e-mail info@ECSEonline.com; internet www.ecseonline.com; f. 2001; regional securities market designed to facilitate the buying and selling of financial products for the 8 mem. territories—Anguilla, Antigua and Barbuda, Dominica, Grenada, Montserrat, Saint Christopher and Nevis, Saint Lucia, and Saint Vincent and the Grenadines; Chair. Sir K. DWIGHT VENNER; Gen. Man. TREVOR E. BLAKE.

INSURANCE

Several foreign insurance companies operate in Grenada and the other islands of the group. Principal locally owned companies include the following:

Gittens Insurance Brokerage Co Ltd: Benoit Bldg, Grand Anse, POB 1695, St George's; tel. 439-4408; fax 439-4462; internet www .cisgrenada.com/gittensinsurance; f. 2003; Chair. PHILLIP McLAWRENCE GITTENS; CEO PHILLIP ARTHUR GITTENS.

Grenada Motor and General Insurance Co Ltd: Scott St, POB 152, St George's; tel. 440-3379; fax 440-7977; e-mail g500z@hotmail .com; Gen. Man. GABRIEL OLOUYNE.

Grenadian General Insurance Co Ltd: Cnr of Young and Scott Sts, POB 47, St George's; tel. 440-2434; fax 440-6618; e-mail ggicoltd@spiceisle.com; Dir KEITH RENWICK.

GTM Grenada (Guyana and Trinidad Mutual Group of Insurance Companies): Church St, St George's; tel. 440-2839; internet www .gtm-gy.com/grenada; f. 1909; headquarters in Guyana; Country Man. SHONETTE INNISS-HOYTE.

Pan-American Life Insurance Co of the Eastern Caribbean: Modern Photo Studio Bldg, St George's; tel. 435-0058; fax 435-0060; internet www.palig.com; f. 2012; part of Pan-American Life Insurance Group (USA); CEO and Man. Dir (Caribbean) WILLIAM R. SCHULZ, Jr; Man. PEARLY CHARLES.

Trade and Industry

CHAMBER OF COMMERCE

Grenada Chamber of Industry and Commerce, Inc (GCIC): Bldg 11, POB 129, Frequente, St George's; tel. 440-2937; fax 440-6627; e-mail gcic@grenadachamber.org; internet www .grenadachamber.org; f. 1921, incd 1947; 170 mems; Pres. AINE BRATHWAITE; Exec. Dir HAZELANN HUTCHINSON.

INDUSTRIAL AND TRADE ASSOCIATIONS

Grenada Cocoa Association (GCA): Kirani James Blvd, POB 3649, St George's; tel. 440-2234; fax 440-1470; e-mail gca@spiceisle .com; f. 1964; Chair. RAMSEY RUSH; Man. ANDREW HASTICK.

Grenada Co-operative Nutmeg Association (GCNA): Lagoon Rd, POB 160, St George's; tel. 440-2117; fax 440-6602; e-mail gcna .nutmeg@caribsurf.com; f. 1947; processes and markets all the nutmeg and mace grown on the island; includes the production of nutmeg oil; Chair. DENIS FELIX; Gen. Man. MARLON CLYNE.

Grenada Industrial Development Corporation (GIDC): Frequenté Industrial Park, Grand Anse, St George's; tel. 444-1035; fax 444-4828; e-mail invest@grenadaidc.com; internet www.grenadaidc .com; f. 1985; Chair. LESLIE ANN SEON; CEO RONALD THEODORE.

Marketing and National Importing Board (MNIB): Young St, POB 652, St George's; tel. 440-1791; fax 440-4152; e-mail mnib@ spiceisle.com; internet www.mnib.gd; f. 1974; govt-owned; imports basic food items, incl. sugar, rice and milk; also exports fresh produce; Chair. CLAUDIA ALEXIS; Gen. Man. FITZROY JAMES.

EMPLOYERS' ORGANIZATION

Grenada Employers' Federation: Bldg 11, Frequenté Industrial Park, Grand Anse, POB 129, St George's; tel. 440-1832; fax 440-6627; e-mail gef@spiceisle.com; internet www.grenadaemployers.com; f. 1962; Pres. MICHAEL PHILBERT; Exec. Dir CECIL EDWARDS; 60 mems.

UTILITIES

Electricity

Grenada Electricity Services Ltd (Grenlec): Halifax St, POB 381, St George's; tel. 440-2097; fax 440-4106; e-mail customersupport@grenlec.com; internet www.grenlec.com; f. 1960; generation and distribution; majority privately owned (61% by WRB Enterprises, USA), 10% govt-owned; Chair. G. ROBERT BLANCHARD, Jr; Man. Dir and CEO VERNON LAWRENCE.

Water

National Water and Sewerage Authority (NAWASA): The Carenage, POB 392, St George's; tel. 440-2155; fax 440-4107; f. 1969; Chair. TERRENCE SMITH; Gen. Man. CHRISTOPHER HUSBANDS.

TRADE UNION

Grenada Trade Union Council (GTUC): Green St, POB 411, St George's; tel. and fax 440-3733; e-mail gtuc@caribsurf.com; Pres. MADONNA HARFORD; Gen. Sec. RAY ROBERTS; 8,000 mems (2011).

Transport

RAILWAYS

There are no railways in Grenada.

ROADS

There were approximately 1,127 km (700 miles) of roads, of which 61% were paved. Following the completion of the first phase of the Agricultural Feeder Roads Project, funded by the OPEC Fund for International Development, work on the second phase of the project, at a cost of EC $45.4m., began in May 2013. Funding for the second phase was provided by the Kuwait Fund for Arab Economic Development.

SHIPPING

The main port is St George's, with accommodation for two ocean-going vessels of up to 500 ft. A number of shipping lines call at St George's. The Melville Street Cruise Terminal became operational in 2004. Grenville, on Grenada, and Hillsborough, on Carriacou, are used mostly by small craft. An ambitious EC $1,600m. development at Port Louis, to include a 350-slipway marina with yachting facilities, was completed in 2009. In December 2014 Grenada's flag registered fleet comprised nine vessels, with an aggregate displacement of some 1,931 grt.

Grenada Ports Authority: POB 494, The Pier, St George's; tel. 440-7678; fax 440-3418; e-mail grenport@caribsurf.com; internet www.grenadaports.com; f. 1981; state-owned; Chair. NIGEL JOHN; Gen. Man. AMBROSE PHILLIP.

CIVIL AVIATION

Maurice Bishop International Airport (formerly Point Salines International Airport) is 10 km (6 miles) from St George's and has scheduled flights to most Eastern Caribbean destinations, including Venezuela, and to the United Kingdom and North America. There is an airfield at Pearls, 30 km (18 miles) from St George's, and Lauriston Airport, on the island of Carriacou, offers regular scheduled services to Grenada, Saint Vincent and Palm Island (Grenadines).

Grenada is a shareholder in the regional airline LIAT (see chapter on Antigua and Barbuda).

Grenada Airports Authority: Maurice Bishop Int. Airport, POB 385, St George's; tel. 444-4101; fax 444-4838; e-mail gaa@mbiagrenada.com; e-mail www.mbiagrenada.com; f. 1985; Chair. JOAN GILBERT.

Tourism

Grenada has the attractions of white sandy beaches and a scenic, mountainous interior with an extensive rainforest. There are also sites of historical interest, and the capital, St George's, is a noted beauty spot. In 2013 there were 112,777 stop-over arrivals and 197,308 cruise ship passengers. In that year tourism earned an estimated EC $327.5m.

Grenada Hotel and Tourism Association Ltd: Ocean House Bldg, Morne Rouge Rd, Grand Anse, POB 440, St George's; tel. 444-1353; fax 444-4847; e-mail mail@ghta.org; internet www.ghta.org; f. 1961; Pres. IAN FIELDEN DA BREO; Exec. Dir PANCY CHANDLER CROSS.

Grenada Tourism Authority: Burns Point, POB 293, St George's; tel. 440-2279; fax 440-6637; e-mail gbt@spiceisle.com; internet www.grenadagrenadines.com; f. 1991 as Grenada Board of Tourism; upgraded to an authority in 2013; Chair. RICHARD STRACHAN.

Defence

A regional security unit was formed in 1983, modelled on the British police force and trained by British officers. A paramilitary element, known as the Special Service Unit and trained by US advisers, acts as the defence contingent and participates in the Regional Security System, a defence pact with other Eastern Caribbean states.

Commissioner of Police: WINSTON JAMES (acting).

Education

Education is free and compulsory for children between the ages of five and 16 years. Primary education begins at five years of age and lasts for seven years. Secondary education, beginning at the age of 12, lasts for a further five years. In 2009 enrolment at primary schools included 87% of children in the relevant age-group. In 2009/10 some 13,663 pupils attended primary school while 11,500 students attended secondary school. Enrolment at all secondary schools included 91% of pupils in the relevant age-group in 2008/09. In 2006 there were 2,710 full-time enrolled students at the T. A. Marryshow Community College. The Extra-Mural Department of the University of the West Indies has a branch in St George's and there is also St George's University, which had 5,880 students in 2012. The combined capital expenditure on education and human resources development was budgeted at EC $109.6m. in 2012 (equivalent to 10.7% of total capital expenditure).

GUATEMALA

Introductory Survey

LOCATION, CLIMATE, LANGUAGE, RELIGION, FLAG, CAPITAL

The Republic of Guatemala lies in the Central American isthmus, bounded to the north and west by Mexico, with Honduras and Belize to the east and El Salvador to the south. It has a long coastline on the Pacific Ocean and a narrow outlet to the Caribbean Sea. The climate is tropical in the lowlands, with an average temperature of 28°C (83°F), and more temperate in the central highland area, with an average temperature of 20°C (68°F). The official language is Spanish, but more than 20 indigenous languages are also spoken. Almost all of the inhabitants profess Christianity: the majority are Roman Catholics, while an estimated 40% are Protestants. A large proportion of the population also follows traditional Mayan beliefs. The national flag (proportions 5 by 8) has three equal vertical stripes, of blue, white and blue, with the national coat of arms (depicting a quetzal, the 'bird of freedom', and a scroll, superimposed on crossed rifles and sabres, encircled by a wreath) in the centre of the white stripe. The capital is Guatemala City.

CONTEMPORARY POLITICAL HISTORY

Historical Context

Under Spanish colonial rule, Guatemala was part of the Viceroyalty of New Spain. Independence was obtained from Spain in 1821, from Mexico in 1824 and from the Federation of Central American States in 1838. Subsequent attempts to revive the Federation failed and, under a series of dictators, there was relative stability, tempered by periods of disruption. A programme of social reform was begun by Juan José Arévalo (President in 1944–50) and his successor, Col Jacobo Arbenz Guzmán. In 1954 Arbenz was overthrown in a coup led by Col Carlos Castillo Armas, who invaded the country with US assistance. Castillo became President but was assassinated in 1957. The next elected President, Gen. Miguel Ydígoras Fuentes, took office in 1958 and ruled until he was deposed in 1963 by a military coup, led by Col Enrique Peralta Azurdia. He suspended the Constitution and dissolved the legislature. A Constituent Assembly introduced a new Constitution in 1965. Dr Julio César Méndez Montenegro was elected President in 1966, and in 1970 the candidate of the Movimiento de Liberación Nacional (MLN), Col (later Gen.) Carlos Araña Osorio, was elected President. Despite charges of fraud in the elections of 1974, Gen. Kjell Laugerud García of the MLN took office as President.

President Laugerud sought to discourage extreme right-wing violence and claimed some success, although it was estimated that 50,000–60,000 people were killed in political violence between 1970 and 1979. In 1978 Gen. Fernando Romeo Lucas García was elected President. The guerrilla movement increased in strength in 1980–81, while the Government was accused of the murder and torture of civilians and, particularly, persecution of the country's indigenous Indian inhabitants, who comprised 60% of the population.

Domestic Political Affairs

In the presidential election of March 1982, from which the left-wing parties were absent, the Government's candidate, Gen. Angel Aníbal Guevara, was declared the winner; however, the election was denounced as fraudulent. A coup followed on 23 March, in which Gen. José Efraín Ríos Montt was installed as leader of a three-man junta. The Congreso Nacional (National Congress) was closed, and the Constitution and political parties suspended. In June Gen. Ríos Montt dissolved the junta and assumed the presidency. He attempted to fight corruption, reorganized the judicial system and disbanded the secret police. The number of violent deaths diminished. However, after initially gaining the support of the national university, the Roman Catholic Church and the labour unions, Ríos Montt declared a state of siege and imposed censorship of the press. The war against the guerrillas intensified, and a civil defence force of Indians was established. Villages were burned, and many inhabitants killed, in order to deter the Indians from supporting the

guerrillas. Ríos Montt's fragile hold on power was threatened in 1982 by several attempted coups, which he managed to forestall.

In January 1983 the US Government announced the resumption of arms sales to Guatemala, suspended since 1977 as a result of human rights violations. However, independent reports claimed that the human rights situation had deteriorated, and revealed that 2,600 people had been killed during the first six months of Ríos Montt's rule. In March the army was implicated in the massacre of 300 Indian peasants at Nahulá, and there was a resurgence in the activity of both left- and right-wing 'death squads'. The President declared a 30-day amnesty for guerrillas and political exiles, and lifted the state of siege. The Government's 'guns and beans' policy provided food and medicine in exchange for recruitment to the Patrullas de Autodefensa Civil (PAC), a pro-Government peasant militia.

By mid-1983 opposition to the President was widespread. In August Gen. Oscar Humberto Mejía Victores, the Minister of Defence, led a successful coup against Ríos Montt. Mejía ended press censorship and announced an amnesty for guerrillas. Urban and rural terrorism continued to escalate, however. Following the murder in northern Guatemala of six US aid workers, the USA suspended US $50m. in aid in 1984. Elections for a Constituent Assembly were held in July, at which the centre groups, including the newly formed Unión del Centro Nacional (UCN), obtained the greatest number of votes. Under the system of proportional representation, however, the right-wing coalition of the MLN and the Central Auténtica Nacionalista obtained a majority of seats in the Assembly.

Guatemala's new Constitution was promulgated in 1985. The main contest in the November presidential election was between Jorge Carpio Nicolle of the UCN and Mario Vinicio Cerezo Arévalo of the Partido Democracia Cristiana Guatemalteca (PDCG). As neither candidate obtained the requisite majority, a second round of voting was held in December, which Cerezo won. The PDCG won the majority of seats in the concurrent election to the new Congress. The US Administration increased economic aid and resumed military aid to Guatemala, in support of the new civilian Government.

Immediately prior to the transfer of power in January 1986, the outgoing military Government decreed a general amnesty for those suspected of involvement in abuses of human rights since 1982. A government commission to investigate 'disappearances' was created in 1987. In August a peace plan for the region was signed in Guatemala City by the Presidents of Costa Rica, El Salvador, Guatemala, Honduras and Nicaragua. Subsequently, a Commission of National Reconciliation (CNR) was formed. In October representatives of the Government and the main guerrilla grouping, the Unidad Revolucionaria Nacional Guatemalteca (URNG), met in Spain, but the peace negotiations ended without agreement. Right-wing pressure on the Government, and an attempted coup in May 1988, forced Cerezo to postpone further negotiations with the URNG. By this time there were also frequent reports of torture and killings by right-wing death squads as discontent with the Government's liberal policies increased.

Guerrilla activity intensified in 1989. Many political figures and labour leaders fled the country after receiving death threats from paramilitary groups. Meanwhile, Cerezo refused to negotiate with the URNG while its members remained armed. In September the URNG made further proposals for negotiations, following the signing of the Tela Agreement (the Central American peace plan accord), but these were rejected. Despite Cerezo's promise to restrict the unlawful activities of the armed forces and right-wing death squads, the number of murders and 'disappearances' escalated in 1990. Following discussions with the CNR, the URNG agreed to participate in a constituent assembly to reform the Constitution.

None of the nominees obtained an absolute majority in the first round of the presidential election of November 1990. A second ballot in January 1991 between the two leading candidates was won by Jorge Serrano Elías of the Movimiento de Acción Solidaria (MAS). The MAS failed to secure a majority in the legislative election, however, and Serrano invited the Partido de

Avanzada Nacional (PAN) and the Partido Socialista Democrático (PSD) to participate in a coalition Government.

In April 1991 direct talks between the URNG and the Government began in Mexico City. However, in an attempt to destabilize efforts at national reconciliation, some members of the state security forces launched a campaign of violence, directing death threats against leaders of trade unions and human rights organizations, and murdering a PSD politician. In late 1991 the ombudsman, Ramiro de León Carpio, secured the resignation of the Director of the National Police, Col Mario Enrique Paíz Bolanos, who was alleged to be responsible for the use of torture.

Further negotiations in Mexico City in 1992 led to concessions by the Government, which agreed to curb the expansion of the PAC. The URNG, which maintained that *campesinos* were forcibly enlisted into the PAC, included in its conditions for a peace agreement the immediate dissolution of the patrols. In November the Government accepted renewed proposals by the URNG for the establishment of a commission on past human rights violations, but only if the rebels signed a definitive peace accord. Talks were suspended in May 1993. The URNG announced a unilateral ceasefire as a gesture of goodwill to the incoming President, Ramiro de León Carpio, in June (see below). In August, in a concession to the URNG, de León announced the reform of the Estado Mayor Presidencial, a military body accused of human rights offences. Talks finally resumed in Mexico in January 1994.

Constitutional coup of 1993

Unrest at economic austerity measures escalated in May 1993. With the MAS no longer able to effect a constructive alliance in the Congress, on 25 May Serrano, with the support of the military, suspended parts of the Constitution and dissolved the Congress and the Supreme Court. A ban was imposed on the media and Serrano announced that he would rule by decree pending the drafting of a new constitution by a constituent assembly, to be elected within 60 days. The constitutional coup provoked almost unanimous international condemnation, with the USA immediately suspending aid. The military reappraised its position and forced the resignation of Serrano. The Minister of National Defence, Gen. José Domingo García Samayoa, assumed control of the country pending an election. The entire Cabinet, excluding García and the Minister of the Interior, Francisco Perdomo Sandoval, resigned on 3 June. Two days later the Congress reconvened to conduct a presidential ballot. The Instancia Nacional de Consenso (INC), a broad coalition of political parties, business leaders and trade unions, elected Ramiro de León Carpio, the former human rights ombudsman, as President. The USA subsequently restored its aid programme to the country.

In August 1993, as an initial measure in a campaign to eradicate corruption from state institutions, de León requested the voluntary resignation of the Congress and the Supreme Court. The request caused a serious division in the legislature, which separated into two main factions, the Gran Grupo Parlamentario (GGP), which included members of the MAS, UCN, PAN and the Frente Republicano Guatemalteco (FRG) and supported the dismissal of 16 deputies identified by the INC as corrupt, and a group, including members of the PDCG and independents, which supported the resignation of all 116 deputies. In September the GGP defied a suspension of a legislative session and elected a new congressional President. The GGP also threatened to boycott any further sessions convened by the previous speaker, Fernando Lobo Dubón (a PDCG member). In November a compromise was reached between the Government and the legislature, involving a series of constitutional reforms. These were subsequently approved by a referendum, although less than 20% of the electorate participated. The reforms took effect in April 1994, and fresh legislative elections were to be held in August. The new Congress, which was to serve until January 1996, was to appoint the members of a new, enlarged Supreme Court of Justice. Other reforms included a reduction in the terms of office of the President, legislature and municipal authorities, and of the Supreme Court justices, and a reduction in the number of congressional seats.

In March 1994 the Government and the URNG agreed a timetable of formal negotiations aimed at achieving a definitive peace agreement by the end of the year. In addition, a general human rights agreement was signed, providing guarantees, including a government commitment to eliminate illegal security corps, strengthen national human rights institutions and cease obligatory military recruitment. Agreement was also reached on the establishment of a UN deputation, the Human Rights Verification Mission in Guatemala (MINUGUA), to verify the implementation of the accord. Further talks resulted in the signing, in June, of agreements on the resettlement of people displaced by the civil war (estimated to number some 1m.), and on the establishment of a commission to investigate human rights violations committed during the 33-year conflict.

In August 1994 the URNG withdrew from the peace negotiations and accused the Government of failing to observe the agreed human rights provisions. Talks remained deadlocked until February 1995, when a new timetable for negotiations, achieved with UN mediation, was announced. The issue of the identity and rights of indigenous peoples was finally resolved, but talks continued beyond the agreed deadline without agreement on other substantive issues, including socio-economic reform and the incorporation of URNG guerrillas into civilian life.

At the legislative election of August 1994 only some 20% of the electorate exercised their vote. Despite winning the greatest number of seats in the 80-seat legislature, the FRG, led by Gen. (retd) José Efraín Ríos Montt, was excluded from the 12-member congressional directorate by an alliance of the PAN, PDCG, MLN and Unión Democrática. However, in December the PDCG transferred its allegiance to the FRG and Ríos Montt was subsequently elected President of the Congress. His inauguration in January 1995 provoked demonstrations by human rights organizations, which considered him responsible for the deaths of as many as 15,000 civilians as a result of counter-insurgency operations conducted during his period as de facto ruler in 1982–83.

The presidential and legislative elections of November 1995 were notable for the return to the electoral process, for the first time for more than 40 years, of the left wing, represented by the Frente Democrático Nueva Guatemala (FDNG). In addition, the URNG declared a unilateral ceasefire to coincide with the electoral campaign and urged people to vote. The two leading presidential candidates, Alvaro Enrique Arzú Irigoyen of the PAN and Alfonso Antonio Portillo Cabrera of the FRG, contested a second round of voting in January 1996, at which Arzú secured a narrow victory. The PAN also secured a majority of seats in the Congress.

The new President implemented a comprehensive reorganization of the military high command, replacing those officers who were not in favour of a negotiated peace settlement. In March 1996 the Congress ratified the International Labour Organization's Convention on the rights of indigenous peoples. However, the document was amended by the Congress, prompting protests by Indian organizations. On 20 March the URNG announced an indefinite unilateral ceasefire. Arzú immediately ordered the armed forces to suspend counter-insurgency operations. In May the Government and the URNG signed an agreement on agrarian and socio-economic reforms. In the following month the Congress adopted legislation that made members of the armed forces accountable to civilian courts for all but strictly military crimes. In September the Government and the URNG signed an agreement on the strengthening of civilian power and the role of the armed forces. Under the terms of the accord, all military and intelligence services were to be placed under the authority of the Government. The police force was to be reorganized, with the creation of a new national civilian force (Policía Nacional Civil—PNC). Also confirmed in the accord was the abolition of the PAC. A general amnesty law was approved by the Congress in December.

1996 peace treaty

On 29 December 1996 the Government and the URNG signed the definitive peace treaty in Guatemala City, bringing to an end some 36 years of civil war, during which an estimated 140,000 people had died. The demobilization of URNG guerrillas, estimated to number some 3,250, was supervised by MINUGUA and completed in May 1997. In the following month the URNG registered as a political party.

In April 1998 the auxiliary bishop of the metropolitan diocese of Guatemala City, Juan José Gerardi Conedera, was murdered. Gerardi had been a founder of the Roman Catholic Church's Oficina de Derechos Humanos del Arzobispado (ODHA—Archbishopric's Human Rights Office), and a prominent critic of the armed forces. Days before his death Gerardi had presented a report by the ODHA documenting human rights abuses during the civil conflict, of which army personnel were found responsible for some 80%. In what the Church and human rights groups interpreted as an attempt to conceal the truth, a priest, Mario

Orantes Nájera, was formally charged with Gerardi's murder in October. In February 1999 the presiding judge ordered the release of Orantes on grounds of insufficient evidence; the judge withdrew from the case in the following month after allegedly receiving death threats. In 2001 former intelligence chief Col (retd) Disrael Lima Estrada, his son, Capt. Byron Lima Oliva, and a former member of the presidential guard, José Obdulio Villanueva, were convicted of Gerardi's murder; Orantes was convicted of conspiring in his death. However, in 2002 a Court of Appeal overturned the convictions and ordered a retrial. At the retrial in 2003 the sentences were upheld by the Supreme Court. Nevertheless, in 2005 a Court of Appeal amended the convictions of Lima Estrada and Lima Oliva to accessory to murder, reducing their sentences from 30 years' to 20 years' imprisonment, and in July 2012 Lima Oliva was released.

In August 1999, in what was widely regarded as a test case for the judicial system, 25 members of the armed forces convicted of the massacre in 1995 of 11 civilians in Xamán, Alta Verapaz, received minimum sentences of five years' imprisonment. The case was the first in which military personnel accused of killing civilians had been tried by a civilian court, and the decision, which provoked public outrage, greatly undermined confidence in the courts' ability to administer justice in the remaining 625 cases of massacres attributed to the security forces. A December 1999 MINUGUA report stated that commitments made by the Arzú administration under the 1996 peace treaty to reduce the influence of the military remained unfulfilled. In the following year MINUGUA asserted that the number of extrajudicial executions had doubled between 1996 and 2000.

In February 1999 the human rights investigative commission published its final report, in which it attributed more than 93% of human rights violations committed during the civil conflict to the armed forces and state paramilitaries. It announced that 200,000 people had been killed or had 'disappeared' between 1962 and 1996, the majority of them Mayan Indians. It also concluded that the USA had financed and trained Guatemalan forces responsible for atrocities. The report recommended that compensation be provided for the families of victims, that prosecutions be brought against those suspected of crimes against humanity and that a purge of the armed forces be implemented. The Government described the Commission's findings as controversial, and did not express any intention of pursuing its recommendations.

In October 1998 the Congress approved constitutional reforms provided for in the 1996 peace accords. The reforms, which concerned the rights of indigenous peoples, the role of the armed forces and the police, and the strengthening of the courts, were subject to ratification in a referendum. However, at the plebiscite, in May 1999, 56% of participating voters rejected the constitutional amendments. The turnout was extremely low, at 19%, and observers attributed the result to a lack of information and to mistrust of the political establishment rather than to the rejection of the peace accords themselves. At presidential and legislative elections, conducted in November, voter participation, at some 40%, was greatly improved. The two leading presidential candidates, Alfonso Portillo of the FRG and Oscar Berger Perdomo of the PAN, contested a second round of voting in December, in which Portillo secured victory. The FRG secured an outright majority in the election to the newly enlarged legislature.

The Portillo Government

The new administration of President Portillo, which took office in January 2000, immediately undertook the promised demilitarization of the upper echelons of government. However, disputes between the Government and the Congress resulted in virtual paralysis in policymaking. Furthermore, throughout 2001 the Government was beset by allegations of corruption. In March 2002 a congressional commission was formed to investigate claims that President Portillo and Vice-President Francisco Reyes López had established bank accounts in Panama for the purpose of money-laundering. The allegations provoked mass protests in Guatemala City. However, in June the investigation by the congressional commission collapsed, owing to a lack of evidence.

The US Government expressed its concern at levels of corruption, drugs-trafficking and continuing human rights abuses in Guatemala in 2002. In March the leader of the opposition Partido Patriótico, Jorge Rosal Zea, was assassinated. President Portillo subsequently announced a number of reforms to the security forces, including the dissolution of the Department of Anti-Narcotics Operations and the creation of a new unit, Unidades

Móviles Operativas, to combat drugs-trafficking and terrorism. Nevertheless, in 2003 the USA added Guatemala to the list of nations it considered unco-operative in combating drugs-trafficking.

In May 2003 Oscar Berger Perdomo, hitherto the PAN's candidate in the forthcoming presidential election, announced that he would stand as the nominee of the Gran Alianza Nacional (GANA), a small, centre-right alliance comprising the Partido Patriota (PP), the Movimiento Reformador and the Partido Solidaridad Nacional. Ríos Montt was to be the FRG's nominee, but in July the Supreme Court barred his candidacy, prompting violent protests. At the end of the month the Constitutional Court overruled the supreme court decision and allowed Ríos Montt to register as a candidate.

Presidential and legislative elections of 2003

Presidential and legislative elections took place in November 2003. Berger and Alvaro Colom Caballeros of the Unidad Nacional de la Esperanza (UNE) contested a second round of voting in December, in which Berger narrowly secured the presidency. GANA won the largest number of seats in the expanded assembly, although it failed to secure a majority.; GANA agreed a governability pact with the UNE and the PAN in January 2004.

In February 2004 the Constitutional Court lifted Ríos Montt's parliamentary immunity. The following month he was charged with premeditated murder, coercion and threats in connection to the violence outside the Supreme Court in 2003 and placed under house arrest; the charges were dismissed in 2006. Also in February 2004, former President Portillo and former Vice-President Reyes similarly lost their immunity from prosecution. Shortly afterwards, Portillo left the country for Mexico. An injunction for his arrest on charges of money-laundering and misuse of public funds was requested. Reyes was arrested in July and charged with fraud, embezzlement and abuse of authority. In May 2007 the Constitutional Court ordered that the case against Portillo be abandoned. Nevertheless, in 2008 Portillo surrendered to Mexican authorities to be extradited. On arrival in Guatemala, however, he was controversially released on bail. Portillo was arrested again in January 2010 after an extradition request by the USA (on money-laundering charges). In August, however, Portillo was ordered to stand trial in Guatemala on the embezzlement charges. The trial of Portillo, together with his former Minister of National Defence, Eduardo Arévalo, and his former Minister of Public Finance, Manuel Maza, in 2011 resulted in all three men being exonerated, prompting criticism from CICIG (see below). (This judgment was upheld by a Court of Appeal in April 2013.) Nevertheless, in November 2011 Portillo's extradition to the USA was ratified by President Colom, and he was transferred to US custody in May 2013. In 2014 Portillo was sentenced to almost six years' imprisonment after having admitted accepting US $2.5m. in bribes from Taiwan while in office; he was released in February 2015.

Internal political conflicts and the defection of congressional deputies impeded the Berger Government's efforts to implement its legislative agenda. In an attempt to secure opposition support for proposed fiscal reforms, in May 2004 President Berger met with Ríos Montt. However, the meeting prompted the withdrawal of the UNE and the PAN from the governability pact and the PP left GANA in protest. In late 2004 a MINUGUA report noted that government efforts to reform the criminal justice system had been largely ineffective. Upon its withdrawal from Guatemala in December, MINUGUA reported that the Government still had to overcome three major challenges: public security; judicial reform; and discrimination against indigenous peoples. Following legislative approval, an office of the UN's High Commission for Human Rights was opened in the country in 2005.

Political tensions escalated into violence in early 2006. A number of activists were assassinated, including a UNE deputy and the co-ordinator of the nascent political party Encuentro por Guatemala. The lynching of four people in two separate attacks in April prompted the mobilization of 11,000 members of the armed forces to assist the police in maintaining order. In February 2007 three Salvadorean deputies were found murdered on the outskirts of Guatemala City. Three days later four Guatemalan police officers who had confessed to the murders were arrested; however, they too were later killed. A vote of no confidence in the Minister of the Interior, Carlos Vielmann, was approved by the Congress in March. The crisis provoked by the assassinations facilitated, in August, the overwhelming approval by the Congress of legislation to create the International Commission against Impunity in Guatemala

(CICIG—Comisión Internacional contra la Impunidad en Guatemala). The independent body was to comprise a panel of international experts who would assist the Guatemalan authorities in the investigation and dismantling of paramilitary security forces and other criminal organizations linked to state institutions. CICIG officially began its operations in January 2008.

Presidential and legislative elections of 2007

Security issues dominated the campaign for the presidential and legislative elections held on 9 September 2007. The vote was preceded by the most violent electoral campaign since the end of the civil war, in which more than 40 people were killed. In the presidential ballot no candidate received enough votes for a first round victory. At a second round of voting in November, the UNE's Colom defeated the PP candidate, Gen. (retd) Otto Fernando Pérez Molina, with 53% of the valid votes cast. In elections to the Congress the UNE increased its representation to 50 seats, becoming the largest party in the legislature. Colom was inaugurated in January 2008, becoming the first centre-left President since 1954.

Colom's electoral campaign included a pledge to improve internal security and reduce impunity. Upon assuming office, the new President introduced the 'Plan Cuadrante', intended to reduce high crime rates, and announced that he planned gradually to decrease army participation in civilian security operations. In a decision welcomed by human rights activists, Colom also declared that previously unseen military archives would be released to the public. Reluctance from military personnel, however, led to delays in the files becoming available. (In June 2011 over 99% of the military's archives were finally declassified, although it had earlier been revealed that the documents covering 1980–85 had disappeared.) Nevertheless, in September 2008 the President announced plans to increase the size of the army to 25,000 to bolster the police force. Colom inaugurated a new security council in November, to co-ordinate and supervise Guatemala's security institutions. In December Colom undertook further changes to the Guatemalan military with the dismissal of many important army officials and the replacement of the Minister of National Defence.

Efforts to improve security

CICIG's 2008 report conceded a lack of tangible progress in reducing crime and levels of impunity, largely owing to opposition from Guatemalan authorities. Colom replaced Francisco Jiménez Irungaray at the Ministry of the Interior with a more hard-line candidate, Salvador Gándara, in January 2009 and made renewed promises to improve security. In March the President announced the creation of an anti-impunity commission intended to complement CICIG's investigations, and in April he signed a national security and justice accord with the President of the Congress and the acting President of the Supreme Court. Notable provisions of the accord included the creation of a public security ministry and the extension of CICIG's mandate. Meanwhile, at the end of March the Congress approved long-awaited gun control legislation.

The President's efforts to reduce violent crime were overshadowed in May 2009 by allegations that he was involved in the killing of a prominent lawyer, Rodrigo Rosenberg Marzano. In a video recording made prior to his death, Rosenberg had claimed that Colom and other senior officials were plotting his murder. Colom requested that CICIG conduct an investigation into the allegations, which he vehemently denied, accusing his opponents of attempting to destabilize his Government. Thousands of people subsequently participated in protests in Guatemala City to demand Colom's resignation, while demonstrations in support of the President were also well attended. In January 2010 CICIG exonerated Colom, concluding that Rosenberg had orchestrated his own assassination. In July eight people were convicted in connection with the killing.

Meanwhile, CICIG continued to encounter resistance from officials while conducting its investigations. In June 2009 the commission filed a formal complaint against a judge who was seeking to terminate its involvement in the case against former President Portillo. The Congress approved a two-year extension of CICIG's mandate in July. With the violent murder rate continuing to rise, Gándara resigned as Minister of the Interior in the same month; he was succeeded by Raúl Antonio Velásquez Ramos. Gándara's decision to replace the leadership of the PNC with retired police officials in the previous month had been criticized by human rights groups. In August Velásquez dismissed the PNC officials appointed by Gándara for alleged

involvement in drugs-trafficking. Following objections by CICIG to several of the Congress's nominees to the Supreme Court, as well as criticism from UN officials over a lack of transparency, in October the legislature revised the list of new judges. CICIG achieved a significant victory in January 2010, when it facilitated the arrest of Portillo (see above).

In the first such conviction since the end of the civil war, in August 2009 Felipe Cusanero Coj, a former member of the PAC, was found guilty of the forced 'disappearances' of six Mayan citizens in 1982–84 and sentenced to 150 years' imprisonment. In December a retired army officer, Marco Antonio Sánchez, received a 53-year prison sentence for the 'disappearances' of eight farm workers.

Three ministers were dismissed in February 2010: the Minister of Agriculture, Livestock and Food, Mario Aldana, owing to irregularities in the tendering process for the supply of fertilizers; the Minister of Education, Bienvenido Argueta, for failing to reveal information about the beneficiaries of Mi Familia Progresa, a social programme that some opposition members suspected had been used to reward government supporters; and Minister of the Interior Velásquez as a result of corruption allegations. In March the PNC Director, Baltázar Gómez Barrios, the head of the PNC's counter-narcotics division, Nelly Bonilla, and the latter's deputy were arrested on suspicion of alleged collusion with drugs-traffickers. The resignation of Rubén Morales as Minister of the Economy in mid-June was followed later that month by those of the Minister of Energy and Mines, Carlos Meany, and the Minister of Public Finance, Juan Alberto Fuentes Knight. Fuentes' replacement, Edgar Balsells, was removed from the Government in November; he reportedly claimed that he had been dismissed for seeking to reduce expenditure on social programmes overseen by Colom's wife, Sandra Torres de Colom. The Government's ability to pursue its legislative agenda had been severely hampered by the UNE's lack of a congressional majority, the party's position having been weakened further by the defection of a number of its deputies to Libertad Democrática Renovada (LIDER), a dissident legislative bloc created in 2009.

The director of CICIG, Carlos Castresana Fernández, resigned in June 2010, expressing frustration with the Government's failure to co-operate in the commission's efforts and urging Colom to dismiss the recently appointed Attorney-General, Conrado Reyes, who he alleged had strong links to organized crime. The Constitutional Court subsequently ruled that the selection process leading to the appointment of Reyes had been unconstitutional, resulting in his removal from the post. The naming of Claudia Paz y Paz Bailey, a lawyer and human rights activist, as Attorney-General in December was welcomed by civil society groups. Also in that month, a further extension of CICIG's mandate, to 2013, was approved by the UN. (A further, final, extension of the mandate, to September 2015, was granted in 2013.)

President Colom declared a 30-day state of siege in the northern department of Alta Verapaz in December 2010, in response to reports that much of the department was under the control of a Mexican drugs cartel, Los Zetas. A further state of siege was enforced in Petén in May following the massacre of 27 people by Los Zetas. (Nine Los Zetas members were sentenced to between 106 and 114 years' imprisonment for the murders in February 2014.) The arrest in mid-2011 of several former high-ranking members of the security forces indicated that progress was being made in bringing to justice the alleged perpetrators of serious human rights violations during the civil conflict. Moreover, in an unprecedented ruling, four former soldiers were sentenced to life imprisonment in August after being found guilty of massacring over 200 villagers in 1982; a fifth suspect also received a life sentence in March 2012. Later in March four former PAC members and an ex-military officer were jailed for life for participating in a separate 1982 massacre, which claimed the lives of 256 indigenous Guatemalans. Meanwhile, a former high-ranking police official, Pedro García Arredondo, was given a 70-year gaol term in August 2012 for orchestrating the 'disappearance' of a student in 1981. In January 2015 García Arredondo was also found guilty of organizing a deadly attack on the Spanish embassy in 1980, in which almost 40 people were killed, and was sentenced to a further 40 years in gaol. Furthermore, García Arredondo was held responsible for the deaths of two students in a separate incident, for which his sentence was increased by an additional 50 years.

Pérez Molina in office

Despite a constitutional provision barring those related to the incumbent President from contesting the presidency, in March 2011 Colom's wife, Sandra Torres de Colom, announced that she intended to compete in the upcoming election as the candidate of the UNE and GANA. Ostensibly to facilitate this objective, Torres and Colom divorced in the following month. However, the Supreme Electoral Tribunal regarded this move as a fraudulent attempt to bypass the Constitution and in June rejected Torres' candidacy. This ruling was endorsed by the Supreme Electoral Court and the Supreme Court in July and the Constitutional Court in August. With Torres' legal options exhausted and the registration deadline expired, the UNE-GANA coalition was unable to field a presidential candidate in the 11 September election.

The presidential and legislative polls took place peacefully, although the pre-election period had been marred by political violence. In the general election, the PP gained control of 56 seats in the 158-seat Congress, while the UNE-GANA (which terminated their alliance later that month) secured 48, LIDER and the Unión del Cambio Nacional 14 each, and Compromiso, Renovación y Orden 12; the remaining 14 seats were distributed among six smaller parties and coalitions. No candidate secured an outright victory in the presidential contest, so a second round of voting between the two leading contenders—the PP's Gen. (retd) Otto Fernando Pérez Molina and Manuel Antonio Baldizón Méndez of LIDER—was held 6 November. Pérez Molina triumphed in the run-off election, receiving 53.7% of the valid votes cast. The rate of participation by the electorate was recorded at 69.3% in the legislative poll and at 69.4% and 60.8% in the first and second rounds, respectively, of the presidential election.

Pérez Molina was sworn in as President on 14 January 2012, becoming the first head of state with a military background since the end of the civil conflict. His new Government was dominated by the PP, although the foreign affairs and agriculture portfolios were allocated to members of the Visión con Valores-Encuentro por Guatemala. A new Ministry of Social Development was also established, which was to focus on poverty reduction initiatives.

To address the country's crime problems, in January 2012 Pérez Molina announced plans for the further involvement of the military in police operations, in spite of the fact that this was in breach of the 1996 peace treaty. He also proposed recruiting an additional 10,000 police officers. Anti-crime measures introduced in mid-2012 included the establishment of a training facility for senior police officials to boost professionalism in the force, the creation of two additional military bases, and the temporary, but controversial, deployment of a contingent of US troops, who were to aid the Guatemalan authorities in combating drugs-smuggling. The PNC reported that the number of murders had declined to 5,174 in 2012, down from 5,681 in 2011 and 6,498 in 2009. The number of recorded homicides rose slightly in 2013, to 5,259, before decreasing to 4,998 in 2014.

In January 2012 Ríos Montt, whose immunity from prosecution had expired with the end of his term as a deputy in the previous Congress, was charged with genocide and other serious crimes dating from his 1982–83 presidency. This development, along with the concurrent ratification of the Rome Statute of the International Criminal Court, alleviated some of the concerns expressed by Pérez Molina's critics, who feared that the new President might obstruct the ongoing investigations into military abuses committed during the civil war. The trial of Ríos Montt finally began in March 2013, after delays caused by a series of appeals submitted by his defence team. In April, however, the trial was suspended after a further appeal by the former dictator's defence team. Nevertheless, in early May Ríos Montt was found guilty of crimes against humanity and sentenced to 80 years' imprisonment, although 10 days later the Constitutional Court overturned this verdict on the basis that the trial should not have resumed until all the defence appeals had been heard. The decision was condemned internationally and by human rights organizations. Nevertheless, the Court ruled that the proceedings of the trial remained valid. The trial of the former dictator recommenced in January 2015, but was immediately suspended following a defence appeal over the impartiality of one of the presiding judges.

The death of an environmental activist in Santa Cruz Barillas, Huehuetenango, in May 2012 prompted rioting and the declaration of a 30-day state of siege in the municipality, although this was rescinded later that month following anti-Government demonstrations. There was also unrest in the capital in July, when a protest against proposed education reforms (which would increase the cost of teacher-training courses) turned violent; the Ministers of Education and the Interior were injured during the disturbances. In October the military resorted to the use of deadly force against six indigenous demonstrators during a march in Totonicapán organized by social activists and opponents of the Government's education plans. In spite of this atrocity, which generated widespread outrage as well as further questions regarding the propriety of the administration's hard-line security strategy, Pérez Molina continued to defend the use of soldiers as auxiliary police officers. Following violent clashes between anti-mining demonstrators and the police in San Rafael Las Flores, Santa Rosa, another 30-day state of siege was announced in May 2013, affecting several municipalities within Santa Rosa and Jalapa. Further social unrest was reported during 2013–14, with numerous demonstrations staged in protest against the Government's education, energy, mining and rural development policies. In late May 2014 the Office of the UN High Commissioner for Human Rights censured the Guatemalan authorities for violently suppressing an anti-mining demonstration near Guatemala City earlier that month; 28 people sustained injuries as a result of the police operation. In September a temporary state of prevention, which imposed limitations on the right to assemble, was declared in San Juan Sacatepéquez after 11 people lost their lives in violent clashes between protesters and proponents of controversial plans to establish a large-scale cement plant and a major highway in the municipality.

Meanwhile, in August 2012 Pérez Molina proposed a series of constitutional changes, providing for judicial reform, a reduction in the number of congressional seats and the increased use of the military in civilian policing. However, political and popular reaction to these proposals was subdued, and in November Pérez Molina suspended the constitutional review process in the Congress, citing funding concerns. The President was more successful in his efforts to reduce high-level corruption, with an anti-graft bill receiving legislative approval in October. Pérez Molina reorganized the Cabinet in January 2013, appointing Luis Fernando Carrera Castro as Minister of Foreign Affairs and Elmer Alberto López Rodríguez as Minister of Agriculture, Livestock and Food. Ostensibly in response to an upturn in the murder rate, in July the President also replaced the Director-General of the PNC and the Minister of National Defence. In a further cabinet reorganization in January 2014, María Concepción Castro Mazariegos was named as the new Minister of Public Finance and Michelle Martínez received the environment and natural resources portfolio. More controversially, in the following month the Constitutional Court upheld an appeal, submitted by a businessman with links to several right-wing parties, that resulted in Attorney-General Paz y Paz's four-year mandate being reduced by seven months. The judgment elicited expressions of concern from CICIG and civil liberties groups, which feared that Paz y Paz's successor would be less willing to address the issue of impunity. Thelma Esperanza Aldana Hernández, a conservative, was installed as the new Attorney-General in May. Also in that month, the Congress adopted a controversial resolution asserting that no acts of genocide had been committed during the civil conflict—a move that attracted criticism from Amnesty International and the Inter-American Commission on Human Rights. Castro was succeeded as Minister of Public Finance by Dorval Carías in June. Further cabinet changes were announced in September; most notably, Carlos Raúl Morales Moscoso was designated as the new Minister of Foreign Affairs and Luis Enrique Monterroso became Minister of Public Health and Social Welfare.

Recent developments: 2015 elections

Presidential and legislative polls were due to be held in September 2015. The UNE selected Torres as its presidential candidate in mid-2013, while the ruling PP nominated Alejandro Sinibaldi, the minister responsible for communications, in early 2014. Baldizón was again chosen to contest the presidential election as LIDER's representative. In December investigators in Brazil uncovered documents that intimated that a Brazilian construction company, OAS, which had been involved in development projects in Guatemala, had made illegal donations (totalling US $1m.) to Sinibaldi's election campaign through the Brazilian Banco Nacional do Desenvolvimento Econômico e Social (BNDES). Sinibaldi rejected this accusation. Later that month the Government severed ties with the BNDES in an apparent attempt to distance the PP and its presidential candidate from these potentially damaging allegations. However, in April 2015 Sinibaldi resigned from the PP. Later that month anti-

Government demonstrations took place in protest at corruption in government. The protests followed the arrests of several senior officials, including the head of the tax agency, on smuggling charges, following an investigation by CICIG.

Foreign Affairs

Until the return to civilian government in 1986, Guatemala remained steadfast in its claims to the neighbouring territory of Belize. However, Guatemala's new Constitution did not include Belize in its delineation of Guatemalan territory. In 1991 Guatemala and Belize signed an accord under the terms of which Belize pledged to legislate to reduce its maritime boundaries and to allow Guatemala access to the Caribbean Sea and use of its port facilities. In return, Guatemala officially recognized Belize as an independent state and established diplomatic relations. Nevertheless, in 1994 Guatemala formally reaffirmed its territorial claim to Belize. In 2000 the Organization of American States (OAS, see p. 392) established a panel of negotiators to supervise the process of bilateral negotiations. Talks in 2001 focused on the issue of Guatemalans living in the disputed border area; an agreement was later reached to relocate the families.

In 2002 relations with Belize appeared to improve following further OAS-mediated discussions on the border issue; proposals were outlined for a solution to the dispute. These included the provision that Guatemala would recognize Belize's land boundary as set out in the Treaty of 1859, and the creation of a model settlement for peasants and landless farmers in the disputed area. In 2003 the foreign ministers of both countries signed a co-operation agreement pending a final settlement of the dispute. In 2004 delegations from the two countries participated in OAS-sponsored negotiations to establish a series of initiatives designed to promote mutual confidence, and in 2005 Guatemala and Belize signed an Agreement on a Framework of Negotiation and Confidence Building Measures. A partial free trade accord entered into force in 2009. In 2008 the ministers of foreign affairs of Guatemala and Belize signed an agreement, subject to ratification by referendum, to submit the dispute to the International Court of Justice (ICJ). In September 2010 the Guatemalan Congress approved the agreement. In November 2011 the ministers responsible for foreign affairs of Guatemala and Belize agreed that concurrent referendums on the issue would be conducted; the date for the plebiscite was set for October 2013, although this was later postponed at Guatemala's request. An agreement was signed by both countries in January 2014 that established a 'roadmap' for bolstering ties, but it remained unclear when the referendums would be held.

In May 2013 Guatemala was granted permission to join Venezuela's Petrocaribe initiative, whereby Caribbean countries were able to purchase petroleum from Venezuela on preferential terms. However, in November Guatemala revealed that it was withdrawing from the accession proceedings owing to concerns over repayment rates.

CONSTITUTION AND GOVERNMENT

Under the 1986 Constitution (revised in 1994), legislative power is vested in the unicameral Congreso de la República (Congress), with 158 members elected for four years by universal adult suffrage. Of the total seats, 127 are filled by departmental representation and 31 according to national listing. Executive power is held by the President (also directly elected for four years), assisted by a Vice-President and an appointed Cabinet. Judicial power is exercised by the Supreme Court of Justice and other tribunals. For the purposes of local administration the country comprises 22 departments, which are divided into 330 municipalities.

REGIONAL AND INTERNATIONAL CO-OPERATION

Guatemala is a member of the Central American Common Market (see p. 228), of the Organization of American States (see p. 392), and of the Community of Latin American and Caribbean States (see p. 460), which was formally inaugurated in December 2011. Guatemala, El Salvador and Honduras signed a free trade agreement with Mexico in 2000, and a more expansive Central America-Mexico free trade pact came into force in September 2013. In 2004 the Presidents of Guatemala, El Salvador, Honduras and Nicaragua signed an agreement creating a Central American customs union. The Dominican Republic-Central American Free Trade Agreement (CAFTA-DR), between Guatemala, Costa Rica, El Salvador, Honduras, Nicaragua, the Dominican Republic and the USA,

came into effect in 2006. CAFTA-DR entailed the gradual elimination of tariffs on most industrial and agricultural products over a period of 10 and 20 years, respectively. A free trade agreement between Guatemala, with other Central American countries, and the European Union, entered into effect in 2013, while a similar agreement with Peru was ratified. In November 2014 Guatemala, with El Salvador and Honduras, initiated the Plan Alianza para la Prosperidad, a regional economic initiative intended to counter migration to the USA.

Guatemala was a founder member of the UN in 1945. As a contracting party to the General Agreement on Tariffs and Trade, Guatemala joined the World Trade Organization (see p. 431) shortly after its establishment in 1995.

ECONOMIC AFFAIRS

In 2013, according to estimates by the World Bank, Guatemala's gross national income (GNI), measured at average 2011–13 prices, was US $51,626m., equivalent to $3,340 per head (or $7,130 per head on an international purchasing-power parity basis). During 2004–13, it was estimated, the population increased by an average of 2.5% per year, while gross domestic product (GDP) per head increased, in real terms, by an average of 1.1% per year. Overall GDP increased, in real terms, at an average annual rate of 3.6% in 2004–13; according to official preliminary figures, GDP grew by an estimated 3.7% in 2013.

Agriculture, including hunting, forestry and fishing, contributed a preliminary 10.9% of GDP in 2013 and engaged 31.9% of the employed population in April 2014. The principal cash crops are sugar (which accounted for 9.4% of export earnings in 2013), coffee (7.1%) and bananas (6.0%). In recent years the country has successfully expanded production of less traditional crops, such as mangoes, berries and green beans. During 2004–13, according to official preliminary figures, agricultural GDP increased, in real terms, by an estimated average of 3.1% per year; agricultural GDP increased by 4.7% in 2013.

Industry, including mining, manufacturing, construction and power, contributed a preliminary 28.1% of GDP in 2013 and engaged 19.4% of the working population in April 2014. According to official preliminary figures, industrial GDP increased by an estimated average of 2.5% per year in 2004–13. Industrial GDP grew by an estimated 3.4% in 2013.

Mining contributed an estimated 1.9% of GDP in 2013 and employed 0.1% of the working population in 2006. The most important mineral exports are precious metals and stones, which accounted for 4.8% of total export earnings in 2013, and petroleum, which contributed 2.8% of the value of exports in the same year. In addition, copper, antimony, lead, zinc and tungsten are mined on a small scale. There are also deposits of nickel, gold and silver. It was estimated that mining GDP increased by an average of 3.1% per year during 2004–13. The sector decreased by an estimated 19.3% in 2012, but recorded a growth of 3.5% in 2013.

Manufacturing contributed an estimated 19.6% of GDP in 2013 and manufacturing and mining together employed 14.8% of the working population in April 2014. Guatemala's *maquila*, or clothing assembly, sector was an important economic contributor, accounting for 12.7% of the value of exports in 2013. Manufacturing GDP increased by an estimated average of 2.6% per year in 2004–13, according to official preliminary figures. The sector's GDP grew by an estimated 3.4% in 2013.

The construction sector contributed a preliminary 4.2% of GDP in 2013 and engaged 4.6% of the employed labour force in April 2014. During 2004–13 the GDP of the sector decreased at an estimated average annual rate of 0.6%. Construction GDP increased by an estimated 1.7% in 2013.

Energy is derived principally from mineral fuels and hydro-electric power. Hydroelectric power was responsible for a decreasing proportion of total power output, accounting for 39.8% of electricity generation in 2011, compared with 57.6% in 1997, while power generation from coal sources increased from 0.7% in 1999 to 14.4% in 2011. Petroleum provided 18.7% of electric energy in 2011. Guatemala is a marginal producer of petroleum and, in 2013, produced on average 14,000 barrels per day. According to estimates, proven petroleum reserves amounted to 83m. barrels in 2014, while reserves of natural gas totalled some 110,000m. cu ft in 2006. Imports of mineral products comprised 19.7% of the value of total imports in 2012. Efforts have been made in recent years to reduce Guatemala's dependency on oil; some US $1,800m. was invested in the construction of three coal-based generators and five hydroelectric plants by 2014, although plans for the latter met with opposition from local communities affected by construction. The Comision Nacional de Energía Eléctrica in 2013 announced plans to increase 'clean' energy use to 80% of total usage by 2026.

In 2013 the services sector contributed a preliminary 60.9% of GDP and employed 48.7% of the working population in April 2014. The GDP of the services sector increased by an estimated average of 4.9% per year in 2004–13; growth in the sector was an estimated 4.1% in 2013.

In 2013 Guatemala recorded a visible merchandise trade deficit of US $6,165.2m., and there was a deficit of $1,514.4m. on the current account of the balance of payments. In 2013 the principal source of imports (37.0%) was the USA; other major suppliers were Mexico and the People's Republic of China. The USA was the principal market for exports (taking 37.7% of exports in that year); other significant purchasers were El Salvador, Honduras and Nicaragua. The main exports in 2013 were clothing, sugar, coffee, bananas, and precious metals and stones. The principal imports were electrical machinery and apparatus, diesel oil, vehicles and transport equipment, motor gas, and plastics. Remittances from citizens working abroad represented the second largest hard currency inflow into the country, after non-traditional exports. According to Banco de Guatemala, in 2014 remittances from the USA totalled $5,544.1m.

In 2013 there was a preliminary budgetary deficit of 9,009.8m. quetzales, equivalent to some 2.1% of GDP. Guatemala's general government gross debt was 104,083m. quetzales in 2013, equivalent to 24.6% of GDP. In 2012 Guatemala's total external debt stood at US $14,975m., of which $6,145m. was public and publicly guaranteed debt. In that year, the cost of servicing long-term public and publicly guaranteed debt and repayments to the IMF was equivalent to 10.9% of the value of exports of goods, services and income (excluding workers' remittances). In 2004–13 the average annual rate of inflation was 6.0%. Consumer prices increased by an average of 4.3% in 2013. An estimated 2.9% of the labour force were unemployed in April 2014, and a further 14.4% were described as underemployed.

The Dominican Republic-Central American Free Trade Agreement (CAFTA-DR) with the USA was considered vital to the future development of the Guatemalan economy, which suffered from large trade deficits. The implementation of CAFTA-DR brought greater access to US markets and encouraged economic diversification. Given the price volatility of agricultural goods exported by Guatemala, the steady inflow of remittances from abroad (primarily the USA) tended to offset shortfalls in foreign exchange earnings. Major obstacles to economic growth included the country's weak human capital base, high rates of violent crime and rampant corruption, all of which deterred foreign investment. The economy was also overly dependent on the performance of the US economy, with the USA accounting for almost 40% of exports. In 2012 the Congress approved legislation to restructure the taxation system, which was expected to lead to a further increase in tax receipts. Measures were also introduced to reduce the high levels of tax evasion. Real GDP growth rose to 3.7% in 2013 (from 3.0% in 2012), owing to the strength of the tourism sector, domestic consumption, remittance inflows and increased foreign direct investment (FDI). A falling murder rate (although remaining relatively high) was also expected to boost tourism and FDI, although persistent perceived widespread corruption and high levels of poverty continued to offset this improvement. Domestic demand remained robust in 2014, and FDI and remittances continued to increase. However, the agricultural sector was negatively affected by a severe drought from mid-2014, which threatened to undermine food security in many parts of the country. In August the Government announced a state of emergency in 16 departments, and emergency measures remained in place in early 2015. The IMF estimated that the economy expanded by 3.4% in 2014 and projected further growth of 3.7% in 2015.

PUBLIC HOLIDAYS

2016: 1 January (New Year's Day), 24–25 March (Maundy Thursday and Good Friday), 1 May (Labour Day), 1 July (for Anniversary of the Revolution), 15 August (Assumption, Guatemala City only), 16 September (for Independence Day), 14 October (for Columbus Day), 21 October (for Revolution Day), 1 November (All Saints' Day), 24 December (Christmas Eve, afternoon only), 25 December (Christmas Day), 31 December (New Year's Eve, afternoon only).

Statistical Survey

Sources (unless otherwise stated): Banco de Guatemala, 7a Avda 22-01, Zona 1, Apdo 365, Guatemala City; tel. 2429-6000; fax 2253-4035; internet www.banguat .gob.gt; Instituto Nacional de Estadística, Edif. América, 4°, 8a Calle 9-55, Zona 1, Guatemala City; tel. 2232-6212; e-mail info-ine@ine.gob.gt; internet www.ine .gob.gt.

Area and Population

AREA, POPULATION AND DENSITY

Area (sq km)	
Land	108,429
Inland water	460
Total	108,889*
Population (census results)†	
17 April 1994	8,322,051
24 November 2002	
Males	5,496,839
Females	5,740,357
Total	11,237,196
Population (official estimates at mid-year)	
2012	15,073,375
2013	15,438,384
2014	15,806,675
Density (per sq km) at mid-2014	145.8

* 42,042 sq miles.
† Excluding adjustments for underenumeration.

POPULATION BY AGE AND SEX
(official estimates at mid-2014)

	Males	Females	Total
0–14 years	3,211,309	3,106,183	6,317,492
15–64 years	4,174,203	4,600,640	8,774,843
65 years and over	333,884	380,456	714,340
Total	7,719,396	8,087,279	15,806,675

DEPARTMENTS
(official estimates at mid-2014)

Alta Verapaz . .	1,219,585		Quetzaltenango .	844,906
Baja Verapaz . .	291,903		Quiché	1,053,737
Chimaltenango .	666,938		Retalhuleu . .	325,556
Chiquimula . .	397,202		Sacatepéquez . .	336,606
El Progreso . . .	166,397		San Marcos . .	1,095,997
Escuintla . . .	746,309		Santa Rosa . . .	367,569
Guatemala . . .	3,306,397		Sololá	477,705
Huehuetenango .	1,234,593		Suchitepéquez . .	555,261
Izabal	445,125		Totonicapán . .	521,995
Jalapa	345,926		Zacapa	232,667
Jutiapa	462,714			
Petén	711,585		**Total**	15,806,675

PRINCIPAL TOWNS
(official population estimates at mid-2014)

Guatemala City .	993,815	San Juan Sacatepéquez .	231,721
Villa Nueva . . .	552,535	Escuintla . . .	158,456
Mixco	491,619	Quetzaltenango .	157,559
Cobán	250,675	Jalapa . . .	156,419
San Pedro Carcha .	235,213	Totonicapán . .	141,751

BIRTHS, MARRIAGES AND DEATHS

	Registered live births		Registered marriages		Registered deaths	
	Number	Rate (per 1,000)	Number	Rate (per 1,000)	Number	Rate (per 1,000)
2006 . .	368,399	28.3	57,505	4.4	69,756	5.4
2007 . .	366,128	26.8	57,003	4.3	70,030	5.2
2008 . .	369,769	26.4	52,315	3.8	70,233	5.1
2009 . .	351,628	25.1	62,104	4.4	67,284	4.8
2010 . .	361,906	25.2	73,124	5.1	72,748	5.1
2011 . .	373,692	25.4	78,286	5.3	72,354	4.9
2012 . .	388,613	25.8	84,253	5.6	72,657	4.8
2013 . .	387,342	25.2	80,750	5.2	76,639	5.0

Life expectancy (years at birth): 71.7 (males 68.2; females 75.3) in 2012 (Source: World Bank, World Development Indicators database).

ECONOMICALLY ACTIVE POPULATION
(population aged 15 years and over, employment and income survey at April 2014)

	Males	Females	Total
Agriculture, forestry, hunting and fishing	1,681,195	229,429	1,910,624
Mining and quarrying; manufacturing	522,835	363,827	886,662
Construction	274,061	3,426	277,487
Wholesale and retail trade; transport and storage; hotels and restaurants	817,099	786,796	1,603,895
Information and communications .	35,781	8,547	44,328
Financial and insurance services .	34,315	32,011	66,326
Real estate activities . . .	1,833	2,981	4,814
Professional, scientific, administrative and support services	116,251	58,140	174,391
Public administration and defence; education; health; social assistance	255,539	296,941	552,480
Other services	120,981	346,187	467,168
Total employed	3,859,890	2,128,285	5,988,175
Unemployed	96,866	83,429	180,295
Total labour force	3,956,756	2,211,714	6,168,470

Health and Welfare

KEY INDICATORS

Total fertility rate (children per woman, 2012)	3.8
Under-5 mortality rate (per 1,000 live births, 2012) . . .	32
HIV/AIDS (% of persons aged 15–49, 2013)	0.6
Physicians (per 1,000 head, 2009)	0.9
Hospital beds (per 1,000 head, 2010)	0.6
Health expenditure (2011): US $ per head (PPP)	329
Health expenditure (2011): % of GDP	6.7
Health expenditure (2011): public (% of total)	35.4
Access to water (% of persons, 2012)	94
Access to sanitation (% of persons, 2012)	80
Total carbon dioxide emissions ('000 metric tons, 2010) .	11,118.3
Carbon dioxide emissions per head (metric tons, 2010) . .	0.8
Human Development Index (2013): ranking	125
Human Development Index (2013): value	0.628

For sources and definitions, see explanatory note on p. vi.

Agriculture

PRINCIPAL CROPS
('000 metric tons)

	2011	2012	2013
Maize	1,672.2	1,723.8	1,731.8
Potatoes	493.0	507.4	521.9
Sugar cane	20,586.1	23,653.0	26,334.7
Oil palm fruit*	1,260.0	1,440.0	1,480.0
Tomatoes	305.4	314.9	320.3
Watermelons*	128.3	130.0	128.0
Cantaloupes and other melons .	497.2	540.0	569.1
Bananas	2,679.9	3,078.6	3,188.1
Plantains	188.8	197.5	197.1
Lemons and limes	120.7	120.8	120.9
Guavas, mangoes and mangosteens	116.3	113.5	114.6
Pineapples	234.5	243.5	243.6
Coffee, green	265.4	272.7	253.2
Tobacco, unmanufactured* . .	22.4	24.0	24.5

* FAO estimate(s).

Aggregate production ('000 metric tons, may include official, semi-official or estimated data): Total cereals 1,752.8 in 2011, 1,799.9 in 2012, 1,808.8 in 2013; Total pulses 244.4 in 2011, 265.9 in 2012, 271.8 in 2013; Total roots and tubers 511.5 in 2011, 527.5 in 2012, 542.0 in 2013; Total vegetables (incl. melons) 1,599.0 in 2011, 1,680.4 in 2012, 1,724.6 in 2013; Total fruits (excl. melons) 3,900.8 in 2011, 4,313.7 in 2012, 4,422.9 in 2013.

Source: FAO.

LIVESTOCK
('000 head, year ending September)

	2011	2012	2013
Horses*	128	130	130
Asses*	9.9	10.0	10.0
Mules*	38.7	39.0	39.0
Cattle	3,323	3,340	3,367
Sheep*	612	614	616
Pigs	2,734	2,743	2,769
Goats*	130	132	134
Chickens*	34,000	35,000	36,000

* FAO estimates.

LIVESTOCK PRODUCTS
('000 metric tons)

	2011	2012	2013
Cattle meat*	81.0	83.0	83.4
Pig meat*	60.0	61.5	61.5
Chicken meat	190.5	189.8†	192.3†
Cows' milk	463.1	484.4	496.2
Hen eggs†	224.5	231.7	238.5
Honey*	3.5	3.6	3.7

* FAO estimates.
† Unofficial figure(s).

Source: FAO.

Forestry

ROUNDWOOD REMOVALS
('000 cubic metres, excl. bark)

	2011	2012	2013
Sawlogs, veneer logs and logs for sleepers	837	528	651
Other industrial wood	15	15	15
Fuel wood*	18,410	18,768	19,133
Total*	19,262	19,311	19,799

* FAO estimates.

Source: FAO.

SAWNWOOD PRODUCTION
('000 cubic metres, incl. railway sleepers, FAO estimates)

	2011	2012	2013
Coniferous (softwood) . . .	40	39	39
Broadleaved (hardwood) . . .	103*	55	90
Total	143*	94	129

* Unofficial figure.

Source: FAO.

Fishing

('000 metric tons, live weight)

	2010	2011	2012
Capture*	21.9	19.7	19.6
Freshwater fishes*	2.3	2.3	2.3
Skipjack tuna	7.0	6.7	7.3*
Yellowfin tuna	5.6	6.3	6.2*
Bigeye tuna	3.7	2.0*	2.0*
Penaeus shrimps	0.7	0.6	0.3
Pacific seabobs	1.3	0.9	0.5
Aquaculture	22.8	21.5*	17.7*
Other tilapias	0.8	5.5	5.4
Penaeus shrimps	21.9	15.9	12.3
Total catch*	44.7	41.2	37.3

* FAO estimate(s).

Source: FAO.

Mining

('000 metric tons unless otherwise indicated)

	2010	2011	2012
Crude petroleum ('000 barrels) .	4,363	3,995	4,000*
Gold (kg)	9,213	11,898	6,473
Silver (kg)	194,683	272,771	204,555
Limestone	4,910	n.a.	2,000*
Sand and gravel ('000 cu m) . .	88	81	261

* Estimated figure.

Source: US Geological Survey.

Industry

SELECTED PRODUCTS
('000 metric tons unless otherwise indicated)

	2009	2010	2011
Sugar (raw)	2,382	2,495	2,346
Cement*	1,500	1,500	1,600
Electric energy (million kWh) .	9,039	8,832	8,146

* Estimates from US Geological Survey.

Cement ('000 metric tons, US Geological Survey estimates): 1,700 in 2012.

Source (unless otherwise indicated): UN Industrial Commodity Statistics Database.

Finance

CURRENCY AND EXCHANGE RATES

Monetary Units
100 centavos = 1 quetzal.

Sterling, Dollar and Euro Equivalents (31 December 2014)
£1 sterling = 11.855 quetzales;
US $1 = 7.595 quetzales;
€1 = 9.222 quetzales;
1,000 quetzales = £84.35 = $131.66 = €108.44.

Average Exchange Rate (quetzales per US dollar)
2012   7.8336
2013   7.8568
2014   7.7322

Note: In December 2000 legislation was approved to allow the circulation of the US dollar and other convertible currencies, for use in a wide range of transactions, from 1 May 2001.

BUDGET
(central government operations, million quetzales)

Revenue	2011	2012	2013*
Current revenue	43,165.2	45,855.1	49,250.3
Tax revenue	40,292.2	42,819.8	46,335.5
Direct taxes	12,710.5	13,453.7	16,052.8
Excise taxes	27,581.7	29,366.1	30,282.7
Non-tax revenue	2,873.0	3,035.3	2,914.8
Social Security	1,214.4	1,273.6	1,273.6
Current transfers	587.8	587.8	587.8
Capital revenue	12.9	18.7	8.8
Total	43,178.1	45,873.8	49,259.2

Expenditure	2011	2012	2013*
Current expenditure	38,774.2	42,307.5	45,555.3
Wages and salaries . . .	14,155.7	15,080.6	16,967.9
Use of goods and services . .	7,218.2	8,760.5	8,709.6
Interest	5,475.7	6,022.3	6,569.0
Discounts and rewards . .	184.9	170.8	228.5
Transfers	8,592.6	8,967.5	9,499.4
Social benefits	3,147.1	3,305.9	3,580.9
Capital expenditure	14,736.8	13,012.0	12,713.7
Total	53,511.0	55,319.6	58,269.0

* Preliminary figures.

Source: Ministry of Finance, Guatemala City.

INTERNATIONAL RESERVES
(US $ million at 31 December)

	2011	2012	2013
Gold (national valuation) . . .	348.9	368.8	266.3
IMF special drawing rights . .	266.4	267.6	270.5
Foreign exchange	5,568.5	6,057.4	6,731.8
Total	6,183.8	6,693.8	7,268.6

Source: IMF, *International Financial Statistics*.

MONEY SUPPLY
(million quetzales at 31 December)

	2011	2012	2013
Currency outside depository corporations	20,510.5	21,227.0	21,964.9
Transferable deposits	52,138.2	56,655.2	60,706.0
Other deposits	88,477.4	98,176.5	110,332.2
Securities other than shares . .	5,135.4	5,766.0	6,179.7
Broad money	166,261.5	181,824.7	199,182.8

Source: IMF, *International Financial Statistics*.

COST OF LIVING
(Consumer Price Index at December; base: December 2010 = 100)

	2011	2012	2013
Food and non-alcoholic beverages .	112.1	118.8	129.3
Housing, water, electricity and gas	105.8	105.6	110.4
Clothing and footwear	103.0	106.2	108.2
All items (incl. others) . . .	106.2	109.9	114.7

All items (Consumer Price Index, annual averages; base: December 2010 = 100): 104.2 in 2011; 108.2 in 2012; 112.9 in 2013.

NATIONAL ACCOUNTS
(million quetzales at current prices)

Expenditure on the Gross Domestic Product

	2011	2012*	2013*
Government final consumption expenditure	37,803.2	40,844.9	44,637.9
Private final consumption expenditure	316,528.2	339,236.0	366,018.6
Increase in stocks	1,592.1	649.6	–1,127.0
Gross fixed capital formation .	54,910.0	58,379.5	60,433.7
Total domestic expenditure	410,833.5	439,110.0	469,963.2
Exports of goods and services .	98,783.4	98,162.5	100,248.6
Less Imports of goods and services	138,605.4	142,549.4	147,105.2
GDP in purchasers' values .	371,011.6	394,723.0	423,106.6
GDP at constant 2001 prices .	207,776.0	213,946.6	221,820.0

Gross Domestic Product by Economic Activity

	2011	2012*	2013*
Agriculture, hunting, forestry and fishing	41,088.7	41,657.8	44,988.0
Mining and quarrying	10,512.2	8,604.2	7,813.2
Manufacturing	69,183.1	75,472.7	80,720.7
Electricity, gas and water . .	7,546.0	8,736.3	9,790.7
Construction	14,738.8	16,446.1	17,278.2
Trade, restaurants and hotels .	75,455.2	82,900.1	92,428.4
Transport, storage and communications	29,105.0	30,515.0	31,820.0
Finance, insurance and real estate	11,518.9	12,953.7	14,301.0
Ownership of dwellings . . .	30,448.4	31,712.8	33,018.4
General government services .	24,374.0	25,670.3	27,226.4
Other community, social and personal services	44,334.5	47,513.4	51,705.6
Sub-total	358,304.7	382,182.5	411,090.7
Less Financial intermediation services indirectly measured (FISIM)	10,646.4	11,591.4	12,829.9
Gross value added in basic prices	347,658.3	370,591.1	398,260.8
Taxes on imports, less subsidies .	23,353.3	24,131.9	24,845.8
GDP in purchasers' values .	371,011.6	394,723.0	423,106.6

* Preliminary figures.

BALANCE OF PAYMENTS
(US $ million)

	2011	2012	2013
Exports of goods	10,518.7	10,102.7	10,190.3
Imports of goods	–15,482.1	–15,837.7	–16,355.6
Balance on goods	–4,963.5	–5,735.0	–6,165.2
Exports of services	2,238.8	2,435.0	2,523.9
Imports of services	–2,516.8	–2,539.4	–2,725.4
Balance on goods and services	–5,241.4	–5,839.5	–6,366.7
Primary income received . . .	413.6	447.0	453.5
Primary income paid . . .	–1,904.7	–1,562.2	–1,550.2
Balance on goods, services and primary income	–6,732.5	–6,954.7	–7,463.4
Secondary income received . .	5,092.6	5,632.7	5,988.3
Secondary income paid . . .	–32.0	–29.6	–39.3

—*continued*	2011	2012	2013
Current balance	–1,671.8	–1,351.5	–1,514.4
Capital account (net) . . .	2.6	—	—
Direct investment assets . .	–130.8	–58.1	–75.1
Direct investment liabilities . .	1,139.7	1,263.6	1,350.1
Portfolio investment assets .	–143.4	–8.7	5.9
Portfolio investment liabilities .	–297.7	–1.5	11.0
Other investment assets . .	–648.7	78.0	–282.1
Other investment liabilities . .	2,058.7	256.4	1,091.9
Net errors and omissions . . .	–224.4	–453.5	–349.5
Reserves and related items .	84.1	–275.3	237.7

Source: IMF, *International Financial Statistics*.

External Trade

PRINCIPAL COMMODITIES
(US $ million)

Imports c.i.f.	2011	2012	2013
Textile materials	667.0	635.7	640.5
Gas-diesel (distillate fuel) oil . .	1,178.2	1,248.6	1,252.7
Motor spirit (gasoline)	991.1	1,029.0	1,067.5
Other petroleum derivatives . .	622.4	599.4	494.3
Chemical products	625.7	661.2	684.1
Pharmaceutical products . . .	503.2	528.3	595.9
Plastics and manufactures thereof	959.7	922.3	998.6
Transmitting and receiving apparatus	442.4	421.5	491.4
Electrical machinery and apparatus	1,405.1	1,531.4	1,621.3
Vehicles and transport equipment	1,133.7	1,273.7	1,190.6
Total (incl. others)	16,613.0	16,994.0	17,514.7

Exports f.o.b.	2011	2012	2013
Coffee	1,174.2	958.1	714.5
Bananas	475.3	499.9	601.5
Beverages, spirits and vinegar .	222.9	321.5	337.5
Sugar	648.8	803.0	941.9
Edible fats and oils	330.9	361.0	361.8
Natural rubber	397.4	295.0	239.5
Crude petroleum	335.4	291.7	277.3
Articles of clothing	1,216.4	1,189.5	1,270.8
Plastics and manufactures thereof	270.7	299.2	290.4
Precious metals and stones . .	941.6	612.9	482.7
Total (incl. others)	10,400.9	9,978.7	10,031.2

PRINCIPAL TRADING PARTNERS
(US $ million)

Imports c.i.f.	2011	2012	2013
Argentina	91.4	162.5	186.9
Brazil	274.7	250.8	249.3
China, People's Republic . . .	1,144.2	1,265.0	1,438.5
Colombia	596.8	551.4	767.6
Costa Rica	455.5	476.8	519.8
Ecuador	184.0	224.2	134.7
El Salvador	820.4	777.0	820.0
Germany	256.1	278.1	289.4
Honduras	344.7	367.1	394.8
Hong Kong	169.4	193.7	194.1
India	162.1	242.7	241.0
Japan	303.9	276.3	255.1
Korea, Republic	369.0	427.2	405.0
Mexico	1,858.9	1,915.7	1,860.3
Panama	476.8	544.4	584.9
Spain	171.9	186.5	222.1
USA	6,508.6	6,460.4	6,488.8
Total (incl. others)	16,613.0	16,994.0	17,514.7

Exports f.o.b.	2011	2012	2013
Belgium	110.2	75.1	62.2
Canada	158.7	149.4	159.5
Chile	135.6	130.1	107.7
China, People's Republic	28.8	34.7	167.2
Costa Rica	404.3	424.5	396.2
Dominican Republic	127.2	115.5	127.6
El Salvador	1,132.3	1,110.7	1,108.8
Germany	145.2	119.6	88.1
Honduras	814.7	795.5	791.0
Italy	106.5	84.6	61.4
Japan	212.2	176.7	188.7
Korea, Republic	125.0	53.1	151.5
Mexico	512.3	550.1	469.6
Netherlands	136.2	169.2	252.6
Nicaragua	459.1	473.4	486.9
Panama	247.4	246.4	237.3
USA	4,307.5	3,955.0	3,786.1
Total (incl. others)	10,400.9	9,977.6	10,031.2

Tourism

TOURIST ARRIVALS BY COUNTRY OF ORIGIN

	2011	2012	2013
Belize	35,960	35,481	40,303
Canada	42,719	53,696	52,955
Costa Rica	42,039	44,984	46,417
El Salvador	542,316	604,871	638,058
Honduras	223,010	235,680	220,497
Mexico	132,661	144,076	152,506
Nicaragua	74,362	77,238	77,691
USA	429,216	434,175	446,814
Total (incl. others)	1,822,663	1,951,173	2,000,126

Tourism receipts (US $ million, excl. passenger transport): 937.2 in 2011; 986.8 in 2012; 1,020.6 in 2013.

Source: Guatemalan Institute of Tourism.

Transport

ROAD TRAFFIC
(motor vehicles in use)

	2011	2012	2013
Passenger cars	555,785	576,821	601,343
Buses and coaches	97,748	99,579	101,623
Lorries and vans	484,090	505,576	521,603
Motorcycles and mopeds	656,590	756,438	863,991
Total (incl. others)	2,222,182	2,389,240	2,562,925

SHIPPING

Flag Registered Fleet
(at 31 December)

	2012	2013	2014
Number of vessels	6	6	9
Total displacement ('000 grt)	3.0	3.0	5.4

Source: Lloyd's List Intelligence (www.lloydslistintelligence.com).

CIVIL AVIATION
(traffic on scheduled services)

	1997	1998	1999
Kilometres flown (million)	5	7	5
Passengers carried ('000)	508	794	506
Passenger-km (million)	368	480	342
Total ton-km (million)	77	50	33

Source: UN, *Statistical Yearbook*.

Passengers carried ('000): 326.1 in 2011; 288.0 in 2012; 301.3 in 2013 (Source: World Bank, World Development Indicators database).

Communications Media

	2011	2012	2013
Telephones ('000 main lines in use)	1,626.3	1,743.8	1,863.1
Mobile cellular telephones ('000 subscribers)	19,479.1	20,787.1	21,716.4
Broadband subscribers ('000)	n.a.	273.7	278.8

Internet users ('000) 2,279.4 in 2009.

Source: International Telecommunication Union.

Education

(2010/11 unless otherwise indicated)

	Institutions	Teachers	Students
Pre-primary	11,859*	26,126	537,265
Primary	17,499*	100,600	2,644,683
Secondary	4,874*	76,850	1,113,881
Tertiary	1,946†	3,843*	233,885‡

* 2005/06.
† 2003/04.
‡ 2006/07.

Source: mainly UNESCO Institute for Statistics.

Pupil-teacher ratio (primary education, UNESCO estimate): 26.3 in 2010/11 (Source: UNESCO Institute for Statistics).

Adult literacy rate (UNESCO estimates): 78.3% (males 84.8%; females 72.4%) in 2012 (Source: UNESCO Institute for Statistics).

Directory

The Government

HEAD OF STATE

President: Gen. (retd) Otto Fernando Pérez Molina (took office 14 January 2012).

Vice-President: Ingrid Roxana Baldetti Elías.

CABINET
(April 2015)

The Government is formed by the Partido Patriota (PP) and the Visión con Valores-Encuentro por Guatemala (VIVA-EG) coalition.

Minister of Foreign Affairs: Carlos Raúl Morales Moscoso.

Minister of the Interior: Mauricio López Bonilla (PP).

Minister of National Defence: Brig.-Gen. Manuel Augusto López Ambrosio (PP).

Minister of Public Finance: Dorval Carías.

Minister of the Economy: Sergio de la Torre (PP).

Minister of Public Health and Social Welfare: Luis Enrique Monterroso.

Minister of Communications, Infrastructure, Transport and Housing: Víctor Enrique Corado Valdez.

Minister of Agriculture, Livestock and Food: José Sebastián Marcucci Ruíz.

Minister of Education: Cynthia del Aguila (PP).

Minister of Energy and Mines: Erick Archila (PP).

Minister of Culture and Sport: Dwight Pezzarossi.

Minister of the Environment and Natural Resources: MICHELLE MARTÍNEZ.

Minister of Social Development: EDGAR LEONEL RODRÍGUEZ LARA (PP).

Minister of Labour and Social Security: CARLOS CONTRERAS SOLÓRZANO (PP).

MINISTRIES

Ministry of Agriculture, Livestock and Food: Edif. Monja Blanca, Of. 306, 3°, 7a Avda 12-90, Zona 13, Guatemala City; tel. 2413-7000; fax 2413-7352; e-mail infoagro@maga.gob.gt; internet www.maga.gob.gt.

Ministry of Communications, Infrastructure, Transport and Housing: Edif. Antiguo Cocesna, 8a Avda y 15 Calle, Zona 13, Guatemala City; tel. 2223-4000; fax 2362-6059; e-mail relpublicas@micivi.gob.gt; internet www.civ.gob.gt.

Ministry of Culture and Sport: Calle 7, entre Avda 6 y 7, Centro Histórico, Palacio Nacional de la Cultura, Zona 1, Guatemala City; tel. 2239-5000; fax 2253-0540; e-mail info@mcd.gob.gt; internet www.mcd.gob.gt.

Ministry of the Economy: 8a Avda 10-43, Zona 1, Guatemala City; tel. 2412-0439; fax 2412-0200; e-mail infonegocios@mineco.gob.gt; internet www.mineco.gob.gt.

Ministry of Education: 6a Calle 1-87, Zona 10, Guatemala City; tel. 2411-9595; fax 2361-0350; e-mail info@mineduc.gob.gt; internet www.mineduc.gob.gt.

Ministry of Energy and Mines: Diagonal 17, 29-78, Zona 11, Las Charcas, Guatemala City; tel. 2419-6464; fax 2476-2007; e-mail informatica@mem.gob.gt; internet www.mem.gob.gt.

Ministry of the Environment and Natural Resources: Edif. MARN, 20 Calle 28-58, Zona 10, Guatemala City; tel. 2423-0500; e-mail sip@marn.gob.gt; internet www.marn.gob.gt.

Ministry of Foreign Affairs: 2a Avda La Reforma 4-17, Zona 10, Guatemala City; tel. 2410-0010; fax 2410-0011; e-mail webmaster@minex.gob.gt; internet www.minex.gob.gt.

Ministry of the Interior: Antiguo Palacio de la Policía Nacional Civil, 6a Avda 13-71, Zona 1, Guatemala City; tel. 2413-8888; fax 2413-8587; e-mail info@mingob.gob.gt; internet www.mingob.gob.gt.

Ministry of Labour and Social Security: Edif. Torre Empresarial, 7 Avda 3-33, Zona 9, Guatemala City; tel. 2422-2500; fax 2422-2503; e-mail ministro@mintrabajo.gob.gt; internet www.mintrabajo.gob.gt.

Ministry of National Defence: Antiguas Escuela Politécnica, Avda La Reforma 1-45, Zona 10, Guatemala City; tel. 2269-4924; fax 2360-9919; e-mail dip@mindef.mil.gt; internet www.mindef.mil.gt.

Ministry of Public Finance: Centro Cívico, 8a Avda y 21 Calle, Zona 1, Guatemala City; tel. 2248-5005; fax 2248-5054; e-mail info@minfin.gob.gt; internet www.minfin.gob.gt.

Ministry of Public Health and Social Welfare: Escuela de Enfermería, 3°, 6a Avda 3-45, Zona 1, Guatemala City; tel. 2475-2121; fax 2475-1125; e-mail info@mspas.gob.gt; internet www.mspas.gob.gt.

Ministry of Social Development: 3a Avda 6-44, Zona 1, Guatemala City; tel. 2491-0900; internet www.mides.gob.gt.

President and Legislature

PRESIDENT

Presidential Election, 11 September and 6 November 2011

Candidate	First round % of votes	Second round % of votes
Gen. (retd) Otto Fernando Pérez Molina (PP)	36.10	53.74
Manuel Antonio Baldizón Méndez (LIDER)	22.68	46.26
José Eduardo Suger Cofiño (CREO)	16.62	—
Mario Amilcar Estrada Orellana (UCN)	8.72	—
Harold Osberto Caballeros López (VIVA-EG)	6.24	—
Rigoberta Menchú Tum (WINAQ-URNG—MAIZ-ANN)	3.22	—
Juan Guillermo Gutiérrez Strauss (PAN)	2.76	—
Patricia de Arzú (Partido Unionista)	2.19	—
Alejandro Eduardo Giammattei Falla (CASA)	1.05	—
Adela Camacho de Torrebiarte (ADN)	0.42	—
Total valid votes	**100.00**	**100.00**

CONGRESS
(Congreso de la República)

President: ARÍSTIDES CRESPO.

General Election, 11 September 2011

	% of votes	Seats*
Partido Patriota (PP)	26.37	56
Unidad Nacional de la Esperanza-Gran Alianza Nacional (UNE-GANA)	22.24	48
Unión del Cambio Nacional (UCN)	9.48	14
Libertad Democrática Renovada (LIDER)	8.66	14
Compromiso, Renovación y Orden (CREO)	8.77	12
Visión con Valores-Encuentro por Guatemala (VIVA)	7.84	6
WINAQ-Unidad Revolucionaria Nacional Guatemalteca—Movimiento Amplio de Izquierdas-Alternativa Nueva Nación	3.20	3
Partido de Avanzada Nacional (PAN)	3.08	2
Frente Republicano Guatemalteco (FRG)†	2.72	1
Partido Unionista	2.67	1
VICTORIA	1.62	1
Centro de Acción Social	1.10	—
Acción de Desarrollo Nacional (ADN)	0.88	—
Frente de Convergencia Nacional (FCN)	0.53	—
Total valid votes (incl. others)	**100.00**	**158**

* Seats are distributed according to a combination of national lists and departmental and proportional representation.
† Succeeded by the Partido Republicano Institucional in 2013.

Election Commission

Tribunal Supremo Electoral: 6a Avda 0-32, Zona 2, Guatemala City; tel. 2413-0303; e-mail tse@tse.org.gt; internet www.tse.org.gt; f. 1983; independent; Pres. RUDY MARLÓN PINEDA RAMÍREZ.

Political Organizations

Acción de Desarrollo Nacional (ADN): Vía 7, 5-33 Zona 4, Guatemala City; tel. 2339-4000; internet www.adn.com.gt; registration cancelled by the Tribunal Supremo Electoral in 2012; Sec.-Gen. ADELA CAMACHO DE TORREBIARTE.

Alternativa Nueva Nación (ANN): Avda 1-31, 8°, Zona 1, Guatemala City; tel. 2251-2514; e-mail corriente@intelnet.net.gt; contested the 2011 elections in coalition with the URNG—MAIZ (q.v.) and the Movimiento Político WINAQ (q.v.).

Bienestar Nacional (BIEN): 8a Avda 6-40, Zona 2, Guatemala City; tel. 2254-1458; Sec.-Gen. FIDEL REYES LEE.

Compromiso, Renovación y Orden (CREO): Vía 3, 5–27 Zona 4, Antiguo Edif. Manuel, Guatemala City; tel. 2339-4942; internet creo.org.gt; Sec.-Gen. ROBERTO GONZÁLEZ DÍAZ-DURÁN.

Encuentro por Guatemala (EG): 9 Avda 0-71, Zona 4, Guatemala City; tel. 2231-9859; fax 2230-6463; e-mail izaveliz@yahoo.es; internet encuentro.gt; f. 2006; centre-left; promotes indigenous interests; contested the 2011 elections in coalition with Visión con Valores (q.v.); Sec.-Gen. NINETH VERENCA MONTENEGRO COTTOM.

Frente de Convergencia Nacional (FCN): Avda Centroamérica 13-45, Zona 1, Guatemala City; tel. 5908-7848; e-mail soporte@partidofcn.com; internet www.fcnnacion.com; Sec.-Gen. JIMMY MORALES CABRERA.

Gran Alianza Nacional (GANA): 6a Avda, 3-44, Zona 9, Guatemala City; tel. 2331-4811; fax 2362-7512; e-mail info@gana.com.gt; internet www.gana.com.gt; f. 2003 as electoral alliance of PP, Movimiento Reformador and Partido Solidaridad Nacional; registered as a party in 2005 following withdrawal of PP; Sec.-Gen. JAIME ANTONIO MARTÍNEZ LOHAYZA.

Libertad Democrática Renovada (LIDER): 13 Calle, 2-52 Zona 1, Guatemala City; tel. 2463-4942; internet www.baldizon.com; f. 2010; Sec.-Gen. MANUEL BALDIZÓN.

Movimiento Político WINAQ: 33 Avda 3-57, Zona 4 de Mixco Bosques de San Nicolás, Guatemala City; tel. 2436-0939; internet winaq.org.gt; promotes indigenous interests; contested the 2011 elections in coalition with the URNG—MAIZ (q.v.) and the Alternativa Nueva Nación (q.v.); Sec.-Gen. AMILCAR POP.

Partido de Avanzada Nacional (PAN): 3a Avda 18-28, Zona 14, Guatemala City; tel. 2366-1509; fax 2337-2001; e-mail pan.partidodeavanzadanacional@gmail.com; internet www.pan-gt.com; Sec.-Gen. JUAN GUILLERMO GUTIÉRREZ STRAUSS.

Partido Patriota (PP): 11 Calle 11-54, Zona 1, Guatemala City; tel. 2311-6886; e-mail comunicacion@partidopatriota.org; internet www.partidopatriota.com; f. 2002; right-wing; Sec.-Gen. JUAN JOSÉ PORRAS CASTILLO.

Partido Republicano Institucional (PRI): Avda Las Américas 19-60, Zona 13, Guatemala City; tel. 2319-000; internet pri.gt; f. 2013 as successor party to Frente Republicano Guatemalteco (f. 1988); right-wing; Sec.-Gen. LUIS FERNANDO PÉREZ MARTÍNEZ.

Partido Unionista: 5a Avda 'A' 13-43, Zona 9, Guatemala City; tel. 2331-7468; fax 2331-6141; e-mail info@unionistas.com; internet www.unionistas.org; f. 1917; Sec.-Gen. ALVARO ENRIQUE ARZÚ IRIGOYEN.

Unidad Nacional de la Esperanza (UNE): 6a Avda 8-72, Zona 9, Guatemala City; tel. 2334-3451; e-mail ideas@une.org.gt; internet www.une.org.gt; f. 2001 following a split within the PAN; centre-left; Sec.-Gen. SANDRA TORRES DE COLOM.

Unidad Revolucionaria Nacional Guatemalteca—Movimiento Amplio de Izquierdas (URNG—MAIZ): 12a Avda 'B' 6-00, Zona 2, Guatemala City; tel. 2254-0704; fax 2254-7062; e-mail debate@urng-maiz.org.gt; internet www.urng-maiz.org.gt; f. 1982 following unification of principal guerrilla groups; registered as party in 1998; contested the 2011 elections in coalition with the Movimiento Político WINAQ (q.v.) and the Alternativa Nueva Nación (q.v.); Sec.-Gen. ANGEL SÁNCHEZ VIESCA.

Unión del Cambio Nacional (UCN): 5a Calle 5-27, Zone 9, Guatemala City; tel. 2361-6729; e-mail administracion.ucn@gmai.com; f. 2006; Sec.-Gen. MARIO AMILCAR ESTRADA ORELLANA.

Unión Democrática (UD): Casa 9, 5 Calle 12-00, Zona 14, Guatemala City; tel. 2363-5013; fax 2369-3062; e-mail info@uniondemocratica.info; f. 1983; Sec.-Gen. MANUEL EDUARDO CONDE ORELLANA.

VICTORIA: Edif. Crece Condado el Naranjo, Of. 607, 6°, 23 Calle 14-58, Zona 4 de Mixco, Guatemala City; Sec.-Gen. EDGAR ABRAHAM RIVERA SAGASTUME.

Visión con Valores (VIVA): 41 Calle 3-45, Zona 8, Guatemala City; tel. 2243-2999; e-mail contacto@visionconvalores.com; internet www.visionconvalores.com; contested the 2011 elections in coalition with Encuentro por Guatemala (q.v.); Sec.-Gen. HAROLD OSBERTO CABALLEROS LÓPEZ.

Diplomatic Representation

EMBASSIES IN GUATEMALA

Argentina: 5a Avda 6-50, Zona 14, Apdo 120, Guatemala City; tel. and fax 2464-5900; e-mail eguat@mrecic.gov.ar; Ambassador MARÍA MARGARITA AHUMADA.

Belize: Edif. Europlaza Torre II, Of. 1502, 5a Avda 5-55, Zona 14, Guatemala City; tel. 2207-4000; fax 2207-4001; e-mail infobelice@embajadadebelice.org; internet www.cmbajadadebelice.org; Ambassador ALEXIS ROBERTO ROSADO.

Brazil: Edif. Los Arcos, 2a Avda 20-13, Zona 10, Apdo 196-A, Guatemala City; tel. 2321-6800; fax 2366-1762; e-mail brascom@intelnet.net.gt; internet guatemala.itamaraty.gov.br; Ambassador JOSÉ ROBERTO DE ALMEIDA PINTO.

Canada: Edif. Edyma Plaza, 8°, 13a Calle 8-44, Zona 10, Apdo 400, Guatemala City; tel. 2363-4348; fax 2365-1210; e-mail gtmla@international.gc.ca; internet www.canadainternational.gc.ca/guatemala; Ambassador STUART PATRICK SAVAGE.

Chile: 3a Avda 14-33, Zona 14, Guatemala City; tel. 2490-2323; fax 2334-8276; e-mail echilegu@intelnet.net.gt; Ambassador DOMINGO NAMUNCURA.

Colombia: Edif. Europlaza, Torre I, Of. 1603, 5a Avda 5-55, Zona 14, Guatemala City; tel. 2385-3432; fax 2385-3438; e-mail embacolombia@intelett.com; internet www.embajadaenguatemala.gov.co; Ambassador CARLOS MANUEL PULIDO COLLAZOS.

Costa Rica: 5a Avda 9-33, Zona 14, Guatemala City; tel. 2366-4215; fax 2337-1969; e-mail embacosta.gt@gmail.com; internet www.embajadacostaricaguatemala.com; Ambassador JAVIER DÍAZ CARMONA.

Cuba: Avda las Américas 20-72, Zona 13, Guatemala City; tel. 2332-5521; fax 2332-5525; e-mail embajador@gt.embacuba.cu; internet www.cubadiplomatica.cu/guatemala; Ambassador CARLOS JUAN DE CÉSPEDES PIEDRA.

Dominican Republic: Centro Empresarial 'Zona Pradera', Torre II, Of. 1606, 18 Calle 24-69, Zona 10, Guatemala City; tel. 2261-7016; fax 2261-7017; e-mail embardgt@gmail.com; Ambassador Dr ELIC CARRERA FERNÁNDEZ.

Ecuador: 4a Avda 12-04, Zona 14, Guatemala City; tel. 2368-0397; fax 2368-0397; e-mail embecuad@itelgua.com; Ambassador GALO ANDRÉS YÉPEZ HOLGUÍN.

Egypt: Edif. Cobella, 5°, 5a Avda 10-84, Zona 14, Apdo 502, Guatemala City; tel. 2333-6296; fax 2368-2808; e-mail embassy.guatemala@mfa.gov.eg; internet www.mfa.gov.eg/Guatemala_Emb; Ambassador DINA FAROUK IBRAHIM EL SEHY.

El Salvador: Avda las Américas 16-40, Zona 13, Guatemala City; tel. 2360-7660; fax 2332-1228; e-mail emsalva@intelnet.net.gt; Ambassador JORGE ALBERTO PALENCIA MENA.

France: Edif. Cogefar, 5a Avda 8-59, Zona 14, Apdo 971-A, 01014 Guatemala City; tel. 2421-7370; fax 2421-7372; e-mail courrier@ambafrance-gt.org; internet www.ambafrance-gt.org; Ambassador PHILIPPE FRANC.

Germany: Edif. Reforma 10, 10°, Avda La Reforma 9-55, Zona 10, Guatemala City; tel. 2364-6700; fax 2365-2270; e-mail info@guat.diplo.de; internet www.guatemala.diplo.de; Ambassador MATTHIAS SONN.

Holy See: 10a Calle 4-47, Zona 9, Apdo 3041, Guatemala City (Apostolic Nunciature); tel. 2332-4274; fax 2334-1918; e-mail nuntius@itelgua.com; Apostolic Nuncio Most Rev. NICOLAS THEVENIN (Titular Archbishop of Aeclanum).

Honduras: 19 Avda A 20-19, Zona 10, Guatemala City; tel. 2366-5640; fax 2368-0062; e-mail embhond@intelnet.net.gt; Ambassador VIVIAN VERÓNICA PANTING GALO.

India: 16 Calle 4-88, Zona 14, Guatemala City; tel. and fax 2368-2988; e-mail hoc.guatemala@mea.gov.in; Ambassador SUBRATA BHATTACHARJEE.

Israel: 13a Avda 14-07, Zona 10, Guatemala City; tel. 2333-6951; fax 2333-6950; e-mail info@guatemala.mfa.gov.il; internet guatemala.mfa.gov.il; Ambassador MOSHÉ BACHAR.

Italy: Edif. Santa Bárbara, 12a Calle 6-49, Zona 14, Guatemala City; tel. 2366-9271; fax 2367-3916; e-mail ambasciata.guatemala@esteri.it; internet www.ambguatemala.esteri.it; Ambassador FABRIZIO PIGNATELLI DELLA LEONESSA.

Japan: Edif. Torre Internacional, 10°, Avda de la Reforma 16-85, Zona 10, Guatemala City; tel. 2382-7300; fax 2382-7310; e-mail info@japon.net.gt; internet www.gt.emb-japan.go.jp; Ambassador EIICHI KAWAHARA.

Korea, Republic: Edif. Europlaza, Torre III, 7°, 5a Avda 5-55, Zona 14, Guatemala City; tel. 2382-4051; fax 2382-4057; e-mail korembsy@mofat.go.kr; internet gtm.mofat.go.kr; Ambassador CHOO YEON-GON.

Mexico: 2a Avda 7-57, Zona 10, Apdo 1455, Guatemala City; tel. 2420-3400; fax 2420 3410; e-mail embamcxguat@itelgua.com; internet www.sre.gob.mx/guatemala; Chargé d'affaires a.i. ADRIANA LUCIA ARGAIZ PARRA.

Nicaragua: 13 Avda 14-54, Zona 10, Guatemala City; tel. 2333-4636; fax 2368-2284; e-mail embaguat@terra.com.gt; Ambassador SILVIO MORA MORA.

Norway: Edif. Murano Center, 15°, Of. 1501, 14 Calle 3-51, Zona 10, Apdo 1764, Guatemala City; tel. 2506-4000; fax 2366-5823; e-mail emb.guatemala@mfa.no; internet www.noruega.org.gt; Ambassador JAN GERHARD LASSEN.

Panama: 12a Calle 2-65, Zona 14, Apdo 929-A, Guatemala City; tel. 2366-3336; fax 2366-3338; e-mail panaguate@hotmail.com; internet www.panamaenelexterior.gob.pa/guatemala; Ambassador IRVING ORLANDO CENTENO SANSON.

Peru: 15a Avda A 20-16, Zona 13, Guatemala City; tel. 2339-1060; e-mail embajadadelperu@yahoo.com; Ambassador NILO JÉSUS FIGUEROA CORTAVARRIA.

Russian Federation: 2a Avda 12-85, Zona 14, Guatemala City; tel. 2367-2765; fax 2367-2766; e-mail embajadarusa@gmail.com; internet www.guat.mid.ru; Ambassador NIKOLAY Y. BÁBICH.

Spain: 6a Calle 6-48, Zona 9, Guatemala City; tel. 2379-3530; fax 2379-3533; e-mail emb.guatemala@maec.es; internet www.maec.es/embajadas/guatemala; Ambassador MANUEL MARÍA LEJARRETA LOBO.

Sweden: Edif. Reforma 10, 11°, Avda de la Reforma 9-55, Zona 10, Apdo 966-A, Guatemala City; tel. 2384-7300; fax 2384-7350; e-mail ambassade.guatemala@foreign.ministry.se; internet www.swedenabroad.com/guatemala; Ambassador GEORG BENGT ERIK ANDRÉN.

Switzerland: Edif. Torre Internacional, 14°, 16a Calle 0-55, Zona 10, Apdo 1426, Guatemala City; tel. 2367-5520; fax 2367-5811; e-mail gua.vertretung@eda.admin.ch; internet www.eda.admin.ch/guatemala; Ambassador JÜRG BENZ.

Taiwan (Republic of China): 4a Avda A 13-25, Zona 9, Apdo 897, Guatemala City; tel. 2322-0168; fax 2332-2668; e-mail gtm@mofa.gov.tw; internet www.taiwanembassy.org/gt; Ambassador ADOLFO SUN.

United Kingdom: Edif. Torre Internacional, 11°, Avda de la Reforma, 16a Calle, Zona 10, Guatemala City; tel. 2380-7300; fax 2380-7339; e-mail embassy@intelnett.com; internet ukinguatemala.fco.gov.uk; Ambassador SARAH DICKSON.

USA: Avda de la Reforma 7-01, Zona 10, Guatemala City; tel. 2326-4000; fax 2326-4654; internet guatemala.usembassy.gov; Ambassador TODD D. ROBINSON.

Uruguay: Centro Empresarial Pradera Torre IV, Of. 701, 18 Calle 24-69, Zona 10, Guatemala City; tel. 2261-8001; e-mail uruguatemala@mrree.gub.uy; Ambassador ALFREDO LAFONE RAGGIO.

Venezuela: Edif. Atlantis, Of. 601, 13a Calle 3-40, Zona 10, Apdo 152, Guatemala City; tel. 2317-0703; fax 2317-0705; e-mail embavene@concyt.gob.gt; internet guatemala.embajada.gob.ve; Ambassador ELENA ALICIA SALCEDO POLEO.

Judicial System

The judiciary comprises the Supreme Court, the Courts of Appeal, the Courts of the First Instance and the Justices of Peace. The Supreme Court is the highest court and is responsible for the administration of the judiciary. There are 20 Courts of Appeal throughout the country. There are 10 civil and 12 penal Courts of the First Instance in Guatemala City, and at least one civil and one penal in each of the 21 remaining departments.

Corte Suprema de Justicia: Centro Cívico, 21 Calle 7-70, Zona 1, Guatemala City; tel. 2426-7000; internet www.oj.gob.gt/csj; 13 mems are appointed by Congress; Pres. JOSUÉ FELIPE BAQUIAX.

Attorney-General: THELMA ESPERANZA ALDANA HERNÁNDEZ.

Religion

Almost all of the inhabitants profess Christianity, with a majority belonging to the Roman Catholic Church. In recent years the Protestant churches have attracted a growing number of converts.

CHRISTIANITY

The Roman Catholic Church

For ecclesiastical purposes, Guatemala comprises two archdioceses, 10 dioceses and the Apostolic Vicariates of El Petén and Izabal. Some 60% of the population are Roman Catholics.

Bishops' Conference: Conferencia Episcopal de Guatemala, Secretariado General del Episcopado, Km 15, Calzada Roosevelt 4-54, Zona 7, Mixco, Apdo 1698, Guatemala City; tel. 2433-1832; fax 2433-1834; e-mail ceguatemala@gmail.com; internet www.iglesiacatolica.org.gt; f. 1973; Pres. Rev. RODOLFO VALENZUELA NÚÑEZ (Bishop of La Verapaz).

Archbishop of Guatemala City: OSCAR JULIO VIAN MORALES, Palacio Arzobispal, 7a Avda 6-21, Zona 1, Apdo 723, Guatemala City; tel. 2231-9707; fax 2251-5068; e-mail arzobispado deguatemala@gmail.com; internet www.arzobispado deguatemala.com.

Archbishop of Los Altos, Quetzaltenango-Totonicapán: MARIO ALBERTO MOLINA PALMA, Arzobispado, 11 Avda 6-27, Zona 1, Apdo 11, 09001 Quetzaltenango; tel. 7761-2840; fax 7761-6049.

The Anglican Communion

Guatemala comprises one of the five dioceses of the Iglesia Anglicana de la Región Central de América.

Bishop of Guatemala: Rt Rev. ARMANDO ROMÁN GUERRA SORIA, Avda Castellana 40-06, Zona 8, Apdo 58, Guatemala City; tel. 2473-6828; fax 2472-0764; e-mail agepiscopal@yahoo.com; diocese founded 1967.

Protestant Churches

The largest Protestant denomination in Guatemala is the Full Gospel Church, followed by the Assembly of God, the Central American Church, and the Prince of Peace Church. The Baptist, Presbyterian, Lutheran and Episcopalian churches are also represented.

Convención de Iglesias Bautista de Guatemala (CIBG): Convention of Baptist Churches of Guatemala, 12 Calle 9-54, Zona 1, Apdo 322, 01901 Guatemala City; tel. and fax 2253-9194; e-mail convencion@cibg.org; internet cibg.org; f. 1946; Pres. OTTO ECHEVERRÍA VELÁSQUEZ; 43,876 mems.

Church of Jesus Christ of Latter-day Saints: 12a Calle 3-37, Zona 9, Guatemala City; e-mail contactos@mormones.org.gt; internet www.mormones.org.gt; 17 bishoprics, 9 chapels; Pres. THOMAS S. MONSON.

Conferencia de Iglesias Evangélicas de Guatemala (CIEDEG) (Conference of Protestant Churches in Guatemala): 7a Avda 1-11, Zona 2, Guatemala City; tel. 2232-3724; fax 2232-1609; internet www.nuevociedeg.org; f. 1987; Pres. VITALINO SIMILOX.

Congregación Luterana La Epifanía (Evangelisch-Lutherische Epiphanias-Gemeinde): 2a Avda 15-31, Zona 10, 01010 Guatemala City; tel. 2333-3697; fax 2366-4968; e-mail pfarrer@laepifania.org; internet www.laepifania.org; mem. of Lutheran World Federation; Pres. MARKUS BÖTTCHER; 200 mems.

Iglesia Evangélica Nacional Presbiteriana de Guatemala: Avda Simeón Cañas 7-13, Zona 2, Apdo 655, Guatemala City; tel. 2288-4441; fax 2254-1242; e-mail ienpg@yahoo.com; internet www.ienpg.org.gt; f. 1962; mem. of World Alliance of Reformed Churches; Pres. LAURENCE ELI BARRIOS CIFUENTES; Sec.-Gen. Pastor ISAÍAS GARCÍA CITALÁN; 17,000 mems.

Iglesia Luterana Castillo Fuerte: 19 Avda 6-64, Zona 11, Guatemala City; tel. 2472-0186; fax 2384-0703; e-mail castillofuerte@lycos.com; f. 2000.

Iglesia Luterana El Divino Salvador de Zacapa: 4a Calle, 9-34, Zona 1, Barrio San Marcos, Zacapa; tel. 7941-0574; e-mail hogarluterano@hotmail.com; f. 1946; Pastors GERARDO VENANCIO VÁSQUEZ SALGUERO, ARED RODRÍGUEZ.

Iglesia Nacional Evangélica Menonita Guatemalteca: Guatemala City; tel. 2339-0606; e-mail AlvaradoJE@ldschurch.org; Pres. ALFREDO SIQUIC ACTÉ; 12,000 mems.

Union Church: 12a Calle 7-37, Zona 9, 01009 Guatemala City; tel. 2361-2037; fax 2362-3961; e-mail unionchurchguatemala@gmail.com; internet www.unionchurchguatemala.com; f. 1943; English-speaking church; Pastor JOHN CONNER.

The Press

PRINCIPAL DAILIES

Diario de Centro América: Casa Editora Tipografía Nacional, 18 Calle 6-72, Zona 1, Guatemala City; tel. 2414-9600; e-mail lector@dca.gob.gt; internet www.dca.gob.gt; f. 1880; morning; official; Dir-Gen. HÉCTOR SALVATIERRA; Editor-in-Chief JUAN CARLOS RUIZ CALDERÓN.

Guía Interamericana de Turismo: Edif. Plaza los Arcos, 3°, 20 Calle 5-35, Zona 10, Guatemala City; tel. 2450-6431; e-mail info@guiainter.org; internet www.guiainter.org; f. 1989; online journal; Dir-Gen. MARIO ORINI; Editor ALFREDO MAYORGA.

La Hora: 9 Calle A 1-56, Zona 1, Apdo 1593, Guatemala City; tel. 2423-1800; fax 2423-1837; e-mail lahora@lahora.com.gt; internet www.lahora.com.gt; f. 1920; evening; ind; Dir-Gen. OSCAR CLEMENTE MARROQUÍN; Editor-in-Chief JAVIER ESTRADA TOBAR; circ. 18,000.

Nuestro Diario: 15 Avda 24-27, Zona 13, Guatemala City; tel. and fax 2379-1600; e-mail opinion@nuestrodiario.com.gt; internet www.nuestrodiario.com; Gen. Man. FERNANDO FAHSEN; Gen. Editor MARIO RECINOS.

El Periódico: 15 Avda 24-51, Zona 13, Guatemala City; tel. 2427-2300; fax 2427-2361; e-mail redaccion@elperiodico.com.gt; internet www.elperiodico.com.gt; f. 1996; morning; ind; Pres. JOSÉ RUBÉN ZAMORA MARROQUÍN; Editor TULIO JUÁREZ; circ. 30,000.

Prensa Libre: 13 Calle 9-31, Zona 1, Apdo 2063, Guatemala City; tel. 2230-5096; fax 2251-8768; e-mail nacionales@prensalibre.com.gt; internet www.prensalibre.com.gt; f. 1951; morning; ind; Gen. Man. LUIS ENRIQUE SOLÓRZANO; Editor GONZALO MARROQUÍN GODOY; circ. 120,000.

Siglo Veintiuno: 14 Avda 4-33, Zona 1, Guatemala City; tel. 2423-6100; fax 2423-6346; e-mail suscripciones@siglo21.com.gt; internet www.s21.com.gt; f. 1990; morning; Dir GUILLERMO FERNÁNDEZ; circ. 65,000.

PERIODICALS

Amiga: 13 Calle 9-31, Zona 1, Guatemala City; tel. 2412-5000; fax 2220-5123; e-mail revistas@prensalibre.com.gt; internet www.revistaamiga.com; f. 1988; health; Dir CAROLINA VÁSQUEZ ARAYA; Editor SILVIA LANUZA.

Gerencia: Torre Citigroup, Of. 402, 3a Avda 13-78, Zona 14, Guatemala City; tel. 2427-4900; fax 2427-4971; e-mail jaqueline@agg.org.gt; internet www.agg.org.gt/revista-gerencia-b; f. 1967; monthly; official organ of the Asscn of Guatemalan Managers; Man. ILEANA LÓPEZ AVILA.

El Metropolitano: Plaza Morumbi 7 y 8, 2°, 3a Calle 15-29, Zona 8, San Cristóbal, Guatemala City; e-mail info@elmetropolitano.net; internet www.elmetropolitano.net; Editor JORGE GARCÍA MONTENEGRO.

Mundo Motor: 13a Calle 9-31, Zona 1, Guatemala City; tel. 2412-5000; fax 2220-5123; e-mail evasquez@prensalibre.com.gt; internet www.mundoymotor.com; Dir CAROLINA VÁSQUEZ; Editor NÉSTOR A. LARRAZÁBAL B.

Revista Data Export: 15 Avda 14-72, Zona 13, Guatemala City; tel. 2422-3431; fax 2422-3434; e-mail portal@export.com.gt; internet revistadata.export.com.gt; monthly; foreign trade affairs; organ of the Asociacíon Guatemalteca de Exportadores; Editor FULVIA DONIS.

Revista Industria y Negocios: 6a Ruta 9-21, Zona 4, Guatemala City; tel. 2380-9000; e-mail contactemos@industriaguate.com; internet www.revistaindustria.com; monthly; official organ of the Chamber of Industry; Dir JAVIER ZAPEDA.

Revista Mundo Comercial: 10a Calle 3-80, Zona 1, 01001 Guatemala City; e-mail jbalcarcel@camaradecomercio.org.gt; internet www.negociosenguatemala.com; monthly; business; official organ of the Chamber of Commerce; Gen. Man. JEANNETTE BALCARCEL; circ. 11,000.

Viaje a Guatemala: 13 Calle 9-31, Zona 1, Guatemala City; tel. 2412-5000; fax 2220-5123; internet www.viajeaguatemala.com; Dir-Gen. CAROLINA VÁSQUEZ; Editor-in-Chief SILVIA LANUZA.

PRESS ASSOCIATION

Asociación de Periodistas de Guatemala (APG): 14 Calle 3-29, Zona 1, Guatemala City; tel. 2232-1813; fax 2238-2781; e-mail apege@intelnet.net.gt; internet www.apg-gt.org; f. 1947; affiliated to International Freedom of Expression Exchange and Fed. Latinoamericana de Periodistas; Pres. FREDY HERMÓGENES GARCÍA LEMUS; Sec. VÍCTOR MANUEL RAMÍREZ DONIS.

NEWS AGENCY

Inforpress Centroamericana: Calle Mariscal o Diagonal 21, 6-58, Zona 11, 0100 Guatemala City; tel. and fax 2473-1704; e-mail inforpre@guate.net; internet www.inforpressca.com; f. 1972; ind; publishes 2 weekly news bulletins, in English and Spanish; Dir NURIA VILLANOVA.

Publishers

Cholsamaj: Calle 5, 2-58, Zona 1, Iximulew, Guatemala City; tel. 2232-5402; fax 2232-5959; e-mail editorialcholsamaj@yahoo.com; internet www.cholsamaj.org; Mayan language publs; Pres. KIKAB' CERDER MUX; Exec. Dir ULMIL JOEL MEJIA.

Ediciones Legales Comercio e Industria: 12a Avda 14-78, Zone 1, Guatemala City; tel. 2253-5725; fax 2220-7592; Man. Dir LUIS EMILIO BARRIOS.

Editorial Cultura: Avda 12 11-11, Zona 1, Guatemala City; tel. 2232-5667; fax 2230-0591; e-mail kaxin@tutopia.com; internet www.mcd.gob.gt/editorial-cultura; f. 1987; part of the Ministry of Culture and Sport; Chief Editor FRANCISCO MORALES SANTOS.

Editorial Palo de Hormigo: 0 Calle 16-40, Zona 15, Col. El Maestro, Guatemala City; tel. 2369-3089; fax 2369-8858; e-mail eph_info@palodehormigo.com; f. 1990; Man. Dir RICARDO ULYSSES CIFUENTES.

Editorial Santillana, SA: 7 Avda 11-11, Zona 9, Guatemala City; tel. 2429-4300; fax 2429-4301; e-mail santillana@santillana.com.gt; internet www.gruposantillana.com/gr_gu.htm; f. 1995; subsidiary of Grupo Santillana (Spain); Dir-Gen. ALBERTO POLANCO.

Editorial Universitaria: Universidad de San Carlos de Guatemala, Ciudad Universitaria, Zona 12, Guatemala City; tel. and fax 2418-8070; fax 2419-9641; e-mail editorialusac@usac.edu.gt; internet editorial.usac.edu.gt; literature, social sciences, health, pure and technical sciences, humanities, secondary and university educational textbooks; Dir ANACLETO MEDINA GÓMEZ.

F & G Editores: 31a Avda 'C' 5-54, Zona 7, 01007 Guatemala City; tel. and fax 2439-8358; e-mail informacion@fygeditores.com; internet www.fygeditores.com; f. 1990 as Figueroa y Gallardo; changed name in 1993; law, literature and social sciences; Editor RAÚL FIGUEROA SARTI.

Piedra Santa: 37 Avda 1-26, Zona 7, Guatemala City; tel. 2422-7676; fax 2422-7610; e-mail info@piedrasanta.com; internet www.piedrasanta.com; f. 1947; education, culture; Man. Dir IRENE PIEDRA SANTA.

PUBLISHERS' ASSOCIATION

Consejo Nacional del Libro (CONALIBRO): 11 Avda 11-07, Zona 1, Guatemala City; tel. 2253-0536; fax 2253-0544; e-mail conalibro@gmail.com; f. 1989; Pres. LUIS EDUARDO MORALES.

Broadcasting and Communications

TELECOMMUNICATIONS

Comcel Guatemala (Tigo): Edif. Plaza Tigo, 3°, Km 9.5, Carretera al Salvador, Guatemala City; tel. 2428-0000; fax 2428-1140; e-mail servicioalcliente@tigo.com.gt; internet www.tigo.com.gt; f. 1990;

55% owned by Millicom International Cellular (Luxembourg); CEO VICTOR UNDA.

Telecomunicaciones de Guatemala, SA (Claro): Edif. Central Telgua, 7a Avda 12-39, Zona 1, Guatemala City; tel. 2230-2098; fax 2251-1799; e-mail clientes@claro.com.gt; internet www.claro.com.gt; fmrly state-owned Empresa Guatemalteca de Telecomunicaciones (Guatel); 95% privatized in 1998; owned by América Móvil, SA de CV (Mexico); Dir ANA BEATRIZ GODÍNEZ.

Telefónica Guatemala, SA (Movistar): Edif. Iberoplaza, 1°, Blvd Los Próceres 20-09, Zona 10, Guatemala City; tel. 2379-7979; e-mail servicioalcliente@telefonica.com.gt; internet www.movistar.com.gt; owned by TelefónicaMóviles, SA (Spain); 298,000 customers; Dir SALVADOR MONTES DE OCA.

Regulatory Authority

Superintendencia de Telecomunicaciones de Guatemala: 4 Avda 15-51, Zona 10, Guatemala City; tel. 2321-1000; fax 2321-1074; e-mail informacion@sit.gob.gt; internet www.sit.gob.gt; f. 1996; Supt EDDIE PADILLA.

BROADCASTING

Radio

Central de Radio, SA: Edif. Canal 3, 30 Avda 3-40, Zona 11, Guatemala City; tel. 2410-3150; internet www.centralderadio.com.gt; operates 7 radio stations; Pres. FERNANDO VILLANUEVA CARRERA.

Emisoras Unidas de Guatemala: 4a Calle 6-84, Zona 13, Guatemala City; tel. 2421-5353; fax 2475-3870; e-mail patrullajeinformativo@emisorasunidas.com; internet www.emisorasunidas.com; f. 1964; 6 stations: Yo Sí Sideral, Emisoras-Unidas, Kiss, Atmósfera, Fabustereo and La Grande; Pres. EDGAR ARCHILA MARROQUÍN.

La Marca: 30a Avda 3-40, Zona 11, Guatemala City; tel. 2410-3150; fax 2410-3151; e-mail lamarca@94fm.com.gt; internet www.94fm.com.gt.

Metro Stereo: 14a Avda 14-78, Zona 10, Guatemala City; tel. 2277-7686; fax 2368-2040; e-mail metrored@metrostereo.net; internet www.metrostereo.net; f. 1980; Dir RUGGIERO MAURO-RHODIO.

Radio Corporación Nacional (RCN): Torre Profesional I, Of. 903, 6 Avda 0-60, Centro Comercial Zona 4, Guatemala City; tel. 2411-2000; tel. 2411-2005; internet www.rcn.com.gt; operates 12 radio stations; Pres. SERGIO ROBERTO ALCÁZAR SOLÍS.

Radio Cultural TGN: 1a Avda 30 09 Zona 3, Apdo 601, 01901 Guatemala City; tel. 2207-7700; fax 2207-7600; e-mail tgn@radiocultural.com; internet www.radiocultural.com; f. 1950; religious and cultural station; programmes in Spanish and English, Cakchiquel, Kekchi, Quiché and Aguacateco; Dir ESTEBAN SYWULKA.

Radio Grupo Alius, SA: Torre Profesional II, 10°, 6 Avda 0-60, Zona 4, Guatemala City; tel. 2412-8484; fax 2412-8448; e-mail exa@grupoalius.com; internet www.grupoalius.com; operates 5 radio stations; Pres. EDUARDO ALFONSO LIU.

Radio Nacional TGW (La Voz de Guatemala): 18a Calle 6-72, Zona 1, Guatemala City; tel. 2323-8282; fax 2323-8310; e-mail info@radiotgw.gob.gt; internet www.radiotgw.gob.gt; f. 1930; govt station; Dir (vacant).

Television

Azteca Guatemala: 12 Avda 1-96, Zona 2 de Mixco, Col. Alvarado, Guatemala City; tel. 2411-1231; e-mail festrada@tvaguatemala.tv; internet www.azteca.com.gt; f. 2008 by the merger of Televisión Azteca (Mexico) and Latitud TV; Dir-Gen. MARIO SAN ROMÁN.

Canal Antigua: Of. 12C, 1°, Avda Reforma 13-70, Zona 9, 01009 Guatemala City; tel. 2222-8800; e-mail info@canalantigua.com; internet www.canalantigua.com; f. 2009; commercial; news and opinions; Exec. Dir ANABEL BONAMI.

Guatevisión: Edif. Tikal Futura, Torre Sol, 4°, Calz Roosevelt 22-43, Zona 11, Guatemala City; tel. 2328-6000; e-mail info@guatevision.com; internet www.guatevision.com; f. 2000; Dir HAROLDO SÁNCHEZ.

Radio-Televisión Guatemala, SA: Edif. Canal 3, 30 Avda 3-40, Zona 11, Apdo 1367, Guatemala City; tel. 2410-3000; e-mail telediario@canal3.com.gt; internet www.canal3.com.gt; f. 1956; commercial; part of Albavisión; Pres. MAXIMILIANO KESTLER FARNÉS; Vice-Pres. J. F. VILLANUEVA; operates the following channels:

Teleonce: 20 Calle 5-02, Zona 10, Guatemala City; tel. 2469-0900; fax 5203-8455; e-mail jcof@canalonce.tv; internet canales11y13.blogspot.in; f. 1968; commercial; Gen. Dir JUAN CARLOS ORTIZ.

Televisiete, SA: 30 Avda 3-40, Zona 11, Apdo 1242, Guatemala City; tel. 2410-3000; fax 2369-1393; internet www.canal7.com.gt; f. 1988; commercial; Dir LUIS RABBÉ.

Trecevisión, SA: 20 Calle 5-02, Zona 10, Guatemala City; tel. 2368-2221; e-mail escribanos@canal7.com.gt; internet www

.canaltrece.tv; f. 1978; commercial; f. 1978; Dir FERNANDO VILLANUEVA.

Regulatory Authority

Dirección General de Radiodifusión y Televisión Nacional: Edif. Tipografía Nacional, 3°, 18 Calle 6-72, Zona 1, Guatemala City; tel. 2323-8282; e-mail contacto@radiotgw.gob.gt; internet www .radiotgw.gob.gt; f. 1931; Dir-Gen. JUAN JOSÉ RÍOS.

Finance

(cap. = capital; res = reserves; dep. = deposits; m. = million; brs = branches; amounts in quetzales)

BANKING

Superintendencia de Bancos: 9a Avda 22-00, Zona 1, Apdo 2306, Guatemala City; tel. 2429-5000; fax 2232-0002; e-mail info@sib.gob .gt; internet www.sib.gob.gt; f. 1946; Supt RAMÓN BENJAMÍN TOBAR MORALES.

Central Bank

Banco de Guatemala: 7a Avda 22-01, Zona 1, Apdo 365, Guatemala City; tel. 2429-6000; fax 2253-6086; e-mail webmaster@banguat.gob .gt; internet www.banguat.gob.gt; f. 1946; state-owned; cap. and res 504.1m., dep. 34,384.7m. (Dec. 2009); Pres. JULIO ROBERTO SUÁREZ GUERRA; Gen. Man. SERGIO FRANCISCO RECINOS RIVERA.

State Commercial Bank

Crédito Hipotecario Nacional de Guatemala (CHN): 7a Avda 22-77, Zona 1, Apdo 242, Guatemala City; tel. 2223-0333; fax 2238-2041; e-mail mercadeo@chn.com.gt; internet www.chn.com.gt; f. 1930; govt-owned; cap. 15m., res 594m., dep. 2,402.6m. (Dec. 2013); Pres. WENCESLAO DE MANUEL LEMUS; Gen. Man. GUSTAVO ADOLFO DÍAZ LEÓN; 44 agencies.

Private Commercial Banks

Banco Agromercantil de Guatemala, SA: 7a Avda 7-30, Zona 9, 01009 Guatemala City; tel. 2338-6565; fax 2388-6566; e-mail info@ bam.com.gt; internet www.bam.com.gt; f. 1926; changed name to Banco Agrícola Mercantil in 1948; cap. 1,339m., res 931.2m., dep. 16,781.1m. (Dec. 2013); Pres. JOSÉ LUIS VALDÉS O'CONNELL; Man. CHRISTIAN ROBERTO SCHNEIDER WILL; 237 brs.

Banco de América Central, SA (BAC): Local 6-12, 1°, 7a Avda 6-26, Zona 9, Guatemala City; tel. 2360-9440; fax 2331-8720; internet www.bac.net; f. 1997; Pres. LUIS FERNANDO SAMAYOA DELGADO; Gen. Man. JUAN JOSÉ VIAUD PÉREZ; 20 brs.

Banco Citibank de Guatemala, SA: Torre Citibank, 1°, 3a Avda 13-78, Zona 10, 01010 Guatemala City; tel. 2333-6574; fax 2333-6860; internet www.citibank.com.gt; Citi acquired Banco Cuscatlan and Banco Uno in 2007; Pres. CONSTANTINO GOTSIS; 37 brs.

Banco de Desarrollo Rural, SA: Avda La Reforma 9-30, Zona 9, Guatemala City; tel. 2339-8888; fax 2360-9740; e-mail internacional4@banrural.com.gt; internet www.banrural.com.gt; f. 1971 as Banco de Desarrollo Agrícola; name changed as above in 1998; cap. 1,168.2m., res 1,984.9m., dep. 31,627.3m. (Dec. 2012); Pres. ADOLFO FERNANDO PEÑA PÉREZ; 640 brs.

Banco G & T Continental, SA: Plaza Continental, 6a Avda 9-08, Zona 9, Guatemala City; tel. 2338-6801; fax 2332-2682; e-mail subanco@gytcontinental.com.gt; internet www.gytcontinental.com .gt; f. 2000 following merger of Banco Continental and Banco Granai y Townson; total assets 11.4m. (2000); Gen. Man. FLAVIO MONTENE-GRO; 151 brs.

Banco Industrial, SA (BAINSA): Edif. Centro Financiero, Torre 1, 7a Avda 5-10, Zona 4, Apdo 744, Guatemala City; tel. 2420-3000; fax 2420-3118; e-mail webmaster@bi.com.gt; internet www.bi.com.gt; f. 1968 to promote industrial devt; merged with Banco del Quetzal in 2007; cap. 2,257.7m., res 1,366.9m., dep. 48,188.4m. (Dec. 2013); CEO DIEGO PULIDO ARAGÓN; 1,404 brs.

Banco Inmobilario, SA: Edif. Galerias España, 7a Avda 11-59, Zona 9, Apdo 1181, Guatemala City; tel. 2339-3777; fax 2332-1418; e-mail info@bcoinmob.com.gt; internet www.bancoinmobiliario.com .gt; f. 1958; cap. 77.6m., res 0.4m., dep. 738.6m. (Dec. 2002); Pres. ADEL ABED ANTON TURJUMAN; 44 brs.

Banco Promerica: Edif. Reforma 10, 2°, Avda 9-55Z, 01010 Guatemala City; tel. 2413-9400; e-mail servicio@bancopromerica.com.gt; internet www.bancopromerica.com.gt; f. 1991 as Banco de la Producción, SA (BANPRO), adopted present name in 2007 following merger with Bancasol; Pres. RAMIRO NORBERTO ORTIZ GURDIÁN.

Banco Reformador, SA: 7a Avda 7-24, Zona 9, 01009 Guatemala City; tel. 2362-0888; fax 2332-9595; internet www.bancoreformador .com; cap. 432.5m., res 294.5m., dep. 7,838.7m. (Dec. 2012); merged

with Banco de la Construcción in 2000, acquired Banco SCI in 2007; Pres. ERNESTO CASTEGNARO ODIO; Gen. Man. ROLANDO LUCERO; 100 brs.

Banco de los Trabajadores: Avda Reforma 6-20, Zona 9, 01001 Guatemala City; tel. 2410-2600; fax 2339-4750; e-mail webmaster@ bantrab.net.gt; internet www.bantrab.com.gt; f. 1966; deals with loans for establishing and improving small industries as well as normal banking business; cap. 460.4m., dep. 2,119.5m., total assets 2,897.6m. (Dec. 2005); Pres. SERGIO HERNÁNDEZ; Gen. Man. RONALD GIOVANNI GARCÍA NAVARIJO; 33 brs.

Inter Banco, SA: Torre Internacional, Avda Reforma 15-85, Zona 10, Apdo 2588, Guatemala City; tel. 2277-3666; fax 2366-6743; e-mail info@bco.inter.com; internet www.interbanco.com.gt; f. 1976; cap. 217.5m., res 91m., dep. 3,545.8m. (Dec. 2011); Pres. CÉSAR JOSÉ ANTONIO CORRALES AGUILAR; Gen. Man. FRANCISCO NARANJO MARTÍNEZ; 44 brs.

Banking Association

Asociación Bancaria de Guatemala: Edif. Margarita 2, Torre II, 5°, Of. 502, Diagonal 6, No 10-11, Zona 10, Guatemala City; tel. 2382-7200; fax 2382-7201; internet www.abg.org.gt; f. 1961; represents all state and private banks; Pres. LUIS FERNANDO DELGADO.

STOCK EXCHANGE

Bolsa de Valores Nacional, SA: Centro Financiero, Torre 2, 9°, 7a Avda 5-10, Zona 4, Guatemala City; tel. 2338-4400; fax 2332-1721; e-mail info@bvnsa.com.gt; internet www.bvnsa.com.gt; f. 1987; the exchange is commonly owned (1 share per assoc.) and trades stocks from private cos, govt bonds, letters of credit and other securities; CEO ROLANDO SAN ROMÁN.

INSURANCE

National Companies

Aseguradora La Ceiba, SA: 20 Calle 15-20, Zona 13, Guatemala City; tel. 2379-1800; fax 2334-8167; e-mail aceiba@aceiba.com.gt; internet www.aceiba.com.gt; f. 1978; Man. ALEJANDRO BELTRANENA.

Aseguradora General, SA: 10a Calle 3-71, Zona 10, Guatemala City; tel. 2285-7200; fax 2334-2093; e-mail servicio@generali.com.gt; internet www.generali.com.gt; f. 1967; subsidiary of Grupo Generali, Trieste, Italy; Pres. ENRIQUE NEUTZE AYCINENA; Man. ENRIQUE NEUTZE TORIELLO.

Chartis Seguros Guatemala, SA: Edif. Etisa, 7a Avda 12-23, 3°, Plazuela España, Zona 9, Guatemala City; tel. 2285-5900; fax 2361-3032; e-mail cmg.servicios@aig.com; internet www.chartisinsurance .com; f. 1967 as La Seguridad de Centroamérica; present name adopted 2010; Pres. JAMES W. DWANE.

Cía de Seguros El Roble, SA: Torre 2, 7a Avda 5-10, Zona 4, Guatemala City; tel. 2420-3333; fax 2361-1191; e-mail rerales@ elroble.com; internet www.elroble.com; f. 1973; Gen. Man. HERMANN GIRON.

Departamento de Seguros y Previsión del Crédito Hipotecario Nacional: Centro Cívico, 7a Avda 22-77, Zona 1, Guatemala City; tel. 2223-0333; fax 2253-8584; e-mail vjsc@chn.com.gt; internet www.chn.com.gt; f. 1942; Pres. OSCAR ERASMO VELASQUEZ RIVERA; Man. GUSTAVO ADOLFO DÍAZ LEÓN.

Mapfre Seguros Guatemala, SA: Edif. Reforma 10, Avda 9-55, Zona 10, Guatemala City; tel. 2328-5000; fax 2328-5001; e-mail roberto.ewel@mapfre.com.gt; internet www.mapfre.com.gt; Gen. Man. JOSÉ TULIO URRUTIA.

Pan-American Life Insurance de Guatemala Cía de Seguros, SA: Edif. Plaza Panamericana, 10°, Avda la Reforma 9-00, Zona 9, Guatemala City; tel. 2338-9800; e-mail servicioalclientegt@ panamericanlife.com; internet www.palig.com/Regions/guatemala; f. 1968; Country Man. SALVADOR LEIVA MADRID.

Seguros Columna, SA: 5a. Calle 0-55, Zona 9, Apdo 01009, Guatemala City; tel. 2419-2020; e-mail info@seguroscolumna.com; internet www.seguroscolumna.com; f. 1994; part of Corporación Financiera Cooperativa FENACOAC; Pres. JOSÉ GUILLERMO PER-ALTA ROSA.

Seguros G & T, SA: Edif. Mini, 6a Avda 1-73, Zona 4, Guatemala City; tel. 2338-5778; e-mail tcontacto@gyt.com.gt; internet www .segurosgyt.com.gt; f. 1947; Pres. MARÍO GRANAI ANDRINO; Gen. Man. ENRIQUE RODRÍGUEZ.

Seguros de Occidente, SA: Edif. Corporación de Occidente, 7a Avda 7-33, Zona 9, Guatemala City; tel. 2279-7000; e-mail seguros@ occidentecorp.com.gt; internet www.occidente.com.gt/cdo; f. 1979; Gen. Man. MARIO ROBERTO VALDEAVELLANO MUÑOZ.

Seguros Universales, SA: 4a Calle 7-73, Zona 9, Apdo 01009, Guatemala City; tel. 2384-7400; fax 2332-3372; e-mail info@ segurosuniversales.net; internet www.segurosuniversales.net; f. 1962; Pres. PEDRO NOLASCO SICILIA VALLS; Gen. Man. FELIPE SICILIA.

Insurance Association

Asociación Guatemalteca de Instituciones de Seguros (AGIS): Edif. Reforma 10, Of. 905, Avda La Reforma 9-55, Zona 10, Guatemala City; tel. 2361-7067; fax 2335-2357; e-mail info@agis .com.gt; internet www.agis.com.gt; f. 1953; 12 mems; Pres. SALVADOR LEIVA MADRID; Exec. Dir ENRIQUE MURILLO C.

Trade and Industry

DEVELOPMENT ORGANIZATIONS

Instituto de Fomento de Hipotecas Aseguradas (FHA): Edif. Aristos Reforma, 2°, Of. 207, Avda Reforma 7-62, Zona 9, Guatemala City; tel. 2323-5656; fax 2362-9491; e-mail promocion@fha.gob.gt; internet www.fha.gob.gt; f. 1961; insured mortgage institution; Pres. EDIN HOMERO VELASQUEZ ESCOBEDO; Man. SERGIO ARMANDO IRUNGARAY SUÁREZ.

Instituto Nacional de Administración Pública (INAP): Blvd Los Próceres 16-40, Zona 10, Apdo 2753, Guatemala City; tel. 2419-8181; fax 2419-8126; e-mail informacion@inap.gob.gt; internet www .inap.gob.gt; f. 1964; provides technical experts to assist in administrative reform programmes; provides training for govt staff; research programmes in administration, sociology, politics and economics; Pres. FERNANDO FUENTES MOHR; Man. HÉCTOR HUGO VÁSQUEZ BARREDA.

Secretaría de Planificación y Programación (SEGEPLAN): 9a Calle 10-44, Zona 1, Guatemala City; tel. 2232-6212; fax 2253-3127; e-mail segeplan@segeplan.gob.gt; internet www.segeplan.gob.gt; f. 1954; oversees implementation of the national economic devt plan; Sec. LUIS FERNANDO CARRERA CASTRO.

CHAMBERS OF COMMERCE AND INDUSTRY

Cámara de Comercio de Guatemala (CCG): 10a Calle 3-80, Zona 1, Guatemala City; tel. 2417-2700; fax 2220-9393; e-mail info@ camaradecomercio.org.gt; internet www.negociosenguatemala.com; f. 1894; Pres. JORGE BRIZ.

Cámara Empresarial de Comercio y Servicios (Cecoms): Guatemala City; Pres. GUILLERMO GONZÁLEZ.

Cámara de Industria de Guatemala: 6a Ruta 9-21, 12°, Zona 4, Apdo 214, Guatemala City; tel. 2380-9000; e-mail info@ industriaguate.com; internet www.industriaguate.com; f. 1959; Pres. ANDRÉS CASTILLO; Exec. Dir JAVIER ZEPEDA.

Cámara Oficial Española de Comercio de Guatemala: Edif. Paladium, 14°, 4 Avda 15-70, Zona 10, Guatemala City; tel. 2470-3301; fax 2470-3304; e-mail gerencia@camacoes.org.gt; internet www.camacoes.org.gt; f. 1928; Pres. Dr RAFAEL BRIZ; Gen. Man. SILVIA CAROLINA TAMAYAC MÁRQUEZ.

Comité Coordinador de Asociaciones Agrícolas, Comerciales, Industriales y Financieras (CACIF): Edif. Cámara de Industria de Guatemala, 6a Ruta 9-21, Zona 4, Guatemala City; tel. 2231-0651; fax 2334-7025; e-mail informacion@cacif.org.gt; internet www.cacif.org.gt; 6 mem. chambers; Pres. JORGE BRIZ; Exec. Dir ROBERTO ARDÓN.

INDUSTRIAL AND TRADE ASSOCIATIONS

Asociación de Azucareros de Guatemala (ASAZGUA): Edif. Europlaza, 178°, 5a Avda 5-55, Zona 14, Guatemala City; tel. 2386-2299; fax 2386-2020; e-mail asazgua@azucar.com.gt; internet www .azucar.com.gt; f. 1957; sugar producers' asscn; 15 mems; Pres. MARCO AUGUSTO GARCÍA; Gen. Man. ARMANDO BOESCHE.

Asociación General de Agricultores (AGA): Edif. Rodseguros, 6°, Via 1, 1-67, Zona 4, Guatemala City; tel. 2361-0654; fax 2332-4817; e-mail asistente@aga.org.gt; internet www.aga.org.gt; f. 1920; general farmers' asscn; Pres. PETER FRANK; 350 mems.

Asociación Guatemalteca de Exportadores (AGEXPORT): 15a Avda 14-72, Zona 13, Guatemala City; tel. 2422-3400; fax 2422-3434; e-mail portal@export.com.gt; internet www.export.com.gt; f. 1982; exporters' asscn; Pres. FRANCISCO MENENDEZ; Dir-Gen. LUIS GODOY.

Asociación Nacional de Avicultores (ANAVI): Edif. El Reformador, 4°, Of. 401, Avda La Reforma 1-50, Zona 9, Guatemala City; tel. 2360-3384; fax 2360-3161; e-mail anavi@anaviguatemala.org; internet www.anaviguatemala.com; f. 1964; national asscn of poultry farmers; 60 mems; Pres. MARIA DEL ROSARIO DE FALLA; Gen. Man. PEGGY CONTRERAS.

Asociación Nacional del Café—Anacafé: 5a Calle 0-50, Zona 14, Guatemala City; tel. 2421-3700; e-mail info@email.anacafe.org; internet www.anacafe.org; f. 1960; national coffee asscn; Pres. RICARDO VILLANUEVA CARRERA; Sec. MARTÍN ARÉVALO DE LEÓN.

Cámara del Agro: Edif. Géminis 10, Torre Norte, 9°, Of. 909, 12 Calle, 1-25, Zona 10, Guatemala City; tel. 2219-9021; e-mail camagro@intelnet.net.gt; internet www.camaradelagro.org; f. 1973; Pres. OTTO KUSIEK; Exec. Dir CARLA CABALLEROS.

Gremial de Empresarios Indígenas de Guatemala (Guate-Maya): f. 2012; private sector org. representing 190 indigenous cos; mem. of CACIF (q.v.); Pres. LUIS TEPEU.

Gremial de Huleros de Guatemala: 6a Avda A 12-37, Zona 9, Guatemala City; tel. 2339-1752; fax 2339-1755; e-mail gremhuleger@ guate.net.gt; internet www.gremialdehuleros.org; f. 1970; rubber producers' guild; 125 mems; Pres. JOSÉ MIGUEL EIZAGUIRRE; Gen. Man. CARLOS ALFREDO NÁJERA CASTILLO.

UTILITIES

Regulatory Authority

Comisión Nacional de Energía Eléctrica (CNEE): Edif. Paladium, 12°, 4 Avda 15-70, Zona 10, Guatemala City; tel. 2321-8000; fax 2321-8002; e-mail cnee@cnee.gob.gt; internet www.cnee.gob.gt; f. 1996; Pres. CARMEN URÍZAR.

Electricity

Empresa Eléctrica de Guatemala, SA: 6 Avda 8-14, Zona 1, Guatemala City; tel. 2277-7000; e-mail consultas@eegsa.net; internet www.eegsa.com; f. 1972; 80% privatized; Gen. Man. JORGE ALONZO; subsidiaries include:

> **Comercializadora Eléctrica de Guatemala, SA (COMEGSA):** Avda 6, 8-14, Zona 1, Guatemala City; tel. 2420-4200; fax 2230-5628; e-mail info@comegsa.net; internet www .comegsa.com.gt; f. 1998; Gen. Man. ANGEL GARCÍA.

> **Trelec, SA:** 2 Avda 9-27, Zona 1, Guatemala City; tel. 2420-4235; fax 2420-0409; e-mail trelec@trelec.net; f. 1999; Gen. Man. EDUARDO MANUEL ARITA.

Instituto Nacional de Electrificación (INDE): Edif. La Torre, 7a Avda 2-29, Zona 9, Guatemala City; tel. (2) 2422-1800; e-mail gerencia.general@inde.gob.gt; internet www.inde.gob.gt; f. 1959; fmr state agency for the generation and distribution of hydroelectric power; privatized in 1998; Pres. ERICK ESTUARDO ARCHILA DEHESA; Gen. Man. MARINUS ARIE BOER JOHANNESSEN.

CO-OPERATIVE

Instituto Nacional de Cooperativas (INACOP): Via 6, 6-72, Zona 4, Guatemala City; tel. 2339-1627; fax 2339-1648; e-mail gerentegeneral@inacop.gob.gt; internet www.inacop.gob.gt; technical and financial assistance in planning and devt of co-operatives; Gen. Man. LUIS ALBERTO MONTENEGRO.

TRADE UNIONS

Confederación General de Trabajadores de Guatemala (CGTG): 3 Avda 12-22, Zona 1, Guatemala City; tel. 2232-1010; fax 2251-3212; e-mail info@confederacioncgtg.org; internet www .confederacioncgtg.org; f. 1987; fmrly Central Nacional de Trabajadores (CNT); Sec.-Gen. JOSÉ E. PINZÓN SALAZAR; 60,000 mems (2007).

Federación Sindical de Trabajadores de la Alimentación Agro-Industrias y Similares de Guatemala (FESTRAS): 16 Avda 13-52, Zona 1, Guatemala City; tel. and fax 2251-8091; e-mail festras@gmail.com; internet festras.blogspot.in; f. 1991; Sec.-Gen. JOSÉ DAVID MORALES C.

Unidad de Acción Sindical y Popular (UASP): 10 Avda A 5-40, Zona 1, Guatemala City; tel. 2230-5423; fax 2230-3004; e-mail uaspgt@yahoo.es; internet www.uaspgt.es.tl; f. 1988; coalition of labour and peasant orgs; Co-ordinator NERY ROBERTO BARRIOS DE LEÓN; Sec. NÉLIDA CORADO; includes:

> **Comité de la Unidad Campesina (CUC)** (Committee of Peasants' Unity): 31a Avda A 14-46, Zona 7, Ciudad de Plata II, Apdo 1002, Guatemala City; tel. 2434-9754; fax 2438-1424; e-mail cuc@ intelnett.com; internet www.cuc.org.gt; f. 1978; Sec.-Gen. DANIEL PASCUAL HERNÁNDEZ.

> **Confederación de Unidad Sindical de Guatemala (CUSG):** 12 Calle A, 0-66, Zona 1, Guatemala City; tel. and fax 2220-7875; e-mail info@cusg.com.gt; internet www.cusg.com.gt; f. 1983; Sec.-Gen. CARLOS ENRIQUE MANCILLA GARCÍA; 30,000 mems (2011).

Unión Guatemalteca de Trabajadores (UGT): 13a Calle 11-40, Zona 1, Guatemala City; tel. and fax 2251-1686; e-mail ugt .guatemala@yahoo.com; Sec.-Gen. ADOLFO LACS.

Transport

RAILWAYS

In 2007 there were 885 km of railway track in Guatemala.

Ferrovías Guatemala: 24 Avda 35-91, Zona 12, 01012 Guatemala City; tel. 2412-7200; fax 2412-7205; e-mail info@ferroviasgt.com;

internet www.rrdc.com/op_guatemala_fvg.html; f. 1968 as Ferrocarriles de Guatemala (FEGUA); 50-year concession awarded in 1997 to the US Railroad Devt Corpn (RDC); 784 km from Puerto Barrios and Santo Tomás de Castilla on the Atlantic coast to Tecún Umán on the Mexican border, via Zacapa, Guatemala City and Santa María; in 2007 services were suspended after arbitration claim filed by the RDC under the terms of the DR-CAFTA; claim resolved in 2013, but the services remained suspended; Pres. WILLIAM J. DUGGAN.

ROADS

In 2010 there were 14,118 km of roads, of which just over one-half were paved. The Guatemalan section of the Pan-American highway is 518.7 km long and totally asphalted. In 2010 the 362-km Franja Transversal del Norte highway, linking Huehuetenango and Izabal, was built.

SHIPPING

Guatemala's major ports are Puerto Barrios and Santo Tomás de Castilla on the Gulf of Mexico, San José and Champerico on the Pacific Ocean, and Puerto Quetzal. At 31 December 2014 the flag registered fleet comprised nine vessels, totalling 5,369 grt.

Comisión Portuaria Nacional: 6 Avda A 8-66, Zona 9, Apdo 01009, Guatemala City; tel. 2419-4800; fax 2360-5457; e-mail info@cpn.gob .gt; internet www.cpn.gob.gt; f. 1972; Pres. VIOLETA LUNA; Exec. Dir CARLOS ENRIQUE DE LA CERDA.

Dacotrans de Centroamerica, SA: 24 Avda 41-81, Zona 12, Interior Almacenadora Integrada, Apdo 40, Guatemala City; tel. 2381-1200; fax 2381-1244; e-mail dacotrans@dacotrans.com.gt; internet www.dacotrans.com.gt; f. 1969; part of Grupo Dacotrans Grosskopf GMBH & Co (Germany); Gen. Man. MATHIAS REHE.

Empresa Portuaria Nacional de Champerico: Avda del Ferrocarril, frente a la playa, 1000101 Champerico, Retalhuleu; tel. 7773-7223; fax 7773-7221; e-mail vallejo.l@gmail.com; internet www .epnac.blogspot.com; f. 1955; Pres. LUIS ENRIQUE PRADO LUARCA; Man. MARGARITO FLORIAN ESCOBEDO.

Empresa Portuaria Nacional Santo Tomás de Castilla (EMPORNAC): Calle Real de la Villa, 17 Calle 16-43, Zona 10, Guatemala City; tel. 7720-4040; fax 7960-0584; e-mail mercade@ santotomasport.com.gt; internet www.santotomasport.com.gt; Pres. JOSÉ ROBERTO DÍAZ-DÚRAN QUEZADA; Gen. Man. EDGARDO LÓPEZ.

Empresa Portuaria Quetzal: Edif. Torre Azul, 1°, Of. 105, 4 Calle 7-53, Zona 9, 01009 Guatemala City; tel. 2312-5000; fax 2334-8172; e-mail mercadeo@puerto-quetzal.com; internet www.puerto-quetzal .com; port and shipping co; Pres. FELIPE CASTAÑEDA; Gen. Man. RODOLFO KUSHIEK.

Seaboard Marine Ltda: Edif. Galerias Reforma, 4°, Of. 411, Avda La Reforma 8-60, Zona 9, Guatemala City; tel. 2384-3900; fax 2334-0077; e-mail Guillermo_Ortiz@seaboardmarine.com.gt; internet www.seaboardmarine.com; subsidiary of Seaboard Corpn (USA); Rep. GUILLERMO ORTIZ.

Transmares, SA: Torre 2, 8°, Centro Gerencial Las Margaritas, Diagonal 6, 10-01, Zona 10, 01010 Guatemala City; tel. 2429-8100; fax 2429-8148; e-mail henneke.sieveking@transmares.net; internet www.transmares.org; ocean liner and cargo shipping; logistics services under Translogística, SA; Gen. Man. HENNEKE SIEVEKING.

CIVIL AVIATION

There are two international airports, La Aurora in Guatemala City and Mundo Maya in Santa Elena, El Petén.

Dirección General de Aeronáutica Civil: Aeropuerto La Aurora, Zona 13, 01013 Guatemala City; tel. 2362-0216; e-mail direccion@ dgac.gob.gt; internet www.dgacguate.com; f. 1929; Dir JUAN JOSÉ CARLOS SUÁREZ.

Aviones Comerciales de Guatemala (Avcom): Aeropuerto La Aurora, Avda Hincapié 18, Zona 13, Guatemala City; tel. 2331-5821; domestic charter passenger services.

TACA: Aeropuerto La Aurora, Avda Hincapié 12-22, Zona 13, Guatemala City; tel. 2470-8222; e-mail scastillo@taca.com; internet www.taca.com; f. 1945 as AVIATECA; privatized in 1989; domestic services to the USA, Mexico, and within Central America; Gen. Man. MYNOR CORDÓN.

Transportes Aéreos Guatemaltecos, SA (TAG): Avda Hinapie y 18 Calle, Zona 13, Guatemala City; tel. 2380-9494; fax 2334-7205; e-mail tagsa@tag.com.gt; internet www.tag.com.gt; f. 1969; domestic and int. charter services; Gen. Man. JONATHAN LAYTON.

Tourism

Guatemala's main attraction lies in the ancient Mayan ruins. Other tourism highlights include its active steaming volcanos, mountain lakes, pristine beaches and a rich indigenous culture. The number of tourist arrivals reached 2.0m. in 2013, when receipts from tourism were US $1,020.6m.

Instituto Guatemalteco de Turismo (INGUAT) (Guatemala Tourist Institute): Centro Cívico, 7a Avda 1-17, Zona 4, Guatemala City; tel. 2421-2800; fax 2331-4416; e-mail informacion@inguat.gob .gt; internet www.inguat.gob.gt; f. 1967; Dir PEDRO PABLO DUCHEZ.

Defence

As assessed in November 2014, Guatemala's active armed forces numbered an estimated 17,300: army 15,550, navy 900 and air force 850. Reserve forces totalled 63,850. In addition, there were paramilitary forces of 25,000. Military service is by selective conscription for 30 months.

Defence Budget: an estimated 2,080m. quetzales in 2014.

Chief of Staff of National Defence: Gen. CARLOS EDUARDO ESTRADA PERÉZ.

Education

Elementary education is free and compulsory between seven and 14 years of age. Primary education begins at the age of seven and lasts for six years. Secondary education, beginning at 13 years of age, lasts for up to six years, comprising two cycles of three years each. Enrolment at primary schools in 2011 included 93% of children in the relevant age-group. The comparable ratio for secondary education in that year was 46%. There are 12 universities, of which 11 are privately run. In 2012 expenditure on education by the central Government was projected at 11,097.7m. quetzales, equivalent to 18.6% of total spending.

GUINEA

Introductory Survey

LOCATION, CLIMATE, LANGUAGE, RELIGION, FLAG, CAPITAL

The Republic of Guinea lies on the west coast of Africa, with Sierra Leone and Liberia to the south, Senegal and Guinea-Bissau to the north, and Mali and Côte d'Ivoire inland to the east. The climate on the coastal strip is hot and moist, with temperatures ranging from about 32°C (90°F) in the dry season to about 23°C (73°F) in the wet season (May–October). The interior is higher and cooler. The official language is French, but Soussou, Manika and six other national languages are widely spoken. Most of the population are Muslims, but some follow traditional animist beliefs. Around 3% are Roman Catholics. The national flag (proportions 2 by 3) consists of three equal vertical stripes, of red, yellow and green. The capital is Conakry.

CONTEMPORARY POLITICAL HISTORY

Historical Context

The Republic of Guinea (formerly French Guinea, part of French West Africa) became independent on 2 October 1958, after 95% of voters rejected the Constitution of the Fifth Republic under which the French colonies became self-governing within the French Community. The new state was the object of punitive reprisals by the outgoing French authorities: all aid was withdrawn, and the administrative infrastructure destroyed. The Parti Démocratique de Guinée—Rassemblement Démocratique Africain (PDG—RDA) became the basis for the construction of new institutions. Its leader, Ahmed Sékou Touré, became President, and the PDG—RDA the sole political party. Sékou Touré pursued vigorous policies of socialist revolution. Following an abortive invasion by Portuguese troops and Guinean exiles in 1970, many of those convicted of involvement were executed.

In November 1978 it was announced that the functions of the PDG—RDA and the state were to be merged, and the country was renamed the People's Revolutionary Republic of Guinea. There was, none the less, a general move away from rigid Marxism and a decline in relations with the USSR, as Guinea sought a political and economic rapprochement with its African neighbours, with France and with other Western powers.

Domestic Political Affairs

Sékou Touré died in March 1984, while undergoing surgery in the USA. In April, before a successor had been chosen by the ruling party, the armed forces seized power in a bloodless coup. A Comité Militaire de Redressement National (Military Committee for National Recovery—CMRN) was appointed, headed by Col (later Gen.) Lansana Conté; the PDG—RDA and the legislature were dissolved; and the Constitution was suspended. The Second Republic of Guinea was proclaimed in May. In December Conté, as President, assumed the posts of Head of Government and Minister of Defence.

In late 1989 Conté announced that, following a referendum on a proposed new constitution, a joint civilian and military Comité Transitoire de Redressement National (Transitional Committee for National Recovery—CTRN) would replace the CMRN. After a transitional period of not more than five years, civilian rule would be established, with an executive and legislature directly elected within a two-party system. The draft Constitution of what was designated the Third Republic was reportedly endorsed by 98.7% of the 97.4% of the electorate who voted in a referendum in December 1990; and the CTRN was inaugurated in February 1991, under Conté's chairmanship.

In October 1991 Conté announced that a law authorizing the registration of an unlimited number of political parties would come into effect in April 1992, and that legislative elections would be held before the end of 1992. The Constitution was promulgated on 23 December 1991, and in January 1992 Conté ceded the presidency of the CTRN, in conformity with the constitutional separation of powers. Most military officers, and all those who had returned from exile after the 1984 coup (termed *Guinéens de l'extérieur*), were subsequently removed from the Council of Ministers.

Some 17 political parties were legalized in April 1992; it was subsequently rumoured that the pro-Conté Parti pour l'Unité et du Progrès (PUP), established by prominent *Guinéens de l'extérieur*, was benefiting from state funds. In December the Government postponed indefinitely the legislative elections which had been scheduled for later that month.

In October 1993 the Supreme Court approved eight candidates for the forthcoming presidential election. According to official results, Conté was elected with 51.7% of the votes cast. His closest rival, Alpha Condé, of the Rassemblement du Peuple de Guinée (RPG), took 19.6% of the votes; Mamadou Boye Bâ, of the Union pour la Nouvelle République (UNR), won 13.4%; and Siradiou Diallo, of the Parti pour le Renouveau et le Progrès (PRP), 11.9%. Conté was inaugurated as President in January 1994.

The delayed legislative elections finally took place in June 1995. Some 846 candidates, from 21 parties, contested the 114 seats in the Assemblée Nationale (National Assembly). As preliminary results indicated that the PUP had won an overwhelming majority in the legislature, the parties of the 'radical' opposition (the RPG, the PRP and the UNR) announced their intention to boycott the assembly, protesting that voting had been conducted fraudulently. According to the final results, which were verified by the Supreme Court in July, the PUP won 71 seats—having taken 30 of the 38 single-member constituencies and 41 of the 76 seats elected on the basis of national lists. Of the eight other parties to win representation, the RPG secured 19 seats, while the PRP and the UNR each won nine. The new legislature was officially inaugurated on 30 August.

In February 1996 Conté was reportedly seized as he attempted to flee the presidential palace during a mutiny by disaffected elements of the military, and was held by rebels for some 15 hours until he made concessions including a doubling of salaries and immunity from prosecution for those involved in the uprising. The Minister of Defence, Col Abdourahmane Diallo, was dismissed, and Conté assumed personal responsibility for defence. In March it was announced that eight members of the military, including four senior officers, had been charged with undermining state security in connection with the coup attempt. In July Conté announced the appointment of a non-partisan economist, Sidya Touré, as Prime Minister, the first time that position had existed under the Third Republic.

In June 1997 it was announced that a State Security Court was to be established to deal with matters of exceptional jurisdiction, and that its first task would be to try the alleged leaders of the previous year's mutiny. In September 38 people charged with offences related to the 1996 attempted coup were sentenced by the new court to custodial sentences of up to 15 years.

The official results of the December 1998 presidential election confirmed a decisive victory for Conté, with 56.1% of the valid votes cast. Bâ, contesting the election for the Union pour le Progrès et le Renouveau (UPR, formed by a merger of the UNR and the PRP), won 24.6%; and Condé, for the RPG, 16.6%. Condé was arrested shortly after the election and subsequently charged with plotting against the Conté regime. In March 1999 Lamine Sidimé, hitherto Chief Justice of the Supreme Court, was appointed Prime Minister.

Opposition groups and human rights organizations campaigned throughout 1999 and 2000 for the release of Condé and other activists detained at the time of the 1998 presidential election. In September 2000 Condé was found guilty of sedition by the State Security Court and sentenced to five years' imprisonment; a further seven defendants were given custodial sentences of between 18 months and three years.

In September 2000 an armed rebellion in south-east Guinea reportedly resulted in at least 40 deaths. Instability subsequently intensified in regions near the borders with Sierra Leone and Liberia. By mid-October fighting between armed groups and Guinean soldiers was reported to have caused around 360 deaths. The Guinean authorities attributed the upsurge in violence to forces supported by the Governments of Liberia and Burkina Faso, and to members of the Sierra Leonean rebel Revolutionary United Front (RUF, see Sierra Leone), in alliance with Guinean dissidents. In November a series of cross-border attacks was reportedly conducted by former members of a faction of a dissolved Liberian dissident group, the United Liberation Movement of Liberia for Democracy (ULIMO), ULIMO—K (see Liberia), which President Conté had previously supported. In December rebel attacks on the southern towns of Guéckédou and Kissidougou led to more than 230 deaths, and the almost complete destruction of Guéckédou. The Government estimated that some 94,000 people had been displaced as a result of fighting in the region, and aid agencies withdrew from south-east Guinea later in the month as a result of the heightened instability.

Constitutional changes

A constitutional referendum took place in November 2001. According to official results, 98.4% of voters approved a series of amendments that removed the restriction on the number of terms the President could serve; allowed candidates aged over 70 years to contest the presidency; and extended the presidential term of office from five years to seven, with effect from the presidential election due in 2003. Turnout was put at 87.2% of the registered electorate. Prior to the vote, there were violent clashes between security forces and opponents of the proposed changes. Opposition members disputed the results, claiming that less than 20% of the electorate had voted.

In April 2002 President Conté issued decrees scheduling legislative elections, which had been repeatedly delayed, for 30 June; and establishing a supervisory Conseil National Electoral. Concerns were expressed that the short period between the establishment of the election council and the forthcoming polls would be insufficient to ensure transparency of conduct, and the European Union (EU, see p. 271) subsequently withheld funding for the elections. In May four opposition parties that had announced their intention to boycott the legislative elections— including the RPG and the Union des Forces Républicaines— formed a political alliance, the Front de l'Alternance Démocratique (FRAD). A split in the UPR became increasingly apparent between a faction led by the current party President, Siradiou Diallo, who sought to engage with the electoral process, and a group led by Mamadou Boye Bâ, its honorary President, who pledged allegiance to the FRAD.

At the June 2002 elections, the PUP increased its majority in the National Assembly, winning 85 of the 114 seats. The governing party was unopposed in all 38 single-member constituencies, and took 47 of the 76 seats allocated by proportional representation. The UPR became the second largest party in the legislature, with 20 seats. Opposition parties, both those that had contested the elections and those of the FRAD, alleged that there had been widespread fraud in the conduct of the polls, and the US ambassador to Guinea expressed concern at apparent electoral irregularities. In October Bâ became President of a new party, the Union des Forces Démocratiques de Guinée (UFDG).

In September 2003, shortly after the formal nomination of Conté as the presidential candidate of the PUP, the FRAD announced that negotiations between the Government and opposition parties on the conduct of the forthcoming election had broken down. In November both the FRAD and the UPR announced that they would boycott the election. Meanwhile, the National Assembly approved legislation providing for an amnesty for persons convicted of political crimes—notably including Alpha Condé, who would thereby nominally be permitted to contest the presidential election. In the event, however, the only candidate who was approved to challenge the incumbent was Mamadou Bhoye Barry, of the Union pour le Progrès National—Parti pour l'Unité et le Développement.

Voting in the presidential election proceeded in December 2003. In the absence of any significant opposition, Conté was re-elected for a further (now seven-year) term of office, with 95.3% of the votes cast, according to official results. Although the opposition claimed that turnout had been as low as 15%, official figures indicated a rate of participation of approximately 82% of the registered electorate.

In February 2004 Conté dismissed Lamine Sidimé and appointed a substantially reorganized Government, with François Lonsény Fall as Prime Minister. In April, however, it was announced that Fall had resigned and had fled Guinea; the former premier subsequently claimed that his Government had been obstructed in its attempts to implement economic and judicial reforms. The post of Prime Minister remained vacant until the appointment in December of Cellou Dalein Diallo, previously Minister of Fisheries and Aquaculture.

Diallo announced a comprehensive government reorganization in April 2006, involving new appointments to most ministerial positions. Notably, responsibility for the economy and finance, for planning and international co-operation, and for economic and financial control was transferred to the office of the Prime Minister. However, it emerged that President Conté (constitutionally Head of Government, as well as Head of State) had not authorized the changes. Diallo was dismissed and the reorganization was countermanded. Conté restructured the Government in May, nominating six ministers of state with responsibility for key portfolios including foreign affairs, the economy and finance, and presidential affairs. No Prime Minister was appointed.

Domestic unrest

In June 2006 the country's two principal trade unions, the Confédération Nationale des Travailleurs de Guinée (CNTG) and the Union Syndicale des Travailleurs de Guinée (USTG), organized a widely observed general strike, demanding, *inter alia*, reductions in the prices of fuel and rice. Clashes between protesters and security forces reportedly resulted in the deaths of some 20 people. The strike was brought to an end after the Government agreed to increase public sector salaries and allowances for rent and transportation, as well as to lower the cost of rice.

The CNTG and the USTG commenced a further general strike in January 2007, supported by a number of opposition parties, non-governmental organizations (NGOs) and civil society groups. Initially, the action again focused on prices of basic foodstuffs and fuel, as well as the return to gaol of two former prominent politicians, accused of financial impropriety, whose release had been secured by the President in the previous month. However, following violent clashes between demonstrators and security forces, in which five people were killed and several hundred were arrested, the unions extended their demands to include the resignation of Conté and his administration. Conté dismissed the Minister of State for Presidential Affairs, El Hadj Fodé Bangoura, but protests continued, and further deaths were reported across the country. Both the UN and the African Union (AU, see p. 188) urged the Government to commence negotiations with the trade unions. After almost two weeks trade union leaders, who had been briefly detained meanwhile, were invited to talks with Conté, who indicated his willingness to appoint a 'consensus' Prime Minister. The strike was halted in late January, after Conté agreed to nominate a new Prime Minister. However, Conté's subsequent choice of Eugène Camara (who had succeeded Bangoura as Minister of State for Presidential Affairs) as Prime Minister was rejected by the trade unions and the political opposition, The unions recommended the general strike in mid-February, again demanding the President's resignation. In response, the President declared a 'state of siege', imposing martial law and a nationwide curfew. In negotiations with the Government, the trade unions rejected Conté's proposal to maintain Camara as interim Prime Minister. The National Assembly subsequently voted to terminate martial law and the curfew; and in late February, following further negotiations brokered by the Economic Community of West African States (ECOWAS, see p. 258), Conté announced that he would select a new Prime Minister from a list of candidates drawn up by the trade unions and opposition parties. Lansana Kouyaté, a career diplomat and the former Executive Secretary of ECOWAS, was duly appointed Prime Minister, and the industrial action was brought to an end. By this time, at least 130 people were reported to have been killed in the violence since January.

Kouyaté was sworn in as Prime Minister at the beginning of March 2007. He subsequently named a Council of Ministers (composed largely of technocrats, notably excluding ministers from the previous administration), in which the former Deputy Chief of Staff of the Armed Forces, Gen. Arafan Camara, became Minister of National Defence. However, Camara was (together with the Chief of Staff of the Armed Forces) replaced following a two-week uprising by members of the armed forces in May, involving widespread intimidation of civilians. The military had been demanding the payment of salary arrears, in some cases dating back as far as 11 years, and protesting against several senior defence appointments made earlier in the year.

In January 2008 Conté dismissed the Minister of Communication and Information Technology, Justin Morel Junior, who had criticized the content of the President's New Year address— in which Conté referred to Prime Minister Kouyaté's administration as a 'disappointment'. Trade unions demanded the minister's reinstatement on the grounds that his dismissal was contrary to the agreement brokered in early 2007, threatening renewed industrial action. Following negotiations led by

Kouyaté with trade unions and civil society representatives, a planned general strike was deferred pending further discussion of a presidential decree, issued in December 2007, whereby Conté had reassumed a number of powers previously devolved to the Prime Minister. Tensions escalated once again in May 2008 after Conté dismissed Kouyaté and replaced him with a close personal ally, Ahmed Tidiane Souaré. Conté also dismissed Gen. Bailo Diallo, the successor to Arafan Camara as Minister of National Defence, following a further uprising by soldiers to demand the payment of salary arrears. At least three people were killed in violence in Conakry, and it was reported that the army Chief of Staff had briefly been held hostage. There were renewed security concerns in June, when a protest by police in Conakry led to clashes with armed forces personnel. A civilian, Almany Kabèle Camara, was appointed in place of Gen. Diallo in the new Government named in that month. In October legislative elections were postponed for a third time, because of insufficient funds and incomplete preparations. In the following month at least four people were killed after security forces opened fire on demonstrators who were demanding lower fuel prices.

Military takeover following the death of Conté

President Conté, who was thought to have been in poor health for some time, died on 22 December 2008. Although Aboubacar Somparé, the Speaker of the National Assembly, stated that he should assume the presidency pending an election, a group of junior army officers, led by Capt. Moussa Dadis Camara, swiftly seized power. Camara proclaimed the formation of a 32-member Conseil National pour la Démocratie et le Développement (National Council for Democracy and Development—CNDD), the suspension of the Constitution and the dissolution of all state institutions. The CNDD banned all political and trade union activities. The coup was widely condemned by the international community, and the AU, followed by ECOWAS, announced the suspension of Guinea's membership pending the return of constitutional order. At the end of December an economist, Kabiné Komara, was appointed as Prime Minister. A new Government was named in January 2009, including Gen. Sékouba Konaté as Minister at the Presidency, in charge of National Defence; Justin Morel Junior was notably reappointed as Minister of Information and Culture. Meanwhile, Camara, who pledged to eradicate corruption and improve living standards, made a commitment to hold legislative and presidential elections within 12 months, stating that he did not intend to contest the latter. A number of former ministers, including Ousmane Doré, and several prominent business executives appeared before a commission charged with investigating corruption during the Conté era. The ban on political and trade union activity was revoked in February. In April two army officers were detained, on suspicion of plotting a coup as Camara prepared to leave the country for the first time since taking power.

A revised election timetable was announced in August 2009, whereby the presidential election was to be held in January 2010, followed by legislative elections in March. Despite an earlier undertaking that members of the military would be precluded from seeking elected office, Camara subsequently indicated his intention to contest the presidency. In response to Camara's announcement, opposition parties organized a protest rally at a stadium in Conakry in September 2009, attended by some 10,000 people. Security forces opened fire on demonstrators, killing more than 150. In October the UN Secretary-General announced that an international Commission of Inquiry would be established to investigate the incident. Meanwhile, ECOWAS imposed an arms embargo on Guinea, and the AU, the EU and the USA imposed targeted sanctions on members of the CNDD. Several government ministers resigned in protest against the killings. The presidential election was subsequently rescheduled for July 2010, with legislative elections to follow at an unspecified date.

Camara's decision to delay the elections, and his apparent intention to stand as a presidential candidate, coupled with international pressure on Camara to bring to justice those believed to be responsible for the Conakry killings, led to growing disaffection within the military regime. In December 2009 there was an assassination attempt against Camara, who suffered a gunshot wound to the head and was transferred to Morocco for medical treatment. Konaté was installed as interim President. The perpetrator of the attack, Lt Abubakar 'Toumba' Diakite—who, it was subsequently reported, was to have been handed over to the authorities to be prosecuted for his alleged role in the events of September—meanwhile evaded capture and fled the country.

The UN Commission of Inquiry into the September 2009 massacre submitted its report in December. The inquiry found that crimes against humanity had been committed, and that there were reasonable grounds to allege individual criminal responsibility on the part of key members of Guinea's military regime—including Capt. Camara and Lt Diakite. The investigation recorded 156 deaths, 109 documented rapes and 40 reported 'disappearances', together with widespread illegal arrests and detentions, and torture of detainees. The Commission recommended, *inter alia*, that cases of crimes against humanity be taken up by the International Criminal Court, and that the Office of the UN High Commissioner for Human Rights (OHCHR) monitor the situation in Guinea. (Accordingly, OHCHR began operations in Conakry in May 2010.)

In January 2010 Konaté pledged to restore civilian rule, and indicated the CNDD's willingness to appoint a transitional government of national unity with a Prime Minister from the political opposition. Following negotiations hosted by the President of Burkina Faso, Blaise Compaoré, involving Camara (who had now been transferred from Morocco to Burkina), senior members of the CNDD and representatives of the opposition, it was agreed that Camara would remain outside Guinea on a 'leave of absence' to continue his convalescence. Jean-Marie Doré, the leader of the Union pour le Progrès de la Guinée, was sworn in as Prime Minister in late January. His new Government, appointed in February, included a number of military members of the outgoing administration, together with representatives of opposition parties, trade unionists and members of civil society. Meanwhile, also in late January, Konaté installed the Secretary-General of the CNTG, Rabiatou Serah Diallo, as President of a Conseil National de Transition (National Transitional Council—CNT). This new body was to oversee the transition from military to civilian rule; its 155 members, including representatives of civil society, political parties and religious groups, as well as members of the CNDD, were appointed in March. Konaté announced in that month that the presidential election would be held on 27 June, and confirmed that he would not be a candidate.

The CNT presented a draft Constitution (replacing that suspended in December 2008) to Konaté in April 2010. Under the terms of the new document, which was adopted by decree on 7 May, a new President and legislature were to be elected for a term of five years, with the presidential mandate to be renewable only once; the minimum age for presidential candidates was set at 35 years.

Alpha Condé elected President

The first round of the presidential election proceeded on 27 June 2010, with 24 candidates. The following day the Commission Electorale Nationale Indépendante (CENI) acknowledged widespread technical failings, but ECOWAS observers assessed that the election had been conducted without malpractice. Provisional results, released by the CENI in early July, indicated that Cellou Dalein Diallo (the candidate of the UFDG) and Alpha Condé (representing the RPG) would proceed to a second round. Protests ensued from several other candidates, in particular from the third-placed Sidya Touré and his supporters. On 20 July the Supreme Court declared revised election results, according to which Diallo, with 43.7% of the votes, and Condé, with 18.3%, were to proceed to a second round. Voter turnout was recorded at about 52% of the registered electorate. Touré subsequently urged his supporters to vote for Diallo, while Lansana Kouyaté, who had been placed fourth in the first round, declared his support for Condé. Gen. Konaté subsequently announced that the second round of the presidential election (originally scheduled for 18 July) would take place on 19 September.

In September 2010 the head of the CENI, Ben Sékou Sylla, and its Director of Planning, Boubacar Diallo, were found guilty of fraudulent activity during the first round of the election, and sentenced to one year's imprisonment. The announcement of their conviction provoked violent clashes between supporters of Diallo and Condé, in which one person was killed and at least 50 others were injured. The authorities suspended the election process and banned all demonstrations. In October the second round was again deferred after Diallo accused the newly appointed head of the CENI, Louceny Camara, of favouring Condé, prompting his replacement by a Malian general, Siaka Toumany Sangaré. The poll was finally rescheduled for 7 November.

International electoral observers declared that the second round of the presidential election, which duly took place on

7 November 2010, had been conducted successfully. In mid-November the CENI announced that Condé had been elected to the presidency, with about 52.5% of votes cast. Diallo again alleged malpractice, and announced that he would challenge the results at the Supreme Court. Following the declaration of the election results, violent clashes erupted between supporters of the two candidates in Conakry and the western cities of Pita and Labé, in which some 10 people were killed and 200 injured. The election of Condé, a member of the Malinké ethnic group, was reported to have exacerbated long-standing tensions between the Malinké and Peul (or Fulani), Diallo's ethnic group. In response to the deterioration in the security situation, Konaté imposed a national state of emergency.

The results of the presidential election were confirmed by the Supreme Court in early December 2010. The AU subsequently restored Guinea's membership and ended all other sanctions in force. The state of emergency was subsequently ended, and Konaté urged the country's armed forces to support the new President. Condé was inaugurated on 21 December. A hitherto relatively unknown economist, Mohamed Saïd Fofana, was appointed Prime Minister. Kerfala Yansané, the Minister of the Economy and Finance in the transitional administration, remained in post, while Condé assumed personal responsibility for defence.

In April 2011, in anticipation of the return of Diallo to Conakry, Condé imposed a ban on demonstrations. Protesters defied the ban, and there were violent clashes with security forces in which, according to the UFDG, three activists were killed and 60 wounded. In July there was an apparent assassination attempt against Condé, when a rocket-propelled grenade landed in the presidential residence, killing at least one bodyguard and wounding several others. The Government blamed the attacks on senior army officers close to the previous regime.

Meanwhile, in June 2011 the CENI stated that legislative elections would be held by the end of the year, contingent on the Government and opposition reaching agreement on the voters' register. In September it was announced that the poll would be held on 29 December. Opposition groups objected that the schedule would not allow for required electoral reforms. In late September, on the eve of what had been planned as a day of national reconciliation in remembrance of the violent events of September 2009, opposition supporters clashed with police in demonstrations over the issues of the timing of the elections and voters' list reform. At least two protesters were reported to have been killed, and the authorities stated that 322 people had been arrested.

In December 2011 numerous casualties were reported when security forces dispersed a meeting of Lansana Kouyaté's Parti de l'Espoir pour le Développement National (PEDN) in Kankan. On 20 December it was announced that the scheduled legislative elections would be postponed. At the same time, 15 opposition activists convicted for their involvement in the violence in September were pardoned. Talks scheduled for early January 2012 to agree a date for elections were subsequently boycotted by the opposition.

It was stated in February 2012 that the legislative elections would take place in May, but in March Lounceny Camara (meanwhile reappointed head of the CENI) confirmed 8 July as the election date. The opposition again asserted that this did not allow sufficient time for the full revision of electoral lists, and in April President Condé announced a further postponement. In May the opposition held demonstrations to demand electoral reforms, and to protest against what they considered to be a pro-Condé bias on the part of the CENI; violent clashes with the security forces ensued, leading to mass arrests and the imposition of a ban on subsequent demonstrations. Further arrests of opposition activists were reported in August, following another anti-Government rally. Two PEDN cabinet ministers resigned in protest against the detentions. The taut political climate fuelled ethnic tensions, and there were outbreaks of violence between Malinké and Peul communities in Conakry during September. Camara, stood down as head of the CENI in September, thus fulfilling a key opposition demand. A new CENI, with increased opposition representation, was inaugurated in November, with Bokary Fofana as its President. In December the new CENI announced that the legislative elections would, provisionally, be held in May 2013.

Condé reorganized the Council of Ministers in October 2012, dismissing the remaining cabinet members who had been involved in the 2008 military coup as well as two ministers accused of corruption. Among new appointees was former Prime Minister Fall, who took the foreign affairs portfolio.

The Chief of Staff of the Armed Forces, Gen. Souleymane Kelefa Diallo, was one of 11 people killed in February 2013, when the aircraft in which they were travelling crashed in Liberia. Gen. Diallo, who had been regarded as an important ally of President Condé, responsible for key armed forces reforms, was succeeded by Brig.-Gen. Namory Traoré, previously Deputy Chief of Staff.

The 2013 legislative elections

There was renewed violence from February 2013, an initial catalyst for which was an opposition-led demonstration in Conakry to demand transparency in the forthcoming legislative elections. Both the UN Secretary-General and OHCHR appealed for calm, but the situation escalated, apparently fuelled by inter-ethnic tensions between Malinké and Peul groups. In mid-April the Secretary-General's Special Representative for West Africa, Saïd Djinnit, was mandated to facilitate a dialogue between the Guinean Government and opposition (after the previous nominee, a Senegalese retired army general, failed to meet the approval of Guinea's opposition groups). Also in mid-April President Condé issued a decree whereby the elections were again postponed until 30 June. The announcement provoked renewed violence, as police intervened in the capital to disperse opposition activists who were protesting against what they considered to be a unilateral decision on the part of the administration. Among opposition demands were that the South African company awarded the contract for revising the electoral register, together with its local partner, be replaced; and that members of the Guinean diaspora be permitted to vote in the national elections. By the end of April at least 12 people were reported to have been killed, and more than 300 injured, in two months of unrest, and a further 12 people were killed, and 100 injured, during a further protest in late May. In response to these latest incidents, Condé dismissed the Minister of Security and Civil Protection, Mouramany Cissé, replacing him with Madifing Diané; a former senior police officer and latterly Guinea's ambassador to Senegal. In late June, by which time the number of deaths reportedly exceeded 50, Condé announced a further postponement of the elections until 28 July. Opposition parties, which had meanwhile withdrawn from the dialogue with the Government in protest against the shooting by police of three political activists at a demonstration by supporters of Cellou Dalein Diallo, returned to negotiations under Djinnit's mediation in early July, and in mid-July a presidential decree was issued setting an election date of 24 September. Agreement was reached whereby the existing contract for the electoral register would remain in place, and that Guineans abroad would be eligible to vote. A monitoring committee, led by the head of the Court of Appeal and including representatives of the CENI, the Government, political parties and representatives of the UN, the EU, the AU, ECOWAS and the Organisation Internationale de la Francophonie (La Francophonie), was established to support the CENI's work in ensuring that the elections were free, fair and credible.

Meanwhile, in June 2013 a senior figure in the former CNDD, Col Claude Pivi, was indicted on charges including murder, rape, arson and destruction of property in connection with the 2009 stadium massacre. At the time of his indictment, Col Pivi was responsible for presidential security in the Condé administration. Hitherto, none of the seven members of the military who had been charged as a result of the investigation into the stadium incident and related events had been brought to trial.

In July 2013, following a six-month trial, five people were sentenced to life imprisonment, having been convicted of involvement in the attempt to assassinate President Condé two years earlier. Among those sentenced were a former head of the late Lansana Conté's presidential guard, Commdr Alpha Oumar Boffa Diallo, and Mamadou Oury Bah (a founder of the UFDG, now living in exile in France), who was one of three defendants convicted *in absentia*. Security forces were deployed to N'Zérékoré, in the Forestière region of south-eastern Guinea, in July, following clashes between rival Guerze and Konianke groups in which at least 57 people were killed and more than 160 injured.

One week before the National Assembly elections were due to take place, the Government and opposition agreed, with UN mediation, to postpone voting for four days in order for final preparations to be completed. The legislative elections—the first in Guinea since 2002—finally proceeded according to this latest schedule on 28 September 2013, with some 33 parties contesting the National Assembly's 114 seats. Voting was reported to have taken place in an atmosphere of calm, despite further violence in preceding days. Cellou Dalein Diallo, whose UFDG was considered as presenting the greatest challenge to Condé's RPG Arc-en-ciel alliance, asserted that logistical problems and anomalies had not been resolved; and at the beginning of October the main opposition parties, alleging widespread fraud, withdrew their representatives from oversight of the counting process and demanded that the elections be annulled. The opposition also subsequently withdrew from the UN-facilitated dialogue once again. In early October a joint statement by the various observer groups—including representatives of ECOWAS, the UN and the EU, together with French and US diplomatic missions—expressed concern that the validity of certain results could be undermined by irregularities observed in eight of the 38 single-member constituencies. None the less, the UN Secretary-General and ECOWAS, along with other members of the international community, commended the release of provisional results by the CENI on 18 October. These showed that the RPG Arc-en-ciel alliance had won the largest number of seats, with 53 of the total 114 (including 18 in the single-member constituencies). The UFDG won 37 seats (including 14 single-member seats), and the Union des Forces Républicaines (UFR) of Sidya Touré 10 (of which five were in single-member constituencies); 12 other parties also secured representation. Turnout was recorded at some 64% of the eligible electorate. Opposition parties maintained their demand that the results be annulled on grounds of fraud. On 15 November, however, the Supreme Court rejected all complaints lodged against the outcome of the elections and formally declared the results unchanged from those previously announced by the CENI. A week later at least one person was killed in clashes with police during an opposition protest against the declared outcome. In mid-December opposition parties confirmed that they would take up their seats in the National Assembly, despite their continued objections to the election results.

The new legislature was sworn in on 13 January 2014 (formally succeeding the CNT), with deputies electing Claude Kory Kondiano, the preferred candidate of the RPG, as President of the National Assembly. Mohamed Saïd Fofana was reappointed as Prime Minister on 18 January, having formally resigned three days earlier. The composition of the new, 35-member Council of Ministers was announced on 20 January, including six members with the rank of Minister of State. Key ministers from the outgoing administration were retained in the RPG-dominated Government, among them Kerfala Yansané as Minister of State, Minister of Mines and Geology. He was succeeded as Minister of the Economy and Finance by Mohamed Diaré, previously a deputy minister responsible for the budget. Fall remained as Minister of Foreign Affairs and Guineans Abroad, with the rank of Minister of State; and Diané retained his post as Minister of Security and Civil Protection. Among 15 new appointees was Cheick Sakho, a lawyer latterly based in France, as Minister of State, Minister of Justice and Keeper of the Seals, and Idrissa Thiam, hitherto a special adviser at the presidency, as Minister of Energy and Water. President Condé retained personal responsibility for defence.

Concerns remained regarding the security situation and increasing frustration on the part of Guineans at the Condé administration's perceived failure to improve economic and social conditions. There were violent clashes in Conakry in mid-February 2014 as police intervened to disperse protests against power failures; at least two people were killed during one day of rioting. At the end of the month government buildings and a police station were ransacked by protesters in Fria, north of Conakry, following the death of a young man in police custody there.

In March 2014 the Governor of Conakry, Commdr Sékou Resco Camara, was dismissed, apparently in connection with a judicial investigation—in response to a complaint brought in 2012 by human rights organizations, together with 17 individuals—into alleged acts of torture conducted in 2010. Camara had been indicted in February 2013; Gen. Nouhou Thiam (who remained in detention while awaiting trial in connection with the attack on the presidential residence in 2011) was charged in the same case later that month, and Commdr Aboubacar Sidiki Camara, head of the presidential guard under the interim administration of Sékouba Konaté, was indicted at the end of July.

Recent developments: *Ebola Virus Disease epidemic*

An outbreak of Ebola Virus Disease (EVD) in south-eastern Guinea was officially reported to the Guinean authorities in March 2014 (it was later recorded that the first case had occurred in a small village in December 2013). The World Health Organization (WHO) formally declared the outbreak on 23 March, and an international appeal was launched on 4 April. Although neighbouring states closed their borders with Guinea, confirmed cases of EVD were reported in Liberia by the end of March, Sierra Leone by May, Nigeria by July, Senegal by August and Mali by October (and through aid workers in Europe and the USA late that year). WHO and the Governments of Sierra Leone, Guinea and Liberia launched a joint US $100m. response plan at the beginning of August. On 14 August President Condé declared a national health emergency and announced a number of medical measures intended to combat the virus in Guinea. Efforts to contain EVD were reported to be hampered by local community suspicions of medical workers: in August riots erupted in N'Zérékoré over rumours that health workers had infected people with Ebola, causing the Government to dispatch security forces to the area; and in September it was reported that eight members of a health care team, including three journalists, had been murdered by local villagers in the south-eastern town of Womey, near N'Zérékoré.

In October 2014 President Condé effected a reorganization of the Government in which Mahmoudou Cissé replaced Diané as Minister of Security and Civil Protection and Idrissa Thiam was dismissed from his position as Minister of Energy and Water. Cheikh Taliby Sylla was appointed to this portfolio while Dr Ibrahima Kassory Fofana became Minister of State in the Presidency, responsible for Public-Private Investments.

Meanwhile, amid the continued crisis, the Guinean authorities undertook preparations for the next presidential election in 2015, which necessitated the prior organization of long-delayed local elections (originally scheduled for early 2014). The opposition accused the authorities of capitalizing on the EVD outbreak and, following the suspension of a political dialogue, staged anti-Government demonstrations in January 2015 to reiterate demands for electoral reform. The arrest of a local imam in connection with conditions at a funeral he had conducted precipitated violent protests in Conakry in early February, which were suppressed by police. By late February the number of deaths in Guinea attributed to EVD totalled 2,113, with 3,190 suspected and confirmed cases (according to WHO figures); while the regional epidemic had been reduced significantly, reported case incidence continued to fluctuate in Guinea. President Condé and his Liberian and Sierra Leonean counterparts, meeting in Conakry on 15 February, declared a common strategy with the intention of eradicating the disease by April. On 25 February the President replaced the longstanding Minister of Territorial Administration and Decentralization, Alassane Condé, with an army general, Bouréma Condé; the opposition protested at the appointment to the post of a military figure, who would be involved in the organization of the planned elections.

Foreign Affairs
Regional relations

Relations between Guinea and several of its neighbours have frequently been strained, most notably during the civil conflicts in Liberia and Sierra Leone. Relations between Guinea and Sierra Leone were further complicated in the early 2000s by an ongoing dispute over ownership of the border town of Yenga, in a reputedly diamond-rich region of Sierra Leone, which Guinean troops had occupied in 1998. In 2004 the two countries issued a joint statement that recognized Yenga as belonging to Sierra Leone, on the basis of a border agreement of 1912 between the British and French colonial powers. Guinea and Sierra Leone concluded an agreement in March 2012 to delineate their maritime boundaries, and in August the two countries pledged to withdraw all military personnel from Yenga and negotiate a peaceful settlement to the dispute.

The protracted conflicts in Liberia and Sierra Leone, as well as the civil conflict in Côte d'Ivoire from 2002, resulted in the presence in Guinea of large numbers of refugees, at times variously estimated to represent 5%–15% of the total population. At mid-2014 the office of the UN High Commissioner for Refugees (UNHCR) recorded a population of concern of 8,696 refugees in Guinea (of whom 6,598 originated from Côte d'Ivoire). During that year the ongoing Ebola epidemic and quarantine measures hampered UNHCR refugee operations and increased the need for food assistance.

Other external relations

The risk of insecurity in Guinea undermining stabilization efforts in neighbouring countries has been of significant concern to the international community, particularly following the seizure of power by the military at the end of 2008. An International Contact Group on Guinea was formed in early 2009, comprising the permanent and African members of the UN Security Council, the EU, La Francophonie and the Mano River Union (see p. 448), and there was close co-operation with the AU and ECOWAS in the process culminating in the election of President Alpha Condé in late 2010. These organizations also worked together in facilitating and overseeing the legislative elections that eventually took place in September 2013, with the UN Secretary-General's Special Representative for West Africa assuming the role of mediator between the Government and opposition from April that year. In December the EU, which had partially suspended development co-operation in late 2008, announced that conditions had been fulfilled for the complete resumption of co-operation with Guinea. President Condé's stated intention of promoting good governance in the management of Guinea's resources received the support of the international community, although a review, from 2011, of the terms of existing mining contracts, together with the adoption of a new mining code (see Economic Affairs) were considered to have contributed to subsequent slow progress in major projects in the sector.

After WHO confirmed the outbreak of EVD in Guinea, at the end of March 2014 the US Centers for Disease Control and Prevention dispatched a five-person team to assist the country's Ministry of Health. A US command centre was established in Liberia later that year, from where US military personnel provided regional support and training for medical workers. In August the AU authorized a humanitarian mission to the region. In a demonstration of support, French Prime Minister François Hollande visited Conakry in November, while the French Government pledged €100m. in financial assistance, and agreed to establish a military hospital in the country to assist efforts against the disease.

CONSTITUTION AND GOVERNMENT

The Constitution adopted on 7 May 2010 defines the clear separation of the powers of the executive, the legislature and the judiciary. The President of the Republic, who is Head of State, must be elected by an absolute majority of the votes cast, and a second round of voting is held should no candidate obtain such a majority at a first round. The duration of the presidential mandate is five years, renewable only once, and elections are by universal adult suffrage. The President appoints a Prime Minister, who is Head of Government, and proposes the structure and composition of the Government for approval by the President. Legislative power is vested in the National Assembly; 38 of its 114 members are elected in single-member constituencies, and 76 from national lists. The legislature is elected, by universal suffrage, with a five-year mandate.

Local administration is based on eight administrative entities (the city of Conakry and seven administrative regions) each under the authority of an appointed Governor; the country is sub-divided into 33 prefectures. Conakry, which comprises a separate administrative unit, is divided into five communes. The 33 prefectures outside of Conakry are sub-divided into 303 communes.

REGIONAL AND INTERNATIONAL CO-OPERATION

Guinea is a member of the African Union (see p. 188) and of the Economic Community of West African States (ECOWAS, see p. 258). Guinea is also a member of the Gambia River Basin Development Organization (OMVG, see p. 447), of the Africa Rice Center (AfricaRice, see p. 441) and of the Mano River Union (see p. 448).

Guinea became a member of the UN in 1958 and was admitted to the World Trade Organization (WTO, see p. 431) in 1995. Guinea is a member of the International Coffee Organization (see p. 442).

ECONOMIC AFFAIRS

In 2013, according to estimates by the World Bank, Guinea's gross national income (GNI), measured at average 2011–13 prices, was US $5,418m., equivalent to $460 per head (or $1,160 on an international purchasing-power parity basis). During 2004–13, it was estimated, the population increased at an average annual rate of 2.5%, while gross domestic product (GDP) per head increased, in real terms, by an average of 0.1%

per year. Overall GDP increased, in real terms, at an average annual rate of 2.7% in 2004–13; it grew by 2.5% in 2013.

According to provisional figures from the African Development Bank (AfDB), agriculture (including hunting, forestry and fishing) contributed 22.0% of GDP in 2013. About 77.5% of the labour force were employed in the agricultural sector in mid-2015, according to FAO estimates. The principal cash crops are fruits, oil palm, groundnuts and coffee. Important staple crops include rice, cassava, maize and plantains. The attainment of self-sufficiency in rice and other basic foodstuffs remains a priority. The food supply is supplemented by the rearing of cattle and other livestock. The Government has made efforts towards the commercial exploitation of Guinea's forest resources and substantial fishing stocks. According to the World Bank, during 2004–11 agricultural GDP increased at an average annual rate of 3.2%; according to provisional figures from the AfDB, growth in agricultural GDP in 2013 was 6.3%.

Industry (including mining, manufacturing, construction and power) contributed an estimated 40.1% of GDP in 2013, according to provisional AfDB figures. An estimated 5.8% of the employed labour force were engaged in the industrial sector at the time of the 1996 census. According to the World Bank, industrial GDP increased at an average annual rate of 2.9% in 2004–11; growth in 2011 was 4.5%.

According to provisional AfDB figures, mining contributed an estimated 18.2% of GDP in 2013. Only 1.1% of the employed labour force were engaged in the sector at the time of the 1996 census. Guinea is the world's foremost exporter of bauxite and the second largest producer of bauxite ore (from which aluminium is extracted), possessing between one-quarter and one-third of known reserves of the mineral. However, in 2013, the aluminium ores and concentrates accounted for only 6.2% of the country's total export earnings, compared with 26.3% in 2011. Gold, which is also mined, accounted for 62.8% of total exports in 2013. Guinea also has valuable deposits of iron ore. Plans for the development of reserves of more than 2,000m. metric tons of high-grade ore at Simandou, in the south-east of the country include construction of a 650-km railway to transport mined ore to the coast, and development of a new deep-water port south of Conakry. However, the scheme has been subject to a series of delays owing to contractual and economic uncertainties, as well as security concerns. Development of reserves of high-grade iron ore at Mt Nimba, near the border with Liberia and Côte d'Ivoire, has similarly been long delayed. The Anglo-Australian BHP Billiton announced its intention to sell its 40% holding there in 2012. Guinea also has diamond deposits. The GDP of the mining sector increased at an average annual rate of 2.0% in 2000–06, according to the IMF. According to provisional figures from the AfDB, the sector's GDP declined by 2.1% in 2012 and by 7.4% in 2013.

The manufacturing sector remains largely undeveloped, contributing only a provisional 7.7% of GDP in 2013, according to the AfDB. At the time of the 1996 census, 2.8% of the employed labour force were engaged in the manufacturing sector. There is an alumina smelter at Fria; however, production there, which was halted by its operator, United Company RUSAL, in April 2012, in response to strike action, remained suspended in early 2015. Most other industrial companies are involved in import-substitution, including the processing of agricultural products and the manufacture of construction materials. According to the World Bank, manufacturing GDP increased at an average annual rate of 2.0% in 2004–11. It increased by 2.5% in 2013, according to provisional AfDB figures.

The construction sector contributed a provisional 13.6% of GDP in 2013, according to the AfDB. At the time of the 1996 census, the sector engaged 1.8% of the employed labour force. According to provisional figures from the AfDB, construction GDP grew by 8.7% in 2013.

Electricity generation is, at present, insufficient to meet demand, and power failures outside the mining and industrial sectors (in which the largest operators generate their own power supplies) have been frequent. However, Guinea possesses considerable hydroelectric potential. The 75-MW Garafiri dam project was inaugurated in 1999, and a further major scheme (with a capacity of 240 MW), at Kaléta, was scheduled for completion in the mid-2010s. In the mean time, some 600,000 metric tons of hydrocarbons are imported annually, and in 2013 imports of mineral fuels accounted for 17.1% of the value of total merchandise imports.

According to the AfDB, the services sector contributed a provisional 37.9% of GDP in 2012. According to the World

Bank, during 2004–11 the sector's GDP increased at an average annual rate of 1.6%; it increased by 3.1% in 2011.

In 2013 Guinea recorded a visible merchandise trade deficit of US $250.3m. and there was a deficit of $1,240.3m. on the current account of the balance of payments. The principal suppliers of imports in 2013 were the Netherlands (which supplied 16.1% of the total), the People's Republic of China, France and India. The principal markets for exports in that year were France (which took 33.5% of exports), Switzerland and the United Arab Emirates. The principal exports in 2013 were gold, natural rubber and petroleum oils. The principal imports included machinery, mechanical appliances and electrical equipment, mineral fuels, rice, chemicals and related products, vehicles, aircraft, vessels and associated transport equipment, iron and steel, other base metals and articles of base metal, and prepared foodstuffs, beverages, spirits, vinegar, tobacco and articles thereof.

In 2014 Guinea's overall programmed budget deficit was 2,804,000m. FG. Guinea's general government gross debt was 26,239,220m. FG in 2011, equivalent to 77.8% of GDP. The country's total external debt was US $1,097m. at the end of 2012, of which $842m. was public and publicly guaranteed debt. In that year the cost of debt-servicing long-term public and publicly guaranteed debt and repayments to the IMF was equivalent to 7.0% of the value of exports of goods, services and income (excluding workers' remittances). Annual inflation averaged 17.8% in 2005–13, according to the AfDB; consumer prices increased by an average of 11.9% in 2013.

Guinea's potential for the attainment of wealth is substantial, owing to its valuable mineral deposits; however, the economy remains overdependent on revenue from bauxite reserves and on external assistance. The inauguration of Alpha Condé as President in December 2010 allowed the reintegration of Guinea into the international community and the resumption of financial assistance. The IMF approved a three-year Extended Credit Facility (ECF) of about US $198.9m. in February 2012. The 'Paris Club' of sovereign creditors agreed to restructure the country's debt commitments in the same year; and extensive debt relief was confirmed by the IMF and the World Bank after Guinea successfully completed its obligations under the Heavily Indebted Poor Countries initiative. A new mining code was adopted in 2011, with terms enabling the Guinean Government

to assume a 15% stake in any mining project without recompense, and to acquire a further 20% on commercial terms. Under an ongoing review of all mining licences contracted by previous administrations, initiated in 2011, the Government in April 2014 revoked two licenses held by a joint venture of Vale SA of Brazil and Israeli-owned BSG Resources Ltd (BSGR) to exploit the large-scale iron-ore reserves at Simandou, on the grounds that they had been obtained fraudulently. BSGR subsequently submitted an international arbitration request; the dispute and expected revocation of other mining licenses continued to impede development in the mining sector, and contribute to lower GDP growth. An outbreak of Ebola Virus Disease in south-eastern Guinea (see *Domestic Political Affairs*) was officially declared a national health emergency in August. The IMF announced in September that Guinea would receive emergency funding of $41m., while the World Bank extended a grant totalling $105m. for the affected countries. Following its fifth review of economic performance under the ECF, which was released in February 2015, the IMF approved the immediate disbursement of around $63.6m., and extended the arrangement to the end of the year; the authorities were urged to continue structural reforms, including in the civil service. In the same month the IMF announced the further extension of debt relief totalling $100m. for Liberia, Sierra Leone and Guinea, under a newly established Catastrophe Containment and Relief Trust. At that time, when the Ebola outbreak continued (with a reduced number of cases), the fiscal impact on Guinea remained severe: estimated GDP growth fell to only 0.5% in 2014, and a small contraction was forecast for 2015.

PUBLIC HOLIDAYS

2016: 1 January (New Year's Day), 28 March (Easter Monday), 1 May (Labour Day), 6 July* (Id al-Fitr, end of Ramadan), 27 August (Anniversary of Women's Revolt), 28 September (Referendum Day), 2 October (Republic Day), 1 November (All Saints' Day), 22 November (Day of 1970 Invasion), 11 December* (Mouloud, Birth of Muhammad), 25 December (Christmas).

* These holidays are determined by the Islamic lunar calendar and may vary by one or two days from the dates given.

Statistical Survey

Source (unless otherwise stated): Direction Nationale de la Statistique, BP 221, Conakry; tel. 300-21-33-12; e-mail dnstat@biasy.net; internet www.stat-guinee.org.

Area and Population

AREA, POPULATION AND DENSITY

Area (sq km)	245,857*
Population (census results)	
31 December 1996†	7,156,406
1 March–2 April 2014‡	
Males	5,142,088
Females	5,486,884
Total	10,628,972
Population (UN estimate at mid-year)§	
2015	12,347,766
Density (per sq km) at mid-2015	50.2

* 94,926 sq miles.
† Including refugees from Liberia and Sierra Leone (estimated at 640,000).
‡ Preliminary figures.
§ Source: UN, *World Population Prospects: The 2012 Revision*; estimate not adjusted to take account of results of 2014 census.

POPULATION BY AGE AND SEX
(UN estimates at mid-2015)

	Males	Females	Total
0–14 years	2,602,357	2,559,805	5,162,162
15–64 years	3,407,428	3,395,619	6,803,047
65 years and over	176,789	205,768	382,557
Total	**6,186,574**	**6,161,192**	**12,347,766**

Note: Estimates not adjusted to take account of 2014 census results.

Source: UN, *World Population Prospects: The 2012 Revision*.

ADMINISTRATIVE DIVISIONS
(population at 2014 census, preliminary)

Region	Area (sq km)	Population	Density (per sq km)
Boké	31,186	1,081,445	34.7
Conakry	450	1,667,864	3,706.4
Faranah	35,581	942,733	26.5
Kankan	72,156	1,986,329	27.5
Kindia	28,873	1,559,185	54.0
Labé	22,869	995,717	43.5
Mamou	17,074	732,117	42.9
N'Zérékoré	37,668	1,663,582	44.2
Total	**245,857**	**10,628,972**	**43.2**

PRINCIPAL LOCALITIES

(population of prefectures at 2014 census)

Conakry (capital) .	1,667,864	Mandiana . . .	339,527
Siguiri	695,449	Dubreka . . .	328,418
Kankan	472,112	Beyla	325,482
Boké	449,405	Mamou	318,738
Kindia . . .	438,315	Labé	318,633
N'Zérékoré . . .	396,118		

BIRTHS AND DEATHS

(annual averages, UN estimates)

	2000–05	2005–10	2010–15
Birth rate (per 1,000) . . .	41.1	39.2	35.4
Death rate (per 1,000) . . .	14.9	12.7	11.5

Source: UN, *World Population Prospects: The 2012 Revision*.

Life expectancy (years at birth): 55.8 (males 55.1; females 56.6) in 2012 (Source: World Bank, World Development Indicators database).

ECONOMICALLY ACTIVE POPULATION

('000, FAO estimates at mid-year)

	2013	2014	2015
Agriculture, etc.	4,470	4,571	4,675
Total labour force (incl. others) .	5,697	5,862	6,032

Source: FAO.

Health and Welfare

KEY INDICATORS

Total fertility rate (children per woman, 2012) . . .	5.0
Under-5 mortality rate (per 1,000 live births, 2012) . . .	101
HIV/AIDS (% of persons aged 15–49, 2013)	1.7
Physicians (per 1,000 head, 2005)	0.1
Hospital beds (per 1,000 head, 2011)	0.3
Health expenditure (2011): US $ per head (PPP)	62
Health expenditure (2011): % of GDP	6.0
Health expenditure (2011): public (% of total)	24.3
Access to water (% of persons, 2012)	75
Access to sanitation (% of persons, 2012)	19
Total carbon dioxide emissions ('000 metric tons, 2010) . .	1,235.8
Carbon dioxide emissions per head (metric tons, 2010) . .	0.1
Human Development Index (2013): ranking	179
Human Development Index (2013): value	0.392

For sources and definitions, see explanatory note on p. vi.

Agriculture

PRINCIPAL CROPS

('000 metric tons)

	2011	2012	2013
Rice, paddy*	1,670	1,919	2,053
Maize*	611	641	672
Fonio	409*	429*	429†
Sweet potatoes†	227.1	230.0	230.0
Cassava (Manioc)	1,112.6*	1,200.0†	1,200.0†
Taro (Cocoyam)† . . .	28	30	30
Yams†	24.5	26.0	26.0
Sugar cane†	283	295	300
Pulses†	56	57	57
Groundnuts, with shell* . . .	290.0	300.0	260
Coconuts	51.4*	51.0*	50.0†
Oil palm fruit†	830	830	830
Bananas†	210.0	215.0	215.9
Plantains†	463.0	470.0	467.8
Guavas, mangoes and mangosteens	157.7*	165.0†	166.8†
Pineapples	118.6*	120.0	123.8
Seed cotton†	40	42	42
Coffee, green	29.5†	30.0	18.0

* Unofficial figure(s).
† FAO estimate(s).

Aggregate production ('000 metric tons, may include official, semi-official or estimated data): Total cereals 2,947.0 in 2011, 3,260.0 in 2012, 3,434.0 in 2013; Total roots and tubers 1,403.2 in 2011, 1,498.0 in 2012, 1,498.0 in 2013; Total vegetables (incl. melons) 557.7 in 2011, 537.9 in 2012, 524.2 in 2013; Total fruits (excl. melons) 1,237.3 in 2011, 1,261.0 in 2012, 1,264.8 in 2013.

Source: FAO.

LIVESTOCK

('000 head, year ending September)

	2011*	2012†	2013†
Cattle	4,672	4,965	4,965
Sheep	1,410	1,700	1,700
Goats	1,751	1,800	1,800
Pigs	91.0	103.0	103.0
Chickens	15,090	15,000	15,000

* Unofficial figures.
† FAO estimates.

Source: FAO.

LIVESTOCK PRODUCTS

('000 metric tons, FAO estimates)

	2011	2012	2013
Cattle meat	52.3	55.7	56.1
Chicken meat	6.5	6.6	6.8
Sheep meat	6.0	6.1	6.7
Goat meat	8.7	8.9	9.0
Game meat	5.8	6.0	6.0
Cows' milk	115.2	116.0	117.0
Goats' milk	12.8	12.9	12.8
Hen eggs	24.5	24.5	24.5

Source: FAO.

Forestry

ROUNDWOOD REMOVALS

('000 cubic metres, excl. bark, FAO estimates)

	2011	2012	2013
Sawlogs, veneer logs and logs for sleepers	138	138	138
Other industrial wood	513	513	513
Fuel wood	12,010	12,063	12,117
Total	12,661	12,714	12,768

Source: FAO.

SAWNWOOD PRODUCTION
('000 cubic metres, incl. railway sleepers, FAO estimates)

	2009	2010	2011
Total (all broadleaved) . . .	81	81	91

2012–13: Production assumed to be unchanged from 2011 (FAO estimates).

Source: FAO.

Fishing

('000 metric tons, live weight)

	2010	2011	2012
Freshwater fishes*	16.0	18.0	20.0
Sea catfishes	9.0	6.7*	4.5
Bobo croaker	6.9	6.2*	5.6
West African croakers . . .	5.1	4.1*	3.2
Sardinellas	5.1	5.4*	5.7
Bonga shad	39.4	49.5*	59.7
Total catch (incl. others)* . .	113.5	122.5	132.2

*FAO estimate(s).

Source: FAO.

Mining

('000 metric tons unless otherwise indicated)

	2010	2011	2012
Bauxite (dry basis)*| . .	15,300	15,300	16,041
Gold (kilograms) . .	15,217	15,695	14,790
Salt (unrefined)†	15	15	n.a.
Diamonds ('000 carats)‡ . . .	374	304	267

* Estimated to be 7% water.
† Estimate.
‡ Including artisanal production.

Source: US Geological Survey.

Industry

SELECTED PRODUCTS
('000 metric tons unless otherwise indicated)

	2010	2011	2012
Palm oil (unrefined)*†	50	50	50
Beer of barley*‡	7.9	23.2	23.2
Alumina (calcined equivalent)§ .	597	574	150
Electric energy (million kWh)‖ .	952	878	n.a.

* Data from FAO.
† Unofficial figures.
‡ FAO estimates.
§ Data from the US Geological Survey.
‖ Data from UN Industrial Commodity Statistics Database.

Finance

CURRENCY AND EXCHANGE RATES
Monetary Units
  100 centimes = 1 franc guinéen (FG or Guinean franc).

Sterling, Dollar and Euro Equivalents (31 December 2014)
  £1 sterling = 11,280.942 Guinean francs;
  US $1 = 7,227.666 Guinean francs;
  €1 = 8,775.110 Guinean francs;
  100,000 Guinean francs = £8.86 = $13.84 = €11.40.

Average Exchange Rate (Guinean francs per US $)
  2012   6,985.8
  2013   6,907.9
  2014   7,014.1

BUDGET
('000 million Guinean francs)

Revenue*	2012	2013	2014†
Mining-sector revenue . . .	1,607	1,489	1,451
Other revenue	6,368	6,416	7,392
Tax revenue	5,993	6,130	6,931
Taxes on domestic production and trade	2,765	2,943	3,468
Taxes on international trade .	1,452	1,703	1,932
Non-tax revenue	375	286	461
Total	7,975	7,905	8,843

Expenditure‡	2012	2013	2014†
Current expenditure	6,291	6,954	8,168
Wages and salaries . . .	1,757	2,102	2,355
Other goods and services . .	2,356	2,499	2,599
Subsidies and transfers . .	1,505	1,860	2,081
Interest due on external debt .	271	72	104
Interest due on domestic debt .	402	421	434
Ebola Virus Disease (EVD) expenditure	—	—	595
Capital expenditure	3,801	3,822	5,800
Domestically financed . . .	2,674	2,184	3,213
Externally financed	1,113	1,620	2,557
Capital transfer	14	17	30
Total	10,092	10,776	13,968

* Excluding grants received ('000 million Guinean francs): 1,071 in 2012; 639 in 2013; 2,485 in 2014 (programmed figure).
† Programmed figures.
‡ Excluding lending minus repayments ('000 million Guinean francs): 251 in 2012 (estimate); 9 in 2013; 164 in 2014 (programmed figure).

Source: IMF, *Guinea: Requests for Disbursement Under the Rapid Credit Facility and for Modification of Performance Criteria Under the Extended Credit Facilit, Arrangement-Staff Report; Press Release; and Statement by the Executive Director For Guinea* (September 2014).

INTERNATIONAL RESERVES
(US $ million at 31 December)

	2010	2011
Gold (national valuation)	10.02	8.60
IMF special drawing rights	116.16	94.34
Reserve position in IMF	0.12	0.12
Foreign exchange	n.a.	8.70
Total	n.a.	111.76

2012: IMF special drawing rights 120.60; Reserve position in IMF 0.12.

2013: IMF special drawing rights 107.10; Reserve position in IMF 0.08.

Source: IMF, *International Financial Statistics*.

MONEY SUPPLY
(million Guinean francs at 31 December)

	2009	2010	2011
Currency outside banks . . .	2,123,925	3,987,512	3,296,217
Demand deposits at commercial banks	1,944,782	4,785,300	5,490,842
Total (incl. others)	4,398,032	8,814,784	9,783,878

Source: IMF, *International Financial Statistics*.

COST OF LIVING
(Consumer Price Index; base: 2002 = 100)

	2011	2012	2013
Foodstuffs, beverages and tobacco.	730.8	845.1	952.0
Clothing and shoes	294.1	350.8	402.0
Housing, water, electricity and gas	354.3	399.4	459.7
All items	491.1	565.8	633.1

NATIONAL ACCOUNTS
('000 million Guinean francs at current prices, provisional)

Expenditure on the Gross Domestic Product

	2011	2012	2013
Government final consumption expenditure	3,355.3	4,118.2	4,959.0
Private final consumption expenditure	30,722.7	35,922.6	41,634.1
Gross fixed capital formation . .	6,741.4	8,786.2	8,567.3
Changes in inventories . . .	5.1	5.5	3.7
Total domestic expenditure .	40,824.5	48,832.5	55,164.1
Exports of goods and services . .	10,951.3	11,291.2	11,423.2
Less Imports of goods and services	18,036.3	20,532.2	21,108.3
GDP at market prices . . .	33,739.5	39,591.6	45,479.0

Gross Domestic Product by Economic Activity

	2011	2012	2013
Agriculture, livestock, forestry and fishing	5,768.5	7,032.9	8,963.9
Mining and quarrying	7,761.2	7,476.3	7,415.4
Manufacturing	2,268.7	2,741.2	3,147.3
Electricity, gas and water . . .	126.9	194.6	207.6
Construction	3,620.7	4,548.8	5,528.0
Trade, restaurants and hotels .	6,620.6	7,990.9	9,088.1
Transport and communications .	1,734.3	2,103.3	2,394.6
Public administration and defence	1,848.0	1,956.0	2,368.2
Other services	1,109.5	1,330.2	1,555.8
GDP at factor cost	30,858.3	35,374.3	40,668.8
Indirect taxes	2,881.1	4,217.3	4,810.2
GDP at purchasers' values .	33,739.5	39,591.6	45,479.0

Notes: Deduction for imputed bank service charge assumed to be distributed at origin. Totals may not be equal to the sum of components, owing to rounding.

Source: African Development Bank.

BALANCE OF PAYMENTS
(US $ million)

	2011	2012	2013
Exports of goods	1,428.4	1,927.6	1,886.3
Imports of goods	−2,097.1	−2,244.0	−2,136.5
Balance on goods	−668.8	−316.4	−250.3
Exports of services	77.4	159.1	103.5
Imports of services	−576.1	−891.8	−696.9
Balance on goods and services	−1,167.5	−1,049.1	−843.6
Primary income received . . .	22.2	31.5	3.6
Primary income paid	−155.6	−153.5	−408.8
Balance on goods, services and primary income	−1,300.8	−1,171.1	−1,248.8
Secondary income received . .	353.7	242.4	230.4

	2011	2012	2013
—continued			
Secondary income paid . . .	−268.0	−172.9	−221.8
Current balance	−1,215.2	−1,101.5	−1,240.3
Capital account (net)	138.9	78.5	77.9
Direct investment assets . . .	−0.8	−1.9	−0.1
Direct investment liabilities . .	956.1	0.1	3.3
Portfolio investment assets . .	211.6	−3.1	—
Other investment assets . . .	−186.5	−98.4	−98.7
Other investment liabilities . .	755.6	126.6	761.7
Net errors and omissions . .	−40.1	235.8	311.8
Reserves and related items .	619.6	−763.9	−184.2

Source: IMF, *International Financial Statistics*.

External Trade

PRINCIPAL COMMODITIES
(distribution by HS, US $ million)

Imports c.i.f.	2011	2012	2013
Vegetables and vegetable products	255.7	269.2	259.1
Cereals	193.6	187.0	173.2
Rice	184.3	186.7	171.2
Milling products, malt, starches, inulin, wheat gluten . . .	52.6	70.2	74.8
Wheat or meslin flour . . .	48.5	67.3	72.2
Prepared foodstuffs; beverages, spirits, vinegar; tobacco and articles thereof .	109.7	98.1	113.8
Mineral products	529.5	401.3	399.3
Salt, sulphur, earth, stone, plaster, lime and cement	54.4	68.8	58.2
Cements, portland, aluminous, slag, supersulfate and similar hydraulic materials . . .	45.3	59.9	48.0
Mineral fuels, oils, distillation products, etc.	475.1	332.4	338.5
Petroleum oils, not crude . .	472.4	322.1	332.4
Chemicals and related products	144.9	163.4	177.1
Pharmaceutical products . . .	58.9	71.1	92.4
Medicament mixtures . . .	48.2	51.8	72.4
Plastics, rubbers, and articles thereof	48.8	63.2	59.1
Textiles and textile articles .	32.0	35.9	62.4
Iron and steel, other base metals and articles of base metal	105.8	117.6	129.6
Machinery and mechanical appliances; electrical equipment; parts thereof .	422.6	548.1	418.5
Machinery, boilers, etc. . . .	313.5	388.7	223.2
Self-propelled bulldozers, angledozers, graders, excavators, etc.	60.2	71.4	22.5
Machine parts	97.5	146.1	50.0
Electrical, electronic equipment .	109.1	159.4	195.3
Vehicles, aircraft, vessels and associated transport equipment	156.8	173.5	152.9
Vehicles other than railway, tramway	151.7	165.0	118.3
Cars (incl. station wagons) . .	50.9	61.7	41.5
Total (incl. others)	1,952.5	2,038.9	1,943.0

Exports f.o.b.	2011	2012	2013
Mineral products	483.8	151.0	133.5
Ores, slag and ash	467.1	43.7	120.9
Aluminum ores and concentrates	467.1	43.3	94.0
Mineral fuels, oils, distillation products, etc.	16.6	107.1	12.6
Petroleum oils, not crude . .	16.6	107.0	12.5
Chemicals and related products	176.3	53.7	2.8
Inorganic chemicals, precious metal compound, isotopes . .	174.6	51.3	1.2
Aluminium oxide (incl. artificial corundum); aluminium hydroxide	174.6	51.3	—
Plastics, rubber, and articles thereof	34.6	303.1	36.8
Rubber and articles thereof . .	21.5	289.4	21.0
Natural rubber, balata, gutta-percha, etc.	21.4	289.4	20.7
Pulp of wood, paper and paperboard, and articles thereof	73.0	92.7	236.7
Printed books, newspapers, pictures, etc.	72.8	92.7	236.6
Unused stamps; cheque forms, banknotes, bond certificates, etc.	72.8	92.7	236.6
Pearls, precious stones, metals, coins, etc.	857.7	1,425.1	987.0
Gold, unwrought or in semi-manufactured forms	821.5	1,386.2	951.5
Machinery and mechanical appliances; electrical equipment; parts thereof .	69.4	55.1	44.1
Machinery, boilers, etc.	24.0	54.0	42.3
Total (incl. others)	1,776.5	2,139.2	1,514.1

Source: Trade Map-Trade Competitiveness Map, International Trade Centre, www.intracen.org/marketanalysis.

PRINCIPAL TRADING PARTNERS
(US $ million)

Imports c.i.f.	2011	2012	2013
Australia	33.2	75.4	14.8
Belgium	146.9	131.8	96.0
Brazil	39.6	19.5	14.3
China, People's Republic . . .	169.1	257.2	297.1
Côte d'Ivoire	26.2	11.7	10.3
France (incl. Monaco)	140.7	162.3	174.6
Greece	21.2	9.8	5.5
Germany	14.4	26.4	38.7
India	57.2	130.1	140.1
Italy	30.1	41.5	23.1
Japan	10.9	30.9	15.8
Malaysia	28.3	46.2	24.4
Korea, Republic	9.6	19.8	22.1
Mali	27.8	27.2	14.3
Malta	35.2	23.1	21.4
Morocco	40.5	69.5	78.9
Myanmar	17.7	41.3	42.2
Netherlands	353.7	300.4	312.9
Pakistan	60.1	19.4	18.3
Portugal	40.9	32.4	6.2
Senegal	24.2	17.8	16.2
Singapore	34.8	17.1	22.3
South Africa	38.7	59.7	39.1
Spain	13.4	35.8	35.6
Sweden	21.0	10.7	12.8
Switzerland	4.2	12.0	20.4
Thailand	21.5	9.7	5.1
Turkey	23.1	27.7	40.0
United Arab Emirates	51.9	45.8	61.5
United Kingdom	72.3	32.9	31.7
USA	86.6	75.8	61.5
Viet Nam	59.4	17.7	38.4
Total (incl. others)	1,952.5	2,038.9	1,943.0

Exports f.o.b.	2011	2012	2013
Belgium	48.9	355.7	34.3
Canada	55.1	0.9	3.2
China, People's Republic . . .	6.1	5.3	28.3
France (incl. Monaco)	513.5	527.8	507.4
Germany	63.8	3.8	9.4
India	14.7	7.2	38.0
Ireland	86.2	117.1	11.1
Italy	7.3	83.0	1.6
Mali	53.0	10.0	11.2
Russia	150.4	41.2	—
Sierra Leone	8.0	104.3	19.4
Spain	112.9	3.6	20.4
Switzerland	384.1	579.5	493.9
Ukraine	40.8	41.9	41.6
United Arab Emirates	56.2	124.8	155.2
USA	79.8	24.7	17.9
Total (incl. others)	1,776.5	2,139.2	1,514.1

Source: Trade Map-Trade Competitiveness Map, International Trade Centre, www.intracen.org/marketanalysis.

Transport

ROAD TRAFFIC
('000, motor vehicles in use, estimates)

	2010	2011
Private vehicles	150.0	190.0
Public vehicles	100.0	109.2
Total	250.0	299.2

SHIPPING

Flag Registered Fleet
(at 31 December)

	2012	2013	2014
Number of vessels	37	37	36
Total displacement ('000 grt) . .	28.8	28.8	24.4

Source: Lloyd's List Intelligence (www.lloydslistintelligence.com).

International Seaborne Freight Traffic
(Port of Conakry, '000 metric tons)

	2009	2010	2011
Goods loaded	3,409	3,759	3,814
Goods unloaded	2,539	3,118	3,357

CIVIL AVIATION
(traffic at Conakry-Gbèssia airport)

	2009	2010	2011
Passengers carried ('000) . . .	248.5	247.6	325.3
Freight handled ('000 metric tons)	3.0	233.2	4.4

Tourism

FOREIGN VISITOR ARRIVALS*

Country of origin	2011	2012	2013
Belgium	2,752	1,721	1,511
Canada	3,136	1,984	1,229
China, People's Republic	5,906	2,739	4,447
Côte d'Ivoire	6,376	3,648	3,268
France	28,400	19,714	10,141
Germany	2,340	1,116	1,012
Mali	5,194	3,838	1,931
Senegal	9,686	8,644	4,012
Sierra Leone	2,710	2,710	1,214
USA	7,860	3,751	3,937
Total (incl. others)†	131,070	96,064	56,146

* Arrivals of non-resident tourists at national borders, by nationality.
† Air arrivals at Conakry-Gbèssia airport.

Receipts from tourism (US $ million, excl. passenger transport): 2.0 in 2010; 2.0 in 2011; 1.4 in 2012.

Source: World Tourism Organization.

Communications Media

	2011	2012	2013
Telephones ('000 main lines in use)	18	—	—
Mobile cellular telephones ('000 subscribers)	4,861	5,585	7,436
Broadband subscribers	6,000	7,000	8,000

Source: International Telecommunication Union.

Education

(2011/12 unless otherwise indicated)

	Institutions	Teachers	Students ('000)		
			Males	Females	Total
Pre-primary	202*	3,599†	77.8‡	73.7‡	151.5‡
Primary	8,313	36,731	874.3	725.5	1,599.8
Secondary	1,253	21,501	412.9	256.1	669.0
General	n.a.	19,880	395.1	240.6	635.7
Tertiary	52	6,221	74.2	27.0	101.2

* 1996/97.
† 2009/10.
‡ 2010/11.

Source: partly UNESCO Institute for Statistics.

Pupil-teacher ratio (primary education, UNESCO estimate): 43.6 in 2011/12 (Source: UNESCO Institute for Statistics).

Adult literacy rate (UNESCO estimates): 25.3% (males 36.8%; females 12.2%) in 2010 (Source: UNESCO Institute for Statistics).

Directory

The Government

HEAD OF STATE

President and Minister of National Defence: ALPHA CONDÉ (inaugurated 21 December 2010).

COUNCIL OF MINISTERS
(April 2015)

Prime Minister: MOHAMED SAÏD FOFANA.

Minister of State, responsible for Mines and Geology: KERFALA YANSANÉ.

Minister of State, responsible for Justice: CHEICK SAKHO.

Minister of State, responsible for Foreign Affairs and Guineans Abroad: FRANÇOIS LONSÉNY FALL.

Minister of State, responsible for Telecommunications, Posts and New Information Technologies: OYÉ GUILAVOGUI.

Minister of State, responsible for the Economy and Finance: MOHAMED DIARÉ.

Minister of State, responsible for Higher Education and Scientific Research: BAILO TÉLIWEL DIALLO.

Minister of State in the Presidency, responsible for Public-Private Investments: Dr IBRAHIMA KASSORY FOFANA.

Minister of Health: Col REMY LAMAH.

Minister of Security and Civil Protection: MAHMOUDOU CISSÉ.

Minister of Energy and Water: CHEICK TALIBY SYLLA.

Minister of Territorial Administration and Decentralization: Gen. BOURÉMA CONDÉ.

Minister of Agriculture: JACQUELINE SULTAN.

Minister of Employment, Labour, Technical Education and Vocational Training: ALBERT DAMANTANG CAMARA.

Minister of Urban Development and Territorial Management: IBRAHIMA BANGOURA.

Minister of the Civil Service, State Reform and Administrative Modernization: SÉKOU KOUROUMA.

Minister of Sport: DOMANI DORÉ.

Minister of International Co-operation: Dr KOUTOUB MOUSTAPHA SANO.

Minister of Communication: ALHOUSSENI KAKÉ MANAKANÉRA.

Minister of Commerce: MARC YOMBOUNO.

Minister of Fisheries and Aquaculture: LOUSENY CAMARA.

Minister of Transport: ALIOUNE DIALLO.

Minister of Pre-university Education and Literacy: Dr IBRAHIMA KOUROUMA.

Minister of Public Works: MOHAMED TRAORÉ.

Minister of the Environment, Water and Forests: KADIATOU N'DIAYE.

Minister of Tourism, Hotels and Handicrafts: MOUSSA CONDÉ.

Minister of Stockbreeding: THIERNO OUSMANE DIALLO.

Minister of Planning: SÉKOU TRAORÉ.

Minister of Industry, Small and Medium-sized Enterprises and the Promotion of the Private Sector: FATOUMATA BINTA DIALLO.

Minister of Culture, Arts and Heritage: AHMED TIDIANE CISSÉ.

Minister of Social Affairs, the Promotion of Women and Children: CAMARA SANABA KABA.

Minister of Human Rights and Public Freedom: KALIFA GASSAMA DIABY.

Minister of Youth and Youth Employment: MOUSTAPHA NAITÉ.

Minister-delegate for National Defence: Commdr ABDOUL KABÉLÉ CAMARA.

Minister-delegate for the Budget: ANSOUMANE CONDÉ.

Minister-delegate for Guineans Abroad: SANOUSSY BANTAMA SOW.

MINISTRIES

Office of the President: BP 1000, Boulbinet, Conakry; tel. 664-87-96-59 (mobile); fax 300-41-16-73; internet www.presidence.gov.gn.

Office of the Prime Minister: BP 5141, Conakry; tel. 300-41-51-19; fax 300-41-52-82.

Office of the Secretary-General at the Presidency: Conakry.

Ministry of Agriculture: face à la Cité du Port, BP 576, Conakry; tel. 601-55-36-76 (mobile); e-mail dourasano@hotmail.com.

Ministry of Commerce: Conakry.

Ministry of Communication: Conakry.

Ministry of Culture, Arts and Heritage: Conakry.

Ministry of the Economy and Finance: blvd du Commerce, Conakry; tel. 300-45-17-95; fax 300-41-30-59; e-mail mef.mdb@finances.gov.gn; internet www.finances.gov.gn.

Ministry of Employment, Technical Education and Vocational Training: Conakry; tel. 628-20-58-58 (mobile).

Ministry of Energy: route du Niger, Coléah, Conakry; tel. 601-22-50-54 (mobile).

Ministry of the Environment, Water and Forests: Conakry.

Ministry of Fisheries and Aquaculture: face à la Cité du Port, BP 307, Conakry; tel. 300-41-12-58; fax 300-41-43-10; e-mail minipaq.jpl@eti-bull.net; internet www.fis.com/guinea.

Ministry of Foreign Affairs and Guineans Abroad: Quartier Almamya, face au Port Autonome de Conakry, Commune de Kaloum, BP 2519, Conakry; tel. 657-16-45-05 (mobile); fax 300-41-16-21; internet www.mae.gov.gn.

Ministry of Health and Public Hygiene: blvd du Commerce, BP 585, Conakry; tel. 300-41-20-32; fax 300-41-41-38.

Ministry of Higher Education and Scientific Research: face à la Cathédrale Sainte-Marie, BP 964, Conakry; tel. 300-45-12-17; fax 300-41-20-12.

Ministry of Human Rights and Public Freedom: Conakry.

Ministry of Industry and Small and Medium-sized Enterprises: Conakry.

Ministry of Information: Conakry.

Ministry of International Co-operation: BP 1210, Conakry; internet mci-guinee.net.

Ministry of Justice: face à l'Immeuble 'La Paternelle', Almamya, Conakry; tel. 300-41-29-60.

Ministry of Labour and the Civil Service: Boulbinet, Conakry; tel. 300-45-20-01.

Ministry of Literacy and the Promotion of National Languages: Conakry.

Ministry of Mines and Geology: BP 295, Conakry; tel. 300-41-38-33; fax 300-41-49-13.

Ministry of National Defence: Camp Samory-Touré, Conakry; tel. 300-41-11-54.

Ministry of Planning: BP 221, Conakry; tel. 300-44-37-15; fax 300-41-43-50.

Ministry of Pre-university Education: Boulbinet, BP 2201, Conakry; tel. 300-45-19-17.

Ministry of Public Works and Transport: BP 715, Conakry; tel. 300-41-36-39; fax 300-41-35-77.

Ministry of Security, Civil Protection and the Reform of Security Services: Coléah-Domino, Conakry; tel. 300-41-45-50.

Ministry of Social Affairs, the Promotion of Women and Children: Corniche-Ouest, face au Terminal Conteneurs du Port de Conakry, BP 527, Conakry; tel. 300-45-45-39; fax 300-41-46-60.

Ministry of Telecommunications, Posts and New Information Technologies: BP 3000, Conakry; tel. 300-43-17-81; fax 300-45-18-96.

Ministry of Territorial Administration and Decentralization: face aux Jardins du 2 Octobre, Tombo, BP 2201, Conakry; tel. 300-41-15-10; fax 300-45-45-07.

Ministry of Tourism, Hotels and Handicrafts: BP 1304, Conakry; tel. 300-44-26-06; fax 300-44-49-90.

Ministry of Urban Development and Territorial Management: Conakry.

Ministry of Youth, Youth Employment and Sports: ave du Port Secrétariat, BP 262, Conakry; tel. 669-67-91-06 (mobile); fax 300-41-19-26; e-mail info@jeunesse.gov.gn; internet jeunesse.gov.gn.

President

Presidential Election, First Round, 27 June 2010

Candidate	% of votes
Cellou Dalein Diallo (UFDG)	43.69
Alpha Conde (RPG)	18.25
Sidya Touré (UFR)	13.02
Lansana Kouyaté (PEDN)	7.04
Papa Koly Kourouma (RDR)	5.74
Ibrahima Abe Sylla (NGR)	3.23
Jean-Marc Telliano (RDIG)	2.33
Others*	6.70
Total	**100.00**

* There were 17 other candidates.

Presidential Election, Second Round, 7 November 2010

Candidate	Votes	% of votes
Alpha Condé (RPG)	1,474,973	52.52
Cellou Dalein Diallo (UFDG)	1,333,666	47.48
Total	**2,808,639**	**100.00**

Legislature

National Assembly: Palais du Peuple, BP 414, Conakry; tel. 300-41-28-04; fax 300-45-17-00; e-mail s.general@assemblee.gov.gn; internet www.assemblee.gov.gn.

President: CLAUDE KORY KONDIANO.

General Election, 28 September 2013

Party	Constituency seats	National list seats	Total seats
Rassemblement du Peuple de Guinée Arc-en-ciel	18	35	53
Union des Forces Démocratiques de Guinée	14	23	37
Union des Forces Républicaines .	5	5	10
Union pour le Progrès de la Guinée	1	1	2
Parti de l'Espoir pour le Développement National . .	–	2	2
Others*	–	10	10
Total	**38**	**76**	**114**

* The Génération pour la Réconciliation, l'Union et le Prospérité, Guinée pour Tous, Guinée Unie pour le Développement, the Nouvelle Génération pour la République, the Parti Guinéen pour la Renaissance et le Progrès, the Parti National pour le Renouveau, the Parti du Travail et de la Solidarité, the Rassemblement pour le Développement Intégré de la Guinée, the Union Guinéenne pour la Démocratie et le Développement and the Union pour le Progrès et le Renouveau were all allocated one national list seat each.

Election Commission

Commission Electorale Nationale Indépendante (CENI): Villa 17, Cité des Nations, Conakry; tel. 664-24-22-06 (mobile); e-mail bensekou@ceniguinee.org; internet www.ceniguinee.org; f. 2005; comprises 10 representatives of the parliamentary majority, 10 representatives of the parliamentary opposition, three representatives of civil society and two representatives of the state administration; Pres. BAKARY FOFANA; Sec.-Gen. BOKAR CISSOKO.

Advisory Council

Economic and Social Council: Immeuble FAWAZ, Corniche Sud, Coléah, Matam, BP 2947, Conakry; tel. 300-45-31-23; fax 300-45-31-24; e-mail ces@sotelgui.net.gn; f. 1997; 45 mems; Pres. MICHEL KAMANO; Sec.-Gen. MAMADOU BOBO CAMARA.

Political Organizations

Alliance Nationale pour le Progrès (ANP): Conakry; Leader Dr SAGNO MOUSSA.

Génération pour la Réconciliation, l'Union et le Prospérité (GRUP): Conakry; Pres. PAPA KOLY KOUROUMA.

Guinée pour Tous (GPT): Conakry; Pres. IBRAHIMA KASSORY FOFANA.

Guinée Unie pour le Développement (GUD): Conakry, f. 2002; Pres. Dr SÉKOU BENNA CAMARA.

Nouvelle Génération pour la République (NGR): Kissosso; tel. 664-29-05-72 (mobile); Leader IBRAHIMA ABE SYLLA.

Parti Démocratique de Guinée—Rassemblement Démocratique Africain (PDG—RDA): Conakry; f. 1946; revived 1992; Sec.-Gen. MOHAMED TOURÉ.

Parti Dyama: Conakry; e-mail mansourkaba@yahoo.fr; internet www.guinea-dyama.com; moderate Islamist party; Pres. MOHAMED MANSOUR KABA.

Parti Écologiste de Guinée (PEG—Les Verts): BP 3018, Quartier Boulbinet, 5e blvd, angle 2e ave, Commune de Kaloum, Conakry; tel. 300-44-37-01; Leader OUMAR SYLLA.

Parti de l'Espoir pour le Développement National (PEDN): Commune Ratoma, BP 1403, Conakry; tel. 655-55-00-00 (mobile); e-mail info@pednespoirl.org; internet www.pednespoir.com; Pres. LANSANA KOUYATÉ.

Parti Guinéen pour la Renaissance et le Progrès (PGRP): Conakry; Pres. ALPHA IBRAHIMA SILA BAH.

Parti National pour le Renouveau: Conakry; Pres. ALPHA SOULEYMANE BAH FISHER.

Parti du Peuple de Guinée (PPG): BP 1147, Conakry; socialist; Leader CHARLES-PASCAL TOLNO.

Parti du Travail et de la Solidarité (PTS): Pres. MAMADOU DIAWARA.

Parti de l'Unité et du Progrès (PUP): Camayenne, Conakry; Pres. (vacant); Sec.-Gen. El Hadj Dr SÉKOU KONATÉ.

Rassemblement pour la Défense de la République (RDR): Leader PAPA KOLY KOUROUMA.

Rassemblement pour le Développement Intégré de la Guinée (RDIG): Leader JEAN-MARC TELLIANO.

Rassemblement du Peuple de Guinée (RPG): Conakry; e-mail admin@rpgguinee.org; internet www.rpgguinee.org; f. 1980 as the Rassemblement des Patriotes Guinéens; socialist; Pres. ALPHA CONDÉ.

Union Démocratique de Guinée (UDG): Dixinn Centre, Conakry; tel. 601-52-40-26 (mobile); f. 2009; Leader El Hadj MAMADOU SYLLA.

Union des Forces Démocratiques (UFD): BP 3050, Conakry; tel. 300-34-50-20; e-mail ufdconakry@yahoo.fr; internet www.ufd-conakry.com; Pres. MAMADOU BAADIKKO BAH.

Union des Forces Démocratiques de Guinée (UFDG): Carrefour Chinois, Belle-Vue, BP 3036, Conakry; e-mail baggelmalal@yahoo.fr; internet www.ufdg.org; f. 2002 by faction of UPR in protest at that party's participation in elections to National Assembly; Pres. CELLOU DALEIN DIALLO.

Union des Forces Républicaines (UFR): Immeuble 'Le Golfe', 4e étage, BP 6080, Conakry; tel. 664-30-47-50 (mobile); fax 300-45-42-31; e-mail contact@ufrguinee.com; internet www.ufrguinee.com; f. 1992; liberal-conservative; Pres. SIDYA TOURÉ; Sec.-Gen. BAKARY GOYO ZOUMANIGUI.

Union Guinéenne pour la Démocratie et le Développement (UGDD): BP 4600, Conakry; tel. 640-00-00-23 (mobile); e-mail info@ugdd.org; internet ugdd.org; Sec.-Gen. KEAMOU BOGOLA HABA.

Union pour le Progrès de la Guinée (UPG): Conakry; Leader JEAN-MARIE DORÉ.

Union pour le Progrès et le Renouveau (UPR): BP 690, Conakry; tel. 300-25-26-01; e-mail basusmane@mirinet.net.gn; internet www.uprguinee.org; f. 1998 by merger of the Parti pour le Renouveau et le Progrès and the Union pour la Nouvelle République; Pres. OUSMANE BAH.

Union pour le Progrès National—Parti pour l'Unité et le Développement (UPN—PUD): Conakry; Leader MAMADOU BHOYE BARRY.

Diplomatic Representation

EMBASSIES IN GUINEA

Algeria: Cité des Nations, Quartiers Kaloum, BP 1004, Conakry; tel. 664-00-00-95 (mobile); fax 300-41-15-35; Ambassador RABAH FASSIH.

Angola: Conakry; tel. 664-56-24-21 (mobile); Ambassador EDUARDO RUAS DE JESUS MANUEL.

Brazil: Résidence 2000, Immeuble de l'Administration el de la DHL, 5e étage, Conakry; tel. 664-20-21-11 (mobile); e-mail brasemb .conacri@itamaraty.gov.br; Chargé d'affaires e.p. ALIRIO RAMOS.

China, People's Republic: Quartier Donka, Cité Ministérielle, Commune de Dixinn, BP 714, Conakry; tel. 664-00-80-00 (mobile); fax 300-46-95-83; e-mail chinaemb_gn@mfa.gov.cn; internet gn .chineseembassy.org; Ambassador BIAN JIANQIANG.

Congo, Democratic Republic: Quartier Almamya, ave de la Gare, Commune du Kaloum, BP 880, Conakry; tel. 300-45-15-01.

Côte d'Ivoire: blvd du Commerce, BP 5228, Conakry; tel. 622-13-38-01 (mobile); fax 300-45-10-79; e-mail acign@ambaci-guinee.org; Ambassador DIARRASSOUBA M. YOUSSOUF.

Cuba: Cité Ministérielle, Quartier Donka, Commune de Dixinn, Conakry; tel. 664-20-87-73 (mobile); fax 300-46-95-28; e-mail embagcon@sotelgui.net.gn; Ambassador MAITÉ RIVERO TORRES.

Egypt: Corniche Sud 2, BP 389, Conakry; tel. 300-46-85-08; fax 300-46-85-07; e-mail ambconakry@hotmail.com; Ambassador TAMER AL MAWAZINI.

France: ave du Commerce, BP 373, Conakry; tel. 621-00-00-10 (mobile); tel. 300-47-10-15; e-mail ambafrance.conakry@diplomatie .gouv.fr; internet www.ambafrance-gn.org; Ambassador BERTRAND COCHERY.

Germany: 2e blvd, Kaloum, BP 540, Conakry; tel. 621-22-17-06 (mobile); fax 300-45-22-17; e-mail amball@sotelgui.net.gn; internet www.conakry.diplo.de; Ambassador HARTMUT KRAUSSER.

Ghana: Immeuble Ex-Urbaine et la Seine, BP 732, Conakry; tel. 622-66-47-45 (mobile); Ambassador BEATRICE ROSA BROBBEY.

Guinea-Bissau: Quartier Bellevue, Commune de Dixinn, BP 298, Conakry; tel. 628-97-13-05 (mobile); Ambassador Elhadj BRAIMA EMBALO.

Holy See: La Minière, DI 777, BP 2016, Conakry; tel. 664-58-49-59 (mobile); e-mail nunziaturaguinea@gmail.com; Apostolic Nuncio Most Rev. SANTO ROCCO GANGEMI.

Iran: Donka, Cité Ministérielle, Commune de Dixinn, BP 310, Conakry; tel. 300-01-03-19; fax 300-47-81-84; e-mail ambiran@yahoo.com; Ambassador KHALIL SADATI-AMIRI.

Japan: Quartier Landréah Port, Corniche Nord, Commune de Dixinn, BP 895, Conakry; tel. 628-68-38-38 (mobile); internet www .gn.emb-japan.go.jp; Ambassador NAOTSUGU NAKANO.

Korea, Democratic People's Republic: BP 723, Conakry; Ambassador RI KYONG SON.

Liberia: Cité Ministérielle, Donka, Commune de Dixinn, BP 18, Conakry; tel. 666-41-46-51 (mobile); Ambassador KRUBO KOLLIE.

Libya: Commune de Kaloum, BP 1183, Conakry; tel. 300-41-41-72; Ambassador B. AHMED.

Malaysia: Quartier Mafanco, Corniche Sud, BP 5460, Conakry; tel. 300-22-17-54; e-mail malconakry@kln.gov.my; internet www.kln .gov.my/web/gin_conakry/home; Ambassador MOHAMED SAMPIL.

Mali: rue D1–15, Camayenne, Corniche Nord, BP 299, Conakry; tel. 300-46-14-18; fax 300-46-37-03; e-mail ambamaliguinee@yahoo.fr; Ambassador HASSANE BARRY.

Morocco: Cité des Nations, Villa 12, Commune du Kaloum, BP 193, Conakry; tel. 300-41-36-86; fax 300-41-38-16; e-mail sifamgui@biasy .net; Ambassador MAJID HALIM.

Nigeria: Corniche Sud, Quartier de Matam, BP 54, Conakry; tel. 666-37-59-19 (mobile); fax 300-46-27-75; Ambassador Dr AISHA LARABA ABDULLAHI.

Russian Federation: Matam-Port, km 9, BP 329, Conakry; tel. 631-40-52-22 (mobile); fax 300-47-84-43; e-mail ambrusgui@mid.ru; internet www.guinee.mid.ru; Ambassador ALEXANDER V. BREGADZE.

Saudi Arabia: BP 611, Conakry; tel. 300-46-70-75; e-mail gnemb@mofa.gov.sa; internet embassies.mofa.gov.sa/sites/Guinea; Ambassador AMJAD BIN HOSAIN BIN ABDUL HAMEED AL-BEDAIWI.

Senegal: bâtiment 142, Coléah, Corniche Che Sud, BP 842, Conakry; tel. 300-44-61-32; fax 300-46-28-34; Ambassador YAKHAM DIOP.

Sierra Leone: Quartier Bellevue, face aux cases présidentielles, Commune de Dixinn, BP 625, Conakry; tel. 631-35-82-03 (mobile); fax 300-41-23-64; Ambassador ADIKALIE FODAY SUMAH.

South Africa: Coléah, Mossoudougou, Conakry; tel. 664-29-92-33 (mobile); fax 300-49-08-79; e-mail conakrys@foreign.gov.za; Ambassador NOMASONTO MARIA SIBANDA-THUSI.

Spain: Plaza Almany Samory Touré, Immeuble R2000, BP 706, Conakry; tel. 631-35-87-30 (mobile); e-mail emb.conakry@maec.es; Ambassador GUILLERMO ARDIZONE GARCÍA.

Ukraine: Commune de Dixinn, Corniche Nord, Cité Ministérielle, Rue DI 256, BP 1350, Conakry; tel. 622-35-38-01 (mobile); fax 622-35-38-03 (mobile); e-mail ambukra@gmail.com; internet www.mfa.gov .ua/guinea; Ambassador ANDRIY ZAYATS.

United Kingdom: Villa 1, Residence 2000, Corniche Sud, Conakry; tel. 631-35-53-29 (mobile); fax 631-35-90-59 (mobile); e-mail britembconakry@hotmail.com; Ambassador CATHERINE INGLEHEARN (designate).

USA: Koloma, Ratoma, BP 603, Conakry; tel. 655-10-40-00 (mobile); fax 655-10-42-97 (mobile); e-mail conconakry@state.gov; internet conakry.usembassy.gov; Ambassador ALEXANDER MARK LASKARIS.

Judicial System

The judicial system comprises a Supreme Court, two Courts of Appeal, 10 Tribunals of First Instance and 26 Tribunals of Justice of Peace. The Constitution of 7 May 2010 embodies the principle of the independence of the judiciary, and delineates the competencies of each component of the judicial system, including the Supreme Court and the Revenue Court.

Supreme Court (Cour Suprême): Corniche-Sud, Camayenne, Conakry; tel. 300-41-29-28; Pres. MAMADOU SYLLA.

Court of Appeal (Cour d'Appel): Conakry: First Pres. SEYDOU KEITA; Kankan: First Pres. MOHAMED SAÏD DIOP.

Religion

It is estimated that 85% of the population are Muslims and 8% Christians, while 7% follow animist beliefs.

ISLAM

National Islamic League: BP 386, Conakry; tel. 300-41-23-38; f. 1988; Sec.-Gen. (vacant).

CHRISTIANITY

The Roman Catholic Church

Guinea comprises one archdiocese and two dioceses. About 3% of the population are Roman Catholics.

Bishops' Conference: Conférence Episcopale de la Guinée, BP 1006 bis, Conakry; tel. and fax 300-41-32-70; e-mail dhewara@eti.met.gn; Pres. Most Rev. VINCENT COULIBALY (Archbishop of Conakry).

Archbishop of Conakry: Most Rev. VINCENT COULIBALY, Archevêché, BP 2016, Conakry; tel. and fax 300-43-47-04; e-mail conakriensis@yahoo.fr.

The Anglican Communion

Anglicans in Guinea are adherents of the Church of the Province of West Africa, comprising 15 dioceses. The diocese of Guinea was established in 1985 as the first French-speaking diocese in the Province. The Primate and Metropolitan of the Province is the Bishop of The Gambia.

Bishop of Guinea: Rt Rev. JACQUES BOSTON, Cathédrale Toussaint, BP 1187, Conakry; tel. 631-20-46-60 (mobile); e-mail agomezd@yahoo.fr.

BAHÁ'Í FAITH

Assemblée Spirituelle Nationale: BP 2010, Conakry 1; e-mail asngunee@yahoo.fr; Sec. MAMMA TRAORÉ.

The Press

REGULATORY AUTHORITY

Haute Autorité de la Communication (HAC): en face Primature, BP 2955, Conakry; tel. 300-45-54-82; fax 300-41-23-85; f. 2010; regulates the operations of the press, and of radio and television; regulates political access to the media; nine mems; Pres. MARTINE CONDÉ.

NEWSPAPERS AND PERIODICALS

Bingo: Mifergui, ave du Port, face à la Douane, Almamya, Kaloum, Conakry; tel. 622-91-60-74; e-mail journalbingo@gmail.com; fortnightly; political and social satire; Dir of Publication BEN BARRY YOUSSOUF; Editor PROSPER DORÉ.

Le Démocrate: Quartier Ratoma Centre, Commune de Ratoma, BP 2427, Conakry; tel. 601-20-01-01 (mobile); e-mail mamadoudianb@yahoo.fr; weekly; Dir of Publication and Editor-in-Chief MAMADOU DIAN BALDÉ.

Le Diplomate: BP 2427, Conakry; tel. 655-51-51-51; e-mail hawasanouci@yahoo.fr; internet www.lediplomateguinee.com; f. 2002; weekly; Dir SANOU KERFALLAH CISSÉ.

L'Enquêteur: Coléah Lanséboundji, Commune de Matam, BP 6474, Conakry; tel. 657-94-46-97; e-mail habib@boubah.com; internet www.enqueteur-gn.info; f. 2001; weekly; Editor HABIB YAMBERING DIALLO.

Fonike: BP 341, Conakry; daily; sport and general; state-owned; Dir IBRAHIMA KALIL DIARE.

Horoya (Liberty): Enceinte de RTG, Boulbinet, Kaloum, BP 191, Conakry; tel. 628-21-47-32; e-mail horoye2010@yahoo.fr; govt daily; Dir OUSMANE CAMARA.

L'Indépendant: Quartier Ratoma Centre, Commune de Ratoma, BP 2427, Conakry; tel. 601-20-01-01 (mobile); e-mail lindependant@afribone.net.gn; weekly; also *L'Indépendant Plus*; Dir of Publication and Editor-in-Chief MAMADOU DIAN BALDÉ.

Le Jour: Immeuble Baldé Zaïre, Sandervalia, Kaloum, Conakry; tel. 669-16-48-64; e-mail lejourinfo@gmail.com; internet www.lejour.info; fortnightly; Dir of Publication OUMAR YACINE BAH.

Journal Officiel de Guinée: BP 156, Conakry; fortnightly; organ of the Govt.

La Lance: Immeuble Baldé Zaïre, BP 4968, Conakry; tel. and fax 300-41-23-85; weekly; general information; Dir SOULEYMANE E. DIALLO.

Le Lynx: Immeuble Baldé Zaïre Sandervalia, BP 4968, Conakry; tel. 628-25-27-82; e-mail contact@lelynx.net; internet lelynx.net; f. 1992; weekly; satirical; Editor SOULEYMANE DIALLO.

La Nouvelle Tribune: blvd Diallo Tally, entre 5e et 6e ave, BP 35, Conakry; tel. 300-22-33-02; e-mail abdcond@yahoo.fr; internet www.lanouvelletribuneguinee.com; weekly, Tuesdays; independent; general information and analysis; Dir of Publ. and Editing ABDOULAYE CONDÉ.

L'Observateur: Immeuble Baldé, Conakry; tel. 300-40-05-24; e-mail ibrahimanouhou@yahoo.fr; internet www.observateur-guinee.com; weekly; independent; Dir NOUHOU BALDÉ.

Sanakou: Labé, Foutah Djallon, Moyenne-Guinée; tel. 620-31-55-11; e-mail info@tabaldefouta.org; f. 2000; monthly; general news; Publr IDRISSA SAMPIRING DIALLO; Editor-in-Chief YAMOUSSA SOUMAH; circ. 1,000.

Le Standard: 4e ave, Boulbinet, Kaloum, Conakry; tel. 601-20-01-01; weekly; Dir of Publication HASSANE KABA.

3P Plus (Parole-Plume-Papier) Magazine: 7e ave Bis Almamyah, BP 5122, Conakry; tel. 631-35-04-90; fax 300-45-29-31; e-mail 3p-plus@mirinet.net.gn; internet www.3p-plus.net; f. 1995; journal of arts and letters; supplements *Le Cahier de l'Economie* and *Mag-Plus: Le Magazine de la Culture*; monthly; Pres. MOHAMED SALIFOU KEÏTA; Editor-in-Chief SAMBA TOURÉ.

NEWS AGENCY

Agence Guinéenne de Presse: BP 1535, Conakry; tel. 300-41-14-34; e-mail info@agpguinee.net; internet www.agpguinee.org; f. 1960; Dir-Gen. ALPHA KABINET DOUMBOUYA.

PRESS ASSOCIATION

Association Guinéenne des Editeurs de la Presse Indépendante (AGEPI): Conakry; f. 1991; an assen of independent newspaper publishers; Chair. HASSANE KABA.

Publishers

Les Classiques Guinéens (SEDIS sarl): 545 rue KA020, Mauquepas, BP 3697, Conakry; e-mail cheick.sedis@mirinet.net.gn; f. 1999; art, history, youth literature; Dir CHEICK ABDOUL KABA.

Editions du Ministère de l'Education Nationale: BP 561, Conakry; tel. 300-43-02-66; e-mail dnrst@mirinet.net.gn; f. 1959; general and educational; Deputy Dir Dr TAMBA TAGBINO.

Editions Ganndal (Knowledge): BP 542, Conakry; tel. and fax 300-46-35-07; e-mail ganndal@mirinet.net.gn; f. 1992; educational, youth and children, general literature and books in Pular; Dir MAMADOU ALIOU SOW.

Société Africaine d'Edition et de Communication (SAEC): Belle-Vue, Commune de Dixinn, BP 6826, Conakry; tel. 300-29-71-41; e-mail dtniane@yahoo.fr; social sciences, reference, literary fiction; Editorial Assistant OUMAR TALL.

Broadcasting and Communications

TELECOMMUNICATIONS

In 2013 there were five providers of mobile cellular telephone services and one provider of fixed-line telephone services in Guinea.

Areeba Guinée: Quartier Almamya, Commune de Kaloum, BP 3237, Conakry; tel. 664-22-22-22 (mobile); fax 664-33-33-33 (mobile); internet www.areeba.com.gn; f. 2005; mobile cellular telephone provider; 75% owned by MTN (South Africa); Dir-Gen. P. J. PHIKE.

Cellcom Guinée: Immeuble WAQF-BID, Almamya, C/Kaloum, BP 6567, Conakry; tel. 655-10-01-00 (mobile); fax 655-10-01-01 (mobile); e-mail info@gn.cellcomgsm.com; internet www.gn.cellcomgsm.com; f. 2008; Dir-Gen. AVISHAY MARZIANO.

Intercel: Immeuble Intercel, Quartier Almamya, rue KA 038, BP 965, Conakry; tel. 631-35-35-35 (mobile); fax 300-40-92-92; e-mail info@gn.intercel.net; internet www.intercel-guinee.com; mobile cellular telephone operator; fmrly Telecel Guinée; acquired by Sudatel (Sudan) in 2011; Dir-Gen. DJIBRIL TOBE.

Orange Guinée: Conakry; tel. 622-77-00-00 (mobile); e-mail serviceclientguinee@orange-sonatel.com; internet www.orange-guinee.com; f. 2007; 85% owned by Groupe Sonatel (Senegal); Dir-Gen. ALASSANE DIÈNE.

Société des Télécommunications de Guinée (SOTELGUI): 4e blvd, BP 2066, Conakry; tel. 300-45-27-50; fax 300-45-03-06; e-mail vickycu@sotelgui.net.gn; f. 1992; state-owned; provides fixed-line services; 12,000 fixed-line subscribers and 549,713 mobile subscribers (2010); Dir-Gen. MOUSSA KEITA.

Lagui: Conakry; wholly owned subsidiary of SOTELGUI providing mobile telephone services.

Regulatory Authority

Autorité de Régulation des Postes et des Télécommunications (ARPT): BP 1500, Conakry; tel. 657-66-66-11 (mobile); e-mail contact@arptguinee.org; internet www.arpt.gov.gn; f. 2008; Dir-Gen. DIABY MOUSTAPHA MAMY.

BROADCASTING

Regulatory Authority

Haute Autorité de la Communication (HAC): see The Press.

Radio

Espace FM: Quartier Matoto, Immeuble Mouna, BP 256, Conakry; tel. 664-20-20-92 (mobile); e-mail services@espacefmguinee.info; internet espacefmguinee.info; Dir-Gen. LAMINE GUIRASSY.

Milo FM: BP 215, Kankan; tel. 300-72-00-82; e-mail info@milo-fm.com; internet www.milo-fm.com; Dir-Gen. LANCINÉ KABA.

Radiodiffusion-Télévision Guinéenne (RTG): BP 391, Conakry; tel. 300-44-22-01; fax 300-41-50-01; broadcasts in French, English, Créole-English, Portuguese, Arabic and local languages; Dir-Gen. YAMOUSSA SIDIBÉ; Dir of Radio ISSA CONDÉ.

Radio Rurale de Guinée: BP 391, Conakry; tel. 300-42-11-09; fax 300-41-47-97; e-mail ruralgui@mirinet.net.gn; network of rural radio stations.

Television

Radiodiffusion-Télévision Guinéenne (RTG): see Radio; transmissions in French and local languages; one channel; f. 1977.

Finance

(cap. = capital; res = reserves; dep. = deposits; m. = million; brs = branches; amounts in Guinean francs)

BANKING

In 2013 there were 14 banks operating in Guinea.

Central Bank

Banque Centrale de la République de Guinée (BCRG): 12 blvd du Commerce, BP 692, Kaloum, Conakry; tel. 300-41-26-51; fax 300-41-48-98; e-mail gouv.bcrg@eti-bull.net; internet www.bcrg-guinee.org; f. 1960; bank of issue; cap. 50,000m., res 20,881m., dep. 7,171,432m. (Dec. 2009); Gov. LOUNCENY NABÉ; First Deputy Gov. YÉRO BALDÉ BALDÉ.

Commercial Banks

Banque Internationale pour le Commerce et l'Industrie de la Guinée (BICIGUI): ave de la République, BP 1484, Conakry; tel. 300-41-45-15; fax 300-41-39-62; e-mail dg.bicigui@africa.bnpparibas.com; internet bicigui.org; f. 1985; 30.8% owned by BNP Paribas BDDI Participations (France), 15.1% state-owned; Pres. IBRAHIMA SOUMAH; Dir-Gen. MANGA FODÉ TOURÉ.

Banque Populaire Maroco-Guinéenne (BPMG): Immeuble BPMG, blvd du Commerce, Kaloum, BP 4400, Conakry 01; tel. 300-41-36-93; fax 300-41-32-61; e-mail bpmg@sotelgui.net.gn; f. 1991; 55% owned by Crédit Populaire du Maroc, 42% state-owned; Pres. EMMANUEL GNAN; Dir-Gen. AHMED IRAQUI HOUSSAINI.

Ecobank Guinée: Immeuble Al Iman, ave de la République, BP 5687, Conakry; tel. 631-70-14-34 (mobile); fax 300-45-42-41; e-mail ecobankgn@ecobank.com; internet www.ecobank.com; f. 1999; wholly owned by Ecobank Transnational Inc. (Togo); cap. 117,500.7m., res 43,413.0m., dep. 1,910,568.4m. (Dec. 2013); Pres. MOHAMED CAMARA; Man. Dir MOUKARAM CHANOU ALAO; 9 brs.

International Commercial Bank SA: Ex-cité du Chemin de Fer, Immeuble Mamou, BP 3547, Conakry; tel. 300-41-25-90; fax 300-41-54-50; e-mail enquiry@icbank-guinea.com; internet www.icbank-guinea.com; f. 1997; acquired by FirstBank of Nigeria Ltd in Nov. 2013; Pres. JOSÉPHINE PREMLA; Man. Dir HAMZA BIN ALIAS.

Orabank Guinée: 6e ave de la République, angle 5e blvd, BP 324, Conakry; tel. 620-35-90-90 (mobile); fax 300-97-26-30; e-mail info-gn@orabank.net; f. 1988; fmrly the Union Internationale de Banques en Guinée, present name adopted in 2011; 54.0% owned by Oragroup SA (Togo), 14.3% owned by Orabank Tchad; cap. 25,000m., res −1,139.1m., dep. 259,713.9m. (Dec. 2009); Pres. PATRICK MESTRALLET; Dir-Gen. MAMADOU SENE; 7 brs.

Société Générale de Banques en Guinée (SGBG): Immeuble Boffa, Cité du Chemin de Fer, BP 1514, Conakry; tel. 300-45-60-00; fax 300-41-25-65; e-mail contact@sgbg.net.gn; internet www.sgbg.net; f. 1985; 53% owned by Société Générale (France); Pres. GÉRALD LACAZE; Dir-Gen. MARC LEGUEVAQUES.

Islamic Bank

Banque Islamique de Guinée: Immeuble Nafaya, 6 ave de la République, BP 1247, Conakry; tel. 664-00-44-66 (mobile); fax 300-41-50-71; e-mail bigconakry@biasy.net; internet www.big-bank.com; f. 1983; 50.01% owned by Tamweel Africa Holding, 49.99% owned by Islamic Development Bank (Saudi Arabia); Pres. MOHAMED HABIB DJARRAYA; Dir-Gen. YAYA DIONG.

INSURANCE

In 2011 there were eight insurance companies in Guinea.

Gras Savoye Guinée: 4e ave, angle 4e blvd, Quartier Boulbinet, Commune de Kaloum, BP 6441, Conakry; tel. 300-45-58-43; fax 300-45-58-42; e-mail gsguinee@sotelgui.net.gn; affiliated to Gras Savoye (France); Man. CHÉRIF BAH.

International Insurance Co: Immeuble Sony, ave de la République, Kaloum, BP 4476, Conakry; tel. 622-03-81-05 (mobile); e-mail contact@iicguinea.com; internet www.iicguinea.com; f. 2007; Dir-Gen. KABINET KONDÉ.

Mutragui: BP 1189, Conakry; tel. 657-05-00-00 (mobile); e-mail info@mutragui.com; internet mutragui.com.

Société Nouvelle d'Assurances de Guinée (SONAG): Cité du Chemin de Fer, Kindia, BP 3363, Conakry; tel. 657-29-09-33 (mobile); e-mail sonag@sonag-assurances.com; internet www.assurances-sonag.com.

Sunu Assurances IARD Guinée: Immeuble Mansarena, face Ecole Dixinn Centre II, BP 1618, Conakry; tel. 666-10-10-27; e-mail guinee.iard@sunu-group.com; internet www.sunu-group.com; Dir-Gen. RAPHAËL TOURÉ.

Union Guinéenne d'Assurances et de Réassurances (UGAR): 14 pl. des Martyrs, BP 179, Conakry; tel. 656-96-00-10 (mobile); fax 300-41-17-11; e-mail ugar@ugar.com.gn; internet www.ugarassurance.com; f. 1989; 40% owned by AXA (France), 35% state-owned; cap. 2,000m.; Pres. ISMAËL BANGOURA; Man. Dir RENÉ BUÉE.

LGV: BP 1786, Conakry; tel. 601-52-99-10 (mobile); life insurance; Dir-Gen. MANGA FODÉ TOURÉ.

Trade and Industry

GOVERNMENT AGENCIES

Agence de Promotion des Investissements Privés-Guichet Unique (APIP–GUINEE): BP 2024, Conakry; tel. 300-41-49-85; fax 300-41-39-90; e-mail dg@apiguinee.org; internet www.apiguinee.org; f. 1992; promotes private investment; Dir-Gen. MOHAMED LAMINE BAYO.

Centre de Promotion et de Développement Miniers (CPDM): BP 295, Conakry; tel. 300-41-15-44; fax 300-41-49-13; e-mail cpdm@mirinet.net.gn; f. 1995; promotes investment and co-ordinates devt strategy in mining sector; Dir MOCIRÉ SYLLA.

Entreprise Nationale Import-Export (IMPORTEX): BP 152, Conakry; tel. 300-44-28-13; state-owned import and export agency; Dir MAMADOU BOBO DIENG.

DEVELOPMENT ORGANIZATIONS

Agence Française de Développement (AFD): 5e ave, KA022, BP 283, Conakry; tel. 300-41-25-69; fax 300-41-28-74; e-mail afdconakry@afd.fr; internet www.afd.fr; Country Dir YAZID BENSAID.

France Volontaires: BP 570, Conakry; tel. 300-35-08-60; internet www.france-volontaires.org; f. 1987; name changed as above in 2009; devt and research projects; Nat. Rep. ERIK HOUINSOU.

Service de Coopération et d'Action Culturelle: BP 373, Conakry; tel. 300-41-23-45; fax 300-41-43-56; administers bilateral aid; Dir in Guinea TOBIE NATHAN.

CHAMBERS OF COMMERCE

Chambre de Commerce, d'Industrie et de l'Artisanat de la Guinée (CCIAG): Quartier Tombo, Commune de Kaloum, BP 545, Conakry; tel. 601-26-02-31 (mobile); fax 300-47-70-58; e-mail cciag@sotelgui.net.gn; internet www.cciag.org; f. 1985; Pres. MORLAYE DIALLO.

Chambre Economique de Guinée: BP 609, Conakry.

Chambre des Mines: BP 2624, Conakry; tel. 622-58-26-89 (mobile); e-mail tbarry@chambredesminesgn.org; internet chambredesminesgn.org; f. 1997; Pres. MAMADY YOULA; 66 mems.

TRADE AND EMPLOYERS' ASSOCIATIONS

Association des Commerçants de Guinée: BP 2468, Conakry; tel. 664-21-92-42; e-mail thouca_acic@yahoo.fr; f. 1976; Sec.-Gen. THIERNO OUMAR CAMARA.

Association des Femmes Entrepreneurs de Guinée (AFEG): BP 104, Kaloum, Conakry; tel. 657-28-02-95 (mobile); e-mail afeguine@yahoo.fr; f. 1987; Pres. HADJA RAMATOULAYE SOW.

Conseil National du Patronat Guinéen (CNPG): Dixinn Bora, BP 6403, Conakry; tel. and fax 300-41-24-70; e-mail msylla@leland-gn.org; f. 1992; Pres. SÉKOU CISSÉ (acting); Exec. Vice-Pres. ANSOUMANE KABA.

UTILITIES
Electricity

Electricité de Guinée (EDG): BP 1463, Conakry; tel. 300-45-18-56; fax 300-45-18-53; e-mail di.sogel@biasy.net; f. 2001 to replace Société Guinéenne d'Electricité; majority state-owned; production, transport and distribution of electricity; Dir-Gen. NAVA TOURÉ.

Water

Service National d'Aménagement des Points d'Eau (SNAPE): BP 2064, Conakry; tel. 300-41-18-93; fax 300-41-50-58; e-mail snape@mirinet.net.gn; supplies water in rural areas; Dir-Gen. Dr ALPHA IBRAHIMA NABÉ.

Société des Eaux de Guinée (SEG): Quartier Almamya, BP 150, Conakry; tel. 601-29-01-50 (mobile); fax 300-41-43-69; e-mail info@segguinee.com; internet segguinee.com; f. 2001 to replace SONEG; national water co; Coordinator Gen. MAMADOU DIOULDÉ DIALLO.

TRADE UNIONS

Confédération Nationale des Travailleurs de Guinée (CNTG): Bourse du Travail, Corniche Sud 004, BP 237, Conakry; tel. 300-41-50-44; fax 11-45-49-96; e-mail cntg60@yahoo.fr; f. 1984; Sec.-Gen. AMADOU DIALLO.

Organisation Nationale des Syndicats Libres de Guinée (ONSLG): BP 559, Conakry; tel. 300-41-52-17; fax 300-43-02-83; e-mail onslguinee@yahoo.fr; 27,000 mems (1996); Sec.-Gen. YAMOUDOU TOURÉ.

Union Syndicale des Travailleurs de Guinée (USTG): BP 1514, Conakry; tel. 300-41-25-65; fax 300-41-25-58; e-mail fofil1952@yahoo.fr; independent; 64,000 mems (2001); Sec.-Gen. IBRAHIMA FOFANA.

Transport
RAILWAYS

There are 1,086 km of railways in Guinea, including 662 km of 1-m gauge track from Conakry to Kankan in the east of the country, crossing the Niger at Kouroussa. Three lines for the transport of bauxite link Sangaredi with the port of Kamsar in the west, via Boké, and Conakry with Kindia and Fria, a total of 383 km. In 2012 the Government announced plans to construct a new 670-km railway, which was to connect the iron ore deposits in the Simandou area with a new port in the Forecariah area (yet to be built); it was hoped that the project would be completed by 2015.

Office National des Chemins de Fer de Guinée (ONCFG): BP 589, Conakry; tel. 300-44-46-13; fax 300-41-35-77; f. 1905; Man. Dir NABY BADRA YOULA.

> **Chemin de Fer de Boké:** BP 523, Boké; operations commenced 1973.

> **Chemin de Fer Conakry–Fria:** BP 334, Conakry; operations commenced 1960; Gen. Man. A. CAMARA.

> **Chemin de Fer de la Société des Bauxites de Kindia:** BP 613, Conakry; tel. 300-41-38-28; operations commenced 1974; Gen. Man. K. KEITA.

ROADS

The road network comprised 43,348 km of roads (of which 7,625 km were highways, main or national roads) in 2011. In 2009 an estimated 35% of all roads were paved. An 895-km cross-country road links Conakry to Bamako, in Mali, and the main highway connecting Dakar (Senegal) to Abidjan (Côte d'Ivoire) also crosses Guinea. The road linking Conakry to Freetown (Sierra Leone) forms part of the Trans West African Highway, extending from Morocco to Nigeria.

La Guinéenne-Marocaine des Transports (GUIMAT): Conakry; f. 1989; owned jtly by Govt of Guinea and Hakkam (Morocco); operates nat. and regional transport services.

Société Générale des Transports de Guinée (SOGETRAG): Conakry; f. 1985; 63% state-owned; bus operator.

SHIPPING

Conakry and Kamsar are the international seaports. The port of Conakry handled 7.2m. metric tons of freight in 2011. The country's flag registered fleet at 31 December 2014 numbered 36 vessels, totalling 24,402 grt.

Getma Guinée: Immeuble KASSA, Cité des Chemins de Fer, BP 1648, Conakry; tel. 300-41-26-66; fax 300-41-42-73; e-mail info@getmaguinee.com.gn; internet www.getma.com; f. 1979; fmrly Société Guinéenne d'Entreprises de Transports Maritimes et Aeriens; marine transportation; cap. 1,100m. FG; Chair. and CEO JEAN-JACQUES GRENIER; 135 employees.

Port Autonome de Conakry (PAC): BP 805, Conakry; tel. 300-41-27-28; fax 300-41-26-04; e-mail pac@eti-bull.net; internet www.biasy.net/~pac; haulage, porterage; Gen. Man. MAMADOUBA SAKHON.

Société Navale Guinéenne (SNG): BP 522, Conakry; tel. 300-44-29-55; fax 300-41-39-70; f. 1968; state-owned; shipping agents; Dir-Gen. MAMADI TOURÉ.

Transmar: 33 blvd du Commerce, Kaloum, BP 3917, Conakry; tel. 300-43-05-41; fax 300-43-05-42; e-mail elitegn@gmail.com; shipping, stevedoring, inland transport.

CIVIL AVIATION

There is an international airport at Conakry-Gbèssia, and some 13 smaller airfields elsewhere in the country. In 2009 renovation and extension work was begun at Conakry airport, with the aim of increasing its annual handling capacity from some 300,000 passengers to more than 1m. passengers. In 2010 plans were under consideration regarding the possible construction of a new international airport, at Matakang.

Air Guinée International: Conakry; f. 2010 to replace Air Guinée (f. 1960); regional and internal services; Dir-Gen. MOHAMED EL-BORAÏ.

Société de Gestion et d'Exploitation de l'Aéroport de Conakry (SOGEAC): BP 3126, Conakry; tel. 300-46-48-03; f. 1987; manages Conakry-Gbessia int. airport; 51% state-owned; Dir-Gen. OULABA KABASSAN KEÏTA.

Union des Transports Aériens de Guinée (UTA): scheduled and charter flights to regional and int. destinations.

Tourism

Some 56,146 tourists visited Guinea in 2013; receipts from tourism in 2012 totalled US $1.4m. (excluding passenger transport).

Office National du Tourisme: Immeuble al-Iman, 6e ave de la République, BP 1275, Conakry; tel. 300-45-51-63; fax 300-45-51-64; e-mail ibrahimabakaley@yahoo.fr; f. 1997; Dir-Gen. Elhadj IBRAHIMA KILLÉ SOW.

Defence

As assessed at November 2014, Guinea's active armed forces numbered 9,700, including an army of 8,500, a navy of 400 and an air force of 800. Paramilitary forces comprised a republican guard of 1,600 and a 1,000-strong gendarmerie, as well as a reserve 'people's militia' of 7,000. Military service is compulsory and lasts for two years.

Defence Expenditure: Estimated at 275,000m. Guinean francs in 2013.

Chief of Staff of the Armed Forces: Gen. NAMORY TRAORÉ.

Chief of Staff of the Army: Commdr MORIBA ABEL MARA.

Chief of Staff of the Air Force: Col ALPHA SOUMAH.

Chief of Staff of the Navy: Vice-Adm. ZÉZÉ ONIVUGUI.

Chief of Staff of the National Gendarmerie: Gen. IBRAHIM BALDÉ.

Education

Education is provided free of charge at every level in state institutions. Primary education, which begins at seven years of age and lasts for six years, is officially compulsory. According to UNESCO estimates, in 2012 enrolment in primary education included 74% of children in the relevant age-group (males 80%; females 69%), while in 2011 enrolment at secondary schools included 30% of children in the appropriate age-group (boys 37%; girls 23%). Secondary education, from the age of 13, lasts for seven years, comprising a first cycle (collège) of four years and a second (lycée) of three years. There are universities at Conakry and Kankan, and other tertiary institutions at Manéyah, Boké and Faranah; a total of some 101,200 students were enrolled at tertiary institutions in 2011/12. In 2012 spending on education represented 11.8% of total budgetary expenditure.

GUINEA-BISSAU

Introductory Survey

LOCATION, CLIMATE, LANGUAGE, RELIGION, FLAG, CAPITAL

The Republic of Guinea-Bissau lies on the west coast of Africa, with Senegal to the north and Guinea to the east and south. The climate is tropical, although maritime and Sahelian influences are felt. The average temperature is 20°C (68°F). The official language is Portuguese, of which the locally spoken form is Creole (Crioulo). There are 19 local languages, of which the most widely spoken are Balanta-Kentohe, Pulaar (Fula), Mandjak, Mandinka and Papel. The principal religious beliefs are animism and Islam. There is a small minority of Roman Catholics and other Christian groups. The national flag (proportions 1 by 2) has two equal horizontal stripes, of yellow over light green, and a red vertical stripe, with a five-pointed black star at its centre, at the hoist. The capital is Bissau.

CONTEMPORARY POLITICAL HISTORY

Historical Context

Portuguese Guinea (Guiné) was colonized by Portugal in the 15th century. Nationalist activism began to emerge in the 1950s. Armed insurgency commenced in the early 1960s, and by 1972 the Partido Africano da Independência da Guiné e Cabo Verde (PAIGC) was in control of two-thirds of the country. The independence of the Republic of Guinea-Bissau was unilaterally proclaimed in September 1973, with Luís Cabral (the brother of the founder of the PAIGC, Amílcar Cabral) as President of the State Council. Hostilities ceased following the military coup in Portugal in April 1974, and on 10 September Portugal recognized the independence of Guinea-Bissau under the leadership of Luís Cabral.

The PAIGC regime introduced measures to establish a single-party socialist state. At elections in December 1976 and January 1977 voters chose regional councils from which a new Assembleia Nacional Popular (National People's Assembly—ANP) was later selected. In 1978 the Chief State Commissioner, Francisco Mendes, died; he was succeeded by Commdr João Vieira, hitherto State Commissioner for the Armed Forces and President of the ANP.

The PAIGC initially supervised both Cape Verde and Guinea-Bissau, the Constitutions of each remaining separate but with a view to eventual unification. These arrangements were terminated in November 1980, when President Cabral was deposed in a coup organized by Vieira, who was installed as Chairman of the Council of the Revolution. Diplomatic relations between Guinea-Bissau and Cape Verde were restored after the release of Cabral from detention in 1982.

Domestic Political Affairs

In May 1983 the ANP, which had been dissolved following the 1980 coup, was re-established, and the Council of the Revolution was replaced by a 15-member Conselho de Estado (Council of State), selected from among the members of the ANP. Vieira was subsequently elected as President of the Council of State and Head of State. The ANP immediately ratified a new Constitution, and formally abolished the position of Prime Minister.

In December 1990 the Central Committee of the PAIGC agreed to the adoption of a multi-party system, following a period of transition, and the holding of a presidential election in 1993. In May 1991 a series of constitutional amendments ending one-party rule were approved by the ANP, terminating the political monopoly of the PAIGC. In addition, all links between the PAIGC and the armed forces were severed, and the introduction of a free-market economy was guaranteed. New legislation in October accorded greater freedom to the press and permitted the formation of new trade unions. In November the Frente Democrática (FD) became the first opposition party to obtain official registration.

In December 1991 a major government reshuffle took place, in which the office of Prime Minister was restored. Carlos Correia was appointed to the post. In late 1991 and early 1992 three further opposition parties obtained legal status: the Resistência da Guiné-Bissau—Movimento Bah-Fatah (RGB—MB); the Frente Democrática Social (FDS); and the Partido Unido Social Democrático (PUSD). Following a split in the FDS, a further party, the Partido para a Renovação Social (PRS), was established in January 1992 by the former Vice-Chairman of the FDS, Kumba Yalá. In the same month four opposition parties—the PUSD, FDS, RGB—MB and the Partido da Convergência Democrática (PCD), led by Vítor Mandinga—agreed on the establishment of a 'democratic forum', whose demands included the dissolution of the political police, the creation of an electoral commission and an all-party consultation on the setting of election dates. Legislation preparing for the transition to a multi-party democracy was approved by the ANP in February 1993, and in the following month a commission was appointed to supervise the forthcoming presidential and legislative elections.

The elections, originally scheduled for March 1994, were subsequently postponed, owing to financial and technical difficulties. In May six opposition parties, the FD, the FDS, the Movimento para a Unidade e a Democracia, the Partido Democrático do Progresso, the Partido de Renovação e Desenvolvimento and the Liga Guinéense de Protecção Ecológica (LIPE), formed a coalition, the União para a Mudança (UM). The elections took place on 3 July, although voting was extended for two days, owing to logistical problems. The PAIGC secured a clear majority in the ANP, winning 62 of the 100 seats, while in the presidential election Vieira obtained 46.3% of the votes, and his nearest rival, Yalá, secured 21.9%. The two candidates contested a second round of polling on 7 August in which Yalá was narrowly defeated, securing 48.0% of the votes. International observers declared the elections to have been free and fair. Vieira was inaugurated as President on 29 September and appointed Manuel Saturnino da Costa (the Secretary-General of the PAIGC) as Prime Minister in October. The Council of Ministers was appointed in November, comprising solely members of the PAIGC.

Guinea-Bissau attained membership of the Union Economique et Monétaire Ouest-Africaine (see p. 327) in March 1997 and entered the Franc Zone in April. The national currency was replaced by the franc CFA, and the Banque Centrale des Etats de l'Afrique de l'Ouest assumed central banking functions. In May da Costa was dismissed. Correia was subsequently again appointed Prime Minister, and a new Council of Ministers was inaugurated in June. In March 1998, following protests by opposition parties at delays in the organization of legislative elections, an independent national elections commission was established.

Attempted coup

In June 1998 rebel troops, led by Brig. (later Gen.) Ansumane Mané, who had recently been dismissed as Chief of Staff of the Armed Forces, seized control of the Brá military barracks in the capital and the international airport. Mané subsequently formed a military junta and demanded the resignation of Vieira and his administration. With the support of Senegalese and Guinean soldiers, troops loyal to the Government attempted unsuccessfully to regain control of rebel-held areas of the city, and heavy fighting ensued. Some 200,000 residents of Bissau fled the city.

On 26 July 1998, following mediation by a delegation from the lusophone commonwealth body, the Comunidade dos Países de Língua Portuguesa (CPLP, see below), the Government and the rebels agreed to implement a truce. In August representatives of the Government and the rebels met, under the auspices of the CPLP and the Economic Community of West African States (ECOWAS, see p. 258), and an agreement was reached to transform the existing truce into a ceasefire. However, the rebels' demand that all Senegalese and Guinean forces be withdrawn from the country as a prerequisite to a definitive peace agreement was rejected by the Government and in October the ceasefire collapsed. On 20 October the Government imposed a nationwide curfew. By that time almost all of the government troops had defected to the rebels, who were thought to control some 99% of the country. On 23 October Mané agreed to abide by a further truce. Subsequent negotiations, held under the aegis of ECOWAS, resulted in the signing of a peace accord on 1 November. Under the terms of the accord, the two sides reaffirmed the ceasefire of August, and resolved that the withdrawal of Senegalese and Guinean troops be conducted simultaneously with the deployment of an ECOMOG (ECOWAS Ceasefire Monitoring Group) interposition force, which would guarantee security on the border with Senegal. It was also agreed that a government of national unity would be established, to include representatives of the rebel junta, and that presidential and legislative elections would be held no later than March 1999. In November 1998 agreement was reached on the composition of a Joint Executive Commission to implement the peace accord. In December Francisco José Fadul was appointed Prime Minister, and Vieira and Mané reached agreement on the allocation of portfolios to the two sides.

Hostilities resumed in the capital at the end of January 1999; however, in February talks between the Government and the rebels produced agreement on a renewed ceasefire and on the immediate withdrawal of Senegalese and Guinean troops. On 20 February the new Government of National Unity was announced. The disarmament of rebel troops and those loyal to the President began in March and the withdrawal of Senegalese and Guinean troops was completed that month. On 30 April the UN Secretary-General established the UN Peacebuilding Support Office in Guinea-Bissau (UNOGBIS); its mandate was regularly extended in subsequent years.

Vieira overthrown

In May 1999 Vieira announced that the delayed elections would take place on 28 December. However, on 7 May, to international condemnation, Vieira was overthrown by the rebel military junta, which claimed that its actions had been prompted by Vieira's refusal to allow his presidential guard to be disarmed. Vieira signed an unconditional surrender and the President of the ANP, Malam Bacai Sanhá, was appointed acting President of the Republic pending a presidential election. In June Vieira went into exile in Portugal where he was offered political asylum. In July constitutional amendments were introduced limiting the tenure of presidential office to two terms and abolishing the death penalty. It was also stipulated that the country's principal offices of state could only be held by Guinea-Bissau nationals born of Guinea-Bissau parents. In September an extraordinary congress of the PAIGC voted to expel Vieira and six others from the party. The incumbent Minister of Defence and Freedom Fighters, Francisco Benante, was appointed President of the party. In October the Attorney-General, Amine Michel Saad, announced that he had sufficient evidence to prosecute Vieira for crimes against humanity and expressed his intention to seek Vieira's extradition from Portugal.

Presidential and legislative elections took place on 28 November 1999. Of the 102 seats in the enlarged legislature, the PRS secured 38, the RGB—MB 28, the PAIGC 24, the Aliança Democrática (AD, an alliance of the FD and the PCD) four, the UM three, the Partido Social Democrata (PSD) three, and the FDS and the União Nacional para Democracia e Progresso one each. As no candidate received the necessary 50% of the votes to win the presidential election outright, the leading candidates, Yalá of the PRS and Sanhá of the PAIGC, contested a second round of voting on 16 January 2000, at which Yalá secured victory with 72% of the votes cast. Yalá was inaugurated on the following day and installed a new Council of Ministers, which included members of several former opposition parties, later that month. Caetano N'Tchama of the PRS was appointed Prime Minister. The election was subsequently judged by international observers to have been 'free and fair'. In October Yalá appointed a State Council, comprising members of all parliamentary political parties, which was to have an advisory role.

Demonstrations organized by the PAIGC, in support of demands for the resignation of the Government, took place in Bissau in November 2000. In late November Mané declared himself Commander-in-Chief of the armed forces, following renewed violence in Bissau, instigated by soldiers loyal to him. However, government troops quickly suppressed the insurgency, and a number of opposition leaders were arrested. Mané fled the capital, and was subsequently killed by the security forces.

In October 2001 a motion of no confidence in Yalá was approved by the ANP; the vote had been instigated by opposition parties in response to what they considered to be increasingly unconstitutional actions by the President. A demonstration against Yalá in Bissau followed further demands for the President's resignation by a coalition of opposition parties. Prime Minister Faustino Fudut Imbali was dismissed in December and was replaced by Almara Nhassé, a member of the PRS and hitherto Minister of Internal Administration. Nhassé immediately formed a new Government, composed solely of members of the ruling coalition. Nhassé was subsequently elected President of the PRS, in place of Yalá.

The developing political uncertainty in the country intensified in November 2002, when Yalá dissolved the ANP and dismissed the Government, citing its incompetence in addressing the economic crisis. Legislative elections were scheduled for February 2003. Mario Pires was appointed as Prime Minister, to head a transitional Government that was dominated by the PRS. Several political coalitions opposing the PRS were formed in preparation for the legislative elections, which were subsequently subject to repeated postponements. In December 2002 the PSD, the LIPE, the Partido da Renovação e Progresso and the Partido Socialista Guinéense created the União Eleitoral (UE). In February 2003 the Plataforma Unida—Mufunessa Larga Guiné was formed by the AD, the FDS, the Frente para a Libertação e Independência da Guiné and the Grupo de Democratas Independentes, which had been established by former members of the RGB—MB.

Seabra depoes Yalá

On 14 September 2003 President Yalá was detained by the armed forces in a bloodless coup, which was widely welcomed within Guinea-Bissau. The Chief of Staff of the Armed Forces, Gen. Veríssimo Correia Seabra, who led the coup, stated that the seizure of power had been in response to the worsening political and economic situation. Seabra proclaimed himself interim President of Guinea-Bissau, and President of a Military Committee for the Restoration of Constitutional and Democratic Order. On 17 September Yalá officially resigned from the presidency, and on 28 September Henrique Pereira Rosa, a business executive, and Artur Sanhá were sworn in as interim President and Prime Minister, respectively. On 2 October a transitional civilian Government was appointed, in accordance with an agreement signed by political organizations and the military authorities. A 56-member National Transition Council, composed of representatives of political and civil groups and the army, was to monitor government policy. In November the Government resumed payment of civil servants' salaries, and schools were reopened, having been closed for much of the previous two years owing to a series of strikes by unpaid teachers. In December the Council announced that legislative elections would be held on 28 March 2004, with the presidential election expected to be held one year later (in accordance with a Transitional Charter drafted in October 2003).

Elections to the ANP took place on 28 and 30 March 2004, with a voter turnout of 74.6%. The PAIGC won 45 of the 100 seats while the PRS secured 35 and the PUSD 17. The PAIGC reached an agreement with the PRS, whereby the latter undertook to support the Government in return for senior positions in the ANP, governmental departments and other state institutions. PAIGC President Carlos Gomes Júnior took office as Prime Minister on 10 May. The new Council of Ministers was sworn in on 12 May.

On 6 October 2004 Seabra and another senior military official were taken hostage and killed by a group of disaffected soldiers, led by Maj. Buate Yanta Namam, in protest against the nonpayment of salaries. On 6 and 7 October the soldiers, who emphasized that they were not seeking to overthrow the Government, presented their demands, which included an improvement in army conditions and the payment of salary arrears. Gomes Júnior attributed the unrest to political forces dissatisfied with the outcome of the April elections (widely assumed as referring to members of the PRS). On 10 October a Memorandum of Understanding was signed by Gomes Júnior, Yanta Naman and Maj.-Gen. Baptista Tagmé Na Wai, representing the armed forces, according to which the soldiers would return to their barracks and salary arrears would be paid. An amnesty was to be granted to the mutineers and later in October Gomes Júnior announced that nearly all salary arrears had been settled. A new military high command, reportedly chosen by the mutineers, was also installed. Na Wai became Chief of Staff of the Armed Forces, while José Americo Bubo Na Tchuto was appointed Navy Chief of Staff.

It was announced in March 2005 that a presidential election would take place on 19 June. Malam Bacai Sanhá, who served as acting President in 1999, was chosen as the candidate for the PAIGC. Meanwhile, both Vieira (who was standing as an independent) and Yalá, representing the PRS, announced their candidacies. According to the Transitional Charter, both Yalá and Vieira were subject to five-year bans from political activity;

however, in April their candidacies were approved by the Supreme Court.

The return of Vieira

At the presidential election on 19 June 2005, Sanhá secured 35.5% of the votes cast, while Vieira took 28.9% and Yalá 25.0%. A second round of voting, contested by Sanhá and Vieira, followed on 24 July, when Vieira was elected with 52.4% of votes cast. The rate of voter participation was 87.6% in the first round and 78.6% in the second round, and international observers declared the election to have been free and fair.

Despite allegations of widespread electoral fraud and Sanhá's demands that the results of the election be annulled, the outcome was upheld by the Supreme Court and Vieira took office on 1 October 2005. Tensions continued, however, among the pro-Vieira members of the PAIGC and the pro-Sanhá, governing faction of the party. In mid-October 14 PAIGC deputies resigned from the party and declared themselves independents, and several members of that party, together with the PRS and the PUSD, formed a pro-Vieira alliance, the Forúm de Convergência para o Desenvolvimento (FCD), with the intention of precipitating the collapse of Gomes Júnior's Government. Members of the FCD claimed to have a majority in the ANP.

In late October 2005, following continued demands by the FCD for the dismissal of the Prime Minister, Vieira dissolved the Government. Aristides Gomes, the former Vice-President of the PAIGC, was appointed Prime Minister on 2 November. Meanwhile, civil unrest exacerbated tensions, resulting in the temporary allocation to Aristides Gomes of the economy and finance portfolios, in order to facilitate the payment of civil service salaries. The new Government, which was sworn in on 9 November, comprised members of the PAIGC, the PRS, the PUSD, the PCD and the UE, and independents, the majority of whom were former PAIGC members. The PAIGC challenged the constitutional legitimacy of the appointment of Aristides Gomes, claiming that as the party that held the largest number of seats in the legislature, it had the right to propose the new Prime Minister; however, in January 2006 the Supreme Court ruled that Vieira had acted in accordance with the Constitution.

In November 2006 Yalá was re-elected as leader of the PRS, following one year's absence from the country; he announced that he no longer recognized the FCD and sought early elections. In mid-March 2007 the PAIGC, the PRS and the PUSD announced that they had signed a National Stability Pact (NSP), which aimed to precipitate the formation of a new government of national unity. The PRS and the PUSD also confirmed their withdrawal from the FCD. President Vieira initially refused to accede to demands to dismiss the Government; however, on 19 March 54 deputies approved a motion of no confidence in Prime Minister Gomes, who tendered his resignation 10 days later. Also in late March it was reported that the PUSD had withdrawn its support for the NSP. On 10 April Vieira nominated Martinho N'Dafa Cabi, a senior member of the PAIGC, who had held the positions of Deputy Prime Minister and Minister of National Defence in the Gomes Júnior administration, as the new Prime Minister. A new Government of national unity was installed in mid-April. Legislative elections were subsequently scheduled for November 2008.

In August 2008 a number of senior ministers were dismissed, prompting the PAIGC to withdraw from the Government. In anticipation of the forthcoming elections, Vieira dissolved the ANP and appointed Carlos Correia as Prime Minister of a new Government largely comprising former PAIGC members loyal to him. Political tensions remained high and later that month it was revealed that an attempted coup to overthrow the President had been averted. Nevertheless, preparations for the legislative elections continued and the ballot duly took place as scheduled on 16 November. According to official results, the PAIGC won 67 seats in the ANP, securing 49.8% of the votes cast, while the PRS took 28 seats with 25.3% of the votes. The newly formed Partido Republicano para a Independência e o Desenvolvimento, led by Aristides Gomes, took three seats and the Partido para a Nova Democracia and the AD won one seat each. However, a further failed coup attempt in late November—a number of mutinous soldiers were reported to have forced their way into the presidential palace, killing one member of the presidential guard—highlighted the growing instability in the country. A new Council of Ministers was named in December, with Gomes Júnior returning to the post of Prime Minister.

The assassination of Vieira

In January 2009 Na Wai accused members of the special presidential militia of attempting to assassinate him after a shooting incident, and ordered that they be disarmed. Relations between Na Wai and President Vieira subsequently deteriorated, and Na Wai was killed in a bomb explosion at the army headquarters on 1 March. Vieira was then assassinated in an attack on his private residence in the early hours of 2 March, which was reported to have been carried out by soldiers seeking to avenge the killing of Na Wai. In the days immediately after Vieira's death senior army figures insisted that no coup had been carried out. On 3 March Raimundo Pereira, President of the ANP, was sworn in as Interim President, pending a presidential election that was, in accordance with the Constitution, to be held within 60 days. The Government subsequently announced that it would hold a judicial inquiry into the deaths of Na Wai and Vieira. The events in Guinea-Bissau were condemned by the African Union (AU), the UN, the European Union (EU, see p. 271) and ECOWAS, and the latter declared that it was to deploy a multi-disciplinary group to monitor and co-ordinate security sector reform in the country. In April Pereira issued a decree stipulating that the presidential election would take place on 28 June.

On 5 June 2009 Baciro Dabo, a close ally of Vieira and a former government minister who had announced his intention to contest the forthcoming presidential election as an independent candidate, was shot dead in his residence by armed men, and a second candidate, former Prime Minister Imbali, was reportedly abducted. With the security situation worsening—the former Minister of Defence, Helder Proenca, was also killed in early June—Pedro Nfanda withdrew from the presidential poll. Requests were filed with the Supreme Court for the election to be postponed and while the Constitution stipulated that the ballot should be delayed in the event of the death of a candidate, Interim President Pereira announced that the poll would proceed as scheduled. Malam Bacai Sanhá, again representing the PAIGC, won 39.6% of votes cast, while Mohamed Yalá Embaló (as Kumba Yalá, who had converted to Islam in 2008, had become known) took 29.4% and Henrique Rosa secured 24.2%. At a second round of voting, which took place on 26 July, Sanhá secured 63.3% of the votes cast, while Yalá Embaló, took 36.7%. Shortly after the election results were announced, Commdr José Zamora Induta, formerly the Navy Chief of Staff, was confirmed as Chief of Staff of the Armed Forces.

Sanhá was sworn in as President on 8 September 2009 and a new Council of Ministers, again headed by Gomes Júnior, was appointed in late October. Maria Adiatú Djaló Nandingna, Minister of Foreign Affairs in the outgoing administration, was appointed Minister of the Presidency of the Council of Ministers, Social Communication and Parliamentary Affairs, the most senior cabinet post after the Prime Minister.

In December 2009 former Navy Chief of Staff Na Tchuto, who had fled to The Gambia following his alleged involvement in the coup attempt of August 2008, returned to the country, prompting the Government to order that he be arrested and prosecuted. Claiming to fear for his personal safety, Na Tchuto was granted refuge in the headquarters of UNOGBIS (which upon completion of its mandate was formally replaced on 1 January 2010 by UNIOGBIS, the UN Integrated Peacebuilding Office in Guinea-Bissau).

Attempted military coup and continuing instability

On 1 April 2010 dissident members of the armed forces, led by the Deputy Army Chief of Staff, Gen. (later Maj.-Gen.) António Indjai, staged a coup attempt. Early that day rebel soldiers entered the UNIOGBIS compound to release Na Tchuto, who joined Indjai. Induta was seized, together with the head of military intelligence, Samba Djaló, and a number of other officers, after which he was transferred to a military compound outside of Bissau, where he remained in detention. After assuming control over the armed forces, Indjai and his entourage arrested Prime Minister Gomes Júnior at the government headquarters. Upon news of his detention, demonstrations were staged in the capital to express support for Gomes Júnior and rejection of the attempted coup. Indjai responded by announcing in a radio broadcast that he would kill Gomes Júnior unless his supporters dispersed. Shortly afterwards, however, the Prime Minister was released, and returned to his office. The international community condemned the attempted coup and urged that the Constitution be respected. On 8 April the US Department of State issued a statement accusing Na Tchuto and Ibraima Papá Camara, the Chief of Staff of the Air Force, of involvement in drugs-trafficking, and announced the freezing of their assets in the USA. Although both Na Tchuto and Camara denied the accusations, the decision increased speculation that the coup attempt was linked to resistance within some elements of the armed forces to efforts to reform the country's security forces.

Throughout April 2010 there were rumours of further attempts to arrest the Prime Minister. Gomes Júnior fled the country and remained abroad for over one month, allegedly for health reasons, returning in June. In late June Sanhá appointed Indjai as the new Chief of Staff of the Armed Forces (the post having been left officially vacant since the ousting of Induta). In the same month the EU announced that it was to end its security sector reform mission in Guinea-Bissau (with effect from the end of September), in view of Na Tchuto and Camara's alleged involvement in narcotics-trafficking and Indjai's appointment. On 1 June Na Tchuto was formally acquitted by a military court of all the charges pending against him, and in October he was reinstated by Sanhá as Navy Chief of Staff (prompting criticism from the USA). In October Gomes Júnior suspended the Minister of the Interior, Hadja Satu Camara Pinto, from office, after she appointed police officers in defiance of a decree issued by the Prime Minister prohibiting this on the grounds that it would disrupt reforms in the armed and security forces. In December Camara Pinto tendered her resignation, complaining that President Sanhá (who had been admitted to hospital in Paris, France) had failed to support her in the dispute with Gomes Júnior. (Dinis Na Fantchamena was subsequently appointed as the new Minister of the Interior.)

In November 2010 the UN Security Council approved a resolution authorizing the extension of UNIOGBIS's mandate in the country until the end of 2011 (subsequently renewed until February 2013), expressing its concern at continuing instability in Guinea-Bissau. The Government had also requested the deployment of an international stabilization force, which was to be established by the AU and ECOWAS to assist in post-conflict reconstruction and development. In December Induta, together with Djaló, were released from detention, shortly after the EU threatened to impose sanctions against the Government.

Following the withdrawal of EU support for Guinea-Bissau's security sector reform programme, a replacement plan proposed by ECOWAS and the CPLP was endorsed by the Council of Ministers in March 2011. In particular, the ECOWAS-CPLP 'roadmap' envisaged a reduction in the size of the military. In the same month Angola, which had assumed a leading role in the ECOWAS-CPLP mission, transferred some 200 troops to Guinea-Bissau to assist in the training and restructuring of the security forces—representing the first phase of an expected deployment of 600 ECOWAS-CPLP personnel.

In May 2011 the official investigation into the June 2009 murders of Dabo and Proença was suspended, ostensibly because of insufficient evidence, while the judicial inquiry examining the deaths of Na Wai and Vieira in March 2009 had only made limited progress by mid-2011. Opposition parties organized several anti-Government demonstrations during July in response. Sanhá effected an extensive cabinet reorganization in the following month, but rejected opposition demands to replace Gomes Júnior as Prime Minister.

The death of Sanhá and the subsequent military coup

Sanhá travelled to Senegal in September 2011, reportedly to receive medical treatment for diabetes. He returned to Guinea-Bissau three weeks later, but in late November was again hospitalized in Senegal, before being transferred to a French hospital shortly thereafter. Amid growing concern for Guinea-Bissau's stability, on 26 December reports emerged from the capital of intra-military clashes. Gomes Júnior fled to the Angolan embassy during the unrest, and at least one fatality was recorded. The Government declared on the following day that Na Tchuto and a number of his associates had been arrested after attempting to stage a coup. (However, other sources claimed that a military pay dispute had precipitated the violence.) The Government announced its intention to launch an inquiry into the alleged uprising. Sanhá died in Paris on 9 January. In compliance with the Constitution, ANP President Raimundo Pereira again became Interim President. Pereira subsequently proclaimed that a presidential election would be held on 18 March.

In early February 2012 Gomes Júnior resigned the premiership and announced his intention to stand for the presidency as the candidate of the PAIGC; Djaló Nandingna was appointed Acting Prime Minister. Among the other eight candidates to contest the presidential election, which was duly held on 18 March, were Yalá Embaló and Henrique Rosa. According to official results, Gomes Júnior won 49.0%, while Yalá Embaló was placed second with 23.4% and Manuel Serifo Nhamadjo took 15.7%. The rate of voter participation was put at 55% of the registered electorate. A run-off election was scheduled to be held on 29 April. However, Yalá Embaló maintained that he would boycott the second round of voting, in protest at alleged irregularities that took place during the first round.

On 12 April 2012 members of the military seized power and detained Pereira and Gomes Júnior. It was reported that the coup was carried out in reaction to plans by Gomes Júnior to use Angolan troops to remove certain elements of the Guinea-Bissau armed forces. A 'Military Command' (Comando Militar) was formed, under the leadership of the army Deputy Chief of Staff, Gen. Mamadu Ture Kuruma, and on 18 April the establishment of a National Transitional Council (Conselho Nacional de Transição) was announced, after 22 political parties, although notably excluding the PAIGC, and the military junta agreed upon a timeframe towards new elections. The Government was dissolved. The AU announced the suspension of Guinea-Bissau from the organization, pending the restoration of democratic rule, while the World Bank and the African Development Bank also suspended their development programmes. On 21 April the junta stated that the transitional period would be reduced from two years to one. Despite this concession and the release from custody of Pereira and Gomes Júnior on 27 April, ECOWAS, which had also suspended Guinea-Bissau's membership, confirmed the imposition of diplomatic and financial sanctions on the country on 30 April. By late April Indjai had become a key figure in negotiations between the junta and ECOWAS, and he was widely believed to have planned the overthrow of the institutions of state.

Following further dialogue with ECOWAS, in mid-May 2012 Nhamadjo was installed as interim President, while former Minister of Finance Rui Duarte de Barros was nominated as Prime Minister. On 19 May a roadmap agreement on the return to civilian rule was signed by the Military Command and 25 political parties (although the PAIGC again declined to participate), and on 22 May the junta formally transferred power to a transitional Government. Celestino do Carvalho, who had been involved in the coup, was controversially included in the new Council of Ministers as the minister responsible for defence; former Prime Minister Imbali received the foreign affairs portfolio. Gomes Júnior denounced the transitional administration as illegitimate. Indeed, some observers noted that, by supporting a Government that excluded Pereira, Gomes Júnior and the PAIGC, ECOWAS had, in effect, upheld the main objectives of the coup. The EU withheld official recognition of the transitional Government and on 31 May expanded its sanctions regime (first introduced on 3 May) against the coup leaders. UN Security Council Resolution 2048, approved earlier that month, also provided for sanctions against senior junta members. Meanwhile, the ECOWAS Mission in Guinea-Bissau (ECOMIB), comprising 629 security personnel, was deployed from late May. ECOMIB replaced the ECOWAS-CPLP Angolan contingent upon its withdrawal in early June, with a six-month mandate (which was subsequently renewed) to stabilize the security situation and monitor the transitional process.

A military base near the capital came under attack by armed men on 21 October 2012, resulting in the deaths of at least seven people. The transitional Government regarded the raid as an attempted counter coup and claimed that it had been orchestrated by Portugal and its allies in the CPLP, which had maintained a firmly pro-Gomes Júnior stance since the April coup. The Guinea-Bissau authorities suspected that Capt. Pansau N'Tchama had overseen the attack, and he was placed in detention in late October. It was also revealed at this time that Guinea-Bissau had requested the extradition of Gomes Júnior from Portugal.

In November 2012 an agreement on restarting the military reform programme was signed by the transitional Government and ECOWAS, which authorized US $63m. in funding for the initiative. In January 2013 the former President of Timor-Leste, José Ramos Horta, was named as the Special Representative of the Secretary-General to Guinea-Bissau and Head of UNIOGBIS; in February UNIOGBIS's mandate was extended until the end of May. Meanwhile, a multi-party political transition accord was concluded in January following negotiations between the transitional Government and the PAIGC.

In April 2013 Na Tchuto (who had been released by the transitional authorities in June 2012) was apprehended on a vessel in international waters, following an operation carried out by US federal officials. Na Tchuto was transferred to custody in New York, USA, along with four other suspects, where they were charged with drugs-trafficking offences. Indjai, who remained in Guinea as Chief of Staff of the Armed Forces, was also formally charged with involvement in the drugs-trafficking conspiracy to supply armaments to a Colombian rebel group. On 22 May 2013 the UN Security Council extended the mandate of UNIOGBIS for a further year, and tasked the mission, under an amended mandate, to support the organization of elections.

Delays in the transitional programme

Political discussions conducted throughout May 2013 resulted in the signature and entry into force of a political agreement between the various parties and a new transitional programme. In early June Nhamadjo reorganized the transitional Government, notably appointing Fernando Delfim da Silva as Minister of Foreign Affairs and Gino Mendes as Minister of Finance; the military succeeded in retaining control over the ministries of national defence and of the interior. On 28 June Nhamadjo announced that the delayed legislative and presidential elections would take place on 24 November.

In mid-November 2013 Nhamadjo announced that the elections had been postponed until 16 March 2014, due to logistical difficulties. Later in November Ramos Horta reported a deterioration in the security situation in the country. In December da Silva and the Minister of the Interior, Antonio Suka Tchama, resigned their government posts after it emerged that a Portuguese national airline plane had been obliged to transport 74 Syrian refugees with false documentation from Bissau to Lisbon, Portugal. The Portuguese Government criticized the incident as a breach of security, while Portugal temporarily suspended flights to Guinea-Bissau.

On 21 February 2014 Nhamadjo issued a decree rescheduling the elections for 13 April, after announcing that a voter registration exercise scheduled to be conducted during the previous December was still incomplete. Later in February the UN Security Council urged the authorities to adhere to the transitional programme and again warned of the possible imposition of sanctions. Nhamadjo announced in early March that, in accordance with the transitional agreements, he would not seek the presidency. The PAIGC finally selected a former Minister of Finance, José Mário Vaz 'Jomav', as its presidential candidate, rather than former premier Gomes Júnior. Attorney-General Abdú Mané subsequently urged the Supreme Court to prohibit Vaz from contesting the poll, on the grounds that an investigation into embezzlement allegations against him was ongoing. However, in mid-March the Supreme Court released a list of 13 approved presidential candidates, including Vaz; 15 of 22 applicant parties had secured registration to contest the legislative elections.

Recent developments: presidential and legislative elections

The elections finally took place peacefully on 13 April 2014. According to official results, the PAIGC secured 48.0% of the votes cast and 57 seats in the 102-member ANP, while the PRS received 30.8% of the votes and 41 seats. In the concurrent presidential election, Vaz secured about 40.9% of the votes cast, Nuno Gomes Nabiam, an independent candidate (and former head of the civil aviation authority) who was supported by the military, 24.8%, an independent and former World Bank official, Paulo Gomes, 10.4% and the PRS candidate, Abel Incada, 7.0%. A voter turnout of more than 88% was reported. A presidential second round between Vaz and Nabiam took place on 18 May, when Vaz was elected to the presidency, with 61.9% of votes cast. Since the conduct of the elections was deemed satisfactory, Guinea-Bissau was readmitted to the AU on 17 June, and relations with all other international institutions were normalized. Upon his inauguration on 23 June, Vaz issued pledges to restore stabilization to the country. On 4 July Vaz appointed a new Government, under the premiership of Domingos Simões Pereira of the PAIGC; his administration comprised 19 representatives of the PAIGC, six of the PRS, one member of each of three smaller parties and three independents.

Following his indictment by the US authorities the previous year, in September 2014 Indjai was removed by President Vaz from the post of Chief of Staff of the Armed Forces; the decision was welcomed by the international community as significant progress in security sector reform. Indjai was replaced by Brig.-Gen. Biague Na Ntam, hitherto head of the presidential guard. The Minister of Internal Administration, Botche Candé, was obliged to tender his resignation in November, after inadvertently entering rebel-held territory while visiting the area bordering Senegal. He was succeeded in March 2015 by Octávio Alves. Meanwhile, on 11 November 2014 the ANP adopted a resolution reactivating a commission for constitutional review (originally established in 2010), comprising parliamentary deputies and civil society representatives, and preparations were initiated for the convening of a national conference on reconciliation in 2015. Tensions within the PAIGC leadership, including between Vaz and Prime Minister Pereira were reported during early 2015. Following official reports that the security situation in Guinea-Bissau remained fragile, on 18 February the UN Security Council extended the mandate of UNIOGBIS until the end of February 2016, under a revised mandate to support the strengthening of democratic institutions in the country.

Foreign Affairs

Regional relations

In 1989 a dispute arose between Guinea-Bissau and Senegal over the demarcation of maritime borders. Guinea-Bissau began proceedings against Senegal in the International Court of Justice (ICJ) after rejecting an international arbitration tribunal's ruling in favour of Senegal. In November 1991 the ICJ ruled that a 1960 agreement regarding the demarcation of maritime borders between Guinea-Bissau and Senegal remained valid. In October 1993 the Presidents of Guinea-Bissau and Senegal signed an agreement providing for the joint management and exploitation of the countries' maritime zones; its ratification was authorized by the legislature in December 1995, after the ICJ announced that Guinea-Bissau had halted all proceedings regarding the border dispute with Senegal.

During 1995 the Senegalese air force bombarded border villages in Guinea-Bissau on at least three occasions, apparently in error, prompting the Guinea-Bissau legislature to form a commission of inquiry to investigate such incidents. In April 2000 there were renewed reports of incidents on the border between Senegal and Guinea-Bissau. In August an agreement was signed by Yalá and President Abdoulaye Wade of Senegal providing for the establishment of a joint military force to patrol the border area. Following the signing of a peace accord between the Senegalese Government and the Casamance separatists in December 2004, security in the region improved. However, a dissident faction of the separatists renewed disruption and from March 2006 further skirmishes occurred with Guinea-Bissau troops. In December 2014 the Guinea-Bissau Government announced the reopening of the border with Guinea, after a four-month closure owing to an outbreak of the Ebola virus in that country.

Relations between Guinea-Bissau and The Gambia were severely strained in June 2002, when President Yalá accused the Government of The Gambia of harbouring and training Casamance rebels and former associates of Gen. Mané, the leader of the coup of 1998 and attempted coup of 2000. With specific reference to the alleged attempted coup of May 2002, Yalá threatened invasion of The Gambia if support for the rebels continued. A visit to The Gambia by Guinea-Bissau's Minister of Foreign Affairs in mid-June eased tensions somewhat, and was followed by UN intervention in July, which recommended the reactivation of a joint commission of the two countries. An improvement in relations was signalled by a visit by Yalá to The Gambia in October. In January 2015 the Guinea-Bissau Government condemned an attempted coup that had been staged in The Gambia, while denying reports that Gambian soldiers had been arrested in Guinea-Bissau in connection with the incident.

Other external relations

The People's Republic of China has been active in promoting good economic relations with Guinea-Bissau since the mid-2000s and funded various public projects, particularly following a visit by President Vieira to Beijing in 2006. This was regarded as undermining the unified approach of the rest of the international donor community in eliciting commitments to reform in return for aid. China benefited from maritime treaties and fishing rights in Guinea-Bissau territorial waters.

In July 1996 Guinea-Bissau was among the five lusophone African nations that, along with Brazil and Portugal, officially established the CPLP, a lusophone grouping intended to benefit each member state by means of joint co-operation in technical, cultural and social matters. Portugal provided Guinea-Bissau with considerable funding and other aid. Guinea-Bissau was a signatory to the 'Luanda Declaration' in November 2011, which pledged greater co-operation between the CPLP member states in the fields of, *inter alia*, security, crime prevention and immigration.

After democratic elections were conducted in Guinea-Bissau in April–May 2014 (see *Domestic Political Affairs*), the EU announced the resumption of full co-operation during a visit by Prime Minister Pereira to Brussels, Belgium, in July. Following a visit to Portugal by Pereira in November, the Portuguese authorities pledged emergency assistance of €6.8m. towards the support of governance in Guinea-Bissau. The International Contact Group on Guinea-Bissau (established in 2006), which had suspended meetings shortly after the coup of April 2012, convened in New York, USA, on 18 November 2014, subsequently issuing a communiqué welcoming the Government's planned reforms.

CONSTITUTION AND GOVERNMENT

Under the terms of the 1984 Constitution (revised in 1991, 1996 and 1999), Guinea-Bissau is a multi-party state, although the formation of parties on a tribal or geographical basis is prohibited. Legislative power is vested in the Assembleia Nacional Popular (National People's Assembly), which comprises 102 members, elected by universal adult suffrage for a term of four years. Executive power is vested in the President of the Republic, who is Head of State and who governs with the assistance of an appointed Council of Ministers, led by the Prime Minister. The President is elected by universal adult suffrage for a term of five years.

REGIONAL AND INTERNATIONAL CO-OPERATION

Guinea-Bissau is a member of the African Union (see p. 188), of the Economic Community of West African States (ECOWAS, see p. 258) and of the West African organs of the Franc Zone (see p. 327). In 2004 Guinea-Bissau became a member of the Community of Sahel-Saharan States (see p. 446).

Guinea-Bissau became a member of the UN in 1974 and was admitted to the World Trade Organization (WTO, see p. 431) in 1995.

ECONOMIC AFFAIRS

In 2013, according to estimates by the World Bank, Guinea-Bissau's gross national income (GNI), measured at average 2011–13 prices, was US $884m., equivalent to $520 per head (or $1,240 on an international purchasing-power parity basis). During 2004–13, it was estimated, the population increased at an average annual rate of 2.3%, while gross domestic product (GDP) per head increased, in real terms, by an average of 0.2% per year. Overall GDP increased, in real terms, at an average annual rate of 2.5% in 2004–13; it decreased by 1.5% in 2012, but increased by 0.3% in 2013.

Agriculture (including forestry and fishing) contributed a provisional 43.7% of GDP in 2013, according to official figures. and the sector engaged an estimated 77.6% of the economically active population in mid-2015, according to FAO. The main cash crops are cashew nuts (production of which in 2012 was estimated by FAO at 130,000 metric tons, with export earnings in that year totalling 60.0m. francs CFA) and cotton. Other crops produced include rice, oil palm fruit, cassava, plantains, coconuts, sorghum, maize and millet. Livestock and timber production are also important. The fishing industry developed rapidly during the 1990s, and earnings from fishing exports and the sale of fishing licences are a significant source of government revenue (revenue from fishing licences was 7,515m. francs CFA in 2005, equivalent to 26.9% of total revenue). A study conducted in 2004 revealed that the potential annual fishing catch was 96,000 tons, although in 2012 the total catch recorded by FAO amounted to only 6,550; in 2006 the Minister of Fisheries and the Maritime Economy estimated that 40,000 tons of fish were stolen from Guinea-Bissau waters annually. According to provisional official figures, agricultural GDP increased, in real terms, by an average of 3.2% per year in 2007–13; agricultural GDP declined by 0.6% in 2012, but increased by 3.2% in 2013.

Industry (including mining, manufacturing, construction and power) employed an estimated 4.1% of the economically active population at mid-1994 and, according to provisional official figures, provided 16.5% of GDP in 2013. Industrial GDP grew, in real terms, by an average of 5.0% per year in 2007–13, according to provisional figures; growth of 2.5% was recorded in 2013.

The mining sector is underdeveloped, although Guinea-Bissau possesses reserves of bauxite, phosphates, diamonds and gold. In 2003 recoverable petroleum reserves were estimated at 2,000m. barrels per day. According to provisional official figures, mining provided less than 0.1% of GDP in 2013.

The sole branches of the manufacturing sector are food-processing, brewing and timber and cotton-processing, while there are plans to develop fish-processing. According to provisional official estimates, manufacturing contributed 14.2% of GDP in 2013. Manufacturing GDP increased, in real terms, by an average of 4.2% per year in 2007–13; the GDP of the sector grew 0.6% in 2013.

The construction sector contributed 1.4% of GDP in 2013, according to provisional official figures. The sector grew, in real terms, by an average of 1.6% per year in 2007–13; construction GDP increased by 62.5% in 2013.

Energy is derived principally from thermal and hydroelectric power. Imports of petroleum and petroleum products comprised 20.3% of the value of total imports in 2012. Energy production since 1999 has been insufficient to supply demand in Bissau, mainly owing to fuel shortages caused by government-set low prices, and to equipment failures caused by poor maintenance. As a result, most energy is currently supplied by private generators.

Services employed an estimated 19.4% of the economically active population at mid-1994, and, according to provisional official figures, provided 39.8% of GDP in 2013. According to the World Bank, the combined The GDP of the service sector increased, in real terms, by an average of 3.6% per year in 2007–13; services GDP declined by 0.3% in 2013.

In 2013 Guinea-Bissau recorded a trade deficit of 17,300m. francs CFA, and there was a deficit of 19,400m. francs CFA on the current account of the balance of payments, according to the IMF. In 2012 the principal source of imports was Senegal (17.5%). In that year India was the principal market for exports (72.9%). In 2012 the principal export was cashew nuts. The principal imports in that year were petroleum and petroleum products.

According to the IMF, in 2013 there was a budgetary deficit of 50,300m. francs CFA, equivalent to 8.8% of GDP. Guinea-Bissau's general government gross debt was 298,554m. francs CFA in 2011, equivalent to 57.3% of GDP. Guinea-Bissau's total external debt was US $280m. at the end of 2012, of which $213m. was public and publicly guaranteed debt. In 2010 the cost of servicing long-term public and publicly guaranteed debt and repayments to the IMF was equivalent to 9.5% of the value of exports of goods, services and income (excluding workers' remittances). In 2004–13 the average annual rate of inflation was 2.1%. Consumer prices decreased by 1.7% in 2012, but increased by 1.1% in 2013.

The economy of Guinea-Bissau is largely dependent on the export of cashew nuts, and foreign financing accounts for a significant part of budget revenue. Relations with donors have, however, been uneasy since the early 2000s, amid chronic political instability in the country, and support has periodically been withheld. Meanwhile, the People's Republic of China has financed and undertaken a number of large-scale projects, including the construction of a large-scale dam 200 km from the capital, at a cost of US $60m. In May 2010 the IMF approved a three-year Extended Credit Facility of $33.3m. to support the Government's economic programme, and in December Guinea-Bissau was pronounced by the IMF to have met the requirements to reach completion point under the initiative for heavily indebted poor countries. The IMF and the World Bank subsequently announced their decision to support $1,200m. in debt relief for Guinea-Bissau. The 'Paris Club' of creditor nations, and other bilateral and multilateral creditors cancelled large proportions of Guinea-Bissau's debt during 2011. However, the military coup of April 2012 led to widespread economic disruption, and a contraction in real GDP. The suspension of financial assistance programmes by many of Guinea-Bissau's international partners compounded economic hardship. Nevertheless, the prospects for economic stabilization improved significantly following the successful organization of elections in April (see *Domestic Political Affairs*). International sanctions were removed, and in June Guinea-Bissau was readmitted to the African Union (see p. 188) (following the suspension of its membership in response to the coup). In September the IMF approved a Rapid Credit Facility (RCF) amounting to funds of $5.4m. for Guinea-Bissau. The total emergency financial assistance available under the RCF was disbursed to support budgetary and balance-of-payments deficits in November, when the IMF commended government plans to reform the operations of the national cashew fund. Despite the restoration of constitutional order, the Government's success in the payment of public sector wage arrears, a significant recovery in cashew exports and prices, and an increase in the country's GDP growth to an estimated 2.1% in 2014, economic activity remained weak. Renewed appeals for donor assistance were issued in early 2015 and an international donor conference was to be convened in Brussels (Belgium) in March.

PUBLIC HOLIDAYS

2016: 1 January (New Year's Day), 20 January (Death of Amílcar Cabral), 8 March (International Women's Day), 1 May (Labour Day), 6 July* (Korité, end of Ramadan), 3 August (Anniversary of the Killing of Pidjiguiti), 12 September* (Tabaski, Feast of the Sacrifice), 24 September (National Day), 14 November (Anniversary of the Movement of Readjustment), 25 December (Christmas Day).

*These holidays are dependent on the Islamic lunar calendar and may vary by one or two days from the dates given.

Statistical Survey

Source (unless otherwise stated): Instituto Nacional de Estatística Guiné-Bissau, Av. Amílcar Cabral, CP 6, Bissau; tel. 3225457; e-mail inec@mail.gtelecom.gw; internet www.stat-guinebissau.com.

Area and Population

AREA, POPULATION AND DENSITY

Area (sq km)	36,125*
Population (census results)	
1 December 1991	983,367
15–29 March 2009	
Males	737,634
Females	783,196
Total	1,520,830
Population (official estimates at mid-year)	
2013	1,499,277
2014	1,514,451
2015	1,530,673
Density (per sq km) at mid-2015	42.4

* 13,948 sq miles.

POPULATION BY AGE AND SEX
(official estimates at mid-2015)

	Males	Females	Total
0–14 years	337,634	328,121	665,755
15–64 years	397,699	432,861	830,560
65 years and over	14,786	19,572	34,358
Total	750,119	780,554	1,530,673

POPULATION BY REGION
(2009 census)

Bafatá	. . .	210,007	Quinará	. . .	63,610
Biombo	. . .	97,120	Sector Autónomo		
Bolama/Bijagós	. .	34,563	Bissau (SAB)	.	387,909
Cacheu	. . .	192,508	Tombali	. .	94,939
Gabú	. . .	215,530	**Total**	. . .	1,520,830
Oio	. . .	224,644			

PRINCIPAL TOWNS
(population at 2009 census)

Bissau (capital)	.	365,097*	Bigene	. . .	51,412
Gabú†	. . .	81,495	Farim	. . .	48,264
Bafatá	. . .	68,956	Mansôa	. . .	46,046
Bissorã	. . .	56,585	Pitche	. . .	45,594

* Figure for Sector Autónomo Bissau (SAB) administrative division.
† Formerly Nova Lamego.

Mid-2014 (incl. suburbs, UN estimate): Bissau (capital) 473,349 (Source: UN, *World Urbanization Prospects: The 2014 Revision*).

BIRTHS AND DEATHS

	2009	2010	2011
Birth rate (per 1,000)	38.7	38.7	37.9
Death rate (per 1,000)	17.0	16.7	16.4

Source: African Development Bank.

Life expectancy (years at birth): 54.0 (males 52.5; females 55.6) in 2012 (Source: World Bank, World Development Indicators database).

ECONOMICALLY ACTIVE POPULATION
('000, FAO estimates at mid-2015)

	Males	Females	Total
Agriculture, etc.	281	238	519
Total labour force (incl. others) .	415	254	669

Source: FAO.

Health and Welfare

KEY INDICATORS

Total fertility rate (children per woman, 2012)	5.0
Under-5 mortality rate (per 1,000 live births, 2012) . .	129
HIV/AIDS (% of persons aged 15–49, 2013)	3.7
Physicians (per 1,000 head, 2009)	0.1
Hospital beds (per 1,000 head, 2009)	1.0
Health expenditure (2011): US $ per head (PPP) . . .	72
Health expenditure (2011): % of GDP	6.3
Health expenditure (2011): public (% of total)	26.8
Access to water (% of persons, 2011)	72
Access to sanitation (% of persons, 2011)	19
Total carbon dioxide emissions ('000 metric tons, 2010) . .	238.4
Carbon dioxide emissions per head (metric tons, 2010) . .	0.2
Human Development Index (2013): ranking	177
Human Development Index (2013): value	0.396

For sources and definitions, see explanatory note on p. vi.

Agriculture

PRINCIPAL CROPS
('000 metric tons)

	2011	2012	2013
Rice, paddy	175.2	198.5	209.7
Maize*	8.0	10.0	7.3
Millet	14.0	17.0	18.1
Sorghum	19.0*	24.0	26.9
Cassava	60.3	68.3	23.0
Sugar cane†	6.3	6.3	6.3
Cashew nuts†	128.7	130.0	n.a.
Groundnuts, with shell	35.4	45.2	46.0†
Coconuts	42.2*	42.2*	43.0†
Oil palm fruit†	80.0	80.0	80.5
Plantains†	49.6	51.0	51.9
Oranges†	6.4	6.5	6.5

* Unofficial figure(s).
† FAO estimate(s).

Aggregate production ('000 metric tons, may include official, semi-official or estimated data): Total cereals 218.2 in 2011, 248.3 in 2012, 264.2 in 2013; Total roots and tubers 118.3 in 2011, 168.3 in 2012, 123.3 in 2013; Total vegetables (incl. melons) 34.6 in 2011, 35.5 in 2012, 35.2 in 2013; Total fruits (excl. melons) 100.1 in 2011, 103.5 in 2012, 104.9 in 2013.

Source: FAO.

LIVESTOCK
('000 head, year ending September)

	2011	2012*	2013*
Cattle	650*	650	670
Pigs	462	460	460
Sheep	460*	460	470
Goats	732	750	750
Chickens	1,721	1,750	1,900

* FAO estimate(s).

Source: FAO.

LIVESTOCK PRODUCTS
('000 metric tons, FAO estimates)

	2011	2012	2013
Cattle meat	6.5	6.7	6.7
Pig meat	15.0	15.2	15.2
Cows' milk	17.3	17.5	17.5
Goats' milk	4.0	4.0	4.0

Source: FAO.

Forestry

ROUNDWOOD REMOVALS
('000 cubic metres, excluding bark, FAO estimates)

	2011	2012	2013
Sawlogs, veneer logs and logs for sleepers	1.9	1.9	1.9
Other industrial wood	130.0	130.0	130.0
Fuel wood	2,637.4	2,675.2	2,713.5
Total	2,769.3	2,807.1	2,845.4

Source: FAO.

SAWNWOOD PRODUCTION
('000 cubic metres, including railway sleepers, FAO estimates)

	2011	2012	2013
Total	16	16	16

Note: Annual production assumed to be unchanged from 1971.

Source: FAO.

Fishing

(metric tons, live weight, FAO estimates)

	2010	2011	2012
Freshwater fishes	150	150	150
Marine fishes	2,700	2,650	2,650
Sea catfishes	380	380	380
Meagre	240	240	240
Mullets	1,500	1,500	1,500
Sompat grunt	230	230	230
Lesser African threadfin	420	420	420
Total catch (incl. others)	6,584	6,549	6,550

Source: FAO.

Industry

SELECTED PRODUCTS
('000 metric tons unless otherwise indicated)

	2001	2002	2003
Hulled rice	69.1	68.4	67.7
Groundnuts (processed)	6.8	6.7	6.6
Bakery products	7.6	7.7	7.9
Frozen fish	1.7	1.7	1.7
Dry and smoked fish	3.6	3.7	3.8
Vegetable oils (million litres)	3.6	3.6	3.7
Beverages (million litres)	3.5	0.0	0.0
Dairy products (million litres)	1.1	0.9	0.9
Wood products	4.7	4.5	4.4
Soap	2.6	2.5	2.4
Electric energy (million kWh)	18.9	19.4	15.8

Source: IMF, *Guinea-Bissau: Selected Issues and Statistical Appendix* (March 2005).

Electric energy (million kWh, estimates): 30 in 2008; 31 in 2009; 32 in 2010 (Source: UN Industrial Commodity Statistics Database).

Finance

CURRENCY AND EXCHANGE RATES

Monetary Units
100 centimes = 1 franc de la Communauté Financière Africaine (CFA).

Sterling, Dollar and Euro Equivalents (31 December 2014)
£1 sterling = 843.273 francs CFA;
US $1 = 540.283 francs CFA;
€1 = 655.957 francs CFA;
10,000 francs CFA = £11.86 = $18.51 = €15.24.

Average Exchange Rate (francs CFA per US $)
2012   510.290
2013   494.040
2014   494.415

Note: An exchange rate of 1 French franc = 50 francs CFA, established in 1948, remained in force until January 1994, when the CFA franc was devalued by 50%, with the exchange rate adjusted to 1 French franc = 100 francs CFA. This relationship to French currency remained in effect with the introduction of the euro on 1 January 1999. From that date, accordingly, a fixed exchange rate of €1 = 655.957 francs CFA has been in operation.

BUDGET
('000 million francs CFA)

Revenue*	2013	2014†	2015†
Tax revenue	35.4	36.0	42.5
Non-tax revenue	5.7	21.4	14.5
Total	41.1	57.4	57.0

Expenditure	2013	2014†	2015†
Current expenditure	79.8	74.5	79.2
Wages and salaries	30.4	30.8	32.6
Goods and services	10.9	12.7	13.5
Transfers	14.6	14.6	15.4
Other current expenditures .	23.4	14.1	14.9
Scheduled interest payments .	0.5	2.4	2.7
Capital expenditure and net lending	29.4	31.5	32.7
Total	109.2	106.0	111.9

* Excluding budget grants received ('000 million francs CFA): 17.8 in 2013; 41.0 in 2014 (projection); 28.0 in 2015 (projection).
† Projections.

Source: IMF, *Guinea-Bissau: Request for Disbursement Under the Rapid Credit Facility-Staff Report; Press Release; and Statement by the Executive Director for Guinea-Bissau* (November 2014).

CENTRAL BANK RESERVES
(US $ million at 31 December)

	2011	2012	2013
IMF special drawing rights . .	19.02	19.04	19.07
Reserve position in IMF . . .	0.32	0.39	0.44
Foreign exchange	200.66	145.16	166.74
Total	220.00	164.59	186.25

Source: IMF, *International Financial Statistics*.

MONEY SUPPLY
(million francs CFA at 31 December)

	2011	2012	2013
Currency outside banks . . .	85,912	83,385	90,956
Demand deposits at deposit money banks	69,032	48,195	65,752
Total money (incl. others) . .	156,519	131,731	156,936

Source: IMF, *International Financial Statistics*.

COST OF LIVING
(Consumer Price Index; base: 2003 = 100 unless otherwise indicated)

	2010	2011	2012
Food*	99.4	106.7	110.1
All items (incl. others) . . .	122.2	128.3	131.1

* Base: 2008=100.

Source: ILO.

All items (Consumer Price Index for Bissau; base: 2010 = 100): 105.0 in 2011; 107.3 in 2012; 108.0 in 2013 (Source: IMF, *International Financial Statistics*).

NATIONAL ACCOUNTS
(million francs CFA at current prices)

Expenditure on the Gross Domestic Product

	2011	2012	2013*
Government final consumption expenditure	68,188	64,049	53,454
Private final consumption expenditure	444,982	475,768	515,287
Gross fixed capital formation .	27,431	33,365	38,729
Change in inventories	547	4,150	546
Total domestic expenditure .	541,148	577,332	608,016
Exports of goods and services .	139,392	78,595	98,070
Less Imports of goods and services	160,409	129,817	136,187
GDP in purchasers' values .	520,132	526,111	569,899
GDP at constant 2005 prices .	399,156	392,200	398,218

Gross Domestic Product by Economic Activity

	2011	2012*	2013*
Agriculture, hunting, forestry and fishing	233,168	247,138	246,108
Mining and quarrying	85	95	164
Manufacturing	57,254	65,377	79,939
Electricity, gas and water . .	7,647	5,836	5,497
Construction	3,109	3,834	7,160
Trade, restaurants and hotels .	103,834	97,145	130,894
Finance, insurance and real estate	8,343	8,424	9,120
Transport, storage and communications	25,997	26,475	29,629
Public administration and other services	70,255	62,413	54,205
Sub-total	509,692	516,737	562,716
Less Financial intermediation services indirectly measured .	9,773	10,703	10,910
GDP at factor cost	499,919	506,034	551,806
Indirect taxes, less subsidies . .	20,213	18,465	17,085
GDP at purchasers' values .	520,132	524,499	568,891

* Provisional figures.

BALANCE OF PAYMENTS
('000 million francs CFA)

	2011	2012	2013
Exports of goods f.o.b.	110.5	72.4	73.6
Imports of goods f.o.b.	−113.3	−92.8	−90.9
Trade balance	−2.8	−20.4	−17.3
Exports of services	21.1	11.1	11.5
Imports of services	−47.0	−37.0	−33.2
Balance on goods and services	−28.9	−46.3	−39.0
Other income (net)	−0.3	−0.5	−0.58
Balance on goods, services and income	−29.2	−46.8	−39.6
Official current transfers . . .	15.8	9.3	4.0
Private current transfers . . .	12.2	14.7	16.1
Current balance	−1.2	−22.8	−19.4
Capital account (net)	26.9	3.1	14.1
Financial account (net)	−10.3	27.6	9.0
Statistical discrepancy	14.9	−38.3	3.4
Overall balance	30.3	−30.4	7.1

Source: IMF, *Guinea-Bissau: Request for Disbursement Under the Rapid Credit Facility-Staff Report; Press Release; and Statement by the Executive Director for Guinea-Bissau* (November 2014).

External Trade

PRINCIPAL COMMODITIES
(million francs CFA)

Imports c.i.f.	2010	2011	2012
Cereals and cereal preparations .	17,656	20,563	17,030
Beverages	3,989	4,646	3,848
Petroleum and petroleum products	30,125	35,085	29,058
Iron and steel	4,627	6,807	n.a.
Road vehicles	4,376	5,029	n.a.
Total (incl. others)	148,173	160,409	143,463

Exports f.o.b.	2010	2011	2012
Cashew nuts	51,800	105,619	59,986
Total (incl. others)	83,742	139,392	89,745

Source: African Development Bank.

PRINCIPAL TRADING PARTNERS
(million francs CFA)

Imports	2009	2010	2011
China, People's Republic . . .	7,470	4,374	6,815
Italy	3,389	4,361	5,077
Netherlands	8,431	4,300	5,333
Portugal	17,766	727	1,409
Senegal	19,133	22,330	28,118
Total (incl. others)	100,727	148,173	160,409

Exports	2009	2010	2011
India	50,503	52,471	101,627
Portugal	701	727	1,409
Singapore	1,333	1,374	2,664
USA	3,552	3,668	7,085
Total (incl. others)	57,438	83,742	139,392

2012: Total imports 143,463; Total exports 89,745.

Source: African Development Bank.

Transport

ROAD TRAFFIC
(motor vehicles in use at 31 December)

	2008
Passenger cars	42,222
Buses and coaches	289
Vans and lorries	9,323
Motorcycles and mopeds	4,936

Source: IRF, *World Road Statistics*.

SHIPPING
Flag Registered Fleet
(at 31 December)

	2012	2013	2014
Number of vessels	12	12	12
Total displacement (grt) . . .	2,903	2,903	2,903

Source: Lloyd's List Intelligence (www.lloydslistintelligence.com).

Tourism

TOURIST ARRIVALS BY NATIONALITY

	2005	2006	2007
Cabo Verde	159	401	1,498
China, People's Republic . . .	46	659	1,488
Cuba	29	329	309
France	599	834	2,984
Italy	213	343	1,871
Korea, Republic	36	523	1,289
Portugal	1,552	2,599	2,245
Senegal	235	921	2,798
Spain	324	231	1,458
USA	57	320	265
Total (incl. others)	4,978	11,617	30,092

Receipts from tourism (US $ million, excl. passenger transport): 2.8 in 2006; 28.4 in 2007; 38.2 in 2008.

Source: World Tourism Organization.

Communications Media

	2011	2012	2013
Telephones ('000 main lines in use)	5.0	5.0	5.0
Mobile cellular telephones ('000 subscribers)	733	1,049	1,263

Source: International Telecommunication Union.

Education

(2009/10 unless otherwise indicated, UNESCO estimates)

	Teachers	Students		
		Males	Females	Total
Pre-primary . .	309	4,360	4,590	8,950
Primary	5,371	144,075	134,815	278,890
Secondary: general .	} 1,913* {	46,445	31,581	78,026
Secondary: technical and vocational . .		656†	239†	895†
Tertiary† . . .	32	399	74	473

* 1999.
† 2000/01.

Institutions (1999): Pre-primary 54; Primary 759.

Students (2005/06): Primary 269,287; Secondary 55,176; Tertiary 3,689.

Teachers (2005/06): Primary 4,327; Secondary 1,480; Tertiary 25.

Pupil-teacher ratio (primary education, UNESCO estimate): 51.9 in 2009/10 (Source: UNESCO Institute for Statistics).

Adult literacy rate (UNESCO estimates): 56.7% (males 69.8%; females 43.9%) in 2012.

Source: UNESCO Institute for Statistics.

Directory

The Government

HEAD OF STATE

President: José Mário Vaz (inaugurated 23 June 2014).

COUNCIL OF MINISTERS
(April 2015)

Prime Minister: Domingos Simões Pereira.

Minister of the Presidency of the Council of Ministers and Parliamentary Affairs: Dr Baciro Djá.

Minister of Internal Administration: Octávio Alves.

Minister of Foreign Affairs, International Co-operation and Communities: Dr Mário Lopes da Rosa.

Minister of Natural Resources: Daniel Gomes.

Minister of the Economy and Finance: Dr Geraldo João Martins.

Minister of National Defence: Cadi Seide.

Minister of Public Works, Construction and Town Planning: Eng. José António Cruz Almeida.

Minister of Public Health: Valentina Mendes.

Minister of National Education: Odete Costa Semedo.

Minister of Agriculture and Rural Development: João Aníbal Pereira.

Minister of Women, Families and Social Cohesion: Bilony Nhama Nantamba Nhassé.

Minister of Energy and Industry: Florentino Mendes Pereira.

Minister of Justice: Carmelita Pires.

Minister of Social Communication: Dr Agnelo Regala.

Minister of the Civil Service and Administrative Reform: Dr Ademir Nelson Belo.

Minister of Trade and Handicrafts: Dr António Serifo Embaló.

In addition, there were 15 Secretaries of State.

MINISTRIES

Office of the President: Bissau; internet www.presidencia-gw.org.

Office of the Prime Minister: Av. dos Combatentes da Liberdade da Pátria, CP 137, Bissau; tel. 3211308; fax 3201671.

Ministry of Agriculture and Rural Development: Av. dos Combatentes da Liberdade da Pátria, CP 102, Bissau; tel. 3221200; fax 3222483.

Ministry of the Civil Service and Administrative Reform: Bissau.

Ministry of the Economy and Finance: Av. dos Combatentes da Liberdade da Pátria, CP 67, Bissau; tel. 3203670; fax 3203496; e-mail info@mail.guine-bissau.org; internet www.guine-bissau.org.

Ministry of Energy and Industry: CP 311, Bissau; tel. 3215659; fax 3223149.

Ministry of Foreign Affairs, International Co-operation and Communities: Av. dos Combatentes da Liberdade da Pátria, Bissau; tel. 3204301; fax 3202378.

Ministry of Internal Administration: Av. Unidade Africana, Bissau; tel. 3203781.

Ministry of Justice: Av. Amílcar Cabral, CP 17, Bissau; tel. 3202185; internet mj-gb.org.

Ministry of National Defence: Amura, Bissau; tel. 3223646.

Ministry of National Education: Rua Areolino Cruz, Bissau; tel. 3202244.

Ministry of Natural Resources: Bissau.

Ministry of the Presidency of the Council of Ministers and Parliamentary Affairs: Bissau.

Ministry of Public Health: CP 50, Bissau; tel. 3204438; fax 3201701.

Ministry of Public Works, Construction and Town Planning: Av. dos Combatentes da Liberdade da Pátria, CP 14, Bissau; internet www.minisinfraestruturas-gov.com; tel. 3206575; fax 3203611.

Ministry of Social Communication: Bissau.

Ministry of Trade and Handicrafts: 34A Av. Pansau na Isna, Bissau; tel. and fax 3206062; e-mail turismom@yahoo.com; internet www.minturgb-gov.com.

Ministry of Women, Families and Social Cohesion: Bissau.

President

Presidential Election, First Round, 13 April 2014

Candidate	Valid votes	% of valid votes
José Mário Vaz 'Jomav' (PAIGC) . . .	257,572	40.89
Nuno Gomes Nabiam (Ind.)	156,163	24.79
Paulo Gomes (Ind.)	65,490	10.40
Abel Incada (PRS)	43,890	6.97
Mamadu Iaia Djaló (PND)	28,535	4.53
Ibrahima Sori Djalo (PRN)	19,497	3.09
António Afonso Té (PRID)	18,808	2.99
Others*	39,971	6.34
Total	**629,926†**	**100.00**

* There were six other candidates.
† In addition, there were 39,532 blank and 22,982 spoiled ballots.

Presidential Election, Second Round, 18 May 2014

Candidate	Valid votes	% of valid votes
José Mário Vaz 'Jomav' (PAIGC) . . .	364,394	61.92
Nuno Gomes Nabiam (Ind.)	224,089	38.08
Total	**588,483***	**100.00**

* In addition, there were 7,884 blank and 10,025 spoiled ballots.

Legislature

Assembleia Nacional Popular: Palácio Colinas de Boé, Av. Francisco Mendes, CP 219, Bissau; tel. 3201991; fax 3206725; internet www.anpguinebissau.org.

President: Cipriano Cassama.

General Election, 13 April 2014

Party	Valid votes	% of valid votes	Seats
Partido Africano da Independência da Guiné e Cabo Verde (PAIGC) . .	281,408	47.98	57
Partido para a Renovação Social (PRS)	180,432	30.76	41
Partido para a Nova Democracia (PND) . . .	28,581	4.87	1
Partido da Convergência Democrática (PCD) . . .	19,757	3.37	2
União para a Mudança (UM) .	10,803	1.84	1
Others	65,543	11.17	—
Total	**586,524**	**100.00**	**102**

Election Commission

Comissão Nacional de Eleições (CNE): Av. Unidade Africana, CP 44, Bissau; tel. 6900976; fax 3203601; e-mail cne.guinebissau@hotmail.com; internet www.cne-guinebissau.org; Pres. Augusto Mendes.

Political Organizations

Centro Democrático (CD): Bissau; tel. and fax 452517; e-mail empossaie@centrodemocratico.com; internet www.cd.empossaie.com; f. 2006; Pres. Empossa Ié; Sec.-Gen. Victor Djelombo.

Partido Africano da Independência da Guiné e Cabo Verde (PAIGC): CP 106, Bissau; internet www.paigc.org; f. 1956; fmrly the ruling party in both Guinea-Bissau and Cabo Verde; although Cabo Verde withdrew from the PAIGC following the coup in Guinea-Bissau in Nov. 1980, Guinea-Bissau has retained the party name and initials; Pres. Domingos Simões Pereira; Sec. Augusto Olivais.

Partido da Convergência Democrática (PCD): Bissau; Pres. Vicente Fernandes.

Directory

Partido Democrático Guinéense (PDG): f. 2007; Pres. EUSEBIO SEBASTIAO DA SILVA.

Partido Democrático Socialista (PDS): Bissau; f. 2006; Pres. JOÃO SECO MAMADÚ MANÉ.

Partido Democrático Socialista de Salvação Guineense: Leader SERIFO BALDÉ.

Partido para a Nova Democracia (PND): Bissau; f. 2007; Pres. IBRAIMA DJALÓ.

Partido Popular Democrático (PPD): Bissau; f. 2006; Pres. MARIA LUIZA EMBALÓ.

Partido da Reconciliação Nacional (PRN): Bissau; f. 2004; Leader ALMARA NHASSÉ; Sec.-Gen. OLUNDO MENDES.

Partido para a Renovação Social (PRS): c/o Assembleia Nacional Popular, Bissau; f. 1992; Pres. ALBERTO NAMBEIA EMBALÓ.

Partido Republicano para a Independência e o Desenvolvimento (PRID): Bissau; f. 2008; Pres. ARISTIDES GOMES.

Partido Social Democrata (PSD): c/o Assembleia Nacional Popular, Bissau; f. 1995; Pres. ANTONIO SAMBA BALDÉ.

Partido Socialista-Guiné Bissau (PS-GB): Bissau; f. 1994; Pres. CIRILO OLIVEIRA RODRIGUES.

Partido dos Trabalhadores (PT): Bissau; e-mail contact@nodjuntamon.org; internet www.nodjuntamon.org; f. 2002; left-wing; Pres. ARREGADO MANTENQUE TÉ.

Partido Unido Social Democrático (PUSD): Bissau; f. 1991; officially registered in Jan. 1992; Pres. AUGUSTO BARAI MANGO.

União para a Mudança (UM): Bissau; Pres. AGNELO REGALA.

União Nacional para Democracia e Progresso (UNDP): Bissau; f. 1998; Pres. ABUBACAR BALDÉ.

União Patriótica Guinéense (UPG): Bissau; f. 2004 by dissident members of the RGB; Pres. FRANCISCA VAZ TURPIN.

Diplomatic Representation

EMBASSIES IN GUINEA-BISSAU

Angola: Bissau; Ambassador DANIEL ANTÓNIO ROSA.

Brazil: Rua São Tomé, Esquina Rua Moçambique, CP 29, Bissau; tel. 3212549; fax 3201317; e-mail emb_brasil_bxo@hotmail.com; Ambassador JORGE GERALDO KADRI.

China, People's Republic: Av. Francisco João Mendes, Bissau; tel. 3203637; fax 3203590; e-mail chinaemb_gw@mail.mfa.gov.cn; internet gw.china-embassy.org/chn; Ambassador LI BAOJUN.

Cuba: Rua Joaquim N'Com 1, y Victorino Costa, CP 258, Bissau; tel. 3213579; fax 3201301; e-mail embcuba@sol.gtelecom.gw; Ambassador ELIS ALBERTO GONZÁLEZ POLANCO.

France: Bairro de Penha, Av. dos Combatentes da Liberdade da Pátria, Bissau; tel. 3257400; fax 3257421; e-mail cad.bissao-amba@diplomatie.gouv.fr; internet www.ambafrance-gw.org; Ambassador MICHEL FLESCH.

The Gambia: 47 Victorino Costa, Chao de Papel, CP 529, 1037 Bissau; tel. 3205085; fax 3251099; e-mail gambiaembbissau@hotmail.com; Ambassador CHERNO B. TOURAY.

Guinea: Rua 14, No. 9, CP 396, Bissau; tel. 3212681; Ambassador TAMBA TIENDO MILLIMONO.

Korea, Democratic People's Republic: Bissau; Ambassador KIM KYONG SIN.

Nigeria: 6 Av. 14 de Novembro, CP 199, Bissau; tel. 3201018; fax 3202564; Ambassador AHMED MAIGIDA ADAMS.

Libya: Rua 16, CP 362, Bissau; tel. 3212006; Representative DOKALI ALI MUSTAFA.

Portugal: Av. Cidade de Lisboa, CP 76, 1021 Bissau; tel. 3201261; fax 3201269; e-mail embaixada@bissau.dgaccp.pt; internet www.consulado-pt-gb.org; Ambassador Dr ANTÓNIO LEÃO ROCHA.

Russian Federation: Av. 14 de Novembro, CP 308, Bissau; tel. 3251050; fax 3251028; e-mail russiagb@eguitel.com; Ambassador MIKHAIL VALINSKIY.

Senegal: Rua Omar Torrijos 43A, Bissau; tel. 3212944; fax 3201748; Ambassador Gen. ABDOULAYE DIENG.

South Africa: c/o Bissau Palace Hotel, Rm No. 9, Av. 14 de Novembro, CP 1334, Bissau; tel. 6678910; e-mail bissau@dirco.gov.za; Ambassador LOUIS MNGUNI.

Spain: Praza Dos Hèroes Naçionais; tel. 6722246; fax 3207656; e-mail emb.bissau@maec.es; Ambassador ALFONSO LÓPEZ PERONA.

Judicial System

The judicial system comprises a Supreme Court, a Court of Appeal, nine Regional Courts (of which five are functional) and 42 Sectoral Courts (of which 21 are functional). The Supreme Court is the final court of appeal in criminal and civil cases and consists of nine judges. The Regional Courts are courts of first instance and deal with felony cases and major civil cases. They also hear appeals from the Sectoral Courts. The Sectoral Courts hear minor civil cases with maximum fines of 1m. francs CFA and criminal cases punishable by sentences of up to three years' imprisonment. There are plans to establish a second Court of Appeal in Bafatá and other Regional and Sectoral Courts envisaged by law.

Supreme Court (Supremo Tribunal de Justiça): Rua Guerra Mendes, CP 341, Bissau; tel. 3211003; fax 3201365; Pres. PAULO SANHA.

Attorney-General of the Republic: HERMENEGILDO PEREIRA.

Religion

ISLAM

Associação Islâmica Nacional: Bissau; Sec.-Gen. Alhaji ABDÚ BAIO.

Conselho Superior dos Assuntos Islâmicos da Guiné-Bissau (CSAI-GB): Bissau; Exec. Sec. MUSTAFA RACHID DJALÓ.

CHRISTIANITY

The Roman Catholic Church

Guinea-Bissau comprises two dioceses, directly responsible to the Holy See. The Bishops participate in the Episcopal Conference of Senegal, Mauritania, Cabo Verde and Guinea-Bissau, currently based in Senegal. Approximately 10% of the total population are adherents of the Roman Catholic Church.

Bishop of Bafatá: Rev. CARLOS PEDRO ZILLI, CP 17, Bafatá; tel. 3411507; e-mail domzilli@yahoo.com.br.

Bishop of Bissau: JOSÉ CÂMNATE NA BISSIGN, Av. 14 de Novembro, CP 20, 1001 Bissau; tel. 3251057; fax 3251058; e-mail diocesebissau@yahoo.it.

The Press

REGULATORY AUTHORITY

Conselho Nacional de Comunicação Social (CNCS): Bissau; f. 1994; dissolved in 2003, recreated in November 2004; Pres. AUGUSTO MENDES.

NEWSPAPERS AND PERIODICALS

Banobero: Rua José Carlos Schwarz, CP 760, Bissau; tel. 3230702; fax 3230705; e-mail banobero@netscape.net; weekly; Dir FERNANDO JORGE PEREIRA.

Comdev Negócios (Community Development Business): Av. Domingos Ramos 21, 1° andar, Bissau; tel. 3215596; f. 2006; independent; business; Editor FRANCELINO CUNHA.

Diário de Bissau: Rua Vitorino Costa 29, Bissau; tel. 3203049; daily; Owner JOÃO DE BARROS.

Expresso de Bissau: Rua Vitorino Costa 30, Bissau; tel. 6666647; e-mail expressobissau@hotmail.com.

Fraskera: Bairro da Ajuda, 1ª fase, CP 698, Bissau; tel. 3253060; fax 3253070; weekly.

Gazeta de Notícias: Av. Caetano Semeao, CP 1433, Bissau; tel. 3254733; e-mail gn@eguitel.com; internet www.gaznot.com; f. 1997; weekly; Dir HUMBERTO MONTEIRO; circ. 1,000.

Jornal Nô Pintcha: Av. do Brasil, CP 154, Bissau; tel. 3213713; Dir SRA CABRAL; circ. 6,000.

Kansaré: Edifico Sitec, Rua José Carlos Schwarz, Bissau; e-mail kansare@eguitel.com; internet www.kansare.com; f. 2003; Editor FAFALI KOUDAWO.

Última Hora: Av. Combatentes da Liberdade da Pátria (Prédio Suna Ker), Bissau; tel. 5932236; e-mail damil@portugalmail.com; Dir ATHIZAR PEREIRA; circ. 500.

Voz de Bissau: Rua Eduardo Mondlane, Apdo 155, Bissau; tel. 3202546; twice weekly.

Wandan: Rua António M'Bana 6, CP 760, Bissau; tel. 3201789.

NEWS AGENCY

Agência de Notícias da Guiné-Bissau (ANG): Av. Domingos Ramos, CP 248, Bissau; tel. 2605200; fax 2605256.

Publisher

Ku Si Mon Editora: Bairro d'Ajuda, Rua José Carlos Schwarz, CP 268, Bissau; tel. 6605565; e-mail kusimon@kusimon.com; internet www.kusimon.com; f. 1994; Portuguese language; Dir ABDULAI SILA.

Broadcasting and Communications

REGULATORY AUTHORITY

Autoridade Reguladora Nacional das Tecnologias de Informação (ARN): Av. Domingos Ramos 53, Praça Cheguevara, CP 1372, Bissau; tel. 3204874; fax 3204876; e-mail geral@arn-gb.com; internet arn-gb.com; f. 2010 to replace Instituto das Comunicações da Guiné-Bissau; also manages radio spectrum; Pres. GIBRIL MANÉ.

TELECOMMUNICATIONS

In 2013 there was one fixed–line telephone operator (5,000 subscribers) and three mobile telephone operators (1.3m. subscribers) in Guinea-Bissau.

Guiné Telecom (GT): Bissau; tel. 3202427; internet www.gtelecom.gw; f. 2003 to replace the Companhia de Telecomunicações da Guiné-Bissau (Guiné Telecom—f. 1989); state-owned; privatization pending; 4,844 subscribers (2011).

  Guinetel: Bissau; f. 2003; mobile operator; CEO JOÃO FREDERICO DE BARROS; 104,749 subscribers (2011).

MTN Guinea Bissau: 7 Av. Unidade Africana, CP 672, Bissau; tel. 3207000; fax 6600111; e-mail contact@mtn-bissau.com; internet www.mtn-bissau.com; f. 2007; mobile operator; CEO ANTHONY MASOZERA; 110 employees; 443,750 subscribers (2011).

Orange Bissau: Praça dos Herois Nacionais, BP 1087, Bissau; tel. 5603030; e-mail abdul.dapiedadeTMP@orange-sonatel.com; internet orange-bissau.com; f. 2007; mobile operator; 244,677 (subscribers 2011).

RADIO AND TELEVISION

Radiodifusão Nacional da República da Guiné-Bissau (RDN): Av. Domingos Ramos, Praça dos Martires de Pindjiguiti, CP 191, Bissau; tel. 3212426; fax 3253070; e-mail rdn@eguitel.com; f. 1974; govt-owned; broadcasts in Portuguese on short-wave, MW and FM; Dir-Gen. LAMINE DJATA.

Rádio Bafatá: CP 57, Bafatá; tel. 3411185.

Rádio Bombolom: Bairro Cupelon, CP 877, Bissau; tel. 3201095; f. 1996; independent; Dir AGNELO REGALA.

Rádio Jovem: Bairro de Ajuda, Bissau; internet www.radiojovem.info.

Rádio Mavegro: Rua Eduardo Mondlane, CP 100, Bissau; tel. 3201216; fax 3201265.

Televisão da Guiné-Bissau (TGB): Bairro de Luanda, CP 178, Bissau; tel. 3221920; fax 3221941; internet www.televisao-gb.net; f. 1997; Dir-Gen. LUÍS DOMINGOS CAMARÁ DE BARROS.

Finance

(cap. = capital; res = reserves; dep. = deposits; m. = million; brs = branches; amounts in francs CFA)

BANKING

Central Bank

Banque Centrale des Etats de l'Afrique de l'Ouest (BCEAO): Av. dos Combatentes da Liberdade da Pátria, Brá, CP 38, Bissau; tel. 3256325; fax 3256300; internet www.bceao.int; HQ in Dakar, Senegal; f. 1955; bank of issue for the mem. states of the Union Economique et Monétaire Ouest-Africaine (UEMOA, comprising Benin, Burkina Faso, Côte d'Ivoire, Guinea-Bissau, Mali, Niger, Senegal and Togo); cap. 134,120m., res 1,474,195m., dep. 2,124,051m. (Dec. 2009); Gov. KONÉ TIÉMOKO MEYLIET; Dir in Guinea-Bissau JOÃO ALAGE MAMADU FADIA.

Other Banks

Banco da África Ocidental, SARL: Rua Guerra Mendes 18, CP 1360, Bissau; tel. 3203418; fax 3203412; e-mail bao@baogb.com; internet bancodaafricaocidental.com; f. 2000; 15% owned by International Finance Corporation, 15% Grupo Montepio Geral (Portugal), 15% Carlos Gomes Júnior; Man. Dir RÓMULO PIRES.

Banco da União (BDU): Av. Domingos Ramos 3, CP 874, Bissau; tel. 3207160; fax 3207163; e-mail info@bdu-sa.com; internet www.bdu-sa.com; f. 2005; 70% owned by Banque de Développement du Mali; CEO HUGO DOS REIS BORGES.

Caixa de Crédito da Guiné: Bissau; govt savings and loan institution.

Caixa Económica Postal: Av. Amílcar Cabral, Bissau; tel. 3212999; postal savings institution.

Ecobank Guinea-Bissau: Av. Amílcar Cabral, BP 126, Bissau; tel. 3207360; fax 3207363; e-mail ecobankgw@ecobank.com; internet www.ecobank.com; total assets 43,453m. (Dec. 2012); Chair. JOÃO JOSÉ SILVA MONTEIRO; Man. Dir ADAMA SENE CISSÉ; 5 brs.

Orabank Bissau: Rua Justino Lopes 70, Bissau; tel. 6672907 (mobile); fax 3207113; e-mail info-gw@orabank.net; fmrly Banco Regional de Solidariedade; present name adopted 2014; 3 brs.

STOCK EXCHANGE

In 1998 a regional stock exchange, the Bourse Régionale des Valeurs Mobilières, was established in Abidjan, Côte d'Ivoire, to serve the member states of UEMOA.

INSURANCE

GUINEBIS—Guiné-Bissau Seguros: Rua Dr Severino Gomes de Pina 36, Bissau; tel. 3211458; fax 3201197.

Instituto Nacional de Segurança Social: Av. Domingos Ramos 12, CP 62, Bissau; tel. and fax 3201494; e-mail nacionalpsocial@ymail.com; internet www.inpsgb.com; state-owned; Dir-Gen. MAMADU IAIA DJALÓ.

NSIA Assurances: Bissau; tel. 5803131; e-mail amadou.thiam@groupensia.com; Dir-Gen. AMADOU THIAM.

Trade and Industry

DEVELOPMENT ORGANIZATION

Ajuda de Desenvolvimento de Povo para Povo ná Guiné Bissau (ADPP): CP 420, Bissau; tel. 6853323; e-mail adppartemisa@eguitel.com.

CHAMBER OF COMMERCE

Câmara de Comércio, Indústria, Agricultura e Serviços da Guiné-Bissau (CCIAS): Av. Amílcar Cabral 7, CP 361, Bissau; tel. 3212844; fax 3201602; f. 1987; Pres. BRAIMA CAMARÁ; Sec.-Gen. SALIU BA.

INDUSTRIAL AND TRADE ASSOCIATIONS

Associação Comercial, Industrial e Agricola (ACIA): CP 88, Bissau; tel. 3222276.

Direcção de Promoção do Investimento Privado (DPIP): Rua 12 de Setembro, Bissau Velho, CP 1276, Bissau; tel. 3205156; fax 3203181; e-mail dpip@mail.bissau.net.

Fundaçao Guineense para o Desenvolvimento Empresarial Industrial (FUNDEI): Rua Gen. Omar Torrijos 49, Bissau; tel. 3202470; fax 3202209; e-mail fundei@fundei.bissau.net; internet www.fundei.net; f. 1994; industrial devt org.; Pres. MACÁRIA BARAI.

Procajú: Bissau; private sector association of cashew producers.

UTILITIES

Gas

Empresa Nacional de Importação e Distribuição de Gás Butano: CP 269, Bissau; state gas distributor.

TRADE UNIONS

Confederação Geral dos Sindicatos Independentes da Guiné-Bissau (CGSI-GB): Rua nº10, Bissau Apartado 693, Bissau; tel. 3204110; fax 3204114; e-mail cgsi-gb@hotmail.com; internet www.lgdh.org/CONFEDERACAOGERALDOSSINDICATOSINDEPENDENTES.htm; Sec.-Gen. FILOMENO CABRAL.

União Nacional dos Trabalhadores da Guiné (UNTG): 13 Av. Ovai di Vievra, CP 98, Bissau; tel. and fax 3207138; e-mail untgcs.gb@hotmail.com; Pres. DESEJADO LIMA DA COSTA; Sec.-Gen. ESTÊVÃO GOMES CÓ.

Transport

RAILWAYS

There are no railways in Guinea-Bissau. However, the proposed construction of a railway line by Bauxite Angola, linking the bauxite extraction site in Boé with the future deep-water port at Buba, was announced in 2008. These plans were put on hold following the coup in April 2012.

ROADS

According to the Government, there are 2,755 km of 'classified' roads in Guinea-Bissau, of which 770 km are paved. There are plans in place for a further 300 km to be paved by 2020.

SHIPPING

Plans have been announced to build a major deep-water port at Buba, the capacity of which will make it one of the largest in West Africa. However, following the coup in April 2012, these plans were postponed. At 31 December 2014 the flag registered fleet comprised 12 vessels, totalling 2,903 grt.

Empresa Nacional de Agências e Transportes Marítimos: Rua Guerva Mendes 4–4A, CP 244, Bissau; tel. 3212675; fax 3213023; state shipping agency; Dir-Gen. M. LOPES.

CIVIL AVIATION

There is an international airport at Bissau, which there are plans to expand, and 10 smaller airports serving the interior. Senegal Airlines, Royal Air Maroc and Transportes Aéreos de Cabo Verde (TACV) fly to Bissau.

Tourism

There were 30,092 tourist arrivals in 2007. Receipts from tourism totalled US $38.2m. in 2008.

Central de Informação e Turismo: CP 294, Bissau; tel. 3213905; state tourism and information service.

Direcção Geral do Turismo: CP 1024, Bissau; tel. 3202195; fax 3204441.

Defence

As assessed at November 2014, the armed forces officially totalled an estimated 4,450 men (army 4,000, navy 350, air force 100), and there was a paramilitary gendarmerie of 2,000 men. Military service was made compulsory from 2007, as part of a programme of reform for the armed forces. Following the seizure of power by the military in April 2012 the ECOWAS Mission in Guinea-Bissau (ECOMIB), comprising 629 security personnel, was deployed in May. ECOMIB's mandate was formalized and extended for a further six months in November 2012. The mission's mandate was subsequently renewed until June 2015.

Defence Expenditure: Budgeted at 13,000m. francs CFA in 2013.

Chief of Staff of the Armed Forces: Brig.-Gen. BIAGUE NA NTAM.

Army Chief of Staff: Gen. AUGUSTO MÁRIO CÓ.

Navy Chief of Staff: Capt. SANHA CLUSSÉ (acting).

Chief of Staff of the Air Force: Brig.-Gen. IBRAIMA PAPÁ CAMARA.

Education

Education is officially compulsory only for the period of primary schooling, which begins at six years of age and lasts for seven years. Secondary education, beginning at the age of 13, lasts for up to five years (a first cycle of three years and a second of two years). According to UNESCO estimates, in 2010 enrolment at primary schools included 70% of children in the relevant age-group (males 71%; females 68%), while enrolment at secondary schools in 2006 was equivalent to only 34% of children in the relevant age-group. In 2000/01 473 students were enrolled in tertiary education. There are three tertiary level institutions in Guinea-Bissau: the Universidade Amílcar Cabral (public); the Universidade Colinas do Boé (private); and the Faculdade de Direito de Bissau (a law school funded and run within the ambit of Portuguese co-operation). According to the 2005 budget, expenditure on education was forecast at 15.0% of total spending.

GUYANA

Introductory Survey

LOCATION, CLIMATE, LANGUAGE, RELIGION, FLAG, CAPITAL

The Co-operative Republic of Guyana lies on the north coast of South America, between Venezuela to the west and Suriname to the east, with Brazil to the south. The narrow coastal belt has a moderate climate with two wet seasons, from April to August and from November to January, alternating with two dry seasons. Inland, there are tropical forests and savannah, and the dry season lasts from September to May. The average annual temperature is 27°C (80°F), with average rainfall of 1,520 mm (60 ins) per year inland, rising to between 2,030 mm (80 ins) and 2,540 mm (100 ins) on the coast. English is the official language but Hindi, Urdu and Amerindian dialects are also spoken. The principal religions are Christianity (which is professed by about 50% of the population), Hinduism (about 28%) and Islam (7%). The national flag (proportions 3 by 5 when flown on land, but 1 by 2 at sea) is green, with a white-bordered yellow triangle (apex at the edge of the fly) on which is superimposed a black-bordered red triangle (apex in the centre). The capital is Georgetown.

CONTEMPORARY POLITICAL HISTORY

Historical Context

Guyana was formerly British Guiana, a colony of the United Kingdom, formed in 1831 from territories finally ceded to Britain by the Dutch in 1814. A new Constitution, providing for universal adult suffrage, was introduced in 1953. The elections of April of that year were won by the left-wing People's Progressive Party (PPP), led by Dr Cheddi Bharat Jagan. In October, however, the British Government, claiming that a communist dictatorship was threatened, suspended the Constitution. An interim administration was appointed. The PPP split in 1955, and in 1957 a number of former members founded a new party, the People's National Congress (PNC), under the leadership of Forbes Burnham. The PNC drew its support mainly from the African-descended population, while PPP support came largely from the Asian-descended 'East' Indian community.

Domestic Political Affairs

A revised Constitution was introduced in December 1956 and an election was held in August 1957. The PPP won and Jagan became Chief Minister. Another Constitution, providing for internal self-government, was adopted in July 1961. The PPP won an election in August and Jagan was appointed premier. In the election of December 1964, held under the system of proportional representation, the PPP won the largest number of seats in the Legislative Assembly, but not a majority. A coalition Government was formed by the PNC and The United Force (TUF), with Burnham as Prime Minister. This coalition led the colony to independence, as Guyana, on 26 May 1966.

The PNC won elections in 1968 and in 1973, although the results of the latter, and every poll thenceforth until the defeat of the PNC in 1992, were disputed by the opposition parties. Guyana became a co-operative republic on 23 February 1970, and Arthur Chung was elected non-executive President in March. In 1976 the PPP, which had boycotted the National Assembly since 1973, offered the Government its 'critical support'. Following a referendum in July 1978 that gave the Assembly power to amend the Constitution, elections to the Assembly were postponed. The legislature assumed the role of a constituent assembly, established in November 1978, to draft a new constitution. In October 1980 Burnham declared himself executive President of Guyana, and a new Constitution was promulgated.

Internal opposition to the PNC Government increased after the assassination in 1980 of Walter Rodney, leader of the Working People's Alliance (WPA). The Government was widely believed to have been involved in the incident. All opposition parties except the PPP and TUF boycotted the December 1980 elections to the National Assembly. The PNC received 78% of the votes, according to official results, although allegations of substantial electoral malpractice were made, both within the country and by international observers. None the less, Burnham was inaugurated as President in January 1981.

In 1981 arrests and trials of opposition leaders continued, and in 1982 the Government's relations with human rights groups, and especially the Christian churches, deteriorated further. Editors of opposition newspapers were threatened, political violence increased, and the Government was accused of interference in the legal process. Industrial unrest and public discontent continued in 1983 and 1984, as Guyana's worsening economic situation increased opposition to the Government, and led to growing disaffection in the trade union movement and the PNC.

Burnham died in August 1985 and was succeeded as President by Desmond Hoyte, hitherto the First Vice-President and Prime Minister. The PNC won the December election, although opposition groups, including the PPP and WPA, denounced the poll as fraudulent. In 1986 five of the six opposition parties formed the Patriotic Coalition for Democracy (PCD).

Outside the formal opposition of the political parties, the Government also experienced pressure from members of the Guyana Human Rights Association, business leaders and prominent religious figures. This culminated, in 1990, in the formation of a movement for legal and constitutional change, Guyanese Action for Reform and Democracy (Guard), which initiated a series of mass protests, urging the Government to accelerate the process of democratic reform. To counter this civic movement, the PNC began mobilizing its own newly established Committees to Re-elect the President (Creeps). Guard accused the Creeps of orchestrating violent clashes at Guard rallies, and of fomenting racial unrest in an attempt to regain support from the Afro-Guyanese population.

In January 1991 the date of the forthcoming general election was postponed, following the approval of legislation extending the term of office of the National Assembly by two months. In March a further two-month extension provoked the resignation of TUF and PPP members from the National Assembly (WPA members had resigned a month earlier). Similar extensions followed in May and July, owing to alleged continuing electoral reform problems. The National Assembly was finally dissolved in September. The publication of a revised electoral register in that month, however, revealed widespread inaccuracies, including the omission of an estimated 100,000 eligible voters. In November several opposition parties announced a boycott of the general election, which had been rescheduled for December. However, in November Hoyte declared a state of emergency (subsequently extended until June 1992) in order to legitimize a further postponement of the poll. A further revised electoral register was approved by the Elections Commission in August 1992. The election finally took place on 5 October and resulted in a narrow victory for the PPP in alliance with the Civic alliance (a social and political movement of businessmen and professionals). The result, which signified an end to the PNC's 28-year period in government, provoked riots by the mainly Afro-Guyanese PNC supporters in Georgetown. However, international observers were satisfied that the elections had been fairly conducted, and Dr Cheddi Bharat Jagan took office as President. Jagan appointed Samuel Hinds, an industrialist who was not a member of the PPP, as Prime Minister.

In August 1995 a serious environmental incident resulted in the temporary closure of Omai Gold Mines Ltd (OGML). The company was responsible for a massive increase in Guyana's gold production since it began production in 1993 and was Guyana's largest foreign investor. However, a breach in a reservoir at its gold mine resulted in the spillage of some 3.5m. cu m of cyanide-tainted water, of which a large volume flowed into the Omai river, a tributary of the Essequibo river. OGML resumed operations in 1996 following the implementation of government-approved environmental safeguards.

In March 1997, following the death of Jagan, Prime Minister Hinds succeeded to the presidency, in accordance with the provisions of the Constitution. Hinds appointed Janet Jagan, the widow of the former President, as Prime Minister. Following the PPP/Civic's success in the December general election, Jagan, who was that alliance's nominee, was inaugurated as President.

In January 1998 the Government accepted a proposal by private sector leaders for an international audit of the election to be conducted. However, the PNC rejected the proposal and demanded instead the holding of fresh elections. In mid-January the Chief Justice ruled that it was beyond the jurisdiction of the High Court to prohibit Jagan from exercising her presidential functions pending a judicial review of the election. The ruling provoked serious disturbances in Georgetown. Public protests by PNC supporters continued in defiance of a ban on demonstrations in the capital. However, following mediation by a three-member Caribbean Community and Common Market (CARICOM) commission, it was announced that an accord (the Herdmanston Agreement) had been signed by Jagan and Hoyte, which provided for the organization of fresh elections within 36 months and the creation of a commission to make recommendations on constitutional reform, to be submitted to a national referendum and a legislative vote. The agreement also made provision for an independent audit of the 1997 election. In June 1998 the CARICOM commission upheld the published results of the December poll.

In January 1999 a 20-member Constitutional Reform Commission was established, comprising representatives of the country's principal political parties and community groups. The Commission's report included proposals (submitted by the PPP/Civic alliance) that the country should be renamed the Republic of Guyana, that the President should be limited to two consecutive terms of office, and that the President should no longer be empowered to dissolve the National Assembly should he/she be censured by the Assembly. The Commission further proposed that the President should no longer have the power to dismiss a public officer in the public interest, and the President and Cabinet should be collectively responsible to the National Assembly and should resign if defeated in a vote of no confidence.

President Jagan retired in August 1999. She was replaced by the erstwhile Minister of Finance, Bharrat Jagdeo. The appointment of Jagdeo, whose relative youth (he was 35 years of age), reported willingness to reach across the political divide, and strong background in economics all contributed to his popularity, was widely welcomed.

The general and regional elections of 2001 were preceded by demonstrations over the late distribution of voter identification cards. The PPP/Civic obtained a majority in the National Assembly, with 34 seats, while the PNC (which contested the elections as the PNCReform) won 27 seats. Some 90% of the registered electorate participated. International observers declared the elections to be generally free and fair. Jagdeo was inaugurated for a second term as President.

A period of social unrest, accompanied by a high incidence of violent crime, began in 2002, as a result of ongoing hostilities between the Government and opposition. During that period large numbers of people were killed or 'disappeared'. The disorder culminated in July in an attack by opposition protesters on the presidential offices during a meeting of CARICOM heads of government. The security forces opened fire on the protesters, killing two and wounding 15. While condemning the violence, the PNCReform leadership announced their support for the demonstrators' grievances of racial discrimination and police brutality.

Robert Corbin was elected leader of the PNCReform in February 2003 following the death of Hoyte. Corbin pledged a policy of 'constructive engagement' with the PPP and in May Jagdeo and Corbin signed an agreement on a number of issues, including local government reform and opposition representation on state bodies, particularly the government-owned media. In the same month the PNCReform ended its boycott of the National Assembly. In December agreement was reached by the two parties on the establishment of four constitutional commissions to oversee reform of the judiciary, the police, the civil service and the teaching sector.

Crime, in particular violent crime, continued to increase during Jagdeo's presidency. Following an increase in the number of abductions in 2003, the National Assembly approved legislation to extend the terms of imprisonment for those convicted of kidnap. In December a parliamentary report referred to the possible existence of a clandestine, government-run paramilitary group. It was claimed that the group targeted suspected criminals and persons linked to known criminals. The allegations were supported in the following month by George Bacchus, who claimed he had been an informant for the so-called 'death squad', which had been allegedly responsible for more than 40

extra-judicial killings in 2003. Bacchus alleged that the Minister of Home Affairs, Ronald Gajraj, had orchestrated the group's operations. In May 2004 a three-member commission was appointed to investigate the allegations. However, in June, on the day that he was scheduled to testify before the commission, Bacchus was killed. In April 2005 a Presidential Commission of Inquiry cleared Gajraj of involvement in the activities of the death squads. He was immediately reinstated to his cabinet post; however, following international pressure and vociferous criticism from the opposition PNCReform, at the end of the month Gajraj resigned.

The problem of violent crime was brought into dramatic focus in April 2006 when Minister of Agriculture Satyadeow Sawh was shot dead at his home.

The re-election of Jagdeo

The PPP/Civic secured a comfortable victory at the general election on 28 August 2006. The party increased its representation in the National Assembly to 36, while the People's National Congress Reform-One Guyana (PNCR-1G, as PNCReform had been restyled) obtained 22 seats. The recently formed Alliance for Change (AFC) won five seats. The rate of voter participation, at 69%, was the lowest since independence. Jagdeo made nine new ministerial appointments.

A series of strikes, reportedly involving up to 10,000 sugar industry workers, were organized during 2010 by the Guyana Agricultural and General Workers' Union (GAWU) to demand a 15% pay increase from the state-owned Guyana Sugar Corpn (GuySuCo). Following negotiations between GAWU and GuySuCo, in December sugar workers accepted 5% pay rise.

In December 2010 the National Assembly adopted legislation to postpone the local elections (due since 1997) for another year. Jagdeo argued that the state lacked the resources necessary to organize local elections, and blamed the opposition, holding them responsible for a lack of progress on local government reform—a prerequisite for the staging of fresh local elections. In March 2014 a joint statement was issued by foreign embassies in the country and civil society and legal organizations urging all political parties in Guyana to co-operate in holding local elections by 1 August. It was announced in January 2015 that local elections would be held on 11 May, at the same time as the general election (see below).

Ramotar in office

The PPP/Civic secured a narrow victory and its fifth consecutive win at the general election of 28 November 2011. However, the party lost its overall majority in the National Assembly, securing 32 seats. It garnered 48.6% of votes cast, while A Partnership for National Unity (APNU)—the coalition of opposition parties comprising the PNCR, the Guyana Action Party, the National Front Alliance and the Working People's Alliance, formed to contest the elections—obtained 26 seats and 40.8% of the ballot. The AFC won seven seats. The rate of voter participation was 73%.

As Jagdeo was constitutionally prohibited from seeking a third term in office, the PPP/Civic's candidate was party Secretary-General Donald Ramotar. Ramotar was inaugurated as President on 3 December 2011. Given that the PPP/Civic would be forming a minority government (the first of its kind in Guyana), Ramotar emphasized the importance of national unity and co-operation. However, the new administration included only PPP/Civic members and remained largely unchanged from the previous administration. Significantly, the President created a new ministry—of Natural Resources and the Environment—to which he appointed former agriculture minister Robert Persaud.

Opposition supporters protested against the election results, leading to the police firing rubber bullets and injuring some demonstrators in the capital on 6 December 2011. The opposition leader David Granger alleged irregularities in the election process, while the APNU called on the Chairman of the Guyana Elections Commission and the Chief Elections Officer to resign.

The two main opposition parties obtained a one-seat majority over the PPP/Civic, so they were able to control the legislative branch of government. Thus, in January 2012 AFC leader Raphael Trotman was installed as parliamentary Speaker. In April the opposition used their majority to reject the Government's proposed budget and to approve one with significantly lower levels of expenditure.

In July 2012 demonstrations took place in Linden, Guyana's second largest town, against the Government's decision to remove electricity subsidies, which was to result in increases of up to 300% in residents' bills. In clashes with police three protesters were shot dead and some 20 injured. On 31 July the National Assembly passed a vote of no confidence in the home affairs minister, Clement Rohee. Despite an agreement to reverse the proposed cuts, disturbances continued and led to the temporary suspension of bauxite production in the area. The Government accused the opposition of prolonging the unrest in the area, which has strategic border crossings with Brazil, in an attempt to destabilize the administration.

Increasing animosity between the Government and the opposition during 2012 culminated in December in the submission of a government document to the Organization of American States (OAS), which warned of the threat of political instability to the country by the opposition. It accused the opposition of using its one-seat majority to subvert a number of parliamentary conventions, such as the selection of committee members and appointments to key parliamentary positions, including Speaker. The Government also repeated the assertion that the opposition leader Granger was exploiting long-standing racial divisions within the country for political purposes.

Meeting anti-money laundering standards

In June 2013 it was announced that a deadline set by the Caribbean Financial Action Task Force (CFATF) for Guyana to conform to international anti-money laundering standards had been postponed to November, following the Government's failure to win majority support for its Anti-Money Laundering and Countering Financing of Terror Bill (AML-CFT bill) by the original deadline of 27 May. The opposition-dominated National Assembly also failed to pass four bills presented by Clement Rohee, having pledged not to support any proposed legislation from the home affairs ministry while he remained in office. In July the Government rejected a report on human trafficking by the US Department of State, although in July 2014 it announced the creation of the Ministerial Task Force on Trafficking in Persons Plan in an effort to address the problem.

Guyana was accused by the CFATF in November 2013 of not having taken sufficient measures to improve its compliance with international standards, following the defeat of the AML-CFT bill earlier that month. While Minister of Finance Ashni Singh warned that the country's credibility in the international community could be severely damaged if the law was not passed, the CFATF advised its members to consider implementing countermeasures to protect their own financial system from the risks emanating from Guyana. In December a new select committee was appointed with the aim of expediting the passage of the bill by February 2014. In mid-February the Financial Action Task Force (FATF—based in Paris, France) decided against blacklisting Guyana because the failure of the legislation was not the fault of the Government. None the less, in June the CFATF referred Guyana to the FATF to review the country's non-compliance with anti-money laundering standards. In October the FATF placed Guyana on a list of countries requiring an ongoing review of compliance with anti-money laundering standards, but refrained from blacklisting it; the AML-CFT bill had still to be approved by the National Assembly, which was not in session (see below), in early 2015.

In October 2013 the Cabinet rejected a Leadership and Democracy Project worth US $13.1m. to be funded by the US Agency for International Development. However, it was subsequently reported that aspects of the project were none the less being implemented, a move that was described by the head of the Presidential Secretariat as an affront to Guyana's sovereignty. In January 2014 the Minister of Local Government and Regional Development, Ganga Persaud, resigned, citing personal reasons.

Recent developments: parliament prorogued

In November 2014 President Ramotar prorogued the National Assembly, reportedly to avoid a vote of no confidence, which the majority opposition coalition had threatened to call in protest at some US $22.5m. of government expenditure that had been made without parliamentary approval, despite having successfully introduced amendments to make significant reductions in spending before the budget had been passed in April. In December Ramotar announced that he intended to call a general election, although he stated that he would specify the date for polls only in early 2015. Both the OAS and the High Commissioner of the United Kingdom to Guyana urged Ramotar to reconvene the National Assembly as soon as possible. In July the outgoing US ambassador to Guyana had criticized the country for failing to hold local government elections, which were last staged in 1994, and in September 2014 demonstrations on the issue were held in Georgetown and the other five municipalities.

Eventually, in late January 2015, Ramotar announced that local and national elections would be held on 11 May.

Foreign Affairs
Regional relations

Guyana has been involved in long-running border disputes with Venezuela and Suriname. Following the restoration of diplomatic links with Suriname in 1979 relations improved. However, in 2000 Suriname claimed that Guyana had violated its territorial integrity by granting a concession to a Canadian company to explore for petroleum and gas. Negotiations to settle the dispute ended inconclusively, and in 2002 the Presidents of the two countries met to discuss a production-sharing agreement. However, in the same year the Surinamese navy forcibly ejected a rig that had been authorized by Guyana to drill in disputed waters. Guyana referred the dispute to the UN's International Tribunal for the Law of the Sea (ITLOS), in Hamburg, Germany, and in 2007 the Tribunal ruled in favour of Guyana, granting sovereignty over 33,152 sq km (12,800 sq miles) of coastal waters; Suriname was awarded 17,891 sq km (6,900 sq miles).

In 2008 the seizure by the Surinamese military of a Guyanese ship provoked serious confrontation between the two countries. The ship and its crew were eventually released after payment of a small fine. In 2010 Jagdeo and new Surinamese President Desiré (Desi) Bouterse agreed to put aside any unresolved border issues and concentrate instead on enhancing bilateral co-operation in trade and security. In 2012 the two countries agreed to seek finance from the Inter-American Development Bank for a feasibility study of the construction of a bridge across the Corentyne river. In a further display of co-operation the two countries agreed to establish a joint border security committee in an attempt to deter cross-border crime, particularly the smuggling of gold. In December 2013 the announcement that Guyana had granted permission for a Brazilian company to conduct a geological survey of a disputed area, the New River Triangle (or Tigri, as it is known in Suriname), provoked a heightening of nationalist sentiment in both countries. In April 2014 Guyana withdrew from an international mining conference in Suriname after a conference document was circulated that depicted the New River Triangle as part of the latter country.

In 1962 Venezuela renewed its claim to 130,000 sq km (50,000 sq miles) of land west of the Essequibo river (nearly two-thirds of Guyanese territory). The area was accorded to Guyana in 1899 by an international tribunal, but Venezuela based its claim on a papal bull of 1493. The Port of Spain Protocol of 1970 put the issue in abeyance until 1982. Guyana and Venezuela referred the dispute to the UN in 1983, and in 1989 the two countries agreed to a mutually acceptable intermediary. In 1999 Guyana and Venezuela established a joint commission, intended to expedite the resolution of the territorial dispute and to promote mutual co-operation. In 2004 Venezuelan President Hugo Chávez met President Jagdeo with the aim of increasing bilateral co-operation, and in the following year Guyana signed the Petrocaribe energy accord with Venezuela, which offered favourable terms on the price of petroleum. Moreover, Guyana was to settle its debt to Venezuela for energy imports by exporting crops such as rice. The agreement began in 2010.

Relations became strained in 2007 when Guyana accused Venezuelan troops of crossing into its territory and blowing up two gold-mining dredges. The Venezuelan Government subsequently expressed regret for the incident. In 2010 Jagdeo and Chávez concluded a number of trade agreements and agreed to restart UN-mediated negotiations on their territorial dispute, which had been in abeyance since 2007. Bilateral relations were strained further in September 2011 after Guyana applied to the UN to extend its continental shelf by 150 nautical miles (from 200 to 350 miles). (Owing to the long-standing territorial dispute the two countries' maritime boundaries had yet to be defined.) Venezuela objected that Guyana had not informed it of the application beforehand, and that Guyana had claimed that the area of the extension was not under dispute. In August 2013, following the death of Chávez, new Venezuelan President Nicolas Maduro made an official visit to Guyana during which he expressed a commitment to strengthening ties and resolving the territorial dispute. Two months later, however, relations were strained when the Venezuelan navy intercepted a research vessel conducting a survey of the sea floor on behalf of a US oil company. Although Venezuela claimed that the vessel had entered its territory, Guyana declared that it was well within its own exclusive economic zone. The UN subsequently presented a plan to accelerate the resolution of the dispute.

Guyana's relations with Brazil continued to improve through trade and military agreements. In 2003 the Government approved a request by the Brazilian authorities for a partial abolition of visas for both countries. A bridge across the Takutu river between the two countries was completed in 2009. In September 2014 Brazil reaffirmed its commitment to the construction of road and hydroelectricity projects in Guyana.

Other external relations

In 2010 President Jagdeo held talks in Moscow with his Russian counterpart. The negotiations were aimed at extending economic and humanitarian co-operation between the two countries. In the same month Jagdeo made an official visit to Iran during which he signed two co-operation agreements.

Guyana was the first CARICOM country to establish diplomatic relations with the People's Republic of China, in 1972. Political and economic co-operation between the two countries culminated in 2004 in the signing of a bilateral investment treaty. In 2012 two agreements were signed that would provide Guyana with a total of US$9.6m. in support from China, in addition to a $130m. loan agreement for the improvement of Guyana's international airport. In 2013 the Government was criticized after reports that it had agreed to allow the Shanghai Construction Group to employ only Chinese workers on the $61m. construction of the Marriott Hotel in Georgetown. The announcement was followed by a series of attacks and robberies against the Chinese community in Guyana. In July 2014 President Ramotar was invited to the summit of the BRICS group (comprising Brazil, Russia, India, China and South Africa) in Brazil, and held bilateral meetings with officials from China and India, including on co-operation in mining, construction, shipping and exploring hydrocarbon resources. In October Guyana and China signed an agreement to provide for the training of Guyanese doctors.

In January 2015 the British High Commissioner to Guyana, Andrew Ayre, announced that the United Kingdom was considering the suspension of development aid to the country, in protest at President Ramotar's prorogation of parliament in November 2014 (see *Recent developments*), and urged Ramotar to allow parliamentary activity to resume.

CONSTITUTION AND GOVERNMENT

Guyana became a republic, within the Commonwealth, on 23 February 1970. A new Constitution was promulgated in October 1980, and amended in 1998, 2000 and 2001. Legislative power is held by the unicameral National Assembly, with 65 members elected for five years by universal adult suffrage, on the basis of proportional representation: 40 members are elected from national lists, and a further 25 members are elected from regional constituency lists. Executive power is held by the President, who leads the majority party in the Assembly and holds office for its duration. The President appoints and heads a Cabinet, which includes the Prime Minister, and may include up to four Ministers who are not elected members of the Assembly. The Cabinet is collectively responsible to the National Assembly. Guyana comprises 10 regions.

REGIONAL AND INTERNATIONAL CO-OPERATION

Guyana is a founder member of CARICOM (see p. 222). It was also one of the six founder members of CARICOM's Caribbean Single Market and Economy, established in 2006, but yet to be implemented by 2015. Guyana became a member of the UN in 1966. As a contracting party to the General Agreement on Tariffs and Trade, Guyana joined the World Trade Organization (see p. 431) on its establishment in 1995. The country is a member of the Commonwealth (see p. 234). In 2001 Guyana was one of 11 Caribbean states to sign an agreement establishing a jointly administered regional court. The Caribbean Court of Justice, inaugurated in Trinidad and Tobago in 2005, replaced the Privy Council in the United Kingdom as Guyana's highest appellate body. Guyana also participated in the third meeting of South American Presidents in Cusco, Peru, in 2004, which created the Comunidad Sudamericana de Naciones (South American Community of Nations, which was renamed Unión de Naciones Suramericanas, UNASUR—Union of South American Nations, see p. 464—in 2007), intended to promote greater regional economic integration. In February 2011 Guyana was a signatory to the Caribbean Basin Security Initiative between CARICOM and the USA. The country is also a member of the Community of Latin American and Caribbean States (see p. 460), which was formally inaugurated in December 2011. In July 2013 Guyana (with Suriname) signed a framework agreement to join the Southern Common Market (Mercado Común del Sur—MERCOSUR, see p. 426).

ECONOMIC AFFAIRS

In 2013, according to estimates by the World Bank, Guyana's gross national income (GNI), measured at average 2011–13 prices, was US $3,002m., equivalent to US $3,750 per head (or US $6,550 per head on an international purchasing-power parity basis). During 2004–13, it was estimated, the population increased at an average annual rate of 0.6%, while gross domestic product (GDP) per head increased, in real terms, by an average of 2.1% per year. According to official figures, overall GDP increased, in real terms, at an average annual rate of 4.6% in 2006–13; real GDP increased by 5.2% in 2013.

Agriculture (including forestry and fishing) provided an estimated 18.2% of GDP in 2013 and, according to FAO, employed an estimated 15.1% of the total labour force in mid-2015. The principal cash crops are rice and sugar cane (sugar provided an estimated 8.3% of the value of total domestic exports in 2013). The sugar industry, which accounted for 3.1% of GDP in 2013, was affected by the gradual ending from 2006 of the European Union's (EU) preferential price regime. In spite of a US $180m. project to upgrade the Skeldon sugar refinery in Berbice and to construct a 30-MW co-generation facility from 2009, sugar output continued to fall, reaching just 186,771 metric tons in 2013, below the 235,000 tons needed to meet local and EU needs. The Caribbean Development Bank in December 2014 authorized a loan of $7.5m. to the beleaguered sector. Vegetables and fruit are cultivated for the local market, and livestock-rearing is being developed. Fishing is also important (particularly shrimp), and accounted for an estimated 2.1% of GDP in 2013. Agricultural production increased by an average annual rate of 1.4% during 2006–13. The sector's GDP increased by 2.3% in 2013.

Timber resources in Guyana are extensive and underdeveloped. In 2013 the forestry sector contributed 2.7% of GDP. About three-quarters of the country's total land area consists of forest and woodland. In 2013 timber shipments provided an estimated 2.8% of total domestic exports. The forestry sector's GDP declined at an average annual rate of 2.3% in 2006–13; the output from the sector decreased by 4.3% in 2012, but increased by 5.0% in 2013.

Industry (including mining, manufacturing, construction and power) provided an estimated 34.4% of GDP in 2013 and engaged 25.4% of the employed labour force in 2002. Industrial GDP increased at an average annual rate of 4.8% in 2006–13. The sector's GDP increased by 2.6% in 2012 and further by 12.2% in 2013.

Mining contributed an estimated 17.3% of GDP in 2013 and employed 4.1% of the total working population in 2002. The registered production of gold accounted for 47.1% of domestic exports in 2013 (compared with 51.4% in the previous year). In 2011 Guyana Goldfields Inc announced it had discovered up to 6m. troy ounces of high-quality gold in Aurora, in the north-west of the country. In 2000 the gold industry was estimated directly to employ some 32,000 people. Bauxite, which is used for the manufacture of aluminium, is also a valuable export. Production fluctuated following the withdrawal in 2002 of the US-based aluminium company Alcoa from the Aroaima bauxite and aluminium mine: output increased by 22% in 2012, but decreased by 23% in 2013. In that latter year a total of 1.7m. metric tons of bauxite was exported, generating 9.8% of the total value of exports. There are also some petroleum reserves and significant diamond resources. In 2013 diamond production stood at 63,961 metric carats, compared with 40,763 metric carats in 2012. The GDP of the mining sector was estimated to have increased by an average of 6.5% per year in 2006–13; the sector increased by 8.0% in 2013.

Manufacturing accounted for an estimated 6.5% of GDP in 2013 and, in 2002, employed 13.3% of the total working population. The main activities are the processing of bauxite, sugar, rice and timber. Manufacturing GDP increased at an average annual rate of 2.8% in 2006–13. Output from the sector increased by 8.0% in 2013.

Construction accounted for an estimated 8.6% of GDP in 2013 and, in 2002, employed 7.0% of the total working population. According to official figures, construction GDP (including engineering) increased at an average annual rate of 4.6% in 2006–13.

Output from the sector decreased by 11.0% in 2012, but increased by 22.6% in 2013.

Energy requirements are almost entirely met by imported hydrocarbon fuels. In 2013 fuels and lubricants constituted 31.3% of the total value of imports (mainly from Venezuela and Trinidad and Tobago). Guyana was a signatory to the Petrocaribe agreement, under which Venezuela accorded petroleum concessions. Guyana is believed to possess substantial petroleum deposits. The Government was exploring the potential of bioenergy production; to this end it signed memorandums of understanding with foreign investors for feasibility studies in 2013. Construction of a hydroelectric plant on the Amaila river was scheduled to begin in 2015.

The services sector contributed an estimated 47.4% of GDP in 2013 and engaged 52.4% of the employed labour force in 2002. The GDP of the services sector increased by an average of 6.0% per year in 2006–13. Services GDP increased, in real terms, by 2.8% in 2013.

In 2013 Guyana recorded a visible merchandise trade deficit of US $471.4m. and a deficit of US $425.3m. on the current account of the balance of payments. In 2012 the principal source of imports was the USA (24.7%), followed by Venezuela, the People's Republic of China and Suriname. Canada was the principal market for exports (35.9% of total exports in 2012), followed by the USA, Venezuela and the United Kingdom. The principal exports in 2013 were gold, rice, bauxite and sugar, and the principal imports were fuel and lubricants, building materials, agricultural machinery and industrial machinery.

In 2013 the overall budget deficit was an estimated $ G21,129.5m. (equivalent to 3.4% of GDP). Guyana's general government gross debt was $ G364,509m. in 2012, equivalent to 62.6% of GDP. According to World Bank estimates, by the end of 2012 Guyana's external debt totalled US $1,974m., of which US $1,215m. was public and publicly guaranteed debt. In 2012 the cost of servicing long-term public and publicly guaranteed debt and repayments to the IMF was equivalent to 8.7% of the value of exports of goods, services and income (excluding workers' remittances). According to the IMF, the annual rate of inflation averaged 5.3% in 2004–13. Consumer prices increased by some 1.9% in 2013, according to official sources. According to census figures the rate of unemployment in 2002 was 11.7%.

The Guyanese economy's reliance on sugar meant that the gradual withdrawal of the EU's Sugar Protocol in 2009 (combined with the removal of sugar duties in 2008) posed an enormous challenge to the authorities. Financial assistance provided by the EU in 2012, worth some US $40m., was intended for the modernization of sugar production facilities in the country. However, in 2013 sugar production reached its lowest levels since 1990 as a result of industrial action, mechanical problems and the movement of workers to other sectors, leading to a growing debate about the future of the sugar industry. A source of further concern was the announcement in mid-2013 that the EU would abolish sugar quotas in 2017, three years earlier than agreed by the European Parliament earlier in the year. In 2013 the Government reached an agreement with the CARICOM Development Fund that would provide $7.3m. in funding for the country's agricultural sector and in December 2014 the Caribbean Development Bank authorized a loan of $7.5m. for the sugar sector. Compared with most of its neighbours in the region, Guyana demonstrated an impressive resilience when confronted by the global economic downturn, registering its eighth consecutive year of GDP growth in 2013, when GDP growth of 5.2% was recorded. The Government predicted growth of 4.5% for 2014, underpinned by rising gold and rice production and renewed infrastructure sector expansion. Large projects, most notably the Amaila Falls hydroelectric power project, which received finance totalling some $506m. from US and Chinese interests, were expected to stimulate the economy, although the project suffered a reverse in 2013 when the US developer withdrew from the venture, citing the failure of the National Assembly to reach a consensus on financing. In October 2014 the Inter-American Development Bank and the EU agreed to provide $96m. in funding to Guyana to improve its water and electricity infrastructure.

PUBLIC HOLIDAYS

2016: 1 January (New Year's Day), 2 January* (Yum an-Nabi, birth of the Prophet), 23 February (Mashramani, Republic Day), 25 March (Good Friday), 28 March (Easter Monday), 4 May (for Labour Day), 5 May (Indian Heritage Day), 2 July (CARICOM Day), 6 July* (Id al-Fitr, end of Ramadan), 1 August (Freedom Day), 12 September* (Id al-Adha, feast of the Sacrifice), 11 December* (Yum an-Nabi, birth of the Prophet), 25–26 December (Christmas).

* These holidays are dependent on the Islamic lunar calendar and may vary by one or two days from the dates given.

In addition, the Hindu festivals of Holi Phagwah (usually in March) and Diwali (October or November) are celebrated. These festivals are dependent on sightings of the moon and their precise date is not known until two months before they take place.

Statistical Survey

Sources (unless otherwise stated): Bank of Guyana, 1 Church St and Ave of the Republic, POB 1003, Georgetown; tel. 226-3250; fax 227-2965; e-mail communications@bankofguyana.org.gy; internet www.bankofguyana.org.gy; Bureau of Statistics, Ministry of Finance, Main and Urquhart Sts, Georgetown; tel. 227-1114; fax 226-1284; internet www.statisticsguyana.gov.gy.

AREA AND POPULATION

Area: 214,969 sq km (83,000 sq miles).

Population: 751,223 at census of 15 September 2002; 747,884 (males 372,547, females 375,337) at census of 15 September 2012 (preliminary). *2015* (UN estimate at mid-year): 807,611 (Source: UN, *World Population Prospects: The 2012 Revision*).

Density (at mid-2015): 3.8 per sq km.

Population by Age and Sex (UN estimates at mid-2015): *0–14 years:* 278,549 (males 146,303, females 132,246); *15–64 years:* 500,342 (males 253,764, females 246,578); *65 years and over:* 28,720 (males 10,134, females 18,586); *Total* 807,611 (males 410,201, females 397,410) (Source: UN, *World Population Prospects: The 2012 Revision*).

Population by Ethnic Group (self-declaration at 2002 census): 'East' Indians 326,277; Africans 227,062; Mixed 125,727; Amerindians 68,675; Portuguese 1,497; Chinese 1,396; White 477; Total (incl. others) 751,223. Note: Classification of ethnicity reflects national census methodology.

Regions (population at 2012 census, preliminary): Barima–Waini 26,941; Pomeroon–Supenaam 46,810; Essequibo Islands–West Demerara 107,416; Demerara–Mahaica 313,429; Mahaica–Berbice 49,723; East Berbice–Corentyne 109,431; Cuyuni–Mazaruni 20,280; Potaro–Siparuni 10,190; Upper Takutu–Upper Essequibo 24,212; Upper Demerara–Berbice 39,452; *Total* 747,884.

Principal Towns (population at 2012 census, preliminary): Georgetown (capital) 118,363; Linden 27,277; New Amsterdam 17,329; Corriverton 11,386. *Mid-2014* ('000, incl. suburbs, UN estimate): Georgetown 124 (Source: UN, *World Urbanization Prospects: The 2014 Revision*).

Births, Marriages and Deaths (2013): Birth rate 18.5 per 1,000; Marriages 4,667 (marriage rate 6.3 per 1,000); Deaths 4,527 (death rate 6.6 per 1,000).

Life Expectancy (years at birth): 66.0 (males 63.5; females 68.7) in 2012. Source: World Bank, World Development Indicators database.

Economically Active Population (persons aged 15 years and over, census of 2002): Agriculture, hunting and forestry 45,378; Fishing 5,533; Mining and quarrying 9,374; Manufacturing 30,483; Electricity, gas and water 2,246; Construction 16,100; Trade, repair of motor vehicles and personal and household goods 37,690; Restaurants and hotels 5,558; Transport, storage and communications 16,790; Financial intermediation 3,074; Real estate, renting and business services 7,384; Public administration, defence and social security 14,995; Education 13,015; Health and social work 5,513; Other community, social and personal service activities 9,599; Private households with employed persons 6,156; Extraterritorial organizations and bodies 477; *Sub-total* 229,365; Activities not adequately defined 1,489; *Total employed* 230,854 (males 162,596, females 68,258); Unemployed 30,533; *Total labour force* 261,387 (males 180,946, females 80,441). *2013:* Central government 12,056; Rest of the public sector 16,941; Total public sector employment 28,997. *Mid-2015* ('000, estimates): Agriculture, etc. 51; Total labour force 383 (Source: FAO).

HEALTH AND WELFARE

Key Indicators

Total Fertility Rate (children per woman, 2012): 2.6.

Under-5 Mortality Rate (per 1,000 live births, 2012): 35.

HIV/AIDS (% of persons aged 15–49, 2013): 1.4.

Physicians (per 1,000 head, 2010): 0.2.

Hospital Beds (per 1,000 head, 2009): 2.0.

Health Expenditure (2011): US $ per head (PPP): 217.

Health Expenditure (2011): % of GDP: 6.8.

Health Expenditure (2011): public (% of total): 67.3.

Access to Water (% of persons, 2012): 98.

Access to Sanitation (% of persons, 2012): 84.

Total Carbon Dioxide Emissions ('000 metric tons, 2010): 1,701.5.

Total Carbon Dioxide Emissions Per Head (metric tons, 2010): 2.2.

Human Development Index (2013): ranking: 121.

Human Development Index (2013): value: 0.638.

For sources and definitions, see explanatory note on p. vi.

AGRICULTURE, ETC.

Principal Crops ('000 metric tons, 2013): Rice, paddy 824; Cassava (Manioc) 8; Sugar cane 2,460; Coconuts 75 (FAO estimate); Bananas 5; Plantains 15. *Aggregate Production* ('000 metric tons, may include official, semi-official or estimated data): Total cereals 827.8; Vegetables (incl. melons) 61; Fruits (excl. melons) 44.9.

Livestock ('000 head, year ending September 2013, FAO estimates): Horses 2.5; Asses 1.0; Cattle 113; Sheep 132; Pigs 13; Goats 82; Chickens 25,200.

Livestock Products ('000 metric tons, 2013): Cattle meat 2.3; Sheep meat 0.6; Pig meat 0.6; Chicken meat 29.3; Cows' milk 45.0; Hen eggs 0.9 (unofficial figure).

Forestry ('000 cubic metres, 2013, FAO estimates): *Roundwood Removals:* Sawlogs, veneer logs and logs for sleepers 399, Pulpwood 100, Other industrial wood 21, Fuel wood 840; Total 1,360. *Sawnwood Production:* Total (all broadleaved) 74.

Fishing ('000 metric tons, live weight, 2012): Capture 53.8 (Marine fishes 24.9; Atlantic seabob 24.8; Whitebelly prawn 0.6); Aquaculture 0.3; *Total catch* 54.1. Note: Figures exclude crocodiles: the number of spectacled caimans caught in 2012 was 18,920.

Source: FAO.

MINING

Production (2013): Bauxite 1,713,242 metric tons; Gold 14,964 kg; Diamonds 63,961 metric carats.

INDUSTRY

Selected Products (2013): Raw sugar 186,771 metric tons; Rice 535,439 metric tons; Rum 40,835 hl; Beer and stout 173,612 hl; Logs 304,601 cu m; Margarine 2,318 metric tons; Biscuits 1,211,100 kg; Paint 26,949 hl; Electricity 711m. kWh.

FINANCE

Currency and Exchange Rates: 100 cents = 1 Guyana dollar ($ G). *Sterling, US Dollar and Euro Equivalents* (31 December 2014): £1 sterling = $ G322.305; US $1 = $ G206.500; €1 = $ G250.712; $ G1,000 = £3.10 = US $4.84 = €3.99. *Average Exchange Rate* ($ G per US $): 204.358 in 2012; 205.386 in 2013; 206.449 in 2014.

Budget ($ G million, 2013): *Revenue:* Tax revenue 154,826.5 (Income tax 57,268.9; Value-added tax 42,673.7; Trade taxes 16,319.8); Other current revenue 10,777.7; Capital revenue (incl. grants) 9,091.0; Total 174,695.2. *Expenditure:* Current expenditure 142,731.9 (Personnel emoluments 47,517.3; Other goods and services 87,837.8; Interest 7,376.8); Capital expenditure 53,092.8; Total 195,824.7.

International Reserves (US $ million at 31 December 2013): IMF special drawing rights 6.73; Foreign exchange 776.89; *Total* 783.62. Source: IMF, *International Financial Statistics*.

Money Supply ($ G million at 31 December 2013): Currency outside depository corporations 60,616; Transferable deposits 75,805; Other deposits 275,914; *Broad money* 412,335. Source: IMF, *International Financial Statistics*.

Cost of Living (Urban Consumer Price Index for Georgetown; base: December 2009 = 100): All items 107.7 in 2011; 109.7 in 2012; 111.8 in 2013.

Expenditure on the Gross Domestic Product ($ G million at current prices, 2013): Government final consumption expenditure 87,236; Private final consumption expenditure 578,782; Gross capital formation 114,211; *Total domestic expenditure* 780,228; Net imports of goods and services −166,099; *GDP in purchasers' values* 614,130.

Gross Domestic Product by Economic Activity ($ G million at current prices, 2013): Agriculture, forestry and fishing 101,553 (Sugar 17,384); Mining and quarrying 96,922; Manufacturing 36,166; Construction 48,037; Electricity, gas and water 11,316; Wholesale and retail trade 77,090; Transport, storage, information and communications 61,424; Finance and insurance 25,986; Real estate and renting 5,632; Public administration 47,592; Education 18,847; Health and social welfare 8,829; Other services 19,866; *Subtotal* 559,260; *Less* Financial intermediation services indirectly measured 21,833; *Gross value added in basic prices* 537,428; Indirect taxes, less subsidies 76,702; *GDP in purchasers' values* 614,130.

Balance of Payments (US $ million, 2013): Exports of goods f.o.b. 1,375.9; Imports of goods f.o.b. −1,847.3; *Trade balance* −471.4; Services (net) −307.1; *Balance on goods and services* −778.5; Transfers (net) 353.2; *Current balance* −425.3; Capital account (net) 314.8; Net errors and omissions −8.9; *Overall balance* −119.5.

EXTERNAL TRADE

Principal Commodities (US $ million, 2013): *Imports c.i.f.:* Agricultural machinery 87.8; Building materials 90.7; Chemicals 76.9; Fuel and lubricants 574.7; Industrial machinery 84.5; Transport machinery 70.0; Motor cars 39.4; Total (incl. others) 1,838.3. *Exports f.o.b.:* Fish and shrimps 76.0; Rice 239.8; Sugar 114.2; Timber 38.5; Bauxite 134.6; Gold 648.5; Total (incl. others, incl. re-exports) 1,375.9.

Principal Trading Partners (US $ million, 2012): *Imports:* Canada 43.0; China, People's Republic 194.5; Japan 77.9; Suriname 143.8; Trinidad and Tobago 269.4; United Kingdom 48.9; USA 486.0; Venezuela 336.0; Total (incl. others) 1,969.7. *Exports:* Canada 501.3; Germany 60.0; Jamaica 42.7; Trinidad and Tobago 54.8; Ukraine 23.4; United Kingdom 118.8; USA 295.2; Venezuela 145.9; Total (incl. others) 1,395.7. *2013* (US $ million): Total imports 1,838.3; Total exports 1,375.9.

TRANSPORT

Road Traffic (vehicles in use, 2008): Passenger cars 44,739; Lorries and vans 28,122; Motorcycles and mopeds 37,069. Source: IRF, *World Road Statistics*.

Shipping: *Flag Registered Fleet* (at 31 December 2014): Vessels 60; Total displacement 32,127 grt. Source: Lloyd's List Intelligence (www.lloydslistintelligence.com).

Civil Aviation ('000, 2013): Passengers carried 192.0. Source: World Bank, World Development Indicators database.

TOURISM

Tourist Arrivals: 151,926 in 2010; 156,871 in 2011; 176,642 in 2012.

Tourism Receipts (US $ million, excl. passenger transport): 80 in 2010; 95 in 2011; 64 in 2012.

Source: World Tourism Organization.

COMMUNICATIONS MEDIA

Telephones (2013): 156,805 main lines in use.

Mobile Cellular Telephones (2013): 555,035 subscribers.

Internet Subscribers (2010): 16,400.

Broadband Subscribers (2013): 36,900.

Source: International Telecommunication Union.

EDUCATION

Pre-primary (2011/12): Institutions 442; Teachers 1,601 (males 4, females 1,597); Students 25,543 (males 13,003, females 12,540).

Primary (2011/12): Institutions 436; Teachers 3,635 (males 418, females 3,217); Students 88,106 (males 44,737, females 43,369).

General Secondary (2011/12): Institutions 110; Teachers 3,204 (males 791, females 2,413); Students 67,548 (males 32,791, females 34,757).

Special Education (2011/12): Institutions 6; Teachers 36 (males 2, females 34); Students 647 (males 407, females 240).

Technical and Vocational (2011/12): Institutions 8; Teachers 239 (males 147, females 92); Students 4,548 (males 2,663, females 1,885).

Teacher Training (2011/12): Institutions 1; Teachers 184 (males 67, females 117); Students 1,795 (males 253, females 1,542).

University (2011/12): Institutions 1; Teachers 491 (males 288, females 203); Students 7,338 (males 2,783, females 4,555).

Private Education (2011/12 unless otherwise indicated): Institutions 58 (2009/10); Teachers 1,113 (males 249, females 864); Students 15,777 (males 7,668, females 8,109).

Source: Ministry of Education.

Pupil-Teacher Ratio (primary education, UNESCO estimate): 23.2 in 2011/12 (Source: UNESCO Institute for Statistics).

Adult Literacy Rate (UNESCO estimates): 85.0% (males 82.4%; females 87.3%) in 2009. Source: UN Development Programme, *Human Development Report*.

Directory

The Government

HEAD OF STATE

President: DONALD RAMOTAR (sworn in 3 December 2011).

CABINET
(April 2015)

The PPP/Civic alliance forms the Government.

Prime Minister and Minister of Parliamentary Affairs and Energy: SAMUEL A. HINDS.

Minister of Foreign Affairs: Dr CAROLYN RODRIGUES-BIRKETT.

Minister of Finance: Dr ASHNI K. SINGH.

Minister of Agriculture: Dr LESLIE RAMSAMMY.

Minister of Amerindian Affairs: PAULINE CAMPBELL-SUKHAI.

Minister of Home Affairs: CLEMENT J. ROHEE.

Minister of Legal Affairs and Attorney-General: ANIL NANDLALL.

Minister of Education: PRIYA DEVI MANICKCHAND.

Minister of Health: Dr BHERI S. RAMSARAN.

Minister of Housing and Water: IRFAAN ALI.

Minister of Labour: Dr NANDA K. GOPAUL.

Minister of Human Services and Social Security: JENNIFER I. M. WEBSTER.

Minister of Local Government and Regional Development: NORMAN WHITTAKER.

Minister of Public Service: Dr JENNIFER WESTFORD.

Minister of Public Works: ROBESON BENN.

Minister of Culture, Youth and Sport: Dr FRANK C. S. ANTHONY.

Minister of Natural Resources and the Environment: ROBERT M. PERSAUD.

Minister of Tourism, Industry and Commerce: IRFAAN ALI (acting).

Head of the Presidential Secretariat: Dr ROGER LUNCHEON.

Minister in the Ministry of Finance: JUAN A. EDGHILL.

Minister in the Ministry of Agriculture: ALLI BAKSH.

MINISTRIES

Office of the President: New Garden St, Bourda, Georgetown; tel. 225-7051; fax 226-3395; e-mail opmed@op.gov.gy; internet www.op.gov.gy.

Office of the Prime Minister: Oranapai Towers, Wights Lane, Kingston, Georgetown; tel. 226-6955; fax 226-7573; e-mail opm@networksgy.gy.

Ministry of Agriculture: Regent Rd and Shiv Chanderpaul Dr., POB 1001, Bourda, Georgetown; tel. 227-5049; fax 227-2978; e-mail info@agriculture.gov.gy; internet www.agriculture.gov.gy.

Ministry of Amerindian Affairs: 251–252 Thomas and Quamina Sts, South Cummingsburg, Georgetown; tel. 227-5067; fax 223-1616; e-mail ministryofamerindian@networksgy.com; internet www.amerindian.gov.gy.

Ministry of Culture, Youth and Sport: 71 Main St, North Cummingsburg, Georgetown; tel. 227-7860; fax 225-5067; e-mail mincys@guyana.net.gy; internet www.mcys.gov.gy.

Ministry of Education: 26 Brickdam, Stabroek, POB 1014, Georgetown; tel. 226-3094; fax 225-5570; e-mail moegyweb@yahoo.com; internet www.education.gov.gy.

Ministry of Finance: 49 Main and Urquhart Sts, Kingston, Georgetown; tel. 225-6088; fax 226-1284; e-mail minister@finance.gov.gy; internet www.finance.gov.gy.

Ministry of Foreign Affairs: 254 South Rd and Shiv Chanderpaul Dr., Bourda, Georgetown; tel. 226-1606; fax 225-9192; e-mail minfor@guyana.net.gy; internet www.minfor.gov.gy.

Ministry of Health: Brickdam, Stabroek, Georgetown; tel. 226-5861; fax 225-4505; e-mail moh@sdnp.org.gy; internet www.health.gov.gy.

Ministry of Home Affairs: 6 Brickdam, Stabroek, Georgetown; tel. 225-7270; fax 227-4806; e-mail info@moha.gov.gy; internet moha.gov.gy.

Ministry of Housing and Water: 41 Brickdam and United Nations Pl., Stabroek, Georgetown; tel. 225-7192; fax 227-3455; e-mail minister_housing@yahoo.com; internet www.chpa.gov.gy.

Ministry of Labour, Human Services and Social Security: 1 Water St and Corhill St, Stabroek, Georgetown; tel. 225-0655; fax 227-1308; e-mail psmlhsss@yahoo.com; internet www.mlhsss.gov.gy.

Ministry of Legal Affairs and Office of the Attorney-General: 95 Carmichael St, North Cummingsburg, Georgetown; tel. 226-2616; fax 225-4809; e-mail legalaffairsps@yahoo.com; internet legalaffairs.gov.gy.

Ministry of Local Government and Regional Development: De Winkle Bldg, Fort St, Kingston, Georgetown; tel. 225-8621; fax 226-5070; e-mail mlgrdps@telsnetgy.net.

Ministry of Natural Resources and the Environment: Shiv Chanderpaul Dr., Bourda, Georgetown; tel. 225-5285; fax 223-0969; e-mail minister@nre.gov.gy; internet www.nre.gov.gy.

Ministry of Public Service: 164 Waterloo St, North Cummingsburg, Georgetown; tel. 227-1193; fax 227-2700; e-mail psm@sdnp.org.gy.

Ministry of Public Works: Wights Lane, Kingston, Georgetown; tel. 226-1875; fax 225-6954; e-mail minoth@networksgy.com.

Ministry of Tourism, Industry and Commerce: 229 South Rd, Lacytown, Georgetown; tel. 226-2505; fax 225-9898; e-mail ministry@mintic.gov.gy; internet www.mintic.gov.gy.

President and Legislature

NATIONAL ASSEMBLY

Speaker: RAPHAEL TROTMAN.

Election, 28 November 2011

Party	% of votes	Seats
People's Progressive Party/Civic	48.6	32
A Partnership for National Unity*	40.8	26
Alliance for Change	10.3	7
The United Force	0.2	—
Total	100.0	65

* A coalition comprising the Guyana Action Party, the National Front Alliance, the People's National Congress Reform and the Working People's Alliance.

Under Guyana's system of proportional representation, the nominated candidate of the party receiving the most number of votes is elected to the presidency. Thus, on 3 December 2011 the candidate of the PPP/Civic alliance, DONALD RAMOTAR, was inaugurated as President.

Election Commission

Guyana Elections Commission (GECOM): 41 High and Cowan Sts, Kingston, Georgetown; tel. 225-0277; fax 226-0924; e-mail gecomfeedback@webworksgy.com; internet www.gecom.org.gy; f. 2000; appointed by the Pres., partly in consultation with the leader of the opposition; Chair. Dr STEVE SURUJBALLY; Chief Elections Officer KEITH LOWENFIELD.

Political Organizations

Alliance for Change (AFC): 139 Fourth St, Campbellville, Georgetown; tel. 231-8183; fax 225-0455; e-mail office@voteafc.com; internet www.afcguyana.com; f. 2005; contesting 2015 elections in alliance with the Partnership for National Unity; Leader KHEMRAJ RAMJATTAN.

Healing the Nation Theocracy Party (HTNT): Georgetown; f. 2015; Pres. ALFRED PARK; Gen. Sec. RAS LEON SAUL.

A Partnership for National Unity (APNU): 121 Regent Rd, Bourda, Georgetown; e-mail info@apnuguyana.com; internet www.apnuguyana.com; f. 2011; contesting 2015 elections in coalition with Alliance for Change; Leader Brig.-Gen. (retd) DAVID GRANGER; comprises the following parties:

Guyana Action Party (GAP).

National Front Alliance: Georgetown; f. 2000; comprises the National Democratic Movt and National Republican Party.

People's National Congress Reform (PNCR): Congress Pl., Sophia, POB 10330, Georgetown; tel. 225-7852; fax 225-2704; e-mail pnc@guyana-pnc.org; internet www.pncrguyana.com; f. 1957 as People's National Congress following split with the PPP; present name adopted in 2006; Leader ROBERT H. O. CORBIN; Chair. BISHWAISHWAR RAMSAROOP; Gen. Sec. OSCAR E. CLARKE.

Working People's Alliance (WPA): Walter Rodney House, 80 Croal St, Stabroek, Georgetown; tel. and fax 225-3679; originally popular pressure group, became political party 1979; independent Marxist; Leaders Dr CLIVE THOMAS, Dr RUPERT ROOPNARINE.

People's Progressive Party/Civic (PPP/Civic): Freedom House, 41 Robb St, Lacytown, Georgetown; tel. 227-2095; fax 227-2096; e-mail pr@ppp-civic.org; internet www.ppp-civic.org; f. 1950; Marxist-Leninist; Gen. Sec. DONALD RAMOTAR.

Organisation for the Victory of the People (OVP): Georgetown; Leader GERALD A. PERREIRA.

The United Force (TUF): Unity House, 95 Robb and New Garden Sts, Bourda, Georgetown; tel. 226-2596; fax 225-2973; f. 1960; right-wing; Leader MANZOOR NADIR.

The United Republican Party, the Independent Party and the National Independence Party also registered to contest the 2015 general election.

Diplomatic Representation

EMBASSIES AND HIGH COMMISSIONS IN GUYANA

Argentina: 66 Brummel Pl., Stabroek, Georgetown; tel. 231-9521; fax 231-9505; e-mail eguya@mrecic.gov.ar; Ambassador LUIS MARTINO.

Brazil: 308 Church St, Queenstown, POB 10489, Georgetown; tel. 225-7970; fax 226-9063; e-mail brasemb@networksgy.com; Ambassador LINEU PUPO DE PAULA.

Canada: High and Young Sts, POB 10880, Georgetown; tel. 227-2081; fax 225-8380; e-mail grgtn@international.gc.ca; internet www.canadainternational.gc.ca/guyana; High Commissioner NICOLE GILES.

China, People's Republic: Lot 2, Botanic Gardens, Mandela Ave, Georgetown; tel. 227-1651; fax 225-9228; e-mail prcemb@networks.gy.com; internet gy.china-embassy.org/eng; Ambassador ZHANG LIMIN.

Cuba: 46 High St, POB 10268, Kingston, Georgetown; tel. 225-1883; fax 226-1824; e-mail emguyana@networksgy.com; internet www.cubadiplomatica.cu/guyana; Ambassador JULIO CÉSAR GONZÁLES MARCHANTE.

India: 307 Church St, Queenstown, Georgetown; tel. 226-3996; fax 225-7012; e-mail hoc.georgetown@mea.gov.in; internet www.hcigeorgetown.org.gy; High Commissioner VENKATACHALAM MAHALINGAM.

Mexico: 44 Brickdam, Stabroek, Georgetown; tel. 226-3987; fax 226-3722; e-mail mexicoembassygy@gmail.com; internet embamex.sre.gob.mx/guyana; Ambassador FRANCISCO OLGUIN.

Russian Federation: 3 Public Rd, Kitty, Georgetown; tel. 226-9773; fax 227-2975; e-mail embrus.guyana@mail.ru; internet www.guyana.mid.ru; Ambassador NIKOLAY SMIRNOV.

Suriname: 171 Peter Rose and Crown Sts, Queenstown, Georgetown; tel. 226-7844; fax 225-0759; e-mail surnmemb@gol.net.gy; Ambassador NISHA KURBAN-BABU.

United Kingdom: 44 Main St, POB 10849, Georgetown; tel. 226-5881; fax 225-3555; e-mail bhcguyana@networksgy.com; internet ukinguyana.fco.gov.uk; High Commissioner JAMES GREGORY QUINN.

USA: 100 Young and Duke Sts, POB 10507, Kingston, Georgetown; tel. 225-4900; fax 225-8497; e-mail usembassy@hotmail.com; internet georgetown.usembassy.gov; Chargé d'affaires a.i. BRYAN D. HUNT.

Venezuela: 296 Thomas St, South Cummingsburg, Georgetown; tel. 226-1543; fax 225-3241; e-mail embveguy@gol.net.gy; Ambassador REINA MARGARITA ARRATIA DIAZ.

Judicial System

The Judicature of Guyana comprises the Supreme Court of Judicature, which consists of the Court of Appeal and the High Court (both of which are superior courts of record), and a number of Courts of Summary Jurisdiction.

The Court of Appeal consists of the Chancellor as President, the Chief Justice, and such number of Justices of Appeal as may be prescribed by the National Assembly.

The High Court of the Supreme Court consists of the Chief Justice as President of the Court and Puisne Judges. Its jurisdiction is both original and appellate. It has criminal jurisdiction in matters brought before it on indictment. The High Court of the Supreme Court has unlimited jurisdiction in civil matters and exclusive jurisdiction in probate, divorce and admiralty and certain other matters. In April 2005 the Caribbean Court of Justice was inaugurated, in Port of Spain, Trinidad and Tobago, as Guyana's highest court of appeal.

A magistrate has jurisdiction to determine claims where the amount involved does not exceed a certain sum of money, specified by law. Appeal lies to the Full Court.

Chancellor of the Judiciary: CARL SINGH (acting).

Chief Justice: IAN CHANG (acting).

Attorney-General: ANIL NANDLALL.

Religion

CHRISTIANITY

Guyana Council of Churches: 26 Durban St, Lodge, Georgetown; tel. 227-5126; e-mail bishopedghill@hotmail.com; f. 1967 by merger of the Christian Social Council (f. 1937) and the Evangelical Council (f. 1960); 15 mem. churches, 1 assoc. mem.; Chair. Rev. FRANCIS DEAN ALLEYNE.

The Anglican Communion

Anglicans in Guyana are adherents of the Church in the Province of the West Indies, comprising eight dioceses. The Archbishop of the Province is the Bishop of the North Eastern Caribbean and Aruba, resident in St John's, Antigua and Barbuda. The diocese of Guyana also includes French Guiana and Suriname. According to the latest available census figures, Anglicans constitute 7% of the population.

Bishop of Guyana: Rt Rev. CORNELL JEROME MOSS, Church House, 49 Barrack St, POB 10949, Georgetown 1; tel. and fax 226-4183; e-mail dioofguy@networksgy.com.

The Baptist Church

Baptist Convention of Guyana: POB 10149, Georgetown; tel. 226-0428; 33 mem. churches, 1,823 mems.

The Lutheran Church

Evangelical Lutheran Church in Guyana: Lutheran Courts, Berbice, POB 40, New Amsterdam; tel. and fax 333-6479; e-mail sjgoolsarran@gmail.com; internet www.elcguyana.org; f. 1947; 13,000 mems; Pres. Rev. MOSES PRASHAD.

The Roman Catholic Church

Guyana comprises the single diocese of Georgetown, suffragan to the archdiocese of Port of Spain, Trinidad and Tobago. According to the latest available census (2002), some 8% of the population are Roman Catholics. The Bishop participates in the Antilles Episcopal Conference Secretariat, currently based in Port of Spain, Trinidad.

Bishop of Georgetown: FRANCIS DEAN ALLEYNE, Bishop's House, 27 Brickdam, POB 101488, Stabroek, Georgetown; tel. 226-4469; fax 225-8519; e-mail rcbishop@networksgy.com; internet www.rcdiocesegy.org.

Seventh-day Adventists
According to the 2002 census, 5% of the population are Seventh-day Adventists. The Guyana Conference is a member of the Caribbean Union Conference and comprises two congregations and 137 churches.

Guyana Conference: 222 Peter Rose and Lance Gibbs Sts, Queenstown, POB 10191, Georgetown; tel. 226-3313; fax 223-8142; e-mail info@guyanaconference.org; internet guyanaconference.org; 50,291 mems in 2007; 173 churches in 23 pastoral districts; Pres. Pastor RICHARD JAMES.

Other Christian Churches
According to the 2002 census, 17% of the population are Pentecostal Christians. Other denominations active in Guyana include the African Methodist Episcopal Church, the African Methodist Episcopal Zion Church, the Church of God, the Church of the Nazarene, the Ethiopian Orthodox Church, the Guyana Baptist Mission, the Guyana Congregational Union, the Guyana Presbyterian Church, the Hallelujah Church, the Methodist Church in the Caribbean and the Americas, the Moravian Church, and the Presbytery of Guyana.

HINDUISM
According to the 2002 census, Hindus constitute 28% of the population.

Guyana Hindu Dharmic Sabha (Hindu Religious Centre): 392–393 Ganges St, Prashad Nagar, Demerara-Mahaica; tel. 227-6181; e-mail ghds@ymail.com; f. 1974; Pres. VINDHYA VASINI PERSAUD.

ISLAM
Muslims in Guyana comprise 7% of the population, according to the 2002 census.

Central Islamic Organization of Guyana (CIOG): M.Y.O. Bldg, Woolford Ave, Thomas Lands, POB 10245, Georgetown; tel. 225-8654; fax 227-2475; e-mail contact@ciog.org.gy; internet www.ciog.org.gy; Pres. Haji S. M. NASIR; Dir of Education QAYS ARTHUR.

Guyana United Sad'r Islamic Anjuman: 157 Alexander St, Kitty, POB 10715, Georgetown; tel. 226-9620; e-mail khalid@gusia.org; f. 1936; 120,000 mems; Pres. Haji A. HAFIZ RAHAMAN.

BAHÁ'Í FAITH
National Spiritual Assembly: 220 Charlotte St, Bourda, Georgetown; tel. and fax 226-5952; e-mail secretariat@gy.bahai.org; internet gy.bahai.org; incorporated in 1976; Nat. Sec. CHRISTINE BRISPORT.

The Press
DAILIES
Guyana Chronicle: 2A Lama Ave, Bel Air Park, POB 11, Georgetown; tel. 227-5204; fax 227-5208; e-mail gm@guyanachronicle.com; internet www.guyanachronicleonline.com; f. 1881; govt-owned; also produces weekly *Sunday Chronicle* (tel. 226-3243); Gen. Man. MICHAEL GORDON; Editor-in-Chief MAHENDRA (MARK) RAMOTAR; circ. 23,000 (weekdays), 43,000 (Sun.).

Guyana Times: 238 Camp and Quamina Sts, Georgetown; tel. 225-5128; fax 225-5134; e-mail news@guyanatimesgy.com; internet www.guyanatimesgy.com; f. 2008; owned by Queen's Atlantic Investment Inc; Editor NIGEL WILLIAMS.

Kaieteur News: 24 Saffon St, Charlestown, Georgetown; tel. 225-8465; fax 225-8473; e-mail kaieteurnews@yahoo.com; internet www.kaieteurnewsonline.com; f. 1994; independent; Editor-in-Chief ADAM HARRIS; Publr GLENN LALL; daily circ. 19,000, Fri. 25,000, Sun. 32,000.

Stabroek News: E1/2 46–47 Robb St, Lacytown, Georgetown; tel. 227-5197; fax 226-2549; e-mail stabroeknews@stabroeknews.com; internet www.stabroeknews.com; f. 1986; also produces weekly *Sunday Stabroek*; liberal independent; Editor-in-Chief ANAND PERSAUD; circ. 14,100 (weekdays), 26,400 (Sun.).

WEEKLIES AND PERIODICALS
The Catholic Standard: 222 South and Wellington Sts, Queenstown, POB 10720, Georgetown; tel. 226-2195; fax 226-2292; e-mail catholicstandardgy@gmail.com; f. 1905; organ of the Roman Catholic church; weekly; Editor COLIN SMITH; circ. 4,000.

The Official Gazette of Guyana: Guyana National Printers Ltd, Lot 1, Public Rd, La Penitence, Georgetown; tel. 226-2616; fax 225-4809; internet www.officialgazette.gov.gy; govt-owned; weekly; circ. 450.

PRESS ASSOCIATION
Guyana Press Association (GPA): 82C Duke St, Kingston, Georgetown; tel. 623-5430; fax 223-6625; e-mail gpaexecutive@gmail.com; f. 1945; affiliated with the Asscn of Caribbean Media Workers; Pres. GORDON MOSELEY.

NEWS AGENCY
Guyana Government Information Agency: Area B, Homestretch Ave, D'Urban Backlands, Georgetown; tel. 226-6715; fax 226-4003; e-mail gina@gina.gov.gy; internet www.gina.gov.gy; f. 1993; Dir NEAZ SUBHAN.

Publishers
Guyana National Printers Ltd: 1 Public Rd, La Penitence, POB 10256, Greater Georgetown; tel. 225-3623; e-mail gnpl@guyana.net.gy; f. 1939; govt-owned.

Guyana Publications Inc: E 1/2 46–47 Robb St, Lacytown, Georgetown; tel. 226-5197; fax 226-3237; e-mail info@stabroeknews.com; internet www.stabroeknews.com; publrs of *Stabroek News* and *Sunday Stabroek*; Chair. Dr IAN MCDONALD.

Broadcasting and Communications
TELECOMMUNICATIONS
Broadband Inc: Georgetown; tel. 226-4114; e-mail support@bbgy.com; internet www.bbgy.com; f. 2002; internet service provider; Exec. Dir NAVINDRA NARINE.

Digicel Guyana: Fort & Barrack St, Kingston, Georgetown; tel. 669-2677; e-mail guy_ccfrontoffice@digicelgroup.com; internet www.digicelguyana.com; f. 1999 as Trans-World Telecom; acquired by Digicel in 2006; operates Celstar and U-Mobile brands; CEO GREGORY DEAN.

E-Networks Inc: 220 Camp St, North Cummingsburg, Georgetown; tel. 225-1461; fax 225-1412; e-mail info@ewirelessgy.com; internet www.ewirelessgy.com; f. 2004; internet service provider; Man. Dir VISHOK PERSAUD.

Guyana Telephones and Telegraph Company (GT & T): 79 Brickdam, POB 10628, Georgetown; tel. 226-0053; fax 226-7269; e-mail pubcomm@gtt.co.gy; internet www.gtt.co.gy; f. 1991; fmrly state-owned Guyana Telecommunications Corpn; 80% owned by Atlantic Tele-Network (USA); CEO JOSEPH GOVINDA SINGH.

Regulatory Authority
National Frequency Management Unit (NFMU): 190 Charlotte St, Bourda, Georgetown; tel. 226-2233; fax 226-7661; e-mail info@nfmu.gov.gy; internet www.nfmu.gov.gy; f. 1990.

BROADCASTING
Radio
Hits and Jams 94.1 Boom FM: 206 Lance Gibbs St, Queenstown, Georgetown; tel. 227-0580; f. 2013; part of the HJ Entertainment Group; Dirs RAWLE FERGUSON, KERWIN BOLLERS.

National Communications Network (NCN): see Television; operates 3 channels: Hot FM, Radio Roraima and Voice of Guyana.

Radio Guyana Inc. (RGI): TVG, Camp and Quamina St, South Cummingsburg, Georgetown; internet radioguyanafm89.com; f. 2012; part of Queens Atlantic Investment Inc (QAII); Pres. Dr RANJISINGHI (BOBBY) RAMROOP.

Television
The transition from analogue to digital television was scheduled to begin in 2016 and to be completed by 2020.

CNS Television Six (CNS6): 43 Robb and Wellington Sts, Lacytown, Georgetown; tel. 226-5462; fax 227-3050; e-mail sharma@cns6.tv; internet www.cns6.tv; f. 1992; privately owned; Man. Dir CHANDRANARINE SHARMA.

Multi Technology Vision Inc (Channel 14/Cable 65): 218 Upper Oronoque and Charlotte Sts, Georgetown; tel. 226-3593; f. 2012; Gen. Man. MARTIN GOOLSARRAN.

National Communications Network (NCN): Homestretch Ave, D'Urban Park, Georgetown; tel. 227-1566; fax 226-2253; e-mail feedback@ncnguyana.com; internet www.ncnguyana.com; f. 2004 following merger of Guyana Broadcasting Corpn (f. 1979) and Guyana Television and Broadcasting Co (f. 1993); govt-owned; operates 3 radio channels and 6 TV channels; CEO RAYMOND AZEEZ (acting).

Regulatory Authority

Guyana National Broadcast Authority (GNBA): Georgetown; f. 2012; licensing authority; Chair. BIBI SAFORA SHADDICK.

Finance

(cap. = capital; res = reserves; dep. = deposits; m. = million; brs = branches; amounts in Guyana dollars)

BANKING

Central Bank

Bank of Guyana: 1 Church St and Ave of the Republic, POB 1003, Georgetown; tel. 226-3250; fax 227-2965; e-mail communications@bankofguyana.org.gy; internet www.bankofguyana.org.gy; f. 1965; cap. 1,000m., res 1,125.8m., dep. 140,694.3m. (Dec. 2009); central bank of issue; acts as regulatory authority for the banking sector; Gov. Dr GOBIND GANGA.

Commercial Banks

Bank of Baroda (Guyana) Inc (India): 10 Ave of the Republic and Regent St, POB 10768, Georgetown; tel. 226-4005; fax 225-1691; e-mail bobinc@networksgy.com; internet www.bankofbaroda.com; f. 1966; Man. Dir RAJENDRA KUMAR.

Citizens' Bank Guyana Inc (CBGI): 201 Camp St and Charlotte St, Lacytown, Georgetown; tel. 226-1705; fax 226-1719; e-mail info@citizensbankgy.com; internet www.citizensbankgy.com; f. 1994; 51% owned by Banks DIH; total assets 18,773m. (Sept. 2007); Chair. CLIFFORD B. REIS; Man. Dir ETON M. CHESTER; 4 brs.

Demerara Bank Ltd: 230 Camp and South Sts, POB 12133, Georgetown; tel. 225-0610; fax 225-0601; e-mail banking@demerarabank.com; internet www.demerarabank.com; f. 1994; cap. 450.0m., res 345.7m., dep. 17,899.9m. (Sept. 2007); Chair. YESU PERSAUD; CEO PRAVINCHANDRA S. DAVE.

Guyana Bank for Trade and Industry Ltd (GBTI): High and Young Sts, Kingston, POB 10280, Georgetown; tel. 231-4401; fax 231-4411; e-mail banking@gbtibank.com; internet www.gbtibank.com; f. 1987 to absorb the operations of Barclays Bank; cap. 800m., res 486.9m., dep. 84,348m. (Dec. 2013); Chair. ROBIN STOBY; CEO JOHN TRACEY; 9 brs.

Republic Bank (Guyana): Promenade Court, 155–156 New Market St, North Cummingsburg, Georgetown; tel. 223-7938; fax 227-2921; e-mail email@republicguyana.com; internet www.republicguyana.com; f. 1984; 51% owned by Republic Bank Ltd, Port of Spain, Trinidad and Tobago; acquired Guyana National Co-operative Bank in 2003; name changed from National Bank of Industry and Commerce in 2006; cap. 300m., res 1,531.3m., dep. 117,307m. (Sept. 2013); Chair. NIGEL M. BAPTISTE; Man. Dir JOHN N. ALVES; 10 brs.

Scotiabank (Canada): 104 Carmichael St, POB 10631, Georgetown; Georgetown; tel. 225-9222; fax 225-9309; e-mail bns.guyana@scotiabank.com; internet www.guyana.scotiabank.com; f. 1968; Country Man. AMANDA ST AUBYN; 5 brs.

Merchant Bank

Guyana Americas Merchant Bank Inc (GAMBI): GBTI Bldg, 138 Regent St, Lacytown, Georgetown; tel. 223-5193; fax 223-5195; e-mail gambi@networksgy.com; f. 2001; fmrly known as Guyana Finance Corpn Ltd; Man. Dir RICHARD ISAVA.

STOCK EXCHANGE

Guyana Association of Securities Companies and Intermediaries Inc (GASCI): Hand-in-Hand Bldg, 1 Ave of the Republic, Georgetown; tel. 223-6176; fax 223-6175; e-mail info@gasci.com; internet www.gasci.com; f. 2001; Chair. NIKHIL RAMKARRAN; Gen. Man. GEORGE EDWARDS.

INSURANCE

Caricom General Insurance Co Inc: Lot A, Ocean View Dr., Ruimzeight Gardens, Ruimzeight, West Coast Demerara; tel. 269-0020; fax 269-0022; e-mail mail@guyanainsurance.com; internet www.caricominsurance.com; f. 1997; fmrly Guyana Fire, Life & General Insurance Co Ltd; CEO SAISNARINE KOWLESSAR; Pres. KULWANTIE SOOKRAM.

Demerara Mutual Life Assurance Society Ltd: 61–62 Robb St and Ave of the Republic, Georgetown; tel. 225-8991; fax 225-8995;

e-mail demlife@demeraramutual.com; internet demeraramutual.net; f. 1891; Chair. RICHARD B. FIELDS; CEO KEITH CHOLMONDELEY.

Diamond Fire and General Insurance Inc: 44B High St, Kingston, Georgetown; tel. 223-9771; fax 223-9770; e-mail diamondins@solutions2000.net; f. 2000; privately owned; Asst Man. RABINDRA-NAUTH BASIL.

Guyana Co-operative Insurance Service (GCIS): 47 Main St, Georgetown; tel. 225-9153; f. 1976; 67% owned by the Hand-in-Hand Group.

Guyana and Trinidad Mutual Group of Insurance Companies (GTM): 27–29 Robb and Hinck St, Georgetown; tel. 225-7910; fax 225-9397; e-mail gtmgroup@gtm-gy.com; internet www.gtm-gy.com; f. 1880; Chair. HAROLD DAVIS; Man. Dir ROGER YEE.

Hand-in-Hand Mutual Fire and Life Group: Hand-in-Hand Bldg, 1–4 Ave of the Republic, POB 10188, Georgetown; tel. 225-1865; fax 225-7519; e-mail info@hihgy.com; internet www.hihgy.com; f. 1865; fire and life insurance; Chair. JOHN G. CARPENTER; CEO KEITH EVELYN.

Association

Insurance Association of Guyana: South 0.5, 14 Pere St, Kitty, Georgetown; tel. 226-3514; f. 1968.

Trade and Industry

GOVERNMENT AGENCIES

Environmental Protection Agency, Guyana: Ganges St, Sophia, Georgetown; tel. 225-5467; fax 225-5481; e-mail epa@epaguyana.org; internet www.epaguyana.org; f. 1988 as Guyana Agency for the Environment; renamed 1996; Exec. Dir INDARJIT RAMDASS.

Guyana Marketing Corporation: 87 Robb and Alexander Sts, Lacytown, Georgetown; tel. 226-8255; fax 227-4114; e-mail info@newgmc.com; internet www.newgmc.com; Gen. Man. NIZAM HASSAN.

Guyana Office for Investment (Go-Invest): 190 Camp and Church Sts, Georgetown; tel. 225-0653; fax 225-0655; e-mail goinvest@goinvest.gov.gy; internet www.goinvest.gov.gy; f. 1994; CEO KEITH BURROWES.

National Industrial and Commercial Investment Ltd (NICIL): 126 Barrack St, Kingston, Georgetown; tel. 226-0576; e-mail winston.brassington@gmail.com; internet www.privatisation.gov.gy; f. 1991; state-run privatization unit; Exec. Dir WINSTON BRASSINGTON.

DEVELOPMENT ORGANIZATION

Institute of Private Enterprise Development (IPED): 253–254 South Rd, Bourda, Georgetown; tel. 225-8949; fax 226-4675; e-mail iped@solutions2000.net; internet www.ipedgy.com; f. 1986; total loans provided $ G1,400m. (2007); Chair. YESU PERSAUD; Exec. Dir RAMESH PERSAUD.

CHAMBER OF COMMERCE

Georgetown Chamber of Commerce and Industry (GCCI): 156 Waterloo St, North Cummingsburg, Georgetown; tel. 225-5846; fax 226-3519; e-mail info@gcci.gy; internet www.gcci.gy; f. 1889; Pres. LANCE HINDS; 130 mems.

INDUSTRIAL AND TRADE ASSOCIATIONS

Guyana Rice Development Board: 116–17 Cowan St, Kingston, Georgetown; tel. 225-8717; fax 225-6486; internet www.grdb.gy; f. 1994 to assume operations of Guyana Rice Export Board and Guyana Rice Grading Centre; Gen. Man. JAGNARINE SINGH.

National Dairy and Development Programme (NDDP): c/o Lands and Surveys Bldg, 22 Upper Hadfield St, Durban Backlands, POB 10367, Georgetown; tel. 225-7107; fax 226-3020; e-mail nddp@sdnp.org.gy; f. 1984; aims to increase domestic milk and beef production; Programme Dir MEER BACCHUS.

EMPLOYERS' ASSOCIATIONS

Consultative Association of Guyanese Industry Ltd: 157 Waterloo St, POB 10730, North Cummingsburg, Georgetown; tel. 225-7170; fax 227-0725; e-mail info@cagi.org.gy; internet www.cagi.org.gy; f. 1962; Chair. YESU PERSAUD; Exec. Dir SAMUEL JERRY GOOLSARRAN; 62 mems.

Forest Products Association of Guyana: 157 Waterloo St, Cummingsburg, Georgetown; tel. 226-9848; fax 226-2832; e-mail fpasect@guyana.net.gy; internet www.fpaguyana.org; f. 1944; 62 mem. cos; Pres. KHALAWAN CORT; Exec. Officer JANICE CRAWFORD.

Guyana Manufacturing and Services Association Ltd (GMSA): National Exhibition Centre, Sophia, Georgetown; tel.

219-0072; fax 219-0073; e-mail gma_guyana@yahoo.com; f. 1967 as the Guyana Mfrs' Asscn; name changed in 2005 to reflect growth in services sector; 190 mems; Pres. CLINTON WILLIAMS.

Guyana Rice Producers' Association (GRPA): 126 Parade and Barrack St, Georgetown; tel. 226-4411; fax 223-7249; e-mail grpa.riceproducers@networksgy.com; f. 1946; non-govt org.; 18,500 mems; Pres. LEEKHA RAMBRICH; Gen. Sec. DHARAMKUMAR SEERAJ.

UTILITIES
Regulatory Authority

Guyana Energy Agency (GEA): 295 Quamina St, POB 903, South Cummingsburg, Georgetown; tel. 226-0394; fax 226-5227; e-mail gea@gea.gov.gy; internet www.gea.gov.gy; f. 1998 as successor to Guyana National Energy Authority; CEO MAHENDRA SHARMA.

Electricity

Guyana Power and Light Inc (GPL): 40 Main St, POB 10390, Georgetown; tel. 224-4618; fax 227-1978; e-mail bharat.dindyal@gplinc.com; internet www.gplinc.com; f. 1999; fmrly Guyana Electricity Corpn; state-owned; Chair. WINSTON BRASSINGTON; CEO BHARAT DINDYAL; 1,200 employees.

Water

Guyana Water Inc (GWI): Vllissengen Rd and Church St, Bel Air Park, Georgetown; tel. 227-8701; fax 227-8718; e-mail customercallcentre@gwi.gy; internet www.gwiguyana.com; f. 2002 following merger of Guyana Water Authority and Georgetown Sewerage and Water Comm.; operated by Severn Trent Water International (United Kingdom); Chair. Dr RAMESH DOOKHOO; CEO SHAIK BAKSH.

TRADE UNIONS

Federation of Independent Trade Unions of Guyana (FITUG): Georgetown; f. 1988; c. 35,000 mems; Pres. CARVIL DUNCAN; Gen. Sec. KENNETH JOSEPH.

Guyana Trades Union Congress (GTUC): Critchlow Labour College, Woolford Ave, Non-pareil Park, Georgetown; tel. 226-2481; fax 227-0254; e-mail gtucorg@yahoo.com; f. 1940; national trade union body; 13 affiliated unions; c. 15,000 mems; affiliated to the International Trade Union Confederation; Pres. LESLIE GONSALVES; Gen. Sec. LINCOLN LEWIS.

Transport
RAILWAY

There are no public railways in Guyana. Until the early 21st century the 15-km Linmine Railway was used for the transportation of bauxite from Linden to Coomaka.

ROADS

The coastal strip has a well-developed road system. There were an estimated 7,970 km (4,952 miles) of paved and good-weather roads and trails. A bridge across the Takutu river, linking Guyana to Brazil, was inaugurated in 2009, while a bridge over the Berbice river was completed in the previous year. In 2012 Guyana and Suriname asked the Inter-American Development Bank (IDB) to fund a feasibility study of a bridge across the Corentyne river. The IDB approved another US $66m. for a road network upgrade and expansion programme in the same year.

SHIPPING

Guyana's principal ports are at Georgetown and New Amsterdam. The port at Linden serves for the transportation of bauxite products. A ferry service is operated between Guyana and Suriname. Communications with the interior are chiefly by river, although access is hindered by rapids and falls. There are 1,077 km (607 miles) of navigable rivers. At 31 December 2014 the flag registered fleet comprised 60 vessels, totalling 32,127 grt.

Transport and Harbours Department: Water St, Stabroek, Georgetown; tel. 225-9350; fax 227-8445; e-mail t&hd@solutions2000.net; Gen. Man. MARCLENE MERCHANT.

Shipping Association of Guyana Inc (SAG): 10–11 Lombard St, Werk-en-Rust, Georgetown; tel. 226-2169; fax 226-9656; e-mail saginc@networksgy.com; internet www.shipping.org.gy; f. 1952; non-governmental forum; Chair. ANDREW ASTWOOD; Sec. IAN D'ANJOU; members:

Guyana National Industrial Company Inc (GNIC): 1–9 Lombard St, Charlestown, POB 10520, Georgetown; tel. 225-5398; fax

226-0432; e-mail gnicadmin@futurenetgy.com; metal foundry, ship building and repair, agents for a number of international transport cos; privatized in 1995; CEO CLINTON WILLIAMS; Port Man. ALBERT SMITH.

Guyana National Shipping Corporation Ltd: 5–9 Lombard St, La Penitence, POB 10988, Georgetown; tel. 226-1840; fax 225-3815; e-mail agencydivision@gnsc.com; internet www.gnsc.com; fmrly Bookers Shipping Transport and Wharves Ltd; govt-owned since 1976; Man. Dir ANDREW ASTWOOD (acting).

John Fernandes Ltd: 24 Water St, POB 10211, Georgetown; tel. 227-3344; fax 226-1881; e-mail philip@jf-ltd.com; internet www.jf-ltd.com; f. 1959; ship agents, pier operators and stevedore contractors; part of the John Fernandes Group of Cos; Chair. and CEO CHRIS FERNANDES.

CIVIL AVIATION

The main airport, Cheddi Jaggan International Airport, is at Timehri, 42 km (26 miles) from Georgetown. Ogle International Airport, six miles east of Georgetown, also accepts international flights; construction of a 4,000-ft runway was completed in 2013. The regional airline LIAT (based in Antigua and Barbuda, and in which Guyana is a shareholder) provides scheduled passenger and cargo services.

Roraima Airways: R8 Epring Ave, Bel Air Park, Georgetown; tel. 225-9650; fax 225-9648; e-mail ral@roraimaairways.com; internet www.roraimaairways.com; f. 1992; flights to Venezuela and 4 domestic destinations; Man. Dir Capt. GERALD GOUVEIA.

Trans Guyana Airways: Ogle Aerodrome, Ogle, East Coast Demerara; tel. 222-2525; e-mail commercial@transguyana.net; internet www.transguyana.net; f. 1956; internal flights to 22 destinations; Dir Capt. GERARD GONSALVES.

Tourism

Despite the beautiful scenery in the interior of the country, Guyana has limited tourist facilities, although during the 1990s the country began to develop its considerable potential as an eco-tourism destination. The total number of visitors to Guyana in 2012 was 176,642. Expenditure by tourists amounted to some US $64m. in the same year.

Guyana Tourism Authority: National Exhibition Centre, Sophia, Georgetown; tel. 219-0094; fax 219-0093; e-mail info@guyana-tourism.com; internet www.guyana-tourism.com; f. 2003; state-owned; Dir INDRANAUTH HARALSINGH.

Tourism and Hospitality Association of Guyana (THAG): 157 Waterloo St, Georgetown; tel. 225-0807; fax 225-0817; e-mail thag@networksgy.com; internet www.exploreguyana.com; f. 1992; Pres. PAUL STEPHENSON; Exec. Dir TREINA BUTTS.

Defence

The armed forces are united in a single service, the Combined Guyana Defence Force, which consisted of some 1,100 men (of whom 900 were in the army, 100 in the air force and about 100 in the navy), as assessed at November 2014. In addition there were reserve forces numbering some 670 (army 500, navy 170). The Guyana People's Militia, a paramilitary reserve force, totalled about 1,500. The President is the Commander-in-Chief.

Defence Budget: An estimated $ G7,930m. (US $37m.) in 2014.

Chief-of-Staff: Brig.-Gen. MARK PHILLIPS.

Education

Education is free and compulsory for children aged between five years and 15 years of age. Children receive primary education for a period of six years; enrolment at primary schools in 2012 included 72% of children in the relevant age-group. Secondary education, beginning at 12 years of age, lasts for up to seven years in a general secondary school. In 2011/12 an estimated 67,548 pupils were enrolled in state secondary schools. Higher education is provided by eight technical and vocational schools and one teacher training college, in all of which 6,343 students were enrolled in 2011/12. The state-run University of Guyana offers degrees, as does the private GreenHeart Medical University. An estimated $ G32,200m. was allocated to the education sector in 2014.

HAITI

Introductory Survey

LOCATION, CLIMATE, LANGUAGE, RELIGION, FLAG, CAPITAL

The Republic of Haiti occupies the western part of the Caribbean island of Hispaniola (the Dominican Republic occupies the remaining two-thirds) and some smaller offshore islands. Cuba, to the west, is less than 80 km away. The climate is tropical but the mountains and fresh sea winds mitigate the heat. Temperatures vary little with the seasons, and the annual average in Port-au-Prince is about 27°C (80°F). The rainy season is from May to November. The official languages are French and Creole. About 55% of the population belong to the Roman Catholic Church, the country's official religion, and other Christian churches are also represented. The folk religion is Voodoo (vodou), a fusion of beliefs involving communication with the spirit world through the medium of trance. The national flag (proportions variable) has two equal horizontal stripes, of dark blue and red. The state flag (proportions 3 by 5) has, in addition, a white rectangular panel containing the national coat of arms (a palm tree, surmounted by a Cap of Liberty and flanked by flags and cannons) in the centre. The capital is Port-au-Prince.

CONTEMPORARY POLITICAL HISTORY

Historical Context

Haiti was first colonized in 1659 by the French, who named the territory Saint-Domingue. French sovereignty was formally recognized by Spain in 1697. Following a period of internal unrest, a successful uprising, begun in 1794 by African-descended slaves, culminated in 1804 with the establishment of Haiti as an independent state, ruled by Jean-Jacques Dessalines, who proclaimed himself Emperor. Hostility between the black population and the mulattos continued throughout the 19th century until, after increasing economic instability, the USA intervened militarily and supervised the government of the country from 1915 to 1934. Mulatto interests retained political ascendancy until 1946, when a black President, Dumarsais Estimé, was installed following a military coup. Following the overthrow of two further administrations, Dr François Duvalier was elected President in 1957.

Domestic Political Affairs

The Duvalier administration soon became a dictatorship, maintaining its authority by means of a notorious private army, popularly called the Tontons Macoutes (Creole for Bogeymen), who used intimidation to crush opposition to the President's rule. In 1964 Duvalier became President-for-Life, and at his death in April 1971 he was succeeded by his 19-year-old son and designated successor, Jean-Claude Duvalier.

At elections held in 1979 almost all seats were won by the official government party, the Parti de l'Unité Nationale. The first municipal elections for 25 years, in 1983, were overshadowed by allegations of fraud and Duvalier's obstruction of opposition parties. No opposition candidates were permitted to contest the general election of February 1984.

In April 1985 Duvalier announced a programme of constitutional reforms, including the eventual appointment of a Prime Minister and the formation of political parties, subject to certain conditions. In September Roger Lafontant, the minister most closely identified with government repression, was dismissed. However, protests organized by the Roman Catholic Church and other religious groups gained momentum, and further measures to curb continued disorder were adopted in January 1986. Duvalier declared martial law.

In February 1986, following intensified public protests, Duvalier fled to exile in France, leaving a National Council of Government (Conseil National Gouvernemental), led by the Chief of Staff of the army, Gen. Henri Namphy, to succeed him. The military-civilian Council appointed a new Cabinet. The National Assembly was dissolved, the Constitution was suspended, and the Tontons Macoutes were disbanded. Namphy announced a timetable to restore constitutional government by February 1988.

The election of members of a Constituent Assembly to revise the Constitution took place in October 1986. The new Constitution was approved by 99.8% of voters in a referendum held in March 1987. An independent Conseil Electoral Provisoire (CEP—Provisional Electoral Council) was subsequently appointed. Presidential and legislative elections were cancelled three hours after voting had begun on 29 November, owing to renewed violence, for which former members of the Tontons Macoutes were believed to be responsible. Elections were rescheduled for 17 January 1988. Leslie Manigat of the Rassemblement des Démocrates Nationaux et Progressistes (RDNP) was declared the winner of the presidential ballot. Opposition leaders alleged that there had been extensive fraud and malpractice.

The Manigat Government was overthrown by disaffected members of the army in June 1988. Gen. Namphy, whom Manigat had attempted to replace as army Chief of Staff, assumed the presidency and appointed a military Cabinet. The Constitution of 1987 was abrogated, and Duvalier's supporters returned to prominence, as did the Tontons Macoutes.

In September 1988 Namphy was ousted in a coup, led by Brig.-Gen. Prosper Avril. In March 1989 Avril partially restored the 1987 Constitution and restated his intention to hold democratic elections. In the following month the Government survived two coup attempts by the Leopard Corps, the country's élite anti-subversion squadron, and the Dessalines battalion, based in Port-au-Prince. Avril resigned as President in March 1990 in response to sustained popular opposition, together with diplomatic pressure from the USA. Power was ceded to the Chief of the General Staff, Hérard Abraham, who subsequently transferred authority to Ertha Pascal-Trouillot, a member of the Supreme Court. Pascal-Trouillot shared power with a 19-member Council of State.

Presidential and legislative elections took place in December 1990. Fr Jean-Bertrand Aristide, a left-wing Roman Catholic priest representing the Front National pour le Changement et la Démocratie (FNCD), won an overwhelming victory in the presidential ballot. His closest rival was Marc Bazin, the candidate of the centre-right Mouvement pour l'Instauration de la Démocratie en Haïti (MIDH). However, the FNCD failed to win a majority of seats in either the Sénat (Senate) or the Chambre des Députés (Chamber of Deputies).

Aristide initiated proceedings in early 1991 to secure the extradition from France of Duvalier to face charges that included embezzlement, abuse of power and murder. Aristide also undertook the reform of the armed forces, and in July Gen. (later Lt-Gen.) Raoul Cédras replaced Abraham as Commander-in-Chief and René Garcia Préval was appointed Prime Minister.

Military coup of 1991

On 30 September 1991 a military junta, led by Gen. Cédras, overthrew the Government. Following international diplomatic intervention, Aristide was allowed to go into exile. The coup was condemned internationally, and an economic embargo was imposed on Haiti by the Organization of American States (OAS, see p. 392). Many hundreds of people were reported to have been killed during the coup. On 7 October military units assembled 29 members of the legislature and coerced them into approving the appointment of Joseph Nerette as interim President.

During the following months the OAS, which continued to recognize Aristide as the legitimate head of state, attempted to negotiate a settlement. However, the two sides remained deadlocked over the conditions for Aristide's return. In February 1992, following OAS-supervised talks in Washington, DC, USA, between Aristide and members of a Haitian legislative delegation, an agreement was signed providing for the installation of René Théodore, leader of the Mouvement pour la Reconstruction Nationale, as Prime Minister. He was to govern in consultation with the exiled Aristide and facilitate his return. However, in March politicians opposed to the accord withdrew from a joint session of the legislature, leaving it inquorate. Following an appeal by Nerette, the Supreme Court declared the agreement null and void, on the grounds that it violated the Constitution by endangering the country's sovereignty. In response, the OAS increased economic sanctions against Haiti.

In May 1992 an agreement providing for the appointment of a new Prime Minister and a multi-party government of national consensus was ratified by the Senate. In June the legislature, in the absence of the FNCD, approved the nomination of Bazin to be Prime Minister. The presidency was left vacant, ostensibly to allow for Aristide's return. A Cabinet, comprising members of most major parties (with the exception of the FNCD), was installed, with the army retaining control of the interior and defence. The appointment of the new Government provoked worldwide condemnation. In September the Government agreed to allow the presence of an OAS commission in Haiti to help to guarantee human rights and assess progress towards a resolution of the crisis.

In June 1993 the USA imposed sanctions against Haiti. Shortly afterwards Bazin resigned as Prime Minister following a loss of legislative support. In July, following OAS- and UN-sponsored talks between Cédras and Aristide, a peace accord was signed, delineating a 10-point agenda for Aristide's reinstatement. Under the terms of the accord, the embargo was to be revoked following the installation of a new Prime Minister (to be appointed by Aristide), Cédras would retire, and a new Commander-in-Chief of the armed forces would be appointed. The accord was approved by Haiti's main political parties. Legislation providing for a series of political and institutional reforms, as required by the accord, was to be enacted, including provision for the transfer of the police force to civilian control.

In August 1993 the legislature ratified the appointment by Aristide of Robert Malval as Prime Minister. In September a concerted campaign of political violence and intimidation by police auxiliaries, known as 'attachés', threatened to undermine the accord. With the upsurge of a Duvalierist tendency, largely embodied by the attachés, a new political party, the Front Revolutionnaire pour l'Avancement et le Progrès d'Haïti (FRAPH), was founded in opposition to any attempt to reinstate Aristide. In September the UN Security Council approved a resolution providing for the immediate deployment of a UN Mission in Haiti. The campaign of political violence by the attachés escalated in October. In response, the US Government ordered six warships into Haitian territorial waters to enforce the reimposed UN embargo. Malval resigned as Prime Minister in December.

A National Reconciliation Conference, proposed by Aristide and excluding the military, took place in Miami, Florida, USA, in January 1994. Following the military regime's failure to meet a revised UN deadline to comply with the terms of the accord, the USA unilaterally imposed further sanctions. In April the US Government abandoned its attempts to effect a compromise solution to the crisis in Haiti in favour of more rigorous economic sanctions. In May the UN Security Council approved a resolution introducing sanctions banning all international trade with Haiti, excluding food and medicine, reducing air links with the country and preventing members of the regime from gaining access to assets held outside Haiti.

In early 1994 the Senate declared the presidency of the Republic vacant, invoking Article 149 of the Constitution, which provides that, in case of prolonged absence by the Head of State, the position may be assumed by the President of the Court of Cassation. In May, with the support of the armed forces, an inquorate legislature appointed Émile Jonassaint provisional President. The appointment by Jonassaint of a new Cabinet was denounced as illegal by the international community. In the following month the USA increased sanctions against Haiti.

In July 1994 the Haitian junta issued an order providing for the expulsion of the UN/OAS international civil commission. On 31 July the UN Security Council approved a resolution authorizing 'all necessary means' to remove the military regime from power and providing for the deployment of a UN peacekeeping force, once stability had been achieved, to remain in Haiti until February 1996, when Aristide's presidential term expired. In August leaders of the Caribbean Community and Common Market (CARICOM, see p. 222) agreed to support a US-led military invasion.

Agreement on a return to civilian rule, 1994

On 19 September 1994 a nominally multinational force composed almost entirely of US troops began a peaceful occupation of Haiti. Under a compromise agreement, the Haitian security forces were to co-operate with the multilateral force in effecting a transition to civilian rule. All sanctions were to be lifted and the military junta granted 'early and honourable retirement' follow-

ing legislative approval of a general amnesty law, or by 15 October at the latest (the date when Aristide was to return from exile to resume his presidency). In September the USA announced the suspension of its unilateral sanctions. A few days later the UN Security Council approved a resolution ending all sanctions against Haiti with effect from the day after the return of Aristide. In October Aristide authorized the amnesty of those involved in the 1991 coup. Later that month the USA formally ended its freeze on the assets of the Haitian military regime. On 12 October Robert Malval resumed office as interim Prime Minister following the resignation of the Jonassaint administration.

Aristide returned to Haiti on 15 October 1994 and appointed Smarck Michel as premier. A new Cabinet, comprising mainly members of the pro-Aristide Organisation Politique Lavalas (OPL), was inaugurated in November. Later that month the legislature approved the separation of the police from the army. In December the formation of a new CEP was completed. In the following month two commissions were established for the restructuring of the armed forces and the new civilian police force.

In January 1995 the UN Security Council adopted a resolution authorizing the deployment of a UN force of 6,000 troops and 900 civil police to succeed the multinational force. The UN Mission in Haiti (UNMIH) was to be responsible for reducing the strength of the army and training both the army and the 4,000-strong (subsequently increased to 6,000) civilian police force, as well as maintaining the 'secure and stable' environment. On 31 March authority was officially transferred to UNMIH.

The first round of legislative, local and municipal elections was held on 25 June 1995. All of the seats were won by the Plateforme Politique Lavalas (PPL), a three-party alliance of the OPL, the Mouvement d'Organisation du Pays (MOP) and the Pati Louvri Baryè (PLB). The results were rejected by the majority of opposition parties, which announced a boycott of the electoral process. In August the FNCD, MIDH and the Parti National Progressiste Révolutionnaire withdrew their respective representatives from the Government in protest against the unresolved electoral dispute. In October Michel resigned as Prime Minister, and was succeeded by Claudette Werleigh.

Presidential election of 1995

At a presidential election held on 17 December 1995, which was boycotted by all the main opposition parties, the candidate endorsed by Aristide, René Préval, was elected with some 88% of the votes cast. He was inaugurated as President in February 1996, and later that month the legislature approved the appointment of Rosny Smarth as Prime Minister.

Partial legislative elections were held in April 1997. The elections were boycotted by many opposition parties, and less than 5% of the electorate participated in the poll. Of the seats contested only two, in the Senate, were decided, both of which were secured by the new political party established by Aristide, La Fanmi Lavalas (FL). The OPL, the majority party in the governing coalition, alleged that members of the CEP had manipulated the election results in favour of the FL. OAS observers supported the claims of electoral irregularities, and, following international pressure, the CEP postponed indefinitely the second round ballot.

Smarth resigned from office on 9 June 1997. However, Préval's nomination of Ericq Pierre as his replacement was rejected by the Chamber of Deputies. In November Préval nominated Hervé Denis, a former minister in the Malval Government, as Prime Minister and announced the establishment of an electoral commission, comprising three independent legal experts, to resolve the electoral deadlock. In January 1998 the legislature rejected the nomination of Denis. In March, following negotiations with supporters of Aristide in the lower house, the OPL (renamed the Organisation du Peuple en Lutte) withdrew its demands for the annulment of the April 1997 elections as a precondition for the approval of a new Prime Minister, and proposed three candidates. However, Préval renominated Denis, whose candidacy was again rejected. In July Préval finally agreed to OPL demands to replace the CEP, subsequently receiving the party's support for the nomination of the Minister of National Education, Jacques-Edouard Alexis, as Prime Minister. Conversely, Aristide's supporters opposed the nomination of Alexis. In August the FL announced that it had formally gone into opposition to the Préval administration.

In December 1998 Alexis was finally declared eligible to become Prime Minister, subject to his nomination being approved by the legislature (which did not occur until November 2000). On 25 March 1999 Préval appointed by decree a new

Cabinet headed by Alexis and including representatives of five small opposition parties. The OPL was not included in the new administration. In June a new CEP announced that it would disregard the results of the flawed partial legislative elections of April 1997; Préval signed a decree annulling the elections in July.

Disputed legislative and presidential elections of 2000

The first round of legislative and municipal elections was held on 21 May 2000; an estimated 60% of the electorate participated. Opposition parties alleged that the results had been manipulated in favour of the FL and demanded the conduct of a fresh ballot. The CEP rejected these claims, but in June the CEP President, Léon Manus, fled to the Dominican Republic, claiming that he had received death threats following his refusal to validate the first round results. According to official first round results, the FL won 16 of the 19 contested seats in the Senate and 26 of the 83 seats in the lower house. The results were criticized as inaccurate by the UN, the OAS and numerous foreign governments. Nevertheless, a second round of voting went ahead on 9 July. A boycott by the 15-party opposition coalition, the Convergence Démocratique (CD), resulted in a low rate of voter participation (an estimated 10%). The FL won 72 seats in the Chamber of Deputies and 18 of the 19 seats contested in the 27-seat upper house. The party also secured control of some 80% of the local councils.

Elections to the presidency and to renew the remaining eight senate seats were held in November 2000 and boycotted by the CD. Aristide was elected President with some 92% of the votes cast. CARICOM estimated a 30% rate of voter participation. The FL also won the eight seats contested in the Senate and the one remaining seat in the Chamber of Deputies.

An eight-member Transition Committee was established in December 2000 to oversee the transfer of power. However, on 7 December the CD announced the formation of an alternative, provisional Government, the Front Alternatif, with the intention of holding fresh elections within two years, provoking widespread violent demonstrations by Aristide supporters. In February 2001 seven of the senators controversially awarded seats in the May 2000 elections resigned. President Aristide named Jean-Marie Chérestal as Prime Minister, and in March a new Cabinet was appointed. In the same month, in an attempt to end the political impasse, Aristide appointed a new CEP to investigate the results of the disputed 2000 elections. The CD was not represented on the Council. In March 2001 it was announced that legislative elections would be held one year early, in November 2002, in order to satisfy international and opposition criticism and to restore the flow of foreign aid, suspended since May 2000. Three days later violent protests broke out in Port-au-Prince, which continued over the following months, and a number of opposition party members were arrested on treason and terrorism charges. In July 2001, following further OAS mediation, the Government stated that legislative and local elections would be held in 2002; an accord was also reached on the composition of the new CEP. The CEP would additionally organize an election to the seven Senate seats vacated in February.

In January 2002 Prime Minister Chérestal resigned his post, following criticism over his inability to resolve the crisis. On 15 March Aristide appointed Senate speaker and prominent FL member Yvon Neptune as Prime Minister. In June Aristide met opposition leaders for the first time in two years, but the talks achieved little progress. Meanwhile, Haiti's accession to full membership of CARICOM in July increased international pressure on Aristide to bring about an end to political instability in the country.

Political unrest intensifies

Political unrest intensified as the November 2002 deadline for the creation of a new CEP passed unfulfilled. Five of the nation's civil groups chose representatives to the CEP in November, but the opposition continued to refuse to do so. In December a general strike led by the opposition was joined by members of Haiti's private sector. Opposition parties united in demanding the resignation of Aristide as the demonstrations continued. Frustrated by the continued political instability, some 184 business and civil society organizations formed the 'Group of 184', which subsequently emerged as a major element of the opposition to Aristide.

The political stalemate between the Government and the opposition remained unresolved in 2003, despite OAS efforts. Most nominees to the nine-member CEP refused to assume their posts, claiming that they were unconvinced that the Government

would not resort to fraudulent practices in future legislative elections, as it had done in 2000. In October at least four people died as a result of violent clashes between police and anti-Government demonstrators in Gonaïves. In December three ministers resigned in protest at the Government's increasing use of violence to suppress the continuing demonstrations.

In January 2004 the mandates of all the members of the Chamber of Deputies and 12 of the 27 members of the Senate expired, leaving Haiti effectively without a legislature and entitling President Aristide to rule by decree. The President pledged to hold legislative elections within six months, an offer rejected by the opposition. CARICOM threatened to impose economic sanctions on Haiti unless President Aristide satisfied a number of conditions, including the formation of a new electoral council and the holding of elections. Aristide subsequently agreed to create a neutral electoral council within two months.

In February 2004, however, anti-Government forces took control of Gonaïves and several other cities in the north of the country. Shortly afterwards, former members of the Haitian armed forces joined the insurrection, enlisting with the rebels to form the Front pour la Libération et la Reconstruction Nationales (FLRN). President Aristide appealed to the international community for assistance in suppressing the rebellion. A plan to end the violence, proposed by France, CARICOM and the OAS, was rejected by the opposition as it failed to provide for the President's departure. At a meeting of the UN Security Council in late February, Caribbean nations called for a multilateral force to be sent to the country in an attempt to bring an end to the violence. However, the USA and France insisted that a political settlement would have to be reached before any forces were deployed to Haiti.

President Aristide finally resigned on 29 February 2004, largely owing to international pressure, and fled to the Central African Republic. In accordance with the Constitution, the President of the Supreme Court, Boniface Alexandre, was sworn in as interim President. On the same day the UN Security Council, acting in response to a request from Alexandre, authorized the establishment of a Multinational Interim Force (MIF) to help to secure law and order prior to the deployment of a larger peacekeeping mission. The MIF eventually comprised around 3,600 troops from the USA, France, Canada and Chile. On 9 March Alexandre and the recently established Council of Elders appointed Gérard Latortue as Prime Minister. The installation of a new Cabinet, composed of independents and technocrats, was generally welcomed by the international community, although CARICOM refused to recognize the new Government.

In April 2004 Latortue, the seven members of the Council of Elders, representatives of the main political organizations (with the exception of the FL) and leaders of civil society organizations signed an agreement on political transition, which provided for the organization of presidential, legislative and municipal elections in 2005, leading to the inauguration of a new administration by February 2006. The agreement also provided for a new CEP, which was inaugurated in May 2004. The FL refused to designate a representative to the CEP, demanding that alleged persecution of its supporters cease.

In April 2004 the UN Secretary-General, Kofi Annan, accused Aristide of having formed an alliance with armed groups, *chimères*, in order to reinforce his position in power and of having condoned their engagement in organized crime, including drugs-smuggling. Aristide went into exile in South Africa in May.

UN peacekeeping force established

A UN peacekeeping force, the UN Stabilization Mission in Haiti (MINUSTAH), was officially established on 1 June 2004 and replaced the MIF later that month. MINUSTAH, which had an authorized strength of 6,700 military personnel and 1,622 civilian police, was to assist the interim administration with preparations for elections and the disarmament and demobilization of armed militias. Meanwhile, the OAS General Assembly approved a resolution declaring Aristide's removal from power to be unconstitutional, although it continued to recognize Latortue's Government.

Former Prime Minister Neptune was arrested in June 2004 in connection with the deaths of demonstrators in the uprising against Aristide's administration in February. In July the Latortue Government issued a deadline of 15 September for armed groups to surrender their weapons. However, the deadline for the surrender of weapons passed unfulfilled.

In September 2004 violence broke out between the police and supporters of Aristide at a rally in Port-au-Prince in support of the former President's return from exile. Clashes continued, and by November at least 80 people had been killed. Tensions were exacerbated by the arrival in the capital of more than 200 former soldiers, intent on confronting the so-called *chimères*. Three members of the FL, including the former President of the Senate, Yvon Feuillé, were arrested in October on suspicion of inciting the violence, and 75 suspected members of the *chimères* were also detained by the national police and MINUSTAH troops in a joint operation. By October only around 2,100 troops of the 6,700-strong authorized MINUSTAH force had been deployed.

In November 2004 the President of the CEP, Roselaure Julien, resigned, claiming that pressure had been exerted on her, particularly by the Group of 184, to allow manipulation of the electoral process. Later that month a five-member Anti-Corruption Commission was established to investigate alleged corruption in 2001–04, as envisaged in the agreement on political transition signed in April. Also in November, CARICOM reaffirmed its decision not to recognize Latortue's Government. Later in the month the UN Security Council approved the extension of MINUSTAH's mandate until 1 June 2005. In December 2004, amid continuing political violence and civil unrest, MINUSTAH troops successfully seized control of two police stations and other official buildings occupied by the *chimères* in the Cité Soleil area of Port-au-Prince. Meanwhile, the authorities provisionally released the three FL members arrested in October.

In January 2005 the CEP announced that the municipal elections were to take place on 9 October, followed by legislative and presidential elections in two rounds, on 13 November and 18 December. A permanent register of voters was to be compiled prior to the elections, and national identity cards were to be issued. It was hoped that proposed mediation by the African Union (see p. 188) would result in the participation of the FL, which continued to demand the release of former officials of the Aristide administration and other 'political' prisoners. In February the Government created a National Disarmament Commission to facilitate the recovery of illegal weapons.

Escalation of violence

An escalation in fighting between MINUSTAH troops and rebel groups was evident from March 2005. Many of the rebels who had helped to oust Aristide from power had subsequently turned against the interim Government. A number of UN peacekeeping troops and rebels were killed in confrontations in the following months.

In May 2005 Neptune was formally charged for his alleged role in political killings during the uprising against Aristide's administration; in April Neptune had begun a hunger strike to protest against his detention without charge. Human rights organizations claimed that hundreds of Aristide supporters had similarly been detained without charge for almost a year.

In June 2005 Paul-Henri Mourral, the French honorary consul, was shot dead and numerous others were also killed as gangs ran amok in the capital. Later that month the UN Security Council decided to extend MINUSTAH's mandate by a further eight months and to deploy an additional 1,000 peacekeeping troops in the country. MINUSTAH subsequently intensified military operations against the rebel gangs and denied allegations that civilians had been killed by UN troops. In July the prominent Haitian journalist Jacques Roches was killed. Later that month demonstrators marched through the capital to protest against the interim Government, MINUSTAH and the collective failure of both to address adequately the security situation in Haiti.

In August 2005 local elections were postponed until December, to allow the authorities to concentrate on preparations for legislative and presidential elections, which in turn were delayed, on account of extremely low voter registration and divisions in the electoral council. The elections were further postponed on three subsequent occasions, with a revised date of 7 February 2006 eventually being set; Latortue also announced that he was to resign as Prime Minister on that date.

Presidential and legislative elections of 2006

On 7 February 2006 presidential and legislative elections were finally held. Voter participation was higher than expected, at 60% of the total electorate, in the presidential poll. It was announced that former President Préval, representing Fwon Lespwa (Front de l'Espoir), had obtained 49% of the vote, marginally short of the overall majority required to avoid a second round of voting. Incensed by what they perceived to be an attempt by the interim Government to force a run-off vote,

and with tempers further inflamed by the discovery of thousands of burnt ballot papers (many of which were reported to be marked in favour of Préval) in a dump near Port-au-Prince, thousands of Préval supporters marched through the capital in protest. It was announced on 16 February that Préval had in fact secured an outright victory and was consequently to be declared President. The announcement followed emergency talks between the interim Government and electoral officials, during which it was agreed to share out the 91,219 blank ballots (4.4% of the total votes cast) proportionately among the candidates, thereby increasing Préval's percentage of the vote to 51%. The RDNP representative, former President Leslie Manigat—the second-placed candidate (with only 12% of the vote)—denounced the outcome, as did the third-placed Respè nominee, Charles Henri Baker. However, the international community—including, significantly, the UN, CARICOM, the OAS and the USA—did recognize Préval's victory. Préval was formally sworn into office on 14 May.

Elections to a newly enlarged 30-seat Senate and 99-seat Chamber of Deputies were also held on 7 February 2006. However, most of the results were inconclusive, necessitating a second round of voting, eventually held on 21 April, a delay attributed by the CEP to the need to investigate numerous claims of voting irregularities. According to partial, provisional results, Préval's Fwon Lespwa won the largest number of seats in both legislative chambers (13 in the Sénat and 24 in the Chamber of Deputies), although the party failed to secure a majority in either house. The Fusion des Sociaux-Démocrates Haïtiens alliance was placed second, with four seats in the upper house and 18 in the lower chamber, while the OPL won three senate seats and 11 seats in the Chamber of Deputies.

President Préval nominated Jacques-Edouard Alexis as Prime Minister. The proposed return of Alexis to his former role was subsequently approved by both legislative chambers, and in June 2006 a new 18-member coalition cabinet, with representatives from six political parties, was sworn into office. Alexis declared that he would give consideration to the plight of political prisoners enduring lengthy detentions without being put on trial. A few days later it was announced that Privert had been released on parole, and in July Neptune was released on health grounds (the charges against him were withdrawn in 2009). Meanwhile, the period of relative calm that had followed Préval's election victory was fractured in June, when a rise in street violence and kidnappings prompted MINUSTAH to increase its presence in Port-au-Prince. Between June and August approximately 100 people were reported to have been killed in the capital. In August the President and the Prime Minister issued an ultimatum to the gang leaders, ordering them to hand in their weapons or be killed. In September the Government appointed a new commission designed to disarm gang members by offering them food, financial support and training.

In August 2006 the UN Security Council voted unanimously to extend MINUSTAH's mandate until February 2007. In November and December 2006 angry protesters amassed in Cité Soleil to demonstrate against the continued presence of MINUSTAH, accusing UN troops of using indiscriminate force to quell civil unrest. Despite the opposition, MINUSTAH's mandate was extended until October 2008. Joint operations by MINUSTAH and Haitian police contributed to a significant improvement in security in Port-au-Prince during 2007, with a reported 70% reduction in kidnappings compared with the previous year. MINUSTAH's mandate was extended for a further 12 months in October 2008.

Continuing political unrest

In early April 2008 violent demonstrations by thousands of protesters against a sharp increase in the cost of food resulted in the deaths of five people and the murder of a MINUSTAH peacekeeper. On 12 April the Senate approved a motion to dismiss Alexis as Prime Minister over his handling of the crisis. Préval nominated Ericq Pierre as Prime Minister, but this was rejected by the Chamber of Deputies, as was Préval's subsequent nomination, Robert Manuel. In June Préval nominated Michèle Pierre-Louis, an economist and director of a charitable foundation, and, following legislative approval, she was eventually sworn in on 29 August, bringing to an end some four months without a functioning Government.

Delayed elections to renew one-third of the seats in the Senate were held in April 2009. In February it had been revealed by the CEP that all candidates from Aristide's FL were to be excluded from the elections on the grounds that two rival FL factions had both submitted lists of candidates. Thousands of FL supporters took to the streets on 28 February in protest against the decision, which had also prompted expressions of concern from the OAS and the US embassy, and to mark the fifth anniversary of Aristide's exile. The first round of the elections, on 19 April, was marked by a low rate of voter participation, of only 11.8%, and violent demonstrations caused polling to be cancelled in the Centre department. As no candidate obtained the required 50% majority, a second round of voting was eventually conducted on 21 June. Fwon Lespwa won five of the 11 seats contested, giving the party a total of 12 of the Senate's 30 seats. However, the turnout was reported to be even lower than in the first round, prompting the FL to declare that the results should be annulled.

At a conference held in Washington, DC, in April 2009, international donors pledged to disburse US $324m. in development aid for Haiti. Following a continued improvement in security in 2008–09, the UN began to broaden the focus of its activities in Haiti, and in May the UN Secretary-General, Ban Ki-Moon, appointed former US President Bill Clinton as his first Special Envoy for the country, with a remit to secure further international support for economic and social recovery.

The Senate adopted a motion to dismiss Pierre-Louis as Prime Minister on 30 October 2009, on the grounds that her Government's efforts to address Haiti's economic difficulties had been insufficient. Noting that Pierre-Louis had succeeded in securing the support of bilateral and multilateral donors during her 14 months in office, observers speculated that her removal was in fact politically motivated. Préval nominated Jean-Max Bellerive as Prime Minister. His new Cabinet retained 11 of the 18 ministers from the previous administration.

In November 2009 the CEP announced that the FL would not be permitted to contest the legislative elections scheduled to be held in 2010, citing the party's alleged failure to meet the legal requirements for registration. Meanwhile, following the dissolution of Fwon Lespwa (at Préval's behest), a new movement in support of the President, Inite (Unité), was formed by several organizations, including the MOP, the PLB and the Union Nationale Chrétienne pour la Reconstruction d'Haïti. Inite's main opposition was the Alternative pour le Progrès et la Democratie (Altenativ), a new electoral alliance created by Alyans, the Fusion des Sociaux-Démocrates Haïtiens and the OPL.

Earthquake of January 2010

More than 230,000 people were estimated to have been killed and more than 300,000 injured in Port-au-Prince and surrounding areas on 12 January 2010 in an earthquake with a magnitude of 7.0. The UN estimated that some 10% of the buildings in the capital had been destroyed, while at least 1.5m. people had been made homeless. On 15 January the UN appealed for US $562m. (subsequently raised to $577m.) in emergency relief to assist an estimated 3m. affected people; one-half of this amount was to be used to provide food aid. The Government's response to the disaster was hampered by the destruction of the presidential palace, the parliament building, the police headquarters and many of its ministries, as well as by the death of public officials and civil servants. International organizations based in the capital were similarly affected: the headquarters of MINUSTAH collapsed and the head of the mission and his deputy were among those killed. Logistical difficulties, resulting from the damage to transport infrastructure and also from the scale of the aid required, delayed the distribution of supplies. A state of emergency was declared on 17 January (and extended for a further 18 months in April). A resolution approved by the UN Security Council on 19 January authorized the deployment to Haiti of an additional 2,000 military personnel and 1,500 police officers. In late January FAO appealed to international donors to support an 18-month plan for the investment of $700m. in the Haitian agricultural sector in order to repair infrastructure, to stimulate food production and to create employment for people (subsequently estimated to number 661,000) fleeing the Port-au-Prince area. Those who did not leave the capital settled in more than 1,300 camps created in the earthquake-affected area.

A government report published in March 2010 estimated the total value of damage and losses caused by the earthquake at $7,860m. (equivalent to around 120% of gross domestic product) and the cost of the long-term reconstruction of the country at $11,500m. The report also advocated a development strategy focused on greater decentralization, noting that 65% of Haiti's economic activity had hitherto been located in the Port-au-Prince area. At a conference held in New York at the end of March, international donors pledged $9,900m. in support of the Haitian Government's Action Plan for National Recovery and Develop-ment, to be disbursed during 2010–12. An Interim Haiti Recovery Commission, co-chaired by Prime Minister Bellerive and Bill Clinton, was established in April to co-ordinate the implementation of the Plan and to monitor the distribution of funds.

The legislative elections were postponed indefinitely in February 2010. In May the Chamber of Deputies and the Senate approved legislation allowing President Préval, whose term was due to end on 7 February 2011, to remain in office until 14 May of that year. The extension of Préval's term prompted demands for the President's resignation at opposition-organized demonstrations in Port-au-Prince. In June 2010, however, Préval signed a decree scheduling both the legislative and the presidential elections for 28 November.

The UN Security Council approved a resolution authorizing the deployment of an additional 680 police officers in Haiti in June 2010, recognizing the need for MINUSTAH to assist the Haitian national police force in protecting the population, amid reports of increased crime and sexual violence in the temporary settlements for displaced people. There were also concerns about a rise in the activity of criminal gangs, which was partly linked to the escape following the earthquake of 5,409 prisoners. (Joint operations between MINUSTAH and the Haitian police resulted in at least 629 prisoners being recaptured during 2010.) The UN Security Council extended MINUSTAH's mandate for a further year in October.

Haiti suffered a further severe setback in October 2010, with the confirmation of an outbreak of cholera in the Artibonite and Centre departments, which subsequently spread throughout the country. Allegations that Nepalese peacekeepers were the source of the outbreak led to unrest and demonstrations against MINUSTAH's presence in Haiti in November. One protester was killed in clashes with UN troops in the northern city of Cap-Haïtien, although the UN suggested that the violence had been orchestrated by those seeking to disrupt the forthcoming elections. Meanwhile, the UN appealed for US $175m. in international aid to combat the cholera epidemic. By November 2013 some 689,500 cases of cholera, including just under 8,500 fatalities, had been recorded.

In January 2013 the President claimed that the disaster had caused damages of nearly US $13,000m. and urged donors to co-operate more closely with the Haitian Government. Of the estimated total of $6,430m. in humanitarian and recovery funding that had been disbursed in 2010–12 to assist Haiti, only an estimated 9.1% had been channelled through the Haitian Government. In June 2013 it was reported that around 4,000 people displaced by the earthquake had been forced out of temporary camps since the start of the year, most of the camps being located on private property, with a further 75,000 facing threats of eviction. In October, according to the UN, the number of Haitians living in camps was some 172,000, down from 1.5m. immediately following the disaster.

2010 and 2011 elections

The presidential and legislative elections were held, as scheduled, on 28 November 2010. Voter participation was extremely low, at just 22.8%. Immediately after the elections, 12 of the 19 presidential candidates alleged that fraud had been perpetrated in favour of Inite's candidate, Jude Célestin, but a joint OAS-CARICOM mission concluded that the irregularities were not sufficiently serious to invalidate the vote. According to preliminary results released by the CEP on 7 December, the RDNP candidate, Mirlande Manigat, an academic and wife of former President Leslie Manigat, secured the largest share of the presidential ballot, with 31.4%, followed by Célestin, with 22.5%, and Michel Martelly, a musician representing Repons Peyizan (Réponse des Paysans), with 21.8%. A second round of voting between the two leading nominees was to be held on 16 January 2011. However, the US embassy cast doubt on the CEP's preliminary results, noting that they were 'inconsistent' with those published by a national election observation organization, which placed Martelly in second place, and violent protests by supporters of Martelly resulted in five deaths. In December 2010, in response to increasing international pressure, President Préval requested OAS assistance in reviewing the disputed results. The second round of voting (in both the presidential and legislative elections) was consequently suspended by the CEP. The OAS electoral experts issued their report in January 2011, concluding that Martelly was the second-placed presidential candidate, ahead of Célestin. In February, without releasing detailed results of the first round, the CEP announced that Manigat and Martelly would contest the run-off presidential ballot, which was to be held on 20 March, concurrently with the second round of the legislative elections (only four of the 11 seats contested in the Senate and 18 of the 99 seats in the lower house having thus far been filled). Meanwhile, former President Duvalier unexpectedly returned to Haiti in January, after 25 years in exile; he was swiftly charged with corruption and misappropriation of funds. Moreover, on the eve of the run-off ballot, Aristide, whose FL had been excluded from the elections, also returned from exile.

International observers asserted that the run-off presidential ballot of 20 March 2011 was better conducted than the first round of voting. Martelly defeated Manigat, winning 67.6% of the valid votes cast, his victory reflecting his popularity among younger voters and public disenchantment with more traditional politicians. The electoral turnout was only 22.5%. Following voting in the second round of the legislative election, Inite was by far the largest party in the legislature, holding 17 of the 30 seats in the Sénat and 46 of the 99 seats in the Chamber of Deputies, according to official results. Martelly's Repons Peyizan took only three seats in the Chamber of Deputies and failed to gain representation in the upper chamber. However, the results of 19 legislative seats (17 in the lower house and two in the Senate), 16 of which had been allocated to Inite, were subsequently disputed. In April, having examined each case at the request of President Préval, the joint OAS-CARICOM electoral observation mission recommended the reinstatement of preliminary results, which had attributed 33 seats in the Chamber of Deputies to Inite. On 11 May the CEP announced the reversal of 15 of the 19 challenged results, with Inite retaining just four of the seats in question.

Martelly in office

President Martelly took office on 14 May 2011, pledging to accelerate stalled reconstruction efforts, to address the cholera epidemic, to restore security, to boost employment and to introduce free education. More controversially, he also proposed the re-establishment of the armed forces, which had been disbanded by Aristide in 1995, suggesting that it could eventually replace MINUSTAH, and mooted granting amnesty to Aristide and Duvalier. Meanwhile, the legislature voted against a proposed amendment to the Constitution, which would have allowed Presidents to serve two consecutive five-year terms.

The President's ability to implement his plans was constrained by his weak position in the legislature and consequent failure to secure approval for his choice of Prime Minister. Martelly designated businessman Daniel-Gérard Rouzier as premier, but this was rejected in June 2011 by the Chamber of Deputies, in which Inite had joined with other parties to form the Groupe des parlementaires pour le renouveau, an alliance claiming to comprise some 70 deputies. Martelly's second nominee, Bernard Gousse, a former Minister of Justice in the administration of Gérard Latortue (2004–06), was rejected by the Senate in August. Finally, on 4 October, the appointment of Martelly's third nominee, Garry Conille, until recently chief of staff to UN Special Envoy Bill Clinton, was endorsed by the Senate, having been accepted by the Chamber of Deputies on 16 September. On 15 October the lower house approved Conille's programme for government—including plans to attract foreign aid and investment, to resettle the homeless, and to create 1.5m. jobs over a period of five years—as well as the composition of his Cabinet, which included three Inite ministers, and took office three days later.

In January 2012 President Martelly announced that a civilian commission that he had appointed had recommended the restoration of the army with a remit to safeguard territorial integrity, respond to natural disasters and combat drugs-trafficking. However, there were concerns among the opposition, and internationally, regarding the financial burden involved (estimated at some US $95m.) and the poor human rights record of the previous military. Hundreds of uniformed former soldiers, many of them armed, began to occupy disused military bases from January, demanding the re-establishment of the army and the payment of some $15m. in wages that they claimed to be owed. Following a series of protest marches in May, a number of former soldiers were arrested and charged with forming a rogue army, and police raided bases that they had refused to vacate. In October 2013 it was announced by the defence ministry that no former members of the armed forces of Haiti would be part of the new civil defence force.

The mandate of the Interim Haiti Recovery Commission expired in October 2011. In August the Commission had notably approved a US $78m. project proposed by the President, which was expected to create some 4,500 jobs and to rehabilitate 16

neighbourhoods of Port-au-Prince to allow the return of some 30,000 people from six particularly vulnerable camps. In September President Martelly announced the creation of a 32-member Presidential Advisory Council on Economic Growth and Investment, comprising eight former heads of state of various countries, as well as business executives; co-chaired by Bill Clinton, the Council was charged with attracting foreign investment and to revitalize the country's economy.

The UN Security Council approved an extension of MINUSTAH's mandate for a further year in October 2011, but reduced its maximum authorized strength to pre-earthquake levels (some 7,340 troops and 3,241 police officers), in view of the completion of the presidential and legislative elections and the gradual curtailment of large-scale humanitarian operations. In the previous month, meanwhile, clashes had occurred in Port-au-Prince between police and hundreds of protesters who were demanding MINUSTAH's withdrawal from Haiti, amid growing anger regarding the source of the ongoing cholera epidemic.

The Minister of Justice and Public Security, Josué Pierre-Louis, was forced to resign from office in November 2011, after he ordered the arrest of Arnel Bélizaire, an opposition member of the Chamber of Deputies. In December the Senate established a committee of inquiry into the nationality of Martelly and members of his Government, following allegations that the President and several ministers held foreign citizenship, in contravention of the Constitution.

In January 2012, in a report to the Attorney-General's office, the judge handling the case against Duvalier recommended that the former dictator should be tried on charges of embezzlement of public funds, but that the statute of limitations had expired with regard to human rights abuses committed during his regime. However, a group of alleged victims of such abuses and their relatives appealed against the latter ruling, arguing that, under international law, the statute of limitations did not apply to crimes against humanity. A hearing into the appeal took place on 28 February at which the former President denied responsibility for abuses carried out during his time in office, including the murder and torture of political opponents; Duvalier died on 4 October 2014; amid vigorous media debate, it was decided not to accord him a state funeral. At his cremation on 11 October a small number of protesters gathered outside the Citizens Protection Office, which had documented abuses carried out under Duvalier's regime.

Prime Minister Conille resigned from office on 24 February 2012. His departure followed a deterioration in relations with President Martelly, particularly after Conille's decision to establish a commission to examine the awarding of construction contracts in the wake of the 2010 earthquake. On 1 March 2012 Martelly nominated close ally and Minister of Foreign Affairs and Religion Laurent Lamothe to succeed Conille, a nomination that received legislative approval. Lamothe formally took office on 16 May, retaining the foreign affairs and religion portfolio. The new Prime Minister pledged to increase security measures and to introduce an anti-poverty strategy entailing free tuition and vaccination for children of primary school age. The Government revoked 39 construction contracts in July, following the completion of the investigation initiated by Conille.

The revised Constitution, as amended by the legislature in May 2011, was finally published in June 2012, allowing its entry into force. In addition to according dual nationality to Haitians living abroad, the changes provided for the creation of three new institutions: a constitutional court; a Supreme Council of Judicial Power (Conseil Supérieur du Pouvoir Judiciaire—CSPJ), which was duly inaugurated in July; and a Permanent Electoral Council (Conseil Electoral Permanent) to replace the discredited CEP, the members of which had been dismissed in December 2011. The establishment of a new electoral council was particularly urgent, as municipal polls and elections to renew one-third of the members of the Senate were overdue, with the mandates of 10 senators having expired in May 2012. Six of the nine members of the Permanent Electoral Council, representing the executive and the judiciary, were installed in August, but the two legislative chambers could not agree on a process to select its nominees, partly owing to the depleted nature of the Senate. In October, moreover, the CSPJ designated three new representatives to the electoral council, following complaints that its existing members had been elected by minority vote, although the installed members refused to stand aside for their replacements. In December, in an attempt to overcome the impasse, the executive and legislative branches of government signed an agreement on the formation of a Transitional College of the

Permanent Electoral Council to organize the next elections, after which its mandate would end. This body would comprise the six members already nominated to the Permanent Electoral Council (with further negotiations to be held to decide which of the CSPJ representatives were legitimate) and three still to be appointed by the legislature. However, this arrangement appeared to be widely regarded as unsatisfactory.

Meanwhile, Lamothe announced a cabinet reorganization in August 2012, notably ceding the foreign affairs and religion portfolio to his erstwhile secretary of state, Pierre Richard Casimir, while assuming responsibility for planning and external co-operation. In September Lamothe announced the establishment of a new mechanism for co-ordinating international assistance: the Aid Effectiveness Committee (Comité de l'Efficacité de l'Aide, CEA).

MINUSTAH's mandate was extended for a further year in October 2012, although its maximum authorized strength was to be reduced to 6,270 troops and 2,601 police officers by June 2013; one of its principal priorities was to assist in the implementation of a plan to increase the Haitian national police force to a minimum of 15,000 serving officers by 2016 (from around 10,000 in 2012). Also in October, plans were announced to boost the government education fund created from levying taxes on international telephone calls and money transfers by some US $100m. through the imposition of additional taxes on alcohol, cigarettes and gambling. However, public discontent with the Government was evident in mid-October, when hundreds of protesters demonstrated in Port-au-Prince against the high cost of living, with some demanding the resignation of President Martelly, whom they accused of corruption and failing to alleviate poverty.

Haiti's difficulties were exacerbated later in October 2012 when Hurricane Sandy struck, killing 54 people, leaving more than 30,000 homeless and inflicting severe damage on the agricultural sector, with an estimated 70% of crops destroyed. The country had already suffered significantly as a result of Tropical Storm Isaac in August, when 24 people were killed, over 81,000 ha of crops damaged and 1,105 homes destroyed. A one-month state of emergency was declared in response to Sandy, while the UN and the Government appealed for an additional US $39.9m. in funding for humanitarian assistance over the following year, amid rising concerns regarding food insecurity in particular. An increase in the number of cholera cases was also reported. The recent revelation by a US cholera expert—who was a member of the panel established by the UN in December 2010 to investigate the outbreak of the disease in Haiti (see *Earthquake of January 2010*)—that newly available data demonstrated that the strain of cholera in Haiti exactly matched a strain prevalent in Nepal in 2010 appeared to strengthen the case of those seeking compensation from the UN. Some 5,000 victims and their families had lodged an official claim with the UN, on the grounds that Nepalese UN peacekeepers were the source of the cholera outbreak, demanding $100,000 for those who had died (who numbered more than 8,000 to date). In February 2013, however, the UN formally rejected the compensation claims, invoking its legal immunity in the countries in which it operates. In May the UN was informed by the Institute for Justice and Democracy in Haiti (IJDH—based in Boston, Massachusetts, USA) that it had 60 days in which to initiate compensation talks with the families of the cholera victims. The Institute filed a new complaint against the UN, in an attempt to lift its diplomatic immunity, in a federal court in New York in October; however, the US Government rejected the claim in March 2014. In the same month a new class action was initiated against the UN. In October 2013 the UN Security Council voted to extend MINUSTAH's mandate until 15 October 2014. UN Secretary-General Ban Ki-Moon announced in July 2014 the launch of a 10-year sanitation programme worth some $2,200m., to reduce the spread of cholera and improve access to potable water in Haiti and the Dominican Republic. In August a vaccination programme began in Haiti, which aimed to inoculate some 200,000 people in areas at most risk of the disease. In October the IJDH presented its case to a district court in New York. In the same month the UN Security Council voted to extend MINUSTAH's mandate for a further year, and authorized a reduction in the number of military personnel from 5,021 to 2,370. In January 2015 the district court in New York ruled that the UN could not be held accountable for criminal negligence in relation to victims of the cholera outbreak.

Amid mounting international concern regarding the continued delay in organizing the overdue municipal and partial senatorial elections, and persistent public discontent over rising food prices and alleged government corruption among other issues, the Cabinet was reorganized again in January 2013. Most significantly, Saint Cyr was succeeded as Minister of the Interior and Territorial Collectivities by David Bazile, an ally of Martelly who had previously served as Secretary of State for Public Security. Marie-Carmelle Jean-Marie, the Minister of the Economy and Finance, resigned in April, as did Minister of Communications Régine Godefroy; they were replaced, respectively, by Wilson Laleau and Josette Darguste (in an acting capacity).

The death of Judge Jean Serge Joseph on 13 July 2013 caused a significant political controversy. The judge had been investigating charges of corruption against Martelly's wife and son. It was alleged that Joseph had been ordered to call off the investigation by, among others, the President, the Prime Minister and the Minister of Justice and Public Security, Jean Renel Sanon, all of whom denied the allegations. Joseph died of a brain haemorrhage, the causes of which were reported to be either stress or poison. A report published on 8 August, following a Senate inquiry into the judge's death, recommended that Lamothe and Sanon be removed from office and that Martelly be impeached for high treason for having lied to the nation. An inquiry conducted by the lower house made similar recommendations.

In January 2014 nine people were charged with the murder of Jean Dominique, a prominent radio broadcaster and political analyst, and a security guard in April 2000. The suspects included several allies of Aristide who was leader of the opposition when the murder took place. In May 2013 thousands of the former President's supporters defied a ban in order to greet him as he appeared in court to give evidence at the trial. Aristide was not indicted as having been part of the conspiracy despite evidence that the organizer of Dominique's murder, former FL senator Mirlande Libérus, had been acting on his orders. In April 2014 the authorities in Argentina arrested a further suspect wanted in relation to the murder of Dominique and in June he was extradited to Haiti; four further suspects were facing extradition from the USA in early 2015.

Recent developments: the long road to elections

On 11 April 2013 a presidential decree was finally published on the formation of the Transitional College of the Permanent Electoral Council. The College was to comprise nine members, three each appointed by the executive, the legislature and the judiciary. In May the Senate approved the country's first ever anti-corruption law; however, the Chamber of Deputies failed to approve the new legislation. In August it was reported that the President of the lower house was to introduce drastic measures to ensure that its members participated in the sessions; no law had been passed since June owing to the lack of quorum. The preliminary draft of the electoral law was submitted to the President in July; it was passed by the Senate in October, ratified by the Chamber of Deputies in late November and promulgated on 14 December. Apart from the passage of the electoral law, the work of the Chamber of Deputies in the second half of 2013 was obstructed by persistent absenteeism.

Representatives of the executive, legislature and political parties began negotiations towards an agreement on the holding of elections began in January 2014 in the El Rancho hotel in Pétionville. On 14 March an accord was reached, which provided for elections to be held to two-thirds of the Senate and the entire Chamber of Deputies by the end of the year, but preferably by 26 October. This was approved by the legislature on 1 April. Later that month the OAS and members of the US Congress urged Haiti to pass legislation expediting the elections. President Martelly issued an executive order to appoint a new Transitional College of the Permanent Electoral Council in May. US Secretary of State, John Kerry, welcomed the measure, as well as anti-corruption legislation signed by Martelly in the same month.

As part of the so-called 'El Rancho' agreement, in April 2014 President Martelly effected a cabinet reshuffle, in order that a wider range of political parties were represented in government. Notably, Marie-Carmelle Jean-Marie was reappointed to the economy and finance ministry, while Duly Brutus, Haiti's erstwhile ambassador to the OAS, was appointed Minister of Foreign Affairs and Religion. In August local politicians urged Senators to cease refusing to attend sessions of the legislature, thereby preventing the upper house from reaching a quorum and facilitating legislation intended to allow for legislative and local elections to be held. Meanwhile, in the same month an investigating judge issued an arrest warrant for former President

Aristide and four associates on charges committed during 2001–04, including embezzlement of public funds, drugs-trafficking and money-laundering, and criticized the police force for failing to arrest him. Aristide's lawyer attempted to have the warrant revoked on the grounds of the judge's impartiality. On 9 September Aristide was placed under house arrest. On 30 September supporters of Aristide protested in Port-au-Prince to mark the 23rd anniversary of the coup which removed him from power; they were dispersed by the police with tear gas and water cannons. Two days later a pro-Government rally in support of Martelly and Prime Minister Lamothe was held in Cap-Haïtien attended by up to 100,000 people.

In early November 2014 members of six opposition parties refused to attend a meeting with President Martelly to discuss passing legislation to enable legislative and local elections to be held; the mandate of the Senate was due to expire on 12 January 2015, after which time only 10 Senators would be eligible to vote and the President could issue a decree for elections to be held. The political impasse led to civil unrest and in-mid November 2014 three people were shot by police officers attempting to disperse anti-Government protesters in Port-au-Prince. Further demonstrations took place in the north-eastern city of Fort Liberé, where some 13 protesters who were calling for electricity to be supplied to their neighbourhood from a nearby power station were shot and injured by police officers attempting to disperse the crowd; and in Ouanaminthe, where a child was killed when a truck driven by a Dominican man lost control after he was attacked by demonstrators. The incident led to attacks on the local consulate of the Dominican Republic.

Amid increasing anti-Government protests in Port-au-Prince, where MINUSTAH troops fired on violent protesters on 12 December 2014, and a demonstrator was shot dead on the following day, as well as demonstrations in Cap-Haïtien and Gonaïves, Prime Minister Laurent Lamothe and his administration resigned on 14 December, following the recommendations of the Transitional Council of the Permanent Electoral Council. The outgoing Minister of Health, Florence Duperval Guillaume, was appointed interim Prime Minister on 21 December, although Martelly nominated Evans Paul as Prime Minister as his favoured candidate on 25 December. However, parliament refused to ratify his appointment, although he remained as de facto premier and promised that elections would be held within 120 days of the installation of a new electoral council. In early January 2015 Martelly and opposition Senators failed to reach an agreement, proposed by the USA, allowing for an extension to the terms of members of the House of Deputies until April, and the Senate until September, during which time electoral legislation could be passed and a new elections council appointed. Parliament was dissolved on 13 January and Martelly ruled by decree until 16 January, when a 'consensus' Government led by Paul was sworn in, which included seven members of the outgoing administration; key allies of Martelly were also appointed, including Yves Germain Joseph as Minister of Planning, and Carel Alexandre as Secretary of State for Public Security, while only one member was appointed who was aligned to the opposition, which questioned the constitutionality of consensus administration, as it had not been ratified by parliament. In the following week the opposition organized demonstrations calling for Martelly to resign and for the formation of a provisional government; violent clashes between protesters and police officers were reported in Port-au-Prince.

A new Provisional Electoral Council (CEP) was sworn in on 23 January 2015. In early March the CEP announced a provisional schedule for elections, which was confirmed by presidential decree two days later: a legislative ballot would be held on 9 August, with a second round scheduled for 25 October, to coincide with a presidential election. Any second round presidential vote would be held on 27 December, with local elections following on 31 December.

Foreign Affairs

Regional relations

Relations between Haiti and its neighbour on the island of Hispaniola, the Dominican Republic, have traditionally been tense owing to the use of the border area by anti-Government guerrillas, smugglers and illegal migrants, resulting in the periodic closure of the border. In March 1996, following an official visit to the Dominican Republic by Préval, the first by a Haitian President since 1935, a joint communiqué was issued establishing a bilateral commission to promote improved co-operation. In 1998 agreement was reached to establish joint border patrols to combat the traffic of drugs and other contraband. In November 1999 Préval submitted a formal protest to the Dominican Republic following a spate of summary deportations of Haitians from the neighbouring country. A protocol was signed in December limiting the repatriations.

Relations between Haiti and the Dominican Republic suffered a marked deterioration in 2005. The Dominican Republic's army forcibly repatriated thousands of Haitian immigrants, a process that was intensified following the murder of a Dominican woman, allegedly by two Haitians, in May. Human rights organizations alleged that the Dominican army was acting indiscriminately and had deported not only illegal immigrants but also many legal immigrants and Dominicans of Haitian origin; the army strenuously denied such claims. In December a visit to Haiti by Dominican President Leonel Fernández was abruptly curtailed after violent demonstrations in protest against the alleged abuse of Haitians in the Dominican Republic broke out. Tensions rose again in 2009, following the murder of a Haitian migrant in the Dominican capital. Following the earthquake in 2010, the Dominican authorities provided humanitarian assistance to the country and suspended the repatriation of Haitian immigrants. In 2011, however, deportations of illegal immigrants resumed and border controls were tightened, in an attempt to curtail the spread of cholera from Haiti, where several thousand deaths from the disease had been recorded (see *Domestic Political Affairs*). President-elect Martelly visited the Dominican Republic in May. Talks with President Fernández focused on border security issues and the status of the estimated 1m. undocumented Haitians living in the Dominican Republic. In June 2012 Haiti briefly recalled its ambassador from the Dominican Republic, amid concerns regarding the effect on Haitian migrants of new legislation regulating foreign workers in the Dominican Republic. However, relations subsequently improved and the new Dominican President, Danilo Medina, reaffirmed a desire to negotiate a free trade agreement with Haiti. In February 2013, moreover, the Haitian and Dominican Governments agreed to connect their electricity systems, with the aim of improving energy security and lowering prices, although work on the project, which would require external financing, was not expected to begin for two years. In June the Haitian authorities imposed a ban on the import of eggs and poultry from its neighbour, citing an outbreak of avian flu across the border, a claim that was strenuously denied by the Dominican Republic. The following month, despite assurances that there would be no reprisals for the ban, the Dominican Republic expelled 157 Haitians without complying with repatriation procedures; further expulsions occurred over a period of several months. Relations between the two countries deteriorated further in September, following an order issued by the Dominican Republic's Constitutional Court whereby the citizenship of the descendants of Haitians born in the Dominican Republic after 1929 was to be removed, rendering thousands of people stateless. Tensions escalated further after the murder of an elderly Dominican couple in Neiba, Dominican Republic, allegedly by a group of Haitians, and the subsequent revenge killing of a Haitian. In November it was reported that more than 1,000 Haitian fugitives, who had escaped their country at the time of the 2010 earthquake, were still at large in the Dominican Republic. In January 2014 a series of talks between the two countries resulted in the lifting of the poultry ban and the expression of commitment on both sides to enact measures to safeguard the rights of Haitians living in the Dominican Republic. In June the Minister responsible for Haitians abroad, François Guillame, announced funding of US $10m. to provide identification documents to around 300,000 undocumented Haitians living in the Dominican Republic. The programme, which was to cost each applicant $80, was due to begin in the Dominican Republic cities of Santo Domingo and Barahona but was to be extended to Haitians living in remote parts of that country, as well as the Bahamas, the Turks and Caicos Islands, Suriname and Miami, USA. The OAS offered its technical support. In the following month, following protests from Haitians living in the Dominican Republic, the Haitian Government reduced the fee to $25 and agreed to assist Haitians to attain legal residency in the Dominican Republic. In February 2015 bilateral relations again deteriorated after a Haitian man was murdered in Santo Domingo; a march against perceived Dominican racism against Haitians was attended by an estimated 10,000 people in Port-au-Prince, and the Haitian ambassador to the Dominican Republic, Fritz Cinéas, resigned in protest.

Other external relations

The USA contributed some 1,900 troops to the Multinational Interim Force deployed in Haiti following the resignation of Aristide in February 2004. In 2006 President-elect Préval visited the USA, meeting US President George W. Bush and addressing the UN Security Council. In October, in recognition of government efforts to introduce peace and stability to the country, the USA partially lifted its arms embargo against Haiti, imposed in 1991. Relations improved under Prime Minister Réné Préval, who met Secretary of State Hillary Clinton in 2009. Clinton emphasized US President Barack Obama's commitment to assisting Haiti during talks with Préval in Port-au-Prince in April. Following the earthquake of January 2010, the USA dispatched more than 22,000 military personnel to the country to assist in the distribution of relief supplies and temporarily to assume control of the international airport. Clinton expressed strong support for President-elect Martelly when he visited Washington, DC, in April 2011. In October 2014 President Obama announced that the processing of residency visas for Haitians with relatives in the USA, who were US citizens or permanent residents, would be expedited. In January 2015 US Vice-President Joe Biden commended attempts by Martelly to negotiate an agreement with parliament and opposition parties to hold legislative elections.

CONSTITUTION AND GOVERNMENT

The March 1987 Constitution was amended in June 2012. It provided for a bicameral legislature, elected by universal adult suffrage. Executive power is held by the President, who is elected by universal adult suffrage for a five-year term and cannot not stand for immediate re-election. The amended Constitution of 2012 provided for the creation of a constitutional court and a permanent electoral council to replace the discredited Provisional Electoral Council.

There are 10 departments, subdivided into arrondissements and communes.

REGIONAL AND INTERNATIONAL CO-OPERATION

Haiti is a member of the Caribbean Community and Common Market (see p. 222), the Association of Caribbean States (see p. 444), of the Latin American Economic System (see p. 448), and of the Community of Latin American and Caribbean States (see p. 460), which was formally inaugurated in December 2011. Haiti is also a member of the International Coffee Organization (see p. 442). Haiti was a founder member of the UN in 1945. Having been a contracting party to the General Agreement on Tariffs and Trade since 1950, Haiti joined the World Trade Organization (see p. 431) in 1996. Haiti is also a signatory to the European Union's Cotonou Agreement (see p. 321).

ECONOMIC AFFAIRS

In 2013, according to estimates by the World Bank, Haiti's gross national income (GNI), measured at average 2011–13 prices, was US $8,397m., equivalent to $810 per head (or $1,710 per head on an international purchasing-power parity basis). In 2004–13 the population increased at an average annual rate of 1.4%, while gross domestic product (GDP) per head increased, in real terms, by an average of 0.6% per year. Overall GDP increased, in real terms, at an average annual rate of 2.0% in 2004–13; according to official estimates, real GDP increased by a provisional 2.7% in 2013/14.

Agriculture (including hunting, forestry and fishing) contributed a provisional 21.9% of GDP, at constant prices, in 2013/14. About 56.1% of the total labour force were engaged in agricultural activities in mid-2015, according to FAO estimates. The principal cash crop, traditionally, was coffee, although production decreased significantly in recent years and was overtaken by mangoes and cocoa. The export of essential oils for cosmetics and pharmaceuticals has become increasingly important, and crayfish are also an important export commodity. The main food crops are sugar, cassava, bananas, yams, sweet potatoes, maize and rice. The World Bank released US $50m. in aid for the agriculture sector in 2012. According to official estimates, agricultural GDP increased at an average annual rate of 0.1% during 2009/10–2013/14. The sector's GDP increased by 4.3% in 2012/13, before decreasing by 1.5% in 2013/14.

Industry (including mining, manufacturing, construction and power) contributed a provisional 19.0% of GDP, at constant prices, in 2013/14. About 11.5% of the employed labour force were engaged in the sector in 2007/08. According to official estimates, industrial GDP increased at an average annual

rate of 7.3% during 2009/10–2013/14; sectoral GDP increased by 5.3% in 2013/14.

Mining contributed a provisional 0.1% of GDP, at constant prices, in 2013/14. About 0.3% of the employed labour force were engaged in extractive activities in 2007/08. Marble, limestone and calcareous clay are mined. There are also unexploited copper, silver and gold deposits. According to official estimates, mining GDP increased at an average annual rate of 2.8% during 2009/10–2013/14. The sector's GDP increased by 5.6% in 2013/14

Manufacturing contributed a provisional 7.9% of GDP, at constant prices, in 2013/14. Some 7.7% of the employed population were engaged in the sector in 2007/08. The most important branches of manufacturing were food-processing, textiles (including apparel, leather and fur products, and footwear), chemicals (including rubber and plastic products) and tobacco. According to official estimates, manufacturing GDP increased at an average annual rate of 7.1% during 2009/10–2013/14; the sector's GDP increased by 2.2% in 2013/14.

Construction contributed an estimated 10.5% of GDP, at constant prices, in 2013/14. Some 3.3% of the employed population were engaged in the sector in 2007/08. According to official estimates, manufacturing GDP increased at an average annual rate of 7.9% during 2009/10–2013/14; the sector's GDP increased by 7.9% in 2013/14.

In 2011 some 79.0% of the country's public electricity came from petroleum, while 16.7% came from hydroelectric power. Overall electricity production was believed to amount to just one-10th of the capital's requirements. Haiti participated in the Petrocaribe initiative (whereby Caribbean countries were able to purchase petroleum from Venezuela on preferential terms). Imports of mineral fuels and related products accounted for 26.6% of the total value of imports in 2012/13.

The services sector contributed an estimated 59.2% of GDP, at constant prices, in 2013/14 and engaged 50.4% of the employed labour force in 2007/08. According to official estimates, services GDP increased by an average annual rate of 4.1% during 2009/10 2013/14; the sector's GDP increased by 3.9% in 2013/14.

In 2012/13 Haiti recorded a visible merchandise trade deficit of US $2,445.5m., and there was a deficit of $1,293.4m. on the current account of the balance of payments. The principal source of imports was the USA (35% in 2004); the USA was also the principal market for exports (81% in the same year). Other significant trading partners in recent years include France, Canada, Japan and the Dominican Republic. The principal export in 2012/13 was manufactured goods (87.5%); agricultural products were also significant. However, the most significant revenue stream came from the re-export, to the USA, of assembled goods (valued at $802.9m. in 2012/13), with income more than double that from domestic exports. The principal imports in 2012/13 were mineral fuels and lubricants (26.6%), basic manufactures, food products, machinery and transport equipment, miscellaneous manufactured goods, and chemical products.

In the financial year ending 30 September 2014 there was an estimated budgetary deficit of 37,928m. gourdes. Haiti's general government gross debt was 77,719m. gourdes in 2013, equivalent to 21.3% of GDP. At the end of 2012 Haiti's total external debt was US $1,154m., of which $985m. was public and publicly guaranteed debt. In that year the cost of servicing long-term public and publicly guaranteed debt and repayments to the IMF was equivalent to 0.3% of the total value of exports of goods, services and income (excluding workers' remittances). The annual rate of inflation averaged 8.8% per year in 2004–13. Consumer prices increased by an average of 5.9% in 2013. Some 60% of the labour force were estimated to be unemployed in 2001. According to the Inter-American Development Bank (IDB), remittances from Haitians living abroad amounted to approximately $2,017m. in 2013 (equivalent to almost 25% of GDP in that year).

In terms of average income, Haiti is the poorest country in the Western hemisphere, and there is extreme inequality of wealth. Over 70% of the population lives on less than US $2 a day. Economic progress has been impeded by political instability and a series of natural disasters, most notably the 2010 earthquake, which caused damage and losses equivalent to more than 120% of GDP. Substantial emergency assistance was pledged to Haiti, and the IMF cancelled the country's outstanding debts and made available a three-year Extended Credit Facility (ECF). The Group of Seven most industrialized nations agreed to cancel Haiti's bilateral debts, and international donors pledged to provide aid of $5,373m. by 2013. There were concerns that much of the money allocated to Haiti by the international community was not reaching its target; in June 2014 Haiti announced plans to open a bureau to facilitate the disbursement of humanitarian donations. The attraction of foreign investment was a key government priority, as were economic decentralization and the promotion of Haiti as a tourist destination (including the construction of the Marriott Hotel in Port-au-Prince, scheduled to open in 2015). In late 2012, in a significant move towards decentralization, the Government inaugurated an industrial park in Caracol, near Cap-Haïtien, one of the poorest areas of the country. It was envisaged that the park would eventually provide jobs for 20,000 workers, as well as attracting foreign investment and increasing export volumes. In December 2014 the IDB allocated some $55m. in grants for development of the park. In 2013 the IMF agreed to a further disbursement of $2.5m. and an extension of the ECF arrangement until August 2014 (at which time the ECF was again extended, to December 2017), in order to support the Government in its completion of key reforms, particularly in the fiscal area. The IMF forecast growth of 3.5% for 2015. The World Bank signed agreements worth $130m. in July 2014 for regional and community development, and tourism and educational projects, and commended Haiti for rehousing people who had been living in camps since 2010, and for reducing the rate of poverty. It was hoped that the holding of long overdue legislative elections in 2015 would finally facilitate foreign investment.

PUBLIC HOLIDAYS

2016: 1 January (Independence Day), 2 January (Heroes of Independence), 8 February (Shrove Monday, half-day), 9 February (Shrove Tuesday), 25 March (Good Friday), 14 April (Pan-American Day), 1 May (Labour and Agriculture Day), 18 May (Flag and University Day), 26 May (Corpus Christi), 15 August (Assumption), 17 October (Death of J.-J. Dessalines), 24 October (United Nations Day), 1 November (All Saints' Day), 2 November (All Souls' Day), 18 November (Army Day and Commemoration of the Battle of Vertières), 25 December (Christmas Day).

Statistical Survey

Sources (unless otherwise stated): Banque de la République d'Haïti, angle rues du Pavée et du Quai, BP 1570, Port-au-Prince; tel. 2299-1202; fax 2299-1145; e-mail brh@brh.net; internet www.brh.net; Institut Haitien de Statistique et d'Informatique, Ministère de l'Economie et des Finances, 1 angle rue Joseph Janvier et boulevard Harry S Truman, Port-au-Prince; tel. 2514-3789; fax 2221-5812; e-mail info@ihsi.ht; internet www.ihsi.ht.

Area and Population

AREA, POPULATION AND DENSITY

Area (sq km)	27,065*
Population (census results)	
30 August 1982†	5,053,792
7 July 2003	
Males	4,039,272
Females	4,334,478
Total	8,373,750
Population (UN estimates at mid-year)‡	
2013	10,317,461
2014	10,461,408
2015	10,603,731
Density (per sq km) at mid-2015	391.8

* 10,450 sq miles.
† Excluding adjustment for underenumeration.
‡ Source: UN, *World Population Prospects: The 2012 Revision.*

Note: It was estimated that approximately 220,000 people were killed as a result of a powerful earthquake that devastated the country's capital, Port-au-Prince, in January 2010. No reliable official estimates of total population have been published since the earthquake.

POPULATION BY AGE AND SEX
(UN estimates at mid-2015)

	Males	Females	Total
0–14 years	1,844,482	1,779,174	3,623,656
15–64 years	3,178,475	3,316,495	6,494,970
65 years and over	216,378	268,727	485,105
Total	5,239,335	5,364,396	10,603,731

Source: UN, *World Population Prospects: The 2012 Revision.*

DEPARTMENTS
(official population projections at mid-2009)

	Area (sq km)	Population	Density (per sq km)	Capital
L'Artibonit (Artibonite) . .	4,886.9	1,571,020	321.5	Gonaïves
Centre	3,487.4	678,626	194.6	Hinche
Grand'Anse . .	1,911.9	425,878	222.8	Jérémie
Nippes	1,267.8	311,497	245.7	Miragoâne
Nord	2,115.2	970,495	458.8	Cap-Haïtien
Nord-Est . . .	1,622.9	358,277	220.8	Fort Liberté
Nord-Ouest . .	2,102.9	662,777	315.2	Port-de-Paix
Ouest	4,982.6	3,664,620	735.5	Port-au-Prince
Sud	2,653.6	704,760	265.6	Les Cayes
Sud-Est . . .	2,034.1	575,293	282.8	Jacmel
Total	27,065.3	9,923,243	366.6	—

PRINCIPAL TOWNS
(official projected population at mid-2009)

Port-au-Prince (capital) . . .	897,859	Delmas	359,451
Carrefour . . .	465,019		

Mid-2014 (urban agglomeration, UN estimate): Port-au-Prince (incl. Carrefour and Delmas) 2,375,910 (Source: UN, *World Urbanization Prospects: The 2014 Revision*).

BIRTHS AND DEATHS
(UN estimates)

	2000–05	2005–10	2010–15
Crude birth rate (per 1,000) . .	29.7	27.7	23.9
Crude death rate (per 1,000) . .	10.6	9.4	8.5

Source: UN, *World Population Prospects: The 2012 Revision.*

Life expectancy (years at birth): 62.7 (males 60.9; females 64.6) in 2012 (Source: World Bank, World Development Indicators database).

ECONOMICALLY ACTIVE POPULATION
('000, FAO estimates at mid-year)

	2013	2014	2015
Agriculture, etc.	2,323	2,346	2,368
Total labour force (incl. others) .	4,064	4,144	4,223

Source: FAO.

2007/08 (national survey of employment and the informal economy, sample survey of persons aged 10 years and over, primary occupation, percentage distribution): Agriculture 36.8; Fishing 1.3; Mining and quarrying 0.3; Manufacturing 7.7; Electricity, gas and water 0.2; Construction 3.3; Wholesale and retail trade, vehicle repairs 27.2; Hotels and restaurants 3.8; Transport, storage and communications 3.0; Financial intermediation 0.6; Real estate, renting and other business activities 1.0; Public administration and compulsory social security 1.1; Education 4.8; Health and social welfare 1.9; Other community, social and personal services 2.3; Other services 4.7; Total employed 100.0.

Health and Welfare

KEY INDICATORS

Total fertility rate (children per woman, 2012)	3.2
Under-5 mortality rate (per 1,000 live births, 2012) . . .	76
HIV/AIDS (% of persons aged 15–49, 2013)	2.0
Physicians (per 1,000 head, 1998)	0.3
Hospital beds (per 1,000 head, 2007)	1.3
Health expenditure (2011): US $ per head (PPP)	101
Health expenditure (2011): % of GDP	8.5
Health expenditure (2011): public (% of total)	21.5
Access to water (% of persons, 2012)	62
Access to sanitation (% of persons, 2012)	24
Total carbon dioxide emissions ('000 metric tons, 2010) . .	2,119.5
Carbon dioxide emissions per head (metric tons, 2010) . .	0.2
Human Development Index (2013): ranking	168
Human Development Index (2013): value	0.471

For sources and definitions, see explanatory note on p. vi.

Agriculture

PRINCIPAL CROPS
('000 metric tons)

	2011	2012	2013
Rice, paddy	144*	148	169
Maize	360*	202	336
Sorghum	126†	92*	108
Sweet potatoes	240†	543	600
Cassava (Manioc)	450†	295	418
Yams	323†	298	425
Sugar cane†	1,150	1,200	1,200
Avocados†	52	53	53
Bananas†	265	270	270
Plantains†	265	267	267
Guavas, mangoes and mangosteens†	199	205	205

* Unofficial figure.
† FAO estimate(s).

Aggregate production ('000 metric tons, may include official, semi-official or estimated data): Total cereals 630 in 2011, 441 in 2012, 613 in 2013; Total roots and tubers 1,086 in 2011, 1,211 in 2012, 1,547 in 2013; Total vegetables (incl. melons) 149 in 2011, 155 in 2012–13; Total fruits (excl. melons) 930 in 2011, 950 in 2012–13.

Source: FAO.

LIVESTOCK
('000 head, year ending September, FAO estimates)

	2011	2012	2013
Horses	500	500	500
Asses	210	210	210
Mules	80	80	80
Cattle	1,460	1,465	1,465
Pigs	1,001	1,001	1,001
Sheep	154	154	154
Goats	1,910	1,950	1,950
Chickens	5,650	5,700	5,700
Turkeys	195	195	195
Ducks	190	190	190

Source: FAO.

LIVESTOCK PRODUCTS
('000 metric tons, FAO estimates)

	2011	2012	2013
Cattle meat	45.5	46.5	46.5
Goat meat	5.5	5.5	5.6
Pig meat	33.0	33.0	33.0
Horse meat	5.6	5.6	5.6
Chicken meat	8.0	8.0	8.1
Cows' milk	64.0	65.0	65.0
Goats' milk	28.1	28.2	28.2
Hen eggs	5.0	5.0	5.0

Source: FAO.

Forestry

ROUNDWOOD REMOVALS
('000 cubic metres, excl. bark, FAO estimates)

	2011	2012	2013
Sawlogs, veneer logs and logs for sleepers*	224	224	224
Other industrial wood* . . .	15	15	15
Fuel wood	2,050	2,060	2,070
Total	2,289	2,299	2,309

* Production assumed to be unchanged since 1971.

Source: FAO.

SAWNWOOD PRODUCTION
('000 cubic metres, incl. railway sleepers, FAO estimates)

	2010	2011	2012
Coniferous (softwood)	8	8	8
Broadleaved (hardwood) . . .	6	6	6
Total	14	14	14

2013: Production assumed to be unchanged from 1971 (FAO estimates).
Source: FAO.

Fishing

('000 metric tons, live weight)

	2010*	2011	2012*
Capture	13.7	16.5*	16.5
Freshwater fishes	0.5	0.6*	0.6
Marine fishes	12.5	15.2*	15.1
Marine crabs	0.1	0.2*	0.2
Caribbean spiny lobster . .	0.4	0.3	0.3
Natantian decapods . .	0.1	0.1*	0.1
Stromboid conchs	0.2	0.2*	0.2
Aquaculture	0.4	0.6	0.7
Total catch	14.1	17.1*	17.2

* FAO estimate(s).

Note: Figures exclude corals and madrepores (FAO estimates, metric tons): 10 in 2010–12.

Source: FAO.

Industry

SELECTED PRODUCTS
(estimates)

	2009	2010	2011
Cement ('000 metric tons) . . .	290.0	290.0	n.a.
Electric energy (million kWh) .	721	587	718

Sources: US Geological Survey; UN Industrial Commodity Statistics Database.

Finance

CURRENCY AND EXCHANGE RATES

Monetary Units
100 centimes = 1 gourde.

Sterling, Dollar and Euro Equivalents (31 December 2014)
£1 sterling = 72.964 gourdes;
US $1 = 46.748 gourdes;
€1 = 56.756 gourdes;
1,000 gourdes = £13.71 = $21.39 = €17.62.

Average Exchange Rate (gourdes per US $)
2012   41.950
2013   43.463
2014   45.216

Note: The official rate of exchange was maintained at US $1 = 5 gourdes until September 1991, when the central bank ceased all operations at the official rate, thereby unifying the exchange system at the 'floating' free market rate.

BUDGET
(million gourdes, year ending 30 September)

Revenue	2011	2012*	2013†
Current revenue	38,893	41,970	46,475
Domestic taxes	24,460	28,076	29,242
Customs duties	13,672	13,721	14,230
Other current revenue . . .	761	174	3,002
Grants	27,428	34,803	29,380
Total	66,321	76,774	75,855

Expenditure	2011	2012*	2013†
Current expenditure	35,232	39,006	43,158
Wages and salaries	14,809	16,706	20,007
Goods and services	7,525	11,406	11,320
Interest payments	1,272	1,359	1,711
Transfers and subsidies . .	11,626	9,534	10,120
Capital expenditure	42,120	53,484	57,051
Domestically financed . . .	17,642	19,252	31,190
Foreign-financed	24,478	34,232	25,861
Total	77,352	92,490	100,208

* Provisional figures.
† Estimates.

Source: IMF, *Haiti: Seventh Review Under the Extended Credit Facility, Requests for Waiver of Nonobservance of Performance Criterion, and Modification of Performance Criteria-Staff Report; Press Release; and Statement by the Executive Director for Haiti* (April 2014).

2014 (million gourdes, year ending 30 September): *Imports:* Direct taxes 15,094; Indirect taxes 36,808 (Taxes on production 7,221, Taxes on international trade 25,680, Taxes on petroleum products 3,907); Other domestic taxes 1,827; Total revenue 53,730 (excl. grants 32,127). *Expenditure:* Current expenditure 46,241 (Wages and salaries 24,034, Goods and services 15,051, Transfers and subsidies 5,679, Interest payments 1,477); Capital expenditure 77,543; Total expenditure 123,785 (Source: Ministry of Economy and Finance, Port-au-Prince).

INTERNATIONAL RESERVES
(US $ million at 31 December)

	2011	2012	2013
IMF special drawing rights . .	105.7	105.8	106.0
Reserve position in IMF . . .	0.1	0.1	0.1
Foreign exchange	1,088.9	1,178.6	1,617.5
Total	1,194.7	1,284.5	1,723.6

Source: IMF, *International Financial Statistics*.

MONEY SUPPLY
(million gourdes at 31 December)

	2011	2012	2013
Currency outside depository corporations	21,701.5	23,263.3	25,055.4
Transferable deposits	51,487.1	56,449.7	61,340.5
Other deposits	67,360.0	70,875.0	75,609.1
Broad money	140,548.6	150,588.0	162,005.0

Source: IMF, *International Financial Statistics*.

COST OF LIVING
(Consumer Price Index for metropolitan areas, base: 2000 = 100)

	2011	2012	2013
Food	438.2	467.3	497.5
All items (incl. others) . . .	406.4	431.9	457.2

Source: ILO.

NATIONAL ACCOUNTS
(million gourdes, year ending 30 September)

Expenditure on the Gross Domestic Product
(at current prices)

	2011/12*	2012/13†	2013/14†
Final consumption expenditure .	350,070	381,296	401,596
Gross capital formation . . .	96,925	109,586	121,212
Total domestic expenditure .	446,995	490,882	522,808
Exports of goods and services .	55,466	66,544	72,521
Less Imports of goods and services	174,400	192,900	206,520
GDP in purchasers' values .	328,061	364,526	388,809
GDP at constant 1986/87 prices	14,407	15,019	15,432

Gross Domestic Product by Economic Activity
(at constant 1986/87 prices)

	2011/12*	2012/13†	2013/14†
Agriculture, hunting, forestry and fishing	3,220	3,360	3,311
Mining and quarrying	17	18	19
Manufacturing	1,150	1,175	1,201
Electricity and water	69	69	70
Construction	1,345	1,470	1,586
Trade, restaurants and hotels	3,954	4,147	4,322
Transport, storage and communications	1,078	1,117	1,158
Business services	1,638	1,692	1,779
Other services	1,629	1,672	1,705
Sub-total	14,100	14,720	15,151
Less Imputed bank service charge	853	909	967
Taxes, less subsidies, on products	1,161	1,209	1,248
GDP in purchasers' values	14,407	15,019	15,432

* Provisional figures.
† Estimates.

BALANCE OF PAYMENTS
(US $ million, year ending 30 September)

	2010/11	2011/12	2012/13
Exports of goods	768.1	778.8	883.7
Imports of goods	−3,314.5	−3,079.3	−3,329.2
Balance on goods	−2,546.4	−2,300.5	−2,445.5
Exports of services	543.6	549.0	652.3
Imports of services	−1,119.0	−1,116.0	−1,090.3
Balance on goods and services	−3,121.7	−2,867.5	−2,883.5
Primary income received	44.2	72.4	71.8
Primary income paid	−3.2	−4.0	−15.0
Balance on goods, services and primary income	3,080.8	−2,799.1	−2,826.7
Secondary income received	1,551.4	1,612.3	1,781.0
Secondary income paid	−240.2	−231.9	−247.7
Current balance	−1,769.6	−1,418.7	−1,293.4
Capital account (net)	170.0	75.7	20.0
Direct investment liabilities	119.0	156.0	185.8
Other investment assets	−55.6	93.4	−3.5
Other investment liabilities	−203.8	356.3	845.5
Net errors and omissions	−74.1	7.6	−473.2
Reserves and related items	−1,814.1	−729.8	−718.8

Source: IMF, *International Financial Statistics*.

External Trade

PRINCIPAL COMMODITIES
(US $ million, year ending 30 September, provisional figures)

Imports c.i.f.	2010/11	2011/12	2012/13
Food products	551.3	523.0	622.5
Mineral fuels, lubricants, etc.	770.4	820.5	951.0
Chemical products	129.6	106.6	220.4
Basic manufactures	843.1	673.1	643.2
Machinery and transport equipment	292.5	224.4	543.7
Miscellaneous manufactured goods	502.3	434.3	410.9
Total (incl. others)	3,240.9	2,881.1	3,579.8

Exports f.o.b.*	2010/11	2011/12	2012/13
Coffee	7.0	8.4	1.3
Cocoa	6.9	9.3	4.9
Mangoes	10.6	10.1	—
Essential oils	16.4	14.3	15.7
Manufactured goods	267.8	273.7	314.4
Total (incl. others)	321.7	328.7	359.2

* Excluding re-export of assembled goods to the USA (US $ million, year ending 30 September, provisional figures): 686.3 in 2010/11; 706.0 in 2011/12; 802.9 in 2012/13.

PRINCIPAL TRADING PARTNERS
(US $ million, year ending 30 September)*

Imports c.i.f.	1989/90	1990/91	1991/92
Belgium	3.4	3.7	2.9
Canada	22.0	31.9	15.2
France	24.5	32.4	17.2
Germany, Federal Republic	14.6	19.2	10.0
Japan	23.6	31.2	17.7
Netherlands	11.2	13.9	8.7
United Kingdom	5.6	6.7	4.2
USA	153.1	203.2	126.7
Total (incl. others)	332.2	400.5	277.2

Exports f.o.b.†	1989/90	1990/91	1991/92
Belgium	15.9	19.5	6.0
Canada	4.5	4.7	2.3
France	17.4	21.6	6.1
Germany, Federal Republic	5.4	6.6	2.4
Italy	16.5	20.7	8.7
Japan	2.4	2.9	0.9
Netherlands	3.4	4.3	1.4
United Kingdom	2.3	2.3	0.7
USA	78.3	96.3	39.7
Total (incl. others)	163.7	198.7	74.7

* Provisional figures.
† Excluding re-exports.

Source: Administration Générale des Douanes, Port-au-Prince.

Transport

SHIPPING

Flag Registered Fleet
(at 31 December)

	2012	2013	2014
Number of vessels	4	4	3
Total displacement ('000 grt)	1.4	1.4	1.3

Source: Lloyd's List Intelligence (www.lloydslistintelligence.com).

CIVIL AVIATION

Traffic (international flights, 2012): Passengers arriving 615,191; Passengers departing 639,946.

Tourism

TOURIST ARRIVALS BY COUNTRY OF ORIGIN

	2009	2010	2011
Canada	31,017	20,119	19,568
Dominican Republic	9,910	3,168	4,487
France	12,508	14,261	18,432
USA	268,224	183,243	267,422
Total (incl. others)	387,218	254,732	348,755

Total tourist arrivals ('000): 349 in 2012; 420 in 2013 (provisional).

Receipts from tourism (US $ million, excl. passenger transport): 169 in 2010; 162 in 2011; 170 in 2012.

Source: World Tourism Organization.

Communications Media

	2011	2012	2013
Telephones ('000 main lines in use)	50.0	50.0	41.0
Mobile cellular telephones ('000 subscribers)	4,200.0	6,094.9	7,160.2
Broadband subscribers ('000)	16.7	n.a.	n.a.

Internet users ('000): 1,000 in 2009.

Source: International Telecommunication Union.

Education

(1994/95)

	Institutions	Teachers	Students
Pre-primary	n.a.	n.a.	230,391*
Primary	10,071	30,205	1,110,398
Secondary	1,038	15,275	195,418
Tertiary	n.a.	654*	6,288*

* 1990/91 figure.

Adult literacy rate (UNESCO estimates): 62.1% (males 60.1%; females 64.0%) in 2007 (Source: UNESCO Institute for Statistics).

Directory

The Government

HEAD OF STATE

President: MICHEL JOSEPH MARTELLY (took office on 14 May 2011).

CABINET
(April 2015)

In January 2015 President Michel Martelly appointed a 'consensus government', in accordance with the recommendations of a Presidential Consultative Commission.

Prime Minister: EVANS PAUL.

Minister of Foreign Affairs and Religion: DULY BRUTUS (until 31 May 2015).

Minister of Justice and Public Security: PIERRE RICHARD CASIMIR.

Minister of the Interior and Territorial Collectivities: ARIEL HENRY.

Minister of the Economy and Finance: WILSON LALEAU.

Minister of Public Works, Transport and Communications: JACQUES ROUSSEAU.

Minister of Public Health and the Population: Dr FLORENCE DUPERVAL GUILLAUME.

Minister of Agriculture, Natural Resources and Rural Development: JEAN FRANÇOIS THOMAS.

Minister of Trade and Industry: HERVEY DAY.

Minister of Tourism and Creative Industries: STÉPHANIE BALMIR VILLEDROUIN.

Minister of National Education and Vocational Training: NESMY MANIGAT.

Minister of Youth and Sports: JIMMY ALBERT.

Minister of Planning and External Co-operation: YVES GERMAIN JOSEPH.

Minister of Social Affairs and Labour: VICTOR BENOIT.

Minister of Culture: DITHNY JOAN RATON.

Minister of Communication: ROTCHILD FRANÇOIS, Jr.

Minister of Women's Affairs and Women's Rights: YVES ROSE MORQUETTE.

Minister of National Defence: LENER RENAULD.

Minister of Haitians Residing Abroad: PIERICHE OLICIER.

Minister of the Environment: JEAN MARIE CLAUDE GERMAIN.

Minister-delegate to the Prime Minister, in charge of Electoral Issues: JEAN FRITZ JEAN-LOUIS.

MINISTRIES

Office of the President: Palais National, ave de la République, Champs de Mars, Port-au-Prince; tel. 2222-3024; e-mail webmestre@palaisnational.info; internet www.lapresidence.ht.

Office of the Prime Minister: 33 blvd Harry S Truman, BP 6114, Port-au-Prince; tel. 2221-0013; e-mail primature@primature.gouv.ht; internet www.primature.gouv.ht.

Ministry of Agriculture, Natural Resources and Rural Development: Route Nationale 1, Damien, BP 1441, Port-au-Prince; tel. 2510-3916; fax 2222-3591; internet www.agriculture.gouv.ht.

Ministry of Communication: 4 rue Magny, Port-au-Prince; tel. 2223-5514.

Ministry of Culture: angle des rues de la République et Geffrard 509, Port-au-Prince; tel. 2221-3238; fax 2221-7318; e-mail contact4@ministereculture.gouv.ht; internet www.ministereculture.gouv.ht.

Ministry of the Economy and Finance: Palais des Ministères, rue Mgr Guilloux, Port-au-Prince; tel. 2223-7113; fax 2223-1247; e-mail mef@mefhaiti.gouv.ht; internet www.mefhaiti.gouv.ht.

Ministry of the Environment: 11 rue Pacot, Port-au-Prince; tel. 2943-0520.

Ministry of Foreign Affairs and Religion: blvd Harry S Truman, Cité de l'Exposition, Port-au-Prince; tel. 2222-8482; fax 2223-1668; e-mail webmaster@maehaitiinfo.org; internet www.mae.gouv.ht.

Ministry of Haitians Residing Abroad: 87 ave Jean-Paul II, Turgeau, BP 6113, Port-au-Prince; tel. 2245-1116; fax 2245-0287; e-mail info@mhave.gouv.ht; internet www.mhave.gouv.ht.

Ministry of the Interior and Territorial Collectivities: Palais des Ministères, Champs de Mars, Port-au-Prince; tel. 2223-0204; fax 2222-8057; e-mail info@mict.gouv.ht; internet www.mict.gouv.ht.

Ministry of Justice and Public Security: 19 ave Charles Summer, Port-au-Prince; tel. 2245-9737; fax 2245-0474; internet www.mjsp.gouv.ht.

Ministry of National Defence: 2 rue Bazelais, Delmas 60, BP 1106, Pétionville; tel. 3454-0501; e-mail haitidefense@gmail.com.

Ministry of National Education and Vocational Training: rue Dr Audain, Port-au-Prince; tel. 2222-1036; fax 2245-3400; e-mail menfp_info@eduhaiti.gouv.ht; internet www.eduhaiti.gouv.ht.

Ministry of Planning and External Co-operation: ave John Brown, route de Bourdon 347, Port-au-Prince; tel. 2228-2512; fax 2222-0226; e-mail info@mpce.gouv.ht; internet www.mpce.gouv.ht.

Ministry of Public Health and the Population: 111 rue Saint Honoré, Port-au-Prince; tel. 2223-6248; fax 2222-4066; e-mail info@mspp.gouv.ht; internet www.mspp.gouv.ht.

Ministry of Public Works, Transport and Communications: rue Toussaint Louverture, Delmas 33, Port-au-Prince; tel. 2222-2528; fax 2223-4519; e-mail secretariat.communications@mtptc.gouv.ht; internet www.mtptc.gouv.ht.

Ministry of Social Affairs and Labour: 16 rue de la Révolution, Port-au-Prince; tel. 2222-1244; fax 2221-0717.

Ministry of Tourism: 8 rue Légitime, Champs de Mars, Port-au-Prince; tel. 2949-2010; fax 2949-2011; e-mail info@haititourisme.gouv.ht; internet www.haititourisme.gouv.ht.

Ministry of Trade and Industry: Bureau du Ministre, 23 ave l'Amartinière, BP 6114, Port-au-Prince; tel. 2943-4488; fax 2943-1868; e-mail secretariatdumiistre@mci.gouv.ht; internet www.mci.gouv.ht.

Ministry of Women's Affairs and Women's Rights: ave Magny 4, Port-au-Prince; tel. 2224-9152; e-mail contact@mcfdf.ht; internet www.mcfdf.ht.

Ministry of Youth and Sports: Ranch de la Croix-des-Bouquets, route de Meyer, route Nationale 3, 18 route de Frères, Pétionville.

Office of the Minister-delegate to the Prime Minister, in charge of Parliamentary Relations: Delmas 48, 5 rue François, Port-au-Prince; tel. 2246-9912.

President and Legislature

PRESIDENT

Election, first round, 28 November 2010*

Candidates	Valid votes cast	%
Mirlande Manigat (RDNP)	336,878	31.37
Jude Célestin (Inite)	241,462	22.48
Michel Joseph Martelly (Repons Peyizan)	234,617	21.84
Jean Henry Ceant (Renmen Ayiti) .	87,834	8.18
Jacques-Edouard Alexis (MPH) . .	32,932	3.07
Charles Henri Baker (Respè) . . .	25,512	2.38
Total (incl others)	1,074,066	100.00

* Preliminary results from the Provisional Electoral Council. A report issued by the Organization of American States in January 2011 stated that Martelly, not Célestin, was the second-placed candidate. In February the Provisional Electoral Council announced that Manigat would face Martelly in the run-off ballot, held on 20 March.

Election, second round, 20 March 2011

Candidates	Valid votes cast	%
Michel Joseph Martelly (Repons Peyizan)	716,986	67.57
Mirlande Manigat (RDNP) . .	336,747	31.74
Total*	1,061,089	100.00

* Including 7,356 blank ballots.

LEGISLATURE

Senate
(Sénat)

President: SIMON DIEUSEUL DESRAS (Oganizasyon Lavni).

Distribution of Seats, August 2012*

	Seats
Inite	15
Alternative pour le Progrès et la Democratie (Altenativ) .	5
Fusion des Sociaux-Démocrates Haïtiens	3
Ayiti an Aksyon (AAA)	2
Konbit pou Bati Ayiti (KONBA)	1
Pou Nou Tout (PONT)	1
Organisation du Peuple en Lutte (OPL)	1
La Fanmi Lavalas (FL)	1
Oganizasyon Lavni (LAVNI)	1
Total	30

* The last elections to the Senate were held on 28 November 2010 and 20 March 2011. The terms of office of all remaining senators expired on 12 January 2015.

Chamber of Deputies
(Chambre des Députés)

President: STEVENSON JACQUES TIMOLÉON.

Elections, 28 November 2010 and 20 March 2011*

	Seats
Inite	32
Alternative pour le Progrès et la Democratie (Altenativ) .	11
Ansanm Nou Fò	10
Ayiti an Aksyon (AAA)	8
Oganizasyon Lavni (LAVNI)	7
Rasanble	4
Repons Peyizan	3
Konbit pou Refè Haïti (KONBIT)	3
Pou Nou Tout (PONT)	3
Mouvement Chrétien pour une Nouvelle Haïti (MOCHRENHA)	3
Plateforme Liberation	2
Plateforme des Patriotes Haïtiens (PLAPH) . . .	2
Mouvement Action Socialiste (MAS)	2
Mouvement Démocratique pour la Libération d'Haïti-Parti Revolutionnaire Démocratique d'Haïti (MODELH-PRDH)	1
Respè	1
Veye Yo	1
Independent	2
Vacant	4
Total	99

* The terms of office of all deputies expired on 12 January 2015.

Election Commission

The Provisional Electoral Council was dissolved in December 2011. A constitutional amendment of 19 June 2012 allowed for the formation of a new electoral body, the Permanent Electoral Council. According to the Constitution, the nine-member commission would comprise three representatives from each of the three branches of government. A Memorandum of Understanding on 24 December 2012 formed the Transitional College of the Permanent Electoral Council. In May 2014 the Permanent Electoral Council was renamed the Provisional Electoral Council and in July the nine members of the Council were appointed; however, in December the Council resigned following the recommendation of a Presidential Consultative Commission. A new Electoral Council was appointed in January 2015. The new body was to organize the overdue legislative elections.

Conseil Electoral Provisoire (CEP): Port-au-Prince; f. 2015; 9 mems; Pres. PIERRE LOUIS OPONT.

Political Organizations

Action Démocratique pour Bâtir Haïti (ADEBHA): 509 route de Delmas, entre Delmas 103 et 105, Port-au-Prince; tel. 2256-6739; fax 3446-6161; e-mail versun_etatdedroit@yahoo.fr; internet www.adebha.populus.org; f. 2004; Pres. RENÉ JULIEN.

Alliance pour la Libération et l'Avancement d'Haïti (ALAH): Haut Turgeau 95, BP 13350, Port-au-Prince; tel. 2245-0446; fax 2257-4804; e-mail reynoldgeorges@yahoo.com; f. 1975; Leader REYNOLD GEORGES.

Alternative pour le Progrès et la Democratie (Altenativ): f. 2010; grouping of more than 70 legislative candidates; Mems of Exec. Cttee ROSNY SMART, EDGARD LEBLANC FILS, VICTOR BENOÎT, SERGE GILLES.

Ansanm Nou Fò: Leader LESLIE VOLTAIRE.

Ayiti an Aksyon (AAA): Port-au-Prince; internet ayitianaksyon.net; Pres. YOURI LATORTUE.

La Fanmi Lavalas (FL): blvd 15 Octobre, Tabarre, Port-au-Prince; tel. 2256-7208; internet www.hayti.net; f. 1996 by Jean-Bertrand Aristide; barred from contesting the 2010 elections.

Force Patriotique pour le Respect de la Constitution (FOPARC): Port-au-Prince; mem. of the opposition movt Table de Concertation de l'Opposition Radicale; Leaders RONY TIMOTHÉE, BIRON ODIGÉ.

Fòs Patriotik ou Respè Konstitsyon an (FOPARK) (Patriotic Force for the Respect of the Constitution): Port-au-Prince; opposition coalition; Nat. Dir BIRON ODIGE.

Front pour la Reconstruction Nationale (FRN): Gonaïves; f. 2004; Sec.-Gen. GUY PHILIPPE.

Fusion des Sociaux-Démocrates Haïtiens (FUSION): Port-au-Prince; opposition party; Pres. EDMONDE SUPPLICE BEAUZILE.

Grand Rassemblement pour l'Evolution d'Haïti (GREH): Port-au-Prince; f. 2003; Leader Col (retd) HIMLER RÉBU.

Inite: Port-au-Prince; f. 2009 to replace Lespwa (l'Espoir, f. 2005); opposition party; Leaders PAUL DENIS, SOREL JACINTHE.

KONAKOM (Congrès National des Mouvements Démocratiques): Bois Verna, Port-au-Prince; tel. 2245-6228; f. 1987; social democratic; Leader DUNOIS ERICK CANTANDE.

Konbit pou Bati Ayiti (KONBA): Port-au-Prince; f. 2005.

Konbit pou Refè Haïti (KONBIT): Port-au-Prince.

Konfyans: Port-au-Prince; centre-left; Leader RUDY HÉRIVEAUX.

Kontra Pèp La: Port-au-Prince; opposition party; Leader JEAN WILLIAM JEANTY.

Konvansyon Inite Demokratik (KID): 14 rue Camille Leon, Port-au-Prince; tel. 245-0185; f. 1986; fmrly Konfederasyon Inite Demokratik; Sec.-Gen. Dr ENOLD JOSEPH.

Mobilisation pour le Progrès Haïtien (MPH): Port-au-Prince; Leader JACQUES-EDOUARD ALEXIS.

Mouvement Action Socialiste (MAS): Hinche.

Mouvement Chrétien pour une Nouvelle Haïti (MOCHRENHA): rue M 7 Turgeau, Carrefour, Port-au-Prince; tel. 3443-3120; e-mail mochrenha@hotmail.com; f. 1998; Leaders LUC MÉSADIEU, GILBERT N. LÉGER.

Mouvement Démocratique pour la Libération d'Haïti-Parti Revolutionnaire Démocratique d'Haïti (MODELH-PRDH): Leader FRANÇOIS LATORTUE.

Mouvement Indépendant pour la Réconciliation Nationale (MIRN): Port-au-Prince; Leader LUC FLEURINORD.

Mouvement de Liberté d'Égalité des Haitiens pour la Fraternité (MOLEGHAF): Port-au-Prince; mem. of the opposition movt Table de Concertation de l'Opposition Radicale.

Mouvement Patriotique de l'Opposition Démocratique (MOPOD): Port-au-Prince; f. as umbrella opposition movt, registered as political party in 2014; mem. of the opposition movt Table de Concertation de l'Opposition Radicale; Gen. Co-ordinator JEAN ANDRÉ VICTOR.

Nouveau Parti Communiste Haïtien (NPCH): Grand Rue 1, Nan Gonmye; e-mail vanialubin@yahoo.fr; internet www.npch.net; Marxist-Leninist.

Oganizasyon Lavni (LAVNI): Leader YVES CHRISTALIN.

Organisation du Peuple en Lutte (OPL): 105 ave L'Amartinière, Bois Verna, Port-au-Prince; tel. 2245-4214; f. 1991 as Organisation Politique Lavalas; name changed as above 1998; formed an alliance with Alyans and the Fusion des Sociaux-Démocrates Haïtiens to contest the 2010 elections; Leader SAUVEUR PIERRE ETIENNE; Nat. Co-ordinator EDGARD LEBLANC FILS.

Parti Agricole Industriel National (PAIN): f. 1956; Pres. HÉBERT DOCTEUR.

Parti pour l'Evolution Nationale d'Haïti (PENH): Port-au-Prince; Leader ERIC SMARKI CHARLES.

Parti Haïtien Tèt Kale: Port-au-Prince; f. 2014 by Pres. Michel Martelly (fmrly of the Repons Peyizan); Pres. ANN VALÉRIE TIMOTHÉE MILFORT.

Parti des Industriels, Travailleurs, Agents du Développement et Commercants d'Haïti (PITACH): Port-au-Prince.

Parti Nationale Démocratique Progressiste d'Haïti (PNDPH): Port-au-Prince; reactivated 2014; Pres. TURNEB DELPÉ.

Plateforme Liberation: Port-au-Prince.

Plateforme des Patriotes Haïtiens (PLAPH): Cap-Haïtien.

Pou Nou Tout (PONT): Port-au-Prince.

Rasanble: Port-au-Prince.

Rassemblement des Démocrates Nationaux et Progressistes (RDNP): 234 route de Delmas, Delmas, Port-au-Prince; tel. 2246-3313; f. 1979; centre party; Sec.-Gen. MIRLANDE MANIGAT.

Regwoupman Sitwayen pou Espwa (Respè): Port-au-Prince; f. 2009; centre party; Pres. CHARLES HENRI BAKER.

Renmen Ayiti: Port-au-Prince; e-mail info@renmenayiti.org; internet www.renmenayiti.org; Leader JEAN HENRY CEANT.

Union de Citoyens Ayisyen pour la Démocratie, le Développement et l'Education (UCADDE): Miragoâne.

Veye Yo: Cap-Haïtien.

Diplomatic Representation

EMBASSIES IN HAITI

Argentina: 48 rue Metellus, Pétionville, Port-au-Prince; tel. 2940-6711; fax 2940-6714; e-mail ehait@mrecic.gov.ar; internet ehait.mrecic.gov.ar; Ambassador ALEJANDRO GUILLERMO ESCOBAL.

Bahamas: 12 rue Boyer, Pétionville, Port-au-Prince; tel. 2257-8782; fax 2256-5759; e-mail bahamasembassy@hainet.net; Ambassador GODFREY GORDON ROLLE.

Brazil: Immeuble Héxagone, 3ème étage, angle des rues Clerveaux et Darguin, Pétionville, BP 15845, Port-au-Prince; tel. 2256-0900; fax 2510-6111; e-mail brasemb1@accesshaiti.com; internet portoprincipe.itamaraty.gov.br; Ambassador JOSÉ LUIZ MACHADO E COSTA.

Canada: route de Delmas, entre Delmas 71 et 75, BP 826, Port-au-Prince; tel. 2249-9000; fax 2249-9920; e-mail prnce@international.gc.ca; internet www.canadainternational.gc.ca/haiti; Ambassador PAULA CALDWELL ST-ONGE.

Chile: 2 rue Coutilien et rue Delmas 60, Musseau, Port-au-Prince; tel. 2813-1613; fax 2813-1708; e-mail embajadachile_haiti@hotmail.com; internet chileabroad.gov.cl/haiti; Ambassador RAUL FERNÁNDEZ DAZA.

Cuba: 3 rue Marion, Peguy Ville, Pétionville, POB 15702, Port-au-Prince; tel. 2256-3503; fax 2257-8566; e-mail secretaria@ht.embacuba.cu; internet www.cubadiplomatica.cu/haiti; Ambassador RICARDO SOTERO GARCÍA NÁPOLES.

Dominican Republic: rue Panaméricaine 121, BP 56, Pétionville, Port-au-Prince; tel. 2813-0887; fax 3257-0383; e-mail embrepdomhai@yahoo.com; Ambassador RUBÉN SILIÉ VALDEZ.

France: 51 rue de Capois, BP 1312, Port-au-Prince; tel. 2999-9000; fax 2999-9001; e-mail ambafrance@hainet.net; internet www.ambafrance-ht.org; Ambassador PATRICK NICOLOSO.

Germany: 2 impasse Claudinette, Bois Moquette, Pétionville, BP 1147, Port-au-Prince; tel. 2949-0202; fax 2257-4131; e-mail info@port-au-prince.diplo.de; internet www.port-au-prince.diplo.de; Ambassador KLAUS PETER SCHICK.

Holy See: rue Louis Pouget, Morne Calvaire, BP 326, Port-au-Prince; tel. 2257-6308; fax 2257-3411; e-mail nonciatureap@hughes.net; Apostolic Nuncio Most Rev. EUGENE MARTIN NUGENT (Titular Archbishop of Domnach Sechnaill).

Japan: Hexagone, 2ème étage, angle rues Clerveaux et Darguin, Pétionville, Port-au-Prince; tel. 2256-3333; fax 2256-9444; internet www.ht.emb-japan.go.jp; Ambassador TAKASHI FUCHIGAMI (resident in the Dominican Republic).

Mexico: rue Métélus 48, Pétionville, BP 327, Port-au-Prince; tel. 2813-0089; fax 2256-6528; e-mail embhaiti@sre.gob.mx; internet embamex.sre.gob.mx/haiti; Ambassador JOSÉ LUIS ALVARADO GONZÁLEZ.

Panama: 157 rue Panaméricaine, Pétionville, Port-au-Prince; tel. 2813-1295; fax 3864-4881; e-mail panaembahaiti@yahoo.com; internet www.panamaenelexterior.gob.pa/Haiti; Ambassador JOHN EVANS ATHERLEY.

Spain: 50 rue Metellus, Pétionville, BP 386, Port-au-Prince; tel. 2940-0952; e-mail Emb.PuertoPrincipe@maec.es; internet www.maec.es/embajadas/puertoprincipe; Ambassador MANUEL LORENZO GARCÍA ORMAECHEA.

Taiwan (Republic of China): 22 rue Lucien Hubert, Morne Calvaire, Pétionville, Port-au-Prince; tel. 3775-0109; fax 2256-8067; e-mail haiti888@gmail.com; internet www.taiwanembassy.org/HT; Ambassador PETER HWANG.

United Kingdom: rue Delmas 73–75, Port-au-Prince; tel. 2812-9191; Ambassador STEVEN FISHER (resident in the Dominican Republic), SHARON CAMPBELL (from Oct. 2015).

USA: Tabarre 41, blvd 15 Octobre, Port-au-Prince; tel. 2229-8000; fax 2229-8028; internet haiti.usembassy.gov; Ambassador PAMELA WHITE.

Venezuela: blvd Harry S Truman, Cité de l'Exposition, BP 2158, Port-au-Prince; tel. 3443-4127; fax 2223-7672; e-mail embavenezhaiti@hainet.net; Ambassador PEDRO ANTONIO CANINO GONZÁLEZ.

Judicial System

Law is based on the French Napoleonic Code, substantially modified during the presidency of François Duvalier.

Courts of Appeal and Civil Courts sit at Port-au-Prince and the three provincial capitals: Gonaïves, Cap-Haïtien and Port de Paix. In principle each commune has a Magistrates' Court. Judges of the Supreme Court and Courts of Appeal are appointed by the President. Constitutional amendments in 2012 created a Supreme Council of

Judicial Power and a constitutional court (which was yet to be appointed in early 2015).

Conseil Supérieur du Pouvoir Judiciaire (Supreme Council of Judicial Power): la route de Frères, Port-au-Prince; f. 2012 to oversee judicial system, ensure separation of powers; 9 mems; Pres. (vacant).

Cour de Cassation (Supreme Court): Port-au-Prince; Pres. (vacant).

Citizens' Rights Defender: FLORENCE ÉLIE.

Religion

Roman Catholicism and the folk religion Voodoo (vodou) are the official religions. There are various Protestant and other denominations.

CHRISTIANITY

The Roman Catholic Church

For ecclesiastical purposes, Haiti comprises two archdioceses and eight dioceses. Some 55% of the population are Roman Catholics, according to the 2003 census.

Bishops' Conference: Conférence Episcopale de Haïti, angle rues Piquant et Lammarre, BP 1572, Port-au-Prince; tel. 222-5194; fax 223-5318; e-mail ceh56@hotmail.com; internet ceh.ht; f. 1977; Pres. Cardinal CHIBLY LANGLOIS (Bishop of Les Cayes).

Archbishop of Cap-Haïtien: Most Rev. MAX LEROY MÉSIDOR, Archevêché, rue 19–20 H, BP 22, Cap-Haïtien; tel. 262-0071; fax 262-1278.

Archbishop of Port-au-Prince: GUIRE POULARD, Archevêché, rue Dr Aubry, BP 538, Port-au-Prince; tel. 2943-4446; e-mail guypoulard@hotmail.com; internet archidiocesedepaup.org.

The Anglican Communion

Anglicans in Haiti fall under the jurisdiction of a missionary diocese of Province II of the Episcopal Church in the USA.

Bishop of Haiti: Rt Rev. JEAN ZACHÉ DURACIN, Eglise Episcopale d'Haïti, BP 1309, Port-au-Prince; tel. 2257-1624; fax 2257-0412, e-mail epihaiti@egliseepiscopaledhaiti.org; internet www .egliseepiscopaledhaiti.org.

Other Christian Churches

According to the 2003 census, some 15% of the population were Baptists and 8% were Pentecostalists.

Baptist Convention: Route Nationale 1, Cazeau BP 2601, Port-au-Prince; tel. 3195-4664; e-mail conventionbaptiste@yahoo.com; f. 1964; Gen. Sec. EMMANUEL PIERRE.

Evangelical Lutheran Church of Haiti: Eglise Evangélique Luthérienne d'Haïti, 29 Route de Frère, Impasse Perpignant 8, Port-au-Prince; tel. 2947-2347; e-mail info@lutheranchurchofhaiti .org; internet www.lutheranchurchofhaiti.org; f. 1975; Pres. Rev. JOSEPH LIVENSON LAUVANUS; 9,000 mems.

Other denominations active in Haiti include Methodists, Church of the Latter-Day Saints (Mormons) and the Church of God 'Eben-Ezer'.

VOODOO

Konfederasyon Nasyonal Vodou Ayisyen (KNVA): Le Péristyle de Mariani, Mariani; tel. 3458-1500; f. 2008; Supreme Leader FRANÇOIS MAX GESNER BEAUVOIR.

The Press

DAILY

Le Nouvelliste: 198 rue du Centre, Port-au-Prince; tel. 2222-4754; fax 2224-2061; e-mail manigapier@lenouvelliste.com; internet www .lenouvelliste.com; f. 1898; evening; French; ind; Editor-in-Chief FRANTZ DUVAL; Publr JEAN MAX CHAUVET; circ. 10,000.

PERIODICALS

Ayiti Fanm: Centre National et International de Documentation, d'Information et de Défense des Droits des Femmes en Haïti, 16 rue de La Ligue Féminine, BP 6114, Port-au-Prince; tel. 2245-0346; fax 2244-1841; e-mail ayitifanm@enfofanm.net; internet www .ayitifanm.org; f. 1991; monthly; publ. by ENFOFANM; Creole; Founder and Editor-in-Chief CLORINDE ZÉPHIR; Dir MYRIAM MERLET.

Haïti en Marche: 74 bis, rue Capois, Port-au-Prince; tel. 3454-0126; e-mail melodiefm@gmail.com; internet www.haitienmarche.com; f. 1986; weekly; Editors MARC GARCIA, ELSIE ETHÉART.

Haïti Observateur: 98 ave John Brown, 3ème étage, Port-au-Prince; tel. 2223-0782; e-mail contact@haiti-observateur.net;

internet www.haiti-observateur.net; f. 1971; weekly; Editor RAY-MOND JOSEPH; circ. 75,000.

Haïti Progrès: 61, Rue Capois, Port-au-Prince; tel. 3446-1957; fax 3680-9397; e-mail editor@haiti-progres.com; internet www .haiti-progres.com; f. 1983; weekly; French, English, Spanish and Creole; Dir MAUDE LEBLANC.

Le Matin: 3 rue Goulard, Pétionville, Port-au-Prince; tel. 4688-3876; e-mail lematinpublicite@gmail.com; internet www.lematinhaiti .com; f. 1907; French; publ. every other week from Jan. 2010; ind; Editor-in-Chief DALY VALET; Publr RÉGINALD BOULOS; circ. 5,000.

Le Moniteur: Presses Nationales d'Haïti, rue Hammerton Killick 231, BP 1746 bis, Port-au-Prince; tel. 2222-1744; fax 2223-1026; e-mail pndh-moniteur@hainet.net; f. 1845; 2 a week; French; official state gazette; Dir-Gen. WILLEMS EDOUARD; circ. 2,000.

Le Septentrion: Cap-Haïtien; weekly; ind; Editor NELSON BELL; circ. 2,000.

NEWS AGENCIES

Agence Haïtienne de Presse (AHP): 6 rue Fernand, Port-au-Prince; tel. 2245-7222; fax 2245-5836; e-mail ahp@yahoo.com; internet www.ahphaiti.org; f. 1989; publishes daily news bulletins in French and English; Dir-Gen. GEORGES VENEL REMARAIS.

AlterPresse: 38 Delmas 8, BP 19211, Port-au-Prince; tel. 2249-9493; e-mail alterpresse@medialternatif.org; internet www .alterpresse.org; f. 2001; independent; owned by Alternative Media Group; Dir GOTSON PIERRE.

Haiti Press Network: 14 rue Lamarre, Pétionville, Port-au-Prince; tel. 2511-6555; fax 2256-6197; e-mail hpnhaiti@yahoo.fr; internet www.hpnhaiti.com; Dir CLARENS RENOIS.

Publishers

Editions des Antilles: route de l'Aéroport, Delmas, Port-au-Prince; tel. 2940-0217; fax 2249-1225; e-mail editiondesantilles@yahoo.com.

Editions Caraïbes, SA: 57 rue Pavéo, BP 2010, Port-au-Prince; tel. 2222-0002; e-mail piereh@yahoo.fr; Man. PIERRE J. ELIE.

Editions CUC-Université Caraïbe: 7, Delmas 29, Port-au-Prince; tel. 2246-5531; e-mail editions@universitecaraibe.com; internet www.editionsuniversitecaraibe.com.

Editions Les Presses Nationales d'Haïti: 61 rue Goulard, Pétion-Ville; tel. 2941-7909; fax 2223-1026; e-mail info@pressesnationales .ht; internet www.pressesnationales.ht.

Imprimerie Roland Theodore, SA: Delmas 1A, No 19, Delmas; tel. 2940-7200; e-mail info@imprimerie-theodore.com; internet www .imprimerie-theodore.com; Gen. Man. HENRI THEODORE.

Maison Henri Deschamps—Les Entreprises Deschamps Frisch, SA: 25 rue Dr Martelly Seïde, BP 164, Port-au-Prince; tel. 2223-2215; fax 2223-4976; e-mail entdeschamps@gdfhaiti.com; internet www.maisonhenrideschamps.com; f. 1898; education and literature; divisions include Editions Hachette-Deschamps and Imprimerie Henri Deschamps; Man. Dir JACQUES DESCHAMPS, Jr; CEO HENRI R. DESCHAMPS.

Broadcasting and Communications

REGULATORY BODY

Conseil National des Télécommunications (CONATEL): 4 ave Christophe, BP 2002, Port-au-Prince; tel. 2511-3940; fax 2223-9229; e-mail info@conatel.gouv.ht; internet www.conatel.gouv.ht; f. 1969; govt communications licensing authority; Dir-Gen. JEAN MARIE GUILLAUME.

TELECOMMUNICATIONS

Digicel Haiti: 151 angle ave John Paul II et Impasse Duverger, BP 15516, Port-au-Prince; tel. 3711-3444; e-mail customercarehaiti@ digicelgroup.com; internet www.digicelhaiti.com; f. 2005; owned by Digicel (Ireland); mobile telephone network provider; Group Chair. DENIS O'BRIEN; CEO, Haiti DAMIAN BLACKBURN.

HaiTel (Haiti Telecommunications International, SA): 17 rue Darguin, 3ème étage, Pétionville, Port-au-Prince; tel. 3510-1201; fax 3510-6273; f. 1999; part-owned by US-based MCI WorldCom; mobile telecommunications provider; Pres. FRANCK CINÉ.

Multilink Haiti: Autoroute de Delmas, angle Delmas 18, 1er étage, Port-au-Prince; tel. 2813-0231; fax 2949-2929; e-mail info@multilink .ht; internet www.multilink.ht; f. 1999; internet service provider; Gen. Man. PAOLO CHILOSI.

Natcom (National Télécom, SA): angle ave Martin Luther King et rue Fernand, Pont-Morin, BP 814, Port-au-Prince; tel. 2222-8888;

fax 3939-3939; e-mail info@haititeleco.com; internet www.natcom .com.ht; fmrly Télécommunications d'Haiti (Haiti Téléco); renamed as above in 2010; 60% owned by Viettel (Viet Nam), 40% govt-owned; landline provider; Dir YVES ARMAND.

BROADCASTING

Radio

La Brise FM 104.9: Camp Perrin, Les Cayes, Sud; tel. 3709-6021; e-mail contact@labrisefm.com; internet www.labrisefm.com; f. 2007; music station; Dir MAX ALAIN LOUIS.

Radio Antilles International: 75 rue du Centre, BP 2335, Port-au-Prince; tel. 3433-0712; fax 2222-0260; e-mail jacquessampeur@yahoo .com; f. 1984; independent; Dir-Gen. JACQUES SAMPEUR.

Radio Caraïbes: 45 rue Chavannes, Port-au-Prince; tel. 3558-9110; e-mail radiocaraibesfm@yahoo.fr; internet radiotelevisioncaraibes .com; f. 1949; owned by Moussignac Group; broadcasts in Port-au-Prince area; Dir PATRICK MOUSSIGNAC.

Radio Galaxie: 17 rue Pavée, Port-au-Prince; tel. 2432-4473; e-mail info@radiogalaxiehaiti.com; internet www.radiogalaxiehaiti.com; f. 1990; independent; Dir YVES JEAN-BART.

Radio Ginen: 28 bis, Delmas 31, BP 6120, Port-au-Prince; tel. 2249-9292; fax 2511-1737; e-mail info@rtghaiti.com; internet www .rtghaiti.com; f. 1994; Dir JEAN LUCIEN BORGES.

Radio Ibo: 51 route du Canapé-Vert, BP 15174, Pétionville, Port-au-Prince; tel. 3557-5214; fax 2245-9850; e-mail ibo@radioibo.net; internet radioibo.net; Dir HÉROLD JEAN FRANÇOIS.

Radio Kiskeya: 42 rue Villemenay, Boisverna, Port-au-Prince; tel. 2244-6605; e-mail admin@radiokiskeya.com; internet radiokiskeya .com; f. 1994; Dir MARVEL DANDIN.

Radio Lumière: Côte-Plage 16, Carrefour, BP 1050, Port-au-Prince; tel. 2234-0331; fax 2234-3708; e-mail rlumiere@ radiolumiere.org; internet www.radiolumiere.org; f. 1959; Protestant; independent; Dir VARNEL JEUNE.

Radio Mélodie: 74 bis, rue Capois, Port-au-Prince; tel. 2452-0428; e-mail melodiefm@gmail.com; internet radiomelodiehaiti.com; f. 1998; Dir MARCUS GARCIA.

Radio Metropole: 8 route de Delmas 52, BP 62, Port-au-Prince; tel. 2246-2626; fax 2249-2020; e-mail informations@naskita.com; internet www.metropolehaiti.com; f. 1970; independent; Pres. HERBERT WIDMAIER; Dir-Gen. RICHARD WIDMAIER.

Radio Nationale d'Haïti: see Télévision Nationale d'Haïti.

Radio Nirvana FM: Cap-Haïtien; tel. 2431-5784; e-mail pdg@ radionirvanafm.com; internet www.radionirvanafm.com; Dir-Gen. RAPHAEL ABRAHAM.

Radio Port-au-Prince Plus: Stade Sylvio Cator, BP 863, Port-au-Prince; tel. 3927-3182; e-mail contactus@radioportauprinceplus .com; internet www.radioportauprinceplus.com; f. 1979; independent; broadcasts in Creole and English; religious programming; Dir-Gen. MAX PRINCE.

Radio Superstar: Delmas 68, angle rues Safran et C. Henri, Pétionville, Port-au-Prince; tel. 3734-2254; fax 2257-3015; e-mail info@radiosuperstarhaiti.com; internet www.superstarhaiti.com; f. 1987; independent; Dir ALBERT CHANCY, Jr.

Radio Tele Megastar: 106 rue de la Réunion, Port-au-Prince; tel. 3711-1197; e-mail jcharleus0@yahoo.com; internet www .radiotelemegastar.com; f. 1991; Pres. and Dir-Gen. JEAN-EDDY CHARLEUS.

Radio Télé Venus: 106 rue 5 et 6 E, Cap-Haïtien; tel. 2262-2742; fax 3780-8053; internet www.radiotelevenushaiti.com; f. 1994.

Radio Vision 2000: 184 ave John Brown, BP 13247, Port-au-Prince; tel. 2813-1875; e-mail info@radiovision2000.com; internet www .radiovision2000haiti.net; f. 1991; Dir LÉOPOLD BERLANGER.

Sans Souci FM: 57, rue 26, blvd Carénage, Cap-Haïtien; tel. 2813-1874; fax 3701-5913; e-mail sanssoucifm@radiosanssouci.com; internet www.radiosanssouci.com; f. 1998; Dir IVES MARIE CHANEL.

Signal FM: 127 rue Louverture, Pétionville, BP 391, Port-au-Prince; tel. 2256-4368; fax 2256-4396; e-mail info@signalfmhaiti.com; internet www.signalfmhaiti.com; f. 1991; independent; Dir-Gen. MARIO VIAU.

Television

CanalSat Haïti: angle des rues Faustin 1er et Chériez, Canapé-Vert, Port-au-Prince; tel. 2946-4141; internet www.emitelsa.com; f. 2011; satellite broadcaster, 46 European channels and 10 radio stations, mostly in French; Exec. Dir RÉGINALD BAKER.

NU TV: 57 rue Clerveaux, Pétionville, Port-au-Prince; tel. 4438-1204; e-mail ialerte@nu-tv.com; internet www.nu-tv.com; f. 2012; 90 Haitian, European, North American and Spanish-language TV channels via satellite; CEO PATRICE TURNIER.

Télé Caraïbes: 45 rue Chavannes, Port-au-Prince; tel. 3558-9110; e-mail radiocaraibesfm@yahoo.fr; internet www .radiotelevisioncaraibes.com; broadcasts in Port-au-Prince area; owned by Moussignac Group; Dir PATRICK MOUSSIGNAC; Exec. Dir WEIBERT ARTHUS.

Télé Eclair: 526 route de Delmas, Port-au-Prince; tel. 2256-4505; fax 2256-3828; f. 1996; independent; Dir PATRICK ANDRÉ JOSEPH.

Télé Ginen: 28 bis, Delmas 31, BP 6120, Port-au-Prince; tel. 2949-2407; fax 2511-1737; e-mail info@rtghaiti.com; internet www .rtghaiti.com; nationwide transmission; Owner, Dir and Gen. Man. JEAN LUCIEN BORGES.

Télé Haïti (Société Haïtienne de Télévision par Satellites, SA): blvd Harry S Truman, Bicentenaire, BP 1126, Port-au-Prince; tel. 2222-3887; fax 2222-9140; e-mail info@telhaiti.com; internet www .telehaiti.net; f. 1959; bldg destroyed by 2010 earthquake, recommenced broadcasts in 2012; pay cable station with 128 international channels; broadcasts in French, Spanish and English; Pres. ALLEN BAYARD.

Télé Metropole: 8 route de Delmas 52, BP 62, Port-au-Prince; tel. 2246-2626; fax 2249-2020; e-mail informations@naskita.com; internet www.metropolehaiti.com; f. 2007; broadcasts to Port-au-Prince area, mainly in French; Pres. HERBERT WIDMAIER; Dir-Gen. RICHARD WIDMAIER.

Télémax: 3 Delmas 19, Port-au-Prince; tel. 246-2002; fax 2246-1155; f. 1994; independent; Dir ROBERT DENIS.

Télévision Nationale d'Haïti: Delmas 33, BP 13400, Port-au-Prince; tel. 2246-2325; fax 2246-0693; e-mail info@tnh.ht; internet www.tnhtv.ht; f. 1979; merged with Radio Nationale d'Haïti in 1987; govt-owned; cultural; 4 channels in Creole, French and Spanish; administered by 4-mem. board; Dir-Gen.(Television) EMMANUEL MÉNARD; Dir-Gen. (Radio) HARRISON ERNEST.

Finance

(cap. = capital; m. = million; res = reserves; dep. = deposits; brs = branches; amounts in gourdes)

BANKING

Central Bank

Banque de la République d'Haïti: angle rues du Pavée et du Quai, BP 1570, Port-au-Prince; tel. 2299-1202; fax 2299-1145; e-mail webmaster@brh.net; internet www.brh.net; f. 1911 as Banque Nationale de la République d'Haïti; name changed as above in 1979; bank of issue; administered by 5-mem. board; cap. 50m., res 3,053.4m., dep. 55,355.2m. (Sept. 2009); Gov. CHARLES CASTEL; Gen. Man. MARC HÉBERT IGNACE.

Commercial Banks

Banque Nationale de Crédit: angle rues du Quai et des Miracles, BP 1320, Port-au-Prince; tel. 2299-4081; fax 2299-4076; internet www.bnconline.com; f. 1979; cap. 25m., dep. 729.9m. (Sept. 1989); Pres. JEAN PHILIPPE VIXAMAR; Dir-Gen. JOSEPH EDY DUBUISSON.

Banque Populaire Haïtienne: angle rues Aubran et Gabart, Pétionville, Port-au-Prince; tel. 2299-6080; fax 2299-6076; e-mail bphinfo@brh.net; f. 1973; state-owned; cap. and res 72.9m., dep. 819m. (Mar. 2007); Dirs-Gen. JESLY LÉVÊQUE, MYRIAM JEAN; 3 brs.

Banque de l'Union Haïtienne: angle rues du Quai et Bonne Foi, BP 275, Port-au-Prince; tel. 2299-8500; fax 2299-8517; e-mail contact@buhsa.com; internet www.buh.ht; f. 1973; cap. 30.1m., res 6.2m. (Sept. 1997), dep. 1,964.3m. (Sept. 2004); Pres. MARCEL FONTIN; 12 brs.

Capital Bank: 38 rue Flaubert, Pétionville, BP 2464, Port-au-Prince; tel. 2299-6700; fax 2299-6520; e-mail capitalbank@brh.net; internet www.capitalbankhaiti.com; f. 1985; fmrly Banque de Crédit Immobilier, SA; cap. 270m., res 141.9m., dep. 6,903.3m. (Sept. 2011); Pres. BERNARD ROY; Gen. Man. LILIANE C. DOMINIQUE.

Scotiabank Haiti (Canada): 360 blvd J. J. Dessalines, BP 686, Port-au-Prince; tel. 2941-3001; e-mail bns.haiti@scotiabank.com; f. 1972; Country Man. CHESTER A. S. HINKSON; 4 brs.

Sogebank, SA (Société Générale Haïtienne de Banque, SA): route de Delmas, BP 1315, Port-au-Prince; tel. 2229-5000; fax 2229-5022; e-mail sogebanking@sogebank.com; internet www.sogebank.com; f. 1986; part of Groupe Sogebank; cap. 1,050m., res. 1,252.4m., dep 38,539.5m. (Sept. 2013); CEO ROBERT MOSCOSO; 35 brs.

Unibank: 157 rue Flaubert, Pétionville, BP 46, Port-au-Prince; tel. 2299-2057; fax 2299-2069; e-mail info@unibankhaiti.com; internet www.unibankhaiti.com; f. 1993; cap. 2,093.4m., res 837.1m., dep. 43,280.6m. (Sept. 2013); Pres. F. CARL BRAUN; 20 brs.

INSURANCE

Principal Companies

Alternative Insurance, SA: 4 rue Jean Gilles, blvd Toussaint Louverture, Port-au-Prince; tel. 2229-6300; fax 2250-1461; e-mail info@aic.ht; internet www.aic.ht; Dir-Gen. OLIVIER BARREAU.

Les Assurances Léger, SA (ALSA): 40 rue Lamarre, BP 2120, Port-au-Prince; tel. 2816-8888; fax 2223-8634; e-mail alsa@alsagroup.com; f. 1994; headquarters in France; Man. S. ABDALLAH.

Compagnie d'Assurances d'Haïti, SA (CAH): étage Dynamic Entreprise, route de l'Aéroport, BP 1489, Port-au-Prince; tel. 2250-0700; fax 2250-0236; e-mail info@groupedynamic.com; internet www.groupedynamic.com/cah.php; f. 1978; subsidiary of Groupe Dynamic SA; Group Chair. and CEO PHILIPPE R. ARMAND.

Excelsior Assurance, SA: rue 6, no 24, Port-au-Prince; tel. 2245-8881; fax 2245-8598; e-mail ingesanon@yahoo.fr; Dir-Gen. EMMANUEL SANON.

Haïti Sécurité Assurance, SA: 352 ave John Brown, BP 1754, Bourdon, Port-au-Prince; tel. 3489-3444; fax 3489-3423; e-mail admin@haiti-securite.com; internet www.haiti-securite.com; f. 1985; Dir-Gen. WILLIAM PHIPPS.

MAVSA Multi Assurances, SA: étage Dynamic Entreprise, route de l'Aéroport, BP 1489, Port-au-Prince; tel. 2250-0700; fax 2250-0236; e-mail info@groupedynamic.com; internet www.groupedynamic.com/mavsa.php; f. 1992; subsidiary of Groupe Dynamic SA; credit life insurance and pension plans; Group Chair. and CEO PHILIPPE R. ARMAND.

National d'Assurance, SA (NASSA): 25 rue Ferdinand Canapé-Vert, BP 532, Port-au-Prince, HT6115; tel. 2245-9800; fax 2245-9701; e-mail nassa@nassagroup.com; internet www.nassagroup.com; f. 1989; specializing in property, medical and life insurance; Pres. FRITZ DUPUY.

National Western Life Insurance: 13 rue Pie XII, Cité de l'Exposition, Port-au-Prince; tel. 2223-0734; e-mail intlmktg@globalnw.com; headquarters in USA; Chair. and CEO ROBERT L. MOODY; Pres. ROSS R. MOODY.

Office National d'Assurance Vieillesse (ONA): 21 angle des rue Grégoire et Villate, Pétionville, Port-au-Prince; tel. 2256-6272; fax 2256-6274; e-mail ona@ona.ht; internet www.ona.ht; f. 1965; Dir-Gen. EMMANUEL MÉNARD.

Société de Commercialisation d'Assurance, SA (SOCOMAS): étage Complexe STELO, 56 route de Delmas, BP 636, Port-au-Prince; tel. 2246-4768; fax 2246-4874; e-mail socomashaiti@hotmail.com; Dir-Gen. JEAN DIDIER GARDÈRE.

Association

Association des Assureurs d'Haïti: 153 rue des Miracles, Port-au-Prince; tel. 2223-0796; fax 2223-8634; e-mail harold.cadet@alsagroup.com; Pres. FRITZ DECATALOGNE.

Trade and Industry

GOVERNMENT AGENCIES

Centre de Facilitation des Investissements (CFI): 8 rue Légitime, Champs de Mars, BP 6110, Port-au-Prince; tel. 2514-5792; fax 2224-8990; e-mail fihaiti@gmail.com; internet www.cfihaiti.net; f. 2006; foreign investment promotion; Dir-Gen. NORMA POWELL.

Centre National des Équipements (CNE): Port-au-Prince; state-run construction co; Dir-Gen. JUDE CÉLESTIN.

Conseil de Modernisation des Entreprises Publiques (CMEP): Palais National, Port-au-Prince; tel. 2222-4111; fax 2222-7761; internet www.cmep.gouv.ht; f. 1996; oversees modernization and privatization of state enterprises; Dir-Gen. YVES BASTIEN.

DEVELOPMENT ORGANIZATIONS

Fonds de Développement Industriel (FDI): 12 angle rue Butte et impasse Chabrier, BP 2597, Port-au-Prince; tel. 2244-9728; fax 2244-9727; e-mail fdi@fdihaiti.com; internet www.fdihaiti.com; f. 1981; Dir-Gen. LHERMITE FRANÇOIS.

Mouvman Peyizan Papay (MPP): Papaye, Hinche; internet www.mpphaiti.org; f. 1973; peasant org., chiefly concerned with food production and land protection; Leader CHAVANNES JEAN-BAPTISTE.

Société Financière Haïtienne de Développement, SA (SOFIHDES): 11 blvd Harry S Truman, BP 1399, Port-au-Prince; tel. 2250-1427; fax 2250-1436; e-mail info@sofihdes.com; internet www.sofihdes.com; f. 1983; industrial and agro-industrial project-financing; Chair. FRANTZ BERNARD CRAAN; Man. Dir THONY MOÏSE.

Société Nationale des Parcs Industriels (SONAPI) (National Society of Industrial Parks): Port-au-Prince; manages industrial parks for housing cos; owns the Caracol Industrial Park (PIC) and the Metropolitan Industrial Park (PIM); Dir-Gen. BERNARD SCHETTINI.

CHAMBERS OF COMMERCE

Chambre Américaine de Commerce en Haïti (AMCHAM): 18 rue Moïse, Pétionville, Delmas, BP 13486, Port-au-Prince; tel. 2511-3024; fax 2940-3024; e-mail psaintcyr@amchamhaiti.com; internet amchamhaiti.com; f. 1979; Pres. PHILIPPE ARMAND; Exec. Dir PHILIPPE SAINT-CYR.

Chambre de Commerce et d'Industrie d'Haïti (CCIH): blvd Harry S Truman, Cité de l'Exposition, BP 982, Port-au-Prince; tel. and fax 3512-5141; e-mail ccih@ccih.ht; internet www.ccih.org.ht; f. 1895; 10 departmental chambers; Pres. HERVÉ DENIS; Sec. JOVENEL MOISE.

Chambre de Commerce et d'Industrie Haitiano-Canadienne (CCIHC): rue des Nimes, Port-au-Prince; tel. 2813-0773; e-mail direction@ccihc.com; internet ccihc.com; Pres. MICHEL LAMARRE; Exec. Dir MARTINE CHANDLER.

Chambre Franco-Haïtienne de Commerce et d'Industrie (CFHCI): 5 rue Goulard, Pétionville, 6140 Port-au-Prince; tel. and fax 2510-8965; e-mail cfhci@yahoo.fr; internet www.chambrefrancohaitienne.com; f. 1987; Pres. GRÉGORY BRANDT; Exec. Dir KETTLY FOURON; 109 mems.

INDUSTRIAL AND TRADE ORGANIZATIONS

Association des Exportateurs de Café (ASDEC): rue Barbancourt, BP 1334, Port-au-Prince; tel. 2249-2160; fax 2249-2142; e-mail asdec@primexsa.com; Pres. JULIEN ETIENNE.

Association Haïtienne pour le Développement des Technologies de l'Information et de la Communication (AHTIC): 18 rue Moise, Pétionville, Port-au-Prince; tel. 2454-1498; e-mail sbruno@websystems.ht; Pres. REYNOLD GUERRIER; Exec. Dir STÉPHANE BRUNO.

Association Haïtienne des Economistes (AHE): rue Lamarre, 26 étage, BP 15567, Pétionville; tel. 2512-4005, e-mail haiti_economistes@yahoo.fr; Pres. EDDY LABOSSIÈRE.

Association des Industries d'Haïti (ADIH): 21 rue Borno, Pétionville, BP 15199, Port-au-Prince; tel. 3776-1211; fax 2514-0184; e-mail administration@adih.ht; internet www.adih.ht; f 1980; Pres. CARL FRÉDÉRIC MADSEN; Exec. Dir MARIE-LOUISE AUGUSTIN RUSSO.

Association Nationale des Distributeurs de Produits Pétroliers (ANADIPP): Centre Commercial Dubois, route de Delmas, Bureau 401, BP 1379, Port-au-Prince; tel. 2246-1414; fax 2245-0698; e-mail moylafortune@hotmail.com; f. 1979; Pres. ALAIN MAX ROMAIN.

Association Nationale des Exportateurs de Mangues (ANEM): 5 Santo 20, Route Nationale 3, Croix des Bouquets; tel. 2510-2636; e-mail anem@mango-haiti.com; Pres. JEAN-MAURICE BUTEAU; Man. BERNARD CRAAN.

Association Nationale des Institutions de Microfinance d'Haïti (ANIMH): 87 rue Wallon, Plc Boyer, BP 15321, Pétionville; tel. 2941-6464; e-mail info@animhaiti.org; internet www.animhaiti.org; f. 2002; Pres. PIERRE MAXIME JEROME; Exec. Dir FRANTZ ELYZEE.

Association Professionnelles des Banques (APB): 133 rue Faubert, Pétionville; tel. 2299-3298; fax 2257-2374; e-mail apbhaiti@yahoo.com; Pres. MAXIME CHARLES; Exec. Dir VLADIMIR FRANÇOIS.

UTILITIES

Electricity

Electricité d'Haïti (EDH): angle rue Charéron, blvd Harry S Truman, Cité de l'Exposition, Port-au-Prince; tel. 2813-1641; e-mail info@edh.ht; internet www.edh.ht; f. 1971; state energy co; 6 sub-stations; Dir-Gen. JEAN ERROL MOROSE.

Water

Direction Nationale d'Eau Potable et de l'Assainissement (DINEPA): angle rue Metellus et route Ibo lélé, No 4, Pétionville, 6140 Port-au-Prince; tel. 2256-4770; fax 2940-0873; e-mail communication@dinepa.gouv.ht; internet www.dinepa.gouv.ht; fmrly Service Nationale d'Eau Potable (SNEP); Dir-Gen. JOSEPH LIONEL DUVALSAINT.

TRADE UNIONS

Batay Ouvriye (Workers' Struggle): Delmas, BP 13326, Port-au-Prince; tel. 2222-6719; e-mail batay@batayouvriye.org; internet www.batayouvriye.org; f. 2002; independent umbrella org.; Co-ordinator YANNICK ETIENNE.

Centrale Autonome des Travailleurs Haïtiens (CATH): 93 rue des Casernes, Port-au-Prince; tel. 3875-1044; e-mail cath.cath17@ yahoo.com; f. 1980; Sec.-Gen. Louis Fignolé Saint-Cyr.

Coalition des Syndicats de Transporteurs Haïtiens (CSTH): Port-au-Prince; umbrella org. of 13 transport worker unions.

Confédération Nationale des Educateurs d'Haïti (CNEH): impasse Noë 17, ave Magloire Ambroise, BP 482, Port-au-Prince; tel. 3421-5777; fax 3812-4576; e-mail cnehaiti@haitiworld.com; f. 1986; Sec.-Gen. Lourdes Edith Joseph Délouis.

Confédération des Travailleurs Haïtiens (CTH): 138 route de Fréres, Pétionville; tel. 2223-9216; fax 2223-7430; e-mail cthhaiti@ gmail.com; internet haiticth.org; f. 1989; comprises 11 federations; Sec.-Gen. Loulou Chéry.

Transport

RAILWAYS

The railway service closed in the early 1990s.

ROADS

The total road network of 3,608 km comprises 950 km of primary roads (linking the main cities), 1,315 km of secondary roads and 1,343 km of tertiary or rural roads. The Inter-American Development Bank in November 2013 approved a US $50m. grant for a five-year road improvement project.

SHIPPING

The two principal ports are Port-au-Prince and Cap-Haïtien. In December 2014 the flag registered fleet comprised three vessels, totalling 1,277 grt.

Autorité Portuaire Nationale: blvd La Saline, BP 616, Port-au-Prince; tel. 2223-2440; fax 2221-3479; e-mail apnpap@hotmail.com; internet www.apn.gouv.ht; f. 1978; Dir-Gen. Jean Evens Charles.

Adeko Enterprises: 33–35 blvd Harry S Truman, ave Marie-Jeanne, Port-au-Prince; tel. 3445-0617; e-mail info@adeko-ht.com; internet www.adeko-ht.com; air and sea freight forwarders and maritime agency; Pres. Jean Marc Antoine; Gen. Man. Marc Kinson Antoine.

AI Shipping International: Apt No 1, Sonadim Bldg, blvd Toussaint Louverture and Patrice Lumumba, Port-au-Prince; tel. 2940-5476; fax 2941-5476; e-mail info@aishippingintl.com; internet www .aishippingintl.com; f. 1981; freight forwarder and maritime agency; Pres. Antoine Ilanes.

CIVIL AVIATION

The Toussaint Louverture International airport, situated 8 km (5 miles) outside Port-au-Prince, is the country's principal airport. There is also an airport at Cap-Haïtien, which opened to international flights in 2013 following an upgrade. In the same year it was renamed the Hugo Chávez International Airport after the late Venezuelan President. Antoine-Simon airport at Les Cayes opened in 2005 and, following an extension of the runway and the building of a new terminal in 2013, was also expected to open to international flights. Construction of a new airport on the island of Ile à Vache began in 2013, while a project to build an international airport at the airfield at Jérémie got under way in late 2014. There are also airfields at Jacmel and Port-de-Paix.

Autorite Aéroportuaire Nationale (AAN): Aéroport International Toussaint Louverture, Port-au-Prince; tel. 3443-0250; fax 2250-5866; e-mail dgaan@haitiworld.com; internet papaeroportauthority.org; Dir-Gen. Pierre André Laguerre.

Haiti Aviation: Aeroport Toussaint Louverture, Port-au-Prince; tel. 2812-2812; e-mail Info@Haitiaviation.com; internet haitiaviation.com.

Office National de l'Aviation Civile (OFNAC): Aéroport International Toussaint Louverture, Delmas, BP 1346, Port-au-Prince; tel. 2246-0052; fax 2246-0998; e-mail lpierre@ofnac.org; Dir-Gen. Jean Marc Flambert.

Sunrise Airways: 12 Impasse Besse, rue Panamericaine, Pétionville; tel. 2816-0616; fax 2811-2222; e-mail info@sunriseairways.net; internet sunriseairways.net; f. 2009 as charter carrier; began

scheduled flights within Haiti in 2012, flights to the Turks and Caicos in 2013 and Jamaica in 2014; Pres. Philippe Bayard.

Tortug' Air: Port-au-Prince; tel. 2511-4613; e-mail info@tortugair .com; internet www.tortugair.com; f. 2003; operates in partnership with Aerodynamics, Inc (USA); Vice-Pres. Nicolas Ntahiraja; 200 employees.

Vision Air Haiti: Aérogare Guy Malary, Port-au-Prince; tel. 3886-2420; internet visionairhaiti.com; f. 2010; domestic flights; Gen. Man. Jean Jiha, Jr.

Tourism

Tourism was formerly Haiti's second largest source of foreign exchange. However, as a result of political instability, the number of cruise ships visiting Haiti declined considerably. In 2013 tourist arrivals totalled a provisional 420,000 and receipts from tourism totalled US $170m. in 2012. In 2013 Best Western International opened a $15m. hotel in Pétionville. Further hotels, including a 173-room Marriott hotel in Port-au-Prince, were also under construction.

Association Haïtienne des Agences de Voyages (ASHAV): 17 rue des Miracles, Port-au-Prince; tel. 3445-5903; fax 2511-2424; e-mail ashav@hainet.net; f. 1988; Pres. Pierre Chauvet, Fils.

Association Touristique d'Haïti (ATH): rue Moise 18, Pétionville, BP 2562, Port-au-Prince; tel. 2946-8484; fax 3906-8484; e-mail athaiti@gmail.com; internet www.haiticherie.ht; f. 1951; Pres. Richard Buteau; Exec. Dir Valerie Louis.

Defence

The armed forces were effectively dissolved in 1995, although officially they remained in existence pending an amendment to the Constitution providing for their abolition. In 2004 the UN Stabilization Mission in Haiti (MINUSTAH) assumed peacekeeping responsibilities in the country. Following the 2010 earthquake, MINUSTAH's authorized capacity was increased. As of February 2015, MINUSTAH comprised 4,618 troops, 2,189 civilian police, 1,475 international and local civilian staff (as of 30 November 2014), and 126 UN Volunteers. The MINUSTAH budget for 2014/15 was an estimated US $580.1m. In 2012 the Governments of Brazil and Ecuador agreed to assist Haiti in the formation of a new army, to number 1,500, which, it was hoped, would eventually replace MINUSTAH. As assessed at November 2014, the army numbered 70. There was also a coastguard of 50. In 2013 Haiti inaugurated a naval base at Les Cayes, intended primarily to counter drugs-trafficking activities.

Education

Education is provided by the state, by the Roman Catholic Church and by other religious organizations. Teaching is based on the French model, and French is the language of instruction. Primary education, which normally begins at six years of age and lasts for six years, is officially compulsory. Secondary education usually begins at 12 years of age and lasts for a further six years, comprising two cycles of three years each. According to UNICEF estimates, in 2011 the primary attendance ratio included 48% of male and 52% of female children in the relevant age-group, while at secondary schools it included 18% of male and 21% of female students in the relevant age-group. Higher education is provided by 18 technical and vocational centres, 42 domestic science schools, by the Université d'Etat d'Haïti and by the Université Roi Henri Christophe (inaugurated in 2012). More than 1,300 educational institutions were destroyed in the 2010 earthquake. In 2011 the National Fund for Education (FNE) was launched to provide more than 500,000 children with access to education. Some US $70m. was made available in 2012 to the FNE. In late 2014 the Inter-American Development Bank approved US $24m. in funding for education in the country. In 2010/11 an estimated 8,504m. gourdes was allocated to education, representing 8% of the total spending.

HONDURAS

Introductory Survey

LOCATION, CLIMATE, LANGUAGE, RELIGION, FLAG, CAPITAL

The Republic of Honduras lies in the middle of the Central American isthmus. It has a long northern coastline on the Caribbean Sea and a narrow southern outlet to the Pacific Ocean. Its neighbours are Guatemala to the west, El Salvador to the south-west and Nicaragua to the south-east. The climate ranges from temperate in the mountainous regions to tropical in the coastal plains: temperatures in the interior range from 15°C (59°F) to 24°C (75°F), while temperatures in the coastal plains average about 30°C (86°F). There are two rainy seasons in upland areas, May–July and September–October. The national language is Spanish. Almost all of the inhabitants profess Christianity, and about 82% of the population are adherents of the Roman Catholic Church. The national flag (proportions 1 by 2) has three horizontal stripes, of blue, white and blue, with five blue five-pointed stars, arranged in a diagonal cross, in the centre of the white stripe. The capital is Tegucigalpa.

CONTEMPORARY POLITICAL HISTORY

Historical Context

Honduras was ruled by Spain from the 16th century until 1821 and became a sovereign state in 1838. From 1939 the country was ruled as a dictatorship by Gen. Tiburcio Carías Andino, leader of the Partido Nacional (PN), who had been President since 1933. In 1949 Carías was succeeded as President by Juan Manuel Gálvez, also of the PN. In 1954 the leader of the Partido Liberal (PL), Dr José Ramón Villeda Morales, was elected President, but was immediately deposed by Julio Lozano Díaz, himself overthrown by a military junta in 1956. The junta organized elections in 1957, when the PL secured a majority in Congress and Villeda was re-elected President. He was overthrown in 1963 by Col (later Gen.) Oswaldo López Arellano, who, following elections held on the basis of a new Constitution, was appointed President in 1965.

A presidential election in 1971 was won by Dr Ramón Ernesto Cruz Uclés, the PN candidate. In December 1972, however, Cruz was deposed in a bloodless coup, led by former President López. In 1974 President López was replaced as Commander-in-Chief of the Armed Forces by Col (later Gen.) Juan Melgar Castro, who was appointed President in 1975. President Melgar was forced to resign in 1978, and was replaced by a military junta. The Commander-in-Chief of the Armed Forces, Gen. Policarpo Paz García, assumed the role of Head of State.

Domestic Political Affairs

Military rule was ended officially when, in April 1980, elections to a Constituent Assembly were held. The PL won 52% of the votes but was unable to assume power. Gen. Paz was appointed interim President. At a general election in 1981 the PL, led by Dr Roberto Suazo Córdova, secured an absolute majority in the Congreso Nacional (National Congress). Suazo was sworn in as President, but real power lay in the hands of Col (later Gen.) Gustavo Alvarez Martínez, who became Commander-in-Chief of the Armed Forces. Alvarez suppressed increasing political unrest by authorizing the arrests of trade union activists and left-wing sympathizers; 'death squads' were allegedly also used. In 1984 Gen. Alvarez was deposed as Commander-in-Chief by a group of army officers.

At the 1985 presidential election the leading candidate of the PN, Rafael Leonardo Callejas Romero, obtained 42% of the votes cast, but the PL's leading candidate, José Simeón Azcona del Hoyo (who had obtained only 27% of the votes cast), was declared the winner because, in accordance with a new electoral law, the combined votes of the PL's candidates secured the requisite majority of 51% of the total votes.

A report by the human rights organization Amnesty International in 1988 gave evidence of an increase in violations of human rights by the armed forces and by right-wing death squads. The Inter-American Court of Human Rights (an organ of the Organization of American States—OAS, see p. 392) found the Honduran Government guilty of the 'disappearances' of Honduran citizens during 1981–84. The PL secured a majority of seats in the National Congress at the 1989 general election, while Callejas of the PN won the concurrent presidential ballot. The Callejas administration adopted economic austerity measures, provoking widespread social unrest.

In 1993, in response to increasing pressure by human rights organizations, the Government established a special commission to investigate allegations of human rights violations by the armed forces. The commission recommended, *inter alia*, the replacement of the armed forces' much-criticized secret counter-intelligence organization, the División Nacional de Investigaciones (DNI), with a body under civilian control. Legislation replacing the DNI with a new ministry, the Dirección de Investigación Criminal, was approved in December.

At elections in November 1993 the PL's Carlos Roberto Reina Idiáquez was elected President. The PL also obtained a clear majority in the Congress. Reina, a former President of the Inter-American Court of Human Rights, committed to reforming the judicial system and the armed forces. In 1994 the Congress approved a constitutional reform abolishing compulsory military service (the amendment was ratified in 1995). In July 4,000 members of indigenous organizations occupied the Congress building and secured an agreement with the Government granting rights and social assistance to the country's indigenous community. The following months were characterized by growing social and political tension. Concern was raised by human rights organizations that instability was being fomented by the armed forces in an attempt to stem the rapid diminution of its powers. An increase in crime and violent demonstrations led the Government to declare a state of national emergency in August and to deploy the armed forces to maintain order.

In May 1997, following the killing of two ethnic minority leaders in the previous month, more than 3,000 members of the indigenous community marched from the western departments of Copán and Ocotepeque to the capital in protest. As a result, Reina agreed to conduct a full investigation into the killings and to accelerate the distribution of some 7,000 ha of land to the indigenous community. However, the killing of a further two indigenous leaders later that month led to accusations by human rights groups that attempts were being made to eliminate minority autonomous organizations.

At the election held in November 1997 Carlos Roberto Flores Facussé, the candidate of the ruling PL, was elected President. The PL also obtained a majority in the Congress. In May 1998 control of the police force, widely suspected of perpetrating human rights abuses, was transferred from the military to the civilian authorities. Nevertheless, reports of human rights abuses continued.

The Maduro presidency

The PN candidate, Ricardo Maduro Joest, emerged victorious in the presidential election of November 2001. The PN also gained a majority in the Congress in the concurrent legislative ballot.

President Maduro faced increasing industrial unrest during his term in office. Public dissatisfaction with reductions in public expenditure culminated with a 'March for Dignity', in which some 10,000 people converged on Tegucigalpa in August 2003.

Despite the implementation of increased security measures by the Maduro administration, Honduras experienced rising levels of violent crime in the 2000s. In January 2003, in response to increasing conflict between street gangs (*maras*), 10,000 army troops had been deployed on to the streets of several cities. Controversial legislation approved in August introduced prison sentences of between nine and 12 years for members of the *maras*, which were held responsible for much of the crime in the country. In 2004 the Government introduced further legislation, increasing the maximum prison sentence for gang membership and extending the period of detention without charge. However, President Maduro's strict policies towards criminals also raised fears of human rights abuses.

The 2005 elections

The presidential election held on 27 November 2005 was narrowly won by the PL's José Manuel Zelaya Rosales. The PL also won a narrow majority in the National Congress. The delay in announcing the final results was severely criticized by observers, who denounced the electoral process as the worst in 25 years of democracy.

The assassination, in March 2007, of Rigoberto Aceituno, the second most senior police official in Honduras, served as a stark reminder of the continuing influence of the country's drugs gangs. Violent crime persisted as a serious problem, with the assassination in 2008 of several political figures, including the Vice-President of the Congress, Mario Fernando Hernández, in November.

The ratification, in October 2008, of Honduras' accession to what became known as the Bolivarian Alliance for the Peoples of our America-People's Trade Treaty (Alianza Bolivariana para los Pueblos de Nuestra América-Tratado de Comercio de los Pueblos—ALBA-TCP, see p. 459), a Venezuelan-led economic and social integration initiative, created some tension within the National Congress. In order to win the support of the legislature, President Zelaya agreed to endorse the campaign of the speaker, Roberto Micheletti Baín, for the presidential election due in November 2009, and created a development fund worth US \$19.5m. to support the congressional campaigns of PL deputies who voted in favour of ratification. The PN decried the misuse of public funds and abstained from voting.

The 2009 constitutional crisis

President Zelaya provoked considerable controversy in March 2009 when he ordered the National Statistics Institute to organize a referendum on convening a constituent assembly to revise the Constitution. The PN and several prominent members of the PL opposed the proposal, amid speculation that Zelaya was seeking a reform that would allow him to remain in office beyond the expiry of his term in January 2010, while the office of the Attorney-General insisted that only the Tribunal Supremo Electoral (TSE—Supreme Electoral Court) had the power to conduct a referendum.

On 23 June 2009, five days before the plebiscite was scheduled to be held, political tensions escalated when the National Congress attempted to thwart Zelaya's plans by approving legislation prohibiting the holding of referendums 180 days before or after a general election. The Chairman of the Joint Chiefs of Staff, Gen. Romeo Vásquez Velásquez, consequently refused to provide logistical support for the vote on the grounds that it was unlawful, leading to his dismissal by Zelaya, which, in turn, prompted the resignation of several senior military officials and of Edmundo Orellana as Minister of National Defence. The Supreme Court, meanwhile, insisted that Vásquez be reinstated. However, Zelaya refused to comply with the Court's demand and proceeded with preparations for the non-binding referendum, without the support of the military and in defiance of both the judiciary and the legislature, which commenced discussions on the possibility of impeaching the President.

Shortly before voting was due to begin, on 28 June 2009, President Zelaya was seized at his residence by members of the armed forces and forced into exile in Costa Rica; it subsequently emerged that the Supreme Court had authorized the detention of Zelaya on 18 charges, including treason and abuse of authority. Later that day the Congress voted to remove Zelaya from the presidency, on the grounds that he had repeatedly violated the Constitution and failed to observe court orders, and Micheletti was sworn in to act as President until the end of the current term in January 2010; prior to the vote, the Congress had been read an alleged letter of resignation from Zelaya (which he denied having signed). An interim Cabinet was appointed on 29 June 2009. Micheletti, who maintained that Zelaya had been legally removed from office in what he termed a 'constitutional succession', declared that the presidential and legislative elections would be conducted, as scheduled, on 29 November. However, the ousting of Zelaya was denounced internationally, with both the UN General Assembly and the OAS adopting resolutions condemning what they deemed to be a coup and demanding the restoration of Zelaya to the presidency. The OAS also suspended the right of Honduras to participate in the Organization and designated Costa Rican President Oscar Arias Sánchez to lead diplomatic efforts to mediate a resolution to the country's political crisis. Meanwhile, demonstrations both for and against Zelaya's reinstatement as President took place nationwide. Zelaya attempted to return to Honduras on 5 July, but the aircraft in which he was travelling was prevented from landing; at least two people were reportedly killed in clashes between the security forces and supporters of the deposed President.

Arias brokered talks between the two sides in Costa Rica, in July 2009, but Micheletti's representatives repeatedly rejected a proposed arrangement that would involve Zelaya returning to serve the remainder of his presidential term as head of a unity government. An OAS delegation of foreign ministers visited Tegucigalpa in late August, but failed to persuade Micheletti's de facto Government to accept the US-supported accord devised by Arias. The Supreme Court also rejected the terms of the accord. The OAS and the US Department of State both announced that they would not recognize the outcome of polls conducted under Micheletti's administration.

Zelaya made an unexpected return to Honduras on 21 September 2009, taking refuge in the Brazilian embassy in Tegucigalpa, outside which thousands of his supporters subsequently gathered before being dispersed by the security forces. The de facto Government imposed a temporary curfew and, on the following day, adopted a decree suspending five constitutional articles, including those guaranteeing freedom of expression, freedom of association and of assembly, and freedom of movement, for a period of 45 days. The decree prompted widespread condemnation, not only internationally, but also from domestic political and business figures, many of whom had previously supported Zelaya's removal from office, including the two main presidential candidates, Porfirio Lobo Sosa of the PN and Elvin Santos for the PL. Micheletti repealed the decree in October.

Representatives of Micheletti and Zelaya held a series of talks in Tegucigalpa in October 2009, under the auspices of the OAS. The main point of contention was Zelaya's proposed restitution to office. On 30 October, following the intervention of the US Department of State, the Tegucigalpa/San José Accord was signed. Under the terms of the Accord, an interim government of unity and national reconciliation was to be formed to oversee the election on 29 November and the transition to a new administration. Also, a congressional vote was to be held on the restoration of executive power to those in office prior to 28 June. A Verification Commission was established to monitor compliance with the commitments contained in the Accord, and a Truth and Reconciliation Commission was to be created. However, amid dissent regarding the timing of the legislative vote on the potential reinstatement of Zelaya, Micheletti announced on 5 November that he was proceeding unilaterally with the appointment of the new interim government owing to the failure of the deposed President to nominate ministers. The US Department of State adopted a different approach from the OAS, meanwhile, stating that the Honduran state institutions should determine how to implement the agreement and confirming that it would recognize the forthcoming elections.

Lobo was victorious in the presidential election of November 2009, securing 57% of the valid votes cast, compared with 38% for Santos. In the concurrent legislative elections, Lobo's PN also won a large majority in the Congress, taking 71 of the 128 seats, while the PL obtained 45 seats, the Partido Demócrata Cristiano de Honduras (PDCH) five, the Partido de Unificación Democrática (PUD) four and the Partido Innovación y Unidad—Social Demócrata (PINU—SD) three. The PN's strong performance was largely attributed to public disenchantment with the divided PL, the party of both Micheletti and Zelaya. The results were recognized by the USA and a number of Latin American countries, including Colombia, Costa Rica and Panama, although the OAS, ALBA-TCP, the Mercado Común del Sur (MERCOSUR) and other members of the international community refused to accept the legitimacy of the vote.

President-elect Lobo's most immediate challenge was to secure international support for his incoming administration, particularly in view of the urgent need for a resumption of foreign aid and lending to Honduras, largely suspended since June 2009. This task was made more difficult on 2 December, when the legislature voted overwhelmingly against the reinstatement of Zelaya (who remained in the Brazilian embassy), pending Lobo's inauguration in January 2010. Lobo subsequently came under significant international pressure to persuade Micheletti to resign as acting President in order to allow the formation of a government of national unity and reconciliation, and to secure a safe passage out of Honduras for Zelaya. However, Micheletti resolutely refused to stand down before Lobo's investiture and insisted that Zelaya would only be permitted to leave Honduras without answering the charges against him if he accepted political asylum in a country outside Central America. In early January the Chairman of the Joint Chiefs of Staff, Gen. Vásquez, and five other senior military officials were charged with abuse of authority in connection with the forced expulsion of Zelaya from

Honduras. On 20 January Lobo signed an agreement with President Leonel Fernández of the Dominican Republic on the safe passage of the deposed President to that country following Lobo's investiture; Zelaya accepted the arrangement.

Lobo in office

Lobo was sworn in as President on 27 January 2010. The new Congress approved a decree granting amnesty for any political offences committed by Zelaya and those involved in his removal from power, while the Supreme Court acquitted the six senior military officials charged with abuse of authority. Lobo's Cabinet included the defeated presidential candidates of the PDCH, the PUD and the PINU—SD, although the most senior posts were allocated to members of the PN.

The primary focus of President Lobo's first months in office was the restoration of relations with the international community. To this end, he continued efforts to fulfil the requirements of the Tegucigalpa/San José Accord. The World Bank and the US Government subsequently announced that they would resume the provision of aid to Honduras. However, human rights groups expressed concern in March 2010 over the murder of several journalists and a series of attacks on political activists, particularly members of the Frente Nacional de Resistencia Popular (FNRP), a broad alliance of organizations and movements that had opposed Zelaya's removal from office. Lobo subsequently sought to demonstrate his commitment to protecting human rights by creating a new government post of Minister Adviser on Human Rights. Meanwhile, Zelaya and four former ministers and officials from his administration were charged in February with fraud, falsification of documents and abuse of authority in relation to the alleged misuse of 30m. lempiras from the Honduran social investment fund. The charges against Zelaya complicated Lobo's efforts to gain recognition of his administration from the countries of ALBA-TCP and MERCOSUR, which demanded that the former President be permitted to return to political life in Honduras. (The charge of abuse of authority was later dismissed, in accordance with the recently approved amnesty decree.)

The Truth and Reconciliation Commission commenced work in May 2010. The FNRP, which continued to seek Zelaya's return and to advocate the creation of a constituent assembly to amend the Constitution, questioned the independence of the Commission, claiming that its purpose was to exonerate the coup leaders, and established an alternative truth commission in June. An OAS commission tasked with assessing the political situation in Honduras issued its report in July. It recommended the termination of legal proceedings involving Zelaya and his associates; the application by Zelaya for membership of the Central American Parliament (Parlacen) in order to secure recognition of his status as Lobo's predecessor as constitutional President of Honduras; the adoption of measures to protect journalists, members of the FNRP and judges who had opposed the coup; the cessation of impunity for human rights violations; and the organization of a national dialogue with the participation of all political sectors. In May the Supreme Court had provoked controversy by dismissing four judges who had criticized the removal of Zelaya from office and the Court's role in this.

Meanwhile, in June 2010 a joint committee of the TSE and the National Congress was established to consider, and consult the public on, a range of proposed political reforms, including a constitutional amendment to ease the conditions for holding a referendum. In October Lobo initiated a national dialogue to discuss the convening of a constituent assembly to reform the Constitution. However, most FNRP members rejected the President's invitation to participate in the dialogue on the grounds that they would not engage with a Government that they did not recognize. A commission charged with drafting reforms to the article of the Constitution regulating referendums was subsequently created. In February 2011 the Congress adopted the proposed constitutional amendments, which not only eased the conditions for initiating a referendum, but also removed a restriction preventing referendums on a provision that forbade the revision of a number of other constitutional articles, including those relating to the length of the presidential term and the ban on presidential re-election. Despite favouring constitutional reform, the FNRP expressed opposition to the amendments, continuing to demand that a constituent assembly be convened.

Amid mounting concern regarding increasing insecurity in Honduras, in early 2011 Lobo ordered some 2,000 troops to participate in joint patrols with the police force in an effort to combat organized crime, particularly drugs-trafficking. The murder rate had risen to 82 per 100,000 persons in 2010. In November 2011 the Government announced a further joint police-military deployment, and measures were introduced to address endemic police corruption. Nevertheless, the declining security situation led the Government in December to declare a 90-day state of emergency, which, in accordance with a controversial constitutional amendment adopted by the legislature in the previous month, granted the military extensive powers to carry out policing duties. (The military's mandate was extended during 2012.) Some observers raised questions about the appropriateness of using soldiers to perform functions usually conducted by trained police officers. The UN reported that the murder rate increased to 92 per 100,000 persons in 2011. A commission of inquiry into police and judicial corruption and potential security reforms was established in early 2012, and a purge of corrupt police officers was effected during the second half of the year.

In May 2011, following pressure from the Government, the Supreme Court revoked the corruption charges against Zelaya, and shortly thereafter Lobo and Zelaya, with Colombian-Venezuelan mediation, concluded a formal reconciliation agreement. As a result, the former President returned to Honduras at the end of the month. This successful process of reconciliation fulfilled a key demand of Lobo's critics in the region, precipitating Honduras' readmission to the OAS in June and the normalization of the country's diplomatic relations. In July the Truth and Reconciliation Commission released its report on the events of 28 June 2009, concluding that Zelaya's letter of resignation had been fabricated and that his deposition had constituted a coup. The Commission therefore adjudged Micheletti's administration to have been illegal, but also criticized Zelaya for having increased institutional tensions prior to the coup. The report recommended that the Constitution be amended to permit presidential impeachment, thus providing the Honduran institutions with a legitimate alternative to military intervention in cases where the head of state was suspected of acting unlawfully. Six senior military officers accused of abuse of authority for their involvement in the 2009 coup were controversially exonerated by the Supreme Court in October 2011. Zelaya denounced this decision, claiming that those responsible for deposing him were being 'protected'.

With support from the FNRP and defectors from the PL, in October 2011 Zelaya established a new political party, the Partido Libertad y Refundación (LIBRE). However, even though the former President had been removed from power before the completion of his full term of office, the Constitution prohibited him from contesting another presidential election. Consequently, Zelaya's wife, Xiomara Castro de Zelaya, announced she would stand as LIBRE's candidate in the 2013 election.

With violent crime still prevalent, in September 2011 Lobo replaced Minister of Public Security Oscar Alvarez with Pompeyo Bonilla. In the same government reorganization, Arturo Corrales Alvarez was appointed Minister of Foreign Affairs. Further cabinet changes were implemented in February 2012: Héctor Guillén received the finance portfolio, Marlon Oniel Escoto became the new Minister of Education, and José Adonis was given responsibility for industry and commerce. Guillén resigned in August and was replaced by Wilfredo Cerrato.

In an attempt to ease long-standing tensions between peasants and landowners in the north of the country, the Government announced a land redistribution scheme in June 2012, while in August a disarmament initiative was implemented in Colón. Nevertheless, land invasions and violent attacks against peasants continued to be reported in the region. In November primary elections were conducted to determine the main parties' representatives in the upcoming presidential poll. Juan Orlando Hernández Alvarado, the President of the National Congress and a close associate of President Lobo, was elected as the PN's candidate, Mauricio Villeda was to represent the PL, and Castro de Zelaya was endorsed as LIBRE's nominee.

Tensions between the Lobo administration and the Supreme Court, which had been escalating since 2010 owing to the latter's repeated rejection of the Government's legislative initiatives, culminated in December 2012 when the Congress approved the replacement of four members of the Court's constitutional branch who had recently voted against legislation on police reform. Legislators claimed that the magistrates had not acted in the national interest. The domestic and international reaction to this politically motivated, and arguably unconstitutional, intervention in the functioning of the Supreme Court was largely subdued, however, and an appeal by the dismissed justices was denied in February 2013. The Constitution was modified in January to incorporate more robust procedures for the impeachment of the President and other high-ranking public figures; the amendments to the charter also, *inter alia*, provided for a reduction in the decision-making powers of the constitutional chamber.

The public security portfolio was reassigned again in April 2013; Corrales was named as Bonilla's replacement, while Mireya Agüero was given responsibility for foreign affairs. New anti-crime measures announced in 2013 included an increase in prison sentences for those convicted of violent crimes, the implementation of structural reforms within the police force and the formation of several specialized security units, while in early 2014 controversial aircraft interception legislation was also adopted by the outgoing Congress. The new law would allow the military to shoot down aircraft suspected of drugs-trafficking. (Approval of this law, however, prompted the USA to suspend radar co-operation with Honduras and also, allegedly, to obstruct Honduran efforts to recondition its fighter aircraft fleet.) In addition, in mid-2013 the Catholic Church and the OAS brokered a provisional truce between the major *maras*. The murder rate fell to 86 per 100,000 people in 2012, to 84 per 100,000 in 2013 and to approximately 66 per 100,000 in 2014. Honduras' murder rate remained, nevertheless, one of the highest in the world.

Recent developments: Hernández in office

Hernández attracted 36.9% of the votes cast in the presidential election conducted on 24 November 2013, defeating Castro de Zelaya (28.8%), Villeda (20.3%) and Salvador Nasralla of the recently formed Partido Anticorrupción (PAC—13.4%). In the concurrent legislative polls, Hernández's PN garnered 48 of the 128 seats in the National Congress; LIBRE won 37 seats, the PL 27, the PAC 13 and smaller parties the remaining three. Despite some electoral irregularities and disquiet about campaign financing, the results were endorsed by international observers. LIBRE, however, denounced the presidential poll as illegitimate and mounted an unsuccessful legal challenge.

Hernández assumed the presidency on 27 January 2014, and several members of the Lobo administration—including Agüero, Cerrato and Corrales—were reappointed to the new Cabinet. In addition, complementary portfolios were to be grouped together into seven consolidated 'superministries' in an attempt to improve government efficiency. Jorge Ramón Hernández Alcerro was named as Co-ordinator-General of the Government and was tasked with overseeing the sectoral ministries. Although the PN had lost its majority in the Congress, commentators deemed it likely that the PL would provide the ruling party with the requisite votes to implement its manifesto.

Hernández reorganized his Cabinet in January 2015, appointing Corrales as Secretary of Foreign Affairs, Gen. (retd) Julián Pacheco Tinoco as Secretary of Public Security, and Ricardo Cardona as Secretary of Development and Social Inclusion. Also in that month, Hernández announced his intention to stage a referendum on a proposed constitutional amendment to institutionalize permanently the Policía Militar de Orden Público (the military police force), which, he claimed, had been largely responsible for the marked decrease in the murder rate in 2014. An earlier attempt to effect this constitutional change through regular legislative procedures had been unsuccessful.

Foreign Affairs

Regional relations

In 1987 Honduras, Costa Rica, El Salvador, Guatemala and Nicaragua signed a Central American peace plan, the Esquipulas agreement, the crucial provisions of which included the implementation of simultaneous ceasefires in Nicaragua and El Salvador, a halt to foreign assistance to rebel groups, and the establishment of national reconciliation commissions in each of the Central American nations. The Government agreed to the establishment by the UN and the OAS of an international commission to oversee the voluntary repatriation or removal to a third country of the rebel forces; in return, the Nicaraguan Government agreed to abandon the action that it had initiated against Honduras at the International Court of Justice (ICJ).

In 1995 Honduras and Nicaragua signed an accord providing for the visible demarcation of each country's territorial waters in the Gulf of Fonseca, and the establishment of a joint naval patrol to police the area. However, in 1999 Nicaragua severed commercial ties with Honduras following a dispute over the Caribbean Sea Maritime Limits Treaty, which granted Colombia

territorial rights to areas of the Caribbean historically claimed by Nicaragua. In 2000, following OAS mediation, the two countries agreed to establish a maritime exclusion zone in the disputed area. Representatives of Honduras and Nicaragua also signed an accord on joint patrols in the Caribbean, pending a ruling by the ICJ, and on combined operations in the Gulf of Fonseca, as well as the withdrawal of forces from the land border area. Following further talks under OAS auspices, in 2001 the two countries agreed to allow monitors into the disputed area to verify troop deployment. The ICJ ruled on a revised maritime border approximately midway between the two countries in 2007. In November 2012 the ICJ settled a disagreement between Colombia and Nicaragua over their boundaries in the Caribbean Sea. The Honduran Government supported the ICJ's judgment, even though, according to some interpretations, the settlement would entail the transfer of approximately 14,000 sq km of Caribbean waters from Honduras to Nicaragua.

A long-standing dispute between Honduras and El Salvador, regarding the demarcation of the two countries' common border and rival claims to three islands in the Gulf of Fonseca, caused hostilities to break out between the two countries in 1969. Although armed conflict soon subsided, the Honduran and Salvadorean Governments did not sign a peace treaty until 1980. In 1992 the ICJ awarded Honduras sovereignty over some two-thirds of the disputed mainland territory and over one of the disputed islands in the Gulf of Fonseca. A convention governing the acquired rights and nationality of those people was finally signed by the Presidents of both countries in 1998. Honduras, El Salvador and Nicaragua created a commission in December 2012 to support the peaceful development of the Gulf of Fonseca region. However, another boundary dispute in the Gulf of Fonseca resurfaced in August 2013 when the Honduran military landed on the tiny Conejo Island, sovereignty over which was asserted by both Honduras and El Salvador, and planted a Honduran flag. The Salvadorean authorities submitted a formal complaint to Honduras in September, but Honduran activity on the island increased during that month. El Salvador's acquisition of 10 attack aircraft in October further exacerbated the situation. Honduras dismissed another Salvadorean complaint in March 2014. A change of leadership in El Salvador in mid-2014 precipitated an easing of bilateral tensions. The new Salvadorean President, Salvador Sánchez Cerén, appeared eager to repair relations with Honduras and adopted a non-confrontational stance towards the Conejo Island dispute. The Honduran, Salvadorean and Nicaraguan leaders concluded several agreements in August on the peaceful development of the Gulf of Fonseca region, while in February 2015 Honduras, El Salvador and Guatemala announced plans to establish a customs union.

Relations with other Latin American countries, in particular Venezuela, were strengthened by the admission of Honduras, in 2007, to the Petrocaribe initiative (whereby Caribbean countries were able to purchase petroleum from Venezuela on preferential terms), and by the country's accession to ALBA-TCP (see above) in 2008. Petroleum supplies to Honduras under Petrocaribe were suspended in 2009 following the removal from office of President Zelaya. Moreover, ALBA-TCP refused to recognize the November elections. In January 2010 the outgoing National Congress ratified a decree issued by de facto President Micheletti withdrawing Honduras from ALBA-TCP. President Lobo swiftly succeeded in gaining recognition for his administration from other Central American countries, with the notable exception of Nicaragua, but many South American countries, including Argentina, Brazil and Venezuela, witheld their support for the restoration of OAS membership rights to Honduras until 2011, when a reconciliation agreement was signed by Lobo and Zelaya. The country was permitted to rejoin the OAS in June. Honduras was readmitted to the Petrocaribe programme in May 2013, although diplomatic relations with Ecuador were not restored until March 2014.

Other external relations

The US Administration of Barack Obama condemned the removal from power of Zelaya in 2009, suspending all military co-operation and some development aid in response. None the less, the USA opted to recognize the elections held in November, and the resumption of US aid was announced in 2010. The USA included Honduras for the first time in 2010 on its list of major illicit drugs-transit or drugs-producing countries. The US Drug Enforcement Administration (DEA) is involved in counter-trafficking operations in Honduras, although its activities in the country are often controversial. Violent demonstrations were staged in Gracias a Dios in May 2012 in protest against a DEA-backed drugs raid that, according to local residents, had resulted in the deaths of several innocent civilians.

There was a dramatic upturn in mid-2014 in the number of unaccompanied minors from the Central American region (most of whom originated from Honduras, El Salvador and Guatemala) attempting to gain illegal entry into the USA. A number of meetings between regional leaders were subsequently arranged in an effort to resolve the migration crisis. In November 2014 Honduras, with El Salvador and Guatemala, initiated the Plan Alianza para la Prosperidad, a regional economic initiative intended to counter migration to the USA. The USA, meanwhile, pledged to increase aid to Central America and to ease certain immigration restrictions, which would allow some children to enter the USA legally as refugees.

CONSTITUTION AND GOVERNMENT

A new Constitution was promulgated in January 1982, and has been amended from time to time. Under the provisions of the Constitution, the President is elected by a simple majority of the voters. The President holds executive power and has a single four-year mandate. Legislative power is vested in the Congreso Nacional (National Congress), with 128 members elected by universal adult suffrage for a term of four years. Judicial power is exercised by the Supreme Court, the Courts of Appeal and various lesser tribunals. The country is divided into 18 local departments, which are subdivided into 298 autonomous municipalities.

REGIONAL AND INTERNATIONAL CO-OPERATION

Honduras is a member of the Central American Common Market (see p. 228), of the Organization of American States (OAS, see p. 392), of the Association of Caribbean States (see p. 444), and of the Community of Latin American and Caribbean States (see p. 460), which was formally inaugurated in December 2011. The Dominican Republic-Central American Free Trade Agreement (CAFTA-DR), between the Dominican Republic, the Central American countries of Costa Rica, Honduras, El Salvador, Guatemala and Nicaragua, and the USA, entered force in Honduras in 2006. CAFTA-DR, which aims to foster export-orientated growth in the region, was to entail the gradual elimination of tariffs on most industrial and agricultural products over a period of 10 and 20 years, respectively. In 2010 an association agreement, covering trade, political dialogue and co-operation, was concluded between Costa Rica, El Salvador, Guatemala, Honduras, Nicaragua and Panama and the European Union (EU). These countries also concluded a free trade agreement with the EU in 2012. A free trade agreement with Mexico entered into force in 2013 and Honduras concluded a free trade agreement with Canada at the end of that year. Honduras was a founder member of the UN in 1945. As a contracting party to the General Agreement on Tariffs and Trade, Honduras joined the World Trade Organization (see p. 431) on its establishment in 1995.

ECONOMIC AFFAIRS

In 2013, according to estimates by the World Bank, Honduras' gross national income (GNI), measured at average 2011–13 prices, was US $17,671m., equivalent to $2,180 per head (or $4,270 per head on an international purchasing-power parity basis). During 2004–13, it was estimated, the population increased at an average annual rate of 2.0%, while gross domestic product (GDP) per head increased, in real terms, by an average of 1.8% per year. Overall GDP increased, in real terms, at an average annual rate of 3.8% in 2004–13; real GDP increased by 2.6% in 2013, according to central bank estimates.

Agriculture (including hunting, forestry and fishing) contributed an estimated 12.4% of GDP and employed 35.8% of the economically active population in 2013. The principal cash crop is traditionally coffee, although an outbreak of coffee leaf rust in 2013–14 severely affected the sector and coffee exports decreased to 19.6% of the total value of exports (excluding gold and *maquila* exports) in 2013, compared with 32.8% in 2012. Exports of bananas contributed 12.8% of total export earnings in 2013. The main subsistence crops include maize, plantains, beans, rice, sugar cane and citrus fruit. Exports of shellfish make a significant contribution to foreign earnings (lobsters and prawns provided 7.0% of total export earnings in 2013). According to official estimates, agricultural GDP increased at an average annual rate of 3.7% during 2004–13; the sector increased by 4.3% in 2013.

Industry (including mining, manufacturing, construction and power) contributed an estimated 25.8% of GDP and employed 18.8% of the economically active population in 2013. According to official estimates, industrial GDP increased at an average annual rate of 2.9% during 2004–13; it increased by 1.2% in 2013.

Mining contributed an estimated 0.9% of GDP and employed 0.3% of the economically active population in 2013. Gold was the major mineral export, contributing an estimated 1.3% of total export earnings in 2013. Lead, zinc, silver, copper and low-grade iron ore are also mined. In addition, small quantities of petroleum derivatives are exported. The GDP of the mining sector decreased by an average of 5.2% per year in 2004–13; it declined by an estimated 1.2% in 2013.

Manufacturing contributed an estimated 17.7% of GDP and employed 12.7% of the economically active population in 2013. Value added by the *maquila* sector contributed an estimated 22,489.6m. lempiras to the economy in 2013. According to official estimates, manufacturing GDP increased at an average annual rate of 2.7% during 2004–13. The sector's GDP increased by 2.3% in 2013.

Construction contributed an estimated 6.0% of GDP and employed 5.3% of the economically active population in 2013. According to official estimates, the GDP of the construction sector increased at an average annual rate of 0.8% during 2004–13; it increased by 2.4% in 2012, but decreased by 2.4% in 2013.

Petroleum accounted for 54.7% of electrical energy output in 2011, while most of the remainder (39.5%) was derived from hydroelectric power. Imports of mineral fuels and lubricants accounted for 25.2% of the value of total imports in 2013. El Cajón dam, the largest in Central America, provided 300 MW of hydroelectricity. The 102 MW Cerro de Hula wind farm south of Tegucigalpa began operating in 2011. Construction of a hydroelectricity plant on the Patuca river in eastern Honduras had been expected to recommence in 2014 after receiving Chinese funding, although further delays meant construction was put back to 2015.

The services sector contributed an estimated 61.8% of GDP and engaged 45.5% of the working population in 2013. The GDP of the services sector increased by an average of 6.0% per year in 2004–13, according to official estimates; it increased by 3.8% in 2013.

In 2013 Honduras recorded a visible merchandise trade deficit of US $4,479.4m., while there was a deficit of $1,655.1m. on the current account of the balance of payments. Workers' remittances from abroad constitute an important source of income: according to central bank estimates, remittances totalled some $3,120.5m. in 2013. The majority of remittances came from the USA. The USA was the principal market for exports (35.8%, excluding *maquila* goods) in 2013; other significant purchasers were El Salvador, Germany, Guatemala and Nicaragua. In the same year the principal source of imports (43.4%) was also the USA; other major suppliers were Guatemala, El Salvador and Mexico. The principal exports (excluding *maquila* goods) in 2013 were coffee, bananas, palm oil, and lobsters and prawns. Exports from the *maquila* sector totalled $3,981.2m. in 2013. The principal imports in that year were mineral fuels and lubricants, machinery and electrical appliances, and chemicals and related products.

In 2013 there was an estimated budgetary deficit of 13,682.8m. lempiras, equivalent to 3.6% of GDP. Honduras' general government gross debt was 164,213m. lempiras in 2013, equivalent to 43.5% of GDP. Honduras' external debt totalled US $4,987m. at the end of 2012, of which $3,645m. was public and publicly guaranteed debt. In that year, the cost of servicing long-term public and publicly guaranteed debt and repayments to the IMF was equivalent to 13.8% of the value of the exports of goods, services and income (excluding workers' remittances). The annual rate of inflation averaged 6.4% in 2005–14. Consumer prices increased by an annual average of 6.1% in 2014. Some 3.9% of the labour force were registered as unemployed in May 2013; it was estimated that around one-quarter of the workforce was underemployed.

Honduras is among the poorest nations in the Americas, and poverty and violent crime are pervasive. Vigorous domestic consumption contributed to economic growth of 4.1% in 2012, although there was a downturn in the *maquila* sector and increased government spending undermined the fiscal position. IMF funding ended in March, and subsequent discussions with the Fund failed to yield a replacement stand-by arrangement. Consequently, the Government issued bonds valued at

US \$1,000m. in 2013. Honduras rejoined the Petrocaribe programme in mid-2013; regaining access to cheaper Venezuelan petroleum was expected to alleviate some of the pressure on the current account. Real GDP growth moderated to an estimated 2.6% in that year as the coffee sector was seriously undermined by an epidemic of the coffee leaf rust fungal disease. The consequent decline in coffee shipments resulted in the current account deficit widening, despite a rise in remittances (which traditionally account for a significant portion of GDP). The budget deficit also increased in 2013, partly owing to ongoing financial problems at the state-run utility Empresa Nacional de Energía Eléctrica. A series of fiscal austerity reforms was adopted by the legislature in December, although some of the measures envisaged were revoked by the incoming administration in January 2014 following public outcry. The IMF put economic growth at 3.0% in 2014. Remittance inflows rose again during that year, and the fiscal and current account deficits both narrowed, although agricultural performance was negatively affected by an acute drought from mid-2014 that threatened to undermine the food security situation. The Government announced a state of emergency in several western departments in July. The IMF authorized an economic stabilization programme for Honduras in December, which entailed a \$113m. stand-by arrangement and a \$75m. stand-by credit facility; the Government, for its part, agreed to intensify its fiscal consolidation efforts. The Fund projected that real GDP would increase by 3.1% in 2015.

PUBLIC HOLIDAYS

2016: 1 January (New Year's Day), 14 April (Pan-American Day/Bastilla's Day), 24–26 March (Easter), 1 May (Labour Day), 15 September (Independence Day), 3 October (Morazán Day), 12 October (Columbus Day), 21 October (Army Day), 25 December (Christmas).

Statistical Survey

Sources (unless otherwise stated): Department of Economic Studies, Banco Central de Honduras, Avda Juan Ramón Molina, 1a Calle, 7a Avda, Apdo 3165, Tegucigalpa; tel. 2237-2270; fax 2237-1876; e-mail jreyes@bch.hn; internet www.bch.hn; Instituto Nacional de Estadística, Edif. Plaza Guijarro, 5°, Lomas de Guijarro, Tegucigalpa; e-mail info@ine.hn.org; internet www.ine.gob.hn.

Note: The metric system is in force, although some old Spanish measures are used, including: 25 libras = 1 arroba; 4 arrobas = 1 quintal (46 kg).

Area and Population

AREA, POPULATION AND DENSITY

Area (sq km)	112,492*
Population (census results)†	
29 May 1988	4,614,377
1 August 2001	
Males	3,230,958
Females	3,304,386
Total	6,535,344
Population (official estimates at mid-year)	
2013	8,555,072
2014	8,725,111
2015	8,894,975
Density (per sq km) at mid-2015	79.1

* 43,433 sq miles.
† Excluding adjustments for underenumeration, estimated to have been 10% at the 1974 census.

POPULATION BY AGE AND SEX
(UN estimates at mid-2015)

	Males	Females	Total
0–14 years	1,474,952	1,414,544	2,889,496
15–64 years	2,560,008	2,587,016	5,147,024
65 years and over	181,203	206,194	387,397
Total	4,216,163	4,207,754	8,423,917

Source: UN, *World Population Prospects: The 2012 Revision*.

PRINCIPAL TOWNS
('000, official population estimates in 2013)

Tegucigalpa—Distrito Central (capital)	1,195.6	Juticalpa	129.4
San Pedro Sula	753.9	Comayagua	127.0
Choloma	320.0	Catacamas	122.6
El Progreso	223.1	Puerto Cortés	117.8
La Ceiba	201.8	Olanchito	99.9
Danlí	194.5	Siguatepeque	92.8
Choluteca	183.6	Tela	87.7
Villanueva	155.3	Tocoa	86.0

BIRTHS AND DEATHS
(UN estimates)

	2000–05	2005–10	2010–15
Birth rate (per 1,000)	30.0	27.7	26.0
Death rate (per 1,000)	5.3	5.1	4.7

Source: UN, *World Population Prospects: The 2012 Revision*.

Life expectancy (years at birth): 73.5 (males 71.2; females 76.0) in 2012 (Source: World Bank, World Development Indicators database).

EMPLOYMENT
('000 persons)

	2011	2012	2013
Agriculture, hunting, forestry and fishing	1,180	1,240	1,248
Mining and quarrying	7	12	9
Manufacturing	433	434	443
Electricity, gas and water	16	14	17
Construction	169	174	185
Trade, restaurants and hotels	732	710	842
Transport, storage and communications	98	107	118
Financing, insurance, real estate and business services	101	95	105
Community, social, personal and other services	491	459	521
Total employed	3,226	3,244	3,487

Health and Welfare

KEY INDICATORS

Total fertility rate (children per woman, 2012)	3.1
Under-5 mortality rate (per 1,000 live births, 2012) . . .	23
HIV/AIDS (% of persons aged 15–49, 2013)	0.5
Physicians (per 1,000 head, 2005)	0.4
Hospital beds (per 1,000 head, 2010)	0.8
Health expenditure (2011): US $ per head (PPP)	335
Health expenditure (2011): % of GDP	8.4
Health expenditure (2011): public (% of total)	49.4
Access to water (% of persons, 2012)	90
Access to sanitation (% of persons, 2012)	80
Total carbon dioxide emissions ('000 metric tons, 2010) . .	8,107.7
Carbon dioxide emissions per head (metric tons, 2010) . .	1.1
Human Development Index (2013): ranking	129
Human Development Index (2013): value	0.617

For sources and definitions, see explanatory note on p. vi.

Agriculture

PRINCIPAL CROPS
('000 metric tons)

	2011	2012	2013
Maize	545	525	596
Sorghum	40	42	40*
Sugar cane	5,725	5,861	6,082†
Beans, dry	89	91	104
Oil palm fruit	1,867	1,989	2,004†
Tomatoes	138	141	144†
Melons	416	375	377†
Bananas	830	880	880†
Plantains	97	99	99†
Oranges	272	276	280†
Pineapples	140	138	139†
Coffee, green	284	343	273

* Unofficial figure.
† FAO estimate.

Aggregate production ('000 metric tons, may include official, semi-official or estimated data): Total cereals 635.5 in 2011, 621.6 in 2012, 686.7 in 2013; Total vegetables (incl. melons) 793.8 in 2011, 768.5 in 2012, 775.4 in 2013; Total fruits (excl. melons) 1,495.7 in 2011, 1,560.6 in 2012, 1,567.5 in 2013.

Source: FAO.

LIVESTOCK
('000 head, year ending September)

	2011	2012	2013*
Cattle	2,687	2,742	2,774
Sheep*	16	16	16
Goats*	25	25	25
Pigs	455	486	487
Horses*	181	182	182
Mules*	70	70	70
Chickens	42,650	44,388	44,500

* FAO estimates.
Source: FAO.

LIVESTOCK PRODUCTS
('000 metric tons)

	2011	2012	2013*
Cattle meat	65.0	62.3	63.0
Pig meat	12.1	13.4	13.4
Chicken meat	146.1	154.6	150.7
Cows' milk*	656.2	675.8	695.0
Hen eggs	47.6*	51.0	51.1

* FAO estimate(s).
Source: FAO.

Forestry

ROUNDWOOD REMOVALS
('000 cubic metres, excl. bark)

	2011	2012	2013
Sawlogs, veneer logs and logs for sleepers	485	367	476
Other industrial wood	14	14	6
Fuel wood*	8,535	8,497	8,462
Total	9,034	8,878	8,944

* FAO estimates.
Source: FAO.

SAWNWOOD PRODUCTION
('000 cubic metres, incl. railway sleepers)

	2011	2012	2013
Coniferous (softwood)	230	242	258
Broadleaved (hardwood) . . .	4	4	5
Total	234	246	263

Source: FAO.

Fishing

('000 metric tons, live weight)

	2010	2011	2012
Capture*	11.1	9.2	8.4
Marine fishes*	2.0	2.1	2.1
Caribbean spiny lobster . . .	3.2	3.3	1.6
Penaeus shrimps	2.1	2.0	1.1
Stromboid conchs	1.6	1.6	1.6
Aquaculture	27.5	37.0*	34.0
Nile tilapia	16.5	20.0*	7.8
Penaeus shrimps	11.1	17.0	27.0
Total catch*	38.6	46.1	43.3

* FAO estimate(s).
Source: FAO.

Mining

(metal content)

	2010	2011	2012
Lead (metric tons)	16,944	16,954	12,400
Zinc (metric tons)	33,839	26,000	26,000
Silver (kg)	58,158	53,167	50,605
Gold (kg)	2,197	1,893	1,858

Source: US Geological Survey.

Industry

SELECTED PRODUCTS

	2011	2012	2013
Raw sugar ('000 quintales) . .	9,410	10,657	11,084
Cement ('000 bags of 42.5 kg) .	40,255	40,337	38,838
Cigarettes ('000 packets of 20) .	286,568	267,605	232,951
Beer ('000 12 oz bottles) . . .	257,031	256,198	273,631
Soft drinks ('000 12 oz bottles) .	2,065,687	2,154,163	2,277,755
Wheat flour ('000 quintales) . .	3,319	3,624	3,687
Fabric ('000 sq m)	1,210,844	1,155,006	1,100,741
Liquor and spirits ('000 litres) .	18,628	18,723	18,555
Vegetable oil and butter ('000 libras)	405,399	514,903	512,342
Electric energy (million kWh) .	7,122	7,503	7,833

Finance

CURRENCY AND EXCHANGE RATES

Monetary Units
100 centavos = 1 lempira.

Sterling, Dollar and Euro Equivalents (28 November 2014)
£1 sterling = 33.734 lempiras;
US $1 = 21.425 lempiras;
€1 = 26.745 lempiras;
1,000 lempiras = £29.64 = $46.67 = €37.39.

Average Exchange Rate (lempiras per US $)
2010   18.895
2011   18.917
2012   19.502

GOVERNMENT FINANCE
(general government transactions, non-cash basis, million lempiras)

Summary of Balances

	2010	2011	2012*
Revenue	69,351.7	77,473.7	83,887.8
Less Expense	68,561.8	74,687.9	84,386.7
Gross operating balance . .	789.9	2,785.7	−499.0
Less Net acquisition of non-financial assets	10,880.1	12,644.4	12,087.1
Net lending/borrowing . . .	−10,090.2	−9,858.6	−12,586.1

Revenue

	2010	2011	2012*
Taxes	45,388.6	51,808.7	55,493.8
Taxes of income, profits and capital gains	13,241.3	16,677.7	17,300.8
Taxes of goods and services .	26,432.2	29,640.1	32,498.7
Social contributions	8,671.1	9,653.5	10,934.2
Grants	4,162.6	3,676.7	3,550.2
Other revenue	11,129.4	12,334.8	13,909.5
Total	69,351.7	77,473.7	83,887.8

Expense by economic type†

	2010	2011	2012*
Compensation of employees . .	39,585.8	39,971.7	42,630.1
Wages and salaries	36,232.2	37,097.6	39,352.5
Social contributions	3,353.6	2,874.1	3,277.6
Use of goods and services . . .	10,961.8	12,183.9	14,904.0
Interest	2,560.5	4,072.4	5,538.9
Subsidies	318.2	557.5	1,091.4
Social benefits	406.3	364.8	226.8
Other expense	14,561.3	17,337.2	19,707.4
Grants	167.9	200.4	288.2
Total (incl. others)	68,561.8	74,687.9	84,386.7

* Preliminary.
† Including purchases of non-financial assets.

Source: IMF, *Government Finance Statistics Yearbook*.

2012 (general government budget, million lempiras, projections): *Revenue:* Current 60,316.4 (Taxes on profits and income 55,495.4); Other revenue 200.0; Grants 3,204.3; Total revenue 63,720.7; *Expenditure:* Current 64,879.4 (Wages and Salaries 34,974.0, Goods and services 8,931.7, Interest 6,466.6, Transfers and subsidies 14,507.1); Capital 15,004.0; Total expenditure 79,883.4 (excl. net lending −25.7).

2013 (general government budget, million lempiras, budget figures): *Revenue:* Current 63,603.7 (Taxes on profits and income 61,247.7); Other revenue 500.0; Grants 2,644.8; Total revenue 66,748.5; *Expenditure:* Current 67,394.8 (Wages and Salaries 36,651.1, Goods and services 9,268.2, Interest 8,391.5, Transfers and subsidies 13,084.0); Capital 13,010.7; Total expenditure 80,405.5 (excl. net lending −25.8).

CENTRAL BANK RESERVES
(US $ million at 31 December)

	2011	2012	2013
Gold (national valuation) . . .	35.02	38.79	26.57
IMF special drawing rights . .	154.20	148.08	142.08
Foreign exchange	2,582.30	2,333.90	2,826.50
Reserve position in IMF . . .	13.24	13.26	13.28
Total	2,784.76	2,534.03	3,008.43

Source: IMF, *International Financial Statistics*.

MONEY SUPPLY
(million lempiras at 31 December)

	2011	2012	2013
Currency outside depository corporations	16,199	16,426	17,062
Transferable deposits	30,804	29,102	29,795
Other deposits	122,947	136,336	150,672
Securities other than shares . .	2,222	2,411	2,458
Broad money	172,172	184,275	199,988

Source: IMF, *International Financial Statistics*.

COST OF LIVING
(Consumer Price Index, base: 1999 = 100)

	2012	2013	2014
Food and non-alcoholic beverages .	222.7	233.9	249.7
Rent, water, fuel and power . .	288.2	303.5	318.4
Clothing and footwear	218.9	232.0	250.9
All items (incl. others) . . .	247.3	260.1	276.0

NATIONAL ACCOUNTS
(million lempiras at current prices)

Expenditure on the Gross Domestic Product

	2011	2012	2013*
Government final consumption expenditure	53,820	58,545	63,538
Private final consumption expenditure	260,106	284,080	305,974
Changes in inventories . . .	5,224	698	−10,424
Gross fixed capital formation .	81,883	88,064	96,293
Total domestic expenditure .	401,034	431,387	455,381
Exports of goods and services .	171,728	183,937	181,775

—*continued*	2011	2012	2013*
Less Imports of goods and services	237,733	253,975	260,854
GDP in purchasers' values .	335,028	361,348	376,302
GDP at constant 2000 prices .	165,958	172,810	177,353

Gross Domestic Product by Economic Activity

	2011	2012	2013*
Agriculture, hunting, forestry and fishing	47,640	49,022	46,145
Mining and quarrying	3,329	3,502	3,421
Manufacturing	57,606	63,909	65,619
Electricity, gas and water . .	5,044	5,247	4,267
Construction	20,506	21,703	22,352
Wholesale and retail trade . .	46,247	50,017	53,325
Hotels and restaurants . . .	9,874	10,821	11,595
Transport and storage . . .	10,127	11,287	12,558
Communications	10,527	11,579	12,773
Finance and insurance . . .	20,253	22,300	24,704
Owner-occupied dwellings . .	17,361	18,577	20,166
Business activities	15,247	16,565	17,907
Education services	23,692	25,589	27,250
Health	11,474	12,679	13,635
Public administration and defence	20,638	22,184	24,344
Other services	9,568	10,221	11,021
Sub-total	329,132	355,199	371,081
Less Financial intermediation services indirectly measured .	17,745	19,595	21,342
GDP at factor cost	311,388	335,604	349,739
Indirect taxes, *less* subsidies . .	23,640	25,744	26,563
GDP in purchasers' values .	335,028	361,349	376,302

* Preliminary.

BALANCE OF PAYMENTS
(US $ million)

	2011	2012	2013
Exports of goods	3,977.6	4,409.1	3,950.3
Imports of goods	−8,355.9	−8,698.0	−8,429.7
Balance on goods	4,378.4	−4,288.9	−4,479.4
Exports of services	2,254.0	2,257.5	2,424.5
Imports of services	−1,447.8	−1,515.0	−1,641.5
Balance on goods and services	−3,572.3	−3,546.4	−3,696.3
Primary income received . . .	58.6	80.3	58.5
Primary income paid	−1,032.3	−1,355.5	−1,359.7
Balance on goods, services and primary income	−4,545.9	−4,821.5	−4,997.5
Secondary income received . .	3,220.5	3,315.9	3,466.1
Secondary income paid . . .	−82.8	−81.3	−123.6
Current balance	−1,408.3	−1,586.9	−1,655.1
Capital account (net)	166.2	101.2	132.5
Direct investment assets . . .	−30.3	−63.7	−35.7
Direct investment liabilities . .	1,042.6	1,067.6	1,069.0
Portfolio investment assets . .	45.8	−11.8	−0.2
Portfolio investment liabilities .	41.9	12.9	1,007.0
Other investment assets . . .	−436.6	137.3	−106.4
Other investment liabilities . .	428.1	315.6	590.2
Net errors and omissions . . .	184.4	−242.8	−520.4
Reserves and related items .	33.8	−270.6	481.0

Source: IMF, *International Financial Statistics*.

External Trade

PRINCIPAL COMMODITIES
(US $ million)

Imports c.i.f.*	2011	2012	2013
Vegetables and fruit	434.8	414.1	410.1
Food products	812.2	907.9	950.2
Mineral products	2,155.5	2,284.0	2,305.9
Fuels and lubricants . . .	2,103.9	2,242.2	2,264.3
Chemicals and related products .	1,227.8	1,281.9	1,179.5
Plastic and manufactures . . .	508.2	558.6	533.1
Paper, paperboard and manufactures	395.5	352.7	394.3
Metal and manufactures . . .	614.6	611.4	556.0
Machinery and electrical appliances	1,380.8	1,359.5	1,342.6
Transport equipment	497.3	573.4	483.9
Total (incl. others)	9,016.2	9,385.3	9,152.3

* Excluding imports destined for the *maquila* sector (US $ million): 2,879.7 in 2011; 2,780.8 in 2012; 2,698.8 in 2013.

Exports f.o.b.*	2011	2012	2013
Bananas	397.8	442.4	490.1
Cigars and cigarettes	81.4	92.2	92.6
Coffee	1,358.4	1,402.4	749.8
Lead and zinc	65.3	51.6	44.4
Melons and watermelons . . .	54.0	50.9	58.8
Palm oil	270.1	304.2	286.4
Lobsters and prawns	205.8	211.5	268.8
Soaps and detergents	68.9	82.1	97.0
Tilapia	62.8	61.7	65.2
Paper and paperboard	63.7	148.7	138.3
Plastics and articles thereof . .	78.4	94.7	90.1
Total (incl. others)	3,866.4	4,281.3	3,830.9

* Excluding exports of gold, and of *maquila* goods (US $ million): 4,092.6 in 2011; 3,974.1 in 2012; 3,981.2 in 2013.

PRINCIPAL TRADING PARTNERS
(US $ million, excluding *maquila* goods)

Imports c.i.f.	2011	2012	2013
Brazil	83.9	95.5	86.5
China, People's Republic . . .	337.2	436.1	452.8
Colombia	317.0	272.2	331.2
Costa Rica	364.5	384.8	355.5
Ecuador	226.8	238.3	182.5
El Salvador	485.7	554.9	521.3
Germany	143.0	132.2	152.0
Guatemala	798.4	801.0	827.7
Japan	111.1	119.0	85.6
Korea, Republic	85.8	90.0	75.7
Mexico	488.8	538.0	514.5
Panama	346.9	359.6	336.2
Peru	27.5	75.2	101.2
Spain	80.4	95.7	80.1
USA	4,207.2	4,131.1	3,969.3
Total (incl. others)	9,016.2	9,385.3	9,152.3

Exports

Exports f.o.b.*	2011	2012	2013
Belgium	251.8	296.1	135.8
Canada	100.8	67.9	82.3
China, People's Republic	102.6	113.7	130.0
Costa Rica	116.3	103.4	109.4
Dominican Republic	40.7	46.2	51.1
El Salvador	298.5	293.7	334.5
France	61.2	53.2	43.7
Germany	416.1	498.4	273.9
Guatemala	235.4	218.5	259.9
Italy	68.2	80.5	42.2
Japan	52.5	34.2	27.7
Mexico	133.9	122.4	136.7
Netherlands	61.4	137.2	111.8
Nicaragua	157.2	202.3	204.3
Panama	24.8	52.8	61.8
Spain	39.1	55.1	44.9
United Kingdom	92.2	76.4	69.8
USA	1,269.1	1,494.8	1,404.8
Total (incl. others)	3,959.8	4,391.1	3,929.4

* Including exports of gold (US $ million): 93.4 in 2011; 109.7 in 2012; 98.5 in 2013.

Transport

ROAD TRAFFIC
(licensed vehicles in use)

	2001	2002	2003
Passenger cars	345,931	369,303	386,468
Buses and coaches	20,380	21,814	22,514
Lorries and vans	81,192	86,893	91,230
Motorcycles and bicycles	36,828	39,245	41,852

2008 (vehicles in use): Passenger cars 213,643; Buses and coaches 51,233; Vans and lorries 427,503; Motorcycles and mopeds 122,397 (Source: IRF, *World Road Statistics*).

SHIPPING

Flag Registered Fleet
(at 31 December)

	2012	2013	2014
Number of vessels	677	664	654
Total displacement ('000 grt)	665.3	755.1	573.3

Source: Lloyd's List Intelligence (www.lloydslistintelligence.com).

CIVIL AVIATION
('000)

	2011	2012	2013
Passengers carried	424	422	426

Source: World Bank, World Development Indicators database.

Tourism

TOURIST ARRIVALS BY COUNTRY OF ORIGIN

	2011	2012	2013
Canada	18,530	17,086	17,339
Costa Rica	22,825	21,629	20,199
El Salvador	150,343	142,961	133,256
Germany	12,219	16,583	15,626
Guatemala	115,768	110,230	103,115
Italy	20,977	27,739	26,358
Mexico	22,968	21,045	21,423
Nicaragua	110,299	104,904	97,233
Spain	15,459	20,821	19,599
United Kingdom	11,742	15,889	14,923
USA	275,117	253,887	257,276
Total (incl. others)	871,468	894,677	863,012

Receipts from tourism (US $ million, excl. passenger transport): 637 in 2011; 661 in 2012; 698 in 2013.

Source: World Tourism Organization.

Communications Media

	2011	2012	2013
Telephones ('000 main lines in use)	614.3	610.5	619.1
Mobile cellular telephones ('000 subscribers)	8,062.2	7,370.0	7,767.2
Broadband subscribers ('000)	57.9	61.3	68.1

Internet subscribers: 72,400 in 2009.

Education

(2013)

	Institutions	Students
Pre-primary	11,336	237,944
Primary	12,573	1,297,804
Secondary	1,699	547,419
Adult	253	10,512
Total	25,861	2,093,679

Teachers (2009/10 unless otherwise indicated): Pre-primary 8,837 (2008/09); Primary 37,370 (2008/09); Secondary 16,667 (2003/04); Higher (incl. university) 8,593 (Source: UNESCO Institute for Statistics).

Pupil-teacher ratio (primary education, UNESCO estimate): 33.9 in 2008/09 (Source: UNESCO Institute for Statistics).

Adult literacy rate (UNESCO estimates): 85.4% (males 85.7%; females 85.1%) in 2012 (Source: UNESCO Institute for Statistics).

Directory

The Government

HEAD OF STATE

President: JUAN ORLANDO HERNÁNDEZ ALVARADO (took office 27 January 2014).

CABINET
(April 2015)

The Government is comprised of members of the Partido Nacional. In addition to the ministers listed below, there are seven sectoral ministries, responsible for the following areas: governability and decentralization, development and social inclusion, economic development, infrastructure, security and defence, competition and economic regulation, and foreign affairs.

Co-ordinator-General of the Government: JORGE RAMÓN HERNÁNDEZ ALCERRO.

Secretary of Human Rights, Justice, Government and Decentralization: RIGOBERTO CHANG CASTILLO.

Secretary of the Presidency: REINALDO SÁNCHEZ.

Secretary of Finance: WILFREDO CERRATO.

Secretary of Health: YOLANI BATRES.

Secretary of Public Security: Gen. (retd) JULIÁN PACHECO TINOCO.

Secretary of National Defence: SAMUEL ARMANDO REYES RENDÓN.

Secretary of Foreign Affairs: ARTURO CORRALES ALVAREZ.

Secretary of Infrastructure and Public Services: ROBERTO ORDÓÑEZ.

Secretary of Economic Development: ALDEN RIVERA.

Secretary of Education: MARLON ESCOTO.

Secretary of Energy, Natural Resources, Environment and Mines: JOSÉ ANTONIO GALDÁMEZ.

Secretary of Agriculture and Livestock: JACOBO PAZ BODDEN.

Secretary of Development and Social Inclusion: RICARDO CARDONA.

Secretary of Communications and Strategy in the Office of the President: HILDA HERNÁNDEZ.

MINISTRIES

Office of the President: Palacio José Cecilio del Valle, Blvd Francisco Morazán, Tegucigalpa; tel. 2290-5010; fax 2231-0097; e-mail diseloalpresidente@presidencia.gob.hn; internet www.presidencia.gob.hn.

Secretariat of Agriculture and Livestock: Avda La FAO, Blvd Centroamérica, Col. Loma Linda, Tegucigalpa; tel. 2232-5029; fax 2231-0051; e-mail infoagro@infoagro.hn; internet www.sag.gob.hn.

Secretariat of Development and Social Inclusion: Edif. Ejecutivo, Las Lomas Anexo II, frente a Ferretería INDUFESA, Blvd Juan Pablo II, Tegucigalpa; tel. 2239-8005; internet sedis.gob.hn.

Secretariat of Economic Development: Edif. San José, Col. Humuya, Blvd José Cecilio del Valle, Tegucigalpa; tel. 2235-3699; fax 2235-3686.

Secretariat of Education: 1 Avda, entre 2 y 3 Calle, Comayagüela, Tegucigalpa; tel. 2238-4325; fax 2222-8571; e-mail webmaster@se.gob.hn; internet www.se.gob.hn.

Secretariat of Energy, Natural Resources, Environment and Mines: 100 m al sur del Estadio Nacional, Apdo 1389, Tegucigalpa; tel. 2232-1386; fax 2232-6250; e-mail sdespacho@yahoo.com; internet www.serna.gob.hn.

Secretariat of Finance: Edif. SEFIN, Avda Cervantes, Barrio El Jazmin, Tegucigalpa; tel. 2222-0112; fax 2238-2309; e-mail sgeneral@sefin.gob.hn; internet www.sefin.gob.hn.

Secretariat of Foreign Affairs: Centro Cívico Gubernamental, Antigua Casa Presidencial, Blvd Kuwait, Contiguo a la Corte Suprema de Justicia, Tegucigalpa; tel. 2230-4156; fax 2230-5664; e-mail cancilleria.honduras@gmail.com; internet www.sre.gob.hn.

Secretariat of Health: 2 Calle, Avda Cervantes, Tegucigalpa; tel. 2222-8518; fax 2238-6787; e-mail comunicacionessalud@yahoo.com; internet www.salud.gob.hn.

Secretariat of Human Rights, Justice, Government and Decentralization: Residencia La Hacienda, Calle La Estancia, Tegucigalpa; tel. 2232-5995; fax 2232-0226; e-mail francis.caceres@seip.gob.hn; internet www.seip.gob.hn.

Secretariat of Infrastructure and Public Services: Barrio La Bolsa, Comayagüela, Tegucigalpa; tel. 2225-2690; fax 2225-5003.

Secretariat of National Defence: Blvd Suyapa, Col. Florencia Sur, frente a Iglesia Colegio Episcopal, Tegucigalpa; tel. 2239-2330; e-mail transparencia@sedena.gob.hn; internet www.sedena.gob.hn.

Secretariat of Public Security: Cuartel General de Casamata, subida al Picacho, Tegucigalpa; tel. 2220-4298; fax 2220-1711; e-mail info@seguridad.gob.hn; internet www.seguridad.gob.hn.

President and Legislature

PRESIDENT

Election, 24 November 2013

Candidate	Valid votes cast	% of valid votes
Juan Orlando Hernández Alvarado (PN)	1,149,302	36.89
Xiomara Castro de Zelaya (LIBRE)	896,498	28.78
Mauricio Villeda (PL)	632,320	20.30
Salvador Nasralla (PAC)	418,443	13.43
Others	18,885	0.61
Total*	**3,115,448**	**100.00**

* In addition, there were 108,171 spoiled votes and 51,727 blank votes.

NATIONAL CONGRESS
(Congreso Nacional)

President: MAURICIO OLIVA.

General Election, 24 November 2013

	Seats
Partido Nacional (PN)	48
Partido Libertad y Refundación (LIBRE)	37
Partido Liberal (PL)	27
Partido Anticorrupción (PAC)	13
Partido Innovación y Unidad—Social Demócrata (PINU—SD)	1
Partido de Unificación Democrática (PUD)	1
Partido Demócrata Cristiano de Honduras (PDCH)	1
Total	**128**

Election Commission

Tribunal Supremo Electoral (TSE): Col. El Prado, frente a Edif. Syre, Tegucigalpa; tel. 2239-1058; fax 2239-3060; e-mail centroinformacion@tse.hn; internet www.tse.hn; f. 2004 as successor to Tribunal Nacional de Elecciones; Pres. DAVID ANDRÉS MATAMOROS BATSÓN.

Political Organizations

Alianza Patriótica Hondureña (La Alianza): Tegucigalpa; tel. 2213-8091; fax 2213-2367; e-mail contacto@laalianza.hn; internet www.laalianza.hn; f. 2011; right-wing; Pres. Gen. (retd) ROMEO VÁSQUEZ VELÁSQUEZ.

Frente Amplio Político Electoral en Resistencia (FAPER): Tegucigalpa; internet partido-faper.blogspot.co.uk; f. 2012; contested the 2013 elections; Pres. ANDRÉS PAVÓN.

Partido Anticorrupción (PAC): Tegucigalpa; e-mail honduras@salvadornasralla.com; internet www.salvadornasralla.com; f. 2011; centre-left; Pres. SALVADOR NASRALLA.

Partido Demócrata Cristiano de Honduras (PDCH): Col. San Carlos, Tegucigalpa; tel. 2236-5969; fax 2236-9941; e-mail pdch@hondutel.hn; internet www.pdch.hn; legally recognized in 1980; Pres. AUGUSTO CRUZ ASENCIO.

Partido Innovación y Unidad—Social Demócrata (PINU—SD): 2a Avda, entre 9 y 10 calles, Apdo 105, Comayagüela, Tegucigalpa; tel. 2220-4224; fax 2220-4232; e-mail pinusd@amnettgu.com; internet pinusd.hn; f. 1970; legally recognized in 1978; Pres. GUILLERMO VALLE MARICHAL; Sec. JORGE RAFAEL AGUILAR PAREDES.

Partido Liberal (PL): Col. Miramontes, atrás de Supermercado la Col. No 1, Tegucigalpa; tel. 2232-0822; e-mail info@partidoliberaldehonduras.hn; internet www.partidoliberal.hn; f. 1891; Pres. MAURICIO VILLEDA BERMÚDEZ.

Partido Libertad y Refundación (LIBRE): Tegucigalpa; internet libre.hn; f. 2011; party of 2013 presidential candidate Xiomara Castro de Zelaya; Pres. JOSÉ MANUEL ZELAYA ROSALES.

Partido Nacional (PN): Paseo el Obelisco, Comayagüela, Tegucigalpa; tel. 2237-7310; fax 2237-7365; e-mail partidonacional@partidonacional.net; internet www.partidonacional.net; f. 1902; traditional right-wing party; Pres. GLADIS AURORA LÓPEZ CALDERÓN.

Partido de Unificación Democrática (PUD): Col. los Almendros, Blvd Morazón, atrás del Restaurante Las Reses, Tegucigalpa; tel. and fax 2236-6868; e-mail partidoudhonduras@yahoo.es; internet www.partidoud.com; f. 1992 following merger of Partido Revolucionario Hondureño, Partido Renovación Patriótica, Partido para la Transformación de Honduras and Partido Morazanista; left-wing; Pres. DAVID ADOLFO CÉSAR HAM PEÑA.

Diplomatic Representation

EMBASSIES IN HONDURAS

Argentina: Calle Palermo 302, Col. Rubén Darío, Apdo 3208, Tegucigalpa; tel. 2232-3376; fax 2231-0376; e-mail ehond@mrecic.gov.ar; internet embajadaargentinaenhonduras.org; Ambassador GUILLERMO ROBERTO ROSSI.

Belize: Area Comercial del Hotel Honduras Maya, Col. Palmira, Tegucigalpa; tel. 2238-4614; fax 2238-4617; e-mail vesahonduras@gmail.com; Chargé d'affaires a.i. RICHARD CLARK VINELLI REISMAN.

Brazil: Col. Palmira, Calle República del Brasil, Apdo 341, Tegucigalpa; tel. 2221-4432; fax 2236-5873; e-mail brastegu@clarotv.com.hn; internet tegucigalpa.itamaraty.gov.br; Ambassador ZENIK KRAWCTSCHUK.

Chile: Torres Metrópolis 1, 16°, Of. 11608, Blvd Suyapa, Tegucigalpa; tel. 2232-4106; fax 2232-2114; e-mail embachilehonduras@clarotv.com.hn; internet chileabroad.gov.cl/honduras; Ambassador JAIME BRAVO OLIVA.

Colombia: Edif. Palmira, 3°, Col. Palmira, Apdo 468, Tegucigalpa; tel. 2239-9709; fax 2232-9324; e-mail ehonduras@cancilleria.gov.co; internet www.embajadaenhonduras.gov.co; Ambassador FRANCISCO CANOSSA GUERRERO.

Costa Rica: Residencial El Triángulo, Calle 3451, Lomas del Guijarro, Apdo 512, Tegucigalpa; tel. 2232-1768; fax 2232-1054; e-mail embacori@amnettgu.com; Ambassador MARÍA GUTIÉRREZ VARGAS.

Cuba: Col. Lomas del Guijarro, Calle Los Eucaliptos, No 3720, Tegucigalpa; tel. 2235-3349; fax 2235-7624; e-mail admon@hn.embacuba.cu; internet www.cubadiplomatica.cu/honduras; Ambassador SERGIO OLIVA GUERRA.

Dominican Republic: Plaza Miramontes, 2°, Local No 6, Col. Miramontes, Tegucigalpa; tel. 2239-0130; fax 2239-1594; e-mail joacosta@serex.gov.do; Ambassador JOSÉ OSVALDO LEGER AQUINO.

Ecuador: Bloque F, Casa 2968, Sendero Senecio, Col. Lomas del Castaños Sur, Apdo 358, Tegucigalpa; tel. 2221-4906; fax 2221-1049; e-mail mecuahon@multivisionhn.net; Ambassador CARMEN IRINA CABEZA RODRÍGUEZ.

El Salvador: Col. Altos de Miramontes, Casa 2952, Diagonal Aguan, Tegucigalpa; tel. 2239-7015; fax 2239-6556; e-mail embasalhonduras@rree.gob.sv; internet embajadahonduras.rree.gob.sv; Ambassador CARLOS DE JESÚS POZO.

France: Col. Palmira, Avda Juan Lindo, Callejón Batres 337, Apdo 3441, Tegucigalpa; tel. 2236-6800; fax 2236-8051; e-mail info@ambafrance-hn.org; internet www.ambafrance-hn.org; Ambassador PHILIPPE ARDANAZ.

Germany: Avda República Dominicana 925, Sendero Santo Domingo, Col. Lomas del Guijarro, Apdo 3145, Tegucigalpa; tel. 2232-3161; fax 2239-9018; e-mail info@tegucigalpa.diplo.de; internet www.tegucigalpa.diplo.de; Ambassador BEATRIX CHRISTINA KANIA.

Guatemala: Casa No 0440, Bloque B, Calle Londres, Col. Lomas del Guijarro Sur, Tegucigalpa; tel. 2232-5018; fax 2239-9809; e-mail embhondurasgt@gmail.com; Ambassador HUGO RENÉ HEMMERLING GONZÁLEZ.

Holy See: Palacio de la Nunciatura Apostólica, Col. Palmira, Avda Santa Sede 401, Apdo 324, Tegucigalpa; tel. 2238-6013; fax 2238-6257; e-mail nunziohn@hotmail.com; Apostolic Nuncio Most Rev. NOVATUS RUGAMBWA.

Italy: Torre Lafise, 3°, Avda Los Próceres, Centro Corporativo, Col. San Carlos, Tegucigalpa; tel. 2221–4963; fax 2221–4953; e-mail ambasciata.tegucigalpa@esteri.it; internet www.ambtegucigalpa.esteri.it; Ambassador GIOVANNI ADORNI BRACCESI CHIASSI.

Japan: Col. San Carlos, Calzada Rep. Paraguay, Apdo 3232, Tegucigalpa; tel. 2236-5511; fax 2236-6100; e-mail keikyo1@multivisionhn.net; internet www.hn.emb-japan.go.jp; Ambassador KENJI OKADA.

Korea, Republic: Edif. Plaza Azul, 5°, Col. Lomas del Guijarro Sur, Tegucigalpa; tel. 2235-5561; fax 2235-5564; e-mail coreaembajada@mofat.go.kr; internet hnd.mofat.go.kr; Ambassador KIM RAI-HYUG.

Mexico: Col. Lomas del Guijarro, Avda Eucalipto 1001, Tegucigalpa; tel. 2232-4039; fax 2232-4719; e-mail embamexhonduras@gmail.com; internet www.sre.gob.mx/honduras; Ambassador VÍCTOR HUGO MORALES.

Nicaragua: Col. Tepeyac, Bloque M-1, Avda Choluteca 1130, Apdo 392, Tegucigalpa; tel. 2231-1966; fax 2231-1412; e-mail embanic@amnettgu.com; Ambassador MARIO JOSÉ DUARTE ZAMORA.

Panama: Edif. Palmira, 3°, Col. Palmira, Apdo 397, Tegucigalpa; tel. 2239-5508; fax 2232-8147; e-mail ephon@multivisionhn.net; Ambassador BETZAIDA GUERRERO MORENO.

Peru: Col. Linda Vista, Calle Principal 3301, Tegucigalpa; tel. 2236-7994; fax 2221-4596; e-mail embajadadelperu@cablecolor.hn; Ambassador GUILLERMO GONZÁLEZ ARICA.

Spain: Col. Matamoros, Calle Santander 801, Apdo 3221, Tegucigalpa; tel. 2236-6875; fax 2236-8682; e-mail emb.tegucigalpa@maec.es; internet www.maec.es/Embajadas/Tegucigalpa; Ambassador MIGUEL ALBERO SUÁREZ.

Taiwan (Republic of China): Col. Lomas del Guijarro, Calle Eucaliptos 3750, Apdo 3433, Tegucigalpa; tel. 2239-5837; fax 2232-0532; e-mail hnd@mofa.gov.tw; internet www.taiwanembassy.org/hn; Ambassador JOSEPH Y. L. KUO.

USA: Avda La Paz, Apdo 3453, Tegucigalpa; tel. 2236-9320; fax 2236-9037; internet honduras.usembassy.gov; Ambassador JAMES D. NEALON.

Venezuela: Col. Rubén Darío, 2116 Circuito Choluteca, Apdo 775, Tegucigalpa; tel. 2232-1879; fax 2232-1016; e-mail info@venezuelalabolivariana.com; internet venezuelalabolivariana.com; Ambassador FILINTO DURÁN CHUECOS.

Judicial System

Justice is administered by the Supreme Court, five Courts of Appeal, and departmental courts (which have their own local jurisdiction).

Tegucigalpa has two Courts of Appeal, the first of which has jurisdiction in the department of Francisco Morazán, and the second of which has jurisdiction in the departments of Choluteca Valle, El Paraíso and Olancho.

The Appeal Court of San Pedro Sula has jurisdiction in the department of Cortés; that of Comayagua has jurisdiction in the departments of Comayagua, La Paz and Intibucá; and that of Santa Bárbara in the departments of Santa Bárbara, Lempira and Copán.

Supreme Court: Edif. Palacio de Justicia, contiguo Col. Miraflores, Centro Cívico Gubernamental, Tegucigalpa; tel. 2275-7183; fax 2233-6784; e-mail comunicaciones@poderjudicial.gob.hn; internet www.poderjudicial.gob.hn; comprises 4 courts: constitutional, labour, civil and penal; Pres. JORGE RIVERA AVILÉS.

Attorney-General: OSCAR FERNANDO CHINCHILLA.

Religion

The majority of the population are Roman Catholics; the Constitution guarantees toleration of all forms of religious belief.

CHRISTIANITY

The Roman Catholic Church

Honduras comprises one archdiocese and seven dioceses. Some 82% of the population are Roman Catholics.

Bishops' Conference: Conferencia Episcopal de Honduras, Blvd Estadio Suyapa, Apdo 3121, Tegucigalpa; tel. 2229-1111; fax 2229-1144; e-mail ceh@unicah.edu; internet www.iglesiahn.org; f. 1929; Pres. Cardinal OSCAR ANDRÉS RODRÍGUEZ MARADIAGA (Archbishop of Tegucigalpa).

Archbishop of Tegucigalpa: Cardinal OSCAR ANDRÉS RODRÍGUEZ MARADIAGA, Arzobispado, 3a y 2a Avda 1113, Apdo 106, Tegucigalpa; tel. 2236-2849; fax 2236-2967; e-mail oficina@arquitegucigalpa.org; internet www.arquitegucigalpa.org.

The Anglican Communion

Honduras comprises a single missionary diocese, in Province IX of the Episcopal Church in the USA.

Bishop of Honduras: Rt Rev. LLOYD EMMANUEL ALLEN, Diócesis de Honduras, 23 Avda C, 21 St Colony Trejo, San Pedro Sula; tel. 2556-6155; fax 2556-6467; e-mail obispoallen@yahoo.com; internet honduras.fedigitales.org.

The Baptist Church

Convención Nacional de Iglesias Bautistas de Honduras (CONIBAH): Apdo 2176, Tegucigalpa; tel. and fax 2221-4024; e-mail conibah@sigmanet.hn; internet www.ublaonline.org/paises/honduras.htm; Pres. Pastor TOMÁS MONTOYA; 24,142 mems.

Other Churches

Church of Jesus Christ of Latter-Day Saints (Mormons): Residenciales Roble Oeste, Blvd Roble Oeste, 3ra Calle Sur, Comayagüela; tel. 2264-1212; internet www.lds.org; 154,207 mems.

Iglesia Cristiana Luterana de Honduras (Lutheran): Barrio Villa Adela, 19 Calle entre 5a y 6a Avda, Apdo 2861, Tegucigalpa; tel. 2225-4464; fax 2225-4893; e-mail iclh@cablecolor.hn; internet iclh.wordpress.com; Pres. Rev. JOSÉ MARTIN GIRÓN; 1,500 mems.

BAHÁ'Í FAITH

National Spiritual Assembly: Sendero de los Naranjos 2801, Col. Castaños, Apdo 273, Tegucigalpa; tel. 2232-6124; fax 2231-1343; e-mail sdooki@tropicohn.com; internet www.bahaihonduras.net; Co-ordinator SOHEIL DOOKI; 40,000 mems resident in more than 500 localities.

The Press

DAILIES

La Gaceta: Empresa Nacional de Artes Gráficas, Col. Miraflores, Tegucigalpa; tel. 2230-1339; fax 2230-3026; internet www.lagaceta.hn; f. 1830; morning; official govt paper; Gen. Man. MARTHA ALICIA

GARCÍA CASCO; Co-ordinator MARCO ANTONIO RODRÍGUEZ CASTILLO; circ. 3,000.

El Heraldo: Avda los Próceres, Frente al Pani, Barrio San Felipe, Apdo 1938, Tegucigalpa; tel. 2236-6000; e-mail contactos@elheraldo .hn; internet www.elheraldo.hn; f. 1979; morning; independent; Editor FERNANDO BERRÍOS; circ. 50,000.

La Prensa: Guamilito, 3a Avda, 6–7 Calles No 34, Apdo 143, San Pedro Sula; tel. 2553-3101; fax 2553-0778; e-mail redaccion@ laprensa.hn; internet www.laprensa.hn; f. 1964; morning; independent; Editor NELSON GARCÍA; Exec. Dir MARÍA ANTONIA MARTÍNEZ DE FUENTES; circ. 50,000.

El Tiempo: 1 Calle, 5a Avda 102, Barrio Santa Anita, Cortés, Apdo 450, San Pedro Sula; tel. 2553-3388; fax 2553-4590; e-mail web .tiempo@continental.hn; internet www.tiempo.hn; f. 1960; morning; left-of-centre; Pres. JAIME ROSENTHAL OLIVA; circ. 35,000.

La Tribuna: Col. Santa Bárbara, Carretera al Primer Batallón de Infantería, Comayagüela, Apdo 1501, Tegucigalpa; tel. 2234-3206; fax 2234-3050; e-mail tribuna@latribuna.hn; internet www .latribuna.hn; f. 1976; morning; independent; Dir ADÁN ELVIR FLORES; Editor OLMAN MANZANO; circ. 45,000.

PERIODICALS

Comercio Global: Cámara de Comercio e Industrias de Tegucigalpa, Blvd Centroamérica, Apdo 3444, Tegucigalpa; tel. 2232-4200; fax 2232-0759; e-mail mercadeo@ccit.hn; internet www.ccit.hn; f. 1970; 4 a year; commercial and industrial news; Publr DANIELA ZELAYA.

Cromos: Torre Libertad, Blvd Suyapa, Tegucigalpa; tel. 2239-3916; fax 2239-7008; e-mail editor@cromos.hn; internet www.cromos.hn; f. 1999; society; monthly; publishes specialized edns *Cromos Gourmet, Cromos Bodas, Cromos Seniors, Cromos Hogar, Cromos Fashion* and *Cromos Ellos* annually; Publr REGINA MARÍA WONG; Editors ALEJANDRA PAREDES, EMMA MIDENCE.

Estilo: Tegucigalpa; tel. 2553-3101; fax 2558-1273; e-mail revista@ estilo.hn; internet www.estilo.hn; f. 1996; lifestyle; monthly; Pres. JORGE CANAHUATI LARACH; Editor BLANCA BENDECK.

Hablemos Claro: Edif. Torre Libertad, Blvd Suyapa, Residencial La Hacienda, Tegucigalpa; tel. 2232-8058; fax 2239-7008; e-mail rwa@hablemosclaro.com; internet www.hablemosclaro.com; f. 1990; weekly; Editor RODRIGO WONG ARÉVALO; circ. 9,000.

Honduras Weekly: Centro Comercial Villa Mare, Blvd Morazán, Apdo 1323, Tegucigalpa; tel. 2239-0285; fax 2232-2300; e-mail editor@hondurasweekly.com; internet www.hondurasweekly.com; f. 1988; weekly; English language; tourism, culture and the environment; Bureau Chief NICOLE MUÑOZ; Editor MARCO CÁCERES.

El Libertador: Tegucigalpa; internet www.ellibertador.hn; Dir JHONNY LAGOS; Editor DELMER MEMBREÑO.

PRESS ASSOCIATION

Asociación de Prensa Hondureña: Casa del Periodista, Avda Gutemberg 1525, Calle 6, Barrio El Guanacaste, Apdo 893, Tegucigalpa; tel. 2239-2970; fax 2237-8102; f. 1930; Pres. CARLOS ORTIZ; Sec.-Gen. FELA ISABEL DUARTE.

Publishers

Centro Editorial: Apdo 1683, San Pedro Sula; tel. and fax 2558-6282; e-mail centroeditorialhn@gmail.com; f. 1987; Dir JULIO ESCOTO.

Ediciones Ramses: Edif. Chiminike, 2°, Blvr Fuerzas Armadas de Honduras, Tegucigalpa; tel. 2225-6630; fax 2225-6633; e-mail servicioalcliente@edicionesramses.hn; internet www .edicionesramses.hn; educational material.

Editorial Coello: Avda 9, Calle 4, 64a, Barrio El Benque, San Pedro Sula; tel. 2553-1680; fax 2557-4362; e-mail tcoello@globalnet.hn; Dir AUGUSTO C. COELLO.

Editorial Pez Dulce: 143 Paseo La Leona, Barrio La Leona, Tegucigalpa; tel. and fax 222-1220; e-mail pezdulce@yahoo.com; Dir RUBÉN IZAGUIRRE.

Editorial Universitaria de la Universidad Nacional Autónoma de Honduras: Blvd Suyapa, Tegucigalpa; tel. and fax 2232-4772; f. 1847; Dir SEGISFREDO INFANTE.

Guaymuras: Avda Zaragoza, Apdo 1843, Barrio La Leona, Tegucigalpa; tel. 2237-5433; fax 2238-4578; e-mail ediguay@123.hn; internet www.guaymuras.hn; f. 1980; Dir ISOLDA ARITA MELZER.

Broadcasting and Communications
REGULATORY AUTHORITY

Comisión Nacional de Telecomunicaciones (Conatel): Edif. Conatel, Col. Modelo, 6 Avda Suroeste, Comayagüela, Apdo 15012, Tegucigalpa; tel. 2232-9600; fax 2234-8611; e-mail info@conatel.gob .hn; internet www.conatel.gob.hn; f. 1995; Pres. (vacant).

TELECOMMUNICATIONS

The monopoly of the telecommunications sector by Hondutel ceased at the end of 2005, when the fixed line and international services market was opened to domestic and foreign investment.

Claro Honduras: Col. San Carlos, Avda República de Colombia, Tegucigalpa; tel. 2205-4222; fax 2205-4337; e-mail clientes@claro .com.hn; internet www.claro.com.hn; f. 2003; operated by Servicios de Comunicaciones de Honduras (Sercom Honduras), a subsidiary of América Móvil, SA de CV (Mexico) since 2004; mobile cellular telephone operator; Gen. Man. LUIS DEL SID.

Empresa Hondureña de Telecomunicaciones (Hondutel): Edif. Gerencia Los Almendros, Residencial Montecarlo, Tegucigalpa; tel. 2221-0411; fax 2216-7800; e-mail miguel.velez@hondutelnet.hn; internet www.hondutel.hn; f. 1976; scheduled for privatization; Gen. Man. Gen. (retd) ROMEO VÁSQUEZ VELÁSQUEZ.

Multifon: Tegucigalpa; tel. 206-0607; e-mail sac@multifon.net; f. 2003; subsidiary of MultiData; awarded govt contract with UT Starcom (q.v.) for fixed telephone lines in 2003; Pres. JOSÉ RAFAEL FERRARI; CEO JOSÉ LUIS RIVERA.

Telefónica Celular (CELTEL) (Tigo): Edif. Celtel, contiguo a la Iglesia Episcopal, Blvd Suyapa, Col. Florencia Norte Hondureña, Tegucigalpa; tel. 2235-7966; fax 2220-7060; e-mail info@mail.celtel .net; internet www.tigo.com.hn; f. 1996; mobile cellular telephone company; wholly owned subsidiary of Millicom International Cellular (Luxembourg); Pres. ANTONIO TAVEL OTERO.

UT Starcom (USA): Edif. Plaza Azul, 6°, Calle Viena, Avda Berlin, Col. Lomas del Guijarro Sur, Tegucigalpa; tel. 2239-8289; fax 2239-9161; e-mail services@utstar.com; internet www.utstar.com; awarded govt contract with Multifon (q.v.) for fixed telephone lines in 2003; Pres. and CEO JACK LU.

BROADCASTING
Radio

HRN, La Voz de Honduras: Blvd Suyapa, contiguo a Televicentro, Apdo 642, Tegucigalpa; tel. 2232-5100; fax 2232-5109; e-mail contacto@radiohrn.hn; internet www.radiohrn.hn; commercial station; f. 1933; part of Grupo Emisoras Unidas; broadcasts 12 channels; 23 relay stations; Gen. Man. NAHÚN EFRAÍN VALLADARES.

Power FM: Edif. Power FM, Blvd del Norte Costado Sur, 105 Brigada, Apdo 868, San Pedro Sula; tel. 2564-0500; fax 2564-0529; e-mail info@powerfm.hn; internet www.powerfm.hn; Gen. Man. XAVIER SIERRA.

Radio América: Col. Alameda, frente a la Droguería Mandofer, Apdo 259, Tegucigalpa; tel. 2290-4950; fax 2232-1009; e-mail info@ americamultimedios.net; internet www.radioamericahn.net; commercial station; broadcasts Radio San Pedro, Radio Continental, Radio Monderna, Radio Universal, Cadena Radial Sonora, Super Cien Stereo, Momentos FM Stereo and 3 regional channels; f. 1948; 13 relay stations; Gen. Man. JULIO ARÉVALO.

Radio Club Honduras: Salida Chamelecon, Apdo 273, San Pedro Sula; tel. 2556-6173; fax 2617-1151; e-mail hr2rch@yahoo.com; internet www.hr2rch.com; f. 1958; amateur radio club; Pres. NOE OLIVA.

Radio Juticalpa: Juticalpa, Olancho; tel. 2785-2277; fax 2785-5063; internet www.radiojuticalpa.com; Gen. Man. MARTHA ELENA RUBÍ H.

Radio Nacional de Honduras: Avda La Paz, Col. Lomas Del Mayab, detras del edif. del Ministerio de la Presidencia, Tegucigalpa; tel. 2235-6723; fax 2235-6678; e-mail radio@rnh.hn; internet www .rnh.hn; f. 1976; official station, operated by the Govt; Exec. Dir GUSTAVO BLANCO.

Radio la Voz del Atlántico: 12 Calle, 2–3 Avda, Barrio Copen, Apdo 21301, Puerto Cortés; tel. 2665-5166; fax 2665-2401; e-mail administracion@lavozdelatlantico.com; internet www .lavozdelatlantico.com; f. 1955; Dir FRANCISCO ANDRÉS GRIFFIN BOQUIN.

Super K: Entrada Principal, Barrio La Ceiba, San Lorenzo del Valle; tel. 2781-2001; e-mail superk_895fm@yahoo.com; internet www .lasuperkfm.com; f. 2008; Dir MARVIN ESTRADA.

Television

Televicentro: Edif. Televicentro, Blvd Suyapa, Col. Florencia, Apdo 734, Tegucigalpa; tel. 2207-5514; fax 2232-5514; e-mail tvcoperaciones@televicentro.hn; internet www.televicentrotv.net; f. 1987; 11 stations, including Telecadena 7 y 4 (f. 1985), Telesistema Hondureño, Canal 3 y 7 (f. 1967) and Megatv; Pres. JOSÉ RAFAEL FERRARI SAGASTUME.

Canal 5: tel. 2232-7835; fax 2232-0097; f. 1959; Gen. Man. RENATO ALVAREZ.

Televisión Nacional de Honduras (TNH): Edif. Ejecutivo 2, 4°, Frente Casa Presidencial, Tegucigalpa; e-mail info@tnh.gob.hn; internet www.tnh.gob.hn; f. 1962; channels include TVN–8, Telenacional, Cadena 1, Primera Cadena and TNH–8; Dir ARMANDO VALDÉZ.

VICA Television: 9a Calle, 10a Avda 64, Barrio Guamilito, Apdo 120, San Pedro Sula; tel. 2552-4478; fax 2557-3257; e-mail info@ mayanet.hn; internet www.vicatv.hn; f. 1986; operates regional channels 2, 9 and 13; Pres. RIGEL SIERRA.

Finance

(cap. = capital; res = reserves; dep. = deposits; m. = million; brs = branches; amounts in lempiras unless otherwise stated)

BANKING

Central Bank

Banco Central de Honduras (BANTRAL): Avda Juan Ramón Molina, 7a Avda y 1a Calle, Apdo 3165, Tegucigalpa; tel. 2222-3422; fax 2237-4502; e-mail Carlos.Espinoza@bch.hn; internet www.bch.hn; f. 1950; bank of issue; cap. 212.5m., res 1,192m., dep. 39,232.9m. (Dec. 2009); Pres. MARLÓN TÁBORA MUÑOZ; Gen. Man. HÉCTOR MENDÉZ; 4 brs.

Commercial Banks

BAC Honduras: Blvd Suyapa, frente a Emisoras Unidas, Apdo 116, Tegucigalpa; tel. 2216-0200; fax 2239-4509; internet www.bac.net/ honduras; bought by Grupo Aval de Colombia in Dec. 2010; fmrly Banco Mercantil, SA, then BAC BAMER; Gen. Man. JACOBO ATALA.

Banco Atlántida, SA (BANCATLAN): Plaza Bancatlán, Blvd Centroamérica, Apdo 3164, Tegucigalpa; tel. 2280-0000; fax 2232-6120; e-mail webmaster@bancatlan.hn; internet www.bancatlan.hn; f. 1913; cap. 4,500m., res 22.7m. dep. 37,043.5m. (Dec. 2013); Pres. GILBERTO GOLDSTEIN RUBINSTEIN; 186 brs.

Banco Continental, SA (BANCON): Centro Comercial Novaprisa, 9–10 Avda NO, Blvd Morazán, San Pedro Sula; tel. 2550-0880; fax 2550-2750; e-mail imontoya@continental.hn; internet www.bancon.hn; f. 1974; cap. 500m., res 19.5m., dep. 5,541.8m. (Dec. 2012); Pres. JAIME ROSENTHAL OLIVA; 77 brs.

Banco Davivienda Honduras, SA: Intersección Blvd Suyapa y Blvd Juan Pablo II, Apdo 344, Tegucigalpa; tel. 2240-0909; fax 2240-4873; internet www.davivienda.com.hn; f. 1947 as Capitalizadora Hondureña, became BANCAHSA in 1968; known as Banco HSBC from 2007 until 2012, when it was bought by Banco Davivienda (Colombia); part of the Grupo Financiero Bolívar Honduras, SA; cap. 1,280m., res 254.5m., dep. 13,694.8m. (Dec. 2013); CEO JONATHAN HARTLEY; 78 brs.

Banco Financiera Comercial Hondureña (Banco FICOHSA): Edif. Plaza Victoria, Col. Las Colinas, Blvd Francia, Tegucigalpa; tel. 2239-6410; fax 2239-6420; e-mail ficobanc@ficohsa.hn; internet www.ficohsa.com; Pres. JAVIER ATALA; 101 brs.

Banco de Honduras, SA: Blvd Suyapa, Col. Loma Linda Sur, Tegucigalpa; tel. 2232-6122; fax 2290-0123; internet www.bancodehonduras.citibank.com; f. 1889; subsidiary of Citibank NA (USA); cap. 250.0m., res 6.8m., dep. 1,940.9m. (2008); Gen. Man. CONSTANTINO GOTSIS; 2 brs.

Banco de Occidente, SA (BANCOCCI): Calle Centenario, 1 Avda sur este, esq. opuesta al Parque Central, Santa Rosa de Copán, Apdo 208, Copán; tel. 2662-0159; fax 2662-0692; e-mail info@bancocci.hn; internet www.bancocci.hn; f. 1951; cap. 1,600m., res 493.1m., dep. 29,907.9m. (Dec. 2012); Pres. and Gen. Man. JORGE BUESO ARIAS; Vice-Pres. EMILIO MEDINA R.; 158 brs.

Banco del País (BANPAIS): Edif. Torre del País, Blvd José Antonio Peraza, Calle Banpais esq., San Pedro Sula; tel. 2566-2020; fax 2566-2040; internet www.banpais.hn; f. 1969; acquired Banco Sogerin and client portfolio of Banco de las Fuerzas Armadas in 2003; cap. 1,400m., res 101.3m., dep. 13,072m. (Dec. 2010); Pres. JUAN MIGUEL TORREBIARTE; 109 brs.

Banco de los Trabajadores, SA (BANCOTRAB): 3a Avda, 13a Calle, Comayagüela, Apdo 3246, Tegucigalpa; tel. 2238-4421; fax 2238-0077; internet www.btrab.com; f. 1967; cap. 204.8m. (Dec. 2002); Pres. JOSÉ ADONIS LAVAIRE; Gen. Man. GUSTAVO ADOLFO ZELAYA CHÁVEZ; 34 brs.

Development Banks

Banco Centroamericano de Integración Económica: Edif. Sede BCIE, Blvd Suyapa, Apdo 772, Tegucigalpa; tel. 2240-2231; fax 2240-2185; e-mail echinchi@bcie.hn; internet www.bcie.org; f. 1960 to finance the economic devt of the Central American Common Market and its mem. countries; mems: Costa Rica, El Salvador, Guatemala, Honduras, Nicaragua; cap. and res US $1,020.0m. (June 2003); Gov. WILFREDO RODRÍGUEZ.

Banco Financiera Centroamericana, SA (FICENSA): Edif. FICENSA, Blvd Morazán, Apdo 1432, Tegucigalpa; tel. 2238-1661; fax 2221-3855; e-mail webmaster@ficensa.com; internet www.ficensa.com; f. 1974; private org. providing finance for industry, commerce and transport; Exec. Vice-Pres. and Gen. Man. ROQUE RIVERA RÍBAS; 41 brs.

Banco Hondureño del Café, SA (BANHCAFE): Calle República de Costa Rica, Blvd Juan Pablo II, Col. Lomas del Mayab, Apdo 583, Tegucigalpa; tel. 2232-8370; fax 2232-8782; e-mail banhcafe@banhcafe.hn; internet www.banhcafe.com; f. 1981 to help finance coffee production; owned principally by private coffee producers; cap. 425m., res 69.1m., dep. 2,507.4m. (Dec. 2013); Pres. MIGUEL ALFONSO FERNÁNDEZ RÁPALO; Gen. Man. CÉSAR A. ZAVALA L.; 41 brs.

Banco Nacional de Desarrollo Agrícola (BANADESA): 4 Avda y 5 Avda, 13 Calle, contiguo al Estado Mayor, Barrio el Obelisco, Apdo 212, Comayagüela; tel. 2237-2201; fax 2237-5187; e-mail banadesa@banadesa.hn; internet www.banadesa.hn; f. 1980; govt devt bank; loans to agricultural sector; cap. 9m., res 811.7m., dep. 1,095.8m. (Dec. 2012); Pres. JORGE JOHNY HANDAL HAWIT; 37 brs.

Banking Associations

Asociación Hondureña de Instituciones Bancarias (AHIBA): Edif. AHIBA, Blvd Suyapa, Apdo 1344, Tegucigalpa; tel. 2235-6770; fax 2239-0191; e-mail ahiba@ahiba.hn; internet www.ahiba.hn; f. 1957; 21 mem. banks; Pres. ROQUE RIBERA RIVAS; Exec. Dir MARÍA LYDIA SOLANO.

Comisión Nacional de Bancos y Seguros (CNBS): Edif. Santa Fé, Col. Castaño Sur, Paseo Virgilio Zelaya Rubí, Bloque C, Apdo 20074, Tegucigalpa; tel. 2290-4500; fax 2237-6232; e-mail rbarahona@cnbs.gov.hn; internet www.cnbs.gov.hn; Dir JOSÉ ADONIS LAVAIRE.

STOCK EXCHANGE

Bolsa Centroamericana de Valores: Edif. Torre Alianza 2, 5°, Frente a Gasolinera Puma, Blvd San Juan Bosco, Col. Lomas del Guijarro Sur, Apdo 3885, Tegucigalpa; tel. 2271-0400; fax 2271-0403; internet www.bcv.hn; Pres. JOSÉ ARTURO ALVARADO.

INSURANCE

American Home Assurance Co (Chartis Honduras): Edif. Los Castaños, 4°, Blvd Morazán, Apdo 3220, Tegucigalpa; tel. 2202-8300; fax 2239-9169; e-mail honduras.sugerencias@aig.com; internet www.chartisinsurance.com; f. 1958; Gen. Man. JOSÉ EDGARDO FLORES RIVEIRO.

Ficohsa Seguros, SA: Edif. Plaza Victoria, Torre II, Col. Las Colinas, Blvd Francia, Tegucigalpa; tel. 2232-4747; fax 2232-2255; internet www.ficohsaseguros.com; f. 1957; fmrly Interamericana de Seguros, SA; part of Grupo Financiero Ficohsa; Pres. LEONEL GIANNINI; Gen. Man. LUIS ALBERTO ATALA FARAJ.

Mapfre Honduras, SA: Edif. El Planetario, 4°, Avda París, Col. Lomas del Guijarro Sur, Calle Madrid, Apdo 312, Tegucigalpa; tel. 2216-2672; fax 2216-2680; e-mail info@mapfre.com.hn; internet www.mapfre.com.hn; f. 1954; fmrly Aseguradora Hondureña, SA; Gen. Man. GERARDO CORRALES.

Pan American Life Insurance Co (PALIC): Edif. PALIC, Avda República de Chile 804, Col. Palmira, Apdo 123, Tegucigalpa; tel. 2216-0909; fax 2239-3437; e-mail servicioalclientehn@panamericanlife.com; internet www.palig.com/Regions/honduras; f. 1944; Pres. SALVADOR ORTEGA (Central America); CEO JOSÉ S. SUQUET.

Seguros Atlántida: Edif. Sonisa, Costado Este de Plaza Bancatlan, Tegucigalpa; tel. 2232-4014; fax 2232-3688; e-mail info@seatlan.com; internet www.segurosatlantida.com; f. 1985; Pres. ROBERT VINELLI; Gen. Man. JUAN MIGUEL ORELLANA.

Seguros Continental, SA: Edif. Continental, 4°, 3a Avda SO, 2a y 3a Calle, Apdo 605, San Pedro Sula; tel. 2550-0880; fax 2550-2750; e-mail seguros@continental.hn; internet www.seguros.continental.hn; f. 1968; Pres. JAIME ROLANDO ROSENTHAL OLIVA; Gen. Man. MARIO ROBERTO SOLÍS DACOSTA.

Seguros Crefisa: Edif. Banco Ficensa, 1°, Blvd Morazán, Apdo 3774, Tegucigalpa; tel. 2238-1750; fax 2238-1714; e-mail info@crefisa.com; internet www.crefisa.com; f. 1993; Gen. Man. MARIO BATRES PINEDA.

Seguros del País: Edif. IPM Anexo, 4°, Blvd Centroamérica, Tegucigalpa; tel. 2239-7077; fax 2232-4216; internet www.segpais .com; f. 2000; Pres. JUAN MIGUEL TORREBIARTE.

Insurance Association

Cámara Hondureña de Aseguradores (CAHDA): Edif. Casa Metromedia, 3°, Col. San Carlos, Apdo 3290, Tegucigalpa; tel. 2545-1212; fax 2221-5356; e-mail info@cahda.org; internet www .cahda.org; f. 1974; Pres. PEDRO BARQUERO; Gen. Man. TETHEY MARTINEZ.

Trade and Industry

GOVERNMENT AGENCIES

Fondo Hondureño de Inversión Social (FHIS): Antiguo Edif. I.P.M., Col. Godoy, Comayagüela, Apdo 3581, Tegucigalpa; tel. 2234-5231; fax 2534-5255; e-mail dgarcia@fhis.hn; internet www.fhis.hn; social investment fund; Exec. Dir GUNTHER BUSTAMENTE.

Suplidora Nacional de Productos Básicos (BANASUPRO): Edif. IHMA, Blvd Kennedy entrada a Col. las Palmas, Col. Kennedy, Tegucigalpa; tel. 2230-1628; fax 2230-5056; e-mail gerencia@ banasupro.org; internet www.banasupro.org; govt-run; sale of grains and other basic foods; Gen. Man. LUIS COLINDRES.

DEVELOPMENT ORGANIZATIONS

Dirección Ejecutiva de Fomento a la Minería (DEFOMIN): Edif. DEFOMIN, 3°, Blvd Miraflores, Avda la FAO, Apdo 981, Tegucigalpa; tel. 2232-6721; fax 2232-6044; e-mail miguel.mejia@ defomin.gob.hn; internet www.defomin.gob.hn; promotes the mining sector; Exec. Dir ALDO SANTOS.

Instituto Hondureño del Café (IHCAFE): Edif. El Faro, Col. Las Minitas, Apdo 40-C, Tegucigalpa; tel. 2237-3130; fax 2238-2368; e-mail gerencia@ihcafe.2hn.com; internet www.cafedehonduras.org; f. 1970; coffee devt programme; Pres. ASTERIO REYES; Gen. Man. VICTOR HUGO MOLINA.

Instituto Hondureño de Mercadeo Agrícola (IHMA): Apdo 727, Tegucigalpa; tel. 2235-3193; fax 2235-5719; e-mail yohanyleticia@ yahoo.com; internet www.ihma.gob.hn; f. 1978; agricultural devt agency; Gen. Man. JOSÉ CARLOS ARÍSTIDES GIRÓN AYALA.

Instituto Nacional Agrario (INA): Col. La Almeda, 4a Avda, entre 10a y 11a Calles, No 1009, Apdo 3391, Tegucigalpa; tel. 2232-4893; fax 2232-7398; e-mail transparencia@ina.hn; internet www.ina.hn; agricultural devt programmes; Minister of the INA NEPTALÍ MEDINA AGURCIA.

Instituto Nacional de Conservación Forestal (INCF): Salida Carretera del Norte, Zona El Carrizal, Col. Brisas de Olancho, Comayagüela, Apdo 1378, Tegucigalpa; tel. 2223-7303; fax 2223-8587; e-mail direccion@icf.gob.hn; internet www.icf.gob.hn; f. 2008 to replace Corporación Hondureña de Desarrollo Forestal (f. 1974); control of the forestry industry and conservation of forest resources; Dir JOSÉ TRINIDAD SUAZO BULNES.

CHAMBERS OF COMMERCE

Cámara de Comercio e Industrias de Copán: Edif. Comercial Romero, 2°, Barrio Mercedes, Santa Rosa de Copán; tel. 2662-0843; fax 2662-1783; e-mail info@camaracopan.com; internet www .camaracopan.com; f. 1940; Pres. RAMÓN DE JESÚS FLORES.

Cámara de Comercio e Industrias de Cortés (CCIC): Barrio Las Brisas, 22 y 24 Calle, Apdo Postal 14, San Pedro Sula; tel. 2561-6100; fax 2566-0344; e-mail cie@ccichonduras.org; internet www .ccichonduras.org; f. 1931; Pres. EMÍN JORGE ABUFELE.

Cámara de Comercio e Industrias de Tegucigalpa (CCIT): Blvd Centroamérica, Apdo 3444, Tegucigalpa; tel. 2232-4200; fax 2232-5764; e-mail asuservicio@ccit.hn; internet www.ccit.hn; Pres. MIGUEL R. MOURRA; Exec. Dir MARIO BUSTILLO.

Cámara Hondureña de la Industria de la Construcción (Chico): Casa 2525, 2da Calle, entre 1era y 2da Avda, al par de Kinder Happy Faces, Col. Florencia Sur, Tegucigalpa; tel. 2239-2039; internet www.chicoorg.org; f. 1968; Pres. JOSÉ ALEJANDRO ALVAREZ ALVARADO; Gen. Man. SILVIO LARIOS BONES.

Federación de Cámaras de Comercio e Industrias de Honduras (FEDECAMARA): Edif. Castaño, 2°, 6a Avda, Col. Los Castaños, Apdo 3393, Tegucigalpa; tel. 2232-1870; fax 2232-6083; e-mail fedecamara.direccion@amnettgu.com; internet www .fedecamara.org; f. 1948; 1,200 mems; Pres. AMÍLCAR BULNES; Co-ordinator JUAN FERRERA LÓPEZ.

Fundación para la Inversión y Desarrollo de Exportaciones (FIDE) (Foundation for Investment and Development of Exports): Col. La Estancia, Plaza Marte, final del Blvd Morazán, Apdo 2029, Tegucigalpa; tel. 2221-6304; fax 2221-6316; e-mail vsierra@

fidehonduras.com; internet www.hondurasinfo.hn; f. 1984; non-profit; Exec. Pres. VILMA SIERRA DE FONSECA.

Honduran American Chamber of Commerce (Amcham Honduras): Commercial Area Hotel Honduras Maya, POB 1838, Tegucigalpa; tel. 2232-6035; fax 2232-2031; e-mail amcham@ amchanhonduras.org; internet www.amchamhonduras.org; f. 1981; Pres. JOSÉ EDUARDO ATALA; Exec. Dir ARACELY BATRES.

INDUSTRIAL AND TRADE ASSOCIATIONS

Asociación Hondureña de Maquiladores (AHM): Altia Business Park, 12°, Blvd Armenta, San Pedro Sula; tel. 2516-9100; internet www.ahm-honduras.com; f. 1991; non-profit asscn for the *maquila* industry; Pres. DANIEL FACUSSÉ.

Consejo Hondureño de la Empresa Privada (COHEP): Edif. 8, Calle Yoro, Col. Tepeyac, Apdo 3240, Tegucigalpa; tel. 2235-3336; fax 2235-3345; e-mail consejo@cohep.com; internet www.cohep.com; f. 1968; represents 52 private sector trade asscns; Pres. ALINE FLORES PAVÓN; Exec. Dir ARMANDO URTECHO.

Asociación Hondureña de Productores de Café (AHPRO-CAFE) (Coffee Producers' Association): Edif. AHPROCAFE, Avda La Paz, Apdo 959, Tegucigalpa; tel. 2236-8286; fax 2236-8310; e-mail ahprocafe@amnet.tgu.com; Pres. ASTERIO REYES.

Asociación Nacional de Acuicultores de Honduras (ANDAH) (Aquaculture Association of Honduras): Empacadora San Lorenzo, Puerto Viejo, contiguo a Banco de Occidente, San Lorenzo, Valle; tel. 2782-0986; fax 2782-3848; e-mail andahn@ hondutel.hn; f. 1986; 136 mems; Pres. MARCO POLO MICHELETTI.

Asociación Nacional de Exportadores de Honduras (ANEX-HON) (National Association of Exporters): Industrias Panavisión, salida nueva a la Lima Frente a Sigmanet, San Pedro Sula; tel. 2553-3029; fax 2557-0203; e-mail roberto@ipsa.hn; comprises 104 private enterprises; Pres. ROBERTO PANAYOTTI.

Asociación Nacional de Industriales (ANDI) (National Association of Manufacturers): Torre Alliance, 10°, Col. Lomas del Guijarro Sur, Blvd San Juan Bosco, Apdo 3447, Tegucigalpa; tel. 2271-0084; fax 2271-0085; e-mail andi@andi.hn; internet www .andi.hn; f. 1958; Pres. ADOLFO FACUSSÉ; Exec. Dir FERNANDO GARCÍA MERINO.

Asociación de Productores de Azúcar de Honduras (APAH): Edif. Palmira, 5°, Módulo E y B, Tegucigalpa; tel. 2239-4933; fax 2239-4934; e-mail apah@cablecolor.hn; internet www.azucar.hn; Pres. CARLOS MELARA.

Federación Nacional de Agricultores y Ganaderos de Honduras (FENAGH) (Farmers' and Livestock Breeders' Association): Col. Miramontes, Avda Principal, 7a Calle 1557, Tegucigalpa; tel. 2239-1303; fax 2231-1392; e-mail jlizardo@ fenagh.net; internet www.fenagh.net; Pres. LEOPOLDO DÚRAN; Exec. Dir JOSÉ LIZARDO REYES.

UTILITIES

Electricity

Empresa Nacional de Energía Eléctrica (ENEE) (National Electrical Energy Co): Edif. EMAS, 4°, Bo El Trapiche, Tegucigalpa; tel. 2235-2934; fax 2235-2969; e-mail informatica@enee.hn; internet www.enee.hn; f. 1957; state-owned electricity co; Pres. RIGOBERTO CUELLAR; Man. ROBERTO ORDÓÑEZ (Secretary of Infrastructure and Public Services, acting).

Luz y Fuerza de San Lorenzo, SA (LUFUSSA): Edif. Comercial Los Próceres, Final Avda Los Próceres 3917, Tegucigalpa; tel. 2236-6545; fax 2236-5826; e-mail lufussa@lufussa.com; internet www .lufussa.com; f. 1994; generates thermoelectric power; Pres. EDUARDO KAFIE.

TRADE UNIONS

Central General de Trabajadores de Honduras (CGTH) (General Confederation of Labour of Honduras): Barrio La Granja, antiguo Local CONADI, Apdo 1236, Comayagüela, Tegucigalpa; tel. 2239-7383; fax 2225-2525; e-mail cgt@123.hn; f. 1970; legally recognized from 1982; attached to Partido Demócrata Cristiano de Honduras; Sec.-Gen. DANIEL A. DURÓN; 250,000 mems (2011).

Confederación Hondureña de Cooperativas (CHC): Edif. I.F.C., 3001 Blvd Morazán, Apdo 3265, Tegucigalpa; tel. 2232-2890; fax 2231-1024; f. 1971; Pres. JOSÉ FRANCISCO ORDÓÑEZ.

Confederación de Trabajadores de Honduras (CTH) (Workers' Confederation of Honduras): Edif. Beige, 2°, Avda Juan Ramón Molina, Barrio El Olvido, Apdo 720, Tegucigalpa; tel. 2220-1757; fax 2237-8575; e-mail organizationcth@yahoo.es; f. 1964; Sec.-Gen. JOSÉ HILARIO ESPINOZA; 55,000 mems (2007).

Confederación Unitaria de Trabajadores de Honduras (CUTH): Barrio Bella Vista, 10a Calle, 8a y 9a Avda, Casa 829, Tegucigalpa; tel. and fax 2220-4732; e-mail sgeneral@cuth.hn; f. 1992; Sec.-Gen. JOSÉ LUIS BAQUEDANO; 295,000 mems (2011).

Transport

RAILWAYS

The railway network is confined to the north of the country and most lines are used for fruit cargo. There are 995 km of railway track in Honduras, of which 349 km are narrow gauge. In 2010 the Government allocated 15m. lempiras to revive three railway routes serving San Pedro Sula, Choloma, Villanueva and Puerto Cortés. There are plans to restructure the train stations and coaches, as well as to set up additional railway routes to serve banana plantations.

Ferrocarril Nacional de Honduras (National Railway of Honduras): 1a Avda entre 1a y 2a Calle, Apdo 496, San Pedro Sula; tel. and fax 2552-8001; f. 1870; govt-owned; Gen. Man. LESTER AGUILAR.

ROADS

According to Fondo Vial de Honduras, in 2011 there were an estimated 14,044 km of roads in Honduras, of which only 21.2% were paved. A further 3,156 km of roads have been constructed by the Fondo Cafetero Nacional, and some routes have been built by the Corporación Hondureña de Desarrollo Forestal to facilitate access to coffee plantations and forestry development areas. In 2010 the Inter-American Development Bank (IDB) approved a US $30m. loan for a rapid bus transit system in Tegucigalpa. The IDB approved a further $17m. loan in 2013 to improve the main highway.

Dirección General de Carreteras: Barrio La Bolsa, Comayagüela, Tegucigalpa; tel. 2225-1703; fax 2225-2469; e-mail dgc@soptravi.gob.hn; internet www.soptravi.gob.hn/Carreteras; f. 1915; highways board; Dir WALTER MALDONADO.

SHIPPING

The principal port is Puerto Cortés on the Caribbean coast, which is the largest and best-equipped port in Central America. Other ports include Tela, La Ceiba, Trujillo/Castilla, Roatán, Amapala and San Lorenzo; all are operated by the Empresa Nacional Portuaria. There are several minor shipping companies. A number of foreign shipping lines call at Honduran ports. In December 2014 the flag registered fleet comprised 654 vessels, totalling 573,292 grt, of which three were gas tankers and 294 were general cargo ships.

Empresa Nacional Portuaria (National Port Authority): Apdo 18, Puerto Cortés; tel. 665-0987; fax 665-1402; e-mail gerencia@enp.hn; internet www.enp.hn; f. 1965; has jurisdiction over all ports in Honduras; a network of paved roads connects Puerto Cortés and San Lorenzo with the main cities of Honduras, and with the principal cities of Central America; Gen. Man. LEO CASTELLÓN.

CIVIL AVIATION

Local airlines in Honduras compensate for the deficiencies of road and rail transport, linking together small towns and inaccessible districts. There are four international airports: Golosón airport in La Ceiba, Ramón Villeda Morales airport in San Pedro Sula, Toncontín airport in Tegucigalpa and Juan Manuel Gálvez airport in Roatán. A new airport at Río Amarillo, Copán, near the Copán Ruinas archaeological park, commenced operations in 2011.

Dirección General Aeronáutica Civil: Apdo 30145, Tegucigalpa; tel. 2234-0263; fax 2233-0258; e-mail contactos@dgachn.org; internet www.dgachn.org; airport infrastructure and security; Dir-Gen. MANUEL ENRIQUE CÁCERES.

Isleña Airlines: Edif. Taragon, 2°, Avda Circunvalacion, San Pedro Sula; tel. 2552-9910; fax 2552-9964; e-mail info.islena@taca.com; internet www.flyislena.com; subsidiary of TACA, El Salvador; domestic service and service to the Cayman Islands; Pres. and CEO ARTURO ALVARADO WOOD.

Tourism

Tourists are attracted by the Mayan ruins, the fishing and boating facilities in Trujillo Bay and Lake Yojoa, near San Pedro Sula, and the beaches on the northern coast. Honduras received 863,012 tourists in 2013, when tourism receipts (excluding passenger transport) totalled US $698m.

Asociación Hotelera y Afines de Honduras (AHAH): Hotel Escuela Madrid, Suite 402, Col. 21 de Octubre-Los Girasoles, Tegucigalpa; tel. 2221-5805; fax 2221-4789; e-mail asociacionhotelerahn@yahoo.com; Pres. LUZ MEJÍA AMADOR; Exec. Dir NORMA MENDOZA.

Asociación Nacional de Agencias de Viajes y Turismo de Honduras: Blvd Morazán, frente a McDonald's, Tegucigalpa; tel. 2232-2308; e-mail scarlethmoncada@yahoo.com; Pres. SCARLETH DE MONCADA.

Asociación de Operadores de Turismo Receptivo de Honduras (OPTURH): Col. San Carlos, Avda Ramon E. Cruz, Tegucigalpa; tel. 2236-9704; e-mail secretaria@opturh.com; internet www.opturh.com; f. 1996; Pres. ROBERTO BANDES.

Cámara Nacional de Turismo de Honduras: Calle Paris, Avda Niza, Casa 1233, Col. Lomas del Guijarro Sur, Tegucigalpa; tel. 2232-1937; fax 2235-8355; e-mail canaturh@canaturh.org; internet www.canaturh.org; f. 1976; Pres. EPAMINONDAS MARINAKYS.

Instituto Hondureño de Turismo: Edif. Europa, 5°, Col. San Carlos, Apdo 3261, Tegucigalpa; tel. and fax 2222-2124; e-mail tourisminfo@iht.hn; internet www.iht.hn; f. 1972; Exec. Vice-Pres. SYNTIA BENNETT SALOMON; Sec.-Gen. MÓNICA HÍDALGO.

Defence

Military service is voluntary. Active service lasts eight months, with subsequent reserve training. As assessed at November 2014, the armed forces numbered 12,000: army 8,300, navy 1,400 and air force some 2,300. Paramilitary public security and defence forces numbered 8,000. There were also 60,000 joint reserves. In addition, some 360 US troops were based in Honduras.

Defence Budget: 4,550m. lempiras (US $216m.) in 2014.

Chairman of the Joint Chiefs of Staff: Gen. FREDY SANTIAGO DÍAZ ZELAYA.

Commander-General of the Army: Col FRANCISCO ISAÍAS ALVAREZ URBINA.

Commander-General of the Air Force: Col JORGE ALBERTO FERNÁNDEZ LÓPEZ.

Commander-General of the Navy: Capt. HÉCTOR ORLANDO CABALLERO ESPINOZA.

Education

Primary education, beginning at six years of age and comprising three cycles of three years, is officially compulsory and is provided free of charge. Secondary education, which is not compulsory, begins at the age of 15 and lasts for three years. In 2012 enrolment at primary schools included 94% of children in the relevant age-group, while enrolment at secondary schools in 2012 was equivalent to 73% of children (66% of boys; 80% of girls) in the appropriate age-group. There are three universities, including the Autonomous National University in Tegucigalpa. Estimated spending on education in 2012 was 23,000m. lempiras, representing 15.9% of the total budget.

HUNGARY

Introductory Survey

LOCATION, CLIMATE, LANGUAGE, RELIGION, FLAG, CAPITAL

Hungary lies in central Europe, bounded to the north by Slovakia, to the east by Ukraine and Romania, to the south by Serbia and Croatia, and to the west by Slovenia and Austria. Its climate is continental, with long, dry summers and severe winters. Temperatures in Budapest are generally between −3°C (27°F) and 28°C (82°F). The language is Hungarian (Magyar). There is a large Romany community (numbering between 500,000 and 700,000 people), and also Croat, German, Romanian, Serb, Slovak, Slovene and Jewish minorities. Most of the inhabitants profess Christianity, and the largest single religious denomination is the Catholic Church, representing about 58% of the population. Other Christian groups include Calvinists (20%), Lutherans (5%), Pentecostals, and the Eastern Orthodox Church. The national flag (proportions 2 by 3) consists of three equal horizontal stripes, of red, white and green. The capital is Budapest.

CONTEMPORARY POLITICAL HISTORY

Historical Context

Although Hungary entered the Second World War on the side of Nazi Germany in 1941, when it sought to break the alliance in 1944 the country was occupied by German forces. In January 1945 Hungary was invaded by Soviet troops and signed an armistice, restoring pre-1938 frontiers. It became a republic in February 1946, and nationalization measures began in December. In the 1947 elections, the communists became the largest single party, with 22.7% of the votes. The communists merged with the Social Democrats to form the Magyar Dolgozók Pártja (MDP—Hungarian Workers' Party) in June 1948. A People's Republic was established in August 1949.

As First Secretary of the MDP, Mátyás Rákosi became the leading political figure, and opposition was removed by means of purges and political trials. Rákosi became Prime Minister in 1952; in 1953 he was replaced by the more moderate Imre Nagy. Rákosi, however, remained as First Secretary, and in 1955 forced Nagy's resignation. Following increasing dissension between the Rákosi and Nagy factions, in July 1956 Rákosi was forced to resign, but was replaced by a close associate, Ernő Gerő. Demonstrations against communist domination ensued, and in October fighting broke out. Nagy was reinstated as Prime Minister; he renounced membership of the Warsaw Pact (the defence grouping of the Soviet bloc) and promised other controversial reforms. In November Soviet troops, stationed in Hungary under the 1947 peace treaty, intervened, and the uprising was suppressed. A new Soviet-supported Government, led by János Kádár, was installed. Some 20,000 participants in the uprising were arrested, of whom 2,000 were subsequently executed, including Nagy and four associates. Kádár, who was appointed the leader of the reconstituted Magyar Szocialista Munkáspárt (MSzMP—Hungarian Socialist Workers' Party), held the premiership until January 1958, and from September 1961 until July 1965.

In March 1985 Kádár was re-elected as leader of the MSzMP. The legislative elections in June were conducted under the system of mandatory multiple nominations. In May 1988 Kádár was succeeded as MSzMP General Secretary of the Central Committee by Károly Grósz (Chairman of the Council of Ministers since June 1987), and appointed to the new, ceremonial post of party President. About one-third of the members of the Central Committee were replaced by younger politicians. In November 1988 Miklós Németh, a prominent member of the MSzMP, replaced Grósz as Chairman of the Council of Ministers.

Following Grósz's appointment as leader of the MSzMP, there was a relaxation of censorship laws, and independent political groups were formally established. In January 1989 the right to strike was fully legalized. In the same month the Országgyülés (National Assembly) enacted legislation guaranteeing the right to demonstrate and to form independent associations and political parties. In February the MSzMP agreed to abandon the constitutional clause upholding the party's leading role in society.

During 1989 there was increasing evidence of dissension within the MSzMP between conservative and reformist members. In May the Council of Ministers declared its independence from the MSzMP; Kádár was removed from the presidency and the Central Committee of the party. After a radical restructuring of the MSzMP, the new Chairman, Rezső Nyers, emerged as the party's leading figure. At a provincial by-election in July 1989, a joint candidate of the centre-right Magyar Demokrata Fórum (MDF—Hungarian Democratic Forum), the liberal Szabad Demokraták Szövetsége (SzDSz—Alliance of Free Democrats) and the Fiatal Demokraták Szövetsége (Fidesz—Federation of Young Democrats) became the first opposition deputy since 1947 to win representation in the legislature. Four further by-elections were won by opposition candidates in July–September 1989. Following popular pressure and continued anti-Government demonstrations, in September the MSzMP and the opposition agreed that the Constitution and electoral law be fundamentally amended. At an MSzMP Congress in October, the party was reconstituted as Magyar Szocialista Párt (MSzP—Hungarian Socialist Party).

Domestic Political Affairs

On 18 October 1989 the National Assembly elected Mátyás Szűrös, the parliamentary President (Speaker), to the newly created post of President of the Republic, on an interim basis. On 23 October (the anniversary of the 1956 uprising) the Republic of Hungary was proclaimed. Multi-party elections were held, in two rounds, on 25 March and 8 April 1990. The MDF received the largest proportion of the total votes cast (42.7%) and 165 of the 386 seats in the National Assembly, followed by the SzDSz, with 23.8% of the votes and 92 seats. The Független Kisgazda Párt (FKgP—Independent Smallholders' Party) and Kereszténydemokrata Néppárt (KDNP—Christian Democratic People's Party), both of which contested the second round of polling in alliance with the MDF, secured 43 and 21 seats, respectively. The MSzP secured 33 seats, while Fidesz obtained 21 seats. The MSzMP failed to secure the 4% of the votes required for representation.

A coalition Government was formed in May 1990, comprising members of the MDF, the FKgP, the KDNP and three independents. József Antall, the Chairman of the MDF, had earlier been elected to chair the new Council of Ministers. The new Government declared commitment to membership of the European Community (now European Union—EU, see p. 271) and transition to a market economy. In the same month Gyula Horn, the outgoing Minister of Foreign Affairs, replaced Nyers as leader of the MSzP. In August Árpád Göncz, a member of the SzDSz, was elected President of the Republic by the legislature. At local elections in September and October, a coalition of the SzDSz and Fidesz won control of Budapest and many other cities. In May 1991 the National Assembly approved legislation to provide compensation for persons killed, imprisoned or deported, or whose property had been expropriated for political reasons in 1939–89.

In February 1992 the Chairman of the FKgP, József Torgyán, frustrated at his party's perceived lack of political influence, announced that it was to withdraw from the Government. However, many FKgP deputies disagreed with this decision and the party divided. In September some 50,000 people demonstrated in Budapest against extreme nationalist figures within the MDF, including the Vice-Chairman of the party, István Csurka. Csurka was expelled from the MDF in July 1993, and subsequently founded the Magyar Igazság és Élet Pártja (MIÉP—Hungarian Justice and Life Party). Antall died in December, and was succeeded as Prime Minister by Dr Péter Boross, an independent, and hitherto the Minister of the Interior. Meanwhile, legislation was approved in early 1993 to allow prosecutions in connection with crimes committed under the communist regime.

Democratic consolidation

Elections to the National Assembly, held on 8 and 29 May 1994, resulted in a parliamentary majority for the MSzP, which received 33.0% of the votes cast for regional party lists and won 209 of the 386 legislative seats. The SzDSz won 19.8% of the votes and 70 seats, while the MDF won only 11.7% of the votes and 37 seats. The FKgP, the KDNP and Fidesz also secured parliamentary seats. The MSzP and the SzDSz signed a coalition agreement in June. Horn was invested as Prime Minister in July.

In January 1995 the Minister of Finance, László Bekesi, resigned, following disagreements with Horn regarding economic reform; he was replaced by Lajos Bokros. Economic austerity measures, adopted in March, prompted strong domestic criticism, and the ministers responsible for public health and for national security resigned shortly afterwards. On 19 June the National Assembly re-elected Göncz President of the Republic. Dissent over the economic programme continued, and the Minister of Labour tendered her resignation in October. Bokros resigned in February 1996, and a banker, Péter Medgyessy, was appointed as Minister of Finance. Following the election of Sándor Lezsák to the MDF leadership, a split in the party ensued in March, with the departure of those who discerned an increasingly nationalistic tendency. In December the MDF established an electoral alliance with the reconstituted Fiatal Demokraták Szövetsége—Magyar Polgári Szövetség (Federation of Young Democrats—Hungarian Civic Party, which continued to be known as Fidesz).

Elections took place to the National Assembly in May 1998. Fidesz, with 147 seats, obtained the largest representation, ahead of: the MSzP, with 134; the FKgP, with 48; the SzDSz, with 24; the MDF, with 18; and the MIEP, with 14. In June Fidesz signed a coalition agreement with the MDF and the FKgP (which was later renamed the Független Kisgazda, Földmunkás és Polgári Párt—Independent Smallholders', Agrarian Workers' and Civic Party). In July the National Assembly elected Viktor Orbán, the Chairman of Fidesz, as Prime Minister of a Government dominated by Fidesz representatives. In September, following the resignation of Horn from the leadership of the MSzP, a former minister, László Kovács, was elected Chairman. In January 2000 László Kövér replaced Orbán as leader of Fidesz. In June Ferenc Mádl, the sole candidate, secured the requisite two-thirds' majority to be elected President of the Republic. He took office on 4 August.

In the legislative elections held in April 2002, although an alliance of Fidesz and the MDF won 48.7% of the total votes cast (and 188 seats), a left-wing coalition of the MSzP (which obtained 46.1% of the votes and 178 seats) and the SzDSz (5.2% of the votes and 20 seats) secured an overall majority in the National Assembly. Péter Medgyessy of the MSzP was sworn in as Prime Minister on 27 May; the Council of Ministers comprised eight further members of the MSzP, four members of the SzDSz, and three independents.

In June 2002 media allegations prompted Medgyessy to reveal that he had served as a counter-intelligence agent at the Ministry of Finance in 1977–82; he insisted that he had sought to protect sensitive economic information from the KGB (the Soviet secret service), in order to negotiate Hungarian membership of the IMF (which it joined in 1982). In July 2002 two parliamentary commissions were established to investigate the alleged links of post-communist government officials with the Soviet-era security service. Meanwhile, in early July the leader of Fidesz, Zoltán Pokorni, who had led demands for Medgyessy's resignation, relinquished his own party and parliamentary posts, after his father's role as a communist informer was revealed. It subsequently emerged that several members of Fidesz (which had emphasized its anti-communist past during campaigning for the legislative elections) had counter-intelligence associations. Local elections took place on 20 October, in which the governing coalition consolidated its position.

In December 2002 the National Assembly voted to adopt a number of constitutional amendments, which were required to permit the country to become a full member of the European Union (EU, see p. 271). In May 2003 Fidesz was re-formed as Fidesz—Magyar Polgári Szövetség (Fidesz—Hungarian Civic Alliance), with Orbán as its leader. In January 2004 the Minister of Finance, Csaba László, left office when it was revealed that the fiscal results for 2003 had failed to meet government targets. Tibor Draskovics (an independent), succeeded László in February, implementing a financial austerity plan shortly afterwards. On 1 May Hungary acceded to full membership of the EU.

On 18 August 2004 Medgyessy resigned as Prime Minister following a decline in support and a severe dispute with the SzDSz over proposed changes to the Council of Ministers. On 24 August the MSzP nominated one of the country's wealthiest business executives, Ferenc Gyurcsány, hitherto the Minister of Children, Youth and Sports, as Prime Minister. Following Gyurcsány's installation as Prime Minister on 4 October, he appointed seven new ministers. Gyurcsány made further adjustments to the Council of Ministers in April 2005: Draskovics was dismissed as Minister of Finance, and replaced by a prominent MSzP member, János Veres. On 7 June László Sólyom, an independent politician endorsed by the main opposition parties, was elected as President, after three rounds of legislative voting. He took office on 5 August.

At legislative elections, held on 9 and 23 April 2006, the governing MSzP-SzDSz coalition secured 210 of the 386 seats in the National Assembly and 54.4% of the votes. A coalition of Fidesz and the KDNP, with 42.5% of the votes, secured 164 seats, the MDF took 11 seats (with 2.9% of the votes) and one seat was won by an independent candidate. In early June, after prolonged negotiations, a new Government, led by Gyurcsány and comprising members of the MSzP and the SzDSz, was formed. On the following day Gyurcsány announced stringent fiscal adjustment measures, intending to reduce the budget deficit.

On 17 September 2006 the media broadcast of a clandestine recording of a post-election speech by Gyurcsány to his party members, in which he admitted having intentionally misled the electorate during the campaign, precipitated mass anti-Government protests in Budapest. Protesters surrounded government buildings and temporarily seized control of the state television headquarters; some 300 people were injured in the rioting and the ensuing confrontations with the police. On 27 September Gyurcsány issued an apology for the Government's delay in addressing the economic situation. At municipal elections on 2 October, Fidesz made significant gains, securing the mayoralties of 15 of Hungary's 23 largest cities and majorities in 18 of the 19 county councils. Nevertheless, in early October a parliamentary motion of confidence in the Government, proposed by Gyurcsány, was supported by 207 votes in the National Assembly.

Official celebrations on 23 October 2006, the 50th anniversary of the 1956 uprising against Soviet rule, were marred by anti-Government demonstrations, organized by the leadership of Fidesz, which demanded Gyurcsány's resignation. Security forces suppressed ensuing riots, in which about 170 people were injured, and a total of 130 protesters were arrested. In February 2007 a commission investigating the rioting issued a report strongly criticizing Fidesz's increasingly populist stance for implying support for the protesters, who were predominantly associated with extreme nationalist groups, while concluding that the police had employed excessive force in suppressing the violence.

In June 2007 Gyurcsány reorganized the Government in support of his reform programme. In December Csaba Kákossy became the new Minister of Economy and Transport, following the resignation of János Kóka, who had been elected as Chairman of the SzDSz in March. Despite strenuous protests, including strike action by public sector workers in November, health care reforms proposed by the Government were finally approved by the National Assembly in February 2008 (overturning an earlier veto by President Sólyom). Fidesz organized a national referendum to seek support for the abolition of newly introduced fees for doctors' visits and hospital stays, and of university fees. At the referendum, held on 9 March, more than 80% of the votes, cast by some 50.5% of the electorate, were in favour of the abolition of these fees. Gyurcsány duly announced that the fees would be abandoned from 1 April, but that the Government was unable to subsidize health and higher education institutions.

At the end of March 2008 Gyurcsány dismissed the Minister of Health, who was an SzDSz representative, prompting the party to withdraw from the governing coalition (which henceforth lacked a parliamentary majority). An extensive government reorganization was approved in the National Assembly in May, when Gordon Bajnai, a close associate of Gyurcsány and hitherto the Minister of Local Government and Regional Development, became Minister of National Development and the Economy. In June Gábor Fodor was elected as the new Chairman of the SzDSz, following divisions within the party and the emergence of a faction opposed to Kóka (who, however, remained leader of the party's parliamentary caucus).

The adverse effects of the international financial crisis in Hungary, further exacerbated anti-Government sentiment. At an MSzP congress in March 2009, Gyurcsány announced his intention to resign as Prime Minister, citing concern that he had become an 'obstacle' to further economic reform, and relinquished the party leadership. The National Assembly elected Bajnai, an independent candidate nominated by the MSzP, Prime Minister on 14 April; he affirmed his commitment to austerity measures, and subsequently formed a new Council of Ministers. However, Fidesz boycotted the parliamentary vote, and a demonstration was staged in Budapest to demand early legislative elections.

Fidesz enact major constitutional changes

At elections to the European Parliament, held on 7 June 2009, Fidesz, in coalition with the KDNP, secured 56.4% of the votes cast and 14 of the 22 contested seats, the MSzP 17.4% of the votes cast and four seats, an extreme nationalist movement, Jobbik Magyarországért Mozgalom (Jobbik—Movement for a Better Hungary), obtained 14.8% of votes and three seats, and the MDF 5.3% of votes and one seat; the rate of electoral participation was 36.3%. The relative success of Jobbik at these polls generated concern both domestically and internationally, particularly owing to the close association of the party with a proscribed nationalist group, the Hungarian Guard (see *Minority affairs*), and to the frequent public expression of anti-Semitic and anti-Roma sentiments by numerous senior party officials. Fodor resigned as Chairman of the SzDSz, following the party's failure to obtain European representation; in July a party congress elected Attila Retkes as his successor. In December Draskovics resigned as Minister of Justice and Law Enforcement; he was succeeded by Imre Forgács.

In the elections to the National Assembly on 11 and 25 April 2010, Fidesz, again in coalition with the KDNP, secured 263 of the 386 elective seats (giving it narrowly in excess of the two-thirds of seats required to permit constitutional amendments). The MSzP was the second-placed party, with 59 seats, followed by Jobbik (which secured national representation for the first time), with 47 seats; a newly formed environmentalist party, Lehet Más a Politika! (LMP—Politics Can Be Different!), obtained 16 seats. Later in April President Sólyom confirmed the nomination of Orbán as Prime Minister. The National Assembly approved a new Government formed by Orbán, in which the number of ministries was reduced from 12 to eight, on 29 May. Tibor Navracsics of Fidesz became Deputy Prime Minister and Minister of Public Administration and Justice, and Zsolt Semjén of the KDNP Deputy Prime Minister and Minister without Portfolio. Other principal new appointments included that of György Matolcsy of Fidesz as Minister of the National Economy. On 29 June the National Assembly voted to elect Pál Schmitt of Fidesz (parliamentary Chairman since May), as President of the Republic, in succession to Sólyom. Schmitt formally assumed office on 6 August. In local government elections, which were conducted on 3 October, Fidesz secured 22 of the 23 mayoralties, including that of Budapest (where the long-standing SzDSz mayor was replaced by a Fidesz-supported candidate, István Tarlós), and majorities in all 19 county assemblies. Gyurcsány subsequently announced the establishment of a group, known as the Demokratikus Koalíció (DK—Democratic Coalition), within the MSzP, following the latter's defeat.

In October 2010 a dispute erupted between the Government, which had adopted a number of controversial fiscal measures, and the Constitutional Court, after the Court reversed new legislation retroactively imposing a 98% tax on large severance payments in the public sector. In November the National Assembly adopted legislation restricting the powers of the Constitutional Court to rule on the state budget, taxes and other financial matters. (Despite its reduced powers, the Constitutional Court ruled again, in May 2011, that the imposition of retroactive tax demands was unconstitutional.) In December 2010 new media legislation, whereby a regulatory authority, comprising five members nominated by the ruling coalition, was empowered to impose large fines on print, broadcast and internet outlets for violating 'public interest, public morals or order', prompted a protest by students in Budapest. The legislation, which entered into effect at the beginning of 2011, continued to attract strenuous criticism, and the European Commission pronounced it to be in violation of EU regulations on freedom of expression. In December the Constitutional Court vetoed parts of the media legislation.

On 18 April 2011 the National Assembly approved a new Constitution, to enter into effect from January 2012, with 262 votes cast in favour, 44 against and one abstention. The text renamed the country 'Hungary', rather than the 'Republic of Hungary'. The Constitution included a new preamble, protecting human life from the moment of conception (despite abortion being provided legally in Hungary), and reaffirming the defin-

ition of marriage as the union of one man and one woman. The new basic law also introduced financial restrictions, including a legal limit, equivalent to 50% of GDP, on the permitted level of national debt, attracting further criticism from political opponents. President Schmitt signed the new Constitution on 25 April.

During 2011 a series of legislative reforms was introduced by Fidesz, and Orbán was re-elected as Chairman in July, as the ruling party attempted to consolidate its balance of power. In December new legislation was approved reducing the number of members of the National Assembly from 386 to 199. A new, two-tier (replacing a three-tier) parliamentary election system was introduced, providing for 106 seats to be filled in single-member districts and 93 from national party lists. Voting rights were introduced for Hungarian citizens not permanently resident in Hungary. Meanwhile, in October the DK broke away from the MSzP to become an independent political organization.

The new Constitution entered into force on 1 January 2012, amid large protests in Budapest. In February the European Parliament adopted a resolution expressing serious concerns about the new Constitution and announced that it was investigating whether the new legislation was in breach of democratic standards. The European Commission requested that Hungary submit proposals for amendments to three specific laws affecting the independence of the Central Bank and the national data office, and imposing a mandatory retirement age on judges and prosecutors. The Commission also opened an inquiry against the Hungarian authorities, citing political interference in the judiciary, the Central Bank and data protection laws. In March, at a rally to commemorate the anniversary of the 1848 uprising against Austrian rule, Orbán denounced what he termed the 'colonialism' of the EU, shortly after the European Commission announced the suspension of funding to Hungary (see *Economic Affairs*).

Meanwhile, in late 2011 allegations emerged that the President had committed plagiarism in the composition of his doctoral thesis, which had been awarded by Semmelweis University in Budapest in 1992. The university subsequently announced that it had withdrawn Schmitt's doctoral award. On 2 April Schmitt resigned as President. Later in the month Orbán nominated János Ader, a senior member of Fidesz, deputy of the European Parliament and former President of the National Assembly, as a presidential candidate. A presidential election took place in the National Assembly on 2 May, and Ader was duly elected as the new President.

In September 2012 Gyurcsány and two other members of the DK staged a one-week hunger strike outside the parliamentary building, in protest against a proposed change to the electoral law that would require voters to register no later than 15 days before an election. In the same month the Budapest Court of Appeals overturned a decision by the Media Council (a five-member body appointed by the National Assembly within the new media authority) rejecting an application by opposition radio station Klubradio for a broadcasting licence. In October the new electoral law adopted by the National Assembly; however, it was subsequently referred by President Ader to the Constitutional Court. A large, pro-Government rally was staged on 23 October, the anniversary of the 1956 uprising against Soviet rule, while at a concurrent opposition demonstration Bajnai announced the creation of a new, centrist alliance, Együtt 2014 (Together 2014). In January 2013 the Constitutional Court ruled against the new voter registration regulations, together with other proposed provisions in the electoral law that imposed restrictions on the broadcasting of political advertisements in the public media.

At the beginning of March 2013 Orbán nominated Matolcsy, a close associate, as the new Governor of the Central Bank; a former Minister of Finance, Mihály Varga, was appointed to succeed Matolcsy as Minister of the National Economy. Meanwhile, radical constitutional changes proposed by the Government prompted mass protests in Budapest; in addition to the adoption of restrictions on political advertisements and the imposition of a number of social measures, rulings made by the Constitutional Court prior to 2012 were to be overturned and its future powers limited. Orbán dismissed criticism by the EU and the USA, amid concerns that the proposed constitutional amendments represented an attempt by the Government to reintroduce changes already deemed to be contrary to European law, and opposed by the Constitutional Court. The controversial amendments were approved in the National Assembly on 11 March 2013, with opposition deputies boycotting the vote. A further protest was staged in Budapest later that month. In

April the Monitoring Committee of the Parliamentary Assembly of the Council of Europe (PACE) recommended that democracy in Hungary be formally monitored. On 11 June the National Assembly adopted legislation that restricted citizens' access to information held by the State, including data on public expenditure.

In response to EU pressure, on 16 September 2013 the National Assembly adopted further constitutional amendments that, *inter alia*, permitted election campaigning by political parties in both state-funded and private media, thereby reversing a principal restrictive measure adopted in March. In November the European Commission officially ended legal proceedings that had been launched against Hungary over the forced early retirement of judges and public prosecutors, after the National Assembly, in March, amended legislation gradually to increase the retirement age to 65 (rather than 62).

Recent developments: the 2014 elections

In January 2014 several leftist opposition parties, including the MSzP, Bajnai's Együtt 2014 and Gyurcsány's DK, signed an agreement to establish a coalition, Összefogás (Unity), to contest legislative elections on 6 April. In March the trial began of Béla Biszku, a former interior minister in the Kádár administration, who was charged with responsibility for the shooting of protesters in 1956. The legislative elections on 6 April 2014 were the first to be conducted under the 2012 Constitution: the coalition of Orbán's Fidesz and the KDNP, while registering a loss in support, won 133 seats in the smaller, 199-member National Assembly (narrowly retaining its two-thirds' majority). The MSzP-led Összefogás secured 38 seats, Jobbik obtained 23 seats and the LMP won five seats. A voter turnout of 61.7% was recorded.

At elections to the European Parliament on 25 May 2014, the Fidesz-KDNP alliance secured 51.5% of the votes cast and 12 of the 21 seats allocated to Hungary. Jobbik was placed second, with 14.7% of the votes and three seats, followed by the MSzP, with 10.9% and two seats, and the DK, with 9.8% and two seats. Two groups each received one seat: an alliance of Együtt 2014 and an environmentalist party formed by former members of the LMP, Párbeszéd Magyarországért (Dialogue For Hungary), which received a total of 7.3% of the votes cast; and the LMP, with 5.0%. The rate of participation was 28.9%.

After local government elections held on 12 October 2014, the Fidesz-KDNP alliance controlled the office of mayor in 19 of the 23 principal cities, as well as retaining of all 19 county assemblies: Tarlós was re-elected mayor of Budapest and the coalition gained control of 17 of 23 districts in the capital. The number of mayoralties held by Jobbik in towns and villages increased to 14 (notably including the northern town of Ózd, with a large Roma population). The official voter turnout was 44.3%. In November the National Assembly adopted legislation that significantly strengthened the powers of the mayor of Budapest over the city's council, which would henceforth not be directly elected, but would rather comprise the mayors of each of the city's 23 districts, in addition to nine unsuccessful district mayoral candidates. Meanwhile, at the end of October Orbán announced the decision to cancel a proposed tax on the transfer of internet data, following large-scale protests in central Budapest. In February 2015 a pro-EU demonstration of some 2,000 was staged in Budapest, prior to a visit by Russian President Vladimir Putin (see *Other external relations*).

The resignation of Fidesz parliamentary deputy Navracsics to become an EU commissioner resulted in a by-election in the western town of Veszprém on 22 February 2015, which was won by Zoltán Kész, an independent candidate. Kész's victory ended the Fidesz-led alliance's two-thirds' parliamentary majority that had enabled it to adopt constitutional legislation without support from any other parliamentary faction. In April, at another by-election, Jobbik won its first single-member constituency mandate in the National Assembly; the other deputies of the party had been elected from the party's national list.

Minority affairs

There has been considerable activism within Hungary by the country's ethnic minorities for the protection of their rights. In July 1993 the National Assembly adopted legislation guaranteeing the cultural, civil and political rights of 12 minority groups and prohibiting ethnic discrimination. From 1994 ethnic minorities were able to elect their own local ethnic authorities, with consultative roles on cultural and educational issues affecting the community. In February 1995 Hungary signed the Council of Europe (see p. 250) Convention on the Protection of National Minorities. In April the Roma of Hungary elected their own governing body, the National Autonomous Authority of the Romany Minority, which was empowered to administer funds and deliberate issues affecting the Roma. In December 2008 the Metropolitan Court in Budapest ordered the dissolution of the extreme nationalist Magyar Gárda Mozgalom (Hungarian Guard Movement), established in August 2007, closely associated with the Jobbik political party, and which was responsible for attacks and discriminatory behaviour against the Roma community. This dissolution of the Guard was confirmed by the Supreme Court in December 2010. (However, former Hungarian Guard members continued to convene, and attempted to reconstitute the movement as a civil service association.) In October 2012 fighting involving Roma residents in the western town of Devecser was followed by an anti-Roma rally organized by Jobbik that degenerated into violent rioting. In January 2013 two Roma men, who as children had been placed in a school for the education of those identified as having special needs, won a discrimination case against Hungary at the European Court of Human Rights. In August three nationalist extremists were sentenced to life imprisonment and a fourth received a 13-year term for killing six Roma in nine attacks in north-eastern Hungary during 2008–09.

In March 2010 legislation that criminalized the denial or 'questioning' of the Holocaust (*shoah*) of the Jews during the Second World War was signed into law in Hungary. Although the law was widely supported among the Jewish community of Hungary, concerns were expressed that the legislation might become a focus of extreme nationalist agitation. Remarks by a Jobbik parliamentary deputy in November 2012, suggesting that lists of citizens of Jewish ancestry should be compiled in the interests of national security, prompted protests outside the National Assembly. In April 2013 a protest against an increase in anti-Semitism in Hungary was staged in Budapest. In early May the annual World Jewish Congress, usually held in Jerusalem, Israel, was convened in Budapest to demonstrate concerns at anti-Semitism in the country. Around 1,000 people attended a rally that was organized by Jobbik in Budapest, in protest at the holding of the Congress in the capital, after an earlier government prohibition on the rally had been overturned by a court ruling; protesters demanded that officials holding dual Hungarian-Israeli citizenship should resign. In February 2014 a rally organized by Jobbik in a former synagogue in the northern town of Esztergom prompted further protests.

Foreign Affairs

Regional relations

A principal factor governing Hungary's relations with several neighbouring states—particularly Romania and Slovakia—has been the presence in those countries of a substantial population of ethnic Hungarians. In September 1996 Hungary and Romania signed a bilateral treaty, guaranteeing the inviolability of the joint border between the two countries and the rights of minority ethnic groups. In May 1997 President Árpád Göncz made an official visit to Romania (the first by a Hungarian Head of State). In June 2001 the Hungarian National Assembly approved legislation that, with effect from January 2002, granted ethnic Hungarians living in adjacent countries education, employment and medical rights in Hungary. This legislation, referred to as the 'status' law, prompted protests from Romania (and Slovakia—see below) that it discriminated against their non-ethnic Hungarian populations and constituted a violation of sovereignty. In December 2001 a memorandum of understanding was signed by Viktor Orbán and Prime Minister Adrian Năstase of Romania, which extended the short-term employment rights offered to ethnic Hungarians under the terms of the law to all Romanian citizens. Finally, in September 2003 a bilateral agreement on the implementation of the 'status' law in Romania was signed in the Romanian capital, Bucharest, by Péter Medgyessy and Năstase.

Relations between Hungary and Slovakia were also strained by a dispute over the Gabčíkovo-Nagymaros hydroelectric project (a joint Hungarian-Czechoslovak scheme initiated in 1977). In 1989 Hungary announced that it was to abandon the scheme, following pressure from environmentalists. In 1991 Czechoslovakia decided to proceed unilaterally with the project, prompting the Hungarian Government to abrogate the 1977 treaty in May 1992. In April 1993 it was agreed to refer the case to the International Court of Justice (ICJ). In March 1995 Prime Minister Horn and his Slovak counterpart, Vladimír Mečiar, signed a Treaty of Friendship and Co-operation, according to which the two countries undertook to guarantee the rights of minority ethnic groups and to recognize the inviolability of their common border. The Treaty came into effect in May 1996. In August 1997 discussions between Horn and Mečiar resulted in an agreement that a joint committee be established to monitor the standard of human rights of ethnic Hungarians resident in Slovakia and the Slovak community in Hungary. In September the ICJ concluded proceedings regarding the dispute over the Gabčíkovo-Nagymaros hydroelectric project, ruling that both countries had contravened international law. Both Hungary and Slovakia were required to pay compensation for damages incurred, and to resume negotiations regarding the further implementation of the agreement. In February 2006 it was announced that Slovakia and Hungary had agreed to implement the 1997 ICJ ruling.

A bilateral agreement was signed by the Ministers of Foreign Affairs of Hungary and Slovakia in December 2003 on the implementation of the Hungarian 'status' law in Slovakia. However, tensions between Hungary and Slovakia were again apparent in August 2009, when the Hungarian President, László Sólyom, was prohibited from entering Slovakia on the instructions of the Slovak Ministry of Foreign Affairs. Sólyom's intended visit to unveil a statue to St István (Stephen), the first King of Hungary, in a predominantly ethnically Hungarian town in southern Slovakia was condemned by the Slovakian Government, on the grounds that it was planned for the anniversary of the 1968 invasion of Czechoslovakia by Warsaw Pact (including Hungarian) troops. Legislation that took effect in Slovakia from September 2009, placing restrictions on the use of languages other than Slovak in an official context, was a further source of controversy. Slovakia and Hungary subsequently agreed that the Organization for Security and Co-operation in Europe (OSCE, see p. 385) would oversee the implementation of the law to ensure that it complied with international norms.

On 26 May 2010 the National Assembly approved controversial legislation, regarded as an extension of the 'status' law, which would permit ethnic Hungarians resident outside the country to apply for Hungarian citizenship, with effect from January 2011. It was also legislated that ethnic Hungarians residing permanently in neighbouring states, with Hungarian as their first language, would remain eligible for benefits, regardless of whether they held Hungarian citizenship. The Prime Minister of Slovakia, Robert Fico, described the legislation as representing a security threat to his country, and on the same day the Slovakian legislature adopted an amendment to the country's law on citizenship, under which Slovak citizenship would be removed from those who applied for citizenship of a second country. (That law was amended by a new Slovakian Government in February 2011.) In March 2014 premiers Orbán and Fico inaugurated an EU-financed Hungarian-Slovak natural gas interconnector pipeline, which linked the two countries' gas networks.

In November 1990 Hungary became a member of the Council of Europe. In March 1996 Hungary was admitted to the Organisation for Economic Co-operation and Development (OECD, see p. 377). Meanwhile, Hungary's associate membership of the EU entered into effect in February 1994, and in April Hungary became the first post-communist state to apply for full EU membership. In December 2002 Hungary was one of 10 countries formally invited to join the EU in May 2004. At a national referendum, held on 12 April 2003, Hungarian membership of the EU was endorsed by 83.8% of the votes cast (with 45.6% of the electorate participating). In December 2007 Hungary implemented the EU's Schengen Agreement, enabling its citizens to travel to and from other member states, without border controls. In the same month Hungary became the first EU member state to ratify the draft Treaty of Lisbon. German Chancellor Angela Merkel visited Hungary in February 2015, when she urged Prime Minister Orbán to continue to observe democratic freedoms, following increasing concerns about numerous recent political developments in Hungary, and in response to a speech made by Orbán in July 2014, when he had praised what he termed the 'illiberal' practices of several states, including the People's Republic of China, Russia and Turkey.

Other external relations

Following a North Atlantic Treaty Organization (NATO, see p. 367) summit meeting in July 1997, Hungary was invited to enter into discussions regarding its application for membership of the Alliance. A national referendum on the country's entry into NATO was conducted in November, at which its accession was approved by 85.3% of the votes cast, with the participation of 49% of the electorate. Hungary was formally admitted to NATO in March 1999. In early 2003 an air base at Taszar, in southwestern Hungary, was used by the USA for the training of Iraqi opposition forces, in relation to the US-led military campaign in Iraq. Hungary subsequently contributed 300 soldiers to the international peacekeeping force in Iraq. Following considerable public and political opposition, these were withdrawn in March 2005.

In August 2012 Armenia suspended diplomatic relations with Hungary, following the Hungarian Government's extradition to Azerbaijan of an Azerbaijani soldier who had murdered an Armenian fellow participant during a NATO 'Partnership for Peace' course in Budapest in 2004. Hungary's action, at the request of the Azerbaijani President (who immediately pardoned and released the soldier from custody), prompted protests in Budapest and international criticism.

In October 2014 Hungary's relations with the USA became strained, after the US Government refused entry to several Hungarian officials accused of corruption. In December one of the affected officials, the head of the tax authority, lodged a legal case against the then US Chargé d'affaires in Budapest, André Goodfriend, for slander, as a result of an interview in which he made allegations of fraudulent activities within the authority. However, in January 2015 the USA refused a request by the Hungarian Government that Goodfriend's diplomatic immunity be withdrawn (his departure from the country was announced in February).

In March 2009 Russian gas producer Gazprom signed an agreement in the Russian capital, Moscow, with the Hungarian Development Bank, in the presence of Prime Minister Gyurcsány and Russian premier Vladimir Putin, on the establishment of a joint venture for its 'South Stream' pipeline project on Hungarian territory. In July Hungary was also one of five countries to sign an agreement on the establishment of the proposed EU- and US-supported Nabucco pipeline, which was to supply gas from various Central Asian states to Europe. In April 2012, however, the Hungarian Oil and Gas Company announced its withdrawal from the Nabucco consortium (the Nabucco project was subsequently abandoned). In November the Hungarian Government finalized the investment agreement with Gazprom on the 'South Stream' project. Following discussions between Russian President Putin and Prime Minister Orbán in January 2014, it was announced that a subsidiary of Russian nuclear agency Rosatom had secured a contract to construct a further two units at the nuclear power installation at Paks, in central Hungary. The nuclear co-operation agreement, under which the Russian Government was to provide 80% of the project's costs, was approved by the Hungarian legislature in February.

Following Russia's annexation of the Crimean peninsula in March 2014 (see the chapter on Ukraine), the Hungarian Government complied with sanctions imposed by the EU against Russia, but was subsequently highly critical of their regional impact. Shortly after a meeting between the head of Gazprom and Orbán in September, Hungary suspended the flow of gas supplies received from Russia to Ukraine, in support of a Russian embargo on fuel to that country (amid Russian involvement in continued conflict in parts of eastern Ukraine). The Hungarian Government reacted with consternation to an announcement by President Putin in December that the 'South Stream' project had been abandoned; however, Hungary was a possible participant state in a proposed alternative pipeline that would link Russia with Turkey. In February 2015 Putin made an official visit to Hungary (his first to an EU state since the previous June), when it was agreed that the gas supply contract between the two countries would be renewed. Orbán subsequently increased his criticism of the EU's stance against Russia. Under legislation adopted in March, on grounds of national security, the details of Rosatom's nuclear contract in Hungary were to remain secret for 30 years.

CONSTITUTION AND GOVERNMENT

On 1 January 2012 a new Constitution entered into force, renaming the country from the Republic of Hungary to simply Hungary; constitutional amendments were approved by the legislature in March 2013. Legislative power is held by the unicameral National Assembly (Országgyűlés), which, under the new Constitution comprises 199 members, elected for a term of four years by universal adult suffrage, under a mixed system of proportional and direct representation. The President of the Republic (Head of State) is elected by the National Assembly for a term of five years. The President may be re-elected for a second term. The Council of Ministers, the highest organ of state administration, is elected by the Assembly on the recommendation of the President. Judicial power is exercised by local courts, labour courts, county courts (or the Metropolitan Court) and the Supreme Court. All judicial offices are filled by election. For local administrative purposes, Hungary is divided into 19 counties (*megyei*) and the capital city (with 23 districts). A 53-member National Autonomous Authority of the Romany Minority is empowered to administer funds disbursed by the central Government.

REGIONAL AND INTERNATIONAL CO-OPERATION

Hungary became a full member of the European Union (EU, see p. 271) in May 2004. It is also a member of the North Atlantic Treaty Organization (NATO, see p. 367), the Council of Europe, the Organization for Security and Co-operation in Europe (OSCE, see p. 385) and the Organisation for Economic Co-operation and Development (OECD, see p. 377).

Hungary joined the UN in 1955 and became a member of the World Trade Organization (WTO, see p. 431) in 1995.

ECONOMIC AFFAIRS

In 2013, according to estimates by the World Bank, Hungary's gross national income (GNI), measured at average 2011–13 prices, was US $123,462m., equivalent to $12,450 per head (or $21,000 per head on an international purchasing-power parity basis). During 2004–13, it was estimated, the population decreased at an average annual rate of 0.2%, while gross domestic product (GDP) per head increased, in real terms, by an average of 0.6% per year. Overall GDP increased, in real terms, at an average annual rate of 0.4% during 2004–13; real GDP decreased by 1.7% in 2012, but increased by 1.1% in 2013.

Agriculture (including hunting, forestry and fishing) contributed 4.4% of GDP and engaged 4.7% of the employed labour force in 2013. The principal crops are maize, wheat, sunflower seeds, barley and sugar beet. Viticulture is also important. During 2004–12, according to UN estimates, real agricultural GDP decreased at an average annual rate of 4.8%. The GDP of the sector increased by 11.8% in 2011, but decreased by 18.9% in 2012.

Industry (including mining, manufacturing, construction and power) contributed 30.2% of GDP and engaged 29.9% of the employed labour force in 2013. According to UN estimates, real industrial GDP decreased at an average annual rate of 0.1% in 2004–12. Industrial GDP increased by 0.4% in 2011, but decreased by 2.0% in 2012.

Mining and quarrying accounted for 0.2% of GDP and engaged 0.2% of the employed labour force in 2013. Hungary's most important mineral resources are lignite (brown coal) and natural gas. Petroleum, bauxite and hard coal are also exploited. At the end of 2013 Hungary's proven coal reserves stood at 1,660m. metric tons. According to UN estimates, real mining GDP (along with utilities) decreased by 1.9% during 2004–12; sectoral GDP decreased by 3.8% in 2011 and by a further 7.0% in 2012.

The manufacturing sector contributed 22.8% of GDP in 2013 and engaged 21.0% of the employed labour force in 2013. According to UN estimates, manufacturing GDP increased, in real terms, at an average annual rate of 1.0% in 2004–12. Manufacturing GDP increased by 0.8% in 2011, but decreased by 0.4% in 2012.

The construction sector contributed 4.0% of GDP and engaged 6.3% of the labour force in 2013. According to UN estimates, real construction GDP decreased by 3.7% in 2004–12. Sectoral GDP increased by 2.0% in 2011, but decreased by 6.3% in 2012.

In 2012 some 45.9% of Hungary's electricity production was generated by nuclear power, 26.7% by natural gas and 18.8% by coal. Imports of fuels and electricity represented 12.5% of the value of total imports in 2013.

The services sector has a significant role, contributing 65.4% of GDP and engaging 65.3% of the employed labour force in 2013. According to UN estimates, the GDP of the services sector increased, in real terms, at an average rate of 0.7% per year in 2004–12. The GDP of the services sector increased by 1.9% in 2011, but decreased by 0.3% in 2012.

In 2013 Hungary recorded a visible merchandise trade surplus of US $3,806m. and a surplus of $3,904m. on the current account of the balance of payments. In that year the principal source of imports was Germany (accounting for 25.0% of the total); other major sources were Russia, Austria, Slovakia and the People's Republic of China. Germany was also the principal market for exports in that year (taking 25.9% of the total); other important purchasers were Romania, Austria and Slovakia. The principal exports in 2013 were machinery and transport equipment, basic manufactures, and food, beverages and tobacco. The main imports in that year were machinery and tranport equipment, basic manufactures, fuels and electricity, and food, beverages and tobacco.

According to official figures, in 2013 Hungary's overall budgetary deficit was estimated at 979,800m. forint, equivalent to 3.3% of GDP. Hungary's general government gross debt was 23,068,250m. forint in 2013, equivalent to 79.3% of GDP. The country's total external debt was an estimated US $203,757m. at the end of 2012, of which $62,140m. was long-term public debt. In that year the cost of debt-servicing was equivalent to 84.6% of the value of exports of goods and services. The annual rate of inflation averaged 5.2% in 2003–12; consumer prices increased by 5.7% in 2012. The rate of unemployment was 10.2% in 2013, according to official figures.

In early 2012 the European Union (EU, see p. 271) suspended the release of funds to Hungary, stating that it had failed to address excessive budgetary deficit and external debt levels. Nevertheless, in September the Government rejected fiscal adjustment measures, including the abolition of the high tax rates imposed on banks, which were required by the IMF. In October the Government announced the extension of the tax measures in force in the financial sector, and the introduction of further taxes on foreign energy enterprises and public utilities, despite the IMF opposing these policies as they regarded them as inimical to private sector investment and growth. The EU excessive deficit procedure against Hungary was officially ended in June 2013, after the fiscal consolidation efforts had successfully reduced the general government deficit. In August (ahead of schedule) Hungary repaid outstanding obligations totalling US $2,850m. to the IMF. The Central Bank announced in September that it had signed a three-year currency exchange agreement amounting to $1,620m. with the Central Bank of the People's Republic of China, which was to facilitate bilateral trade and investment. A nuclear co-operation agreement, under which a subsidiary of the Russian state nuclear agency Rosatom was to construct a further two units at Hungary's only nuclear power installation, secured legislative approval in February 2014 and was confirmed in December (following the adoption of legislation removing the requirement to hold a public tender). In a report issued in June, the IMF considered that the authorities had demonstrated strong commitment to restraining the budget deficit, which was subsequently estimated at 2.6% of GDP in 2014 (lower than the official target). The Government in November obliged Hungarian banks to make financial arrangements to convert some $12,000m. in foreign-currency mortgages, largely denominated in Swiss francs, into local currency, thereby averting a potential increase in household debt in real terms. Following a contraction in 2012, modest GDP growth in 2013 strengthened to an estimated 3.2% in 2014 and the current account continued to be in robust surplus; however, the value of the forint had fallen significantly. Although Hungary participated in EU sanctions imposed against Russia from March 2014, its gas supply contract with Russia was renewed in February 2015.

PUBLIC HOLIDAYS

2016: 1 January (New Year's Day), 15 March (Anniversary of 1848 uprising against Austrian rule), 28 March (Easter Monday), 1 May (Labour Day), 16 May (Whit Monday), 20 August (Constitution Day), 23 October (Day of the Proclamation of the Republic), 1 November (All Saints' Day), 25–26 December (Christmas).

Statistical Survey

Source (unless otherwise stated): Központi Statisztikai Hivatal (Hungarian Central Statistical Office), 1525 Budapest, Keleti Károly u. 5–7; tel. (1) 345-6136; fax (1) 345-6378; e-mail erzsebet.veto@office.ksh.hu; internet www.ksh.hu.

Area and Population

AREA, POPULATION AND DENSITY

Area (sq km)	93,024*
Population (census results)	
1 February 2001	10,198,315
1 October 2011	
Males	4,718,479
Females	5,219,149
Total	9,937,628
Population (official estimates at 1 January)	
2012	9,931,925
2013	9,908,798
2014	9,877,365
Density (per sq km) at 1 January 2014	106.2

* 35,908 sq miles.

POPULATION BY AGE AND SEX
(official estimates at 1 January 2014)

	Males	Females	Total
0–14 years	732,203	693,613	1,425,816
15–64 years	3,326,519	3,393,219	6,719,738
65 years and over	644,669	1,087,142	1,731,811
Total	4,703,391	5,173,974	9,877,365

ADMINISTRATIVE DIVISIONS
(official population estimates at 1 January 2014)

	Area (sq km)	Population	Density (per sq km)	County town (with population)
Counties:				
				Kecskemét (112,071)
Bács-Kiskun . .	8,445	516,892	61.2	
Baranya . . .	4,430	373,984	84.4	Pécs (146,581)
Békés . . .	5,630	355,199	63.1	Békéscsaba (60,571)
Borsod-Abaúj-Zemplén . .	7,247	674,999	93.1	Miskolc (161,265)
Csongrád . . .	4,263	407,389	95.6	Szeged (161,921)
Fejér	4,358	419,506	96.3	Székesfehérvár (99,060)
Győr-Moson-Sopron . .	4,208	450,318	107.0	Győr (128,902)
Hajdú-Bihar . .	6,211	539,507	86.9	Debrecen (203,914)
Heves . . .	3,637	303,503	83.4	Eger (54,527)
Jász-Nagykun-Szolnok . . .	5,582	383,489	68.7	Szolnok (73,106)
Komárom-Esztergom . .	2,264	300,677	132.8	Tatabánya (67,043)
Nógrád . . .	2,545	198,392	78.0	Salgótarján (36,497)
Pest	6,391	1,220,748	191.0	Érd (63,294)
Somogy . . .	6,065	315,512	52.0	Kaposvár (64,872)
Szabolcs-Szatmár-Bereg . .	5,936	561,379	94.6	Nyíregyháza (118,164)
Tolna . . .	3,703	227,996	61.6	Szekszárd (33,373)
Vas	3,336	254,580	76.3	Szombathely (77,566)
Veszprém . . .	4,463	349,007	78.2	Veszprém (60,788)
Zala	3,784	279,623	73.9	Zalaegerszeg (59,275)
Capital city				
Budapest* . .	525	1,744,665	3323.2	—
Total . . .	93,024	9,877,365	106.2	—

* Budapest has separate county status.

PRINCIPAL TOWNS
(official population estimates at 1 January 2014)

Budapest (capital) .	1,744,665	Pécs	146,581
Debrecen . . .	203,914	Győr	128,902
Szeged	161,921	Nyíregyháza . .	118,164
Miskolc	161,265	Kecskemét . . .	112,071

BIRTHS, MARRIAGES AND DEATHS

	Registered live births		Registered marriages		Registered deaths	
	Number	Rate (per 1,000)	Number	Rate (per 1,000)	Number	Rate (per 1,000)
2006 . .	99,871	9.9	44,528	4.4	131,603	13.1
2007 . .	97,613	9.7	40,842	4.1	132,938	13.2
2008 . .	99,149	9.9	40,105	4.0	130,027	13.0
2009 . .	96,442	9.6	36,730	3.7	130,414	13.0
2010 . .	90,335	9.0	35,520	3.6	130,456	13.0
2011 . .	88,050	8.8	35,812	3.6	128,795	12.9
2012 . .	90,269	9.1	36,161	3.6	129,440	13.0
2013 . .	88,689	9.0	36,986	3.7	126,778	12.8

Life expectancy (years at birth): 75.1 (males 71.6; females 78.7) in 2012 (Source: World Bank, World Development Indicators database).

ECONOMICALLY ACTIVE POPULATION
(labour force surveys, '000 persons aged 15 to 74 years)

	2011	2012	2013
Agriculture, hunting, forestry and fishing	184.6	192.7	184.6
Mining and quarrying	11.1	9.1	7.5
Manufacturing	800.1	789.2	819.3
Electricity, gas and water supply .	89.5	99.3	92.8
Construction	260.7	243.2	245.5
Wholesale and retail trade; repair of motor vehicles, motorcycles and personal and household goods	534.7	539.3	528.6
Hotels and restaurants . . .	157.5	161.8	158.0
Transport, storage and communications	344.8	360.5	370.5
Financial intermediation . . .	90.7	91.6	96.1
Real estate, renting and business activities	266.5	285.4	306.3
Public administration and defence; compulsory social security . .	308.1	322.4	365.8
Education	317.7	315.6	309.5
Health and social work . . .	251.1	263.9	261.6
Other community, social and personal service activities . .	142.2	153.2	146.7
Total employed	3,759.1	3,827.2	3,892.8
Unemployed	466.0	473.2	441.0
Total labour force	4,225.0	4,300.4	4,333.8
Males	2,272.5	2,310.9	2,343.0
Females	1,952.5	1,989.5	1,990.8

Health and Welfare

KEY INDICATORS

Total fertility rate (children per woman, 2012) . . .	1.4
Under-5 mortality rate (per 1,000 live births, 2012) . . .	6.0
HIV/AIDS (% of persons aged 15–49, 2011)	<0.1
Physicians (per 1,000 head, 2011)	3.0
Hospital beds (per 1,000 head, 2009)	7.1
Health expenditure (2011): US $ per head (PPP)	1,690
Health expenditure (2011): % of GDP	7.9
Health expenditure (2011): public (% of total)	65.0
Total carbon dioxide emissions ('000 metric tons, 2010) . .	50,582.6
Carbon dioxide emissions per head (metric tons, 2010) . .	5.1
Human Development Index (2013): ranking	43
Human Development Index (2013): value	0.818

For sources and definitions, see explanatory note on p. vi.

Agriculture

PRINCIPAL CROPS
('000 metric tons)

	2011	2012	2013
Wheat	4,107.0	3,740.0	5,095.8
Barley	988.0	995.7	1,071.1
Maize	7,992.0	4,741.5	6,724.8
Rye	75.2	78.8	106.1
Oats	129.1	137.2	134.8
Triticale (wheat-rye hybrid) . .	345.7	345.1	458.5
Potatoes	600.0	511.1	443.1
Sugar beet	856.0	769.7	949.7
Peas, dry	42.6	42.5	43.6
Soybeans (Soya beans) . . .	95.0	67.8	82.1
Sunflower seed	1,374.8	1,316.5	1,469.6
Rapeseed	526.8	414.6	527.4
Cabbages and other brassicas .	101.1	82.9	57.9
Tomatoes	163.3	108.8	138.1
Cucumbers and gherkins . .	35.9	33.9	20.0
Chillies and peppers, green . .	128.0	92.6	95.0
Onions, dry	57.6	57.2	62.0
Peas, green	99.1	92.4	78.0
Carrots and turnips . . .	65.1	74.7	63.4
Maize, green	427.3	433.6	540.1*
Watermelons	202.9	182.7	183.9
Apples	292.8	650.6	552.4
Sour (Morello) cherries . . .	61.7	53.4	53.3
Peaches and nectarines . . .	43.1	16.9	43.3
Plums and sloes	37.3	43.3	49.0
Grapes	450.9	356.4	494.3
Tobacco, unmanufactured . .	10.9	9.3	8.4

* Unofficial figure.

Aggregate production ('000 metric tons, may include official, semi-official or estimated data): Total cereals 13,678.1 in 2011, 10,072.6 in 2012, 13,621.0 in 2013; Total roots and tubers 600.0 in 2011, 511.1 in 2012, 443.1 in 2013; Total vegetables (incl. melons) 1,475.3 in 2011, 1,363.1 in 2012, 1,441.4 in 2013; Total fruits (excl. melons) 973.0 in 2011, 1,189.5 in 2012, 1,280.2 in 2013.

Source: FAO.

LIVESTOCK
('000 head, year ending September)

	2011	2012	2013
Cattle	682	698	760
Pigs	3,169	3,044	2,989
Sheep	1,181	1,120	1,185
Goats	75	79	89
Horses	65	74	76
Chickens	31,848	32,860	30,075
Ducks	5,813	4,433	4,484
Geese	1,384	1,085	1,189
Turkeys	3,168	2,999	2,798

Source: FAO.

LIVESTOCK PRODUCTS
('000 metric tons)

	2011	2012	2013
Cattle meat	26.4	25.4	23.5
Sheep meat	1.0	1.1	0.9
Pig meat	434.7	393.7	368.2
Chicken meat	235.7	253.8	244.2
Duck meat	59.3	61.4	64.1
Rabbit meat	5.7	6.5	6.6
Cows' milk	1,712.5	1,812.8	1,758.5
Sheep's milk	1.6	1.7	1.4*
Goats' milk	3.9	3.9	3.9
Hen eggs	136.6	133.9	139.3
Other poultry eggs*	3.9	3.9	3.9
Honey	24.5	17.5	18.5
Wool, greasy	3.8	3.8	3.8

* FAO estimate(s).

Source: FAO.

Forestry

ROUNDWOOD REMOVALS
('000 cu metres, excl. bark)

	2011	2012	2013
Sawlogs, veneer logs and logs for sleepers	1,232	1,196	1,163
Pulpwood	959	1,073	1,133
Other industrial wood	827	718	873
Fuel wood	3,215	2,959	2,858
Total	**6,232**	**5,946**	**6,027**

Source: FAO.

SAWNWOOD PRODUCTION
('000 cu metres, incl. railway sleepers)

	2011	2012	2013
Coniferous (softwood)	122	90	33
Broadleaved (hardwood) . . .	100	212	175*
Total	**222**	**302**	**208***

* Unofficial figure.

Source: FAO.

Fishing

(metric tons, live weight)

	2010	2011	2012
Capture	6,216	7,048	6,717
Common carp	3,247	3,855	3,688
Silver carp	350	455	336
Other cyprinids	1,113	1,219	1,223
Aquaculture	14,245	15,584	15,133
Common carp	9,927	10,807	9,985
Grass carp	437	437	502
Silver carp	1,081	1,545	1,681
North African catfish . . .	1,810	1,913	1,852
Freshwater fishes	619	407	640
Total catch	**20,461**	**22,632**	**21,850**

Source: FAO.

Mining

('000 metric tons unless otherwise indicated)

	2010	2011	2012
Brown coal	911	758	859
Lignite	8,203	8,801	8,438
Crude petroleum ('000 barrels)* .	5,025	4,470	4,410
Bauxite	365	278	255
Natural gas (million cu metres)† .	2,600	2,667	2,280

* Estimates.
† Marketed production.
Source: US Geological Survey.

Industry

SELECTED PRODUCTS
('000 metric tons unless otherwise indicated)

	2010	2011	2012
Crude steel*	1,678	1,746	1,543
Cement*†	2,100	2,000	1,900
Nitrogenous fertilizers‡ . . .	273	303	303
Refined sugar	133	130	n.a.
Electric energy (million kWh) .	37,371	35,983	n.a.
Radio receivers ('000) . . .	1,577	1,106	n.a.

* Source: US Geological Survey.
† Estimates.
‡ Production in terms of nitrogen (Source: FAO).

Non-rubber footwear ('000 pairs): 5,340 in 2007

Source: mainly UN Industrial Commodity Statistics Database.

Finance

CURRENCY AND EXCHANGE RATES

Monetary Units
100 fillér = 1 forint.

Sterling, Dollar and Euro Equivalents (31 December 2014)
£1 sterling = 404.450 forint;
US $1 = 259.130 forint;
€1 = 314.610 forint;
1,000 forint = £2.47 = $3.86 = €3.18.

Average Exchange Rate (forint per US dollar)
2012   225.104
2013   223.695
2014   232.602

BUDGET
('000 million forint)

Revenue	2012	2013	2014*
Payments of economic units . .	1,157.2	1,152.1	1,351.7
Corporate taxes	342.3	322.5	358.8
Simplified business tax . . .	146.5	110.0	67.0
Gambling tax	52.4	30.9	33.0
Other central payments . .	172.0	233.2	343.2
Taxes on consumption . . .	3,702.7	4,055.3	4,316.7
Value-added tax	2,747.4	2,809.6	3,014.1
Excises and tax on consumption	943.1	912.9	948.2
Payments of households† . . .	1,609.4	1,654.4	1,700.1
Personal income tax revenue of the central budget . . .	1,498.4	1,504.6	1,550.0
Fees	109.6	107.4	110.0
Central budgetary institutions and chapter-administered appropriations	2,603.6	3,443.4	2,903.6
Payments of general government sub-systems	68.0	240.7	72.2
Payments of extra-budgetary funds	—	15.1	10.0
Payments related to state property	69.8	205.7	209.9
Revenue related to debt service and other revenues	172.0	179.3	110.6
Transfers from the European Union	20.8	37.0	32.4
Total	**9,403.6**	**10,967.8**	**10,697.3**

Expenditure	2012	2013	2014*
Subsidies to economic units . .	259.5	279.9	282.6
Support to the media	61.8	66.6	69.9
Social policy subsidy for fares .	—	94.8	104.0
Consumer price subsidy . . .	96.9	—	—
Housing grants	124.0	131.2	150.2
Family benefits and social subsidies	817.0	746.3	714.5
Family benefits	445.8	434.6	446.2
Income-supplement benefits .	62.7	62.3	66.8
Payments of central budgetary institutions and chapter-administered appropriations	5,067.2	6,670.6	6,421.2
Transfers to general government sub-systems†	1,852.2	1,933.5	1,750.2
Contribution to social-security funds	690.9	986.6	917.4
Transfers to local governments .	1,066.7	674.8	715.9
Transfer to non-profit organizations	3.8	3.8	9.8
Debt service related expenditures and interest expenditures . .	1,202.4	1,277.9	1,165.0
Reserves	—	—	289.2
Subsidy for local governments' debt repayments	73.7	33.9	64.0
State property expenditures . .	137.4	260.3	180.9
Extraordinary and other expenditures	43.4	148.6	127.1
Government guarantees redeemed	40.8	27.1	32.3
Contribution to the European Union budget	234.9	272.3	288.7
Total	**10,014.8**	**11,947.6**	**11,658.6**

* Budget estimates.
† Including personal income tax ceded to local governments.

INTERNATIONAL RESERVES
(US $ million at 31 December)

	2011	2012	2013
Gold (national valuation) . . .	154	164	119
IMF special drawing rights . .	842	365	21
Reserve position in IMF . . .	113	113	114
Foreign exchange	47,725	44,028	46,254
Total	**48,834**	**44,670**	**46,508**

Source: IMF, *International Financial Statistics*.

MONEY SUPPLY
('000 million forint at 31 December)

	2011	2012	2013
Currency outside depositary corporations	2,551.5	2,553.9	3,000.5
Transferable deposits	4,791.3	4,743.4	5,897.5
Other deposits	8,049.3	7,903.7	6,976.4
Securities other than shares	2,530.8	1,864.8	2,488.1
Broad money	17,922.8	17,065.7	18,362.6

Source: IMF, *International Financial Statistics*.

COST OF LIVING
(Consumer Price Index; base: 2000 = 100)

	2010	2011	2012
Food	191.7	204.3	216.4
All items (incl. others)	173.1	179.9	190.1

Source: ILO.

NATIONAL ACCOUNTS
('000 million forint at current prices)
Expenditure on the Gross Domestic Product

	2011	2012	2013
Government final consumption expenditure	5,838.7	5,753.2	5,937.8
Private final consumption expenditure*	14,736.4	15,353.8	15,725.2
Changes in inventories	181.0	25.5	−32.4
Gross fixed capital formation	5,551.7	5,458.4	5,949.2
Total domestic expenditure	26,307.8	26,590.9	27,579.8
Exports of goods and services	24,540.1	24,956.2	26,491.9
Less Imports of goods and services	22,812.9	22,998.4	24,225.5
GDP in purchasers' values	28,035.0	28,548.8	29,846.3

* Includes non-profit institutions serving households.

Gross Domestic Product by Economic Activity

	2011	2012	2013
Agriculture, hunting, forestry and fishing	1,106.3	1,088.1	1,098.8
Mining and quarrying	60.2	59.3	59.3
Manufacturing	5,261.2	5,419.4	5,719.4
Electricity, gas and water supply	880.4	905.2	820.4
Construction	955.7	906.7	994.0
Wholesale and retail trade; repair of motor vehicles	2,462.1	2,462.5	2,683.0
Hotels and restaurants	378.6	340.4	373.8
Transport, storage and communications	2,692.5	2,711.6	2,933.8
Financial intermediation	1,076.2	1,031.2	980.9
Real estate, renting and business activities	4,183.7	4,223.8	4,415.9
Public administration, defence and compulsory social security	2,058.4	2,024.3	2,207.7
Education	1,063.4	1,091.3	1,031.1
Health and social work	934.3	1,025.7	1,097.0
Other community, social and personal service activities	675.6	669.4	712.1
Gross value added in basic prices	23,788.6	23,959.0	25,127.2
Taxes *less* subsidies on products	4,246.5	4,589.8	4,719.0
GDP in market prices	28,035.0	28,548.8	29,846.3

BALANCE OF PAYMENTS
(US $ million)

	2011	2012	2013
Exports of goods	97,770	88,373	95,192
Imports of goods	−94,535	−86,549	−91,386
Balance on goods	3,235	1,824	3,806
Exports of services	22,753	22,772	23,240
Imports of services	−17,202	−15,872	−16,672
Balance on goods and services	8,786	8,725	10,374
Primary income received	14,078	13,177	13,215
Primary income paid	−22,909	−21,446	−21,097
Balance on goods, services and primary income	−45	456	2,491
Secondary income received	3,726	3,526	4,494
Secondary income paid	−3,004	−3,073	−3,082
Current balance	676	909	3,904
Capital account (net)	3,170	3,319	4,505
Direct investment assets	−8,616	−6,946	816
Direct investment liabilities	10,500	9,779	−732
Portfolio investment assets	2,289	939	557
Portfolio investment liabilities	6,392	1,434	3,557
Financial derivatives and employee stock options assets	7,016	6,032	5,207
Financial derivatives and employee stock options liabilities	−8,053	−5,650	−4,424
Other investment assets	3,023	2,448	997
Other investment liabilities	−8,023	−13,562	−7,084
Net errors and omissions	−2,824	1,920	1,040
Reserves and related items	5,550	621	8,342

Source: IMF, *International Financial Statistics*.

External Trade

PRINCIPAL COMMODITIES
('000 million forint)

Imports c.i.f.	2011	2012	2013
Food, beverages and tobacco	1,088.3	1,122.3	1,123.8
Crude materials	521.5	537.1	522.7
Fuels and electricity	2,511.4	2,759.6	2,776.6
Basic manufactures	6,800.1	7,096.1	7,531.7
Machinery and transport equipment	9,442.5	9,706.0	10,208.0
Total	20,363.9	21,221.0	22,162.8

Exports f.o.b.	2011	2012	2013
Food, beverages and tobacco	1,683.2	1,887.2	1,938.3
Crude materials	681.4	790.9	737.9
Fuels and electricity	810.3	935.6	869.8
Basic manufactures	6,537.5	7,192.9	7,659.3
Machinery and transport equipment	12,630.2	12,336.5	12,912.6
Total	22,342.5	23,143.1	24,117.8

PRINCIPAL TRADING PARTNERS
('000 million forint)*

Imports c.i.f.	2011	2012	2013
Austria	1,342.3	1,493.7	1,478.7
Belgium	427.4	451.8	484.6
China, People's Republic	1,226.4	1,218.9	1,191.6
Czech Republic	698.2	753.8	908.1
France	740.5	765.9	843.9
Germany	4,852.1	5,221.3	5,536.3
Hong Kong	228.6	178.0	149.7
Italy	915.0	938.3	976.7
Japan	318.0	286.7	275.4
Korea, Republic	423.7	326.7	252.7
Netherlands	850.3	851.6	854.8
Poland	944.2	988.3	1,075.1
Romania	651.5	594.3	629.7

Imports c.i.f.—*continued*	2011	2012	2013
Russia	1,780.8	1,859.5	1,895.0
Slovakia	1,104.9	1,197.6	1,275.3
Slovenia	228.0	226.5	265.8
Spain	239.2	253.0	296.0
Sweden	224.9	230.5	215.1
Taiwan	263.7	265.1	219.8
Ukraine	275.3	352.0	365.6
United Kingdom	416.1	402.9	409.8
USA	390.7	428.5	473.5
Total (incl. others)	20,363.9	21,221.0	22,162.8

Exports f.o.b.	2011	2012	2013
Austria	1,260.1	1,329.3	1,343.3
Belgium	318.1	337.4	365.5
China, People's Republic . . .	337.7	407.2	444.2
Croatia	322.9	367.4	330.2
Czech Republic	831.7	897.0	907.8
France	1,041.7	1,067.0	1,073.2
Germany	5,529.9	5,785.0	6,236.8
Italy	1,113.8	1,076.7	1,140.8
Netherlands	555.3	640.9	687.3
Poland	856.8	876.4	937.3
Romania	1,361.7	1,377.5	1,366.5
Russia	717.4	740.5	749.9
Serbia	301.7	360.3	352.4
Slovakia	1,312.3	1,359.2	1,295.5
Slovenia	247.7	265.0	279.4
Spain	587.1	540.2	598.3
Sweden	223.3	245.6	234.5
Turkey	375.4	351.1	420.1
Ukraine	456.0	514.6	575.4
United Arab Emirates	393.6	267.4	228.3
United Kingdom	1,023.0	961.0	937.9
USA	457.0	553.2	731.1
Total (incl. others)	22,342.5	23,143.1	24,117.8

* Imports by country of origin; exports by country of destination.

Transport

RAILWAYS
(traffic)

	2011	2012	2013
Passengers carried (million) .	145.7	147.8	148.5
Passenger-kilometres (million) .	7,806	7,806	7,842
Freight carried ('000 metric tons) .	47,424	46,884	49,085
Net ton-kilometres (million) . .	9,118	9,230	9,722

ROAD TRAFFIC
(motor vehicles in use at 31 December)

	2011	2012	2013
Passenger cars	2,967,792	2,986,028	3,040,732
Buses and coaches	17,366	17,301	17,569
Lorries and vans	415,424	414,405	419,031
Motorcycles and mopeds . . .	147,382	151,405	157,178
Road tractors	50,262	52,596	56,089

SHIPPING
Flag Registered Fleet
(at 31 December)

	2012	2013	2014
Number of vessels	2	3	2
Total displacement (grt) . . .	15	1,315	15

Source: Lloyd's List Intelligence (www.lloydslistintelligence.com).

INLAND WATERWAYS
(traffic)

	2011	2012	2013
Freight carried ('000 metric tons) .	7,175	8,135	7,857
Freight ton-km (million) . . .	1,840	1,982	1,924

CIVIL AVIATION
(traffic)

	2010	2011
Kilometres flown (million)	127	142
Passengers carried ('000)	11,787	12,970
Passenger-km (million)	14,984	17,021
Total ton-km	1,377	1,562

Source: UN, *Statistical Yearbook.*

2013 ('000): Passengers carried 13,500 (Source: World Bank, World Development Indicators database).

Tourism

TOURISTS BY COUNTRY OF ORIGIN
('000 arrivals, including visitors in transit)

	2011	2012	2013
Austria	6,649	7,233	7,117
Bulgaria	1,380	1,443	1,174
Czech Republic	916	1,041	1,188
Croatia	934	756	824
Germany	3,026	3,188	2,848
Poland	1,331	1,603	1,812
Romania	7,575	7,901	7,282
Serbia	2,964	2,658	3,344
Slovakia	8,825	9,971	10,015
Ukraine	1,831	1,863	1,901
Total (incl. others)	41,304	43,565	43,611

Tourist receipts (million forint): 1,200,139 in 2011; 1,208,547 in 2012; 1,263,957 in 2013.

Communications Media

	2011	2012	2013
Telephones ('000 main lines in use)	2,933.3	2,960.6	2,978.0
Mobile cellular telephones ('000 subscribers)	11,689.9	11,579.4	11,590.3
Internet subscribers ('000) . .	2,221.5	n.a.	n.a.
Broadband subscribers ('000) . .	2,208.1	2,281.1	2,401.1
Book production: titles	12,456	12,080	11,957
Book production: copies ('000) .	34,251	30,649	27,590

Source: mainly International Telecommunication Union.

Education

(2013/14, preliminary, full- and part-time education)

	Institutions	Teachers	Students
Pre-primary	4,532	30,873	330,184
Primary	3,605	73,906	750,333
Vocational	877	10,129	125,606
Secondary	1,848	36,299	459,543
General	869	17,680	220,472
Vocational	979	18,619	239,071
Tertiary	66	21,137	320,124

Pupil-teacher ratio (primary education, UNESCO estimate): 10.5 in 2011/12 (Source: UNESCO Institute for Statistics).

Adult literacy rate (UNESCO estimates): 99.4% (males 99.4%; females 99.4%) in 2012 (Source: UNESCO Institute for Statistics).

Directory

The Government

HEAD OF STATE

President of the Republic: János Áder.

COUNCIL OF MINISTERS
(April 2015)

Principally comprising members of Fidesz—Magyar Polgári Szöevetség (Fidesz) and the Kereszténydemokrata Néppárt (KDNP).

Prime Minister: Viktor Orbán (Fidesz).

Deputy Prime Minister, Minister without Portfolio: Dr Zsolt Semjén (KNDP).

Minister in charge of the Prime Minister's Office: János Lázár (Fidesz).

Minister of the Interior: Dr Sándor Pintér (Independent).

Minister of Human Resources: Zoltán Balog (Fidesz).

Minister of Agriculture: Dr Sándor Fazekas (Fidesz).

Minister of Defence: Dr Csaba Hende (Fidesz).

Minister of Justice: László Trócsányi (Independent).

Minister of Foreign Affairs and Trade: Péter Szijjártó (Fidesz).

Minister of the National Economy: Mihály Varga (Fidesz).

Minister of National Development: Miklós Seszták (KNDP).

MINISTRIES

Office of the President: 1014 Budapest, Sándor-Palace, Szent György tér 1; tel. (1) 224-5000; fax (1) 784-9181; e-mail ugyfelkapu@keh.hu; internet www.keh.hu.

Office of the Prime Minister: 1357 Budapest, pf. 6; tel. (1) 795-5000; fax (1) 795-0381; e-mail titkarsag@me.gov.hu; internet www.kormany.hu.

Ministry of Agriculture: 1055 Budapest, Kossuth Lajos tér 11; tel. (1) 795-2000; fax (1) 795-0200; e-mail miniszter@vm.gov.hu; internet www.kormany.hu/hu/foldmuvelesugyi-miniszterium.

Ministry of Defence: 1055 Budapest, Balaton u. 7–11; tel. (1) 236-5111; fax (1) 474-1335; e-mail hmugyfelszolgalat@hm.gov.hu; internet www.kormany.hu/hu/honvedelmi-miniszterium.

Ministry of Foreign Affairs and Trade: 1027 Budapest, Bem rakpart 47; tel. (1) 458-1000; fax (1) 212-5918; e-mail kozkapcsolat@kum.gov.hu; internet www.kormany.hu/hu/kulgazdasagi-es-kulugyminiszterium.

Ministry of Human Resources: 1055 Budapest, Szalay u. 10–14; tel. (1) 795-1200; fax (1) 795-0012; e-mail info@nefmi.gov.hu; internet www.kormany.hu/hu/emberi-eroforrasok-miniszteriuma.

Ministry of the Interior: 1051 Budapest, József Attila u. 2–4; tel. (1) 441-1000; fax (1) 441-1437; e-mail ugyfelszolgalat@bm.gov.hu; internet www.kormany.hu/hu/belugyminiszterium.

Ministry of Justice: 1055 Budapest, Kossuth Lajos tér 4; tel. (1) 795-1000; fax (1) 795-0002; e-mail lakossag@kim.gov.hu; internet www.kormany.hu/hu/igazsagugyi-miniszterium.

Ministry of National Development: 1011 Budapest, Fő u. 44–50; tel. (1) 795-1700; fax (1) 795-0697; e-mail ugyfelszolgalat@nfm.gov.hu; internet www.kormany.hu/hu/nemzeti-fejlesztesi-miniszterium.

Ministry of the National Economy: 1051 Budapest, József Nádor tér 2–4; tel. (1) 374-2700; fax (1) 374-2925; e-mail ugyfelszolgalat@ngm.gov.hu; internet www.kormany.hu/hu/nemzetgazdasagi-miniszterium.

President

In an election conducted in the National Assembly (which at that time comprised 386 deputies) on 2 May 2012 János Áder, the sole candidate, was duly elected as President, receiving the support of 262 deputies; 40 deputies opposed his nomination, five invalid votes were cast, and 79 deputies did not vote.

Legislature

National Assembly
(Országgyülés)

1055 Budapest, Kossuth tér 1–3; 1357 Budapest, POB 2; tel. (1) 441-4000; fax (1) 441-5000; internet www.parlament.hu.

President: László Kövér.

General Election, 6 April 2014

Parties and coalitions	Seats		
	A*	B*	Total
Fidesz—KDNP coalition	96	37	133
Összefogás†	10	28	38
Jobbik	—	23	23
LMP	—	5	5
Total	106	93	199

* The 199 seats comprise 106 (A) elected in single-member constituencies and 93 (B) elected on the basis of national lists.
† A coalition of the MSzP, Együtt 2014, the DK, the PM and the MLP.

Election Commission

Országos Választási Iroda (OVI) (National Election Office): 1357 Budapest, POB 2; tel. (1) 795-3303; fax (1) 795-0143; e-mail visz@otm.gov.hu; internet www.valasztas.hu; Chair. András Patyi.

Political Organizations

Demokratikus Koalíció (DK) (Democratic Coalition): 1081 Budapest, Népszínház u. 42–44; tel. (1) 300-1000; e-mail ugyfelszolgalat@dk365.hu; internet www.demokratikuskoalicio.hu; f. 2011 by fmr mems of Magyar Szocialista Párt (q.v.); social democratic; contested 2014 legislative elections as mem. of Összefogás (Unity) coalition; Chair. Ferenc Gyurcsány.

Együtt 2014 (Together 2014): 1122 Budapest, Városmajor utca 48/b; tel. (1) 919-1414; e-mail info@hazaeshaladas.org; internet www.egyutt2014.hu; f. 2013; alliance of three civil society organizations; contested 2014 legislative elections as mem. of Összefogás (Unity) coalition; Pres. Viktor Szigetvári.

Fidesz—Magyar Polgári Szöevetség (Fidesz) (Federation of Young Democrats—Hungarian Civic Alliance): 1062 Budapest, Lendvay u. 28; tel. (1) 555-2000; fax (1) 441-5463; e-mail fidesz@fidesz.hu; internet www.fidesz.hu; f. 1988 as Fiatal Demokraták Szövetsége (Federation of Young Democrats); renamed April 1995; re-formed as an alliance in 2003; Chair. Viktor Orbán; 10,000 mems.

Jobbik Magyarországért Mozgalom (Jobbik) (Jobbik—Movement for a Better Hungary): 1113 Budapest, Villányi ú. 20A; tel. and fax (1) 365-1488; e-mail jobbik@jobbik.hu; internet www.jobbik.hu; f. 2003; extreme nationalist; Pres. Gábor Vona.

Jólét és Szabadság Demokrata Közösség (JESz) (Democratic Community of Welfare and Freedom): 1026 Budapest, Szilágyi Erszébet fasor 73; tel. (1) 225-2280; fax (1) 225-2290; e-mail kis.jozsef@jesz.hu; internet www.jesz.hu; f. 1987; fmrly Magyar Demokrata Fórum (Hungarian Democratic Forum); present name adopted 2011; centre-right; Chair. Zsolt Makay.

Kereszténydemokrata Néppárt (KDNP) (Christian Democratic People's Party): 1141 Budapest, Bazsarózsa u. 69; tel. (1) 489-0880; fax (1) 489-0879; e-mail kdnp@kdnp.hu; internet www.kdnp.hu; f. 1989 as revival of pre-communist-era party; formed an electoral alliance with Fidesz—Magyar Polgári Szöevetség (q.v.) to contest the 2010 and 2014 legislative elections; Chair. Zsolt Semjén.

Lehet Más a Politika! (LMP) (Politics Can Be Different!): 1136 Budapest, Hegedus Gyula u. 36; 1386 Budapest, POB 959; tel. and fax (30) 962-6868; e-mail info@lehetmas.hu; internet www.lehetmas.hu; f. 2009; environmentalist; Sec. Attila Vida.

Magyar Liberális Párt (MLP) (Hungarian Liberal Party): 1051 Budapest, Sas u. 10-12; tel. (1) 784-3680; e-mail liberalisok@liberalisok.hu; internet liberalisok.hu; f. 2013; contested 2014 legislative elections as mem. of Összefogás (Unity) coalition; Chair. Gábor Fodor.

Magyarországi Szociáldemokrata Párt (MSzDP) (Hungarian Social Democratic Party): 1535 Budapest; tel. (1) 214-9496; fax (1) 214-9497; e-mail mszdp@mszdp.hu; internet www.mszdp.hu; f. 1988 as revival of party originally founded in 1890; Chair. László Andráska.

Magyar Szocialista Párt (MSzP) (Hungarian Socialist Party): 1066 Budapest, Jókai u. 6; tel. (1) 459-7200; e-mail info@mszp.hu; internet www.mszp.hu; f. 1989 to replace Magyar Szocialista Munkáspárt (Hungarian Socialist Workers' Party); contested 2014 legislative elections as mem. of Összefogás (Unity) coalition; Pres. József Tóbiás.

Párbeszéd Magyarországért (PM) (Dialogue For Hungary): Budapest; tel. (1) 441-5260; e-mail info@parbeszedmagyar orszagert.hu; internet parbeszedmagyarorszagert.hu; f. 2013 by fmr members of LMP; environmentalist; contested 2014 legislative elections as mem. of Összefogás (Unity) coalition; Leader BENEDEK JÁVOR.

Diplomatic Representation

EMBASSIES IN HUNGARY

Albania: 1062 Budapest, Andrássy u. 132; tel. and fax (1) 336-1098; fax 336-1098; e-mail embassy.budapest@mfa.gov.al; internet www.ambasadat.gov.al/hungary; Ambassador MIRA HOXHA.

Algeria: 1121 Budapest, Zugligeti u. 27; tel. (1) 392-0510; fax (1) 200-6781; e-mail ambalbud@t-online.hu; internet www.algerianembassy.hu; Ambassador LOUNÈS MAGRAMANE.

Angola: 1124 Budapest, Sirály u. 3; tel. (1) 487-7680; fax (1) 487-7699; e-mail embanhun@angolaembassy.hu; internet www.angolaembassy.hu; Ambassador LIZETH SATUMBO PENA.

Argentina: 1023 Budapest, Vérhalom u. 12–16; tel. (1) 325-0492; fax (1) 326-0494; e-mail eungr@mrecic.gov.ar; Ambassador CLAUDIO ALBERTO GIACOMINO.

Austria: 1068 Budapest, Benczúr u. 16; tel. (1) 479-7010; fax (1) 352-8795; e-mail budapest-ob@bmeia.gv.at; internet www.aussenministerium.at/budapest; Ambassador RALPH SCHEIDE.

Azerbaijan: 1067 Budapest, Eötvös u. 14; tel. (1) 374-6070; fax (1) 302-3535; e-mail budapest@azembassy.hu; internet www.azembassy.hu; Ambassador VILAYAT GULIYEV.

Belarus: 1126 Budapest, Agárdi u. 3B; tel. (1) 214-0553; fax (1) 214-0554; e-mail hungary@mfa.gov.by; internet www.hungary.mfa.gov.by; Ambassador ALYAKSANDR KHAINOVSKY.

Belgium: 1015 Budapest, Toldy Ferenc u. 13; tel. (1) 457-9960; fax (1) 375-1566; e-mail budapest@diplobel.fed.be; internet www.diplomatie.belgium.be/hungary; Ambassador JOHAN INDEKEU.

Bosnia and Herzegovina: 1026 Budapest, Verseghy Ferenc u. 4; tel. (1) 212-0106; fax (1) 212-0109; e-mail bihambud@yahoo.com; Ambassador NIKOLA ĐUKIĆ.

Brazil: 1054 Budapest, Szabadság tér 7; tel. (1) 351-0060; fax (1) 202-0740; e-mail brasemb.budapest@itamaraty.gov.br; internet budapeste.itamaraty.gov.br; Ambassador VALTER PECLY MOREIRA.

Bulgaria: 1062 Budapest, Andrássy u. 115; tel. (1) 322-0824; fax (1) 322-5215; e-mail embassy.budapest@mfa.bg; internet www.mfa.bg/embassies/hungary; Ambassador BISERKA BENISHEVA.

Canada: 1027 Budapest, Ganz u. 12–14; tel. (1) 392-3360; fax (1) 392-3390; e-mail bpest@international.gc.ca; internet www.canadainternational.gc.ca/hungary-hongrie; Ambassador LISA HELFAND.

Central African Republic: 1056 Budapest, Molnár u. 19; tel. (1) 484-7590; fax (1) 421-8558; e-mail ambassaderca@yahoo.fr; Ambassador BERNARD LECLERC.

Chile: 1024 Budapest, Rózsahegy u. 1B; tel. (1) 326-3054; fax (1) 326-3056; e-mail embajada@embachile.hu; internet chileabroad.gov.cl/hungria; Ambassador RODRIGO NIETO MATURANA.

China, People's Republic: 1068 Budapest, Városligeti fasor 20–22; tel. (1) 413-2400; fax (1) 413-2451; e-mail chinaemb_hu@mfa.gov.cn; internet hu.chineseembassy.org; Ambassador XIAO QIAN.

Croatia: 1063 Budapest, Munkácsy Mihály u. 15; tel. (1) 354-1315; fax (1) 354-1319; e-mail croemb.bp@mvep.hr; internet hu.mvp.hr; Ambassador GORDAN GRLIĆ RADMAN.

Cuba: 1121 Budapest, Normafa u. 55A; tel. (1) 325-7290; fax (1) 325-7586; e-mail recepcion@embacuba.hu; internet www.cubadiplomatica.cu; Ambassador JULIO CÉSAR CANCIO FERRER.

Cyprus: 1051 Budapest, Dorottya u. 3; tel. (1) 266-1330; fax (1) 266-0538; e-mail cypembhu@axelero.hu; internet www.mfa.gov.cy/mfa/embassies/embassy_budapest.nsf; Ambassador ANTONIOS THEOCHAROUS.

Czech Republic: 1064 Budapest, Rózsa u. 61; tel. (1) 462-5011; fax (1) 351-9189; e-mail budapest@embassy.mzv.cz; internet www.mzv.cz/budapest; Ambassador JURAJ CHMIEL.

Denmark: 1122 Budapest, Határőr u. 37; tel. (1) 487-9000; fax (1) 487-9045; e-mail budamb@um.dk; internet ungarn.um.dk; Ambassador TOM NØRRING.

Ecuador: 1061 Budapest, Andrássy u. 20 1/2; tel. (1) 315-2124; fax (1) 315-2104; e-mail embajada@ecuador.hu; Ambassador JAIME AUGUSTO BARBERIS MARTINEZ.

Egypt: 1124 Budapest, Istenhegyi u. 7B; tel. (1) 225-2150; fax (1) 225-8596; e-mail egyptembassybudapest@yahoo.com; Ambassador ASSEM MAHMOUD EL-MAGHRABY.

Finland: 1118 Budapest, Kelenhegyi u. 16A; tel. (1) 279-2500; fax (1) 385-0843; e-mail sanomat.bud@formin.fi; internet www.finland.hu; Ambassador PASI TUOMINEN.

France: 1062 Budapest, Lendvay u. 27; tel. (1) 374-1100; fax (1) 374-1140; e-mail consulat.budapest-amba@diplomatie.gouv.fr; internet www.ambafrance-hu.org; Ambassador ROLAND GALHARAGUE.

Georgia: 1125 Budapest, Virányos u. 6B; tel. (1) 202-3390; fax (1) 214-3299; e-mail budapest.emb@mfa.gov.ge; internet www.hungary.mfa.gov.ge; Ambassador ZAZA KANDELAKI.

Germany: 1014 Budapest, Úri u. 64–66; tel. (1) 488-3500; fax (1) 488-3505; e-mail info@budapest.diplo.de; internet www.budapest.diplo.de; Ambassador LIESELORE CYRUS.

Greece: 1063 Budapest, Szegfű u. 3; tel. (1) 413-2600; fax (1) 342-1934; e-mail gremb.bud@mfa.gr; internet www.greekembassy.hu; Ambassador SPYRIDON N. GEORGILES.

Holy See: 1126 Budapest, Gyimes u. 1–3; tel. (1) 355-8979; fax (1) 355-6987; e-mail nuntbud@communio.hcbc.hu; Apostolic Nuncio ALBERTO BOTTARI DE CASTELLO (Titular Archbishop of Opitergium).

India: 1025 Budapest, Búzavirág u. 14; tel. (1) 325-7742; fax (1) 325-7745; internet www.indianembassy.hu; Ambassador MALAY MISHRA.

Indonesia: 1068 Budapest, Városligeti fasor 26; tel. (1) 413-3800; fax (1) 322-8669; e-mail embassy@indonesianembassy.hu; internet www.indonesia.hu; Ambassador WENING ESTHYPROBO.

Iran: 1143 Budapest, Stefánia u. 97; tel. (1) 460-9260; fax (1) 460-9430; e-mail embiran@nextra.hu; internet www.iran-embassy.hu; Ambassador Dr REZA MORSHEDZADEH.

Iraq: 121 Budapest, Bölöni György u. 3; tel. (1) 392-5120; fax (1) 392-5133; e-mail budemb@iraqmofamail.net; Ambassador JASIM M. HUSAIN.

Ireland: 1054 Budapest, Szabadság tér, Bank Center; tel. (1) 301-4960; fax (1) 302-9599; e-mail budapestembassy@dfa.ie; internet www.embassyofireland.hu; Ambassador KEVIN DOWLING.

Israel: 1026 Budapest, Fullánk u. 8; tel. (1) 392-6200; fax (1) 200-0783; e-mail info@budapest.mfa.gov.il; internet embassies.gov.il/budapest; Ambassador ILAN MOR.

Italy: 1143 Budapest, Stefánia u. 95; tel. (1) 460-6200; fax (1) 460-6260; e-mail ambasciata.budapest@esteri.it; internet www.ambbudapest.esteri.it; Ambassador MARIA ASSUNTA ACCILI.

Japan: 1125 Budapest, Zalai u. 7; tel. (1) 398-3100; fax (1) 275-1281; e-mail administration@japanembassy.hu; internet www.hu.emb-japan.go.jp; Ambassador JUNICHI KOSUGE.

Kazakhstan: 1025 Budapest, Kapy u. 59; tel. (1) 275-1300; fax (1) 275-2092; e-mail kazak@t-online.hu; internet www.kazembassy.hu; Ambassador NURBAKH RUSTEMOV.

Korea, Republic: 1062 Budapest, Andrássy u. 109; tel. (1) 462-3080; fax (1) 351-1182; e-mail korcom@t-online.hu; internet hun.mofat.go.kr; Ambassador YIM GEUN HYEONG.

Kosovo: 1054 Budapest, Szabadság tér 7; tel. (1) 688-7872; fax (1) 688-7875; e-mail embassy.hungary@ks-gov.net; internet www.ambasada-ks.net/hu; Ambassador SAMI UKELLI.

Kuwait: 1122 Budapest, Székács u. 16; tel. (1) 202-3335; fax (1) 202-3387; e-mail kuwait.emb@kuwaitembassy.hu; Ambassador Dr HAMAD BURHAMA.

Latvia: 1124 Budapest, Vas Gereben u. 20; tel. (1) 310-7262; fax (1) 249-2901; e-mail embassy.hungary@mfa.gov.lv; Ambassador IMANTS VIESTURS LIEĢIS.

Lebanon: 1112 Budapest, Sasadi u. 160; tel. (1) 249-0900; fax (1) 249-0901; e-mail amblib@t-online.hu; Ambassador NOEL FATTAL.

Libya: 1143 Budapest, Stefánia u. 111; tel. (1) 364-9332; fax (1) 364-9330; e-mail libiaemb@tripoli.axelero.net; Ambassador ABDURHMAN BEN OMRAN.

Lithuania: 1052 Budapest, Deák Ferenc u. 15; tel. (1) 224-7910; fax (1) 202-3995; e-mail amb.hu@urm.lt; internet hu.mfa.lt; Ambassador RASA KAIRIENÉ.

Macedonia, former Yugoslav republic: 1062 Budapest, Andrássy u. 130, 1/1-2; tel. (1) 336-0510; fax (1) 315-1921; e-mail budapest@mfa.gov.mk; internet www.missions.gov.mk/budapest; Ambassador IGOR ESMEROV.

Malaysia: 1026 Budapest, Pasaréti u. 29; tel. (1) 488-0810; fax (1) 488-0824; e-mail malbdpest@kln.gov.my; internet www.kln.gov.my/perwakilan/budapest; Ambassador MOHAMAD SADIK KETHERGANY.

Mexico: 1024 Budapest, Rómer Flóris u. 58; tel. (1) 326-0447; fax (1) 326-0485; e-mail consulmex@t-online.hu; internet embamex.sre.gob.mx/hungria; Ambassador ISABEL BÁRBARA TÉLLEZ ROSETE.

Moldova: 1024 Budapest, Ady Endre u. 16; tel. (1) 336-3450; fax (1) 209-1195; e-mail budapesta@mfa.md; internet www.ungaria.mfa.md; Chargé d'affaires a.i. VLADIMIR RUSNAC.

Mongolia: 1022 Budapest II, Bogár u. 14C; tel. (1) 212-4579; fax (1) 212-5731; e-mail mongolemb@t-online.hu; Ambassador TÖGSJARGALYN GANDI.

Montenegro: 1051 Budapest, Arany János 15; tel. (1) 373-0300; fax (1) 269-4475; e-mail hungary@mfa.gov.me; Ambassador MIRSAD BIBOVIĆ.

Morocco: 1026 Budapest, Sodrás u. 11; tel. (1) 391-4310; fax (1) 275-1437; e-mail sifamabudap@t-online.hu; Ambassador NOUREDDINE BENOMAR.

Netherlands: 1022 Budapest, Füge u. 5–7; tel. (1) 336-6300; fax (1) 326-5978; e-mail bdp@minbuza.nl; internet hungary.nlembassy.org; Ambassador GAJUS SCHELTEMA.

Nigeria: 1023 Budapest, Rómer Flóris u. 57; tel. (1) 212-2021; fax (1) 212-2025; e-mail embassy@nigerianembassy.hu; internet www.nigerianembassy.hu; Ambassador EDDY ONUOHA.

Norway: 1015 Budapest, Ostrom u. 13; tel. (1) 325-3300; fax (1) 325-3399; e-mail emb.budapest@mfa.no; internet www.norvegia.hu; Ambassador TOVE SKARSTEIN.

Pakistan: 1125 Budapest, Adonis u. 3A; tel. (1) 355-8017; fax (1) 375-1402; e-mail parepbudapest@yahoo.com; internet www.mofa.gov.pk/hungary; Ambassador IFTEKHAR AZIZ.

Philippines: 1026 Budapest, Gábor Áron u. 58; tel. (1) 391-4300; fax (1) 200-5528; e-mail phbuda@philembassy.hu; internet www.philippineembassy.hu; Ambassador ELEANOR L. JAUCIAN.

Poland: 1068 Budapest, Városligeti fasor 16; tel. (1) 413-8200; fax (1) 351-1722; e-mail budapeszt.amb.sekretariat@msz.gov.pl; internet budapeszt.msz.gov.pl; Ambassador ROMAN KOWALSKI.

Portugal: 1123 Budapest, Alkotás u. 53, MOM Park Bldg C, 4th Floor; tel. (1) 201-7617; fax (1) 201-7619; e-mail embport@t-online.hu; Ambassador ANTÓNIO AUGUSTO JORGE MENDES.

Qatar: 1025 Budapest, Cseppkő u. 27B; tel. (1) 392-1010; fax (1) 392-1020; e-mail budapest@mofa.gov.qa; internet www.qatarembassy.hu; Ambassador ABDULLAH HUSSAIN AL-JABER.

Romania: 1146 Budapest, Thököly u. 72; tel. (1) 384-8394; fax (1) 384-5535; e-mail budapesta@mae.ro; internet budapest.mae.ro; Ambassador ALEXANDRU VICTOR MICULA.

Russian Federation: 1062 Budapest, Bajza u. 35; tel. (1) 302-5230; fax (1) 353-4164; e-mail rusemb@t-online.hu; internet www.hungary.mid.ru; Ambassador VLADIMIR N. SERGEYEV.

Saudi Arabia: 1016 Budapest, Bérc u. 16; tel. (1) 436-9500; fax (1) 453-3554; e-mail huemb@mofa.gov.sa; internet www.saudiembassy.org.hu; Ambassador ABDULHADI M. AL-MATRAFI.

Serbia: 1068 Budapest, Dózsa György u. 92 B; tel. (1) 322-9838; fax (1) 322-1438; e-mail budapest@amb.srbije.net; internet budapest.mfa.gov.rs; Ambassador RADE DROBAC.

Slovakia: 1143 Budapest, Stefánia u. 22–24; tel. (1) 460-9010; fax (1) 460-9020; e-mail emb.budapest@mzv.sk; internet www.mzv.sk/budapest; Ambassador RASTISLAV KÁČER.

Slovenia: 1025 Budapest, Cseppkő u. 68; tel. (1) 438-5600; fax (1) 325-9187; e-mail vbp@goy.si; internet budimpesta.veleposlanistvo.si; Ambassador KSENIJA ŠKRILEC.

South Africa: 1026 Budapest, Gárdonyi Géza u. 17; tel. (1) 392-0999; fax (1) 200-7277; e-mail budapest.admin@dirco.gov.za; Ambassador J. MARX.

Spain: 1067 Budapest, Eötvös u. 11B; tel. (1) 202-4006; fax (1) 202-4206; e-mail emb.budapest@maec.es; internet www.exteriores.gob.es/embajadas/budapest; Ambassador JOSÉ ÁNGEL LÓPEZ JORRIN.

Sweden: 1027 Budapest, Kapás u. 6–12; tel. (1) 460-6020; fax (1) 460-6021; e-mail ambassaden.budapest@gov.se; internet www.swedenabroad.com/budapest; Ambassador NICLAS TROUVÉ.

Switzerland: 1143 Budapest, Stefánia u. 107; tel. (1) 460-7040; fax (1) 384-9492; e-mail bud.vertretung@eda.admin.ch; internet www.swissembassy.hu; Ambassador JEAN-FRANÇOIS PAROZ.

Thailand: 1025 Budapest, Verecke u. 79; tel. (1) 438-4020; fax (1) 438-4023; e-mail info@thaiembassy.hu; internet www.thaiembassy.org/budapest; Chargé d'affaires a.i. ORACHA TANAKORN.

Tunisia: 11126 Budapest, Nárcisz u. 36; tel. (1) 336-1616; fax (1) 325-7291; e-mail at.budapest@t-online.hu; Ambassador ABDERRAOUF BETBAIEB.

Turkey: 1062 Budapest, Andrássy u. 123; tel. (1) 478-9100; fax (1) 344-5143; e-mail embassy.budapest@mfa.gov.tr; internet budapest.emb.mfa.gov.tr; Ambassador ŞAKIR FAKILI.

Ukraine: 1125 Budapest, Istenhegyi u. 84B; tel. (1) 422-4120; fax (1) 220-9873; e-mail emb_hu@mfa.gov.ua; internet hungary.mfa.gov.ua; Chargé d'affaires a.i. MYKHAILO YUNHER.

United Kingdom: 1051 Budapest, Harmincad u. 6; tel. (1) 266-2888; fax (1) 266-0907; e-mail info@britemb.hu; internet ukinhungary.fco.gov.uk; Ambassador JONATHAN KNOTT.

USA: 1054 Budapest, Szabadság tér 12; tel. (1) 475-4400; fax (1) 475-4764; e-mail publicaffairsbudapest@state.gov; internet hungary.usembassy.gov; Ambassador COLLEEN BELL.

Venezuela: 1063 Budapest, Szegfű u. 6; tel. (1) 326-0460; fax (1) 326-0450; e-mail embavenezhu@t-online.hu; Ambassador RAÚL JOSÉ BETANCOURT SEELAND.

Viet Nam: 1146 Budapest, Thököly u. 41; tel. (1) 342-5583; fax (1) 352-8798; e-mail vp-budapest@mofa.gov.vn; internet www.vietnamembassy-hungary.org; Ambassador NGUYEN THANH TUAN.

Yemen: 1026 Budapest, Bimbó út 179/a; tel. (1) 212-3991; fax (1) 212-3883; e-mail yemen22may@t-online.hu; Chargé d'affaires HAMMAD DAHAN.

Judicial System

The system of court procedure in Hungary is based on an act that came into effect in 1953, as subsequently revised. Notably, since 2013, all rulings of the Constitutional Court taken prior before the introduction of the 2012 Constitution have been deemed to be of no legal effect.

The system of jurisdiction is based on local courts, labour courts, county courts (or the Metropolitan Court) and the Kúria. In the legal remedy system of two instances, appeals against the decisions of city and district courts can be lodged with the competent county court and the Metropolitan Court of Budapest, respectively. Against the judgment of first instance of the latter, appeal is to be lodged with the Kúria.

The President of the Kúria, the supreme judicial body, is elected from among its members by the National Assembly for a period of nine years. Judges are appointed by the President of Hungary for an indefinite period, but may not serve beyond the legal age of retirement. Assessors are elected by the local municipal councils. The Supreme Prosecutor is elected by the National Assembly upon the recommendation of the President of Hungary.

Kúria: 1055 Budapest, Markó u. 16; tel. (1) 268-4749; fax (1) 268-4748; e-mail kuria@kuria.birosag.hu; internet www.kuria-birosag.hu; Pres. Dr PÉTER DARÁK.

Supreme Prosecutor: Dr PÉTER POLT.

Constitutional Court (Alkotmánybíróság): 1015 Budapest, Donáti u. 35–45; tel. (1) 488-3100; fax (1) 212-1170; internet www.mkab.hu; Pres. BARNABÁS LENKOVICS.

Religion

CHRISTIANITY

The Roman Catholic Church

Hungary comprises five archdioceses (including one for Catholics of the Byzantine Rite), nine dioceses (including one for Catholics of the Byzantine Rite), one apostolic exarchate of the Byzantine Rite and one territorial abbacy (directly responsible to the Holy See).

Bishops' Conference: 1071 Budapest, Városligeti fasor 45, POB 79; tel. (1) 342-6959; fax (1) 342-6957; e-mail pkt@katolikus.hu; internet www.katolikus.hu; Pres. Cardinal PÉTER ERDŐ (Archbishop of Esztergom-Budapest).

Archbishop of Eger: Most Rev. CSABA TERNYÁK, 3301 Eger, Széchenyi u. 1; tel. (36) 517-589; fax (36) 517-751.

Archbishop of Esztergom-Budapest: Cardinal PÉTER ERDŐ, 1014 Budapest, Úri u. 62; tel. (33) 225-2590; fax (33) 202-5458; e-mail egombp@katolikus.hu.

Archbishop of Hajdúdorog (Byzantine Rite): PÉTER FÜLÖP KOCSIS, 4400 Nyíregyháza, Bethlen Gábor u. 5; tel. (42) 415-901; fax (42) 415-911; internet www.gorogkatolikus.hu.

Archbishop of Kalocsa-Kecskemét: Most Rev. BALÁZS BÁBEL, 6301 Kalocsa, Szentháromság tér 1; tel. (78) 462-166; fax (78) 465-279; e-mail hivatal@asztrik.hu.

Archbishop of Veszprém: Most Rev. GYULA MÁRFI, 8201 Veszprém, Vár u. 19; tel. (88) 462-088; fax (88) 466-287; e-mail ersekseg@ersekseg.veszprem.hu.

Protestant Churches

Evangelical Lutheran Church in Hungary (Magyarországi Evangélikus Egyház): 1085 Budapest, Üllöi u. 24; tel. (1) 483-2260; fax (1) 486-3554; e-mail szerkesztoseg@lutheran.hu; internet www.lutheran.hu; Presiding Bishop PÉTER GÁNCS; 213,125 mems (2010).

Reformed Church in Hungary—Presbyterian (Magyarországi Református Egyház): 1146 Budapest, Abonyi u. 21; tel. (1) 343-7870; e-mail info@reformatus.hu; internet www.reformatus.hu; Pres. of Gen. Synod Bishop Dr GUSZTÁV BÖLCSKEI.

The Eastern Orthodox Church

The Bulgarian, Romanian, Russian and Serbian Orthodox Churches are all represented in Hungary.

ISLAM

There are about 3,000 Muslims in Hungary.

Hungarian Islamic Community (Magyar Iszlám Közösség): 1135 Budapest, Róbert Karoly krt. 104; tel. (30) 272-9865; internet www.magyariszlam.hu; Pres. ZOLTÁN BOLEK.

JUDAISM

The Jewish community in Hungary is estimated to number around 120,000 people. Some 80% of Hungary's Jewish community resides in Budapest.

Federation of Jewish Communities in Hungary (Magyarországi Zsidó Hitközségek Szövetsége): 1075 Budapest, Síp u. 12; tel. and fax (1) 413-5504; internet mazsihisz.hu; 120,000 mems; 40 active synagogues; Orthodox and Conservative; Exec. Dir GUSZTAV ZOLTAI; Chief Rabbi of Hungary ROBERT DEUTSCH.

The Press

Budapest dailies circulate nationally. The most popular are: *Népszabadság*, *Nemzeti Sport* and *Népszava*. *Népszabadság*, the most influential daily, was formerly the central organ of the Hungarian Socialist Workers' Party, but is now independent.

PRINCIPAL DAILIES

24 Óra (24 Hours): 2800 Tatabánya, Fő tér 4; tel. (34) 514-010; fax (34) 514-011; e-mail kemma@kemma.hu; internet www.24ora.hu; Editor-in-Chief ZOLTÁN TAKÁCS; circ. 17,023 (2010).

Békés Megyei Hírlap (Békés County News): 5600 Békéscsaba, Kiss Ernő u. 3; tel. (66) 527-200; fax (66) 527-231; e-mail beol@beol.hu; internet www.bmhirlap.hu; f. 1945; Editor-in-Chief JÁNOS NÁNÁSI; circ. 23,279 (2010).

Blikk: 1082 Budapest, Futó u. 35–37; tel. (1) 460-2400, fax (1) 460-2501; e-mail online@blikk.hu; internet www.blikk.hu; f. 1994; colour tabloid; Editor-in-Chief GERGELY KOMÁROMI; circ. 192,182 (2010).

Délmagyarország (Southern Hungary): 6740 Szeged, Szabadkai 20; tel. (62) 567-800; fax (62) 567-881; e-mail szerkesztoseg@delmagyar.hu; internet www.delmagyar.hu; Editor-in-Chief GÁBOR TÓTH; circ. 27,199 (2010).

Észak-Magyarország (Northern Hungary): 3526 Miskolc, Zsolcai kapu 3; tel. (46) 502-900; fax (46) 501-262; e-mail info@eszak.hu; internet www.eszak.hu; Editor-in-Chief LÁSZLÓ KISS; circ. 44,615 (2010).

Fejér Megyei Hírlap (Fejér County Journal): 8000 Székesfehérvár, Ady Endre u. 15; tel. (22) 542-703; fax (22) 542-719; e-mail szerk@fmh.plt.hu; internet www.fmh.hu; Editor-in-Chief ELEKES ANDRÁS; circ. 37,053 (2010).

Hajdú-Bihari Napló (Hajdú-Bihar Diary): 4031 Debrecen, Balmazújvárosi u. 11; tel. (40) 424-424; e-mail info@naplo.hu; internet www.naplo.hu; f. 1944; Editor-in-Chief LÁSZLÓ KISS; circ. 60,000.

Heves Megyei Hírlap (Heves County Journal): 3301 Eger, Trinitárius u. 1; tel. (36) 513-600; e-mail heol@heol.hu; internet www.hevesmegyeihirlap.hu; Editor-in-Chief ISTVÁN STANGA; circ. 15,276 (2010).

Kisalföld: 9021 Győr, Újlak u. 4A; tel. (96) 504-555; fax (96) 504-414; e-mail szerkesztoseg@kisalfold.hu; internet www.kisalfold.hu; Editor-in-Chief CSABA NYERGES; circ. 70,257 (2010).

Magyar Hírlap (Hungarian Journal): 1145 Budapest, Thököly u. 105–107; tel. (1) 887-3230; fax (1) 887-3253; e-mail levelezes@magyarhirlap.hu; internet www.magyarhirlap.hu; f. 1968; Editor-in-Chief ISTVÁN STEFKA; circ. 13,858 (2010).

Magyar Nemzet (Hungarian Nation): 1089 Budapest; tel. (1) 476-2131; fax (1) 215-3197; e-mail szerk@mno.hu; internet www.mno.hu; Editor-in-Chief GÁBOR ÉLŐ; circ. 48,877 (2010).

Metropol: 1134 Budapest, Tüzér u. 39-41; tel. (1) 431-6401; fax (1) 431-6401; e-mail g.izbeki@metropol.hu; internet www.metropol.hu; fmrly *Metro*, current name adopted in Aug. 2008; five issues a week; distributed free of charge; Editor-in-Chief GÁBOR IZDÉKI; circ. 274,105 (2010).

Napló (Diary): 8200 Veszprém, Almádi u. 3; 8201 Veszprém, POB 161; tel. (20) 241-1655; fax (88) 579-432; e-mail bartak.peter@naplo.plt.hu; internet veol.hu; Editor-in-Chief PÉTER BARTÁK; circ. 40,744 (2010).

Nemzeti Sport (National Sport): 1082 Budapest, Futó u. 35-37; tel. (1) 460-2600; fax (1) 460-2601; e-mail szerkesztoseg@nemzetisport.hu; internet www.nemzetisport.hu; Editor-in-Chief JÓZSEF BUZGÓ; circ. 69,607 (2010).

Népszabadság (People's Freedom): 1591 Budapest; tel. (1) 460-2740; fax (1) 436-4619; e-mail szerkesztoseg@nepszabadsag.hu; internet www.nol.hu; f. 1942; independent; Editor LEVENTE TÓTH (acting); circ. 72,502 (2010).

Népszava (Voice of the People): 1146 Budapest, Thököly u. 127; tel. (1) 688-7030; fax (1) 477-9033; e-mail online@nepszava.hu; internet www.nepszava.hu; f. 1873; Editor PÉTER NÉMETH; circ. 19,099 (2010).

Petőfi Népe: 1122 Budapest, Városmajor u. 11; tel. (76) 518-200; e-mail baon@baon.hu; internet www.petofinepe.hu; Editor-in-Chief ERNŐ KIRÁLY; circ. 27,938 (2010).

Somogyi Hírlap (Somogy Journal): 7400 Kaposvár, Kontrássy u. 2A; tel. (82) 528-104; fax (82) 528-155; e-mail sonline@sonline.hu; internet www.somogyihirlap.hu; Editor ATTILA CZENE; circ. 25,478 (2010).

Tolnai Népújság (Tolna News): 7100 Szekszárd, Liszt Ferenc tér 3; tel. (74) 511-510; fax (74) 511-500; e-mail teol@teol.hu; internet www.tolnainepujsag.hu; Editor-in-Chief FERENC NIMMERFROH; circ. 16,601 (2010).

Új Dunántúli Napló: 1122 Budapest, Városmajor u. 11; tel. (72) 505-060; fax (72) 505-034; e-mail hirportal_fejlesztes@axelspringer.hu; internet www.dunantulinaplo.hu; f. 1948; Editor FERENC NIMMERFROH; circ. 34,677.

Új Néplap (New People's Paper): 5000 Szolnok, Mészáros Lőrinc út 2; tel. (56) 516-753; e-mail szoljon@szoljon.hu; internet www.ujneplap.hu; Editor-in-Chief ATTILA MOLNÁR; circ. 22,338 (2010).

Vas Népe (Vas People): 9700 Szombathely, Moszkva tér 40; tel. (94) 528-309; fax (94) 522-596; e-mail vasnepe@vn.plt.hu; internet www.vasnepe.hu; Editor-in-Chief MIKLÓS HALMÁGYI; circ. 48,672 (2010).

Zalai Hírlap (Zala Journal): 8901 Zalaegerszeg, Ady Endre u. 62; tel. (92) 502-231; fax (92) 502-240; e-mail zalaihirlap@zh.plt.hu; internet www.zalaihirlap.hu; Editor-in-Chief ZSOLT VIRRASZTÓ; circ. 47,979 (2010).

WEEKLIES

The Budapest Times/Budapester Zeitung: 1037 Budapest, Kunigunda útja 18; tel. (1) 453-0752, fax (1) 240 7583; e-mail erlag@bzt.hu; internet www.budapesttimes.hu; internet www.budapester.hu; f. 1999 (*Budapester Zeitung*); f. 2003 (*The Budapest Times*); English and German edns; Editors ALLAN BOYKO (*The Budapest Times*), JAN MAINKA (*Budapester Zeitung*).

Élet és Irodalom (Life and Literature): 1089 Budapest, Rezso tér 15; tel. (1) 303-9211; fax (1) 303-9241; e-mail es@es.hu; internet www.es.hu; f. 1957; literary and political; Editor ZOLTÁN KOVÁCS; circ. 22,000.

Élet és Tudomány (Life and Science): 1088 Budapest, Bródy u. 16; tel. (1) 327-8950; fax (1) 327-8969; e-mail eltud@eletestudomany.hu; internet www.eletestudomany.hu; f. 1946; popular science; Editor-in-Chief ÁKOS GÓZON; circ. 20,000.

Evangélikus Élet (Evangelical Life): 1085 Budapest, Üllői u. 24; tel. (1) 317-1108; fax (1) 486-1195; e-mail evelet@lutheran.hu; internet www.evangelikuselet.hu; f. 1933; Evangelical Lutheran Church newspaper; Editor KÁROLY T. PINTÉR; circ. 4,000 (2012).

Figyelő (Observer): 1053 Budapest, Kecskeméti u. 5; tel. (1) 437-3957; fax (1) 437-1420; e-mail online@figyelo.hu; internet www.figyelo.hu; f. 1957; Thursdays; business; Editor-in-Chief GÁBOR LAMBERT; circ. 15,932 (2010).

Heti Világgazdaság (World Economy Weekly): 1037 Budapest, Montevideo u. 14; tel. (1) 436-2000; fax (1) 436-2045; e-mail hvg.hu@hvg.hu; internet www.hvg.hu; f. 1979; Editor GÁBOR GAVRA.

Ľudové Noviny (People's News): 1135 Budapest, Csata u. 17; tel. (1) 878-1431; fax (1) 878-1432; e-mail ludove@luno.hu; internet www.luno.hu; in Slovak; Editor IVETT HORVÁTHOVÁ.

Magyar Mezőgazdaság (Hungarian Agriculture): 1141 Budapest, Mírtusz u. 2; tel. (1) 470-0411; fax (1) 470-0410; e-mail kiado@magyarmezogazdasag.hu; internet www.magyarmezogazdasag.hu; f. 1946; Editors LÁSZLÓ BÁRDOS, DÁNIEL HAFNER; circ. 24,000.

Neue Zeitung (New Paper): 1062 Budapest, Lendvay u. 22; tel. and fax (1) 302-6877; e-mail neuezeitung@t-online.hu; internet www.neue-zeitung.hu; f. 1957; in German; Editor-in-Chief JOHANN SCHÜTH; circ. 2,000 (2014).

Reformátusok Lapja: 1113 Budapest, Tas vezér u. 13; tel. (1) 217-6809; fax (1) 217-8386; e-mail szerk@reflap.hu; internet www.reflap.hu; f. 1957; Reformed Church paper for the laity; Editor-in-Chief and Publr LÁSZLÓ T. NÉMETH.

RTV Részletes (Radio and TV News): 1801 Budapest; tel. (1) 328-7321; fax (1) 328-7691; e-mail terjesztes.kiadoi.kft@mtva.hu; internet www.rtvreszletes.hu; f. 1924; circ. 50,000 (2013).

Szabad Föld (Free Earth): 1036 Budapest, Lajos u. 48–66; tel. (1) 489-8800; e-mail info@szabadfold.hu; internet www.szabadfold.hu; f. 1945; Editor LÁSZLÓ HORVÁTH; circ. 720,000.

Új Ember (New Man): 1053 Budapest, Kossuth Lajos u. 1; tel. (1) 317-3933; fax (1) 317-3471; e-mail ujember@katolikus.hu; internet ujember.katolikus.hu; f. 1945; weekly; Roman Catholic; Editor TAMÁS PAPP; circ. 40,000.

OTHER PERIODICALS
(published monthly, unless otherwise indicated)

Beszélő (The Speaker): 1364 Budapest, POB 143; tel. (1) 756-4416; e-mail beszelo@enternet.hu; internet beszelo.c3.hu; f. 1981; political and cultural; Editor-in-Chief LÁSZLÓ NEMÉNYI.

Budapest Business Journal (BBJ): 1075 Budapest, Madách Imre u. 13-14; tel. (1) 398-0344; fax (1) 398-0345; e-mail recepcio@amedia.hu; internet www.bbj.hu; every two weeks; English; Editor-in-Chief TOM POPPER; circ. 10,000 (2014).

Ezermester 2000 (Handyman 2000): 1145 Budapest, Mexikói u. 35A; tel. (1) 222-6392; fax (1) 220-9065; e-mail ezermester@ezermester.hu; internet www.ezermester2000.hu; f. 1957; do-it-yourself magazine; Editor JÓZSEF PERÉNYI; circ. 50,000.

Gramofon—Klasszikus: 1023 Budapest, Fergeteg u. 11; tel. (1) 430-2870; fax (1) 436-0101; e-mail kovacs.veronika@gramofon.hu; internet www.gramofon.hu; f. 1996; classical, jazz and 'world' music; 4 a year; Editor-in-Chief TAMÁS VÁRKONYI; circ. 3,000 (2009).

Közgazdasági Szemle (Economic Review): 1112 Budapest, Budaörsi u. 45; tel. (1) 319-3165; fax (1) 319-3166; e-mail kszemle@econ.core.hu; internet www.kszemle.hu; f. 1954; publ. by Cttee for Economic Sciences of Hungarian Academy of Sciences; Editor-in-Chief TAMÁS HALM; circ. 1,000.

Magyar Közlöny (Official Gazette): 1055 Budapest, Kossuth Lajos tér 4; tel. (1) 112-1236; e-mail info.magyarkozlony@kim.gov.hu; internet kozlony.magyarorszag.hu; publ. by Office of the Prime Minister; Chief of Editorial Bd Dr ANDRÁS LEVENTE GÁL; circ. 90,000.

Magyar Tudomány (Hungarian Science): Hungarian Academy of Sciences, 1051 Budapest, Nádor u. 7; tel. and fax (1) 317-9524; e-mail matud@hefka.iif.hu; internet www.matud.iif.hu; f. 1846; multi-disciplinary science review; Chief Editor VILMOS CSÁNYI.

Új Élet (New Life): Magyarországi Zsidó Hitközségek Szövetsége, 1075 Budapest, Síp u. 12; tel. (1) 413-5564; fax 413-5504; f. 1945; every two weeks; Jewish interest; Editor Dr PÉTER KARDOS; circ. 5,000.

NEWS AGENCIES

HavariaPress News Agency: 1152 Budapest, Vécsey u. 15; tel. (1) 321-5538; e-mail havaria@havaria.hu; internet www.havariapress.hu; f. 1994; independent.

Hungarian News Agency Co (Magyar Távirati Iroda Rt—MTI): 1016 Budapest, Naphegy tér 8; tel. (1) 441-9000; fax (1) 318-8297; e-mail info@mti.hu; internet www.mti.hu; f. 1880; 20 brs in Hungary; 10 bureaux abroad; Chief Exec. ISTVÁN GALAMBOS.

Independent News Agency (Független Hírügynökség—FH): 1137 Budapest, Szent István Park 3; tel. (1) 382-0310; fax (1) 382-0309; e-mail info@fuggetlenhir.hu; f. 2004; Editor-in-Chief PÉTER KÖVESDI.

PRESS ASSOCIATIONS

Hungarian Newspaper Publishers' Association: 1016 Budapest, Naphegy tér 8; tel. (1) 368-8674; fax (1) 212-5025; e-mail mle@t-online.hu; internet www.mle.org.hu; f. 1990; Gen. Sec. KATALIN HAVAS; 47 mems.

National Association of Hungarian Journalists (Magyar Újságírók Országos Szövetsége—MÚOSZ): 1064 Budapest, Vörösmarty u. 47A; tel. (1) 478-9040; e-mail info@muosz.hu; internet www.muosz.hu; f. 1896; Pres. TÓTH KÁROLY; 7,000 mems.

Publishers
PRINCIPAL PUBLISHING HOUSES

Akadémiai Kiadó: 1117 Budapest, Prielle Kornélia u. 19/D; tel. (1) 464-8200; fax (1) 464-8201; e-mail ak@akkrt.hu; internet www.akkrt.hu; f. 1828; economics, humanities, social, political, natural and technical sciences, dictionaries, textbooks and journals; Hungarian and English; Dir BUCSI SZABÓ ZSOLT.

Corvina Kiadó: 1086 Budapest, Dankó u. 4–8; tel. (1) 411-2410; fax (1) 318-4410; e-mail corvina@lira.hu; internet www.corvinakiado.hu; f. 1955; art and educational books, general non-fiction, tourist guides and cookery books; Dir LÁSZLÓ KUNOS.

EMB Music Publisher: 1132 Budapest, Victor Hugo u. 11–15; tel. (1) 236-1100; fax (1) 236-1101; e-mail emb@emb.hu; internet www.emb.hu; f. 1950; sheet music and books on musical subjects; Dir ANTAL BORONKAY.

Európa Könyvkiadó: 1055 Budapest, Kossuth Lajos tér 13–15; tel. (1) 353-2328; fax (1) 331-4162; e-mail info@europakiado.hu; internet www.europakiado.hu; f. 1946; world literature translated into Hungarian; Dir IMRE BARNA.

Helikon Kiadó: 1027 Budapest, Horvát u. 14–24/V; tel. (1) 225-4300; fax (1) 225-4320; e-mail helikon@helikon.hu; internet www.helikon.hu; bibliophile books; Dir KATALIN BERGER.

Kossuth Kiadó: 1043 Budapest, Csányi László u. 36; tel. (1) 370-0607; fax (1) 370-0602; f. 1944; social sciences, educational and philosophy publs, information technology books; Man. ANDRÁS SÁNDOR KOCSIS.

Közgazdasági és Jogi Könyvkiadó: Budapest; tel. (1) 112-6430; fax (1) 111-3210; f. 1955; business, economics, law, sociology, psychology, tax, politics, education, dictionaries; Man. Dir DAVID G. YOUNG.

Magvető Könyvkiadó: 1806 Budapest, Dankó u. 4–8; 1086 Budapest, POB 123; tel. (1) 235-5032; e-mail magveto@lira.hu; internet www.lira.hu/kiado/magveto; f. 1955; literature; Dir GÉZA MORCSÁNYI.

Medicina Könyvkiadó: 1072 Budapest, Rákóczi u. 16; tel. (1) 312-2650; fax (1) 312-2450; e-mail medkiad@euroweb.hu; internet www.medicina-kiado.hu; f. 1957; medicine, health care, tourism; Dir FRIGYESNÉ FARKASVÖLGYI.

Mezőgazda Kiadó: 1165 Budapest, Koronafürt u. 44; tel. (1) 407-1018; fax (1) 407-1012; e-mail mezoig@mezogazdakiado.hu; internet www.mezogazdakiado.hu; ecology, natural sciences, environmental protection, food industry; Man. Dr LAJOS LELKES.

Móra Könyvkiadó Zrt: 1134 Budapest, Váci u. 19; tel. (1) 320-4740; fax (1) 320-5382; e-mail mora@mora.hu; internet www.mora.hu; f. 1950; fiction and non-fiction; Pres. Dr JÁNOS JANIKOVSZKY.

Műszaki Könyvkiadó: 1033 Budapest, Szentendre u. 89–93; tel. (1) 437-2405; fax (1) 437-2404; e-mail lakatosz@muszakikiado.hu; internet www.muszakikiado.hu; f. 1955; scientific and technical, vocational, and general textbooks; Man. SÁNDOR BÉRCZI.

Nemzeti Tankönyvkiadó (National Textbook Publishing House): 1143 Budapest, Szobránc u. 6–8; tel. (1) 460-1800; fax (1) 460-1869; e-mail public@ntk.hu; internet www.ntk.hu; f. 1949; school and university textbooks, pedagogical literature and language books; Gen. Man. JÓZSEF PÁLFI.

PUBLISHERS' ASSOCIATION

Hungarian Publishers' and Booksellers' Association (Magyar Könyvkiadók és Könyvterjesztők Egyesülése): 1073 Budapest, Kertész u. 41 I/4; 1367 Budapest, POB 130; tel. (1) 343-2540; fax (1) 343-2541; e-mail mkke@mkke.hu; internet www.mkke.hu; f. 1795; Pres. LÁSZLÓ PÉTER ZENTAI; Sec.-Gen. MARTINA BUDAY.

Broadcasting and Communications
TELECOMMUNICATIONS

At May 2011 there were 11 fixed-line telephone operators and three providers of mobile cellular telecommunications services in Hungary. In 2013 there were 3.0m. main telephone lines in use in Hungary, and 11.6m. subscriptions to mobile cellular telecommunications services.

Magyar Telekom: 1013 Budapest, Krisztina krt 55; tel. (1) 458-0000; fax (1) 458-7176; e-mail investor.relations@telekom.hu; internet www.telekom.hu; f. 1991 as Matáv Hungarian Telecommunications Co; name changed as above in May 2005; 59.2% owned by Deutsche Telekom AG (Germany); merged with T-Mobile Magyarország in Dec. 2005; mobile telecommunications and internet service provider; CEO CHRISTOPHER MATTHEISEN; 11,653 employees (2012).

Telenor Magyarorszag (Telenor Hungary): 2045 Törökbálint, Pannon u. 1; tel. (1) 464-6000; fax (1) 464-6100; e-mail sajto@telenor.hu; internet www.telenor.hu; f. 1994 as Pannon GSM Telecommunications; 100% stake acquired by Telenor (Norway) in 2002; rebranded as above in May 2010; mobile telecommunications and internet service provider; CEO CHRISTOPHER LASKA; 3.5m. subscribers (2013).

Vodafone Hungary: 1476 Budapest, POB 350; tel. (1) 288-3288; fax (1) 288-3149; e-mail ugyfelszolgalat.hu@vodafone.com; internet www.vodafone.hu; f. 1999; mobile cellular telecommunications and internet service provider; owned by Vodafone (UK); Chair. Dr GYÖRGY BECK; Chief Exec. DIEGO MASSIDDA; more than 2m. subscribers (May 2007).

Regulatory Authority

National Media and Communications Authority (Nemzeti Média- és Hírközlési Hatóság): 1525 Budapest, POB 75; tel. (1) 457-7100; fax (1) 356-5520; e-mail info@nmhh.hu; internet www.nmhh.hu; f. 2010, by the merger of the National Communications Authority and the National Radio and Television Commission; responsible to the legislature; Pres. Dr MONIKA KARAS.

BROADCASTING

Antenna Hungária Rt: 1119 Budapest, Petzvál József u. 31–33; tel. (1) 464-2464; fax (1) 464-2525; e-mail antennah@ahrt.hu; internet www.ahrt.hu; f. 1998; radio and television; 100% owned by TDF, SAS (France); Chief Exec. ANDRÁS PILLER.

Radio

Class FM: 1089 Budapest, Üllői u. 102; tel. (1) 555-55-00; e-mail classfm@classfm.hu; internet classfm.hu; f. 2009; owned by Advenio Zrt; nationwide commercial broadcaster and the most widely listened radio station in Hungary in 2013; approx. 2.1m. listeners.

Hungarian Radio (Magyar Rádió zrt): 1016 Budapest, Naphegy tér 8; tel. (1) 328-7000; fax (1) 328-7447; e-mail info@radio.hu; internet www.radio.hu; f. 1925; stations: Radio Kossuth, Radio Petőfi, Radio Bartók (classical music), MR4 (regional and minority interest), MR5 (parliamentary sessions) and MR6 (regional programmes); CEO ISTVÁN JÓNÁS.

Radio C: 1086 Budapest, Teleki László tér 7; tel. (1) 492-0240; e-mail radioc@radioc.hu; internet www.radioc.hu; f. 2001; Roma radio station; Man. Dir FÁTYOL TIVADAR.

Television

Hungarian Television Rt (Magyar Televízió): 1054 Budapest, Naphegy tér 8; tel. (1) 441-9353; fax (1) 373-4133; e-mail ujmedia@mti.hu; internet premier.mtv.hu; f. 1957; state-owned; three channels (M1, M2, M3); Editor ALEXANDER KORDA.

Finance

(cap. = capital; res = reserves; dep. = deposits; m. = million; brs = branches; amounts in forint)

In 2010 there were 30 commercial banks in operation in Hungary. Responsibility for bank supervision is held by the Central Bank of Hungary (into which the Hungarian Financial Supervisory Authority was absorbed in October 2013).

BANKING

Central Bank

Central Bank of Hungary (Magyar Nemzeti Bank): 1850 Budapest, Szabadság tér 8–9; tel. (1) 429-2600; fax (1) 428-8000; e-mail info@mnb.hu; internet www.mnb.hu; f. 1924; bank of issue; conducts international transactions; supervises banking system; Hungarian Financial Supervisory Authority merged with the Central Bank in October 2013; cap. 10,000m., res 261,768m., dep. 4,912,097m. (Dec. 2009); Gov. Dr GYÖRGY MATOLCSY.

Other Banks

Bank of Hungarian Savings Co-operatives (Magyar Takarékszövetkezeti Bank): 1122 Budapest, Pethényi köz 10, POB 775; tel. (1) 457-8907; fax (1) 225-4280; e-mail info@tbank.hu; internet www.takarekbank.hu; f. 1989; 63.72% owned by savings co-operatives, 31.27% owned by DZ Bank AG (Germany); cap. 2,735m., res 5,861m., dep. 40,632m. (Dec. 2012); Chair. of Bd IMRE HARTMANN; CEO PÉTER CSICSÁKY.

Budapest Credit and Development Bank: 1138 Budapest, POB 1852, Váci u. 188; tel. (1) 450-6000; fax (1) 450-6001; e-mail info@budapestbank.hu; internet www.budapestbank.hu; f. 1987; cap. 19,346m., res 21,919m., dep. 744,616m. (Dec. 2012); 99.7% owned by GE Capital International Financing Corpn (USA); Pres. and CEO SEAN MORRISSEY; 101 brs.

CIB Bank Ltd: 1027 Budapest, Medve u. 4–14, POB 394; tel. (1) 423-1000; fax (1) 489-6500; e-mail cib@cib.hu; internet www.cib.hu; f. 1979; 89.1% owned by Intesa Holding International, SA (Luxembourg); name changed as above Jan. 2008, following merger with Inter-Európa Bank Zrt; cap. 145,000m., res 101,692m., dep. 1,745,854m. (Dec. 2012); Chair. Dr GYÖRGY SURÁNYI; CEO TOMAS SPURNY.

Citibank Zrt: 1367 Budapest, POB 123; tel. (1) 374-5000; fax (1) 374-5100; internet www.citibank.hu; f. 1985; owned by Citibank Europe Plc; cap. 13,005m., res 7,295m., dep. 364,493m. (Dec. 2006); Country Chief Officer SAJJAD RAZVI.

Commerzbank Zrt: 1054 Budapest, Széchenyi rkp 8; tel. (1) 374-1000; fax (1) 269-4574; e-mail info.budapest@commerzbank.hu; internet www.commerzbank.hu; f. 1993; cap. 2,467m., res 19,976m., dep. 252,838m. (Dec. 2011); Pres. and Chair. of Supervisory Bd WILHELM NÜSE; Chair. and Chief Exec. KOZMA ANDRÁS.

Erste Bank Hungary Zrt: 1138 Budapest, Népfürdo u. 24–26; tel. (1) 298-0221; fax (1) 272-5160; e-mail uszolg@erstebank.hu; internet www.erstebank.hu; f. 1987; present name adopted 1998; absorbed Postbank and Savings Bank Corpn—Postabank in 2004; 99.9%

owned by Erste Group Bank (Austria); cap. 101,000m., res 189,248m., dep. 2,457,567m. (Dec. 2012); CEO EDIT PAPP; 143 brs.

Hungarian Export-Import Bank (EXIMBANK): 1065 Budapest, Nagymező u. 46–48; tel. (1) 374-9100; fax (1) 269-4476; e-mail eximh@eximbank.hu; internet www.eximbank.hu; f. 1994; state-owned; cap. 10,100m., res 7,154m., total assets 258,569m. (Dec. 2012); CEO ROLAND NÁTRÁN.

K&H Bank Zrt: 1095 Budapest, Lechner Ödön fasor 9; tel. (1) 328-9000; fax (1) 328-9696; e-mail bank@kh.hu; internet www.kh.hu; f. 1987 as Kereskedelmi és Hitelbank Nyrt; name changed as above 2008; owned by KBC Bank NV (Belgium); cap. 140,978m., res 61,329m., dep. 1,999,026m. (Dec. 2012); Chair. DANNY DE RAYMAEKER; CEO HENDRIK SCHEERLINCK; 219 brs.

MagNet Bank—Magyar Közösségi Bank (Hungarian Community Bank): 1062 Budapest, Andrássy u. 98; tel. (1) 428-8888; fax (1) 428-8889; e-mail info@magnetbank.hu; internet www.magnetbank.hu; f. 2006; fmrly HBW Express Bank; present name adopted 2010; cap. 2,000m., res 2,129m., dep. 76,152m. (Dec. 2012); Chair. ZSOLT FÁY.

MFB Hungarian Development Bank (Magyar Fejlesztési Bank): 1051 Budapest, Nádor u. 31; tel. (1) 428-1400; fax (1) 428-1490; e-mail mfb@mfb.hu; internet www.mfb.hu; f. 1991 as an investment company; authorized as a bank 1993; name changed as above 2007; state-owned; cap. 114,500m., res 112,529m., dep. 563,966m. (Dec. 2012); Pres. DÁNIEL LONTAI; CEO CSABA NAGY.

MKB Bank Zrt: 1056 Budapest, Váci u. 38; tel. (1) 327-8600; fax (1) 327-8700; e-mail mkb@mkb.hu; internet www.mkb.hu; f. 1950; commercial banking; 89.6% owned by Bayerische Landesbank (Germany); absorbed Konzumbank in 2003; present name adopted 2007; cap. 108,936m., res 224,350m., dep. 1,800,817m. (Dec. 2012); Chair. and CEO TAMÁS ERDEI; 80 brs.

OTP Bank (Országos Takarékpénztár Bank): 1051 Budapest, Nádor u. 16; tel. (1) 473-5000; fax (1) 473-5955; e-mail otpbank@otpbank.hu; internet www.otpbank.hu; f. 1949 as Hungarian National Savings Bank; name changed as above 2006; savings deposits, credits, foreign transactions; privatized in 1996; cap. 28,000m., res –98,418m., dep. 7,352,490m. (Dec. 2012); Chair. and Chief Exec. Dr SÁNDOR CSÁNYI; 405 brs.

Raiffeisen Bank Zrt: 1054 Budapest, Akadémia u. 6; tel. (1) 484-4400; fax (1) 484-4444; e-mail info@raiffeisen.hu; internet www.raiffeisen.hu; f. 1986; present name adopted 1999; 100% owned by Raiffeisen Banking Group (Austria); cap. 165,023m., res –4,405m., dep. 1,726,187m. (Dec. 2012); Pres. Dr HERBERT STEPIC; Man. Dir Dr PÉTER FELCSUTI; 120 brs.

UniCredit Bank Hungary Zrt: 1054 Budapest, Szabadság tér 5–6; tel. (1) 269-0812; fax (1) 353-4959; e-mail info@unicreditbank.hu; internet www.unicreditbank.hu; f. 2001 by merger of Bank Austria Creditanstalt Hungary RT and Hypovereinsbank Hungary RT; name changed as above 2007; 100% owned by Bank Austria Creditanstalt AG; cap. 24,118m., res 47,308m., dep. 1,360,433m. (Dec. 2012); CEO Dr MIHÁLY PATAI.

STOCK EXCHANGE

Budapest Stock Exchange (Budapesti Értéktőzsde—BET): 1062 Budapest, Andrássy u. 93; tel. (1) 429-6700; fax (1) 429-6800; e-mail info@bse.hu; internet www.bse.hu; f. 1991; partly owned by a consortium comprising: UniCredit Bank Hungary (25.2%), Wiener Börse (Vienna Stock Exchange, Austria, 12.5%) and Österreichische Kontrollbank AG (Austria, 12.5%); allied with the Wiener Börse from May 2004; Pres. MIHÁLY PATAI; Chief Exec. GYÖRGY MOHAI.

INSURANCE

In 2013 there were 32 insurance companies. The following were among the most important:

AB-AEGON Általános Biztosító: 1091 Budapest, Üllői u. 1; tel. (1) 477-4800; fax (1) 476-5710; e-mail ugyfelszolg@aegon.hu; internet www.aegon.hu; f. 1949; present name adopted 1992; pensions, life and property insurance, insurance of agricultural plants, co-operatives, foreign insurance, etc.; Gen. Man. Dr GÁBOR KEPECS.

Allianz Hungária Insurance Co (Hungária Biztosító): 1087 Budapest, Könyves Kálmán u. 48-52; tel. (1) 301-6565; fax (1) 301-6100; e-mail ugyfelszolgalat@allianz.hu; internet www.allianz.hu; f. 1986; handles international insurance, industrial and commercial insurance, and motor car, marine, life, household, accident and liability insurance; cap. 4,266m.; Chair. and Chief Exec. PÉTER KISBENEDEK.

ERSTE Vienna Insurance Group Biztosító Zrt: 1134 Budapest, Váci u. 24-26; tel. (1) 484-1778; fax (1) 484-1799; e-mail info@erstebiztosito.hu; internet www.erstebiztosito.hu; f. 2000; life insurance; Chair. GÁBOR LEHEL; Pres. and CEO ZSOLT RAVECZKY.

Generali Esoport: 1066 Budapest, Teréz 39; tel. (1) 301-7100; fax (1) 452-3505; e-mail generali@generali.hu; internet www.generali.hu; f. 1832; CEO MIHÁLY ERDŐS.

Grawe Életbiztosító Zrt: 1126 Budapest, Istenhegyi u. 9B; tel. (1) 202-1211; fax (1) 355-5530; e-mail info@grawe.hu; internet www .grawe.hu; Pres. Dr OTHMAR EDERER.

ING Biztosító Zrt: 1068 Budapest, Dózsa György u. 84B; tel. (1) 255-5757; fax (1) 267-9093; e-mail ing@ing.hu; internet www.ing.hu; f. 2003.

K&H Insurance: 1068 Budapest, Benczúr u. 47; tel. (1) 461-5200; fax (1) 461-5276; e-mail biztosito@kh.hu; internet www.kh.hu; f. 2006; both life and non-life.

MetLife: 1138 Budapest, Népfürdő u. 22; tel. (40) 444-445; fax (1) 391-1660; e-mail info@metlife.hu; internet www.metlife.hu; f. 1996; 100% owned by MetLife, Inc.

UNION Biztosító: 1082 Budapest, Baross u. 1; tel. (1) 486-4343; fax (1) 486-4390; e-mail ugyfelszolgalat@unionbiztosito.hu; internet www.unionbiztosito.hu; f. 2000; mem. of Vienna Insurance Gp (registered in Austria); Pres. and CEO GÁBOR LEHEL.

UNIQA Biztosító Zrt: 1134 Budapest, Róbert Károly 70–74; tel. (1) 544-5555; fax (1) 238-6060; e-mail info@uniqa.hu; internet www .uniqa.hu; f. 1990; name changed as above in 2003; Pres. Dr WOLFGANG KINDL; CEO OTHMAR MICHL.

INSURANCE ASSOCIATION

Association of Hungarian Insurance Companies (Magyar Biztosítók Szövetsége—MABISZ): 1062 Budapest, Andrássy u. 100; tel. (1) 802 8400; fax (1) 802 8499; e-mail info@mabisz.hu; internet www .mabisz.hu; f. 1990; Pres. ANETT PANDURICS; Sec.-Gen. Dr DÁNIEL MOLNOS; 26 mem. cos.

Trade and Industry

GOVERNMENT AGENCY

Hungarian State Holding Co (Magyar Nemzeti Vagyonkezelő Zrt.—MNV Zrt): 1133 Budapest, Pozsonyi u. 56; tel. (1) 237-4400; fax (1) 237-4100; e-mail info@mnv.hu; internet www.mnv.hu; f. 2008; Chair. Dr TIBOR HALASI.

NATIONAL CHAMBERS OF COMMERCE AND OF AGRICULTURE

Hungarian Chamber of Agriculture (Magyar Agrárkamara): 1119 Budapest, Fehérvári u. 89-95; tel. (1) 802-6100; fax (1) 802-0600; e-mail info@agrarkamara.hu; internet www.agrarkamara.hu; f. 1994; Pres. Dr FORGÁCS BARNA.

Hungarian Chamber of Commerce and Industry (Magyar Kereskedelmi és Iparkamara): 1055 Budapest, Kossuth Lajos tér 6–8; tel. (1) 474-5100; fax (1) 474-5105; e-mail hcci@hcci.com; internet www.mkik.hu; f. 1850; central org. of the 23 Hungarian county chambers of commerce and industry; based on a system of voluntary membership; over 46,000 mems; Pres. Dr LÁSZLÓ PARRAGH; Sec.-Gen. PÉTER DUNAI.

EMPLOYERS' ASSOCIATIONS

Confederation of Hungarian Employers and Industrialists (Munkaadók és Gyáriparosok Országos Szövetsége—MGYOSZ): 1055 Budapest, Kossuth L. tér 6–8; tel. (1) 474-2044; fax (1) 474-2065; e-mail mgyosz@mgyosz.hu; internet www.mgyosz.hu; f. 1902; re-est. 1990; 64 member asscns; Sec.-Gen. ISTVÁN WIMMER.

National Asscn of Entrepreneurs and Employers (Vállalkozók és Munkáltatók Országos Szövetsége—VOSZ): 1054 Budapest, Holdu. 21; tel. (1) 414-2181; fax (1) 414-2180; e-mail center@vosz .hu; internet www.vosz.hu; f. 1988; Sec.-Gen. DÁVID FERENC.

INDUSTRIAL AND TRADE ASSOCIATIONS

Hungarian Industrial Asscn (Magyar Iparszövetség—OKISZ): 1146 Budapest, Thököly u. 58–60; tel. (1) 343-5181; fax (1) 343-5521; e-mail okisz@okiszinfo.hu; internet www.okisz.hu; safeguards interests of over 1,100 mem. enterprises (all private); Pres. ISTVÁN TOKÁR.

HUNICOOP Foreign Trade Co for Industrial Co-operation: 1036 Budapest, Galagonya u. 7; tel. (1) 250-8117; fax (1) 250-8121; e-mail hunicoop@axelero.hu; internet www.hunicoop.hu; agency for foreign cos in Hungary, export and import; Dir GÁBOR TOMBÁCZ.

National Asscn of Industrial Corporations (Ipartestületek Országos Szövetsége—IPOSZ): 1054 Budapest, Kálmán Imre u. 20; tel. (1) 354-3140; e-mail titkarsag@iposz.hu; internet www.iposz.hu; Chair. GYÖRGY SZŰCS; 230 mem. orgs.

National Federation of Agricultural Co-operators and Producers (Mezőgazdasági Szövetkezők és Termelők Országos Szövetsége—MOSZ): 1125 Budapest, Istenhegyi u. 59–61; tel. (1) 332-1163; fax (1) 353-2552; e-mail mosztit@mosz.agrar.hu; internet www.mosz .agrar.hu; f. 1967; present name adopted 1989; Pres. TAMÁS NAGY; Sec.-Gen. GÁBOR HORVÁTH; c. 1,300 mem. orgs.

UTILITIES

Supervisory Organization

Hungarian Energy and Public Utility Regulatory Authority (Magyar Energetikai És Közmü-Szabályozási Hivatal): 1081 Budapest, II János Pál Pápa tér 7; tel. (1) 459-7777; fax (1) 459-7766; e-mail mekh@mekh.hu; regulation and supervision of activities performed by gas and electricity cos, price regulation and protection of consumer interest; Pres. LAJOS DORKOTA.

Electricity

Budapest Electricity Co (Budapesti Elektromos Művek—ELMŰ): 1132 Budapest, Váci u. 72–74; tel. (1) 238-1000; fax (1) 238-2822; e-mail elmu@elmu.hu; internet www.elmu.hu; f. 1949; transmission and distribution of electricity; CEO Dr MARIE-THERES THIELL; Chair. of Supervisory Bd EMMERICH ENDRESZ; 3,000 employees.

EDF Démász (South Hungarian Power Supply Co): 6720 Szeged, Klauzál tér 9; tel. (62) 565-565; fax (62) 482-500; e-mail info@edf.hu; internet www.edfdemasz.hu; f. 1951; distributes electricity to south-eastern Hungary; Pres. THIERRY LE BOUCHER.

EDF Émász (North Hungarian Electricity Supply Co): 3525 Miskolc, Dózsa Gy. u. 13; tel. (46) 411-875; fax (46) 411-871; e-mail emasz@emasz.hu; internet www.emasz.hu; majority share owned by EDF (France); Chair. Dr MARIE-THÉRÈSE THIELL.

E.ON Hungária Rt: 1051 Budapest, Széchenyi tér 7-8; tel. (1) 472-2300; e-mail info@eon-hungaria.com; internet www.eon-hungaria .com; f. 2000; 86% owned by E.ON Energie AG (Germany); subsidiary electicity supply cos incl. E.ON Del-dunántúli Áramszolgáltató (south-west Hungary), E.ON Észak-dunántúli Áramszolgáltató (north-west Hungary), E.ON Tiszántúli Áramszolgáltató (north-east Hungary); Chair. of Bd of Dirs KONRAD KRAUSER.

Mátrai Power Plant (Erőmű Részvénytársaság) Co: 3271 Visonta, Erőmű u. 11; tel. (37) 334-000; fax (37) 334-016; e-mail matra@mert.hu; internet www.mert.hu; f. 1965; electricity generation; Chair. JÓZSEF VALASKA; 3,645 employees.

MVM Hungarian Electricity Private Limited Company (MVM Magyar Villamos Művek Zrt.—MVM): 1031 Budapest, Szentendrei u. 207-209; tel. (1) 304-2000; fax (1) 202-1246; e-mail mvm@mvm.hu; internet www.mvm.hu; f. 1963; electricity wholesaler; CEO BAJI CSABA.

MVM Paks Nuclear Power Plant Ltd. (MVM Paksi Atomerőmű Zrt.): 7031 Paks, POB 71; tel. (75) 508-833; fax (75) 506-662; e-mail uzemlatogatas@npp.hu; internet www.npp.hu; f. 1992; electrical energy production; CEO ISTVÁN LÁSZLÓ HAMVAS; 2,500 employees.

Vértesi Power Plant (Erőmű) Co: 2841 Oroszlány, POB 23; tel. (34) 360-255; fax (34) 360-882; e-mail vert@vert.hu; internet www .vert.hu; electricity and heat generation; CEO ANDRÁS ZOLTÁN KOVÁCS.

Gas

Fõgáz—Fővárosi Gázművek (Budapest Gas) Co: 1081 Budapest, II János Pál Pápa tér 20; tel. (1) 477-1111; fax (1) 477-1277; e-mail kommunikacio@fogaz.hu; internet www.fogaz.hu; f. 1856; gas distribution; Pres. Dr TAMÁS BÁN.

GDF SUEZ Energia Magyarorzság Zrt.: 6724 Szeged, Pulz u. 44; tel. (62) 569-600; fax (63) 473-943; e-mail ugyfel@degas.hu; internet www.gdfsuez-energia.hu; fmrly Égáz-Dégáz Zrt; present name adopted 2010; gas supply and services; 99.6% owned by Gaz de France (France); CEO PATRICK EECKELERS.

MOL Hungarian Oil and Gas PLC: 1117 Budapest, Október huszonharmadika u. 18; tel. (1) 209-0000; fax (1) 209-0005; e-mail webmaster@mol.hu; internet www.mol.hu; f. 1991; privatized in 1995; petroleum and gas exploration, processing, transportation and distribution; 34,000 employees; Chair. and CEO ZSOLT HERNÁDI.

Tigáz—Tiszántúli Gázszolgáltató (Tiszá Gas) Co: 4200 Hajdúszoboszló, Rákóczi u. 184; tel. (52) 333-338; fax (52) 361-149; e-mail titkarsaga@tigaz.hu; internet www.tigaz.com; f. 1950; majority share owned by ENI S.p.A (Italy); gas distribution in north-eastern regions of Hungary; Chair. of Bd CESARE CUNIBERTO.

TRADE UNIONS

From 1988, and particularly after the restructuring of the former Central Council of Hungarian Trade Unions (SzOT) as the National Confederation of Hungarian Trade Unions (MSzOSz) in 1990, several new union federations were created. Several unions are affiliated to more than one federation, and others are completely independent.

Trade Union Federations

Association of Hungarian Free Trade Unions (Magyar Szabad Szakszervezetek Szövetsége): 1068 Budapest, Városligeti fasor 46–

48; tel. (1) 323-2686; fax (1) 323-2651; internet www.mszosz.com; f. 1994; Pres. BÉLA BALOGH.

Autonomous Trade Union Confederation (Autonóm Szakszervezetek Svövetsége): 1068 Budapest, Benczúr u. 45; tel. (1) 413-1934; fax (1) 461-2480; e-mail autonom@t-online.hu; internet www.autonomok.hu; Pres. LAJOS FŐCZE; 137,000 mems (2007).

Democratic League of Independent Trade Unions—LIGA (Független Szakszervezetek Demokratikus Ligája): 1146 Budapest, Ajtósi Dürer sor 27/A; tel. (1) 321-5262; fax (1) 321-5405; e-mail info@liganet.hu; internet www.liganet.hu; f. 1988; Pres. ISTVÁN GASKÓ; 110,000 mems (2011).

Federation of Unions of Intellectual Workers (Értelmiségi Szakszervezeti Tömörülés—ÉSzT): 1066 Budapest, Jókai u. 2; tel. (1) 473-1429; fax (1) 331-4577; e-mail eszt@eszt.hu; internet www.eszt.hu; Pres. Dr LÁSZLÓ KUTI.

National Confederation of Hungarian Trade Unions (Magyar Szakszervezetek Országos Szövetsége—MSzOSz): 1086 Budapest, Magdolna u. 5–7; tel. (1) 323-2660; fax (1) 323-2662; e-mail gykiss@mszosz.hu; internet www.mszosz.hu; f. 1898; reorganized 1990; Pres. Dr LÁSZLÓ SÁNDOR; 400,000 mems (2007).

Transport

RAILWAYS

In 2011 the length of railway lines in use totalled 7,906 km, of which 2,996 km were electrified. There is an underground railway in Budapest, the second oldest in the world.

Budapest Transport Company (BKV): 1072 Budapest, Akácfa u. 15; tel. (1) 461-6500; fax (1) 461-6557; e-mail bkv@bkv.hu; internet www.bkv.hu; f. 1968; operates metro system (comprising four lines amounting to 38.2km and including 52 stations in 2015), suburban railway network, trams, trolley buses and conventional buses; Pres. Dr GYULA VÁRSZEGI; Chief Exec. TIBOR BOLLA.

Hungarian State Railways Co (Magyar Államvasutak—MÁV): 1087 Budapest, Kálmán krt. 54-60; tel. (1) 511-3186; fax (1) 511-4931; e-mail sajto@mav.hu; internet www.mav.hu; f. 1993; Pres. and Chief Exec. ZSOLT VÖLGYESI, Gen. Dir ILONA DÁVID.

ROADS

In 2012 there were 201,941 km of roads in Hungary, of which 1,515 km were motorways and 6,836 km were main roads.

SHIPPING AND INLAND WATERWAYS

MAHART—Magyar Hajózás (Hungarian Shipping) Co: 1211 Budapest, Weiss Manfréd u. 5—7; tel. (20) 979-0152; fax (1) 278-3505; e-mail kabinet@mahart.hu; internet www.mahart.hu; f. 1895; transportation of goods on the Rhine–Main–Danube waterway; carries passenger traffic on the Danube; operates port activities at Budapest Csepel National and Free Port (port agency service, loading, storage, handling goods); management of multi-modal and combined transport (cargo-booking, oversized goods, chartering); shipbuilding and ship-repair services; Dir-Gen. Capt. LÁSZLÓ SOMLÓVÁRI.

CIVIL AVIATION

Budapest Ferenc Liszt International Airport (formerly Budapest Ferihegy International Airport) and Balatonkiliti airport, near Siófok, serve international traffic. Other airports are located at Nyíregyháza, Debrecen, Szeged, Pécs, Szombathely and Győr.

National Transport Authority (Nemzeti Közlekedési Hatóság—NKH): 1066 Budapest, Teréz krt. 38; tel. (1) 373-1400; fax (1) 332-6532; e-mail office@nkh.gov.hu; internet www.nkh.gov.hu; f. 2007; as a successor to Civil Aviation Authority; controls civil aviation; Pres. GYULA GYŐRI.

Wizz Air Hungary: 1185 Budapest; tel. (22) 351-9499; e-mail info@wizzair.com; internet www.wizzair.com; f. 2003; wholly owned subsidiary of Wizz Air (UK); mem. of European Low Fares Airline Asscn; Chair. and Chief Exec. JÓZSEF VÁRADI.

Tourism

Lake Balaton is the main holiday centre for boating, bathing and fishing. Hungary's cities have great historical and recreational attractions, and the annual Budapest Spring Festival is held in March. Budapest has numerous swimming pools watered by thermal springs. There were 43.6m. foreign visitors (including those in transit) in 2013, when revenue from tourism amounted to 1,263,957m. forint.

Hungarian Tourism Office: 1115 Budapest, Bartók Béla u. 105-113; tel. (1) 488-8700; fax (1) 488-8600; e-mail info@itthon.hu; internet www.hungarytourism.hu; Gen. Man. DENÉNÉ TÓTH MARIANNA.

Defence

Compulsory military service was abolished in November 2004. As assessed at November 2014, the active armed forces numbered 26,500, including an army of 10,300, an air force of 5,900 and 10,300 joint-forces troops. Reservists totalled 44,000. Paramilitary forces comprised 12,000 border guards. In 1999 Hungary became a member of the North Atlantic Treaty Organization (NATO).

Defence Expenditure: Budgeted at 234,000m. forint for 2014.

Chief of the Defence Staff: Gen. TIBOR BENKŐ.

Education

Children under the age of three years attend crèches (bölcsődék), and those between the ages of three and six years attend kindergartens (óvodák). Education is compulsory between the ages of six and 16 years. Children attend basic or primary school (általános iskola) until the age of 14. In 2010/11 pre-primary enrolment included 84% of children in the relevant age-group. The comparable ratio in the same year for primary education was 93% and that for secondary education was 92%. The majority of children continue with their education after 16 years of age.

In 2012 there were 19 public universities, seven private universities, and nine and 32 public and private colleges of tertiary education, respectively. In 2013/14 some 320,124 students attended 66 institutions of tertiary education. Expenditure on education in 2011 was some 1,077.6m. forint (equivalent to 3.9% of total government expenditure).

ICELAND

Introductory Survey

LOCATION, CLIMATE, LANGUAGE, RELIGION, FLAG, CAPITAL

The Republic of Iceland comprises one large island and numerous smaller ones, situated near the Arctic Circle in the North Atlantic Ocean. The main island lies about 300 km (190 miles) south-east of Greenland, about 1,000 km (620 miles) west of Norway and about 800 km (500 miles) north of Scotland. The Gulf Stream keeps Iceland warmer than might be expected, with average temperatures ranging from 10°C (50°F) in the summer to 1°C (34°F) in winter. Icelandic is the official language. Almost all of the inhabitants profess Christianity: the Evangelical Lutheran Church is the established church and embraces about 74% of the population. The civil flag (proportions 18 by 25) displays a red cross, bordered with white, on a blue background, the upright of the cross being towards the hoist; the state flag (proportions 9 by 16) bears the same design, but has a truncated triangular area cut from the fly. The capital is Reykjavík.

CONTEMPORARY POLITICAL HISTORY

Historical Context

Iceland became independent on 17 June 1944, when the Convention that linked it with Denmark, under the Danish crown, was terminated. Iceland became a founder member of the North Atlantic Treaty Organization (NATO, see p. 367) in 1949, joined the Council of Europe (see p. 250) in 1950, and has belonged to the Nordic Council (see p. 462) since its foundation in 1952. Membership of the European Free Trade Association (EFTA, see p. 446) was formalized in 1970.

From 1959 to 1971 Iceland was governed by a coalition of the Independence Party (IP) and the Social Democratic Party (SDP). Following the general election of June 1971, Olafur Jóhannesson, the leader of the Progressive Party (PP), formed a coalition Government with the left-wing People's Alliance (PA) and the Union of Liberals and Leftists. At the general election held in June 1974 voters favoured right-wing parties, and the IP and the PP subsequently formed a coalition Government under the leader of the IP, Geir Hallgrímsson. However, failure adequately to address economic difficulties resulted in a decline in the coalition's popularity and the Government resigned in June 1978, following extensive electoral gains by the PA and the SDP. In September Jóhannesson formed a coalition of the PP with the PA and the SDP, but this Government resigned in October 1979, when the SDP withdrew from the coalition. An interim administration was formed by Benedikt Gröndal, the leader of the SDP. The results of a general election, held in December, were inconclusive, and in February 1980 Gunnar Thoroddsen of the IP formed a coalition Government with the PA and the PP.

Domestic Political Affairs

In June 1980 Vigdís Finnbogadóttir, a non-political candidate, achieved a narrow victory in the election for the mainly ceremonial office of President. She took office on 1 August 1980, becoming the world's first popularly elected female Head of State. The coalition Government lost its majority in the Lower House of the Alþingi (Althingi—parliament) in September 1982, and a general election took place in April 1983. The IP received the largest share of the votes cast, and a coalition was subsequently formed by the IP and the PP, with Steingrímur Hermannsson (the leader of the PP) as Prime Minister.

A general election for an enlarged, 63-seat Althingi was held in April 1987. The IP and the PP both lost seats, while a new rightwing group, the Citizens' Party (CP) won seven seats. A coalition of the IP, the PP and the SDP was formally constituted in July. Thorsteinn Pálsson, the leader of the IP and hitherto the Minister of Finance, was appointed Prime Minister.

In September 1988 the SDP and the PP withdrew from the Government, following disagreements over economic policy. Later that month Hermannsson became Prime Minister in a centre-left coalition of the PP, the SDP and the PA. In September 1989 a new Government, based on a coalition agreement between the PP, the SDP, the PA, the CP and the Association for Equality and Social Justice, was formed. Hermannsson remained as Prime Minister.

In March 1991 Davíð Oddsson, the mayor of Reykjavík, successfully challenged Pálsson for the leadership of the IP. At a general election in April the IP emerged as the largest single party, securing 26 seats. Although the incumbent coalition would have retained an overall majority of seats, the SDP decided to withdraw from the coalition, chiefly as a result of the failure to reach agreement on Iceland's position in the discussions between EFTA and the European Community (EC, now European Union—EU, see p. 271), with regard to the creation of a European Economic Area (EEA). A new coalition Government was formed in April by the IP and the SDP, with Oddsson as Prime Minister.

In 1991 Iceland's Constitution was amended, ending the system whereby the Althingi was divided into an Upper House (one-third of the members) and a Lower House.

In June 1992 President Finnbogadóttir was elected unopposed for a fourth term in office (she had begun a second term, unopposed, in August 1984 and a third term in June 1988).

Although the IP remained the strongest party with 25 seats following a general election in April 1995, its hitherto coalition partner the SDP obtained only seven. The IP subsequently formed a new coalition Government with the PP. Oddsson remained Prime Minister and Halldór Asgrímsson, the Chairman of the PP, became Minister of Foreign Affairs.

Olafur Ragnar Grímsson, a former leader of the PA, won the presidential election of June 1996, with 41% of the votes cast. (Finnbogadóttir had decided not to seek re-election.) Grímsson secured a second term of office, unopposed, in August 2000.

At a general election in May 1999 the governing coalition retained its majority in the Althingi: the IP and the PP won 26 and 12 seats, respectively. The Social Democratic Alliance (SDA), a left-wing electoral grouping of the PA, the SDP, the People's Movement and the Women's List, won 17 seats. Two new parties also secured representation in the legislature: the Left-Green Movement, established by three former PA deputies, won six seats, while the Liberal Party, founded by a former IP minister, secured two. A new coalition Government comprising the IP and the PP, was formed under Oddsson.

At a general election in May 2003, the IP remained the party with the largest representation in the Althingi, winning 22 seats. The IP renewed its coalition with the PP, which had won 12 seats. Oddsson remained Prime Minister but agreed to relinquish the premiership in September 2004 in favour of PP leader and Minister of Foreign Affairs Asgrímsson. The SDA won 20 seats, the Left-Green Movement five, and the Liberal Party four.

In May 2004 the Althingi narrowly approved a bill to limit media ownership. The legislation provoked uncharacteristic public protests as many perceived the bill to be directed against a particular company, the Baugur Group, whose media outlets had been openly critical of Oddsson. In the first use of the presidential power of veto in the 60-year history of the Republic, President Grímsson refused to sign the bill, stating that it lacked the necessary consensus. Grímsson was re-elected President for a third term on 26 June, with 85.6% of the votes cast. The Althingi rejected an amended version of the media bill in July.

In accordance with the post-election agreement between the IP and PP, Asgrímsson replaced Oddsson as Prime Minister in September 2004. Oddsson resigned from politics in September 2005 and assumed the chairmanship of the Central Bank of Iceland. Geir Haarde, who had replaced him as Minister of Foreign Affairs, was elected leader of the IP.

In June 2006 Asgrímsson resigned as Prime Minister, following the PP's poor performance in municipal elections, and was succeeded by Haarde. Asgrímsson also resigned as Chairman of the PP in August and was replaced by Jón Sigurðsson, whom Haarde had recently appointed Minister of Industry and Commerce.

The IP remained the largest party in the Althingi at elections in May 2007, securing 25 seats. The PP won just seven seats, while the SDA secured 18. The Left-Green Movement became the third largest party in the legislature, increasing its representation from five to nine seats. A new coalition Government comprising the IP and the SDA was subsequently formed. Haarde continued as Prime Minister, while the leader of the SDA, Ingibjörg Sólrún Gísladóttir, became Minister of Foreign Affairs. Guðni Agústsson replaced Sigurðsson as Chairman of the PP. President Grímsson was sworn in to serve a fourth term of office in August 2008, his candidacy having been unopposed.

Collapse of the banking sector

By mid-2008 a sharp contraction of credit on the global financial markets had severely weakened confidence in Iceland's banking sector, which held assets reported to be worth 10 times the country's annual gross domestic product (GDP); meanwhile, the value of the króna declined rapidly during 2008, and the country experienced high levels of inflation. On 6 October the Althingi approved an emergency bill to give the Icelandic Financial Supervisory Authority (Fjármálaeftirlitið—FME) extensive powers to intervene in the country's financial system. The Government assumed control of Iceland's three largest banks—Glitnir Banki, Landsbanki Íslands and Kaupþing Banki—and placed all three in receivership. Relations between the United Kingdom and Iceland were strained when it emerged that, as a consequence of the action taken by the FME, the accounts of some 400,000 British and Dutch savers who had invested in Icesave, a savings brand operated by Landsbanki in the UK and the Netherlands, had been frozen. Amid doubts that the Icelandic Depositors' and Investors' Guarantee Fund had sufficient assets to compensate Landsbanki's foreign creditors, the British Government invoked anti-terrorism legislation in order to seize Landsbanki's assets in the UK. The measure, which was described by Haarde as 'hostile', caused significant popular resentment in Iceland. The Bank of England subsequently granted Landsbanki a loan of £100m. to assist Iceland in repaying British Icesave account holders. The IMF approved a loan of US $2,100m. to Iceland in November, following an announcement that Iceland and EU member states had reached an agreement over compensation for Icesave account holders in the UK and the Netherlands.

In November 2008 the Government defeated a motion of no confidence proposed by the opposition in the Althingi over its handling of the economic crisis. However, this did little to increase public confidence in the administration. A series of demonstrations were staged around Iceland calling for the Government to resign. In January 2009 Haarde scheduled an early general election for 9 May, and announced his intention to stand down as leader of the IP. Two days later the Minister of Business Affairs, Björgvin Sigurðsson, resigned, citing his resolve to take responsibility for the political role he had played in the country's financial decline. Prior to his resignation, he dismissed the director of the FME. The following day Haarde announced the resignation of the Government. On 1 February Jóhanna Sigurðardóttir of the SDA, hitherto Minister of Social Affairs, was sworn in as Iceland's first female Prime Minister and a minority interim coalition Government comprising the SDA, the Left-Green Movement and independents was appointed, pending the general election, which was brought forward to 25 April.

Sigurðardóttir began implementing measures aimed at alleviating Iceland's acute financial situation. In February 2009 the Althingi approved a bill on the reorganization of the senior management of the Central Bank of Iceland, facilitating the dismissal of the bank's Governor, Oddsson, whom many considered responsible for exacerbating the country's economic problems. In the event, Oddsson resigned. In March Gísladóttir resigned as leader of the SDA for health reasons; Sigurðardóttir was elected her successor. Meanwhile, Bjarni Benediktsson was appointed Chairman of the IP, replacing Haarde.

At the general election held on 25 April 2009 the interim coalition parties, the SDA and the Left-Green Movement, won 34 of the 63 seats in the Althingi, the first time left-wing parties had won a majority in parliament. The SDA replaced the IP as the largest party in the Althingi, winning 20 seats, while the Left-Green Movement won 14 seats. The IP won 16 seats, while the PP secured nine. The success of the Citizens' Movement, founded just two months earlier by activists involved in the protests against the Government's handling of the economic crisis, also confounded expectations by winning four seats.

The SDA-Left-Green Movement Coalition

On 10 May 2009 a new Government, led by Sigurðardóttir and largely unchanged from the outgoing interim coalition, took office. Steingrímur J. Sigfússon, the leader of the Left-Green

Movement, remained Minister of Finance. The new administration declared its principal aim to be the achievement of a balanced state budget by 2013. In July the Althingi voted narrowly in favour of applying for accession to the EU (which had gained increasing popular support since the onset of the economic crisis and which had been a central policy of the SDA). A formal application was duly submitted to the European Council. The Government emphasized that, should Iceland be admitted to the EU, the accession treaty would be subject to approval in a referendum.

Meanwhile, negotiations continued with the UK and the Netherlands over the consequences of the collapse of Landsbanki Íslands. In June 2009 it was agreed that the Icelandic Government would guarantee loans of some £2,350m. from the UK and €1,200m. from the Netherlands to the Depositors' and Investors' Guarantee Fund in respect of the compensation that the two countries' Governments had issued to savers who had lost deposits held in Icesave accounts; the loans were to be repaid by 2024, with repayment, at an interest rate of 5.55%, to commence in 2016. The agreement encountered domestic opposition on the grounds that it placed an unduly harsh burden on the Icelandic economy, the amount loaned being equivalent to some US $17,000 per head. None the less, in August 2009 the Althingi approved a bill to ratify the loan agreement, but added stipulations to the effect that Iceland would repay no more than 4% of its annual GDP growth to the UK and 2% to the Netherlands in any one year, and that any portion of the debt not repaid by 2024 would effectively be cancelled. The British and Dutch Governments objected to the amended bill (which was signed into law in September 2009) and demanded further negotiations with Iceland. A revised agreement with the UK and the Netherlands concluded in October, which retained the Althingi's annual limits on repayment but allowed for payments to continue beyond the 2024 deadline if necessary, was narrowly approved by the Althingi in December. However, by 2 January 2010 more than 56,000 people—some 23% of the electorate—had signed a petition urging President Grímsson to veto the bill. In response, on 5 January Grímsson announced that he would not sign the legislation, and that, in accordance with the Constitution, it would thus be subject to a referendum.

In anticipation of a referendum defeat for the Icesave compensation bill, the Government held further talks with the British and Dutch authorities in February 2010. However, the talks collapsed after Iceland rejected as insufficient a British and Dutch offer, estimated to be worth €450m., to waive interest payments for the first two years and to replace the fixed interest rate of 5.55% with a variable one. Sigurðardóttir urged electors not to vote in the referendum, arguing that the offer of revised terms for the loans had already made the bill of December 2009 obsolete. None the less, 62.7% of registered voters participated in the referendum (the first since Iceland's independence) on 6 March 2010, at which 93.2% of votes cast were against the bill. As a result, the payment terms authorized in September 2009 were to remain in force pending further negotiations with the UK and the Netherlands.

A commission established by the Althingi to investigate the collapse of the banking sector in 2008 presented its report in April 2010, accusing the Icelandic Government and regulators of the financial sector of 'extreme negligence' in the period preceding the crisis and concluding that the failure of the banking system had become inevitable as early as the end of 2006. Seven former officials were specifically criticized: from the Government, then Prime Minister Haarde, Minister of Finance Árni Mathiesen and Minister of Business Affairs Björgvin Sigurðsson; from the Central Bank, former Governor Oddsson and two other officials; and from the FME, former Director-General Jónas Jónsson. The report was also highly critical of the management and largest shareholders of the three banks that failed, noting that the owners had 'abnormally easy access to loans in these banks' and were, indeed, their largest borrowers. In September the nine-member commission voted in favour of a recommendation to convene the Landsdómur, a special court for hearing cases against elected officials, to try Haarde, Mathiesen and Sigurðsson, as well as former Minister of Foreign Affairs Ingibjörg Gísladóttir. Later that month the Althingi voted to pursue charges of negligence against Haarde, but not the other three erstwhile ministers.

The Landsdómur was duly convened in February 2011, for the first time since its establishment in 1905. In June Haarde was formally charged on six counts of violating the laws on ministerial responsibility. Appearing before the Landsdómur in

September, Haarde denied all of the charges, claiming that they were a result of a 'political vendetta' against him by the current Government. The Landsdómur subsequently withdrew two of the six charges against Haarde. In April 2012 Haarde was found guilty of a minor charge—of failing to keep his government ministers properly informed of developments prior to the collapse of the banking sector in 2008, for which he faced no punishment—and was cleared of the more serious charges of negligence. Meanwhile, a special prosecutor appointed in early 2009 began to file charges against former bank executives, including Lárus Welding, the former CEO of Glitnir Banki, and Gudmundur Hjaltason, Glitnir's former head of corporate finance, in December 2011, and Hreiðar Már Sigurðsson and Sigurður Einarsson, respectively the former CEO and Chairman of Kaupþing Banki, in February 2012; Sigurjón Árnason, the former CEO of Landsbanki Íslands, was also under investigation. Welding and Hjaltason were convicted of fraud and each sentenced to nine months' imprisonment in December 2012. Meanwhile, Welding and Jón Ásgeir Jóhannesson, the former head of Icelandic investment company Baugur and Glitnir's largest shareholder, were indicted by the special prosecutor in a separate case related to the approval of a 6,000m. krónur loan. Also in December, Welding's predecessor at Glitnir, Bjarni Ármannsson, was formally indicted for tax evasion. In July 2013 charges were filed against another four former employees of Glitnir bank for market manipulation and irregularities surrounding a 3,800m. krónur loan to a company owned by a senior executive at the bank, while in December Sigurðsson and Einarsson of Kaupþing Banki were sentenced to five-and-a-half, and five years' imprisonment, respectively, for fraud. In November 2014 Árnason was sentenced to 12 months' imprisonment for fraud and market manipulation. Two of his former colleagues from Landsbanki received sentences of nine months each.

The second Icesave referendum

Public discontent with the traditional parties was evident at the municipal elections of May 2010 with the success in Reykjavík of a new, satirical political organization, the Best Party, which had been established by a comedian, Jón Gnarr, in November 2009. The party won the largest number of seats on Reykjavík's city council, with Gnarr subsequently becoming mayor.

At a summit held in Brussels, Belgium, in June 2010, EU leaders agreed to open membership negotiations with Iceland, although it was made clear that accession would not be possible while the dispute with the UK and the Netherlands over compensation for savers who had lost Icesave deposits remained unresolved. In the previous month the EFTA Surveillance Authority had ruled that Iceland was obliged to ensure payment of the minimum compensation (€20,000) to British and Dutch savers. Negotiations on Iceland's accession to the EU formally opened in Brussels in July.

Direct elections to a constitutional parliament, which was to propose revisions to the Constitution, took place in November 2010, but were marked by an extremely low turnout of around 36% and were subsequently declared void by the Supreme Court owing to irregularities in the organization of the vote. In February a legislative committee recommended that the 25 people elected to the constitutional parliament should be appointed by the Althingi to a Constitutional Council, which would have a similar role to the planned parliament. The Constitutional Council was duly appointed and convened in April.

In December 2010 Iceland reached a new agreement with the Netherlands and the UK on the repayment of loans related to the compensation of savers who had lost deposits held in Icesave accounts. From Iceland's perspective, the terms of this accord represented a significant improvement on those of the previous one: repayments were to commence in 2016 and to be completed by 2046, while interest was to be paid at a fixed rate of 3.0% to the Netherlands and 3.3% to the UK (reflecting the differing cost to each country of raising funds). Annual repayments would also be limited to no more than the equivalent of 5% of government revenue in the preceding year or 1.3% of GDP (whichever was higher). In February 2011 the Althingi approved the ratification of the agreement, but President Grímsson again vetoed the accord, thus triggering the organization of a referendum, which took place on 9 April, at which the repayment agreement was rejected by 58.9% of those who voted. Opposition to the agreement appeared to centre on the rejection of the principle that the Icelandic taxpayer should be responsible for the debt. The dispute was referred to the Court of Justice of the European Free Trade Association States (EFTA Court), which in January 2013

ruled in Iceland's favour, judging that the relevant European directive did not require the Icelandic state itself to ensure payments to depositors in the Icesave branches in the Netherlands and the UK when the deposit guarantee scheme was unable to meet its obligations. Meanwhile, payments continued to be made from the estate of Landsbanki Íslands to the Governments of the UK and the Netherlands and to other priority creditors, including British and Dutch local authorities, having commenced in December 2011, following a ruling by the Supreme Court in October upholding emergency legislation adopted in 2008 that had given depositors priority status over other creditors for compensation. Although by early 2013 Landsbanki's estate had reportedly paid back a large proportion of the amount that the British and Dutch Governments had advanced to cover the minimum deposit guarantee, repayments to other creditors were expected to take many more years.

Recent developments: EU membership negotiations and constitutional review

Iceland and the EU commenced formal negotiations on the first four of the 35 negotiating chapters of the *acquis communautaire*, the EU's body of law, on 27 June 2011. Two of the chapters were completed that day, an unprecedented development within the EU's enlargement history, which was attributed to the fact that Iceland already largely complied with some two-thirds of EU law through its membership of the EEA.

In July 2011 the Constitutional Council presented its draft bill on a new constitution to the Althingi. The bill notably provided for increased public participation in decision-making (allowing 10% of the electorate to demand a referendum on laws adopted by the Althingi and 2% to submit a legislative proposal); a strengthening of the role of the Althingi; the creation of a Law Council (Lögrétta) to examine the constitutionality of new legislation; and greater autonomy for local authorities. In addition, the President would be limited to serving a maximum of three terms in office and government ministers to holding the same office for eight years, while the Prime Minister would be directly elected by the Althingi following legislative elections.

Grímsson was re-elected to serve a fifth term as President at an election held on 30 June 2012, securing 52.8% of the votes cast.

A non-binding national referendum on the Constitutional Council's draft bill on a new constitution was held on 20 October 2012. A majority of those who participated (48.9% of the electorate) responded positively to all six questions posed. A specific proposal that natural resources not in private ownership should be declared national property received the strongest level of support. In November the Althingi submitted the bill for the consideration of the Venice Commission of the Council of Europe, which criticized some provisions for being too general or unclear. As it became clear that discussions on the draft constitution would not be completed prior to the forthcoming legislative elections, which were scheduled to take place on 27 April, a deputy representing the opposition The Movement (which had been created in 2009 by former members of the Citizens' Movement) submitted a motion of no confidence in the Government owing to its failure to finalize the constitutional review during the current parliamentary term. The Government narrowly survived the vote, by 32 votes to 29. On the final day of its term in office a government amendment was adopted, stipulating that the draft constitution could be approved with the support of two-thirds of the Althingi and 40% of the electorate in a further referendum.

In January 2013 the Government announced that it was suspending the opening of negotiations on new chapters of the EU's *acquis* pending the elections to the Althingi in April. Popular support for EU accession had declined since the submission of Iceland's application for membership in July 2009, amid a recovery in the Icelandic economy and serious financial difficulties in the eurozone. National congresses held by the principal parties in February were dominated by discussions regarding EU accession negotiations, which the IP and PP wished to halt, while the SDA, the Left-Green Movement and Bright Future favoured their completion.

The governing coalition of the SDA and the Left-Green Movement—which had lost its narrow majority following a series of defections—was ousted at the legislative elections on 27 April 2013, with the IP and the PP each securing 19 seats. The Left-Green Movement won seven seats, while new groupings Bright Future, established in early 2012 by members of the Best Party and Guðmundur Steingrímsson, formerly of the PP, won six seats and the Pirate Party, campaigning for political transparency and internet freedom, won three seats. An electoral participation rate of 81.2% was the lowest recorded in the country's history. The PP and the IP agreed on coalition terms in May. Chairman of the PP Sigmundur Gunnlaugsson, whose party had more than doubled its representation at the election, became the youngest Prime Minister in Iceland's history, at 38 years old. Bjarni Benediktsson of the IP was appointed Minister of Finance and Economic Affairs. Both parties had campaigned against the country's bid to join the EU, and one of the first actions of the coalition Government was the announcement of the indefinite suspension of EU accession negotiations. There were protests outside the Althingi in early 2014, after members of the coalition parties in the Althingi voted in favour of suspending EU membership negotiations; opinion polls showed that some 82% of Icelanders wanted the issue of Iceland's application for membership put to the electorate in a referendum, as had been pledged by Benediktsson before the elections. Support for a referendum continued throughout the year; however, the Government announced in March 2015 that it had informed the EU that Iceland no longer considered itself a candidate country for EU membership.

Ongoing negotiations with the foreign creditors of Iceland's failed banks presented a persistent challenge for the new Government. At a meeting in London in September 2013 representatives of Landsbanki asked the British and Dutch Governments for a more lenient repayment schedule, claiming that the regime due to commence in early 2014 was not workable. Moreover, the Central Bank of Iceland had publicly stated that the country's economy could not support the schedule. However, in November 2013 the British and Dutch financial authorities began legal proceedings against the Icelandic Depositors' and Investors' Guarantee Fund over the collapse of Icesave.

Dissatisfaction with the governing coalition, and particularly with Prime Minister Benediktsson (who, according to an opinion poll in mid-2014, enjoyed a public approval rating of less than 40%), was reflected in the results of municipal elections in Reykjavík in May. The SDA won the largest number of votes, securing 32.6% of the total, and formed a coalition with the Left-Green Movement, Bright Future and the Pirate Party under the mayorship of SDA leader Dagur Eggertsson.

Iceland's distinctive cultural heritage was the focus of international interest in early 2015 when it was announced that the country's first pagan temple in about 1,000 years was to be built near Reykjavík. Iceland's main neo-pagan religion, the Asatrúarfélagid (Ásatrú) movement, which practises a modern version of Norse paganism, was reported to be gaining in popularity, its membership having tripled during the previous 10 years to some 2,400 in 2014.

Foreign Affairs

Regional relations

Iceland has strong links to the EU through its participation in the EEA and its membership of the Schengen Agreement on border controls. Negotiations on Iceland's accession to the EU formally opened in July 2010, one year after the country applied for membership, and discussions on the first four of the 35 negotiating chapters of the *acquis communautaire*, the EU's body of legislation, commenced in June 2011. Negotiations on accession to the EU, however, were suspended indefinitely following the general election of April 2013; in March 2015 the Government announced that it had informed the EU that Iceland did not intend to restart accession negotiations and no longer considered itself a candidate country for membership.

The importance of fishing to Iceland's economy, and fears of excessive exploitation of the fishing grounds near Iceland by foreign fleets, caused the Icelandic Government to extend its territorial waters to 12 nautical miles (22 km) in 1964 and to 50 nautical miles (93 km) in 1972. British opposition to these extensions resulted in two 'cod wars'. In October 1975 Iceland unilaterally introduced a fishing limit of 200 nautical miles (371 km), both as a conservation measure and to protect Icelandic interests. The 1973 agreement on fishing limits between Iceland and the UK expired in November 1975, and failure to reach a new agreement led to the third and most serious 'cod war'. Casualties occurred, and in February 1976 Iceland temporarily severed diplomatic relations with the UK, the first diplomatic break between two NATO countries. In June an agreement was reached, and in December the British trawler fleet withdrew from Icelandic waters. In June 1979 Iceland declared its exclusive rights to the 200-mile fishing zone. Following negotiations between the EC and EFTA on the creation of the EEA, an

agreement was reached (in October 1991) allowing tariff-free access to the EC for 97% of Iceland's fisheries products by 1997, while Iceland was to allow EC vessels to catch 3,000 metric tons of fish per year in its waters, in return for some access to EC waters. The EEA agreement was ratified by the Althingi in January 1993 and entered into force in January 1994.

In 1993 a dispute developed between Iceland and Norway over fishing rights in an area of the Barents Sea fished by Iceland, over which Norway claimed jurisdiction. Iceland's case was weakened in 1995, when Canada officially recognized Norway's sovereign rights over the disputed area (a fisheries protection zone extending 200 km around the Svalbard archipelago). A similar dispute arose in 1996 between Iceland and Denmark over fishing rights in an area of the Atlantic Ocean between Iceland and Greenland (a self-governing province of Denmark).

Iceland's relations with the EU and Norway were strained from mid-2010 by a dispute over fishing quotas for mackerel in the north-east Atlantic Ocean. Iceland had unilaterally set itself a mackerel quota of 130,000 metric tons for that year, in the absence of an agreement on the issue between the interested states. Iceland and the Faroe Islands, which also set their own quota, maintained that they had been forced to take this action having been excluded from a bilateral quota arrangement between the EU and Norway and that stocks of mackerel had become more plentiful in their waters as a result of changing migration patterns. Negotiations between officials from the four parties, held in October and November, failed to reach a resolution on quotas for 2011. The Icelandic Government subsequently announced that its mackerel quota for 2011 would be 146,818 tons, prompting threats of sanctions from the European Commission. However, Icelandic officials claimed that the EU and Norway would be primarily responsible for overfishing of mackerel in 2011, having allocated themselves more than 90% of the recommended total allowable catch. Officials from the EU, Norway, Iceland and the Faroe Islands engaged in several rounds of negotiations during 2011–12, but these again ended without agreement. In September 2012 the European Parliament approved a regulation that would allow the imposition of sanctions against countries deemed to be engaging in unsustainable fishing practices, including restrictions on the import of fish from these countries to the EU. The continued dispute over quotas led the Marine Conservation Society to downgrade mackerel from its list of fish suitable to eat. In February 2013 the Icelandic Government announced a 15% reduction in its mackerel quota for that year (compared with 2012), citing its commitment to the long-term sustainability of stocks. As in previous years, the European Commission expressed regret at such unilateral action, and in July 2013 the EU's Fisheries and Maritime Affairs Commissioner threatened to commence infringement action against Iceland. However, no such measures were undertaken and a further meeting between officials from Iceland and the EU in Reykjavík in September ended without agreement. The issue remained unresolved in early 2015.

Other external relations

Iceland has developed close relations with the USA, which was the first country officially to recognize Icelandic independence in 1944. Having joined NATO at its foundation in 1949, in 1951 Iceland concluded a bilateral defence agreement with the USA, which provided for the territorial defence of Iceland by the USA and led to the establishment of the Iceland Defence Force (IDF) at Keflavík airbase, near Reykjavík.

In 2003 it emerged that the USA was planning to withdraw the four remaining fighter jet aircraft stationed at Keflavík, following a review of its international military commitments. The IDF, which was composed of 1,658 US troops, was traditionally viewed as providing protection for Iceland, which had no military of its own; moreover, many Icelanders in the nearby town of Reykjanesbær depended on the Keflavík airbase for their livelihood. Prime Minister Oddsson suggested that if the USA withdrew the aircraft it would have to end its military presence in Iceland altogether—an unpalatable proposition for the USA, which still regarded its reconnaissance of the North Atlantic as a high priority. Concern among Icelanders was such that the Government requested that the Secretary-General of NATO, Lord Robertson of Port Ellen, intervene on their behalf. Following Lord Robertson's subsequent non-partisan representations, the US authorities announced that they had delayed their decision with regard to the aircraft at Keflavík.

In March 2006 the USA announced its intention to withdraw the remaining US troops from Keflavík airbase by October of that year. A subsequent offer by the Icelandic Government to contribute one-half of the annual cost of maintaining the US mission was rejected. In September the new coalition Government signed an agreement with the USA, under which the USA reaffirmed its commitment to defend Iceland as a NATO ally. Iceland was to pay up to 5,000m. krónur to clean contaminated land at the former US airbase and return the site to civilian use. On 30 September the USA completed the withdrawal of its troops from Iceland.

At a meeting of the North Atlantic Council in July 2007 NATO members signed an agreement over the protection of Icelandic airspace, which had been proposed by the Prime Minister, Geir Haarde, in November 2006. Under the accord, the air forces of NATO member countries would undertake military exercises and patrols in Iceland on a rotating basis at intervals of no more than four months, while the Icelandic Government would pay for technical assistance and the use by visiting forces of the facilities at the Keflavík airbase. In May 2008 the Ministry of Foreign Affairs established the Iceland Defence Agency (IDA) to co-ordinate the country's security and defence policy and supervise all NATO matters pertaining to Iceland. In January 2011, however, the IDA was dissolved, with its duties integrated into the interior and foreign affairs ministries.

Iceland strongly criticized the moratorium on commercial whaling, imposed (for conservation purposes) by the International Whaling Commission (IWC, see p. 438) in 1986, and continued to catch limited numbers of whales for scientific purposes. However, in 1989 Iceland halted whaling, following appeals by environmental organizations for an international boycott of Icelandic products. In 1991 Iceland announced its withdrawal from the IWC (with effect from June 1992), claiming that certain species of whales were not only too plentiful to be in danger of extinction, but were also threatening Iceland's stocks of cod and other fish. In 1999 the Althingi voted to end the self-imposed 10-year ban on whaling.

Iceland's application to rejoin the IWC, with an unprecedented exemption that would allow it to disregard the moratorium on commercial whaling, was rejected in July 2001. A further bid was rejected again in May 2002, but it was readmitted in October 2002, when the Government undertook not to allow the resumption of commercial whaling until at least 2006 and after that not to resume commercial whaling while negotiations on a revised management plan were in progress. In August 2003, however, Iceland resumed whaling for research purposes, provoking widespread international criticism. Furthermore, in October 2006 Iceland resumed commercial whaling. However, the suspension of commercial whaling quotas was announced for the 2007/08 fishing season, owing to a lack of consumer demand, meat from the 2006/07 season having remained unsold. By May 2008, however, the Government licensed the capture of 40 minke whales for the 2008/09 season, and in 2009 issued an annual whaling quota of 150 fin whales and 100 minke whales over a five-year period. The only company involved in capturing fin whales, Hvalur, suspended hunting for 2011, owing to weak demand from Japan, its main export market, but 58 minke whales were caught that season. Commercial hunting of minke whales continued in 2012, while hunting for fin whales, which are included on the International Union for the Conservation of Nature's 'red list' of endangered species, remained suspended. However, Hvalur resumed its commercial hunting of the fin whale in June 2013 and by September of that year it had killed 134 fin whales. The resumption of the practice provoked international outrage, with many freight operators refusing to ship the whale meat. A consignment of whale meat en route to Japan was sent back to Iceland from Hamburg, Germany, via Rotterdam, the Netherlands in July, when officials at the port refused to handle the cargo. None the less, the practice continued and a total of 137 fin whales were killed in the 2013/14 season.

In June 2014, following eight years of intermittent negotiations, Iceland and the People's Republic of China concluded a free trade agreement. The accord, which came into effect in July, was expected to increase economic co-operation between the two countries, particularly with regard to hydrocarbon exploration in the Arctic region. Moreover, in November Iceland's Minister of Foreign Affairs, Gunnar Sveinsson, met his Japanese counterpart in Tokyo, Japan, to discuss the possibility of a free trade agreement between the two nations. Japan had been a significant trading partner with Iceland for many years, purchasing a large proportion of the country's fish exports.

CONSTITUTION AND GOVERNMENT

The Constitution came into force in June 1944, when Iceland became an independent republic. Executive power is vested in the President (elected for four years by universal adult suffrage) and the Cabinet, consisting of the Prime Minister and other ministers appointed by the President. In practice, however, the President performs only nominally the functions ascribed in the Constitution to this office, and it is the Cabinet alone that holds real executive power. Legislative power is held jointly by the President and the unicameral Althingi (parliament), with 63 members elected by universal suffrage for four years (subject to dissolution by the President), using a system of proportional representation in eight multi-member constituencies. The Cabinet is responsible to the Althingi. Iceland is divided into 74 municipalities, each with a municipal council and executive. Municipal governments are responsible for education, infrastructure and social services.

REGIONAL AND INTERNATIONAL CO-OPERATION

Iceland is a member of the Nordic Council (see p. 462), the Arctic Council (see p. 444) and the European Free Trade Association (EFTA, see p. 446). It participates in the European Economic Area, and is thus integrated into the internal market of the European Union (EU, see p. 271); it is also a member the EU's Schengen Agreement on border controls by virtue of its membership of the Nordic passport union. Iceland applied for full membership of the EU in July 2009 and accession negotiations formally opened in July 2010. It is also participates in the Council of Europe (see p. 250) and the Organization for Security and Co-operation in Europe (OSCE, see p. 385).

Iceland joined the UN in 1946. As a contracting party to the General Agreement on Tariffs and Trade, it joined the World Trade Organization (WTO, see p. 431) on its establishment in 1995. Iceland was a founder member of the North Atlantic Treaty Organization (NATO, see p. 367) and is a member of the Organisation for Economic Co-operation and Development (OECD, see p. 377).

ECONOMIC AFFAIRS

In 2013, according to estimates by the World Bank, Iceland's gross national income (GNI), measured at 2011–13 prices, was US \$14,190m., equivalent to \$43,930 per head (or \$38,870 per head on an international purchasing-power parity basis). During 2004–13, it was estimated, the population increased at an average annual rate of 1.1%, while gross domestic product (GDP) per head increased, in real terms, by an average of 0.5% per year. Iceland's overall GDP increased, in real terms, at an average annual rate of 1.7% during 2004–13; GDP increased by 1.5% in 2012, and further by 3.3% in 2013.

Agriculture (including fishing) contributed a preliminary 7.6% of GDP in 2012 (fishing contributed 6.5% of GDP and agriculture alone only 1.1%); in 2013 4.6% of the employed labour force were engaged in the agricultural and fishing sectors, with a further 2.9% employed in fish processing. The principal agricultural products are dairy produce and lamb. Marine products accounted for 35.4% of total export earnings in 2013. A cod quota system is in place to avoid the depletion of fish stocks through overfishing as happened in previous years. The decline in the catch of cod has been offset by an increase in the catch of other species, such as haddock and redfish. Capelin remains the most valuable species, accounting for 32.5% of the value of the total catch in 2013, followed by cod (17.3%), herring (11.6%) and mackerel (11.3%). According to UN estimates, during 2004–12 agricultural GDP (including fishing) remained almost constant, with a negligible average annual rate of growth; the sector grew by 5.9% in 2012.

Industry (including mining, manufacturing, construction and power) contributed a preliminary 24.3% of GDP in 2012 and engaged 18.7% of the employed labour force (including the 2.9% employed in fish processing) in 2013. Mining activity is negligible. During 2004–12, according to UN estimates, industrial GDP decreased at an average annual rate of 0.1%; industrial GDP increased by 1.5% in 2011, but declined by 1.0% in 2012.

Manufacturing contributed a preliminary 13.4% of GDP in 2012, and employed 9.1% of the labour force in 2013. The most important sectors are fish processing (which contributed 4.0% of GDP in 2012), the production of aluminium, medical equipment, pharmaceuticals and ferrosilicon. Basic metal processing contributed 2.7% of GDP in 2012. A new aluminium smelter, Alcoa Fjardaál, fuelled by hydroelectric power plants, opened in 2007, with a production capacity of 346,000 metric tons per year.

Construction of an aluminium smelter at Helguvík, with a planned production capacity of 360,000 tons, began in 2008, but was subject to delays. However, the Government announced in May 2013 that it planned to allow construction of the smelter to recommence. During 2004–12 the GDP of the manufacturing sector grew at an average annual rate of 2.0%, according to UN estimates; the sector grew by 3.8% in 2011, but declined by 0.2% in 2012.

The construction sector contributed a preliminary 4.7% of GDP in 2012 and engaged 6.1% of the employed labour force in 2013. According to UN estimates, the GDP of the sector declined at an average annual rate of 4.9% during 2004–12; the GDP of the sector decreased by 0.4% in 2011, but increased by 1.5% in 2012.

Iceland is potentially rich in hydroelectric and geothermal power, although both energy sources have yet to be fully exploited. Hydroelectric power has promoted the development of the aluminium industry, while geothermal energy provides nearly all the country's heating and hot water. In 2013 hydroelectric power provided 71.8% of the country's electricity, geothermal energy 24.0% and fuel 4.1%. Fuel imports comprised 14.7% of the value of merchandise imports in 2013. In 2001 Iceland announced its intention to develop the world's first economy free of carbon dioxide emissions by using hydrogen or methanol-powered fuel cells. Two new hydroelectric power plants in the east of the country, the Kárahnjúkar Hydroelectric Project, built amid much controversy to fuel the Alcoa Fjardaál smelter, were officially opened in June 2007.

Services contributed a preliminary 68.0% of GDP in 2012 and employed 76.7% of the labour force in 2013. Banking was an important sector in Iceland, with the financial sector providing 8.7% of GDP in 2007; however, the sector effectively collapsed in October 2008, when the three largest banks, Glitnir Banki, Landsbanki Íslands and Kaupbing Banki, were placed in receivership. The tourism sector is becoming an increasingly significant source of revenue; the number of overnight stays by foreign visitors in hotels and guest houses totalled 2,231,963 in 2012. Receipts from tourism totalled US $1,059m. in 2013, according to provisional figures from the World Tourism Organization. According to UN estimates, the real GDP of the services sector grew at an average annual rate of 2.5% in 2004–12; the GDP of the sector increased by 2.8% in 2012.

In 2013 Iceland recorded a visible merchandise trade surplus of US $63.1m., while there was a surplus of $1,378.3m. on the current account of the balance of payments. In 2013 the principal sources of imports were Norway (providing 15.6% of total imports), followed by the USA, Germany, the People's Republic of China, Brazil, Denmark and the Netherlands; the principal market for exports was the Netherlands (accounting for 30.0% of total exports), followed by Germany and the UK. In 2013 member countries of the European Economic Area (EEA, see p. 446) provided 60.9% of Iceland's merchandise imports and took 79.1% of its exports. The principal imports in 2013 were industrial supplies, capital goods (except for transport), fuels and lubricants, consumer goods, food and beverages, and transport equipment. The principal exports in the same year were industrial supplies, and food and beverages.

In 2013 there was a budgetary deficit of 30,400m. krónur, equivalent to 1.7% of GDP. Iceland's total external debt was 12,421,840m. krónur at the end of 2013. Iceland's general government gross debt was 1,605,200m. krónur in 2013, equivalent to 72.7% of GDP. According to IMF estimates, the annual rate of inflation averaged 6.5% in 2004–13; consumer prices increased by 3.8% in 2013. The unemployment rate was 5.4% in 2013.

From the late 1990s the Icelandic economy expanded rapidly: the financial sector benefited from the liberalization of capital flows, while high-technology industries were developed and the tourism sector grew strongly. However, the over-extended banking sector experienced major difficulties in 2008 owing to a lack of availability of credit resulting from the international financial crisis, and in October the Government was forced to assume control of the three largest commercial banks. In November Iceland became the first Western nation since 1976 to receive IMF assistance. The stabilization of the currency, the króna, which had depreciated drastically, was the principal aim of the IMF's economic recovery programme. The Government that took office in May 2009 stated its intention to eliminate the fiscal deficit by 2013. The deficit was reduced from 13.5% of GDP in 2008 to 3.8% in 2012 and further to 2.1% in 2013. Despite the Government's original target, similar figures of 2.0% and 2.1% were estimated and predicted for 2014 and 2015, respectively. Meanwhile, the inflation rate decreased from 18.6% in January 2009 to 2.2% by early 2015. However, unemployment rose significantly, peaking at 9.1% in the second quarter of 2009; it fluctuated thereafter, but had declined to 4.3% by December 2014. Following contractions of 6.6% in 2009 and 4.1% in 2010, GDP increased by 2.1%, 1.5% and 3.3% in 2011, 2012 and 2013, respectively; GDP growth was estimated at 2.5% in 2014 and forecast at 3.3% in 2015. Iceland returned to the international credit markets in June 2011, in its first bond issue since 2006, and successfully completed its IMF-supported programme in August 2011, announcing the early repayment of some of its loans in early 2012. The country's relatively rapid recovery was attributed in part to its refusal (and inability) to bail out the failed banks and their foreign creditors and its exchange rate flexibility, which allowed the devaluation of the króna, thereby increasing export competitiveness. However, in early 2015 slow progress in removing capital controls imposed in 2008 continued to inhibit investment in Iceland. It was hoped that the Government's policy of household mortgage debt relief, introduced in mid-2013, would stimulate private spending in the country and further assist economic recovery.

PUBLIC HOLIDAYS

2016: 1 January (New Year's Day), 24 March (Maundy Thursday), 25 March (Good Friday), 28 March (Easter Monday), 21 April (First Day of Summer), 1 May (Labour Day), 5 May (Ascension Day), 16 May (Whit Monday), 17 June (National Day), 1 August (Bank Holiday), 24*–26 December (Christmas), 31 December (New Year's Eve)*.

* Afternoon only.

Statistical Survey

Sources (unless otherwise stated): Statistics Iceland, Borgartúni 21A, 150 Reykjavík; tel. 5281000; fax 5281099; e-mail statice@statice.is; internet www.statice.is; Seðlabanki Íslands (Central Bank of Iceland), Kalkofnsvegur 1, 150 Reykjavík; tel. 5699600; fax 5699605; e-mail sedlabanki@sedlabanki.is; internet www.sedlabanki.is.

AREA AND POPULATION

Area: 103,000 sq km (39,769 sq miles).

Population: 315,556 (males 158,147, females 157,409) at census of 31 December 2011; 325,671 (males 163,318, females 162,353) at 1 January 2014 (national population register).

Density (at 1 January 2014): 3.2 per sq km.

Population by Age and Sex (national population register at 1 January 2014): *0–14 years:* 66,809 (males 34,020, females 32,789); *15–64 years:* 215,820 (males 109,175, females 106,645); *65 years and over:* 43,042 (males 20,123, females 22,919); *Total* 325,671 (males 163,318, females 162,353).

Principal Towns (population at 1 January 2014): Reykjavík (capital) 121,230; Kópavogur 32,308; Hafnarfjörður 27,357; Akureyri 18,103; Reykjanesbær 14,527.

Births, Marriages and Deaths (2013, unless otherwise indicated): Live births 4,326 (birth rate 13.4 per 1,000); Marriages 1,458 (marriage rate 4.6 per 1,000) in 2011; Deaths 2,154 (death rate 6.7 per 1,000).

Life Expectancy (years at birth): 82.9 (males 81.6; females 84.3) in 2012. Source: World Bank, World Development Indicators database.

Economically Active Population (2013, figures rounded to nearest 100 persons): Agriculture 4,700; Fishing 3,600; Manufacturing (excl. fish-processing) 15,900; Fish-processing 5,000; Electricity and water supply 1,300; Construction 10,600; Wholesale and retail trade, repairs 23,700; Restaurants and hotels 10,100; Transport, storage and communications 11,900; Financial intermediation 7,200; Real estate and business services 17,800; Public administration 9,000; Education 20,500; Health services and social work 20,800; Other services not specified 13,100; *Total employed* (incl. unclassified)

174,900; Unemployed 10,000; *Total labour force* 184,900. Note: Totals may not be equal to the sum of components, owing to rounding.

HEALTH AND WELFARE
Key Indicators

Total Fertility Rate (children per woman, 2012): 2.1.

Under-5 Mortality Rate (per 1,000 live births, 2012): 2.

HIV/AIDS (% of persons aged 15–49, 2011): 0.3.

Physicians (per 1,000 head, 2012): 3.5.

Hospital Beds (per 1,000 head, 2007): 5.8.

Health Expenditure (2011): US $ per head (PPP): 3,361.

Health Expenditure (2011): % of GDP: 9.2.

Health Expenditure (2011): public (% of total): 80.7.

Total Carbon Dioxide Emissions ('000 metric tons, 2010): 1,961.8.

Carbon Dioxide Emissions Per Head (metric tons, 2010): 6.2.

Human Development Index (2013): ranking: 13.

Human Development Index (2013): value: 0.895.

For sources and definitions, see explanatory note on p. vi.

AGRICULTURE, ETC.

Principal Crops (metric tons, 2013): Cereals 5,890; Carrots 360; Cabbages 158; Tomatoes 1,560; Cucumbers 1,781; Cauliflower 51; Turnips 670; Peppers 243; Chinese cabbages 71; Mushrooms 585.

Livestock (2013 unless otherwise indicated): Cattle 70,461; Sheep 484,108; Horses 72,626; Goats 877; Pigs 3,651; Hens 215,180; Other poultry 50,820 (2012); Mink 38,800.

Livestock Products (metric tons, 2013, unless otherwise indicated): Cattle meat 9,891; Goat meat 9,891; Pig meat 6,404; Chicken meat 7,897; Milk ('000 litres, processed) 123,178 (2010).

Fishing (metric tons, live weight, 2013): Atlantic cod 236,051; Saithe 57,416; Haddock 45,471; Atlantic redfish 8,961; Capelin 442,780; Atlantic herring 157,446; Total (incl. others) 1,362,790.

INDUSTRY

Selected Products ('000 metric tons, 2012, unless otherwise indicated): Frozen fish 462.8 (demersal catch, 2009); Salted, dried or smoked fish 875.6 (2007); Cement 146.0 (2012); Ferrosilicon 131.8 (2012); Aluminium (unwrought) 802.8 (2012); Electric energy 18,116 million kWh (2013). Source: partly US Geological Survey.

FINANCE

Currency and Exchange Rates: 100 aurar (singular: eyrir) = 1 new Icelandic króna (plural: krónur). *Sterling, Dollar and Euro Equivalents* (31 December 2014): £1 sterling = 198.066 krónur; US $1 = 126.900 krónur; €1 = 154.069 krónur; 1,000 krónur = £5.05 = $7.88 = €6.49. *Average Exchange Rate* (krónur per US $): 125.083 in 2012; 122.179 in 2013; 116.767 in 2014.

Budget (general government finances, '000 million krónur, 2013): *Revenue:* Tax revenue 606.2 (Taxes on income, profits and capital gains 315.6, Taxes on payroll and workforce 6.5, Taxes on property 46.5, Taxes on goods and services 220.8, Taxes on international trade 5.8, Other taxes 11.0); Social contributions 69.9; Grants 2.9; Other revenue 116.8; Total 795.9. *Expenditure:* Current expenditure 825.0 (Compensation of employees 266.5, Use of goods and services 211.1, Consumption of fixed capital 38.3, Interest 94.4, Subsidies 32.3, Grants 4.2, Social benefits 132.6, Other expenditure 45.5); Non-financial assets 1.3; Total 826.3.

International Reserves (US $ million at 31 December 2013): Gold (national valuation) 76.6; IMF special drawing rights 8.3; Reserve position in IMF 28.9; Foreign exchange 4,123.6; Total 4,237.4. Source: IMF, *International Financial Statistics.*

Money Supply (million krónur at 31 December 2013): Currency outside banks 41,617; Transferable deposit 452,894; Other deposit 1,092,906; Broad money 1,587,417. Source: IMF, *International Financial Statistics.*

Cost of Living (Consumer Price Index; base: January 2008 = 100): All items 140.7 in 2012; 146.2 in 2013; 149.2 in 2014.

Gross Domestic Product (million krónur at constant 2005 prices): 1,059,557 in 2011; 1,075,058 in 2012; 1,110,137 in 2013. Source: IMF, *International Financial Statistics.*

Expenditure on the Gross Domestic Product (million krónur at current prices, 2013, preliminary): Government final consumption expenditure 455,735; Private final consumption expenditure 986,500; Changes in inventories −8,012; Gross fixed capital formation 282,749; *Total domestic expenditure* 1,716,971; Exports of goods

and services 1,043,741; *Less* Imports of goods and services 887,699; *Gross domestic product in market prices* 1,873,013.

Gross Domestic Product by Economic Activity (million krónur at current prices, 2012, preliminary): Agriculture, hunting and forestry 17,081; Fishing 102,277; Mining and quarrying 1,030; Manufacturing 209,437; Electricity, gas and water supply 95,442; Construction 73,922; Wholesale and retail trade and repair of vehicles and household goods 142,158; Hotels and restaurants 36,509; Transport, storage and communications 150,466; Financial intermediation 151,174; Real estate, renting and business services 229,157; Public administration and compulsory social security 134,375; Education 67,858; Health and social work 102,321; Other community, social and personal services 46,712; Private households with employed persons 1,107; Activities of extraterritorial organizations and bodies 251; *Sub-total* 1,561,274; Correction item, taxes and subsidies on products 16,359; *Gross value added at basic prices* 1,577,634; Taxes on production and imports 212,132; *Less* Subsidies 15,764; *GDP in market prices* 1,774,001.

Balance of Payments (US $ million, 2013): Exports of goods 4,592.7; Imports of goods −4,529.6; *Balance on goods* 63.1; Exports of services 3,649.0; Imports of services −1,934.8; *Balance on goods and services* 1,777.3; Primary income received 986.4; Primary income paid −1,270.5; *Balance on goods, services and primary income* 1,493.1; Secondary income received 73.1; Secondary income paid −187.9; *Current balance* 1,378.3; Capital account (net) −10.6; Direct investment assets −624.0; Direct investment liabilities 468.7; Portfolio investment assets −1,270.5; Portfolio investment liabilities −4,679.7; Financial derivatives and employee stock options (net) −4.5; Other investment assets 974.8; Other investment liabilities −416.4; Net errors and omissions −104.0; *Reserves and related items* −4,288.0. Source: IMF, *International Financial Statistics.*

EXTERNAL TRADE

Principal Commodities (million krónur, 2013): *Imports c.i.f.:* Food and beverages 58,268.1; Fuels and lubricants 85,673.2 (Motor spirit 16,850.6); Capital goods 133,067.5; Transport equipment 49,922.8 (Passenger cars 18,876.5); Consumer goods 78,711.3 (Semi-durable goods 30,117.8; Non-durable goods 33,814.2); Miscellaneous industrial supplies 176,970.3; Total (incl. others) 583,494.9. *Exports f.o.b.:* Food and beverages 257,685.2; Fuels and lubricants 9,759.8; Capital goods 20,573.7; Consumer goods 19,197.0; Miscellaneous industrial supplies 294,161.6; Total (incl. others) 610,691.6.

Principal Trading Partners (million krónur, country of consignment, 2013): *Imports c.i.f.:* Belgium 7,307.0; Brazil 44,826.3; Canada 5,885.3; China, People's Republic 47,841.6; Czech Republic 5,942.2; Denmark (incl. Faroe Islands and Greenland) 42,335.5; France 13,665.6; Germany 48,812.5; Italy 20,173.2; Japan 8,499.9; Netherlands 30,422.7; Norway 90,870.3; Poland 9,744.9; Spain 7,618.5; Sweden 24,594.9; Switzerland 10,502.3; United Kingdom 27,273.3; USA 58,042.5; Total (incl. others) 583,494.9. *Exports f.o.b.:* Belgium 10,590.0; China, People's Republic 7,020.1; Denmark (incl. Faroe Islands and Greenland) 26,289.0; France 28,341.1; Germany 74,165.5; Italy 13,478.5; Japan 11,442.1; Lithuania 10,508.5; Netherlands 183,402.7; Nigeria 12,134.3; Norway 28,913.1; Poland 7,645.8; Portugal 7,282.8; Russia 20,436.0; Spain 24,057.0; Switzerland 6,557.6; Ukraine 7,892.0; United Kingdom 57,894.5; USA 28,667.3; Total (incl. others) 610,691.6.

TRANSPORT

Road Traffic (registered motor vehicles, 2012): Passenger cars 245,949; Buses and coaches 2,179; Goods vehicles 30,657; Motorcycles 10,213.

Shipping: *Flag Registered Fleet* (registered vessels, 31 December 2014): Vessels 202; Total displacement 160,855 grt. Source: Lloyd's List Intelligence (www.lloydslistintelligence.com).

Civil Aviation (scheduled traffic, 2011): Kilometres flown (million) 37; Passengers carried ('000) 1,804; Passenger-km (million) 4,970; Total ton-km (million) 566. Source: UN, *Statistical Yearbook. Passengers Carried* ('000): 2,604 in 2013 (Source: World Bank, World Development Indicators database).

TOURISM

Foreign Visitors by Country of Origin (overnight stays in hotels and guesthouses, 2012): Canada 44,685; Denmark 105,911; France 161,597; Germany 349,603; Italy 59,736; Netherlands 92,181; Norway 124,981; Spain 66,142; Sweden 103,639; Switzerland 59,968; United Kingdom 351,215; USA 309,228; Total (incl. others) 2,231,963.

Receipts from Tourism (US $ million, excl. passenger transport): 751 in 2011; 865 in 2012; 1,059 in 2013 (Source: World Tourism Organization).

COMMUNICATIONS MEDIA

Telephones (2013): 115,826 main lines in use.

Mobile Cellular Telephones ('000 subscribers, 2013): 356.3.

Internet Subscribers ('000, 2011): 114.8.

Broadband Subscribers ('000, 2013): 115.8.

Books (published, 2010): 1,506 titles (incl. new editions).

Daily Newspapers (2010, unless otherwise specified): 3 (combined circulation 129,750 copies per issue in 2010).

Non-daily Newspapers (2010): 21 (combined circulation 230,792 copies).

Source: partly International Telecommunication Union.

EDUCATION

Institutions (2012 unless otherwise indicated): Pre-primary 256; Primary and secondary (lower level) 169 (2013); Secondary (higher level) 53 (2005); Tertiary (universities and colleges) 23 (2010).

Teachers (incl. part-time, 2012 unless otherwise indicated): Pre-primary 3,544; Primary and secondary (lower level) 4,779 (2013); Secondary (higher level) 1,915 (2011); Tertiary 2,070.

Students (2012 unless otherwise indicated): Pre-primary 19,713 (2013); Primary and Secondary (lower level) 42,734 (2013); Secondary (higher level) 25,460; Tertiary 18,619.

Pupil-teacher Ratio (primary education, UNESCO estimate): 9.7 in 2010/11 (Source: UNESCO Institute for Statistics).

Directory

The Government

HEAD OF STATE

President: ÓLAFUR RAGNAR GRÍMSSON (elected 29 June 1996, took office 1 August 1996; unopposed in 2000, began a second term 1 August 2000; re-elected 26 June 2004, began third term 1 August 2004; unopposed in 2008, began fourth term 1 August 2008; re-elected 30 June 2012, began a fifth term 1 August 2012).

THE CABINET
(April 2015)

A coalition of the Independence Party (IP) and the Progressive Party (PP).

Prime Minister: SIGMUNDUR DAVÍÐ GUNNLAUGSSON (PP).

Minister of Finance and Economic Affairs: BJARNI BENEDIKTSSON (IP).

Minister of Health: KRISTJÁN ÞÓR JÚLÍUSSON (IP).

Minister of Education, Science and Culture: ILLUGI GUNNARSSON (IP).

Minister of Industry and Trade: RAGNHEIÐUR ELÍN ÁRNADÓTTIR (IP).

Minister of Social Affairs and Housing: EYGLÓ HARÐARDÓTTIR (PP).

Minister of Fisheries and Agriculture: SIGURÐUR INGI JÓHANNSSON (PP).

Minister of Environment and Natural Resources: SIGRÚN MAGNÚSDÓTTIR (PP).

Minister for Foreign Affairs and External Trade: GUNNAR BRAGI SVEINSSON (PP).

Minister of the Interior: ÓLÖF NORDAL (IP).

MINISTRIES

Office of the President: Stadastaður, Sóleyjargötu 1, 101 Reykjavík; tel. 5404400; fax 5624802; e-mail forseti@forseti.is; internet www.forseti.is.

Prime Minister's Office: Stjórnarráðshúsinu við Lækjartorg, 101 Reykjavík; tel. 5458400; fax 5624014; e-mail postur@for.is; internet www.forsaetisraduneyti.is.

Ministry of Education, Science and Culture: Sölvhólsgötu 4, 150 Reykjavík; tel. 5459500; fax 5623068; e-mail postur@mrn.is; internet www.menntamalaraduneyti.is.

Ministry for the Environment and Natural Resources: Skuggasundi 1, 150 Reykjavík; tel. 5458600; fax 5624566; e-mail postur@uar.is; internet www.umhverfisraduneyti.is.

Ministry of Finance and Economic Affairs: Arnarhvoli við Lindargötu, 101 Reykjavík; tel. 5459200; fax 5459299; e-mail postur@fjr.is; internet www.fjr.is.

Ministry of Fisheries and Agriculture: Skúlagata 4, 150 Reykjavík; tel. 5459700; fax 5521160; e-mail postur@anr.is; internet www.sjavarutvegsraduneyti.is.

Ministry for Foreign Affairs: Rauðarárstíg 25, 150 Reykjavík; tel. 5459900; fax 5622373; e-mail postur@utn.stjr.is; internet www.mfa.is.

Ministry of Industries and Innovation: Skúlagata 4, 150 Reykjavík; tel. 5459700; fax 5521160; e-mail postur@anr.is; internet www.anr.is.

Ministry of the Interior: Sölvhólsgötu 7, 150 Reykjavík; tel. 5459000; fax 5527340; e-mail postur@irr.is; internet www.innanrikisraduneyti.is.

Ministry of Welfare: Hafnarhúsinu við Tryggvagötu, 101 Reykjavík; tel. 5458100; fax 5519165; e-mail postur@vel.is; internet www.velferdarraduneyti.is.

President and Legislature

PRESIDENT

Presidential Election, 30 June 2012

	% of votes
Ólafur Ragnar Grímsson	52.78
Thóra Arnórsdóttir	33.16
Ari Trausti Guðmundsson	8.64
Herdís Thorgeirsdóttir	2.63
Andrea Johanna Ólafsdóttir	1.80
Hannes Bjarnason	0.98

LEGISLATURE

Althingi
(Alþingi)

v/Austurvöll, 150 Reykjavík; tel. 5630500; fax 5630550; e-mail editor@althingi.is; internet www.althingi.is.

Speaker of the Althingi: EINAR K. GUÐFINNSSON.

Secretary-General (Clerk) of the Althingi: HELGI BERNÓDUSSON.

General Election, 27 April 2013

Party	Votes	% of votes	Seats
Sjálfstæðisflokkurinn (Independence Party)	50,454	26.70	19
Framsóknarflokkurinn (Progressive Party)	46,173	24.43	19
Samfylkingin (Social Democratic Alliance)	24,292	12.85	9
Vinstrihreyfingin–grænt framboð (Left-Green Movement)	20,546	10.87	7
Björt framtíð (Bright Future)	15,583	8.25	6
Píratar (Pirate Party)	9,647	5.10	3
Others*	22,295	11.80	—
Total	**188,990**	**100.00**	**63**

* Including Dögun (Dawn), Flokkur Heimilanna (Households Party), Lýðræðisvaktin (The Democracy Watch), Hægri Grænir Flokkur Fólksins (Right-Green People's Party), Regnboginn (Rainbow), Landsbyggðarflokkurinn (Rural Party), Sturla Jónsson, Húmanistaflokkurinn (Humanist Party) and Alþýðufylkingin (People's Front of Iceland).

Election Commission

Landskjörstjórn (National Electoral Commission): Kirkjustræti 8B, 150 Reykjavík; tel. 5630933; fax 5630905; e-mail thorhallur@althingi.is; internet www.landskjor.is; Sec. ÞÓRHALLUR VILHJÁLMSSON.

Political Organizations

Alþýðufylkingin (People's Front of Iceland—PFI): Hverfisgata 82, 101 Reykjavík; e-mail althydufylkingin@gmail.com; f. 2013; anti-capitalist, anti-euro; Chair. ÞORVALDUR ÞORVALDSSON.

Besti Flokkurinn (Best Party): Holtsgata 20, 101 Reykjavík; e-mail heida@bestiflokkurinn.is; internet www.bestiflokkurinn.is; f. 2009; satirical; won the largest number of seats on Reykjavík city council at municipal elections in 2010; Leader JÓN GNARR.

Björt framtíð (Bright Future): Hverfisgata 98, 101 Reykjavík; e-mail tolvupostur@heimasidan.is; internet www.bjortframtid.is; f. 2012; Leader GUÐMUNDUR STEINGRÍMSSON.

Dögun (Dawn): e-mail xdogun@xdogun.is; internet www.xdogun.is; f. 2012 as an alliance of Borgarahreyfingin, Frjálslyndi flokkurinn and other small parties; Chair. BENEDIKT SIGURÐARSON.

Flokkur Heimilanna (Households Party): f. 2013; a coalition of 8 smaller parties formed to contest the 2013 general election.

Framsóknarflokkurinn (Progressive Party—PP): Hverfisgötu 33, POB 453, 101 Reykjavík; tel. 5404300; fax 5404301; e-mail framsokn@framsokn.is; internet www.framsokn.is; f. 1916 with a programme of social liberalism and co-operation; Chair. SIGMUNDUR DAVÍÐ GUNNLAUGSSON; Parliamentary Leader SIGRÚN MAGNÚS-DÓTTIR.

Frjálslyndi flokkurinn (Liberal Party): Lyngháls 3, 110 Reykja-vík; tel. 4452093; e-mail xf@xf.is; f. 1998 by Sverrir Hermannsson, a former IP cabinet minister; incorporated fmr mems of defunct Nýtt Afl (New Force) in 2006; part of the Dögun alliance; Leader SIGURJÓN ÞÓRÐARSON.

Hægri Grænir Flokkur Fólksins (Right-Green People's Party): Barónsstígur 47, 101 Reykjavík; tel. 5177740; e-mail stjornmalaflokkur@gmail.com; internet www.afram-island.is; f. 2010; Chair. GUÐMUNDUR FRANKLÍN JÓNSSON.

Húmanistaflokkurinn (Humanist Party): Brautarholt 4, 105 Rey-kjavík; tel. 6615621; f. 1984.

Landsbyggðarflokkurinn (Rural Party): f. 2013.

Lýðræðisvaktin (The Democracy Watch): e-mail xlvaktin@xlvaktin.is; f. 2013; Leader Dr THORVALDUR GYLFASON.

Píratar (Pirate Party): e-mail piratar@piratar.is; internet www.piratar.is; f. 2012; Leader BIRGITTA JÓNSDÓTTIR.

Regnboginn (Rainbow): Reykjavík; e-mail regnboginn@regnboginn.is; internet regnboginn.is; f. 2013; Spokesperson JÓN BJARNASON.

Samfylkingin (Social Democratic Alliance—SDA): Hallveigarstíg 1, 101 Reykjavík; tel. 4142200; fax 4142201; e-mail samfylking@samfylking.is; internet www.samfylkingin.is; f. 1999 by merger of Alþýðubandalagið (People's Alliance, f. 1956), Alþýðuflokkurinn (Social Democratic Party, f. 1916), Samtök um kvennalista (Women's List, f. 1983) and Þjóðvaki—hreyfing fólksins (Awakening of the Nation—People's Movement, f. 1994); Chair. ÁRNI PÁLL ÁRNASON; Parliamentary Leader MAGNÚS ORRI SCHRAM.

Sjálfstæðisflokkurinn (Independence Party—IP): Háaleitisbraut 1, 105 Reykjavík; tel. 5151700; fax 5151717; e-mail xd@xd.is; internet www.xd.is; f. 1929 by an amalgamation of the Conservative and Liberal Parties; advocates social reform within the framework of private enterprise and the furtherance of national and individual independence; Leader BJARNI BENEDIKTSSON; Parliamentary Leader RAGNHEIÐUR RÍKHARÐSDÓTTIR; Sec.-Gen. ÞÓRÐUR ÞÓRARINSSON.

Sturla Jónsson: f. 2013; fmrly called Forward Moving Party; Leader STURLA JÓNSSON.

Vinstrihreyfingin–grænt framboð (Left-Green Movement): Suðurgötu 3, POB 175, 101 Reykjavík; tel. 5528872; e-mail vg@vg.is; internet www.vg.is; f. 1999 by dissident mems of the People's Alliance, the Women's List, the Greens and independent left-wingers; around 3,000 mems; Leader KATRÍN JAKOBSDÓTTIR; Parlia-mentary Leader SVANDÍS SVAVARSDÓTTIR; Sec.-Gen. SÓLEY TÓMAS-DÓTTIR.

Diplomatic Representation

EMBASSIES IN ICELAND

Canada: Túngata 14, 101 Reykjavík; POB 1510, 121 Reykjavík; tel. 5756500; fax 5756501; e-mail rkjvk@international.gc.ca; internet www.canadainternational.gc.ca/iceland-islande; Ambassador STEW-ART WHEELER.

China, People's Republic: Bríetartún 1, 105 Reykjavík; tel. 5526751; fax 5626110; e-mail chinaemb@simnet.is; internet is .china-embassy.org; Ambassador ZHANG WEIDONG.

Denmark: Hverfisgata 29, 101 Reykjavík; tel. 5750300; fax 5750310; e-mail rekamb@um.dk; internet island.um.dk; Ambassador KJUEL NIELSEN.

Finland: Túngata 30, 101 Reykjavík; POB 1060, 121 Reykjavík; tel. 5100100; fax 5623880; e-mail sanomat.rey@formin.fi; internet www .finland.is; Ambassador VALTTERI HIRVONEN.

France: Túngata 22, 101 Reykjavík; POB 1750, 121 Reykjavík; tel. 5759600; fax 5759604; e-mail ambafrance@ambafrance.is; internet ambafrance-is.org; Ambassador PHILIPPE O'QUIN.

Germany: Laufásvegur 31, 101 Reykjavík; tel. 5301100; fax 5301101; e-mail info@reykjavik.diplo.de; internet www.reykjavik .diplo.de; Ambassador THOMAS MEISTER.

India: Skúlagata 17, 101 Reykjavík; tel. 5349955; fax 5349959; e-mail gen@indianembassy.is; internet www.indianembassy.is; Ambassador ASHOK DAS.

Japan: Laugavegur 182, POB 5380, 105 Reykjavík; tel. 5108600; fax 5108605; e-mail japan@rk.mofa.go.jp; internet www.is.emb-japan.go .jp; Ambassador MITSUKO SHINO.

Norway: Fjólugötu 17, 101 Reykjavík; tel. 5200700; fax 5529553; e-mail emb.reykjavik@mfa.no; internet www.noregur.is; Ambas-sador CECILIE LANDSVERK.

Poland: Þórunnartún 2, 105 Reykjavik; tel. 5205050; fax 5111120; e-mail reykjavik.info@msz.gov.pl; internet www.reykjavik.msz.gov .pl; Ambassador STEFAN CZMUR (Resident in Oslo, Norway).

Russian Federation: Garðastræti 33, POB 380, 101 Reykjavík; tel. 5515156; fax 5620633; e-mail russemb@itn.is; internet www.iceland .mid.ru; Ambassador ANTON V. VASILIEV.

Sweden: Lágmúla 7, 108 Reykjavík; POB 8136, 128 Reykjavík; tel. 5201230; fax 5201235; e-mail ambassaden.reykjavik@foreign .ministry.se; internet www.swedenabroad.com/reykjavik; Ambas-sador BO WILLIAM HEDBERG.

United Kingdom: Laufásvegur 31, 101 Reykjavík; POB 460, 121 Reykjavík; tel. 5505100; fax 5505105; e-mail info@britishembassy.is; internet ukiniceland.fco.gov.uk; Ambassador STUART GILL.

USA: Laufásvegur 21, 101 Reykjavík; tel. 5629100; fax 5629139; e-mail reykjavikprotocol@state.gov; internet iceland.usembassy .gov; Ambassador ROBERT C. BARBER.

Judicial System

All cases are heard in Ordinary Courts except those specifically within the jurisdiction of Special Courts. The Ordinary Courts include both a lower division of urban and rural district courts presided over by the district magistrates, and the Supreme Court.

Justices of the Supreme Court are appointed by the President and cannot be dismissed except by the decision of a court. The Justices elect the Chief Justice for a period of two years.

Supreme Court: Dómhúsið v. Arnarhól, 150 Reykjavík; tel. 5103030; fax 5623995; e-mail haestirettur@haestirettur.is; internet www.haestirettur.is; Chief Justice MARKÚS SIGURBJÖRNS-SON.

Religion

In early 2015 some 74.0% of the total population were members of the Þjóðkirkja Íslands (Evangelical Lutheran Church of Iceland). The Free Lutheran Churches had a total membership of 4.9% of the population, while 3.6% were members of the Roman Catholic Church. Some 7.1% belonged to 'other and not specified' religious organizations (including religions, such as Judaism, that have been practised in the country for years without requesting official recog-nition), while 5.6% were not part of any religious organization.

CHRISTIANITY

Protestant Churches

Þjóðkirkja Íslands (Evangelical Lutheran Church of Iceland): Biskupsstofa, Laugavegur 31, 150 Reykjavík; tel. 5284000; fax 5284099; e-mail kirkjan@kirkjan.is; internet www.kirkjan.is; the national church, endowed by the state; Iceland forms 1 diocese, with 2 suffragan sees; 272 parishes, 130 pastors; 242,743 mems (2015); Bishop AGNES M. SIGURÐARDÓTTIR.

A further 19 Protestant churches are officially registered, the largest of which are the following:

Fríkirkjusöfnuðurinn í Hafnarfirði (Hafnarfjörður Free Lutheran Church): Linnetsstíg 6–8, 220 Hafnarfjörður; tel. 5653430; e-mail einar@frikirkja.is; internet www.frikirkja.is; f. 1913; 6,416 mems (2015); Head EINAR EYJÓLFSSON.

Fríkirkjusöfnuðurinn í Reykjavík (Reykjavík Free Lutheran Church): Laufásvegi 13, 101 Reykjavík; POB 1671, 121 Reykjavík; tel. 5527270; fax 5527287; e-mail frikirkjan@frikirkjan.is; internet www.frikirkjan.is; f. 1899; Free Lutheran denomination; 9,556 mems (2015); Head HJÖRTUR MAGNI JÓHANNSSON.

Hvítasunnukirkjan á Íslandi (Pentecostal Assemblies): Hátúni 2, 105 Reykjavík; tel. 5354700; e-mail filadelfia@filadelfia.is; internet www.filadelfia.is; f. 1936; 2,108 mems (2015); Head VÖRÐUR LEVÍ TRAUSTASON.

Óhádi söfnuðurinn (Independent Congregation): Háteigsvegi 56, 105 Reykjavík; tel. 5510999; e-mail postur@ohadisofnudurinn.is; internet www.ohadisofnudurinn.is; Free Lutheran denomination; 3,348 mems (2015); Head Rev. PÉTUR ÞORSTEINSSON.

The Roman Catholic Church

Iceland comprises a single diocese, directly responsible to the Holy See. At the beginning of 2015 there were 11,911 adherents in the country (3.5% of the total population).

Bishop of Reykjavík: Rt Rev. PIERRE BÜRCHER, Biskupsstofa, Hávallagata 14, 101 Reykjavík; POB 490, 121 Reykjavík; tel. 5525388; fax 5623878; e-mail catholica@catholica.is; internet www .catholica.is.

ISLAM

Félag múslima á Íslandi (Muslim Asscn of Iceland): Ármúli 38, 3 hæð, 108 Reykjavík; tel. 8951967; e-mail ibrahim@islam.is; internet www.islam.is; f. 1997; 486 mems (2015); Head IBRAHIM SVERRIR AGNARSSON.

BAHÁ'Í FAITH

Bahá'í samfélagið á Íslandi (Bahá'í Community of Iceland): Öldugötu 2, 101 Reykjavík; tel. 5670344; e-mail nsa@bahai.is; internet www.bahai.is; 381 mems (2015); Sec. RÓBERT BADÍ BALDURSSON.

BUDDHISM

Búddistafélag Íslands (Buddhist Association of Iceland): Víghólastíg 21, 200 Kópavogur; 1,022 mems (2015); Head PHAMAHA-PRASIT BOONKAM.

Trúfélagið Zen á Íslandi, Nátthagi (Soto Zen Buddhist Asscn of Iceland): Grensásvegur 8, 108 Reykjavík; e-mail zen@zen.is; internet www.zen.is; 85 mems (2011); Head HELGA JÓAKIMSDÓTTIR.

OTHER RELIGIOUS ORGANIZATION

Ásatrúarfélagið (Asatru): Síðumúla 15, 108 Reykjavík; tel. 5618633; e-mail asatru@asatru.is; internet asatru.is; pagan rite; 2,675 mems (2015); f. 1972; Chair. HALLUR GUÐMUNDSSON.

The Press

PRINCIPAL DAILIES

DV (Dagblaðið-Vísir): DV ehf, Tryggvagötu 11, 101 Reykjavík; tel. 5127000; e-mail ritstjorn@dv.is; internet www.dv.is; f. 1910; independent; Editors REYNIR TRAUSTASON, JON TRAUSTI REYNISSON; circ. 340,000 (2013).

Fréttablaðið (The Newspaper): Skaftahlíð 24, 105 Reykjavík; tel. 5125000; fax 5125301; e-mail ritstjorn@frettabladid.is; internet www.visir.is; f. 2001; distributed free of charge; owned by 365 miðlar ehf; Editor-in-Chief ÓLAFUR Þ. STEPHENSEN; circ. 88,000 (2010).

Morgunblaðið (Morning News): Hádegismóum 2, 110 Reykjavík; tel. 5691100; fax 5691110; e-mail morgunbladid@mbl.is; internet www.mbl.is; f. 1913; owned by Árvakur hf; Editors DAVÍÐ ODDSSON, HARALDUR JOHANNESSEN; circ. 43,250 (2010).

WEEKLIES

Bæjarins besta (BB): Sólgötu 9, 400 Ísafjörður; tel. 4564560; fax 4564564; e-mail bb@bb.is; internet www.bb.is; f. 1984; local; Editor SIGURJÓN J. SIGURÐSSON.

Fiskifréttir: Nóatúni 17, 105 Reykjavík; tel. 5116622; fax 5696692; e-mail vb@vb.is; internet www.fiskifrettir.is; f. 1983; weekly; for the fishing industry; Editor GUÐJÓN EINARSSON; circ. 6,000.

Séð & Heyrt: Lyngás 17, 210 Garðabær; tel. 5155500; fax 5155599; e-mail birtingur@birtingur.is; internet www.birtingur.is; showbusiness and celebrities; Editor LILJA KATRÍN GUNNARSDÓTTIR; circ. 23,000.

Skessuhorn: Kirkjubraut 56, 300 Akranesi; tel. 4335500; fax 4335501; e-mail skessuhorn@skessuhorn.is; internet www .skessuhorn.is; f. 1998; local; Editor MAGNÚS MAGNÚSSON.

Sunnlenska Fréttablaðið: Austurvegi 22, 800 Selfoss; tel. 4823074; fax 4823084; e-mail sunnlenska@sunnlenska.is; internet www.sunnlenska.is; f. 1991; local newspaper; Editor SIGMUNDUR SIGURÐSSON; circ. 6,300.

Vikan: Lyngháls 17, 210 Garðabær; tel. 5155500; fax 5155599; e-mail birtingur@birtingur.is; internet www.birtingur.is; f. 1938; publ. by Birtíngur; women's weekly; Editor ELÍN ARNAR; circ. 17,000.

Víkurfréttir: Grundarvegur 23, 260 Reykjanesbær; tel. 4210000; fax 4210020; e-mail pket@vf.is; internet www.vf.is; f. 1983; local newspaper; Editor PÁLL KETILSSON; circ. 8,700.

Viðskiptablaðið: Nóatún 17, 105 Reykjavík; tel. 5116622; fax 5116692; e-mail mottaka@vb.is; internet www.vb.is; f. 1994; publ. by Myllusetur ehf; business weekly in collaboration with the *Financial Times* (UK); Editor-in-Chief PÉTUR ÁRNI JÓNSSON.

OTHER PERIODICALS

Ægir: Hafnarstræti 82, 600 Akureyri; tel. 5155220; e-mail johann@ athygli.is; internet www.athygli.is; f. 1905; owned by Athygli ehf; publ. by the Fisheries Asscn of Iceland; 10 a year; Editor JÓHANN ÓLAFUR HALLDÓRSSON; circ. 2,500.

Atlantica: Borgartún 23, 105 Reykjavík; tel. 5127575; fax 5618646; e-mail heimur@heimur.is; internet www.heimur.is; f. 1967; 6 a year; in-flight magazine of Icelandair; Editor PÁLL STEFÁNSSON.

Bændablaðið: 107 Reykjavík; tel. 5630300; fax 5623058; e-mail bbl@bondi.is; f. 1995; fortnightly; organ of the Icelandic farmers' union; Editor HÖRÐUR KRISTJÁNSSON; circ. 6,400.

Eiðfaxi: Nóatúni 17, 105 Reykjavík; tel. 5116622; e-mail eidfaxi@ eidfaxi.is; internet www.eidfaxi.is; f. 1977; monthly (Icelandic edn, English and German edns every 2 months); horse-breeding and horsemanship; circ. 7,000.

Freyr, búnaðarblað: Bændahöllin við Hagatorg, 107 Reykjavík; tel. 5630300; fax 5623058; e-mail freyr@bondi.is; internet www .bondi.is; monthly; agriculture; Editor TJORVI BJARNASON; circ. 1,600.

Frjáls Verslun (Free Trade): Borgartún 23, 105 Reykjavík; tel. 5617575; fax 5618646; e-mail jgh@heimur.is; internet www.heimur .is; f. 1939; 10 a year; business magazine; Editor JÓN G. HAUKSSON; circ. 6,000–9,000.

Gestgjafinn: Lyngás 17, 210 Garðabær; tel. 5155500; fax 5155599; e-mail gestgjafinn@frodi.is; internet www.gestgjafinn.is; f. 1981; 12 a year; food and wine; Editor SIGRÍÐUR BJÖRK BRAGADÓTTIR; circ. 13,000–16,000.

Hús og Híbýli: Lyngás 17, 210 Garðabær; tel. 5155500; fax 5155599; e-mail birtingur@birtingur.is; f. 1973; 17 a year; architecture, homes and gardens; Editor SIGRÍÐUR ELÍN ASMUNDSDÓTTIR; circ. 15,000–17,000.

Húsfreyjan (The Housewife): Túngata 14, 101 Reykjavík; tel. 5517044; e-mail husfreyjan@husfreyjan.is; f. 1949; quarterly; the organ of the Federation of Icelandic Women's Societies; Editor HRAFNHILDUR VALGARÐS; circ. 4,000.

Iceland Review: Borgartún 23, 105 Reykjavík; tel. 5127575; e-mail icelandreview@icelandreview.com; internet www.icelandreview .com; f. 1963; quarterly, in English; general; Editor PÁLL STEFÁNSSON.

Lifandi vísindi: Klapparstíg 25, 105 Reykjavík; tel. 5708300; fax 5703809; e-mail lifandi@visindi.is; internet www.visindi.is; popular science; Editor GUÐBJARTUR FINNBJÖRNSSON.

Mannlíf: Lyngás 17, 210 Garðabær; tel. 5155500; fax 5155599; e-mail birtingur@birtingur.is; internet www.birtingur.is; f. 1984; 10 a year; general interest; Dir KARLS STEINARS ÓSKARSSONAR; circ. 16,000.

Myndbönd mánaðarins (Videos of the Month): Reykjavík; tel. 5811280; fax 5811286; e-mail myndmark@islandia.is; f. 1994; monthly; Editor BERGUR ÍSLEIFSSON; circ. 26,000.

Nýtt Líf: Lyngás 17, 210 Garðabær; tel. 5155555; fax 5155599; e-mail nyttlif@birtingur.is; f. 1978; 11 a year; fashion; Editor KOLBRÚN PÁLÍNA HELGADÓTTIR; circ. 13,000–17,000.

Peningamál: Kalkofnsvegur 1, 150 Reykjavík; tel. 5699600; fax 5699605; e-mail sedlabanki@sedlabanki.is; internet www .sedlabanki.is; f. 1999; 4 a year; bulletin published by the Central Bank; Editor THÓRARINN G. PÉTURSSON; circ. 1,000.

The Reykjavík Grapevine: Hafnarstræti 15, 101 Reykjavík; tel. 5403600; fax 5403609; e-mail grapevine@grapevine.is; internet www .grapevine.is; f. 2003; 18 a year; in English; distributed free of charge; owned by Fröken ehf; Publr HILMAR STEINN GRÉTARSSON; Editor HAUKUR S. MAGNÚSSON; circ. 30,000.

Skírnir: Skeifan 3B, 108 Reykjavík; tel. 5889060; fax 5814088; e-mail hib@islandia.is; internet www.hib.is; f. 1827; journal of Hið íslenska bókmenntafélag (Icelandic Literary Society); Editor HALLDÓR GUÐMUNDSSON.

Skutull (Harpoon): Miðtun 16, 400 Isafjörður; tel. 8958270; e-mail skutull@skutull.is; internet skutull.is; f. 1923; monthly; organ of the Social Democratic Alliance in Westfjords; Editor SIGURÐUR PÉTURSSON.

Ský: Borgartún 23, 105 Reykjavík; tel. 5127575; fax 5618646; e-mail benedikt@heimur.is; internet www.heimur.is; complimentary in-flight magazine of Air Iceland; Editors BENEDIKT JÓHANNESSON, JÓN G. HAUKSSON.

Tölvuheimur (PC World Iceland): Borgartún 23, 105 Reykjavík; tel. 5127575; fax 5618646; e-mail tolvuheimur@heimur.is; internet www

.heimur.is; in collaboration with International Data Group; computers; Editor (vacant).

Veiðimaðurinn (The Angler): Borgartún 23, 105 Reykjavík; tel. 5127575; fax 5618646; e-mail heimur@heimur.is; internet www .heimur.is; f. 1984; 3 a year; angling; Editor BJARNI BRYNJÓLFSSON; circ. 5,000–7,000.

Vinnan (Labour): Sætún 1, 105 Reykjavík; tel. 5107500; fax 5107501; e-mail gra@asi.is; internet www.asi.is; 2 a year; f. 1943; publ. by Icelandic Federation of Labour; Editor Dr SNORRI MÁR SKÚLASON; circ. 5,000.

Vísbending: Borgartún 23, 105 Reykjavík; tel. 5127575; fax 5618646; e-mail heimur@heimur.is; internet www.heimur.is; f. 1983; weekly; business; Editor BENEDIKT JÓHANNESSON.

Publishers

Birtíngur útgáfufélag: Lyngás 17, 110 Garðabær; tel. 5155500; fax 5155599; e-mail birtingur@birtingur.is; internet www.birtingur.is; f. 2007; publr of popular magazines: *Gestgjafinn*, *Hús & Híbýli*, *Júlía*, *Nýtt Líf*, *Sagan Öll*, *Séð & Heyrt*, *Vikan* and *WOW*; Dir HREINN LOFTSSON.

Bjartur: Bræðraborgarstíg 9, 101 Reykjavík; tel. 4141450; e-mail bjartur@bjartur.is; internet www.bjartur.is; f. 1990; contemporary fiction, illustrated and children's books; Publr PÉTUR MÁR ÓLAFSSON.

Edda útgáfa hf: Lynghálsi 4, 110 Reykjavík; tel. 5222000; fax 5222022; e-mail edda@edda.is; internet www.edda.is; imprints: Almenna bókafélagið, Forlagið, Iðunn, Mál og menning, Nýja bókafélagið-Þjóðsaga, Vaka-Helgafell; Icelandic fiction and non-fiction, translated fiction, biography, illustrated books, children's books on Iceland, maps; Man. Dir SÆMUNDUR BENEDIKTSSON; Editor GRÉTA BJÖRG JAKOBSDÓTTIR.

Forlagið: Bræðraborgarstíg 7, 101 Reykjavík; tel. 5755600; fax 5755601; e-mail forlagid@forlagid.is; internet www.forlagid.is; general, fiction, biography, reference, illustrated; Dir JÓHANN PÁLL VALDIMARSSON.

Háskólaútgáfan (University of Iceland Press): Dunhagi 18, 107 Reykjavík; tel. 5254003; fax 5255255; e-mail hu@hi.is; internet www .haskolautgafan.hi.is; f. 1988; non-fiction, science, culture, history; Man. Dir JÖRUNDUR GUÐMUNDSSON.

Hið íslenska bókmenntafélag (Icelandic Literary Society): Skeifan 3B, 108 Reykjavík; tel. 5889060; fax 5814088; e-mail hib@islandia .is; internet www.hib.is; f. 1816; literary criticism; Pres. SIGURÐUR LÍNDAL.

Hið íslenska Fornritafélag: Skeifan 3B, 108 Reykjavík; tel. 5889060; fax 5814088; e-mail hib@islandia.is; internet www.hib.is; f. 1928; Pres. J. NORDAL.

Hólar: Hagasel 14, 109 Reykjavík; tel. 5872619; fax 5871180; e-mail holar@holabok.is; internet www.holabok.is; f. 1995; general; Dir GUDJÓN INGI EIRÍKSSON.

Jentas ehf: Austurströnd 10, 170 Seltjarnarnes; tel. 5687054; internet www.jentas.is; f. 1997; fmrly PP Forlag ehf Ísland; general; Dir SIGRÚN HALLDÓRSDÓTTIR.

Krydd í tilveruna: Heiðarhjalli 5, 200 Kópavogur; tel. 8923334; e-mail krydd@simnet.is; f. 1989; children's, cookery; Dir ÆVAR GUÐMUNDSSON.

Námsgagnastofnun (National Centre for Educational Materials): Víkurhvarf 3, 203 Kópavogur; tel. 5350400; fax 5350401; e-mail simi@nams.is; internet www.nams.is; f. 1979; state-owned; Man. Dir INGIBJÖRG ÁSGEIRSDÓTTIR.

Ormstunga: Ránargötu 20, 101 Reykjavík; tel. 5610055; e-mail books@ormstunga.is; internet www.ormstunga.is; f. 1992; Icelandic and foreign fiction and non-fiction; Dir GÍSLI MÁR GÍSLASON.

Salka: Skipholti 50C, 105 Reykjavík; tel. 5222250; fax 5528122; e-mail salka@salka.is; internet www.salka.is; f. 2000; non-fiction, books for, by and about women; Dir HILDUR HERMÓÐSDÓTTIR.

Samhjálp: Stangarhyl 3A, 110 Reykjavík; tel. 5611000; fax 5610050; e-mail heidar@samhjalp.is; internet www.samhjalp.is; religious, pentecostal; Dir HEIDAR GUÐNASON.

Setberg: Akralind 2, 203 Kópavogur; tel. 5517667; fax 5526640; e-mail setberg@setberg.is; internet www.setberg.is; f. 1950; fiction, cookery, juvenile, picture books, activity books and children's books; Dir ARNBJÖRN KRISTINSSON.

Skálholtsútgáfan (National Church Publishing): Laugavegi 31, 101 Reykjavík; tel. 5284200; fax 5621595; e-mail skalholtsutgafan@ skalholtsutgafan.is; internet www.skalholtsutgafan.is; f. 1981; non-fiction, religion, children's; Man. Dir EDDA MÖLLER.

Skjaldborg ehf: Mörkin 1, POB 8427, 108 Reykjavík; tel. 5882400; fax 5888994; e-mail skjaldborg@skjaldborg.is; general; Dir BJÖRN EIRÍKSSON.

Skrudda: Eyjarslóð 9, 101 Reykjavík; tel. 5528866; fax 5528870; e-mail skrudda@skrudda.is; internet www.skrudda.is; f. 2003; fiction, non-fiction, translated fiction, biography, children's; Man. STEINGRIMUR STEINTHORSSON.

Sögufélagið: Skeifunni 3B, 108 Reykjavík; tel. 5889060; e-mail sogufelag@sogufelag.is; internet www.sogufelag.is; f. 1902; non-fiction, history; Dir GUÐNI TH. JÓHANNESSON.

Stofnun Árna Magnússonar í íslenskum fræðum: Árnagarður, Suðurgötu, 101 Reykjavík; tel. 5254010; fax 5254035; e-mail arnastofnun@hi.is; internet www.arnastofnun.is; f. 1972; state-owned; non-fiction; Dir GUÐRÚN NORDAL.

Útgáfufélagið Heimur: Borgartún 23, 105 Reykjavík; tel. 5127575; fax 5618646; e-mail heimur@heimur.is; internet www.heimur.is; f. 2000; magazines, travel books; Man. Dir BENEDIKT JÓHANNESSON.

PUBLISHERS' ASSOCIATION

Félag íslenskra bókaútgefenda (Icelandic Publishers' Asscn): Barónsstíg 5, 101 Reykjavík; tel. 5118020; e-mail fibut@fibut.is; internet www.fibut.is; f. 1889; Pres. EGILL ÖRN JÓHANNSSON; Man. BENEDIKT KRISTJANSSON.

Broadcasting and Communications

TELECOMMUNICATIONS

IceCell ehf: Skúlagata 19, 101 Reykjavík; tel. 6666330; fax 6666331; e-mail info@icecell.is; internet www.icecell.is; mobile telecommunications; CEO ANDREAS FINK.

IMC Island ehf: Borgartún 31, 105 Reykjavík; tel. 6618540; e-mail info@worldcell.com; GSM mobile service provider; wholly owned subsidiary of WorldCell Inc., USA; CEO JEFFREY STARK.

Nova ehf: Lágmúla 9, 108 Reykjavík; tel. 5191000; fax 5190001; e-mail nova@nova.is; internet www.nova.is; f. 2006; mobile telecommunications and broadband internet access; CEO LIV BERGÞÓRSDÓTTIR.

Síminn hf: Ármúli 25, 108 Reykjavík; tel. 5506000; fax 5506009; e-mail siminn@siminn.is; internet www.siminn.is; f. 1998 as Iceland Telecom Ltd; present name adopted 2005 following privatization; offers fixed-line telecommunications, digital TV services and broadband internet access; CEO ORRI HAUKSSON.

Vodafone Iceland: Skútuvogi 2, 104 Reykjavík; tel. 5999000; fax 5999001; e-mail vodafone@vodafone.is; internet www.vodafone.is; f. 2003 as Og Vodafone by merger of Tal, Íslandssími and Halló; renamed as above in 2006; provides mobile and fixed-line telecommunications; CEO STEFÁN SIGURÐSSON.

Supervisory Authority

Póst- og Fjarskiptastofnun (Post and Telecom Administration): Suðurlandsbraut 4, 108 Reykjavík; tel. 5101500; fax 5101509; e-mail pfs@pfs.is; internet www.pfs.is; supervisory authority; Man. Dir HRAFNKELL V. GÍSLASON.

BROADCASTING

Ríkisútvarpið (Icelandic National Broadcasting Service—RÚV): Broadcasting Centre, Efstaleiti 1, 150 Reykjavík; tel. 5153000; fax 5153010; e-mail ruv@ruv.is; internet www.ruv.is; f. 1930; Dir-Gen. MAGNÚS GEIR ÞÓRÐARSON.

Skjárinn: Skipholt 31, 105 Reykjavík; tel. 5956000; e-mail info@ skjarinn.is; internet www.skjarinn.is; f. 2005; owned by Síminn hf; multi-channel digital television service; also operates 3 television channels: Skjáreinn, Skjárbíóand and Skjárheimur; Man. FRIÐRIK FRIÐRIKSSON.

365 miðlar ehf: Skaftahlíð 24, 105 Reykjavík; tel. 5125000; e-mail askrft@stod2.is; internet www.365.is; f. 2005; owns fmr broadcasting assets of Íslenska Sjónvarpsfélagið hf, as well as the daily newspaper *Fréttablaðið*; Chair. INGIBJÖRG STEFANÍA PÁLMADÓTTIR.

Radio

Ríkisútvarpið—Útvarpi (Icelandic National Broadcasting Service—Radio): Radio Division, Efstaleiti 1, 150 Reykjavík; tel. 5153000; fax 5153010; e-mail frettir@ruv.is; internet www.ruv.is; f. 1930; Programmes 1 and 2 are broadcast over a network of 89 transmitters each; Programme 1 is broadcast for 112 hours a week, with the remaining hours simulcast with Programme 2; Programme 2 is broadcast 168 hours a week; 2 long-wave transmitters broadcast the same programme, alternating between Programme 1 and Programme 2; Dir SIGRÚN STEFÁNSDÓTTIR.

Bylgjan: Skaftahlíð 24, 105 Reykjavík; tel. 5125200; e-mail ritstjorn@visir.is; internet bylgjan.visir.is; owned by 365 miðlar ehf; Dir ÁGÚST HEÐINSSON.

FM957: Skaftahlíð 24, 110 Reykjavík; tel. 5110957; e-mail fm957@ fm957.is; internet www.fm957.is; owned by 365 miðlar ehf.

Kristilega útvarpsstöðin Lindin: Krókháls 4A, 110 Reykjavík; tel. 5671818; fax 5671824; e-mail lindin@lindin.is; internet lindin.is; Dir MICHAEL E. FITZGERALD.

Létt Bylgjan: Skaftahlíð 24, 105 Reykjavík; tel. 5125000; fax 5156830; e-mail lettbylgjan@lettbylgjan.is; internet www.bylgjan .is; owned by 365 miðlar ehf; Dir ÁGÚST HEÐINSSON.

Útvarp Saga: Nóatún 17, 105 Reykjavík; tel. 5333943; fax 5881994; e-mail saga@utvarpsaga.is; internet www.utvarpsaga.is; Dir ARNÞRÚÐUR KARLSDÓTTIR.

X 97.7: Skaftahlíð 24, 105 Reykjavík; tel. 5125000; e-mail x977@x977 .is; internet www.x977.is; owned by 365 miðlar ehf.

Television

Ríkisútvarpið—Sjónvarp (Icelandic National Broadcasting Service—Television): Efstaleiti 1, 150 Reykjavík; tel. 5153000; fax 5153010; e-mail istv@ruv.is; internet www.ruv.is; f. 1966; covers 99% of the population; broadcasts daily, total 70 hours a week; Dir SIGRÚN STEFÁNSDÓTTIR.

Bíórásin: Skaftahlíð 24, 105 Reykjavík; tel. 5125000; owned by 365 miðlar ehf.

Omega Kristniboðskirkja: Grensásvegur 8, 108 Reykjavík; tel. 5800700; fax 5800799; e-mail omega@omega.is; internet www.omega .is; f. 1995; broadcasts only in the Reykjavík area; religious; Dir EIRÍKUR SIGURBJÖRNSSON.

PoppTíví: Skaftahlíð 24, 105 Reykjavík; tel. 5125000; f. 1998; owned by 365 miðlar ehf; music station.

Stöð 2: Skaftahlíð 24, 105 Reykjavík; tel. 5125000; fax 5125100; e-mail askrift@stod2.is; internet www.stod2.is; f. 1986; owned by 365 miðlar ehf; 'pay-TV' station; channels include Stöð 2 Sport.

Finance

(cap. = capital; res = reserves; dep. = deposits; m. = million; amounts in krónur; brs = branches)

BANKING

In 1989–90 the number of commercial banks was reduced from seven to three, by amalgamating four banks to form Íslandsbanki; a further restructuring of the banking sector commenced in 2000 with the merger of Íslandsbanki with the recently privatized investment bank FBA. Íslandsbanki was renamed Glitnir Banki in 2006. By early 2003 the Icelandic Government had withdrawn completely from the country's commercial banking sector, having sold its controlling stakes in Bunaðarbanki Íslands and Landsbanki Íslands.

In 2008 the banking sector suffered severe difficulties resulting from a reduction in the availability of credit on global financial markets, and the Icelandic Government was forced to intervene in an attempt to stabilize the economy. In October the Government acquired a 75% stake in Iceland's third largest retail bank, Glitnir Banki, and subsequently announced that it would guarantee the security of all domestic bank deposits held in Icelandic banks. The Althingi (parliament) approved legislation in the same month that granted wide-ranging powers to the Financial Supervisory Authority (Fjármálaeftirlitið—FME), allowing it to take control of financial institutions. The FME subsequently assumed control of Landsbanki Íslands, Glitnir Banki and Kaupþing Banki. Three new banks—Nýi Glitnir Banki (renamed Íslandsbanki in February 2009), Nýi Kaupþing Banki (renamed Arion Banki in November) and NBI (Landsbankinn)—which were fully owned by the Icelandic Government, were created to take control of domestic assets, ensure the provision of normal banking services and safeguard domestic deposits, while the foreign assets and liabilities were retained by the former banks, which were in receivership.

Central Bank

Seðlabanki Íslands (Central Bank of Iceland): Kalkofnsvegur 1, 150 Reykjavík; tel. 5699600; fax 5699605; e-mail sedlabanki@ sedlabanki.is; internet www.sedlabanki.is; f. 1961; cap. 57,501m., res 11,878.2m., dep. 1,019,162.5m. (Dec. 2010); Chair., Supervisory Bd ÓLÖF NORDAL; Gov. MÁR GUÐMUNDSSON.

Principal Banks

Arion Banki: Borgartún 19, 105 Reykjavík; tel. 4446000; fax 4446009; e-mail arionbanki@arionbanki.is; internet www .arionbanki.is; f. 2008 as Nýi Kaupþing Banki hf to assume responsibility for domestic assets and deposits of Kaupþing Banki (f. 2003) after it was nationalized; adopted current name Nov. 2009; 87% owned by creditors of Kaupþing Banki, 13% by Icelandic Govt; cap. 2,000m., res 75,498m., dep. 506,155m. (Dec. 2011); Chair. MONICA CANEMAN; CEO HÖSKULDUR H. ÓLAFSSON; 35 brs.

Íslandsbanki hf: Kirkjusandur, 155 Reykjavík; tel. 4404000; fax 4404001; e-mail islandsbanki@islandsbanki.is; internet www .islandsbanki.is; f. 2008 as Nýi Glitnir Banki to assume responsibility for domestic assets and deposits of Glitnir Banki (f. 1990) after it was nationalized in Oct. 2008; adopted current name Feb. 2009; 95% owned by creditors of Glitnir Banki, 5% by Icelandic Govt; cap. 10,000m., res 57,471m., dep. 543,842m. (Dec. 2012); Chair. FRIÐRIK SOPHUSSON; CEO BIRNA EINARSDÓTTIR; 29 brs.

Landsbankinn hf (Nýi Landsbanki Íslands—Landsbankinn): Austurstræti 11, 155 Reykjavík; tel. and fax 5606600; e-mail info@ landsbank.is; internet www.landsbank.is; f. 2008; 81.3% owned by Icelandic Govt; est. to assume responsibility for domestic assets and deposits of Landsbanki Íslands (f. 1885) after it was nationalized in Oct. 2008; present name adopted 2011; cap. 23,618m., res 127,746m., dep. 456,662m. (Dec. 2013); Chair. GUNNAR HELGI HÁLFDÁNARSON; CEO STEINÞÓR PÁLSSON; 33 brs.

MP Banki hf: Ármúli 13A, 108 Reykjavík; tel. 5403230; fax 5403201; e-mail info@mp.is; internet www.mp.is; f. 1999 as a brokerage firm under name MP Verðbref; status changed to investment bank in 2003 and name changed to MP Fjárfestingarbanki; granted a commercial licence in Oct. 2008 and adopted current name; cap. 5,550m., res 49.9m., dep. 42,402.4m. (Dec. 2012); Chair. ÞORSTEINN PÁLSSON; CEO SIGURÐUR ATLI JÓNSSON.

STOCK EXCHANGE

NASDAQ OMX Nordic Exchange Iceland: Laugavegur 182, 105 Reykjavík; tel. 5252800; fax 5252888; internet www.nasdaqomx .com; f. 2006 by merger of Kauphöll Íslands and OMX AB (Sweden); part of OMX Nordic Exchange with Copenhagen (Denmark), Helsinki (Finland) and Stockholm (Sweden) exchanges; acquired by NASDAQ Stock Market, Inc (USA) in 2008; Group CEO ROBERT GREIFELD.

INSURANCE

Tryggingastofnun ríkisins (Social Insurance Administration): Laugavegi 114, 105 Reykjavík; tel. 5604400; fax 5604451; e-mail tr@tr.is; internet www.tr.is; f. 1936; Chair. STEFÁN ÓLAFSSON; Dir-Gen. SIGRIÐUR LILLÝ BALDURSDÓTTIR.

Private Insurance Companies

Líftryggingafélag Íslands hf (Lífís): Ármúla 3, 108 Reykjavík; tel. 5605100; fax 5605108; e-mail vis@vis.is; internet www.lifis.is; f. 1990; owned by holding co of Vátryggingafélag Íslands hf (VÍS); life; CEO SIGRÚN RAGNA ÓLAFSDÓTTIR.

Líftryggingamiðstöðin hf: Síðumúla 24, 108 Reykjavík; tel. 5152000; fax 5152020; f. 2005; subsidiary of Tryggingamiðstöðin hf (TM); Gen. Man. HJÁLMAR SIGURÞÓRSSON.

Sjóvá-Almennar tryggingar hf (Marine-General Insurance Co): Kringlan 5, 103 Reykjavík; tel. 4402000; fax 4402020; e-mail sjova@ sjova.is; internet www.sjova.is; f. 1988; all branches except life; Chair. ERNA GÍSLADÓTTIR; Gen. Man. HERMANN BJÖRNSSON.

Tryggingamiðstöðin hf (TM): Síðumúla 24, 108 Reykjavík; tel. 5152000; fax 5152020; e-mail tm@tm.is; internet www.tm.is; f. 1956; acquired Trygging hf in 1999; Chair. SIGURÐUR VIÐARSSON.

Vátryggingafélag Íslands hf (VÍS): Ármúla 3, 108 Reykjavík; tel. 5605000; fax 5605108; e-mail vis@vis.is; internet www.vis.is; f. 1989; non-life; Chair. FRIÐRIK HALLBJÖRN KARLSSON; CEO SIGRÚN RAGNA ÓLAFSDÓTTIR.

Viðlagatrygging Íslands: Hlidasmari 14, 201 Kopavogur; tel. 5753300; fax 5753303; e-mail vidlagatrygging@vidlagatrygging.is; internet vidlagatrygging.is; f. 1976; CEO HULDA RAGNHEIDUR.

Vörður tryggingar hf: Borgartún 25, 105 Reykjavík; tel. 5141000; fax 5141001; e-mail vordur@vordur.is; internet www.vordur.is; f. 1926; as Vörður; life and non-life; Chair. JENS ERIK CHRISTENSEN.

Supervisory Authority

Fjármálaeftirlitið (FME) (Financial Supervisory Authority): Höfðatún 2, 105 Reykjavík; tel. 5203700; fax 5203727; e-mail fme@ fme.is; internet www.fme.is; f. 1999 by merger of Insurance Supervisory Authority and Bank Inspectorate of the Central Bank of Iceland; Chair. HALLA SIGRÚN; Dir-Gen. UNNUR GUNNARSDÓTTIR.

Trade and Industry

GOVERNMENT AGENCIES

Íslandsstofa (Promote Iceland): Sundagarðar 2, 104 Reykjavík; tel. 5114000; fax 5114040; e-mail islandsstofa@islandsstofa.is; internet www.islandsstofa.is; promotes Icelandic exports; partnership between govt and private enterprise; Chair. VILBORG EINARSDÓTTIR.

Invest in Iceland: Borgartúni 35, 105 Reykjavík; tel. 5615200; fax 5114040; e-mail info@invest.is; internet www.invest.is; f. 1995; promotes foreign investment; managed by Promote Iceland and Ministry of Industries and Innovation; Man. Dir THORDUR H. HILMARSSON.

Orkustofnun (National Energy Authority): Grensásvegur 9, 108 Reykjavík; tel. 5696000; fax 5688896; e-mail os@os.is; internet www.os.is; f. 1967; part of the Ministry of Industries and Innovation; 2 main divisions: hydrological research unit and energy administration unit; contracts and supervises energy research projects financed by the national budget, monitors energy consumption and publishes forecasts for energy market; operates United Nations Geothermal Training Programme as independent entity; licenses and monitors exploration for oil and gas in Icelandic waters; Dir-Gen. Dr GUÐNI A. JOHANNESSON.

CHAMBER OF COMMERCE

Viðskiptaráð Íslands (Iceland Chamber of Commerce): Kringlan 7, 103 Reykjavík; tel. 5107100; fax 5686564; e-mail mottaka@vi.is; internet www.vi.is; f. 1917; fmrly Verslunarráð Íslands; Chair. HREGGVIÐUR JÓNSSON; 370 mems.

INDUSTRIAL AND TRADE ASSOCIATIONS

Fiskifélag Íslands (Fisheries Asscn of Iceland): POB 8214, 128 Reykjavík; tel. 5910308; fax 5910301; e-mail fi@fiskifelag.is; internet www.fiskifelag.is; f. 1911; conducts technical and economic research and services for fishing vessels and for the fishing industry; Chair. ELÍNBJÖRG MAGNÚSDÓTTIR.

Samtök Fiskvinnslustöðva (Federation of Icelandic Fish Processing Plants): Borgartúni 35, 105 Reykjavík; tel. 5910350; fax 5910358; e-mail sf@sf.is; internet www.sf.is; f. 1975; represents all enterprises in fish processing and distribution; merged with Icelandic Fishing Vessel Owners' Fedn in 2014; Chair. ARNAR SIGURMUNDSSON.

Samtök Iðnaðarins (SI) (Federation of Icelandic Industries): Borgartúni 35, 105 Reykjavík; tel. 5910100; fax 5910101; e-mail mottaka@si.is; internet www.si.is; f. 1993 by merger of Federation of Icelandic Industries (f. 1933), Federation of Icelandic Crafts and Industries (f. 1932) and 4 other employers' orgs; Chair. GUÐRÚN HAFSTEINSDÓTTIR; 1,200 mems.

EMPLOYERS' ORGANIZATION

Samtök Atvinnulífsins (SA) (Confederation of Icelandic Employers): Borgartúni 35, 105 Reykjavík; tel. 5910000; fax 5910050; e-mail sa@sa.is; internet www.sa.is; f. 1934; 7 mem. asscns; Chair. BJÖRGÓLFUR JÓHANNSSON; Man. Dir Dr VILHJÁLMUR EGILSSON.

UTILITIES

Electricity

HS Orka hf: Brekkustíg 36, POB 225, 260 Reykjanesbær; tel. 5209300; fax 4214727; e-mail hsorka@hsorka.is; internet www.hsorka.is; f. 2008 by division of Hitaveita Suðurnesja hf (HS, f. 1974) into HS Orka hf and HS Veitur hf; produces and sells geothermal electricity; 66.6% shares owned by Magma Energy Sweden A.B. and 33.4% owned by Jarðvarmi slhf; CEO ASGEIR MARGEIRSSON.

HS Veitur hf: Brekkustíg 36, POB 225, 260 Reykjanesbær; tel. 4225200; fax 4214727; e-mail hs@hs.is; internet www.hsveitur.is; f. 2008 by division of Hitaveita Suðurnesja hf (HS); produces and distributes hot water heating and electricity for the Suðurnes region; Chair. BÖÐVAR JÓNSSON.

Landsvirkjun (National Power): Háaleitisbraut 68, 103 Reykjavík; tel. 5159000; fax 5159007; e-mail landsvirkjun@landsvirkjun.com; internet www.landsvirkjun.com; f. 1965; generates and sells electricity from renewable energy sources to public distribution systems and industrial enterprises; state-owned; Chair. JÓNAS ÞÓR GUÐMUNDSSON; Pres. and CEO HÖRDUR ARNARSON.

Orkubú Vestfjarða ohf (Westfjord Power Co): Stakkanesi 1, 400 Isafjördur; tel. 4503211; fax 4563204; e-mail orkubu@ov.is; internet www.ov.is; f. 1978; produces, distributes and sells electrical energy in the Westfjords area; state-owned; Man. Dir KRISTJÁN HARALDSSON.

Orkuveita Reykjavíkur (OR) (Reykjavík Energy): Bæjarháls 1, 110 Reykjavík; tel. 5166000; fax 5166709; e-mail or@or.is; internet www.or.is; f. 1999; produces and distributes geothermal hot-water for central heating, cold water and electricity for the city of Reykjavík and regions in south-western Iceland; owned by city of Reykjavík and other local authorities; Chair. HARALDUR FLOSI TRYGGVASON; CEO BJARNI BJARNASON.

RARIK ohf (Iceland State Electricity): Dvergshöfða 2, 110 Reykjavík; tel. 5289000; fax 5289009; e-mail rarik@rarik.is; internet www.rarik.is; f. 1947 as Rafmagnsveitur Ríkisins; produces, procures, distributes and sells electrical energy; also provides consultancy services; Chair. and CEO TRYGGVI ÞÓR HARALDSSON.

TRADE UNIONS

Alþýðusamband Íslands (ASÍ) (Icelandic Confederation of Labour): Guðrúnartúni 1, 105 Reykjavík; tel. 5355600; fax 5355601; e-mail asi@asi.is; internet www.asi.is; f. 1916; affiliated to ITUC, ETUC and the Council of Nordic Trade Unions; Pres. GYLFI ARNBJÖRNSSON; c. 109,000 mems.

Bandalag Háskólamanna (BHM) (Asscn of Academics): Borgartún 6, 105 Reykjavík; tel. 5955100; fax 5955101; e-mail bhm@bhm.is; internet www.bhm.is; f. 1958; asscn of 26 trade unions; publishes *BHM-tíðindi* (annual); Chair. PÁLL HALLDÓRSSON; Gen. Man. STEFÁN AÐALSTEINSSON; 11,000 mems.

Bandalag Starfsmanna Ríkis og Bæja (BSRB) (Municipal and Government Employees' Asscn): Grettisgötu 89, 105 Reykjavík; tel. 5658300; fax 5258309; e-mail bsrb@bsrb.is; internet www.bsrb.is; f. 1942; Chair. ELÍN BJÖRG JÓNSDÓTTIR; 22,000 mems.

Blaðamannafélag Íslands (Union of Icelandic Journalists): Síðumúla 23, 108 Reykjavík; tel. 5539155; fax 5539177; e-mail bi@press.is; internet www.press.is; f. 1897; Chair. HJÁLMAR JÓNSSON; 575 mems.

Transport

Samgöngustofa (Icelandic Transport Authority—ICETRA): Ármúli 2, 108 Reykjavík; tel. 4806000; fax 4806001; e-mail icetra@icetra.is; internet www.icetra.is; f. 2013; responsible for all areas of transport, jncl. road, aviation and maritime transport; Dir-Gen. ÞÓRÓLFUR ÁRNASON.

RAILWAYS

There are no railways in Iceland.

ROADS

Much of the interior is uninhabited and the main road largely follows the coastline. Regular motor coach services link the main settlements. In 2012 Iceland had 12,936 km of national roads, of which 4,385 km were main roads. Approximately one-third of the main roads are paved. The construction of three tunnels was approved in 2012, including a 7.5-km tunnel between Eskifjörður and Neskaupstaður in eastern Iceland, which was to be built by 2016 to replace a one-lane tunnel that was deemed to be hazardous.

Vegagerðin (Icelandic Road and Coastal Administration—IRCA): Borgartún 5–7, 105 Reykjavík; tel. 5221009; e-mail vegagerdin@vegagerdin.is; internet www.vegagerdin.is; part of the Icelandic Transport Authority (ICETRA); oversees the construction and maintenance of roads; since 2013 also responsible for harbour and lighthouse operations of the Icelandic Maritime Administration; Gen. Dir HREINN HARALDSSON.

Bifreiðastöð Íslands hf (BSÍ) (Iceland Motor Coach Service): Umferðarmiðstöðinni, Vatnsmýrarveg 10, 101 Reykjavík; tel. 5621011; e-mail bsi@bsi.is; internet www.bsi.is; f. 1936; 45 scheduled bus lines throughout Iceland; also operates sightseeing tours and excursions; Chair. ÓSKAR SIGURJÓNSSON; Man. Dir GUNNAR SVEINSSON.

SHIPPING

Heavy freight is carried by coastal shipping. The principal seaport for international shipping is Reykjavík. At 31 December 2014 the Icelandic flag registered fleet numbered 202 vessels, with a combined displacement of 160,855 grt, of which 164 were fishing vessels and 5 were general cargo ships.

Port Authority

Faxaflóahafnir sf (Associated Icelandic Ports): POB 382, 121 Reykjavík; Harbour Bldg, Tryggvagata 17, 101 Reykjavík; tel. 5258900; fax 5258990; e-mail hofnin@faxaports.is; internet faxafloahafnir.is; f. 2005 by merger of ports of Akranes, Borgarnes, Grundartangi and Reykjavík; Chair. KRISTIN SOFFIA JONSDOTTIR; Dir GISLI GISLASON.

Principal Companies

Eimskip (Iceland Steamship Co Ltd): Korngörðum 2, 104 Reykjavík; tel. 5257000; fax 5257009; e-mail info@eimskip.com; internet www.eimskip.com; f. 1914 as Eimskipafélag Íslands; subsidiary of Avion Group; transportation and logistics services between Iceland and the UK, Scandinavia, the rest of Europe, the USA and Canada; Chair. BRAGI RAGNARSSON; Pres. and CEO GYLFI SIGFÚSSON.

Nesskip hf (Austurströnd 1, 170 Seltjarnarnes; tel. 5639900; fax 5639919; e-mail operations@nesskip.is; internet www.nesskip.is; f. 1974; bulk cargo shipping services to the USA, Canada, Russia, Scandinavia, the Baltic countries and other parts of Europe; agency and chartering for vessels in all Icelandic ports; Chair. OYVING GJERDE; Man. Dir GARÐAR JÓHANNSSON.

Samskip hf: Kjalarvogur, 104 Reykjavík; tel. 4588000; fax 4588100; e-mail samskip@samskip.is; internet www.samskip.is; services to Europe, the USA, South America and the Far East; Chair ÓLAFUR ÓLAFSSON.

CIVIL AVIATION

Air transport is particularly important to Iceland and is used to convey both people and agricultural produce from remote districts. More than 90% of passenger traffic between Iceland and other countries is by air. There are regular air services between Reykjavík and outlying townships. There is an international airport at Keflavík, 47 km from Reykjavík.

Air Atlanta Icelandic: Hlíðasmára 3, 201 Kópavogur; tel. 4584000; fax 4584001; e-mail info@airatlanta.com; internet www.airatlanta .com; f. 1986; leases cargo and passenger aircraft; CEO HANNES HILMARSSON.

Air Iceland: Reykjavík Airport, 101 Reykjavík; tel. 5703000; fax 5703001; e-mail service@airiceland.is; internet www.airiceland.is; part of Icelandair Group; scheduled regional flights; 96% owned by Icelandair; Man. Dir ÁRNI GUNNARSSON.

Eagle Air (Flugfélagið Ernir ehf): Reykjavík Airport, 101 Reykjavík; tel. 5624200; fax 5624202; e-mail info@eagleair.is; internet www .eagleair.is; f. 1970; charter and domestic scheduled services; Pres. and CEO HÖRÐUR GUÐMUNDSSON.

Icelandair (Flugleiðir hf): Reykjavík Airport, 101 Reykjavík; tel. 5050757; fax 5050758; e-mail postmaster@icelandair.is; internet www.icelandair.is; f. 1973 as the holding co for the 2 principal Icelandic airlines, Flugfélag Íslands (f. 1937) and Loftleiðir (f. 1944); took over all licences, permits and authorizations previously held by Flugfélag Íslands and Loftleiðir in 1979; operates flights from Reykjavík to 9 domestic airfields and more than 20 destinations in Europe and North America; CEO BIRKIR HÓLM GUÐNASON.

WOW Air: Höfðatún 12, 105 Reykjavík; tel. 5903000; e-mail wowair@wow.is; internet www.wowiceland.co.uk; f. 2011; took over Iceland Express flight operations in Oct. 2012; Chair. LIV BERGÞÓRS-DÓTTIR; Pres. and CEO SKÚLI MOGENSEN.

Tourism

Iceland's main attraction for tourists lies in the rugged beauty of the landscape, with its geysers and thermal springs. In 2013 receipts from tourism, excluding passenger transport, totalled US $1,059m.

Overnight stays by foreign visitors in hotels and guesthouses amounted to some 2.2m. in 2012.

Iceland Tourist Board: Geirsgata 9, 101 Reykjavík; tel. 5355500; e-mail upplysingar@ferdamalastofa.is; internet www .ferdamalastofa.is; Gen. Dir ÓLÖF ÝRR ATLADÓTTIR.

Höfuðborgarstofa (Visit Reykjavík): Aðalstræti 2, 101 Reykjavík; tel. 5901500; fax 5901501; e-mail info@visitreykjavik.is; internet www.visitreykjavik.is; tourism marketing and events for the city of Reykjavík; Dir EINAR ÞÓR BÁRÐARSON.

Defence

Apart from a 180-strong coastguard, Iceland has no defence forces of its own, but it is a member of the North Atlantic Treaty Organization (NATO). Until 2006 there were units of US forces at Keflavík airbase, which was used for observation of the North Atlantic Ocean, under a bilateral agreement made in 1951 between Iceland and the USA. In September 2006 the USA withdrew its forces from Iceland, but maintained its commitment to defend Iceland as a fellow member of NATO. In November 2012 Denmark, Finland, Iceland, Sweden and Norway agreed to operate military transport aircraft jointly. (Iceland does not currently own military aircraft, but was to contribute funds towards joint purchases.)

Defence Expenditure: Budgeted at 4,510m. krónur (coastguard only) for 2014.

Education

Education starts at the pre-primary level, which is non-compulsory for pupils aged between one and six years of age. Education is compulsory and free for 10 years between six and 16 years of age (primary and lower secondary levels). Upper secondary education begins at 16 years of age and usually lasts for four years. In 2011/12, enrolment in pre-primary schools included 97% of children in the relevant age-group. In the same year, enrolment in primary schools included 98% of children in the relevant age-group, while enrolment in secondary education included 88% of children in the relevant age-group. Higher education is provided by universities and select institutions offering a limited number of study programmes. Iceland had 23 institutions providing tertiary-level education in 2010. In 2012 there were 18,619 students enrolled in tertiary-level education. Public expenditure on education was 7.02% of gross domestic product in 2013. Local communities finance compulsory education.

INDIA

Introductory Survey

LOCATION, CLIMATE, LANGUAGE, RELIGION, FLAG, CAPITAL

The Republic of India forms a natural sub-continent, with the Himalaya mountain range to the north. Two sections of the Indian Ocean—the Arabian Sea and the Bay of Bengal—lie to the west and east, respectively. India's neighbours are Tibet (the Xizang Autonomous Region of the People's Republic of China), Bhutan and Nepal to the north, Pakistan to the north-west and Myanmar (formerly Burma) to the north-east, while Bangladesh is surrounded by Indian territory except for a short frontier with Myanmar in the east. Near India's southern tip, across the Palk Strait, is Sri Lanka. India's climate ranges from temperate to tropical, with an average summer temperature on the plains of approximately 27°C (85°F). Annual rainfall varies widely, but the summer monsoon brings heavy rain over much of the country in June and July. The official language is Hindi, spoken by about 30% of the population. English is used as an associate language for many official purposes. The Indian Constitution also recognizes 18 regional languages, of which the most widely spoken are Telugu, Bengali, Marathi, Tamil, Urdu and Gujarati. In addition, many other local languages are used. According to the 2001 census, about 81% of the population are Hindus and 13% Muslims. There are also Christians, Sikhs, Buddhists, Jains and other minorities. The national flag (proportions 2 by 3) has three equal horizontal stripes, of saffron, white and green, with the Dharma Chakra (Wheel of the Law), in blue, in the centre of the white stripe. The capital is New Delhi.

CONTEMPORARY POLITICAL HISTORY

Historical Context

After a prolonged struggle against British colonial rule, India became independent, within the Commonwealth, on 15 August 1947. The United Kingdom's Indian Empire was partitioned, broadly on a religious basis, between India and Pakistan. The principal nationalist movement that had opposed British rule was the Indian National Congress (later known as the Congress Party). At independence the Congress leader, Jawaharlal Nehru, became India's first Prime Minister. Sectarian violence, the movement of 12m. refugees, the integration of the former princely states into the Indian federal structure and a territorial dispute with Pakistan over Kashmir presented major problems to the new Government.

India became independent as a dominion, with the British monarch as head of state, represented by an appointed Governor-General. In November 1949, however, the Constituent Assembly approved a republican Constitution, providing for a President (with mainly ceremonial functions) as head of state. Accordingly, India became a republic on 26 January 1950, although remaining a member of the Commonwealth. France transferred sovereignty of Chandernagore to India in May, and ceded its four remaining Indian settlements in 1954.

In December 1961 Indian forces overran the Portuguese territories of Goa, Daman and Diu, which were immediately annexed by India. Border disputes with the People's Republic of China escalated into a brief military conflict in 1962. Nehru died in May 1964 and was succeeded by Lal Bahadur Shastri. India and Pakistan fought a second war over Kashmir in 1965. Following mediation by the USSR, Shastri and President Ayub Khan of Pakistan signed a joint declaration, aimed at a peaceful settlement of the Kashmir dispute, on 10 January 1966. However, Shastri died on the following day and Nehru's daughter, Indira Gandhi, became Prime Minister.

Domestic Political Affairs

Indira Gandhi dominates Indian politics (1966–84)

Following the presidential election of August 1969, when two factions of Congress supported different candidates, the success of Indira Gandhi's candidate split the party. The Organization (Opposition) Congress, led by Morarji Desai, emerged in November, but at the next general election to the lower house of the legislature, the Lok Sabha (House of the People), held in March 1971, Indira Gandhi's wing of Congress won 350 of the 515 elective seats.

Border incidents led to a 12-day war with Pakistan in December 1971. The Indian army rapidly occupied East Pakistan, which India recognized as the independent state of Bangladesh. Indira Gandhi and President Zulfikar Ali Bhutto of Pakistan held a summit conference at Shimla in June–July 1972, when the two leaders agreed that their respective forces should respect the ceasefire line in Kashmir, and that India and Pakistan should resolve their differences through bilateral negotiations or other peaceful means. In 1975 the former protectorate of Sikkim became the 22nd state of the Indian Union, leading to tensions in India's relations with Nepal.

A general election to the Lok Sabha was held in March 1977, when the number of elective seats was increased to 542. The election resulted in victory for the Janata (People's) Party, chaired by Morarji Desai, who became Prime Minister. The Janata Party and an allied party, the Congress for Democracy, together won 298 of the 540 seats where polling took place. Congress obtained 153 seats. In January 1978 Indira Gandhi became leader of a new breakaway political group, the Congress (Indira) Party, known as Congress (I).

In 1979 the Government's ineffectual approach to domestic problems provoked a wave of defections by Lok Sabha members of the Janata Party. Many joined Raj Narain, who formed a new, secular party, the Lok Dal. Congress (I) lost its position as official opposition party after defections from its ranks to the then official Congress Party by members who objected to Indira Gandhi's perceived authoritarianism. The resignation of Desai's Government in July was followed by the departure from the Janata Party of Charan Singh, who became the leader of the Lok Dal and, shortly afterwards, Prime Minister in a coalition with both Congress parties. When Congress (I) withdrew its support, Singh's 24-day administration collapsed, and Parliament was dissolved. A general election to the Lok Sabha was held in January 1980. Congress (I) won an overwhelming majority (352) of the elective seats; the Janata Party and the Lok Dal won only 31 and 41 seats, respectively. Indira Gandhi was reinstated as Prime Minister. Presidential rule was imposed in nine states, hitherto governed by opposition parties, in February.

By-elections in June 1981 for the Lok Sabha and state assemblies (to which elections were held in June 1980) were notable for two reasons: the overwhelming victory that Rajiv Gandhi, the Prime Minister's son, obtained in the former constituency of his late brother (killed in an air crash in 1980); and the failure of the fragmented Janata Party to win any seats. In February 1983 Rajiv Gandhi became a General Secretary of Congress (I).

Indira Gandhi's Government faced serious problems, as intercommunal disturbances in several states (particularly Assam and Meghalaya) continued in 1982–83, with violent protests against the presence of Bengali immigrants. Election defeats in Andhra Pradesh, Karnataka and Tripura represented a series of setbacks for the Prime Minister. Alleged police corruption and the resurgence of caste violence (notably in Bihar and Gujarat) caused further problems for the Government.

There was also unrest in the Sikh community of the Punjab, despite the election to the Indian presidency in July 1982 of Giani Zail Singh, the first Sikh to hold the position. Demands were made for greater religious recognition, for the settlement of grievances over land and water rights, and over the sharing of the state capital at Chandigarh with Haryana; in addition, a minority called for the creation of a separate Sikh state ('Khalistan'). In October 1983 the state was brought under presidential rule. However, the violence continued, and followers of an extremist Sikh leader, Jarnail Singh Bhindranwale, established a terrorist stronghold inside the Golden Temple (the Sikh holy shrine) at Amritsar. An army assault against the extremists resulted in the death of Bhindranwale and hundreds of his supporters, and serious damage to sacred buildings.

Rajiv Gandhi assumes power (1984–89)

In October 1984 Indira Gandhi was assassinated by militant Sikh members of her personal guard. Her son, Rajiv Gandhi, was immediately sworn in as Prime Minister, despite his lack of ministerial experience. The widespread communal violence that erupted throughout India, resulting in more than 2,000 deaths, was curbed by prompt government action. Congress (I) achieved a decisive victory in elections to the Lok Sabha in December. Including the results of the January 1985 polling, the party won 403 of the 513 contested seats.

In February 1986 there were mass demonstrations and strikes throughout India in protest against government-imposed increases in the prices of basic commodities. The opposition parties united against Rajiv Gandhi's policies, and Congress (I) suffered considerable reversals in the indirect elections to the upper house of the legislature, the Rajya Sabha (Council of States), in March. In April Rajiv Gandhi attempted to purge Congress (I) of critics calling themselves 'Indira Gandhi loyalists', and, in a major government reorganization, he appointed Sikhs to two senior positions. The Prime Minister survived an assassination attempt by three Sikhs in October.

Laldenga, the leader of the Mizo National Front (MNF), signed a peace agreement with Rajiv Gandhi in June 1986, thus ending Mizoram's 25 years of rebellion. The accord granted Mizoram limited autonomy in the drafting of local laws, independent trade with neighbouring foreign countries and a general amnesty for all Mizo rebels. In February 1987 Mizoram and Arunachal Pradesh were officially admitted as the 23rd and 24th states of India, and in May the Union Territory of Goa became India's 25th state.

During 1987 Congress (I) sustained defeats in a number of state elections, and political tensions were intensified by an open dispute between the Prime Minister and the outgoing President, Giani Zail Singh. Public concern was aroused by various accusations of corruption and financial irregularities made against senior figures in the ruling party. Several ministers resigned from the Government, among them the Minister of Defence, Vishwanath Pratap (V. P.) Singh, who was also, with three other senior politicians, expelled from Congress (I) in July for 'anti-party activities'. V. P. Singh soon emerged as the leader of the Congress (I) dissidents, and in October formed a new political group, the Jan Morcha (People's Front), advocating radical social change.

In 1988 a more confrontational style was adopted by the central administration towards non-Congress (I) state governments, and presidential rule was imposed in states suffering political instability. The opposition forces attained a degree of unity when four major centrist parties, the Indian National Congress (S), the Jan Morcha, the Janata Party and the Lok Dal, and three major regional parties formed a coalition National Front (Rashtriya Morcha), to oppose Congress (I) at the next election. Three of the four centrist parties formed a new political grouping, the Janata Dal (People's Party), which was to work in collaboration with the National Front. V. P. Singh, who was widely regarded as Rajiv Gandhi's closest rival, was elected President of the Janata Dal.

The Janata Dal Government (1989–91)

At elections to the Lok Sabha in November 1989, Congress (I) lost its overall majority. Of the 525 contested seats, it won 193, the Janata Dal and its electoral allies in the National Front won 141 and three, respectively, and the right-wing Hindu nationalist Bharatiya Janata Party (BJP) won 88. In December, after the National Front had been promised the support of the communist parties and the BJP, V. P. Singh was sworn in as the new Prime Minister. He appointed Devi Lal, the populist Chief Minister of Haryana and President of Lok Dal (B), as Deputy Prime Minister, and a Kashmiri Muslim, Mufti Mohammed Sayeed, as Minister of Home Affairs. At elections held in February 1990, Congress (I) lost power in eight of 10 state assemblies that it had formerly controlled, and there was a notable increase in support for the BJP. In July Devi Lal was dismissed as Deputy Prime Minister, accused of nepotism and disloyalty, and making unsubstantiated accusations of corruption against ministerial colleagues.

The BJP withdrew its support for the National Front in October 1990, following the arrest of its President, Lal Krishna (L. K.) Advani, as he led a controversial procession of Hindu devotees to the holy town of Ayodhya, in Uttar Pradesh, to begin the construction of a Hindu temple on the site of a disused ancient mosque, the Babri Masjid. V. P. Singh accused the BJP leader of deliberately inciting inter-communal hatred by exhorting Hindu extremists to join him in illegally tearing down the mosque. Paramilitary troops were sent to Ayodhya, and thousands of Hindu activists were arrested. Following repeated clashes between police and crowds, Hindu extremists stormed the mosque and laid siege to it for several days.

In November 1990 one of the Prime Minister's leading rivals in the Janata Dal, Chandra Shekhar (with the support of Devi Lal), formed his own dissident faction, the Janata Dal (Socialist) or Janata Dal (S), (which merged with the Janata Party in April 1991 to become the Samajwadi Party). The Lok Sabha convened for a special session, at which the Government overwhelmingly lost a vote of confidence. V. P. Singh immediately resigned, and the President invited Rajiv Gandhi, as leader of the largest parliamentary party, to form a new government. Gandhi refused the offer, in favour of Shekhar. Although the Janata Dal (S) held only about 60 seats in the Lok Sabha, Congress (I) had earlier offered it unconditional parliamentary support. On 10 November Chandra Shekhar was sworn in as Prime Minister. A new Council of Ministers was appointed, with Devi Lal becoming Deputy Prime Minister. Although Shekhar succeeded in initiating talks between the two sides in the Ayodhya dispute, Hindu–Muslim violence increased throughout India in December.

In January 1991 Prime Minister Shekhar imposed direct rule in Tamil Nadu in response to the increased activity of Sri Lankan Tamil militants in the state, which had led to the breakdown of law and order. In the resultant riots more than 1,000 arrests were made. In February five cabinet ministers were forced to resign when they lost their seats in the Lok Sabha for violating India's anti-defection laws: they had left the Janata Dal to join the Janata Dal (S). In March Congress (I) deputies boycotted Parliament, following the revelation that Rajiv Gandhi's house had been kept under police surveillance. Shekhar unexpectedly resigned, but accepted the President's request that he remain as head of an interim Government pending a fresh general election.

The return of Congress to power (1991–96)

As the general election, which was to take place over three days in May 1991, approached, it seemed likely that no party would win an outright majority and that the political stalemate would continue. On 21 May, however, after the first day's polling, Rajiv Gandhi was assassinated while campaigning in Tamil Nadu, allegedly by members of the Sri Lankan Tamil separatist group, the Liberation Tigers of Tamil Eelam (LTTE). Consequently, the remaining elections were postponed until June. The final result gave Congress (I) 227 of the 511 seats contested. The BJP, which almost doubled its share of the vote compared with its performance in the 1989 general election, won 119 seats, while the Janata Dal gained only 55 seats. P. V. Narasimha Rao, who had been elected as acting President of Congress (which had gradually shed its 'I' suffix) following Rajiv Gandhi's assassination, assumed the premiership and appointed a new Council of Ministers. The new Government's main priority on assuming power was to attempt to solve the country's severe economic crisis, caused by an enormous foreign debt, high inflation, a large current account deficit and an extreme shortage of foreign exchange reserves. The new Minister of Finance, Dr Manmohan Singh, launched a far-reaching programme of economic liberalization and reform, including the dismantling of bureaucratic regulations and the encouragement of private and foreign investment. In September 1991 the Government announced the adoption of the recommendations of the 12-year-old Mandal Commission that 27% of government jobs and institutional places be reserved for certain lower castes, in addition to the 22.5% already reserved for those from a Dalit ('untouchable') background and tribal people. (In November 1992 the Supreme Court ruled that non-Hindus, such as Christians and Sikhs, who were socially disadvantaged were also entitled to job reservations.) In July 1992 the Congress candidate, Dr Shankar Dayal Sharma, was elected to the presidency.

Following the collapse of talks in November 1992 between the Vishwa Hindu Parishad (VHP—World Hindu Council) and the All India Babri Masjid Action Committee regarding the Ayodhya dispute—see *The Janata Dal Government (1989–91)*—the VHP and the BJP appealed for volunteers to begin the construction of a Hindu temple on the site of the existing mosque. Despite the dispatch of paramilitary troops to Ayodhya, in December the temple/mosque complex was stormed by large numbers of Hindu activists, who proceeded to tear down the remains of the ancient mosque. This highly inflammatory action provoked widespread communal violence throughout India, which resulted in more than 1,200 deaths and prompted worldwide censure, notably from the neighbouring Islamic states of Pakistan and Bangladesh, where violent anti-Hindu demonstrations were held. The central Government also strongly condemned the demolition of the holy building and pledged to rebuild it. The leaders of the BJP, including L. K. Advani and the party's President, Dr Murli Manohar Joshi, and those of the VHP were arrested. The BJP Chief Minister of Uttar Pradesh resigned, the state legislature was dissolved and Uttar Pradesh was placed under presidential rule. The security forces took full control of Ayodhya, including the disputed complex. The Government banned five communal organizations, including the VHP and two Muslim groups, on the grounds that they promoted religious disharmony. In an attempt to prevent any further acts of Hindu militancy, the central Government dismissed the BJP administrations in Madhya Pradesh, Rajasthan and Himachal Pradesh and placed these states under presidential rule. In late December the Government announced plans to acquire all the disputed areas in Ayodhya. The land would be made available to two trusts, which would be responsible for the construction of a new Hindu temple and a new mosque.

However, in January 1993 there was a resurgence of Hindu–Muslim violence in India's commercial centre, Mumbai (then still known as Bombay), and in Ahmedabad, necessitating the imposition of curfews and the dispatch of extra paramilitary troops to curb the unrest. In an effort to prevent a proposed mass rally of Hindu activists taking place in the centre of New Delhi in February, thousands of BJP members were arrested throughout India and the crowds that did gather in the capital were dispersed by the security forces. In March there were a number of bomb explosions in Mumbai, resulting in some 250 casualties.

In July 1993 Narasimha Rao narrowly survived a vote of no confidence, which was supported in the Lok Sabha by virtually all the opposition parties. However, an apparent decline in the BJP's popularity was highlighted by its inability in November to win state elections in three of the four northern states where BJP governments had been dismissed in December 1992. Despite the Government's economic reforms continuing to show positive results, and the opposition suffering from fragmentation, in late 1994 and early 1995 Congress suffered damaging defeats in several state elections.

In January 1996 the Central Bureau of Investigation (CBI) charged seven leading politicians, including L. K. Advani and Devi Lal, and sought the prosecution of three Union ministers (who subsequently resigned) for allegedly accepting large bribes from a Delhi-based industrialist, Surendra Jain. The sheer scale of the so-called Hawala (illegal money transfer) scandal, in terms of the sums involved and the number of people implicated, led to widespread public disillusionment with politicians in general. Three more cabinet ministers resigned in February after their names had been linked to the scandal, further damaging Congress's hopes of retaining power in the forthcoming general election.

Political instability under the United Front (1996–98)

The results of the general election held in April–May 1996 gave no party or group an overall majority. The largest party was the BJP, which won 160 seats and, with the support of Shiv Sena (a right-wing Hindu nationalist party based in Mumbai) and other smaller allies, could count on an overall legislative strength of 194 seats. Congress secured 136 seats. The National Front (comprising the Janata Dal and its allies) and Left Front (representing the two major communist parties) together obtained 179 seats, with the remainder won by minor parties and independents. On 15 May the President asked the BJP under its new parliamentary leader, Atal Bihari Vajpayee, to form the new government and to prove its majority support within two weeks. The latter task proved impossible, and Vajpayee resigned on 28 May in anticipation of his Government's inevitable defeat in a parliamentary vote of confidence. Meanwhile, the National and Left Fronts had merged to form the United Front (UF), an informal coalition of 13 parties, with the Janata Dal, the Samajwadi Party, the two communist parties and the regional Dravida Munnetra Kazhagam (DMK) and the Telugu Desam Party (TDP) as its major components. With Congress prepared to lend external support, the UF was able to form a Government at the end of May, led by former Chief Minister of Karnataka H. D. Deve Gowda.

In September 1996 Narasimha Rao resigned from the leadership of Congress after he was ordered to stand trial on charges of cheating and criminal conspiracy; separate charges of forgery and criminal conspiracy (dating back to his tenure of the external

affairs ministry in the 1980s) were later made against Rao, who was replaced as Congress's president and parliamentary leader by the veteran politician Sitaram Kesri.

In April 1997 Deve Gowda resigned following the defeat of the UF administration in a vote of confidence. Inder Kumar Gujral, hitherto Minister of External Affairs, was sworn in as Prime Minister on 22 April. In May Sonia Gandhi, the widow of former Prime Minister Rajiv Gandhi, joined Congress as a 'primary member', and in the following month Kesri was re-elected President of the party in Congress's first contested leadership poll since 1977. In July 1997 Kocheril Raman Narayanan was elected as India's new President, notably the first person of Dalit origins to reach this position. In September the results of a five-year investigation into the destruction of the mosque at Ayodhya in 1992 led to charges of criminal conspiracy and incitement to riot being filed against senior BJP and religious leaders, including L. K. Advani and the leader of Shiv Sena, Balashaheb 'Bal' Thackeray.

Prime Minister Gujral was forced to resign in November 1997, when Congress withdrew its support for the Government over Gujral's refusal to expel the Tamil Nadu-based DMK (which was alleged to be indirectly implicated in the 1991 assassination of Rajiv Gandhi) from the coalition. President Narayanan dissolved the Lok Sabha in December following the inability of both Congress and the BJP to form an alternative coalition government. Gujral retained the premiership in an acting capacity pending a fresh general election in early 1998.

In an apparent attempt to halt the fragmentation of the Congress party, which had suffered internal discord and defections, Sonia Gandhi agreed to campaign in the run-up to the election, although she refused to stand for parliamentary office. In January 1998 26 Tamil militants implicated in the murder of Rajiv Gandhi were sentenced to death by a court in Chennai (Madras). (In May 1999, however, the Supreme Court in New Delhi acquitted 19 defendants and commuted the sentences of three others. In February 2014 the Supreme Court commuted the final three death sentences in the case to life imprisonment, on the grounds of unreasonable delays in settling the convicts' pleas for clemency. However, the Court subsequently blocked a decision by the government of Tamil Nadu to release the remaining seven prisoners convicted in the case, including the three whose death sentences had just been commuted.)

The BJP heads coalition governments (1998–2004)

At the general election held in February–March 1998, the BJP won 182 of the 545 seats in the Lok Sabha, while Congress secured 142 seats; shortly after the election Sonia Gandhi replaced Kesri as Congress's President. BJP parliamentary leader Atal Bihari Vajpayee was appointed Prime Minister by the President and, with the support of the All-India Anna Dravida Munnetra Kazhagam (AIADMK), the TDP (which eventually left the UF) and a number of other minor groups, he formed a coalition Government that secured a legislative vote of confidence on 28 March. None the less, it was immediately apparent that Vajpayee's 14-party coalition had a fragile hold on power.

In May 1998 the Government shocked both India and the rest of the world by authorizing a series of underground nuclear test explosions. This provocative action was initially greeted with massive popular enthusiasm, but Pakistan's retaliatory tests and a rapid realization of the negative international consequences (particularly the imposition of economic sanctions by the USA) soon tempered domestic approval.

Two AIADMK ministers resigned from the Government in April 1999, following a dispute over the dismissal of the Chief of Staff of the Navy. When the Government narrowly lost a resultant parliamentary vote of confidence, the President invited Sonia Gandhi to assemble a new coalition, which she was unable to do. Consequently, the Lok Sabha was dissolved and fresh elections were called, with Vajpayee's Government remaining in power in an acting capacity.

In May 1999 Congress's erstwhile parliamentary leader, Sharad Pawar, who had earlier publicly criticized Sonia Gandhi's foreign (Italian) origins, announced the formation of a breakaway party, entitled the Nationalist Congress Party (NCP); the NCP absorbed the Indian National Congress (S) in June. Meanwhile, the assertion of Indian military dominance following an outbreak of hostilities between Indian and Pakistani troops in the Kargil area of Kashmir in mid-1999 (see *Foreign Affairs*) boosted the BJP's standing and, in particular, that of acting premier Vajpayee, who was widely perceived to have responded with firmness and commendable restraint in the face of Pakistani provocation.

The BJP contested the general election, held in September–October 1999, at the head of the 24-member National Democratic Alliance (NDA), which comprised numerous minor regional and national parties with little shared ideology. The NDA won an outright majority in the Lok Sabha, with 299 of the 545 seats, while Congress and its electoral allies obtained 134 seats. Although Sonia Gandhi won both of the seats that she herself contested in Karnataka and Uttar Pradesh, her lack of political experience, weak grasp of Hindi and foreign birth all contributed to Congress's worst electoral defeat since India's independence. Following his appointment as leader of the NDA, Vajpayee was sworn in as Prime Minister, for a third term, at the head of a large coalition Government.

Legislation establishing the states of Chhattisgarh, Jharkhand and Uttaranchal was approved by Parliament in August 2000; the new states came into being in November. In October former Prime Minister Narasimha Rao was convicted of corruption and sentenced to three years' imprisonment. (His conviction was overturned by the High Court in New Delhi in March 2002, however.)

Following a devastating earthquake in Gujarat in January 2001, which claimed the lives of more than 30,000 people and rendered more than 1m. people homeless, both the central and state Governments were criticized for their tardy reaction to the disaster. During 2001 a new series of political and financial scandals exposed continuing corruption at the highest levels of government and commerce, and further undermined popular confidence in the BJP. In March videotaped evidence emerged of senior government and army officials accepting bribes from journalists posing as facilitators seeking to secure a bogus defence contract. BJP President Bangaru Laxman and Samata Party leader Jaya Jaitly both resigned from their posts following the revelations, as did the Minister of Defence, George Fernandes. Fernandes, by then leader of the Samata Party, was reappointed Minister of Defence in October. In April 2012 Laxman was convicted of bribery in connection with the case and sentenced to four years' imprisonment.

In February 2002 communal violence broke out in Gujarat after a train carrying members of the VHP returning from the disputed religious site at Ayodhya, where illegal construction of a temple was scheduled to commence in March, was set alight by a suspected group of Muslims in the town of Godhra. The attack, in which 59 Hindu activists were killed, was followed by a cycle of communal violence throughout Gujarat that lasted for several weeks and resulted in the deaths of up to 2,000 people, the majority of whom were Muslims. The Indian army was drafted in to quell the riots. Opposition members demanded the resignation of the Minister of Home Affairs, L. K. Advani, and the Chief Minister of Gujarat, Narendra Modi, for failing to control the riots. In April a report by the European Union on the situation in Gujarat concluded that the riots and killings had been, contrary to the official account, not in reaction to the attack on the train, but in fact an organized massacre of Muslims, and that the security forces had been ordered not to intervene. Modi eventually resigned and recommended the dissolution of the state assembly in July; he was requested to continue as leader of an interim administration until state elections were held in December.

In July 2002 the Government's candidate, A. P. J. Abdul Kalam, a South Indian Muslim who was closely involved in the development of the country's missile and nuclear programmes, won a convincing victory in the presidential election. At state elections in Gujarat in December, the BJP secured 126 of the 182 seats, while Congress won 51 seats. Interim Chief Minister Narendra Modi was confirmed in the post. Meanwhile, in September two armed assailants forced entry into a Hindu temple in Gujarat and shot dead 29 worshippers; three commandos were also killed in the attack, which was believed to have been carried out in retaliation for the deaths of Gujarati Muslims in the recent riots.

In March 2003 the Allahabad High Court ordered the Archaeological Survey of India to carry out an excavation at the disputed site in Ayodhya to ascertain whether an earlier Hindu temple existed beneath the Babri Masjid; issued in August, the report indicated that there was indeed evidence of a temple-like structure existing from the 10th century. However, a group of independent archaeologists and historians claimed that the Survey had misused or falsified evidence for political reasons. Meanwhile, in May the CBI filed new charges against L. K.

Advani and seven other leading politicians in connection with the destruction of the Ayodhya mosque in 1992. In September 2003 a special court exonerated Advani of any role in provoking the demolition of the mosque or encouraging communal agitation, but sustained the charges against the seven other defendants.

In January 2004, encouraged by the BJP's recent victories in state elections, a surging economy and an improvement in relations with Pakistan, Vajpayee announced that a general election would be held by the end of April, five months earlier than scheduled. Nevertheless, the BJP lost support from the DMK, the Marumalarchi Dravida Munnetra Kazhagam (MDMK) and Pattali Makkal Katchi; the AIADMK, meanwhile, announced that it would form an alliance with the BJP to contest the forthcoming election. In the same month the NCP split into two factions; the faction led by Sharad Pawar entered into an alliance with Congress, while Purno Shangma's group agreed to support the NDA.

Congress returned to power: the 2004 and 2009 general elections

At the general election held in April–May 2004, Congress defeated the NDA, securing, together with its allies, a total of 222 seats in the 545-member Lok Sabha, compared with 186 for the NDA. Congress alone won 145 seats, while the BJP secured 138. Left Front parties also performed well, with the Communist Party of India—Marxist (CPI—M) winning 43 seats. Shortly after the election Sonia Gandhi refused the appointment of Prime Minister, despite being unanimously endorsed as a candidate by Congress, its allies and the Left Front. However, she remained President of Congress, and was elected Chairwoman of the newly formed Congress-led coalition, the United Progressive Alliance (UPA). The respected Sikh economist and former Minister of Finance Dr Manmohan Singh was subsequently appointed as India's first non-Hindu Prime Minister. Meanwhile, Congress secured victory at state elections in Andhra Pradesh in May, and in Maharashtra and Arunachal Pradesh later in the year.

At the first session of the newly elected Lok Sabha, in June 2004, the BJP protested against the UPA's appointment of three ministers—all members of the Bihar-based Rashtriya Janata Dal—who had been charged variously with corruption and attempted murder, most notably the new Minister of Railways, Lalu Prasad Yadav, who continued to face corruption charges related to his tenure as Chief Minister of Bihar in 1997. (In April 2005 Yadav was formally charged with embezzlement during his tenure as Chief Minister; he received a five-year prison term in October 2013, having been found guilty of corruption and criminal conspiracy.) In July 2004 the Government dismissed the Governors of Goa, Gujarat, Haryana and Uttar Pradesh, owing to their alleged links to the fundamentalist Hindu group Rashtriya Swayamsevak Sangh (RSS—National Volunteer Organization).

India was one of the countries worst affected by the devastating tsunami generated by a huge earthquake in the Indian Ocean on 26 December 2004. The states of Tamil Nadu, Kerala and Andhra Pradesh and the Union Territory of Pondicherry on the east coast were all affected, together with the Andaman and Nicobar Islands, which were severely damaged. The disaster resulted in the loss of around 16,000 lives and numerous homes and livelihoods.

Subsequent to the general election, L. K. Advani took over as the BJP's parliamentary leader and later also as President of the party. However, in July 2005 charges were brought against Advani (and seven others) in connection with the riots at Ayodhya in 1992, overturning the ruling in September 2003 that had exonerated him of blame. Advani's resignation from the party leadership in December 2005 was believed to be largely a result of pressure from the RSS, which had close links with the BJP. Rajnath Singh, a former Chief Minister of Uttar Pradesh and a federal minister in the Government of Atal Bihari Vajpayee, was subsequently appointed as Advani's successor.

The Minister of External Affairs, K. Natwar Singh, was forced to resign in November 2005, having been implicated as a beneficiary of corrupt practices following an investigation into the UN's 'oil-for-food' programme in Iraq; Prime Minister Manmohan Singh subsequently assumed the external affairs portfolio. In December 10 legislators from the Lok Sabha and one from the Rajya Sabha were expelled from Parliament, having been filmed in the process of accepting bribes, apparently in exchange for asking certain questions in the chamber. Six of those expelled were BJP legislators. The expulsion was the largest to have taken place in India since independence.

In March 2006 Sonia Gandhi resigned as a member of the Lok Sabha and as Chairperson of the National Advisory Council (NAC), following assertions regarding the alleged illegality of her holding both positions simultaneously. Legislation was subsequently approved that categorized the chairmanship of the NAC and numerous other posts as non-'office of profit' positions. In May Sonia Gandhi was re-elected to the Lok Sabha in a by-election in Rae Bareilly. At state elections in April and May Congress, with the support of its allies, retained power in Assam (Asom) and in Pondicherry (renamed as Puducherry in October 2006), but was defeated by a CPI—M alliance in Kerala and West Bengal. During 2007–08 Congress obtained mixed results at various state elections, being voted into government in states including Manipur, Rajasthan and Mizoram. The BJP appeared to experience a resurgence, with victories in several states including Uttarakhand, Himachal Pradesh and Gujarat and, significantly, the southern state of Karnataka.

In August 2006 the regional party Telangana Rashtra Samithi (TRS) withdrew from the UPA, expressing its dissatisfaction with the Government's apparent lack of commitment to creating an independent Telangana state in Andhra Pradesh. In February 2007 the Samajwadi Party also withdrew from the UPA coalition; this was followed by the withdrawal of the MDMK in March and the Bahujan Samaj Party (BSP) in June 2008. In July 2007, upon the expiry of A. P. J. Abdul Kalam's presidential term, the UPA candidate and erstwhile Governor of Rajasthan, Pratibha Patil, was sworn in to succeed him, thus becoming the first female President of India. In September the rapid rise to political prominence of Rahul Gandhi, the son of Sonia Gandhi and Rajiv Gandhi, continued with his appointment as a General Secretary of Congress.

In July 2008 the Left Front bloc withdrew its support from the UPA Government in protest against the ratification of a nuclear co-operation agreement with the USA (see *Foreign Affairs*). The Government survived a parliamentary vote of confidence, called by Prime Minister Singh, later that month, gaining the support of the Samajwadi Party and others to secure a total of 275 votes against the opposition's 256 votes.

Meanwhile, in 2007 the establishment of Special Economic Zones (SEZs) was a major point of controversy in a number of states, including West Bengal, where activists and local residents protested against the forcible seizure of land for industrial development. In May 2008 protests staged by Gujjar tribespeople in Rajasthan against their official caste status escalated into violence, resulting in the deaths of more than 40 people and causing disruption in other states. Violence against Christians increased dramatically in 2008, with attacks on churches in Orissa and Karnataka and the displacement of thousands of people.

In the general election held in five phases during April–May 2009, the UPA won a decisive victory, taking 262 seats in the 543-seat Lok Sabha, while the NDA achieved 159 seats and the Third Front (a newly formed electoral alliance comprising the Left Front and a number of major regional parties—including the AIADMK, the BSP and the TDP) garnered only 79 seats. Many observers interpreted Congress's comfortable victory as a sign of the Indian public's overriding wish for stability and continuity at a time of worldwide economic crisis. Manmohan Singh was reappointed Prime Minister (the first Indian premier since Jawaharlal Nehru to be returned to office following a full five-year term) and a new coalition Government, dominated by Congress members, was installed on 22 May. Congress retained power in Maharashtra, Haryana and Arunachal Pradesh following state legislative elections in October.

In April 2010 the opposition called a 12-hour general strike in protest against the Government's failure adequately to address the issue of rising food prices, which severely affected transport services and business operations in a number of states, including West Bengal and Kerala. Another 12-hour strike, over rising fuel prices, was called by the opposition in July following the Government's decision to eliminate state petrol subsidies in a bid to tackle the fiscal deficit. The announcement in August of significant increases to parliamentarians' salaries and parliamentary expenses allowances further exacerbated a sense of public anger. Further protests against food price inflation and unemployment took place in February 2011, with at least 100,000 trade union members reported to have marched through the streets of Delhi. Meanwhile, a historic piece of legislation came into effect in April

2010, which made free and elementary education a fundamental right for all children in India between the ages of six and 14 years.

In September 2010 the Allahabad High Court ruled that the disputed Ayodhya holy site should be divided equally between Hindus and Muslims within three months, and that the razed mosque should not be rebuilt. However, both Hindu and Muslim groups filed appeals against the ruling. In May 2011 the Supreme Court suspended the High Court's verdict, noting that neither party had sought the partitioning of the site. Pending a final ruling, both sides were to be prohibited from engaging in any construction activities at the disputed site.

Mounting corruption scandals put pressure on the Congress-led Government

During 2010–11 a number of corruption scandals diminished public confidence in the Congress-led Government. In April 2010 allegations emerged that the Government had covertly monitored the mobile telephone calls of prominent political figures, including the Minister of Agriculture and of Food Processing Industries, Sharad Pawar, without the required authorization. Furore over the allegations, which the Government adamantly denied, precipitated the adjournment of both legislative chambers. In December, following further revelations concerning the widespread use of telephone surveillance measures by government agencies, Prime Minister Singh defended the use of such practices as essential to national security and the prevention of money-laundering and tax evasion; none the less, the premier ordered an inquiry into the use of telephone surveillance by law enforcement agencies.

The Government was criticized by the Supreme Court in October 2010 for alleged inaction in response to claims that in 2008 the Minister of Communications and Information Technology, Andimuthu Raja of the DMK, had sold mobile telephone licences at grossly undervalued rates to a select group of companies, instead of organizing appropriate commercial bidding processes. Critics claimed that the Prime Minister's reluctance to intervene was borne out of a fear of alienating the DMK, one of Congress's main coalition partners. A leaked report by the office of the Comptroller and Auditor General in November 2010 deemed Raja to be personally responsible for the scandal, which it alleged had cost the Government as much as US $37,000m. in lost revenue. Raja resigned later in November, but denied the accusations against him, insisting that he had merely sought to increase competition and reduce tariff prices in the burgeoning telecommunications industry. The Government resisted opposition demands for a full, joint inquiry into the allegations, underlining that impartial agencies—the CBI and the Supreme Court—were already investigating the case. In the same month a report published by the US-based Global Financial Integrity claimed that India had lost some $462,000m. in illegal capital outflows since acceding to independence in 1947, with a marked increase since economic liberalization began in 1991.

Prime Minister Singh effected a cabinet reorganization in January 2011, amid rising public anger over the corruption scandals and food price inflation. The most prominent portfolios remained unchanged, however. During a rare press conference in February, Singh reiterated his commitment to eradicating corruption at all levels of the political system. On the following day, in a *volte-face* that was welcomed by the opposition, the Prime Minister announced that a joint parliamentary committee was to be launched to investigate the circumstances surrounding the telecommunications scandal.

In March 2011 the Supreme Court ruled that the appointment of P. J. Thomas as head of the Central Vigilance Commission, an organization charged with monitoring public corruption, had been inappropriate, in light of corruption allegations against him dating back to 1992, as well as his having worked in the Ministry of Communications and Information Technology during the telecommunications scandal. Thomas duly tendered his resignation, while refuting the charges against him as baseless. Further controversy was provoked following the online release, in March 2011, by WikiLeaks—an organization publishing leaked private and classified content—of a US diplomatic cable in which it was alleged that an aide to a senior Congress leader had shown a US embassy official cash that was intended to buy votes in advance of a vote of no confidence in 2008 over a controversial nuclear agreement with the USA (see *Foreign Affairs*). In August 2011 four legislators were charged with each having accepted bribes worth US $2.5m. in return for their support in the vote of no confidence, and in September a former aide of L. K. Advani was arrested in connection with the scandal; all denied any wrongdoing.

In April 2011 Andimuthu Raja—who had been arrested by the CBI in February—was formally indicted on a series of charges including conspiracy, forgery and abuse of official position; eight other individuals, including two officials from the Ministry of Communications and Information Technology and senior executives from the telecommunications industry, were also indicted on similar charges. The trial of Raja and his co-accused commenced in November, with the proceedings still ongoing in early 2015. Meanwhile, the scandal led to a second ministerial resignation in July 2011, when the Minister of Textiles, Dayanidhi Maran of the DMK, left his post amid allegations of coercion in relation to the mis-selling of the mobile telephone licences during his tenure as Minister of Communications and Information Technology in 2004–08. In February 2012 the Supreme Court ordered the cancellation of 122 licences awarded by Raja during 2008.

As a popular anti-corruption movement gained momentum, two figures rose to prominence: Swami Ramdev (popularly known as Baba Ramdev), a well-known yoga guru who had become increasingly renowned for his political and social activism, and Kisan Baburao Hazare (popularly known as Anna Hazare), a social campaigner. Ramdev and Hazare both used widely publicized hunger strikes to force action on corruption, and attracted large numbers of supporters for protests. In response to the public mood, in July 2011 the Government proposed the establishment of an independent ombudsman—the Lokpal—which would have the authority to investigate and prosecute public officials suspected of corruption; however, neither serving Prime Ministers, senior members of the judiciary nor the conduct of legislators within Parliament would fall within its remit. In August, after being arrested and briefly held in custody, Hazare commenced a new hunger strike in Delhi in support of more comprehensive anti-corruption reforms. Hazare ended his hunger strike, on its 12th day, after members of Parliament, apparently taken aback by the extent of public support for the activist, approved a resolution in favour of tabling tougher anti-corruption legislation. The resulting Lokpal and Lokayuktas Bill (the jurisdiction of which was to cover most categories of government officials, including the Prime Minister) was approved by the Lok Sabha in December, but the legislation subsequently foundered in the Rajya Sabha. After the introduction of a number of amendments, the Bill was finally adopted by both houses of Parliament, with broad cross-party support, in December 2013.

Meanwhile, the 2010 Commonwealth Games, which were hosted by New Delhi in October of that year (the largest international sporting event ever to be held in India), were plagued by poor planning and delays in the construction of stadiums and other amenities, highlighting India's infrastructural deficiencies and damaging its international reputation. A number of senior members of the event's organizing committee were arrested between November 2010 and April 2011 in connection with ongoing investigations into allegations of corruption and mismanagement surrounding the Games. (In February 2013 Suresh Kalmadi, the Chairman of the organizing committee, was charged with corruption, along with the Secretary-General and the Director-General of the Games, and seven others.)

Legislative elections were held in several states in April–May 2011; notably, the CPI—M was defeated both in Kerala, where it lost to the Congress-led United Democratic Front, and in West Bengal, where its uninterrupted period of rule since 1977 was ended by the All India Trinamool Congress (AITC). The AITC Chairwoman and federal Minister of Railways, Mamata Banerjee, became West Bengal's first female Chief Minister, heading a coalition government that also comprised Congress.

Meanwhile, in February 2011 31 people were convicted on charges of criminal conspiracy and murder in connection with the 2002 Godhra train attack—see *The BJP heads coalition governments (1998–2004)*—of whom 11 were sentenced to death and 20 were imprisoned for life. Several trials relating to the communal violence in Gujarat that followed the train attack concluded during 2011 and 2012: more than 80 people, many of whom received life sentences, were convicted of involvement in the violence. In April 2012 the Chief Minister of Gujarat, Narendra Modi, was formally cleared of complicity in one of the worst atrocities of the 2002 riots, in which 69 mainly Muslim residents of the Gulbarg housing complex in Ahmedabad were killed. However, in August 2012 a former Gujarat state minister and aide to Modi, Maya Kodnani, was sentenced to 28 years'

imprisonment for her involvement in the massacre of almost 100 Muslims in Naroda Patiya, a suburb of Ahmedabad. (Kodnani was released on bail by the Gujarat High Court in July 2014, on grounds of ill health, while her legal representatives prepared to launch an appeal against her conviction.)

In September 2011 six people were killed when police in Tamil Nadu opened fire on a group of Dalit protesters in the town of Paramakudi who were demanding the release of the Tamizhaga Makkal Munnetra Kazhagam (TMMK—Tamil People's Progressive Federation) leader, John Pandian, who had been arrested earlier in the month. State authorities insisted that the police had acted in self-defence after coming under attack by the protesters. Later in the month 17 police and government officials were convicted of rape, while 252 others were convicted of 'atrocities against Dalits' in connection with an incident in the Tamil Nadu village of Vachathi in June 1992, when officials had raided the village following reports that villagers were involved in sandalwood-smuggling. More than 100 Dalits were reported to have been abused, 18 women were raped, and homes and livestock were destroyed.

Meanwhile, the majority of elected representatives from the northern Telangana region of Andhra Pradesh and 12 Telangana members of the national Parliament tendered their resignations in July 2011, in protest at the state government's failure to introduce a bill on the formation of the proposed new state of Telangana. (The resignations, however, were rejected in November by the Speaker of the Lok Sabha on procedural grounds.) Also in July pro-Telangana activists staged a 48-hour strike in support of their demands for the new state, bringing Andhra Pradesh's capital city, Hyderabad, and other towns and cities in the state to a virtual standstill. A session of the Lok Sabha in November was disrupted by angry protests following the approval by the Uttar Pradesh state assembly of a resolution, introduced by Chief Minister Kumari Mayawati, in support of the division of Uttar Pradesh into four smaller states—Avadh Pradesh, Bundelkhand, Paschim Pradesh and Purvanchal. Disagreements over the proposal (which was widely interpreted as an attempt by the ruling BSP to bolster its popular support in advance of state legislative elections due in February–March 2012) led to the temporary adjournment of both the Lok Sabha and the Rajya Sabha. Meanwhile, with effect from 1 November 2011, the state of Orissa was officially redesignated as Odisha.

Political events in advance of the 2014 general election
At state elections held in January–March 2012, Congress, whose election campaign was led by Rahul Gandhi, retained power in Manipur and emerged as the largest party in Uttarakhand, forming a state administration with the support of independent candidates. However, Congress recorded only a marginal increase of seats and remained a minor party in Uttar Pradesh, India's most populous state, where the left-wing Samajwadi Party ousted Mayawati's BSP. The BJP replaced Congress as Goa's government, and maintained a majority at municipal elections in Delhi, while the ruling Shiromani Akali Dal-BJP coalition retained control of the state assembly in the Punjab.

In July 2012 Pranab Mukherjee, the erstwhile Minister of Finance in the UPA cabinet, won a convincing victory in a presidential election. Mukherjee's extensive political experience was expected to transform the ceremonial post into a position of greater influence. In the same month the NCP's Sharad Pawar and Praful Patel, Minister of Agriculture and Minister of Heavy Industries and Public Enterprises, respectively, submitted their resignations, citing dissatisfaction with Congress's management of the coalition. In response, Congress agreed to the establishment of a coalition co-ordination committee, forestalling the ministers' departure. At the end of July the Prime Minister announced a cabinet reorganization, allocating the finance portfolio to P. Chidambaram, and appointing Sushilkumar Shinde, the erstwhile Minister of Power, to replace Chidambaram as Minister of Home Affairs. Chidambaram's appointment in particular was seen as addressing mounting criticism of government inertia in the area of economic policy.

In August 2012 a report published by the Comptroller and Auditor General (CAG) asserted that between 2005 and 2009 coalfields were allocated without the necessary auction procedure, resulting in losses of approximately US $33,000m. Prime Minister Singh, who had held responsibility for the coal portfolio at the time, was not accused of misconduct by the CAG; nevertheless, the BJP demanded his immediate resignation and the cancellation of the original allocations, causing an interruption to parliamentary proceedings that lasted 13 days. Discord within the UPA coalition was evident in September when the AITC withdrew its ministers from Government in protest over the latter's decision to allow majority foreign investment in multi-sector retail, a policy that had also proved unpopular with the opposition; however, the Government did secure parliamentary support for the measure in December.

In October 2012 Singh announced major alterations to the composition of the Council of Ministers, introducing or promoting several younger Congress members. The external affairs portfolio, which had recently been vacated by S. M. Krishna, was given to Salman Khurshid, who was replaced as Minister of Law and Justice by Ashwani Kumar.

Several missile tests were performed in 2012, including that of a long-range missile capable of reaching China or Europe; India was reported to have become the largest importer of military equipment in the world. The country was also financing a major expansion of its space programme, with an unmanned mission to Mars announced in August 2012. In July, meanwhile, a massive power failure resulted in an electricity 'blackout' for approximately 670m. Indians in 20 states in the north, west and east of the country, causing large-scale disruption and considerable embarrassment for the Government.

State elections were held in Himachal Pradesh and Gujarat in late 2012. Congress defeated the incumbent BJP government in Himachal Pradesh in November; former union minister Virbhadra Singh became Chief Minister of the state for the sixth time. In Gujarat the BJP retained power in December, winning almost twice as many seats as Congress. Narendra Modi was sworn in for a fourth term as Chief Minister amid heightened speculation over his potential as a future Prime Minister. Congress's performance in assembly elections in the north-eastern states of Meghalaya, Tripura and Nagaland in February 2013 was poorer than anticipated and did not bode well for the forthcoming national election (although the party did remain in power in the former state, with the support of independents and smaller parties). In January the party had appointed Rahul Gandhi as its Vice-President.

Meanwhile, in January 2013 the National President of the India National Lok Dal and former Chief Minister of Haryana, Om Prakash Chautala, was convicted of corruption and sentenced to 10 years' imprisonment. His son Ajay Singh Chautala, the Secretary-General of the party, received the same sentence. In the same month Rajnath Singh was elected as President of the BJP (having previously served in the position until 2009), to replace Nitin Gadkari, who was under investigation for alleged corruption.

In December 2012 the rape and murder of a woman on a private bus in Delhi by a group of men provoked large-scale protests and outrage, highlighting the mistreatment of women in Indian society and the shortcomings of the legal system. Five men and a juvenile male were subsequently arrested in connection with the case. In February 2013 the country's rape laws were amended, with longer minimum sentences and the provision of the death penalty in cases where rape leads to death. However, in March, in what was described as a 'major lapse in security', one of the suspects in the rape case died in prison, having reportedly committed suicide. In August the juvenile male was convicted of rape and murder and sentenced to three years' imprisonment, the maximum available sentence under India's juvenile justice legislation. In September the four remaining adult suspects were convicted of rape, murder, unnatural offences and destruction of evidence, and were sentenced to death. However, the executions were postponed in March and July 2014, pending appeal hearings with the Supreme Court.

Meanwhile, in March 2013 the Tamil Nadu-based DMK—which held five cabinet posts—withdrew its support from the ruling coalition. The regional party accused the Government of a weak response to ongoing allegations that the Government of Sri Lanka committed human rights violations against its Tamil citizens during that country's civil war (see *Other regional relations*). Following the resignations in May of the federal Minister of Railways, Pawan Kumar Bansal, and the Minister of Law and Justice, Ashwani Kumar, amid allegations of corruption, in June Prime Minister Singh carried out a further significant reorganization of the Council of Ministers, with eight new ministers (all of whom were members of Congress) being appointed to the Government.

Despite recent setbacks, Congress achieved an outright majority at state elections held in the formerly BJP-controlled state of Karnataka in May 2013. The party won 121 out of 224 seats, compared with 40 seats each for the BJP and the Janata Dal (Secular). K. Siddaramaiah was chosen by Congress as the new Chief Minister of Karnataka.

In July 2013 the UPA approved the division of Andhra Pradesh to create a separate state of Telangana, which would thereby become India's 29th state. The announcement led to a series of protests and strikes being held in coastal and southern districts of Andhra Pradesh by those opposed to the bifurcation of the state; many inhabitants of the existing state feared that the change would bring economic disruption and that Maoist insurgents in Telangana would threaten the region's security. In October several Congress ministers from Andhra Pradesh tendered their resignations from the federal cabinet (although these were not accepted), while several legislators from Congress and the TDP withdrew from Parliament. The draft legislation was endorsed by the Lok Sabha in February 2014, having received the support of the BJP as well as the UPA; it was approved by the Rajya Sabha later that month. Under the proposals, the neighbouring states would share the capital city of Hyderabad for an initial period of 10 years. Government officials denied opposition claims that the decision to proceed with the creation of Telangana was intended to attract regional votes at the forthcoming general election. At the Lok Sahba vote in February, there were violent disturbances in the chamber as legislators protested against the Government's proposals for the region. In late February Kiran Kumar Reddy tendered his resignation as Chief Minister of Andhra Pradesh in protest against the imminent division of the state; Reddy also announced his departure from Congress. On 1 March, following the failure of Congress officials in the state to reach agreement on a successor to Reddy, presidential rule was imposed in Andhra Pradesh. President Mukherjee signed the Telangana bill into law on the same day, and a few days later the Government announced that the new state of Telangana would officially be created on 2 June.

State elections were held in Chhattisgarh, Madhya Pradesh and Rajasthan, and in the National Capital Territory of Delhi, during November–December 2013. Congress candidates fared extremely badly, while the BJP secured outright majorities in the three states, winning by significant margins in Madhya Pradesh and Rajasthan. The BJP also won the most seats in the Delhi territorial election, although no party achieved a majority in the capital and thus the formation of a new government proved to be problematic (see below). Securing an absolute majority in the small state of Mizoram in December provided little consolation for the Congress leadership.

While the BJP performed strongly in the December 2013 Delhi election—increasing its representation in the assembly to 31 seats, from 23 seats at the previous election in 2008—the most notable result of the polls was the success of the recently formed Aam Aadmi Party (AAP), which had emerged from the popular anti-corruption movement and was contesting its first-ever election; the AAP secured 28 seats in the assembly. Congress was relegated to third place with just eight seats (compared with 43 seats in 2008); Sheila Dixit of Congress, who since 1998 had served three consecutive terms as Chief Minister, tendered her resignation. Given the inconclusive outcome of the Delhi polls, Kejriwal's AAP formed a minority government in the territory, with conditional support from Congress. The AAP's leader Arvind Kejriwal, a social activist and former civil servant with no political experience, was sworn in as Chief Minister of Delhi in late December. However, in February 2014, after less than two months in office, Kejriwal resigned following the failure of both Congress and the BJP to support the introduction of tough anti-corruption legislation in the territory—the AAP's flagship policy; Kejriwal's resignation led to the imposition of presidential rule in Delhi.

Meanwhile, in June 2013 Narendra Modi was appointed Chairman of the BJP's election committee in preparation for the 2014 legislative elections, despite opposition from L. K. Advani. Advani threatened to resign from his official BJP posts, but eventually accepted Modi's prime ministerial candidacy, which was officially announced in September 2013. While Modi attracted extensive popular support, in particular for his record on promoting economic development in Gujarat, there were also concerns that his controversial handling of communal tensions in his home state would make him a divisive leader who could potentially alienate many of India's non-Hindu citizens. In January 2014 Manmohan Singh confirmed that he would not continue in political office after the forthcoming general election. In the same month Rahul Gandhi was appointed chief of Congress's general election campaign. In February 11 left-leaning and regional parties—including the CPI—M, the Samajwadi

Party, Janata Dal (Secular), Biju Janata Dal, Asom Gana Parishad and the AIADMK—announced the formation of a Third Front to contest the general election. However, the proposed alliance proved to be precarious and the parties were unable to present a unified agenda; some of the constituent parties, including the AIADMK, subsequently withdrew from the Front.

Recent developments: the BJP wins the 2014 general election

Final results of the general election, held in nine phases between 7 April and 12 May 2014 were announced by the Election Commission on 16 May. The NDA, led by Modi's BJP, secured a resounding victory over the Congress-led UPA, whose decade in government was thus to come to an end. Prime Minister Singh conceded defeat to his rival long before all the votes had been counted, formally resigning as premier on 17 May. The BJP alone secured 282 of the 543 elected seats in the Lok Sabha, 10 more than the number required to secure an overall parliamentary majority; its allies in the NDA received a further 55 seats. By contrast, Congress won only 44 seats, and its allies in the UPA a further 15. Other parties and independents garnered 147 seats. Electoral turnout was recorded at 66.4%. The BJP's victory represented the first time that a party had won an outright majority at an Indian general election since 1984. Among the non-allied parties, the Tamil Nadu-based AIADMK and the West Bengal-based AITC performed well, securing 37 seats and 34 seats, respectively; both of the influential regional parties increased their representation in the Lok Sabha considerably. The AAP, competing in its first general election, secured four seats in Punjab. Although the anti-corruption party polled some 33% of the votes cast in Delhi, it failed to secure any seats in the national capital. Indeed, a notable feature of the election results was the frequent disparity between the share of the popular vote and the number of seats garnered by individual parties. For example, the BJP acquired its overwhelming victory with a more modest 31.0% share of the popular vote, while Congress's disappointing share of the vote (19.3%) translated into just 8.1% of the elective parliamentary seats. Analysts attributed this to the increasing fragmentation of Indian politics, with a growing number of smaller regional parties attracting significant shares of the vote.

The overwhelming defeat of Congress at the polls—the party's worst electoral performance since independence—was widely attributed to public disillusionment over the state of the economy, the high level of official corruption and the perceived ineffectiveness of its recent administrations. Both Rahul and Sonia Gandhi offered to resign from the leadership of the party in the immediate aftermath of the election, although their resignations were not accepted. A new NDA administration, led by Prime Minister Modi, dominated by the BJP and including one member from each of the Lok Jan Shakti Party, the TDP, Shiv Sena and Shiromani Akali Dal, was installed on 26 May. The BJP was allocated the key portfolios, with Rajnath Singh and Sushma Swaraj appointed Minister of Home Affairs and Minister of External Affairs and Overseas Indian Affairs, respectively, and Arun Jaitley awarded responsibility for the defence and finance portfolios. (Rajnath Singh was replaced as President of the BJP by Amit Shah, hitherto the party's General Secretary, in July.) Following the death of Gopinath Munde, the newly appointed Minister of Rural Development, of Panchayati Raj, and of Drinking Water and Sanitation, in a car accident in early June, responsibility for Munde's portfolios was awarded to the Minister of Road Transport and Highways, Nitin Gadkari. A few days later Sumitra Mahajan of the BJP was unanimously elected Speaker of the Lok Sabha.

Meanwhile, in mid-May 2014 Modi was replaced as Chief Minister of Gujarat by Anandiben Patel of the BJP, who thus became the state's first female Chief Minister, while T.R. Zeliang of the Naga People's Front was appointed to replace Neiphiu Rio as Chief Minister of Nagaland following Rio's election to the Lok Sabha. Nitish Kumar resigned as Chief Minister of Bihar in response to the poor performance of his Janata Dal (United) party in the general election, and Jitan Ram Manjhi was inaugurated as his replacement.

At state legislative elections held concurrently with the general election in April–May 2014, Congress, Biju Janata Dal and the Sikkim Democratic Front retained control of Arunachal Pradesh, Odisha and Sikkim, respectively. The new state of Telangana was officially created as scheduled on 2 June, thereby becoming India's 29th state, with 10 districts (compared with 13 in the remaining areas of Andhra) and Hyderabad serving as the capital of both Telangana and the residual Andhra Pradesh state for the next 10 years. K. Chandrasekhar Rao of the TRS was inaugurated as Chief Minister of Telangana, the TRS having secured 63 seats in the 119-seat Telangana legislative assembly. N. Chandrababu Naidu of the TDP was sworn in as Chief Minister of Andhra Pradesh in the following week after his party won 102 of the 175 seats in the state assembly.

In July 2014 D. V. Sadananda Gowda, the new Minister of Railways, proposed allowing foreign investment and a greater number of public-private partnerships in the country's rail sector, in order to accelerate the much-needed modernization of the country's rail network. In August Modi launched an initiative to provide a bank account for every Indian household, to help the poor gain greater economic independence and reduce the influence of informal financing channels operating outside the control of the central bank; at that time nearly two-fifths of the population were estimated not to have a bank account. Analysts noted that the ability to transfer state benefits directly into bank accounts in a greater number of cases would reduce waste and corruption.

Three founding members of the BJP—Atal Bihari Vajpayee, L. K. Advani and Dr Murli Manohar Joshi—were for the first time excluded from the party's parliamentary board (its highest decision-making body) in August 2014, a development that was widely interpreted as evidence of a generational shift taking place under the premiership of Modi. The BJP performed well in state legislative elections in Haryana and Maharashtra, both formerly Congress strongholds, in October. In Haryana, the BJP secured 47 of the 90 seats to gain control of the state for the first time, with Manohar Lal Khattar appointed Chief Minister. In Maharashtra, Congress was relegated to third place with 42 seats, allowing the BJP, which won 122 of the 288 seats, to form a coalition government with Shiv Sena, which had secured 63 seats; Devendra Fadnavis was appointed Chief Minister.

Amid criticism that some ministers were overburdened with responsibility for multiple portfolios, in November 2014 Modi effected a comprehensive expansion and reorganization of the cabinet, with four new ministers and 17 new ministers of state appointed. Notable changes included the transfer of the defence portfolio from Arun Jaitley to Manohar Parrikar, with Jaitley retaining the finance and corporate affairs portfolios and gaining concurrent responsibility for information and broadcasting, and the appointment of Suresh Prabhu as Minister of Railways.

Following state elections in Jharkhand and Jammu and Kashmir (see *Foreign Affairs*) in November–December 2014, the BJP emerged as the largest party and formed coalition governments in both states. Raghubar Das was appointed Chief Minister of the former state, while in the latter, after lengthy political negotiations, Mufti Mohammad Sayeed of the regional People's Democratic Party was appointed Chief Minister in February 2015. Also in February the AAP secured a resounding victory in elections in Delhi, winning 67 of the 70 seats in the territorial assembly; the BJP took the remaining three seats. Arvind Kejriwal was sworn in to his former post of Chief Minister in mid-February. Speculation subsequently emerged of divisions within the AAP, with some members reportedly concerned about Kejriwal's dual role as party leader and Chief Minister of Delhi. In the same month Jitan Ram Manjhi resigned as Chief Minister of Bihar in advance of a planned vote of confidence on his leadership; he was replaced by his predecessor, Nitish Kumar, who expressed regret for his decision to resign following the 2014 general election.

Meanwhile, at the end of December 2014 Modi's Government promulgated an ordinance exempting certain industrial and infrastructural projects from land-acquisition restrictions imposed by the former UPA administration in January, arguing that the restrictions were a hindrance to industrial development. Draft legislation seeking permanently to amend the existing land acquisition act was formally introduced to Parliament in February 2015. Members of the opposition (led by Congress) and thousands of farmers staged a protest march upon Parliament, arguing that the proposed legislation would be detrimental to the agricultural sector, which employed more than one-half of the total workforce; the protesters were repelled by police using batons and water cannons. Nevertheless, the controversial bill, with a few minor amendments incorporated to mollify the opposition, was approved by the Lok Sabha, on account of the BJP's comfortable majority, in mid-March. However, the Government failed to garner sufficient support for the bill in the opposition-controlled Rajya Sabha and at the end of March, with the ordinance due to expire on 5 April, Modi prorogued the upper house in order to reintroduce the land-acquisition ordinance and gain more time in which to secure parliamentary approval of the legislation. In mid-April the apparent public suicide of a farmer from Rajasthan at a political rally in New Delhi, organized by the AAP to protest against the proposed land bill, resulted in heightened scrutiny of and opposition to the Government's proposed legislation. Meanwhile, legislation increasing the cap on foreign investment in the insurance sector (from 26% to 49%) and two separate pieces of legislation pertaining to mining received parliamentary approval in mid-March.

Internal Unrest and the Threat of Terrorism

In the aftermath of the devastating terrorist attacks on the US mainland on 11 September 2001, for which the USA held the militant Islamist al-Qa'ida organization responsible, the Indian Government sought to emphasize its own uncompromising response to the activities of illegal organizations. In October the Government promulgated the controversial Prevention of Terrorism Act (POTA), which broadened the definitions of terrorist activity, proscribed indefinitely 23 organizations engaged in principally separatist activities, and granted special powers of response to the authorities, including the power to detain terrorist suspects for up to 180 days before filing formal charges against them. The Act was passed by a joint session of Parliament in March 2002, having earlier met with resistance in the Rajya Sabha. A series of audacious terrorist attacks perpetrated by Kashmiri separatists severely tested the resolve of the Government in late 2001 and early 2002 (see *Foreign Affairs*), resulting in an unexpected consolidation of popular and political support for the ruling coalition.

A number of bomb explosions occurred in Mumbai in December 2002–August 2003, killing more than 65 people. In June 2004 five people were charged under the POTA in connection with the bombings. Shortly after coming to power, in September 2004 the United Progressive Alliance (UPA) Government approved the repeal of the controversial POTA, which many critics claimed had been primarily used to harass minority groups, including Muslims, Dalits and tribal people. During 2005–08 there was a series of terrorist attacks against civilian targets in various locations across India. In October 2005 a number of bomb attacks in the national capital, New Delhi, resulted in the deaths of more than 60 people. In November police announced that they had arrested a man suspected of having financed and planned the bombings; he was believed to be a member of the Pakistan-based militant group Lashkar-e-Taiba (LeT). In March 2006 a number of bombs exploded in the holy city of Varanasi in Uttar Pradesh, killing at least 14 people. Several suspects, allegedly linked to the Bangladeshi wing of the Islamist militant group Harakat-ul-Jihad-i-Islami (HUJI—the Movement for Islamic Jihad, which was founded in the 1980s and was also active in Pakistan), were subsequently arrested. On 11 July some 187 people were killed and hundreds more injured in a series of bomb blasts on the Mumbai train network. In November 28 people were charged with involvement in the bombings, including 15 suspects who had not yet been apprehended. Among those charged were several with alleged links to the banned Students' Islamic Movement of India (SIMI—which was alleged to be linked to both al-Qa'ida and the militant Hizbul Mujahideen, see *Foreign Affairs*) and a little-known, affiliated group, the Indian Mujahideen. (The authorities subsequently failed to capture any of those charged *in absentia*, and trial proceedings against the 13 detainees were subject to lengthy delays and controversy regarding the credibility of evidence presented by the prosecution. By early 2015 the specially convened court hearing the case had yet to issue its verdict.) Another series of bomb explosions, at a Muslim cemetery in Malegaon, Maharashtra, killed at least 37 people in September 2006. By the end of November several suspects, with alleged links to the SIMI, had been arrested. In August 2007 two bomb explosions in the southern city of Hyderabad killed some 42 people. Six bomb explosions targeting three courts in Uttar Pradesh claimed the lives of 18 people in November; the Indian Mujahideen claimed responsibility for the attacks.

Further attacks were carried out in May 2008 in Jaipur, Rajasthan, resulting in the deaths of more than 80 people. In July bombings in Bangalore, Karnataka, which caused two fatalities, were followed by a series of explosions in the Gujarati city of Ahmedabad, killing some 50 people. In September, a month after Prime Minister Singh had identified 'terrorism, extremism, communalism and fundamentalism' as the 'major challenges to the unity and integrity' of the country, bomb attacks resulted in the deaths of more than 20 people in Delhi.

The Indian Mujahideen claimed responsibility for each of the four series of attacks.

In November 2008 some 166 people were killed in co-ordinated offensives carried out by 10 gunmen against public targets in Mumbai, including two hotels, a hospital, a railway station and a Jewish centre. Following the attacks and subsequent siege, which lasted for several days in some locations, and in which all but one of the gunmen were killed, the Minister of Home Affairs, Shivraj V. Patil, resigned on 30 November; he was replaced by the incumbent Minister of Finance, P. Chidambaram. As public criticism of the Government's handling of the attacks increased, in December the Chief Minister of Maharashtra, Vilasrao Deshmukh, was also forced to step down. In the same month the establishment of the National Investigation Agency was announced as part of a government campaign for greater internal security. In May 2010 the sole surviving gunman of the 2008 Mumbai attacks—Pakistani national Mohammed Ajmal Amir Kasab, who was allegedly a member of LeT—was convicted on five charges, including murder, terrorist activity and waging war against the nation, and sentenced to death; he was hanged in November 2012.

From December 2008 the authorities in Pakistan arrested several militants suspected of involvement in planning the 2008 Mumbai attacks; these included Zaki-ur-Rehman Lakhvi, a senior leader of LeT. However, Pakistan resisted Indian demands for the suspects to be extradited to India. Seven suspects, including Lakhvi, were charged in connection with the attacks under Pakistani anti-terrorism laws in November 2009; all seven denied the charges against them. Nine others were charged *in absentia*. In December the Indian Government announced plans to overhaul and strengthen its security services by recruiting 400,000 more police officers, establishing a national intelligence database and creating a national counter-terrorism centre. In June 2012 another alleged planner of the Mumbai attacks was arrested in New Delhi, while in January 2013 David Headley, a US-Pakistani associate of LeT, was sentenced in the USA to 35 years in prison for his role in planning the attacks. In accordance with a Pakistani court order overruling his ongoing detention, Lakhvi was released on bail in April 2015. The move caused consternation in India, although trial proceedings against Lakhvi and his co-defendants in the Mumbai attacks case were scheduled to continue.

Three co-ordinated bomb explosions in busy districts of Mumbai in July 2011 claimed the lives of 26 people and injured many others. No individuals or groups claimed responsibility for the attacks. Some officials attributed blame for the attacks to the Indian Mujahideen, while others contended that the attacks had been orchestrated by LeT or other elements seeking to derail the Indo-Pakistani peace process; other observers argued that the attacks may have been linked to the criminal underworld. In September, while Prime Minister Singh was on a state visit to Bangladesh, a bomb exploded outside the High Court in Delhi, killing 12 people. The Indian Mujahideen and HUJI both claimed responsibility for the attack; HUJI's senior leader, Ilyas Kashmiri, was reported to have died in a US unmanned drone strike in north-western Pakistan in June. The UPA Government drew growing criticism for its failure adequately to contain the threat of terrorist attacks on Indian soil. Later in September the Indian Mujahideen became the first Indian-based group to be formally designated as a foreign terrorist organization by the US Department of State.

In February 2013 17 people were killed and more than 100 injured following a pair of bomb attacks in Hyderabad. Although the identity of the perpetrators was unknown, numerous reports speculated that the attacks were related to an upsurge in unrest in Jammu and Kashmir in the same month (see *Relations with Pakistan and the Kashmir issue*).

In a video message released in September 2014, al-Qa'ida leader Ayman al-Zawahiri announced the creation of an Indian branch of the militant network—al-Qa'ida in the Indian Subcontinent—which sought to 'rescue' Muslims from alleged injustice and oppression in the Indian states of Assam, Gujarat, and Jammu and Kashmir, as well as in Bangladesh and Myanmar. In November, a few days after a suicide bomb attack on the Pakistani side of the Wagah border crossing (see *Foreign Affairs*), Indian security agencies claimed to have intercepted communications indicating growing operational links between the Indian Mujahideen and al-Qa'ida, as well as Afghan and Pakistani militant groups, prompting concerns of major terrorist plots targeting India.

Gurkha Separatist Movement

Regional issues continue to play an important role in Indian political affairs. In 1986 the Gurkhas (of Nepalese stock) in West Bengal launched a campaign for a separate autonomous homeland in the Darjiling (Darjeeling) region and the recognition of Nepali as an official language. The violent separatist campaign, led by the Gurkha National Liberation Front (GNLF), was prompted by the eviction of about 10,000 Nepalis from the state of Meghalaya, where the native residents feared that they were becoming outnumbered by immigrants. In an attempt to arrest the GNLF-led unrest and strikes, in 1987 the central Government instituted tripartite talks with the GNLF's leader, Subhas Ghising, and the Chief Minister of West Bengal. The Prime Minister rejected the GNLF's demand for an autonomous Gurkha state, but Ghising agreed to the establishment of a semi-autonomous Darjiling Gorkha Hill Council (DGHC), which was inaugurated in August 1988. Following elections to the DGHC in November, the GNLF won 26 of the 28 elective seats (the 14 remaining members of the Council were to be nominated) and Ghising was elected Chairman of the Council. However, the GNLF continued to demand the establishment of a fully autonomous Gurkha state. In 1992 a constitutional amendment providing for the recognition of Nepali as an official language was adopted.

In February 2008 a splinter group of the GNLF, the Gorkha Janmukti Morcha (GJM—the Gurkha People's Liberation Front), blockaded entry routes into Darjiling to protest against a new autonomy agreement drawn up between the DGHC and the state and federal authorities. Following the resignation of Ghising in March, the GJM rapidly became the dominant force representing Gurkha separatism. A series of GJM-orchestrated strikes and protests severely disrupted the key tourism and tea industries in the area. In August 2009 the central Government initiated a series of tripartite talks involving the GJM and the West Bengal state authorities, following which the Government agreed to repeal the legislation creating the DGHC, while the GJM pledged to remain 'peaceful and democratic'. After Mamata Banerjee of the All India Trinamool Congress became Chief Minister of West Bengal, an agreement was signed between the state government and the GJM in July 2011 providing for the creation of a semi-autonomous Gorkhaland Territorial Administration (GTA), which was to comprise Darjiling, Kalimpong and Kurseong and have various administrative, executive and financial powers, as well as the authority to regulate its tea plantations. In October the GJM proposed the enlargement of the GTA to include a number of subdivisions in Terai and Dooars inhabited primarily by Gurkhas or Adivasis (also of Nepalese stock), whereby the GTA's official designation would change to the Gorkhaland and Adivasi Territorial Administration. In March 2013 a GJM delegation travelled to Delhi to meet with President Pranab Mukherjee. The GJM reiterated its demands for an autonomous Gurkha state ('Gorkhaland'), and complained about the West Bengal state government's interference in GTA affairs. In August, as the Government was proceeding with plans to create an independent state of Telangana out of Andhra Pradesh, the GJM declared an indefinite strike in Darjiling to protest against the failure of the federal authorities to establish a separate Gurkha state; the strike again had a serious effect on the economy of West Bengal. In a firm statement against bifurcation, Chief Minister Banerjee stressed in March 2014 that Darjiling was an integral part of West Bengal and accused the GJM of engaging in 'divisive politics' for its own vested interests rather than out of concern for the development of the area.

Unrest in Assam

From 1979 a popular movement emerged in the north-eastern state of Assam, which aimed to combat and reverse the flow of allegedly illegal immigrants into the state, mostly from neighbouring Bangladesh. The leaders of the movement claimed that successive waves of immigration were undermining Assam's economy and threatening the (Hindu) cultural and social traditions of the state. Spearheaded by the All Assam Students' Union and the All Assam Gana Sangram Parishad, the movement began as a programme of peaceful agitation, but gradually resulted in rising sectarian violence. In August 1985 events culminated in the signing of an agreement between the central Government and the Assamese activists, which limited the voting rights of immigrants (mainly Bangladeshis) to Assam. When the accord was announced, Bangladesh stated that it would not take back Bengali immigrants from Assam and denied that it had allowed illegal refugees to cross its borders into

Assam. In December an election for the state assembly was won by the Asom Gana Parishad (AGP—Assam People's Council), a new political party formed by the leaders of the anti-immigrant movement.

Another disaffected Indian tribal group, the Bodos of Assam, demanded a separate state of Bodoland. In February 1989 the Bodos, under the leadership of the All Bodo Students' Union (ABSU), intensified their separatist campaign by organizing strikes, bombings and violent demonstrations. The central Government dispatched armed forces to the state. In August the ABSU held talks with state and central government officials, agreeing to suspend its violent activities, while the Assam government agreed to suspend emergency security measures.

The situation became more complicated in 1989, when a militant Maoist group, the United Liberation Front of Assam (ULFA), re-emerged. The ULFA demanded the outright secession of the whole of Assam from India. In 1990 the ULFA claimed responsibility for about 90 assassinations, abductions and bombings. In November, when the violence began to disrupt the state's tea industry, the central Government placed Assam under direct rule, dispatched troops to the state and outlawed the ULFA. In the 1991 state elections the AGP was defeated, and Congress (I) took power. In September, following the breakdown of talks with the ULFA, the Government launched a new offensive against the separatist guerrillas and declared the entire state a disturbed area. Meanwhile, following the suspension of violence by the ABSU, the Bodo Security Force assumed the leading role in the violent campaign for a separate state of Bodoland. The Bodo Security Force was outlawed by the central Government in November 1992. At a tripartite meeting attended by the Minister of State for Home Affairs, the Chief Minister of Assam and the President of the ABSU in Guwahati in February 1993, a memorandum was signed providing for the establishment of a 40-member Bodoland Autonomous Council, which would be responsible for the socio-economic and cultural affairs of the Bodo people. However, attacks leading to substantial loss of life were made by Bodo and ULFA activists in the second half of the 1990s, both on the security forces and on non-tribal groups in the area. In March 2000 the Government and the Bodo Liberation Tigers (BLT—a group that had waged a violent campaign for a separate state for the Bodo people since 1996) agreed to a ceasefire.

In 2002 the Assam state assembly passed a resolution granting a degree of autonomy to the Bodo people through the creation of a territorial council for the Bodos comprising four western districts of the state. The Bodoland Territorial Council was established in December 2003 and the Bodo militants surrendered their weapons to mark the formal disbanding of the BLT. However, the ULFA continued its campaign of violence, and inter-tribal clashes also occurred in the state. In August 2004 the ULFA was believed to have been responsible for the bombing of an Independence Day parade in the town of Dhemaji, which killed 16 people. In October a series of violent incidents in Assam and neighbouring Nagaland was attributed to the ULFA and the National Democratic Front of Bodoland (NDFB), another militant group operating in the region. In May 2005 the NDFB signed a one-year ceasefire agreement with both the government of Assam and the Union Government. The ULFA also agreed subsequently to conduct peace negotiations with the Union Government; by September 2006, however, negotiations had collapsed, and in subsequent months the Government dispatched further troops to the region to curb the escalating violence. There was also an increase in attacks on migrant workers in Assam, allegedly perpetrated by the ULFA, together with a new strategy of targeting Congress officials.

Co-ordinated bomb attacks, most of them in Guwahati, resulted in more than 80 fatalities in October 2008. In the same month violence between Bodos and settlers caused dozens of deaths in the state. In November 2009 several senior ULFA leaders were arrested by the Bangladeshi authorities and transferred into Indian custody. A marked reduction in militant activity was evident from 2010, and, to facilitate peace talks with the central Government, the ULFA announced a unilateral ceasefire in July 2011.

Violence broke out between Bodos and Muslim settlers in the Kokrajhar district in July 2012, leading to some 95 deaths and the internal displacement of hundreds of thousands of people. Further displacement was reported in southern cities, including Bangalore and Chennai, as north-eastern migrants fearing further violence fled. In February 2013 the holding of local elections precipitated clashes between protesters and the police, resulting in 19 fatalities. A curfew was imposed in the districts of Baksa and Kokrajhar in May 2014 following a series of attacks attributed to the NDFB (Sangbijit) faction, in which more than 30 Muslims were killed; survivors of the attacks claimed that they had been targeted in revenge following the election of a non-Bodo independent candidate in Kokrajhar—formerly a stronghold of the Bodoland People's Front (BPF—a successor organization to the BLT)—in the recent Lok Sabha elections. The electoral loss of the BPF, which ended its long-standing alliance with Congress in June, appeared to inject fresh impetus to demands for a separate Bodoland state. In December another curfew was imposed and solders were deployed in several districts following further attacks attributed to the NDFB (Sangbijit), which, together with retaliatory attacks against Bodos, claimed the lives of more than 70 people.

'Greater Nagaland'

Elsewhere in north-eastern India, violence—separatist, inter-tribal (particularly against ethnic Bengali settlers) and anti-Government—continued in Nagaland, Tripura, Bihar, Mizoram and Manipur during the 2000s, leading to an alarming increase in the number of civilian deaths. In 1997 the central Government entered a ceasefire agreement with the National Socialist Council of Nagaland (Issak Muivah)—NSCN (IM)—a rebel organization that advocated the creation of a 'greater Nagaland', which, in addition to the state of Nagaland, would include districts in Assam, Manipur and Arunachal Pradesh. In June 2001 the Government extended the scope of the existing ceasefire in Nagaland to include the National Socialist Council of Nagaland (Khaplang)—NSCN (K)—along with all underground organizations in north-eastern India, and offered to involve the NSCN (K) and the NSCN (IM) in peace negotiations. The decision to extend the ceasefire to Naga groups in the neighbouring states of Assam, Manipur and Arunachal Pradesh gave rise to fears of the creation of a 'greater Nagaland' as part of an eventual settlement at the expense of the other states. Strikes and violent protests took place in Manipur. In July, in an effort to curb the violence, the national Government agreed to limit the ceasefire arrangement to the state of Nagaland. In November 2002 the central Government lifted its ban on the NSCN (IM) and agreed to hold negotiations on the political status of Nagaland. In 2007, at India's request, security forces in Myanmar took action against NSCN (K) bases inside Myanma territory. In 2010 regional tensions about the creation of a greater Naga territory erupted in crisis. In April a Naga student group linked to the NSCN (IM) conducted a blockade of the main roads into Manipur, in protest at elections to a tribal hill council in the neighbouring state, causing shortages and hardship in the region. In the mean time, the Naga nationalist movement has increasingly been riven by factional violence and further internal splits in both the NSCN (IM) and the NSCN (K). In March 2015 it was reported that the NSCN (K) was preparing to revoke its long-standing ceasefire agreement with the central Government, owing to a lack of progress towards its political goals.

Naxalite Insurgency

The Naxalites are a myriad group of Maoist insurgents who emerged in the late 1960s in West Bengal. Since then the rebels, who claim to be fighting for the rights of the rural poor, have spread into less developed areas of central and eastern India (popularly known as the 'Red Corridor'). In mid-2012 the Ministry of Home Affairs estimated the total number of Naxalite cadres at 46,600, of whom 8,600 were described as well-armed.

In mid-2004 the state government of Andhra Pradesh agreed a ceasefire with the People's War Group, a faction of the Communist Party of India (Marxist-Leninist), which had been waging a sporadic violent campaign in the state since 1980. The Naxalite rebels demanded the creation of a communist state comprising tribal areas in Andhra Pradesh, Maharashtra, Orissa, Bihar and Chhattisgarh. In September 2004 the People's War Group merged with another militant separatist group, the Maoist Communist Centre, to become the Communist Party of India (Maoist)—CPI (Maoist). Peace negotiations commenced between the rebels and the Andhra Pradesh state authorities in October, but collapsed in early 2005, leading to escalating violence in the region. In August the state government imposed a fresh ban on the CPI (Maoist), after rebels murdered nine people in the town of Narayanpet.

In September 2005 an Inter-State Joint Task Force was established to co-ordinate operations against Naxalite rebels across state borders, with the assistance of the Union Government. In the same month the government of Chhattisgarh outlawed all Naxalite organizations, following a recent increase

in insurgent activity in the state. In April 2006 Prime Minister Manmohan Singh stated that the Naxalite insurgency posed the 'single biggest internal security challenge' to India, and called for further co-operation between the main affected states. In 2007 insurgents were allegedly involved in road blockades and attacks on infrastructure staged in protest against the establishment of Special Economic Zones in states such as West Bengal. During 2006–07 Naxalite attacks and clashes between rebels and security forces in Chhattisgarh reportedly resulted in several hundred deaths, including many civilians. Despite concerted action by the security forces, the number of deaths resulting from Naxalite violence increased from 721 in 2008 to 908 in 2009, and by early 2010 it was estimated that the Naxalite insurgency had spread to at least 20 of India's 28 states.

In April 2010 more than 70 paramilitary troops were killed by Naxalite rebels in Chhattisgarh. After a landmine killed more than 30 people (the majority of whom were civilians) in the same state in May, the Government announced that it was reviewing its strategy against the rebels. In an apparent case of sabotage later that month, more than 80 people were killed when a train travelling from Calcutta to Mumbai derailed. Naxalite leaders denied involvement in the derailment, but pledged to launch an investigation and to punish any 'rogue' units found to have been involved; police claimed to have substantial evidence indicating the responsibility of a local Naxalite militia. In June Minister of Home Affairs P. Chidambaram set out the Government's pre-conditions for initiating peace talks with Naxalite rebels, demanding the total cessation of violent activities for a 72-hour period, following which security forces would refrain from targeting them; the initiative was reported to have been cautiously welcomed by Naxalite rebels, but the violence continued unabated, and a number of rebels were reported to have been killed during July–August. The number of deaths resulting from Naxalite violence increased to 1,005 in 2010. However, the ministry noted a marked decline, to 611 persons, in 2011, and attributed this to the Government's ongoing counter-insurgency efforts. Enhanced co-operation between the various authorities across state borders and significant improvements in intelligence-gathering were believed to have played key roles in the significant reduction of casualties.

Although the number of fatalities caused by Naxalite militants decreased further in 2012 and 2013, to an estimated 414 and 397, respectively, violent incidents continued to be reported. In May 2013 Maoist militants attacked a convoy of political activists in Chhattisgarh, killing 28 people, including 12 senior Congress officials. In June nine states that faced security threats from Maoist insurgents, including Bihar and Chhattisgarh, announced the implementation of a new, united policy to tackle the problem. An estimated 40,000 members of the security forces in eight of the states commenced a four-day military operation in December to attempt to defeat the insurgency. It became apparent in the second half of 2013, with further fatal Maoist attacks having taken place in Bihar and Jharkhand in June and July, respectively, that the insurgents were increasingly targeting the civilian population as well as government and military targets. An estimated 309 fatalities were caused by Naxalite militants in 2014, including a total of 22 police officers killed in two attacks by Maoist rebels in Chhattisgarh in February and March, and a further seven officers killed when Maoist rebels detonated a landmine in Maharashtra in May.

Foreign Affairs

Upon assuming office in May 2014, the Government of Prime Minister Narendra Modi seemed committed to consolidating relations with India's regional neighbours, in an apparent effort to counterbalance increasing Chinese influence within South Asia. Invitations to Modi's inauguration ceremony in May were extended to the leaders of the seven other member states of the South Asian Association for Regional Co-operation (SAARC, see p. 417). Six of the seven invited leaders accepted the invitation—including Muhammad Nawaz Sharif, the Prime Minister of India's longtime adversary, Pakistan—while Bangladesh's parliamentary Speaker attended the ceremony in place of Prime Minister Sheikh Hasina, who was in Japan on an official visit.

Relations with Pakistan and the Kashmir issue

Relations with Pakistan deteriorated in the late 1970s and early 1980s, aggravated by Pakistan's potential capability for the development of nuclear weapons and its significant purchases of US armaments. The Indian Government believed that such developments would upset the balance of power in the region and precipitate an 'arms race'. Pakistan's President, Gen. Mohammad Zia ul-Haq, visited India in 1985, when he and Rajiv Gandhi announced their mutual commitment not to attack each other's nuclear installations and to negotiate the sovereignty of the disputed Siachen glacier region in Kashmir. Pakistan continued to demand a settlement of the Kashmir problem in accordance with earlier UN resolutions, prescribing a plebiscite under UN auspices in the two parts of the state, now divided between India and Pakistan. India argued that the problem should be settled in accordance with the Shimla Agreement of 1972, which required that all Indo–Pakistani disputes be resolved through bilateral negotiations. In late 1989 the outlawed Jammu and Kashmir Liberation Front (JKLF) and several other militant Islamist groups intensified their campaigns of civil unrest, strikes and terrorism, demanding an independent Kashmir or unification with Pakistan. The Indian Government dispatched troops to the region and placed the entire Srinagar valley under curfew. Pakistan denied India's claim that the militants were trained and armed in Pakistan-held Kashmir (known as Azad Kashmir). In January 1990 Jammu and Kashmir was placed under Governor's rule, and in July under President's rule. By 1996 the total death toll resulting from the conflict in Jammu and Kashmir was estimated at up to 20,000. However, the situation improved somewhat when elections for the national parliamentary seats were held in the troubled state shortly after the general election of April–May 1996. State elections (the first to be held since 1987) were conducted in Jammu and Kashmir in September 1996 and attracted a turnout of more than 50%, despite being boycotted by the majority of the separatist groups. The moderate Jammu and Kashmir National Conference (JKNC), led by Dr Farooq Abdullah, won the majority of seats in the state assembly and subsequently offered to instigate talks with the separatist leaders.

Official Indo-Pakistani negotiations resumed in March 1997 after a three-year hiatus, but yielded little progress. Following the collapse of the Indian United Front Government in late 1997, Pakistan rejected talks with the new administration of Atal Bihari Vajpayee unless the Kashmir issue was to be afforded substantive attention. Meanwhile, tension increased in September when a large-scale outbreak of artillery exchanges along the Line of Control (LoC) in Kashmir (a ceasefire line drawn up in 1949) resulted in about 40 civilian deaths. Relations were further impeded in May 1998 when both countries conducted controversial nuclear test explosions (see *Domestic Political Affairs*). Formal talks regarding Kashmir and other issues resumed in Islamabad, the Pakistani capital, in October 1998. In February 1999 Prime Minister Vajpayee made a historic bus journey over the border to Lahore, in eastern Pakistan, inaugurating the first passenger bus service between India and Pakistan. He and his Pakistani counterpart, Muhammad Nawaz Sharif, proceeded to hold a rare summit meeting, at which they signed the Lahore Declaration on peace and nuclear security. The contentious subject of Jammu and Kashmir was, however, largely avoided.

Despite the apparent rapprochement, in April 1999 both India and Pakistan carried out tests on their latest missiles, which were capable of carrying nuclear warheads. In May the situation deteriorated drastically after Islamist guerrilla groups, reinforced by regular Pakistani troops, occupied strategic positions on the Indian side of the LoC in the Kargil area of Kashmir. The Indian army was forced to wage an expensive and lengthy campaign, during which more than 480 Indian soldiers were killed, but in July Indian military dominance combined with US diplomatic pressure led to a Pakistani withdrawal.

In August 1999 the Hizbul Mujahideen, one of the main Kashmiri militant groups, ended a brief ceasefire because of the Indian Government's opposition to instigating tripartite negotiations including representatives of Pakistan. In April 2000 there were indications that the Indian Government was willing to re-establish dialogue with Kashmiri militants. Leaders of the All-Party Hurriyat Conference (APHC), an organization that acted as a quasi-political voice for some of the militant groups, were released in April and May. The Government suspended combat operations against Kashmiri militants between November 2000 and May 2001, but the militant groups refused to enter into tripartite discussions and continued their campaign of violence; Indian security forces were authorized to retaliate if fired upon. More than 1,000 people were estimated to have been killed in Kashmir-related violence during the unilateral ceasefire.

Relations with Pakistan appeared to improve following the earthquake in Gujarat in January 2001, when Pakistan offered humanitarian relief to India. In May Vajpayee issued an unexpected invitation to the Pakistani President, Gen. Pervez Musharraf, to attend bilateral negotiations in Agra in July. However, the two leaders failed to agree to a joint declaration on Kashmir; the divergent views of the two sides on the priority issue in the dispute (cross-border terrorism according to India, and Kashmiri self-determination in the opinion of Pakistan) appeared to be more firmly entrenched than ever. Violence increased in the region as a result of the disappointment engendered by the meeting. A guerrilla-style attack on the state assembly building in Srinagar in October, responsibility for which was claimed by the Pakistan-based militant group Jaish-e-Mohammed (JeM), killed 38 people.

On 13 December 2001 five armed assailants attempted to launch an apparent suicide attack on the Union Parliament building in New Delhi. Although no parliamentary deputies were hurt in the attack, 14 people (including the assailants) were killed. The Indian authorities attributed responsibility for the attack to JeM and another Pakistan-based militant group, Lashkar-e-Taiba (LeT), although the latter denied any involvement. Afzal Guru, a member of JeM arrested in Kashmir, subsequently admitted to involvement in the incident and alleged publicly that Pakistani security and intelligence agencies had provided support to those directly responsible. (Guru, however, subsequently alleged that his confession had been extracted under torture.) India recalled its High Commissioner from Islamabad and announced the suspension of overground and aviation transport services between the two countries. Mindful of the potential detriment to security at Pakistan's border with Afghanistan that could result from an escalation in conflict in Kashmir, the USA applied increased pressure on the Pakistani Government to adopt a more conciliatory attitude towards India's security concerns, and in late December the Pakistani authorities followed the US Government's lead in freezing the assets of JeM and LeT. The leaders of the two groups were later detained by the Pakistani authorities, but the Indian Government continued to dismiss much of the Pakistani response as superficial and demanded that the two leaders be extradited to stand trial in India. In December 2002 a special court convicted three Kashmiri Muslims—two of whom were reportedly members of JeM and the third a member of the JKLF—of organizing the attack on the Union Parliament and sentenced them to death. (However, a High Court ruling overturned the convictions of two of the men following an appeal in October 2003.)

In January 2002 Musharraf yielded to international pressure by publicly condemning the activities of militant extremists based in Pakistan and announcing the introduction of a broad range of measures to combat terrorist activity and religious zealotry, including the proscription of five extremist organizations (among them JeM and LeT). However, further attacks by suspected Islamist militants in January and May, which the Indian authorities linked to Pakistan, caused another stand-off along the LoC. Relations deteriorated further following the assassination of Abdul Ghani Lone, the leader of the APHC, in May, by suspected Islamist militants. As a result of international efforts to defuse the situation, in June India withdrew five naval ships from patrol of the coast of Pakistan and allowed Pakistani civilian aircraft to enter its airspace, in response to Pakistani pledges to halt cross-border infiltration, and both sides subsequently scaled down their troop numbers along the international border.

State elections in Jammu and Kashmir, scheduled for September–October 2002, were boycotted by the APHC, who demanded that a referendum on independence should first be held. Violence continued throughout the election period, with at least 730 people reportedly killed. Following the elections, in which no single party won an outright majority, Congress and the regional People's Democratic Party (PDP) reached a power-sharing arrangement, under which PDP leader Mufti Mohammed Sayeed was to be appointed Chief Minister for a three-year term, followed by local Congress President Ghulam Nabi Azad for the next three years.

In early 2003 Indo-Pakistani tensions were exacerbated by mutual accusations of diplomatic espionage, India's latest round of 'routine' ballistic missile tests without advance warning (Pakistan responded in kind), ongoing violence in Kashmir, and India's recent strategic partnership agreement and arms deals with Russia (see *Other external relations*). The killing of 24 Kashmiri Hindus, including women and children, in a village south of Srinagar by suspected Islamists in March provoked widespread condemnation and posed a setback to Chief Minister Sayeed's reconciliation programme. Nevertheless, in May the

Indian and Pakistani premiers agreed to restore the recently severed diplomatic relations. Two months later the bus service between Lahore and New Delhi was restored.

In August 2003 the assassination in Srinagar of Ghazi Baba, the chief commander of JeM and alleged mastermind of the December 2001 attack on the Union Parliament building, provoked a surge in violence in Kashmir.In October the Indian Minister of External Affairs, Yashwant Sinha, announced 12 confidence-building measures to improve and normalize relations with Pakistan, while emphasizing that no direct talks on Kashmir would take place until Pakistan halted cross-border infiltration by Islamist militants. In November a bilateral ceasefire along the LoC came into effect. In December Indian and Pakistani officials signed a three-year agreement on the restoration of a train service between New Delhi and Lahore. Direct aviation links between the two countries were resumed on 1 January 2004.

At a ground-breaking SAARC summit meeting in Islamabad in January 2004, Musharraf assured Vajpayee that he would not permit any territory under Pakistan's control to be used to support terrorism; in return Vajpayee agreed to begin negotiations on all bilateral issues, including Kashmir. The APHC called for a boycott of the general election, held in April–May, and a series of violent attacks directed at all politicians campaigning in Jammu and Kashmir resulted in several deaths. Overall electoral turnout in Kashmir was 35%, although this declined to less than 19% in Srinagar. In June Indian and Pakistani officials meeting in New Delhi agreed to restore their diplomatic missions to full strength. An agreement was also reached that each country would, in future, notify the other of any forthcoming missile tests. In September India and Pakistan held their first, official, ministerial-level talks in more than three years in New Delhi, agreeing to implement a series of confidence-building measures.

In November 2004 Prime Minister Manmohan Singh ordered a 'substantial' reduction in the number of Indian troops deployed in Kashmir. In early 2005 Jammu and Kashmir held its first municipal elections in 27 years. At the same time, tensions resurfaced, with India and Pakistan accusing each other of violating the ongoing ceasefire along the LoC. However, in February the two countries agreed to open a bus service across the LoC, linking Srinagar with Muzaffarabad, in Azad Kashmir. In April Musharraf travelled to New Delhi for further peace talks with Prime Minister Singh. In June a delegation of APHC leaders travelled to Muzaffarabad, where they held discussions with Pakistani Kashmiri leaders. The visit represented the first time since 1946 that Indian Kashmiri politicians had been permitted to traverse the LoC. In September, in a symbolic gesture, the Government began to withdraw paramilitary Border Security Force (BSF) troops from Srinagar; responsibility for security in the city was subsequently assumed by the Central Reserve Police Force (CRPF).

In October 2005 a massive earthquake centred in Azad Kashmir resulted in widespread loss of life and destruction, particularly on the Pakistani side of the LoC. Pakistan accepted an Indian offer of aid and, following a series of negotiations, the two countries subsequently agreed to open a number of crossing-points on the LoC, in order to permit the reunification of divided families. In February 2006 a second rail link was opened between India and Pakistan, linking the town of Munabao in Rajasthan to the Pakistani town of Khokrapar in Sindh.

Relations between India and Pakistan were strained by the Mumbai train bombings in July 2006 (see *Internal Unrest and the Threat of Terrorism*). Although President Musharraf condemned the attacks, Prime Minister Singh suggested that those responsible had links to Pakistan. Bilateral peace talks were postponed, and in September the Mumbai police claimed that LeT was responsible for the July bombings and had apparently been aided in the attacks by Pakistan's Inter-Services Intelligence agency (an accusation swiftly denied by the Pakistani authorities). In November India and Pakistan agreed to share information on anti-terrorism measures. In February 2007, however, explosions on the Samjhauta Express train, which was bound for Lahore, Pakistan, from Delhi, caused a devastating fire on board, killing at least 67 passengers, the majority of whom were Pakistani nationals. The attack was viewed by many as an attempt to hinder the peace process; none the less, later in the month India and Pakistan signed an agreement designed to prevent inadvertent nuclear conflict between the two countries.

In mid-2008 a decision by the state government of Jammu and Kashmir to transfer land (on a permanent basis) to a board

managing a popular Hindu shrine precipitated large-scale protests, prompting the government to rescind its offer. However, the issue had already served to intensify hostility between Muslim separatists and Hindu nationalists, and Chief Minister Ghulam Nabi Azad resigned in July. Following legislative elections in November, the JKNC was forced to form a coalition with Congress in order to secure a majority. Omar Abdullah, the son of Dr Farooq Abdullah, was sworn in as Chief Minister in January 2009. According to official statistics, militancy-related fatalities in Jammu and Kashmir in 2009 fell to 386 (the lowest level in 20 years), compared with 3,035 in 1995.

Relations with Pakistan were severely damaged by terrorist attacks on Indian targets during 2008. In July a suicide bombing at the Indian embassy in Kabul, Afghanistan, resulted in more than 40 fatalities; the Indian Government intimated that the plot had originated in Pakistan. In the aftermath of the November Mumbai attacks (see *Internal Unrest and the Threat of Terrorism*), the Indian Government suggested that the perpetrators were all from Pakistan, a claim that the Pakistani authorities initially denied; however, they subsequently conceded that the sole gunman captured alive was indeed a Pakistani national. Moreover, in an unexpected turnaround, a senior official of the Pakistan Government publicly admitted in February 2009 that the Mumbai attacks had been partly planned in Pakistan and stated that seven suspects belonging to LeT had been arrested. The Indian Government welcomed the admission but demanded that the suspects be extradited to India; however, Pakistan insisted that any prosecutions be carried out internally.

In February 2010 India and Pakistan held their first high-level direct talks since the 2008 Mumbai attacks; however, the discussions proved fruitless, with both sides accusing each other of supporting terrorism and of tolerating human rights abuses. In June 2010 the Indian Minister of Home Affairs, P. Chidambaram, visited Islamabad, urging the Pakistani Government to intensify its efforts against LeT members thought to have been involved in the planning of the attacks. In July a visit to Islamabad by the Indian Minister of External Affairs, S. M. Krishna, was initially hailed by both sides as having been a 'constructive' resumption of high-level talks, but the meeting culminated in mutual recriminations. Prior to the summit the Indian Home Secretary had accused Pakistan's intelligence agency of having co-ordinated the Mumbai attacks.

In March 2011 Pakistani Prime Minister Yousaf Raza Gilani accepted an invitation from his Indian counterpart to attend the semi-final of the Cricket World Cup, between India and Pakistan, in Mohali, India. During Gilani's visit, the premiers held positive discussions that apparently encompassed 'all outstanding issues' concerning bilateral relations. A two-day meeting involving the Indian and Pakistani Home Secretaries had preceded the summit, resulting in a range of measures to enhance co-operation in counter-terrorism.

Following a ministerial summit in September 2011 in New Delhi, the two countries pledged to double bilateral trade (to around US $6,000m.) within three years. A commitment by Pakistan to confer the status of 'most favoured nation' (MFN) upon India in November (having previously insisted that this would require a resolution to the ongoing dispute over Kashmir) was hailed by both sides as a reflection of improving ties; however, in the event, MFN status was withheld owing to considerable domestic opposition to the proposal within Pakistan. In April 2012, during what was ostensibly a private visit to India, Pakistani President Asif Ali Zardari met with Prime Minister Singh for informal discussions on bilateral issues. However, relations again became strained in early 2013 over ceasefire violations in Kashmir. In January India accused the Pakistani army of beheading one of its soldiers; two Indian soldiers and three Pakistani soldiers were killed in that month. In February unrest erupted in Kashmir following the execution, after a protracted legal contest, of Afzal Guru, a Kashmiri Muslim who had been convicted in 2002 of organizing the attack a year earlier on the parliament building in New Delhi (see above). Five CRPF officers and two militants were killed during a suicide attack in Srinagar a few days later.

Prime Minister Singh was swift to congratulate Muhammad Nawaz Sharif upon his victory in Pakistan's general election of May 2013, thereby securing an historic third term as Prime Minister. Many Indians hoped that the change of Pakistani leadership might lead to an easing of tensions between the two countries, since the new premier outlined improved relations with India as one of the priorities of his administration. However, bilateral ties continued to be threatened by actions carried out by militant Islamist groups from Pakistan and by mutual accusations of ceasefire violations in Kashmir, including fatalities on both sides. Nevertheless, a meeting between the Indian and Pakistani Prime Ministers at the UN General Assembly in New York, USA, at the end of September was said by Indian sources to have been 'useful' in terms of the ongoing effort by both Governments to stem the violence.

As with Sharif's return to power, Nahendra Modi's assumption of the Indian premiership in May 2014 prompted hopes of an improvement in Indian-Pakistani relations. On the day following Sharif's attendance at Modi's inauguration ceremony in late May, the two leaders held amicable talks to discuss the future direction of the bilateral relationship. However, the initial goodwill appeared largely to have evaporated by August, when Modi visited Jammu and Kashmir for the second time since becoming Prime Minister (the first Indian premier to have visited the contested region since 1999); addressing troops during his visit, Modi criticized Pakistan for waging a 'proxy war of terrorism' against India, drawing the ire of the Pakistani Government. In the same month Modi cancelled scheduled talks between the two countries' respective foreign secretaries, due to have been held in Islamabad at the end of the month, in response to recent discussions between the Pakistani high commissioner to India and Kashmir-based separatists, which the Indian Government denounced as unacceptable. The dispute appeared to trigger a marked increase in the incidence, and severity, of border incursions and exchanges of fire across the LoC; in October civilian casualties were reported to have been incurred on both sides in Kashmir. Nevertheless, there were some instances of successful bilateral co-operation during 2014, including mutual offers of assistance by Modi and Sharif following flash floods that claimed more than 500 lives in Kashmir in September, and the signing in October of a bilateral gas pricing agreement that cleared the way for the export to Pakistan of natural gas from India, via a pipeline to be constructed between Jalandhar, in the Indian state of Punjab, and Lahore.

A suicide attack near a Pakistani security checkpoint at Wagah, the only official land border crossing between India and Pakistan, in early November 2014, which was reported to have claimed the lives of 55 people and injured at least 100 others, raised concerns within India of further terrorist attacks along its border (see the chapter on Pakistan for further details). In January 2015 the Pakistani authorities, citing heightened security risks, restricted the bus service between Lahore and New Delhi, with the service to terminate at Wagah henceforth.

Despite ongoing unrest and sporadic violence in the region, elections to the Jammu and Kashmir state legislature were held in five phases during November–December 2014. No party gained an overall majority at the polls: the PDP and the BJP overtook the JKNC, with 28 and 25 seats, respectively; the JKNC, which had ended its alliance with Congress in July, secured just 15 seats, representing a loss of 13 seats from 2008, while Congress won 12 seats, a loss of five. Following protracted political negotiations, a BJP-PDP coalition government was finally inaugurated in the state at the beginning of March 2015, with Mufti Mohammad Sayeed of the PDP as Chief Minister.

In February 2015 the Indian and Pakistani premiers agreed to the resumption of formal high-level talks, which had remained suspended since August 2014. The two sides' respective Foreign Secretaries met in Islamabad in early March 2015, whereupon they agreed to strive for common ground.

Other regional relations

India's military intervention in the civil war involving East and West Pakistan in 1971 helped East Pakistan to break away and form Bangladesh. None the less, issues of border policing and demarcation, and water-sharing disputes have provoked sporadic tensions in Indo-Bangladeshi relations. In 1992 the Indian Government, under the provisions of an accord signed with Bangladesh in 1974, formally leased the Tin Bigha Corridor (a small strip of land covering an area of only 1.5 ha) to Bangladesh for 999 years. India maintained sovereignty over the Corridor, but the lease gave Bangladesh access to its enclaves of Dahagram and Angarpota. The transfer of the Corridor occasioned protests from right-wing quarters in India, who also made an issue over the presence in Delhi and other cities of illegal immigrants from Bangladesh and claimed that the Bangladeshi Government had done little to protect its Hindu minority. In December 1996 India signed an 'historic' treaty with Bangladesh, which was to be in force for 30 years, regarding the sharing of the Ganga waters. In April 2001 some 16 members of the Indian BSF and three

members of the Bangladesh Rifles were killed during fighting on the Bangladeshi border with the Indian state of Meghalaya—the worst strife between the two countries since serious border clashes in 1976.

Bilateral tensions were exacerbated by India's decision not to attend a planned summit of SAARC in Bangladesh in February 2005, citing security concerns; this forced the postponement of the meeting. Further clashes between the border patrols of the two countries aggravated the situation, which had deteriorated as a result of India's continued construction of a fence along the joint border, in contravention of its obligations under a 1974 treaty.

Relations between India and Bangladesh improved following the return to power of the Bangladesh Awami League in December 2008, partly because the new Bangladeshi Government began to take action against the Indian groups that maintained bases in Bangladesh (including the arrest and transfer to the Indian authorities of a number of ULFA leaders—see *Unrest in Assam*). Following a successful visit to New Delhi by the Bangladeshi Prime Minister, Sheikh Hasina, in January 2010, it was reported that Bangladesh and India aimed to remove all barriers to mutual trade in an effort to improve economic co-operation and as a precursor to the conclusion of a bilateral free trade agreement. The two countries later announced an agreement providing for a US $1,000m. loan by India to Bangladesh for infrastructural development. In October India eliminated tariffs on 61 local products imported by Bangladesh, including textiles. In November the two countries held the first bilateral border talks in five years, which was interpreted by some observers as a tacit acknowledgement from India of the importance of ensuring continued growth and development in Bangladesh in order to safeguard the development and security of India's north-eastern states. Following a joint border survey of disputed frontier areas, in August 2011 Bangladesh and India began the process of approving border maps, officially recognizing their 4,156-km frontier (a 6.5-km stretch of the border remained disputed).

An interim bilateral agreement on the sharing of waters from the Teesta river was one of several significant deals that had been expected to be concluded during an official visit to the Bangladeshi capital Dhaka in September 2011 by Manmohan Singh—the first state visit to Bangladesh by an Indian Prime Minister in 12 years. However, reportedly owing to objections from Mamata Banerjee, the Chief Minister of West Bengal, Singh withdrew the proposed deal. The two countries consequently failed to reach agreement on a land transit agreement that would have granted India overland access to its landlocked north-eastern states through Bangladeshi territory. Nevertheless, a border agreement, resolving demarcation of the remaining 6.5-km stretch of the bilateral frontier, and an agreement providing for the exchange of 111 Indian enclaves within Bangladesh and 51 Bangladeshi enclaves within India, were signed. However, the agreement remained unratified by the Indian Parliament owing to the Government's failure to garner sufficient parliamentary support, with the Bharatiya Janata Party (BJP) and the All India Trinamool Congress among those opposed to it. During a visit to Tripura in January 2012 Prime Minister Sheikh Hasina urged the Indian Government to be more flexible in order to facilitate the resolution of outstanding bilateral issues, including the issue of water-sharing. In July it was announced that India would help to locate and return to Bangladesh the remains of some 2,400 Bangladeshi fighters who were believed to have been buried along the border during the Bangladesh war of liberation in 1971. Following a visit by Sheikh Hasina to New Delhi in January 2013, in April India and Bangladesh signed a major joint venture agreement to build two coal-fired power stations in the south of Bangladesh by 2018; the project was estimated to cost some US $1,600m. A joint power transmission plant was opened in October 2013 to enable India to supply electricity to Bangladesh. Also in 2013 plans were finalized for the construction of a 15-km rail link between eastern Bangladesh and Tripura, which would greatly improve rail connectivity between the Indian mainland and its north-eastern states.

Following the BJP's victory in the 2014 general election, Prime Minister Narendra Modi moved swiftly to tackle the problem of illegal immigrants from Bangladesh, in keeping with a pledge made during the electoral campaign period, and imposed new restrictions on Bangladeshi nationals applying for visas upon arrival in India. During a visit to Bangladesh in June by Minister of External Affairs Sushma Swaraj, a number of bilateral deals were signed, including an agreement to ease visa restrictions for children and the elderly, while the formation of a special economic zone in Bangladesh for Indian investors was proposed. A long-running Indo–Bangladeshi maritime dispute was resolved in July when the Permanent Court of Arbitration—arbitrating at the formal request in 2009 of Bangladesh, under the UN Convention on the Law of the Sea—awarded Bangladesh nearly 80% of a disputed area stretching over 25,000 sq km in the Bay of Bengal; the ruling was accepted by both sides. Meeting with Sheikh Hasina on the sidelines of a SAARC summit in Nepal in November 2014, Modi stated that firm efforts were being made to resolve the disputes over the land boundary and the sharing of waters from the Teesta river; the two leaders also pledged to continue bilateral efforts to combat terrorism.

Relations between India and Nepal deteriorated in 1989, when India decided not to renew two bilateral treaties determining trade and transit, insisting that a common treaty covering both issues be negotiated. Nepal refused, stressing the importance of keeping the treaties separate on the grounds that Indo-Nepalese trade issues were negotiable, whereas the right of transit was a recognized right of landlocked countries. India responded by closing most of the transit points through which Nepal's trade was conducted. The dispute was aggravated by Nepal's acquisition of Chinese-made military equipment, which, according to India, violated the Treaty of Peace and Friendship of 1950. However, in June 1990 India and Nepal signed an agreement restoring trade relations and reopening the transit points. New, separate bilateral transit and trade treaties were concluded in December 1991 (and were subsequently amended and renewed on several occasions). In June 1997 the Indian Prime Minister, Inder Kumar Gujral, made a visit to Nepal and announced the opening of a transit route through north-eastern India between Nepal and Bangladesh.

In February 2005 relations with Nepal were seriously affected when the Nepalese King orchestrated a coup, dismissing the Government and declaring a state of emergency in the country. It was feared that Maoist rebels from Nepal might infiltrate the country's border with India's fractious north-eastern states, a concern borne out to an extent by a reported decision by the CPI (Maoist) and Nepalese rebels to co-operate in promoting the spread of communism in both countries. India subsequently ceased provision of all military aid to Nepal and intensified security along the shared border. In July India resumed non-lethal military aid to Nepal. In June 2006, following the reinstatement of Parliament, the newly appointed Nepalese Prime Minister, G. P. Koirala, paid an official visit to India, during which India pledged to increase aid to Nepal. In August 2009 the two countries signed a new trade treaty (replacing that concluded in December 1991) and India pledged to assist its neighbour with development projects, including road and rail links. During a visit to New Delhi in October 2011 by the recently appointed Nepalese premier Baburam Bhattarai, a 10-year Bilateral Investment Promotion and Protection Agreement was signed. It was announced in June 2013 that India and Nepal had pledged to co-operate in efforts to tighten border security and to tackle the problems of militancy and organized crime such as people- and drugs-trafficking. At the end of an official visit to Nepal in August 2014—the first such visit by an Indian premier since 1997—Prime Minister Modi and his Nepalese counterpart, Sushil Koirala, who had assumed office in February 2014, issued a joint statement noting their shared resolve to review and update the 1950 Treaty of Peace and Friendship in order to modernize the bilateral relationship. Modi also pledged up to US $1,000m. in concessional loans for infrastructure projects in Nepal. A bus service linking Delhi with the Nepalese capital Kathmandu, which was expected to boost bilateral trade and tourism, was inaugurated during Modi's second visit to Nepal, in November 2014.

Since 1983 India's relations with Sri Lanka have been threatened by conflicts between the latter's Sinhalese and Tamil communities, in which India has sought to arbitrate. In July 1987 Rajiv Gandhi and the Sri Lankan President, Junius Jayewardene, signed an accord aimed at settling the conflict. An Indian Peacekeeping Force (IPKF) was dispatched to Sri Lanka, but encountered considerable resistance from the Tamil separatist guerrillas. Following the gradual implementation of the peace accord, the IPKF troops completed their withdrawal in March 1990. However, violence flared up again and by late 1991 the number of Sri Lankans living in refugee camps in Tamil Nadu was estimated at more than 200,000. The assassination of Rajiv Gandhi in May 1991, allegedly by members of the Liberation Tigers of Tamil Eelam (LTTE), completed India's disen-

chantment with the latter organization. Measures were subsequently taken by the Tamil Nadu government to suppress LTTE activity within the state, and also to begin the protracted process of repatriating refugees. In May 1992 the LTTE was officially banned in India. A new Indo-Sri Lankan bilateral free trade agreement came into effect in March 2000. During the 2000s India refrained from any direct involvement in the Sri Lankan conflict, but, after the escalation in hostilities in 2008 following the collapse of a ceasefire, insisted that a negotiated political settlement rather than a military solution be sought. India subsequently extended its ban on the LTTE at regular intervals, most recently in November 2014 for a further five-year period.

Following the defeat of the LTTE in 2009, India played a role in the resettlement and rehabilitation of thousands of displaced Tamil civilians and in the reconstruction of the war-ravaged north-east of Sri Lanka. India opened two new consulates in Sri Lanka (in Hambantota and Jaffna) during 2010. Bilateral relations were threatened by the shooting, allegedly by members of the Sri Lankan navy, of two Indian fishermen in separate incidents in January 2011. Nevertheless, ferry services between the two countries resumed in June, having been suspended in the 1980s as a result of the Sri Lankan conflict. A serious strain was placed on bilateral ties following India's decision In March 2012 to support a US-sponsored resolution at the UN Human Rights Council (UNHRC), which urged the Sri Lankan Government to investigate allegations of human rights violations in the final stages of the Sri Lankan civil conflict. India's stance, which appeared to contravene a traditional policy of abstaining on country-specific UNHRC resolutions, was widely interpreted as a response to pressure exerted on the federal Government by its political partners in Tamil Nadu. Sri Lankan President Mahinda Rajapaksa paid an official visit to India in September, meeting with the Indian President, Pranab Mukherjee, and Prime Minister Manmohan Singh. The leader of the Tamil MDMK party, Vaiko, was arrested for leading a protest march against Rajapaksa's visit. India supported a second US-sponsored resolution, adopted by UNHRC in March 2013, which recommended that an independent investigation be conducted into the claims of human rights violations. The DMK had withdrawn from India's coalition Government earlier that month in protest at its perceived weakness in dealing with its Sri Lankan counterpart on the issue. Prime Minister Singh boycotted a summit meeting of Commonwealth heads of government held in Colombo, Sri Lanka, in November, in order to demonstrate India's dissatisfaction at Sri Lanka's recent record on human rights. However, in March 2014 the Indian authorities opted to abstain from a stronger UNHRC resolution on Sri Lanka, which demanded the establishment of an independent, international investigation into alleged human rights abuses. Following his election in January 2015, the new Sri Lankan President, Maithripala Sirisena, chose India as the destination for his first foreign state trip. During his visit in February, Sirisena and Prime Minister Modi hailed a 'new beginning' in bilateral relations, and four co-operation agreements, on agriculture, cultural issues, education and nuclear energy, were signed, while both sides also pledged to increase defence co-operation. In March Modi became the first Indian premier to visit Sri Lanka since Rajiv Gandhi in 1987; addressing the Sri Lankan Parliament, Modi underscored the need to expand maritime co-operation in order to combat terrorism.

In the early 1980s there was an improvement in India's relations with the People's Republic of China. Both countries agreed to try to resolve their Himalayan border dispute and to seek to normalize relations, and a number of working groups were subsequently established. Following an official visit to India by the Chinese Premier, Li Peng, in December 1991 (the first such visit by a Chinese Premier for 31 years), bilateral border trade was resumed in July 1992. Sino-Indian relations were further strengthened as a result of a visit to India by the Chinese President, Jiang Zemin, in November 1996 (the first ever visit by a Chinese head of state to India). However, despite the gradual improvement in relations, India has frequently expressed concern over the nuclear asymmetry between the two countries and the transfer by China of missiles and missile technology to Pakistan. Sino-Indian relations deteriorated following India's 1998 nuclear tests, partly because China believed that India was using a fabricated threat from China to justify its actions. In June 1999 the Indian Minister of External Affairs visited the Chinese capital Beijing to restore Sino-Indian dialogue. Border negotiations between the two countries were held in

November 2000. Prime Minister Vajpayee made a state visit to China in June 2003, during which a number of agreements were signed, the most significant being India's official recognition of Chinese sovereignty over Tibet (the Xizang Autonomous Region). China also agreed to trade with the north-eastern Indian state of Sikkim, thus implicitly acknowledging India's control of that area.

In January 2005 India and China held their first-ever strategic dialogue, in New Delhi, agreeing, *inter alia*, to attempt to resolve their boundary dispute in a fair and mutually satisfactory manner. In April Chinese Premier Wen Jiabao visited India, agreeing to plans for the resolution of the boundary dispute and the expansion of bilateral trade. In July 2006 the reopening of the historic border trading post of Nathu La (which was once part of the ancient Silk Road) highlighted the ongoing improvement in bilateral relations, which were further strengthened by high-level visits including that of the Chinese President, Hu Jintao, to India in November, when the two countries agreed to co-operate in several fields, including nuclear energy. However, a number of issues continued to undermine cordial relations, including India's deepening ties with the USA, and in August 2010 India suspended all bilateral defence exchanges, in protest at the refusal by the Chinese authorities to grant a visa to an Indian army general from Kashmir—China has long maintained a claim to the Shaksam Valley and Aksai Chin areas of Kashmir. Furthermore, during a state visit to India in December, Premier Wen's refusal to condemn the 2008 Mumbai attacks was widely interpreted as reflecting a wish not to alienate Pakistan, China's other firm ally in South Asia; in response, India refused to reiterate its adherence to the 'one China' policy. Nevertheless, during Wen's visit 48 bilateral commercial contracts, collectively worth an estimated US $16,000m., were signed and the two leaders pledged to increase bilateral trade to some $100,000m. by 2015. In April 2011 India and China agreed to resume bilateral defence exchanges, and in January 2012 an agreement was signed providing for the establishment of a joint border-management mechanism. In March President Hu Jintao attended talks with Prime Minister Singh in Delhi; the two leaders declared 2012 to be the year of 'India-China friendship and co-operation'.

Shortly after becoming China's new Premier, Li Keqiang undertook an official visit to India in May 2013, during which eight bilateral agreements were signed covering various fields including culture, trade and water resources. Trade between the two countries had reportedly increased from US $2,090m. in 2001/02 to $67,830m. in 2012/13. In October 2013 a Border Defence Co-operation Agreement was signed in an effort to improve Sino-Indian understanding and minimize the risk of further incidents taking place such as had occurred in April, when a contingent of Chinese soldiers temporarily established a camp in the disputed territory of Aksai Ching. The incident had led to an increase in bilateral tensions prior to the withdrawal of the Chinese troops three weeks later. In a further sign of improving relations, the two countries' armed forces held 10 days of joint counter-terrorism exercises in Chengdu, south-western China, in November—the first time that such exercises had been staged since 2008.

The decision to invite the head of the Tibetan government-in-exile to Prime Minister Modi's inauguration ceremony in May 2014 provoked the consternation of the People's Republic. Nevertheless, meeting on the sidelines of the annual summit of BRICS (the grouping of major emerging economic powers involving Brazil, Russia, India, China and South Africa) hosted by Brazil in July 2014, Chinese President Xi Jinping invited Modi to attend the Asia-Pacific Economic Co-operation (APEC) summit scheduled to be held in Beijing in November 2015; it would be the first time that Indian representation had attended a summit of the regional trade forum, membership of which India was keen to attain in order to boost its economic prospects. At the BRICS summit, India, China and the three other member states signed an agreement providing for the establishment of a joint development bank and emergency reserve fund.

A stand-off arose in September 2014 between hundreds of Indian and Chinese troops in the disputed Himalayan border area of Ladakh, following the commencement by the Chinese of road construction in an area contested by India, while Chinese troops disrupted the construction by Indian soldiers of a canal in similarly disputed territory. The confrontation coincided with a state visit to India by President Xi, during which he met with Modi; despite the ongoing tensions, the two sides signed 12 agreements, including a deal providing for Chinese investment of some US $20,000m. in Indian infrastructure over five years and an agreement to establish industrial parks in Gujarat and Maharashtra. The stand-off in Ladakh came to an end after two weeks with both sides agreeing to pull back troops from the disputed border.

In October 2004 the Chairman of Myanmar's ruling body, the State Peace and Development Council, Field Marshal Than Shwe, paid the first visit to India by a Myanma head of state in 24 years. The visit was illustrative of improving relations between the two countries, deemed necessary if India was to combat successfully the problem of insurgents in north-eastern India establishing bases across the border in Myanmar. In April 2008 India signed an agreement worth US $120m. to construct a seaport at Sittway in north-western Myanmar and to improve roads and waterways elsewhere in the country. In return for its help with infrastructure development, it was widely believed that India was hoping for preferential access (as was China) to Myanmar's reserves of petroleum and natural gas. During Than Shwe's second visit to India in July 2010 the two countries signed five bilateral agreements intended to enhance co-operation in the fields of energy, defence, counter-terrorism and transnational crime prevention. In October 2011 Myanma President Thein Sein paid a visit to India, during which a series of agreements intended to bolster bilateral trade and investment, including the provision by India of a $500m. grant for infrastructural development projects in Myanmar, was signed. In May 2012 Manmohan Singh paid the first official visit to Myanmar by an India Prime Minister since Rajiv Gandhi in 1987; 12 co-operation agreements were signed on, *inter alia*, air transport, border area development and the establishment of a joint trade and investment forum. In November 2012 the Myanma opposition leader Aung San Suu Kyi attended talks with Singh in Delhi; she appealed for India's backing for Myanmar's nascent democratization process. India's Ministry of External Affairs proposed in August 2013 that India and Myanmar should establish a Joint Border Working Group in order to resolve any border incidents that occurred between the two countries. Talks between Thein Sein and Modi during a visit to Myanmar by the Indian premier in November 2014 were described as positive. Discussions regarding the introduction of a bus route between Imphal, in Manipur, and Mandalay, in central Myanmar, were reported to be at an advanced stage in early 2015.

As relations between Afghanistan and Pakistan deteriorated amid Afghan allegations of Pakistani support for a series of violent attacks against the Afghan authorities during 2011 (see the chapter on Afghanistan), India appeared keen to enhance its own ties with Afghanistan. In May, during a visit to the Afghan capital, Kabul, Prime Minister Singh announced that India was to grant US $500m. over a six-year period (in addition to the $1,500m. that it had already pledged) to Afghanistan, to be disbursed on a range of development projects, with a focus on agriculture, infrastructure and social programmes. Bilateral relations were further consolidated during a reciprocal visit to India by Afghan President Hamid Karzai in October 2011 with the signing of a strategic partnership agreement, which was intended to enhance co-operation in the fields of trade, counter-terrorism, and political and cultural engagement. Under the terms of the accord, India also pledged to provide security training and equipment to support the Afghan authorities as they prepared to assume full responsibility for national security by the end of 2014, and to undertake efforts to facilitate Afghanistan's economic integration within South Asia as a whole. In 2013 the Afghan leadership was reported to be seeking closer military ties with India: during a visit to New Delhi in May, President Karzai discussed with Prime Minister Singh the possibility of India supplying Afghanistan with a range of heavy weaponry and other military equipment, including tanks and helicopters. However, the Indian Government kept to its long-standing pledge to provide only 'non-lethal military assistance' to the Karzai administration. In July India's Minister of External Affairs, Salman Khurshid, advocated dialogue with all groups in Afghanistan, including militant organizations such as the Taliban, thereby indicating a reversal of India's previous foreign policy with regard to Afghanistan. A series of attacks on Indian establishments in Afghanistan in 2014, including that on the Indian consulate building in Herat in May, was attributed by some analysts to Pakistan-based militants displeased by burgeoning Indian-Afghan relations; some cited the timing of the consulate attack, three days prior to Prime Minister Modi's inauguration, as an indication that the assault was staged by elements seeking to warn the Pakistani Government against forging closer relations with the incoming Indian Government.

Other external relations

Prior to its disintegration in December 1991, the USSR was a major contributor of economic and military assistance to India. The President of Russia, Boris Yeltsin, made an official visit to India in 1993, during which he signed a Treaty of Friendship and Co-operation. In October 1996 India and Russia signed a defence co-operation agreement, and in December India signed a US $1,800m. contract to purchase 40 fighter aircraft from Russia. In June 1998 Russia defied a Group of Eight (G8) ban on exporting nuclear technology to India by agreeing to supply the latter with two nuclear reactors. In October 2000 the newly elected Russian President, Vladimir Putin, visited India. The two countries signed a declaration of 'strategic partnership', which involved co-operation on defence, economic matters and international terrorism issues. India signed a contract to purchase a further 50 fighter aircraft from Russia, with a licence to manufacture around 150 more, and in February 2001 India agreed to buy 310 Russian tanks. In June the two countries successfully conducted tests of a new, jointly developed supersonic cruise missile, the PJ-10. In November it was announced that Russia had been awarded a contract to construct a nuclear power reactor in Kudankulam in Tamil Nadu (this was later extended to two reactors). During a visit to India by the Russian President in January 2007, Putin and Prime Minister Manmohan Singh focused on the key bilateral issues of energy and trade, and announced that Russia was to assist India with the construction of four more nuclear power reactors at Kudankulam. In March 2010 Putin, in his new role as Russia's Prime Minister, paid an official visit to India, during which an important agreement was signed by the two countries regarding Russia's pledge to construct 16 new nuclear reactors in India. A further 30 bilateral deals were signed during a visit to India by Russian President Dmitrii Medvedev in December, including two framework agreements that provided for the construction of two additional nuclear reactors in India; Medvedev also offered Russian support for Indian aspirations to gain a permanent seat on the UN Security Council. (In October India had secured election to the 15-member Council for a two-year term commencing in January 2011.) Following talks between Medvedev and Singh in Moscow in December 2011, the former expressed the support of the Russian Government for India's bid to secure full membership of the Shanghai Cooperation Organization. Further defence agreements were signed during a visit by President Putin to India in December 2012. Following protracted delays and widespread opposition to the plant within Tamil Nadu, the production of nuclear energy at the Kudankulam plant finally commenced in October 2013. Bilateral relations were given a significant boost following a visit to India by Putin in December 2014, during which 20 co-operation agreements were signed, including a deal providing for the construction by Russia of up to 12 additional nuclear reactors in India, at an estimated cost of US $40,000m., and the purchase by India of 10m. metric tons of oil per year from Russian oil company Rosneft. (These agreements came at a time when several Russian officials and organizations, including Rosneft, were being targeted by the USA and the European Union with economic sanctions, in respone to Russia's involvement in political unrest in Ukraine.) Putin and Prime Minister Narendra Modi also agreed in principle on the supply to India of military helicopters produced by Russia in Indian factories, with Russia appearing keen to regain its former position (recently ceded to the USA) as India's primary weapons provider; under the terms of the mooted agreement, India would be free to export the helicopters to third countries.

Meanwhile, in mid-1996, in a move that provoked widespread international condemnation, India decided not to be party to the Comprehensive Test Ban Treaty (CTBT), which it had earlier supported, so long as the existing nuclear powers were unwilling to commit themselves to a strict timetable for full nuclear disarmament. In May 1998 India's controversial decision to explode five nuclear test devices and to claim thereby its new status as a nuclear-weapons state led to a rapid escalation in the 'arms race' with Pakistan (which responded with its own series of nuclear tests). The USA, with limited support from other countries, subsequently imposed economic sanctions on both India and Pakistan until such time as they had signed the Nuclear Non-Proliferation Treaty (NPT) and the CTBT and taken steps to reverse their nuclear programmes. Immediately after the tests, India announced a self-imposed moratorium on further testing and launched itself into intense diplomatic activity. During 1998–99 the USA lifted some of the sanctions imposed on India and Pakistan, while reiterating its requests that the two countries sign the CTBT and exercise restraint in their respective missile programmes.

Following the collapse of the USSR, the Indian Government sought to strengthen its ties with the USA. In 1992 discussions were held between Indian and US officials regarding military co-operation and ambitious joint defence projects. However, the USA remained concerned about the risks of nuclear proliferation across South Asia and India's ongoing refusal to sign the NPT, and, despite India's adoption of a programme of economic liberalization, conflicts over trade and related issues remained. During a visit to India by the US Secretary of Defense in 1995, a 'landmark' agreement on defence and security co-operation was signed by the two countries. US President Bill Clinton made an official visit to India in March 2000 (the first by a US President since 1978), which was widely considered as the launch of a new era in bilateral relations. In September Prime Minister Vajpayee visited the USA, asserting that consensus among Indian ministers had to be reached before a decision on the CTBT could be made. In late September 2001 US President George W. Bush announced an end to the military and economic sanctions imposed against India and Pakistan in 1998. The decision followed the renewal of high-level military contacts between the USA and India in mid-2001, and Pakistan's co-operation with US counter-terrorism initiatives against neighbouring Afghanistan in the aftermath of the terrorist attacks carried out on US mainland targets on 11 September. In July 2003 India declined a request by the USA to contribute peacekeeping troops to the US-led forces in Iraq.

During a visit to the USA in July 2005, Prime Minister Manmohan Singh signed a historic outline agreement with President Bush regarding future nuclear co-operation. In return for an Indian pledge to separate its civilian and military nuclear programmes, to allow international monitoring of its civilian nuclear programme, and not to conduct further nuclear weapons tests or to transfer nuclear technology to other countries, the US Government proposed to share civilian nuclear technology with India. The agreement was finalized during a visit to India by President Bush in March 2006. In August 2007, however, the agreement met with opposition not only from the Bharatiya Janata Party, but also from the United Progressive Alliance coalition's allies, the left-wing parties comprising the Left Front, which feared the possibility of US intervention in India's foreign policy and other areas. In July 2008, despite the withdrawal of support by the Left Front, the Government was able to win a parliamentary vote of confidence and to proceed with the agreement, which, having subsequently received the endorsement of the International Atomic Energy Agency and the Nuclear Suppliers Group (NSG), as well as the approval of the US Congress, was signed into law by President Bush in October. In November 2010, during his first state visit to India following his inauguration as US President in January 2009, Barack Obama furthered the promises of the civilian nuclear pact by announcing that export controls on sensitive dual-use technologies—those that have both civilian and military uses—were to be lifted; the controls were formally rescinded in January 2011. In addition, Obama underscored the US view that the Kashmir issue was an internal affair and pledged not to intervene unless requested to do so by India. A series of relatively minor bilateral agreements was signed during the visit, but Obama hailed the breadth and sheer number of deals, collectively estimated to be worth some US $10,000m., as a sign of burgeoning bilateral relations. During his visit, Obama also expressed US support for India's quest to attain a permanent seat on the UN Security Council—an endorsement that was denounced as 'incomprehensible' by Pakistan. Counter-terrorism operations, bilateral trade and investment, and Indian concerns about the USA's withdrawal from Afghanistan formed the focus of a visit to New Delhi by US Secretary of State Hillary Clinton in July. Clinton appealed for a deepening of bilateral security and nuclear energy co-operation, while noting the US Government's positive response to the renewed dialogue between India and Pakistan. Clinton paid another visit to India in May 2012, during which she urged India to reduce its oil imports from Iran. Despite a visit by Singh to the USA for talks with President Obama in September 2013, and evidence that diplomatic and economic relations were continuing to grow, India's relationship with the USA was damaged in December when the Indian Deputy Consul-General in New York was arrested on suspicion of visa fraud and allegedly mistreated by US officials. In response to the incident, the Indian authorities demanded an unequivocal apology from the USA and withdrew various diplomatic privileges enjoyed by US diplomats in India.

In July 2014 the Indian Government was accused by the Obama Administration of bringing the World Trade Organization (WTO) to 'the brink of crisis', owing to the former's unexpected refusal to accede to a WTO trade facilitation agreement until an ongoing dispute over its food security programme had been resolved. The trade facilitation agreement—to which all 159 of the WTO's members, including India, had signed up in December 2013—provided for the global streamlining of the cross-border flow of goods, and represented the first time that the WTO had concluded an agreement involving all of its members. The USA and other member states firmly censured India's apparent attempt to renegotiate its position after the conclusion of the agreement and contested that it represented a severe threat to the credibility of the WTO. Following protracted negotiations, an end to the impasse was secured in November 2014 when India agreed to adhere to the trade agreement in exchange for US assurances that a 'peace clause' effectively barring any challenge at the WTO to India's system of agricultural subsidies (which had been due to expire in 2017) would be extended. (India views its system of subsidies for cereal farmers as vital for its national food security, while the USA and other countries insist that such extensive state aid for food production violates WTO rules.) The issue was among those discussed by Modi and Obama during a visit by the Indian premier to Washington, DC, in September 2014, a visit that was widely perceived to have injected fresh impetus into bilateral relations. During a reciprocal visit by Obama to New Delhi in January 2015, the US President and Modi signed a joint strategic document pledging to forge closer relations and to expand defence and economic co-operation, with a view to promoting greater regional stability; Obama also pledged support for India's bid for a seat on the UN Security Council as well as for membership of both the Asia-Pacific Economic Cooperation forum and the NSG. Meanwhile, the Indian Government welcomed a report published by the US Department of Defense in October 2014 that was explicit in its criticism of Pakistan's alleged use of militants as proxy forces to counter India's superior military strength.

During a state visit to Delhi in December 2010 by French President Nicolas Sarkozy, India and France signed a range of bilateral agreements, including a co-operation deal providing for the construction by the French company Areva of two nuclear reactors, each worth approximately US $10,000m., and for a new nuclear plant in Jaitapur, in the western Indian state of Maharashtra. Meanwhile, India and Canada signed a nuclear co-operation deal in June 2010, which provided for the opening up of the Indian market to Canadian nuclear exports, as well as enhanced co-operation in the field of nuclear waste management.

In January 2015 UN Secretary-General Ban Ki-Moon urged India and Italy to find a mutually acceptable solution to a protracted dispute involving two Italian navy marines arrested by the Indian authorities in February 2012 for the killing of two Indian fishermen; the marines, who had been contracted to guard an Italian-flagged vessel, contested that they had mistaken the fishermen for pirates and fired warning shots. The Italian authorities demanded that the two men be released to stand trial in Italy since the incident took place in international waters, while the Indian authorities insisted that it had jurisdiction in the case as the victims were Indians on board an Indian vessel. The Supreme Court of India subsequently authorized the transfer of the marines from Indian custody to the Italian embassy in New Delhi pending trial, and in August 2014 the Court allowed one of the marines to return to Italy on medical grounds. The decision by the European Parliament in January 2015 to adopt a resolution appealing for the two marines to be allowed permanently to return to Italy, and for the case to be settled under Italian jurisdiction or through international arbitration, was criticized by the Indian Government as unwarranted interference in a bilateral dispute.

CONSTITUTION AND GOVERNMENT

The Constitution of India, adopted by the Constituent Assembly on 26 November 1949, was inaugurated on 26 January 1950. India is a federal republic. Legislative power is vested in Parliament, consisting of the President and two Houses. The Council of States (Rajya Sabha) has 245 members, most of whom are indirectly elected by the state assemblies for six years (one-third retiring every two years), the remainder being nominated by the President for six years. The House of the People (Lok Sabha) has up to 550 elected members, serving for five years (subject to dissolution). A small number of members of the Lok Sabha may be nominated by the President to represent the Anglo-Indian community, while the 550 members are directly elected by universal adult suffrage in single-member constituencies. The President is a constitutional head of state, elected for five years by an electoral college comprising elected members of both Houses of Parliament and the state legislatures. The President exercises executive power on the advice of the Council of Ministers, which is responsible to Parliament. The President appoints the Prime Minister and, on the latter's recommendation, other ministers.

India contains 29 self-governing states, each with a governor (appointed by the President for five years), a legislature (elected for five years) and a council of ministers headed by the chief minister. Bihar, Jammu and Kashmir, Karnataka, Maharashtra, Telangana and Uttar Pradesh have bicameral legislatures, the other state legislatures being unicameral. Each state has its own legislative, executive and judicial machinery, corresponding to that of the Indian Union. In the event of the failure of constitutional government in a state, presidential rule can be imposed by the Union. There are also six Union Territories and a National Capital Territory, administered by lieutenant-governors or administrators, all of whom are appointed by the President. The territories of Delhi and Puducherry also have elected chief ministers and state assemblies. In February 2014 Parliament approved the bifurcation of Andhra Pradesh to create a new state of Telangana; India's 29th state was formally established on 2 June.

REGIONAL AND INTERNATIONAL CO-OPERATION

India is a member of the Asian Development Bank (ADB, see p. 206), the South Asian Association for Regional Cooperation (SAARC, see p. 417) and the Colombo Plan (see p. 445).

Having joined the UN on its foundation in 1945, India is a member of the Economic and Social Commission for Asia and the Pacific (ESCAP, see p. 30). As a contracting party to the General Agreement on Tariffs and Trade (GATT), India joined the World Trade Organization (WTO, see p. 431) on its establishment in 1995. India is also member of the Commonwealth (see p. 234).

ECONOMIC AFFAIRS

In 2013, according to estimates by the World Bank, India's gross national income (GNI), measured at average 2011–13 prices, was US $1,960,072m., equivalent to $1,570 per head (or $5,350 per head on an international purchasing-power parity basis). During 2004–13, it was estimated, the population increased at an average annual rate of 1.3%, while gross domestic product (GDP) per head grew, in real terms, by an average of 6.0% per year. According to official figures, overall GDP increased, in real terms, at an average annual rate of 7.5% in 2004/05–2013/14; the rate of growth was estimated at 4.7% in 2013/14.

Agriculture (including forestry and fishing) contributed an estimated 18.2% of GDP in 2013/14. According to FAO estimates, about 52.1% of the economically active population were expected to be engaged in agriculture in mid-2015. The principal cash crops are cotton (which accounted for 3.2% of total export earnings in 2013/14), sugar cane, rice, groundnuts, spices and tea. Coffee and jute production are also important. Agricultural performance is affected by volatile climatic conditions. According to official figures, the average annual growth rate in the output of the agricultural sector was 3.9% in 2004/05–2013/14; agricultural GDP increased by 4.7% in 2013/14.

Industry (including mining, manufacturing, power and construction) contributed an estimated 24.8% of GDP in 2013/14. According to estimates by the Asian Development Bank (ADB), about 24.3% of the working population were employed in the industrial sector in 2011. According to official figures, industrial GDP increased at an average annual rate of 6.8% in 2004/05–2013/14; industrial GDP grew by 0.4% in 2013/14.

Mining contributed an estimated 2.1% of GDP in 2013/14, and employed an estimated 2.1% of the working population in 2010. Iron ore and cut diamonds are the major mineral exports. Coal, limestone, zinc and lead are also mined. In 2013 India was the third largest coal producer in the world after the People's Republic of China and the USA. Substantial uranium deposits have been discovered in Andhra Pradesh; according to the Atomic Energy Commission of India, following the completion of exploratory work total reserves at the Tumalapalli mine were estimated to amount to some 150,000 metric tons, which would render it the largest uranium mine in the world. According to official figures, mining GDP increased at an estimated average annual rate of 2.6% during 2004/05–2013/14; sectoral GDP decreased by an estimated 1.4% in 2013/14.

Manufacturing contributed an estimated 12.9% of GDP in 2013/14, and employed an estimated 8.9% of the working population in 2010. According to official figures, the GDP of the manufacturing sector increased at an average annual rate of 7.3% during 2004/05–2013/14; manufacturing GDP rose by 1.1% in 2012/13, but declined by an estimated 0.7% in 2013/14.

Construction contributed an estimated 7.8% of GDP in 2013/14, and employed 7.5% of the working population in 2010. According to official figures, the GDP of the construction sector increased at an average annual rate of 7.2% during 2004/05–2013/14; construction GDP rose by an estimated 1.6% in 2013/14.

Production of electricity rose from 912,057m. kWh in 2012/13 to 967,150m. kWh in 2013/14. In 2013/14 thermal plants (including renewable energy sources) accounted for an estimated 81.9% of total power generation and hydroelectric plants (often dependent on monsoons) for 13.9%. Nuclear plants accounted for 3.5% of total power generation. However, the Government has proposed plans to increase this to 25% of total power generation by 2050, which would involve the establishment of 30 nuclear reactors. Imports of mineral fuels, lubricants, etc., comprised 40.4% of the cost of total imports in 2013/14.

The services sector, which is dominated by the rapidly expanding data-processing business, the growing number of business call centres and the tourism industry, contributed an estimated 57.0% of GDP in 2013/14. According to estimates by the ADB, the service sector engaged 26.8% of the economically active population in 2011. By the early 2000s business call centres had become the fastest growing industry in India and an increasing number of multinational companies were transferring their call centre operations to the country, largely owing to cheaper labour costs and low long-distance telephone charges. More than 550,000 people were employed in the outsourcing industry in 2006/07. According to official figures, the GDP of the services sector increased by an average of 9.1% per year in 2004/05–2013/14; the rate of growth reached 6.8% in 2013/14.

In 2013/14 India reported a visible merchandise trade deficit of US $147,609m. and a deficit of $32,397m. on the current account of the balance of payments, according to preliminary official figures. In that year the principal source of imports was China (providing 11.4% of total imports), followed by Saudi Arabia, the United Arab Emirates (UAE) and the USA. The principal market for exports (accounting for 12.4% of total exports) was the USA, followed by the UAE. The principal exports in 2013/14 were mineral fuels, mineral oils and products of their distillation, and natural or cultured pearls, precious and semi-precious stones and precious metals. The principal imports in that year were mineral fuels and lubricants, pearls, precious and semi-precious stones, electrical machinery and equipment, and aircraft, spacecraft and parts thereof.

In the financial year ending 31 March 2015 there was a projected budgetary deficit of Rs 5,286,309m. According to the ADB, the overall fiscal deficit of the central Government amounted to the equivalent of 5.9% of GDP in 2013/14. In 2008, according to the UN Development Programme, India received a total of US $2,108m. in official development assistance. General government gross debt was Rs 69,827,200m. in 2013, equivalent to 61.5% of GDP. According to the ADB, India's total external debt was $400,250m. at the end of 2013. The cost of debt-servicing in that year was equivalent to 6.2% of earnings from the exports of goods and services. According to figures by the International Labour Organization, the average annual rate of inflation was 8.4% in 2004–13. According to the ADB, consumer prices increased by 5.9% in 2013. A labour force survey for 2009/10 indicated that the rate of unemployment stood at about 9.4% (with the rate in urban areas at 7.3%, and that in rural areas in excess of 11%).

The process of wide-ranging economic reform initiated in 1991, including trade and investment liberalization, industrial deregulation, gradual privatization of public enterprises, and financial and tax reforms, has continued despite several changes in government. Following the creation in 2004 of an Investment Commission for the purpose of encouraging domestic and foreign investment, total foreign direct investment (FDI) inflows increased from US $4,322m. in 2003/04 to a peak of $46,556m.

in 2011/12, according to the Department of Industrial Policy and Promotion, before a marked decline, to $34,298m., in 2012/13; however, FDI inflows increased to $36,396m. in 2013/14 and were projected to increase further in 2014/15. India was ranked the fourth most-favoured destination for worldwide investors in the UN Conference on Trade and Development's World Investment Report for 2014. In December 2012, despite strong public and political opposition, legislation permitting 51% FDI in the previously protected multi-brand retail sector gained parliamentary approval; however, by mid-2014 only one foreign investment had been approved in the sector. Following the victory of the Bharatiya Janata Party in the 2014 general election, the new Government announced that it intended to disallow FDI in multi-brand retail, although at early 2015 no moves to rescind the legislation had been reported. Meanwhile, in 2011 the Government launched a National Manufacturing Policy, which aimed to increase the sector's contribution to GDP from 13.5% in 2012/13 to around 25% by 2022 and envisaged the creation of some 100m. new jobs. Ongoing attempts to address India's unwieldy fiscal deficit (traditionally exacerbated by the country's modest tax base and cumbersome local government apparatus) have been largely frustrated by the repeated stalling of the divestment programme, internal security concerns, volatile foreign relations and the costs associated with natural disasters; nevertheless, the deficit declined to 4.5% of GDP in 2013/14 from in excess of 6% in 2009/10, and was projected at 4.1% of GDP for 2014/15. The budget for 2014/15 provided for the establishment of the Expenditure Management Commission, charged with recommending reforms to reduce the fiscal deficit to more manageable levels. Hopes of fiscal consolidation were further boosted by the introduction to Parliament in December 2014 of draft legislation that, if approved, would facilitate the implementation by 2016 of a long-mooted goods and services tax, which could significantly boost revenue generation. The trade deficit declined to $73,200m. in the first half of 2014/15, from $83,800m. in the corresponding period of 2013/14, while the current account deficit declined to $17,900m., from $26,900m. Following a series of increases to the national interest rate between March 2010 and October 2011 in an effort to control rising inflation, the central bank announced four national interest rate reductions between April 2012 and May 2013 in an attempt to stimulate economic growth; however, GDP growth slowed to 4.5% in 2012/13, the lowest figure in a decade. With inflation having increased to in excess of 10%, the bank implemented three increases in the interest rate between September 2013 and January 2014, before effecting a 0.25% reduction, to 7.75%, in January 2015 as part of a wider monetary easing policy, inflation having slowed to a nine-year low of 4.4% in November 2014. According to the Government's 2014/15 Economic Survey, GDP growth was estimated to have recovered marginally in 2013/14, to 4.7%, and was projected to increase further in 2014/15, to 5.9%. However, in early 2015 the Government released revised economic estimates which suggested significantly higher rates of recent growth than those previously published. According to the revised data, GDP growth projections were raised to 5.1% and 6.9% for 2012/13 and 2014/15, respectively—the higher estimates resulted from a change in the base year for calculating the national accounts from 2004/05 to 2011/12 and the use of a wider range of data.

PUBLIC HOLIDAYS

The public holidays observed in India vary locally. The dates given below apply to Delhi. There are, in addition, numerous restricted (or optional) holidays.

2016: 26 January (Republic Day), 23 March (Holi), 15 April (Ram Navami), 19 April (Mahavir Jayanti), 29 April (Good Friday), 21 May (Buddha Purnima), 6 July (Rath Yatra), 15 August (Independence Day), 25 August (Janmashtami), 12 September (Id ul-Zuha, Feast of the Sacrifice), 2 October (Mahatma Gandhi's Birthday and Muharram, Islamic New Year), 11 October (Dussehra), 30 October (Diwali), 14 November (Guru Nanak Jayanti), 11 December (Milad-un-Nabi, Birth of the Prophet), 25 December (Christmas).

Note: A number of Hindu, Muslim and Buddhist holidays depend on lunar sightings.

Statistical Survey

Source (unless otherwise stated): Central Statistical Organization, Ministry of Statistics and Programme Implementation, Sardar Patel Bhavan, Patel Chowk, New Delhi 110 001; tel. (11) 23742150; fax (11) 23344689; e-mail moscc@bol.net.in; internet mospi.nic.in.

Area and Population

AREA, POPULATION AND DENSITY*

Area (sq km)	3,166,414†
Population (census results)	
1 March 2001‡	1,028,610,328
1 March 2011	
Males	623,270,258
Females	587,584,719
Total	1,210,854,977
Population (official estimate at mid-year)§	
2012	1,213,370,000
Density (per sq km) at mid-2012	383.2

* Including the Indian-held part of Jammu and Kashmir.
† 1,222,559 sq miles.
‡ Including estimates for certain areas in the states of Gujarat and Himachal Pradesh where the census could not be conducted owing to recent natural disasters, but excluding data for Mao-Maram, Paomata and Purul subdivisions of Senapati district of Manipur.
§ Data rounded to nearest thousand persons.

Source: Office of the Registrar General of India, Ministry of Home Affairs, New Delhi.

POPULATION BY AGE AND SEX
('000 persons at 2011 census)

	Males	Females	Total
0–14 years	194,351.4	178,092.7	372,444.1
15–64 years	394,175.9	373,559.8	767,735.7
65 years and over	32,370.1	33,815.2	66,185.3
Total*	620,897.4	585,467.8	1,206,365.2

* Excluding persons of unknown or undeclared age: 4,489,800 (males 2,372,900, females 2,116,900).

Note: Totals may not be equal to the sum of components, owing to rounding.

STATES AND TERRITORIES
(official estimates at mid-2012)

	Area (sq km)	Population ('000)	Density (per sq km)	Capital
States				
Andhra Pradesh .	275,045	85,744	311.7	Hyderabad
Arunachal Pradesh . . .	83,743	1,260	15.0	Itanagar
Assam	78,438	31,071	396.1	Dispur
Bihar	94,163	99,457	1,056.2	Patna
Chhattisgarh .	135,191	24,695	182.7	Raipur
Goa	3,702	1,834	495.4	Panaji
Gujarat . . .	196,024	60,062	306.4	Gandhinagar
Haryana . . .	44,212	25,994	587.9	Chandigarh*
Himachal Pradesh	55,673	6,878	123.5	Shimla
Jammu and Kashmir† .	101,387	11,915	117.5	Srinagar/Jammu
Jharkhand .	79,714	32,050	402.1	Ranchi
Karnataka .	191,791	60,229	314.0	Bangalore‡
Kerala	38,863	34,882	897.6	Thiruvananthapuram (Trivandrum)
Madhya Pradesh .	308,245	73,730	239.2	Bhopal
Maharashtra .	307,713	114,697	372.7	Mumbai (Bombay)
Manipur . . .	22,327	2,487	111.4	Imphal
Meghalaya . .	22,429	2,662	118.7	Shillong
Mizoram . . .	21,081	1,020	48.4	Aizawl
Nagaland . . .	16,579	2,284	137.8	Kohima
Orissa§ . . .	155,707	41,224	264.8	Bhubaneswar
Punjab	50,362	28,083	557.6	Chandigarh*
Rajasthan . .	342,239	69,250	202.3	Jaipur
Sikkim . . .	7,096	622	87.7	Gangtok
Tamil Nadu . .	130,058	68,002	522.9	Chennai (Madras)

—continued	Area (sq km)	Population ('000)	Density (per sq km)	Capital
Tripura . .	10,486	3,672	350.2	Agartala
Uttarakhand‖ .	53,483	10,131	189.4	Dehradun
Uttar Pradesh .	240,928	205,426	852.6	Lucknow
West Bengal . .	88,752	90,595	1,020.8	Kolkata (Calcutta)
Territories				
Andaman and Nicobar Islands	8,249	512	62.1	Port Blair
Chandigarh* . .	114	1,532	13,438.6	Chandigarh
Dadra and Nagar Haveli . .	491	376	765.8	Silvassa
Daman and Diu .	112	285	2,544.6	Daman
Delhi . . .	1,483	19,164	12,922.5	Delhi
Lakshadweep . .	32	77	2,406.3	Kavaratti
Puducherry (Pondicherry) .	479	1,471	3,071.0	Puducherry (Pondicherry)
Total¶ . . .	3,166,414	1,213,370	383.2	—

* Chandigarh forms a separate Union Territory, not within Haryana or the Punjab. As part of a scheme for a transfer of territory between the two states, Chandigarh was due to be incorporated into the Punjab on 26 January 1986, but the transfer was postponed.
† Figures refer only to the Indian-held part of the territory.
‡ Renamed Bengaluru from November 2014.
§ Renamed Odisha from November 2011.
‖ Uttaranchal prior to 2007.
¶ Area data exclude contested area of Jammu and Kashmir (120,849 sq km), a disputed area between Puducherry and Andhra Pradesh (13 sq km) and two as yet undemarcated areas of Madhya Pradesh (7 sq km) and Chhattisgarh (3 sq km).

Note: Totals may not be equal to the sum of components, owing to rounding.

Note: The creation of a new state, Telangana, from territory formerly part of Andhra Pradesh, was announced in June 2014.

Source: Office of the Registrar General of India, Ministry of Home Affairs, New Delhi.

PRINCIPAL TOWNS
(population at 2011 census, provisional*)

Greater Mumbai (Bombay) . . .	12,478,447		Guwahati . . .	963,429
Delhi	11,007,835		Chandigarh . . .	960,787
Bengaluru (Bangalore) . .	8,425,970		Solapur	951,118
Hyderabad . . .	6,809,970		Hubli-Dharwad .	943,857
Ahmedabad . . .	5,570,585		Bareilly	898,167
Chennai (Madras) .	4,681,087		Moradabad . . .	889,810
Kolkata (Calcutta) .	4,486,679		Mysuru (Mysore) .	887,446
Surat	4,462,002		Gurgaon . . .	876,824
Pune (Poona) . .	3,115,431		Aligarh	872,575
Jaipur (Jeypore) .	3,073,350		Jalandhar . . .	862,196
Lucknow . . .	2,815,601		Tiruchirappalli . .	846,915
Kanpur (Cawnpore).	2,767,031		Bhubaneswar . .	837,737
Nagpur	2,405,421		Salem	831,038
Indore	1,960,631		Mira-Bhayander .	814,655
Thane	1,818,872		Thiruvananthapuram . .	752,490
Bhopal	1,795,648		Bhiwandi . . .	711,329
Visakhapatnam (Vizag) . . .	1,730,320		Saharanpur . . .	703,345
Pimpri-Chinchwad .	1,729,359		Gorakhpur . . .	671,048
Patna	1,683,200		Guntur	651,382
Vadodara (Baroda) .	1,666,703		Bikaner	647,804
Ghaziabad . . .	1,636,068		Amravati . . .	646,801
Ludhiana . . .	1,613,878		Noida	642,381
Agra	1,574,542		Jamshedpur . .	629,659
Nashik	1,486,973		Bhilai Nagar . .	625,697
Faridabad Complex .	1,404,653		Warangal . . .	620,116
Meerut	1,309,023		Cuttack	606,007
Rajkot	1,286,995		Firozabad . . .	603,797
Kalyan-Dombivli .	1,246,381		Kochi (Cochin) . .	601,574
Vasai Virar . . .	1,221,233		Bhavnagar . . .	593,768
Varanasi (Banaras).	1,201,815		Dehradun . . .	578,420
Srinagar . . .	1,192,792		Durgapur . . .	566,937

Aurangabad	. .	1,171,330	Asansol		564,491
Dhanbad	. .	1,161,561	Nanded Waghala	.	550,564
Amritsar	. .	1,132,761	Kolapur . . .		549,283
Navi Mumbai	. .	1,119,477	Ajmer		542,580
Allahabad	. .	1,117,094	Gulbarga . . .		532,031
Ranchi .	. .	1,073,440	Jamnagar . . .		529,308
Haora . .	. .	1,072,161	Ujjain		515,215
Coimbatore	. .	1,061,447	Loni		512,296
Jabalpur					
(Jubbulpore)	. .	1,054,336	Siliguri		509,709
Gwalior .	. .	1,053,505	Jhansi		507,293
Vijayawada					
(Vijayavada)	. .	1,048,240	Ulhasnagar . . .		506,937
Jodhpur .	. .	1,033,918	Nellore		505,258
Madurai .	. .	1,016,885	Jammu . . .		503,690
			Sangli Miraj		
Raipur .	. .	1,010,087	Kupwad . . .		502,697
Kota . .	. .	1,001,365			

* Figures refer to the city proper in each case.

Capital: New Delhi, provisional population 249,998 at 2011 census.

Population of principal urban agglomerations at 2011 census, provisional: Greater Mumbai 18,414,288; Delhi 16,314,838; Kolkata 14,112,536; Chennai 8,696,010; Bengaluru (Bangalore) 8,499,399; Hyderabad 7,749,334; Ahmedabad 6,352,254; Pune 5,049,968; Surat 4,585,367; Kanpur 2,920,067; Lucknow 2,901,474; Nagpur 2,497,777; Ghaziabad 2,358,525; Indore 2,167,447; Coimbatore 2,151,466; Kochi 2,117,990; Patna 2,046,652; Kozhikode 2,030,519; Bhopal 1,883,381; Thrissur 1,854,783; Vadodara 1,817,191; Agra 1,746,467; Malappuram 1,698,645; Thiruvananthapuram 1,687,406; Kannur 1,642,892; Nashik 1,562,769; Vijayawada 1,491,202; Madurai 1,462,420; Varanasi 1,435,113; Meerut 1,424,908; Rajkot 1,390,933; Jamshedpur 1,337,131; Srinagar 1,273,312; Jabalpur 1,267,564; Asansol 1,243,008; Allahabad 1,216,719; Dhanbad 1,195,298; Aurangabad 1,189,376; Amritsar 1,183,705; Jodhpur 1,137,815; Ranchi 1,126,741; Raipur 1,122,555; Kollam 1,110,005; Gwalior 1,101,981; Durg-Bhilainagar 1,064,077; Chandigarh 1,025,682; Tiruchirappalli 1,021,717.

Population of urban agglomeration at mid-2015 (incl. suburbs, UN estimate): Delhi 25,703,168 (Source: UN, *World Urbanization Prospects: The 2014 Revision*).

BIRTHS AND DEATHS
(estimates based on Sample Registration Scheme)

	2011	2012	2013
Birth rate (per 1,000)	21.8	21.6	21.4
Death rate (per 1,000)	7.1	7.0	7.0

Life expectancy (years at birth): 66.2 (males 64.5; females 68.0) in 2012 (Source: World Bank, World Development Indicators database).

ECONOMICALLY ACTIVE POPULATION
(persons aged five years and over, 1991 census, excluding Jammu and Kashmir)

	Males	Females	Total
Agriculture, hunting, forestry and fishing	139,361,719	51,979,110	191,340,829
Mining and quarrying . . .	1,536,919	214,356	1,751,275
Manufacturing	23,969,433	4,702,046	28,671,479
Construction	5,122,468	420,737	5,543,205
Trade and commerce . .	19,862,725	1,433,612	21,296,337
Transport, storage and communications	7,810,126	207,620	8,017,746
Other services	23,995,194	5,316,428	29,311,622
Total employed	221,658,584	64,273,909	285,932,493
Marginal workers	2,705,223	25,493,654	28,198,877
Total labour force	224,363,807	89,767,563	314,131,370

Unemployment (work applicants at 31 December, '000 persons aged 14 years and over): 41,466 (males 29,685, females 11,781) in 2006; 39,974 (males 27,972, females 12,002) in 2007; 39,112 (males 26,785, females 12,327) in 2008 (Source: ILO).

2011 census: Cultivators 118,692,640 (males 82,706,724, females 35,985,916); Agricultural labourers 144,329,833 (males 82,740,351, females 61,589,482); Household industry workers 18,336,307 (males 9,775,635, females 8,560,672); Other 200,384,531 (males 156,643,220, females 43,741,311); Total employed 481,743,311 (incl. 119,296,891 marginal workers).

Mid-2015 (FAO estimates in '000): Agriculture, etc. 278,435; Total labour force 534,751 (Source: FAO).

Health and Welfare

KEY INDICATORS

Total fertility rate (children per woman, 2012) . . .	2.5
Under-5 mortality rate (per 1,000 live births, 2012) . . .	56
HIV/AIDS (% of persons aged 15–49, 2013)	0.3
Physicians (per 1,000 head, 2012)	0.7
Hospital beds (per 1,000 head, 2005)	0.9
Health expenditure (2011): US $ per head (PPP) . . .	146
Health expenditure (2011): % of GDP	3.9
Health expenditure (2011): public (% of total)	30.5
Access to water (% of persons, 2012)	93
Access to sanitation (% of persons, 2012)	36
Total carbon dioxide emissions ('000 metric tons, 2010) .	2,008,822.9
Carbon dioxide emissions per head (metric tons, 2010) . .	1.7
Human Development Index (2013): ranking	135
Human Development Index (2013): value	0.586

For sources and definitions, see explanatory note on p. vi.

Agriculture

PRINCIPAL CROPS
('000 metric tons, year ending 30 June)

	2011/12	2012/13	2013/14*
Total cereals	242,200	238,790	245,500
Rice, milled	105,300	105,240	106,540
Sorghum (Jowar) . . .	5,980	5,280	5,390
Cat-tail millet (Bajra) . . .	10,280	8,740	9,180
Maize	21,760	22,260	24,350
Finger millet (Ragi) . . .	1,930	1,570	1,880
Small millets	450	440	450
Wheat	94,880	93,510	95,900
Barley	1,620	1,750	1,810
Chick-peas (Gram)	7,700	8,830	9,880
Pigeon-peas (Tur)	2,650	3,020	3,290
Dry beans, dry peas, lentils and other pulses	6,740	6,490	6,100
Total food grains	259,290	257,130	264,770
Groundnuts (in shell)	6,964	4,695	9,673
Sesame seed	810	685	675
Rapeseed and mustard . . .	6,604	8,029	7,960
Linseed	152	149	143
Castorseed	2,295	1,964	1,689
Total edible oilseeds (incl. others)	29,799	30,943	32,877
Cotton lint†	35,200	34,220	36,590
Jute and kenaf‡	11,399	10,930	11,580
Sugar cane: production cane . .	361,037	341,200	350,022

* Estimates.
† Production in '000 bales of 170 kg each.
‡ Production in '000 bales of 180 kg each.

Source: Directorate of Economics and Statistics, Ministry of Agriculture.

Tea ('000 metric tons): 967 in 2011; 1,000 in 2012 (FAO estimate); n.a. in 2013 (Source: FAO).

Tobacco, unmanufactured ('000 metric tons): 830 in 2011; 875 in 2012 (FAO estimate); n.a. in 2013 (Source: FAO).

Potatoes ('000 metric tons): 42,339 in 2011; 41,483 in 2012; 45,344 in 2013 (Source: FAO).

LIVESTOCK
('000 head, year ending September)

	2011	2012	2013
Cattle*	210,824	212,615	214,350
Sheep†	74,500	75,000	75,500
Goats†	157,000	160,000	162,000
Pigs†	9,500	9,400	9,300
Horses†	520	525	528
Asses†	296	294	292
Mules†	105	105	104
Buffaloes*	112,916	114,485	115,420
Camels†	440	438	436
Chickens†	942,000	947,000	950,000
Ducks†	26,500	27,000	27,500

* Unofficial figures.
† FAO estimates.
Source: FAO.

LIVESTOCK PRODUCTS
('000 metric tons)

	2011	2012	2013
Cattle meat*	984.7	975.8	966.6
Buffalo meat*	1,559.4	1,573.2	1,610.0
Sheep meat*	247.4	242.0	237.6
Goat meat*	517.0	513.0	509.0
Pig meat*	64.0	357.0	353.5
Chicken meat*	2,235.0	2,278.0	2,328.0
Duck meat*	33.0	31.2	29.9
Cows' milk	57,770	59,805	60,600*
Buffaloes' milk	65,352	67,675	70,000*
Goats' milk	4,782	4,950	5,000*
Hen eggs	3,466	3,655	3,835
Wool, greasy	44.4	46.1	46.5*

* FAO estimate(s).
Source: FAO.

Forestry

ROUNDWOOD REMOVALS
('000 cubic metres, excl. bark, FAO estimates)

	2011	2012	2013
Sawlogs, veneer logs and logs for sleepers	47,804	47,804	47,804
Pulpwood	1,332	1,332	1,332
Other industrial wood	381	381	381
Fuel wood	308,776	308,244	307,709
Total	358,293	357,761	357,226

Source: FAO.

SAWNWOOD PRODUCTION
('000 cubic metres, incl. railway sleepers)

	2005	2006	2007
Coniferous sawnwood	9,900	9,900	2,000
Broadleaved sawnwood	4,889	4,889	4,889
Total	14,789	14,789	6,889

2008–13: Figures assumed to be unchanged from 2007 (FAO estimates).
Source: FAO.

Fishing
('000 metric tons, live weight)

	2010	2011	2012
Capture	4,689.3	4,311.1	4,862.9
Bombay-duck (Bummalo)	156.2	136.8	188.3
Croakers and drums	238.5	264.2	278.3
Indian oil-sardine (Sardinella)	320.2	381.7	404.3
Giant tiger prawn	155.5	189.6	180.0
Aquaculture	3,785.8	3,673.1*	4,209.4
Roho labeo	279.0	645.3	627.7
Mrigal carp	87.7	131.8	165.8
Catla	2,705.2	2,148.4	2,458.8
Silver carp	129.8	103.3	123.2
Total catch	8,475.1	7,984.2*	9,072.3

* FAO estimate.
Source: FAO.

Mining
('000 metric tons, unless otherwise indicated)

	2011/12	2012/13	2013/14
Coal	539,950	556,402	563,085
Lignite	42,332	46,453	44,275
Iron ore*	168,582	136,618	152,433
Manganese ore*	2,412	2,342	2,588
Bauxite	13,600	16,612	21,666
Chalk (Fireclay)	179	176	126
Kaolin (China clay)	3,077	4,259	4,753
Dolomite	5,969	7,234	7,109
Gypsum	3,979	3,557	2,930
Limestone	262,568	278,725	285,030
Crude petroleum	38,090	37,862	37,778
Chromium ore*	2,923	2,834	2,853
Phosphorite	2,260	1,941	1,384
Kyanite	4	1	2
Magnesite	224	224	195
Steatite	998	972	865
Copper ore*	3,479	3,636	3,778
Lead concentrates*	162	184	194
Zinc concentrates*	1,414	1,493	1,491
Mica—crude (metric tons)	1,899	1,256	1,610
Gold (kg)	2,194	1,588	1,564
Diamonds (carats)	18,490	31,988	37,515
Natural gas (million cu m)†	47,559	40,679	34,412

* Figures refer to gross weight. The estimated metal content is: Iron 63%; Manganese 40%; Chromium 30%; Copper 1.2%; Lead 70%; Zinc 60%.
† Figures refer to gas utilized.
Source: Indian Bureau of Mines.

Industry

SELECTED PRODUCTS
('000 metric tons, unless otherwise indicated)

	2008/09	2009/10	2010/11
Refined sugar*	18,407	17,303	22,535
Cotton cloth (million sq metres) .	26,898	28,517	30,659
Paper and paper board . . .	6,543	7,067	n.a.
Soda ash	1,989	2,051	2,298
Fertilizers	14,334	16,224	n.a.
Motor spirit	16,020	15,970	17,509
Cement	181,400	200,651	209,660
Pig-iron	6,206	5,796	5,585
Stainless steel	2,680	2,881	3,737
Aluminium ingots (metric tons) .	784,755	745,542	n.a.
Diesel engines—stationary (number)	3,337,682	3,377,819	n.a.
Television receivers (number) .	7,574,271	9,622,186	n.a.
Electric fans (number)	11,541,791	14,074,284	n.a.
Passenger cars	1,516,791	1,910,465	2,452,819
Commercial vehicles (number) .	416,491	566,585	752,597
Motorcycles, mopeds and scooters (number)	8,361,411	10,510,331	13,376,451
Bicycles (number)	11,123,734	12,651,846	n.a.

* Figures relate to crop year (beginning November) and are in respect of cane sugar only.

Finance

CURRENCY AND EXCHANGE RATES

Monetary Units
100 paise (singular: paisa) = 1 Indian rupee (R).

Sterling, Dollar and Euro Equivalents (31 December 2014)
£1 sterling = Rs 98.848;
US $1 = Rs 63.332;
€1 = Rs 76.891;
1,000 Indian rupees = £10.12 = $15.79 = €13.01.

Average Exchange Rate (rupees per US $)
2012	53.437
2013	58.598
2014	61.026

UNION BUDGET
(Rs million, rounded, year ending 31 March)

Revenue	2012/13	2013/14*	2014/15†
Tax revenue (net)	7,402,558	8,360,260	9,864,173
Customs receipts . . .	1,653,462	1,750,560	2,013,140
Union excise duties . . .	1,765,354	1,795,373	2,005,850
Corporation tax	3,563,260	3,936,770	4,510,050
Other taxes on income . .	2,014,865	2,416,910	3,064,660
Other taxes and duties . .	1,365,402	1,689,443	2,198,294
Less States' share of tax revenue	2,915,466	3,182,296	3,877,321
Less Surcharge transferred to National Calamity Contingency Fund . .	44,319	46,500	50,500
Other current revenue . .	1,373,569	1,932,257	1,807,136
Interest receipts (net) . .	207,630	210,178	197,291
Dividends and profits . .	537,607	881,879	772,293
Receipts of Union Territories .	11,171	10,970	11,107
External grants . . .	23,110	31,350	24,050
Other receipts (net) . . .	594,050	797,880	802,400
Non-debt capital revenue . . .	421,573	366,438	674,522
Total	9,197,700	10,658,955	12,345,831

Expenditure	2012/13	2013/14*	2014/15†
Central Ministries/Departments .	12,967,363	14,664,582	14,196,621
Agriculture and co-operation (incl. agricultural research and education)	158,544	189,819	116,339
Atomic energy	74,713	82,365	104,466
Defence	2,306,421	2,534,760	2,792,029
Drinking water and sanitation .	129,686	120,062	2,379
Economic affairs	3,585,826	4,355,060	4,918,364
External affairs	101,148	117,937	141,304
Fertilizers	656,383	680,090	681,000
Food and public distribution .	862,198	929,270	1,156,568
Health and family welfare . .	251,333	275,310	99,721
Home affairs	477,781	550,232	608,286
School education and literacy .	456,315	501,363	60,639
Petroleum and natural gas .	974,230	855,661	635,430
Railways	241,319	270,000	290,000
Road transport and highways .	201,862	273,671	286,142
Rural development	501,874	593,557	76,023
Urban development	84,670	95,482	125,295
State plans	1,041,974	1,135,721	3,307,435
Union territories	94,334	104,039	128,084
Total	14,103,671	15,904,341	17,632,140
Current‡	12,435,089	13,995,398	15,500,538
Capital	1,668,582	1,908,944	2,131,602

* Estimates.
† Budget figures.
‡ Including interest payments (Rs million): 3,131,690 in 2012/13; 3,800,660 in 2013/14 (estimate); 4,270,110 in 2014/15 (budget figure).

Source: Government of India, Union Budget 2014/15.

Note: From 2014/15 disbursement of funds to several ministries and departments (including those governing drinking water and sanitation, health and family welfare, school education and literacy, and rural development) was transferred from the central budgetary plan to state budgets. As a result, figures for Union Budget departmental expenditure for 2014/15 are not comparable with those for previous years. Total departmental expenditure (including expenditure by states) for 2014/15 was estimated as follows (Rs million): drinking water and sanitation 152,669; health and family welfare 351,630; school education and literacy 551,151; rural development 800,933.

INTERNATIONAL RESERVES
(US $ million at 31 December)

	2011	2012	2013
Gold (national valuation) . . .	26,620	27,220	19,725
IMF special drawing rights . .	4,429	4,436	4,447
Reserve position in IMF . . .	3,923	4,494	4,344
Foreign exchange	262,933	261,656	267,703
Total	297,905	297,806	296,218

Source: IMF, *International Financial Statistics*.

MONEY SUPPLY
(Rs '000 million, last Friday of year ending 31 March)

	2011/12	2012/13	2013/14
Currency with the public . . .	10,236.7	11,410.6	12483.4
Demand deposits with banks . .	7,109.0	7,532.3	8,043.9
Other deposits with Reserve Bank	28.2	32.4	19.7
Time deposits	56474.4	64,922.9	74,426.3
Broad money	73,848.3	83,898.2	94,973.3

Source: Reserve Bank of India.

COST OF LIVING
(Consumer Price Index; base: 2010 = 100)

	2011	2012	2013
Food, beverages and tobacco . .	109.8	121.1	135.6
Clothing, bedding and footwear .	115.3	128.5	141.0
Fuel and lighting	113.1	123.9	133.7
Housing	105.4	118.0	120.4
All items (incl. others) . . .	109.6	120.3	132.4

NATIONAL ACCOUNTS
(Rs '000 million at current prices, year ending 31 March)

National Income and Product

	2011/12	2012/13	2013/14*
Domestic factor incomes . . .	75,117.95	83,727.44	92,993.45
Consumption of fixed capital .	8,798.96	10,161.32	11,734.62
Gross domestic product at factor cost	83,916.91	93,888.76	104,728.07
Indirect taxes, less subsidies .	6,180.31	7,244.05	8,822.66
GDP in purchasers' values .	90,097.22	101,132.81	113,550.73
Net factor income from abroad .	−768.30	−1,167.66	−1,283.00
Gross national product . .	89,328.92	99,965.15	112,267.73
Less Consumption of fixed capital	8,798.96	10,161.32	11,734.62
National income in market prices	80,529.96	89,803.83	100,533.11

* Provisional estimates.

Expenditure on the Gross Domestic Product

	2011/12	2012/13	2013/14*
Government final consumption expenditure	10,258.95	11,891.32	13,413.41
Private final consumption expenditure	51,418.96	57,720.59	64,850.37
Increase in stocks	1,705.96	1,711.84	1,867.97
Gross fixed capital formation .	28,610.62	30,715.43	32,111.14
Acquisitions, less disposals, of valuables	2,466.73	2,664.82	1,705.48
Total domestic expenditure .	94,461.22	104,704.00	113,948.37
Exports of goods and services .	21,503.26	24,268.07	28,177.73
Less Imports of goods and services	27,219.47	31,084.30	32,260.89
Statistical discrepancy . . .	1,352.21	3,245.04	3,685.52
GDP in purchasers' values .	90,097.22	101,132.81	113,550.73
GDP at constant 2004/05 prices	56,330.50	58,998.47	61,958.42

* Provisional estimates.

Gross Domestic Product by Economic Activity

	2010/11	2011/12	2012/13
Agriculture	11,435.17	13,005.69	14,174.68
Forestry and logging	1,188.98	1,316.67	1,494.05
Fishing	572.71	668.62	780.53
Mining and quarrying	2,048.66	2,227.16	2,224.16
Manufacturing	10,724.89	12,361.82	13,209.07
Electricity, gas and water supply	1,195.60	1,356.70	1,571.32
Construction	5,715.35	6,897.98	7,599.90
Trade, hotels and restaurants .	12,504.72	14,575.65	16,158.65
Transport, storage and communications	5,291.58	6,147.07	7,088.30
Banking and insurance . . .	4,104.07	4,814.95	5,495.00
Real estate and business services .	7,548.36	9,000.29	10,675.76
Public administration and defence	4,421.20	4,983.46	5,671.93
Other services	5,737.30	6,560.85	7,745.41
GDP at factor cost	72,488.59	83,916.91	93,888.76
Indirect taxes, less subsidies . .	5,352.55	6,180.31	7,244.05
GDP in market prices . . .	77,841.15	90,097.22	101,132.81

2013/14 (provisional estimates): Agriculture, forestry and fishing 19,063.48; Mining and quarrying 2,226.52; Manufacturing 13,500.39; Electricity, gas and water supply 2,030.49; Construction 8,184.32; Trade, hotels and restaurants, transport, storage and communications 25,099.07; Finance, insurance, real estate and business services 19,394.82; Community, social and personal services 15,228.98; **GDP at factor cost** 104,728.07; Indirect taxes, less subsidies 8,822.66; **GDP in market prices** 113,550.73.

BALANCE OF PAYMENTS
(US $ million)

	2011/12	2012/13	2013/14*
Exports of goods f.o.b.	309,774	306,581	318,607
Imports of goods f.o.b.	−499,533	−502,237	−466,216
Trade balance	−189,759	−195,656	−147,609
Services (net)	64,098	64,915	72,965
Balance on goods and services	−125,661	−130,741	−74,644
Other income (net)	−15,988	−21,455	−23,028
Balance on goods, services and income	−141,649	−152,196	−97,672
Current transfers (net) . . .	63,494	64,034	65,276
Current balance	−78,155	−88,163	−32,397
Direct investment abroad . . .	−10,892	−7,134	−9,199
Direct investment from abroad .	32,952	26,953	30,763
Portfolio investment assets . .	17,409	27,770	5,029
Portfolio investment liabilities .	−239	−878	−207
Net loans	19,307	31,124	7,765
Banking capital (net)	16,226	16,570	25,449
Rupee debt service	−79	−58	−52
Other capital (net)	−6,929	−5,047	−10,761
Net errors and omissions . . .	−2,432	2,689	−882
Overall balance	−12,831	3,826	15,508

* Preliminary figures.

Source: Reserve Bank of India.

External Trade

PRINCIPAL COMMODITIES
(Rs million, year ending 31 March)

Imports c.i.f.	2011/12	2012/13	2013/14
Animal and vegetable oils, fats and waxes	465,681	616,301	571,528
Mineral fuels, mineral oils and products of their distillation .	8,279,657	9,860,856	10,983,116
Organic chemicals	691,442	854,391	1,031,569
Natural or cultured pearls, precious and semi-precious stones, precious metals and articles thereof; imitation jewellery; coin	4,345,985	4,558,560	3,450,296
Iron and steel	657,494	741,253	549,082
Boilers, machinery, mechanical appliances and parts thereof .	1,800,016	1,917,361	1,852,701
Electrical machinery and equipment and parts thereof; sound and television apparatus	1,573,375	1,622,670	1,764,610
Aircraft, spacecraft, and parts thereof	198,111	256,914	260,337
Total (incl. others)	23,454,632	26,691,620	27,154,339

Exports f.o.b.	2011/12	2012/13	2013/14
Cereals	306,249	525,678	635,429
Ores, slag and ash	262,173	129,154	133,451
Mineral fuels, mineral oils and products of their distillation	2,743,870	3,375,673	3,923,831
Organic chemicals	561,793	659,150	728,605
Pharmaceutical products	408,169	547,737	674,037
Iron and steel	397,592	440,421	560,483
Articles of iron or steel	339,877	404,776	412,565
Cotton	436,017	485,143	604,866
Articles of apparel and clothing accessories, knitted or crocheted	276,385	302,382	403,386
Articles of apparel and clothing accessories, not knitted or crocheted	381,001	402,907	504,456
Natural or cultured pearls, precious and semi-precious stones, precious metals and articles thereof; imitation jewellery; coin	2,262,909	2,384,585	2,521,754
Boilers, machinery, mechanical appliances and parts thereof	520,508	628,467	731,699
Electrical machinery and equipment and parts thereof; sound and television apparatus	553,766	591,441	624,282
Vehicles other than railway or tramway rolling stock, and parts and accessories thereof	525,568	663,992	785,698
Total (incl. others)	14,659,594	16,343,188	19,050,111

Source: Ministry of Commerce and Industry.

PRINCIPAL TRADING PARTNERS
(Rs million, year ending 31 March)

Imports c.i.f.	2011/12	2012/13	2013/14
Angola	318,685	389,464	366,514
Australia	746,196	712,171	589,576
Belgium	497,573	545,368	646,723
China, People's Republic	2,654,656	2,843,846	3,092,350
Colombia	27,231	128,125	299,963
Germany	748,406	779,337	782,096
Hong Kong	495,702	430,301	441,071
Indonesia	704,199	809,657	890,354
Iran	665,522	630,256	627,984
Iraq	905,315	1,045,964	1,116,377
Italy	245,094	256,524	251,406
Japan	576,710	675,472	572,117
Korea, Republic	615,703	713,373	752,826
Kuwait	794,495	901,843	1,033,626
Malaysia	453,850	541,988	559,021
Nigeria	701,039	656,222	857,672
Qatar	618,638	854,578	950,054
Saudi Arabia	1,531,099	1,846,848	2,205,155
Singapore	397,085	407,640	410,635
South Africa	524,460	483,196	358,583
Switzerland	1,663,834	1,745,118	1,123,382
Thailand	253,248	291,130	323,800
United Arab Emirates	1,756,375	2,129,233	1,741,267
United Kingdom	340,939	342,312	360,430
USA	1,123,629	1,372,386	1,356,135
Venezuela	321,301	768,345	843,844
Total (incl. others)	23,454,632	26,691,620	27,154,339

Exports f.o.b.	2011/12	2012/13	2013/14
Bangladesh	183,867	279,826	374,113
Belgium	342,061	299,264	386,869
Brazil	275,769	328,720	338,706
China, People's Republic	874,708	735,296	905,611
France	220,208	271,059	309,513
Germany	379,653	394,081	455,194
Hong Kong	618,772	668,982	772,410
Indonesia	321,007	289,961	293,399
Iran	115,117	182,548	300,566
Israel	193,266	203,467	227,571
Italy	232,717	237,793	318,872
Japan	305,113	332,142	412,535
Kenya	109,872	205,257	235,955
Korea, Republic	207,678	228,702	254,709
Malaysia	191,032	241,435	254,136
Nepal	131,302	168,056	217,702
Netherlands	439,073	573,726	487,445

Exports f.o.b.—*continued*	2011/12	2012/13	2013/14
Saudi Arabia	272,082	532,444	738,639
Singapore	803,630	739,950	749,662
South Africa	227,297	278,034	307,699
Sri Lanka	209,515	216,877	276,437
Taiwan	159,862	165,551	120,605
Tanzania	n.a.	117,329	209,071
Thailand	142,535	203,102	224,311
Turkey	168,940	215,244	270,424
United Arab Emirates	1,722,685	1,978,321	1,847,787
United Kingdom	411,402	468,782	592,192
USA	1,664,554	1,967,408	2,365,898
Viet Nam	180,850	215,628	332,533
Total (incl. others)	14,659,594	16,343,188	19,050,111

Source: Ministry of Commerce and Industry.

Transport

RAILWAYS
(million, year ending 31 March)

	2010/11	2011/12	2012/13
Passengers	7,651	8,224	8,421
Passenger-km	978,508	1,046,522	1,098,103
Freight (metric tons)	921.7	969.1	1,008.1
Freight (metric ton-km)	626,473	668,618	692,637

Source: Railway Board, Ministry of Railways and Indian Railways.

ROAD TRAFFIC
('000 motor vehicles in use at 31 March)

	2010	2011	2012
Private cars, jeeps and taxis	17,109	19,231	21,568
Buses and coaches	1,527	1,604	1,677
Goods vehicles	6,432	7,064	7,658
Motorcycles and scooters	91,598	101,865	115,419
Others	11,080	12,102	13,169
Total	127,746	141,866	159,491

Source: Ministry of Road Transport and Highways.

SHIPPING

Flag Registered Fleet
(at 31 December)

	2012	2013	2014
Number of vessels	1,378	1,553	1,577
Total displacement ('000 grt)	9,587.8	9,740.1	9,652.5

Source: Lloyd's List Intelligence (www.lloydslistintelligence.com).

CIVIL AVIATION
(all Indian carriers, traffic on scheduled services)

	2010/11	2011/12	2012/13
Passengers carried ('000)	67,001	75,217	69,430
Passenger-km (million)	103,171	112,794	99,972
Freight carried (metric tons)	620,000	602,200	561,800
Freight ton-km (million)	1,646	1,750	1,529
Mail carried (metric tons)	25,000	18,500	7,000
Mail ton-km (million)	48	45	49

Source: Directorate General of Civil Aviation.

Tourism

FOREIGN VISITORS BY COUNTRY OF ORIGIN

	2011	2012	2013
Australia	192,592	202,105	218,967
Bangladesh	463,543	487,397	524,923
Canada	259,017	256,021	255,222
China, People's Republic	142,218	168,952	174,712
France	231,423	240,674	248,379
Germany	240,235	254,783	252,003
Japan	193,525	220,015	220,283
Malaysia	208,196	195,853	242,649
Russia	144,312	177,526	259,120
Sri Lanka	305,853	296,983	262,345
United Kingdom	798,249	788,170	809,444
USA	980,688	1,039,947	1,085,309
Total (incl. others)	6,309,222	6,577,745	6,967,601

Receipts from tourism (US $ million, provisional): 16,564 in 2011; 17,737 in 2012; 18,445 in 2013.

Source: Ministry of Tourism.

Communications Media

	2011	2012	2013
Telephones ('000 main lines in use)	32,685.2	31,080.0	28,894.2
Mobile cellular telephones ('000 subscribers)	893,862.5	864,720.0	886,304.2
Internet subscribers ('000)	22,390	n.a.	n.a.
Broadband subscribers ('000)	13,350	14,980	14,540

Daily newspapers (2009/10): 9,355 (circulation 162,313,000 copies).

Non-daily newspapers and other periodicals (2009/10): 68,029 (circulation 146,504,000 copies).

Sources: International Telecommunication Union; Register of Newspapers for India; Ministry of Information and Broadcasting.

Education

(2011/12 unless otherwise indicated)

	Institutions	Teachers	Students
Pre-primary	61,499	72,850	6,073,502
Primary	712,437	2,253,767	139,869,904
Upper primary	474,294	2,073,993	63,006,313
Secondary (high school)			
Higher secondary (new pattern)	212,512	2,465,962	55,060,146
Intermediate/pre-degree/ junior college			
Higher education*	33,634†	817,000‡	25,191,000‡

* Includes colleges for general and professional education, universities and institutions of national importance.
† At August 2011.
‡ Rounded figure.

Source: Ministry of Human Resource Development.

Pupil-teacher ratio (primary education, UNESCO estimate): 35.2 in 2010/11 (Source: UNESCO Institute for Statistics).

Adult literacy rate (UNESCO estimates): 66.0% (males 76.9%; females 54.5%) in 2007 (Source: UNESCO Institute for Statistics).

Directory

The Government

HEAD OF STATE

President: PRANAB MUKHERJEE (sworn in 25 July 2012).

Vice-President: MOHAMMAD HAMID ANSARI (sworn in 12 August 2007; re-elected 7 August 2012).

COUNCIL OF MINISTERS
(April 2015)

The Government is formed by the Bharatiya Janata Party (BJP), the Lok Jan Shakti Party (LJSP), the Telugu Desam Party (TDP), Shiv Sena and Shiromani Akali Dal (SAD).

Prime Minister and Minister-in-charge of Personnel, Public Grievances and Pensions, of Atomic Energy and of Space: NARENDRA MODI (BJP).

Minister of Home Affairs: RAJNATH SINGH (BJP).

Minister of External Affairs and of Overseas Indian Affairs: SUSHMA SWARAJ (BJP).

Minister of Finance, of Corporate Affairs and of Information and Broadcasting: ARUN JAITLEY (BJP).

Minister of Urban Development, of Housing and Urban Poverty Alleviation, and of Parliamentary Affairs: M. VENKAIAH NAIDU (BJP).

Minister of Road Transport and Highways, and of Shipping: NITIN JAIRAM GADKARI (BJP).

Minister of Defence: MANOHAR PARRIKAR (BJP).

Minister of Railways: SURESH PRABHU (BJP).

Minister of Law and Justice: D. V. SADANANDA GOWDA (BJP).

Minister of Water Resources, River Development and Ganga Rejuvenation: UMA BHARTI (BJP).

Minister of Minority Affairs: NAJMA A. HEPTULLA (BJP).

Minister of Consumer Affairs, Food and Public Distribution: RAMVILAS PASWAN (LJSP).

Minister of Micro, Small and Medium Enterprises: KALRAJ MISHRA (BJP).

Minister of Women and Child Development: MANEKA SANJAY GANDHI (BJP).

Minister of Chemicals and Fertilizers: ANANTH KUMAR (BJP).

Minister of Communications and Information Technology: RAVI SHANKAR PRASAD (BJP).

Minister of Health and Family Welfare: JAGAT PRAKASH NADDA (BJP).

Minister of Civil Aviation: ASHOK GAJAPATHI RAJU PUSAPATI (TDP).

Minister of Heavy Industries and Public Enterprises: ANANT GEETE (Shiv Sena).

Minister of Food Processing Industries: HARSIMRAT KAUR BADAL (SAD).

Minister of Mines, and of Steel: NARENDRA SINGH TOMAR (BJP).

Minister of Rural Development, of Panchayati Raj, and of Drinking Water and Sanitation: CHAUDHARY BIRENDER SINGH (BJP).

Minister of Tribal Affairs: JUAL ORAM (BJP).

Minister of Agriculture: RADHA MOHAN SINGH (BJP).

Minister of Social Justice and Empowerment: THAAWAR CHAND GEHLOT (BJP).

Minister of Human Resource Development: SMRITI ZUBIN IRANI (BJP).

Minister of Science and Technology, and of Earth Sciences: HARSH VARDHAN (BJP).

Ministers of State with Independent Charge

Minister of State for Statistics and Programme Implementation, and Minister of State in the Ministry of External Affairs and the Ministry of Overseas Indian Affairs: Gen. (retd) V. K. SINGH (BJP).

Minister of State for Planning, and Minister of State in the Ministry of Defence: RAO INDERJIT SINGH (BJP).

Minister of State for Textiles: SANTOSH KUMAR GANGWAR (BJP).

Minister of State for Labour and Employment: BANDARU DATTATREYA (BJP).

Minister of State for Skill Development and Entrepreneurship, and for Parliamentary Affairs: RAJIV PRATAP RUDY (BJP).

Minister of State for Ayurveda, Yoga and Naturopathy, Unani, Siddha and Homeopathy, and for Health and Family Welfare: SHRIPAD YASSO NAIK (BJP).

Minister of State for Petroleum and Natural Gas: DHARMENDRA PRADHAN (BJP).

Minister of State for Youth Affairs and Sports: SARBANANDA SONOWAL (BJP).

Minister of State for Environment, Forest and Climate Change: PRAKASH JAVADEKAR (BJP).

Minister of State for Power, for Coal and for New and Renewable Energy: PIYUSH GOYAL (BJP).

Minister of State for the Development of the North-Eastern Region, and Minister of State in the Prime Minister's Office, the Ministry of Personnel, Public Grievances and Pensions, the Department of Atomic Energy and the Department of Space: JITENDRA SINGH (BJP).

Minister of State for Commerce and Industry: NIRMALA SITHARAMAN (BJP).

Minister of State for Culture, for Tourism and for Civil Aviation: MAHESH SHARMA (BJP).

There were, in addition, 26 Ministers of State without independent charge.

MINISTRIES AND GOVERNMENT OFFICES

President's Office: Rashtrapati Bhavan, New Delhi 110 004; tel. (11) 23015321; fax (11) 23017290; e-mail presidentofindia@rb.nic.in; internet www.presidentofindia.nic.in.

Vice-President's Office: 6 Maulana Azad Rd, New Delhi 110 011; tel. (11) 23016344; fax (11) 23018124; e-mail vpindia@nic.in; internet vicepresidentofindia.nic.in.

Prime Minister's Office: 152 South Blk, Raisina Hill, New Delhi 110 011; tel. (11) 23012312; fax (11) 23016857; e-mail pmindia@pmindia.nic.in; internet www.pmindia.nic.in.

Ministry of Agriculture: Krishi Bhavan, Dr Rajendra Prasad Rd, New Delhi 110 001; tel. (11) 23383370; fax (11) 23384129; e-mail secy-agri@nic.in; internet agricoop.nic.in.

Ministry of Ayurveda, Yoga and Naturopathy, Unani, Siddha and Homeopathy (AYUSH): Ayush Bhavan, Block B, GPO Complex, INA, New Delhi 110 023; tel. (11) 24651710; e-mail minister-ayush@nie.in; internet indianmedicine.nic.in.

Ministry of Chemicals and Fertilizers: Shastri Bhavan, Dr Rajendra Prasad Rd, New Delhi 110 001; tel. (11) 23386519; fax (11) 23384020; e-mail mincf.cpc@sb.nic.in; internet chemicals.gov .in; internet fert.nic.in; internet pharmaceuticals.gov.in.

Ministry of Civil Aviation: Rajiv Gandhi Bhavan, Safdarjung Airport, New Delhi 110 023; tel. (11) 24610358; fax (11) 24602397; e-mail secy.moca@nic.in; internet civilaviation.nic.in.

Ministry of Coal: Shastri Bhavan, Dr Rajendra Prasad Rd, New Delhi 110 001; tel. (11) 23384884; fax (11) 23381678; e-mail secy .moc@nic.in; internet coal.nic.in.

Ministry of Commerce and Industry: 45C Udyog Bhavan, New Delhi 110 011; tel. (11) 23062261; fax (11) 23063418; e-mail csoffice@nic.in; internet commerce.nic.in.

Ministry of Communications and Information Technology: Electronic Niketan, CGO Complex, Lodhi Rd, New Delhi 110 003; tel. (11) 24301851; fax (11) 24363101; e-mail secretary@deity.gov.in; internet deity.gov.in.

Ministry of Consumer Affairs, Food and Public Distribution: 179 Krishi Bhavan, New Delhi 110 001; tel. (11) 23097018; fax (11) 23386052; e-mail secy-food@nic.in; internet fcamin.nic.in.

Ministry of Corporate Affairs: 'A' Wing, Shastri Bhavan, Dr Rajendra Prasad Rd, New Delhi 110 001; tel. (11) 23384660; fax (11) 23073806; e-mail hq.delhi@mca.gov.in; internet www.mca.gov .in.

Ministry of Culture: 'C' Wing, Shastri Bhavan, Dr Rajendra Prasad Rd, New Delhi 110 001; tel. (11) 23386995; fax (11) 23385115; e-mail secy-culture@nic.in; internet indiaculture.nic.in.

Ministry of Defence: South Blk, New Delhi 110 011; tel. (11) 23019030; fax (11) 23015403; e-mail ak.antony@sansad.nic.in; internet www.mod.nic.in.

Ministry of Development of North Eastern Region: Vigyan Bhavan Annexe, Maulana Azad Rd, New Delhi 110 011; tel. (11) 23022020; fax (11) 23022024; e-mail secydoner@nic.in; internet mdoner.gov.in.

Ministry of Drinking Water and Sanitation: 'A' Wing, 2nd Floor, Nirman Bhavan, New Delhi 110 001; tel. (11) 23061207; fax (11) 23062715; e-mail secydws@nic.in; internet ddws.gov.in.

Ministry of Earth Sciences: Prithvi Bhavan, IMD Campus, Lodhi Rd, New Delhi 110 003; tel. (11) 24629771; fax (11) 24629777; e-mail secretary@moes.gov.in; internet moes.gov.in.

Ministry of Environment, Forest and Climate Change: Indira Paryavaran Bhavan, Jor Bagh Rd, New Delhi 110 003; tel. (11) 24362064; fax (11) 24362222; e-mail envisect@nic.in; internet envfor .nic.in.

Ministry of External Affairs: South Blk, New Delhi 110 011; tel. (11) 23011127; fax (11) 23013254; e-mail eam@mea.gov.in; internet www.mea.gov.in.

Ministry of Finance: North Blk, 1st Floor, New Delhi 110 001; tel. (11) 23092611; fax (11) 23094075; e-mail secy-dea@nic.in; internet finmin.nic.in.

Ministry of Food Processing Industries: Panchsheel Bhavan, August Kranti Marg, New Delhi 110 049; tel. (11) 26493225; fax (11) 26493012; e-mail secy.hub@nic.in; internet mofpi.nic.in.

Ministry of Health and Family Welfare: Nirman Bhavan, Maulana Azad Rd, New Delhi 110 011; tel. and fax (11) 23061647; fax (11) 23062358; e-mail secyhfw@nic.in; internet mohfw.nic.in.

Ministry of Heavy Industries and Public Enterprises: Udyog Bhavan, New Delhi 110 011; tel. (11) 23061854; fax (11) 23062207; e-mail singh.rk1967@nic.in; internet dhi.nic.in.

Ministry of Home Affairs: North Blk, Central Secr., New Delhi 110 001; tel. (11) 23092011; fax (11) 23093750; e-mail websitemhaweb@nic.in; internet mha.nic.in.

Ministry of Housing and Urban Poverty Alleviation: Nirman Bhavan, Maulana Azad Rd, New Delhi 110 011; tel. (11) 23061444; fax (11) 23061991; e-mail secy-mhupa@nic.in; internet mhupa.gov .in.

Ministry of Human Resource Development: Shastri Bhavan, Dr Rajendra Prasad Rd, New Delhi 110 001; tel. (11) 23383936; fax (11) 23381355; e-mail dsel-mhrd@nic.in; internet mhrd.gov.in.

Ministry of Information and Broadcasting: 'A' Wing, Shastri Bhavan, Dr Rajendra Prasad Rd, New Delhi 110 001; tel. (11) 23382639; fax (11) 23386530; e-mail secy.inb@nic.in; internet mib .gov.in.

Ministry of Labour and Employment: Shram Shakti Bhavan, Rafi Marg, New Delhi 110 001; tel. (11) 23710265; fax (11) 23718730; e-mail m.sarangi@nic.in; internet labour.nic.in.

Ministry of Law and Justice: 'A' Wing, 4th Floor, Shastri Bhavan, Dr Rajendra Prasad Rd, New Delhi 110 001; tel. (11) 23387557; fax (11) 23384241; e-mail vnathan@nic.in; internet lawmin.nic.in.

Ministry of Micro, Small and Medium Enterprises: Udyog Bhavan, Rafi Marg, New Delhi 110 011; tel. (11) 23061431; fax (11) 23063045; e-mail js.sme@nic.in; internet msme.gov.in.

Ministry of Mines: 'A' Wing, 3rd Floor, Shastri Bhavan, Dr Rajendra Prasad Rd, New Delhi; tel. (11) 23385173; fax (11) 23384682; e-mail secy-mines@nic.in; internet mines.nic.in.

Ministry of Minority Affairs: Paryavaran Bhavan, 11th Floor, CGO Complex, Lodhi Rd, New Delhi 110 003; tel. (11) 24364272; fax (11) 24364285; e-mail secy-mma@nic.in; internet minorityaffairs.gov .in.

Ministry of New and Renewable Energy: Blk 14, CGO Complex, Lodhi Rd, New Delhi 110 003; tel. (11) 24361481; fax (11) 24367329; e-mail secy-mnre@nic.in; internet mnes.nic.in.

Ministry of Overseas Indian Affairs: Akbar Bhavan, Chanakyapuri, New Delhi 110 021; tel. (11) 24197900; fax (11) 24197919; e-mail info@moia.nic.in; internet moia.gov.in.

Ministry of Panchayati Raj: Krishi Bhavan, Dr Rajendra Prasad Rd, New Delhi 110 001; tel. (11) 23074309; fax (11) 23389028; e-mail secy-mopr@nic.in; internet www.panchayat.gov.in.

Ministry of Parliamentary Affairs: 87 Parliament House, New Delhi 110 001; tel. (11) 23034844; fax (11) 23017557; e-mail secympa@nic.in; internet mpa.nic.in.

Ministry of Personnel, Public Grievances and Pensions: North Blk, New Delhi 110 001; tel. (11) 23094848; fax (11) 23092432; e-mail secy_mop@nic.in; internet persmin.nic.in.

Ministry of Petroleum and Natural Gas: Shastri Bhavan, Dr Rajendra Prasad Rd, New Delhi 110 001; tel. (11) 23382583; fax (11) 23383100; e-mail jsm.png@nic.in; internet petroleum.nic.in.

Ministry of Power: Shram Shakti Bhavan, Rafi Marg, New Delhi 110 001; tel. (11) 23710271; fax (11) 23721487; e-mail p .umashankar@nic.in; internet powermin.nic.in.

Ministry of Railways: Rail Bhavan, Raisina Rd, New Delhi 110 001; tel. (11) 23385227; fax (11) 23382068; e-mail secyrb@rb.railnet .gov.in; internet www.indianrailways.gov.in.

Ministry of Road Transport and Highways: Parivahan Bhavan, 1 Parliament St, New Delhi 110 001; tel. (11) 23739085; fax (11) 23356669; e-mail wim.rth@nic.in; internet morth.nic.in.

Ministry of Rural Development: Krishi Bhavan, Dr Rajendra Prasad Rd, New Delhi 110 001; tel. (11) 23382230; fax (11) 23382408; e-mail secyrd@nic.in; internet rural.nic.in.

Ministry of Science and Technology: Technology Bhavan, New Mehrauli Rd, New Delhi 110 016; tel. (11) 26567373; fax (11) 26864570; e-mail dstinfo@nic.in; internet dst.gov.in.

Ministry of Shipping: Transport Bhavan, 1 Parliament St, New Delhi 110 001; tel. (11) 23710220; fax (11) 23356713; e-mail secyship@nic.in; internet shipping.gov.in.

Ministry of Skill Development and Entrepreneurship: 2nd Floor, Annexe Bldg Shivaji Stadium, Shaheed Bhagat Singh Marg, Connaught Place, New Delhi 110 001; tel. (11) 23450837; e-mail secy-dsde@nic.in; internet www.skilldevelopment.gov.in.

Ministry of Social Justice and Empowerment: Shastri Bhavan, Dr Rajendra Prasad Rd, New Delhi 110 001; tel. (11) 23382683; fax (11) 23385180; e-mail secywel@nic.in; internet socialjustice.nic.in.

Ministry of Statistics and Programme Implementation: Sardar Patel Bhavan, Patel Chowk, New Delhi 110 001; tel. (11) 23340884; fax (11) 23340138; e-mail srikantjena3@gmail.com; internet mospi.gov.in.

Ministry of Steel: Udyog Bhavan, New Delhi 110 107; tel. (11) 23063417; fax (11) 23063236; e-mail ric-steel@nic.in; internet steel .nic.in.

Ministry of Textiles: Udyog Bhavan, New Delhi 110 011; tel. (11) 23061338; fax (11) 23063711; e-mail secy-ub@nic.in; internet texmin .nic.in.

Ministry of Tourism: Transport Bhavan, Rm 109, 1 Parliament St, New Delhi 110 001; tel. (11) 23711792; fax (11) 23717890; e-mail sectour@nic.in; internet tourism.gov.in.

Ministry of Tribal Affairs: Shastri Bhavan, Dr Rajendra Prasad Rd, New Delhi 110 001; tel. (11) 23388482; fax (11) 23070577; e-mail dirit@tribal.nic.in; internet www.tribal.nic.in.

Ministry of Urban Development: Nirman Bhavan, Maulana Azad Rd, New Delhi 110 011; tel. (11) 23062377; fax (11) 23061459; e-mail secyurban@nic.in; internet moud.gov.in.

Ministry of Water Resources, River Development and Ganga Rejuvenation: Shram Shakti Bhavan, Rafi Marg, New Delhi 110 001; tel. and fax (11) 23715919; e-mail secy-mowr@nic.in; internet wrmin.nic.in.

Ministry of Women and Child Development: Shastri Bhavan, Dr Rajendra Prasad Rd, New Delhi; tel. (11) 23383586; fax (11) 23381495; e-mail secy.wcd@nic.in; internet wcd.nic.in.

Ministry of Youth Affairs and Sports: Shastri Bhavan, Dr Rajendra Prasad Rd, New Delhi 110 001; tel. (11) 23384183; fax (11) 23381898; e-mail minister.yas@nic.in; internet yas.nic.in.

Department of Atomic Energy: Anushakti Bhavan, Chatrapathi Shivaji Maharaj Marg, Mumbai 400 001; tel. (22) 22862702; fax (22) 22048476; e-mail info@dae.gov.in; internet www.dae.gov.in.

Department of Space: Antariksh Bhavan, New BEL Rd, Bengaluru 560 231; tel. (80) 22172296; fax (80) 23511984; e-mail dir.ppr@ isro.gov.in; internet dos.gov.in.

Legislature

PARLIAMENT

Rajya Sabha
(Council of States)

Most of the members of the Rajya Sabha are indirectly elected by the state assemblies for six years, with one-third retiring every two years. The remaining members are nominated by the President.

Rajya Sabha: Parliament House Annexe, New Delhi 110 001; tel. (11) 23034695; fax (11) 23792940; e-mail secygen.rs@sansad.nic.in; internet rajyasabha.nic.in.

Chairman: MOHAMMAD HAMID ANSARI.

Deputy Chairman: P. J. KURIEN.

Distribution of Seats, April 2015

Party	Seats
Congress	68*
Bharatiya Janata Party	47
Samajwadi Party	15
All India Trinamool Congress	12
Janata Dal (United)	12
All-India Anna Dravida Munnetra Kazhagam	11
Bahujan Samaj Party	10
Communist Party of India (Marxist)	9
Biju Janata Dal	7
Nationalist Congress Party	6
Telugu Desam	6
Dravida Munnetra Kazhagam	4
Shiv Sena	3
Shiromani Akali Dal	3
Jammu and Kashmir People's Democratic Party	2
Independents and others	18
Nominated	10
Vacancy	1
Total	**244**

* Including two nominated members.

Lok Sabha
(House of the People)

Lok Sabha: Parliament House Annexe, New Delhi 110 001; tel. (11) 23017465; fax (11) 23792107; e-mail vnathan@sansad.nic.in; internet loksabha.nic.in.

Speaker: SUMITRA MAHAJAN.

Deputy Speaker: MUNISAMY THAMBIDURAI.

General Election, 7, 9–12, 17, 24 and 30 April, and 7 and 12 May 2014

Party	% of votes	Seats
Bharatiya Janata Party *	31.0	282
Congress †	19.3	44
All India Anna Dravida Munnetra Kazhagam	3.3	37
All India Trinamool Congress	3.8	34
Biju Janata Dal	1.7	20
Shiv Sena *	1.9	18
Telugu Desam Party *	2.5	16
Telangana Rashtra Samithi	1.2	11
Communist Party of India (Marxist)	3.2	9
Y. S. R. Congress Party	2.5	9
Nationalist Congress Party †	1.6	6
Lok Jan Shakti Party *	0.4	6
Samajwadi Party	3.4	5
Aam Aadmi Party	2.0	4
Rashtriya Janata Dal †	1.3	4
Shiromani Akali Dal *	0.7	4
All India United Democratic Front	0.4	3
Jammu and Kashmir People's Democratic Party *	<0.1	3
Rashtriya Lok Samta *	0.2	3
Apna Dal *	0.1	2
Indian National Lok Dal	0.5	2
Janata Dal (Secular)	0.7	2
Janata Dal (United)	1.1	2
Jharkhand Mukti Morcha †	0.3	2
Indian Union Muslim League †	0.2	2
Others ‡	13.7	10
Independents	3.0	3
Nominated	—	2§
Total	**100.0**	**545**

* Member of the National Democratic Alliance.

† Member of the United Progressive Alliance.

‡ Other parties elected, with a single seat, included All India Majlis-e-Ittehadul Muslimeen, All India N. R. Congress, Communist Party of India, Kerala Congress (M), Naga People's Front, National People's Party, Pattali Makkal Katchi, Revolutionary Socialist Party, Sikkim Democratic Front and Swabhimani Paksha.

§ Nominated by the President to represent the Anglo-Indian community; as of April 2015 the two Anglo-Indian representatives to the 16th Lok Sabha had yet to be nominated and the seats remained vacant.

State Governments

(Note: Distribution of seats in the state legislatures reflect the results of the most recent state election, except where otherwise indicated.)

ANDHRA PRADESH
(Capital—Hyderabad)

Governor: E. S. L. NARASIMHAN (also Governor of Telangana).

Chief Minister: CHANDRABABU NAIDU (Telugu Desam Party).

Legislative Assembly: 175 seats (at April 2015: Telugu Desam 102, YSR Congress 67, Bharatiya Janata Party 4, Navodyam Party 1, independents 1); last election April–May 2014; following the bifurcation of Andhra Pradesh and the formation of the state of Telangana on 2 June 2014, 119 assembly members were transferred to a new Legislative Assembly of Telangana.

Legislative Council: revived April 2007; 47 seats (at April 2015: Telugu Desam 10, Congress 9, YSR Congress 3, Communist Party of India 1, independents 10, nominated 5, vacant 9).

ARUNACHAL PRADESH
(Capital—Itanagar)

Governor: NIRBHAY SHARMA.

Chief Minister: NABAM TUKI (Congress).

Legislative Assembly: 60 seats (Congress 42, Bharatiya Janata Party 11, People's Party of Arunachal 5, independents 2); last election April 2014.

ASSAM (ASOM)
(Capital—Dispur)

Governor: PADMANABHA BALAKRISHNA ACHARYA.

Chief Minister: TARUN GOGOI (Congress).

Legislative Assembly: 126 seats (at April 2015: Congress 78, All India United Democratic Front 18, Bodoland Peoples Front 12, Asom Gana Parishad 10, Bharatiya Janata Party 5, All India Trinamool Congress 1, independents 2); last election April 2011.

BIHAR
(Capital—Patna)

Governor: KESHARI NATH TRIPATHI.

Chief Minister: NITISH KUMAR (Janata Dal—United).

Legislative Assembly: 243 seats (at April 2015: Janata Dal—United 111, Bharatiya Janata Party 86, Rashtriya Janata Dal 24, Congress 5, Communist Party of India 1, independents 5, vacant 11); last election Oct.–Nov. 2010.

Legislative Council: 75 seats.

CHHATTISGARH
(Capital—Raipur)

Governor: BALRAMJI DASS TANDON.

Chief Minister: Dr RAMAN SINGH (Bharatiya Janata Party).

Legislative Assembly: 91 seats (Bharatiya Janata Party 49, Congress 39, Bahujan Samaj Party 1, independent 1, nominated 1); last election Nov. 2013.

GOA
(Capital—Panaji)

Governor: MRIDULA SINHA.

Chief Minister: LAXMIKANT PARSEKAR (Bharatiya Janata Party).

Legislative Assembly: 40 seats (Bharatiya Janata Party 21, Congress 9, Maharashtrawadi Gomantak Party 3, Goa Vikas Party 2, independents 5); last election March 2012.

GUJARAT
(Capital—Gandhinagar)

Governor: OM PRAKASH KOHLI.

Chief Minister: ANANDIBEN PATEL (Bharatiya Janata Party).

Legislative Assembly: 182 seats (Bharatiya Janata Party 115, Congress 61, Nationalist Congress Party 2, Gujarat Parivartan Party 2, Janata Dal—United 1, independent 1); last election Dec. 2012.

HARYANA
(Capital—Chandigarh)

Governor: KAPTAN SINGH SOLANKI.

Chief Minister: MANOHAR LAL KHATTAR (Bharatiya Janata Party).

Legislative Assembly: 90 seats (Bharatiya Janata Party 47, Indian National Lok Dal 19, Congress 15, Haryana Janhit Congress 2, Bahujan Samaj Party 1, Shiromani Akali Dal 1, independents 5); last election Oct. 2014.

HIMACHAL PRADESH
(Capital—Shimla)

Governor: KALYAN SINGH (acting).

Chief Minister: VIRBHADRA SINGH (Congress).

Legislative Assembly: 68 seats (at April 2015: Congress 36, Bharatiya Janata Party 27, Himachal Lokhit Party 1, independents 4,); last election Nov. 2012.

JAMMU AND KASHMIR
(Capitals—Srinagar (Summer), Jammu (Winter))

Governor: NARENDRA NATH VOHRA.

Chief Minister: Mufti MOHAMMAD SAYEED (People's Democratic Party).

Legislative Assembly: 87 seats (People's Democratic Party 28, Bharatiya Janata Party 25, Jammu and Kashmir National Conference 15, Congress 12, Communist Party of India (Marxist) 1, Jammu and Kashmir People's Democratic Front 1, independents and others 5, nominated 2); last election Nov.–Dec. 2014.

Legislative Council: 36 seats.

JHARKHAND
(Capital—Ranchi)

Governor: Dr SYED AHMED.

Chief Minister: RAGHUBAR DAS (Bharatiya Janata Party).

Legislative Assembly: 81 seats (Bharatiya Janata Party 37, Jharkhand Mukti Morcha 19, Jharkhand Vikas Morcha (Prajatantrik) 8, Congress 6, All Jharkhand Students' Union 5, others 6); last election Nov.–Dec. 2014.

KARNATAKA
(Capital—Bangalore)

Governor: VAJUBHAI RUDABHAI VALA.

Chief Minister: K. SIDDARAMAIAH (Congress).

Legislative Assembly: 225 seats (at January 2015: Congress 122, Bharatiya Janata Party 46, Janata Dal—Secular 40, Badavara Shramikara Raitara (Congress) Party 4, Maharashtra Ekikarana Samiti 2, independents and others 10, nominated 1); last election May 2013.

Legislative Council: 75 seats.

KERALA
(Capital—Thiruvananthapuram)

Governor: P. SATHASIVAM.

Chief Minister: OOMMEN CHANDY (Congress).

Legislative Assembly: 140 seats (Communist Party of India (Marxist) 45, Congress 38, Muslim League Kerala State Committee 20, Communist Party of India 13, Kerala Congress (M) 9, Janata Dal (Secular) 4, National Congress Party 2, Revolutionary Socialist Party 2 and others 7); last election April 2011.

MADHYA PRADESH
(Capital—Bhopal)

Governor: RAM NARESH YADAV.

Chief Minister: SHIVRAJ SINGH CHOUHAN (Bharatiya Janata Party).

Legislative Assembly: 230 seats (Bharatiya Janata Party 165, Congress 58, Bahujan Samaj Party 4, independents 3); last election Nov. 2013.

MAHARASHTRA
(Capital—Mumbai)

Governor: C. VIDYASAGAR RAO.

Chief Minister: DEVENDRA FADNAVIS (Bharatiya Janata Party).

Legislative Assembly: 288 seats (Bharatiya Janata Party 122, Shiv Sena 63, Congress 42, Nationalist Congress Party 41, Bahujan Vikas Aghadi 3, Peasants' and Workers' Party 3, All-India Majlis-e-Ittehadul Muslimeen 2, Bharipa Bahujan Mahasangh 1, Communist Party of India—Marxist 1, Maharashtra Navnirman Sena 1, Rashtriya Samaj Paksha 1, Samajwadi Party 1, independent 7); last election Oct. 2014.

Legislative Council: 78 seats.

MANIPUR
(Capital—Imphal)

Governor: KRISHAN KANT PAUL.

Chief Minister: OKRAM IBOBI SINGH (Congress).

Legislative Assembly: 60 seats (Congress 42, All India Trinamool Congress 7, Manipur State Congress Party 5, Naga People's Front 4, Lok Jan Shakti Party 1, Nationalist Congress Party 1); last election Jan. 2012.

MEGHALAYA
(Capital—Shillong)

Governor: KESHARI NATH TRIPATHI.

Chief Minister: Dr MUKUL M. SANGMA (Congress).

Legislative Assembly: 60 seats (Congress 29, United Democratic Party 8, Hill State People's Democratic Party 4, Nationalist Congress Party 2, National People's Party 2, independents and others 15); last election Feb. 2013.

MIZORAM
(Capital—Aizawl)

Governor: KESHARI NATH TRIPATHI.

Chief Minister: LAL THANHAWLA (Congress).

Legislative Assembly: 40 seats (Congress 34, Mizo National Front 5, Mizo People's Conference 1); last election Nov. 2013.

NAGALAND
(Capital—Kohima)

Governor: PADMANABHA BALAKRISHNA ACHARYA.

Chief Minister: T. R. ZELIANG (Naga People's Front).

Legislative Assembly: 60 seats (at April 2015: Naga People's Front 38, Congress 8, Bharatiya Janata Party 4, Nationalist Congress Party 1, Janata Dal (United) 1, independents 8); last election Feb. 2013.

ODISHA
(Capital—Bhubaneswar)

Governor: S. C. JAMIR.

Chief Minister: NAVEEN PATNAIK (Biju Janata Dal).

Legislative Assembly: 147 seats (Biju Janata Dal 117, Congress 16, Bharatiya Janata Party 10, Communist Party of India 1, Samata Kranti Dal 1, independents 2); last election April 2014.

PUNJAB
(Capital—Chandigarh)

Governor: KAPTAN SINGH SOLANKI (also Administrator of Chandigarh ex officio).

Chief Minister: PARKASH SINGH BADAL (Shiromani Akali Dal).

Legislative Assembly: 117 seats (at April 2015: Shiromani Akali Dal 59, Congress 43, Bharatiya Janata Party 12, independents 3); last election Jan. 2012.

RAJASTHAN
(Capital—Jaipur)

Governor: KALYAN SINGH.

Chief Minister: VASUNDHARA RAJE (Bharatiya Janata Party).

Legislative Assembly: 200 seats (at April 2015: Bharatiya Janata Party 160, Congress 24, National People's Party 4, Bahujan Samaj Party 3, National Unionist Zamindara Party 2, independents 7); last election Dec. 2013.

SIKKIM
(Capital—Gangtok)

Governor: SHRINIWAS DADASAHEB PATIL.

Chief Minister: PAWAN KUMAR CHAMLING (Sikkim Democratic Front).

Legislative Assembly: 32 seats (Sikkim Democratic Front 22, Sikkim Krantikari Morcha 10); last election April 2014.

TAMIL NADU
(Capital—Chennai)

Governor: KONIJETI ROSAIAH.

Chief Minister: O. PANNEERSELVAM (All India Anna Dravida Munnetra Kazhagam).

Legislative Assembly: 235 seats, (All India Anna Dravida Munnetra Kazhagam 150, Desiya Murpokku Dravida Kazhagam 29, Dravida Munnetra Kazhagam 23, Communist Party of India (Marxist) 10, Communist Party of India 9, Congress 5, Pattali Makkal Katchi 3, All India Forward Bloc 1, others 4, nominated 1); last election April 2011.

TELANGANA

Governor: E. S. L. NARASIMHAN (also Governor of Andhra Pradesh).

Chief Minister: K. CHANDRASEKHAR RAO (Telangana Rashtra Samithi).

Legislative Assembly: 119 seats (Telangana Rashtra Samithi 65, Congress 21, Telugu Desam Party 15, All India Majlis-e-Ittehadul Muslimeen 7, Bharatiya Janata Party 5, YSR Congress 3, Communist Party of India (Marxist) 1, Communist Party of India 1, independent 1); last election April–May 2014; following the establishment of Telangana on 2 June 2014, 119 members elected to the Andhra Pradesh Legislative Assembly were transferred to a new Legislative Assembly of Telangana.

Legislative Council: 40 seats.

TRIPURA
(Capital—Agartala)

Governor: PADMANABHA BALAKRISHNA ACHARYA.

Chief Minister: MANIK SARKAR (Communist Party of India—Marxist).

Legislative Assembly: 60 seats (Communist Party of India—Marxist 49, Congress 10, Communist Party of India 1); last election Feb. 2013.

UTTAR PRADESH
(Capital—Lucknow)

Governor: RAM NAIK.

Chief Minister: AKHILESH YADAV (Samajwadi Party).

Legislative Assembly: 404 seats (at April 2015: Samajwadi Party 229, Bahujan Samaj Party 79, Bharatiya Janata Party 40, Congress 28, Rashtriya Lok Dal 8, Peace Party 4, Qaumi Ekta Dal 2, Apna Dal 1, Nationalist Congress Party 1, Ittehad-e-Millat Council 1, All India Trinamool Congress 1, independents 6, nominated 1, vacant 3); last election Feb.–March 2012.

Legislative Council: 100 seats.

UTTARAKHAND
(Capital—Dehradun)

Governor: KRISHAN KANT PAUL.

Chief Minister: HARISH RAWAT (Congress).

Legislative assembly: 71 seats (at April 2015: Congress 36, Bharatiya Janata Party 28, Bahujan Samaj Party 2, Uttarakhand Kranti Dal 1, independents 3, nominated 1); last election Jan. 2012.

WEST BENGAL
(Capital—Kolkata)

Governor: KESHARI NATH TRIPATHI.

Chief Minister: MAMATA BANERJEE (All India Trinamool Congress).

Legislative Assembly: 295 seats (All India Trinamool Congress 184, Congress 42, Communist Party of India—Marxist 40, All India Forward Bloc 11, Revolutionary Socialist Party 6, Gorkha Janmukti Morcha 3, Communist Party of India 2, others 6, nominated 1); last election April–May 2011.

UNION TERRITORIES

Andaman and Nicobar Islands (Headquarters—Port Blair): Lt-Gov. Lt-Gen. (retd) A. K. SINGH.

Chandigarh (Headquarters—Chandigarh): Administrator KAPTAN SINGH SOLANKI (Governor of the Punjab ex officio); Chandigarh was to be incorporated into the Punjab state on 26 January 1986, but the transfer was postponed indefinitely.

Dadra and Nagar Haveli (Headquarters—Silvassa): Administrator ASHISH KUNDRA.

Daman and Diu (Headquarters—Daman): Administrator ASHISH KUNDRA.

Lakshadweep (Headquarters—Kavaratti): Administrator H. RAJESH PRASAD.

Puducherry (Capital—Puducherry): Lt-Gov. Lt-Gen. (retd) A. K. SINGH; Chief Minister THIRU. N. RANGASAMY (All India NR Congress); Legislative Assembly: 30 seats (Congress 7, All India Anna Dravida Munnetra Kazhagam 5, Dravida Munnetra Kazhagam 2 and others 16).

NATIONAL CAPITAL TERRITORY

Delhi (Headquarters—Delhi): Lt-Gov. NAJEEB JUNG; Chief Minister ARVIND KEJRIWAL (Aam Aadmi Party); Legislative Assembly: 70 seats (Aam Aadmi Party 67, Bharatiya Janata Party 3); last election Feb. 2015.

Election Commission

Election Commission of India: Nirvachan Sadan, Ashoka Rd, New Delhi 110 001; tel. (11) 23717391; fax (11) 23717075; e-mail feedbackeci@gmail.com; internet eci.nic.in; f. 1950; independent; Chief Election Commr S. NASIM ZAIDI.

Political Organizations

MAJOR NATIONAL POLITICAL ORGANIZATIONS

Bahujan Samaj Party (Majority Society Party): 12 Gurudwara Rakabganj Rd, New Delhi 110 001; internet www.bspindia.org; f. 1984; promotes the rights of the *Harijans* ('Untouchables') of India; Founder KANSHI RAM; Pres. KUMARI MAYAWATI.

Bharatiya Janata Party (BJP) (Indian People's Party): 11 Ashoka Rd, New Delhi 110 001; tel. (11) 23005700; fax (11) 23005787; e-mail webmaster@bjp.org; internet www.bjp.org; f. 1980 as a breakaway group from Janata Party; right-wing Hindu party; Pres. and Chair. of Parliamentary Party AMIT SHAH; Gen. Secs P. MURALIDHAR RAO, RAM MADHAV, SUSHREE SAROJ PANDEY, BHUPENDER YADAV, RAM LAL; c. 88m. mems.

Communist Party of India (CPI): 15 Ajoy Bhavan, Indrajit Gupta Marg, New Delhi 110 002; tel. (11) 23232801; fax (11) 23235543; e-mail cpiofindia@gmail.com; internet www.communistparty.in; f. 1925; advocates the establishment of a socialist society led by the working class, and ultimately of a communist society; 9-mem. cen. secr; Leader GURUDAS DASGUPTA; Gen. Sec. S. SUDHAKAR REDDY; 486,578 mems (2004).

Communist Party of India—Marxist (CPI—M): A. K. Gopalan Bhavan, 27–29 Bhai Vir Singh Marg, New Delhi 110 001; tel. (11) 23344918; fax (11) 23747483; e-mail cc@cpim.org; internet www .cpim.org; f. 1964; est. after split in the CPI; maintains an ind. position; managed by a cen. cttee of 89 mems and a politburo of 15 mems; Leaders BUDDHADEV BHATTACHARYA, PRAKASH KARAT, SITARAM YECHURY; Gen. Sec. SITARAM YECHURY; 1,044,833 mems (2011).

Indian National Congress (Congress): 24 Akbar Rd, New Delhi 110 011; tel. (11) 23019080; fax (11) 23017047; e-mail connect@inc.in; internet www.inc.in; f. in 1885 as a forum for political debate; subsequently played an active role in the struggle for independence; following independence in 1947, the party remained the dominant force in Indian politics for three decades, under the leadership of Jawaharlal Nehru, Indira Gandhi and others; following a split in the party in 1969, a separate faction was est. under Indira Gandhi, originally known as Indian National Congress (R), then as Indian National Congress (I); name of party gradually reverted to Indian National Congress or, simply, Congress in the early to mid-1990s; Pres. SONIA GANDHI; Vice-Pres. RAHUL GANDHI; Gen. Secs MUKUL WASNIK, JANARDAN DWIVEDI, DIGVIJAYA SINGH, B. K. HARIPRASAD, MADHUSUDAN MISTRY, AJAY MAKEN, AMBIKA SONI, C. P. JOSHI, GURUDAS KAMAT, MOHAN PRAKASH, SHAKEEL AHMED, P. C. CHACKO, V. NARAYANSAMY; 35m. mems (1998).

Nationalist Congress Party (NCP): 10 Dr Bishambhar Das Marg, New Delhi 110 001; tel. (11) 23314414; fax (11) 23352112; e-mail info@ncp.org.in; internet www.ncp.org.in; f. 1999; est. as breakaway faction of Indian National Congress; split into two factions—one headed by Sharad Pawar and the other by Purno Sangma—in Jan. 2004, but was reunified in 2006; Pres. SHARAD PAWAR; Gen. Secs TARIQ ANWAR, T. P. PEETHAMBARAN MASTER, Prof. DEVI PRASAD TRIPATHI, Dr V. RAJESHWARAN, GOVINDRAO ADIK.

MAJOR REGIONAL POLITICAL ORGANIZATIONS

Aam Aadmi Party (AAP): Ground Floor, A-119, Kaushambi, Ghaziabad 201 010; tel. (971) 8500606; e-mail contact@ aamaadmiparty.org; internet www.aamaadmiparty.org; f. 2012; campaigns on an anti-corruption platform; made its electoral debut at the Dec. 2013 legislative assembly elections in Delhi, following which the party briefly headed a minority government in the territory; secured a majority at the Delhi legislative assembly elections of Feb. 2015; Leader ARVIND KEJRIWAL.

All India Anna Dravida Munnetra Kazhagam (AIADMK) (All-India Anna Dravidian Progressive Asscn): 226 Avvai Shanmugam Salai, Roayapettah, Chennai 600 014; tel. (44) 28132266; fax (44) 28133510; e-mail info@aiadmk.com; internet aiadmk.com; f. 1972; breakaway group from the DMK; Leader and Gen. Sec. JAYARAM JAYALALITHA.

All India Trinamool Congress (AITC): 30B Harish Chatterjee St, Kolkata 700 026; tel. (33) 24540881; fax (33) 24540880; e-mail aitmc@ aitmc.org; internet aitmc.org; f. 1998, following split from the Indian National Congress; based in West Bengal; Chair. MAMATA BANERJEE; Gen. Secs MUKUL ROY.

All India United Democratic Front (AIUDF): 3 Friends Path, Hatigaon, Guwahati 781038; f. 2005; fmrly the Assam United Demo-cratic Front; active in Assam and West Bengal; Leader Maulana BADRUDDIN AJMAL.

Asom Gana Parishad (AGP) (Assam People's Council): Gopinath Bordoloi Rd, Guwahati 781 001; tel. and fax (361) 2600536; e-mail party.agp@gmail.com; internet www.asomganaparishad.org; f. 1985; est. as the spearhead political party for groups opposed to illegal immigration into Assam (primarily from Bangladesh); advo-cates constitutional safeguards for Assamese cultural and linguistic identities; Pres. ATUL BORA.

Biju Janata Dal: 6R/3, Unit 6, Forest Park, Bhubaneswar 751 006; tel. and fax (674) 2395979; e-mail president@bijujanatadal.net; internet www.bjdodisha.org.in; f. 1997; dominant party in the legislative assembly of Odisha; Pres. NAVEEN PATNAIK.

Dravida Munnetra Kazhagam (DMK): Anna Arivalayam, 367–369 Anna Salai, Chennai 600 018; e-mail thedmk@vsnl.com; internet www.dmk.in; f. 1949; aims at full autonomy for states (primarily Tamil Nadu) within the Union; Pres. MUTHUVEL KARUNANIDHI; Gen. Sec. K. ANBAZHAGAN; more than 4m. mems.

Indian National Lok Dal: 18 Janpath, New Delhi 110 001; e-mail inldchandigarh@gmail.com; internet www.inld.co.in; fmrly mem. of the National Democratic Alliance; promotes the cause of farmers and labourers of Haryana; Nat. Pres. OM PRAKASH CHAUTALA; Sec.-Gen. AJAY SINGH CHAUTALA.

Jammu and Kashmir National Conference (JKNC): Mujahid Manzil, Nawa-i-Subh Complex Zero Bridge, Srinagar 190 002; tel. (194) 2452326; e-mail contact@jknc.in; internet www.jknc.in; fmrly All Jammu and Kashmir Nat. Conference; f. 1931; renamed 1939, reactivated 1975; state-based party campaigning for internal autonomy and responsible self-govt; Pres. Dr FAROOQ ABDULLAH; Gen. Sec. ALI MOHAMMAD SAGAR; 1m. mems.

Jammu and Kashmir People's Democratic Party: 2 Circuit House, Emporium Lane, Residency Rd, Srinagar; tel. (194) 2483422; internet jkpdp.org; f. 1999; advocates self-rule for Jammu and Kashmir; Pres. MEHBOOBA MUFTI SAYEED.

Janata Dal—Secular (People's Party—Secular): 5 Safdarjung Lane, New Delhi 110 003; tel. (11) 23794499; e-mail jdsecular2013@gmail.com; internet www.jds.ind.in; f. 2000 following split of Janata Dal; active in Karnataka and Kerala; Pres. H. D. DEVE GOWDA; Sec.-Gen. KUNWAR DANISH ALI.

Janata Dal—United (People's Party—United): 7 Jantar Mantar Rd, New Delhi 110 001; tel. (11) 23368833; fax (11) 23368138; e-mail info@janatadalunited.org; internet www.janatadalunited.org; f. 2000; est. following split of Janata Dal; merged with Samata Party in 2003; fmr mem. of National Democratic Alliance; main power base is in Bihar; advocates non-alignment, eradication of poverty, unemployment and wide disparities in wealth, and protec-tion of minorities; Pres. SHARAD YADAV; Leader NITISH KUMAR.

Jharkhand Mukti Morcha: Bariatu Rd, Ranchi 834 009; tel. and fax (651) 2542990; fax (651) 6453012; internet www .jharkhandmuktimorcha.org; aligned with national ruling coalition, the United Progressive Alliance; Leader SHIBU SOREN.

Lok Jan Shakti Party (LJSP): 12 Janpath, Firoz Shah Marg, New Delhi, 110 001; tel. (11) 23015249; fax (11) 23017681; e-mail lokjanshaktiparty@gmail.com; internet www.lokjanshaktiparty.in; f. 2000; est. as breakaway faction of Janata Dal—United; left-wing; Pres. RAM VILAS PASWAN; Sec. Gen. ABDUL KHALIQ.

Rashtriya Janata Dal (RJD) (National People's Party): 13 V. P. House, Rafi Marg, New Delhi 110 001; tel. (11) 23357182; e-mail info@rjd.co.in; internet www.rjd.co.in; f. 1997; est. by breakaway mems of Janata Dal; Leader LALU PRASAD YADAV.

Rashtriya Lok Samta Party: Mohanpur, Punaichak, Boring Canal Rd, Patna 1; f. 2013; active in Bihar; participated in the Nat. Democratic Alliance for 2014 Lok Sabha elections; Chair. UPENDRA KUSHWAHA.

Samajwadi Party (Socialist Party): 18 Copernicus Lane, New Delhi; tel. (11) 23386842; fax (11) 23382430; e-mail samajwadi partynewdelhi@gmail.com; internet www.samajwadiparty.in; f. 1991; the major regional party in Uttar Pradesh; also active in Maharashtra; Pres. MULAYAM SINGH YADAV.

Shiromani Akali Dal (SAD): Blk 6, Madhya Marg, Sector 28, Chandigarh; e-mail contact@shiromaniakalidal.org.in; internet www.shiromaniakalidal.org.in; f. 1920; largest of 6 splinter groups, each of which claims to be the 'real' Akali Dal; a major political force in Punjab province; Pres. (Shiromani Akali Dal—Badal) SUKHBIR SINGH BADAL; Sec.-Gen. SUKHDEV SINGH DHINDSA.

Shiv Sena (Army of Shiv): Shiv Sena Bhavan, Ram Ganesh Gadkari Chowk, Dadar, Mumbai 400 028; tel. (22) 24328181; e-mail mazamaharashtra@shivsena.org; internet www.shivsena.org; f. 1966; militant Hindu group; Bharatiya Kamgar Sena (Indian Workers' Army) affiliated to the party; Pres. UDDHAV THACKERAY.

Sikkim Democratic Front: Upper Deorali, Gangtok, East Sikkim; internet sikkimdemocraticfront.org; f. 1993; Pres. Dr PAWAN KUMAR CHAMLING.

Telangana Rashtra Samithi: Telangana Bhavan, Rd 10, Banjara Hills, Hyderabad 500 034; f. 2001; campaigned for the creation of a new Telangana state through the bifurcation of Andhra Pradesh; Pres. K. CHANDRASEKHAR RAO.

Telugu Desam Party (Telugu Nation): NTR Bhavan, Rd 2, Banjara Hills, Hyderabad 500 034; tel. (40) 30699999; fax (40) 23542108; e-mail contact@telugudesam.org; internet www.telugudesam.org; f. 1983; state-based party (Andhra Pradesh); Pres. N. CHANDRABABU NAIDU; 8m. mems.

YSR Congress Party (Bharathiya Yuvatha, Samatha, Rashtriyatha Congress): Plot 883–884, Rd 45, Jubilee Hills, Hyderabad 500033; tel. (40) 23609191; e-mail helpdesk@ysrcongress.com; internet www.ysrcongress.com; f. 2009; est. mainly by fmr mems of Indian National Congress in Andhra Pradesh; initially supported the est. of the new state of Telangana, but eventually campaigned for a united Andhra Pradesh; Pres. JAGANMOHAN REDDY.

Diplomatic Representation

EMBASSIES AND HIGH COMMISSIONS IN INDIA

Afghanistan: 5/50F Shanti Path, Chanakyapuri, New Delhi 110 021; tel. (11) 26883601; fax (11) 26875439; e-mail delhi@afghanistan-mfa.net; internet www.afghanembassy.in; Ambassador SHAIDA MOHAMMAD ABDALI.

Algeria: 2/2 Shanti Niketan, New Delhi 110 021; tel. (11) 24117585; fax (11) 24117590; e-mail embalgindia@hotmail.com; internet www.embalgindia.com; Ambassador MOHAMMED HACENE ECHARIF.

Angola: 5 Poorvi Marg, Vasant Vihar, New Delhi 110 057; tel. (11) 26146195; fax (11) 26146184; e-mail angolaembassyindia@gmail.com; internet www.angolaembassyindia.com; Ambassador MANUEL EDUARDO DOS SANTOS E SILVA BRAVO.

Argentina: A-2/6 Vasant Vihar, New Delhi 110 057; tel. (11) 41661982; fax (11) 41661988; e-mail embargentindi@yahoo.com; Ambassador RAUL IGNACIO GUASTAVINO.

Armenia: D-133 Anand Niketan, New Delhi 110 057; tel. (11) 24112851; fax (11) 24112853; e-mail info@armenian.co.in; internet www.armenian.co.in; Ambassador ARA HAKOBYAN.

Australia: 1/50G Shanti Path, Chanakyapuri, POB 5210, New Delhi 110 021; tel. (11) 41399900; fax (11) 41494490; e-mail austhighcom.newdelhi@dfat.gov.au; internet www.india.embassy.gov.au; High Commissioner PATRICK MICHAEL SUCKLING.

Austria: EP-13 Chandragupta Marg, Chanakyapuri, New Delhi 110 021; tel. (11) 24192700; fax (11) 26886929; e-mail new-delhi-ob@bmeia.gv.at; internet www.aussenministerium.at/newdelhi; Ambassador BERNHARD WRABETZ.

Azerbaijan: 41 Paschimi Marg, Vasant Vihar, New Delhi 110 057; tel. (11) 24652228; fax (11) 24652227; e-mail newdelhi@mission.mfa.gov.az; internet www.azembassy.in; Ambassador IBRAHIM ASSAD OGLU HAJIYEV.

Bahrain: 42 Poorvi Marg, Vasant Vihar, New Delhi 110 057; tel. (11) 26154153; fax (11) 26146731; e-mail bahrainembindia@yahoo.com; internet www.bahrainembassyindia.com; Ambassador Maj. Gen. TARIQ MUBARAK BIN DAINEH.

Bangladesh: EP-39 Dr S. Radhakrishnan Marg, Chanakyapuri, New Delhi 110 021; tel. (11) 24121389; fax (11) 26878953; e-mail email@bhcdelhi.org; internet www.bhcdelhi.org; High Commissioner Syed MUAZZEM ALI.

Belarus: F-6/8B Vasant Vihar, New Delhi 110 057; tel. (11) 40529338; fax (11) 40529336; e-mail india@mfa.gov.by; internet india.mfa.gov.by/eng; Ambassador VITALY A. PRIMA.

Belgium: 50N Shanti Path, Chanakyapuri, New Delhi 110 021; tel. (11) 42428000; fax (11) 42428002; e-mail newdelhi@diplobel.fed.be; internet www.diplomatie.be/newdelhi; Ambassador JAN LUYKX.

Benin: K-26, Jangpura, New Delhi 110 014; tel. (11) 43074470; fax (11) 43074472; e-mail ambabenindelhi@yahoo.fr; internet www.beninembassy.in; Ambassador ANDRE SANRA.

Bhutan: Chandragupta Marg, Chanakyapuri, New Delhi 110 021; tel. (11) 26889807; fax (11) 26876710; e-mail bhutan@vsnl.com; Ambassador Maj.-Gen. VETSOP NAMGYEL.

Bolivia: A-2/7 Ground Floor, Vasant Vihar, New Delhi 110 057; tel. (11) 46060934; fax (11) 46060935; e-mail coco.cardenas@gmail.com; Ambassador JORGE CÁRDENAS ROBLES.

Bosnia and Herzegovina: E-9/11 Vasant Vihar, New Delhi 110 057; tel. (11) 41662481; fax (11) 41662482; e-mail abhind@gmail.com; Ambassador Dr SABIT SUBASIC.

Botswana: F-8/3 Vasant Vihar, New Delhi 110 057; tel. (11) 46537000; fax (11) 46036191; e-mail botind@gov.bw; internet www.botswanahighcom.in; High Commissioner LESEGO ETHEL MOTSUMI.

Brazil: 8 Aurangzeb Rd, New Delhi 110 011; tel. (11) 23017301; fax (11) 23793684; e-mail brasindi@eth.net; internet www.brazilembassy.in; Ambassador CARLOS SERGIO SOBRAL DUARTE.

Brunei: 4 Poorvi Marg, Vasant Vihar, New Delhi 110 057; tel. (11) 26148340; fax (11) 26142101; e-mail newdelhi.india@mfa.gov.bn; High Commissioner Haji SIDEK BIN Haji ALI.

Bulgaria: 16/17 Chandragupta Marg, Chanakyapuri, New Delhi 110 021; tel. (11) 26115549; fax (11) 26876190; e-mail embassy.delhi@mfa.bg; internet www.mfa.bg/embassies/india; Ambassador PETKO DOYKOV.

Burkina Faso: F2/4 Vasant Vihar, New Delhi 110 057; tel. (11) 26140641; fax (11) 26140630; e-mail embassy@burkinafasoindia.org; internet www.burkinafasoindia.org; Ambassador (vacant).

Burundi: B-4/1, Vasant Vihar, New Delhi 110 057; tel. (11) 46151947; fax (11) 49503170; e-mail ambabudelhi@yahoo.fr; internet www.burundiembassy.in; Ambassador RUBUKA ALOYS.

Cambodia: W-112 Greater Kailash Part II, New Delhi 110 048; tel. (11) 29214435; fax (11) 46016117; e-mail camemb.ind@mfa.gov.kh; Ambassador YOUS MAKANA.

Canada: 7/8 Shanti Path, Chanakyapuri, New Delhi 110 021; tel. (11) 41782000; fax (11) 41782020; e-mail delhi@international.gc.ca; internet www.india.gc.ca; High Commissioner NADIR PATEL.

Chile: A-16/1 Vasant Vihar, New Delhi 110 057; tel. (11) 43100400; fax (11) 43100431; e-mail embassy@chileindia.com; internet chileabroad.gov.cl/india; Ambassador ANDRES BARBE GONZALEZ.

China, People's Republic: 50D Shanti Path, Chanakyapuri, New Delhi 110 021; tel. (11) 26112345; fax (11) 26885486; e-mail chinaemb_in@mfa.gov.cn; internet in.chineseembassy.org; Ambassador LE YUCHENG.

Colombia: 85 Poorvi Marg, Vasant Vihar, New Delhi 110 057; tel. (11) 43202100; fax (11) 43202199; e-mail eindia@cancilleria.gov.co; internet india.embajada.gov.co; Ambassador JUAN ALFREDO PINTO SAAVEDRA.

Congo, Democratic Republic: B-3/61 Safdarjung Enclave, New Delhi 110 029; tel. (11) 26183354; fax (11) 41663152; e-mail poliad@drcembassyinindia.org; internet www.drcembassyinindia.org; Ambassador BALUMUENE NKUNA FRANCOIS.

Costa Rica: C-25, 3rd Floor, Anand Niketan, New Delhi 110 021; tel. (11) 41080810; fax (11) 41080809; e-mail embajadacostarica.india@gmail.com; Ambassador UBALDO GARCIA RUIZ.

Côte d'Ivoire: 63 Poorvi Marg, Vasant Vihar, New Delhi 110 057; tel. (11) 46043000; fax (11) 46043031; e-mail embassy@amb2ci-inde.org; internet www.amb2ci-inde.org; Ambassador SAINY TIEMELE.

Croatia: A-15 West End, New Delhi 110 021; tel. (11) 41663101; fax (11) 24116873; e-mail croemb.new-delhi@mvpei.hr; Ambassador AMIR MUHAREMI.

Cuba: W-124A Greater Kailash Part I, New Delhi 110 048; tel. (11) 29242467; fax (11) 26232469; e-mail embcuind@ndf.vsnl.net.in; internet www.cubadiplomatica.cu/india; Ambassador ABELARDO RAFAEL CUETO SOSA.

Cyprus: D-64, Malcha Marg, Chanakyapuri, New Delhi 110 021; tel. (11) 26111156; fax (11) 26111160; e-mail delhihc@mfa.gov.cy; internet www.mfa.gov.cy/mfa/highcom/highcom_newdelhi.nsf; High Commissioner MARIA MICHAEL.

Czech Republic: 50M Niti Marg, Chanakyapuri, New Delhi 110 021; tel. (11) 24155200; fax (11) 24155270; e-mail newdelhi@embassy.mzv.cz; internet www.mfa.cz/newdelhi; Ambassador MILOSLAV STAŠEK.

Denmark: 11 Golf Links, New Delhi 110 003; tel. (11) 42090700; fax (11) 24602019; e-mail delamb@um.dk; internet www.indien.um.dk; Ambassador FREDDY SVANE.

Djibouti: E-12/6 Vasant Vihar, New Delhi 110 057; tel. (11) 41354491; fax (11) 41354490; e-mail embassyofdjibouti@airtelmail.in; Ambassador SAI ABSIEH WARSAMA.

Dominican Republic: B-1/20, Ground Floor, Vasant Vihar, New Delhi 110 057; tel. (11) 43425000; fax (11) 43425050; e-mail embadom@dr-embassy-india.com; internet www.dr-embassy-india.com; Ambassador FRANK HANS DANNENBERG CASTELLANOS.

Ecuador: B-9/1A Vasant Vihar, New Delhi 110 057; tel. (11) 46011801; fax (11) 46011804; e-mail eecuindia@mmrree.gov.ec; internet www.embassyofecuadortoindia.com; Ambassador FRANK HANS DANNENBERG CASTELLANOS.

Egypt: 1/50M Niti Marg, Chanakyapuri, New Delhi 110 021; tel. (11) 26114096; fax (11) 26885355; e-mail india_emb@mfa.gov.eg; internet www.mfa.gov.eg/english/embassies/egyptian_embassy_india/pages/default.aspx; Ambassador HATEM EL-SAYED TAGELDIN.

El Salvador: F-48, Munirka Marg, Vasant Vihar, New Delhi 110 057; tel. (11) 46088400; fax (11) 46011688; e-mail esembassy@gmail.com; internet embajadaindia.rree.gob.sv; Ambassador GUILLERMO RUBIO FUNES.

Eritrea: C-7/9 Vasant Vihar, New Delhi 110 057; tel. (11) 26146336; fax (11) 26146337; e-mail eriindia@yahoo.co.in; internet www.eritreaembindia.com; Ambassador ALEM TSEHAYE WOLDEMARIAM.

Estonia: C-15 Malcha Marg, Chanakyapuri, New Delhi 110 021; tel. (11) 49488650; fax (11) 49488651; e-mail Embassy.New-Delhi@mfa.ee; internet www.newdelhi.vm.ee; Ambassador VILJAR LUBI.

Ethiopia: 7/50G Satya Marg, Chanakyapuri, New Delhi 110 021; tel. (11) 26119513; fax (11) 26875731; e-mail delethem@yahoo.com; internet www.ethiopianembassy.org.in; Ambassador GENET ZEWDIE.

Fiji: C-1/10, Ground Floor, Vasant Vihar, New Delhi 110 057; tel. (11) 46564574; fax (11) 46564573; e-mail info@fijihc-india.in; internet www.fijihc-india.in; High Commissioner YOGESH KARAN.

Finland: E-3 Nyaya Marg, Chanakyapuri, New Delhi 110 021; tel. (11) 41497500; fax (11) 41497555; e-mail sanomat.nde@formin.fi; internet www.finland.org.in; Ambassador AAPO PÖLHÖ.

France: 2/50E Shanti Path, Chanakyapuri, New Delhi 110 021; tel. (11) 24196100; fax (11) 43196119; e-mail webmaster@france-in-india.org; internet www.ambafrance-in.org; Ambassador FRANÇOIS RICHIER.

Gabon: E-84 Paschimi Marg, Vasant Vihar, New Delhi 110 057; tel. (11) 41012513; fax (11) 41012512; e-mail gabonambainde@yahoo.fr; internet www.gabonembassynewdelhi.com; Ambassador DESIRE KOUMBA.

The Gambia: 7 Olof Palme Marg, 1st Floor, Vasant Vihar, New Delhi 110 057; tel. (11) 46120472; fax (11) 46120471; e-mail gamhighcomdel@hotmail.com; Ambassador DEMBO BADJIE.

Georgia: 115 Jor Bagh, New Delhi 110 003; tel. (11) 47078602; fax (11) 47078603; e-mail delhi.emb@mfa.gov.ge; internet india.mfa.gov.ge; Ambassador LEVAN NIZHARADZE.

Germany: 6/50G Shanti Path, Chanakyapuri, POB 613, New Delhi 110 021; tel. (11) 44199199; fax (11) 26888010; e-mail info@new-delhi.diplo.de; internet www.new-delhi.diplo.de; Ambassador MICHAEL STEINER.

Ghana: 50N Satya Marg, Chanakyapuri, New Delhi 110 021; tel. (11) 24193500; fax (11) 24193525; e-mail ghcindia@vsnl.net; internet www.ghana-mission.co.in; High Commissioner SAMUEL PANYIN YALLEY.

Greece: EP-32 Dr S. Radhakrishnan Marg, Chanakyapuri, New Delhi 110 021; tel. (11) 26880700; fax (11) 26888010; e-mail gremb.del@mfa.gr; internet www.mfa.gr/india; Ambassador IOANNIS E. RAPTAKIS.

Guinea-Bissau: 26 Poorvi Marg, Vasant Vihar, New Delhi 110 057; tel. (11) 46540211; fax (11) 46544440; e-mail ambaguineedelhi@gmail.com; Ambassador ALEXANDRE CECE LOUA.

Guyana: E-7/19 Vasant Vihar, New Delhi 110 057; tel. (11) 41669717; fax (11) 41669714; e-mail hcommguy.del@gmail.com; High Commissioner JAIRAM RONALD GAJRAJ.

Holy See: 50C Niti Marg, Chanakyapuri, New Delhi 110 021 (Apostolic Nunciature); tel. (11) 26889187; fax (11) 26874286; e-mail nuntius@apostolicnunciatureindia.com; internet apostolicnunciatureindia.com; Nuncio Most Rev. SALVATORE PENNACCHIO (Titular Archbishop of Montemarano).

Hungary: Plot 2, 50M Niti Marg, Chanakyapuri, New Delhi 110 021; tel. (11) 26114737; fax (11) 26886742; e-mail mission.del@kum.hu; internet www.mfa.gov.hu/emb/newdelhi; Ambassador SZILVESZTER BUS.

Iceland: 10 Munirka Marg, Vasant Vihar, New Delhi 110 057; tel. (11) 43530300; fax (11) 43530311; e-mail emb.newdelhi@mfa.is; internet www.iceland.org/in; Ambassador THORIR IBSEN.

Indonesia: 50A Kautilya Marg, Chanakyapuri, New Delhi 110 021; tel. (11) 26118642; fax (11) 26886763; e-mail administrasi@indonesianembassy.in; internet www.kemlu.go.id/newdelhi; Ambassador RIZALI WILMAR INDRAKESUMA.

Iran: 5 Barakhamba Rd, New Delhi 110 001; tel. (11) 23329600; fax (11) 23325493; e-mail info@iran-embassy.org.in; internet www.newdelhi.mfa.ir; Ambassador GHOLAMREZA ANSARI.

Iraq: A-15/14 Vasant Vihar, New Delhi 110 057; tel. (11) 26150081; fax (11) 26150083; e-mail dlh1emb@iraqmfamail.com; Ambassador AHMAD TAHSIN AHMAD BERWARI.

Ireland: C-17, Malcha Marg, Chanakyapuri, New Delhi 110 021; tel. (11) 49403200; fax (11) 40591898; e-mail newdelhiembassy@dfa.ie; internet www.embassyofireland.in; Ambassador FEILIM McLAUGHLIN.

Israel: 3 Aurangzeb Rd, New Delhi 110 011; tel. (11) 30414500; fax (11) 30414555; e-mail info@newdelhi.mfa.gov.il; internet delhi.mfa.gov.il; Ambassador DANIEL CARMON.

Italy: 50E Chandragupta Marg, Chanakyapuri, New Delhi 110 021; tel. (11) 26114355; fax (11) 26873889; e-mail ambasciata.newdelhi@esteri.it; internet www.ambnewdelhi.esteri.it; Ambassador DANIELE MANCINI.

Japan: Plots 4–5, 50G Shanti Path, Chanakyapuri, New Delhi 110 021; tel. (11) 26876581; fax (11) 26885587; e-mail jpembjic@nd.mofa.go.jp; internet www.in.emb-japan.go.jp; Ambassador TAKESHI YAGI.

Jordan: N-14 Panchsheel Park, New Delhi 110 017; tel. (11) 24653318; fax (11) 24653353; e-mail jordan@jordanembassyindia.org; internet www.jordanembassyindia.org; Ambassador HASSAN MAHMOUD MUHAMMAD AL-JAWARNEH.

Kazakhstan: 61 Poorvi Marg, Vasant Vihar, New Delhi 110 057; tel. (11) 46007700; fax (11) 46007701; e-mail office@kazembassy.in; internet www.kazakhembassy.in; Ambassador BULAT SARSENBAYEV.

Kenya: D-1/27 Vasant Vihar, New Delhi 110 057; tel. (11) 26146537; fax (11) 26146550; e-mail info@kenyahicom-delhi.com; internet www.kenyahicom-delhi.com; High Commissioner FLORENCE IMISA WECHE.

Korea, Democratic People's Republic: E-455 Greater Kailash Part II, New Delhi 110 048; tel. (11) 29219644; fax (11) 29219645; e-mail dprk194899@yahoo.com; Ambassador KYE CHUN YONG.

Korea, Republic: 9 Chandragupta Marg, Chanakyapuri Ext., New Delhi 110 021; tel. (11) 42007000; fax (11) 26884840; e-mail india_visa@mofa.go.kr; internet ind.mofa.go.kr; Ambassador LEE JOON-GYU.

Kuwait: 5A Shanti Path, Chanakyapuri, New Delhi 110 021; tel. (11) 24100791; fax (11) 26873516; e-mail new_delhi@mofa.gov.kw; internet www.kuwaitembassy.in; Ambassador SAMI MOHAMMAD AL-SULAIMAN.

Kyrgyzstan: 78 Poorvi Marg, Vasant Vihar, New Delhi 110 057; tel. (11) 26149582; fax (11) 24118009; e-mail delhi@kgzembind.in; internet www.kgzembind.in; Ambassador. SAMARGIUL ADAMKULOVA.

Laos: A-104/7 Parmanand Estate, Maharani Bagh, New Delhi 110 065; tel. (11) 41327352; fax (11) 41327353; e-mail boualyrone_delhi@yahoo.com; Ambassador SOUTHAM SAKONNINHOM.

Lebanon: H-1 Anand Niketan, New Delhi 110 021; tel. (11) 24110919; fax (11) 24110818; e-mail lebemb2013@gmail.com; Ambassador WAJIB ABDEL SAMAD.

Lesotho: 26 Poorvi Marg, New Delhi 110 057; tel. (11) 41660713; fax (11) 26141636; e-mail lesotho.newdelhi@gov.ls; High Commissioner BOTHATA TSIKOANE.

Libya: 22 Golf Links, New Delhi 110 003; tel. (11) 24697717; fax (11) 24633005; e-mail libya_bu_ind@yahoo.com; Ambassador ALI ABD AL-AZIZ AL-ISAWI.

Lithuania: D-129 C-93 Anand Niketan, New Delhi 110 021; tel. (11) 43132200; fax (11) 43132222; e-mail amb.in@urm.lt; internet in.mfa.lt; Ambassador LAIMONAS TALAT KELPŠA.

Luxembourg: 84 Jor Bagh, New Delhi 110 003; tel. (11) 49986600; fax (11) 41525201; e-mail newdelhi.amb@mae.etat.lu; internet newdelhi.mae.lu; Ambassador SAM SCHREINER.

Macedonia, former Yugoslav republic: A-15/30, Blk A, Vasant Vihar, New Delhi 110 057; tel. (11) 46142603; fax (11) 46142604; e-mail embassy.macedonia@gmail.com; internet www.macedoniaindia.com; Ambassador TONI ATANASOVSKI.

Madagascar: 781 Nikka Singh Block, Asian Games Village, New Delhi 110 049; tel. (11) 41067747; fax (11) 66173222; e-mail contact@madagascar-embassy.in; Chargé d'affaires a.i. MARIE LEONTINE RAZANADRASOA.

Malawi: C-6/11, Vasant Vihar, New Delhi 110 057; tel. (11) 26706000; fax (11) 26706010; e-mail malawihcindia@gmail.com; internet www.malawi-india.org; High Commissioner Dr PERKS M. LIGOYA.

Malaysia: 50M Satya Marg, Chanakyapuri, New Delhi 110 021; tel. (11) 26111291; fax (11) 26881538; e-mail maldelhi@kln.gov.my; internet www.kln.gov.my/perwakilan/newdelhi; High Commissioner Datuk NAIMUN ASHAKLI MOHAMMAD.

Maldives: B-2 Anand Niketan, New Delhi 110 021; tel. (11) 41435701; fax (11) 41435709; e-mail admin@maldiveshighcom.in; internet www.maldiveshighcom.in; High Commissioner AHMED MOHAMED (designate).

Mali: A-2/29 Safdarjung Enclave, New Delhi 110 029; tel. (11) 41090624; fax (11) 41090620; e-mail info@maliembassy.co.in; internet www.maliembassy.co.in; Ambassador OUSMANE TANDIA.

Malta: N-60 Panchsheel Park, New Delhi 110 017; tel. (11) 47674900; fax (11) 47674949; e-mail maltahighcommission.newdelhi@gov.mt; High Commissioner JOHN AQUILINA.

Mauritius: EP-41 Jesus and Mary Marg, Chanakyapuri, New Delhi 110 021; tel. (11) 24102161; fax (11) 24102194; e-mail mhcnd@bol.net.in; High Commissioner ARYE KUMAR JAGESSUR.

Mexico: C-8 Anand Niketan, New Delhi 110 021; tel. (11) 24107182; fax (11) 24117193; e-mail contact@embmexin.com; internet embamex.sre.gob.mx/india/index.php/en; Ambassador JAIME NUALART.

Mongolia: 34 Archbishop Makarios Marg, New Delhi 110 003; tel. (11) 24631728; fax (11) 24633240; e-mail mongemb@vsnl.net; Ambassador SANJAASÜRENGIIN BAYARA.

Morocco: 46 Sunder Nagar, New Delhi 110 003; tel. (11) 24355582; fax (11) 24355579; e-mail ambassador@moroccoembassyin.org; Ambassador LARBI REFFOUH.

Mozambique: B-3/24 Vasant Vihar, New Delhi 110 057; tel. (11) 26156663; fax (11) 26156665; e-mail hcmozind@hclinfinet.com; High Commissioner JOSÉ MARÍA DA SILVA VIEIRA MORAIS.

Myanmar: 3/50F Nyaya Marg, Chanakyapuri, New Delhi 110 021; tel. (11) 24678822; fax (11) 24678824; e-mail myandelhi@gmail.com; internet myanmedelhi.com; Ambassador AUNG KHIN SOE.

Namibia: E-86 Paschimi Marg, Vasant Vihar, New Delhi 110 057; tel. (11) 26140389; fax (11) 26146120; e-mail nam@nhcdelhi.com; internet www.nhcdelhi.com; Ambassador PIUS DUNAISKI.

Nepal: Barakhamba Rd, New Delhi 110 001; tel. (11) 23327361; fax (11) 23329647; e-mail mail@nepalembassy.in; internet www.nepalembassy.in; Chargé d'affaires a.i. KRISHNA PRASAD DHAKAL.

Netherlands: 6/50F Shanti Path, Chanakyapuri, New Delhi 110 021; tel. (11) 24197600; fax (11) 24197710; e-mail nde@minbuza.nl; internet india.nlembassy.org; Ambassador ALPHONSUS H. M. STOELINGA.

New Zealand: Sir Edmund Hillary Marg, Chanakyapuri, New Delhi 110 021; tel. (11) 46883170; fax (11) 46883165; e-mail nzhcindia@gmail.com; internet www.nzembassy.com/india; High Commissioner GRAHAME MORTON.

Nigeria: EP-4 Chandragupta Marg, Chanakyapuri, New Delhi 110 021; tel. (11) 24122142; fax (11) 24122138; e-mail nhcnder@nigeriahighcommissionindia.org; internet www.nigeriahighcommissionindia.org; High Commissioner NDUBUISI VITUS AMAKU.

Norway: 50C Shanti Path, Chanakyapuri, New Delhi 110 021; tel. (11) 41779200; fax (11) 41363200; e-mail emb.newdelhi@mfa.no; internet www.norwayemb.org.in; Ambassador EIVIND S. HOMME.

Oman: EP-10/11 Chandragupta Marg, Chankyapuri, New Delhi 110 021; tel. (11) 26885622; fax (11) 26885621; e-mail newdelhi@mofa.gov.om; internet www.omanembassy.in; Ambassador Sheikh HAMED BIN SAIF BIN ABDUL AZIZ AL-RAWAHI.

Pakistan: 2/50G Shanti Path, Chanakyapuri, New Delhi 110 021; tel. (11) 26110601; fax (11) 26872339; e-mail pahicnewdelhi@mofa.gov.pk; High Commissioner ABDUL BASIT.

Panama: 3D Palam Marg, Vasant Vihar, New Delhi 110 057; tel. (11) 26148268; fax (11) 26148261; e-mail panaind@bol.net.in; Ambassador JULIO DE LA GUARDIA ARROCHA.

Papua New Guinea: B-2/19 Vasant Vihar, 1st Floor, New Delhi 110 057; tel. (11) 46012813; fax (11) 46012812; e-mail kundund@yahoo.com; internet www.pnghcdelhi.in; High Commissioner TARCISIUS A. ERI.

Paraguay: B-11 Vasant Marg, Vasant Vihar, New Delhi 110 057; tel. (11) 42705671; fax (11) 42705672; e-mail delhi@embaparindia.in; internet www.paraguayembassy.in; Ambassador BRIGIDO LEZCANO.

Peru: F-3/16, Vasant Vihar, New Delhi 110 057; tel. (11) 46163333; fax (11) 46163301; e-mail admin@embassyperuindia.in; internet www.embassyperuindia.in; Ambassador JAVIER MANUAL PAULINICH VELARDE.

Philippines: 50N Nyaya Marg, Chanakyapuri, New Delhi 110 021; tel. (11) 26889091; fax (11) 26876401; e-mail newdelhipe@bol.net.in; internet www.newdelhipe.com; Ambassador BENITO B. VALERIANO.

Poland: 50M Shanti Path, Chanakyapuri, New Delhi 110 021; tel. (11) 41496900; fax (11) 26871914; e-mail info@newdelhi.polemb.net; internet www.newdelhi.polemb.net; Ambassador TOMASZ LUKASZUK.

Portugal: 4 Panchsheel Marg, Chanakyapuri, New Delhi 110 021; tel. (11) 46071001; fax (11) 4607103; e-mail embassy@portugal-india.com; internet www.portugal-india.com/en; Ambassador JORGE ROZA DE OLIVEIRA.

Qatar: EP-31A Chandragupta Marg, Chanakyapuri, New Delhi 110 021; tel. (11) 26117988; fax (11) 26886080; e-mail newdelhi@mofa.gov.qa; Ambassador AHMED IBRAHIM ABDULLA AL-ABDULLA.

Romania: D-6/6 Vasant Vihar, New Delhi 110 057; tel. (11) 26140447; fax (11) 26140611; e-mail newdelhi@mae.ro; internet newdelhi.mae.ro; Chargé d'affaires a.i. RADU OCTAVIAN DOBRE.

Russian Federation: Shanti Path, Chanakyapuri, New Delhi 110 021; tel. (11) 26873799; fax (11) 26876823; e-mail rucoembassy.in; internet www.india.mid.ru; Ambassador ALEXANDER M. KADAKIN.

Rwanda: 41 Paschimi Marg, Vasant Vihar, New Delhi 110 057; tel. (11) 28661604; fax (11) 28661605; e-mail rwandaembassy@yahoo.com; internet india.embassy.gov.rw; High Commissioner ERNEST RWAMUCYO.

Saudi Arabia: 2 Paschimi Marg, Vasant Vihar, New Delhi 110 057; tel. (11) 43244444; fax (11) 26144244; e-mail inemb@mofa.gov.sa; internet www.saudiembassy.org.in; Ambassador SAUD BIN MOHAMMED AL-SATI.

Senegal: D-6/32, Vasant Vihar, New Delhi 110 057; tel. (11) 26734400; fax (11) 26142422; e-mail embassy@seninindia.org; internet www.embseninindia.org; Ambassador AMADOU MOUSTAPHA DIOUF.

Serbia: 3/50G Niti Marg, Chanakyapuri, New Delhi 110 021; tel. (11) 26873661; fax (11) 26885535; e-mail embassyofserbianewdelhi@hotmail.com; internet www.newdelhi.mfa.gov.rs; Ambassador VLADMIR MARIC.

Seychelles: F-4 Anand Niketan, New Delhi 110 021; tel. (11) 26658853; fax (11) 26658852; e-mail seychelleshighcommission@gmail.com; High Commissioner WAVEN WILLIAM.

Singapore: E-6 Chandragupta Marg, Chanakyapuri, New Delhi 110 021; tel. (11) 46000800; fax (11) 46016413; e-mail singhc_del@sgmfa.gov.sg; internet www.mfa.gov.sg/newdelhi; High Commissioner LIM THUAN KUAN.

Slovakia: 50M Niti Marg, Chanakyapuri, New Delhi 110 021; tel. (11) 26889071; fax (11) 26877941; e-mail emb.delhi@mzv.sk; internet www.newdelhi.mfa.sk; Ambassador ŽIGMUND BERTÓK.

Slovenia: A-5/4, Vasant Vihar, New Delhi 110 057; tel. (11) 41662891; fax (11) 41662895; e-mail vnd@gov.si; internet newdelhi.embassy.si; Ambassador DARJA BAVDAZ KURET.

Somalia: D-47, Anand Niketan, New Delhi 110 021; tel. (11) 28034177; fax (11) 45510250; e-mail webmaster@somaligov.net; internet www.india.somaligov.net; Ambassador EBYAN LADANE.

South Africa: B-18 Vasant Marg, Vasant Vihar, New Delhi 110 057; tel. (11) 26149411; fax (11) 26148605; e-mail highcommissioner@sahc-india.com; internet southafricainindia.wordpress.com; High Commissioner FRANCE KOSINYANE MORULE.

South Sudan: Farm House, 50D Radhey Mohan Dr., Bandh Rd, Jonapur, New Delhi 110 047; tel. (11) 66545656; fax (11) 66545666; e-mail embassyssindia@gmail.com; Ambassador DANIEL PETER OTHOL.

Spain: 12 Prithviraj Rd, New Delhi 110 011; tel. (11) 41293000; fax (11) 41293020; e-mail emb.nuevadelhi@maec.es; Ambassador GUSTAVO MANUEL DE ARISTEGUI Y SAN ROMAN.

Sri Lanka: 27 Kautilya Marg, Chanakyapuri, New Delhi 110 021, tel. (11) 23010201; fax (11) 23793604; e-mail lankacomnd@mea.gov.lk; internet www.slhcindia.org; High Commissioner SUDARSHAN SENEVIRATNE.

Sudan: Plot 3, Shanti Path, Chanakyapuri, New Delhi 110 021; tel. (11) 26873785; fax (11) 26883758; e-mail admin@sudanembassyindia.org; internet www.sudanembassyindia.org; Ambassador HASSAN EISA EL TALIB.

Suriname: A-15/27, Vasant Vihar, New Delhi 110 057; tel. (11) 26150153; fax (11) 26150150; e-mail amb.india@foreignaffairs.gov.sr; internet www.embsurnd.com; Ambassador AASHNA WANDANI RADHA KANHAI.

Sweden: 4–5 Nyaya Marg, Chanakyapuri, New Delhi 110 021; tel. (11) 44197100; fax (11) 44197101; e-mail ambassaden.new-delhi@foreign.ministry.se; internet www.swedenabroad.se/newdelhi; Ambassador HARALD SANDBERG.

Switzerland: Nyaya Marg, Chanakyapuri, New Delhi 110 021; tel. (11) 49959500; fax (11) 49959509; e-mail ndh.vertretung@eda.admin.ch; internet www.eda.admin.ch/newdelhi; Ambassador LINUS VON CASTELMUR.

Syria: D-5/8 Vasant Vihar, New Delhi 110 057; tel. (11) 26140233; fax (11) 26143107; e-mail embsyriadel@rediffmail.com; Ambassador RIAD KAMEL ABBAS.

Tajikistan: E-13/2 Vasant Vihar, New Delhi 110 057; tel. and fax (11) 26154282; fax 26154282; e-mail tajembindia@gmail.com; internet www.tajikembassy.in; Ambassador MIRZOSHARIF JALOLOV.

Tanzania: EP-15C Chanakyapuri, New Delhi 110 021; tel. (11) 24122864; fax (11) 24122862; e-mail info@tanzrepdelhi.com; internet www.tanzrepdelhi.com; High Commissioner JOHN W. H. KIJAZI.

Thailand: D-1/3 Vasant Vihar, New Delhi 110 057; tel. (11) 26150130; fax (11) 26150128; e-mail thaidel@mfa.go.th; internet www.thaiemb.org.in; Ambassador CHALIT MANITYAKUL.

Trinidad and Tobago: B-3/26 Vasant Vihar, New Delhi 110 057; tel. (11) 46007500; fax (11) 46007505; e-mail info@hctt.in; internet www.hctt.net; High Commissioner CHANDRADATH SINGH.

Tunisia: B-1/2 Vasant Vihar, New Delhi 110 057; tel. (11) 26145346; fax (11) 26145301; e-mail tunisiaembassy@airtelbroadband.in; Ambassador TAREK AZOUZ.

Turkey: 50N Nyaya Marg, Chanakyapuri, New Delhi 110 021; tel. (11) 26890054; fax (11) 26881409; e-mail embassy.newdelhi@mfa.gov.tr; internet yenidelhi.be.mfa.gov.tr; Ambassador Dr BURAK AKCAPAR.

Turkmenistan: C-11 West End Colony, Chanakyapuri, New Delhi 110 021; tel. (11) 24116527; fax (11) 24116526; e-mail tmemb.ind2@

gmail.com; internet www.turkmenembassy.in; Ambassador PARA-KHAT HOMMADOVICH DURDYEV.

Uganda: B-3/26, Vasant Vihar, New Delhi 110 057; tel. (11) 26144413; fax (11) 26144405; e-mail ughcom@ndb.vsnl.net.in; High Commissioner ELIZABETH PAULA NAPEYOK.

Ukraine: E-1/8 Vasant Vihar, New Delhi 110 057; tel. (11) 26146041; fax (11) 26146043; e-mail emb_in@mfa.gov.ua; internet india.mfa .gov.ua; Ambassador OLEKSANDR D. SHEVCHENKO.

United Arab Emirates: EP-12 Chandragupta Marg, Chanakya-puri, New Delhi 110 021; tel. (11) 26111111; fax (11) 26873272; e-mail newdelhi@mofa.gov.ae; internet www.uaeembassy-newdelhi.com; Chargé d'affaires a.i. SAEED MUHAMMAD AL-MOUHAIRI.

United Kingdom: Shanti Path, Chanakyapuri, New Delhi 110 021; tel. (11) 24192100; fax (11) 24192411; e-mail web.newdelhi@fco.gov .uk; internet www.gov.uk/world/india; High Commissioner JAMES BEVAN.

USA: Shanti Path, Chanakyapuri, New Delhi 110 021; tel. (11) 24198000; fax (11) 24190017; e-mail ndwebmail@state.gov; internet newdelhi.usembassy.gov; Ambassador RICHARD RAHUL VERMA.

Uruguay: B-8/3 Vasant Vihar, New Delhi 110 057; tel. (11) 26151991; fax (11) 26144306; e-mail uruind@del3.vsnl.net.in; Ambassador CARLOS E. ORLANDO BONET.

Uzbekistan: EP-40 Dr S. Radhakrishnan Marg, Chanakyapuri, New Delhi 110 021; tel. (11) 24670774; fax (11) 24670773; e-mail info@uzbekembassy.in; internet www.uzbekembassy.in; Ambas-sador Dr SALIKH INAGAMOV.

Venezuela: E-106 Malcha Marg, Chanakyapuri, New Delhi 110 021; tel. (11) 41680218; fax (11) 41750743; e-mail embassy@ embaveneindia.com; internet www.embaveneindia.com; Ambas-sador MILENA SANTANA-RAMÍREZ.

Viet Nam: 20 Kautilya Marg, Chanakyapuri, New Delhi 110 021; tel. (11) 26879852; fax (11) 26879869; e-mail ebsvnin@yahoo.com.vn; internet www.mofa.gov.vn/vnemb.india; Ambassador TON SINH THANH.

Yemen: D-2/5 Vasant Vihar, New Delhi 110 057; tel. (11) 42705723; fax (11) 42705725; e-mail info@yemeninindia.com; Ambassador KHADIJA RADMAN MOHAMED GHANEM.

Zambia: D-5/4, Vasant Vihar, New Delhi 110 057; tel. (11) 26145883; fax (11) 26145764; e-mail zambiand@sify.com; High Commissioner Brig. Gen. PATRICK RUMEDYO TEMBO.

Zimbabwe: 4 Aradhana Enclave, Sector 13, R. K. Puram, New Delhi 110 066; tel. (11) 26110430; fax (11) 26114316; e-mail info@zimdelhi .com; internet zimdelhi.net; Ambassador JONATHAN WUTAWUNASHE.

Judicial System

THE SUPREME COURT

The Supreme Court, consisting of a Chief Justice and a maximum of 30 other judges appointed by the President, exercises exclusive jurisdiction in any dispute between the Union and the states (although there are certain restrictions where an acceding state is involved). It has appellate jurisdiction over any judgment, decree or order of the High Court where that Court certifies that either a substantial question of law or the interpretation of the Constitution is involved. The Supreme Court can enforce fundamental rights and issue writs covering habeas corpus, mandamus, prohibition, quo warranto and certiorari. The Supreme Court is a court of record and has the power to punish for its contempt.

Provision is made for the appointment by the Chief Justice of India of judges of High Courts as ad hoc judges at sittings of the Supreme Court for specified periods, and for the attendance of retired judges at sittings of the Supreme Court. The Supreme Court has advisory jurisdiction in respect of questions which may be referred to it by the President for opinion. The Supreme Court is also empowered to hear appeals against a sentence of death passed by a State High Court in reversal of an order of acquittal by a lower court, and in a case in which a High Court has granted a certificate of fitness.

The Supreme Court also hears appeals that are certified by High Courts to be fit to be heard, subject to rules made by the Court. Parliament may, by law, confer on the Supreme Court any further powers of appeal.

The judges hold office until the age of 65 years.

Supreme Court: Tilak Marg, New Delhi 110 001; tel. (11) 23388942; fax (11) 23381508; e-mail supremecourt@nic.in; internet supremecourtofindia.nic.in.

Chief Justice: HANDYALA L. DATTU.

Attorney-General: MUKUL ROHATGI.

Solicitor-General: RANJIT KUMAR.

HIGH COURTS

The High Courts are the Courts of Appeal from the lower courts, and their decisions are final except in cases where appeal lies with the Supreme Court.

LOWER COURTS

Provision is made in the Code of Criminal Procedure for the consti-tution of lower criminal courts called Courts of Session and Courts of Magistrates. The Courts of Session are competent to try all persons duly committed for trial, and inflict any punishment authorized by the law. The President and the local government concerned exercise the prerogative of mercy.

The constitution of inferior civil courts is determined by regula-tions within each state.

Religion

BUDDHISM

The Buddhists in Ladakh (Jammu and Kashmir) are followers of the Dalai Lama. The Buddhists in Sikkim are followers of Mahayana Buddhism. In 2001 there were 8.0m. Buddhists in India, represent-ing 0.8% of the population.

Mahabodhi Society of India: 4-A, Bankim Chatterjee St, Kolkata 700 073; tel. and fax (33) 22415214; fax (33) 22199294; e-mail info@ mahabodhisociety.in; internet www.mahabodhisociety.in; f. 1891; 11 centres in India, 5 centres worldwide; Pres. PRASANNA JAYASURIYA; Gen. Sec. P. SEEWALEE THERO.

HINDUISM

In 2001 there were 827.6m. Hindus in India, representing 80.5% of the population.

Rashtriya Swayamsevak Sangh (RSS) (National Volunteer Organization): Keshav Kunj, Jhandewala, D. B. Gupta Marg, New Delhi 110 055; tel. (11) 23611372; fax (11) 23611385; e-mail contactus@rss.org; internet www.rss.org; f. 1925; 934,000 service centres in tribal, rural and urban slum areas; 58,000 working centres; Pres. MOHAN BHAGWAT; Gen. Sec. SURESH BHAIYYAJI JOSHI.

Sarvadeshik Arya Pratinidhi Sabha: 15 Hanuman Rd, New Delhi 110 001; tel. (11) 23274771; e-mail aryasabha@seshik.com; internet www.thearyasamaj.org/sarvadeshiksabha; f. 1875 by Maharishi Dayanand Saraswati; the international body for Arya Samaj temples propagating reforms in all fields on the basis of Vedic principles; Pres. ACHARYA BALDEV; Sec. PRAKASH ARYA Adv.

Vishwa Hindu Parishad (VHP) (World Hindu Council): Sankat Mochan Ashram, Ramakrishna Puram Sector 6, New Delhi 110 022; tel. (11) 26178992; fax (11) 26195527; e-mail info@vhp.org; internet www.vhp.org; f. 1964, banned in Dec. 1992–June 1993 for its role in the destruction of the Babri mosque in Ayodhya; Pres. G. RAGHAVENDRA REDDY; Sec.-Gen. CHAMPAT RAI.

ISLAM

Muslims are divided into two main sects, Shi'as and Sunnis. Most of the Indian Muslims are Sunnis. At the 2001 census Islam had 138.2m. adherents (13.4% of the population).

Jamiat Ulama-i-Hind (Assembly of Muslim Religious Leaders of India): 1 Bahadur Shah Zafar Marg, New Delhi 110 002; tel. (11) 23311455; fax (11) 23316173; e-mail jamiat@vsnl.com; internet www .jamiatulamaihind.net; f. 1919; Pres MAULANA QARI MOHAMMAD USMAN MANSOORPURI; Gen. Sec. Maulana MAHMOOD MADANI.

SIKHISM

In 2001 there were 19.2m. Sikhs (comprising 1.9% of the population), the majority living in the Punjab.

Shiromani Gurdwara Parbandhak Committee: Darbar Sahab, Amritsar 143 001; tel. (183) 2553957; fax (183) 2553919; e-mail info@ sgpc.net; internet www.sgpc.net; f. 1925; highest authority in Sikhism; Pres. Jathedar AVTAR SINGH; Sec. SARDAR DALMEGH SINGH.

CHRISTIANITY

According to the 2001 census, Christians represented 2.3% of the population in India.

National Council of Churches in India: Christian Council Lodge, Civil Lines, POB 205, Nagpur 440 001; tel. (712) 2531312; fax (712) 2520554; e-mail ncci@nccindia.in; internet www.nccindia.in; f. 1914; mems: 30 protestant and orthodox churches, 17 regional Christian councils, 17 all-India ecumenical orgs, 7 related agencies and 3 autonomous bodies; represents c. 13m. mems; Pres. Bishop Dr TARANATH S. SAGAR; Gen. Sec. Bishop Dr ROGER GAIKWAD.

Orthodox Churches

Malankara Orthodox Syrian Church: Devalokam, Kottayam 686 038; tel. (481) 2578500; fax (481) 2570569; e-mail catholicos@mosc.in; internet malankaraorthodoxchurch.in; c. 3m. mems (2012); 31 bishops, 30 dioceses, 2,000 parishes; Catholicos of the East and Malankara Metropolitan HH BASELIOS MARTHOMA PAULOSE II.

Mar Thoma Syrian Church of Malabar: Tiruvalla 689 101; tel. (469) 2630449; fax (469) 2630327; e-mail sabhaoffice@marthoma.in; internet www.marthomasyrianchurch.org; c. 1m. mems (2001); Valiya Metropolitan Most Rev. Dr PHILIPOSE MAR CHRYSOSTOM; Sec. Rev. P. T. THOMAS.

The Malankara Jacobite Syrian Orthodox Church is also represented.

Protestant Churches

Church of North India (CNI): CNI Bhavan, 16 Pandit Pant Marg, New Delhi 110 001; tel. (11) 43214000; fax (11) 43214006; e-mail alwanmasih@cnisynod.org; internet www.cnisynod.org; f. 1970 by merger of the Church of India (Anglican—fmrly known as the Church of India, Pakistan, Burma and Ceylon), the Council of the Baptist Churches in Northern India, the Methodist Church (British and Australasian Conferences), the United Church of Northern India (a union of Presbyterians and Congregationalists, f. 1924), the Church of the Brethren in India, and the Disciples of Christ; comprises 27 dioceses; c. 1.5m. mems (2014); Moderator Most Rev. Dr PRADEEP KUMAR SAMANTAROY (Bishop of Amritsar); Gen. Sec. ALWAN MASIH.

Church of South India (CSI): CSI Centre, 5 Whites Rd, Chennai 600 014; tel. (44) 28521566; fax (44) 28523528; e-mail info@csisynod.com; internet www.csisynod.com; f. 1947 by merger of the Weslyan Methodist Church in South India, the South India United Church (itself a union of churches in the Congregational and Presbyterian/Reformed traditions) and the 4 southern dioceses of the (Anglican) Church of India; comprises 22 dioceses (incl. one in Sri Lanka); c. 3.8m. mems (2009); Moderator Most Rev. G. DYVASIRVADAM; Gen. Sec. Rev. D. R. SADANANDA.

Methodist Church in India: Methodist Centre, 21 YMCA Rd, Mumbai 400 008; tel. (22) 23094316; fax (22) 23074137; e-mail gensecmci@vsnl.com; f. 1856 as the Methodist Church in Southern Asia; 648,000 mems (2005); Gen. Sec. Rev. MUNNAGI ALFRED DANIEL.

Samavesam of Telugu Baptist Churches: A. D. M. Compound, Kavali 524 201; tel. (8626) 241363; fax (8626) 241847; e-mail stbcpabc@yahoo.com; f. 1962; comprises 2,000 independent Baptist churches; 578,295 mems (1995); Gen. Sec. Dr J. M. FRANKLIN.

United Evangelical Lutheran Churches in India: Martin Luther Bhavan, 95 Purasawalkam High Rd, Kilpauk, Chennai 600 010; tel. (44) 26430008; fax (44) 26611364; e-mail augustinejkumar@uelci.org; internet www.uelci.org; f. 1975; 12 constituent denominations: Andhra Evangelical Lutheran Church, Arcot Lutheran Church, Evangelical Lutheran Church in Madhya Pradesh, Evangelical Lutheran Church in the Himalayan States, Good Shepherd Evangelical Lutheran Church, Gossner Evangelical Lutheran Church in Chotanagpur and Assam (Asom), India Evangelical Lutheran Church, Jeypore Evangelical Lutheran Church, Nepal Northern Evangelical Lutheran Church, Northern Evangelical Lutheran Church, South Andhra Lutheran Church and Tamil Evangelical Lutheran Church; more than 4.5m. mems; Pres. Rt Rev. GODWIN NAG; Exec. Sec. Rev. Dr A. G. AUGUSTINE JEYAKUMAR.

Other denominations active in the country include the Assembly of the Presbyterian Church in North East India, the Bengal-Odisha-Bihar Baptist Convention (6,000 mems), the Chaldean Syrian Church of the East, the Convention of the Baptist Churches of Northern Circars, the Council of Baptist Churches of North East India, the Council of Baptist Churches of Northern India, the Hindustani Convent Church and the Mennonite Church in India.

The Roman Catholic Church

India comprises 30 archdioceses and 134 dioceses. These include five archdioceses and 25 dioceses of the Syro-Malabar rite, and two archdioceses and six dioceses of the Syro-Malankara rite. The archdiocese of Goa and Daman is also the seat of the Patriarch of the East Indies. The remaining archdioceses are metropolitan sees. In 2011 there were an estimated 15.5m. adherents of the Roman Catholic faith in the country.

Catholic Bishops' Conference of India (CBCI): CBCI Centre, 1 Ashok Place, nr Gole Dakkhana, New Delhi 110 001; tel. (11) 23344470; fax (11) 23364615; e-mail cbcisec@gmail.com; internet www.cbci.in; f. 1944; Pres. Cardinal CLEEMIS CATHOLICOS (Archbishop of Trivandrum); Sec.-Gen. Most Rev. ALBERT D'SOUZA (Archbishop of Agra).

Latin Rite

Conference of Catholic Bishops of India (CCBI): CCBI Centre, 2nd Cross, Hutchins Rd, POB 8490, Bangalore 560 084; tel. (80) 25498282; fax (80) 25498180; e-mail ccbi@airtelmail.in; internet www.ccbi.in; f. 1994; Pres. Cardinal TELESPHORE TOPPO (Archbishop of Ranchi).

Syro-Malabar Rite

In 2012 there were some 4.2m. Syro-Malabar Catholics in India.

Major Archbishop of the Syro-Malabar Church: MAR GEORGE Cardinal ALENCHERRY (Archbishop of Ernakulam-Angamaly), Archdiocesian Curia, Mount St Thomas, POB 2580, Kakkand, Kochi 682 031; tel. (484) 2352629; fax (484) 2355010; e-mail curia@ernakulamarchdiocese.org; internet www.ernakulamarchdiocese.org.

Archbishop of Changanasserry: Most Rev. MAR JOSEPH PERUMTHOTTAM, Archbishop's House, POB 20, Changanasserry 686 101; tel. (481) 2420040; fax (481) 2422540; e-mail abpchry@sancharnet.in; internet www.archdiocesechanganacherry.org.

Archbishop of Kottayam: Most Rev. MATHEW MOOLAKKATTU, Archbishop's House, POB 71, Kottayam 686 001; tel. (481) 2563527; fax (481) 2563327; e-mail cbhktym@hotmail.com; internet www.kottayamad.org.

Archbishop of Tellicherry: Most Rev. GEORGE NJARALAKATT, Archbishop's House, POB 70, Tellicherry 670 101; tel. (490) 2341058; fax (49) 2341412; e-mail archbishopgeorgev@gmail.com; internet www.archdioceseoftellicherry.org.

Archbishop of Trichur: Most Rev. MAR ANDREWS THAZHATH, Archbishop's House, Trichur 680 005; tel. (487) 2333325; fax (487) 2338204; e-mail info@trichurarchdiocese.org; internet www.trichurarchdiocese.org.

Syro-Malankara Rite

Major Archbishop of Trivandrum: Cardinal BASELIOS CLEEMIS CATHOLICOS, Major Archbishop's House, Pattom, Thiruvananthapuram 695 004; tel. (471) 2541643; fax (471) 2541635; e-mail malankaracc@gmail.com; internet www.malankaracatholicchurch.net.

BAHÁ'Í FAITH

National Spiritual Assembly: Bahá'í House, 6 Shrimant Madhavrao Scindia Rd, POB 19, New Delhi 110 001; tel. (11) 23387004; fax (11) 23782178; e-mail admin@bahai.in; internet www.bahai.in; f. 1923; c. 2m. mems; Sec.-Gen. Dr A. K. MERCHANT.

OTHER FAITHS

Jainism: 4.2m. adherents (2001 census), 0.4% of the population.

Zoroastrianism: In 2001 69,601 Parsis practised the Zoroastrian religion, compared with 76,382 in 1991.

The Press

India has a thriving and dynamic newspaper industry and despite the gradual growth of the digital news media, circulation, readership and advertising revenues in the print sector have all risen over recent years. According to research by the World Association of Newspapers and News Publishers, the total number of paid-for daily publications increased by almost 90% between 2007 and 2011, rising from 2,337 titles to 4,396. During that period average daily circulation per issue increased by 11.2% (to 109,937). According to the Registrar of Newspapers for India, there were 94,067 registered publications as of 31 March 2013 (12,511 newspapers and 81,556 periodicals), with a total average circulation of more than 405m. copies in 2012/13.

English-language dailies attract the largest share of advertising revenues, and the English-language *Times of India* remains the largest newspaper by paid circulation. However, the non-English market is growing faster than the English segment, and in recent years Hindi-language dailies have overtaken their English counterparts in terms of circulation and readership.

The majority of publications in India are under individual ownership, and they claim a large part of the total circulation. The most powerful groups, owned by joint stock companies, publish most of the large English dailies and frequently have considerable private commercial and industrial holdings. Some of the major groups are listed below.

PRINCIPAL NEWSPAPER GROUPS

Ananda Bazar Patrika Group: 6 Prafulla Sarkar St, Kolkata 700 001; tel. (33) 22345374; fax (33) 22253241; internet www.abp.in; f. 1922; dailies: *Ananda Bazar Patrika* and *The Telegraph*; periodicals incl.: *Business World, Anandamela, Desh, Anandalok* and

Sananda; Chair. ASHOK S. GANGULY; Chief Editor AVEEK SARKAR PURKAYASTHA; Man. Dir and CEO DIPANKAR DAS PURKAYASTHA.

Dainik Bhaskar Group: Synergy Media Entertainment Ltd, D-143, Sector 63, Noida 201301; tel. (120) 4227670; internet www .dainikbhaskargroup.com; dailies: *Dainik Bhaskar, Divya Bhaskar, Divya Marathi, Saurashtra Samachar, DB Star*; other activities incl. an FM radio station and several magazines; Chair. RAMESH CHANDRA AGARWAL; Man. Dir SUDHIR AGARWAL.

Hindustan Times Media Group: 18–20 Kasturba Gandhi Marg, New Delhi 110 001; tel. (11) 23361234; fax (11) 66561270; e-mail feedback@hindustantimes.com; internet www.htmedia.in; f. 1924; dailies: the *Hindustan Times* and *Mint* (English), and *Hindustan* (Hindi); periodicals: *Nandan* and *Kadambini* (Hindi); Chair. SHOBHANA BHARTIA; CEO RAJIV VERMA.

Indian Express Group: Express Towers, Nariman Point, Mumbai 400 021; tel. (22) 22022627; fax (2) 22022139; internet expressgroup .indianexpress.com; publishes dailies incl. the *Indian Express* and the *Financial Express* (English), *Jansatta* (Hindi), *Lokasatta* (Marathi), *Dinamani* (Tamil), *Andhra Prabha* (Telugu), *Kannada Prabha* (Kannada); periodicals incl. *Screen* (English), *Lokprabha* (Marathi), and *Dinamani Kadir* (Tamil); Chair. and Man. Dir VIVECK GOENKA.

Times of India Group (Bennett, Coleman and Co Ltd): Times House, 7 Bahadur Shah Zafar Marg, New Delhi 110 103; tel. (11) 23302000; internet www.timesgroup.com; publishes 13 newspapers and 18 periodicals from 11 regional centres; dailies incl.: *The Times of India* and the *Mumbai Mirror* (English), the *Economic Times* (in English, Hindi and Gujarati), the *Nav Bharat Times* and the *Sandhya Times* (Hindi) and the *Maharashtra Times* (Marathi); periodicals incl.: the English fortnightly *Femina* and monthly *Filmfare*, and the Bengali monthlies *Aamar Somoy* and *Ami Udita*; Chair. INDU JAIN; Man. Dir VINEET JAIN.

PRINCIPAL DAILIES

Circulation figs are for 2009 unless otherwise stated.

Delhi (incl. New Delhi)

The Asian Age: S-7, Green Park, Main Market, New Delhi 110 016; tel. (11) 26530001; fax (11) 26530030; e-mail delhidesk@asianage .com; internet www.asianage.com; f. 1994; morning; English; also publ. from Ahmedabad, Bengaluru, Kolkata, Mumbai and London (United Kingdom); Editor-in-Chief VENKATTRAM REDDY; circ. 46,895.

Business Standard: Nehru House, 4 Bahadur Shah Zafar Marg, New Delhi 110 002; tel. (11) 23720202; fax (11) 23720201; e-mail letters@business-standard.com; internet www.business-standard .com; morning; English; also publ. from Kolkata, Ahmedabad, Bengaluru, Chennai, Hyderabad, Chandigarh, Pune, Kochi, Lucknow, Bhubaneswar and Mumbai; Editor-in-Chief A. K. BHATTACHARYA; circ. 26,390.

Daily Milap: Milap Niketan, 8A Bahadur Shah Zafar Marg, New Delhi 110 002; tel. (11) 23317651; fax (11) 23319166; e-mail milap4mail@gmail.com; internet www.milap.com; f. 1923; Urdu; nationalist; also publ. in Hindi; publ. also from Jullundur and Hyderabad; Man. Editor PUNAM SURI; Editor NAVIN SURI; circ. 36,295.

Daily Pratap: Pratap Bhavan, 5 Bahadur Shah Zafar Marg, New Delhi 110 002; tel. (11) 23317938; fax (11) 41509555; e-mail admin@ dailypratap.com; internet www.dailypratap.com; f. 1919; Urdu; Chief Editor ANIL NARENDRA; CEO S. M. AFIF AHSEN; circ. 65,866.

The Economic Times: 7 Bahadur Shah Zafar Marg, New Delhi 110 002; tel. (11) 23492234; fax (11) 23491248; internet economictimes .indiatimes.com; f. 1961; English; also publ. from Kolkata, Ahmedabad, Bengaluru, Hyderabad, Chennai and Mumbai; Editorial Dir RAHUL JOSHI; circ. 175,438.

Financial Express: Express Bldg, The Indian Express Online Media (Pvt) Ltd, 9–10 Bahadur Shah Zafar Marg, New Delhi 110 002; tel. (11) 23702100; fax (11) 23702141; e-mail editor@ expressindia.com; internet www.financialexpress.com; f. 1961; morning; English; also publ. from Ahmedabad (in Gujarati), Mumbai, Bengaluru, Kolkata and Chennai; Man. Editor SUNIL JAIN; circ. 31,383.

Hindustan: 18–20 Kasturba Gandhi Marg, 2nd Floor, New Delhi 110 001; tel. (11) 23704600; fax (11) 66561445; e-mail feedback@ hindustantimes.com; internet www.livehindustan.com; f. 1936; morning; Hindi; also publ. from Patna, Muzaffarpur, Bhagalpur, Ranchi, Jamshedpur, Dhanbad, Lucknow, Varanasi, Meerut, Agra, Kanpur and Chandigarh; Editor-in-Chief SHASHI SHEKHAR; combined circ. 2,237,243 (2013).

Hindustan Times: 18–20 Kasturba Gandhi Marg, New Delhi 110 001; tel. (11) 23361234; fax (11) 66561270; e-mail feedback@ hindustantimes.com; internet www.hindustantimes.com; f. 1924; morning; English; also publ. from Mumbai, Lucknow, Patna, Ranchi and Kolkata; Editor-in-Chief SANJOY NARAYAN; combined circ. 1,321,807 (2013).

Jansatta: 9–10 Bahadur Shah Zafar Marg, New Delhi 110 002; tel. (11) 23702100; fax (11) 23702141; e-mail feedback@expressindia .com; f. 1983; Hindi; also publ. from Kolkata and Raipur; Editor OM THANVI; circ. 43,612.

Nav Bharat Times: 7 Bahadur Shah Zafar Marg, New Delhi 110 002; tel. (11) 23492041; fax (11) 23492168; internet navbharattimes .indiatimes.com; f. 1947; Hindi; also publ. from Mumbai; Editor RAM KRIPAL SINGH; circ. 409,584.

The Pioneer: Link House, 3 Bahadur Shah Zafar Marg, New Delhi 110 002; tel. (11) 23755271; fax (11) 23755275; e-mail info@ dailypioneer.com; internet www.dailypioneer.com; f. 1865; also publ. from Lucknow, Bhopal, Bhubaneswar, Ranchi, Kochi, Chandigarh and Dehradun; Editor CHANDAN MITRA; circ. 96,332.

Punjab Kesari: Plot No. 2, Printing Press Complex, Ring Rd, nr Wazirpur Bus Depot, Delhi 110 035; tel. (11) 27193719; fax (11) 27194470; e-mail sales@punjabkesari.com; internet www .punjabkesari.com; f. 1983; Hindi; also publ. from Jalandhar and Ambala; circulated in Haryana, Rajasthan, Uttar Pradesh, Uttarakhand, Madhya Pradesh, Punjab, Himachal Pradesh, Maharashtra, Bihar and Gujarat; Resident Editor ASHWANI KUMAR; circ. 348,890.

Rashtriya Sahara: Navrang House, 12th Floor, 21 Kasturba Gandhi Marg, New Delhi 110 001; tel. (11) 43596017; fax (11) 23352370; e-mail rsahara@saharasamay.com; internet rashtriyasahara.samaylive.com; morning; Hindi; also publ. from Lucknow, Gorakhpur, Kanpur, Dehradun and Patna; Resident Editor SWATANTRA MISHRA; circ. 97,625 (2011).

Sandhya Times: 7 Bahadur Shah Zafar Marg, New Delhi 110 002; tel. (11) 23492162; fax (11) 23492047; f. 1979; Hindi; evening; Editor SAT SONI; circ. 34,756.

The Statesman: Statesman House, 148 Barakhamba Rd, New Delhi 110 001; tel. (11) 23315911; fax (11) 23315295; e-mail thestatesman@ vsnl.com; internet www.thestatesman.net; f. 1931; English; also publ. from Bhubaneswar, Kolkata and Siliguri; Editor and Man. Dir RAVINDRA KUMAR; circ. 7,598.

The Times of India (New Delhi): 7 Bahadur Shah Zafar Marg, New Delhi 110 002; tel. (11) 23302000; fax (11) 23351606; internet timesofindia.indiatimes.com; f. 1838; English; also publ. from 12 other regional centres incl. Mumbai, Bengaluru, Kolkata, Chennai, Hyderabad, Pune, Ahmedabad and Lucknow; Editorial Dir JAIDEEP BOSE.

Andhra Pradesh

Hyderabad

Andhra Jyothi: Andhra Jyothi Bldg, Plot No. 76, HUDA Heights, Rd No. 70, Journalist Colony, Jubilee Hills, Hyderabad 500 033; tel. (40) 23558233; fax (40) 23558288; e-mail editor@andhrajyothy.com; internet www.andhrajyothy.com; f. 1960; Telugu; also publ. from 13 other regional centres; Editor K. SRINIVAS; combined circ. 91,896.

Andhra Prabha: 16-1-28, Kolandareddy Rd, Poornanandampet, Vijayawada 520 003; tel. (866) 2571351; e-mail info@andhraprabha .com; internet www.prabhanews.com; f. 1938; Telugu; also publ. from Bengaluru, Hyderabad, Chennai and Visakhapatnam; Editor VASUDEV DEKSHITILU; circ. 68,590.

Deccan Chronicle: 36 Sarojini Devi Rd, Hyderabad 500 003; tel. (40) 27803930; fax (40) 27803870; e-mail advt@deccanmail.com; internet www.deccanchronicle.com; f. 1938; English; also publ. from 6 other regional centres; Editor-in-Chief A. T. JAYANTI; circ. 45,748.

Eenadu: Somajiguda, Hyderabad 500 082; tel. (40) 23318181; fax (40) 23392530; e-mail editor@eenadu.net; internet www.eenadu.net; f. 1974; Telugu; also publ. from 22 other towns; Chief Editor RAMOJI RAO; combined circ. 1,801,213 (2013).

Rahnuma-e-Deccan: 12-2-837/A/3, Asif Nagar, Hyderabad 500 028; tel. (40) 23534943; fax (40) 23534945; e-mail jameelnews@ gmail.com; internet www.rahnumadeccan.com; f. 1949; morning; Urdu; independent; Chief Editor SYED VICARUDDIN; circ. 26,293.

Siasat Daily: Jawaharlal Nehru Rd, Hyderabad 500 001; tel. (40) 24744180; fax (40) 24603188; e-mail contact@siasat.com; internet www.siasat.com; f. 1949; morning; Urdu; Editor ZAHID ALI KHAN; circ. 44,073.

Assam (Asom)

Amar Asom: G. S. Rd, Ulubari, Guwahati 781 007; tel. (361) 2521467; fax (361) 2521620; e-mail glpghy2009@hotmail.com; internet amarasom.glpublications.in; f. 1997; Assamese; also publ. from Jorhat and Lakhimpur; Editor HOMEN BORGOHAIN; circ. 59,995.

Asomiya Pratidin: Maniram Dewan Rd, Chandmari, Guwahati 781 003; tel. (361) 2660420; fax (361) 2666377; e-mail mail@ pratidingroup.com; internet www.asomiyapratidin.co.in; morning; Assamese; also publ. from Dibrugarh, Barpari and Kamrup; Editor NITYA BORA; circ. 74,460.

Assam Tribune: GNB Rd, Guwahati 781 003; tel. (361) 2661357; fax (361) 2666398; e-mail editoratribune@gmail.com; internet www

.assamtribune.com; f. 1939; English; also publishes Assamese edn, Dainik Assam; Man. Dir and Editor P. G. BARUAH; circ. 90,815 (2011).

Dainik Agradoot: Agradoot Bhavan, Dispur, Guwahati 781 006; tel. (361) 2261923; fax (361) 2260655; e-mail agradoot@gmail.com; internet www.dainikagradoot.com; f. 1995; Assamese; Editor K. S. DEKA; circ. 66,409.

Dainik Janmabhumi: Tulsi Narayan Sarma Rd, Jorhat 785 001; tel. (376) 2320033; fax (376) 2321713; e-mail janambhumiadvt@gmail.com; internet www.dainikjanambhumi.co.in; f. 1972; Assamese; also publ. from Tinsukia, Guwahati and Tezpur; Editor HEMANTA BARMAN; Man. Partner SUBROTO SHARMA; circ. 29,163.

Dainik Jugasankha: 13 Green Path, G. S. Rd, Guwahati 781 007; tel. (361) 2526670; fax (361) 2450496; e-mail dainikjugasankha@yahoo.com; internet www.dainikjugasankha.in; f. 1950; Bengali; also publ. from Silchar; Editor-in-Chief BIJOY KRISHNA NATH; Editor ARIJIT ADITYA; circ. 75,650.

The North East Times: G. S. Rd, Ulubari, Guwahati 781 007; tel. (361) 2458395; fax (361) 2521620; e-mail guwahatiglpghy@hotmail.com; internet net.glpublications.in; English; Editor G. L. AGARWALLA; circ. 34,891.

The Sentinel: G. S. Rd, Six Mile, Dispur, Guwahati 781 022; tel. (361) 2229330; fax (361) 2229110; e-mail thesentinel@satyam.net.in; internet www.sentinelassam.com; f. 1983; English; Editor SHANKAR RAJKHEWA; circ. 58,751.

Chhattisgarh

Deshbandhu: Deshbandhu Complex, Ramsagar Para, Raipur 492 001; tel. (771) 4288888; e-mail deshbandhuraipur@gmail.com; internet www.deshbandhu.co.in; f. 1959; Hindi; also publ. from Jabalpur, Satna, Bilaspur, Indore, New Delhi and Bhopal; publishes an evening edn, Highway Channel, from Raipur, Jabalpur and Bilaspur; Chief Editor LALIT SURJAN; circ. 84,357 (Raipur), 24,289 (Satna), 46,785 (Bhopal), 50,468 (Jabalpur), 59,013 (Bilaspur).

Nava Bharat: Nava Bharat Bhavan Press Complex, G. E. Rd, Raipur 492 001; tel. (771) 2535544; fax (771) 2534936; internet www.navabharat.biz; Hindi; also publ. from 6 other regional centres; Editor PRAKASH MAHESHWARI; circ. 189,186 (2011).

Goa

Gomantak Times: Gomantak Bhavan, St Inez, Panaji, Goa 403 001; tel. (832) 2422700; fax (832) 2422701; internet www.dainikgomantak.com; f. 1962; morning; Marathi and English edns; Exec. Editor DERRICK ALMEIDA; circ. 24,906 (Marathi).

Navhind Times: Navhind Bhavan, Rua Ismail Gracias, POB 161, Panaji, Goa 403 001; tel. (832) 2224920; fax (832) 2463050; e-mail navhind@navhindtimes.com; internet www.navhindtimes.in; f. 1963; morning; English; Editor ARUN SINHA; circ. 34,835.

O Heraldo: Herald Publications Pvt Ltd, AF/1-4, Campal Trade Centre, Panjim 403 001; tel. (832) 2224202; fax (832) 2225622; e-mail editor@herald-goa.com; internet www.heraldgoa.in; f. 1900; English; Editor-in-Chief R. F. FERNANDES; Editor SUJAY GUPTA; circ. 61,587 (2011).

Gujarat

Ahmedabad

Gujarat Samachar: Gujarat Samachar Bhavan, Khanpur, Ahmedabad 380 001; tel. (79) 5508001; fax (79) 5502000; e-mail editor@gujaratsamachar.com; internet www.gujaratsamachar.com; f. 1930; morning; Gujarati; also publ. from Surat, Rajkot, Baroda, Bhavnagar, Mumbai, London and New York; Editor SHREYANSH SHAH; circ. 537,029.

Lokasatta—Janasatta: Mirzapur Rd, POB 188, Ahmedabad 380 001; tel. (79) 25507307; fax (79) 25507708; f. 1953; morning; Gujarati; also publ. from Rajkot and Vadodara; Man. Editor VIVEK GOENKA; circ. 49,161.

Sandesh: Sandesh Bhavan, Lad Society Rd, Ahmedabad 380 054; tel. (79) 40004000; fax (79) 40004242; e-mail advt@sandesh.com; internet sandesh.com; f. 1923; Gujarati; also publ. from Bhavnagar, Vadodara, Rajkot and Surat; Editor FALGUNBHAI C. PATEL; circ. 346,553.

Western Times: 301 Gala Argos, 3rd Floor, nr Kalgi Char Rasta, Gujarat College Rd, Ellisbridge, Ahmedabad 380 006; tel. (79) 26402880; fax (79) 26402882; e-mail gujarati@westerntimes.co.in; internet www.westerntimes.co.in; f. 1967; English and Gujarati edns; also publ. (in Gujarati) from 8 other towns; Editor NIKUNJ PATEL; total circ. more than 200,000.

Bhuj

Kutchmitra: Kutchmitra Bhavan, nr Indirabai Park, Bhuj 370 001; tel. (2832) 252090; fax (2832) 250271; e-mail info@kutchmitradaily.com; internet www.kutchmitradaily.com; f. 1947; Gujarati; Propr Saurashtra Trust; Man. SHAILESH KANSARA; circ. 47,882 (2011).

Rajkot

Jai Hind: Jai Hind Press Bldg, Babubhai Shah Rd, POB 59, Rajkot 360 001; tel. (281) 3048684; fax (281) 2448677; e-mail editor@jaihinddaily.com; internet www.jaihinddaily.com; f. 1948; morning and evening (in Rajkot as Sanj Samachar); Gujarati; also publ. from Ahmedabad; Editor Y. N. SHAH; combined circ. 107,300.

Phulchhab: Phulchhab Bhavan, Phulchhab Marg, Rajkot 360 001; tel. (281) 2444611; fax (281) 2448751; e-mail editor@janmabhoominewspapers.com; internet phulchhab.janmabhoominewspapers.com; f. 1950; morning; Gujarati; Propr Saurashtra Trust; Editor DINESH RAJA; circ. 84,500.

Surat

Gujaratmitra and Gujaratdarpan: Gujaratmitra Bhavan, nr Old Civil Hospital, Sonifalia, Surat 395 003; tel. (261) 2599992; fax (261) 2599990; e-mail mitra@gujaratmitra.in; internet www.gujaratmitra.in/web; f. 1863; morning; Gujarati; Editor B. P. RESHAMWALA; circ. 91,000.

Haryana

Bharat Janani: Sonipat Rd, Rohtak; tel. and fax (1262) 427191; f. 1971; Hindi; morning; also publ. from Rewari; Editor Dr R. S. SANTOSHI; circ. 56,360.

Himachal Pradesh

Dainik Himachal Sewa: Hans Kutir, Khalini, Shimla 171 002; tel. (177) 2224119; fax (177) 2260187; f. 1986; Hindi; Editor-in-Chief Dr R. S. SANTOSHI; circ. 60,000.

Himachal Times: Himachal Times Complex, 64–66 The Mall, Shimla 171 001; tel. and fax (177) 2811555; e-mail devkpandhi@gmail.com; internet himachaltimesgroup.com; f. 1948; English; Chief Editor VIJAY PANDHI.

Jammu and Kashmir

Daily Excelsior: Excelsior House, Excelsior Lane, Janipura, Jammu Tawi 180 007; tel. (191) 2537055; fax (191) 2537831; e-mail editor@dailyexcelsior.com; internet www.dailyexcelsior.com; f. 1965; English; Publr and Editor NEERAJ ROHMETRA.

Greater Kashmir: 6 Pratap Park, Residency Rd, Srinagar 190 001; tel. (194) 2455435; fax (194) 2477782; e-mail editor@greaterkashmir.com; internet www.greaterkashmir.com; f. 1993; English; Chief Editor FAYAZ AHMED KALOO; circ. 81,068.

Kashmir Times: Residency Rd, Jammu 180 001; tel. (191) 2543676; fax (191) 2542028; e-mail editor@kashmirtimes.com; internet www.kashmirtimes.com; f. 1955; morning; English and Hindi; Editor-in-Chief PRABODH JAMWAL.

Srinagar Times: Badshah Bridge, Srinagar; internet www.srinagartimes.net; f. 1969; Urdu; Editor S. F. MOHAMMED; circ. 14,000.

Jharkhand

Aaj: 15–16 Namkum Industrial Area, Ranchi; Hindi; morning; also publ. from 8 other cities; Publr AMITAV CHAKRAVORTHY; circ. 59,267 (Ranchi).

Hindustan: Circular Court, Circular Rd, Ranchi 834 001; tel. (651) 2205811; Hindi; morning; also publ. from Patna, Delhi, Bhagalpur, Lucknow, Varanasi and Muzaffarpur; Editor SHASHI SHEKHAR.

Prabhat Khabar: 15-P, Kokar Industrial Area, Kokar, Ranchi 834 001; tel. (651) 3053100; fax (651) 254006; e-mail ranchi@prabhatkhabar.in; internet www.prabhatkhabar.com; f. 1984; Hindi; also publ. from Dhanbad, Kolkata, Jamshedpur, Siliguri, Deoghar and Patna; Chief Editor HARIVANSH; circ. 120,162 (Ranchi).

Ranchi Express: 55 Baralal St, Ranchi 834 001; tel. (651) 2206320; fax (651) 2206213; e-mail news@ranchiexpress.com; internet ranchiexpress.com; f. 1963; Hindi; morning; Editor AJAY MAROO; circ. 57,959.

Karnataka

Bengaluru

Deccan Herald: 75 Mahatma Gandhi Rd, POB 5331, Bengaluru 560 001; tel. (80) 25588000; fax (80) 25880165; e-mail ads@deccanherald.co.in; internet www.deccanherald.com; f. 1948; morning; English; also publ. from Hubli-Dharwar, Mangalore, Dhavangere and Gulbarga; Editor K. N. TILAK KUMAR; circ. 163,221.

Kannada Prabha: Express Bldgs, 1 Queen's Rd, Bengaluru 560 001; tel. (80) 22866893; fax (80) 22866617; e-mail anisikeprabha@gmail.com; internet www.kannadaprabha.com; f. 2005; morning;

Kannada; also publ. from Belgaum, Mangalore, Gulbarga, Hubali and Shimoga; Editor VISHWESHWAR BHAT; circ. 96,485 (2011).

Prajavani: 75 M. G. Rd, POB 5331, Bengaluru 560 001; tel. (80) 25880000; fax (80) 25880165; e-mail ads@deccanherald.co.in; internet www.prajavani.net; f. 1948; morning; Kannada; also publ. from Mysore, Gulbarga, Mangalore and Dharwad; Editor-in-Chief K. N. SHANTH KUMAR; circ. 56,240.

Hubballi-Dharwad

Samyukta Karnataka: POB 30, Koppikar Rd, Hubli 580 020; tel. (836) 2364303; fax (836) 2362760; e-mail skhubli@gmail.com; f. 1933; Kannada; also publ. from Bengaluru, Davangere, and Gulbarga; Editor A. C. GOPAL; circ. 100,337.

Vijay Karnataka: Giriraj Annexe, Circuit House Rd, Hubli 580 029; tel. (836) 2237556; fax (836) 2253630; internet www .vijaykarnatakaepaper.com; f. 1999; Kannada; also publ. from Bengaluru, Gangavati, Gulbarga, Mangalore, Mysore, Bagalkot, Chitradurga and Shimoga; Printer and Publr VIJAY SANKESHWAR; circ. 69,201.

Manipal

Udayavani: Manipal Media Network, New Udayavani Bldg, Manipal 576 119; tel. (820) 2571151; fax (820) 2570563; e-mail udayavanionline@manipalmedia.com; internet www.udayavani .com; f. 1970; Kannada; also publ. from Manipal-Udupi and Mumbai; Group Editor RAVI HEGDE; circ. 21,739.

Kerala

Deepika: POB 7, Kottayam 686 001; tel. (481) 3012001; fax (481) 3012222; e-mail editor@deepika.com; internet www.deepika.com; f. 1887; Malayalam; independent; also publ. from Kannur, Kochi, Kozhikode, Thiruvananthapuram and Thrissur; Chief Editor Fr BOBY ALEX MANNAMPLACKAL; circ. 47,520.

Deshabhimani: Deshabhimani Bldg, Kaloor, Kochi 682 017; tel. (484) 2530346; fax (484) 2530006; e-mail kochi@deshabhimani.com; internet www.deshabhimani.com; f. 1946; Malayalam; morning; publ. by the CPI (M); also publ. from Kochi, Kottayam, Thrissur, Calicut, Malappuram and Thiruvananthapuram; Chief Editor V. V. DAKSHINAMOORTHY; circ. 57,530.

Kerala Kaumudi: Kaumudi Bldgs, Pettah, Thiruvananthapuram 695 024; tel. (471) 2461010; fax (471) 2461985; e-mail editor@ ekaumudi.com; internet news.keralakaumudi.com; f. 1911; Malayalam; also publ. from Kollam, Alappuzha, Kochi, Kannur, Kozhikode and Bengaluru; Editor-in-Chief M. S. RAVI; Man. Editor DEEPU RAVI; circ. 60,036.

Malayala Manorama: K. K. Rd, POB 26, Kottayam 686 001; tel. (481) 2563646; fax (481) 2562479; e-mail editor@malayalamanorama .com; internet www.manoramaonline.com; f. 1890; Malayalam; publ. from 10 other regional centres in Kerala and one in Delhi; morning; Man. Dir and Editor MAMMEN MATHEW; combined circ. 2,239,527 (2014).

Mathrubhumi: M. J. Krishnamohan Memorial Bldg, K. P. Kesava Menon Rd, POB 46, Kozhikode 673 001; tel. (495) 2366655; fax (495) 2366656; e-mail mbiclt@mpp.co.in; internet www.mathrubhumi .com; f. 1923; Malayalam; also publ. from Thiruvananthapuram, Kozhikode, Kannur, Thrissur, Kollam, Malappuram, Pallakad, Alappuzha, Kottayam, Kochi, Bengaluru, Chennai, New Delhi and Mumbai; Editor M. KESAVA MENON; circ. 1,458,796 (2013).

Madhya Pradesh

Dainik Bhaskar: 6 Dwarka Sadan, Press Complex, M. P. Nagar, Bhopal; tel. (755) 3988884; fax (755) 270466; e-mail editorbhaskar@ bhaskar.com; internet www.bhaskar.com; f. 1958; morning; Hindi; also publ. from 36 other regional centres across 12 states; Chief Editor KALPESH YAGNIK; combined circ. 3,557,269 (2014).

Naidunia: 60/1 Babu Labhchand Chhajlani Marg, Indore 452 009; tel. (731) 4711000; fax (731) 4711111; e-mail response@naidunia .com; internet www.naidunia.com; f. 1947; morning; Hindi; also publ. from Jabalpur, Gwalior and Bhopal; Editor-in-Chief SHRAVAN GARG; combined circ. 412,904.

Maharashtra

Kolhapur

Pudhari: 2318, 'C' Ward, Bhausingji Rd, Kolhapur 416 002; tel. (231) 2543111; fax (231) 2543124; e-mail news.kop@pudhari.co.in; internet www.pudhari.com; f. 1974; Marathi; Editor PRATAP SINGH JADHAV; circ. 721,649 (2013).

Mumbai (Bombay)

Afternoon Despatch & Courier: Janmabhoomi Bhavan, 3rd Floor, Janmabhoomi Marg, Fort, Mumbai 400 001; tel. (22) 40768999; fax (22) 40768916; e-mail afternoonnews@gmail.com; internet www.afternoondc.in; evening; English; Editor CAROL ANDRADE.

Bombay Samachar: Red House, S. A. Brelvi Rd, Horniman Circle, Fort, Mumbai 400 001; tel. (22) 22045531; fax (22) 22046642; e-mail samachar.bombay@gmail.com; internet www.bombaysamachar .com; f. 1822; morning and Sun.; Gujarati; political, social and commercial; Editor JEHANBUX DHANJISHA DARUWALA; circ. 89,931 (2013).

Daily News and Analysis (DNA): 11th Floor, Tower 3, India Bulls Finance Centre, Senapati Bapat Marg, Elphinstone (West), Mumbai 400 013; tel. (22) 39888888; fax (22) 39801000; internet www .dnaindia.com; f. 2005; English; also publ. from Bengaluru, Pune, Ahmedabad, Surat, Jaipur and Indore; Chief. Editor C. P. SUREN-DRAN; circ. 397,147.

Dainik Saamana: Sadguru Darshan, Nagu Sayaji Wadi, Dainik Saamana Marg, Prabhadevi, Mumbai 400 028; tel. (22) 24370591; fax (22) 24224181; e-mail response@saamana.com; internet www .saamana.com; f. 1989; Marathi; Exec. Editor SANJAY RAUT; circ. 102,900.

The Economic Times: Times of India Bldg, Dr Dadabhai Naoroji Rd, Mumbai 400 001; tel. (22) 22733535; fax (22) 22731344; e-mail etbom@timesgroup.com; internet economictimes.indiatimes.com; f. 1961; also publ. from New Delhi, Kolkata, Ahmedabad, Hyderabad, Chennai and Bengaluru; English; Editor RAHUL JOSHI; combined circ. 405,940 (2013).

Financial Express: Express Towers, Nariman Point, Mumbai 400 021; tel. (22) 6740000; fax (11) 22022139; e-mail editor@expressindia .com; internet www.financialexpress.com; f. 1961; morning; English; also publ. from New Delhi, Bengaluru, Kolkata, Coimbatore, Ahmedabad (Gujarati) and Chennai; Man. Editor VIVECK GOENKA; Editor SHOBHANA SUBRAMANIAN; circ. 22,427 (English).

The Free Press Journal: Free Press House, 215 Free Press Journal Rd, Nariman Point, Mumbai 400 021; tel. (22) 22874566; fax (22) 22874688; e-mail mail@fpj.co.in; internet www.freepressjournal.in; f. 1930; English; also publ. from Indore, Kolkata, Bhopal, Chennai and New Delhi; Man. Editor GIRDHARILAL LAKHOTIA.

Hindustan Times: Mahalaxmi Industrial Estate, 2nd Floor, L. J. Coross Rd No. 1, Mumbai 400 016; tel. (22) 24368012; fax (22) 24303625; e-mail feedback@hindustantimes.in; internet www .hindustantimes.com; f. 1924; also publ. from Delhi, Lucknow, Bhopal, Kolkata and Chandigarh; Editor-in-Chief SANJOY NARAYAN; Editor SOUMYA BHATTACHARYA; circ. 279,372.

Indian Express: Express Tower, 1st and 2nd Floors, Nariman Point, Mumbai 400 021; tel. (22) 67440000; fax (22) 22835726; f. 1940; English; also publ. from 8 regional centres; Man. Editor VIVECK GOENKA; Chief Editor RAJ KAMAL JHA; circ. 75,020.

Inquilab: 156 D. J. Dadajee Rd, Tardeo, Mumbai 400 034; tel. (22) 71221450; fax (22) 24183171; e-mail inquilab@mid-day.com; internet www.inquilab.com; f. 1938; morning; Urdu; Editor SHAHID LATIF; circ. 31,640.

Janmabhoomi: Janmabhoomi Bhavan, Janmabhoomi Marg, Fort, POB 62, Mumbai 400 001; tel. (22) 22870831; fax (22) 22874097; e-mail info@janmabhoominewspapers.com; internet www .janmabhoominewspapers.com; f. 1934; evening; Gujarati; Propr Saurashtra Trust; Editor KUNDAN R. VYAS; circ. 18,464.

Lokasatta: Express Towers, Ramnath Goenka Marg, Nariman Point, Mumbai 400 021; tel. (22) 22022627; fax (22) 22822187; e-mail pratikriya@expressindia.com; internet www.loksatta.com; f. 1948; morning (incl. Sun.); Marathi; also produces editions for New Delhi, Pune, Thane, Nashik, Nagpur, Aurangabad, Navi Mumbai and Ahmedmangar; Editor GIRISH KUBER; circ. 206,975.

Maharashtra Times: Dr Dadabhai Naoroji Rd, POB 213, Mumbai 400 001; tel. (22) 22733636; fax (22) 22731175; internet maharashtratimes.indiatimes.com; f. 1962; Marathi; Editor ASHOK PANVALKAR; circ. 312,614.

Mid-Day: Peninsula Centre, Dr S. S. Rao Rd, opp. Mahatma Gandhi Hospital, Parel, Mumbai 400 012; tel. (22) 67017171; fax (22) 24150009; e-mail cs@mid-day.com; internet www.mid-day.com; f. 1979; daily and Sun.; English; also publ. from New Delhi, Pune and Bengaluru; Editor SACHIN KALABAG; circ. 121,342.

Mumbai Mirror: The Times of India Bldg, Dr Dadabhai Naoroji Rd, Mumbai 400 001; tel. (22) 26005555; e-mail mumbai.mirror@ timesgroup.com; internet www.mumbaimirror.com; f. 2005; English; Editor PANKAJ UPADHYAYA; circ. 708,687.

Navakal: 13 Shenviwadi, Khadilkar Rd, Girgaun, Mumbai 400 004; tel. (22) 23880181; fax (22) 23860989; f. 1923; Marathi; Exec. Editor ROHIT PANDE; circ. 172,466.

Navbharat Times: Dr Dadabhai Naoroji Rd, Mumbai 400 001; tel. (22) 22733535; fax (22) 22731144; internet navbharattimes .indiatimes.com; f. 1950; Hindi; also publ. from New Delhi, Jaipur, Patna and Lucknow; Chief Editor SUNDER CHAND THAKUR; circ. 159,578 (Mumbai).

Navshakti: Free Press House, 215 Nariman Point, Mumbai 400 021; tel. (22) 22853335; fax (22) 22874566; e-mail editor@navshakti.co.in; internet navshakti.co.in; f. 1932; Marathi; Man. Editor G. L. LAKHOTIA; Editor PRAKASH KULKARNI; circ. 16,719.

Sakal: Sakal Bhavan, Plot No. 42-B, Sector No. 11, CBD Belapur, Navi Mumbai 400 614; tel. (22) 66843000; fax (22) 27574280; e-mail editor.mumbai@esakal.com; internet www.esakal.com; f. 1970; Marathi; also publ. from Pune, Aurangabad, Nasik, Kolhapur and Solapur; Chief Editor PADMABHUSHAN B. DESHPANDE; circ. 88,094.

The Times of India: The Times of India Bldg, Dr Dadabhai Naoroji Rd, Mumbai 400 001; tel. (22) 56353535; fax (22) 22731444; e-mail toieditorial@timesgroup.com; internet www.timesofindia.com; f. 1838; morning; English; publishes 13 regional editions from centres incl. Mumbai, New Delhi, Bengaluru, Kolkata, Chennai, Hyderabad, Pune, Ahmedabad and Lucknow; Editor DERICK B. D'SA; combined circ. 3,321,702 (2013).

Nagpur

The Hitavada: Pandit Jawaharlal Nehru Marg, POB 201, Dhantoli, Nagpur 440 012; tel. (712) 2435737; fax (712) 2422362; e-mail twinkleclub@thehitavada.com; internet thehitavada.com; f. 1911; morning; English; also publ. from Raipur, Jabalpur and Bhopal; Editor-in-Chief BANWARILAL PUROHIT; Editor V. PHANSHIKAR; circ. 73,550.

Lokmat: Lokmat Bhavan, Wardha Rd, Nagpur 440 012; tel. (712) 2523527; fax (712) 2445555; e-mail editorial@lokmat.com; internet www.lokmat.com; also publ. from Jalgaon, Pune and Nasik; Marathi; Lokmat Samachar (Hindi) publ. from Nagpur, Akola and Aurangabad; Lokmat Times (English) publ. from Nagpur and Aurangabad; Chair. VIJAY DARDA; Chief Editor SURESH DWADASHIWAR; combined circ. 1,476,900 (2013).

Nava Bharat: Nava Bharat Bhavan, Cotton Market, Nagpur 440 018; tel. (712) 2726677; fax (712) 2723444; internet www.navabharat .biz; f. 1934; morning; Hindi; also publ. from 15 other cities; Editor-in-Chief R. G. MAHESWARI; circ. 133,495.

Tarun Bharat: 28 Farmland, Ramdaspeth, Nagpur 440 010; tel. (712) 6653120; fax (712) 2531758; e-mail tbadvt@gmail.com; internet tarunbharat.net; f. 1941; Marathi; independent; also publ. from Belagavi; Editor GAJANAN SHRIDHAR NIMDEO; Chief Editor KIRAN THAKUR; circ. 53,617 (Nagpur).

Pune

Kesari: 560 Narayan Peth, Pune 411 030; tel. (20) 4459250; fax (20) 4451677; e-mail kesari@giaspn01.vsnl.net.in; internet www .dailykesari.com; f. 1881; Marathi; also publ. from Solapur, Chiplun, Ahmednagar and Sangli; Editor DEEPAK TILAK; circ. 41,191.

Sakal: 595 Budhawar Peth, Pune 411 002; tel. (20) 24455500; fax (20) 24450583; e-mail webeditor@esakal.com; internet www.esakal.com; f. 1932; daily; Marathi; also publ. from 10 other regional centres; Chief Editor SHRIRAM PAWAR; Man. Editor PRATAP PAWAR; circ. 410,932.

Manipur

Naharolgi Thoudang: Keishampat Airport Rd, Imphal 795 001; tel. (385) 2449086; fax (385) 2440353; e-mail nthoudang@yahoo.co .in; internet www.naharolgithoudang.com; f. 1996; daily; Manipuri; Editor LOYALAKPA KHOIROM; circ. 27,420.

Poknapham: Keishampat Junction, Keishampat Thiyam Leirak, Imphal 795 001; tel. (385) 2459175; fax (385) 2442981; e-mail poknaphamdaily@yahoo.co.in; internet www.poknapham.in; f. 1975; daily; Manipuri; also publ. from Silchar; Editor A. ROBINDRO SHARMA; Assoc. Editor BIJOY KAKCHINGTABAM; circ. 32,566.

The Sangai Express: Sega Rd, Thouda Bhabok Leikai, Imphal 795 001; tel. (385) 2458133; fax (385) 2444881; e-mail sangaiinfo@gmail .com; internet www.thesangaiexpress.com; f. 1999; daily; Manipuri and English; Editor RAJESH HIJAM; circ. 27,513 (Manipuri) and 11,817 (English).

Meghalaya

Mawphor: Mawkhar, Mavis Dunn Rd, Shillong 793 002; tel. (364) 2545043; fax (364) 2548433; e-mail mawphordailynews@yahoo.com; internet mawphor.com; f. 1989; Khasi; Editor D. L. SIANGSHAI; circ. 53,072.

The Shillong Times: Rilbong, Shillong 793 004; tel. (364) 2223488; fax (364) 2220188; e-mail letters@theshillongtimes.com; internet www.theshillongtimes.com; f. 1945; English; Editor PATRICIA MUKHIM; circ. 30,899.

Nagaland

The Morung Express: 4 Duncan Basti, Dimapur 797 112; tel. (3862) 36871; fax (3862) 35194; e-mail morung@gmail.com; internet

www.morungexpress.com; f. 2005; Man. Dir and Editor AKUM LONGCHARI; circ. 25,593.

Nagaland Post: Nagaland Post Bldg, POB 59, Circular Rd, Dimapur 797 112; tel. (3862) 248489; fax (3862) 248500; e-mail npdesk@ gmail.com; internet www.nagalandpost.com; f. 1990; English; Editor GEOFFREY YADEN; circ. 50,450 (2011).

Odisha

Dharitri: B-15 Industrial Estate, Rasulgarh, POB 144, Bhubaneswar 751 010; tel. (674) 2549302; fax (674) 2549854; e-mail advt@ dharitri.com; internet www.dharitri.com; f. 1974; evening and morning; Oriya; Editor TATHAGATA SATPATHY; circ. 210,986.

Pragativadi: 178B, Mancheswar Industrial Estate, Bhubaneswar 751 010; tel. (674) 2588297; fax (674) 2582709; e-mail pragativadi@ yahoo.com; internet www.pragativadi.com; f. 1973; Exec. Editor SAMAHIT BAL; circ. 215,388.

Samaja: Gopabandhu Bhavan, Buxibazar, Cuttack 753 001; tel. (671) 2301994; fax (671) 2301086; e-mail printer_publisher@samaja .in; internet www.thesamaja.com; f. 1919; Oriya; also publ. from Sambalpur, Vizag, Bhubaneswar, Rourkela, Baleswar, Berhampur and Kolkata; Working Editor SUSANT KUMAR MOHANTY; circ. 14,927.

The Samaya: Plot No. 44 and 54, Sector A, Zone D, Mancheswar Industrial Estate, Bhubaneswar 751 017; tel. (674) 2585740; fax (674) 2586665; e-mail thesamaya@yahoo.com; internet odishasamaya.com; f. 1966; Oriya; Chief Editor SATAKADI HOTA; Man. Editor RANJIB BISWAL; circ. 226,668.

Sambad: B-27 Industrial Estate, Rasulgarh, Bhubaneswar 751 010; tel. (674) 2548902; fax (674) 2588905; e-mail sambadadvt@ easternmedia.in; internet sambadepaper.com; f. 1984; Oriya; also publ. from 7 other regional centres; Editor S. R. PATNAIK; circ. 94,903.

Punjab

Ajit: Ajit Bhavan, Nehru Garden Rd, Jalandhar 144 001; tel. (181) 2455961; fax (181) 2455960; e-mail ajit@ajitjalandhar.com; internet www.ajitjalandhar.com; f. 1955; Punjabi; Chief Editor BARJINDER SINGH HAMDARD; CEO SARVINDER KAUR; circ. 369,474.

Daily Hind Samachar: Civil Lines, Jalandhar 144 001; tel. (181) 3067320; fax (181) 2280113; e-mail punjabkesari@vsnl.com; internet hindsamachar.in; f. 1948; Urdu; also publ. from Ambala Cantt and Jammu; Editor-in-Chief VIJAY KUMAR CHOPRA; combined circ. 30,041.

Jag Bani: ER-129 Pucca Bagh, Jalandhar; tel. (181) 2280104; fax (181) 2280111; e-mail feedback@jagbani.com; internet www.jagbani .in; f. 1978; morning; Punjabi; Publr VIJAY KUMAR; circ. 302,988.

Punjab Kesari: Civil Lines, Pucca Bagh, Jalandhar 144 001; tel. (181) 2280104; fax (181) 2280111; e-mail contact@thepunjabkesari .com; internet www.thepunjabkesari.com; f. 1965; morning; Hindi; also publ. from Jalandhar, Ludhiana, Amritsar, Ambala, Panipat, Hisar, Palampur and Jammu; Editor-in-Chief VIJAY KUMAR CHOPRA; Jt Editor AVINASH CHOPRA.

The Tribune: The Tribune Trust, Sector 29C, Chandigarh 160 030; tel. (172) 2655066; fax (172) 2651293; e-mail letters@tribuneindia .com; internet www.tribuneindia.com; f. 1881 (English edn), f. 1978 (Hindi and Punjabi edns); Editor-in-Chief RAJ CHENGAPPA; Editor (Hindi edn) SANTOSH TEWARI; Editor (Punjabi edn) VARINDER WALIA; circ. in 2011 161,231 (English), 59,846 (Punjabi), 1,010 (Hindi).

Rajasthan

Rajasthan Patrika: Kesargarh, Jawaharlal Nehru Marg, Jaipur 302 004; tel. (141) 3327700; fax (141) 2566011; e-mail info@epatrika .com; internet www.rajasthanpatrika.com; f. 1956; Hindi edn also publ. from 17 other towns; Chief Editor GULAB KOTHARI; combined circ. 1,735,083 (2013).

Rashtradoot: M.I. Rd, POB 30, Jaipur 302 001; tel. (141) 2372634; fax (141) 2373513; f. 1951; Hindi; also publ. from Kota, Udaipur, Ajmer, Bikaner, Jalore, Hindaun and Churu; CEO SOMESH SHARMA; Chief Editor RAJESH SHARMA; circ. 204,878.

Tamil Nadu

Chennai (Madras)

Daily Thanthi: 86 E.V.K. Sampath Rd, POB 467, Chennai 600 007; tel. (44) 26618661; fax (44) 26618797; e-mail managerms@dt.co.in; internet www.dailythanthi.com; f. 1942; Tamil; also publ. from 14 other regional centres; Chief Gen. Man. (Admin) RENGASAMY CHANDRASEKARAN; Editor J. P. VIJAYARAJ; combined circ. 1,738,183 (2013).

Dinakaran: 229 Kutchery Rd, Mylapore, POB 358, Chennai 600 004; tel. (44) 42209191; fax (44) 24951008; e-mail dotcom@dinakaran .com; internet www.dinakaran.com; f. 1977; Tamil; also publ. from Madurai, Tiruchirapalli, Vellore, Tirunelveli, Salem, Coimbatore and Puducherry (Pondicherry); Man. Dir KALANIDHI MARAN; Editor R. M. R. RAMESH; circ. 246,487.

Dinamalar: 39 Whites Rd, Chennai 600 014; tel. (44) 28540001; fax (44) 28540010; e-mail dmrae@dinamalar.in; internet www.dinamalar.com; f. 1951; Tamil; also publ. from 10 other towns; Editor Dr R. KRISHNAMURTHY; circ. 128,436.

Dinamani: Express Estates, Mount Rd, Chennai 600 002; tel. (44) 23457601; fax (44) 23457619; e-mail webmani@dinamani.com; internet www.dinamani.com; f. 1934; morning; Tamil; also publ. from Madurai, Coimbatore, Thiruchirapalli, Vellore, Tirunelveli and Bengaluru; Editor K. VAIDYANATHAN; circ. 37,981.

The Hindu: Kasturi Bldgs, 859/860 Anna Salai, Chennai 600 002; tel. (44) 28576300; fax (44) 28415325; e-mail letters@thehindu.co.in; internet www.thehindu.com; f. 1878; morning; English; independent; also publ. from 12 other regional centres; Editor-in-Chief MALINI PARTHASARATHY; circ. 1,314,016 (2014).

The Hindu (Tamil): Kasturi Bldg, 859–60, Anna Salai, Chennai 600 002; tel. (44) 30899000; e-mail editor@thehindutamil.co.in; internet tamil.thehindu.com; f. 2013; Tamil; Editor K. ASOKAN.

The Hindu Business Line: 859 Anna Salai, Chennai 600 002; tel. (44) 28413344; fax (44) 28415325; e-mail bleditor@thehindu.co.in; internet www.thehindubusinessline.com; f. 1994; morning; English; also publ. from 12 other regional centres; Editor D. SAMPATH KUMAR; circ. 178,520.

Murasoli: Tantara Foundation, 180 Kodambakkam High Rd, Chennai 600 034; tel. (44) 28270044; fax (44) 28217515; internet www.murasoli.in; f. 1960; organ of the DMK; Tamil; Editor S. SELVAM; circ. 54,000.

New Indian Express: 29 Express Gardens, Ambattur Industrial Estate, Chennai 600 058; tel. (44) 23457601; fax (44) 23457619; e-mail writetous@newindianexpress.com; internet expressbuzz.com; f. 1932 as *Indian Express*; morning; English; also publ. from 12 other cities, incl. Bengaluru, Bhubaneswar, Hyderabad, Kochi and Vijayawada; Chair. and Man. Dir MANOJ KUMAR SONTHALIA; Exec. Editor V. SUDARSHAN; circ. (Chennai edn) 103,247.

Tripura

Dainik Sambad: 11 Jagannath Bari Rd, POB 2, Agartala 799 001; tel. (381) 2326676; fax (381) 2324845; e-mail dainik2@sanchar.net.in; internet www.dainiksambad.net; f. 1966; Bengali; morning; Editor SANJAY GUPTA; circ. 56,922.

Uttar Pradesh

Agra

Amar Ujala: Sikandra Rd, Agra 282 007; tel. (562) 2321600; fax (562) 2322181; e-mail editor@amarujala.com; internet www.amarujala.com; f. 1948; Hindi; also publ. from Bareilly, Allahabad, Jhansi, Kanpur, Moradabad, Chandigarh and Meerut; Editor AJAY K. AGARWAL.

Kanpur

Dainik Jagran: Jagran Bldg, 2 Sarvodaya Nagar, Kanpur 208 005; tel. (512) 2216161; fax (512) 2216972; e-mail kanpur@knpcom; internet in.jagran.yahoo.com; f. 1942; Hindi; also publ. from 37 other cities and districts; Editorial Dir MAHENDRA MOHAN GUPTA; Chief Editor SANJAY GUPTA; combined circ. 3,034,140 (2014).

I Next: Krishna Tower, 9th Floor, Civil Lines, Kanpur 208 001; tel. (512) 2216161; fax (512) 2216972; internet epaper.inextlive.com; f. 2006; Hindi daily in bilingual format; publ. from Agra, Allahabad, Bareilly, Gorakhpur, Lucknow, Meerut, Varanasi; also publ. from 5 other cities in Uttarakhand, Bihar, Jharkhand and Madhya Pradesh; Editor ALOK SANWAL.

Lucknow

The Pioneer: Sahara Shopping Centre, Faizabad Rd, Lucknow 226 016; tel. (522) 2346444; fax (522) 2345582; internet www.dailypioneer.com; f. 1865; English; also publ. from Bhopal, Bhubneshwar, Chandigarh, Dehradun, Ranchi and New Delhi; Editor CHANDAN MITRA; circ. 86,913.

Swatantra Bharat: 1 Jopling Rd, 2nd Floor, Lucknow 226 001; tel. (522) 2204306; fax (522) 2208071; e-mail swatantrabharat47@gmail.com; internet swatantrabharat.com; f. 1947; Hindi; also publ. from Kanpur and Delhi; Editor K. K. SRIVASTAVA; circ. 73,317 (Lucknow), 73,689 (Kanpur).

Varanasi

Aj: Aj Bhavan, Sant Kabir Rd, Kabirchaura, Varanasi 221 001; tel. (542) 2393981; fax (542) 2393989; e-mail ajhindidaily@gmail.com; f. 1920; Hindi; also publ. from Gorakhpur, Patna, Allahabad, Ranchi, Agra, Bareilly, Lucknow, Jamshedpur, Haldwani and Kanpur; Editor SHARDUL VIKRAM GUPTA; circ. 45,314.

West Bengal

Kolkata (Calcutta)

Aajkaal: BP-7, Sector 5, Bidhannagar, Kolkata 700 091; tel. (33) 30110800; fax (33) 23675502; e-mail aajkaal@cal.vsnl.net.in; internet www.aajkaal.net; f. 1981; morning; Bengali; also publ. from Agartala and Siliguri; also publishes evening edn (*Sandhya Aajkaal*); Chief Editor ASHOK DASGUPTA; circ. 152,123.

Ananda Bazar Patrika: 6 Prafulla Sarkar St, Kolkata 700 001; tel. (33) 22374880; fax (33) 22253241; internet www.anandabazar.com; f. 1922; morning; Bengali; also publ. from Mumbai; Chief Editor AVEEK SARKAR; circ. 1,263,259.

Bartaman: Bartaman Pvt Ltd, 6 J. B. S. Haldane Ave, Kolkata 700 105; tel. (33) 23000291; fax (33) 23234030; e-mail info@bartamanpatrika.com; internet www.bartamanpatrika.com; f. 1984; also publ. from Barddhaman and Siliguri; Editor SUBHA DUTTA; circ. 534,603.

Business Standard: Saraf Bldg, 3rd Floor, 4/1 Red Cross Pl., Kolkata 700 001; tel. (33) 22101314; fax (33) 22101599; e-mail letters@business-standard.com; internet www.business-standard.com; f. 1975; morning; also publ. from Mumbai, Delhi, Patna, Lucknow, Bhopal and Chandigarh; English; Editor A. K. BHATTA-CHARYA; circ. 13,217.

Ganashakti: 74A A. J. C. Bose Rd, Kolkata 700 016; tel. (33) 22278950; fax (33) 2278090; e-mail mail@ganashakti.co.in; internet www.ganashakti.com; f. 1967; owned by Communist Party of India (Marxist), West Bengal State Cttee; morning; Bengali; also publ. from Durgapur and Siliguri; Editor NARAYAN DATTA; circ. 176,812.

Sangbad Pratidin: 20 Prafulla Sarkar St, Kolkata 700 072; tel. (33) 22128400; fax (33) 22126031; e-mail mail@sangbadpratidin.org; internet sangbadpratidin.in; f. 1992; morning; Bengali; also publ. from Ranchi and Siliguri; Chief Editor SRINJOY BOSE; circ. 299,876.

Sanmarg: 160B Chittaranjan Ave, Kolkata 700 007; tel. (33) 30615000; fax (33) 22415087; e-mail sanmarghindi@gmail.com; internet www.sanmarg.in; f. 1948; Hindi; also publ. from Varanasi, Patna, Ranchi and Bhubaneswar; Editor HARI RAM PANDEY; circ. 115,049.

The Statesman: Statesman House, 4 Chowringhee Sq., Kolkata 700 001; tel. (33) 22127070; fax (33) 22126181; e-mail thestatesman@vsnl.com; internet www.thestatesman.net; f. 1875; morning; English; independent; also publ. from New Delhi, Siliguri and Bhubaneswar; Editor RAVINDRA KUMAR; circ. 177,113.

The Telegraph: 6 Prafulla Sarkar St, Kolkata 700 001; tel. (33) 22345374; fax (33) 22253243; e-mail ttedit@abpmail.com; internet www.telegraphindia.com; f. 1982; English; also publ. from Guwahati, Jamshedpur, Ranchi and Siliguri; Editor AVEEK SARKAR; circ. 555,869.

Uttar Banga Sambad: 7 Old Court House St, Kolkata 700 001; tel. (33) 22435663; fax (33) 22435618; e-mail uttarmail@sify.com; internet www.uttarbangasambad.com; f. 1980; Bengali; circ. 143,177; Editor SABYASACHI TALUKDAR.

Vishwamitra: 74 Lenin Sarani, Kolkata 700 013; tel. (33) 22651139; fax (33) 22656393; e-mail vismtra@vsnl.com; f. 1915; morning; Hindi; commercial; Editor PRAKASH CHANDRA AGRAWALA; circ. 99,911.

SELECTED PERIODICALS

Circulation figs are for 2009, unless otherwise stated.

Delhi and New Delhi

Alive: Delhi Press Bldg, E-3 Jhandewala Estate, Rani Jhansi Rd, New Delhi 110 055; tel. (11) 23529557; fax (11) 41398888; e-mail delpress@bol.net.in; internet www.caravanalive.com; f. 1940 as *Caravan*; renamed as above in 1983; monthly; English; general interest; Editor, Publr and Printer DIVESH NATH.

Business Today: Videocon Towers, E-1 Jhandelwalan Extn, New Delhi 110 055; tel. (11) 23684800; fax (11) 23684819; e-mail Mukta.Saigal@intoday.com; internet businesstoday.intoday.in; f. 1992; fortnightly; English; Editor PROSENJIT DATTA; circ. 111,806.

Catholic India: CBCI Centre, 1 Ashok Place, Goldakkhana, New Delhi 110 001; tel. and fax (11) 23344470; fax (11) 23364615; e-mail editor@cbci.in; internet cbci.in; bi-annual; Fr GEORGE PLATHOTTAM.

Competition Refresher: 4739/23 UGF, Ansari Rd, Daryaganj, New Delhi 110 002; tel. (11) 23283226; fax (11) 23269227; e-mail editorial@brightpublications.com; internet www.brightpublications.com; f. 1984; monthly; English; Chief Editor, Publr and Man. Dir PRITAM SINGH BRIGHT; circ. 165,612 (2014).

Competition Success Review (CSR): 604 Prabhat Kiran Bldg, Rajendra Place, Delhi 110 008; tel. (11) 45113300; fax (11) 25825391; e-mail info@competitionreview.com; internet www.competitionreview.com; f. 1964; monthly; English; Editor S. K. SACHDEVA; circ. 184,999 (2014).

Employment News: Government of India, East Blk IV, Level 5, R. K. Puram, New Delhi 110 066; tel. (11) 26174975; fax (11) 26105875; e-mail empnews@bol.net.in; internet www.employmentnews.gov.in; f. 1976; weekly; Hindi, Urdu and English edns; Gen. Man. and Chief Editor PUSHPINDER KAUR; Editor RAKESH RENU; combined circ. 305,229 (2014).

Grihshobha: Delhi Press Bldg, E-3 Jhandewala Estate, Rani Jhansi Rd, New Delhi 110 055; tel. (11) 51398888; fax (11) 51540714; e-mail editorial@delhipressgroup.com; f. 1979; fortnightly Hindi and Bangla edns; monthly Tamil, Telugu, Kannada, Marathi, Malayalam and Gujarati edns; women's interests; Editor, Publr and Printer PARESH NATH; circ. 236,378 (Hindi edn, 2014).

India Perspectives: 152, 'A' Wing, Shastri Bhavan, New Delhi 110 001; tel. (11) 23389471; fax 23385549; internet www .indiaperspectives.in; f. 1988; culture; publ. by Ministry of External Affairs; Editor SYED AKBARUDDIN.

India Today: F-14/15, Connaught Place, New Delhi 110 001; tel. (11) 23315801; fax (11) 23316180; e-mail ratnam@intoday.com; internet www.india-today.com; f. 1975; weekly; English, Tamil, Telugu, Malayalam, Bengali and Hindi; Editor M. J. AKBAR; Editor-in-Chief AROON PURIE; circ. 120,171 (Hindi edn, 2014).

Indian Railways: 411 Rail Bhavan, Raisina Rd, New Delhi 110 001; tel. (11) 23384481; fax (11) 23383540; e-mail editorir@rb.railnet.gov .in; f. 1956; monthly; English; publ. by the Ministry of Railways (Railway Board); Editor M. R. KALYANI; circ. 7,000.

Junior Science Refresher: 4739/23 UGF, Ansari Road, Daryaganj, New Delhi 110 002; tel. (11) 23282226; fax (11) 23269227; e-mail editorial@brightpublications.com; internet www.brightpublications .com; f. 1987; monthly; English; Chief Editor, Publr and Man. Dir PRITAM SINGH BRIGHT; circ. 114,450 (2014).

Kadambini: Hindustan Times House, 18–20 Kasturba Gandhi Marg, New Delhi 110 001; tel. (11) 66561234; fax (11) 66561270; e-mail vnagar@hindustantimes.com; f. 1960; monthly; Hindi; Editor VIJAY KISHORE MANAV; Exec. Editor VISHNU NAGAR; circ. 31,530.

Krishak Samachar: Bharat Krishak Samaj, Dr Panjabrao Deshmukh Krishak Bhavan, A-1 Nizamuddin West, New Delhi 110 013; tel. (11) 24619508; fax (11) 24359509; e-mail publication@bks.org.in; internet bks.org.in/krishak-samachar; f. 1957; monthly; English and Hindi edns; agriculture; Editor Dr KRISHAN BIR CHAUDHARY; circ. 6,970 (English), 22,728 (Hindi).

Kurukshetra: Soochna Bhawan, CGO Complex, Lodhi Rd, New Delhi 110 003; tel. (11) 23015014; fax (11) 23386879; monthly; English and Hindi; rural development; Publr KAILASH CHAND MEENA; circ. 18,056 (English), 21,146 (Hindi).

Liberation: U-90 Shakarpur, New Delhi 110 092; tel. and fax (11) 22521067; fax (11) 22442790; e-mail mail@cpiml.org; internet www .cpiml.org; f. 1967; monthly; Editor in Chief DIPANKAR BHATTACHARYA; organ of Communist Party of India (Marxist-Leninist).

Mainstream: 145/1D Shahpur Jat, 1st Floor, nr Asiad Village, New Delhi 110 049; tel. (11) 26497188; fax (11) 26569382; e-mail mainlineweekly@yahoo.com; internet www.mainstreamweekly.net; English; weekly; politics and current affairs; Editor SUMIT CHAKRAVARTTY.

Maxim India: Media Transasia (India) Ltd, K-35, Green Park, New Delhi 110 016; tel. (11) 26862687; fax (11) 26867641; internet www .maximindia.in; f. 2005; monthly; English; men's lifestyle; CEO and Publr PIYUSH SHARMA; Editor-in-Chief VIVEK PAREEK.

Mayapuri: A-5, Mayapuri Phase 1, New Delhi 110 064; tel. (11) 28116120; fax (11) 41833139; e-mail info@mayapurigroup.com; internet www.mayapurigroup.com/mayapuri.htm; f. 1974; weekly; Hindi; cinema; Editor A. P. BAJAJ.

New Age Weekly: Ajoy Bhavan, 15 Comrade Indrajeet Gupta Marg, Delhi 110 002; tel. (11) 23230762; fax (11) 23235543; e-mail cpindia@ del2.vsnl.net.in; internet www.newageweekly.com; f. 1953; main organ of the Communist Party of India; weekly; English; Editor SHAMEEM FAIZEE; Man. N. S. NEGI; circ. 215,000.

Organiser: Sanskriti Bhavan, D. B. Gupta Rd, Jhandewala, New Delhi 110 055; tel. (11) 47642022; fax (11) 47642023; e-mail editor .organiser@bpdl.in; internet www.organiser.org; f. 1947; weekly; English; Editor PRAFULLA KETKAR; circ. 44,100.

Outlook: AB-10 Safdarjung Enclave, New Delhi 110 029; tel. (11) 33505500; fax (11) 26191420; e-mail outlook@outlookindia.com; internet www.outlookindia.com; f. 1995; weekly; Hindi and English edns; Publr MAHESHWER PERI; Editor-in-Chief VINOD MEHTA; circ. 250,000.

Panchjanya: Sanskriti Bhavan, Deshbandhu Gupta Marg, Jhandewala, New Delhi 110 055; tel. (11) 47642013; fax (11) 47642015; e-mail editor.panchjanya@gmail.com; internet www.panchjanya .com; f. 1947; weekly; Hindi; general interest; nationalist; Editor HITESH SHANKAR; circ. 41,573.

Punjabi Digest: 209 Hemkunt House, 6 Rajendra Place, POB 2549, New Delhi 110 008; tel. (11) 25715225; fax (11) 25761053; e-mail info@punjabidigest.com; internet www.punjabidigest.com; f. 1971; literary monthly; Gurmukhi; Chief Editor Sardar S. B. SINGH; circ. 55,000.

Sainik Samachar: Blk L-1, Church Rd, New Delhi 110 001; tel. (11) 23094668; e-mail sainiksamachar@gmail.com; internet sainiksamachar.nic.in; f. 1909; pictorial fortnightly for India's armed forces; English, Hindi, Urdu, Tamil, Punjabi, Telugu, Marathi, Kannada, Gorkhali, Malayalam, Bengali, Assamese and Oriya edns; Editor-in-Chief HASIBUR RAHMAN; circ. 20,000.

Saras Salil: Delhi Press Bldg, E-3 Jhandewala Estate, Rani Jhansi Rd, New Delhi 110 055; tel. (11) 41398888; fax (11) 41540714; e-mail editorial@delhipressgroup.com; internet www.delhipress.in; f. 1993; fortnightly; Hindi, Telugu, Tamil, Gujarati and Marathi edns; Editor, Publr and Printer PARESH NATH; combined circ. 683,676.

Sarita: Delhi Press Bldg, E-3 Jhandewala Estate, Rani Jhansi Rd, New Delhi 110 055; tel. (11) 41398888; fax (11) 23625020; e-mail editorial@delhipressgroup.com; internet www.delhipress.in; f. 1945; fortnightly; Hindi; family magazine; Editor, Publr and Printer PARESH NATH; circ. 75,735.

Tehelka: M-76, M-Block Market, 2nd Floor, Greater Kailash Pt 2, New Delhi 110 048; tel. and fax (11) 40575757; e-mail editor@tehelka .com; internet www.tehelka.com; f. 2004; weekly; English; current affairs, business and culture; Editor MATHEW SAMUEL.

Vigyan Pragati: CSIR-NISCAI, Dr K. S. Krishnan Marg, New Delhi 110 012; tel. (11) 25841769; fax (11) 25847062; e-mail vp@ niscair.res.in; internet www.niscair.res.in; f. 1952; monthly; Hindi; popular science; Editor PRADEEP SHARMA; circ. 37,000.

Woman's Era: Delhi Press Bldg, E-3 Jhandewala Estate, Rani Jhansi Rd, New Delhi 110 055; tel. (11) 41398888; fax (11) 23625020; e-mail delpress@bol.net.in; internet www.womansera .com; f. 1973; fortnightly; English; women's interests; Editor, Publr and Printer PARESH NATH; circ. 66,200.

Yojana: Soochna Bhavan, Lodhi Rd, New Delhi 110 003; tel. (11) 23717910; fax (11) 24362971; e-mail yojana@techpilgrim.com; internet www.yojana.gov.in; f. 1957; monthly; economic issues; English, Tamil, Bengali, Marathi, Gujarati, Assamese, Malayalam, Telugu, Kannada, Punjabi, Urdu, Oriya and Hindi edns; Chief Editor DEEPIKA KACHHAL; circ. 29,032 (English).

Andhra Pradesh

Andhra Bhoomi Sachitra Masa Patrika: 36 Sarojini Devi Rd, Secunderabad 500 003; tel. (842) 27802340; fax (842) 27805256; f. 1977; fortnightly; Telugu; Editor T. VENKATRAM REDDY; circ. 34,817.

Andhra Jyoti Sachitra Vara Patrika: Vijayawada 520 010, tel. (866) 2474532; f. 1967; weekly; Telugu; Editor PURANAM SUBRAMANYA SARMA; circ. 59,000.

Andhra Prabha Illustrated Weekly: 591 Lower Tank Bund Rd, Express Centre, Domalaguda, Hyderabad 500 029; tel. (40) 2233586; e-mail info@apweekly.com; internet www.apweekly.com; weekly; Telugu; publ. by Indian Express Group.

Swati Saparivara Patrika: Anil Bldgs, Suryaraopet, POB 339, Vijayawada 520 002; tel. (866) 2431862; fax (866) 2430433; e-mail advt_swati@sify.com; internet www.swatipublications.com; f. 1984; weekly; Telugu; Editor VEMURI BALARAM; circ. 252,100.

Assam (Asom)

Agradoot: Agradoot Bhavan, Dispur, Guwahati 781 006; tel. (361) 2261923; fax (361) 2260655; e-mail agradoot@sify.com; f. 1971; bi-weekly; Assamese; Editor KANAK SEN DEKA; circ. 29,463.

Asam Bani: Tribune Bldg, MRD Rd, Chandmari, Guwahati 781 003; tel. (361) 2660102; e-mail editor@asambani.com; internet www .asambani.com; f. 1955; weekly; Assamese; Editor DILEEP CHANDAN; circ. 6,153.

Sadin: Maniram Dewan Rd, Chandmari, Guwahati 781 003; tel. (361) 2524594; fax (361) 2524634; e-mail sadin@pratidinassam.com; internet www.pratidinassam.com/sadin; weekly; Assamese; Editor ANURADHA SHARMA PUJARI; circ. 33,082.

Bihar

Hamara Dinmaan: Trading Co Pvt Ltd, Bandhuk Bhawan, Station Rd, Patna; monthly; Hindi; Publr MAHESH KUMAR SINGH; circ. 53,700.

Kewal Sach: East Ashok Nagar, 14 Kankarbagh Rd, Patna 800 020; tel. (612) 3240075; e-mail info@kewalsach.com; internet www .kewalsach.com; monthly; Hindi; Publr BRAJESH MISHRA; circ. 24,035.

Lok Prasang: 102 Park View Apt, Srikrishna Puri, Patna 800 001; tel. (612) 2540662; internet www.lokprasang.com; monthly; Hindi; current affairs; Editor SHYAMAKANT JHA.

Ubharta Bihar: C-49 Housing Colony, Lohiya Nagar, Kankadbagh, Patna 800020; internet ubhartabihar.com; monthly; Hindi; Publr RAJIV RANJAN; circ. 23,550.

Gujarat

Sakhi: Sakhi Publications, Jai Hind Press Bldg, nr Gujarat Chamber, Ashram Rd, Navrangpura, Ahmedabad 380 009; tel. (79) 26581734; fax (79) 26587681; internet www.jagran.com/sakhi-hindi.html; f. 1984; fortnightly; Gujarati; women's interests; Man. Editor NITA Y. SHAH; Editor Y. N. SHAH.

Stree: Sandesh Bhavan, Lad Society Rd, Ahmedabad 380 054; tel. (79) 40004242; e-mail stree@sandesh.com; internet www.sandesh.com; f. 1962; weekly; Gujarati; Editor FALGUNBHAI PATEL; circ. 42,000.

Karnataka

Mayura: 75 Mahatma Gandhi Rd, Bengaluru 560 001; tel. (80) 25588999; fax (80) 25587179; e-mail ads@deccanherald.co.in; f. 1968; monthly; Kannada; Editor-in-Chief K. N. SHANTH KUMAR; circ. 20,512 (2011).

Sudha: 75 Mahatma Gandhi Rd, Bengaluru 560 001; tel. (80) 25588999; fax (80) 25587179; e-mail ads@deccanherald.co.in; f. 1965; weekly; Kannada; Editor-in-Chief K. N. HARI KUMAR; circ. 61,300.

Taranga: New Udayavani Bldg, Press Corner, Manipal 576 104; tel. (820) 2571151; fax (820) 2570563; e-mail tarangaonline@manipalmedia.com; internet www.udayavani.com; f. 1983; weekly; Kannada; Editor T. SATISH; circ. 69,510.

Kerala

Arogya Masika: Mathrubhumi Bldgs, K. P. Kesava Menon Rd, Kozhikode 673 001; tel. (495) 2765381; fax (495) 2760138; e-mail arogyamasika@mpp.co.in; internet www.mathrubhumi.com; owned by Mathrubhumi Printing and Publishing Co Ltd; monthly; Malayalam; health; Man. Editor P. V. CHANDRAN; circ. 270,281 (2014).

Grihalakshmi: Mathrubhumi Bldgs, K. P. Kesava Menon Rd, POB 46, Kozhikode 673 001; tel. (495) 2366655; fax (495) 2366656; e-mail mathrclt@md2.vsnl.net.in; internet www.mathrubhumi.org; f. 1979; monthly; Malayalam; women's interests; Editor K. K. SREEDHARAN NAIR; circ. 309,391 (2014).

Kalakaumudi: Kaumudi Bldgs, Pettah, Thiruvananthapuram 695 024; tel. (471) 2443531; fax (471) 2442895; e-mail vellinakshatram@gmail.com; internet www.kalakaumudi.com; f. 1975; weekly; Malayalam; Chief Editor M. S. MANI; Editor N. R. S. BABU; circ. 73,000.

Kerala Sabdam: Andamukkam, Kollam 691 001; tel. (474) 2745772; fax (474) 2751010; e-mail sabdam@vsnl.com; internet www.nanaonline.in; f. 1962; weekly; Malayalam; Man. Editor B. A. RAJAKRISHNAN; circ. 66,600.

Manorama Weekly: K. K. Rd, POB 26, Kottayam 686 001; tel. (481) 2587405; fax (481) 2565398; e-mail subscription@mm.co.in; internet eweekly.manoramaonline.com; f. 1937; weekly; Malayalam; Editor-in-Chief MAMMEN MATHEW; circ. 459,314 (2014).

Thozhilvartha: Mathrubhumi Bldgs, K. P. Kesava Menon Rd, Kozhikode 673 001; tel. (495) 2366655; fax (495) 2366656; e-mail mbiclt@mpp.co.in; internet www.mathrubhumi.org; f. 1992; weekly; Malayalam; employment; Editor K. K. SREEDHARAN NAIR; circ. 406,267 (2014).

Vanitha: MM Publications Ltd, POB 226, Kottayam 686 001; tel. (481) 2563721; fax (481) 2564393; e-mail vanitha@mmp.in; f. 1975; women's fortnightly; Malayalam (monthly) and Hindi edns; Chief Editor PREMA MAMMEN MATHEW, MARIAM MAMMEN MATHEW; Gen. Man. V. SAJEEV GEORGE; circ. (2014) 762,112 (Malayalam), 181,415 (Hindi).

Vellinakshatram: Kaumudi Bldgs, Pettah, Thiruvananthapuram 695 024; tel. (471) 2443531; fax (471) 2442895; e-mail kalakaumudi@vsnl.net; internet www.vellinakshatram.com; f. 1987; film weekly; Malayalam; Editor PRASAD LAKSHMANAN; Chief Editor SUKUMARAN MANI; circ. 65,000.

The Week: Malayala Manorama Bldgs, POB 4278, Kochi 682 036; tel. (484) 2316285; fax (484) 2315745; e-mail editor@the-week.com; internet week.manoramaonline.com; f. 1982; weekly; English; current affairs; Man. Editor PHILIP MATHEW; circ. 210,452 (2014).

Madhya Pradesh

Krishak Jagat: 14 Indira Press Complex, M. P. Nagar, POB 37, Bhopal 462 011; tel. (755) 3013605; fax (755) 2571449; e-mail info@krishakjagat.org; internet www.krishakjagat.org/krishak/; f. 1946; weekly; Hindi; agriculture; also publ. in Jaipur and Raipur; Chief Editor VIJAY KUMAR BONDRIYA; Editor SUNIL GANGRADE; circ. 73,950.

Maharashtra

Mumbai (Bombay)

Abhiyaan: Sambhaav Media Ltd, 4 AB, Government Industrial Estate, Charkop, Kandivli (W), Mumbai 400 067; tel. (22) 28687515; fax (22) 28680991; e-mail rajeshpathak@sambhaav.com; internet www.sambhaav.com; f. 1986; weekly; Gujarati; Chief Man. Dir KIRAN VADODARIA; Group Editor DEEPAL TREVEDIE; circ. 68,883.

Bhavan's Journal: Kulapati Dr K. M. Munshi Marg, Chowpatty, Mumbai 400 007; tel. (22) 23631261; fax (22) 23630058; e-mail bhavan@bhavans.info; internet www.bhavans.info; f. 1954; fortnightly; English; literature, philosophy, culture and spirituality; Exec. Sec. H. N. DASTUR; Editor V. N. NARAYANAN; circ. 40,000.

Bombay Samachar: Red House, Sayed Abdulla Brelvi Rd, Mumbai 400 001; tel. (22) 22045531; fax (22) 22046642; e-mail samachar.bombay@gmail.com; internet bombaysamachar.com; f. 1822; weekly; Gujarati; Editor NILESH DAVE; circ. 77,774 (2011).

Business India: Nirmal, 14th Floor, Nariman Point, Mumbai 400 021; tel. (22) 22883943; fax (22) 22883940; e-mail biedit.mumbai@businessindiagroup.com; internet www.businessindiagroup.com; f. 1978; fortnightly; English; Publr ASHOK ADVANI; circ. 75,700.

Business World: B-2/C-2, Paragon Condominium Asscn, P. Budhkar Marg, Worli, Mumbai 400 013; tel. (22) 24962587; fax (22) 24962596; e-mail bwonline@bworldmail.com; internet www.businessworld.in; f. 1980; weekly; English; Editor PROSENJIT DATTA; circ. 146,500.

Chitralekha: 25 Andheri Industrial Estate, off Veera Desai Rd, Mumbai 400 053; tel. (22) 67309898; fax (22) 26730858; e-mail mumbai@chitralekha.com; internet www.chitralekha.com; f. 1950; weekly; Gujarati and Marathi; Editors BHARAT GHELANI, GYANESH MAHARAO; circ. 113,344 (Gujarati, 2014).

Cine Blitz: A/3, Sangam Bhavan, Ground Floor, Brahma Kumaris Rd, nr Strand Cinema, Colaba, Mumbai 400 005; tel. (22) 22830668; fax (22) 22830672; e-mail cbedit@sify.com; internet www.cineblitz.in; f. 1974; fortnightly; English; Editor NICHOLA PAIS; circ. 41,611.

Citadel: Magna Publishing Co Ltd, Magna House, 100E Old Prabhadevi Rd, Prabhadevi, Mumbai 400 025; tel. (22) 24362270; fax (22) 24306523; e-mail citadel@magnamags.com; internet www.magnamags.com/citadel; monthly; English; lifestyle; Editor RAJESHWARI RAJIMWALE.

Economic and Political Weekly: 320–321, A to Z Industrial Estate, Ganapatrao Kadam Marg, Lower Parel, Mumbai 400 013; tel. (22) 40638282; fax (22) 24934515; e-mail epw.mumbai@gmail.com; internet epw.in; f. 1966; English; Editor C. RAMMANOHAR REDDY; circ. 12,500.

Femina: Times of India Bldg, Dr Dadabhai Naoroji Rd, Mumbai 400 001; tel. and fax (22) 22733535; fax (22) 22731585; e-mail contactfemina@wwm.co.in; internet www.femina.in; f. 1959; fortnightly (English), monthly (Hindi); Editor-in-Chief PETTY S. FATIMAH; circ. 260,157 (English, 2014).

Filmfare: Times of India Bldg, 4th Floor, Dr Dadabhai Naoroji Rd, Mumbai 400 001; tel. (22) 22733535; fax (22) 22731585; e-mail rahul.nanda@wwm.co.in; internet www.filmfare.com; f. 1952; monthly; English; Exec. Editor JITESH PILLAI; circ. 136,604 (2014).

Janmabhoomi-Pravasi: Janmabhoomi Bhavan, Janmabhoomi Marg, Fort, POB 62, Mumbai 400 001; tel. (22) 22870831; fax (22) 22874097; e-mail bhoomi@bom3.vsnl.net.in; internet pravasi.janmabhoominewspapers.com; f. 1939; weekly; Gujarati; Propr Saurashtra Trust; Editor KUNDAN VYAS; circ. 27,709.

Meri Saheli: C-14 Royal Industrial Estate, 5-B Naigaum Cross Rd, Wadala, Mumbai 400 031; tel. (22) 24182797; fax (22) 24133610; e-mail woman17@zediffmail.com; internet www.merisaheli.com; f. 1987; monthly; Hindi; women's lifestyle; Editor HEMA MALINI; circ. 327,820 (2014).

New Woman: C-14 Royal Industrial Estate, 5-B Naigaum Cross Rd, Wadala, Mumbai 400 031; tel. (22) 43448000; fax (22) 24133610; e-mail newwomanmag@gmail.com; f. 1996; monthly; English; Editor HEMA MALINI; circ. 72,800.

Onlooker: Free Press House, 215 Free Press Journal Marg, Nariman Point, Mumbai 400 021; tel. (22) 22874566; f. 1939; fortnightly; English; news magazine; Exec. Editor K. SRINIVASAN; circ. 61,000.

Reader's Digest: 12th Floor, Tower 2A, One India Bulls, Parel West, Mumbai 400 001; tel. (22) 66523337; e-mail editor.india@rd.com; internet readersdigest.co.in; f. 1954; monthly; English; Editor-in-Chief MOHAN SIVANAND; circ. 384,870.

Screen: Express Tower, Nariman Point, Mumbai 400 021; tel. (22) 22022627; fax (22) 22022139; e-mail iemumbai@expressindia.co.in; internet www.screenindia.com; f. 1950; film weekly; English; circ. 8,379.

Society: Magna Publishing Co Ltd, Magna House, 100E Old Prabhadevi Rd, Prabhadevi, Mumbai 400 025; tel. (22) 67091234; fax (22) 67091208; e-mail info@magnamags.com; internet www.magnamags.com/society; f. 1979; monthly; English; Editorial Dir FAHEEM RUHANI; circ. 29,302.

Vyapar: Janmabhoomi Bhavan, Janmabhoomi Marg, POB 62, Fort, Mumbai 400 001; tel. (22) 22870831; fax (22) 22874097; e-mail jbhoomi@yahoo.com; internet vyapar.janmabhoominewspapers.com; f. 1949; (Gujarati), 1987 (Hindi); Gujarati (2 a week) and

Hindi (weekly); commerce; propr Saurashtra Trust; Editor RAJESH M. BHAYANI; circ. 8,933 (Gujarati), 5,017 (Hindi), 1,438 (English).

Nagpur

All India Reporter: AIR Ltd, Congress Nagar, POB 209, Nagpur 440 012; tel. (712) 2534321; fax (712) 2526283; e-mail info@ airwebworld.com; internet www.airwebworld.com; f. 1914; weekly and monthly; English; law journals and court reports; Chief Editor V. R. MANOHAR; circ. 55,500.

Manipur

The Eastern Frontier: Kwakeithel Thiyam Leikai, Imphal; monthly; Manipuri; Editor LOITONGBAM BINODKUMAR SINGH.

Rajasthan

Itwari Patrika: Kesargarh, Jawahar Lal Nehru Marg, Jaipur 302 004; tel. (141) 2561582; fax (141) 2566011; e-mail ads@ rajasthanpatrika.com; weekly; Hindi; circ. 12,000.

Rashtradoot Saptahik: M.I. Rd, POB 30, Jaipur 302 001; tel. (141) 2372634; fax (141) 2373513; e-mail info@rashtradoot.com; f. 1983; Hindi; also publ. from Kota and Bikaner; Chief Editor and Man. Editor RAJESH SHARMA; CEO SOMESH SHARMA; combined circ. 324,721.

Tamil Nadu

Chennai (Madras)

Ananda Vikatan: 757 Anna Salai, Chennai 600 002; tel. (44) 28524074; fax (44) 28523819; e-mail ennangal@vikatan.com; internet www.vikatan.com; f. 1924; weekly; Tamil, Editor R. KANNAN; Man. Dir B. SRINIVASAN; circ. 275,871 (2014).

Aval Vikatan: 757 Anna Salai, Chennai 600 002; tel. (44) 28524074; fax (44) 28523819; e-mail aval@vikatan.com; internet www.vikatan .com; f. 1998; fortnightly; Tamil; Editor and Man. Dir B SRINIVASAN; circ. 210,388 (2014).

Chandamama: B-3, Lunic Industry, Cross Road B, M.I.D.C., Andheri East, Mumbai 4000093; tel. (22) 28311849; fax (22) 28311872; e-mail online@chandamama.com; internet www .chandamama.com; f 1947; children's monthly; publ. in 13 languages incl. Hindi, Gujarati, Telugu, Kannada, English, Tamil, Malayalam; Editor PRASHANT MULEKAR; combined circ. 420,000.

Frontline: Kasturi Bldgs, 859/860 Anna Salai, Chennai 600 002; tel. (44) 28413344; fax (44) 28415325; e-mail frontline@thehindu.co.in; internet www.flonnet.com; f. 1984; fortnightly; English; current affairs; independent; Editor and Publr N. RAM; circ. 73,442.

Junior Vikatan: 757 Anna Salai, Chennai 600 002; tel. (44) 28524074; fax (44) 28523819; e-mail junior@vikatan.com; internet www.vikatan.com; f. 1983; twice a week; Tamil; Editor and Man. Dir B. SRINIVASAN; circ. 180,447.

Kumudam: 151 Purasawalkam High Rd, Chennai 600 010; tel. (44) 26422146; fax (44) 26425041; e-mail kumudam@hotmail.com; internet www.kumudam.com; f. 1947; weekly; Tamil; Editor Dr S. A. P. JAWAHAR PALANIAPPAN; circ. 265,772 (2014).

Kungumam: 93A Kodambakkam High Rd, Chennai 600 034; tel. (44) 28268177; e-mail kannappan@dinakaran.com; internet www .kungumam.co.in; f. 1978; weekly; Tamil; Editor PARASAKTHI; circ. 146,391 (2014).

Rani Muthu: 86 Periyar E.V.R. High Rd, Chennai 600 007; tel. (44) 25324771; fax (44) 26426884; e-mail raniweekly@vsnl.net; f. 1969; fortnightly; Tamil; Editor RAGUPATHY BASKARAN; circ. 35,175.

Rani Weekly: 86 Periyar E.V.R. High Rd, Chennai 600 007; tel. (44) 25324771; fax (44) 26426884; e-mail raniweekly@vsnl.net; f. 1962; Tamil; Editor RAGUPATHY BASKARAN; circ. 141,911.

Thuglak: 46 Greenways Rd, Chennai 600 028; tel. (44) 42606228; fax (44) 24936915; e-mail webmaster@thuglak.com; internet www .thuglak.com; f. 1970; weekly; Tamil; Editor CHO S. RAMASWAMY; circ. 66,087.

Uttar Pradesh

Cosmopolitan: Mediaplex, FC-8, Sector 16A, Film City, Noida 201 301; tel. (120) 4807100; e-mail nandini.bhalla@intoday.com; internet cosmo.intoday.in; monthly; English; women's lifestyle; Editor NANDINI BHALLA; circ. 31,149.

Nutan Kahaniyan: 15 Sheo Charan Lal Rd, Allahabad 211 003; tel. (532) 2400612; f. 1975; monthly; Hindi; Chief Editor K. K. BHARGAVA; circ. 31,655.

West Bengal

Kolkata (Calcutta)

All India Appointment Gazette: 7 Old Court House St, Kolkata 700 001; tel. (33) 22435663; fax (33) 22435618; e-mail sambadmail@ sify.com; f. 1973; weekly; English; circ. 22,713.

Anandalok: 6 Prafulla Sarkar St, Kolkata 700 001; tel. (33) 22374880; fax (33) 22253241; f. 1975; fortnightly; Bengali; film; Editor PAULAMI SENGUPTA; circ. 71,707.

Contemporary Tea Time: c/o Contemporary Brokers Pvt Ltd, 1 Old Court House Corner, POB 14, Kolkata 700 001; tel. (33) 22307241; fax (33) 22435753; e-mail webmaster@contemporary.co .in; internet www.contemporarybrokers.com/teatime.aspx; f. 1988; quarterly; English; tea industry.

Desh: 6 Prafulla Sarkar St, Kolkata 700 001; tel. (33) 22374880; fax (33) 22253240; e-mail desh@abpmail.com; f. 1933; fortnightly; Bengali; literary; Editor HARSHA DATTA; circ. 99,881.

Global Reach Newsletter: 7W The Millennium, 235/2A A. J. C. Bose Rd, Kolkata 700 020; tel. (33) 22835537; fax (33) 22835538; e-mail ravi@globalreachonline.com; internet www.globalreach.in; f. 1991; monthly; English; education magazine for those planning to study abroad; Editor RAVI LOCHAN.

Nabakallol: 11 Jhamapookur Lane, Kolkata 700 009; tel. (33) 23504294; f. 1960; monthly; Bengali; Editor HARSHA DUTTA; circ. 29,500.

Prabuddha Bharata (Awakened India): 5 Dehi Entally Rd, Kolkata 700 014; tel. (33) 22640898; e-mail mail@advaitaashrama.org; internet advaitaashrama.org/pbmonthly; f. 1896; monthly; art, culture, religion, humanities and philosophy; Publr Swami BODHA-SARANANDA; Editor Swami NARASIMHANANDA; circ. 7,500.

Saptahik Bartaman: 6 J. B. S. Haldane Ave, Kolkata 700 105; tel. (33) 23000101; fax (33) 23234030; e-mail bartaman@satyam.net.in; f. 1988; weekly; Bengali; Editor KAKOLI CHAKRABORTY; circ. 154,803 (2014).

NEWS AGENCIES

Press Trust of India Ltd: PTI Bldg, 4 Parliament St, New Delhi 110 001; tel. (11) 23716621; fax (11) 23718714; e-mail trans@pti.in; internet www.ptinews.com; f. 1947; re-established 1978; Editor-in-Chief and CEO M. K. RAZDAN.

United News of India (UNI): 9 Rafi Marg, New Delhi 110 001; tel. (11) 23710522; fax (11) 23355841; e-mail uninet@uniindia.com; internet www.uniindia.com; f. 1959; national and international news service in English, Hindi (UNIVARTA) and Urdu; photograph and graphics service; brs in 67 centres in India; Chair. VISHWAS TRIPATHI; Chief Editor and Gen. Man. ASHOK TUTEJA.

CO-ORDINATING BODIES

Press Council of India: Soochna Bhavan, 8 C. G. O. Complex, Ground Floor, Lodhi Rd, New Delhi 110 003; tel. (11) 24366746; fax (11) 24368726; e-mail pcibpp@gmail.com; internet www .presscouncil.nic.in; f. 1979; est. under an Act of Parliament to preserve the freedom of the press and maintain and improve the standards of newspapers and news agencies in India; 28 mems; Chair. Justice C. K. PRASAD; Sec. VIBHA BHARGAVA.

Press Information Bureau: Shastri Bhavan, Dr Rajendra Prasad Rd, New Delhi 110 001; tel. (11) 23383643; fax (11) 23383203; e-mail pib@alpha.nic.in; internet www.pib.nic.in; f. 1946 to co-ordinate govt press affairs; represents newspaper managements, journalists, news agencies, parliament; has power to examine journalists under oath and may censor objectionable material; Prin. Information Officer DEEPAK SANDHU.

Registrar of Newspapers for India: Ministry of Information and Broadcasting, West Block 8, Wing 2, Ramakrishna Puram, New Delhi 110 066; tel. (11) 26107504; fax (11) 26189801; e-mail rni.hub@ nic.in; internet rni.nic.in; f. 1956 as a statutory body to collect press statistics; maintains a register of all Indian newspapers; Press Registrar MOHAN CHANDAK.

PRESS ASSOCIATIONS

All-India Newspaper Editors' Conference: 36–37 Northend Complex, Rama Krishna Ashram Marg, New Delhi 110 001; tel. (11) 23364519; fax (11) 23317947; f. 1940; c. 300 mems; Pres. VISHWA BANDHU GUPTA; Sec.-Gen. BISHAMBER NEWAR.

All India Small and Medium Newspapers' Federation: 26-F Rajiv Gandhi Chowk (Connaught Pl.), New Delhi 110 001; tel. (11) 23326000; fax (11) 23320906; e-mail indian.observer@gmail.com; c. 9,200 mems; Pres. GURINDER SINGH; Gen. Secs B. C. GUPTA, B. M. SHARMA, VIJAY SOOD.

The Foreign Correspondents' Club of South Asia: AB-19 Mathura Rd, opp. Pragati Maidan Gate 3, New Delhi 110 001; tel. (11) 23385518; fax (11) 23385517; e-mail fcc@fccsouthasia.net;

internet www.fccsouthasia.net; f. 1992; over 400 mems; Pres. Dr WAIEL S. H. AWWAD.

Indian Federation of Working Journalists: Garud Vihar, Connaught Place, New Delhi 110 001; tel. and fax (11) 23418871; e-mail ifwj.media@gmail.com; internet www.ifwj.in; f. 1950; 31,570 mems; Pres. K. VIKRAM RAO; Sec.-Gen. PARMANAND PANDEY.

Indian Journalists' Association: New Delhi; Pres. VIJAY DUTT; Gen. Sec. A. K. DHAR.

Indian Languages Newspapers' Association: Bhasha Bhavan, Badruddin Tyabji Marg, J. J. School of Arts, Mumbai 400 001; tel. (22) 22691587; internet www.ilnaindia.org; f. 1941; 320 mems; Pres. PARESH NATH; Hon. Gen. Secs CHAITANYA KASHYAP, SARVINDER KAUR, RAVI KUMAR BISHNOI.

Indian Newspaper Society: INS Bldg, Rafi Marg, New Delhi 110 001; tel. (11) 23715401; fax (11) 23723800; e-mail indnews@sify.com; internet www.indiannewspapersociety.org; f. 1939; 685 mems; Pres. RAVINDRA KUMAR.

National Union of Journalists (India): 7 Jantar Mantar Rd, 2nd Floor, New Delhi 110 001; tel. and fax (11) 23368610; e-mail nujindia@ndf.vsnl.in; internet education.vsnl.com/nujindia; f. 1972; 12,000 mems; Pres. J. K. GUPTA; Sec.-Gen. M. D. GANGWAR.

Press Club of India: 1 Raisina Rd, New Delhi 110 001; tel. (11) 23719844; fax (11) 23357048; e-mail contact@pressclubofindia.org; internet www.pressclubofindia.org; f. 1958; Pres. ANAND KISHORE SAHAY; 4,500 mems.

Press Institute of India: Rind Premises, Second Main Rd, Taramani, CPT Campus, Chennai 600 113; tel. (44) 22542344; fax (44) 22542323; e-mail editorpiirind@gmail.com; internet www .pressinstitute.in; f. 1963; 32 mem. newspapers and other orgs; Chair. K. N. SHANTH KUMAR; Dir and Editor SASHI NAIR.

Publishers

DELHI AND NEW DELHI

Affiliated East-West Press (Pvt) Ltd: G-1/16 Ansari Rd, Daryaganj, New Delhi 110 002; tel. (11) 23264180; fax (11) 23260538; e-mail affiliat@vsnl.com; internet www.aewpress.com; textbooks and reference books; also represents scientific societies; Dirs SUNNY MALIK, KAMAL MALIK.

Aleph Book Co: 161 B/4, Ground Floor, Gulmohar House, Yusuf Sarai Community Centre, New Delhi 110 049; tel. (11) 49226666; e-mail publicity@alephbookcompany.com; internet www .alephbookcompany.com; f. 2011; literary fiction, history, biography, popular culture; Man. Dir DAVID DAVIDAR.

Atlantic Publishers and Distributors (Pvt) Ltd: 7/22 Ansari Rd, Darya Ganj, New Delhi 110 002; tel. (11) 40775252; fax (11) 23285873; e-mail editorial@atlanticbooks.com; internet www .atlanticbooks.com; f. 1977; academic, professional and general non-fiction; co-publishing and distribution arrangements with numerous int. publrs; Man. Dir MANISH KUMAR GUPTA.

B. I. Publications Pvt Ltd: B. I. House, 54 Janpath, New Delhi 110 001; tel. (11) 46209999; fax (11) 23323138; e-mail bipgroup@vsnl .com; internet www.bipgroup.com; f. 1959; academic, general and professional; Man. Dir SHASHANK BHAGAT.

Book Circle: 19A Ansari Rd, Daryaganj, New Delhi 110 002; tel. (11) 23264444; fax (11) 23263050; e-mail bookcircle@vsnl.net; f. 2001; social sciences, arts and architecture, technical, medical, scientific; Propr and Dir HIMANSHU CHAWLA.

Cambridge University Press India (Pvt) Ltd: Cambridge House, 4381/4 Ansari Rd, Daryaganj, New Delhi 110 002; e-mail cupdel@ cambridge.org; internet cambridgeindia.org; branch offices in Mumbai, Kolkata, Chennai, Bengaluru, Hyderabad, Pune and Thiruvananthapuram; academic and educational books; Man. Dir MANAS SAIKIA.

S. Chand and Co Ltd: 7361 Ram Nagar, Qutab Rd, nr New Delhi Railway Station, New Delhi 110 055; tel. (11) 23672080; fax (11) 23677446; e-mail info@schandgroup.com; internet www .schandgroup.com; f. 1917; educational and general in English and Hindi; also book exports and imports; Man. Dir RAVINDRA KUMAR GUPTA.

Children's Book Trust: Nehru House, 4 Bahadur Shah Zafar Marg, New Delhi 110 002; tel. (11) 23316970; fax (11) 23721090; e-mail cbtnd@vsnl.com; internet www.childrensbooktrust.com; f. 1957; children's books in English and other languages of India; Editor C. G. R. KURUP; Gen. Man. RAVI SHANKAR.

Concept Publishing Co: A/15–16, Commercial Block, Mohan Garden, New Delhi 110 059; tel. (11) 25351794; fax (11) 25357109; e-mail publishing@conceptpub.com; internet www.conceptpub.com; f. 1974; social sciences, management, psychology, community development; Chair. and Man. Dir ASHOK KUMAR MITTAL; CEO NITIN MITTAL.

Delhi Press: E-3, Rani Jhansi Rd, Jhandewalan, New Delhi 110 055; tel. (11) 41398888; fax (11) 23625020; internet www.delhipress.in; f. 1939; publr of 32 magazine titles in 9 languages, incl. *Grihshobha*, *Sarita*, *Saras Salil* and *Champak*; Dir ANANT NATH.

Frank Bros & Co (Publishers) Ltd: 4675A Ansari Rd, 21 Daryaganj, New Delhi 110 002; tel. (11) 23263393; fax (11) 23269032; e-mail connect@frankbros.com; internet www.frankbros.com; f. 1930; children's, educational and management; Chair. and Man. Dir R. C. GOVIL.

Heritage Publishers: 19A Ansari Rd, Daryaganj, New Delhi 110 002; tel. (11) 23266633; fax (11) 23263050; e-mail heritage@nda.vsnl .net.in; internet www.meditechbooks.com; f. 1973; social sciences, art and architecture, technical, medical, scientific; Propr and Dir B. R. CHAWLA.

Hindustan Publishing Corpn (India): 4805/24 Bharat Ram Rd, 102, Daryaganj, New Delhi 110 002; (11) 43580512; e-mail hpcedu@rediffmail.com; archaeology, anthropology, business management and applied sciences, geology, mathematics, physics, sociology; publ. *Demography India* and *Journal of Economic Geology and Georesource Management*; exporter of Indian journals and periodicals, Indian and foreign books; Man. Partner B. B. JAIN.

Lalit Kala Akademi: Rabindra Bhavan, New Delhi 110 001; tel. (11) 23009200; fax (11) 23009292; e-mail lka@lalitkala.gov.in; internet www.lalitkala.gov.in; books on Indian art; Chair. BALAN NAMBIAR.

Lancers Books: POB 4236, New Delhi 110 048; tel. (11) 26241617; fax (11) 26992063; e-mail lancersbooks@hotmail.com; internet www .lancersbooks.net; f. 1977; politics (with special emphasis on northeast India), defence; Propr S. KUMAR.

Motilal Banarsidass Publishers (Pvt) Ltd: A-44, Naraina Industrial Area, Phase 1, New Delhi 110 028; tel. (11) 25795180; fax (11) 25797221; e-mail web@mlbd.com; internet www.mlbd.com; f. 1903; religion, philosophy, astrology, yoga, linguistics, history, art, architecture, literature, music and dance, alternative medicine; English and Sanskrit; offices in Bengaluru, Chennai, Kolkata, Mumbai, Patna, Pune and Varanasi; Man. Dir N. P. JAIN.

Munshiram Manoharlal Publishers Pvt Ltd: 54 Rani Jhansi Rd, POB 5715, New Delhi 110 055; tel. (11) 23671668; fax (11) 23612745; e-mail info@mrmlonline.com; internet www.mrmlonline.com; f. 1952; Indian art, architecture, archaeology, religion, music, law, medicine, dance, dictionaries, travel, history, politics, numismatics, Buddhism, philosophy, sociology, etc.; Man. Dir ASHOK JAIN.

National Book Trust: 5 Nehru Bhavan, Institutional Area, Vasant Kunj, Phase 2, New Delhi 110 070; tel. (11) 26707700; fax (11) 26121883; e-mail office.nbt@nic.in; internet www.nbtindia.org.in; f. 1957; autonomous organization established by the Ministry of Human Resource Development to produce and encourage the production of good literary works; Chair. BALDEV SHARMA.

National Council of Educational Research and Training (NCERT): Sri Aurobindo Marg, New Delhi 110 016; tel. (11) 26560620; fax (11) 26868419; e-mail ncert.media@gmail.com; internet www.ncert.nic.in; f. 1961; school textbooks, teachers' guides, research monographs, journals, etc.; Dir Prof. P. SINCLAIR.

Neeta Prakashan: A-4 Ring Rd, South Extension Part I, POB 3853, New Delhi 110 049; tel. (11) 24636010; fax (11) 24636011; e-mail info@neetaprakashan.com; internet www.neetaprakashan.com; f. 1960; educational, children's, general; Dir RAJESH GUPTA.

New Age International Pvt Ltd: 4835/24 Ansari Rd, Daryaganj, New Delhi 110 002; tel. (11) 23276802; fax (11) 23267437; e-mail info@newagepublishers.com; internet www.newagepublishers.com; f. 1966; science, engineering, technology, management, humanities, social sciences; Man. Dir SAUMYA GUPTA.

Oxford University Press: YMCA Library Bldg, 1st Floor, 1 Jai Singh Rd, POB 43, New Delhi 110 001; tel. (11) 43600300; fax (11) 23360897; e-mail admin.in@oup.com; internet www.oup.co.in; f. 1912; educational, scientific, medical, general, humanities and social sciences, dictionaries and reference; Man. Dir MANZAR KHAN.

Penguin Books India (Pvt) Ltd: 11 Community Centre, Panchsheel Park, New Delhi 110 017; tel. (11) 26494401; fax (11) 26494403; e-mail penguin@del2.vsnl.net.in; internet www.penguinbooksindia .com; f. 1987; Indian literature and general non-fiction in English; CEO ANDREW PHILLIPS; Pres. THOMAS ABRAHAM.

PHI Learning: M-97 Connaught Circus, New Delhi 110 001; tel. (11) 22143344; fax (11) 23417179; e-mail phi@phindia.com; internet www .phindia.com; f. 1963 as Prentice-Hall of India (Pvt) Ltd; university-level text and reference books; Man. Dir A. K. GHOSH.

Pitambar Publishing Co Pvt Ltd: 888 East Park Rd, Karol Bagh, New Delhi 110 005; tel. (11) 23676058; fax (11) 23676058; e-mail pitambar@bol.net.in; academic, children's books, textbooks and general; Man. Dir ANAND BHUSHAN; 5 brs.

Pustak Mahal: J-3/16 Daryaganj, New Delhi 110 002; tel. (11) 23272783; fax (11) 23260518; e-mail pustak@pustakmahal.com;

internet www.pustakmahal.com; children's, general, computers, religious, encyclopedias; Chair. R. A. GUPTA; Man. Dir ASHOK GUPTA.

Rajkamal Prakashan (Pvt) Ltd: 1B Netaji Subhas Marg, Daryaganj, New Delhi 110 002; tel. (11) 23274463; fax (11) 23278144; e-mail info@rajkamalprakashan.com; internet www.rajkamalprakashan.com; f. 1947; Hindi; literary; also literary journal and monthly trade journal; Man. Dir ASHOK KUMAR MAHESHWARI.

Rajpal and Sons: 1590 Madrasa Rd, Kashmere Gate, Delhi 110 006; tel. (11) 23865483; fax (11) 23867791; e-mail mail@rajpalpublishing.com; internet www.rajpalpublishing.com; f. 1891; humanities, social sciences, art, juvenile; Hindi; Chair. MEERA JOHRI.

Research and Information System for Developing Countries: Zone IV-B, 4th Floor, India Habitat Centre, Lodhi Rd, New Delhi 100 003; tel. (11) 24682177; fax (11) 24682173; e-mail publication@ris.org.in; internet www.ris.org.in; f. 1983; trade and development issues; Dir-Gen. Dr BISWAJIT DHAR.

Roli Books (Pvt) Ltd: M-75 Greater Kailash Part II Market, New Delhi 110048; tel. (11) 40682000; e-mail info@rolibooks.com; internet www.rolibooks.com; f. 1978; general fiction and non-fiction, children's books; Publisher PRAMOD KAPOOR.

Rupa & Co: 7/16 Ansari Rd, Daryaganj, POB 7017, New Delhi 110 002; tel. (11) 23278586; fax (11) 23277294; e-mail info@rupapublications.com; internet www.rupapublications.com; f. 1936; Chief Exec. R. K. MEHRA.

Sage Publications India Pvt Ltd: B-1/I-1, Mohan Co-operative Industrial Estate, Mathura Rd, Post Bag 7, New Delhi 110 044; tel. (11) 40539222; fax (11) 40539234; e-mail info@sagepub.in; internet www.sagepub.in; f. 1981; social sciences, development studies, business and management studies; Man. Dir and CEO VIVEK MEHRA.

Sahitya Akademi: Rabindra Bhavan, 35 Ferozeshah Rd, New Delhi 110 001; tel. (11) 23386626; fax (11) 23382428; e-mail secy@ndb.vsnl.net.in; internet www.sahitya-akademi.gov.in; f. 1954; bibliographies, translations, monographs, encyclopedias, literary classics, etc.; Pres. SUNIL GANGOPADHYAY; Sec. A. KRISHNA MURTHY.

Scholar Publishing House (Pvt) Ltd: 85 Model Basti, New Delhi 110 005; tel. (11) 23541299; fax (11) 23676565; e-mail info@scholar.ws; internet www.scholar.ws; f. 1968; educational; Man. Dir RAMESH RANADE.

Sterling Publishers (Pvt) Ltd: A-59 Okhla Industrial Area, Phase II, New Delhi 110 020; tel. (11) 26387070; fax (11) 26383788; e-mail mail@sterlingpublishers.com; internet www.sterlingpublishers.com; f. 1964; academic books on the humanities and social sciences, children's books, trade paperbacks; Chair. and Man. Dir S. K. GHAI; Dirs VIKAS GHAI, GAURAV GHAI.

Taylor & Francis Books India Pvt Ltd: YMCA Library Bldg, 2nd & 3rd Floor, 1 Jai Singh Rd, POB 43, New Delhi 110 001; tel. (11) 23712131; fax (11) 23342132; e-mail inquiry@tandfindia.com; internet www.taylorandfrancisgroup.com; f. 2004; Man. Dir NITASHA DEVASAR.

Vitasta Publishing: 2/15 Ansari Rd, New Delhi 110 002; tel. (11) 23283024; fax (11) 23263522; e-mail info@vitastapublishing.com; internet www.vitastapublishing.com; f. 2004; science, technology and management; Man. Dir RENU KAUL KUMAR.

Women Unlimited: K-36, Hauz Khas Enclave, Ground Floor, New Delhi 110 016; tel. (11) 26964947; fax (11) 26496597; e-mail womenunltd@vsnl.net; internet www.womenunlimited.net; f. 2003; feminism; Head RITU MENON.

Zubaan: 128B, 1st Floor, Shahpur Jat, New Delhi 110 019; tel. (11) 26494617; e-mail contact@zubaanbooks.com; internet www.zubaanbooks.com; f. 2003; women's studies, social sciences, humanities, general non-fiction, fiction, etc.; Dir URVASHI BUTALIA; Editor PREETI GILL.

CHENNAI (MADRAS)

Emerald Publishers: 15A Casa Major Rd, 1st Floor, Egmore, Chennai 600 008; tel. (44) 28193206; fax (44) 28192380; e-mail info@emeraldpublishers.com; internet www.emeraldpublishers.com; English textbooks, self-help and examination skills; CEO G. OLIVANNAN.

Eswar Press: Archana Arcade, 16 Natesan St, T. Nagar, Chennai 600 017; tel. (44) 24345902; fax (44) 24339590; e-mail enquiry@eswar.com; internet www.eswar.com; science and technology; CEO M. PERIYASAMY.

New Horizon Media: 177/103 Ambal's Bldg, 1st Floor, Lloyds Rd, Royapettah, Chennai 600 014; tel. (92) 44411119; fax (44) 43009701; e-mail nhm-shop@nhm.in; internet www.nhm.in; f. 2004; fiction and non-fiction in Tamil, English and Malayalam; Man. Dir BADRI SESHADRI.

Scitech Publications (India) (Pvt) Ltd: 7/3-C Madley Rd, T. Nagar, Chennai 600 017; tel. (44) 24311113; e-mail scitech@md5.vsnl.net.in; internet www.scitechpublications.com; f. 1998; sci-

ence, technology, management, reference, etc.; Man. Dir M. R. PURUSHOTHAMAN.

Sura Books (Pvt) Ltd: 1620 J Block, 16th Main Rd, Anna Nagar, Chennai 600 040; tel. (44) 26162126; fax (44) 26162173; e-mail enquiry@surabooks.com; internet www.surabooks.com; children's books, dictionaries, examinations guides, tourist guides, Indology, etc.; Man. Dir V. K. SUBBURAJ.

JAIPUR

Neelkanth Publishers: C-93, Jagraj Marg, Bapu Nagar, Jaipur 302 015; tel. (141) 2702517; e-mail info@neelkanthpublishers.in; internet www.neelkanthpublishers.in; f. 2005; academic textbooks and reference books; Dir KULDEEP GOYAL.

Pointer Publishers: 807 Vyas Bldg, S.M.S. Highway, Jaipur 302 003; tel. and fax (141) 2578159; e-mail info@pointerpublishers.com; internet www.pointerpublishers.com; f. 1986; sciences, commerce, economics, education, literature, history, journalism, law, philosophy, psychology, sociology, tourism; in English and Hindi; Contact VIPIN JAIN.

Rajasthan Hindi Granth Akademi: Plot No. 1, Jhalana Institutional Area, Jaipur 302 004; tel. (141) 2711129; fax (141) 2710341; e-mail hindigranth@indiatimes.com; internet www.rajhga.com; engineering, agriculture, science, social sciences, law, education, fine arts and journalism; Dir Dr R. D. SAINI.

Shyam Prakashan: 1926 Nataniyon Ka Rasta, Jaipur 302 003; tel. (141) 2317659; fax (141) 2326554; e-mail ankit_146@sify.com; internet www.shyamprakashan.com; Propr OM PRAKASH AGRAWAL.

KOLKATA (CALCUTTA)

Academic Publishers: 5A Bhawani Dutta Lane, Kolkata 700 073; tel. (33) 22571071; fax (33) 22572489; e-mail info@academicpublishers.in; internet www.academicpublishers.in; f. 1958; textbooks, management, medical, technical; Man. Partner B. K. DHUR.

Advaita Ashrama: 5 Dehi Entally Rd, Kolkata 700 014; tel. (33) 22164000; e-mail mail@advaitaashrama.org; internet www.advaitaashrama.org; f. 1800; religion, philosophy, spiritualism, Vedanta; publication centre of Ramakrishna Math and Ramakrishna Mission; Editor PRABUDDHA BHARATA.

Ananda Publishers (Pvt) Ltd: 45 Beniatola Lane, Kolkata 700 009; tel. (33) 22414352; fax (33) 22193856; e-mail ananda@cal3.vsnl.net.in; internet www.anandapub.com; literature, general; owned by ABP Group (internet www.abp.in); Man. Dir S. MITRA.

Assam Review Publishing Co: 27A Waterloo St, 1st Floor, Kolkata 700 069; tel. (33) 22482251; fax (33) 22482251; e-mail assamrev@yahoo.co.in; f. 1926; publrs of *The Assam Review and Tea News* (monthly) and *The Assam Directory and Tea Areas Handbook* (annually); Chief Exec. GOBINDALAL BANERJEE.

Dev Sahitya Kutir: 21 Jhamapukur Lane, Kolkata 700 009; tel. (33) 23507887; e-mail dev_sahitya@rediffmail.com; children's, general; Dir ARUN CHANDRA MAZUMDER.

Dey's Publishing: 13 Bankim Chatterjee St, Kolkata 700 073; tel. (33) 22412330; fax (33) 22192041; e-mail deyspublishing@hotmail.com; internet deyspublishing.com; academic books, religion, philosophy, general; Dir SUDHANGSHU KUMAR DEY.

Eastern Law House (Pvt) Ltd: 54 Ganesh Chunder Ave, Kolkata 700 013; tel. (33) 22151989; fax (33) 22150491; e-mail elh.cal@gmail.com; internet www.elh.co.in; f. 1918; legal, commercial and accountancy; Dir ASOK DE; br. in New Delhi.

Firma KLM Private Ltd: 257B B. B. Ganguly St, Kolkata 700 012; tel. and fax (33) 22217294; e-mail info@firmaklm.net; internet www.firmaklm.net; f. 1950; Indology, scholarly, alternative medicine; in English, Bengali, Sanskrit and Hindi; Man. Dir S. MUKHERJI.

Indian Museum: 27 Jawaharlal Nehru Rd, Kolkata 700 016; tel. (33) 22861702; fax (33) 22861696; e-mail imbot@cal12.vsnl.net.in; internet www.indianmuseumkolkata.org; social sciences and humanities; Dir ANUP K. MATILAL.

Naya Udyog: 206 Bidhan Sarani, Kolkata 700 006; tel. (33) 22413540; e-mail nayaudyog@yahoo.in; f. 1992; books in English and Bengali; agriculture, horticulture, social sciences, history, botany; distributes Naya Prokash publications; Man. Dir PARTHA SANKAR BASU.

Punthi Pustak: 136/4B Bidhan Sarani, Kolkata 700 004; tel. and fax (33) 25555573; e-mail info@punthipustak.com; f. 1956; religion, history, philosophy; Propr P. K. BHATTACHARYA.

Samya: 16 Southern Ave, Kolkata 700 026; tel. (33) 24660812; fax (33) 24644614; e-mail streesamya.manager@gmail.com; internet www.stree-samyabooks.com; f. 1996; owned by joint partnership, Bhatkal and Sen; social change, cultural studies, caste studies and Dalit writings; Dir MANDIRA SEN.

Seagull Books (Pvt) Ltd: 31A S. P. Mukherjee Rd, Kolkata 700 025; tel. (33) 24765869; fax (33) 22805143; e-mail books@seagullindia

.com; internet www.seagullindia.com; f. 1982; academic, literary, general; CEO NAVIN KISHORE.

Shishu Sahitya Samsad: 32A Acharya Prafulla Chandra Rd, Kolkata 700 009; tel. (33) 23507669; fax (33) 23603508; e-mail contact@samsadbooks.com; internet www.samsadbooks.com; f. 1951; children's, reference, science, literature; Man. Dir DEBAJYOTI DATTA.

Stree-Samya: 16 Southern Ave, Kolkata 700 026; tel. (33) 24660812; fax (33) 24644614; e-mail streesamya@gmail.com; internet www .stree-samyabooks.com; f. 1990 (Stree), 1996 (Samya); imprints publ. by joint venture of Harsha Bhatkal, Popular Prakashan and Mandira Sen; social and women's issues and caste writings in English and Bengali; Dir MANDIRA SEN.

MUMBAI (BOMBAY)

Allied Publishers (Pvt) Ltd: 15 J. N. Heredia Marg, Mumbai 400 001; tel. (22) 42126930; fax (22) 22617928; e-mail arjunsachdev@ alliedpublishers.com; internet alliedpublishers.com; f. 1934; academic and general; Dir ARJUN SACHDEV.

Bharatiya Vidya Bhavan: Munshi Sadan, Kulapati K. M. Munshi Marg, Mumbai 400 007; tel. (22) 23631261; fax (22) 23630058; e-mail bhavans@bhavans.info; internet www.bhavans.info; f. 1938; art, literature, culture, education, philosophy, religion, history of India; various periodicals in English, Hindi, Sanskrit and other Indian languages; Pres. SURENDRALAL G. MEHTA; Dir-Gen. H. N. DASTUR.

Himalaya Publishing House: Dr Bhalerao Marg (Kelewadi), Girgaon, Mumbai 400 004; tel. (22) 23860170; fax (22) 23877178; e-mail himpub@vsnl.com; internet www.himpub.com; f. 1976; textbooks and research work; Publr MEENA PANDEY.

India Books and Magazines Distributors (Pvt) Ltd: Arch No 30, Below Mahalaxmi Bridge, nr Race Course, Mahalaxmi; tel. (22) 40497401; e-mail contact@ibhworld.com; internet www.ibhworld .com; Man. Dir ABIZAR SHAIKH.

International Book House (Pvt) Ltd: Indian Mercantile Mansions (Extension), Madame Cama Rd, Mumbai 400 039; tel. (22) 66242222; fax (22) 22851109; e-mail info@ibhbookstore.com; internet www.ibhbookstore.com; f. 1941; children's, general, educational, scientific, technical, engineering, social sciences, humanities and law; Dir ROHIT GUPTA; Dir SANJEEV GUPTA.

Jaico Publishing House: A2, Jash Chambers, Sir P. M. Rd, Fort, Mumbai 400 001; tel. (22) 40306767; fax (22) 22656412; e-mail jaicowbd@vsnl.com; internet www.jaicobooks.com; f. 1947; general paperbacks, management, computer and engineering books, etc.; imports scientific, medical, technical and educational books; Man. Dir ASHWIN J. SHAH.

Popular Prakashan (Pvt) Ltd: 301 Mahalaxmi Chambers, 22 Bhulabhai Desai Rd, Mumbai 400 026; tel. (22) 23530303; fax (22) 24945294; e-mail info@popularprakashan.com; internet www .popularprakashan.com; f. 1968; sociology, biographies, religion, philosophy, fiction, arts, music, current affairs, medicine, history, politics and administration in English and Marathi; CEO HARSHA BHATKAL.

Sheth Publishing House: G-12 Suyog Industrial Estate, nr LBS Marg, Vikhroli (W), Mumbai 400 083; tel. (22) 25773707; fax (22) 25774200; e-mail shethpublishinghouse@gmail.com; internet www .indiamart.com/shethpublishinghouse; educational, children's; Man. PURVISH SHETH.

Somaiya Publications (Pvt) Ltd: 172 Mumbai Marathi Granthasangrahalaya Bldg, M.M.G.S. Marg, Dadar (E), Mumbai 400 014; tel. (22) 24130230; fax (22) 22047297; e-mail somaiyabooks@rediffmail .com; internet www.somaiya.com; f. 1967; economics, sociology, history, politics, mathematics, sciences, language, literature, education, psychology, religion, philosophy, logic; Chair. Dr S. K. SOMAIYA.

Vora Medical Publications: 6 Princess Bldg, E. R. Rd, Mumbai 400 003; tel. (22) 23754161; fax (22) 23704053; e-mail voramedpub@ yahoo.co.in; internet www.voramedicalpublications.com; medicine, nursing, management, spiritualism, general knowledge; Propr R. K. VORA.

OTHER TOWNS

Anada Prakashan (Pvt) Ltd: 1756 Gandhi Rd, Ahmedabad 380 001; tel. (79) 2169956; fax (79) 2139900; e-mail anadaad1@ sancharnet.in; internet www.anada.com; children's, educational, dictionaries; Man. Dir B. R. ANADA.

Bharati Bhawan: Thakurbari Rd, Kadamkuan, Patna 800 003; tel. (612) 2670325; fax (612) 2670010; e-mail sales.bbpddel@gmail.com; internet bharatibhawan.in; f. 1942; educational and juvenile; Man. Partner TARIT KUMAR BOSE.

Books for Change: 139 Richmond Rd, Bengaluru 560 025; tel. (80) 25580346; fax (80) 25586284; e-mail bfc@bookforchange.info; internet www.booksforchange.info; f. 1997; operated by ActionAid

Karnataka Projects; publr and distributor of books and other media relating to social issues; Publr and Chief Editor SHOBA RAMACHANDRAN.

DC Books: DC Kizhakemuri Edam, Good Shepherd St, POB 214, Kottayam 686 001; tel. (481) 2563114; fax (481) 2564758; e-mail info@ dcbooks.com; internet www.dcbooks.com; f. 1974; fiction, general and reference books in Malayalam; CEO RAVI DEECEE.

HarperCollins Publishers India (Pvt) Ltd: A-53, Sector 57, Noida; tel. (120) 4044800; e-mail sapana.solanki@ harpercollins-india.com; internet www.harpercollins.co.in; f. 2003; general fiction and non-fiction, children's and reference; imprints incl. Collins, Avon, Harper Vantage, Fourth Estate; CEO P. M. SUKUMAR.

Hind Pocket Books (Pvt) Ltd: B-13, Sector 81, Phase II, Noida 201305; tel. (120) 3093992; fax (120) 2563983; e-mail gbp@del2.vsnl .net.in; f. 1958; fiction and non-fiction paperbacks in English, Hindi, Punjabi, Malayalam and Urdu; Chair DINA NATH MALHOTRA; Man. Dir SHEKHAR MALHOTRA.

Indica Books: D-40/18 Godowlia, Varanasi 221 001; tel. (542) 3094999; fax (542) 2452258; e-mail indicainfo@indicabooks.com; internet www.indicabooks.com; Indology, philosophy, religion, culture; Propr DILIP KUMAR JAISWAL.

Kalyani Publishers: 1/1 Rajinder Nagar, Civil Lines, Ludhiana 141 008; tel. (161) 2745756; fax (161) 2745872; e-mail kalyanibooks@ yahoo.co.in; textbooks; Dir RAJ KUMAR.

Krishna Prakashan Media (Pvt) Ltd: Krishna House, 11 Shivaji Rd, Meerut 250 001; tel. (121) 2644766; fax (121) 2642946; e-mail info@krishnaprakashan.com; internet www.krishnaprakashan .com; f. 1942; textbooks; Exec. Dir SUGAM RASTOGI; Dir S. K. RASTOGI.

Law Publishers: 18 A. Sardar Patel Marg, Civil Lines, POB 1077, Allahabad; tel. (532) 262374; fax (532) 2622781; e-mail sai@ lawpublisherindia.com; internet www.lawpublisherindia.com; f. 1929; legal texts in English; Dir NARESH SAGAR.

Macmillan Publishers India Ltd: 315/316 Raheja Chambers, 12 Museum Rd, Bengaluru 560 001; tel. (80) 25586563; fax (80) 25588713; e-mail rberi@macmillan.co.in; internet www .macmillanindia.com; school and university books in English; general; Pres. and Man. Dir RAJIV BERI.

Madhubun Educational Books: E-28, Sector 8, Noida 201 301; tel. (120) 4078900; fax (120) 4078999; e-mail info@madhubunbooks.com; internet madhubunbooks.com; f. 1969; school books, children's books; Dir SAJILI SHIRODKAR.

Mapin Publishing (Pvt) Ltd: 706B Kaivanna, Panchvati, Ellisbridge, Ahmedabad 380 006; tel. (79) 40228228; fax (79) 40228201; e-mail mapin@mapinpub.com; internet www.mapinpub.com; f. 1984; illustrated books on Indian art, culture, history, architecture, photography, crafts and literature; collaborates with art book publrs and museums to provide custom packaging services; Man. Dir BIPIN SHAH.

Navajivan Publishing House: PO Navajivan, Ahmedabad 380 014; tel. (79) 7540635; f. 1919; Gandhiana and related social sciences; in English, Hindi and Gujarati; Man. Trustee JITENDRA DESAI; Sales Man. KAPIL RAWAL.

Orient Blackswan (Pvt) Ltd: 3-6-752 Himayat Nagar, Hyderabad 500 029; tel. (40) 27665466; fax (40) 27645046; e-mail centraloffice@ orientblackswan.com; internet www.orientblackswan.com; f. 1948 as Orient Longman (Pvt) Ltd; educational, technical, general and children's in English and almost all Indian languages; Chair. SHANTA RAMESHWAR RAO; Dirs Dr NANDINI RAO, J. KRISHNADEV RAO.

Parikalpana Prakashan: D-68 Nirala Nagar, Lucknow 226 010; tel. (522) 2786782; fax (522) 2786782; e-mail janchetna@rediffmail .com; internet janchetnaaa.blogspot.in; f. 1996; fiction, poetry, literary criticism, history, political sciences, philosophy; Hindi and English; Pres. KATYAYANI.

Pilgrims Publishing: Pilgrims Book House, B27/98-A-8 Nawabganj Rd, Durga Kund, Varanasi 221 001; tel. (542) 2314060; fax (542) 2314059; e-mail pilgrims@satyam.net.in; internet www .pilgrimsbooks.com; f. 1986; publishes fiction and reference books on subjects including history, travel, Nepal, Tibet, India and the Himalayas; also operates Pilgrims Book House in India and Nepal; Editor CHRISTOPHER N. BURCHETT.

Punjabi University Publication Bureau: Punjabi University, Patiala 147 002; tel. (175) 3046093; fax (175) 2283073; e-mail head_publication@pbi.ac.in; internet www.punjabiuniversity.ac.in; f. 1966; university-level text and reference books, and other general interest books; Punjabi, English and other languages; Head of Bureau Dr S. K. SHARMA.

Ram Prasad and Sons: Hospital Rd, Agra 282 003; tel. (562) 2461904; fax (562) 2460920; e-mail rpsons@sancharnet.in; f. 1905; agricultural, arts, history, commerce, education, general, computing, engineering, pure and applied science, economics, sociology; Man. S. N. AGARWAL; br. in Bhopal.

Random House India: Windsor IT Park, 7th Floor, Tower-B, A-1, Sector 125, Noida 201 301; tel. (120) 4607500; fax (120) 4607518; e-mail contact@randomhouse.co.in; internet www.randomhouse.co.in; f. 2005; part of United Kingdom-based Random House Group; Man. Dir GAURAV SHRINAGESH.

Sahitya Bhawan Publications: Agra-Mathura Bypass Rd, Agra 282 002; tel. (562) 4042977; fax (562) 2858183; e-mail sbpd.publications@gmail.com; internet sahityabhawan.com; social sciences, humanities; Propr RAJEEV BANSAL.

Samvad Prakashan: 233 Rajlaxmi Society, nr Shivmahal Palace, Old Padra Rd, Vadodara 390015; tel. (265) 2312747; e-mail samvadprakashan@yahoo.co.in; internet www.samvadprakashan.co.in; books and magazines in Gujarati; Propr YUYUTSU PANCHAL.

Simon and Schuster India: 2316, Tower A, The Corenthum, A-41, Sector 62, Noida 201 301; tel. 9810173662 (mobile); e-mail rahul.srivastava@simonandschuster.com; f. 2011; Dir RAHUL SRIVASTAVA.

Tata McGraw-Hill Publishing Co Ltd: B-4, Sector 63, Noida 2010301; tel. (120) 4383400; fax (120) 4383401; e-mail editorial_india@mcgraw-hill.com; internet www.tatamcgrawhill.com; f. 1970; engineering, computers, sciences, medicine, management, humanities, social sciences; Chair. Dr F. A. MEHTA; Man. Dir Dr N. SUBRAHMANYAM.

Universities Press (India) (Pvt) Ltd: 3-6-747/1/A and 3-6-754/1 Himayat Nagar, Hyderabad 500 029; tel. (40) 27662849; fax (40) 27645046; e-mail info@universitiespress.com; internet www.universitiespress.com; academic and educational books on science, technology, management; Man. Dir MADHU REDDY.

Vikas Publishing House Pvt Ltd: E-28, Sector 8, Noida 201 301; tel. (120) 4078900; fax (120) 4078999; e-mail helpline@vikaspublishing.com; internet www.vikaspublishing.com; f. 1969; computers, management, commerce, sciences, engineering textbooks; Dir PIYUSH CHAWLA.

Vishwavidyalaya Prakashan: Vishalakshi Bldg, POB 1149, Chowk, Varanasi 221 001, Uttar Pradesh; tel. (542) 2413741; fax (542) 2413082; e-mail vvp@vsnl.net; internet www.vvpbooks.com; f. 1950; Hindu and Sanskrit literature, Indology, history, art and culture, spiritualism, religion, philosophy, education, sociology, psychology, music, journalism, mass communication, science and social science; Partner ANURAG KUMAR MODI.

GOVERNMENT PUBLISHING HOUSE

Publications Division: Ministry of Information and Broadcasting, Govt of India, Patiala House, New Delhi 110 001; tel. and fax (11) 24366670; e-mail dpd@sb.nic.in; internet publicationsdivision.nic.in; f. 1941; culture, art, literature, planning and development, general; also 21 periodicals in English and 13 Indian languages; Dir-Gen. K. GANESAN.

PUBLISHERS' ASSOCIATIONS

Association of Publishers in India: c/o Cambridge University Press, Cambridge House, 4381/4, 3rd Floor, Ansari Rd, Daryaganj, New Delhi 110 002; e-mail info@api.org; internet www.publishers.org.in; f. 2001; represents the interests of foreign publishers operating in India; 27 mem. cos; Pres. P. M. SUKUMAR; Sec. ROHIT KUMAR.

Bombay Booksellers' and Publishers' Association: No. 25, 6th Floor, Bldg No. 3, Navjivan Commercial Premises Co-op Society Ltd, Dr Bhadkamkar Marg, Mumbai 400 008; tel. (22) 23088691; e-mail bbpassn@yahoo.co.in; internet www.bbpassn.org; f. 1961; 400 mems; Pres. ANIL KUMAR PANDEY; Hon. Gen. Sec. B. S. FERNANDES.

Delhi State Booksellers' and Publishers' Association: 4760-61/23 Ansari Rd, Daryaganj, New Delhi 110 002; tel. (11) 43502211; fax (11) 43502212; e-mail info@dsbpa.in; internet www.dsbpa.in; f. 1941; 450 mems; Pres. K. K. SAXENA; Sec. SURYA MITTAL.

Federation of Indian Publishers: Federation House, 18/1-C Institutional Area, nr JNU, New Delhi 110 067; tel. (11) 26964847; fax (11) 26864054; e-mail fipl@satyam.net.in; internet www.fipindia.org; 18 affiliated asscns; 190 mems; Pres. ANAND BHUSHAN; Hon. Gen. Sec. SHAKTI MALIK.

Federation of Publishers' and Booksellers' Associations in India: 84 Daryaganj, 2nd Floor, New Delhi 110 002; tel. (11) 23272845; fax (11) 23281227; e-mail fpbaidelhi@gmail.com; internet www.fpbai.org; f. 1955; 12 affiliated asscns; 507 mems; Pres. S. C. SETHI; Hon. Sec. J. L. KUMAR.

Publishers' and Booksellers' Guild: Guild House, 2B Jhamapukur Lane, Kolkata 700 009; tel. (33) 23544417; fax (33) 23604566; e-mail guildpb@gmail.com; internet www.kolkatabookfaironline.com; f. 1975; 39 mems; organizes annual internationally recognized Kolkata Book Fair; Pres. JAYANT MANAKTALA; Hon. Gen. Sec. TRIDIB KR. CHATTERJEE.

Broadcasting and Communications

TELECOMMUNICATIONS

The telecommunications sector has expanded rapidly in recent years. Mobile cellular subscriptions increased from 52.2m. in 2004 to 952.3m. at the end of January 2015 (representing the second largest market in the world in terms of subscribers); of these, 842.4m. were described as active subscriptions. The mobile telephone penetration rate was measured at 76.0% of the population. At that time there were an estimated 26.9m. fixed-line telephone subscribers and 94.5m. broadband internet subscribers.

Regulatory Authority

Telecom Regulatory Authority of India (TRAI): Mahanagar Doorsanchar Bhavan (next to Zakir Hussain College), Jawaharlal Nehru Marg (Old Minto Rd), New Delhi 110 002; tel. (11) 23236308; fax (11) 23213294; e-mail ap@trai.gov.in; internet www.trai.gov.in; f. 1997; Chair. RAHUL KHULLAR.

Service Providers

Aircel Ltd: Dishnet Wireless Ltd, Bldg 10A, 2nd Floor, DLF Cyber City, Phase II, Gurgaon 122 022; tel. (124) 4765000; fax (124) 4290524; e-mail care.haryana@aircel.co.in; internet www.aircel.com; f. 1999; 74% owned by Maxis Communications Bhd (Malaysia); 78.6m. subscribers (Dec. 2014); Chair. SUNEETA REDDY.

Bharat Sanchar Nigam Ltd (BSNL): Bharat Sanchar Bhavan, Harish Chandra Mathur Lane, Janpath, New Delhi 110 001; tel. (11) 23372424; fax (11) 23372444; e-mail cmdbsnl@bsnl.co.in; internet www.bsnl.co.in; f. 2000; fmrly Dept of Telecom Operations; state-owned; 81.3m. subscribers (Dec. 2014); Chair. and Man. Dir ANUPAM SHRIVASTAVA.

Bharti Airtel Ltd: Bharti Crescent, 1 Nelson Mandela Rd, Vasant Kunj, Phase 2, New Delhi 110 070; tel. (11) 46666100; fax (11) 46666411; internet www.airtel.in; f. 1995; India's first privately owned telephone network; provides mobile, fixed-line, direct-to-home and internet protocol TV services; 217m. subscribers (Dec. 2014); Chair. and Man. Dir SUNIL BHARTI MITTAL.

Idea Cellular: Idea Cellular Ltd, 5th Floor, Windsor CST Rd, Kalina Santa Cruz (East), Mumbai 400 098; tel. 9594004000 (mobile); fax 9594003181 (mobile); e-mail rajat.mukarji@idea.adityabirla.com; internet www.ideacellular.com; f. 1995; 49% owned by Aditya Birla Group; 150.5m. subscribers (Dec. 2014); Chair. KUMAR MANGALAM BIRLA; Man. Dir HIMANSHU KAPANIA.

Mahanagar Telephone Nigam Ltd (MTNL): Jeevan Bharati Bldg, 124 Connaught Circus, New Delhi 110 001; tel. (11) 23719020; fax (11) 23314243; e-mail cmd@bol.net.in; internet www.mtnl.net.in; f. 1986; 56% state-owned; owns and operates telecommunications and information technology services in Mumbai and Delhi; 8.8m. subscribers (Jan. 2011); Chair. and Man. Dir P. K. PURWAR.

Reliance Communications Ltd: Blk H, 1st Floor, Dhirubhai Ambani Knowledge City, Navi Mumbai 400 709; tel. (22) 30373333; fax (22) 30388005; e-mail customercare@relianceada.com; internet www.rcom.co.in; f. 1999; provides mobile and fixed-line telephony services throughout India; 106.2m. subscribers (Dec 2014); Chair. ANIL D. AMBANI; CEO VINOD SAWHNY.

Sistema Shyam TeleServices Ltd: MTS Towers, 334 Udyog Vihar, Phase IV, Gurgaon 122 001; tel. (12) 44812500; e-mail ceo@mtsindia.in; internet www.mtsindia.in; f. 1993; offers services under the brand MTS; 9.1m. subscribers (Jan. 2011); Pres. and CEO MIKHAIL SHAMOLIN.

Tata Group: operates Tata Teleservices Ltd, Tata Communications (fmrly VSNL) and Tatanet; 87.2m. subscribers (Jan 2011); Chair. CYRUS P. MISTRY.

Tata Communications: Plots C-21 and C-36, Blk G, Bandra Kurla Complex, Bandra (East), Mumbai 400 098; tel. (22) 66578765; fax (22) 66591912; e-mail ravindran.s@tatacommunications.com; internet www.tatacommunications.com; f. 1986 as Videsh Sanchar Nigam Ltd (VSNL); enterprise data services, broadband internet and overseas communications; Man. Dir VINOD KUMAR.

Tata Teleservices Ltd: A, E and F Blks, Voltas Premises, T. B. Kadam Marg, Chinchpokli, Mumbai 400033; tel. (22) 66671414; fax (22) 66605335; internet www.tatateleservices.com; f. 1996; 66.1m. mobile subscribers (Dec. 2014); Chair. CYRUS P. MISTRY; Man. Dir and CEO SRINATH NARASIMHAN.

Telewings Communications Services Ltd (Uninor): Unitech Wireless (Tamil Nadu) Pvt Ltd, Ground Floor, Masterpiece, Sector 54, DLF Golf Course Rd, Gurgaon 122 002; tel. (12) 43329000; e-mail sharad.goswami@uninor.in; internet www.uninor.in; f. 2009; subsidiary of Telenor Group, Norway; 43.6m. subscribers (Dec. 2014); Man. Dir VIVEK SOOD.

Videocon Telecommunications Ltd: 248 Udyog Vihar, Phase IV, Gurgaon 122 015; e-mail 121@videocon.com; internet www.videocon .com; f. 2010; 8.6m. subscribers (Nov. 2014); Chair. VENUGOPAL DHOOT.

Vodafone Essar Ltd (Hutch): Peninsula Corporate Park, Ganpatrao Kadam Marg, Lower Parel, Mumbai 400 013; tel. 9619215000 (mobile); fax (22) 24963645; e-mail vodafonecare.mum@vodafone .com; internet www.vodafone.in; f. 1994; Vodafone (United Kingdom) acquired controlling 67% share from Hutchison Telecommunications International (Hong Kong) in Feb. 2007, 33% owned by Essar Group; 178.6m. subscribers (Dec. 2014); CEO MARTEN PIETERS.

Other mobile telephone operators include: Loop Mobile and S Tel.

Other Companies

ITI Ltd: ITI Bhavan, Doorvaninagar, Bengaluru 560 016; tel. (80) 25614466; fax (80) 25617525; e-mail secretary@itiltd.co.in; internet www.itiltd-india.com; f. 1948; govt undertaking; mfrs of all types of telecommunication equipment, incl. telephones, automatic exchanges and long-distance transmission equipment; also produces optical fibre equipment and microwave equipment; will manufacture all ground communication equipment for the 22 earth stations of the Indian National Satellite; in conjunction with the Post and Telegraph Department, a newly designed 2,000-line exchange has been completed; Chair. and Man. Dir K. L. DHINGRA.

BROADCASTING

Prasar Bharati (Broadcasting Corpn of India): Doordarshan Bhavan, Copernicus Marg, New Delhi 110 001; tel. (11) 23737603; fax (11) 23352549; e-mail webadmin@dd.nic.in; internet www .prasarbharati.gov.in; f. 1997; autonomous body; oversees operations of state-owned radio and television services; Chair. MRINAL PANDE; CEO JAWHAR SIRCAR.

Radio

Guidelines for the licensing of private FM radio stations were first introduced in 1999. By November 2012 there were some 245 privately owned FM radio channels operating in 85 cities.

All India Radio (AIR): Akashvani Bhavan, Sansad Marg, New Delhi 110 001; tel. (11) 23710300; fax (11) 23421956; e-mail dgair@air .org.in; internet allindiaradio.org; broadcasting is controlled by the Ministry of Information and Broadcasting and is primarily govt-financed; operates a network of 277 stations and 432 transmitters (grouped into 4 zones—north, south, east and west), covering almost the entire population and over 99% of the total area of the country; Dir-Gen. F. SHEHARYAR; The News Services Division of AIR, centralized in New Delhi, is one of the largest news organizations in the world. It has 44 regional news units, which broadcast 647 bulletins daily in 75 languages. Daily broadcasts include: 178 bulletins in 33 languages in the Home Services; 187 regional bulletins in 65 languages and dialects; and 66 bulletins in 26 languages in the External Services.

Television

India represents the third largest television market in the world, after China and the USA, with some 146m. households using a television set in 2012. According to the Ministry of Information and Broadcasting, the total number of television channels grew from 69 in 2002 to 850 (including 96 foreign operators) in 2012. Private satellite television channels were first permitted to operate in 2000.

Doordarshan India (Television India): Mandi House, Doordarshan Bhavan, Copernicus Marg, New Delhi 110 001; tel. (11) 23385958; fax (11) 23386507; e-mail webadmin@dd.nic.in; internet www.ddindia .gov.in; f. 1976; broadcasting is controlled by the Ministry of Information and Broadcasting and is govt-financed; programmes: 280 hours weekly; 5 all-India channels, 16 regional-language satellite channels, 5 state networks and 1 international channel; Dir-Gen. VIJAYALAXMI CHABBRA.

NDTV Network: NDTV Ltd, 207 Okhla Industrial Estate, Phase III, New Delhi 110 020; tel. (11) 26446666; fax (11) 41037119; e-mail feedback@ndtv.com; internet www.ndtv.com; f. 1988; 3 news channels: NDTV 24x7 (English), NDTV India (Hindi) and NDTV Profit (Business); also NDTV Lifestyle, NDTV Convergence, NDTV Good Times and NDTV Worldwide; 23 offices and studios; Chair. and Dir Dr PRANNOY ROY; CEO VIKRAMADITYA CHANDRA.

Network 18 Group: 503, 504 and 507, 5th Floor, Mercantile House, 15 Kasturba Gandhi Marg, New Delhi 110 001; tel. (11) 41506112; fax (11) 41506115; internet www.network18online.com; f. 1993; owns news channels, incl. CNN-IBN, CNBC-TV18, IBN 7 and IBN Lokmat (Marathi); also operates, in a jt venture with Viacom, Inc. of the USA, entertainment channels incl. Colors, MTV, VH1 and Nick; CEO A. P. PARIGI.

Sony Entertainment Television (Multi Screen Media Pvt. Ltd): Multi Screen Media Pvt. Ltd, 3rd Floor, Bldg No. 7, Malad Link Rd,

Malad (West), Mumbai 400 064; tel. (22) 67081111; fax (22) 66434748; e-mail feedback.set@setindia.com; internet www .setindia.com; f. 1995; channels incl. Sony Entertainment Television, SAB TV, SET Max, Sony Aath, SET PIX, Sony MIX, AXN and Animax India; owned by MSM Pvt. Ltd, fmrly SET India Pvt. Ltd; CEO N. P. SINGH.

Star TV: Star India Pvt. Ltd, Star House, Dr E. Moses Rd, Mahalaxmi, Mumbai 400 011; tel. (22) 66305555; fax (22) 66305050; internet www.startv.com; f. 1991; 35 channels in 7 languages, incl. Star World, Star Movies, Star Plus, Star One, Star Utsav, Star Gold, Star News, ESPN, Star Sports, Channel V, National Geographic Channel, etc.; CEO UDAY SHANKAR.

TV Today Network: Videocon Tower, 8th Floor, E-1 Jhandewalan Extn, New Delhi 110 055; tel. (11) 23684878; fax (11) 23684895; e-mail info@aajtak.com; internet www.indiatodaygroup.com; f. 1975; owns news channels incl. Aaj Tak (Hindi), Headlines Today (English), Tez (Hindi) and Dilli Aaj Tak (Hindi) news channel; Chair. AROON PURIE; CEO JOY CHAKRABORTHY.

Zee Entertainment Enterprises Ltd: 135 Continental Bldg, Dr Annie Beasant Rd, Worli, Mumbai 400 018; tel. (22) 66971234; fax (22) 24900302; e-mail inquiry@zeenetwork.com; internet www .zeetelevision.com; f. 1992; owns more than 30 news and entertainment channels, incl. Zee TV, Zee Cinema, Ten Sports, Zee Studio, Zee News, Zee Business, 9X, etc.; Chair. SUBHASH CHANDRA; CEO PUNIT GOENKA.

Finance

(cap. = capital; p.u. = paid up; res = reserves; dep. = deposits; m. = million; br.(s) = branch(es); amounts in rupees unless otherwise stated)

BANKING

Scheduled commercial banks are grouped under the following categories: the State Bank of India and its associates; state-owned commercial banks; foreign banks; regional rural banks; and private scheduled commercial banks. At the end of March 2013 there were 151 scheduled commercial banks in operation in India (including 41 foreign banks and 64 regional rural banks). At that time scheduled commercial banks held aggregate deposits of an estimated Rs 74,295,324m. and operated a network of 92,114 branches and offices.

State Banks

Reserve Bank of India: Central Office Bldg, Shahid Bhagat Singh Rd, POB 10007, Mumbai 400 001; tel. (22) 22661602; fax (22) 22658269; e-mail helpprd@rbi.org.in; internet www.rbi.org.in; f. 1934; nationalized 1949; sole bank of issue; cap. 50m., res 65,000m., dep. 3,754,115m. (June 2010); Gov. RAGHURAM G. RAJAN; Dep. Govs SUBHASH SHEORATAN MUNDRA, R. GANDHI, URJIT PATEL, H. R. KHAN; 19 regional offices and 9 sub-offices.

State Bank of India: Corporate Centre, Madame Cama Rd, POB 10121, Mumbai 400 021; tel. (22) 22022426; fax (22) 22851391; e-mail gm.gbu@sbi.co.in; internet www.statebankofindia.com; f. 1955; cap. 6,840.3m., res 1,055,400.1m., dep. 16,274,026.1m. (March 2013); 5 associates, 7 domestic subsidiaries/affiliates, 3 foreign subsidiaries, 4 jt ventures abroad; Chair. ARUNDHATI BHATTACHARYA; Man. Dirs P.PRADEEP KUMAR, A. KRISHNA KUMAR; 9,593 brs (incl. 52 overseas brs and rep. offices in 34 countries).

State-owned Commercial Banks

Fourteen of India's major commercial banks were nationalized in 1969 and a further six in 1980. They are managed by 15-member boards of directors (two directors appointed by the central Government, one employee director, one representing employees who are not workmen, one representing depositors, three representing farmers, workers, artisans, etc., five representing persons with special knowledge or experience, one Reserve Bank of India official and one Government of India official). The Department of Banking of the Ministry of Finance controls all banking operations.

Allahabad Bank: 2 Netaji Subhas Rd, Kolkata 700 001; tel. (33) 22319144; fax (33) 22107425; e-mail gmpd@allahabadbank.in; internet www.allahabadbank.com; f. 1865; nationalized 1969; cap. 5,000.3m., res 98,663.4m., dep. 1,787,339.4m. (March 2013); Chair. and Man. Dir RAKESH SETHI; Exec. Dirs T. R. CHAWLA, J. K. SINGH KHARB; 2,020 brs.

Andhra Bank: Andhra Bank Bldgs, Saifabad, 5-9-11 Secretariat Rd, Hyderabad 500 004; tel. (40) 23252000; fax (40) 23232419; e-mail customerser@andhrabank.co.in; internet www.andhrabank.in; f. 1923; nationalized 1980; cap. 5,595.8m., res 66,100.1m., dep. 1,237,964.5m. (March 2013); Chair. and Man. Dir C.V.R. RAJENDRAN; Exec. Dir S. K. KALRA; 1,128 brs and 113 extension counters.

Bank of Baroda: Baroda Corporate Centre, C-26, G Blk, Bandra-Kurla Complex, Bandra (East), Mumbai 400 051; tel. (22) 26985000; fax (22) 26523000; e-mail customerservice@bankofbaroda.com; internet www.bankofbaroda.com; f. 1908; nationalized 1969; merged with Benares State Bank in 2002; cap. 4,225.1m., res 278,762.9m., dep. 4,826,388.9m. (March 2013); Chair. and Man. Dir (vacant); Exec. Dirs RANJAN DHAWAN, BHUWANCHANDRA B. JOSHI, P. SRINIVAS; 2,773 brs in India, 38 brs overseas.

Bank of India: Star House, C-5, G Blk, 3rd Floor, Bandra-Kurla Complex, Bandra (East), Mumbai 400 051; tel. (22) 66684444; fax (22) 56684558; e-mail headoffice.god@bankofindia.co.in; internet www .bankofindia.com; f. 1906; nationalized 1969; cap. 5,966.4m., res 210,544.7m., dep. 3,831,309.9m. (March 2013); Chair. and Man. Dir V. R. IYER; 2,883 brs in India, 21 brs overseas.

Bank of Maharashtra: 'Lokmangal', 1501 Shivajinagar, Pune 411 005; tel. (20) 25532731; fax (20) 25533246; e-mail bomcopln@ mahabank.co.in; internet www.bankofmaharashtra.in; f. 1935; nationalized 1969; cap. 12,494.7m., res 39,523m., dep. 943,302.1m. (March 2013); Chair. and Man. Dir SUSHIL MUHNOT; Exec. Dirs R. K. GUPTA, R. ATHMARAM; 1,291 brs.

Bharatiya Mahila Bank Ltd: IFCI Tower, 9th Floor, 61 Nehru Pl., New Delhi 110 019; tel. (11) 47472100; e-mail ruchi.singhal@bmb.co .in; internet www.bmb.co.in; f. 2013; nat. women's bank; cap. 10,000m.; Chair. and Man. Dir USHA ANANTHASUBRAMANIAN; 50 brs (March 2015).

Canara Bank: 112 Jayachamarajendra Rd, POB 6648, Bengaluru 560 002; tel. (80) 22221581; fax (80) 22223168; internet www .canarabank.com; f. 1906; nationalized 1969; cap. 4,430m., res 217,637.2m., dep. 3,556,846.3m. (March 2013); Chair. and Man. Dir V. S. KRISHNAKUMAR; Exec. Dirs HARIDEESH KUMAR B., PRADYUMAN SINGH RAWAT; 2,744 brs.

Central Bank of India: Chandermukhi, Nariman Point, Mumbai 400 021; tel. (22) 66387777; fax (22) 22044336; e-mail chairman@ centralbank.co.in; internet www.centralbankofindia.co.in; f. 1911; nationalized 1969; cap. 26,615.7m., res 126,355m., dep. 2,262,190.6m. (March 2013); Chair. and Man. Dir RAJEEV RISHI; Exec. Dirs RAJ KUMAR GOYAL, ANIMESH CHAUHAN, B. K. DIVAKARA; 3,130 brs.

Corporation Bank: Mangaladevi Temple Rd, POB 88, Mangaluru 575 001; tel. (824) 2426416; fax (824) 2440964; e-mail query@ corpbank.co.in; internet www.corpbank.com; f. 1906; nationalized 1980; cap. 1,529.1m., res 80,063.5m., dep. 1,659,984.4m. (March 2013); Chair. and Man. Dir S. R. BANSAL; Exec. Dirs AMAR LAL DAULTANI, BIBHAS KUMAR SRIVASTAV; 617 brs.

Dena Bank: C 10, G Blk, Bandra-Kurla Complex, Bandra (East), Mumbai 400 051; tel. (22) 26545035; fax (22) 26545761; e-mail cmd@ denabank.co.in; internet www.denabank.com; f. 1938 as Devkaran Nanjee Banking Co Ltd; nationalized 1969; cap. 3,500.6m., res 46,035.7m., dep. 972,071.5m. (March 2013); Chair. and Man. Dir ASHWANI KUMAR; Exec. Dir R. K. TAKKAR, TRISHNA GUHA; 1,122 brs.

Indian Bank: 254 Avvai Shanmugam Salai, POB 5555, Royapettah, Chennai 600 014; tel. (44) 28134300; fax (44) 25231278; e-mail indmail@indianbank.co.in; internet www.indian-bank.com; f. 1907; nationalized 1969; cap. 8,297m., res 110,941.3m., dep. 1,419,677.3m. (March 2013); Chair. and Man. Dir T. M. BHASIN; Exec. Dirs B. RAJ KUMAR, MAHESH KUMAR JAIN; 1,960 brs.

Indian Overseas Bank: 763 Anna Salai, POB 3765, Chennai 600 002; tel. (44) 28524212; fax (44) 28523595; e-mail investor@iobnet.co .in; internet www.iob.in; f. 1937; nationalized 1969; merged with Bharat Overseas Bank Ltd in 2007; cap. 9,241m., res 119,660.3m., dep. 2,021,353.4m. (March 2013); Chair. and Man. Dir R. KOTEES-WARAN; Exec. Dirs PAWAN KUMAR BAJAJ, ATUL AGARWAL; 1,496 brs.

Oriental Bank of Commerce: Harsha Bhavan, E Blk, Connaught Place, POB 329, New Delhi 110 001; tel. (11) 47651186; fax (11) 23321514; e-mail bdncmd@obcindia.com; internet www.obcindia.co .in; f. 1943; nationalized 1980; cap. 2,917.6m., res 124,836m., dep. 1,758,975.2m. (March 2013); Chair. and Man. Dir ANIMESH CHAUHAN; Exec. Dirs SURESH N. PATEL, BHUPINDER NAYYAR; 1,772 brs.

Punjab National Bank: 7 Bhikaiji Cama Place, Africa Ave, New Delhi 110 066; tel. (11) 26102303; fax (11) 26196456; e-mail cmd@pnb .co.in; internet www.pnbindia.com; f. 1895; nationalized 1969; merged with New Bank of India in 1993; cap. 3,534.7m., res 286,978.8m., dep. 3,990,001.6m. (March 2013); Chair. and Man. Dir (vacant); Exec. Dirs GAURI SHANKAR, RAKESH SETHI, K. VEERA BRAHMAJI RAO; 3,833 brs.

Punjab & Sind Bank: Bank House, 21 Rajendra Place, New Delhi 110 008; tel. (11) 25719082; fax (11) 25723793; e-mail ho.pr@psb.org .in; internet www.psbindia.com; f. 1908; nationalized 1980; cap. 4,540.2m., res 26,070m., dep. 706,415m. (March 2013); Chair. and Man. Dir JATINDERBIR SINGH; Exec. Dir MUKESH KUMAR JAIN; 866 brs.

Syndicate Bank: POB 1, Manipal 576 119; tel. (825) 2571181; fax (825) 2570266; e-mail idcb@syndicatebank.com; internet www .syndicatebank.com; f. 1925; est. as Canara Industrial and Banking Syndicate Ltd; name changed as above 1964; nationalized 1969; cap. 6,019.5m., res 90,587.8m., dep. 1,853,508m. (March 2013); Chair. and Man. Dir (vacant); Exec. Dirs RAVI SHANKER PANDEY, T. K. SRIVASTAVA; 2,127 brs.

UCO Bank: 10 Biplabi Trailokya Maharaj Sarani (Brabourne Rd), POB 2455, Kolkata 700 001; tel. (33) 22254120; fax (33) 22253986; e-mail ucobank@vsnl.net; internet www.ucobank.com; f. 1943; est. as United Commercial Bank Ltd; name changed as above 1985; nationalized 1969; cap. 25,756.2m., res 49,922m., dep. 1,734,310.4m. (March 2013); Chair. and Man. Dir ARUN KAUL; Exec. Dirs S. CHANDRASEKHARAN, JAI KUMAR GARG; 1,849 brs.

Union Bank of India: Union Bank Bhavan, 239 Vidhan Bhavan Marg, Nariman Point, Mumbai 400 021; tel. (22) 22892000; fax (22) 22824689; e-mail ibd@unionbankofindia.com; internet www .unionbankofindia.co.in; f. 1919; nationalized 1969; cap. 7,078m., res 146,013.8m., dep. 2,636,815.5m. (March 2013); Chair. and Man. Dir ARUN TIWARI; Exec. Dirs KISHOR KHARAT, K. SUBRAHMANYAM, RAKESH SETHI; 2,082 brs.

United Bank of India: 11 Hemant Basu Sarani, Kolkata 700 001; tel. (33) 2487471; fax (33) 2485852; e-mail homail@unitedbank.co.in; internet www.unitedbankofindia.com; f. 1950; nationalized 1969; cap. 11,747m., res 43,171m., dep. 1,006,515.4m. (March 2013); Chair. and Man. Dir P. SRINIVAS; Exec. Dir SANJAY ARYA; 1,354 brs.

Vijaya Bank: 41/2 Mahatma Gandhi Rd, Bengaluru 560 001; tel. (80) 25584066; fax (80) 25584142; e-mail ibd@vijayabank.co.in; internet www.vijayabank.com; f. 1931; nationalized 1980; cap. 16,955.4m., res 29,041.2., dep. 970,172m. (March 2013); Chair. and Man. Dir KISHORE KUMAR SANSI; Exec. Dir K. RAMADAS SHENOY, B. S. RAMA RAO; 1,200 brs.

Principal Private Banks

Bombay Mercantile Co-operative Bank Ltd: 78 Mohammed Ali Rd, Mumbai 400 003; tel. (22) 23425961; fax (22) 23482387; e-mail bmcit@vsnl.net; internet bmcbankltd.com; f. 1939; cap. 404m., res 962.5m., dep. 21,833.5m. (March 2012); Man. Dir Dr MUHAMMAD SHAHALAM KHAN; 52 brs.

Catholic Syrian Bank Ltd: St Mary's College Rd, POB 502, Trichur 680 020; tel. (487) 2333020; fax (487) 2333435; e-mail pdd@csb.co.in; internet www.csb.co.in; f. 1920; cap. 419m., res 6,829.8m., dep. 123,416.2m. (March 2013); Chair. S. SANTHANAK RISHNAN; Man. Dir and CEO RAKESH BHATIA; 380 brs.

City Union Bank Ltd: 149 TSR (Big) St, Kumbakonam 612 001; tel. (435) 2432322; fax (435) 2431746; e-mail co@cityunionbank.com; internet www.cityunionbank.com; f. 1904; cap. 474.4m., res 12,646m., dep. 203,047m. (March 2013); Chair. S. BALASUBRAMANIAN; Man. Dir and CEO N. KAMAKODI; 125 brs.

The Federal Bank Ltd: Federal Towers, POB 103, Alwaye 683 101; tel. (484) 2623620; fax (484) 2622672; e-mail nrihelp@federalbank.co .in; internet www.federalbank.co.in; f. 1931; cap. 1,710.5m., res 50,597.4m., dep. 576,111.7m. (March 2013); Man. Dir and CEO SHYAM SRINIVASAN; Exec. Dirs ABRAHAM CHACKO; 606 brs.

HDFC Bank: HDFC Bank House, Senapati Bapat Marg, Lower Parel, Mumbai, 400 013; tel. (22) 66521000; fax (22) 24960739; e-mail corporatecommunications@hdfcbank.com; internet www.hdfcbank .com; merged with Centurion Bank of Punjab in 2008; cap. 4,758.8m., res 246,909m., dep. 2,960,917m. (March 2013); Chair. C. M. VASUDEV; Man. Dir ADITYA PURI; 1,412 brs.

ICICI Bank Ltd: ICICI Towers, South Tower, 4th Floor, Bandra-Kurla Complex, Bandra (East), Mumbai 400 051; tel. (22) 26531414; fax (22) 26531124; e-mail info@icicibank.com; internet www .icicibank.com; f. 1994; cap. 15,036.3m., res 572,793.1m., dep. 3,157,614.2m. (March 2013); merged with Sangli Bank in 2007 and with The Bank of Rajasthan Ltd in 2010; CEO and Man. Dir CHANDRA D. KOCHHAR; Chair. K. V. KAMATH; 1,400 brs.

IndusInd Bank Ltd: One Indiabulls Centre, Tower 1, 8th Floor, 841 S. B. Marg, Elphinstone Rd, Mumbai 400 013; tel. (22) 24231999; fax (22) 24231998; e-mail mktg@indusind.com; internet www.indusind .com; f. 1994; cap. 5,228.6m., res 48,586.1m., dep. 541,167.1m. (March 2012); Chair. R. SESHASAYEE; Man. Dir ROMESH SOBTI; 209 brs.

ING Vysya Bank Ltd: 22 M. G. Rd, Bengaluru 560 001; tel. (80) 25005000; fax (80) 25588442; e-mail ingvysyabank@ingvysyabank .com; internet www.ingvysyabank.com; f. 1930; cap. 1,548.5m., res 30,960.3m., dep. 413,290.4m. (March 2012); Chair. ARUN THIAGAR-AJAN; Man. Dir and CEO SHAILENDRA BHANDARI; 404 brs.

Jammu and Kashmir Bank Ltd: Corporate Headquarters, M. A. Rd, Srinagar 190 001; tel. (194) 2481930; fax (194) 2481923; e-mail jkbcosgr@jkbmail.com; internet jkbank.net; f. 1938; cap. 484.9m., res 37,612.1m., dep. 642,121.8m. (March 2013); Chair. MUSHTAQ AHMAD; 556 brs.

Karnataka Bank Ltd: POB 599, Kodialbail, Mangaluru 575 003; tel. (824) 2228222; fax (824) 2228284; e-mail info@ktkbank.com; internet www.karnatakabank.com; f. 1924; cap. 1,883.5m., res

23,206.1m., dep. 360,562.2m. (March 2013); Chair. and CEO ANANTHAKRISHNA; Man. Dir and CEO P. JAYARAMA BHAT; 370 brs.

The Karur Vysya Bank Ltd: Erode Rd, POB 21, Karur, Tamil Nadu 639 002; tel. (4324) 226520; fax (4324) 225700; e-mail kvbpdd@ kvbmail.com; internet www.kvb.co.in; f. 1916; cap. 1,071.8m., res 24,259m., dep. 386,529m. (March 2013); Chair. K. P. KUMAR; Man. Dir and CEO K. VENKATARAMAN; 312 brs.

Lakshmi Vilas Bank Ltd: Kathaparai, Salem Rd, POB 2, Karur 639 006; tel. (4324) 220051; fax (4324) 220068; e-mail info@lvbank .com; internet www.lvbank.com; f. 1926; cap. 975m., res 8,252m., dep. 156,189m. (March 2013); Man. Dir and CEO RAKESH SHARMA; 291 brs.

South Indian Bank Ltd: SIB House, T. B. Rd, Mission Quarters, Thrissur 680 001; tel. (487) 2420020; fax (487) 2442021; e-mail sibcorporate@sib.co.in; internet www.southindianbank.com; f. 1929; cap. 1,344m., res 26,915m., dep. 474,910.8m. (March 2014); Man. Dir and CEO V. A. JOSEPH; 450 brs.

Tamilnad Mercantile Bank Ltd: 57 Victoria Extension Rd, Tuticorin 628 002; tel. (461) 2321932; fax (461) 2322994; e-mail bd@ tnmbonline.com; internet www.tmb.in; f. 1921; est. as Nadar Bank; name changed as above 1962; cap. 2.8m., res 13,201.4m., dep. 171,104.4m. (March 2012); Man. Dir and CEO K. B. NAGENDRA MURTHY; 304 brs.

Banking Organizations

Indian Banks' Association: World Trade Centre Complex, Centre I Bldg, 6th Floor, Cuffe Parade, Mumbai 400 005; tel. (22) 22174040; fax (22) 22184222; e-mail webmaster@iba.org.in; internet www.iba .org.in; 156 mems; Chair. ALOK K. MISRA.

Indian Institute of Banking and Finance: 2 Kohinoor City Commercial, Tower 1, 2nd and 3rd Floors, Kirol Rd, Kurla (West), Mumbai 400 070; tel. (22) 25039746; fax (22) 25037332; e-mail mem-services@iibf.org.in; internet www.iibf.org.in; f. 1928; 343,202 mems; 4 zonal offices; CEO R. BHASKARAN; Pres. M. D. MALLYA.

National Institute of Bank Management: NIBM Post Office, Kondhwe Khurd, Pune 411 048; tel. (20) 26716000; fax (20) 26834478; e-mail director@nibmindia.org; internet www .nibmindia.org; f. 1969; Gov. Dr D. SUBBARAO; Dir ALLEN C. A. PEREIRA.

DEVELOPMENT FINANCE ORGANIZATIONS

Agricultural Finance Corporation Ltd: Dhanraj Mahal, 1st Floor, Chhatrapati Shivaji Maharaj Marg, Mumbai 400 001; tel. (22) 22029517; fax (22) 22028966; e-mail afcl@afcindia.org.in; internet www.afcindia.org.in; f. 1968; est. by consortium of 45 public and private sector commercial banks incl. devt finance institutions; aims to increase the flow of investment and credit into agriculture and rural devt projects; provides project consultancy services to commercial banks, Union and state govts, public sector corpns, int. financial institutions, and to individuals; publishes quarterly journal *Financing Agriculture*; Chair. Y. C. NANDA; Man. Dir A. K. GARG; 3 regional offices and 9 br. offices.

Export-Import Bank of India: Centre One Bldg, Floor 21, World Trade Centre Complex, Cuffe Parade, Mumbai 400 005; tel. (22) 22172600; fax (22) 22182572; e-mail cag@eximbankindia.in; internet www.eximbankindia.in; f. 1982; cap. 22,999.9m., res 32,301.7m., dep. 31,566.1m. (March 2012); Chair. and Man. Dir T. C. A. RANGANATHAN; 14 offices worldwide.

Housing Development Finance Corpn Ltd (HDFC): Ramon House, 169 Backbay Reclamation, Churchgate, Mumbai 400 020; tel. (22) 66316000; fax (22) 22048834; e-mail info@hdfc.com; internet www.hdfc.com; f. 1977; provides loans to individuals and corporate bodies; cap. p.u. 2,844.5m., res 128,529.4m., dep. 193,746.7m. (March 2009); Chair. C. M. VASUDEV; Man. Dir RENU SUD KARNAD; 173 brs (incl. one overseas br.).

IDBI Bank Ltd (Industrial Development Bank of India): IDBI Tower, World Trade Centre Complex, Cuffe Parade, Mumbai 400 005; tel. (22) 66553355; fax (22) 22188137; e-mail pro@idbi.co.in; internet www.idbi.com; f. 1964; reorg. 1976; merged with The United Western Bank Ltd in 2006; 76.5% govt-owned; provides direct finance, refinance of industrial loans and bills, finance to large- and medium-sized industries, extends financial services, such as merchant banking and forex services, to the corporate sector; cap. 12,783.8m., res 158,031m., dep. 2,102,441.7m. (March 2012); Chair. and Man. Dir R. M. MALLA; 5 zonal offices and 36 br. offices.

Small Industries Development Bank of India: SIDBI Tower, 15 Ashok Marg, Lucknow 226 001; tel. (522) 2288547; fax (522) 2288548; e-mail cmdsecttlho@sidbi.com; internet www.sidbi.in; f. 1990; wholly owned subsidiary of IDBI; promotes, finances and develops small-scale industries; cap. 4,500m., res 57,974.9m., dep. 157,342m. (March 2012); Chair. and Man. Dir SUSHIL MUHNOT; 39 offices.

IFCI Ltd: IFCI Tower, 61 Nehru Place, New Delhi 110 019; tel. (11) 41792800; fax (11) 26488471; e-mail helpdesk@ifciltd.com; internet www.ifciltd.com; f. 1948, as Industrial Finance Corpn of India; renamed as above in 1999; CEO and Man. Dir ATUL K. RAI.

Industrial Investment Bank of India: 19 Netaji Subhas Rd, Kolkata 700 001; tel. (33) 22209941; fax (33) 22208049; e-mail iibiho@vsnl.com; Chair. and Man. Dir BHASKAR SEN; Exec. Dir V. K. DHINGRA.

National Bank for Agriculture and Rural Development: Plot C-24, G Blk, Bandra-Kurla Complex, Bandra (East), Mumbai 400 051; tel. (22) 26525068; fax (22) 26530050; e-mail contact@nabard .org; internet www.nabard.org; f. 1982; est. to provide credit for agricultural and rural devt through commercial, co-operative and regional rural banks; cap. p.u. 20,000m., res 52,910m. (March 2004); held 50% each by cen. Govt and Reserve Bank; Chair. PRAKASH BAKSHI; 30 regional offices, 10 sub-offices and 4 training establishments.

STOCK EXCHANGES

In mid-2014 there were 21 stock exchanges in India. The two most important exchanges are the Bombay Stock Exchange and the National Stock Exchange.

Ahmedabad Stock Exchange: Kamdhenu Complex, opp. Sahajanand College, Panjarapole, Ambawadi, Ahmedabad 380 015; tel. (79) 26307971; fax (79) 26308877; e-mail info@agipt.org; internet www.aselindia.org; f. 1894; 2,000 mems; Chair. HEMANTSINGH JHALA; Man. Dir K. K. MISHRA.

Bombay Stock Exchange (BSE): Phiroze Jeejeebhoy Towers, 25th Floor, Dalal St, Fort, Mumbai 400 001; tel. (22) 22721233; fax (22) 22721919; e-mail info@bseindia.com; internet www.bseindia.com; f. 1875; 5,112 listed cos (Dec. 2011); Chair. S. RAMADORAI; Man. Dir and CEO ASHISH KUMAR CHAUHAN.

Calcutta Stock Exchange Association Ltd: 7 Lyons Range, Kolkata 700 001; tel. (33) 40253000; fax (33) 22104500; e-mail cseadmn@cse-india.com; internet www.cse-india.com; f. 1908; 917 mems; Chair. SUNIL MITRA; Man. Dir and CEO B. MADHAV REDDY.

Delhi Stock Exchange Ltd: DSE House, 3/1 Asaf Ali Rd, New Delhi 110 002; tel. (11) 46470000; fax (11) 46740053; e-mail contact@ dseindia.org.in; internet www.dseindia.org.in; f. 1947; some 2,750 listed cos (Feb. 2013); Sec. SUNIL BHATIA.

Ludhiana Stock Exchange Association Ltd: Feroze Gandhi Market, Ludhiana 141 001; tel. (161) 2405756; fax (161) 2404748; e-mail lse@satyam.net.in; internet lse.co.in; f. 1981; 295 mems; Chair. PADAM PARKASH KANSAL.

Madras Stock Exchange Ltd: Exchange Bldg, 30 Second Line Beach, POB 183, Chennai 600 001; tel. (44) 25228951; fax (44) 25244897; e-mail info@mseindia.in; internet www.mseindia.in; f. 1937; 222 mems; Man. Dir K. N. RAMANATH.

National Stock Exchange of India Ltd (NSE): Exchange Plaza, Bandra-Kurla Complex, Bandra (East), Mumbai 400 051; tel. (22) 26598100; fax (22) 26598120; e-mail cc_nse@nse.co.in; internet www .nseindia.com; f. 1994; 1,640 listed cos (Dec. 2011); New York Stock Exchange, Goldman Sachs, General Atlantic (all of the USA) and SoftBank Asian Infrastructure Fund (Hong Kong) each acquired a 5% share in Jan. 2007; Chair. S. B. MATHUR; CEO CHITRA RAMKRISHNA.

Uttar Pradesh Stock Exchange Association Ltd (UPSE): Padam Towers, 14/113 Civil Lines, Kanpur 208 001; tel. (512) 2293115; fax (512) 2293175; e-mail upstockexchange@gmail.com; internet www.upse-india.com; 540 mems; Chair. K. D. GUPTA; Man. Dir BHARAT KUMAR NADHANI.

Other recognized stock exchanges include: Madhya Pradesh (Indore), Pune, Guwahati, Jaipur, Bhubaneswar (Odisha), Meerut, Vadodara, the OTC Exchange and the Inter-connected Stock Exchange (ISE).

Regulatory Authority

Securities and Exchange Board of India: Plot No. C4-A, 'G' Block, Bandra Kurla Complex, Bandra (East), Mumbai 400 051; tel. (22) 26449000; fax (22) 26449019; e-mail sebi@sebi.gov.in; internet www.sebi.gov.in; f. 1992; Chair. U. K. SINHA.

INSURANCE

In January 1973 all Indian and foreign insurance companies were nationalized. The Insurance Regulatory and Development Authority Bill, approved by the legislature in December 1999, established a regulatory authority for the insurance sector and henceforth permitted up to 26% investment by foreign companies in new domestic, private sector insurance companies. At the end of September 2014 there were 28 general insurance companies, 24 life insurance companies and one reinsurance company registered in India.

Bajaj Allianz: GE Plaza, Airport Rd, Yerawada, Pune 411 006; tel. (20) 66026777; fax (20) 66026789; e-mail info@bajajallianz.co.in;

internet www.bajajallianz.com; f. 2001; life and general insurance; private sector; Chair. RAHUL BAJAJ; Man. Dir and CEO TAPAN SINGHEL.

General Insurance Corpn of India (GIC): 'Suraksha', 170 J. Tata Rd, Churchgate, Mumbai 400 020; tel. (22) 22867000; fax (22) 22899600; e-mail info@gicofindia.com; internet www.gicofindia .com; f. 1972; Chair. and Man. Dir ASHOK KUMAR ROY.

HDFC ERGO General: Leela Business Park, 6th Floor, Andheri Kurla Rd, Andheri (East), Mumbai 400 059; tel. (22) 66383600; fax (22) 66383699; e-mail care@hdfcergo.com; internet www.hdfcergo .com; f. 2002; general insurance; private sector; Chair. DEEPAK S. PAREKH; Man. Dir and CEO RITESH KUMAR; 78 brs.

ICICI Lombard: 401 and 402, Interface Bldg, 11 Link Rd, Malad (West), Mumbai 400 064; internet www.icicilombard.com; f. 2001; general insurance; private sector; Chair. CHANDA KOCHHAR; Man. Dir and CEO BHARGAV DASGUPTA; 350 brs.

ICICI Prudential: ICICI Pru Life Towers, 1,089 Appasaheb Marathe Marg, Prabhadevi, Mumbai 400 025; tel. (22) 40391600; e-mail lifeline@iciciprulife.com; internet www.iciciprulife.com; f. 2000; life insurance; private sector; Chair. CHANDA KOCHHAR; Man. Dir and CEO SANDEEP BAKHSHI.

IFFCO—Tokio: IFFCO Tower, 4th and 5th Floors, Plot 3, Sector 29, Gurgaon 122 001; internet www.iffcotokio.co.in; f. 2000; general insurance; private sector; Man. Dir YOGESH LOHIYA.

Life Insurance Corpn of India (LIC): 'Yogakshema', Jeevan Bima Marg, Mumbai 400 021; tel. (22) 26137545; fax (22) 22810680; e-mail co_pgs@licindia.com; internet www.licindia.in; f. 1956; leading insurance co; public sector; Chair. S. K ROY; Man. Dirs Thomas MATHEW, SUSHOBHAN SARKER; 109 divisional offices, 2,048 brs, 8 zonal offices and 992 satellite offices.

National Insurance Co Ltd: 3 Middleton St, Kolkata 700 071; tel. (33) 22831705; fax (33) 22831712; e-mail website.administrator@nic .co.in; internet www.nationalinsuranceindia.com; f. 1906; general insurance; public sector; Chair. and Man. Dir N. S. R. CHANDRA PRASAD; 1,000 brs.

New India Assurance Co Ltd: 87 Mahatma Gandhi Rd, Fort, Mumbai 400 001; tel. (22) 22708220; fax (22) 22652811; e-mail cmd .nia@newindia.co.in; internet www.newindia.co.in; f. 1919; general insurance; public sector; 26 regional offices, 393 divisional offices, 614 br. offices, 34 direct agent brs and 19 overseas brs; Chair. and Man. Dir G. SRINIVASAN.

The Oriental Insurance Co Ltd: Oriental House, A-25/27 Asaf Ali Rd, New Delhi 110 002; tel. (11) 23279221; internet www .orientalinsurance.org.in; general insurance; public sector; Chair. and Man. Dir Dr A. K. SAXENA.

Sahara India Life Insurance Co Ltd: Sahara India Centre, 2 Kapoorthala Complex, Lucknow 226 024; tel. (522) 2337777; fax (522) 2332683; e-mail life@life.sahara.co.in; internet www.saharalife.com; f. 2004; was the first wholly Indian-owned insurance co; pvt sector; Chair. SUBRATA ROY SAHARA; Dir and CEO N. P. BALI.

SBI Life Insurance Co Ltd: Natraj, M.V. Rd and Western Express Highway Junction, Andheri (East), Mumbai 400 069; e-mail info@ sbilife.co.in; internet www.sbilife.co.in; f. 2001; jt venture between State Bank of India and BNP Paribas Assurance; Man. Dir and CEO M. N. RAO; 430 brs.

United India Insurance Co Ltd: 24 Whites Rd, Chennai 600 014; tel. (44) 28520161; internet www.uiic.co.in; f. 1938; general insurance; public sector; Chair. and Man. Dir MILIND A. KHARAT; 1,340 brs.

Regulatory Authority

Insurance Regulatory and Development Authority: Parisrama Bhavan, 3rd Floor, Basheer Bagh, Hyderabad 500 004; tel. (40) 23381100; fax (40) 66823334; internet www.irda.gov.in; f. 2000; Chair. T. S. VIJAYAN.

Trade and Industry

GOVERNMENT AGENCIES AND DEVELOPMENT ORGANIZATIONS

Cotton Corpn of India Ltd: Plot No. 3A, Sector No. 10, CBD Belapur, Navi Mumbai 400 614; tel. (22) 27579217; fax (22) 27576030; e-mail headoffice@cotcorp.com; internet www.cotcorp .gov.in; f. 1970 as an agency in the public sector for the purchase, sale and distribution of home-produced cotton and imported cotton staple fibre; exports long-staple cotton; Chair. and Man. Dir B. K. MISHRA.

Export Credit Guarantee Corpn of India Ltd (ECGC): Express Towers, 10th Floor, Nariman Point, POB 11677, Mumbai 400 021; tel. (22) 66590500; fax (22) 66590517; e-mail webmaster@ecgc.in; internet www.ecgc.in; f. 1957 to insure for risks involved in exports

on credit terms and to supplement credit facilities by issuing guarantees, etc.; Chair. and Man. Dir GEETHA MURALIDHAR; 29 brs.

Food Corpn of India: DDA Complex, Ground Floor, Rajendra Pl., Rajendra Bhavan, New Delhi 110 008; tel. (11) 25710962; fax (11) 25750670; e-mail fci-gmhq@lsmgr.nic.in; internet www.fciweb.nic .in; f. 1965 to undertake trading in food grains on a commercial scale but within the framework of an overall govt policy; to provide farmers an assured price for their produce; to supply food grains to the consumer at reasonable prices; also purchases, stores, distributes and sells food grains and other foodstuffs and arranges imports and handling of food grains and fertilizers at the ports; distributes sugar in a number of states and has set up rice mills; Chair. and Man. Dir C. VISWANATH; c. 26,000 employees (2013).

Handicrafts and Handlooms Exports Corpn of India Ltd: Jawahar Vyapar Bhavan Annexe, 5th Floor, 1 Tolstoy Marg, New Delhi 110 001; tel. (11) 23701086; fax (11) 23701051; e-mail hhecnd@ bol.net.in; internet www.hhecworld.com; f. 1958; govt undertaking dealing in export of handicrafts, handloom goods, ready-to-wear clothes, carpets, jute, leather and precious jewellery, and import of bullion and raw silk; promotes exports and trade development; Chair. and Man. Dir NIRMAL SINHA.

Housing and Urban Development Corpn Ltd: HUDCO Bhavan, India Habitat Centre, Lodhi Rd, New Delhi 110 003; tel. (11) 24649610; fax (11) 24625308; e-mail mail@hudco.org; internet www.hudco.org; f. 1970 to finance and undertake housing and urban development programmes including the establishment of new or satellite towns and building material industries; 21 brs; Chair. and Man. Dir M. RAVI KANTH.

India Trade Promotion Organisation (ITPO): Pragati Bhavan, Pragati Maidan, Lal Bahadur Shastri Marg, New Delhi 110 001; tel. (11) 23371540; fax (11) 23371492; e-mail info@itpo.gov.in; internet www.indiatradefair.com; f. 1992 following merger; promotes selective development of exports of high-quality products; arranges investment in export-orientated ventures undertaken by India with foreign collaboration; organizes trade fairs; operates Trade Information Centre; regional offices in Bengaluru, Mumbai, Kolkata and Chennai, and international offices in Brazil, Germany, Japan, Russia and the USA; Chair. and Man. Dir J. S. DEEPAK; Exec. Dir MALAY SHRIVASTAVA.

Jute Corpn of India Ltd: 15-N, Nellie Sengupta Sarani, 7th Floor, Kolkata 700 087; tel. (33) 22527027; fax (33) 22526771; e-mail jutecorp@vsnl.net; internet www.jci.gov.in; f. 1971; objects: (i) to undertake price support operations in respect of raw jute; (ii) to ensure remunerative prices to producers through efficient marketing; (iii) to operate a buffer stock to stabilize raw jute prices; (iv) to handle the import and export of raw jute; (v) to promote the export of jute goods; Chair. and Man. Dir ARUN KUMAR CHAKRABORTY.

Minerals and Metals Trading Corpn of India Ltd (MMTC): SCOPE Complex, Core 1, 7 Institutional Areas, Lodhi Rd, New Delhi 110 003; tel. (11) 24368426; fax (11) 24366274; e-mail mmtc@ mmtclimited.com; internet www.mmtclimited.com; f. 1963; export of iron and manganese ore, ferro-manganese, finished stainless steel products, engineering, agricultural and marine products, textiles, leather items, chemicals and pharmaceuticals, mica, coal and other minor minerals; import of steel, non-ferrous metals, rough diamonds, fertilizers, etc. for supply to industrial units in the country; 11 regional offices in India; foreign offices in Japan, the Republic of Korea, Jordan and Romania; Chair. and Man. Dir VED PRAKASH.

National Co-operative Development Corpn: 4 Siri Institutional Area, Hauz Khas, New Delhi 110 016; tel. (11) 26569246; fax (11) 26962370; e-mail editor@ncdc.in; internet www.ncdc.in; f. 1963 to plan, promote and finance country-wide programmes through co-operative societies for the production, processing, marketing, storage, export and import of agricultural produce, foodstuffs and notified commodities and minor forest produce; also programmes for the development of poultry, dairy, fish products, coir, handlooms, distribution of consumer articles in rural areas, industrial and service co-operatives, water conservation work, irrigation, micro-irrigation, animal care, health, disease prevention, agricultural insurance and credit, rural sanitation, etc.; 18 regional directorates; Pres. RADHA MOHAN SINGH (Minister of Agriculture); Man. Dir VASUDHA MISHRA.

National Mineral Development Corpn Ltd: Khanij Bhavan, 10-3-311/A Castle Hills, Masab Tank, POB 1352, Hyderabad 500 028; tel. (40) 23538713; fax (40) 23538711; e-mail hois@nmdc.co.in; internet www.nmdc.co.in; f. 1958; to exploit minerals in the public sector; cen. govt undertaking; two iron ore mines at Bailadila in Chhattisgarh, and one at Donimalai in Karnataka, producing 30m. metric tons in 2013; diamond mines at Panna in Madhya Pradesh; new iron ore mines at Bailadila and Kumaraswamy (Karnataka) scheduled for completion in 2015; other operations incl. steel production, pellets and wind turbines; Chair. and Man. Dir NARENDRA KOTHARI; 5,664 employees (2014).

National Productivity Council: Utpadakta Bhavan, 5–6 Institutional Area, Lodhi Rd, New Delhi 110 003; tel. (11) 24690331; fax (11) 24615002; e-mail npcinfo@npcindia.gov.in; internet www.npcindia.gov.in; f. 1958 to increase productivity and to improve quality by improved techniques which aim at efficient and proper utilization of available resources; autonomous body representing national orgs of employers and labour, govt ministries, professional orgs, local productivity councils, small-scale industries and other interests; 13 regional professional management groups, 1 training institute; 75 mems; Chair. AMITABH KANT; Sec. HARBHAJAN SINGH.

National Research Development Corpn: 20–22 Zamroodpur Community Centre, Kailash Colony Extension, New Delhi 110 048; tel. (11) 29240401; fax (11) 29240409; e-mail write2@nrdcindia.com; internet www.nrdcindia.com; f. 1953 to stimulate development and commercial exploitation of new inventions with financial and technical aid; finances development projects to set up demonstration units in collaboration with industry; exports technology; Chair. and Man. Dir H. PURUSHOTHAM.

National Seeds Corpn Ltd: Beej Bhavan, Pusa, New Delhi 110 012; tel. (11) 25846292; fax (11) 25846462; e-mail nsc@indiaseeds.com; internet www.indiaseeds.com; f. 1963 to improve and develop the seed industry; Chair. and Man. Dir VINOD KUMAR GAUR.

National Small Industries Corpn Ltd: NSIC Bhavan, Okhla Industrial Estate, New Delhi 110 020; tel. (11) 26926275; fax (11) 26932075; e-mail pro@nsic.co.in; internet www.nsic.co.in; f. 1955 to aid, advise, finance and promote the interests of small industries; establishes and supplies machinery for small industries in other developing countries on turnkey basis; all shares held by the Govt; Chair. and Man. Dir RAVINDRA NATH.

PEC Ltd: 'Hansalaya', 15 Barakhamba Rd, New Delhi 110 001; tel. (11) 23316397; fax (11) 23314797; e-mail pec@peclimited.com; internet www.peclimited.com; f. 1971; export of engineering, industrial and railway equipment; undertakes turnkey and other projects and management consultancy abroad; countertrade, trading in agrocommodities, construction materials (steel, cement, clinkers, etc.) and fertilizers; Chair. and Man. Dir RAJANI RANJAN RASHMI.

Power Finance Corpn Ltd: Urjanidhi Bldg, 1 Barakhamba Lane, Connaught Pl., New Delhi 110 001; tel. (11) 23456000; internet www.pfcindia.com; f. 1986; provides funding for power sector projects; Chair. and Man. Dir M. K. GOEL.

State Farms Corpn of India Ltd: Farm Bhavan, 14–15 Nehru Place, New Delhi 110 019; tel. (11) 26446903; fax (11) 26226898; e-mail sfci-moa@nic.in; internet sfci.nic.in; f. 1969 to administer the central state farms; activities include the production of quality seeds of high-yielding varieties of wheat, paddy, maize, bajra and jowar; advises on soil conservation, reclamation and development of waste and forest land; consultancy services on farm mechanization; Chair. and Man. Dir Brig. VINOD KUMAR GAUR.

State Trading Corpn of India Ltd: Jawahar Vyapar Bhavan, Janpath Road, Tolstoy Marg, New Delhi 110 001; tel. (11) 23313177; fax (11) 23701191; e-mail co.stc@gov.in; internet stc.gov.in; f. 1956; govt undertaking dealing in exports and imports; 6 regional brs, 6 sub-brs and 1 office overseas; Chair. and Man. Dir KHALEEL RAHIM.

Steel Authority of India Ltd (SAIL): Ispat Bhavan, Lodhi Rd, POB 3049, New Delhi 110 003; tel. (11) 24367481; fax (11) 24367015; e-mail sail.co@vsnl.com; internet www.sail.co.in; f. 1973 to provide co-ordinated development of the steel industry in the public sector; 75% govt-owned (following sale of 5% stake in late 2014); integrated steel plants at Bhilai (Chhattisgarh), Burnpur and Durgapur (West Bengal), Bokaro (Jharkhand), Rourkela (Odisha); stainless and alloy steel plants at Karnataka, Maharashtra, West Bengal and Tamil Nadu; 11 jt venture power- and steel-related cos; subsidiaries: SAIL Refractory Co Ltd (Tamil Nadu); combined crude steel capacity is almost 14m. metric tons annually; Chair. CHANDRA SHEKHAR VERMA; 97,897 employees (2014).

Tea Board of India: 14 B. T. M. Sarani (Brabourne Rd), POB 2172, Kolkata 700 001; tel. (33) 22351331; fax (33) 22215715; internet teaboard.gov.in; provides financial assistance to tea research stations; sponsors and finances independent research projects in universities and tech. institutions to supplement the work of tea research establishments; also promotes tea production and export; Chair. SIDDHARTH.

CHAMBERS OF COMMERCE

Associated Chambers of Commerce and Industry of India (ASSOCHAM): 5 Sardar Patel Marg, Chanakyapuri, New Delhi 110 021; tel. (11) 46550555; fax (11) 23017008; e-mail assocham@nic.in; internet www.assocham.org; f. 1920; central org. of over 450 chambers of commerce and industry and industrial asscns representing more than 100,000 cos throughout India; 5 promoter chambers, 115 ordinary mems, 45 patron mems and 500 corporate associates; Pres. RANA KAPOOR; Sec.-Gen. D. S. RAWAT.

Federation of Indian Chambers of Commerce and Industry (FICCI): Federation House, Tansen Marg, New Delhi 110 001; tel. (11) 23738760; fax (11) 23320714; e-mail ficci@ficci.com; internet www.ficci.com; f. 1927; more than 1,500 corporate mems, 500 chamber of commerce and business asscn mems; Pres. JYOTSNA SURI; Sec.-Gen. ALWYN DIDAR SINGH.

International Chamber of Commerce (ICC) India: Federation House, Tansen Marg, New Delhi 110 001; tel. (11) 23322472; fax (11) 23320714; e-mail iccindia@iccindiaonline.org; internet www.iccindiaonline.org; f. 1929; 43 org. mems, 375 corporate mems, 8 patron mems, 130 cttee mems; Pres. SANDIP SOMANY; Exec. Dir ASHOK UMMAT.

Associated Chambers of Commerce and Industry of Uttar Pradesh: Alaknanda Enclave, Laulai Indira Canal Rd, Chinhat, Lucknow 226 010; tel. (522) 2301957; fax (522) 2301958; e-mail asochamup@yahoo.com; internet asochamup.org.in; f. 1994; 405 mems; Pres. ANIL RATHI; Sec.-Gen. S. B. AGRAWAL.

Bengal Chamber of Commerce and Industry: Royal Exchange, 6 Netaji Subhas Rd, Kolkata 700 001; tel. (33) 22303711; fax (33) 22301289; e-mail bencham@bengalchamber.com; internet www.bengalchamber.com; f. 1853; more than 300 mems; Pres. ALOK ROY.

Bengal National Chamber of Commerce and Industry: BNCCI House, 23 Sir R. N. Mukherjee Rd, Kolkata 700 001; tel. (33) 22482951; fax (33) 22487058; e-mail bncci@bncci.com; internet www.bncci.com; f. 1887; 500 mems, 35 affiliated industrial and trading asscns; Pres. ARUN KUMAR SARKAR; Sec. D. P. NAG.

Bharat Chamber of Commerce: 9 Park Mansions, 2nd Floor, 57-A Park St, Kolkata 700 016; tel. (33) 22299591; fax (33) 22294947; e-mail info@bharatchamber.com; internet www.bharatchamber.com; f. 1900; c. 500 mems; Pres. SAJJAN BHAJANKA; Sec.-Gen. K. SARMA.

Bihar Chamber of Commerce: Khem Chand Chaudhary Marg, Patna 800 001; tel. (612) 3200646; fax (612) 2677505; e-mail info@biharchamber.org; internet www.biharchamber.org; f. 1926; 552 ordinary mems; Pres. O. P. SAH.

Bombay Chamber of Commerce and Industry: Mackinnon Mackenzie Bldg, 3rd Floor, 4 Shoorji Vallabhdas Rd, Ballard Estate, POB 473, Mumbai 400 001; tel. (22) 49100200; fax (22) 49100213; e-mail bcci@bombaychamber.com; internet www.bombaychamber.com; f. 1836; 935 ordinary mems, 650 assoc. mems, 75 hon. mems; Pres. HASIT B. JOSHIPURA; Vice-Pres. R. MUKUNDAN.

Calcutta Chamber of Commerce: 18H Park St, Stephen Court, Kolkata 700 071; tel. (33) 22290758; fax (33) 22298236; e-mail calchamb@bsnl.in; internet www.calcuttachamber.com; 300 mems; Pres. S. P. SAHARIA; Sr Vice-Pres. P. K. AGRAWAL.

Chamber of Commerce and Industry (Regd) Jammu: OB 31, Rail Head Complex, Jammu 180 012; tel. (191) 2472266; fax (191) 2472255; e-mail ccijammu@yahoo.com; internet jammuchamber.org; f. 1932; 1,069 mems; Pres. RAKESH GUPTA; Sec.-Gen. ARUN GUPTA.

Cochin Chamber of Commerce and Industry: Bristow Rd, Willingdon Island, POB 503, Kochi 682 003; tel. (484) 2668650; fax (484) 2668651; e-mail secretary@cochinchamber.org; internet www.cochinchamber.org; f. 1857; 245 mems; Pres. C. S. KARTHA; Vice-Pres. SHAJI VARGHESE.

Delhi Chamber of Commerce: 49 Rani Jhansi Rd, New Delhi 110055; tel. (11) 23518994; fax (11) 23628847; e-mail info@delhichamber.com; internet www.delhichamber.com; f. 1950; Pres. DAVINDER KUMAR; Sec.-Gen. JASBIRENDRA S. SODHBANS.

Federation of Andhra Pradesh Chambers of Commerce and Industry: Federation House, FAPCCI Marg, 11-6-841, Red Hills, POB 14, Hyderabad 500 004; tel. (40) 23395515; fax (40) 23395525; e-mail info@fapcci.in; internet www.fapcci.in; f. 1917; 3,300 mems; Pres. SHIV KUMAR RUNGTA; Sec.-Gen. SHRIPAD BHALERAO.

Federation of Karnataka Chambers of Commerce and Industry: Federation House, K. G. Rd, POB 9996, Bengaluru 560 009; tel. (80) 22262355; fax (80) 22251826; e-mail president@fkcci.in; internet www.fkcci.org; f. 1916; 2,100 mems; Pres. S. SAMPATHRAMAN; Sr Vice-Pres. TALLAM R. DWARAKANATH.

Federation of Madhya Pradesh Chambers of Commerce and Industry: Udyog Bhavan, 129A Malviya Nagar, Bhopal 462 003; tel. (755) 2573612; fax (755) 4292647; e-mail fmpcci@yahoo.co.in; internet fmpcci.com; f. 1975; 500 ordinary mems, 58 asscn mems; Pres. RAMESH CHANDRA AGRAWAL.

Goa Chamber of Commerce and Industry: Narayan Rajaram Bandekar Bhavan, Rua de Ormuz, POB 59, Panaji 403 001; tel. (832) 2422635; fax (832) 2425560; e-mail goachamber@goachamber.org; internet www.goachamber.org; f. 1908 as Associacao Commercial da India Portuguesa; more than 500 mems; Pres. NARAYAN BANDEKAR; Dir-Gen. Air Cmmdr (retd) R. S. KAMAT.

Gujarat Chamber of Commerce and Industry: Shri Ambica Mills, Gujarat Chamber Bldg, Ashram Rd, POB 4045, Ahmedabad 380 009; tel. (79) 26582301; fax (79) 26587992; e-mail gcci@gujaratchamber.org; internet www.gujaratchamber.org; f. 1949; 7,713 mems; Pres. RAKESH R. SHAH; Sr Vice-Pres. ROHITBHAI J. PATEL.

Indian Chamber of Commerce: ICC Towers, 4 India Exchange Place, Kolkata 700 001; tel. (33) 22203242; fax (33) 22213377; e-mail ceo@indianchamber.net; internet www.indianchamber.org; f. 1925; 500 corporate group mems, more than 1,200 mem. cos; Pres. ROOPEN ROY; Dir-Gen. RAJEEV SINGH.

Indian Chamber of Commerce and Industry—Cochin: Indian Chamber Rd, Mattancherry, POB 236, Kochi 682002; tel. (484) 2224335; fax (484) 2224203; e-mail info@iccicochin.com; internet www.iccicochin.com; f. 1897; Pres. RAJKUMAR GUPTA; Sec. K. RAGHU.

Indian Merchants' Chamber: IMC Bldg, IMC Marg, Churchgate, Mumbai 400 020; tel. (22) 22046633; fax (22) 22048508; e-mail imc@imcnet.org; internet www.imcnet.org; f. 1907; 185 asscn mems, 2,915 mem. firms; Pres. PRABODH THAKKER; Dir-Gen. ARVIND PRADHAN.

Karnataka Chamber of Commerce and Industry: G. Mahadevappa Karnataka Chamber Bldg, Jayachamraj Nagar, Hubballi 580 020; tel. (836) 2218234; fax (836) 2360933; e-mail kccihubli@rediffmail.com; internet www.kccihubli.org; f. 1928; 2,500 mems; Pres. VASANT N. LADWA; Hon. Sec. SIDDHESHWAR G KAMMAR.

Madras Chamber of Commerce and Industry (MCCI): Karumuttu Centre, 1st Floor, 634 Anna Salai, Chennai 600 035; tel. (44) 24349452; fax (44) 24349164; e-mail madraschamber@madraschamber.in; internet www.madraschamber.in; f. 1836; 374 mem. firms, 20 affiliated, 8 hon.; Pres. S. G. PRABHAKHARAN; Sec.-Gen. K. SARASWATHI.

Maharashtra Chamber of Commerce, Industry and Agriculture: Oricon House, 6th Floor, 12 K. Dubhash Marg, Fort, Mumbai 400 001; tel. (22) 22855859; fax (22) 22855861; e-mail sec.general@maccia.org.in; internet www.maccia.org.in; f. 1927; more than 3,500 mems; more than 800 affiliated trade asscns and professional bodies; Pres. RAMCHANDRA BHOGALE; Sr Vice Pres. SHANTANU BHADKAMKAR.

Mahratta Chamber of Commerce, Industries and Agriculture: MCCIA Trade Tower, 505, A-Wing, ICC Complex, 403 Senapati Pabat Rd, Pune 411 016; tel. (20) 25709000; fax (20) 25709021; e-mail info@mcciapune.com; internet www.mcciapune.com; f. 1934; more than 3,000 mems; Pres. SATISH MAGAR; Dir-Gen. ANANT SARDESHMUKH.

Merchants' Chamber of Uttar Pradesh: 14/76 Civil Lines, Kanpur 208 001; tel. (512) 2530877; fax (512) 2531306; e-mail info@merchantschamber-up.com; internet www.merchantschamberup.com; f. 1932; 222 mems; Pres. I. M. ROHTAGI; Sec. A. K. SINHA.

PHD Chamber of Commerce and Industry (PHDCCI): PHD House, 4/2 Siri Institutional Area, August Kranti Marg, New Delhi 110 016; tel. (11) 26863801; fax (11) 26855450; e-mail phdcci@phdcci.in; internet www.phdcci.in; f. 1905; 1,760 mems, 150 asscn mems; Pres. ALOK B. SHRIRAM; Sec.-Gen. SAURABH SANYAL.

Rajasthan Chamber of Commerce and Industry: Rajasthan Chamber Bhavan, M. I. Rd, Jaipur 302 002; tel. (141) 2565163; fax (141) 2561419; e-mail info@rajchamber.com; internet www.rajchamber.com; 575 mems; Pres. MAHENDRA SINGH DAGA; Hon. Sec.-Gen. K. L. JAIN.

Southern India Chamber of Commerce and Industry (SICCI): Indian Chamber Bldgs, 6 Esplanade, POB 1208, Chennai 600 108; tel. (44) 25342228; fax (44) 25341876; e-mail info@sicci.in; internet sicci.in; f. 1909; 1,000 mems; Pres. JAWAHAR VADIVELU; Sec. S. RAGHAVAN.

Utkal Chamber of Commerce and Industry Ltd: N/6, IRC Village, Nayapalli, Bhubaneswar 751 015; tel. (674) 2362598; fax (674) 2557598; e-mail contact@utkalchamber.com; internet www.utkalchamber.in; f. 1963; 250 mems; Pres. RAMESH MOHAPATRA; Hon. Sec. DEBABRATA DASH.

INDUSTRIAL AND TRADE ASSOCIATIONS

Ahmedabad Textile Mills' Association: Ashram Rd, Navrangpura, POB 4056, Ahmedabad 380 009; tel. (79) 26582273; fax (79) 26588574; e-mail atma@atmaahd.com; internet www.atmaahd.com; f. 1891; 19 mems; Pres. CHINTAN N. PARIKH; Sec.-Gen. ABHINAVA SHUKLA.

All India Federation of Master Printers: 605 Madhuban, 6th Floor, 55 Nehru Place, New Delhi 110 019; tel. (11) 26451742; fax (11) 26451743; e-mail fopaid11@gmail.com; internet www.aifmp.com; f. 1953; 59 affiliates, 900 mems; Pres. DEV NAIR; Hon. Gen. Sec. ANAND V. LIMAYE.

All India Manufacturers' Organization (AIMO): Jeevan Sahakar, 4th Floor, Sir P.M. Rd, Fort, Mumbai 400 001; tel. (22) 22615858; fax (22) 22615656; e-mail aimoindia@aimoindia.com; internet www.aimoindia.com; f. 1941; 800 mems; Pres. N. TARACHAND DUGAR; Sr Vice-Pres. SUDARSHAN SAREEN.

All India Plastics Manufacturers' Association: AIPMA House, A-52, St No. 1, MIDC, Andheri (East), Mumbai 400 093; tel. (22) 67778899; fax (22) 28216390; e-mail office@aipma.net; internet www.aipma.net; f. 1947; 2,500 mems; Pres. RITURAJ GUPTA.

All India Shippers' Council: Federation House, Tansen Marg, New Delhi 110 001; tel. (11) 23487492; fax (11) 23320736; e-mail aisc.india@gmail.com; internet www.aisc.in; f. 1967; 82 mems; Chair. RAMU S. DEORA; CEO and Sec. MANAB MAJUMDAR.

Association of Man-made Fibre Industry of India: Resham Bhavan, 78 Veer Nariman Rd, Mumbai 400 020; tel. (22) 22040009; fax (22) 22049172; e-mail amfiirayon@hotmail.com; internet www.viscoserayonindia.com; f. 1954; 8 mems; Pres. LALIT NAIK; Sec. M. P. JOSEPH.

Automotive Component Manufacturers' Association of India: The Capital Court, 6th Floor, Olof Palme Marg, Munirka, New Delhi 110 067; tel. (11) 26160315; fax (11) 26160317; e-mail acma@acma.in; internet www.acmainfo.com; 600 mems; Pres. RAMESH SURI; Exec. Dir VISHNU MATHUR.

Automotive Tyre Manufacturers' Association: PHD House, opp. Asian Games Village, Siri Fort Institutional Area, New Delhi 110 016; tel. (11) 26851187; fax (11) 26864799; e-mail atma@atmaindia.org; internet www.atmaindia.org; f. 1975; 10 mems; Chair. RAGHUPATI SINGHANIA; Dir-Gen. RAJIV BUDHRAJA.

Bharat Krishak Samaj (Farmers' Forum, India): Dr Panjabrao Deshmukh Krishak Bhavan, A-1 Nizamuddin West, New Delhi 110 013; tel. (11) 65650384; e-mail ho@bks.org.in; internet www.farmersforum.in; f. 1954; national farmers' org.; 5m. ordinary mems, 100,000 life mems; Chair. AJAY VIR JAKHAR; Pres. RAM NIWAS MIRDHA.

Bombay Metal Exchange Ltd: 88/90 Kika St, 1st Floor, Gulalwadi, Mumbai 400 004; tel. (22) 22421964; fax (22) 22422640; e-mail bme@bom8.vsnl.net.in; internet www.bme.in; f. 1950; promotes trade and industry in non-ferrous metals; 386 mems; Pres. ASHOK G. BAFNA; Sr Vice-Pres MAHENDRA H. SHAH.

Calcutta Tea Traders' Association: 6 Netaji Subhas Rd, Kolkata 700 001; tel. (33) 22301574; fax (33) 22301289; e-mail ctta@cal3.vsnl.net.in; f. 1886; 1,300 mems; Chair. SANGEETA KICHLU; Vice-Chair. L. N. GUPTA.

Cement Manufacturers' Association: CMA Tower, A-2E, Sector 24, Noida 201 301; tel. (95120) 2411955; fax (95120) 2411956; e-mail cmand@cmaindia.org; internet cmaindia.org; f. 1961; 54 mems; 126 major cement plants; Pres. M. A. M. R. MUTHIAH; Sec.-Gen. N. A. VISWANATHAN.

Confederation of Indian Industry (CII): 23 Institutional Area, Lodi Rd, New Delhi 110 003; tel. (11) 24629994; fax (11) 24626149; e-mail info@cii.in; internet www.cii.in; f. 1974; 7,500 mem. cos; Pres. AJAY S. SHRIRAM; Dir-Gen. CHANDRAJIT BANERJEE.

Consumer Electronics and Appliances Manufacturers' Association (CEAMA): F-4/23, 4th Floor, 1st Silver Tower, Sector 18, Noida 201 301; tel. (11) 4265697; e-mail info@ceama.in; internet www.ceama.in; f. 1978; 106 mems; Pres. ANIRUDH V. DHOOT; Sec.-Gen. AMIT CHADHA.

Cotton Association of India: Cotton Exchange Bldg, 2nd Floor, Cotton Green, Mumbai 400 033; tel. (22) 30063400; fax (22) 23700337; e-mail cai@caionline.in; internet www.caionline.in; f. 1921; 465 mems; Pres. DHIREN N. SHETH; Sec. AMAR SINGH.

Darjeeling Tea Association: Royal Exchange, 6 Netaji Subhas Rd, Kolkata 700 001; tel. and fax (33) 22102408; fax (33) 22102408; internet www.darjeelingtea.com; Chair. S. S. BAGARIA.

ELCINA Electronic Industries Association of India: ELCINA House, 422 Okhla Industrial Estate, New Delhi 110 020; tel. (11) 26924597; fax (11) 26923440; e-mail info@elcina.com; internet www.elcina.com; f. 1967; fmrly Electronic Component Industries Association; 255 mems; Pres. T. VASU; Sec.-Gen. RAJOO GOEL.

Federation of Automobile Dealers Associations: 805 Surya Kiran, 19 Kasturba Gandhi Marg, New Delhi 110 001; tel. (11) 23320095; fax (11) 23320093; e-mail fada@fada.in; internet www.fadaindia.org; f. 1964; Pres. K. V. S. PRAKASH RAO; Sec.-Gen. VINAY SANGHI; 1,500 mems.

Federation of Gujarat Industries: Gotri-Sevasi Rd, Khanpur, Vadodara 390 101; tel. (265) 2372901; fax (265) 2372904; e-mail info@fgi.co.in; internet www.fgibaroda.com; f. 1918; Pres. AMIT PATEL; 415 mems.

Federation of Hotel and Restaurant Associations of India (FHRAI): B-82 Himalaya House, 23 Kasturba Gandhi Marg, New Delhi 110 001; tel. (11) 40780780; fax (11) 40780777; e-mail fhrai@vsnl.com; internet www.fhrai.com; f. 1955; 3,961 mems; Pres. T. S. WALIA; Sec.-Gen. M. D. KAPOOR.

Federation of Indian Export Organisations: Niryat Bhavan, Rao Tula Ram Marg, opp. Army Hospital Research and Referral, New Delhi 110 057; tel. (11) 46042112; fax (11) 26150112; e-mail fieo@nda.vsnl.net.in; internet www.fieo.org; f. 1965; 17,500 mems; Pres. M. RAFEEQUE AHMED; Dir-Gen. and CEO AJAY SAHAI.

Federation of Indian Mineral Industries (FIMI): B-311, Okhla Industrial Area, Phase 1, New Delhi 110 020; tel. (11) 26814596; fax (11) 26814593; e-mail fimi@fedmin.com; internet www.fedmin.com; f. 1966; 350 mems; Pres. H. C. DAGA.

The Fertiliser Association of India: 10 Shaheed Jit Singh Marg, New Delhi 110 067; tel. (11) 26567144; fax (11) 26960052; e-mail general@faidelhi.org; internet www.faidelhi.org; f. 1955; 1,406 mems; Chair. S. S. NANDURDIKAR; Dir-Gen. SATISH CHANDER.

Indian Drug Manufacturers' Association: 102B Poonam Chambers, Dr A. B. Rd, Worli, Mumbai 400 018; tel. (22) 24944625; fax (22) 24950723; e-mail admin@idmaindia.com; internet www.idma-assn .org; f. 1961; 800 mems; Pres. S. V. VEERRAMANI; Hon. Sec.-Gen. B. PATEL.

Indian Electrical and Electronics Manufacturers' Association (IEEMA): 501 Kakad Chambers, 132 Dr Annie Besant Rd, Worli, Mumbai 400 018; tel. (22) 24930532; fax (22) 24932705; e-mail mumbai@ieema.org; internet www.ieema.org; f. 1948; 650 mems; Pres. VISHNU AGARWAL; Dir-Gen. SUNIL MISHRA.

Indian Jute Mills Association: Royal Exchange, 6 Netaji Subhas Rd, Kolkata 700 001; tel. (33) 22309918; fax (33) 22313836; e-mail ijma@ijma.org; internet www.ijma.org; sponsors and operates export promotion, research and product development; regulates labour relations; 33 mems; Chair. RAGHAVENDRA GUPTA; Exec. Vice-Chair. SUMANT PODDAR.

Indian Leather Products Association: Suite 6, Chatterjee International Centre, 14th Floor, 33-A, Jawaharlal Nehru Rd, Kolkata 700 071; tel. (33) 22267102; fax (33) 22468339; e-mail ilpa@cal2.vsnl .net.in; internet www.ilpaindia.org; 145 mems; Pres. SANKAR DAWN; Exec. Dir P. P. RAY CHAUDHURI.

Indian Machine Tool Manufacturers' Association: 10th Mile, Tumkur Rd, Madavara Post, Bengaluru 562 123; tel. (80) 66246600; fax (80) 66246661; e-mail imtma@imtma.in; internet www.imtma.in; 500 mems; Pres. VIKRAM SIRUR; Dir-Gen. V. ANBU.

Indian Motion Picture Producers' Association: IMPPA House, Dr Ambedkar Rd, Bandra (West), Mumbai 400 050; tel. (22) 26486344; fax (22) 26480757; e-mail imppa1937@gmail.com; internet www.indianmotionpictures.com/imppa/index.html; f. 1938; 14,400 mems; Pres. T. P. AGGARWAL.

Indian National Shipowners' Association: 22 Maker Tower F, Cuffe Parade, Mumbai 400 005; tel. (22) 22182105; fax (22) 22182104; e-mail insa@insa.org.in; internet insa.in; f. 1929; 36 mems; Pres. ATUL J. AGARWAL; Sec.-Gen. S. S. KULKARNI.

Indian Oilseeds & Produce Export Promotion Council (IOPEA): 78/79 Bajaj Bhavan, Nariman Point, Mumbai 400 021; tel. (22) 22023225; fax (22) 22029236; e-mail info@iopepc.org; internet www.iopepc.org; f. 1956; export promotion council; 350 mems; Chair. KISHORE TANNA; CEO SURESH RAMRAKHIANI.

Indian Refractory Makers' Association: 5 Lala Lajpat Rai Sarani, 4th Floor, Kolkata 700 020; tel. (33) 22810868; fax (33) 22814357; e-mail irmaindia@hotmail.com; internet www.irmaindia .org; 77 mems; Chair. A. K. JAIN; Exec. Dir P. DASGUPTA.

Indian Soap and Toiletries Makers' Association: 614 Raheja Centre, 6th Floor, Free Press Journal Marg, Nariman Point, Mumbai 400 021; tel. (22) 22824115; fax (22) 22853649; e-mail istmamum@ gmail.com; internet istma.internetindia.com/index.htm; f. 1937; 28 mems; Pres. HEMANT BAKSHI; Sec.-Gen. O. P. AGARWAL.

Indian Sugar Mills' Association: Ansal Plaza, 2nd Floor, C-Blk, Andrews Ganj, New Delhi 110 049; tel. (11) 26262294; fax (11) 26263231; e-mail isma@indiansugar.com; internet www .indiansugar.com; f. 1932; 250 mems; Pres. A. VELLAYAN.

Indian Tea Association: Royal Exchange, 6 Netaji Subhas Rd, Kolkata 700 001; tel. (33) 22102474; fax (33) 22434301; e-mail ita@ indiatea.org; internet www.indiatea.org; f. 1881; 202 mem. cos; 482 tea estates; Chair. A. N. SINGH; Sec.-Gen. MONOJIT DASGUPTA.

Indian Woollen Mills' Federation: Churchgate Chambers, 7th Floor, 5 New Marine Lines, Mumbai 400 020; tel. (22) 22624372; fax (22) 22624675; e-mail mail@iwmfindia.com; internet www .iwmfindia.com; f. 1948; 50 mems; Chair. S. L. POKHARNA; Sec.-Gen. MAHESH N. SANIL.

National Association of Software and Service Companies (NASSCOM): International Youth Centre, Teen Murti Marg, Chanakyapuri, New Delhi 110 021; tel. (11) 23010199; fax (11) 23015452; e-mail info@nasscom.in; internet www.nasscom.in; 1,200 mems; Pres. R. CHANDRASHEKHAR; Chair. R. CHANDRASEKARAN.

Organisation of Pharmaceutical Producers of India (OPPI): Peninsular Corporate Park, Peninsular Chambers, Ground Floor, Ganpatrao Kadam Marg, Lower Parel, Mumbai 400 013; tel. (22) 24918123; fax (22) 24915168; e-mail indiaoppi@vsnl.com; internet www.indiaoppi.com; f. 1965; 45 mems; Pres. SHAILESH AYYANGAR; Dir-Gen. RANJANA SMETACEK.

Society of Indian Automobile Manufacturers: Core 4B, 5th Floor, India Habitat Centre, Lodhi Rd, New Delhi 110 003; tel. (11) 24647810; fax (11) 24648222; e-mail siam@vsnl.com; internet www.siamindia.com; f. 1960; 36 mems; Pres. VIKRAM S. KIRLOSKAR; Dir-Gen. VISHNU MATHUR.

Southern India Mills' Association: 41 Race Course, Coimbatore 641 018; tel. (422) 4225333; fax (422) 4225366; e-mail info@simamills .com; internet www.simamills.com; f. 1933; 360 mems; Chair. T. RAJKUMAR; Sec.-Gen. Dr K. SELVARAJAU.

Surgical Manufacturers' and Traders' Association: 60 Darya Ganj, New Delhi 110 002; tel. (11) 23271027; fax (11) 23258576; e-mail info@smta.in; internet www.smta.in; f. 1951; Pres. S. B. SAWHNEY; Sec. RAJESH SAWHNEY.

Synthetic and Art Silk Mills' Research Association Ltd (SAS-MIRA): Sasmira Bldg, Sasmira Marg, Worli, Mumbai 400 030; tel. (22) 24935351; fax (22) 24930225; e-mail sasmira@vsnl.com; internet www.sasmira.org; f. 1950; 100 mems; Pres. MAGANLAL H. DOSHI; Exec. Dir U. K. GANGOPADHYAY.

Telecom Equipment Manufacturers' Association of India (TEMA): PHD House, 4th Floor, Khel Gaon Marg, Hauz Khas, New Delhi 110 016; tel. (11) 26859621; fax (11) 26859620; e-mail tema@eth.net; internet tematelecom.in; f. 1990; Pres. RAHUL SHARMA; Sec.-Gen. PUNEET JAIN.

The Textile Association (India): Pathare House, Room 6, 2nd Floor, 67 Ranade Rd, Dadar West, Mumbai 400 028; tel. (22) 24461145; fax (22) 24474971; e-mail taicnt@mtnl.net.in; internet www.textileassociationindia.org; f. 1939; 27 regional units, of which the Mumbai unit is the largest (www.textileassociationindia.com); Pres. ARVIND SINHA; Chair. V. D. ZOPE; c. 23,000 mems.

The United Planters' Association of Southern India (UPASI): Glenview, POB 11, Coonoor 643 101; tel. (423) 2230270; fax (423) 2232030; e-mail upasi@upasi.org; internet www.upasi.org; f. 1893; 749 mems; Pres. VIJAYAN RAJES; Sec.-Gen. ULLAS MENON.

EMPLOYERS' ORGANIZATIONS

Council of Indian Employers: Federation House, Tansen Marg, New Delhi 110 001; tel. (11) 23316121; fax (11) 23320714; e-mail secretariat@aioe.com; f. 1956; Pres. SAROJ KUMAR PODDAR; comprises:

> **All India Organisation of Employers (AIOE):** Federation House, Tansen Marg, New Delhi 110 001; tel. (11) 23316121; fax (11) 23320714; e-mail aioe@ficci.com; internet www.aioe.in; f. 1932; 50 affiliated asscns and 149 corporate mems; Pres. SANJAY BHATIA.

> **Employers' Federation of India (EFI):** Army and Navy Bldg, 148 Mahatma Gandhi Rd, Mumbai 400 023; tel. (22) 22844232; fax (22) 22843028; e-mail efisolar@mtnl.net.in; internet www .efionline.in; f. 1933; 28 asscn mems, 182 ordinary mems, 18 hon. mems; Pres. R. MUKUNDAN; Sec.-Gen. SHARAD S. PATIL.

> **Standing Conference of Public Enterprises (SCOPE):** Core 8, SCOPE Complex, 1st Floor, 7 Lodhi Rd, New Delhi 110 003; tel. (11) 24362604; fax (11) 24361371; e-mail scopedg@yahoo.com; internet www.scopeonline.in; f. 1973; representative body of all central public enterprises in India; advises the Govt and public enterprises on matters of major policy and co-ordination; trade enquiries, regarding imports and exports of commodities, carried out on behalf of mems; 211 mems; Chair. C. S. VERMA.

Employers' Federation of Southern India: 33 Hindi Prachar Sabha St, T Nagar, Chennai 600 017; tel. (44) 24320801; fax (44) 24322750; e-mail efsi@vsnl.net; internet www.efsi.org.in; f. 1920; 735 mems (2013); Pres. ANAND SUNDARESAN; Sec. T. M. JAWAHARLAL.

UTILITIES

Electricity

Central Electricity Authority (CEA): Sewa Bhavan, R. K. Puram, New Delhi 110 066; tel. (11) 26732500; fax (11) 26105619; e-mail cea-edp@hub.nic.in; internet www.cea.nic.in; responsible for technical co-ordination and supervision of electricity programmes; advises Ministry of Power on all technical, financial and economic issues; Chair. NEERJA MATHUR.

Essar Power Ltd: Essar House, 11 Keshavrao Khadye Marg, Mahalaxmi, Mumbai 400 034; tel. (22) 66601100; fax (22) 66601809; e-mail essarpower@essar.com; internet www.essar.com; Man. Dir and CEO SUSHIL MAROO.

National Hydroelectric Power Corpn: Sector 33, Faridabad 121 003; tel. (129) 2588500; fax (129) 2277941; e-mail webmaster@nhpc .nic.in; internet www.nhpcindia.com; f. 1975; Chair and Man. Dir R. S. T. SAI.

NTPC Ltd: Core 7, SCOPE Complex, Lodhi Rd, New Delhi 110 003; tel. (11) 24360100; fax (11) 24361018; e-mail info@ntpc.co.in; internet www.ntpc.co.in; f. 1975 as National Thermal Power Corpn; renamed as above 2005; operates 17 coal-fired and 7 gas-fired power stations throughout India; Chair. and Man. Dir ARUP ROY CHOUDHURY; 24,546 employees.

Nuclear Power Corpn of India Ltd: Commerce Center-1, 16th Floor, World Trade Centre, Cuffe Parade, Mumbai 400 005; tel. (22)

22182171; fax (22) 22180109; e-mail info@npcil.co.in; internet www .npcil.nic.in; Chair. and Man. Dir K. C. PUROHIT.

Power Grid Corpn of India Ltd: Saudamani, Plot No. 2, Sector 29, Gurgaon 122 001; tel. (124) 2571700; fax (124) 2571760; internet www.powergridindia.com; f. 1989; responsible for formation of national power grid; Chair. and Man. Dir R. N. NAYAK.

Reliance Energy: Reliance Energy Centre, Santacruz (East), Mumbai 400 055; tel. (22) 30099999; fax (22) 30099536; e-mail corporate.communication@relianceada.com; internet www .relianceenergy.in; f. 1929 as Bombay Suburban Electric Supply Ltd, merged with the Reliance Group in 2003; generates, transmits and distributes power in Maharashtra, Goa and Andhra Pradesh; Chair. and Man. Dir ANIL AMBANI.

Rural Electrification Corpn Ltd: Core-4, SCOPE Complex, 7 Lodhi Rd, New Delhi 110 003; tel. (11) 24365161; fax (11) 24360644; e-mail recorp@recl.nic.in; internet www.recindia.com; f. 1969; provides support to rural electrification projects; Chair. and Man. Dir RAJEEV SHARMA.

Tata Power Co Ltd: Bombay House, 24 Homi Mody St, Mumbai 400 001; tel. (22) 66658282; fax (22) 66658801; e-mail tatapower@ tatapower.com; internet www.tatapower.com; generation, transmission and distribution of electrical energy; Chair. CYRUS P. MISTRY; Man. Dir ANIL SARDANA.

Gas

Gas Authority of India Ltd: 16 Bhikaji Cama Place, R. K. Puram, Delhi 110 066; tel. (11) 26172580; fax (11) 26185941; internet gail.nic .in; f. 1984; 65% state-owned; transports, processes and markets natural gas; constructing gas-based petrochemical complex; subsidiaries incl.: GAIL Gas Ltd, GAIL Global (Singapore) Pte Ltd; Chair. and Man. Dir B. C. TRIPATHI; 3,480 employees (2009).

Gujarat Gas Co Ltd: 2 Shanti Sadan Society, Ellis Bridge, Ahmedabad 380 006; tel. (79) 26462980; fax (79) 26466249; internet www .gujaratgas.com; Chair. D. JAGATHEESA PANDIYAN; CEO P. P. G. SHARMA.

Indraprastha Gas Ltd: IGL Bhavan Plot No. 4, Community Centre Sector 9, R. K. Puram, New Delhi 110 022; tel. (11) 46074607; fax (11) 26171860; internet www.iglonline.net; Chair. M. RAVINDRAN, Man. Dir NARENDRA KUMAR.

Water

Central Water Commission: 313S Sewa Bhavan, R. K. Puram, New Delhi 110 066; tel. (11) 26187232, fax (11) 26195516; e-mail secy-cwc@nic.in; internet www.cwc.nic.in; responsible for co-ordination of nat. water policy and projects; provision of research, promotion and advice on water resources devt; Chair. ASHWIN B. PANDYA.

Chennai Metropolitan Water Supply and Sewerage Board: No. 1 Pumping Station Rd, Chintadripet, Chennai 600 002; tel. (44) 28451300; fax (44) 28458181; internet www.chennaimetrowater.tn .nic.in; f. 1978; Man. Dir B. CHANDRA MOHAN.

Delhi Jal Board: Varunalaya Phase II, Karol Bagh, New Delhi 110 005; tel. and fax (11) 23516261; e-mail prodjb306@gmail.com; internet www.delhijalboard.nic.in; f. 1957 as Delhi Water Supply and Sewage Disposal Undertaking, reconstituted as above in 1998; part of the Delhi Municipal Corpn; production and distribution of potable water and treatment and disposal of waste water in Delhi; Chair. MANISH SISODIA.

Karnataka Rural Water Supply and Sanitation Agency: E Blk, 2nd Floor, KHB Complex, Cauvery Bhavan, K. G. Rd, Bengaluru 560 009; tel. (80) 22246508; fax (80) 22240509; e-mail krwssa@gmail.com; Dir SALMA K. FAHIM.

Karnataka Urban Water Supply and Drainage Board: 6 Jalabhavan 1st Stage, 1st Phase, BTM Layout, Bannerghatta Rd, Bengaluru 560 029; tel. (80) 26539003; fax (80) 26539206; internet www.kuwsdb.org; Chair. G. C. CHANDRA SHEKHAR; Man. Dir MANIVANNAN P.

Kolkata Municipal Corpn (Water Supply Department): 5 S. N. Banerjee Rd, Kolkata 700 013; tel. (33) 22861000; fax (33) 22861444; e-mail dgwskmc@rediffmail.com; internet www.kolkatamycity.com; f. 1870; Dir-Gen. (Water Supply) BIBHAS KUMAR MAITI.

TRADE UNIONS

In 2008 there were 11 Central Trade Union Organizations (CTUO) recognized by the Indian Ministry of Labour and Employment. The major unions were:

All-India Trade Union Congress (AITUC): 24 Canning Lane, New Delhi 110 001; tel. (11) 23387320; fax (11) 23386427; e-mail aitucong@bol.net.in; internet www.aituc.org; f. 1920; affiliated to WFTU; 4.6m. mems, 2,272 affiliated unions; 28 state brs, 21 national feds; Pres. J. CHITHARANJAN; Gen. Sec. GURUDAS DASGUPTA.

All India United Trade Union Centre: 77/2/1 Lenin Sarani, Kolkata 700 013; tel. (33) 22659085; fax (33) 22645605; e-mail aiutuc@gmail.com; f. 1958; fmrly the United Trade Union Centre— Lenin Sarani (UTUC—LS); changed to present name in 2008; labour wing of the Socialist Unity Party of India; 600 affiliated unions; 1.3m. mems in 2002; Pres. KRISHNA CHAKRABORTY; Gen. Sec. SHANKAR SAHA.

Bharatiya Mazdoor Sangh: Dattopant Thengadi Bhawan, 27 Deen Dayal Upadhyay Marg, New Delhi 110 002; tel. (11) 23562654; fax (11) 23582648; e-mail bms@bms.org.in; internet www.bms.org.in; f. 1955; 4,700 affiliated unions with a total membership of 8.5m.; 27 state brs; 34 nat. feds; Pres. C. K. SAJINARAYANAN; Gen. Sec. BAIJ NATH RAI.

Centre of Indian Trade Unions: BTR Bhavan, 13 A Rouse Ave, New Delhi 110 002; tel. (11) 23221288; fax (11) 23221284; e-mail citu@bol.net.in; internet www.citucentre.org; f. 1970; 3.37m. mems; 25 state and union territory brs; 4,300 affiliated unions, 12 nat. feds; Major affiliated unions incl. All India Coal Workers' Fed., All India Road Transport Workers' Fed., Steel Workers' Fed. of India, Water Transport Workers' Fed. of India; Pres. A. K. PADMANABHAN; Gen. Sec. TAPAN SEN.

Hind Mazdoor Sabha (HMS): 120 Babar Rd, New Delhi 110 001; tel. (11) 23413519; fax (11) 23411037; e-mail hms1gs@gmail.com; internet www.hmsindia.org.in; f. 1948; affiliated to ITUC; 5.8m. mems from more than 2,775 affiliated unions; 25 state councils; 16 nat. industrial feds; Major affiliated unions incl. Mumbai Port Trust Dock and General Employees' Union, South Central Railway Mazdoor Union, Transport and Dock Workers' Union, Western Railway Employees' Union; Pres. SHARAD RAO; Gen. Sec. UMRAOMAL PUROHIT.

Indian National Trade Union Congress (INTUC): 4 Bhai Veer Singh Marg, New Delhi 110 001; tel. (11) 23747767; fax (11) 23364244; e-mail info@intuc.net; internet www.intuc.net; f. 1947; 4,411 affiliated unions with a total membership of 7.93m.; affiliated to ICFTU; 32 state brs and 29 nat. feds; Pres. G. SANJEEVA REDDY; Gen. Sec. RAJENDRA PRASAD SINGH.

Major affiliated unions include:

Indian National Mineworkers' Federation: CJ 49 Salt Lake, Kolkata 700 091; tel. and fax (33) 23372158; e-mail imme@vsnl .com; f. 1949; 351,454 mems in 139 affiliated unions; Pres. RAJENDRA P. SINGH; Sec.-Gen. S. Q. ZAMA.

Indian National Textile Workers' Federation: 27 Burjorji Bharucha Marg, Fort, Mumbai 400 023; tel. (22) 22671577; f. 1948; 400 affiliated unions; 363,790 mems; Pres. SACHINBHAU AHIR; Gen. Sec. P. L. SUBHAIH.

Indian National Transport Workers' Federation: Bus Mazdoor Karyalaya, L/1, Hathital Colony, Jabalpur 482 001; tel. (761) 2429210; 357 affiliated unions; 379,267 mems; Pres. G. SANJEEVA REDDY; Gen. Sec. K. S. VERMA.

United Trades Union Congress (UTUC): 249 Bipin Behari Ganguly St, 1st Floor, Kolkata 700 012; tel. (33) 22259234; fax (33) 22375609; f. 1949; 1.2m. mems from 387 affiliated unions; 12 state brs and 6 nat. feds; Pres. SHANKARAN NAIR; Gen. Sec. ABANI ROY.

Other principal trade unions:

All India Bank Employees' Association (AIBEA): Prabhat Nivas, Singapore Plaza, 164 Linghi Chetty St, Chennai 600 001; tel. (44) 25351522; fax (44) 25358853; e-mail aibeahq@gmail.com; internet www.bankunionaibea.in; 32 state units, 710 affiliated unions, 525,000 mems; Pres. RAJEN NAGAR; Gen. Sec. C. H. VENKATACHALAM.

All India Defence Employees' Federation (AIDEF): Survey No. 81, Elphinstone Rd, Khadki, Pune 411 003; tel. (20) 25818761; f. 1953; 358 affiliated unions; 200,000 mems; Pres. S. N. PATHAK; Gen. Secs S. BHATTACHARYA, C. SRIKUMAR.

All India Railwaymen's Federation (AIRF): 4 State Entry Rd, New Delhi 110 055; tel. (11) 23365912; fax (11) 23363167; e-mail airfindia@gmail.com; internet www.airfindia.com; f. 1924; c. 1m. mems (2010); 24 affiliated unions; Pres. UMRAOMAL PUROHIT; Gen. Sec. SHIVA GOPAL MISHRA.

Confederation of Central Government Employees and Workers: Manishinath Bhavan, A-2-95 Rajouri Garden, New Delhi 110 027; tel. (11) 25105324; e-mail confederation06@yahoo.co.in; internet confederationhq.blogspot.com; 1.2m. mems; Pres. S. K. VYAS; Sec.-Gen. K. K. N. KUTTY.

Affiliated union:

National Federation of Postal Employees (NFPE): D-7, North Ave Post Office Bldg, 1st Floor, New Delhi 110 001; tel. and fax (11) 23092771; e-mail nfpehq@gmail.com; internet nfpe .blogspot.com; f. 1954 as National Federation of Post and Telegraph Employees, reconstituted as above in 1986; 400,000 mems from 7 affiliated unions; Pres. R. N. CHAUDHARY; Sec.-Gen. M. KRISHNAN.

Electricity Employees' Federation of India (EEFI): B. T. R. Bhavan, 13A Rouse Ave, New Delhi 110 002; tel. 9830264170 (mobile); fax (11) 23219670; e-mail eefederation@gmail.com; internet www.eefi.org; f. 1984; largest electricity union in India; 45 affiliated unions; Pres. K. O. HABIB; Gen. Sec. PRASANTA N. CHOWDHURY.

National Federation of Indian Railwaymen (NFIR): 3 Chelmsford Rd, New Delhi 110 055; tel. (11) 23343305; fax (11) 23744013; e-mail nfir@satyam.net.in; f. 1953; 26 affiliated unions; 925,500 mems (2003); Pres. GUMAN SINGH; Gen. Sec. M. RAGHAVAIAH.

Transport

RAILWAYS

India's railway system is the largest in Asia and the fourth largest in the world. In March 2014 the total length of the railways was 65,808 route-km. In 2013/14 the network carried an estimated 8,397m. passengers and 1,058.8m. metric tons of freight traffic. The Government exercises direct or indirect control over all railways through the Railway Board. India's largest railway construction project of the 20th century, the 760-km Konkan railway line, was officially opened in 1998. The construction of a 345-km Jammu–Udhampur–Srinagar–Baramulla line, linking Jammu and Kashmir with the national rail network, was declared a project of national importance in 2002. By early 2010 two of the project's four phases had been completed. However, owing to technical challenges presented by the difficult terrain, the project was unlikely to be completed before 2016. In February 2015 the Government allocated some US $137,000m. to a major, five-year programme of modernization and development of the ageing railway network.

A 16.5-km underground railway was completed in Kolkata in 1995 and extended to 22.2 km in 2009. The network carries more than 1m. people daily. The country's second metro system, in New Delhi, became operational in 2004. Following the completion of work on the second phase of the system in early 2011, the network comprised 142 stations across a route length of 189 km, carrying 1.3m. people daily. A third metro system, in Bengaluru (Bangalore), became operational in late 2011. On completion of the first phase of the project, the system was to comprise 41 stations across a route length of 42.3 km. The first phase of a 12-km metro rail system in Gurgaon, a fast-developing satellite city of New Delhi, was opened in November 2013. In February 2014 a 9-km metropolitan monorail line was inaugurated in Mumbai; a second line was also under construction.

Ministry of Railways (Railway Board): Rail Bhavan, Raisina Rd, New Delhi 110 001; tel. (11) 23384010; fax (11) 23384481; e-mail crb@rb.railnet.gov.in; internet www.indianrailways.gov.in; Chair. A. K. MITTAL.

Zonal Railways

The railways are grouped into 17 zones:

Central Railway: Chhatrapati Shivaji Terminus (Victoria Terminus), Mumbai 400 001; tel. (22) 22697311; fax (22) 22612354; e-mail gmcr@bom2.vsnl.net.in; internet www.cr.indianrailways.gov.in; Gen. Man. S. K. SOOD.

East Central Railway: Hajipur 844 101; tel. (6224) 274728; fax (6224) 274738; internet www.ecr.indianrailways.gov.in; f. 1996; Gen. Man. MADHURESH KUMAR.

East Coast Railway: Rail Vihar, Chandrasekhar Pur, Bhubaneswar 751 023; tel. (674) 2300773; fax (674) 2300196; e-mail gm@eastcoastrailway.gov.in; internet www.eastcoastrail.indianrailways.gov.in; f. 1996; Gen. Man. RAJIV VISHNOI.

Eastern Railway: 17 Netaji Subhas Rd, Kolkata 700 001; tel. (33) 22307596; fax (33) 22480370; internet www.er.indianrailways.gov.in; Gen. Man. RAM KUMAR GUPTA.

Metro Railway, Kolkata: Metro Rail Bhavan, 8th Floor, 33/1 J. L. Nehru Rd, Kolkata 700 071; tel. (33) 22267280; fax (33) 22264581; e-mail com@mtp.railnet.gov.in; internet www.mtp.indianrailways.gov.in; f. 1995; Gen. Man. RADHEY SHYAM.

North Central Railway: Allahabad 211 001; tel. (532) 2230200; fax (532) 2603900; e-mail secy@ncr.railnet.gov.in; internet www.ncr.indianrailways.gov.in; f. 1996; Gen. Man. PRADEEP KUMAR.

North Eastern Railway: Gorakhpur 273 012; tel. (551) 2201041; fax (551) 2201299; e-mail gm@ner.railnet.gov.in; internet www.ner.indianrailways.gov.in; Gen. Man. RAJIV MISRA.

North Western Railway: Nr Jawahar Circle, Jaipur; tel. 9001195127 (mobile); fax (141) 2725833; e-mail cio@nwr.railnet.gov.in; internet www.nwr.indianrailways.gov.in; Gen. Man. ANIL SINGHAL.

Northeast Frontier Railway: Maligaon, Guwahati 781 011; tel. (361) 2676000; fax (361) 2570580; e-mail gm@nfr.railnet.gov.in; internet www.nfr.indianrailways.gov.in; f. 1958; Gen. Man. RANJIT SINGH VIRDI.

Northern Railway: NOCR Bldg, State Entry Rd, New Delhi 110 001; tel. (11) 23363469; fax (11) 23363469; e-mail gm@nr.railnet.gov.in; internet www.nr.indianrailways.gov.in; Gen. Man. A. K. PUTHIA.

South Central Railway: Rm 312, 3rd Floor, Rail Nilayam, Secunderabad 500 071; tel. (40) 27822874; fax (40) 27833203; e-mail gm@scr.railnet.gov.in; internet www.scr.indianrailways.gov.in; Gen. Man. P. K. SRIVASTAVA.

South East Central Railway: R. E. Complex, Bilaspur 495 004; tel. (7752) 47102; e-mail webmaster@secr.railnet.gov.in; internet www.secr.indianrailways.gov.in; Gen. Man. RAJIV VISHNOI.

South Eastern Railway: 11 Garden Reach Rd, Kolkata 700 043; tel. (33) 24393532; fax (33) 24397831; e-mail gm@ser.railnet.gov.in; internet www.ser.indianrailways.gov.in; Gen. Man. RADHEY SHYAM.

South Western Railway: Club Rd, Keshwapur, Hubli 580 023; tel. (836) 2360747; fax (836) 2365209; e-mail cpro@swr.railnet.gov.in; internet www.swr.indianrailways.gov.in; f. 1996; Gen. Man. PRADEEP KUMAR SAXENA.

Southern Railway: Park Town, Chennai 600 003; tel. (44) 25353455; fax (44) 25354950; e-mail srailway@gmail.com; internet www.sr.indianrailways.gov.in; Gen. Man. ASHOK K. AGARWAL.

West Central Railway: Jabalpur 482 001; tel. (761) 2627444; fax (761) 2607555; e-mail osdwcr@yahoo.com; internet www.wcr.indianrailways.gov.in; f. 1996; Gen. Man. RAMESH CHANDRA.

Western Railway: Churchgate, Mumbai 400 020; tel. (22) 22005670; fax (22) 22068545; e-mail secygm@wr.railnet.gov.in; internet www.wr.indianrailways.gov.in; Gen. Man. MAHESH KUMAR.

ROADS

In 2012 there were an estimated 4.9m. km of roads in India, 241,178 km of which were national or state highways; 55.5% of the total road network was paved. In 1999 the Government launched the ambitious Rs 500,000m. National Highways Development Project, which included plans to build a circuit of roads linking the four main cities of Mumbai, Chennai, Kolkata and New Delhi (Phase I), as well as an east–west corridor linking Silchar with Porbandar and a north–south corridor linking Kashmir with Kanyakumari (Phase II). The majority of work on the first two phases had been completed by 2010. The third phase of the project, the widening and upgrading of an estimated 12,000 km of national highways, was scheduled for completion by late 2016. Under four other organized plans (Phases III to VI), the Government has approved construction work on expressways and highways across the country. In 2007 the Government pledged Rs 480,000m. for the upgrade of India's rural road network with the stated aim of connecting 66,000 villages; the allocation represented part of the four-year Bharat Nirman initiative (at an estimated cost of Rs 1,740,000m.) to enhance infrastructure and rural incomes by increasing connectivity with roads, telecommunications and drinking water.

Border Roads Organisation: Seema Sadak Bhavan, Ring Road Naraina, Delhi 110 010; e-mail bro-edp@nic.in; internet www.bro.nic.in; f. 1960 to accelerate the economic development of the north and north-eastern border areas; has constructed 31,061 km and improved 37,077 km of roads, and built permanent bridges totalling a length of 19,544 m in the border areas.

National Highways Authority of India: G-5 and 6, Sector 10, Dwarka, New Delhi 110 075; tel. (11) 25074100; fax (11) 25093507; e-mail chairman@nhai.org; internet www.nhai.org; f. 1995; responsible for the planning, construction and maintenance of the national highways system, and implementation of the National Highways Development Project; the 172 national highways constitute India's main trunk roads, connecting the state capitals and major ports, and linking with the highway systems of neighbouring countries; under the Ministry of Road Transport and Highways; Chair. R. P. SINGH.

INLAND WATERWAYS

About 14,500 km of rivers are navigable by power-driven craft, and 3,700 km by large country boats. Services are mainly on the Ganga and Brahmaputra and their tributaries, the Godavari, the Mahanadi, the Narmada, the Tapti and the Krishna. About 55m. metric tons of cargo is moved annually by certified vessels. In addition, a substantial volume of cargo and passengers is transported in the unorganized sector.

Central Inland Water Transport Corpn Ltd: 4 Fairlie Pl., Kolkata 700 001; tel. (33) 22435718; fax (33) 22436164; e-mail ciwtc@cal3.vsnl.net.in; internet www.ciwtcltd.com; f. 1967; inland water transport services in Bangladesh and the east and north-east Indian states; also ship-building and -repairing, general engineering, lightering of ships and barge services; Chair. and Man. Dir PRAFUL TAYAL.

Inland Waterways Authority of India: A-13, Sector 1, Noida 201 301; tel. (120) 2544036; fax (120) 2544041; e-mail iwainoi@nic.in; internet iwai.nic.in; f. 1986; devt and regulation of inland waterways for shipping and navigation; under Ministry of Shipping; Chair. AMITABH VERMA.

SHIPPING

The major ports are Chennai, Haldia, Jawaharlal Nehru (at Nhava Sheva near Mumbai), Kandla, Kochi, Kolkata, Mormugao, Mumbai, New Mangalore, Paradip (Paradeep), Tuticorin and Visakhapatnam. At 31 December 2014 India's flag registered fleet had a total of 1,577 ships, including 359 general cargoes, 108 bulk carriers, 40 fishing tankers and 19 gas tankers, with a total displacement of 9.65m. grt.

Port Authorities and Supervisory Bodies

Chennai Port Trust: 1 Rajaji Salai, Chennai 600 001; tel. (44) 25362201; fax (44) 25361228; e-mail info@chennaiport.gov.in; internet www.chennaiport.gov.in; f. 1881; under the Ministry of Shipping; Chair. ATULYA MISRA.

Cochin Port Trust: Willingdon Island, Cochin 682 009; tel. (484) 2668200; fax (484) 2666417; e-mail mail@cochinport.gov.in; internet www.cochinport.com; f. 1926; under the Ministry of Shipping; manages infrastructure around Ernakulam and Mattancherry wharfs; Chair. PAUL ANTONY.

Indian Ports Association: South Tower, 1st Floor, NBCC Place, Bhisham Pitamah Marg, Lodi Rd, New Delhi 110 003; tel. (11) 24365632; fax (11) 24365866; e-mail ipa@nic.in; internet ipa.nic.in; f. 1966; supervisory and advisory body; Man. Dir A. JANARDHANA RAO.

Indian Register of Shipping: 52A, Adi Shankaracharya Marg, Powai, Mumbai 400 072; tel. (22) 71199400; fax (22) 25703611; e-mail mumbai@irclass.org; internet www.irclass.org; f. 1975; ship classification society; provides technical inspection and certification services for marine craft and structures; Chair. ARUN SHARMA.

Kolkata Port Trust: 15 Strand Rd, Kolkata 700 001; tel. (33) 22303451; fax (33) 22304901; e-mail calport@kopt.in; internet www.kolkataporttrust.gov.in; f. 1870; operates Kolkata and Haldia dock systems; handles cargo and maintains vessel traffic; Chair. R. P. S. KAHLON.

Mumbai Port Trust: Port House, S. V. Marg, Mumbai 400 001; tel. (22) 22621234; fax (22) 66564011; e-mail chairman@mbptmail.com; internet www.mumbaiport.gov.in; f. 1873; works to improve infrastructure facilities and manages port traffic; Chair. R. M. PARMAR.

Visakhapatnam Port Trust: Port Area, Visakhapatnam 530 035; tel. (891) 2876001; fax (891) 2565023; e-mail info@vizagport.com; internet www.vizagport.com; f. 1964; handles 3 harbours: outer (200 ha with 6 berths), inner (100 ha with 18 berths) and a fishing harbour; Chair. M. T. KRISHNA BABU.

Shipping Companies

Kolkata

Apeejay Shipping Ltd: Apeejay House, 15 Park St, Kolkata 700 016; tel. (33) 44035455; fax (33) 22179596; e-mail solcal@apeejaygroup.com; internet www.apeejayshipping.com; f. 1948; shipowners; Chair. KARAN PAUL; CEO S. S. MAHAPATRA.

India Steamship Co Ltd: Birla Bldg, 9th Floor, 9/1 R. N. Mukherjee Rd, Kolkata 700 001; tel. (33) 71071000; fax (33) 22624191; e-mail iss@indiasteamship.com; internet www.indiasteamship.com; f. 1928; cargo services; Pres. K. SATISHCHANDRA; br in Delhi.

Mumbai

Chowgule Brothers (Pvt) Ltd: Malhotra House, 3rd Floor, POB 1770, Mumbai 400 001; tel. (22) 22675579; fax (22) 22610659; e-mail mumbai.cb@chowgule.co.in; internet www.chowgulebrothers.com; Dir JAYWANT CHOWGULE.

Essar Shipping Ltd: Essar House, 11 Keshavrao Khadye Marg, Mahalaxmi, Mumbai 400 034; tel. (22) 66601100; fax (22) 66601809; e-mail contactshipping@essar.com; internet www.essar.com; f. 1969; Chair. SHASHI RUIA; Man. Dir A. R. RAMAKRISHNAN.

The Great Eastern Shipping Co Ltd: Indiabulls Finance Centre, Tower 3, 23rd Floor, Senapati Bapat Marg, Elphinstone Rd, Mumbai 400 013; tel. (22) 67207500; fax (22) 66517428; e-mail marketing@greatshipglobal.com; internet www.greatshipglobal.com; f. 1948; shipping; Exec. Chair. BHARAT K. SHETH; Man. Dir ALOK MAHAJAN; brs in Singapore, Mauritius, Australia and the United Kingdom.

Mercator Ltd: Mittal Tower, 3rd Floor, B Wing, Nariman Point, Mumbai 400 021; tel. (22) 66373333; fax (22) 66373344; e-mail mercator@mercator.in; internet www.mercator.in; f. 1983; cargo shipping; fmrly Mercator Lines Ltd; Chair. H. K. MITTAL; Man. Dir ATUL J. AGARWAL.

Shipping Corpn of India Ltd: Shipping House, 245 Madame Cama Rd, Mumbai 400 021; tel. (22) 22026666; fax (22) 22026905; e-mail isd@sci.co.in; internet www.shipindia.com; f. 1961 as a govt undertaking; Chair. and Man. Dir A. K GUPTA; brs in Kolkata, New Delhi, Chennai and London.

Tolani Shipping Co Ltd: 10A Bakhtawar, Nariman Point, Mumbai 400 021; tel. (22) 56568989; fax (22) 22870697; e-mail tmi@tolani.edu; internet www.tolani-shipping.com; f. 1974; Chair. and Man. Dir Dr NANDLAL PRIBHDAS TOLANI.

Varun Shipping Co Ltd: Laxmi Bldg, 3rd Floor, 6 Shoorji Vallabhdas Marg, Ballard Estate, Mumbai 400 001; tel. (22) 66350100; fax (22) 66350274; e-mail isd@varunship.com; internet www.varunship.com; f. 1971; Chair. and Man. Dir YUDHISHTHIR D. KHATAU.

CIVIL AVIATION

In January 2015 there were 21 designated international airports under the jurisdiction of the Airports Authority of India (AAI)—12 managed by the AAI, six operated by private consortiums and three civil enclaves. In addition, there were about 60 domestic airports in operation and six customs airports. Overall annual passenger-handling capacity of AAI airports increased from 101.2m. in 2009 to 233m. in 2012. According to the Directorate General of Civil Aviation, India's domestic airlines carried 76.4m. passengers in 2014. Since 2006 contracts to manage and modernize several international airports, including Mumbai, New Delhi and Hyderabad, have been awarded to public-private partnerships. A new terminal at Indira Gandhi International Airport in New Delhi was inaugurated in 2010, increasing the airport's annual handling capacity to 37m. passengers. In February 2014 a major new terminal was opened at Mumbai's Chhatrapati Shivaji International Airport with a handling capacity of some 40m. passengers annually.

Airports Authority of India: Rajiv Gandhi Bhavan, Safdarjung Airport, New Delhi 110 003; tel. (11) 24632950; fax (11) 24641088; e-mail aaichmn@vsnl.com; internet www.aai.aero; f. 1972; responsible for air traffic management and devt of airport infrastucture; manages 125 international and domestic airports; Chair. S. RAHEJA.

Directorate General of Civil Aviation (DGCA): Aurbindo Marg, New Delhi 110 003; tel. (11) 24627830; fax (11) 24652760; e-mail dgoffice.dgca@nic.in; internet www.dgca.nic.in; Dir-Gen. M. SATHIYAVATHY.

Air India: Air India Bldg, 218 Backbay Reclamation, Nariman Point, Mumbai 400 021; tel. (22) 22023031; fax (22) 22021096; e-mail eCommerce@airindia.in; internet www.airindia.in; f. 1932 as Tata Airlines; renamed Air-India in 1946; in 1953 became a state corpn responsible for international flights; merged with Indian Airlines in 2007 to form the National Aviation Company of India, operating as Air India; operates domestic flights under the brand name Air India Regional and low-cost services under the Air India Express brand (internet www.airindiaexpress.in); carried an estimated 15.4m. passengers in 2013/14; Chair. and Man. Dir ROHIT NANDAN.

Blue Dart Express: 88–89 Old International Terminal, Meenambakkam Airport, Chennai 600 027; tel. (44) 22568200; fax (44) 22568385; e-mail radhag@bluedart.com; internet www.bluedart.com; f. 1983 as Blue Dart Courier Services; name changed as above in 1990; air express transport co; operates a fleet of 7 aircraft; Chair. SHARAD UPASANI; Man. Dir ANIL KHANNA.

Go Air: C-1, Wadia Int. Centre, 1st Floor, Pandurang Budhkar Marg, Worli, Mumbai 400 025; tel. (22) 67410000; fax (22) 67420001; e-mail feedback@goair.in; internet www.goair.in; f. 2005; low-cost passenger services to domestic destinations; Man. Dir JEHANGIR 'JEH' WADIA.

Indigo Airlines: Tower C, Level 1, Global Business Park, Mehrauli-Gurgaon Road, Gurgaon 122 002; tel. (124) 4352500; fax (124) 4068536; e-mail sakshi.batra@bm.com; internet www.goindigo.in; f. 2005; private co; passenger services to domestic destinations; int. services to Oman, Singapore, Thailand and the United Arab Emirates launched in 2011; Chair. RAHUL BHATIA; Pres. ADITYA GHOSH.

Jagson Airlines: Vandana Bldg, 3rd Floor, 11 Tolstoy Marg, New Delhi 110 001; tel. (11) 23721594; fax (11) 23324693; e-mail jagson-id@eth.net; internet www.jagsongroup.com; f. 1991; a small regional airline operating scheduled and charter passenger services to domestic destinations; Chair. JAGDISH GUPTA.

Jet Airways (India) Ltd: Siroya Centre, Sahar Airport Rd, Andheri (East), Mumbai 400 099; tel. (22) 61211000; fax (22) 29201313; internet www.jetairways.com; f. 1992; commenced operations 1993; acquired Air Sahara in 2007; private co; operates scheduled passenger services to 51 domestic and 22 int. destinations; operates a fleet of 116 aircraft; Chair. and Man. Dir NARESH GOYAL; CEO CRAMER BALL.

SpiceJet: 319 Udyog Vihar, Phase IV, Gurgaon 122 016; tel. 9871803333 (mobile); e-mail custrelations@spicejet.com; internet www.spicejet.com; f. 2005; low-cost domestic passenger service; Chair. AJAY SINGH; CEO SANJIV KAPUR.

Tourism

The tourist attractions of India include sub-Himalayan scenery in the north and the east; diverse fauna, including the Bengal tiger, the peacock and the Asiatic elephant; myriad wildlife sanctuaries and national parks; historic monuments, including forts, palaces and temples; various cultural and religious festivals; and many other vibrant urban and rural attractions. India possesses 28 UNESCO World Heritage sites, including the Taj Mahal. Tourism infrastructure has recently been expanded by the provision of additional luxury hotels and improved means of transport. In 2013 there were an estimated 7.0m. foreign visitors to India, an increase of 5.9% compared with the previous year. In that year revenue from tourism rose by 4.0%, compared with the previous year, to reach an estimated US $18,445m. In 2013 the USA and the United Kingdom were the most important sources of tourist arrivals, providing 15.6% and 11.6% of total arrivals, respectively.

Ministry of Tourism: internet www.incredibleindia.org; (see Ministries and Government Offices); formulates and administers govt policy for promotion of tourism; plans the org. and devt of tourist facilities; operates tourist information offices in India and overseas; Sec. LALIT K. PANWAR.

India Tourism Development Corpn Ltd: SCOPE Complex, Core-8, 7 Lodhi Rd, New Delhi 110 003; tel. (11) 24360303; fax (11) 24360233; e-mail contact@itdc.com; internet www.theashokgroup .com; f. 1966; operates Ashok Group of hotels, resort accommodation, tourist transport services, duty-free shops and a travel agency and provides consultancy and management services; Chair. and Man. Dir Dr GIRISH SHANKAR.

Travel Agents' Association of India: 2D Lawrence and Mayo House, 276 Dr D. N. Rd, Mumbai 400 001; tel. (22) 40836786; fax (22) 40836767; e-mail taai@taai.in; internet travelagentsofindia.com; 2,341 mems; Pres. SUNIL KUMAR R. (acting); Hon. Sec.-Gen. HARMANDEEP SINGH ANAND.

Defence

As assessed at November 2014, India's total armed forces numbered 1,346,000: army 1,150,900, navy 58,350 (including naval air force), air force 127,200, coastguard 9,550. Active paramilitary forces totalled 1,403,700 members, including the 230,000-strong Border Security Force (based mainly in the troubled state of Jammu and Kashmir). Military service is voluntary, although the Constitution states that every citizen has a fundamental duty to perform national service when called upon to do so.

Defence Budget (2013/14): Estimated at Rs 2,040,000.

Chief of the Air Staff: Air Chief Marshal ARUP RAHA.

Chief of the Army Staff: Lt Gen. DALBIR SINGH SUHAG.

Chief of the Naval Staff: Adm. ROBIN DHOWAN.

Education

Under the Constitution, education in India is primarily the responsibility of the individual state governments, although the central Government has several direct responsibilities, including responsibility for the Central Universities, all higher institutions, promotion and propagation of Hindi, co-ordination and maintenance of higher education standards, scientific and technological research and welfare of Indian students abroad.

Education in India is administered centrally by the Department of Education (Ministry of Human Resource Development). At state level, there is an Education Minister. There are facilities for free primary education (lower and upper stages) in each of the states. An amendment to the Constitution, which came into effect in 2010, ensures free and compulsory education for children from the age of six to 14. In addition, the historic legislation seeks to ensure universal education by requiring private schools to reserve no less than one-quarter of placements for children from impoverished backgrounds, by creating new state-run neighbourhood schools, by removing school admission fees and by providing for the creation of schools for children with disabilities. Central government expenditure on education and literacy for 2013/14 was estimated at Rs 501,363m. (equivalent to 3.2% of total spending).

ELEMENTARY EDUCATION

The notable characteristic of elementary education in India is the use of what is known as basic education. There is an activity-centred curriculum which educates through socially useful, productive activities such as spinning, weaving, gardening, leather work, book craft, domestic crafts, pottery, elementary engineering, etc. Emphasis has been placed on introducing important features of basic education in non-basic schools. Basic education is the national pattern of all elementary education and all elementary schools will ultimately be brought over to the basic system.

In pre-primary and primary classes, for children between six and 11 years of age, the total number of pupils increased from 50m. in 1965 to an estimated 195.8m. in 2013/14. Enrolment in higher primary or middle schools (age-group 11–14 years) in the latter year was 62.1m. Similarly, the number of primary (lower and higher) schools increased from 466,862 in 1965/66 to more than 1.2m. in 2010/11. Enrolment at primary schools in 2011 included 93% of pupils in the relevant age-group.

SECONDARY EDUCATION

Education at this level is provided for those between the ages of 14 and 18. There were an estimated 200,184 secondary schools, higher secondary schools and junior colleges in 2010/11, with some 51.2m. pupils and 2.5m. teachers. In 2011 enrolment at secondary schools was equivalent to 69% of pupils in the relevant age-group (71% of boys; 66% of girls).

Most schools follow what is known as the 'three-language formula', which comprises teaching of the regional language or dialect, Hindi and English. Much emphasis is now also being laid on physical training, which has become a compulsory subject.

HIGHER AND ADULT EDUCATION

The universities are for the most part autonomous with regard to administration. The University Grants Commission is responsible for the promotion and co-ordination of university education and has the authority to make appropriate grants and to implement development schemes.

India had a total of 564 universities and institutions with university status in 2010/11, and some 33,634 colleges of higher education by August 2011. In 2010/11, by some estimates, university enrolment was equivalent to some 14.1% of students in the relevant age-group. In that year an estimated 25.2m. students were enrolled in institutions of higher education.

INDONESIA

Introductory Survey

LOCATION, CLIMATE, LANGUAGE, RELIGION, FLAG, CAPITAL

The Republic of Indonesia consists of a group of more than 18,000 islands (including rocks, reefs, sandbanks, etc.), lying between the mainland of South-East Asia and Australia. The archipelago is the largest in the world, and it stretches from the Malay peninsula to New Guinea. The principal islands are Java, Sumatra, Kalimantan (comprising more than two-thirds of the island of Borneo), Sulawesi (Celebes), Papua (formerly Irian Jaya, comprising the western part of the island of New Guinea), the Maluku Islands (the Moluccas) and West Timor (comprising part of the island of Timor). Indonesia's only land frontiers are with Papua New Guinea (PNG), to the east of Papua, with the Malaysian states of Sarawak and Sabah, which occupy northern Borneo, and with Timor-Leste (formerly East Timor), to the east of West Timor. The climate is tropical, with an annual average temperature of 26°C (79°F) and heavy rainfall during most seasons. Rainfall averages 706 mm (28 in) annually in Indonesia, although there are large variations throughout the archipelago; the heaviest annual rainfall (averaging 2,286 mm or 90 in) is along the equatorial rain belt, which passes through Sumatra, Borneo and Sulawesi. The official language is Bahasa Indonesia (a form of Malay); there are an estimated 583 other languages and dialects spoken in the archipelago, including Javanese, Sundanese, Arabic and Chinese. Around 88% of the inhabitants profess adherence to Islam. About 10% of the population are Christians, and most of the remainder are either Hindus or Buddhists. The national flag (proportions 2 by 3) has two equal horizontal stripes, of red and white. The capital is Jakarta, on the island of Java.

CONTEMPORARY POLITICAL HISTORY

Historical Context

Indonesia was formerly the Netherlands East Indies (except for the former Portuguese colony of East Timor, which became known as Timor-Leste following its accession to independence in 2002—see *Provincial Affairs and Separatist Tensions*). Dutch occupation began in the 17th century and gradually extended over the whole archipelago. Nationalist opposition to colonial rule emerged in the early 20th century. During the Second World War the territory was occupied by Japanese forces from March 1942. On 17 August 1945, three days after the Japanese surrender, a group of nationalists proclaimed the independence of Indonesia. The first President of the self-proclaimed republic was Dr Sukarno, a leader of the nationalist movement since the 1920s. The declaration of independence was not recognized by the Netherlands, which attempted to restore its pre-war control of the islands. After four years of intermittent warfare and negotiations between the Dutch authorities and the nationalists, agreement was reached on a formal transfer of power. On 27 December 1949 the United States of Indonesia became legally independent, with Sukarno continuing as President. Initially, the country had a federal Constitution, which gave limited self-government to the 16 constituent regions. In August 1950, however, the federation was dissolved, and the country became the unitary Republic of Indonesia. The 1949 independence agreement excluded West New Guinea (subsequently Irian Jaya and known as Papua from 1 January 2002), which remained under Dutch control until October 1962; however, following a brief period of UN administration, it was transferred to Indonesia in May 1963.

Domestic Political Affairs

Sukarno followed a policy of extreme nationalism, and his regime became increasingly dictatorial. His foreign policy was sympathetic to the People's Republic of China but, under his rule, Indonesia also played a leading role in the Non-aligned Movement (see p. 462). Inflation and widespread corruption provoked opposition to Sukarno's regime; in September–October 1965 there was an abortive military coup, in which the Partai Komunis Indonesia (PKI—Indonesian Communist Party) was strongly implicated. A massacre of alleged PKI members and supporters

ensued. In March 1966 Sukarno was forced to transfer emergency executive powers to military commanders, led by Gen. Suharto, Chief of Staff of the Army, who outlawed the PKI. In February 1967 Sukarno transferred full power to Suharto. In March the Majelis Permusyawaratan Rakyat (MPR—People's Consultative Assembly) removed Sukarno from office and named Suharto acting President. He became Prime Minister in October 1967 and, following his election by the MPR, he was inaugurated as President in March 1968. In July 1971, in the first general election since 1955, the government-sponsored Sekretariat Bersama Golongan Karya (Joint Secretariat of Functional Groups), known as Golkar, won a majority of seats in the Dewan Perwakilan Rakyat (DPR—House of Representatives). Suharto was re-elected to the presidency in March 1973.

Under Suharto's 'New Order', real power passed from the legislature and the Cabinet to a small group of army officers and to the Operation Command for the Restoration of Order and Security (Kopkamtib), the internal security organization. Left-wing movements were suppressed, and a liberal economic policy was adopted. A general election in May 1977 gave Golkar a legislative majority, and Suharto was re-elected President (unopposed) in March 1978. Golkar won an increased majority in the election of May 1982. In March 1983 Suharto was re-elected, again unopposed, as President.

During 1984 Suharto's attempt to introduce legislation requiring all political, social and religious organizations to adopt *Pancasila*, the five-point state philosophy (belief in a supreme being; humanitarianism; national unity; democracy by consensus; social justice), as their only ideology encountered violent opposition, allegedly instigated by Muslim opponents of the proposed legislation; many Muslims were tried and imprisoned. All political parties had accepted *Pancasila* by July 1985. At the April 1987 general election, despite international allegations of corruption and human rights abuse, Golkar won 299 of the 400 elective seats in the 500-seat DPR (100 seats being allocated to the military).

In February 1988 new legislation reaffirmed the *dwifungsi*, or 'dual (i.e. military and socio-economic) function', of the Angkatan Bersenjata Republik Indonesia (ABRI—Armed Forces of the Republic of Indonesia). In March Suharto was again re-elected unopposed as President. Lt-Gen. (retd) Sudharmono, the Chairman of Golkar, was subsequently appointed Vice-President, to the consternation of ABRI since, under Sudharmono's chairmanship of Golkar, there had been a shift away from military dominance in the grouping. In October Sudharmono resigned as party Chairman and was replaced by Gen. (retd) Wahono.

In 1989 Suharto promoted legislation whereby decisions made by Islamic courts no longer required confirmation by civil courts, and in December 1990 the President opened the symposium of the newly formed Ikatan Cendekiawan Muslim Indonesia (ICMI—Association of Indonesian Muslim Intellectuals), an organization that united a broad spectrum of Islamic interests. ABRI was opposed to the establishment of ICMI because it regarded the polarization of politics by religion as a threat to stability.

During 1991 several new organizations were formed to promote freedom of expression and other democratic values. As labour unrest grew, arrests and the alleged intimidation of political activists curbed expressions of dissent, and political campaigns were banned on university campuses. In September Suharto removed several of the most outspoken members of Golkar from the list of candidates to contest the next legislative elections. During the campaign period, political parties were prohibited from addressing religious issues, the question of the dominant role of the ethnic Chinese community in the economy, or any subject that might present a threat to national unity. However, the opposition parties did exploit the increasing public resentment about the rapidly expanding businesses of Suharto's children. In the general election of June 1992, which attracted a turnout of 90.4%, Golkar secured 282 of the 400 elective seats, the Partai Persatuan Pembangunan (PPP—United Development Party) won 62 seats and the Partai Demokrasi Indonesia (PDI—Indonesian Democratic Party) took 56.

In March 1993 the DPR elected Suharto and Gen. Try Sutrisno, the former Commander-in-Chief of the Armed Forces, to the posts of President and Vice-President, respectively, the election of the latter appearing to consolidate ABRI's position following considerable public debate over its active involvement in political affairs and, in particular, concern over whether the appointment of 100 members of ABRI to the DPR remained justifiable. However, Suharto's new Cabinet constituted a slight decline in ABRI representation, and included several members of ICMI, whose Chairman, Prof. Dr Ir Bucharuddin Jusuf (B. J.) Habibie, was deeply unpopular with the military.

In October 1993, at the party congress, the Minister of Information, Harmoko, became the first civilian to be elected to the chairmanship of Golkar. In an unprecedented development, Suharto had openly endorsed Harmoko's candidacy. Also at the congress, Suharto's family entered active national politics; his son, Bambang Trihatmodjo, and daughter, Siti Hardijanti Rukmana (known as Mbak Tutut), who had both been appointed to the MPR in 1992, were elected to positions of responsibility within Golkar.

Meanwhile, in July 1993 the incumbent Chairman of the PDI, Soerjadi, was re-elected to the post at a fractious party congress. However, the Government invalidated the election of Soerjadi, who had campaigned during the 1992 elections for a limited presidential term of office, and appointed a 'caretaker board' pending new elections. An extraordinary congress of the PDI ended inconclusively in December owing to the unexpected candidacy for the chairmanship of Megawati Sukarnoputri, the daughter of former President Sukarno. Despite government pressure to elect a senior party official, Megawati received overwhelming support from the congressional participants, and the 'caretaker board' prevented a vote from taking place. The Government then ordered the holding of a new PDI congress, at which Megawati was elected Chairman.

Suppression of political and civil unrest, 1993–98

In June 1993, in response to pressure from the USA for Indonesia to improve workers' rights or lose trade privileges, the Government adopted reforms to the only officially recognized trade union, the Serikat Pekerja Seluruh Indonesia (All Indonesia Workers' Union), substantially increased the minimum wage and revoked the controversial 1986 Labour Law, which allowed the intervention of the armed forces in labour disputes. However, workers subsequently went on strike, accusing employers of failing to pay the new minimum wage and demanding improved working conditions. In February 1994 the unrecognized Serikat Buruh Sejahtera Indonesia (SBSI—Indonesian Prosperous Labour Union) appealed for a one-hour national work stoppage. The General Secretary of the SBSI, Muchtar Pakpahan, was charged with inciting hatred against the Government and temporarily detained. In April riots broke out in Medan, Sumatra, over workers' continuing demands, rapidly degenerating into attacks on ethnic Chinese property and business executives, who were widely perceived to have benefited disproportionately from the country's rapid economic growth. Three members of the SBSI surrendered to the authorities in May and admitted to having organized the protests. Further strikes took place in other parts of northern Sumatra. In August Pakpahan was rearrested; he was given a three-year prison sentence in November for inciting labour unrest (later extended to four years).

In January 1995 the armed forces announced that 300 members of the PDI were to be investigated for links to the 1965 coup attempt, following allegations that many party members had relatives or contacts in the banned PKI. In a further apparent bid to discredit the opposition grouping, the authorities attempted to ascribe social unrest to communist subversion. In September the Chief of Staff of the Armed Forces named several prominent dissidents, including Pakpahan (whose conviction for incitement had been rescinded by the Supreme Court in that month), as members of 'formless organizations', which, he claimed, had infiltrated pressure groups to promote the revival of communism. In November 300 alleged subversives were arrested in Java.

In July 1995, in response to widespread condemnation of Indonesia's human rights violations, Suharto announced that three prisoners detained for their complicity in the 1965 coup attempt would be released to coincide with the 50th anniversary of independence in August. The administration also subsequently announced that the code ET (which stood for *Eks Tahanan Politik*—former political prisoner) was to be removed from identity papers following the anniversary. The measure affected about 1.3m. citizens, most of whom had been arrested following the 1965 coup attempt, but released without trial; ET

status had subjected them to certain restrictions (for example, in employment) and to widespread discrimination. In October 1995 30 members of an extreme right-wing group, the Islamic State of Indonesia, were arrested in western Java for attempting to overthrow 'the unitary state of Indonesia'. In January 1996 in Bandung, West Java, thousands took part in demonstrations against the disproportionately wealthy ethnic Chinese.

In January 1996 the Government abolished permit requirements for political meetings (police permission was still necessary for public gatherings and demonstrations). In April the Government restored voting rights to more than 1.1m. people who had been associated with the PKI. However, the Government's increasing concern over potential opposition subsequently resulted in a return to more authoritarian practices.

In June 1996, in response to the increasing popularity of Megawati's leadership of the PDI, government supporters within the party organized a party congress in the northern Sumatran town of Medan, which removed Megawati as leader, and re-installed Soerjadi as Chairman. PDI members loyal to Megawati organized demonstrations in her support. In July members of Soerjadi's PDI faction and the armed forces forcibly removed Megawati and her supporters from the PDI headquarters, prompting violence in which five people were killed. The Government declared the minor, Marxist-influenced Partai Rakyat Demokrasi (PRD) to be responsible for the rioting, and renewed its campaign against communism. In September the Government proscribed the PRD, and Megawati's new party headquarters in eastern Jakarta were closed down.

In October 1996 Suharto ordered ABRI to suppress all political dissent. In November the Government declared that it would take action against non-governmental organizations (NGOs) that violated Indonesian law and the *Pancasila* ideology. In December the DPR ratified legislation granting the Government extensive powers to revoke the broadcasting permits of private television and radio stations. In the same month a government decree banned mass rallies during campaigning for the forthcoming legislative elections. In April 1997 thousands of supporters of Megawati rallied outside the DPR to protest against the exclusion from the final list of candidates of those nominated by her faction.

In the worst incident of pre-election violence, 125 people were killed when a shopping centre was set alight during clashes between supporters of Golkar and the PPP in the provincial capital of Kalimantan, Banjarmasin; more than 150 others were killed in various other incidents across the country. The elections were held on 29 May 1997. However, riots in Madura, fuelled by PPP claims that ballots had not been counted, resulted in an unprecedented repeat of voting at 86 polling stations several days later. The final results of the elections, which continued to attract allegations of fraud, revealed that Golkar had secured 325 of the 425 elective seats, the PPP 89 seats, and Soerjadi's PDI only 11 (compared with 56 in 1992); the remaining 75 seats were allocated to the military.

Widespread social unrest continued throughout 1997, as a result of religious tension, income disparity between social and ethnic groups and the repercussions of the central Government's transmigration programme, which had been initiated in 1971 in an effort to reduce population pressure on the most densely populated islands, particularly Java.

In August 1997 two Muslim leaders, Abdurrahman Wahid, the Chairman of the country's largest Islamic organization, the Nahdlatul Ulama (NU—Revival of the Islamic Scholars), and Amien Rais, the head of Indonesia's second largest Islamic grouping, Muhammadiyah, were excluded from the list of 500 civilian and military appointees to the MPR. Amien Rais had been forced to resign from a board of experts in ICMI in February for publicly criticizing the controversial Freeport mine in Irian Jaya (now Papua).

Following a massive decline in the value of the Indonesian currency between August and October 1997, President Suharto was forced to accept a rescue programme from the IMF. However, he subsequently failed to implement the requisite reforms, fearing that they would provoke unrest and adversely affect the business interests of his family and friends. At an unprecedented gathering of Muslim leaders and intellectuals (including members of ICMI) held in December, participants rejected Suharto's leadership and rallied around Amien Rais, who had already offered himself as a presidential candidate. Wahid subsequently joined Amien Rais and Megawati (who had entered an informal alliance) in demanding Suharto's resignation. In a largely symbolic gesture, in January 1998 Megawati also presented herself as a presidential candidate.

Nevertheless, at the presidential election, held in March 1998, Suharto was re-elected unopposed. He then endorsed the nomination of Habibie as the new Vice-President. Suharto's new Cabinet included a number of his immediate circle of friends and family. (Prior to his re-election, Suharto had also appointed his son-in-law, Lt-Gen. Prabowo Subianto, as Commander of Kostrad—the Indonesian army's strategic reserve.) In May riots erupted in Jakarta, precipitated by a large increase in fuel prices. The following month Indonesia's leading human rights group claimed that at least 1,188 people had died in Jakarta alone, while hundreds were believed to have perished during unrest elsewhere. Indonesia's ethnic Chinese minority was the target for much of the violence: an indeterminate number of Chinese were murdered, numerous Chinese women were raped, and Chinese homes and businesses were looted and burned.

The presidencies of Habibie and Wahid

On 21 May 1998, following sustained pressure (including an unprecedented demand for his resignation by Golkar Chairman Harmoko, and the resignation of 14 cabinet ministers), Suharto stepped down as President. Vice-President Habibie was sworn in as Suharto's successor, and subsequently appointed a new 'reform Cabinet', which nevertheless retained some ministers from the previous administration. The new President also announced the release of a number of political prisoners (including the union leader Pakpahan), encouraged government departments to sever links with enterprises owned by Suharto's family, and supported the dismissal of Lt-Gen. Prabowo as Commander of Kostrad. In June an investigation into the assets of Suharto and other government officials was announced, and Habibie expelled 41 members of the MPR, including several close associates of Suharto, on account of alleged corruption, nepotism and collusion. Seven members of Suharto's family were removed from their seats in the MPR the following month.

Unrest continued across the archipelago throughout the latter half of 1998, exacerbated by dissatisfaction at the pace of change under the new administration and at severe food shortages. During a four-day special session of the MPR in Jakarta in November at least 16 people were killed and many injured when demonstrators clashed with soldiers outside the building. At least 14 people died during clashes between Muslims and Christians in further riots. In the same month a report was published containing the findings of a panel appointed by the Government to investigate the riots that had occurred in May. The panel found that elements of the military had acted as 'provocateurs' during the riots, with particular suspicion falling on Kostrad. Lt-Gen. Prabowo had been formally dismissed from the army in August owing to the role that he had played as the then Commander of the unit. In December Suharto was questioned at the Higher Prosecutor's Office over allegations of corruption.

In December 1998 it was announced that legislative elections would be held in June 1999 and that the MPR (including 200 additional delegates) would convene in August to elect a new President (although this was subsequently postponed until November). Elections to the DPR would be conducted under a new electoral system, combining both district and proportional voting, but only parties presenting candidates in the requisite number of districts would be permitted to contest the poll. Civil servants were no longer to be obliged to support Golkar; the number of seats in the DPR allocated to the military was to be reduced from 75 to 38; and the membership of the MPR was to be reduced from 1,000 to 700.

At least 159 people were killed during clashes between Muslims and Christians on the island of Ambon, in the province of Maluku, in early 1999. The Habibie Government continued to pursue an extensive programme of reform. In April the police force—part of the Indonesian military since 1962—was formally separated from the armed forces (while remaining under the control of the Ministry of Defence), and the armed forces reassumed their revolutionary-era name, Tentara Nasional Indonesia (TNI—Indonesian National Defence Forces), instead of ABRI. The Subversion Law, introduced in 1963 and previously applied in the suppression of political dissidents, was repealed by the MPR (although some prohibitions were retained). In May 1999 a presidential decree removed a ban on the use and teaching of the Mandarin Chinese language and also outlawed discrimination on the grounds of ethnic origin.

President Habibie was nominated as the sole presidential candidate of Golkar in May 1999, despite some concerns regarding his close association with former President Suharto. The

three leading opposition parties—Megawati's Partai Demokrasi Indonesia Perjuangan (PDI—P, Indonesian Democratic Struggle Party), Wahid's Partai Kebangkitan Bangsa (PKB—National Awakening Party), and Amien Rais's Partai Amanat Nasional (PAN—National Mandate Party)—created an informal electoral alliance to stand against Golkar; however, the alliance appeared unstable from an early stage. At the legislative elections in June, which attracted a turnout of 91%, the PDI—P was victorious, securing 154 seats; the second largest share of the vote was unexpectedly won by Golkar, which took 120 seats, performing poorly in the cities but strongly in the outer islands. The PKB secured 59 seats, while the PAN won 35.

Megawati and Habibie thus emerged initially as the main candidates for the presidency. However, in October 1999, following the rejection of his presidential record by the MPR in a secret ballot, Habibie withdrew his candidacy. Contrary to widespread expectation, Megawati failed to win the presidential contest, receiving 313 votes, against the 373 secured by Wahid, the only other serious candidate, who had received the endorsement of a number of Islamic parties, as well as the support of Golkar. Wahid's victory provoked outrage among Megawati's supporters, and violent protests erupted in Jakarta and elsewhere. The MPR voted to appoint Megawati as Vice-President. The new Cabinet reflected the conciliatory and inclusive approach of the incoming President, incorporating both Islamic and nationalist representatives, as well as representatives of non-Javanese groups. Gen. Wiranto was replaced as Minister of Defence by former Minister of Education and Culture Juwono Sudarsono, the first civilian to hold the post.

The newly appointed Attorney-General, Marzuki Darusman, announced that the investigation into the allegations of corruption made against former President Suharto was to be reopened. The apparent commitment of the new administration to addressing corruption was further emphasized in November 1999, when Wahid urged the investigation of three government ministers, one of whom, the Co-ordinating Minister for People's Welfare and leader of the PPP, Hamzah Haz, subsequently resigned from the Cabinet.

Following Wahid's election to the presidency, there was further unrest across the archipelago. Ethnic violence continued on the island of Ambon in Maluku province where, according to official estimates published in December 1999, more than 750 people had died and from where many thousands more had fled since the renewal of violent clashes between Muslims and Christians in January. (Aid agencies estimated the total number of dead to be much higher.) Despite the dispatch of additional troops to the region to supplement the 2,500 already deployed there, and despite the formal separation of the predominantly Muslim northern districts of Maluku as the new province of North Maluku in late 1999, at least 265 people were believed to have been killed in clashes between Christians and Muslims on the island of Halmahera at the end of December, with violence also reported on other islands.

In January 2000 Indonesia's National Human Rights Commission released the results of its investigation into the role of the Indonesian armed forces in human rights abuses in the former Indonesian province of East Timor (now Timor-Leste—see *Provincial Affairs and Separatist Tensions*). Thirty-three military officers, including Gen. Wiranto, who had been Commander-in-Chief of the armed forces in 1998–99, were implicated; Wiranto resigned from the Cabinet in May 2000. In January, meanwhile, a reorganization took place within the TNI, in which officers loyal to Wiranto were removed from high-ranking positions. A second reorganization of senior military personnel was announced in February. In August doubts concerning the commitment of the Indonesian Government to the trial of military personnel suspected of involvement in gross human rights violations in East Timor were provoked when the MPR introduced a constitutional amendment excluding military personnel from prosecution for crimes committed prior to the enactment of the relevant legislation. In September, furthermore, Wiranto was not included on the Attorney-General's list of 19 suspects.

In April 2000 President Wahid dismissed from the Cabinet the Minister of State for Investment and Development of State Enterprises, Laksamana Sukardi of the PDI—P, and the Minister of Trade and Industry, Muhammad Jusuf Kalla of the pro-Habibie wing of Golkar, subsequently suggesting that both were guilty of corruption. In July Wahid was heavily criticized by the DPR for refusing adequately to explain the reasons for these dismissals. Meanwhile, general misgivings about Wahid's style of government also increased. In August Wahid announced that he was to delegate the daily administration of the Government to Vice-President Megawati. Constitutional amendments approved by the MPR in that month included articles defining explicitly the remit of the DPR, particularly regarding the body's questioning and investigating of government activities; legislation was also enacted to extend military representation in the MPR until 2009, four years after the date at which the military had been scheduled to relinquish its remaining 38 seats in the chamber. In August 2000 President Wahid announced the formation of a new Cabinet, which included considerably fewer representatives of Megawati's PDI—P and allocated a number of the most influential posts to Wahid loyalists: Gen. (retd) Susilo Bambang Yudhoyono was appointed Co-ordinating Minister for Political, Legal and Security Affairs.

In August 2000 Suharto was formally charged with corruption. In September, however, the charges against him were dismissed after an independent medical team declared the former President mentally and physically unfit to stand trial, provoking violent protests in Jakarta. (In May 2006 criminal charges against Suharto were formally abandoned owing to his deteriorating health, but a civil case was subsequently instigated—see *The first direct presidential election*.) In September 2000 President Wahid ordered the arrest of Suharto's youngest son, Hutomo Mandala Putra (commonly known as Tommy Suharto), in connection with a series of bomb threats and explosions in Jakarta. In one such attack in September at least 15 people were killed when a bomb exploded at the Jakarta Stock Exchange; two men were subsequently convicted of carrying out the bombing and were both sentenced to 20 years' imprisonment. At the end of September the Supreme Court overruled Tommy Suharto's previous acquittal from an unrelated charge of fraudulent activity in 1999, and sentenced him to 18 months' imprisonment. In July 2001 the judge who had presided over the proceedings, Justice Syafiuddin Kartasasmita, was shot dead. Two suspects subsequently confessed to the murder, but admitted in custody that Suharto's son had financed them and supplied the weapons used in the attack; both were convicted and sentenced to life imprisonment. In an unexpected development, a Supreme Court panel rescinded the original fraud charge in October. However, Tommy Suharto was arrested in the following month in connection with the murder of Syafiuddin. In July 2002 he was convicted of arranging Syafiuddin's murder, illegal possession of a weapon and attempting to evade justice, and was sentenced to 15 years' imprisonment. Following a successful appeal, this was subsequently reduced to a 10-year term, and in October 2006 he was granted conditional early release.

The transfer of power to Megawati

In September 2000 the DPR appointed a commission to investigate two financial scandals with which President Wahid had been linked: the first involved the irregular diversion of US $4.1m. from the funds of the Badan Urusan Logistic (BULOG—National Logistics Agency), allegedly to finance the Golkar party election campaign in 1999, while the second concerned a donation of $2m. made by Sultan Hassanal Bolkiah of Brunei. The President, denying any wrongdoing on his part, initially refused to be questioned on either matter. In January 2001 the commission concluded that Wahid 'could be suspected of playing a role' in the theft of BULOG funds by his personal masseur and that the President had been deliberately inconsistent in his explanations of how the donation from the Sultan (originally intended for social welfare) had been spent; however, the commission was unable to present clear evidence that Wahid had personally benefited from either situation. In February the DPR voted overwhelmingly to censure Wahid formally over his alleged involvement in the scandals. Wahid was given three months in which to provide a satisfactory explanation of his actions to the DPR. Tens of thousands of pro-Wahid demonstrators took to the streets in Surabaya and elsewhere in East Java (President Wahid's home province), and protesters set fire to the regional offices of Golkar, which had supported the vote to censure Wahid. Later in the same month Wahid offered himself for questioning by police investigating the two scandals. In March 2001 more than 12,000 students held a demonstration in Jakarta to demand the President's resignation. In view of Wahid's unsatisfactory reply to his first censure, in April the DPR issued a second censure and requested that the MPR convene a special session to begin impeachment proceedings. Violent pro-Wahid demonstrations took place in East Java. Despite the abandonment of all charges against Wahid in May, following the ruling by Attorney-General Marzuki Darus-

man that there was no evidence to implicate the President in either of the financial scandals, later that month the DPR voted by a huge majority to instruct the MPR to instigate an impeachment hearing. In response, in June the President reorganized his Cabinet, dismissing the Co-ordinating Minister for Political, Legal and Security Affairs, Yudhoyono. The Chief of Police, Gen. Surojo Bimantoro, was suspended. In the following month the President threatened to declare a state of emergency if no compromise were reached, and effected another cabinet reorganization. He also appointed a new Chief of Police without the endorsement of the legislature. A special session of the MPR was convened to which the President was summoned to give an account of his 21 months in power. President Wahid deemed the session illegal and refused to attend. He suspended the legislature, declaring a state of civil emergency, and urged that new elections be held in one year's time. However, the military refused to support the declaration, and the MPR stated that the President did not have the constitutional authority to dissolve it.

On 23 July 2001 Wahid was deposed as President following an impeachment hearing. He was replaced by Vice-President Megawati. Legislators elected the leader of the PPP, Hamzah Haz, to act as the new President's deputy, and in August Megawati announced the composition of her first Cabinet. Of its 32 members, only four were former military men, in sharp contrast to previous practice, and Yudhoyono was reinstated as Co-ordinating Minister for Political, Legal and Security Affairs.

In October 2001 the Speaker of the DPR and Chairman of Golkar, Akbar Tandjung, was questioned in court regarding the alleged misappropriation of BULOG funds. In September 2002 Tandjung was convicted of corruption and sentenced to a three-year prison term; in February 2004, however, the Supreme Court overruled his conviction.

Meanwhile, on 1 January 2001 new legislation took effect devolving increased financial and administrative control to Indonesia's regional governments. The central Government was to retain control over justice, defence, foreign affairs and monetary policy.

The first direct presidential election

In August 2002 a series of constitutional amendments was approved by the MPR. These provided for the direct election of both the President and Vice-President at the next national poll, scheduled to be held in 2004, and for the abolition of all seats held by non-elected representatives, effectively terminating military involvement in the legislature five years earlier than planned. The amendments also provided for a bicameral legislature through the creation of an upper house representing the regions, the Dewan Perwakilan Daerah (DPD—House of Representatives of the Regions), which, together with the DPR, would form the MPR. A total of 14 amendments (constituting the 'Fourth Amendment' to the Constitution) received legislative assent, and were ratified by the DPR in 2003.

The legislative elections held in April 2004 were contested by 24 parties; turnout was estimated at 84% of the electorate. Golkar secured 128 of the 550 seats in the expanded DPR, replacing the PDI—P, which won 109 seats, as the largest parliamentary grouping. Of the smaller parties, the PPP won 58 seats, the Partai Democrat (PD—Democratic Party) 57, and the PAN and the PKB each secured 52 seats.

At the inaugural direct presidential and vice-presidential election held in July 2004, the presidential candidate of the PD, Yudhoyono, secured 33.6% of the votes cast, followed by the incumbent Megawati, with 26.6%, and Golkar's candidate, Gen. (retd) Wiranto, with 22.2%; Amien Rais and Vice-President Hamzah Haz also contested the election on behalf of their respective parties, the PAN and the PPP. As no candidate won more than 50% of the votes, Yudhoyono and Megawati proceeded to a second round of voting, which was held in September: despite Golkar's declared support for the incumbent, Yudhoyono (whose vice-presidential candidate was Muhammad Jusuf Kalla, the Co-ordinating Minister for People's Welfare) emerged victorious, securing 60.6% of the votes cast. Estimated voter turnout in the second round was 75%, compared with 78% in the first. The new President, who was inaugurated in October, included representatives of several political organizations in his Cabinet. Among the notable new appointees were Adm. (retd) Widodo Adi Sutjipto, the former Commander-in-Chief of the TNI, as Co-ordinating Minister for Political, Legal and Security Affairs, and Aburizal Bakrie, of Golkar, as Co-ordinating Minister for Economic Affairs; Hassan Wirajuda, the Minister of Foreign

Affairs, was one of five ministers retained from Megawati's administration.

Vice-President Kalla was elected as Chairman of Golkar in December 2004, defeating the incumbent, Akbar Tandjung. As a result, it was anticipated that Golkar would henceforth broadly support the Government, enabling Yudhoyono to secure legislative approval for his policies. In late December Abdullah Puteh, the Governor of Aceh, became the first person to be prosecuted by the recently formed Komisi Pemberantasan Korupsi (KPK—Corruption Eradication Commission). Puteh, who was suspended from office, was charged with corruption in relation to the purchase of a Russian helicopter in 2002. He was convicted in April 2005 and sentenced to 10 years' imprisonment.

In November 2004 it emerged that Munir Said Thalib, a leading Indonesian human rights activist who had died during a flight to the Netherlands in September, had been poisoned with arsenic. Munir had been an outspoken critic of Indonesia's military and Badan Inteligen Negara (BIN—State Intelligence Agency). In January 2008 Pollycarpus Priyanto, an airline pilot of the state-owned Garuda Indonesia who had been on Munir's flight while off duty, was convicted of the activist's murder and sentenced to 20 years' imprisonment, and in February Indra Setiawan, the former CEO of Garuda, was convicted of assisting in Munir's murder and given a 12-month sentence; both men claimed to have been carrying out orders issued to them by BIN. In August Maj.-Gen. Muchdi Purwopranjono, the deputy head of BIN at the time of Munir's murder, went on trial, charged with ordering the killing of the activist. Human rights groups welcomed the development, which represented the first prosecution of a senior BIN official. However, Purwopranjono was acquitted in December owing to a lack of evidence.

Meanwhile, on 26 December 2004 Indonesia, in particular the region of Aceh, was devastated by a series of tsunamis caused by a massive earthquake in the Indian Ocean. The regional capital, Banda Aceh, was severely damaged, while the town of Meulaboh, 150 km from the epicentre of the earthquake, was completely destroyed. Large-scale operations were launched to distribute food, medical supplies and shelter to survivors. Aceh had been under emergency rule prior to the disaster, owing to a separatist insurgency (see *Provincial Affairs and Separatist Tensions*), and largely closed to foreign agencies and the international media. According to official estimates, in Aceh alone as many as 170,000 people had died; more than 400,000 were made homeless.

In July 2005 the Majelis Ulama Indonesia (MUI—Indonesian Ulama Council) issued 11 *fatwa* (religious edicts), the most controversial of which outlawed secularism, pluralism and liberal Islamic teachings. The issue of the *fatwa* was thought to be in response to the activities of two moderate, progressive Islamic organizations: the Jaringan Islam Liberal (JIL—Liberal Islam Network) and the Muhammadiyah Youth Intellectuals Network. Meanwhile, ongoing criticism of the Ahmadiyah sect (which maintained that its founder, Mirza Ghulam Ahmad, rather than the Prophet Muhammad, was the final prophet) continued; although deemed an heretical group, the sect was believed to have 200,000 followers in Indonesia. In July thousands of members of the so-called Indonesian Muslim Solidarity group attacked the Ahmadiyah compound in Jakarta, citing an edict issued in 1980 by the MUI, which had declared members of Ahmadiyah to be deviants. The edict was renewed in August 2005. Ahmadis in Bandung and other Javanese cities were also targeted. In April 2008, after a government panel recommended that the group be banned, a large protest was held in Jakarta demanding the expulsion of Ahmadis from Indonesia. A series of attacks on Ahmadiyah mosques prompted the Government to demand that Ahmadis cease 'spreading interpretations and activities which deviate from the principal teachings of Islam' and to warn of prison terms for offenders. It was subsequently reported that the police had helped local Islamic extremists forcibly to shut down several mosques owned by the sect in a village in West Java. The leniency of sentences handed down by a district court in July 2011 to the perpetrators of a violent mob attack against a group of Ahmadis at a mosque in another West Javan village, during which three Ahmadis had been killed (attendant police officers having apparently failed to intervene), elicited much criticism from human rights groups and the wider international community. The defendants, none of whom were charged with murder, received short prison terms, having been convicted only of relatively minor offences.

In December 2005, meanwhile, President Yudhoyono effected a cabinet reorganization, which focused predominantly on economic personnel. Co-ordinating Minister for Economic Affairs

Aburizal Bakrie, who had attracted much criticism for his failure to halt the rapid decline in the value of the rupiah, was replaced by Prof. Dr Boediono, Minister of Finance during Megawati's presidency. Further ministerial changes were required in May 2007 following the dismissal of the Minister of Justice and Human Rights Affairs, Hamid Awaluddin, and State Secretary Yusril Ihza Mahendra, as a result of their alleged involvement in the illegal transfer of US $10m. to Tommy Suharto from a bank account in the United Kingdom.

In July 2007 a civil case was filed against former President Suharto, in the hope of recovering some US $440m. that he had allegedly misappropriated from funds ostensibly allocated to an educational foundation. However, Suharto died in January 2008. Although the former President was posthumously acquitted in March, his charitable foundation, Supersemar, was found guilty and directed to reimburse some $100m. to the state. In August the Government seized $150m. from Timor Putra Nasional, a now-defunct motor vehicle company belonging to Tommy Suharto, amid ongoing investigations into allegations that he had illegally sold assets from Timor Putra Nasional to five of his other companies.

Meanwhile, Jakarta's first direct gubernatorial election took place in August 2007 (in accordance with legislation introduced in 2005 providing for local leaders—including mayors, provincial governors and regents—to be elected by direct popular vote rather than being appointed by local assemblies). The election, which attracted a turnout of 65%, was won by the incumbent Deputy Governor, Fauzi Bowo, who received nearly 58% of the votes cast, there being only one other candidate. In June 2008 Minister of Finance and State Enterprises Development Dr Sri Mulyani Indrawati assumed concurrent responsibility for the economic affairs portfolio, following the departure of Prof. Dr Boediono from the Cabinet.

In October 2008 Burhanuddin Abdullah, the former Governor of Bank Indonesia, was sentenced to five years' imprisonment, after being convicted of embezzling funds in order to bribe legislators and to engage lawyers in an attempt to defend officials of the central bank against corruption allegations.

The 2009 legislative and presidential elections

In April 2008 it was announced that the legal status of 24 new political parties had been recognized. A total of 38 national parties were now deemed eligible to participate in the 2009 legislative elections. Under new legislation approved in October 2008, political parties were required to secure at least 20% of the seats or 25% of the votes cast in the legislative elections in order to nominate a presidential candidate.

At the legislative elections in April 2009, which attracted a turnout of 71%, the number of seats in the DPR was increased from 550 to 560. For the first time, under Indonesia's system of proportional representation, electors were able to vote for specific candidates within each party. Polling for the 132 (hitherto 128) regional delegates of the DPD also took place, along with local elections. A major issue was the rapid deterioration in the country's economy. The PD won 20.8% of the votes cast (nearly tripling the share of the votes it received at the 2004 elections) to secure 148 of the 560 seats in the DPR, thereby enabling the incumbent President Yudhoyono formally to present his candidacy for the presidential election scheduled for July. Golkar secured 108 seats (14.4% of the vote), reduced from 128 at the last elections, while the PDI—P won 93 seats (14.0%), compared with 109 five years previously.

In May 2009, having failed to fulfil the criteria required to nominate a presidential candidate, Golkar and the PDI—P announced the formation of a 10-party electoral coalition, thus enabling them to present Kalla and Megawati as their respective candidates for the presidential election, which was held in July. Incumbent President Yudhoyono, with Prof. Dr Boediono as his vice-presidential running candidate, achieved a resounding victory, attracting 60.8% of the votes cast. Megawati and Lt-Gen. Prabowo secured 26.8% of the ballot, while Kalla and Gen. (retd) Wiranto obtained just 12.4%. Yudhoyono was sworn in for his second consecutive term as President in October. The incoming Cabinet retained 10 ministers from the previous administration, including Indrawati as Minister of Finance. Notable new appointees included Air Chief Marshal (retd) Djoko Suyanto as Co-ordinating Minister for Political, Legal and Security Affairs and Hatta Radjasa as Co-ordinating Minister for Economic Affairs.

Aburizal Bakrie was elected as the new Chairman of Golkar at a party congress in October 2009; the former Co-ordinating

Minister for People's Welfare defeated three other candidates, including Tommy Suharto (who failed to secure a single vote).

Declining support for Yudhoyono

An alleged plot to sabotage the KPK was a significant contributory factor in a rapid decline in the popularity of President Yudhoyono from late 2009. In October the integrity of the KPK had been called into question when two of its Deputy Chairmen were arrested on suspicion of bribery. However, both were released in November, and the charges against them were withdrawn in December, after the pair submitted covert recordings of conversations between several people widely accepted to have been senior police officers and the Attorney-General's office, which revealed that those speaking, angered by the KPK's successful investigation and charging of numerous officials, intended to attempt to destroy the reputation of the anti-corruption commission. Two of the officials linked to the plot, Deputy Attorney-General Abdul Hakim Ritonga and Chief Detective Susno Duadji, tendered their resignations, following numerous protests demanding the dismissal of those involved. In March 2011 Susno Duadji was sentenced to three-and-a-half years' imprisonment, having been convicted of accepting bribes and embezzling public funds. However, as of late 2014, no proceedings appeared to have been instigated against Susno—or any other individual—in connection with the alleged plot against the KPK. Many Indonesians were disillusioned by the perceived failure of Yudhoyono to intervene, and questioned his commitment to his pre-election pledge to take firm action against vice and corruption.

Meanwhile, the controversy surrounding the alleged plot against the KPK intensified further in February 2010 when the former head of the commission, Antasari Azhar, was convicted of arranging the murder of an Indonesian businessman and sentenced to 18 years' imprisonment. The conviction of Antasari (who had been Chairman of the KPK at the time of his arrest in May 2009) came despite claims made by a witness during the trial that he had been forced to co-operate with a police-instigated plot to incriminate the former KPK head. An appeal lodged by Antasari was rejected by the Supreme Court in September 2010. However, his many supporters continued to insist that he had been the victim of an ongoing attempt by the police to discredit the KPK and obstruct anti-corruption efforts.

The Government's controversial rescue programme for a failing financial institution, PT Bank Century Tbk, was another source of considerable contention. Legislators and the general public alike were angered by the revelation in late 2009 that the takeover of the bank in November 2008 had cost taxpayers the equivalent of US $720m., more than four times the amount originally agreed by the Government and the DPR. Opposition parliamentarians argued that Vice-President Boediono (Governor of Bank Indonesia at the time of the intervention) and Minister of Finance Indrawati had abused their positions to protect the interests of Bank Century, which was renamed PT Bank Mutiara Tbk in October 2009, without first securing the approval of the DPR. (Subsequently, many of the bank's wealthy clients were alleged to have made sizeable donations to the election campaign of Yudhoyono and Boediono.) A parliamentary inquiry into 'Centurygate', as the scandal had become known, was initiated in late 2009. In March 2010 the committee published its final report: although it stated that it had found no evidence of Bank Century money being used to support any political campaign, it did criticize the decision-making process, including the actions of Boediono and Indrawati, and urged the Government to pursue the possibility of prosecutions. However, Yudhoyono contested that the rescue programme had been 'essential to saving the banking system' and declared that he saw no need for any action to be taken against Boediono or Indrawati, who both denied any wrongdoing. A forensic audit of the bank was carried out by the Badan Pemeriksa Keuangan (BPK—Supreme Audit Agency) in mid-2011 at the request of the DPR. However, the report submitted by the BPK in December was inconclusive and was widely criticized for its perceived failure fully to explain how all of the rescue programme funding had been spent.

In April 2010 the Constitutional Court rejected appeals to overrule controversial legislation implemented in 1967 allowing for criminal penalties and bans on individuals or groups that 'distort' the central tenets of Indonesia's six officially recognized religions—Buddhism, Christianity (both Catholicism and Protestantism), Confucianism, Hinduism and Islam—declaring that the law was in accordance with the Constitution and was vital to religious harmony. It had been hoped that the legislation might be reviewed to allow the official establishment of new religions and sects. According to a local human rights organization, there was a notable rise in the number of reported attacks on religious freedom in Indonesia in the first half of 2010; many of the attacks were attributed to the Front Pembela Islam (FPI—Islamic Defenders' Front), which demanded the implementation of Islamic law (*Shari'a*) across the archipelago. Critics of the Yudhoyono Government claimed that the President had failed to intervene since Islamic parties formed the core of his parliamentary support.

In May 2010 Indrawati, who was widely credited for the macroeconomic reforms that had helped Indonesia to withstand the effects of the international financial crisis of 2008/09, resigned as Minister of Finance in order to assume a senior position at the World Bank; she was replaced by former banking executive Agus Martowardojo.

Yudhoyono's reputation as an anti-corruption reformist suffered a further reverse during the trial of former tax official Gayus Tambunan, who in January 2011 was convicted of corruption; the defendant's testimony during court proceedings suggested endemic levels of corruption within the judiciary, the police force and the prison service. Also in January, the Minister of Home Affairs, Gamawan Fauzi, expressed concern at the apparent escalation in corruption, noting that some 155 regional leaders had been named as suspects in investigations since 2004; of these, 17 were either current or former governors.

In a more positive development, in October 2010 the Constitutional Court rescinded legislation that allowed the Attorney-General's office unilaterally to prohibit the publication and supply of books that were deemed to be 'offensive' or a 'threat to public order', ruling that the power to impose such bans should henceforth be accorded to the judiciary. The revocation of the legislation, which had been implemented in 1963 and had been used to silence opposition during the Suharto era, was welcomed as symbolically significant.

Also in October 2010, the Government came under intense criticism following a tsunami that claimed the lives of more than 400 people and left some 13,000 homeless. Indonesia's early warning system, which had been implemented at great expense after the 2004 disaster, failed to alert the authorities to the impending tsunami, generated by a major earthquake off the coast of Sumatra; the system was reported to have fallen into disrepair owing to inadequate maintenance. Yudhoyono oversaw the subsequent rescue operation, together with a separate operation to provide relief to those affected by a series of volcanic eruptions by Mount Merapi, which began one day after the tsunami and killed more than 200 people. However, the authorities' perceived mishandling of the response to the tsunami disaster, with reports of shortages of basic medical and food supplies, prompted widespread anger.

New, more stringent, legislation to combat human-trafficking was approved by the legislature in April 2011. The development was widely welcomed, both domestically and further afield, particularly by the Australian Government, which had for some time been pressing Indonesia to adopt a firmer stance on the issue, with many thousands of illegal migrants and asylum seekers using Jakarta as a transit point en route to Australia.

Further corruption allegations emerged in April 2011, with the Treasurer of the PD, Muhammad Nazaruddin, accused of soliciting bribes amounting to US $2.8m. from a construction company, in exchange for a contract to build athletes' accommodation for the Southeast Asian Games, which Indonesia hosted in November. However, Nazaruddin refuted the claims, alleging the involvement in the scandal of other legislators and PD officials—including the Secretary-General of the PD, Edhie 'Ibas' Baskoro Yudhoyono (the President's son), and PD Chairman Anas Urbaningrum. Having thereby fomented division within the PD leadership, Nazaruddin was dismissed from his party role, although he was allowed to retain his parliamentary seat pending further investigation by the KPK. He fled the country in May, but was arrested in Colombia in August and was extradited to Indonesia. In April 2012 Nazaruddin was found guilty of bribery and sentenced to four years and 10 months in prison. The episode, and particularly concerns regarding how Nazaruddin had been able to flee the country despite the gravity of the claims against him, wreaked considerable damage upon the reputation of both the PD and the Yudhoyono administration, and cast further doubt on the latter's commitment to tackling corruption.

Meanwhile, the appointment in June 2011 of Gen. Pramono Edhie Wibowo, Yudhoyono's brother-in-law, as Chief of Staff of the Army provoked accusations of nepotism. Of further consternation to critics of the appointment was the alleged involvement of Gen. Wibowo in human rights abuses in East Timor in 1999 (see *Provincial Affairs and Separatist Tensions*).

A cabinet reorganization effected by Yudhoyono in October 2011 was widely interpreted as an attempt to restore public confidence in the President's administration. Opinion polls conducted in that month suggested that Yudhoyono's popularity had sunk to its lowest ebb; the President's perceived failure effectively to combat corruption and to address the country's economic challenges were two of the principal factors cited in the decline.

In December 2011 a student activist, Sondang Hutagalung, set himself on fire outside the presidential buildings; he subsequently died from his injuries. While Sondang's motivation remained unclear, the local media was quick to speculate that the student's self-immolation had been driven by deep discontent with the Government and endemic corruption. President Yudhoyono suffered a further setback in December 2012 when the Minister of State for Youth and Sports Affairs, Andi Mallarangeng, was forced to resign following allegations of his complicity in financial irregularities surrounding the construction of a sports complex in Hambalang, West Java. Mallarangeng's suspected involvement in the scandal was of particular embarrassment to Yudhoyono since he was the first serving government minister to be accused of corruption by the KPK since the commission's establishment in 2003. The President's problems mounted in February 2013 when the Chairman of the PD, Anas Urbaningrum, stood down from his post following accusations by the KPK that he too had been involved in the sports complex scandal; Yudhoyono was elected unopposed to the chairmanship at an extraordinary party congress the following month. (In July 2014 Mallarangeng was found guilty of accepting bribes and sentenced to four years' imprisonment, and in September Urbaningrum received an eight-year sentence after being convicted of corruption charges.)

Meanwhile, Jakarta's second direct gubernatorial election was held in September 2012. The candidate supported by the majority of the opposition parties, Joko Widodo, defeated the incumbent Fauzi Bowo (who had the backing of the central Government) in a fiercely contested poll. In January 2013 the new, populist Governor was forced to declare a temporary state of emergency in the capital following severe flooding that left 32 people dead and inundated much of the city.

In October 2012 the number of provinces in Indonesia increased from 33 to 34 following the establishment of Kalimantan Utara (North Kalimantan), which was formed from four regencies of Kalimantan Timur (East Kalimantan) on the island of Borneo.

Following his assumption of the governorship of the central bank in May 2013, Agus Martowardojo was replaced as Minister of Finance by Dr Muhammad Chatib Basri. The reputation of the Government was once again tarnished by allegations of high-level corruption when Rudi Rubiandini, the chairman of the state petroleum and gas regulatory agency, SKK Migas, and former cabinet minister, was arrested by the KPK in August on suspicion of bribery. Furthermore, in September a former senior police officer, Inspector Gen. Djoko Susilo, was sentenced to 10 years in prison on corruption charges, and in the following month the Chief Justice of the Constitutional Court, Dr Akil Mochtar, was forced to resign in the wake of bribery allegations.

Recent developments: the 2014 legislative and presidential elections

The legislative elections of 9 April 2014, which attracted a turnout of some 73%, were contested by 12 political parties nationally, with a further three local parties running in the province of Aceh (see below). Polling for the 136 regional delegates of the DPD (up from 132 in 2009) took place concurrently, along with local elections. There was no outright winner in the elections to the DPR; the PDI—P won 109 seats with some 19.0% of the votes cast, Golkar 91 seats (14.8%) and the Partai Gerakan Indonesia Raya (Gerindra—Great Indonesia Movement Party)—headed by the former Commander of Kostrad, Lt-Gen. Prabowo Subianto—73 seats (11.8%, compared with just 4.5% in 2009). Support for the PD of the outgoing President, Yudhoyono, who was constitutionally barred from seeking a third presidential term, was halved, to around 10.2% of the vote, with the party securing only 61 seats. Support for most of the Islamic parties remained steady (with the PAN, the PKS and the PPP all receiving around 7% of the vote), with the exception of the PKB, whose share of the vote rose from 4.9% in 2009 to 9.0%

in 2014. Since none of the parties achieved the requisite 25% of the vote or 20% of DPR seats to be eligible formally to present its own candidate for the presidential election, which was due to be held in July, intensive negotiations were conducted during April in an attempt to establish parliamentary alliances that would enable a number of presidential nominees to be put forward. An early pledge by the Partai NasDem (National Democratic Party), which secured around 6.7% of the vote, to back the PDI—P ensured that the presidential nominee of the latter party, the populist Governor of Jakarta, Joko Widodo ('Jokowi'), would be able to contest the forthcoming poll; the PDI—P subsequently also won the backing of the Partai Hati Nurani Rakyat (People's Conscience Party) and the PKB. Gerindra's presidential nominee, Prabowo, gained the support of several major parties that had earlier failed to secure electoral deals with Widodo, including the PAN, the PPP and Golkar, although Widodo notably selected Muhammad Jusuf Kalla of Golkar as his vice-presidential running mate.

At the presidential election, which was held on 9 July 2014 and was contested by only two candidates, Widodo—whose election campaign focused on ending the government corruption, nepotism and intolerance that, he claimed, had prevailed under Suharto—secured victory over Prabowo in a divisive and hard-fought contest by 53.2% to 46.8%. Prabowo refused to accept the official result presented by the Komisi Pemilihan Umum (General Elections Commission) and appealed to the Constitutional Court, alleging large-scale electoral fraud. Following the Court's prompt dismissal of these accusations, Prabowo reluctantly accepted the outcome of the poll. Widodo and Kalla took office on 20 October. A new minority coalition Cabinet—which held only about 37% of the seats in the lower legislative chamber—was sworn in on 27 October. Among the notable appointments were Retno Marsudi as Minister of Foreign Affairs, Tjahjo Kumolo as Minister of Home Affairs and Bambang Brodjonegoro as Minister of Finance. The following month Basuki Tjahaja Purnama was sworn in as the new Governor of Jakarta, following the resignation of Widodo from the post in early October.

Meanwhile, in late September 2014, in a highly controversial move, the DPR approved legislation, by 226 votes to 135, abolishing direct regional elections (for mayors, regents and provincial governors)—a system introduced in 2005 as part of Indonesia's post-Suharto democratization; local leaders were henceforth to be appointed by local assemblies, as they had been prior to 2005. Opponents of the measure, including Widodo (himself a directly elected governor and former mayor) and Yudhoyono, protested that it represented a retrograde step for Indonesian politics in that it would perpetuate nepotism and cronyism within the country's larger parties while keeping the smaller parties out of power. Before standing down from the presidency, Yudhoyono issued a decree to overturn the legislation; in January 2015 the new DPR, which was inaugurated in October 2014, reversed its predecessor's decision by voting unanimously to uphold the presidential decree to retain the direct election of local leaders.

The Threat of Terrorism

An ongoing challenge for successive Indonesian governments has been the threat posed by terrorist activity, at both domestic and regional level. In October 2002 the Government's response to this threat was tested when two bombs exploded outside a nightclub in the tourist resort of Kuta, on the island of Bali. The explosions resulted in the deaths of 202 people, many of whom were Australian tourists. In its first admission that Islamist fundamentalists were operative within Indonesia, the Government initially attributed the attack to the international network of al-Qa'ida, which it believed had collaborated with local terrorists. The DPR authorized two emergency decrees, bringing into effect several previously delayed anti-terrorism measures, including a law permitting suspects to be detained for up to seven days without charge. The Muslim cleric Abu Bakar Bashir, commander of the Majelis Mujahidin Indonesia (MMI—Indonesian Mujahideen Council) and allegedly the spiritual head of the regional Islamist organization Jemaah Islamiah (JI), was detained in connection with the attack. (He had been questioned by police in January over alleged links to al-Qa'ida but had been released without charge.) The USA and the UN announced that they had designated JI a terrorist entity and frozen its financial assets. The police made several further arrests as the investigation into the bombings proceeded and in November one of the suspects, Amrozi bin Nurhasyim, confessed to his involvement and to having strong links to JI, as well as implicating several others in the attack. Later in the same month Imam Samudra was arrested on suspicion of having organized the attack. He confessed to being a member of JI and to having planned earlier attacks, including the bombing of churches across the archipelago in December 2000 (see *Provincial Affairs and Separatist Tensions*), together with the operational leader of JI, Riduan Isamuddin (alias Hambali). In December 2002 Ali Gufron (alias Mukhlas), who had apparently succeeded Hambali as JI operational leader, was also arrested and confessed to having helped to plan the Bali attack.

In March 2003 the DPR endorsed legislation specifically designating terrorism as a crime and providing for detention without trial for terrorist suspects. The legislation was enacted retrospectively in order to cover the Bali bombings. In April the trial of Bashir on charges of, *inter alia*, subversion, immigration violations, and involvement in several terrorist attacks, including the December 2000 church bombings, began in Jakarta. In September 2003 Bashir was convicted of the subversion charges against him but, owing to insufficient evidence, was acquitted of any involvement in terrorist attacks and of being the spiritual leader of JI. He was sentenced to a four-year prison term, which on appeal was later twice reduced, to three years and then just 18 months, although the remaining charges against him were upheld. In April 2004, immediately after his release from prison, Bashir was rearrested on suspicion of terrorism. Meanwhile, Idris (alias Jhoni Hendrawan), suspected of involvement in the Bali bombings, was reported to have been arrested in June 2003, and in August the Thai authorities announced that they had finally captured Hambali, who was subsequently taken into custody by the USA. Also in August Amrozi became the first person to be convicted in connection with the Bali bombings; his appeal against the death sentence was subsequently rejected. In the following month Imam Samudra was also convicted and sentenced to death; a further suspect, Ali Imron, was sentenced to life imprisonment, having expressed some remorse for his actions. In October Mukhlas was convicted of having helped to plan the attacks and was sentenced to death. (Amrozi, Imam Samudra and Mukhlas were executed in November 2008, their final appeals against the death sentence having been rejected by the Supreme Court during 2007.) In July 2004 the Constitutional Court declared that the counter-terrorism legislation approved in 2003 and used to convict a number of those responsible for the Bali bombings should not have been applied retroactively. The Minister of Justice and Human Rights Affairs stated that the ruling did not rescind the convictions already secured, but made it impossible to apply the law in future cases for crimes committed before its enactment.

In August 2003 an explosive device detonated by a suicide bomber outside the Marriott Hotel in Jakarta resulted in the deaths of 12 people. The police apprehended a number of suspects, all of whom were believed to be members of JI. In the first half of 2004 two of the detainees were convicted of involvement in the attack and sentenced to prison terms (of 10 years and seven years). In August Idris was sentenced to 10 years' imprisonment for his part in the hotel bombing, but charges against him in connection with the Bali bombings were withdrawn, owing to the Constitutional Court's July ruling, despite an earlier confession of his involvement.

A bomb exploded outside the Australian embassy in Jakarta in September 2004, killing nine people and injuring more than 180 others. JI was held responsible for the attack, and a number of suspects were subsequently detained. In October the trial of Bashir on charges of conspiring and inciting acts of terrorism, including the Bali and Marriott bombings, commenced in Jakarta; he was again accused of being the spiritual leader of JI. In relation to the Bali attacks, Bashir was to be tried under the criminal code. In March 2005 Bashir was found guilty of conspiracy over the Bali attacks and sentenced to a prison term of two-and-a-half years, although he was acquitted of involvement in the Marriott bombing. Australia and the USA immediately expressed their disappointment at the leniency of the sentence. An appeal by Bashir against the verdict was rejected by the Supreme Court in August. However, Bashir's sentence was reduced as part of Indonesia's 60th anniversary of independence celebrations, and he was released from prison in June 2006. He again appealed against the original verdict, and in January 2007 his conviction was overruled by the Supreme Court on the grounds of insufficient evidence. Meanwhile, in the latter half of 2005 four men were tried in connection with the bombing of the Australian embassy in September 2004; two of them received the death penalty, while the two others were given prison sentences.

In October 2005 Bali was again struck by terrorist activity. Three bombs were detonated at tourist locations on the island, killing 23 people, including the bombers, and injuring more than 100 others. In November one of JI's senior leaders, the Malaysian bomb-maker Azahari Husin, who was suspected of organizing the previous month's bombings with fellow Malaysian Noordin Mohammad Top, was killed during an Indonesian police operation in Batu, near Malang, in East Java. In January 2006 Noordin released a statement claiming responsibility for the 2005 Bali attacks. In his message, Noordin also claimed to have formed a new South-East Asian Islamist militant organization, Tanzim Qaedat al-Jihad (Organization for the Basis of Jihad). In September 2006 four suspects were convicted of involvement in the 2005 Bali bombings and were sentenced to between eight and 18 years' imprisonment. In November eight members of JI were found guilty of carrying out and supporting terrorist activity; they received prison terms of between six years and life. In March 2007 police arrested several suspected JI members in the Javanese city of Yogyakarta; the militants were believed to have links to Abu Dujana, who, according to some reports, had become the commander of JI's military operations. In June Abu Dujana was one of eight suspects apprehended by the authorities in Central Java. On the same day, Zarkasih (also known as Nuaim or Mbah, among other aliases), who had acted as the head of JI since 2004, was also arrested. Both members of JI admitted their involvement with the organization and in April 2008 were sentenced to 15 years' imprisonment: Abu Dujana on charges of plotting terrorist activities and of sheltering other militants; and Zarkasih on charges of conspiring to commit terrorism and of supplying weapons and training to JI members. Meanwhile, two senior members of JI—Abdul Rohim, who was alleged to have replaced Zarkasih as JI leader following the latter's arrest, and Agus Purwanto—were apprehended in Malaysia in January and subsequently extradited to Indonesia.

In July 2009 the Marriott Hotel suffered a second terrorist attack when suicide bombers launched near-simultaneous strikes on the Marriott and Ritz-Carlton hotels in Jakarta. Six foreign tourists and one Indonesian were killed, as well as the two bombers themselves; more than 50 others were seriously injured. The bombers were widely believed to have links to JI, although no claim of responsibility was reported. In September the Indonesian authorities announced that Noordin Mohammad Top had been killed during a police operation in Central Java. The trials of three men accused of involvement in the Marriott and Ritz-Carlton bombings commenced in February 2010; in June the defendants each received prison sentences of between 18 months and eight years.

In July 2010 the Government formally established a new national anti-terrorism agency, which was to be responsible for all existing anti-terrorism divisions across the Government, the police force and the military. Meanwhile, in early 2010 the authorities announced the discovery in Aceh of a military training camp with purported links to Jemaah Ansharut Tauhid (JAT), a new terrorist network thought to have been established by Amar Usman (alias Dulmatin), a senior JI leader suspected of involvement in the 2002 Bali bombings. In February 2010 members of the cell were reported to have shot dead three police officers, and in the following month three suspected militants (one of whom was later confirmed to be Dulmatin) were killed in two separate police operations near Jakarta. Abdullah Sonata was subsequently reported to have replaced Dulmatin as leader of JAT, but was arrested in Java, together with two other suspected militants, in June. More than 100 other individuals had already been detained on suspicion of connection with the network. In August Abu Bakar Bashir was rearrested on suspicion of having helped to establish and fund JAT; in December he was charged with multiple counts of terrorist involvement. Bashir was convicted in June 2011 and sentenced to 15 years' imprisonment. Following an appeal, in October the Jakarta High Court reduced Bashir's prison term to nine years 'on humanitarian grounds', prompting widespread anger. However, in February 2012 the Supreme Court overturned the High Court ruling, reinstating Bashir's 15-year sentence.

One of the main suspects in the 2002 Bali bombings, Umar Patek, an Indonesian national, was arrested in Pakistan in January 2011, and was extradited to Indonesia in August. Patek, who was alleged to have made the explosives used in the Bali attacks and to have had close links with Dulmatin, was charged with murder rather than terrorism in connection with the 2002 bombings, owing to the Constitutional Court's outlawing of the retroactive use of the 2003 counter-terrorism legislation (see above); however, he was also charged with, *inter alia*, assisting JAT in terrorist activities. Patek's trial commenced in February 2012, and in June, having been found guilty of murder, bomb-making and complicity in the church attacks of December 2000, he was sentenced to 20 years in prison.

Another suspect in the 2002 Bali bombings, Heru Kuncoro, was arrested in Central Java in June 2011, after the authorities uncovered a new terrorist plot (involving cyanide) against the police force. Although the Government's crackdown on JI following the Bali bombings in 2002 was generally held to have proved relatively successful, a number of new, smaller terrorist organizations were reported to have been established and there were also incidents of attacks being organized by lone extremists. In October 2012 11 people were arrested on suspicion of planning bomb attacks on Western targets in Indonesia, including the US embassy in Jakarta and the offices of the mining company Freeport. The detainees were allegedly members of an Islamic group known as the Harakah Sunniyah Untuk Masyarakat Islami (HASMI—Sunni Movement for Islamic Society), which had been established in around 2009. HASMI denied any involvement in terrorism activity, claiming that it was engaged solely in peaceful activities such as education. The trial of five Islamist activists accused of plotting to carry out a bomb attack on the Myanma embassy in Jakarta in May 2013 commenced in November; the defendants, who were allegedly part of a network called the Negara Islam Indonesia (Islamic State of Indonesia), were reported to have been seeking revenge for the deaths of Rohingya Muslims during a period of prolonged communal unrest in Myanmar in 2012. In January 2014 the ringleader of the group was convicted of committing an act of terrorism and was sentenced to seven-and-a-half years in prison.

In response to the emergence and increasing power of the extremist militant group the Islamic State in Iraq and the Levant (subsequently renamed Islamic State—IS) in Syria and Iraq during 2013–14, the Indonesian authorities attempted to curb the group's rising profile within Indonesia by announcing a ban on any public displays of support for IS in August 2014 and by arresting suspected sympathizers. However, in December the head of the state anti-terrorism agency, Saud Usman Nasution, claimed that more than 500 Indonesians had travelled to Iraq and Syria to join IS.

Provincial Affairs and Separatist Tensions

From 2000 a major challenge confronting successive governments was the escalation of communal violence across the archipelago, together with separatist tensions in individual regions such as Aceh and Irian Jaya (now Papua). Some of the worst such violence occurred in the provinces of Maluku and North Maluku, arising from the ongoing conflict between the region's Christian and Muslim populations. By mid-2000 more than 4,000 people were reported to have been killed and some 300,000 displaced. In June President Wahid declared a state of civil emergency in the two provinces and it was announced that around 1,400 of the 10,200 members of the armed forces in the region were to be replaced because they had become involved in the conflict. In the case of at least one outbreak of serious violence it was reported that evidence had emerged of the military's collusion with elements of the militant Muslim paramilitary organization Laskar Jihad, which had travelled to the region to participate in the campaign of violence. On 24 December 18 people were reported to have been killed and more than 80 others injured in a series of bombings of Christian churches in nine towns and cities across Indonesia, including Jakarta. In June 2002 an Iraqi citizen, Omar al-Faruq, who claimed to be the South-East Asian representative of al-Qa'ida, was arrested and allegedly confessed to having participated in carrying out the bombings. Following the bombings in Bali, a senior operative of JI also confessed to involvement in the church attacks. In a television broadcast in April 2004 four Malaysians detained in Indonesia admitted involvement in the church bombings and membership of JI. However, human rights groups claimed that the statements had been obtained through coercion.

Following negotiations between the warring Muslim and Christian factions in Maluku and North Maluku, the 'Malino II Agreement', which urged the expulsion of external groups such as Laskar Jihad from the area, was signed in February 2002. A series of bombings in the city of Ambon between February and April was condemned by the Government, but it insisted that the attacks did not signify the failure of the peace agreement. In the latter month Alex Manuputty, the leader of the Christian separatist organization Front Kedaulatan Maluku (FKM—the Maluku Sovereignty Front), was arrested and charged with treason

for planning to raise a flag to commemorate the 52nd anniversary of the proclamation of the South Maluku Republic. On 25 April FKM members raised flags in Ambon in remembrance of the anniversary, prompting the leader of Laskar Jihad, Ja'far Umar Thalib, to urge all Muslims in the region to renew their war against the Christian community. (In October 14 FKM members were sentenced to terms of imprisonment for raising the flags.) Violence broke out again in Ambon at the end of April, resulting in the deaths of 14 Christians. Thalib was arrested in May and was subsequently charged with inciting hatred and rebellion and defaming the President and Vice-President; he was later acquitted of all charges. In October, following the Bali bombings, Laskar Jihad reportedly disbanded and left the region; Thalib claimed that the decision had been taken owing to the group's increasing political involvement and denied that it had any connection to events in Bali. In January 2003 Manuputty and another Christian leader, Samuel Waileruny, were convicted of subversion and sentenced *in absentia* to three-year prison terms, later increased to four years. Later that year Manuputty fled to the USA; the Government's subsequent request for his deportation to Indonesia was turned down.

In April 2003 supporters of the separatist movement in Maluku were again alleged to have flown flags in commemoration of the anniversary of the proclamation of the South Maluku Republic; more than 120 people were subsequently prosecuted on charges of subversion. However, owing to the relative peace that had been maintained in the province since the signing of the Malino II Agreement, in September it was reported that the Government had revoked the state of civil emergency in Maluku; several battalions of peacekeeping troops would continue to be stationed in the province. The civil emergency status in North Maluku had been revoked in the previous year. In January 2004 nine men were sentenced to prison terms of up to 15 years for membership of the FKM. At least 40 people were killed and around 150 injured in violent clashes in Ambon in April, following a rally by a predominantly Christian separatist group on the island. More than 1,000 police officers and troops were dispatched in an attempt to quell the unrest. In May one person was killed and at least 22 others injured in a series of bomb explosions on Ambon. These events led some observers to question the long-term success of the peace treaty. In November Moses Tuanakotta, an FKM leader, was convicted of subversion and sentenced to nine years in prison for instigating the rally in April.

Meanwhile, in late 2001 violence also broke out on the island of Sulawesi, where ongoing religious tensions had caused approximately 1,000 deaths over the previous two years. In the first week of December at least seven people were killed and thousands left homeless following clashes between armed Muslim groups and Christians. The violence was believed to have been precipitated by the recent arrival of members of Laskar Jihad on the island, and more than 2,000 police and troop reinforcements were sent to the area. A peace agreement was concluded between the involved parties in late December, but explosions at four churches in the capital of Central Sulawesi, Palu, during New Year celebrations highlighted the continuing political instability on the island. In June 2002 a bomb exploded on a bus travelling towards Poso, Central Sulawesi, killing four people, and in December, two bombs exploded in Makassar, the capital of South Sulawesi, resulting in the deaths of three people.

In October 2003 an estimated 11 people died as a result of an outbreak of sectarian violence in Poso. There was speculation that the renewal of violence in Sulawesi had been co-ordinated by JI to coincide with the anniversary of the bombings in Bali. In the following month at least four more people died following an outbreak of anti-Christian violence in the city. In January 2004 a bomb exploded in the town of Palopo, South Sulawesi, killing four people. A subsequent series of attacks in Central Sulawesi included a bomb explosion on a bus in Poso in November 2004, which killed six people, and two explosions in a busy market in the predominantly Christian town of Tentena in May 2005, which claimed the lives of 21 people and injured dozens more. In July 24 alleged members of JI were arrested in connection with these attacks, as well as with the Bali bombings of 2002. In October 2005 religious tensions were further exacerbated in Central Sulawesi by the beheading, allegedly by Islamist militants, of three Christian schoolgirls near Poso. In 2007 six suspected Islamist militants were convicted in connection with the murders and sentenced to terms of imprisonment ranging from 10 to 20 years.

In September 2006 three Christian men were executed following their convictions on charges of inciting an attack on an Islamic school in Poso, in which approximately 200 people had been killed in May 2000. Many Christians alleged that the three men were not the perpetrators of the attack, and demonstrations ensued. In October 2006 a Christian priest who had been one of the leaders of the protests against the executions was shot dead in Palu. In late 2007 several Muslim militants were convicted of carrying out attacks in Central Sulawesi—including the murder of the priest in October 2006 and the Tentena market bombings in May 2005—and were sentenced to lengthy terms in prison.

In April 2011 19 people were arrested on suspicion of planning a terrorist attack on Good Friday, following the discovery of a large unexploded bomb near a Catholic church in Jakarta. A suicide bomb attack at a church in Solo, Central Java, in September claimed the lives of at least two people and injured several others. In April 2012 the authorities in the Singkil region of southern Aceh ordered the closure of 20 Christian churches, and later that year the provincial government demanded the closure of nine more churches and five Buddhist temples. In a further indication of the rising levels of religious intolerance in Indonesia, two members of a minority Shi'a community in Madura, East Java, were killed and more than a dozen wounded in August in an unprovoked attack by several hundred anti-Shi'a fanatics armed with machetes. The previous month the religious leader of Madura's Shi'a community had been sentenced to two years' imprisonment after having been found guilty of blasphemy on the grounds of his religious teachings. Human rights groups claimed that the Indonesian Government was failing adequately to clamp down on the perpetrators of religious violence and that the relatively small number of individuals who were actually convicted of such offences were given overly lenient sentences.

However, in October 2014 the newly installed Government of President Widodo proposed a series of ground-breaking legislative reforms aimed at protecting religious minorities from ill-treatment and giving them equal religious rights (including freedom of worship). Among the proposals were plans to allow people to leave the religious affiliation column on their national identity cards blank and to make it easier for minority groups to obtain permits for building places of worship. Preparation of the draft bill was expected to be completed within six months.

East Timor (Timor-Leste)

During 1974 several parties emerged within the small Portuguese colony of East Timor (which became known as Timor-Leste following its accession to independence on 20 May 2002), with aims ranging from full independence to integration with Indonesia or Australia. Indonesia, which had never presented a claim to East Timor, initially showed little interest in the territory. In 1975 Portuguese forces withdrew from the colony, and the territory's capital, Dili, was occupied by the forces of the left-wing Frente Revolucionária do Timor Leste Independente (Fretilin), which advocated independence for East Timor. To prevent Fretilin from gaining full control of the island of Timor, Indonesian troops intervened and established a provincial government. (In December 2001 the declassification of US state papers relating to the Indonesian occupation revealed that the US Government had endorsed the invasion in the belief that it would curb the spread of communism in the region.) In July 1976 East Timor was declared the 27th province of Indonesia. Human rights organizations subsequently claimed that as many as 200,000 people, from a total population of 650,000, might have been killed by the Indonesian armed forces during the annexation. The UN continued officially to recognize Portugal as the administrative power in East Timor. In February 1983 the UN Commission on Human Rights adopted a resolution affirming East Timor's right to independence and self-determination. In November 1990 the Indonesian Government rejected proposals by the military commander of Fretilin, José Alexandre (Xanana) Gusmão, for unconditional peace negotiations aimed at ending the armed struggle in East Timor. In August 1992 the UN General Assembly adopted its first resolution condemning Indonesia's violations of human rights in East Timor.

Following the downfall of President Suharto, in August 1998 it was announced that Indonesia and Portugal had agreed to hold discussions on the possibility of 'wide-ranging' autonomy for East Timor. In January 1999 the Indonesian Government unexpectedly announced that if the East Timorese voted to reject Indonesia's proposals for autonomy, it would consider granting independence to the province. Although the Government was initially opposed to a referendum on the issue of independence

for East Timor, it signed an agreement with Portugal in May, giving its assent to a process of 'popular consultation' to take the form of a UN-supervised poll. The referendum proceeded on 30 August, and resulted in an overwhelming rejection, by 78.5% of voters, of the Indonesian Government's proposals for autonomy and in an endorsement of independence for East Timor. The announcement of the result of the referendum led to a rapid deterioration in the territory's security situation. In late September Indonesia and Portugal reiterated their agreement for the transfer of authority in East Timor to the UN. Also in late September the Indonesian armed forces formally relinquished responsibility for security in the territory to the UN peacekeeping force, the International Force for East Timor (Interfet); the last Indonesian troops left East Timor in late October. In the same month the result of the referendum was ratified by the Indonesian MPR, thus permitting East Timor's accession to independence to proceed (see Timor-Leste). In September 2000 Indonesia drew criticism from the UN and the international community following the murder of three UN aid workers by pro-Jakarta militias in West Timor. The militia groups were widely believed to be receiving the support of the Indonesia military. In December 2001 10 members of a pro-Indonesia militia became the first individuals to be convicted by the UN-sponsored Special Panel for Serious Crimes (SPSC) in Dili of crimes against humanity in connection with the violence of 1999. However, the Indonesian Government continued to obstruct efforts to bring all those culpable to justice, blocking attempts to extradite an 11th suspect to stand trial.

In January 2002 the Government established a special court in Jakarta to try those suspected of contravening human rights in East Timor in 1999. A total of 18 pro-Jakarta militiamen and Indonesian soldiers were prosecuted by the tribunal, the first trials of which began in March 2002. Prior to its disbandment the tribunal passed just six convictions, prompting widespread international condemnation, with many observers insisting that the acquittal of 12 of the 18 defendants represented a gross miscarriage of justice. The six convicted men included former Governor of East Timor Abílio Soares, who was found guilty of failing to prevent violence involving his subordinates; Eurico Guterres, head of the youth wing of President Megawati's PDI—P; Lt-Col Soejarwo, Indonesia's military commander in Dili in 1999; and Maj.-Gen. Adam Damiri, the most senior military officer to have been charged. However, by August 2004 all six convictions had been overturned.

Meanwhile, in February 2003 the SPSC in Dili indicted Gen. (retd) Wiranto, Abílio Soares and 56 other Indonesian generals for crimes committed in East Timor; the Indonesian Government continued to refuse to hand over any of the accused for trial. The SPSC issued an arrest warrant for Wiranto in May 2004. In December Indonesia and Timor-Leste announced the establishment of a joint Commission of Truth and Friendship (CTF) to investigate human rights violations during the violence in East Timor in 1999. In the previous month the UN Security Council had expressed concern at Indonesia's failure to punish those responsible. The first hearing of the CTF opened on Bali in February 2007. Its 10 members were drawn from both Indonesia and Timor-Leste and included experts in the fields of law and human rights. In its final report, which was published in July 2008, the CTF concluded that the Indonesian Government, military and police bore 'institutional responsibility for gross human rights violations'. President Yudhoyono responded by stating his remorse, but critics were dissatisfied with the lack of a clear apology or of punishment for the perpetrators.

Aceh

In the mid-1970s dissent re-emerged in Aceh, which, at the end of the war of independence, had held the status of a full province of the Republic of Indonesia but which had subsequently had this status removed before being made a 'special district' (Daerah Istimewa) with considerable autonomy in religious and educational affairs. The dissent was provoked by the central Government's exploitation of Aceh's natural resources and the subsequent lack of benefits from these operations received by the region itself. A sense of the erosion of Aceh's autonomy was heightened by the migration and transmigration of other Indonesians into the region and by the increasing power of the central Government, and in 1976 the Gerakan Aceh Merdeka (GAM—Free Aceh Movement) was formed by Hasan di Tiro, who declared independence in 1977. This small-scale rebellion was swiftly suppressed by the armed forces; Tiro later established a government-in-exile in Sweden.

INDONESIA

In 1989 opposition to the central Government arose again, this time led by the National Liberation Front Acheh Sumatra. The region was made a 'military operations zone' in 1990, thus allowing the armed forces far greater freedom to counter the uprising. By mid-1991 the rebellion had been largely suppressed; however, it was estimated that about 1,000 Acehnese had been killed in the process. The number of deaths continued to rise in subsequent years, and in 1993 the human rights organization Amnesty International estimated that about 2,000 Acehnese had been killed since 1989, with hundreds of others having 'disappeared'.

Aceh's status as a 'military operations zone' was revoked in June 1998, following the downfall of President Suharto in May, and an apology for past military excesses was made by Gen. Wiranto. However, the subsequent intended withdrawal of Indonesian troops from the territory was suspended following rioting in Aceh in September. Decentralization measures introduced by President Habibie failed to defuse resentment in the region, and public opinion in Aceh became increasingly sympathetic towards the notion of independence. In 1999 the discovery of several mass graves of people killed by the armed forces during security operations further exacerbated tension in the territory. Violence continued to escalate following the legislative elections in June as GAM guerrillas intensified their campaign for independence for Aceh.

In November 1999, following the rejection by legislators in the regional assembly of demands for the holding of a referendum on self-determination for Aceh, a local government building in western Aceh was set on fire during a demonstration by 5,000 protesters. While much of the ongoing widespread violence in the territory was attributed to the separatist movement, some believed that a degree of the unrest was being initiated by 'provocateurs' acting to destabilize Aceh and undermine the separatist movement. Despite the Indonesian Government and Acehnese rebel negotiators reaching agreement in May 2000 on a ceasefire, which took effect the following month and was subsequently extended indefinitely, violence continued throughout the territory; Acehnese human rights groups estimated that more than 1,000 civilians died in clashes between the Indonesian military and Acehnese rebels during 2000. In December thousands of Acehnese protesters rallied peacefully in Banda Aceh, demanding independence for the territory. However, it was reported that at least 34 (and possibly as many as 200, according to human rights groups) unarmed civilians had been killed in the days preceding the rally as the result of military action to target Acehnese en route to the demonstration.

In April 2001 President Abdurrahman Wahid signed a decree authorizing the security forces to assist the military in restoring law and order in Aceh by targeting armed separatist organizations. This brought an end to the uneasy truce prevailing in the region. In July one of President Megawati's first official actions was to sign into law a special autonomy plan for Aceh intended to assuage the separatist movement. However, while generous in its scope, the legislation was criticized for failing to address the problems posed by the continued military presence in the area. Critics' concerns were borne out when some 30 civilians were massacred on an Aceh palm oil plantation in August. According to GAM, the military had carried out the attack as retribution for an earlier assault on a military post that had left several soldiers dead.

In January 2002 the commander of GAM, Abdullah Syafei, was killed during a gun battle with security forces on Sumatra; six other GAM members also died. Further fighting prompted the Government to resume a separate military command for Aceh, a decision denounced by both GAM and human rights groups. In May, following the instigation of peace discussions in Geneva, Switzerland, the Government and GAM agreed to work towards a ceasefire. However, the violence continued. Aceh's Legal Aid Institute claimed that 771 people had been killed in the region's conflict during the first six months of 2002.

In December 2002 government and GAM representatives finally signed a peace agreement in Geneva. As well as establishing an immediate ceasefire, the deal provided for free elections (to be held in 2004), which would establish an autonomous, although not independent, government, and included the granting of permission by the central Government to the Acehnese authorities to implement partial *Shari'a* law (Aceh's first *Shari'a* court was inaugurated in March 2003). The new regional government would retain 70% of all fuel revenues. In return, all rebels in the territory would disarm in designated areas. Following the signing of the peace accord, international peace

monitors established a Joint Security Committee in Aceh. In February 2003 GAM rebels began surrendering their weapons, but by April the peace agreement was close to collapsing. Offices occupied by the international monitors had been attacked and, in one instance, burned down. At peace talks held in May in Tokyo, Japan, GAM negotiators refused to accept the Government's demands that the movement abandon its goal of independence, accept a special autonomy agreement and complete the disarmament of its forces. President Megawati immediately authorized the imposition of martial law in Aceh, initially for a six-month period, and the recommencement of military action against GAM. Owing to the restrictions placed on media reporting of the conflict, little independent information was available as to its progress throughout the succeeding months. In November the Government announced that it would extend its military operations in Aceh indefinitely, prompting international criticism. In December a bomb exploded at a market in the eastern town of Pereulak, killing 10 people.

The Government downgraded the status of martial law in Aceh to a state of civil emergency in May 2004, restoring power to the civilian Governor. The security forces, which were to remain in the territory, claimed to have killed some 2,000 suspected GAM rebels and arrested a further 3,000 since launching the military offensive against the separatist movement a year earlier. Human rights groups alleged that at least 300 of those killed had been civilians. In November President Yudhoyono extended the state of civil emergency in Aceh by up to six months and, during a visit to the territory, offered an amnesty to all GAM rebels who surrendered their weapons.

Following the tsunami disaster that devastated Aceh in December 2004, GAM and the Government agreed to an informal ceasefire to facilitate relief efforts. In mid-January 2005, however, the Chief of Staff of the Army announced that during the previous two weeks the security forces had killed 120 GAM rebels who had been stealing aid intended for victims of the tsunamis; GAM dismissed the claims of theft. None the less, the natural disaster appeared to have provided a new impetus for GAM and the Indonesian Government to seek a resolution to their conflict, and in late January formal talks between the two sides were held in Helsinki, Finland. After several rounds of negotiations, the two sides reached agreement in July upon the terms of a draft accord, which was formally signed on 15 August. GAM agreed to give up its long-standing claims for independence and the Indonesian Government was to allow GAM to operate as an official political party, a concession that would require constitutional change (existing laws decreed that all political parties be based in Jakarta and that branches be maintained in at least one-half of the country's then 33 provinces). Furthermore, as agreed in 2002, Aceh was to be allocated up to 70% of the revenues earned from the exploitation of its natural resources (including petroleum and natural gas). In late August 2005 the Indonesian authorities released approximately 200 Acehnese detainees, including four senior GAM members, and the Government began a phased withdrawal of its 24,000 troops based in the region; by the end of the year almost 10,000 troops had departed. Meanwhile, GAM effected a process of complete disarmament within three months of the signing of the agreement. In July 2006 legislation was introduced granting Aceh partial autonomy and allowing for the formation of political parties in the territory. Although GAM agreed to its terms, critics argued that the law was strongly biased in favour of the central Government, which was to monitor all the affairs of the Acehnese administration; furthermore, management of petroleum and gas in Aceh was to be conducted jointly by the regional administration and the central Government.

In December 2006 Aceh held its first direct gubernatorial and district elections, formally marking the culmination of the peace process. The polls, which attracted a turnout of 85%, passed without incident. Irwandi Yusuf, an independent candidate and former GAM spokesman, secured the position of regional Governor, obtaining 38% of the total votes cast. In the same month the Indonesian Government finalized draft legislation providing for the establishment of local political parties in Aceh, although candidates would only be allowed to stand for seats within the House of Representatives in Jakarta if they secured the support of national parties and would be required to relinquish membership of their local party once nominated. In October 2008 Hasan di Tiro, the founder of GAM, returned to Aceh, thereby ending three decades of self-imposed exile; he died in June 2010. Zaini Abdullah, the former GAM 'foreign minister', was elected as Aceh's second Governor in gubernatorial and district elections held in April 2012, securing nearly 56% of the votes cast, and defeating the incumbent Yusuf (who won some 29% of the vote) and three other candidates. In March 2013 the Acehnese authorities approved the use of the former GAM flag as the official flag of Aceh, prompting tensions with the central Government, which subsequently demanded that the flag be changed on the grounds that it violated a law banning separatist symbols. A report published by Amnesty International in April claimed that the failure of the central Government to establish a 'truth commission' to investigate alleged human rights abuses perpetrated by both sides during the conflict between GAM and the Indonesian military constituted a breach of the commitments made under the 2005 peace accord. In December 2013 the newly elected Wali Nanggroe ('guardian of the state') of Aceh, Malik Mahmud al-Haytar, who was reportedly a former leader of GAM, was inaugurated as the head of a new bureaucracy set up to safeguard Acehnese culture and values.

Three local parties from Aceh were authorized to take part in the general election of 9 April 2014, in accordance with the 2005 peace agreement. Both the dominant local party, the Partai Aceh (PA), which controlled the provincial assembly in Aceh, and Yusuf's Partai Nasional Aceh (PNA) comprised many former GAM combatants. Rivalry between the PA and the PNA led to the deaths of several people in politically motivated violence during the campaign period. As local parties were unable to field candidates at national level, the PA formed an alliance with Gerindra to contest the national elections. (In the 2009 elections it had allied itself with Yudhoyono's PD.)

Papua

In May 1977 a rebellion in the province of Irian Jaya (annexed to Indonesia in 1963—see *Historical Context*) was reported to have been staged by the Organisasi Papua Merdeka (OPM—Free Papua Movement), which sought unification with PNG. Fighting continued until December 1979, when Indonesia and PNG finalized a new border administrative agreement. However, frequent border incidents ensued, and in early 1984 fighting broke out in Jayapura, the capital of Irian Jaya. As a result, about 10,000 refugees fled over the border into PNG. In October Indonesia and PNG signed a five-year agreement establishing a joint border security committee; at the end of 1985 Indonesians were continuing to cross into PNG, but a limited number of repatriations took place in 1986. There was also concern among native Irian Jayans (who are of Melanesian origin) at the introduction of large numbers of Javanese into the province, under the central Government's transmigration scheme. This was interpreted as an attempt to reduce the Melanesians to a minority and thus to stifle opposition. In 1986 it was announced that the Government intended to resettle 65m. people over a 20-year period, despite protests by human rights and conservation groups. Relations with PNG improved when the Prime Minister, Paias Wingti, visited Suharto in January 1988. However, cross-border action by the Indonesian armed forces during October and November, in an attempt to capture Melanesian separatists operating on the border, led to renewed tension between the two countries. In October 1990 the Governments of Indonesia and PNG renewed the basic accord on joint border security arrangements. In September 1992 the two countries agreed to facilitate the passage of border trade, and in the following month an Indonesian consulate was established in Vanimo, PNG.

In April 1995 the Australian Council for Overseas Aid (ACFOA) alleged that 37 Irian Jayans had been killed by security forces near the copper and gold mine operated by PT Freeport Indonesia (a subsidiary of the US conglomerate Freeport-McMoran) between June 1994 and February 1995. In August the ACFOA's claims were reiterated by NGOs, which lodged a complaint with the National Commission on Human Rights in Jakarta about summary executions, arbitrary detentions and torture in the province between mid-1994 and mid-1995. In November 1995 four members of the Indonesian armed forces were arrested in an investigation into the killing in May of 11 unarmed civilians at a prayer meeting. The widespread perception that Freeport bore a large degree of responsibility for the situation in Irian Jaya arose from its role as civil administrator in the area of the mine and also because the indigenous inhabitants' campaigns against Freeport's indiscriminate exploitation of natural resources in the area often resulted in their being killed by security forces as suspected members of the OPM.

In December 1995 clashes between Indonesian forces and the OPM intensified, forcing hundreds of refugees to cross into PNG. Four people were killed in riots in Jayapura in March 1996. Riots near the Grasberg mine in the same month were the result of

problems similar to those experienced by residents in the area around the Freeport mine (relating principally to the lack of any benefit from the mining project to the local community and to the potential adverse impact of the project on the local environment). There were also tensions among the local Irianese, Indonesians from other provinces and commercial operators. In April Freeport agreed to allocate 1% of revenue over a period of 10 years to community development programmes for tribal groups living around the mine, and to improve environmental safeguards.

Seven people were reported to have been killed in outbreaks of violence in Jayapura and the island of Biak in July 1998. In October the Government revoked the status of Irian Jaya as a 'military operations zone' following the conclusion of a ceasefire agreement with the OPM in September, but this was not followed by the withdrawal of troops from the region. In February 1999 Irian Jayan tribal leaders raised the issue of independence for the province at a meeting with President Habibie. (A referendum on self-determination for the province had been promised by the Indonesian Government prior to the territory's annexation in 1963; however, while a vote was eventually held in 1969, only tribal chiefs selected by Jakarta were allowed to participate and the result was widely discredited.) The independence movement in the province continued to strengthen throughout 1999, and was encouraged by the achievements of the East Timorese independence movement. In December independence demonstrations took place throughout Irian Jaya. A delegation from the DPR visited the province and announced that the administration of the newly elected President Abdurrahman Wahid had agreed to the popular demand that the province's name be changed from Irian Jaya to West Papua, although it was emphasized that this decision should not be construed as implying the Government's approval of any action towards the province's secession from Indonesia. (However, it was subsequently reported that the proposed change had not been approved by the Indonesian legislature.)

In mid-2000 the Papuan People's Congress, held in Jayapura, adopted a five-point resolution reinstating a unilateral declaration of independence for West Papua originally made in 1961, before the province's annexation to Indonesia. However, the declaration was immediately rebuffed by the Indonesian Government. In October 2000 30–40 people were killed and many others injured in clashes between police and West Papuan separatists in the town of Wamena when police attempted to remove a Morning Star independence flag being flown by the separatists. Although President Wahid had previously decreed that the flying of the Morning Star flag was allowed, provided that the flag was flown alongside, and slightly lower than, the Indonesian flag, following the violence the Government introduced a ban on the flying of the controversial flag. In November and December the Indonesian military severely clamped down on the separatists; seven people were shot dead by the armed forces in an outbreak of violence in the town of Merauke, and dozens of separatist sympathizers, including the pro-independence leader of the Presidium Dewan Papua (PDP—Papua Presidium Council), Theys Eluay, were arrested.

In March 2001 five West Papuan separatist leaders, including Eluay, were released on bail to await trial on charges of treason. In October the DPR approved legislation giving Irian Jaya greater autonomy and a larger share of tax revenues. Furthermore, the so-called Special Autonomy Law for Papua also proposed that the region be officially known as Papua and provided for a bicameral Papuan People's Council, intended to safeguard indigenous interests. However, the separatist PDP swiftly rejected the legislation as it failed to grant Irian Jaya complete independence. In November Eluay was found dead in his car. He was believed to have been assassinated and military involvement was suspected. In December hundreds of students occupied the parliament building in Jayapura to demand a referendum on independence and to express their anger at the authorities' failure to find the killer of Eluay. The protest took place just days before the autonomy reforms came into force on 1 January 2002, when the province officially became known as Papua.

In August 2002 two US citizens and an Indonesian were killed following an ambush near the Freeport mine. In November it was alleged by police that Kopassus soldiers had been involved in the attack. (In June 2004 the US authorities indicted *in absentia* Anthonius Wamang, an Indonesian, for murdering the two US citizens, describing him as an operational commander for the OPM, although human rights groups reportedly claimed that Wamang had close links to the Kopassus special forces.) In April 2003 four Kopassus officers and three soldiers were convicted of the abduction, torture and murder of Eluay and were sentenced to short prison terms. The trial was criticized both for the leniency of the sentences and for its failure fully to investigate the reasons behind the murder of Eluay. Meanwhile, in January 2003 the central Government approved legislation to divide Papua into three smaller provinces—Central Papua, East Papua and West Irian Jaya. The proposal angered local leaders, who claimed that such action would threaten the region's autonomy. Following reports that six people had died during fighting in Timika, the designated capital of Central Papua, the formal creation of Central Papua was postponed. However, the appointment of a Governor for West Irian Jaya was approved in November. In November 2004 the Constitutional Court simultaneously overruled the law dividing Papua province into three and ratified the creation of the province of West Irian Jaya (which was formally renamed West Papua—or Papua Barat—in April 2007) as an established fact; the original province of Papua was, therefore, now composed of two constituent parts—the provinces of West Irian Jaya and Papua. Meanwhile, in the latter half of 2003 it was reported that 10 members of the OPM had been killed in clashes with government troops in Papua. In December the appointment of Brig.-Gen. Timbul Silaen to the post of regional police commander was criticized by the USA, owing to Silaen's indictment for crimes against humanity in East Timor. In March 2004 it was reported that Leo Warisman, a leader of the OPM, had been killed in a gunfight with security forces in Papua. Another OPM leader, Yance Hembring, was sentenced to 10 years' imprisonment by a court in Jayapura in August for advocating Papua's independence. In December at least five people were injured and 18 arrested during violent clashes between protesters and police at a pro-independence rally in Jayapura.

In October 2005 the Papuan People's Council (Majelis Rakyat Papua—MRP) was formally established; it was charged primarily with the issue of the partition of Papua and with the forthcoming gubernatorial elections. Originally scheduled to be held in November, the elections were twice postponed, owing to poor administrative planning, but finally proceeded in March 2006. Barnabas Suebu was subsequently pronounced Governor of Papua. Meanwhile, in January more than 200 demonstrators forced their way into the local legislative building and demanded the immediate withdrawal of all Indonesian military personnel from the province. In February the Minister of Defence, Juwono Sudarsono, conceded that some members of the Indonesian military and police force had committed human rights abuses, including torture and rape, against local residents in Papua. In the same month the Constitutional Court officially reaffirmed the legitimacy of West Irian Jaya's status as a separate province, maintaining that the 2001 Special Autonomy Law for Papua could not be applied retroactively. In March 2006 five members of the security forces were killed in Jayapura by demonstrators reiterating demands for the closure of the Freeport mine, which continued to be regarded locally as a symbol of oppression, and in the following month four people, including two soldiers, were killed in an assault on an army post in Papua.

In February 2007 the international NGO Human Rights Watch drew attention to the continued imprisonment of 18 Papuan activists, who were reported to have received substantial sentences following their peaceful protests in support of Papuan self-determination. The organization urged the Indonesian Government to release these prisoners and to abandon charges against other political detainees who had yet to be brought to trial. In July Human Rights Watch accused the Papuan police force of perpetrating, with apparent impunity, extrajudicial killings and other serious abuses.

A number of people were killed and dozens injured during several days of fighting in October 2007 between rival tribal groups near the Freeport mine. The mine was the scene of another attack, in July 2009, when an Indonesian police officer and an Australian security guard were fatally shot in an attack attributed by the police to the OPM (although subsequent revelations cast doubt on this theory and the OPM denied any involvement). In December a senior leader of the OPM, Kelly Kwalik, who the authorities claimed had been involved in a series of attacks, including the 2002 Freeport ambush, was killed during a police operation in Timika; his death prompted a wave of anti-Indonesian protests and demands for self-determination for Papuans. A three-month strike by employees at the Freeport mine in late 2011, which severely hindered production, was finally concluded in December after the company agreed to a substantial increase in wages and improved staff benefits.

Meanwhile, in June 2010 the lower house of the MRP voted to reject Special Autonomy status for Papua. In July an estimated 50,000 Papuans took to the streets of Jayapura, and urged the upper house of the provincial legislature to endorse the decision. Demands for full autonomy intensified following the release on the internet in October of a video recording showing two members of the Indonesian army torturing indigenous Papuan civilians; in January 2011 a military tribunal sentenced the two men, as well as their sergeant, to short prison terms.

In August 2011 thousands of Papuans marched on the parliament building in Jayapura, demanding the holding of a referendum on the question of Papuan self-determination. In October Indonesian troops fired tear gas and warning shots at members of the Third Papuan People's Congress gathered in Abepura and arrested dozens of attendees; the authorities claimed that the Congress had issued a declaration of independence and announced the formation of a transitional government for Papua. Although it was reported that three people had been killed, the authorities denied that there had been any casualties. The trial of five activists accused of treason in connection with the incident began in January 2012; having been convicted in March, they each received sentences of three years' imprisonment. The situation in Papua remained tense throughout the remainder of the year and into 2013, with a series of violent incidents reportedly taking place between separatists and the security forces. The OPM was widely believed to have been responsible for the deaths of eight soldiers in two separate attacks on military posts in the Puncak Jaya district in February 2013. According to Australian media reports, at least 11 OPM supporters were killed by Indonesian counter-terrorist troops in a village in the central highlands of Papua in May. It was reported that in November at least one person was killed and others injured when Indonesian police opened fire on a crowd of around 800 demonstrators in Jayapura. The protest had been staged by the Komite Nasional Papua Barat (KNPB—West Papua National Committee), which demanded the holding of a referendum on Papuan independence. In February 2014 five men who had been arrested in May 2013 for raising the banned Morning Star flag at a ceremony commemorating the 50th anniversary of Indonesia's annexation of West Papua were sentenced to terms of imprisonment ranging from 22 months to three years. Several violent clashes between the security forces and separatists were reported during 2014, resulting in a number of fatalities on both sides.

During an official visit to Indonesia by Prime Minister Peter O'Neill of PNG in June 2013, the two countries signed a controversial extradition treaty, which, some claimed, would be used by Indonesia primarily to demand the extradition of separatist activists from Papua province seeking refuge in PNG.

Foreign Affairs

Regional relations

Indonesia's foreign policy has focused on its leading role in the regional grouping of the Association of Southeast Asian Nations (ASEAN, see p. 210), which it founded, together with Malaysia, the Philippines, Singapore and Thailand, in 1967. Indonesia supported the organization's opposition to Viet Nam's military presence in Cambodia and played a prominent role in attempts to find a political solution to the situation in Cambodia (q.v.). In 1989 Indonesia was also one of the founding members of the Asia-Pacific Economic Cooperation (APEC, see p. 200). In October 2008 Indonesia became the final member state to ratify the ASEAN charter, which declared among its purposes the promotion of democracy and good governance, and the creation of a single market. Indonesia assumed the annually rotating chair of ASEAN in 2011. At the ASEAN summit meeting held in Bali in November, President Susilo Bambang Yudhoyono asserted that the regional grouping had recorded a number of positive developments under Indonesia's chairmanship, including the signing of the Bali Declaration on the ASEAN Community in a Global Community of Nations (commonly known as the Bali Concord III), which pledged increased co-operation in the fields of, *inter alia*, politics, security, economics and culture, at both regional and global level; the agreement also defined development issues pertaining to the implementation, by 2015, of an ASEAN Economic Community and the promotion of ASEAN's full integration into the global economy. The 25th summit meeting of APEC was held in Bali in October 2013.

Diplomatic relations with China, suspended since 1967 owing to its alleged complicity in the 1965 attempted coup in Indonesia, were finally restored in 1990 following an Indonesian undertaking to settle financial debts incurred with China by the Sukarno regime. Bilateral relations suffered a reverse in 1998 following the violence perpetrated against ethnic Chinese Indonesians at the time of the removal of President Suharto in May. China issued a strong diplomatic protest; President Habibie publicly expressed his sympathy for the plight of the ethnic Chinese victims of violence. In May 1999, as part of a programme of general reform, Habibie removed a ban on the use and teaching of the Mandarin Chinese language within Indonesia. The two countries signed a strategic partnership agreement, intended to promote bilateral trade, investment and maritime co-operation, in April 2005; a further agreement, aimed at enhancing co-operation in the political, legal and security fields, was signed in January 2010. Between 2003 and 2010 Sino-Indonesian bilateral trade increased almost tenfold. The strengthening ties between Indonesia and China were clearly illustrated when, during a visit to Jakarta in October 2013, the new Chinese President, Xi Jinping, became the first foreign political leader ever to address the Indonesian legislature. Joko Widodo's first official visit abroad following his assumption of the Indonesian presidency was to the Chinese capital of Beijing in November 2014 to attend the APEC annual summit. During his visit, Widodo held talks with both President Xi Jinping and the Chinese Premier, Li Keqiang.

Indonesia and Australia restored defence co-operation links in April 1990, following a four-year hiatus. In September 1994 Vice-President Try Sutrisno became the first senior Indonesian official to visit Australia since Suharto's final visit in 1975. However, in the latter half of the 1990s relations between the two countries were strained by Australia's decision to investigate claims of new evidence about the killing of six Australia-based journalists, in two separate incidents, during the annexation of East Timor in 1975. The Indonesian Government claimed that the journalists had died in crossfire. However, separate reports published by the Australian Government, in June 1996, and by Switzerland-based human rights organization International Commission of Jurists, in 1998, concluded that the journalists had been killed by Indonesian troops, in order to conceal Indonesia's invasion of East Timor; in October 1998 it was announced that Australia was to reopen a judicial inquiry into the killings. In November 2007 the Australian judiciary ruled that five of the journalists (the 'Balibo five') had been deliberately killed by Indonesian special forces, declaring that there was sufficient evidence for the case to constitute a war crime.

Meanwhile, in October 1996 the Australia-Indonesia Development Area was created to develop bilateral economic links, and in March 1997 Indonesia and Australia signed a treaty defining permanent maritime boundaries between the two countries. Following the downfall of Suharto in May 1998, relations between Indonesia and Australia continued to be affected by the issue of East Timor. In January 1999 the Indonesian Government expressed its 'deep regret' at Australia's announcement earlier in that month that it was to change its policy on East Timor and actively promote 'self-determination' in the territory. Following the vote in favour of independence held in East Timor in August, Australia committed 4,500 peacekeeping troops to Interfet, which was formed by the UN to restore order in the territory following the violence perpetrated by pro-Jakarta militias after the announcement of the result of the poll. A military co-operation agreement signed between Indonesia and Australia in December 1995 was reported, in October 1999, to have been cancelled as a result of the Indonesian Government's displeasure at Australia's leading involvement in the peacekeeping operation.

In November 2000 the Australian ambassador to Indonesia was physically attacked by a pro-Jakarta mob in Makassar, Sulawesi. The Australian Government accepted the Indonesian Government's apology for the incident. In June 2001 President Abdurrahman Wahid paid an official visit to Australia, the first by an Indonesian head of state for 26 years. In August the Australian Prime Minister, John Howard, became the first foreign leader to make an official visit to Indonesia following President Megawati's assumption of power.

However, relations were strained once again later in August 2001 when a cargo ship carrying hundreds of mainly Afghan asylum seekers became stranded in the international waters between the two countries. Neither country agreed to accept responsibility for the refugees. In September the Australian Minister for Foreign Affairs, Alexander Downer, arrived in Jakarta for discussions with Indonesian ministers on the problems caused by illegal trafficking of immigrants. In October more

than 350 refugees, believed to be heading for Australia, drowned when their boat sank off the Indonesian coast, and in the same month a missing boat carrying approximately 170 Iraqi and Afghan asylum seekers was found on the Indonesian island of Wera. In February 2002 Indonesia and Australia co-hosted the inaugural 'Bali Process' regional ministerial summit on people-smuggling, human-trafficking and related transnational crime. (Four further such summit meetings were co-hosted by Indonesia and Australia between 2003 and 2013, by which time more than 50 countries, as well as numerous international organizations, were participating in the 'Bali Process'.)

Both the Speaker of the DPR and the Speaker of the MPR cancelled scheduled meetings with Howard during his visit to Indonesia in February 2002; during the Australian Prime Minister's stay, students protested in response to allegations that Australia was providing funding for separatist groups in Aceh and Papua. Howard denied such charges and signed an agreement with President Megawati concerning counter-terrorism measures. In May, following an initiative proposed during Howard's visit, the inaugural Australia-Indonesia dialogue was held in Bogor, where Minister of Foreign Affairs Hassan Wirajuda met with his Australian counterpart, Downer.

In October 2002 Indonesia's relations with Australia were seriously affected by the bomb attacks on the island of Bali, a popular destination for Australian tourists, which resulted in the deaths of almost 90 Australian citizens. While the Australian Government immediately offered assistance to Indonesia, a subsequent series of raids on the homes of Indonesian Muslims resident in Australia prompted Vice-President Hamzah Haz to warn that such an offensive could damage bilateral relations. In February 2004 Australia and Indonesia co-hosted the Bali Regional Ministerial Meeting on Counter-Terrorism on Bali; a second such conference was co-hosted by the two countries in Jakarta in March 2007. In December 2004, however, bilateral relations were strained by the Australian Government's announcement that it was to create a coastal security zone extending five times as far as its territorial waters.

Following the tsunami disaster of December 2004, Australia dispatched some 1,000 troops to assist with relief operations in the province of Aceh and pledged US $773m. in aid to the Indonesian Government. Prime Minister Howard visited Aceh in February 2005. In the same month, however, the lenience of Abu Bakar Bashir's sentence for his role in the 2002 Bali bombings (see *The Threat of Terrorism*) was heavily criticized by the Australian Government. In April 2005 President Yudhoyono and Prime Minister Howard signed a Joint Declaration on Comprehensive Partnership, which addressed economic, trade, security and reconstruction issues.

Indonesia's relations with Australia were threatened in February 2006 by the conviction of the 'Bali nine'—a group of nine Australians who had been arrested by the Indonesian authorities in April 2005 for attempting to smuggle a large quantity of heroin into Australia from the Indonesian island. The two ringleaders of the group were sentenced to death by firing squad, while the seven drugs couriers were all sentenced to life imprisonment. At March 2015 the two ringleaders, having lost a number of judicial appeals, were awaiting execution. The Indonesian Government declined a request made by the Australian Minister for Foreign Affairs that month for a prisoner transfer arrangement to allow the two to serve prison terms in Australia. Appeals for clemency had been rejected in January by President Widodo, who appeared to be escalating the use of executions to deter drugs-trafficking. An unofficial four-year moratorium on executions had ended in May 2013, with the execution of three convicted murderers. In January 2015 the first six executions took place under Widodo's leadership (see below).

In January 2006 a dispute arose over the case of 43 Papuans who had fled to Australia by boat in search of asylum; the refugees claimed that in Papua they had been tortured while imprisoned without charge, and that they had witnessed the shooting of friends and relatives. Following the Australian Government's announcement in March that all but one of the asylum seekers were to be granted temporary visas, Indonesia recalled its ambassador from Canberra, accusing Australia of tacitly supporting the Papuan separatist movement. The ambassador returned to Australia in June, prior to Prime Minister Howard's visit to the Indonesian island of Batam to meet with President Yudhoyono, and in July the remaining detainee was finally granted a temporary visa.

In November 2006 Indonesian Minister of Foreign Affairs Wirajuda and his Australian counterpart, Downer, signed a security pact to promote co-operation in law enforcement and counter-terrorism. Yudhoyono met with the new Australian Prime Minister, Kevin Rudd, during the latter's visit to Indonesia in June 2008, when the two leaders agreed to collaborate in the areas of defence, the economy and the environment. Relations were further consolidated by a number of senior-level bilateral visits during 2010, including that of Yudhoyono to Australia in March, and a reciprocal visit by Prime Minister Julia Gillard (who had replaced Rudd in June) in November. The two countries drew up a disaster management plan in late 2011 to help co-ordinate the region's response to natural disasters. Negotiations on a proposed Indonesia-Australia Comprehensive Economic Partnership Agreement commenced in Jakarta in September 2012. In November Prime Minister Gillard organized an historic trilateral meeting in Bali between herself, President Yudhoyono and the Prime Minister of Timor-Leste, Kay Rala (Xanana) Gusmão, on the sidelines of the fifth annual Bali Democracy Forum.

Following his resumption of the Australian premiership in June 2013, Prime Minister Rudd travelled to Indonesia to hold talks with President Yudhoyono, including on the pressing issue of people-smuggling and deepening trade ties. In response to the recent sharp increase in asylum seekers arriving in Australia via Indonesia, Yudhoyono offered to host a regional meeting—involving countries of origin, transit and destination—to address the problem. However, relations between Indonesia and Australia soured somewhat when, shortly after assuming power in September, the new Australian Prime Minister, Tony Abbott, announced that asylum seekers setting out for Australia from Indonesia by boat would now be intercepted en route by the Australian navy and returned to their point of departure. The Indonesian authorities claimed that such action could potentially constitute a violation of their country's sovereignty. During an official visit by Abbott to Jakarta in late September (notably, his first official foreign visit) the new Australian Prime Minister attempted to assuage these concerns by stressing that his country respected Indonesia's sovereignty and territorial integrity. Relations deteriorated markedly in November, however, following allegations that Australian embassies (including that in Jakarta) had been used as part of a US-led spying network in Asia; the Australian Government declined to comment on the reports, which were based on leaked official US documents. In the wake of further revelations later that month that Australian espionage agencies had monitored the telephone calls of President Yudhoyono, his wife, Vice-President Boediono and other senior ministers in 2009, the Indonesian ambassador to Australia was recalled and Indonesia suspended co-ordinated military co-operation (including anti-people-smuggling operations) with Australia. In January 2014 the Indonesian authorities claimed that the Australian navy had violated Indonesia's sovereignty on several occasions during operations to turn back boats carrying asylum seekers. However, the normalization of relations between the two countries was signalled in August by their signing an intelligence code of conduct. In November the Australian authorities clamped down further on asylum seekers by introducing a new policy whereby anyone registering as a refugee with the UN High Commissioner for Refugees in Indonesia on or after 1 July 2014 would no longer be eligible for resettlement in Australia. The Australian Minister for Immigration and Border Protection further angered human rights groups by also announcing that from 2015 his country's annual intake of refugees from Indonesia would be reduced to 450 individuals; around 1,400 refugees were accepted in 2014.

The forced repatriation in early 1998 of thousands of Indonesian workers from Malaysia as a result of the regional economic crisis placed a strain on relations between the two countries. Relations were further exacerbated in October when the Indonesian Government condemned the treatment received in custody by the former Malaysian Deputy Prime Minister and Minister of Finance, Anwar Ibrahim (see Malaysia), breaking with a tradition among ASEAN countries of non-interference in the internal affairs of other member countries. In May 2002 Indonesia signed a trilateral security pact with Malaysia and the Philippines, enabling the signatories to exchange intelligence and launch joint police operations to combat terrorism in the region; Cambodia and Thailand later also acceded to the agreement.

In August 2002 relations with Malaysia were affected by that country's introduction of stringent anti-immigration laws, which resulted in the forced deportation of many illegal immigrants, most of whom were Indonesian, and provoked protests outside the Malaysian embassy in Jakarta. In early February 2005 Malaysia extended an amnesty for illegal immigrants to leave the country if they were to avoid legal action, in response to a written request from President Yudhoyono. In the same month Yudhoyono visited both Malaysia and Singapore to meet with Malaysian Prime Minister Abdullah Badawi and Singaporean Prime Minister Lee Hsien Loong; this was the first visit to Singapore by an Indonesian head of state since 1974. In April 2007 Indonesia concluded agreements with Singapore relating to extradition and defence co-operation.

Indonesia's relations with both Malaysia and Singapore were placed under considerable strain in mid-2013 as a result of the record high levels of air pollution experienced in the two countries caused by a persistent smog from the fires used in illegal land-clearing practices in Sumatra. President Yudhoyono offered an official apology to both countries for the hazardous haze and stated that extensive efforts were being made to extinguish the fires. In May 2014, following some 20 years of negotiations, the ministers responsible for foreign affairs of Indonesia and the Philippines signed an historic agreement defining the maritime borders of the two countries' exclusive economic zones where they overlap in the Mindanao and Celebes Seas.

Meanwhile, in May 2002 President Megawati attracted criticism when she attended celebrations in Timor-Leste to mark the territory's official accession to nation status; in February Indonesia and East Timor had agreed to establish full diplomatic relations following independence. The inaugural meeting of the Indonesia-Timor-Leste Joint Ministerial Commission for Bilateral Co-operation took place in Jakarta in October. In April 2005, during an official visit to Timor-Leste, President Yudhoyono met with Timorese President Gusmão; the two heads of state signed a border agreement concluding the demarcation of approximately 96% of the land borders between the two countries.

Indonesia signed an important free trade agreement with Japan in August 2007 during a state visit by Prime Minister Shinzo Abe to Jakarta. The agreement envisaged the eventual removal of most bilateral import taxes (with the notable exception of Japanese imports of rice). Indonesia also confirmed its supplies of liquefied natural gas to Japan. The Japan-Indonesia Economic Partnership Agreement entered into force in July 2008.

Other external relations

In response to the Dili massacre in November 1991, the US Congress imposed a ban on International Military Education and Training (IMET) to Indonesia in 1992; in March 1996 the ban was relaxed to allow members of ABRI, excluding military officers, to attend IMET courses. However, in September 1999 US President Bill Clinton announced the suspension of military assistance to Indonesia following ABRI's 'campaign of destruction' in East Timor. Later that month the US Senate passed legislation banning all military co-operation, including IMET, for Indonesia until that country honoured the results of the August 1999 referendum and allowed independence to be granted to East Timor. In October/November 2000 Muslim groups rallied outside the US embassy in Jakarta, calling for *jihad*; threats were made against US citizens in Indonesia; US companies in the country were attacked; and it was reported that the Indonesian Government had requested the immediate removal and replacement of the recently appointed US ambassador, Robert Gelbard, for his alleged interference in Indonesian domestic affairs.

President Megawati visited Washington, DC, in September 2001, becoming the first leader of a predominantly Muslim country to meet with US President George W. Bush in the aftermath of the terrorist attacks of 11 September 2001; the two heads of state issued a joint statement in which they agreed to 'strengthen bilateral co-operation on counter-terrorism'. However, following the commencement of air strikes against the Taliban regime in Afghanistan in October, fundamentalist Muslims in Indonesia threatened violence if the Indonesian Government did not sever diplomatic relations with the USA. In October the Front Pembela Islam (FPI—Islamic Defenders' Front) warned that if British and US citizens did not leave the country immediately their safety could not be guaranteed. Megawati, under pressure from Muslim groups and Vice-President Hamzah Haz, indirectly condemned the US attacks in Afghanistan for the first time.

In April 2002 Indonesia and the USA held sensitive security talks, during which measures to combat terrorism and to strengthen civilian control over the armed forces were discussed.

In July the US Senate voted to remove restrictions on the provision of IMET to Indonesia, pending congressional approval. In August, during a visit to Indonesia, US Secretary of State Colin Powell granted some $50m. of funding for Indonesia's police and counter-terrorism units over a three-year period. However, following the murders in the same month of two US citizens in Papua and the 'insufficient co-operation' with the resultant investigation on the part of the Indonesian Government and military, the US Congress voted against the restoration of normal military relations, including any further relaxation of IMET. In early 2003 the USA placed Indonesia on a list of countries whose citizens were required to register with the US immigration authorities if they visited the country. Nevertheless, in October President Bush visited Indonesia and announced plans for a $157m. programme to improve education in the country in an attempt to create a system that would discourage the development of Islamist extremism.

The USA took an active part in relief operations in Indonesia following the tsunami disaster of December 2004, notably deploying some 13,000 military personnel in the region. In February 2005 US Secretary of State Condoleezza Rice announced a full resumption of IMET for Indonesia (although this excluded the training of Indonesia's élite special forces, Kopassus), stating that Indonesian co-operation in the investigation of the two murdered US citizens in Papua had 'met the conditions set by Congress'. In May President Yudhoyono made an official visit to the USA, during which he held talks with President Bush covering a wide range of issues. In November military bilateral relations between the two countries were normalized when the USA resumed Foreign Military Financing for Indonesia and the export to that country of lethal defence articles (having done likewise with non-lethal defence articles in the previous month).

The election in November 2008 of US President Barack Obama, who had lived in Indonesia for several years during childhood, was warmly welcomed by the Indonesian Government and public alike. In February 2009 the new US Secretary of State, Hillary Clinton, visited Indonesia, holding discussions with Indonesian Minister of Foreign Affairs Wirajuda on a number of issues, including security, trade and counter-terrorism. In June 2010 Indonesia and the USA signed the Framework Arrangement on Cooperative Activities in the Field of Defense, a wide-ranging agreement that was intended to integrate existing collaboration between the two countries.

In July 2010 US Secretary of Defense Robert Gates announced that the USA was gradually to resume the training of Kopassus, owing to positive reforms within Indonesia's military. Human Rights Watch and other rights organizations expressed reservations about the announcement, claiming that individuals still active within Kopassus were guilty of human rights transgressions and did not appear likely ever to be brought to justice. During a short visit to Indonesia by Obama in the course of a tour of Asia in November, the US President emphasized Indonesia's global importance as a rising economic power, while appealing for increased co-operation in efforts to address the challenge posed by religious extremism. In September 2012, as part of an extensive tour of South-East Asia, US Secretary of State Clinton held talks with President Yudhoyono and her Indonesian counterpart in Jakarta.

Meanwhile, in December 1999, with the issue of the status of East Timor having been resolved, Indonesia and Portugal formally re-established full diplomatic relations. In August 1995 Queen Beatrix of the Netherlands, the former colonial power in Indonesia, visited Indonesia (the first Dutch monarch to do so for 24 years) and spoke of her regret for the suffering caused to Indonesians by Dutch rule. In December 2011 the Dutch Government extended a formal apology for a massacre perpetrated by its soldiers in the Indonesian village of Rawagede (subsequently renamed Balongsari) in 1947, which claimed the lives of several hundred Indonesian men, and pledged financial compensation for the surviving widows of those killed in the atrocity. At an official ceremony held in the Dutch embassy in Jakarta in September 2013 the Dutch ambassador made another, more general, formal apology for the 'excesses committed by Dutch forces' in Indonesia between 1945 and 1949. Relations with the Netherlands and Brazil were strained in January 2015, when the execution of one of each of their citizens in Indonesia for drugs offences prompted both countries to recall their ambassadors from Jakarta for consultations. A further deterioration in ties with Brazil occurred in February, following a last-minute decision by that country's President, Dilma Rousseff, to delay the acceptance of the credentials of the new Indonesian ambassador to Brazil; in response, President Widodo ordered the immediate return of the diplomat to Indonesia.

During a visit to Moscow in April 2003 President Megawati signed an agreement to buy Russian defence equipment to the value of US $197m., which was to be partly financed by the bartering of Indonesian palm oil. In September 2007 President Vladimir Putin of Russia visited Jakarta, where he concluded an agreement with President Yudhoyono providing for further purchases of Russian armaments and fighter aircraft. This arrangement was to be financed by a 10-year loan of $1,000m. from Russia.

Indonesia has appeared keen in recent years to develop its relations with a number of Middle Eastern and South Asian countries. During a tour of the Middle East in April–May 2006, Yudhoyono reached preliminary energy and investment agreements, worth many millions of dollars, and expressed Indonesia's support for the creation of an independent Palestinian state. During his first official visit to Indonesia, in October 2007, the Palestinian President, Mahmud Abbas, signed several co-operation agreements with his host country, covering areas such as education and communications. In July 2010 the Indonesian Minister of Defence and his Pakistani counterpart signed a defence co-operation agreement, entailing joint military exercises between the armed forces of both countries, intelligence sharing on terrorism and military student exchanges.

Relations with Saudi Arabia were threatened in the early years of the 2010s by a number of reports of Indonesian maids being maltreated (and, in one case, allegedly being killed) by their Saudi employers. Bilateral tensions were exacerbated by the execution in June 2011 of an Indonesian maid who had been convicted of murdering her Saudi employer, after allegedly suffering months of abuse at her hands and having been denied permission to leave her employment and return to her family in Indonesia. The Minister of Foreign Affairs expressed particular displeasure at the Saudi Government's failure to inform the Indonesian authorities or the woman's family that she was to be executed until after the event. Despite assurances by Saudi officials that such an occurrence would not be repeated, at the end of June the Indonesian Government announced a moratorium prohibiting its nationals from working as domestic servants in Saudi Arabia, effective from 1 August. In response, the Saudi Government announced that it was to cease issuing new work permits to Indonesian domestic workers, effective from 2 July. In June 2012 around 17,000 Indonesian migrant workers were imprisoned in Saudi Arabia, and at April 2014, according to the Indonesian foreign ministry, some 41 Indonesian maids faced possible death sentences there. In February 2014 Indonesia and Saudi Arabia signed an agreement which guaranteed better terms of employment for Indonesian domestic employees working in the Gulf state; however, the Indonesian authorities planned to retain the moratorium on the recruitment of new domestic workers from Indonesia until they were certain that the new agreement was being properly implemented.

CONSTITUTION AND GOVERNMENT

Executive power rests with the President, who is elected for five years by the Majelis Permusyawaratan Rakyat (MPR—People's Consultative Assembly), which is the highest authority of the state. The President governs with the assistance of an appointed Cabinet; the Cabinet is responsible to the President. In 2002 the MPR approved a series of amendments to the Constitution. These provided for: the direct election of the President and Vice-President; the termination of all non-elected representation in the Dewan Perwakilan Rakyat (DPR—House of Representatives) and the MPR; and the creation of the Dewan Perwakilan Daerah (DPD—House of Representatives of the Regions), which, together with the DPR, henceforth comprised the MPR. The MPR consists of 692 members serving for five years. The MPR incorporates all 560 members of the DPR, the country's legislative organ, and the 136 elected regional representatives of the DPD.

There are 34 provinces, and local government is through a three-tier system of provincial, regency and village assemblies. Each province is headed by a governor, who is elected to a five-year term of office by direct popular vote (prior to 2005 provincial governors were appointed by the provincial assemblies). Jakarta, Aceh and Yogyakarta are designated as 'special districts'.

REGIONAL AND INTERNATIONAL CO-OPERATION

Indonesia is a member of the Association of Southeast Asian Nations (ASEAN, see p. 210), of the Asian Development Bank (ADB, see p. 206) and of Asia-Pacific Economic Cooperation (APEC, see p. 200). It is also a member of the UN's Economic and Social Commission for Asia and the Pacific (ESCAP, see p. 30) and of the Colombo Plan (see p. 445), which promotes economic and social development in Asia and the Pacific.

Indonesia became a member of the UN in 1950. As a contracting party to the General Agreement on Tariffs and Trade (GATT), Indonesia joined the World Trade Organization (WTO, see p. 431) upon its establishment in 1995. The country is a member of the International Labour Organization (ILO, see p. 139) and of the Non-aligned Movement (see p. 462). In January 2009 Indonesia suspended its membership of the Organization of the Petroleum Exporting Countries (OPEC, see p. 406).

ECONOMIC AFFAIRS

In 2013, according to estimates by the World Bank, Indonesia's gross national income (GNI), measured at average 2011–13 prices, was US $894,967m., equivalent to $3,580 per head (or $9,260 per head on an international purchasing-power parity basis). During 2004–13, it was estimated, the population increased at an average annual rate of 1.4%, while gross domestic product (GDP) per head grew, in real terms, by an average of 4.5% per year. According to figures from the Asian Development Bank (ADB), overall GDP increased, in real terms, by an average of 5.9% per year in 2004–13; GDP expanded by 5.8% in 2013.

Agriculture, forestry and fishing contributed 14.4% of GDP in 2013, according to preliminary figures, and engaged 34.0% of the employed labour force at August 2014. Principal crops for domestic consumption include rice, cassava and maize. Although Indonesia remains a major exporter of rubber and palm oil, these commodities' contributions to the country's export earnings have declined. Other important cash crops are sugar cane, coconut, banana, coffee, spices, tea, cocoa and tobacco. A large percentage of Indonesia's land area remains covered by tropical rainforests. However, illegal logging practices have been widespread, leading to serious environmental damage. During 2004–13, according to figures from the ADB, agricultural GDP increased by an average of 3.6% per year; the GDP of the agricultural sector expanded by 3.8% in 2013.

Industry (including mining, manufacturing, construction and utilities) provided 45.7% of GDP in 2013, according to preliminary figures, and engaged 21.2% of the employed labour force at August 2014. During 2004–13, according to ADB data, industrial GDP increased by an average of 4.6% per year; the GDP of the industrial sector grew by 4.9% in 2013.

Mining contributed 11.2% of GDP in 2013, according to preliminary figures, but engaged just 1.3% of the employed labour force at August 2014. Indonesia's principal mineral resource is petroleum, and the country is a leading exporter of liquefied natural gas. At the end of 2013 proven reserves of petroleum amounted to 4,000m. barrels, sufficient to sustain production at that year's rate for nearly 12 years. Indonesia suspended its membership of the Organization of the Petroleum Exporting Countries (OPEC) in January 2009 on the grounds that the country was no longer a net oil exporter. Prior to that, Indonesia was subject to annual quotas for petroleum production as agreed within OPEC. The Government aimed to increase crude petroleum production from an estimated 978,000 barrels per day (b/d) in 2008 to 1.1m. b/d by 2015; however, crude petroleum output fell to 826,000 b/d in 2013, according to the ADB. In 2013, according to industry sources, natural gas production was 70,402m. cu m, from proven reserves amounting to 300,000m. cu m at the end of that year, sufficient to sustain production at that year's rate for more than 42 years. In 2013 coal production reached 375m. metric tons. Indonesia is one of the world's largest producers of tin, with output of ore amounting to 32,251 tons in 2013. Bauxite, nickel, copper, gold and silver are also mined. During 2004–13, according to figures from the ADB, mining GDP increased at an average annual rate of 2.3%; the GDP of the sector expanded by 1.6% in 2013.

Manufacturing contributed 23.7% of GDP in 2013, according to preliminary figures, and engaged 13.3% of the employed labour force at August 2014. Apart from petroleum refineries, the main branches of the sector include food products, textiles, clothing and footwear, transport equipment, electrical machinery and electronic equipment. According to ADB data, manufacturing GDP increased by an average of 4.6% per year in 2004–13; sectoral GDP grew by 5.6% in 2013.

Construction contributed 10.0% of GDP in 2013, according to preliminary figures, and engaged 6.4% of the employed labour force at August 2014. According to figures from the ADB, construction GDP increased by an average of 7.3% per year in 2004–13; the sector's GDP grew by 5.9% in 2013.

From the 1980s Indonesia broadened the base of its energy supplies to include gas, coal, hydroelectricity and geothermal energy, in addition to the traditional dependence on petroleum. In 2011, of total electricity produced, coal accounted for 44.4%, petroleum 23.2% and natural gas 20.3%. In 2013 imports of mineral fuels and lubricants comprised 24.4% of the total value of merchandise imports. Government plans for the construction of a 30-MW nuclear power plant at Serpong, in the province of Banten, were reported in February 2014.

Services (including trade, transport and communications, finance and tourism) provided 39.9% of GDP in 2013, according to preliminary figures, and engaged 44.8% of the employed labour force at August 2014. Tourism is normally a major source of foreign exchange. Revenue from tourism (excluding passenger transport) reached an estimated US $9,337m. in 2013. The number of tourist arrivals totalled 8.8m. in that year, according to preliminary figures. According to figures from the ADB, the GDP of the services sector expanded by an average of 7.8% per year in 2004–13; the sector's GDP increased by 7.1% in 2013.

In 2013, according to IMF figures, Indonesia recorded a visible merchandise trade surplus of US $5,833.2m. and a deficit of $29,129.5m. on the current account of the balance of payments. In 2013 the principal source of imports was the People's Republic of China (which supplied 16.0% of the total), followed by Singapore, Japan, Malaysia, the Republic of Korea and Thailand. Japan was the principal market for exports in that year (purchasing 14.8%). Other major purchasers were China, Singapore, the USA, India, the Republic of Korea and Malaysia. The principal exports in 2013 were solid fuels manufactured from coal, petroleum gases, palm oil and its fraction, electrical and electronic equipment, crude petroleum oils, and rubber and rubber products. The principal imports were mineral fuels and lubricants, machinery, nuclear reactors and boilers, electrical and electronic equipment, and iron and steel.

Budget proposals for 2014 projected revenue of Rp. 1,661,148,000m. and expenditure of Rp. 1,230,304,000m. According to the ADB, a budget deficit of Rp. 209,523,000m. was recorded in 2013, equivalent to 2.3% of GDP. Indonesia's general government gross debt was Rp. 2,371,400,000m. in 2013, equivalent to 26.1% of GDP. According to the ADB, Indonesia's external debt was estimated at US $264,060m. at the end of 2013. In that year the cost of servicing external public debt was equivalent to 42.7% of the value of exports of goods and services. The annual rate of inflation averaged 7.3% in 2004–13. Consumer prices increased by 7.0% in 2013. The rate of unemployment stood at 5.9% of the labour force in August 2014, while the level of underemployment and part-time employment remained very high, at 29.4% of the labour force at August 2014.

Amid declining international commodity prices and export demand resulting from the emerging global financial crisis, in February 2009 the Government announced a Rp. 73,300,000m. stimulus programme, which aimed to maintain consumer spending and to create employment opportunities through infrastructure projects. Following a sharp decrease in 2009, foreign direct investment (FDI) recovered strongly thereafter, rising from US $15,292.0m. in 2010, according to World Bank figures, to $23,286.8m. in 2013. Although GDP contracted in the fourth quarter of 2008, for the year as a whole the economy recorded positive growth, which was maintained in 2009 and 2010, partly owing to strengthening consumer demand on the large domestic market. Following GDP growth of 6.5% in 2011 (the highest annual rise in 15 years), there was a slight deceleration to 6.2% in 2012. Despite weaker export growth in 2012, resulting from a slowdown in the key market of the People's Republic of China and the generally sluggish recovery of the global economy (notably in the USA and the eurozone), the Indonesian economy remained robust, with FDI, tax revenue and government expenditure continuing to rise and private consumption remaining buoyant. Strong economic growth helped to generate thousands of new jobs in the formal sector, and there was a slight fall in the incidence of poverty. The rate of growth of GDP moderated to 5.8% in 2013 as external demand decreased, the current account deficit widened to a record high, and the rate of inflation rose to 7.0% (largely owing to increases in fuel and food prices and a sharp depreciation in the rupiah). In January 2014 the Government announced measures further to boost FDI, including tax incentives and the opening up of a number of profitable market sectors that had previously been closed to overseas investment. However, the rate of economic growth continued to decelerate in 2014 (to 5.0%, the lowest level recorded since 2009), largely as a result of the faltering global economic recovery (particularly in the eurozone and Japan), the decline in prices of Indonesia's main commodity exports and subdued investment spending, although there was a slight narrowing in the current account deficit. Shortly after assuming power in October, the new Government of President Joko Widodo raised subsidized fuel prices by an average of 34% in an attempt to reduce the burgeoning budget deficit (which, owing to a shortfall in tax revenue, threatened to exceed the legally binding limit of 3% of GDP in that year) and to enable greater expenditure on development, health and social welfare. This measure was expected to result in a rise in the average annual rate of inflation to around 7.5% in 2015. The World Bank forecast that GDP growth would rebound slightly, to 5.2%, in 2015. The relatively slow rate of economic growth was expected to lead to a correspondingly slow rate of reduction in the national poverty level, which stood at 11.3% at March 2014.

PUBLIC HOLIDAYS

2016: 1 January (New Year's Day), 8 February (Chinese New Year), 25 March (Good Friday), 4 May* (Ascension of the Prophet Muhammad), 5 May (Ascension Day), 21 May (Waisak Day), 6 July* (Id al-Fitr, end of Ramadan), 17 August (Independence Day), 12 September* (Id al-Adha, Feast of the Sacrifice), 2 October* (Muharram, Islamic New Year), 11 December* (Mouloud, Prophet Muhammad's Birthday), 25 December (Christmas Day).

* These holidays are dependent on the Islamic lunar calendar and may vary by one or two days from the dates given.

Statistical Survey

Source (unless otherwise stated): Badan Pusat Statistik (Central Bureau of Statistics/Statistics Indonesia), Jalan Dr Sutomo 6–8, Jakarta 10710; tel. (21) 3507057; fax (21) 3857046; e-mail bpshq@bps.go.id; internet www.bps.go.id.

Area and Population

AREA, POPULATION AND DENSITY

Area (sq km)	1,910,931*
Population (census results)	
30 June 2000	206,264,595
31 May 2010	
Males	119,630,913
Females	118,010,413
Total	237,641,326
Population (UN estimates at mid-year)†	
2013	249,865,631
2014	252,812,245
2015	255,708,785
Density (per sq km) at mid-2015	133.8

* 737,814 sq miles.
† Source: UN, *World Population Prospects: The 2012 Revision.*

POPULATION BY AGE AND SEX
(UN estimates at mid-2015)

	Males	Females	Total
0–14 years	36,793,046	34,935,075	71,728,121
15–64 years	85,630,810	84,474,814	170,105,624
65 years and over	6,176,285	7,698,755	13,875,040
Total	128,600,141	127,108,644	255,708,785

Source: UN, *World Population Prospects: The 2012 Revision.*

ISLANDS AND PROVINCES
(population at mid-2013)*

	Area (sq km)	Population ('000)	Density (per sq km)
Jawa (Java) and Madura . .	129,438	141,985.6	1,096.9
DKI Jakarta†	664	9,969.9	15,014.9
Jawa Barat	35,378	45,340.8	1,281.6
Jawa Tengah	32,801	33,264.3	1,014.1
DI Yogyakarta†	3,133	3,594.9	1,147.4
Jawa Timur	47,800	38,363.2	802.6
Banten	9,663	11,452.5	1,185.2
Sumatera (Sumatra) . . .	480,793	53,539.0	111.4
Nanggroe Aceh Darussalem† .	57,956	4,811.1	83.0
Sumatera Utara	72,981	13,590.3	186.2
Sumatera Barat . . .	42,013	5,066.5	120.6
Riau	87,024	6,033.3	69.3
Jambi	50,058	3,286.1	65.6
Sumatera Selatan . . .	91,592	7,828.7	85.5
Bangkulu	19,919	1,814.4	91.1
Lumpung	34,624	7,932.1	229.1
Kepulauan Bangka-Belitung .	16,424	1,315.1	80.1

—continued	Area (sq km)	Population ('000)	Density (per sq km)
Kepulauan Riau	8,202	1,861.4	226.9
Sulawesi (Celebes) . . .	188,522	18,216.9	96.6
Sulawesi Utara . . .	13,852	2,360.4	170.4
Sulawesi Tengah . . .	61,841	2,785.5	45.0
Sulawesi Selatan . . .	46,717	8,342.0	178.6
Sulawesi Tenggara . .	38,068	2,396.7	63.0
Gorontalo	11,257	1,098.0	97.5
Sulawesi Barat . . .	16,787	1,234.3	73.5
Kalimantan	544,150	14,751.4	27.1
Kalimantan Barat . . .	147,307	4,641.4	31.5
Kalimantan Tengah . .	153,565	2,384.7	15.5
Kalimantan Selatan . .	38,744	3,854.5	99.5
Kalimantan Timur . . .	204,534	3,870.8	18.9
Nusa Tenggara and Bali‡ . .	73,070	13,721.1	187.8
Nusa Tenggara Barat . .	18,572	4,710.8	253.7
Nusa Tenggara Timur . .	48,718	4,954.0	101.7
Bali	5,780	4,056.3	701.8
Maluku (Moluccas) and Papua§	494,957	6,604.1	13.3
Maluku	46,914	1,628.4	34.7
Maluku Utara	31,983	1,114.9	34.9
Papua Barat†	97,024	828.3	8.5
Papua†	319,036	3,032.5	9.5
Total	1,910,931	248,818.1	130.2

* Figures refer to provincial divisions, organized according to geography, island or island groupings.
† Province with special status.
‡ The Nusa Tenggara provinces comprise most of the Lesser Sunda Islands, principally Flores, Lombok, Sumba, Sumbawa and part of Timor.
§ The Papua provinces were formerly known as Irian Jaya (West Papua).

A new province, Kalimantan Utara, was created in October 2012 from part of the former territory of the province of Kalimantan Timur.

PRINCIPAL TOWNS
(UN estimates at mid-2015)

Jakarta (capital) . .	10,323,142	Bandar Lampung . .	965,241
Surabaya	2,853,237	Padang	903,224
Bandung	2,543,742	Samarinda	865,034
Medan	2,204,005	Malang	856,090
Semarang	1,629,599	Tasikmalaya . . .	786,810
Ujung Pandang			
(Makassar) . . .	1,488,630	Banjarmasin . . .	682,120
Palembang	1,455,256	Balikpapan	655,425
Batam	1,390,546	Jambi	604,088
Pekanbaru	1,120,893	Pontianak	603,350
Denpasar	1,106,593	Surakarta	504,211
Bogor	1,075,563		

Source: UN, *World Urbanization Prospects: The 2014 Revision.*

BIRTHS AND DEATHS
(annual averages, UN estimates)

	2000–05	2005–10	2010–15
Birth rate (per 1,000)	21.5	21.0	17.0
Death rate (per 1,000)	6.7	6.4	6.2

Source: UN, *World Population Prospects: The 2012 Revision*.

Life expectancy (years at birth): 70.6 (males 68.6; females 72.7) in 2012 (Source: World Bank, World Development Indicators database).

ECONOMICALLY ACTIVE POPULATION
(persons aged 15 years and over, at August)

	2012	2013	2014
Agriculture, hunting, forestry and fishing	39,590,054	39,220,261	38,973,033
Mining and quarrying	1,602,706	1,426,454	1,436,370
Manufacturing	15,615,386	14,959,804	15,254,674
Electricity, gas and water . . .	251,162	252,134	289,193
Construction	6,851,291	6,349,387	7,280,086
Trade, restaurants and hotels .	23,517,145	24,105,906	24,829,734
Transport, storage and communications	5,052,302	5,096,987	5,113,188
Financing, insurance, real estate and business services . . .	2,696,090	2,898,279	3,031,038
Public services	17,328,732	18,451,860	18,420,710
Total employed	112,504,868	112,761,072	114,628,026
Unemployed	7,344,866	7,410,931	7,244,905
Total labour force . . .	119,849,734	120,172,003	121,872,931

Health and Welfare

KEY INDICATORS

Total fertility rate (children per woman, 2012)	2.4
Under-5 mortality rate (per 1,000 live births, 2012) . . .	31
HIV/AIDS (% of persons aged 15–49, 2013)	0.5
Physicians (per 1,000 head, 2012)	0.20
Hospital beds (per 1,000 head, 2010)	0.60
Health expenditure (2011): US $ per head (PPP)	132
Health expenditure (2011): % of GDP	2.9
Health expenditure (2011): public (% of total)	37.9
Access to water (% of persons, 2012)	85
Access to sanitation (% of persons, 2012)	59
Total carbon dioxide emissions ('000 metric tons, 2010) . .	433,989.5
Carbon dioxide emissions per head (metric tons, 2010) . .	1.8
Human Development Index (2013): ranking	108
Human Development Index (2013): value	0.684

For sources and definitions, see explanatory note on p. vi.

Agriculture

PRINCIPAL CROPS
('000 metric tons)

	2011	2012	2013
Rice, paddy	65,757	69,056	71,280
Maize	17,643	19,387	18,512
Potatoes	995	1,094	1,023
Sweet potatoes	2,192	2,483	2,387
Cassava (Manioc)	24,044	24,177	23,937
Beans, dry	341	284	205
Sugar cane*	24,000	28,700	33,700
Cashew nuts, with shell . . .	115	117	117
Soybeans (Soya beans) . . .	851	843	780
Groundnuts, with shell† . . .	1,150	1,251	1,340
Coconuts*	17,500	19,400	18,300
Oil palm fruit†	105,000	113,000	120,000
Cabbages and other brassicas .	1,364	1,450	1,406
Tomatoes	954	893	947
Pumpkins, squash and gourds .	428	428	372
Cucumbers and gherkins . .	522	511	468
Aubergines (Eggplants) . . .	519	519	509
Chillies and peppers, green . .	1,903	1,657	1,726

—*continued*	2011	2012	2013
Onions, dry	893	964	959
Beans, green	885	871	882
Carrots and turnips	527	466	479
Oranges	1,819	1,612	1,411
Avocados	276	294	276
Mangoes, mangosteens and guavas	2,131	2,376	2,059
Pineapples	1,541	1,782	1,837
Bananas	6,133	6,189	5,359
Papayas	958	906	871
Coffee, green	639	691	699
Cocoa beans	712	741	778
Tea	150	143	148
Cinnamon	90	90	90
Cloves	72	100	99
Ginger	95	115	233
Tobacco, unmanufactured . . .	215	261	260
Natural rubber	2,990	3,012	3,108

* Unofficial figure.
† FAO estimates.

Aggregate production ('000 metric tons, may include official, semi-official or estimated data): Total cereals 83,400.2 in 2011, 88,443.1 in 2012, 89,791.6 in 2013; Total roots and tubers 27,615.5 in 2011, 28,155.1 in 2012, 27,767.0 in 2013; Total vegetables (incl. melons) 10,097.9 in 2011, 10,464.7 in 2012, 10,243.9 in 2013; Total fruits (excl. melons) 17,472.6 in 2011, 17,880.7 in 2012, 16,003.1 in 2013.

Source: FAO.

LIVESTOCK
('000 head)

	2011	2012	2013
Cattle	14,824	15,981	16,607
Sheep	11,791	13,420	14,560
Goats	16,946	17,906	18,570
Pigs	7,525	7,900	8,246
Horses	409	437	454
Buffaloes	1,305	1,438	1,484
Chickens	1,566,967	1,657,684	1,793,022
Ducks	43,488	49,295	50,931

Source: FAO.

LIVESTOCK PRODUCTS
('000 metric tons)

	2011	2012	2013
Cattle meat	485.3	505.5	545.6
Buffalo meat	35.3	37.0	40.3
Sheep meat	46.8	44.4	45.7
Goat meat	66.3	65.2	67.0
Pig meat*	721.1	728.8	742.5
Chicken meat	1,664.8	1,734.0	1,837.9
Cows' milk	974.6	959.7	981.6
Goats' milk*	281.4	282.0	282.8
Hen eggs	1,027.8	1,139.9	1,223.7
Other poultry eggs	256.2	276.2	280.0
Wool, greasy*	30.8	30.8	30.8

* FAO estimates.

Note: Figures for meat refer to inspected production only, i.e. from animals slaughtered under government supervision.

Source: FAO.

Forestry

ROUNDWOOD REMOVALS
('000 cubic metres, excl. bark, FAO estimates)

	2011	2012	2013
Sawlogs, veneer logs and logs for sleepers	28,000	28,000	28,000
Pulpwood	28,000	29,900	29,900
Other industrial wood	4,706	4,706	4,706
Fuel wood	57,288	54,917	52,627
Total	117,994	117,523	115,233

Source: FAO.

SAWNWOOD PRODUCTION
('000 cubic metres, incl. railway sleepers, unofficial figures)

	2006	2007	2008
Total (all broadleaved) . . .	4,330	4,330	4,169

2009–13: Production assumed to be unchanged from 2008.
Source: FAO.

Fishing

('000 metric tons, live weight)

	2010	2011	2012
Capture	5,374.6	5,701.4	5,813.8
Scads	351.2	405.8	427.5
Goldstripe sardinella . . .	255.6	246.2	161.8
'Stolephorus' anchovies . . .	175.7	204.8	203.2
Skipjack tuna	361.2	372.7	402.4
Indian mackerels	17.8	19.7	44.2
Aquaculture	2,304.8*	2,718.4	3,067.7
Common carp	282.7	332.2	374.4
Milkfish	422.1	467.3	482.9
Total catch	7,679.4*	8,419.9	8,881.5

* FAO estimate.

Note: Figures exclude aquatic plants ('000 metric tons): 3,917.7 (capture 2.7, aquaculture 3,915.0) in 2010; 5,175.7 (capture 5.5, aquaculture 5,170.2) in 2011; 6,522.5 (capture 7.6, aquaculture 6,514.9) in 2012. Also excluded are crocodiles, recorded by number rather than by weight. The number of crocodiles caught was: 11,752 in 2010; 16,780 in 2011; 15,267 in 2013.
Source: FAO.

Mining

('000 metric tons unless otherwise indicated)

	2010	2011	2012
Crude petroleum (million barrels)*	341.0	340.0†	342.0†
Natural gas (million cu m) . .	77,741	80,000†	79,000†
Bauxite†	27.0	40.0	29.0
Coal (bituminous)	137,801	150,000†	140,000†
Nickel‡	235.8	218.2	228.0
Copper‡	878.4	542.7	360.0†
Tin ore (metric tons)‡ . . .	43,258	42,000†	41,000†
Gold (kg)§	106,316	96,100	58,800
Silver (kg)§	271,534	310,400	250,000†

* Including condensate.
† Estimate(s).
‡ Figures refer to the metal content of ores and concentrates.
§ Including gold and silver in copper concentrate.
Source: US Geological Survey.

2013 ('000 metric tons unless otherwise indicated, estimates): Crude petroleum (million barrels) 301.4; Bauxite 55.7; Tin ore (metric tons) 32,251.

Industry

SELECTED PRODUCTS
('000 metric tons unless otherwise indicated)

	2009	2010	2011
Raw sugar (centrifugal)[1] . . .	2,740	2,450	2,500
Palm oil[1,2]	19,324	19,760	21,449
Veneer sheets ('000 cu m)[1] . .	685	737	816
Plywood ('000 cu m)[1,2] . . .	4,150	4,850	4,850
Paper and paperboard[1,3] . . .	86	86	87
Jet fuel	1,911	1,791	2,152
Motor spirit (petrol)	9,243	8,350	9,326
Naphthas	1,921	1,731	3,423
Kerosene	3,794	2,478	1,857
Gas-diesel oil	13,769	13,338	16,272
Residual fuel oils	2,803	2,271	8,833
Lubricating oils	388	283	432
Liquefied petroleum gas . . .	1,425	1,825	1,581
Rubber tyres ('000)[4] . . .	36,811	n.a.	n.a.
Cement (hydraulic)[5,3] . . .	22,195	28,000	29,000
Aluminium (unwrought)[5,6] . .	258	253	244
Tin (unwrought, metric tons)[5,6]	51,418	43,832	43,000
Electric energy (million kWh) .	157,516	186,594	182,384

2012 ('000 metric tons unless otherwise stated): Palm oil 23,672 (unofficial figure)[1,2]; Veneer sheets ('000 cu m) 891[1]; Plywood ('000 cu m) 5,178[1]; Paper and paperboard 89[1]; Cement (hydraulic) 29,000[3,5]; Aluminium (unwrought) 244[5]; Tin (unwrought, metric tons) 43,000[3,5].

2013 ('000 metric tons unless otherwise stated): Veneer sheets ('000 cu m) 816[1,2]; Plywood ('000 cu m) 5,268[1,2]; Paper and paperboard 89[1]; Cement (hydraulic) 29,000[3,5].

[1] Source: FAO.
[2] Unofficial figure.
[3] Provisional or estimated production.
[4] For road motor vehicles, excluding bicycles and motorcycles.
[5] Source: US Geological Survey.
[6] Primary metal production only.

Source (unless otherwise indicated): UN Industrial Commodity Statistics Database.

Finance

CURRENCY AND EXCHANGE RATES

Monetary Units
100 sen = 1 rupiah (Rp.).

Sterling, Dollar and Euro Equivalents (31 December 2014)
£1 sterling = 19,416.4 rupiah;
US $1 = 12,440.0 rupiah;
€1 = 15,103.4 rupiah;
100,000 rupiah = £5.15 = $8.04 = €6.62.

Average Exchange Rate (rupiah per US $)
2012   9,386.6
2013   10,461.2
2014   11,865.2

GOVERNMENT FINANCE
(central government operations, '000 million rupiah)

Summary of Balances

	2012	2013	2014*
Revenue	1,332,323	1,497,521	1,661,148
Less Expenditure and net lending	1,010,558	1,196,828	1,230,304
Overall balance	321,765	300,693	430,844

Revenue and Grants

	2012	2013	2014*
Tax revenue	980,518	1,148,365	1,310,219
Income tax	465,070	538,760	591,621
Value-added tax (VAT) on goods and services, and tax on sales of luxury goods	337,584	423,708	518,879
Tax of rights in land and building	28,969	27,344	25,541
Excise duties	95,028	104,730	114,284
Import duties	28,418	30,812	33,937
Export taxes	21,238	17,609	19,978
Other taxes	4,211	5,402	5,980
Non-tax revenue	351,805	349,156	350,930
Total	1,332,323	1,497,521	1,661,148

Expenditure and Net Lending

	2012	2013	2014*
Personnel expenditure . . .	197,864	232,979	276,678
Material expenditure . . .	140,885	206,507	203,654
Interest payments	100,516	112,518	119,533
Domestic interest . . .	70,211	96,759	107,687
External interest . . .	30,305	15,759	11,846
Subsidies	346,420	348,119	336,242
Petroleum subsidies . .	306,478	299,830	284,660
Non-petroleum subsidies . .	39,942	48,289	51,582
Social expenditure	75,621	82,488	55,865
Capital expenditure	145,104	192,600	205,843
Other expenditure	4,073	19,271	28,946
Grant expenditures	75	2,346	3,543
Total	1,010,558	1,196,828	1,230,304

* Budget proposals.

INTERNATIONAL RESERVES
(US $ million at 31 December)

	2011	2012	2013
Gold (market prices)	3,598	3,940	3,023
IMF special drawing rights . .	2,704	2,707	2,712
Reserve position in IMF . . .	223	224	224
Foreign exchange	103,611	105,907	93,427
Total	110,136	112,778	99,386

Source: IMF, *International Financial Statistics.*

MONEY SUPPLY
('000 million rupiah at 31 December)

	2011	2012	2013
Currency outside depository corporations	307,760	361,967	399,589
Transferable deposits . . .	568,499	662,060	729,838
Other deposits	1,986,573	2,270,198	2,575,463
Securities other than shares . .	14,388	10,420	22,805
Broad money	2,877,220	3,304,645	3,727,696

Source: IMF, *International Financial Statistics.*

COST OF LIVING
(Consumer Price Index; base: 2000 = 100)

	2011	2012	2013
Food	268.1	283.8	317.7
All items (incl. others) . . .	239.3	249.6	267.0

Source: ILO.

NATIONAL ACCOUNTS
('000 million rupiah at current prices)

Expenditure on the Gross Domestic Product

	2011	2012*	2013*
Government final consumption expenditure	669,000	733,269	827,243
Private final consumption expenditure	4,053,364	4,496,373	5,071,094
Changes in inventories . .	70,774	170,310	179,778
Gross fixed capital formation .	2370,273	2,688,884	2,876,253
Total domestic expenditure .	7,163,411	8,088,836	8,954,368
Exports of goods and services .	1,955,821	1,999,254	2,156,809
Less Imports of goods and services	1,851,070	2,127,726	2,338,119
Statistical discrepancy . .	151,025	269,075	310,914
GDP in purchasers' values .	7,419,187	8,229,439	9,083,972
GDP at constant 2000 prices .	2,464,566	2,618,938	2,770,345

Gross Domestic Product by Economic Activity

	2011	2012*	2013*
Agriculture, forestry and fishing .	1,091,447	1,193,453	1,311,037
Mining and quarrying	876,984	970,824	1,020,773
Manufacturing	1,806,141	1,972,524	2,152,593
Electricity, gas and water . .	55,882	62,235	70,075
Construction	753,555	844,091	907,267
Trade, hotels and restaurants .	1,023,725	1,148,691	1,301,506
Transport, storage and communications	491,287	549,105	636,888
Finance, insurance, real estate and business services	535,153	598,523	683,010
Public administration	433,371	486,315	541,191
Other services	351,643	403,679	459,631
Total	7,419,187	8,229,439	9,083,972

* Preliminary figures.

BALANCE OF PAYMENTS
(US $ million)

	2011	2012	2013
Exports of goods	191,108.7	187,346.5	182,080.2
Imports of goods	−157,283.7	−178,667.0	−176,256.0
Balance of goods	33,825.0	8,679.5	5,833.2
Exports of services	21,888.2	23,660.2	22,944.1
Imports of services	−31,691.4	−34,224.4	−35,015.9
Balance on goods and services	24,021.7	−1,884.7	−6,238.5
Primary income received . . .	2,581.1	2,649.6	2,602.4
Primary income paid . . .	−29,128.3	−29,277.5	−29,452.5
Balance on goods, services and primary income	−2,525.4	−28,512.5	−33,088.6
Secondary income received . .	7,635.6	8,066.7	8,289.3
Secondary income paid . . .	−3,425.1	−3,972.4	−4,330.1
Current balance	1,685.1	−24,418.1	−29,129.5
Capital account (net)	32.9	50.6	21.0
Direct investment assets . . .	−9,036.5	−7,484.6	−9,617.7
Direct investment from liabilities .	20,564.9	21,200.8	23,286.8
Portfolio investment assets . .	−1,189.4	−5,467.0	−1,272.8
Portfolio investment liabilities .	4,995.8	14,673.4	10,803.8
Financial derivatives and employee stock options (net)	69.4	13.0	−334.4
Other investment assets . . .	−6,754.5	−5,353.0	−3,427.4
Other investment liabilities . .	4,953.7	7,275.4	2,503.1
Net errors and omissions . . .	−3,465.7	−275.7	−158.1
Reserves and related items .	11,855.6	214.8	−7,325.0

Source: IMF, *International Financial Statistics.*

External Trade

PRINCIPAL COMMODITIES
(distribution by HS, US $ million)

Imports c.i.f.	2011	2012	2013
Vegetables and vegetable products	8,906.0	7,611.8	6,923.3
Prepared foodstuffs; beverages, spirits, vinegar; tobacco and articles thereof	5,903.7	6,741.6	7,326.9
Mineral products	42,337.8	44,218.9	47,118.2
Mineral fuels, oils, distillation products, etc.	40,840.2	42,764.2	45,544.7
Crude petroleum oils	11,154.5	10,803.3	13,585.8
Non-crude petroleum oils	27,721.8	28,038.2	27,850.9
Chemicals and related products	16,359.3	17,519.3	17,139.1
Organic chemicals	6,634.8	6,883.0	7,011.5
Plastics, rubber, and articles thereof	9,034.2	9,615.2	9,855.6
Plastics and articles thereof	6,687.5	6,990.9	7,642.7
Textiles and textile articles	8,530.5	8,143.6	8,472.7
Iron and steel, other base metals and articles of base metal	17,247.7	20,481.1	19,291.6
Iron and steel	8,580.5	10,138.9	9,553.6
Machinery and mechanical appliances; electrical equipment; parts thereof	42,974.0	47,334.3	45,491.6
Machinery, boilers, etc.	24,728.8	28,429.6	27,290.5
Electrical and electronic equipment	18,245.2	18,904.7	18,201.1
Vehicles, aircraft, vessels and associated transport equipment	13,108.6	16,192.0	11,106.9
Vehicles other than railway and tramway	7,602.8	9,757.0	7,914.8
Total (incl. others)	177,435.6	191,690.9	186,628.6

Exports f.o.b.	2011	2012	2013
Animal, vegetable fats and oils, cleavage products, etc.	21,655.3	21,299.8	19,224.9
Palm oil and its fraction	17,261.2	17,602.2	15,838.9
Mineral products	76,428.8	68,580.8	64,128.5
Ores, slag and ash	7,342.6	5,082.6	6,544.1
Mineral fuels, oils, distillation products, etc.	68,921.1	63,385.1	57,413.3
Solid fuels manufactured from coal	25,523.2	24,293.2	22,773.2
Crude petroleum oils	13,828.7	12,293.4	10,204.7
Petroleum gases	22,871.5	20,520.5	18,129.2
Chemicals and related products	10,689.7	10,239.6	10,264.9
Plastics, rubber, and articles thereof	16,865.9	12,911.7	11,922.1

Exports f.o.b.—*continued*	2011	2012	2013
Rubber and articles thereof	14,352.2	10,475.2	9,394.2
Natural rubber, balata, gutta-percha, etc.	11,766.2	7,864.5	6,910.7
Pulp of wood, paper and paperboard, and articles thereof	5,769.4	5,517.8	5,644.0
Textiles and textile articles	13,256.8	12,461.7	12,679.5
Iron and steel, other base metals and articles of base metal	11,965.8	9,387.4	8,614.8
Machinery and mechanical appliances; electrical equipment; parts thereof	16,894.9	16,867.9	16,406.9
Machinery, boilers, etc.	5,749.5	6,103.1	5,968.5
Electrical and electronic equipment	11,145.4	10,764.8	10,438.4
Vehicles, aircraft, vessels and associated transport equipment	4,787.9	5,914.4	5,694.0
Total (incl. others)	203,496.6	190,031.8	182,551.8

Source: Trade Map-Trade Competitiveness Map, International Trade Centre, www.intracen.org/marketanalysis.

PRINCIPAL TRADING PARTNERS
(US $ million)*

Imports c.i.f.	2011	2012	2013
Australia	5,177.1	5,297.6	5,038.2
Brazil	1,898.1	1,971.0	2,216.0
Canada	2,015.8	1,810.7	2,067.5
China, People's Republic	26,212.2	29,387.1	29,849.5
France (incl. Monaco)	2,007.4	1,926.2	1,594.5
Germany	3,393.8	4,188.5	4,426.3
Hong Kong	2,465.2	1,930.2	2,092.4
India	4,322.0	4,305.6	3,964.0
Japan	19,436.6	22,767.8	19,284.6
Korea, Republic	12,999.8	11,970.4	11,592.6
Kuwait	1,407.9	2,181.5	1,440.9
Malaysia	10,404.9	12,243.6	13,322.5
Nigeria	1,626.9	2,770.7	3,122.4
Russia	1,680.9	2,505.7	2,593.6
Saudi Arabia	5,426.6	5,199.4	6,526.4
Singapore	25,964.7	26,087.3	25,581.5
Taiwan	4,259.5	4,692.8	4,480.5
Thailand	10,405.1	11,437.2	10,703.1
Viet Nam	2,382.9	2,595.0	2,722.6
USA	10,834.0	11,614.2	9,081.8
Total (incl. others)	177,435.6	191,690.9	186,628.6

Exports f.o.b.	2011	2012	2013
Australia	5,582.5	4,905.4	4,370.5
China, People's Republic	22,941.0	21,659.5	22,601.5
Germany	3,304.7	3,075.0	2,883.4
Hong Kong	3,215.4	2,633.9	2,693.3
India	13,335.7	12,496.3	13,031.3
Italy	3,168.3	2,277.0	2,128.6
Japan	33,714.7	30,135.1	27,086.3
Korea, Republic	16,388.8	15,049.9	11,422.5
Malaysia	10,995.8	11,280.3	10,666.6
Netherlands	5,132.5	4,664.3	4,106.0
Philippines	3,699.0	3,707.6	3,817.0
Singapore	18,443.9	17,135.0	16,686.2
Spain	2,427.9	2,069.3	1,810.4
Taiwan	6,584.9	6,242.5	5,862.4
Thailand	5,896.7	6,635.1	6,061.9
USA	16,497.6	14,910.2	15,741.1
Viet Nam	2,354.2	2,273.7	2,400.9
Total (incl. others)	203,496.6	190,031.8	182,551.8

* Imports by country of production, exports by country of consumption; figures include trade in gold.

Source: Trade Map-Trade Competitiveness Map, International Trade Centre, www.intracen.org/marketanalysis.

Transport

RAILWAYS
(traffic)

	2011	2012	2013*
Passengers embarked ('000) . .	199,337	202,179	216,010
Passenger-km (million) . . .	19,024	17,154	16,860
Freight loaded ('000 metric tons) .	20,438	23,619	26,755
Total ton-km (million)	6,643	6,951	8,190

* Preliminary figures.

ROAD TRAFFIC
(motor vehicles registered)

	2011	2012	2013
Passenger cars	9,548,866	10,432,259	11,484,514
Trucks	4,958,738	5,286,061	5,615,494
Buses	2,254,406	2,273,821	2,286,309
Motorcycles	68,839,341	76,381,183	84,732,652
Total	85,601,351	94,373,324	104,118,969

SHIPPING

Flag Registered Fleet
(at 31 December)

	2012	2013	2014
Number of vessels	6,138	6,781	7,133
Displacement ('000 grt) . . .	15,085.0	16,547.9	17,636.6

Source: Lloyd's List Intelligence (www.lloydslistintelligence.com).

Seaborne Freight Traffic
('000 metric tons)

	2011	2012	2013
International:			
goods loaded	376,652	488,264	510,699
goods unloaded	78,836	69,645	89,512
Domestic:			
goods loaded	238,940	312,599	303,881
goods unloaded	284,292	327,715	336,063

CIVIL AVIATION
(traffic on scheduled services)

	2010	2011
Kilometres flown (million)	440	518
Passengers carried ('000)	56,774	67,795
Passenger-km (million)	60,649	73,098
Total ton-km (million)	5,797	6,964

Source: UN, *Statistical Yearbook*.

Passengers carried ('000): 79,406 in 2012; 85,103 in 2013 (Source: World Bank, World Development Indicators database).

Tourism

FOREIGN TOURIST ARRIVALS

Country of residence	2011	2012	2013*
Australia	933,376	952,717	1,024,806
China, People's Republic . . .	594,997	726,088	887,990
France	171,736	184,273	208,081
Germany	149,110	158,212	177,813
India	181,791	196,983	250,528
Japan	423,113	463,486	569,230
Korea, Republic	320,596	328,989	392,726
Malaysia	1,173,351	1,269,089	1,496,142
Netherlands	163,268	152,749	167,829
Philippines	210,029	236,866	192,300
Singapore	1,324,839	1,324,706	1,658,399
Taiwan	228,922	217,708	264,750
United Kingdom	201,221	219,726	238,286
USA	203,205	217,599	261,732
Total (incl. others)	7,649,731	8,044,462	8,802,129

* Preliminary figures.

Receipts from tourism (US $ million, excl. passenger transport): 7,997 in 2011; 8,324 in 2012; 9,337 in 2013 (provisional) (Source: World Tourism Organization).

Communications Media

	2011	2012	2013
Telephones ('000 main lines in use)	38,617.5	37,982.9	40,165.0
Mobile cellular telephones ('000 subscribers)	236,799.5	281,963.7	303,606.2
Broadband subscribers ('000) . .	2,736.4*	2,983.0	3,251.8

* Estimate.

Internet subscribers: 1,707,200 in 2008.

Source: International Telecommunication Union.

Education

(2012/13)

	Institutions	Teachers	Pupils and Students
Kindergarten	71,356	213,823	3,993,929
Primary schools	148,272	1,533,991	26,769,680
General junior secondary schools .	35,527	552,083	9,653,093
General senior secondary schools .	12,107	252,405	4,272,860
Vocational senior secondary schools	10,673	176,856	4,189,519
Tertiary institutions	3,189	206,641	5,822,143

Source: Ministry of Education and Culture.

Pupil-teacher ratio (primary education, UNESCO estimate): 18.6 in 2011/12 (Source: UNESCO Institute for Statistics).

Adult literacy rate (UNESCO estimates): 92.8% (males 95.6%; females 90.1%) in 2011 (Source: UNESCO Institute for Statistics).

Directory

The Government

HEAD OF STATE

President: JOKO WIDODO (elected 9 July 2014; took office 20 October 2014).

Vice-President: MUHAMMAD JUSUF KALLA.

CABINET
(April 2015)

The Government includes members of the Partai Demokrasi Indonesia Perjuangan (PDI—P), Partai Hati Nurani Rakyat (Hanura), Partai NasDem and Partai Kebangkitan Bangsa (PKB), along with numerous unaffiliated members.

Co-ordinating Minister for Political, Legal and Security Affairs: TEDJO EDHY PURDIJATNO.

Co-ordinating Minister for Economic Affairs: SOFJAN DJALIL.

Co-ordinating Minister for Maritime Affairs and the Environment: INDROYONO SUSILO.

Co-ordinating Minister for Human Development and Culture: PUAN MAHARANI.

Minister of Home Affairs: TJAHJO KUMOLO.

Minister of Foreign Affairs: RETNO MARSUDI.

Minister of Defence: RYAMIZARD RYACUDU.

Minister of Law and Human Rights: YASONA H. LAOLY.

Minister of Finance: BAMBANG BRODJONEGORO.

Minister of Energy and Mineral Resources: SUDIRMAN SAID.

Minister of Industry: SALEH HUSIN.

Minister of Trade: RAHMAT GOBEL.

Minister of Environment and Forestry: SITI NURBAYA.

Minister of Agriculture: AMRAN SULAIMAN.

Minister of Agrarian and Spatial Planning: Drs FERRY MUSYIDAN BALDAN.

Minister of Transportation: IGNASIUS JONAN.

Minister of Maritime Affairs and Fisheries: SUSI PUDJIASTUTI.

Minister of Manpower: HANIF DHAKIRI.

Minister of Public Works and Public Housing: BASUKI HADIMULJONO.

Minister of Health: NILA MOELOEK.

Minister of Culture and Elementary and Secondary Education: ANIES BASWEDAN.

Minister of Social Affairs: KHOFIFAH INDAR PARAWANSA.

Minister of State for Religious Affairs: LUKMAN HAKIM SAIFUDDIN.

Minister of Communications and Information: RUDIANTARA.

Minister of Research and Technology and Higher Education: M. NASIR.

Minister of Women's Empowerment and Child Protection: YOHANA SUSANA YEMBISE.

Minister of Administrative and Bureaucratic Reform: YUDDY CHRISNANDI.

Minister of Villages, Disadvantaged Regions and Transmigration: MARWAN JAFAR.

Minister of National Development Planning: ANDRINOF CHANIAGO.

Minister of State-Owned Enterprises: RINI SOEMARNO.

Minister of Co-operatives and Small and Medium Enterprises: ANAK AGUNG GEDE NGURAH PUSPAYOGA.

Minister of Tourism: ARIEF YAHYA.

Minister of State for Youth and Sports Affairs: IMAM NAHRAWI.

Officials with the rank of Minister of State:

Chief of Staff: LUHUT BINSAR PANJAITAN.

Attorney-General: H. M. PRASETYO.

State Secretary: PRATIKNO.

MINISTRIES

Office of the President: Istana Merdeka, 2nd Floor, Jakarta 10110; tel. (21) 3840946; internet www.presidenri.go.id.

Office of the Vice-President: Istana Wakil Presiden, Jalan Medan Merdeka Selatan 14, Jakarta 10110; tel. (21) 34830565; fax (21) 3503940; e-mail tirta_hidayat@yahoo.go.id; internet www.setwapres.go.id.

Office of the Attorney-General: Jalan Sultan Hasanuddin 1, Kebayoran Baru, Jakarta Selatan; tel. (21) 7221269; fax (21) 7392576; e-mail webmaster@kejaksaan.go.id; internet www.kejaksaan.go.id.

Office of the Cabinet Secretary: 4th Floor, Jalan Veteran 18, Jakarta Pusat 10110; tel. (21) 3846463; fax (21) 3866579; e-mail itcp@setkab.go.id; internet www.setkab.go.id.

Office of the Co-ordinating Minister for Economic Affairs: Jalan Lapangan Banteng Timur 2–4, Jakarta 10710; tel. (21) 3521974; fax (21) 3521985; e-mail humas@ekon.go.id; internet www.ekon.go.id.

Office of the Co-ordinating Minister for People's Welfare: Jalan Merdeka Barat 3, Jakarta Pusat; tel. (21) 3459444; fax (21) 3453289; internet www.menkokesra.go.id.

Office of the Co-ordinating Minister for Political, Legal and Security Affairs: Jalan Medan Merdeka Barat 15, Jakarta 10110; tel. (21) 3521121; fax (21) 3450918; e-mail dkpt@polkam.go.id; internet www.polkam.go.id.

Office of the State Secretary: Jalan Veteran 17–18, Jakarta 10110; tel. (21) 3849043; fax (21) 3452685; e-mail webmaster@setneg.go.id; internet www.setneg.go.id.

Ministry of Agriculture: Gedung D, 4th Floor, Jalan Harsono R. M. 3, Ragunan, Pasar Minggu, Jakarta Selatan 12550; tel. (21) 7804056; fax (21) 7804237; e-mail webmaster@deptan.go.id; internet www.deptan.go.id.

Ministry of Communications and Information Technology: Jalan Medan Merdeka Barat 9, Jakarta Pusat 10110; tel. (21) 3844227; fax (21) 3867600; e-mail info@depkominfo.go.id; internet www.depkominfo.go.id.

Ministry of Defence: Jalan Medan Merdeka Barat 13–14, Jakarta Pusat 10200; tel. (21) 3456184; fax (21) 3440023; e-mail webmaster@dephan.go.id; internet www.dephan.go.id.

Ministry of Education and Culture: Jalan Jenderal Sudirman, Senayan, Jakarta Pusat 10270; tel. (21) 57950226; fax (21) 5733125; e-mail pengaduan@kemdikbud.go.id; internet www.kemdiknas.go.id.

Ministry of Energy and Mineral Resources: Jalan Medan Merdeka Selatan 18, Jakarta 10110; tel. and fax (21) 3519881; e-mail pie@esdm.go.id; internet www.esdm.go.id.

Ministry of Finance: Jalan Lapangan Banteng Timur 2–4, Jakarta 10710; tel. (21) 3841067; fax (21) 3808395; e-mail helpdesk@depkeu.go.id; internet www.depkeu.go.id.

Ministry of Foreign Affairs: 10th Floor, Jalan Taman Pejambon 6, Jakarta Pusat 10110; tel. (21) 3441508; fax (21) 3857316; e-mail dipten@deplu.go.id; internet www.deplu.go.id.

Ministry of Forestry: Gedung Manggala Wanabakti, Blok I, 3rd Floor, Jalan Jenderal Gatot Subroto, Senayan, Jakarta 10270; tel. (21) 5704501; fax (21) 5720216; e-mail pusdata@dephut.go.id; internet www.dephut.go.id.

Ministry of Health: Blok X5, Jalan H. R. Rasuna Said, Kav. 4–9, Jakarta 12950; tel. (21) 5201590; fax (21) 5201591; internet www.depkes.go.id.

Ministry of Home Affairs: Gedung Utama, 4th Floor, Jalan Medan Merdeka Utara 7, Jakarta Pusat 10110; tel. (21) 3450038; fax (21) 3851193; e-mail pusdatinkomtel@depdagri.go.id; internet www.depdagri.go.id.

Ministry of Industry: Jalan Jenderal Gatot Subroto, Kav. 52–53, Jakarta Selatan 12950; tel. (21) 5252194; fax (21) 5261086; internet www.depperin.go.id.

Ministry of Justice and Human Rights: Jalan H. R. Rasuna Said, Kav. 6–7, Kuningan, Jakarta Selatan; tel. (21) 5253004; fax (21) 5253139; e-mail pullahta@depkumham.go.id; internet www.depkumham.go.id.

Ministry of Manpower and Transmigration: Jalan Jenderal Gatot Subroto, Kav. 51, Jakarta Selatan 12950; tel. (21) 5255683; fax (21) 7974488; e-mail redaksi_balitfo@nakertrans.go.id; internet www.depnakertrans.go.id.

Ministry of Marine Affairs and Fisheries: Gedung Humpus, Jalan Medan Merdeka Timur 16, Jakarta 10110; tel. (21) 3500023; fax (21) 3519133; e-mail mail@kkp.go.id; internet www.kkp.go.id.

Ministry of Public Works: Jalan Pattimura 20, Kebayoran Baru, Jakarta Selatan 12110; tel. (21) 7392262; fax (21) 7200793; e-mail sekjen@pu.go.id; internet www.pu.go.id.

Ministry of Religious Affairs: Jalan Lapangan Banteng Barat 3–4, Jakarta Pusat 10710; tel. (21) 3843005; fax (21) 3812306; e-mail pikda@depag.go.id; internet www.depag.go.id.

Ministry of Social Affairs: Jalan Salemba Raya 28, Jakarta 10430; tel. (21) 3103591; fax (21) 3103783; e-mail setjend@kemsos.go.id; internet www.depsos.go.id.

Ministry of Tourism and Creative Economy: Gedung Sapta Pesona, Jalan Medan Merdeka Barat 17, Jakarta Pusat 10110; tel. (21) 3838167; fax (21) 3849715; e-mail pusdatin@budpar.go.id; internet www.budpar.go.id.

Ministry of Trade: 2nd Floor, Jalan Jenderal Gatot Subroto, Kav. 52–53, Jakarta 12950; tel. (21) 5256548; fax (21) 5229592; internet www.depdag.go.id.

Ministry of Transportation: Jalan Medan Merdeka Barat 8, Jakarta 10110; tel. (21) 3811308; fax (21) 3862371; e-mail pusdatin@dephub.go.id; internet www.dephub.go.id.

Office of the Minister of State for Administrative and Bureaucratic Reform: Jalan Jenderal Sudirman, Kav. 69, Jakarta Selatan 12190; tel. (21) 7398381; internet www.menpan.go.id.

Office of the Minister of State for Co-operatives and Small and Medium-Sized Businesses: Jalan H. R. Rasuna Said, Kav. 3–5, POB 177, Jakarta Selatan 12940; tel. (21) 5204366; fax (21) 5204378; e-mail bagdat@depkop.go.id; internet www.depkop.go.id.

Office of the Minister of State for Development of Disadvantaged Regions: Jalan Abdul Muis 7, Jakarta Pusat 10110; tel. (21) 3500334; internet www.kemenegpdt.go.id.

Office of the Minister of State for the Environment: Gedung A, 6th Floor, Jalan D. I. Panjaitan, Kav. 24, Kebon Nanas, Jakarta 13410; tel. (21) 8580067; fax (21) 8517184; e-mail edukom@menlh.go.id; internet www.menlh.go.id.

Office of the Minister of State for Research and Technology: Gedung BPP Teknologi II, 5th–8th Floors, Jalan M. H. Thamrin 8, Jakarta Pusat 10340; tel. (21) 3169119; fax (21) 3101952; e-mail webmstr@ristek.go.id; internet www.ristek.go.id.

Office of the Minister of State for State Enterprises: Jalan Medan Merdeka Selatan 13, Jakarta 10110; e-mail sekretariat@bumn.go.id; internet www.bumn.com.

Office of the Minister of State for Women's Empowerment: Jalan Medan Merdeka Barat 15, Jakarta 10110; tel. (21) 3805563; fax (21) 3805562; e-mail biroren@menegpp.go.id; internet www.menegpp.go.id.

Office of the Minister of State for Youth and Sports Affairs: Jalan Gerbang Pemuda Senayan, Jakarta 10270; internet www.kemenpora.go.id.

OTHER GOVERNMENT BODIES

Badan Pemeriksa Keuangan (BPK) (Supreme Audit Board): Jalan Gatot Subroto 31, Jakarta 10210; tel. (21) 25549000; fax (21) 57854096; internet www.bpk.go.id; Chair. Drs HADI POERNOMO; Vice-Chair. HASAN BISRI.

National Economic Council: Jakarta; f. 1999; 13-mem. council formed to advise the President on economic policy; Chair. CHAIRUL TANJUNG.

President and Legislature

PRESIDENT

Presidential Election, 9 July 2014

Candidate	Votes	% of votes
Joko Widodo (PDI—P)	70,997,833	53.15
Prabowo Subianto (Gerindra) . . .	62,576,444	46.85
Total	**133,574,277**	**100.00**

LEGISLATURE

People's Consultative Assembly
(Majelis Permusyawaratan Rakyat)

Jalan Jenderal Gatot Subroto 6, Jakarta 10270; tel. (21) 57895049; fax (21) 57895048; e-mail kotaksurat@mpr.go.id; internet www.mpr.go.id.

In late 2002 the Constitution was amended to provide for the direct election of all members of the Majelis Permusyawaratan Rakyat (MPR—People's Consultative Assembly) at the next general election, held in 2004. The MPR thus became a bicameral institution comprising the Dewan Perwakilan Daerah (DPD—House of Representatives of the Regions) and the Dewan Perwakilan Rakyat (DPR—House of Representatives). The MPR subsequently consisted of the 550 members of the DPR and 128 regional delegates, increasing to 560 and 132, respectively, at the 2009 election; the number of regional delegates increased further at the 2014 election, to 136.

Speaker: ZULKIFLI HASAN.

	Seats
Members of the Dewan Perwakilan Rakyat . . .	560
Regional representatives	136
Total	**696**

House of Representatives
(Dewan Perwakilan Rakyat)

Jalan Gatot Subroto 16, Jakarta; tel. (21) 586833; e-mail humas@dpr.go.id; internet www.dpr.go.id.

Speaker: SETYA NOVANTO.

Legislative Elections, 9 April 2014

Party	Votes	% of votes	Seats
Partai Demokrasi Indonesia Perjuangan (PDI—P)	23,681,471	18.95	109
Partai Golongan Karya (Golkar) . .	18,432,312	14.75	91
Partai Gerakan Indonesia Raya (Gerindra)	14,760,371	11.81	73
Partai Demokrat (PD)	12,728,913	10.19	61
Partai Amanat Nasional (PAN) . .	9,481,621	7.59	49
Partai Kebangkitan Bangsa (PKB) .	11,298,957	9.04	47
Partai Keadilan Sejahtera (PKS) .	8,480,204	6.79	40
Partai Persatuan Pembangunan (PPP)	8,157,488	6.53	39
Partai NasDem (NasDem) . . .	8,402,812	6.72	35
Partai Hati Nurani Rakyat (Hanura).	6,579,498	5.26	16
Partai Bulan Bintang (PBB) . .	1,825,750	1.46	—
Partai Keadilan dan Persatuan Indonesia (PKPI)	1,143,094	0.91	—
Total	**124,972,491**	**100.00**	**560**

Election Commission

Komisi Pemilihan Umum (KPU): Jalan Imam Bonjol 29, Jakarta 10310; tel. (21) 31937223; fax (21) 3157759; e-mail redaktur@kpu.go.id; internet www.kpu.go.id; f. 1999; govt body; Chair. HUSNI KAMIL MANIK.

Political Organizations

All parties must adhere to the state philosophy of *Pancasila* and reject communism. A total of 12 national parties contested the legislative elections of April 2014.

Partai Amanat Nasional (PAN) (National Mandate Party): Rumah PAN, Jalan Raya Warung Buncit 17, Jakarta Selatan; tel. (21) 7975588; fax (21) 7975632; internet www.pan.or.id; f. 1998; aims to achieve democracy, progress and social justice, to limit the length of the presidential term of office, and to increase autonomy in the provinces; Chair. ZULKIFLI HASAN; Sec.-Gen. TAUFIK KURNIAWAN.

Partai Bulan Bintang (PBB) (Crescent Moon and Star Party): Jalan Raya Pasar Minggu 1B, Km 18, Jakarta Selatan; tel. (21) 79180734; fax (21) 79180765; internet bulan-bintang.org; f. 1998; Leader M. S. KABAN; Sec.-Gen. B. M. WIBOWO.

Partai Demokrasi Indonesia Perjuangan (PDI—P) (Indonesian Democratic Struggle Party): Jalan Lenteng Agung 99, Jakarta Selatan; tel. (21) 7806028; fax (21) 7814472; internet www.pdiperjuangan.or.id; est. by Megawati Sukarnoputri, fmr PDI leader, following her removal from PDI leadership by Govt in 1996; Chair. MEGAWATI SUKARNOPUTRI; Sec.-Gen. TJAHJO KUMOLO.

Partai Demokrat (PD): Jalan Kramat Raya 146, Jakarta Pusat 10450; tel. (21) 31907999; fax (21) 31908999; internet www.demokrat.or.id; f. 2001; Chair. Gen. (retd) SUSILO BAMBANG YUDHOYONO; Sec.-Gen. EDHIE 'IBAS' BASKORO YUDHOYONO.

Partai Gerakan Indonesia Raya (Gerindra) (Great Indonesia Movement Party): Jalan Harsono R. M. 54, Ragunan, Jakarta Selatan 12160; tel. (21) 7892377; fax (21) 7819712; e-mail badankomunikasi@partaigerindra.or.id; internet www.partaigerindra.or.id; f. 2008; Chair. (vacant); Sec.-Gen. AHMAD MUZANI.

Partai Golongan Karya (Golkar) (Party of Functional Groups): Jalan Anggrek Nellimurni, Jakarta 11480; tel. (21) 5302222; fax (21) 5303380; e-mail info@golkar.or.id; internet www.golkar.or.id; f. 1964; reorg. 1971; Pres. and Chair. ABURIZAL BAKRIE; Sec.-Gen. IDRUS MARHAM.

Partai Hati Nurani Rakyat (Hanura) (People's Conscience Party): Jalan Tanjung Karang 7, Menteng, Jakarta 10310; tel. (21) 31935334; fax (21) 3922054; e-mail info@hanura.or.id; internet www .hanura.com; f. 2006; Chair. H. WIRANTO; Sec.-Gen. YUS USMAN SUMANEGARA.

Partai Keadilan dan Persatuan Indonesia (PKPI) (Justice and Unity Party): Jalan Diponegoro 63, Menteng, Jakarta Pusat 10310; tel. (21) 31922733; fax (21) 31922822; e-mail info@pkpindonesia.or .id; internet pkpindonesia.or.id; f. 2002; Chair. H. SUTIYOSO; Sec.-Gen. LUKMAN F. MOKOGINTA.

Partai Keadilan Sejahtera (PKS) (Prosperous Justice Party): Jalan T. B. Simatupang 82, Pasar Minggu, Jakarta 21520; tel. (21) 78842116; fax (21) 78846456; e-mail partai@pks.or.id; internet www .pks.or.id; f. 2002; Islamic party; Chair. ANIS MATTA; Sec.-Gen. MUHAMMAD TAUFIK RIDHO.

Partai Kebangkitan Bangsa (PKB) (National Awakening Party): Jalan Raden Saleh 9, Jakarta Pusat 10430; tel. (21) 3145328; fax (21) 3145329; e-mail dpp@pkb.or.id; internet www.dpp.pkb.or.id; f. 1998; nationalist Islamic party; Chair. MUHAIMIN ISKANDAR; Sec.-Gen. ABDUL KADIR KARDING.

Partai NasDem (National Democratic Party): Jalan R. P. Soeroso 44, Menteng, Jakarta 10350; tel. (21) 31927141; fax (21) 31927039; internet www.partainasdem.org; f. 2011; supports the creation of a welfare state; Chair. SURYA PALOH; Sec.-Gen. PATRICE RIO CAPELLA.

Partai Persatuan Pembangunan (PPP) (United Development Party): Jalan Diponegoro 60, Jakarta Pusat 10310; tel. (21) 31936338; fax (21) 3142558; e-mail info@ppp.or.id; internet www .ppp.or.id; f. 1973; est. by merger of 4 Islamic parties; Chair. M. ROMAHURMUZIY; Sec.-Gen. AUNUR ROFIQ.

In accordance with the 2005 peace agreement, Aceh is the only province that permits local parties. Three local parties were authorized to contest the elections of 9 April 2014 in the province: the Partai Aceh (PA—Aceh Party; f. 2008; Leader Muzakkir Manaf), the Partai Nasional Aceh (PNA—Aceh National Party; f. 2012; Chair. Irwansyah; Sec.-Gen. Muharram Idris) and the Partai Damai Aceh (PDA—Aceh Peace Party). The PA and the PNA both comprised many former combatants of the separatist group the Gerakan Aceh Merdeka (GAM—Free Aceh Movement). Since local parties could not field candidates at national level, the dominant local party, the PA, formed an alliance with Gerindra for the national elections.

Diplomatic Representation

EMBASSIES IN INDONESIA

Afghanistan: Jalan Dr Kusuma Atmaja 15, Jakarta Pusat 10310; tel. (21) 3143169; fax (21) 31935390; e-mail afghanembassy_jkk@ yahoo.com; Ambassador GHULAM SAKHI GHAIRAT.

Algeria: Jalan H. R. Rasuna Said, Kav. 10-1, Kuningan, Jakarta 12950; tel. (21) 5254719; fax (21) 5254654; e-mail ambaljak@cbn.net .id; internet www.embalgeria-id.org; Ambassador ABDELKRIM BELARBI.

Argentina: Menara Thamrin, Suite 1705, 17th Floor, Jalan M. H. Thamrin, Kav. 3, Jakarta 10250; tel. (21) 2303061; fax (21) 2303962; e-mail eisia@mrecic.gov.ar; internet www.eisia.mrecic.gov.ar; Ambassador RICARDO LUIS BOCALANDRO.

Armenia: Jalan Denpasar II 49, Kuningan, Jakarta; tel. (21) 5276549; fax (21) 29675166; e-mail armindonesiaembassy@mfa .am; Ambassador ANNA AGHAJANYAN.

Australia: Jalan H. R. Rasuna Said, Kav. C15–16, Kuningan, Jakarta 12940; tel. (21) 25505555; fax (21) 25505467; e-mail public-affairs-jakt@dfat.gov.au; internet www.indonesia.embassy .gov.au; Ambassador PAUL GRIGSON.

Austria: Jalan Diponegoro 44, Menteng, Jakarta 10310; tel. (21) 23554005; fax (21) 31904881; e-mail jakarta-ob@bmeia.gv.at; internet www.austrian-embassy.or.id; Ambassador Dr ANDREAS KARABACZEK.

Azerbaijan: Jalan Karang Asem Tengah, Blok C-5, Kav. 20, Kuningan Timur, Jakarta 12950; tel. (21) 25554408; fax (21) 25554409; e-mail jakarta@mission.mfa.gov.az; internet www .azembassy.or.id; Ambassador TAMERLAN KARAYEV.

Bangladesh: Jalan Karang Asem Utara, Blok C4, No. 12, Kav. 42, Jakarta Selatan 12950; tel. (21) 5262173; fax (21) 5262174; e-mail bdootjak@yahoo.com; internet www.bdembassyjakarta.org; Ambassador NIZAMUL QUAUNINE.

Belarus: Jalan Patra Kuningan VII 3, Kuningan, Jakarta Selatan 12950; tel. (21) 5251388; fax (21) 52960207; e-mail indonesia@mfa .gov.by; internet www.belembassy.org/eng/06.html; Ambassador VLADIMIR LOPATO-ZAGORSKY.

Belgium: Deutsche Bank Bldg, 16th Floor, Jalan Imam Bonjol 80, Jakarta 10310; tel. (21) 3162030; fax (21) 3162035; e-mail jakarta@ diplobel.fed.be; internet www.diplomatie.be/jakarta; Ambassador PATRICK HERMANN.

Bosnia and Herzegovina: Menara Imperium, 11th Floor, Suite D-2, Metropolitan Kuningan Super Blok, Kav. 1, Jalan H. R. Rasuna Said, Jakarta 12980; tel. (21) 83703022; fax (21) 83703029; Ambassador FUAD SABETA.

Brazil: Menara Mulia, Suite 1602, Jalan Jenderal Gatot Subroto, Kav. 9–11, Jakarta 12390; tel. (21) 5265656; fax (21) 5265659; e-mail brasemb.jacarta@itamaraty.gov.br; Ambassador PAULO ALBERTO DA SILVEIRA SOARES.

Brunei: Jalan Teuku Umar 9, Menteng, Jakarta Pusat 10350; tel. (21) 31906080; fax (21) 31905070; e-mail kbjindo@cbn.net.id; Ambassador Dato' Paduka MAHMUD Haji SAIDIN.

Bulgaria: Jalan Imam Bonjol 34–36, Menteng, Jakarta Pusat 10310; tel. (21) 3904048; fax (21) 3904049; e-mail embassy .jakarta@mfa.bg; internet www.mfa.bg/embassies/indonesia; Ambassador SERGEY MICHEV.

Cambodia: Jalan T. B. Simatupang, Kav. 13, Jakarta Selatan 12520; tel. (21) 7812523; fax (21) 7812524; e-mail camemb.jkt@mfa .gov.kh; Ambassador KAN PHARITH.

Canada: World Trade Center, 6th Floor, Jalan Jenderal Sudirman, Kav. 29–31, POB 8324/JKS.MP, Jakarta 12920; tel. (21) 25507800; fax (21) 25507811; e-mail canadianembassy.jkrta@international.gc .ca; internet www.canadainternational.gc.ca/indonesia-indonesie; Ambassador DONALD BOBIASH.

Chile: City Tower Bldg, 27th Floor, Jalan M. H. Thamrin 81, Jakarta Pusat 10310; tel. (21) 31997201; fax (21) 31997204; e-mail emchijak@ cbn.net.id; internet chileabroad.gov.cl/indonesia; Ambassador EDUARDO RUIZ ASMUSSEN.

China, People's Republic: Jalan Mega Kuningan 2, Karet Kuningan, Jakarta 12950; tel. (21) 5761039; fax (21) 5761034; e-mail chinaemb_id@mfa.gov.cn; internet id.china-embassy.org; Ambassador XIE FENG.

Colombia: Plaza Central Bldg, 12th Floor, Jalan Jenderal Sudirman, Kav. 47, Jakarta 12190; tel. (21) 57903560; fax (21) 52905217; e-mail eindonesia@cancilleria.gov.co; Ambassador ALFONSO GARZÓN MÉNDEZ.

Croatia: Menara Mulia, Suite 2801, Jalan Gatot Subroto, Kav. 9–11, Jakarta 12930; tel. (21) 5257822; fax (21) 5204073; e-mail jakarta@ mvep.hr; internet www.croatemb.or.id; Ambassador ŽELJKO CIMBUR.

Cuba: Jalan Logan, Blok D-58, Permata Hijau, Jakarta 12210; tel. (21) 5485902; fax (21) 5328174; e-mail cubaindo@cbn.net.id; Ambassador ENNA ESTHER VIANT VALDÉS.

Czech Republic: Jalan Gereja Theresia 20, Menteng, Jakarta Pusat 10350; tel. (21) 2396112; fax (21) 3904078; e-mail jakarta@ embassy.mzv.cz; internet www.mfa.cz/jakarta; Ambassador TOMÁŠ SMETÁNKA.

Denmark: Menara Rajawali, 25th Floor, Jalan Mega Kuningan, Lot 5.1, Jakarta 12950; tel. (21) 5761478; fax (21) 5761535; e-mail jktamb@um.dk; internet indonesien.um.dk; Ambassador CASPER KLYNGE.

Ecuador: World Trade Center, 16th Floor, Jalan Jenderal Sudirman, Kav. 31, Jakarta 12920; tel. (21) 5211484; fax (21) 5226954; e-mail ecuadorinindonesia@gmail.com; Ambassador RODRIGO GUILLERMO RIOFRIO MACHUCHA.

Egypt: Jalan Teuku Umar 68, Menteng, Jakarta Pusat 10310; tel. (21) 3143440; fax (21) 3145073; e-mail Jakarta_emb@mfa.gov.eg; internet www.mfa.gov.eg/Jakarta_Emb; Ambassador BAHAA BAHGAT IBRAHIM DESSOUKI AL DEEN.

Fiji: Menara Topaz, 14th Floor, Jalan M. H. Thambrin, Kav. 9, Jakarta 10350; tel. (21) 3902543; fax (21) 3902544; e-mail stui_cavuilati@yahoo.com; Ambassador RATU SEREMAIA TUI CAVUILATI.

Finland: Menara Rajawali, 9th Floor, Lot 5.1, Jalan Mega Kuningan, Kawasan Mega Kuningan, Jakarta 12950; tel. (21) 29393000; fax (21) 5761631; e-mail sanomat.jak@formin.fi; internet www .finland.or.id; Ambassador PÄIVI HILTUNEN-TOIVIO.

France: Jalan M. H. Thamrin, 40th Floor, 1 Jakarta Pusat 10310; tel. (21) 23557600; fax (21) 23557602; e-mail contact@ambafrance-id .org; internet www.ambafrance-id.org; Ambassador CORINNE BREUZE.

Georgia: Jalan Karang Asem Tengah, Block C5, No. 22, Kuningan, Jakarta Selatan 12950; tel. (21) 29410842; fax (21) 29410694; e-mail jakarta.emb@mfa.gov.ge; internet www.indonesia.mfa.gov.ge; Ambassador ZURAB ALEKSIDZE.

Germany: Jalan M. H. Thamrin 1, Jakarta Pusat 10310; tel. (21) 39855000; fax (21) 39855130; e-mail kontakt-pr@jaka.diplo.de; internet www.jakarta.diplo.de; Ambassador Dr GEORG WITSCHEL.

Greece: Plaza 89, 12th Floor, Suite 1203, Jalan H. R. Rasuna Said, Kav. X-7 No. 6, Kuningan, Jakarta Selatan 12940; tel. (21) 5207776;

fax (21) 5207753; e-mail grembas@cbn.net.id; internet www
.greekembassy.or.id; Ambassador GEORGIOS VEIS.

Holy See: Jalan Merdeka Timur 18, POB 4227, Jakarta Pusat
(Apostolic Nunciature); tel. (21) 3841142; fax (21) 3841143; e-mail
vatjak@cbn.net.id; Apostolic Nuncio ANTONIO GUIDO FILIPAZZI (Titular Archbishop of Sutrium).

Hungary: Jalan H. R. Rasuna Said 36, Kav. X-3, Kuningan, Jakarta
12950; tel. (21) 5203459; fax (21) 5203461; e-mail mission.jkt@kum
.hu; internet www.mfa.gov.hu/kulkepviselet/id; Ambassador JUDIT
NEMETH-PACH.

India: Jalan H. R. Rasuna Said, Kav. S-1, Kuningan, Jakarta 12950;
tel. (21) 5204150; fax (21) 5204160; e-mail ambasador@net-zap.com;
internet www.indianembassyjakarta.com; Ambassador GURJIT
SINGH.

Iran: Jalan Hos Cokroaminoto 110, Menteng, Jakarta Pusat 10310;
tel. (21) 31931378; fax (21) 3107860; e-mail irembjkt@indo.net.id;
internet www.iranembassy.or.id; Ambassador MOHAMMADI NASRA-
BADI.

Iraq: Jalan Teuku Umar 38, Jakarta 10350; tel. (21) 3904067; fax
(21) 3904066; e-mail iraqembi@rad.net.id; Ambassador ABDULLAH
HASSAN SALIH.

Ireland: Jakarta Stock Exchange Bldg Tower I, Jakarta 12190; tel.
and fax (21) 5151977; e-mail irelandhonconsul.indonesia@gmail
.com; Ambassador KYLE O'SULLIVAN.

Italy: Jalan Diponegoro 45, Menteng, Jakarta Pusat 10310; tel. (21)
31937445; fax (21) 31937422; e-mail ambasciata.jakarta@esteri.it;
internet www.ambjakarta.esteri.it; Ambassador FEDERICO FAILLA.

Japan: Jalan M. H. Thamrin 24, Jakarta Pusat 10350; tel. (21)
31924308; fax (21) 31925460; internet www.id.emb-japan.go.jp;
Ambassador YASUAKI TANIZAKI.

Jordan: Artha Graha Tower, 9th Floor, Sudirman Central Business
District, Jalan Jenderal Sudirman, Kav. 52–53, Jakarta 12190; tel.
(21) 5153483; fax (21) 5153482; e-mail jordanem@scbd.net.id;
internet www.jordanembassy.or.id; Ambassador WALID ABDEL RAH-
MAN AL-HADID.

Korea, Democratic People's Republic: Jalan Teluk Betung 1–2,
Jakarta Pusat 12050; tel. (21) 31908425; fax (21) 31908427; e-mail
dprkorea@rad.net.id; Ambassador RI JONG RYUL.

Korea, Republic: Plaza Office Tower, 30th Floor, Jalan M. H.
Thamrin, Kav. 28-30, Jakarta Pusat 10350; tel. (21) 5201915; fax
(21) 5254159; e-mail koremb_in@mofat.go.kr; internet idn.mofat.go
.kr; Ambassador CHO TAI-YOUNG.

Kuwait: Jalan Mega Kuningan Barat III, Kav. 16–17, Jakarta; tel.
(21) 5764159; fax (21) 5764561; e-mail jakarta@mofa.gov.kw;
Ambassador NASER BAREH SHAHER EL-ENEZI.

Laos: Jalan Patra Kuningan XIV 1A, Kuningan, Jakarta 12950; tel.
(21) 5229602; fax (21) 5229601; e-mail laoembjktof@hotmail.com;
Ambassador KOUILY A. SOUPHAKET.

Lebanon: Jalan YBR V 82, Kuningan, Jakarta 12950; tel. (21)
5253074; fax (21) 5207121; e-mail lebanon_embassy_jkt@yahoo
.com; Ambassador VICTOR ZMETER.

Libya: Jalan Kintamani Raya II, Blok C-17, Kav. 6–7, Kuningan
Timur, Jakarta Selatan 12950; tel. (21) 52920033; fax (21) 52920036;
e-mail gsplaj@cbn.net.id; Chargé d'affaires a.i. ABDUSSAMEE HARB.

Malaysia: Jalan H. R. Rasuna Said, Kav. X-6 Nos 1–3, Kuningan,
Jakarta 12950; tel. (21) 5224947; fax (21) 5224974; e-mail
maljakarta@kln.gov.my; internet www.kln.gov.my/web/
idn_jakarta; Ambassador Datuk Seri ZAHRAIN MOHAMED HASHIM.

Mexico: Menara Mulia, Suite 2306, Jalan Jenderal Gatot Subroto,
Kav. 9–11, Jakarta Selatan 12930; tel. (21) 5203980; fax (21)
5203978; e-mail embmexico@gmail.com; internet embamex.sre.gob
.mx/indonesia; Ambassador MARY MELBA PRIA OLAVARRIETA.

Mongolia: The East Tower, 38th Floor, Suite 3, Jalan Mega
Kuningan, Kav. 1, Jakarta 12950; tel. (21) 57958140; fax
57958141; e-mail jakarta@mfa.gov.mn; Ambassador SHAGDAR BATT-
SEGSEG.

Montenegro: Jakarta; Ambassador BRANKO PEROVIC.

Morocco: Jalan Denpasar Raya, Blok A-13, Kav. 1, Kuningan,
Jakarta 12950; tel. (21) 5200773; fax (21) 5200586; e-mail
sifamaind@gmail.com; Ambassador MOHAMED MAJDI.

Mozambique: Jalan Karang Asem II, Blok C-10, Kav. 2–3, Kuningan Timur, Jakarta 12950; tel. (21) 5227955; fax (21) 5227954; e-mail
embamoc@cbn.net.id; Ambassador (vacant).

Myanmar: Jalan Haji Agus Salim 109, Menteng, Jakarta 10350; tel.
(21) 327684; fax (21) 327204; e-mail myanmar@cbn.net.id; Ambassador SAN MYINT OO.

Netherlands: Jalan H. R. Rasuna Said, Kav. S-3, Kuningan,
Jakarta 12950; tel. (21) 5248200; fax (21) 5700734; e-mail jak@
minbuza.nl; internet indonesia.nlembassy.org; Ambassador ROB
SWARTBOL.

New Zealand: Sentral Senayan 2, 10th Floor, Jalan Asia Afrika 8,
Gelora Bung Karno, Jakarta Pusat 10270; tel. (21) 29955800; fax (21)
57974578; e-mail nzembjak@cbn.net.id; internet www.nzembassy
.com/indonesia; Ambassador TREVOR MATHESON.

Nigeria: Jalan Taman Patra XIV 11, Kuningan Timur, POB 3649,
Jakarta Selatan 12950; tel. (21) 5260922; fax (21) 5260924; e-mail
embnig@centrin.net.id; Ambassador MUHAMMAD LAWAL SULAIMAN.

Norway: Menara Rajawali, 20th Floor, Kawasan Mega Kuningan,
Jakarta 12950; tel. (21) 29650000; fax (21) 29650001; e-mail emb
.jakarta@mfa.no; internet www.norway.or.id; Ambassador STIG
INGEMAR TRAAVIK.

Pakistan: Jalan Mega Kuningan, Blok E-3.9, Kav. 5–8, Kawasan
Mega Kuningan, Jakarta Selatan 12950; tel. (21) 57851836; fax (21)
57851645; e-mail embassy@parepjakarta.com; internet www.mofa
.gov.pk/indonesia; Ambassador ATTIYA MAHMOOD.

Panama: World Trade Center, 13th Floor, Jalan Jenderal Sudirman, Kav. 29–31, Jakarta 12920; tel. (21) 5711867; fax (21) 5711933;
e-mail panaemb@net2cyber.web.id; Ambassador VICTOR LUIS NG
CHAN.

Papua New Guinea: Panin Bank Centre, 6th Floor, Jalan Jenderal
Sudirman 1, Jakarta 10270; tel. (21) 7251218; fax (21) 7201012;
e-mail kdujkt@cbn.net.id; Ambassador ALPHA DIALLO.

Peru: Menara Rajawali, 12th Floor, Jalan Mega Kuningan, Lot 5.1,
Kawasan Mega Kuningan, Jakarta Selatan 12950; tel. (21) 5761820;
fax (21) 5761825; e-mail embaperu@cbn.net.id; Ambassador
ROBERTO SEMINARIO PORTOCARRERO.

Philippines: Jalan Imam Bonjol 6–8, Jakarta Pusat 10310; tel. (21)
3100334; fax (21) 3151167; e-mail phjkt@indo.net.id; internet
philembjkt.com; Ambassador MARIA LUMEN BANZON INSLETA.

Poland: Jalan H. R. Rasuna Said, Blok IV-3, Kav. X, Jakarta Selatan
12950; tel. (21) 2525938; fax (21) 2525958; e-mail dzakarta.amb
.sekretariat@msz.gov.pl; internet www.dzakarta.msz.gov.pl;
Ambassador TADEUSZ ANDRZEJ SZUMOWSKI.

Portugal: Jalan Indramayu 2A, Menteng, Jakarta 10310; tel. (21)
31908030; fax (21) 31908031; e-mail porembjak@cbn.net.id; internet
www.embassyportugaljakarta.or.id; Ambassador JOAQUIM MOREIRA
DE LEMOS.

Qatar: Lot E 2.3, Jalan Mega Kuningan Barat, Kawasan Mega
Kuningan, Jakarta 12950; tel. (21) 57906065; fax (21) 57906564;
e-mail jakarta@mofa.gov.qa; Ambassador MUHAMMAD KHATER IBRA-
HIM AL-KHATER.

Romania: Jalan Teuku Cik Di Tiro 42A, Menteng, Jakarta Pusat;
tel. (21) 3900489; fax (21) 3106241; e-mail romind@indosat.net.id;
internet jakarta.mae.ro; Ambassador VALERICA EPURE.

Russian Federation: Jalan H. R. Rasuna Said, Kav. X-7 Nos 1–2,
Jakarta 12940; tel. (21) 5222912; fax (21) 5222916; e-mail rusemb
.indonesia@mid.ru; internet www.indonesia.mid.ru; Ambassador
MIKHAIL Y. GALUZIN.

Saudi Arabia: Jalan M. T. Haryono, Kav. 27, Cawang Atas, Jakarta
13630; tel. (21) 8011533; fax (21) 8011527; e-mail idemb@mofa.gov
.sa; Ambassador MUSTAFA IBRAHIM AL-MUBARAK.

Serbia: Jalan Hos Cokroaminoto 109, Jakarta Pusat 10310; tel. (21)
3143560; fax (21) 3143613; e-mail embjakarta@serbian-embassy
.org; internet www.jakarta.mfa.rs; Ambassador JOVAN JOVANOVIĆ.

Singapore: Jalan H. R. Rasuna Said, Blok X-4, Kav. 2, Kuningan,
Jakarta 12950; tel. (21) 5201489; fax (21) 5201486; e-mail
singemb_jkt@sgmfa.gov.sg; internet www.mfa.gov.sg/jkt; Ambassador ANIL KUMAR NAYAR.

Slovakia: Jalan Prof. Mohammed Yamin 29, POB 1368, Menteng,
Jakarta Pusat 10310; tel. (21) 3101068; fax (21) 3101180; e-mail emb
.jakarta@mzv.sk; internet www.mzv.sk/jakarta; Ambassador
MICHAL SLIVOVIČ.

Solomon Islands: Jakarta; Ambassador SALANA KALU.

Somalia: Jalan Permata Hijau Raya, Blok T, No. 8, Kebayoran
Lama, Jakarta Selatan 12210; tel. (21) 8311506; fax (21) 8352586;
e-mail somalirep_jkt@yahoo.com; internet www.indonesia
.somaligov.net; Ambassador MOHAMED OLOW BAROW.

South Africa: Wisma GKBI, Suite 705, Jalan Jenderal Sudirman
28, Jakarta 10210; tel. (21) 5740660; fax (21) 5740655; e-mail
saembpol@centrin.net.id; internet www.dirco.gov.za/jakarta;
Ambassador NOEL NOA LEHOKO.

Spain: Jalan H. Agus Salim 61, Menteng, Jakarta 10350; tel. (21)
3142355; fax (21) 31935134; e-mail emb.yakarta@mae.es; Ambassador FRANCISCO JOSÉ VIQUEIRA NIEL.

Sri Lanka: Jalan Diponegoro 70, Jakarta 10320; tel. (21) 3161886;
fax (21) 3107962; e-mail lankaemb@telkom.net; Ambassador ANOJA
WIJEYESEKERA.

Sudan: Jalan Lembang 7, Menteng, Jakarta Pusat 10310; tel. (21)
3908234; fax (21) 3908235; e-mail sudanind@cbn.net.id; Ambassador
ABD AL-RAHIM AL-SIDDIQ MOHAMED OMAR.

Suriname: Jalan Padalarang 9, Menteng, Jakarta Pusat 10310; tel. (21) 3154437; fax (21) 3154556; e-mail ambassador@srembassyjkt .org; Ambassador TITI AMINA PARDI.

Sweden: Menara Rajawali, 9th Floor, Jalan Mega Kuningan, Lot 5.1, Kawasan Mega Kuningan, Jakarta Selatan 12950; tel. (21) 55535900; fax (21) 5762691; e-mail ambassaden.jakarta@foreign .ministry.se; internet www.swedenabroad.com/jakarta; Ambassador JOHANNA BRISMAR SKOOG.

Switzerland: Jalan H. R. Rasuna Said, Blok X-3 No. 2, Kuningan, Jakarta Selatan 12950; tel. (21) 5256061; fax (21) 5202289; e-mail jak .vertretung@eda.admin.ch; internet www.eda.admin.ch/jakarta; Ambassador YVONNE BAUMANN.

Syria: Jalan Karang Asem I 8, Jakarta 12950; tel. (21) 5255991; fax (21) 5202511; e-mail syrianemb@cbn.net.id; internet syrianembassy .or.id; Chargé d'affaires a.i. BASSAM AL-KHATIB.

Thailand: Jalan Imam Bonjol 74, Jakarta Pusat 10310; tel. (21) 3904052; fax (21) 3107469; e-mail thaijkt@indo.net.id; internet www .thaiembassy.org/jakarta; Ambassador PASKORN SIRIYAPHAN.

Timor-Leste: Gedung Surya, 11th Floor, Jalan M. H. Thamrin, Kav. 9, Jakarta Pusat 10350; tel. (21) 3902678; fax (21) 3902660; e-mail manser_tl@yahoo.com; Ambassador MANUEL SERRANO.

Tunisia: Jalan Karang Asem Tengah, Blok C-5, Kav. 15, Kuningan, Jakarta Selatan 12950; tel. (21) 52892328; fax (21) 5255889; e-mail atjkt@uninet.net.id; Ambassador MOURAD BELHASSEN.

Turkey: Jalan H. R. Rasuna Said, Kav. 1, Kuningan, Jakarta 12950; tel. (21) 5256250; fax (21) 5226056; e-mail embassy.jakarta@mfa.gov .tr; internet jakarta.emb.mfa.gov.tr; Ambassador ZEKERIYA AKÇAM.

Ukraine: Jalan Jenderal Sudirman, Kav. 27, Mayapada Tower 2, 8th Floor, Jakarta 12920; tel. (21) 2500801; fax (21) 2500802; e-mail emb_id@mfa.gov.ua; internet www.mfa.gov.ua/indonesia; Ambassador VOLODYMYR PAKHIL.

United Arab Emirates: Jalan Prof. Dr Satrio, Blok C-4, Kav. 16–17, Jakarta 12950; tel. (21) 5206518; fax (21) 5206526; e-mail jakarta@mofa.gov.ae; internet www.uaeembassyjakarta.org/index .php; Ambassador AHMED ABDULLAH MUHAMMED AL-MUSALLI.

United Kingdom: Jalan Patra Kuningan Raya, Blok L5-6, Jakarta 12950; tel. (21) 23565200; fax (21) 23565351; e-mail Jakarta.MCS@ fco.gov.uk; internet ukinindonesia.fco.gov.uk; Ambassador MOAZ-ZAM MALIK.

USA: Jalan Medan Merdeka Selatan 3–5, Jakarta 10110; tel. (21) 34359000; fax (21) 3862259; e-mail jakconsul@state.gov; internet jakarta.usembassy.gov; Ambassador ROBERT BLAKE.

Uzbekistan: Jalan Daksa III 14, Kebayoran Baru, Jakarta; tel. (21) 7200950; fax (21) 5222582; e-mail inbox@uzbemb.or.id; internet www.uzbemb.or.id; Ambassador SHAVKAT DJAMOLOV.

Venezuela: Menara Mulia, 20th Floor, Suite 2005, Jalan Jenderal Gatot Subroto, Kav. 9–11, Jakarta Selatan 12930; tel. (21) 5227547; fax (21) 5227549; e-mail evenjakt@indo.net.id; Chargé d'affaires a.i. MARÍA VIRGINIA MENZONES LICCIONI.

Viet Nam: Jalan Teuku Umar 25, Jakarta Pusat 10350; tel. (21) 3100358; fax (21) 3149615; e-mail jakarta@mofa.gov.vn; internet www.vietnamembassy-indonesia.org; Ambassador NGUYEN XUAN THUY.

Yemen: Jalan Subang 18, Menteng, Jakarta Pusat 10310; tel. (21) 3108029; fax (21) 3904946; e-mail yemb-jakarta@mofa.gov.ye; Ambassador ALI AL-SOSWA.

Zimbabwe: Jalan Patra Kuningan VII 5, Jakarta Selatan 12950; tel. (21) 5221378; fax (21) 5250365; e-mail zimjakarta@yahoo.com; Ambassador ALICE MAGEZA.

Judicial System

There is one codified criminal law for the whole of Indonesia. In December 1989 the Islamic Judicature Bill, giving wider powers to *Shari'a* courts, was approved by the Dewan Perwakilan Rakyat (House of Representatives). The new law gave Muslim courts authority over civil matters, such as marriage. Muslims may still choose to appear before a secular court. Europeans are subject to the Code of Civil Law published in the State Gazette in 1847. Alien orientals (i.e. Arabs, Indians, etc.) and Chinese are subject to certain parts of the Code of Civil Law and the Code of Commerce. The work of codifying this law has started, but, in view of the great complexity and diversity of customary law, it may be expected to take a considerable time to achieve. In June 2005 a judicial commission was established; the seven-member body, appointed by the House of Representatives, was charged with reforming the judiciary and with nominating Supreme Court justices, including the Chief Justice.

Supreme Court (Mahkamah Agung): Jalan Merdeka Utara 9–13, Jakarta 10110; tel. (21) 3843348; fax (21) 3811057; e-mail info@ma-ri .go.id; internet www.mahkamahagung.go.id; final court of appeal; comprised 49 judges at Nov. 2012; Chief Justice HATTA ALI.

Constitutional Court (Mahkamah Konstitusi): Jalan Medan Merdeka Barat 6, Jakarta 10110; tel. (21) 23529000; fax (21) 3520177; e-mail humas@mahkamahkonstitusi.go.id; internet www .mahkamahkonstitusi.go.id; f. 2003; adjudicates the following matters: constitutionality of a law; impeachment; dissolution of a political party; disputes between state agencies; and disputes concerning election results; composed of nine justices, of whom three each are appointed by the President, the Supreme Court and the House of Representatives; Chief Justice ARIEF HIDAYAT.

High Courts in Jakarta Surabaya, Medan, Makassar, Banda Aceh, Padang, Palembang, Bandung, Semarang, Banjarmasin, Menado, Denpasar, Ambon and Jayapura deal with appeals from the District Courts. District Courts deal with marriage, divorce and reconciliation.

Religion

All citizens are required to state their religion. The Ministry of Religious Affairs accords official status to six religions—Islam, the Christian faiths of Protestantism and Catholicism, Hinduism, Buddhism and Confucianism. According to a survey in 2000, 88.2% of the population were Muslims, while 5.9% were Protestant, 3.1% were Roman Catholic, 1.8% were Hindus, 0.8% were Buddhists and 0.2% professed adherence to other religions, such as other Christian denominations and Judaism, which remains unrecognized.

National religious councils—representing the official religious traditions—were established to serve as liaison bodies between religious adherents and the Government and to advise the Government on the application of religious principles to various elements of national life.

ISLAM

Indonesia has the world's largest Muslim population.

Majelis Ulama Indonesia (MUI) (Indonesian Ulama Council): Jalan Proklamasi 51, Menteng, Jakarta Pusat; tel. (21) 31902666; fax (21) 31905266; e-mail mui-online@mui.or.id; internet www.mui .or.id; central Muslim org.; Chair. Dr SAHAL MAHFUDH; Sec.-Gen. ICHWAN SAM.

Muhammadiyah: Jalan Menteng Raya 62, Jakarta Pusat 10340; tel. (21) 3903021; fax (21) 3903024; e-mail pp_muhammadiyah@ yahoo.com; internet www.muhammadiyah.or.id; f. 1912; 28m. mems; second largest Muslim org. in Indonesia; incorporates the Muhammadiyah Youth Asscn and 'Aisyiyah', a women's org.; religious, charitable and educational activities; has established more than 5,000 Islamic schools; Chair. Dr DIN SYAMSUDDIN; Sec.-Gen. Dr AGUNG DANARTO.

Nahdlatul Ulama (NU) (Revival of the Islamic Scholars): Jalan Kramat Raya 164, Jakarta 10430; tel. (21) 3914014; fax (21) 3914013; internet www.nu.or.id; f. 1926; 30m. mems; largest Muslim org. in Indonesia; promotes Islamic teachings, as well as culture, education and economic devt; directly involved in politics from the mid-1950s until 1984; Chair. Dr SAID AQIL SIRADJ; Sec.-Gen. Dr MARSUDI SYUHUD.

CHRISTIANITY

Persekutuan Gereja-Gereja di Indonesia (Communion of Churches in Indonesia): Jalan Salemba Raya 10, Jakarta Pusat 10430; tel. (21) 3150451; fax (21) 3150457; e-mail pgi@bit.net.id; internet www.pgi.or.id; f. 1950; 81 mem. churches; Chair. Rev. ROYKE OCTAVIAN RORING; Gen. Sec. GOMAR GULTOM.

The Roman Catholic Church

Indonesia comprises 10 archdioceses and 27 dioceses. At 31 December 2007 there were an estimated 6,537,062 adherents in Indonesia, representing 3.9% of the population.

Bishops' Conference: Konferensi Waligereja Indonesia (KWI), Jalan Cut Meutia 10, POB 3044, Jakarta 10340; tel. and fax (21) 31925757; e-mail dokpen@kawali.org; internet www.kawali.org; f. 1973; Pres. IGNATIUS SUHARYO.

Archbishop of Ende: Most Rev. VICENTIUS SENSI, Keuskupan Agung, POB 210, Jalan Katedral 5, Ndona-Ende 86312, Flores; tel. (381) 21176; fax (381) 21606; e-mail uskup@ende.parokinet.org.

Archbishop of Jakarta: Most Rev. IGNATIUS SUHARYO HARDJOAT-MODJO, Keuskupan Agung, Jalan Katedral 7, Jakarta 10710; tel. (21) 3813345; fax (21) 3855681.

Archbishop of Kupang: Most Rev. PETER TURANG, Keuskupan Agung Kupang, Jalan Thamrin, Oepoi, Kupang 85111, Timor NTT; tel. (380) 826199; fax (380) 833331.

Archbishop of Makassar: Most Rev. JOHANNES LIKU ADA', Keuskupan Agung, Jalan Thamrin 5–7, Makassar 90111, Sulawesi Selatan; tel. (411) 315744; fax (411) 326674; e-mail sekr_kams@ yahoo.com.

Archbishop of Medan: Most Rev. Bongsu Antonius Sinaga, Jalan Imam Bonjol 39, POB 1191, Medan 20152, Sumatra Utara; tel. (61) 4519768; fax (61) 4145745; e-mail sekrkam@hotmail.com.

Archbishop of Merauke: Most Rev. Nicolaus Adi Septura, Keuskupan Agung, Jalan Mandala 30, Merauke 99602, Papua; tel. (971) 321011; fax (971) 321311.

Archbishop of Palembang: Most Rev. Aloysius Sudarso, Keuskupan Agung, Jalan Tasik 18, Palembang 30135; tel. (711) 350417; fax (711) 314776; e-mail alva@mdp.net.id.

Archbishop of Pontianak: Most Rev. Agustinus Agus, Keuskupan Agung, Jalan A. R. Hakin 92A, POB 1119, Pontianak 78011, Kalimantan Barat; tel. (561) 732382; fax (561) 738785; e-mail kap@pontianak.wasantara.net.id.

Archbishop of Samarinda: Most Rev. Florentinus Sului Hajang Hau, Keuskupan Agung, POB 1062, Jalan Gunung Merbabu 41, Samarinda 75010; tel. (541) 741193; fax (541) 203120.

Archbishop of Semarang: Most Rev. Johannes Maria Trilaksyanta Pujasumarta, Keuskupan Agung, Jalan Pandanaran 13, Semarang 50244; tel. (24) 8312276; fax (24) 8414741; e-mail uskup@semarang.parokinet.org.

Other Christian Churches

Protestant Church in Indonesia (Gereja Protestan di Indonesia): Jalan Medan Merdeka Timur 10, Jakarta 10110; tel. (21) 3519003; fax (21) 34830224; consists of 12 churches of Calvinistic tradition; 3,047,300 mems, 4,808 congregations; Chair. Rev. Dr Samuel B. Hakh.

Numerous other Protestant communities exist throughout Indonesia, organized mainly on a local basis.

BUDDHISM

All-Indonesia Buddhist Association: Jakarta.

Indonesian Buddhist Council: Jakarta; Head Siti Hartati Tjakra Murdaya.

HINDUISM

Hindu Dharma Council: Jakarta; Chair. Maj.-Gen. (retd) Sang Nyoman Suwisma.

The Press

PRINCIPAL DAILIES

Bali

Harian Pagi Umum (Bali Post): Jalan Kepundung 67A, Denpasar 80232; tel. (61) 225764; fax (61) 249483; e-mail iklan@balipost.co.id; internet www.balipost.co.id; f. 1948; daily (Indonesian edn), weekly (English edn); Editor-in-Chief Nyoman Wirata; circ. 25,000.

Java

Berita Buana: RT 14/9, Johar Baru Village, District Johar Baru, Central Jakarta; tel. (21) 95316544; fax (21) 4203376; internet beritabuana.co; f. 1970; relaunched 1990; Indonesian; Editor-in-Chief Dada Sugandi; Editor Mufi al Akhyari; circ. 150,000.

Bisnis Indonesia: Wisma Bisnis Indonesia, Jalan K. H. Mas Mansyur 12A, Karet, Jakarta 10220; tel. (21) 57901023; fax (21) 57901025; e-mail redaksi@bisnis.co.id; internet www.bisnis.com; f. 1985; available online; Indonesian; Editor-in-Chief Arif Budisusilo; circ. 72,000.

Harian Pelita: Jalan Minangkabau 35B-C Manggarai, Jakarta Selatan 12970; tel. (21) 83706765; fax (21) 83706771; e-mail redaksi@pelitaonline.com; internet www.harianpelita.com; f. 1974; 6 a week; Indonesian; Muslim; Chief Editor A. Basori.

Harian Terbit: Jalan Pulogadung 15, Kawasan Industri Pulogadung, Jakarta 13920; tel. (21) 4603973; fax (21) 4603970; e-mail terbit@harianterbit.com; internet www.harianterbit.com; f. 1972; Indonesian; Editor-in-Chief Tarman Azzam; Man. Editor Ali Akbar Coal; circ. 120,000.

The Jakarta Post: Jalan Palmerah Barat 142–143, Jakarta 10270; tel. (21) 5300476; fax (21) 5350050; e-mail editorial@thejakartapost.com; internet www.thejakartapost.com; f. 1983; English; Exec. Dir Riyadi Suparno; Chief Editor Meidyatama Suryodiningrat; circ. 85,000.

Jawa Pos: Graha Pena Bldg, 4th Floor, Achmad Yani 88, Surabaya 60234; tel. (31) 8283333; fax (31) 8285555; e-mail digital@jawapos.co.id; internet www.jawapos.co.id; f. 1949; Indonesian; Pres. Dir Azrul Ananda; Chief Editor Leak Kustiya; circ. 400,000.

Kedaulatan Rakyat: Jalan P. Mangkubumi 40–44, Yogyakarta; tel. (274) 565685; fax (274) 563125; internet krjogja.com; f. 1945; Indonesian; independent; Chief Editor Octo Lampito; circ. 50,000.

Kompas: Gedung Kompas Gramedia, Unit II, Lantai 5, Jalan Palmerah Selatan 26–28, Jakarta 10270; tel. (21) 5350377; fax (21) 5360678; e-mail redaksikcm@kompas.co.id; internet www.kompas.com; f. 1965; Indonesian; Man. Editor Tri Wahono; circ. 550,000.

Koran Tempo: Gedung Tempo, Jalan H. R. Rasuna Said, Kav. C-17, Kuningan, Jakarta 10770; tel. (21) 5201022; fax (21) 5200092; e-mail interaktif@tempo.co.id; internet www.korantempo.com; f. 2001; Indonesian; Editor-in-Chief Bambang Harymurti.

Media Indonesia Daily: Jalan Pilar Mas Raya, Kav. A–D, Kedoya Selatan, Kebon Jeruk, Jakarta 11520; tel. (21) 5812088; fax (21) 5812105; e-mail miol@mediaindonesia.co.id; internet www.mediaindo.co.id; f. 1989; fmrly *Prioritas*; Indonesian; Publr Surya Paloh; Editor Djafar H. Assegaff; circ. 2,000.

Pikiran Rakyat: Jalan Asia-Afrika 77, Bandung 40111; tel. (22) 51216; e-mail pdr@pikiran-rakyat.com; internet www.pikiran-rakyat.com; f. 1950; Indonesian; independent; Editor Bram M. Darmaprawira; circ. 150,000.

Pos Kota: Yayasan Antar Kota, Jalan Gajah Mada 100, Jakarta 10130; tel. and fax (21) 5652603; e-mail editor@poskotanews.com; internet www.poskota.co.id; f. 1970; Indonesian; Editor-in-Chief H. Joko Lesteri; circ. 500,000.

Rakyat Merdeka: Graha Pena, 9th Floor, Jalan Raya Kebayoran Lama 12, Jakarta Selatan 12210; tel. (21) 5348460; fax (21) 53671716; e-mail redaksi@rakyatmerdeka.co.id; internet www.rakyatmerdeka.co.id; f. 1945; Indonesian; independent; Chief Editor Teguh Santosa; circ. 300,000.

Republika: Jalan Warung Buncit Raya 37, Jakarta Selatan 12510; tel. (21) 7803747; fax (21) 7800649; e-mail sekretariat@republika.co.id; internet www.republika.co.id; f. 1995; organ of the Assen of Indonesian Muslim Intellectuals (ICMI); Chief Editor Nasihin Masha.

Sin Chew Daily Indonesia: Jalan Toko Tiga Seberang 21, POB 4755, Jakarta 11120; tel. (21) 6295948; fax (21) 6297830; internet indonesia.sinchew.com.my; f. 1966; Chinese; fmrly *Harian Indonesia*; Indonesia's first Chinese-language newspaper; Editor W. D. Sukisman; Dir Hadi Wibowo; circ. 50,000.

Solo Pos: Griya SOLOPOS, Jalan Adisucipto 190, Solo 57145; tel. (271) 724811; fax (271) 724833; internet www.solopos.co.id; Editor-in-Chief Sunyoto Ya.

Suara Karya: Jalan Bangka Raya 2, Kebayoran Baru, Jakarta Selatan 12720; tel. (21) 7192656; fax (21) 71790746; e-mail redaksi@suarakarya-online.com; internet www.suarakarya-online.com; f. 1971; Indonesian; Chief Editor Ricky Rachmadi; Man. Editor Djunaedi Tjunti Agus; circ. 300,000.

Suara Merdeka: Jalan Pandanaran 30, Semarang 50241; tel. (24) 8412600; fax (24) 8411116; e-mail redaksi@suaramerdeka.info; internet www.suaramerdeka.com; f. 1950; Indonesian; Publr Ir H. Tommy Hetami; Editor-in-Chief Iwan Kelana; circ. 200,000.

Suara Pembaruan: Citra Graha Bldg, 11th Floor, Jalan Jenderal Gatot Subroto, Kav. 35–36, Jakarta 12950; tel. (21) 57851555; fax (21) 5200072; e-mail koransp@suarapembaruan.com; internet www.suarapembaruan.com; f. 1987; Chief Editor Primus Dorimulu; CEO Sachin Gopalan.

Surabaya Post: Ruko Rich Palace, Kav. 19–20, Jalan Mayjend Sungkono 149–150, Surabaya; tel. (31) 5667000; fax (31) 5635000; e-mail redaksi@surabayapost.co.id; internet www.surabayapost.co.id; f. 1953; independent; afternoon; Chief Editor and Dir Bambang Hariawan; Man. Editor Agustina Widyawati; circ. 120,000.

Surya: Jalan Rungkut Industri III, 68 & 70 SIER, Surabaya 60293; tel. (31) 8419000; fax (31) 8414024; e-mail redaksi.suryaonline@gmail.com; internet www.surya.co.id; Editor-in-Chief Dahlan Dahi.

Kalimantan

Banjarmasin Post: Gedung HJ Djok Mentaya, Jalan AS Musyaffa 16, Banjarmasin 70111; tel. (511) 3354370; fax (511) 4366123; e-mail redaksi@banjarmasinpost.co.id; internet www.banjarmasinpost.co.id; f. 1971; Indonesian; Editor-in-Chief Yusran Pare; circ. 48,000.

Kaltim Post: Jalan Jenderal Sudirman RT XVI 82, Balikpapan 76144; tel. (542) 736459; fax (542) 735242; e-mail redaksi@kaltimpost.net; internet www.kaltimpost.co.id; f. 1988; fmrly *Manuntung*; Editor-in-Chief Drs H. Bambang Isnoto.

Pontianak Post: Pontianak Post Group, Jalan Gajah Mada 2–4, Pontianak 78121; tel. (561) 735071; fax (561) 736607; e-mail redaksi@pontianakpost.com; internet www.pontianakpost.com; f. 1972; CEO Dr Untung Sukarti.

Maluku

Pos Maluku: Jalan Raya Pattimura 19, Ambon; tel. (911) 44614; daily.

Suara Maluku: Komplek Perdagangan Mardikas, Blok D3/11A, Ternate; tel. (911) 44590.

Nusa Tenggara

Pos Kupang: Jalan Kenari 1, Kupang 85115; tel. (380) 833820; fax (380) 831801; e-mail poskpg@yahoo.com; internet kupang .tribunnews.com; Chief Editor DION D. B. PUTRA.

Papua

Cenderawasih Post: Jalan Cenderawasih 10, Kelapa II, Entrop, Jayapura 99013; tel. (967) 532417; fax (967) 532418; e-mail cepos_jpr@yahoo.com; internet www.cenderawasihpos.com; Editor-in-Chief N. LUCKY IREEUW; Man. Editor WENNY FIRMAN.

Teropong: Jalan Soeprapto Sintuvu 38, Palu 94000; tel. (451) 427783; e-mail majalahteropong@ymail.com; internet www .teropongpapua.com.

Riau

Batam Pos: Gedung Graha Pena, 2nd Floor, Jalan Raya Batam Centre, Batam 29461; tel. (778) 460000; fax (778) 462162; e-mail redaksi@batampos.co.id; internet www.batampos.co.id; Editor-in-Chief HASAN ASPAHANI.

Riau Pos: Jalan H. R. Subrantas, Km 10.5, Pekanbaru, Riau 28294; tel. (761) 64633; fax (761) 64640; e-mail redaksi@riaupos.com; internet www.riaupos.co.id; Group Head Editor RAJA ISYAM ANWAR; Editor-in-Chief NAZIR MUHAMMAD FAHMI; circ. 40,000.

Sulawesi

Fajar (Dawn): Gedung Graha Pena, Lantai 4, Jalan Urip Sumoharjo 21, Makassar 90231; tel. (411) 441441; fax (411) 441224; e-mail redaksi@fajar.co.id; internet www.fajar.co.id; Editor-in-Chief ALWI HAMU; circ. 35,000.

Manado Post: Manado Post Centre, Manado Town Sq., Blok B, Kav. 14–15, Manado; tel. (431) 855558; fax (431) 860398; e-mail editor@ mdopost.com; internet www.mdopost.com; Editor-in-Chief SUHENDRO BOROMA.

Suluh Merdeka: Jalan R. W. Mongsidi 4/96, POB 1105, Manado 95110; tel. and fax (431) 866150.

Tegas: Jalan H. A. Mappanyukki 28, Makassar; tel. (411) 3960.

Sumatra

Harian Analisa: Jalan Ahmad Yani 35–49, Medan 20111; tel. (61) 4513554; fax (61) 4151436; internet www.analisadaily.com; f. 1972; Indonesian; Editor H. ALI SOEKARDI; circ. 75,000.

Harian Berita Sore: Jalan Letjen Suprapto 1, Medan 20151; tel. (61) 4158787; fax (61) 4150383; e-mail redaksi@beritasore.com; internet www.beritasore.com; Indonesian; Publr SAID PRABUDI SAID; Editor-in-Chief H. TERUNA JASA SAID.

Harian Haluan: Komplek Bandara Tabing, Jalan Hamka, Padang; tel. (51) 4488700; e-mail aluanpadang@gmail.com; internet www .harianhaluan.com; f. 1948; Publr BASRIZAL KOTO; Editor-in-Chief YON ERIZON; circ. 54,000.

Harian Umum Nasional Waspada: Jalan Letjen Suprapto, cnr Jalan Brigjenderal Katamso 1, Medan 20151; tel. (61) 4150858; fax (61) 4510025; e-mail redaksi.online@waspada.co.id; internet www .waspada.co.id; f. 1947; Indonesian; Editor-in-Chief AVIAN E. TUMENGKOL.

Mimbar Umum: Merah, Medan; tel. (61) 517807; e-mail mimbarumum@yahoo.com; internet www.mimbarumumberita .com; f. 1947; Indonesian; independent; Editor MOHD LUD LUBIS; circ. 55,000.

Padang Ekspres: Jalan Proklamasi Tarandam 5D, Padang, Sumatra Barat; tel. (751) 841300; fax (751) 841904; e-mail redaksi@ padang-today.com; internet www.padang-today.com; Indonesian; Editor SHI MUSLIM.

Serambi Indonesia: Jalan Raya Lambaro, Km 4.5, Tanjung Permai, Manyang PA, Banda Aceh; tel. (651) 635544; fax (651) 637180; e-mail redaksi@serambinews.com; internet www.serambinews.com; Editor-in-Chief MAWARDI IBRAHIM.

Sinar Indonesia Baru: Jalan Brigjenderal Katamso 66, Medan 20151; tel. (61) 4512530; fax (61) 4538150; e-mail redaksi@hariansib .com; internet www.hariansib.com; f. 1970; Indonesian; Chief Editor G. M. PANGGABEAN; circ. 150,000.

Sriwijaya Post: Jalan Jenderal Basuki Rahmat 1608 B–D, Palembang; tel. (711) 310088; fax (711) 312888; e-mail redaksi@sripoku .com; internet www.suararakyat.net; f. 2002; Editor-in-Chief HADI PRAYOGO.

Waspada: Jalan Letjen Suprapto, cnr Jalan Brigjenderal Katamso 1, Medan 20151; tel. (61) 4150868; fax (61) 4510025; e-mail waspada@waspada.co.id; internet www.waspada.co.id; f. 1947; Indonesian; Editor-in-Chief AVIAN TUMENGKOL; circ. 60,000 (daily), 55,000 (Sun.).

PRINCIPAL PERIODICALS

Amanah: Jalan Garuda 69, Kemayoran, Jakarta; tel. (21) 410254; fortnightly; Indonesian; Muslim current affairs; Man. Dir MASKUN ISKANDAR; circ. 180,000.

Ayahbunda: Jalan H. R. Rasuna Said, Blok B, Kav. 32–33, Jakarta 12910; tel. (21) 5253816; fax (21) 5262131; e-mail kontak@ ayahbunda.co.id; internet www.ayahbunda.co.id; fortnightly; family magazine.

Berita Negara: Jalan Pertjetakan Negara 21, Kotakpos 2111, Jakarta; tel. and fax (21) 4207251; f. 1951; 2 a week; official gazette.

Bobo (PT Penerbitan Sarana Bobo): Gramedia Magazine Bldg, 2nd Floor, Jalan Panjang 8A, Kebon Jeruk, Jakarta 11530; tel. (21) 5330150; fax (21) 5320681; f. 1973; subsidiary of Gramedia Group; weekly; children's magazine; Editor KOES SABANDIYAH; circ. 85,315.

Bola: Gedung Kompas Gramedia, Jalan Palmerah Barat 33–37, Jakarta 10270; tel. (21) 53677835; fax (21) 5303400; e-mail redaksi@ bolanews.com; internet www.bolanews.com; f. 1984; 3 a week; Mon., Thur. and Sat.; Indonesian; Chief Editor ARIEF KURNIAWAN; circ. 715,000.

Buana Minggu: Jalan Tanah Abang Dua 33–35, Jakarta Pusat 10110; tel. (21) 364190; weekly; Sun.; Indonesian; Editor WINOTO PARARTHO; circ. 193,450.

Business News: Jalan H. Abdul Muis 70, Jakarta 10160; tel. (21) 3848207; fax (21) 3454280; f. 1956; 3 a week (Indonesian edn), 2 a week (English edn); Chief Editor SANJOTO SASTROMIHARDJO; circ. 15,000.

Cita Cinta: Jalan H. R. Rasuna Said, Blok B, Kav. 32–33, Jakarta 12910; tel. (21) 5254206; fax (21) 5262131; e-mail citacinta@ feminagroup.com; internet www.citacinta.com; f. 2000; teenage lifestyle magazine.

Citra: Gramedia Bldg, Unit 11, 5th Floor, Jalan Palmerah Selatan 24–26, Jakarta 10270; tel. (21) 5483008; fax (21) 5494035; e-mail citra@gramedia-majalah.com; f. 1990; weekly; TV and film programmes, music trends and celebrity news; Chief Editor H. MAMAN SUHERMAN; circ. 239,000.

Depthnews Indonesia: Jalan Jatinegara Barat III/6, Jakarta 13310; tel. (21) 8194994; fax (21) 8195501; f. 1972; weekly; publ. by Press Foundation of Indonesia; Editor SUMONO MUSTOFFA.

Dunia Wanita: Jalan Brigjenderal 1 Katamso, Medan; tel. (61) 4150858; fax (61) 4510025; e-mail waspada@indosat.net.id; internet www.dunia-wanita.com; f. 1949; fortnightly; Indonesian; women's tabloid; Chief Editor Dr RAYATI SYAFRIN; circ. 10,000.

Economic Review: Bank BNI, Strategic Planning Division, Gedung Bank BNI, Jalan Jenderal Sudirman, Kav. 1, POB 2955, Jakarta 10220; tel. (21) 5728692; fax (21) 5728456; e-mail renkek01@ bni.co.id; f. 1946; 3 a year; English; economic and business research and analysis; Editor-in-Chief DARWIN SUZANDI.

Ekonomi Indonesia: Jalan Merdeka, Timur 11–12, Jakarta; tel. (21) 494458; monthly; English; economic journal; Editor Z. ACHMAD; circ. 20,000.

Eksekutif: Jalan R. S. Fatmawati 20, Jakarta 12430; tel. (21) 7659218; fax (21) 7504018; internet eksekutif.com.

Femina: Jalan H. R. Rasuna Said, Blok B, Kav. 32–33, Jakarta Selatan 12910; tel. (21) 5209370; fax (21) 5209366; e-mail redaksi@ feminagroup.com; internet www.femina.co.id; f. 1972; weekly; women's magazine; CEO SVIDA ALISJAHBANA; Editor-in-Chief PETTY S. FATIMAH; circ. 170,000.

Gadis: Jalan H. R. Rasuna Said, Blok B, Kav. 32–33, Jakarta 12910; tel. (21) 5253816; fax (21) 5262131; e-mail palupi.ambardini@ feminagroup.com; internet www.gadis.co.id; f. 1973; 3 a month; Indonesian; teenage lifestyle magazine; Editor-in-Chief PALUPI AMBARDINI; circ. 150,000.

Gatra: Gedung Gatra, Jalan Kalibata Timur IV/15, Jakarta 12740; tel. (21) 7973535; fax (21) 79196941; e-mail redaksi@gatra.com; internet www.gatra.com; est. by fmr employees of *Tempo* (banned 1994–98); Man. Editor NUR HIDAYAT; Editor-in-Chief HEDDY LUGITO.

Gugat (Accuse): Surabaya; politics, law and crime; weekly; circ. 250,000.

Hai: Jalan Panjang 8A, Kebon Jeruk, Jakarta Barat; tel. (21) 5330170; fax (21) 5220070; e-mail hai_magazine@ gramedia-majalah.com; internet www.hai-online.com; f. 1973; weekly; youth magazine; Man. Editor JUNIOR EKA PUTRO; circ. 42,000.

Indonesia Business News: Wisma Bisnis Indonesia, 7th Floor, Jalan K. H. Mas Mansyur 12A, Karet, Jakarta 10220; tel. (21) 57901023; fax (21) 57901025; e-mail redaksi@bisnis.co.id; internet www.bisnis.co.id; Indonesian and English.

Indonesia Business Weekly: Wisma Bisnis Indonesia, Jalan Letjenderal S. Parman, Kav. 12, Slipi, Jakarta 11410; tel. (21) 5304016; fax (21) 5305868; English; Editor TAUFIK DARUSMAN.

Indonesia Magazine: Jalan Merdeka Barat 20, Jakarta; tel. (21) 352015; f. 1969; monthly; English; Chair. G. DWIPAYANA; Editor-in-Chief HADELY HASIBUAN; circ. 15,000.

Intisari (Digest): Gramedia Bldg, Unit II, 5th Floor, Jalan Palmerah Selatan 24–26, Jakarta 10270; tel. (21) 5483008; fax (21) 53696525; e-mail intisari@gramedia-majalah.com; internet www .intisari-online.com; f. 1963; monthly; Indonesian; popular science, health, technology, crime and general interest; Editors AL. HERU KUSTARA, IRAWATI; circ. 141,000.

Jakarta Jakarta: Gramedia Bldg, Unit II, 5th Floor, Jalan Palmerah Selatan 24–26, Jakarta 10270; tel. (21) 5483008; fax (21) 5494035; f. 1985; weekly; food, fun, fashion and celebrity news; circ. 70,000.

Jurnal Indonesia: Jalan Hos Cokroaminoto 49A, Jakarta 10350; tel. (21) 31901774; fax (21) 3916471; e-mail jurnal@cbn.net.id; monthly; political, economic and business analysis.

Keluarga: Jalan Sangaji 11, Jakarta; fortnightly; women's and family magazine; Editor S. DAHONO.

Kontan: Gedung Kontan, Jalan Kebayoran Lama 3119, Jakarta 12210; tel. (21) 5357636; fax (21) 5357633; e-mail red@kontan.co.id; internet www.kontan.co.id; weekly; Indonesian; business news-paper; Editor-in-Chief ARDIAN TAUFIK GESURI.

Majalah Ekonomis: POB 4195, Jakarta; monthly; English; busi-ness; Chief Editor S. ARIFIN HUTABARAT; circ. 20,000.

Majalah Kedokteran Indonesia (Journal of the Indonesian Med-ical Asscn): Jalan Kesehatan 111/29, Jakarta 11/16; tel. (21) 31937910; fax (21) 3900465; e-mail yapenidi@yahoo.com; internet mki.idionline.org; f. 1951; monthly; Indonesian, English.

Manglé: Jalan Lodaya 19–21, 40262 Bandung; tel. (22) 411438; f. 1957; weekly; Sundanese; Chief Editor Drs OEJANG DARAJATOEN; circ. 74,000.

Matra: Grafity Pers, Kompleks Buncit Raya Permai, Kav. 1, Jalan Warung, POB 3476, Jakarta; tel. (21) 515952; f. 1986; monthly; men's magazine; general interest and current affairs; Editor-in-Chief SRI RUSDY; circ. 100,000.

Mimbar Kabinet Pembangunan: Jalan Merdeka Barat 7, Ja-karta; f. 1966; monthly; Indonesian; publ. by Dept of Information.

Mutiara: Jalan Dewi Sartika 136D, Cawang, Jakarta Timur; gen-eral interest; Publr H. G. RORIMPANDEY.

Nova: Gedung Kompas Gramedia, Lantai 3, Jalan Panjang 8A, Kebon Jeruk, Jakarta Barat 11530; tel. (21) 5330150; fax (21) 5321020; e-mail admin@tabloidnova.com; internet www .tabloidnova.com; weekly; Wed.; Indonesian; women's interest; Publr SAMINDRA UTAMA; circ. 618,267.

Oposisi: Jakarta; weekly; politics; circ. 400,000.

Otomotif: Gedung Kompas Gramedia, Lantai 7, Jalan Panjang 8A, Kebon Jeruk, Jakarta Barat 11530; tel. (21) 5330170; fax (21) 5330185; e-mail otomotifnet@gramedia-majalah.com; internet www.otomotifnet.com; f. 1990; weekly; automotive specialist tabloid; Editor-in-Chief AGUS SULISTRIYONO; circ. 215,763.

PC Magazine Indonesia: Jalan H. R. Rasuna Said, Blok B, Kav. 32–33, Jakarta 12910; tel. (21) 5209370; fax (21) 5209366; computers; Editor-in-Chief SVIDA ALISJAHBANA.

Peraba: Bintaran Kidul 5, Yogyakarta; weekly; Indonesian and Javanese; Roman Catholic; Editor W. KARTOSOEHARSONO.

Pertani PT: Jalan Pasar Minggu, Kalibata, POB 247/KBY, Jakarta Selatan; tel. (21) 793108; f. 1974; monthly; Indonesian; agricultural; Pres. Dir Ir RUSLI YAHYA.

Petisi: Surabaya; weekly; Editor CHOIRUL ANAM.

Rajawali: Jakarta; monthly; Indonesian; civil aviation and tourism; Dir R. A. J. LUMENTA; Man. Editor KARYONO ADHY.

Selecta: Kebon Kacang 29/4, Jakarta; fortnightly; illustrated; Editor SAMSUDIN LUBIS; circ. 80,000.

SWA Sembada: Jalan Taman Tanah Abang, III/23, Jakarta 10610; tel. (21) 3523839; fax (21) 3457338; internet www.swa.co.id; business information; Editor-in-Chief KEMAL EFFENDI GANI.

Tempo: Gedung Temprint, Lantai 2, Jalan Palmerah Barat 8, Jakarta 12210; tel. (21) 5360409; fax (21) 5360412; e-mail interaktif@tempo.co.id; internet www.tempointeractive.com; f. 1971; weekly; Editor-in-Chief ARIEF ZULKIFLI.

Tiara: Gramedia Bldg, Unit 11, 5th Floor, Jalan Palmerah Selatan 24–26, Jakarta 10270; tel. (21) 5483008; fax (21) 5494035; f. 1990; fortnightly; lifestyles, features and celebrity news; circ. 47,000.

Ummat: Jakarta; Islamic; sponsored by ICMI.

Wenang Post: Jalan R. W. Mongsidi 4/96, POB 1105, Manado 95115; tel. and fax (431) 866150; weekly.

NEWS AGENCIES

ANTARA (Indonesian News Agency): Wisma Antara, Lantai 19, 17 Jalan Medan Merdeka Selatan, POB 1257, Jakarta 10110; tel. (21) 3802383; fax (21) 3522178; e-mail newsroom@antaranews.com; internet www.antaranews.com; f. 1937; 33 brs in Indonesia, 5 overseas brs; 800 bulletins in Indonesian and in English; monitoring service of stock exchanges worldwide; photo service; CEO M. SAIFUL HADI; Chief Editor AHMAD KUSAENI.

Kantorberita Nasional Indonesia (KNI News Service): Jalan Jatinegara Barat III/6, Jakarta Timur 13310; tel. (21) 811003; fax (21) 8195501; f. 1966; independent national news agency; foreign and domestic news in Indonesian; Dir and Editor-in-Chief Dr SUMONO MUSTOFFA; Exec. Editor HARIM NURROCHADI.

PRESS ASSOCIATIONS

Aliansi Jurnalis Independen (AJI) (Alliance of Independent Journalists): Jalan Kembang Raya 6 Kwitang, Senen, Jakarta Pusat 10420; tel. (21) 3151214; fax (21) 3151261; e-mail office@ajiindonesia .org; internet www.ajiindonesia.org; f. 1994; unofficial; aims to promote freedom of the press; Pres. EKO MARYADI; Sec.-Gen. SUWARJONO.

Jakarta Foreign Correspondents' Club: Plaza Gani Djemat, Lantai 4, Jalan Imam Bonjol 76–78, Jakarta 10310; tel. (21) 3903628; fax (21) 3917453; e-mail office@jfcc.info; internet www.jfcc.info; more than 400 mems; Pres. JOE COCHRANE; Exec. Dir THEODORA TRISNAWATI.

Persatuan Wartawan Indonesia (PWI) (Indonesian Journalists' Asscn): Gedung Dewan Pers, Lantai 4, Jalan Kebon Sirih 34, Jakarta 10110; tel. (21) 3453131; fax (21) 3453175; e-mail pwi@pwi.or.id; internet www.pwi.or.id; f. 1946; govt-controlled; 14,000 mems (Feb. 2009); Chair. MARGIONO; Gen. Sec. HENDRY BANGUN.

Serikat Penerbit Suratkabar (SPS) (Indonesian Newspaper Publishers' Asscn): Gedung Dewan Pers, 6th Floor, Jalan Kebon Sirih 34, Jakarta 10110; tel. (21) 3459671; fax (21) 3862373; e-mail spspusat@spsindonesia.or.id; f. 1946; mems: 451 publrs; Exec. Chair. DAHLAN IKSAN; Sec.-Gen. SUKARDI DARMAWAN.

Publishers

JAKARTA

Aries Lima/New Aqua Press PT: Jalan Rawagelan II/4, Jakarta Timur; tel. (21) 4897566; general and children's; Pres. TUTI SUNDARI AZMI.

Bhratara Niaga Media PT: Jalan Cipinang Bali 17, Jakarta Timur 13420; tel. (21) 8520319; fax (21) 8191858; f. 1986; fmrly Bhratara Karya Aksara; university and educational textbooks; Man. Dir ROBINSON RUSDI.

Bulan Bintang PT: Jalan Kramat Kwitang I/8, Jakarta 10420; tel. (21) 3901651; fax (21) 3901652; e-mail bukubulanbintang@gmail .com; internet www.bulanbintang.co.id; f. 1954; Islamic, social sciences, natural and applied sciences, art; Man. Dir FAUZI AMELZ.

Bumi Aksara PT: Jalan Sawo Raya 18, Rawamanguu, Jakarta 13220; tel. (21) 4717049; fax (21) 4700989; e-mail info@bumiaksara .co.id; internet www.bumiaksara.co.id; f. 1990; university textbooks; Dir LUCYA ANDAM DEWI.

Cakrawala Cinta PT: Jalan Minyak I/12B, Duren Tiga, Jakarta 12760; tel. (21) 7990725; fax (21) 7974076; f. 1984; science; Dir Drs M. TORSINA.

Centre for Strategic and International Studies (CSIS): Jalan Tanah Abang III 23–27, Jakarta 10160; tel. (21) 3865532; fax (21) 3847517; e-mail csis@csis.or.id; internet www.csis.or.id; f. 1971; economic, political and social sciences; Exec. Dir RIZAL SUKMA.

Cipta Adi Pustaka: Graha Compaka Mas Blok C 22, Jalan Cem-paka Putih Raya, Jakarta Pusat; tel. (21) 4213821; fax (21) 4269315; f. 1986; encyclopaedias; Dir BUDI SANTOSO.

Dian Rakyat PT: Jalan Rawa Girang 8, Kawasan Industri Pulo-gadung, Jakarta; tel. (21) 4604444; fax (21) 4609115; f. 1966; general; Pres. Dir MARIO ALISJAHBANA.

Dunia Pustaka Jaya: Jalan Kramat Raya 5K, Komp. Maya Indah, Jakarta 10450; tel. (21) 3909322; fax (21) 3909320; f. 1971; fiction, religion, essays, poetry, drama, criticism, art, philosophy and chil-dren's; Man. A. RIVAI.

EGC Medical Publishers: Jalan Agung Timur 4, No. 39 Blok 0–1, Jakarta 14350; tel. (21) 65306283; fax (21) 6518178; e-mail mktg@ egc-arcan.com; internet www.egcmedbooks.com; f. 1978; medical and public health, nursing, dentistry; Dir IMELDA DHARMA.

Erlangga PT: Kami Melayani II, Pengetahuan, Jalan H. Baping 100, Ciracas, Jakarta 13740; tel. (21) 8717006; fax (21) 87794609; e-mail webmaster@erlangga.co.id; internet www.erlangga.co.id; f. 1952; secondary school and university textbooks; Man. Dir GUNAWAN HUTAURUK.

Gaya Favorit Press: Jalan H. R. Rasuna Said., Kav. B 32–33, Jakarta 12910; tel. (21) 5209370; fax (21) 5209366; f. 1971; fiction, popular science, lifestyle and children's; Vice-Pres. MIRTA KARTOHA-DIPRODJO; Man. Dir WIDARTI GUNAWAN.

Gema Insani Press: Jalan Kalibata Utara II/84, Jakarta 12740; tel. (21) 7984391; fax (21) 7984388; e-mail penerbitan@gemainsani.co.id; internet www.gemainsani.co.id; f. 1986; Islamic; Dir UMAR BASYAR-AHIL.

Ghalia Indonesia: Jalan Pramuka Raya 4, Jakarta 13140; tel. (21) 8581814; fax (21) 8564784; f. 1972; children's and general science, textbooks; Man. Dir LUKMAN SAAD.

Gramedia Widyasarana Indonesia: Gramedia Bldg, 3rd Floor, Jalan Palmerah Barat 33–37, Jakarta 10270; tel. (21) 53650110; fax (21) 53698098; internet www.grasindo.co.id; f. 1973; university textbooks, general non-fiction, children's and magazines; Man. JAROT YUDHOPRATOMO.

Gunung Mulia PT: Jalan Kwitang 22–23, Jakarta 10420; tel. (21) 3901208; fax (21) 3901633; e-mail publishing@bpkgm.com; internet www.bpkgunungmulia.com; f. 1946; general, children's, Christian; Man. Dir STEPHEN Z. SATYAHADI.

Hidakarya Agung PT: Jalan Percetakan Negara D51, Jakarta Pusat; tel. (21) 4219786; fax (21) 4247128; Dir MAHDIARTI MACHMUD.

Ichtiar: Jalan Majapahit 6, Jakarta Pusat; tel. (21) 3841226; f. 1957; textbooks, law, social sciences, economics; Dir JOHN SEMERU.

Indira PT: Jalan Borobudur 20, Jakarta 10320; tel. (21) 3148868; fax (21) 3921079; f. 1953; general science, general trade and children's; Dir BAMBANG P. WAHYUDI.

Kinta CV: Jalan Kemanggisan Ilir V/110, Pal Merah, Jakarta Barat; tel. (21) 5494751; f. 1950; textbooks, social sciences, general; Man. Drs MOHAMAD SALEH.

Midas Surya Grafindo PT: Jalan Kesehatan 54, Cijantung, Jakarta 13760; tel. (21) 8400414; fax (21) 8400270; f. 1984; children's; Dir Drs FRANS HENDRAWAN.

Mutiara Sumber Widya PT: Gedung Maya Indah, Jalan Kramat 55C, Jakarta 10450; tel. (21) 3909864; fax (21) 3160313; f. 1951; textbooks, Islamic, social sciences, general and children's; Pres. FADJRAA OEMAR.

Penebar Swadya PT: Jalan Gunung Sahari III/7, Jakarta Pusat; tel. (21) 4204402; fax (21) 4214821; agriculture, animal husbandry, fisheries; Dir Drs ANTHONIUS RIYANTO.

Penerbit Universitas Indonesia: Jalan Salemba Raya 4, Jakarta; tel. (21) 335373; f. 1969; science; Man. S. E. LEGOWO.

Pustaka Binaman Pressindo: Jalan Kembang Raya 8, Jakarta Pusat 10030; tel. (21) 2303157; fax (21) 2302051; e-mail pustaka@bit .net.id; f. 1981; management; Dir Ir MAKFUDIN WIRYA ATMAJA.

Pustaka Sinar Harapan PT: Jalan Dewi Sartika 136D, Jakarta 13630; tel. and fax (21) 8006982; e-mail marketing@penerbitsinarharapan.co.id; internet penerbitsinarharapan.co.id; f. 1981; general science, fiction, comics, children's; Dir W. M. NAIDEN.

Pustaka Utma Grafiti PT: 25 Jalan Kramat VI, Jakarta Pusat 10250; tel. (21) 31903006; fax (21) 31906649; f. 1981; social sciences, humanities and children's books; Dir ZULKIFLY LUBIS.

Rajagrafindo Persada PT: Jalan Pelepah Hijau IV TN-1 14–15, Kelapa Gading Permai, Jakarta 14240; tel. (21) 4520951; fax (21) 4529409; f. 1980; general science and religion; Dir Drs ZUBAIDI.

Rineka Cipta PT: Kompang Perkantoran Mitra Matraman, 148 Jalan Matraman Raya B 1–2, Jakarta; tel. (21) 85918080; fax (21) 85918143; f. 1990; est. by merger of Aksara Baru (f. 1972) and Bina Aksara; general science and university texts; Dir Dr H. SUARDI.

Rosda Jayaputra PT: Jalan Kembang 4, Jakarta 10420; tel. (21) 3904984; fax (21) 3901703; f. 1981; general science; Dir H. ROZALI USMAN.

Sastra Hudaya: Jalan Kalasan 1, Jakarta Pusat; tel. (21) 882321; f. 1967; religious, textbooks, children's and general; Man. ADAM SALEH.

Tintamas Indonesia: Jalan Kramat Raya 60, Jakarta 10420; tel. and fax (21) 3911459; f. 1947; history, modern science and culture, especially Islamic; Man. MARHAMAH DJAMBEK.

Tira Pustaka: Jalan Cemara Raya 1, Kav. 10D, Jaka Permai, Jaka Sampurna, Bekasi 17145; tel. (21) 8841277; fax (21) 8842736; e-mail Tirapus@cbn.net.id; f. 1977; translations, children's; Dir ROBERT B. WIDJAJA.

Toko Buku Walisongo PT: Gedung Idayu, Jalan Kwitang 13, Jakarta 10420; tel. (21) 3154890; fax (21) 3154889; e-mail edp@tokowalisongo.com; f. 1986; fmrly Masagung Group; general, Islamic, textbooks, science; Pres. H. KETUT ABDURRAHMAN MASA-GUNG.

Widjaya: Jalan Pecenongan 48C, Jakarta Pusat; tel. (21) 3813446; f. 1950; textbooks, children's, religious and general; Man. DIDI LUTHAN.

Yasaguna: Jalan Minangkabau 44, POB 422, Jakarta Selatan; tel. (21) 8290422; f. 1964; agricultural, children's, handicrafts; Dir HIL-MAN MADEWA.

BANDUNG

Alumni PT: Jalan Bukit Pakar Timur II/109, Bandung 40197; tel. (22) 2501251; fax (22) 2503044; f. 1968; university and school textbooks; Dir EDDY DAMIAN.

Armico: Jalan Madurasa Utara 10, Cigereleng, Bandung 40253; tel. (22) 5202234; fax (22) 5201972; f. 1980; school textbooks; Dir Ir ARSIL TANJUNG.

Citra Aditya Bakti PT: Jalan Geusanulun 17, Bandung 40115; tel. (22) 438251; fax (22) 438635; e-mail cab@citraaditya.com; internet www.citraaditya.com; f. 1985; general science; Dir Ir IWAN TANUAT-MADJA.

Diponegoro Publishing House: Jalan Mohammad Toha 44–46, Bandung 40252; tel. and fax (22) 5201215; e-mail dpnegoro@indosat .net.id; internet www.penerbitdiponegoro.com; f. 1963; Islamic, textbooks, fiction, non-fiction, general; Dir HADIDJAH DAHLAN.

Epsilon Group: Jalan Marga Asri 3, Margacinta, Bandung 40287; tel. (22) 7567826; f. 1985; school textbooks; Dir Drs BAHRUDIN.

Eresco PT: Jalan Megger Girang 98, Bandung 40254; tel. (22) 5205985; fax (22) 5205984; f. 1957; scientific and general; Man. Drs ARFAN ROZALI.

Ganeca Exact Bandung: Kawasan Industri MM 2100, Jalan Selayar Kav. A5, Bekasi 17520; tel. (22) 89981946; fax (22) 89981947; e-mail presdir@ganeca-exact.com; internet www .ganeca-exact.com; f. 1982; school textbooks; Dir Ir KETUT SUARDHARA LINGGIH.

Mizan Pustaka PT: Jalan Cinambo 135, Bandung 40294; tel. (22) 7834310; fax (22) 7834311; e-mail info@mizan.com; internet www .mizan.com; f. 1983; Islamic and general books; Pres. Dir HAIDAR BAGIR.

Putra A. Bardin: Jalan Kembar Timur II 3, Bandung 40254; tel. (22) 5208305; fax (22) 7300879; f. 1998; textbooks, scientific and general; Dir NAI A. BARDIN.

Sarana Panca Karya Nusa PT: Jalan Kopo 633, Km 13/4, Bandung 40014; e-mail spkn641@yahoo.com; f. 1986; general; Dir WIMPY S. IBRAHIM.

Tarsito PT: Jalan Guntur 20, Bandung 40262; tel. (22) 7304915; fax (22) 7314630; academic; Dir T. SITORUS.

FLORES

Nusa Indah: Jalan El Tari, Ende 86318, Nusa Tenggara Timur, Flores; tel. (381) 21502; fax (381) 23974; e-mail namkahu@yahoo .com; f. 1970; religious and general; Dir LUKAS BATMOMOLIN.

KUDUS

Menara Kudus: Jalan Menara 4, Kudus 59315; tel. (291) 437143; fax (291) 436474; f. 1958; Islamic; Man. CHILMAN NAJIB.

MEDAN

Hasmar: Jalan Letjenderal Haryono M. T. 1, POB 446, Medan 20231; tel. (61) 4144581; fax (22) 4533673; f. 1962; primary school textbooks; Dir FAUZI LUBIS; Man. AMRAN SAID RANGKUTI.

Impola: Jalan H. M. Joni 46, Medan 20217; tel. (61) 711415; f. 1984; school textbooks; Dir PAMILANG M. SITUMORANG.

Madju Medan Cipta PT: Jalan Amaliun 37, Medan 20215; tel. (61) 7361990; fax (61) 7367753; e-mail koboi@indosat.net; f. 1950; textbooks, children's and general; Pres. H. MOHAMED ARBIE; Man. Dir Drs DINO IRSAN ARBIE.

Masco: Jalan Sisingamangaraja 191, Medan 20218; tel. (61) 713375; f. 1992; school textbooks; Dir P. M. SITUMORANG.

SEMARANG

Intan Pariwara: Jalan Ki Hajar Dewantoro, Kotak Pos III, Kotif Klaten, Jawa-Tengah; tel. (272) 322441; fax (272) 322607; e-mail intan@intanpariwara.co.id; internet www.intanpariwara.co.id; school textbooks; Pres. CHRIS HARJANTO.

Mandira PT: Jalan Letjenderal M. T. Haryono 501, Semarang 50241; tel. (24) 8316150; fax (24) 8415092; f. 1962; Dir Ir A. HARIYANTO.

SOLO

Pabelan PT: Jalan Raya Solo, Kertasura, Km 8, Solo 57162; tel. (271) 743975; fax (271) 714775; f. 1983; school textbooks; Dir AGUNG SASONGKO.

Tiga Serangkai Pustaka Mandiri, PT: Jalan Dr Supomo 23, Solo 57141, Central Java; tel. (271) 714344; fax (271) 713607; internet www.tigaserangkai.com; e-mail tspm@tigaserangkai.co.id; f. 1959; school textbooks, general textbooks; Pres. ABDULLAH SITI AMINAH.

SURABAYA

Bina Ilmu PT: Jalan Tunjungan 53E, Surabaya 60275; tel. (31) 5323214; fax (31) 5315421; f. 1973; school textbooks, Islamic; Pres. ARIEFIN NOOR.

Bintang: Jalan Potroagung III/41C, Surabaya; tel. (31) 3770687; fax (31) 3715941; school textbooks; Dir AGUS WINARNO.

Grip PT: Jalan Rungkut Permai II/C11, Surabaya; tel. (31) 22564; f. 1958; textbooks and general; Man. SURIPTO.

Jaya Baya: Jalan Embong Malang 69H, POB 250, Surabaya 60001; tel. (31) 41169; f. 1945; religion, philosophy and ethics; Man. TADJIB ERMADI.

Sinar Wijaya: Jalan Raya Sawo VII/58, Bringin-Lakarsantri, Surabaya; tel. (31) 7406616; general; Dir DULRADJAK.

YOGYAKARTA

BPFE PT: Jalan Gambiran 37, Yogyakarta 55161; tel. (274) 373760; fax (274) 380819; f. 1984; university textbooks; Dir Drs INDRIYO GITOSUDARMO.

Centhini Yayasan: Gedung Bekisar UH V/716 E1, Yogyakarta 55161; tel. (274) 383148; f. 1984; Javanese culture; Chair. H. KARKONO KAMAJAYA.

Gadjah Mada University Press: Jalan Grafika 1, Kampus UGM, Bulaksumur, Yogyakarta 55281; tel. and fax (274) 561037; e-mail gmupress@ugm.ac.id; internet www.gmup.ugm.ac.id; f. 1971; university textbooks; Chair. Dr SURATMAN.

Indonesia UP: Gedung Bekisar UH V/716 E1, Yogyakarta 55161; tel. (274) 383148; f. 1950; general science; Dir H. KARKONO KAMAJAYA.

Kanisius Printing and Publishing: Jalan Cempaka 9, Deresan, Yogyakarta 55281; tel. (274) 588783; fax (274) 563349; e-mail office@kanisiusmedia.com; internet www.kanisiusmedia.com; f. 1922; philosophy, children's, textbooks, Christian and general; Pres. Dir AUGUSTINUS SARWANTO.

Kedaulatan Rakyat PT: Jalan P. Mangkubumi 40–42, Yogyakarta; tel. (274) 2163; Dir DRONO HARDJUSUWONGSO.

Penerbit Tiara Wacana Yogya: Jalan Kaliurang, Km 7, 8 Kopen 16, Banteng, Yogyakarta 55581; tel. and fax (274) 880083, f. 1986; university textbooks and general science; Dir SITORESMI PRABUNINGRAT.

PUBLISHERS' ASSOCIATION

Ikatan Penerbit Indonesia (IKAPI) (Assen of Indonesian Book Publishers): Jalan Kalipasir 32, Jakarta Pusat 10330; tel. (21) 31902532; fax (21) 31926124; e-mail sekretariat@ikapi.org; internet www.ikapi.org; f. 1950; 1,126 mems (2013); Pres. LUYA ANDAM DEWI; Gen. Sec. HUSNI SYAWIE.

Broadcasting and Communications

TELECOMMUNICATIONS

PT AXIS Telekom Indonesia (AXIS): Jalan Jenderal Gatot Subroto, Kav. 35–36, Jakarta Selatan 12950; tel. (21) 5760880; fax (21) 5760809; e-mail cs@axisworld.co.id; internet www.axisworld.co.id; f. 2001; cellular telephone network operator; provides GSM 1800 and 3G video services; 80.1% owned by Saudi Telecom Co; Pres. Dir and CEO ERIK AAS.

PT Hutchison 3 Indonesia (H3I): Jalan Jenderal Gatot Subroto, Kav. 9–11, Jakarta Selatan 12950; tel. (21) 52906800; fax (21) 52906900; e-mail 3Care@three.co.id; internet tri.co.id; f. 2003; est. as PT Cyber Access Communications; present name adopted 2013; subsidiary of Hutchison Telecommunications International Ltd; cellular telephone network operator providing GSM 1800 and third generation (3G) video services; Pres. and CEO RAJIV SAWHNEY.

PT Indonesian Satellite Corporation Tbk (INDOSAT): Jalan Medan Merdeka Barat 21, POB 2905, Jakarta 10110; tel. (21) 54388888; fax (21) 5449501; e-mail publicrelations@indosat.com; internet www.indosat.com; f. 1967; telecommunications; partially privatized in 1994; 41.94% stake sold to Singapore Technologies Telemedia in 2002; 40.81% share sold to QTEL in 2008; Pres. Dir and CEO ALEXANDER RUSLI; Pres. Commr Dr NASSER MOHAMMED MARAFIH.

PT SmartFren Telecom Tbk: Jalan H. Agus Salim 45, Sabang, Jakarta Pusat 10340; e-mail customercare@smartfren.com; internet www.smartfren.com; f. 2010 by merger of PT Mobile-8 and PT Smart Telecom; Pres. Commr GANDI SULISTIYANTO SOEHERMAN; Pres. Dir RUDOLFO PANTOJA.

PT Telekomunikasi Indonesia Tbk (TELKOMSEL): Corporate Office, Jalan Japati 1, Bandung 40133; tel. (22) 2500000; fax (22) 4240313; internet www.telkom.co.id; domestic telecommunications;

24.2% of share capital was transferred to the private sector in 1995; Pres. Commr HENDRI SAPARINI; Pres. Dir ALEX JANANGKIH SINAGA.

PT Telekomunikasi Selular (TELKOMSEL): Wisma Mulia, 12th Floor, Jalan Jenderal Gatot Subroto, Kav. 42, Jakarta Selatan 12710; tel. (21) 5240811; fax (21) 52906121; e-mail investor@telkomsel.co.id; internet www.telkomsel.com; f. 1995; provides domestic cellular services with international roaming available through 356 network partners; jt venture between PT Telekomunikasi Indonesia Tbk (65%) and Singapore Telecommunications Ltd (35%); Pres. Commr ALEX JANANGKIH SINAGA; Pres. Dir RIRIEK ADRIANSYAH.

PT XL Axiata Tbk (XL Axiata): Jalan Dr Ide Anak Agung Gde Agung, Blok 6.2, Kawasan Mega Kuningan, Jakarta 12950; tel. (21) 5761881; fax (21) 5761880; e-mail corpsec@xl.co.id; internet www.xl.co.id; f. 1996; fixed-line and cellular telephone network provider; Pres. Dir HASNUL SUHAIMI.

Regulatory Authority

Directorate-General of Posts and Informatics Resources (SDPPI): Gedung Sapta Pesona, Jalan Medan Merdeka Barat 17, Jakarta 10110; tel. (21) 3835955; fax (21) 3860754; e-mail admin@postel.go.id; internet www.postel.go.id; Dir-Gen. MUHAMMAD BUDI SETIAWAN.

BROADCASTING

Radio

KBR68H: Jalan Utan Kayu 68H, Jakarta Timur 13120; tel. (21) 8513386; fax (21) 8513002; e-mail redaksi@kbr68h.com; internet www.kbr68h.com; Man. Dir TOSCA SANTOSO.

PT Radio Prambors 102.2 FM: Jalan Adityawarman 71, Kebayoran Baru, Jakarta 12160; tel. (21) 7202238; fax (21) 7222058; e-mail info@pramborsfm.com; internet pramborsfm.com; Gen. Man. NOOR KAMIL.

Radio Republik Indonesia (RRI): Jalan Medan Merdeka Barat 4–5, Jakarta 10110; tel. (21) 3846817; fax (21) 3457134; internet rri.co.id; f. 1945; 49 stations; Pres. Dir ROSARITA NIKEN WIDIASTUTI.

Voice of Indonesia: Jalan Medan Merdeka Barat 4–5, POB 1157, Jakarta; tel. (21) 3450811; fax (21) 3500990; e-mail voi@rri-online.com; internet www.voi.co.id; f. 1945; international service provided by Radio Republik Indonesia; daily broadcasts in Arabic, English, French, German, Bahasa Indonesia, Japanese, Bahasa Malaysia, Mandarin, Spanish and Thai.

Television

In March 1989 Indonesia's first private commercial television station began broadcasting to the Jakarta area. In 2014 there were 12 privately owned television stations in operation and 54 local television stations.

PT Cakrawala Andalas Televisi (ANTEVE): Gedung Sentra Mulia, 18th Floor, Jalan H. R. Rasuna Said, Kav. X-6 No. 8, Jakarta Selatan 12940; tel. (21) 5222086; fax (21) 5229174; e-mail humas@an.tv; internet www.an.tv; f. 1993; private channel; broadcasting to 10 cities; Pres. Commr ANINDYA N. BAKRIE; Pres. Dir ERICK THOHIR.

MNCTV: Jalan Pintu II—Taman Mini Indonesia Indah, Pondok Gede, Jakarta Timur 13810; tel. (21) 8412473; fax (21) 8412470; e-mail info@tpi.tv; internet www.mnctv.com; f. 1991; private channel funded by commercial advertising; Pres. Dir S. N. WIDODO; Pres. Commr HARY TANOESOEDIBJO.

PT Rajawali Citra Televisi Indonesia (RCTI): Jalan Raya Pejuangan 3, Kebon Jeruk, Jakarta 11000; tel. (21) 5303540; fax (21) 5320906; e-mail webmaster@rcti.tv; internet www.rcti.tv; f. 1989; first private channel; 22-year licence; Pres. Dir HARY TANOESOEDIBJO; Vice-Pres. Commr POSMA LUMBAN TOBING.

PT Surya Citra Televisi (SCTV): SCTV Tower, Senayan City, Jalan Asia Afrika, Lot 19, Jakarta 10270; tel. (21) 27935555; fax (21) 27935444; e-mail stephanus@sctv.co.id; internet www.sctv.co.id; f. 1990; private channel broadcasting nationally; Pres. Dir SUTANTO HARTONO.

Rajawali Televisi (RTV): Gedung Mulia, 18th Floor, Jalan H. R. Rasuna Said, Kav. B.10-11, Jakarta Selatan 12910; tel. (21) 29306677; fax (21) 29306678; e-mail sales@rtv.co.id; internet www.rtv.co.id.

Televisi Republik Indonesia (TVRI): TVRI Senayan, Jalan Gerbang Pemuda, Senayan, Jakarta 10270; tel. (21) 5704720; fax (21) 5733122; e-mail humas@tvri.co.id; internet www.tvri.co.id; f. 1962; fmrly state-controlled; became independent in 2003; Pres. Dir SUMITA TOBING.

Regulatory Authority

Komisi Penyiaran Indonesia—KPI (Indonesian Broadcasting Commission): Lantai 6, Jalan Gajah Mada 8, Jakarta 10120; tel.

(21) 6340713; fax (21) 6340667; internet www.kpi.go.id; f. 2002; ind. broadcasting regulatory authority; Sec. M. SI MARULI MATONDANG.

Finance

(cap. = capital; p.u. = paid up; res = reserves; dep. = deposits; m. = million; brs = branches; amounts in rupiah)

BANKING

In October 2013 there were four state banks and 117 private banks operating in Indonesia.

Central Bank

Bank Indonesia (BI): Jalan M. H. Thamrin 2, Jakarta Pusat 10350; tel. (21) 2310108; fax (21) 3501867; e-mail humasbi@bi.go.id; internet www.bi.go.id; f. 1828; nationalized as central bank in 1953; cap. 16,876,926m., res 41,555,776m. (Dec. 2011); Gov. AGUS MARTOWARDOJO; 42 brs.

State Banks

PT Bank Mandiri (Persero): Plaza Mandiri, Jalan Jenderal Gatot Subroto, Kav. 36–38, Jakarta 12190; tel. (21) 52997777; fax (21) 52997735; internet www.bankmandiri.co.id; f. 1998; est. following merger of 4 state-owned banks—PT Bank Bumi Daya, PT Bank Dagang Negara, PT Bank Ekspor Impor Indonesia and PT Bank Pembangunan Indonesia; cap. 11,666,667m., res 16,833,988m., dep. 497,582,793m. (Dec. 2012); Chair. EDWIN GERUNGAN; Pres. Dir BUDI GUNADI SADIKIN; 909 local brs, 6 overseas brs.

PT Bank Negara Indonesia (Persero) Tbk: Jalan Jenderal Sudirman, Kav. 1, Jakarta 10220; tel. (21) 2511946; fax (21) 5728805; e-mail investor.relations@bni.co.id; internet www.bni.co.id; f. 1946; commercial bank; specializes in credits to the industrial sector; cap. 9,054,807m., res 18,936,953m., dep. 260,906,084m. (Dec. 2012); Pres. Commr PETER B. STOK; Pres. Dir and CEO GATOT MUDIANTORO SUWONDO; 919 local brs, 5 overseas brs.

PT Bank Rakyat Indonesia (Persero): Gedung BRI 1, Jalan Jenderal Sudirman, Kav. 44–46, POB 94, Jakarta 10210; tel. (21) 2510244; fax (21) 2500077; internet www.bri.co.id; f. 1895; present name since 1946; commercial and foreign exchange bank; specializes in agricultural smallholdings and rural devt; cap. 6,167,291m., res 11,971,824m., dep. 442,465,775m. (Dec. 2012); Pres. Commr BUNASOR SANIM; Pres. Dir SOFYAN BASIR; 326 brs.

PT Bank Tabungan Negara (Persero): Menara Bank BTN, 10th Floor, Jalan Gajah Mada 1, Jakarta 10130; tel. (21) 26533555; e-mail webadmin@btn.co.id; internet www.btn.co.id; f. 1964; commercial bank; state-owned; cap. 5,178.2m., res 3,736,689m., dep. 81,483,537m. (Dec. 2012); Pres. Commr ZAKI BARIDWAN; Pres. Dir MARYONO; 44 brs.

PT BPD Jawa Timur (Bank Jatim): Jalan Basuki Rachmad 98–104, Surabaya; tel. (31) 5310090; fax (31) 5470159; e-mail humas@bankjatim.co.id; internet www.bankjatim.co.id; f. 1961; cap. 942,123m., res 1,437,417m., dep. 20,388,367m. (Dec. 2011); Pres. Commr MULJANTO; Pres. Dir HADI SUKRIANTO.

Indonesia Eximbank: Gedung Bursa Efek, Menara II, Lantai 8, Jalan Jenderal Sudirman, Kav. 52–53, Jakarta 12190; tel. (21) 5154638; fax (21) 5154639; e-mail corpsec@indonesiaeximbank.go.id; internet www.indonesiaeximbank.go.id; fmrly PT Bank Ekspor Indonesia (Persero); cap. 6,321,586m., res 629,035m., dep. 1,856,763m. (Dec. 2012); Chair. MADE GDE ERATA; Man. Dir ARIFIN INDRA SULISTYANTO.

Commercial Banks

PT Bank ANZ Indonesia: ANZ Tower, 8th Floor, Jalan Jenderal Sudirman, Kav. 33A, Jakarta 10220; tel. (21) 5750300; fax (21) 5735054; e-mail customercare.id@anz.com; internet www.anz.com/indonesia; f. 1973; est. as Westpac Panin Bank; present name adopted 1993; 85% owned by Australia and New Zealand Banking Group Ltd; cap. 1,650,000m., res 14,690m., dep. 22,503m. (Dec. 2012); CEO JOSEPH ABRAHAM.

PT Bank Artha Graha Internasional Tbk: Bank Artha Graha Tower, 5th Floor, Jalan Jenderal Sudirman, Kav. 52–53, Jakarta 12190; tel. (21) 5152168; fax (21) 5153470; e-mail agraha@rad.net.id; internet www.arthagraha.com; f. 1967; est. as PT Bank Bandung; merged with PT Bank Arta Pratama in 1999 and with PT Bank Inter-Pacific in 2005; cap. 950,804.4m., res 418,787.2m., dep. 16,889,059m. (Dec. 2011); Pres. Dir ANDY KASIH; Pres. Commr KIKI SYAHNAKRI; 78 brs.

PT Bank Central Asia Tbk (BCA): Menara BCA, Grand Indonesia, Jalan M. H. Thamrin 1, Jakarta 10310; tel. (21) 23588000; fax (21) 23588300; e-mail halobca@bca.co.id; internet www.bca.co.id; f. 1957; 51% share sold to Farallon Capital Management (USA) in March 2002; cap. 1,540,938m., res 4,751.6m., dep. 373,866.3m. (Dec.

2012); Pres. Commr DJOHAN EMIR SETIJOSO; Pres. Dir JAHJA SETIAATMADJA; 760 local brs.

PT Bank Chinatrust Indonesia: Wisma Tamara, Lantai 15–17, Jalan Jenderal Sudirman, Kav. 24, Jakarta 12920; tel. (21) 5206848; fax (21) 5206767; e-mail ctcbjak@rad.net.id; internet www.chinatrust.co.id; f. 1995; cap. 150,000m., dep. 3,675,976m. (Dec. 2011); Pres. Commr JACK LEE; Pres. Dir JOSEPH SHIH.

PT Bank CIMB Niaga Tbk: Graha Niaga, Jalan Jenderal Sudirman, Kav. 58, Jakarta 12190; tel. (21) 5460555; fax (21) 2505205; e-mail corsec@cimbniaga.co.id; internet www.cimbniaga.com; f. 1955; cap. 1,612,257m., res 7,715,582m., dep. 133,568,414m. (Dec. 2011); Pres. Commr Dato' Sri NAZIR RAZAK; Pres. Dir ARWIN RASYID; 227 brs.

PT Bank Danamon Indonesia Tbk: Menara Danamon, Lantai 6, Jalan Prof. Dr Satrio 6, Kav. E-4, Mega Kuningan, Jakarta 12950; tel. (21) 57991001; fax (21) 57991445; e-mail danamon.access@danamon.co.id; internet www.danamon.co.id; f. 1956; placed under supervision of Indonesian Bank Restructuring Agency in April 1998; merged with PT Bank Tiara Asia, PT Tamara Bank, PT Bank Duta and PT Bank Nusa Nasional in 2000; 51% share sold to consortium led by Singapore's Temasek Holdings in May 2003; cap. 5,901,122m., res 7,556,830m., dep. 91,340,427m. (Dec. 2011); Pres. Commr NG KEE CHOE; Pres. Dir HENRY HO HON CHEONG; 483 brs.

PT Bank ICB Bumiputera Tbk: Menara ICB Bumiputera, Jalan Probolinggo 18, Menteng, Jakarta Pusat 10350; tel. (21) 3919898; fax (21) 3919797; e-mail bank@icbbumiputera.co.id; internet www.icbbumiputera.co.id; f. 1989; cap. 548,607m., res 130,230m., dep. 6,413,520m. (Dec. 2011); Pres. Commr Dato MAT AMIR BIN JAFFAR; Pres. Dir EDDY RAINAL SINULINGGA.

PT Bank Internasional Indonesia Tbk (BII): Gedung Sentral Senayan 3, Jalan Asia Afrika 8, Gelora Bung Karno, Jakarta 10270; tel. (21) 29228888; fax (21) 29039051; e-mail cs@bii.co.id; internet www.bii.co.id; cap. 3,407,411m., res 2,147.1m., dep. 88,491.2m. (Dec. 2012); Pres. Commr Tan Sri Dato' MEGAT ZAHARUDDIN BIN MEGAT MOHAMMAD NOR; Pres. Dir TASWIN ZAKARIA; 368 local brs; 3 overseas brs.

PT Bank KEB Indonesia: Wisma GKBI, Lantai 20, Suite 2002, Jalan Jenderal Sudirman, Kav. 28, Jakarta 10210; tel. (21) 5741030; fax (21) 5741031; e-mail contact.center@kebi.co.id; owned by KEB Seoul (99%) and PT Clemont Finance Indonesia (1%); f. 1990; fmrly PT Korea Exchange Bank Danamon; cap. 150,000m., res 30,000m., dep. 2,522,105m. (Dec. 2011); Pres. Commr OO YEOUNG JEONG; Pres. Dir CHO YONG WOO.

PT Bank Mayapada Internasional Tbk: Menara Mayapada, Jalan Jenderal Sudirman, Kav. 28, Jakarta 12920; tel. (21) 5212288; fax (21) 5211965; e-mail mayapada@bankmayapada.com; internet www.bankmayapada.com; f. 1989; cap. 464,486m., res 836m., dep. 15,165.6m. (Dec. 2012); Chair. Dato' Sri JONATHAN TAHIR; Pres. Dir HARIYONO TJAHJARIJADI; 41 brs.

PT Bank Mizuho Indonesia: Plaza BII, Lantai 24, Menara 2, Jalan M. H. Thamrin 51, Jakarta 10350; tel. (21) 3925222; fax (21) 3926354; internet www.mizuhobank.co.id; f. 1989; fmrly PT Bank Fuji International Indonesia; name changed as above in 2001; cap. 1,323,574m., res 7,847.6m., dep. 10,501.6m. (Dec. 2012); Pres. Commr RUSDI ABDULLAH DJAMIL; Pres. Dir SAMBUTAN DARI.

PT Bank Muamalat Indonesia (BMI): Gedung Arthaloka, Jalan Jenderal Sudirman 2, Jakarta 10220; tel. (21) 2511414; fax (21) 2511453; internet www.muamalatbank.com; Indonesia's first Islamic bank; cap. 821,843m., res 515,251.9m., dep. 39,669,316.8m. (Dec. 2012); Pres. Dir Ir ARVIYAN ARIFIN; Pres. Commr WIDIGDO SUKARMAN.

PT Bank Mutiara Tbk: Gedung International Financial Centre, Jalan Jenderal Sudirman, Kav. 22–23, Jakarta 12920; tel. (21) 29261111; fax (21) 5224670; e-mail corsec@mutiarabank.co.id; internet www.mutiarabank.co.id; f. 1989 as PT Bank Century Tbk; renamed as above in 2009; cap. 8,973,675m., res 274,862m., dep. 13,475,784m. (Dec. 2012); Pres. Commr PONTAS RIYANTO SIAHAAN; Pres. Dir SUKORIYANTO SAPUTRO.

PT Bank OCBC NISP Tbk: Menara Bank OCBC NISP, Jalan Prof. Dr Satrio, Kav. 25, Jakarta 12940; tel. (21) 25533888; fax (21) 57944000; internet www.ocbcnisp.com; f. 1941; 81.9% owned by OCBC Bank, Singapore; cap. 1,068,615m., res 3,711,000m., dep. 61,309,975m. (Dec. 2012); Pres. Commr PRAMUKTI SURJAUDAJA; Pres. Dir PARWATI SURJAUDAJA; 168 brs.

PT Bank Permata Tbk: Menara PermataBank I, Lantai 17, Jalan Jenderal Sudirman, Kav. 27, Jakarta 12920; tel. (21) 5237899; fax (21) 5237253; e-mail isaptono@permatabank.co.id; internet www.permatabank.com; f. 1954; est. as Bank Persatuan Dagang Indonesia; became PT Bank Bali in 1971 and PT Bank Bali Tbk in 1990; name changed as above Sept. 2002 following merger with PT Bank Prima Express, PT Bank Universal Tbk, PT Arthamedia Bank and PT Bank Patriot; cap. 1,667,159m., res 9,454,526m., dep. 106,919,167m. (Dec. 2012); Pres. Commr NEERAJ SWAROOP; Pres. Dir DAVID MARTIN FLETCHER; 288 brs.

PT Bank Rabobank International Indonesia: Plaza 89, Lantai 9, Jalan H. R. Rasuna Said, Kav. X-7 No. 6, Jakarta 12940; tel. (21) 2520876; fax (21) 2520875; e-mail indonesia@rabobank.com; internet www.rabobank.co.id; f. 1990; est. as PT Rabobank Duta Indonesia; name changed as above in 2001 when Rabobank Nederland secured sole ownership; cap. 715,000m., res 1,990m., dep. 11,441,190m. (Dec. 2012); Pres. Commr ROELOF JAN DEKKER; Pres. Dir HENK MULDER.

PT Bank Sumitomo Mitsui Indonesia: Gedung Summitmas II, Lantai 10, Jalan Jenderal Sudirman, Kav. 61–62, Jakarta 12190; tel. (21) 5227011; fax (21) 5227022; f. 1989; fmrly PT Bank Sumitomo Indonesia; merged with PT Bank Sakura Swadharma in April 2001; cap. 2,873,942m., res 107,095m., dep. 12,585,800m. (Dec. 2012); Pres. Commr MASAYUKI SHIMURA; Pres. Dir MASAYA HIRAYAMA; 1 br.

PT Bank UOB Indonesia: UOB Plaza, Jalan M. H. Thamrin 10, Jakarta 10230; tel. (21) 23506000; fax (21) 29936682; e-mail squ@uob.co.id; internet www.uob.co.id; f. 1956; est. as PT Bank Buana Indonesia Tbk; name changed to PT Bank UOB Buana in 2009; above name adopted in 2011; cap. 2,388,471m., res 2,105,419m., dep. 44,219,714m. (Dec. 2011); Pres. Commr WEE CHO YAW; Pres. Dir ARMAND B. ARIEF; CEO WEE EE CHEONG; 32 brs.

PT Pan Indonesia Tbk (Panin Bank): Panin Bank Centre, Lantai 11, Jalan Jenderal Sudirman, Kav. 1, Senayan, Jakarta 10270; tel. (21) 2700545; fax (21) 2700340; e-mail panin@panin.co.id; internet www.panin.co.id; f. 1971; est. as a result of the merger of 3 private national banks; cap. 2,408,765m., res 3,452,496m., dep. 109,477,500m. (Dec. 2012); Pres. Commr JOHNNY N. WIRAATMADJA; Pres. Dir Drs H. ROSTIAN SJAMSUDIN; 250 local brs, 2 overseas brs.

PT Woori Bank Indonesia: Jakarta Stock Exchange Bldg, Lantai 16, Jalan Jenderal Sudirman, Kav. 52–53, Jakarta 12190; tel. (21) 5151919; fax (21) 5151477; e-mail indonesia@wooribank.com; internet id.wooribank.com; fmrly PT Hanvit Bank Indonesia; cap. 170,000m., res 34,000m., dep. 3,561,858m. (Dec. 2011); Pres. Dir LIM CHOI-JIN.

Banking Association

The Association of Indonesian National Private Commercial Banks (Perhimpunan Bank-Bank Umum Nasional Swasta—PERBANAS): Griya Perbanas, Lantai 1, Jalan Perbanas, Karet Kuningan, Setiabudi, Jakarta 12940; tel. (21) 5223038; fax (21) 5223037; e-mail sekretariat@perbanas.org; internet www.perbanas.org; f. 1952; 78 mems; Chair. SIGIT PRAMONO; Sec.-Gen. FARID RAHMAN.

STOCK EXCHANGE

Indonesia Stock Exchange (IDX): Indonesia Stock Exchange Bldg, Menara 1, Jalan Jenderal Sudirman, Kav. 52–53, Jakarta 12190; tel. (21) 5150515; fax (21) 5150330, e-mail callcenter@idx.co.id; internet www.idx.co.id; fmrly Jakarta Stock Exchange; name changed as above upon merger with Surabaya Stock Exchange in 2007; 125 securities houses constitute the mems and the shareholders of the exchange, each company owning one share; CEO ITO WARSITO.

Regulatory Authority

Badan Pengawas Pasar Modal (BAPEPAM) (Capital Market Supervisory Agency): Gedung Sumitro Djojohadikusumo, Jalan Lapangan Banteng Timur 1–4, Jakarta 10710; tel. (21) 3858001; fax (21) 3857917; e-mail bapepam@bapepam.go.id; internet www.bapepam.go.id; Chair. A. FAUD RAHMANY; Exec. Sec. NGALIM SAWEGA.

INSURANCE

In September 2012 there were 235 insurance companies, including 101 non-life companies, 83 general insurance, 45 life companies, four reinsurance companies and two social insurance companies.

Selected Life Insurance Companies

PT AIA Financial: Menara Matahari, Lantai 8, Jalan Bulevar Palem Raya 7, Lippo Karawaci 1200, Tangerang 15811; tel. (21) 54218777; fax (21) 5475409; e-mail id.customer@aia.com; internet www.aia-financial.co.id; f. 1983; CEO and Pres. Dir PETER J. CREWE.

PT Asuransi Allianz Life Indonesia: Gedung Summitmas II, Lantai 1, Jalan Jenderal Sudirman, Kav. 61–62, Jakarta 12190; tel. (21) 25989999; fax (21) 30003400; e-mail contactus@allianz.co.id; internet www.allianz.co.id; f. 1996; CEO JOACHIM WESSLING.

Asuransi Jiwa Bersama Bumiputera 1912: Wisma Bumiputera, Lantai 18–21, Jalan Jenderal Sudirman, Kav. 75, Jakarta 12910; tel. (21) 2512154; fax (21) 2512172; e-mail bp1912@bumiputera.com; internet www.bumiputera.com; Chair. Dr H. SUGIHARTO; Pres. Dir MADJDI ALI.

PT Asuransi Jiwa Central Asia Raya: Blue Dot Center, Blok A–C, Jalan Gelong Baru Utara 5–8, Jakarta Barat 11440; tel. (21) 56961929; fax (21) 56961939; e-mail lancar@car.co.id; internet www.car.co.id; Pres. Commr ANTHONI SALIM; Pres. Dir FREDDY THAMRIN.

PT Asuransi Jiwasraya (Persero): Jalan H. Juanda 34, Jakarta 10120; tel. (21) 3845031; fax (21) 3862344; e-mail asuransi@jiwasraya.co.id; internet www.jiwasraya.co.id; f. 1959; Pres. Commr DJONNY WIGUNA; Pres. Dir HENDRISMAN RAHIM.

PT Asuransi Panin Life: Panin Life Center, Lantai 6, Jalan Letjenderal S. Parman, Kav. 91, Jakarta 11420; tel. (21) 25566888; fax (21) 25566711; e-mail customer@paninlife.co.id; internet www.paninlife.co.id; Pres. Dir HERU YUWONO.

Selected Non-life Insurance Companies

PT Asuransi Bina Dana Arta Tbk: Plaza ABDA, Lantai 27, Jalan Jenderal Sudirman, Kav. 59, Jakarta 122190; tel. (21) 51401688; fax (21) 51401698; e-mail contactus@abda.co.id; internet www.abda.co.id; Pres. Commr TJAN SOEN ENG; Pres. Dir CANDRA GUNAWAN.

PT Asuransi Bintang Tbk: Jalan R. S. Fatmawati 32, Jakarta Selatan 12430; tel. (21) 75902777; fax (21) 7656287; e-mail bintang@asuransibintang.com; internet www.asuransibintang.com; f. 1955; general insurance; Pres. Commr SHANTI POESPOSOETJIPTO; Pres. Dir ZAFAR DINESH IDHAM.

PT Asuransi Buana Independen: Jalan Pintu Besar Selatan 78, Jakarta 11110; tel. (21) 6266286; fax (21) 6263005; e-mail headoffice@buanaindependent.co.id; internet buanaindependent.co.id; Pres. Commr ISHAK SUMARNO; Pres. Dir MADE MARKA.

PT Asuransi Central Asia: Wisma Asia, Lantai 12–15, Jalan Letjenderal S. Parman, Kav. 79, Slipi, Jakarta Barat 11420; tel. (21) 56998288; fax (21) 5638029; e-mail info@aca.co.id; internet www.aca.co.id; Pres. Commr ANTHONY SALIM; Pres. Dir TEDDY HAILAMSAH.

PT Asuransi Dayin Mitra: Jalan Raden Saleh Raya, Kav. 1B–1D, Jakarta 10430; tel. (21) 3153577; fax (21) 3912902; e-mail nuning@dayinmitra.co.id; internet www.dayinmitra.co.id; f. 1982; general insurance; Man. Dir LARSOEN HAKER.

PT Asuransi Indrapura: Menara Chase Plaza, Lantai 4, Jalan Jenderal Sudirman, Kav. 21, Jakarta 12920; tel. (21) 5200338; fax (21) 5200175; e-mail insure@indrapura.co.id; internet www.indrapura.co.id; f. 1954; Pres. Commr A. WAHYUHADI; Pres. Dir MINTARTO HALIM.

PT Asuransi Jasa Indonesia: Jalan Letjenderal M. T. Haryono, Kav. 61, Jakarta 12041; tel. (21) 7994508; fax (21) 7995364; e-mail jasindo@jasindo.co.id; internet www.jasindo.co.id; Pres. Commr MOELYADI; Pres. Dir Drs EKO BUDIWIYONO.

PT Asuransi Jasa Tania: Wisma Jasa Tania, Jalan Teuku Cik Ditiro 14, Jakarta 10350; tel. (21) 3101850; fax (21) 31923089; e-mail ajstania@jasatania.co.id; internet www.jasatania.co.id; Pres. Dir DASRAN DAMANIK (acting).

PT Asuransi Maipark Indonesia: Gedung Setiabudi Atrium, Lantai 4, Suite 408, Jalan H. R. Rasuna Said, Kav. 62, Jakarta 12920; tel. (21) 5210803; fax (21) 5210738; e-mail maipark@maipark.com; internet www.maipark.com; fmrly PT Maskapai Asuransi Indonesia; Chair. and CEO KORNELIUS SIMANJUNTAK.

PT Asuransi Parolamas: Komplek Golden Plaza, Blok G 39–42, Jalan R. S. Farmawati 15, Jakarta 12420; tel. (21) 7508983; fax (21) 7506339; internet www.parolamas.co.id; Chief Commr TJUT ROEKMA RAFFLI; Pres. Dir Drs SYARIFUDDIN HARAHAP.

PT Asuransi Ramayana: Jalan Kebon Sirih 49, Jakarta 10340; tel. (21) 31937148; fax (21) 31934825; e-mail info@ramayanains.com; internet ramayanainsurance.com; f. 1965; Pres. Commr A. WINOTO DOERIAT; Pres. Dir SYAHRIL.

PT Asuransi Tri Pakarta: Jalan Paletehan I/18, Jakarta 12160; tel. (21) 7222717; fax (21) 7394748; internet www.tripakarta.co.id; Chair. SAIFUDIEN HASAN; Pres. TEDDY PUSPITO.

PT Asuransi Wahana Tata: Jalan H. R. Rasuna Said, Kav. C-4, Jakarta 12920; tel. (21) 5203145; fax (21) 5203149; e-mail aswata@aswata.co.id; internet www.aswata.co.id; Chair. RUDY WANANDI; Pres. Dir CHRISTIAN WANANDI.

PT Berdikari Insurance: Jalan Merdeka Barat 1, Jakarta 10110; tel. (21) 3440266; fax (21) 3440586; e-mail ho@berdikariinsurance.com; internet www.berdikariinsurance.com; Pres. ANGGIAT ISIDORUS SITOHANG.

PT Tugu Pratama Indonesia: Wisma Tugu I, Jalan H. R. Rasuna Said, Kav. C8–9, Kuningan, Jakarta Selatan 12920; tel. (21) 52961777; fax (21) 52961555; e-mail tpi@tugu.com; internet www.tugu.com; f. 1981; general insurance; Pres. Commr FEREDERICK SIAHAAN; Pres. Dir EVITA M. TAGOR.

Joint Ventures

PT Asuransi AIG Life: Matahari AIG Lippo Cyber Tower, 5th–7th Floors, Jalan Bulevar Palem Raya 7, Lippo Karawaci 1200, Tangerang 15811; tel. (21) 54218888; fax (21) 5475415; e-mail service@aig-life.co.id; internet www.aig-life.co.id; jt venture between American International Group, Inc, and PT Asuransi Lippo Life; life insurance; Dep. Pres. Dir S. BUDISUHARTO.

PT Asuransi Allianz Utama Indonesia: Gedung Summitmas II, 9th Floor, Jalan Jenderal Sudirman, Kav. 61–62, Jakarta Selatan 12190; tel. (21) 2522470; fax (21) 2523246; e-mail general@allianz.co.id; internet www.allianz.co.id; f. 1989; non-life insurance; Chair. EDI SUBEKTI; Pres. Dir VOLKER MISS.

PT Asuransi Jiwa Manulife Indonesia: Menara Selatan, Lantai 3, Jalan Jenderal Sudirman, Kav. 45, Jakarta 12930; tel. (21) 25557788; fax (21) 25557799; e-mail communication_id@manulife.com; internet www.manulife-indonesia.com; f. 1985; life insurance; Pres. Dir ALAN MERTEN.

PT Asuransi Jiwa Sinarmas: Wisma EKA Jiwa, Lantai 8, Jalan Mangga Dua Raya, Jakarta 10730; tel. (21) 6257808; fax (21) 6257837; e-mail cs@sinarmaslife.co.id; internet www.sinarmaslife.com; fmrly PT Asuransi Jiwa EKA Life; Pres. Commr INDRA WIDJAJA; Pres. Dir IVENA WIDJAJA.

PT Asuransi MSIG Indonesia: Gedung Summitmas II, Lantai 15, Jalan Jenderal Sudirman, Kav. 61–62, Jakarta 12190; tel. (21) 2523110; fax (21) 2524307; e-mail msig@id.msig-asia.com; internet www.msig.co.id; f. 1975; est. as PT Asuransi Mitsui Marine Indonesia; name changed to PT Asuransi Mitsui Sumitomo Indonesia in 2003, following merger with PT Asuransi Sumitomo Marine and Pool; present name adopted 2007; Chair. RUDY WANANDI; Pres. Dir TADASHI MAEKAWA.

PT Asuransi Tokio Marine Indonesia: Sentral Senayan I, Lantai 4, Jalan Asia Afrika 8, Jakarta 10270; tel. (21) 5725772; fax (21) 5724005; e-mail cp@tokiomarine.co.id; internet www.tokiomarine.co.id; jt venture between Tokio Marine Asia Pte Ltd and PT Asuransi Jasa Indonesia; Pres. Dir MITSUTAKA SATO.

PT Chartis Insurance Indonesia: Indonesia Stock Exchange Bldg, Menara II, Lantai 3A, Jalan Jenderal Sudirman, Kav. 52–53, Jakarta 12190; tel. (21) 52914888; fax (21) 52914889; e-mail contact.us@chartisinsurance.com; internet www.chartisinsurance.co.id; f. 1970; fmrly PT Asuransi AIU Indonesia; Pres. Dir MICHAEL BLAKEWAY.

Insurance Associations

Asosiasi Asuransi Jiwa Indonesia (Indonesia Life Insurance Association): The Plaza Office Tower, Lantai 19, Jalan M. H. Thamrin, Kav. 28–30, Jakarta 10350; tel. (21) 29922929; fax (21) 29922828; e-mail aaji.info@aaji.or.id; internet www.aaji.or.id; f. 2002; 49 mems; Chair. HENDRISMAN RAHIM; Exec. Dir ROSA C. GINTING.

Asosiasi Asuransi Umum Indonesia (General Insurance Association of Indonesia): Permata Kuningan Bldg, 2nd Floor, Jalan Kuningan Mulia, Kav. 9C, Jakarta 12960; tel. (21) 2906980; fax (21) 29069828; e-mail secretary@aaui.or.id; internet aaui.or.id; f. 1957; est. as Dewan Asuransi Indonesia (Insurance Council of Indonesia); present name adopted 2003; Chair. KORNELIUS SIMANJUNTAK; Exec. Dir JULIAN NOOR.

Trade and Industry

GOVERNMENT AGENCIES

Badan Pengatur Hilir Minyak dan Gas Bumi (BPH Migas): Gedung BPH Migas, Jalan Captain P. Tendean 28, Jakarta Selatan 12710; tel. (21) 5255500; fax (21) 5223210; e-mail humas@bphmigas.go.id; internet www.bphmigas.go.id; f. 2002; regulates downstream petroleum and gas industry; Chair. TUBAGUS HARYONO.

Badan Pengembangan Industri Strategis (BPIS) (Agency for Strategic Industries): Gedung Arthaloka, 3rd Floor, Jalan Jenderal Sudirman 2, Jakarta 10220; tel. (21) 5705335; fax (21) 3292516; f. 1989; co-ordinates production of capital goods.

Badan Pengkajian dan Penerapan Teknologi (BPPT) (Agency for the Assessment and Application of Technology): Jalan M. H. Thamrin 8, Jakarta 10340; tel. (21) 3168200; fax (21) 3904573; e-mail humas@bppt.go.id; internet www.bppt.go.id; Chair. Dr Ir MARZAN A. ISKANDAR.

Badan Tenaga Nuklir Nasional (BATAN) (National Nuclear Energy Agency): Jalan Kuningan Barat, Mampang Prapatan, Jakarta 12710; tel. (21) 5251109; fax (21) 5251110; e-mail humas@batan.go.id; internet www.batan.go.id; Chair. Dr SOEDYARTOMO.

Badan Urusan Logistik (BULOG) (National Logistics Agency): Jalan Jenderal Gatot Subroto, Kav. 49, Jakarta 12950; tel. and fax (21) 5256482; e-mail redaksiweb@bulog.co.id; internet www.bulog.co.id; Dir-Gen. SUTARTO ALIMOESO.

National Agency for Export Development (NAFED): Jalan M. I. Ridwan Rais 5, 3rd Floor, Jakarta 10110; tel. (21) 3858171; fax (21) 23528662; e-mail nafed@nafed.go.id; internet www.nafed.go.id; Chair. HESTI INDAH KRESNARINI.

National Economic Council: Jakarta; f. 1999; 13-mem. council formed to advise the President on economic policy; Chair. CHAIRUL TANJUNG.

Satuan Kerja Khusus Sementara Pelaksana Kegiatan Usaha Hulu Minyak dan Gas Bumi (SKK Migas) (Special Task Force for Upstream Oil and Gas Business Activities): Gedung Wisma Mulia, Lantai 35, 42 Jalan Gatot Subroto, Jakarta 12710; tel. (21) 29241607; fax (21) 29249999; e-mail hupmas@skspmigas-esdm.go.id; internet www.skspmigas-esdm.go.id; f. 2012 to replace Badan Pelaksana Kegiatan Usaha Hulu Minyak dan Gas Bumi (BP Migas), disbanded by a ruling of the Constitutional Court; regulates upstream petroleum and natural gas industry; Chair. RUDI RUBIANDINI.

DEVELOPMENT ORGANIZATIONS

Badan Koordinasi Penanaman Modal (BKPM) (Investment Co-ordinating Board): Jalan Jenderal Gatot Subroto 44, POB 3186, Jakarta 12190; tel. (21) 52921334; fax (21) 5264211; e-mail info@bkpm.go.id; internet www.bkpm.go.id; f. 1976; Chair. MUHAMAD CHATIB BASRI.

Badan Perencanaan Pembangunan Nasional (Bappenas) (National Development Planning Board): Jalan Taman Suropati 2, Jakarta 10310; tel. (21) 3905650; fax (21) 3145374; e-mail admin@bappenas.go.id; internet www.bappenas.go.id; formulates Indonesia's economic devt plans; Chair. Dr ARMIDA ALISJAHBANA.

CHAMBER OF COMMERCE

Kamar Dagang dan Industri Indonesia (KADIN) (Indonesian Chamber of Commerce and Industry): Menara Kadin Indonesia, Lantai 29, Jalan H. R. Rasuna Said X5, Kav. 2–3, Jakarta 12950; tel. (21) 5274484; fax (21) 5274331; e-mail kadin@kadin-indonesia.or.id; internet www.kadin-indonesia.or.id; f. 1968; 33 provincial-level chambers and 442 district-level chambers; Chair. SURYO BAMBANG SULISTO; Exec. Dir Drs RAHARDJO JAMTOMO.

INDUSTRIAL AND TRADE ASSOCIATIONS

Association of Indonesian Automotive Industries (GAIKINDO): Jalan Hos Cokroaminoto 6, Jakarta Pusat 10350; tel. (21) 3157178; fax (21) 3142100; e-mail gaikindo@cbn.net.id; internet www.gaikindo.org; Chair. BAMBANG TRISULO.

Association of Indonesian Beverage Industries (ASRIM): 8/F, Wisma GKBI, Jalan Jenderal Sudirman 28, Jakarta 10210; tel. (21) 5723838; fax (21) 5740817; e-mail sekertariat.asrim@gmail.com; 22 mems; Chair. WILLY SIDHARTA; Sec.-Gen. SUROSO NATAKUSUMA.

Association of Indonesian Coffee Exporters (AIKE): Gedung AIKE, Lantai 3, Jalan R. P. Soeroso 20, Jakarta 10350; tel. (21) 3106765; fax (21) 3144115; e-mail bphaeki@yahoo.com; 800 mems; Chair. HASSAN WIDJAYA; Sec.-Gen. RACHIM KARTABRATA.

Association of State-owned Companies: CTC Bldg, Jalan Kramat Raya 94–96, Jakarta; tel. (21) 346071; co-ordinates the activities of state-owned enterprises; Pres. ODANG.

BANI Arbitration Center (BANI): Wahana Graha, Lantai 2, Jalan Mampang Prapatan 2, Jakarta 12760; tel. (21) 7940542; fax (21) 7940543; e-mail bani-arb@indo.net.id; internet www.bani-arb.org; f. 1977; resolves business disputes; Chair. Prof. Dr H. PRIYATNA ABDURRASYID; Sec.-Gen. N. KRISNAWENDA.

Electric and Electronic Appliance Manufacturers' Association: Jalan Pangeran, Blok 20A-1D, Jakarta; tel. (21) 6480059.

Importers' Association of Indonesia (GINSI): Wisma Kosgoro Bldg, 8th Floor, Jalan M. H. Thamrin 53, Jakarta 10350; tel. (21) 39832510; fax (21) 39832540; f. 1956; 2,921 mems (1996); Chair. AMIRUDIN SAUD; Sec.-Gen. DEDDY BINTANG.

Indonesia National Shippers' Council (INSC): Jalan Cempaka Putih, Barat 6, Jakarta Pusat 10520; tel. (21) 4254677; fax (21) 4206303; e-mail depalindo@yahoo.com; Chair. SUARDI ZEN; Sec.-Gen. RACHIM KARTABRATA.

Indonesian Cement Association (ICA): Graha Irama Bldg, Lantai 11, Suite 11G, Jalan H. R. Rasuna Said, Blok X-1, Kav. 1–2, Jakarta Selatan 12950; tel. (21) 5261105; fax (21) 5261108; e-mail info@asi.or.id; internet www.asi.or.id; f. 1969; Chair. URIP TIMURYONO.

Indonesian Coal Mining Association (APBI-ICMA): Menara Kuningan, Lantai 1, Jalan H. R. Rasuna Said, Blok X-7, Kav. 5, Jakarta 12940; tel. (21) 30015935; fax (21) 30015936; e-mail apbi-icma@indo.net.id; internet www.apbi-icma.com; 109 mems; Chair. BOB KAMANDANU; Exec. Dir SUPRIATNA SUHALA.

Indonesian Cocoa Association (ASKINDO): Jalan Pungkur 115, Bandung 40262; tel. (22) 4262235; fax (22) 4214084; e-mail info@askindo.or.id; internet www.askindo.or.id; Chair. ZULHEFI SIKUMBANG.

Indonesian Exporters' Federation: Menara Sudirman, 8th Floor, Jalan Jenderal Sudirman, Kav. 60, Jakarta 12190; tel. (21) 5226522; fax (21) 5203303; Chair. HAMID IBRAHIM GANIE.

Indonesian Food and Beverages Association (GAPMMI): Kantor Pusat Kementerian Pertanian, Ground Floor, Lot 2, Jalan Harsono, Rm 3, 224A Ragunan, Pasarminggu, Jakarta 12550; tel. (21) 70322627; fax (21) 7804347; e-mail gapmmi@cbn.net.id; internet www.gapmmi.or.id; f. 1976; 260 mems; Chair. ADHI SISWAJA LUKMAN.

Indonesian Footwear Association (APRISINDO): Gedung Adis Dimension Footwear, Jalan Tanah Abang III/18, Jakarta Pusat 10160; tel. (21) 3447575; fax (21) 3447572; e-mail aprisindo@vision.net.id; internet www.aprisindo.info; 95 mems; Chair. EDDY WIJANARKO; Sec.-Gen. YUDHI KOMARUDIN.

Indonesian Furniture Industry and Handicraft Association (ASMINDO): Jalan Pegambiran 5A, 3rd Floor, Rawamangun Jakarta 13220; tel. (21) 47864028; fax (21) 47864031; e-mail asmindo@indo.net.id; internet www.asmindo.or.id; f. 1988; Chair. TAUFIK GANI; Exec.-Dir LISMAN SUMARDJANI.

Indonesian Nutmeg Exporters' Association: c/o PT Berdirari (Persero) Trading Division, Jalan Yos Sudarso 1, Jakarta; tel. (21) 4301625; e-mail bnuina@indosat.net.id.

Indonesian Palm Oil Producers' Association (GAPKI): Sudirman Park Rukan, Blok B, Jalan K. H. Mas Mansyur 18, Kav. 35, Jakarta 10220; tel. (21) 57943871; fax (21) 57943872; internet www.gapki.or.id; Chair. JOEFLY J. BAHROENY.

Indonesian Precious Metals Association: Galva Bldg, 5th Floor, Jakarta Pusat, Jakarta 10120; tel. (21) 3451202; fax (21) 3812713.

Indonesian Pulp and Paper Association: Jalan Cimandiri 6, Flat I/2, Jakarta 10330; tel. (21) 326084; fax (21) 3140168; Chair. M. MANSUR.

Indonesian Tea Association (ATI): Jalan Polombangkeng 15, Kebayoran Baru, Jakarta; tel. (21) 7260772; fax (21) 7205810; e-mail insyaf@hotmail.com; internet www.indotea.org; Chair. SUGIAT; Gen. Sec. ATIK DHARMADI.

Indonesian Textile Association (API): Panin Bank Centre, 3rd Floor, Jalan Jenderal Sudirman 1, Jakarta Pusat 10270; tel. (21) 7396094; fax (21) 7396341; f. 1974; Sec.-Gen. DANANG D. JOEDONAGORO.

Indonesian Tobacco Association: Jalan H. Agus Salim 85, Jakarta 10350; tel. (21) 3140627; fax (21) 325181; Pres. H. A. ISMAIL.

Masyarakat Perhutanan Indonesia (MPI) (Indonesian Forestry Community): Gedung Manggala Wanabakti, 9th Floor, Wing B, Blok IV, Jalan Jenderal Gatot Subroto, Jakarta Pusat 10270; tel. (21) 5733010; fax (21) 5732564; f. 1974; 9 mems; Pres. M. HASAN.

Rubber Association of Indonesia (Gapkindo): Jalan Cideng Barat 62A, Jakarta 10150; tel. (21) 3501510; fax (21) 3500368; e-mail karetind@indosat.net.id; internet www.gapkindo.org; 161 mems; Chair. DAUD HUSNI BASTARI; Exec. Dir Dr RUSDAN DALIMUNTHE.

UTILITIES

Electricity

PT Perusahaan Listrik Negara (Persero) (PLN): Jalan Trunojoyo, Blok M1/135, Kebayoran Baru, Jakarta Selatan 12160; tel. (21) 7251234; fax (21) 7204929; e-mail kontakkami@pln.co.id; internet www.pln.co.id; state-owned electricity co; Pres. Dir NUR PAMUDJI.

Gas

PT Perusahaan Pertambangan Minyak dan Gas Bumi Negara (PERTAMINA): Jalan Medan Merdeka Timur 1A, Jakarta 10110; tel. (21) 3815111; fax (21) 3843882; e-mail pcc@pertamina.com; internet www.pertamina.com; f. 1968; state-owned petroleum and natural gas mining enterprise; Pres. Dir and CEO KAREN AUGUSTIAWAN.

Perusahaan Gas Negara (PGN) (Public Gas Corporation): Jalan K. H. Zainul Arifin 20, Jakarta 11140; tel. (21) 6334838; fax (21) 6333080; e-mail contact.center@pgn.co.id; internet www.pgn.co.id; monopoly of domestic gas distribution; Pres. Dir HENDI PRIO SANTOSO.

Water

PDAM DKI Jakarta (PAM JAYA): Jalan Penjernihan II, Pejompongan, Jakarta 10210; tel. (21) 5704250; fax (21) 5711796; internet www.pamjaya.co.id; f. 1977; responsible for the water supply systems of Jakarta; govt-owned; Pres. Dir SRIWIDAYANTO KADERI.

PDAM Kodya Dati II Bandung: Jalan Badaksinga 10, Bandung 40132; tel. (22) 2509030; fax (22) 2508063; e-mail pdambdg@olga.net.id; f. 1974; responsible for the water supply and sewerage systems of Bandung; Pres. Dir Ir SUENITIYOSO HADI PRATIKTO.

PDAM Tirtanadi Medan: Jalan Sisingamangaraja 1, Medan 20212; tel. (61) 4571666; fax (61) 4572771; e-mail tirtanadi@pdamtirtanadi.co.id; internet www.pdamtirtanadi.co.id; f. 1979; manages the water supply of Medan and nearby towns and cities; Man. Dir Ir AZZAM RIZAL.

Konfederasi Serikat Pekerja Seluruh Indonesia (KSPSI) (Confederation of All Indonesian Trades Unions): Jalan Raya Pasar Minggu 9, Km 17, Jakarta Selatan 12740; tel. (21) 7974359; fax (21) 7974361; f. 1973; renamed 2001; sole officially recognized Nat. Industrial Union; 5.1m. mems in June 2005; Gen. Chair. JACOB NUWA WEA; Gen. Sec. LATIEF NASUTION.

Konfederasi Serikat Buruh Sejahtera Indonesia (KSBSI) (Confederation of Indonesia Prosperity Trade Unions): Jalan Cipinang Muara Raya 33, Jatinegara, Jakarta Timur 13420; tel. (21) 70984671; fax (21) 8577646; e-mail ksbsi@pacific.net.id; internet www.ksbsi.or.id; f. 1998; application for official registration rejected in May 1998; 1,228,875 mems in 168 branches in 27 provinces throughout Indonesia; Pres. REKSON SILABAN; Sec.-Gen. IDIN ROSIDIN.

Transport

RAILWAYS

There are railways on Java, Madura and Sumatra. In 2006 the Japanese Government agreed to provide a US $741m. loan to finance a Mass Rapid Transport (MRT) rail system in Jakarta. Construction commenced in May 2013, with completion of the first phase of the project expected by early 2018.

Directorate General of Railways: Ministry of Transportation, Jalan Medan Merdeka Barat 8, Jakarta 10110; tel. (21) 3800349; fax (21) 3860758; e-mail bagrenka_dephub@yahoo.com; internet perkeretaapian.dephub.go.id; Dir-Gen. TUNDJUNG INDERAWAN.

PT Kereta Api Indonesia (Persero) (KAI): Jalan Perintis Kermedekaan 1, Bandung 40117; tel. (22) 4230031; fax (22) 4203342; e-mail kontak_pelanggan@kereta-api.co.id; internet www.kereta-api.co.id; 6 regional offices; transferred to the private sector in 1991; Chief Commr IMAN HARYATNA; Chief Dir IGNASIUS JONAN.

ROADS

There is an adequate road network on Java, Sumatra, Sulawesi, Kalimantan, Bali and Madura, but on many of the other islands traffic is by jungle track or river boat. In 2012 Indonesia had a total road length of 501,969 km, of which 38,570 km were highways, and 53,642 km were regional roads. In 2013 the Ministry of Public Works announced the allocation of US $390m. for the improvement of regional road networks, proposing to construct up to 281.4 km of new national roads and 7,164 m of bridges.

Directorate General of Land Transportation: Ministry of Transportation, Jalan Medan Merdeka Barat 8, Jakarta 10110; tel. (21) 3502971; fax (21) 3503013; e-mail info@hubdat.web.id; internet www.hubdat.web.id; Dir-Gen. SUROYO ALIMOESO.

SHIPPING

In December 2014 Indonesia's flag registered fleet numbered 7,133 vessels, with a combined displacement of 17.6m. grt, including 1,284 general cargo carriers, 655 tank ships, 57 gas tankers and 71 fishing vessels. The four main ports are Tanjung Priok (near Jakarta), Tanjung Perak (near Surabaya), Belawan (near Medan) and Makassar (formerly Ujung Pandang, in South Sulawesi). More than 100 of Indonesia's ports and harbours are classified as capable of handling ocean-going shipping.

Directorate-General of Sea Transportation: Ministry of Transportation, Jalan Medan Merdeka Barat 8, Jakarta 10110; tel. (21) 3456332; internet kemhubri.dephub.go.id/hubla.

Indonesian National Ship Owners' Association (INSA): Jalan Tanah Abang III, No. 10, Jakarta Pusat; tel. (21) 3850993; fax (21) 3849522; e-mail info@insa.or.id; internet insa.or.id; Chair. CARMELITA HARTOTO; Sec.-Gen. PAULIS A. DJOHAN.

Shipping Companies

PT Admiral Lines: POB 1476, Jakarta 10014; tel. (21) 4247908; fax (21) 4206267; e-mail setper@admiral.co.id; internet admirallines.net; f. 1966; fmrly PT Pelayaran Samudera Admiral Lines; Pres. Dir BOBBY ADI PRABAWA MOELJADI.

PT Djakarta Lloyd: Jalan Senen Raya 44, Jakarta 10410; tel. (21) 3456208; fax (21) 3441401; internet www.djakartalloyd.co.id; f. 1950; services to USA, Europe, Japan, Australia and the Middle East; Commr Dr Ir TJUK SUKARDIMAN; Dir SYAHIL JAPARIN.

PT Karana Line: Wisma Kalimanis, 12th and 13th Floors, Jalan M. T. Haryono, Kav. 33, Jakarta 12770; tel. (21) 7985914; fax (21) 7985913; Pres. Dir BAMBANG EDIYANTO.

PT Pelayaran Bahtera Adhiguna (Persero): Jalan Kalibesar Timur 10–12, POB 4313, Jakarta 11110; tel. (21) 6912547; fax (21) 6901450; e-mail pelba@bahteradhiguna.co.id; internet www

.bahteradhiguna.co.id; f. 1971; Pres. Commr BINARTO BEKTI MAHARD-JANA; Pres. Dir BIMA PUTRAJAYA.

PT Pelayaran Nasional Indonesia (PELNI): Jalan Gajah Mada 14, Jakarta 10130; tel. (21) 6334342; fax (21) 63854130; e-mail humas@pelni.co.id; internet www.pelni.co.id; state-owned; national shipping co; Pres. Dir JUSSABELLA SAHEA.

PT Pertamina (Persero): Downstream Directorate for Shipping, Jalan Yos Sudarso 32–34, POB 14020, Tanjung Priok, Jakarta Utara 14320; tel. (21) 43930325; fax (21) 4370161; e-mail pcc@pertaminashipping.com; internet www.pertaminashipping.com; f. 1959; state-owned; maritime business services; Pres. Dir KAREN AGUSTIAWAN.

PT Perusahaan Pelayaran Gesuri Lloyd: Gesuri Lloyd Bldg, Jalan Tiang Bendera IV/45, Jakarta 11230; tel. (21) 6904000; fax (21) 6925987; e-mail operation_agency@gesuri.co.id; internet www.gesuri.co.id; f. 1963; Pres. Dir ANTONIUS NURIMBA.

PT Perusahaan Pelayaran Nusantara (PANURJWAN): Jalan Raya Pelabuhan Nusantara, POB 2062, Jakarta 10001; tel. (21) 494344; internet www.panurjwan.co.id; Pres. Dir A. J. SINGH.

PT Perusahaan Pelayaran Samudera 'Samudera Indonesia': Jalan Yos Sudarso 1, Blok A1-7, Tanjung Priok, Jakarta 14320; tel. (21) 4301150; fax (21) 43930116; internet www.samudera.com; Chair. SHANTI L. POESPOSOETJIPTO; Pres. Dir MASLI MULIA.

PT Perusahaan Pelayaran Samudera Trikora Lloyd: Graha Satria, 4th Floor, Jalan R. S. Fatmawati 5, Jakarta Selatan, Jakarta 12430; tel. (21) 75915381; fax (21) 75915385; e-mail tkldir@cbn.net.id; internet www.boedihardjogroup.com/shipping/trikora_lloyd.htm; f. 1964; Pres. Dir GANESHA SOEGIHARTO; Man. Dir P. R. S. VAN HEEREN.

CIVIL AVIATION

Sukarno-Hatta Airport, at Cengkareng, serves Jakarta. An extensive expansion to increase passenger capacity at Ngurah Rai Airport, in Denpasar (Bali), was completed in September 2013. Other international airports include Kuala Namu Airport, replacing Polonia Airport, in Medan (North Sumatra), Juanda Airport, near Surabaya (East Java), Sam Ratulangi Airport, in Manado (North Sulawesi), Hasanuddin Airport, near Makassar (formerly Ujung Pandang, South Sulawesi), and Frans Kaisepo Airport, in Papua (formerly Irian Jaya). Syamsudin Noor Airport, in Banjarbaru (South Kalimantan), began international operations in 2014. A second international airport was planned for Buleleng, Bali, with construction scheduled to start in 2018 and finish in 2021. There are numerous other commercial airports.

Directorate General of Civil Aviation: Jalan Medan Merdeka Barat 8, Jakarta Pusat 10110; tel. (21) 3505550; fax (21) 3505139; e-mail hubud@dephub.go.id; internet hubud.dephub.go.id; Dir-Gen. HERRY BAKTI.

Deraya Air Taxi (DRY): Terminal Bldg, 1st Floor, Rm 150/HT, Halim Perdanakusuma Airport, Jakarta 13610; tel. (21) 80899401; fax (21) 8095770; e-mail admderaya@deraya.co.id; internet www.deraya.co.id; f. 1967; scheduled and charter passenger and cargo services to domestic and regional destinations; Pres. Dir ATTY BOEDIMILYARTI.

PT Garuda Indonesia: Gedung Area Perkantoran, Jalan M1, Garuda City Center, Sukarno-Hatta Airport, Cenkareng; tel. (21) 25601001; fax (21) 55915639; e-mail cs@garuda-indonesia.com; internet www.garuda-indonesia.com; f. 1949; 67% state-owned; operates scheduled domestic, regional and international services to destinations in Europe, the USA, the Middle East, Australasia and the Far East; Pres. and CEO EMIRSYAH SATAR; Chair. HADIYANTO.

Citilink: Juanda Business Centre, Jalan Juanda 1, Blok C2, Gedangan, Sidoarjo; tel. (31) 8549860; internet www.citilink.co.id; f. 2001; subsidiary of PT Garuda Indonesia; low-cost carrier providing shuttle services between 7 domestic destinations; Dir MOHAMMAD ARIF WIBOWO.

PT Merpati Nusantara Airlines: Jalan Angkasa, Blok B-15, Kav. 2–3, Jakarta 10720; tel. (21) 6548888; fax (21) 6540620; e-mail contactcenter@merpati.co.id; internet www.merpati.co.id; f. 1962; subsidiary of PT Garuda Indonesia; domestic and regional services to Australia and Malaysia; Pres. Dir EKANUGRAHA EKANUGRAHA; Chief Commr EDDI HARIYADHI.

Indonesia AirAsia: No. 10, Blok LA–4, Kelapa Gading, Jakarta 14200; tel. (21) 2927 0999; internet www.airasia.com/id; CEO SUNU WIDYATMOKO.

PT Lion Mentari Airlines (Lion Air): Lion Air Tower, Jalan Gajah Mada 7, Jakarta Pusat; tel. (21) 6338345; fax (21) 6335669; e-mail info@lionair.co.id; internet www.lionair.co.id; f. 1999; budget carrier providing domestic and international services; Pres. Dir RUSDI KIRANA.

Batik Air: Lion Air Tower, Jaland Gajah Mada 7, Jakarta Pusat; tel. (21) 6338345; fax (21) 6335669; internet www.batikairlines.com; f. 2013; subsidiary of PT Lion Mentari Airlines; licensed to provide long-haul services to 66 domestic and 20 int. destinations, incl. to Australia and East Asia; Pres. Dir ACHMAD LUTHFIE.

Wings Abadi Airlines (Wings Air): Lion Air Tower, Jalan Gajah Mada 7, Jakarta Pusat; tel. (21) 6326039; fax (21) 6348744; f. 2003; subsidiary co of Lion Air; budget carrier providing scheduled domestic and international passenger services.

Pelita Air Service: Jalan Abdul Muis 52–56A, Jakarta 10160; tel. (21) 2312030; fax (21) 2312216; e-mail marketing@pelita-air.com; internet www.pelita-air.com; f. 1970; subsidiary of state oil co Pertamina; domestic scheduled and charter passenger and cargo services; Pres. Dir ANDJAR WIBAWANUN.

Premiair: Halim Perdanakusuma Airport Terminal Bldg, Ground Floor, Jakarta 13610; tel. (21) 8091255; fax (21) 8002060; e-mail sales@flypremiair.com; internet www.flypremiair.com; f. 1989; domestic and international charter services; CEO Capt. ARI DARYATA SINGGIH.

Sriwijaya Air: No. 13, Blok B8–10, Jalan Gunung Sahari Raya, Jakarta; tel. (21) 55917777; fax (21) 55912888; internet www.sriwijayaair.co.id; f. 2003; domestic services; Pres. Dir CHANDRA LIE; Pres. Commr HENDRY LIE.

Tourism

Indonesia's tourism industry is based mainly on the islands of Java, famous for its volcanic scenery and religious temples, and Bali, renowned for its scenery and Hindu/Buddhist temples and religious festivals. Lombok, Sumatra and Sulawesi are also increasingly popular. Domestic tourism within Indonesia has also increased significantly. According to provisional figures, revenue from tourism (excluding passenger transport) amounted to US $9,337m. in 2013. The number of tourist arrivals in that year totalled an estimated 8.8m.

Indonesia Tourism Promotion Board: Wisma Nugra Santana, 9th Floor, Jalan Jenderal Sudirman 8, Jakarta 10220; tel. (21) 5704879; fax (21) 5704855; e-mail itpb@cbn.net.id; private body; promotes national and international tourism; Chair. WIRYANT SUKAMDANI.

Defence

As assessed at November 2014, the total strength of the armed forces was an estimated 395,500: army 300,400, navy 65,000, and air force 30,100; paramilitary forces comprised some 281,000, including a police 'mobile brigade' of 14,000. Reserve forces numbered 400,000, including an estimated 40,000 trainees of KAMRA (People's Security). Military service, which is selective, lasts for two years. In support of international peacekeeping efforts, at November 2014 1,287 Indonesian troops were stationed in Lebanon, 175 in the Democratic Republic of the Congo and 168 in the Central African Republic.

Defence Budget: Rp. 94,900,000m. for 2015.

Commander-in-Chief of the Armed Forces: Gen. MOELDOKO.

Chief of Staff of the Army: Lt-Gen. GATOT NURMANTYO.

Chief of Staff of the Navy: Adm. ADE SUPANDI.

Chief of Staff of the Air Force: Air Chief Marshal AGUS SUPRIATNA.

Education

Education is administered mainly by the Ministry of Education and Culture, but the Ministry of Religious Affairs also operates Islamic religious schools (*madrasahs*) at the primary level.

Primary education, beginning at seven years of age and lasting for six years, was made compulsory in 1987. In 1993 it was announced that compulsory education was to be expanded to nine years. Secondary education begins at 13 years of age and lasts for a further six years, comprising three years of junior secondary education and a further three years of senior secondary education. A further three years of academic level or five years of higher education may follow. In July 2013 the Government implemented compulsory 12-year education for all Indonesian children.

In 2012/13 there were 26,769,680 pupils enrolled at 148,272 primary schools, 9,653,093 pupils enrolled at 35,527 general junior secondary schools, and 4,272,860 pupils at 12,107 general senior secondary schools. Enrolment at primary level in 2010/11 included 94% of pupils in the relevant age-group; enrolment at secondary level in the same year included 75% of children in the relevant age-group. Vocational subjects have been introduced in the secondary schools. There were 4,189,519 pupils at 10,673 vocational senior secondary schools in 2012/13. In the same year there were 3,189 tertiary institutions, with enrolment totalling 5,822,143. The Government's budget for 2009 allocated Rp. 244,440,000m., representing 20% of total expenditure, to education.

IRAN

Introductory Survey

LOCATION, CLIMATE, LANGUAGE, RELIGION, FLAG, CAPITAL

The Islamic Republic of Iran lies in western Asia, bordered by Armenia, Azerbaijan and Turkmenistan to the north, by Turkey and Iraq to the west, by the Persian (Arabian) Gulf and the Gulf of Oman to the south, and by Pakistan and Afghanistan to the east. The climate is one of great extremes. Summer temperatures of more than 55°C (131°F) have been recorded, but in the winter the great altitude of much of the country results in temperatures of −18°C (0°F) and below. The principal language is Farsi (Persian), spoken by about 50% of the population. Turkic-speaking Azeris form about 27% of the population, and Kurds, Arabs, Baluchs and Turkomans form less than 25%. The great majority of Persians and Azeris are Shi'a Muslims, while the other ethnic groups are mainly Sunni Muslims. There are also small minorities of Christians (mainly Armenians), Zoroastrians and Jews. The Bahá'í faith, which originated in Iran, has been severely persecuted, being denied rights given to other recognized religious minorities. The national flag (proportions 4 by 7) comprises three unequal horizontal stripes, of green, white and red, with the emblem of the Islamic Republic of Iran (the stylized word Allah) centrally positioned in red, and the inscription 'Allaho Akbar' ('God is Great') written 11 times each in white Kufic script on the red and green stripes. The capital is Tehran.

CONTEMPORARY POLITICAL HISTORY

Historical Context

Iran, called Persia until 1935, was formerly a monarchy, ruled by a Shah (Emperor). In 1925, having seized power in a military coup, Reza Khan, a Cossack officer, was elected Shah, adopting the title Reza Shah Pahlavi. In 1941 British and Soviet forces occupied Iran, and the Shah (who favoured Nazi Germany) was forced to abdicate in favour of his son, Muhammad Reza Pahlavi. British and US forces left Iran in 1945, and Soviet forces in 1946. The United Kingdom retained considerable influence through the Anglo-Iranian Oil Co, which controlled much of Iran's extensive petroleum reserves. In March 1951, however, the Majlis (National Consultative Assembly) approved the nationalization of the petroleum industry. The leading advocate of nationalization, Dr Muhammad Mussadeq, who became Prime Minister in May 1951, was deposed in August 1953 in a military coup engineered by the US and British intelligence services. The Shah assumed dictatorial powers in 1963 with the so-called 'White Revolution'. Large estates were redistributed to small-scale farmers, and women were granted the right to vote. In 1965 Prime Minister Hassan Ali Mansur was assassinated, reportedly by a follower of Ayatollah Ruhollah Khomeini, a fundamentalist Shi'a Muslim leader strongly opposed to the Shah. (Khomeini had been deported in 1964 for his opposition activities, and was living in exile in Iraq.)

There followed a period of political stability and strong economic growth, based on substantial petroleum revenues which funded expenditure on defence equipment and infrastructure projects. However, a declining economy from late 1977 and the repressive nature of the Shah's rule led to widespread anti-Government protests by the end of 1978. These involved both left-wing and liberal opponents of the Shah, as well as Islamist activists, but the most effective opposition came from supporters of Ayatollah Khomeini (who was now based in France). The growing unrest forced the Shah to leave Iran in January 1979. Khomeini arrived in Tehran on 1 February, and effectively assumed power 10 days later. A 15-member Islamic Revolutionary Council was formed to govern the country, in co-operation with a Provisional Government, and on 1 April Iran was declared an Islamic republic. Supreme authority was vested in the Wali Faqih, a religious leader (initially Khomeini) appointed by the Shi'a clergy. Executive power was to be vested in a President, to which post Abolhasan Bani-Sadr was elected in January 1980. Elections to a 270-member Majlis—renamed the Majlis-e-Shura-e Islami (Islamic Consultative Assembly)—took place in March and May. The Islamic Republican Party (IRP), which was identified with Khomeini and traditionalist Muslims, won some 60 seats, and subsequently increased its support base.

Domestic Political Affairs

In November 1979 Iranian students seized 63 hostages at the US embassy in Tehran. The original purpose of the siege was to force the USA (where the Shah was undergoing medical treatment) to return the former ruler to Iran to face trial. The Shah died in Egypt in July 1980, by which time Iran had made other demands, notably for a US undertaking not to interfere in its affairs. Intense diplomatic activity led to the release of the 52 remaining hostages in January 1981, others having been freed two weeks into the siege. However, a failed rescue operation by the US military in April 1980 had resulted in the deaths of eight US servicemen.

The prolonged hostage crisis had forced the resignation of the moderate Provisional Government, and during 1980 a rift became apparent between President Bani-Sadr and his modernist allies on the one hand, and the IRP and traditionalist elements on the other. In June 1981 clashes between their rival supporters escalated into sustained fighting between members of the Mujahidin-e-Khalq (an Islamist guerrilla group that supported Bani-Sadr) and troops of the Islamic Revolutionary Guards Corps. The Majlis voted to impeach the President, who was subsequently dismissed by Khomeini. Bani-Sadr fled to France, as did the leader of the Mujahidin, Massoud Rajavi. A presidential election in July resulted in victory for the Prime Minister, Muhammad Ali Rajani, who was himself replaced by Muhammad Javar Bahonar. In August, however, both the President and Prime Minister were killed in a bomb attack attributed to the Mujahidin-e-Khalq. A further presidential election, held in October, was won by Hojatoleslam Sayed Ali Khamenei. Mir Hossein Mousavi was appointed Prime Minister.

Mousavi's attempts to implement nationalization and land reform were continually obstructed by the predominantly conservative, clerical Majlis. Elections to the second Majlis in April and May 1984 resulted in an easy victory for the IRP. The elections were boycotted by the sole opposition party to have a degree of official recognition, Nehzat-e Azadi-ye Iran (Liberation Movement of Iran), led by Dr Mehdi Bazargan (Prime Minister in the 1979 Provisional Government), which cited the undemocratic conditions prevailing in Iran. Prior to the August 1985 presidential election, the Council of Guardians (responsible for the supervision of elections) rejected almost 50 candidates, including Bazargan. Khamenei was elected President for a second four-year term, with 85.7% of the votes cast. Mousavi was reconfirmed as Prime Minister in October.

The Iran–Iraq War

For most of the 1980s Iran's domestic and foreign policy was dominated by the war with Iraq. In September 1980, ostensibly to assert a claim of sovereignty over the disputed Shatt al-Arab waterway, Iraqi forces invaded Iran along a 500-km front. The Iranian military offered strong resistance, and began a counter-offensive in early 1982; by June Iraq had been forced to withdraw from Iranian territory, and Iranian troops subsequently entered Iraq. A conflict of attrition thus developed, in which petroleum reserves, installations and transshipment facilities were targeted. From 1984 Iraq began attacking tankers using Iran's Kharg Island oil terminal in the Persian (Arabian) Gulf, and Iran retaliated by targeting Saudi Arabian and Kuwaiti tankers, as well as neutral vessels using Kuwait. Despite UN efforts to broker peace negotiations, Iran's conditions for peace were the removal from power of the Iraqi President, Saddam Hussain, as well as agreement by Iraq to pay war reparations. The war had left Iran in virtual diplomatic isolation, although in late 1986 it emerged that the USA had made secret shipments of weapons, allegedly in exchange for Iranian assistance in securing the release of US hostages held by Shi'a groups in Lebanon and an Iranian undertaking to relinquish involvement in international terrorism.

In April 1988 Iraq recaptured the Faw peninsula, forcing the Iranian military to withdraw across the Shatt al-Arab; in June Iraq also retook Majnoun Island. In July an IranAir passenger flight, apparently mistaken for an attacking fighter jet, was shot down by a US aircraft carrier in the Strait of Hormuz; all 290 people on board were killed. In that month Iraqi troops crossed into Iranian territory for the first time since 1986, and the last Iranian troops on Iraqi territory were dislodged. On 18 July 1988 Iran unexpectedly announced its unconditional acceptance of UN Security Council Resolution 598, adopted one year earlier. This urged an immediate ceasefire, the withdrawal of military forces to international boundaries, and the co-operation of Iran and Iraq in mediation efforts to achieve a peace settlement. More than 1m. people were estimated to have died in the eight-year conflict. A ceasefire came into effect on 20 August, and UN-sponsored peace negotiations began shortly afterwards in Geneva, Switzerland. In the same month a UN Iran-Iraq Military Observer Group (UNIIMOG) was deployed in the region. However, the negotiations soon became deadlocked in disputes regarding the sovereignty of the Shatt al-Arab waterway, the exchange of prisoners of war and the withdrawal of armed forces to within international boundaries. The pursuit of a comprehensive peace settlement was rapidly overshadowed by Iraq's invasion of Kuwait at the beginning of August 1990. Saddam Hussein sought an immediate, formal peace with Iran, accepting all the claims that Iran had pursued since the ceasefire declaration (including the reinstatement of the Algiers Agreement of 1975, dividing the Shatt al-Arab), and Iraq immediately began to redeploy troops from its border with Iran to Kuwait. Prisoner exchanges took place, and Iran and Iraq restored diplomatic relations in September 1990. In February 1991 the withdrawal of all armed forces to internationally recognized boundaries was confirmed by UNIIMOG, the mandate of which was terminated shortly afterwards.

Iran denounced Iraq's invasion of Kuwait, and observed the economic sanctions imposed by the UN on Iraq. However, it was unequivocal in its condemnation of the deployment of a US-led multinational force in the Gulf region. Relations between Iran and Iraq deteriorated after the liberation of Kuwait in February 1991. Iran protested strongly against the Baathist regime's suppression of the Shi'a-led rebellion in southern and central Iraq, and renewed its demand for Saddam Hussein's resignation. Iraq, in turn, accused Iran of supporting the rebellion. Nevertheless, in late 1993 high-level bilateral talks recommenced on the exchange of remaining prisoners of war, under the terms of Resolution 598.

Political developments following the death of Ayatollah Khomeini

Elections to the Majlis in April and May 1988 apparently provided a stimulus to more reformist elements in the Government (identified with Ali Akbar Hashemi Rafsanjani, since 1980 the Speaker of the Majlis, and Prime Minister Mousavi) by producing an assembly strongly representative of their views. (The elections were the first not to be contested by the IRP, which had been dissolved in 1987.) In June 1988 Rafsanjani was re-elected as Speaker, and Mousavi was overwhelmingly endorsed as Prime Minister. In February 1989, however, Ayatollah Khomeini referred explicitly to a division in the Iranian leadership between reformers (who sought a degree of Western participation in Iran's post-war reconstruction) and conservatives (who opposed such involvement), and declared that he would never permit the reformers to prevail. A number of prominent reformists, among them Ayatollah Ali Hossein Montazeri (who had been designated as Khomeini's successor by the Assembly of Experts in 1985), subsequently resigned from the Iranian leadership.

Ayatollah Khomeini died on 3 June 1989. In an emergency session on 4 June the Assembly of Experts elected President Khamenei to succeed Khomeini as Iran's spiritual leader (Wali Faqih). The presidential election, scheduled for mid-August, was brought forward to 28 July, to be held simultaneously with a referendum on proposed amendments to the Constitution. Both conservatives and reformers within the leadership apparently united in support of Rafsanjani's candidacy for the presidency, and Rafsanjani (opposed only by a 'token' candidate) was overwhelmingly elected with 95.9% of the votes cast. A similar proportion of voters approved the constitutional amendments, which included the abolition of the post of Prime Minister (and a consequent increase in the powers of the President).

President Rafsanjani appointed a Government balancing conservatives, reformers and technocrats, and its endorsement by the Majlis in August 1989 was viewed as a mandate for Rafsanjani to conduct a more conciliatory policy towards the West. In

October 1990, with the co-operation of Ayatollah Khamenei, Rafsanjani was able to prevent the election of many powerful conservatives to the Assembly of Experts. An estimated 70% of deputies elected to the fourth Majlis in April–May 1992 were, broadly speaking, pro-Rafsanjani. However, economic reform was lowering the living standards of the traditional constituency of the Islamic regime, the urban lower classes, leading to serious rioting in several cities. Rafsanjani was re-elected in June 1993, but his share of the vote (against three ostensibly 'token' candidates) fell to 63.2%. In August 1995 it was reported that political parties, associations and groups were free to conduct political activities in Iran on condition that they honoured the country's Constitution, although Nehzat-e Azadi was subsequently refused formal registration as a political party.

Elections to the fifth Majlis, in March–April 1996, provided an important measure of the shifting balance of power between more reformist, or liberal, and conservative elements in Iranian politics. At the first round of voting, candidates of the pro-Rafsanjani Servants of Iran's Construction faction were reported to have won some 70% of the seats. However, the conservative Society of Combatant Clergy, with the unofficial patronage of Ayatollah Khamenei, claimed that its candidates had achieved an equally conclusive victory. After the second round of voting, unofficial sources suggested that the Society of Combatant Clergy would command the loyalty of 110–120 deputies in the 270-seat Majlis, and the Servants of Iran's Construction that of 90–100 deputies.

President Khatami's first term of office

In March 1997 Rafsanjani, whose presidential mandate was due to expire, was appointed Chairman of the Council to Determine the Expediency of the Islamic Order for a further five-year term. (He was reappointed as head of the Expediency Council—which arbitrates in disputes between the Majlis and the Council of Guardians—in 2002, 2007 and March 2012.) In May 1997 the Council of Guardians approved four candidatures for that month's presidential election, rejecting 234. It had been widely expected that Ali Akbar Nateq Nouri, the Majlis Speaker favoured by the Society of Combatant Clergy, would secure an easy victory, but the more liberal Sayed Muhammad Khatami (a presidential adviser and former Minister of Culture and Islamic Guidance) emerged as a strong contender immediately prior to the election. Khatami—supported by the Servants of Iran's Construction as well as by intellectuals, professionals, and women's and youth groups—took some 69.1% of the total votes cast; Nateq Nouri took 24.9%.

Taking office in August 1997, President Khatami emphasized his commitment to fostering sustained growth in the political, economic and social spheres. In foreign affairs, he undertook to promote the principle of mutual respect, but pledged that Iran would stand up to any power that sought to subjugate Iranian sovereignty. A notable moderate appointee in Khatami's first Council of Ministers was Dr Massoumeh Ebtekar as Vice-President and Head of the Organization for the Protection of the Environment (the first woman to be appointed to such a senior government post since the Islamic Revolution). In the months following his election, Khatami appeared conciliatory towards the West, while Khamenei continued to denounce the West's military and cultural ambitions, particularly those of the USA and Israel.

The Khatami administration moved to formalize its support base during 1998, primarily through the registration or establishment of reformist parties such as the Servants of Construction, the Islamic Iran Solidarity Party (Hezb-e Hambastegi-ye Iran-e Islami) and the Islamic Iran Participation Front (Jebbeh-ye Mosharekat-e Iran-e Islami—which counted Ebtekar among its leaders). In June the Majlis voted to dismiss Abdollah Nuri as Minister of the Interior, a group of conservative deputies having initiated impeachment on the grounds that he had made provocative statements and permitted dissident rallies. Conservatives retained overwhelming control of the Assembly of Experts at elections in October. Khatami's Government suffered a further setback in February 1999 with the resignation of Qorbanali Dorri Najafabadi, the Minister of Information, after it was admitted that agents of his ministry had been responsible for the murder of several intellectuals and dissident writers in late 1998.

Iran's first local government elections since the Islamic Revolution took place in February 1999. Reformist candidates had notable success in Tehran, Shiraz and Esfahan, while conservatives secured control of councils in their traditional strongholds of Qom and Mashhad.

During 1998–99 Ayatollah Khamenei and conservative Majlis deputies sought action against journalists and publications that they perceived as abusing freedom of speech to weaken Islamic beliefs. A small demonstration by students at the University of Tehran, to protest against the closure, in July 1999, of a newspaper with close links to President Khatami, was dispersed with considerable violence by police. This action, in conjunction with a raid on student dormitories by security forces, aided by vigilantes of the semi-official Ansar-e Hezbollah paramilitary (in which at least one student died), provoked five days of rioting in Tehran and other cities, resulting in some 1,400 arrests. Within a year both the national and Tehran chiefs of police had been dismissed.

Pro-reform candidates secured notable victories at elections to the newly expanded, 290-seat Majlis in February 2000: by mid-2000 reformist or liberal deputies were believed to hold some 200 seats. Reformist deputies immediately drafted legislation to replace a new law, endorsed by the outgoing Majlis, that would further restrict freedom of the press. However, Ayatollah Khamenei instructed the new Majlis not to debate proposed amendments to the press law, on the grounds that these would endanger state security and religious faith.

Khatami's second presidential term

Khatami was re-elected as President in June 2001, with some 76.9% of the total votes cast. Despite this apparent endorsement of his programme of political and economic reforms, there were evident conflicts of interest between Khatami's more reformist supporters in the Majlis and ultra-conservative elements, particularly in the Council of Guardians. Furthermore, the judiciary intensified its actions against pro-reform activists, with mass arrests, public floggings and even public executions in the ostensible interests of reducing crime and encouraging stronger morality. Following what was reported to be the largest political trial in Iran since 1979, 33 activists of Nehzat-e Azadi received custodial sentences of up to 10 years in July 2002, and the movement was formally banned. In early 2003 the Council refused to ratify two reform bills that aimed to reduce the powers of the ultra-conservatives, including by transferring to the Ministry of the Interior the prerogative of the Council of Guardians to approve or disqualify election candidates.

At the beginning of 2004 the Council of Guardians announced that more than 2,000 candidates (from a preliminary list of around 8,200) for the forthcoming elections to the seventh Majlis would be barred from standing. Khatami and several of his ministers threatened to resign in protest, as did Iran's 27 regional governors, and about 100 deputies joined a sit-in at the Majlis, but attempts to reverse the disqualifications were largely unsuccessful. Voting proceeded in February, but turnout was estimated to be only 51%. A second round was held in May for 61 of the 290 seats that remained vacant after the first round. Conservatives were confirmed as having achieved a majority in the legislature, with some 195 seats overall; reformists held fewer than 50, with the remainder being held by nominally independent deputies. In the same month the Council of Guardians formally approved new legislation that had been adopted by the Majlis to ban the use of torture.

Mahmoud Ahmadinejad's first term of office

Voting to elect President Khatami's successor took place in June 2005. Former President Rafsanjani, who had projected himself in the middle ground between reformers and hardliners, received the largest number of votes, with 21.0% of the total. Less expected was the success of Mahmoud Ahmadinejad, the mayor of Tehran, who was placed second with 19.5% of votes cast. Since none of the seven candidates received an outright majority, the election proceeded to an unprecedented second round. At the second round, Ahmadinejad—whose populist campaign promising greater economic equality, reduced corruption and a return to the values of the Islamic Revolution was strongly supported by poorer Iranians—was elected with a decisive 61.7% of votes cast. He was inaugurated in August.

Elections took place in December 2006 both to the Assembly of Experts and for more than 113,000 municipal councillors. Unexpectedly, associates of the President failed to win control of any municipal council. In Tehran, notably, Ahmadinejad's allies secured just two of the 15 council seats; allies of the hard-line mayor Muhammad Baqir Qalibaf won eight seats, reformists' four, and an independent candidate one. Former President Rafsanjani was among candidates elected to the Assembly of Experts; he was elected as Speaker of the Assembly in September 2007.

In January 2007 it was reported that 50 members of the Majlis had signed a document demanding that President Ahmadinejad answer questions in the legislature concerning his increasingly confrontational stance on the issue of Iran's nuclear programme. Moreover, 150 Majlis deputies were said to have signed a letter holding Ahmadinejad responsible for the country's high levels of inflation and unemployment. The introduction of petrol rationing in June, following price increases the previous month, in an effort to reduce the burden of fuel subsidies on the budget, provoked a number of attacks on petrol stations and other state buildings in Tehran and elsewhere. In early 2008 Ayatollah Khamenei overruled the President's decision not to supply subsidized gas to Iranians in rural areas who were suffering shortages owing to extreme weather conditions.

Prior to the 2008 elections to the eighth Majlis, it was reported that the political conservatives had divided into separate electoral lists: the United Principlist Front was formed by traditionalists who supported Ahmadinejad's policies; while the Broad Principlist Coalition included those who were more critical of the President's foreign and economic policies (among them so-called 'revisionists' Ali Larijani, Mohsen Rezai and Muhammad Baqir Qalibaf). Meanwhile, at least 1,700 reformist candidates (of 7,168 registered candidates) were disqualified. At the first legislative ballot, held on 14 March, 208 of the 290 seats were reportedly filled. However, reformists asserted that the election had been neither free nor fair, since so many of their candidates had been disqualified; the opposition also considered that Iran's state-controlled media had been noticeably biased in favour of pro-Ahmadinejad candidates during the election campaign. Both the USA and the European Union (EU, see p. 271) were also strongly critical of the conduct of the election. A second round of voting for the undecided seats was held on 25 April. Overall, according to official reports, conservatives consolidated their control of the Majlis, with some 198–200 seats (including 29 of the 30 seats for Tehran); reformists secured 46–50 seats, and 40–43 seats were held by independents. Around one-third of the conservatives were understood to be members of the Broad Principlist Coalition. Larijani was elected Speaker of the Majlis in May.

It was reported in January 2009 that 16 police officers who had been kidnapped in Sistan and Baluchestan province in mid-2008 had all been killed by the militant Sunni People's Resistance Movement of Iran (PRMI); the group had demanded the release from detention of 200 of its members. More than 20 people were killed in a suicide bomb attack on a Shi'a mosque in Zahedan in May 2009. Responsibility for the attack was claimed by the PRMI, which stated that a secret meeting involving senior members of the Revolutionary Guards had been taking place at the mosque. Assertions by the Iranian Government that the attack had been sponsored by the USA were vehemently denied by President Barack Obama. In late May three members of the PRMI were publicly executed, having allegedly confessed to involvement in planning the Zahedan bombing. In June some 14 suspected PRMI members were extradited from Pakistan; 13 were executed in July for involvement in militant activity. The 14th suspect was executed in May 2010. The PRMI leader, Abdolmalek Rigi, was executed in June, having been found guilty of 79 charges relating to the PRMI's campaign of violence against the Iranian authorities.

The 2009 presidential election

The Council of Guardians approved just four of 475 prospective candidates for the June 2009 presidential election. These were: Mahmoud Ahmadinejad; Mir Hossein Mousavi, the former Prime Minister who was supported by former President Khatami; former Majlis Speaker Mahdi Karrubi, considered a reformist; and Mohsen Rezai, a conservative former Revolutionary Guards commander opposed to the President's economic policies. Following the election, on 12 June, at which an estimated 85% of registered voters participated, Ahmadinejad was officially pronounced to have won 62.6% of the vote. Mousavi took 33.8%, Rezai 1.7% and Karrubi 0.9%. The defeated candidates demanded that the result be annulled, alleging irregularities in the conduct of the election. Violent clashes broke out between anti-Government protesters and security forces in Tehran, and hundreds of thousands of opposition supporters in Tehran defied an official ban on unauthorized demonstrations to march in protest against what they believed was a rigged election. The protests also spread to cities including Shiraz and Esfahan. The unprecedented wave of public protests in Iran in the following weeks became known as the 'Green Movement', with demonstrators wearing green items of clothing in reference to the predominant colour in Mousavi's election campaign material. There were reports of members of the Basij paramilitary volunteer force being deployed to suppress the protests. Official Iranian figures subsequently put the number of deaths as a result of the post-election protests at 36, while the opposition claimed that more than 80 supporters of the Green Movement had been killed.

Meanwhile, on 19 June 2009 Ayatollah Khamenei declared the election valid. He ordered an immediate end to the demonstrations, accusing foreign powers of fomenting unrest within Iran. Following an inquiry into allegations of voting irregularities, the Council of Guardians announced that the number of votes cast had exceeded the number of eligible voters in as many as 50 constituencies. However, the Council ruled that these and other discrepancies were insufficient to affect the outcome of the election. On 24 June Rezai withdrew his opposition to the election result. Intermittent violent clashes between protesters and security forces continued in subsequent weeks. Established divisions within the Iranian political hierarchy were apparently deepened as a result of the disputed election. In July, notably, Rafsanjani—now head of both the Expediency Council and the Assembly of Experts—alleged that the authorities had lost the trust of the people, and urged the lifting of restrictions on the media and the release of hundreds of detainees. Ahmadinejad was sworn in for a second term as President on 5 August, but the inauguration ceremony was boycotted by Mousavi and Karrubi, as well as by former Presidents Rafsanjani and Khatami, and by as many as 50 parliamentary deputies.

In September 2009 the Majlis approved 18 of Ahmadinejad's 21 ministerial nominees, five of whom retained the posts they had held in the outgoing cabinet. Marzieh Vahid Dastjerdi, the new Minister of Health and Medical Education, became the first woman to join the Council of Ministers since the Islamic Revolution. The appointment of Brig.-Gen. Ahmad Vahidi as Minister of Defence and Armed Forces Logistics provoked international criticism: Vahidi, a former Revolutionary Guards commander, was accused by the authorities in Argentina of involvement in the bombing of a Jewish cultural centre in Buenos Aires in 1994, which caused the deaths of 85 people. Nominees for the three outstanding ministerial positions received parliamentary approval in November 2009.

Meanwhile, in August 2009 the trial took place of more than 100 detainees, including numerous prominent reformist figures, during which several defendants were reported to have confessed to involvement in fomenting the post-election unrest and a conspiracy to overthrow the Islamic Republic in collusion with various foreign agencies. Many of Ahmadinejad's critics and political rivals, including Mousavi, Khatami and Rafsanjani, were implicated in the alleged conspiracy. Opposition leaders and international human rights organizations protested that the confessions had been extracted under duress. In October three defendants were reported to have been sentenced to death for their role in the unrest; another five received the death sentence in November. Two dissidents who had been convicted in August were executed in January 2010. Both were alleged to have participated in a pro-royalist plot to overthrow the Islamic Republic. In February former Deputy Minister for Foreign Affairs Mohsen Aminzadeh and another former government minister, Mohsen Behzad, were sentenced to six and five years' imprisonment, respectively. In June Ayatollah Khamenei pardoned, or commuted, the prison sentences of 81 people who had been convicted of crimes during the post-election unrest; the opposition considered this to be an attempt to pre-empt any large-scale protests on the first anniversary of Ahmadinejad's re-election. In January 2011 two further dissidents were executed, having been convicted of distributing footage of the 2009 demonstrations via the internet, and of promoting the proscribed Mujahidin-e-Khalq.

It was reported in October 2009, meanwhile, that Karrubi was to be investigated by a special judicial committee, after he alleged that security forces had tortured and sexually abused political prisoners following the post-election unrest. In November more than 100 people were arrested following violent clashes in Tehran between security forces and participants in a Green Movement protest: demonstrators demanded the removal of Ahmadinejad, and chanted slogans against Ayatollah Khamenei. It was subsequently disclosed that Khamenei, in response to the civil unrest, had sanctioned the creation of a new intelligence agency under the auspices of the Revolutionary Guards. There were further large demonstrations in Tehran at the end of December, on the occasion of the Ashoura festival; eight

opposition activists (including a nephew of Mousavi) were reported to have died during clashes with security forces.

More than 40 people, including at least five senior Revolutionary Guards commanders, were killed in a suicide bomb attack in Sistan and Baluchestan province in October 2009, responsibility for which was claimed by the PRMI. The Iranian Government again accused the USA and the United Kingdom of providing support to the Baluchi militants, and also claimed that the militants maintained bases in Pakistan and had received assistance from Pakistani intelligence agents. In July 2010 some 28 people, again including Revolutionary Guards personnel, were killed in a suicide bombing at a Shi'a mosque in Zahedan. The PRMI claimed that it had carried out the attack in revenge for the execution of Abdolmalek Rigi. In November the US Department of State formally designated the PRMI as a terrorist organization. At least 33 people were killed in a bomb attack conducted by the PRMI at a mosque in the south-eastern port city of Chabahar in December.

The Islamic Iran Participation Front, which had denounced Ahmadinejad's victory in the 2009 election as a '*coup d'état*', complained in March 2010 that the judiciary had barred it from holding its annual party conference. In April both the Participation Front and the Organization of the Mujahidin of the Islamic Revolution, which had also supported Mousavi in the presidential election, were said to have been 'dissolved' for reasons of undermining national security.

Increased tensions within the political establishment

In April 2010 the Majlis approved legislation to reduce its powers to review orders issued by the Council of Guardians, the Assembly of Experts, the Expediency Council and the Supreme National Security Council (SNSC). This apparently exemplified the growing influence of these mainly non-elected bodies over the elected parliament. It became apparent that even conservative politicians were becoming increasingly concerned by the authoritarianism of Ahmadinejad's regime. In December it was announced that the Minister of Foreign Affairs, Manouchehr Mottaki, had been removed from office and replaced on an interim basis by the Vice-President and Head of the Atomic Energy Organization, Ali Akbar Salehi. Mottaki was reported to have disagreed with Ahmadinejad over the ongoing negotiations concerning Iran's nuclear programme. In January 2011 the formal nomination of Salehi as Minister of Foreign Affairs was approved by the Majlis, and in February Fereydoun Abbasi Davani, a leading nuclear scientist who had been the target of an attempted assassination in 2010, assumed Salehi's former post.

In February 2011 two people were reportedly killed after Green Movement activists took part in protests in Tehran, apparently in support of the popular uprisings in Tunisia and Egypt. Karrubi and Mousavi were reportedly placed under house arrest in an attempt to prevent their participation in the protests. Both men remained in detention in early 2015, as did Mousavi's wife, Zahra Rahnavard, although the terms of their detention had partially been eased (see below).

In March 2011 Ayatollah Muhammad Reza Mahdavi Kani became Chairman of the Assembly of Experts. Rafsanjani had declined to seek a further term, citing concern for national unity. In April it was reported that Ahmadinejad had forced the resignation of the Minister of Intelligence and Security, Heydar Moslehi, but that Ayatollah Khamenei had intervened to order that Moslehi remain in office. In apparent protest, Ahmadinejad declined to attend meetings of the Council of Ministers for several days. In May Ahmadinejad dismissed the Ministers of Petroleum, of Industries and Mines, and of Welfare and Social Security, stating that he wished to reduce the number of government ministers; Ahmadinejad subsequently named himself as interim Minister of Petroleum. He was prevented from formally assuming the post, on grounds of unconstitutionality, both by the Council of Guardians and by a large majority in the Majlis. The Majlis did, however, endorse Ahmadinejad's plan eventually to reduce the number of ministries from 21 to 17. In August Brig.-Gen. Rostam Ghasemi was named as Minister of Petroleum. As a member of the Revolutionary Guards, Ghasemi was subject to US and EU sanctions. (For details of sanctions imposed against Iran, see *The Nuclear Issue*.)

In June 2011, meanwhile, the resignation was announced of the newly appointed Deputy Minister of Foreign Affairs, Muhammad Sharif Malekzadeh. A close ally of both the President and his adviser Esfandiar Rahim-Mashai, Malekzadeh was accused by conservative deputies of acting against the clerical hierarchy. Shortly after resigning, he was arrested in connection with a financial scandal that reportedly involved some of the country's largest banks. In October the Deputy Governor of the central bank, Sayed Hamid Pour-Mohammadi (another close associate of the President), was detained by police on suspicion of involvement in the alleged fraud. A number of Majlis deputies formally requested that President Ahmadinejad be examined by a parliamentary committee in relation to the affair. The trial of 39 defendants accused of involvement in the alleged fraud began in February 2012. In July four were given death sentences for their role in the scandal; two others were sentenced to life imprisonment; and the remaining defendants received gaol terms of up to 25 years.

A Green Movement rally in Tehran in June 2011, on the second anniversary of the disputed presidential election, was forcibly disrupted by security forces and a number of protesters were reportedly arrested. Human rights groups monitoring the situation in Iran noted a significant increase in the number of executions during 2011: more than 600 people were reported to have been executed (a figure rejected by the Iranian Government), many of whom had been convicted of crimes in connection with drugs-trafficking.

In November 2011 an apparent bomb attack at a Revolutionary Guards missile base in Bigdaneh, east of Tehran, was reported to have killed 17 members of the corps; among the dead was Maj.-Gen. Hassan Moghaddam, who was said to be a leading figure in Iran's missiles programme. Although the Iranian authorities described the explosion as an accident, there was widespread speculation regarding the possible involvement of Israel's foreign intelligence agency, Mossad.

In March 2012 Ahmadinejad became the first serving President since the establishment of the Islamic Republic to appear before the Majlis for questioning. Principally under scrutiny was his management of the economy, although some deputies also intended to question him about the state of relations with Ayatollah Khamenei and about recent disputes concerning the appointment or dismissal of government officials.

The 2012 legislative elections

A number of dissidents, journalists and intellectuals were reportedly arrested in early 2012, in advance of elections to the ninth Majlis, scheduled for March, and the Government apparently tried to block public internet access to sites critical of the regime. At the first round of voting, on 2 March, around 3,400 candidates contested the 290 parliamentary seats. At least one-third of the original 5,000 candidates had been barred from standing by the Council of Guardians; many of these were mainly reformist deputies in the outgoing Majlis, and several prominent supporters of President Ahmadinejad were also understood to have been disqualified. Iran's most prominent pro-reform parties boycotted the elections, in continuing protest against the disputed presidential election of 2009 and the subsequent crackdown on opposition groups. It was reported that conservatives won 143 seats, while reformists took 59. Candidates representing religious minorities secured 14 seats, and independents nine. A second round of voting took place for the remaining 65 seats on 4 May, at which conservatives won 41 further seats, reformists 13, and independents 11. According to the Ministry of the Interior, the rate of voter participation was 64.2%. The outcome suggested that Ayatollah Khamenei was likely to receive more support from the new Majlis than was Ahmadinejad.

In December 2012 the Majlis adopted a bill proposing to introduce more stringent requirements for presidential candidates, in advance of the election scheduled to take place in June 2013. Ahmadinejad criticized the bill as handing too much power to the legislature concerning the election process. In January 2013 the Council of Guardians rejected the proposals concerning presidential candidates. The revised election reform bill notably transferred responsibility for the organization and monitoring of elections from the Ministry of the Interior to a central election board, to include, *inter alia*, representatives of the executive, legislature and judiciary.

As part of government changes in December 2012, Ahmadinejad appointed Esfandiar Rahim-Mashai as head of the Secretariat of the Non-Aligned Movement. The appointment increased speculation that the President was seeking to assist his close ally in a bid for the presidency in 2013. Ahmadinejad was also reported to have dismissed the Minister of Health and Medical Education, Marzieh Vahid Dastjerdi (who had remained the only woman in the Council of Ministers), over disagreement about government policy.

In February 2013 the Majlis voted to impeach the Minister of Labour and Social Affairs, Abdolreza Sheikholeslami, in connection with his role in appointing former prosecutor-general Saeed Mortazavi as head of the country's social security fund. Mortazavi, who was regarded as a supporter of the President, had in 2010 been identified by a parliamentary investigation as being principally responsible for the deaths of three students at the Kahrizak detention centre in Tehran after the Green Movement protests in 2009. Ahmadinejad subsequently appointed Sheikholeslami as Vice-President for Social Affairs. Meanwhile, Mortazavi was arrested and tried in February 2013, on charges of participation in the murder of anti-Government protesters. The court's ruling, issued in July, indicated that Mortazavi and two other defendants had been permanently dismissed from positions within the judiciary, and had been barred from holding any government office for five years. Mortazavi was acquitted of participation in murder, but was fined for false reporting.

Recent developments: the 2013 presidential election

It was announced in May 2013 that the Council of Guardians had approved eight candidates (of 686 who had registered) for the following month's presidential election: Saeed Jalili, the Secretary of the SNSC and Iran's principal negotiator on the nuclear issue; Hassan Rouhani, head of the SNSC in 1989–2005 and also, in this capacity, chief nuclear negotiator; former Minister of Foreign Affairs Ali Akbar Velayati; Muhammad Baqir Qalibaf, the mayor of Tehran; former Revolutionary Guards commander Mohsen Rezai; former Majlis Speaker Gholam-Ali Haddad-Adel; Muhammad Reza Aref, who had served as First Vice-President under President Khatami; and Muhammad Gharazi, who had held ministerial office under Presidents Khamenei and Rafsanjani. Notable among the disallowed candidates were both former President Rafsanjani and Ahmadinejad's ally Rahim-Mashai. (The Council had also previously announced that, under the terms of the Constitution, women were ineligible to stand as candidates—30 women having registered.) With Rafsanjani disallowed, and with both Mousavi and Karrubi remaining in detention, initially it was widely assumed that the election would be dominated by conservative or principlist candidates loyal to Ayatollah Khamenei. As the election approached, however, moderate and reformist support coalesced around Rouhani, who urged greater engagement with the West, and undertook to ease economic hardship as a result of international sanctions and mismanagement under the Ahmadinejad regime, release political prisoners and institute media reforms. Muhammad Reza Aref, hitherto regarded as the most reformist of the approved candidates, withdrew from the contest shortly before the poll—apparently at the request of former President Khatami, who, together with Rafsanjani, urged support for Rouhani. (The conservative Haddad-Adel had also meanwhile withdrawn.)

Voting in the presidential election (held concurrently with municipal elections) proceeded on 14 June 2013, with an official turnout of 72.7%. According to the results published by the Ministry of the Interior, Rouhani was elected outright with 50.7% of the total votes cast. Muhammad Baqir Qalibaf was placed second, with 16.6%, and Saeed Jalili third, with 11.4%. Conservatives performed strongly in the municipal elections, reportedly securing control of 70% of some 1,230 local councils nationwide; reformists took 20%, and about 9% came under moderate control.

Rouhani was sworn in as President on 4 August 2013, having been formally endorsed by Ayatollah Khamenei the previous day. In his inaugural address before the Majlis, Rouhani emphasized that voters had chosen moderation, and pledged, *inter alia*, to promote women's rights and to reduce state interference in the lives of the Iranian people. In international affairs, he urged engagement through dialogue rather than sanctions. Notably, representatives of the international community were invited to attend the inauguration for the first time since the Islamic Revolution.

On the day of his inauguration, Rouhani presented his first list of ministerial nominations for parliamentary approval. All but three of his 18 nominees were endorsed by the Majlis in mid-August 2013. (The rejected candidates were deemed to have been too close to the Green Movement protests in 2009; the Majlis approved the final three nominees in October and November 2013.) Most prominent among the nine Vice-Presidents appointed by Rouhani was Ali Akbar Salehi, who became Vice-President and Head of the Atomic Energy Organization. Expectations that the new President was likely to accord greater authority in international nuclear talks to the new Minister of Foreign Affairs, Muhammad Javad Zarif, who had been Iran's permanent representative at the UN in 2002–07, were confirmed in September 2013, when Rouhani announced that the Ministry of Foreign Affairs—rather than the SNSC, regarded as close to Ayatollah Khamenei—would lead future nuclear negotiations on behalf of Iran.

In September 2013, meanwhile, prior to the new President's highly anticipated visit to address the UN General Assembly in New York, USA, it was officially announced that 80 prisoners had been pardoned. These were understood to include a group of 11 political prisoners, among them Mohsen Aminzadeh and a prominent human rights lawyer, Nasrin Sotoudeh, whose release had been reported the previous week. Meanwhile, there were indications that the terms of house arrest of Mahdi Karrubi, Mir Hossein Mousavi and Zahra Rahnavard had been eased.

Cross-border tensions with Pakistan were raised from 2013. In October at least 14 Iranian border guards were killed in an attack near the border with Pakistan, which was attributed to the Sunni Islamist group, Jaish al-Adl (Army of Justice), based in Sistan and Baluchestan province. Some 16 prisoners held on terrorism charges were hanged by the Iranian authorities in the following week in Zahedan, the capital of the province. In November Jaish al-Adl militants shot dead a local prosecutor and his driver, and in December three Revolutionary Guards were killed in a bomb attack. Jaish al-Adl militants took five Iranian border guards hostage in February 2014, holding them captive in Pakistan, and demanded that the Iranian authorities release 300 Sunni prisoners held by Iran and Syria; the militant group announced that it had executed one of the hostages in March, but the other four were released in April. Further violence on the Iranian-Pakistani border took place throughout 2014, including a co-ordinated truck bomb attack and assault by 70 Sunni militants on an Iranian military base in September. In early October three Iranian police officers were killed near Saravan by suspected Jaish al-Adl militants, who then crossed the border and killed a Pakistani border guard. The Iranian Government condemned the Pakistani authorities for their inability to control Islamist militants. Tensions between the two governments escalated further on 18 October when some 30 Iranian border guards crossed into Pakistan in pursuit of Jaish al-Adl militants; in the ensuing exchange of gunfire a Pakistani border guard was killed. Iranian and Pakistani armed forces were also reported to have exchanged mortar fire the following week. The Iranian Deputy Minister of Foreign Affairs subsequently visited his counterpart in Pakistan where both parties agreed to increase co-operation on security matters.

Despite some early signs of cautious change under Rouhani—including suggestions by the Minister of Culture and Islamic Guidance, Ali Jannati, that internet social networks should be made more freely accessible to the Iranian public—uncertainty remained as to the likely tolerance within Iran's conservative institutions of such measures. In January 2014, notably, the Prosecutor-General, Gholam-Hossein Mohseni Ejeie, criticized comments made by Jannati concerning the need to ease restrictions on areas such as the media and arts, stating that it was not within the minister's authority to define the responsibilities of the judiciary. Meanwhile, the judiciary continued to curtail the activities of reformist news media outlets. By February four reformist or pro-Rouhani newspapers had been banned for alleged violations of Islamic principles, and ultra-conservative members of the Majlis were reportedly proposing legislation to ban permanently journalists who had worked for reformist publications which had been closed down. In August the Minister of Science, Research and Technology, Reza Faraji-Dana, was impeached by the Majlis for 'politicizing the academic environment'. The impeachment proceedings had reportedly been prompted by allegations that Faraj-Dana had allowed students who had participated in the election protests of 2009–10 to resume their education in public universities, and had appointed senior university officials from among those who had participated in the protests. He was replaced by Muhammad Farhadi. In November 2014 the Chairman of the Assembly of Experts, Mahdavi Kani, died. At the election for his replacement in early March 2015, Ayatollah Muhammad Yazdi defeated former President Rafsanjani by 47 votes to 24.

The Nuclear Issue

Following President Khatami's announcement in February 2003 regarding the discovery and successful extraction of uranium, the USA urged the International Atomic Energy Agency (IAEA) to declare Iran to be in violation of the nuclear non-proliferation treaty (NPT), and appealed for Russia to end its collaboration with Iran on construction of the Bushehr nuclear power plant, in south-western Iran. In June the Director-General of the IAEA,

Dr Mohammed el-Baradei, called on Iran to open its nuclear programme to a more rigorous system of inspections. Iran responded that it would comply with this request only if it were given access to the nuclear technology it required. Despite Khatami's assurances that Iran's nuclear programme was 'entirely peaceful', the IAEA (with US support) adopted a resolution in September giving Iran until the end of October to disclose full details of its programme. This followed the discovery of enriched uranium at a processing plant south of Tehran. In late October it was announced that Iran would accept a more rigorous system of inspections at its nuclear facilities.

However, the IAEA reported in February 2004 that it had found evidence of undeclared facilities that could be used for the enrichment of uranium. The Agency adopted a resolution condemning Iran for the secrecy of its nuclear activities in March, and a further resolution on 18 June criticizing Iran for failing to co-operate with the inspections process. In late June the Iranian leadership announced that, although it would adhere to its pledge to suspend actual uranium enrichment, it would recommence the testing and assembly of centrifuges. Moreover, Iran criticized France, Germany and the United Kingdom for not supplying it with the technology and trade they had promised in return for this pledge. In October 2004 Russia and Iran completed the construction of the Bushehr nuclear plant, although Russian officials also pressed the Islamic regime to cease uranium enrichment. (The plant was not formally opened until 2011.) Iran also tested a long-range satellite-launching rocket, the *Shahab-4*, asserting that it would only use its missiles in self-defence. In November Iran complied with IAEA demands to suspend temporarily its enrichment programme.

In August 2005 Iran resumed the conversion of uranium to gas (the stage before enrichment) at the Esfahan conversion facility, having previously rejected a set of compensatory proposals put forward by France, Germany and the United Kingdom in exchange for abandoning its enrichment programme. The IAEA subsequently adopted a resolution in mid-August expressing 'serious concern' at the resumption of nuclear activities at Esfahan, and urging Iran to reinstate suspension. Also in August President Ahmadinejad appointed Ali Larijani, believed to be a close ally of Ayatollah Khamenei, as Secretary of the SNSC and chief nuclear negotiator. A further IAEA resolution in late September found Iran guilty of 'non-compliance'. However, Iran announced in January 2006 that it had reopened its uranium enrichment research facility at Natanz, south of Tehran, after a two-year moratorium; it subsequently confirmed that small-scale uranium enrichment had recommenced. In March el-Baradei transmitted his latest IAEA report on Iran's nuclear programme to the UN Security Council, which, later that month, called on Iran to suspend all uranium enrichment activities within 30 days. In April Ahmadinejad announced that Iran had successfully enriched uranium for the first time, although he insisted that his country had no intention of developing nuclear weapons. Meanwhile, the US Administration revealed that it was allocating US $75m. to fund Iranian dissident groups.

In April 2006 el-Baradei delivered a report to the UN Security Council which concluded that Iran had failed to comply with the 30-day deadline imposed by the Council to halt its uranium enrichment activities. In response, the US ambassador to the UN, John Bolton, called on the Security Council to invoke Chapter VII of the UN Charter, which contained provision for the use of military action—a demand that was immediately rejected by the People's Republic of China and Russia. Meeting in Brussels, Belgium, in May, EU ministers responsible for foreign affairs responded by proposing trade and technical incentives for Iran to halt its nuclear programme. However, the offer was firmly rejected by the Iranian leadership. Further economic incentives were offered by the EU in June, following an agreement reached by the five permanent members of the UN Security Council together with Germany (the so-called P5+1 group), concerning new proposals to encourage Iran to renounce enrichment. These included an offer of nuclear technical assistance and the removal of certain US economic sanctions.

In July 2006 the UN Security Council approved a resolution (No. 1696), which expressed 'serious concern' regarding Iran's refusal to co-operate with the IAEA and warned that the country could face 'appropriate measures' unless it halted its uranium enrichment programme by 31 August. In late August 2006 Larijani described Iran's enrichment activities as an 'inalienable right'. The IAEA reported to the UN Security Council on 31 August that Iran had failed to meet its requirement to cease uranium enrichment and in December the Security Council adopted Resolution 1737, which imposed a series of limited sanctions on the Iranian regime—including a ban on the trade of nuclear-related technology and materials, and a freeze on the assets of leading individuals and companies involved in the nuclear programme. Iran was granted 60 days in which to cease all enrichment activities and thus avoid further sanctions. However, President Ahmadinejad rejected Resolution 1737, and the Majlis adopted legislation that urged an acceleration of Iran's nuclear energy programme. In January 2007 Iran announced that it was barring 38 IAEA inspectors from the country, in retaliation for the imposition of sanctions.

In his report to the IAEA in February 2007, el-Baradei affirmed that Iran had failed to meet the deadline to cease uranium enrichment and had actually expanded the enrichment programme. In March the UN Security Council adopted Resolution 1747, which again required Iran to suspend all enrichment-related activities and to grant IAEA inspectors full access to its nuclear sites. Resolution 1747 imposed, *inter alia*, an embargo on the sale of arms to and from Iran, and a ban on the transfer of funds to Iran by state and international financial institutions (excluding those intended for humanitarian or development aid). The UN granted Iran 60 days to comply with the measures. However, in April Ahmadinejad boasted that Iran had joined the 'nuclear club of nations'. Following an inspection of the Natanz nuclear facility, IAEA inspectors asserted that Iran had commenced the process of enriching uranium, but were uncertain as to whether all of the 1,300 centrifuges at Natanz were actually in operation. The day before the Security Council's deadline of 24 May, el-Baradei declared that he believed Iran to possess the capability to build a nuclear weapon in three to eight years, but asserted that he did not have evidence that Iran was seeking to produce such weapons of mass destruction.

Following a meeting between Iranian and IAEA officials in Vienna, Austria, in July 2007, Iran agreed to provide information about previous nuclear experiments, to allow inspectors to visit a plutonium-producing reactor being built at Arak and to decelerate its uranium enrichment programme at Natanz. In August el-Baradei agreed a 'work plan' with Iranian officials, whereby Iran was given a three-month deadline by which to end any technical ambiguities concerning its nuclear programme. However, the US Administration continued to demand an immediate cessation of uranium enrichment. In October Saeed Jalili, Iran's Deputy Foreign Minister for European and American Affairs, replaced Larijani as Secretary of the SNSC and principal negotiator on the nuclear issue. Towards the end of October the USA imposed further unilateral sanctions against Iran, which principally targeted Iranian state-owned banks and agencies deemed to be involved in a clandestine nuclear programme or to sponsor terrorism abroad, and in particular named affiliates of the Revolutionary Guards and its élite Quds Force.

In November 2007 el-Baradei informed the IAEA that the Iranian authorities were continuing to restrict inspectors' access to nuclear plants and confirmed that Iran had an estimated 3,000 centrifuges in operation. The US Administration insisted in December that a joint report published by the US intelligence agencies, in which they disclosed their findings that Iran had in fact suspended its nuclear weapons development programme in 2003, would not lead the USA to re-evaluate its policy towards the Islamic Republic. Ahmadinejad reiterated his assertion that Iran had never sought to develop a clandestine nuclear weapons programme.

In March 2008 the UN Security Council adopted Resolution 1803, which tightened the sanctions already imposed on Iran with regard to the financial assets and ability to travel of officials and institutions allegedly involved in nuclear activities. It also prohibited the trade in so-called 'dual-use' goods or technologies which could be employed for civilian or military purposes. In May the latest IAEA report issued by el-Baradei affirmed that Iranian officials had again failed to co-operate with the Agency in answering vital questions about its nuclear programme, and indeed that 500 centrifuges had been added at Natanz.

The EU led a delegation from the P5+1 group to Tehran in June 2008 to offer Iran a new package of incentives and proposed that the UN Security Council would delay any further imposition of sanctions against the Iranian regime in return for Iran's agreement to suspend the installation of extra centrifuges at its nuclear facilities, while continuing current levels of uranium enrichment for a six-week period only. Under the proposals, which sought the cessation of Iran's expansion of its enrichment programme as a precondition for the start of formal negotiations,

the international community would assist with the construction of light-water reactors for electricity generation. Further talks were held by the EU and Iran in Geneva in July, notably in the presence of the USA's Undersecretary of State for Political Affairs, William Burns; these represented the most senior diplomatic contacts between the USA and Iran since 1979. However, by early August 2008 Iran had not sufficiently clarified its stance towards the incentives offered by the international delegation. After the EU had imposed new financial and trade sanctions against Iran, in mid-August further US sanctions were introduced targeting companies with links to the nuclear industry.

In September 2008 the UN Security Council adopted Resolution 1835, requiring Iran to comply with its obligations concerning its nuclear programme as outlined in earlier UN resolutions. In his report to the IAEA Board in November, el-Baradei stated that Iran's stockpiles of enriched uranium were growing at a rapid rate, and therefore that by early 2009 the country might achieve nuclear 'breakout capacity'—meaning that in theory it had the capability to produce a sufficient level of enriched uranium to build a nuclear weapon.

President Ahmadinejad inaugurated Iran's first nuclear fuel manufacturing plant at Esfahan in April 2009. Ahmadinejad also announced that tests had commenced on new centrifuges with enhanced enrichment capacity. In June an IAEA quarterly report on Iran revealed that the number of installed centrifuges had increased to 7,221, with almost 5,000 in operation at that time. A subsequent report, issued in August, revealed that IAEA inspectors had been granted access to the Arak nuclear reactor site, which was under construction, for the first time in more than a year, and that improved monitoring arrangements had been introduced at the Natanz facility. None the less, the report noted Iran's continuing refusal to suspend its enrichment activity and highlighted its failure to co-operate with the Agency in connection with a possible military dimension to its nuclear programme.

In September 2009 it emerged that a second uranium enrichment facility, the Fordo plant, was close to completion at a site near Qom. The Iranian authorities, who had hitherto concealed the plant, informed the IAEA of its existence just days before the leaders of the USA, the United Kingdom and France planned to disclose details of the facility at a meeting of the Group of 20 leading industrialized and developing nations (G20) in Pittsburgh, USA. The site had reportedly been monitored by Western intelligence agencies for two years. Ahmadinejad insisted that, as the facility was more than six months from completion, Iran was not obliged to report its existence to the IAEA. Later that month the Revolutionary Guards test-fired a number of *Shahab-3* and *Sajjil-2* rockets, which have a range of up to 1,300 miles and could thus reach targets in Israel as well as US military bases in the Gulf region.

Direct negotiations involving Jalili and the international negotiating group took place in Geneva at the beginning of October 2009. The international negotiators stipulated that Iran should suspend its enrichment programme immediately in order to forestall the introduction of further economic sanctions. Iran's negotiators confirmed that they would facilitate an IAEA inspection of the Fordo enrichment plant and agreed to enter into substantive negotiations on the nuclear issue. However, Jalili insisted that these should be linked to a broad package of agreements on regional and international security and global nuclear disarmament. In the first direct senior-level engagement between US and Iranian officials since the Islamic Revolution, Jalili held bilateral talks with Burns during the summit. On 3 October the *New York Times* newspaper published details of a confidential IAEA dossier which alleged that Iran was in possession of sufficient knowledge to create an effective nuclear missile. However, the following day el-Baradei emphasized that there was still no concrete evidence of an Iranian military nuclear programme. El-Baradei hosted further talks in Vienna on 20–21 October, during which a draft agreement was finalized on the proposal for transferring low-enriched uranium from Iran to Russia and France for conversion into higher-grade fuel. An Iranian counter-proposal received by the IAEA on 29 October involved Iran retaining most of its stock of low-enriched uranium and importing higher-grade fuel from abroad. Meanwhile, in November the IAEA confirmed that around 3,000 centrifuges had been installed at the Fordo nuclear facility.

In November 2009 the IAEA adopted a resolution calling on Iran to suspend construction of the Fordo facility and to confirm whether any other nuclear facilities were under development. In a defiant response, President Ahmadinejad announced plans for a major escalation of Iran's nuclear programme: some 10 new uranium enrichment plants were reportedly scheduled for construction. In early February 2010, in response to the stalled uranium transfer negotiations, Salehi confirmed that Iran had commenced production of 20%-enriched uranium. Previously, Iran had processed only 3.5%-enriched uranium, a grade sufficient for the production of nuclear power, while the higher-grade fuel was required for the production of isotopes for use in medical research and diagnosis. (Uranium enriched to 90% would be required for the production of atomic weapons.) In mid-February the new Director-General of the IAEA, Yukiya Amano noted that the regime was still refusing to co-operate regarding IAEA inspections, and was continuing to expand its uranium enrichment activities. In May Amano additionally stated that, with further enrichment, Iran now had sufficient nuclear fuel ultimately to produce two atomic weapons.

The acceleration of Iran's nuclear activities resulted in further international pressure on the Government either to accept the terms of the original IAEA uranium transfer proposal or to cease enrichment entirely. On 17 May 2010 the so-called Tehran Declaration, signed by Iran, Turkey and Brazil, agreed a new uranium transfer proposal whereby Iran would send 1,200 kg of its stockpile of low-enriched uranium to Turkey, in exchange for 120 kg of nuclear reactor fuel. Yet the deal, which would require further agreement to be reached with the Western negotiating governments, failed to prevent a fourth round of sanctions against Iran from being adopted by the UN Security Council in June (although Turkey and Brazil opposed the motion). Resolution 1929 involved more stringent military and economic penalties against Iran, focusing on the possible transport by Iranian-owned ships of proscribed materials and on financial institutions suspected of having links with nuclear activities, as well as freezing the assets of, and imposing travel bans on, companies and individuals connected with the Revolutionary Guards and Iran's wider defence establishment. China and Russia had apparently been persuaded to support a new round of sanctions following reassurances that their bilateral trade relations with Iran, in particular concerning the oil and gas sector, would not be jeopardized.

President Obama promulgated further unilateral US sanctions against Iran at the beginning of July 2010. The latest US measures specifically targeted the Post Bank of Iran (making it the 16th Iranian bank to be blacklisted by the US Administration), shipping and financial companies, and those providing the country with much needed fuel imports. The EU also announced new economic sanctions against Iran later that month. On the same day Iran informed the IAEA that it was prepared to resume discussions regarding the proposed transfer of uranium without preconditions. In August the US Administration extended its sanctions to include several institutions suspected of assisting radical organizations in the region such as the Islamic Resistance Movement (Hamas) in the Palestinian territories and Hezbollah in Lebanon.

In November 2010 the Iranian authorities declared that the loading of fuel into the nuclear reactor at the Bushehr power plant was complete, the reactor having finally been launched in August. Further talks between negotiators from the P5+1 group of countries and the Iranian team led by Jalili were held in Geneva in December and in Istanbul, Turkey, in January 2011; however, no breakthrough was achieved. Earlier that month Salehi had announced that Iran now possessed the capability to manufacture fuel plates and rods to be used in its nuclear reactors. In Amano's sixth report to the IAEA board in May, the Director-General suggested that an Iranian nuclear weapons programme might be under development. In July the Iranian authorities stated that the installation of a new range of centrifuges would accelerate the process by which uranium could be enriched. In early September Amano's seventh report to the IAEA, which again included suggestions of a possible military dimension to Iran's nuclear programme, prompted Abbasi Davani, Vice-President and Head of the Atomic Energy Organization of Iran, to promise full access to Iran's nuclear sites by IAEA inspectors if the sanctions in place against Tehran were lifted. On 12 September the Bushehr plant was officially opened.

The IAEA issued a report in early November 2011 which used detailed evidence to indicate that the Islamic regime had, as recently as 2010, been involved in the 'development of a nuclear explosive device' and found that some of these actions 'may still be ongoing'. This was the first time that the Agency had indicated directly that Iran was engaged in such efforts. A resolution passed by the IAEA Board in mid-November sought to increase the pressure on Iran by urging it to comply with the terms of previous UN Security Council resolutions. Iranian officials swiftly repeated assertions that the programme was solely for civilian purposes. However, in that month both the USA and the United Kingdom announced a new range of sanctions affecting Iranian banks and the energy sector. (For further details on sanctions imposed in late 2011 and 2012, see *Foreign Affairs*.)

IAEA officials confirmed in early January 2012 that scientists at the Fordo enrichment plant had begun to enrich uranium to 20% and thus were getting closer to weapons-grade capacity. The US Administration accused Iran of 'escalating' its violation of UN Security Council resolutions. In late January President Ahmadinejad surprised some Western observers by offering to resume discussions on its nuclear programme. It was reported in mid-February that the Turkish Government had again offered to host negotiations between Iranian and P5+1 officials. Iran's ambassador to the UN, Muhammad Khazaii, declared in February that Iran would enter new talks without preconditions, but reiterated that his country would not cede any of its 'inalienable rights'. Later that month Ahmadinejad was present at a ceremony held at the Tehran research reactor (which manufactures isotopes for medical usage), where for the first time the reactor was loaded with domestically produced nuclear fuel rods. During early 2012 Iran again prevented IAEA inspectors from carrying out their work without hindrance.

Discussions finally resumed between the P5+1 group and an Iranian delegation in Istanbul in April 2012. Further high-level talks were held in Baghdad, Iraq, in May and in Moscow, Russia, in June. However, Iranian officials rejected the Western nations' offer to ease certain sanctions and provide fuel rods for the research reactor in Tehran in exchange for transporting its 20%-enriched uranium to a foreign country, agreeing to end such enrichment and shutting down the Fordo facility. Moreover, in his 10th report to the IAEA issued in June, Amano stated that in May IAEA inspectors at the Fordo plant had found evidence of uranium enrichment up to the higher level of 27%.

In September 2012 the IAEA again reported Iran's non-compliance with its nuclear inspections team, expressing 'serious concern' over the country's continued enrichment of uranium. Moreover, a report published by the US-based Institute for Science and International Security in October, using evidence taken from IAEA inspections of Iran's nuclear facilities, found that the Iranian authorities—should this be their intention—were probably between two to four months away from producing a sufficient quantity of highly enriched uranium to manufacture a nuclear bomb and a further eight to 10 months away from the construction of such a device. In November the IAEA's quarterly report on Iran's nuclear programme alleged that the number of centrifuges in operation at the Fordo facility could be rapidly doubled by the Iranian authorities from some 700 to around 1,400 (of a total 2,784 centrifuges). Following his re-election to the US presidency in November, Obama had pledged that his Administration would seek to revive the stalled negotiations between Iran and the international negotiators. There was also speculation in the US media that Iranian and US officials might be prepared to begin direct talks on the nuclear issue, although in early February 2013 Ayatollah Khamenei reportedly rejected the offer of such talks. However, negotiations between Iran and the P5+1 group took place in Almatı, Kazakhstan, in late February. It was reported that the P5+1 group had presented an offer to remove some economic sanctions currently imposed on Iran in return for the suspension of uranium enrichment activity at the Fordo plant, although no agreement was reached. Meanwhile, in January IAEA officials resumed their discussions with their Iranian counterparts, amid growing frustration over the Iranian authorities' refusal to allow them access to Parchin, a military complex close to Tehran, where it was alleged that research into nuclear weapons had taken place. Following a round of expert-level talks in Istanbul in March the EU announced that it had issued proposals to Iran designed to end the stand-off. Iran submitted its own proposals at a meeting in Almatı in April.

In June 2013, following initial denials by the Iranian authorities that a series of earthquakes in April and May had caused any damage, it was announced that cracks had appeared in one section of the Bushehr power plant. In August President Rouhani appointed Ali Akbar Salehi as head of the Atomic Energy Organization (see *Recent developments*). At the end of the month the UN announced that Iran had increased its nuclear capacity, having completed the installation of a further 1,000 advanced uranium enrichment centrifuges. In September Rouhani announced that nuclear negotiations would be led by the Ministry of Foreign Affairs, in place of the SNSC, which was under the control of Khamenei, thus allowing Rouhani greater influence over Iran's stance in the talks. Iran presented a new set of proposals specifying an 'endgame' to the dispute at a round of talks with the P5+1 group in Geneva in November. Although the position of neither side was made public, it was reported that the P5+1 negotiators' demand for the suspension of construction at Arak was the most contentious. Despite the talks being extended, no deal was reached. On 11 November, however, Iran and the IAEA reached an agreement on future co-operation that would allow the IAEA to send inspectors to the Arak site and the Gachin uranium mine. On 24 November Iran and the P5+1 group announced an interim agreement, officially titled the Joint Plan of Action (JPA), whereby Iran pledged to halt all uranium enrichment above 5% and to neutralize its existing stock of nearly 20%-enriched uranium to below 5% by 24 July 2014. In addition, Iran pledged not to install new centrifuges for enrichment or to commission the Arak reactor, while also permitting the strict monitoring of its programme. For its part, the P5+1 agreed to relieve some US $7,200m. of economic sanctions, primarily pertaining to the trading of gold and precious metals, and the petrochemical and automobile sectors. It was envisaged that implementation of the interim agreement would begin in January 2014 and that a final agreement would be concluded by July. An IAEA monitoring team duly arrived in Tehran in January. Iran subsequently began disabling centrifuges at two of its nuclear facilities and later that month disagreements over the order in which sanctions should be revoked and uranium enrichment slowed down were resolved following talks in Geneva.

Preliminary negotiations on a final settlement began in Vienna in mid-February 2014, in advance of a third meeting between the senior negotiators in Vienna in late March, after which the IAEA reported that Iran intended to start conversion of enriched uranium stockpiles to below 5% in April. Prior to the March discussions, the High Representative of the EU for Foreign Affairs, Catherine Ashton, visited Iran for the first time since 2008 and met with civil rights organizations without government approval; Zarif subsequently cancelled a planned meeting with Ashton. The IAEA reported in April that Iran had neutralized one-half of its 20%-enriched uranium stockpile, in accordance with the JPA. However, US Secretary of State, John Kerry, stated that Iran had the ability to produce enough weapons-grade uranium for a nuclear bomb within two months, although he qualified his statement by adding that Iran did not necessarily have a warhead or suitable delivery system. The fourth round of negotiations took place in Vienna in mid-May, at which the P5+1 negotiators insisted that Iran scale back its enrichment programme and extend the 'breakout' time required for building a nuclear bomb to one year; Iran, for its part, insisted that it needed at least 19,000 centrifuges to meet its civilian energy needs. The Iranian and US delegations also held a bilateral meeting in Vienna, although they made little progress in drafting a final agreement, scheduling instead a fifth round of negotiations in June. Meanwhile, in May the IAEA announced a new set of actions to be completed by Iran before 25 August, including providing information regarding its previous alleged military experiments. The IAEA also published a report in that month stating that Iran had reduced its stockpile of 20%-enriched uranium by around four-fifths, although the conversion of low-enriched uranium (up to 5%) to oxide powder, to which Iran had agreed under the Geneva interim agreement, had not commenced. At the fifth round of negotiations in June in Vienna Iran and the P5+1 remained at an impasse, particularly over demands for Iran to reduce its number of centrifuges. The IAEA board met in that month, and Amano confirmed that Iran had been complying with the terms of the JPA and that the IAEA's investigation into the pending concerns over the country's nuclear programme was making progress.

A sixth and final round of negotiations began in July 2014 in Vienna, at which Iran tentatively offered to freeze its current capacity for seven years, on condition that it would then be free to operate without special restrictions, although the P5+1 insisted on reducing Iran's enrichment capacity, freezing it in place for 10 years and imposing strict conditions on use thereafter; therefore no agreement was reached. Iran and the USA again held bilateral discussions, at which Zarif reported that a heavy-water reactor nearing completion near Arak had been sabotaged by an unnamed 'foreign power'. None the less, the Iranian delegation reported that progress was made and announced that it had

convinced the P5+1 to extend the deadline for the JPA to 24 November; moreover, the USA offered to unfreeze US $2,800m. in Iranian funds in exchange for a commitment from Iran to convert some of its 20%-enriched uranium into fuel for a research reactor. The parties revealed additional actions that Iran would take, namely the conversion of 25 kg of 20%-enriched uranium powder into fuel plates and the dilution of approximately three tons of enriched uranium to less than 2%. In August Iran announced that negotiations with the P5+1 would continue alongside the UN General Assembly session scheduled for early September. Also in that month Iran reported that it had intercepted an Israeli unmanned aerial vehicle (or drone) near the uranium enrichment site in Natanz. The IAEA confirmed that since January Iran had not enriched uranium above 5% and had neutralized one-half of its higher-enriched uranium, and announced that a uranium conversion plant required to fulfil obligations under the JPA had been inaugurated on 23 August. In that month Rouhani criticized hardline members of parliament for attempting to derail diplomatic efforts, including the detention of the Tehran correspondent of the *Washington Post* in late July. Khamenei made a speech in mid-August reiterating his pessimism about the prospects of a nuclear agreement. At the end of that month the USA extended sanctions to more than 30 entities, including Iranian-owned banks, airlines and shipping and energy companies, citing the entities' connections to the funding of terrorism and Iran's covert nuclear programme. In September the IAEA reported that Iran had failed to give a satisfactory explanation of its research at Parchin into detonators that could be used to trigger a nuclear weapon, and had failed to provide sufficient information on 'possible military dimensions' of past nuclear research. On a more positive note, the JPA stipulated that a short-term suspension of parts of Iran's nuclear programme would be effected in exchange for an easing of economic sanctions on the country. As Iran had fulfilled this requirement, during the first six-month implementation phase Iran reportedly received 'sanctions relief' equivalent in value to approximately $550m., in addition to a further $900m. that was released following the dilution of its 20%-enriched uranium stockpile.

In early September 2014 the UN Security Council received the quarterly report from the IAEA on the implementation of the NPT Safeguards Agreement and relevant provisions of Council resolutions on Iran. According to the report, Iran had implemented only three of five practical measures agreed with the IAEA in May under the Framework of Co-operation initially agreed in November 2013. The two outstanding measures related to information sharing on its research into high-explosive detonators, and studies that could be relevant in calculating the explosive yield of a nuclear weapon. The IAEA also reported that Iran had still to propose new practical measures. However, on 23 September UN Security Council members received a report on the status of Iran's implementation of the JPA and concluded that Iran had continued to comply with the measures agreed under the plan. Two workers were killed at the Parchin military complex in early October; the complex was suspected of housing military nuclear research, raising suspicion of a covert operation to sabotage the facility. An eighth round of talks took place in Vienna in mid-October, at which the Russian representative of the P5+1 stated that the issues of Iran's enrichment programme, the lifting of economic sanctions and the future of the reactor in Arak were not settled and that the subject of inspections and the duration of an eventual agreement had not yet been agreed. Tensions increased later that month when Iran refused to issue an entry visa to a member of the IAEA inspection team. Nevertheless, a ninth round of talks took place over two days in Muscat, Oman, in November. It was reported that Iran and Russia had signed an agreement for Russia to build two nuclear reactors at the nuclear plant in Bushehr, under the auspices of the IAEA, with the option to construct a further six. Russia promised to supply uranium fuel for the reactors and take possession of it for reprocessing. A 10th and final round of negotiations took place in Vienna in mid-November, which were due to end by the revised deadline of 24 November. At an IAEA meeting on 20 November in Vienna, Amano reported that Iran had not provided any explanations that enabled the IAEA to clarify outstanding practical measures. The deadline for fulfilment of the JPA on 24 November passed without agreement on enrichment capacity, and both parties agreed to extend the deadline to 1 July 2015, although both expressed their desire that a broad political agreement would be in place by 1 March; it was also announced that expert-level discussions would resume in December and that Iran would henceforth receive around US $700m. in previously frozen assets each month. In early December 2014 a confidential UN report accused Iran of making illicit purchases of equipment for the heavy-water reactor at Arak, although the USA maintained that the purchases were not in contravention of the JPA.

An eleventh round of negotiations (the first since the extension agreed in November 2014) took place in mid-December in Geneva. The Russian representative, Deputy Minister of Foreign Affairs, Sergei Ryabkov, stated that the heavy-water reactor at Arak and sanctions imposed on Iran were the key issues to be resolved before a final agreement could be made. A twelfth round of talks took place in mid-January 2015, following four days of bilateral discussions between Iran and the USA, although no major breakthrough was reported. Zarif noted that allowing Russia greater influence in discussions could expedite the process, while acknowledging that the USA was willing to reach a comprehensive agreement. A thirteenth round of talks was convened in Lausanne, Switzerland, in mid-March in an attempt to reach a broad agreement by the end of that month. Those discussions were subsequently extended, and on 2 April a 'framework agreement' was signed by the negotiating parties. Under the terms of the agreement, Iran was to reduce its stockpile of enriched uranium from 10 metric tons to 300 kg, limit any further enrichment to 3.67%, and reduce the total number of centrifuges from 19,000 to 5,060 for a period of 10 years. Enrichment activity at Fordo was to be suspended for 15 years. Iran also agreed to allow inspections by the IAEA of its entire nuclear 'supply chain' for a period of at least 20 years, while also pledging to remove or destroy the reactor in Arak and to sell any excess heavy water produced at that plant on international markets for a period of 15 years. For their part, the P5+1 negotiators agreed to the gradual removal of sanctions against the Iranian economy. First, the EU would remove its sanctions, while measures imposed by the USA and the UN would be eased 'simultaneously' with verification of Iran's compliance with the agreed measures. Talks were, meanwhile, to continue with the aim of securing a final agreement by 30 June. A fourteenth round of talks duly began in Vienna on 22 April.

Foreign Affairs

Relations with the USA

Relations with the USA since the end of the Iran–Iraq War have continued to be characterized by mutual suspicion. In April 1995 US efforts to isolate Iran internationally culminated in the announcement that all US companies and their overseas subsidiaries would be banned from investing in, or trading with, Iran (with the subsequent exception of US oil companies in the Caucasus and Central Asia involved in marketing petroleum from the countries of the former USSR). In mid-1996 the US Congress approved legislation (termed the Iran-Libya Sanctions Act—ILSA) to penalize companies operating in US markets that were investing US $40m. (subsequently amended to $20m.) or more in energy projects in prescribed countries deemed to be sponsoring terrorism. However, these 'secondary' economic sanctions received little international support.

A notable development following Khatami's election to the Iranian presidency in mid-1997 was the designation by the USA, in October, of the opposition Mujahidin-e-Khalq as one of 30 proscribed terrorist organizations. (The Mujahidin-e-Khalq's parent organization, the National Council of Resistance of Iran, also based in France, was proscribed by the USA in October 1999.) In December 1997 Khatami expressed his desire to engage in a 'thoughtful dialogue' with the USA. However, the announcement, in July 1998, that Iran had successfully test-fired a new ballistic missile capable of striking targets at a distance of 1,300 km (thus potentially Israel or US forces in the Gulf), caused renewed tensions. US concerns regarding what it perceived as Iran's efforts to acquire weapons of mass destruction remained a principal cause of mutual suspicion.

In March 2000 US Secretary of State Madeleine Albright announced an end to restrictions on imports from Iran of several non-hydrocarbons items. This substantive step towards the normalization of relations was in recognition of what the US Administration under President Bill Clinton regarded as trends towards democracy under President Khatami. Albright furthermore offered what amounted to an apology for the role played by the USA in the coup of 1953, as well as for US support for Iraq in the Iran–Iraq War. Relations between Iran and the USA deteriorated in June 2001 after 14 men were indicted *in absentia* by the US Government, having been charged in connection with the bomb attack at al-Khobar, Saudi Arabia in 1996 (see *Regional*

relations). US officials reiterated allegations that members of the Iranian Government were behind the bombing. In August 2001 the new Administration of President George W. Bush, inaugurated in January, confirmed that ILSA was to be extended for a further five years. However, in March 2005 President Bush announced a series of economic incentives, including the withdrawal of its veto on Iran's membership of the World Trade Organization (WTO), provided that Iran agreed permanently to suspend its nuclear energy programme. However, accession negotiations had not begun by early 2015.

President Khatami offered his condolences to the USA following the suicide attacks in New York and Washington, DC, on 11 September 2001. Although Ayatollah Khamenei also condemned the terrorist attacks, he and Iran's 'conservative' press warned against any large-scale US military offensive targeting the Taliban regime and militants of the radical Islamist al-Qa'ida network—widely believed to have perpetrated the attacks—in Afghanistan. In 2002 the Iranian administration denied accusations by the USA that it was permitting fleeing al-Qa'ida and Taliban fighters to cross the Afghan border into Iran. Relations deteriorated abruptly in January, when, in his annual State of the Union address, the US President referred to Iran as forming (together with Iraq and the Democratic People's Republic of Korea—North Korea) an 'axis of evil', explicitly accusing Iran of aggressively pursuing the development of weapons of mass destruction and of 'exporting terror'. Khatami accused his US counterpart of 'warmongering', and in May urged reformist deputies in the Majlis not to attempt to hold discussions with US officials. Meanwhile, the US Department of State again designated Iran as the world's 'most active' sponsor of terrorism (as the country was also termed during 2003–12). President Khatami, for his part, openly condemned US plans to use military force to bring about 'regime change' in Iraq, warning that such action posed a serious risk to regional stability.

Iran had been host to many Iraqi groups-in-exile, most notably the Shi'a-dominated Supreme Council for the Islamic Revolution in Iraq (renamed the Islamic Supreme Council of Iraq in 2007) and its military wing, the Badr Brigade. Therefore, following the conflict in Iraq which began in March 2003 and the removal from power of President Saddam Hussain by the US-led coalition in April, the US Administration warned Iran not to interfere in Iraqi affairs, fearing that the Iranian leadership sought a political settlement that would favour the Shi'a Muslim majority and lead to the formation of a Shi'ite bloc in the Middle East antipathetic to US interests. However, in May it became necessary for the USA and Iran to instigate UN-sponsored talks in Geneva to discuss the return of Iraqi exiles and refugees in Iran, as well as the presence in Iraq of the Mujahidin-e-Khalq and its military wing, the National Liberation Army (NLA—see *Regional relations*). The talks collapsed after Ayatollah Khamenei described them as 'tantamount to surrender', and when US officials accused Iran of interfering in Iraqi internal affairs and of sheltering al-Qa'ida militants suspected of masterminding suicide bombings at expatriate compounds in Saudi Arabia, earlier that month.

After a devastating earthquake in the city of Bam in December 2003, the US Administration agreed to ease financial sanctions and restrictions on the export of technical apparatus to Iran in order to facilitate the reconstruction process. In April 2004 Iranian officials rejected suggestions that the USA had asked Iran for assistance in its struggle to defeat the insurgency in Iraq or that any Iranian element was supporting the radical Shi'a movement led by Hojatoleslam Muqtada al-Sadr. An Iranian diplomatic mission, supposedly dispatched upon the request of the United Kingdom to mediate between US troops and al-Sadr's forces around the Iraqi city of Najaf, was withdrawn following the assassination of the first secretary of the Iranian embassy in Baghdad. In July Iran criticized the USA's decision to declare a group of 3,800 members of the Mujahidin-e-Khalq interned in Iraq to be protected persons under the Geneva Convention. The introduction to the US Senate in August of the Iran Freedom and Support Act of 2004, which was designed to promote 'regime change' in Iran and to provide US $10m. in support of pro-democracy opposition groups, was seen as further evidence of the desire of President Bush's Administration to use military force against Iran. Meanwhile, the Iranian regime undoubtedly benefited from the success of Shi'a parties in the elections to Iraq's new permanent legislature in December 2005.

The election of the 'ultra-conservative' Mahmoud Ahmadinejad to the Iranian presidency in June 2005 caused concern in US political circles. Rumours circulated in the US media that

Ahmadinejad had, as a student, been involved in the taking of hostages at the US embassy in Tehran in 1979, although the Iranian Government denied the allegations. Bilateral tensions also increased markedly as a result of Iran's resumption of uranium enrichment. In May 2006 President Ahmadinejad sent an 18-page letter to Bush, proposing 'new solutions' for the two states to settle their differences. The letter, which was dismissed by US officials, was reported to be the first direct communication between an Iranian President and his US counterpart since the 1979 Islamic Revolution. In September 2006 the US Administration blacklisted the state-owned Bank Saderat Iran, following accusations that the bank was involved in the transfer of money to terrorist organizations, including Hezbollah in Lebanon.

In January 2007 US troops detained five Iranians during a raid on an Iranian liaison office in the northern Iraqi town of Irbil (Arbil). The USA accused the officials of being linked to the Revolutionary Guards, whom they alleged to be training insurgents within Iraq. The Iranian Government, for its part, accused the USA of having made illegal arrests, stating that the officials held diplomatic immunity. Also in January the US Administration froze the assets of Iran's Bank Sepah, accusing the bank of acting as the conduit for an agreement with a North Korean organization that allegedly provided missile technology to Iran. Yet, despite the considerable tension in Iranian–US relations during mid-2007, exacerbated by military exercises being carried out by US naval forces in the Gulf, three rounds of direct talks concerning the sectarian conflict in Iraq were held by the US and Iranian ambassadors to Baghdad. (These discussions were halted by Iran in May 2008, in response to a recent operation by US and Iraqi forces against Shi'a militias in Iraq.)

After the inauguration of Barack Obama as US President in late January 2009, President Ahmadinejad stated in early February that he was willing to enter into a dialogue with the new US Administration. President Obama had indicated during his election campaign that his Administration would be far more open to constructive discussions with Iran than had the Bush Administration. Nevertheless, the USA continued to view Iran as a threat to its national security and extended the sanctions against the Islamic regime for another year from March.

President Obama condemned the violent repression of demonstrators during the unrest that followed the presidential election in June 2009 and rejected allegations that the USA was complicit in fomenting the unrest. However, his Administration continued to pursue a policy of engagement with Iran and did not dispute the legitimacy of Ahmadinejad's presidency. The USA's engagement policy was most evident in its participation in direct negotiations over Iran's nuclear programme, initiated in October, during which US and Iranian officials held their most senior-level summit since the Islamic Revolution. However, from late 2009, following a lack of progress in the nuclear talks, the Obama Administration actively campaigned for a new package of UN Security Council sanctions against Iran. In February 2010 the US Administration extended its unilateral sanctions against businesses connected to the Revolutionary Guards. Meanwhile, earlier that month the US Central Command confirmed that the imminent deployment of major new US-manufactured missile defence systems in Bahrain, Kuwait, Qatar and the United Arab Emirates (UAE) was designed to counter the growing threat of a conflict with Iran. The USA imposed two further packages of unilateral sanctions against Iran in July and August, as bilateral relations continued to be dominated by US suspicions of a covert Iranian nuclear agenda and objections to Iranian interference in Iraq.

In October 2011 the US Administration accused Iran of having plotted to assassinate Saudi Arabia's ambassador to Washington, DC, and to have planned to detonate bombs at the embassies of both Saudi Arabia and Israel in the US capital; Iranian officials strongly rejected the claims. Following further suggestions by the IAEA that Iran might have a covert nuclear agenda, in November the USA extended its bilateral sanctions to target firms engaged in business deals with the Iranian oil and petrochemical sectors. Further sanctions imposed at the end of 2011 were intended to make it harder for Iran to sell petroleum by placing restrictions on foreign companies that engage in business with the Central Bank. The Central Bank sanctions were expanded in February 2012, while President Obama also announced a freeze on all Iranian government assets in the USA. Specific sanctions were imposed on Iran's Ministry of Intelligence, which was alleged by the US Administration to be sponsoring militant Islamist groups and violating Iranians'

human rights. Meanwhile, in early 2012 the USA twice sent an aircraft carrier through the Strait of Hormuz, in an apparent gesture of defiance in response to Iran's recent threats that it would close the vital transit route. Sanctions introduced in June sought to prevent foreign companies from assisting Iran in defying the embargo on oil and petrochemical exports. By late September, as the likelihood of Israel launching a pre-emptive military strike against Iran's nuclear facilities was thought to be increasing, the US Administration had sent a significant number of military vessels to the Gulf. In that month naval forces from some 25 countries—including the USA, the United Kingdom, Saudi Arabia and the UAE—held large-scale naval exercises to prepare for a possible Iranian retaliation in the form of closing the Strait of Hormuz.

In August 2013, following the release of declassified documents of the US Central Intelligence Agency, the Majlis approved a bill requiring the Iranian Government to sue the USA over its role, along with the British intelligence services, in the overthrow of Muhammad Mussadeq in 1953. In November 2013 the Obama Administration successfully persuaded the US Congress to reject a proposal by some of its members to impose further sanctions, citing the potential of such measures to undermine the USA's position in negotiations over the nuclear issue. (For further details of Iranian–US relations, see *The Nuclear Issue*.) Tensions were exacerbated in April 2014 when the US Congress passed emergency legislation preventing the issue of a visa to Iran's nominee for permanent representative to the UN in New York, Hamid Aboutalebi, citing his alleged involvement in the siege at the US embassy in Tehran in 1979–81. Iran selected another nominee for the role in January 2015. Moreover, although Iran's relations with the USA had improved somewhat following Rouhani's election, several matters of bilateral contention remained active. Saeed Abedini, a Christian pastor with dual Iranian-American citizenship who had been imprisoned in Iran in 2012 for reportedly attempting to convert Muslims to Christianity, remained in gaol in early 2015 despite a request for his release from President Obama. In addition, in April 2014 a former US marine, Amir Hekmati, who had been in Iranian custody since August 2011 on charges of espionage, was sentenced to 10 years' imprisonment by a secret court after being found guilty of 'practical collaboration with the US Government'. None the less, Iran and the USA held bilateral talks in Geneva in June 2014, where Aboutalebi stated that only Iran and the USA could neutralize the threat of the militant Islamist group Islamic State (formerly Islamic State in Iraq and the Levant), while US Secretary of State John Kerry suggested that co-operation could be 'constructive'; however, Supreme Leader Khamanei refused US requests for military co-operation in September. None the less, Kerry welcomed reports of air strikes by Iran against Islamic State targets in northern Iraq in December, although Iranian officials denied co-operating with the USA in carrying out the attacks. In his State of the Union address in January 2015, President Obama announced that he did not intend to impose further economic sanctions on Iran, as they would isolate the country and jeopardize the chance of reaching a diplomatic solution to the nuclear issue.

Regional relations

In October 2000 Kamal Kharrazi became the first Iranian Minister of Foreign Affairs to visit Iraq for a decade, and the two countries agreed to reactivate a 1975 border and security agreement that had been in abeyance since 1980. However, tensions between the two sides increased in April 2001, when Iran launched a heavy missile attack against Iraqi military bases used by the Mujahidin-e-Khalq, apparently in response to repeated attacks by the armed opposition group on Iranian targets. By early 2002 a general thaw in bilateral relations was evident, despite a protest lodged with the UN by Iraq in June stating that Iran was continuing to violate agreements reached at the end of the Iran–Iraq War.

Following the removal from power of the Iraqi regime under Saddam Hussain by the US-led coalition in early 2003, large numbers of Iraqis-in-exile returned to their homeland. The UN High Commissioner for Refugees (UNHCR) estimated that, by December 2004, an estimated 107,000 Iraqi refugees—more than one-half of the pre-conflict total in Iran—had returned home; a further 56,000 returned to Iraq in 2005. After US-led coalition aircraft had launched attacks against training camps of the NLA, in April 2003 the Mujahidin-e-Khalq and its military wing (which had been based in Iraq since 1986) agreed a ceasefire with the occupying forces in Iraq, a move that was condemned by Iran. In November 2005 President Jalal Talabani became the first Iraqi head of state for over 30 years to visit Iran, and a high-profile reciprocal visit by President Ahmadinejad to Iraq took place in March 2008. In November Iran and Iraq exchanged the remains of 241 troops killed in the 1980–88 conflict. However, in December 2009 the Iraqi Government accused Iranian troops of occupying a section of the al-Fakkah oilfield in south-eastern Iraq. Moreover, following Iraq's legislative elections of March 2010, Iran was accused of interference in the protracted negotiations to form a new coalition government in order to guarantee the success of certain Shi'a parties. In December 2011 an agreement was reached between the Iraqi Government and the UN whereby some 3,000 members of the Mujahidin-e-Khalq would be relocated to enable officials to verify their refugee status. In September 2012 the US Department of State formally removed the Mujahidin-e-Khalq from its list of proscribed terrorist organizations, in recognition of the group's decision to renounce violence. In July 2013 Iran and Iraq signed an agreement whereby Iran was to supply natural gas via a new pipeline to Basra province over four years. The value of the agreement to Iran was estimated at some US $3,700m. per year. In March 2014 Iranian officials indicated that exports would commence by the middle of that year. Meanwhile, in September 2013 some 52 members of the Mujahidin-e-Khalq were killed in an attack in Baghdad. It was alleged by the residents of the camp that Iraqi security forces had carried out the attack. In June 2014 President Rouhani announced that Iran was ready to assist the Iraqi Government in curbing the influence of Sunni insurgents in northern and western Iraq, and it was reported that Revolutionary Guards units and senior military officers were providing military training to the Iraqi armed forces, and increasingly involved in frontline combat. Qassem Suleimani, the commander of the Quds Force, part of the Revolutionary Guards, had been deeply involved in operations to wrest control of a number of besieged Shi'a towns from Sunni militants, including Samarra in June. In August Iran publicly endorsed the Iraqi Prime Minister-designate, Haider al-Abadi, and Minister of Foreign Affairs Zarif made an official visit to al-Abadi in Baghdad in that month. Iran reportedly carried out air strikes against Islamic State militants in northern Iraq from December.

Amid the continuing international disquiet over the country's nuclear ambitions in recent years, Iran has fuelled further outrage by its frequent statements about Israel and the Holocaust. Remarks by President Ahmadinejad in October 2005, in which he reiterated the demand of Ayatollah Khomeini that Israel be 'wiped off the map', were condemned in a statement by the UN Security Council. Subsequent public statements by Ahmadinejad in December, to the effect that the Holocaust was a 'fabrication' and that the Jewish state should be moved outside the Middle East, were similarly condemned by Israel, the USA and the EU as illustrating the dangers of allowing Iran to develop military nuclear capabilities. Hostility between Iran and Israel was exacerbated by the victory of Hamas in the Palestinian legislative elections of January 2006 and Iran's subsequent offer of financial support to the Hamas-led administration.

Iran was also viewed as having played a leading role in the conflict between Israel and the militant Lebanese organization Hezbollah in July–August 2006; however, while the Iranian leadership admitted its support for Hezbollah, it denied that Iran was providing the group with military assistance. In November a spokesman from the Iranian Ministry of Foreign Affairs warned that any pre-emptive military strikes launched by Israel against Iran's nuclear facilities would be met with a swift and powerful military response. In July 2008 the Iranian regime apparently responded to Israeli military exercises being held over the Mediterranean Sea by conducting a series of missile tests, which included testing a new *Shahab-3* ballistic missile. A new long-range missile, the *Sajjil*, was test-fired by Iran in November, and further tests conducted in May 2009 demonstrated that the country possessed missiles with sufficient range to target Israel and the USA's military bases in the region.

Meanwhile, following his appointment as Prime Minister of Israel in February 2009, Binyamin Netanyahu indicated that significant progress in the stalled Middle East peace process would not be possible until the threat posed by Iran's nuclear programme had been negated. In November it was announced that Israeli forces had intercepted a cargo ship in the Mediterranean Sea, en route to Syria, which Israel claimed was carrying a large consignment of Iranian armaments destined for Hezbollah militants in Lebanon. During his first official visit to Lebanon in October 2010, President Ahmadinejad provoked controversy by visiting towns near the country's border with Israel, where

fighting had been most intense during the war between Israel and Hezbollah in 2006.

Iran has accused Israel's external intelligence service, Mossad, of being responsible—together with the USA's Central Intelligence Agency and the British Secret Intelligence Service—for the actual and attempted assassinations of several of its leading nuclear scientists. For example, Mostafa Ahmadi-Roshan, who worked at the Natanz nuclear plant, was killed in a car bomb explosion in Tehran in January 2012. In mid-February a spokesman for Iran's Ministry of Foreign Affairs denied allegations by Netanyahu that Iran and Hezbollah were jointly responsible for a bomb attack in the Indian capital, New Delhi, and an attempted bombing in the Georgian capital, Tbilisi; in both cases, Israeli diplomats were the apparent targets. Police in the Thai capital, Bangkok, also accused Iran of being behind the attempted assassination of two Israeli diplomats on the following day. A suicide bombing carried out on a bus in Bulgaria in July, in which five Israeli tourists and a Bulgarian died, was similarly blamed on Iran and Hezbollah; a report published by Bulgarian investigators in January 2013 found that at least two of the three men suspected of carrying out the attack were connected to Hezbollah. During 2012 there were growing international concerns that, should the expansion of Iran's nuclear programme continue at such a rapid rate Israel might launch unilateral pre-emptive military action against Iran. Netanyahu reiterated his Government's stance that Israel had the right to take such action in the interests of national security. However, US President Barack Obama was known to favour delaying any military action until all diplomatic means had been exhausted. In September 2013, during an address to the UN General Assembly, President Rouhani condemned the Holocaust as a 'reprehensible crime', prompting hopes of a relaxation of tensions on the part of Iran. In March 2014, however, the interception of a ship in the Red Sea by Israeli security forces provoked further tension. Israel claimed that the ship had been transporting surface-to-air missiles from Iran, bound ultimately for use by Islamic Jihad and other Palestinian militant groups in the Gaza Strip. Iran denied any knowledge of the shipment. Relations were further strained in January 2015 when Iran confirmed that a general from the Revolutionary Guards had been killed in an Israeli air strike against Hezbollah militants (six of whose members were also killed) in the Syrian-controlled part of the Golan Heights.

Despite Iran's extremely close relationship with Syria and its military and financial support for the regime of President Bashar al-Assad, President Ahmadinejad surprised many in the West by urging Assad, in September 2011, to end the violence being perpetrated by Syrian government forces in their crackdown on the political uprising against Assad's rule, and to begin talks with representatives of the Syrian opposition. However, in September 2012 the Commander of the Revolutionary Guards, Brig.-Gen. Muhammad Ali Jafari, admitted that some members of the Quds Force were assisting President Assad's forces in their efforts to halt the anti-Government rebellion. In November 2013 some 25 people were killed in a suicide bomb attack outside the Iranian embassy in Beirut. Responsibility for the attack was claimed by a Sunni militant group, the Abdullah Azzam Brigades, which was thought to have been involved in other attacks against both Iranian and Lebanese Shi'a interests. Despite expressions of support for Assad by President Rouhani following his election, in January 2014 the Iranian Government was formally invited to participate in the Syrian peace talks in Geneva under UN auspices. On the conclusion of that round of talks, it was announced that the goal of the negotiations would be to establish a transitional governing body in Syria, an objective that Iran had previously been opposed to on the grounds that it was likely to exclude Assad. In December the Minister of Foreign Affairs, Zarif, held talks with his Syrian and Iraqi counterparts in Tehran in an effort to find a regional solution to the ongoing conflict. Later that month Zarif hosted the Syrian Prime Minister, Wael Nader al-Halqi, the Speaker of the Iraqi Council of Representatives, Salim al-Jaburi, and the Turkish Minister of Foreign Affairs, Mevlüt Çavuşoğlu, for discussions on combating the threat posed by Islamic State.

Relations between Iran and Saudi Arabia were frequently strained after the Islamic Revolution of 1979. A period of particularly hostile relations, following the deaths of 275 Iranian pilgrims as a result of clashes with Saudi security forces in the Islamic holy city of Mecca during the *Hajj* (annual pilgrimage) in July 1987, culminated in the suspension of diplomatic relations in April 1988. Links were not restored until March 1991. Allegations of Iranian involvement in the bombing of a US military housing complex at al-Khobar, Saudi Arabia, in June 1996 again strained relations. However, the installation of a new Iranian Government in August 1997 facilitated rapprochement, perhaps reflecting the desire of the two countries, as the region's principal petroleum producers, to co-operate in maintaining world oil prices and in efforts to curtail over-production by members of the Organization of the Petroleum Exporting Countries (OPEC). An Iranian delegation led by former President Rafsanjani visited Saudi Arabia in February 1998, at the end of which the formation of a joint ministerial committee for bilateral relations was announced. Several co-operation agreements were subsequently signed, including a Saudi-Iranian security accord in April 2001. During late 2003 Iran countered US accusations that certain suspected al-Qa'ida militants who remained in Iranian custody had been involved in plotting suicide attacks against expatriate compounds in Riyadh in May.

In March 2007 President Ahmadinejad held discussions with King Abdullah in Saudi Arabia, where the two leaders sought to demonstrate that perceived differences between their countries as a result of recent sectarian tensions in Iraq and Lebanon had been exaggerated. Nevertheless, Saudi officials outlined their opposition to Iran's nuclear activities and warned that Saudi Arabia would also seek to develop a nuclear weapons capability should it be discovered that Iran had done so. Diplomatic relations were damaged following the dispatch by the Cooperation Council of the Arab States of the Gulf (Gulf Cooperation Council—GCC) of a contingent of (principally Saudi) military forces to assist the Sunni Muslim authorities in Bahrain in quelling the largely Shi'a anti-Government protests which erupted there in February 2011. Saudi Arabia accused Iran of being behind much of the unrest in Bahrain. Bilateral tensions have also been heightened by the ongoing conflict in Syria, with Iran continuing to support the Assad regime and Saudi Arabia providing military assistance to the anti-Government rebels. Moreover, the Saudi Government has accused the Iranian authorities of encouraging dissent among its Shi'a minority, who staged several anti-Government demonstrations in Saudi Arabia's Eastern Province during 2011–12. Tensions were raised in October 2014 when the Iranian Minister of Petroleum, Bijan Namdar Zanganeh, urged the organization of an emergency summit of OPEC members to address the rapidly declining international price of oil. Observers suggested that Iran had criticized Saudi Arabia for maintaining a high level of production and thus allowing the price of oil to fall, in an attempt to inflict economic harm on Iran, which needed to maintain a high price to cover its production costs.

Both the Khatami and Ahmadinejad administrations have sought improved relations with Saudi Arabia's fellow members of the GCC, although a long-standing territorial dispute with the UAE remains unresolved. In March 1992 Iran occupied those parts of Abu Musa island and the Greater and Lesser Tunbs that had remained under the control of the emirate of Sharjah since the original occupation in 1971. In December 1994 the UAE announced its intention to refer the dispute to the International Court of Justice (ICJ) in The Hague, Netherlands. In June 1997, after Iran had in 1996 opened an airport on Abu Musa and a power station on Greater Tunb, the UAE complained to the UN; UAE officials protested that Iran was repeatedly violating the emirates' territorial waters. During the 2000s the UAE remained an important trading partner of Iran and political relations generally improved. However, reports in July 2010 that the UAE's ambassador to the USA had appeared to encourage the idea of a pre-emptive US military strike against Iran in order to prevent the Islamic regime from building a nuclear weapon precipitated a deterioration in diplomatic relations. Difficulties persisted in 2011–12, amid allegations of Iranian interference in Bahrain and the UAE's support for the international sanctions imposed against Iran; however, joint economic initiatives continued to be pursued. In April 2012 the UAE withdrew its ambassador from Tehran in protest against a controversial visit by President Ahmadinejad to Abu Musa, which holds a strategic location in the Strait of Hormuz, during which he revived Iran's historical claim of ownership over the island. In November Iran was reported to have opened a new naval base close to the island.

Victories achieved by the Sunni fundamentalist Taliban in the Afghan civil war in September 1996 prompted Iran, which supported the Government of President Burhanuddin Rabbani, to express fears for its national security, and to accuse the USA of interference in Afghanistan's internal affairs. In June 1997 the Taliban accused Iran of espionage, and ordered the closure of the Iranian embassy in Kabul. Iran retaliated by halting all trade across its border with Afghanistan. In September 1998, as it

emerged that nine Iranian diplomats missing since August had been murdered by Taliban militia as they stormed the city of Mazar-i-Sharif, 500,000 Iranian troops were reportedly placed on full alert in readiness for conflict with Afghanistan. In an attempt to defuse the crisis, in October the Taliban agreed to free all Iranian prisoners being held in Afghanistan and to punish those responsible for the killing of the nine diplomats. Following the suicide attacks on the USA in September 2001, as the USA began preparations for military action against al-Qa'ida and its Taliban hosts, Iran closed its eastern border with Afghanistan and sent a large contingent of troops there in order to prevent a further influx of Afghan refugees. In October, however, when the US-led military action began, Iran reportedly agreed to the establishment of eight refugee camps within its borders to provide shelter for some 250,000 Afghan refugees. Although Iran refused to give military assistance to the US-led coalition, it actively supported the Western-backed opposition forces, collectively known as the United National Islamic Front for the Salvation of Afghanistan (the Northern Alliance), and welcomed their swift victory over the Taliban.

A programme allowing for voluntary repatriations of Afghan refugees under the auspices of UNHCR was inaugurated by the Iranian and Afghan authorities in April 2002, although UNHCR put the number of 'spontaneous' repatriations prior to that date at 57,000. More than 1.5m. Afghan refugees in Iran were estimated by UNHCR to have returned to Afghanistan by November 2005. By the end of 2011 the total number of refugees in Iran had fallen slightly, to 882,700; those fleeing Afghanistan (840,200) now accounted for virtually all of the refugees, with the number of Iraqis totalling 42,500. In August 2002 President Khatami became the first Iranian head of state to visit Afghanistan for 40 years. In June 2011 Brig.-Gen. Ahmad Vahidi, the Minister of Defence and Armed Forces Logistics, undertook an historic visit to Kabul for discussions with his Afghan counterpart.

Closer relations were developed with Turkey during the 1990s, despite periodic tensions arising, particularly from Turkish allegations of Iranian support for the Kurdish separatist Kurdistan Workers' Party (Partiya Karkeren Kurdistan—PKK) in its conflict with the armed forces in south-eastern Turkey. In 1997 Iran was a founder member of the Developing Eight (D-8) group of Islamic countries, based in Istanbul. Since 2010 the Turkish Government has played a more significant role in attempts to resolve the dispute between Iran and Western countries concerning Iran's nuclear programme, even hosting formal discussions in Istanbul between Iran and international negotiators in January 2011 and April 2012. However, tensions in the bilateral relationship were evident in the latter part of 2012 as a result of Iran's continued support for the Syrian regime under President Assad and Turkey's growing military assistance to Syrian opposition forces. In January 2014 Turkish premier Recep Tayyip Erdoğan visited Tehran, in an attempt to ease recent tensions between the two countries, capitalizing ostensibly upon the apparent rapprochement between Iran and Western governments over the Syrian conflict and the Iranian nuclear programme. However, in a speech in October Erdoğan, who had been elected as President of Turkey in August, criticized Iran for its support of the regime of Assad. On a visit to Tehran in December, the Turkish Minister of Foreign Affairs, Mevlüt Çavuşoğlu, announced that Turkey intended to increase the value of bilateral trade to some US $30,000m. a year. Trade between the two countries had totalled $21,800m. in 2012 but declined sharply to $13,800m. in 2013, due in part to economic sanctions imposed on Iran by the USA and the EU. Çavuşoğlu added that President Erdoğan intended to visit Tehran for a meeting on high-level strategic co-operation in early 2015.

Meanwhile, considerable political and economic advantage has been perceived arising from Iran's potential as a transit route for hydrocarbons from the former Soviet republics of Central Asia, and since the early 1990s Iran has sought to strengthen its position in Central Asia through bilateral economic, security and cultural agreements as well as institutions such as the Tehran-based Economic Cooperation Organization. Relations between Iran and Azerbaijan—already tense owing to disagreement over a contested section of the Caspian Basin— deteriorated in July 2001, when Iran ordered a military patrol boat into the disputed waters in order to prevent foreign companies from undertaking oil exploration there. Subsequent meetings of the five littoral states (Iran, Russia, Azerbaijan, Kazakhstan and Turkmenistan) failed to resolve the dispute regarding the legal status of the Caspian. An improvement in relations between Iran and Azerbaijan was evident later in the decade, and moves towards the imposition of wider economic sanctions against Iran were of concern to Azerbaijan, owing to Iran's large ethnic Azeri population, as well as the energy agreements in place between the two countries. However, in February 2012 bilateral relations deteriorated after Azerbaijan announced that it was to purchase military equipment from Israel. In March Azerbaijan denied reports that it had agreed to allow the Israeli air force access to airfields within Azerbaijan in the event of Israeli military action against Iranian nuclear facilities. In November 2013 Azerbaijan closed a section of its border with Iran following an incident in which an Azerbaijani government vehicle was reported to have been fired upon from the Iranian side of the border; Iran reciprocated later that month with the closure of two further crossings.

Other external relations

The EU pursued a policy of 'critical dialogue' with Iran during the 1990s, despite US pressure as well as tensions between Iran and certain EU states. Notably, a lengthy period of strained relations with the United Kingdom developed after Ayatollah Khomeini issued a *fatwa* (edict) in February 1989, imposing a death penalty against a British writer, Salman Rushdie, for material deemed offensive to Islam in his novel *The Satanic Verses*. 'Critical dialogue' was suspended in April 1997, after a German court ruled that the Iranian authorities had ordered the assassination of four prominent members of the dissident Democratic Party of Iranian Kurdistan in Berlin in September 1992. Germany withdrew its ambassador to Tehran (as did other EU members) and expelled four Iranian diplomats. In November 1997, following the inauguration of President Khatami, a compromise arrangement was finally reached allowing the readmission of all EU ambassadors, and in February 1998 EU foreign ministers agreed to resume senior-level ministerial contacts with Iran. Despite assurances given to the British Department for Foreign and Commonwealth Affairs in September by the Iranian Government that it had no intention of threatening the life of Rushdie, 'conservative' clerics maintained that the *fatwa* issued by Ayatollah Khomeini was irrevocable. President Khatami became the first Iranian head of state to visit the West since the Islamic Revolution when, in March 1999, he travelled to Italy and the Vatican. In December 2002 the EU commenced negotiations with Iran regarding a trade and co-operation agreement, with the stipulation that the accord be linked with consideration of human rights and terrorism.

A crisis erupted in relations with the United Kingdom in June 2004, when Iran captured three British patrol craft and detained eight Royal Navy personnel on the Shatt al-Arab waterway dividing Iran from Iraq. Iran asserted that the vessels had entered Iranian territorial waters, but the sailors, who were released four days later, alleged that they had been 'forcibly escorted' into Iranian waters. In October 2005 British officials accused the Iranians of supplying explosives to and running training camps for Iraqi Shi'a insurgents operating in the British-controlled region of southern Iraq. In March 2007 some 15 British Royal Navy and Royal Marines personnel were captured and detained by Iranian Revolutionary Guards while patrolling the Shatt al-Arab waterway. As in 2004, Iran claimed that the sailors had trespassed into Iranian territorial waters; however, British naval officials insisted that the two crews were operating in Iraqi waters at the time of their arrest. Following discussions between Iranian and British officials in April 2007, the 15 sailors were finally released from detention 13 days after their capture. The British Government denied that a deal had been agreed with Iran to secure the sailors' release. However, several commentators noted that shortly before the pardon five diplomats who had been seized by US forces at the Iranian consulate in Arbil, Iraq, in January had been granted consular access; moreover, a senior diplomat at the Iranian embassy in Baghdad, who had been abducted by gunmen in February, had also recently been released.

Relations between Iran and the United Kingdom deteriorated in the aftermath of the disputed Iranian presidential election in June 2009. The Iranian authorities alleged that British agents had travelled to Iran prior to the election to plan civil unrest, and that the British Broadcasting Corporation's Persian-language service had encouraged protests against the result of the election. Two British diplomats were expelled from Iran on 22 June. The British Government retaliated with the expulsion of two Iranian diplomats. On 27 June nine Iranian employees from the British embassy in Tehran were arrested for their alleged role in the post-election unrest. Although by July all had been released from custody, trial proceedings subsequently began against one

senior employee, political counsellor Hossein Rassam. During a court hearing in early August, he reportedly admitted distributing information on the post-election unrest. The hearing was one of a series of mass trials of political prisoners that took place during August. In October Rassam was convicted of espionage and fomenting unrest, and sentenced to four years' imprisonment; however, following an appeal, his prison term was commuted to a suspended sentence in October 2010.

Amid an intensification of the dispute concerning Iran's nuclear programme during 2011, the EU extended its list of Iranian individuals and companies whose assets were frozen. On 29 November, two days after Iranian legislators voted to downgrade Iran's diplomatic ties with the United Kingdom, hundreds of Iranian demonstrators attacked the British embassy in Tehran to protest against the imposition by the British Government on 22 November of further economic sanctions—which included a virtual ban on British banks doing business with Iranian banks and on firms involved in Iran's energy sector. This followed the IAEA's strongly worded report detailing suspicions that Iran was engaged in the development of a nuclear weapons programme (see *The Nuclear Issue*). In response, on 30 November the United Kingdom closed its embassy and gave Iranian diplomats in London two days to leave the country. In January 2012 the EU (which accounts for some 20% of Iranian oil exports) banned imports of crude petroleum from the Islamic Republic with effect from 1 July. The Union also froze assets belonging to the Central Bank. The Iranian leadership warned that it would close the Strait of Hormuz if the country was 'seriously threatened', and in February 2012 announced that it was ending all oil exports to the United Kingdom and France with immediate effect. In October, after no breakthrough had been made in discussions on how to resolve the nuclear crisis, EU member states introduced tougher sanctions against the Iranian regime. The measures included further asset freezes on Iranian companies, as well as a ban on imports of natural gas and on transactions with Iranian banks, unless these were for the purpose of providing food or medicines. In March 2013 it was announced that the Iranian Government was in discussions with the United Kingdom regarding the resumption of consular activities between the two countries; representatives of both governments met at the nuclear talks in Geneva in October, following which it was announced that chargés d'affaires would be appointed. In September the European Court of Justice voted to reject sanctions imposed by the EU on a number of Iranian companies for their alleged links to Iran's nuclear energy programme. However, the European Parliament passed a resolution in April 2014 condemning human rights violations in Iran and calling for the release of prisoners of conscience, although it commended Rouhani's administration for the release of human rights lawyer Nasrin Sotoudeh in September 2013. In June the British Ministry of Foreign and Commonwealth Affairs announced its intention to re-open its embassy in Tehran, although it was still closed in March 2015, amid reports that the British Home Office was demanding that some 4,000 Iranian citizens residing illegally in the United Kingdom were deported, before it would open a consular section issuing visas in Tehran; it also expected Iran to pay compensation for damage caused to the British embassy by Iranian protesters in November 2011.

In March 2001 Russia pledged to assist Iran with the completion of the nuclear plant at Bushehr (see *The Nuclear Issue*), and in May Russian officials reportedly agreed to supply Iran with advanced cruise missiles. The two countries signed a military co-operation pact in October, believed to amount to annual sales to Iran of Russian weapons worth some US $300m. In July 2002 Russia and Iran concluded a draft 10-year development and co-operation accord, which was reported to include the construction of a further three nuclear reactors at Bushehr. Construction of the Bushehr plant was completed in October 2004, and in February 2005 Russia agreed to supply Iran with nuclear fuel for the plant; however, following international pressure, the deal required that Iran return to Russia spent fuel rods, which could be used to produce nuclear weapons, from the site. As the diplomatic crisis over Iran's nuclear programme intensified during that year, Russia proposed that sensitive elements of Iran's nuclear programme, such as uranium enrichment, could be conducted on Russian territory; this proposal was rejected by the Iranian administration in early 2006.

In March 2007 the Russian Government rejected a deadline by which it was to deliver nuclear fuel to the Bushehr plant, claiming that Iran had failed to make the requisite payments; Russia also warned Iran that it would continue to withhold the provision of fuel until Iran agreed to suspend uranium enrichment, as demanded by the UN Security Council. However, in October President Vladimir Putin expressed his opposition to any US-led military strike against Iran's nuclear facilities. The first shipment of Russian nuclear fuel to the Bushehr reactor arrived in December, after Russia and Iran had finally agreed on a timetable for completion of the project (for further details, see *The Nuclear Issue*). After a fourth round of UN sanctions were adopted against Iran in June 2010, the Russian Government declared that it was required to cancel the planned delivery of an *S-300* air defence missile system to Iran. By early 2012 senior Russian officials suggested that any new sanctions imposed against Iran would merely harm the Iranian people rather than persuade the Government to end its nuclear programme. In January the two countries agreed henceforth to use their respective currencies, rather than the US dollar, for the purposes of bilateral trade. In July Iranian officials stated their intention to double the level of Iran's trade with Russia from the equivalent of US \$4,000m. to \$8,000m., and in February 2013 mutual pledges were made to increase co-operation in the fields of agriculture and energy. In January 2015 Sergei Shoigu made the first visit by a Russian Minister of Defence to Iran since 2000 and signed a military co-operation agreement with his Iranian counterpart, Hossein Dehghan, who emphasized the need to counter the influence of the USA in the region.

Iranian exports to the People's Republic of China (including oil exports) have risen considerably as Chinese demand has increased, and a growing number of Chinese companies are now investing in large-scale Iranian infrastructure projects, often replacing Western businesses which have withdrawn their interests as a consequence of sanctions imposed by the UN, the USA and the EU. Although China has voted for certain UN Security Council resolutions imposing stricter penalties against the Iranian regime, the Chinese have expressed support for Iran's right to develop a civil nuclear energy programme. In 2009 China was reported to have become Iran's largest trading partner, with the value of bilateral trade estimated at US \$21,200m. in that year, compared with a mere \$400m. 15 years previously. In June 2012 China was among 20 oil importers that were given a temporary exemption from new US sanctions against foreign hydrocarbons firms which traded with Iran. In May 2014 China and Iran agreed to increase co-operation in defence and security.

CONSTITUTION AND GOVERNMENT

A draft constitution for the Islamic Republic of Iran was published on 18 June 1979. It was submitted to an Assembly of Experts, elected by popular vote on 3 August, to debate the various clauses and to propose amendments. The amended Constitution was approved by a referendum on 2–3 December 1979. A further 45 amendments to the Constitution were approved by a referendum on 28 July 1989.

Legislative power is vested in the Islamic Consultative Assembly (Majlis-e-Shura-e Islami), with 290 members. The chief executive of the administration is the President. The Majlis and the President are both elected by universal adult suffrage for a term of four years. There is no limit on the total number of terms a President may serve. However, no candidate may hold office for more than two consecutive terms. A 12-member Council of Guardians supervises elections and ensures that legislation is in accordance with the Constitution and with Islamic precepts. The Council to Determine the Expediency of the Islamic Order, created in February 1988 and formally incorporated into the Constitution in 1989, rules on legal and theological disputes between the Majlis and the Council of Guardians. In October 2005 the powers of the Expediency Council were extended, allowing it to supervise all branches of government. The executive, legislative and judicial wings of state power are subject to the authority of the Wali Faqih (supreme religious leader). Iran is divided into 31 provinces, each with an appointed Governor.

REGIONAL AND INTERNATIONAL CO-OPERATION

Iran became a member of the UN upon its foundation in October 1945. A working party was established in May 2005 to examine Iran's application to join the World Trade Organization (WTO); however, accession negotiations had not begun by early 2015. Iran is also a member of the Organization of Islamic Cooperation (OIC), of the Organization of the Petroleum Exporting Countries (OPEC), of the Developing Eight group of Islamic countries (D-8), and of the Group of 15 developing countries (G15). The headquarters of the Economic Cooperation Organization (ECO) are located in Tehran.

ECONOMIC AFFAIRS

In 2013, according to estimates by the World Bank, Iran's gross national income (GNI), measured at average 2011–13 prices, was US \$447,534m., equivalent to \$5,780 per head (or \$15,600 per head on an international purchasing-power parity basis). During 2004–13, it was estimated, the population increased at an average annual rate of 1.2%, while gross domestic product (GDP) per head increased, in real terms, by an average of 1.9% per year. According to the Central Bank of Iran, overall GDP increased, in real terms, at an average annual rate of 2.6% between 2004/05 and 2013/14. GDP declined by a preliminary 1.9% in 2013/14 (Iranian year to March).

Agriculture (including forestry and fishing) contributed a provisional 9.0% of GDP in 2013/14. About 19.6% of the employed labour force were engaged in agriculture in the first quarter of 2014/15 (Iranian year to March), according to official figures. The principal cash crops are fresh and dried fruit and nuts, which accounted for 7.6% of non-petroleum export earnings in 2012/13. Wheat, rice, sugar cane potatoes, sugar beet and barley are the main subsistence crops. Imports of cereals comprised some 11.9% of the value of total imports in 2012/13. Production of fruit and vegetables is also significant. According to the central bank, agricultural GDP increased by an average of 1.7% per year in 2004/05–13/14; the sector's GDP grew by 4.7% in 2013/14.

Industry (including manufacturing, construction and power, but excluding mining) contributed a provisional 22.2% of GDP in 2013/14, and, according to official estimates, (including mining) engaged some 33.0% of the employed labour force in the first quarter of 2014/15. In 2004/05–13/14 industrial GDP increased by an average of 3.7% per year; sectoral GDP declined by 2.9% in 2013/14, according to the central bank.

Mining (including petroleum-refining) contributed 22.7% of GDP in 2010/11, although the sector engaged only an estimated 0.5% of the working population in 2010. Metal ores are the major non-hydrocarbon mineral exports, and coal, magnesite and gypsum are also mined. The sector is dominated by the hydrocarbons sector, which contributed a preliminary 17.0% of GDP in 2013/14. At the end of 2013 Iran's proven reserves of petroleum were estimated at 157,000m. barrels, sufficient to maintain the 2013 rate of production—estimated at 3.6m. barrels per day (b/d)—for more than 100 years. As a member of the Organization of the Petroleum Exporting Countries (OPEC, see p. 406), Iran is subject to production quotas agreed by the Organization's Conference. Iran's proven reserves of natural gas (33,780,000m. cu m at the end of 2013) are the second largest in the world, after those of Russia. Since late 2008 Iran, Russia and Qatar have increased their co-operation on gas projects. A deal was concluded in June 2010 for the construction of a pipeline, at a cost of US \$7,600m., through which Iran would export natural gas from its South Pars offshore gasfield (an extension of Qatar's North Field) to Pakistan's southern provinces of Balochistan and Sindh. The project was officially inaugurated in March 2013, at which time the Iranian section of the pipeline was nearing completion. However, the Pakistani section was delayed until at least 2016 owing to financial difficulties. In July 2011 an agreement worth \$10,000m. was signed by Iran, Iraq and Syria, involving the construction, by 2014–16, of a pipeline that would transport gas from the South Pars field to the latter countries and eventually via Lebanon to the Mediterranean Sea. According to the central bank, the GDP of the mining sector increased by an average of 10.6% per year in 2004/05–13/14; mining GDP declined by 2.5% in 2012/13, but increased by 0.9% in 2013/14.

Manufacturing (excluding petroleum-refining) contributed 11.7% of GDP in 2013/14, and engaged about 17.1% of the employed labour force in 2010. The most important sectors, in terms of value added, are textiles, food-processing and transport equipment. The sector's GDP increased by an average of 3.7% per year in 2004/05–13/14; real GDP of the sector declined by 3.9% in 2013/14, according to the central bank.

The construction sector contributed a provisional 9.2% of GDP in 2013/14, and engaged 13.7% of the employed labour force in 2010. The GDP of the sector increased at an average annual rate of 2.9% during 2004/05–13/14; the sector contracted by 3.1% in 2013/14, according to the central bank.

Principal sources of energy are natural gas (providing around 66.8% of total electricity production in 2011) and petroleum (some 27.8% in the same year). Imports of mineral fuels and lubricants comprised just 1.4% of the value of total imports in 2011. The first phase of Iran's South Pars gasfield was brought on stream in 2004, and a total of 29 phases were planned. Gas reserves in the South Pars field are estimated at more than

14,000,000m. cu m, with a production capacity in late 2012 of 300m. cu m of gas per day.

The services sector contributed a provisional 52.8% of GDP in 2013/14, and engaged an estimated 47.3% of the employed labour force in the first quarter of 2014/15, according to official estimates. According to the Central Bank of Iran, during 2004/05 and 2013/14, the GDP of the services sector increased by an average of 4.8% per year; growth in the sector was about 1.1% in 2012/13, but contracted by 1.5% in 2013/14.

According to preliminary figures from the Central Bank of Iran, in the year ending March 2014 Iran recorded a visible trade surplus of US $32,968m., and there was a surplus of $27,965m. on the current account of the balance of payments. In 2010/11 the principal source of imports was the United Arab Emirates (UAE, which supplied 32.9% of total imports); other major suppliers included the People's Republic of China, Germany, Turkey, Switzerland and the Republic of Korea (South Korea). China and Iraq (taking 17.2% and 17.1%, respectively) were the principal markets for Iranian exports in 2010/11; the UAE, India and Afghanistan were also important export markets. Other than petroleum and natural gas, Iran's principal exports in 2012/13 were plastic goods, organic chemicals, fresh and dried fruit and nuts, and iron and steel. Exports of petroleum and gas comprised 67.7% of the value of total exports in that year, according to preliminary figures. The principal imports in that year were machinery and transport equipment, food and live animals, basic manufactures, and chemicals and related products.

According to IMF estimates, the budget deficit for the financial year ending March 2014 totalled IR 81,818m. Iran's general government gross debt was IR 1,023,049,760m. in 2013, equivalent to 11.3% of GDP. Iran's total external debt was US $11,477m. at the end of 2012, of which $4,003m. was public and publicly guaranteed debt. The annual rate of inflation averaged 17.2% in 2003/04–12/13; consumer prices increased by an estimated average of 34.8% in 2013/14. According to the Central Bank, the rate of unemployment was 10.7% in the first quarter of 2014/15.

By early 2015 Iran's economy was hampered by a number of significant challenges, including the over-reliance on revenue from the petroleum sector, high rates of inflation and unemployment, and, moreover, the effects of economic and technological sanctions imposed by the UN, the USA and the EU. Thus, while Iran possessed the world's second largest proven reserves of both crude oil and natural gas, sanctions on its hydrocarbons industry required the Government to reduce its dependency on the sector, and to seek new export markets for its petroleum sales. The rapid decline in oil production and exports, the latter accounting for around 80% of foreign revenue, together with US and EU restrictions placed on firms dealing with Iran's financial institutions—including the Central Bank—also had a dramatic impact on the value of Iran's currency. The rial reached a record

low against the US dollar in October 2012: it lost an estimated 50% of its value as a result of sanctions. An average annual growth rate of 8% was projected in the Government's Fifth Five-Year Development Plan (2010–15). However, as the effects of the economic sanctions intensified, GDP growth rates remained below this target: according to the central bank, growth was recorded at 6.5% in 2010/11 and 4.3% in 2011/12. GDP contracted by 6.8% in 2012/13. The election of Hassan Rouhani as President of Iran in June 2013, and the signing of an interim agreement on the country's nuclear programme in November between Iran and the P5+1 group of countries, had a slight positive effect on Iran's economic prospects. The IMF forecast a return to GDP growth, at 1.5%, in 2014, and 2.2% in 2015, while the rate of inflation was expected to be around 20% in 2015. None the less, despite limited sanctions relief as a result of the November 2013 agreement, restrictions on oil exports and on the banking sector remained in place at March 2015, pending the conclusion of a permanent accord. In the budget for 2014/15, which was presented in December 2014, the average price of a barrel of oil was forecast at US $100; however, by January 2015 the actual price had fallen below $50, and the Government was likely to need to seek loans from the National Development Fund, or expedite its privatization programme, to cover current expenditure. Meanwhile, the rial weakened further against the US dollar in late 2014 and the price of bread rose by 30% in December after the Government reduced subsidies for certain foodstuffs in an attempt to reduce expenditure.

PUBLIC HOLIDAYS

The Iranian year 1394 runs from 21 March 2015 to 19 March 2016, and the year 1395 from 20 March 2016 to 20 March 2017.

2016: 11 February (Victory of the Islamic Revolution), 19 March (Day of Oil Industry Nationalization), 20–23 March† (Norouz, Iranian New Year), 12 March (Martyrdom of Hazrat Fatemeh), 31 March (Islamic Republic Day), 1 April (Sizdah-bedar, Nature Day—13th Day of Norouz), 20 April (Birth of Imam Ali), 4 May* (Prophet Muhammad receives his calling), 22 May* (Birth of Imam Mahdi), 3 June (Death of Imam Khomeini), 4 June (1963 Uprising), 26 June* (Martyrdom of Imam Ali), 6–7 July* (Eid-e Fitr, end of Ramadan), 30 July* (Martyrdom of Imam Jafar Sadeq), 12 September* (Qorban, Feast of the Sacrifice), 20 September* (Eid-e Ghadir Khom), 10 October* (Tassoua), 11 October* (Ashoura), 20 November* (Arbain), 28 November (Demise of Prophet Muhammad and Martyrdom of Imam Hassan), 30 November* (Martyrdom of Imam Reza), 16 December (Birth of Prophet Muhammad and Birth of Imam Jafar Sadegh),

* These holidays are dependent on the Islamic lunar calendar and may vary by one or two days from the dates given.

† This festival begins on the date of the Spring Equinox.

Statistical Survey

The Iranian year runs from approximately 21 March to 20 March

Sources (except where otherwise stated): Statistical Centre of Iran, POB 14155-6133, Dr Fatemi Ave, Tehran 14144; tel. (21) 88965061; fax (21) 88963451; e-mail sci@sci.org.ir; internet www.amar.org.ir; Bank Markazi Jomhouri Islami Iran (Central Bank), POB 15875-7177, 144 Mirdamad Blvd, Tehran; tel. (21) 29954855; fax (21) 29954780; e-mail g.secdept@cbi.ir; internet www.cbi.ir.

Area and Population

AREA, POPULATION AND DENSITY

Area (sq km)	1,648,195*
Population (census results)	
28 October 2006	70,495,782
24 October 2011	
Males	37,905,669
Females	37,244,000
Total	75,149,669
Population (UN estimates at mid-year)†	
2013	77,447,170
2014	78,470,223
2015	79,476,308
Density (per sq km) at mid-2015	48.2

* 636,372 sq miles.
† Source: UN, *World Population Prospects: The 2012 Revision.*

POPULATION BY AGE AND SEX
(UN estimates at mid-2015)

	Males	Females	Total
0–14 years	9,787,172	9,353,643	19,140,815
15–64 years	28,016,036	27,929,879	55,945,915
65 years and over	2,112,564	2,277,014	4,389,578
Total	**39,915,772**	**39,560,536**	**79,476,308**

Source: UN, *World Population Prospects: The 2012 Revision.*

PROVINCES
(population at 2011 census)

Province (Ostan)	Area (sq km)*	Population	Density (per sq km)	Provincial capital
Alborz†	5,122	2,412,513	471.0	Karaj
Ardebil	17,800	1,248,488	70.1	Ardebil
Azarbayejan-e-Gharbi (West Azerbaijan) . .	37,411	3,080,576	82.3	Orumiyeh
Azarbayejan-e-Sharqi (East Azerbaijan) . .	45,651	3,724,620	81.6	Tabriz
Bakhtaran (Kermanshah) .	25,009	1,945,227	77.8	Bakhtaran
Bushehr	22,743	1,032,949	45.4	Bushehr
Chaharmahal and Bakhtiyari . .	16,328	895,263	54.8	Shahr-e-Kord
Esfahan	107,018	4,879,312	45.6	Esfahan
Fars	122,608	4,596,658	37.5	Shiraz
Gilan	14,042	2,480,874	176.7	Rasht
Golestan	20,367	1,777,014	87.2	Gorgan
Hamadan	19,368	1,758,268	90.8	Hamadan
Hormozgan . . .	70,697	1,578,183	22.3	Bandar Abbas
Ilam	20,133	557,599	27.7	Ilam
Kerman	180,726	2,938,988	16.3	Kerman
Khuzestan	64,055	4,531,720	70.7	Ahvaz
Kohgiluyeh and Boyrahmad . .	15,504	658,629	42.5	Yasuj
Kordestan (Kurdistan) . .	29,137	1,493,645	51.3	Sanandaj
Lorestan	28,294	1,754,243	62.0	Khorramabad
Markazi (Central) .	29,127	1,413,959	48.5	Arak
Mazandaran . .	23,842	3,073,943	128.9	Sari
North Khorasan .	28,434	867,727	30.5	Bojnurd

Province (Ostan)— *continued*	Area (sq km)*	Population	Density (per sq km)	Provincial capital
Qazvin	15,567	1,201,565	77.2	Qazvin
Qom	11,526	1,151,672	99.9	Qom
Razavi Khorasan .	118,851	5,994,402	50.4	Mashhad
Semnan . . .	97,491	631,218	6.5	Semnan
Sistan and Baluchestan . .	181,785	2,534,327	13.9	Zahedan
South Khorasan .	95,385	662,534	6.9	Birjand
Tehran (Teheran)† .	13,692	12,183,391	889.8	Tehran (Teheran)
Yazd	129,285	1,074,428	8.3	Yazd
Zanjan	21,773	1,015,734	46.7	Zanjan
Total	**1,628,771**	**75,149,669**	**46.1**	**—**

* Excluding inland water; densities are calculated on basis of land area only.
† In June 2010 the legislature enacted a law dividing the existing province of Tehran to create a new province, Alborz, with the city of Karaj as its capital.

PRINCIPAL TOWNS
(population at 2011 census)

Tehran (Teheran, the capital) . .	8,154,051	Kerman	534,441
Mashhad (Meshed) .	2,766,258	Hamadan	525,794
Esfahan (Isfahan) .	1,756,126	Yazd	486,152
Karaj	1,614,626	Arak	484,212
Tabriz	1,494,998	Ardabil (Ardebil) .	482,632
Shiraz	1,460,665	Bandar Abbas . .	435,751
Ahvaz	1,112,021	Eslamshahr (Islam Shahr)	389,102
Qom	1,074,036	Zanjan	386,851
Bakhtaran (Kermanshah) .	851,405	Qazvin	381,598
Orumiyeh . . .	667,499	Sanandaj . . .	373,987
Rasht	639,951	Khorramabad . .	348,216
Zahedan . . .	560,725		

Mid-2014 ('000, incl. suburbs, UN estimate): Tehran 8,352,930 (Source: UN, *World Urbanization Prospects: The 2014 Revision*).

BIRTHS, MARRIAGES AND DEATHS
(annual averages, UN estimates)

	2000–05	2005–10	2010–15
Birth rate (per 1,000)	18.9	18.8	16.6
Death rate (per 1,000)	5.2	5.3	5.2

Source: UN, *World Population Prospects: The 2012 Revision.*

Births ('000): 1,239 in 2005/06; 1,254 in 2006/07; 1,287 in 2007/08; 1,300 in 2008/09; 1,349 in 2009/10; 1,364 in 2010/11; 1,382 in 2011/12; 1,422 in 2012/13; 1,472 in 2013/14.

Marriages ('000): 788 in 2005/06; 778 in 2006/07; 841 in 2007/08; 882 in 2008/09; 890 in 2009/10; 892 in 2010/11; 875 in 2011/12; 830 in 2012/13; 775 in 2013/14.

Deaths ('000): 355 in 2004/05; 364 in 2005/06; 409 in 2006/07; 413 in 2007/08; 418 in 2008/09; 394 in 2009/10; 441 in 2010/11; 383 in 2011/12; 368 in 2012/13; 372 in 2013/14.

Life expectancy (years at birth). 73.8 (males 71.9, females 75.7) in 2012 (Source: World Bank, World Development Indicators database).

ECONOMICALLY ACTIVE POPULATION
('000 persons aged 10 years and over, excl. armed forces, 2010)

	Males	Females	Total
Agriculture, hunting and forestry .	2,939.7	966.1	3,906.0
Fishing	63.8	0.4	64.0
Mining and quarrying	102.4	9.5	111.8
Manufacturing	2,727.3	795.0	3,522.3
Electricity, gas and water supply .	188.5	9.1	197.7
Construction	2,789.5	30.9	2,820.4
Wholesale and retail trade; repair of motor vehicles, motorcycles and personal and household goods	3,006.5	226.2	3,232.7
Hotels and restaurants . . .	231.2	15.3	246.5
Transport, storage and communications	2,084.5	41.1	2,125.6
Financial intermediation . . .	205.2	37.3	242.5
Real estate, renting and business activities	523.0	141.4	664.4
Public administration and defence; compulsory social security . .	1,143.8	110.5	1,254.3
Education	607.0	626.3	1,233.4
Health and social work . . .	255.6	236.4	492.0
Other community, social and personal service activities . .	327.0	183.0	510.0
Private households with employed persons	28.4	2.8	31.2
Extraterritorial organizations and bodies	0.6	—	0.6
Sub-total	17,198.4	3,457.0	20,655.4
Activities not adequately defined .	1.3	—	1.3
Total employed	17,199.7	3,457.0	20,656.7
Unemployed	2,326.0	892.4	3,218.3
Total labour force	19,525.7	4,349.4	23,875.0

Source: ILO.

2014 (labour force survey, March–June 2014, '000 persons aged 10 years and over, incl. armed forces and unpaid family workers): Agriculture 4,139.7; Industry 6,975.1; Services 9,990.9; Total employed 21,105.7 (males 17,953.4, females 3,152.3); Unemployed 2,530.1 (males 1,772.1, females 757.9); Statistical discrepancy 1.5; Total labour force 23,637.3 (males 19,727.0, females 3,910.3).

Health and Welfare

KEY INDICATORS

Total fertility rate (children per woman, 2012)	1.9
Under-5 mortality rate (per 1,000 live births, 2012) . . .	18
HIV/AIDS (% of persons aged 15–49, 2013)	0.1
Physicians (per 1,000 head, 2005)	0.9
Hospital beds (per 1,000 head, 2009)	1.7
Health expenditure (2011): US $ per head (PPP)	874
Health expenditure (2011): % of GDP	4.6
Health expenditure (2011): public (% of total)	49.5
Access to water (% of persons, 2012)	96
Access to sanitation (% of persons, 2012)	89
Total carbon dioxide emissions ('000 metric tons, 2010) . .	571,612.0
Carbon dioxide emissions per head (metric tons, 2010) . .	7.7
Human Development Index (2013): ranking	75
Human Development Index (2013): value	0.749

For sources and definitions, see explanatory note on p. vi.

Agriculture

PRINCIPAL CROPS
('000 metric tons)

	2011	2012	2013
Wheat	12,339.4	13,800.0*	14,000.0*
Rice, paddy	2,746.6	2,400.0*	2,900.0*
Barley	2,853.6	3,400.0*	3,200.0*
Maize	2,746.6	1,223.0*	2,540.0*
Potatoes	5,577.6	5,400.0†	5,560.0†
Sugar cane†	5,850.0	6,000.0	6,200.0
Sugar beet†	4,100.0	4,150.0	4,185.0
Beans, dry	257.7	250.0†	253.0†
Chick-peas†	290.2	315.0	295.0
Lentils	71.8	85.0†	73.0†
Almonds, with shell . . .	92.5	100.0†	87.3†
Walnuts, with shell . . .	390.0	450.0†	454.0†
Pistachios†	472.1	472.1	478.6
Soybeans (Soya beans) . .	170.0*	200.0*	186.0
Cabbages and other brassicas† .	508.6	550.0	574.5
Lettuce and chicory† . . .	550.8	570.0	569.0
Tomatoes	5,565.2	6,000.0†	6,174.2†
Pumpkins, squash and gourds† .	951.2	965.0	897.3
Cucumbers and gherkins . .	1,532.8	1,600.0†	1,570.1†
Aubergines (Eggplants)† . . .	1,215.0	1,300.0	1,570.1
Chillies and peppers, green† . .	65.0	65.0	62.1
Onions, dry	2,168.0	2,260.0	2,381.6†
Garlic†	90.2	90.9	90.9
Watermelons	3,786.3	3,800.0†	3,947.1†
Cantaloupes and other melons† .	1,400.0	1,450.0	1,501.4
Oranges	1,412.2	1,285.0†	1,192.3†
Tangerines, mandarins, clementines and satsumas† .	800.0	825.0	837.3
Lemons and limes† . . .	560.1	600.0	584.6
Apples	1,843.0	1,700.0†	1,693.4†
Pears	106.7	147.0†	136.3†
Apricots	226.5	460.0†	457.3†
Sweet cherries	151.2*	200.0†	200.0†
Peaches and nectarines . .	476.4	500.0†	515.0†
Plums and sloes	288.7	295.0†	305.3†
Grapes	2,112.7	2,150.0†	2,046.4†
Figs	67.4	78.0†	78.4†
Dates	1,053.9	1,066.0†	1,083.7†
Tea	103.9	158.0†	160.0†

* Unofficial figure.
† FAO estimate(s).

Aggregate production ('000 metric tons, may include official, semi-official or estimated data): Total cereals 20,695.8 in 2011, 22,010.0 in 2012, 22,650.1 in 2013; Total roots and tubers 5,577.6 in 2011, 5,400.0 in 2012, 5,560.0 in 2013; Total vegetables (incl. melons) 22,486.1 in 2011, 23,498.7 in 2012, 23,651.6 in 2013; Total fruits (excl. melons) 11,743.3 in 2011, 11,971.7 in 2012, 11,806.5 in 2013.

Source: FAO.

LIVESTOCK
('000 head, FAO estimates, unless otherwise indicated)

	2011	2012	2013
Horses	140	140	140
Asses	1,600	1,600	1,600
Mules	175	175	175
Cattle	8,600	8,650	8,670
Buffaloes	192	166*	135
Camels	86†	85	66
Sheep	50,000	50,215†	50,220
Goats	22,000	22,094	22,100
Chickens	900,000	925,000	927,200
Ducks	1,600	1,600	1,650
Geese and guinea fowl . . .	1,000	1,000	1,000
Turkeys	2,000	2,000	2,000

* Unofficial figure.
† Official figure.

Source: FAO.

LIVESTOCK PRODUCTS
('000 metric tons)

	2011	2012	2013
Cattle meat	250	248	249*
Buffalo meat	4	5	5*
Sheep meat	104	126	127*
Goat meat*	142	143	143
Chicken meat	1,907	1,950*	1,956*
Turkey meat*	6	6	6
Cows' milk*	6,940	6,800	6,850
Buffaloes' milk*	85	80	65
Goats' milk	205	225*	228*
Hen eggs	559	625*	665*
Honey*	48	45	44
Wool: greasy*	61	62	62

* FAO estimate(s).

Source: FAO.

Forestry

ROUNDWOOD REMOVALS
('000 cubic metres, excl. bark)

	2010	2011	2012
Sawlogs, veneer logs and logs for sleepers	263	254	286
Pulpwood	199	176	196
Other industrial wood	235	230	248
Fuel wood	53	46	52
Total	750	706	782

2013: Production assumed to be unchanged from 2012 (FAO estimates).

Source: FAO.

SAWNWOOD PRODUCTION
('000 cubic metres, incl. railway sleepers)

	2010	2011	2012
Total (all broadleaved) . . .	32	31	33

2013: Production assumed to be unchanged from 2012 (FAO estimate).

Source: FAO.

Fishing

('000 metric tons, live weight)

	2010	2011	2012
Capture	443.7	487.8	542.4
Caspian sprat	27.1	20.7	24.1
Indian oil sardine	20.8	35.4	33.3
Kawakawa	16.3	22.2	26.2
Skipjack tuna	22.3	17.4	27.1
Longtail tuna	64.5	80.9	76.3
Yellowfin tuna	31.5	28.8	35.1
Aquaculture	220.0	247.3	296.6
Silver carp	66.9	72.7	85.0
Rainbow trout	91.5	106.4	131.0
Total catch	663.7	735.1	839.0

Source: FAO.

Production of caviar (metric tons, year ending 20 March): 6 in 2011/12; 4 in 2012/13; 4 in 2013/14.

Mining

CRUDE PETROLEUM
('000 barrels per day, year ending 20 March)

	2010/11	2011/12	2012/13
Total production	3,536	3,619	3,742

Total production ('000 barrels per day, estimate): 3,558 in 2013 (Source: BP, *Statistical Review of World Energy*).

NATURAL GAS
(excluding reinjection gas; million cu metres, year ending 20 March)

	2005/06	2006/07	2007/08
Consumption (domestic)* . . .	102,200	109,800	122,500
Flared	15,800	15,100	15,000
Regional uses and wastes . . .	7,400	5,000	7,300
Gas for export	4,800	5,700	5,600
Less Net imports	5,200	6,300	6,200
Total production	125,000	129,300	144,200

* Includes gas for household, industrial, generator and refinery consumption.

Natural gas consumption (domestic): 150,800 in 2010/11; 152,700 in 2011/12; 152,000 in 2012/13.

Gas injection (year ending 20 March, million cu metres): 26,663 in 2006/07; 25,971 in 2007/08; 28,448 in 2008/09; 28,840 in 2009/10.

OTHER MINERALS
('000 metric tons, unless otherwise indicated, year ending 20 March)

	2009/10	2010/11	2011/12*
Iron ore: gross weight	35,000*	44,355	50,000
Iron ore: metal content* . . .	16,500	20,900	24,000
Copper concentrates*† . . .	257	259	260
Bauxite	681	818	820
Lead concentrates*†	25	40	40
Zinc concentrates*†	80	105	105
Manganese ore‡	132	194	200
Chromium concentrates§ . . .	45	418	400
Molybdenum concentrates (metric tons)*†	3,900	3,400	3,900
Gold (kilograms)*†	2,000	2,000	2,500
Bentonite	350	377	400
Kaolin	1,480	2,000*	1,500
Other clays*	550	550	550
Magnesite	127	173	170
Fluorspar (Fluorite)	72*	56	60
Feldspar	652	577	580
Barite (Barytes)	326	271	270
Salt (unrefined)	3,291	2,715	3,000
Gypsum (crude)	11,914	14,657	15,000
Mica (metric tons)	2,860	7,130	7,000
Talc	96	59	60
Turquoise (kilograms)* . . .	20,000	20,000	21,000
Coal	2,300*	2,499	1,300

* Estimate(s).

† Figures refer to the metal content of ores and concentrates.

‡ Figures refer to gross weight. The estimated metal content ('000 metric tons) was: 46 in 2009/10, 68 in 2010/11, 70 in 2011/12.

§ Figures refer to gross weight. The estimated chromic oxide content ('000 metric tons) was: 22 in 2009/10, 200 in 2010/11, 190 in 2011/12.

Source: US Geological Survey.

Industry

PETROLEUM PRODUCTS
(average cu m per day, year ending 20 March)

	2007/08	2008/09	2009/10
Liquefied petroleum gas . . .	7,723	8,071	8,362
Motor spirit (petrol) . . .	45,080	51,496	59,515
Burning oil (for electricity) . .	21,680	21,347	18,519
Jet fuel	3,426	3,519	4,188
Gas-diesel (distillate fuel) oil . .	81,549	84,957	88,702
Residual fuel oils	73,020	77,132	76,101
Petroleum bitumen (asphalt) . .	976	616	698

OTHER PRODUCTS
(year ending 20 March)

	2009/10	2010/11	2011/12
Refined sugar ('000 metric tons) .	1,409	1,846	1,846
Soft drinks (million bottles) . .	3,849	3,024	3,458
Malt liquor (million bottles) . .	870	1,001	1,405
Cigarettes (million)	26,898	22,354	21,708
Threads ('000 metric tons) .	324	374	412
Finished fabrics (million metres) .	293	280	246
Machine-made carpets ('000 sq m)	75,642	77,245	5,462
Hand-woven carpets (moquette— '000 sq m)	71,995	59,609	66,936
Paper ('000 metric tons) . .	466	487	493
Detergent powder ('000 metric tons)	594	541	575
Soap (metric tons)	57,750	82,869	78,879
Cement ('000 metric tons) . .	49,471	57,181	63,205
Washing machines ('000) . .	667	690	333
Radio receivers ('000) . . .	656	356	555
Television receivers ('000) . .	389	519	406
Water meters ('000) . . .	1,611	556	498
Electricity meters ('000) . . .	1,757	904	3,755
Passenger cars and jeeps ('000) .	1,442	1,428	1,628
Electric energy (million kWh) .	221,314	232,994	240,064

Electric energy (million kWh): 248,166 in 2012/13.

Finance

CURRENCY AND EXCHANGE RATES

Monetary Units
100 dinars = 1 Iranian rial (IR).

Sterling, Dollar and Euro Equivalents (31 December 2014)
£1 sterling = 42,357.0 rials;
US $1 = 27,138.0 rials;
€1 = 32,948.2 rials;
100,000 Iranian rials = £2.36 = $3.68 = €3.04.

Average Exchange Rate (rials per US $)
2012   12,175.55
2013   18,414.45
2014   25,941.66

Note: In March 1993 the former multiple exchange rate system was unified, and since then the exchange rate of the rial has been market-determined. The foregoing information on average exchange rates refers to the base rate, applicable to receipts from exports of petroleum and gas, payments for imports of essential goods and services, debt-servicing costs and imports related to large national projects. There was also an export rate, set at a mid-point of US $1 = 3,007.5 rials in May 1995, which applied to receipts from non-petroleum exports and to all other official current account transactions not effected at the base rate. In addition, a market rate was determined by transactions on the Tehran Stock Exchange: at 31 January 2002 it was US $1 = 7,924 rials. The weighted average of all exchange rates (rials per US $, year ending 20 December) was: 3,206 in 1997/98; 4,172 in 1998/99; 5,731 in 1999/2000. A new unified exchange rate, based on the market rate, took effect from 21 March 2002.

BUDGET
(consolidated accounts of central government and Oil Stabilization Fund—OSF, '000 million rials, year ending 20 March)

Revenue	2007/08	2008/09*	2009/10†
Oil and gas revenue	578,708	569,951	436,159
Budget revenue	444,278	559,589	498,071
Transfers from OSF . . .	209,098	184,235	223,099
Revenues transferred to OSF .	134,430	10,362	−61,912
Non-oil budgetary revenue . .	237,893	283,918	354,315
Tax revenue	162,579	203,042	240,454
Taxes on income, profits and capital gains	97,097	130,453	153,994
Domestic taxes on goods and services	16,663	15,900	29,771
Taxes on international trade and transactions	48,819	56,689	56,689
Non-tax revenue	75,314	80,876	113,861
Non-oil OSF revenues	4,551	6,038	6,223
Total	821,152	859,906	796,697

Expenditure	2007/08	2008/09*	2009/10†
Central government expenditures	710,022	841,093	884,798
Current expenditure . . .	562,306	595,254	676,682
Wages and salaries . . .	151,583	211,000	229,000
Interest payments . . .	7,371	5,982	5,982
Subsidies	62,862	61,000	68,000
Goods and services . . .	39,119	55,000	71,600
Grants	13,823	50,800	28,700
Social benefits	64,492	139,605	181,000
Gasoline imports	33,820	60,867	34,300
Other expenses	189,236	11,000	58,100
Capital expenditure	147,716	245,839	208,116
OSF expenditures	40,289	19,148	—
Total	750,311	860,240	884,798

* Estimates.
† Projections.

Source: IMF, *Islamic Republic of Iran: 2009 Article IV Consultation-Staff Report; Staff Supplement; Public Information Notice on the Executive Board Discussion; and Statement by the Executive Director for Iran* (March 2010).

2011/12 ('000 million rials): *Revenue:* Tax revenue 359,451 (Taxes on income, profits and capital gains 207,505; Domestic taxes on goods and services 60,104; Taxes on international trade and transactions 78,930); Other revenue 844,263 (Property income 731,636); Total 1,203,714. *Expenditure:* Current expenditure 904,225; Net acquisition of non-financial assets 287,560; Total 1,191,784 (Source: IMF—see below).

2012/13 ('000 million rials): *Revenue:* Tax revenue 395,169 (Taxes on income, profits and capital gains 232,385; Domestic taxes on goods and services 70,487; Taxes on international trade and transactions 76,403); Other revenue 620,634; Total 1,015,803. *Expenditure:* Current expenditure 889,974; Net acquisition of non-financial assets 149,282; Total 1,039,256 (Source: IMF—see below).

2013/14 ('000 million rials, estimates): *Revenue:* Tax revenue 469,745 (Taxes on income, profits and capital gains 271,296; Domestic taxes on goods and services 123,829; Taxes on international trade and transactions 53,463); Other revenue 788,217; Total 1,257,962. *Expenditure:* Current expenditure 1,232,400; Net acquisition of non-financial assets 107,380; Total 1,339,780 (Source: *Islamic Republic of Iran: 2014 Article IV Consultation-Staff Report; Press Release; and Statement by the Executive Director for the Islamic Republic of Iran*—April 2014).

INTERNATIONAL RESERVES
(US $ million at 31 December)*

	2011	2012	2013
IMF special drawing rights . .	2,359	2,368	2,390

* No official figures have been available for reserves of gold or foreign exchange since 1982 (when the value of foreign exchange reserves was US $5,287m.), although together these were believed to be worth more than US $100,000m. in 2013.

Source: partly IMF, *International Financial Statistics*.

MONEY SUPPLY
('000 million rials at 20 December)

	2008	2009	2010
Currency outside banks . . .	122,603	147,878	210,289
Non-financial public enterprises' deposits at Central Bank . .	16,978	15,496	18,353
Demand deposits at commercial banks	300,451	317,415	150,432
Total money	440,031	480,790	379,073

Source: IMF, *International Financial Statistics*.

COST OF LIVING
(Consumer Price Index in urban areas, year ending 20 March; base: 2011/12 = 100)

	2010/11	2012/13	2013/14
Food and non-alcoholic beverages .	79.4	144.6	204.9
Clothing and footwear	81.9	147.8	219.4
Housing, water, electricity, gas, and other fuels	84.6	112.9	135.7
All items (incl. others) . . .	82.3	130.5	175.9

NATIONAL ACCOUNTS
('000 million rials at current prices, year ending 20 March, preliminary)

Expenditure on the Gross Domestic Product

	2011/12	2012/13	2013/14
Final consumption expenditure .	3,409,775	4,254,537	5,674,162
Private	2,778,553	3,546,398	4,690,756
Public	631,222	708,140	983,406
Changes in inventories . . .	553,658	758,470	494,883*
Gross fixed capital formation .	1,648,671	1,973,068	2,528,109
Total domestic expenditure .	5,612,104	6,986,075	8,697,154
Exports of goods and services .	1,612,985	1,598,714	2,588,373
Less Imports of goods and services	1,039,833	1,482,252	1,864,313
Statistical discrepancy . . .	99,999	47,058	—
GDP at market prices . . .	6,285,255	7,149,595	9,421,216
GDP at constant 2004/05 prices	2,157,934	2,011,554	1,972,852

* Changes in inventories in 2013 includes statistical discrepancy.

Gross Domestic Product by Economic Activity

	2011/12	2012/13	2013/14
Hydrocarbon GDP	1,564,360	1,164,713	1,589,633
Non-hydrocarbon GDP . . .	4,681,406	5,926,676	7,753,438
Agriculture	367,196	558,475	843,647
Industry	1,338,222	1,768,256	2,165,098
Mining	47,827	73,237	94,078
Manufacturing	689,284	893,743	1,090,953
Construction	491,697	691,705	863,908
Electricity, gas and water . .	109,414	109,571	116,159
Services	3,142,750	3,798,693	4,930,060
Transport, storage and communication	510,053	620,582	791,150
Banking and insurance . . .	221,832	273,762	268,931
Trade, restaurants and hotels .	877,350	1,064,238	1,361,692
Real estate and professional services	824,903	1,004,185	1,384,695
Public services	518,415	597,818	805,110
Private services	190,197	238,108	318,482
Less Imputed bank service charge.	166,762	198,747	185,367
GDP at factor prices . . .	6,245,766	7,091,389	9,343,071
Net indirect taxes	39,489	58,207	78,145
GDP at market prices . . .	6,285,255	7,149,595	9,421,216

BALANCE OF PAYMENTS
(US $ million, year ending 20 March)

	2011/12	2012/13	2013/14*
Exports of goods f.o.b. . . .	144,874	98,033	93,015
Petroleum and gas . . .	118,232	68,135	64,789
Non-petroleum and gas exports	26,642	29,899	28,226
Imports of goods f.o.b. . . .	−77,805	−67,058	−60,047
Trade balance	67,069	30,975	32,968
Exports of services	8,621	6,687	6,593
Imports of services	−17,053	−12,979	−13,283
Balance on goods and services	58,637	24,683	26,277
Income received	2,171	2,469	2,354
Income paid	−1,849	−1,431	−1,248
Balance on goods, services and income	58,960	25,721	27,382
Transfers (net)	423	552	583
Current balance	59,383	26,272	27,965
Capital account (net) . . .	−684	−249	} −26,621
Financial account (net) . . .	−37,291	−21,799	
Overall balance	21,409	4,224	1,344

* Preliminary.

External Trade

PRINCIPAL COMMODITIES
(US $ million, year ending 20 March)

Imports c.i.f. (distribution by SITC)	2010/11	2011/12	2012/13
Food and live animals . . .	6,790	7,388	11,517
Cereals and cereal preparations .	2,278	2,998	6,370
Crude materials (inedible) except fuels	2,156	2,300	1,805
Mineral products	3,867	3,920	1,538
Animal and vegetable oils and fats	1,444	1,625	2,041
Vegetable oils and fats . . .	1,440	1,620	2,035
Chemicals and related products	7,011	7,441	6,773
Chemical elements and compounds	1,434	1,440	1,444
Plastic, cellulose and artificial resins	2,190	2,536	2,082
Basic manufactures	14,231	13,442	10,631
Iron and steel	9,235	8,357	6,121
Machinery and transport equipment	20,713	22,136	16,271
Non-electrical machinery . . .	10,692	10,291	7,579
Electrical machinery, apparatus, etc.	4,400	5,456	4,845
Transport equipment	5,620	6,388	3,847
Miscellaneous manufactured articles	1,788	1,809	1,536
Total (incl. others)	64,450	61,808	53,451

Exports f.o.b.*	2010/11	2011/12	2012/13
Agricultural and traditional goods	5,056	5,181	5,560
Carpets	557	559	427
Fruits (fresh and dried) . . .	2,194	2,204	2,482
Industrial manufactures . .	20,194	27,590	25,137
Oil and gas products	4,892	8,485	5,149
Iron and steel	1,015	1,522	1,804
Organic chemicals	2,818	3,770	3,432
Plastic materials and products .	2,860	3,380	3,643
Total (incl. others)	26,551	33,819	32,567

* Excluding exports of crude petroleum and associated gas (US $ million): 90,191 in 2010/11; 118,232 in 2011/12; 68,135 in 2012/13 (preliminary).

2013/14 Total imports 49,422; Total exports 31,332.

Note: Imports include registration fee, but exclude defence-related imports and imports of refined petroleum products.

PRINCIPAL TRADING PARTNERS
(US $ million, year ending 20 March)

Imports c.i.f.	2008/09	2009/10	2010/11
Austria	1,131	736	728
Belgium	994	569	642
Brazil	570	614	634
Canada	672	312	n.a.
China, People's Republic	4,945	4,846	5,804
France	1,992	1,688	2,042
Germany	5,369	4,688	4,590
India	1,819	1,793	1,297
Italy	1,979	1,898	1,746
Japan	1,344	1,423	1,568
Korea, Republic	3,105	3,468	3,643
Netherlands	535	1,092	1,031
Russia	1,405	1,016	1,167
Singapore	882	1,015	1,188
Sweden	716	600	865
Switzerland	3,542	2,137	3,772
Turkey	1,508	2,025	3,996
United Arab Emirates	13,491	16,187	21,182
United Kingdom	2,039	1,654	732
Total (incl. others)	56,042	55,287	64,450

Exports f.o.b.	2008/09	2009/10	2010/11
Afghanistan	633	1,047	1,378
Azerbaijan	369	374	375
Belgium	406	509	439
China, People's Republic	2,051	3,126	4,571
Ecuador	224	n.a.	n.a.
Germany	319	349	347
Hong Kong	150	200	451
India	1,159	1,264	1,822
Indonesia	321	368	610
Iraq	2,762	4,560	4,539
Italy	325	436	337
Japan	589	360	443
Korea, Republic	821	543	576
Malaysia	186	97	n.a.
Netherlands	346	298	284
Pakistan	296	435	551
Philippines	108	222	235
Russia	358	333	331
Saudi Arabia	388	177	n.a.
Spain	175	169	177
Syria	316	379	524
Taiwan	376	184	426
Tajikistan	187	163	190
Turkey	530	593	1,056
Turkmenistan	249	358	415
United Arab Emirates	2,322	2,934	3,336
Total (incl. others)	18,334	21,891	26,551

Note: Exports exclude crude petroleum and associated gas.

2011/12: Total imports 61,808; Total exports 33,819.

2012/13: Total imports 53,451; Total exports 32,567.

2013/14: Total imports 49,422; Total exports 31,332.

Transport

RAILWAYS
(traffic, year ending 20 March)

	2011/12	2012/13	2013/14
Passengers carried ('000)	28,560	27,015	25,533
Passenger-km (million)	17,877	17,172	17,409
Freight carried ('000 metric tons)	33,104	34,276	32,693
Freight ton-km (million)	21,008	22,604	22,400

ROAD TRAFFIC
(registered motor vehicles, year ending 20 March)

	2011/12	2012/13	2013/14
Passenger cars*	1,378,860	739,330	691,740
Pick-ups and light trucks	200,035	136,982	98,651
Motorcycles	813,386	418,733	312,594
Total (incl. others)	2,482,718	1,333,609	1,127,361

* Including ambulances.

SHIPPING

Flag Registered Fleet
(at 31 December)

	2012	2013	2014
Number of vessels	619	757	787
Total displacement ('000 grt)	2,394.7	3,416.9	3,418.3

Source: Lloyd's List Intelligence (www.lloydslistintelligence.com).

International Seaborne Freight Traffic
(year ending 20 March, '000 metric tons)*

	2011/12	2012/13	2013/14
Goods loaded	57,188	57,439	64,678
Crude petroleum and petroleum products	21,029	16,877	19,849
Goods unloaded	64,471	66,673	61,319
Petroleum products	20,605	21,302	23,599

* Cargo loaded onto and from vessels with a capacity of 1,000 metric tons or greater only.

CIVIL AVIATION
(year ending 20 March)

	2011/12	2012/13	2013/14
Passengers ('000):			
domestic flights	16,481	16,655	16,617
international arrivals	4,379	4,079	3,001
international departures	4,404	4,138	3,070
Freight (excl. mail, metric tons):			
domestic flights	56,413	13,581	11,157
international arrivals	61,221	41,230	34,235
international departures	24,806	26,017	17,544
Mail (metric tons):			
domestic flights	3,843	3,005	2,676
international arrivals	7,842	1,124	934
international departures	4,180	1,271	944

Tourism

FOREIGN TOURIST ARRIVALS

Country of nationality	2011	2012	2013
Afghanistan	202,369	308,183	392,559
Azerbaijan	732,201	677,457	1,077,713
Iraq	589,074	1,055,447	1,603,920
Pakistan	187,920	170,754	151,470
Saudi Arabia	74,275	111,049	155,196
Turkey	419,853	392,615	391,283
Turkmenistan	135,683	141,533	169,618
Total (incl. others)	3,353,713	3,833,577	4,768,836

Tourism receipts (US $ million, excl. passenger transport): 2,707 in 2010; 2,381 in 2011; 1,114 in 2012.

Source: World Tourism Organization.

Communications Media

	2011	2012	2013
Telephones ('000 main lines in use)	27,766.9	28,758.5	29,688.6
Mobile cellular telephones ('000 subscribers)	56,043.0	58,157.5	65,246.2
Internet subscribers ('000)	5,240.2	n.a.	n.a.
Broadband subscribers ('000)	1,772.9	3,076.2	4,351.2
Book production*:			
titles	61,724	58,236	60,076
copies ('000)	173,592	152,135	135,435

* Twelve months beginning 21 March of year stated.

Newspapers and periodicals (number of titles, year ending 20 March 2006): Daily 183; Other 4,528.

Source: partly International Telecommunication Union.

Education

(2013/14 unless otherwise indicated)

	Institutions	Teachers	Students ('000)		
			Males	Females	Total
Special	1,644	15,306	45.0	27.7	72.7
Pre-primary	16,010	1,898*	271.6	260.3	531.9
Primary	60,066	284,271	3,610.9	3,407.4	7,018.3
Lower secondary:					
mainstream	22,765	130,961	1,085.2	986.0	2,071.2
adult	848		13.1	8.7	21.8
Upper secondary:					
mainstream	21,793	199,911	1,696.6	1,591.6	3,288.2
adult	5,233		160.3	242.1	402.4
Pre-university:					
mainstream	8,593	n.a.	177.3	263.3	440.6
adult*	1,068		24.1	19.3	43.4
Teacher training*	98	n.a.	16.6	18.9	35.5
Islamic Azad University	n.a.	93,186	1,008.4	628.4	1,636.8
Other higher	n.a.	192,879	1,541.8	1,625.4	3,167.2

* 2011/12.

Pupil-teacher ratio (primary education, UNESCO estimate): 20.5 in 2008/09 (Source: UNESCO Institute for Statistics).

Adult literacy rate (UNESCO estimates): 84.3% (males 89.4%; females 79.2%) in 2012 (Source: UNESCO Institute for Statistics).

Directory

The Government

SUPREME RELIGIOUS LEADER

Wali Faqih: Ayatollah SAYED ALI KHAMENEI.

HEAD OF STATE

President: Dr HASSAN ROUHANI (assumed office 3 August 2013).

First Vice-President: ESHAQ JAHANGIRI.

Head of the Presidential Office and Chief of Staff: MUHAMMAD NAHVANDIAN.

Executive Vice-President: MUHAMMAD SHARIATMADARI.

Vice-President in charge of Legal Affairs: ELHAM AMINZADEH.

Vice-President for Legal and Parliamentary Affairs: MAJEAD ANSARI.

Vice-President for Science and Technology: SORENA SATTARI.

Vice-President for Women and Family Affairs: SHAHINDOKHT MOLAVERDI.

Vice-President for Supervision and Strategic Affairs: MUHAMMAD BAGHER NOBAKHT.

Vice-President and Head of the Cultural Heritage, Handicrafts and Tourism Organization: MASSOUD SULTANIFAR.

Vice-President and Head of the Atomic Energy Organization: ALI AKBAR SALEHI.

Vice-President and Head of the Martyrs' and Self-Sacrificers' Affairs Foundation: SEYED MUHAMMAD ALI SHAHIDI.

Vice-President and Head of the Organization for the Protection of the Environment: MASSOUMEH EBTEKAR.

COUNCIL OF MINISTERS
(April 2015)

Minister of Education: ALI ASGHAR FANI.

Minister of Communications and Information Technology: MAHMOUD VAEZI.

Minister of Intelligence: MAHMOUD ALAVI.

Minister of Economic Affairs and Finance: ALI TAYEBNIA.

Minister of Foreign Affairs: MUHAMMAD JAVAD ZARIF.

Minister of Health and Medical Education: HASSAN QAZIZADEH HASHEMI.

Minister of Labour, Co-operatives and Social Affairs: ALI RABEI.

Minister of Agricultural Jihad: MAHMOUD HOJJATI.

Minister of Justice: MOSTAFA POUR-MUHAMMADI.

Minister of Defence: HOSSEIN DEHQAN.

Minister of Roads and Urban Development: ABBAS AHMAD AKHOUNDI.

Minister of Industries, Mines and Trade: MUHAMMAD REZA NEMATZADEH.

Minister of Culture and Islamic Guidance: ALI JANNATI.

Minister of the Interior: ABDOLREZA RAHMANI FAZLI.

Minister of Science, Research and Technology: MUHAMMAD FARHADI.

Minister of Petroleum: BIJAN NAMDAR ZANGANEH.

Minister of Energy: HAMID CHITCHIAN.

Minister of Sport and Youth Affairs: MAHMOUD GOUDARZI.

MINISTRIES

Office of the President: POB 1423-13185, Pasteur Ave, Tehran 13168-43311; tel. (21) 64451; e-mail webmaster@president.ir; internet www.president.ir.

Ministry of Agricultural Jihad: 20 Malaei Ave, Vali-e-Asr Sq., Tehran; tel. (21) 64583101; fax (21) 66412123; e-mail pr@maj.ir; internet www.maj.ir.

Ministry of Communications and Information Technology: POB 15875-4415, Shariati St, Tehran 16314; tel. (21) 88114315; fax (21) 88467210; e-mail khajeh@ict.gov.ir; internet www.ict.gov.ir.

Ministry of Culture and Islamic Guidance: POB 5158, Baharestan Sq., Tehran 11365; tel. (21) 38512583; fax (21) 33117535; e-mail info@ershad.gov.ir; internet www.farhang.gov.ir.

Ministry of Defence: Shahid Yousuf Kaboli St, Sayed Khandan Area, Tehran; tel. (21) 26126988; e-mail info@mod.ir; internet www.mod.ir.

Ministry of Economic Affairs and Finance: Bab Homayoon St, Imam Khomeini Sq., Tehran; tel. (21) 39909; fax (21) 33967205; e-mail mzandi22@yahoo.com; internet mefa.ir.

Ministry of Education: Si-e-Tir St, Imam Khomeini Sq., Tehran; tel. (21) 82281111; fax (21) 88805431; e-mail negah@medu.ir; internet www.medu.ir.

Ministry of Energy: POB 19968-32611, Niayesh Highway, Vali-e-Asr Ave, Tehran; tel. (21) 81606000; fax (21) 81606132; e-mail info-portal@moe.org.ir; internet www.moe.gov.ir.

Ministry of Foreign Affairs: Imam Khomeini Sq., Tehran; tel. (21) 61151; fax (21) 66743149; e-mail info@mfa.gov.ir; internet www.mfa.gov.ir.

Ministry of Health and Medical Education: POB 310, Jomhouri Islami Ave, Hafez Crossing, Tehran 11344; tel. (21) 88363560; fax (21) 88364111; e-mail webmaster@mohme.gov.ir; internet www.mohme.gov.ir.

Ministry of Industries, Mines and Trade: Shahid Kalantari, Ostad Negatollahi St, Ferdosi Sq., Tehran; tel. (21) 88906563; fax (21) 88903650; e-mail info@mimt.gov.ir; internet www.mimt.gov.ir.

Ministry of Intelligence: POB 16765-1947, Second Negarestan St, Pasdaran Ave, Tehran; tel. (21) 233031; fax (21) 23305.

Ministry of the Interior: Jahad Sq., Fatemi St, Tehran; tel. (21) 84861; fax (21) 88964678; e-mail ravabetomomi@moi.gov.ir; internet www.moi.ir.

Ministry of Justice: Panzdah-e-Khordad Sq., Tehran 14158-55139; tel. (21) 88383201; fax (21) 3904986; e-mail info@justice.ir; internet www.justice.ir.

Ministry of Labour, Co-operatives and Social Affairs: Azadi St, Tehran; tel. (21) 66580031; e-mail infopack@mcls.gov.ir; internet www.mcls.gov.ir.

Ministry of Petroleum: Hafez Crossing, Taleghani Ave, Tehran 15936-57919; tel. (21) 61651; fax (21) 88939304; e-mail info@mop.ir; internet www.mop.ir.

Ministry of Roads and Urban Development: Dadman Tower, Africa Blvd, Tehran; tel. (21) 88646130; internet www.mrud.ir.

Ministry of Science, Research and Technology: POB 15875-4375, Central Bldg, Ostad Nejatollahi Ave, Tehran; tel. (21) 82231000; fax (21) 88827234; e-mail zahedi@msrt.ir; internet www.msrt.ir.

Ministry of Sport and Youth Affairs: Tehran.

President

Presidential Election, 14 June 2013

Candidates	Votes	%
Hassan Rouhani	18,613,329	50.71
Muhammad Baqir Qalibaf	6,077,292	16.56
Saeed Jalili	4,168,946	11.36
Mohsen Rezai	3,884,412	10.58
Ali Akbar Velayati	2,268,753	6.18
Muhammad Gharazi	446,015	1.22
Total	**36,704,156***	**100.00**

* Including 1,245,409 invalid votes (3.39% of total votes cast).

Legislature

MAJLIS-E-SHURA-E ISLAMI—ISLAMIC CONSULTATIVE ASSEMBLY

Elections to the eighth Majlis took place in early 2008. Prior to the elections the Council of Guardians and the Ministry of the Interior barred at least 1,700 of the 7,168 registered candidates from standing, including a number of current Majlis deputies. The majority of the barred candidates were recognized as being 'reformists'. At the first round of voting, held on 14 March, 208 deputies received a sufficient number of votes to be elected directly to the Majlis; at the second round, on 25 April, a further 79 deputies were elected. Three seats remained vacant following both rounds, after election officials had annulled the results for unspecified reasons; by-elections for these seats were to be held at a later date. According to official reports, 'conservatives' controlled the eighth Majlis, with an estimated 198–200 seats; 'reformists' secured around 46–50 seats, and some 40–43 seats were held by 'independents'. A reported 29 of the 30 seats in Tehran were filled by 'conservatives', with only one seat going to a 'reformist' candidate. However, despite the 'conservatives' having consolidated their control of the Majlis, some of the new deputies were reported to be critical of President Mahmoud Ahmadinejad's policies. On 2 March 2012 the first round of elections to the ninth Majlis took place. Of the 290 seats, 'conservatives' secured 143 seats, while 'reformists' took 59 seats. Candidates representing religious minorities held 14 seats and nine seats went to 'independents'. A second round of voting for the 65 remaining seats was held on 4 May, at which 'conservatives' secured 41 seats, 'reformists' secured 13 seats and 11 seats went to 'independents'.

Islamic Consultative Assembly: Baharestan Sq., Tehran; tel. (21) 33440236; fax (21) 33440309; e-mail islamic@parliran.ir; internet www.parliran.ir.

Speaker: ALI ARDESHIR LARIJANI.

SHURA-YE ALI-YE AMNIYYAT-E MELLI—SUPREME NATIONAL SECURITY COUNCIL

Formed in July 1989 (in place of the Supreme Defence Council) to co-ordinate defence and national security policies, the political programme and intelligence reports, and social, cultural and economic activities related to defence and security. The Council is chaired by the President and includes a representative of the Wali Faqih, the Minister of the Interior, the Speaker of the Majlis, the Head of the Judiciary, the Chief of the Supreme Command Council of the Armed Forces, the Minister of Foreign Affairs, the Head of the Management and Planning Organization, and the Minister of Intelligence.

Secretary: Rear Adm. ALI SHAMKHANI.

MAJLIS-E KHOBREGAN—ASSEMBLY OF EXPERTS

Elections were held on 10 December 1982 to appoint an Assembly of Experts which was to choose an eventual successor to the Wali Faqih (then Ayatollah Khomeini) after his death. The Constitution provides for a three- or five-man body to assume the leadership of the country if there is no recognized successor on the death of the Wali Faqih. The Council comprises 86 clerics, who are elected by direct suffrage for an eight-year term. Elections to a fourth term of the Council were held on 15 December 2006.

Assembly of Experts: Tehran—e-mail info@majleskhobregan.com; internet www.majlesekhobregan.ir.

Chairman: Ayatollah MUHAMMAD YAZDI.

SHURA-E-NIGAHBAN—COUNCIL OF GUARDIANS

The Council of Guardians, composed of six qualified Muslim jurists appointed by Ayatollah Khomeini and six lay Muslim lawyers, appointed by the Majlis from among candidates nominated by the Head of the Judiciary, was established in 1980 to supervise elections and to examine legislation adopted by the Majlis, ensuring that it accords with the Constitution and with Islamic precepts.

Chairman: Ayatollah AHMAD JANNATI.

SHURA-YE TASHKHIS-E MASLAHAT-E NEZAM— COUNCIL TO DETERMINE THE EXPEDIENCY OF THE ISLAMIC ORDER

Formed in February 1988, by order of Ayatollah Khomeini, to arbitrate on legal and theological questions in legislation approved by the Majlis, in the event of a dispute between the latter and the supervisory Council of Guardians. Its permanent members, defined in March 1997, are Heads of the Legislative, Judiciary and Executive Powers, the jurist members of the Council of Guardians, and the Minister or head of organization concerned with the pertinent arbitration. In October 2005 the powers of the Expediency Council were extended, allowing it to supervise all branches of government. Former President Ali Akbar Hashemi Rafsanjani was reappointed as Chairman of the Council in March 2012; the members of the Council are appointed for a term of five years.

Chairman: Hojatoleslam ALI AKBAR HASHEMI RAFSANJANI.

Political Organizations

Numerous political organizations were registered in the late 1990s, following the election of former President Khatami, and have tended to be regarded as either 'conservative' or 'reformist', the principal factions in the legislature. There are also a small number of centrist political parties. Under the Iranian electoral system, parties do not field candidates *per se* at elections, but instead back lists of candidates, who are allowed to be members of more than one party. In the mid-2000s there were estimated to be more than 100 registered political organizations, some of which are listed below:

Democratic Coalition of Reformists: Tehran; f. 2010; Sec.-Gen. MASSOUMEH EBTEKAR.

Eslahteleban-e Motedel (Moderate Reformists): Tehran; Leader ALI MOTAHARI.

Jebhe-ye Besiret ve Bidari-ye Eslami (Insight and Islamic Awakening Front): Tehran; Leader SHAHABEDDIN SADRI.

Jebhe-ye Istadegi (Resistance Front): Tehran.

Jebhe-ye Mottehed-e Osulgeraian (United Front of Principalists): Tehran; officially formed in 2008; reformed in 2012.

Jebhe-ye Paydari-ye Enghelab-e Eslami (Front of Islamic Revolution Stability): Tehran; internet www.jebhepaydari.ir; f. 2011; Leader GHOLAM-HUSSEIN ELHAM; Sec.-Gen. MORTEZA AGHA-TEHRANI.

Jebhe-ye Seda-ye Mellet (People's Voice Front): Tehran; f. 2011; Leader MOHSEN REZAI; Sec.-Gen. ALI MOTAHARI.

Jebhe-ye Touhid ve Edalet (Monotheism and Justice Front): Tehran; f. 2012; Leader MANOUCHEHR MOTTAKI; Sec.-Gen. ESFANDIAR RAHIM-MASHAI.

Labour Coalition (LC): Tehran; f. 2000; Leader HOSSEIN KAMALI; Sec.-Gen. SOHEILA JOLODARZADEH.

Most of the following are either registered political parties that have boycotted elections to the Majlis-e-Shura-e Islami (Islamic Consultative Assembly) in the 2000s, or are unregistered organizations or guerrilla groups:

Ansar-e Hezbollah (Helpers of the Party of God): f. 1995; militant, ultra-conservative youth movement; pledges allegiance to the Wali Faqih (supreme religious leader).

Daftar-e Tahkim-e Vahdat (Office for Strengthening Unity): Tehran; f. 1979; org. of Islamist university students who supported Khatami in the presidential election of 1997 and reformist candidates in the Majlis elections of 2000; Sec.-Gen AHMAD ZEIDABADI.

Democratic Party of Iranian Kurdistan: 17 ave d'Italie, Paris 75013, France; tel. 1-45-85-64-31; fax 1-45-85-20-93; e-mail pdkiran@club-internet.fr; internet www.pdki.org; f. 1945; seeks a federal system of govt in Iran, in order to secure the national rights of the Kurdish people; consultative mem. of the Socialist International; 95,000 mems; Sec.-Gen. MUSTAFA HIJRI.

Fedayin-e-Khalq (Organization of the Iranian People's Fedayeen—Majority): Postfach 260268, 50515 Köln, Germany; e-mail info@fadai.org; internet www.fadai.org; f. 1971; Marxist; Leader BEHROUZ KHALIQ.

Fraksion-e Hezbollah: f. 1996 by deputies in the Majlis who had contested the 1996 legislative elections as a loose coalition known as the Society of Combatant Clergy; Leader ALI AKBAR HOSSAINI.

Free Life Party of Kurdistan (Parti Jiyani Azadi Kurdistan—PJAK): f. 2004; militant org. that operates in mountainous areas of Iran and northern Iraq; apparently has close links with the Kurdistan Workers' Party (PKK—Partiya Karkeren Kurdistan) of Turkey; seeks a federal, secular system of govt in Iran, in order to secure the national rights of the Kurdish people; Sec.-Gen. RAHMAN HAJI AHMADI.

Hezb-e Etemad-e Melli (National Confidence Party—NCP): Tehran; tel. (21) 88373305; fax (21) 88373306; e-mail info@etemademelli.ir; f. 2005 by Mahdi Karrubi, fmrly of the Militant Clergy Association, shortly after his defeat in the presidential election of June; reformist, centrist; Sec.-Gen. MAHDI KARRUBI.

Hezb-e Hambastegi-ye Iran-e Islami (Islamic Iran Solidarity Party): f. 1998; reformist; Sec.-Gen. EDRAHIM ASGHARZADEH.

Hezb-e-Komunist Iran (Communist Party of Iran): POB 70445, 107 25 Stockholm, Sweden; e-mail cpi@cpiran.org; internet www.cpiran.org; f. 1979 by dissident mems of Tudeh Party; Sec.-Gen. 'AZARYUN'.

Iran National Front (Jebhe Melli Iran): US Section, POB 136, Audubon Station, New York, NY 10032, USA; e-mail contact@jebhemelli.net; internet www.jebhemelli.net; f. late 1940s by the late Dr Muhammad Mussadeq; secular, pro-democracy opposition group, which also seeks to further religious freedom within Iran; Leader ADIB BOROUMAND.

Jame'e-ye Eslaami-e Mohandesin (Islamic Society of Engineers): f. 1988; conservative; mems incl. fmr President Mahmoud Ahmadinejad; Sec.-Gen. MUHAMMAD REZA BAHONAR.

Jebbeh-ye Mosharekat-e Iran-e Islami (Islamic Iran Participation Front): e-mail mail.emrooz@gmail.com; f. 1998; reformist, leftist; reportedly proscribed by the Iranian authorities in March 2010; Sec.-Gen. MOHSEN MIRDAMADI.

Komala Party of Iranian Kurdistan: e-mail secretariat@komala.org; internet www.komala.org; f. 1969; Kurdish wing of the Communist Party of Iran; Marxist-Leninist; Sec.-Gen. ABDULLAH MOHTADI.

Marze Por Gohar (Glorious Frontiers Party): 1351 Westwood Blvd, Suite 111, Los Angeles, CA 90024, USA; tel. (310) 473-4763; fax (310) 477-8484; e-mail info@marzeporgohar.org; internet www.marzeporgohar.org; f. 1998 in Tehran; nationalist party advocating a secular republic in Iran; Chair. ROOZBEH FARAHANIPOUR.

Mujahidin-e-Khalq (Holy Warriors of the People): e-mail mojahed@mojahedin.org; internet www.mojahedin.org; Marxist-Islamist guerrilla group opposed to clerical regime; since June 1987 comprising the National Liberation Army; mem. of the National Council of Resistance of Iran; based in Paris, France 1981–86 and in Baghdad, Iraq, 1986–2003; Leaders MARYAM RAJAVI, MASSOUD RAJAVI.

Nehzat-e Azadi-ye Iran (Liberation Movement of Iran): e-mail nehzateazadi1340@gmail.com; f. 1961; emphasis on basic human rights as defined by Islam; Sec.-Gen. Dr IBRAHIM YAZDI.

Pan-Iranist Party: POB 31535-1679, Karaj; e-mail iran@paniranism.info; internet www.paniranist.org; calls for a Greater Persia; Leader REZA KERMANI.

Sazeman-e Mujahidin-e Enqelab-e Islami (Organization of the Mujahidin of the Islamic Revolution): reformist; Sec.-Gen. MUHAMMAD SALAMATI.

Sazeman e-Peykar dar Rahe Azadieh Tabaqe Kargar (Organization Struggling for the Freedom of the Working Class): Marxist-Leninist.

Tudeh Party of Iran (Party of the Masses): POB 100644, 10566 Berlin, Germany; tel. and fax (30) 3241627; e-mail mardom@tudehpartyiran.org; internet www.tudehpartyiran.org; f. 1941; declared illegal 1949; resumed legal activities 1979; banned April 1983; First Sec., Cen. Cttee ALI KHAVARI.

The National Council of Resistance (NCR) was formed in Paris, France, in October 1981 by former President Abolhasan Bani-Sadr and Massoud Rajavi, the leader of the Mujahidin-e-Khalq in Iran. In 1984 the Council comprised 15 opposition groups, operating either clandestinely in Iran or from exile abroad. Bani-Sadr left the Council in that year because of his objection to Rajavi's growing links with the Iraqi Government. The French Government asked Rajavi to leave Paris in June 1986 and he moved his base of operations to Baghdad, Iraq. In June 1987 Rajavi, Secretary of the NCR, announced the formation of a 10,000–15,000-strong National Liberation Army as the military wing of the Mujahidin-e-Khalq. However, the status of the Mujahidin was initially uncertain following the invasion of Iraq by the US-led coalition in March 2003 (see the chapter on Iraq) and firmer measures being taken against the activities of the organization by the authorities in Paris in mid-2003. In July 2004 the USA declared a group of 3,800 members of the Mujahidin-e-Khalq interned in Iraq to have 'protected status' under the Geneva Convention. There is also a National Movement of Iranian Resistance, based in Paris.

Diplomatic Representation

EMBASSIES IN IRAN

Afghanistan: Dr Beheshti Ave, cnr of 4th St, Pakistan St, Tehran; tel. (21) 88737050; fax (21) 88735600; e-mail info@afghanembassy.ir; internet www.afghanembassy.ir; Ambassador Dr NASIR AHMADNOUR.

Algeria: No. 6, 16th Alley, Velenjak Ave, Velenjak, Tehran; tel. (21) 22420015; fax (21) 22420017; e-mail ambalg_teheran@yahoo.fr; Ambassador SOFIANE MIMOUNI.

Argentina: POB 15875-4335, 11 Ghoo Alley, Yar Mohammadi Ave, Darrous, Tehran; tel. (21) 22577433; fax (21) 22577432; e-mail eiran@mrecic.gob.ar; internet www.eiran.mrecic.gob.ar; Chargé d'affaires GUILLERMO NICOLÁS.

Armenia: 32 Ostad Shahriar St, Razi St, Jomhouri Islami Ave, Tehran 11337; tel. (21) 66704833; fax (21) 66700657; e-mail armiranembassy@mfa.am; Ambassador ARTASHES TUMANYAN.

Australia: POB 15875-4334, No. 2, 23rd St, Khalid Islambuli Ave, Tehran 15139-34113; tel. (21) 83863666; fax (21) 88720484; e-mail dfat-tehran@dfat.gov.au; internet www.iran.embassy.gov.au; Ambassador PAUL FOLEY.

Austria: 6–8 Bahonar St, Moghaddasi St, Ahmadi Zamani St, Tehran; tel. (21) 22750040; fax (21) 22705262; e-mail teheran-ob@bmeia.gv.at; internet www.bmeia.gv.at/botschaft/teheran; Ambassador Dr FRIEDRICH STIFT.

Azerbaijan: 16 Ratovan St, Sherzad Ave, Ehteshamie, Tehran; tel. (21) 22563146; fax (21) 22558183; e-mail az.embassy.ir@gmail.com; internet www.azembassy.ir; Ambassador JAVANSHIR AKHUNDOV.

Bahrain: POB 33111-15186, Tehran; tel. (21) 88773383; fax (21) 88880276; e-mail tehran.mission@mofa.gov.bh; internet www.mofa.gov.bh/tehran; Ambassador RASHID BIN SAAD AL-DOSARI.

Bangladesh: POB 11365-3711, Bldg 58, cnr Maryam Alley, Vanak St, Tehran; tel. (21) 88063073; fax (21) 88039965; e-mail info@bangladoot.ir; Ambassador KHANDAKAR ABDUS SATTAR.

Belarus: House 1, Azar Alley, Shahid Taheri St, Fallahi St, Zafaranieyeh Ave, Tehran 19887; tel. (21) 22752229; fax (21) 22751382, e-mail iran@mfa.gov.by; internet iran.mfa.gov.by; Ambassador VIKTOR RYBAK.

Belgium: POB 11365-115, 82–157 Shahid Fayyaz Bakhsh Ave, Elahieh, Tehran 16778; tel. (21) 22391909; fax (21) 22247313; e-mail teheran@diplobel.fed.be; internet www.diplomatie.be/tehran; Ambassador FRANÇOIS DELHAYE.

Bosnia and Herzegovina: No. 485, Aban Alley, 4th St, Iran Zamin Ave, Shahrak-e-Ghods, Tehran; tel. (21) 88086929; fax (21) 88092120; e-mail bhembasy@parsonline.net; Ambassador EDIB BEGOVIĆ.

Brazil: POB 19886-33854, 2 Yekta St, Vali-e-Asr Ave, Zafaranieh, Tehran; tel. (21) 22753108; fax (21) 22752009; e-mail brasemb .teera@itamaraty.gov.br; internet teera.itamaraty.gov.br; Ambassador SANTIAGO IRAZABAL MOURÃO.

Brunei: No. 7 Mina Blvd, Africa Ave, Tehran; tel. (21) 88797946; fax (21) 88770162; e-mail tehran.iran@mfa.gov.bn; Ambassador Haji MULOK BIN Haji JUMAT.

Bulgaria: POB 11365-7451, Vali-e-Asr Ave, Tavanir Ave, 40 Nezami-e-Ganjavi St, Tehran; tel. (21) 88775662; fax (21) 88779680; e-mail embassy.tehran@mfa.bg; internet www.mfa.bg/ embassies/iran; Chargé d'affaires STILIYAN VARBANOV.

China, People's Republic: POB 11365-3937, 13 Narenjestan 7th, Pasdaran Ave, Tehran; tel. (21) 22291240; fax (21) 22290690; e-mail chinaemb_ir@mfa.gov.cn; internet ir.chineseembassy.org; Ambassador PANG SEN.

Comoros: No. 10 Malek St, Shariati Ave, Tehran; tel. (21) 77624400; fax (21) 77624411; e-mail ambacomoresthn@yahoo.fr; Ambassador AHMAD NADJID AL-MARZOUQI.

Croatia: No. 25, 1st Behestan, Pasdaran St, Tehran; tel. (21) 22589923; fax (21) 22549199; e-mail vrhteh@mvpei.hr; Ambassador STRIBOR KIKEREC.

Cuba: Bldg 54, 17th West, Khodaverdi St, Niavaran Sq., Tehran; tel. and fax (21) 22282749; e-mail embajada@embacuba.ir; internet www .cubadiplomatica.cu/iran; Ambassador VLADIMIR ANDRÉS GONZÁLEZ QUESADA.

Cyprus: POB 18348-44681, 328 Shahid Karimi, Dezashib, Tajrish, Tehran; tel. (21) 22219842; fax (21) 22219843; e-mail cyprus@ parsonline.net; internet www.mfa.gov.cy/embassytehran; Ambassador ANDREAS P. KOUZOUPIS.

Czech Republic: POB 11365-4457, No. 36, Nastaran Alley, Bostan St, North Pasdaran Ave, Upper Farmaniyeh Crossroads, Tehran; tel. (21) 26118851; fax (21) 22802079; e-mail teheran@embassy.mzv.cz; internet www.mzv.cz/tehran; Chargé d'affaires PETR ŠTĚPÁNEK.

Denmark: POB 19395-5358, 10 Dashti St, Dr Shariati Ave, Hedayat St, Tehran 1914861144; tel. (21) 28155000; fax (21) 22640007; e-mail thramb@um.dk; internet iran.um.dk; Ambassador ANDERS CHRISTIAN HOUGÅRD.

Finland: POB 19395-1733, No. 2, Haddadian Alley, Mirzapour St, Dr Shariati Ave, Tehran 19336; tel. (21) 23512000; fax (21) 22215822; e-mail sanomat.teh@formin.fi; internet www.finland.org.ir; Ambassador HARRI KÄMÄRÄINEN.

France: 64–66 Neauphle-le-Château Ave, Tehran; tel. (21) 64094000; fax (21) 64094092; e-mail contact@ambafrance-ir.org; internet www.ambafrance-ir.org; Ambassador BRUNO FOUCHER.

The Gambia: No. 10, Malek St, Shariati Ave, Tehran; tel. (21) 77500074; fax (21) 77529515; e-mail gambiaembassy_tehran@yahoo .co.uk; Ambassador SAEED ZARE.

Georgia: 92, 2nd Golestan St, Pasdaran Ave, Tehran; tel. and fax (21) 22782386; fax (21) 22542692; e-mail tehran.emb@mfa.gov.ge; internet www.iran.mfa.gov.ge; Ambassador IOSEB CHAKHVASHVILI.

Germany: POB 11365-179, 320–324 Ferdowsi Ave, Tehran; tel. (21) 39990000; fax (21) 39991890; e-mail info@tehe.diplo.de; internet www.teheran.diplo.de; Ambassador MICHAEL FREIHERR VON UNGERN-STERNBERG.

Greece: POB 11155-1151, 43 Esfandiar Ave, Africa Expressway, Tehran 19679; tel. (21) 22050533; fax (21) 22057431; e-mail gremb .teh@mfa.gr; internet www.mfa.gr/tehran; Ambassador GEORGIOS AYFANTIS.

Guinea: POB 11365-4716, Dr Shariati Ave, Malek St, No. 10, Tehran; tel. (21) 77535744; fax (21) 77535743; e-mail ambaguinee_thr@hotmail.com; Ambassador BANGALI DIAKHABI.

Holy See: Apostolic Nunciature, POB 11155-178, 84 Razi Ave, Crossroad Neauphle-le-Château Ave, Tehran; tel. (21) 66403574; fax (21) 66419442; e-mail nuntius_fars@fastmail.fm; Apostolic Nuncio LEO BOCCARDI (Titular Archbishop of Bittetum).

Hungary: POB 6363-19395, No. 16, Shadloo St, Hedayat Sq., Darrous, Tehran; tel. (21) 22550460; fax (21) 22550503; e-mail mission.thr@mfa.gov.hu; internet www.mfa.gov.hu/kulkepviselet/ ir; Ambassador GYULA PETHŐ.

India: POB 15875-4118, 22 Mir-Emad St, cnr of 9th St, Dr Beheshti Ave, Tehran; tel. (21) 88755103; fax (21) 88755973; e-mail hoc .tehran@mea.gov.in; internet www.indianembassy-tehran.ir; Ambassador DINKAR PRAKASH SRIVASTAVA.

Indonesia: POB 11365-4564, Ghaem Magham Farahani Ave, No. 180, Tehran; tel. (21) 88716865; fax (21) 88718822; e-mail tehran .kbri@kemlu.go.id; internet tehran.kemlu.go.id; Ambassador DIAN WIRENGJURIT.

Iraq: Vali-e-Asr Ave, Vali-e-Asr Sq., Tehran; tel. (21) 88938865; fax (21) 88938877; e-mail info@iraqembassy.ir; internet www .iraqembassy.ir; Ambassador MUHAMMAD MAJID ABBAS AL-SHEIKH.

Italy: POB 4813-4863, 66–68 Neauphle-le-Château Ave, Tehran 1134834814; tel. (21) 66726958; fax (21) 66726961; e-mail segreteria .teheran@esteri.it; internet www.ambteheran.esteri.it; Ambassador MAURO CONCIATORI.

Japan: POB 11365-814, Bucharest Ave, cnr of 5th St, Tehran; tel. (21) 88717922; fax (21) 88713515; e-mail infoeoj@th.mofa.go.jp; internet www.ir.emb-japan.go.jp; Ambassador KOJI HANEDA.

Jordan: No. 1553, 2nd Alley, North Zarafshan, Phase 4, Shahrak-e-Ghods, Tehran; tel. (21) 88088356; fax (21) 88080496; e-mail tehran@ fm.gov.jo; Ambassador ABDULLAH SULAIMAN ABDULLAH ABU RUMMAN.

Kazakhstan: 82 North Hedayet St, cnr of Masjed Alley, Darrous, Tehran; tel. (21) 22565933; fax (21) 22546400; e-mail iran@mfa.kz; Ambassador BAGDAD K. AMREYEV.

Kenya: POB 19395-4566, 46 Golshar St, Africa Ave, Tehran; tel. (21) 22049355; fax (21) 22025792; e-mail info@kenyaemb-tehran.com; Ambassador RUQYAH AHMAD SUBU.

Korea, Democratic People's Republic: 349 Shahid Dastjerdi Ave, Africa Ave, Tehran; tel. (21) 22357300; fax (21) 22089718; Ambassador KANG SAM HYON.

Korea, Republic: POB 11155-3581, No. 2, West Daneshvar St, Shaikhbahai Ave, Vanak Sq., Tehran; tel. (21) 88054900; fax (21) 88064899; e-mail emb-ir@mofa.go.kr; internet irn.mofa.go.kr; Ambassador SONG WOONG-YEOB.

Kuwait: Africa Ave, Mahiyar St, No. 15, Tehran; tel. (21) 88785997; fax (21) 88788257; Ambassador MAJDI AL-DHUFAIRI.

Kyrgyzstan: POB 19579-35611, Bldg 12, 5th Naranjestan Alley, Pasdaran St, Tehran; tel. (21) 22830354; fax (21) 22281720; e-mail krembiri.mydatak@gmail.com; Ambassador ASANBEYK OSMANALIEV.

Lebanon: POB 11365-3753, No. 31, Shahid Kalantari St, Gharani Ave, Tehran; tel. (21) 88908451; fax (21) 88907345; Ambassador FADI HAJALI.

Libya: 2 Maryam Alley, South Kamranieh St, Tehran; tel. (21) 22201677; fax (21) 22236649; Ambassador SAAD MOJBAR.

Macedonia, former Yugoslav republic: No. 7, 4th Alley, Intifada Ave, Tehran; tel. and fax (21) 88720810; Ambassador CVETKO SOFKOVSKI.

Malaysia: No. 6, Changizi Alley, Alef St, Mahmoodieh, Tehran; tel. (21) 22046873; fax (21) 22046972; e-mail mwtehran@kln.gov.my; internet www.kln.gov.my/web/irn_tehran; Ambassador RAJA NUSH-IRWAN ZAINAL ABIDIN.

Mali: No. 16, Aroos Alley, Istanbul St, Shariati Ave, Tehran; tel. (21) 22207278; fax (21) 22234631; e-mail malimissiontehran@yahoo.com; Ambassador (vacant).

Mexico: POB 19156, No. 12, Golfam St, Africa Ave, Tehran; tel. (21) 22057586; fax (21) 22057589; e-mail embiran@sre.gob.mx; internet embamex.sre.gob.mx/iran; Ambassador ULISES CANCHOLA GUTIÉRREZ.

Netherlands: POB 11155-138, No. 7 Sonbol, Tehran; tel. (21) 23660000; fax (21) 23660190; e-mail teh@minbuza.nl; internet iran.nlambassade.org; Ambassador JOS DOUMA.

New Zealand: No. 1, 2nd Park Alley, 34 Sousan St, North Golestan Complex, Aghdassiyeh Ave, Niavaran, Tehran; tel. (21) 26122175; fax (21) 26121973; e-mail nzembassytehran@hotmail.co.nz; internet www.nzembassy.com/iran; Ambassador EAMONN O'SHAUGHNESSY.

Nicaragua: Tehran; tel. (21) 88685070; fax (21) 88685073; e-mail mbarquero@cancilleria.gob.ni; Ambassador MARIO BARQUERO.

Nigeria: 11 Sarvestan St, Elahieh, Tehran; tel. (21) 22009119; fax (21) 88799783; e-mail ngrembtehran@yahoo.com; Ambassador TUKUR MANI.

Norway: No. 54, Dr Lavasani St, cnr of Salmanpoor Zahir St, Tehran 1953694483; tel. (21) 22291333; fax (21) 22292776; e-mail emb .tehran@mfa.no; internet www.norway-iran.org; Ambassador AUD LISE NORHEIM.

Oman: No. 12, Tandis Alley, Africa Ave, Tehran; tel. (21) 22128352; fax (21) 22044672; e-mail tehran@mofa.gov.om; Ambassador SAUD BIN AHMAD BIN KHALID AL-BIRWANI.

Pakistan: No. 1, Ahmed Eitmadzadeh St, West Dr Fatemi Ave, Tehran 14118; tel. (21) 66941388; fax (21) 66944898; e-mail eoptehran@gmail.com; Ambassador NOOR MOHAMMAD JADMANI.

Philippines: POB 19395-4797, 5 Khayyam St, Vali-e-Asr Ave, Tehran; tel. (21) 22668774; fax (21) 22668990; e-mail tehranpe@ yahoo.com; Ambassador EDUARDO MARTIN R. MEÑEZ.

Poland: POB 11155-3489, No. 2, Pirouz St, Africa Expressway, Tehran; tel. (21) 88787262; fax (21) 88788774; e-mail teheran.amb .sekretariat@msz.gov.pl; internet teheran.msz.gov.pl; Ambassador JULIUSZ JACEK GOJŁO.

Portugal: No. 13, Rouzbeh St, Hedayat Ave, Darrous, Tehran; tel. (21) 22582760; fax (21) 22552668; e-mail teerao@mne.pt; internet www.portugueseembassy.ir; Ambassador Dr MARIO FERNANDO DAMAS NUNES.

Qatar: POB 11155-1631, No. 4, Golazin St, Africa Ave, Tehran; tel. (21) 22029336; fax (21) 22058453; e-mail tehran@mofa.gov.qa; Ambassador Dr ALI BIN HAMAD AL-SULAITI.

Romania: 89 Shahid Meshki, Baharestan Ave, Tehran; tel. (21) 77647570; fax (21) 77535291; e-mail teheran@mae.ro; Ambassador CRISTIAN TEODORESCU.

Russian Federation: 39 Neauphle-le-Château Ave, Tehran; tel. (21) 66701161; fax (21) 66701652; e-mail teheran@dks.ru; internet iran.mid.ru; Ambassador LEVAN S. DZHAGARYAN.

Saudi Arabia: No. 1, Niloufar St, Boustan St, Pasdaran Ave, Tehran; tel. (21) 22288543; fax (21) 22294691; e-mail iremb@mofa.gov.sa; Ambassador ABD AL-RAHMAN BIN GHARMAN AL-SHAHRI.

Serbia: POB 11365-118, Velenjak Ave, No. 9, 9th St, Tehran 19858; tel. (21) 22412571; fax (21) 22402869; e-mail serbembteh@parsonline.net; Ambassador ALEXANDER TASIĆ.

Sierra Leone: POB 11365-1689, No. 4, Bukan St, Sadeghi Ghomi St, Bahonar Ave, Niavaran, Tehran; tel. (21) 22721474; fax (21) 22721485; e-mail slembsy_tehran@yahoo.com; Ambassador MUHAMMAD FUFANA.

Slovakia: POB 19395-6341, 34 Sarlashgar Fallahi St, Tehran 19887; tel. (21) 22666601; fax (21) 22666605; e-mail emb.tehran@mzv.sk; internet www.tehran.mfa.sk; Ambassador JÁN BÓRY.

Somalia: 1 Hadaiyan St, Mirzapour St, Dr Shariati Ave, Tehran; tel. and fax (21) 22245146; e-mail safarian@hotmail.com; Ambassador KHALIFA MOUSSA.

South Africa: POB 11365-7476, 5 Yekta St, Bagh-e-Ferdows, Vali-e-Asr Ave, Tehran; tel. (21) 22702866; fax (21) 22716192; e-mail tehran.admin@foreign.gov.za; Ambassador WILLIAM MAX WHITEHEAD.

Spain: No. 10 Shadi St Abbas Asadi St, Sharzad Blvd, Darrous, Tehran; tel. (21) 22568681; fax (21) 22568018; e-mail emb.teheran@maec.es; internet www.exteriores.gob.es/embajadas/teheran/es/paginas/inicio.aspx; Ambassador PEDRO ANTONIO VILLENA PÉREZ.

Sri Lanka: No. 66, Kafiabadi Alley, Shahid Fallahi St, Zafaranieh, Tehran; tel. (21) 22569179; fax (21) 22175471; e-mail slemb@aframail.com; Ambassador MUHAMMAD FEISAL RAZIN.

Sudan: No. 39, Babak Bahrami St, Africa Ave, Tehran; tel. (21) 88781183, fax (21) 88792331, e-mail sudanembassy_tehran@yahoo.com; internet www.sudanembassyir.com; Ambassador SULEIMAN ABD AL-TAWAB ZEIN.

Sweden: POB 19575-458, 27 Nastaran St, Boostan Ave, Tehran; tel. (21) 23712200; fax (21) 22296451; e-mail ambassaden.teheran-visum@gov.se; internet www.swedenabroad.com/tehran; Ambassador PETER TEJLER.

Switzerland: POB 19395-4683, 2 Yasaman St, Sharifimanesh Ave, Elahieh, Tehran 19649; tel. (21) 22008333; fax (21) 22006002; e-mail teh.vertretung@eda.admin.ch; internet www.eda.admin.ch/tehran; Ambassador GIULIO HAAS; also represents interests of the USA in Iran.

Syria: 19 Iraj St, Africa Ave, Tehran; tel. (21) 22052780; fax (21) 22059409; e-mail tehran@mofa.gov.sy; Ambassador Dr ADNAN MAHMOUD.

Tajikistan: No. 10, 3rd Alley, Shahid Zeynali St, Niavaran, Tehran; tel. (21) 22299584; fax (21) 22809299; e-mail tajemb-iran@tajikistanir.com; internet www.tajembiran.tj; Ambassador NEMATOLLAH IMAMZADA.

Thailand: POB 11495-111, No. 4 Esteghlal Alley, Baharestan St, Tehran; tel. (21) 77531433; fax (21) 77532022; e-mail info@thaiembassy-tehran.org; internet www.thaiembassy-tehran.org; Ambassador ADISORNDEJ SUKHASVASTI.

Tunisia: No. 12, Shahid Lavasani Ave, Farmanieh, Tehran; tel. (21) 2706699; fax (21) 22631994; e-mail at-teheran@neda.net; Ambassador GHAZI BEN SALEH.

Turkey: POB 11365-8758, No. 337 Ferdowsi Ave, Africa Ave, Tehran; tel. (21) 35951100; fax (21) 33117928; e-mail embassy.tehran@mfa.gov.tr; internet tehran.emb.mfa.gov.tr; Ambassador RIZA HAKAN TEKIN.

Turkmenistan: 5 Barati St, Vatanpour St, Tehran; tel. (21) 22206731; fax (21) 22206732; e-mail tmnteh@afranet.com; Ambassador AKHMED GURBANOV.

Uganda: 3rd Floor, 10 Malek St, Shariati Ave, Tehran; tel. (21) 77643335; fax (21) 77643337; e-mail uganda_teh@yahoo.com; Ambassador Dr MUHAMMAD AHMAD KISULE.

Ukraine: 120 Vanak St, Vanak Sq., Tehran; tel. (21) 88039476; fax (21) 88063074; e-mail emb_ir@mfa.gov.ua; internet mfa.gov.ua/iran; Chargé d'affaires SERHIJ B. KRASNOSHAPKA.

United Arab Emirates: POB 19395-4616, No. 337, Vahid Dastjerdi Ave, Vali-e-Asr Ave, Tehran; tel. (21) 88788515; fax (21) 88789084; e-mail tehran@mofa.gov.ae; Ambassador SAIF MUHAMMAD OBAID AL-ZAABI.

Uruguay: POB 19395-4718, No. 6, Mina Blvd, Africa Ave, Tehran; tel. (21) 88679690; fax (21) 88782321; e-mail uruter@uruter.com; Ambassador JUAN CARLOS OJEDA VIGLIONE.

Uzbekistan: No. 6, Nastaran Alley, Boustan St, Pasdaran Ave, Tehran; tel. (21) 22299780; fax (21) 22299158; internet www.uzbekembassy.ir; Ambassador ELHAM AKRAMOV.

Venezuela: No. 17 Tajiki St, Kamranieh St North, Tehran; tel. (21) 22284450; fax (21) 26124886; e-mail embve.irthr@mre.gob.ve; internet emveniran.net; Ambassador AMENHOTEP ZAMBRANO CONTRERAS.

Viet Nam: No. 6, East Ordibehesht, Zaferanieh, Peysian St, M. Ardabili Vali-e-Asr Ave, Tehran; tel. (21) 22411670; fax (21) 22416045; e-mail vnemb.ir@mofa.gov.vn; internet www.vietnamembassy-iran.org; Ambassador NEGVIN HUNG TACH.

Yemen: No. 15, Golestan St, Africa Ave, Tehran; tel. (21) 22042701; e-mail yem.emb.ir@neda.net; Ambassador JAMAL ABDULLAH AL-SOLAL.

Zimbabwe: 6 Shad Avar St, Mogghadas Ardabili, Tehran; tel. (21) 22027555; fax (21) 22049084; e-mail zimtehran@yahoo.com; Ambassador NICHOLAS KITIKITI.

Judicial System

In August 1982 the Supreme Court revoked all laws dating from the previous regime that did not conform with Islam; in October all courts set up prior to the Islamic Revolution of 1979 were abolished. In June 1987 Ayatollah Khomeini ordered the creation of clerical courts to try members of the clergy opposed to government policy. A new system of *qisas* (retribution) was established, placing the emphasis on swift justice. Islamic codes of correction were introduced in 1983, including the amputation of a hand for theft, flogging for fornication and violations of the strict code of dress for women, and stoning for adultery. The Islamic revolutionary courts try those accused of crimes endangering national security, corruption, drugs-trafficking, and moral and religious offences. The Supreme Court has 33 branches, each of which is presided over by two judges.

Supreme Court: Chief Justice Ayatollah MOHSENI GORKANI.

Head of the Judiciary: Hojatoleslam SADEQ ARDESHIR LARIJANI.

Prosecutor-General: Hojatoleslam Sayed EBRAHIM RA'ISI.

Religion

According to the 1979 Constitution, the official religion is Islam of the Ja'fari sect (Shi'a), but other Islamic sects, including Zeydi, Hanafi, Maleki, Shafe'i and Hanbali, are valid and will be respected. Zoroastrians, Jews and Christians will be recognized as official religious minorities. According to the 2006 census, there were 70,097,741 Muslims, 109,415 Christians (mainly Armenian), 19,823 Zoroastrians and 9,252 Jews in Iran.

ISLAM

The great majority of the Iranian people are Shi'a Muslims, but there is a minority of Sunni Muslims. Persians and Azerbaijanis are mainly Shi'a, while the other ethnic groups are mainly Sunni.

CHRISTIANITY

The Roman Catholic Church

Armenian Rite

Bishop of Esfahan: (vacant), Armenian Catholic Bishopric, POB 11318, Khiaban Ghazzali 65, Tehran; tel. (21) 66707204; fax (21) 66727533; e-mail arcaveso@yahoo.com.

Chaldean Rite

Archbishop of Ahvaz: HANNA ZORA, Archbishop's House, 334 Suleiman Farsi St, Ahvaz; tel. (61) 2224980.

Archbishop of Tehran: RAMZI GARMOU, Archevêché, Enghelab St, Sayed Abbas Moussavi Ave 91, Tehran 15819; tel. (21) 88823549; fax (21) 88308714.

Archbishop of Urmia (Rezayeh) and Bishop of Salmas (Shah-pour): THOMAS MERAM, Khalifagari Kaldani Katholiq, POB 338, 7 Mirzaian St, Orumiyeh 57135; tel. (441) 2222739; fax (441) 2236031; e-mail thmeram@yahoo.com.

Latin Rite

Archbishop of Esfahan: IGNAZIO BEDINI, Consolata Church, POB 11155-445, 73 Neauphle-le-Château Ave, Tehran; tel. (21) 66703210; fax (21) 66724749; e-mail latin.diocese@gmail.com.

The Anglican Communion

Anglicans in Iran are adherents of the Episcopal Church in Jerusalem and the Middle East, formally inaugurated in January 1976. The Bishop in Cyprus and the Gulf is resident in Cyprus.

Bishop in Iran: Rt Rev. AZAD MARSHALL, POB 135, 81465 Esfahan; tel. (21) 88801383; fax (21) 88906908; internet dioceseofiran.org; diocese founded 1912.

Presbyterian Church

Synod of the Evangelical (Presbyterian) Church in Iran: POB 14395-569, Assyrian Evangelical Church, Khiaban-i Hanifnejad, Khiaban-i Aramanch, Tehran; tel. (21) 88006135; Moderator Rev. ADEL NAKHOSTEEN.

OTHER COMMUNITIES

Communities of Armenians, and somewhat smaller numbers of Zoroastrians, Jews, Assyrians, Greek Orthodox Christians, Uniates and Latin Christians are also found as officially recognized faiths. The Bahá'í faith, which originated in Iran, has about 300,000 Iranian adherents, although at least 10,000 are believed to have fled since 1979 in order to escape persecution. The Government banned all Bahá'í institutions in August 1983.

The Press

Tehran dominates the media, as many of the daily papers are published there, and the bi-weekly, weekly and less frequent publications in the provinces generally depend on the major metropolitan dailies as a source of news. A press law announced in August 1979 required all newspapers and magazines to be licensed, and imposed penalties of imprisonment for insulting senior religious figures. Offences against the Act will be tried in the criminal courts. Under the Constitution, the press is free, except in matters that are contrary to public morality, insult religious belief, or slander the honour and reputation of individuals. An intense judicial campaign since the late 1990s has sought to curb freedom of the press; some sources estimate that more than 100 publications were closed down during Muhammad Khatami's presidency (1997–2005).

PRINCIPAL DAILIES

Aftab-e-Yazd (Sun of Yazd): POB 13145-1134, Tehran; tel. (21) 66495833; fax (21) 66495835; e-mail aftab.yz@gmail.com; internet www.aftabeyazd.ir; f. 2000; Farsi; pro-reform; Chief Editor SAYED MOJTABA VAHEDI; circ. 100,000.

Alik: POB 11365-953, 16 Shahid Mohebi Ave, North Sohrevardi Ave, Tehran 155588; tel. (21) 88768567; fax (21) 88760994; e-mail info@alikonline.ir; internet www.alikonline.ir; f. 1931; afternoon; Armenian; political, literary, cultural, social, sport; Editor DERENIK MELIKIAN; circ. over 4,500.

Donya-e-Eqtesad (Economic World): POB 14157-44344, Tehran; tel. (21) 87762511; fax (21) 87762515; e-mail info@donya-e-eqtesad.com; internet www.donya-e-eqtesad.com; Farsi; Editor ALI MIRZAKHANI.

Entekhab (Choice): 12 Noorbakhsh Ave, Vali-e-Asr Ave, Tehran; tel. (21) 88893954; fax (21) 89773382; e-mail info@entekhab.ir; internet www.entekhab.ir; online only; Farsi; centrist; Man. Dir MOSTAFA FAQIHI.

Etemad (Confidence): e-mail info@etemaad.com; internet www.etemaad.ir; Farsi; pro-reform; Man. Dir ELIAS HAZRATI; Editor BEHROUZ BEHZADI.

Ettela'at (Information): Ettela'at Bldg, Mirdamad Ave, South Naft St, Tehran 15499; tel. (21) 29999; fax (21) 22258022; e-mail ettelaat@ettelaat.com; internet www.ettelaat.com; f. 1925; evening; Farsi; political and literary; operates under the direct supervision of *wilayat-e-faqih* (religious jurisprudence); Editor SAYED MAHMOUD DO'AYI; circ. 500,000.

Hambastegi (Solidarity): Tehran; e-mail info@hambastegi-news.com; internet www.hambastegidaily.com; Farsi; pro-reform; Editor SALEH ABADI.

Ham-Mihan (Compatriot): Tehran; e-mail info@hammihan.com; internet www.hammihan.com; f. 2000; Farsi; independent, pro-reform; Founder and Man. Dir GHOLAMHOSSEIN KARBASCHI; Chair. of Bd MUHAMMAD ATRIANFAR; Editor MUHAMMAD GHOUCHANI.

Hamshahri (Citizen): POB 19395-5446, Tehran; tel. (21) 23023453; fax (21) 23023455; e-mail contact@hamshahri.org; internet www.hamshahrilinks.org; f. 1993; Farsi; conservative; economics, society and culture; owned by the Municipality of Tehran; Editor-in-Chief HOSSEIN GORBANZADEH; circ. 400,000.

Iran: POB 15875-5388, Tehran; tel. (21) 88761720; fax (21) 88761254; e-mail iran-newspaper@iran-newspaper.com; internet www.iran-newspaper.com; Farsi; conservative; connected to the Islamic Republic News Agency; Man. Dir HOSSEIN ZIYAEI; Editor-in-Chief BIJAN MOGHADDAM.

Iran Daily: Iran Cultural and Press Institute, 208 Khorramshahr Ave, Tehran; tel. (21) 88755761; fax (21) 88761869; e-mail iran-daily@iran-daily.com; internet www.iran-daily.com; English.

Iran News: POB 15875-8551, No. 13, Pajouhesh Lane, Golestan St, Marzdaran Blvd, Tehran; tel. (21) 44253401; fax (21) 44253478; e-mail info@irannewsdaily.com; internet www.irannewsdaily.com; f. 1994; English; Man. Dir MAJID AQAZADEH; circ. 35,000.

Jam-e Jam: Tehran; tel. (21) 22222511; fax (21) 22226252; e-mail info@jamejamonline.ir; internet www.jamejamonline.ir; online only; Farsi, English and French; conservative; linked to Islamic Republic of Iran Broadcasting; Man. Editor B. MOGHADDAM.

Jomhouri-e-Eslami (Islamic Republic): tel. (21) 33916111; fax (21) 33117552; e-mail info@jomhourieslami.com; internet www.jomhourieslami.com; f. 1980; Farsi; conservative; Man. Dir MASIH MOHAJERI.

Kayhan (Universe): Institute Kayhan, POB 11365-3631, Shahid Shahcheraghi Alley, Ferdowsi Ave, Tehran 11444; tel. (21) 33110251; fax (21) 33111120; e-mail kayhan@kayhannews.ir; internet www.kayhannews.ir; f. 1941; evening; Farsi; political; also publishes *Kayhan International* (f. 1959; daily; English; Editor HAMID NAJAFI), *Kayhan Arabic* (f. 1980; daily; Arabic), *Kayhan Persian* (f. 1942; daily; Farsi), *Zan-e Rooz* (Today's Woman; f. 1964; weekly; Farsi), *Kayhan Varzeshi* (World of Sport; f. 1955; daily and weekly; Farsi), *Kayhan Bacheha* (Children's World; f. 1956; weekly; Farsi), *Kayhan Farhangi* (World of Culture; f. 1984; monthly; Farsi); owned and managed by Mostazafin Foundation from October 1979 until January 1987, when it was placed under the direct supervision of *wilayat-e-faqih* (religious jurisprudence); Editor-in-Chief HOSSEIN SHARIATMADARI; circ. 350,000.

Khorasan: Mashhad; Head Office: Khorasan Daily Newspapers, 14 Zohre St, Mobarezan Ave, Tehran; tel. (511) 7634000; fax (511) 7624395; e-mail info@khorasannews.com; internet www.khorasannews.com; f. 1948; Farsi; Propr MUHAMMAD SADEGH TEHERANIAN; Editor MUHAMMAD SAEED AHADI; circ. 40,000.

Quds Daily: POB 91735-577, Khayyam Sq., Sajjad Blvd, Mashhad; tel. (51) 7685011; fax (511) 7684004; e-mail info@qudsdaily.com; internet www.qudsdaily.com; f. 1987; Farsi; owned by Astan Quds Razavi, the org. that oversees the shrine of Imam Reza at Mashhad; also publ. in Tehran; Man. Dir GHOLAMREZA GHALANDARIAN; Editor-in-Chief MUHAMMAD HADI ZAHEDI.

Resalat (The Message): POB 11365-777, 53 Ostad Nejatollahi Ave, Tehran; tel. (21) 88902642; fax (21) 88900587; e-mail info@resalat-news.com; internet www.resalat-news.com; f. 1985; organ of right-wing group of the same name; Farsi; conservative; political, economic and social; Propr Resalat Foundation; Man. Dir SAYED MORTEZA NABAVI; circ. 100,000.

Shargh (East): Tehran; internet www.sharghdaily.ir; f. 2003; Farsi; reformist; publ. suspended in August 2009, allowed to resume in March 2010; Man. Dir MEHDI RAHMANIAN; Editor AHMAD GHOLAMI.

Tehran Times: POB 14155-4843, 32 Bimeh Alley, Ostad Nejatollahi Ave, Tehran; tel. (21) 88800789; fax (21) 88800788; e-mail info@tehrantimes.com; internet www.tehrantimes.com; f. 1979; English; independent; Man. Dir ALI ASGARI; Editor-in-Chief ABOLFAZI AMOUEI.

PRINCIPAL PERIODICALS

Acta Medica Iranica: Bldg No. 8, Faculty of Medicine, Tehran University of Medical Sciences, Poursina St, Tehran 14174; tel. (21) 42910700; e-mail acta@tums.ac.ir; internet acta.tums.ac.ir; f. 1956; monthly; English; Editor-in-Chief AHMAD REZA DEHPOUR; circ. 2,000.

Ashur (Assyria): Ostad Motahari Ave, 11–21 Kuhe Nour Ave, Tehran; tel. (21) 622117; f. 1969; Assyrian; monthly; Founder and Editor Dr WILSON BET-MANSOUR; circ. 8,000.

Bukhara: POB 15655-166, Tehran; tel. 9121300147 (mobile); fax (21) 88958697; e-mail info@bukharamag.com; internet www.bukharamag.com; bi-monthly; Farsi; arts, culture and humanities; Editor ALI DEHBASHI.

Bulletin of the National Film Archive of Iran: POB 11155, Baharestan Sq., Tehran 11499-43381; tel. (21) 38512583; fax (21) 38512710; e-mail khoshnevis_nfai@yahoo.com; f. 1989; English; Editor M. H. KHOSHNEVIS.

Daneshmand (Scientist): POB 15875-3649, Tehran; tel. (21) 88497883; fax (21) 88497880; e-mail info@daneshmandonline.ir; f. 1963; monthly; Farsi; owned by Mostazafari Foundation; science and technology in Iran and abroad; CEO YAGHOUB MOSHFEGH; Editor-in-Chief MINOO MEHRALI.

Donya Varzesh (World of Sports): Tehran; tel. (21) 3281; fax (21) 33115530; internet www.donyayevarzesh.com; weekly; sport; Editor G. H. SHABANI; circ. 200,000.

The Echo of Iran: POB 14155-1168, 4 Hourtab Alley, Hafez Ave, Tehran; tel. (21) 22930477; e-mail info@iranalmanac.com; internet www.iranalmanac.com; f. 1952; monthly; English; news, politics and economics; Man. FARJAM BEHNAM; Editor JAHANGIR BEHROUZ.

Echo of Islam: POB 14155-3899, Tehran; tel. (21) 88897663; fax (21) 88902725; e-mail info@echoofislam.com; internet www.echoofislam .com; quarterly; English; publ. by the Islamic Thought Foundation; Man. Dir Dr MAHDI GOLJAN; Editor-in-Chief S. MOUSAVI.

Economic Echo: POB 14155-1168, 4 Hourtab Alley, Hafez Ave, Tehran; tel. (21) 22930477; e-mail info@iranalmanac.com; internet www.iranalmanac.com; f. 1998; English; Man. FARJAM BEHNAM.

Ettela'at Haftegi: 11 Khayyam Ave, Tehran; tel. (21) 311238; fax (21) 33115530; f. 1941; general weekly; Farsi; Editor F. JAVADI; circ. 150,000.

Ettela'at Javanan: POB 15499-51199, Ettela'at Bldg, Mirdamad Ave, South Naft St, Tehran; tel. (21) 29999; fax (21) 22258022; f. 1966; weekly; Farsi; youth; Editor M. J. RAFIZADEH; circ. 120,000.

Farhang-e-Iran Zamin: POB 19575-583, Niyavaran, Tehran; tel. (21) 283254; annual; Farsi; Iranian studies.

Film International, Iranian Film Quarterly: POB 11365-875, Tehran; tel. (21) 66709374; fax (21) 66719971; e-mail info@ film-international.com; internet www.film-international.com; f. 1993; quarterly; English; Editor-in-Chief MASSOUD MEHRABI; circ. 15,000.

Iran Almanac: POB 14155-1168, 4 Hourtab Alley, Hafez Ave, Tehran; tel. and fax (932) 9139201; e-mail info@iranalmanac.com; internet www.iranalmanac.com; f. 2000; English; reference; history, politics, trade and industry, tourism, art, culture and society; Researcher and Editor FARJAM BEHNAM.

Iran Tribune: POB 111244, Tehran; e-mail matlab@iran-tribune .com; internet www.iran-tribune.com; monthly; English and Farsi; socio-political and cultural.

Iran Who's Who: POB 14155-1168, 4 Hourtab Alley, Hafez Ave, Tehran; e-mail info@iranalmanac.com; internet www.iranalmanac .com; annual; English; Editor FARJAM BEHNAM

Iranian Cinema: POB 11155, Baharestan Sq., Tehran 11499-43381; tel. (21) 35812583; fax (21) 35812710; e-mail khoshnevis-nfai@yahoo.com; f. 1985; annual; English.

Kayhan Bacheha (Children's World): Institute Kayhan, POB 11365 3631, Shahid Shahcheraghi Alley, Ferdowsi Ave, Tehran 11444; tel. (21) 33110251; fax (21) 333900025; internet www .kayhanbacheha.ir; f. 1956; weekly; illustrated magazine for children; circ. 150,000.

Kayhan Varzeshi (World of Sport): Instituto Kayhan, POB 11365-3631, Shahid Shahcheraghi Alley, Ferdowsi Ave, Tehran 11444; tel. (21) 33110246; fax (21) 33114228; e-mail info@kayhanvarzeshi.com; internet www.kayhanvarzeshi.com; f. 1955; weekly; Farsi; Dir MAHMAD MONSETI; circ. 125,000.

Mahjubah: POB 14155-3899, Tehran; tel. (21) 88899663; fax (21) 88902725; e-mail info@mahjubah.com; internet www.mahjubah .com; Islamic family magazine; publ. by the Islamic Thought Foundation; Editor-in-Chief TURAN JAMSHIDIAN.

Soroush: POB 15875-1163, Soroush Bldg, Motahari Ave, Mofattch Crossroads, Tehran; tel. and fax (21) 88847602; e-mail cultural@ soroushpress.com; internet www.soroushpress.com; f. 1972; one weekly magazine; four monthly magazines, one for women, two for adolescents and one for children; one quarterly review of philosophy; all in Farsi; Editor-in-Chief ALI AKBAR ASHARI.

Tavoos: POB 19395-6434, 6 Asgarian St, East Farmanieh Ave, Tehran 19546-44755; tel. (21) 22817700; fax (21) 22825447; e-mail info@tavoosmag.com; internet www.tavoosonline.com; quarterly; Farsi and English; arts; Man. Dir MANIJEH MIREMADI; circ. 5,000.

Tchissta: POB 13145-593, Tehran; tel. (21) 678581; e-mail daneshvamardom@tchissta.com; internet tchissta.com; Farsi; politics, society, science and literature; Editor-in-Chief PARVIZ SHAHRIARI.

ZamZam: POB 14155-3899, Tehran; tel. (21) 88897663; fax (21) 88902725; internet www.zamzam-mag.com; children's magazine; English; publ. by the Islamic Thought Foundation; Man. Dir Dr MAHDI GOLJAN; Editor-in-Chief SHAGHAYEGH GHANDEHARI.

Zan-e Rooz (Today's Woman): Institute Kayhan, POB 11365-3631, Shahid Shahcheraghi Alley, Ferdowsi Ave, Tehran 11444; tel. (21) 33911575; fax (21) 33911569; e-mail kayhan@istn.irost.com; f. 1964; weekly; women's; circ. over 60,000.

NEWS AGENCIES

Fars News Agency: Tehran; e-mail info@farsnews.ir; internet www .farsnews.com; f. 2003; independent; news in Farsi and English; Man. Dir SEYED NEZAMODDIN MOUSSAVI.

Iranian Quran News Agency (IQNA): 97 Bozorgmehr St, Qods Ave, Tehran; tel. (21) 66470212; fax (21) 66970769; e-mail info@iqna .ir; internet www.iqna.ir; f. 2003; general news and news on Koranic activities.

Islamic Republic News Agency (IRNA): POB 764, 873 Vali-e-Asr Ave, Tehran; tel. (21) 88902050; fax (21) 88905068; e-mail irna@irna .com; internet www.irna.com; f. 1934; state-controlled; Man. Dir MUHAMMAD KHODADI.

Mehr News Agency: 32 Bimeh Alley, Nejatollahi St, Tehran; tel. (21) 88809500; fax (21) 88805801; e-mail info@mehrnews.com; internet www.mehrnews.com; f. 2003; news in Farsi, English and Arabic; Man. Dir ALI ASGARI.

PRESS ASSOCIATION

Association of Iranian Journalists: No. 87, 7th Alley, Shahid Kabkanian St, Keshavarz Blvd, Tehran; tel. (21) 88956365; fax (21) 88963539; e-mail generalsecretary@aoij.org; Pres. RAJABALI MAZROOEI; Sec. BADRALSADAT MOFIDI.

Publishers

Amir Kabir Book Publishing and Distribution Co: POB 11365-4191, Jomhouri Islami Ave, Esteghlal Sq., Tehran; tel. (21) 33900751; fax (21) 33903747; e-mail info@amirkabir.net; internet www.amirkabir.net; f. 1948; historical, philosophical, social, literary and children's books; Dir AHMAD NESARI.

Avayenoor Publications: 31 Roshan Alley, Vali-e-Asr Ave, Tehran; tel. (21) 55136353; fax (21) 88907452; e-mail info@avayenoor .com; internet www.avayenoor.com; f. 1988; sociology, politics and economics; Editor-in-Chief SAYED MUHAMMAD MIRHOSSEINI.

Caravan Books Publishing House: POB 186-14145, 18 Salehi St, Sartip Fakouri Ave, Northern Karegar Ave, Tehran 14136; tel. (21) 88007421; fax (21) 88029486; e-mail info@caravan.ir; internet caravan.ir; f. 1997; fiction and non-fiction; Chief Editor ARASH HEJAZI.

Echo Publishers & Printers: POB 14155-1168, 4 Hourtab Alley, Hafez Ave, Tehran; tel. and fax (21) 22930477; e-mail info@ iranalmanac.com; internet www.iranalmanac.com; f. 2000; politics, economics and current affairs; Man. FARJAM BEHNAM.

Eghbal Publishing Organization: 273 Dr Ali Shariati Ave, Tehran 16139; tel. (21) 77500973; fax (21) 7768113; f. 1903; Man. Dir SAEED ECHBAL.

Farhang Moaser: 43 Khiaban Daneshgah, Tehran 13147; tel. (21) 66465520; fax (21) 66417018; e-mail info@farhangmoaser.com; internet www.farhangmoaser.com; dictionaries.

Gooya Publications: 139 Karimkhan-e Zand Ave, Tehran 15856; tel. (21) 8838453; fax (21) 8842987; e-mail info@gooyabooks.com; internet www.gooyabooks.com; f. 1981; art; Dir NASER MIR BAGHERI.

Iran Chap Co: Ettela'at Bldg, Mirdamad Ave, South Naft St, Tehran; tel. (21) 29999; fax (21) 22258022; e-mail ettelaat@ ettelaat.com; internet www.ettelaat.com; f. 1966; newspapers, books, magazines, book-binding and colour printing; Man. Dir MAHMOUD DOAEI.

Iran Exports Publication Co Ltd: POB 16315-1773, 41 First Mehr Alley, Mirzapour St, Shariati Ave, Tehran; tel. (21) 22200646; fax (21) 22888505; e-mail info@iranexportsmagazine.com; internet www .iranexportsmagazine.com; f. 1987; business and trade publs in English; Editor-in-Chief and Dir of Int. Affairs AHMAD NIKFARJAM.

Ketab Sara Co: POB 15117-38951, Tehran; tel. (21) 88711321; fax (21) 88717819; e-mail ketabsara@ketabsara.org; internet www .ketabsara.ir; f. 1980; Dir SADEGH SAMII.

Kowkab Publishers: POB 19575-511, Tehran; tel. (21) 22949834; fax (21) 22949834; e-mail info@kkme.com; internet www.kkme.com; engineering, science, medicine, humanities, reference; Man. Dir Dr AHMAD GHANDI.

The Library, Museum and Documentation Center of the Islamic Consultative Assembly (Ketab-Khane, Muze va Markaz-e Asnad-e Majlis-e-Shura-e Islami): POB 11365-866, Ketab-Khane Majlis-e-Shura-e Islami No. 2, Baharestan Sq., Tehran; tel. (21) 33130911; fax (21) 33130920; e-mail info@majlislib.com; internet www.majlislib.com; f. 1912 as Majlis Library; renamed as above in 1996; arts, humanities, social sciences, politics, Iranian and Islamic studies; Dir SAYED MOHAMMAD ALI AHMADI ABHARI.

Ofoq Publishers: 181 Nazari St, 12th Farvardin St, Tehran 13145-1135; tel. (21) 66413367; fax (21) 66414285; e-mail info@ofoqco.com; internet www.ofoqco.com; f. 1990; illustrated books for children and teenagers, adult fiction and non-fiction; Dir REZA HASHEMINEJAD.

Qoqnoos Publishing House: 111 Shohadaye Jandarmeri St, Enghelab Ave, Tehran; tel. (21) 66408640; fax (21) 66413933; e-mail pub@qoqnoos.ir; internet www.qoqnoos.ir; f. 1977; fiction, history, philosophy, law, sociology and psychology; privately owned; Owner and Gen. Man. AMIR HOSSEINZADEGAN; Editor-in-Chief ARSALAN FASIHI.

Sahab Geographic and Drafting Institute: POB 11365-617, 30 Somayeh St, Hoquqi Crossroads, Dr Ali Shariati Ave, Tehran 16517;

tel. (21) 77535651; fax (21) 77535876; internet www.sahabmap.com; f. 1936; maps, atlases, and books on geography, science, history and Islamic art; Man. Dir MUHAMMAD REZA SAHAB.

Soroush Press: POB 15875-1163, Soroush Bldg, Motahari Ave, Mofatteh Crossroads, Tehran; tel. and fax (21) 88847602; fax (21) 88300760; e-mail cultural@soroushpress.com; internet www .soroushpress.ir; part of Soroush Publication Group, the publs dept of Islamic Republic of Iran Broadcasting; publishes books, magazines and multimedia products on a wide range of subjects; Man. Dir ALI AKBAR ASHARI.

Tehran University Press: 16th St, North Karegar St, Tehran; tel. (21) 88012080; fax (21) 88012077; e-mail press@ut.ac.ir; internet press.ut.ac.ir; f. 1944; univ. textbooks; Man. Dir Dr MUHAMMAD SHEKARCIZADEH.

Broadcasting and Communications

TELECOMMUNICATIONS

The Mobile Communications Company of Iran, a subsidiary of the Telecommunications Company of Iran, previously had a monopoly over the provision of mobile cellular telecommunications services in the country. However, in February 2004 Iran's second GSM licence was awarded to Irancell, a consortium led by Turkcell (Turkey). The contract was subsequently revised by the Majlis and the Council of Guardians to require that domestic firms hold a majority stake in the consortium, and Turkcell was replaced as the foreign partner by the second-placed bidder, the South African company MTN. The licence award was eventually signed in November 2005, and initial services commenced in October 2006. A consortium led by the Emirates Telecommunications Corpn (Etisalat—United Arab Emirates) was named as the successful bidder for Iran's third GSM licence in January 2009. However, in May the award was revoked by the regulatory authority. In April 2010 the third GSM licence was reallocated to Tamin Telecom, an Iranian company that had formed part of the previous Etisalat-led consortium. Tamin began offering third-generation mobile telecommunications services, under the brand name RighTel, in 2013.

Telecommunications Company of Iran (TCI): POB 3316-17, Dr Ali Shariati Ave, Tehran; tel. (21) 88113938; fax (21) 88405055; e-mail info@tci.ir; internet tci.ir; fmrly 100% state-owned; 51% stake acquired by Etemad-e-Mobin consortium Sept. 2009; 24.3m. fixed-line subscribers (Sept. 2008); Chair. SEYYED MUSTAFA SEYYED HASHEMI; Man. Dir MUZAFAR POURRANJBAR.

> **Mobile Communications Company of Iran (MCCI):** 88 Hamrah Tower, Vanak St, Vanak Sq., Tehran, 1991954651; fax (21) 88641012; e-mail info@mci.ir; internet www.mci.ir; f. 2004; wholly owned subsidiary of TCI; 27.8m. subscribers (Sept. 2008); CEO VAHID SADOUGHI.

MTN Irancell: 12 Anahita Alley, Africa St, Tehran; internet www .irancell.ir; f. 2004 as Irancell, name changed as above 2005; mobile telecommunications; consortium of Iran Electronic Devt Co (51%) and MTN (South Africa—49%); 18.2m. subscribers (March 2009); Chair. Dr IBRAHIM MAHMOUDZADEH; Man. Dir ALIREZA GHALAMBOR DEZFOULI.

Regulatory Authority

Radio Communications and Regulations Organization: f. 2005; affiliated to the Ministry of Communications and Information Technology (see Ministries).

BROADCASTING

Article 175 of Iran's Constitution prohibits the establishment of private television channels and radio stations that are deemed to be 'un-Islamic'. However, in addition to the channels operated by the state-controlled Islamic Republic of Iran Broadcasting, many Iranians have access to foreign television programmes transmitted via satellite dishes (although ownership of these is officially banned).

Islamic Republic of Iran Broadcasting (IRIB): POB 19395-3333, Jam-e Jam St, Vali-e-Asr Ave, Tehran; tel. (21) 22041093; fax (21) 22014802; e-mail infopr@irib.ir; internet www.irib.ir; semi-autonomous authority, affiliated with the Ministry of Culture and Islamic Guidance; non-commercial; operates seven national and 30 provincial television stations, and nine national radio networks; broadcasts worldwide in 27 languages; launched Al-Alam (international Arabic-language news channel) in 2002 and Press TV (English-language satellite channel) in 2007; Pres. SAYED EZZATOLLAH ZARGHAMI.

Radio

Radio Network 1 (Voice of the Islamic Republic of Iran): Covers the whole of Iran and also reaches Europe, Asia, Africa and part of the USA via short-wave and the internet; medium-wave

regional broadcasts in local languages: Arabic, Armenian, Assyrian, Azerbaijani, Balochi, Bandari, Dari, Farsi, Kurdish, Mazandarani, Pashtu, Turkish, Turkoman and Urdu; external broadcasts in English, French, German, Spanish, Italian, Turkish, Bosnian, Albanian, Russian, Georgian, Armenian, Azeri, Tajik, Kazakh, Arabic, Kurdish, Urdu, Pashtu, Dari, Hausa, Bengali, Hindi, Japanese, Mandarin, Kiswahili, Indonesian and Hebrew.

Television

Television Network 1 (Vision of the Islamic Republic of Iran): 625-line, System B; Secam colour; two production centres in Tehran producing for national networks and 30 local television stations.

Finance

(cap. = capital; res = reserves; dep. = deposits; brs = branches; m. = million; amounts in rials, unless otherwise stated)

BANKING

Banks were nationalized in June 1979 and a revised commercial banking system was introduced consisting of nine banks (subsequently expanded to 11). Three banks were reorganized, two (Bank Tejarat and Bank Mellat) resulted from mergers of 22 existing small banks, three specialize in industry and agriculture, and one, the Islamic Bank of Iran (now Islamic Economy Organization), set up in May 1979, was exempt from nationalization. The 10th bank, the Export Development Bank, specializes in the promotion of exports. Post Bank of Iran became the 11th state-owned bank upon its establishment in 2006. A change-over to an Islamic banking system, with interest (forbidden under Islamic law) being replaced by a 4% commission on loans, began on 21 March 1984. All short- and medium-term private deposits and all bank loans and advances are subject to Islamic rules.

A partial liberalization of the banking sector was implemented by the administration of former President Khatami during 1997–2005, beginning with the establishment of four private banks after 2001. Two further private banks were granted licences to commence operations in 2005. Notable banks included in the Government's privatization programme are Mellat, Refah, Saderat, Tejarat and Post Bank of Iran.

Central Bank

Bank Markazi Jomhouri Islami Iran (Central Bank): POB 15875-7177, 144 Mirdamad Blvd, Tehran; tel. (21) 29954855; fax (21) 29954780; e-mail g.secdept@cbi.ir; internet www.cbi.ir; f. 1960; Bank Markazi Iran until Dec. 1983; issuing bank, govt banking; cap. 15,000,000m., res 102,794,098m., dep. 782,499,933m. (March 2009); Gov. Dr VALIOLLAH SEIF.

State-owned Commercial Banks

Bank Keshavarzi (Agricultural Bank): POB 14155-6395, 247 Patrice Lumumba Ave, Jalal al-Ahmad Expressway, Tehran 14454; tel. (21) 84895593; fax (21) 88253625; e-mail icd@agri-bank .com; internet www.agri-bank.com; f. 1980 by merger of Agricultural Co-operative Bank of Iran and Agricultural Devt Bank of Iran; cap. 8,021,118m., res 10,660,488m., dep. 328,337,431m. (March 2013); Chair. and Man. Dir Dr MUHAMMAD TALEBI; 1,870 brs.

Bank Mellat (Nation's Bank): Head Office Bldg, 327 Taleghani Ave, Tehran 15817; tel. (21) 82962043; fax (21) 88834417; e-mail info@ bankmellat.ir; internet www.bankmellat.ir; f. 1980 by merger of 10 fmr private banks; cap. 16,000,000m., res 5,685,685m., dep. 534,498,512m. (March 2011); Chair. and Man. Dir ALI DIVANDARI; 1,905 brs in Iran, 5 abroad.

Bank Melli Iran (National Bank of Iran): POB 11365-171, Ferdowsi Ave, Tehran; tel. (21) 66731382; fax (21) 66738606; e-mail intlrel@ bankmelli-iran.com; internet www.bankmelli-iran.com; f. 1928; present name since 1943; cap. 22,400,000m., res 7,460,824m., dep. 508,409,899m. (March 2009); Chair. and Man. Dir Dr ABDOLNASER HEMMATI; 3,300 brs in Iran, 16 abroad.

Bank Refah Kargaran: 186 Northern Shiraz Ave, Molla Sadra Ave, Vanak Sq., Tehran 19917; tel. and fax (21) 88653991; fax (21) 42504292; e-mail info@bankrefah.ir; internet www.refah-bank.ir; f. 1960; cap. 895,000m., res 302,259m., dep. 56,545,320m. (March 2008); Chair. and Man. Dir SAYYED ZIA IMANI; 1,117 brs.

Bank Saderat Iran: POB 15745-631, Bank Saderat Tower, 43 Somayeh Ave, Tehran; tel. (21) 88302699; fax (21) 88839539; e-mail info@bsi.ir; internet www.bsi.ir; f. 1952; cap. 20,164,000m., res 8,445,000m., dep. 465,818,000m. (March 2011); Chair. MUHAMMAD REZA PISHRO; 3,300 brs in Iran, 21 abroad.

Bank Sepah: 7 Africa Ave, Argentina Sq., Tehran 15149-47111; tel. (21) 84433161; fax (21) 88646951; e-mail info@banksepah.ir; internet www.banksepah.ir; f. 1925; nationalized in June 1979; cap. 8,559,365m., res 1,870,563m., dep. 328,705,912m. (March 2013);

Chair. and Man. Dir KAMEL TAGHAVI NEJAD; 1,891 brs in Iran, 3 abroad.

Bank Tejarat (Commercial Bank): POB 11365-5416, 130 Taleghani Ave, Nejatoullahie, Tehran 15994; tel. (21) 88826690; fax (21) 88893641; internet www.tejaratbank.ir; f. 1979 by merger of 12 banks; cap. 13,568,599m., res 6,345,677m., dep. 361,381,210m. (March 2011); Chair. and Man. Dir Dr MAJID REZA DAVARI; 1,971 brs in Iran, 2 abroad.

Post Bank of Iran (PBI): 229 Motahari Ave, Tehran 15876-18118; tel. (21) 88502024; fax (21) 88502025; e-mail info@postbank.ir; internet www.postbank.ir; f. 2006; cap. 561,143m., res 11,559m., dep. 8,236,617m. (March 2009); Chair. MAHMOUD HASSANZADEH; Man. Dir ALI ZIAEI.

Private Commercial Banks

Bank Pasargad: POB 19697-74511, 430 Mirdamad Ave, Tehran; tel. (21) 88649502; fax 88649501; e-mail info@bankpasargad.com; internet fa.bpi.ir; f. 2005; cap. 27,258,000m., res 4,841,393m., dep. 172,188,341m. (March 2012); Chair. SAYED KAZEM MIRVALAD; CEO Dr GHASEMI; 233 brs.

Eghtesad Novin Bank (EN Bank): 28 Esfandiar Blvd, Vali-e-Asr Ave, Tehran 196865-5944; tel. (21) 82330000; fax (21) 88880166; e-mail info@enbank.ir; internet www.en-bank.com; f. 2001; granted operating licence in 2001; cap. 5,500,000m., res 1,585,908m., dep. 120,235,940m. (March 2011); Chair. BAHRAM FATHALI; CEO Dr HASSAN MOTAMEDI; 280 brs.

Karafarin Bank: POB 1966916461, No. 97, West Nahid St, Valiasr Ave, Tehran; tel. (21) 26215000; fax (21) 26214995; e-mail info@karafarinbank.com; internet www.karafarinbank.com; f. 1999 as Karafarin Credit Institute; converted into private bank in 2001; cap. 3,000,000m., res 1,026,021m., dep. 33,776,307m. (March 2011); Chair. ATAOLAH AYATOLAHI; Man. Dir FAZLOLAH MOAZAMI; 81 brs.

Parsian Bank: 4 Zarafshan St, Farahzadi Blvd, Shahrak Ghods, Tehran 146779-3811; tel. (21) 81151000; fax (21) 88362744; e-mail info@parsian-bank.ir; internet www.parsian-bank.com; f. 2002; cap. US $897m., res $567m., dep. $21,764m. (March 2012); Chair. Dr GHOLAMREZA SULEIMANI AMIRI; Man. Dir ALI DIVANDARI; 155 brs.

Saman Bank Corpn: Bldg No. 1, 879 Kaledge Junction, Engheleb St, Tehran; tel. (21) 23095100; fax (21) 26210911; e-mail info@sb24.com; internet www.sb24.com; f. 2001; cap. 6,573,503m., res 979,056m., dep. 118,650,030m. (March 2013); Chair. ALLAHVERDI RAJAEE SALMASI; 54 brs.

Sarmaye Bank: POB 19395-6415, 24 Arak St, Gharani Ave, Tehran; tel. (21) 88803632; fax (21) 88890839; e-mail info@sbank.ir; internet www.sbank.ir; f. 2005; cap. 3,535,000m., res 965,425m., dep. 37,242,086m. (March 2012), Chair. PARVIZ KAZEMI; CEO SHAHABEDDIN GHANDALI; 61 brs.

Development Banks

Bank of Industry and Mine (BIM): POB 15875-4456, Firouzeh Tower, 2917 Vali-e-Asr Ave (above Park Way Junction), Tehran; tel. (21) 22029811; fax (21) 22031904; e-mail info@bim.ir; internet w3.bim.ir; f. 1979 by merger of Industrial Credit Bank, Industrial and Mining Devt Bank of Iran, Devt and Investment Bank of Iran, and Iranian Bankers Investment Co; state-owned; cap. 20,722,472m., res 3,749,028m., dep. 48,449,128m. (March 2012); Chair. and Man. Dir ALI ASHRAF AFKHAMI; 31 brs.

Export Development Bank of Iran (EDBI): POB 151674-7913, Tose'e Tower, 15th St, Ahmad Ghasir Ave, Argentina Sq., Tehran; tel. (21) 88702130; fax (21) 88798259; e-mail info@edbi.ir; internet www.edbi.ir; f. 1991; state-owned; cap. 16,418,554m., res 6,325,389m., dep. 41,972,684m. (March 2012); Chair. and Man. Dir BAHMAN VAKILI; 34 brs.

Housing Bank

Bank Maskan (Housing Bank): POB 19947-63811, 14 Attar St, Vanak Sq., Tehran; tel. (21) 88797822; fax (21) 82932735; e-mail intl_div@bank-maskan.ir; internet bank-maskan.ir; f. 1979; state-owned; cap. 30,735,134m., res 3,615,729m., dep. 766,090,576m. (March 2013); provides mortgage and housing finance; Chair. and Man. Dir GHODRATOLLAH SHARIFI; 1,214 brs.

STOCK EXCHANGE

Tehran Stock Exchange: 192 Hafez Ave, Tehran 11355; tel. (21) 66719535; fax (21) 66710111; e-mail int@tse.ir; internet www.tse.ir; f. 1967; cap. US $122,845m. (Nov. 2014); 315 listed cos (May 2014); Chair. HAMID REZA RAFIEI KESHTELI; CEO and Pres. Dr HASSAN GHALIDAF ASL.

INSURANCE

The nationalization of insurance companies was announced in June 1979. However, as part of the reforms to the financial sector undertaken by the former Khatami administration, four new private insurance companies were licensed to commence operations in May 2003. In 2011 there were 24 privately owned insurance and reinsurance companies operating in Iran. There was also one state-owned insurance company in operation, Bimeh Iran.

Bimeh Alborz (Alborz Insurance Co): POB 4489-15875, Alborz Bldg, 234 Sepahboad Garani Ave, Tehran; tel. (21) 88803821; fax (21) 88908088; e-mail info@alborzins.com; internet www.alborzinsurance.ir; f. 1959; all types of insurance; Chair. and Man. Dir MUHAMMAD EBRAHIM AMIN; 39 brs.

Bimeh Asia (Asia Insurance Co): POB 15815-1885, Asia Insurance Bldg, 299 Taleghani Ave, Tehran; tel. (21) 88800950; fax (21) 88898113; e-mail info@bimehasia.ir; internet www.bimehasia.com; f. 1959; all types of insurance; Man. Dir A. HAJFATALIHA; 83 brs.

Bimeh Dana (Dana Insurance Co): 25 15th St, Ghandi Ave, Tehran 151789-5511; tel. (21) 88770971; fax (21) 88792997; e-mail info@dana-insurance.com; internet www.dana-insurance.com; f. 1988; 56% govt-owned; life, personal accident and health insurance; Chair. and Man. Dir H. O. HOSSEIN.

Bimeh Day (Day Insurance Co): 241 Mirdamad Blvd, Tehran; tel. (21) 22900551; fax (21) 22900516; e-mail info@dayins.com; internet www.dayins.com; f. 2004; privately owned; all types of insurance.

Bimeh Iran (Iran Insurance Co): POB 14155-6363, 107 Dr Fatemi Ave, Tehran; tel. (21) 88954712; e-mail info@iraninsurance.ir; internet www.iraninsurance.ir; f. 1935; state-owned; all types of insurance; Chair. and Man. Dir JAVAD SAHAMIAN MOGHADDAM; 246 brs in Iran, 14 brs abroad.

Bimeh Karafarin (Karafarin Insurance Co): POB 15875-8475, No. 9, 17th St, Ahmad Ghasir Ave, Argentina Sq., Tehran; tel. (21) 88723830; fax (21) 88723840; e-mail karafarin@karafarin-insurance.com; internet www.karafarin-insurance.com; f. 2003; privately owned; all types of insurance; 14 brs; Chair. Dr PARVIZ AGHILI-KERMANI; Man. Dir ABDOLMAHMOUD ZARRABI.

Bimeh Novin (Novin Insurance Co): POB 19119-33183, 11 Behrouz St, Madar (Mohseni) Sq., Mirdamad Blvd, Tehran; tel. (21) 22258046; fax (21) 22923844; e-mail info@novininsurance.com; internet www.novininsurance.com; f. 2006; privately owned; all types of insurance; Chair. Dr GHOLAMALI GHOLAMI.

Bimeh Saman (Saman Insurance Co): 113 Khaled Eslamboli Ave, Tehran 15138-13119; tel. (21) 88700205; fax (21) 88700204, e-mail info@samaninsurance.com; internet www.samaninsurance.com; f. 2005; privately owned; Chair. MUHAMMAD ZRABYH.

Bimeh Sina (Sina Insurance Co): 343 Beheshti Ave, Tehran; tel. (21) 88706701; fax (21) 88709654; e-mail info@sinainsurance.com; internet www.sinainsurance.com; f. 2003; privately owned.

Mellat Insurance Co: 48 Shahid Haghani Expressway, Vanak Sq., Tehran; tel. and fax (21) 88878814; e-mail info@mellatinsurance.com; internet www.mellatinsurance.com; privately owned; property, life, engineering, aviation and marine insurance; Chair. ABDOLHOSSEIN SABET; Man. Dir MASOUD HAJJARIAN KASHANI.

Regulatory Authority

Bimeh Markazi Iran (Central Insurance of Iran): POB 19395-5588, 72 Africa Ave, Tehran 19157; tel. (21) 22050001; fax (21) 22054099; e-mail pr@centinsur.ir; internet www.centinsur.ir; f. 1971; regulates and supervises the insurance market and tariffs for new types of insurance cover; the sole state reinsurer for domestic insurance cos, which are obliged to reinsure 50% of their direct business in life insurance and 25% of business in non-life insurance with Bimeh Markazi Iran; Pres. Dr JAVAD FARSHBAF MAHERIYAN.

Trade and Industry

CHAMBERS OF COMMERCE

Iran Chamber of Commerce, Industries and Mines: 254 Taleghani Ave, Tehran 15875-4671; tel. (21) 88846031; fax (21) 88825111; e-mail dsg@iccim.ir; internet www.iccim.ir; supervises the affiliated 32 local chambers; Pres. Dr MUHAMMAD NAHAVANDIAN.

Esfahan Chamber of Commerce, Industries and Mines: POB 81656-336, Feyz Sq., Tehran; tel. (311) 6611467; fax (311) 6615099; e-mail m.eslamian@eccim.com; internet www.eccim.com; Pres. KHORSO KARAEIYAN.

Shiraz Chamber of Commerce, Industries and Mines: Zand St, Shiraz; tel. (711) 6294901; fax (711) 6294910; e-mail info@sccim.org; internet www.sccim.ir; Chair. FERIDOUN FORGHANI.

Tabriz Chamber of Commerce, Industries and Mines: 65 North Artesh Ave, Tabriz; tel. (411) 5264111; fax (411) 5264115; e-mail info@tzccim.ir; internet www.tzccim.ir; f. 1906; privately owned; Chair. RAHIM SADEGHIAN.

Tehran Chamber of Commerce, Industries and Mines: 285 Motahari Ave, Tehran; tel. (21) 88701912; fax (21) 88715661; e-mail into@tccim.ir; internet www.tccim.ir; Chair. Dr YAHYA ALE-ESHAGH.

INDUSTRIAL AND TRADE ASSOCIATIONS

National Iranian Industries Organization (NIIO): POB 15875-1331, No. 11, 13th Alley, Miremad St, Tehran; tel. (21) 88744198; fax (21) 88757126; f. 1979; owns 400 factories in Iran; Man. Dir ALI TOOSI.

National Iranian Industries Organization Export Co (NECO): No. 8, 2nd Alley, Bucharest Ave, Tehran; tel. (21) 44162384; fax (21) 212429.

STATE HYDROCARBONS COMPANIES

The following are subsidiary companies of the Ministry of Petroleum:

National Iranian Gas Co (NIGC): POB 6394-4533, 7th Floor, No. 401, Saghitaman, Taleghani Ave, Tehran; tel. (21) 88133347; fax (21) 88133456; e-mail webmaster@nigc.org; internet www.nigc.ir; f. 1965; Chair. BIJAN NAMDAR ZANGANEH (Minister of Petroleum); Man. Dir JAVAD OJI.

National Iranian Oil Co (NIOC): POB 1863, Taleghani Ave, Tehran 15875-1863; tel. (21) 66154975; fax (21) 66154977; e-mail public-relations@nioc.com; internet www.nioc.com; f. 1948; controls all upstream activities in the petroleum and natural gas industries; incorporated April 1951 on nationalization of petroleum industry to engage in all phases of petroleum operations; in Feb. 1979 it was announced that in future Iran would sell petroleum directly to the petroleum companies, and in Sept. 1979 the Ministry of Petroleum assumed control of the NIOC; Chair. BIJAN NAMDAR ZANGANEH (Minister of Petroleum); Man. Dir SEIFOLLAH JASHNSAZ; subsidiary cos include the following:

> **Iranian Offshore Oil Co (IOOC):** POB 5591, 38 Tooraj St, Vali-e-Asr Ave, Tehran 19395; tel. (21) 22664402; fax (21) 22664216; e-mail M.Khandan@iooc.co.ir; internet www.iooc.co.ir; f. 1980; devt, exploitation and production of crude petroleum, natural gas and other hydrocarbons in all offshore areas of Iran in the Persian (Arabian) Gulf and the Caspian Sea; Chair. Dr MUHAMMAD JAVAD ASEMI POOR; Man. Dir MAHMOUD ZIRAKCHIAN ZADEH.

> **Pars Oil and Gas Co (POGC):** POB 14141-73111, 1 Parvin Etesami Alley, Dr Fatemi Ave, Tehran; tel. (21) 88966031; fax (21) 88989273; e-mail info@pogc.ir; internet www.pogc.ir; f. 1999; Man. Dir ALI VAKILI.

National Iranian Oil Refining and Distribution Co (NIORDC): POB 15815-3499, NIORDC Bldg, 140 Ostad Nejatollahi Ave, Tehran 15989; tel. (21) 88801001; fax (21) 66152138; e-mail info@niordc.ir; internet www.niordc.ir; f. 1992 to assume responsibility for refining, pipeline distribution, engineering, construction and research in the petroleum industry from NIOC; Chair. BIJAN NAMDAR ZANGANEH (Minister of Petroleum); Man. Dir NOUREDDIN SHAHNAZIZADEH.

National Iranian Petrochemical Co (NIPC): POB 19395-6896, North Sheikh Bahaei St, Tehran; tel. (21) 88620000; fax (21) 88059702; e-mail webmaster@nipc.net; internet www.nipc.net; f. 1964; oversees the devt and operation of Iran's petrochemical sector; directs activities of over 50 subsidiaries; Chair. BIJAN NAMDAR ZANGANEH (Minister of Petroleum); Man. Dir ABDOLHOSSEIN BAYAT.

CO-OPERATIVES

Central Union of Rural and Agricultural Co-operatives of Iran: POB 14155-6413, 78 North Palestine St, Opposite Ministry of Energy, Tehran; tel. (21) 84082200; fax (21) 88964166; internet www.trocairan.com; f. 1963; educational, technical, commercial and credit assistance to rural co-operative societies and unions; Chair. and Man. Dir SAYED MUHAMMAD MIRMUHAMMADI.

UTILITIES

Electricity

Iran Power Generation, Transmission and Distribution Co (Tavanir): POB 19988-36111, Tavanir Blvd, Rashid Yasami St, Vali-e-Asr Ave, Tehran; tel. (21) 88774088; fax (21) 88778437; e-mail info@tavanir.org.ir; internet www.tavanir.org.ir; f. 1979; state-owned; operates a network of 16 regional electricity cos, 27 generating cos and 42 distribution cos; also responsible for electricity transmission; Man. Dir HOMAYOUN HAERI.

Water

Iran Water Resources Management Co: 517 Felestin Ave, Tehran; tel. (21) 88905003; fax (21) 88801555; e-mail waterpr@wrm.ir; internet www.wrm.ir; f. 2003; govt agency reporting to the Ministry of Energy; in charge of Iran's Regional Water Authorities; Man. Dir MUHAMMAD HAJRASOULIHA.

Transport

RAILWAYS

In 2010 the total length of Iranian railways was 6,073 route-km. In 2007 it was reported that the Government planned to expand the rail network to 28,000 km by 2020. However, the expansion programme has been severely impeded by a shortage of foreign investment and the impact of US-led sanctions. None the less, construction of a 506-km rail link between Esfahan and Shiraz was completed in June 2009. In the same month a 250-km Zahedan–Kerman line was inaugurated, linking the rail networks of Iran and Pakistan and facilitating the launch of a direct Islamabad (Pakistan)–Tehran–Istanbul (Turkey) freight service in August. Construction of a 1,350-km railway along Iran's eastern border, linking Mashhad, in the north-east, with Chabahar on the Persian (Arabian) Gulf, commenced in May 2010. A 51-km railway linking Khorramshahr with Basra in southern Iraq was also under construction. In February 2011 a US $12,860m. contract to build eight new lines—totalling some 5,300 km—was awarded to the People's Republic of China.

Islamic Republic of Iran Railways: Railways Central Bldg, Argentina Sq., Africa Blvd, Tehran; tel. (21) 88646568; fax (21) 88646570; e-mail iranrai@rai.ir; internet www.rai.ir; f. 1934; affiliated to Ministry of Roads and Urban Development; Pres. Dr MOHSEN POUR SEYED AGHAEI.

Raja Passenger Trains Co: POB 15875-1363, 1 Sanaie St, Karimkhan Zand Ave, Tehran; tel. (21) 88310880; fax (21) 88834340; e-mail info@raja.ir; internet www.raja.ir; f. 1996; state-owned; affiliated to Islamic Republic of Iran Railways; Chair. and Man. Dir SEYED HASSAN MOSAVI NEJAD.

Underground Railway

Construction of the Tehran underground railway system commenced in 1977. By 2015 the system consisted of five lines: Line 1, a 34-km line linking north and south Tehran; Line 2, a 24-km line running east–west across the city; Line 3, initially a 7-km line between two stations in the city centre (eventually to become a 35-km line running south-east to north-east); Line 4, a 16-km line running east–west through the centre; and Line 5, a 41.5-km suburban line, linking Tehran with the satellite city of Karaj. A further two lines—6 and 7—were under construction. In March 2010 the Tehran Urban and Suburban Railway Company announced plans for an additional six underground lines—8 and 9, and four suburban lines linking central Tehran to satellite cities. It was envisaged that construction work on these additional lines would commence in 2018, following the completion of existing projects.

Tehran Urban and Suburban Railway Co (Tehranmetro) (TUSRC): 37 Mir Emad St, Tehran 15878-13113; tel. (21) 88740110; fax (21) 88740114; e-mail info@tehranmetro.com; internet www.tehranmetro.com; f. 1976; CEO HABIL DARVISH.

ROADS

In 2010 there were an estimated 276,597 km of roads, including 2,166 km of motorways, 34,203 km of highways, main or national roads, 44,454 km of secondary or regional roads and 195,775 km of other roads. There is a paved highway (A1, 2,089 km) from Bazargan on the Turkish border to the Afghanistan border. The A2 highway runs 2,473 km from the Iraq border to Mir Javeh on the Pakistan border. A new highway linking the eastern city of Dogharun to Herat in Afghanistan was opened in January 2005.

INLAND WATERWAYS

Lake Urmia (formerly Lake Rezaiyeh): 80 km west of Tabriz in north-western Iran; from Sharafkhaneh to Golmankhaneh there is a regular service of tugs and barges for the transport of passengers and goods.

Karun River: Flowing south through the oilfields into the Shatt al-Arab waterway, and thence to the head of the Persian (Arabian) Gulf near Abadan; there is a regular cargo service, as well as daily motorboat services for passengers and goods.

SHIPPING

The main oil terminal on the Persian (Arabian) Gulf is at Kharg Island. The principal commercial non-oil ports are Bandar Shahid Rajai (which was officially inaugurated in 1983 and handles a significant proportion of the cargo passing annually through Iran's Gulf ports), Bandar Imam Khomeini, Bushehr, Bandar Abbas and Chabahar. The Bandar Abbas port complex, which predates the 1979 Islamic Revolution, comprises two separate ports, Shahid Rajai and Shahid Bahonar. A major expansion of Chabahar port, which was expected to increase annual handling capacity from 100,000 to 500,000 20-ft equivalent units, was under way in 2015. Iran's principal ports on the Caspian Sea include Bandar Anzali (formerly Bandar Pahlavi) and Bandar Nowshahr.

At 31 December 2014 Iran's flag registered fleet comprised 787 vessels, with an aggregate displacement of 3.4m. grt, of which 37 were bulk carriers, 36 were fish carriers and 215 were general cargo ships.

Port Authority

Ports and Maritime Organization (PMO): POB 158754574-158753754, South Didar St, Shahid Haghani Highway, Vanak Sq.,

Tehran; tel. (21) 88809280; fax (21) 84932279; e-mail info@pmo.ir; internet www.pmo.ir; f. 1960 as Ports and Shipping Org.; affiliated to Ministry of Roads and Urban Development; Man. Dir MUHAMMAD SAEIDNEJAD.

Principal Shipping Companies

Bonyad Shipping Agencies Co (BOSCO): POB 15875-3794, 24 Gandhi Ave, 15177 Tehran; tel. (21) 88795211; fax (21) 88776951; e-mail bosaco@bosaco.ir; internet www.bosacoir.com; f. 1991; Man. Dir ALI SAFARALI.

Iran Marine Services: 151 Mirdamad Blvd, Tehran 19116; tel. (21) 22053927; fax (21) 26204158; e-mail center@ims-ir.com; internet www.ims-ir.com; f. 1981; Chair. and Man. Dir MUHAMMAD AHMADI BAFANDEH.

Irano–Hind Shipping Co (IHSC): POB 15875-4647, 18 Sedaghat St, Vali-e-Asr Ave, Tehran; tel. (21) 22058095; fax (21) 22057739; e-mail admin@iranohind.com; f. 1974; jt venture between Islamic Republic of Iran and Shipping Corpn of India; Man. Dir Capt. C. P. ATHAIDE.

Islamic Republic of Iran Shipping Lines (IRISL): POB 19395-1311, 37 Asseman Tower, Sayyad Shirazee Sq., Pasdaran Ave, Tehran; tel. (21) 20100369; fax (21) 20100367; e-mail e-pr@irisl .net; internet www.irisl.net; f. 1967; Man. Dir MUHAMMAD HOSSEIN DAJMAR.

National Iranian Tanker Co (NITC): POB 19395-4833, 67–68 Atefis St, Africa Ave, Tehran; tel. (21) 66153220; fax (21) 22224537; e-mail souri@nitc.co.ir; internet www.nitc.co.ir; Chair. and Man. Dir ALI AKBAR SAFAEI.

CIVIL AVIATION

The principal international airport is the Imam Khomeini International Airport (IKIA), to the south of Tehran. IKIA opened fully in May 2005, and, by mid-2006, had taken over all international flights from Mehrabad airport (west of Tehran). There are several other international airports, including those at Esfahan, Mashhad, Shiraz and Tabriz.

Civil Aviation Organization (CAO): POB 13445-1798, Taleghani Ave, Tehran; tel. (21) 66025131; fax (21) 44665496; e-mail info@cao .ir; internet www.cao.ir; affiliated to Ministry of Roads and Urban Development; Pres. ALI REZA JAHANGIRIAN.

Caspian Airlines: 5 Sabonchi St, Shahid Beheshti Ave, Tehran; tel. (21) 88751671; fax (21) 887516676; e-mail info@caspianairlines.com; internet www.caspian.aero; f. 1992; operates more than 50 flights per week from Tehran to other cities in Iran, as well as scheduled flights to the United Arab Emirates, Lebanon, Syria, Turkey and several European destinations; rep. offices abroad; Gen. Dir Capt. ASGAR RAZZAGHI.

IranAir (Airline of the Islamic Republic of Iran): POB 13185-755, IranAir HQ, Mehrabad Airport, Tehran; tel. (21) 46624255; fax (21) 46628222; e-mail pr@iranair.com; internet www.iranair.com; f. 1962; serves the Middle East and Persian (Arabian) Gulf area, Europe, Asia and the Far East; Chair. and Man. Dir FARHAD PARVARESH.

   Iran Airtours: POB 1587997811, 183 Motahari St, Dr Mofatteh Cross Rd, Tehran; tel. (21) 89317813; fax (21) 89317080; e-mail info@iranairtours.com; internet iranairtours.ir; f. 1992; low-cost subsidiary of IranAir, offering flights from Tehran and Mashhad; serves domestic routes and the wider Middle East; Chair. ABBAS POUR-MUHAMMADI; Man. Dir SIROUS BAHERI.

Iran Aseman Airlines: POB 141748, Mehrabad Airport, Tehran 13145-1476; tel. (21) 66035310; fax (21) 66030413; e-mail public@iaa .ir; internet www.iaa.ir; f. 1980 as result of merger of Air Taxi Co (f. 1958), Pars Air (f. 1969), Air Service Co (f. 1962) and Hoor Asseman; domestic routes and charter services to destinations in Central Asia and the Middle East; Man. Dir ABBAS RAHMATIAN.

Kish Air: POB 19395-4639, 215 Africa Ave, Tehran 19697; tel. (21) 44665639; fax (21) 44665221; e-mail info@kishairline.com; internet www.kishairline.com; f. 1989, under the auspices of the Kish Devt Org.; domestic routes and flights to the United Arab Emirates and Turkey; Chair. and CEO Capt. REZA NAKHJAVANI.

Mahan Air: POB 14515-411, Mahan Air Tower, 21 Azadegan St, Karaj Highway, Tehran 14816-55761; tel. (21) 48384838; fax (21) 48381450; e-mail international@mahanairlines.com; internet www .mahan.aero; f. 1992; domestic routes and charter services to other Middle Eastern, Asian and European destinations; Man. Dir HAMID ARABNEJAD.

Qeshm Air: 17 Ghandi Ave, Tehran; tel. (21) 88776012; fax (21) 88786252; e-mail info@qeshm-air.com; internet qeshm-air.com; operates regular flights from Qeshm Island to the Iranian mainland and the United Arab Emirates.

Saha Airlines: POB 13865-164, Karadj Old Rd, Tehran 13873; tel. (21) 66696200; fax (21) 66698016; e-mail saha2@iran-net.com; f. 1990; owned by the Iranian Air Force; operates passenger and cargo charter domestic flights and services to Europe, Asia and Africa; Man. Dir Capt. MANSOUR NIKUKAR.

Tourism

Iran's principal attraction for tourists is its wealth of historical sites, notably Esfahan, Shiraz, Persepolis, Tabriz and Shush (Susa). The country also possesses a wide variety of natural landscapes, and skiing or hiking are popular activities in the Alborz Mountains close to Tehran. In 2006 it was announced that Iran was seeking to attract tourists from neighbouring Muslim countries by developing the tourism industry on Kish island, declared a free trade zone in 1992. The Government plans to attract 20m. foreign tourists each year to Iran by 2018. Tourist arrivals totalled 4.8m. in 2013. Receipts from tourism in 2012 were recorded at US $1,114m. (excluding passenger transport).

Iran Tourism and Touring Organization (ITTO): 154 Keshavarz Blvd, Tehran; tel. (21) 88737065; fax (21) 88736800; e-mail info@ itto.org; internet www.itto.org; f. 1985; administered by Ministry of Culture and Islamic Guidance.

Defence

Secretary of the Supreme National Security Council: Rear Adm. ALI SHAMKHANI.

Chief of Staff of the Armed Forces: Maj.-Gen. HASSAN FIROUZABADI.

Commander of the Army: Brig.-Gen. ATAOLLAH SALEHI.

Commander of the Air Force: Brig.-Gen. HASSAN SHAHSAFI.

Commander of the Navy: Rear-Adm. HABIBOLLAH SAYYARI.

Chief of Staff of the Islamic Revolutionary Guards Corps (Pasdaran Inqilab): Brig.-Gen. MUHAMMAD ALI JAFARI.

Commander of the Islamic Revolutionary Guards Corps Ground Forces: Brig.-Gen. MUHAMMAD PAKPOUR.

Commander of the Islamic Revolutionary Guards Corps Air Force: Brig.-Gen. AMIR ALI HEJIZADEH.

Commander of the Islamic Revolutionary Guards Corps Navy: Rear-Adm. ALI FADAVI.

Commander of Basij (Mobilization) War Volunteers Corps: Brig.-Gen. MUHAMMAD REZA NAGHDI.

Budgeted defence expenditure (2013): (year ending 20 March) est. IR 366,000,000m.

Total armed forces: As assessed at November 2014, Iran's regular armed forces totalled an estimated 523,000 (excluding 350,000 reserves): army 350,000 men; navy 18,000; air force 30,000; Islamic Revolutionary Guards Corps (*Pasdaran Inqilab*, which has its own land, navy and marine units) some 125,000; membership of Basij War Volunteers Corps estimated to include up to 1m. combatants; there were also some 40,000 paramilitary forces under the command of the Ministry of the Interior.

Education

PRIMARY AND SECONDARY EDUCATION

Primary education, beginning at the age of six and lasting for five years, is compulsory for all children and provided free of charge. Secondary education, from the age of 11, lasts for up to seven years, comprising a first cycle of three years and a second of four years. According to the Government, 24,000 schools were built between the 1979 Revolution and 1984. According to official figures, 6,851,000 pupils were enrolled in primary education in 2012/13, while 5,843,300 were engaged in secondary education. In 2006/07, according to UNESCO estimates, primary enrolment included 99% of children in the relevant age-group, while in 2011 enrolment at secondary schools included 79% of the appropriate age-group.

HIGHER EDUCATION

Iran has 39 universities, including 16 in Tehran. Universities were closed by the Government in 1980 but have been reopened gradually since 1983. According to official sources, some 2,853,300 students were enrolled at Iran's public colleges and universities in the 2012/13 academic year, in addition to the 1,582,400 students enrolled at the Islamic Azad University. Apart from Tehran, there are universities in Bakhtaran, Esfahan, Hamadan, Tabriz, Ahwaz, Babolsar, Meshed, Kermanshah, Rasht, Shiraz, Zahedan, Kerman, Shahrekord, Urmia and Yazd. There are c. 50 colleges of higher education, c. 40 technological institutes, c. 80 teacher-training colleges, several colleges of advanced technology, and colleges of agriculture in Hamadan, Zanjan, Sari and Abadan. Vocational training schools also exist in Tehran, Ahwaz, Meshed, Shiraz and other cities. Budgetary expenditure on education by the central Government in the financial year 2004/05 was IR 31,518,000m. (8.2% of total spending).

IRAQ

Introductory Survey

LOCATION, CLIMATE, LANGUAGE, RELIGION, FLAG, CAPITAL

The Republic of Iraq is an almost landlocked state in western Asia, with a narrow outlet to the sea on the Persian (Arabian) Gulf. Its neighbours are Iran to the east, Turkey to the north, Syria and Jordan to the west, and Saudi Arabia and Kuwait to the south. The climate is extreme, with hot, dry summers, when temperatures may exceed 43°C (109°F), and cold winters, especially in the highlands. Summers are humid near the Gulf coast. The official language is Arabic, spoken by about 80% of the population; about 15% speak Kurdish, while there is also a small Turkoman-speaking minority. Some 95% of the population are Muslims, of whom about 60% belong to the Shi'a sect. In January 2008 the Council of Representatives approved the design of a new, temporary national flag, which was to be replaced by a permanent one within one year. However, by early 2015 a permanent flag had not been selected, largely owing to political differences between the Arab and Kurdish parties. The temporary flag (proportions 2 by 3) has three equal horizontal stripes, of red, white and black, and the inscription 'Allahu Akbar' ('God is Great') written in green Kufic script on the central white stripe. The capital is Baghdad.

CONTEMPORARY POLITICAL HISTORY

Historical Context

Iraq was formerly part of Turkey's Ottoman Empire. During the First World War (1914–18), when Turkey was allied with Germany, the territory was captured by British forces. In 1920 Iraq was placed under a League of Nations mandate, administered by the United Kingdom. In 1921 Amir Faisal ibn Hussain, a member of the Hashimi (Hashemite) dynasty of Arabia, was proclaimed King of Iraq. After prolonged negotiations, a 25-year Anglo-Iraqi Treaty of Alliance was signed in 1930. The British mandate ended on 3 October 1932, when Iraq became fully independent.

During its early years the new kingdom was confronted with Kurdish revolts (1922–32) and with border disputes in the south. Gen. Nuri al-Said became Prime Minister in 1930 and held the office for seven terms over a period of 28 years. He strongly supported Iraq's close links with the United Kingdom and with the West in general. After the death of King Faisal I in 1933, the Iraqi monarchy remained pro-British in outlook, and in 1955 Iraq signed the Baghdad Pact, a British-inspired agreement on collective regional security. However, following the overthrow of King Faisal II (the grandson of Faisal I) during a military revolution on 14 July 1958, which brought to power a left-wing, nationalist regime headed by Brig. (later Lt-Gen.) Abd al-Karim Kassem, the 1925 Constitution was abolished, the legislature was dissolved, and in March 1959 Iraq withdrew from the Baghdad Pact. Kassem, who had become increasingly isolated, was assassinated in February 1963 during a coup by members of the armed forces. The new Government of Col (later Field Marshal) Abd al-Salem Muhammad Aref was more pan-Arab in outlook, and sought closer relations with the United Arab Republic (Egypt). Following his death in March 1966, President Aref was succeeded by his brother, Maj.-Gen. Abd al-Rahman Muhammad Aref, who was deposed on 17 July 1968 by members of the Arab Renaissance (Baath) Socialist Party. Maj.-Gen. (later Field Marshal) Ahmad Hassan al-Bakr, a former Prime Minister, became President and Prime Minister, and supreme authority was vested in the Revolutionary Command Council (RCC), of which President al-Bakr was also Chairman.

Domestic Political Affairs

On 16 July 1979 the Vice-Chairman of the RCC, Saddam Hussain, who had long exercised real power in Iraq, replaced al-Bakr as RCC Chairman and as President of Iraq. Shortly afterwards several members of the RCC were executed for their alleged role in a coup plot. The suspicion of Syrian involvement in the attempted putsch, exacerbated by the rivalry between both countries' Baathist movements, resulted in the suspension of discussions concerning political and economic union between Iraq and Syria. During 1979 the Iraqi Communist Party (ICP) broke away from the National Progressive Front, an alliance of Baathists, Kurdish groups and Communists, claiming that the Baathists were conducting a 'reign of terror'. In February 1980 Saddam Hussain announced a National Charter, reaffirming the principles of non-alignment. In June elections took place for a 250-member legislative National Assembly; these were followed in September by the first elections to a 50-member Kurdish Legislative Council in the Kurdish Autonomous Region (which had been established in 1970).

In 1982 Saddam Hussain consolidated his positions as Chairman of the RCC and Regional Secretary of the Baath Party by conducting a purge throughout the administration. Kurdish rebels became active in northern Iraq, occasionally supporting Iranian forces in the war with Iraq. Another threat was posed by the Supreme Council for the Islamic Revolution in Iraq (SCIRI, renamed the Islamic Supreme Council of Iraq—ISCI—in May 2007), formed in the Iranian capital, Tehran, in November 1982 by the exiled Shi'a leader Hojatoleslam Muhammad Baqir al-Hakim. None the less, the majority of Iraq's Shi'a community was not attracted by the fundamentalist Shi'a doctrine of Ayatollah Khomeini of Iran, remaining loyal to Iraq and its Sunni President, while Iranian-backed militant groups (such as the predominantly Shi'a Islamic Dawa Party—Hizb al-Da'wa al-Islamiya—which made numerous attempts to assassinate Saddam Hussain) were ineffective.

Relations with Iran, precarious for many years, descended into full-scale war in September 1980. Iraq had become increasingly dissatisfied with the 1975 Algiers Agreement, which had defined the southern border between Iran and Iraq as the mid-point of the Shatt al-Arab waterway, and also sought the withdrawal of Iranian forces from Abu Musa and the Tunb islands, which Iran had occupied in 1971. The Iranian Revolution of 1979 exacerbated these grievances, and Iran accused Iraq of encouraging Arab demands for autonomy in Iran's Khuzestan ('Arabistan') region. In September 1980, following clashes on the border, Iraq abrogated the Algiers Agreement and its forces advanced into Iran. Fierce Iranian resistance led to military deadlock until mid-1982, when Iranian counter-offensives led to the retaking of the port of Khorramshahr and the withdrawal of Iraqi troops from territory occupied in 1980. In July 1982 the Iranian army crossed into Iraq. However, the balance of military power in the war moved in Iraq's favour in 1984, and the USA and the USSR provided financial aid. (Diplomatic relations between the USA and Iraq were restored in November 1984, having been suspended since the Arab–Israeli War of 1967.) In July 1988 Iraqi forces crossed into Iran for the first time since 1986. Iran announced its unconditional acceptance of UN Security Council Resolution 598, and by August a UN-monitored ceasefire was in force. However, negotiations on the full implementation of the resolution had made little progress by the time of Iraq's invasion of Kuwait in August 1990, at which point Saddam Hussain abruptly sought a formal peace agreement with Iran—accepting all the claims that Iran had pursued since the ceasefire, including the reinstatement of the Algiers Agreement. (For a fuller account of the 1980–88 Iran–Iraq War and of subsequent bilateral relations, see the chapter on Iran.)

In the second half of the 1980s Saddam Hussain consolidated his control over the country. In 1988 the President announced political reforms, including the introduction of a multi-party system, and in January 1989 declared that these would be incorporated into a new permanent constitution. In April 1989 elections took place to the 250-seat National Assembly, as a result of which more than 50% of deputies were reported to be Baathists. In July the National Assembly approved a new draft Constitution, under the terms of which a 50-member Consultative Assembly was to be established; both institutions would assume the duties of the RCC, which was to be abolished after a presidential election.

During the 1980s representatives of Iraq's 2.5m.–3m. Kurds demanded greater autonomy. Resources were repeatedly diverted from the war with Iran to control Kurdish insurgency in the north-east of Iraq. Saddam Hussain sought an accommodation with the Kurds, and, after a ceasefire had been agreed with Jalal Talabani, the leader of the Patriotic Union of Kurdistan (PUK), discussions began in December 1983. However, they excluded the other main Kurdish group, the Kurdistan Democratic Party (KDP), led by Masoud Barzani. Negotiations collapsed in May 1984, and armed conflict resumed in Kurdistan in January 1985 between PUK guerrillas and government troops, with Kurdish and Iranian forces repeatedly collaborating in raids against Iraqi military and industrial targets. In February 1988 KDP and PUK guerrillas (assisted by Iranian forces) made inroads into government-controlled territory in Iraqi Kurdistan. In March the Iraqi Government retaliated by using chemical weapons against the Kurdish town of Halabja, killing up to 5,000 people. In May the KDP and the PUK announced the formation of a coalition of six organizations to continue the struggle for Kurdish self-determination and to co-operate militarily with Iran. The ceasefire in the Iran–Iraq War in August allowed Iraq to launch a new offensive to overrun guerrilla bases near the borders with Iran and Turkey, again allegedly employing chemical weapons. By September there were reported to be more than 200,000 Kurdish refugees in Iran and Turkey. In that month the Iraqi Government offered a full amnesty to all Iraqi Kurds inside and outside the country, excluding only Jalal Talabani. By October 1989 it had also created a 30-km uninhabited 'security zone' along the whole of Iraq's border with Iran and Turkey by evacuating inhabitants of the Kurdish Autonomous Region to the interior of Iraq, prompting the PUK to announce a nation-wide urban guerrilla campaign against the Government. In September elections had proceeded to the legislative council of the Kurdish Autonomous Region.

The 1990–91 Gulf War

In mid-1990 the Iraqi Government criticized countries (principally Kuwait and the United Arab Emirates—UAE) that had persistently produced petroleum in excess of the quotas imposed by the Organization of the Petroleum Exporting Countries (OPEC, see p. 406). Iraq also accused Kuwait of violating the Iraqi border in order to secure petroleum resources, and demanded that Kuwait waive repayments of Iraq's vast debt to the emirate, incurred during the Iran–Iraq War. Direct negotiations between Iraq and Kuwait concerning their territorial and debt disputes failed, and on 2 August Iraqi forces invaded Kuwait, taking control of the country and establishing a provisional 'free government'. The UN Security Council unanimously adopted Resolution 660, demanding the immediate and unconditional withdrawal of Iraqi forces from Kuwait. Subsequent resolutions imposed mandatory economic sanctions against Iraq and occupied Kuwait (No. 661), and declared Iraq's annexation of Kuwait null and void (No. 662). At a meeting of the League of Arab States (the Arab League, see p. 359) on 3 August, 14 of the 21 members condemned the invasion and demanded an unconditional withdrawal by Iraq; after Iraq announced its formal annexation of Kuwait on 8 August, 12 member states voted to send an Arab deterrent force to the region of the Persian (Arabian) Gulf. On 7 August the US Government dispatched troops and aircraft to Saudi Arabia, at the request of King Fahd, in order to secure the country's border with Kuwait against a possible Iraqi attack; other countries quickly lent their support to what was designated 'Operation Desert Shield', and a multinational force was formed to defend Saudi Arabia.

In November 1990 the UN Security Council adopted Resolution 678, authorizing member states to use 'all necessary means' to enforce an Iraqi withdrawal if all Iraqi forces had not left Kuwait by 15 January 1991. 'Operation Desert Storm'—in effect, war with Iraq—began on the night of 16–17 January, with air attacks on Baghdad by the multinational force, and by the end of January the allied force had achieved air supremacy. Although Iraq managed to launch Scud missiles against Saudi Arabia and Israel, the latter's refusal to retaliate was the result of considerable diplomatic pressure aimed at ensuring Arab unity in the coalition. In February Iraq formally severed diplomatic relations with Egypt, France, Italy, Saudi Arabia, Syria, the United Kingdom and the USA. During the night of 23–24 February the multinational force began a successful ground offensive for the liberation of Kuwait: Iraqi troops surrendered in large numbers. A ceasefire was declared by the US Government on 28 February. Iraq agreed to renounce its claim to Kuwait, to release prisoners of war and to comply with all pertinent UN Security Council resolutions. Resolution 687, adopted in April, provided for the establishment of a commission to demarcate the border between Iraq and Kuwait. The resolution also linked the removal of sanctions imposed on Iraq following its invasion of

Kuwait to the elimination of non-conventional weaponry, to be certified by a UN Special Commission (UNSCOM), and required that Iraq accept proposals for the establishment of a war reparation fund to be derived from Iraqi petroleum reserves. Later that month the UN Security Council approved Resolution 689, which established a demilitarized zone between the two countries.

Within Iraq, the war was followed by domestic unrest: in March 1991 rebel forces, including Shi'a Muslims and disaffected soldiers, were reported to have taken control of Basra and other southern cities, although the rebellion was soon crushed by troops loyal to Saddam Hussain. In the north, Kurdish separatists overran a large area of Kurdistan. However, the Kurdish guerrillas were unable to resist the onslaught of the Iraqi armed forces and an estimated 1m.–2m. Kurds fled across the mountains into Turkey and Iran. UN Security Council Resolution 688, adopted in April 1991, condemned the repression of Iraqi civilians and provided for the establishment of an international effort to provide relief to displaced persons and to secure designated 'safe havens' on Iraqi territory north of latitude 36°N. In support of Resolution 688, a corresponding air exclusion zone was established by the USA, with the support of France and the United Kingdom.

A second air exclusion zone, south of latitude 32°N, was established by those countries plus Russia in August 1992, with the aim of protecting the southern Iraqi Shi'a communities, including the semi-nomadic Ma'dan (Marsh Arabs). In July 1993 Iraqi armed forces were reported to have renewed the Government's offensive against the inhabitants of the marshlands. In May 1996 government forces launched a major offensive against the Shi'a opposition and tribes in Basra governorate, which led to armed clashes between Iraqi security forces and the Shi'a opposition throughout the southern regions.

Conflict in the Kurdish Autonomous Region

Meanwhile, in April 1991 the PUK leader, Talabani, announced that President Saddam Hussain had agreed in principle to implement the provisions of a 15-point peace plan concluded by Kurdish leaders and the Iraqi Government in 1970. However, negotiations subsequently became deadlocked over the Kurdish demand for the inclusion of Kirkuk in the Kurdish Autonomous Region. In October 1991 the Iraqi Government effectively subjected the Kurds to an economic blockade. The various Kurdish factions proceeded to organize elections, in May 1992, to a 105-member Iraqi Kurdistan National Assembly, and for a paramount Kurdish leader. The outcome of voting, in which none of the smaller Kurdish parties achieved representation, was that the KDP and the PUK agreed to share equally the number of seats in the new assembly. The election for an overall Kurdish leader was deemed inconclusive, with Barzani, the KDP leader, receiving 47.5% of the votes cast, and Talabani 44.9%.

Armed conflict between partisans of the PUK and the KDP led, in May, to the division of the northern Kurdish-controlled enclave into two zones. In June 1995 the Islamic League of Kurdistan (or Islamic Movement of Iraqi Kurdistan—IMIK) withdrew from the Iraqi National Congress (INC—a broad coalition of largely foreign-based opposition groups), and in July there was renewed fighting between PUK and KDP forces, as a result of which scheduled elections to the Iraqi Kurdistan National Assembly were postponed. The two parties finally agreed, in October, to hold the elections in May 1996.

However, hostilities escalated in August 1996. At the end of the month Iraqi military support for the KDP in the recapture of the PUK-held towns of Irbil (Arbil) and Sulaimaniya in the Kurdish area of northern Iraq provoked a new international crisis. In September the USA unilaterally launched retaliatory 'limited' air strikes on air defence and communications targets in southern Iraq, and extended the southern air exclusion zone from latitude 32°N to latitude 33°N (thereby incorporating some southern suburbs of Baghdad). Turkey, which had refused to allow the use of its air bases for the US operation, deployed some 20,000 troops to reinforce its border with Iraq. Meanwhile, the KDP gained control of all three Kurdish provinces. The Iraqi Government subsequently announced the restoration of Iraqi sovereignty over Kurdistan, and offered an amnesty to its Kurdish opponents. In late September the KDP formed a coalition administration which included the IMIK, the Kurdistan Communist Party and representatives of the northern Assyrian and Turkoman communities. In October PUK fighters were reported to have recaptured much of the territory that they had ceded to the KDP, having regained control of Sulaimaniya and Halabja. Concern that Iran's alleged involvement in the conflict would provoke direct Iraqi intervention in the north prompted renewed diplomatic efforts on the part of the USA and Turkey, and US-sponsored peace talks in Ankara, Turkey, in late October resulted in a truce agreement. A new air surveillance programme—conducted by British, Turkish and US forces—began in January 1997.

The KDP withdrew from the peace negotiations in March 1997, and in May around 50,000 Turkish troops entered northern Iraq, where, apparently in co-operation with the KDP, they launched a major offensive against bases maintained by the Kurdistan Workers' Party (Partiya Karkeren Kurdistan—PKK). As Turkey began to withdraw its armed forces in October, the PUK launched a massive military offensive against the KDP, which subsequently alleged that the assault had been co-ordinated by Iran and supported by the PKK. By mid-1998, amid a fragile ceasefire between the PUK and the KDP, the two organizations agreed to exchange prisoners. In September a formal peace agreement was signed in Washington, DC, USA, which, *inter alia*, provided for: Kurdish legislative elections in 1999 (although these did not take place); a unified regional administration; the sharing of local revenues; and an end to hostilities. A new Kurdish coalition government was appointed by the Iraqi Kurdistan National Assembly in December 1999.

Political developments after the Gulf War

After Iraq's defeat by the US-led coalition forces in 1991, Saddam Hussain strengthened his control over the country by placing family members and close supporters in the most important government positions. In September Hussain was re-elected Secretary-General of the Baath Party's powerful Regional Command at its 10th Congress, and in May 1994 he assumed the post of Prime Minister. Unsuccessful coups reportedly took place in January and March 1995; the latter was instigated by the former head of Iraqi military intelligence and supported by Kurdish insurgents in the north and Shi'a rebels in the south. In September the RCC approved an interim amendment of the Constitution whereby its elected Chairman would automatically assume the presidency of the Republic, subject to approval by the National Assembly and endorsement by national plebiscite. Saddam Hussain's candidature was duly approved by the Assembly, and endorsed by 99.96% of the votes cast at a referendum held on 15 October.

The first elections to the Iraqi National Assembly since 1989 took place in March 1996, when 689 government-approved candidates contested 220 of the Assembly's 250 seats: the remaining 30 seats were reserved for representatives of the Autonomous Regions of Arbil, D'hok and Sulaimaniya, and were filled by presidential decree. The elections were denounced by the INC, based in London, United Kingdom, and by other groups opposed to the Government.

Following reports in late 1997 that Saddam Hussain had ordered the execution of a number of senior military officers, Baath Party members and prisoners, internal unrest continued during 1998. According to SCIRI, a renewed government offensive against the Shi'a in southern Iraq resulted in the execution of some 60 people during March. Later in 1998 two senior Shi'a religious leaders, Ayatollah Murtada al-Burujirdi and Grand Ayatollah Mirza Ali al-Gharawi, were both assassinated. In February 1999 the killing of Iraq's Shi'a leader, Grand Ayatollah Muhammad Sadiq al-Sadr, provoked widespread demonstrations which were brutally suppressed by units of the Sunni-dominated Iraqi Special Republican Guard. Meanwhile, in October 1998 the US Congress approved the Iraq Liberation Act, permitting the US President to provide up to US $97m. in military assistance to Iraqi opposition groups in exile.

Elections took place on 27 March 2000 for 220 seats in the National Assembly. Official results stated that 165 seats had been won by members of the Baath Party, and the remaining 55 elective seats by independent candidates; a further 30 independents were nominated by the Government to fill the seats reserved for representatives of the Kurdish areas of the north. Saddam Hussain's elder son, Uday, was elected to the legislature for the first time. In May 2001 Saddam Hussain was re-elected Secretary-General of the Baath Party Regional Command at the organization's 12th Congress, while his younger son, Qusay, was elected to the party Command.

At a national referendum held on 15 October 2002 to decide whether President Saddam Hussain should remain in office for a further seven-year term, the Iraqi leader was officially reported to have received 100% of the votes. A general amnesty for prisoners held in Iraqi gaols was subsequently announced by the authorities; however, opposition groups maintained that there were still thousands of political prisoners in Iraq. This proved to be the last major internal political development under the Baath regime prior to the US-led coalition's military campaign of early 2003, which led to the removal of Saddam Hussain's Government.

The UN's sanctions regime and international monitoring of Iraq's weapons programme

Issues of the maintenance of sanctions originally imposed under UN Security Council Resolution 661 and of Iraqi non-compliance with its obligations under Resolution 687 with regard to its weapons capabilities remained inextricably linked in the decade following the Gulf conflict. Resolution 692, adopted in May 1991, provided for the establishment of the UN Compensation Commission for victims of Iraqi aggression (both governments and individuals), to be financed by a levy (subsequently fixed at 30%) on Iraqi petroleum revenues. In August the Security Council adopted Resolution 706 (approved in Resolution 712 in September), proposing that Iraq should be allowed to sell petroleum worth up to US $1,600m. over a six-month period, the revenue from which would be controlled by the UN. Part of this revenue was to be made available to Iraq for the purchase of food, medicines and essential supplies. Iraq rejected the UN's terms for the resumption of petroleum exports, and in February 1992 withdrew from further negotiations, but in October Resolution 778 permitted the confiscation of oil-related Iraqi assets to the value of $500m.

UN Security Council Resolution 707, adopted in August 1991, condemned Iraq's failure to comply with UN weapons inspectors, and demanded that Iraq: disclose details of all non-conventional weaponry; allow members of UNSCOM and of the International Atomic Energy Agency (IAEA) unrestricted access to necessary areas and records; and halt all nuclear activities. In early 1994, having reportedly agreed to co-operate with UN weapons inspectors, the Iraqi Government engaged in a campaign of diplomacy to obtain the removal of economic sanctions. However, the USA and the United Kingdom refused to join the other members of the UN Security Council in acknowledging Iraq's increased co-operation with UN agencies. Following a stand-off between Iraq and the US and British military, prompted by the movement of Iraqi forces near the border with Kuwait, the Iraqi National Assembly voted in November to recognize Kuwait within the border defined by the UN in April 1992.

Economic sanctions imposed on Iraq were renewed on a 60-day basis from 1995. In May 1996 the Iraqi Government accepted a revised UN proposal (contained in Security Council Resolution 986) for the partial resumption of crude petroleum exports to generate funds under what was designated an 'oil-for-food' programme. The memorandum of understanding (MOU) signed by the two sides permitted Iraq to sell some 700,000 barrels per day (b/d) of petroleum over an initial period of six months. Of every US $1,000m. realized through the sales, $300m. would be paid into the UN reparations fund; $30m.–$50m. would contribute to the costs of UN operations in Iraq; and $130m.–$150m. would go towards funding UN humanitarian operations in Iraq's Kurdish governorates. Remaining revenues would be used for the purchase and distribution of humanitarian goods in Iraq. The UN emphasized that the embargo on sales of Iraqi petroleum would not be fully revoked until all the country's weapons of mass destruction had been accounted for and destroyed.

In October 1997 the initial report of UNSCOM to the UN Security Council asserted that Iraq had failed to produce a credible account of its biological, chemical and nuclear warfare programmes and was continuing to hinder UNSCOM's work. In November the Security Council unanimously adopted a resolution (No. 1137) that imposed a travel ban on Iraqi officials deemed to be responsible for obstructing UNSCOM weapons inspectors. The confrontation deepened in January 1998, when Iraq prohibited inspections by an UNSCOM team led by a former US marine officer, Scott Ritter, claiming that Ritter was spying for the US Central Intelligence Agency.

However, the UN Security Council remained divided on the issue of weapons inspections: the USA, supported by the United Kingdom, indicated that it was prepared to respond militarily to Iraq's continued non-co-operation, while China, France and Russia opposed the use of force. In February 1998 the five permanent members of the Security Council approved a compromise formula whereby a group of diplomats, specially appointed by the UN Secretary-General, Kofi Annan, would be allowed unrestricted access to the eight so-called presidential sites. The compromise was accepted by Iraq, and in March the Security

Council unanimously approved Resolution 1154, warning of 'extreme consequences' should Iraq renege on the agreement. Members of the special group began visiting the presidential sites later in the month, but in April the head of UNSCOM concluded that the destruction of Iraq's chemical and biological weapons was incomplete.

UNSCOM reportedly informed the UN Security Council in June 1998 that US military tests on weaponry recently dismantled showed that Iraq had chemical weapons capability prior to the Gulf conflict. In August negotiations between UNSCOM and Iraqi Deputy Prime Minister Tareq Aziz collapsed, Iraq suspended arms inspections, and Saddam Hussain announced new terms and conditions for their resumption, including the establishment of a new executive bureau to supervise UNSCOM's operations. In September the Security Council unanimously adopted a resolution (No. 1194) demanding that the Iraqi Government co-operate fully with UNSCOM and suspending for an indefinite period any review of the sanctions regime. This prompted the Government to halt all co-operation with UNSCOM indefinitely. In November the Security Council unanimously adopted a British-drafted resolution (No. 1205) demanding that Iraq immediately and unconditionally resume co-operation with UNSCOM. US and British military enforcements were again dispatched to the Gulf region to prepare for possible air strikes against Iraqi targets. Egypt, Saudi Arabia and Syria, while opposing the threat of force, urged Iraq to resume co-operation. Later in November Iraq declared that UNSCOM would be permitted unconditionally to resume the weapons inspection programme.

However, in early December 1998 a weapons inspection team conducting a new series of what were termed 'surprise' inspections was denied access to the Baath Party headquarters in Baghdad. On the night of 16–17 December, following the withdrawal from Iraq of UNSCOM and IAEA personnel, the USA and the United Kingdom commenced a campaign of air strikes against Iraqi targets; 'Operation Desert Fox' was terminated on 20 December, with US and British forces claiming to have caused significant damage to Iraqi military installations. France, Russia and China contended that the military action had been undertaken without UN Security Council authorization; however, the USA and the United Kingdom maintained that Resolution 1154, adopted in March, provided sufficient legitimacy. In January 1999 Iraqi ground forces launched attacks on US aircraft engaged in policing the air exclusion zone over southern Iraq.

The US Administration of President George W. Bush, which assumed office in January 2001, swiftly adopted an uncompromising stance with regard to Iraq. In February US and British fighter aircraft launched a renewed attack on air defence targets near Baghdad to enforce the northern and southern air exclusion zones. Iraq protested that the air strikes had targeted residential areas of Baghdad, while Western media reports suggested that three people had been killed in the attacks. US and British military aircraft launched air strikes against Iraqi air defence installations in both exclusion zones during late 2001 and in September 2002; Iraqi officials claimed that a number of civilians had died in the raids.

Meanwhile, the campaign of air strikes conducted against Iraqi targets in December 1998 was regarded as marking the collapse of UNSCOM's mission. Later that month the Security Council adopted a resolution (No. 1284) providing for the establishment of a UN Monitoring, Verification and Inspection Commission (UNMOVIC) as a successor body to UNSCOM. The resolution also provided for the suspension of the economic sanctions in force against Iraq for renewable 120-day periods (on the condition that Iraq co-operated fully with the new weapons inspectorate and the IAEA), and effectively removed restrictions on the maximum amount of petroleum that Iraq was permitted to sell under the oil-for-food programme. In January 2000 the Security Council endorsed the appointment of Hans Blix, a former Director-General of the IAEA, as head of UNMOVIC. In his first report to the UN Security Council in March 2000, Blix emphasized that, should Iraq permit the return of weapons inspectors, UNMOVIC would resume 'surprise' inspections of Iraqi sites. In the same month Tareq Aziz decisively rejected the terms of Resolution 1284. In March 2001 it was reported that, according to a recent UNMOVIC assessment, Iraq might still have stocks of, and the ability to deploy, biological and chemical weapons.

The 'oil-for-food' programme

Exports of Iraqi crude petroleum, under the terms of Resolution 986, had recommenced in December 1996, and continued until immediately prior to the US-led military intervention to remove the regime of Saddam Hussain in March 2003. The first supplies of food purchased with the revenues from these exports arrived in Iraq in March 1997. In February 1998 the UN Security Council raised the maximum permitted revenue from exports of petroleum to US $5,200m. in the six months to the end of July, of which Iraq would be permitted to spend some $3,550m. on humanitarian goods. Following concerns about the deterioration of its oil production facilities, in June the Security Council approved a resolution allowing Iraq to import essential spare parts to the value of $300m. for the oil sector. Under the oil-for-food programme, from December 2000 Iraq was allocated a maximum of $525m. for the costs of maintaining the oil industry. In September 2000 the UN Security Council approved the payment to Kuwait of $15,900m. in compensation for lost production and sales of petroleum as a result of the 1990–91 occupation.

In early 2001 the Bush Administration emphasized its commitment to maintaining the sanctions regime pending the full implementation of Resolution 1284. The USA swiftly undertook to secure implementation of a revised sanctions regime, with a view to resolving humanitarian concerns, by means of allowing the direct sale or supply to Iraq of most consumer goods without prior UN approval, while maintaining strict controls on the supply of goods with potential military applications. In November the Security Council continued to extend the oil-for-food programme every six months. In mid-March 2003, immediately prior to the start of the US-led military campaign in Iraq, the UN announced a temporary suspension of the oil-for-food programme. However, amid a sharp deterioration in the living conditions of Iraqi citizens following the outbreak of hostilities, at the end of March the UN Security Council adopted Resolution 1472, granting Secretary-General Annan the authority to implement existing contracts and to facilitate the delivery of aid for an initial 45-day period, which was subsequently extended until the beginning of June. In May the UN Security Council passed Resolution 1483, which removed sanctions against Iraq; the oil-for-food programme was formally discontinued in November.

Negotiations with UNMOVIC and the increasing threat of military intervention

After the defeat of the Taliban regime in Afghanistan (q.v.) in late 2001, there was considerable speculation that the USA would seek 'regime change' in Iraq as part of its declared 'war on terror'. In response to demands by George W. Bush that Iraq readmit UN inspectors to prove that it was not developing weapons of mass destruction, the Iraqi authorities reiterated that UN sanctions should first be ended and the air exclusion zones revoked. Tensions were heightened in January 2002 when, in his State of the Union address, President Bush assessed Iraq as forming what he termed an 'axis of evil' (with Iran and the Democratic People's Republic of Korea) seeking to develop weapons of mass destruction.

In March 2002 Annan met with the Iraqi Minister of Foreign Affairs, Naji Sabri, in New York, USA, for talks on the implementation of Security Council resolutions adopted since 1990. In August 2002 the UN Security Council declined an offer by the Iraqi Government to resume negotiations on the return of weapons inspectors, stating that Iraq should not impose any preconditions on the resumption of inspections. At the same time the USA pursued attempts to secure a UN resolution that would authorize military action in Iraq, while indicating that it would be prepared to act unilaterally. In September the British Government published a dossier outlining its case against the regime of Saddam Hussain and the perceived threat posed by Iraq's 'illicit weapons programmes' to the security of both the West and the Middle East. Shortly afterwards the US Secretary of Defense, Donald Rumsfeld, reiterated US claims that Iraq had provided assistance in the training of Islamist militants from the al-Qa'ida network. In early October Blix stated that Iraq had agreed to allow inspectors 'unrestricted access' to all relevant sites, but that no new agreement had been reached concerning access to the presidential palaces. The USA and the United Kingdom were keen for the Security Council to approve a new resolution that would strengthen the mandate under which the UN inspectors were to operate. China, France and Russia all maintained that—in the event of Iraq's failure to comply with the terms of a future resolution concerning Iraqi disarmament—a second UN resolution should be adopted prior to any military action being taken against the Iraqi regime.

In mid-October 2002 President Bush signed a resolution approved by the US Congress authorizing the use of force, if necessary unilaterally, to disarm Saddam Hussain's regime. On 8 November the UN Security Council unanimously adopted Resolution 1441, which demanded, *inter alia*, that Iraq permit weapons inspectors from UNMOVIC and the IAEA unrestricted access to sites suspected of holding illegal weapons (including the presidential palaces) and required the Iraqi leadership to make a full declaration of its chemical, biological, nuclear and ballistic weapons within 30 days. The resolution affirmed that Iraq would face 'serious consequences' in the event of non-compliance with the UN inspectors. On 13 November the RCC announced its unconditional acceptance of the terms of the resolution. Iraqi officials, however, stated that they did not possess any weapons of mass destruction.

Iraq presented UNMOVIC officials with a 12,000-page declaration of its weapons programmes in early December 2002. In mid-December, however, the USA stated that Iraq was in 'material breach' of UN Resolution 1441 since it had failed to give a complete account of its weapons capabilities, citing in particular Iraq's failure to account for stocks of biological weapons. In January 2003 UNMOVIC personnel to the south of Baghdad reported the discovery of several empty chemical warheads, which had reportedly not been included in Iraq's recent declaration. Meanwhile, Iraqi officials dismissed suggestions by some Arab states (including Saudi Arabia and Egypt) that Saddam Hussain either stand down or go into exile.

During January 2003 the USA and the United Kingdom ordered a massive deployment of troops to the Gulf region, while asserting that a conflict was not inevitable if Iraq complied with the UN's disarmament terms. Both the French and German Governments, meanwhile, were vociferous in their opposition to military action and advocated an extension of the UN inspectors' mandate. In late January the ministers responsible for foreign affairs of Turkey, Syria, Iran, Jordan, Egypt and Saudi Arabia, meeting in Istanbul, Turkey, issued a joint communiqué urging Iraq to co-operate fully with UN inspectors in order to avoid a new conflict in the region. On 27 January, 60 days after the resumption of UN weapons inspections in Iraq (as stipulated under Resolution 1441), Blix and the Director-General of the IAEA, Muhammad el-Baradei, briefed the UN Security Council on the progress of inspections. El-Baradei stated that IAEA inspectors had found no evidence that Iraq had restarted its nuclear weapons programme, but requested more time for the organization to complete its research, while Blix claimed that there was no evidence that Iraq had destroyed known stocks of illegal chemical and ballistic weapons.

Eight European countries (including the United Kingdom, Italy and Spain) signed a joint statement at the end of January 2003 expressing support for the USA's militant stance with regard to Iraq. In February the British Prime Minister, Tony Blair, accelerated his efforts to secure a second UN Security Council resolution authorizing a US-led campaign in Iraq should UNMOVIC inspectors continue to report Baghdad's non-compliance. President Bush asserted that, although he favoured the adoption of a second resolution, Resolution 1441 had given the USA the authority to disarm Iraq by military means. The US Secretary of State, Colin Powell, had, on 5 February, presented to the Security Council what the USA claimed to be overwhelming evidence of Iraq's attempts to conceal its possession of weapons of mass destruction, and outlined its alleged links with international terrorist groups, including al-Qa'ida. In his report on UNMOVIC's inspections to the Security Council on 14 February, Blix stated that the monitoring process should continue in order to determine whether Iraq did possess undeclared weapons of mass destruction.

On 24 February 2003 the USA, the United Kingdom and Spain presented a draft resolution to the UN Security Council effectively proposing a US-led military campaign against Saddam Hussain's regime, in response to Baghdad's failure to disarm peacefully. The resolution stated that a deadline of 17 March would be set, by which time Iraq should prove that it was disarming; however, no specific mention was made of consequent military action in the event of the deadline not being met, apparently in an effort by the US-led coalition to persuade France, Russia and China not to exercise their right of veto. Officials from France, Russia and Germany presented an alternative proposal involving an extended timetable of weapons inspections in order to avert a war. At the beginning of March

Turkey's Grand National Assembly voted to allow US military aircraft to enter Turkish airspace in the event of a campaign being waged against the Iraqi regime, while rejecting a plan for US forces to use Turkey's military bases. Shortly afterwards France and Russia pledged to veto a second UN resolution authorizing the use of force to disarm Saddam Hussain. On 11 March President Bush rejected a suggested 45-day postponement of any decision to go to war by six countries that had the power to influence the Security Council vote. On 15 March, in anticipation of a probable US-led invasion, Iraq's RCC issued a decree dividing the country into four military commands, under the overall leadership of Saddam Hussain. On 17 March the USA, the United Kingdom and Spain withdrew their draft resolution from the UN, stating that they reserved the right to take their own action to ensure Iraqi disarmament. On the same day President Bush issued an ultimatum giving Saddam Hussain and his two sons 48 hours to leave Baghdad or face military action; the Iraqi National Assembly rejected the ultimatum.

The overthrow of Saddam Hussain

Shortly after the expiry of President Bush's deadline, on 20 March 2003 US and British armed forces launched a campaign (code-named 'Operation Iraqi Freedom') to oust the regime of Saddam Hussain. An initial series of air strikes intended to target leading members of the regime in Baghdad were unsuccessful. Meanwhile, US-led coalition forces crossed into Iraq from Kuwait and began a steady advance towards the capital. At the same time a series of air strikes were launched against selected military bases, government buildings, and broadcasting and communications headquarters in and around Baghdad. US and British forces adopted a simultaneous campaign of distributing leaflets and broadcasting radio messages, in an effort to persuade Iraqi citizens to abandon their support for the Baath regime. British troops were principally engaged in securing towns in southern Iraq, including Iraq's second city of Basra, after the US-led coalition had seized control of the key southern port of Umm Qasr and the Al-Faw Peninsula. The coalition hoped that the Shi'a Muslim population of Basra would initiate an uprising against the regime of Saddam Hussain, as had occurred following the Gulf War in 1991. Although fighting between US-led troops and Iraqi armed forces was often intense, resistance from the Iraqi army and from a number of *fedayeen* (martyrs) and volunteers from other Arab countries was generally lighter than had been anticipated by the allies. Moreover, there were widespread reports of Iraqi soldiers surrendering to the advancing forces. In late March 2003 US forces opened a second front in the Kurdish-controlled regions of northern Iraq, where Kurdish forces joined US troops in targeting bases of Ansar al-Islam, a militant Islamist group suspected of having links with al-Qa'ida.

At an emergency summit meeting of Arab League states in Cairo, Egypt, on 24 March 2003, representatives of the 17 member states in attendance (except Kuwait) issued a resolution condemning the US-led invasion of Iraq and demanding the withdrawal of all foreign forces. By 7 April US armed forces had entered central Baghdad, including its presidential palaces. The disintegration of the Baath regime appeared to be complete on 9 April, when crowds of Iraqis staged street demonstrations denouncing Saddam Hussain and destroying images and statues of him. Kurdish *peshmerga* fighters gained control of the northern town of Kirkuk on 10 April, while the town of Mosul was seized by Kurdish and US forces on the following day. Also on 11 April the USA issued a 'most wanted' list of 55 members of the deposed regime whom it sought to arrest: one of the most high-profile of these, Tareq Aziz, surrendered to US forces two weeks later. The seizure by US troops of Saddam Hussain's birthplace and power base, Tikrit (to the north of Baghdad), on 14 April was widely viewed as the last strategic battle of the US-led campaign to remove the Baathist regime. On 1 May President Bush officially declared an end to 'major combat operations' in Iraq.

On 15 April 2003 a US-sponsored meeting of Iraqi opposition groups took place in the southern city of Nasiriya. While the participants produced a 13-point resolution detailing proposals for a transition to a democratic, sovereign government, it became clear that in the interim period the practical responsibilities of rebuilding and maintaining the material infrastructure of Iraq, as well as combating emerging 'resistance' groups, would fall to the US-led coalition. Retired US army general Jay Garner, Director of the USA's Office of Reconstruction and Humanitarian Assistance (ORHA), arrived in the country on 21 April to manage the restoration of basic services to the Iraqi population and to enforce law and order. However, the ORHA was subsequently replaced by the Coalition Provisional Authority (CPA), headed by US diplomat L. Paul Bremer, III. Bremer assumed his responsibilities on 12 May, his first act being to outlaw the Baath Party and related organizations, to demobilize the Iraqi armed forces and security apparatus, and dissolve the Ministry of Defence.

UN Security Council Resolution 1483, adopted on 22 May 2003, recognized the CPA as the legal occupying power in Iraq, and mandated it to establish a temporary Iraqi governing authority. On 13 July the inaugural meeting of the 25-member Iraqi Governing Council was held in Baghdad; members of the Governing Council were appointed in direct proportion to the principal ethnic and religious groups in Iraq: 13 Shi'a Arabs, five Sunni Arabs, five Kurds, one Assyrian Christian and one Turkoman. They were mostly drawn from the main parties that had been in opposition to Saddam Hussain's regime, notably Ahmad Chalabi of the INC, Dr Ayad Allawi of the Iraqi National Accord (INA), Talabani of the PUK, Barzani of the KDP and Abd al-Aziz al-Hakim of SCIRI. The Governing Council had no executive powers, but could appoint ministers, set a date for the holding of free elections, and formulate a new constitution. At the end of July the Governing Council adopted a system of rotating presidency, under which Ibrahim al-Ja'fari of the predominantly Shi'a Islamic Dawa Party, was chosen as Iraq's first President of the post-Baathist era. In August the UN Security Council approved a resolution 'welcoming', but not formally recognizing, the establishment of the Iraqi Governing Council. On 1 September the Governing Council announced the formation of a 25-member interim Cabinet, appointed along the same ethnic and religious lines, which was to administer the country until the holding of legislative elections. Finally, on 15 November a timetable for the transition of power to an elected, sovereign government was published by the CPA and the Governing Council. The plan was threefold: these two authorities were to be dissolved and replaced by an Iraqi Transitional National Assembly by 30 June 2004; a constitutional convention was to take place by mid-2005, after which a popular referendum would be held on the new constitution; and, by the end of 2005, national elections were to be held to select a new Iraqi government.

Increasing violence following the end of US-led combat operations

In the aftermath of the war, Iraq's security situation remained extremely volatile. Armed resistance to US-led coalition forces was waged by militants loyal to the former Baathist regime, even despite the arrest or elimination of several leading establishment figures. Moreover, the UN, diplomatic missions, Shi'a clergy and members of the interim Cabinet were also targeted by militant groups. In early August 2003 the Jordanian embassy in Baghdad was severely damaged by a car bomb, which killed up to 19 people. The militant Islamist group Ansar al-Islam was initially held to be responsible. (In November 2007 a military court in Jordan sentenced to death a Jordanian national found to have plotted the embassy bombing on the orders of al-Qa'ida in Iraq.) The UN Special Representative for Iraq, Sergio Vieira de Mello, and some 20 others were killed in late August 2003, when the UN compound in Baghdad was bombed. A previously unknown Islamist group, the Armed Vanguards of the Second Muhammad Army, claimed responsibility for the explosion, which resulted in most of the UN's foreign personnel being withdrawn from Iraq. At the end of that month a car bomb exploded in the holy city of Najaf, killing the Shi'a cleric Hojatoleslam Muhammad Baqir al-Hakim and up to 125 of his followers. It was evident from mid-2003 that Iraq's various Shi'a factions were fighting among themselves in order to establish a dominant position among the majority Shi'a population.

In July 2003 US special forces shot dead Saddam Hussain's two sons, Uday and Qusay, at a house in Mosul where they had apparently been hiding. In December Saddam Hussain was captured by US special forces in the village of al-Dawr, near the former President's hometown of Tikrit. Saddam Hussain was accorded prisoner-of-war status and detained in US military custody. In July 2004 Hussain, along with 11 co-defendants, appeared in front of a special US-appointed court in Baghdad to face charges including the use of chemical weapons against Kurds in Halabja in 1988 and the invasion of Kuwait in 1990. However, the former Iraqi leader declared the proceedings to be illegal. In October 2004 US investigators seeking evidence as part of preparations for war crime trials against Saddam Hussain and former senior Iraqi officials found a mass grave in Hatra, near the ancient city of Nineveh, in which they uncovered

the bodies of hundreds of Kurds apparently killed in late 1987–early 1988.

Meanwhile, in September 2004 a report issued by the Iraq Survey Group—a team of experts appointed by the US-led coalition to locate Iraq's alleged weapons of mass destruction—concluded that the Baathist regime's involvement with chemical or biological agents prior to the 2003 invasion had been restricted to small quantities of poisons, probably for use in assassinations. While no illegal stockpiles of weapons had been found, and there was no evidence of attempts to recommence Iraq's nuclear weapons programme, it did appear that Saddam Hussain's regime had intended to reintroduce its illegal weapons programmes if the UN lifted sanctions against the country. However, subsequent to the release of the report, the IAEA announced that buildings used during Iraq's nuclear programme prior to the Gulf War in 1991 had been dismantled, and that material that could be utilized to produce nuclear weapons had disappeared. The US Administration announced an end to the search for weapons of mass destruction in January 2005.

By January 2004 US-led forces had apprehended or killed 42 of the 55 'most wanted' former Baathists. However, at the end of the month some 105 people, mostly Kurds, were killed in suicide bomb attacks directed against the offices of the principal Kurdish parties—the KDP and the PUK—in Arbil. Meanwhile, the insurgents were now targeting Iraqis working with the occupying forces: in February 2004 nearly 100 people were killed in two separate attacks against the Iraqi police and army in Iskandariya and Baghdad, respectively. In early March a series of bombs exploded among crowds of Shi'a who had gathered in Baghdad and Karbala to celebrate the festival of Ashoura, resulting in more than 180 deaths. The CPA claimed that Abu Musab al-Zarqawi, a Jordanian national believed to have ties with al-Qa'ida, was responsible for the bombings and the majority of attacks on coalition and civilian targets in Iraq. Bremer announced the re-establishment of the Ministry of Defence in March.

The Transitional Administrative Law (TAL) was signed by the Governing Council on 8 March 2004; it outlined a new timetable for the establishment of a permanent legislature and sovereign government (see *Constitution and Government*), which superseded that previously set out in the agreement published on 15 November 2003. This development was interpreted as evidence of the growing influence on the political process of Iraq's most senior Shi'a cleric, Grand Ayatollah Ali al-Husaini al-Sistani: in particular, plans to elect a transitional national assembly by regional caucuses were replaced by proposals to hold national elections to an interim (and likely Shi'a-dominated) legislature.

In May 2004 the Independent Electoral Commission of Iraq (IECI) was formed by the CPA to organize elections to a 275-member Transitional National Assembly (TNA), which were subsequently scheduled for 30 January 2005. Key functions of the TNA were to draft, by 15 August 2005, a permanent constitution, to be submitted to a popular referendum by 15 October; and to elect a state Presidency Council responsible for appointing a Prime Minister and cabinet. Under the timetable for Iraq's political transition, constitutionally elected organs of government were to be installed by 15 December. In early December 2004 the PUK and the KDP announced that they had agreed to form a joint list—the Kurdistan Alliance List (or Democratic Patriotic Alliance of Kurdistan). Subsequently, major Shi'a groups, backed by al-Sistani, announced that they too would be campaigning on a shared list, to be known as the United Iraqi Alliance (UIA). In late December, after failing to secure a delay in the holding of the ballot (citing security concerns), the Sunni Iraqi Islamic Party (IIP—al-Hizb al-Islami al-Iraqi) and various other Sunni groups withdrew from the campaign, advocating a boycott of the polls.

Meanwhile, the CPA closed down the Baghdad newspaper *Al-Hawza al-Natiqa* in March 2004 for allegedly inciting violence against the US-led coalition. The newspaper was closely associated with Hojatoleslam Muqtada al-Sadr, a Shi'a cleric whose father had been assassinated by the previous regime in February 1999 and who was a suspect in the murder of a moderate Shi'a cleric in Najaf in 2003. Several of al-Sadr's supporters had formed a militia known as the 'Mahdi Army', and protests outside the newspaper offices were the precursor to a nationwide upsurge in violence against coalition forces. After four US private security contractors were killed in an ambush in the Sunni-dominated town of Fallujah, to the west of Baghdad in Anbar province, in early April 2004, US forces surrounded and effectively blockaded the town; around 450 Iraqis (including many civilians) and 40 US soldiers died in the ensuing violence. A scandal developed in late April, when photographs taken by US guards of US soldiers coercing Iraqi prisoners into performing degrading acts were broadcast worldwide. One soldier received a 10-year gaol sentence in January 2005 in connection with the abuse of prisoners at the Abu Ghraib prison, west of Baghdad, while other implicated officers received lesser sentences. In early 2005 four British soldiers were discharged from the army and sentenced to short prison terms, having been convicted of the abuse of Iraqi prisoners at a military base near Basra in May 2003.

The transfer of power to the Iraqi Interim Government

In mid-May 2004 Sunni insurgents in central Baghdad assassinated the President of the Governing Council, Izzadine Salim, who was replaced by the Sunni Sheikh Ghazi Mashal Ajil al-Yawar. The INA Secretary-General, Dr Ayad Allawi, was appointed interim Prime Minister of Iraq in late May, and in early June Ghazi al-Yawar was named as President of the Interim Government, to which power was to be transferred from the CPA on 30 June. However, amid security fears following an intensification of insurgent attacks, and the kidnapping and killing of foreign workers, the date for the granting of sovereignty to the Interim Government was secretly moved forward to 28 June. Shortly after the ceremony in Baghdad, Bremer left Iraq; the CPA and the Governing Council were both dissolved. Around 140,000 US soldiers remained in Iraq following the handover of power. In August delegates to a national conference in Baghdad declared the appointment of a 100-member transitional national council that was to govern Iraq in conjunction with the Interim Government until the January 2005 elections.

Following a decision by the CPA to re-employ former Baathist security officials, the US military had, in April 2004, arranged for an Iraqi security force led by one of Saddam Hussain's former generals to replace the US Marine Corps in Fallujah. In May coalition forces launched major assaults against the Mahdi Army, and particularly heavy fighting was reported in Sadr City (a predominantly Shi'a suburb of Baghdad), Karbala and Najaf. In June nine of Iraq's leading political factions reached agreement with Dr Allawi to disband their militias by January 2005. According to the agreement, some 100,000 fighters (but excluding members of the Mahdi Army) would join the security forces or return to civilian life. Meanwhile, after US forces reached an accommodation with al-Sadr to end his insurgency, in July 2004 the ban on the *Al-Hawza al-Natiqa* newspaper was lifted. However, a Sunni uprising in Najaf and in other southern cities from early August led to renewed fighting in that month, with many fatalities being reported. Grand Ayatollah al-Sistani, accompanied by thousands of Iraqi Shi'a, travelled to Najaf, where he negotiated a ceasefire with al-Sadr. Meanwhile, Abu Musab al-Zarqawi declared that he had managed a spate of co-ordinated attacks across Iraq in June, including five car bomb explosions in Mosul, which had killed about 100 people. In July the Interim Government introduced new legislation granting it wider powers to control the insurgency by enabling the Prime Minister to declare a state of emergency for periods of up to 60 days. The death penalty was reintroduced for certain crimes in August, having been suspended by the CPA in early 2003.

The Mahdi Army announced a ceasefire in October 2004 and stated that it would begin to disarm, provided that the Interim Government released its prisoners. In mid-October insurgents managed to penetrate central Baghdad's heavily fortified International Zone—an area still commonly known by its original name, the Green Zone —and launch a suicide attack, which killed at least 10 people (including four US civilians). The Green Zone contained the headquarters of the Iraqi Government and the US and British embassies. Al-Zarqawi's group, which had recently named itself Tanzim Qa'idat al-Jihad fi Bilad al-Rafidain (Base of Holy War in Mesopotamia, also known as al-Qa'ida in Iraq), claimed responsibility for the attack, and for the killing in late October of 49 unarmed National Guard soldiers in Diyala province, near the Iranian border. It was estimated later in the month that 100,000 Iraqi civilians had died in the period since the US-led invasion, principally as a result of air strikes by coalition forces.

Allawi declared a 60-day state of emergency in early November 2004, closing Baghdad airport and imposing martial law across most of the country as an estimated 15,000 US troops and 3,000 Iraqi troops attempted to end the ongoing insurgency in Fallujah. By mid-November US troops claimed to be in control of the city, having killed an estimated 1,200 insurgents, with losses of a reported 38 US and six Iraqi military. Heavy civilian and military casualties were recorded during a spate of suicide car bomb attacks and insurgent raids in Karbala, Najaf, Mosul and the area around Baghdad in December 2004 and early January 2005. The number of insurgents at this time was estimated at 200,000, greater than the number of coalition troops. In response to the growing violence and in advance of the forthcoming legislative elections, in January the Interim Government extended the state of emergency for another month, closed Iraq's borders and imposed a strict curfew. Al-Zarqawi, who had castigated Shi'a Muslims for assisting the occupying forces, vowed in the week before the poll to launch an offensive against the elections. Five days before the scheduled ballot, 37 US troops were killed—the highest single death toll for US forces since March 2003.

The January 2005 election to the Transitional National Assembly

Despite the boycott by many Sunni political groups and the poor security situation, the legislative election took place as scheduled on 30 January 2005. At least 44 people died in attacks across Iraq during polling. In the election to the TNA, the UIA took 47.6% of the total votes, winning 140 of the 275 seats, the Kurdistan Alliance List won 75 seats (with 25.4% of the votes) and the Iraqi List, a bloc led by Dr Allawi, secured 40 seats (with 13.6% of the votes); nine other parties achieved representation in the interim legislature. Voting for the TNA was held simultaneously with elections to 18 provincial assemblies and to a new Iraqi Kurdistan National Assembly, where the Kurdistan Democratic List won 104 of the 111 seats. In February some 125 people were killed in a suicide bomb attack in the predominantly Shi'a city of Hilla.

On 6 April 2005 the TNA voted to appoint the PUK leader, Talabani, to the post of President. A Sunni, Ghazi al-Yawar (previously the President of the Interim Government), and a Shi'a, Adil Abd al-Mahdi (hitherto the Minister of Finance), were appointed Vice-Presidents. The three, together constituting a state Presidency Council, were sworn in on 7 April, whereupon they appointed Ibrahim al-Ja'fari to the post of Prime Minister. On 28 April the TNA overwhelmingly approved al-Ja'fari's new Council of Ministers, which was sworn in on 3 May. By the end of May more than 1,000 people were reported to have been killed in various insurgent attacks across the country following the approval of the new Transitional Government. On 12 June the Iraqi Kurdistan National Assembly voted unanimously to appoint Barzani, leader of the KDP, to the post of President of the Kurdish Autonomous Region.

Meanwhile, under the schedule outlined by the TAL, a draft constitution drawn up by the transitional administration was to be agreed by a constitutional committee and submitted to the TNA for approval by 15 August 2005. Sunni representation on the committee was increased in an attempt to reach an agreeable consensus. Significant points of disagreement included: the degree of federalism to be incorporated into the new state; the distribution of oil revenue; the question of 'de-Baathification' of the official sphere; and the role of Islam as a source of legislation. The agreed deadline was twice missed, largely because of Sunni objections on these key issues, before a final text was submitted to the TNA for approval on 28 August. The text was subsequently submitted to the UN on 14 September. On the same day a series of car bombings in Baghdad, apparently perpetrated by al-Zarqawi's al-Qa'ida in Iraq, caused the deaths of some 150 people. At a nationwide referendum held on 15 October, the Constitution was ratified with the support of 78.6% of the valid votes cast.

On 19 October 2005 the new Supreme Iraqi Criminal Tribunal began trial proceedings against former Iraqi President Saddam Hussain. Together with his seven co-defendants, Hussain pleaded not guilty to charges of organizing the killing of 148 Iraqi Shi'a in the town of Dujail, where he had survived an assassination attempt in 1982. The trial was adjourned until late November 2005, by which time two defence lawyers had been killed. In January 2006 the appointment of a Kurd from Halabja (where Hussain's Government had used chemical weapons in 1988) as the new presiding judge compounded the objections of the defence team that the trial was incapable of impartiality.

In November 2005 US troops discovered more than 170 prisoners, many showing signs of torture, in the basement of the Shi'a-dominated Ministry of the Interior. The IIP, with the support of the USA, demanded an inquiry into the practices of the Ministry's officials. In January 2006 some 28 people were killed in a suicide bomb attack on the Ministry building, which al-Qa'ida in Iraq announced it had carried out in revenge for the mistreatment of Sunni prisoners.

The formation of a permanent Council of Representatives

Following the approval of the Constitution, several Sunni groups that had boycotted the elections of January 2005 declared that they would participate in the elections to the first permanent Council of Representatives, which were due to be held on 15 December. Three major Sunni groups, including the IIP, formed the Iraqi Accord Front (IAF—Jabhat al-Tawafuq al-Iraqiya) in October, in a bid to engage Sunnis in the political process. Another Sunni coalition, the Iraqi Front for National Dialogue (Hewar National Iraqi Front), was formed from parties that disagreed with the IIP's acceptance of the Constitution. Meanwhile, the UIA announced a 17-party list dominated once again by Shi'a, including supporters of al-Sadr alongside the Islamic Dawa Party and SCIRI. However, the INC, which had been transformed since 2003 from a multi-party coalition into a political party headed by Deputy Prime Minister Ahmad Chalabi, declined to run on the UIA list, creating instead the National Congress Coalition. In contrast to his support for the UIA in January 2005, Grand Ayatollah al-Sistani indicated his neutrality in the elections. Former Prime Minister Allawi established a secular coalition, the Iraqi National List (INL), including his own INA, the Iraqis party of Ghazi al-Yawar and the ICP, while the PUK and the KDP maintained the Kurdistan Alliance List. The voting on 15 December was only marginally disrupted by violence. The final election results, released on 10 February 2006, gave the UIA 41.2% of votes cast and 128 of the Council's 275 seats. The Kurdistan Alliance List secured 53 seats with 21.7% of votes, while the IAF won 15.1% of the votes and 44 seats. Allawi's INL won 25 seats, and 11 seats were allocated to the Iraqi Front for National Dialogue. Chalabi's coalition failed to win a seat.

On 22 February 2006, with negotiations ongoing over the composition of the new government, two bombs were exploded inside the al-Askari Mosque (or Golden Mosque) in Samarra, destroying the dome of one of Iraq's holiest Shi'a shrines. The attack caused a sharp increase in sectarian violence across the country (including retaliatory attacks on Sunni mosques), which resulted in the deaths of at least 300 people within a week, according to official sources; independent media reports suggested that more than 1,000 had died. Following the upsurge in violence, Kurdish, Sunni and secular factions increased their opposition to the continued premiership of al-Ja'fari, who had narrowly won the nomination of the UIA to the post of Prime Minister in February. On 13 March some 85 bodies were reportedly discovered by Iraqi police in various parts of Baghdad, apparently the victims of increasingly common execution-style killings by sectarian 'death squads'. The Council of Representatives eventually convened for the first time in Baghdad's Green Zone on 16 March.

Seeking to resolve the impasse in negotiations over the new government, on 20 April 2006 al-Ja'fari withdrew his candidacy for the post of Prime Minister. On the following day the UIA nominated Nuri Kamal (Jawad) al-Maliki of the Islamic Dawa Party, as their replacement candidate. At the second session of the Council of Representatives on 22 April, President Talabani was elected for a second term. Talabani subsequently invited al-Maliki to form a permanent government within 30 days. Meanwhile, the Kurdish region's first unified Cabinet, led by Barzani, assumed office on 7 May.

On 20 May 2006 the Council of Ministers was sworn into office. This Government of national unity represented the first permanent Iraqi Government since the removal of Saddam Hussain's regime in 2003, and it constituted the first administration since that date to include the principal Sunni factions. In all, the new Council of Ministers included 20 Shi'a, eight Kurds, eight Sunni Arabs and one Christian. Of the 275 seats in the Council of Representatives, the Government—composed principally of the UIA, the Kurdish Alliance, the IAF and the INL—plus three smaller parties, controlled 240.

The new Government appeared initially to have been strengthened by reports on 7 June 2006 that Abu Musab al-Zarqawi, the leader of al-Qa'ida in Iraq, had been killed during a US air strike close to the town of Baquba. It was claimed by the Ministry of Health that almost 1,400 civilians had been killed in Baghdad in May. On 14 June al-Maliki's administration ordered a new military strategy involving thousands of Iraqi and US forces, code-named 'Operation Together Forward'. Meanwhile, it

was claimed that Abu Ayyub al-Masri, also known as Abu Hamza al-Muhajir, had been appointed to succeed al-Zarqawi as the leader of al-Qa'ida in Iraq. Al-Maliki also appealed for a dialogue with Sunni insurgents, and on 25 June announced a 'national reconciliation plan' offering an amnesty to members of certain militant groups who renounced violence, and outlining plans to disarm the country's various militias. However, the violence perpetrated by both Sunni insurgents and Shi'a militias continued relentlessly, prompting Grand Ayatollah al-Sistani to declare that he would no longer act as a political leader and was powerless to prevent civil war. Nevertheless, the formal hand-over of control of Iraq's armed forces from the US-led coalition to the Iraqi Government did occur on 7 September.

Also in September 2006 the Council of Representatives began to debate the controversial issue of federal devolution, which some feared might eventually lead to Iraq's dissolution along ethnic lines. The UIA stated that it favoured the division of Iraq into autonomous regions, thereby permitting the oil-rich Shi'a south to be governed along the lines of the Kurdish north. While Sunni politicians had previously opposed the move, fearing that it would leave them with only the resource-poor centre and west of the country, they now hinted that they might support the 'administrative application of federalism' so long as a strong central Government remained in place. By late September a compromise had emerged: a parliamentary committee was to be set up immediately to draft constitutional amendments to ensure that national oil revenues were shared fairly and to limit the potential of regions to secede from the central state. On 26 September both Kurdish and Shi'a legislators tabled federalism bills. The Kurdish bill (which showed the disputed, oil-rich city of Kirkuk as belonging to the Kurdish Autonomous Region) was rejected, but the Shi'a-proposed draft was given a first reading. The draft made provisions for Iraq's 18 provinces to hold referendums on whether they wanted to merge with neighbouring areas, thus forming larger areas with powers of self-rule. On 11 October a law was adopted unanimously by the Council of Representatives; however, the two largest Sunni blocs and two factions making up the Shi'a alliance refused to attend the session.

A UN report issued in late September 2006 showed that some 6,600 Iraqi civilians had been killed during July and August. British and Iraqi forces operating in Basra initiated a campaign, code-named 'Operation Sinbad', which was aimed at preventing the infiltration of some of the city's police units by Shi'a militants. In October al-Maliki announced the establishment of local security committees to monitor the violence in their respective areas. However, amid worsening violence, Sunni leaders from Anbar province, west of Baghdad, began to form their own security forces. Many Iraqis fled their homes and sought refuge either in other parts of the country or in neighbouring states.

The trial of Saddam Hussain and seven co-defendants accused of involvement in the murder of 148 Iraqi Shi'a in Dujail in 1982 was marred by numerous setbacks during 2006, including the murder of a third defence lawyer in June. On 5 November Hussain and two of his co-defendants—Awad Hamed al-Bandar (former head of the Revolutionary Court under the Baathist regime) and Barzan Ibrahim al-Tikriti (half-brother of the former President)—were found guilty of crimes against humanity in connection with the killing of the 148 Shi'a, and were sentenced to death. Former Vice-President Taha Yassin Ramadan was sentenced to life imprisonment, while three others received 15-year custodial sentences; one defendant was acquitted owing to a lack of evidence. The verdict provoked a mixed reaction in Iraq, with thousands defying a curfew to express publicly either their support for Hussain or to celebrate the verdict. Nevertheless, many commentators and human rights organizations questioned the impartiality of the trial, and Hussain's lawyers immediately lodged an appeal against the verdict.

In November 2006 at least 215 people died when a series of car bombs and mortar rounds exploded in Sadr City, followed by mortar attacks on Sunni areas of Baghdad. Prime Minister al-Maliki imposed an indefinite curfew in the capital, but the killings continued, prompting a group led by Muqtada al-Sadr to threaten withdrawal from the unity Government, in which his followers held six cabinet posts. This threat was carried out when al-Maliki flew to the Jordanian capital, Amman, to discuss Iraq's security situation with US President Bush—a move that al-Sadr's group described as 'a provocation to the Iraqi people and a violation of their constitutional rights'. On 6 December the US cross-party Iraq Study Group published a report demanding 'urgent action' to prevent Iraq from sliding towards chaos. The report recommended that, rather than conducting a combat mission and massively increasing troop numbers, US forces should be used to train Iraqis; it also appealed for direct dialogue on Iraq's future with Syria and Iran.

The execution of Saddam Hussain

Saddam Hussain was executed by hanging on 30 December 2006, following the rejection of his appeal against the death sentence imposed by the Supreme Iraqi Criminal Tribunal in November. While some in Iraq celebrated the death of the deposed leader, many Sunnis described Saddam Hussain as a martyr, and protests against the hanging were held in Baghdad, Samarra and his hometown of Tikrit. A statement issued by the Baath Party at the start of January 2007 named Izzat Ibrahim al-Douri as its new Secretary-General. In mid-January Saddam Hussain's two aides, al-Bandar and al-Tikriti, were hanged, and in March former Vice-President Ramadan was also executed, after the Court of Appeal recommended that his sentence of life imprisonment was too lenient.

At the time of Saddam Hussain's death, trial proceedings (initiated in August 2006) were ongoing against the former President and six co-defendants on charges of genocide and crimes against humanity in relation to an offensive in the Anfal region during 1987–88 in which, according to the prosecution, more than 180,000 Iraqi Kurds were killed. When the trial resumed in January 2007, the charges against Hussain were abandoned. In June Gen. Ali Hassan al-Majid, a cousin of Saddam Hussain and former regional commander, was sentenced to death by the Supreme Iraqi Criminal Tribunal, having been convicted of genocide, war crimes and crimes against humanity for his role in the Anfal operation. Two of al-Majid's co-defendants received the same sentence, while a further two were sentenced to life imprisonment; the sixth defendant was acquitted owing to a lack of evidence. In August al-Majid received an additional death sentence following his conviction on charges of involvement in the violent suppression of thousands of Shi'a rebels in southern Iraq following the Gulf conflict of 1990–91. Al-Majid received a third death sentence in March 2009 for the killing of Shi'as protesting against the assassination of Grand Ayatollah Muhammad Sadiq al-Sadr in 1999. In mid-January 2010 al-Majid received a further death sentence for his role in the attacks involving chemical weapons that killed thousands of Kurds in Halabja in 1988, and he was executed by hanging on 25 January.

In 2007 there were growing fears concerning the large exodus of Iraqi citizens, both to neighbouring states and through regional displacement. According to estimates by the office of the UN High Commissioner for Refugees (UNHCR), by September between 2.1m. and 2.5m. Iraqis had become refugees in neighbouring countries, notably Syria (1.2m.–1.4m.) and Jordan (500,000–750,000), while around 2.3m. Iraqis were displaced internally. Aid agencies, meanwhile, warned that many neighbouring countries were starting to impose severe limitations on the number of Iraqi refugees allowed to enter. UNHCR also expressed concern in September 2007 regarding the estimated 13,000 Palestinian refugees who were believed to remain in Iraq, as well as the Christian and other minority communities.

Prime Minister al-Maliki announced a new security plan for Baghdad on 9 January 2007; this centred on the deployment of additional Iraqi forces, including Kurdish troops, with US backing. Sunni leaders denounced the plan as unconstitutional since it had not been referred to the Council of Representatives for debate. The following day US President Bush confirmed that the USA would send an additional 21,000 troops to Iraq. Bush's new so-called 'surge' strategy also included the following provisions: the Iraqi Government was to appoint a new military commander for Baghdad; there was to be accelerated training of Iraqi security forces, leading to them being brought under Iraqi control by November; provincial elections were to be held later that year; and increased diplomacy was to be sought with Iraq's neighbours, excluding Iran and Syria (from where insurgents were allegedly crossing into Iraq).

On 16 January 2007 at least 70 people—most of them female students—were killed in a double bomb attack at Baghdad's Mustansiriyah University. Six days later more than 130 people were killed in and around the capital. None the less, the ending of the two-month political boycott by followers of al-Sadr appeared to suggest a greater unity among Iraq's Shi'a factions. Security forces subsequently claimed to have captured 600 members of al-Sadr's reportedly 60,000-strong Mahdi Army. In late January officials announced that some 300 insurgents, reportedly from a militant group called the Army of Heaven, had been killed in

battles near Najaf. Some news reports, however, claimed that those killed were Shi'a pilgrims. In early February more than 130 people were killed in a lorry bombing at a central Baghdad marketplace. The attack coincided with the launch of the new Iraqi-US security initiative in the capital, 'Operation Law and Order' (or the Baghdad Security Plan). In the second week of February insurgents marked the first anniversary of the bombing of the Samarra shrine by launching a series of fatal explosions in Baghdad. In the first week of March more than 110 Shi'a pilgrims on their approach to Karbala were killed by militants in central Iraq.

The six cabinet ministers of Muqtada al-Sadr's faction resigned from their posts in mid-April 2007, in protest against Prime Minister al-Maliki's failure to agree a timetable for the withdrawal of coalition forces from Iraq. Four days earlier at least one Iraqi legislator was killed in a suicide bomb attack inside the Council of Representatives building, adjacent to Baghdad's Green Zone. An international conference to discuss reconstruction and security in Iraq was convened in the Egyptian resort of Sharm el-Sheikh in May. At the conference, a five-year framework for the country's future development, the International Compact with Iraq, was launched by al-Maliki. By June it appeared that Operation Law and Order was not achieving significant results in curbing sectarian violence in Baghdad. During July violence also intensified in the north of the country, particularly in Kirkuk, possibly as a result of the tightening of security by Iraqi-US forces in the capital. In one incident, the headquarters of the PUK were targeted, with militants clearly attempting to influence any future decision regarding the status of Kirkuk. Meanwhile, on 29 June 2007 the UN Security Council adopted Resolution 1762, which, *inter alia*, ended the mandate of UNMOVIC, on the grounds that Iraq's known weapons of mass destruction had now been rendered harmless and that the new Iraqi Government had declared itself to be in favour of non-proliferation.

The perilous state of the Iraqi administration was demonstrated on 1 August 2007, when the IAF withdrew its six ministers from the national unity Government, resulting in an even weaker participation by Sunni politicians in the country's decision-making processes. Moderate Kurdish and Shi'a political parties responded to this announcement by establishing a new alliance aimed at assisting the Prime Minister in pushing forward important legislation; this new grouping included the PUK and the KDP, together with al-Maliki's Islamic Dawa Party and the Islamic Supreme Council of Iraq (ISCI—as SCIRI had been renamed in May).

The UN Security Council voted on 10 August 2007 to expand the organization's operations in Iraq, having played a minimal role in Iraq's political affairs following the attack against its Baghdad headquarters in August 2003. The mandate of the UN Assistance Mission for Iraq was subsequently extended at regular intervals, most recently for 12 months in late July 2013. On 14 August 2007 an estimated 400–500 people from the minority (primarily Kurdish) Yazidi community in northern Iraq were killed as the result of co-ordinated suicide bombings; US military officials asserted that al-Qa'ida in Iraq had been responsible for the blasts. Muqtada al-Sadr, meanwhile, declared at the end of the month that his Mahdi Army was to suspend its campaign against rival militias and US-led forces for a six-month period; this truce was extended for a further six months in February 2008.

The withdrawal of British troops from Basra

British armed forces withdrew from their remaining base in the city of Basra on 3 September 2007, transferring military control of the city centre to Iraqi troops and police. The formal handover of security from British to Iraqi forces in the remainder of Basra province took place on 16 December, thereby transferring to Iraqi authority the last of the four southern provinces controlled by the British military since 2003. It was reported in 2007 that large numbers of Iraqi refugees were returning to the country, particularly from neighbouring countries such as Syria. In December the UN Secretary-General's Special Representative for Iraq, Staffan de Mistura, launched a plan worth US $11,400m. to provide assistance to thousands of refugees and internally displaced families who had chosen to return home. It was reported in October 2007 that 22 Iraqi insurgent groups had agreed to establish a new coalition, the Supreme Command for Jihad and Liberation, to be led by the Baath Party's Izzat Ibrahim al-Douri.

After a period of lesser violence in Baghdad, on 1 February 2008 an estimated 100 people were killed in two massive suicide bomb attacks. Despite Basra having been noticeably calmer since the withdrawal of British forces, in March al-Maliki ordered a major offensive—code-named 'Operation Charge of the Knights'—against Shi'a militias in the city (including factions of al-Sadr's Mahdi Army) in an effort to reduce levels of criminal and militant activity. Some 210 people reportedly died during the operation, which involved more than 40,000 Iraqi troops assisted by coalition forces, and was concluded on 30 March when a truce was agreed between the Government and al-Sadr. Meanwhile, fierce fighting was reported in several cities in southern Iraq and also in the Sadr City district of Baghdad. A joint Iraqi-US military operation against the Mahdi Army in Sadr City began on 6 April and, after seven weeks—when al-Sadr again declared a ceasefire—had led to around 1,000 (mainly civilian) deaths. On 12 May al-Sadr agreed to allow Iraqi troops to enter Sadr City, pledging that his forces would end mortar and rocket attacks against Baghdad's Green Zone.

By mid-2008 violence across the country had generally shown a significant decline since the overthrow of Saddam Hussain in 2003. One explanation given for the decline in sectarian killings in Baghdad was that the capital was now essentially divided into separate Shi'a and Sunni districts. Another reason for the improved security in Sunni provinces of Iraq (such as Anbar) was the policy adopted by the US Administration whereby former Sunni militias involved in the insurgency against coalition forces were encouraged to form so-called Awakening Councils, receiving the support of US troops in order to fight extremist Islamist groups such as al-Qa'ida in Iraq.

Meanwhile, on 12 January 2008 the Council of Representatives approved a law permitting former middle- and low-ranking members of the Baath Party who had not been charged with crimes to reclaim positions of public office, effectively repealing the CPA's de-Baathification legislation adopted in 2003, which had resulted in the dismissal of thousands of Baathist officials. In July 2008 the six IAF ministers who had left the national unity Government in August 2007 rejoined the cabinet. The IAF had reportedly been satisfied by recent government actions such as the approval of an amnesty law involving thousands of Sunni prisoners and the clampdown on Shi'a militias. Moreover, four independent members of the UIA replaced the ministers from al-Sadr's faction, who continued to boycott the Government.

Following numerous delays, on 24 September 2008 the Council of Representatives approved legislation stipulating that provincial elections originally scheduled to have taken place by 1 October should now be held in most parts of Iraq by the end of January 2009, and that a parliamentary committee would review the status of Kirkuk. The new law was approved by the Presidency Council on 3 October 2008. Meanwhile, in July 2008 Kirkuk council members voted to permit a referendum to be held among the province's population to decide whether or not the city would join the Kurdish Autonomous Region; Turkmen and Arab members boycotted the vote.

President Bush declared in September 2008 that some 8,000 US forces would leave Iraq by February 2009—far fewer than had been anticipated—with some 138,000 troops remaining after that date. On 1 October 2008 the Iraqi Government assumed responsibility for directing and funding members of the Sunni Awakening Councils in Baghdad; by the end of that month 13 of Iraq's 18 provinces were under Iraqi security control. Meanwhile, on 9 October Saleh al-Auqaeili, a Shi'a member of the Council of Representatives affiliated with Muqtada al-Sadr, died in a roadside explosion in Sadr City. There was speculation that the ISCI's armed faction, the Badr Organization (founded in Tehran in 1983 as the Badr Brigade), might have been responsible for al-Auqaeili's murder, owing to the rivalry between its umbrella group and al-Sadr's followers. On 15 October US military chiefs claimed recently to have killed Abu Qaswarah (also known as Abu Sara), the second-in-command of al-Qa'ida in Iraq, during a military offensive in Mosul. In late 2008 al-Sadr was reported to have fled to Iran following the issuing of a warrant for his arrest.

The Status of Forces Agreement

The Status of Forces Agreement (SOFA) was signed by the US ambassador in Baghdad, Ryan Crocker, and the Iraqi Minister of Foreign Affairs, Hoshyar al-Zibari, on 17 November 2008, and was subsequently endorsed by the Council of Representatives and Presidency Council. Under the terms of the security pact, which was to be put to a nationwide referendum by the end of July 2009, all US armed forces were to withdraw from urban areas of the country by 30 June 2009; the remaining forces would leave by 31 December 2011. However, the timetable was depend-

ent on the successful assumption of control by Iraqi security forces. The Sadrist bloc insisted that the US military should withdraw from Iraq immediately. On 23 December 2008 the Iraqi parliament agreed to allow the Government to extend the mandate for non-US foreign forces to remain in the country after the expiry on 31 December of the UN mandate for the US-led multinational force, provided that these troops were withdrawn by July 2009. The number of US troops killed in Iraq was reported to have declined to some 314 in 2008, compared with 904 in 2007. On 1 January 2009, when the SOFA entered effect, control of the Green Zone in Baghdad was handed from the Iraqi to US authorities. At the same time, responsibility for the 145,700 US forces was transferred to the Iraqi Government.

At the elections finally held on 31 January 2009 in 14 of Iraq's 18 provinces (the three Kurdish provinces and Kirkuk being excluded from the vote), the official rate of voter participation was just 51%; however, turnout in certain mainly Sunni areas was higher than expected, and the elections were hailed as demonstrating the return of Sunni Arab political parties to the democratic system. The vote was relatively free of violence, compared with 2005, although six prospective candidates were killed in advance of polling. Allies of Prime Minister al-Maliki—standing as the State of Law coalition—secured notable successes, particularly in southern Shi'a areas of Iraq. While al-Maliki's coalition won a majority of votes in Baghdad and nine other provinces, the ISCI—previously dominant in Shi'a areas—failed to win in any provinces.

In February 2009 the recently inaugurated US President, Barack Obama, declared that his Administration intended to withdraw the majority of US troops from Iraq by the end of August 2010. President Obama stated that between 35,000 and 50,000 US forces would remain in the country after that date in order to advise Iraqi security forces and protect US interests. All US forces would have withdrawn from Iraq by the end of 2011, as stipulated under the terms of the SOFA. During April 2009 scores of Iraqis were killed in violent attacks perpetrated by al-Qa'ida in Iraq and other militant groups in Baghdad and elsewhere; many Iranian pilgrims also died in an explosion targeting the revered Shi'a Imam Musa al-Kadhim shrine in the capital.

The withdrawal of coalition forces and continuing violent insurgency

On 30 April 2009 the United Kingdom's combat mission in Iraq was officially declared to have been completed. By the end of July the withdrawal had been effected of the majority of the 4,100-strong British force in southern Iraq, as well as all other non-US coalition forces in the country. An estimated 400 British troops were to remain to provide specialist training to the Iraqi security forces. A bilateral maritime agreement under which the United Kingdom's navy would protect offshore petroleum facilities and provide training for Iraq's navy entered into force in November. (In May 2011 the last remaining British navy personnel were withdrawn from Iraq, signalling the formal end of the British military's operations in Iraq, during which a total of 179 British troops had been killed.) Meanwhile, on 30 June 2009, according to the terms of the SOFA, US combat forces initiated their withdrawal from Baghdad and other urban centres. Henceforth, US forces would fulfil a non-combative support role in the cities, while serving as a partner in Iraqi-led combat operations elsewhere.

Frequent incidents of sectarian violence occurred in mid-2009, particularly in Baghdad and Mosul. Confidence in the Iraqi security forces was severely undermined following a series of bomb and mortar attacks on 19 August, which targeted official buildings near Baghdad's Green Zone, including the Ministries of Foreign Affairs and of Finance. At least 101 people were killed in the attacks. On 23 August a former Baathist police officer claimed responsibility for organizing one of the bombs, and alleged that the operation had been directed by two senior Iraqi Baath party officials exiled in Syria, a claim that provoked a diplomatic confrontation with Syria (see *Regional relations*). Nevertheless, in late August Islamic State in Iraq, a network of Sunni militant groups suspected of links with al-Qa'ida, claimed that it had perpetrated the attacks. Islamic State in Iraq also alleged that it had organized two suicide car bombs in Baghdad on 25 October, one of which targeted the Ministry of Justice. At least 155 people died in the bombings, which raised concerns that the security forces were susceptible to infiltration by insurgents. By the end of October more than 60 security officers had reportedly been arrested and questioned in connection with the attacks. Meanwhile, in that month the Ministry of Human

Rights reported that 85,694 people had been killed in violence between the beginning of 2004 and October 2008, almost 150,000 people had been injured and an estimated 10,000 were missing.

Amid reports of divisions in the Shi'a UIA coalition—the largest parliamentary grouping—in August 2009 the formation was announced of a new Shi'a electoral list, the Iraqi National Alliance. The new grouping, which excluded Prime Minister al-Maliki's Islamic Dawa Party, was dominated by supporters of al-Sadr (who remained in self-imposed exile in Iran) and also included the ISCI.

Meanwhile, on 24 June 2009 a draft Constitution for the Kurdish Autonomous Region was approved by the Iraqi Kurdistan Parliament (the National Assembly having adopted the name Parliament in February). The document, which identified Islamic *Shari'a* as the basis for the region's legal system, also included territorial claims to Kirkuk and other disputed regions. However, a planned referendum on the draft Constitution was subsequently postponed; no date had been set for the referendum by early 2015. Following elections to the Iraqi Kurdistan Parliament held on 25 July 2009, the Kurdistani List—comprising the PUK and the KDP—secured 59 of the 111 seats. A new reformist party, the Movement for Change (Gorran), which had been established by former PUK members in 2006, received 25 seats. In a concurrent election for the regional presidency, Barzani was re-elected with 69.6% of the valid votes cast. In August 2009 Barham Salih, of the PUK, resigned as Deputy Prime Minister in the central Government to assume the post of Prime Minister of the Kurdish Autonomous Region.

The March 2010 legislative elections

Revised legislation concerning the forthcoming national legislative elections was approved by the Council of Representatives on 7 November 2009. The negotiations had been protracted owing to disagreement over voter registration in the disputed city of Kirkuk. The law also provided for: an increase in the number of Council seats from 275 to 323, partly to accommodate claims for increased representation by Kurds and Sunnis; an allocation of 5% of seats for representatives of minorities (including Christians) and displaced Iraqis; and the adoption of an open electoral list system. However, on 18 November Vice-President Tariq al-Hashimi vetoed the bill on the grounds that it provided inadequate representation for the vast numbers of Iraqis displaced in Syria and Jordan, many of whom were Sunnis. (According to figures published by the respective Governments, by January 2010 there were an estimated 1,054,466 Iraqi refugees living in Syria, and a further 450,756 in Jordan.) As a result, the Independent High Electoral Commission (IHEC) declared that it would not be possible to hold the election by the constitutional deadline of the end of January 2010. An amended electoral law, which increased the number of seats in the Council to 325 and accorded displaced Iraqis the right to vote for candidates in their province of origin, received parliamentary approval on 7 December 2009. Al-Hashimi rescinded his veto, and the election was subsequently rescheduled for 7 March 2010. On 8 December 2009 five car bombs were directed at targets in Baghdad including the Ministry of the Interior and a university campus; at least 127 people were killed in the attacks, for which Islamic State in Iraq again claimed responsibility.

In mid-January 2010 the IHEC announced that it was to bar more than 500 candidates and up to 15 political organizations from participating in the forthcoming election. The proscribed list reportedly included more than 170 candidates who had been identified as having alleged links to the Baath Party or to Saddam Hussain's former security apparatus. Following claims by Sunni Arab leaders that the ruling would exacerbate sectarian tensions and diminish the legitimacy of the election, in early February a special appeals panel ruled that, instead, any elected candidates with Baath Party associations should be scrutinized after the election. However, the Government insisted that candidates be fully investigated prior to the ballot. On 11 February some 26 previously barred candidates were reinstated.

A day of early voting on 4 March 2010 was marked by three separate attacks on polling stations in Baghdad, in which at least 17 people died. Nevertheless, some 62.4% of eligible voters participated in the election on 7 March. Final results were announced by the IHEC on 26 March. Following the allocation of compensatory seats, the Iraqi National Movement of former interim Prime Minister Allawi emerged as the largest party, with 89 seats (plus two compensatory seats) in the 325-seat Council of Representatives. This new electoral bloc, widely known as Iraqiya, had replaced Allawi's INL, and included the INA and the Iraqi Front for National Dialogue. The State of Law

alliance of incumbent premier al-Maliki won 87 seats (plus two compensatory seats). The Shi'a Iraqi National Alliance secured 68 seats (with an additional two seats subsequently being allocated) and the Kurdistan Alliance list of the PUK and KDP 42 (plus one compensatory seat). Al-Maliki refused to accept the outcome and demanded a full recount of the votes; the IHEC announced on 19 April that a recount would take place in the Baghdad area. Meanwhile, owing to the lack of overall majority for either of the leading coalitions, lengthy coalition negotiations ensued. On 25 March 2010 the Federal Supreme Court had confirmed that, constitutionally, the leader of the largest coalition in parliament was entitled to form a new administration, leaving open the possibility of a post-election merger of the State of Law alliance with former allies in the Iraqi National Alliance. On 26 April it was ruled that a further 52 former Baathist candidates should not have been permitted to contest the elections.

The political uncertainty, as well as the approach to the end of US combat operations in August 2010, again prompted a deterioration in Iraq's security situation. On 19 April 2010 the respective leaders of Islamic State in Iraq and of al-Qa'ida in Iraq, Abu Omar al-Baghdadi and Abu Ayyub al-Masri, were reportedly killed in a joint Iraqi-US security operation near Tikrit. Another al-Qa'ida leader, Ahmad al-Obeidi (also known as Abu Suhaib), was also reported killed in Nineveh on 20 April. The killings led to a wave of fatal revenge attacks across Iraq, and militants sought to widen the divisions between the country's Sunni and Shi'a communities. On 10 May more than 100 people were killed as bombs were detonated in Hilla, gunmen attacked Iraqi soldiers and police officers in Baghdad, and attacks were carried out in Basra, Fallujah and Mosul. On 14 May Islamic State in Iraq announced the appointment of al-Masri's successor, Abu Suleiman al-Nasser (also known as Noman Salman), as its new 'Minister of War', and warned that the organization had begun a new military campaign against Iraqi Shi'a and security forces. (On 25 February 2011 Iraqi security forces claimed to have killed Abu Suleiman during a military raid near Baghdad.)

Meanwhile, in an effort to defeat Allawi's victorious Iraqiya faction in its attempt to form Iraq's next government, on 4 May 2010 al-Maliki's State of Law alliance agreed to form a unified parliamentary bloc with the Iraqi National Alliance, to be called the National Alliance (NA). The merger of the two Shi'a alliances into a new 'super-bloc' was formally announced on 11 June, shortly before the first session of the new legislature. Al-Maliki was also reported to be participating in coalition discussions with the Kurdistan Alliance. However, Iraqiya insisted that, as the winner of the largest number of seats, it should be entitled to seek to form an administration first. Moreover, despite commanding a total of 159 seats in the Council of Representatives—and thus requiring only four more seats to hold a parliamentary majority of 163 in the 325-seat legislature—the constituent parties of the NA were unable to agree on a prime ministerial candidate, with the ISCI and the Sadrists refusing to accept al-Maliki's continuation in that role.

An inaugural session of the Council of Representatives took place on 14 June 2010. However, although Iraq's new deputies were sworn in, the session was declared to be left open but suspended, pending an agreement between the various political factions on the formation of a new government. On 24 October the Supreme Court ordered the parliament to resume its functions. Meanwhile, on 17 May 2010 a court of appeal reinstated nine successful electoral candidates, eight of whom belonged to Allawi's faction, after they had previously been barred as part of the de-Baathification process. On 24 May a deputy from Iraqiya was attacked by unidentified gunmen outside his house in Mosul and subsequently died.

The formation of a new Government

As the US Administration sought to exert pressure on Allawi's Iraqiya faction and al-Maliki's State of Law alliance in order to reach a power-sharing deal before the USA withdrew its combat troops, the agreement between al-Maliki's bloc and the Iraqi National Alliance began to falter in August 2010. Smaller Shi'a movements in the NA, such as the Sadrists, still refused to back al-Maliki's renomination as Prime Minister. For his part, Allawi—whose Iraqiya coalition also ruled out joining a government under al-Maliki—had held a meeting with al-Sadr in Damascus, Syria, in July, in an effort to accelerate the formation of a viable administration. On 16 August it was reported that discussions between Iraqiya and the State of Law alliance had been suspended, after the incumbent Prime Minister described

Iraqiya as being a 'Sunni bloc'. Moreover, al-Maliki refused to step down as Prime Minister in favour of Allawi.

President Obama formally declared the end of the US combat mission in Iraq, known as Operation Iraqi Freedom, on 31 August 2010. He confirmed that almost 50,000 US forces would remain in the country in order to 'advise and assist' Iraq's security forces and defend US interests, but that the US military would be completely withdrawn by 31 December 2011, under the terms of the SOFA. (The Iraqi Chief of Staff of the Joint Armed Forces, Lt-Gen. Babakir Zebari, had warned in early August 2010 that Iraqi troops might not be adequately prepared to guarantee the security of Iraq until 2020, and suggested that US forces should in fact remain until that date.) A ceremony was held in Baghdad on 1 September 2010 to commemorate the start of the 'final phase' of the USA's mission in Iraq, code-named 'Operation New Dawn'. The weeks preceding the end of US combat operations had been marked by a wave of attacks being perpetrated against Iraqi police and security targets and ordinary civilians; the continuing pattern of Sunni–Shi'a violence was also evident.

During the latter part of 2010 the campaign being waged by radical Islamist organizations against Iraq's Christian community intensified, resulting in a further exodus of Christians either to the relative safety of northern Iraq or abroad. On 3 November Islamic State in Iraq issued a statement threatening to expel all Christians from the country, describing the Christian religion as a 'legitimate target' for Islamist attacks. This followed an incident on 31 October 2010 when gunmen entered the Syrian Catholic church in central Baghdad during a mass, holding around 100 worshippers hostage and reportedly demanding the release of al-Qa'ida detainees from Iraqi prisons. At least 58 people were killed, most as a result of suicide bombs detonated by the attackers as security forces entered the church in an attempt to free the hostages.

Meanwhile, on 1 October 2010 it was announced that the NA had finally decided to support al-Maliki's continuing as Prime Minister at the head of a new administration, amid reports that a deal had been brokered by the Iranian Government. On 10 November the leaders of Iraq's principal factions in the Council of Representatives formally signed a power-sharing agreement under which a coalition government would again be led by al-Maliki (a Shi'a), while a new foreign policy and security council, the National Council for Strategic Policies (NCSP), would be run by Allawi (a secular Shi'a). The coalition agreement followed a power-sharing deal which had been reached between the NA and both the Kurdistan Alliance and Iraqiya in early November. On 11 November a session of the Council of Representatives was duly held, at which Talabani (a Kurd) was re-elected as President, while a Sunni Arab member of Iraqiya, Osama al-Nujaifi, was elected as the Speaker. Al-Maliki was officially named by President Talabani as Prime Minister-designate on 25 November. Meanwhile, it emerged in late October 2010 that, apparently as part of the Iranian-brokered agreement reached between al-Maliki and al-Sadr, large numbers of militants from the latter's Mahdi Army had been released from gaol. The Mahdi Army was reported to have been dissolved by al-Sadr in mid-2008 and succeeded by a civilian organization, Al-Mumahidun (Supporters of the Mahdi). (Al-Sadr returned to Iraq in January 2011, after more than three years' self-imposed exile in Iran.)

On 17 November 2010 President Talabani refused to approve the execution order for Saddam Hussain's former Deputy Prime Minister, Tareq Aziz, after Aziz had on 26 October been sentenced to death by the Federal Supreme Court for his involvement in the persecution of Shi'a politicians during the 1980s; two other senior Baathists, including the former Minister of the Interior and Director of Iraqi Intelligence, Saadoun Shaker, were also given a death sentence. (Aziz had already been sentenced to a 15-year gaol term and a further seven-year term for separate offences.) Announcing his decision, Talabani cited the fact that Aziz was 74 years old and a Christian. Although a prime ministerial aide indicated in December 2011 that Aziz would in fact be executed during the course of 2012, following the completion of the US troop withdrawal, the execution had yet to occur by early 2015.

The legislature finally approved the new Council of Ministers submitted by al-Maliki, in which all the major blocs were represented, on 21 December 2010. Al-Maliki was to take temporary charge of the defence, national security and interior portfolios, amid disagreement about possible nominees to these crucial ministries. On 13 February 2011 eight further nominees, including a permanent Minister of Trade, received parliamentary approval. In August some 12 ministries were disbanded, including those of marsh lands and tribal affairs.

Following protracted disagreements between the leading parliamentary groups regarding the establishment and authority of the new foreign policy and security council, Allawi announced in March 2011 that he no longer wished to preside over the NCSP, citing the Prime Minister's decision to assume interim responsibility for the defence, national security and interior portfolios, together with the protracted delay in appointing permanent ministers, as evidence of his 'lack of commitment to national partnership'.

During February 2011, as social and political unrest spread across large parts of the Middle East and North Africa, spontaneous protests were held in several Iraqi cities by people demonstrating against official corruption, poor provision of basic services, high unemployment and the lack of civil liberties. The protesters called for 25 February to be a 'day of rage', and at least nine people were reportedly killed in clashes with security forces in cities outside the capital. Al-Maliki, who apparently described the demonstrations as a 'Baathist plot', had attempted to prevent the uprisings in Tunisia and Egypt—which had resulted in the ouster of both countries' governing regimes—from spreading to Iraq by announcing in early February that he would not stand for a third term of office in 2014 and pledged to pursue constitutional reform. In late February 2011 al-Maliki warned government ministers that he would reorganize the Council of Ministers if there had not been a tangible improvement in ministerial performance after 100 days. The Prime Minister also announced that US $900m. of funds that had been allocated to the purchase of fighter aircraft were to be redirected towards the provision of food for the poor, with a further $400m. reserved to pay for fuel to power air conditioners during the hot summer months, and initiated a series of infrastructure projects intended to improve Iraq's dilapidated road and sewerage systems.

However, the protests continued into April 2011, principally in the Kurdish Autonomous Region. In late April security forces in Sulaimaniya opened fire on protesters who were demanding the resignation of the regional administration. Days later Iraqi troops and *peshmerga* fighters entered the city in an attempt to quell the protests. By the end of April it was reported that up to 36 people had been killed across Iraq as a result of the unrest. In June protests took place against the Government's failure to achieve meaningful reform, amid demands for an improvement in public services, particularly the supply of electricity.

Completion of the withdrawal of US troops

There was an escalation of attacks targeting US troops before the scheduled completion of the military withdrawal, due by 31 December 2011 under the terms of the SOFA. Some 18 US soldiers were killed during a six-week period in June–July 2011, forcing the US military back into active combat despite the formal conclusion of the combat operation in August 2010. In mid-August 2011 co-ordinated bomb attacks by Islamic State in Iraq, targeting largely Shi'a areas across Iraq as well as government compounds in Karbala and Najaf, killed more than 70 people; the attacks led to renewed concern about the Iraqi authorities' ability to manage national security in the absence of US assistance. In September Muqtada al-Sadr marked the imminent end of the US mission by ordering his supporters to halt attacks on US troops.

In July 2011 the Iraqi authorities assumed control of the Development Fund for Iraq, which had been established following the ouster of Saddam Hussain's regime in 2003 and contained billions of dollars of oil revenues set aside by the UN. Meanwhile, in June 2011 a US official investigating the disappearance of US $6,600m. from the Fund, which had been airlifted into Iraq by the Bush Administration during 2003–04 as part of a $20,000m. reconstruction package, suggested that the money might have been stolen by elements within the Iraqi interim administration at the time.

During a joint press conference held on 12 December 2011, al-Maliki and President Obama reaffirmed their mutual commitment to a long-term comprehensive partnership between Iraq and the USA, including plans to bolster co-operation in the fields of defence and security, as well as trade and economic development and institution-building. Although al-Maliki hailed the imminent completion of the US withdrawal as an indication of the successful defeat of terrorism and the beginning of a 'new chapter' for Iraq, Obama cautioned of the heightened risk of attacks in the coming months by elements seeking to 'derail Iraq's progress'. Many observers also noted that the US withdrawal would render Iraq more susceptible to increasing Iranian influence. Following the completion of its withdrawal, the USA was to have no military bases within Iraq, although a small number of military personnel would remain in the country to assist with arms sales, together with some 16,000 personnel to assist in the establishment of effective diplomatic, civilian and military ties.

A ceremony was staged in Baghdad on 15 December 2011 to mark the formal end of the US mission, attended by the US Secretary of Defense, Leon Panetta. On 18 December the final convoy of 500 US troops withdrew from Iraq, thereby concluding a campaign that had claimed the lives of 4,484 US troops and cost the US Government an estimated US $800,000m. since its inception in March 2003. According to Iraq Body Count, an estimated 4,144 civilians died as a result of violence during 2011, representing a slight increase on the previous year.

The feared escalation in sectarian violence soon became apparent across Iraq, leading many Iraqis to fear a return to the intense sectarian conflict seen in the country during 2006–07. According to Iraqi security officials, by late January 2012 some 434 people (mainly Shi'as) had been killed since the completion of the US withdrawal. Attacks against the national security forces also intensified, with a spate of attacks targeting police officers in January. A series of fatal gun and bomb attacks was launched by Sunni insurgents during 2012, with reciprocal attacks by militant Shi'a groups also being reported.

Meanwhile, in December 2011 Prime Minister al-Maliki signed a warrant for the arrest of Vice-President al-Hashimi on charges of terrorism, and issued a concurrent request to the Council of Representatives to remove Deputy Prime Minister Salih al-Mutlaq from office on the grounds of incompetence. Al-Mutlaq had recently referred to al-Maliki as a 'dictator', and he was barred from participating in cabinet meetings. Al-Hashimi, who subsequently fled to northern Iraq, was alleged by an investigative committee established by the Ministry of the Interior to have ordered bodyguards to carry out terrorist attacks against government and security officials, as well as Shi'a pilgrims, for a number of years. Al-Maliki demanded that the President of the Kurdistan Autonomous Region Barzani, and Iraqi President Talabani transfer al-Hashimi to the custody of the Iraqi judiciary in Baghdad. In protest at the action taken against two of its members, who were both Sunnis, Iraqiya subsequently withdrew its participation from the Council of Ministers and announced a concomitant boycott of the Council of Representatives. The dispute between the Shi'a Prime Minister and the nominally secular but Sunni-dominated Iraqiya threatened further to exacerbate sectarian divisions. Iraqiya ended its parliamentary boycott in January 2012, and in February also resumed its participation in cabinet meetings. However, in April the Higher Judicial Council announced that al-Hashimi—who had sought refuge in Istanbul, Turkey—would be tried *in absentia* on charges of murder from 3 May.

In late January 2012 the UN Office of the High Commissioner for Human Rights stated that at least 63 people had been executed by the Iraqi authorities in the preceding two months, and expressed reservations about the 'due process and fairness of trials' in Iraq. Pillay's comments echoed concerns expressed in an Amnesty International report in late 2011, which claimed that at least 1,300 prisoners were on death row in Iraq at that time, that trials 'consistently failed to satisfy international standards for fair trial', and that torture and other abuse of detainees within Iraqi prisons was 'rife'. At the beginning of February 2012 the Ministry of Justice confirmed that more than 50 people had been executed in Iraq during January—although some human rights groups claimed that the actual figure might be significantly higher.

Renewed sectarian violence amid rising political tensions

In April 2012 the leaders of the Kurdistan Alliance, Iraqiya and the Sadrist movement held talks in Arbil in an effort to force Prime Minister al-Maliki from office. Following the meeting, they presented a nine-point ultimatum letter to al-Maliki, which included the demands that a premier be permitted to serve only two consecutive terms of office and that the role of the Council of Representatives be expanded. However, the subsequent lack of political consensus among the various opposition groups meant that they were deemed to be unable to achieve a sufficient number of votes to remove al-Maliki from office in a parliamentary vote of no confidence.

It was announced in late May 2012 that al-Mutlaq would resume his participation in the Government. In early September

Vice-President al-Hashimi was found guilty *in absentia* of two charges of planning and facilitating murder, and sentenced to death by a court in Baghdad. However, al-Hashimi rejected the verdict, claiming that the proceedings had been instigated by the Prime Minister for political reasons. The Turkish Prime Minister, Recep Tayyip Erdoğan, indicated that Turkey would refuse to extradite al-Hashimi. By mid-December al-Hashimi had been given a total of five death sentences, all *in absentia*, having additionally been convicted of crimes including plotting to explode a car bomb targeting Shi'a pilgrims and planning to assassinate an official at the Ministry of the Interior; al-Hashimi's son-in-law, Ahmad Qahtan, was also sentenced to death on similar charges. In mid-October 2013 al-Hashimi stated that he would be prepared to return to Iraq, provided that he received a fair trial.

During 2012 Iraq Body Count estimated the number of violent civilian deaths to be 4,573—representing a 10% increase compared with the previous year. In June a series of bomb attacks targeted Shi'a districts of Baghdad and other cities, with some estimates claiming that 280 people had been killed. Islamic State in Iraq claimed responsibility for a significant number of the deaths. In a single day in early September more than 100 Iraqis were reportedly killed as a result of the co-ordinated bombings of principally Shi'a targets; the same militant group was again held responsible. In February 2013 militants launched a series of car bombings in Shi'a-dominated areas of Baghdad and other Iraqi towns, apparently to disrupt preparations for the country's first ballot to be held since the legislative polls of March 2010. Provincial elections were scheduled to take place across Iraq, with the exclusion of the three Kurdish provinces, on 20 April 2013. On 19 March at least 60 people were killed in a series of co-ordinated bombings and shootings in Shi'a districts of Baghdad. Later that day the Government announced that provincial elections in Anbar and Nineveh provinces were to be postponed, owing to concerns over security; these polls were later scheduled for June. Meanwhile, President Talabani was reported to have suffered a serious stroke in mid-December 2012 and was flown to Germany for emergency medical treatment.

From late 2012 there was an escalation of protests being held by Sunni Iraqis against the Shi'a-led Government; some observers noted the evident loss of Talabani's ability to mediate between Iraq's rival Shi'a, Sunni and Kurdish groups. Supporters of the Iraqiya movement had begun anti-Government protests in cities including Fallujah and Ramadi in December, following the arrest by the authorities of 10 bodyguards employed to protect the Sunni Minister of Finance, Dr Rafie al-Issawi, a senior member of Iraqiya; the men were all accused of involvement in terrorism. However, al-Maliki denied that he had personally ordered the arrests. The protests subsequently spread to majority Sunni districts of Baghdad, as well as Baquba, Mosul and Kirkuk. Counter-demonstrations were held by Shi'a supporters of the Government across Iraq, including in Basra and Karbala, in early January 2013. In mid-January a Sunni member of the Council of Representatives was killed, together with two of his bodyguards, in a suicide bombing in Fallujah. In late February demonstrators gathered in central Baghdad to protest at the failure of parliament to approve the Government's draft budget for that year. Iraqiya demanded that a certain level of funding was allocated to develop Iraq's provinces, while the Kurdistan Alliance sought financial assistance from the central Government to pay the foreign oil firms operating in the region, as well as to carry out vital reconstruction projects. The budget was finally approved by the Council of Representatives on 7 March 2013, although the parliamentary session was boycotted by Kurdish deputies in protest at what they regarded as the unfair distribution of oil revenues. Meanwhile, at the beginning of March it was reported that al-Issawi had resigned from the Government, citing his opposition to the 'sectarian' nature of al-Maliki's administration. A week later Minister of Agriculture Ezz al-Din Ahmad Hussein al-Dawla—also a member of Iraqiya—announced his resignation, following allegations that the security forces had shot dead a Sunni demonstrator in Mosul. At least 40 people were killed in Hawija, close to Kirkuk, on 23 April. In late April the Government suspended the operating licences of some 10 television channels, including the Qatar-based Al Jazeera, accusing them of inciting violence. At the end of April the Government claimed to have evidence that senior officials from the former Baathist regime, including Izzat Ibrahim al-Douri, were leading the protests.

Despite the ongoing unrest, provincial elections were held as scheduled in 12 of Iraq's 18 provinces on 20 April 2013. Polls in the majority Sunni provinces of Anbar and Nineveh were held on 20 June 2013, while no elections were held in the three Kurdish provinces or in Kirkuk, the status of which continued to be disputed by Iraq's various political factions. Some violent incidents were reported at polling stations, but the elections were largely peaceful. The IHEC recorded an overall voter turnout of 50%; however, the rate was said to be as low as 33% in Baghdad. Although al-Maliki's State of Law coalition received the largest number of council seats and won a majority of votes in seven provinces (including Baghdad and Basra), it was required to govern in coalition with other, smaller parties. Commentators attributed the State of Law's loss of votes to other Shi'a parties and the Sadrist movement to public disillusionment with the Prime Minister, notably his failure to reduce unemployment and to stem the tide of sectarian violence across Iraq. Meanwhile, a new grouping led by the Speaker of the Council of Representatives, Osama al-Nujaifi, called the Uniters, took a significant number of votes from Allawi's Iraqiya coalition. During 15–21 May 2013 an estimated 450 people died as the result of sectarian bomb and gun attacks in northern and central areas of the country.

By the second half of 2013 the violence had reached a level of intensity not seen since the 2006–08 period. A number of bomb attacks were perpetrated by extremist Sunni militant groups against both Shi'a and Christian targets. On 21 July more than 500 detainees, many of whom were said to be senior members of al-Qa'ida in Iraq, escaped from Baghdad Central Prison and the nearby Taji prison in a co-ordinated assault by the militant group using both gunmen and suicide bombers. An estimated 41 people (20 security guards and 21 prisoners) died during the operation, which was claimed by the umbrella group Islamic State in Iraq and the Levant (ISIL; renamed Islamic State in June 2014)—formed in April by jihadist fighters to co-ordinate militant attacks in both Iraq and Syria. Almost 200 people were killed across Iraq in late July and early August by Sunni militants targeting Shi'as. In mid-August a crossing on Iraq's border with Syria was opened, allowing some 50,000 (mainly Kurdish) Syrian refugees who were escaping fighting between Kurdish groups and Islamist rebels to enter the Kurdish Autonomous Region of northern Iraq. By November there were reported to be more than 200,000 Syrian refugees in Iraq. Meanwhile, many Iraqis who had fled to Syria during the Iraqi conflict were returning to the country, with Iraqi Red Cross officials stating that more than 70,000 had returned to Iraq since the start of the Syrian uprising in early 2011.

Iraq Body Count assessed on 1 September 2013 that between 120,809 and 133,960 civilians had died as a result of violence during the entire period since the US-led invasion in 2003. It was alleged on the same day that Iraqi security forces had entered Camp Ashraf, north-east of Baghdad, and killed some 52 members of the Iranian dissident group Mujahidin-e-Khalq. In mid-September 2013 it was revealed that the remaining inhabitants of the camp had been moved to another centre close to the capital, from where they would be permanently resettled. Later that month Arbil, in the Kurdish Autonomous Region, became the target of further bombings by militant Islamists. Islamic State in Iraq and the Levant claimed that it was waging a campaign of violence against the Kurdish people as a result of their support for Syrian Kurds who were engaged in fighting Islamist groups in that country's civil conflict.

At elections to the Iraqi Kurdistan Parliament on 21 September 2013, the KDP emerged as the leading party, securing 38 seats. Gorran became the second largest party, with 24 seats, while the PUK came third, winning only 18 seats. However, although these polls were expected to have been held concurrently with a presidential ballot, on 30 June 2013 the Kurdish legislature had voted to postpone elections for the regional presidency until August 2015. The decision was condemned by Kurdish opposition parties, who insisted that Kurdish President Barzani (elected in 2005 and re-elected in 2009) had now served the permitted two terms in office. However, KDP and PUK officials asserted that the delay would enable an agreement to be reached on the new Kurdish constitution prior to the vote taking place. After Prime Minister al-Maliki had convened a cabinet meeting in Arbil for the first time in June 2013, in July Barzani held talks in Baghdad with al-Maliki; their discussions reportedly focused on disputes concerning the exploitation of Iraq's vast hydrocarbon resources.

It was announced in early October 2013 that elections to the Iraqi Council of Representatives would take place in April 2014. Meanwhile, the sectarian violence continued: during 5–6 October

2013 more than 100 people died as a result of militant attacks, including 51 Shi'a pilgrims in a Baghdad suicide bombing and 12 children in a car bomb attack on their school in Mosul. Further attacks launched by Sunni militants in Shi'a areas of the Iraqi capital throughout the month led to scores of fatalities. In late December a group of Christians attending Christmas Day services in two churches in Baghdad were the victims of bomb attacks, with more than 35 worshippers being killed.

According to UN estimates, 7,157 people died as the result of violent incidents in Iraq during 2013—more than double the figure of 3,238 recorded in 2012. UN figures for January 2014 showed that at least 1,013 people had been killed. The number of fatalities was thus three times greater in that month than during January 2013, and indicated that the sectarian violence had deteriorated to a level last seen in 2008. The anti-Government protests led by Sunnis continued into 2014, and were met with a harsh response from the Iraqi authorities. In January security forces in the western province of Anbar, assisted by local Sunni tribesmen from the province's Awakening Council, were engaged in fierce gun battles with Sunni militias allied with Islamic State in Iraq and the Levant, who had seized control of parts of Fallujah and Ramadi in the previous month. The unrest had been provoked by the arrest on terrorism charges of a leading Sunni member of the Iraqiya faction in the legislature, Ahmad al-Alwani, in Ramadi in December 2013. The Government regained control of Ramadi, but struggled to defeat the militants in Fallujah. It had been reported in mid-2013 that the US Administration was preparing to send specialist forces to Iraq to assist the al-Maliki Government in its struggle to defeat militant groups allied with al-Qa'ida in Iraq, who were believed to be acting together with extremist Sunni groups seeking to topple the Syrian regime of President Bashar al-Assad. On 30 December the Government forcibly ended the sit-in that had been initiated by Sunni protesters in Ramadi in late 2012; at least 10 people died as a result of this action, leading 44 (mainly Sunni) members of the Iraqi parliament to tender their resignations in protest.

The 2014 legislative elections

The IHEC in March 2014 discussed the postponement of the forthcoming legislative elections in Anbar province, owing to continued conflict between government forces and Sunni militants, particularly in Ramadi and Fallujah, and the resulting displacement of some 400,000 people from the province. On 25 March commissioners from the IHEC resigned, citing political and judicial 'interference' in the electoral process, although the resignations were later withdrawn following appeals from the UN. Meanwhile, at least 45 people were killed in a car bomb attack in Hilla on 9 March, and 33 people were killed in a series of bombings in Baghdad on 27 March.

Despite the ongoing violence in northern and western parts of the country, the legislative elections went ahead as scheduled on 30 April 2014, with turnout reported at 62% of eligible voters. Official results published by the IHEC some three weeks later confirmed that al-Maliki's State of Law party had emerged with the largest share of parliamentary seats. Including affiliated lists, that group's representation increased from 89 of 325 seats at the previous poll, to 94 of 328 seats in the new, expanded Council of Representatives. Elsewhere among the principal Shi'a lists, the Sadrist bloc gained 31 seats, and the ISCI increased its allocation from 21 to 30 seats, while the Sadrist party al-Fadhila (Islamic Virtue Party) secured six. Among the main Sunni lists, Mutahhidun confirmed its status as the dominant political movement among Sunni voters, winning a total of 28 seats. Notably, the party appeared to have regained lost ground in its stronghold of Nineveh province, more than doubling its share of the vote compared with the 2013 provincial election. Elsewhere, the INL/Wataniya list obtained 21 seats, 10 of which were in Baghdad, while al-Arabiya secured 11 seats. Among the various Kurdish parties, the KDP emerged with the largest share of seats with 25, while the PUK, with 19 seats, improved considerably on its poor performance in the elections to the Kurdish parliament in 2013. The PUK's share of seats was increased by the fact that an election was held in Kirkuk, the party's stronghold, for the first time since 2005, and it secured one-half of Kirkuk's 12 seats. The other Kurdish parties obtaining parliamentary seats were Gorran (nine), the Kurdistan Islamic Union (four) and the Islamic Group of Kurdistan (three), bringing the total Kurdish representation to 62 seats. Moreover, the disintegration of large coalitions such as Iraqiya and the National Alliance meant that potential opposition to a continuation of al-Maliki's tenure was divided. The main Kurdish parties scored overwhelming victories in Kurdish-populated areas, the Shi'a lists won almost all the seats on offer south of Baghdad and only a handful of seats to the north, and the Sunni parties won almost all the seats in Sunni regions north and west of Baghdad, indicating that Iraqi politics was still ordered primarily by ethnicity and religious sect. Polling day was followed by a number of bombings, including one on 22 May in which 35 Shi'a pilgrims were killed, and a series of bombings nationwide on 28 May which resulted in the deaths of 74 people.

On 11 July 2014 Hussain al-Shahristani was appointed acting Minister of Foreign Affairs in place of Hoshyar al-Zibari, one of a number of Kurdish ministers who withdrew from the Government earlier that month after al-Maliki accused the Kurdistan Regional Government (KRG) of harbouring extremists belonging to Islamic State in Arbil; however, al-Zibari was reinstated in his former role in mid-August along with other Kurdish ministers, upon the assumption of the premiership by Haidar al-Abadi (q.v.). The inaugural session of the new parliament on 1 July ended after Kurdish and Sunni deputies boycotted the session and caused its adjournment owing to a lack of a quorum. Unlike after previous elections, the three most senior positions—Speaker, Prime Minister and President—were elected sequentially, rather than as part of a single agreement. First, in mid-July parliament elected the Sunni Arab politician Salim al-Jaburi as Speaker. A critic of al-Maliki, al-Jaburi was endorsed by parliament, winning 194 votes. The following week, the Kurdish politician Fouad Masoum was overwhelmingly endorsed to succeed Jalal Talabani as President, thus activating the constitutionally mandated 15-day deadline for the nomination and approval of a Prime Minister. As leader of the largest parliamentary bloc, al-Maliki was considered likely to win a third successive term, but faced strong opposition from Sunnis, Kurds and even many within his own Shi'a community. On 25 July, however, Grand Ayatollah al-Sistani issued a statement urging Iraq's leaders not to 'cling to power', regarded as a reference to al-Maliki's efforts to retain his post. Al-Sistani's stance was subsequently endorsed by Iran's Supreme Religious Leader, Seyed Ali Khamenei. The effect of this statement was to divide the State of Law alliance. Ultimately, in early August the State of Law group nominated Haidar al-Abadi in preference to al-Maliki by a vote of 50 to 45. However, al-Maliki announced on 10 August that he would be filing a complaint against Masoum, and security forces loyal to al-Maliki seized strategic areas around Baghdad, including installations in the Green Zone. On 11 August Iraq's highest federal court ruled that as leader of the largest parliamentary bloc, al-Maliki could remain as Prime Minister. However, al-Abadi's nomination was confirmed by President Masoum, despite the protestations of al-Maliki, who initially indicated that he would refuse to recognize the legitimacy of any government formed by al-Abadi. However, following apparent pressure from the USA and Iran, al-Maliki agreed to resign on 14 August. Al-Abadi's administration was approved by the legislature and took office on 8 September. The new premier concurrently assumed the leadership of the Islamic Dawa Party. Allawi, al-Maliki and al-Nujaifi were appointed as Vice-Presidents. Ibrahim al-Ja'fari was appointed as Minister of Foreign Affairs. Riyad Ghareeb and Jaber al-Jaberi were initially nominated for the defence and interior portfolios, respectively, but were rejected by parliament (as were nominees for finance, tourism and women's affairs); the positions had been vacant since late 2010. On 18 October parliament approved the nominations of Khalid al-Obeidi as Minister of Defence and Muhammad Salem al-Ghabban as Minister of the Interior, as well as nominees for the other vacant portfolios. Al-Zibari was sworn in as Minister of Finance.

Meanwhile, sectarian violence continued: in August 2014 some 47 people were killed in a car bomb in a Shi'a district of Baghdad, Shi'a militiamen killed around 70 Sunni worshippers in Diyala province and around 20 people were killed in a suicide bomb attack on the headquarters of the intelligence services in Baghdad. A further two suicide bombings in Baghdad in September killed at least 65 people, and in October large numbers of people were killed in a series of suicide bombings, mainly in Shi'a neighbourhoods in and around Baghdad. These violent attacks continued in November in Baghdad and, in Arbil, six people were killed in a suicide bombing on 19 November. Prime Minister al-Abadi's efforts to restructure the armed forces attracted criticism: in September he disbanded the office of the Commander in Chief of the Armed Forces, which had been dominated by loyalists of al-Maliki, and in October he established the National Defence Guard, which was tasked with fighting Islamic State

(formerly ISIL) using Sunni recruits from the affected provinces; this policy was opposed by factions which advocated reliance on Shi'a militia to defeat Islamic State. In November al-Abadi also introduced plans to reform the security services and reportedly dismissed some 26 military commanders.

Tensions between the central Government and the KRG increased in July 2014 after Kurdish *peshmerga* seized oil production facilities in Kirkuk province, which had hitherto been run by the central Government. Relations improved, however, by November 2014, when the Iraqi Minister of Oil, Adel Abd al-Mahdi, and the Prime Minister of the KRG, Nechirvan Barzani, began an initiative to resolve ongoing disputes, including over unauthorized oil exports by the KRG and outstanding payments to the KRG of its share of hydrocarbons revenue. The two governments agreed in December that the KRG would export 250,000 barrels of oil per day through central government-controlled infrastructure in Baghdad (having agreed the previous month that the KRG would receive an initial US $500m. from the central Government), while the central Government agreed to resume payments of 17% of the national budget to the KRG.

Recent developments: the rise of Islamic State

In June 2014 the ascent of Islamic State (previously ISIL) in the north and west of the country escalated, when a series of victories by the insurgent group resulted in Iraq's security forces losing control of large parts of the north-west of the country. Under the leadership of Abu Bakr al-Baghdadi, the group had emerged as the successor to the Islamic State in Iraq and changed its name to ISIL following its expansion into Syria in 2013. The leadership of al-Qa'ida officially disowned ISIL in February 2014, following military confrontations between ISIL and the al-Qa'ida affiliated Jabhat al-Nusra (al-Nusra Front) in Syria. ISIL became the largest and most well-funded insurgent organization operating in Iraq, estimated to comprise up to 10,000 individual fighters and to possess funds in excess of US $2,000m. Its financial resources were reported to derive from its control of oilfields, the sale of natural resources and stolen antiquities, kidnapping, protection rackets and bank robberies. In Iraq ISIL capitalized on the discontent manifest in the Sunni protest movement to present itself as a champion of Sunni interest against the perceived Shi'a dominance of Baghdad. In some areas, notably Ramadi, ISIL faced the hostility of local tribes and other insurgent groups, but in Fallujah ISIL co-operated with local tribal groups in January 2014 to take control of the city. As the military wing of the so-called Military Council of Tribal Revolutionaries which governed Fallujah, ISIL fought successfully against Iraqi security forces attempting to retake the city later that year. For their part, the security forces' strategy of surrounding the city and conducting daily shelling and missile strikes proved counterproductive. An estimated 450 inhabitants of Fallujah died as a result of indiscriminate bombing in the first half of 2014, which appeared further to solidify opposition to the Iraqi Government in the city.

By June 2014 it was estimated that ISIL was responsible for some four-fifths of all insurgent attacks in Iraq. In that month ISIL began to implement its stated strategy of seizing control of territory in the region. On 5 June the group launched a full-scale military assault on the city of Samarra in Salah al-Din province. The attackers took control of five of the city's seven districts before being driven out by the security forces. None the less, on the following day ISIL launched an attack against Mosul and within three days the security forces and the local police had abandoned their positions and ISIL had taken control of the city, seizing military equipment, including helicopters, and freeing hundreds of prisoners from the city's main gaol. On 10 June ISIL also took control of Tikrit and by mid-June controlled large parts of the provinces of Anbar, Nineveh, Kirkuk, Salah al-Din and Diyala. At the end of the month the group announced that it had changed its name from ISIL to Islamic State, following its proclamation of a new caliphate stretching 'from Aleppo to Diyala', with al-Baghdadi as caliph. The threat posed by the group led to the active participation in the conflict of the Quds Force of the Iranian Revolutionary Guards and the re-mobilization of Shi'a militia groups, while a fatwa issued by Grand Ayatollah al-Sistani was interpreted as calling for a Shi'a defensive *jihad* against Sunni insurgents. Meanwhile, the leadership of the KRG moved quickly to capitalize on the weakening of central Government authority to reoccupy disputed territory, including Kirkuk in June. In early July, moreover, Kurdish President Masoud Barzani described Iraq as 'effectively partitioned', and charged members of the Kurdish regional parliament with forming an electoral commission to prepare for a referendum on Kurdish independence before the end of 2014. (However, upon the formation of a new government under al-Abadi in September, which included Kurdish ministers, Barzani agreed to put the referendum on hold.) In August 2014 Kurdish forces suffered a significant defeat when Islamic State launched a large-scale assault on the Kurdish-controlled district of Sinjar in Nineveh province; large numbers of civilians were reported to have been killed, while up to 200,000 people fled the district. Although theoretically in place to protect the district's Yazidi population, up to 10,000 *peshmerga* withdrew from their positions, leaving the civilian population undefended. Significant numbers of Yazidi civilians fled for the safety of the Sinjar mountains, creating a potential humanitarian disaster, and prompting intervention from the USA and other Western countries.

On 7 August 2014 President Obama announced that the USA would commence air strikes against Islamic State targets in northern Iraq, with the aim of defending US military and civilian personnel stationed in Iraq, blocking an Islamic State advance on Arbil and preventing a 'potential act of genocide' against Yazidi civilians in Sinjar. The first air strikes were confirmed by the US Department of Defense on 8 August. US military aircraft had undertaken the delivery of humanitarian aid to Yazidi refugees earlier that week. In mid-August the US air force provided support to Kurdish fighters in their attempts to regain control of the strategic Mosul dam from Islamic State, and to end the siege of Sinjar. By the end of that month it was reported that some 1,000 US troops were stationed in Iraq, and that the USA had conducted nearly 120 air strikes against Islamic State targets. In early September Obama announced that the scope of the USA's intervention would be widened to include Syria, while several other countries, including a group of Arab states led by Saudi Arabia, indicated their willingness to contribute to the military personnel and equipment. In September the United Kingdom and France joined the US-led coalition, and carried out air strikes in northern Iraq. During that month more than 350 Iraqi soldiers were reportedly killed by Islamic State forces after an attack on an army camp in Saqlawiyah, north of Fallujah.

In October 2014 Islamic State militants advanced into Anbar province around the provincial capital of Ramadi, seizing control of the town of Heet and displacing some 180,000 civilians, according to the UN. Provincial officials appealed for urgent military assistance. More than 200 Sunni tribesmen opposed to Islamic State were executed by members of the group in late October. However, during that month Kurdish forces gained territory in the north under the cover of coalition air strikes, including the town of Zumar on 25 October; on the same day Iraqi government forces and Shi'a militia captured the town of Jurf al-Sakhar, near Baghdad. However, Islamic State also made advances in Anbar province in November, killing around 75 members of various Sunni tribes. Meanwhile, the USA and Iran competed to provide military assistance and increase their influence in Anbar: in early November Obama authorized the deployment of 1,500 additional US troops to fight within Iraqi units, while Iranian-backed Shi'a militias offered support to Sunni tribal leaders. In December Islamic State captured the town of al-Wafa in Anbar province, although Kurdish forces made advances in northern Iraq, including the breaking of the siege of Sinjar mountain on 18 December. The city of Sinjar was retaken in the following days, while it was also reported that *peshmerga* were advancing towards Islamic State's military base in Tal Afar, west of Mosul, to which its militants had withdrawn. On the same day the USA claimed that it had killed three senior Islamic State leaders in air strikes that month, including the group's deputy leader, Abu Musallam al-Turkmani, and the following week further US air strikes destroyed oil-producing infrastructure under Islamic State control in northern Iraq. In late December the Iraqi police force reported that Hassan Saeed al-Jabouri, the Islamic State member acting as Governor of Mosul, had been killed in a coalition air strike. Meanwhile, al-Abadi requested further training assistance for Iraqi troops from NATO while visiting Brussels, Belgium in early December. According to the UN, some 12,282 civilians were killed in violent incidents in Iraq during 2014 (some 5,000 more than the previous year), owing to the activities of Islamic State and an increase in violence around the legislative elections in April.

By January 2015 the US-led coalition against Islamic State was reported to have launched more than 900 separate air strikes against militants in Iraq since August 2014. In mid-January 2015 Islamic State was reported to be attempting to regain control of the Kurdish town of Gwer, near Mosul, which had been taken by Iraqi Government forces in August 2014. On 21 January 2015 *peshmerga* fighters began an operation to regain Mosul, disrupting essential Islamic State supply routes between Mosul and Syria. Under the cover of US air strikes, some 200 Islamic State fighters were reportedly killed on the first day of the campaign, as well as the recently installed Islamic State Governor of Nineveh province. The following day the US air force increased the number of air strikes on Islamic State positions in Mosul. However, Kurdish officials stated that they did not intend to move beyond primarily Kurdish areas, and that retaking Mosul was the responsibility of the Iraqi national army. Nevertheless, on 27 January Islamic State forces launched a surprise attack on Kirkuk, reportedly in an attempt to draw *peshmerga* fighters away from Mosul. Kurdish forces repelled the attack and regained some of their lost territory, while the US air force increased its air strikes on positions within Kirkuk at the beginning of February.

Regional relations

In June 2005 Egypt became the first Arab state to nominate an ambassador to Baghdad since the US-led invasion; however, the abduction and murder of the ambassador, Ihab al-Sherif, in July made other Arab countries unwilling to send envoys to Iraq. Al-Qa'ida in Iraq claimed responsibility for the killing of al-Sherif, together with the subsequent abduction and killing of two Algerian diplomats later in July. However, as the security situation improved, by mid-2008 several Arab countries had chosen to resume full diplomatic relations with Iraq and to return ambassadors to Baghdad. The UAE also cancelled some US $7,000m. of Iraqi debt in July. In November 2009 the new Egyptian ambassador to Iraq, Sherif Kamal Shahin, arrived in Baghdad. Saudi Arabia finally appointed a non-resident ambassador to Iraq, Fahd al-Zaid (its envoy to Jordan), in February 2012. In March a historic summit meeting of the Arab League was held in the Iraqi capital. However, many Arab governments opted to send a low-level delegation to the summit, in protest at the Iraqi Government's close relations with Iran and its apparently 'neutral' position on the Syrian crisis. Iraq's relations with Saudi Arabia subsequently deteriorated amid disagreement over the Saudi authorities' decision to advocate the provision of weapons to rebels engaged in fighting government forces in Syria. In June and July 2014 Saudi Arabia deployed troops to its border with Iraq, after the Iraqi Government lost control of or withdrew forces from strategic crossing points which had come under the control of Islamic State. Relations improved after the appointment in August of Iraqi Prime Minister, Haidar al-Abadi, who Saudi Arabia considered to be more independent of Iranian influence than his predecessor, Nuri al-Maliki. President Fouad Masoum made an official visit to Saudi Arabia for talks with King Abdullah in November. A delegation from the Saudi Government visited Baghdad in January 2015 to commence preparations for the re-opening of its embassy there, which was scheduled to take place in March; Saudi Arabia also intended to open a consulate in Arbil in the Kurdish Autonomous Region.

In October 2008 Ali Muhammad al-Momen became the first Kuwaiti ambassador to Iraq since diplomatic relations were abruptly severed in 1990. In February 2010 the UN confirmed that it had been engaged in intensive efforts to promote progress on all outstanding issues between Iraq and Kuwait, including the issue of Kuwaiti missing persons. At the end of May Muhammad Hussain Bahr al-Ulum, Iraq's first ambassador to Kuwait since 1990, assumed his diplomatic post. In May 2010 the Iraqi Government had announced the gradual dissolution of the national airline, Iraqi Airways, in an effort to avoid paying US $1,200m. in compensation to Kuwait for 10 Kuwait Airways planes that it had appropriated after the 1990 invasion; however, in May 2011 it announced that the dissolution had been halted. Having frequently attempted to seize Iraqi Airways planes at foreign airports, later that month the Kuwaiti authorities took control of the airline's office in Amman, after obtaining a court ruling in Jordan. Despite the removal of Iraq's Baathist regime in 2003, the Kuwaiti Government has consistently refused to agree to the cancellation of this debt. The attendance of Sheikh Sabah al-Ahmad al-Jaber al-Sabah, the Amir of Kuwait, at the Arab League summit held in Baghdad in March 2012 was widely heralded as marking a significant breakthrough in bilateral relations. In November the Iraqi Government endorsed the terms of a financial settlement agreed with its Kuwaiti counterpart in the previous month; Iraq would pay $500m. to Kuwait Airways to resolve the long-running dispute, in return for which the Kuwaiti authorities would cancel all legal action currently in place against Iraqi Airways. Following ratification of the deal by the Kuwaiti National Assembly in January 2013, the $500m. payment was duly transferred. In December 2014 the Kuwaiti Government announced that it intended to open consulates in Arbil and Basra.

In August 2008 King Abdullah of Jordan made the first visit to Baghdad by an Arab head of state since the fall of Saddam Hussain in 2003, and in the following month an agreement governing the supply of subsidized Iraqi oil to Jordan was announced. In October Nayef al-Zaidan took up his post as Jordan's ambassador to Iraq—the previous ambassador having been withdrawn following the bombing of the Jordanian embassy in August 2003. In January 2009 the Iraqi Government welcomed a directive from King Abdullah to ease the restrictions on Iraqis entering and residing in Jordan. The two countries also agreed, in June 2011, to increase the volume of bilateral trade, with Iraq pledging to raise the volume of oil supply to Jordan. In January 2013 the Iraqi and Jordanian authorities pledged to expedite the creation of a free trade zone that had been agreed in 2009. In January 2014 the respective Governments launched a joint project involving the construction of a double pipeline to transport oil and gas between Basra and the Jordanian city of Aqaba; the project, costing an estimated US $18,000m., was expected to be completed in 2017. The trade route between Jordan and Iraq was severely affected by the deteriorating security situation in Anbar province in 2014, where Islamic State seized large areas of territory and imposed taxes on vehicles carrying goods between the two countries.

After Iraq and Syria declared in November 2006 that they would restore diplomatic ties that had been severed in 1982, in the following month they opened embassies in each other's capitals. Iraqi officials hoped that the resumption in relations with Syria would assist in stemming the flow of insurgents across their joint border. In January 2007 Talabani became the first Iraqi President to visit Syria for nearly three decades. In February Iraq accused Syria of harbouring fugitive militants and refusing refuge for genuine Iraqi refugees. Syria finally named an ambassador to Baghdad, Nawaf al-Fares, in September 2008. However, al-Fares and the newly appointed Iraqi ambassador in Syria, Dr Ala'a al-Jawadi, were both temporarily recalled from their respective embassies in August 2009, following Iraqi allegations that the latter was harbouring two men suspected of involvement in a series of bombings that had targeted government buildings in Baghdad earlier that month, killing more than 100 people (see *Domestic Political Affairs*); Syria adamantly denied the claims. Despite a number of conciliatory gestures by the Iraqi Government during 2011 in response to mounting international calls for President Assad to tender his resignation amid widespread popular protests in Syria (q.v.), in September Prime Minister al-Maliki urged Assad to step down. During the Arab League summit held in Baghdad in March 2012, al-Maliki sought to dissuade member states from providing military assistance to either side in the Syrian conflict, warning that such action risked turning it into a 'regional and international proxy war'. Nevertheless, during 2013 Western governments claimed to have evidence that the Iraqi authorities were permitting Iranian planes to use Iraqi airspace in order to provide military assistance to Syrian government forces. Observers noted that the Iraqi Government was afraid that a radical Sunni Islamist government might eventually replace the Assad regime. In December 2013 the Iraqi Government closed its border with Syria following the commencement of military operations against al-Qa'ida militants in desert areas of Anbar province in the west of Iraq. The rise of Islamic State in 2014 and its de facto control over large areas of Iraqi territory in the north and west of the country led to the Iraqi authorities losing control of numerous border crossings with Syria. This allowed the free passage of Islamic State militants in both directions, as well as the movement of refugees between the two countries, notably Yazidis fleeing from Nineveh province in Iraq into Syria in mid-2014.

Iraq and Iran resumed diplomatic relations in September 2004, although many issues relating to the 1980–88 War remained unresolved. In November 2005 President Talabani became the first Iraqi head of state to visit Tehran in over 30 years. In the same month an Iraqi passenger flight landed in the Iranian capital for the first time since 1980. Iran hosted security talks on Iraq in November 2006. Although the Iranian leadership pledged to assist Iraq by any possible means, it warned that the restoration of security was dependent on the withdrawal of US troops. Following discussions between the US and Iranian ambassadors to Baghdad concerning co-operation to end the

sectarian violence, the first meeting of their joint sub-committee was held in August 2007. The Iranian President, Mahmoud Ahmadinejad, undertook an official visit to Baghdad in March 2008, where he signed seven MOUs relating to bilateral co-operation with his Iraqi counterpart. During the visit Ahmadinejad denied persistent US claims that Iran was providing military and financial assistance to Iraqi Shi'a militias. In July 2011 Iranian forces crossed the border into northern Iraq in pursuit of fighters belonging to the separatist group the Party of Free Life in Kurdistan. Several Iraqi Kurds were reportedly killed and hundreds displaced during the offensive. Also in July Iraq, Iran and Syria signed an MOU providing for the construction of a 6,000-km natural gas pipeline, which would extend under Iraqi, Syrian and Lebanese territory and transport gas from Assalouyeh, in southern Iran, to the European market. Construction of the Iranian section of the US $10,000m. pipeline project reportedly commenced in November 2012. As the extent of trading between Iran and Iraq continued to increase, it was reported in mid-2014 that the value of this bilateral trade had exceeded US $12,000m. in 2013 and was expected to rise to $15,000m. in 2014. Iran's influence in Iraq grew in 2014 as the Iraqi Government proved unable effectively to confront the threat posed by Islamic State. In addition to Iran's ongoing training and co-ordination of Shi'a militia groups to counter Sunni militants, the Iranian air force commenced air strikes against Islamic State targets in Diyala province in November, apparently at the request of the Iraqi Government. Iran emphasized that its combat operations in Iraq were separate from those of the US-led coalition.

In September 2007 Turkey and Iraq signed a security co-operation pact intended to curb the military activities of the Kurdish separatist organization the Kurdistan Workers' Party (Partiya Karkeren Kurdistan—PKK). However, although the pact did not include Turkey's principal demand that its military be permitted to enter Iraqi territory in pursuit of Kurdish fighters, in December Turkish troops began an offensive against PKK bases in Iraq's northern region, in response to a series of cross-border raids by armed separatists to carry out bomb attacks against Turkish soldiers in south-eastern Turkey. The President of the Kurdish Autonomous Region, Barzani, described Turkey's actions as a violation of Iraqi sovereignty. In February 2008 Turkey ordered a further military incursion into northern Iraq, with the additional launching of air strikes against PKK militant bases. Dozens of PKK militants were killed in the week-long offensive, together with several Turkish soldiers. The Iraqi Government again asserted that it had not given its approval for the offensive. However, during a visit to Iraq by Turkey's Prime Minister, Recep Tayyip Erdoğan, in July 2008 several accords on energy and border security were also signed. The inaugural meeting of the Iraq-Turkey High-Level Strategic Co-operation Council was convened in İstanbul in September 2009.

In March 2011 Erdoğan became the first Turkish premier to visit Iraq's Kurdish Autonomous Region, where he held talks with Barzani regarding co-operation in combating the PKK. In May the Iraqi Government declared that the Turkish authorities' restriction of water supply from Turkey to Iraq via the Euphrates and Tigris rivers was 'unacceptable', claiming that a series of dams constructed on both rivers allowed Turkey to monopolize the waters. An Iraqi government spokesperson insisted that the Council of Representatives would not recognize the strategic co-operation council with Turkey until a bilateral water-sharing agreement was successfully concluded. Bilateral relations deteriorated in late 2011, after the Iraqi authorities' issuing of an arrest warrant for Vice-President al-Hashimi and his subsequent arrival in Turkey (see *Domestic Political Affairs*). Moreover, the Turkish Government was strongly criticized by its Iraqi counterpart in May 2012, when it agreed to begin importing crude petroleum from Iraq's Kurdish Autonomous Region via a new pipeline from 2013. During mid-2012 Turkey intensified its military campaign against the PKK, launching air strikes against militant bases in northern Iraq in response to a series of fatal PKK attacks against its soldiers. The Turkish Government claimed that the civil conflict in Syria had made it easier for the PKK, assisted by affiliated Kurdish groups inside Syria, to launch operations against Turkey from the border areas. However, despite ongoing tensions, in October 2013 the Iraqi and Turkish Ministers of Foreign Affairs, Hoshyar al-Zibari and Ahmet Davutoğlu, pledged henceforth to hold more intensive discussions on contentious issues. Davutoğlu, who had been appointed Prime Minister in August 2014, made an official visit to Baghdad in November, the first visit to Iraq by a Turkish premier in four years. An agreement was reached regarding joint security measures against Islamic State, although observers noted that Turkey would be unlikely to commit significant resources to assisting Iraq, owing to the perception that the Shi'a-majority Iraqi Government was aligned with Iran and Syria.

CONSTITUTION AND GOVERNMENT

Prior to the ousting of Saddam Hussain's regime by the US-led coalition in April 2003, Iraq was divided into 18 governorates (including three Autonomous Regions). In the immediate aftermath of the war, a US-led Coalition Provisional Authority (CPA) was established to govern the country in the absence of an elected sovereign government. On 13 July the CPA formed a 25-member interim Governing Council, the members of which were selected in proportion to Iraq's main ethnic and religious groups. It had no executive power, but could appoint ministers and diplomatic representatives, draw up a new constitution and set a date for free elections. The Governing Council decided upon a rotating presidency, commencing in September, with nine members of the council each serving for one month. In the same month 25 ministers were appointed to serve in an interim Cabinet, also chosen according to ethnicity and creed. On 15 November the CPA and Governing Council published a plan for the creation of a democratically elected, sovereign government and constitution by the end of 2005. However, this plan was superseded by the Transitional Administrative Law (TAL) signed on 8 March 2004. Under the terms of the TAL, an Iraqi Interim Government assumed power on 28 June 2004 (two days earlier than planned), and the CPA and Governing Council were dissolved. The Interim Government was replaced by an Iraqi Transitional Government, consisting of a state Presidency Council and a Prime Minister and Cabinet to be appointed by the Council, in April 2005, following elections to the 275-member Transitional National Assembly (TNA), which took place on 30 January. Members of the TNA were required to produce a draft constitution by 15 August 2005, to be approved by national referendum by 15 October. In the event, disagreements over key issues delayed the submission of the draft Constitution to the TNA until 28 August 2005, and a further amended text was presented to the UN on 14 September. The draft Constitution was ratified following its endorsement at a national referendum on 15 October. National elections for a permanent legislature, the 325-seat Council of Representatives, took place on 15 December. The size of the legislature was expanded to 328 seats at elections held on 30 April 2014.

REGIONAL AND INTERNATIONAL CO-OPERATION

Iraq is a member of the League of Arab States (the Arab League) and the Organization of Arab Petroleum Exporting Countries. It joined the UN on 21 December 1945. The country was granted observer status at the World Trade Organization (WTO) in February 2004, and working party discussions to negotiate the country's eventual membership of the WTO began in May 2007. Iraq also participates in the Organization of Islamic Cooperation (OIC), the Organization of the Petroleum Exporting Countries (OPEC), and the Group of 77 developing countries (G77).

ECONOMIC AFFAIRS

In 2013, according to estimates by the World Bank, Iraq's gross national income (GNI), measured at average 2011–13 prices, was US $224,177m., equivalent to $6,710 per head (or $15,220 per head on an international purchasing-power parity basis). During 2004–13, it was estimated, the population increased at an average annual rate of 2.5%, while gross domestic product (GDP) per head increased, in real terms, by an average of 3.8% per year. Overall GDP increased, in real terms, at an average annual rate of 6.4% during 2004–13; real GDP increased by 9.2% in 2012, and only by 4.0% in 2013.

Agriculture (including hunting, forestry and fishing) contributed 4.0% of GDP in 2013. According to FAO estimates, 4.1% of the labour force was engaged in agriculture in mid-2015. Dates are the principal cash crop. Other crops include wheat, tomatoes, maize, cucumbers and gherkins, and barley. Production of eggs, milk and poultry meat is also important. According to the World Bank, during 2004–13, the real GDP of the agricultural sector increased by an average of 2.3% per year; agricultural GDP increased by 11.9% in 2013.

Industry (including mining, manufacturing, construction and power) provided 59.6% of GDP in 2013, according to official figures. The sector engaged 18.2% of the employed population in 2008. According to the World Bank, industrial GDP increased, in real terms, by an average annual rate of 6.6% in 2004–13; the sector's GDP increased by 0.8% in 2013.

The mining sector accounted for 47.0% of GDP in 2013 and employed 0.4% of the working population in 2008. Iraq had proven reserves of 150,000m. barrels of petroleum at the end of 2013 (the fifth largest in the world, after Venezuela, Saudi Arabia, Canada and Iran), as well as 3,587,745m. cu m of natural gas. In addition, Iraq is believed to possess considerable undiscovered reserves of petroleum. It was reported by the Ministry of Oil in November 2014 that the production rate had reached 3.00m. barrels per day (b/d). According to oil industry data, the rate of petroleum production in 2013 was 3.14m. b/d. Reserves of phosphates, sulphur, gypsum and salt are also exploited. According to official estimates, during 2006–11 the sector's GDP increased, in real terms, by an average annual rate of 7.1%; the sector's GDP increased by 1.0% in 2010 and by some 12.5% in 2011.

Manufacturing contributed just 2.7% of GDP in 2013 and engaged 4.9% of the employed population in 2008. Since the outbreak of conflict in Iraq in 2003, the development of the manufacturing sector has been severely hindered by issues such as fuel shortages, damaged and outdated equipment, poor security, and communication problems. According to the World Bank, manufacturing GDP increased, in real terms, at an average annual rate of 7.1% during 2004–13; sectoral GDP increased by an estimated 16.5% in 2012, but contracted by 10.9% in 2013.

Construction contributed 8.4% of GDP in 2013 and employed 10.8% of the working population in 2008. During 2006–11, according to official estimates, the sector's GDP increased at an average annual rate of 17.7%. As reconstruction efforts increased following the end of the conflict, the sector expanded rapidly; construction GDP increased by some 56.8% in 2010. However, sectoral growth slowed to just 0.3% in 2011.

Energy is derived principally from natural gas, which accounted for an estimated 62.1% of total electricity generation in 2011. Since 2003 power shortages and rationing have been a persistent feature in Iraq, particularly in Baghdad. Actual electricity-generating capacity has been lower than Iraq's official installed capacity, owing to outdated technology, insurgent attacks on power stations and disruptions in fuel supplies. In order to meet demand, additional electricity has been imported from Iran and Turkey. In 2012 the Iraqi Government launched a master plan for the energy sector, which involved the renovation of existing power plants and the installation of new ones to provide an additional 24,400 MW of electricity-generating capacity by 2017. With ongoing reconstruction of the means of generation, transmission and distribution, the country's installed generating capacity had reached an estimated 13,000 MW by the end of 2013. Iraq had become self-sufficient in electricity production by October 2013, according to the Ministry of Electricity, which pledged to provide 24-hour power supplies to households for the first time in two decades.

The services sector contributed 36.4% of GDP in 2013 and engaged 58.3% of the working population in 2008. During 2004–13, according to the World Bank, the sector's GDP increased, in real terms, by an average annual rate of 7.2%; services GDP increased by an estimated 7.0% in 2013.

In 2012, according to IMF figures, Iraq recorded a visible merchandise trade surplus of US $44,052.0m., and there was a surplus of $29,541.0m. on the current account of the balance of payments. Crude petroleum was by far the most important export prior to the imposition of international economic sanctions in 1990. According to figures from the Central Bank, mineral fuels and lubricants constituted 99.3% of Iraqi exports in 2013. The principal imports in the same year were machinery and transport equipment, miscellaneous manufactured articles, basic manufactures, mineral fuels and lubricants, chemicals, animal and vegetable oils and fats, and food and live animals.

Budget proposals for 2013 forecast expenditure of ID 121,800,000m. and revenue of ID 126,100,000m. Iraq's general government gross debt was ID 8,759,548m. in 2013, equivalent to 31.3% of GDP. According to Central Bank estimates, Iraq's total external debt was US $87,700m. in 2010, equivalent to 106.7% of GDP. During 2007–13 the average annual rate of inflation was 6.1%, according to official figures. Consumer prices increased by an average of 1.9% in 2013. Iraq's official rate of unemployment was recorded at around 11.9% in mid-2013;

however, the rate of youth unemployment was reported to be twice this figure, and many sources suggested that the real unemployment rate was in fact much higher.

In December 2010 the Government outlined details of a US $186,000m., five-year National Development Plan, the principal objectives of which were economic diversification, job creation, poverty reduction and sustained GDP growth through the completion of some 2,800 projects focusing on the agricultural, hydrocarbons, construction, power and transport sectors. In early 2014 the IMF forecast growth of 6% for that year, but the instability caused by the Islamic State insurgency in the north and west of the country led to a downward revision by the Fund later that year; a contraction of 2.7% was forecast for 2014, before a modest return to growth, at 1.5%, in 2015. Moreover, by early 2015 the Government's draft hydrocarbons law, proposed in February 2007, had still to be approved by the Iraqi parliament, owing to its politically sensitive nature. In December 2014 the Iraqi Government agreed a deal with the Kurdish regional government that allowed petroleum exports of up to 550,000 b/d through Turkey, including 250,000 b/d from the Kurdish Autonomous Region. The opening of the Iraqi oil sector to international oil companies from October 2008, including the award in June 2009 of a 20-year development contract for the giant Rumaila oilfield to British-based BP and the China National Petroleum Co, led the Ministry of Oil to forecast that production capacity could be increased from its 2010 level of 2.5m. b/d to 12m. b/d by 2017. However, many industry analysts claimed that this was an unrealistic target, owing to Iraq's ongoing political and security problems, and in January 2014 the Deputy Prime Minister announced a new target of 4.7m. b/d by 2015 and 9.0m. b/d by 2020; production was estimated at 4.0m. b/d at the end of 2014.

Oil exports increased to 2.9m. b/d in 2014, from 2.4m. b/d in 2013. In recent years Asia has become an increasingly important market for Iraqi oil exports, while European demand has declined. Iraq's budget for 2015, approved by the Council of Ministers in late January, amounted to an estimated $105,000m., a reduction of almost one-third compared with 2014, owing in part to the significant decline in the international price of oil, and projected a fiscal deficit of over $23,000m; the amount allocated to defence was increased to around 20% in order to finance the military campaign against Islamic State. The Government intended to finance the deficit by issuing debt, drawing funds from the IMF through its Special Drawing Right, and imposing taxes on imported cars, mobile telephone SIM cards and internet access. Meanwhile, Kuwait agreed to defer one year's payment of reparations for the invasion by Iraq in 1990.

PUBLIC HOLIDAYS

2016: 1 January (New Year's Day), 6 January (Army Day), 17 April (FAO Day), 1 May (Labour Day), 4 May* (Leilat al-Meiraj, ascension of Muhammad), 6 July* (Id al-Fitr, end of Ramadan), 14 July (Republic Day, commemorating overthrow of the Hashemite monarchy in 1958), 8 August (Ceasefire Day, commemorating end of the Iran–Iraq War in 1988), 12 September* (Id al-Adha, Feast of the Sacrifice), 2 October* (Muharram, Islamic New Year), 3 October (National Iraqi Day, commemorating Iraq joining League of Nations in 1932), 11 October* (Ashoura), 11 December* (Mouloud, Birth of Muhammad).

* These holidays are dependent on the Islamic lunar calendar and may vary by one or two days from the dates given.

Statistical Survey

Sources (unless otherwise indicated): Central Organization for Statistics and Information Technology (COSIT), Ministry of Planning, 929/29/6 Arrasat al-Hindiya, Baghdad; tel. and fax (1) 885-3653; e-mail iraqmop@mop.gov.iq; internet cosit.gov.iq; Central Bank of Iraq, POB 64, al-Rashid St, Baghdad; tel. (1) 816-5170; fax (1) 816-6802; e-mail cbi@cbi.iq; internet www.cbi.iq.

Area and Population

AREA, POPULATION AND DENSITY

Area (sq km)	434,128*
Population (census results)	
17 October 1987	16,335,199
17 October 1997	
Males	10,987,252
Females	11,058,992
Total	22,046,244
Population (UN estimates at mid-year)†	
2013	33,765,232
2014	34,768,760
2015	35,766,702
Density (per sq km) at mid-2015	82.4

* 167,618 sq miles. This figure excludes 924 sq km (357 sq miles) of territorial waters and also the Neutral Zone, of which Iraq's share is 3,522 sq km (1,360 sq miles). The Zone lies between Iraq and Saudi Arabia, and is administered jointly by the two countries. Nomads move freely through it, but there are no permanent inhabitants.

† Source: UN, *World Population Prospects: The 2012 Revision.*

2012 (official estimate): Total population 34,207,248 (males 17,419,724, females 16,787,524).

POPULATION BY AGE AND SEX
(UN estimates at mid–2015)

	Males	Females	Total
0–14 years	7,213,179	6,819,346	14,032,525
15–64 years	10,361,936	10,239,928	20,601,864
65 years and over	498,329	633,984	1,132,313
Total	18,073,444	17,693,258	35,766,702

Source: UN, *World Population Prospects: The 2012 Revision.*

GOVERNORATES
(official population estimates at 2012)

	Area (sq km)*	Population	Density (per sq km)
Nineveh	37,323	3,353,875	89.9
Salah al-Din	24,363	1,441,266	59.2
Al-Ta'meem (Kirkuk)	9,679	1,432,747	148.0
Diyala	17,685	1,477,684	83.6
Baghdad	4,555	7,255,278	1,592.8
Al-Anbar (Anbar)	137,808	1,598,822	11.6
Babylon	5,119	1,864,124	364.2
Karbala	5,034	1,094,281	217.4
Al-Najaf (Najaf)	28,824	1,319,608	45.8
Al-Qadisiya	8,153	1,162,485	142.6
Al-Muthanna	51,740	735,905	14.2
Thi-Qar	12,900	1,883,160	146.0
Wasit	17,153	1,240,935	72.3
Maysan	16,072	997,410	62.1
Al-Basrah (Basra)	19,070	2,601,790	136.4
Kurdish Autonomous Region			
D'hok	6,553	1,158,633	176.8
Irbil (Arbil)	15,074	1,657,684	110.0
Al-Sulaimaniya (Sulaimaniya) .	17,023	1,931,561	113.5
Total	434,128	34,207,248	78.8

* Excluding territorial waters (924 sq km).

PRINCIPAL TOWNS
(population at 1987 census)

Baghdad (capital) . .	3,841,268	Al-Sulaimaniya (Sulaimaniya) . .	364,096
Al-Mawsil (Mosul) . .	664,221	Al-Najaf (Najaf) . .	309,010
Irbil (Arbil)	485,968	Karbala	296,705
Kirkuk	418,624	Al-Hillah (Hilla) . .	268,834
Al-Basrah (Basra) . .	406,296	Al-Nasiriyah (Nasiriya)	265,937

Source: UN, *Demographic Yearbook.*

Mid-2014 (incl. suburbs, UN estimate): Baghdad 6,483,210 (Source: UN, *World Urbanization Prospects: The 2014 Revision*).

BIRTHS AND DEATHS
(annual averages, UN estimates)

	2000–05	2005–10	2010–15
Birth rate (per 1,000)	35.2	33.3	31.3
Death rate (per 1,000)	5.1	5.6	5.2

Source: UN, *World Population Prospects: The 2012 Revision.*

Registered marriages: 245,022 in 2010; 230,470 in 2011; 234,495 in 2013.

Life expectancy (years at birth): 69.2 (males 65.7; females 73.0) in 2012 (Source: World Bank, World Development Indicators database).

EMPLOYMENT
(labour force survey, '000)

	2006	2007	2008
Agriculture, hunting and forestry .	1,925.7	1,066.2	1,759.9
Fishing	22.8	10.0	21.7
Mining and quarrying	43.4	84.4	32.4
Manufacturing	376.3	522.3	369.4
Electricity, gas and water . . .	76.6	130.5	161.6
Construction	665.0	797.2	823.5
Wholesale and retail trade; repair of motor vehicles, motorcycles and personal and household goods	961.8	1,117.6	1,167.2
Hotels and restaurants . . .	52.9	105.4	62.6
Transport, storage and communications	616.5	707.5	608.1
Financial intermediation . . .	26.9	26.4	20.8
Real estate, renting and business activities	40.6	285.8	35.1
Public administration and defence; compulsory social security . .	727.3	677.6	1,003.3
Education	556.1	612.9	686.7
Health and social work . . .	146.2	196.8	218.2
Community, social and personal services	312.7	520.8	618.5
Households with employed persons	1.5	—	9.7
Extraterritorial organizations and bodies	4.7	—	7.3
Sub-total	6,557.2	6,861.4	7,606.1
Activities not adequately defined .	—	255.3	—
Total employed	6,557.2	7,116.7	7,606.1

Source: ILO.

Mid-2015 (estimates in '000): Agriculture, etc. 394; Total labour force 9,495 (Source: FAO).

Health and Welfare

KEY INDICATORS

Total fertility rate (children per woman, 2012)	4.1
Under-5 mortality rate (per 1,000 live births, 2012) . . .	34
HIV/AIDS (% of persons aged 15–49, 2003)	<0.1
Physicians (per 1,000 head, 2010)	0.6
Hospital beds (per 1,000 head, 2010)	1.3
Health expenditure (2011): US $ per head (PPP)	110
Health expenditure (2011): % of GDP	2.7
Health expenditure (2011): public (% of total)	75.1
Access to water (% of persons, 2012)	85
Access to sanitation (% of persons, 2012)	85
Total carbon dioxide emissions ('000 metric tons, 2010) . .	114,667.1
Carbon dioxide emissions per head (metric tons, 2010) . .	3.7
Human Development Index (2013): ranking	120
Human Development Index (2013): value	0.642

For sources and definitions, see explanatory note on p. vi.

Agriculture

PRINCIPAL CROPS
('000 metric tons)

	2011	2012	2013
Wheat	2,809	3,062	4,178
Rice, paddy	235	361	452
Barley	820	832	1,003
Maize	336	503	831
Potatoes	557	560*	580*
Sugar cane	11	10	8
Chick peas	0.9	1	1
Tomatoes	1,060	768	904
Cauliflowers and broccoli . . .	25	24	29
Pumpkins, squash and gourds .	165	168	164
Cucumbers and gherkins . . .	496	414	406
Aubergines (Eggplants) . . .	452	422	511
Onions, dry	90	125	129
Watermelons	340	406	416
Canteloupes and other melons .	161	172	196
Grapes	227	242	270
Oranges	91	92	113
Tangerines, mandarins, clementines and satsumas . .	4	4	4
Apples	46	52	62
Apricots	21	23	26
Peaches and nectarines . . .	2	2	2
Plums	10	10	12
Dates	619	655	676

* FAO estimate.

Aggregate production ('000 metric tons, may include official, semi-official or estimated data): Total cereals 4,270 in 2011, 4,791 in 2012, 6,501 in 2013; Total roots and tubers 557 in 2011, 560 in 2012, 580 in 2013; Total vegetables (incl. melons) 3,851 in 2011, 3,983 in 2012, 3,825 in 2013; Total fruits (excl. melons) 1,127 in 2011, 1,167 in 2012, 1,279 in 2013.

Source: FAO.

LIVESTOCK
('000 head, year ending September)

	2011	2012	2013
Horses	49	50*	52*
Asses*	380	380	380
Mules*	11	11	12
Cattle	2,707	2,720*	2,780*
Buffaloes	300	305*	307*
Camels*	62	65	65
Sheep	8,183	8,200*	8,250*
Goats	1,565	1,580*	1,600*
Chickens*	38,000	38,000	38,000

* FAO estimate(s).

Source: FAO.

LIVESTOCK PRODUCTS

('000 metric tons)

	2011	2012	2013
Cattle meat	50.1*	50.3*	51.3†
Buffalo meat†	1.0	1.3	1.3
Sheep meat†	44.0	47.2	47.2
Goat meat†	11.4	11.5	11.6
Chicken meat	87.2	87.2†	88.0†
Cows' milk†	233.0	234.9	238.0
Buffaloes' milk	27.2	28.5†	32.0†
Sheep's milk	55.8	60.0†	56.0†
Goats' milk	18.8	20.0†	18.0†
Hen eggs	50.9	53.0†	54.0†
Wool, greasy†	17.0	17.0	17.0
Cattle and buffalo hides† .	3.7	3.7	3.7

* Unofficial figure.
† FAO estimate(s).
Source: FAO.

Forestry

ROUNDWOOD REMOVALS

('000 cubic metres, excl. bark, FAO estimates)

	2011	2012	2013
Sawlogs, veneer logs and logs for sleepers	25.0	25.0	25.0
Other industrial wood . . .	34.0	34.0	34.0
Fuel wood	118.0	118.0	118.0
Total	177.0	177.0	177.0

Note: Annual production assumed to be unchanged from 1998.
Source: FAO.

SAWNWOOD PRODUCTION

('000 cubic metres, incl. railway sleepers, FAO estimates)

	2011	2012	2013
Total (all broadleaved) . . .	12	12	12

Note: Annual production assumed to be unchanged from 1998.
Source: FAO.

Fishing

('000 metric tons, live weight)

	2010	2011	2012
Capture	19.3	31.5	51.1
Cyprinids (incl. Common carp) .	1.2	10.5	20.2
Freshwater siluroids . . .	3.0	1.1	2.4
Other freshwater fishes . . .	8.0	3.6	18.8
Marine fishes	1.7	0.2	3.2
Aquaculture	20.3	16.3	25.0
Common carp	16.8	13.2	20.9
Total catch	39.6	47.8	76.1

Source: FAO.

Mining

('000 metric tons unless otherwise indicated)

	2010	2011	2012
Crude petroleum	121,479	136,678	152,498
Natural gas (million cu m)* . .	16,885	18,692	20,496
Ammonia (nitrogen content) . .	126	143	143
Sulphur†‡	20	20	20
Salt (unrefined)‡	102	136	143

* Figures refer to gross production.
† Figures refer to native production and by-products of petroleum and natural gas processing.
‡ Estimated figures.

Crude petroleum: 153,242 in 2013.

Sources: BP, *Statistical Review of World Energy*; US Geological Survey.

Industry

SELECTED PRODUCTS

('000 metric tons unless otherwise indicated)

	2009	2010	2011
Naphtha	550	774	498
Motor spirit (petrol)	2,496	2,472	3,226
Kerosene	2,056	2,100	2,258
Jet fuel	159	295	308
Gas-diesel (distillate fuel) oil . .	4,220	5,213	6,365
Residual fuel oils	11,526	13,458	13,621
Paraffin wax	33	26	43
Petroleum bitumen (asphalt) . .	379	412	596
Liquefied petroleum gas:			
from natural gas plants . . .	1,003	1,081	1,111
from petroleum refineries . .	211	278	283
Cement*†	7,000	8,000	10,000
Electric energy (million kWh) .	46,065	48,909	52,240

* Source: US Geological Survey.
† Estimated figures.

Cement ('000 metric tons, estimates): 10,000 in 2012.

Source (unless otherwise indicated): UN Industrial Commodity Statistics Database.

Finance

CURRENCY AND EXCHANGE RATES

Monetary Units
  1,000 fils = 20 dirhams = 1 new Iraqi dinar (ID).

Sterling, Dollar and Euro Equivalents (31 December 2014)
  £1 sterling = 1,819.9 Iraqi dinars;
  US $1 = 1,166.0 Iraqi dinars;
  €1 = 1,415.6 Iraqi dinars;
  10,000 Iraqi dinars = £5.49 = $8.58 = €7.06.

Average Exchange Rate (Iraqi dinars per US $)
  2012   1,166.17
  2013   1,166.00
  2014   1,166.00

Note: Following the overthrow of the regime of Saddam Hussain in 2003, the new Coalition Provisional Authority established an exchange rate of US $1 = 1,400 dinars. A new dinar currency, the new Iraqi dinar (ID), was introduced on 15 October to replace both the 'Swiss' dinar (at ID 1 = 150 'Swiss' dinars), the currency in use in the Kurdish autonomous regions of northern Iraq since 1991, and the 'Saddam' dinar (at par), the official currency of the rest of Iraq. The new currency was to be fully convertible.

BUDGET
(ID '000 million)

Revenue	2011	2012*	2013†
Revenues	102,400	119,400	126,100
Crude petroleum export revenues	93,400	109,400	117,900
Grants	2,100	0	0
Total	104,600	119,400	126,100

Expenditure	2011	2012*	2013†
Current expenditure	66,800	75,800	81,800
Salaries and pensions . . .	33,900	34,900	41,000
Goods and services	12,000	17,500	17,600
Transfers	14,700	16,600	15,200
Interest payments . . .	1,600	1,000	1,900
War reparations	4,600	5,500	5,500
Capital expenditure	27,400	33,600	40,000
Total	94,300	109,400	121,800

* Preliminary.
† Budget projections.
Source: IMF, *Iraq: 2013 Article IV Consultation* (July 2013).

INTERNATIONAL RESERVES
(US $ million at 31 December)

	2011	2012	2013
Gold (national valuation) . .	296.9	1,593.6	1,631.0
IMF special drawing rights . .	1,743.8	1,724.4	1,552.4
Reserve position in IMF . .	262.7	263.0	263.5
Foreign exchange	58,737.9	66,746.1	74,296.3
Total	61,041.3	70,327.1	77,743.2

Source: IMF, *International Financial Statistics*.

MONEY SUPPLY
(ID '000 million at 31 December)

	2010	2011	2012
Currency outside depository corporations	24,342.2	28,296.0	30,593.7
Transferable deposits	30,039.2	37,991.9	37,059.4
Other deposits	7,011.6	7,810.1	9,489.1
Broad money	61,393.1	74,098.0	77,142.2

Source: IMF, *International Financial Statistics*.

COST OF LIVING
(Consumer Price Index; base: 2007 = 100)

	2011	2012	2013
Food and non-alcoholic beverages .	138.4	147.4	148.0
Clothing and footwear	126.7	136.3	144.8
Housing, water, electricity, gas and other fuels	140.9	153.6	159.3
All items (incl. others) . . .	132.1	140.1	142.7

NATIONAL ACCOUNTS
National Income and Product
(ID '000 million at current prices, provisional estimates)

	2004	2005	2006
Compensation of employees . .	7,866.1	10,394.6	16,573.7
Operating surplus	33,857.9	45,296.7	67,543.7
Domestic factor incomes . .	41,723.9	55,691.2	84,117.4
Consumption of fixed capital . .	6,234.6	8,308.9	11,470.6
Gross domestic product (GDP) at factor cost	47,958.6	64,000.1	95,588.0
Indirect taxes (net)	−10,909.3	−14,009.4	−15,128.5
GDP in purchasers' values . .	37,049.3	49,990.7	80,459.4
Net factor income from abroad* .	76.2	1,089.0	1,314.1
Gross national product (GNP) .	37,125.5	51,079.7	81,773.6
Less Consumption of fixed capital .	6,234.6	8,308.9	11,470.6
National income in market prices	30,890.8	42,770.8	70,303.0

* Figures obtained as residuals.

Gross Domestic Product by Economic Activity
(ID '000 million at current prices, provisional estimates)

	2004	2005	2006
Agriculture, hunting, forestry and fishing	3,539.4	4,248.8	5,569.0
Mining and quarrying . . .	30,543.0	39,366.3	53,030.9
Crude petroleum	30,496.0	39,316.0	n.a.
Manufacturing	770.9	1,220.9	1,473.2
Electricity and water . . .	263.3	393.1	779.4
Construction	468.3	2,932.4	3,449.7
Trade, restaurants and hotels .	3,070.5	4,083.5	6,350.0
Transport, storage and communications	3,687.7	4,911.3	6,742.9
Finance, insurance and real estate	663.0	931.4	7,945.8
Government, community, social and personal services . .	5,200.4	6,139.9	10,726.2
Sub-total	48,206.5	64,227.6	96,067.2
Less Imputed bank service charge	248.0	227.5	479.2
GDP at factor cost . . .	47,958.5	64,000.1	95,588.0
Indirect taxes . . . . . } *Less* Subsidies . . . . . }	−10,909.3	−14,009.4	−15,128.5
GDP in market prices . .	37,049.3	49,990.7	80,459.4

2011 (ID '000 million at current prices, preliminary): Agriculture, hunting, forestry and fishing 9,918.3; Mining and quarrying 115,999.4; Manufacturing 6,132.8; Construction 10,358.5; Electricity and water 3,443.1; Transport, storage and communications 10,175.9; Trade, restaurants and hotels 14,115.7; Finance, insurance and real estate 17,955.2; Education 8,265.7; Health and social work 3,455.9; Public administration and defence; compulsory social security 15,878.0; Other community, social and personal services activities 2,919.2; Private households with employed persons 0.1; *Sub-total* 218,617.8; *Less* Imputed bank service charge 1,290.7; *Gross domestic product at factor cost* 217,327.1. *Gross domestic product at constant 1988 prices* 63.7.

2012 (ID '000 million at current prices, preliminary): Agriculture, hunting, forestry and fishing 9,990.7; Mining and quarrying 130,064.4; Manufacturing 4,221.5; Construction 13,785.6; Electricity and water 2,429.2; Transport, storage and communications 11,582.9; Trade, restaurants and hotels 15,626.5; Finance, insurance and real estate 21,506.7; Government, community, social and personal services 36,527.8; *Sub-total* 245,735.2; *Less* Imputed bank service charge 1,232.5; *Gross domestic product at factor cost* 244,502.6. *Gross domestic product at constant 1988 prices* 68.1.

2013 (ID '000 million at current prices, preliminary): Agriculture, hunting, forestry and fishing 10,742.4; Mining and quarrying 126,750.5; Manufacturing 7,288.0; Construction 22,738.5; Electricity and water 3,991.1; Transport, storage and communications 15,063.3; Trade, restaurants and hotels 17,688.3; Finance, insurance and real estate 22,143.2; Government, community, social and personal services 43,242.5; *Sub-total* 269,647.9; *Less* Imputed bank service charge 2,252.3; *Gross domestic product at factor cost* 267,395.6. *Gross domestic product at constant 1988 prices* 73.2.

BALANCE OF PAYMENTS
(US $ million)

	2010	2011	2012
Exports of goods	51,760.3	79,684.0	94,207.0
Imports of goods	−37,328.0	−40,633.0	−50,155.0
Balance on goods	14,432.3	39,051.0	44,052.0
Exports of services	2,833.6	2,822.0	2,833.0
Imports of services	−9,863.5	−11,124.0	−13,291.0
Balance on goods and services	7,402.4	30,749.0	33,594.0
Primary income received	2,079.9	1,172.0	2,080.0
Primary income paid	−486.7	−1,409.0	−1,021.0
Balance on goods, services and primary income	8,995.6	30,512.0	34,653.0
Secondary income received	240.8	371.0	413.0
Secondary income paid	−2,748.1	−4,757.0	−5,525.0
Current balance	6,488.3	26,126.0	29,541.0
Capital account (net)	25.3	11.0	7.0
Direct investment assets	−124.9	−366.0	−490.0
Direct investment liabilities	1,396.2	2,082.0	3,400.0
Portfolio investment assets	727.1	−6,573.0	−5,679.0
Portfolio investment liabilities	56.5	43.0	7.0
Other investment assets	5,310.4	−8,226.0	−4,976.0
Other investment liabilities	337.8	566.0	−8,448.0
Net errors and omissions	−9,150.6	−3,738.0	−4,116.2
Reserves and related items	5,066.1	9,924.2	9,254.8

Source: IMF, *International Financial Statistics*.

External Trade

PRINCIPAL COMMODITIES
(US $ million)

Imports c.i.f.	2011	2012	2013
Food and live animals	2,581	3,186	3,175
Beverages and tobacco	622	767	764
Crude materials (inedible) except fuels	860	1,062	1,058
Mineral fuels, lubricants, etc.	4,685	5,783	5,762
Animal and vegetable oils and fats	3,059	3,776	3,763
Chemicals	3,203	3,954	3,939
Basic manufactures	5,450	6,727	6,703
Machinery and transport equipment	18,404	22,717	22,637
Miscellaneous manufactured articles	7,553	9,323	9,290
Total (incl. others)	47,803	59,006	58,796

Exports c.i.f.	2011	2012	2013
Food and live animals	223	264	251
Crude materials (inedible) except fuels	120	141	135
Mineral fuels, lubricants, etc.	79,083	93,503	89,096
Chemicals	8	9	9
Basic manufactures	40	47	45
Machinery and transport equipment	191	226	215
Total (incl. others)	79,681	94,209	89,769

PRINCIPAL TRADING PARTNERS
(US $ million)

Imports c.i.f.	1988	1989	1990
Australia	153.4	196.2	108.7
Austria	n.a.	1.1	50.9
Belgium-Luxembourg	57.6	68.2	68.3
Brazil	346.0	416.4	139.5
Canada	169.9	225.1	150.4
China, People's Republic	99.2	148.0	157.9
France	278.0	410.4	278.3
Germany	322.3	459.6	389.4
India	32.3	65.2	57.5
Indonesia	38.9	122.7	104.9
Ireland	150.4	144.9	31.6

Imports c.i.f.—*continued*	1988	1989	1990
Italy	129.6	285.1	194.0
Japan	533.0	621.1	397.2
Jordan	164.3	210.0	220.3
Korea, Republic	98.5	123.9	149.4
Netherlands	111.6	102.6	93.8
Romania	113.3	91.1	30.1
Saudi Arabia	37.2	96.5	62.5
Spain	43.4	129.0	40.5
Sri Lanka	50.1	33.5	52.3
Sweden	63.0	40.6	64.8
Switzerland	65.7	94.4	126.6
Thailand	22.3	59.2	68.9
Turkey	874.7	408.9	196.0
USSR	70.7	75.7	77.9
United Kingdom	394.6	448.5	322.1
USA	979.3	1,001.7	658.4
Yugoslavia	154.5	182.0	123.1
Total (incl. others)	5,960.0	6,956.2	4,833.9

Exports f.o.b.	1988	1989	1990*
Belgium-Luxembourg	147.5	249.6	n.a.
Brazil	1,002.8	1,197.2	n.a.
France	517.4	623.9	0.8
Germany	122.0	76.9	1.7
Greece	192.5	189.4	0.3
India	293.0	438.8	14.7
Italy	687.1	549.7	10.6
Japan	712.1	117.1	0.1
Jordan	28.4	25.2	101.6
Netherlands	152.9	532.3	0.2
Portugal	120.8	125.8	n.a.
Spain	370.0	575.7	0.7
Turkey	1,052.6	1,331.0	83.5
USSR	835.7	1,331.7	8.9
United Kingdom	293.1	167.0	4.4
USA	1,458.9	2,290.8	0.2
Yugoslavia	425.4	342.0	10.4
Total (incl. others)	10,268.3	12,333.7	392.0

* Excluding exports of most petroleum products.

Source: UN, *International Trade Statistics Yearbook*.

2011 (US $ million): *Imports by regions:* Arab nations 11,903; North and South America 4,101; European Union 4,881; Other Europe 13,925; Asia 12,615; Other countries 378; Total imports 47,803. *Exports by region:* Arab nations 2,853; North and South America 24,024; European Union 13,801; Other Europe 2,279; Asia 36,310; Other countries 414; Total exports 79,681.

2012 (US $ million): *Imports by regions:* Arab nations 12,816; North and South America 4,190; European Union 5,918; Other Europe 20,929; Asia 14,864; Other countries 289; Total imports 59,006. *Exports by region:* Arab nations 3,156; North and South America 25,314; European Union 15,846; Other Europe 405; Asia 46,784; Other countries 2,704; Total exports 94,209.

2013 (US $ million): *Imports by regions:* Arab nations 12,770; North and South America 4,175; European Union 5,897; Other Europe 20,855; Asia 14,811; Other countries 288; Total imports 58,796. *Exports by region:* Arab nations 3,007; North and South America 24,121; European Union 15,099; Other Europe 386; Asia 44,580; Other countries 2,576; Total exports 89,769.

Transport

RAILWAYS
(traffic)

	2011	2012	2013
Passengers carried ('000)	178.0	148.0	134
Freight carried ('000 tons)	660.0	850.0	1,703.0
Passenger-km (million)	89.8	74.9	68.0
Freight ton-km (million)	199.0	203.0	231.0

ROAD TRAFFIC
(estimates, '000 motor vehicles in use)

	2006
Passenger cars	784.8
Buses and coaches	112.1
Lorries and vans	1,345.4
Total	2,242.3

Source: IRF, *World Road Statistics*.

SHIPPING
Flag Registered Fleet
(at 31 December)

	2012	2013	2014
Number of vessels	78	83	84
Total displacement ('000 grt) . .	128.0	149.5	140.0

Source: Lloyd's List Intelligence (www.lloydslistintelligence.com).

CIVIL AVIATION
(passenger traffic)

	2011	2012	2013
Passengers carried ('000) . . .	761.8	784.9	512.2

Source: World Bank, World Development Indicators database.

Tourism

ARRIVALS AT FRONTIERS OF VISITORS FROM ABROAD*

Country of nationality	2011	2012	2013
India	17,949	37,530	25,726
Iran	1,430,908	989,787	787,195
Pakistan	23,594	38,259	38,081
Total (incl. others)	1,510,174	1,111,492	891,836

* Including same-day visitors.

Tourism receipts (US $ million, excl. passenger transport): 1,620 in 2010; 1,836 in 2011; 2,281 in 2012.

Source: World Tourism Organization.

Communications Media

	2010	2011	2012
Telephones ('000 main lines in use)	1,720.6	1,794.0	1,871.0
Mobile cellular telephones ('000 subscribers)	23,264	25,519	26,756
Internet subscribers ('000) . .	0.3	n.a.	n.a.
Broadband subscribers ('000) . .	100	n.a.	n.a.

2013: Telephones ('000 main lines in use) 1,900.0; Mobile cellular telephones ('000 subscribers) 32,450.

Source: International Telecommunication Union.

Education

(2013/14 unless otherwise indicated)

	Institutions	Teachers	Students
Pre-primary	1,041	7,971	202,525
Primary	15,807	287,502	5,558,674
Secondary:			
academic	7,083	160,323	2,528,133
vocational*	298	12,745	58,689
Teacher training*	105	3,033	20,042
Higher†	65	14,700	240,000‡

* 2012/13.
† 2002/03.
‡ Figure for undergraduates only.

Sources: Ministries of Education, and of Higher Education and Scientific Research.

Pupil-teacher ratio (primary education, UNESCO estimate): 17.0 in 2006/07 (Source: UNESCO Institute for Statistics).

Adult literacy rate (UNESCO estimates): 79.0% (males 85.8%; females 72.2%) in 2011 (Source: UNESCO Institute for Statistics).

Directory

The Government

HEAD OF STATE

President: FOUAD MASOUM (assumed office 24 July 2014).
Vice-Presidents: AYAD ALLAWI, NURI KAMAL (JAWAD) AL-MALIKI, OSAMA AL-NUJAIFI.

COUNCIL OF MINISTERS
(April 2015)

Prime Minister: HAIDAR AL-ABADI.
Deputy Prime Ministers: BAHA ARRAJI, SALIH AL-MUTLAQ, ROZH NURI SHAWAIS.
Minister of Agriculture: FALAH HASSAN AL-ZAIDAN.
Minister of Communications: KADHIM HASSAN RASHED.
Minister of Construction and Housing: TARIQ AL-KHIKANI.
Minister of Culture: FARYAD RAWANDOZI.
Minister of Defence: KHALID AL-OBEIDI.
Minister of Education: MUHAMMAD IQBAL OMAR.
Minister of Electricity: KASSIM AL-FADHAWI.
Minister of the Environment: QUTAIBA AL-JABURI.
Minister of Finance: HOSHYAR AL-ZIBARI.
Minister of Foreign Affairs: IBRAHIM AL-JA'FARI.
Minister of Health: ADILA HAMMOUD.

Minister of Higher Education and Scientific Research: HUSSAIN AL-SHAHRISTANI.
Minister of Human Rights: MUHAMMAD MAHDI AL-BAYATI.
Minister of Industry and Minerals: NASSER KAZEM AL-ISSAWI.
Minister of the Interior: MUHAMMAD SALEM AL-GHABBAN.
Minister of Justice: HAIDAR AL-ZAMILI.
Minister of Labour and Social Affairs: MUHAMMAD SHAYAA AL-SUDANI.
Minister of Municipalities and Public Works: ABD AL-KARIM YOUNIS.
Minister of Oil: ADEL ABD AL-MAHDI.
Minister of Planning: SALMAN AL-JUMAILI.
Minister of Science and Technology: FARIS YOUSUF JAJO.
Minister of Trade: ABD AL-KARIM MLASS AL-KASNAZANI.
Minister of Transportation: BAYAN JABR AL-ZUBAIDI.
Minister of Tourism: ADEL FAHD AL-SHIRSHAB.
Minister of Water Resources: MOHSEN ASFOUR.
Minister of Women's Affairs: BAYAN NOURI.
Minister of Youth and Sports: ABD AL-HUSSAIN ABTAN.
Minister of State for Provincial Affairs and for Council of Representatives Affairs: AHMAD ABDULLAH AL-JABURI.

MINISTRIES

Ministry of Agriculture: Khulafa St, Khullani Sq., Baghdad; tel. (1) 719-5381; e-mail minis_of_agr@moagr.org; internet www.zeraa .gov.iq.

Ministry of Communications: Baghdad; tel. (1) 718-4555; e-mail info@moc.gov.iq; internet www.moc.gov.iq.

Ministry of Construction and Housing: Baghdad; tel. (1) 537-2381; e-mail moch@imariskan.gov.iq; internet www.moch.gov.iq.

Ministry of Culture: POB 624, Qaba bin Nafi Sq., Sadoun St, Baghdad; tel. (1) 538-3171; internet www.mocul.gov.iq.

Ministry of Defence: Baghdad; e-mail webmaster@mod.mil.iq; internet www.mod.mil.iq.

Ministry of Education: Saad State Enterprises Bldg, nr the Convention Centre, Baghdad; tel. (1) 883-2571; e-mail general@moedu .gov.iq; internet www.moedu.gov.iq.

Ministry of Electricity: Baghdad; e-mail infocen@moelc.gov.iq; internet www.moelc.gov.iq.

Ministry of Energy Affairs: Baghdad.

Ministry of the Environment: POB 10026, Baghdad; e-mail enviro_center@yahoo.com; internet www.moen.gov.iq.

Ministry of Finance: Khulafa St, nr al-Russafi Sq., Baghdad; tel. (1) 887-4871; e-mail iraqmof@mof.gov.iq; internet www.mof.gov.iq.

Ministry of Foreign Affairs: opp. State Organization for Roads and Bridges, Karradat Mariam, Baghdad; tel. (1) 537-0091; e-mail press@iraqmfamail.com; internet www.mofa.gov.iq.

Ministry of Health: Baghdad; e-mail minister office@moh.gov.iq; internet www.moh.gov.iq.

Ministry of Higher Education and Scientific Research: 52 Rusafa St, Baghdad; tel. and fax (1) 717-0709; e-mail info@mohesr .gov.iq; internet www.mohesr.gov.iq.

Ministry of Human Rights: Baghdad; tel. 7812753736 (mobile); e-mail shakawa@humanrights.gov.iq; internet www.humanrights .gov.iq.

Ministry of Industry and Minerals: POB 5815, Baghdad; tel. (1) 816-2006; e-mail admin@industry.gov.iq; internet www.industry .gov.iq.

Ministry of the Interior: Baghdad; tel. (1) 817-3101; e-mail media@moi.gov.iq; internet www.moi.gov.iq.

Ministry of Justice: Baghdad; fax (1) 537-2269; internet www.moj .gov.iq.

Ministry of Labour and Social Affairs: Baghdad; e-mail info@ molsa.gov.iq; internet www.molsa.gov.iq.

Ministry of Municipalities and Public Works: Baghdad; e-mail dma@mmpw.gov.iq; internet www.mmpw.gov.iq.

Ministry of Oil: Oil Complex Bldg, Port Said St, Baghdad; tel. (1) 817-7000; fax (1) 747-0341; e-mail minister.office@oil.gov.iq; internet www.oil.gov.iq.

Ministry of Planning: 929/29/6 Arrasat al-Hindiya, Baghdad; tel. (1) 778-3899; e-mail iraqmop@mop.gov.iq; internet www.mop.gov.iq.

Ministry of Science and Technology: Baghdad; e-mail inprb@ most.gov.iq; internet www.most.gov.iq.

Ministry of State for Council of Representatives Affairs: Baghdad.

Ministry of State for Provincial Affairs: Baghdad.

Ministry of Trade: POB 5833, Khullani Sq., Baghdad; tel. (1) 887-2681; fax (1) 790-1907; e-mail motcenter@motiraq.org; internet www .mot.gov.iq.

Ministry of Transportation: nr Martyr's Monument, Karradat Dakhil, Baghdad; tel. (1) 776-6041; e-mail mt_office@motrans.gov.iq; internet www.motrans.gov.iq.

Ministry of Water Resources: Palestine St, Baghdad; tel. (1) 772-0240; fax (1) 774-0672; e-mail waterresmin@yahoo.co.uk; internet www.mowr.gov.iq.

Ministry of Youth and Sports: Baghdad; internet www.moys.gov .iq.

Legislature

COUNCIL OF REPRESENTATIVES

Elections to an expanded, 328-seat Council of Representatives were held on 30 April 2014, the results of which were confirmed by the Higher Judicial Council on 11 June. The State of Law alliance secured the largest representation, with 94 seats (including affiliates), while the Sadrist Movement took 31 seats and the Islamic Supreme Council of Iraq 30 seats. The largely Sunni Muslim Mutahhidun bloc of former parliamentary speaker Osama al-Nujaifi won 28 seats, while Ayad Allawi's Wataniya group obtained 21 seats. Among the main Kurdish parties, the Kurdistan Democratic Party won 25 seats, the Patriotic Union of Kurdistan 19 and the Movement for Change (Gorran) nine. However, the election of four deputies was not ratified, owing to them being the subject of ongoing legal proceedings.

Council of Representatives: Baghdad International Zone Convention Center, Baghdade-mail press@parliament.iq; internet www .parliament.iq.

Speaker: SALIM AL-JABURI.

Kurdish Autonomous Region

A 15-article accord signed by the Iraqi Government and Kurdish leaders in 1970 provided for: the creation of a unified autonomous area for the Kurdish population, comprising the administrative departments of Sulaimaniya, D'hok and Irbil (Arbil), and the Kurdish sector of the city of Kirkuk; and the establishment of a 50-member Kurdish Legislative Council. Following the recapture of Kuwait from Iraqi forces by a multinational military coalition in early 1991, renewed negotiations between the Iraqi Government (under Saddam Hussain) and Kurdish groups stalled over the status of Kirkuk, and in October 1991 the Government effectively severed all economic and administrative support to the region. In May 1992 the Kurdish Iraqi Front (KIF), an alliance of several Kurdish factions—including the two largest, the Patriotic Union of Kurdistan (PUK) and the Kurdistan Democratic Party (KDP)—established in 1988, organized elections to a new 105-member Iraqi Kurdistan National Assembly. However, by September 1996 bitter factional disputes had led to the effective disintegration of the KIF, and prompted the Government to reassert full Iraqi sovereignty over the Kurdish areas. At a meeting in Washington, DC, USA, in September 1998, representatives of the PUK and the KDP reached a formal peace agreement, which provided for a unified regional administration, the sharing of local revenues and co-operation in implementing the UN-sponsored 'oil-for-food' programme. In December 1999 the KDP announced the composition of a new 25-member coalition administration (comprising the KDP, the Iraqi Communist Party, the Assyrian Movement, the Independent Workers' Party of Kurdistan, the Islamic Union and independents) for the areas under its control, principally the departments of Arbil and D'hok. Municipal elections (to select 571 officials) were conducted in the KDP-administered region in May 2001; according to official KDP sources, KDP candidates received 81% of votes cast. Negotiations between representatives of the KDP and the PUK for the full implementation of the Washington accord were held during 2002, and resulted in the resumption of a transitional joint session of the Iraqi Kurdistan National Assembly in October. The autonomous regions retained their status following the removal of the regime of Saddam Hussain in early 2003, but the status of Kirkuk remained highly controversial.

THE PRESIDENCY OF THE KURDISH AUTONOMOUS REGION

President: MASOUD BARZANI.

THE CABINET
(April 2015)

A coalition comprising the Kurdistan Democratic Party (KDP), the Patriotic Union of Kurdistan (PUK), Movement for Change (Gorran), the Kurdistan Islamic Union (Yakgrtui Islami Kurdistan), the Islamic Group (Komaleh Islami) and independents.

Prime Minister: NECHIRVAN IDRIS BARZANI.

Deputy Prime Minister: QUBAD JALAL TALABANI.

Minister of Agriculture and Water Resources: ABD AL-STAR MAJEED.

Minister of Culture and Youth: KHALID DOSKI.

Minister of Education: PISHTIWAN SADIQ.

Minister of Electricity: SALAHADDIN BABAKIR.

Minister of Endowment and Religious Affairs: KAMAL MUSLIM.

Minister of Finance and the Economy: REBAZ MUHAMMAD.

Minister of Health: REKAWT HAMA RASHEED.

Minister of Higher Education and Scientific Research: YOUSIF MUHAMMAD.

Minister of Housing and Reconstruction: DARBAZ KOSRAT RASUL.

Minister of Justice: SINAN ABD AL-KHALIQ CHALABI.

Minister for the Interior: ABD AL-KARIM SULTAN SINJARI.

Minister of Labour and Social Affairs: MUHAMMAD QADIR.

Minister of Martyrs and Anfal Affairs: MAHMOUD HAJI SALIH.

Minister of Municipalities and Tourism: NEWROZ MAWLOOD AMIN.

Minister of Natural Resources: ABDULLAH ABD AL-RAHMAN ABDULLAH.

Minister of Peshmerga Affairs: MUSTAFA SAYID KADIR.

Minister of Planning: ALI SINDI.

Minister of Trade and Industry: SAMAL SARDAR.

Minister of Transport and Communications: JONSON SIYAWASH.

Minister of State for Environmental Affairs: ABD AL-RAHMAN ABD AL-RAHIM HAMA REZA.

Minister of State for Parliamentary Affairs: MAWLOOD MURAD MOHYELDIN.

The President of the Divan of the Council of Ministers, the Secretary of the Cabinet, the Chief of Staff of the Presidency, the Head of the Department of Foreign Relations and the Chairman of the Investment Board also have full ministerial status.

LEGISLATURE

In May 1992 negotiations with the Iraqi Government over the full implementation of the 1970 accord on Kurdish regional autonomy having stalled, the KIF unilaterally organized elections to a 105-member Iraqi Kurdistan National Assembly, in which almost the entire electorate of 1.1m. participated. The KDP and the PUK were the only parties to achieve representation in the new Assembly, and subsequently agreed to share seats equally (50 seats each—five having been reserved for two Assyrian Christian parties). However, the subsequent disintegration of the KIF and prolonged armed conflict between elements of the KDP and the PUK prevented the Assembly from becoming properly instituted. Relations between the KDP and the PUK improved following the Washington, DC, agreement of September 1998, and on 8 September 2002 representatives of the two parties signed an agreement providing for the inauguration of a transitional joint parliamentary session (with representation based on the results of the May 1992 elections) before the end of the year. On 4 October 2002 a joint session of the Iraqi Kurdistan National Assembly was convened for the first time since 1996.

Following the removal of the regime of Saddam Hussain by US-led forces in early 2003, elections to a new Iraqi Kurdistan National Assembly took place on 30 January 2005, concurrently with elections to the Transitional National Assembly. The Kurdistan Democratic List won 104 of the 111 seats. On 12 June the new Kurdish legislature voted unanimously to appoint Masoud Barzani, leader of the KDP, to the post of President of the Kurdish Autonomous Region. The Government, led by Barzani, assumed office on 7 May 2006, and represented the region's first unified Cabinet. Prior to a unification agreement signed in January 2006, Sulaimaniya had been governed by the PUK, while Arbil and D'hok were administered by the KDP. In February 2009 the Iraqi Kurdistan National Assembly was renamed the Iraqi Kurdistan Parliament. A draft Constitution for the Kurdish Autonomous Region, which included territorial claims to Kirkuk and other disputed regions, was approved by the Iraqi Kurdistan Parliament on 24 June 2009. However, a planned referendum on the draft Constitution was subsequently postponed, owing to opposition from the Independent High Electoral Commission and the Iraqi parliament. At elections to the Iraqi Kurdistan Parliament held on 25 July, the Kurdistani List, which comprised the PUK and the KDP, secured 59 of the 111 seats in the legislature. The significant reduction in the two main parties' majority was largely due to the success of the Movement for Change (Gorran), which received 25 seats; the group had been established in 2006 by former members of the PUK, and campaigned on a pro-reform and anti-corruption platform. Meanwhile, in a concurrent election for the regional presidency, Barzani was re-elected with 69.6% of the valid votes cast. At legislative elections held on 21 September 2013, the KDP emerged as the leading party, winning 38 seats, according to official results announced on 2 October. Gorran became the second largest party, with 24 seats, surpassing the PUK, which took just 18 seats.

Iraqi Kurdistan Parliament: Erbil (Hewlêr), Kurdistan, Iraq e-mail office@perleman.org; internet www.perleman.org.

Speaker: YOUSUF MUHAMMAD SADIQ.

Election, 21 September 2013

	Seats
Kurdistan Democratic Party (KDP)	38
Movement for Change (Gorran)	24
Patriotic Union of Kurdistan (PUK)	18
Kurdistan Islamic Union	10
Islamic Group of Kurdistan	6
Islamic Movement in Iraqi Kurdistan	1
Kurdistan Communist Party	1
Kurdistan Socialist Democratic Party	1
Kurdistan Toilers Party	1
Seats reserved for minority groups*	11
Total	**111**

*Includes five seats reserved for parties representing the Assyrian, Chaldean and Syriac communities, five seats for representatives of the Turkoman community and one seat for the Armenian community.

Election Commission

Independent High Electoral Commission (IHEC): POB 55074, Baghdad; tel. (1) 743-2519; e-mail ihec.media@yahoo.com; internet www.ihec.iq; f. 2004 as Independent Electoral Comm. of Iraq by fmr Coalition Provisional Authority; renamed as above 2007; Chair. SARBAST RASHEED.

Political Organizations

Following the removal from power of the Baathist regime, restrictions were effectively lifted on opposition political organizations that were either previously declared illegal, forced to operate clandestinely within Iraq or were based abroad. Some 306 political parties were reported to have participated in the election to the Council of Representatives held on 7 March 2010.

Arab Baath Socialist Party: revolutionary Arab socialist movement founded in Damascus, Syria, in 1947; governed Iraq during 1968–2003 as principal constituent of ruling coalition, the Nat. Progressive Front (NPF); the NPF was removed from power by US-led forces in May 2003, whereupon membership of the Baath Party was declared illegal and former party mems were barred from govt and military posts; subsequently thought to be involved in insurgent activities in Iraq; in Feb. 2008 new legislation was ratified permitting certain former Baathists to be reinstated to official posts; in Jan. 2007, following the execution of former Iraqi President Saddam Hussain, former Vice-President IZZAT IBRAHIM AL-DOURI was named as the party's new leader.

Assyrian Democratic Movement (Zowaa Dimuqrataya Aturaya—Zowaa): e-mail info@zowaa.org; internet www.zowaa.org; f. 1979; seeks recognition of Assyrian rights within framework of democratic national govt; Sec.-Gen. YOUNADAM YOUSUF KANNA.

Assyrian Socialist Party: Baghdad; e-mail gaboatouraya@yahoo .co.uk; internet asp2.no.sapo.pt; f. 2002 (refounded); advocates the establishment of an Assyrian nation.

Constitutional Party: Baghdad; f. 2004; Shi'a; Founder and Leader JAWAD AL-BULANI.

Al-Ezediah Movement for Progress and Reform: Yazidi grouping; Leader AMIN FARHAN JEJO.

Independent Democratic Gathering: f. 2003; seeks a secular and democratic govt of Iraq; part of the State of Law alliance; Leader MAHDI AL-HAFEZ.

Iraqi Accord (Jabhat al-Tawafuq al-Iraqiya): internet www .altawafoq.org; e-mail info@altawafoq.com; f. 2005 as the Iraqi Accord Front; reformed to contest the March 2010 legislative elections; mainly Sunni; secular; coalition of the Iraqi Islamic Party and the Nat. Gathering of the People of Iraq.

Iraqi Communist Party (ICP): Baghdad; e-mail info@iraqicp.com; internet www.iraqicp.com; f. 1934; became legally recognized in July 1973 on formation of NPF; left NPF March 1979; First Sec. HAMID MAJID MOUSSA.

Iraqi Constitutional Movement: Baghdad; f. 1993; fmrly Constitutional Monarchy Movement.

Iraqi Front for National Dialogue (Hewar National Iraqi Front): f. 2005 as breakaway party from Iraqi Nat. Dialogue Council; coalition of minor Sunni parties; Founder and Leader SALEH AL-MUTLAQ.

Iraqi Islamic Party (IIP) (al-Hizb al-Islami al-Iraqi): e-mail iraqiparty@iraqiparty.com; internet www.iraqiparty.com; f. 1960; Sunni; branch of the Muslim Brotherhood; contested March 2010 legislative election as part of the Iraqi Accord list; Sec.-Gen. AYAD AL-SAMARRAI.

Iraqi National Accord (INA): e-mail wifaq_ina@hotmail.com; internet www.wifaq.com; f. 1990; contested March 2010 legislative election as mem. of Iraqi Nat. Movement; Founder and Sec.-Gen. Dr AYAD ALLAWI .

Iraqi National Alliance: list of mainly Shi'a parties, incl. the ISCI, the Sadr II Movement, the Iraqi Nat. Congress, the Nat. Reform Movement and the Islamic Virtue Party, which contested the March 2010 legislative elections as a single coalition; Leader IBRAHIM AL-JA'FARI.

Iraqi National Congress (INC): e-mail info@inciraq.com; internet inciraq.com; f. 1992 in London, United Kingdom, as a multi-party coalition supported by the US Govt; following the removal of the regime of Saddam Hussain, the INC moved to Baghdad and was transformed into a distinct political party; formed Nat. Congress Coalition before 2005 legislative elections, at which it failed to win any seats; contested March 2010 election as part of the Iraqi Nat. Alliance; Leader AHMAD CHALABI.

Iraqi National Foundation Congress (INFC): Baghdad; f. 2004; multi-party coalition incl. Nasserites, pre-Saddam Hussain era Baathists, Kurds, Christians, Sunnis and Shi'ites; seeks secular govt of national unity; opposed to presence of US-led coalition in Iraq, and consequently boycotted the electoral process initiated by the coalition; led by 25-mem. secretariat; Gen. Sec. Sheikh JAWAD AL-KHALISI.

Iraqi National Movement (Iraqiya): secular electoral list formed to contest the March 2010 legislative election, comprising a no. of political orgs, incl. the INA, the Iraqi Front for Nat. Dialogue, the Renewal List and Iraqis; Leader Dr AYAD ALLAWI.

Iraqi Turkmen Front (Irak Türkmen Cephesi): Arbil; internet www.kerkuk.net; f. 1995; coalition of Turkmen groups; seeks autonomy for Turkmen areas in Iraq and recognition of Turkmen as one of main ethnic groups in Iraq, and supports establishment of multi-party democratic system in Iraq; contests status of Kirkuk with Kurds; Leader ERŞAT SALIH; Sec.-Gen. YUNUS BAYRAKTAR.

Iraqi Unity Coalition: f. 2009 to contest the March 2010 legislative election; electoral alliance comprising 38 parties, incl. the Constitutional Party and the Iraqi Awakening Conference.

Iraqis (Iraqiyun): f. 2004; moderate; includes both Sunnis and Shi'a; Leader OSAMA AL-NUJAYFI.

Islamic Dawa Party (Hizb al-Da'wa al-Islamiya): Baghdad; e-mail info@islamicdawaparty.org; internet www.islamicdawaparty.org; f. 1957 in Najaf; banned 1980; fmrly based in Tehran, Iran, and London, United Kingdom; re-established in Baghdad 2003; part of State of Law coalition; predominantly Shi'a, but with Sunni mems; advocates govt centred on the principles of Islam; Gen. Sec. NURI KAMAL (JAWAD) AL-MALIKI.

Islamic Group of Kurdistan (Komaleh Islami): Khurmal; f. 2001; splinter group of IMIK; moderate Islamist, aligned with the PUK; Founder and Leader Mullah ALI BAPIR.

Islamic Movement of Kurdistan (IMK): Halabja; e-mail bzotnawa@yahoo.com; f. 1987; Islamist movement seeking to obtain greater legal rights for Iraqi Kurds; Founder and Leader IRFAN ABD AL-AZIZ.

Islamic Supreme Council of Iraq (ISCI): Najaf; e-mail info@almejlis.org; internet www.almejlis.org; f. 1982 as the Supreme Council for the Islamic Revolution in Iraq; name changed as above in 2007; Shi'a; seeks govt based on principle of *wilayat-e-faqih* (guardianship of the jurisprudent); armed faction, the Badr Organization (fmrly Badr Brigade), assisted coalition forces in Iraq after the removal of Saddam Hussain's regime; Leader AMMAR AL-HAKIM.

Islamic Virtue Party (Hizb al-Fadhila al-Islamiya—IVP): Basra; e-mail info@alfadhela.net.iq; internet www.alfadhela.net.iq; Shi'a; an offshoot of the Sadrist movement; follows the spiritual leadership of Ayatollah al-Sayyid Muhammad al-Ya'qubi; Sec.-Gen. HASHIM AL-HASHIMI.

Kurdistan Democratic Party (KDP): European Office (Germany), 10749 Berlin, POB 301516; tel. (30) 79743741; fax (30) 79743746; e-mail party@kdp.se; internet www.kdp.se; f. 1946; seeks to protect Kurdish rights and promote Kurdish culture and interests through regional political and legislative autonomy, as part of a federative republic; Pres. MASOUD BARZANI; Vice-Pres. NECHIRVAN BARZANI.

Kurdistan Islamic Union (Yakgrtui Islami Kurdistan): e-mail info@kurdiu.org; internet kurdiu.org; f. 1991; seeks establishment of an Islamic state in Iraq that recognizes the rights of Kurds; branch of the Muslim Brotherhood; Sec.-Gen. MUHAMMAD FARAJ.

Kurdistan Socialist Democratic Party (KSDP): Sulaimaniya; e-mail info@psdkurdistan.org; f. 1994; splinter group of the KDP, aligned with the PUK; Sec.-Gen. MUHAMMAD HAJI MAHMOUD.

Kurdistan Toilers Party (Hizbi Zahmatkeshani Kurdistan): f. 1985; advocates a federal Iraq; closely associated with the KSDP; Sec.-Gen. BALEN ABDULLAH.

Movement for Change (Gorran): e-mail info@gorran.net; internet gorran.net; f. 2006; established by fmr members of the PUK; advocates political and economic reform, anti-corruption measures and the independence of the judiciary; advocates a federal Iraq; Leader NAWSHIRWAN MUSTAFA.

National Gathering of the People of Iraq: f. 2004 as the Iraqi People's Conference; name changed in 2009; Sunni; Leader KHALED AL-BARAA.

National Rafidain List: e-mail info@alrafedainlist.com; internet www.alrafedainlist.com; f. 2004; Assyrian-Christian list headed by the Assyrian Democratic Movement; Leader YOUNADAM KANA.

National Reform Movement: f. 2008 by fmr mems of Islamic Dawa Party; Shi'a; Leader IBRAHIM AL-JA'FARI.

National Tribal Gathering: f. 2007; Sunni; Leader OMAR AL-HAYKAL.

Patriotic Union of Kurdistan (PUK): European Office (Germany), 10502 Berlin, POB 210213; tel. (30) 34097850; fax (30) 34097849; e-mail puk@puk.org; internet www.puk.org; f. 1975; seeks to protect and promote Kurdish rights and interests through self-determination; Sec.-Gen. JALAL TALABANI.

Reconciliation and Liberation Bloc (Kutla al-Musalaha wa't-Tahrir): Mosul; f. 1995 in Jordan as Iraqi Homeland Party (Hizb al-Watan al-Iraqi); moved to Damascus, Syria, and to Mosul in 2003; liberal, secular Sunni; advocates withdrawal of coalition troops and partial rehabilitation of mems of the former Baathist regime; publishes *Al-Ittijah al-Akhar* newspaper; Leader MISHAAN AL-JUBURI.

Sadr II Movement (Jamaat al-Sadr al-Thani): Najaf; f. 2003; Shi'a; opposes presence of US-led coalition in Iraq; military wing is Imam al-Mahdi Army; Leader Hojatoleslam MUQTADA AL-SADR.

State of Law (Dawlat al-Kanoon): f. prior to 2009 provincial elections; predominantly Shi'a alliance of parties and independent candidates, incl. the Islamic Dawa Party, the Independent Arab Movement and the Anbar Salvation Nat. Front.

Major militant groups that have launched attacks against Iraqis and the US-led coalition include: **Fedayeen Saddam** (Saddam's Martyrs; f. 1995 by mems of the former Baathist regime; paramilitary group); **Ansar al-Islam** (f. 1998; splinter group of IMIK; Islamist; suspected of having links with al-Qa'ida); **Hezbollah** (Shi'a Marsh Arab; Leader ABD AL-KARIM MAHMOUD MOHAMMEDAWI—' ABU HATEM'); **Ansar al-Sunnah** (f. 2003 by mems of Ansar al-Islam; Islamist); **Imam al-Mahdi Army** (armed wing of the Sadr II Movement—Jamaat al-Sadr al-Thani); **Base of Holy War in Mesopotamia** (Tanzim Qa'idat al-Jihad fi Bilad al-Rafidain; Sunni insurgent network, also known as al-Qa'ida in Iraq; Leader AL-NASSER LIDEEN ALLAH ABU SULEIMAN, who was reported to have been killed in Feb. 2011); **Islamic State** (al-Dawlat al-Islamiyya; network of Sunni insurgent groups; in de facto control of territory in Anbar, Kirkuk, Nineveh and Salah al-Din provinces—including the city of Mosul—since June 2014; also controls territory in northern Syria; proclaimed an independent Islamic state (or 'caliphate') in those areas under its control in June 2014, changing its name from Islamic State in Iraq and the Levant; Leader ABU BAKR AL-BAGHDADI AL-HUSSEINI AL-QURASHI).

Diplomatic Representation

EMBASSIES IN IRAQ

Algeria: Hay al-Mansour, Baghdad; tel. (1) 543-4137; fax (1) 542-5829; e-mail ambalgabaghdad@yahoo.com; Ambassador (vacant).

Australia: International Zone, Baghdad; tel. 7809237565 (mobile); e-mail austemb.baghdad@dfat.gov.au; internet www.iraq.embassy.gov.au; Ambassador LYNDALL SACHS.

Bahrain: 41/6/605 Hay al-Mutanabi, Baghdad; tel. (1) 7815808306 (mobile); fax (1) 541-2027; e-mail baghdad.mission@mofa.gove.bh; internet www.mofa.gov.bh/baghdad; Ambassador SALAH AL-MALIKI.

Bangladesh: 6/14/929 Hay Babel, Baghdad; tel. (1) 719-0068; fax (1) 718-6045; Ambassador REZA NOOR RAHMAN KHAN.

Bulgaria: 12/25/624 al-Ameriya, Baghdad; tel. (1) 556-8197; fax (1) 556-4182; e-mail embassy.baghdad@mfa.bg; Chargé d'affaires KRASIMIR GEORGIEV.

Canada: International Zone, Baghdad; Chargé d'affaires ROBERT BISSETT.

China, People's Republic: POB 2386, al-Jadryaa Post Office, Baghdad; tel. 7901912315 (mobile); e-mail chinaemb_iq@mfa.gov.cn; internet iq.chineseembassy.org; Ambassador WANG YONG.

Czech Republic: POB 27124, 37/11/601 Hay al-Mansour, Baghdad; tel. (1) 542-4868; fax (1) 214-2621; e-mail baghdad@embassy.mzv.cz; internet www.mzv.cz/baghdad; Ambassador ALEXANDR LANGER.

Egypt: 103/11/601 Hay al-Mansour, Baghdad; tel. (1) 543-0572; fax (1) 556-6346; e-mail egypt@uruklink.net; Ambassador AHMAD HASSAN IBRAHIM.

France: POB 118, 7/55/102 Abu Nawas, Baghdad; tel. (964) 718-1996; fax (964) 718-1997; e-mail info@ambafrance-iq.org; internet www.ambafrance-iq.org; Ambassador MARC BARETY.

Germany: POB 2036, Hay al-Mansour, Baghdad; tel. 7901922526 (mobile); fax (1) 543-5840; e-mail info@bagdad.diplo.de; internet www.bagdad.diplo.de; Ambassador EKKEHARD BROSE.

Greece: 63/31/913, Jadriyah University Sq., Hay Babel, Baghdad; tel. 7801372165 (mobile); e-mail gremb.bag@mfa.gr; Ambassador DIONYSSIOS KYVETOS.

Holy See: Apostolic Nunciature, POB 2090, 904/2/46 Saadoun St, Baghdad; tel. (1) 718-2083; e-mail nuntiusiraq@yahoo.com; Apostolic Nuncio Most Rev. GIORGIO LINGUA (Titular Archbishop of Tuscania).

India: House 18, St 16, Mohalla 609, Al-Mansour, Baghdad; tel. 7704439731 (mobile); e-mail amb.baghdad@mea.gov.in; Ambassador AJAY KUMAR.

Iran: POB 39095, Salehiya, Karadeh Maryam, Baghdad; tel. (1) 884-3033; fax (1) 537-5636; Ambassador HASSAN DANAFAR.

Italy: International Zone, Baghdad; tel. 7505010505 (mobile); e-mail ambasciata.baghdad@esteri.it; internet www.ambbaghdad.esteri.it/ambasciata_baghdad; Ambassador MASSIMO MAROTTI.

Japan: International Zone, Baghdad; tel. (1) 776-6791; e-mail azza_fh@yahoo.com; internet www.iraq.emb-japan.go.jp; Ambassador KAZUYA NASHIDA.

Jordan: POB 6314, 145/49/617 Hay al-Andalus, Baghdad; tel. (1) 541-2892; fax (1) 541-2009; e-mail jordan@uruklink.net; Ambassador MUHAMMAD QARAAN.

Korea, Republic: House 11, Babylon Hotel St, al-Jadriya, Baghdad; tel. 7707252006 (mobile); e-mail kembiraq@mofat.go.kr; internet irq.mofat.go.kr; Ambassador JO JANG-WON.

Kuwait: International Zone, Baghdad; tel. 7435309666 (mobile); Ambassador GHASSAN YOUSEF AL-ZAWAWI.

Lebanon: Bldg 51, al-Askari St, 116 al-Sarafiya Area, Baghdad; tel. (1) 414-2711; fax (1) 885-6731; e-mail lebembbaghadad@yahoo.com; Chargé d'affaires NAWAF SHARIF HAZZA.

Netherlands: POB 2064, 7/15/215 International Zone, Baghdad; tel. (1) 778-2571; fax (1) 776-3513; e-mail bag@minbuza.nl; internet iraq.nlembassy.org; Ambassador JEANNETTE SEPPEN.

Pakistan: 14/7/609 Hay al-Mansour, Baghdad; fax 7812369544 (mobile); e-mail pakembbag@yahoo.com; Ambassador MUHAMMAD IFTIKHAR ANJUM.

Philippines: POB 3236, 4/22/915 Hay al-Jamiyah, al-Jadriya, Baghdad; tel. (1) 788-9761; fax (1) 719-3228; e-mail baghdad.pe@dfa.gov.ph; Ambassador EDSEL BARBA BOUMBERADA.

Poland: 38/75 Karadat Mariam International Zone, Baghdad; tel. (1) 7902354765 (mobile); e-mail bagdad.amb.sekretariat@msz.gov.pl; internet www.bagdad.msz.gov.pl; Chargé d'affaires a.i. ANDRZEJ MAŚNICA.

Romania: POB 2571, Arassat al-Hindia St, 452A/31/929 Hay Babel, Baghdad; tel. (1) 778-2860; fax (1) 778-7553; e-mail bagdad@mae.ro; Ambassador IACOB PRADA.

Russian Federation: 4/5/605 Hay al-Mutanabi, Baghdad; tel. and fax (1) 541-4754; e-mail rusiraq@mail.ru; internet www.iraq.mid.ru; Ambassador ILYA A. MORGUNOV.

Serbia: POB 2061, 16/35/923 Hay Babel, Baghdad; tel. (1) 778-7887; fax (1) 778-0489; e-mail embrbag@yahoo.com; internet www.baghdad.mfa.rs; Ambassador RADISAV PETROVIĆ.

Slovakia: 94/28/923 Hay Babel, Baghdad; tel. (1) 776-7367; fax (1) 776-7368; Ambassador LUBOMÍR MACKO.

Spain: POB 2072, 50/1/609 al-Mansour, Baghdad; e-mail emb.bagdad@maec.es; internet www.cxteriores.gob.es/embajadas/bagdad; Ambassador JOSÉ MARÍA FERRÉ DE LA PEÑA.

Sweden: POB 3475, Karadat Mariam, Baghdad; tel. 7801987450; e-mail ambassaden.bagdad@gov.se; internet www.swedenabroad.com/baghdad; Ambassador JÖRGEN LINDSTRÖM.

Syria: Hay al-Mansour, Baghdad; Ambassador SATTAM JAD'AN AL-DANDAH.

Tunisia: 1/49/617 Hay al-Andalus, Baghdad; tel. (1) 542-4569; Ambassador SAMIR JUMAIE ABDULLAH.

Turkey: POB 14001, 2/8 Waziriya, Baghdad; tel. (312) 218-6010; fax (312) 218-6110; e-mail embassy.baghdad@mfa.gov.tr; internet www.baghdad.emb.mfa.gov.tr; Ambassador FARUK KAYMAKCI.

Ukraine: POB 15192, 50/1/609 al-Mansour, al-Yarmouk, Baghdad; tel. 7904167152 (mobile); fax 543-9849; e-mail emb_iq@mfa.gov.ua; internet iraq.mfa.gov.ua; Ambassador ANATOLII MARYNETS.

United Arab Emirates: 81/34/611 Hay al-Andalus (al-Daoudi), Baghdad; tel. (1) 543-9174; fax (1) 543-9093; Ambassador ABDULLAH IBRAHIM AL-SHEHHI.

United Kingdom: International Zone, Baghdad; e-mail britishconsulbaghdad@yahoo.co.uk; tel. 7901926280 (mobile); internet www.gov.uk/government/world/iraq; Ambassador FRANK BAKER.

USA: Al-Kindi St, International Zone, Baghdad; e-mail baghdadirc@state.gov; internet iraq.usembassy.gov; Ambassador STUART E. JONES.

Yemen: 4/36/904 Hay al-Wahada, Baghdad; tel. (1) 718-6682; fax (1) 717-2318; Ambassador ZAID HASSAN AL-WARITH.

Judicial System

Supreme Iraqi Criminal Tribunal: Following the ousting of the Baath regime, the judicial system was subject to a process of review and de-Baathification. In June 2003 the former Coalition Provisional Authority (CPA) established a **Judicial Review Committee**, the task of which was to review and repair the material status of the courts and to assess personnel. In December the Governing Council created the **Iraqi Special Tribunal**, in order to bring to trial those senior members of the former regime accused of war crimes, crimes against humanity and genocide. The statute of the Tribune was amended by the former Transitional National Assembly in October 2005, when it was renamed the **Supreme Iraqi Criminal Tribunal**.

Central Criminal Court of Iraq: Consists of an **Investigative Court** and a **Trial Court**. It was created by the CPA in July 2003 as the senior court in Iraq, with jurisdiction over all crimes committed in the country since 19 March 2003. With a few exceptions, the application of justice was to be based upon the 1969 Penal Code of Iraq and the 1971 Criminal Proceedings Code of Iraq.

Higher Judicial Council: tel. (1) 538-4406; fax (1) 537-2267; e-mail iraqinfocenter@yahoo.com; internet www.iraqja.iq; Pres. HASSAN IBRAHIM HUSSEIN HUMAIRI.

Religion

ISLAM

About 95% of the population are Muslims, some 60% of whom are of the Shi'a sect. The Arabs of northern Iraq, the Bedouins, the Kurds, the Turkomans and some of the inhabitants of Baghdad and Basra are mainly of the Sunni sect, while the remaining Arabs south of the Diyali are Shi'a.

CHRISTIANITY

There are Christian communities in all the principal towns of Iraq, but their main villages lie mostly in the Mosul district. The Christians of Iraq comprise three groups: the free Churches, including the Nestorian, Gregorian and Syrian Orthodox; the churches known as Uniate, since they are in union with the Roman Catholic Church, including the Armenian Uniates, Syrian Uniates and Chaldeans; mixed bodies of Protestant converts, New Chaldeans and Orthodox Armenians. There are estimated to be 500,000–700,000 Christians of various denominations in Iraq; however, there has been an exodus to neighbouring countries such as Syria and Jordan since the mid-2000s, as a result of the ongoing sectarian conflict.

The Assyrian Church

Assyrian Christians, an ancient sect having sympathies with Nestorian beliefs, were forced to leave their mountainous homeland in northern Kurdistan in the early part of the 20th century. The estimated 550,000 members of the Apostolic Catholic Assyrian Church of the East are now exiles, mainly in Iraq (about 50,000 adherents), Syria, Lebanon and the USA. Their leader is the Catholicos Patriarch, His Holiness MAR DINKHA IV.

The Orthodox Churches

Armenian Apostolic Church: Diocese of the Armenian Church of Iraq, POB 2280, al-Jadriya, Tayaran Sq., Baghdad; tel. (1) 815-1856; fax (1) 815-1857; e-mail iraqitem@yahoo.com; internet www.iraqitem.org; f. 1639; Primate Archbishop AVAK ASADOURIAN; 12 churches (four in Baghdad); 14,562 mems.

Syrian Orthodox Church: Syrian Orthodox Archbishopric, POB 843, al-Seenah St, Baghdad; tel. (1) 719-6320; fax (1) 719-7583; Archbishop of Baghdad and Basra SEVERIUS JAMIL HAWA; 12,000 adherents in Iraq.

The Greek Orthodox Church is also represented in Iraq.

The Roman Catholic Church

Armenian Rite

Archbishop of Baghdad: Most Rev. EMMANUEL DABBAGHIAN, 27/903 Archevêché Arménien Catholique, POB 2344, Karrada Sharkiya, Baghdad; tel. (1) 719-2461; e-mail dabbaghianemm@hotmail.com.

Chaldean Rite

Iraq comprises the patriarchate of Babylon, five archdioceses (including the patriarchal see of Baghdad) and five dioceses (all of which are suffragan to the patriarchate). Altogether, the Patriarch has jurisdiction over 21 archdioceses and dioceses in Iraq, Egypt, Iran, Lebanon, Syria, Turkey and the USA, and the Patriarchal Vicariate of Jerusalem.

Patriarch of Babylon of the Chaldeans: Cardinal EMMANUEL III DELLY, POB 6112, Patriarcat Chaldéen Catholique, al-Mansour, Baghdad; tel. (1) 537-9164; fax (1) 537-8556; e-mail info@st-addayyahoo.com.

Archbishop of Arbil: Most Rev. BASHAR WARDA, Archevêché Catholique Chaldéen, Ainkawa, Arbil; tel. (665) 225-0009.

Archbishop of Baghdad: the Patriarch of Babylon (q.v.).

Archbishop of Basra: Most Rev. IMAD AZIZ AL-BANNA, Archevêché Chaldéen, POB 217, Ashar-Basra; tel. (40) 613427; e-mail efather2006@yahoo.com.

Archbishop of Kirkuk: Most Rev. LOUIS SAKO, Archevêché Chaldéen, POB 490, Kirkuk; tel. (50) 220525; fax (50) 213978; e-mail luis_sako2@yahoo.com.

Archbishop of Mosul: Most Rev. EMIL SHIMOUN NONA, Archevêché Chaldéen, POB 757, Mayassa, Mosul; tel. (60) 815831; fax (60) 816742; e-mail archdioceseofmossul@yahoo.com.

Latin Rite

The archdiocese of Baghdad is directly responsible to the Holy See.

Archbishop of Baghdad: Most Rev. JEAN BENJAMIN SLEIMAN, Archevêché Latin, POB 35130, Hay al-Wahda—Mahallat 904, rue 8, Immeuble 44, 12906 Baghdad; tel. (1) 719-9537; fax (1) 717-2471; e-mail jbsleiman@yahoo.com.

Melkite Rite

The Greek-Melkite Patriarch of Antioch (GRÉGOIRE III LAHAM) is resident in Damascus, Syria.

Patriarchal Exarchate of Iraq: Exarchat Patriarchal Grec-Melkite, Karradat IN 903/10/50, Baghdad; tel. (1) 719-1082; 100 adherents (2006); Exarch Patriarchal (vacant).

Syrian Rite

Iraq comprises two archdioceses and the Patriarchal Exarchate of Basra.

Archbishop of Baghdad: Most Rev. ATHANASE MATTI SHABA MATOKA, Archevêché Syrien Catholique, 903/2/1 Baghdad; tel. (1) 719-1850; fax (1) 719-0166; e-mail mattishaba@yahoo.com.

Archbishop of Mosul: Most Rev. BOUTROS MOSHE, Archevêché Syrien Catholique, Hosh al-Khan, Mosul; tel. (60) 762160; fax (60) 771439; e-mail syrcam2003@yahoo.com.

The Anglican Communion

Within the Episcopal Church in Jerusalem and the Middle East, Iraq forms part of the diocese of Cyprus and the Gulf. Expatriate congregations in Iraq meet at St George's Church, Baghdad. The Bishop in Cyprus and the Gulf is resident in Cyprus.

JUDAISM

A tiny Jewish community, numbering only eight people in late 2008, remains in Baghdad.

OTHERS

About 550,000 Yazidis and a smaller number of Sabians and Shebeks reside in Iraq.

Sabian Community: al-Nasiriyah (Nasiriya); 20,000 adherents; Mandeans, mostly in Nasiriya; Head Sheikh DAKHIL.

Yazidis: Ainsifni; Leader TASHIN SAID ALI.

The Press

Since the overthrow of the regime of Saddam Hussain by US-led coalition forces in early 2003, the number of publications has proliferated: by the end of 2003 an estimated 250 newspapers and periodicals were in circulation, although only some 100 of these were reportedly still being published in 2008. Many newspapers are affiliated with political or religious organizations; however, the daily *Al-Sabah* is controlled by the Iraqi Government, with coalition backing. Security issues have resulted in severe distribution problems, and some newspaper offices have either relocated or chosen to publish online-only editions following threats being issued against journalists by militant groups, militias and security forces. A selection of publications is given below.

DAILIES

Al-Adala (Justice): Baghdad; e-mail aliisadik@yahoo.com; internet www.aladalanews.net; f. 2004; twice weekly; Arabic; organ of the Islamic Supreme Council of Iraq; publ. by the Al-Adala Group for Press, Printing and Publishing; Owner Dr ADIL ABD AL-MAHDI.

Baghdad: al-Zeitoun St, al-Harthiya, Baghdad; e-mail baghdadwifaq@yahoo.com; f. 1991; organ of the Iraqi Nat. Accord; Publr AYAD ALLAWI.

Al-Bayan (The Manifesto): Baghdad; f. 2003; Arabic; organ of Islamic Dawa Party; Man. Editor SADIQ AL-RIKABI.

Dar al-Salam (House of Peace): Baghdad; Arabic; organ of Iraqi Islamic Party.

Al-Dustur (The Constitution): Baghdad; f. 2003; Arabic; politics; independent; publ. by Al-Dustur Press, Publishing and Distribution House; Chair. BASIM AL-SHEIKH; Editor-in-Chief ALI AL-SHARQI.

Al-Jarida (The Newspaper): Baghdad; f. 2003; Arabic; organ of the Iraqi Arab Socialist Movement; Editor Prof. QAYS AL-AZZAWI.

Kul al-Iraq (All Iraq): Baghdad; e-mail info@kululiraq.com; internet www.kululiraq.com; f. 2003; Arabic; independent; Editor-in-Chief Dr ABBAS AL-SIRAF.

Al-Mada: 41/1 Abu Nuwas St, Baghdad; fax (1) 881-3256; e-mail info@almadapaper.net; internet www.almadapaper.com; f. 2004; Arabic; independent; publ. by Al-Mada Foundation for Media, Culture and Arts; Editor-in-Chief FAKHRI KARIM.

Al-Mannarah (Minarets): Basra; tel. (40) 315758; e-mail almannarah@almannarah.com; Arabic; publ. by South Press, Printing and Publishing Corpn; Editor-in-Chief Dr KHALAF AL-MANSHADI.

Al-Mashriq: Baghdad; e-mail info@almashriqnews.com; internet www.al-mashriq.net; f. 2004; Arabic; independent; publ. by Al-Mashriq Institution for Media and Cultural Investments; circ. 25,000.

Al-Mutamar (Congress): Baghdad; e-mail almutamer@yahoo.com; internet www.inciraq.com/index_paper.php; f. 1993; Arabic; publ. by Iraqi Nat. Congress; Editor-in-Chief LUAY BALDAWI.

Al-Sabah: Baghdad; e-mail sabah@alsabaah.com; f. 2003; Arabic and English; state-controlled; publ. by the Iraqi Media Network; Deputy Editor-in-Chief ADNAN SHERKHAN.

Al-Sabah al-Jadid (New Morning): Baghdad; e-mail info@newsabah.com; internet www.newsabah.com; f. 2004; Arabic; independent; Editor-in-Chief ISMAIL ZAYER.

Sawt al-Iraq (Voice of Iraq): Baghdad; e-mail admin@sotaliraq.com; internet www.sotaliraq.com; online only; Arabic; independent.

Al-Taakhi (Brotherhood): e-mail badirkhansindi@yahoo.com; f. 1967; Kurdish and Arabic; organ of the Kurdistan Democratic Party (KDP); publ. by Al-Taakhi Publishing and Printing House; Editor-in-Chief Dr BADIRKHAN SINDI; circ. 20,000 (Baghdad).

Tariq al-Sha'ab (People's Path): Saadoun St, Baghdad; e-mail altareeq_1934@yahoo.com; f. 1974; Arabic and English; organ of the Iraqi Communist Party; Editor ABD AL-RAZZAK AL-SAFI.

Xebat: Arbil; e-mail info@xebat.net; internet www.xebat.net; f. 1959; Arabic and Kurdish; organ of the KDP; Editor-in-Chief SALAM ABDULLAH.

Al-Zaman (Time): Baghdad; tel. (1) 717-7587; e-mail postmaster@azzaman.com; internet www.azzaman.com; f. 1997 in the United Kingdom, f. 2003 in Baghdad; Arabic, with some news translated into English; Editor-in-Chief SAAD AL-BAZZAZ.

WEEKLIES

Al-Ahali (The People): Baghdad; e-mail info@ahali-iraq.net; internet www.ahali-iraq.net; Arabic; politics; Editor HAVAL ZAKHOUBI.

Alif Baa al-Iraq: Baghdad; Arabic and English; general, social and political affairs.

Habazbuz fi Zaman al-Awlamah (Habazbuz in the Age of Globalization): Baghdad; f. 2003; Arabic; satirical; Editor ISHTAR AL-YASIRI.

Iraq Today: Baghdad; f. 2003; English; current affairs; Founder and Editor-in-Chief HUSSAIN SINJARI.

Al-Iraq al-Yawm (Iraq Today): Baghdad; e-mail iraqtoday@iraqtoday.net; Arabic and English; Editor ISRA SHAKIR.

Al-Ittihad (Union): Baghdad and Sulaimaniya; tel. (1) 543-8954; e-mail alitthad@alitthad.com; internet www.alitthad.com; Arabic and Kurdish; publ. by the Patriotic Union of Kurdistan; Editor ABD AL-HADI; circ. 30,000 (Baghdad).

Al-Ittijah al-Akhar (The Other Direction): Baghdad; tel. (1) 776-3334; fax (1) 776-3332; e-mail alitijahalakhar@yahoo.com; Arabic; organ of Reconciliation and Liberation Bloc; Chair. and Editor MISHAAN AL-JUBURI.

Kurdish Globe: Salah al-Din Highway, Pirzeen, Arbil; tel. 7507747784 (mobile); e-mail info@kurdishglobe.net; internet www.kurdishglobe.net; f. 2005; English; Kurdish news and issues; Exec. Editor GAZI HASSAN; circ. 40,000.

Majallati: POB 8041, Children's Culture House, Baghdad; Arabic; children's newspaper; Editor-in-Chief Dr SHAFIQ AL-MAHDI.

Al-Muajaha (The Witness): 6/41/901, Karrada Dakhil, Baghdad; e-mail almuajaha@riseup.net; f. 2003; Arabic and English; current affairs; independent; Editor RAMZI MAJID JARRAR.

Al-Nahda (Renaissance): Basra; f. 2003; Arabic; organ of the Independent Democratic Gathering; Publr ADNAN PACHACHI.

Regay Kurdistan: Arbil; e-mail regaykurdistan@gmail.com; internet www.regaykurdistan.com; Arabic and Kurdish; organ of the Iraqi and Kurdistan Communist Parties; Editor-in-Chief HANDREN AHMAD.

Al-Sina'i (The Industrialist): Baghdad; Arabic; general; publ. by the Nat. Industrialist Coalition; Editor-in-Chief Dr ZAYD ABD AL-MAJID BILAL.

Al-Waqai al-Iraqiya (Official Gazette of the Republic of Iraq): Ministry of Justice, Baghdad; tel. (1) 537-2023; e-mail Hashim_Jaffar_alsaieg@yahoo.com; f. 1922; Arabic and English; Dir HASHIM N. JAFFAR; circ. 5,000.

PERIODICALS

Hawlati: e-mail hawlati2000@yahoo.com; internet hawlati.co; f. 2001; fortnightly; Kurdish, Arabic and English; independent, privately owned; mainly Kurdish politics; Publr TARIQ FATIH; Editor KAMAL RAOUF.

Majallat al-Majma' al-'Ilmi al-Iraqi (Journal of the Academy of Sciences): POB 4023, Waziriya, Baghdad; tel. (1) 422-4202; fax (1) 422-2066; e-mail iraqacademy@yahoo.com; internet www .iraqacademy.iq; f. 1950; quarterly; Arabic; scholarly magazine on Arabic Islamic culture; Editor-in-Chief Prof. Dr AHMAD MATLOUB.

Al-Sa'ah (The Hour): Baghdad; twice weekly; Arabic; organ of the Iraqi Unified Nat. Movement; Publr AHMAD AL-KUBAYSI; Editor NI'MA ABD AL-RAZZAQ.

Sawt al-Talaba (Voice of the Students): Baghdad; fortnightly; Arabic; publ. by New Iraq Youth and Students' Org; Editor MUSTAFA AL-HAYIM.

NEWS AGENCIES

National Iraqi News Agency: Baghdad; tel. (1) 717-2251; e-mail news@ninanews.com; internet www.ninanews.com; f. 2005; Arabic and English; independent; Chair. Dr FARID AYAR; Man. Dir ABD AL-MUHSEN HUSSAIN JAWAD.

PRESS ORGANIZATION

Iraqi Union for Journalists: POB 14101, nr al-Resafah Bldg, al-Waziriya, Baghdad; tel. (1) 537-0762; fax (1) 422-6011; e-mail iraqiju@yahoo.com; Chair. MUAID AL-LAMI.

Publishers

Afaq Arabiya Publishing House: POB 4032, Adamiya, Baghdad; tel. (1) 443-6044; fax (1) 444-8760; publr of literary monthlies, periodicals and cultural books; Chair. Dr MOHSIN AL-MUSAWI.

Dar al-Ma'mun for Translation and Publishing: POB 24015, Karradat Mariam, Baghdad; tel. (1) 538-3171; publr of newspapers and magazines.

Al-Hurriyah Printing Establishment: Karantina, Sarrafiya, Baghdad; f. 1970.

Al-Jamaheer Press House: POB 491, Sarrafiya, Baghdad; tel. (1) 416-9341; fax (1) 416-1875; f. 1963; publr of a number of newspapers and magazines; Pres. SAAD QASSEM HAMMOUDI.

Kurdish Culture and Publishing House: Baghdad; f. 1976.

Al-Ma'arif Ltd: Mutanabi St, Baghdad; f. 1929; publishes periodicals and books in Arabic, Kurdish, Turkish, French and English.

Al-Mada Foundation for Media, Culture and Arts: 141 Abu Nuwas St, Baghdad; tel. 7702799999 (mobile); e-mail info@ almadapaper.net; internet www.almadapaper.net; f. 1994; Dir FAKHRI KARIM.

Al-Muthanna Library: POB 14019, Mutanabi St, Baghdad; tel. 770-3649664 (mobile); e-mail mail@almuthannabooks.com; internet www.almuthannabooks.com; f. 1936; booksellers and publrs of books and monographs in Arabic and oriental languages; Propr ANAS AL-RAJAB; Dir IBRAHIM AL-RAJAB.

Al-Nahdah: Mutanabi St, Baghdad; tel. (1) 416-2689; e-mail yehya_azawy@yahoo.com; politics, Arab affairs.

National House for Publishing, Distribution and Advertising: POB 624, al-Jumhuriya St, Baghdad; tel. (1) 425-1846; f. 1972; publishes books on politics, economics, education, agriculture, sociology, commerce and science in Arabic and other Middle Eastern languages; Dir-Gen. M. A. ASKAR.

Al-Thawra Printing and Publishing House: POB 2009, Aqaba bin Nafi's Sq., Baghdad; tel. (1) 719-6161; f. 1970; Chair. (vacant).

PUBLISHERS' ASSOCIATION

Iraqi Publishers' Association: Baghdad; tel. (1) 416-9279; fax (1) 416-7584; e-mail al_nasheren@yahoo.com; Chair. Dr ABD AL-WAHAB AL-RADI.

Broadcasting and Communications

REGULATORY AUTHORITY

Communications and Media Commission (CMC): POB 2044, Hay Babel, al-Masbah, Baghdad; tel. (1) 718-0009; fax (1) 719-5839; e-mail enquiries@cmc.iq; internet www.cmc.iq; f. 2004 by fmr Coalition Provisional Authority; independent telecoms and media regulator; responsibilities include the award and management of telecommunications licences, broadcasting, media and information services, as well as spectrum allocation and management; CEO Dr SAFAA AL-DIN RABEE.

TELECOMMUNICATIONS

Under the former Baathist regime, the Iraqi Telecommunications and Posts Co was the sole provider of telecommunications and postal services. Following the removal from power of Saddam Hussain, in 2003 the Coalition Provisional Authority issued three short-term licences for the provision of mobile telephone services to stimulate competition in the sector. Asiacell, led by the Iraqi Kurdish Asiacell Co for Telecommunication Ltd, was awarded the licence for the northern region; the licence for Baghdad and the central region was won by Orascom Telecom Iraq Corpn (Iraqna), led by Orascom Telecom of Egypt; and Atheer Telecom Iraq (MTC Atheer), led by the Mobile Telecommunications Co of Kuwait, won the licence for Basra and the southern region. In August 2007 Asiacell, Korek Telecom Ltd and MTC Atheer (which subsequently acquired 100% of Iraqna shares and was renamed Zain) won the auction launched by the Government for three new national licences to provide mobile telephone services over a 15-year period; Iraqna withdrew from the bidding process.

Asiacell: Headquarters Bldg, Sulaimaniya; e-mail customercare@ asiacell.com; internet www.asiacell.com; f. 1999; 51% owned by Asiacell Co for Telecommunication Ltd, 40% by Wataniya Telecom (Kuwait) and 9% owned by United Gulf Bank (Bahrain); 6.0m. subscribers (Dec. 2008); Chair. of Bd FAROUK MUSTAFA RASOUL.

Iraqi Telecommunications and Posts Co (ITPC): POB 2450, Abu Nuwas St, Baghdad; tel. (1) 886-2372; e-mail itpcmedia@yahoo .com; internet www.itpc.gov.iq; state-owned; Dir-Gen. SALEH HASSAN ALI.

Korek Telecom: Kurdistan St, Pirmam, Arbil; tel. (66) 243-3455; e-mail media.pr@korektel.com; internet korektel.com; f. 2001; 44% owned by jt-venture of Agility Logistics (Kuwait) and France Telecom—Orange; CEO GHADA GEBARA.

Zain: Bldg 47, St 14, Hay al-Mutanabi, al-Mansoor, Baghdad; e-mail info@iq.zain.com; internet www.iq.zain.com; f. 2003 as MTC Atheer, a subsidiary of Mobile Telecommunications Co (Kuwait); acquired Iraqna Co for Mobile Phone Services Ltd (operated by Orascom Telecom Holding—Egypt) in Dec. 2007; name changed to above in Jan. 2008; 13.8m. subscribers (Dec. 2014); Chair. and Acting CEO MUHAMMAD AL-CHARCHAFCHI.

BROADCASTING

The Iraqi Media Network (IMN) was established by the former Coalition Provisional Authority (CPA) to replace the Ministry of Information following the ousting of the former regime. The IMN established new television and both FM and AM radio stations. In January 2004 the CPA announced that a consortium led by the US-based Harris Corpn had been awarded the contract to take over from the IMN the control of 18 television channels, two radio stations and the *Al-Sabah* daily newspaper.

Iraqi Media Network (IMN): Baghdad; e-mail info@imn.iq; internet www.imn.iq; f. 2003.

Al-Iraqiya Television: Baghdad; internet www.imn.iq/pages/ iraqia-tv; terrestrial and satellite television.

Iraq Media Network—Southern Region: internet www.imnsr .com.

Republic of Iraq Radio: Baghdad; e-mail rir.info@ iraqimedianet.net; internet www.imn.iq/pages/radio-iraqia/.

Radio

Hawler Radio: Shorsh St, Next to Shangri-La Hotel, Arbil; tel. 7507361177 (mobile); e-mail hawlerradio@yahoo.com; internet www .hawlerradio.com; Kurdish—language; covers Arbil, D'hok, Kirkuk and Sulaimaniya.

Radio Dijla: House 3, Hay al-Jamia Zone 635/52, Baghdad; tel. (0) 533-271-901; e-mail post@radiodijla.com; internet www.radiodijla .com; f. 2004; privately owned; first talk radio station to be established in post-invasion Iraq; also broadcasts music programmes; Founder Dr AHMAD AL-RIKABI.

Voice of Iraq: Baghdad; e-mail admin@voiraq.com; internet www .voiraq.com; f. 2003; privately owned AM radio station; broadcasts music, news and current affairs programmes in Arabic, Turkmen and English.

Other independent radio stations include Radio Al Bilad, Radio Nawa, Radio Shafak and Sumer FM.

Television

Al Sharqiya: 10/13/52 Karrada Kharj, Baghdad; tel. (88216) 6775-1380 (satellite); e-mail alsharqiya@alsharqiya.com; internet www .alsharqiya.com; f. 2004; privately owned; independent; broadcasts news and entertainment programming 24 hours a day terrestrially and via satellite; Founder and CEO SAAD AL-BAZZAZ.

Alsumaria TV: POB 3311, Baghdad; tel. and fax (1) 717-6023; e-mail communication-department@alsumaria.tv; internet www .alsumaria.tv; f. 2004; privately owned, independent satellite network; broadcasts news, entertainment and educational programming 24 hours a day.

Finance

(cap. = capital; res = reserves; dep. = deposits; brs = branches; m. = million; amounts in Iraqi dinars, unless otherwise stated)

All banks and insurance companies in Iraq, including all foreign companies, were nationalized in July 1964. The assets of foreign companies were taken over by the state. In May 1991 the Government announced its decision to end the state's monopoly in banking, and during 1992–2000 17 private banks were established; however, they were prohibited by the former regime from conducting international transactions. Following the establishment of the Coalition Provisional Authority in 2003, efforts were made to reform the state-owned Rafidain and Rashid Banks, and in October the Central Bank allowed private banks to begin processing international transactions. In January 2004 the Central Bank of Iraq announced that three foreign banks—HSBC and Standard Chartered (both of the United Kingdom), and the National Bank of Kuwait—had been awarded licences to operate in Iraq, the first such licences awarded for 40 years. A further five foreign banks had also been granted licences by mid-2005. There were six public sector and 37 private sector banks operating in Iraq in 2011.

BANKING

Central Bank

Central Bank of Iraq (CBI): POB 64, al-Rashid St, Baghdad; tel. (1) 816-5170; fax (1) 816-6802; e-mail cbi@cbi.iq; internet www.cbi.iq; f. 1947 as Nat. Bank of Iraq; name changed as above 1956; has the sole right of note issue; cap. 100,000m., res 246,026m., dep. 28,479,125m. (Dec. 2009); Gov. Dr ABD AL-BASET TURKI SAEED; 4 brs.

State-owned Commercial Banks

Rafidain Bank: POB 11360, Banks St, Baghdad; tel. (1) 816-0287; fax (1) 816-5035; e-mail emailcenter9@yahoo.com; internet www .rafidain-bank.org; f. 1941; cap. 25,000m., res 203,198m., dep. 30,021,687m. (Dec. 2012); Dir-Gen. HABIB ZIA ALCKHEON; 147 brs in Iraq, 8 brs abroad.

Rashid Bank: al-Rashid St, Baghdad; tel. (1) 818-8921; fax (1) 882-6201; e-mail natbank@uruklink.net; internet www.rasheedbank .gov.iq; f. 1988; cap. 2,000m., res 39,628m., dep. 15,938,638m. (Dec. 2011); total assets US $750m. (2003); Chair. KADHIM M. NASHOOR; 161 brs.

Private Commercial Banks

Babylon Bank: al-Amara St, Baghdad; tel. (1) 717-3686; fax (1) 719-1014; e-mail info@babylonbank-iq.com; internet www .babylonbank-iq.com; f. 1999; cap. and res 31,310m., total assets 89,981m. (Dec. 2007); Chair. MUHAMMAD QASSIM AL-NADOSI; Gen. Dir TARIQ ABD AL-BAKI ABOUD; 6 brs.

Bank of Baghdad: POB 3192, al-Karada St, Alwiya, Baghdad; tel. (1) 717-5007; fax (1) 717-5006; internet www.bankofbaghdad.com; f. 1992; 50.6% stake owned by Burgan Bank (Kuwait); cap. 175,000m., res 7,153m., dep. 1,046,719m. (Dec. 2012); Chair. IMAD ISMAEL SHARIF; Man. Dir ADNAN AL-CHALABI; 5 brs.

Commercial Bank of Iraq PSC (CBIQ): Saadoun St, Alwiya, Baghdad; tel. (1) 740-5583; fax (1) 718-4312; e-mail cb.iraq@ ahliunited.com; internet www.ahliunited.com/bh_aub_cbiq.html; f. 1992; Ahli United Bank BSC (Bahrain) acquired 49% stake in Dec. 2005; cap. US $60m., dep. $59.6m., total assets $124.3m. (2006); Chair. FAHAD AL-RAJAAN; CEO and Man. Dir ADEL A. AL-LABBAN; 10 brs.

Credit Bank of Iraq: POB 3420, Saadoun St, Alwiya, Baghdad; tel. (1) 718-2198; fax (1) 717-0156; e-mail creditbkiq@yahoo.com; internet www.creditbankofiraq.com; f. 1998; 75% owned by Nat. Bank of Kuwait SAK, 10% by World Bank's Int. Finance Corpn and

15% by private investors; cap. 1,250m., res 528m., dep. 16,376.9m. (Dec. 2002); Chair. FOUAD M. MUSTAFA; Man. Dir BASIL H. AL-DHAHI; 12 brs.

Gulf Commercial Bank: POB 3101, nr Baghdad Hotel, Saadoun St, Alwiya, Baghdad; tel. (1) 719-8534; fax (1) 778-8251; e-mail admn@ gulfbankiraq.com; f. 2000; cap. 37,500m. (Jan. 2009); Chair. ABU TALIB HASHIM; 14 brs.

National Bank of Iraq (al-Ahli al-Iraqi Bank): Saadoun St, nr Firdos Sq., Baghdad 11194; tel. (1) 717-7735; e-mail info@nbirq.com; internet www.nbirq.com; f. 1995; 61.9% owned by Capital Bank of Jordan; cap. 250,000m. (Dec. 2013); Chair. TALAL FANAR AL-FAISAL; 3 brs.

Sumer Commercial Bank: POB 3876, Hay al-Riad, Section 908, St 16, Baghdad; tel. (1) 719-6472; internet www.sumerbankiq.com; cap. 10,200m., res 531m., dep. 7,500m. (Aug. 2005); Chair. KHALIL KHAIRALLAH S. AL-JUMAILI; Man. Dir FOUAD HAMZA AL-SAEED; 9 brs.

Specialized Banks

Agricultural Co-operative Bank of Iraq: POB 2421, al-Rashid St, Baghdad; tel. (1) 886-4768; fax (1) 886-5047; e-mail agriculturalcoopbank@yahoo.com; internet www.agriculturalbank .gov.iq; f. 1936; state-owned; Dir-Gen. MUHAMMAD H. AL-KHAFAJI; 32 brs.

Basra International Bank for Investment: Watani St, Ashar, Basra; tel. (40) 616955; internet www.basrahbank.net; cap. 55,000m., res 10,320m., dep. 110,850m. (Dec. 2007); Chair. HUSSEIN GHALIB KUBBA; Man. Dir HASSAN GHALIB KUBBA; 12 brs.

Dar el-Salaam Investment Bank: POB 3067, al-Saadoun Park 103/41/3, Alwiya, Baghdad; tel. (1) 719-6488; e-mail info@desiraq .com; internet www.desiraq.com; f. 1999; 70.1% share acquired by HSBC (United Kingdom) in 2005; total assets 35,562m. (Aug. 2005); 14 brs.

Economy Bank for Investment and Finance (EBIF): 14 Ramadan St, al-Mansour Sq., Baghdad; tel. (1) 298-7712; fax (1) 298-7713; e-mail info@economybankiraq.com; internet www .economybankiraq.com; f. 1997; CEO HOUSSAM OBEID ALI; 23 brs.

Industrial Bank of Iraq: POB 5825, al-Sinak, Baghdad; tel. (1) 887-2181; fax (1) 888-3047; e-mail bank2004@maktoob.com; f. 1940; state-owned; total assets US $34.7m. (2003); Dir-Gen. BASSIMA ABD AL-HADDI AL-DHAHIR; 9 brs.

Investment Bank of Iraq: POB 3724, 902/2/27 Hay al-Wahda, Alwiya, Baghdad; tel. (1) 719-9042; fax (1) 719-8505; e-mail info@ ibi-bankiraq.com; internet www.ibi-bankiraq.com; f. 1993; cap. 100,000m., res 7,819m., dep. 193,307m. (Dec. 2012); Chair. HUSSEIN SALIH SHARIF; Gen. Man. HAMZA DAWOUD SALMAN HALBOUN; 18 brs.

Iraqi Islamic Bank for Investment and Development: 609/18/67, al-Mansour, Baghdad; tel. (1) 416-4939; fax (1) 414-0697; e-mail info@iraqiislamicb.com; internet www.iraqiislamicb.com; f. 1992; Chair. Dr TARIQ KHALAF AL-ABDULLAH.

Iraqi Middle East Investment Bank: POB 10379, Bldg 65, Hay Babel, 929 Arasat al-Hindiya, Baghdad; tel. (1) 717-5545; e-mail cendep@iraqimdlestbank.com; internet www.iraqinet.net/com/3/ mdlestbank.htm; f. 1993; cap. 100,000m., res 12,172m., dep. 505,117m. (Dec. 2011); Man. Dir M. F. AL-ALOOSI; Exec. Man. SUDAD A. AZIZ; 19 brs.

Kurdistan International Bank for Investment and Development: 70 Abd al-Salam Barzani St, Arbil; tel. (66) 223-0822; fax (66) 253-1369; e-mail info@kibid.com; internet www.kibid.com; f. 2005; private bank; cap. 300,000m., res 67,912m., dep. 574,719m. (Dec. 2012); Chair. SALAR MUSTAFA HAKIM; 4 brs.

Mosul Bank for Development and Investment: POB 1292, al-Markaz St, Mosul; tel. (60) 813-090; fax (60) 815-411; e-mail mosul_bank@yahoo.com; internet www.mosulbank.com.

Real Estate Bank of Iraq: POB 8118, 29/222 Haifa St, Baghdad; tel. (1) 885-3212; fax (1) 884-0980; e-mail estatebank194@yahoo.com; internet www.reb-iraq.com; f. 1949; state-owned; gives loans to assist the building industry; acquired the Co-operative Bank in 1970; total assets US $10m. (2003); Dir-Gen. ABD AL-RAZZAQ AZIZ; 25 brs.

United Bank for Investment: 906/14/69, al-Wathiq Sq., Hay al-Wehda, Baghdad; tel. (1) 888-112; e-mail unitedbank2004@yahoo .com; internet www.unitedbank–iq.net; f. 1995; cap. 250,000m., res 9,717m., dep. 246,693m. (Dec. 2012); Chair. IBRAHIM HASSAN AL-BADRI; Man. Dir ZIAD ABBAS HASHEM; 8 brs.

Warka Bank for Investment and Finance: POB 3559, 902/14/50, Hay al-Wehda, Baghdad; tel. (1) 717-4970; fax (1) 717-9555; e-mail info@warka-bank-iq.com; internet www.warka-bank.com; f. 1999; private bank; cap. 24,000m. (2006); Chair. and CEO SAAD SAADOUN AL-BUNNIA; 130 brs.

Trade Bank

Trade Bank of Iraq (TBI): POB 28445, Bldg 20, St 1, 608 al-Yarmouk District, Baghdad; tel. (1) 543-3561; fax (1) 543-3560;

e-mail info@tbiraq.com; internet www.tbiraq.com; f. 2003 by fmr Coalition Provisional Authority to facilitate Iraq's exports of goods and services and the country's reconstruction; independent of Cen. Bank of Iraq; cap. US \$427m., res \$240m., dep. \$13,700m. (Dec. 2011); Chair. HAMDIYAH MAHMOOD FARAJ AL-JAFF; 7 brs.

INSURANCE

Iraqi Insurance Diwan: Ministry of Finance, 147/6/47 Hay al-Eloom, Baghdad; tel. (1) 416-8030; e-mail IraqiInsuranceDiwan@iraqinsurance.org; internet www.iraqinsurance.org; f. 2005 as independent regulator for the insurance sector.

Ahlia Insurance Co: al-Tahreeat Sq., Baghdad; tel. (790) 4565829 (mobile); e-mail info@aic-iraq.com; internet www.aic-iraq.com; f. 2001; privately owned; general, marine, engineering, motor, health and life insurance; Chair. SAADOUN KUBBA; Gen. Man. SAADOUN M. KHAMIS AL-RUBAI.

Al-Hamra'a Insurance Co: POB 10491, Karrada, Baghdad; tel. (1) 717-7573; fax (1) 717-7574; e-mail info@alhamraains.com; internet www.alhamraains.com; f. 2001; private co; general and life insurance; CEO Dr YASIR RAOOF.

Iraq Insurance Co: POB 989, Khaled bin al-Walid St, Aqaba bin Nafi Sq., Baghdad; tel. (1) 719-2185; fax (1) 719-2606; state-owned; life, fire, accident and marine insurance.

Iraq Reinsurance Co: POB 297, Aqaba bin Nafi Sq., Khalid bin al-Waleed St, Baghdad; tel. (1) 719-5131; fax (1) 719-1497; e-mail iraqre@yahoo.com; f. 1960; state-owned; transacts reinsurance business on the international market; Chair. and Gen. Man. SAID ABBAS M. A. MIRZA.

National Insurance Co: POB 248, National Insurance Co Bldg, al-Khullani St, Baghdad; tel. (1) 885-3026; fax (1) 886-1486; f. 1950; state-owned; cap. 20m.; all types of general and life insurance, reinsurance and investment; Chair. and Gen. Man. MUHAMMAD HUSSAIN JAAFAR ABBAS.

STOCK EXCHANGE

Iraq Stock Exchange (ISX): Baghdad; tel. 7711211522 (mobile); fax (1) 717 4461; e-mail info-isx@isx-iq.net; internet www.isx-iq.net, f. 2004, following the closure of the fmr Baghdad Stock Exchange by the Coalition Provisional Authority in March 2003; 84 cos listed in Jan. 2015; CEO TAHA AHMAD AL-RUBAYE.

Trade and Industry

DEVELOPMENT ORGANIZATION

Iraq Foreign Investment Board: e-mail info@ishtargate.org; internet www.ishtargate.org; seeks to attract inward private sector investment into Iraq and to stimulate domestic capital resources for growth and innovation, as well as promote Iraqi businesses; Senior Advisor WILLIAM C. DAHM.

CHAMBERS OF COMMERCE

Federation of Iraqi Chambers of Commerce: POB 3388, Saadoun St, Alwiya, Baghdad; tel. (1) 717-1798; fax (1) 719-2479; e-mail ficcbaghdad@yahoo.com; internet www.ficciraqbag.org; f. 1969; all 18 Iraqi chambers of commerce are affiliated to the Federation; Chair. JAAFAR AL-HAMADANI.

Arbil Chamber of Commerce and Industry: Chamber of Commerce and Industry Bldg, Aras St, Arbil; tel. (66) 2222014; e-mail erbilchamberofcommerce@yahoo.com; internet www.erbilchamber .org; f. 1966; Chair. DARA JALIL KHAYAT.

Baghdad Chamber of Commerce: POB 5015, al-Sanal, Baghdad; tel. (1) 880-220; fax (1) 816-3347; e-mail baghdad_chamber@yahoo .com; internet www.baghdadchamber.com; f. 1926; Chair. AMJAD ABD AL-KARIM AL-JUBURI.

Basra Chamber of Commerce: Manawi Pasha, Ashar, Basra; tel. (40) 614630; e-mail info@bcoc-iraq.net; internet www.bcoc-iraq.net; f. 1926; Chair. MAKKI HASSAN HAMADI AL-SUDANI.

Kirkuk Chamber of Commerce: Kirkuk; e-mail kirkukchamber@yahoo.com; f. 1957; Chair. SABAH AL-DIN MUHAMMAD AL-SALIHI.

Mosul Chamber of Commerce: POB 35, Mosul; tel. (60) 774771; fax (60) 771359; e-mail mcc19262000@yahoo.com; Chair. MUKBIL SIDIQ AL-DABAGH.

Sulaimaniya Chamber of Commerce and Industry: Sulaimaniya; e-mail info@sulcci.com; internet www.sulcci.com; Chair. HASSAN BAQI HORAMI.

EMPLOYERS' ORGANIZATION

Iraqi Federation of Industries: 191/22/915 al-Zaweya, Karada, Baghdad; tel. (1) 778-3502; fax (1) 776-3041; e-mail info@fediraq.org;

internet www.fediraq.org; f. 1956; 35,000 mems; Pres. HASHIM THANOUN AL-ATRAKCHI.

PETROLEUM AND GAS

Ministry of Oil: Oil Complex Bldg, Port Said St, Baghdad; tel. (1) 727-0710; e-mail oilministry@oil.gov.iq; internet www.oil.gov.iq; merged with INOC in 1987; affiliated cos: Oil Marketing Co, Oil Projects Co, Oil Exploration Co, Oil Products Distribution Co, Iraqi Oil Tankers Co, Gas Filling Co, Oil Pipelines Co, Iraqi Drilling Co, North Oil Co, South Oil Co, Missan Oil Co, North Refineries Co, Midland Refineries Co, South Refineries Co, North Gas Co, South Gas Co.

Iraq National Oil Co (INOC): POB 476, Khullani Sq., Baghdad; tel. (1) 887-1115; f. 1964; reorg. upon nationalization of Iraq's petroleum industry, and became solely responsible for exploration, production, transportation and marketing of Iraqi crude petroleum and petroleum products; merged with Ministry of Oil in 1987, and remained under its authority following the overthrow of the regime of Saddam Hussain in 2003; draft legislation providing for the reconstitution of INOC as an independent entity was approved by the Council of Ministers in July 2009; under the proposed reorganization, INOC would be responsible for the management and development of Iraq's petroleum industry and would assume control of the existing state-run oil and gas cos.

UTILITIES

Electricity

Electricity production in Iraq has been greatly diminished as a result of the US-led military campaign in 2003, subsequent looting and sabotage by Baathist loyalists, and disruptions in fuel supplies to power stations. Power outages are common, especially in Baghdad and the surrounding area, and the Government has resorted to power-rationing. With ongoing reconstruction of the means of generation, transmission and distribution, the Ministry of Electricity was achieving peak production levels of 6,750 MW by early 2009, supplying intermittent power for only 14 hours per day.

Water

The Ministry of Water Resources manages the supply of water throughout Iraq. Water resources are diminishing, and a large-scale investment programme is currently under way, which includes funding for new dam and irrigation projects, repairs to damaged facilities, and improvements in technology. Following years of neglect during the period of UN sanctions, infrastructure has also been damaged since the US-led military campaign in 2003, largely as a result of vandalism and looting. The Baghdad Water Authority is responsible for the management of water resources in the capital.

TRADE UNIONS

General Federation of Iraqi Workers (GFIW): POB 3049, Tahrir Sq., al-Rashid St, Baghdad; fax (1) 670-4200; e-mail abdullahmuhsin@iraqitradeunions.org; internet www .iraqitradeunions.org; f. 2005 by merger of Gen. Fed. of Trade Unions, Gen. Fed. of Trade Unions of Iraq (an offshoot of the former) and Iraqi Fed. of Workers' Trade Unions; covers all of Iraq's provinces except the three Kurdish Autonomous Regions; Pres. ALI RAHEEM ALI; Vice-Pres. HADI ALI LAFTA.

There are also unions of doctors, pharmacologists, jurists, writers, journalists, artists, engineers, electricity and railway workers.

Transport

RAILWAYS

In 2010 the total length of Iraqi railways was 2,025 route-km. A line covers the length of the country, from Rabia, on the Syrian border, via Mosul, to Baghdad (534 km), and from Baghdad to Basra and Umm Qasr (608 km), on the Persian (Arabian) Gulf. A 404-km line links Baghdad, via Radi and Haditha, to Husaibah, near the Iraqi–Syrian frontier. Baghdad is linked with Arbil, via Khanaqin and Kirkuk, and a 252-km line (designed to serve industrial projects along its route) runs from Kirkuk to Haditha, via Baiji (though this was rendered out of action in mid-2006, as a result of bombing by US forces). A 638-km line runs from Baghdad, via al-Qaim (on the Syrian border), to Akashat (with a 150-km line linking the Akashat phosphate mines and the fertilizer complex at al-Qaim). A regular international service between Baghdad and İstanbul, Turkey, was suspended following the US-led invasion in 2003; however, services on a section of the line, between Mosul and Gaziantep, resumed in early 2010. Passenger rail services between Mosul and Aleppo, Syria, resumed in August 2000 after an interruption of almost 20 years, but were closed again in 2004 after repeated insurgent attacks. Passenger rail services between Baghdad and Basra resumed in late 2007, and a Baghdad–Ramadi passenger service recommenced in May 2009. The railway system was due to be repaired and upgraded as part of the reconstruction of Iraq following the removal from power of Saddam Hussain's regime in 2003. Eventually, it was planned that the system would be divided, with the infrastructure being kept as a state asset, while operations were to be privatized. It was reported in 2006 that the Ministry of Transportation hoped to add an additional 2,300 km to the existing rail network, although concerns remained over funding. In 2013 the French company Alstom signed a contract with the Baghdad Governorate for the design and construction of the first phase of a monorail project in the capital city. Upon completion, the first phase of the monorail will comprise a 25-km line with 14 stations, at an estimated cost of US $1,500m.

General Co for Railways: Ministry of Transportation, nr Martyr's Monument, Karradat Dakhil, Baghdad; e-mail iraqitransport@yahoo.com; internet www.scr.gov.iq.

Iraqi Republic Railways Co (IRRC): West Station, Baghdad; tel. (1) 537-0011; e-mail d1_g_office@iraqrailways.com; internet www.iraqrailways.com; f. 1914; Dir-Gen. RAFIL YUSSEF ABBAS.

ROADS

In 2012, according to estimates by the International Road Federation, Iraq's road network extended over 59,623 km.

The most important roads are: Baghdad–Mosul–Tel Kotchuk (Syrian border), 521 km; Baghdad–Kirkuk–Arbil–Mosul–Zakho (border with Turkey), 544 km; Kirkuk–Sulaimaniya, 160 km; Baghdad–Hilla–Diwaniya–Nasiriya–Basra, 586 km; Baghdad–Kut–Nasiriya, 186 km; Baghdad–Ramadi–Rurba (border with Syria), 555 km; Baghdad–Kut–Umara–Basra–Safwan (border with Kuwait), 660 km; and Baghdad–Baqaba–Kanikien (border with Iran). Most sections of the six-lane, 1,264-km international Express Highway, linking Safwan (on the Kuwaiti border) with the Jordanian and Syrian borders, had been completed by June 1990. Studies have been completed for a second, 525-km Express Highway, linking Baghdad and Zakho on the Turkish border. A complex network of roads was constructed behind the war front with Iran in order to facilitate the movement of troops and supplies during the 1980–88 conflict. The road network was included in the US-led coalition's programme of reconstruction following the ousting of the Baathist regime in 2003.

Iraqi Land Transport Co: Baghdad; internet sclt.gov.iq; f. 1988 to replace State Org. for Land Transport; fleet of more than 1,000 large trucks; Dir-Gen. ABBAS OMRAN MUSA.

State Organization for Roads and Bridges: POB 917, Karradat Mariam, Karkh, Baghdad; tel. (1) 32141; responsible for road and bridge construction projects under the Ministry of Construction and Housing.

SHIPPING

The ports of Basra and Umm Qasr are usually the commercial gateway of Iraq. They are connected by various ocean routes with all parts of the world, and constitute the natural distribution centre for overseas supplies. The Iraqi General Company for Maritime Transport maintains a regular service between Basra, the Persian (Arabian) Gulf and north European ports. There is also a port at Khor al-Zubair, which came into use in 1979.

For the inland waterways, there are 1,036 registered river craft, 48 motor vessels and 105 motorboats.

The port at Umm Qasr was heavily damaged during the early part of the US-led coalition's campaign to oust Saddam Hussain. A large-scale project to redevelop the port is under way. In July 2009 contracts to lease and develop new commercial berths at Umm Qasr were awarded to two foreign port operators. In February 2011 the UAE-based firm Gulftainer signed a US $150m. contract to construct and operate a dry port north of Umm Qasr. In August 2012 16 bids were received for the first phase in the construction of a new deep-sea port at Faw in Basra province. It was anticipated that the new $6,300m. facility would, upon completion, replace Umm Qasr as Iraq's main commercial port.

At 31 December 2014 Iraq's flag registered fleet totalled 84 vessels, with an aggregate displacement of 139,965 grt, of which two were fish carriers and five were general cargo ships.

Port and Regulatory Authorities

General Co of Iraqi Ports (IPA): Malik bin Dinar St, Basra; tel. (40) 041-3211; e-mail info@scp.gov.iq; internet scp.gov.iq; Dir-Gen. OMRAN RADI.

State Enterprise for Iraqi Water Transport: POB 23016, Airport St, al-Furat Quarter, Baghdad; f. 1987, when State Org. for Iraqi Water Transport was abolished; responsible for the planning, supervision and control of six nat. water transportation enterprises, incl. General Co for Maritime Transport (see below).

Principal Shipping Companies

Arab Bridge Maritime Navigation Co: Aqaba, Jordan; tel. (3) 2092000; fax (3) 2092001; e-mail info@abmaritime.com.jo; internet www.abmaritime.com.jo; f. 1987; jt venture by Egypt, Iraq and Jordan to improve economic co-operation; an expansion of the co established a ferry link between the ports of Aqaba, Jordan, and Nuweibeh, Egypt, in 1985; six vessels; cap. US $75m. (2010); Chair. SALMAN SADDAM JASEM; Vice-Chairs. Eng. LAITH DABABNEH, Capt. HASSAN ABD AL-QADER FALAH; Man. Dir HUSSEIN AL-SOUOB.

General Co for Maritime Transport: POB 13038, al-Jadriya al-Hurriya Ave, Baghdad; Basra office: POB 766, 14 July St, Basra; tel. (1) 776-3201; e-mail watertrans@motrans.gov.iq; internet scmt.gov.iq; f. 1952 as State Enterprise for Maritime Transport; renamed as above 2009; Dir-Gen. SAMIR ABD AL-RAZZAQ.

Gulf Shipping Co: POB 471, Basra; tel. (40) 776-1945; fax (40) 776-0715; f. 1988; imports and exports goods to and from Iraq.

Al-Masar al-Iraqi Co LLC: Manawi Pasha St, nr Manawi Pasha Hotel, POB 85885, Basra; tel. 7704926113 (mobile); e-mail operation@iraqilogistic.com; internet www.iraqilogistic.com; provides a range of freight and shipping agency services.

CIVIL AVIATION

There are international airports at Baghdad, Basra and Mosul. Baghdad's airport, previously named Saddam International Airport, reopened in August 2000, after refurbishment necessitated by damage sustained during the war with the multinational force in 1991. However, international air links were virtually halted by the UN embargo imposed in 1990. Internal flights, connecting Baghdad to Basra and Mosul, recommenced in November 2000. In April 2003 the capital's airport was renamed Baghdad International Airport by US forces during their military campaign to oust the regime of Saddam Hussain. Following a programme of reconstruction, the airports at Baghdad and Basra were reopened to commercial flights from late 2003; Mosul International Airport reopened for civilian flights in December 2007. The expansion of Arbil International Airport (including the construction of a new passenger terminal and runway) was completed in mid-2010. In July 2008 Al-Hamza airport in Najaf (formerly a military airport) was inaugurated for civilian use, as increasing numbers of pilgrims were visiting the shrines of that holy city.

Iraq Civil Aviation Authority (ICAA): Baghdad; tel. 7905-319779 (mobile); fax (1) 543-0689; e-mail info@iraqcaa.com; internet www.iraqcaa.com; f. 1987; Dir-Gen. Capt. NASER HUSSEIN BANDAR.

Iraqi Airways Co: Baghdad International Airport, Baghdad; tel. (1) 537-2002; e-mail info@iraqiairways.co.uk; internet www.iraqiairways.co.uk; f. 1945; operates flights to other Arab countries, Iran, Turkey, Greece and Sweden; Dir-Gen. Capt. SAAD AL-KHAFAJY.

Tourism

Arrivals of foreign nationals totalled 891,836 in 2013; tourist receipts in 2012 were estimated at US $2,281m. Following the US-led invasion of Iraq in 2003, the site housing the ruins of the ancient civilization of Babylon became part of a US military base; several other places of interest became military or refugee camps, and, amid the protracted period of conflict since 2003, tourists have been deterred from visiting the country's many cultural and religious sites. Nevertheless, in August 2006 the relatively peaceful Kurdish Autonomous Region launched a tourism campaign, with advertisements broadcast on US television. Since 2008 religious tourism has been growing, with increasing numbers of pilgrims using the newly renovated airport in Najaf (see Transport) to visit the Islamic holy shrines of both that city and nearby Karbala.

Iraq Tourism Board: POB 7783, Haifa St, Baghdad; tel. (1) 543-3912; Chair. HAMOUD MOHSEN AL-YACOUBI.

Defence

The US-led Coalition Provisional Authority (CPA) dissolved Iraq's armed forces and security organizations in place under Saddam Hussain in May 2003, following the ousting of the regime in the previous month. In August the CPA promulgated the establishment of the New Iraqi Army.

Chief of Staff of the Joint Armed Forces: Lt-Gen. KURSHID RASHID.

Commander of the Ground Forces: Lt-Gen. RIAD AL-KOTAIRI.

Commander of the Air Force: Lt-Gen. ANWAR HAMAD AMIN AHMAD.

Commander of the Navy: Rear Adm. ALI HUSSEIN ALI.

Defence Budget (2014): ID 22,000,000m.

Total Armed Forces (as assessed at November 2014): 177,600: army 100,000; navy 3,600; air force 5,000; air defence 4,000 plus 65,000 support; At November 2013, there were 531,000 Ministry of the Interior Forces (including 302,000 members of the Iraqi Police Service, 44,000 members of the Iraqi Federal police, 95,000 members of the Facilities Protection Service, 60,000 members of the Border Enforcement forces and 30,000 members of the Oil Police).

Education

Following the establishment of the Republic in 1958, there was a marked expansion in education at all levels, and spending on education increased substantially. During the mid-1970s free education was established at all stages from pre-primary to higher, and private education was abolished; all existing private schools were transformed into state schools. However, military conflict and economic sanctions during the 1980s and 1990s undermined much of the progress made in education during the previous two decades.

Primary education, beginning at six years of age, lasts for six years. Enrolment at primary schools of children in the relevant age-group had declined to 76% by 1995, but reportedly rose again, to 91%, in 2000/01. According to UNESCO estimates, in 2006/07 enrolment at primary schools included 88% of pupils in the relevant age-group. Secondary education, from 12 years of age and lasting for up to six years, is divided into two cycles of three years each. Enrolment at secondary schools in 2006/07 included some 43% of children in the appropriate age-group, according to UNESCO. Following the change of regime in Iraq in April 2003, a comprehensive reform of the country's education system was implemented. In the 2011/12 academic year there were estimated to be 20,715 primary and secondary schools in Iraq, with a total enrolment of 7,335,678 pupils. There are 43 technical institutes and colleges, two postgraduate commissions and 20 universities. In 2002/03 there were approximately 240,000 undergraduates attending institutions of higher education. In 2010 government expenditure on education amounted to US $4,310m., equivalent to 6.0% of total government spending.

IRELAND

Introductory Survey

LOCATION, CLIMATE, LANGUAGE, RELIGION, FLAG, CAPITAL

Ireland consists of 26 of the 32 historic counties that comprise the island of Ireland. The remaining six counties, in the north-east, form Northern Ireland, which is part of the United Kingdom. Ireland lies in the Atlantic Ocean, about 80 km (50 miles) west of Great Britain. The climate is mild and equable, with temperatures generally between 0°C (32°F) and 21°C (70°F). Irish (Gaeilge) is the official first language, but its use as a vernacular is now restricted to certain areas, collectively known as the Gaeltacht, mainly in the west of Ireland. English is the second official language and is almost universally spoken. The majority of the inhabitants profess Christianity: about 84% of the population are Roman Catholics. The national flag (proportions 1 by 2) consists of three equal vertical stripes, of green, white and orange. The capital is Dublin.

CONTEMPORARY POLITICAL HISTORY

Historical Context

The whole of Ireland was formerly part of the United Kingdom. In 1920 the island was partitioned, the six north-eastern counties remaining part of the UK, with their own government. In 1922 the 26 southern counties achieved dominion status, under the British Crown, as the Irish Free State. The dissolution of all remaining links with Great Britain culminated in 1937 in the adoption of a new Constitution, which gave the Irish Free State full sovereignty within the Commonwealth. Formal ties with the Commonwealth were ended in 1949, when the 26 southern counties became a republic. The partition of Ireland remained a contentious issue, and in 1969 a clandestine organization, calling itself the Provisional Irish Republican Army (IRA—see United Kingdom), initiated a violent campaign to achieve reunification.

Domestic Political Affairs

At the general election of February 1973, the Fianna Fáil party, which had held office, with only two interruptions, since 1932, was defeated. Jack Lynch, who had been Taoiseach (Prime Minister) since 1966, resigned, and Liam Cosgrave formed a coalition between his own party, Fine Gael, and the Labour Party. The Irish Government remained committed to power-sharing in the six counties, but opposed any British military withdrawal from Northern Ireland. Following the assassination of the British Ambassador to Ireland by the Provisional IRA in July 1976, the Irish Government introduced stronger measures against terrorism. Fianna Fáil won the general election of June 1977 and Lynch again became Prime Minister. He resigned in December 1979 and was succeeded by Charles Haughey. In June 1981, following an early general election, Dr Garret FitzGerald of Fine Gael became Prime Minister in a coalition of Fine Gael and the Labour Party. However, the rejection by the Dáil (the lower house of the legislature) of the coalition's budget proposals precipitated a further general election in February 1982, in which Haughey was returned to power. The worsening economic situation, however, made the Fianna Fáil Government increasingly unpopular, and in November Haughey lost the support of two independent members of the Dáil, precipitating an early general election, at which Fianna Fáil failed to gain an overall majority. In December FitzGerald formed a new Fine Gael-Labour Party coalition.

During 1986 FitzGerald's coalition lost support, partly due to the formation of a new party, the Progressive Democrats (PD), by disaffected members of Fianna Fáil. A government proposal to end a constitutional ban on divorce was defeated by national referendum in June and a series of defections led to the loss of the coalition's parliamentary majority. In January 1987 the Labour Party refused to support Fine Gael's budget proposals and the coalition collapsed. Following a general election in February, Fianna Fáil, led by Haughey, formed a minority Government.

Prior to the general election of June 1989 Fine Gael and the PD concluded an electoral pact to oppose Fianna Fáil. Severe reductions in public expenditure and continuing problems of unemployment and emigration eroded Fianna Fáil's electoral support, and it obtained only 77 of the 166 seats in the Dáil, while Fine Gael won 55 seats and the PD six seats. Following lengthy negotiations, a Fianna Fáil-PD coalition Government, led by Haughey, was formed.

In October 1991 the Government narrowly defeated a motion of no confidence, prompted by a series of financial scandals involving public officials. In November, however, a group of Fianna Fáil members of the Dáil proposed a motion demanding Haughey's removal as leader of the party. Albert Reynolds, the Minister for Finance and a former close associate of Haughey, and Pádraig Flynn, the Minister for the Environment, announced their intention to support the motion, and were immediately dismissed from office. The attempt to depose Haughey was defeated by a substantial majority of the Fianna Fáil parliamentary grouping. However, the PD made their continued support of the Government conditional on Haughey's resignation. In February 1992 Reynolds replaced Haughey as leader of Fianna Fáil and assumed the premiership.

In June 1992 the leader of the PD, Desmond O'Malley, criticized Reynolds' conduct as Minister for Industry and Commerce before a parliamentary inquiry into allegations of fraud and political favouritism during 1987–88. In October 1992, in his testimony to the inquiry, the Prime Minister accused O'Malley of dishonesty. Following Reynolds' refusal to withdraw the allegations, in early November the PD left the coalition, and the Government was defeated on the following day in a motion of no confidence. A general election took place in November, concurrent with three constitutional referendums on abortion. Fianna Fáil and Fine Gael both suffered a substantial loss of support, while the Labour Party more than doubled its seats and the PD increased its representation. Following prolonged negotiations, in January 1993 Fianna Fáil and the Labour Party agreed to form a coalition Government. Reynolds retained the premiership, while Dick Spring, the leader of the Labour Party, was allocated the foreign affairs portfolio, as well as the post of Deputy Prime Minister (Tánaiste).

In November 1994 the Labour Party withdrew from the coalition after Reynolds and the Fianna Fáil members of the Cabinet approved the appointment of the Attorney-General, Harry Whelehan, to the High Court, in the absence of the Labour Party ministers, who had opposed Whelehan's nomination. Reynolds relinquished the Fianna Fáil leadership and was succeeded by the Minister for Finance, Bertie Ahern. Whelehan, meanwhile, resigned as President of the High Court. Following extensive talks, a new coalition of Fine Gael, the Labour Party and a small party, the Democratic Left, took office in December. The leader of Fine Gael, John Bruton, became Prime Minister, while Spring regained the role of Deputy Prime Minister and Minister for Foreign Affairs.

In November 1996 the Minister for Transport, Energy and Communications, Michael Lowry, resigned following allegations that he had received personal financial gifts from a business executive, Ben Dunne. During 1997 an inquiry into other political donations by Dunne revealed that payments totalling some IR£1.3m. had been made to Haughey during his premiership. Haughey later admitted the allegations, although he insisted that he had no knowledge of the donations until he resigned from office.

The Government of Bertie Ahern

At a general election held in June 1997 none of the main political parties secured an overall majority in the Dáil and Sinn Féin (the political wing of the IRA) won its first seat. After Bruton conceded that he could not form a majority coalition administration, Ahern formed a Government composed of Fianna Fáil and the PD. The leader of the PD, Mary Harney, was appointed Deputy Prime Minister. In September the President, Mary Robinson, who had been elected in November 1990 as an independent candidate, resigned from her position in order to assume the role of United Nations High Commissioner for Human Rights. In the ensuing election in October 1997, the Fianna Fáil candidate, Dr Mary McAleese, was elected President (the country's first head of state from Northern Ireland), receiving 45.2% of the first-preference votes cast.

During 2000 independent judicial inquiries investigating corruption among politicians implicated many senior political figures. An inquiry into planning irregularities in County Dublin in the early 1990s, headed by Justice Feargus Flood, heard that the Fine Gael leader, Bruton, knew that a member of his party had demanded payment for voting in favour of a planning decision, and had himself benefited from the decision. In January 2001 Fine Gael members of the Dáil passed a motion of no confidence in Bruton, who resigned as party leader. He was replaced by Michael Noonan, a former Minister for Health and Children. In March 2001 the inquiry revealed that former Minister for Foreign Affairs Ray Burke had held money in offshore accounts while a minister, and had conducted international financial transactions without first requesting the necessary permission from the Central Bank. He also admitted to misleading the Dáil regarding his financial affairs. Moreover, in September 2002 Justice Flood reported that Burke had received several 'corrupt payments' between 1974 and 1989. Ahern came under intense political pressure regarding his appointment of Burke as Minister for Foreign Affairs. Justice Alan Mahon replaced Flood as chairman of the Tribunal in June 2003. In December Burke was formally charged with making false tax returns, and in January 2005 he was sentenced to six months' imprisonment.

Meanwhile, a new tribunal chaired by Justice Michael Moriarty was established to investigate further payments made to politicians and the sources of specific offshore bank accounts that had been used by Haughey. In May 2000 the tribunal heard that between 1979 and 1996 Haughey had received payments totalling IR£8.5m., a much larger figure than had previously been acknowledged. In March 2003 Haughey agreed to pay the Revenue Commissioners €5m. in settlement of his outstanding tax liabilities resulting from undisclosed payments made to him. Haughey died in June 2006. A subsequent report by Justice Moriarty stated that, between 1979 and 1996, funds totalling IR£9.1m. had been made available for Haughey's personal use.

In June 2001 a referendum was held on the ratification of the Treaty of Nice, which proposed structural reforms to the institutions of the European Union (EU, see p. 271) prior to the enlargement of the Union from 2004. The treaty was rejected by 53.9% of those who voted, an embarrassing reverse for the Government, which had campaigned in favour of it. The defeat was attributed to fears that ratification of the treaty would result in Irish participation in the EU's proposed rapid reaction force, thus undermining Ireland's neutrality, and concerns that Ireland would receive reduced funding and assistance from the EU. The Government suffered a further reverse when, at a referendum on abortion held in March 2002, 50.4% of the electorate voted against proposals to remove the constitutional protection of the lives of suicidal pregnant women wishing to terminate their pregnancies, and would have made abortion a criminal offence.

The elections of 2002 and 2007

At the general election in May 2002 Fianna Fáil increased its parliamentary representation to 81 seats, and thus only narrowly failed to achieve an overall majority in the Dáil. Fine Gael won only 31 seats, while the PD and Sinn Féin increased their representation to eight seats and five seats, respectively, and the Green Party obtained six seats. Noonan resigned as leader of Fine Gael and was succeeded by Enda Kenny. In the same month Fianna Fáil and the PD concluded a new coalition agreement, following which Ahern was re-elected Prime Minister.

In June 2002 the Government won support at an EU summit meeting for formally declaring that Ireland's participation in the EU rapid reaction force would be limited to those operations with a UN mandate, approved by the Government and sanctioned by the Dáil. For their part, Ireland's EU partners issued a complementary declaration reiterating that neither the Treaty of Nice nor previous EU treaties compromised Ireland's traditional neutrality and that no member state envisaged the rapid reaction force as a future European army. At a referendum in October, 62.9% of participating voters approved the final ratification of the Treaty of Nice, and the prohibition of Irish participation in any future common European defence force.

At another referendum in June 2004 a constitutional amendment removing the automatic entitlement to Irish citizenship of children born in Ireland (including Northern Ireland) was approved by 79.2% of voters. The plebiscite followed a ruling by the Irish Supreme Court in the previous year, which declared that non-national parents of Irish-born children were not entitled to live in Ireland by virtue of having an Irish-born child. The Government had endorsed the amendment, citing the need to deter immigrants from exploiting Irish law to gain entitlement to residency in any EU member state. Ireland was the only EU country with an automatic right to citizenship at birth, which had been enshrined in the Constitution in 1999 as a consequence of the Good Friday Agreement for peace in Northern Ireland (see *The peace process in Northern Ireland*).

At the general election held on 24 May 2007 Fianna Fáil remained the largest party in the Dáil, with 78 seats. Fine Gael increased its representation substantially, to 51 seats, while the Labour Party won 20 seats and the Green Party six. Sinn Féin's representation declined to four seats, and that of the PD to only two. In June 2007 a coalition agreement was signed between Fianna Fáil, the PD and the Green Party, under the premiership of Ahern.

In September 2007 a vote of no confidence in Ahern, brought by Fine Gael and the Labour Party in response to concerns about the veracity of evidence he had presented to the Mahon tribunal, concerning his personal finances, was defeated. (From September 2006 the tribunal had investigated allegations that, during his period of office as Minister for Finance between 1991 and 1993, Ahern had granted favours in return for loans or donations.)

The Government of Brian Cowen

In April 2008 Ahern announced his resignation as Prime Minister and leader of Fianna Fáil. Brian Cowen, Deputy Prime Minister and Minister for Finance, was elected unopposed as leader of Fianna Fáil, and was duly elected as Prime Minister by the Dáil on 7 May.

On 12 June 2008 a referendum was held on the ratification of the Treaty of Lisbon, which sought to reform the institutions of the EU and was intended to supersede the defunct EU constitutional treaty. Despite a campaign in favour of ratification supported by all the principal political parties except Sinn Féin, the treaty was rejected by 53.4% of those who voted. Widespread public uncertainty about the implications of the treaty, and concerns that it might compromise Ireland's neutrality or affect its policies on taxation or ethical issues, such as abortion, were thought to have contributed to the result.

In November 2008 the PD voted at its conference to dissolve the party, after the leadership argued that it had no viable future. The PD, which had espoused many controversial liberal policies, on issues such as divorce and contraception, was formally disbanded in November 2009. The sole PD member of the Cabinet, Harney, retained her ministerial position as an independent.

During 2008 it became clear that the economic prosperity enjoyed by Ireland over the previous decade was coming to an end. Affected by the international credit crisis and the economic decline that was being experienced throughout much of the developed world, the Irish economy became the first in the eurozone to move into recession. Property prices, which had increased dramatically during the decade to 2006, when Irish banks made large loans to developers and builders for speculative projects, now declined rapidly. In September 2008 the Government announced that it would guarantee the deposits in six banks and building societies. In January 2009 it was obliged to nationalize Anglo Irish Bank (which had specialized in large-scale lending for property development) in order to maintain market confidence, and in February it agreed to provide new capital for Allied Irish Banks and the Bank of Ireland. In April the Government announced the establishment of a National Asset Management Agency (NAMA), which would purchase non-performing loans at a discount. Meanwhile, unpopular austerity measures were announced as part of the budget for 2009. Despite failing to reach an agreement with the Irish Congress of Trade Unions, the Government announced further austerity measures, including a pension levy on the wages of public sector workers.

In June 2009 Cowen announced that a second referendum on the Treaty of Lisbon would be held in October. The European Council had agreed on a document intended to address Irish concerns over the treaty, including formal guarantees, which were to be given force of law by their incorporation into the next EU accession treaty, to the effect that the Treaty of Lisbon would in no way affect any member state's neutrality or its competencies in relation to taxation or family law. At the referendum, on 2 October, ratification of the treaty was approved by 67.1% of voters, with 59.0% of the electorate participating. It was believed that the economic crisis had contributed to the strong increase in support for the treaty by strengthening popular enthusiasm for EU membership.

In October 2009 the Ceann Comhairle (Chairman) of the Dáil, John O'Donoghue of Fianna Fáil, was forced to resign following revelations of his extravagant official expenses. Séamus Kirk, also of Fianna Fáil, was elected to replace him. The incident represented a further loss of authority for the Government, which in August had lost its official majority in the Dáil after two Fianna Fáil members resigned from the parliamentary party in protest at the closure of a hospital unit in their constituency. In November some 250,000 public sector workers staged a strike in protest against proposed pay reductions and other austerity measures. The Government was weakened further in February 2010 by the resignation of Willie O'Dea, the Minister for Defence, and Trevor Sargent, a Minister of State and the former leader of the Green Party, over improprieties.

Financial assistance from the EU and the IMF

During 2010 hopes of an economic recovery proved premature: levels of unemployment and emigration remained high, while the enormous cost to taxpayers of alleviating the banking crisis, necessitating substantial reductions in other budgetary spending, caused considerable resentment. In September fresh assistance for Allied Irish Banks, Anglo Irish Bank and the Irish Nationwide Building Society brought the total cost of supporting the financial system to at least €45,000m.; in addition, Irish banks owed some €130,000m. to the European Central Bank. By October the total budgetary deficit for 2010, including support for the banks, was estimated to be equivalent to 32% of gross domestic product (GDP—compared with the limit of 3% required by the EU). Meanwhile, the cost to Ireland of borrowing on the international bond markets increased as a result of uncertainty over the country's financial stability. Minister for Finance Brian Lenihan insisted that the programme of support for the banks was now complete and that the cost was manageable, that a four-year austerity programme would restore the budgetary deficit to acceptable levels, and that Ireland was not about to default on its debts. Nevertheless, under pressure from other EU governments, anxious to ensure the stability of the euro, in November the Irish Government finally made a formal application for financial assistance from the EU and the IMF, and was granted support totalling €85,000m. The UK, Sweden and Denmark also pledged assistance in the form of bilateral loans. Of this total, Ireland itself was to provide €17,500m. from its National Pension Reserve Fund and from cash reserves. The assistance was conditional upon a reorganization of the banking system, and upon the four-year budgetary adjustment programme that aimed to reduce the budgetary deficit to less than 3% of GDP by 2015. The budget for 2011 envisaged savings of €6,000m., with reductions in welfare, public sector pensions and the minimum wage, together with tax increases and the introduction of taxation for the lower-paid. The bailout agreement was widely perceived as a national humiliation and as imposing an unfair burden on the least well-off.

The 2011 general election

In November 2010 the Green Party, deploring the proposed economic adjustment programme, announced that it would leave the coalition by the end of January 2011. The budget was adopted in December with the support of independent members. In January 2011 Cowen's principal critic within Fianna Fáil, the Minister for Foreign Affairs, Micheál Martin, resigned from his post and urged Cowen to resign, following revelations about previously undisclosed contacts with Sean Fitzpatrick, the former chairman of Anglo Irish Bank, prior to the Government's controversial guarantee to the banks in September 2008. However, Cowen, who denied any impropriety, retained the leadership of Fianna Fáil in a self-imposed vote of confidence among party members in the legislature. Cowen attempted to reorganize the Cabinet, replacing five other ministers who had resigned on the grounds that they would not be candidates in the forthcoming general election to be held on 11 March. However, the Green Party refused to accept the reorganization and Cowen was obliged to withdraw the appointments and transfer the former ministers' portfolios to other members of the Cabinet. Following further loss of support within Fianna Fáil, on 22 January he resigned as leader of the party, while stating that he would remain as Prime Minister until the election. The Green Party then withdrew from the coalition, although it undertook to support the remaining budgetary legislation (on which depended the release of funds from the emergency assistance provided by the EU and the IMF). Later in January Martin was elected leader

of Fianna Fáil. On 1 February Cowen announced the dissolution of the legislature and the holding of a general election on 25 February

At the general election in February 2011, Fine Gael won 76 seats, while the Labour Party also increased its representation to 37 seats. Fianna Fáil secured only 20 seats (having won 78 in 2007), and its former coalition partner, the Green Party, lost all six of the seats it had held. Sinn Féin won 14 seats (compared with four in 2007). Fine Gael and the Labour Party agreed to form a coalition Government, with Enda Kenny, the leader of Fine Gael, as Prime Minister. Kenny announced a Cabinet of 10 Fine Gael and five Labour members. Eamon Gilmore, the leader of the Labour Party since 2007, became Deputy Prime Minister and Minister for Foreign Affairs and Trade. Michael Noonan (Fine Gael) was appointed Minister for Finance, while some of the previous responsibilities of this post were transferred to a new Ministry for Public Expenditure and Reform, allocated to Brendan Howlin (Labour). The new administration undertook to renegotiate the terms of the assistance programme that had been agreed with the EU and the IMF (in particular the high interest rates being charged on some of the loans), while implementing for at least two years most of the austerity measures introduced by the previous Government in order to reduce the budget deficit.

Recent developments: the Enda Kenny Government

During 2011 the IMF acknowledged the Irish Government's 'resolute implementation' of the economic adjustment programme, reporting that the reduction of the budgetary deficit and the restructuring of the banking sector were proceeding according to schedule. Moderate economic growth was resumed, although unemployment remained high. In February 2012 it was announced that it would be legally necessary to hold a referendum on a proposed EU 'fiscal compact' (the Treaty on Stability, Co-ordination and Governance) whereby participating countries would accept legally binding limits on future budgetary deficits, and incur penalties imposed by the European Court of Justice if they exceeded the limits. Kenny urged approval of the treaty (which he signed in March, as did representatives of all other EU governments except the Czech Republic and the UK) as being in the national interest. Fianna Fáil and the Green Party also declared their support. Sinn Féin urged voters to reject the treaty, declaring that approval would represent a vote for austerity. At the referendum, in May, the treaty was approved by 60.3% of those voting.

In October 2011 a presidential election was held, to replace Mary McAleese after the expiry of her second term of office. The successful candidate was Michael D. Higgins, a former Labour member of the Dáil.

In July 2011, meanwhile, the latest in a series of reports on the sexual abuse of children by Roman Catholic clergy in Ireland was published. The report, dealing with the Cloyne diocese, stated that diocesan officials, including the former bishop, had not followed the Church's own guidelines on reporting suspected abusers to the police. Kenny strongly criticized the Vatican's alleged role in concealing the extent of the abuse. Widespread support for his stance suggested a profound change in the nation's traditionally deferential attitude to the Church. The Papal Nuncio (the diplomatic representative of the Holy See in Ireland) was recalled for consultations and later replaced. In May 2012 the leader of the Roman Catholic Church in Ireland, Cardinal Sean Brady, was criticized by senior politicians following accusations that he had failed to respond adequately to allegations of child abuse perpetrated by a priest in the 1970s; the Cardinal made a public apology to the victims, but rejected demands to resign. In November a referendum was held on amending the Irish Constitution to include provisions on the state's responsibilities in protecting the rights and welfare of children: some 58% of those voting approved the amendment, which was supported by all the main political parties. In February 2013, following the publication of an official report into the Magdalene Laundries (workhouses run by religious orders), Kenny made a formal apology on behalf of the state for its role in forcibly consigning some 10,000 women and girls between 1922 and 1996 to work in the laundries without pay. The discovery in mid-2014 of the remains of some 800 babies and young children at the site of a former home for unmarried mothers in Tuam, County Galway, run by religious orders between 1926 and 1961, prompted further questions about the role of the Roman Catholic Church in alleged historical human rights abuses.

In March 2012 the report of the Mahon tribunal on allegations of corruption in development planning (originally the Flood tribunal, initiated in 1997) was finally published: it found that corrupt payments had been received by the former minister and European Commissioner Pádraig Flynn and by two former Fianna Fáil members of the Dáil. Although the tribunal did not find that the former Prime Minister, Bertie Ahern, had received corrupt payments, it stated that he had failed truthfully to explain the source of money in his bank accounts. Ahern denied any wrongdoing, but after Fianna Fáil began proceedings to expel him for 'conduct unbecoming', he resigned from the party, as did Flynn. The Government referred the tribunal's report to the police.

During 2013 there was controversy over proposed changes to Ireland's legislation on abortion, which had hitherto only permitted the practice when the mother's physical or mental health was endangered; a credible threat of suicide was now proposed as additional grounds for abortion. Bishops of the Roman Catholic Church condemned the proposal as morally unacceptable, but the Government maintained that it was intending to clarify, rather than change, the law; supporters of the bill pointed out that, in any case, hundreds of Irish women were travelling to Britain for abortions every year. The legislation was approved by the Dáil in July.

In October 2013 a referendum took place on the proposed abolition of the upper house of the legislature, the Seanad (Senate) as part of the Government's programme of institutional reforms. The Government argued that the body was ineffectual, the selection process for members unsatisfactory, and that abolition would save some €20m. a year in public expenditure. Opponents argued that the Seanad played a useful role in amending legislation. Despite support for abolition by all the main political parties except Fianna Fáil, 51.7% of those voting rejected the proposal, a result viewed as an embarrassment for the Government. In the same referendum, voters approved the establishment of a Court of Appeal to hear appeals from the High Court (hitherto heard by the Supreme Court).

During 2013 and 2014 representatives of the EU and the IMF continued to report favourably on Ireland's restructuring of its banking system and on the implementation of austerity measures to reduce its budgetary deficit, but the social cost of this success was high, with the rate of unemployment remaining above 11% during 2014, while some 400,000 people had emigrated from Ireland during the five years to early 2014. In December 2013 Ireland made a formal exit from the bailout programme: the Minister for Finance, Noonan, while celebrating the fact that Ireland had been 'handed back her purse' warned that austerity policies would have to continue in order to reduce the still unacceptably high public debt and budgetary deficit. New charges introduced for water (which had previously been financed by central and local government taxes) during 2014 were among the most unpopular measures, prompting a series of demonstrations. In December an estimated 100,000 people surrounded the Dáil to protest against the imposition of the charges and some become involved in clashes with the police. The Government promised to help pensioners with the charge but insisted that the policy would remain.

Meanwhile, at local and European elections in May 2014 the Labour Party performed badly, reflecting wider popular dissatisfaction with the governing coalition. Gilmore resigned immediately after the elections and was replaced by Joan Burton as Labour Party leader and Deputy Prime Minister.

The announcement by Kenny in December 2014 of a referendum on the introduction of same-sex marriage appeared to acknowledge the increased acceptance of liberal social attitudes among the Irish people. Despite strong opposition from the Catholic Church, the proposal was supported by all the main political parties and, according to opinion polls, by a majority of the electorate. Moreover, in the following month, the Minister of Health, Leo Varadkar, became the first member of an Irish government publicly to announce his homosexuality. The referendum, which was also to include a proposal to lower the minimum age for presidential candidates from 35 to 21 years, was scheduled to take place on 22 May 2015.

The peace process in Northern Ireland

Consultations between the UK and Ireland on the future of Northern Ireland resulted, in November 1985, in the signing of the Anglo-Irish Agreement, which provided for regular participation in Northern Ireland affairs by the Irish Government on political, legal, security and cross-border matters. The Agreement maintained that no change in the status of Northern Ireland would be made without the assent of the majority of its population. The terms of the Agreement were approved by

both the Irish and the UK Parliaments. Under the provisions of the Agreement, the Irish Government pledged co-operation in enhanced cross-border security, in order to suppress IRA operations. Despite underlying tensions, the ensuing co-ordination between the Garda Síochána (Irish police force) and the Northern Ireland police force, the Royal Ulster Constabulary (RUC), was broadly successful. In February 1989 a permanent joint consultative assembly, comprising 25 British MPs and 25 Irish members of the Dáil, was established. The representatives were selected in October. The assembly's meetings, the first of which began in February 1990, were to take place twice a year, alternately in Dublin and London.

In May 1990, following a British Government initiative, the unionists agreed to hold direct discussions with the Irish Government, an unprecedented concession. Discussions on the restoration of devolution to Northern Ireland (abandoned in 1974) between the Northern Ireland parties commenced in June 1991, with the inclusion of the Irish Government in April and September 1992. The principal point of contention was the unionists' demand that Ireland hold a referendum on Articles 2 and 3 of its Constitution, which laid claim to the territory of Northern Ireland. Ireland was unwilling to make such a concession except as part of an overall settlement. The negotiations formally ended in November.

In October 1993 the new Irish Prime Minister, Albert Reynolds, and his British counterpart, John Major, issued a joint statement setting out the principles on which future discussions were to be based, including, notably, that Sinn Féin permanently renounce violence before being admitted to the negotiations. In December the Prime Ministers jointly issued the Downing Street Declaration, which referred to the possibility of a united Ireland and accepted the legitimacy of self-determination, but insisted on majority consent within Northern Ireland. While Sinn Féin and the unionist parties considered their response to the Declaration, Reynolds received both groups' conditional support for his proposal to establish a 'Forum for Peace and Reconciliation', which was to encourage both sides to end violent action. In August 1994 the IRA announced that it had ceased all military operations; this was followed in October by a similar suspension on the part of loyalist organizations.

An international panel, chaired by George Mitchell (a former US Senator), recommended in January 1996 that weapons decommissioning should take place in parallel with all-party talks, and that their destruction should be monitored by an independent commission. The British and Irish Governments accepted those recommendations, but the Irish Government rejected proposals for elections to be held to a Northern Ireland assembly, which would provide the framework for all-party negotiations. In February 1996, following a bomb explosion in London, the British and Irish Governments suspended official contacts with Sinn Féin.

In May 1997 the Irish Prime Minister, John Bruton, met the newly elected British premier, Tony Blair, and the new Secretary of State for Northern Ireland, Mo Mowlam, and a fresh initiative to proceed with weapons decommissioning, while simultaneously pursuing negotiations for a constitutional settlement, was announced. In July the newly elected Irish Prime Minister, Bertie Ahern, confirmed his commitment to the peace initiative. Following the IRA's subsequent restoration of its ceasefire, the Irish Government reinstated official contacts with Sinn Féin and resumed the policy of considering convicted IRA activists for early release from prison. Sinn Féin agreed to accept the outcome of the peace process and to renounce violence, providing for the party's participation in all-party talks. A procedural agreement to pursue negotiations in parallel with the decommissioning of weapons (which was to be undertaken by an Independent International Commission on Decommissioning—IICD, led by Gen. John de Chastelain of Canada) was signed by all the main parties later in September.

On 10 April 1998 the two Governments and eight political parties involved in the talks signed the Good Friday (or Belfast) Agreement at Stormont Castle in the Northern Irish capital. Immediately thereafter the two Governments signed a new British-Irish Agreement, replacing the Anglo-Irish Agreement, committing them to enact the provisions of the Good Friday Agreement, subject to its approval at referendums to be held in Ireland and Northern Ireland in May. The peace settlement provided for changes to the Irish Constitution (notably Articles 2 and 3) and to British constitutional legislation to enshrine the principle that a united Ireland could be achieved only with the consent of the majority of the people of both Ireland and Northern

Ireland. The Good Friday Agreement provided for a new Northern Ireland Assembly and Executive Committee, together with North/South and British-Irish institutions. In addition, provision was made for the early release of paramilitary prisoners affiliated to organizations that established a complete and unequivocal ceasefire. On 22 May, at referendums held simultaneously in Ireland and Northern Ireland, 94.4% and 71.1% of voters, respectively, voted in favour of the Good Friday Agreement.

Elections to the Assembly were conducted in June 1998; the Assembly convened in July and elected the leader of the Ulster Unionist Party (UUP), David Trimble, as First Minister. The peace process was threatened with disruption by sectarian violence and by the detonation of an explosive device in August in Omagh, Northern Ireland by a republican splinter group, the Real IRA, which caused 29 deaths. A dispute between unionists and Sinn Féin concerning weapons decommissioning meant that the deadlines for the formation both of the Executive Committee and the North/South body, and for the devolution of powers to the new Northern Ireland institutions, were not met. In June 1999 the two Prime Ministers presented a compromise plan that envisaged the immediate establishment of the Executive Committee prior to the surrender of paramilitary weapons, with the condition that Sinn Féin guarantee that the IRA complete decommissioning by May 2000. Negotiations effectively collapsed in July 1999 and a review of the peace process, headed by George Mitchell, began in September. In November Mitchell secured agreement providing for the devolution of powers to the Executive Committee, after the IRA committed to enter discussions with the IICD. On 2 December power was officially transferred to the new Northern Ireland Executive. On the same day, in accordance with the Good Friday Agreement, the Irish Constitution was amended to remove the state's territorial claim over Northern Ireland.

In December 1999 the Irish Cabinet attended the inaugural meeting, in Armagh, of the North South Ministerial Council. The British and Irish Governments engaged in intensive negotiations in an effort to avert the collapse of the peace process, which was threatened by the IRA's failure to disarm. Despite assurances given by the IRA that its ceasefire would not be broken, in February 2000 legislation came into effect returning Northern Ireland to direct rule. The IRA subsequently announced its withdrawal from discussions with the IICD. Following the resumption of direct talks between the Irish and British Governments in May 2000, the IRA offered to 'initiate a process that will completely and verifiably put arms beyond use' and on 30 May power was again transferred to the Northern Ireland institutions.

In July 2001 Trimble resigned as First Minister in protest at the lack of progress on IRA decommissioning; Sir Reg Empey assumed the role of acting First Minister. A package of non-negotiable proposals presented by Ahern and Blair did not meet with the approval of the pro-Agreement parties, and on 10 August the British Government suspended the Assembly for 24 hours, thereby delaying the appointment of a new First Minister for a further six weeks. The Assembly was again suspended on 22 September as the deadlock continued, and in October the three UUP ministers and two Democratic Unionist Party (DUP) ministers resigned. Having retracted its offer to 'put arms beyond use' in August, the IRA resumed the process in October, and the IICD confirmed the 'significant' disposal of IRA weapons. The unionist ministers therefore reassumed their posts and Trimble was re-elected as First Minister. In November the RUC was replaced by the Police Service of Northern Ireland (PSNI).

In October 2002 Sinn Féin's offices at the Assembly were raided by police, who suspected that the IRA had infiltrated the Northern Ireland Office and gained access to large numbers of confidential documents. In consequence, Northern Ireland was returned to direct rule. Blair and Ahern announced that the devolved institutions would only be restored if Sinn Féin ended its link with paramilitary organizations. The IRA responded by suspending all contact with the IICD. Talks aimed at resolving the impasse continued into 2003. The IRA failed to respond to the British Government's demand for a definitive cessation of paramilitary activities, and in May Blair postponed the elections to the Assembly indefinitely. In the same month the British and Irish Governments published a Joint Declaration containing their proposals for reinstating the Northern Ireland institutions and demanding a full and permanent cessation of all paramilitary activity. Talks continued, and in October, following further

acts of decommissioning of IRA weapons, elections to the Assembly were scheduled for the following month.

At elections to the Assembly in November 2003, the DUP secured 30 of the 108 seats, thus becoming the largest party. In talks with Ahern in January 2004 the leader of the DUP, Rev. Ian Paisley, remained insistent that his party would not conduct direct talks with Sinn Féin until the IRA had disbanded. In May Blair and Ahern agreed the basis of a 'roadmap' to restore the suspended Northern Ireland Assembly and Executive by October. A DUP demand for changes to the functioning of the Assembly and the Executive before it would enter a government with Sinn Féin led to deadlock in September. The British and Irish Governments passed their proposals for restoring the power-sharing Executive to the DUP and Sinn Féin for consultation in November.

In February 2005 Ahern and Blair warned the IRA that its failure to demilitarize was the only obstacle to reaching an agreement on power-sharing; the following day the IRA withdrew its commitment to decommissioning. However, in July the IRA announced the end of its armed campaign and in September the IICD confirmed that the IRA's weapons had been fully decommissioned. Talks with the Northern Ireland parties continued during early 2006.

On 15 May 2006 the Assembly was restored; however, there were no nominations for the roles of First Minister and Deputy First Minister. In October the International Monitoring Commission (IMC) reported that, despite the IRA's commitment to the peace process, members both of loyalist and republican paramilitary groups continued to engage in criminal activity. The DUP remained sceptical concerning the progress of the disbandment of the IRA. On 13 October, following talks in St Andrews, Scotland, Ahern and Blair announced an agreement (the St Andrews Agreement) that was intended to precipitate the restoration of a power-sharing Executive, and set a deadline of 10 November by which the Northern Ireland main parties were to agree to adhere to its provisions, which included support by all parties for the PSNI and the Northern Ireland Policing Board, and the formation of a North-South Inter-parliamentary Forum. Devolution was restored on 24 November when the Assembly convened; however, Paisley refused to accept his nomination as First Minister, while hinting that he would assume the role after elections, scheduled to be held in early March 2007, should Sinn Féin formally signal its support for the PSNI and the Policing Board. Following lengthy discussions, Sinn Féin voted to support the policing institutions in January.

In elections to the Assembly on 7 March 2007 the DUP secured 36 seats and Sinn Féin 28, thereby confirming their status as the main parties in Northern Ireland. On 26 March Paisley and the Sinn Féin President, Gerry Adams, held their first direct meeting, during which an agreement was reached for a power-sharing Executive, which was duly installed on 8 May. Paisley became First Minister and Sinn Féin's Martin McGuinness was appointed as Deputy First Minister. Meanwhile, in April Bertie Ahern met Paisley in Dublin to discuss arrangements for future co-operation between the Executive and the Irish Government.

From mid-2009 the functioning of the Executive was disrupted by disagreements between Sinn Féin and the DUP (led since June 2008 by Peter Robinson, who had also succeeded Paisley as First Minister) over a timetable for the transfer of powers over policing and justice, which constituted the final area of responsibility due to be devolved under the Good Friday Agreement. In January 2010, following the collapse of negotiations between the two parties aimed at ending the impasse, Brian Cowen (Irish Prime Minister from May 2008) and his British counterpart, Gordon Brown, travelled to Belfast in order to mediate in the dispute. After intensive talks, the DUP and Sinn Féin concluded an agreement that envisaged the transfer of policing and justice powers to the Executive on 12 April; the agreement also addressed other issues of contention between the parties, including a mechanism for resolving disputes over the routes of traditional parades by Protestant orders. The transfer of powers took place as scheduled on 12 April, when the Assembly elected a Minister of Justice to form part of the Executive.

During 2010–13 police in the Irish Republic seized weapons and explosives in a number of raids on suspected dissident republicans who were believed to be planning violent attacks in Northern Ireland in protest at the peace process. A Northern Ireland police officer was killed in an explosion in Omagh in April 2011, for which the Provisional IRA claimed responsibility. In November 2012 a Northern Ireland prison officer was murdered by a group calling itself the IRA, believed to be an amalgamation of dissident republican groups. In November 2013 the report of a long-running inquiry into the murder of two senior RUC officers by the Provisional IRA in 1989 was finally submitted to the Dáil: the inquiry, chaired by Justice Peter Smithwick, had been established by the Irish legislature in 2005 to investigate allegations that members of the Garda Síochána had colluded in the killings by alerting the perpetrators to the whereabouts of the RUC officers. The report concluded that there had been collusion by the Garda, but did not identify any individual officer as responsible.

Ongoing sectarian tensions in Northern Ireland were illustrated by violent street protests in Belfast in December 2012 after the city council voted to fly the Union flag on official buildings only for 18 days per year, instead of daily: the Union flag and the Irish tricolour flag, displayed officially and unofficially, had become emotive symbols for unionists and nationalists respectively. Violent actions attributed to dissident republicans continued in 2013, and stocks of weapons, ammunition and explosives believed to have been amassed by them were discovered by police on both sides of the border. In May the First Minister and Deputy First Minister announced the formation of a panel comprising members of the five parties represented in the Northern Ireland Executive, to consider ways of reducing sectarianism and promoting reconciliation. The panel began its work in July under the chairmanship of Richard Haass, an American diplomat who had been the US special envoy to Northern Ireland in 2001–03. It considered three sources of division, namely parades, commemorations and related protests; flags and emblems; and contending with the past (referring chiefly to the lack of prosecutions for almost 3,300 of the killings, totalling some 3,500, that had taken place during the 'Troubles'). A draft agreement produced in December proposing the replacement of the existing Parades Commission by an Office for Parades, Select Commemorations and Related Protests, which could refer contentious events to an Authority for Public Events Adjudication. The panel admitted failure to reach consensus on the display of flags and emblems, but proposed establishing a Commission on Identity, Culture and Tradition to hold public discussions on such matters. It also recommended the establishment of a Historical Investigations Unit to examine past sectarian violence, leading to prosecution where the evidence warranted it, and an Independent Commission for Information Retrieval to allow victims and survivors access to information about conflict-related events, while providing informants with limited immunity from prosecution, since the information provided would not be admissible as evidence in court. An Implementation and Reconciliation Group would be established to monitor the agreement's implementation.

The Haass agreement was accepted by the Social Democratic and Labour Party (SDLP—see United Kingdom) and Sinn Féin, but elements of it were rejected by the unionist parties. The process was severely affected in February 2014 when a judge at the High Court in London ruled that a former IRA member, John Downey, could not be prosecuted in connection with the deaths of four members of the Household Cavalry in a bomb attack in Hyde Park, London, in July 1982, because Downey had received a letter from the British Northern Ireland Office in 2007 stating that he would not face criminal charges in Northern Ireland and (mistakenly) that he was not wanted for questioning by any other police force in the UK. To the outrage of unionists it was then revealed that, under an agreement between the British Government and Sinn Féin, similar letters had been sent to more than 180 paramilitary republicans who were suspected of having committed conflict-related crimes, including suspects linked to some 300 murders, before the Good Friday Agreement (or had been convicted and later escaped): the aim was to clarify the legal status of so-called 'On the Runs'. An investigation into the affair, led by Lady Justice Hallett, concluded in July 2014 that the scheme was 'unprecedented and flawed' with 'significant systemic failures' but that the letters were lawful and did not constitute an amnesty for those who received them. However, in September the British Secretary of State for Northern Ireland, Theresa Villiers, stated that former IRA members who had received the letters should no longer rely upon them as a defence, as their accuracy had subsequently been called into question. In late 2014 Villiers and Irish foreign minister Charlie Flanagan took part in 10 weeks' of cross-party talks aimed at resolving some of the outstanding issues of identity, particularly relating to parades. These talks were resumed in February 2015.

Meanwhile, a series of counter-terrorism operations during 2014, and the notable discovery of a large cache of explosives near the border in October, indicated the persistence of Irish Republican dissident groups opposed to the peace process.

Foreign Affairs

Ireland became a member of the European Community (EC—now the European Union—EU, see p. 271) in 1973. At a referendum in 1987 the country affirmed its commitment to the EC when, in a referendum, 69.9% of Irish voters supported adherence to the Single European Act, providing for closer economic and political co-operation between EC member states (including the creation of a single market by 1993). In December 1991 Ireland agreed to the far-reaching Treaty on European Union (the Maastricht Treaty). Ireland secured a special provision within the treaty (which was signed by all parties in February 1992), guaranteeing that Ireland's constitutional position on abortion would be unaffected by any future EC legislation. Ratification of the treaty was endorsed at a referendum held in June 1992. A referendum conducted in May 1998 approved the Amsterdam Treaty, which had been signed by EU ministers in October 1997, amending the Maastricht Treaty. The common European currency, the euro, was adopted by Ireland at the beginning of 2002. In October of that year the Treaty of Nice, which provided for the impending enlargement of the EU, was approved in a national referendum, despite having been rejected in an earlier referendum held in 2001. As President of the Council of the European Union, Bertie Ahern led negotiations between the leaders of the member states over a draft constitutional treaty, which was concluded in June 2004. The treaty required ratification by all 25 member states either by parliamentary vote or referendum, and its rejection in national referendums in France and the Netherlands in mid-2005 led to the indefinite postponement of further referendums in EU countries yet to ratify the treaty, including Ireland. During 2007 member states agreed to replace the constitutional treaty with the Treaty of Lisbon, which was rejected at a referendum in Ireland in June 2008. However, the ratification process continued across Europe, and in June 2009 Brian Cowen achieved a series of formal guarantees from the European Council addressing Irish concerns regarding aspects of the treaty. It was approved by a substantial majority at a second referendum in October, and subsequently entered into force across the EU in December.

In July 2006 an amendment to previous defence legislation was promulgated following a vote in the Dáil. Under the amended legislation, Irish troops could join EU 'battlegroups' in emergency humanitarian, reconnaissance and training missions prior to receiving a UN mandate or approval from the Dáil, thus circumventing the so-called 'triple-lock' that required any deployment of Irish troops abroad to be mandated by the UN and approved by the Irish Government and Parliament. However, if either or both declined to approve such a mission, troops would be withdrawn.

In November 2010 the Irish Government accepted emergency assistance from the EU after the country's budgetary deficit far exceeded the limits stipulated by the EU (see *Economic Affairs*). In March 2012 the Government signed the EU Treaty on Stability, Co-ordination and Governance (more often referred to as the 'fiscal compact'), and adherence to the treaty, which envisaged legally binding limits on national budgetary spending, was approved by a national referendum in May.

In May 2011 Queen Elizabeth II paid a state visit to Ireland, becoming the first British monarch to visit the country since its independence. In acts perceived as being of great symbolic importance, the Queen laid wreaths at memorials to those who had died in the struggle for Irish independence, and in the First World War, and in a speech she expressed 'deep sympathy' with victims of the 'troubled past'. The visit was seen as evidence of a more mature and cordial relationship between the two countries, following the successful outcome of the peace process in Northern Ireland. In the following year, during a visit to the UK, Irish Prime Minister Enda Kenny signed a Joint Statement of Co-operation with his British counterpart, David Cameron: the statement referred to a 'uniquely close' relationship between the two countries, and the two Governments undertook to reinforce their co-operation over the next decade, especially with regard to economic recovery, research, energy supply, EU relations and the implementation of the peace agreements for Northern Ireland. In December 2013 Kenny and Cameron jointly visited memorials in Belgium to the dead of the First World War, including those from Ireland who had fought in the British army. In March 2014 Kenny visited London to discuss with Cameron the implementation of the Haass agreement (see *The peace process in Northern Ireland*). President Higgins paid a state visit to the UK in April, the first such visit by an Irish head of state.

Ireland has strong historic links with the USA through emigration, and from 1995 the special envoy of the US President undertook an important diplomatic role in negotiations on the future of Northern Ireland (see *The peace process in Northern Ireland*). The USA is a major trading partner (Ireland's largest individual export market in 2013) and the country's principal source of foreign direct investment, attracted by a skilled English-speaking labour force and a low corporate tax rate: in 2014 there were more than 700 US companies operating in Ireland, employing more than 115,000 people. However, the US Senate criticized Irish taxation policy following an investigation it carried out in mid-2013, which revealed that US technology company Apple had paid less than 2% tax on US $74,000m. of its income by exploiting an anomaly in Irish law allowing corporations to remain 'stateless' for tax purposes. The policy also attracted criticism from the European Commission and from several EU member states, particularly France, which claimed that it amounted to state aid for multinational corporations.

A visit by the then Chinese Vice-President, Xi Jinping, in February 2012, during which various agreements on trade and investment were concluded, indicated that the Chinese Government regarded Ireland as an important entry point in its dealings with the EU. Kenny led a trade mission to China in the following month and in mid-2014 a US $100m. investment fund was created with the aim of assisting Irish technology companies with interests in China. In December 2014 the Chinese President, Xi Jinping, accepted a formal invitation by Irish President Higgins to visit Ireland, although no date was set.

The Irish Government attracted criticism from Israel when in December 2014 the Dáil voted to recognize Palestine as an independent state.

CONSTITUTION AND GOVERNMENT

The Constitution took effect in 1937. Legislative power is vested in the bicameral Oireachtas (National Parliament), comprising the Seanad Eireann (Senate) and the Dáil Eireann (House of Representatives). The Senate has 60 members, including 11 nominated by the Taoiseach (Prime Minister) and 49 indirectly elected for five years. The House of Representatives has 166 members, elected by universal adult suffrage for five years (subject to dissolution) by means of the single transferable vote, a form of proportional representation.

The Uachtarán (President) is the constitutional head of state, elected by direct popular vote for seven years; re-election is permitted only once. Executive power is effectively held by the Cabinet, led by the Prime Minister, who is appointed by the President on the nomination of the Dáil. The President appoints other Ministers on the nomination of the Prime Minister with the previous approval of the Dáil. The Cabinet is responsible to the Dáil.

Local government in Ireland consists of a number of democratically elected local and regional authorities at three levels: two regional assemblies, eight regional authorities and 29 county councils, five city councils, five borough councils and 75 town councils.

REGIONAL AND INTERNATIONAL CO-OPERATION

Ireland is a member of the European Union (EU, see p. 271) and uses the single currency, the euro; however, it does not participate in the Schengen Agreement on open borders. It is a member of the Council of Europe (see p. 250) and the Organization for Security and Co-operation in Europe (OSCE, see p. 385).

Ireland joined the UN in 1955. As a contracting party to the General Agreement on Tariffs and Trade, it joined the World Trade Organization (WTO, see p. 431) on its establishment in 1995. Ireland is also a member of the Organisation for Economic Co-operation and Development (OECD, see p. 377) and participates in the Partnership for Peace framework of the North Atlantic Treaty Organization (NATO, see p. 367).

ECONOMIC AFFAIRS

In 2012, according to estimates by the World Bank, Ireland's gross national income (GNI), measured at average 2010–12 prices, was US $179,390m., equivalent to $39,110 per head (or $35,090 on an international purchasing-power parity basis). During 2004–13, it was estimated, the population increased at an average annual rate of 1.4%, while gross domestic product (GDP) per head decreased, in real terms, by an average of 0.4% per year. According to the World Bank, overall GDP increased, in

real terms, at an average annual rate of 0.9% in 2004–13; in 2012 GDP increased by 0.2%, but decreased by 0.3% in 2013, measured at constant prices. According to chain-linking methodologies, GDP decreased by 0.3% in 2012, but increased by a preliminary 0.2% in 2013.

Agriculture (including forestry and fishing) contributed a preliminary 2.4% of GDP in 2013 and employed an estimated 5.7% of the working population in the third quarter of 2014. Beef and dairy production dominate Irish agriculture. Principal crops include barley, wheat and potatoes. According to UN estimates, agricultural GDP decreased by an average of 3.8% per year during 2004–12; sectoral GDP decreased by 10.0% in 2012. In 2013, according to chain-linking methodologies, agricultural GDP decreased by 3.9% in 2012, but increased by a preliminary 5.5% in 2013.

Industry (comprising mining, manufacturing, construction and utilities) provided a preliminary 23.7% of GDP in 2013 and employed 18.3% of the working population in the third quarter of 2014. Industrial GDP, according to UN estimates, decreased by an average of 1.7% per year during 2004–12; it decreased by 1.5% in 2012. According to chain-linking methodologies, in 2013 industrial GDP decreased by a preliminary 1.4%

Mining (including quarrying and turf production) provided employment to 0.4% of the working population in 2006. Ireland possesses substantial deposits of lead-zinc ore and recoverable peat, both of which are exploited. Natural gas is produced from the Kinsale field off the south coast of Ireland (although production is declining) and from the Seven Heads field that came on stream in 2003. Substantial gas supplies were discovered at the Corrib field situated off the west coast of Ireland; the project was delayed owing to local objections to a proposed pipeline to bring the gas onshore. Small quantities of coal are also extracted. Offshore reserves of petroleum have also been located and several licences awarded to foreign-owned enterprises to undertake further exploration.

According to World Bank estimates, manufacturing contributed 23.1% of GDP in 2012. The manufacturing sector comprises many high-technology, largely foreign-owned, capital-intensive enterprises. In the year to February 2010 the value of manufacturing output declined by 2.6%.

Construction engaged 5.9% of the employed labour force in the third quarter of 2014. According to UN estimates, construction GDP decreased, in real terms, at an average annual rate of 3.8% in 2004–12; sectoral GDP decreased by 7.4% in 2012. The construction sector declined by 6.0% in 2012, but expanded by a preliminary 11.9% in 2013, according to chain-linking methodologies.

Electricity is derived principally from natural gas, which provided 49.7% of total requirements in 2012, while coal provided 20.0% and petroleum 1.5%. There was potential for the further development of wind-generated energy, which was increasing in importance. In 2013 imports of mineral fuels were 13.9% (by value) of total merchandise imports.

Service industries (including commerce, finance, transport and communications and public administration) contributed a preliminary 73.9% of GDP in 2013 and employed 76.0% of the working population in the third quarter of 2014. The financial sector expanded rapidly in the 2000s, however, in 2008–11 there was a crisis in the banking system, following the global financial crisis and the collapse in domestic property prices. Tourism is one of the principal sources of foreign exchange. Revenue from the tourism and travel sector amounted to an estimated €4,610m. in 2011; it decreased to €4,412m. in 2012, but increased to €4,463 in 2013. The GDP of the services sector increased by an average of 2.0% per year during 2004–12, but declined by 0.8% in 2012, according to UN estimates.

In 2013, according to IMF statistics, Ireland recorded a visible merchandise trade surplus of US $49,990m. with a surplus of $14,438m. on the current account of the balance of payments. In 2013 the principal source of imports was the United Kingdom (31.5%). The European Union (EU, see p. 271) as a whole accounted for 64.7% of imports; the USA, Germany, the People's Republic of China and the Netherlands were also important suppliers. The USA was the principal market for exports (21.2%); the EU accounted for 57.0% of exports, while other major purchasers included the UK, Germany and Switzerland. In 2013 principal imports included machinery and transport equipment, chemicals and related products, mineral fuels and lubricants, miscellaneous manufactured articles, and food and live animals. Principal exports included chemicals and related products, miscellaneous manufactured articles, machinery and transport equipment, and food and live animals.

There was a general government deficit of €11,700m. in 2013, equivalent to 6.7% of GDP. Ireland's general government gross debt was €202,920m. at the end of 2013, equivalent to 116.1% of GDP. The annual rate of inflation averaged 1.6% in 2004–13. Consumer prices decreased by 1.7% in 2012 and by 0.5% in 2013. The unemployment rate averaged 11.3% in the third quarter of 2014.

In the late 1990s the Irish economy enjoyed an unprecedentedly high rate of growth, which was attributed largely to prudent fiscal and monetary management and low taxation, aided by a substantial increase in foreign direct investment. Continuing high levels of growth were sustained in 2004–07 by the rapid expansion of the construction sector (assisted by banks and building societies which provided loans on extremely liberal terms) and high levels of consumer spending. However, in 2008 the Irish economy became the first in the eurozone to enter recession, as the effects of the global financial crisis coincided with, and exacerbated, a correction in domestic property prices. The subsequent collapse in property prices and sharp decline in investment led to a contraction in consumer spending, while the high value of the euro against the pound sterling resulted in a decline in exports. Moreover, Ireland's banking sector, which was affected by the lack of available credit caused by the global financial crisis, was also exposed to the collapse in domestic property prices, which resulted in borrowers' inability to meet repayment obligations on lending. The Government's decision in September 2008 to guarantee deposits in six financial institutions, was to require support for the banking system totalling at least €45,000m. Meanwhile, the effects of the downturn led to a rapid deterioration of government finances; the budgetary deficit was equivalent to some 32% of GDP in 2010 (compared with the maximum of 3% stipulated by the EU for countries belonging to the eurozone). Moreover, uncertainty over the country's financial stability meant that the cost to Ireland of borrowing on the international bond markets increased to levels that were widely regarded as unsustainable. In November, under pressure from fellow members of the EU, concerned for the stability of the euro, the Irish Government was finally obliged to make a formal application for assistance from the EU and the IMF. Under the resulting bailout agreement a total of €85,000m. was made available to Ireland, including €10,000m. for the recapitalization of the banks, with a further €25,000m. as a contingency reserve for the banking system. The assistance was conditional upon the restructuring of the banking system, and the adoption of a four-year programme of austerity measures, involving reductions in expenditure of €10,000m. and increases in taxation totalling €5,000m. Successive annual budgets imposed reductions in social benefits, health services and public sector pay, and increases in tax income (including the introduction of income tax for the lower-paid). Ireland's traditionally low rate of corporation tax (12.5%) was maintained, however (despite pressure from other EU member states), in order to encourage foreign investment. In 2011 Ireland's GDP increased by 1.4%, after three years of decline. Monitoring by the European Commission, the European Central Bank (ECB) and the IMF in 2011–13 showed that Ireland was consistently meeting its targets for restructuring the banking system and reducing the budgetary deficit. None the less, the deficit remained high in 2012, at more than 8% of GDP and levels of unemployment exceeded 14% of the labour force. The Government's capital investment programme for 2012–16 aimed to stimulate growth and provide employment, envisaging public and private investment amounting to more than €19,000m. In March 2013 Ireland returned to the international bond markets with a successful sale of 10-year bonds, and in December the country made a formal exit from the EU/IMF assistance programme, a significant step in its economic recovery. However, GDP declined by 0.3% in 2013, before increasing by 4.8% in 2014, although the rate of unemployment remained high at 11.1% in the latter year. The budget for 2015 was the first since the start of the crisis to include an easing of the austerity programme, with modest increases in child benefit and spending on social housing, as well as a small reduction in the upper rate of tax. The introduction of new water charges for all householders proved extremely controversial and prompted large-scale protests. A budget deficit equivalent to 2.7% of GDP was predicted for that year. A marked increase in export revenue, partly attributable to the low value of the euro, contributed to GDP growth of 4.8% in 2014 and a forecast growth rate of 3.5% for 2015. While Ireland's economy was the fastest growing in the eurozone in 2014, its debt remained one of the highest in the EU, equivalent to 115% of GDP.

PUBLIC HOLIDAYS

2016: 1 January (New Year), 17 March (St Patrick's Day), 28 March (Easter Monday), 2 May (May Bank Holiday), 6 June (June Bank Holiday), 1 August (August Bank Holiday), 31 October (October Bank Holiday), 25 December (Christmas Day), 26 December (St Stephen's Day).

Statistical Survey

Source (unless otherwise stated): Central Statistics Office, Skehard Rd, Cork; tel. (21) 4535000; fax (21) 4535555; e-mail information@cso.ie; internet www.cso.ie.

Area and Population

AREA, POPULATION AND DENSITY

Area (sq km)	70,182*
Population (census results)	
23 April 2006	4,239,848
10 April 2011	
Males	2,272,699
Females	2,315,553
Total	4,588,252
Population (official estimates at 30 April)†	
2012	4,585,407
2013	4,593,125
2014‡	4,609,600
Density (per sq km) at 30 April 2014	65.7

* 27,097 sq miles.
† Preliminary.
‡ Rounded figure.

POPULATION BY AGE AND SEX
('000, official estimates at 30 April 2014, preliminary)

	Males	Females	Total
0–14 years	518.0	497.7	1,015.7
15–64 years	1,490.7	1,516.6	3,007.3
65 years and over	271.1	315.6	586.7
Total	**2,279.7**	**2,329.9**	**4,609.6**

Note: Totals may not be equal to the sum of components, owing to rounding.

ADMINISTRATIVE DIVISIONS
(population at 2011 census)

Province/County	Area (sq km)	Population	Density (per sq km)
Connacht	17,713	542,547	30.6
Galway	6,151	250,653	40.7
Galway City . .	51	75,529	1,481.0
Galway County . .	6,010	175,124	29.1
Leitrim	1,589	31,798	20.0
Mayo	5,588	130,638	23.4
Roscommon	2,548	64,065	25.1
Sligo	1,837	65,393	35.6
Leinster	19,774	2,504,814	126.7
Carlow	898	54,612	60.8
Dublin	921	1,273,069	1,382.3
Dublin City . .	118	527,612	4,471.3
Dún Laoghaire-Rathdown . .	127	206,261	1,624.1
Fingal	453	273,991	604.8
South Dublin . .	223	265,205	1,189.3
Kildare	1,694	210,312	124.2
Kilkenny	2,072	95,419	46.1
Laoighis	1,719	80,559	46.9
Longford	1,091	39,000	35.7
Louth	832	122,897	147.7
Meath	2,335	184,135	78.9
Offaly	1,990	76,687	38.5
Westmeath	1,825	86,164	47.2
Wexford	2,365	145,320	61.4
Wicklow	2,033	136,640	67.2
Munster	24,608	1,246,088	50.6
Clare	3,442	117,196	34.0
Cork	7,508	519,032	69.1
Cork City . . .	40	119,230	2,980.8
Cork County . .	7,468	399,802	53.5
Kerry	4,735	145,502	30.7
Limerick	2,760	191,809	69.5
Limerick City* . .	20	57,106	2,855.3
Limerick County* .	2,740	134,703	49.2
Tipperary	4,304	158,754	36.9
Tipperary North . .	2,046	70,322	34.4
Tipperary South . .	2,258	88,432	39.2
Waterford	1,859	113,795	61.2
Waterford City . .	42	46,732	1,112.7
Waterford County .	1,817	67,063	36.9
Ulster (part)	8,087	294,803	36.5
Cavan	1,932	73,183	37.9
Donegal	4,860	161,137	33.2
Monaghan	1,296	60,483	46.7
Total	**70,182**	**4,588,252**	**65.4**

* The boundary of Limerick City was expanded at the 2011 census to include the electoral division Limerick North Rural, but revised area details were not available.

PRINCIPAL TOWNS
(population at 2011 census)

Dublin (capital) .	527,612	Limerick . . .	57,106
Cork	119,230	Waterford . . .	46,732
Galway	75,529		

BIRTHS, MARRIAGES AND DEATHS

	Registered live births		Registered marriages		Registered deaths	
	Number	Rate (per 1,000)	Number	Rate (per 1,000)	Number	Rate (per 1,000)
2006 .	64,237	15.2	22,089	5.2	27,479	6.5
2007 .	70,620	16.3	22,756	5.2	28,050	6.5
2008 .	75,724	17.1	22,187	5.0	28,192	6.4
2009 .	74,928	16.8	21,627	4.8	28,898	6.5
2010 .	74,976	16.8	20,635	4.6	27,565	6.2
2011 .	74,650	16.3	19,879	4.3	28,995	6.3
2012 .	72,225	15.8	21,245	4.6	28,848	6.3
2013 .	68,930	15.0	21,770	4.7	30,018	6.5

Life expectancy (years at birth): 80.9 (males 78.7; females 83.2) in 2012 (Source: World Bank, World Development Indicators database).

IMMIGRATION AND EMIGRATION
('000, year ending April, official estimates, preliminary)

Immigrants

Country of origin	2011/12	2012/13	2013/14
United Kingdom	8.4	9.7	9.7
Other EU	19.5	22.1	21.0
USA	4.9	3.6	2.6
Rest of the world	19.9	20.5	27.2
Total	**52.7**	**55.9**	**60.6**

Emigrants

Country of destination	2011/12	2012/13	2013/14
United Kingdom	19.0	21.9	17.9
Other EU	24.0	25.7	24.9
USA	8.6	6.2	6.9
Rest of the world	35.6	35.2	32.2
Total	**87.1**	**89.0**	**81.9**

Note: Data for immigrants include large numbers of Irish nationals returning from permanent residence abroad ('000, preliminary): 20.6 in 2011/12; 15.7 in 2012/13; 11.6 in 2013/14.

ECONOMICALLY ACTIVE POPULATION
('000 persons, quarterly labour force survey, July–September, estimates)

	2012	2013	2014
Agriculture, forestry and fishing	85.6	110.6	109.7
Mining and quarrying . . .			
Manufacturing	231.1	242.0	238.8
Electricity, gas and water . .			
Construction	101.1	105.4	112.4
Wholesale and retail trade; repair of motor vehicles and motorcycles	272.7	273.3	275.2
Hotels and restaurants . . .	123.1	137.7	139.8
Transport, storage and communications	168.5	170.2	166.8
Finance, insurance and real estate activities . . .	102.3	101.5	103.1
Professional, scientific and technical activities . .	100.4	111.3	116.9
Administrative and support service activities . . .	66.6	64.7	65.2
Public administration and defence; compulsory social security	99.7	96.1	98.1
Education	140.6	140.8	144.1
Health and social work . .	245.0	243.6	249.5
Other services	101.9	99.9	101.6
Sub-total	**1,838.5**	**1,897.2**	**1,921.1**
Activities not adequately defined	2.8	2.1	5.8
Total employed	**1,841.3**	**1,899.3**	**1,926.9**
Unemployed	324.5	282.9	245.5
Total labour force . . .	**2,165.8**	**2,182.2**	**2,172.4**

Health and Welfare

KEY INDICATORS

Total fertility rate (children per woman, 2012)	2.0
Under-5 mortality rate (per 1,000 live births, 2012) . . .	4
HIV/AIDS (% of persons aged 15–49, 2011)	0.3
Physicians (per 1,000 head, 2012)	2.7
Hospital beds (per 1,000 head, 2008)	4.9
Health expenditure (2011): US $ per head (PPP)	3,703
Health expenditure (2011): % of GDP	8.8
Health expenditure (2011): public (% of total)	67.0
Total carbon dioxide emissions ('000 metric tons, 2010) . .	39,999.6
Carbon dioxide emissions per head (metric tons, 2010) . .	8.9
Access to sanitation (% of persons, 2012)	99
Human Development Index (2013): ranking	11
Human Development Index (2013): value	0.899

For sources and definitions, see explanatory note on p. vi.

Agriculture

PRINCIPAL CROPS
('000 metric tons)

	2011	2012	2013
Wheat	929.0	708.0	545.0
Oats	168.0	157.0	193.0
Barley	1,412.0	1,261.0	1,663.0
Potatoes	357.8	232.0	410.0
Carrots and turnips	39.0	33.4	37.1
Cabbages and other brassicas* .	59.5	62.0	61.8

* FAO estimates.

Aggregate production ('000 metric tons, may include official, semi-official or estimated data): Total cereals 2,511.8 in 2011, 2,128.4 in 2012, 2,403.4 in 2013; Total roots and tubers 356.0 in 2011, 232.0 in 2012, 410.0 in 2013; Total vegetables (incl. melons) 231.1 in 2011, 233.6 in 2012, 234.6 in 2013; Total fruits (excl. melons) 62.2 in 2011, 52.6 in 2012, 53.2 in 2013.

Source: FAO.

LIVESTOCK
('000 head at June)

	2011	2012	2013
Cattle	6,493.0	6,754.1	6,902.6
Sheep	4,694.7	5,170.0	5,110.6
Pigs	1,549.0	1,570.6	1,552.0
Chickens*	14,000	14,500	15,000

* FAO estimates.

Source: FAO.

LIVESTOCK PRODUCTS
('000 metric tons)

	2011	2012	2013
Cattle meat	545.9	495.4	517.6
Sheep meat	48.1	53.7	57.5
Pig meat	234.7	241.5	239.3
Chicken meat*	87.0	88.0	89.0
Cows' milk	5,536.7	5,387.8	5,583.7
Hen eggs*	46.0	46.5	47.0

* FAO estimates.

Source: FAO.

Forestry

ROUNDWOOD REMOVALS
('000 cubic metres, excluding bark)

	2011	2012	2013
Sawlogs, veneer logs and logs for sleepers	1,391	1,418	1,472
Pulpwood	936	831	970
Other industrial wood	113	126	108
Fuel wood	195	205	209
Total	2,635	2,580	2,760

Source: FAO.

SAWNWOOD PRODUCTION
('000 cubic metres, including railway sleepers)

	2011	2012	2013
Coniferous (softwood)	760	781	824
Broadleaved (hardwood) . . .	1	1	1
Total	761	782	825

Source: FAO.

Fishing

('000 metric tons, live weight)

	2010	2011	2012
Capture	318.9	214.0	276.0
Blue whiting	8.3	1.2	7.6
Atlantic herring	26.7	24.8	28.7
Atlantic horse mackerel . . .	44.5	38.5	45.3
Atlantic mackerel	58.2	61.7	63.2
Edible crab	8.2	6.7	6.3
Norway lobster	7.8	7.9	10.4
Aquaculture	46.5	44.3	36.1
Atlantic salmon	15.7	12.2	12.4
Blue mussel	22.2	22.7	15.2
Total catch	365.4	258.2	312.1

Note: Figures exclude aquatic plants ('000 metric tons, FAO estimates): 29.5 (North Atlantic rockweed 28.0) in 2010–12.

Source: FAO.

Mining

('000 metric tons unless otherwise indicated)

	2010	2011	2012
Natural gas (million cu m) . .	402	356	350
Lead*	39.1	50.7	47.0
Zinc*	342.5	344.0	337.5
Peat†	4,991	3,707	3,700‡

* Figures refer to the metal content of ores mined.
† Excluding peat for horticultural use ('000 metric tons, estimates): 600 in 2010–12.
‡ Estimate.

Source: US Geological Survey.

Industry

SELECTED PRODUCTS
('000 metric tons unless otherwise indicated)

	2009	2010	2011
Motor spirit (gasoline)	481	463	506
Gas-diesel oil (distillate fuel oil) .	975	1,070	1,047
Mazout (residual fuel oil) . . .	949	969	1,071
Electric energy (million kWh) .	28,313	28,612	27,655

Source: UN Industrial Commodity Statistics Database.

Finance

CURRENCY AND EXCHANGE RATES

Monetary Units
100 cent = 1 euro (€).

Sterling and Dollar Equivalents (31 December 2014)
£1 sterling = €1.286;
US $1 = €0.824;
€10 = £7.78 = $12.14.

Average Exchange Rate (euros per US $)
2012	0.7783
2013	0.7532
2014	0.7537

Note: The national currency was formerly the Irish pound (or punt). From the introduction of the euro, with Irish participation, on 1 January 1999, a fixed exchange rate of €1 = 78.7564 pence was in operation. Euro notes and coins were introduced on 1 January 2002. The euro and local currency circulated alongside each other until 9 February, after which the euro became the sole legal tender.

BUDGET
(€ '000 million)

Revenue	2013	2014*	2015*
Tax revenue	41.4	43.3	45.4
Personal income tax . . .	15.8	16.5	17.2
Corporate income tax . . .	4.3	4.5	4.9
Value-added tax	10.3	10.5	10.9
Excise tax	4.7	4.9	5.1
Others	6.1	6.8	7.1
Social contributions . . .	10.2	10.5	10.8
Non-tax revenue	7.3	6.8	7.0
Total	**58.9**	**60.7**	**63.2**

Expenditure†	2013	2014*	2015*
Current expenditure	67.9	66.3	65.5
Interest payments	7.7	8.0	8.5
Wages and salaries	18.4	18.3	17.5
Goods and services	8.3	8.2	8.1
Social benefits	28.6	27.9	27.1
Subsidies	1.5	1.4	1.5
Other expenses	3.5	2.6	2.7
Gross fixed capital formation . .	2.7	2.7	2.8
Total	**70.6**	**69.0**	**68.3**

* Projections.
† Excluding bank support costs (€ '000 million): 0.0 in 2013; 0.1 in 2014 (projection); 0.1 in 2015 (projection).

Source: IMF, *Ireland: First Post-Program Monitoring Discussions; Staff Report; Staff Supplements; and Press Release on the Executive Board discussion* (June 2014).

INTERNATIONAL RESERVES
(US $ million at 31 December)

	2011	2012	2013
Gold (Eurosystem valuation) . .	304	321	232
IMF special drawing rights . .	976	986	1,001
Reserve position in IMF . . .	397	397	398
Foreign exchange	27	3	4
Total	**1,704**	**1,707**	**1,635**

Source: IMF, *International Financial Statistics*.

MONEY SUPPLY
(incl. shares, depository corporations, national residence criteria, € million at 31 December)

	2011	2012	2013
Currency issued	13,673	13,999	14,726
Central Bank of Ireland . .	29,062	29,940	31,203
Demand deposits	77,719	79,377	100,440
Other deposits	86,141	88,842	82,065
Securities other than shares . .	95,484	81,363	61,103
Money market fund shares . .	49,846	64,925	44,823
Shares and other equity . . .	129,376	138,608	134,647
Other items (net)	−10,088	−16,552	−17,885
Total	**442,151**	**450,562**	**419,919**

Source: IMF, *International Financial Statistics*.

COST OF LIVING
(Consumer Price Index; base: December 2011 = 100)

	2011	2012	2013
Food and non-alcoholic beverages .	99.8	100.3	101.4
Clothing and footwear	97.5	97.3	94.4
Housing, water, electricity, gas and other fuel	97.2	97.8	98.5
All items (incl. others) . . .	**99.4**	**101.1**	**101.6**

NATIONAL ACCOUNTS
(€ million at current prices)

National Income and Product

	2011	2012	2013*
Gross domestic product in market prices	171,042	172,755	174,791
Net factor income from abroad .	−32,127	−30,310	−26,262
Gross national product in market prices	138,915	142,445	148,529
Subsidies paid by the EU . . .	1,700	1,632	1,450
Less Taxes paid to the EU . .	240	242	247
Gross national income in market prices	140,376	143,835	149,733
Net current transfers from abroad (excl. EU subsidies and taxes) .	−2,643	−3,808	−3,665
Gross national disposable income	137,732	140,027	146,067

Expenditure on the Gross Domestic Product

	2011	2012	2013*
Government final consumption expenditure	26,111	25,922	25,956
Private final consumption expenditure	82,969	82,467	83,334
Changes in inventories . . .	780	288	837
Gross fixed capital formation .	24,841	26,923	26,541
Total domestic expenditure .	**134,701**	**135,600**	**136,668**
Exports of goods and services .	167,086	182,506	184,056
Less Imports of goods and services	−132,398	−147,079	−147,694
Statistical discrepancy . . .	1,654	1,728	1,761
GDP in market prices . . .	**171,042**	**172,755**	**174,791**

Gross Domestic Product by Economic Activity

	2011	2012	2013*
Agriculture, forestry and fishing	3,972	3,798	3,815
Mining and quarrying . . .			
Manufacturing			
Electricity, gas and water supply	42,731	42,306	37,987
Construction			
Wholesale and retail trade, repair and hotels and restaurants	39,452	40,958	43,917
Transport, storage and communications			
Public administration and defence	6,683	6,462	6,303
Other services	65,304	65,709	68,223
Statistical discrepancy . . .	−1,654	−1,728	−1,761
Gross value added at factor cost	**156,489**	**157,506**	**158,484**
Taxes (excl. taxes on products) .	1,900	2,095	2,298
Less Subsidies (excl. subsidies on products)	−2,196	2,120	1,990
Gross value added in basic prices	**156,192**	**157,481**	**158,792**
Taxes on products	15,939	16,334	16,968
Less Subsidies on products . .	1,088	1,061	968
GDP in market prices . .	**171,042**	**172,755**	**174,791**

* Preliminary figures.

BALANCE OF PAYMENTS
(US $ million)

	2011	2012	2013
Exports of goods f.o.b.	127,471	119,321	116,091
Imports of goods f.o.b.	−67,195	−63,628	−66,101
Balance on goods	60,277	55,693	49,990
Exports of services	104,146	107,041	118,405
Imports of services	−115,641	−111,955	−117,704
Balance on goods and services	48,782	50,779	50,691
Primary income received . . .	79,471	73,559	73,496
Primary income paid	−123,734	−113,555	−107,900
Balance on goods, services and primary income	4,519	10,783	16,287
Secondary transfers received . .	7,448	7,164	6,005
Secondary transfers paid . . .	−9,139	−8,701	−7,854
Current balance	2,828	9,245	14,438
Capital account (net)	−357	−2,634	20
Direct investment assets . . .	1,536	−21,340	−37,588
Direct investment liabilities . .	23,665	40,962	49,960
Portfolio investment assets . .	−4,170	−95,816	−125,797
Portfolio investment liabilities .	41,379	94,077	68,734
Financial derivatives and employee stock options (net)	554	−14,536	−3,804
Other investment assets . . .	4,234	91,754	65,971
Other investment liabilities . .	−71,043	−102,435	−35,202
Net errors and omissions . . .	−16,266	−7,747	−1,154
Reserves and related items .	−17,640	−8,470	−4,422

Source: IMF, *International Financial Statistics.*

External Trade

PRINCIPAL COMMODITIES
(distribution by SITC, € million)

Imports c.i.f.	2011	2012	2013
Food and live animals . . .	5,019	5,589	6,050
Mineral fuels, lubricants, etc. .	6,946	7,160	6,885
Petroleum and petroleum products	5,321	5,475	5,021
Natural gas	1,354	1,450	1,576
Chemicals and related products	10,415	10,265	10,875
Organic chemicals	2,456	2,485	2,545
Medicinal and pharmaceutical products	4,387	4,164	4,509
Basic manufactures	3,712	3,713	3,848
Machinery and transport equipment	12,414	12,560	12,063
Office machines and automatic data-processing equipment . .	2,693	2,648	2,823
Other electrical machinery, apparatus, etc.	2,102	1,927	1,966
Road vehicles and parts (excl. tyres, engines and electrical parts) .	1,699	1,598	1,863
Other transport equipment . .	2,347	2,494	1,008
Miscellaneous manufactured articles	6,013	6,069	6,027
Total (incl. others)*	48,302	49,151	49,635

* Including transactions not classified by commodity.

Exports f.o.b.	2011	2012	2013
Food and live animals . . .	7,874	8,132	8,748
Meat and meat preparations . .	2,762	2,979	3,019
Chemicals and related products	56,031	55,045	50,418
Organic chemicals	19,969	20,053	18,291
Medicinal and pharmaceutical products	26,393	24,551	21,617
Essential oils, perfume materials and toilet and cleansing preparations	5,777	6,245	6,250
Machinery and transport equipment	10,370	10,314	10,430
Office machines and automatic data-processing equipment . .	3,562	3,501	3,998
Electrical machinery, apparatus, etc.	2,873	2,614	2,277
Miscellaneous manufactured articles	10,231	10,831	10,693
Professional, scientific and controlling apparatus . . .	3,380	3,608	3,583
Total (incl. others)*	91,228	91,688	86,890

* Including transactions not classified by commodity.

PRINCIPAL TRADING PARTNERS
(€ million)*

Imports c.i.f.	2011	2012	2013
Belgium	1,166	955	995
China, People's Republic (incl. Hong Kong and Macao) . . .	2,714	2,760	2,997
Denmark	605	456	683
France	1,994	1,907	2,086
Germany	3,708	3,436	4,053
Italy	775	782	862
Japan	796	733	1,041
Korea, Republic	384	333	405
Netherlands	2,434	2,318	2,667
Nigeria	180	676	211
Norway	1,165	938	1,103
Spain	668	660	770
Switzerland	762	958	838
United Kingdom	15,638	15,403	15,657
USA	5,907	6,441	5,220
Total (incl. others)	48,302	49,151	49,635

Exports f.o.b.	2011	2012	2013
Belgium	13,227	13,619	11,221
China, People's Republic (incl. Hong Kong and Macao) . . .	2,330	1,565	1,418
France	4,951	4,348	4,016
Germany	6,285	7,461	6,572
Italy	2,992	2,656	2,291
Japan	1,743	2,085	1,692
Netherlands	3,123	3,292	3,671
Spain	3,049	2,766	2,693
Switzerland	3,686	5,070	5,116
United Kingdom	12,845	13,682	12,505
USA	21,601	18,157	18,389
Total (incl. others)	91,228	91,688	86,890

* Imports by country of origin; exports by country of final destination.

Transport

RAILWAYS
(traffic, '000)

	2010	2011	2012
Passengers carried	38,070	37,222	36,837
Freight tonnage	568	611	567

ROAD TRAFFIC
(licensed motor vehicles at 31 December)

	2011	2012	2013
Passenger cars	1,887,810	1,882,550	1,910,165
Lorries and vans	320,966	309,219	317,849
Buses and coaches	33,405	32,446	31,452
Motorcycles and mopeds	36,582	35,106	36,623

Source: Department of Transport, Tourism and Sport, Dublin.

SHIPPING

Flag Registered Fleet
(at 31 December)

	2012	2013	2014
Number of vessels	191	186	186
Total displacement (grt)	217,456	239,090	257,603

Source: Lloyd's List Intelligence (www.lloydslistintelligence.com).

Seaborne Freight Traffic
('000 metric tons)

	2011	2012	2013
Goods loaded	15,240	16,458	15,319
Goods unloaded	29,838	31,191	31,403

CIVIL AVIATION
(traffic on scheduled services)

	2010	2011
Kilometres flown (million)	127	128
Passengers carried ('000)	84,784	89,956
Passenger-km (million)	97,834	109,948
Total ton-km (million)	8,959	10,101

Source: UN, *Statistical Yearbook*.

Passengers carried ('000): 92,637 in 2012; 95,585 in 2013 (Source: World Bank, World Development Indicators database).

Tourism

FOREIGN TOURIST ARRIVALS BY ORIGIN
('000)

	2011	2012	2013
Australia and New Zealand	141	158	92
France	400	384	409
Germany	420	437	466
Italy	213	240	226
Spain	237	239	249
United Kingdom*	4,129	3,986	4,444
USA	818	833	924
Total (incl. others)	7,630	7,550	8,261

* Including residents of Northern Ireland.

Tourism receipts ($ million, excl. passenger transport): 4,212 in 2011; 3,867 in 2012; 4,426 in 2013.

Source: World Tourism Organization.

Communications Media

	2011	2012	2013
Telephone lines ('000 in use)*	2,046.6	2,007.7	2,034.5
Mobile cellular telephones ('000 subscribers)*	4,906.4	4,905.9	4,754.7
Internet subscribers ('000)*	1,089.5	n.a.	n.a.
Broadband subscribers ('000)	993.7	1,039.6	1,121.6

* At December.

Personal computers: 2,480,000 (582.1 per 1,000 persons) in 2006.

Source: International Telecommunication Union.

Education

(2013/14 unless otherwise indicated)

	Institutions	Teachers (full-time)	Students (full-time)
National schools*	3,286	32,828	536,317
Secondary schools	373	13,373†	189,446
Vocational schools	256	8,538†	120,473
Community and comprehensive schools	94	4,274†	57,259
Teacher (primary and home economics) training colleges	7‡	127§	6,454
Technology colleges‖	14‡	3,347§	65,039
Universities and other Higher Education Authority Institutions	7‡	3,507§	90,341
Other aided institutions	4‡	71§	3,029

* State-aided primary schools; includes Special National Schools (numbering 141 in 2013/14).
† 2010/11.
‡ 2012/13.
§ 2000/01.
‖ Comprising 13 Institutes of Technology, the Tipperary Institute and the Hotel Training and Catering College, Killybegs, Co Donegal.

Sources: Central Statistics Office, and Department of Education and Skills.

Pupil-teacher ratio (primary education, UNESCO estimate): 16.1 in 2011/12 (Source: UNESCO Institute for Statistics).

Directory

The Government

HEAD OF STATE

Uachtarán (President): MICHAEL D. HIGGINS (assumed office 11 November 2011).

THE CABINET
(April 2015)

A coalition of Fine Gael (FG) and the Labour Party (LP)

Taoiseach (Prime Minister): ENDA KENNY (FG).

Tánaiste (Deputy Prime Minister), Minister for Social Protection: JOAN BURTON (LP).

Minister for Finance: MICHAEL NOONAN (FG).

Minister for Public Expenditure and Reform: BRENDAN HOWLIN (LP).

Minister for Jobs, Enterprise and Innovation: RICHARD BRUTON (FG).

Minister for Agriculture, Food and the Marine, and for Defence: SIMON COVENEY (FG).

Minister for Justice and Equality: FRANCES FITZGERALD (FG).

Minister for Children and Youth Affairs: Dr JAMES REILLY (FG).

Minister for Health: LEO VARADKAR (FG).

Minister for Foreign Affairs and Trade: CHARLES FLANAGAN (FG).

Minister for Education and Skills: JAN O'SULLIVAN (LP).

Minister for the Environment, Community and Local Government: ALAN KELLY (LP).

Minister for Communications, Energy and Natural Resources: ALEX WHITE (LP).

Minister for Transport, Tourism and Sport: PASCHAL DONOHOE (FG).

Minister for Arts, Heritage and the Gaeltacht: HEATHER HUMPHREYS (FG).

MINISTRIES

Office of the President: Áras an Uachtaráin, Phoenix Park, Dublin 8; tel. (1) 6171000; fax (1) 6171001; e-mail info@president.ie; internet www.president.ie.

Department of the Taoiseach: Government Bldgs, Upper Merrion St, Dublin 2; tel. (1) 6194000; fax (1) 6194297; e-mail webmaster@taoiseach.gov.ie; internet www.taoiseach.gov.ie.

Department of Agriculture, Food and the Marine: Agriculture House, Kildare St, Dublin 2; tel. (1) 6072000; fax (1) 6616263; e-mail info@agriculture.gov.ie; internet www.agriculture.gov.ie.

Department of Arts, Heritage and the Gaeltacht: 23 Kildare St, Dublin 2; tel. (1) 6313800; e-mail press.office@ahg.gov.ie; internet www.ahg.gov.ie.

Department of Children and Youth Affairs: 43–49 Mespil Rd, Dublin 4; tel. (1) 6473000; fax (1) 6473101; e-mail omc@dcya.gov.ie; internet www.dcya.gov.ie.

Department of Communications, Energy and Natural Resources: 29–31 Adelaide Rd, Dublin 2; tel. (1) 6782000; fax (1) 6782449; e-mail press.office@dcenr.gov.ie; internet www.dcenr.gov.ie.

Department of Defence: Station Rd, Newbridge, Co Kildare; tel. (45) 492000; fax (45) 492017; e-mail info@defence.ie; internet www.defence.ie.

Department of Education and Skills: Marlborough St, Dublin 1; tel. (1) 8896400; e-mail info@education.gov.ie; internet www.education.ie.

Department of the Environment, Community and Local Government: Custom House, Dublin 1; tel. (1) 8882403; fax (1) 8882888; e-mail minister@environ.ie; internet www.environ.ie.

Department of Finance: Government Bldgs, Upper Merrion St, Dublin 2; tel. (1) 6767571; fax (1) 6789936; e-mail webmaster@finance.gov.ie; internet www.finance.gov.ie.

Department of Foreign Affairs and Trade: 80 St Stephen's Green, Dublin 2; tel. (1) 4082000; fax (1) 4082400; internet www.dfa.ie.

Department of Health: Hawkins House, Hawkins St, Dublin 2; tel. (1) 6354000; fax (1) 6354001; internet www.dohc.ie.

Department of Jobs, Enterprise and Innovation: 23 Kildare St, Dublin 2; tel. (1) 6312121; fax (1) 6312827; e-mail info@entemp.ie; internet www.enterprise.gov.ie.

Department of Justice and Equality: 94 St Stephen's Green, Dublin 2; tel. (1) 6028202; fax (1) 6615461; e-mail info@justice.ie; internet www.justice.ie.

Department of Public Expenditure and Reform: Government Bldgs, Upper Merrion St, Dublin 2; tel. (1) 6767571; fax (1) 6789936; e-mail webmasterper@per.gov.ie; internet per.gov.ie.

Department of Social Protection: Áras Mhic Dhiarmada, Store St, Dublin 1; tel. (1) 7043000; fax (1) 7043870; e-mail info@welfare.ie; internet www.welfare.ie.

Department of Transport, Tourism and Sport: 44 Kildare St, Dublin 2; tel. (1) 6707444; fax (1) 6041185; e-mail info@dttas.ie; internet www.dttas.ie.

Legislature

NATIONAL PARLIAMENT (OIREACHTAS)

Parliament comprises two Houses: Dáil Éireann (House of Representatives), with 166 Teachtaí Dála (members), elected for a five-year term by universal adult suffrage; and Seanad Éireann (Senate), with 60 members serving a five-year term, of whom 11 are nominated by the Taoiseach (Prime Minister) and 49 elected (six by the universities and 43 from specially constituted panels).

Dáil Éireann

Leinster House, Kildare St, Dublin 2; tel. (1) 6183000; fax (1) 6184118; e-mail communications@oireachtas.ie; internet www.oireachtas.ie.

Ceann Comhairle (Chairman): SEÁN BARRETT.

Leas-Cheann Comhairle (Deputy Chairman): MICHAEL KITT.

General Election, 25 February 2011

Party	Votes*	% of votes*	Seats
Fine Gael	801,628	36.10	76
Labour Party	431,796	19.45	37
Fianna Fáil	387,358	17.45	20†
Independents	279,459	12.58	15
Sinn Féin	220,661	9.94	14
Socialist Party	26,770	1.21	2
People Before Profit Alliance	21,551	0.95	2
Green Party	41,039	1.85	—
Total (incl. others)	2,220,359	100.00	166

* The election was conducted by means of the single transferable vote. Figures refer to first-preference votes.
† Including the Ceann Comhairle (Chairman), who is automatically re-elected.

Seanad Éireann

Leinster House, Dublin 2; tel. (1) 6183000; fax (1) 6184118; e-mail info@oireachtas.ie; internet www.oireachtas.ie.

Cathaoirleach (Chairman): PADDY BURKE.

Leas-Chathaoirleach (Deputy Chairman): DENIS O'DONOVAN.

Elections were held to the Seanad Éireann in April 2011, with the closing date for the receipt of votes from the members of five vocational panels (Administrative, Agricultural, Cultural and Educational, Industrial and Commercial, and Labour) being 26 April, and that for the two university panels (National University of Ireland, and University of Dublin) being 27 April. Following the nomination of 11 members by the Taoiseach (Prime Minister) on 20 May, the strength of the parties was as follows:

Party	Elected	Appointed	Total seats
Fianna Fáil	18	1	19
Fine Gael	14	—	14
Labour Party	9	3	12
Sinn Féin	3	—	3
Independents	5	7	12
Total	49	11	60

Political Organizations

Communist Party of Ireland (Páirtí Cumannach na hÉireann): James Connolly House, 43 East Essex St, Dublin 2; tel. and fax (1) 6708707; e-mail cpoi@eircom.net; internet www

.communistpartyofireland.ie; f. 1933; advocates a united, socialist, independent Ireland; Chair. LYNDA WALKER; Gen. Sec. EUGENE MCCARTAN.

Fianna Fáil (The Republican Party) (Soldiers of Destiny): 65–66 Lower Mount St, Dublin 2; tel. (1) 6761551; fax (1) 6785690; e-mail info@fiannafail.ie; internet www.fiannafail.ie; f. 1926; centrist; Pres. and Leader MICHEÁL MARTIN; Gen. Sec. SEÁN DORGAN.

Fine Gael (United Ireland Party) (Family of the Irish): 51 Upper Mount St, Dublin 2; tel. (1) 6198444; e-mail finegael@finegael.com; internet www.finegael.ie; f. 1933; centrist; Leader ENDA KENNY; Chair DAN NEVILLE; Gen. Sec. TOM CURRAN.

Green Party (Comhaontas Glas): 16–17 Suffolk St, Dublin 2; tel. (1) 6790012; fax (1) 6797168; e-mail info@greenparty.ie; internet www.greenparty.ie; f. 1981 as the Ecology Party of Ireland; name changed as above in 1983; advocates a humane, ecological society, freedom of information and political decentralization; Leader EAMON RYAN; Chair. RODERIC O'GORMAN.

Labour Party: 17 Ely Place, Dublin 2; tel. (1) 6784700; fax (1) 6612640; e-mail head.office@labour.ie; internet www.labour.ie; f. 1912; merged with Democratic Left (f. 1992) in 1999; democratic socialist party; affiliated to the Party of European Socialists; Leader JOAN BURTON; Gen. Sec. DAVID LEACH.

Sinn Féin (We Ourselves): 44 Parnell Sq., Dublin 1; tel. (1) 8726100; fax (1) 8733441; e-mail admin@sinnfein.ie; internet www.sinnfein.ie; f. 1905; advocates the termination of British rule in Northern Ireland; seeks a mandate to establish a democratic socialist republic in a reunified Ireland; Pres. GERRY ADAMS; Chair. DECLAN KEARNEY; Gen. Sec. DAWN DOYLE.

Socialist Party: 141 Thomas St, Dublin 8; tel. (1) 6772592; fax (1) 6772686; e-mail info@socialistparty.net; internet www.socialistparty.net; f. 1996; mem. of the Committee for a Workers' International (CWI); advocates a socialist Ireland as part of a free and voluntary socialist federation of Ireland, Scotland, England and Wales; anti-EU; Leader JOE HIGGINS.

Workers' Party: 24A/25 Hill St, Dublin 1; tel. (1) 8740716; fax (1) 8748702; e-mail wpi@indigo.ie; internet workersparty.ie; f. 1905; fmrly Sinn Féin The Workers' Party; name changed as above in 1982; aims to establish a unitary socialist state on the island of Ireland; Pres. MICHAEL FINNEGAN; Gen. Sec. JOHN LOWRY.

Diplomatic Representation

EMBASSIES IN IRELAND

Argentina: 15 Ailesbury Dr., Dublin 4; tel. (1) 2691546; fax (1) 2600404; e-mail embassyofargentina@eircom.net; Ambassador SILVIA PISANO MARÍA MEREGA.

Australia: Fitzwilton House, 7th Floor, Wilton Terrace, Dublin 2; tel. (1) 6645300; fax (1) 6623566; e-mail austremb.dublin@dfat.gov.au; internet www.ireland.embassy.gov.au; Ambassador Dr RUTH P. ADLER.

Austria: 15 Ailesbury Court, 93 Ailesbury Rd, Dublin 4; tel. (1) 2694577; fax (1) 2830860; e-mail dublin-ob@bmeia.gv.at; Ambassador THOMAS NADER.

Belgium: 1 Elgin Rd, Dublin 4; tel. (1) 6315283; fax (1) 6675665; e-mail dublin@diplobel.fed.be; internet www.diplomatie.belgium.be/ireland; Ambassador PHILIPPE ROLAND.

Brazil: Harcourt Centre, Block 8, Charlotte Way, Dublin 2; tel. (1) 4756000; fax (1) 4751341; e-mail info@brazil.ie; internet dublin.itamaraty.gov.br/en-us; Ambassador AFONSO JOSÉ SENA CARDOSO.

Bulgaria: 22 Burlington Rd, Dublin 4; tel. (1) 6603293; fax (1) 6603915; e-mail bulgarianembassydublin@eircom.net; internet www.mfa.bg/embassies/ireland; Ambassador BRANIMIR ZAIMOV.

Canada: 7–8 Wilton Terrace, 3rd Floor, Dublin 2; tel. (1) 2344000; fax (1) 2344001; e-mail dubln@international.gc.ca; internet www.canadainternational.gc.ca/ireland-irlande; Ambassador KEVIN VICKERS.

Chile: 44 Wellington Rd, Dublin 4; tel. (1) 6675094; fax (1) 6675156; e-mail echile.irlanda@minrel.gov.cl; internet www.chileabroad.gov.cl/irlanda; Ambassador LEONEL FERNANDO SEARLE COUVE.

China, People's Republic: 40 Ailesbury Rd, Dublin 4; tel. (1) 2691707; fax (1) 2839938; e-mail chinaemb_ie@mfa.gov.cn; internet ie.china-embassy.org; Ambassador XU JIANGUO.

Croatia: Adelaide Chambers, Peter St, Dublin 8; tel. (1) 4767181; fax (1) 4767183; e-mail croemb.dublin@mvep.hr; internet ie.mfa.hr; Ambassador JASNA OGNJANOVAC.

Cuba: 32B Westland Sq., Pearse St, Dublin 2; tel. (1) 4752999; e-mail infocubadublin@eircom.net; internet www.cubadiplomatica.cu/irlanda; Ambassador HERMES HERRERA HERNÁNDEZ.

Cyprus: 71 Lower Leeson St, Dublin 2; tel. (1) 6763060; fax (1) 6763099; e-mail dublinembassy@mfa.gov.cy; internet www.mfa.gov.cy/embassydublin; Ambassador MICHALIS STAVRINOS.

Czech Republic: 57 Northumberland Rd, Dublin 4; tel. (1) 6681135; fax (1) 6681660; e-mail dublin@embassy.mzv.cz; internet www.mfa.cz/dublin; Ambassador HANA MOTTLOVÁ.

Denmark: Block E, 7th Floor, Iveagh Court, Harcourt Rd, Dublin 2; tel. (1) 4756404; fax (1) 4784536; e-mail dubamb@um.dk; internet www.irland.um.dk; Ambassador CARSTEN SØNDERGAARD.

Egypt: 12 Clyde Rd, Ballsbridge, Dublin 4; tel. (1) 6606566; fax (1) 6683745; e-mail info@embegyptireland.ie; internet www.embegyptireland.ie; Ambassador SHERIF ELKHOLI.

Estonia: Block E, 3rd Floor, Iveagh Court, Harcourt Rd, Dublin 2; tel. (1) 4788888; fax (1) 4788887; e-mail embassy.dublin@mfa.ee; internet www.estemb.ie; Ambassador KRISTI KARELSOHN.

Ethiopia: 26 Upper Fitzwilliam St, Dublin 2; tel. (1) 6787062; fax (1) 6787065; e-mail info@ethiopianembassy.ie; internet www.ethiopianembassy.ie; Ambassador LELA-ALEM GEBREYOHANNES TEDLA.

Finland: Russell House, Stokes Pl., St Stephen's Green, Dublin 2; tel. (1) 4781344; fax (1) 4783727; e-mail sanomat.dub@formin.fi; internet www.finland.ie; Ambassador HILKKA NENONEN.

France: 36 Ailesbury Rd, Ballsbridge, Dublin 4; tel. (1) 2775000; fax (1) 2775001; e-mail chancellerie@ambafrance.ie; internet www.ambafrance-ie.org; Ambassador JEAN-PIERRE THÉBAULT.

Georgia: 5 Marine Rd, Dun Laoghaire, Co Dublin; tel. (1) 9059191; fax (1) 5311190; internet ireland.mfa.gov.ge; Chargé d'affaires GIORGI ZURABASHVILI.

Germany: 31 Trimleston Ave, Booterstown, Blackrock, Co Dublin; tel. (1) 2693011; fax (1) 2693800; e-mail info@dublin.diplo.de; internet www.dublin.diplo.de; Ambassador MATTHIAS HÖPFNER.

Greece: 1 Upper Pembroke St, Dublin 2; tel. (1) 6767254; fax (1) 6618892; e-mail amboffice.dub@mfa.gr; internet www.mfa.gr/dublin; Ambassador CONSTANTINA ZAGORIANOU-PRIFTI.

Holy See: 183 Navan Rd, Dublin 7; tel. (1) 8380577; fax (1) 8380276; e-mail nuncioirl@eircom.net; Apostolic Nuncio Most Rev. CHARLES J. BROWN (Titular Archbishop of Aquileia).

Hungary: 2 Fitzwilliam Pl., Dublin 2; tel. (1) 6612902; fax (1) 6612880; e-mail mission.dub@kum.hu; internet www.mfa.gov.hu/kulkepviselet/ie; Ambassador Dr TAMÁS MAGYARICS.

India: 6 Leeson Park, Dublin 6; tel. (1) 4966792; fax (1) 4978074; e-mail indembassy@eircom.net; internet www.indianembassy.ie; Ambassador RADHIKA LAL LOKESH.

Iran: 72 Mount Merrion Ave, Blackrock, Co Dublin; tel. (1) 2880252; fax (1) 2834246; e-mail iranembassy@indigo.ie; Ambassador JAVAD KACHOUEIAN.

Israel: 122 Pembroke Rd, Ballsbridge, Dublin 4; tel. (1) 2309400; fax (1) 2309446; e-mail info@dublin.mfa.gov.il; internet dublin.mfa.gov.il; Ambassador BOAZ MODAI.

Italy: 63–65 Northumberland Rd, Dublin 4; tel. (1) 6601744; fax (1) 6682759; e-mail ambasciata.dublino@esteri.it; internet www.ambdublino.esteri.it; Ambassador GIOVANNI ADORNI BRACCESI CHIASSI.

Japan: Nutley Bldg, Merrion Centre, Nutley Lane, Dublin 4; tel. (1) 2028300; fax (1) 2838726; e-mail cultural@embjp.ie; internet www.ie.emb-japan.go.jp; Ambassador CHIHIRO ATSUMI.

Kenya: 11 Elgin Rd, Dublin 4; tel. (1) 6136380; fax (1) 6685506; e-mail info@kenyaembassyireland.net; internet www.kenyaembassyireland.net; Ambassador RICHARD ANGULU OPEMBE.

Korea, Republic: 15 Clyde Rd, POB 2101, Dublin 4; tel. (1) 6608800; fax (1) 6608716; e-mail irekoremb@mofat.go.kr; internet irl.mofat.go.kr; Ambassador PARK HAE-YUN.

Latvia: 92 St Stephen's Green, Dublin 2; tel. (1) 4780161; fax (1) 4780162; e-mail embassy.ireland@mfa.gov.lv; internet www.am.gov.lv/en/ireland; Ambassador GINTS APALS.

Lesotho: 52 Upper Mount St, Dublin 2; tel. (1) 6762233; fax (1) 6762258; e-mail info@lesothoembassy.ie; internet www.lesothoembassy.ie; Ambassador PARAMENTE PHAMOTSE.

Lithuania: 47 Ailesbury Rd, Ballsbridge, Dublin 4; tel. (1) 2035757; fax (1) 2839354; e-mail amb.ie@urm.lt; internet ie.mfa.lt; Ambassador RASA ADOMAITIENÉ.

Malaysia: Level 3A–5A Shelbourne House, Shelbourne Rd, Dublin 4; tel. (1) 6677280; fax (1) 6677283; e-mail mwdublin@mwdublin.ie; Ambassador SYED SULTAN BIN MOHD IDRIS.

Malta: 15 Leeson St Lower, Dublin 2; tel. (1) 6762340; fax (1) 6766066; e-mail maltaembassy.dublin@gov.mt; Chargé d'affaires CHANTAL SCIBERRAS.

Mexico: 19 Raglan Rd, Dublin 4; tel. (1) 6673105; fax (1) 6641013; e-mail info@embamex.ie; internet www.sre.gob.mx/irlanda; Ambassador CARLOS EUGENIO GARCIA DE ALBA.

Morocco: 39 Raglan Rd, Dublin 4; tel. (1) 6609449; fax (1) 6609468; e-mail sifamdub@indigo.ie; Ambassador ANAS KHALES.

Netherlands: 160 Merrion Rd, Dublin 4; tel. (1) 2693444; fax (1) 2839690; e-mail dub-info@minbuza.nl; internet www .netherlandsembassy.ie; Ambassador PAUL SCHELLEKENS.

Nigeria: 56 Leeson Park, Dublin 6; tel. (1) 6604366; fax (1) 6604092; e-mail enquiries@nigerianembassydublin.org; internet www .nigerianembassydublin.org; Ambassador BOLERE ELIZABETH KETEBU.

Norway: 34 Molesworth St, Dublin 2; tel. (1) 6621800; fax (1) 6621890; e-mail emb.dublin@mfa.no; internet www.norway.ie; Ambassador ROALD NÆSS.

Pakistan: Ailesbury Villa, 1B Ailesbury Rd, Dublin 4; tel. (1) 2613032; fax (1) 2613007; e-mail pakembassydublin@gmail.com; internet www.pakembassydublin.com; Chargé d'affaires a.i. SYED RIZWAN AHMED.

Poland: 5 Ailesbury Rd, Ballsbridge, Dublin 4; tel. (1) 2830855; fax (1) 2698309; e-mail dublin@msz.gov.pl; internet www.dublin.msz .gov.pl; Ambassador RYSZARD SARKOWICZ.

Portugal: 15 Leeson Park, Dublin 6; tel. (1) 4127040; fax (1) 4970299; e-mail embport@dublin.dgaccp.pt; internet www .embassyportugal.ie; Ambassador BERNARDO FUTSCHER PEREIRA.

Romania: 26 Waterloo Rd, Dublin 4; tel. (1) 6681085; fax (1) 6681761; e-mail ambrom@eircom.net; internet dublin.mae.ro; Ambassador MANUELA BREAZU.

Russian Federation: 184–186 Orwell Rd, Rathgar, Dublin 14; tel. (1) 4922048; fax (1) 4923525; e-mail info@russianembassy.ie; internet www.ireland.mid.ru; Ambassador MAXIM ALEXANDROVICH PESHKOV.

Saudi Arabia: 6–7 Fitzwilliam Sq. East, Dublin 2; tel. (1) 6760704; fax (1) 6760715; e-mail prsedi@gmail.com; Ambassador ABD AL-AZIZ ABD AL-RAHMAN ALDRISS.

Slovakia: 80 Merrion Sq., Dublin 2; tel. (1) 6619594; fax (1) 6619553; e-mail emb.dublin@mzv.sk; internet www.mzv.sk/dublin; Ambassador DUŠAN MATULAY.

South Africa: Alexandra House, 2nd Floor, Earlsfort Centre, Earlsfort Terrace, Dublin 2; tel. (1) 6615553; fax (1) 6615590; e-mail dublin .info@dirco.gov.za; Ambassador AHLANGENE CYPRIAN SIGCAU.

Spain: 17A Merlyn Park, Dublin 4; tel. (1) 2691640; fax (1) 2691854; e-mail emb.dublin.inf@maec.es; internet www.maec.es/embajadas/ dublin; Ambassador JOSÉ MARÍA RODRÍGUEZ COSO.

Switzerland: 6 Ailesbury Rd, Dublin 4; tel. (1) 2186382; fax (1) 2830344, e-mail dub.vertretung@eda.admin.ch; internet www.eda .admin.ch/dublin; Ambassador MARIE-CLAUDE MEYLAN.

Turkey: 8 Raglan Rd, Ballsbridge, Dublin 4; tel. (1) 6144590; fax (1) 6685014; e-mail embassy.dublin@mfa.gov.tr; internet www.dublin .be.mfa.gov.tr; Ambassador NECIP EGÜZ.

Ukraine: 16 Elgin Rd, Ballsbridge, Dublin 4; tel. (1) 6685189; fax (1) 6697917; e-mail ukrembassy@eircom.net; internet www.mfa.gov.ua/ ireland; Ambassador SERGII REVA.

United Arab Emirates: 45–47 Pembroke Rd, Dublin 4; tel. (1) 6600000; fax (1) 2375920; e-mail dublin@mofa.gov.ae; Ambassador Dr SAEED MOHAMED ALI al-SHAMSI.

United Kingdom: 29 Merrion Rd, Dublin 4; tel. (1) 2053700; fax (1) 2053885; e-mail chancery.dublx@fco.gov.uk; internet www .britishembassy.ie; Ambassador. DOMINICK JOHN CHILCOTT.

USA: 42 Elgin Rd, Dublin 4; tel. (1) 6688777; e-mail dublinrsvp@ state.gov; internet dublin.usembassy.gov; Ambassador KEVIN F. O'MALLEY.

Judicial System

Justice is administered in public by judges appointed by the President on the advice of the Government. The judges of all courts are completely independent in the exercise of their judicial functions. The jurisdiction and organization of the courts are dealt with in the Courts (Establishment and Constitution) Act, 1961, and the Courts (Supplemental Provisions) Acts, 1961 to 1981. An amendment to the Constitution, approved by a referendum held in October 2013, established a new Court of Appeal, which came into operation in October 2014, thereby creating an appellate jurisdictional level between the High Court and the Supreme Court.

Attorney-General: MÁIRE WHELAN.

SUPREME COURT

An Chúirt Uachtarach (The Supreme Court): Four Courts, Inns Quay, Dublin 7; tel. (1) 8886568; fax (1) 8732332; e-mail supremecourt@courts.ie; internet www.supremecourt.ie; consisting of the Chief Justice and seven other judges, the Supreme Court is the court of final appeal; it has appellate jurisdiction from decisions of the High Court and the Court of Appeal involving matters of exceptional public importance or which, in the interests of justice, ought to be heard by the Supreme Court; the President of Ireland may, after consultation with the Council of State, refer a bill that has been passed by both Houses of the Oireachtas (other than a money bill or certain others) to the Court to establish whether it or any other provisions thereof are repugnant to the Constitution; the President of the High Court is ex officio a member of the Supreme Court; Chief Justice SUSAN GAGEBY DENHAM.

COURT OF APPEAL

An Chúirt Achomhairc (Court of Appeal): Áras Uí Dhálaigh, Ground Floor, Inns Quay, Dublin 7; tel. (1) 8886120; e-mail courtofappealcivil@courts.ie; f. 2014; established as a result of an amendment to the Constitution to sit between the Supreme Court and the High Court; comprises a President and nine ordinary judges; the Chief Justice and Pres. of the High Court are *ex officio* judges; the Court hears appeals from the High Court in civil cases and from the Circuit Criminal Court, Central Criminal Court and the Special Criminal Court in criminal cases; Pres. SEÁN RYAN.

HIGH COURT

An Ard-Chúirt (The High Court): Four Courts, Inns Quay, Dublin 7; tel. (1) 8886442; fax (1) 8725669; e-mail highcourtcentraloffice@ courts.ie; internet www.courts.ie; comprising the President of the High Court and 36 ordinary judges, the High Court has full original jurisdiction in, and power to determine, all matters and questions whether of law or fact, civil or criminal; the High Court on circuit acts as an appeal court from the Circuit Court; the Central Criminal Court sits as directed by the President of the High Court to try criminal cases outside the jurisdiction of the Circuit Court; the duty of acting as the Central Criminal Court is assigned to a judge, or judges, of the High Court; the Chief Justice and the President of the Circuit Court are ex officio additional Judges of the High Court; Pres. NICHOLAS KEARNS; Master of the High Court EDMUND HONOHAN.

CIRCUIT AND DISTRICT COURTS

The civil jurisdiction of the Circuit Court is limited to claims up to the value of €75,000 in contract and tort and in actions founded on hire-purchase and credit-sale agreements and to a rateable value of €253.95 in equity, and in probate and administration, but where the parties consent the jurisdiction is unlimited. In criminal matters the Court has jurisdiction in all cases except murder, rape, treason, piracy and allied offences. One circuit court judge is permanently assigned to each of the eight circuits with the exception of Dublin, which has 10 judges, and Cork, which has three. The remainder of the 38 judges are not permanently assigned to any circuit. The President of the District Court is ex officio an additional Judge of the Circuit Court. The Circuit Court acts as an appeal court from the District Court, which has a summary jurisdiction in a large number of criminal cases where the offence is not of a serious nature. In civil matters the District Court has jurisdiction where the claim does not exceed €15,000.

All criminal cases, except those dealt with summarily by a judge in the District Court, are tried by a judge and a jury of 12 members. Juries are also used in some civil cases in the High Court. In a criminal case 10 members of the jury may, in certain circumstances, agree on a verdict, and in a civil case the agreement of nine members is sufficient.

President of An Chúirt Chuarda (the Circuit Court): RAYMOND GROARKE.

President of An Chúirt Dúiche (the District Court): ROSEMARY HORGAN.

Religion

CHRISTIANITY

The organization of the churches takes no account of the partition of the island of Ireland into two separate political entities; both Northern Ireland and Ireland are subject to a unified ecclesiastical jurisdiction. The Roman Catholic Primate of All Ireland and the Church of Ireland (Protestant Episcopalian) Primate of All Ireland have their seats in Northern Ireland, at Armagh, and the headquarters of the Presbyterian Church in Ireland is at Belfast, Northern Ireland.

Adherents of the Roman Catholic Church in Ireland were enumerated at 3,861,335 in the 2011 census, representing some 84% of the population. In the same year there were 129,039 adherents of the Church of Ireland, 24,600 of the Presbyterian Church and 6,842 of the Methodist Church. There were 45,223 adherents of Orthodox churches in that year.

Irish Council of Churches (ICC): Inter-Church Centre, 48 Elmwood Ave, Belfast, BT9 6AZ, Northern Ireland; tel. (28) 9066-3145; e-mail info@irishchurches.org; internet www.irishchurches.org;

f. 1922; present name adopted 1966; Pres. Dr DONALD WATTS; Exec. Officer MERVYN MCCULLAGH; 15 mem. churches.

The Roman Catholic Church

The island of Ireland comprises four archdioceses and 22 dioceses. Numerous Roman Catholic religious orders are strongly established in the state; these play an important role, particularly in the spheres of education, health and social welfare.

Irish Episcopal Conference: Ara Coeli, Cathedral Rd, Armagh, BT61 7QY, Northern Ireland; tel. (28) 3752-2045; fax (28) 3752-6182; e-mail admin@aracoeli.com; Pres. Most Rev. EAMON MARTIN.

Archbishop of Armagh and Primate of All Ireland: Most Rev. EAMON MARTIN, Ara Coeli, Cathedral Rd, Armagh, BT61 7QY, Northern Ireland; tel. (28) 3752-2045; fax (28) 3752-6182; e-mail admin@aracoeli.com; internet www.armagharchdiocese.org.

Archbishop of Cashel and Emly: Most Rev. KIERAN O'REILLY, Archbishop's House, Thurles, Co Tipperary; tel. (504) 21512; fax (504) 22680; e-mail office@cashel-emly.ie; internet www.cashel-emly.ie.

Archbishop of Dublin and Primate of Ireland: Most Rev. Dr DIARMUID MARTIN, Archbishop's House, Drumcondra, Dublin 9; tel. (1) 8379253; fax (1) 8360793; e-mail communications@dublindiocese.ie; internet www.dublindiocese.ie.

Archbishop of Tuam: Most Rev. Dr MICHAEL NEARY, Archbishop's House, St Jarlath's, Tuam, Co Galway; tel. (93) 24166; fax (93) 28070; e-mail archdiocesetuam@gmail.com; internet www.tuamarchdiocese.org.

Church of Ireland
(The Anglican Communion)

Ireland (including Northern Ireland) comprises two archdioceses and 10 dioceses.

Representative Body of the Church of Ireland: Church of Ireland House, Church Ave, Rathmines, Dublin 6; tel. (1) 4978422; fax (1) 4978821; e-mail office@rcbdub.org; internet rcb.ireland.anglican.org; Chief Officer and Sec. ADRIAN CLEMENTS.

Archbishop of Armagh and Primate of All Ireland and Metropolitan: Most Rev. Dr RICHARD CLARKE, The See House, Cathedral Close, Armagh, BT61 7EE, Northern Ireland; tel. (28) 3752-2858; fax (28) 3751-0596; e-mail archbishop@armagh.anglican.org; internet armagh.anglican.org.

Archbishop of Dublin and Bishop of Glendalough, Primate of Ireland and Metropolitan: Most Rev. Dr MICHAEL JACKSON, The See House, 17 Temple Rd, Milltown, Dublin 6; tel. (1) 4125663; e-mail archbishop@dublin.anglican.org; internet www.dublin.anglican.org.

Orthodox Churches

Greek Orthodox Church in Ireland: Greek Orthodox Church of the Annunciation, 46 Arbour Hill, Dublin 7; tel. and fax (1) 6779020; Pres. Very Rev. Dr IRENEU IOAN CRACIUN.

Russian Orthodox Church (Moscow Patriarchate) in Ireland: Harold's Cross Rd, Dublin 6; tel. (86) 7347934; e-mail stpeterstpaul@stpeterstpaul.net; internet www.stpeterstpaul.net; f. 2001; Parish Priest Very Rev. Fr MIKHAIL NASONOV.

Other Christian Churches

Association of Baptist Churches in Ireland: The Baptist Centre, 19 Hillsborough Rd, Moira, BT67 0HG, Northern Ireland; tel. (28) 9261-9267; e-mail abc@thebaptistcentre.org; internet www.baptistsinireland.org; Pres. Pastor PHILIP BROWN.

Lutheran Church in Ireland: Lutherhaus, 24 Adelaide Rd, Dublin 2; tel. and fax (1) 6766548; e-mail info@lutheran-ireland.org; internet www.lutheran-ireland.org; f. 1698; Pastors MARTIN WIELEPP.

Methodist Church in Ireland: 1 Fountainville Ave, Belfast, BT9 6AN, Northern Ireland; tel. (28) 9032-4554; fax (28) 9023-9467; e-mail secretary@irishmethodist.org; internet www.irishmethodist.org; Pres. Rev. KENNETH LINDSAY.

Presbyterian Church in Ireland: Assembly Bldgs, 2–10 Fisherwick Place, Belfast, BT1 6DW, Northern Ireland; tel. (28) 9032-2284; fax (28) 9041-7301; e-mail info@presbyterianireland.org; internet www.presbyterianireland.org; Moderator of Gen. Assembly Rev. Dr MICHAEL BARRY; Clerk of Assembly and Gen. Sec. Rev. TREVOR GRIBBEN.

Religious Society of Friends (Quakers) in Ireland: Quaker House, Stocking Lane, Rathfarnham, Dublin 16; tel. (1) 4998003; fax (1) 4998005; e-mail office@quakers.ie; internet www.quakers.ie; Recording Clerk ROSEMARY CASTAGNER.

ISLAM

The Muslim population of Ireland stood at 49,204 at the 2011 census.

Irish Council of Imams: 19 Roebuck Rd, Clonskeagh, Dublin 14; tel. (1) 2080000; fax (1) 2603708; e-mail imamhalawa@islamireland.ie; f. 2006; comprises 14 imams from across Ireland; Chair. Imam Sheikh HUSSEIN HALAWA; Vice-Chair. Sheikh YAHYA AL-HUSSEIN.

Islamic Cultural Centre of Ireland: 19 Roebuck Rd, Clonskeagh, Dublin 14; tel. (1) 2080000; fax (1) 2080001; e-mail info@islamireland.ie; internet www.islamireland.ie; f. 1996; CEO Dr NOOH AL-KADDO; Imam Sheikh HUSSEIN HALAWA.

Islamic Foundation of Ireland: 163 South Circular Rd, Dublin 8; tel. (1) 4533242; fax (1) 4532785; e-mail info@islaminireland.com; internet www.islaminireland.com; f. 1959; religious, cultural, educational and social org.; Imam YAHYA MUHAMMAD AL-HUSSEIN.

JUDAISM

At the 2011 census, the Jewish community numbered 1,984. In 2008 there were a total of three synagogues operating, of which two were Orthodox and one was progressive.

Chief Rabbi: ZALMAN LENT, Herzog House, Zion Rd, Rathgar, Dublin 6; tel. (1) 4923751; fax (1) 4920888; e-mail rabbilent@jewishireland.org; internet www.jewishireland.org.

The Press

A significant feature of the Irish press is the number of weekly and twice-weekly newspapers published in provincial centres.

DAILIES

(Average net circulation figures, including Ireland and the UK, as at December 2011, unless otherwise stated)

Cork

Evening Echo: City Quarter, Lapps Quay, Cork; tel. (21) 4272722; fax (21) 4273846; e-mail news@eecho.ie; internet www.eveningecho.ie; f. 1892; Editor MAURICE GUBBINS; circ. 17,556 (2012).

Irish Examiner: City Quarter, Lapps Quay, Cork; tel. (21) 4272722; fax (21) 4273846; e-mail editor@examiner.ie; internet www.irishexaminer.com; f. 1841; Editor TIM VAUGHAN; circ. 42,083.

Dublin

Evening Herald: Independent House, 27–32 Talbot St, Dublin 1; tel. (1) 7055333; fax (1) 7055497; e-mail hnews@herald.ie; internet www.herald.ie; f. 1891; Editor ALAN STEENSON; circ. 62,411.

Irish Daily Mail: Embassy House, 3rd Floor, Herbert Park Lane, Dublin 4; tel. (1) 6375800; fax (1) 6375880; internet www.dailymail.co.uk; Propr Associated Newspapers (UK); Editor-in-Chief SEBASTIAN HAMILTON; circ. 50,486.

Irish Daily Star: Independent House, 27–32 Talbot St, Dublin 1; tel. (1) 4901228; fax (1) 4907425; e-mail info@thestar.ie; internet www.thestar.ie; Editor GERARD COLLERAN; circ. 61,590 (Jan.—June 2014).

Irish Independent: Independent House, 27–32 Talbot St, Dublin 1; tel. (1) 7055333; fax (1) 8720304; internet www.independent.ie; f. 1905; Editor CLAIRE GRADY; circ. 131,161.

The Irish Times: Irish Times Bldg, 24–28 Tara St, Dublin 2; tel. (1) 6758000; fax (1) 6758035; e-mail newsdesk@irishtimes.com; internet www.irishtimes.com; f. 1859; Editor KEVIN O'SULLIVAN; circ. 96,150.

Metro Herald: Independent House, 1st Floor, 27–32 Talbot St, Dublin 1; tel. (1) 7055055; fax (1) 7055044; e-mail info@metroherald.ie; internet www.metroherald.ie; f. 2009 by merger of *Metro* and *Herald AM* (both f. 2005); distributed free of charge in the Greater Dublin area; Man. Dir PAUL CROSBIE; circ. 60,151.

OTHER NEWSPAPERS

(Average net circulation figures, including Ireland and the UK, as at December 2011, unless otherwise stated)

An Phoblacht: 58 Parnell Sq., Dublin 1; tel. (1) 8733611; fax (1) 8733074; e-mail editor@anphoblacht.com; internet www.anphoblacht.com; f. 1970; organ of Sinn Féin; monthly; Editor JOHN HEDGES; circ. 15,000 (2007).

Anglo-Celt: Station House, Cavan, Co Cavan; tel. (49) 4331100; fax (49) 4332280; e-mail linda@anglocelt.ie; internet www.anglocelt.ie; f. 1846; Thur.; Editor LINDA O'REILLY; circ. 12,310.

Argus: Partnership Court, Park St, Dundalk, Co Louth; tel. (42) 9334632; fax (42) 9331643; e-mail editorial@argus.ie; internet www.argus.ie; f. 1835; Thur.; circ. 11,507 (2007).

Clare Champion: Barrack St, Ennis, Co Clare; tel. (65) 6828105; fax (65) 6820374; e-mail editor@clarechampion.ie; internet www.clarechampion.ie; f. 1903; Thur.; Editor AUSTIN HOBBS; circ. 15,742.

Connacht Tribune: 15 Market St, Galway; tel. (91) 536222; fax (91) 567970; e-mail cormac@ctribune.ie; internet www.galwaynews.ie; f. 1909; Fri.; Group Editor DAVE O'CONNELL; circ. 20,702.

Connaught Telegraph: Cavendish Lane, Castlebar, Co Mayo; tel. (94) 9021711; fax (94) 9024007; e-mail info@con-telegraph.ie; internet www.con-telegraph.ie; f. 1828; Tue.; independent; Editor TOM GILLESPIE; circ. 14,900.

Donegal Democrat: Larkin House, Oldtown Rd, Donegal, Co Donegal; tel. (7491) 28000; e-mail editorial@donegaldemocrat.com; internet www.donegaldemocrat.com; f. 1919; Tue. and Thur.; Editor MICHAEL DALY; circ. 6,618 (Tue.); 9,191 (Thur.).

Drogheda Independent: 9 Shop St, Drogheda, Co Louth; tel. (41) 9838658; fax (41) 9834271; e-mail editorial@drogheda-independent .ie; internet www.drogheda-independent.ie; f. 1884; Thur.; circ. 10,328 (2007).

Dundalk Democrat: 7 Crowe St, Dundalk, Co Louth; tel. (42) 9334058; fax (42) 9331399; e-mail editor@dundalkdemocrat.ie; internet www.dundalkdemocrat.ie; f. 1849; Wed.; Editor ANTHONY MURPHY; circ. 6,500 (2007).

Dungarvan Observer: Shandon, Dungarvan, Co Waterford; tel. (58) 41205; fax (58) 41559; e-mail news@dungarvanobserver.ie; internet www.dungarvanobserver.ie; f. 1912; Editor JAMES A. LYNCH.

The Echo: Slaney Pl., Enniscorthy, Co Wexford; tel. (53) 9259900; fax (53) 9233506; e-mail editor@theecho.ie; internet www.theecho.ie; f. 1902; Wed.; edns for Enniscorthy, Gorey, New Ross and Wexford; Editor TOM MOONEY; circ. 7,210.

Iris Oifigiúil (Official Irish Gazette): 52 St Stephen's Green, Dublin 2; tel. (1) 6476636; fax (1) 6476843; e-mail irisoifigiuil@opw.ie; internet www.irisoifigiuil.ie; f. 1922; twice weekly (Tue. and Fri.); Editor DEIRDRE CARROLL.

Irish Mail on Sunday: Embassy House, 3rd Floor, Herbert Park Lane, Dublin 4; tel. (1) 6375800; fax (1) 4179830; Propr Associated Newspapers (UK); fmrly *Ireland on Sunday*; name changed to current in 2006; Editor-in-Chief CONOR O'DONNELL; circ. 122,231.

The Kerryman: Denny St, Tralee, Co Kerry; tel. (66) 7145500; fax (66) 7145572; e-mail dmalone@kerryman.ie; internet www .kerryman.ie; f. 1904; Thur.; Editor DECLAN MALONE; circ. 26,392 (2007).

Kilkenny People: 34 High St, Kilkenny; tel. (56) 7721015; fax (56) 7721414; e-mail editor@kilkennypeople.ie; internet www .kilkennypeople.ie; f. 1892; weekly; Editor BRIAN KEYES; circ. 11,536.

Leinster Express: Dublin Rd, Portlaoise, Co Laois; tel. (57) 8621666; fax (57) 8620491; e-mail conor.ganly@leinsterexpress.ie; internet www.leinsterexpress.ie; f. 1831; weekly; Editor PAT SOMERS; circ. 11,070 (incl. *Offaly Express*).

Leinster Leader: 19 South Main St, Naas, Co Kildare; tel. (45) 897302; fax (45) 897647; e-mail editor@leinsterleader.ie; internet www.leinsterleader.ie; f. 1880; Tue.; Editor DAVID POWER; circ. 6,497.

Limerick Leader: 54 O'Connell St, Limerick; tel. (61) 214500; fax (61) 401424; e-mail admin@limerick-leader.ie; internet www .limerick-leader.ie; f. 1889; 4 a week; Editor ALAN ENGLISH; circ. 14,851 (weekend edn).

Limerick Post: 97 Henry St, Limerick; tel. (61) 413322; fax (61) 417684; e-mail news@limerickpost.ie; internet www.limerickpost.ie; f. 1986; owned by Carnbeg Limited; distributed free of charge; Thur.; Dir JOHN RYAN; circ. 51,829.

The Mayo News: The Fairgreen, Westport, Co Mayo; tel. (98) 25311; fax (98) 26108; e-mail info@mayonews.ie; internet www.mayonews .ie; f. 1892; Tue.; Man. Editor NEILL O'NEILL; circ. 10,569 (2013).

Midland Tribune: Main St, Birr, Co Offaly; tel. (57) 9120003; fax (57) 9120588; e-mail editor@midlandtribune.ie; internet www .midlandtribune.ie; f. 1881; Wed.; Editor JOHN O'CALLAGHAN; circ. 10,105 (2007).

The Nationalist: Hanover House, Hanover, Carlow; tel. (59) 9170100; fax (59) 9130301; e-mail news@carlow-nationalist.ie; internet www.carlow-nationalist.ie; f. 1883; owned by Thomas Crosbie Holdings; Editor CONAL O'BOYLE.

Offaly Express: Bridge St, Tullamore, Co Offaly; tel. (57) 9321744; fax (57) 9351930; e-mail alan@offalyexpress.ie; internet www .offalyexpress.ie; weekly; Editor ALAN WALSH; circ. 11,070 (incl. *Leinster Express*).

Sligo Champion: Connacht House, Markievicz Rd, Sligo; tel. (71) 9169222; fax (71) 9169040; e-mail editor@sligochampion.ie; internet www.sligochampion.ie; f. 1836; Tue.; Editor JENNY MCCUDDEN; circ. 12,574 (2007).

The Southern Star: Ilen St, Skibbereen, Co Cork; tel. (28) 21200; fax (28) 21071; e-mail info@southernstar.ie; internet www .southernstar.ie; f. 1889; Sat.; Editor CON DOWNING; circ. 14,500 (2007).

Sunday Business Post: 80 Harcourt St, Dublin 2; tel. (1) 6026000; fax (1) 6796496; e-mail info@sbpost.ie; internet www.businesspost .ie; f. 1989; Editor PAT LEAHY (acting); circ. 39,416.

Sunday Independent: Independent House, 27–32 Talbot St, Dublin 1; tel. (1) 7055333; fax (1) 7055779; e-mail sunday.letters@ independent.ie; internet www.independent.ie; f. 1905; Editor COR- MAC BOURKE; circ. 220,565 (2014).

Sunday World: Independent House, 27–32 Talbot St, Dublin 1; tel. (1) 8848900; fax (1) 8849002; e-mail news@sundayworld.com; internet www.sundayworld.com; f. 1973; Editor COLM MCGINTY; circ. 251,455.

Tipperary Star: Friar St, Thurles, Co Tipperary; tel. (504) 21122; e-mail info@tipperarystar.ie; internet www.tipperarystar.ie; f. 1909; Wed.; Editor ANNE O'GRADY; circ. 7,115.

Tuam Herald: Dublin Rd, Tuam, Co Galway; tel. (93) 24183; fax (93) 24478; e-mail editor@tuamherald.ie; internet www.tuamherald.ie; f. 1837; Wed.; Editor DAVID BURKE; circ. 8,482.

Tullamore Tribune: William St, Tullamore, Co Offaly; tel. (5793) 21152; fax (5793) 21927; e-mail editor@tullamoretribune.ie; internet www.tullamoretribune.ie; f. 1978; Wed.; Editor GERARD SCULLY.

Waterford News & Star: Gladstone House, Gladstone St, Water- ford; tel. (51) 874951; fax (51) 855281; e-mail editor@waterford-news .ie; internet www.waterford-news.ie; f. 1848; Thur.; Editor FRANCES RYAN.

Western People: Tone St, Ballina, Co Mayo; tel. (96) 60999; fax (96) 70208; e-mail info@westernpeople.ie; internet www.westernpeople .ie; f. 1883; Tue.; Editor JAMES LAFFEY; circ. 14,166.

Westmeath Examiner: Blackhall Pl., Mullingar, Co Westmeath; tel. (44) 9346700; fax (44) 9330765; e-mail editor@ westmeathexaminer.ie; internet www.westmeathexaminer.ie; f. 1882; weekly; Editor BRIAN O'LOUGHLIN; circ. 5,799.

Wicklow People: Channing House, Upper Row St, Wicklow, Co Wexford; tel. (53) 9140100; fax (53) 9140192; e-mail front.office@ peoplenews.ie; internet www.wicklowpeople.ie; weekly; circ. 13,122 (2007).

SELECTED PERIODICALS

Afloat: 2 Lower Glenageary Rd, Dún Laoghaire, Co Dublin; tel. (1) 2846161; fax (1) 2846192; e-mail info@afloat.ie; internet www.afloat .ie; monthly; sailing and boating; Man. Editor DAVID O'BRIEN.

Banking Ireland: 1 North Wall Quay, Dublin 1; tel. (1) 6116500; fax (1) 6116565; e-mail info@bankers.ie; internet www.instbankers.com/ bi/index.html; f. 1898; quarterly; journal of the Inst. of Bankers in Ireland; circ. 15,500 (Dec. 2006).

Books Ireland: Unit 9, 78 Furze Rd, Sandyford Industrial Estate, Dublin 18; tel. (1) 2933568; e-mail booksireland@wordwellbooks .com; internet www.booksirelandmagazine.com; f. 1976; owned by Wordwell Books Ltd; 6 a year; reviews Irish-interest books; Editor ANTHONY CANAVAN; circ. 2,350 (Dec. 2013).

Business & Finance: Unit 1A, Waters Edge, Charlotte Quay, Dublin 4; tel. (1) 2377000; fax (1) 6602504; e-mail info@ businessandfinance.com; internet www.businessandfinance.com; f. 1964; bi-monthly; Publr IAN HYLAND; Editor NIAMH MAC SWEENEY; circ. 10,000.

Food & Wine: Rosemount House, Dundrum Rd, Dundrum, Dublin 16; tel. (1) 2405300; fax (1) 6619486; e-mail matkins@harmonia.ie; internet www.harmonia.ie; f. 1997; publ. by Harmonia Ltd; Editor MIRIAM ATKINS; circ. 8,607 (2012).

Hot Press: 13 Trinity St, Dublin 2; tel. (1) 2411500; fax (1) 2411538; e-mail info@hotpress.com; internet www.hotpress.com; fortnightly; music, leisure, current affairs; Editor NIALL STOKES; circ. 17,178 (2012).

House and Home: Cunningham House, 130 Francis St, Dublin 8; tel. (1) 4167930; fax (1) 4167901; e-mail info@dyflin.ie; internet www .houseandhome.ie; bi-monthly; published by Dyflin Media Ltd; interior decor.

Image: 22 Crofton Rd, Dún Laoghaire, Co Dublin; tel. (1) 2808415; fax (1) 2808309; e-mail info@image.ie; internet www.image.ie; f. 1975; bi-monthly; women's fashion, lifestyle; Editor MELANIE MORRIS; circ. 21,511.

Ireland's Own: Channing House, Rowe St, Co Wexford; tel. (53) 9140140; fax (53) 9140192; e-mail irelands.own@peoplenews.ie; f. 1902; weekly; family interest; Editors SEAN NOLAN, SHEA TOMPKINS; circ. 38,033 (2011).

The Irish Catholic: St Mary's, Bloomfield Ave, Donnybrook, Dublin 4; tel. (1) 6874020; fax (1) 4276450; e-mail news@irishcatholic.ie; internet www.irishcatholic.ie; f. 1888; publ. by Grace Communica- tions; weekly; Man. Editor MICHAEL KELLY; circ. 30,000 (2012).

Irish Computer: Media House, South County Business Park, Leopardstown, Dublin 18; tel. (1) 2947777; fax (1) 2947799; e-mail info@mediateam.ie; internet www.techcentral.ie; f. 1977; monthly; Editor BILLY HUGGARD; circ. 4,000 (+1,500 to Irish Computer Society members).

Irish Farmers' Journal: Irish Farm Centre, Bluebell, Dublin 12; tel. (1) 4199599; fax (1) 4520876; e-mail jmccarthy@farmersjournal

.ie; internet www.farmersjournal.ie; f. 1948; weekly; Editor JUSTIN MCCARTHY; weekly circ. 70,111 (July–Dec 2012).

The Irish Field: Irish Farm Centre, Bluebell, Dublin 12; tel. (1) 4051100; fax (1) 4554008; e-mail info@theirishfield.ie; internet www.theirishfield.ie; f. 1870; publ. by the Agricultural Trust; weekly; horse racing, breeding and equine leisure; Man. Editor LEO POWELL; circ. 11,117 (July–Dec 2012).

Irish Historical Studies: c/o Dept of History, Trinity College, Dublin 2; tel. (1) 6081020; e-mail info@irishhistoricalstudies.ie; internet www.irishhistoricalstudies.ie; f. 1938; 2 a year; publ. by Irish Historical Studies Publications Ltd; Editors Dr ROBERT ARMSTRONG, Dr ROBERT MCNAMARA.

Irish Journal of Medical Science: Royal Academy of Medicine in Ireland, Setanta House, 2nd Floor, Setanta Pl., Dublin 2; tel. (1) 6334820; fax (1) 6334918; e-mail helenmoore@rcpi.ie; internet www.ijms.ie; f. 1832; quarterly; organ of the Royal Academy of Medicine; Editor Prof. JAMES JONES.

Irish Law Times: Thomson Reuters, Round Hall, 43 Fitzwilliam Pl., Dublin 2; tel. (1) 6625301; fax (1) 6625302; e-mail martin.mccann@thomsonreuters.com; internet www.roundhall.ie; f. 1983; 20 a year; Editor DAVID BOYLE.

Irish Medical Journal: 10 Fitzwilliam Pl., Dublin 2; tel. (1) 6767273; fax (1) 6612758; e-mail lduffy@imj.ie; internet www.imj.ie; f. 1867; 10 a year; journal of the Irish Medical Org; Editor Dr JOHN F. A. MURPHY.

The Irish Skipper: Unit 5, Teach na Rosann, Annagry, Co Donegal; tel. (74) 9548935; fax (74) 9548940; e-mail hugh@maramedia.ie; internet www.irishskipper.net; f. 1964; monthly; journal of the commercial fishing and aquaculture industries; Editor HUGH BONNER.

Irish Tatler: Rosemount House, Dundrum Rd, Dundrum, Dublin 16; tel. (1) 2405300; fax (1) 6619486; internet www.irishtatler.com; f. 1890; monthly; Editor JESSIE COLLINS; circ. 24,919 (July–Dec 2012).

Irish University Review: School of English, Drama and Film, University College Dublin, Belfield, Dublin 4; tel. (1) 7168181; fax (1) 7161174; e-mail john.brannigan@ucd.ie; internet www.irishuniversityreview.ie; f. 1970; 2 a year; literature, history, fine arts, politics, cultural studies; Editor Dr JOHN BRANNIGAN.

Law Society Gazette: Law Society of Ireland, Blackhall Pl., Dublin 7; tel. (1) 6724800; fax (1) 6724801; e-mail gazette@lawsociety.ie; internet www.gazette.ie; f. 1907; 10 a year; publ. by the Law Society of Ireland; Editor MARK MCDERMOTT.

Motoring Life: 48 North Great George's St, Dublin 1; tel. (1) 8780444; fax (1) 8787740; e-mail info@motoringlife.ie; internet www.motoringlife.ie; f. 1946; bi-monthly; Editor GERALDINE HERBERT.

The Phoenix: 44 Lower Baggot St, Dublin 2; tel. (1) 6611062; fax (1) 6624532; e-mail editor@thephoenix.ie; internet www.thephoenix.ie; f. 1983; fortnightly; news and comment, satirical; Editor PADDY PRENDIVILLE; circ. 14,013 (July–Dec 2012).

Poetry Ireland (Éigse Éireann): 32 Kildare St, Dublin 2; tel. (1) 6789815; fax (1) 6789782; e-mail info@poetryireland.ie; internet www.poetryireland.ie; quarterly; Editor VONA GROARKE.

RTÉ Guide: Radio Telefís Éireann, Donnybrook, Dublin 4; tel. (1) 2083111; fax (1) 2083080; internet www.rteguide.ie; weekly; programmes of the Irish broadcasting service; Editor CATHERINE LEE; circ. 61,881 (2012).

ShelfLife: Media House, South County Business Park, Leopardstown, Dublin 18; tel. (1) 2947777; fax (1) 2947799; e-mail shelflife@mediateam.ie; internet www.shelflife.ie; monthly; food, drinks, grocery, consumer goods sectors; owned by Mediateam LTD; Man. Dir JOHN MCDONALD; Editor FIONNUALA CAROLAN; circ. 7,795 (2012).

Studies: An Irish Quarterly Review: 37 Lower Leeson St, Dublin 2; tel. (1) 6767491; fax (1) 6767493; e-mail studies@jesuit.ie; internet www.studiesirishreview.ie; f. 1912; published by the Jesuits In Ireland; quarterly review of letters, history, religious and social questions; Editor Fr BRUCE BRADLEY.

U Magazine: Rosemount House, Dundrum Rd, Dundrum, Dublin 14; tel. (1) 2405300; fax (1) 6619757; e-mail jstevens@harmonia.ie; internet www.harmonia.ie/#/20; f. 1979; every 2 weeks; for young women; Editor JENNIFER STEVENS; circ. 27,819 (2012).

Village Magazine: 6 Ormond Quay Upper, Dublin 7; tel. (1) 8735824; fax (1) 6425001; e-mail editor@villagemagazine.ie; internet www.villagemagazine.ie; f. 2004; monthly; current affairs; Editor MICHAEL SMITH.

Woman's Way: Rosemount House, Dundrum Rd, Dundrum, Dublin 14; tel. (1) 2405300; fax (1) 6628719; e-mail atoner@harmonia.ie; internet www.womansway.ie; f. 1963; 51 a year; Editor AINE TONER; circ. 21,321 (2013).

NEWS AGENCY

Ireland International News Agency: 51 Wellington Quay, Dublin 2; tel. (1) 6712442; fax (1) 6796586; e-mail iina@eircom.net; Man. Dir DIARMAID MACDERMOTT.

PRESS ORGANIZATIONS

National Newspapers of Ireland: Clyde Lodge, 15 Clyde Rd, Dublin 4; tel. (1) 6689099; fax (1) 6689872; e-mail info@nni.ie; internet www.nni.ie; f. 1985; 16 mems; Chair. VINCENT CROWLEY; Co-ordinating Dir DARA MCMAHON.

Regional Newspapers and Printers Association of Ireland: Latt, Cavan; tel. and fax (1) 6779116; e-mail johanlon@localireland.info; internet www.localireland.info; f. 1917; 35 mems; Pres. SEAN MAHON; Dir JOHNNY O'HANLON.

Publishers

Blackhall Publishing: Lonsdale House, Avoca Ave, Dublin; tel. (1) 2785090; fax (1) 2784800; e-mail info@blackhallpublishing.com; internet www.blackhallpublishing.com; f. 1997; law, business, marketing, management.

Boole Press: 19 Silchester Rd, Glenageary, Co Dublin; e-mail info@boolepress.com; internet www.boolepress.com; f. 1979; scientific, technical, medical, scholarly; Man. Dir Dr J. MILLER.

Cló Iar-Chonnachta: Inverin, Connemara, Co Galway; tel. (91) 593307; fax (91) 593362; e-mail eolas@cic.ie; internet www.cic.ie; f. 1985; music, children's books; Gen. Man. DEIRDRE NÍ THUATHAIL.

The Columba Press: 55A Spruce Ave, Stillorgan Industrial Park, Blackrock, Co Dublin; tel. (1) 2942556; fax (1) 2942564; e-mail info@columba.ie; internet www.columba.ie; f. 1985; sport, health, food, music, history, religion, memoirs, politics and fiction; Publr FEARGHAL O'BOYLE.

Comhairle Bhéaloideas Éireann (Folklore of Ireland Council): University College, Belfield, Dublin 4; tel. (1) 7168216; fax (1) 17161144; e-mail info@comhairlebheal.ie; internet comhairlebheal.ie; Editor Prof. RÍONACH UÍ ÓGÁIN.

Cork University Press: Youngline Industrial Estate, Pouladuff Rd, Togher, Cork; tel. (21) 4902980; internet www.corkuniversitypress.com; f. 1925; owned by University College Cork; academic, art, music, geography, literature, history; imprints include Attic Press and Atrium; Publications Dir MIKE COLLINS.

Dedalus Press: 13 Moyclare Rd, Baldoyle, Dublin 13; tel. (1) 8392034; e-mail editor@dedaluspress.com; internet www.dedaluspress.com; f. 1985; Irish and some international poetry, occasional prose; Publr and Editor PAT BORAN.

Dominican Publications: 42 Parnell Sq., Dublin 1; tel. (1) 8731355; fax (1) 8731760; e-mail sales@dominicanpublications.com; internet www.dominicanpublications.com; f. 1897; religious affairs in Ireland and the developing world, pastoral-liturgical aids; Man. Rev. BERNARD TREACY.

CJ Fallon: Block B, Ground Floor, Liffey Valley Office Campus, Dublin 22; tel. (1) 6166400; fax (1) 6166499; e-mail editorial@cjfallon.ie; internet www.cjfallon.ie; f. 1927; educational; CEO BRIAN GILSENAN.

Four Courts Press: 7 Malpas St, Dublin 8; tel. (1) 4534668; fax (1) 4534672; e-mail info@fourcourtspress.ie; internet www.fourcourtspress.ie; f. 1970; philosophy, theology, Celtic and Medieval studies, art, literature, modern history; Editorial Dir MARTIN FANNING; Publr MARTIN HEALY.

The Gallery Press: Loughcrew, Oldcastle, Co Meath; tel. and fax (49) 8541779; e-mail gallery@indigo.ie; internet www.gallerypress.com; f. 1970; poetry, plays, prose by Irish authors; Publr and Editor PETER FALLON.

Gill and Macmillan: Hume Ave, Park West, Dublin 12; tel. (1) 5009500; fax (1) 5009597; e-mail sales@gillmacmillan.ie; internet www.gillmacmillan.ie; f. 1968; literature, biography, history, social sciences, current affairs and textbooks; Chair. MICHAEL GILL.

Hachette Ireland: Unit 8, Castlecourt Centre, Dublin 15; tel. (1) 8246288; e-mail info@hbgi.ie; internet www.hachette.ie; f. 2002 as Hodder Headline Ireland; fiction, non-fiction; div. of Hachette UK; Editorial Dir CIARA DOORLEY.

Irish Academic Press: 8 Chapel Lane, Sallins, Co. Kildare; tel. (45) 895562; e-mail info@iap.ie; internet www.iap.ie; f. 1974; academic and popular, mainly history and Irish studies; Publr CONOR GRAHAM; Man. Editor LISA HYDE.

Liberties Press: 140 Terenure Rd North, Dublin 6; tel. (1) 4151286; e-mail info@libertiespress.com; internet www.libertiespress.com; f. 2003; sport, health, food, music, art, history, religion, politics, fiction, poetry; Publr SEÁN O'KEEFFE.

Lilliput Press: 62/63 Sitric Rd, Arbour Hill, Dublin 7; tel. (1) 6711647; fax (1) 6711233; e-mail info@lilliputpress.ie; internet www.lilliputpress.ie; f. 1985; ecology and environment, literary criticism, biography, memoirs, fiction, Irish history, general; Publr ANTONY FARRELL.

Mentor Books: 43 Furze Rd, Sandyford Industrial Estate, Dublin 18; tel. (1) 2952112; fax (1) 2952114; e-mail admin@mentorbooks.ie; internet www.mentorbooks.ie; f. 1979; adult and children's fiction and non-fiction, educational; Man. Dir DANIEL MCCARTHY.

Mercier Press Ltd: Unit 3B, Oak House, Bessboro Rd, Blackrock, Co Cork; tel. (21) 4614700; fax (21) 4614802; e-mail info@mercierpress.ie; internet www.mercierpress.ie; f. 1944; folklore, history, biography, current affairs, fiction, politics, humour, religious; Man. Dir CLODAGH FEEHAN.

O'Brien Press Ltd: 12 Terenure Rd East, Rathgar, Dublin 6; tel. (1) 4923333; fax (1) 4922777; e-mail books@obrien.ie; internet www.obrien.ie; f. 1974; biography, history, sport, Celtic, politics, travel, crime, children's, literary fiction; Man. Dir IVAN O'BRIEN.

Poolbeg Press: 123 Grange Hill, Baldoyle Industrial Estate, Dublin 13; tel. (1) 8321477; fax (1) 8321430; e-mail info@poolbeg.com; internet www.poolbeg.com; f. 1976; general, poetry, politics, children's; Publr PAULA CAMPBELL.

Royal Irish Academy (Acadamh Ríoga na hÉireann): 19 Dawson St, Dublin 2; tel. (1) 6762570; fax (1) 6762346; e-mail admin@ria.ie; internet www.ria.ie; f. 1785; humanities and sciences; Man. Editor RUTH HEGARTY; Exec. Sec. LAURA MAHONEY.

Thomson Reuters/Round Hall: 43 Fitzwilliam Pl., Dublin 2; tel. (1) 6625301; fax (1) 6625302; e-mail catherine.dolan@thomsonreuters.com; internet www.roundhall.ie; f. 1980 as The Round Hall Press; law books and journals and Westlaw IE online; part of Thomson Reuters; Publr CATHERINE DOLAN.

Veritas Publications: 7–8 Lower Abbey St, Dublin 1; tel. (1) 8788177; fax (1) 8786507; e-mail publications@veritas.ie; internet www.veritas.ie; f. 1969; Christian, religious and educational, theological, liturgical; Dir MAURA HYLAND.

GOVERNMENT PUBLISHING HOUSE

Oifig an tSoláthair/Stationery Office: Government Publications, Office of Public Works, 52 St Stephen's Green, Dublin 2; tel. (1) 6476834; fax (1) 6476843; e-mail publications@opw.ie; internet www.opw.ie; Asst Principal Officer GERRY BURKE.

PUBLISHERS' ASSOCIATION

Publishing Ireland/Foilsiú Éireann: 25 Denzille Lane, Dublin 8; tel. (1) 6394868; e-mail info@publishingireland.com; internet www.publishingireland.com; f. 1970 as CLE—Irish Book Publishers' Association; 100 mem. publishers; Pres. MICHAEL MCLOUGHLIN.

Broadcasting and Communications

TELECOMMUNICATIONS

eircom: 1 Heuston South Quarter, St John's Rd, Dublin 8; tel. (1) 6714444; fax (1) 6716916; e-mail investor.relations@eircom.ie; internet www.eircom.ie; f. 1984; fmrly Telecom Éireann; offers fixed-line telecommunications and internet access; partially privatized in 1999, acquired by BCM Ireland Holdings Ltd in August 2006; Chair. PADRAIG MCMANUS; CEO RICHARD MOAT.

Meteor Mobile Communications Ltd: 1 Heuston South Quarter, St John's Rd, Dublin 8; tel. (1) 4307085; fax (1) 4307013; e-mail info@meteor.ie; internet www.meteor.ie; f. 2001; mobile cellular telecommunications; subsidiary of eircom; 1,065,000 subscribers (March 2010).

Hutchison 3G Ireland Ltd (3 Ireland): 1 Clarendon Row, 3rd Floor, Dublin 2; tel. (1) 5426300; fax (1) 5426301; e-mail customer.services.ie@3mail.com; internet www.three.ie; f. 2005; mobile cellular telecommunications; owned by Hutchison Whampoa Ltd (Hong Kong); 500,000 subscribers (June 2010); CEO ROBERT FINNEGAN.

Telefónica O₂ Ireland Ltd: 28–29 Sir John Rogerson's Quay, Dublin 2; tel. (1) 6095000; e-mail customercare@o2.ie; internet www.o2online.ie; f. 1997; mobile cellular telecommunications and broadband internet access; acquired by Hutchison Whampoa Ltd (Hong Kong) 2014; CEO TONY HANWAY.

Vodafone Ireland: Mountainview, Leopardstown, Dublin 18; tel. (1) 2038232; fax (1) 6708465; e-mail custcare@vodafone.ie; internet www.vodafone.ie; f. 2001, following acquisition of Eircell; mobile cellular telecommunications; subsidiary of Vodafone Group PLC (UK); Chief Exec. ANNE O'LEARY.

Regulatory Authority

Commission for Communications Regulation (ComReg): Block DEF, Abbey Court, Irish Life Centre, Lower Abbey St, Dublin 1; tel. (1) 8049600; fax (1) 8049680; e-mail info@comreg.ie; internet www.comreg.ie; f. 2002; regulatory authority for Ireland's postal and telecommunications sectors; issues licences to service providers; manages the interconnection of telecommunications networks; approves equipment and oversees national telephone numbering; Chair. KEVIN O'BRIEN.

BROADCASTING

The Radio and Television Act of 1988 provided for the establishment of an independent television station, an independent national radio service and a series of local radio stations.

Broadcasting Authority of Ireland (BAI): 2–5 Warrington Pl., Dublin 2; tel. (1) 6441200; fax (1) 6441299; e-mail info@bai.ie; internet www.bai.ie; f. 2009 to replace the Broadcasting Commission of Ireland (f. 1988) and the Broadcasting Complaints Commission (f. 1977); responsible for regulating public service and independent broadcasting in Ireland; also responsible for the licensing of new broadcasting services, as well as the development of codes of programming and advertising standards for television and radio services; Chair. Dr PAURIC TRAVERS.

Radio

Raidió Teilifís Éireann (RTÉ): Donnybrook, Dublin 4; tel. (1) 2083111; fax (1) 2083080; e-mail info@rte.ie; internet www.rte.ie; f. 1960; national public service broadcasting corpn; financed by net licence revenue and sale of advertising time; governed by Board of 12 mems; operates 4 radio networks; Chair. MOYA DOHERTY; Dir-Gen. NOEL CURRAN; Man. Dir of Radio JIM JENNINGS; Man. Dir of Television GLEN KILLANE; Man. Dir of News KEVIN BAKHURST.

   RTÉ lyric fm: Cornmarket Sq., Limerick, Co Limerick; tel. (61) 207300; fax (61) 207390; e-mail lyric@rte.ie; internet www.rte.ie/lyricfm; broadcasts classical and traditional music, jazz, opera; Dir AODÁN Ó DUBHGHAILL.

   RTÉ Radio 1: Donnybrook, Dublin 4; tel. (1) 2083111; e-mail info@rte.ie; internet www.rte.ie/radio1; music news, drama and entertainment programmes; Dir TOM MCGUIRE.

   RTÉ Raidió na Gaeltachta: Casla, Connemara, Co Galway; tel. (91) 506677; fax (91) 506666; e-mail rnag@rte.ie; internet www.rte.ie/rnag; f. 1972; broadcasts in Irish.

   RTÉ 2FM: Donnybrook, Dublin 4; tel. (1) 2083111; e-mail info@rte.ie; internet 2fm.rte.ie; popular music; Head DAN HEALY.

Classic Hits 4FM: Castleforbes House, Ground Floor, Castleforbes Rd, Dublin 1; tel. (1) 4255400; fax (1) 4255444; e-mail info@4fm.ie; internet www.4fm.ie; f. 2009; broadcasting popular music programmes in Co Clare, Co Cork, Co Dublin, Co Galway and Co Limerick; Chief Exec. SEAN ASHMORE.

FM104: Macken House, Mayor St Upper, North Wall, Dublin 1; tel. (1) 5006600; fax (1) 6689401; e-mail sales@fm104.ie; internet www.fm104.ie; broadcasts popular music and entertainment programmes in Co Dublin; owned by UTV (UK); Chief Exec. MARGARET NELSON.

NewsTalk 106–108 FM: Marconi House, Digges Lane, Dublin 2; tel. (1) 6445100; fax (1) 6445101; e-mail info@newstalk.ie; internet www.newstalk.ie; f. 2002; began broadcasting news and talk programmes nationally in 2006; Propr Communicorp Group; Chair. DENIS O'BRIEN; Chief Exec. GERARD WHELAN.

98 FM: South Block, The Malt House, Grand Canal Quay, Dublin 2; tel. (1) 4398800; fax (1) 4398899; e-mail info@98fm.com; internet www.98fm.com; f. 1989; provides news service to independent local radio stations under contract from the BAI; Propr Communicorp Group; CEO KEITH MCCORMACK.

100-102 Today FM: Marconi House, Digges Lane, Dublin 2; tel. (1) 8049000; fax (1) 8049099; e-mail info@todayfm.com; internet www.todayfm.com; f. 1998; national, independent station; acquired by Communicorp Group 2007; Chair. JOHN MCCOLGAN; CEO PETER MCPARTLIN.

There are also local radio stations operating under the supervision of the Independent Radio and Television Commission.

Television

Four television channels, RTÉ 1, RTÉ 2, TV3 and TG4 owned by RTÉ NL (RTÉ Transmissions Network Ltd) transmit free-to-air channels. In October 2012 the transition from analogue to digital broadcasting was completed.

Raidió Teilifís Éireann (RTÉ): see above; operates 2 television channels: RTÉ 1 and RTÉ 2; Man. Dir of Television GLEN KILLANE.

Sky Ireland: Alexandra House, Earlsfort Terrace, Dublin 2; tel. (1) 6147776; internet www.sky.com/ireland; Man. Dir J. D. BUCKLEY.

TG4 (Teilifís na Gaeilge): Baile na hAbhann, Connemara, Co Galway; tel. (91) 505050; fax (91) 505021; e-mail pol.o.gallchoir@tg4.ie;

internet www.tg4.ie; f. 1996; national public service Irish-language broadcaster; fmrly operated under RTÉ, became an independent statutory authority in April 2007; financed by the Govt and sales of commercial airtime; Chief Exec. PÓL Ó GALLCHÓIR.

TV3: Westgate Business Park, Ballymount, Dublin 24; tel. (1) 4193333; fax (1) 4193300; e-mail info@tv3.ie; internet www.tv3.ie; f. 1998; first national, commercial, independent television network; also broadcasts entertainment channel, 3e; CEO DAVID MCREDMOND; Dir of Programming LYNDA MCQUAID; Dir of News ANDREW HANLON.

Finance

(cap. = capital; res = reserves; dep. = deposits; m. = million; brs = branches; amounts in euros, unless otherwise indicated)

BANKING

Under the Central Bank Reform Act 2010, which took effect on 1 October, the Central Bank of Ireland was created as a new unitary body responsible for both central banking and financial regulation. The new structure replaced the previous related entities, the Central Bank and the Financial Services Authority of Ireland and the Financial Regulator.

Central Bank

Central Bank of Ireland (Banc Ceannais na hÉireann): Dame St, POB 559, Dublin 2; tel. (1) 2246000; fax (1) 6716561; e-mail enquiries@centralbank.ie; internet www.centralbank.ie; f. 1942; bank of issue; responsible for regulation of the banking and financial services industry; cap. and res 1,740.1m., dep. 108,408.4m. (Dec. 2009); Gov. PATRICK HONOHAN; Deputy Gov. (Financial Regulation) CYRIL ROUX; Deputy Gov. (Central Banking) STEFAN GERLACH.

Principal Banks

AIB Group (Allied Irish Banks PLC): Bankcentre, POB 452, Ballsbridge, Dublin 4; tel. (1) 6600311; fax (1) 6604715; e-mail aibtoday@aib.ie; internet www.aib.ie; f. 1966; 18.6% shares held by the Govt; nationalized in Dec. 2010; cap. 5,206m., res 5,039m., dep. 63,645m. (Dec. 2012); Exec. Chair. RICHARD PYM; Man. Dir DAVID DUFFY; over 750 brs and offices.

Bank of Ireland Group: Lower Baggot St, Dublin 2; tel. (1) 6615933; fax (1) 6615193; e-mail careline@boimail.com; internet www.bankofireland.ie; f. 1783; cap. 2,452m., res 1,532m., dep. 83,220m. (Dec. 2012); Chair. ARCHIE KANE; CEO RICHIE BOUCHER; 357 brs.

Barclays Bank Ireland PLC: 2 Park Pl., Hatch St, Dublin 2; tel. (1) 6182600; internet www.barclays.ie; CEO ANDREW SASHA WIGGINS.

Danske Bank A/S: National House, Airton Close, Tallaght, Dublin 24; tel. (1) 4840000; fax (1) 6385198; internet www.danskebank.ie; f. 1986 as Northern Bank (Ireland) Ltd; name changed to present in 2012; subsidiary of Danske Bank Group (Denmark); began withdrawal from personal banking in Ireland in early 2014; Chair. PETER STRAARUP; CEO ANDREW HEALY; 61 brs.

DEPFA Bank PLC: 1 Commons St, Dublin 1; tel. (1) 7922222; fax (1) 7922211; e-mail info@depfa.com; internet www.depfa.com; subsidiary of Hypo Real Estate Holding AG (Germany); cap. 1,242m., res 2,602m., dep. 20,032m. (Dec. 2012); CEO TOM GLYNN.

DZ BANK Ireland PLC: International House, 3 Harbourmaster Pl., IFSC, Dublin 1; tel. (1) 6700715; fax (1) 8290298; e-mail info@dzbank.ie; internet www.dzbank.ie; f. 1994; present name adopted 2001; subsidiary of DZ BANK AG Deutsche Zentral-Genossenschaftsbank, (Germany); cap. cap. 6.5m., res 242.2m., dep. 1,244.5m. (Dec. 2013); Man. Dirs Dr TILMANN GERHARDS, MARK JACOB.

EAA Covered Bond Bank PLC: IFSC House, Dublin 1; tel. (1) 6127133; fax (1) 6127175; e-mail bond@westlb.ie; f. 2002 as WestLB Covered Bond Bank PLC; name changed as above following acquisition in 2010; public sector finance; owned by Erste Abwicklungsanstalt (Germany); cap. 6.4m., res 669.8m., dep. 820.4m. (Dec. 2012); Chair. DIETRICH VOIGTLÄNDER; Man. Dir MICHAEL DOHERTY.

Intesa Sanpaolo Bank Ireland PLC: KBC House, 3rd Floor, 4 St George's Dock, IFSC, Dublin 1; tel. (1) 6726720; fax (1) 6726727; e-mail dublin.ie@intesasanpaolo.com; internet www.intesasanpaolo.com; f. 1987; present name adopted 2007; subsidiary of Intesa Sanpaolo SpA (Italy); cap. 400.5m., res 517.2m., dep. 7,709.2m. (Dec. 2012); Chair. STEFANO DEL PUNTA; Man. Dir ENRICO CUCCHIANI.

KBC Bank Ireland PLC: Sandwith St, Dublin 2; tel. (1) 6646000; fax (1) 6646199; e-mail info@kbc.ie; internet www.kbc.ie; f. 1973; fmrly IIB Bank PLC; present name adopted 2008; subsidiary of KBC Bank NV (Belgium); cap. 1,024m., res 407.7m., dep. 2,741.3m. (Dec. 2012); Chair. LUC PHILIPS; CEO JOHN H. REYNOLDS; 5 brs.

JP Morgan Bank (Ireland) PLC: JP Morgan House, IFSC, Dublin 1; tel. (1) 6123000; fax (1) 6123123; internet www.chase.com; f. 1968 as Chase and Bank of Ireland (International) Ltd; name changed as above 2001; owned by JP Morgan International Finance Ltd (USA); cap. US $56.6m., res US $238.1m., dep. US $1,421.9m. (Dec. 2011); Chair. and CEO JAMES DIMON; 1 br.

permanent tsb PLC: Irish Life Centre, Lower Abbey St, Dublin 1; tel. (1) 7041010; fax (1) 7041900; internet www.permanenttsbgroup.ie; f. 1884; present name adopted 2012; brought under state control in 2011; cap. 89m., res 5,255m., dep. 32,894m. (Dec. 2012); Chair. ALAN COOK; Group CEO JEREMY MASDING.

> **permanent tsb:** 56–59 St Stephen's Green, Dublin 2; tel. (1) 2124101; e-mail info@permanenttsb.ie; internet www.permanenttsb.ie; formed by merger of Irish Permanent and TSB Bank; subsidiary of permanent tsb PLC; Group CEO JEREMY MASDING; 101 brs.

Rabobank Ireland PLC: George's Dock House, IFSC, Dublin 1; tel. (1) 6076100; fax (1) 6701724; e-mail fm.ie.dublin.information@rabobank.com; internet www.rabobank.ie; f. 1994; corporate and investment banking; owned by Rabobank International Holding BV (Netherlands); cap. 7.1m., res 308.4m., dep. 12,442.3m. (Dec. 2012); CEO KEVIN KNIGHTLY.

Ulster Bank Ireland Ltd: Ulster Bank Group Centre, George's Quay, Dublin 2; tel. (1) 6777623; fax (1) 6775035; internet www.ulsterbank.com; merged with First Active PLC in early 2010; mem. of Royal Bank of Scotland Group (UK); cap. 3,592m., res 13,648m., dep. 26,208m. (Dec. 2012); Chair. SEAN DORGAN; Chief Exec. JIM BROWN; 132 brs.

UniCredit Bank Ireland PLC: La Touche House, IFSC, Dublin 1; tel. (1) 6702000; fax (1) 6702100; e-mail enquiry@unicreditgroup.ie; internet www.unicreditbank.ie; f. 1995; present name adopted 2007; subsidiary of UniCredit SpA (Italy); cap. 1,343.1m., res 89.8m., dep. 10,964.3m. (Dec. 2012); Man. Dir and CEO STEFANO VAIANI.

Banking Association

Irish Banking Federation: Nassau House, Nassau St, Dublin 2; tel. (1) 6715311; fax (1) 6796680; e-mail info@ibf.ie; internet www.ibf.ie; approx. 70 mems; CEO NOEL BRETT.

STOCK EXCHANGE

Irish Stock Exchange: 28 Anglesea St, Dublin 2; tel. (1) 6174200; fax (1) 6776045; e-mail info@ise.ie; internet www.ise.ie; f. 1793; formed as limited co. 1995; operates under supervision of the Central Bank of Ireland; Chair. PADRAIC O'CONNOR; CEO DEIRDRE SOMERS.

INSURANCE

Principal Companies

Allianz PLC: Allianz House, Elm Park, Merrion Rd, Dublin 4; tel. (1) 6133000; fax (1) 6134444; internet www.allianz.ie; f. 1998; 66.4% owned by Allianz AG (Germany), 30.4% by Irish Life and Permanent PLC; Chief Exec. BRENDAN MURPHY.

Aviva Group Ireland PLC: 1 Park Place, Hatch St, Dublin 2; tel. (1) 8988000; internet www.aviva.ie; f. 1908; subsidiary of Aviva PLC (UK); life and non-life; Chief Exec. ALISON BURNS.

AXA Insurance Ltd: Wolfe Tone House, Wolfe Tone St, Dublin 1; tel. (1) 8726444; fax (1) 8729703; e-mail axa.dublincity@axa.ie; internet www.axa.ie; f. 1967; Chief Exec. JOHN O'NEILL.

Bank of Ireland Life: 40 Mespil Rd, Dublin 4; tel. (1) 6615933; fax (1) 6615671; e-mail info@bankofirelandlife.ie; internet www.bankofirelandlife.ie; f. 1987; present name adopted 2002; part of New Ireland Assurance Co; Group CEO RICHIE BOUCHER.

FBD Insurance PLC: FBD House, Bluebell, Dublin 12; tel. (1) 4639820; e-mail info@fbd.ie; internet www.fbd.ie; motor, property, business; Group CEO ANDREW LANGFORD.

Irish Life Assurance PLC: Lower Abbey St, POB 129, Dublin 1; tel. (1) 7041010; fax (1) 7041900; e-mail customerservice@irishlife.ie; internet www.irishlife.ie; f. 1939; life and non-life; bought by Great-West Lifeco (Canada) and merged with Canada Life (Ireland) in 2014; Chief Exec. GERRY HASSETT.

Liberty Insurance: Dublin Rd, Cavan, Co Cavan; tel. (49) 4324000; fax (49) 4368101; e-mail info@libertyinsurance.ie; internet www.libertyinsurance.ie; f. 1996 as Quinn Insurance; fmrly Quinn Insurance Ltd; acquired by Liberty Mutual Group, Inc (USA) in 2011 and renamed as above; property, motor, health; Chief Exec. PATRICK O'BRIEN.

New Ireland Assurance Co PLC: 9–12 Dawson St, Dublin 2; tel. (1) 6172000; fax (1) 6172075; e-mail info@newireland.ie; internet www.newireland.ie; f. 1918; wholly owned subsidiary of Bank of Ireland Group; Chair. JOHN COLLINS; Man. Dir SEAN CASEY.

permanent tsb: see Banking.

RSA Insurance Ireland Ltd: RSA House, Sandyford Rd, Dundrum, Dublin 16; tel. (1) 2901000; fax (1) 2901001; e-mail patrick

.nally@ie.rsagroup.com; internet www.rsagroup.ie; f. 1721; fmrly Royal & Sun Alliance; non-life; CEO KEN NORGROVE.

Standard Life Ireland: 90 St Stephen's Green, Dublin 2; tel. (1) 6397300; e-mail marketing@standardlife.ie; internet www.standardlife.ie; f. 1834; life assurance, pensions, investments and annuities; Chief Exec. NIGEL DUNNE.

Zurich Insurance PLC: Zurich House, Ballsbridge Park, Dublin 4; tel. (1) 6670666; fax (1) 6670644; e-mail customerhelp@zurich.ie; internet www.zurichinsurance.ie; f. 1919 as Eagle Star Insurance; present name adopted 2009; mem. of the Zürich Financial Services Group (Switzerland); CEO KEN NORGROVE.

Insurance Associations

Insurance Institute of Ireland: 39 Molesworth St, Dublin 2; tel. (1) 6456600; fax (1) 6772621; e-mail info@iii.ie; internet www.iii.ie; f. 1885; Pres. KEN NORGROVE; CEO EAMON SHACKLETON; c. 15,000 mems.

Insurance Ireland: Insurance House, 39 Molesworth St, Dublin 2; tel. (1) 6761820; fax (1) 6761943; e-mail info@insuranceireland.eu; internet www.insuranceireland.eu; f. 1986; Pres. PHILIP SMITH; CEO KEVIN THOMPSON; 63 mems.

Irish Brokers' Association: 87 Merrion Sq., Dublin 2; tel. (1) 6613067; fax (1) 6619955; e-mail info@iba.ie; internet www.iba.ie; f. 1990; Pres. (2014–15) BRENDAN SPRING; CEO CIARAN PHELAN; 500 mems.

Professional Insurance Brokers' Association (PIBA): Unit 14B, Cashel Business Centre, Cashel Rd, Crumlin, Dublin 1; tel. (1) 4922202; fax (1) 4991569; e-mail info@piba.ie; internet www.piba.ie; f. 1995; Chair. LIAM CARBERRY; CEO DIARMUID KELLY; c. 880 mems.

Trade and Industry

GOVERNMENT AGENCIES

An Post (The Irish Post Office): General Post Office, O'Connell St, Dublin 1; tel. (1) 7057000; fax (1) 8723553; e-mail press.office@anpost.ie; internet www.anpost.ie; f. 1984; provides national postal, communications and financial services through c. 1,100 outlets; Chair. CHRISTOPH MUELLER; CEO DONAL CONNELL.

Food Safety Authority of Ireland (FSAI): Abbey Court, Lower Abbey St, Dublin 1; tel. (1) 8171300; fax (1) 8171301; e-mail info@fsai.ie; internet www.fsai.ie; f. 1998; takes all reasonable steps to ensure that food produced, distributed or marketed in Ireland meets the highest standards of food safety and hygiene reasonably available, and to ensure that food complies with legal requirements, or, where appropriate, with recognized codes of good practice; Chair. Prof. MICHAEL GIBNEY; Chief Exec. Prof. ALAN REILLY.

National Economic and Social Council (NESC): 16 Parnell Sq., Dublin 1; tel. (1) 8146300; fax (1) 8146301; e-mail info@nesc.ie; internet www.nesc.ie; f. 1973; analyses and reports on strategic issues relating to the efficient development of the economy and the achievement of social justice; Chair. MARTIN FRASER; Dir Dr RORY O'DONNELL.

DEVELOPMENT ORGANIZATIONS

Enterprise Ireland: East Point Business Park, Dublin 3; tel. (1) 7272000; fax (1) 7272020; e-mail client.service@enterprise-ireland.com; internet www.enterprise-ireland.com; f. 1998; combines the activities of the fmr An Bord Tráchtála, Forbairt and the in-company training activities of FÁS; Chair. TERENCE O'ROURKE; Chief Exec. JULIE SINNAMON.

IDA Ireland (Industrial Development Agency): Wilton Park House, Wilton Pl., Dublin 2; tel. (1) 6034000; fax (1) 6034040; e-mail idaireland@ida.ie; internet www.idaireland.com; f. 1993; govt agency with national responsibility for securing new investment from overseas in manufacturing and international services and for encouraging existing foreign enterprises in Ireland to expand their businesses; Chair. FRANK RYAN; CEO BARRY O'LEARY.

Sustainable Energy Ireland (SEAI): Wilton Park House, Wilton Pl., Dublin 2; tel. (1) 8082100; fax (1) 8082002; e-mail info@seai.ie; internet www.seai.ie; promotes and assists environmentally and economically sustainable production, supply and use of energy, in support of govt policy, across all sectors of the economy; Chair. BRENDAN HALLIGAN; CEO Dr BRIAN MOTHERWAY.

Teagasc (Agriculture and Food Development Authority): Oak Park, Carlow; tel. (59) 9170200; fax (59) 9182097; e-mail info@hq.teagasc.ie; internet www.teagasc.ie; f. 1988; provides research, educational and training services to agri-food sector and rural communities; Chair. Dr NOEL CAWLE; Nat. Dir Prof. GERRY BOYLE.

CHAMBERS OF COMMERCE

Chambers Ireland (CI): Newmount House, 22–24 Lower Mount St, Dublin 2; tel. (1) 4004300; e-mail info@chambers.ie; internet www.chambers.ie; f. 1923; Pres. DÓNALL CURTIN; CEO IAN TALBOT; represents over 13,000 businesses nationwide; 60 chamber mems.

Cork Chamber: Fitzgerald House, Summerhill North, Cork; tel. (21) 4509044; fax (21) 4508568; e-mail info@corkchamber.ie; internet www.corkchamber.ie; f. 1819; Pres. GILLIAN KEATING; Chief Exec. CONOR HEALY; 1000 mems.

Dublin Chamber of Commerce: 7 Clare St, Dublin 2; tel. (1) 6647200; fax (1) 6447234; e-mail info@dubchamber.ie; internet www.dubchamber.ie; f. 1783; Pres. MARTIN MURPHY; Chief Exec. GINA QUIN.

INDUSTRIAL AND TRADE ASSOCIATIONS

Construction Industry Federation (CIF): Construction House, Canal Rd, Dublin 6; tel. (1) 4066000; fax (1) 4966953; e-mail cif@cif.ie; internet www.cif.ie; Pres. MICHAEL STONE; Dir-Gen. TOM PARLON; 37 asscns representing 1,500 mems.

Irish Creamery Milk Suppliers' Association (ICMSA): John Feely House, Dublin Rd, Castletroy, Limerick; tel. (61) 314677; fax (61) 315737; e-mail info@icmsa.ie; internet www.icmsa.ie; f. 1950; Pres. JOHN G. COMER; Gen. Sec. JOHN ENRIGHT.

Irish Farmers' Association (IFA): Irish Farm Centre, Bluebell, Dublin 12; tel. (1) 4500266; fax (1) 4551043; e-mail info@ifa.ie; internet www.ifa.ie; Pres. EDDIE DOWNEY; Gen. Sec. PAT SMITH; 87,000 mems.

Irish Fishermen's Organisation Ltd: Cumberland House, Fenian St, Dublin 2; tel. (1) 6612400; fax (1) 6612424; e-mail irishfish@eircom.net; f. 1974; representative body for Irish commercial fishermen; Chair. EBBIE SHEEHAN.

Irish Grain and Feed Association (IGFA): Lower Main St, Abbeyleix, Co Laois; tel. (57) 8730350; e-mail info@eorna.ie; internet www.igfa.ie; Pres. TONY MANNIX; Dir DEIRDRE WEBB.

EMPLOYERS' ORGANIZATIONS

Irish Business and Employers Confederation (IBEC): Confederation House, 84–86 Lower Baggot St, Dublin 2; tel. (1) 6051500; fax (1) 6381500; e-mail info@ibec.ie; internet www.ibec.ie; f. 1993; represents c. 7,000 cos and orgs; Pres. JOHN KENNEDY; Dir-Gen DANNY MCCOY.

Irish Exporters' Association (IEA): 28 Merrion Sq., Dublin 2; tel. (1) 6612182; fax (1) 6612315; e-mail iea@irishexporters.ie; internet www.irishexporters.ie; f. 1951; Pres. COLIN LAWLOR; CEO SIMON MCKEEVER.

UTILITIES

Regulatory Authority

An Coimisiún um Rialáil Fuinnimh/Commission for Energy Regulation (CER): The Exchange, Belgard Sq. North, Tallaght, Dublin 24; tel. (1) 4000800; fax (1) 4000850; e-mail info@cer.ie; internet www.cer.ie; f. 1999; responsible for licensing and regulating the generation and supply of electricity, water and natural gas, and authorizing construction of new generating plants; designed and implemented cross-border Single Electricity Market with Northern Ireland Authority for Utility Regulation; Chair. GARRETT BLANEY.

Electricity and Gas

Bord Gáis Éireann (BGÉ) (The Irish Gas Board): 6 Lapps Quay, POB 835, Cork, Co Cork; tel. (21) 4658700; fax (21) 4658701; e-mail gasinfo@bge.ie; internet www.bordgais.ie; f. 1975; natural gas transmission and distribution, gas and electricity supply, electricity generation; Chair. ROSE HYNES; CEO MICHAEL MCNICHOLAS.

EirGrid PLC: 160 Shelbourne Rd, Dublin 4; tel. (1) 6771700; fax (1) 6615375; e-mail info@eirgrid.com; internet www.eirgrid.com; f. 2006; manages transmission of Ireland's electricity; state-owned; Chair. JOHN O'CONNOR; CEO FINTAN SLYE.

Electricity Supply Board (ESB): 27 Lower Fitzwilliam St, Dublin 2; tel. (1) 6765831; fax (1) 6760727; e-mail service@esb.ie; internet www.esb.ie; f. 1927; reorg. 1988; supplier of electricity and operator of 15 generating stations; 95% state owned; Chair. LOCHLANN QUINN; CEO PAT O'DOHERTY.

Energia: Mill House, 3rd Floor, Ashtowngate, Navan Rd, Dublin 15; fax (1) 8692050; e-mail customer.service@energia.ie; internet www.energia.ie; f. 1999; generator and supplier of electricity and gas to business customers across Ireland; subsidiary of Viridian Group Ltd (UK); Chief Exec. TOM GILLEN.

Flogas Natural Gas Ltd: Knockbrack House, Matthews Lane, Donore Rd, Drogheda, Co Louth; tel. (41) 9831041; fax (41) 9834652; e-mail info@flogas.ie; internet www.flogasnaturalgas.ie;

supplier of natural gas to residential customers across Ireland; Man. Dir RICHARD MARTIN.

SSE Airtricity: Red Oak South, South County Business Park, Leopardstown, Dublin 18; tel. (1) 6556400; fax (1) 6556444; e-mail info@airtricity.com; internet www.airtricity.com; f. 1997; generator and supplier of electricity, using renewable sources; acquired by Scottish and Southern Energy PLC (UK) in 2008; Man. Dir STEPHEN WHEELER.

Water

Irish Water was established in 2013 with responsibility for the provision and development of water services nationwide. It was to take over from the local authorities, previously responsible for water supply, over an estimated five-year period from January 2014.

Irish Water: Colvill House, 24–26 Talbot St, Dublin 1; tel. (1) 7072828; e-mail press@water.ie; internet www.water.ie; f. 2013; semi-state company; subsidiary of Bord Gáis Éireann; accountable to the Commission for Energy Regulation (CER) and the Environmental Protection Agency; CEO JOHN TIERNEY.

CO-OPERATIVES

Irish Co-operative Organisation Society (ICOS): The Plunkett House, 84 Merrion Sq., Dublin 2; tel. (1) 6764783; fax (1) 6624502; e-mail info@icos.ie; internet www.icos.ie; f. 1894; 3 operating divisions; offices in Dublin, Cork and Brussels (Belgium); Pres. MARTIN KEANE; CEO SEAMUS O'DONOHOE; over 130 mem. co-operatives representing c. 150,000 farmers.

Irish Dairy Board: Grattan House, Lower Mount St, Dublin 2; tel. (1) 6619599; fax (1) 6612778; e-mail idb@idb.ie; internet www.idb.ie; f. 1961; reorg. 1973 as a farmers' co-operative; principal exporter of Irish dairy products; Chair. AARON FORDE; Chief Exec. KEVIN LANE.

TRADE UNIONS

Central Organization

Irish Congress of Trade Unions (ICTU): 31–32 Parnell Sq., Dublin 1; tel. (1) 8897777; fax (1) 8872012; e-mail congress@ictu.ie; internet www.ictu.ie; f. 1894; represents some 770,569 workers in 47 affiliated unions in Ireland and Northern Ireland (2013); Pres. JOHN DOUGLAS; Gen. Sec. PATRICIA KING.

Unions not Affiliated to the ICTU

National Bus and Rail Union (NBRU): 54 Parnell Sq., Dublin 1; tel. (1) 8730411; fax (1) 8730137; e-mail nbru@eircom.net; internet www.nbru.ie; f. 1963; Gen. Sec. DERMOT O'LEARY; 3,000 mems.

Transport

Córas Iompair Éireann (CIÉ) (The Irish Transport Co): Heuston Station, Dublin 8; tel. (1) 7032008; fax (1) 7032276; internet www.cie.ie; f. 1945; state corpn operating rail and road transport services; 3 operating cos: Iarnród Éireann (Irish Rail), Bus Éireann (Irish Bus) and Bus Átha Cliath (Dublin Bus); Chair. VIVIENNE JUPP.

RAILWAYS

In 2013 there were some 2,400 km of track. Railway services are operated by Iarnród Éireann.

Iarnród Éireann (Irish Rail): Connolly Station, Dublin 1; tel. (1) 8363333; fax (1) 8364760; e-mail info@irishrail.ie; internet www.irishrail.ie; f. 1987; division of CIÉ; Chair. PHIL GAFFNEY; Chief Exec. DAVID FRANKS.

INLAND WATERWAYS

The Grand and Royal Canals and the canal link into the Barrow Navigation system are controlled by CIÉ. The Grand Canal and Barrow are open to navigation by pleasure craft, and the rehabilitation and restoration of the Royal Canal is proceeding. The River Shannon, which is navigable from Limerick to Lough Allen, includes stretches of the Boyle, Suck, Camlin and Inny Rivers, the Erne Navigation and the Shannon–Erne Waterway. The total length of Irish navigable waterways is about 700 km.

ROADS

At 31 December 2008 there were an estimated 96,424 km of roads; at 31 December 2012 there were 4,513 km of national roads, of which 2,697 km were national primary roads (including 900 km of motorways). In that year there were also 11,631 km of regional secondary roads.

National Roads Authority: St Martin's House, Waterloo Rd, Dublin 4; tel. (1) 6602511; fax (1) 6680009; e-mail info@nra.ie; internet www.nra.ie; f. 1994; responsible for the planning, super-

vision and maintenance of national road network; Chair. CORMAC O'ROURKE; Chief Exec. FRED BARRY.

Bus Éireann (Irish Buses): Heuston Station, Dublin 8; internet www.buseireann.ie; f. 1987; provides bus and coach services across Ireland, except Dublin area; subsidiary of CIÉ; Chair. PAUL MALLEE; Chief Exec. MARTIN NOLAN.

Dublin Bus (Bus Átha Cliath): 59 Upper O'Connell St, Dublin 1; tel. (1) 8734222; fax (1) 7033177; e-mail info@dublinbus.ie; internet www.dublinbus.ie; f. 1987; provides bus services in Dublin area; subsidiary of CIÉ; Chair. KEVIN BONNER; Chief Exec. PADDY DOHERTY.

SHIPPING

The principal seaports are Dublin, Dún Laoghaire, Cork, Waterford, Rosslare, Limerick, Foynes, Galway, New Ross, Drogheda, Dundalk, Fenit and Whiddy Island. At 31 December 2014 the Irish flag registered fleet numbered 186 vessels, with a combined displacement of 257,603 grt, of which 105 were fishing vessels and 30 were general cargo ships.

Arklow Shipping: North Quay, Arklow, Co Wicklow; tel. (402) 39901; fax (402) 39902; e-mail chartering@asl.ie; internet www.asl.ie; f. 1966; Man. Dir JAMES S. TYRRELL; 37 carriers.

Fastnet Line: Ferry Port, Ringaskiddy, Co Cork; tel. (21) 4378892; fax (21) 4378893; e-mail info@fastnetline.com; internet www.fastnetline.com; f. 2009; owned by West Cork Tourism Co-op; operates car ferry service between Cork and Swansea (Wales, UK); Chair. CONOR BUCKLEY; CEO PHIL JONES.

Irish Continental Group PLC: Ferryport, Alexandra Rd, Dublin 1; tel. (1) 6075700; fax (1) 8552268; e-mail info@icg.ie; internet www.icg.ie; f. 1972; controls Irish Ferries, operating passenger vehicle and ro-ro freight ferry services between Ireland, the UK and continental Europe; Chair. JOHN B. McGUCKIAN; Man. Dir EAMONN ROTHWELL.

Irish Ferries: Ferryport, Alexandra Rd, POB 19, Dublin 1; tel. (81) 8300400; fax (1) 8193942; e-mail info@irishferries.com; internet www.irishferries.com; drive-on/drive-off car ferry and ro-ro freight services between Ireland, the UK and continental Europe, operating up to 109 sailings weekly; Group Man. Dir EAMONN ROTHWELL.

Stena Line: Ferry Terminal, Dún Laoghaire Harbour, Co Dublin; tel. (1) 2047777; fax (1) 2047620; e-mail info@stenaline.com; internet www.stenaline.ie; services between Dún Laoghaire and Dublin Port–Holyhead (Wales, UK) including high-speed catamaran, Rosslare–Fishguard (Wales, UK), Belfast (Northern Ireland) and Stranraer (Scotland, UK), Larne–Fleetwood (England, UK), passengers, drive-on/drive-off car ferry, ro-ro freight services; Man. Dir GUNNAR BLOMDAHL.

Associations

Irish Chamber of Shipping: Port Centre, Alexandra Rd, Dublin Port, Dublin 1; tel. (1) 8559011; fax (1) 8559022; e-mail bks@iol.ie; Pres. JOHN TONER; Dir B. W. KERR.

Irish Ship Agents' Association: Conway House, East Wall Road, Dublin 3; tel. (1) 8556221; fax (1) 8557234; e-mail info@irishshipagents.com; internet www.irishshipagents.com; Pres. MICHAEL COLLINS.

CIVIL AVIATION

There are international airports at Dublin, Shannon, Cork, Kerry and Knock (Ireland West Airport).

Commission for Aviation Regulation: Alexandra House, 3rd Floor, Earlsfort Terrace, Dublin 2; tel. (1) 6611700; fax (1) 6611269; e-mail info@aviationreg.ie; internet www.aviationreg.ie; f. 2001; responsible for licensing the travel trade in Ireland as well as airlines; approves providers of ground handling services under EU regulations; Commissioner CATHAL GUIOMARD.

Dublin Airport Authority PLC (DAA): Dublin Airport, Dublin; tel. (1) 8141111; e-mail info@daa.ie; internet www.daa.ie; state-controlled; responsible for the management of Dublin and Cork airports; Chair. PÁDRAIG Ó. RÍORDÁIN; Chief Exec. KEVIN TOLAND.

Irish Aviation Authority: The Times Bldg, 11–12 D'Olier St, Dublin 2; tel. (1) 6718655; fax (1) 6792934; e-mail info@iaa.ie; internet www.iaa.ie; f. 1994; provides air traffic management, engineering and communications in airspace controlled by Ireland and related air traffic technological infrastructure; also regulates aircraft airworthiness certification and registration, the licensing of personnel and orgs involved in the maintenance of aircraft, as well as the licensing of pilots and aerodromes; Chair. ANNE NOLAN; Chief Exec. EAMONN BRENNAN.

Airlines

Aer Arann: 1 Northwood Ave, Santry, Dublin 9; tel. (1) 8447700; fax (1) 8447701; e-mail info@aerarann.com; internet www.aerarann

.com; f. 1970; regional airline operating flights on 37 routes throughout Ireland, UK and France; CEO SEÁN BROGAN (acting).

Aer Lingus Group PLC: Dublin Airport, Dublin; tel. (1) 8868202; fax (1) 8863832; internet www.aerlingus.com; f. 1936; reorg. 1993; 29.88% owned by Ryanair Holdings PLC, 25.1% govt-owned; domestic and international scheduled services; Chair. COLM BARRINGTON; CEO STEPHEN KAVANAGH.

CityJet: Swords Business Campus, Balheary Rd, Swords, Co Dublin; tel. (1) 8700100; fax (1) 8700115; e-mail info@cityjet.com; internet www.cityjet.com; f. 1994; operates chartered and scheduled passenger routes between Dublin and Belfast (Northern Ireland), London (UK) and destinations in continental Western Europe; owned by Intro Aviation (Germany); CEO CHRISTINE OURMIÈRES.

Ryanair: Dublin Airport, Dublin; tel. (1) 8121212; fax (1) 8121213; internet www.ryanair.com; f. 1985; scheduled and charter passenger services to European and North African destinations; Chair. DAVID BONDERMAN; CEO MICHAEL O'LEARY.

Tourism

Intensive marketing campaigns have been undertaken in recent years to develop new markets for Irish tourism. In addition to many sites of historic and cultural interest, the country has numerous areas of natural beauty, notably the Killarney Lakes and the west coast. In 2013 a total of 8.3m. foreign tourists (including residents of Northern Ireland) visited Ireland. Receipts from tourism (including passenger transport) totalled an estimated €4,463m. in 2013.

Dublin Regional Tourism Authority Ltd (Dublin Tourism): Suffolk St, Dublin 2; tel. (1) 6057700; fax (1) 6057757; internet www.visitdublin.com; Chair. ANN RIORDAN.

Fáilte Ireland (National Tourism Development Authority): 88–95 Amiens St, Dublin 1; tel. (1) 8847700; fax (1) 8556821; e-mail info@failteireland.ie; internet www.failteireland.ie; f. 2003; Chair. MICHAEL CAWLEY; Chief Exec. SHAUN QUINN.

Irish Tourist Industry Confederation (ITIC): Sandyford Office Park, Unit 5, Ground Floor, Dublin 18; tel. (1) 2934950; fax (1) 2934991; e-mail itic@eircom.net; internet www.itic.ie; Chair. PAUL CARTY; CEO EAMONN MCKEON.

Tourism Ireland: Bishop's Sq., 5th Floor, Redmond's Hill, Dublin 2; tel. (1) 4763400; fax (1) 4763666; e-mail corporate.dublin@tourismireland.com; internet www.tourismireland.com; f. 1998; promotes Ireland and Northern Ireland as a tourist destination; jointly funded by the Irish Government and the Northern Ireland Executive; Chair. BRIAN AMBROSE; Chief Exec. NIALL GIBBONS.

Defence

As assessed at November 2014, the regular armed forces totalled 9,350. The army comprised 7,500, the navy 1,050 and the air force 800. There was also a reserve of 4,630. Military service is voluntary. In November 2004 the European Union (EU) ministers responsible for defence agreed to create a number of 'battlegroups' (each comprising about 1,500 men), which could be deployed at short notice to crisis areas around the world. The EU battlegroups, two of which were to be ready for deployment at any one time, following a rotational schedule, reached full operational capacity from 1 January 2007. From January 2008 Ireland was a participant in the EUFOR mission to eastern Chad and the Central African Republic and by February 2009 was the second largest contributor to the mission (which was taken over by the UN in March), with 476 troops. In 2013 Irish troops contributed to the United Nations Interim Force in Lebanon (UNIFIL).

Defence Expenditure: estimated at €885m. in 2015.

Chief of Staff of the Defence Forces: Maj.-Gen. CONOR O'BOYLE.

Education

The Irish state has constitutional responsibility for the national education system. An aided system is in operation: Irish schools are funded by the state, but are under the management (with a few minor exceptions) of community bodies, usually religious groups. Pre-primary education is non-compulsory and aimed at children aged between one and six years. Primary and lower secondary education in Ireland is compulsory for nine years between six and 16 years of age. Primary education may begin at the age of four and lasts for up to eight years, comprising a two-year infant cycle and a six-year primary cycle. In 2005/06 aided primary schools accounted for the education of 98.9% of children in the primary sector. In 2011/12 enrolment at primary level included 99% of children in the relevant age-group, while enrolment at secondary level in 2010/11 included 99% of children in the relevant age-group. Post-primary education begins at 12 years of age and lasts for up to six years, comprising a junior cycle of three years and a senior cycle of two or three years. The Junior Certificate examination is taken after three years in post-primary (second-level) education. The Leaving Certificate examination is taken after a further two or three years and is a necessary qualification for entry into university education. Accreditation for higher education is provided by the Department of Education and Skills. There are four universities in Ireland: the University of Dublin (Trinity College); the National University of Ireland (comprising the University Colleges of Cork, Dublin, Maynooth and Galway); Dublin City University; and the University of Limerick (which obtained university status in 1989). In 2013/14, there were seven university-level institutions, 14 institutes of technology and four other higher education providers.

Government expenditure on education and skills was budgeted at €8,279m. in 2015.

ISRAEL

Introductory Survey

LOCATION, CLIMATE, LANGUAGE, RELIGION, FLAG, CAPITAL

Israel lies in western Asia, occupying a narrow strip of territory on the eastern shore of the Mediterranean Sea. The country also has a narrow outlet to the Red Sea at the northern tip of the Gulf of Aqaba. All of Israel's land frontiers are with Arab countries, the longest being with Egypt to the west and with Jordan to the east. Lebanon lies to the north, and Syria to the north-east. The climate is Mediterranean, with hot, dry summers, when the maximum temperature in Jerusalem is generally between 30°C and 35°C (86°F to 95°F), and mild, rainy winters, with a minimum temperature in the city of about 5°C (41°F). The climate is sub-tropical on the coast but more extreme in the Negev Desert, in the south, and near the shores of the Dead Sea (a lake on the Israeli–Jordanian frontier), where the summer temperature may exceed 50°C (122°F). The official languages are Hebrew and Arabic. Hebrew is spoken by about two-thirds of the population, including most Jews. About 15% of Israeli residents, including Muslim Arabs, speak Arabic, while many European languages (notably Russian) are also spoken. In 2013 some 75.0% of the population professed adherence to Judaism, the officially recognized religion of Israel, while 17.5% were Muslims. The national flag (proportions 8 by 11) has a white background, with a six-pointed blue star composed of two overlapping triangles (the 'Shield of David') between two horizontal blue stripes near the upper and lower edges. Although the Israeli Government has designated the city of Jerusalem (part of which is Jordanian territory annexed by Israel in 1967) as the country's capital, this is not recognized by the UN, and most foreign governments maintain their embassies in Tel-Aviv.

CONTEMPORARY POLITICAL HISTORY

Historical Context

The Zionist movement emerged in Europe in the 19th century in response to the growing sense of insecurity among Jewish minorities in many European countries as a result of racial and religious persecution. The primary objective of Zionism was defined at the First Zionist Congress, held in Basel, Switzerland, in 1897, when Dr Theodor Herzl stated that Zionism sought 'to create for the Jewish people a home in Palestine secured by public law'. Zionists aimed to re-establish an autonomous community of Jews in what was their historical homeland.

Palestine was almost entirely populated by Arabs, and had become part of the Turkish Ottoman Empire in the early 16th century. During the First World War the Ottoman Empire's Arab subjects launched the so-called Arab Revolt, and, following the withdrawal of the Turks, in 1917–18 British troops occupied Palestine. In November 1917 the British Foreign Secretary, Arthur Balfour, declared British support for the establishment of a Jewish national home in Palestine, on condition that the rights of 'the existing non-Jewish communities' there were safeguarded; this became known as the Balfour Declaration and was confirmed by the governments of other countries then at war with Turkey. The British occupation of Palestine continued after the war under the terms of a League of Nations mandate, which also incorporated the Balfour Declaration. (In 1920 Palestine was formally placed under British administration.) British rule in Palestine was hampered by the conflict between the declared obligations to the Jews and the rival claims of the Arab majority. In accordance with the mandate, Jewish settlers were admitted to Palestine only on the basis of limited annual quotas. There was serious anti-Jewish rioting by Arabs in 1921 and 1929. Attempts to restrict immigration led to Jewish-sponsored riots in 1933. The extreme persecution of Jews by Nazi Germany caused an increase in the flow of Jewish immigrants, both legal and illegal, which intensified the unrest in Palestine. In 1937 a British proposal to establish separate Jewish and Arab states, while retaining a British-mandated area, was accepted by most Zionists but rejected by the Arabs, and by the end of that year hostilities between the two communities had descended into open conflict. A British scheme offering eventual independence for a bi-communal Palestinian state was postponed because of the Second World War, during which the Nazis caused the deaths of an estimated 6m. Jews in central and eastern Europe (more than one-third of the world's total Jewish population). The enormity of the Holocaust greatly increased international sympathy for Jewish claims to a homeland in Palestine.

After the war there was strong opposition by Palestinian Jews to continued British occupation. Numerous terrorist attacks were made by Jewish groups against British targets. In November 1947 the UN approved a plan for the partition of Palestine into two states, one Jewish (covering about 56% of the area) and one Arab. The plan was, however, rejected by Arab states and by Palestinian Arab leaders. Meanwhile, the conflict in Palestine escalated into full-scale war.

On 14 May 1948 the United Kingdom terminated its mandate, and Jewish leaders immediately proclaimed the State of Israel, with David Ben-Gurion as Prime Minister. Despite the absence of recognized borders, the new state quickly received international recognition. Neighbouring Arab countries attempted to conquer Israel by military force, and fighting continued until January 1949, when ceasefire agreements left Israel in control of 75% of Palestine, including West Jerusalem. The de facto territory of Israel was thus nearly one-third greater than the area assigned under the original UN partition plan. Jordanian forces controlled most of the remainder of Palestine, the area eventually known as the West Bank (or, to Israelis, as Judea and Samaria) and which was fully incorporated into Jordan in April 1950.

At the end of the British mandate the Jewish population of Palestine was about 650,000 (or 40% of the total). The new State of Israel encouraged further Jewish immigration: the Law of Return, adopted in July 1950, established a right of immigration for all Jews, and resulted in a rapid influx of Jewish settlers. Many former Arab residents of Palestine, meanwhile, had become refugees in neighbouring countries, mainly Jordan and Lebanon. About 400,000 Arabs had evacuated their homes prior to May 1948, and a similar number fled subsequently. In 1964 exiled Palestinian Arabs formed the Palestine Liberation Organization (PLO), with the aim, at that time, of overthrowing Israel.

Israel, with the United Kingdom and France, launched an attack on Egypt in October 1956 following the nationalization of the Suez Canal by President Nasser; Israel seized the Gaza Strip (part of Palestine occupied by Egypt since 1949) and the Sinai Peninsula. After pressure from the UN and the USA, Israeli forces evacuated these areas in 1957, when a UN Emergency Force (UNEF) was established in Sinai. In 1967 the United Arab Republic (Egypt) secured the withdrawal of UNEF from its territory. Egyptian forces immediately reoccupied the garrison at Sharm el-Sheikh, near the southern tip of Sinai, and closed the Straits of Tiran to Israeli shipping, effectively (as in 1956) blockading the Israeli port of Eilat. In retaliation, Israeli forces attacked Egypt, Jordan and Syria, swiftly making substantial territorial gains. The so-called Six-Day War left Israel in possession of all Jerusalem, the West Bank area of Jordan, the Sinai Peninsula in Egypt, the Gaza Strip and the Golan Heights in Syria. East Jerusalem was almost immediately integrated into the State of Israel, while the other conquered areas were regarded as Occupied Territories. In November 1967 the UN Security Council adopted Resolution 242, urging Israel to withdraw from all the recently occupied Arab territories.

Domestic Political Affairs

Ben-Gurion resigned in June 1963 and was succeeded by Levi Eshkol. Three of the parties in the ruling coalition merged to form the Israel Labour Party in 1968. On the death of Eshkol in 1969, Golda Meir was elected Prime Minister. A ceasefire between Egypt and Israel was arranged in August 1970, but other Arab states and Palestinian guerrilla (mainly PLO) groups continued hostilities. Another Arab–Israeli war began on 6 October 1973, as Arab forces invaded Israeli-held territory on the Jewish holy day of Yom Kippur (the Day of Atonement). Egyptian forces crossed the Suez Canal and reoccupied part of Sinai, while Syrian troops launched an offensive on the Golan Heights.

Having successfully repelled these advances, Israel made cease-fire agreements with Egypt and Syria on 24 October. The UN Security Council adopted Resolution 338 in that month, urging a ceasefire and reaffirming the principles of Resolution 242. Gen. Itzhak Rabin succeeded Meir as Prime Minister of a Labour Alignment coalition in 1974. The Labour Alignment was defeated at the May 1977 general election, and the Likud (Consolidation) bloc, led by Menachem Begin of the Herut (Freedom) Party, formed a new coalition Government.

In November 1977 the Egyptian President, Anwar Sadat, visited Israel, indicating tacit recognition of the Jewish State. In September 1978 President Jimmy Carter of the USA, President Sadat and Prime Minister Begin met at the US presidential retreat at Camp David, Maryland, and concluded two agreements: a 'framework for peace in the Middle East', providing for autonomy for the West Bank and Gaza Strip after a transitional period of five years; and a 'framework for the conclusion of a peace treaty between Egypt and Israel'. A formal peace treaty was signed in March 1979 in Washington, DC, USA. In 1980 Egypt became the first Arab country to grant diplomatic recognition to Israel. However, approval by the Israeli Knesset (parliament) of legislation stating explicitly that Jerusalem should be forever the undivided capital of Israel, and, in 1981, Israel's formal annexation of the Golan Heights, impeded prospects of agreement on Palestinian autonomy.

Israel's phased withdrawal from Sinai was completed in April 1982. In June Israeli forces, under 'Operation Peace for Galilee', advanced through Lebanon and surrounded west Beirut, trapping 6,000 PLO fighters. Egypt withdrew its ambassador from Tel-Aviv in protest. Diplomatic efforts resulted in the evacuation of 14,000–15,000 PLO and Syrian fighters from Beirut to various Arab countries. In September Lebanese Phalangists massacred Palestinian refugees in the Sabra and Chatila camps in Beirut (see the chapter on Lebanon); an official Israeli inquiry found the Israeli leadership to be indirectly responsible through negligence, forcing the resignation of Gen. Ariel Sharon as Minister of Defence. In May 1983 Israel and Lebanon concluded a peace agreement, declaring an end to hostilities and envisaging the withdrawal of all foreign forces from Lebanon within three months. However, Syria's refusal to withdraw some 30,000 troops, and the continued presence of about 7,000 PLO fighters in the Beqa'a valley and northern Lebanon, delayed the Israeli withdrawal, although by the end of 1983 the number of Israeli troops in Lebanon had been reduced from 30,000 to 10,000.

In August 1983 Itzhak Shamir succeeded Begin as leader of the Likud bloc and Prime Minister. However, economic difficulties further undermined the Government, and the Labour Party forced a general election in July 1984. Since neither the Labour Alignment nor Likud could form a viable coalition, President Chaim Herzog invited the Labour leader, Shimon Peres, to form a government of national unity with Likud.

Israel's forces finally completed their withdrawal from Lebanon in June 1985, leaving responsibility for policing the occupied southern area of Lebanon to the Israeli-controlled 'South Lebanon Army' (SLA). During 1986 Palestinian guerillas resumed rocket attacks on settlements in northern Israel, provoking Israeli air assaults on Palestinian targets in southern Lebanon. Meanwhile, the Shi'a fundamentalist group Hezbollah intensified attacks on SLA positions within the southern buffer zone. The conflict escalated following the abduction, in July 1989, of a local Shi'a Muslim leader by Israeli agents, and in February 1992, after the assassination by the Israeli air force of the Hezbollah Secretary-General, Sheikh AbbasMoussawi.

In July 1988 King Hussein abrogated Jordan's legal and administrative responsibilities in the West Bank, and declared that he would no longer represent the Palestinians in any international conference on the Palestinian question. King Hussein's decision strengthened the PLO's negotiating position as the sole legitimate representative of the Palestinian people. International attention had been focused on the Palestinian cause since December 1987, following an *intifada* (uprising) against Israeli rule in the Occupied Territories and Israeli attempts to suppress the rebellion. In November 1988 the PLO declared an independent Palestinian state (notionally the West Bank and Gaza Strip), and endorsed UN Security Council Resolution 242, thereby implicitly granting recognition to Israel. The USA refused to accept proposals for a two-state solution put forward by the PLO Chairman, Yasser Arafat, in December, but it did open a dialogue with the organization. Prime Minister Itzhak Shamir (the Likud leader had assumed the Israeli premiership in October 1986, in accordance with the 1984 coalition

agreement) would not negotiate, distrusting the PLO's undertaking to abandon violence. Instead, he appeared to favour the introduction of limited self-rule for the Palestinians of the West Bank and Gaza, as outlined in the 1978 Camp David accords. At the November 1988 general election neither Likud nor Labour secured enough seats in the Knesset to form a viable coalition. A further Government of national unity was formed under Shamir, with Shimon Peres as Deputy Prime Minister and Minister of Finance.

In April 1989 Shamir presented a peace proposal that included plans for the holding of democratic elections in the West Bank and Gaza for Palestinian delegates who would be empowered to negotiate self-rule under Israeli authority. The proposals were unacceptable to the PLO, with which direct talks were precluded. In September President Hosni Mubarak of Egypt offered to host a meeting between Israeli and Palestinian representatives, but Likud ministers rejected any direct contact with PLO delegates. In November Israel provisionally accepted a proposal by the US Secretary of State, James Baker, for a preliminary meeting to discuss the holding of elections in the West Bank and Gaza, on condition that Israel would not be required to negotiate with the PLO. The PLO continued to demand a direct role, and the Baker initiative foundered.

The Likud-Labour coalition was beset in early 1990 with disputes, and in March the Knesset adopted a motion of no confidence in Prime Minister Shamir. Shimon Peres was unable to form a new, Labour-led coalition, and in June Shamir formed a new, right-wing coalition Government, comprising Likud, smaller parties and independents. Shamir emphasized the right of Jews to settle in all parts of 'Greater Israel', his opposition to the creation of an independent Palestinian state and his refusal to negotiate with the PLO—or with any Palestinians other than those resident in the Occupied Territories (excluding East Jerusalem).

Meanwhile, also in March 1990 US President George Bush opposed the granting to Israel of a loan of some US $400m. for the housing of Jewish immigrants from the USSR, since Israel would not guarantee to refrain from constructing new settlements in the Occupied Territories. Violence erupted throughout Israel and the Occupied Territories in May. The PLO's refusal to condemn the violence caused the USA to suspend its dialogue with the organization and to veto a UN Security Council resolution urging that international observers be dispatched to the Occupied Territories. In October some 17 Palestinians were shot dead by Israeli police, following clashes with Jewish worshippers. International outrage at the shootings prompted a UN Security Council vote to send an investigative mission, although Israel agreed only to receive a UN emissary. The invasion of Kuwait by Iraq in August had brought about an improvement in US-Israeli relations. However, Iraqi missile attacks on Israel in January 1991, shortly after the US-led multinational force had begun its offensive against Iraq, threatened the cohesion of the force. US diplomatic efforts, and the installation in Israel of US air defence systems, averted an immediate Israeli response.

The Madrid Peace Conference and the launch of the Middle East peace process

By August 1991 intensive diplomacy by US Secretary of State Baker had secured the agreement of the Israeli, Syrian, Egyptian, Jordanian and Lebanese Governments, and of Palestinian representatives, to attend a regional peace conference, the terms of reference for which would be a comprehensive peace settlement based on UN Security Council Resolutions 242 and 338. An initial, 'symbolic' session was held in Madrid, Spain, in October. However, subsequent talks soon became deadlocked over procedural issues. Israel repeatedly questioned the status of the Palestinian-Jordanian delegation, and the right of the Palestinian component to participate separately in negotiations; furthermore, the Government refused to end construction of new settlements in the Occupied Territories. In February 1992, immediately prior to the fourth session of peace talks, to be held in Washington, DC, Baker demanded a complete halt to Israel's settlement-building programme as a precondition for the granting of loan guarantees to the value of US $10,000m. for the housing of Jewish immigrants from the former USSR. A fifth round of negotiations was held in Washington, DC in April 1992. Israeli representatives presented proposals for the holding of municipal elections in the West Bank and Gaza, and for the transfer of control of health care provision there to the Palestinian authorities. In May the first multilateral negotiations commenced between the parties to the Middle East peace conference; however, the sessions were boycotted by Syria and Lebanon.

A general election was held in June 1992, following the collapse of Shamir's coalition Government in January. The new Chairman of the Labour Party, Itzhak Rabin, subsequently formed a new coalition. This alliance, comprising Labour, Meretz and the ultra-Orthodox Shas, held a total of 62 of the 120 Knesset seats, and also commanded the unofficial support of the two Arab parties. Although international observers generally regarded the installation of the Labour-led coalition as having improved the prospects for peace in the Middle East, the sixth and seventh rounds of bilateral negotiations between Israeli, Syrian, Lebanese and Palestinian-Jordanian delegations, in September–November, failed to achieve any progress.

An eighth round of bilateral negotiations between Israeli and Arab delegations commenced in Washington, DC, in December 1992, but were soon overshadowed by violent confrontations between Palestinians and the Israeli security forces in the Occupied Territories, which led to the withdrawal of the Arab participants. In mid-December, in response to the deaths of five members of the Israeli security forces, and the abduction and murder by the Islamic Resistance Movement (Hamas) of an Israeli policeman, the Rabin Government ordered the deportation to Lebanon of 413 alleged Palestinian supporters of Hamas. The expulsions provoked international outrage, and the UN Security Council, in Resolution 799, demanded the return of the deportees to Israel. Consequently, the ninth round of peace talks was formally suspended. In March 1993, amid a sharp escalation of violence in the West Bank and Gaza, Israel sealed off the territories indefinitely.

The suspended ninth round of bilateral negotiations resumed in Washington, DC, in April 1993. The Palestinian delegation apparently agreed to attend the sessions after Israel had agreed to allow Faisal Husseini, the nominal leader of the Palestinian delegation, to participate. Israel was also reported to have undertaken to halt punitive deportations, and, with the USA, to have reaffirmed its commitment to Resolutions 242 and 338 as the terms of reference for the peace process.

In March 1993, meanwhile, Binyamin Netanyahu was chosen to replace Shamir as the Likud leader. In May Ezer Weizman was inaugurated as Israeli President. In July Israeli armed forces mounted the most intensive air and artillery attacks on targets in Lebanon since Operation Peace for Galilee in 1982, in retaliation for attacks by Hezbollah fighters on settlements in northern Israel.

Declaration of Principles on Palestinian Self-Rule (the Oslo accords)

Following the 10th round of bilateral negotiations, convened in Washington, DC, in June 1993, on 13 September Israel and the PLO signed a Declaration of Principles on Palestinian Self-Rule in the Occupied Territories. The agreement, which entailed mutual recognition by Israel and the PLO, had been elaborated during a series of secret negotiations mediated by Norway (and thus became known as the Oslo accords). The Declaration of Principles established a detailed timetable for Israel's disengagement from the Occupied Territories, stipulating that a permanent settlement of the Palestinian question be in place by December 1998. From 13 October 1993 Palestinian authorities were to assume responsibility for education and culture, health, social welfare, direct taxation and tourism in the Gaza Strip and the Jericho area of the West Bank, and a transitional period of Palestinian self-rule was to begin on 13 December. Although the Declaration of Principles was ratified by the Knesset on 23 September 1993, there was widespread opposition, particularly to Israel's recognition of the PLO, from rightwing Israelis. Rabin and Arafat held their first meeting in the context of the Oslo accords in Cairo, Egypt, on 6 October. A joint PLO-Israeli liaison committee was convened for the first time a week later, with delegations headed, respectively, by Mahmud Abbas and Shimon Peres.

Meanwhile, in September 1993 allegations of corruption against Shas leader Aryeh Der'i prompted the resignation of Shas ministers from the Government, thus reducing the coalition to an alliance between the Labour Party and Meretz. A new coalition agreement was signed with Yi'ud, a breakaway group from the Tzomet party, in July 1994.

Meeting in Cairo on 4 May 1994, Israel and the PLO signed an accord providing for Israel's military withdrawal from the Gaza Strip and Jericho, and for the deployment of a 9,000-strong Palestinian police force. A nominated Palestinian (National) Authority (PA) was to assume control of these areas, with the exception of external security and foreign affairs. Elections for a Palestinian Council were postponed until October. Israel's military withdrawal from Gaza and Jericho was completed on 13 May, and on 17 May the PLO formally assumed control of the Israeli Civil Administration's departments there. On 26–28 May the PA held its first meeting in the Tunisian capital, Tunis. Arafat made a symbolic return to Gaza City on 1 July—his first visit for 25 years—and the PA was formally inaugurated in Jericho on 5 July. In August Israel and the PLO signed an agreement extending the authority of the PA to include education, health, tourism, social welfare and taxation.

In October 1994 an Israeli soldier was abducted near Tel-Aviv by Hamas fighters, who subsequently demanded that Israel release the detained Hamas spiritual leader, Sheikh Ahmad Yassin, and other Palestinian prisoners. Despite Palestinian action to detain some 300 Hamas members in the Gaza Strip, the kidnapped soldier was subsequently killed in the West Bank. Shortly afterwards an attack by a Hamas suicide bomber in Tel-Aviv, in which 22 people died, prompted Israel to close its borders with the Palestinian territories. In November a member of another militant Palestinian organization, Islamic Jihad, was killed in a car bomb attack in Gaza. Three Israeli soldiers were subsequently killed in a suicide bombing in the Gaza Strip, for which Islamic Jihad claimed responsibility. It became clear that Israel's security concerns would continue to delay the redeployment of its armed forces from the West Bank and the holding of Palestinian elections (see *The assassination of Itzhak Rabin*). In January 1995, after a further suicide bombing apparently carried out by Islamic Jihad at Beit Lid, in which 21 Israeli soldiers and civilians died, the Israeli Government again closed the country's borders with the West Bank and Gaza, and postponed the planned release of some 5,500 Palestinian prisoners. In February, meanwhile, Israeli armed forces completed their withdrawal from Jordanian territories, in accordance with the October 1994 bilateral peace treaty.

Despite intensive negotiations, an agreement on the expansion of Palestinian self-rule in the West Bank was not achieved by the target date of 1 July 1995. The principal obstacles remained the question of precisely to where Israeli troops in the West Bank would redeploy, and the exact nature of security arrangements for some 130,000 Jewish settlers who were to remain there. On 28 September the Israeli-Palestinian Interim Agreement on the West Bank and the Gaza Strip was finally signed by Israel and the PLO. Its main provisions were the withdrawal of Israeli armed forces from a further six West Bank towns (Nablus, Ramallah, Jenin, Tulkarm, Qalqilya and Bethlehem) and a partial redeployment from the town of Hebron; national Palestinian legislative elections to an 82-member Palestinian Council and for a Palestinian Executive President; and the phased release of Palestinians detained by Israel. In anticipation of a violent reaction against the Interim Agreement by 'rejectionist' groups within the Occupied Territories, Israel immediately sealed its borders with the West Bank and Gaza.

Meanwhile, bilateral negotiations between Israeli and Syrian delegations resumed in Washington, DC, in January 1994. In September Rabin announced details of a plan for a partial withdrawal of Israeli armed forces from the occupied Golan Heights. The proposals were rejected by President Assad of Syria, although he did state his willingness to work towards peace with Israel. Eventually, in May 1995 Israel and Syria were reported to have agreed to facilitate discussions on security issues. Also in January 1994 Morocco and Tunisia became the second and third Arab states, respectively, to establish diplomatic ties with Israel; the six members of the Cooperation Council for the Arab States of the Gulf (the Gulf Cooperation Council, see p. 245) agreed to revoke the subsidiary elements of the Arab economic boycott of Israel. On 25 July Israel and Jordan signed a joint declaration formally ending the state of war between them and on 26 October the two countries signed a formal peace treaty.

The assassination of Itzhak Rabin

On 4 November 1995 Itzhak Rabin was assassinated in Tel-Aviv by a Jewish student opposed to the peace process, in particular the Israeli withdrawal from the West Bank. The Minister of Foreign Affairs, Shimon Peres, was, with the agreement of Likud, invited to form a new government. The members of the outgoing administration—Labour, Meretz and Yi'ud—subsequently signed a new coalition agreement, and the Cabinet was formally approved by the Knesset in late November. In February 1996 Peres announced that elections to the Knesset, and (for the first time) the direct election of the Prime Minister, would take place in May.

Israeli armed forces completed their withdrawal from the West Bank town of Jenin in November 1995, and in December they withdrew from Tulkaram, Nablus, Qalqilya, Bethlehem and Ramallah. With regard to Hebron, Israel and the PA signed an agreement transferring jurisdiction in some 17 areas of civilian affairs from Israel to the PA. At talks with Arafat in December, Peres confirmed that Israel would release some 1,000 Palestinian prisoners before the forthcoming Palestinian elections.

Peace negotiations between Israel and Syria resumed in December 1995 in Maryland, USA, and were followed by a second round in January 1996. However, the talks were swiftly undermined by a series of suicide bombings in Israel in early 1996, and in March the Israeli negotiators returned home. Meanwhile, King Hussein of Jordan made a visit to Tel-Aviv in January, during which Israel and Jordan signed a number of agreements relating to the normalization of economic and cultural relations.

Palestinian legislative and presidential elections were held in January 1996, leading in principle to the final stage of the peace process, when Palestinian and Israeli negotiators would address such issues as Jerusalem, the rights of Palestinian refugees and the status of Jewish settlements in the Palestinian territories. In February and March, however, more than 50 Israelis died as a result of suicide bomb attacks in Jerusalem, Ashkelon and Tel-Aviv, and talks were suspended. Israel again ordered the closure of its borders with the Palestinian territories. A hitherto unknown group, the 'Yahya Ayyash Units', claimed responsibility for the attacks, to avenge the assassination—by Israeli agents—of Ayyash, a leading Hamas activist. Arafat, now the elected Palestinian President, condemned the bombings, and in late February more than 200 members of Hamas were detained by Palestinian security forces. Israel asserted the right of its armed forces to enter PA-controlled areas when Israeli security was at stake, and an agreement to redeploy troops from Hebron by 20 March was rescinded.

In April 1996 Israeli armed forces began a sustained campaign of intense air and artillery attacks on alleged Hezbollah positions in southern Lebanon and Beirut. The declared aim of the operation (code-named 'Grapes of Wrath') was to achieve the cessation of rocket attacks by Hezbollah on settlements in northern Israel. Some 400,000 Lebanese were displaced northwards, after the Israeli military authorities warned that they would be endangered by the offensive against Hezbollah. Moreover, the shelling by Israeli forces of a base of the UN peacekeeping force at Qana resulted in the deaths of more than 100 Lebanese civilians who had been sheltering there, and of four UN peacekeepers. A ceasefire 'understanding' took effect in late April; this was effectively a compromise confining the conflict to the area of the security zone in southern Lebanon, recognizing both Hezbollah's right to resist Israeli occupation and Israel's right to self-defence.

Israel welcomed the decision of the Palestine National Council (PNC) in late April 1996 to amend the Palestinian National Charter (or PLO Covenant), removing all clauses demanding the destruction of Israel: the Israeli Government had required that the Covenant be amended as a precondition for participation in the final stage of peace negotiations with the PLO.

The first term of Prime Minister Binyamin Netanyahu

The Likud leader, Binyamin Netanyahu, achieved a marginal victory over Shimon Peres in the direct prime-ministerial election, held on 19 May 1996. At the parallel legislative election, an alliance of Likud, the Tzomet party and Gesher secured 32 of the 120 Knesset seats, and Labour 34. Netanyahu proceeded to sign agreements between the Likud alliance and Shas, the National Religious Party (NRP), Israel B'Aliyah, United Torah Judaism and the Third Way, to form a majority coalition in the Knesset. The new Government's statement of policy excluded the possibility of granting Palestinian statehood or, with regard to Syria, of relinquishing de facto sovereignty of the occupied Golan Heights. Moreover, Netanyahu apparently postponed further discussion of the withdrawal of Israeli armed forces from Hebron, where they provided security for some 400 Jewish settlers.

In September 1996 it was announced that Israel's Ministry of Defence had approved plans to construct some 1,800 new homes at existing Jewish settlements in the West Bank. Violent confrontations erupted between Palestinian security forces and civilians, and the Israeli armed forces, in which at least 50 Palestinians and 18 Israelis were killed. Nevertheless, in January 1997 Israel and the PA finally concluded an agreement on the withdrawal of Israeli forces from Hebron. As guarantor of the Hebron agreement, the USA undertook to obtain the release of Palestinian prisoners, and to ensure that Israel continued to engage in negotiations for a Palestinian airport in the Gaza Strip, and on safe passage for Palestinians between the West Bank and Gaza. The USA also undertook to ensure that the PA would continue to combat terrorism, complete the revision of the Palestinian National Charter, and consider Israeli requests to extradite Palestinians suspected of involvement in attacks in Israel.

Progress achieved through the agreement on Hebron was severely undermined in February 1997, when Israel announced that it was to proceed with the construction of 6,500 housing units at Har Homa (Jabal Abu Ghunaim in Arabic) in East Jerusalem. Tensions escalated in March, after Israel decided unilaterally to withdraw its armed forces from only 9% of the West Bank. Israeli intransigence over the Har Homa settlement prompted Palestinians to abandon the 'final status' talks on borders, the Jerusalem issue, Jewish settlements and Palestinian refugees, scheduled to begin on 17 March, and construction at the site began the following day. Riots erupted among Palestinians, and shortly afterwards Hamas carried out a bomb attack in Tel-Aviv, killing four people. In late March the League of Arab States (the Arab League, see p. 359) voted to resume its economic boycott of Israel, suspend moves to establish diplomatic relations, and withdraw from multilateral peace talks. (Jordan, the PA and Egypt were excluded from the resolution, owing to their binding bilateral agreements with Israel.)

In June 1997 Ehud Barak, a former government minister and army chief of staff, was elected to replace Peres as Labour Party Chairman. In July two Hamas suicide bombers killed 14 civilians in Jerusalem, prompting Israel to suspend payment of tax revenues to the PA and again close off the Gaza Strip and the West Bank. Further suicide bombings in West Jerusalem in early September resulted in eight deaths. Following a visit by US Secretary of State Madeleine Albright in mid-September, Israel released further Palestinian assets (one-third of tax revenues owed to the PA had been released in August), while the Palestinians announced the closure of 17 institutions affiliated to Hamas.

Renewed hostilities erupted in northern Israel in August 1997, after Hezbollah launched a rocket attack on civilians in Kiryat Shmona. The attack, made following raids by Israeli commandos in which five Hezbollah members were killed, provoked further air strikes by Israel in southern Lebanon. Violence escalated, with the shelling by the SLA of the Lebanese port of Sidon resulting in at least six deaths. Domestic pressure for an Israeli withdrawal from southern Lebanon increased after 12 Israeli marines were killed south of Sidon in September.

Relations between Jordan and Israel deteriorated in September 1997, after members of the Israeli intelligence force, Mossad, attempted to assassinate Hamas's political leader, Khalid Meshaal, in the Jordanian capital, Amman. Following intensive negotiations between Netanyahu, Crown Prince Hassan of Jordan and US officials, several agreements were reached regarding the release of prisoners: in October Israel freed the Hamas spiritual leader, Sheikh Ahmad Yassin, in return for the release by Jordan of two Mossad agents arrested in connection with the attack on Meshaal.

Bilateral negotiations between Israel and the PA resumed in November 1997. Israel offered to decelerate its construction of Jewish settlements in return for Palestinian approval of a plan to delay further redeployments of Israeli troops from the West Bank. However, the Israeli Government also announced plans to build 900 new housing units in the area. At the end of November the Israeli Cabinet agreed in principle to a partial withdrawal from the West Bank, but specified neither the timing nor the scale of this. In January 1998 Netanyahu announced that he would not make any further decisions regarding the peace process until the Palestinians had demonstrated further efforts to combat terrorism, reduced their security forces from 40,000 to 24,000, and amended their National Charter to recognize Israel's right to exist.

In June 1998 President Weizman (who had been elected for a second term in March) angered Netanyahu by publicly demanding the dissolution of the Knesset and early elections, so that Israelis might choose the future direction of peace talks. Meanwhile, the Cabinet approved Netanyahu's draft plan whereby the municipal boundaries of Jerusalem would be extended to incorporate seven West Bank Jewish settlements—to create a 'Greater

Jerusalem' covering six times the current area of the city. Arab leaders accused Netanyahu of seeking formally to annex parts of the West Bank, and the UN Security Council urged Israel to abandon the proposals.

After nine days of intensive talks with US President Bill Clinton at the Wye Plantation, Maryland, on 23 October 1998 Netanyahu and Arafat signed an agreement (the Wye River Memorandum) that outlined a three-month timetable for the implementation of the 1995 Interim Agreement and signalled the commencement of 'final status' talks—which should have begun in May 1996. With the mediation of Clinton and King Hussein, Israel agreed to redeploy its troops from 13.1% of the West Bank, while the PA agreed to intensify measures to prevent terrorism and to rewrite the Palestinian National Charter. On 11 November 1998, after the postponement of four scheduled meetings (owing to a bombing by Islamic Jihad in Jerusalem and Israeli fears of further attacks by Palestinian militant groups), the Israeli Cabinet approved the Wye Memorandum. Netanyahu subsequently reiterated that a number of conditions would first have to be met by the Palestinians, and threatened effective Israeli annexation of areas of the West Bank if a Palestinian state were to be declared on 4 May 1999. (Arafat continued to reassert his right to declare a Palestinian state on the expiry date of the interim stage defined in Oslo.) The Knesset ratified the Wye Memorandum on 17 November 1998. Three days later the Israeli Government implemented the first stage of renewed redeployment from the West Bank, also releasing 250 Palestinian prisoners and signing a protocol allowing for the opening of an international airport at Gaza.

During December 1998 it became increasingly evident that divisions within Netanyahu's coalition over implementation of the Wye Memorandum were making government untenable. The administration effectively collapsed when the Minister of Finance, Yaacov Ne'eman, announced his resignation. Shortly afterwards the Knesset voted to hold elections to the legislature and premiership in early 1999.

In December 1998 US President Clinton attended a session of the PNC, at which the removal from the Palestinian National Charter of all clauses seeking Israel's destruction was re-affirmed. Netanyahu announced that the second phase of Israeli troop deployment envisaged by the Wye Memorandum, scheduled for 18 December, would not be undertaken, claiming that the Palestinians had not adequately addressed their security commitments. The Knesset subsequently voted to suspend implementation of the Wye Memorandum, thereby effectively suspending the peace process. In late December Arafat freed the Hamas spiritual leader, Sheikh Ahmad Yassin, from house arrest, prompting further Israeli claims that agreed anti-terrorism measures were not being implemented. The US Administration threatened to withhold US $1,200m. promised to Israel to fund its redeployment in the West Bank unless it complied with the terms of the Wye Memorandum. For several months President Clinton refused to hold a private meeting with Netanyahu, while agreeing to meet Arafat in March 1999 to discuss his threatened unilateral declaration of statehood on 4 May; following intense international pressure, the declaration was postponed at the end of April.

Hostilities in southern Lebanon between Israeli forces and Hezbollah persisted throughout 1998. In that year some 23 Israeli soldiers were killed, and there was increasing pressure on Netanyahu for a unilateral withdrawal from the territory. On 1 April the Israeli Security Cabinet voted unanimously to adopt UN Security Council Resolution 425 (of March 1978), urging an immediate withdrawal of Israeli troops from all Lebanese territory provided that the Lebanese army gave security guarantees. However, both Lebanon and Syria demanded an unconditional withdrawal. Fighting escalated in August, when Hezbollah launched rocket attacks on northern Israel in retaliation for an Israeli helicopter attack in which a senior Lebanese military official was killed. Seven Israeli soldiers died in two attacks in November, leading Netanyahu to curtail a European tour in order to hold an emergency cabinet meeting on a possible withdrawal. In December an Israeli air attack in which eight Lebanese civilians were killed was considered to be a violation of the ceasefire 'understanding' reached in April 1996. In February 1999 the commander of the Israeli army unit for liaison with the SLA became the most senior Israeli officer to be killed in southern Lebanon since 1982. Israel responded with its heaviest air raids against Lebanon since the 1996 Grapes of Wrath operation.

The election of Ehud Barak as Prime Minister

At the general election held on 17 May 1999, Ehud Barak was elected Prime Minister with 56.1% of the total votes cast. In the elections to the Knesset, Barak's One Israel alliance (including Gesher and the moderate Meimad) secured 26 seats, while Likud's representation fell from 32 seats to 19. Shas won 17 seats. Netanyahu subsequently resigned from both the Knesset and the Likud leadership, and in September Ariel Sharon was elected as Likud's new Chairman. Barak stated that he would observe four 'security red lines' concerning negotiations with the Palestinians: Jerusalem would remain under Israeli sovereignty; there would be no return to the pre-1967 borders; most West Bank settlers would remain in settlements under Israeli sovereignty; and no 'foreign armies' would be based west of the Jordan river. Following complex negotiations, Barak forged a broad coalition with the Centre Party, Shas, Meretz, Israel B'Aliyah and the NRP, which was endorsed by the Knesset in July 1999. Barak himself took the defence portfolio.

In early September 1999, during a visit to the region by US Secretary of State Albright, Barak and Arafat travelled to Egypt for talks at Sharm el-Sheikh. On 4 September the two leaders signed the Sharm el-Sheikh Memorandum (or Wye Two accords), which outlined a revised timetable for implementation of the outstanding provisions of the original Wye Memorandum in order to facilitate the resumption of 'final status' talks: a new target date—13 September 2000—was set for the conclusion of a comprehensive 'final status' settlement. One important change was the reduction, to 350, of the number of Palestinian prisoners to be released by Israel. On 8 September 1999 the Knesset ratified the Wye Two accords; the following day Israel released some 200 Palestinian prisoners, and on 10 September a further 7% of the West Bank was transferred to Palestinian civilian control. A further 151 Palestinian prisoners were released from Israeli custody in mid-October. On 25 October a southern 'safe passage' for Palestinians travelling between Gaza and Hebron was finally opened.

Despite this apparent progress, Barak encountered severe criticism in late 1999 among left-wing groups and Palestinians over his Government's apparent intention to continue to approve the expansion of Jewish settlements in the West Bank. Barak subsequently angered settler groups with a ruling that several of the 42 'outpost settlements' established in the West Bank under the Likud Government had been built illegally; 12 of the 'outposts' were dismantled in October.

On 8 November 1999 representatives of Israel and the PA commenced talks on 'final status' issues in the West Bank city of Ramallah, although the redeployment of Israeli armed forces from a further 5% of the West Bank on 15 November was delayed. In December Barak and Arafat met on Palestinian territory for the first time, and at the end of the month Israel released some 26 Palestinian 'security' prisoners as a gesture of goodwill. On 6–7 January 2000 Israeli troops withdrew from a further 5% of the West Bank. However, Israel subsequently announced the postponement of a third redeployment (scheduled for 20 January) until Barak had returned from talks with Syrian representatives in the USA. In early February PA officials suspended peace negotiations, following the decision by the Israeli Cabinet to withdraw its armed forces from a sparsely populated 6.1% of the West Bank. The redeployment from a further 6.1% took place on 21 March, facilitating an official resumption of 'final status' talks. In that month a ruling by Israel's Supreme Court that the allocation of state-owned land on the basis of religion, nationality or ethnicity was illegal allowed Israeli Arabs to purchase land for the first time.

Meanwhile, in June 1999 the SLA completed a unilateral withdrawal from the Jezzine enclave. Later that month the outgoing Netanyahu administration launched a series of air attacks on Lebanon, destroying Beirut's main power station and other infrastructure, in response to Hezbollah rocket attacks on northern Israel. In December Israel and Syria reached an 'understanding in principle' to limit the fighting in southern Lebanon. However, the informal ceasefire did not endure, and in February 2000 Israel retaliated for a series of attacks by Hezbollah with further bombing raids on Lebanese infrastructure. Israel also announced a unilateral withdrawal from the 1996 ceasefire agreement.

In March 2000 the Israeli Cabinet voted unanimously to withdraw its forces from southern Lebanon by 7 July, even in the absence of a peace agreement with Syria. The Lebanese Government responded by demanding that Israel also depart from the Shebaa Farms area on the Syrian border. (Shebaa

Farms has been designated by the UN as being part of Syria, and thus subject to the Syrian track of the peace process; Hezbollah, however, considers it to be part of southern Lebanon.) In April Israel released 13 Lebanese prisoners who had been detained without trial for more than a decade, apparently as 'bargaining chips' for Israeli soldiers missing in Lebanon. Fighting between Israeli troops and Hezbollah intensified in May, and on 23 May Israel's Security Cabinet voted to accelerate the withdrawal of its remaining troops from southern Lebanon. By this date Hezbollah had taken control of about one-third of the territory, following the evacuation by the SLA of outposts transferred to its control by the Israeli army. The rapid departure of all Israeli forces from southern Lebanon was completed on 24 May; about 900 Israelis had been killed there since 1978. After the withdrawal several thousand SLA members and their families fled across the border into northern Israel. In June 2000 the UN Security Council confirmed that Israel had completed its withdrawal from Lebanon in compliance with Resolution 425. Following the withdrawal, personnel from the UN Interim Force in Lebanon (UNIFIL) began patrolling the area vacated by Israeli forces, monitoring the line of withdrawal and providing humanitarian assistance.

A third round of 'final status' discussions opened in Eilat on 30 April 2000, but maps presented by Israeli officials to the PA in early May, defining Barak's interpretation of a future Palestinian state, were firmly rejected by the Palestinians. Barak and Arafat held a crisis meeting in Ramallah, at which Barak proposed that Israel transfer to full PA control three Arab villages situated close to Jerusalem, on condition that the third West Bank redeployment (scheduled for June) was postponed until after the conclusion of a final peace settlement. The Knesset subsequently approved the transfer. However, Barak later announced that an Israeli withdrawal from the Arab villages would not be implemented until the PA took appropriate measures to curb unrest in the West Bank, where Palestinians had been protesting in support of gaoled Palestinians on hunger strike.

In May 2000, following an inconclusive police investigation into allegations of fraud, President Weizman announced his intention to resign. In the ensuing presidential election, held on 31 July, Likud's Moshe Katsav unexpectedly secured a narrow victory over Barak's nominee, Shimon Peres. Katsav was duly sworn in as the eighth President of Israel on 1 August, to serve an exceptional seven-year term. In early July, meanwhile, the three right-wing parties (Israel B'Aliyah, the NRP and Shas) withdrew from the coalition Government in protest against what they perceived to be Barak's willingness to concede to PA territorial claims. Despite the loss of six ministers, Barak survived a motion of no confidence in the Knesset and a similar vote immediately after the presidential election. In August, however, the Minister of Foreign Affairs, David Levy, announced his resignation, citing disagreements with Barak over the peace process.

US President Clinton opened the Camp David talks, aimed at reaching a framework agreement for a final peace settlement, on 11 July 2000. Despite intensive mediation efforts, the summit ended on 25 July without agreement. Progress had reportedly been made on the issues of the borders of a future Palestinian entity (to comprise all of the Gaza Strip and at least 90% of the West Bank) and the status of Palestinian refugees, but the two sides were unable to reach a compromise regarding the future status of Jerusalem. In the summit's final communiqué, both sides vowed to continue the pursuit of a 'final status' settlement and to avoid 'unilateral actions'—thereby implying that Arafat would not declare a Palestinian state on 13 September. Shortly before that date the Palestinian legislature voted to delay such a declaration for an indefinite period.

The al-Aqsa intifada

In late September 2000 Barak and Arafat met for the first time since the Camp David summit. The resumption of contacts was swiftly overshadowed by a renewed uprising by Palestinians against Israeli occupation, which resulted in the suspension of the Middle East peace process. On 28 September the Likud leader, Ariel Sharon, made a highly controversial visit to the Temple Mount/Haram al-Sharif compound in Jerusalem (the site of the Dome of the Rock and the al-Aqsa Mosque). Protests there by Palestinians triggered violent unrest throughout the Palestinian territories. For the first time, notably, Israeli Arabs clashed with security forces within Israel. On 7 October the UN Security Council adopted a resolution condemning the 'excessive use of force' by Israeli security forces against Palestinian demonstrators. Israel closed the borders of the Palestinian territories

and Gaza airport, and Barak demanded that Arafat rearrest some 60 militant Islamists who had recently been freed from Palestinian detention.

The crisis escalated in mid-October 2000, after Israeli forces launched rocket attacks on the headquarters of Arafat's Fatah movement in Ramallah and on other PA offices, in response to the murder of two Israeli army reservists by a Palestinian crowd. Despite an emergency summit meeting between Barak and Arafat, convened by US President Clinton, and hosted by Egyptian President Mubarak at Sharm el-Sheikh, at which measures were agreed to end the fighting, violence intensified, and on 22 October Barak announced that Israel was to take a 'time-out' from the peace process. This came as Barak undertook discussions with Likud on the formation of a national unity government prior to the reconvening of the Knesset for the new parliamentary session; however, no compromise was reached, apparently owing to Sharon's demand for a veto on all decisions relating to national security. Barak's decision formally to suspend Israel's participation in the peace process was precipitated by the final communiqué issued by Arab leaders after an emergency summit meeting of the Arab League in Cairo, which declared that Israel bore full responsibility for the recent violence. Morocco, Tunisia and Oman announced that they had severed relations with Israel, and Qatar broke off ties in November.

A suicide bomb attack by Islamic Jihad on an Israeli military target in Gaza at the end of October 2000 led the Israeli army to declare a new strategy of 'targeted killings', of the leaders of such groups, as well as senior Fatah commanders, whom it held responsible for 'terrorist' actions. In early November the Israeli Minister of Regional Co-operation, Shimon Peres, held crisis talks with Arafat in Gaza, at which a ceasefire was agreed. However, the truce was broken almost immediately, when a car bomb planted by Islamic Jihad exploded in Jerusalem, killing two Israelis. In mid-November Israel effectively imposed a complete economic blockade of the Palestinian areas. Later in the month the explosion of a bomb close to a bus carrying Israeli schoolchildren (as a result of which two people died and several children were injured) provoked public outrage, and led Israel to launch further air raids against Fatah targets in Gaza. Egypt responded by announcing that it was recalling its ambassador from Tel-Aviv. (Egypt suspended all direct contact with the Israeli Government in April 2002, other than for negotiations aimed at restoring peace in the region, and did not return an ambassador to Israel until March 2005.)

The accession of Prime Minister Ariel Sharon

At the end of November 2000, in an apparent attempt to secure his increasingly beleaguered Government, Barak unexpectedly called early prime ministerial elections for 2001. The election, held on 6 February 2001, resulted in an overwhelming victory for the Likud leader, Ariel Sharon, with 62.4% of the votes cast. Barak had notably lost the Israeli Arab vote—as the Arab parties had urged their supporters to boycott or abstain in the poll—and his defeat was interpreted as a decisive rejection of the Oslo peace process by the majority of Israelis. Sharon immediately sought the formation of a broad-based government of national unity, essentially to secure a political base in the Knesset (where Likud held only 19 of the 120 seats). Barak announced his resignation as Labour leader; he subsequently declared that he would not enter a government led by Sharon, and that he would withdraw from political life. In late February Labour's Central Committee voted to join a coalition administration, enabling Sharon to conclude agreements principally with the religious and right-wing parties. The national unity Government, approved by the Knesset in early March, included the ultra-Orthodox Shas, Israel B'Aliyah and the extreme right-wing National Union-Israel Beytenu bloc.

Following his election victory, Sharon rejected an appeal by the new US Administration of President George W. Bush, who had been inaugurated in January 2001, for Israel to end its blockade on the West Bank and Gaza Strip and to deliver overdue tax transfers to the PA. In March Arab League heads of state, meeting in Amman, resolved to reinstate the 'secondary' economic boycott of Israel. It was announced in early April that the Israeli Government had issued tenders for the construction of a further 708 housing units in the West Bank. In the same month, in response to a Palestinian mortar attack on the Israeli town of Sderot, Israeli armed forces imposed road blockades, which effectively divided the Gaza Strip into three sections, and sent tanks and bulldozers into the Gazan town of Beit Hanoun; this was Israel's first armed incursion into territory that it had transferred to PA control under the terms of the Oslo accords. Under heavy pressure from the USA, Israel withdrew its forces less than 24 hours later. Hopes of a resumption of the Oslo peace talks were raised in mid-April amid a revival of the 'Egyptian-Jordanian initiative' or Taba plan. The initiative required that the situation on the ground be restored to that prior to the start of the al-Aqsa *intifada* and that Israel agree to halt its settlement programme in the Occupied Territories. Sharon stated that Israel would endorse the Taba plan, on condition that the PA end its demand for a complete freeze on the construction of Jewish settlements, and that all Palestinian violence cease prior to the resumption of peace talks.

In May 2001 the Sharm el-Sheikh Fact-Finding Committee, under the chairmanship of former US Senator George Mitchell, published its recommendations relating to the causes of the Israeli–Palestinian violence. The Mitchell Report referred to the visit of Ariel Sharon to the Islamic holy sites in September 2000 as 'provocative', but declined to single out for blame either Sharon or the PA leadership (which Israeli officials had accused of having orchestrated the violence). The Mitchell Report also demanded that Arafat undertake further measures to curb Palestinian 'terrorist operations', and appealed to Israel to end its economic blockade of the West Bank and Gaza and to halt its settlement expansion programme. In early June 21 Israelis were killed in an attack on a Tel-Aviv nightclub by a Palestinian suicide bomber. In mid-June proposals for a comprehensive ceasefire, brokered by the USA, were approved by Israel and the PA; however, although Israel began to implement provisions to withdraw troops from PA-controlled towns and to ease the economic blockade, the process was hindered by the murder of two West Bank settlers by Palestinian gunmen and the killing of two Israeli soldiers in a suicide bombing in the Gaza Strip.

In late July 2001 two leading Hamas members, alleged by Israel to have been involved in the Tel-Aviv nightclub bombing, were killed during an air raid on Hamas media offices in Nablus. In early August at least 15 Israelis were killed by a Palestinian suicide bomber at a Jerusalem restaurant. The Israeli Government responded to the bombing by taking temporary control of Orient House, the de facto headquarters of the PA in East Jerusalem. At the end of August Abu Ali Moustafa, leader of the Popular Front for the Liberation of Palestine (PFLP), was killed by Israeli security forces at the party's offices in Ramallah. In September the PFLP claimed responsibility for four bomb attacks in Jerusalem. On several occasions during the latter part of the year Israel ordered its forces into PA-controlled towns—among them Hebron, Bethlehem, Jenin and Beit Jala—in response to violent clashes between Israelis and Palestinians. By the time of the first anniversary of the outbreak of the al-Aqsa *intifada*, on 28 September, the violence had led to the deaths of more than 160 Israelis, and at least 600 Palestinians. The massive suicide attacks against New York and Washington, DC, on 11 September 2001 accelerated US and European Union (EU, see p. 271) efforts to urge Israel and the PA to effect a lasting ceasefire.

In October 2001 two ministers resigned after the right-wing National Union-Israel Beytenu bloc withdrew from the governing coalition in protest at the Sharon administration's decision to pull back Israeli armed forces from Hebron. Two days later one of the outgoing ministers, the Minister of Tourism, Rechavam Ze'evi, was assassinated in Arab East Jerusalem by a PFLP militant, in apparent retaliation for the recent assassination of the group's leader. Following the murder of Ze'evi, the National Union-Israel Beytenu bloc maintained its presence in the Government. Sharon suspended all contact with the PA, holding Arafat personally responsible for Ze'evi's death. The Israeli Government also reversed its recent moves to ease the economic restrictions on Palestinians in the West Bank and Gaza, and demanded that the PA immediately extradite the PFLP militants implicated in the assassination. Israeli armed forces entered six Palestinian towns in the West Bank (including Ramallah, Jenin, Nablus and Bethlehem), leading US officials to urge Israel to withdraw its troops from PA-controlled towns. Although Israeli forces duly withdrew from two of the towns (Bethlehem and Beit Jala) at the end of October, Sharon announced that the withdrawal from the remaining four would not take place until the PA arrested more Islamist militants.

The Israeli–Palestinian crisis escalated in December 2001, when Palestinian militants launched suicide attacks in Haifa and Jerusalem, in reprisal for the 'targeted killing' of a Hamas leader: during one weekend some 25 Israelis were killed. Sharon ordered military strikes against Palestinian security targets,

and Israel escalated its operations in the Palestinian territories in mid-December after 10 Israelis died in a bomb attack in the West Bank. Israeli armed forces undertook a 'tactical' withdrawal from areas around Nablus and Ramallah to permit Arafat's security forces to arrest wanted Palestinian militants. However, Arafat remained confined to his headquarters in Ramallah after Israel imposed a travel ban on the Palestinian leader.

In early January 2002 the Israeli administration ordered the partial withdrawal of its forces from some West Bank towns, and the easing of certain restrictions against Palestinians there. Meanwhile, it was announced that Israeli forces in the Red Sea had intercepted a freighter ship, the *Karine-A*, which Israel asserted was carrying Iranian-made heavy weaponry destined for the Gaza Strip. The PA denied all knowledge of the shipment but, none the less, instituted an internal inquiry into the *Karine-A* affair. In mid-January Israeli forces assassinated a leader of the Fatah-affiliated Al-Aqsa Martyrs' Brigades, provoking retaliatory attacks by that organization in Hadera and Jerusalem in which six Israelis died. Israeli forces proceeded to tighten the blockade around Arafat's Ramallah offices. At the end of the month Sharon approved a security plan involving the physical 'separation' of Jerusalem from the West Bank, in order to prevent attacks by Palestinian Islamist groups on Israeli territory.

In early March 2002 the UN Security Council adopted Resolution 1397, affirming its 'vision' of both Israeli and Palestinian states 'within secure and recognized borders'. A peace initiative put forward by Crown Prince Abdullah of Saudi Arabia at the Arab League summit in Beirut in late March, whereby Israel would withdraw from all Arab lands occupied since 1967 in exchange for full recognition of the State of Israel by the Arab states, was rejected by the Israeli Government. Towards the end of March 2002 a Hamas suicide bombing at a Passover celebration in Netanya resulted in the deaths of 30 Israelis. In response, Israeli forces, on 29 March, began a massive campaign of military incursions into West Bank towns—code-named 'Operation Defensive Shield'—with the aim of dismantling the Palestinian 'terrorist infrastructure'. Arafat's presidential compound at Ramallah was surrounded by Israeli troops.

During the first two weeks of April 2002 intense fighting between the Israeli army and Palestinian militias occurred in the Jenin refugee camp—considered by Israel to be a base for Palestinian militants opposed to the Oslo accords. Some 23 Israeli soldiers and an estimated 53 Palestinians were reportedly killed in ambushes and gun battles at the camp. US Secretary of State Colin Powell arrived in Israel in mid-April in an attempt to broker a ceasefire, and the Bush Administration repeated demands for Israel to withdraw from PA-controlled towns. There was a subsequent redeployment of Israeli forces from areas of the West Bank, and Arafat was freed at the beginning of May, after the PA agreed to hand over five men suspected of involvement in the assassination of Rechavam Ze'evi. (For further details of events in the West Bank and Gaza Strip in March–May 2002, see the chapter on the Palestinian Territories.)

The National Union-Israel Beytenu bloc withdrew from the governing coalition in March 2002, in protest against recent concessions made towards the Palestinians. However, the Government was strengthened a month later by the appointment of David Levy of Gesher and two ministers from the NRP as ministers without portfolio. The Central Committee of Likud voted in May categorically to reject the creation of a Palestinian state; this was interpreted as a reverse for Ariel Sharon, who publicly accepted the possibility of Palestinian independence.

In June 2002 Israel commenced the construction of a 'security fence', to extend the entire length of its border with the West Bank, to prevent Palestinian militants from infiltrating Israeli territory. Despite international efforts to bring about a new round of peace talks between Israel and the PA, and reports of a potential US initiative involving the creation of an 'interim' Palestinian state, there was a marked increase in violence at this time. Israel launched a new offensive, code-named 'Operation Determined Path', ordering troops into several West Bank and Gaza towns, in retaliation for another series of suicide attacks by Palestinian militants; and Arafat's headquarters in Ramallah were again blockaded by the Israeli military. In late June senior-level talks resumed between Israel and the PA, while the Quartet group (comprising the USA, Russia, the UN and the EU) held discussions in London, United Kingdom, with the aim of re-activating the Oslo peace process.

Several Israelis died in an attack on a bus near a Jewish settlement in the West Bank in July 2002, for which three

Palestinian militant groups all claimed responsibility. The Israeli response to the latest assaults included suspending plans to ease some of the restrictions imposed on Palestinians in the Territories and proposing to deport a number of relatives of suspected Palestinian militants to the Gaza Strip. In late July an Israeli air strike on a residential building in Gaza City, targeting a leader of Hamas's military wing, reportedly resulted in the deaths of 15 Palestinians. The Gaza air strike precipitated a new round of violence, with four Jewish settlers being killed near Hebron. Israel responded by ordering tanks into the Gaza Strip. At the end of July at least seven Israelis were killed in a suicide bomb attack at the Hebrew University in Jerusalem, for which Hamas claimed responsibility. Following at least 15 further Israeli fatalities in early August, as a result of Palestinian militant attacks, the Israeli Government ordered a total ban on freedom of movement for Palestinians in most West Bank cities, and targeted a number of leading Gazan militants. Israel and the PA agreed at this time to implement a security plan, whereby Israel would withdraw from the Gaza Strip and Bethlehem in return for Palestinian security guarantees and a crackdown on militants. Israel began to withdraw its forces from Bethlehem the following day; however, violence continued and further talks were cancelled. Following two suicide bombings in Um al-Fahm and Tel-Aviv in that month, Israeli forces began demolishing buildings in Arafat's Ramallah compound, claiming that some 20 Palestinian militants were being sheltered there.

Elections to the Knesset were held on 28 January 2003, a few months earlier than scheduled. In October 2002 the Labour Party had withdrawn from Sharon's governing coalition in opposition to provisions in the 2003 budget that allocated funds to Jewish settlements in the West Bank. Sharon and his Likud party won a resounding victory over the left-wing parties at the polls, securing 38 seats in the Knesset. A new coalition Government was announced at the end of February 2003: it comprised Likud, the secularist Shinui party (part of the Meretz alliance from 1992, but re-formed as an independent party in 1997), and the right-wing and religious NRP, National Union and Israel B'Aliyah parties. The former Likud premier, Binyamin Netanyahu, was named as Minister of Finance. In May Amram Mitzna resigned as Labour leader; he was subsequently replaced, initially in an acting capacity, by Shimon Peres.

The 'roadmap' peace plan

President George W. Bush announced in mid-April 2003 that he would publish the Quartet-sponsored 'roadmap' for achieving peace in the Middle East once the newly appointed Palestinian Prime Minister, Mahmud Abbas, had announced a new cabinet. On 30 April the USA presented both the Israeli and Palestinian Prime Ministers with copies of the 'roadmap'—despite a suicide bombing in Tel-Aviv the previous day, as a result of which five people were killed. The three-phase initiative envisaged the creation of a sovereign Palestinian state by 2005–06. The first phase would deal largely with Palestinian issues, namely the cessation of militant operations against Israel and the establishment of a civilian and government infrastructure. Israel would be required to withdraw from areas that it had occupied since 2000, and to dismantle Jewish settlements constructed since 2001. In phase two, Israel would hold peace talks with Lebanon and Syria regarding Palestinian borders. The third and final phase would deal with the issues of Jerusalem and refugees. The roadmap emphasized the importance of UN Security Council Resolutions 242, 338 and 1397 in establishing a two-state settlement, and also reiterated that the Arab states must recognize Israel's right to exist. On 25 May 2003 the Israeli Cabinet accepted the terms of the roadmap, and at the end of the month Sharon made the unprecedented admission that Israel was in occupation of the Palestinian areas.

In early June 2003 Ariel Sharon, Mahmud Abbas and President Bush met in Aqaba, Jordan, to discuss the implementation of the roadmap. On 9 June Israeli troops commenced the dismantlement of settlements in the West Bank, but the renewed peace process was immediately thwarted by a resumption of violence. An attempt by Israel to kill a prominent Hamas leader, Abd al-Aziz al-Rantisi, prompted a suicide attack against a bus in Jerusalem, in which 16 people died. Israeli helicopter gunships were subsequently ordered to attack targets in Gaza. In all, 26 people were killed in the renewed hostilities. However, Israel continued to dismantle the settlements; it also instigated troop withdrawals from the West Bank and Gaza Strip, as well as the release of a number of Palestinian prisoners. By August more than 400 prisoners had been released, including members of

Hamas and Islamic Jihad who were deemed not to have been involved in planning or executing attacks against Israeli targets. These two groups, along with Arafat's Fatah movement, had declared a three-month ceasefire at the end of June.

Meanwhile, there was growing international concern regarding Israel's construction of its 'security fence' in the West Bank: Israel was accused of using the 'fence' to annex Palestinian territory, and it was feared that it would become a permanent border in any future peace settlement. President Bush had urged Sharon to remove the 'security fence' when the two leaders met in July, and the US Administration further threatened to withhold nearly US $10,000m. of essential loan guarantees unless construction ceased. Israel none the less continued to erect the barrier, as well as to maintain its policy of 'targeted killing' of senior Palestinian militants. In August Israeli forces killed a senior Islamic Jihad commander in Hebron, and both Hamas and Islamic Jihad subsequently claimed responsibility for a suicide bomb attack on a bus in Jerusalem, in which 20 Israelis were killed. In retaliation, Israel reimposed road-blocks on the main north–south highway in the Gaza Strip, reversing one of the earliest roadmap initiatives.

In October 2003 the Israeli Cabinet approved the next phase of the 'security fence', which was to enclose settlements in the West Bank completely. Additionally, a tender was issued for the construction of 550 new homes in a settlement close to Jerusalem. The USA announced in November its intention to cut US $290m. from a set of loan guarantees for Israel as a penalty for renewed settlement construction in the West Bank and Gaza. The issue of the settlements was further raised by the authors of a new peace plan, launched by senior Palestinian and Israeli political figures in Geneva, Switzerland, on 1 December. The Geneva Accords, which did not have the official approval of either the Israeli or Palestinian administrations, outlined a two-state solution, including proposals that Palestinians would receive compensation for giving up the right of return; that most settlements in the West Bank and Gaza (except those neighbouring Jerusalem) would be dismantled; and that Jerusalem (which would be the capital of two states) would be divided administratively rather than physically. On 8 December the UN General Assembly adopted a resolution asking the International Court of Justice (ICJ) in The Hague, Netherlands, to issue a (non-binding) ruling on the legality of Israel's 'security fence'; hearings began in February 2004.

Sharon's disengagement plan

In December 2003 Ariel Sharon warned the PA that unless it began disarming and disbanding Palestinian militant groups, Israel would adopt a 'disengagement plan' that would effectively accelerate the construction of the 'security fence' in the West Bank and physically separate Israel from the Palestinian territories. Sharon's speech attracted criticism from right-wing and ultra-Orthodox settler groups when it became clear that disengagement would involve the evacuation of 17 settlements in the Gaza Strip, considered beyond the reach of the 'security fence'. The roadmap required at least 60 settlements in the West Bank and Gaza to be dismantled.

Sharon confirmed in February 2004 that he had drawn up a plan to evacuate all Jewish settlements in the Gaza Strip. The evacuation would reportedly affect 7,500 settlers in 17 settlements. Although the plan was welcomed by the recently appointed Palestinian Prime Minister, Ahmad Quray, the proposed disengagement was overshadowed by the 'targeted killing' of Sheikh Ahmad Yassin, the founder and spiritual leader of Hamas, by Israeli helicopter gunships in March. The action to kill Yassin, which provoked international condemnation, followed a double suicide bombing at the southern port of Ashdod, responsibility for which was claimed jointly by Hamas and the Al-Aqsa Martyrs' Brigades, in which 10 Israelis died. Yassin's successor as leader of Hamas in Gaza, Abd al-Aziz al-Rantisi, was also killed in April in a rocket attack by Israeli helicopter gunships. Hamas kept secret the identity of al-Rantisi's successor, reportedly adopting a policy of 'collective leadership' in order to prevent future known leaders of the organization from being similarly targeted.

The Israeli Prime Minister secured the endorsement of President Bush for his proposal to 'disengage' from Gaza, which also involved the consolidation of six settlements in the West Bank. In May 2004, however, Likud members overwhelmingly rejected the plan. Sharon subsequently made limited modifications to the proposals, and in June dismissed two ministers of the far-right National Union party—the Minister of Transport, Avigdor Lieberman, and the Minister of Tourism, Binyamin

Elon—both of whom were opposed to disengagement from Gaza. A few days later the NRP Minister of Construction and Housing, Efraim Eitam, resigned, after the Cabinet approved in principle Sharon's broad proposals. However, Sharon subsequently lost his Knesset majority when National Union's six deputies resigned, and he entered into negotiations with the Labour Party.

Meanwhile, attacks by Palestinian militants against Israeli soldiers in the Gaza Strip intensified, and in May 2004 Israel launched a large military offensive, code-named 'Operation Rainbow'. The aims of the operation were to locate and dismantle tunnels in the Rafah refugee camps through which militants were able to smuggle weapons from Egypt, and to arrest Palestinians wanted for involvement in attacks against Israelis. Some 40 Palestinians, whom Israel claimed to be terrorists, were reported to have been killed. In June the Israeli Supreme Court ordered the Government to alter the route of part of the 'security fence'. In July the ICJ advised that the barrier contravened international law and effectively constituted the annexation of Palestinian land, and that it disrupted thousands of civilians' lives, frustrating Palestinian attempts to achieve self-determination. The ICJ urged Israel to remove parts of the fence and pay compensation to affected Palestinians; Sharon rejected the ruling. The UN General Assembly subsequently voted to demand that Israel comply with the ICJ ruling and dismantle the barrier. In August Sharon approved the construction of 1,000 new homes in the West Bank.

In October 2004 the Knesset voted to accept Sharon's proposal to dismantle all 21 Israeli settlements in Gaza, and four in the northern West Bank. In November the Cabinet approved a plan to compensate Jewish settlers due to be evacuated from Gaza, and to imprison settlers who resisted evacuation. The NRP's six parliamentary members withdrew from the coalition, in opposition to Sharon's proposals. In early December Sharon dismissed Shinui's five ministers, who had voted against the first reading of the 2005 budget because it pledged US $98m. in subsidies to projects supported by United Torah Judaism. Likud was left with only 40 out of the Knesset's 120 seats. Following negotiations, Labour agreed to form a coalition with Likud. In January 2005 the Knesset narrowly approved the new coalition Government, to be composed principally of Likud, Labour and United Torah Judaism, thereby restoring Sharon's parliamentary majority; the Labour leader, Shimon Peres, was awarded the title of Vice-Premier.

In mid-October 2004, meanwhile, the Israeli army ended a 16-day assault, code-named 'Operation Days of Penitence', in the Gaza Strip; according to UN figures, 135 Palestinians were killed and an estimated 95 homes destroyed. The operation had been prompted by a Hamas rocket that killed two children in Sderot, close to the Gaza Strip. Egypt undertook to provide 750 border guards to replace Israeli troops along the Egypt–Gaza frontier, in an effort to stem arms-smuggling, and to prevent Hamas and other Palestinian militants from firing rockets into Israel in the event of Israeli disengagement.

Following the death of Yasser Arafat in November 2004, Mahmud Abbas was elected Executive President of the PA in January 2005. On 8 February a summit meeting was convened in Sharm el-Sheikh between Sharon, Abbas, Egypt's President Mubarak and King Abdullah of Jordan in Sharm el-Sheikh. Sharon and Abbas shook hands, and issued verbal declarations to end hostilities between their two peoples; however, despite hopes of a breakthrough in the Middle East peace process, no formal ceasefire was agreed, and Hamas and Islamic Jihad refused to be bound by Abbas's declaration. Israel none the less agreed to hand over to PA security control the towns of Jericho, Tulkarm, Bethlehem, Qalqilya and Ramallah in the coming weeks; its forces duly withdrew from Jericho and Tulkarm in March. Moreover, shortly after the Sharm el-Sheikh summit Israel allowed 56 deported Palestinians to return to the West Bank, and also transferred the bodies of 15 Palestinian bombers to the PA. In late February Israel began the release of 500 Palestinian prisoners; a further 400 prisoners were to be freed after a three-month period. Jordan returned its ambassador to Israel in March, as did Egypt.

The Israeli Cabinet gave its final approval in late February 2005 to the Government's planned disengagement from all settlements in the Gaza Strip and four in the West Bank. In March 13 armed Palestinian factions declared a ceasefire until the end of the year, on the condition that Israel refrained from attacks and released 8,000 Palestinian prisoners. The Knesset voted in late March to reject a bill that would require a national referendum to be held prior to any implementation of Sharon's Disengagement Plan.

In July 2005 Israeli and Palestinian officials were reported to have agreed in principle to the establishment of a 'safe passage' between the West Bank and the Gaza Strip following the implementation of Israel's Disengagement Plan. In early August, shortly before the Cabinet voted to implement the first stage of the disengagement, Netanyahu announced his resignation as Minister of Finance, denouncing the plan as a threat to the security of the country and the unity of the nation. Sharon appointed the Vice-Prime Minister and Minister of Industry, Trade and Labour, Ehud Olmert, to replace Netanyahu in an acting capacity. Despite public protests, and the need forcibly to evacuate settlers who refused to leave the territories after the deadline of 17 August, the disengagement was completed ahead of schedule, on 12 September, when the last Israeli forces left Gaza. On 22 September Israeli forces completed their withdrawal from the northern West Bank. In late August, meanwhile, Israel had approved the deployment of Egyptian troops along the Egypt–Gaza frontier. In November Israeli and Egyptian officials agreed to reopen the Rafah border crossing, which was to be managed by the PA.

Soon after the completion of the withdrawal, and in response to a series of rocket attacks on Israel by Hamas militants from Gaza, Israel carried out air strikes on the Gaza Strip, targeting the Hamas leadership, and made a series of arrests. Several fatal attacks against Israelis during October 2005 resulted in the suspension of security contacts with the PA. In November Hamas announced that it would not renew its ceasefire at the end of the year. Sharon continued to assert that Israeli operations against Hamas targets would not cease until Abbas disarmed militants.

The Israeli Supreme Court voted in September 2005 to reject the non-binding ICJ ruling of July 2004 that the 'security fence' contravened international law. The Government had approved the final route of its 'fence' in July 2005, which was to result in four Arab areas of Jerusalem being separated from local schools and hospitals. (New amenities were apparently to be built on the Palestinian side, and transport and crossing-points were to be provided.) Despite the Supreme Court's rejection of the ICJ ruling, justices ordered that a section of the barrier around the settler village of Alfei Menashe in the West Bank be removed, asserting that due consideration had not been given for the rights of Palestinians living in the area. Moreover, following complaints from residents of Palestinian villages near Qalqilya that the 'security fence' isolated them from the rest of the West Bank, the Supreme Court ordered a review of the barrier's route. (After the Supreme Court ruled in 2006 that the route around Qalqilya should be revised, in July 2008 the Israeli Ministry of Defence agreed to remove a section of the barrier to allow Palestinian residents better access to their farmland.)

Formation of Kadima

Having defeated Vice-Premier Shimon Peres in a ballot for the leadership of the Labour Party in November 2005, the Chairman of the Histadrut trade union confederation, Amir Peretz, announced that he would seek the party's withdrawal from the coalition Government, which he claimed had mismanaged the peace process as well as domestic social issues. Eight Labour-Meimad ministers subsequently resigned their posts, including Peres.

At the same time Prime Minister Ariel Sharon announced that he was leaving Likud to establish a new party, Kadima (Forward). The new party, he declared, would aim to pursue a peace agreement with the Palestinians in accordance with the roadmap, and to combat economic and social problems. The Vice-Prime Minister, Ehud Olmert, and the Minister of Immigrant Absorption and of Justice, Tzipi Livni, were among prominent Likud figures to join Kadima. Following a request from the Prime Minister, in late November 2005 President Katsav issued a decree dissolving the legislature, and calling legislative elections (due by November 2006) for 28 March 2006. Shimon Peres announced that he would leave the Labour Party in order to campaign for Kadima. Both the acting Chairman of Likud and Minister without Portfolio, Tzachi Hanegbi, and the Minister of Defence, Lt-Gen. Shaul Mofaz, joined Kadima in December 2005. Netanyahu was confirmed as the new Likud Chairman later that month, and announced plans to withdraw the party from the Government.

In early January 2006 Sharon suffered a stroke (his second in a month), which was to leave him in a coma for eight years (see *Recent developments*). In mid-January, following the withdrawal of Likud members, the Cabinet approved the appointment of three new ministers and the reallocation of various portfolios among existing government members. Acting Prime Minister Olmert adopted the interior portfolio and was also appointed acting leader of Kadima on the same day.

Also in January 2006, the Israeli Cabinet voted unanimously to permit Arab residents of East Jerusalem to participate in that month's elections to the Palestinian Legislative Council (PLC). Hamas—which was contesting the polls as the Change and Reform list in order to circumvent a ban on its direct participation—secured a decisive majority in the PLC. Abbas subsequently confirmed that he would ask Hamas to form a new administration. The president's own Fatah movement announced that it would not join Hamas in government.

Olmert declared that Israel would not deal with what he termed an 'armed terror organization that calls for Israel's destruction'. The Quartet group appealed to Hamas to reject violence and recognize Israel, and President Bush declared that the USA would not negotiate with a Hamas-led administration unless the organization renounced its call to destroy Israel. However, Khalid Meshaal, the head of Hamas's political bureau, asserted that violence was a legitimate form of resistance to Israeli occupation. Hamas was willing to negotiate a long-term truce only if Israel agreed to certain conditions, including a return to the pre-1967 borders. Olmert pledged, under a Kadima administration, to separate Israel from the Palestinians within permanent borders, and to preserve a Jewish majority in Israel: Israel would retain the whole of Jerusalem and the main West Bank settlement blocs of Ma'aleh Adumim, Ariel and Gush Etzion, in addition to the Jordan Valley, but would be willing to relinquish parts of the West Bank where the majority of the population were Palestinian. Meshaal rejected the so-called Convergence Plan as allowing Israel to retain illegally its possession of the largest section of the West Bank and its 'security fence', reject concessions on the status of Jerusalem, and thwart the 'right of return' of Palestinian refugees.

Following the inauguration of the new PLC in February 2006, Israel approved a series of measures intended to weaken the future Hamas-led administration, including withholding monthly tax payments to the PA and a ban on the transfer of equipment to Palestinian security forces. In early March Hamas leaders announced that they would never accept Israel's right to exist. However, they pledged to extend the ceasefire with Israel for another year, on the condition that Israel refrained from the use of force.

At the general election of March 2006, Kadima obtained the largest share of the valid votes cast (22.0%), to win 29 of the 120 seats in the Knesset. Labour-Meimad retained 19 seats, while the depleted Likud held only 12. Shas also secured 12 seats, Israel Beytenu 11 and the Pensioners' Party seven. In mid-April, on the same day that the new Knesset held its inaugural session, a suicide bomber launched an attack in Tel-Aviv, killing himself and nine others; Islamic Jihad claimed responsibility for the attack. In late April Labour-Meimad agreed to join the new, Kadima-led administration, and a coalition agreement with Shas and the Pensioners' Party was concluded in May. Likud, which strongly opposed Olmert's plans for Israel to withdraw from large areas of the West Bank, had ruled out the possibility of joining the coalition. The Knesset voted to approve the new Government, which commanded 67 seats, on 4 May. Olmert became Prime Minister and Minister of Social Affairs. Other notable appointees from Kadima included Shimon Peres as Vice-Premier and Minister for the Development of the Negev and Galilee, and Tzipi Livni as Vice-Prime Minister and Minister of Foreign Affairs. The Labour leader, Amir Peretz, was appointed Deputy Prime Minister and Minister of Defence.

Olmert made immediate efforts to secure diplomatic support for his unilateralist Convergence Plan. However, the likely success of his strategy was severely challenged as violence broke out in the Gaza Strip in June 2006, following the kidnapping of an Israeli soldier, Corporal Gilad Shalit, in a cross-border raid by Hamas militants (in which two other soldiers were killed). Palestinian militant groups issued a statement demanding that Israel release all female Palestinian prisoners and all Palestinian detainees under 18 years of age in exchange for Shalit. Israel responded by launching air strikes on Gaza and entering the southern part of the Strip, in a military operation code-named 'Summer Rains'; Israeli security forces detained dozens of Hamas officials, including cabinet ministers and parliamentarians, in connection with their alleged involvement in attacks against Israeli targets.

Israel's military campaign in southern Lebanon

Regional tensions escalated further in mid-July 2006, after Hezbollah militants kidnapped two Israeli soldiers and killed three others in a raid across Lebanon's border with northern Israel. Five further Israeli soldiers were killed when troops crossed into Lebanon on a rescue mission. Hezbollah declared that it would free the abducted soldiers in exchange for the release of Lebanese prisoners in Israeli gaols. Olmert secured the approval of his Cabinet to undertake a military campaign against Hezbollah targets and Lebanese infrastructure with the aim of securing the release of the soldiers, and forcing the Lebanese Government to disarm Hezbollah. During the month-long conflict Hezbollah, having declared 'open war' on Israel, launched thousands of rockets into Israeli territory. Israel, meanwhile, systematically targeted Lebanese infrastructure, blockading seaports, destroying numerous roads and bridges, and bombing strategic targets such as Beirut International Airport. Prime Minister Olmert expressed his 'deep sorrow' when at least 28 Lebanese (many of them children) died in a bombing raid on an apartment building in Qana, Lebanon, at the end of July; Israeli military chiefs stated that Hezbollah had been using the building in order to launch missile attacks against Israel. In early August Israel sent ground troops deeper into Lebanon—some 30 km north of the Israeli border. (For further details regarding the conflict, see the chapter on Lebanon.)

On 11 August 2006 the UN Security Council adopted Resolution 1701, which sought an immediate and full cessation of hostilities, the extension of the Lebanese Government's authority over the whole country, and the delineation of Lebanon's international boundaries, with particular regard to disputed areas such as Shebaa Farms. The resolution urged the parties involved to address the underlying causes of the conflict, including making efforts towards settling the issue of Lebanese prisoners in Israeli gaols, and pressed Hezbollah to release unconditionally the kidnapped Israeli soldiers. In line with earlier Security Council resolutions, Resolution 1701 also required that all armed groups in Lebanon should disarm. A ceasefire between Israel and Hezbollah took effect on 14 August. By this time, 43 Israeli civilians and 119 soldiers had been killed in the conflict, and more than 1,000 Lebanese had died; the number of Hezbollah militants killed was unknown. Under the terms of the ceasefire, Lebanese government forces and an enhanced UNIFIL contingent were to be deployed in southern Lebanon, while Israel was simultaneously to withdraw its forces from the territory. Israel removed restrictions on air travel to and from Lebanon, and lifted its naval blockade, in September. The final Israeli ground forces were withdrawn from Lebanon on 1 October.

Meanwhile, Israel had established a commission of inquiry under the chairmanship of a retired judge, Dr Eliyahu Winograd, into the military campaign in Lebanon. The Winograd Commission published the initial results of its investigation, covering the period between Israel's withdrawal from southern Lebanon in 2000 to mid-July 2006, at the end of April 2007. This interim report found Olmert and other senior Israeli officials to have demonstrated 'very serious failings' in their handling of the 2006 war with Hezbollah, and found that the declared aims of the Israeli military—i.e. the defeat of Hezbollah—were 'overly ambitious and impossible to achieve'. Following the publication of the Commission's interim report, there were mass protests in Israel to demand the resignation of the Government, while Olmert was subject to three votes of no confidence (all of which he survived) in the Knesset in May 2007.

Political developments after the war in Lebanon

In October 2006 the ultra-nationalist Avigdor Lieberman, of Israel Beytenu, was appointed as Deputy Prime Minister and Minister of Strategic Affairs. In January 2007 the Knesset voted to declare President Moshe Katsav 'temporarily incapacitated' for a three-month period, following a police recommendation that he be charged in connection with a number of serious offences, including rape and sexual harassment, fraud, bribery and obstruction of justice. The Knesset Speaker, Dalia Itzik, was named as acting President. In April Katsav's leave of absence was extended by a further three months, or until the scheduled end of his presidential term in July.

In April 2007 Olmert assumed the finance portfolio in an acting capacity, after the Minister of Finance, Abraham Hirchson, took a temporary leave of absence as a result of police investigations into his failure to report an embezzlement of funds by a former employee. Shortly afterwards the State Comptroller recommended that the Prime Minister be subject to a criminal investigation into allegations that he arranged investment opportunities for an associate while serving as Minister of Industry, Trade and Labour. A new police investigation into Olmert's personal dealings began in September, after it was alleged that, while in office as mayor of Jerusalem, he had acquired a property in the city at a price significantly below its market value, in exchange for the accelerated provision of building permits to a property developer. The office of the Prime Minister strenuously denied the claims. On 13 June 2007 Shimon Peres was elected by the Knesset as President of Israel; he was officially inaugurated on 15 July.

Discussions between Olmert and Abbas

Towards the end of November 2006—following an intensification of Operation Summer Rains from October, and by which time hundreds of Palestinians had been killed in the military campaign—PA President Abbas brokered a ceasefire between Palestinian fighters and Israeli forces, resulting in an Israeli withdrawal from Gaza. Prime Minister Olmert subsequently made it clear that he now favoured the resumption of Middle East peace talks with a view to the eventual creation of a Palestinian state, rather than any further unilateral Israeli withdrawals from the West Bank, and indicated that Israel was prepared to free a substantial number of Palestinian prisoners, in exchange for the release, unharmed, of Corporal Gilad Shalit, whose abduction had precipitated several months of conflict.

Further to an agreement signed between representatives of Hamas and Fatah, in February 2007, to form a Palestinian government of national unity, Israeli officials maintained that they would refuse to have contact with any administration that failed to: recognize Israel's right to exist; renounce violence; and respect existing agreements between Israel and the PA. While Israel maintained its boycott of the Palestinian administration, the USA and some EU governments revealed that they would initiate contacts with non-Hamas ministers. In April 2007 Abbas and Olmert held discussions regarding a future Palestinian state and a possible prisoner exchange, in what was intended to be the first of a series of regular fortnightly meetings between the two. Later in the month, however, Hamas declared the ceasefire brokered five months earlier to be at an end, and launched a number of rockets into Israel from the Gaza Strip. Israel responded with air strikes against alleged militant targets in Gaza. Several Hamas ministers, PLC members and local government officials were detained by Israeli security forces at this time.

President Abbas dissolved the national unity government and appointed an emergency administration in its place in June 2007, after Hamas militants seized control of the Gaza Strip. Although Israel was swift to recognize the new administration (and to show its support for Abbas by agreeing to transfer tax revenues which it had withdrawn following Hamas's election victory in January 2006), the fact that governance of the Palestinian territories was now effectively split between a Cabinet backed by President Abbas of Fatah in the West Bank and a Hamas-led administration in Gaza made the likelihood of a resumption of peace negotiations more remote. In late June, at a meeting in Sharm el-Sheikh, Olmert announced that Israel was to release from gaol 250 Fatah activists.

Olmert and Abbas held discussions in the West Bank town of Jericho in early August 2007—the first meeting on Palestinian territory between Israeli and Palestinian leaders since May 2000. Further talks took place later in August 2007, and again in early September. Israel released another 57 Palestinian prisoners to the West Bank and 29 to the Gaza Strip in October. Later that month, in response to the launching of rockets into northern Israel by Palestinian militants from the Gaza Strip, Israel confirmed a strategy of reducing fuel supplies to Gaza. Meanwhile, Israel and the USA signed a memorandum of understanding in August 2007 concerning the provision to Israel of some US $30,000m. in military assistance during 2008–18.

The Annapolis conference

An international peace meeting, intended officially to relaunch the Middle East peace process, was convened under US auspices in Annapolis, Maryland, on 27 November 2007, following preparatory meetings between US officials and Israeli and Palestinian delegations in the preceding weeks. Representatives of the international Quartet group and the Arab League attended the talks, and Syria notably sent a low-level delegation. At the end of the meeting US President Bush read a statement of Joint Understanding on Negotiations between Olmert and Abbas, both of whom expressed their commitment to achieving a final settlement of the outstanding issues of contention by the end of 2008.

Following the Annapolis meeting, the Israeli authorities released a further 429 Palestinian prisoners as a renewed gesture of support for President Abbas. In December 2007, however, Israel issued tenders for more than 300 new housing units at the Har Homa settlement in East Jerusalem. Moreover, Olmert appeared to indicate that Israel would not be required to conclude a peace treaty with the PA by the end of 2008 if it considered that the Palestinians had not met their security obligations. In mid-December 2007 Israeli forces conducted a series of air strikes against militants in the Gaza Strip, and sent tanks into the southern part of the Strip, in an attempt to prevent the continuing rocket fire against Sderot in northern Israel.

Israel intensified its military offensive in the Gaza Strip after a Palestinian rocket assault on the city of Ashkelon in early January 2008. In response to international criticism regarding the number of Palestinians killed during the offensive, Israel claimed that militants were deliberately firing on Israeli troops from civilian areas. In that month President Bush visited Israel and the West Bank, holding discussions with both Olmert and Abbas. Bush asserted that a future Palestinian state should comprise contiguous territory, rather than separate cantons. He again urged Israel to cease the expansion of existing settlements in the West Bank and to remove illegal outposts, while also stating that the PA must ensure that militant groups be dismantled. Bush surprised some commentators by issuing a firm statement urging Israel to withdraw from Arab territory that its forces had occupied in 1967. Amid concerns about a potential humanitarian crisis in Gaza as a result of virtually a complete blockade, the Olmert administration subsequently agreed to allow the supply of food, medicine and necessary fuel to the territory.

Also in January 2008 the Deputy Prime Minister and Minister of Strategic Affairs, Avigdor Lieberman, withdrew Israel Beytenu from the governing coalition, in protest at Olmert's policy of engaging in peace negotiations with the PA. This left Olmert with a reduced majority in the Knesset, and resulted in the resignation from the Cabinet of Lieberman and the Minister of Tourism, Yitzhak Aharonovitch.

The final report of the Winograd Commission was released at the end of January 2008. Although the Commission described Israel's ground offensive in Lebanon in mid-2006 as a 'serious failure' in both military and political terms, it assessed Prime Minister Olmert as having acted 'in the sincere interest of Israel' in ordering the military action. Many observers expressed surprise at the lack of serious direct criticism of the Prime Minister, particularly since he ordered Israeli armed forces to undertake a large-scale ground offensive in southern Lebanon only hours before the agreed ceasefire was scheduled to take effect: some 33 Israeli soldiers had died during this final stage of the war.

Despite an incident in March 2008, in which a Palestinian gunman killed eight students at a Jewish religious college in West Jerusalem, talks between Olmert and Abbas resumed in April. Shortly after the Jerusalem shooting, Olmert approved a plan to construct a further 330 homes for settlers in the West Bank, and in June 2008 Israel announced two new building projects in East Jerusalem, involving the construction of some 2,200 new homes.

In May 2008 Israeli police began questioning Olmert with regard to the alleged receipt of some US $150,000 in donations from a US businessman to support past election campaigns for both the mayoralty of Jerusalem and the Likud leadership. The Prime Minister subsequently admitted to having received funds, but insisted that these had not been for personal gain. In July 2008, after investigators stated that they intended also to examine allegations that Olmert had been involved in 'serious fraud and other offences', he declared his intention to resign as Prime Minister in September, following the election of a new Kadima leader.

After lengthy negotiations under Egyptian auspices, in mid-June 2008 a formal ceasefire was agreed between Israeli and Hamas representatives in the Gaza Strip. Israel was to end its economic blockade, and cease military action in the territory, on condition that Hamas and other Palestinian militant groups halt cross-border attacks on Israeli targets. The truce was to remain in place for at least six months, and was to take effect in stages. Later in June, however, Israel responded to a rocket attack against the town of Sderot by closing border crossings into Gaza.

The rocket attack was apparently carried out by Islamic Jihad in retaliation for the deaths of two Palestinian militants in an Israeli military raid in the West Bank. In early July Hamas stated that, since Israel was not abiding by the terms of the truce, it had suspended negotiations concerning a proposed prisoner exchange involving the release of Corporal Gilad Shalit.

In August 2008 Olmert was reported to have proposed a new peace plan whereby Israel would, *inter alia*, offer Palestinians 93% of the West Bank, provided that Abbas's security forces regained control of the Gaza Strip from Hamas. In that month the Israeli Government released 198 Palestinian prisoners in a goodwill gesture to Abbas. In September 2008 Tzipi Livni won the leadership of Kadima, narrowly defeating the Deputy Prime Minister and Minister of Transport and Road Safety, Shaul Mofaz. Accordingly, Olmert formally resigned as Prime Minister (although he continued to serve on an interim basis), in order to contest the various corruption charges against him, and President Shimon Peres asked Livni to form a new government. In late October, however, Livni announced that negotiations with potential coalition partners had been unsuccessful, and a general election was thus scheduled for 10 February 2009.

Direct clashes took place in November 2008 between Israeli armed forces and Hamas militants in the Gaza Strip for the first time since the June ceasefire agreement. Israel launched a renewed military campaign in Gaza and reimposed its blockade, to prevent what it claimed to be Hamas's attempts to kidnap Israeli soldiers. Hamas and Islamic Jihad fighters responded by firing rockets into northern Israel. In December, following a meeting between Olmert and Abbas, Israel released some 227 Palestinian prisoners (none of whom were from Hamas or Islamic Jihad) as a confidence-building measure. On 16 December the UN Security Council approved Resolution 1850, which endorsed a two-state solution to the Israeli–Palestinian conflict and affirmed that the peace process was 'irreversible'.

'Operation Cast Lead'

On 19 December 2008 Hamas formally declared an end to its six-month truce with Israel, asserting that Israel had not adhered to its obligations. Rocket and mortar attacks by Palestinian militants against towns in northern Israel resumed. On 27 December Prime Minister Olmert ordered a campaign of intensive air strikes against targets in the Strip, as the first phase of a new offensive code-named 'Operation Cast Lead'. The military campaign initially targeted security headquarters and police stations, as well as the tunnels through which weapons were smuggled into the territory. At least 225 Palestinians were reported to have been killed on the first day of the operation. A meeting of the UN Security Council regarding the escalation of the situation in Gaza urged 'an immediate halt to all violence'.

Having declared an 'all-out war against Hamas', the Deputy Prime Minister and Minister of Defence, Ehud Barak, sanctioned a wider campaign of air strikes, which now targeted government offices, presidential buildings and the Islamic University in Gaza. On 3 January 2009 the Israeli Government ordered a major ground assault into the Strip. The declared aim of the operation, which effectively divided the enclave into two, was to guarantee the long-term security of Israel's citizens by preventing the continued firing of rockets and mortars by Hamas militants against towns in southern Israel; the Israeli military sought to destroy Hamas's infrastructure, weapons factories and supplies. Israeli army reservists were called up to join the ground offensive, and heavy fighting occurred in densely populated districts of Gaza City and other urban centres. There was condemnation from the international community when an Israeli mortar attack close to a UN-administered school in the Jabalia refugee camp resulted in the deaths of 43 Palestinians. In mid-January Israeli forces bombed the headquarters in Gaza City of the UN Relief and Works Agency for Palestine Refugees in the Near East (UNRWA). Israel insisted that, in both instances, the buildings were being used by Hamas militants in order to fire rockets and mortars into Israel.

UN Security Council Resolution 1860, adopted on 8 January 2009, called for an immediate and durable ceasefire between Israeli armed forces and Hamas militants, a complete withdrawal of Israeli forces from the Gaza Strip, the unimpeded provision of humanitarian aid within Gaza and intensified international arrangements to prevent the smuggling of weapons into the territory. (The USA abstained in the vote.) Eventually, on 17 January the Israeli Government declared a unilateral ceasefire, with Olmert asserting that the objectives of Operation Cast Lead had been achieved. The following day Hamas announced a week-long cessation of hostilities against Israeli targets, in order to permit Israel to withdraw its armed forces from the Gaza Strip. Palestinian sources claimed that more than 1,400 Palestinians had been killed, and some 5,000 wounded, during the 22-day offensive; 13 Israelis (including 10 soldiers) were reported to have died. Thousands of Palestinian homes, as well as commercial and industrial buildings, had also been destroyed by Israeli forces. There was a brief re-escalation towards the end of January when an Israeli soldier was killed in a bomb attack while patrolling the border with Gaza. The attack led the Israeli Government to order renewed military action against Hamas targets in Gaza, during which at least one Palestinian was killed.

During January 2009 several countries suspended relations with Israel, and the Qatari Government announced that it was closing Israel's trade office in the capital, Doha, and was suspending political and economic ties. Meanwhile, international diplomatic efforts were ongoing in the region to secure a formal, permanent truce between Israel and Hamas, with the aim of ensuring that arrangements be put in place to prevent the smuggling of weapons into Gaza, and to allow for the unimpeded provision of humanitarian aid within Gaza and the reconstruction of the territory's infrastructure. In April the UN Human Rights Council appointed a committee led by a South African judge and former war crimes prosecutor, Richard Goldstone, to lead an investigation into 'all violations of international humanitarian law' before, during and in the aftermath of Operation Cast Lead.

Netanyahu returns as Prime Minister

Following the general election to the Knesset held in February 2009, Livni, of Kadima (which held 28 of the 120 Knesset seats), and Netanyahu, of Likud (which, on a joint list with the right-wing, nationalist Ahi party, won 27 seats), each declared their ability to undertake successful coalition negotiations. In general, there had been a notable shift in voting towards the more right-wing, nationalist parties: Israel Beytenu won 15 seats, pushing the Labour Party, with 13 seats, into fourth place; the ultra-Orthodox Shas and United Torah Judaism secured 11 and five seats, respectively. A decision made in January by the Knesset and its Central Elections Committee to prevent two Israeli Arab political groupings—Balad (the National Democratic Assembly) and the United Arab List-Arab Movement for Renewal—from contesting the election was later overturned by the Supreme Court. Both groups had been accused, after protests by Israeli Arabs against the Israeli invasion of Gaza, of failing to recognize Israel's right to exist, and of supporting 'terrorist' groups.

President Peres, considering the Likud leader the most likely to forge a coalition agreement, appointed Netanyahu as Prime Minister-designate. At the end of March 2009 Netanyahu presented his Cabinet to parliament. The new administration was a coalition of Likud, Israel Beytenu, Labour, Shas and Jewish Home (HaBayit HaYehudi—a right-wing, nationalist party formed in 2008 as a successor to the NRP). United Torah Judaism also formed part of the Government, although none of its members were appointed to cabinet posts. The Israeli Beytenu leader, Avigdor Lieberman, became Deputy Prime Minister and Minister of Foreign Affairs. The Labour leader, Ehud Barak, remained as Deputy Prime Minister and Minister of Defence, while the Chairman of Shas, Eliyahu Yishai, remained as a Deputy Prime Minister, additionally assuming the interior portfolio.

Netanyahu visited Washington, DC, in May 2009 for his first meeting with the new US President, Barack Obama, who affirmed his determination to foster a revival of the stalled peace process, and declared his commitment to a two-state settlement. Obama identified the expansion of settlements as the chief obstacle to the resumption of peace negotiations. For his part, Netanyahu identified Iran's nuclear ambitions as the main threat to regional peace. In June Netanyahu indicated his acceptance of the idea of a sovereign Palestinian state. However, he insisted that the formation of such a state would be conditional on a complete demilitarization of the Palestinian territories, Arab recognition of Israel as a Jewish state, and an undivided, Israeli capital in Jerusalem. Furthermore, he rejected the 'right of return' of Palestinian refugees. An invitation to resume direct negotiations, issued to Abbas in July, was rejected: the Palestinians refused to resume peace talks, pending the complete cessation of Israeli settlement activity.

In late July 2009 George Mitchell, the US special envoy to the Middle East, visited Israel for discussions on reviving the peace process. Mitchell held further talks with Netanyahu in London in August, during which the principal topic was reported to be the settlements issue. In early September the Israeli Ministry of

Defence announced that approval had been granted for the construction of 455 new housing units in settlements in the West Bank. Later that month President Obama hosted a tripartite meeting involving Netanyahu and Abbas at the UN General Assembly in New York, although all parties acknowledged that the meeting did not signal the resumption of negotiations. During a visit to Jerusalem at the end of October, US Secretary of State Hillary Clinton praised Netanyahu's stance on restraining settlement activity, describing his proposed concessions as 'unprecedented'. Abbas had already rejected a resumption of talks based on a partial suspension of settlement activity.

The Goldstone Report

The UN Fact Finding Mission on the Gaza Conflict, headed by Richard Goldstone, issued its final report in September 2009. The report found evidence of potential war crimes and crimes against humanity committed by both the Israeli armed forces and Palestinian militants. The report proposed that the authorities in Israel and Gaza should conduct fully independent inquiries into the findings within six months. The Israeli authorities, who had refused to co-operate with the investigation, rejected the report as 'propaganda'. Hamas also denied the allegations contained within the report pertaining to its own conduct. The Goldstone Report was endorsed by the UN Human Rights Council in October, and in November the UN General Assembly adopted a resolution demanding that Israel conduct an investigation into allegations that its forces had committed war crimes. In February 2010 the UN Secretary-General confirmed that Israel had submitted a formal response to the Goldstone Report.

In December 2009 Prime Minister Netanyahu announced a 10-month moratorium on settlement-building activity in the West Bank. However, the moratorium applied only to private homes, and excluded as many as 3,000 housing units that were already under construction or for which permission had previously been granted. Moreover, the initiative did not apply to settlements within East Jerusalem, which Netanyahu described as part of Israel's 'sovereign capital'. In February 2010 the Israeli Ministry of Defence confirmed that construction work had continued in some 29 West Bank settlements. The announcement in March that two further developments, in Bethlehem and East Jerusalem, had been approved coincided with a visit to Israel by the US Vice-President, Joe Biden, who warned that it would undermine efforts by the USA to renew peace talks. A scheduled visit to Israel by George Mitchell was subsequently postponed, and no progress was reported on the issue of settlement-building following talks in Washington, DC, between Netanyahu and President Obama during separate visits by the Israeli premier in March and June.

Israel's relations with several Western allies were strained by allegations of Israeli involvement in the assassination, in January 2010 in Dubai, United Arab Emirates, of senior Hamas member Mahmoud al-Mabhouh. The Dubai authorities issued details of 11 suspects, all of whom had travelled to the emirate using false British, Australian, Irish, French and German passports. Hamas accused the Israeli intelligence service, Mossad, of involvement in al-Mabhouh's death. In June the Polish authorities were reported to have arrested, at Germany's request, a suspected Mossad agent on charges relating to the assassination. The Israeli Government, for its part, insisted that there was no proof that its intelligence service had been involved in the incident.

In February 2010 Hamas suspended its participation in negotiations over the release of Gilad Shalit, which had resumed in early 2009, in part owing to the allegations of Israel's involvement in the killing of al-Mabhouh. In June, following protests led by relatives of Shalit, it was announced that Israel had agreed to a prisoner-exchange deal, whereby Hamas would release Shalit in exchange for some 1,000 Palestinian detainees. However, negotiations broke down, following disagreements over which detainees would be released by Israel, which refused to accede to demands by Hamas that the exchange include 450 Palestinians detained on suspicion of violent attacks.

Resumption and suspension of direct Israeli-Palestinian peace talks

On 2 September 2010 Netanyahu and Abbas met in Washington, DC, for the first direct Israeli-Palestinian talks since December 2008; the sessions were chaired by US Secretary of State Clinton, and were also attended by George Mitchell. Hamas refused to recognize the legitimacy of the talks, which had been preceded by further violence in the West Bank in July–August. A second round of direct negotiations began in Sharm el-Sheikh on 14 September and continued in Jerusalem the following day. Progress was reported to have been made in some areas. However, following the expiry of Israel's 10-month moratorium on settlement-building in late September, the PA suspended its involvement in the peace process, stating that it would resume talks only when Israel had agreed to end the construction of settlements and the blockade of Gaza. It was reported in October that construction work had commenced on more than 600 new homes in settlements in the West Bank.

Also in October 2010 the Cabinet endorsed controversial draft legislation, promoted by the Deputy Prime Minister and Minister of Foreign Affairs, Avigdor Lieberman, that would require non-Jewish applicants for Israeli citizenship to pledge their loyalty to Israel as a 'Jewish and democratic state'. Some observers speculated that Netanyahu had supported the measure in exchange for Lieberman's acquiescence on further limits to settlement expansion. Three Likud ministers joined their Labour colleagues in voting against the legislation, which went on to receive Knesset approval in March 2011. Meanwhile, in November 2010 the Knesset approved legislation requiring any proposed withdrawal from territory under Israeli sovereignty—including East Jerusalem and the Golan Heights—to be endorsed by a two-thirds' parliamentary majority, or, failing that, at a national referendum.

Increasing criticism of the Netanyahu administration

In December 2010, following a year-long trial conducted behind closed doors, former President Katsav was convicted on charges of rape and of sexual assault, perpetrated against former employees during his term of office. Katsav was sentenced to seven years' imprisonment in March 2011. An appeal against his conviction was rejected by the Supreme Court in November 2011, and the original sentence was upheld.

Meanwhile, the trial began in February 2010 of former premier Ehud Olmert on corruption charges relating to his tenure as Minister of Industry, Trade and Labour and his two earlier terms as mayor of Jerusalem; the charges included fraud, breach of the public trust and failure to report income. In July 2012 Olmert was acquitted of the two most serious charges of corruption, although he was found to have granted illegal favours to a business associate and ordered to serve four months' community service. In January, meanwhile, Olmert was indicted on fresh charges pertaining to allegations that he had accepted bribes amounting to nearly US $1m. during his tenure as mayor of Jerusalem, in order to facilitate a construction project. Some 17 others, including Olmert's successor as mayor of Jerusalem, Uri Lupolianski, were also charged with offering or receiving associated bribes.

In January 2011 the Deputy Prime Minister and Minister of Defence, Ehud Barak, tendered his resignation as Labour Chairman in order to form a new party, Ha'atzmaut (Independence). The remaining Labour members of the Cabinet also subsequently resigned. A renewed coalition agreement, facilitating the appointment of further Ha'atzmaut representatives to the Government, was approved by the Knesset two days later. The revised Cabinet included four members of Ha'atzmaut, among them Barak, who retained the defence portfolio. Barak's withdrawal from the Labour Party followed months of internal division concerning the party's future involvement in the coalition, prompted by Netanyahu's stance in the peace process. In September Shelly Yachimovich was announced as the new Labour leader.

In response to mass social protests which began in Tel-Aviv in July 2011 and rapidly spread to other cities, Netanyahu ordered the establishment of a committee, chaired by Prof. Manuel Trajtenberg, to examine the issues raised by the protesters, which mainly concerned escalating living costs. The Trajtenberg Committee for Social and Economic Change submitted its recommendations at the end of September. Among proposals adopted were taxation reforms, including the introduction of tax benefits for working parents of children under the age of three, and the extension of free education to pre-primary level.

In November 2011, in the context of elevated tensions between Israel and Iran (see *Regional relations*), the opposition leader, Livni, accused Netanyahu of being overly preoccupied with the perceived threat posed to Israel by Iran. Her comments appeared to confirm reports that Israel's leading military and security experts had made clear their opposition to a possible Israeli attack on Iranian nuclear facilities.

At the end of January 2012 Netanyahu was decisively re-elected as Likud Chairman, securing some 77% of the vote. In

March 2012 Shaul Mofaz was elected to replace Livni as leader of Kadima. Livni resigned as a member of the Knesset in May. Meanwhile, amid growing anticipation of an early general election, a new, secular centrist party, Yesh Atid (There is a Future), was registered at the end of April by a prominent media personality, Yair Lapid.

In early May 2012 Netanyahu, apparently seeking to take advantage of a relatively favourable standing in opinion polls, stated that he would request Knesset approval for a general election to take place in early September. Almost immediately, however, he announced that a new agreement had been reached whereby Kadima would join a broad coalition government, ensuring a stable administration until the scheduled end of the Knesset's term in October 2013. Under the new arrangement, commitment was given to revive the peace process with the Palestinians, and to address the issue of legislation, commonly known as the Tal Law, allowing principally ultra-Orthodox students to defer military conscription. (In February the High Court of Justice had ruled the law in its current form to be unconstitutional: the legislation, introduced in 2002 and renewable every five years, was due to expire in August 2012, and had been deemed by the secular parties to be inequitable.) The new administration, which was to command 94 seats in the 120-member Knesset, was subsequently endorsed by the legislature.

Kadima's participation in the coalition was, however, short-lived. The party withdrew from the Government in July 2012, in disagreement with Netanyahu's proposed compromise arrangement to replace the provisions of the Tal Law: ultra-Orthodox members of the coalition had notably threatened to withdraw their support if seminary students were to lose their exemption from military service. Deeming the compromise, which envisaged a phased drafting into the Israeli military and civil service, insufficient, Kadima's Knesset members voted decisively to leave the coalition, again fuelling expectation of an early general election. In the absence of an agreement, the provisions of the Tal Law formally lapsed at the beginning of August.

In October 2012 Netanyahu finally announced that a general election would take place early the following year. Ehud Barak subsequently confirmed that conscription of those previously exempted under the Tal Law would be deferred pending the election.

Developments in Israeli-Palestinian relations, 2011–12

In May 2011 the Israeli Government announced the temporary suspension of the transfer of tax revenues to the PA, in response to the conclusion of a 'unity' agreement between Fatah and Hamas. The Netanyahu administration stated that the funds could be used to finance Hamas operations against Israeli interests. Reports emerged in July that the Israeli Government had threatened to renounce all previous agreements concluded with the Palestinians, including the Oslo accords, in response to Palestinian proposals unilaterally to seek, through the UN, formal recognition of an independent Palestinian state, on the basis of its pre-1967 borders, and with East Jerusalem as its capital. Tensions were further heightened in September 2011, when the PA formally submitted an application for full membership of the UN as an independent state. (For further details, see the chapter on the Palestinian Territories.) In November Israel and the USA both announced that they were to freeze their funding to UNESCO, in response to the organization's decision, the previous month, to admit 'Palestine' as a full member. Israel again announced that it was to halt the transfer of tax and customs revenues to the PA, and further stated that it was to accelerate the construction of 2,000 new homes in settlements in East Jerusalem and the West Bank. However, Israel subsequently agreed, under international pressure, to resume revenue transfers to the PA.

In October 2011, in an Egyptian-brokered prisoner exchange, Gilad Shalit was released after more than five years in Palestinian detention. The arrangement between Israel and Hamas provided for the release by Israel of 477 predominantly Palestinian prisoners immediately following that of Shalit, and of a further 550 prisoners (including 300 members of Fatah) in December. PA President Abbas welcomed the exchange, but emphasized that the Palestinian authorities would continue to press for the release of all remaining Palestinian prisoners detained in Israel.

In January 2012 the first meetings between Israeli and Palestinian peace negotiators in more than a year were held in Amman, under the auspices of King Abdullah; however, the exploratory talks were reported to have ended without any significant progress. The PA continued to insist that it would not resume formal peace talks until Israel had suspended all settlement-building activity, and Israel maintained that it would not participate until the PA had abandoned all preconditions to the resumption of formal negotiations.

The principal focus of discussions in Washington, DC, between President Obama and Netanyahu, in early March 2012, was Iran. Shortly afterwards, the Secretary-General of the Hamas-aligned Popular Resistance Committees was among several militants killed in what were stated to be preventive Israeli air strikes on Gaza. In the ensuing exchange of retaliatory rocket attacks on Israel and further strikes on Gaza, some 25 Palestinians were killed. In late March the Israeli Government announced the suspension of co-operation with the UN Human Rights Council, after the body voted in favour of sending a mission to Israel to investigate the effect of Israeli settlements on Palestinians' civil, political, economic, social and cultural rights.

In early April 2012 a female Palestinian detainee from Jenin was released from Israeli custody and exiled to Gaza, under an arrangement whereby she ended a hunger strike begun following her detention without trial (so-called 'administrative detention') in mid-February. The detainee, a supporter of Islamic Jihad, had previously been among prisoners released under the terms of the October 2011 agreement, but had been rearrested for alleged involvement in planned attacks by Islamic Jihad. Her forced exile was condemned by the Palestinian authorities, as well as by Israeli human rights activists. The protest against administrative detention (under which some 300 Palestinians were held in custody) escalated during April 2012, with a mass hunger strike extending to some 1,500 Palestinians in Israeli detention by the end of the month. In early May the Supreme Court rejected an appeal against the terms of their imprisonment by two Palestinians, held in administrative detention on security grounds, who had maintained a hunger strike for more than 70 days. In mid-May, following a direct request by President Abbas and mediation assistance by Egypt and Jordan, an agreement was reached to end the mass protest. Among its terms, Israel undertook not to renew detentions without charge in the absence of further evidence. At the end of May, also under terms of the agreement ending the hunger strike, Israel transferred to the PA the remains of 91 Palestinians killed in suicide bombings and other attacks on Israel over a period of more than 35 years.

Direct confrontation was renewed in the second half of June 2012, as a series of Israeli air strikes on militant targets in Gaza provoked retaliatory rocket attacks for which Hamas's military wing—which had effectively refrained from such operations over a prolonged period—claimed responsibility. At least seven Palestinians were killed in the engagements. In late June Hamas stated that a senior member of the organization, Kamal Ghanaja, had been assassinated in the Syrian capital, Damascus. In early August it was reported that an air strike on the Gaza Strip had targeted a militant held responsible for an exchange in June on Israel's border with Egypt, in which an Israeli civilian working on the border fence was killed in an attack from Sinai, along with two assailants.

There was a major escalation in the situation from mid-November 2012, when, in response to protracted rocket fire from Gaza into southern Israel, Israeli forces began an intense series of strikes from the air and sea against Hamas, Islamic Jihad and other militant groups, and their missile capabilities and weapons storage facilities. Among the targets of 'Operation Pillar of Defence' was the head of Hamas's military wing, Ahmed Said Khalil al-Jabari, who was killed in an air strike in Gaza City on 14 November. As the confrontation deepened, Egypt led efforts to bring about a ceasefire. US Secretary of State Clinton travelled to Israel for talks with Netanyahu and other government officials, reaffirming US support for Israel's right to self-defence, and subsequently went on to Ramallah for discussions with Abbas, before meeting with President Muhammad Mursi in Cairo. The Israeli authorities were reported to have come under intense international pressure not to begin a ground offensive in Gaza. The diplomatic initiative was also joined by the UN Secretary-General, and a ceasefire eventually took effect on 21 November. Under its terms, Israel was to cease hostilities and targeted killings, enter discussions on the reopening of border crossings with Gaza, and ease restrictions on the movement of goods and people, while the Palestinian militant organizations were required to halt rocket attacks and border assaults. At the conclusion of hostilities, there had been 158 deaths in Gaza, including 103 civilian deaths; at least 30 children were killed. Six Israelis were killed, four of them civilians. The relatively low numbers of Israeli casualties were ascribed to the efficacy of Israel's missile-defence systems in destroying incoming missiles.

Israel led opposition to the vote of the UN General Assembly, on 29 November 2012, which accorded (by 138 votes to nine, with 41 abstentions) Palestine the status of non-member observer state. Netanyahu denounced the decision and reiterated that there could be no establishment of a Palestinian state in the absence of a settlement guaranteeing Israel's security. The USA voted against the resolution, and Hillary Clinton termed the vote counter-productive. In early December Israel confirmed its intention to proceed with its project to construct 3,000 settlement homes on land effectively separating East Jerusalem from the West Bank; plans also proceeded later in the month with regard to 1,500 housing units announced during US Vice-President Biden's visit in 2010; and planning approval was given for more than 2,600 homes on land between southern Jerusalem and Bethlehem.

The 2013 Knesset elections and the new coalition Government

Likud and Israel Beytenu announced in late October 2012 that they would contest the forthcoming general election in alliance, presenting a joint list of candidates. In late November Tzipi Livni returned to active politics with the establishment of a new, centre-left party, Hatnua (The Movement). In the same month Naftali Bennett, a former chief of staff to Netanyahu, became leader of the right-wing nationalist Jewish Home. Also in late November the Deputy Prime Minister and Minister of Defence, Ehud Barak, announced his intention to retire from party politics; the Ha'atzmaut party subsequently stated that it would not contest the 2013 general election.

In mid-December 2012 Avigdor Lieberman resigned as Deputy Prime Minister and Minister of Foreign Affairs, and waived his right of parliamentary immunity, after it was announced that he was to be prosecuted on charges—which he denied—of breach of trust. The Israel Beytenu leader was accused in connection with the promotion of an Israeli diplomat from whom he had allegedly received confidential documents pertaining to investigations, which had first begun more than a decade earlier, into his activities. However, the principal charges, including alleged money-laundering and bribery, were abandoned on grounds of lack of evidence. Lieberman was indicted at the end of December, and his trial formally opened in February 2013.

The Likud-Israel Beytenu alliance, with 23.3% of valid votes cast, won the largest number of seats at the general election, which took place on 22 January 2013; however, the two parties' joint representation, at 31 of 120 seats, was significantly below their combined representation (43 seats) in the outgoing Knesset, and Netanyahu's own standing was considered to be somewhat weakened by the result. The greatest challenge came from Yesh Atid, which won 19 seats with 14.3% of the vote; the party had focused its campaign on an end to deferred military service and on a revival of the peace process with the Palestinians. The Labour Party won 15 seats (with 11.4%), while the populist rhetoric of Jewish Home's new leader led to its representation increasing to 12 seats (with 9.1%). Shas retained 11 seats, and United Torah Judaism returned seven deputies. Hatnua won six seats, while Kadima retained just two of its previous 28 seats. The rate of participation by voters was officially recorded at 67.8%.

The 19th Knesset was inaugurated on 5 February 2013. In mid-February 2013 it was announced that Netanyahu had reached an agreement with Livni whereby the Hatnua leader would join a new coalition as Minister of Justice, and as Israel's chief negotiator in the peace process (the key focus of her election campaign). At the beginning of March, following the expiry of the original, one-month deadline for the formation of a new government, Peres granted Netanyahu two more weeks to conclude an agreement, and, on 18 March, a new coalition administration, including members of Likud, Israel Beytenu, Yesh Atid, Jewish Home and Hatnua, took office. Prime Minister Netanyahu temporarily held the foreign affairs portfolio, while the Yesh Atid leader, Yair Lapid, became Minister of Finance. Shas and United Torah Judaism were, notably, to remain outside the coalition for the first time since 2005. Early tasks for the new Government included securing Knesset approval of the budget for 2013, and to achieve consensus on the issue of conscription.

The outcome of the election suggested a clear shift in voter sentiment away from the policies of the outgoing administration, not least with regard to Israeli-Palestinian relations. This, in conjunction with the inauguration for a second term of US President Obama, allowed for muted optimism among some commentators regarding the prospect of a renewed impetus in the peace process. Livni's agreement, in February 2013, to join Israel's new coalition Government with a mandate to lead negotiations with the Palestinians was also recognized as a development likely to expedite renewed contacts. At the end of January, none the less, Israel became the first country to fail to attend a mandatory review of the UN Human Rights Council. In that month the Council published a report stating that the outgoing Netanyahu administration had contributed to the consolidation and expansion of settlements, and emphasized that the transfer of Israeli citizens to occupied territory was in violation of international criminal law. The Israeli Government responded that the report was a reminder of the Council's bias against Israel. Meanwhile, the PA had indicated that, should the new Israeli Government proceed with plans to construct settlements east of Jerusalem, it might seek recourse to the International Criminal Court (which it had become eligible to join upon adoption as a non-member observer state at the UN in November 2012).

US President Obama made his first official visit to Israel in March 2013, shortly after the inauguration of Netanyahu's new Government, before proceeding to Ramallah to meet with President Abbas. While in Israel, Obama notably spoke of the need for a viable, independent Palestinian state, and stated that the continued expansion of settlements on occupied land did not advance the cause of peace. However, he emphasized the strength of US-Israeli ties, not least in military and intelligence co-operation. The US President offered no new proposals for reviving peace talks, but stated that Secretary of State John Kerry would begin a new programme of intense diplomacy between Israel and the Palestinians with the aim of renewing negotiations.

In February 2013 violent clashes had broken out between Palestinian protesters and Israeli armed forces in West Bank towns. The protesters were demanding the release of four Palestinians in administrative detention (of a total number of 178 in such detention), who were on hunger strike. Tensions escalated in late February, following the sudden death in custody of a Palestinian from the West Bank who had been arrested on suspicion of stone-throwing. The Israeli authorities stated that the detainee had suffered a heart attack, but Palestinians claimed that there was evidence that he had died as a result of torture; in protest, most Palestinian detainees observed a one-day hunger strike.

Meanwhile, after the expiry of the Tal Law in 2012, a ministerial commission set up to look into the question of the gradual induction of ultra-Orthodox students into the Israeli military and civil service had recommended that only 1,800 of an estimated 40,000 seminary students should be exempted from military conscription. On 23 July 2013 draft legislation to replace the provisions of the Tal Law passed its first reading in the Knesset. Ultra-Orthodox students, with the exception of these 1,800, were thus required to enter military or civil service within a four-year period. Ultra-Orthodox parties in the legislature declared that they would refuse to adhere to the terms of the draft law.

Resumption and collapse of direct negotiations between Israel and the PA

On 29–30 July 2013 preliminary discussions regarding a permanent status accord between Israel and the PA were held in Washington, DC. The talks were hosted by Kerry, and led by Minister of Justice Livni for Israel and Saeb Erakat for the PA. Having reportedly pledged to seek to reach a final status agreement within nine months, Israeli and Palestinian representatives began formal peace negotiations in Jerusalem on 14 August. The talks were expected to take place weekly, and to alternate between Jerusalem and the West Bank town of Jericho. It was agreed at the initial discussions that, provided that progress was being made in the talks, Israel would release 104 long-serving Palestinian prisoners in four stages by 29 April 2014, the deadline for a preliminary agreement to be signed. The PA, for its part, was required to delay any applications for the Palestinian Territories' membership of UN agencies to be upgraded. However, no breakthrough in the peace process had been achieved by February 2014, with Israel's Ministry of Housing and Construction continuing to approve tenders for the building of new Jewish settlements in the West Bank and East Jerusalem. (Shortly before the talks held on 14 August 2013 the Israeli Government freed the first 26 of the Palestinian prisoners; however, it was also announced that the construction of a further 2,000 new settler homes was planned. A further 26 detainees were released on 30 October, despite a recent upsurge in violence between Israeli forces and Hamas militants in the Gaza Strip, and a third group of 26 on 30 December.) In mid-February 2014 Erakat warned that, in the event of a failure in the negotiations by 29 April, the PA would push the international community to impose economic sanctions against Israel, and would bring a series of lawsuits against the Israeli Government at the ICJ and the International Criminal Court, both based in The Hague. Meanwhile, the release of Palestinian prisoners remained a controversial issue among the Israeli electorate, since many of those being freed had been convicted of committing acts of terrorism against Israelis; many Palestinians also complained that the number of prisoners involved was too insignificant to represent a major concession to the PA. Netanyahu was also required to reassure several members of his own Government that he would put any eventual peace deal with the PA to a nationwide referendum; legislation to this effect was approved on 28 July 2013. However, in April 2014 the negotiations appeared to be faltering. In early April Israel announced that it was to suspend the transfer of around US $100m. per month in tax revenues to the PA, in response to the latter's formal accession to some 13 UN institutions. Later that month, following the announcement of a further national unity agreement between Hamas and Fatah, Netanyahu suspended Israel's participation in the peace process just days in advance of the scheduled deadline for a preliminary agreement to be concluded, and sanctioned the PA by preventing ministerial nominees from travelling to the West Bank, and encouraging the international community to cease dealing with it.

Meanwhile, at the conclusion of his trial, on 6 November 2013 Avigdor Lieberman was cleared of the charges of breach of trust that had led to his resignation as Deputy Prime Minister and Minister of Foreign Affairs in December 2012. The Israel Beytenu leader therefore rejoined the Cabinet on 11 November 2013, resuming responsibility for the foreign affairs portfolio. On 11 January 2014 it was announced that Ariel Sharon had died, having been in a coma since January 2006.

In February 2014 Jordan suggested it might reconsider the peace treaty it had signed with Israel in 1994, after members of the Knesset debated a bill concerning the highly controversial issue of declaring Israeli sovereignty over the Temple Mount/Haram al-Sharif compound in Jerusalem (currently administered by Jordan). The debate led a majority of members of the Jordanian parliament to demand the expulsion of the Israeli ambassador and the recall of Jordan's envoy to Tel-Aviv, and also provoked anger in a number of other neighbouring Arab states. Amid heightened tensions at the Jerusalem compound, violent clashes between Israelis and Palestinians had been reported at the site in late September 2013. Jordan recalled its ambassador to Israel in November 2014 for consultations, in a gesture of protest at what it deemed Israeli 'violations' at holy sites in Jerusalem—the first time it had done so since the countries signed a peace agreement in 1994. In that month the US Secretary of State, John Kerry, met Netanyahu and King Abdullah in Amman to discuss measures to defuse tensions at holy sites in Jerusalem.

Despite the abstention of several opposition parties, three controversial legislative bills were approved by the Knesset in March 2014. The so-called governability bill increased the minimum share of the national vote required for representation in the legislature from 2% to 3.25%; critics claimed that the changes would prevent small and minority parties (particularly Israeli Arab parties) from gaining parliamentary seats. The equal burden bill introduced a gradual change in the non-recruitment of ultra-orthodox Yeshiva students into the armed forces from 2017, from which time there the number of Yeshiva students drafted would increase gradually, including a minimum quota serving in the army. Those students considered to be 'exceptional scholars' would, however, be exempt. Liberal opponents of the law criticized it on the grounds that it did not ensure genuine equality, while the ultra-Orthodox parties criticized the legally enforced nature of the measure and the fact that it included criminal penalties for those who avoided the draft. A demonstration by members of the ultra-Orthodox community was held before the final approval of the law on 2 March 2014, in which hundreds of thousands of people participated both in Israel and abroad. Another controversial law was the basic law, which implemented the 2010 referendum law at a constitutional level,

making it more difficult to amend or abolish. According to the law, if an Israeli government subsequently decided to withdraw from territories that were under Israeli jurisdiction, that decision would require approval by a majority of members of the Knesset and at a national referendum.

The issue of corruption marred the campaign for the presidency, the election for which took place in the Knesset on 10 June 2014. The number of candidates seeking election was the highest in Israeli history. However, the Minister of Energy and Water Resources, Silvan Shalom of Likud, withdrew his candidacy before the official campaign began, following allegations of sexual harassment; he was not officially charged with any offence. The former Labour leader Binyamin Ben Eliezer also withdrew after he was investigated by police over allegations regarding his ownership of properties. Finally, five candidates proceeded to contest the election: two former members of the Knesset, Dalia Itzik and Meir Shitrit; former Speaker Reuven Rivlin; former high court judge Dalia Dorner; and Nobel prize winning scientist Prof. Dan Shechtman. After the first round of voting, Rivlin and Shitrit emerged as the leading candidates, and at the second round, Rivlin won with 63 votes. Rivlin was sworn in as the 10th President of Israel on 28 July.

Operations 'Brother's Keeper' and 'Protective Edge'

In early June 2014 three Yeshiva students were kidnapped near Hebron on the West Bank, following which Israel launched 'Operation Brother's Keeper'. The operation's objectives were to find the students, but also to destroy infrastructure used by militant organizations in the Hebron area. During the operation, around 350 Palestinians were detained, while five Palestinians were reportedly killed. Although Mahmud Abbas condemned the act of kidnapping, Israel continued to criticize Fatah's unity agreement with Hamas. The students were found dead at the end of the month, and, although no Palestinian organization formally claimed responsibility for their murder, Israel stated that it ultimately blamed Hamas. In September Israel charged Hussam Qawasmeh over the abduction and murder of the three teenagers from Hebron in June. Although he had been imprisoned in Israel for his involvement with Hamas in the past, Khalid Meshaal claimed that his group had not ordered the abduction of the teenagers. In late September two further suspects were shot dead by Israeli special forces in Hebron, while three others were arrested.

On 7 July 2014 Israel launched 'Operation Protective Edge', which included air strikes and artillery fire against alleged militants and missile-launch sites in Gaza. This followed increased rocket fire into southern Israel from the territory in the preceding weeks. Despite the Israeli action, the firing of missiles continued, and on 17 July Israeli troops entered Gaza, in an attempt to halt rocket fire and to destroy tunnels used by militants to smuggle weapons under the border. On 22 July the UN Human Rights Council initiated an official investigation into allegations that Israel had violated international humanitarian and human rights laws during Operation Protective Edge. (At that time, it was estimated that at least 710 Palestinians and 30 Israelis had been killed.) By 26 July it was estimated that more than 2,000 rockets had been fired at Israel, 422 of which were shot down by Israel's 'Iron Dome' missile defence system. An attempt by Egypt to foster a ceasefire failed at the end of July, as did a separate initiative by US Secretary of State John Kerry. Following continued mediation efforts by Egypt and the USA, a temporary, three-day ceasefire was subsequently agreed. This commenced on 11 August, and on 13 August an agreement was reached to extend the truce by five days. Although low-level rocket fire from Gaza continued, it was subsequently reported that Israel had agreed to relax elements of its blockade against Gaza. However, the ceasefire was broken later that day and fighting ensued for another week. An initial month-long ceasefire was finally accepted by Hamas (and Islamic Jihad) and Israel on 26 August.

On 10 September 2014 Israel's chief military prosecutor ordered criminal investigations into five incidents during the recent conflict in Gaza, including alleged indiscriminate bombing of Rafah during an attempt to rescue an Israeli officer whom it was feared had been kidnapped. Some 130 Palestinians, mostly civilians, were killed in the incident. Both Israel and Hamas were also subject to an investigation by the UN Human Rights Council, and a separate UN inquiry initiated by the Secretary-General, Ban Ki-Moon, in August, into the targeting of UN-operated schools by Israel and the storing of weapons in some of those schools by Hamas. Israel indicated that it was unwilling to co-operate with the UN Human Rights Council inquiry led by the

Canadian judge William Schabas, accusing it of being biased (in February 2015 Schabas resigned from the inquiry, after confirming that he had previously undertaken consultancy work on behalf of the PLO). The inquiry was due to present its report in March 2015.

At an international donor conference held in Cairo in October 2014, some US $5,400m. was pledged for the reconstruction of Gaza, and the Gaza Reconstruction Mechanism was agreed by the Palestinian Authority, Israel and the UN to allow building materials to be imported into Gaza. Qatar committed to provide $1,000m. in aid, while the US Secretary of State, John Kerry, promised a total contribution of $400m. One of the five priorities of the Reconstruction Mechanism was to satisfy Israeli concerns related to the use of construction and so-called dual use materials, particularly for large-scale works including schools and industrial facilities, with Israel being asked to review all project submissions and oversee security measures by UN personnel to prevent cement and other materials from being diverted for military purposes, including tunnel-building.

In early November 2014 Israel reopened two border crossings with Gaza which it had ordered shut for four days after a rocket fired from Gaza struck Israeli territory, without causing any casualties or damage. Also that month the human rights group Amnesty International published a report accusing Israel of committing war crimes during its campaign in Gaza and claimed that its armed forces displayed 'callous indifference' by launching attacks on residential areas without specifying a military target, although it added that war crimes were also committed by Palestinian militants, who had fired rockets indiscriminately onto Israeli territory. On 24 December Israeli forces shot dead a member of Hamas's armed wing after being fired upon by snipers in the southern Gaza Strip along the border with Israel; an Israeli soldier was wounded. In that month the Minister of Foreign Affairs, Lieberman, criticized Prime Minister Netanyahu for his strategy in negotiations with the PA and proposed his own comprehensive peace agreement that included negotiations with Arab states alongside the PA.

Tensions in the West Bank and Jerusalem were raised in October 2014 when Israeli border police began preventing access to male Palestinians under 50 years old from worshipping at the Al-Aqsa mosque in East Jerusalem, leading to clashes between Palestinians and Israeli security forces. Palestinians had claimed that the Israeli authorities in Jerusalem had allowed Jewish worshippers unrestricted access to Temple Mount during the festival of Sukkot, a charge which Netanyahu denied. On 30 October Israel closed access fully to the Al-Aqsa compound to prevent unrest, following the killing of a member of Islamic Jihad, who had attempted to assassinate on the previous day an extreme right-wing Jewish activist campaigning for Jews to be granted free access to the compound and ultimately for the construction of a Jewish temple on the site. Israelis were allowed to access the site during certain hours but were not permitted to worship at the site. Access to the Al-Aqsa compound was reopened to Palestinians on the following day, although men under 50 years old were again prevented from praying. President Abbas, whom Netanyahu blamed for inciting the recent spate of violence, appealed for Palestinians to join a 'day of rage'. On 5 November an Israeli policeman was killed and 13 people were wounded after a Palestinian drove a vehicle into pedestrians on a street in Jerusalem. The assailant was later killed by police officers. Later that day, in a separate incident, a vehicle was driven into a group of Israeli soldiers near Bethlehem, injuring three of them. On 6 November Netanyahu announced that there would be no change in the restrictions on Jewish worshippers at the Temple Mount, despite appeals from his far-right coalition partners. The violence continued into mid-November, when two Palestinian men from East Jerusalem attacked worshippers at a synagogue in the west of the city, killing four rabbis and an Israeli Arab policemen, and injuring eight other people. The two assailants, reportedly affiliated to the PFLP, were shot dead by Israeli security forces.

Recent developments: early elections to the Knesset

In November 2014 President Reuven Rivlin expressed his opposition to a new law proposed by Netanyahu that would define 'national rights' in Israel as reserved for Jews only. The 'Jewish nation-state' bill proposed to recognize Israel's Jewish character, institutionalize Jewish law as a basis for legislation and possibly delist Arabic as a second official language. The proposal attracted criticism from opponents inside Israel as well as from the USA and the EU, who claimed that it threatened to undermine Israel's declaration of independence, which gives equal rights to the country's minorities, including Israeli Arabs, by promoting the idea of Israel as a Jewish state above one that is democratic. For his part, Netanyahu argued that individual civil rights would be guaranteed under existing laws for all, but that 'national rights' should be reserved for Jews. Passage of the bill was delayed after Likud announced on 2 December that it would support a bill for the dissolution of the Knesset and early elections, and later that day Netanyahu dismissed Tzipi Livni, the Minister for Justice, and Yair Lapid, the Minister for Finance, from the Cabinet for opposing government policy, including the proposed 'Jewish nation-state' bill, an increase in the defence budget, the expansion of settlements in East Jerusalem and the West Bank, and the ongoing blockade of the Gaza Strip. Deputies voted to dissolve the Knesset on 8 December, and elections were subsequently scheduled for March 2015. The election was to be the first at which the minimum requirement for parliamentary representation was 3.25% (compared with 2% previously), a measure that some observers contended was a deliberate attempt to limit the representation of small parties such as Livni's Hatnua. In December 2014 the Labour Party, under the leadership of Issac Herzog, and Hatnua announced that they would contest the elections in alliance under the name Zionist Union, while the three main Israeli Arab parties also announced that, for the first time, they would contest the elections as a single list.

Elections to the Knesset were duly held on 17 March 2015. Results published by the Central Elections Committee the following week confirmed that Likud had won, taking 30 seats and 23.4% of the valid votes cast. The opposition Zionist Union took 24 seats and 18.7% of the vote. The Joint List of Israeli Arab parties took 13 seats (10.6%), while Yesh Atid garnered 11 (8.8%). A new party, Kulanu, led by former Likud deputy and government minister Moshe Kahlon, secured 10 seats (7.5%). A further five parties exceeded the increased threshold: Jewish Home won eight seats and 6.7% of the vote; Shas (seven, 5.7%); Israel Beytenu (six, 5.1%); United Torah Judaism (six, 5.0%); and Meretz (five, 3.9%). Voter turnout was recorded at 72.3%. Likud's victory was regarded as somewhat unexpected, as several opinion polls conducted in the days preceding the vote had indicated that the levels of support for Likud and the Zionist Union were almost equal. Furthermore, controversy arose on polling day itself after Prime Minister Netanyahu issued a statement in which he claimed that foreign and left-wing NGOs were transporting large numbers of Israeli Arabs to polling stations in an attempt to disadvantage the right-wing parties. Following the confirmation of the result, it was reported that Kulanu had agreed to support a coalition government under Netanyahu's premiership. Meanwhile, the Zionist Union announced that it would enter into opposition, as did Yesh Atid. President Rivlin formally appointed Netanyahu to form a new government on 25 March. Negotiations over the formation of a new coalition government were ongoing in late April.

Regional relations

In July 1999 Prime Minister Ehud Barak undertook to negotiate a bilateral peace agreement with Syria, based on UN Resolutions 242 and 338: this was interpreted as a signal of his intention to return most of the occupied Golan Heights in exchange for peace and normalized relations. On 20 July Syria ordered a 'ceasefire' with Israel. In December, apparently as a result of diplomatic efforts by US President Bill Clinton and secret meetings between Israeli and Syrian officials, the two sides agreed to a resumption of negotiations from the point at which they had broken off in 1996. Clinton inaugurated peace negotiations between Barak and the Syrian Minister of Foreign Affairs, Farouk al-Shara', in Washington, DC, on 15 December 1999. The talks commenced in the context of rising tensions in southern Lebanon, and resulted only in an agreement to resume discussions in January 2000. Barak, meanwhile, was encountering growing domestic opposition to a possible return of the Golan Heights to Syria. In late December 1999 Israel and Syria agreed an informal 'ceasefire' to curb hostilities in Lebanon. Barak and al-Shara' attended further discussions in January 2000 in Shepherdstown, USA about the normalization of relations. However, Syria announced that it required a commitment from Israel to withdraw from the Golan Heights before negotiations could resume. In mid-January a further scheduled round of talks between Israel and Syria was postponed indefinitely. In April Barak declared that the Israeli Government would resume the construction of settlements in the Golan Heights (following a declared suspension prior to the December 1999 talks).

Following the death of President Hafiz al-Assad in June 2000, his son, Bashar, who assumed the Syrian presidency in July, promised a continuation of his father's policies towards Israel. The Israeli-Syrian track remained deadlocked after Ariel Sharon became Israeli Prime Minister in 2001, and bilateral tensions were subsequently compounded by the US Administration of George W. Bush's references to Syria as a possible target in its 'war on terror'. In October 2003 Israel launched an air strike against an alleged training camp for Palestinian militants near Damascus.

In late 2003 and early 2004 the Israeli President, Moshe Katsav, proposed to President Bashar al-Assad that Syria should commence direct negotiations with Israel 'without preconditions'. However, the Syrian leadership dismissed the offer. In February 2005 Israeli officials stated that they would not resume negotiations with Syria regarding the Golan Heights until Syria had implemented a complete withdrawal of its forces from Lebanon (for further details, see the chapters on Lebanon and Syria). A report published in Israel's *Ha'aretz* newspaper in January 2007 alleged that secret discussions had taken place among Israeli and Syrian representatives between September 2004 and the start of the conflict between Israel and Hezbollah in July 2006, as a result of which important mutual understandings had been reached with regard to the Golan Heights and other contentious issues. The claim was denied by officials from both countries.

Relations between Israel and Syria deteriorated further in September 2007, following an Israeli air strike on a military installation at al-Kibar in Syria. US intelligence indicated in April 2008 that the Israeli military had targeted a covert nuclear facility that was being built with assistance from the Democratic People's Republic of Korea (North Korea). Representatives of the UN International Atomic Energy Agency (IAEA) subsequently undertook investigations of the al-Kibar site, and an IAEA report published in February 2009 asserted that there was a 'low probability' that Israeli missiles used to bomb the installation were the source of traces of uranium that had been found there.

Israeli and Syrian officials confirmed in May 2008 that indirect negotiations aimed at concluding a 'comprehensive peace' between the two countries were being held in the city of Istanbul, Turkey. By August four rounds of Turkish-mediated talks had taken place, although no significant progress had apparently been reached. A fifth round, scheduled for September, was postponed owing to the political uncertainty in Israel, following the resignation of Ehud Olmert, as Prime Minister. Apparently in response to Israel's large-scale military offensive against Hamas targets in the Gaza Strip in December 2008 and January 2009 (which also led to a deterioration in relations between Israel and Turkey), Assad formally suspended the talks with Israel. Following the inauguration of a new Government under Binyamin Netanyahu in March 2009, the new Minister of Foreign Affairs, Avigdor Lieberman, ruled out any Israeli withdrawal from the Golan Heights.

Prospects for a resumption of direct negotiations were further impeded by the popular uprising in Syria from early 2011, and that country's subsequent descent into civil war. In May Israeli troops clashed with hundreds of pro-Palestinian protesters who had broken through a security fence to enter the Golan Heights from Syria. Syrian state media reported in the following month that 12 Palestinians and two Syrians had been killed when Israeli soldiers opened fire at another group of protesters attempting to enter the Golan Heights from across the Syrian border. As the Syrian conflict deepened, Israel was concerned to avoid a mass influx of refugees, but was notably generally cautious in its stance towards both the incumbent Assad regime and the armed opposition. In July 2012, none the less, the then Deputy Prime Minister and Minister of Defence, Ehud Barak, stated that Israel was ready to intervene in Syria should Hezbollah or other militant groups acquire chemical weapons. There was an escalation in tension in February 2013, when President Assad stated that Israel was attempting to destabilize Syria. In January Syria had accused Israel of carrying out an air strike on Syrian territory, understood to involve the targeting of a weapons convoy bound for Hezbollah's use in Lebanon; the Syrian military itself stated that a military research facility had been hit. In subsequent months Israeli officials became increasingly concerned about the emergence of a number of radical Islamist groups among Syria's armed opposition; these fears increased during 2013, when it became evident that the Syrian civil war was also destabilizing Lebanon. In mid-2013 the Israeli leadership denied claims by the Syrian regime that its military

planes had attacked a number of sites in Syria that were being used to store weapons. Meanwhile, in February 2014, following several incidents during the preceding months in which the violence from Syria had crossed into the Golan Heights (see *Israeli Occupied Territories*), the Israeli military announced that it was sending a specialized army division to the border area to respond to security threats originating from Syria.

In September 2014 the Israeli army shot down a Syrian military aircraft that, it was claimed, had violated Israeli airspace. In early December Syria accused Israel of bombing two of its military installations, one near Damascus and the second near the Lebanese border. The Syrian Observatory for Human Rights suggested that the target of the air strikes were ground-to-air missiles. On 18 January 2015 an Israeli helicopter strike in Syria near the border with the occupied Golan Heights killed five members of Hezbollah, including the son of the group's late military leader Imad Mughniyeh, and a senior member of the Quds Force of the Iranian Islamic Revolutionary Guards Corps, who had been deployed to Syria to assist Government forces. The Israeli army claimed that those killed had intended to attack Israel.

Israel's strategic and commercial co-operation with Turkey increased following the upgrading of diplomatic relations to ambassadorial level in 1991. A Security and Secrecy Agreement concerning military and intelligence co-operation was signed in 1994. During 1996 the two countries signed a number of military accords, providing for joint military-training exercises and reciprocal access to airspace. The arrangements, which received support from the USA, stemmed from common concerns about Iran, Iraq and Syria. A bilateral free trade agreement came into force in 1997. In 2002 a 20-year agreement was signed, whereby Turkey would supply Israel with 50m. cu m of water annually.

The Turkish Prime Minister, Recep Tayyip Erdoğan, described the Israeli offensive in Gaza of May 2004 as 'state-sponsored terrorism'. Turkey, which had acted as host and mediator for indirect peace talks between Syria and Israel during 2008, also voiced strong condemnation of Israel's military offensive against Hamas which began in Gaza in December of that year, and which led to the formal suspension of negotiations by Syria. Nevertheless, in March 2009 the foreign ministers of Israel and Turkey held talks on bilateral relations and regional stability during a North Atlantic Treaty Organization (NATO) summit in Brussels, Belgium. Turkey subsequently announced its willingness to resume the role of mediator in Syrian-Israeli peace negotiations. In October, however, Turkey announced the cancellation of Israel's involvement in a scheduled military exercise, as well as plans for a further bilateral military exercise, declaring that the decision had been motivated by disapproval of Israel's operation in Gaza.

Tensions between Israel and Turkey escalated again following a raid, in May 2010, by Israeli naval forces on a ship in international waters. The vessel was part of a flotilla attempting to breach the Israeli blockade of Gaza, purportedly to deliver humanitarian aid and materials to the population there; nine pro-Palestinian Turkish activists were killed in the incident, and many more were injured. Foreign governments and international organizations condemned the Israeli action, despite Israel's claim that its forces had acted in self-defence. An Israeli commission established to investigate the raid subsequently determined that the actions of the Israeli soldiers had 'regrettable consequences of human life losses and physical injuries' but were, none the less, compliant with international law. In June Turkey suspended diplomatic and military ties with Israel, withdrawing its ambassador from Tel-Aviv and insisting that it would not restore full relations until Israel publicly apologized for the incident, compensated the relatives of the victims and agreed to the holding of an independent international inquiry.

Relations deteriorated further following the publication by the UN, in September 2011, of the report of an inquiry into the raid. The report criticized the conduct of both countries over the incident, determining that the decision by the Israeli military to board the vessel with substantial force constituted an 'excessive and unreasonable' action, while recognizing the 'legitimacy' of Israel's blockade as a means of stemming the flow of weapons into Gaza by sea. The Turkish Government, citing Israel's continued refusal formally to apologize for the incident, expelled the Israeli ambassador and his deputy from Ankara and recalled its remaining senior diplomats from its embassy in Tel-Aviv, as diplomatic relations with Israel were downgraded to the level of second secretary. Bilateral military and commercial ties were also suspended. Remarks in February 2013 by the Turkish Prime

Minister in which he characterized Zionism (along with anti-Semitism, fascism and Islamophobia) as a 'crime against humanity' drew strong condemnation from Israel, the UN and the USA. In March, however, at the conclusion of US President Obama's visit to Israel, it was announced that Prime Minister Binyamin Netanyahu had issued an apology to Turkey and agreed to conclude compensation arrangements. The apology, which was accepted by Erdoğan, was deemed to be an initial step towards the normalization of relations between Israel and Turkey. The Israeli Government stated that it had been agreed to exchange ambassadors, and that Turkey would withdraw legal proceedings against members of the Israeli armed forces with regard to the incident. In November 2014 the ICC announced that it would not seek to prosecute Israel for war crimes in relation to the incident.

Israel's relations with Iran have been characterized, particularly under the presidency of Mahmoud Ahmadinejad, by often violent anti-Israeli rhetoric on the part of the Iranian Government, by intense suspicion within Israel of Iran's nuclear ambitions, and of Iranian support for Hamas and Hezbollah. From 2006 Israeli government officials repeatedly urged international leaders to act in order to prevent Iran from developing a nuclear weapons capability, emphasizing that a military attack against Iran's nuclear facilities remained a strategic option. Iran countered with warnings that any pre-emptive military strikes launched by Israel would be met with a swift and powerful military response. In May 2009 Iran conducted tests that appeared to demonstrate that it possessed missiles with sufficient range to target Israel, as well as US military bases in the region. In November it was announced that Israeli forces in the Mediterranean Sea had intercepted a cargo ship en route to Syria, which Israel claimed was carrying a large consignment of Iranian-made weapons destined for Hezbollah militants in Lebanon. In February 2010 the Israeli air force announced the development of a fleet of unmanned aircraft able to launch missile attacks or conduct surveillance operations. Ahmadinejad stated that the aircraft were intended to target Iran, but Prime Minister Netanyahu insisted that Israel had no intention of instigating military action.

In February 2011 two Iranian warships passed through the Suez Canal, for the first time since the 1979 Islamic Revolution, sailing past the Israeli coast en route to Syria; their passage was condemned by the Israeli Government as a deliberate act of provocation. In November Israel test-fired a ballistic missile, intensifying speculation that Israel might be planning to launch a pre-emptive military strike against Iranian nuclear facilities. Such concerns were heightened following the publication by the IAEA of a report noting serious concerns regarding possible military dimensions to Iran's nuclear programme. Israel held Iran and Hezbollah responsible for a series of bomb explosions in February 2012 that apparently targeted staff at the Israeli embassies in India, Georgia and Thailand; the Iranian Government denied any involvement in the attacks. In March Netanyahu again gave indications of Israel's willingness to act unilaterally against Iran's nuclear facilities. Netanyahu held Hezbollah responsible for the deaths of five Israeli tourists in a suicide bombing of a bus in Bulgaria in July, and warned Iran of a strong response to acts of terrorism.

The composition of the new Israeli Government appointed in March 2013 was interpreted by some observers as signalling a change in regional policy. The new Israeli Minister of Defence, Moshe Ya'alon, was initially considered to favour a less confrontational stance with regard to Iran; and some significance was attached to the agreement of Tzipi Livni, who had previously been highly critical of Netanyahu's rhetoric on Iran, to join his new administration. In February 2013 Israel announced that it had successfully tested a new defensive interceptor system, capable of destroying incoming missiles beyond the Earth's atmosphere. In March Israeli naval forces intercepted a cargo ship in the Red Sea, claiming that the vessel was carrying surface-to-air missiles and other weapons from Iran that were intended for use by militant groups in the Gaza Strip. Netanyahu denounced in the strongest terms an interim agreement concerning Iran's nuclear programme that had been reached in November after intensive negotiations between Iran (since August under the presidency of Hassan Rouhani) and the Western negotiating powers in Geneva. The interim accord permitted the Iranian Government to continue the enrichment of uranium, provided that this was not to a sufficiently high grade to permit Iran to construct a nuclear weapon. In return for Iran's commitment regarding uranium enrichment, the five permanent members of the UN Security Council (France, Russia, the People's Republic of China, the United Kingdom and the USA), along with Germany, agreed to lift some of the sanctions imposed on the Iranian Government in recent years. A further, 'framework agreement' signed in April 2015 was also condemned by Netanyahu (see the chapter in Iran for further details). Meanwhile, a senior member of the Quds Force of the Iranian Islamic Revolutionary Guards Corps, who had been deployed to Syria to assist the Government against rebels in the civil war, was killed in an air strike by the Israeli air force in January 2015.

Tensions between Israel and Lebanon remained high following Israel's military campaign in southern Lebanon in mid-2006. In August 2010 there were clashes between Israeli and Lebanese soldiers near the 'Blue Line' (the UN's name for the border between the two countries); this constituted the most serious confrontation between the two countries since 2006. The UN urged both sides to exercise restraint and the governments of each country acted swiftly to reduce tensions.

The discovery in 2009–10 of two huge natural gas reserves in the Mediterranean Sea off the coast of Israel, a short distance from the disputed maritime border with Lebanon, further complicated relations. Israel contended that Lebanon's proposals for the delineation of its maritime border with Israel, submitted to the UN in August 2010, and with Cyprus, submitted in November, encroached upon Israeli territory. Furthermore, while the proposed boundaries did not include the recently discovered Tamar and Leviathan gasfields, they potentially contained significant oil and gas reserves, and contradicted previous maritime border agreements. In July 2011 Israel submitted its own proposal to the UN, insisting that Lebanon agree to bilateral negotiations on all border issues. Lebanon filed a formal complaint with the UN over Israel's proposal for the maritime border in September, stating that it infringed on some 860 sq km of Lebanese sovereign territory. In November there was renewed tension at the land border, when four rocket attacks were launched into northern Israel from Lebanon, in response to which the Israeli military fired artillery shells into Lebanese territory. The militant Islamist organization Abdullah Azzam Brigades, reported to be affiliated with al-Qa'ida, subsequently claimed responsibility for the attacks. The Israeli Government was reported in early 2012 to have begun preparations for the construction of a wall along the northern ceasefire-line with Lebanon, in order to bolster border security. In October Israeli officials stated that an unarmed drone, of Iranian origin, had been shot down over southern Israel, and that it was likely to have been launched from Lebanon by Hezbollah for the purposes of intelligence-gathering.

Following the removal from power of Egyptian President Hosni Mubarak in February 2011, there were fears of a significant deterioration in Israeli-Egyptian relations, which had remained generally stable during Mubarak's tenure. In Egypt the now increasingly influential Muslim Brotherhood, which had close links with Hamas, urged a review of the 1978 peace treaty signed between Israel and Egypt and appealing for an end to normalization with Israel. In June 2011 the arrest in Egypt of a student of dual Israeli and US citizenship, Ilan Grapel, on suspicion of espionage and of working to foment unrest in the aftermath of Mubarak's removal from office prompted angry protests in Israel. In October, following the successful conclusion of the first phase of the prisoner-exchange programme involving Gilad Shalit (see *Developments in Israeli-Palestinian relations, 2011–12*), Grapel was released in exchange for 25 Egyptian prisoners detained in Israeli gaols. Meanwhile, following the killing in August of five Egyptian soldiers by Israeli troops during an exchange of gunfire with suspected Palestinian militants close to the Israeli–Egyptian border, Egypt announced that it was to recall its ambassador from Tel-Aviv pending the completion of a full investigation into the incident by the Israeli Government (although, in the event, this was not carried out). In September protesters, who gathered outside the Israeli embassy in Cairo to demand the expulsion of the Israeli ambassador, penetrated and ransacked the premises, forcing the emergency evacuation to Israel of embassy staff.

Relations with Egypt were further undermined by the success of the Freedom and Justice Party (FJP—founded by the Muslim Brotherhood) at legislative elections held in November 2011–January 2012, and by the election, in June 2012, of the FJP candidate, Muhammad Mursi, as President. However, the Egyptian authorities notably mediated in efforts to end both the mass hunger strike by Palestinian detainees in May and the confrontations between Israeli forces and Palestinian militants in Gaza in June. President Mursi, furthermore, drew praise internationally for his role in bringing about the ceasefire that ended the Israeli offensive and Palestinian counter-strikes in November. However, Mursi was removed from office by the Egyptian military in July 2013 and replaced by an interim administration. The ousting of Mursi and handover of power to the new, military-backed authorities brought a swift end to the burgeoning relationship between Egypt and the Hamas administration in the Gaza Strip. In September, for example, Israeli officials welcomed measures taken by Egypt's interim administration to reduce the presence of militant Islamist groups in the Sinai Peninsula and to prevent the smuggling of weapons into Gaza. Egypt played a significant role in mediating negotiations for a ceasefire between Hamas and the Israeli Government in July–August 2014, and President Abd al-Fatah al-Sisi hosted a conference in Cairo for the reconstruction of Gaza in October. Also in that month two Israeli soldiers in southern Israel were injured by anti-tank fire directed across the border from Sinai in Egypt by Islamic militants (see the chapter on Egypt).

CONSTITUTION AND GOVERNMENT

Israel does not have a formal, written constitution. However, in June 1950 the Knesset (parliament) voted to adopt a state constitution by evolution over an unspecified period. A number of laws, including the Law of Return (1950), the Nationality Law (1952), the State President (Tenure) Law (1952), the Education Law (1953) and the 'Yad-va-Shem' Memorial Law (1953), are considered as incorporated into the state Constitution. Other constitutional laws are: the Law and Administration Ordinance (1948), the Knesset Election Law (1951), the Law of Equal Rights for Women (1951), the Judges Act (1953), the National Service and National Insurance Acts (1953), and the Basic Law (the Knesset—1958).

Supreme authority in Israel rests with the Knesset, with 120 members elected by universal suffrage for four years (subject to dissolution), on the basis of proportional representation. The President, a constitutional head of state, is elected by the Knesset for a maximum of one seven-year term. Executive power lies with the Cabinet, led by a Prime Minister. The Cabinet takes office after receiving a vote of confidence in the Knesset, to which it is responsible. Ministers are usually members of the Knesset, but non-members may be appointed. The country is divided into six administrative districts. Local authorities are elected at the same time as elections to the Knesset. In 2013 there were 75 municipal councils, 126 local councils and 1,000 regional councils.

REGIONAL AND INTERNATIONAL CO-OPERATION

Israel became a member of the UN on 11 May 1949. As a contracting party to the General Agreement on Tariffs and Trade, Israel joined the World Trade Organization (WTO, see p. 431) on its establishment in 1995. The country officially acceded to the Organisation for Economic Co-operation and Development (OECD, see p. 377) in 2010.

ECONOMIC AFFAIRS

In 2013, according to estimates by the World Bank, Israel's gross national income (GNI), measured at average 2011–13 prices, was US $275,024m., equivalent to $34,120 per head (or $32,140 per head on an international purchasing-power parity basis). During 2004–13, it was estimated, the population increased at an average annual rate of 1.9%, while gross domestic product (GDP) per head increased, in real terms, by an average of 2.5% per year. Overall GDP increased, in real terms, at an average annual rate of 4.4% in 2004–13; it grew by 3.3% in 2013.

Agriculture (including hunting, forestry and fishing) contributed a preliminary 1.3% of GDP in 2014, and engaged 1.3% of the employed labour force during the third quarter of 2014. Most agricultural workers live in large co-operatives (*kibbutzim*), of which there were 267 at December 2013, or co-operative smallholder villages (*moshavim*), of which there were 443. Israel is largely self-sufficient in foodstuffs. Citrus fruits constitute the main export crop. Other important crops are tomatoes, vegetables (particularly potatoes, carrots and turnips, chillies and peppers, and cucumbers and gherkins), wheat, melons and apples. The export of exotic fruits, winter vegetables and flowers has increased significantly in recent years. Poultry, livestock and fish production are also important. According to UN figures, the GDP of the agricultural sector increased at an estimated average annual rate of 2.4% in 2004–13; it increased by 0.8% in 2013.

Industry (comprising mining, manufacturing, construction and power) contributed a preliminary 23.0% of GDP in 2014, and engaged 17.3% of the employed labour force during the third quarter of 2014. The state plays a major role in all sectors of industry, and there is a significant co-operative sector. According to UN figures, in 2004–13 industrial GDP increased at an average annual rate of 5.0%; it expanded by an estimated 4.9% in 2013.

The mining and manufacturing sectors together contributed a preliminary 15.2% of GDP in 2014, and engaged 11.7% of the employed labour force during the third quarter of 2014; mining and quarrying employed about 0.2% of the working population in 2008. Israel has small proven reserves of petroleum (of some 3.9m. barrels), from which less than 500 barrels per day are currently produced; however, in 1999 potential new reserves were discovered in central Israel and off the southern coast. Israel's Petroleum Commission has estimated that the country could possess around 5,000m. barrels of oil reserves, most likely located underneath gas reserves, and that offshore gas could supply its short-term energy needs. Production at the offshore Tamar gasfield, the reserves of which were estimated at some 250,000m. cu m, began in March 2013; Tamar was expected to supply 50%–80% of Israel's natural gas consumption within the next decade. Reserves at the offshore Leviathan field, discovered in December 2010, are estimated at some 620,000m. cu m. Production at the Leviathan field was expected to commence by 2017. Phosphates, potash, bromides, magnesium and other salts are mined, and Israel is the world's largest exporter of bromine. The principal branches of manufacturing, measured by gross revenue, are: chemical, petroleum and coal products; food products; scientific, photographic, optical equipment, etc.; metal products; pharmaceutical products; and rubber and plastic products. According to official estimates, in 2003–09 sectoral GDP increased by an average annual rate of 3.9%; it expanded by 6.2% in 2008, before declining by an estimated 6.2% in 2009.

The construction sector contributed a preliminary 5.4% of GDP in 2014. During the third quarter of 2014 the sector engaged 4.8% of the employed labour force. During 2004–13 the GDP of the sector increased at an average annual rate of 5.5%; it increased by 0.4% in 2013, according to UN figures.

Energy is derived principally from coal (accounting for 69.9% of total electricity output in 2012); however, it is intended that natural gas should eventually become Israel's principal energy source. Energy derived from natural gas contributed 20.9% of total electricity output in 2012, up from just 0.1% in 2003. Imports of mineral fuels comprised 20.2% of the total value of imports in 2013.

Services contributed a preliminary 75.7% of GDP in 2014, and engaged 81.5% of the employed labour force in the third quarter of 2014. Tourism is an important source of revenue, although the sector has at times been severely damaged by regional instability. A decline in the number of militant attacks in the late 2000s resulted in an increase in tourist numbers: in 2013 some 3.0m. tourists visited Israel (increased from 2.3m. in 2009), while receipts from tourism were estimated at US $5,667m. in 2013. Financial services are also important: banking, insurance, real estate and business services together contributed a preliminary 18.5% of GDP in 2014, and employed 15.8% of the working population in the third quarter of 2014. According to UN figures, in 2004–13 the GDP of the services sector increased at an average annual rate of 3.8%; it grew by an estimated 3.6% in 2013.

In 2013 Israel recorded a visible merchandise trade deficit of US $9,328.9m.; however, there was a surplus of $6,893.1m. on the current account of the balance of payments. Excluding trade with the West Bank and Gaza Strip, in 2013 the principal source of imports was the USA, which supplied 11.3% of imports to Israel; other major suppliers were the People's Republic of China, Germany, Switzerland-Liechtenstein and Belgium-Luxembourg. The USA was also the principal market for exports, taking 26.2% of Israeli exports in that year; other important purchasers were Hong Kong and the United Kingdom. Israel is the world's largest supplier of polished diamonds. The principal exports in 2013 were basic manufactures (chiefly non-metallic mineral manufactures), machinery and transport equipment, chemicals and related products, miscellaneous manufactured articles, and mineral fuels, lubricants and related products . The principal imports in that year were machinery and transport equipment, basic manufactures, mineral fuels and lubricants (mainly petroleum and petroleum products), basic manufactures (mainly non-metallic mineral manufactures), chemicals and related products, miscellaneous manufactured articles, and food and live animals.

Government revenue each year normally includes some US $8,632m. in economic and military aid from the USA. The Government planned for a balanced budget for 2014, with revenue and expenditure both totalling NIS 406,265m. in that year. Israel's general gross government debt was NIS 697,279m. in 2013, equivalent to 64.1% of GDP. During 2004–13 consumer prices rose at an average annual rate of 2.4%; consumer prices increased by 1.5% in 2013. The unemployment rate was reported at 6.4% during the third quarter of 2014.

A principal task for the new coalition Government that took office in March 2013 was to secure approval of a budget that would balance the need to reduce spending obligations, with the electorate's demands for the reduction of living costs, and the highly sensitive issue of defence commitments. In May the Cabinet approved the new Minister of Finance's austerity budget for the August 2013–December 2014 period, which, *inter alia*, increased personal and corporate taxation, reduced child allowances and imposed a limited cut in defence expenditure; the budget received Knesset approval in July 2013. The continued growth in housing prices—a key focus of the mass social protests of 2011—reflected the shortage of homes relative to demand, as well as the impact of low interest rates in fuelling demand for property investment. The Government approved draft legislation to create a sovereign wealth fund in April 2013, following the commencement of natural gas production from the Tamar gas field in March. The long-term expansion of natural gas production from the Tamar and Leviathan fields was expected to reduce Israel's dependence on fuel imports; moreover, the country was expected to become a net exporter of natural gas by the end of the decade. In June 2013 the Government voted to permit the export of 40% of Israel's gas reserves, with the remaining 60% to be retained for domestic consumption; the decision was ratified by the Supreme Court in October. In December 2014 Israel, Cyprus and Greece appealed to the European Union for funding to construct a pipeline that could eventually annually transport up to 15 billion cubic metres (bcm) of natural gas produced in their territorial waters to the European market. The budget for 2015, which was approved in October 2014, included significant additional spending on health care, and forecast a budget deficit of 3.4%. Following GDP growth of an estimated 2.5% in 2014, the IMF forecast the Israeli economy to grow at 2.8% in 2015, with unemployment expected to decline slightly to 6.0%.

PUBLIC HOLIDAYS

The Sabbath starts at sunset on Friday and ends at nightfall on Saturday. The Jewish year 5776 begins on 14 September 2015 and the year 5777 on 3 October 2016.

2016: 23–30 April (Pesach, Passover—public holidays on first and last days of festival), 12 May (Yom Ha'atzmaut, Independence Day), 12 June (Shavuot, Feast of Weeks), 3–4 October (Rosh Hashanah, Jewish New Year), 12 October (Yom Kippur, Day of Atonement), 17–23 October (Succot, Feast of the Tabernacles), 24 October (Shemini Atzeret, Assembly of the Eighth Day/ Simchat Torah, Celebration of the Torah),

(Observance of the Jewish festivals and fast days begins at sunset in the evening prior to the dates given.)

Islamic holidays are observed by Muslim Arabs, and Christian holidays by the Christian Arab community.

Statistical Survey

Source (unless otherwise indicated): Central Bureau of Statistics, POB 13015, Hakirya, Romema, Jerusalem 91130; tel. 2-6592037; fax 2-6521340; e-mail yael@ cbs.gov.il; internet www.cbs.gov.il.

Area and Population

AREA, POPULATION AND DENSITY

Area (sq km)	
Land	21,643
Inland water	429
Total	22,072*
Population (*de jure*; census results)†	
4 November 1995	5,548,523
27 December 2008	
Males	3,663,910
Females	3,748,270
Total	7,412,180
Population (*de jure*; official estimates at 31 December)†	
2011	7,836,600
2012	7,984,500
2013	8,134,500
Density (per sq km) at 31 December 2013	375.8§

* 8,522 sq miles. Area includes East Jerusalem, annexed by Israel in June 1967, and the Golan sub-district (1,154 sq km), annexed by Israel in December 1981.

† Including the population of East Jerusalem and Israeli residents in certain other areas under Israeli military occupation since June 1967. Figures also include non-Jews in the Golan sub-district, an Israeli-occupied area of Syrian territory. Census results exclude adjustment for underenumeration.

§ Land area only.

Mid-2014 (official estimate): 8,207,800.

POPULATION BY AGE AND SEX
('000, official population estimates, annual averages, 2013)

	Males	Females	Total
0–14 years	1,164.9	1,108.5	2,273.4
15–64 years	2,454.1	2,482.8	4,936.9
65 years and over	372.3	476.9	849.2
Total	**3,991.3**	**4,068.2**	**8,059.5**

POPULATION BY RELIGION
(31 December 2013)

	Number	%
Jews	6,104,500	75.0
Muslims	1,420,300	17.5
Christians*	160,900	2.0
Druze	133,400	1.6
Unclassified†	315,400	3.9
Total	**8,134,500**	**100.0**

* Including Arab Christians.
† Including Lebanese not classified by religion.

Mid-2014: Jews 6,155,700 (75.0%); Total 8,207,800.

DISTRICTS
(31 December 2013)

	Area (sq km)*	Population (rounded)†	Density (per sq km)
Jerusalem‡	653	1,008,400	1,544.3
Northern§	4,473	1,341,500	299.9
Haifa	866	951,900	1,099.2
Central	1,294	1,976,300	1,527.3
Tel-Aviv	172	1,331,300	7,740.1
Southern	14,185	1,168,600	82.4
Total	**21,643**	**8,134,500†**	**375.8**

* Excluding lakes, with a total area of 429 sq km.
† Components exclude, but total includes, Israelis residing in Jewish localities in the West Bank totalling some 356,500 at 31 December 2013.
‡ Including East Jerusalem, annexed by Israel in June 1967.
§ Including the Golan sub-district (area 1,154 sq km, population an estimated 44,900 at 31 December 2013), annexed by Israel in December 1981.

PRINCIPAL TOWNS
(population at 31 December 2012)

Jerusalem (capital)*	815,300	Beersheba . . .	197,300
Tel-Aviv—Jaffa .	414,600	Netanya	192,200
Haifa	272,200	Holon	185,300
Rishon LeZiyyon .	235,100	Bene Beraq . . .	168,800
Ashdod . . .	214,900	Ramat-Gan . . .	148,400
Petach-Tikva . .	213,900	Bat Yam . . .	129,400

* The Israeli Government has designated the city of Jerusalem (including East Jerusalem, annexed by Israel in June 1967) as the country's capital, although this is not recognized by the UN.

Mid-2014 ('000, incl. suburbs, UN estimate): Jerusalem 829,396 (Source: UN, *World Urbanization Prospects: The 2014 Revision*).

BIRTHS, MARRIAGES AND DEATHS*

	Registered live births		Registered marriages		Registered deaths†	
	Number	Rate (per 1,000)	Number	Rate (per 1,000)	Number	Rate (per 1,000)
2006 .	148,170	21.0	44,685	6.3	38,765‡	5.5‡
2007 .	151,679	21.1	46,448	6.5	40,081	5.6
2008 .	156,923	21.5	50,038	6.8	39,484	5.4
2009 .	161,042	21.5	48,997	6.5	38,812	5.2
2010 .	166,255	21.8	47,855	6.2	39,613	5.2
2011 .	166,296	21.4	51,271	6.6	40,889	5.3
2012 .	170,940	21.6	n.a.	n.a.	42,108	5.3
2013 .	171,444	21.1	n.a.	n.a.	41,632	5.1

* Including East Jerusalem.
† Including deaths abroad of Israelis residing outside of Israel less than one year.
‡ Excluding 116 deaths of military personnel resulting from hostilities with militant factions based in Lebanon.

Note: Data include marriages involving a spouse not resident in Israel and those in which spouses may be of different religions.

Life expectancy (years at birth): 81.7 (males 79.9; females 83.6) in 2012 (Source: World Bank, World Development Indicators database).

IMMIGRATION*

	2011	2012	2013
Immigrants on immigrant visas .	14,332	13,479	13,406
Immigrants on tourist visas† . .	2,561	3,075	3,478
Total	**16,893**	**16,554**	**16,884**

* Excluding immigrating citizens (4,085 in 2011; 4,176 in 2012; 3,922 in 2013) and Israeli residents returning from abroad.
† Figures refer to tourists who changed their status to immigrants or potential immigrants.

ECONOMICALLY ACTIVE POPULATION
(sample surveys, July–September, '000 persons aged 15 years and over, excluding armed forces)*

	2012	2013	2014
Agriculture, hunting, forestry and fishing	37.8	39.7	44.4
Industry†	411.7	404.5	407.8
Electricity, gas and water supply .	27.0	26.8	29.0
Construction	152.0	166.0	166.3
Wholesale and retail trade; repair of motor vehicles, motorcycles and personal and household goods	401.6	419.4	406.5
Hotels and restaurants . . .	156.6	159.9	161.4
Transport, storage and communications	299.1	312.9	336.2
Financial intermediation . . .	117.2	116.9	125.3
Real estate, renting and business activities	403.4	423.0	427.7
Public administration and defence; compulsory social security . .	365.5	363.1	366.4
Education	394.5	404.2	412.7
Health and social work . . .	340.5	355.4	386.9
Other community, social and personal service activities . .	149.0	158.7	158.0
Private households with employed persons	69.5	64.0	63.3
Extraterritorial organizations and bodies	2.0	2.0	3.2
Sub-total	**3,327.4**	**3,416.5**	**3,495.1**
Not classifiable by economic activity	66.4	54.1	65.6
Total employed	**3,393.8**	**3,470.6**	**3,560.7**
Unemployed	254.9	231.8	243.2
Total labour force	**3,648.7**	**3,702.5**	**3,803.8**
Males	1,934.7	1,973.0	2,011.4
Females	1,714.1	1,729.5	1,792.5

* Totals may not be equal to the sum of components, owing to independent estimation methodologies.
† Comprising mining and quarrying, and manufacturing.

Health and Welfare

KEY INDICATORS

Total fertility rate (children per woman, 2012)	2.9
Under-5 mortality rate (per 1,000 live births, 2012) . . .	4
HIV/AIDS (% of persons aged 15–49, 2011)	0.2
Physicians (per 1,000 head, 2011)	3.3
Hospital beds (per 1,000 head, 2010)	3.5
Health expenditure (2011): US $ per head (PPP)	2,186
Health expenditure (2011): % of GDP	7.6
Health expenditure (2011): public (% of total)	61.2
Total carbon dioxide emissions ('000 metric tons, 2010) . .	70,655.8
Carbon dioxide emissions per head (metric tons, 2010) . .	9.3
Human Development Index (2013): ranking	19
Human Development Index (2013): value	0.888

For sources and definitions, see explanatory note on p. vi.

Agriculture

PRINCIPAL CROPS
('000 metric tons)

	2011	2012	2013
Wheat	122.0	189.5	151.8
Maize	96.4	85.4	110.1
Potatoes	621.1	565.6	590.5
Olives	66.0	63.0	67.0
Cabbages and other brassicas	57.7	59.8	60.3
Lettuce and chicory	32.2	32.9	31.2*
Tomatoes	411.0	392.1	421.2
Cucumbers and gherkins	105.4	100.8	100.9
Aubergines (Eggplants)	46.1	43.1	47.0
Chillies and peppers, green	226.1	240.7	244.0
Onions, dry	91.8	82.8	84.4
Carrots and turnips	289.3	282.9	292.4
Watermelons	100.6	103.2	97.6
Cantaloupes and other melons	41.5	37.6	36.2
Bananas	101.3	129.5	139.4
Oranges	90.5	111.9	90.2
Tangerines, mandarins, clementines and satsumas	130.6	184.9	160.8
Grapefruit and pomelos	183.7	246.6	210.7
Apples	119.2	131.6	117.6
Peaches and nectarines	54.2	102.3	65.8
Grapes	89.5	94.0	85.1
Avocados	75.3	73.4	91.9

* FAO estimate.

Aggregate production ('000 metric tons, may include official, semi-official or estimated data): Total cereals 253.7 in 2011, 323.4 in 2012, 310.3 in 2013; Total roots and tubers 641.3 in 2011, 582.9 in 2012, 617.1 in 2013; Total vegetables (incl. melons) 1,744.4 in 2011, 1,718.5 in 2012, 1,780.0 in 2013; Total fruits (excl. melons) 1,194.2 in 2011, 1,454.2 in 2012, 1,336.0 in 2013.

Source: FAO.

LIVESTOCK
('000 head, year ending September)

	2011	2012	2013
Cattle	432	435	465
Pigs*	224	224	177
Sheep	486	540	540
Goats	107	100	100
Chickens	40,717	40,247	40,179
Geese and guinea fowls†	1,050	1,000	950
Turkeys	3,685	3,503	3,283
Ducks†	200	190	180

* Unofficial figures.
† FAO estimates.
Source: FAO.

LIVESTOCK PRODUCTS
('000 metric tons)

	2011	2012	2013
Cattle meat	116.7	116.9	132.2
Sheep meat*	9.5	9.7	9.9
Pig meat	19.2	19.4	16.3
Chicken meat	459	482	443
Goose and guinea fowl meat*	3.6	3.6	3.6
Turkey meat	90.0	92.0	83.6
Cows' milk	1,355.7	1,366.4	1,390.8
Sheep's milk	16.5	18.1	19.7
Goats' milk	22.3	25.9	24.7
Hen eggs	120.9	120.3	123.5
Honey	2.9	3.1	3.4

* FAO estimates.
Source: FAO.

Forestry

ROUNDWOOD REMOVALS
('000 cubic metres, excl. bark, FAO estimates)

	2011	2012	2013
Sawlogs, veneer logs and logs for sleepers	11	11	11
Pulpwood	7	7	7
Other industrial wood	7	7	7
Fuel wood	2	2	2
Total	27	27	27

Note: Figures assumed to be unchanged from 2001.
Source: FAO.

Fishing

(metric tons, live weight)

	2010	2011	2012
Capture	2,588	2,650*	2,650*
Carps, barbels, etc.	294	258	258*
Aquaculture*	19,895	20,107	19,743
Common carp	5,629	5,840	5,267
Tilapias	7,662	7,390	7,215
Gilthead seabream	1,240	1,440	2,052
Flathead grey mullet	2,125	2,169	2,338
Total catch*	22,483	22,757	22,393

* FAO estimate(s).
Source: FAO.

Mining

('000 metric tons unless otherwise indicated)

	2010	2011	2012
Crude petroleum ('000 barrels)	12.0	34.0	32.0
Natural gas (million cu m)	3,234	4,318	2,556
Phosphate rock*	3,135	3,105	3,513
Potash salts†	2,636	2,642	3,060
Salt (unrefined, marketed)	421	410	415
Gypsum	99.7	20.4	45.4
Bromine (elemental)	185	202	174

* Figures refer to beneficiated production; the phosphoric acid content (in '000 metric tons) was: 860 in 2010 (estimate); 850 in 2011; 960 in 2012 (estimate).
† Figures refer to K$_2$O content.

Source: US Geological Survey.

Industry

SELECTED PRODUCTS
('000 metric tons unless otherwise indicated)

	2010	2011	2012
Wine*	5.0	5.0	5.2
Sulphuric acid†	630	630	680
Cement	5,139	5,480	5,900
Electric energy (million kWh)	56,102	57,145	61,074

* FAO estimates.
† Sulphuric content; US Geological Survey estimates.

Sources: mainly FAO; US Geological Survey.

Finance

CURRENCY AND EXCHANGE RATES

Monetary Units
100 agorot (singular: agora) = 1 new sheqel (plural: sheqalim) or shekel (NIS).

Sterling, Dollar and Euro Equivalents (31 December 2014)
£1 sterling = NIS 6.070;
US $1 = NIS 3.889;
€1 = NIS 4.722;
NIS 100 = £16.47 = $25.71 = €21.18.

Average Exchange Rate (NIS per US $)
2012   3.8559
2013   3.6107
2014   3.5779

STATE BUDGET*
(NIS million)

Revenue and grants†	2012	2013‡	2014‡
Current receipts	258,804	279,846	286,932
Taxes and compulsory payments	233,826	235,953	259,166
Income and property taxes .	111,800	112,800	126,300
Taxes on expenditure . .	122,026	123,153	132,866
Interest, royalties, etc. . . .	4,366	2,693	2,782
Transfer from loans and capital account receipts . . .	20,613	41,200	24,984
Receipts from loans and capital account	107,111	115,187	119,333
Collection of principal . . .	6,240	5,160	4,983
Miscellaneous	40	13	14
Privatization	1,813	1,132	1,132
Domestic loans	99,786	128,305	118,254
Loans and grants from overseas	17,672	20,546	18,432
Less Transfer to current receipts	18,440	39,968	23,482
Total	365,916	395,033	406,265

Expenditure§	2012	2013‡	2014‡
Civilian consumption	71,155	80,691	84,157
Domestic	46,632	49,998	52,980
Defence consumption . . .	66,610	58,622	57,840
Transfer and support payments	102,736	110,505	113,114
Investments and credit granting .	19,335	25,159	27,569
Interest payments and credit subsidies	38,049	39,473	41,762
Miscellaneous	9,295	9,879	10,859
Reserves	—	7,076	7,401
Debt repayment (principal) . .	88,384	85,489	86,003
Less Revenue-dependent expenditure	19,171	21,860	22,441
Total	376,392	395,033	406,265

* Excluding Bank of Israel.
† Revenue includes grants received from abroad (NIS million): 8,672 in 2012; 8,746 in 2013 (forecast); 8,632 in 2014 (forecast).
‡ Forecasts.
§ Expenditure includes the central Government's credit issuance (NIS million): 1,214 in 2012; 1,943 in 2013 (forecast); 2,030 in 2014 (forecast).

Source: Ministry of Finance, Budget Division.

INTERNATIONAL RESERVES
(excluding gold, US $ million at 31 December)

	2011	2012	2013
IMF special drawing rights . .	1,269.5	1,276.7	1,539.2
Reserve position in IMF . . .	552.6	591.0	655.3
Foreign exchange	73,052.0	74,040.0	79,591.0
Total	74,874.1	75,907.6	81,785.5

Source: IMF, *International Financial Statistics*.

MONEY SUPPLY
(NIS '000 million at 31 December)

	2011	2012	2013
Currency held by public . . .	43.1	48.2	50.7
Current account deposits . . .	58.7	68.6	83.8
Total means of payment . .	101.8	116.8	134.5

COST OF LIVING
(Consumer Price Index; base: 2000 = 100)

	2011	2012	2013
Food	143.4	144.4	151.6
All items (incl. others) . . .	127.9	130.1	132.1

Source: ILO.

NATIONAL ACCOUNTS
(NIS million at current prices)

National Income and Product

	2012	2013	2014*
Gross domestic product in market prices	991,762	1,049,108	1,087,932
Net income paid abroad . . .	−25,082	−22,835	−13,996
Gross national income (GNI) .	966,680	1,026,273	1,073,936
Less Consumption of fixed capital	132,625	136,207	142,834
Net national income . . .	834,054	890,065	931,103

Expenditure on the Gross Domestic Product

	2012	2013	2014*
Final consumption expenditure .	783,556	829,113	866,285
Private	561,206	593,168	618,433
General government . . .	222,350	235,945	247,852
Changes in inventories . . .	5,398	1,335	3,283
Gross fixed capital formation .	201,066	204,245	201,735
Total domestic expenditure	990,020	1,034,693	1,071,303
Exports of goods and services .	359,459	345,418	345,908
Less Imports of goods and services	357,718	331,003	329,279
GDP in market prices . . .	991,762	1,049,108	1,087,932

Gross Domestic Product by Economic Activity

	2012	2013	2014*
Agriculture, hunting, forestry and fishing	13,344	13,131	13,041
Manufacturing, mining and quarrying	144,586	148,577	147,172
Electricity, gas and water supply .	11,231	20,474	22,541
Construction	49,786	51,985	52,537
Wholesale, retail trade, repair of motor vehicles, motorcycles and personal and household goods; hotels and restaurants . . .	91,448	93,854	94,007
Transport, storage and communications	111,873	108,890	117,384
Financial intermediation; real estate, renting and business activities	158,370	174,294	178,469
Public administration and community services† . . .	140,152	148,685	155,567
Housing services	109,659	115,283	123,280
Education; health and social work; arts, entertainment and recreation	56,721	60,012	62,955
Sub-total	887,170	935,185	966,953
Net taxes on products . . .	104,593	113,922	120,999
Statistical discrepancy . . .	−1	1	−20
GDP in market prices . . .	991,762	1,049,108	1,087,932

* Preliminary figures.
† Including non-profit institutions serving households.

BALANCE OF PAYMENTS
(US $ million)

	2011	2012	2013
Exports of goods	64,293.8	62,041.6	61,956.7
Imports of goods	−72,434.9	−71,783.0	−71,285.6
Balance on goods	**−8,141.1**	**−9,741.4**	**−9,328.9**
Exports of services	27,382.7	31,177.6	33,732.4
Imports of services	−20,537.2	−21,013.3	−20,238.7
Balance on goods and services	**−1,295.6**	**422.9**	**4,164.8**
Primary income received . . .	7,766.0	7,572.8	8,105.4
Primary income paid . . .	−11,326.7	−14,064.3	−14,444.1
Balance on goods, services and primary income . . .	**-4,856.3**	**−6,068.6**	**−2,173.9**
Secondary income received . .	10,132.5	9,556.1	10,490.7
Secondary income paid . .	−1,355.6	−1,383.0	−1,423.7
Current balance	**3,920.6**	**2,104.5**	**6,893.1**
Capital account (net) . . .	1,234.0	672.6	1,625.2
Direct investment assets . .	−9,165.0	−3,257.3	−4,670.1
Direct investment liabilities . .	9,094.1	8,055.2	11,804.2
Portfolio investment assets . .	−3,402.0	−8,023.5	−9,415.7
Portfolio investment liabilities .	−5,392.1	−3,330.6	1,755.0
Financial derivatives and employee stock options (net)	−13.6	302.1	461.7
Other investment assets . . .	−677.6	2,489.9	−4,360.9
Other investment liabilities . .	1,680.6	−3,603.2	−1,148.1
Net errors and omissions . . .	7,453.0	4,455.1	1,727.8
Reserves and related items .	**4,732.0**	**−135.2**	**4,672.2**

Source: IMF, *International Financial Statistics*.

External Trade

PRINCIPAL COMMODITIES
(US $ million)

Imports c.i.f.	2011	2012	2013
Food and live animals . . .	4,356.3	4,242.0	4,363.5
Mineral fuels, lubricants, etc. .	13,635.9	16,078.8	14,552.8
Petroleum, petroleum products, etc.	11,709.4	14,309.0	12,856.3
Chemicals and related products	7,961.4	8,344.3	8,058.3
Basic manufactures	18,041.5	15,179.8	16,212.5
Non-metallic mineral manufactures	11,589.0	9,113.7	9,978.7
Machinery and transport equipment	21,146.7	21,039.6	20,236.2
General industrial machinery, equipment and parts . .	2,403.2	2,722.1	2,394.5
Machinery for particular industries	2,893.1	2,172.3	1,232.7
Office machines and automatic data-processing machines . .	1,937.5	1,842.8	1,841.6
Telecommunications and sound equipment	2,751.8	2,320.8	2,286.0
Other electrical machinery, apparatus, etc.	4,455.9	4,974.5	4,962.9
Road vehicles and parts . . .	4,824.0	4,206.6	4,911.1
Miscellaneous manufactured articles	6,082.1	6,175.1	6,442.1
Total (incl. others)	73,536.2	73,121.4	72,000.3

Exports f.o.b.	2011	2012	2013
Food and live animals . . .	1,925.8	1,944.7	2,056.5
Mineral fuels, lubricants and related products	4,046.6	3,257.9	5,569.4
Chemicals and related products	15,398.0	14,735.9	13,601.8
Organic chemicals	1,891.6	2,026.0	1,810.0
Medical and pharmaceutical products	7,083.1	6,598.9	6,096.8
Basic manufactures	24,105.4	20,755.7	22,260.3
Non-metallic mineral manufactures	20,991.0	17,884.4	19,493.2
Machinery and transport equipment	15,013.2	15,404.2	16,147.0
Telecommunications and sound equipment	3,202.2	3,002.4	2,656.9
Other electrical machinery, apparatus, etc.	5,691.1	6,085.9	6,887.1
Road vehicles and other transport equipment and parts . . .	2,131.3	1,903.6	2,206.6
Miscellaneous manufactured articles	5,873.2	5,760.6	6,010.5
Professional, scientific and controlling instruments, etc. .	2,849.7	2,806.7	3,077.3
Total (incl. others)	67,802.2	63,145.3	66,788.4

PRINCIPAL TRADING PARTNERS
(US $ million)*

Imports (excl. military goods) c.i.f.	2011	2012	2013
Belgium-Luxembourg	4,465.0	3,544.9	3,823.4
China, People's Republic . . .	5,450.5	5,322.2	5,660.1
Cyprus	318.9	964.7	463.5
France	1,625.5	1,646.2	1,544.0
Germany	4,566.5	4,621.8	4,667.7
Hong Kong	1,856.2	1,563.9	1,668.4
India	2,154.5	1,936.2	2,121.9
Italy	3,055.9	2,779.5	2,692.8
Ireland	994.5	1,006.0	935.2
Japan	2,402.1	1,727.3	1,118.7
Korea, Republic	1,607.7	1,663.0	1,513.0
Netherlands	2,761.5	2,746.9	2,719.3
Russia	1,052.9	819.4	994.6
Singapore	794.5	773.4	790.2
Spain	1,183.4	1,201.9	1,381.0
Switzerland-Liechtenstein . .	3,970.2	4,055.4	4,397.4
Taiwan	761.5	782.1	814.5
Turkey	2,171.1	2,082.7	2,354.1
United Kingdom	2,776.7	2,598.1	2,420.9
USA	8,706.7	9,398.7	8,153.2
Total (incl. others)	73,536.2	73,121.4	72,000.3

Exports f.o.b.	2011	2012	2013
Belgium-Luxembourg	3,767.5	2,929.7	3,118.3
Brazil	892.6	1,130.9	1,041.9
Canada	807.1	767.7	635.2
China, People's Republic . . .	2,718.3	2,758.2	2,886.4
Cyprus	937.4	905.1	1,126.5
France	1,542.0	1,437.3	1,556.1
Germany	1,950.0	1,631.9	1,763.3
Hong Kong	5,339.1	4,882.8	5,378.2
India	3,036.4	2,460.8	2,237.9
Italy	1,390.5	1,149.9	1,157.6
Japan	900.8	831.8	727.8
Korea, Republic	724.1	700.7	594.0
Malaysia	717.2	763.3	1,457.1
Netherlands	2,160.6	2,248.6	2,095.1
Russia	954.3	1,053.1	1,036.4
Spain	984.2	1,033.4	1,241.1
Switzerland-Liechtenstein . .	1,438.4	1,133.0	1,376.0
Taiwan	776.6	699.4	744.4
Turkey	1,855.7	1,421.4	2,515.6
United Kingdom	3,424.7	3,568.7	3,853.5
USA	19,432.4	17,518.2	17,500.8
Total (incl. others)	67,802.2	63,145.3	66,788.4

* Imports by country of purchase; exports by country of destination.

Transport

RAILWAYS
(traffic)

	2011	2012	2013
Passengers carried ('000 journeys)	35,930	40,373	45,137
Passenger-km (million) . . .	1,927	2,133	n.a.
Freight carried ('000 metric tons) .	6,229	6,265	6,667
Freight ton-km (million) . . .	1,099	1,011	n.a.

ROAD TRAFFIC
(motor vehicles in use at 31 December)

	2011	2012	2013
Private passenger cars	2,164,385	2,246,053	2,338,687
Taxis	19,020	19,222	19,821
Minibuses	14,848	14,492	14,238
Buses and coaches	15,382	15,625	16,917
Lorries, vans and road tractors	347,980	341,859	335,078
Special service vehicles . .	4,318	4,433	4,554
Motorcycles and mopeds . . .	117,254	119,295	121,218

SHIPPING

Flag Registered Fleet
(at 31 December)

	2012	2013	2014
Number of vessels	38	39	40
Displacement ('000 grt) . . .	272.0	273.1	274.8

Source: Lloyd's List Intelligence (www.lloydslistintelligence.com).

International Seaborne Freight Traffic
('000 metric tons)

	2011	2012	2013
Goods loaded	19,554	19,429	20,464
Goods unloaded*	25,392	27,037	28,287

* Including traffic between Israeli ports.

CIVIL AVIATION
(traffic on scheduled services)

	2010	2011
Kilometres flown (million)	109	109
Passengers carried ('000)	5,085	5,151
Passenger-km (million)	18,178	17,926
Total ton-km (million)	2,687	2,688

Source: UN, *Statistical Yearbook*.

Passengers carried ('000): 5,382 in 2012; 5,339 in 2013 (Source: World Bank, World Development Indicators database).

Tourism

TOURIST ARRIVALS
('000)*

Country of residence	2011	2012	2013†
Canada	64.4	62.0	65.3
France	269.5	263.5	292.3
Germany	171.0	158.5	159.8
Italy	113.3	126.2	127.7
Netherlands	58.7	62.0	52.0
Poland	60.4	58.9	67.3
Russia	353.4	380.8	405.0
Spain	51.0	50.1	47.9
Ukraine	106.8	109.2	108.0
United Kingdom	168.0	165.1	173.3
USA	581.0	583.6	597.2
Total (incl. others)	2,820.2	2,885.8	2,961.7

* Excluding arrivals of Israeli nationals residing abroad.
† Provisional.

Tourism receipts (US$ million, excl. passenger transport): 5,304 in 2011; 5,446 in 2012; 5,666 in 2013 (Source: World Tourism Organization).

Communications Media

	2011	2012	2013
Telephones ('000 main lines in use)	3,500	3,594	3,465
Mobile cellular telephones ('000 subscribers)	9,200	9,225	9,500
Broadband subscribers ('000) . .	1,879	1,937	1,985

Source: International Telecommunication Union.

Education

(2013/14 unless otherwise indicated, provisional figures)

	Schools	Pupils	Teachers
Hebrew			
Kindergarten	n.a.	399,543*	18,526
Primary schools	2,049	698,415	60,670
Special needs	211	11,282	n.a.
Intermediate schools†	502	183,414	24,489
Secondary schools	1,493	493,120	65,741
Vocational schools‡ . . .	112	23,485	n.a.
Teacher training colleges . . .	56‡	33,893‡	5,359§
Arab			
Kindergarten	n.a.	96,162*	3,960
Primary schools	596	249,222	20,043
Special needs	69	3,490	n.a.
Intermediate schools†	138	70,463	5,195
Secondary schools	394	178,151	16,379
Vocational schools‡ . . .	24	4,376	n.a.
Teacher training colleges . . .	4‡	2,827‡	491§

* 2012/13 provisional data.
† 2007/08 provisional data.
‡ 2008/09 provisional data.
§ 2006/07 data.

Pupil-teacher ratio (primary education, UNESCO estimate): 12.5 in 2010/11 (Source: UNESCO Institute for Statistics).

Adult literacy rate (UNESCO estimates): 97.8% (males 98.7%; females 96.8%) in 2011 (Source: UNESCO Institute for Statistics).

Directory

The Government

HEAD OF STATE

President: REUVEN RIVLIN (took office 28 July 2014).

THE CABINET
(April 2015)

A coalition of Likud, Israel Beytenu and Jewish Home.

Prime Minister, Minister of Public Diplomacy and Minister of Communications: BINYAMIN NETANYAHU (Likud).

Minister of Public Security: YITZHAK AHARONOVITCH (Israel Beytenu).

Minister for Senior Citizens: (vacant).

Minister of Strategic Affairs, Minister of Intelligence and Minister Responsible for International Relations: YUVAL STEINITZ (Likud).

Minister of Defence: MOSHE YA'ALON (Likud).

Minister of Interior: GILAD ERDAN (Likud).

Minister of Finance: (vacant).

Minister of Foreign Affairs: AVIGDOR LIEBERMAN (Israel Beytenu).

Minister of Health: (vacant).

Minister of the Economy, Minister of Religious Services and Minister for Jerusalem and Diaspora Affairs: NAFTALI BENNETT (Jewish Home).

Minister of Immigration and Absorption: SOFA LANDVER (Israel Beytenu).

Minister of National Infrastructure, Energy and Water, Minister of Regional Co-operation and Minister for the Development of the Negev and Galilee: SILVAN SHALOM (Likud).

Minister of Welfare and Social Services: (vacant).

Minister of Environmental Protection: (vacant).

Minister of Justice: (vacant).

Minister of Housing and Construction: URI YEHUDA ARIEL (Jewish Home).

Minister of Transport and Road Safety: YISRAEL KATZ (Likud).

Minister of Agriculture and Rural Development: YAIR SHAMIR (Israel Beytenu).

Minister of Tourism: UZI LANDAU (Israel Beytenu).

Minister of Education: (vacant).

Minister of Science, Technology and Space: (vacant).

Minister of Culture and Sport: LIMOR LIVNAT (Likud).

Note: The Prime Minister automatically assumes responsibility for any portfolio which becomes vacant, until a permanent or acting minister is appointed.

MINISTRIES

Office of the President: 3 Hanassi St, Jerusalem 92188; tel. 2-6707211; fax 2-5887225; e-mail public@president.gov.il; internet www.president.gov.il.

Office of the Prime Minister: POB 187, 3 Kaplan St, Kiryat Ben-Gurion, Jerusalem 91950; tel. 3-6109898; fax 2-5605000; e-mail pm_eng@pmo.gov.il; internet www.pmo.gov.il.

Ministry of Agriculture and Rural Development: POB 50200, Agricultural Centre, Beit Dagan 50250; tel. 3-9485555; fax 3-9485858; e-mail bellay@moag.gov.il; internet www.moag.gov.il.

Ministry of Communications: 23 Jaffa St, Jerusalem 91999; tel. 2-6706301; fax 2-6240029; e-mail dovrut@moc.gov.il; internet www.moc.gov.il.

Ministry of Culture and Sport: 14 HaMasger St, Tel-Aviv 61575; tel. 3-6367223; fax 3-6883430; e-mail ministerts@most.gov.il; internet www.mcs.gov.il.

Ministry of Defence: Kirya, Tel-Aviv 64734; tel. 3-6975540; fax 3-6976711; e-mail pniot@mod.gov.il; internet www.mod.gov.il.

Ministry for the Development of the Negev and Galilee: 8 Shaul Hamelech Blvd, Tel-Aviv 64733; tel. 3-6060700; fax 3-6958414; e-mail hilap@pmo.gov.il; internet www.vpmo.gov.il.

Ministry of Education: POB 292, 34 Shivtei Israel St, Jerusalem 91911; tel. 2-5602222; fax 2-5602223; e-mail info@education.gov.il; internet www.education.gov.il.

Ministry of the Economy: 5 Bank of Israel St, Jerusalem 91009; tel. 2-6662252; fax 2-6662908; internet www.moit.gov.il.

Ministry of Environmental Protection: POB 34033, 5 Kanfei Nesharim St, Givat Shaul, Jerusalem 95464; tel. 2-6495802; fax 2-6495892; e-mail pniot@environment.gov.il; internet www.environment.gov.il.

Ministry of Finance: POB 13195, 1 Kaplan St, Kiryat Ben-Gurion, Jerusalem 91030; tel. 2-5317215; fax 2-5695347; e-mail dover@mof.gov.il; internet www.mof.gov.il.

Ministry of Foreign Affairs: 9 Yitzhak Rabin Blvd, Kiryat Ben-Gurion, Jerusalem 91950; tel. 2-5303111; fax 2-5303367; e-mail pniot@mfa.gov.il; internet www.mfa.gov.il.

Ministry of Health: POB 1176, 2 Ben-Tabai St, Jerusalem 91010; tel. 2-5081222; fax 2-6787982; e-mail pniot@moh.health.gov.il; internet www.health.gov.il.

Ministry of Housing and Construction: POB 18110, 3 Clermont Ganneau St, Kiryat Hamemshala (East), Jerusalem 91180; tel. 2-5847654; fax 2-5824111; e-mail sar@moch.gov.il; internet www.moch.gov.il.

Ministry of Immigration and Absorption: 6 Ester Hamalka St, Tel-Aviv; tel. 3-5209127; fax 3-5209161; e-mail sar@moia.gov.il; internet www.moia.gov.il.

Ministry of Intelligence: Jerusalem; tel. 2-6705360; fax 2-6703377.

Ministry of Interior: POB 6158, Kiryat Ben-Gurion, Jerusalem 91061; tel. 2-6701400; fax 2-566376; e-mail meda@moin.gov.il; internet www.moin.gov.il.

Ministry of Jerusalem and Diaspora Affairs: Jerusalem; tel. 2-6587100; fax 2-6587118; e-mail yaels@it.pmo.gov.il.

Ministry of Justice: POB 49029, 29 Salahadin St, Jerusalem 91010; tel. 2-6466527; fax 2-6285438; e-mail pniot@justice.gov.il; internet www.justice.gov.il.

Ministry of National Infrastructure, Energy and Water: POB 36148, 216 Yaffo St, Jerusalem 91360; tel. 2-5006780; fax 4-8660189; e-mail pniot@energy.gov.il; internet www.energy.gov.il.

Ministry of Public Security: POB 18182, Bldg 3, Kiryat Hamemshala (East), Jerusalem 91181; tel. 2-5418083; fax 2-5428500; e-mail sar@mops.gov.il; internet www.mops.gov.il.

Ministry of Regional Co-operation: Jerusalem.

Ministry of Religious Services: POB 13059, 7 Kanfei Nesharim St, Jerusalem 95464; tel. 2-5311101; fax 2-5311308; e-mail keren@dat.gov.il; internet www.dat.gov.il.

Ministry of Science, Technology and Space: POB 49100, Kiryat Hamemshala, Hamizrachit, Bldg 3, Jerusalem 91490; tel. 2-5411101; fax 2-5811613; e-mail minister@most.gov.il; internet www.most.gov.il.

Ministry of Senior Citizens: 3 Kaplan St, Kiryat Ben-Gurion, Jerusalem 91919; tel. 02-6547020; fax 02-6547035; internet vatikim.gov.il.

Ministry of Social Affairs and Social Services: POB 915, 2 Kaplan St, Kiryat Ben-Gurion, Jerusalem 91008; tel. 2-6752523; fax 2-5666385; e-mail sar@molsa.gov.il; internet www.molsa.gov.il.

Ministry of Strategic Affairs: Jerusalem; tel. 2-6773750; fax 2-6517299.

Ministry of Tourism: POB 1018, 5 Bank of Israel St, Jerusalem 91009; tel. 2-6664331; fax 2-6514629; e-mail sar@tourism.gov.il; internet www.tourism.gov.il.

Ministry of Transport and Road Safety: POB 867, Government Complex, 5 Bank of Israel St, Jerusalem 91008; tel. 2-6663004; fax 2-6663005; e-mail sar@mot.gov.il; internet www.mot.gov.il.

GOVERNMENT AGENCY

The Jewish Agency for Israel

POB 92, 48 King George St, Jerusalem 91000; tel. 2-6202222; fax 2-6202303; e-mail pniyottzibor@jafi.org; internet www.jewishagency.org.

f. 1929; reconstituted in 1971 as a partnership between the World Zionist Organization and the fund-raising bodies United Israel Appeal, Inc (USA) and Keren Hayesod.

Organization: The governing bodies are: the Assembly, which determines basic policy; the Board of Governors, which sets policy for the Agency between Assembly meetings; and the Executive, responsible for the day-to-day running of the Agency.

Chairman of Executive: NATAN SHARANSKY.

Chairman of Board of Governors: CHARLES HOROWITZ RATNER.

Director-General: ALAN HOFFMANN.

CEO and President of Jewish Agency International Development: MISHA GALPERIN.

Functions: According to the Agreement of 1971, the Jewish Agency undertakes the immigration and absorption of immigrants in Israel, including: absorption in agricultural settlement and immigrant housing; social welfare and health services in connection with immigrants; education, youth care and training; and neighbourhood rehabilitation through project renewal.

Legislature

Knesset: Kiryat Ben-Gurion, Jerusalem 91950; tel. 2-6753809; fax 2-6753665; e-mail mshenkar@knesset.gov.il; internet www.knesset .gov.il.

Speaker: YULI-YOEL EDELSTEIN.

General Election, 17 March 2015

Party	Valid votes cast	% of valid votes	Seats
Likud	985,408	23.40	30
Zionist Union . . .	786,313	18.67	24
Joint List	446,583	10.61	13
Yesh Atid	371,602	8.82	11
Kulanu	315,360	7.49	10
Jewish Home . . .	283,910	6.74	8
Shas	241,613	5.74	7
Israel Beytenu . . .	214,906	5.10	6
United Torah Judaism .	210,143	4.99	6
Meretz	165,529	3.93	5
Others	185,517	4.50	0
Total	**4,210,884***	**100.00**	**120**

* Excluding 43,854 invalid votes.

Election Commission

Central Elections Committee: Knesset, Kiryat Ben-Gurion, Jerusalem 91950; tel. 2-6753407; fax 2-6753737; e-mail doverd@knesset .gov.il; internet www.bechirot.gov.il; independent; Supreme Court elects a Justice as Chair; each parliamentary group nominates representatives to the Cttee in proportion to the group's level of representation in the Knesset; Chair. Justice SALIM JOUBRAN; Dir-Gen. ORLY ADAS.

Political Organizations

Agudat Israel (Union of Israel): POB 513, Jerusalem; tel. 2-5385251; fax 2-5385145; f. 1912; mainly Ashkenazi ultra-Orthodox Jews; stands for introduction of laws and institutions based on Jewish religious law (the Torah); contested 2015 legislative elections as part of the United Torah Judaism list (with Degel Hatorah).

Arab Movement for Renewal (Tnua'a Aravit le'Hitkadshut—Ta'al): Jerusalem; tel. 2-6753333; fax 2-6753927; e-mail atibi@ knesset.gov.il; f. 1996 following split from Balad; contested March 2015 legislative elections as part of the Joint List; Leader Dr AHMAD TIBI.

Balad (National Democratic Assembly): POB 2248, Nazareth Industrial Zone, Nazareth 16000; tel. 4-6455070; fax 4-6463457; e-mail balad@zahav.net.il; f. 1999; united Arab party; contested 2015 legislative elections as part of the Joint List; Leader Dr JAMAL ZAHALKA.

Communist Party of Israel (Miflagah Kommonistit Yisraelit—Maki): POB 26205, 5 Hess St, Tel-Aviv 61261; tel. 3-6293944; fax 3-6297263; e-mail info@maki.org.il; internet www.maki.org.il; f. 1948; Jewish-Arab party descended from the Socialist Workers' Party of Palestine (f. 1919); renamed Communist Party of Palestine 1921, Jewish and Arab sections split 1945, reunited as Communist Party of Israel (Maki) 1948; further split 1965: pro-Soviet predominantly Arab anti-Zionist group formed New Communist Party of Israel (Rakah) 1965, while predominantly Jewish bloc retained name Maki; Rakah joined with other leftist orgs as Hadash 1977; name changed to Maki 1989, as the dominant component of Hadash (q.v.); Gen. Sec. MUHAMMAD NAFA'H.

Degel Hatorah (Flag of the Torah): 103 Rehov Beit Vegan, Jerusalem; tel. 2-6498106; fax 2-6418967; f. 1988 by Lithuanian Jews as breakaway faction from Agudat Israel; mainly Ashkenazi ultra-Orthodox (Haredi) Jews; contested 2015 legislative elections as part of the United Torah Judaism list (with Agudat Israel).

Hadash (Hachazit Hademokratit Leshalom Uleshivyon—Democratic Front for Peace and Equality): POB 26205, Tel-Aviv 61261; tel. 3-6292512; fax 3-6297263; e-mail info@hadash.org.il; internet hadash.org.il; f. 1977 by merger of the New Communist Party of Israel (Rakah) with other leftist groups; party list, the principal

component of which is the Communist Party of Israel (q.v.); Jewish-Arab membership; aims for a socialist system in Israel and a lasting peace between Israel, Arab countries and the Palestinian Arab people; favours full implementation of UN Security Council Resolutions 242 and 338, Israeli withdrawal from all Arab territories occupied since 1967, formation of a Palestinian Arab state in the West Bank and Gaza Strip (with East Jerusalem as its capital), recognition of national rights of State of Israel and Palestinian people, democratic rights and defence of working-class interests, and demands an end to discrimination against Arab minority in Israel and against oriental Jewish communities; contested 2015 legislative elections as part of the Joint List; Chair. MUHAMMAD BARAKEH.

Hatnua (The Movement): 8 HaArb'a St, Tel-Aviv; tel. 3-6333000; internet www.hatnua.org.il; f. 2012; centrist; supports revival of peace talks with the Palestinian (National) Authority based on a two-state solution, increase to the minimum wage, environmental sustainability, extension of national service to all citizens; contested 2015 legislative elections as part of the Zionist Union; Leader TZIPI LIVNI.

Israel Beytenu (Israel Is Our Home/Nash dom Izrail): 78 Yirmiyahu St, Jerusalem 94467; tel. 2-5012999; fax 2-5377188; e-mail gdv7191@hotmail.com; internet www.beytenu.org.il; f. 1999; right-wing immigrant party; joined Nat. Union in 2000, but left to contest March 2006 and Feb. 2009 legislative elections alone; contested 2013 elections on joint list with Likud, but contested March 2015 legislative elections as an individual party; seeks resolution of the Israeli–Palestinian conflict through the exchange of territory and population with the Palestinians, incl. the transfer of Arab Israelis to territory under Palestinian control; membership largely drawn from fmr USSR; 18,000 mems (2006); Leader AVIGDOR LIEBERMAN.

Israel Labour Party (Mifleget HaAvoda HaYisraelit): POB 62033, Tel-Aviv 61620; tel. 3-6899444; fax 3-6899420; e-mail mifkad@ havoda.org.il; internet www.havoda.org.il; f. 1968 as a merger of the three Labour groups, Mapai, Rafi and Achdut Ha'avoda; Am Ehad (One Nation) merged with Labour in 2004; a Zionist democratic socialist party; contested 2015 legislative elections as part of the Zionist Union; Chair. ISSAC HERZOG; Sec.-Gen. YECHIEL BAR.

Jewish Home (HaBayit HaYehudi): Jerusalem; internet baityehudi.org.il; f. 2008 by merger of Nat. Religious Party (NRP; f. 1956), Moledet and Tekuma; however, Moledet and some Tekuma mems subsequently withdrew from new party; right-wing nationalist, Zionist; opposes further Israeli withdrawals from the West Bank and the creation of a Palestinian state; favours strengthening of the state and system of religious education; Leader NAFTALI BENNETT.

Joint List (al-Kaama al-Mushtraka): f. 2015 as an alliance of parties representing Israeli Arab citizens; comprised Balad, Hadash, Arab Movement for Renewal and United Arab List; Leader AYMAN ODEH.

Kadima (Forward): Petach Tikva, Tel-Aviv; tel. 3-9788000; fax 3-9788115; e-mail dovrutkadima@gmail.com; internet www.kadima .org.il; f. 2005; liberal party formed as a breakaway faction from Likud by fmr party Chairman Ariel Sharon; aims to pursue a peace agreement with the Palestinians in accordance with the 'roadmap' peace plan, and to establish Israel's permanent borders, if necessary unilaterally; seeks to combat economic and social problems; Leader SHAUL MOFAZ.

Kulanu (All of Us): ; tel. 8-6117001; internet www.kulanu-party.co .il; f. 2014; centre-right; Leader MOSHE KAHLON.

Likud (Consolidation): 38 Rehov King George, Tel-Aviv 61231; tel. 2-2754231; fax 2-5605000; internet www.likud.org.il; f. Sept. 1973; fmrly a parliamentary bloc of Herut (f. 1948), the Liberal Party of Israel (f. 1961), Laam (For the Nation—f. 1976), Ahdut, Tami (f. 1981; joined Likud in June 1987) and an ind. faction led by Itzhak Modai (f. 1990), which formed the nucleus of a new Party for the Advancement of the Zionist Idea; Herut and the Liberal Party formally merged in Aug. 1988 to form the Likud-Nat. Liberal Movement; Israel B'Aliyah merged with Likud in 2003; contested Feb. 2009 legislative elections on joint list with Ahi (right-wing nationalist; Leader EFRAIM EITAM); contested 2013 elections on joint list with Israel Beytenu; aims: territorial integrity; absorption of newcomers; a social order based on freedom and justice, elimination of poverty and want; economic devt and environmental reforms to improve living standards; Chair. BINYAMIN NETANYAHU.

Meimad: POB 53139, 19 Yad Harutzim St, Jerusalem 91533; tel. 2-6725134; fax 2-6725051; f. 1988; moderate democratic Jewish party; ended alliance with Israel Labour Party and joined list with Green Movement (HaTnuah Hayeruka—f. 2008) prior to Feb. 2009 legislative elections, at which it failed to achieve representation in the Knesset; Leader Rabbi MICHAEL MELCHIOR.

Meretz (Social Democratic Party of Israel): Beit Amot Mishpat, 8th Shaul Hamelech Blvd, Tel-Aviv 64733; tel. 3-6098998; fax 3-6961728; e-mail info@meretz.org.il; internet www.meretz.org.il; f. 2003 as Yahad (Together—Social Democratic Israel) from a merger of Meretz (f. 1992; an alliance of Ratz, Shinui and the United Workers' Party) and Shahar (f. 2002; a breakaway faction of the Israel Labour Party); name changed to above in 2005; Jewish-Arab social democratic party; stands for: civil rights; welfarism; Palestinian self-determination and a return to the 1967 borders, with minor adjustments; a divided Jerusalem, but no right of return for Palestinian refugees to Israel; separation of religion from the state; Chair. ZAHAVA GAL-ON.

Moledet (Homeland): 14 Yehuda Halevi St, Tel-Aviv; tel. 3-654580; e-mail moledet@moledet.org.il; internet www.m-moledet.org.il; f. 1988; right-wing nationalist party; aims include the expulsion ('transfer') of Palestinians living in the West Bank and Gaza Strip; united with Tehiya—Zionist Revival Movement in June 1994 as the Moledet—the Eretz Israel Faithful and the Tehiya; contested Feb. 2009 legislative elections as part of the Nat. Union; Chair. URI BANK.

National Union (Haichud Haleumi): e-mail info@leumi.org.il; f. 1999 as right-wing coalition comprising Herut, Moledet and Tekuma parties; contested March 2006 legislative elections on joint list with Nat. Religious Party, but stood alone (comprising Moledet, Hatikva, Eretz Yisrael Shelanu and fmr Tekuma mems) in Feb. 2009 elections; believes in a 'Greater Israel'; opposed to further withdrawals from the Occupied Territories; stated aim of joint list was the creation of an Israeli society based on the spiritual and social values of Judaism and the retention of an undivided Israel; Leader YAAKOV DOV KATZ.

Pensioners' Party (Gimla'ey Yisrael LaKneset—Gil) (Pensioners of Israel to the Knesset—Age): 100 Ha' Hashmonaim, Tel-Aviv; tel. 3-5611900; fax 3-5611909; e-mail info@gimlaim.org.il; internet www .gimlaim.org.il; stands for pensioners' rights; failed to achieve representation in the Knesset at 2013 legislative elections; Leader RAFI EITAN.

Shas (Sephardic Torah Guardians): POB 34263, Jerusalem 91341; tel. 2-5008888; fax 2-5380226; e-mail p@shas.org.il; internet shas.org .il; f. 1984 by splinter groups from Agudat Israel; ultra-Orthodox Sephardic party; Chair. ARYEH DERI.

United Arab List (Reshima Aravit Me'uchedet—Ra'am): Jerusalem; tel. 9-7997088; fax 9-7996295; e-mail media.amc@gmail.com; internet www.a-m-c.org; f. 1996 by merger of the Arab Democratic Party and individuals from the Islamic Movement and Nat. Unity Front (left-wing Arab parties); supports establishment of a Palestinian state, with East Jerusalem as its capital, and equality for all Israeli citizens; contested 2015 legislative elections as part of the Joint List; Chair. AHMAD TIBI.

United Torah Judaism (Yahadut Hatorah): f. prior to 1992 election; electoral list of four minor ultra-Orthodox parties (Moria, Degel Hatorah, Poale Agudat Israel and Agudat Israel) established to overcome the increase in election threshold from 1% to 1.5% and to seek to counter the rising influence of the secular Russian vote; contested 2003 election composed of Degel Hatorah and Agudat Israel, into which constituent parties it split in early 2005; two parties reunited in late 2005 and contested March 2006 and Feb. 2009 legislative elections together; represents Ashkenazi ultra-Orthodox Jews and advocates the application of religious precepts in all areas of life and government; Chair., Parliamentary Group ISRAEL EICHLER.

Yesh Atid (There's a Future): Tel-Aviv; tel. 3-7715050; fax 3-7715041; e-mail contact@yeshatid.org.il; internet en.yeshatid.org .il; f. 2012; proposes reduction in the size of the Cabinet, reform of the education system, expansion of mandatory national service to include all citizens, increase in housing provision; Founder and Leader YAIR LAPID.

Zionist Union (HaMahane HaZioni): 53 Yigal Alon St, Tel-Aviv 6706206; fax 3-7283616; e-mail mifkad@havoda.org.il; internet hamahanehazioni.co.il; f. 2014; centre-left electoral list comprising Hatnua and the Israel Labour Party.

Diplomatic Representation

EMBASSIES IN ISRAEL

Albania: 54/26 Pinkas St, Tel-Aviv 62261; tel. 3-5465866; fax 3-5444545; e-mail embassy.telaviv@mfa.gov.al; internet www .ambasadat.gov.al/israel; Chargé d'affaires a.i. ELTJON VERLENI.

Angola: 14 Simtat Beit Hashoeva St, Tel-Aviv; tel. 3-6912093; fax 3-6912094; e-mail embangl@zahav.net.il; internet www .angolaembassy.org.il; Ambassador FELICIANO ANTÓNIO DOS SANTOS.

Argentina: 85 Medinat Hayehudim St, 3rd Floor, Herzliya Pituach 46120; tel. 9-9702744; fax 9-9702748; e-mail embarg@netvision.net .il; Ambassador CARLOS FAUSTINO GARCÍA.

Australia: POB 29108, Discount Bank Tower, 28th Floor, 23 Yehuda Halevi St, Tel-Aviv 65136; tel. 3-6935000; fax 3-6935002; e-mail telaviv.embassy@dfat.org.au; internet www.israel.embassy.gov.au; Ambassador DEVANAND NOEL (DAVE) SHARMA.

Austria: Sason Hogi Tower, 12 Abba Hillel St, 4th Floor, Ramat-Gan 52506; tel. 3-6120924; fax 3-7510716; e-mail tel-aviv-ob@bmeia.gv .at; internet www.aussenministerium.at/telaviv; Ambassador Dr FRANZ JOSEF KUGLITSCH.

Belarus: POB 11129, 3 Reines St, Tel-Aviv 64381; tel. 3-5231069; fax 3-5231273; e-mail israel@mfa.gov.by; internet www.israel.mfa.gov .by; Ambassador VLADIMIR SKVORTSOV.

Belgium: 12 Abba Hillel St, 15th Floor, Ramat-Gan 52506; tel. 3-6138130; fax 3-6138160; e-mail telaviv@diplobel.fed.be; internet www.diplomatie.be/telaviv; Ambassador JOHN CORNET D'ELZIUS.

Bosnia and Herzegovina: Yachin Bldg, 10th Floor, 2 Kaplan St, Tel-Aviv; tel. 3-6124499; fax 3-6124488; e-mail embtelaviv@bezeqint .net; Ambassador BRANKO KESIC.

Brazil: 23 Yehuda Halevi St, 30th Floor, Tel-Aviv 65136; tel. 3-7971500; fax 3-6916060; e-mail brasemb.telaviv@itamaraty.gov.br; internet telaviv.itamaraty.gov.br; Ambassador HENRIQUE DA SILVEIRA SARDINHA PINTO.

Bulgaria: 21 Leonardo da Vinci St, Tel-Aviv 64733; tel. 3-6961379; fax 3-6961430; e-mail embassy.telaviv@mfa.bg; internet www.mfa .bg/en/118; Ambassador DIMITAR MIHAILOV.

Cameroon: 28 Moshe Sharet St, Ramat-Gan 52425; tel. 3-5298401; fax 3-6370583; e-mail activ50@yahoo.fr; Ambassador HENRI ETOUNDI ESSOMBA.

Canada: POB 9442, 3/5 Nirim St, Tel-Aviv 67060; tel. 3-6363300; fax 3-6363380; e-mail taviv@international.gc.ca; internet www .canadainternational.gc.ca/israel; Ambassador VIVIAN BERCOVICI.

Chile: 34 Habarzel St, Bldg B, Floor 1, Ramat Hahayal, Tel-Aviv 69710; tel. 3-5102751; fax 3-5100102; e-mail echileil@inter.net.il; internet chileabroad.gov.cl/israel; Ambassador JORGE MONTERO FIGUEROA.

China, People's Republic: POB 6067, 222 Ben Yehuda St, Tel-Aviv 61060; tel. 3-5442638; fax 3-5467251; e-mail chinaemb_il@mfa.gov .cn; internet il.china-embassy.org; Ambassador ZHAN YONGXIN.

Colombia: Hogi Sason Bldg, 8th Floor, Abba Hillel St, Ramat-Gan 12; tel. 3-6953384; fax 3-6957847; e-mail emcolis@netvision.net.il; Ambassador Dr FERNANDO ALZATE DONOSO.

Congo, Democratic Republic: 1 Rachel St, 2nd Floor, Tel-Aviv 64584; tel. 3-5239860; fax 3-5292623; e-mail ambardc_il@yahoo.fr; Chargé d'affaires a.i. MARCEL MAKENGO MA KIMBOKO.

Congo, Republic: POB 12504, 9 Maskit St, Herzliya Pituach 46120; tel. 9-9577130; fax 9-9577216; e-mail guy_itoua@yahoo.fr; Chargé d'affaires a.i. JEAN MARIE NGAKALA.

Costa Rica: Paz Tower, 5-7 Shoham St, 6th Floor, Ramat-Gan 52521; tel. 3-6135061; fax 3-6134779; e-mail embcr-il@rree.go.cr; Chargé d'affaires a.i. FANNY PATRICIA VELÁSQUEZ GONZÁLEZ.

Côte d'Ivoire: South Africa Bldg, 12 Menachim Begin St, Ramat-Gan 52521; tel. 3-6126677; fax 3-6126688; e-mail ambacita@ netvision.net.il; Ambassador JEAN-BAPTISTE GOMIS.

Croatia: 2 Weizman St, Migdal Amot, Tel-Aviv 64239; tel. 3-6403000; fax 3-6438503; e-mail croemb.israel@mvep.hr; Ambassador PJER SIMUNOVIĆ.

Cyprus: Top Tower, 14th Floor, Dizengoff Centre, 50 Dizengoff St, Tel-Aviv 64322; tel. 3-9273000; fax 3-6290535; e-mail ambassador@ cyprusembassytelaviv.com; internet www.mfa.gov.cy/ embassytelaviv; Ambassador DIMITRIS HATZIARGYROU.

Czech Republic: POB 16361, 23 Zeitlin St, Tel-Aviv; tel. 3-6918282; fax 3-6918286; e-mail telaviv@embassy.mzv.cz; internet www.mzv .cz/telaviv; Ambassador IVO SCHWARZ.

Denmark: POB 21080, Museum Tower, 11th Floor, 4 Berkowitz St, Tel-Aviv 61210; tel. 3-6085850; fax 3-6085851; e-mail tlvamb@um .dk; internet israel.um.dk; Ambassador JESPER VAHR.

Dominican Republic: Beit Ackerstein, 3rd Floor, 103 Medinat Hayehudim St, Herzliya Pitauch 46766; tel. 9-9515529; fax 9-9515528; e-mail israel@embajadadominicana.net; Ambassador ALEXANDER DE LA ROSA.

Ecuador: POB 34002, Asia House, 5th Floor, 4 Weizman St, Tel-Aviv 64239; tel. 3-6958764; fax 3-6913604; e-mail eecuisrael@ mmrree.gov.ec; Ambassador GUILLERMO BASSANTE RAMÍREZ.

Egypt: 54 Basel St, Tel-Aviv 62744; tel. 3-5464151; fax 3-5441615; e-mail egypem.ta@zahav.net.il; internet www.mfa.gov.eg/english/ embassies/egyptian_embassy_telaviv/pages/default.aspx; Ambassador ATEF SALEM EL-AHL.

El Salvador: 6 Hamada St, 4th Floor, Herzliya Pituach 46733; tel. 9-9556237; fax 9-9556603; e-mail embassy@elsalvador.org.il; internet www.el-salvador.org.il; Ambassador SUZANA GUN DE HASENSON.

Eritrea: 1 Twin Towers, 33 Jabotinsky St, 11th Floor, Ramat-Gan 52511; tel. 3-6120039; fax 3-5750133; Ambassador TESFAMARIAM TEKESTE.

Estonia: POB 7166, 24th Floor, Menachem Begin Rd 125, 44 Kaplan St, HaYovel Tower, Tel-Aviv 61071; tel. 3-7103910; fax 3-7103919;

e-mail embassy.telaviv@mfa.ee; internet www.telaviv.vm.ee; Ambassador MALLE TALVET-MUSTONEN.

Ethiopia: Bldg B, Floor 8B, 48 Darech Menachem Begin St, Tel-Aviv 66184; tel. 3-6397831; fax 3-6397837; e-mail info@ethioemb.org.il; internet www.ethioemb.org.il; Ambassador HELAWE YOSEF.

Finland: POB 39666, Canion Ramat Aviv, 9th Floor, 40 Einstein St, Tel-Aviv 61396; tel. 3-7456600; fax 3-7440314; e-mail sanomat.tel@formin.fi; internet www.finland.org.il; Ambassador LEENA-KAISA MIKKOLA.

France: 112 Tayelet Herbert Samuel, Tel-Aviv 63572; tel. 3-5208300; fax 3-5208340; e-mail diplomatie@ambafrance-il.org; internet www.ambafrance-il.org; Ambassador PATRICK MAISONNAVE.

Georgia: 3 Daniel Frisch St, Tel-Aviv 64731; tel. 3-6093206; fax 3-6093205; e-mail israel.emb@mfa.gov.ge; internet israel.mfa.gov.ge; Ambassador PAATA KALANDADZE.

Germany: POB 16038, 3 Daniel Frisch St, 19th Floor, Tel-Aviv 64731; tel. 3-6931313; fax 3-6969217; e-mail info@tel-aviv.diplo.de; internet www.tel-aviv.diplo.de; Ambassador ANDREAS MICHAELIS.

Ghana: 12 Abba Hillel St, 7th Floor, Ramat-Gan 52506; tel. 3-5766000; fax 3-7520827; e-mail chancery@ghanaemb.co.il; Ambassador ERNEST SOWATEY LOMOTEY.

Greece: POB 64731, 3 Daniel Frisch St, Tel-Aviv; tel. 3-6953060; fax 3-6951329; e-mail gremb.tlv@mfa.gr; internet www.mfa.gr/telaviv; Ambassador SPYRIDON LAMPRIDIS.

Guatemala: Beit Ackerstein, 4th Floor, 103 Medinat Hayehudim St, Herzliya Pituach 46766; tel. 9-9568707; fax 9-9518506; e-mail embguate@netvision.net.il; Ambassador ALFREDO VASQUEZ RIVERA.

Holy See: 1 Netiv Hamazalot, Old Jaffa 68037; tel. 2-6835658; fax 2-6835659; e-mail vatge@netvision.net.il; Apostolic Nuncio Most Rev. GIUSEPPE LAZZAROTTO (Titular Archbishop of Numana).

Honduras: Aharon Karon St, 3 Rishon le Zion 75262; tel. 3-9642092; fax 9-9577457; e-mail honduras@netvision.net.il; Ambassador JOSÉ ISAIAS BARAHONA HERRERA.

Hungary: POB 21095, 18 Pinkas St, Tel-Aviv 62661; tel. 3-5466985; fax 3-5467018; e-mail mission.tlv@kum.hu; internet www.mfa.gov.hu/emb/telaviv; Ambassador ANDOR NAGY.

India: POB 3368, 140 Hayarkon St, Tel-Aviv 61033; tel. 3-5291999; fax 3-5291953; e-mail indemtel@indembassy.co.il; internet www.indembassy.co.il; Ambassador JAIDEEP SARKAR.

Ireland: The Tower, 17th Floor, 3 Daniel Frisch St, Tel-Aviv 64731; tel. 3-6964166; fax 3-6964160; e-mail telavivembassy@dfa.ie; internet www.embassyofireland.co.il; Ambassador EAMONN CHRISTOPHER MCKEE.

Italy: Trade Tower, 25 Hamered St, Tel-Aviv 68125; tel. 3-5104004; fax 3-5100235; e-mail info.telaviv@esteri.it; internet www.ambtelaviv.esteri.it; Ambassador FRANCESCO MARIA TALÒ.

Japan: Museum Tower, 19th and 20th Floors, 4 Berkowitz St, Tel-Aviv 64238; tel. 3-6957292; fax 3-6910516; e-mail info@tl.mofa.go.jp; internet www.israel.emb-japan.go.jp; Ambassador SHIGEO MATSUTOMI.

Jordan: 14 Abba Hillel, Ramat-Gan 52506; tel. 3-7517722; fax 3-7517712; Ambassador WALID OBAIDAT.

Kazakhstan: 52A Hayarkon St, Tel-Aviv 63432; tel. 3-5163411; fax 3-5163437; e-mail tel-aviv@mfa.kz; internet www.kazakhemb.org.il; Ambassador DOULAT KUANYSHEV.

Kenya: 15 Aba Hillel Silver St, Ramat-Gan 52136; tel. 3-5754633; fax 3-5754788; e-mail info@kenyaembassytlv.org; Ambassador Lt-Gen. AUGUSTIONO NJOROGE.

Korea, Republic: 4 Hasadna'ot St, 3rd Floor, Herzliya Pituach 46278; tel. 9-9510318; fax 9-9569853; e-mail israel@mofat.go.kr; internet isr.mofat.go.kr; Ambassador LEE GUN-TAE.

Latvia: Amot Investments Tower, 15th Floor, 2 Weizman St, Tel-Aviv 64239; tel. 3-7775800; fax 3-6953101; e-mail embassy.israel@mfa.gov.lv; internet www.mfa.gov.lv/en/israel/; Ambassador VILCĀNS ANDRIS.

Lithuania: Amot Mishpat Bldg, 8 Shaul Ha Meleh, Tel-Aviv 64733; tel. 3-6958685; fax 3-6958691; e-mail amb.il@urm.lt; internet il.mfa.lt; Ambassador EDMINAS BAGDONAS.

Macedonia, former Yugoslav republic: Paz Tower, 9th Floor, 5 Shoham St, Ramat-Gan 52136; tel. 3-7154900; fax 3-6124789; e-mail telaviv@mfa.gov.mk; internet www.missions.gov.mk/telaviv; Ambassador PAJO AVIROVIKJ.

Mexico: Trade Tower, 5th Floor, 25 Hamered St, Tel-Aviv 68125; tel. 3-5163938; fax 3-5163711; e-mail communication1@embamex.org.il; internet embamex.sre.gob.mx/israel; Ambassador FEDERICO SALAS.

Moldova: 38 Rembrandt St, Tel-Aviv 64045; tel. 3-5231000; fax 3-5233000; e-mail moldova@barak.net.il; internet www.israel.mfa.md; Ambassador ANATOL VANGHELI.

Myanmar: Textile Centre, 12th Floor, 2 Kaufman St, Tel-Aviv 68012; tel. 3-5170760; fax 3-5163512; e-mail myanmar@zahav.net.il; Ambassador MYO AYE.

Nepal: Textile Centre, 7th Floor, 2 Kaufman St, Tel-Aviv 68012; tel. 3-5100111; fax 3-5167965; e-mail nepal.embassy@012.net.il; internet www.nepalembassy-israel.org; Ambassador PRAHLAD KUMAR PRASAI.

Netherlands: Beit Oz, 13th Floor, 14 Abba Hillel St, Ramat-Gan 52506; tel. 3-7540777; fax 3-7540751; e-mail nlgovtel@012.net.il; internet israel.nlembassy.org; Ambassador CASPAR VELDKAMP.

Nigeria: POB 3339, 34 Gordon St, Tel-Aviv 61030; tel. 3-5222144; fax 3-5248991; e-mail support@nigerianembassy.co.il; internet www.nigerianembassy.co.il; Ambassador DAVID OLADIPO OBASA.

Norway: POB 17575, Canion Ramat Aviv, 13th Floor, 40 Einstein St, Tel-Aviv 69101; tel. 3-7401900; fax 3-7441498; e-mail emb.telaviv@mfa.no; internet www.norway.org.il; Ambassador SVEIN SEVJE.

Panama: 10/3 Hei Be'Iyar St, Kikar Hamedina, Tel-Aviv 62998; tel. 3-6960849; fax 3-6910045; Ambassador HECTOR APARICIO.

Peru: 60 Medinat Hayehudim St, Entrance B, 2nd Floor, Herzliya Pituach 46766; tel. 9-9578835; fax 9-9568495; e-mail emperu@012.net.il; Ambassador GONZALO ANTONIO OTERO ZAPATA.

Philippines: 18 Bnei Dan St, Tel-Aviv 62260; tel. 3-6010500; fax 3-6041038; e-mail filembis@netvision.net.il; internet www.philippine-embassy.org.il; Ambassador NATHANIEL G. IMPERIAL.

Poland: 16 Soutine St, Tel-Aviv 64684; tel. 3-7253111; fax 3-5237806; e-mail telaviv.amb.sekretariat@msz.gov.pl; internet www.telawiw.msz.gov.pl; Ambassador JACEK CHODOROWICZ.

Portugal: 3 Daniel Frisch St, 12th Floor, Tel-Aviv 64731; tel. 3-6956373; fax 3-6956366; e-mail afonso.laginha@mne.pt; Ambassador MIGUEL DE ALMEIDA E SOUSA.

Romania: 24 Adam Hacohen St, Tel-Aviv 64585; tel. 3-5229472; fax 3-5247379; e-mail office_romania@bezeqint.net; internet telaviv.mae.ro; Ambassador ANDREEA PĂSTÂRNAC.

Russian Federation: 120 Hayarkon St, Tel-Aviv 63573; tel. 3-5226736; fax 3-5226713; e-mail consul@russianembassy.org.il; internet russianembassy.org.il; Ambassador SERGEY YA. YAKOVLEV.

Serbia: 10 Bodenheimer St, Tel-Aviv 62008; tel. 3-6045535; fax 3-6049456; e-mail srbambil@netvision.net.il; internet www.telaviv.mfa.gov.rs; Ambassador MILUTIN STANOJEVIC.

Slovakia: POB 6459, 37 Jabotinsky St, Tel-Aviv 62287; tel. 3-5449119; fax 3-5449144; e-mail emb.telaviv@mzv.sk, Ambassador RADOVAN JAVORČIK.

Slovenia: POB 23245, Top Tower, 19th Floor, 50 Dizengoff St, Tel-Aviv 64332; tel. 3-6293563; fax 3-5282214; e-mail vta@gov.si; internet telaviv.veleposlanistvo.si; Ambassador ALENKA SUHADOLNIK.

South Africa: POB 7138, Sason Hogi Tower, 17th Floor, 12 Abba Hilel Silver St, Ramat-Gan 52520; tel. 3-5252566; fax 3-5253230; e-mail info@saemb.org.il; internet www.safis.co.il; Ambassador SISA NGOMBANE.

Spain: Dubnov Tower, 18th Floor, 3 Daniel Frisch St, Tel-Aviv 64731; tel. 3-7697900; fax 3-6965217; e-mail emb.telaviv@maec.es; internet www.exteriores.gob.es/embajadas/telaviv; Ambassador FERNANDO CARDERERA SOLER.

Sri Lanka: 4 Jean Jaurès St, Tel-Aviv 63412; tel. 3-5277635; fax 3-5277634; e-mail srilanka@013.net; Ambassador SARATH DEVESENA WIJESINGHE.

Sweden: Asia House, 4 Weizman St, Tel-Aviv 64239; tel. 3-7180000; fax 3-7180005; e-mail ambassaden.tel-aviv@gov.se; internet www.swedenabroad.com/telaviv; Ambassador CARL MAGNUS NESSER.

Switzerland: POB 6068, 228 Hayarkon St, Tel-Aviv 6106001; tel. 3-5464455; fax 3-5464408; e-mail tel.vertretung@eda.admin.ch; internet www.eda.admin.ch/telaviv; Ambassador ANDREAS BAUM.

Thailand: POB 2125, Mercazim Bldg 2001, 1 Abba Eban Blvd, Herzliya Pituach 46120; tel. 9-9548412; fax 9-9548417; e-mail thaisr@netvision.co.il; internet www.thaiembassy.org/telaviv; Ambassador ANGSANA SIHAPITAK.

Turkey: 202 Hayarkon St, Tel-Aviv 63405; tel. 3-35241101; fax 3-5241390; e-mail turkemb.telaviv@mfa.gov.tr; relations downgraded since Sept. 2011; Chargé d'affaires a.i. DOĞAN FERHAT IŞIK.

Ukraine: 50 Yirmiyahu St, Tel-Aviv 62594; tel. 3-6040242; fax 3-6042512; e-mail emb_il@mfa.gov.ua; internet www.mfa.gov.ua/israel; Ambassador HENNADII NADOLENKO.

United Kingdom: 192 Hayarkon St, Tel-Aviv 63405; tel. 3-7251222; fax 3-5278574; e-mail webmaster.telaviv@fco.gov.uk; internet ukinisrael.fco.gov.uk; Ambassador MATTHEW GOULD.

USA: 71 Hayarkon St, Tel-Aviv 63903; tel. 3-5197575; fax 3-5108093; e-mail nivtelaviv@state.gov; internet israel.usembassy.gov; Ambassador DANIEL B. SHAPIRO.

Uruguay: G.R.A.P. Bldg, 1st Floor, 4 Shenkar St, Industrial Zone, Herzliya Pituach 46725; tel. 9-9569611; fax 9-9515881; e-mail secretaria@emburuguay.co.il; Ambassador BERNARDO GREIVER.

Uzbekistan: 31 Moshe Sharet St, Ramat-Gan 52413; tel. 3-6722371; fax 3-6722621; e-mail admindep@uzbembassy.org.il; internet www .uzbembassy.org.il; Ambassador OYBEK I. ESHONOV.

Viet Nam: Asia Bldg, 4th Floor, 4 Weizman St, Tel-Aviv; tel. 3-6966304; fax 3-6966243; e-mail vnembassy.il@mofa.gov.vn; internet www.vietnamembassy-israel.org; Ambassador TA DUY CHINH.

Judicial System

The law of Israel is composed of the enactments of the Knesset and, to a lesser extent, of the acts, orders-in-council and ordinances that remain from the period of the British Mandate in Palestine (1922–48). The pre-1948 law has largely been replaced, amended or reorganized, in the interests of codification, by Israeli legislation. This legislation generally follows a very similar pattern to that operating in England and the USA. However, there is no jury system.

The Supreme Court: Sha'arei Mishpat St, Kiryat David Ben-Gurion, Jerusalem 91950; tel. 2-6556845; fax 2-6556846; e-mail pniyot@court.gov.il; internet www.court.gov.il; This is the highest judicial authority in the state. It has jurisdiction as an Appellate Court over appeals from the District Courts in all matters, both civil and criminal (sitting as a Court of Civil Appeal or as a Court of Criminal Appeal). In addition, it is a Court of First Instance (sitting as the High Court of Justice) in actions against governmental authorities, and in matters in which it considers it necessary to grant relief in the interests of justice and which are not within the jurisdiction of any other court or tribunal. The High Court's exclusive power to issue orders in the nature of *habeas corpus, mandamus,* prohibition and *certiorari* enables the court to review the legality of, and redress grievances against, acts of administrative authorities of all kinds; Pres. MIRIAM NAOR.

District Courts: There are five District Courts (Jerusalem, Tel-Aviv, Haifa, Beersheba, Nazareth). They have residual jurisdiction as Courts of First Instance over all civil and criminal matters not within the jurisdiction of a Magistrates' Court (e.g. civil claims exceeding NIS 1m.), all matters not within the exclusive jurisdiction of any other tribunal, and matters within the concurrent jurisdiction of any other tribunal so long as such tribunal does not deal with them. In addition, the District Courts have appellate jurisdiction over appeals from judgments and decisions of Magistrates' Courts and judgments of Municipal Courts and various administrative tribunals.

Magistrates' Courts: There are 29 Magistrates' Courts, having criminal jurisdiction to try contraventions, misdemeanours and certain felonies, and civil jurisdiction to try actions concerning possession or use of immovable property, or the partition thereof, whatever may be the value of the subject matter of the action, and other civil claims not exceeding NIS 1m.

Labour Courts: Established in 1969. Regional Labour Courts in Jerusalem, Tel-Aviv, Haifa, Beersheba and Nazareth, composed of judges and representatives of the public; a National Labour Court in Jerusalem; the Courts have jurisdiction over all matters arising out of the relationship between employer and employee or parties to a collective labour agreement, and matters concerning the National Insurance Law and the Labour Law and Rules.

Religious Courts: The Religious Courts are the courts of the recognized religious communities. They have jurisdiction over certain defined matters of personal status concerning members of their respective communities. Where any action of personal status involves persons of different religious communities, the President of the Supreme Court decides which Court will decide the matter. Whenever a question arises as to whether or not a case is one of personal status within the exclusive jurisdiction of a Religious Court, the matter must be referred to a Special Tribunal composed of two Justices of the Supreme Court and the President of the highest court of the religious community concerned in Israel. The judgments of the Religious Courts are executed by the process and offices of the Civil Courts. Neither these Courts nor the Civil Courts have jurisdiction to dissolve the marriage of a foreign subject; Jewish Rabbinical Courts have exclusive jurisdiction over matters of marriage and divorce of Jews in Israel who are Israeli citizens or residents. In all other matters of personal status they have concurrent jurisdiction with the District Courts; Muslim Religious Courts have exclusive jurisdiction over matters of marriage and divorce of Muslims who are not foreigners, or who are foreigners subject by their national law to the jurisdiction of Muslim Religious Courts in such matters. In all other matters of personal status they have concurrent jurisdiction with the District Courts; Christian Religious Courts have exclusive jurisdiction over matters of marriage and divorce of members of their communities who are not foreigners. In all other matters of personal

status they have concurrent jurisdiction with the District Courts; Druze Courts, established in 1963, have exclusive jurisdiction over matters of marriage and divorce of Druze in Israel, who are Israeli citizens or residents, and concurrent jurisdiction with the District Courts over all other matters of personal status of Druze.

Attorney-General: YEHUDA WEINSTEIN.

Religion

JUDAISM

Judaism, the religion of the Jews, is the faith of the majority of Israel's inhabitants. On 31 December 2012 Judaism's adherents totalled 5,999,600, equivalent to 75.1% of the country's population. Its basis is a belief in an ethical monotheism.

There are two main Jewish communities: the Ashkenazim and the Sephardim. The former are the Jews from Eastern, Central or Northern Europe, while the latter originate from the Balkan countries, North Africa and the Middle East.

There is also a community of Ethiopian Jews, the majority of whom have been airlifted to Israel from Ethiopia at various times since the fall of Emperor Haile Selassie in 1974.

The supreme religious authority is vested in the Chief Rabbinate, which consists of the Ashkenazi and Sephardi Chief Rabbis and the Supreme Rabbinical Council. It makes decisions on interpretation of the Jewish law, and supervises the Rabbinical Courts. There are eight regional Rabbinical Courts, and a Rabbinical Court of Appeal presided over by the two Chief Rabbis.

According to the Rabbinical Courts Jurisdiction Law of 1953, marriage and divorce among Jews in Israel are exclusively within the jurisdiction of the Rabbinical Courts. Provided that all the parties concerned agree, other matters of personal status can also be decided by the Rabbinical Courts.

There are over 170 Religious Councils, which maintain religious services and supply religious needs, and about 400 religious committees with similar functions in smaller settlements. Their expenses are borne jointly by the state and the local authorities. The Religious Councils are under the administrative control of the Ministry of Religious Services. In all matters of religion, the Religious Councils are subject to the authority of the Chief Rabbinate. There are 365 officially appointed rabbis. The total number of synagogues is about 7,000, most of which are organized within the framework of the Union of Israel Synagogues.

Head of the Ashkenazi Community: The Chief Rabbi YONA METZGER.

Head of the Sephardic Community: The Chief Rabbi SHLOMO AMAR, Jerusalem; tel. 2-5313131.

Two Jewish sects still loyal to their distinctive customs are:

The Karaites: a sect which recognizes only the Jewish written law and not the oral law of the Mishna and Talmud. The community of about 12,000, many of whom live in or near Ramla, has been augmented by immigration from Egypt.

The Samaritans: an ancient sect mentioned in 2 Kings xvii, 24. They recognize only the Torah. The community in Israel numbers about 500; about one-half of this number live in Holon, where a Samaritan synagogue has been built, and the remainder, including the High Priest, live in Nablus, near Mt Gerazim, which is sacred to the Samaritans.

ISLAM

Muslims in Israel belong principally to the Sunni sect of Islam, and are divided among the four rites: the Shafe'i, the Hanbali, the Hanafi and the Maliki. Before June 1967 they numbered approximately 175,000; in 1971 some 343,900. On 31 December 2012 the total Muslim population of Israel was 1,387,500, equivalent to 17.4% of the country's population.

Mufti of Jerusalem: POB 17412, Jerusalem; tel. 2-283528; Sheikh MUHAMMAD AHMAD HUSSEIN (also Chair. Supreme Muslim Council for Jerusalem); appointed by the Palestinian (National) Authority (PA).

There was also a total of 131,500 Druzes in Israel at 31 December 2012. The official spiritual leader of the Druze community in Israel is Sheikh MUWAFAK TARIF, but his leadership is not widely recognized.

CHRISTIANITY

The total Christian population of Israel (including East Jerusalem) at 31 December 2012 was 158,400.

United Christian Council in Israel: POB 116, Jerusalem 91000; tel. and fax 2-6259012; e-mail ucci@ucci.net; internet www.ucci.net; f. 1956; member of World Evangelical Alliance; over 30 mems (evangelical churches and social and educational insts); Chair. Rev. CHARLES KOPP.

The Roman Catholic Church

Armenian Rite

The Armenian Catholic Patriarch of Cilicia is resident in Beirut, Lebanon.

Patriarchal Exarchate of Jerusalem and Amman: POB 19546, 36 Via Dolorosa, Jerusalem 91190; tel. 2-6284262; fax 2-6272123; e-mail acpejerusalem@yahoo.com; f. 1885; Exarch Patriarchal Mgr RAPHAEL FRANÇOIS MINASSIAN.

Chaldean Rite

The Chaldean Patriarch of Babylon is resident in Baghdad, Iraq.

Patriarchal Exarchate of Jerusalem: Chaldean Patriarchal Vicariate, POB 20108, 7 Chaldean St, Saad and Said Quarter, Jerusalem 91200; tel. 2-6844519; fax 2-6274614; e-mail kolin-p@zahav.net.il; Exarch Patriarchal Mgr MICHEL KASSARJI.

Latin Rite

The Patriarchate of Jerusalem covers Palestine, Jordan and Cyprus.

Bishops' Conference: Conférence des Evêques Latins dans les Régions Arabes, Notre Dame of Jerusalem Center, POB 20531, Jerusalem 91204; tel. 2-6288554; fax 2-6288555; e-mail evcat@palnet.com; f. 1967; Pres. His Beatitude FOUAD TWAL (Patriarch of Jerusalem).

Patriarchate of Jerusalem: Latin Patriarchate of Jerusalem, POB 14152, Jerusalem 91141; tel. 2-6282323; fax 2-6271652; e-mail chancellery@latinpat.org; internet www.lpj.org; Patriarch His Beatitude FOUAD TWAL; Auxiliary Bishop of Jerusalem WILLIAM SHOMALI; Vicar-General for Israel GIACINTO-BOULOS MARCUZZO (Titular Bishop of Emmaus Nicopolis); Vicariat Patriarcal Latin, Street 6191/3, Nazareth 16100; tel. 4-6554075; fax 4-6452416; e-mail latinpat@rannet.com.

Maronite Rite

The Maronite community is under the jurisdiction of the Maronite Patriarch of Antioch (resident in Lebanon).

Patriarchal Exarchate of Jerusalem: Maronite Patriarchal Exarchate, POB 14219, 25 Maronite Convent St, Jaffa Gate, Jerusalem 91141; tel. 2-6282158, fax 2-6272821; Exarch Patriarchal Mgr PAUL NABIL SAYAH (also the Maronite Archbishop of Haifa).

Melkite Rite

The Greek-Melkite Patriarch of Antioch and all the East, of Alexandria and of Jerusalem (GRÉGOIRE III LAHAM) is resident in Damascus, Syria.

Patriarchal Vicariate of Jerusalem

Patriarcat Grec-Melkite Catholique, POB 14130, Porte de Jaffa, Jerusalem 91141; tel. 2-6282023; fax 2-6289606; e-mail gcpjer@p-ol.com; Protosyncellus Archim. Archbishop GEORGES MICHEL BAKAR.

Archbishop of Akka (Acre): ELIAS CHACOUR, Archevêché Grec-Catholique, POB 9450, 33 Hagefen St, 31094 Haifa; tel. 4-8508105; fax 4-8508106; e-mail chacoure@netvision.net.il.

Syrian Rite

The Syrian Catholic Patriarch of Antioch is resident in Beirut, Lebanon.

Patriarchal Exarchate of Jerusalem: Vicariat Patriarcal Syrien Catholique, POB 19787, 6 Chaldean St, Jerusalem 91197; tel. 2-6282657; fax 2-6284217; e-mail st_thomas@bezeqint.net; Exarch Patriarchal Mgr GRÉGOIRE PIERRE MELKI.

The Armenian Apostolic (Orthodox) Church

Patriarch of Jerusalem: Archbishop NOURHAN MANOUGIAN, Armenian Patriarchate of St James, POB 14235, Jerusalem; tel. 2-6264853; fax 2-6264862; e-mail webmaster@armenian-patriarchate.org; internet www.armenian-patriarchate.org.

The Greek Orthodox Church

The Patriarchate of Jerusalem includes Israel, the Occupied Territories, Jordan, Kuwait, Saudi Arabia and the United Arab Emirates.

Patriarch of Jerusalem: THEOPHILOS III, POB 14518, Jerusalem 91145; tel. 2-6274941; fax 2-6282048; e-mail secretariat@jerusalem-patriarchate.info; internet www.jerusalem-patriarchate.info.

The Anglican Communion

Episcopal Diocese of Jerusalem and the Middle East: POB 19122, St George's Cathedral Close, Jerusalem 91191; tel. 2-6271670; fax 2-6273847; e-mail info@j-diocese.org; internet www.j-diocese.org; Bishop The Rt Rev. SUHEIL DAWANI (Anglican Bishop in Jerusalem).

Other Christian Churches

Other denominations include the Coptic Orthodox Church, the Russian Orthodox Church, the Ethiopian Orthodox Church, the Romanian Orthodox Church, the Baptist Church, the Lutheran Church and the Church of Scotland.

The Press

Tel-Aviv is the main publishing centre. Largely for economic reasons, no significant local press has developed away from the main cities; hence all newspapers have tended to regard themselves as national. Friday editions, issued on Sabbath eve, are increased to as much as twice the normal size by special weekend supplements, and experience a considerable rise in circulation. No newspapers appear on Saturday.

Most of the daily papers are in Hebrew, and others appear in Arabic, English, Russian, Polish, Hungarian, Yiddish, French and German. The total daily circulation is 500,000–600,000 copies, or 21 papers per hundred people, although most citizens read more than one daily paper.

Most Hebrew morning dailies have strong political or religious affiliations, and the majority of newspapers depend on subsidies from political parties, religious organizations or public funds. The limiting effect on freedom of commentary entailed by this party press system has provoked repeated criticism. There are around 400 other newspapers and magazines, including some 50 weekly and 150 fortnightly; over 250 of them are in Hebrew, the remainder in 11 other languages.

Ha'aretz is the most widely read of the morning papers, exceeded only by the popular afternoon press, *Ma'ariv* and *Yedioth Ahronoth*. *The Jerusalem Post* gives detailed news coverage in English.

DAILIES

Calcalist (Economist): Tel-Aviv; e-mail mail@calcalist.co.il; internet www.calcalist.co.il; f. 2008; Hebrew; business; publ. by Yedioth Ahronoth Group; Founder and Publr YOEL ESTERON; CEO STEVE SCHUMACHER.

Globes: POB 5126, Rishon le Zion 75150; tel. 3-9538611; fax 3-9525971; e-mail mailbox@globes.co.il; internet www.globes.co.il; f. 1983; evening; Hebrew; business and economics; owned by the Monitin Group; CEO EITAN MADMON; Editor-in-Chief HAGGAI GOLAN; circ. 45,000.

Ha'aretz (The Land): 21 Schocken St, Tel-Aviv 61001; tel. 3-5121333; fax 3-5121349; e-mail contact@haaretz.co.il; internet www.haaretz.co.il; f. 1919; morning; Hebrew and English; liberal; independent; 25% stake acquired by M. DuMont Schauberg (Germany) in 2006; Man. Dir RAMI GUEZ; Editor-in-Chief ALUF BENN; Publr AMOS SCHOCKEN; circ. 72,000 (weekdays), 100,000 (Fri.).

Hamodia (The Informer): 16 A Petach Tikva St, Jerusalem 91012; tel. 2-5389255; fax 2-5003384; e-mail englishweekly@hamodia.com; internet www.hamodia.com; f. 1950; morning; Hebrew, English and French edns; Orthodox; organ of Agudat Israel; Editor HAIM MOSHE KNOPF; international circ. 250,000.

Israel HaYom (Israel Today): 2 Hashlosha St, Tel-Aviv; e-mail hayom@israelhayom.co.il; internet israelhayom.co.il; f. 2007; free daily publ. Sun.–Thur; Hebrew; Publr ASHER BAHARAV; Editor-in-Chief AMOS REGEV; CEO ZIPPI KOREN; circ. 255,000.

Israel Nachrichten (News of Israel): POB 28397, Tel-Aviv 61283; tel. 3-5372059; fax 3-5376166; e-mail info@israelnachrichten.de; f. 1935 as Neueste Nachrichten, renamed as above 1948; morning; German; Editor HELGA MÜLLER-GAZMAWE; circ. 1,500.

Israel Post: 15 HaAchim MeSalvita, Tel-Aviv; f. 2007 as Metro Israel; free daily; afternoon; Hebrew; publ. by Metro Israel Ltd; Co-owners ELI AZUR, DAVID WEISMAN; Editor-in-Chief GOLAN BAR-YOSEF.

Al-Itihad (Unity): POB 104, Haifa; tel. 4-8666301; fax 4-8641407; e-mail aletihad@bezeqint.net; internet www.aljabha.org; f. 1944; Arabic; organ of Hadash; Editor-in-Chief AIDA TOUMA-SLIMAN; circ. 60,000.

The Jerusalem Post: POB 81, The Jerusalem Post Bldg, Romema, Jerusalem 91000; tel. 2-5315666; fax 2-5389527; e-mail feedback@jpost.com; internet www.jpost.com; f. 1932 as The Palestine Post, renamed as above 1950; morning; English; independent; CEO RONIT HASIN-HOCHMAN; Editor-in-Chief STEVE LINDE; circ. 15,000 (weekdays), 40,000 (weekend edn); there is also a weekly international edn (circ. 70,000), and a weekly French edn.

Nasha strana (Our Country): 52 Harakeret St, Tel-Aviv 67770; tel. 3-370011; fax 3-5371921; f. 1970; morning; Russian; Editor S. HIMMELFARB; circ. 35,000.

Novosti nedeli (The Week's News): 15 Ha-Ahim Mi-Slavita St, Tel-Aviv; tel. 3-6242225; fax 3-6242227; Russian; Editor-in-Chief DMITRII LODYZHENSKII.

Al-Quds (Jerusalem): POB 19788, Jerusalem; tel. 2-6272663; fax 2-6272657; e-mail contact@alquds.com; internet www.alquds.com; f. 1968; Arabic; Founder and Publr MAHMOUD ABU ZALAF; Gen. Man. Dr MARWAN ABU ZALAF; circ. 55,000.

Viata Noastra: 49 Tchlenor St, Tel-Aviv 66048; tel. 3-5372059; fax 3-6877142; e-mail viatanoastra2001@yahoo.com; internet viatanoastra.1colony.com; f. 1950; morning; Romanian; Editor NANDO MARIO VARGA; circ. 30,000.

Yated Ne'eman: POB 328, Bnei Brak; tel. 3-6170800; fax 3-6170801; e-mail let-edit@yatedneman.co.il; internet www.yated.com; f. 1986; morning; Hebrew; religious; Editors Rabbi ITZHAK ROTH, Rabbi NOSSON ZE'EV GROSSMAN; circ. 25,000.

Yedioth Ahronoth (The Latest News): 2 Yehuda and Noah Mozes St, Tel-Aviv 61000; tel. and fax 3-6082222; e-mail service@y-i.co.il; internet www.ynet.co.il; f. 1939; evening; Hebrew; independent; Editor-in-Chief SHILO DE BEER; circ. 350,000, Fri. 600,000.

WEEKLIES AND FORTNIGHTLIES

Akhbar al-Naqab (News of the Negev): POB 426, Rahat 85357; tel. 8-9919202; fax 8-9917070; e-mail akhbar@akhbarna.com; internet www.akhbarna.com; f. 1988; weekly; Arabic; educational and social issues concerning the Negev Bedouins; Editor-in-Chief MUHAMMAD YOUNIS.

Aurora: Aurora Ltd, POB 57416, Tel-Aviv 61573; tel. 3-5625216; fax 3-5625082; e-mail aurora@aurora-israel.co.il; internet www.aurora-israel.co.il; f. 1963; weekly; Spanish; Editor-in-Chief ARIE AVIDOR; Director MARIO WAINSTEIN; circ. 20,000.

Bamahane (In the Camp): Military POB 1013, Tel-Aviv; f. 1948; illustrated weekly of the Israel Defence Forces; Hebrew; Editor-in-Chief YONI SHANFELD; circ. 70,000.

B'Sheva: Petach Tikva; internet www.inn.co.il/besheva; f. 2002; Hebrew; religious Zionist newspaper, distributed freely in religious communities; owned by Arutz Sheva (Channel Seven) media network; Editor EMANUEL SHILO; circ. 140,000.

Etgar (The Challenge): POB 35252, Ha'aliyah St, 2nd Floor, Tel-Aviv 61351; tel. 3-5373268; fax 3-5373269; e-mail nir@hanitzoz.org.il; internet www.etgar.info; twice weekly; Hebrew; publ. by Hanitzotz Publishing House; Editor NATHAN YALIN-MOR.

InformationWeek: POB 1161, 13 Yad Harutzim St, Tel-Aviv 61116; tel. 3-7330733; fax 3-7330703; e-mail world@pc.co.il; internet www.pc.co.il; weekly; Hebrew and English; Man. Dirs DAHLIA PELED, PELI PELED; Editor-in-Chief YEHUDA KONFORTES.

The Jerusalem Post International Edition: POB 81, Romema, Jerusalem 91000; tel. 2-5315666; fax 2-5389527; e-mail liat@jpost.com; internet www.jpost.co.il; f. 1959; weekly; English; overseas edn of *The Jerusalem Post* (q.v.); circ. 70,000 to 106 countries; Editor LIAT COLLINS.

Jerusalem Report: POB 1805, Jerusalem 91017; tel. 2-5315660; fax 2-5315631; e-mail jrep@jreport.co.il; f. 1990; bi-weekly; English; publ. under umbrella of *The Jerusalem Post*; Editor-in-Chief ILAN EVYATAR.

Laisha (For Women): POB 28122, 35 Bnei Brak St, Tel-Aviv 66021; tel. 3-6386400; fax 3-6386904; e-mail laisha@laisha.co.il; internet laisha.co.il; f. 1949; Hebrew; women's magazine; Editor-in-Chief ILAM YITZHAK; circ. 100,000.

My Tour-Il Magazine: 15 Lamdan St, Tel-Aviv 6941415; tel. 3-6486611; fax 3-6486622; e-mail ilan777@gmail.com; internet www.mytour-il.co.il; f. 1994; weekly; Hebrew and English; Publr and Editor ILAN SHCHORI; circ. 50,000.

Reshumot: Ministry of Justice, POB 1087, 29 Rehov Salahadin, Jerusalem 91010; f. 1948; Hebrew, Arabic and English; official govt gazette.

Al-Sabar: POB 2647, Nazareth 16126; tel. 4-6462156; fax 4-6462152; e-mail alsabar.mag@gmail.com; internet www.alsabar-mag.com; publ. by the Org. for Democratic Action; Arabic; political and cultural Israeli-Palestinian affairs.

Vesti (News): 2 Homa U'Migdal, Tel-Aviv 67771; tel. 3-6383444; fax 3-6383440; f. 1992; publ. Sun.–Thur; Russian; Editor-in-Chief SERGEI PODRAZHANSKII.

OTHER PERIODICALS

Bitaon Heyl Ha'avir (Israel Air Force Magazine): Military POB 01560, Zahal; tel. 3-6067729; fax 3-6067735; e-mail iaf@inter.net.il; internet www.iaf.org.il; f. 1948; bi-monthly; Hebrew and English; Dep. Editor U. ETSION; Editor-in-Chief MERAV HALPERIN; circ. 30,000.

Al-Bushra (Good News): POB 6228, Haifa 31061; tel. 4-8385002; fax 4-8371612; f. 1935; monthly; Arabic; organ of the Ahmadiyya movement; Editor MUSA ASA'AD O'DEH.

Challenge: POB 35252, Tel-Aviv 61351; tel. 3-5373268; fax 3-5373269; e-mail oda@netvision.net.il; internet www.challenge-mag.com; f. 1989; magazine on the Israeli–Palestinian conflict, publ. by

Hanitzotz Publishing House; online only; English; Editor-in-Chief RONI BEN EFRAT; Editor STEPHEN LANGFUR.

Diamond Intelligence Briefs: POB 3442, Ramat-Gan 52136; tel. 3-5750196; fax 3-5754829; e-mail office@tacy.co.il; internet www.diamondintelligence.com; f. 1985; English; Publr CHAIM EVEN-ZOHAR.

Eastern Mediterranean Tourism/Travel: Israel Travel News Ltd, POB 3251, Tel-Aviv 61032; tel. 3-5251646; fax 3-5251605; e-mail office@itn.co.il; internet www.itn.co.il; f. 1979; monthly; English; Editor GERRY AROHOW; circ. 20,000.

Hamizrah Hehadash (The New East): Israel Oriental Society, The Hebrew University, Mount Scopus, Jerusalem 91905; tel. 2-5883633; e-mail ios49@hotmail.com; f. 1949; annual of the Israel Oriental Society; Middle Eastern, Asian and African Affairs; Hebrew with English summary; Editors HAIM GERBER, ELIE PODEH; circ. 1,500–2,000.

Harefuah (Medicine): POB 3566, 2 Twin Towers, 35 Jabotinsky St, Ramat-Gan 52136; tel. 3-6100444; fax 3-5753303; e-mail harefuah@ima.org.il; internet www.ima.org.il/harefuah; f. 1920; monthly journal of the Israel Medical Asscn; Hebrew with English summaries; also publishes *Israel Medical Asscn Journal*; Editor Prof. YEHUDA SHOENFELD; circ. 16,000.

Hed Hachinuch (Echoes of Education): 2 Tashach St, Tel-Aviv 62093; tel. 3-6091819; fax 3-6094521; e-mail hed@itu.org.il; internet www.itu.org.il; f. 1926; monthly; Hebrew; also publishes Arabic edn; educational; publ. by the Israel Teachers Union; Editor DALIA LACHMAN; circ. 40,000.

Hed Hagan (Echoes of Kindergarten): 8 Ben Saruk St, Tel-Aviv 62969; tel. 3-6922958; e-mail hedhagan@morim.org.il; internet www.itu.org.il; f. 1935; quarterly; Hebrew; early education issues; publ. by the Israel Teachers Union; Editor ILANA MALCHI; circ. 9,000.

Historia: POB 4179, Jerusalem 91041; tel. 2-5650444; fax 2-6712388; e-mail shazar@shazar.org.il; f. 1998; bi-annual; Hebrew, with English summaries; general history; publ. by the Historical Society of Israel; Editors Prof. BILLIE MELMAN, Prof. YURI PINES, Prof. ALEXANDER YAKOBSON, Prof. JOSEPH ZIEGLER; circ. 1,000.

Israel Environment Bulletin: Ministry of Environmental Protection, POB 34033, 5 Kanfei Nesharim St, Givat Shaul, Jerusalem 95464; tel. 2-6553825; fax 2-6554823; e-mail shoshana@sviva.gov.il; internet www.environment.gov.il; f. 1973; bi-annual; English; environmental policy, legislation and news; Editor SHOSHANA GABBAY; circ. 3,500.

Israel Exploration Journal: POB 7041, 5 Avida St, Jerusalem 9107001; tel. 2-6257991; fax 2-6247772; e-mail ies@vms.huji.ac.il; internet israelexplorationsociety.huji.ac.il/iej.htm; f. 1950; bi-annual; English; general and biblical archaeology, ancient history and historical geography of Israel and the Holy Land; Editors SHMUEL AHITUV, AMIHAI MAZAR; circ. 2,500.

Israel Journal of Chemistry: POB 34299, Jerusalem 91341; tel. 2-6522226; fax 2-6522277; e-mail info@israelsciencejournals.com; internet www.sciencefromisrael.com; f. 1951; quarterly; English; publ. by Science from Israel; Editor Prof. EHUD KEINAN.

Israel Journal of Earth Sciences: POB 34299, Jerusalem 91341; tel. 2-6522226; fax 2-6522277; e-mail info@israelsciencejournals.com; internet www.sciencefromisrael.com; f. 1951; quarterly; English; publ. by Science from Israel; Editor-in-Chief Y. ENZEL.

Israel Journal of Ecology and Evolution: POB 34299, Jerusalem 91341; tel. 2-6522226; fax 2-6522277; e-mail info@israelsciencejournals.com; internet www.sciencefromisrael.com; f. 1951 as *Israel Journal of Zoology*; name changed in 2006; quarterly; English; publ. by Science from Israel; Editors LEON BLAUSTEIN, BURT P. KOTLER.

Israel Journal of Mathematics: The Hebrew University Magnes Press, POB 39099, Jerusalem 91390; tel. 2-6586656; fax 2-5633370; e-mail iton@math.huji.ac.il; internet www.ma.huji.ac.il/~ijmath; f. 1951; bi-monthly; English; Editor-in-Chief NATI LINIAL.

Israel Journal of Plant Sciences: POB 34299, Jerusalem 91341; tel. 2-6522226; fax 2-6522277; e-mail info@israelsciencejournals.com; internet www.sciencefromisrael.com; f. 1951 as *Israel Journal of Botany*; quarterly; English; publ. by Science from Israel; Editor-in-Chief NIRIT BERNSTEIN.

Israel Journal of Psychiatry and Related Sciences: Gefen Publishing House Ltd, 6 Hatzvi St, Jerusalem 94386; tel. 2-5380247; fax 2-5388423; e-mail ijp@gefenpublishing.com; f. 1963; quarterly; English; Editor-in-Chief Dr DAVID GREENBERG.

Israel Journal of Veterinary Medicine: POB 22, Ra'nana 43100; tel. 9-7419929; fax 9-7431778; e-mail ivma@zahav.net.il; internet www.ijvm.org.il; f. 1943; fmrly *Refuah Veterinarith*; quarterly of the Israel Veterinary Medical Asscn; English; Editor-in-Chief TREVOR WANER.

Israel Law Review: Minerva Center for Human Rights, Faculty of Law, Hebrew University of Jerusalem, Mt Scopus, Jerusalem 91905;

tel. 2-5881156; fax 2-5819371; e-mail ilr@savion.huji.ac.il; internet law.huji.ac.il/eng/pirsumim.asp; f. 1966; 3 a year; English; Editors-in-Chief Sir NIGEL RODLEY, YUVAL SHANY.

Israel Medical Asscn Journal (IMAJ): POB 3604, 2 Twin Towers, 11th Floor, 35 Jabotinsky St, Ramat-Gan 52136; tel. 3-6100418; fax 3-7519673; e-mail imaj@ima.org.il; internet www.ima.org.il/imaj; f. 1999; monthly English-language journal of the Israel Medical Asscn; also publishes *Harefuah*; Editor-in-Chief Prof. YEHUDA SHOENFELD.

Journal d'Analyse Mathématique: The Hebrew University Magnes Press, POB 39099, Jerusalem 91390; tel. 2-6586656; fax 2-5633370; e-mail magnes@vms.huji.ac.il; internet www.ma.huji.ac.il/jdm; f. 1955; 3 vols a year; French; Exec. Editor A. LINDEN.

Leshonenu: Academy of the Hebrew Language, Givat Ram Campus, Jerusalem 91904; tel. 2-6493555; fax 2-5617065; e-mail ivrit@hebrew-academy.org.il; internet hebrew-academy.huji.ac.il; f. 1929; quarterly; Hebrew; for the study of the Hebrew language and cognate subjects; Editor MOSHE BAR-ASHER.

Leshonenu La'am: Academy of the Hebrew Language, Givat Ram Campus, Jerusalem 91904; tel. 2-6493555; fax 2-5617065; e-mail ivrit@heberw-academy.org.il; internet hebrew-academy.huji.ac.il; f. 1945; quarterly; Hebrew; popular Hebrew philology; Editor MOSHE FLORENTIN.

Lilac: Nazareth; f. 2000 for Christian and Muslim Arab women in the region; monthly; Arabic; Israel's first magazine for Arab women; Founder and Editor-in-Chief YARA MASHOUR.

MB-Yakinton (Yakinton): 157 Yigal Alon St, Tel-Aviv 6744365; tel. 3-5164461; fax 3-5164435; e-mail info@irgun-jeckes.org; internet www.irgun-jeckes.org; f. 1932; 8 a year; monthly journal of the Irgun Jotsei Merkaz Europa (Asscn of Israelis of Central European Origin); Hebrew and German; Editor MICHA LIMOR.

Moznaim (Balance): POB 7098, Tel-Aviv; tel. 3-6953256; fax 3-6919681; f. 1929; monthly; Hebrew; literature and culture; publ. by Hebrew Writers Asscn; Editors ASHER REICH, AZRIEL KAUFMAN; circ. 2,500.

News from Within: POB 31417, Jerusalem 91313; tel. 2-6241159; fax 2-6253151; e-mail bryan@alt-info.org; internet www.alternativenews.org; monthly; joint Israeli-Palestinian publ.; political, economic, social and cultural; publ. by the Alternative Information Centre.

PC Plus: PC Media, POB 11438, 13 Yad Harutzim St, Tel-Aviv 61114; tel. 3-7330733; fax 3-7330703; e-mail tigerlove@pc.co.il; internet www.pc.co.il; f. 1992; monthly; Hebrew; information on personal computers; CEO and Man. Editor DAHLIA PELED; CEO and Editor-in-Chief PELI PELED; circ. 23,000.

Proche-Orient Chrétien: St Anne's Church, POB 19079, Jerusalem 91190; tel. 2-6281992; fax 2-6280764; e-mail mafrpoc@steanne.org; f. 1951; quarterly on churches and religion in the Middle East; publ. in asscn with St Joseph University, Beirut, Lebanon; French; circ. 1,000.

Terra Santa: POB 14038, Jaffa Gate, Jerusalem 91142; tel. 2-6272692; fax 2-6286417; e-mail cicinfo@cicts.org; internet www.cicts.org; f. 1973; bi-monthly; publ. by the Christian Information Centre, which is sponsored by the Custody of the Holy Land (the official custodians of the Holy Shrines); Italian, Spanish, French, English and Arabic edns publ. in Jerusalem by the Franciscan Printing Press, German edn in Munich, Maltese edn in Valletta; Dir Fr JERZY KRAJ.

WIZO Review: Women's International Zionist Organization, 38 Sderot David Hamelech Blvd, Tel-Aviv 64237; tel. 3-6923805; fax 3-6923801; e-mail wreview@wizo.org; internet www.wizo.org; f. 1926; English (3 a year); Man. Editor INGRID ROCKBERGER; circ. 6,000.

PRESS ASSOCIATIONS

Daily Newspaper Publishers' Asscn of Israel: POB 51202, 74 Petach Tikva Rd, Tel-Aviv 61200; fax 3-5617938; safeguards professional interests and maintains standards, supplies newsprint to dailies; negotiates with trade unions; mems all daily papers; affiliated to International Federation of Newspaper Publishers; Pres. SHABTAI HIMMELFARB; Gen. Sec. BETZALEL EYAL.

Foreign Press Asscn: Beit Sokolov, 4 Kaplan St, Tel-Aviv 64734; tel. 3-6916143; fax 3-6961548; e-mail fpa@netvision.net.il; internet www.fpa.org.il; f. 1957; represents journalists employed by international news orgs who report from Israel, the West Bank and the Gaza Strip; private, non-profit org.; almost 500 mems from 30 countries; Chair. LUKE BAKER.

Israel Association of Periodical Press (IAPP): 17 Keilat Venezia St, Tel-Aviv 69400; tel. 3-6449851; fax 3-6449852; e-mail iapp@zahav.net.il; internet www.iapp.co.il; f. 1962; 600 mems; Chair. JOSEPH FRENKEL.

Israel Press Council: Beit Sokolov, 4 Kaplan St, Tel-Aviv; tel. 3-6951437; fax 3-6951145; e-mail moaza@m-i.org.il; internet www.m-i.org.il; f. 1963; deals with matters of common interest to the Press such as drafting the code of professional ethics, which is binding on all journalists; Chair. ORNA LIN; Gen. Sec. AVI WEINBERG.

National Federation of Israeli Journalists (NFIJ): POB 585, 37 Hillet St, Jerusalem 91004; tel. 2-6254351; fax 3-6254353; e-mail office@jaj.org.il; internet www.jaj.org.il; affiliated to International Federation of Journalists; Chair. AHIA HIKA GINOSAR.

Publishers

Achiasaf Publishing House Ltd: 3, Bney Binyamin St, Netanya 4201959; tel. 9-8851390; fax 9-8851391; e-mail info@achiasaf.co.il; internet www.achiasaf.co.il; f. 1937; general; Pres. MATAN ACHIASAF.

Am Oved Publishers Ltd: 22 Mazeh St, Tel-Aviv 65213; tel. 3-6288500; fax 3-6298911; e-mail info@am-oved.co.il; internet www.am-oved.co.il; f. 1942; fiction, non-fiction, reference books, school and university textbooks, children's books, poetry, classics, science fiction; Man. Dir YAAKOV BREY.

Amihai Publishing House Ltd: POB 8448, 19 Yad Harutzim St, Netanya Darom 42505; tel. 9-8859099; fax 9-8853464; e-mail ami1000@bezeqint.net; internet www.amichaibooks.co.il; f. 1948; fiction, general science, linguistics, languages, arts; Dir ITZHAK ORON.

Arabic Publishing House: 93 Arlozorof St, Tel-Aviv; tel. 3-6921674; f. 1960; established by the Histadrut; periodicals and books; Gen. Man. GHASSAN MUKLASHI.

Ariel Publishing House: POB 3328, Jerusalem 91033; tel. 2-6434540; fax 2-6436164; e-mail elysch@netvision.net.il; internet www.arielp.co.il; f. 1976; history, archaeology, religion, geography, folklore; CEO ELY SCHILLER.

Astrolog Publishing House: POB 1231, Hod Hasharon 45111; tel. 3-9190957; fax 3-9190958; e-mail abooks@netvision.net.il; f. 1994; general non-fiction, religion, alternative medicine; Man. Dir SARA BEN-MORDECHAI.

Carta, The Israel Map and Publishing Co Ltd: POB 2500, 18 Ha'uman St, Industrial Area, Talpiot, Jerusalem 91024; tel. 2-6783355; fax 2-6782373; e-mail carta@carta.co.il; internet www.carta-jerusalem.com; f. 1958; the principal cartographic publr; Pres. and CEO SHAY HAUSMAN.

Eliner Library—The World Zionist Organization: POB 10615, Jerusalem 91104; tel. 2-6202137; fax 2-6202792; e-mail eliner@wzo.org.il; internet www.eliner.co.il; f. 1945; education, Jewish philosophy, studies in the Bible, children's books publ. in Hebrew, English, French, Spanish, German, Swedish and Portuguese, Hebrew teaching material; Dir of Publication Division ORIT AVITAL.

Gefen Publishing House Ltd: 6 Hatzvi St, Jerusalem 94386; tel. 2-5380247; fax 2-5388423; e-mail sales@gefenpublishing.com; internet www.israelbooks.com; f. 1981; largest publr of English-language books in Israel; also publishes wide range of fiction and non-fiction; Publr ILAN GREENFIELD.

Globes Publishers: POB 5126, Rishon le Zion 75150; tel. 3-9538611; fax 3-9525971; e-mail mailbox@globes.co.il; internet www.globes.co.il; business, finance, technology, law, marketing; CEO EITAN MADMON; Editor-in-Chief HAGGAI GOLAN.

Gvanim: POB 11138, 29 Bar-Kochba St, Tel-Aviv 61111; tel. 3-5281044; fax 3-6202032; e-mail traklinm@zahav.net.il; internet gvanim-books.com; f. 1992; poetry, belles lettres, fiction; Man. Dir MARITZA ROSMAN.

Hakibbutz Hameuchad—Sifriat Poalim Publishing Group: POB 1432, Bnei Brak, Tel-Aviv 51114; tel. 3-5785810; fax 3-5785811; e-mail info@kibutz-poalim.co.il; internet www.kibutz-poalim.co.il; f. 1939 as Hakibbutz Hameuchad Publishing House Ltd; subsequently merged with Sifriat Poalim; general; Gen. Dir UZI SHAVIT.

Hanitzotz Publishing House: POB 35252, Tel-Aviv 61351; tel. 3-5373268; fax 3-5373269; e-mail oda@netvision.net.il; internet www.hanitzotz.com; f. 1985; 'progressive' booklets and publications, incl. the periodicals *Challenge* (in English), *Etgar* (Hebrew), and *Al-Sabar* (Arabic); also produces documentary films on human and workers' rights; Contact RONI BEN EFRAT.

The Hebrew University Magnes Press: The Hebrew University, The Sherman Bldg for Research Management, POB 39099, Givat Ram, Jerusalem 91390; tel. 2-6586656; fax 2-5660341; e-mail info@magnespress.co.il; internet www.magnespress.co.il; f. 1929; academic books and journals on many subjects, incl. biblical, classical and Jewish studies, social sciences, language, literature, art, history and geography; Dir HAI TSABAR.

Hed Arzi (Ma'ariv) Publishing Ltd: 3A Yoni Netanyahu St, Or-Yehuda, Tel-Aviv 60376; tel. 3-5383333; fax 3-6343205; e-mail shimoni@hed-arzi.co.il; f. 1954 as Sifriat-Ma'ariv Ltd; later known as Ma'ariv Book Guild Ltd; general; Man. Dir ELI SHIMONI.

Hod-Ami—Computer Books Ltd: POB 6108, Herzliya 46160; tel. 9-9564716; fax 9-9571582; e-mail info@hod-ami.co.il; internet www .hod-ami.co.il; f. 1984; information technology, management; translations from English into Hebrew and Arabic; CEO ITZHAK AMIHUD.

Jerusalem Center for Public Affairs: 13 Tel Hai St, Jerusalem 92107; tel. 2-5619281; fax 2-5619112; e-mail info@jcpa.org; internet www.jcpa.org; f. 1976; Jewish political tradition; publishes *Jerusalem Viewpoints, Jerusalem Issue Brief, Jewish Political Studies Review* and other books; Pres. DORE GOLD; Chair. Dr MANFRED GERSTENFELD.

The Jerusalem Publishing House: 2B HaGai St, Beit Hakerem, Jerusalem 96262; tel. 2-6537966; fax 2-6537988; e-mail mh2@017 .net.il; internet jerpub.com; f. 1966; biblical research, history, encyclopedias, archaeology, arts of the Holy Land, cookbooks, guidebooks, economics, politics; CEO MOSHE HELLER; Man. Editor RACHEL GILON.

Jewish History Publications (Israel 1961) Ltd: POB 1232, 29 Jabotinsky St, Jerusalem 92141; tel. 2-5632310; f. 1961; encyclopedias, World History of the Jewish People series.

Keter Publishing House Ltd: POB 7145, Givat Shaul B, Jerusalem 91071; tel. 2-6557822; fax 2-6536811; e-mail info@keterbooks.co .il; internet www.keterbooks.co.il; f. 1959; original and translated works of fiction, encyclopedias, non-fiction, guidebooks and children's books; publishing imprints: Israel Program for Scientific Translations, Keter Books, Domino, Shikmona, Encyclopedia Judaica; Man. Dir YIPHTACH DEKEL.

Kinneret Zmora-Bitan Dvir Publishing House: 10 Hataasiya St, Or-Yehuda 60210; tel. 3-6344977; fax 3-6340953; internet www .kinbooks.co.il; f. 2002 following merger between Kinneret and Zmora Bitan-Dvir publishing houses; adult and children's fiction and non-fiction, history, science, sociology, psychology, current affairs and politics, dictionaries, architecture, travel; Man. Dir YORAM ROZ.

MAP-Mapping and Publishing Ltd (Tel-Aviv Books): POB 56024, 17 Tchernikhovski St, Tel-Aviv 61560; tel. 3-6210500; fax 3-5257725; e-mail info@mapa.co.il; internet www.mapa.co.il; f. 1985; maps, atlases, travel guides, textbooks, reference books; Man. Dir HEZI LEVY.

Ministry of Defence Publishing House: POB 916, Yaakov Dori Rd, Kiryat Ono 55108; tel. 3-7380738; fax 3-7380645; e-mail minuy@ inter.net.il; f. 1958; military literature, Judaism, history and geography of Israel; Dir JOSEPH PERLOVITZ.

M. Mizrachi Publishing House Ltd: 67 Levinsky St, Tel-Aviv 66855; tel. 3-6870936; fax 3-6888185; e-mail mizrahi.co@jmail.com; f. 1960; children's books, fiction, history, medicine, science; Dirs MEIR MIZRACHI, ISRAEL MIZRACHI.

Mosad Harav Kook: POB 642, 1 Maimon St, Jerusalem 91006; tel. 2-6526231; fax 2-6526968; e-mail mosad-haravkook@neto.bezeqint .net; f. 1937; editions of classical works, Torah and Jewish studies; Dir Rabbi YOSEF MOVSHOVITZ.

Otsar Hamoreh: c/o Israel Teachers Union, 8 Ben Saruk, Tel-Aviv 62969; tel. 3-6922983; fax 3-6922988; f. 1951; educational; Man. Dir JOSEPH SALOMAN.

People and Computers Ltd: POB 11438, 53 Derech Asholom St, Givatayim 53454; tel. 3-7330733; fax 3-7330703; e-mail info@pc.co.il; internet www.pc.co.il; information technology; Editor-in-Chief and CEO PELI PELED; Man. Editor and CEO DAHLIA PELED.

Rodney Franklin Agency: POB 37727, 53 Mazeh St, Tel-Aviv 65789; tel. 3-5600724; fax 3-5600479; e-mail rodneyf@netvision.net .il; internet www.rodneyagency.com; f. 1974; exclusive representative of various British, other European and US publrs; e-marketing services for academic and professional journal publrs in 15 countries; Dir RODNEY FRANKLIN.

Rubin Mass Ltd: POB 990, 7 Ha-Ayin-Het St, Jerusalem 91009; tel. 2-6277863; fax 2-6277864; e-mail rmass@barak.net.il; internet www .rubinmass.com; f. 1927; Hebraica, Judaica, export of all Israeli books and periodicals; Man. OREN MASS.

Schocken Publishing House Ltd: POB 57188, 24 Nathan Yelin Mor St, Tel-Aviv 61571; tel. 3-5610130; fax 3-5622668; e-mail gila_g@ haaretz.co.il; internet www.schocken.co.il; f. 1938; general; Publr RACHELI EDELMAN.

Shalem Press: 3 Ha'askan St, Jerusalem 9378010; tel. 2-5605586; fax 2-5605565; e-mail shalempress@shalem.ac.il; internet www .shalempress.co.il; f. 1994; economics, political science, history, philosophy, cultural issues; Pres. DANIEL POLISAR.

Sinai Publishing: 24 Rambam St, Tel-Aviv 65813; tel. 3-5163672; fax 3-5176783; e-mail sinaipub@zahav.net.il; internet www .sinaibooks.com; f. 1853; Hebrew books and religious articles; Dir MOSHE SCHLESINGER.

Steinhart-Katzir: POB 8333, Netanya 42505; tel. 9-8854770; fax 9-8854771; e-mail mail@haolam.co.il; internet www.haolam.co.il; f. 1991; travel; Man. Dir OHAD SHARAV.

Tcherikover Publishers Ltd: 12 Hasharon St, Tel-Aviv 66185; tel. 3-6396099; fax 3-6874729; e-mail barkay@inter.net.il; education, psychology, economics, psychiatry, literature, literary criticism, essays, history, geography, criminology, art, languages, management; Man. Editor S. TCHERIKOVER.

Yachdav United Publishers Co Ltd: POB 20123, 29 Carlebach St, Tel-Aviv 67132; tel. 3-5614121; fax 3-5611996; e-mail info@tbpai.co .il; f. 1960; educational; Chair. EPHRAIM BEN-DOR; Exec. Dir AMNON BEN-SHMUEL.

Yavneh Publishing House Ltd: POB 4781, 4 Mazeh St, Tel-Aviv 65213; tel. 3-6297856; fax 3-6293638; e-mail publishing@yavneh.co .il; internet www.yavneh.co.il; f. 1932; general; Man. Dir NIRA PREISKEL.

Yedioth Ahronoth Books: POB 53494, 10 Kehilat Venezia, Tel-Aviv 61534; tel. 3-7683333; fax 3-7683300; e-mail info@ybook.co.il; internet www.ybook.co.il; f. 1952; non-fiction, politics, Judaism, health, music, dance, fiction, education; Man. Dir DOV EICHENWALD.

S. Zack: 31 Beit Hadfus St, Jerusalem 95483; tel. 2-6537760; fax 2-6514005; e-mail zackmt@bezeqint.net; internet www.zack.co.il; f. 1935; fiction, science, philosophy, Judaism, children's books, educational and reference books, dictionaries, languages; Dir MICHAEL ZACK.

PUBLISHERS' ASSOCIATION

The Book Publishers' Association of Israel: POB 20123, 29 Carlebach St, Tel-Aviv 67132; tel. 3-5614121; fax 3-5611996; e-mail info@tbpai.co.il; internet www.tbpai.co.il; f. 1939; mems: 84 publishing firms; Chair. YARON SADAN; Man. Dir AMNON BEN-SHMUEL.

Broadcasting and Communications

TELECOMMUNICATIONS

013 Netvision: Omega Center, Matam, Haifa 3190501; tel. 4-8560660; fax 4-5201960; e-mail service@netvision013.net.il; internet www.013netvision.net.il; f. 2007 after merger with 013 Barak and GlobCall; CEO RAVIT BARNIV.

Bezeq—The Israel Telecommunication Corpn Ltd: Azrieli Center 2, Tel-Aviv 61620; tel. 3-6262600; fax 3-6262609; e-mail dover@bezeq.co.il; internet www.bezeq.co.il; f. 1984; privatized in May 2005; launched own cellular network, Pelephone Communications Ltd, in 1986; total assets NIS 15,156m. (Dec. 2007) CEO STELLA HANDLER; Chair. SHAUL ELOVITCH.

> **Pelephone Communications Ltd:** 33 Hagvura St, Givatayim, Tel-Aviv 53483; tel. 3-5728881; fax 3-5728111; internet www .pelephone.co.il; f. 1986; launched Esc brand in 2003; 2.85m. subscribers (2010); CEO GIL SHARON.

Cellcom Israel: POB 4060, 10 Hagavish St, Netanya 42140; tel. 52-9990052 (mobile); fax 52-9989700 (mobile); e-mail investors@cellcom .co.il; internet www.cellcom.co.il; f. 1994; mobile telecommunications operator; 3.19m. subscribers (Dec. 2012); Chair. AMI EREL; Pres. and CEO NIR SZTERN.

ECI Telecom Ltd: POB 3038, 30 Hasivim St, Petach-Tikva, Tel-Aviv 49133; tel. 3-9266555; fax 3-9266500; e-mail web.inquiries@ ecitele.com; internet www.ecitele.com; f. 1961; Pres. and CEO DARRYL EDWARDS.

MagicJack VocalTec Ltd (Vocal Tec): 14 Beni Ga'on St, Bldg B2-Rakefet, Netanya 42504; tel. 9-9703888; fax 9-9558175; e-mail info@ vocaltec.com; internet www.vocaltec.com; suppliers of VOIP software; Chair. DONALD A. BURNS; Pres. and CEO GERALD VENTO.

Partner Communications Co Ltd: POB 435, 8 Amal St, Afeq Industrial Park, Rosh Ha'ayin 48103; tel. 54-7814888 (mobile); fax 54-7814999 (mobile); e-mail deborah.margalit@orange.co.il; internet www.orange.co.il; f. 1999; provides mobile telecommunications and Wi-Fi internet services under the Orange brand name; represents about one-third of the mobile-cellular market in Israel; Chair. SHLOMO RODAV; CEO HAIM ROMANO.

BROADCASTING

In 1986 the Government approved the establishment of a commercial radio and television network to be run in competition with the state system.

Radio

Israel Broadcasting Authority (IBA) (Radio): POB 28080, 161 Jaffa Rd, Jerusalem 94342; tel. 2-5015555; e-mail dover@iba.org.il; internet www.iba.org.il; f. 1948; state-owned station in Jerusalem with additional studios in Tel-Aviv and Haifa; broadcasts six programmes for local and overseas listeners on medium-wave, shortwave and VHF/FM in 16 languages: Hebrew, Arabic, English, Yiddish, Ladino, Romanian, Hungarian, Moghrabi, Farsi, French,

Russian, Bukharian, Georgian, Portuguese, Spanish and Amharic; Chair. AMIR GILAT; Dir-Gen. YONI BEN-MENACHEM.

Galei Zahal: MPOB, Zahal; tel. 3-5126666; fax 3-5126760; e-mail radio@galatz.co.il; internet glz.co.il; f. 1950; Israel Defence Force broadcasting station, Tel-Aviv, with studios in Jerusalem; broadcasts 24-hour news, current affairs, music and cultural programmes in Hebrew on FM, medium and short waves; Dir YARON DEKEL.

Kol Israel (The Voice of Israel): POB 1082, 21 Heleni Hamalka, Jerusalem 91010; tel. 1-599509510; e-mail radiodirector@iba.org.il; internet www.iba.org.il/kolisrael; broadcasts music, news and multilingual programmes within Israel and overseas on short wave, AM and FM stereo, in 15 languages, incl. Hebrew, Arabic, French, English, Spanish, Ladino, Russian, Yiddish, Romanian, Hungarian, Amharic and Georgian; Dir SHMUEL BEN-ZVI; Gen. Dir YONI BEN-MENACHEM.

Television

Israel Broadcasting Authority (IBA) (Television): 161 Jaffa Rd, Jerusalem; tel. 2-5301333; fax 2-292944; internet www.iba.org.il; broadcasts began in 1968; station in Jerusalem with additional studios in Tel-Aviv; one colour network (VHF with UHF available in all areas); one satellite channel; broadcasts in Hebrew, Arabic and English; Chair. AMIR GILAT; Dir-Gen. YONI BEN-MENACHEM.

The Council of Cable TV and Satellite Broadcasting: 23 Jaffa Rd, Jerusalem 91999; tel. 2-6702210; fax 2-6702273; e-mail inbard@moc.gov.il; f. 1982; Chair. NATI SCHUBERT.

Israel Educational Television: Ministry of Education, 14 Klausner St, Tel-Aviv 69011; tel. 3-646227; fax 3-6466164; e-mail webmaster@ietv.gov.il; internet www.23tv.co.il; f. 1966 by Hanadiv (Rothschild Memorial Group) as Instructional Television Trust; began transmission in 1966; school programmes form an integral part of the syllabus in a wide range of subjects; also adult education; Dir-Gen. ELDAD KOBLENTZ.

Second Authority for Television and Radio: POB 3445, 20 Beit Hadfus St, Jerusalem 95464; tel. 2-6556222; fax 2-6556287; e-mail rashut@rashut2.org.il; internet www.rashut2.org.il; f. 1991; responsible for providing broadcasts through two principal television channels, Channel 2 and Channel 10, and some 14 radio stations; Chair. ILAN AVISHAR.

Finance

(cap. = capital; res = reserves; dep. = deposits, m. = million; br.(s) = branch(es); amounts in shekels)

BANKING

Central Bank

Bank of Israel: POB 780, Bank of Israel Bldg, Kiryat Ben-Gurion, Jerusalem 91007; tel. 2-6552211; fax 2-6528805; e-mail webmaster@bankisrael.gov.il; internet www.bankisrael.gov.il; f. 1954 as Cen. Bank of the State of Israel; cap. 60m., res 3,925m., dep. 212,688m. (Dec. 2009); Gov. Dr KARNIT FLUG; 1 br.

Principal Commercial Banks

Arab-Israel Bank Ltd: POB 207, 48 Bar Yehuda St, Tel Hanan, Nesher 36601; tel. 4-8205222; fax 4-8205250; e-mail aravi@bll.co.il; internet www.bank-aravi-israeli.co.il; res 315m., dep. 4,948m., total assets 5,761m. (Dec. 2011); subsidiary of Bank Leumi le-Israel BM; Chair. SHMUEL ZUSMAN; Gen. Man. ITZHAK EYAL.

Bank Hapoalim: 50 Rothschild Blvd, Tel-Aviv 61000; tel. 3-5673333; fax 3-5607028; internet www.bankhapoalim.co.il; f. 1921 as Workers' Bank; name changed as above 1961; mergers into the above: American-Israel Bank in 1999, Maritime Bank of Israel in 2003, Mishkan-Hapoalim Mortgage Bank and Israel Continental Bank in 2004; privatized in June 2000; cap. 8,010m., res 851m., dep. 278,055m. (Dec. 2012); Chair. YAIR SEROUSSI; Pres. and CEO ZION KENAN; 325 brs in Israel and 10 brs abroad.

Bank of Jerusalem Ltd: POB 2255, 2 Herbert Samuel St, Jerusalem 91022; tel. 2-6706018; fax 2-6234043; e-mail webmaster@bankjerusalem.co.il; internet www.bankjerusalem.co.il; private bank; cap. 127m., res 100m., dep. 9,877m. (Dec. 2012); Chair. JONATHAN IRONI; CEO PAZ URI; 14 brs.

Bank Leumi le-Israel BM: 34 Yehuda Halevi St, Tel-Aviv 65546; tel. 3-5148111; fax 3-5148656; e-mail pniot@bll.co.il; internet www.bankleumi.co.il; f. 1902 as Anglo-Palestine Co; renamed Anglo-Palestine Bank 1930; reincorporated as above 1951; 34.78% state-owned; cap. 7,059m., res 1,566m., dep. 294,062m. (Dec. 2012); Chair. DAVID BRODET; 242 brs in Israel and 2 abroad.

Bank Otsar Ha-Hayal Ltd: POB 52136, 11 Menachem Begin St, Ramat-Gan 52136; tel. 3-7556000; fax 3-7556007; e-mail ozfrndep@netvision.net.il; internet www.bankotsar.co.il; f. 1946; 68% owned by First Int. Bank of Israel, 24% by Hever Veterans & Pensions Ltd, 8%

by Provident Fund of the Employees of IAILTD; dep. 11,214.8m., total assets 13,638m. (Dec. 2008); Chair. SMADAR BARBER-TSADIK; Gen. Man. ISRAEL TRAU.

First International Bank of Israel Ltd (FIBI): 42 Rothschild Blvd, Tel-Aviv 66883; tel. 3-5196111; fax 3-5100316; e-mail zucker.d@fibi.co.il; internet www.fibi.co.il; f. 1972 by merger between Foreign Trade Bank Ltd and Export Bank Ltd; cap. 927m., res −16m., dep. 82,519m. (Dec. 2010); Chair. RONI HIZKIYAHU; CEO SMADAR BARBER-TSADIK; 182 brs in Israel and abroad (incl. subsidiaries).

Israel Discount Bank Ltd: POB 456, 27–31 Yehuda Halevi St, Tel-Aviv 61003; tel. 3-5145555; fax 3-5146954; e-mail intidb@discountbank.co.il; internet www.discountbank.co.il; f. 1935; name changed as above in 1957; cap. 665m., res 3,970m., dep. 156,660m., total assets 200,880m. (Dec. 2012); Chair. Dr JOSEPH BACHAR; Pres. and CEO LILACH ASHER-TOPILSKY; 126 brs in Israel and abroad.

Mercantile Discount Bank Ltd: POB 1292, 103 Allenby Rd, Tel-Aviv 61012; tel. 3-710550; fax 3-7105532; e-mail fec@mdb.co.il; internet www.mercantile.co.il; f. 1971 as Barclays Discount Bank Ltd, to take over (from Jan. 1972) the Israel brs of Barclays Bank Int. Ltd; Barclays Bank PLC, one of the joint owners, sold its total shareholding to the remaining owner, Israel Discount Bank Ltd, in Feb. 1993, and name changed as above that April; Mercantile Bank of Israel Ltd became branch of the above in March 1997; cap. 51m., res 246m., dep. 22,558m. (Dec. 2012); Chair. Dr JOSEPH BACHAR; Pres. and CEO REUVEN SPIEGEL; 66 brs.

Mizrahi Tefahot Bank Ltd: POB 3450, 7 Jabotinsky St, Ramat-Gan 52136; tel. 3-7559468; fax 3-6234819; e-mail lernerh@umtb.co.il; internet www.mizrahi-tefahot.co.il; f. 1923 as Mizrahi Bank Ltd; mergers into the above: Hapoel Hamizrahi Bank Ltd, as United Mizrahi Bank Ltd; Finance and Trade Bank Ltd in 1990; Tefahot Israel Mortgage Bank Ltd in 2005, when name changed as above; Adanim Mortgage Bank merged into above bank in 2009; cap. 2,108m., res 18m., dep. 143,347m. (Dec. 2013); Chair. MOSHE VIDMAN; Pres. and CEO ELDAD FRESHER, 166 brs.

UBank Ltd: POB 677, 38 Rothschild Blvd, Tel-Aviv 61006; tel. 3-5645645; fax 3-5645285; e-mail gsteiger@u-bank.net; internet www.u-bank.net; f. 1934 as Palestine Credit Utility Bank Ltd; renamed Israel General Bank Ltd 1964; ownership transferred to Investec Bank Ltd (South Africa) 1996; name changed to Investec Clali Bank Ltd 1999, and to Investec Bank (Israel) Ltd 2001; control of bank transferred to First Int. Bank of Israel 2004 and name changed as above 2005; cap. 60m., res 346m., dep. 6,684m. (Dec. 2012); Chair. YORAM SIRKIS; CEO BEDNY RON; 8 brs.

Union Bank of Israel Ltd: 6–8 Ahuzat Bayit St, Tel-Aviv 65143; tel. 3-5191222; fax 3-5191344; e-mail info@ubi.co.il; internet www.ubi.co.il; f. 1951; cap. 952m., res 100m., (Dec. 2012); dep. 30,843m. (Dec. 2013); Chair. ZEEV ABELES; Pres. and CEO HAIM FREILICHMAN; 35 brs.

Mortgage Banks

Discount Mortgage Bank Ltd: POB 2844, 16–18 Simtat Beit Hashoeva, Tel-Aviv 61027; tel. 3-5643311; fax 3-5661704; e-mail contact@discountbank.net; internet www.discountbank.net; f. 1959; subsidiary of Israel Discount Bank Ltd; total assets 10,355m. (Dec. 2005); Chair. SHLOMO ZOHAR; Pres. and CEO GIORA OFFER; 3 brs.

Leumi Mortgage Bank Ltd: POB 69, 31–37 Montefiore St, Tel-Aviv 65201; tel. 3-5648444; fax 3-5648334; f. 1921 as Gen. Mortgage Bank Ltd; subsidiary of Bank Leumi le-Israel BM; res 2,567m., dep. 48,605m., total assets 56,532m. (Dec. 2011); Chair. AVI ZELDMAN; Gen. Man. R. ZABAG; 9 brs.

STOCK EXCHANGE

The Tel-Aviv Stock Exchange: 54 Ahad Ha'am St, Tel-Aviv 65202; tel. 3-5677411; fax 3-5105379; e-mail info@tase.co.il; internet tase.co.il; f. 1953; Chair. SAUL BRONFELD; CEO ESTER LEVANON.

INSURANCE

The Israel Insurance Assen lists 14 member companies; a selection of these are listed below, as are some non-members.

Clal Insurance Enterprise Holdings Ltd: POB 326, 46 Petach Tikva Rd, Tel-Aviv 66184; tel. 3-6387777; fax 3-6387676; e-mail avigdork@clal-ins.co.il; internet www.clalbit.co.il; f. 1962; 55% owned by IDB Group, 10% by Bank Hapoalim and 35% by the public; insurance, pensions and finance; Chair. KAPLAN AVIGDOR.

Dikla Insurance Co Ltd: 1 Ben Gurion Rd, BSR-2 Tower, Bnei Brak 51201; tel. 3-6145555; fax 3-6145566; internet www.dikla.co.il; f. 1976; health and long-term care insurance; Chair. YAIR HAMBURGER.

Eliahu Insurance Co Ltd: 2 Ibn Gvirol St, Tel-Aviv 64077; tel. 3-6920911; fax 3-6952117; e-mail gad.nussbaum@eliahu.com; internet www.eliahu.co.il; f. 1966; Chair. SHLOMO ELIAHU; Man. Dir OFER ELIAHU.

Harel Insurance Investments and Financial Services Ltd: Tel-Aviv; tel. 3-7547000; e-mail infonet@harel-group.co.il; internet www .harel-group.co.il; f. 1935 as Hamishmar Insurance Service; Harel est. 1975, became Harel Hamishmar Investments Ltd 1982, Harel Insurance Investments Ltd 1998 and current name adopted 2007; 39.9% owned by Hamburger family, 20.2% by Sampoerna Capital; Chair. GIDEON HAMBURGER.

Menorah Mivtachim Insurance Co Ltd: POB 927, 15 Allenby St, Tel-Aviv 61008; tel. 3-7107777; fax 3-7107402; e-mail anat-by@ bezeqint.net; internet www.menoramivt.co.il; f. 1935; Chair. MENACHEM GUREWITZ; Gen. Man. SHABTAI ENGEL.

Migdal Insurance Co Ltd: POB 37633, 26 Sa'adiya Ga'on St, Tel-Aviv 67135; tel. 3-5637637; fax 3-9295189; e-mail marketing@ migdal-group.co.il; internet www.migdal.co.il; 70% owned by Generali Group; 10% by Bank Leumi and 20% by the public; f. 1934; Chair. AHARON FOGEL; CEO YONEL COHEN.

Phoenix Insurance Co Ltd: 53 Derech Hashalom St, Givatayim 53454; tel. 3-7332222; fax 3-5735151; e-mail ir@fnx.co.il; internet www.fnx.co.il; f. 1949; controlled by Delek Group; Pres. and CEO EYAL LAPIDOT.

Trade and Industry

DEVELOPMENT ORGANIZATIONS

Galilee Development Authority: POB 2511, Acco 24316; tel. 4-9552426; fax 4-9552440; e-mail judith@galil.gov.il; internet www .galilee.gov.il; f. 1993; statutory authority responsible for the social and economic devt of the Galilee region; Man. Dir MOSHE DAVIDOVITZ.

Jerusalem Development Authority (JDA): 2 Safra Sq., Jerusalem 91322; tel. 2-6297627; e-mail moty@jda.gov.il; internet www.jda .gov.il; f. 1988; statutory authority responsible for the economic devt of Jerusalem; CEO MOTY HAZAN.

Negev Development Authority: Negev; e-mail negev_de@ netvision.net.il; internet www.negev.co.il; f. 1991; statutory authority responsible for the economic and social devt of the Negev region, and co-ordination between govt offices; Chair SHMUEL RIFMAN.

CHAMBERS OF COMMERCE

Federation of Israeli Chambers of Commerce: POB 20027, 84 Ha' Hashmonaim St, Tel-Aviv 67132; tel. 3-5631020; fax 3-5619027; e-mail chamber@chamber.org.il; internet www.chamber.org.il; co-ordinates the Tel-Aviv, Jerusalem, Haifa, Nazareth and Beersheba Chambers of Commerce; Pres. URIEL LYNN.

Israel Federation of Bi-National Chambers of Commerce and Industry with and in Israel: POB 50196, 29 Hamered St, Tel-Aviv 61500; tel. 3-5177737; fax 3-5142881; e-mail felixk@export.gov.il; Chair. JAIME ARON; Man. Dir FELIX KIPPER.

Beersheba Chamber of Commerce: POB 5278, 7 Hamuktar St, Beersheba 84152; tel. 8-6234222; fax 8-6234899; e-mail chamber7@ zahav.net.il; internet www.negev-chamber.org.il.

Chamber of Commerce and Industry of Haifa and the North: POB 33176, 53 Ha'atzmaut Rd, Haifa 31331; tel. 4-8302100; fax 4-8645428; e-mail main@haifachamber.org.il; internet www .haifachamber.com; f. 1921; 850 mems; Pres. GAD SCHAFFER; Man. Dir DOV MAROM.

Israel-British Chamber of Commerce: POB 50321, Industry House, 13th Floor, 29 Hamered St, Tel-Aviv 61502; tel. 3-5109424; fax 3-5109540; e-mail info@ibcc.co.il; internet www.ibcc.co.il; f. 1951; 350 mems; annual bilateral trade of more than US $3,000m; Chair. LEN JUDES; Exec. Dir FELIX KIPPER.

Jerusalem Chamber of Commerce: POB 2083, Jerusalem 91020; tel. 2-6254333; fax 2-6254335; e-mail jerccom@inter.net.il; internet www.jerccom.co.il; f. 1908; 200 mems; Pres. NAHUM WISSMANN.

INDUSTRIAL AND TRADE ASSOCIATIONS

The Centre for International Agricultural Development Cooperation (CINADCO): POB 30, Beit Dagan 50250; tel. 3-9485760; fax 3-9485761; e-mail cinadco@moag.gov.il; shares agricultural experience through the integration of research and project devt; runs specialized training courses, advisory missions and feasibility projects in Israel and abroad, incl. those in co-operation with developing countries; Dir YACOV POLEG.

Israel Dairy Board (IDB): POB 97, 4 Derech Hahoresh, Yahud 56100; tel. 3-9564750; fax 3-9564766; e-mail office@milk.org.il; internet www.israeldairy.com; regulates dairy farming and the dairy industry; implements govt policy on the planning of milk production and marketing; CEO MICHAL KRAUS.

Israel Diamond Exchange Ltd: 3 Jabotinsky Rd, Ramat-Gan 52130; tel. 3-5760301; fax 3-5750652; e-mail ella@isde.co.il; internet www.isde.co.il; f. 1937; production, export, import and finance facilities; exports: polished diamonds US $6,610m., rough diamonds $2,701m. (2006); Pres. and Chair. SHMUEL SCHNITZER; Vice-Pres. BEN ZION SHASHU.

Israel Export and International Co-operation Institute: POB 50084, 29 Hamered St, Tel-Aviv 68125; tel. 3-5142900; fax 3-5162810; e-mail galit@export.gov.il; internet www.export.gov.il; f. 1958; jt venture between the state and private sectors; Chair. RAMZI GABBAY.

The Israeli Cotton Board: POB 384, Herzlia B 46103; tel. 9-9604003; fax 9-9604010; e-mail mali@cotton.co.il; internet www .cotton.co.il; f. 1956 as the Israel Cotton Production and Marketing Board; CEO URI GILAD.

Kibbutz Industries' Asscn: POB 40012, 13 Leonardo da Vinci St, Tel-Aviv 61400; tel. 3-6955413; fax 3-6951464; e-mail kia@kia.co.il; internet www.kia.co.il; f. 1962; liaison office for marketing and export of the goods produced by Israel's kibbutzim; Chair. YONATAN BASI; Man. Dir UDI ORENSTEIN.

Manufacturers' Asscn of Israel: POB 50022, Industry House, 29 Hamered St, Tel-Aviv 61500; tel. 3-5198832; fax 3-5103154; e-mail leor@industry.org.il; internet www.industry.org.il; 1,700 mem. enterprises employing nearly 85% of industrial workers in Israel; Dir AMIR HAYEK; Pres. SHRAGA BROSH.

National Federation of Israeli Journalists: POB 585, Beit Agron, 37 Hillet St, Jerusalem 91004; tel. 2-6254351; fax 3-6254353; e-mail office@jaj.org.il; Chair. AHIYA GENOSAR.

Plants Production and Marketing Board: 46 Derech Ha'macabim, Rishon le Zion 75359; tel. 3-9595666; fax 3-9502211; e-mail plants@plants.org.il; internet www.plants.org.il; includes fruit, citrus fruit, vegetable and olive board.

UTILITIES

Israel Electric Corporation Ltd (IEC): POB 58003, Halechi 17, Bnei-Brak IT School, Haifa 1200; tel. 3-6174944; fax 3-6174922; e-mail ucgia@iec.co.il; internet www.iec.co.il; state-owned; total assets US $21,065m. (Dec. 2009); Chair. YIFTAH RON TAL; Pres. and CEO ELI GLIKMAN.

Mekorot (Israel National Water Co): POB 2012, 9 Lincoln St, Tel-Aviv 61201; tel. 3-6230555; fax 3-6230833; e-mail m-doveret@ mekorot.co.il; internet www.mekorot.co.il; f. 1937; state-owned; sales more than US $700m. (2006); Chair. ALEX WIZNITZER; CEO SHIMON BEN HAMO.

The Histadrut

Histadrut (General Federation of Labour in Israel): 93 Arlozorof St, Tel-Aviv 62098; tel. 3-6921511; fax 3-6921512; e-mail avitals@ histadrut.org.il; internet www.histadrut.org.il; f. 1920; Chair. AVI NISSENKORN.

The Histadrut is the largest labour organization in Israel. It strives to ensure the social security, welfare and rights of workers, and to assist in their professional advancement, while endeavouring to reduce the divisions in Israeli society. Membership of the Histadrut is voluntary, and open to all men and women of 18 years of age and above who live on the earnings of their own labour without exploiting the work of others. These include the self-employed and professionals, as well as housewives, students, pensioners and the unemployed. Workers' interests are protected through a number of occupational and professional unions affiliated to the Histadrut (see below). The organization operates courses for trade unionists and new immigrants, as well as apprenticeship classes. It maintains an Institute for Social and Economic Issues and the International Institute, one of the largest centres of leadership training in Israel, for students from Africa, Asia, Latin America and Eastern Europe, which includes the Levinson Centre for Adult Education and the Jewish-Arab Institute for Regional Co-operation. Attached to the Histadrut is Na'amat, a women's organization which promotes changes in legislation, operates a network of legal service bureaux and vocational training courses, and runs counselling centres for the treatment and prevention of domestic violence; women joining the Histadrut automatically become members of Na'amat.

ORGANIZATION

In 2006 the Histadrut had a membership of 700,000. In addition, over 100,000 young people under 18 years of age belong to the Organization of Working and Student Youth, HaNoar HaOved VeHalomed, a direct affiliate of the Histadrut.

All members take part in elections to the Histadrut Convention (Veida), which elects the General Council (Moetsa) and the Executive Committee (Vaad Hapoel). The latter elects the 41-member Executive Bureau (Vaada Merakezet), which is responsible for day-to-day implementation of policy. The Executive Committee also elects the Secretary-General, who acts as its chairman as well as head of the organization as a whole and chairman of the Executive Bureau. Nearly all political parties are represented on the Histadrut Executive Committee.

The Executive Committee has the following departments: Trade Union, Organization and Labour Councils, Education and Culture, Social Security, Industrial Democracy, Students, Youth and Sports, Consumer Protection, Administration, Finance and International.

TRADE UNION ACTIVITIES

Collective agreements with employers fix wage scales, which are linked with the retail price index; provide for social benefits, including paid sick leave and employers' contributions to sick and pension and provident funds; and regulate dismissals. Dismissal compensation is regulated by law. The Histadrut actively promotes productivity through labour management boards and the National Productivity Institute, and supports incentive pay schemes.

There are unions for the following groups: clerical workers, building workers, teachers, engineers, agricultural workers, technicians, textile workers, printing workers, diamond workers, metal workers, food and bakery workers, wood workers, government employees, seamen, nurses, civilian employees of the armed forces, actors, musicians and variety artists, social workers, watchmen, cinema technicians, institutional and school staff, pharmacy employees, medical laboratory workers, X-ray technicians, physiotherapists, social scientists, microbiologists, psychologists, salaried lawyers, pharmacists, physicians, occupational therapists, truck and taxi drivers, hotel and restaurant workers, workers in Histadrut-owned industry, garment, shoe and leather workers, plastic and rubber workers, editors of periodicals, painters and sculptors, and industrial workers.

Histadrut Trade Union Department: Chair. DANIEL AVI NISSENKORN.

Transport

RAILWAYS

In 2012 Israel's active railway network, including sidings, comprised an estimated 1,138 km of track. Freight traffic consists mainly of grain, phosphates, potash, containers, petroleum and building materials. A rail route serves Haifa and Ashdod ports on the Mediterranean Sea, while a combined rail-road service extends to Eilat port on the Red Sea. Passenger services operate between the main towns: Nahariya, Haifa, Tel-Aviv and Jerusalem. Construction of a high-speed rail link between Jerusalem and Tel-Aviv commenced in 2001. However, owing to technical and financial difficulties, completion of the project was not expected before 2017. The first line of a light railway network intended to ease traffic congestion in Jerusalem was inaugurated in August 2011. The project was a source of considerable controversy owing to the incorporation within the network of disputed Jewish developments in East Jerusalem.

Israel Railways (IR): POB 18085, Central Station, Tel-Aviv 61180; tel. 3-5774000; fax 3-6937443; e-mail israelrailways@tservice.co.il; internet www.rail.co.il; f. 2003 as an ind. govt-owned corpn; prior to that date IR had operated as a unit of the Ports and Railways Authority; CEO BOAZ ZAFRIR.

Underground Railway

Haifa Underground Funicular Railway: 122 Hanassi Ave, Haifa 34633; tel. 4-8376861; fax 4-8376875; e-mail orna@carmelit.com; internet www.carmelit.com; opened 1959; 2 km in operation.

ROADS

In 2012 there were 18,697 km of roads, of which 10,489 km were classified as urban roads, 6,582 km as non-urban roads, and 1,582 km as access roads.

Ministry of Transport, National Infrastructures and Road Safety: see The Government—Ministries

Egged Bus Co-operative: POB 43, Egged Bldg, Airport City 70150; tel. 3-9142000; fax 3-9142237; internet www.egged.co.il; f. 1933; operates 3,057 bus routes throughout Israel; Chair. GIDEON MIZRACHI.

SHIPPING

At 31 December 2014 Israel's flag registered fleet consisted of 40 vessels, with a combined aggregate displacement of 274,842 grt, of which one was a fish carrier and four were general cargo ships.

Haifa and Ashdod are the main ports in Israel. The former is a natural harbour, enclosed by two main breakwaters and dredged to 45 ft below mean sea level. Haifa handled 24.0m. metric tons of cargo and 1.4m. 20-ft equivalent units (TEUs) in 2012. The deep-water port at Ashdod was completed in 1965. A new NIS 3,000m. container terminal, Eitan Port, was inaugurated at Ashdod in 2005. Ashdod

handled 19.5m. tons of cargo and 1.2m. TEUs in 2012. In 2009 the Government approved proposals to sell minority stakes in the Haifa and Ashdod port companies. The three-stage privatization process commenced in early 2010, with 15% of the shares in each company to be sold via a public offering.

The port of Eilat, Israel's gateway to the Red Sea, has storage facilities for crude petroleum. It is a natural harbour, operated from a wharf. In April 2011 the Government announced its intention fully to privatize the Eilat Port Company. The plan was approved by the Knesset in May 2012, and in November Papo Maritime Ltd was awarded a 15-year franchise.

Port Authority and Companies

Israel Ports Development and Assets Co Ltd (IPC): POB 20121, 74 Menachem Begin Rd, Tel-Aviv 61201; tel. 3-5657060; fax 3-5622281; e-mail dovf@israports.co.il; internet www.israports.co.il; f. 1961 as the Israel Ports Authority (PRA); the IPC was established by legislation in 2005 as part of the Israeli Port Reform Program, whereby the PRA was abolished and replaced by four govt-owned cos: the IPC as owner and developer of port and infrastructure, and three port-operating cos responsible for handling cargo in each of Israel's three commercial seaports; responsible for devt and management of Israel's port infrastructure on behalf of the Govt and carries out some of the largest infrastructure projects in the country; CEO SHLOMO BRIEMAN.

Ashdod Port Co Ltd: POB 9001, Ashdod 77191; tel. 8-8517605; fax 8-8517632; e-mail igalbz@ashdodport.co.il; internet www.ashdodport.co.il; provides full range of freight and passenger services; f. 1965; CEO ISAAC BLUMENTHAL.

Haifa Port Co Ltd: Haifa; tel. 4-8518666; fax 4-8518215; internet www.haifaport.co.il; 6.5-km dock, 10.5 m–14 m draught; f. 1933; CEO MENDI ZALTZMAN.

Principal Shipping Companies

XT Shipping: POB 15090, 9 Andre Saharov St, Matam Park, Haifa 31905; tel. 4-8610610; fax 4-8501515; e-mail shipping@xtholdings.com; internet www.oferg.com; f. 1956 as shipping agency, Mediterranean Seaways; fmrly known as Ofer Shipping Group, renamed as above in 2012; part of the XT Group; runs cargo and container services; Chair. UDI ANGEL.

ZIM Integrated Shipping Services Ltd: POB 1723, 9 Andrei Sakharov St, MATAM Park, Haifa 31016; tel. 4-8652111; fax 4-8652956; e-mail shats.avner@il.zim.com; internet www.zim.co.il; f. 1945; 100% owned by the Israel Corpn; international integrated transportation system providing door-to-door services around the world; operates about 100 vessels; estimated 2.5m. TEUs of cargo carried in 2013; Chair. of Bd NIR GILAD; Pres. and CEO RAFI DANIELI.

CIVIL AVIATION

The principal airport is Ben-Gurion International Airport, situated about 15 km from the centre of Tel-Aviv. Limited international services also operate from Ovda Airport in the Negev Desert. The busiest domestic airports are located at Eilat, Haifa, Rosh Pina and Sde Dov (Tel-Aviv). In 2011 the Government approved a proposal to build a new international airport with a capacity of 1.5m. passengers at Timna, north of Eilat, at a projected cost of NIS 1,700m. Construction of the airport, which was to replace the existing airports at Eilat and Ovda, was expected to be completed in 2016.

Israel Airports Authority: POB 137, Ben-Gurion Airport, Tel-Aviv 70100; tel. 3-9752386; fax 3-9752387; e-mail avia@iaa.gov.il; internet www.iaa.gov.il; f. 1977; Chair. ELI OVADIA.

El Al Israel Airlines Ltd: 32 Ben-Yehuda St, Tel-Aviv; tel. 3-9771111; fax 3-6292312; e-mail customer@elal.co.il; internet www.elal.co.il; f. 1948; over 40% owned by Knafaim-Arkia Holdings Ltd; about 31% state-owned; regular services to many European cities, as well as to destinations in North America, Africa and Asia; direct flights to Brazil, with connecting flights to other South American destinations, launched in early 2009; Chair. of Bd AMIKAM COHEN; Pres. and CEO DAVID MAIMON.

Arkia Israeli Airlines Ltd: POB 39301, Dov Airport, Tel-Aviv 61392; tel. 3-6902210; fax 3-6903311; e-mail customer.service@arkia.co.il; internet www.arkia.co.il; f. 1980 by merger of Kanaf-Arkia Airlines and Aviation Services; scheduled passenger services linking Tel-Aviv, Jerusalem, Haifa, Eilat, Rosh Pina, Kiryat Shmona and Yotveta; charter services to many European destinations, Turkey and Jordan; CEO GAD TEPPER.

Israir Airlines: POB 26444, 23 Ben Yehuda St, Tel-Aviv 63806; tel. 3-7954008; fax 3-7954051; e-mail site@israir.co.il; internet www.israir.co.il; f. 1996; domestic flights between Tel-Aviv and Eilat, and international flights to destinations in Europe and the USA; Pres. and CEO DAVID KAMINITZ.

Tourism

Israel possesses a wealth of antiquities and cultural attractions, in particular the historic and religious sites of Jerusalem. The country has a varied landscape, with a Mediterranean coastline, as well as desert and mountain terrain. The Red Sea resort of Eilat has become an important centre for diving holidays, while many tourists visit the treatment spas of the Dead Sea. In 2013 an estimated 3.0m. tourists visited Israel, compared with 2.9m. the previous year. Tourism receipts, including passenger transport, in 2013 totalled US $5,666m., according to provisional figures.

Ministry of Tourism: See The Government—Ministries; Dir-Gen. AMIR HALEVY.

Defence

The General Staff: Consists of the Chiefs of the General Staff, Personnel, Technology and Logistics, Intelligence, Operations, and Plans and Policy Branches of the Defence Forces, the Commanders-in-Chief of the Air Force and the Navy, and the officers commanding the 4 Territorial Commands (Northern, Central, Southern and Home Front). It is headed by the Chief of Staff of the Armed Forces.

Chief of Staff of the Armed Forces: Lt-Gen. GADI EISENKOT.

Chief of Ground Forces Command: Maj.-Gen. GUY ZUR.

Commander-in-Chief of the Air Force: Maj.-Gen. AMIR ESHEL.

Commander-in-Chief of the Navy: Vice Adm. RAM ROTHBERG.

Defence Budget (2014): NIS 71,800m.

Military Service (Jewish and Druze population only; Christians, Circassians and Muslims may volunteer): Officers are conscripted for regular service of 48 months, men 36 months, women 24 months. Annual training as reservists thereafter, to age 40 for men (54 for some specialists), 38 (or marriage/pregnancy) for women.

Total Armed Forces (as assessed at November 2014): 176,500: army 133,000 (107,000 conscripts); navy 9,500 (2,500 conscripts); air force 34,000. Reserves 465,000.

Paramilitary Forces (as assessed at November 2014): est. 8,000.

Education

Israel has high standards of literacy and advanced educational services. Free, compulsory education is provided for all children between five and 15 years of age. Following the recommendations of a committee set up in 2011 to investigate ways to improve socio-economic conditions within Israel, the Government announced that pre-primary education for children aged three and four years in public institutions would be provided free of charge. The changes entered into effect in August 2012, at the beginning of the new academic year. Primary education is provided for all those between five and 10 years of age. There is also secondary, vocational and agricultural education. Post-primary education comprises two cycles of three years. According to UNESCO estimates, enrolment at primary schools in 2010 included 97% of pupils in the relevant age-group, while 98% of pupils in the appropriate age-group were enrolled at secondary schools. There are six universities, as well as the Technion (Israel Institute of Technology) in Haifa and the Weizmann Institute of Science in Rehovot. In 2010 general government expenditure on education totalled NIS 55,015m. (some 15.9% of total spending).

OCCUPIED TERRITORIES

EAST JERUSALEM

LOCATION

Greater Jerusalem includes: Israeli West Jerusalem (99% Jewish); the Old City and Mount of Olives; East Jerusalem (the Palestinian residential and commercial centre); Arab villages declared to be part of Jerusalem by Israel in 1967; and Jewish neighbourhoods constructed since 1967, either on land expropriated from Arab villages or in areas requisitioned as 'government land'. Although the area of the Greater Jerusalem district is 627 sq km, the Old City of Jerusalem covers just 1 sq km.

DEMOGRAPHY

Immediately prior to the 1967 Arab–Israeli War, East Jerusalem and its Arab environs had an Arab population of approximately 70,000, and a small Jewish population in the old Jewish quarter of the city. By contrast, Israeli West Jerusalem had a Jewish population of 196,000. As a result of this imbalance, in the Greater Jerusalem district as a whole the Jewish population was in the majority. Israeli policy following the occupation of East Jerusalem and the West Bank consisted of encircling the eastern sector of the city with Jewish settlements. In contrast to the more politically sensitive siting of Jewish settlements in the old Arab quarter of Jerusalem, the Government of Itzhak Rabin concentrated on the outer circle of settlement-building. Official statistics for the end of 2013 reported that Greater Jerusalem had a total population of 1,008,400, of whom 673,100 were Jews, 306,300 were Muslims and 15,900 were Christians. The Jerusalem Institute for Israel Studies (JIIS) estimated in August 2007 that the growth rate for the Arab population of Greater Jerusalem was almost double that of the Jewish population. According to the JIIS, if this trend continued, the city's population would have a Jewish-Arab ratio of 60:40 by 2020, and of 50:50 by 2035. In May 2007 the mayor of Jerusalem, Uri Lupolianski, suggested easing the restrictions on family reunification for the estimated 10,000 Christian Arabs in Jerusalem, in order to prevent a further decline in their number.

The Old City, within the walls of which are found the ancient quarters of the Jews, Christians, Muslims and Armenians, is predominantly Arab. According to JIIS, the Old City had a total population of 38,700 in 2012.

ADMINISTRATION

Until the 1967 Arab–Israeli War, Jerusalem had been divided into the new city of West Jerusalem—captured by Jewish forces in 1948—and the old city, East Jerusalem, which was part of Jordan. Israel's victory in 1967, however, reunited the city under Israeli control. Two weeks after the fighting had ended, on 28 June, Israeli law was applied to East Jerusalem and the municipal boundaries were extended by 45 km (28 miles). Jerusalem had effectively been annexed. Israeli officials, however, still refer to the 'reunification' of Jerusalem.

Immediately following the occupation, all electricity, water and telephone grids in West Jerusalem were extended to the east. Roads were widened and cleared, and the Arab population immediately in front of the 'Wailing Wall' was forcibly evicted. Arabs living in East Jerusalem became 'permanent residents' and could apply for Israeli citizenship if they wished (in contrast to Arabs in the West Bank and Gaza Strip). However, few chose to do so. None the less, issued with identity cards (excluding the estimated 25,000 Arabs from the West Bank and Gaza living illegally in the city), the Arab residents were taxed by the Israeli authorities, and their businesses and banks became subject to Israeli laws and business regulations. Now controlling approximately one-half of all land in East Jerusalem and the surrounding Palestinian villages (previously communally, or privately, owned by Palestinians), the Israeli authorities allowed Arabs to construct buildings on only 10%–15% of the land in the city, and East Jerusalem's commercial district has been limited to three streets.

In May 1999 the Israeli Government announced its refusal to grant Israeli citizenship to several hundred Arabs living in East Jerusalem, regardless of their compliance with the conditions stipulated under the Citizenship Law. In October, however, Israel ended its policy of revoking the right of Palestinians to reside in Jerusalem if they had spent more than seven years outside the city. Moreover, the Israeli Government announced in March 2000 that Palestinian residents of Jerusalem whose identity cards had been revoked could apply for their restoration.

At the Camp David talks held between Israel and the Palestinian (National) Authority (PA) in July 2000, the issue of who would have sovereignty over East Jerusalem in a future 'permanent status' agreement proved to be the principal obstacle to the achievement of a peace deal. It was reported that the Israeli Government had offered the PA municipal autonomy over certain areas of East Jerusalem (including access to the Islamic holy sites), although sovereignty would remain in Israeli hands; the proposals were rejected by PA President Yasser Arafat. In September the holy sites of East Jerusalem were the initial focal point of a renewed uprising by Palestinians against the Israeli authorities, which became known as the al-Aqsa *intifada* (after Jerusalem's al-Aqsa Mosque). The publication of the internationally sponsored 'roadmap' peace plan in April 2003 offered directions for talks on the Jerusalem issue, although progress was halted by the resumption of attacks by Palestinian militants against Israeli citizens and Israeli counterattacks later that year.

Following a lengthy period during which all negotiations between Israel and the PA were effectively stalled, some optimism was expressed in August 2007 when the Israeli Prime Minister, Ehud Olmert, held direct talks with the PA President, Mahmud Abbas, in the West Bank town of Jericho in preparation for an international Middle East peace conference, which was convened in Annapolis, USA, in November. The US Administration of President George W. Bush declared its intention that a permanent agreement could be reached by the end of the year. However, an increase in attacks on northern Israel by Palestinian militants from the Gaza Strip from January 2008, and a consequent military campaign by Israeli forces in Gaza, resulted in a stalling of negotiations. In February the Israeli Prime Minister angered Palestinians by declaring that talks concerning the final status of Jerusalem, and the key Palestinian demand that East Jerusalem become their capital, would be the last 'core issue' on the agenda to be negotiated by the two parties. Moreover, the Israeli Government continued to issue tenders for hundreds of new housing units at Jewish settlements in East Jerusalem and the West Bank, thereby contravening its obligations under the terms of the roadmap.

Renewed diplomatic efforts followed the inauguration of Barack Obama as US President in January 2009. The Obama Administration demanded a temporary halt to Israel's settlement-building programme as a precondition for the resumption of negotiations. However, although in December the Israeli Government announced the imposition of a 10-month moratorium on settlement-building in the West Bank, building activity in East Jerusalem was exempted. In March 2010 Netanyahu asserted that the settlements were an 'integral and inextricable' part of the city and that building activity in all areas of Jerusalem would continue. Following the expiry in September of the moratorium, the PA suspended its involvement in the peace process, stating that it would resume talks only when the Israeli Government had agreed to end both settlement construction and the blockade of Gaza.

Nevertheless, settlement-building activity continued apace. In August 2011 the Israeli Government approved plans for the construction of 1,600 new homes at Ramat Shlomo, announced in March 2010, and in the following month indicated its intention to authorize the construction of a brand new settlement at Givat Hamatos, to the south of Jerusalem; the new settlement was to incorporate some 2,600 homes. Following the PA's acceptance at the end of October as a full member of UNESCO, the Israeli Government announced that it was to accelerate the construction of around 2,000 homes for settlers in East Jerusalem and the West Bank. Further plans for expansion at the Har Homa and Pisgat Ze'ev settlements were published in January and April 2012. In October the Israeli Government gave its final approval to plans for 797 new homes at Gilo. After the UN General Assembly's decision in November to upgrade the PA's status in the organization to that of a non-member observer state (Abbas having applied for full UN membership in September), Netanyahu announced his Government's intention to accelerate plans for the construction of some 3,000 new homes in the so-called E-1 area between Jerusalem and the Ma'ale Adumim settlement to the east of the city.

During a visit to Jerusalem in March 2013, President Obama appealed for Israel to resume negotiations with the PA. Following subsequent repeated visits to the region by the newly appointed US Secretary of State, John Kerry, preliminary talks were held in Washington, DC, USA, in July between Israel's chief negotiator, Minister of Justice Tzipi Livni, and Saeb Erakat for the PA. The stated aim of those talks was for both parties to reach a limited peace agreement within nine months. Formal discussions, moderated by President Obama's Special Envoy for Israeli-Palestinian

Negotiations, Martin Indyk, commenced in Jerusalem and Jericho in August. However, the prospects of an agreement being reached before the deadline were diminished by ongoing instances of Israeli–Palestinian violence and by the Israeli Government's continuation of its controversial settlement-building programme in East Jerusalem and the West Bank. Moreover, in mid-April 2014 Israel suspended the transfer of tax revenues to the PA over the latter's accession to UN institutions, and later that month Prime Minister Netanyahu suspended Israel's participation in the process following the announcement of a national unity agreement between Hamas and Fatah. A so-called unity administration, with jurisdiction over the Gaza Strip and the West Bank, was appointed in June.

In early October 2014 the Jerusalem Municipality announced that it had approved plans for the construction of 2,500 homes in Givat Hamatos, a development that would complete a band of Jewish housing in East Jerusalem and thus obstruct any future Palestinian state from establishing a capital city there. On a two-day visit to Israel and Palestine in that month, UN Secretary-General Ban Ki-Moon announced that the settlement proposal was a 'clear violation of international law' and urged Netanyahu to make compromises for peace with the Palestinians. However, Israel announced plans later that month for an additional 400 homes in Har Homa and 600 in Ramat Shlomo. The announcement followed a threat by the Minister of the Economy, Naftali Bennett, that his Jewish Home party would destabilize Netanyahu's governing coalition unless he 'unfroze' settlement building. Remarks by Netanyahu during campaigning for the March 2015 legislative elections indicating his renewed opposition to the establishment of a Palestinian state were condemned by opposition parties and by the international community. Amid attempts by Netanyahu to form a new, right-wing coalition government, in late March Israel announced the resumption of revenue transfers to the PA.

THE GOLAN HEIGHTS

LOCATION AND CLIMATE

The Golan Heights, a mountainous plateau that formed most of Syria's Quneitra Province (1,710 sq km) and parts of Dar'a Province, was occupied by Israel after the Arab–Israeli War of June 1967. Following the Disengagement Agreement of 1974, Israel continued to occupy some 70% of the territory (1,176 sq km), valued for its strategic position and abundant water resources (the headwaters of the Jordan river have their source on the slopes of Mount Hermon). The average height of the Golan is approximately 1,200 m above sea level in the northern region and about 300 m above sea level in the southern region, near Lake Tiberias (the Sea of Galilee). Rainfall ranges from about 1,000 mm per year in the north to less than 600 mm per year in the southern region.

DEMOGRAPHY

As a consequence of the Israeli occupation, an estimated 93% of the ethnically diverse Syrian population of 147,613, distributed across 163 villages and towns and 108 individual farms, was expelled. The majority were Arab Sunni Muslims, but the population also included Alawite and Druze minorities and some Circassians, Turkmen, Armenians and Kurds. Approximately 9,000 Palestinian refugees from the 1948 Arab–Israeli War also inhabited the area. At the time of the occupation, 64% of the labour force was employed in agriculture. Only one-fifth of the population resided in the administrative centres. By 1991 the Golan Heights had a Jewish population of about 12,000 living in 21 Jewish settlements (four new settlements had been created by the end of 1992), and a predominantly Druze population of some 16,000 living in the only six remaining villages, of which Majd al-Shams is by far the largest. According to official figures, at the end of 2013 the Golan Heights had a total population of 44,900, of whom 19,400 were Jews, 2,400 were Muslims and 21,800 Druze.

ADMINISTRATION

Prior to the Israeli occupation, the Golan Heights were incorporated by Syria into a provincial administration of which the city of Quneitra, with a population at the time of 27,378, was the capital. The Disengagement Agreement that was mediated by US Secretary of State Henry Kissinger in 1974 (after the 1973 Arab–Israeli War) provided for the withdrawal of Israeli forces from Quneitra. Before withdrawal, however, Israeli army engineers destroyed the city. In December 1981 the Israeli Knesset enacted the Golan Annexation Law, whereby Israeli civilian legislation was extended to the territory of Golan, now under the administrative jurisdiction of the Commissioner for the Northern District of Israel. The Arab-Druze community of the Golan responded immediately by declaring a strike and appealed to the UN Secretary-General to force Israel to rescind the annexation decision. At the seventh round of multilateral talks between Israeli and Arab delegations in Washington, DC, USA, in August 1992, the Israeli Government of Itzhak Rabin for the first time accepted that UN Security Council Resolution 242, adopted in 1967, applied to the Golan Heights. In January 1999 the Knesset approved legislation stating that any transfer of land under Israeli sovereignty (referring to the Golan Heights and East Jerusalem) must be approved by both an absolute majority of Knesset members and by the Israeli electorate at a national referendum. Following the election of Ehud Barak as Israel's Prime Minister in May 1999, peace negotiations between Israel and Syria were resumed in December. However, in January 2000 the talks were postponed indefinitely after Syria demanded a written commitment from Israel to withdraw from the Golan Heights. In July 2001 Ariel Sharon, who had recently been elected as Israeli premier, stated that he would be prepared to resume peace talks with Syria, but that the Israeli occupation of the Golan was 'irreversible'.

In July 2007 the Israeli Ministry of Foreign Affairs confirmed that messages had been relayed between Israel and Syria by third parties for some time, although Israel continued to deny claims that secret discussions had taken place. Both countries confirmed in May 2008 that indirect negotiations aimed at concluding a 'comprehensive peace' were being held through Turkish intermediaries in Istanbul, Turkey. By the second week of August four rounds of the Turkish-mediated discussions had taken place, although no significant progress had apparently been achieved. Despite subsequent claims by President Assad that Israel and Syria were within 'touching distance' of an agreement, a fifth round of talks, scheduled for September, was delayed owing to the political uncertainty in Israel following Ehud Olmert's resignation as premier. Moreover, Syrian President Bashar al-Assad formally suspended the indirect discussions in December, in protest against an Israeli military incursion into the Gaza Strip that month.

The inauguration, in March 2009, of a new, right-wing Israeli Government under Prime Minister Binyamin Netanyahu was widely perceived as an obstacle to hopes of a resumption of bilateral negotiations: Netanyahu had previously declared his opposition to the surrender of the Golan Heights as part of any Israeli-Syrian peace agreement. In November the Knesset approved legislation stating that any Israeli withdrawal from the Golan Heights would require the prior endorsement of Israeli voters in a national referendum.

Hopes of further progress towards a resumption of direct negotiations were put on hold as a result of the popular uprising that emerged in Syria (q.v.) from early 2011. In May Israeli troops clashed with hundreds of pro-Palestinian protesters who had broken through a security fence to enter the Golan Heights from Syria. Syrian state media reported in the following month that 12 Palestinians and two Syrians had been killed when Israeli soldiers opened fire at another group of protesters attempting to enter the Golan Heights from across the Syrian border; according to hospital reports, some 225 others were injured in the incident. The Israeli authorities accused the Assad regime of orchestrating the violence as a means of diverting international attention from the harsh measures employed by Syrian government forces against opposition activists.

From late 2012, with the Syrian domestic unrest having descended into civil conflict, fears increased that the violence could spill over into the Golan Heights. In November a campaign by Syria against opposition fighters located near the border resulted in mortar shells landing close to Israeli army posts in the north of the territory, prompting retaliatory attacks on Syrian government positions by Israeli troops. Several further instances of mortar shells from Syria falling in the Golan Heights were reported during 2013 and early 2014, as the conflict between government and opposition forces in Syria intensified. At the end of June 2013 UN Secretary-General Ban Ki-Moon recommended that the UN Disengagement Observer Force (UNDOF) be expanded and that it be given additional self-defence capabilities. Earlier in that year there had been two separate instances in which UNDOF troops had been abducted by Syrian militant groups, while in early June Austria had announced the withdrawal of its troops from UNDOF (representing one-third of the total), citing concerns over their safety. Exchanges of artillery, mortar and gunfire between Syrian and Israeli troops continued sporadically throughout 2014. In June Israel launched retaliatory strikes against strategic targets inside Syria, in response to a cross-border attack that had resulted in the death of an Israeli teenager in the Golan Heights.

ITALY

Introductory Survey

LOCATION, CLIMATE, LANGUAGE, RELIGION, FLAG, CAPITAL

The Italian Republic comprises a peninsula, extending from southern Europe into the Mediterranean Sea, and a number of adjacent islands. The two principal islands are Sicily, to the south-west, and Sardinia, to the west. The Alps form a natural boundary to the north, where the bordering countries are France to the north-west, Switzerland and Austria to the north and Slovenia to the north-east. The climate is temperate in the north and Mediterranean in the south, with mild winters and long, dry summers. The average temperature in Rome is 7.4°C (45.3°F) in January and 25.7°C (78.3°F) in July. The principal language is Italian. German and Ladin are spoken in the Trentino-Alto Adige (South Tyrol) region on the Austrian border, and French in the Valle d'Aosta region (bordering France and Switzerland), while in southern Italy there are Greek-speaking and Albanian minorities. A dialect of Catalan is spoken in north-western Sardinia. Almost all of the inhabitants profess Christianity: more than 90% are adherents of the Roman Catholic Church. The national flag (proportions 2 by 3) has three equal vertical stripes, of green, white and red. The capital is Rome.

CONTEMPORARY POLITICAL HISTORY

Historical Context

The Kingdom of Italy, under the House of Savoy, was proclaimed in 1861 and the country was unified in 1870. Italy subsequently acquired an overseas empire, comprising the African colonies of Eritrea, Italian Somaliland and Libya. Benito Mussolini, leader of the Fascist Party, became President of the Council (Prime Minister) in October 1922 and assumed dictatorial powers in 1925–26. Relations between the Italian state and the Roman Catholic Church, a subject of bitter controversy since Italy's unification, were codified in 1929 by a series of agreements, including the Lateran Pact, which recognized the sovereignty of the state of the Vatican City (q.v.), a small enclave within the city of Rome, under the jurisdiction of the Pope. Under Mussolini, Italian forces occupied Ethiopia in 1935–36 and Albania in 1939. Italy supported the fascist forces in the Spanish Civil War of 1936–39, and from June 1940 supported Nazi Germany in the Second World War. In 1943, however, as forces from the allied powers invaded Italy, the fascist regime collapsed. In July of that year King Victor Emmanuel III dismissed Mussolini, and the Fascist Party was dissolved.

In April 1945 German forces in Italy surrendered and Mussolini was killed. In June 1946, following a referendum, the monarchy was abolished and Italy became a republic. Until 1963 the Partito della Democrazia Cristiana (DC—Christian Democratic Party) held power continuously, while industry expanded rapidly, supported by capital from the USA. By the early 1960s, however, public discontent was increasing, largely owing to low wage rates and a lack of social reform. In the general election of 1963 the Partito Comunista Italiano (PCI—Italian Communist Party), together with other parties of the extreme right and left, made considerable gains at the expense of the DC. During the next decade there was a rapid succession of mainly coalition governments, involving the DC and one or more of the other major non-communist parties.

Domestic Political Affairs

Aldo Moro's coalition Government of the DC and the Partito Repubblicano Italiano (PRI—Italian Republican Party), formed in 1974, resigned in January 1976, following the withdrawal of support by the Partito Socialista Italiano (PSI—Italian Socialist Party). After the failure of a minority DC administration, the PCI won 228 seats at elections to the 630-member Camera dei Deputati (Chamber of Deputies) in June. The DC remained the largest party, but could no longer govern against PCI opposition in the legislature. However, the DC continued to insist on excluding the PCI from power, and in July formed a minority Government, with Giulio Andreotti as premier. He relied on the continuing abstention of PCI deputies to introduce severe austerity measures in response to the economic crisis. In January 1978 the minority Government was forced to resign under pressure from the PCI, which demanded more active participation in government. However, the new Government that Andreotti subsequently formed with support from the PCI was almost identical to the previous administration. In May former Prime Minister Moro was kidnapped and murdered by the extreme left-wing Brigate Rosse (Red Brigades).

The Andreotti administration collapsed in January 1979, when the PCI withdrew from the official parliamentary majority. A new coalition Government, formed by Andreotti in March, lasted only 10 days before being defeated in a vote of no confidence. Following elections in June, at which its representation in the Chamber of Deputies declined to 201 seats, the PCI returned to opposition. In August Francesco Cossiga of the DC formed a minority coalition Government. However, the new Government was thwarted by obstructionism in Parliament. In April 1980 Cossiga established a majority coalition, comprising members of the DC, the PRI and the PSI. In September, however, the Government resigned after losing a vote on its economic programme. The subsequent coalition Government, assembled by Arnaldo Forlani, the Chairman of the DC, was beset with allegations of corruption; it too was forced to stand down, in May 1981, following revelations that more than 1,000 of Italy's foremost establishment figures belonged to a secret masonic lodge, P-2 ('Propaganda Due'), which had extensive criminal connections both in Italy and abroad. The lodge was linked with many political and financial scandals and with right-wing terrorism, culminating in 1982 with the collapse of one of Italy's leading banks, Banco Ambrosiano, and the death of its President, Roberto Calvi.

In June 1981 the leader of the PRI, Giovanni Spadolini, formed a coalition Government, thus becoming the first non-DC Prime Minister since 1946. Spadolini resigned in November 1982. Amintore Fanfani, a former DC Prime Minister, assembled a new coalition in December which lasted until the PSI withdrew its support in April 1983. At a general election held in June, the DC lost considerable support, winning only 33% of the votes for the Chamber of Deputies. The PSI increased its share of the votes to 11%, and its leader, Bettino Craxi, was subsequently appointed Italy's first socialist Prime Minister, at the head of a coalition. Craxi resigned in June 1986 when his Government lost a vote of confidence in the Chamber of Deputies; Andreotti began talks to form a new government. However, the refusal of other parties to support Andreotti led to Craxi's return to power in July, on condition that he transfer the premiership to a DC member in March 1987. Craxi accordingly submitted his resignation, and that of his Government, as scheduled. After several unsuccessful attempts to form a coalition, a general election was held in June, at which the DC won 34% of the votes cast and the PSI 14%. The PCI suffered its worst post-war electoral result, with 27% of the votes. Giovanni Goria of the DC was appointed Prime Minister of a coalition Government. By the end of the year, however, the Government had lost considerable support, and in March 1988 Goria resigned. Ciriaco De Mita, the Secretary-General of the DC, formed a new coalition with the same five parties that had served in Goria's administration.

Severe criticism by Craxi of De Mita's premiership led to the collapse of the Government in May 1989. In July the coalition partners of the outgoing Government agreed to form a new administration, with Andreotti as Prime Minister. Andreotti resigned the premiership in March 1991, following criticism from the PSI. President Francesco Cossiga (who had taken office in July 1985) none the less nominated Andreotti to form a new government (Italy's 50th since 1945), which comprised the same coalition partners as the outbound administration, apart from the PRI.

In early 1991 the PCI was renamed the Partito Democratico della Sinistra (PDS—Democratic Party of the Left), having transformed itself into a social democratic party. A minority of members of the former PCI refused to join the PDS, and in May they established the Partito della Rifondazione Comunista (PRC—Party of Communist Refoundation).

At the general election held in April 1992, support for the DC declined to less than 30% of the votes cast. The PDS won 16% of the votes, and the PSI 14%. The Lega Nord (LN—Northern League), a grouping of regionalist parties led by Umberto Bossi, performed well in northern Italy. In May Giuliano Amato of the PSI was appointed Prime Minister; the new Government, which was appointed the following month, was composed of the same four parties that had formed the outgoing administration.

The 'Tangentopoli' affair

The uncovering of a corruption scandal in Milan in 1992, which became known as 'Tangentopoli' ('Bribesville'), subsequently assumed wider implications. It was alleged that politicians (mainly of the PSI and DC) and government officials had accepted bribes in exchange for the awarding of large public contracts. In February 1993 the Minister of Justice, Claudio Martelli of the PSI, was obliged to resign, having been placed under formal investigation for alleged complicity in the collapse of Banco Ambrosiano. Shortly afterwards, Craxi stood down as Secretary-General of the PSI, although he continued to deny accusations of fraud. In March 1993 five DC politicians, including Andreotti, were placed under investigation over their alleged links with the Mafia.

Despite the collapse of confidence in his Government, Amato agreed to remain in office until after nationwide referendums had been held in April 1993 on a number of proposed legislative amendments, including a reform of the electoral system for the upper legislative house, the Senato della Repubblica (Senate of the Republic), and the end of state funding of political parties. These amendments, intended to prevent electoral malpractice and, in particular, interference by organized crime, were overwhelmingly approved. (In August Parliament endorsed a similar system for elections to the Chamber of Deputies.) Amato resigned as Prime Minister shortly after the referendums, and Carlo Azeglio Ciampi was invited by President Oscar Luigi Scalfaro, who had taken office in May 1992, to form a new government. Ciampi, hitherto Governor of the Banca d'Italia (the central bank), was the first non-parliamentarian to be appointed to the premiership. His coalition comprised the four parties of the outgoing administration and the PRI.

In May 1993 the Chamber of Deputies voted overwhelmingly to abolish parliamentary immunity in cases of corruption and serious crime. Furthermore, the Senate approved the removal of Andreotti's parliamentary immunity, to allow investigations into his alleged association with the Mafia, although his arrest remained prohibited. Meanwhile, investigations began in April into the activities of former DC Prime Minister Forlani. The investigations were subsequently extended to encompass politicians of the PDS and PRI. In August the Chamber of Deputies voted to allow Craxi to be investigated by magistrates on four charges of corruption. The following month Andreotti was charged with providing the Sicilian Mafia with political protection in exchange for votes in Sicily, and with complicity in the murder of an investigative journalist, Mario Francese, who had allegedly discovered evidence linking Andreotti with the Mafia.

Ciampi resigned in January 1994. A general election was scheduled for March. In January Silvio Berlusconi, the principal shareholder in and former manager of the media-based Fininvest, Italy's third largest private business group, announced the formation of a right-wing organization, Forza Italia (Forward Italy or Come on, Italy!), to contest the election. In subsequent weeks, in response to the collapse in popular support for the previously dominant DC and PSI largely due to the Tangentopoli affair, parties of all leanings formed electoral alliances with an aim to securing a majority in the Chamber of Deputies. Seven left-wing parties—including the PDS and the PRC—established I Progressisti (The Progressives); the Polo delle Libertà e del Buon Governo (commonly known as the Polo delle Libertà—the Freedom Alliance), under the leadership of Berlusconi, was set up by the LN, Forza Italia and the Alleanza Nazionale (AN—National Alliance), which incorporated members of the neo-fascist Movimento Sociale Italiano-Destra Nazionale (MSI-DN—Italian Social Movement-National Right); and the centre-right Patto per l'Italia (Pact for Italy) included the Partito Popolare Italiano (PPI—Italian People's Party), formed from the liberal wing of the DC. The Polo delle Libertà won an outright majority in the Chamber of Deputies and was only three seats short of a majority in the Senate. In May Berlusconi formed a new Government, which included members of the AN, the LN and the MSI-DN.

In November 1994 Berlusconi was placed under investigation for bribery. In the following month Antonio Di Pietro, a high-profile magistrate in Milan who had led the investigation into political corruption in 1992, resigned in protest at increasing government interference in the work of the judiciary. The failure of the Prime Minister to resolve his conflict of business and political interests, together with the growing tension between the Government and the judiciary, precipitated the disintegration of the coalition and Berlusconi's resignation in January 1995. Lamberto Dini, the Minister of the Treasury, formed an interim Government composed of technocrats. In March it was announced that Berlusconi was to be subject to further investigation on charges of financial irregularities.

In October 1995 the Minister of Justice, Filippo Mancuso, refused to resign despite a successful motion of no confidence in him, which had been prompted by his alleged vendetta against anti-corruption magistrates in Milan. President Scalfaro revoked Mancuso's mandate, and transferred responsibility for the justice portfolio to Dini. Shortly afterwards, the Government narrowly defeated a motion of no confidence proposed by Berlusconi and Mancuso, following an agreement whereby PRC deputies abstained from the vote on condition that Dini resign as premier by the end of the year. Dini's resignation, submitted in December, was, however, rejected by Scalfaro. In January 1996 the AN proposed a resolution demanding Dini's resignation, which it was expected to win with the support of parties of the extreme left. Scalfaro was thus obliged to accept Dini's resignation, which the Prime Minister submitted prior to the vote. Elections were scheduled for April.

Meanwhile, in July 1994 Craxi and the former Deputy Prime Minister and Minister of Justice, Martelli, were both sentenced for fraudulent bankruptcy in relation to the collapse of Banco Ambrosiano. Craxi, who claimed to be too ill to return from his residence in Tunisia, was sentenced *in absentia*; in mid-1995 he was formally declared a fugitive from justice. In October all 22 defendants were convicted in a trial concerning illegal funding of political parties. Among those convicted were former Prime Ministers Craxi, who was sentenced *in absentia* to four years' imprisonment, and Forlani, sentenced to 28 months' custody; Bossi received a suspended sentence.

The centre-left in power: 1996–2001

The legislative elections held in April 1996 were won by L'Ulivo (The Olive Tree), a centre-left electoral alliance dominated by the PDS, but also including the PPI and Dini's newly formed, centrist Rinnovamento Italiano (RI—Italian Renewal). The alliance narrowly defeated the Polo per le Libertà (as the Polo delle Libertà had been renamed), securing 284 of the 630 seats in the Chamber of Deputies and 157 of the 315 elective seats in the Senate. President Scalfaro invited Romano Prodi, the leader of L'Ulivo, to form a government.

In December 1997 Berlusconi and four associates were convicted on charges of false accounting with regard to the purchase of a film group in 1988. Later that month Berlusconi and Cesare Previti, a former Minister of Defence and a lawyer for Fininvest, were ordered to stand trial on charges relating to their planned bribery of judges. In two separate trials in July 1998 Berlusconi was convicted of bribing tax inspectors involved in Fininvest audits and of making illicit payments to Craxi and the PSI in 1991.

In June 1998 the Chamber of Deputies approved legislation endorsing the admission to the North Atlantic Treaty Organization (NATO, see p. 367) of Hungary, Poland and the Czech Republic. The vote, which had become an issue of confidence in the Prodi Government as the PRC (on which the coalition relied in parliamentary votes) opposed the eastward expansion of the alliance and thus withdrew its support, was carried with the backing of the new, centrist Unione Democratica per la Repubblica (UDR—Democratic Union for the Republic) and with the abstention of Forza Italia. There was a further political crisis in October, when the PRC again withdrew its support for the Government on the issue of the 1999 budget. The Government lost an ensuing confidence motion by one vote, and Prodi was forced to resign. Massimo D'Alema, the leader of the Democratici di Sinistra (DS—Democrats of the Left—as the PDS had been renamed), was asked to assume the premiership. The new Government comprised members of seven political parties. In May 1999 former Prime Minister Ciampi was elected to succeed Scalfaro as President of the Republic.

In October 1999 Berlusconi's 1998 conviction for making illicit payments to Craxi and the PSI was overturned. In the following month, however, Berlusconi was ordered to stand trial in two cases involving charges of bribery and false accounting. Meanwhile, in June a new trial had been ordered against Craxi on charges of illegal party financing; however, in January 2000 Craxi died in exile in Tunisia.

D'Alema tendered his resignation as Prime Minister in December 1999, following the withdrawal of support by a number of the coalition parties. President Ciampi asked D'Alema to form a new government; D'Alema forged a new coalition of parties of the left and centre, including I Democratici per l'Ulivo (The Democrats for the Olive Tree), founded earlier in that year by Prodi, and the Unione Democratici per l'Europa (UDEUR—Union of Democrats for Europe). However, following the defeat of the new centre-left coalition by a centre-right alliance of Forza Italia and LN at regional elections in April 2000, D'Alema resigned. A new, eight-party, centre-left coalition Government, led by Amato, was subsequently formed.

In May 2000, at a first appeal, Berlusconi was acquitted of one charge of bribing tax inspectors involved in Fininvest audits on which he had been convicted in 1998; the appeals court also invoked the statute of limitations (which, under Italian law, continued to apply even after proceedings had begun) to overturn his convictions on three similar counts. In June 2000 Berlusconi was further acquitted at a pre-trial hearing of bribery charges relating to his acquisition of the Mondadori publishing company in 1991.

Berlusconi's second premiership: 2001–06

At the general election held in May 2001, Berlusconi's Casa delle Libertà (House of Freedoms) alliance—the successor to the Polo per le Libertà—won majorities in both legislative houses. Following his nomination as premier by Ciampi, in June Berlusconi formed a coalition Government composed of Forza Italia, the AN, the LN, the Cristiani Democratici Uniti (CDU—United Christian Democrats), the Centro Cristiano Democratico (CCD—Christian Democratic Centre) and independents. The AN leader, Gianfranco Fini, became Deputy Prime Minister, and the Government also included three members of LN, one being Bossi.

The issue of apparent conflict of interest between Berlusconi's political role and business interests was heightened by the general election. Berlusconi's new position as Prime Minister placed him in effective control of the state broadcasting company, Radiotelevisione Italiana (Rai), and this, coupled with his ownership of the media company Fininvest (which operated Italy's principal private television concern, Mediaset), gave him effective control over the majority of the Italian television network.

In August 2001 legislation to decriminalize fraud associated with false accounting was approved by the Chamber of Deputies. Furthermore, in October legislation was adopted by the Senate which altered regulations governing the use of evidence in criminal cases. Opposition parties protested that Berlusconi would directly benefit from the new regulations, which were likely to invalidate legal proceedings against himself and Previti in respect of allegations that they had bribed judges in return for a favourable court judgment over the sale of state-owned food company SME Meridionale. Prior to the trial's commencement, in January 2002, an attempt by the Minister of Justice to remove one of the three judges on the case caused public and judicial consternation. In October 2001 the Supreme Court of Cassation overturned Berlusconi's 1998 conviction on charges of bribing tax inspectors in exchange for favourable audits of Fininvest.

In April 2002 a 'conflict of interest' bill was passed in the Chamber of Deputies. The legislation, which became law in July 2004, prohibited a figure in public office from active involvement in running a company, but did not forbid ownership, thus permitting Berlusconi's continued possession of Mediaset.

Following the rejection of an appeal by Berlusconi in May 2002 to have his bribery trial moved from Milan (where, he alleged, the judicial system was dominated by communists), several draft bills proposing judicial reform provoked controversy in the legislature and the judiciary, most notably a trial bill, which would allow proceedings to be rescheduled and relocated if there was 'legitimate suspicion' of prosecutorial bias on the part of the judge. Nevertheless, the trial bill was passed by Parliament in November.

In November 2002 an appeals court in Palermo overturned the acquittal of Andreotti on charges of conspiracy to murder the journalist Mario Francese in 1979, and sentenced the former Prime Minister to 24 years' imprisonment. In October 2003 the Supreme Court of Cassation overturned this ruling, acquitting Andreotti of the murder. Meanwhile, in May of that year an appeals court in Sicily upheld a 1999 ruling exonerating Andreotti of charges of association with the Mafia. In October 2004 Andreotti was acquitted by the Supreme Court of Cassation of collusion with the Mafia while in office.

In January 2003, after a further bid to relocate his bribery trial was rejected by the Supreme Court, Berlusconi announced the possible reintroduction of immunity from prosecution for members of Parliament (abolished in 1993), arousing opposition protest. In April Berlusconi's trial opened in Milan. Later that month Previti was sentenced to 11 years' imprisonment for bribing judges to influence two corporate takeovers in the 1990s. However, in June Berlusconi's trial was halted, following the adoption of a bill granting immunity while in office to Italy's five most senior politicians (the President, the Prime Minister, the head of the Constitutional Court and the leaders of the two houses of Parliament). However, the Constitutional Court declared in January 2004 that this legislation was illegal, thus permitting the resumption in April of Berlusconi's bribery trial. Berlusconi was acquitted on one charge in December, and the court ruled that the statute of limitations had expired on the second charge.

In December 2003 President Ciampi refused to sign legislation designed to reduce restrictions on media ownership. Opponents of the bill maintained that it would allow Berlusconi—who, through his direct influence over Rai and his Mediaset company, already controlled more than 90% of Italy's television media—to expand his media holdings and thereby reduce further the freedom of the press. However, the bill was approved by the Chamber of Deputies in February 2004, as the Government linked the vote to a motion of confidence, and received final approval in the Senate in April; Ciampi was constitutionally obliged to sign it into law in May.

In November 2004 employees in the legal profession organized a strike to protest against planned judicial reform which, it was claimed, would reduce the independence of the judiciary and the power of the legal professionals to prosecute politicians for corruption. Although it was adopted by Parliament, on 16 December President Ciampi refused to sign the legislation, stating that it was unconstitutional.

The ruling coalition performed poorly at regional elections in April 2005. The Unione dei Democratici Cristiani e di Centro (UDC—Union of Christian and Centre Democrats, formed in 2002 from a merger of the CDU and the CCD) subsequently withdrew from the governing coalition and the AN threatened to do likewise. Berlusconi resigned in order to form a new Government in late April, which comprised the four parties in the previous coalition: the PRI, the Nuovo Partito Socialista Italiano (Nuovo PSI—New Italian Socialist Party) and independents.

Legislation providing for a return to total proportional representation prior to the elections in 2006 and setting a threshold for the percentage of votes a party needed to win to be eligible for seats in Parliament was approved by the Chamber of Deputies in October 2005. The opposition abstained from voting, claiming that the legislation was designed to reduce the representation of L'Unione (a nine-party coalition created by Prodi and incorporating members of L'Ulivo and the PRC) in the next parliament. The legislation was approved by the Senate in December.

In November 2005 the two parliamentary houses approved legislation reducing the statute of limitations for business-related crimes, including fraud and corruption, and lengthening it for Mafia-related crimes. In January 2006 President Ciampi refused to sign legislation, approved earlier in the month by Parliament, that abolished the right of prosecutors to appeal against an acquittal, claiming that it was unconstitutional. The legislation was widely regarded as being designed to exempt Berlusconi from further prosecution, since a court in Milan was due to begin hearing an appeal of a case in which Berlusconi had been acquitted on four charges of bribing judges; the appeal was rejected in April 2007.

In March 2006 Berlusconi went on trial in Milan, along with 13 other defendants, on charges of tax fraud relating to the purchase of television and film rights by Mediaset in the 1990s. In November a separate trial opened involving Berlusconi and his former lawyer, David Mills (the estranged husband of British government minister Tessa Jowell), in which Berlusconi was accused of paying Mills at least US $600,000 after the latter gave favourable testimony in two corruption trials involving Berlusconi in 1997 and 1998.

Prodi's second Government

At the general election held in April 2006, Prodi's L'Unione coalition won a narrow victory in both houses of Parliament. In the Senate L'Unione obtained 158 seats, while the Casa delle Libertà took 156 seats. New legislation, which automatically awarded 55% of the seats in the lower house to the party or group with the largest number of votes, meant that L'Unione secured

348 seats in the Chamber of Deputies, while Berlusconi's coalition won 281 seats. In May Giorgio Napolitano of the DS was elected to succeed Ciampi as President of the Republic, following which Prodi was inaugurated as Prime Minister. His Government included two former Prime Ministers: D'Alema as Minister of Foreign Affairs and Amato as Minister of Internal Affairs.

In June 2006 a referendum was held on controversial constitutional reforms, introduced by the previous administration and approved by Parliament in November 2005, aimed at granting greater autonomy to Italy's regions and extending the powers of the Prime Minister. The reforms were rejected, by 61.7% of the votes cast. President Ciampi and the centre-left had been severely critical of the proposed measures, claiming that the power of the legislature would be diminished and that the devolution of power to the regions, promoted by the LN, favoured the more affluent northern regions at the expense of their southern counterparts.

In February 2007 the Government was defeated in the Senate on the continued presence of Italian troops in Afghanistan and the expansion of a US military base near Vicenza. Prodi submitted his resignation to the President; however, this was not accepted by Napolitano, who asked the Prime Minister to call confidence votes in Parliament. Prodi went on to win the votes, in the Senate in February and the Chamber of Deputies in March, after persuading all parties in the coalition to agree to a programme that included support for the peacekeeping mission in Afghanistan, as well as measures to liberalize the economy.

In October 2007, in an attempt to consolidate support for the main left-wing parties and to promote a more centrist agenda, the two largest parties in L'Unione—the DS and Democrazia è Libertà—La Margherita (Democracy is Freedom—The Daisy)—and a number of smaller parties merged to form the Partito Democratico (PD—Democratic Party); the Mayor of Rome, former Deputy Prime Minister Walter Veltroni, was elected as National Secretary of the new party.

The ongoing struggle to maintain stability within L'Unione culminated in January 2008 with the resignation of the Minister of Justice, Clemente Mastella, following the arrest of his wife on charges of corruption. Days later Mastella announced the withdrawal from the governing coalition of his UDEUR party, thereby divesting the Government of its narrow majority in the upper house. On 24 January the Government lost a vote of confidence in the Senate that had been prompted by the perceived inadequacy of its response to an ongoing refuse collection crisis in Naples. Prodi submitted the Government's resignation, which was accepted by President Napolitano, who requested that Prodi remain in office on an interim basis pending the formation of a new Government. Napolitano subsequently asked the President of the Senate, Franco Marini, to lead discussions over the formation of a cross-party interim administration with a mandate to pursue electoral reform. However, the main opposition parties refused to agree to such measures, which would have reversed reforms implemented during Berlusconi's second term as Prime Minister. In February Napolitano dissolved Parliament and scheduled a general election for April. Berlusconi and Fini announced that Forza Italia and the AN were to present a joint list of candidates as the Popolo della Libertà, a coalition that was subsequently joined by numerous smaller parties. While ruling out a formal merger, the LN and the Movimento per l'Autonomia agreed to ally themselves with the Popolo della Libertà. The UDC was to contest the election as part of a new coalition, the Unione di Centro (UdC), which it had formed with other centrist, Christian-democratic parties in December 2007.

Meanwhile, in January 2008 a court in Milan acquitted Berlusconi on charges of false accounting, on the grounds that, according to the reforms promulgated in 2001 under Berlusconi's premiership, it was no longer a criminal offence.

Berlusconi's third premiership: 2008–11

At the general election held in April 2008, the number of parties represented in Parliament was greatly reduced, partly owing to the consolidation of the main, centrist alliances. Berlusconi's Popolo della Libertà and its allies secured a majority in both the Chamber of Deputies and the Senate. In the lower house the Popolo della Libertà won 276 seats, while its allies the LN and the Movimento per l'Autonomia obtained 60 and eight seats, respectively, compared with 217 seats for the PD. The Popolo della Libertà won 147 seats in the upper house, while the LN and the Movimento per l'Autonomia secured 25 and two seats, respectively; the PD took 118 seats. The UdC, Antonio Di Pietro's Italia dei Valori (Italy of Principals) and a number of small parties also gained representation in both houses. A high voter turnout of 81.4% was recorded. A coalition Government, led by Berlusconi and comprising the Popolo della Libertà and the LN, took office in May. Franco Frattini (hitherto European Commissioner for Justice) was appointed as Minister of Foreign Affairs, and Roberto Maroni of the LN became Minister of the Interior. Other notable appointments included that of Bossi as Minister without Portfolio for Federal Reform.

The new Government embarked upon a controversial programme of judicial reform, despite criticism from the centre-left opposition, which claimed that the measures were intended to protect Berlusconi against the possibility of conviction in the two ongoing trials in which he was a defendant. In June 2008 both houses of Parliament approved a bill providing for the suspension of all trials involving crimes committed before 2002 for which the maximum sentence was less than 10 years' imprisonment; the Government claimed that this measure was designed to prioritize cases involving serious or violent crimes. Following the promulgation of the legislation, the proceedings against Berlusconi begun in 2006 were suspended. In July 2008 legislation was approved by both houses of Parliament that granted immunity from prosecution while in office, for one legislative term, to the President, the Prime Minister, and the Presidents of the Chamber of Deputies and the Senate. The Government maintained that the new law would overcome the objections raised by the Constitutional Court to similar legislation, enacted in 2003, that had been annulled by the Court in 2004.

Meanwhile, immigration and crime continued to dominate the political agenda. In June 2008 the European Union (EU) and several non-governmental organizations denounced as racial discrimination government proposals to introduce compulsory fingerprinting for all people of Roma origin. The proposals reflected growing anti-Roma sentiment, following a number of widely reported violent incidents involving Roma immigrants. In July Maroni declared a national state of emergency, citing statistics indicating that the number of migrants arriving in Italy had doubled during the first half of 2008, compared with the same period in the previous year. Earlier in July the Government had proposed measures designed to curb illegal immigration and reduce violent crime, under which illegal immigrants convicted of crimes would receive prison sentences of up to one-third longer than those imposed on Italian and other EU citizens. The measures also included powers to deploy up to 3,000 troops to patrol strategic locations in major cities, including railway stations and detention centres, for illegal immigrants, and received final approval from the Senate later that month. In February 2009, following several widely publicized incidents of rape allegedly perpetrated by immigrants, the Government promulgated a decree which provided for a mandatory life sentence for certain rape convictions and introduced other measures relating to sexual violence and harassment; controversially, it also sanctioned the creation of civilian street patrols to apprehend alleged criminals, and extended the period for which illegal immigrants could be held in detention centres. The decree secured parliamentary approval in April, after amendments had been adopted removing the provisions relating to civilian patrols and detention centres. However, these measures were incorporated into a bill also before Parliament that, in addition, sought to make illegal immigration a criminal offence. This legislation was adopted in July despite protests by the opposition, the Roman Catholic Church and human rights groups.

The trend for consolidation among the main parties continued in late 2008, as Forza Italia and the AN prepared to formalize the creation of a single, right-wing party. In November the national executive committee of Forza Italia agreed to dissolve the party into a new party to be named the Popolo della Libertà (PdL), after the existing coalition. In March 2009 AN officials confirmed their party's dissolution prior to joining the new party. and the PdL was established as a single party, under the leadership of Berlusconi, at the end of the month. Eleven small parties joined the new organization, but the LN remained independent. Meanwhile, following its defeat at the April 2008 general election, the centre-left opposition struggled to make an impact. In February 2009 Veltroni resigned as National Secretary of the PD, citing his failure to establish the party as an effective opposition movement; he was replaced by Pier Luigi Bersani in October.

In October 2009 the Constitutional Court overturned the legislation of July 2008 granting immunity from prosecution to the holders of the highest offices of state, principally on the grounds that it violated the constitutional principle that all citizens were equal before the law. The Court's ruling was given in response to an appeal by the prosecutors in the two corruption trials in which Berlusconi was a defendant. As a result, both trials (one relating to the purchase of film rights by Mediaset and the other to the alleged bribery of Mills) resumed in November 2009. Meanwhile, the Government introduced draft legislation in that month which sought to limit the length of trials for which the maximum sentence was less than 10 years' imprisonment, by imposing time limits on each of the three stages of a trial (the initial hearing and two appeals). The bill, which would apply retroactively, and which the Government described as a much-needed reform of Italy's notoriously slow judicial system, was approved by the Senate in January 2010, but subsequently stalled in the Chamber of Deputies. In April both trials involving Berlusconi were suspended again, pending a ruling from the Constitutional Court on the legitimacy of a law passed by Parliament in March, under which the Prime Minister and cabinet ministers were to be granted the automatic suspension of legal process for a maximum of 18 months if they certified that their official commitments constituted a 'legitimate impediment' to their attendance at a trial. Also in April, in a second case involving Mediaset, Berlusconi was accused of tax fraud and embezzlement related to the purchase of film rights by the company's Mediatrade division.

Regional elections held in March 2010 resulted in gains for the centre-right parties—particularly the LN—at the expense of the centre-left. Although the PdL's performance declined slightly in comparison to recent elections, the popularity of the party and of the Prime Minister appeared not to have been significantly damaged by the recent controversies surrounding Berlusconi's confrontation with the judiciary, nor by a series of sex and corruption scandals in which he had been involved since mid-2009.

However, internal divisions (notably between Berlusconi and Fini, the erstwhile leader of the AN and the President of the Chamber of Deputies) and further corruption scandals threatened the stability of the Government in the months following the regional elections. Claudio Scajola resigned as Minister of Economic Development in May 2010, in the wake of allegations that he had purchased a property with financial assistance from an allegedly corrupt businessman. In June the appointment as a Minister without Portfolio of Aldo Brancher, a former business associate of Berlusconi who had been charged with embezzlement, was widely condemned, particularly after he invoked the so-called 'legitimate impediment' law in order to avoid a court hearing. Brancher resigned after just 17 days in office, shortly before an opposition-proposed motion of no confidence in him was due to be debated in Parliament. In July Nicola Cosentino, an under-secretary in the Ministry of the Economy and Finance, also stood down, after being placed under investigation in connection with his alleged involvement in a secret association of PdL officials and supporters seeking to influence political appointments and judicial decisions.

Proposed legislation to restrict the use of telephone-tapping in judicial investigations and to prevent pre-trial reporting of intercepted conversations provoked considerable controversy and further divisions within the PdL in mid-2010. It was claimed that the measures were designed to shield Berlusconi and other government officials from adverse media coverage rather than to protect the privacy of ordinary citizens; the bill was amended in July to allow the publication of transcripts of intercepted conversations when considered relevant by magistrates. However, the Chamber of Deputies subsequently postponed a vote on the proposed legislation (the unamended version of which had been approved by the Senate in June).

Continued tensions between the Prime Minister and the President of the Chamber of Deputies culminated at the end of July 2010 in the adoption by the executive committee of the PdL of a motion censuring Fini for fomenting internal dissent within the PdL and criticizing party decisions. Legislators loyal to Fini consequently formed a new parliamentary group, Futuro e Libertà per l'Italia (FLI—Future and Freedom for Italy). The Government was thus deprived of a majority in the Chamber of Deputies, although Fini stated that the FLI would support government proposals that fulfilled electoral pledges made by the PdL.

In a significant reverse for Berlusconi's administration, the FLI withdrew its four members from the Council of Ministers in November 2010 in response to the Prime Minister's rejection of an ultimatum issued by Fini that he should resign to form a new, broader coalition. Opposition demands for Berlusconi's resigna-

tion had been precipitated by further revelations regarding his personal life. In December the Government defeated motions of no confidence in Berlusconi tabled in both houses of Parliament. Following Berlusconi's narrow survival in the Chamber of Deputies (by three votes), some 50 police officers and 40 anti-Government protesters were injured during violent clashes in Rome.

In January 2011 the Constitutional Court delivered its verdict on the validity of the 'legitimate impediment' law, ruling that the suspension of legal process should not be automatic but should be decided by individual judges. The three corruption trials in which Berlusconi was a defendant (one relating to the alleged bribery of Mills and the other two to the acquisition of film rights by Mediaset and its Mediatrade division) resumed in early 2011. Berlusconi attended court (for the first time since 2003) for proceedings relating to all three cases. In February, moreover, the Prime Minister was ordered to stand trial in a fourth case, in which he was accused of paying for sex with an underage prostitute and of abusing his power by intervening to seek her release from custody after she was arrested on suspicion of theft in May 2010. The trial, which Berlusconi did not attend, opened in April 2011, but was immediately adjourned. In the same month the Government suffered a further setback when its proposals regarding tax reform were rejected by a parliamentary committee.

In April 2011 the Chamber of Deputies passed a bill to shorten the statute of limitations on trials of defendants with no previous convictions. The legislation, which required approval by the Senate, formed part of a broader proposed reform of the judiciary, which Berlusconi insisted was necessary to limit political interference by politically biased magistrates but which critics claimed was to protect the Prime Minister from prosecution and would weaken judicial independence. In October the Prime Minister was cleared of all charges in one of the Mediaset cases, and in February 2012 the Mills case was abandoned, having expired under the statute of limitations.

Berlusconi's political future appeared increasingly uncertain following poor performances (to the benefit of the centre left) by the PdL and the LN in local elections in May 2011; notably, the PdL mayor of Milan was unexpectedly ousted from office by the left-wing candidate, thus ending almost 18 years of centre-right rule in the Prime Minister's home town. Since his return to power in 2008 Berlusconi's approval rating had fallen dramatically, and the problems arising from the ongoing sex scandals and trials were compounded by Italy's ailing economy and its mounting debt crisis. In June 2011 the Prime Minister's political standing suffered a further setback when the electorate voted against government policy in a referendum tabled by the opposition. Despite Berlusconi's appeals for a boycott of the poll, in the first referendum since 1995 to achieve the requisite quorum of more than 51% of the electorate (actual turnout was around 57%), the Italian people overwhelmingly rejected the Government's plans to revive nuclear power production and partially to privatize water utilities, and voted to repeal the controversial 'legitimate impediment' law.

In early July 2011 the Minister of the Economy and Finance, Giulio Tremonti, introduced an austerity package aimed at lowering the country's budget deficit; the proposals, which included a range of expenditure cuts and a new series of privatizations, were approved by the Chamber of Deputies on 15 July. However, later that month Tremonti's political credibility was threatened by revelations of his links to a number of individuals who were under investigation for suspected corruption involving official appointments and state tenders. Also in July, Berlusconi's weakening authority was highlighted by the lower house voting, for the first time, to divest a PdL legislator accused of corruption of his immunity from arrest.

In August 2011 concern mounted that Italy's increasing debt would necessitate an EU bailout or, at worst, lead to the collapse of the eurozone. In response to growing pressure from the European Central Bank, an emergency austerity package was approved by the Government on 12 August; however, much internal dissension ensued regarding the details of the proposals and numerous revisions were enacted before a compromise package was agreed upon. In September there were further damaging revelations regarding Berlusconi's personal life and the Prime Minister's problems were exacerbated by the staging of a general strike in protest at the proposed austerity measures. On 14 September the Chamber of Deputies passed the much-amended austerity package (approved earlier by the Senate), which included a pledge to balance the budget by 2013.

Mario Monti's Government of technocrats

Amid widespread doubts that the Prime Minister was capable of resolving Italy's financial crisis, and following a number of defections from the PdL and the loss of the Government's majority in the Chamber of Deputies in October 2011, Berlusconi—Italy's longest-serving post-war Prime Minister—resigned from office on 12 November. (Parliament had previously approved a stability law incorporating the urgent economic reforms demanded by the EU.) On 13 November President Napolitano appointed Mario Monti, a renowned economist and former EU commissioner, as the country's new Prime Minister. Monti's new Council of Ministers comprised a team of technocrats tasked with addressing the deepening financial crisis. Monti himself assumed responsibility for the economy and finance portfolio (although he transferred responsibility for the ministry to Vittorio Grilli in July 2012). In December 2011 Parliament approved a new package of stringent austerity measures drawn up by Monti.

In April 2012 the treasurer of the LN and close associate of Bossi, Francesco Belsito, was forced to resign following allegations of his improper use of party subsidies (large amounts of which had reportedly been transferred for the personal use of Bossi and his immediate family). While denying any wrongdoing on his part, Bossi resigned as Federal Secretary of the LN and was replaced by former Minister of the Interior Maroni. Bossi was appointed to the honorary position of Federal President for Life of the LN in July.

The extent of the discontent arising from the Government's austerity drive was reflected in the gains made by various protest groups and parties of the centre-left (including the PD), at the expense mainly of the PdL and the scandal-hit LN, in mayoral and local elections held throughout Italy in May 2012. One protest group that performed particularly strongly in northern Italy (notably in Parma) was the MoVimento 5 Stelle (M5S, Five Star Movement), an anti-establishment group founded by the popular comedian and activist Beppe Grillo in 2009; the M5S attracted much of its support from among the younger electorate and had no traditional party structure.

In October 2012 Berlusconi was convicted of tax fraud relating to the purchase of film rights by Mediaset; he was sentenced to four years' imprisonment (subsequently reduced to one year, although, according to legislation introduced by the former Prime Minister, no one older than 70 years could be incarcerated in Italy) and barred from holding political office for five years. Having immediately launched an appeal against the verdict, in December Berlusconi announced that he intended to stand as the prime ministerial candidate of the PdL in the forthcoming elections. (In March 2013 Berlusconi was convicted and sentenced to one year in prison for illegally tapping the telephone of a political rival in 2005.)

The general election of February 2013

On 21 December 2012, following the PdL's withdrawal of parliamentary support earlier that month on the grounds that the Government's austerity measures were harming Italy, Prime Minister Monti resigned, having first overseen, as promised, the approval of the 2013 budget by Parliament. At the President's request, Monti remained as head of an interim administration pending the holding of a general election on 24–25 February 2013. Not surprisingly, the main focus of the election campaign was Italy's ongoing economic crisis: Berlusconi, adopting an anti-austerity stance, pledged to cut (and even refund) taxes, while his party's two main rivals—a centrist coalition, Con Monti per l'Italia (With Monti for Italy), headed by Monti and a centre-left coalition led by Bersani's PD, Italia. Bene Comune (Italy Common Good)—advocated the retention, to varying degrees, of the austerity programme. In the final stages of the campaign M5S rallies attracted large crowds, as many Italians appeared to have become disillusioned with the country's mainstream political parties; Grillo (who did not stand for election himself, owing to a previous conviction) vehemently denounced corruption and austerity, and pledged to hold a referendum on Italy's continued membership of the eurozone.

There was no clear victor in the general election, which attracted a turnout of around 75%, and political deadlock ensued, with no single party or coalition able to form a government (since to do so required a working majority in both houses of the legislature). The PD and its allies secured a majority of 345 seats in the Chamber of Deputies, while the PdL and its centre-right allies won 125 seats, the M5S 109 and the centrist coalition headed by Monti 47. However, no party or coalition won a majority in the Senate: the PD and its allies obtained 123 seats in the upper house, the PdL and its allies 117, the M5S 54 and Monti's coalition 19. The widespread unpopularity of Monti's austerity programme was illustrated by his coalition's poor electoral performance and, conversely, by the extraordinary success achieved by Grillo's protest movement (whose new parliamentarians had little or no previous political experience).

In March 2013 the Minister of Foreign Affairs, Giulio Terzi di Sant'Agata, resigned in protest at the Government's sending back to India for trial of two Italian marines, who were accused of killing two Indian fishermen off the coast of Kerala in February 2012 (the marines, who had been guarding an Italian oil tanker, claimed to have mistaken the fishermen for pirates). The marines had been allowed temporarily to return to Italy in February 2013 to vote in the legislative elections. The Italian Government, which had originally insisted that the marines should be tried in Italy since the incident took place in international waters, agreed to their rendition following the imposition by the Indian Supreme Court of a travel ban on the Italian ambassador in New Delhi.

Meanwhile, as political deadlock persisted, with Bersani failing to form a coalition Government in late March 2013 (largely as a result of his refusal to work with Berlusconi), President Napolitano appointed a commission of 10 experts from the fields of politics, the judiciary and business, the so-called 'wise men', who reported in April on possible political and economic reforms.

At presidential elections held on 18–20 April 2013, the first five rounds of voting failed to produce a clear winner. In response to a cross-party appeal, the widely respected incumbent, Napolitano, who was due to retire in May, presented himself as a candidate in the sixth round. The veteran politician was elected to an unprecedented second term of office, defeating the M5S candidate, Stefano Rodotà, by 738 votes to 217. Bersani resigned as leader of the PD immediately after the eventual conclusion of the presidential election, which had exposed the lack of unity between factions of the PD—many of the parliamentary deputies of the party, including the young mayor of Florence, Matteo Renzi (who had stood against Bersani in the PD leadership contest in October 2009), had refused to support Bersani's preferred presidential candidate. (Guglielmo Epifani replaced Bersani as National Secretary of the PD, on an interim basis, in May.) The re-elected President Napolitano continued efforts to break the political impasse by requesting that the deputy leader of the PD, Enrico Letta, attempt to form a broad coalition. A new 'grand coalition' Government was finally sworn in on 28 April headed by Letta and comprising the PD, PdL, UdC, Scelta Civica (Civic Choice), Radicali Italiani and independent experts; the M5S refused to join the coalition. Noteworthy appointments included that of the Secretary of the PdL, Angelino Alfano, as Deputy Prime Minister and Minister of the Interior and that of the Director-General of the Banca d'Italia, Fabrizio Saccomanni, as Minister of the Economy and Finance.

Recent developments: further political upheaval and proposed electoral and constitutional reform

A notable decline in support for the M5S was indicated by its extremely poor performance in local elections held throughout Italy in May/June 2013; there were also reports of growing internal dissatisfaction with Grillo's leadership: by March 2014 13 M5S senators had either resigned from or been expelled from the organization. In July 2013 Alfano comfortably survived a vote of no confidence held in the Senate in the wake of allegations that he had been involved in the deportation from Italy of the wife and child of a fugitive Kazakh dissident.

In June 2013 Berlusconi was convicted of paying for sex with an underage prostitute in 2010 and of abuse of office; he was sentenced to seven years' imprisonment and a lifelong ban from holding public office. Berlusconi suffered a more serious setback the following month when the Supreme Court of Cassation rejected his final appeal against the custodial sentence imposed on him (for tax fraud) in 2012; the Court also ordered a further judicial review on whether the former Prime Minister should be banned from holding public office. This ruling represented the first of Berlusconi's convictions to be confirmed on appeal in more than 20 years of fighting legal cases; however, rather than being incarcerated, the former Prime Minister was expected to serve house arrest or community service. In accordance with an anti-corruption law passed in 2012, Berlusconi now faced expulsion from the Senate. In protest against such an action, in September 2013 Berlusconi threatened to bring Letta's fragile administration to the verge of collapse by ordering the withdrawal of all PdL deputies from Parliament. The crisis was further compounded at the end of the month when, in an attempt to pre-empt the planned holding of a vote of confidence in the Government (as called for by Letta), Berlusconi ordered the resignation of the five PdL cabinet members, citing his party's opposition to a proposed increase in the sales tax. However, Letta refused to accept the resignations. In the event, amid reports of the ministers' unwillingness to comply with their leader's order that they stand down and of threatened defections from the ranks of the more moderate PdL parliamentarians, Berlusconi carried out a dramatic *volte-face* by supporting the crucial vote of confidence in Letta's Government in early October. Later that month Berlusconi was ordered to stand trial on charges of bribing a senator to defect to his party in 2006 (the trial commenced in February 2014). Berlusconi's political standing appeared further diminished in November 2013 when a group of some 60 PdL dissidents, led by Deputy Prime Minister Alfano, announced the establishment of a new party, the Nuovo Centrodestra (NC—New Centre-Right). The following day Berlusconi officially relaunched the PdL under his party's founding name, Forza Italia. At the end of November Berlusconi formally withdrew Forza Italia from the coalition, while the NC remained as a constituent party. A few days later the Senate voted to expel Berlusconi with immediate effect and barred him from standing in any election for six years; furthermore, without parliamentary immunity, the veteran politician now faced the possibility of being arrested on other criminal charges. In March 2014 the Supreme Court of Cassation upheld a two-year ban on standing for public office which had been imposed on Berlusconi after his conviction for tax fraud. None the less, Berlusconi, who commenced one year's community service at a care home near Milan in May, defiantly pledged to continue his political career from outside parliamentary confines.

In December 2013 Renzi won an overwhelming victory in a leadership contest for the PD. In the same month a series of protests were held across the country against the Government's continuing programme of economic austerity; several of the demonstrations, which attracted a broad cross section of the population, were forcibly dispersed by riot police. Also in December, Prime Minister Letta decreed that state funding of political parties was to be abolished (the proposal had been approved by the Chamber of Deputies in October). In that month the Constitutional Court ruled that two elements of the electoral system that had been used for the 2013 general election—namely the majority bonus and the closed party lists—were unconstitutional and that reform was urgently required in order to avoid future occurrences of political deadlock and uncertainty.

The new PD leader, Renzi, made his debut in national politics by announcing in January 2014 his party's proposals for comprehensive reform of the electoral system and Constitution in a bid to end political instability and weak governance, and speed up the legislative process. The proposals, which—controversially—had earlier been discussed with and had won the support of Berlusconi and his party, included changes to the proportional electoral system to guarantee stable governments with clear parliamentary majorities, and the radical transformation of the Senate by more than halving it in size, drastically limiting its powers and making it effectively a consultative body composed of appointed (rather than directly elected) regional representatives. The Chamber of Deputies would thereby become primarily responsible for lawmaking. Following a decision by the PD to support Renzi's demands for the installation of a new government and against a background of increasing pressure over the country's foundering economy, Letta resigned on 14 February. As widely predicted, President Napolitano asked Renzi to form a new government; at 39 years of age Renzi became the youngest Italian Prime Minister to date. The new coalition of the PD, NC, UdC, Scelta Civica and independents took office later that month. Notable new appointments to the Council of Ministers (one-half of which was female) included Federica Mogherini as Minister of Foreign Affairs, Roberta Pinotti as Minister of Defence and Pier Carlo Padoan, Organisation for Economic Co-operation and Development (OECD, see p. 377) Chief Economist, as Minister of the Economy and Finance. Alfano remained in his post as Minister of the Interior. Renzi's hold over the PD was strengthened by the party's strong performance in the elections to the European Parliament held in May; the PD, which based its electoral campaign on promises of political renewal, secured almost 41% of the votes cast, while M5S won 21% and Forza Italia only 17%. Paolo Gentiloni of the PD assumed responsibility for the foreign affairs ministry at the end of October following the departure from government of Mogherini to take up a new post in the European Commission.

Meanwhile, in March 2014 the Chamber of Deputies endorsed the proposed electoral reform bill, widely known as the 'Italicum', which was then passed on to the Senate for consideration. Later that month, in a separate development, the new Government approved draft legislation covering the proposed constitutional reform—including the divestment from the Senate of its power to hold votes of confidence in the Government and on the budget, and a reduction in its size to 100 members (of whom 95 would be selected by the Regional Councils and five nominated by the President). Despite considerable opposition from within the upper house, the first reading of the bill was approved by the Senate in early August. However, in accordance with the lengthy process involved in amending the Constitution, the bill required approval by the Chamber of Deputies prior to another vote in both parliamentary houses. Furthermore, if the overall endorsement in Parliament was less than a two-thirds' majority, a national referendum on the proposed legislation would be required. In January 2015 the Senate approved the Italicum following the passage of substantial amendments to the original proposals. According to the amended draft legislation any party that won at least 40% of the vote in a general election would automatically be given 340 of the 630 seats in the lower house (a 55% majority). In the event that no party achieved the 40% threshold, a run-off poll would be held between the two most successful parties in the first ballot. The winner of this second contest would be awarded the 55% majority. Other parties would be allocated seats on a proportional basis, provided that they had each secured at least 3% of the vote. Once the amended electoral bill had received final approval from the Chamber of Deputies later that year (as widely expected), it was scheduled to enter into force from July 2016.

On 14 January 2015, citing fatigue and old age, 89-year-old President Napolitano stood down early from his post having served in the presidency for a record nine years; he was replaced, in an acting capacity, by the President of the Senate, Pietro Grasso. Following three inconclusive rounds of voting, the fourth round, held on 31 January, proved successful and was won by a judge of the Constitutional Court and former Minister of Defence, Sergio Mattarella, who was sworn in as the country's new President (and the first to come from Sicily) on 3 February. On assuming power, Mattarella, whose own brother was murdered by the Mafia in 1980, pledged, *inter alia*, to prioritize the fight against corruption and organized crime during his term in office.

Organized Crime

Despite mass trials of Mafia suspects in the late 1980s, the Italian Government continued to experience problems in dealing with organized crime. In 1992 the murders of Salvatore Lima, a Sicilian politician and member of the European Parliament, Giovanni Falcone, a prominent anti-Mafia judge, and Paolo Borsellino, a colleague of Falcone, provoked renewed public outrage, and later that year, following an increase in the powers of the police and the judiciary, hundreds of suspects were detained. In 1993 the judiciary mounted a campaign to seize Mafia funds, and in the course of the year several suspected leading figures in the world of organized crime, including Salvatore Riina, the alleged head of the Sicilian Mafia ('Cosa Nostra'), were arrested. In September 1997 24 influential members of the Mafia, including Riina, were sentenced to life imprisonment for their part in the murder of Falcone. In July 1998 Riina received another conviction, along with 17 others, for complicity in the murder of Lima in 1992; this constituted Riina's 13th sentence of life imprisonment. In April 1999 an official of the treasury ministry was arrested on charges of external complicity with the Mafia; he was the first serving government member to be taken into preventive detention. In December 17 Mafia members were sentenced to life imprisonment for the murder of Borsellino. Emergency measures were decreed in November 2000 in an attempt to prevent the early release from prison of those accused of Mafia-related crimes. The laws followed the discharge, on technical grounds, of 10 detainees accused of involvement in murders attributed to the Mafia. Magistrates were granted greater powers in determining the length of preventive detention for suspects and a ban on plea-bargaining was introduced. Benedetto Spera, reputedly the closest colleague of the head (since 1995) of the Sicilian Mafia, Bernardo Provenzano, was arrested in January 2001; Spera had been convicted *in absentia* for his role in the murders of Falcone and Borsellino. In April Riina, along with six others, was sentenced to 30 years' imprisonment for the murder, in 1979, of the investigative journalist Mario Francese.

Organized crime continued to be problematic during Berlusconi's second term as Prime Minister. Provenzano's closest accomplice, Antonino Giuffrè, was arrested in April 2002 near Palermo. In December Giuffrè directly implicated Berlusconi in the bribing of the Mafia for votes in Sicily in 1993. (In April 2006 Provenzano himself, who had been in hiding since 1963, was arrested in Sicily.) Although a murder charge against Berlusconi was dropped in 2002, a nine-year prison sentence (later reduced to seven years) for Mafia collusion was imposed on his close friend Marcello Dell'Utri in December 2004. Further allegations about Berlusconi's links with the Mafia emerged during Dell'Utri's trial in January 2003, when it was alleged by a Mafia informer that the Mafia had transferred its allegiance from the DC to Berlusconi's Forza Italia after the latter's formation in 1994.

In September 2004 an investigation into the President of the Sicilian regional administration, Salvatore Cuffaro of the UDC, concluded that he had indirectly aided the Mafia by transmitting sensitive information. In January 2008 Cuffaro was convicted and sentenced to five years' imprisonment. Later that month Cuffaro was forced to resign, despite having refused to do so in the aftermath of his conviction. However, pending the appeal process, Cuffaro was re-elected to the Senate in April. Cuffaro's sentence was increased to seven years in January 2010 by an appeals court in Palermo, which convicted him of the additional charge of favouring the Mafia. This verdict was confirmed by the Supreme Court of Cassation a year later, resulting in Cuffaro's imprisonment and the loss of his seat in the Senate.

During 2010–11 the Italian authorities focused their activities against organized crime on seizing control of the various assets of the Mafia, in an attempt to weaken the syndicate's financial structure. One of the most powerful organized crime networks in Italy, the 'Ndrangheta, which is based in the southern region of Calabria, suffered a serious setback in 2010 when police arrested more than 300 suspected members. In March 2012, in a major anti-Mafia operation centred on Naples, the police seized assets worth some US $1,300m. and arrested 16 judges who were alleged to have accepted bribes to issue rulings in favour of the Camorra organized crime group. In an attempt to prevent it from being overrun by suspected Mafia associates, the entire city council of Reggio Calabria was dismissed by the central authorities in October. The alleged head of the 'Ndrangheta, Roberto Pannunzi, who had escaped from custody in Rome in 2010, was arrested in Colombia in mid-2013. In March 2014 the Government decided to deploy 850 army troops to tackle the long-running problem of the illegal dumping of toxic waste in an area north of Naples, allegedly by members of the Camorra.

Foreign Affairs

Regional relations

Italy's foreign policy has traditionally been governed by its firm commitment to Europe, notably through its membership of the European Community (now European Union—EU, see p. 271) and NATO (see p. 367). The heads of state and of government of the EU formally approved the Treaty establishing a Constitution for Europe in October 2004, which required ratification by all of the then 25 member states. Italy ratified the constitutional treaty by parliamentary vote in April 2005. However, the ratification process was stalled, following the treaty's rejection in national referendums in France and the Netherlands in May and June, respectively. A reform treaty, to replace the constitutional treaty, was signed by EU heads of state and of government at a summit meeting in Lisbon, Portugal, in December 2007. The Treaty of Lisbon was ratified by the Italian Parliament in August 2008 and entered into force in December 2009.

Italy's extended coastline and geographical position attract many illegal immigrants from South-Eastern Europe and North Africa. Following Italy's accession to the EU's Schengen Agreement on cross-border travel in October 1997, large numbers of refugees, mainly Turkish and Iraqi Kurds, began arriving in southern Italy, provoking concern among Italy's EU partners. On 1 April 1998 the Schengen Agreement, which had previously been applicable only to air travel between Italy and the other EU member states, was fully implemented, opening the borders with Austria and France. In order to comply with the terms of the agreement, a new law had been promulgated in February, providing for the detention, prior to forcible repatriation, of illegal immigrants. In February 1999 legislation was approved allowing for the detention of illegal immigrants arriving in Italy

without first making an asylum application. In March 2002 a state of emergency was declared following the arrival of 1,000 Kurdish refugees in Sicily. In June legislation was passed allowing for the fingerprinting of non-EU nationals and requiring residence permits to be renewed every two years. Further increases in arrivals of immigrants prompted a government decree in June 2003 enabling the Italian navy to board ships carrying illegal immigrants and divert them away from the Italian coast.

In August 2004 an agreement was reached with Libya on controlling immigration through that country, and in October the Italian Government commenced returning would-be immigrants to Libya. In September 2006 the Italian and Libyan Governments were accused of abusing the human rights of African migrants through forced repatriations. In August 2008 the two countries signed an accord under which Italy was to invest US $5,000m. in Libya over the following 20 years, in recognition of the injustices suffered by Libyans during the colonial era, for which Berlusconi offered an official apology. In May 2009 it was announced that, in accordance with the terms of the 'friendship agreement', joint maritime patrols had begun. The number of boats carrying illegal immigrants from Libya to Italy subsequently declined sharply. Given its extensive business and trade links with Libya, the Italian Government's response to a popular uprising in that country in February 2011 was initially cautious. Nevertheless, the Italian Government condemned the violent repression of the anti-Government demonstrations in Libya and, following the evacuation of its citizens from that country, suspended the 2008 friendship agreement and announced its support for EU sanctions against the regime of the Libyan leader, Col Muammar al-Qaddafi. During 2011 thousands of migrants from Tunisia, Libya and Egypt arrived by boat on the Italian island of Lampedusa following the civil unrest in those countries. Relations between Italy and France deteriorated as France objected to Italy providing thousands of Tunisian migrants with temporary residence permits, which enabled them to travel within the EU (often to France). In April, however, Italy and France agreed to launch joint sea and air patrols in an attempt to limit the influx from North Africa. In the same month the Italian Government committed Italy to joining France, the United Kingdom and the USA in mounting air strikes against Libya. The Italian embassy in the Libyan capital of Tripoli was attacked by Qaddafi loyalists in May. Despite this, talks between 22 countries supporting the rebels in Libya took place in Rome later that month, chaired by Italy and Qatar; it was agreed to establish a non-military fund to help the rebels. Following the collapse of Qaddafi's regime in September and the death of the former dictator the following month, relations between Italy and Libya began to be normalized. Prime Minister Monti visited Tripoli in January 2012 to hold discussions with the transitional administration.

During 2013–14 thousands of migrants continued to attempt the dangerous crossing from North Africa and the Middle East across the Mediterranean to Sicily and other Italian islands. According to official figures, the number of migrants who reached Italy by sea in 2013 totalled almost 43,000, representing an increase of some 325% compared with the previous year. In October at least 366 African migrants (mainly from Eritrea and Somalia) died when the overcrowded boat that was carrying them sank off the coast of Lampedusa. In response to this disaster, the Italian Government announced a 12-month emergency programme, entitled Mare Nostrum ('Our Sea'), to increase the number of sea and air search and rescue missions. According to official estimates, in the 10 months to the end of October 2014 some 153,000 migrants arrived in Italy by sea. Despite widespread concern that the lives of thousands of migrants would thereby be endangered, the Mare Nostrum programme was concluded in November (as scheduled) and was replaced by a more limited 'border protection' mission known as Triton, which was to be jointly operated by Italy and the EU external border agency Frontex.

Other external relations

Under the premiership of Berlusconi in 2001–06 increasing emphasis on promoting national interests was accompanied by a repositioning of Italian foreign policy towards support for the USA in its 'war on terror'. The deployment of some 2,700 Italian troops to assist US military efforts following the September 2001 suicide attacks in the USA, was approved by the Italian Parliament in November. An investigation into the existence of terrorist cells possibly connected with the al-Qa'ida organization led to a number of arrests in Italy in 2002–03. Berlusconi's increasing political allegiance with the group of powers, including the USA, the UK and Spain, which was in favour of military action against the regime of Saddam Hussain in Iraq gave rise to nationwide protests in February 2003. Owing to the level of popular dissent, the Italian Government did not at this stage agree to supply troops for the US-led military campaign in Iraq; it did, however, offer the USA the use of Italy's bases and airspace for logistical purposes. At the onset of armed conflict in Iraq in March, the anti-war movement in Italy gained momentum. In April the Government approved the provision of humanitarian support for Iraq; however, by November Italy had approximately 2,400 troops stationed in the country. In that month a suicide bombing took place at an Italian base in Nasiriyah, Iraq, killing 19 Italian soldiers; this led to renewed calls for Italy to pull out of Iraq. Pressure for the withdrawal of troops increased following the kidnapping and murder of an Italian journalist by Islamist extremists in Iraq in August 2004. In January 2006 the Italian Government announced that all 3,000 Italian troops then stationed in Iraq would be withdrawn by the end of the year; the last Italian troops left Iraq in December.

Following the conflict in Lebanon between Israeli forces and the militant group Hezbollah in mid-2006, Italy sent some 2,500 peacekeeping troops to form part of the UN Interim Force in Lebanon (UNIFIL); at December 2014 the Italian contingent of UNIFIL numbered 1,098 troops. In late 2013 Italy also had around 4,000 troops stationed in Afghanistan as part of the NATO-led peacekeeping force (the International Security Assistance Force—ISAF); in December 2014 ISAF formally concluded its mission and all remaining combat troops were withdrawn from Afghanistan. However, Italy was expected to contribute military personnel to the NATO-led, non-combat mission, Resolute Support, which from January 2015 was to provide training, advice and assistance to the Afghan security forces and institutions.

CONSTITUTION AND GOVERNMENT

Under the 1948 Constitution, legislative power was held by the bicameral Parlamento (Parliament), elected by universal suffrage for five years (subject to dissolution) on the basis of proportional representation. A referendum held in 1993 supported the amendment of the Constitution to provide for the election of 75% of the members of the Senato della Repubblica (Senate of the Republic) by a simple plurality and the remainder under a system of proportional representation, and provided for further electoral reform. In August Parliament approved a similar system for elections to the Camera dei Deputati (Chamber of Deputies). In December 2005 new legislation was enacted providing for the return to full proportional representation. The Senate has 315 elected members (seats allocated on a regional basis) and up to five life senators appointed by the President. The Chamber of Deputies has 630 members. The minimum voting age is 25 years for the Senate and 18 years for the Chamber of Deputies. The two houses have equal power.

The President of the Republic is a constitutional head of state elected for seven years by an electoral college comprising both houses of Parliament and 58 regional representatives. Executive power is exercised by the Council of Ministers. The head of state appoints the President of the Council (Prime Minister) and, on the latter's recommendation, other ministers. The Council is responsible to Parliament.

The country is divided into 20 regions, of which five (Sicily, Sardinia, Trentino-Alto Adige/Südtirol, Friuli-Venezia Giulia and Valle d'Aosta) enjoy a special autonomous status. There is a large degree of regional autonomy. Each region has a legislative Regional Council (known as the Regional Assembly in Sicily and the Council of the Valley in the Valle d'Aosta) elected every five years by universal suffrage and an executive Giunta Regionale which is responsible to the Regional Council. At February 2014 the regions were subdivided into a total of 109 provinces and 8,058 municipalities. In April the Chamber of Deputies approved legislation to create 10 metropolitan cities (città metropolitane) out of the provinces covering the 10 largest cities (and their suburbs) in Italy; each metropolitan city was to be governed by three bodies: a Mayor, a Metropolitan Council and a Metropolitan Conference. The new administrative divisions, the establishment of which entailed a considerable reduction in the total number of provinces, became operational on 1 January 2015.

REGIONAL AND INTERNATIONAL CO-OPERATION

Italy was a founder member of the European Community, now the European Union (EU, see p. 271), and uses the single currency, the euro. It is a member of the Council of Europe (see p. 250), the Central European Initiative (see p. 459) and the Organization for Security and Co-operation in Europe (OSCE, see p. 385).

Italy joined the UN in 1955. As a contracting party to the General Agreement on Tariffs and Trade, Italy joined the World Trade Organization (WTO, see p. 431) on its establishment in 1995. Italy is also a member of the North Atlantic Treaty Organization (NATO, see p. 367), the Organisation for Economic Co-operation and Development (OECD, see p. 377), the Group of Seven major industrialized nations (G7, see p. 460) and the Group of 20 major industrialized and systemically important emerging market nations (G20, see p. 451).

ECONOMIC AFFAIRS

In 2013, according to estimates by the World Bank, Italy's gross national income (GNI), measured at average 2011–13 prices, was US $2,058,172m., equivalent to $34,400 per head (or $34,100 per head on an international purchasing-power parity basis). During 2004–13, it was estimated that the population increased by an average of 0.4% per year, while Italy's gross domestic product (GDP) per head decreased, in real terms, at an average annual rate of 0.9%. Overall GDP decreased, in real terms, at an average annual rate of 0.5% in 2004–13. GDP decreased by 1.9% in 2013, measured both at constant prices and according to chain-linking methodologies.

Agriculture (including forestry and fishing) contributed 2.3% of GDP in 2013, and engaged 3.8% of the employed labour force in July–September 2014. The principal crops are grapes, maize, wheat, tomatoes, olives and sugar beet. Italy is a leading producer and exporter of wine. According to the World Bank, during 2004–13 the real GDP of the agricultural sector increased at an average rate of 1.1% per year; agricultural GDP decreased by 4.3% in 2012, but increased by 0.3% in 2013, measured at constant prices. According to chain-linking methodologies, agricultural GDP decreased by 2.7% in 2012, but grew by 0.6% in 2013.

Industry (including mining, manufacturing, construction and power) contributed 23.3% of GDP in 2013, and engaged 27.2% of the employed labour force in July–September 2014. According to the World Bank, real industrial GDP fell by an average of 1.6% per year during 2004–13; the GDP of the sector declined by 3.8% in 2013.

The mining sector contributed just 0.4% of GDP in 2013, and engaged 0.1% of the employed labour force in the same year. The major product of the mining sector is petroleum, followed by talc, feldspar, rock salt and gypsum. Italy also has reserves of lignite, lead and zinc. According to chain-linking methodologies, mining GDP increased by 2.8% in 2012, but decreased by 9.5% in 2013.

Manufacturing contributed 14.9% of GDP, and engaged 16.4% of the employed labour force in 2013. The most important branches of manufacturing are metals and metal products, non-electrical machinery, food products, textiles and wearing apparel, rubber and plastic products, wood and paper products, and transport equipment. According to the World Bank, in 2004–13 the GDP of the manufacturing sector declined, in real terms, at an average annual rate of 1.2%. Real GDP declined by 3.1% in 2013, measured at constant prices, while according to chain-linking methodologies, manufacturing GDP decreased by 2.8% in 2013.

Construction contributed 5.2% of GDP, and engaged 6.6% of the employed labour force in 2013. According to chain-linking methodologies, the construction sector contracted by 5.8% in 2013.

More than 80% of energy requirements are imported. According to World Bank figures, in 2012 natural gas-fired stations provided 46.1% of electricity production, coal-fired electricity generating stations 16.0%, hydroelectric power stations 14.2% and petroleum 6.3%. In 2004 Libya began delivering natural gas to Sicily through a pipeline financed by Ente Nazionale Idrocarburi (Eni), the main—formerly wholly state-owned—gas provider, and its Libyan counterpart. In 2012, according to the World Bank, fuel imports accounted for 22.9% of the value of total merchandise imports.

Services accounted for 74.4% of GDP in 2013, and engaged 69.0% of the employed labour force in July–September 2014. Tourism is an important source of income; in 2013 50.2m. foreigners visited Italy, compared with 48.7m. in the previous year. Tourism receipts totalled US $43,912m. in 2013. According to the World Bank, the combined GDP of the services sector increased, in real terms, at an estimated average rate of 0.1% per year in 2004–13; sectoral GDP fell by 0.9% in 2013, measured at constant prices.

In 2013, according to IMF data, Italy recorded a visible merchandise trade surplus of US $48,092m., and there was a surplus of $21,272m. on the current account of the balance of payments. According to official provisional figures, in 2013 the principal source of imports was Germany (14.7%); other major suppliers were France, the People's Republic of China, the Netherlands and the Russian Federation. Germany was also the principal market for exports (12.4%); other major purchasers in that year were France, the USA, Switzerland and the United Kingdom. In 2013 Italy's fellow members of the European Union (EU, see p. 271) were the source of 55.3% of Italy's imports and purchased 53.7% of its exports. The principal exports in 2013 were machinery and mechanical equipment, metals and metal products, chemicals and artificial fibres, textile products, transport equipment, electrical equipment, food, beverages and tobacco, and rubber, plastic products and non-metallic minerals. The principal imports were chemicals and artificial fibres, metals and metal products, electrical equipment, crude petroleum, transport equipment, food, beverages and tobacco, textile products, machinery and mechanical equipment, and natural gas.

According to preliminary figures, the budgetary deficit for 2013 was €47,300m., equivalent to 2.9% of annual GDP. Italy's general government gross debt was €2,067,500m. in 2013, equivalent to 132.5% of GDP. According to the International Labour Organization the average annual rate of inflation in 2004–13 was 2.1%. Consumer prices increased by 1.2% in 2013. The rate of unemployment averaged 11.8% in July–September 2014.

Although Italy's economy is the fourth largest in Europe, the country suffers from significant structural problems, including low productivity, an inefficient public sector, and considerable economic disparity between the more industrialized, prosperous north and the impoverished south. Following the deterioration in global economic conditions in 2008, real GDP contracted by 1.3% in 2008 and by a further 5.1% in 2009, largely owing to declines in domestic demand, investment and export revenue, while the budget deficit widened to 2.7% of GDP in 2008 and 5.4% in 2009. In contrast to other advanced economies, the Italian Government was able to introduce only limited fiscal stimulus owing to the country's high public debt. Moderate growth of 1.3% in 2010 was driven mainly by an increase in export revenue, as global demand recovered, and the budget deficit narrowed to 4.6% of GDP in that year. However, the debt-to-GDP ratio continued to rise, reaching 119.0% in 2010 (the second highest in the eurozone after Greece), and unemployment remained high, at 8.6% in

December. Although the budget deficit fell to 3.8% of GDP in 2011, partly as a result of the implementation of a number of austerity measures by Silvio Berlusconi's Government, the rate of overall growth decelerated to 0.4% and the debt-to-GDP ratio had increased to 120.1% by the end of December. Following Berlusconi's resignation in November 2011, an emergency package of stringent fiscal adjustments, including new taxes, drastic cuts in public expenditure, the sale of state assets and controversial pension reform, was introduced by the new Prime Minister, Mario Monti, in December. Although these measures led in 2012 to a further reduction in the budget deficit, to match the EU-mandated ceiling of 3.0% of GDP, the situation deteriorated in other aspects, with the debt-to-GDP ratio rising to 127.0%, a contraction of 2.4% in real GDP, and an increase in the unemployment rate to 10.8% at mid-year. Against a background of political instability and falling output and consumer demand, Italy's economic prospects remained bleak in 2013, with unemployment reaching 12.5% in September (the highest level since official records began in 1977). The high rate of youth unemployment (exceeding 40%) was a source of particular concern. Moreover, in 2013 real GDP declined by a further 1.9% and the debt-to-GDP ratio continued to escalate, reaching 132.5%. With economic prospects appearing uncertain in 2014 against a backdrop of persistently high unemployment and falling inflation (in August consumer prices posted a year-on-year decline for the first time since 1959), the Government of Matteo Renzi, which came to power in February, upheld the austerity programme while at the same time introducing bold measures to reform the labour market in an attempt to increase competitiveness, employment, flexibility and productivity. According to IMF estimates, in 2014 GDP was forecast to contract for a third consecutive year, by 0.1%, while the budget deficit was projected to amount to some 3.0% of GDP (as in both 2012 and 2013). The debt-to-GDP ratio was expected to peak at 136.4% in 2014 prior to falling gradually thereafter as credit conditions improved and the positive effects of large-scale quantitative easing by the European Central Bank (from early 2015) began to be felt within the eurozone.

PUBLIC HOLIDAYS

2016: 1 January (New Year's Day), 6 January (Epiphany), 28 March (Easter Monday), 25 April (Liberation Day), 1 May (Labour Day), 2 June (Republic Day), 15 August (Assumption), 1 November (All Saints' Day), 8 December (Immaculate Conception), 25 December (Christmas Day), 26 December (St Stephen's Day).

There are also numerous local public holidays, held on the feast day of the patron saint of each town.

Statistical Survey

Source (unless otherwise stated): Istituto Nazionale di Statistica, Via Cesare Balbo 16, 00184 Roma; tel. (06) 46731; fax (06) 467313101; e-mail info@istat.it; internet www.istat.it.

Area and Population

AREA, POPULATION AND DENSITY

Area (sq km)	301,336*
Population (census results)†	
21 October 2001	56,995,744
9 October 2011	
Males	28,745,507
Females	30,688,237
Total	59,433,744
Population (official estimates at 1 January)	
2012	59,394,207
2013	59,685,227
2014	60,782,668
Density (per sq km) at 1 January 2014	201.7

* 116,346 sq miles.
† Census figures are *de jure*, in 2001 the de facto population was 57,110,144 (males 27,617,335, females 29,492,809).

POPULATION BY AGE AND SEX
(official population estimates at 1 January 2014)

	Males	Females	Total
0–14 years	4,348,146	4,099,987	8,448,133
15–64 years	19,566,348	19,753,245	39,319,593
65 years and over	5,570,070	7,444,872	13,014,942
Total	29,484,564	31,298,104	60,782,668

REGIONS
(official population estimates at 1 January 2014)

Region	Area (sq km)	Population	Density (per sq km)	Regional capital(s)
Abruzzo	10,763	1,333,939	123.9	L'Aquila
Basilicata	9,995	578,391	57.9	Potenza
Calabria	15,081	1,980,533	131.3	Catanzaro
Campania	13,590	5,869,965	431.9	Napoli (Naples)
Emilia-Romagna	22,117	4,446,354	201.0	Bologna
Friuli-Venezia Giulia	7,858	1,229,363	156.4	Trieste
Lazio	17,236	5,870,451	340.6	Roma (Rome)
Liguria	5,422	1,591,939	293.6	Genova (Genoa)
Lombardia (Lombardy)	23,863	9,973,397	417.9	Milano (Milan)
Marche	9,694	1,553,138	160.2	Ancona
Molise	4,438	314,725	70.9	Campobasso
Piemonte (Piedmont)	25,402	4,436,798	174.7	Torino (Turin)
Puglia	19,358	4,090,266	211.3	Bari
Sardegna (Sardinia)	24,090	1,663,859	69.1	Cagliari
Sicilia (Sicily)	25,711	5,094,937	198.2	Palermo
Toscana (Tuscany)	22,994	3,750,511	163.1	Firenze (Florence)
Trentino-Alto Adige/Südtirol	13,607	1,051,951	77.3	Bolzano/Trento*
Umbria	8,456	896,742	106.0	Perugia
Valle d'Aosta	3,263	128,591	39.4	Aosta
Veneto	18,399	4,926,818	267.8	Venezia (Venice)
Total	301,336	60,782,668	201.7	—

* Bolzano (Bozen) and Trento (Trent) are joint regional capitals of Trentino-Alto Adige/Südtirol.

PRINCIPAL TOWNS
(official population estimates at 1 January 2014, measured by *comune*)

Roma (Rome, the capital)	2,863,322	Livorno (Leghorn)	160,512
Milano (Milan)	1,324,169	Ravenna	158,784
Napoli (Naples)	989,111	Cagliari	154,019
Torino (Turin)	902,137	Foggia	153,143
Palermo	678,492	Rimini	146,856
Genova (Genoa)	596,958	Salerno	133,885
Bologna	384,202	Ferrara	133,423
Firenze (Florence)	377,207	Sassari	127,715
Bari	322,751	Latina	125,375
Catania	315,576	Monza	123,151
Venezia (Venice)	264,534	Siracusa (Syracuse)	122,304
Verona	259,966	Pescara	121,325
Messina	241,997	Giugliano in Campania	120,157
Padova (Padua)	209,678	Bergamo	118,717
Trieste	204,849	Forlí	118,359
Taranto	203,257	Trento (Trent)	117,285
Brescia	193,599	Vicenza	113,655
Prato	191,268	Terni	112,227
Parma	187,938	Bolzano	105,713
Reggio di Calabria	184,937	Novara	104,736
Modena	184,525	Piacenza	102,404
Reggio nell'Emilia	172,525	Ancona	101,742
Perugia	166,030	Andria	100,333

BIRTHS, MARRIAGES AND DEATHS

	Registered live births		Registered marriages		Registered deaths	
	Number	Rate (per 1,000)	Number	Rate (per 1,000)	Number	Rate (per 1,000)
2006	560,010	9.5	245,992	4.2	557,892	9.5
2007	563,933	9.5	250,360	4.2	570,801	9.6
2008	576,659	9.6	246,613	4.1	585,126	9.8
2009	568,857	9.5	230,613	3.8	591,663	9.8
2010	561,944	9.3	217,700	3.6	587,488	9.7
2011	546,607	9.0	204,830	3.5	593,404	9.7
2012	534,186	9.0	207,138	3.5	612,883	10.3
2013	514,308	8.5	194,057	3.2	600,744	10.0

Life expectancy (years at birth): 82.9 (males 80.4; females 85.6) in 2012 (Source: World Bank, World Development Indicators database).

IMMIGRATION AND EMIGRATION

	2011	2012	2013
Immigration	412,344	350,772	307,454
Emigration	96,308	106,216	125,735

EMPLOYMENT
('000 persons aged 15 years and over)

	2011	2012	2013
Agriculture, hunting, forestry and fishing	942.2	913.1	883.5
Mining and quarrying	25.5	24.4	23.7
Manufacturing	4,135.3	4,062.6	3,990.1
Electricity, gas and water	279.1	280.3	282.8
Construction	1,867.6	1,774.4	1,614.6
Wholesale and retail trade; repair of motor vehicles, motorcycles and personal and household goods	3,715.3	3,714.1	3,608.3
Restaurants and hotels	1,329.5	1,383.2	1,361.6
Transportation and storage	1,143.1	1,121.9	1,095.5
Information and communications	595.0	596.1	600.4
Financial intermediation	684.7	685.9	669.7
Real estate, renting and business activities	2,963.1	3,009.1	3,019.7
Public administration and defence; compulsory social security	1,344.8	1,315.9	1,300.3
Education	1,524.7	1,503.5	1,507.4
Health and social work	1,762.7	1,791.4	1,756.9
Other community, social and personal service activities	1,021.7	1,037.5	1,020.5
Private households with employed persons	1,508.4	1,575.3	1,569.1
Total employed	24,842.7	24,788.7	24,304.1

2014 ('000 persons aged 15 years and over, July–September): Agriculture 864; Industry 6,129; Services 15,559; *Total employed* 22,552; Unemployed 3,010; *Total labour force* 25,561.

Health and Welfare

KEY INDICATORS

Total fertility rate (children per woman, 2012)	1.5
Under-5 mortality rate (per 1,000 live births, 2012)	4
HIV/AIDS (% of persons aged 15–49, 2013)	0.3
Physicians (per 1,000 head, 2011)	4.1
Hospital beds (per 1,000 head, 2009)	3.6
Health expenditure (2011): US $ per head (PPP)	3,017
Health expenditure (2011): % of GDP	9.2
Health expenditure (2011): public (% of total)	77.8
Total carbon dioxide emissions ('000 metric tons, 2010)	406,307.3
Carbon dioxide emissions per head (metric tons, 2010)	6.7
Human Development Index (2013): ranking	26
Human Development Index (2013): value	0.872

For sources and definitions, see explanatory note on p. vi.

Agriculture

PRINCIPAL CROPS
('000 metric tons)

	2011	2012	2013
Wheat	6,642	7,767	7,277
Rice, paddy	1,490	1,583	1,339*
Barley	949	960	873
Maize	9,753	8,195	7,900
Oats	297	292	247
Sorghum	300	158	317
Potatoes	1,547	1,598	1,337
Sugar beet	3,548	2,501	2,159
Almonds, with shell	105	90	73
Hazelnuts (Filberts)	129	85	113
Soybeans (Soya beans)	565	422	625

—continued	2011	2012	2013
Olives	3,182	3,018	2,941
Sunflower seed	274	186	286
Cabbages	334	312	308
Artichokes	475	365	548
Lettuce	819	756	796
Tomatoes	5,950	5,132	4,932
Cauliflowers and broccoli .	421	414	382
Pumpkins, squash and gourds .	539	520†	530†
Aubergines (Eggplants) . . .	243	218	220
Chillies and peppers, green . .	229	191	212
Onions, dry	414	337	351
Beans, green	164	134	155
Carrots and turnips . . .	543	482	493
Watermelons	378	347	393
Cantaloupes and other melons .	536	461	480
Oranges	2,470	1,771	1,708
Tangerines, mandarins, clementines and satsumas . .	864	760	650
Lemons and limes	483	346	336
Apples	2,411	1,991	2,217
Pears	927	646	743
Apricots	263	247	198
Sweet cherries	113	105	131
Peaches and nectarines . .	1,637	1,332	1,402
Plums	192	172	210
Strawberries	46	41	40
Grapes	7,445	5,819	8,010
Kiwi fruit	432	385	448
Tobacco, unmanufactured . .	70	51†	50

* Unofficial figure.
† FAO estimate.

Aggregate production ('000 metric tons, may include official, semi-official or estimated data): Total cereals 19,521 in 2011, 19,039 in 2012, 18,084 in 2013; Total roots and tubers 1,557 in 2011, 1,603 in 2012, 1,344 in 2013; Total vegetables (incl. melons) 14,242 in 2011, 12,961 in 2012, 13,049 in 2013; Total fruits (excl. melons) 17,693 in 2011, 13,914 in 2012, 16,371 in 2013.

Source: FAO.

LIVESTOCK
('000 head, year ending September)

	2011	2012	2013
Horses	373	396	394
Asses*	24	24	24
Mules*	9	9	9
Cattle	5,832	6,252	6,092
Buffaloes	354	349	403
Pigs	9,321	9,351	8,662
Sheep	7,900	7,943	7,016
Goats	983	960	892
Chickens*	138,000	140,000	136,000
Turkeys*	24,500	25,000	25,200

* FAO estimates.

Source: FAO.

LIVESTOCK PRODUCTS
('000 metric tons)

	2011	2012	2013
Cattle meat	1,000	958	842
Buffalo meat	11	24	12
Sheep meat	47	46	34
Pig meat	1,602	1,651	1,625
Horse meat	17	18	15
Chicken meat	889	922	905
Turkey meat	309	322	311
Rabbit meat*	255	263	263
Cows' milk	10,479	10,580	10,397
Buffaloes' milk	193	192	195
Sheep's milk	418	406	384
Goats' milk	24	28	27
Hen eggs*	755	765	775

* FAO estimates.

Source: FAO.

Forestry

ROUNDWOOD REMOVALS
('000 cubic metres, excl. bark)

	2009	2010	2011
Sawlogs, veneer logs and logs for sleepers	1,236	1,549	1,000
Pulpwood	594	370	645
Other industrial wood	898	728	711
Fuel wood	5,352	5,197	5,388
Total	8,080	7,844	7,744

2012–13: Production assumed to be unchanged from 2011 (FAO estimates).
Source: FAO.

SAWNWOOD PRODUCTION
('000 cubic metres, incl. railway sleepers)

	2011	2012	2013
Coniferous (softwood) . . .	750	850	860
Broadleaved (hardwood) . . .	500	520	500
Total	1,250	1,370	1,360

Source: FAO.

Fishing
('000 metric tons, live weight)

	2010	2011	2012
Capture	234.7	216.9*	200.8*
European hake	12.0	10.5	9.4
European anchovy . . .	54.1	46.2	42.8
Striped venus	19.7	19.7	20.0
Aquaculture	153.5	164.2*	162.6*
Rainbow trout	33.2	34.4	34.4*
Mediterranean mussel . .	64.3	79.5	79.0*
Clams (Carpet shells) . .	36.7	32.3	31.6*
Total catch	388.1	381.1*	363.4*

* FAO estimate.

Note: Figures exclude aquatic plants (FAO estimates, all capture, '000 metric tons): 1.4 in 2010; 1.2 in 2011; 1.2 in 2012. Also excluded are aquatic mammals (recorded by number rather than weight) and corals. The number of whales and dolphins caught was: 3 in 2010; 12 in 2011; 14 in 2012. Corals landed (metric tons): 10.3 in 2010; 10.5 in 2011; 10.2 in 2012.

Source: FAO.

Mining
('000 metric tons unless otherwise indicated)

	2010	2011	2012
Crude petroleum ('000 barrels) .	35,040	36,201	36,865
Natural methane gas (million cu m)	8,296	8,438	8,400*
Copper (refined, all kinds) . .	1.8	7.6	7.7
Lead (metric tons)*†	800	800	n.a.
Barite (Barytes)*	3.5	3.5	3.5
Feldspar*	4,700	4,700	4,700
Bentonite	111	102	144
Kaolin	6	8	8
Salt	4,006	2,912	3,098
Gypsum	4,441	5,939	2,563
Pumice*‡	30	30	30
Pozzolan*	4,000	4,000	4,000
Talc and steatite	110.0	110.0	110.0

* Estimate(s).
† Metal content of ores and concentrates.
‡ Including pumiceous lapilli.

Source: US Geological Survey.

Industry

SELECTED PRODUCTS
('000 metric tons unless otherwise indicated)

	2002	2003	2004
Wine (thousand hl)*	44,604.1	44,086.1	53,135.2
Cotton yarn	231.8	212.0	193.9
Cotton woven fabrics	209.8	197.1	186.9
Wood pulp, mechanical . . .	309.2	341.4	364.8
Newsprint†	175.1	182.0	193.0
Magazine print	780.0	830.0	945.1
Other printing and writing paper .	2,104.5	2,091.2	2,164.7
Washing powders and detergents .	1,982.0	2,123.8	2,174.5
Jet fuels	2,458.8	2,626.8	2,550.9
Benzene	20,999.1	20,759.4	n.a.
Motor gasoline	37,297.0	38,349.5	38,025.0
Naphthas	3,243.3	4,287.7	3,938.8
Gas-diesel oil	12,286.3	12,166.5	13,278.2
Bitumen	2,942.3	3,274.8	3,496.3
Coke	3,973.9	3,663.1	3,964.6
Tyres for road motor vehicles . .	258.6	265.4	278.9
Glass bottles and other containers of common glass	2,939.8	3,139.5	3,171.1
Cement	41,722.3	43,580.0	45,342.9
Steel	26,301.4	26,832.1	28,385.4
Rolled iron	24,165.6	25,608.6	28,710.6
Other iron and steel-finished manufactures	3,260.2	3,133.9	3,164.8
Refrigerators for household use ('000 units)	7,088.8	6,715.3	6,444.1
Washing machines for household use ('000 units)	8,884.0	9,666.8	9,679.9
Passenger motor cars ('000 units) .	1,125.8	1,026.5	839.2
Lorries (Trucks) ('000 units) . .	266.4	267.4	283.9
Motorcycles, scooters, etc. ('000 units)	588.9	572.5	622.3
Bicycles ('000 units)	597.7	581.6	501.5
Hydroelectric power (million kWh)†	47,262	44,277	n.a.
Thermoelectric power (million kWh)‡	231,069	242,784	n.a.
Other electric power (million kWh)‡	6,066	6,799	n.a.

* Provisional data.
† Source: FAO.
‡ Net production.

2009 ('000 metric tons): Newsprint 211.3; Mechanical wood pulp 259.9; Other printing and writing paper 2,635 (Source: FAO); Crude steel 19,848; Cement 36,317 (Source: US Geological Survey).

2010 ('000 metric tons): Newsprint 181.3; Mechanical wood pulp 278.0; Other printing and writing paper 2,852 (Source: FAO); Crude steel 25,750; Cement 34,408 (Source: US Geological Survey).

2011 ('000 metric tons): Newsprint 193.2; Mechanical wood pulp 281.0; Other printing and writing paper 2,858 (Source: FAO); Crude steel 28,735; Cement 33,120 (Source: US Geological Survey).

2012 ('000 metric tons): Newsprint 127.1; Mechanical wood pulp 269.0; Other printing and writing paper 2,778 (Source: FAO); Crude steel 27,257; Cement 26,200 (Source: US Geological Survey).

2013 ('000 metric tons): Newsprint 51.8; Mechanical wood pulp 269.1; Other printing and writing paper 2,687 (Source: FAO).

Electrical energy (million kWh, including San Marino): 303,699 in 2005; 314,121 in 2006; 313,888 in 2007; 319,130 in 2008; 292,642 in 2009; 302,062 in 2010; 302,570 in 2011; 285,116 in 2012.

Finance

CURRENCY AND EXCHANGE RATES

Monetary Units
100 cent = 1 euro (€).

Sterling, Dollar and Euro Equivalents (31 December 2014)
£1 sterling = 1.286 euros;
US $1 = 0.824 euros;
€10 = £7.78 = $12.14.

Average Exchange Rate (euros per US $)
2012   0.7783
2013   0.7532
2014   0.7537

Note: The national currency was formerly the Italian lira (plural: lire). From the introduction of the euro, with Italian participation, on 1 January 1999, a fixed exchange rate of €1 = 1,936.27 lire was in operation. Euro notes and coins were introduced on 1 January 2002. The euro and local currency circulated alongside each other until 28 February, after which the euro became the sole legal tender.

STATE BUDGET
(€ '000 million)

Revenue	2012*	2013†	2014†
Taxes	473.1	468.4	478.4
Social contributions	216.0	215.0	216.5
Grants	3.0	3.0	3.0
Other revenue	114.2	117.1	120.0
Total	**806.3**	**803.5**	**817.9**

Expenditure	2012*	2013†	2014†
Expense	790.1	793.1	803.3
Compensation of employees .	165.2	164.1	162.9
Use of goods and services . .	86.4	83.4	82.6
Consumption of fixed capital .	−31.4	−30.4	−31.5
Interest	84.6	82.0	81.8
Social benefits	356.6	366.2	376.2
Other expense	128.8	127.9	131.3
Net acquisition of non-financial assets	61.6	57.7	61.7
Total	**851.7**	**850.8**	**865.0**

* Preliminary figures.
† Projections.

Source: IMF, *Italy: 2014 Article IV Consultation* (September 2014).

INTERNATIONAL RESERVES
(US $ million at 31 December)

	2011	2012	2013
Gold (Eurosystem valuation) . .	124,116	131,171	94,713
IMF special drawing rights . .	9,184	9,458	9,434
Reserve position in IMF . . .	5,844	6,225	5,825
Foreign exchange	34,158	34,816	35,516
Total	**173,302**	**181,670**	**145,488**

Source: IMF, *International Financial Statistics*.

MONEY SUPPLY
(incl. shares, depository corporations, national residency criteria, € '000 million at 31 December)

	2011	2012	2013
Currency issued	150.16	154.16	161.78
Banca d'Italia	150.16	154.16	161.78
Demand deposits	736.30	733.23	761.09
Other deposits	626.33	741.33	765.29
Securities other than shares . .	914.23	958.32	878.34
Money market fund shares . .	26.97	9.14	9.55
Shares and other equity . . .	477.89	492.98	481.00
Other items (net)	−463.00	−496.76	−232.03
Total	**2,468.87**	**2,592.40**	**2,825.62**

Source: IMF, *International Financial Statistics*.

COST OF LIVING
(Consumer Price Index; base: 2010 = 100)

	2011	2012	2013
Food (incl. non-alcoholic beverages)	102.4	105.0	107.5
Rent and utilities	105.1	112.6	114.9
Clothing (incl. footwear) . . .	101.7	104.3	105.4
All items (incl. others) . . .	102.8	105.9	107.2

NATIONAL ACCOUNTS
(€ million at current prices)

National Income and Product

	2011	2012	2013
Compensation of employees . .	651,470	650,986	647,963
Operating surplus and mixed income (net)	491,737	463,454	464,460
Domestic factor incomes . .	1,143,208	1,114,440	1,112,423
Consumption of fixed capital . .	291,128	296,570	298,280
Gross domestic product (GDP) at factor cost	1,434,336	1,411,010	1,410,703
Taxes on production and imports .	233,426	248,192	241,581
Less Subsidies	28,904	31,198	33,381
GDP in market prices . . .	1,638,857	1,628,004	1,618,904
Net primary income received from abroad	−5,414	−3,390	−2,773
Gross national product . . .	1,633,443	1,624,614	1,616,131
Less Consumption of fixed capital .	291,128	296,570	298,280
Net national income	1,342,315	1,328,044	1,317,851
Net current transfers from abroad	−18,954	−19,126	−18,009
Net national disposable income	1,323,361	1,308,918	1,299,842

Expenditure on the Gross Domestic Product

	2011	2012	2013
Final consumption expenditure .	1,329,508	1,311,072	1,294,177
Households	999,772	986,483	970,404
Non-profit institutions serving households	8,819	8,924	8,957
General government	320,918	315,665	314,816
Gross capital formation . . .	335,062	302,260	287,836
Changes in inventories . . .	10,913	−3,478	−2,840
Acquisitions, less disposals, of valuables	2,312	2,248	2,068
Gross fixed capital formation .	321,837	303,489	288,609
Total domestic expenditure .	1,664,570	1,613,331	1,582,013
Exports of goods and services . .	442,219	460,071	462,296
Less Imports of goods and services	467,932	445,397	425,405
GDP in market prices . . .	1,638,857	1,628,004	1,618,904

Gross Domestic Product by Economic Activity

	2011	2012	2013
Agriculture, hunting, forestry and fishing	30,880	31,901	33,699
Mining and quarrying	5,467	5,587	5,145
Manufacturing	232,204	219,090	216,520
Construction	82,072	80,448	76,390
Electricity, gas and water . . .	36,220	40,013	40,954
Wholesale and retail trade; repair of motor vehicles, motorcycles and personal and household goods	165,772	165,116	160,566
Hotels and restaurants . . .	53,156	52,767	53,244
Transport, storage and communications	140,501	138,738	138,533
Financial intermediation . . .	78,824	78,286	79,143
Real estate, renting and business activities	335,333	341,382	343,728
Public administration and defence; compulsory social security . .	103,240	101,589	101,746
Education	61,818	61,125	61,204
Health and social work . . .	87,113	86,577	85,449
Other community, social and personal service activities . .	41,064	41,299	41,283
Private households with employed persons	18,065	18,870	19,198
Gross value added in basic prices	1,471,728	1,462,787	1,456,803
Net taxes on products	167,129	165,217	162,101
GDP in market prices . . .	1,638,857	1,628,004	1,618,904

BALANCE OF PAYMENTS
(US $ million)

	2011	2012	2013
Exports of goods	503,886	479,792	501,687
Imports of goods	−524,032	−455,084	−453,594
Balance on goods	−20,145	24,708	48,092
Exports of services	103,453	102,994	113,210
Imports of services	−115,122	−104,968	−107,853
Balance on goods and services	−31,814	22,733	53,449
Primary income received . . .	84,983	69,403	65,515
Primary income paid	−96,958	−78,039	−78,459
Balance on goods, services and primary income	−43,789	14,098	40,505
Secondary income received . .	27,646	25,345	26,527
Secondary income paid . . .	−49,657	−44,971	−45,759
Current balance	−65,800	−5,529	21,272
Capital account (net)	1,244	5,062	−101
Direct investment assets . . .	−47,518	−14,540	−28,619
Direct investment liabilities . .	28,003	6,683	13,127
Portfolio investment assets . .	48,887	79,019	−27,180
Portfolio investment liabilities .	−61,972	−47,438	45,736
Financial derivatives and employee stock options (net)	10,338	−7,388	−3,982
Other investment assets . . .	−59,319	−49,439	39,445
Other investment liabilities . .	177,118	52,071	−69,173
Net errors and omissions . . .	−29,811	−16,619	11,473
Reserves and related items .	1,169	1,881	1,999

Source: IMF, *International Financial Statistics*.

External Trade

Note: Figures refer to the trade of Italy, San Marino and the Vatican City.

PRINCIPAL COMMODITIES
(€ million)

Imports c.i.f.	2011	2012	2013*
Agriculture and fishing . . .	13,013	12,312	12,652
Food, beverages and tobacco . .	27,497	27,295	28,037
Crude petroleum	41,577	44,252	34,990
Natural gas	21,201	24,297	20,199
Textiles, clothing, leather and leather products	28,876	26,526	26,534
Wood and wood products; paper and paper products, printing and publishing	10,158	9,248	9,212
Chemicals and man-made fibres .	55,663	55,525	55,237
Rubber, plastics and non-metal mineral ore products . . .	12,404	11,517	11,687
Metals and metal products . .	42,468	37,782	35,164
Machinery and mechanical equipment	24,138	22,495	22,282
Computers, electrical appliances and electrical equipment . .	44,743	38,773	35,035
Transportation means	38,334	30,578	29,401
Total (incl. others)	401,428	380,292	359,454

Exports f.o.b.	2011	2012	2013*
Food, beverages and tobacco . .	24,419	26,086	27,468
Textiles, clothing, leather and leather products	41,979	43,101	44,971
Wood and wood products; paper and paper products, printing and publishing	7,503	7,635	7,763
Refined oil products	16,845	20,497	16,355
Chemicals and man-made fibres .	40,239	42,583	45,139
Rubber, plastics and non-metal mineral ore manufactures .	22,516	22,597	23,218
Metals and metal products . .	48,386	50,842	45,484
Machinery and mechanical equipment	68,447	70,439	71,597
Computers, electrical appliances and electrical equipment . .	33,244	32,600	32,499
Transportation means	36,518	36,288	37,163
Total (incl. others)	375,904	390,182	389,854

* Provisional data.

PRINCIPAL TRADING PARTNERS
(€ million)*

Imports c.i.f.	2011	2012	2013†
Austria	9,439	8,986	9,001
Belgium	14,568	14,545	15,041
China, People's Republic . . .	29,574	25,006	23,135
Czech Republic	4,901	4,524	4,449
France	33,603	31,580	30,322
Germany	62,388	55,130	52,955
Japan	4,218	3,190	2,567
Netherlands	21,037	20,544	20,678
Poland	7,518	7,121	6,607
Russia	16,904	18,321	20,056
Spain	18,111	16,974	16,176
Switzerland	11,294	10,972	10,520
Turkey	5,979	5,257	5,507
United Kingdom	10,943	9,714	9,570
USA	13,026	12,660	11,541
Total (incl. others)	401,428	380,292	359,454

Exports f.o.b.	2011	2012	2013†
Austria	8,724	8,675	8,463
Belgium	9,633	10,341	11,407
Brazil	4,782	4,997	5,088
China, People's Republic . . .	9,996	8,999	9,852
Czech Republic	n.a.	4,226	4,239
France	43,593	43,237	42,226
Germany	49,267	48,833	48,425
Greece	4,782	4,207	3,737
Japan	4,732	5,632	6,029
Netherlands	9,119	9,285	9,069
Poland	9,418	9,234	9,368
Romania	6,135	5,923	5,936
Russia	9,305	9,979	10,797
Spain	19,890	18,310	17,150
Sweden	3,892	3,773	3,809
Switzerland	20,640	22,878	20,403
Turkey	9,634	10,591	10,084
United Kingdom	17,542	18,957	19,592
USA	22,831	26,640	27,023
Total (incl. others)	375,904	390,182	389,854

* Imports by country of production; exports by country of consignment.
† Provisional data.

Transport

STATE RAILWAYS
(traffic)

	2010	2011	2012
Passenger journeys (million) . .	838.9	847.3	854.8
Passenger-km (million) . . .	47,172	46,845	46,759
Freight carried ('000 metric tons) .	84,435	91,811	88,505
Freight ton-km (million) . . .	18,616	19,787	20,244

ROAD TRAFFIC
(vehicles in use at 31 December)

	2009	2010	2012
Passenger cars	35,871,854	35,871,854	37,033,401
Buses and coaches	98,244	98,666	98,398
Lorries and vans	4,505,348	4,556,648	4,596,121
Motorcycles and mopeds . . .	6,309,992	6,525,820	8,956,535

* Data for 2011 were not available.

Source: IRF, *World Road Statistics*.

SHIPPING

Flag Registered Fleet
(at 31 December)

	2012	2013	2014
Number of vessels	2,232	2,221	2,162
Total displacement ('000 grt) . .	18,963.9	18,522.8	16,762.1

Source: Lloyd's List Intelligence (www.lloydslistintelligence.com).

CIVIL AVIATION
(traffic on scheduled and charter services)

	2010	2011	2012
Passengers carried ('000):			
domestic	59,619	63,703	60,385
international	79,237	84,293	85,703
Freight carried ('000 metric tons):*	878.8	890.1	846.8

* Includes mail.

Freight carried ('000 metric tons): 859.4 in 2013.

Tourism

TOURIST ARRIVALS BY COUNTRY OF ORIGIN
(arrivals in registered accommodation establishments)

	2011	2012	2013
Austria	2,115,524	2,110,605	2,113,848
Belgium	1,079,541	1,103,629	1,136,286
China, People's Republic	1,342,518	1,583,479	1,850,206
France	3,689,634	3,700,775	3,879,255
Germany	9,873,213	10,192,697	10,329,271
Japan	1,410,677	1,449,115	1,432,051
Netherlands	1,933,447	1,959,306	1,925,017
Poland	989,436	919,013	981,351
Russia	1,474,137	1,707,998	1,926,911
Spain	1,929,832	1,711,807	1,614,839
Switzerland-Liechtenstein	1,994,976	2,151,675	2,314,559
United Kingdom	2,746,752	2,890,015	2,955,262
USA	4,466,672	4,442,549	4,542,936
Total (incl. others)	47,460,809	48,738,575	50,263,236

Tourism receipts (US $ million, excl. passenger transport): 43,243 in 2011; 40,960 in 2012; 43,835 in 2013 (Source: World Tourism Organization).

Communications Media

	2011	2012	2013
Telephones ('000 main lines in use)	22,105	21,656	20,926
Mobile cellular telephones ('000 in use)	96,041	97,226	96,904
Broadband subscribers ('000)	13,432	13,483	13,600

Source: International Telecommunication Union.

Education

(state education, 2007/08, unless otherwise indicated)

	Schools	Teachers	Students
Pre-primary	13,629	83,586	975,757
Primary	16,018	245,727	2,579,938
Secondary:			
Scuola Media	7,104	163,159	1,625,651
Scuola Secondaria Superiore	5,128	230,881	2,570,010
of which:			
Technical	1,802	78,411	870,708
Professional	1,425	43,950	540,794
Art Licei and institutes	271	9,261	96,812
Classical, linguistic and scientific Licei	1,630	70,040	1,061,696
Higher*	74	61,929	1,820,221†‡

* Includes private institutions.
† Undergraduates only.
‡ 2006/07 figure.

Source: Ufficio di Statistica, Ministero dell'Istruzione, dell'Università e della Ricerca.

2012/13: Pre-primary (schools 24,036, teachers 81,352, students 1,686,095); Primary (schools 17,413, teachers 201,226, students 2,825,400); Lower secondary (schools 8,150, teachers 139,247, students 1,779,758); Upper secondary (schools 7,105, teachers 204,242, students 2,652,448).

Pupil-teacher ratio (primary education, UNESCO estimate): 10.3 in 2006/07 (Source: UNESCO Institute for Statistics).

Adult literacy rate (UNESCO estimates): 99.0% (males 99.2%; females 98.7%) in 2011 (Source: UNESCO Institute for Statistics).

Directory

The Government

HEAD OF STATE

President of the Republic: SERGIO MATTARELLA (took office 3 February 2015).

COUNCIL OF MINISTERS
(April 2015)

A coalition comprising the Partito Democratico (PD), Nuovo Centrodestra (NC, which was formed after the dissolution of Popolo della Libertà (PdL) in November 2013), Unione di Centro (UdC), Scelta Civica (SC) and independents.

Prime Minister: MATTEO RENZI (PD).

Minister of Foreign Affairs: PAOLO GENTILONI SILVERI (PD).

Minister of the Interior: ANGELINO ALFANO (NC).

Minister of Justice: ANDREA ORLANDO (PD).

Minister of Defence: ROBERTA PINOTTI (PD).

Minister of the Economy and Finance: PIER CARLO PADOAN (Ind.).

Minister of Economic Development: FEDERICA GUIDI (Ind.).

Minister of Infrastructure and Transport: GRAZIANO DELRIO (PD).

Minister of Agricultural, Food and Forestry Policies: MAURIZIO MARTINA (PD).

Minister of the Environment, Land Management and the Sea: GIANLUCA GALLETTI (UdC).

Minister of Labour and Social Policies: GIULIANO POLETTI (Ind.).

Minister of Education, Universities and Research: STEFANIA GIANNINI (SC).

Minister of Cultural Assets and Activities and of Tourism: DARIO FRANCESCHINI (PD).

Minister of Health: BEATRICE LORENZIN (NC).

Minister of Regional Affairs: (vacant).

Minister for Constitutional Reforms and Relations with Parliament: MARIA ELENA BOSCHI (PD).

Minister for Legislative Simplification and Public Administration: MARIA ANNA MADIA (PD).

MINISTRIES

Office of the President: Palazzo del Quirinale, 00187 Roma; tel. (06) 46991; fax (06) 46993125; internet www.quirinale.it.

Office of the Prime Minister: Palazzo Chigi, Piazza Colonna 370, 00187 Roma; tel. (06) 67791; internet www.governo.it.

Ministry of Agricultural, Food and Forestry Policies: Via XX Settembre 20, 00187 Roma; tel. (06) 46651; fax (06) 4742314; e-mail urp@pec.politicheagricole.gov.it; internet www.politicheagricole.gov.it.

Ministry of Cultural Assets and Activities and of Tourism: Via del Collegio Romano 27, 00186 Roma; tel. (06) 67232980; fax (06) 6798441; e-mail urp@beniculturali.it; internet www.beniculturali.it.

Ministry of Defence: Palazzo Baracchini, Via XX Settembre 8, 00187 Roma; tel. (06) 46911; internet www.difesa.it.

Ministry of Economic Development: Via Molise 2, 00187 Roma; tel. (06) 47051; fax (06) 47887770; e-mail segreteria.capogabinetto@ sviluppoeconomico.gov.it; internet www.sviluppoeconomico.gov.it.

Ministry of the Economy and Finance: Via XX Settembre 97, 00187 Roma; tel. (06) 476111; fax (06) 5910993; e-mail portavoce@ tesoro.it; internet www.mef.gov.it.

Ministry of Education, Universities and Research: Via Trastevere 76A, 00153 Roma; tel. (06) 58491; e-mail urp@istruzione.it; internet www.istruzione.it.

Ministry of the Environment, Land Management and the Sea: Via Cristoforo Colombo 44, 00147 Roma; tel. (06) 57221; e-mail segr .ufficiostampa@minambiente.it; internet www.minambiente.it.

Ministry of Foreign Affairs: Piazzale della Farnesina 1, 00194 Roma; tel. (06) 36911; fax (06) 3236210; e-mail ministero .affariesteri@cert.esteri.it; internet www.esteri.it.

Ministry of Health: Viale Giorgio Ribotta 5, 00144 Roma; tel. (06) 59941; fax (06) 59942376; e-mail urpminsalute@sanita.it; internet www.salute.gov.it.

Ministry of Infrastructure and Transport: Piazzale Porta Pia 1, 00198 Roma; tel. (06) 44121; fax (06) 44123205; e-mail ufficio .stampa@mit.gov.it; internet www.mit.gov.it.

Ministry of the Interior: Piazzale del Viminale, Via Agostino Depretis 7, 00184 Roma; tel. (06) 4651; fax (06) 46549599; e-mail segreteriaufficiostampa@interno.it; internet www.interno.it.

Ministry of Justice: Via Arenula 71, 00186 Roma; tel. (06) 68851; fax (06) 68891493; e-mail centrocifra.gabinetto@giustiziacert.it; internet www.giustizia.it.

Ministry of Labour and Social Policies: Via Veneto 56, 00187 Roma; tel. (06) 46831; fax (06) 48161451; e-mail ufficiostampa@ lavoro.gov.it; internet www.lavoro.gov.it.

President

The President of the Republic is elected by the members of both parliamentary chambers, in addition to representations (Grand Electors) of each administrative region, and is required to receive the support of at least two-thirds of the votes cast in the first three rounds of voting, or a simple majority thereafter. SERGIO MATTARELLA was elected President in a fourth round of voting conducted on 31 January 2015, receiving 665 votes (from 995 possible voters present at the session).

Legislature

PARLIAMENT
(Parlamento)

Chamber of Deputies
(Camera dei Deputati)

Palazzo di Montecitorio, Piazza Montecitorio, 00186 Roma; tel. (06) 67601; e-mail dlwebmast@camera.it; internet www.camera.it.

President: LAURA BOLDRINI.

General Election, 24 and 25 February 2013

Parties/Alliances	Total seats
Italia. Bene Comune	345
Partito Democratico (PD)	297
Sinistra Ecologia Libertà (SEL)	37
Centro Democratico (CD)	6
Südtiroler Volkspartei (SVP)	5
Centre-right coalition	125
Popolo della Libertà (PdL)*	98
Lega Nord (LN)	18
Fratelli d'Italia—Centrodestra Nazionale	9
MoVimento 5 Stelle (M5S)	109
Con Monti per l'Italia	47†
Scelta Civica (SC)	37
Unione di Centro (UdC)	8
Movimento Associativo Italiani all'Estero	2
USEI‡	1
Valle d'Aosta	1
Total	**630**

* In November 2013 the PdL split to form two parties: Nuovo Centrodestra and Forza Italia.
† Includes two seats won by Con Monti per l'Italia from expatriate votes.
‡ Unione Sudamericana Emigrati Italiani (South American Union of Italian Emigrants).

Senate
(Senato)

Piazza Madama, 00186 Roma; tel. (06) 67061; e-mail infopoint@ senato.it; internet www.senato.it.

President: PIETRO GRASSO.

General Election, 24 and 25 February 2013

Parties/Alliances	Elective seats
Italia. Bene Comune	123
Partito Democratico (PD)*	113
Sinistra Ecologia Libertà	7
Il Megafono—Lista Crocetta	1
Südtiroler Volkspartei (SVP)*	2
Centre-right coalition	117
Popolo della Libertà (PdL)†	99
Lega Nord (LN)	17
Grande Sud	1
MoVimento 5 Stelle (M5S)	54
Con Monti per l'Italia	19
Movimento Associativo Italiani all'Estero	1
Valle d'Aosta	1
Total‡	**315**

* Partito Democratico (PD), Partito Autonomista Trentino Tirolese (PATT), Südtiroler Volkspartei (SVP) and Unione per il Trentino (UpT) contested the election in alliance in Trentino Tyrol. The PD won four seats while the SVP won two seats in that region.
† In November 2013 the PdL split to form two parties: Nuovo Centrodestra and Forza Italia.
‡ In addition to the 315 elected members, there were, as at March 2015, six life members.

Political Organizations

NATIONAL PARTIES AND COALITIONS

Alleanza per l'Italia (ApI) (Alliance for Italy): Largo della Fontanella di Borghese 84, 00186 Roma; tel. (06) 91712000; fax (06) 68802560; e-mail info@alleanzaperlitalia.it; internet www .alleanzaperlitalia.it; f. 2009; Pres. FRANCESCO RUTELLI; Co-ordinator LORENZO DELLAI.

Centro Democratico–Diritti e Libertà (Democratic Centre–Rights and Freedom): Via Giovanni Pierluigi da Palestrina 63, 00193 Roma; tel. (06) 93570168; e-mail info@ilcentrodemocratico .it; internet www.ilcentrodemocratico.it; f. 2012; centre-left coalition led by the party Diritti e Libertà; contested the 2013 legislative elections as part of Italia. Bene Comune; Pres. BRUNO TABACCI.

Federazione dei Liberali Italiani (Federation of Italian Liberals): Studio Sgobbo, Corso Trieste 61, 00198 Roma; tel. (06) 8418007; fax (06) 8416975; e-mail info@liberali.it; internet www .liberali.it; f. 1994; Pres. RAFFAELLO MORELLI.

Federazione dei Verdi (I Verdi) (Green Party): Via Antonio Salandra 6, 00187 Roma; tel. (06) 4203061; fax (06) 42004600; e-mail federazione@verdi.it; internet www.verdi.it; f. 1986; advocates environmentalist and anti-nuclear policies; contested the 2013 legislative elections as part of Rivoluzione Civile; branch of the European Green movement; Co-Pres ANGELO BONELLI, LUANA ZANELLA.

Forza Italia (FI) (Forward Italy): Via dell'Umiltà 36, 00187 Roma; tel. (06) 6731381; internet www.forzaitalia.it; f. 2013 following the splitting of Popolo della Libertà into two parties; Pres. SILVIO BERLUSCONI.

Fratelli d'Italia—Alleanza Nazionale (Brothers of Italy—National Centre-right): Via Quattro Cantoni 16, 00184 Roma; tel. (06) 4880690; fax (06) 48907931; e-mail info@fratelli-italia.it; internet www.fratelli-italia.it; f. 2012; contested the 2013 legislative elections as part of the centre-right coalition; Pres. GIORGIA MELONI.

Futuro e Libertà per l'Italia (FLI) (Future and Freedom for Italy): Via Poli 29, 00187 Roma; tel. (06) 69773701; internet www .futuroeliberta.it; f. 2011; liberal; contested the 2013 legislative elections as part of Con Monti per l'Italia; Nat. Co-ordinator ROBERTO MENIA.

Italia dei Valori—Lista Di Pietro (IdV) (Italy of Principals—Di Pietro List): Via Santa Maria in Via 12, 00187 Roma; tel. (06) 97848144; fax (06) 97848355; e-mail info@italiadeivalori.it; internet www.italiadeivalori.it; anti-corruption; contested the 2013 legislative elections as part of Rivoluzione Civile; Nat. Sec. IGNATIUS MESSINA.

Liberal Democratici (LD) (Liberal Democrats): Largo della Fontanella di Borghese 84, 00186 Roma; tel. (06) 68808380; fax (06) 68808500; e-mail liberal-democratici@libero.it; internet www

.liberal-democratici.it; f. 2007; liberal centrist; Pres. ITALO TANONI; Co-ordinator ENZO MARRAZZO.

Lista Consumatori (Consumers' List): Via Tagliamento 3, Ardea, 00040 Roma; tel. (06) 23328286; e-mail info@listaconsumatori.it; f. 2004; Pres. RENATO CAMPIGLIA; Nat. Sec. DAVID BADINI.

Il Megafono—Lista Crocetta (The Megaphone—List of Crocetta): e-mail larivoluzionecontinua@gmail.com; f. 2012; contested the 2013 legislative elections as part of Italia. Bene Comune; Leader ROSARIO CROCETTA.

MoVimento 5 Stelle (M5S) (Five Star Movement): internet www .movimento5stelle.it; f. 2009; populist, anti-corruption; Leader BEPPE GRILLO.

Movimento Cristiano sociali (Christian-Social Movement): Via Calabria 56, 00198 Roma; tel. (06) 3210694; fax (06) 68300539; e-mail movcso@alice.it; internet www.cristianosociali.it; f. 1993; Pres. MIMMO LUCÀ.

Movimento Sociale—Fiamma Tricolore (Tricolour Flame): Via Flaminia Vecchia 732I, 00191 Roma; tel. (06) 33221128; fax (06) 233235547; e-mail info@fiammatricolore.com; internet www .fiammatricolore.com; f. 1996; electoral alliance incorporating fmr mems of neo-fascist Movimento Sociale Italiano-Destra Nazionale; Nat. Sec. ATTILIO CARELLI.

Nuovo Centrodestra (NC) (New Centre-Right): Roma; e-mail info@nuovocentrodestra.it; internet www.nuovocentrodestra.it; f. 2013 following the splitting of Popolo della Libertà into two parties; Leader ANGELINO ALFANO.

Partito dei Comunisti Italiani (PdCI) (Party of Italian Communists): Piazza Augusto Imperatore 32, 00186 Roma; tel. (06) 686271; fax (06) 68627230; e-mail direzionenazionale@ comunisti-italiani.org; internet www.comunisti-italiani.it; f. 1998; contested the 2013 legislative elections as part of Rivoluzione Civile; Gen. Sec. CESARE PROCACCINI.

Partito Democratico (PD): Via Sant'Andrea delle Fratte 16, 00187 Roma; tel. (06) 695321; e-mail redazione@partitodemocratico.it; internet www.partitodemocratico.it; f. 2007 by merger of Democratici di Sinistra, Democrazia è Libertà—La Margherita and other left-wing and centrist parties; centre-left; contested the 2013 legislative elections as part of Italia. Bene Comune; Co-Vice-Pres MATTEO RICCI, SANDRA ZAMPA; Nat. Sec. MATTEO RENZI.

Partito Liberale Italiano (PLI) (Italian Liberal Party): Via Uffici del Vicario 43, 2°, 00186 Roma; tel. (06) 45505081; e-mail segretaria@ partitoliberale.it; internet www.partitoliberale.it; Pres. PAOLO GUZZANTI; Nat. Sec. GIANCARLO MORANDI.

Partito Repubblicano Italiano (PRI) (Italian Republican Party): Corso Vittorio Emanuele II 326, 00186 Roma; tel. (06) 6865824; fax (06) 68210234; e-mail info@pri.it; internet www.pri.it; Nat. Pres. FRANCESCO NUCARA.

Partito della Rifondazione Comunista (PRC) (Party of Communist Refoundation): Via degli Scialoja 3, 00196 Roma; tel. (06) 441821; fax (06) 44239231; e-mail segretario@rifondazione.it; internet www.rifondazione.it; f. 1991 by fmr mems of the Partito Comunista Italiano (Italian Communist Party); contested the 2013 legislative elections as part of Rivoluzione Civile; Nat. Sec. PAOLO FERRERO.

Partito Socialista Italiano (PSI) (Italian Socialist Party): Via di Santa Caterina da Siena 57, 00186 Roma; tel. (06) 6878688; fax (06) 68307659; e-mail info@partitosocialista.it; internet www .partitosocialista.it; f. 2007 by fmr leadership of Socialisti Democratici Italiani; contested the 2013 legislative elections as part of Italia. Bene Comune; Nat. Sec. RICCARDO NENCINI.

Patto—Partito dei Liberaldemocratici (The Pact—Liberal Democratic Party): Via Vittorio Veneto 169, 00187 Roma; tel. and fax (06) 4744916; f. 1993 as Patto Segni; liberal party, advocating institutional reform; Nat. Sec. Prof. MARIO SEGNI.

Popolari—UDEUR (Alleanza Popolare—Unione Democratici per l'Europa) (Union of Democrats for Europe): Via Gaetano Donizetti 2, 82100 Benevento; tel. (0824) 24500; e-mail info@ popolariudeur.it; internet www.popolariudeur.it; f. 1999; Sec. CLEMENTE MASTELLA.

Radicali Italiani (RI): Via di Torre Argentina 76, 00186 Roma; tel. (06) 689791; fax (06) 68210375; e-mail segreteria.roma@radicali.it; internet www.radicali.it; f. 2001 as Partito Radicale; Pres. RICCARDO MAGI; Gen. Sec. RITA BERNARDINI.

Scelta Civica (SC) (Civic Choice): tel. (06) 67486222; e-mail info@ sceltacivica.it; internet www.sceltacivica.it; f. 2013; contested the 2013 legislative elections as part of Con Monti per l'Italia; Pres. (vacant).

Sinistra Ecologia Libertà (SEL) (Left Ecology Freedom): Via Goito 39, 00185 Roma; tel. (06) 44700403; fax (06) 4455832; e-mail redazione@sxmail.it; internet www.sinistraecologialiberta.it; f. 2010; socialist party advocating social progressivism; contested

the 2013 legislative elections as part of Italia. Bene Comune; Pres. NICHI VENDOLA.

Unione di Centro (UdC) (Union of the Centre): Via dei Due Macelli 66, 00182 Roma; tel. (06) 69791001; fax (06) 6791574; f. 2008; coalition includes Unione dei Democratici Cristiani e di Centro and Rosa Bianca; contested the 2013 legislative elections as part of Con Monti per l'Italia; Leader PIER FERDINANDO CASINI.

Unione dei Democratici Cristiani e di Centro (UDC) (Union of Christian and Centre Democrats): Via dei Due Macelli 66, 00182 Roma; tel. (06) 69791001; fax (06) 6791574; e-mail info@udc-italia.it; internet www.udc-italia.it; f. 2002 from merger of Centro Cristiano Democratico (f. 1994) and Cristiani Democratici Uniti (f. 1995 after split from Partito Popolare Italiano); Pres. GIANPIERO D'ALIA; Nat. Sec. LORENZO CESA.

Political organizations for Italians abroad include the **Associazioni Italiane in Sud America**, the **Movimento Associativo Italiani all'Estero** and the **Unione Sudamericana Emigranti Italiani**.

REGIONAL PARTIES AND COALITIONS

Autonomie Liberté Démocratie (ALD) (Autonomy Liberty Democracy): f. 2006; coalition of parties active in the Aosta valley.

Lega Nord per l'Indipendenza della Padania (LN) (Northern League for the Independence of Padania): Via Carlo Bellerio 41, 20161 Milano; tel. (02) 662341; fax (02) 6454475; e-mail webmaster@ leganord.org; internet www.leganord.org; f. 1991; advocates federalism and transfer of control of resources to regional govts; in 1996 declared the 'Independent Republic of Padania'; opposes immigration; Eurosceptic; contested the 2013 legislative elections as part of the centre-right alliance; Pres. UMBERTO BOSSI; Sec. MATTEO SALVINI.

Liga Veneta Repubblica (Venetian Republic League): Via Antonio Provolo 2B, 37060 Verona; tel. and fax (045) 8601344; e-mail info@ ligavenetarepubblica.org; internet www.ligavenetarepubblica.org; f. 2001 by merger of Liga Veneta Repubblica—Veneti d'Europa and Fronte Marco Polo; advocates independence for Veneto region; Pres. GIAN PIETRO PIOTTO; Gen. Sec. FABRIZIO COMENCINI.

Movimento per l'Autonomia (MPA) (Autonomy Movement): Via dell'Oca 27, Roma; tel. (06) 3220836; fax (06) 32647632; e-mail sede .roma@autonomia.info; internet www.mpa-italia.it; pro-regional autonomy in the south; Fed. Sec. GIOVANNI PISTORIO.

Partito Autonomista Trentino Tirolese (PATT) (Autonomist Party of Trento and the Tyrol): Via Roma 7, 38100 Trento; tel. (0461) 391399; fax (0461) 394940; e-mail info@patt.tn.it; internet www.patt .tn.it; advocates autonomy for South Tyrol region; Pres. WALTER KASWALDER; Pol. Sec. FRANCO PANIZZA.

Partitu Sardu—Partito Sardo d'Azione (Sardinian Action Party): Piazza Repubblica 18, 09125 Cagliari; tel. and fax (070) 3481434; e-mail info@psdaz.net; internet www.psdaz.net; Pres. GIACOMO SANNA; Nat. Sec. GIOVANNI ANGELO COLLI.

Südtiroler Volkspartei (SVP) (South Tyrol People's Party): Brennerstr. 7A, 39100 Bozen/Bolzano; tel. (0471) 304040; fax (0471) 981473; e-mail info@svp.eu; internet www.svp.eu; regional party of the German and Ladin-speaking people in the South Tyrol; contested the 2013 legislative elections as part of Italia. Bene Comune; Pres. PHILIPP ACHAMMER; Gen. Sec. MANUEL MASSL.

Union Autonomista Ladina (Autonomist Ladin Movement): Strada Dolomites 111, 38036 Pozza di Fassa; tel. and fax (0462) 763396; e-mail ualdefascia@virgilio.it; internet www.movimentual .it; Pres. MICHELE ANESI; Pol. Sec. MANUEL FARINA.

Union Valdôtaine (Aosta Valley Union): Ave des Maquisards 29, 11100 Aosta; tel. (0165) 235181; fax (0165) 364289; e-mail siegecentral@unionvaldotaine.org; internet www.unionvaldotaine .org; f. 1945; promotes interests of the Aosta valley; contested the 2013 legislative elections as part of the Valle d'Aosta list; Pres ENNIO PASTORET.

Other regional parties and coalitions include **Die Freiheitlichen** (South Tyrol), the **Federazione per l'Autodeterminazione della Sicilia-Noi Siciliani, iRS—indipendèntzia Repùbrica de Sardigna, Moderati per il Piemonti**, the **Movimento Triveneto, Nuova Sicilia, Per il Sud, Progetto Nordest, Progetto Sud** and **Sardigna Natzione Indipendentzia**.

Diplomatic Representation

EMBASSIES IN ITALY

Afghanistan: Via Nomentana 120, 00161 Roma; tel. (06) 8611009; fax (06) 86322939; e-mail info@afghanistanembassyitaly.com; internet afghanistanembassy.it; Ambassador ZIA UDDIN NEZAM.

Albania: Via Asmara 5, 00199 Roma; tel. (06) 8622414; fax (06) 86224120; e-mail embassy.rome@mfa.gov.al; internet www .ambasadat.gov.al/italy; Ambassador NERITAN CEKA.

Algeria: Via Bartolomeo Eustachio 12, 00161 Roma; tel. (06) 44202533; fax (06) 44292744; e-mail embassy@algerianembassy.it; internet www.algerianembassy.it; Ambassador RACHID MARIF.

Angola: Via Druso 39, 00184 Roma; tel. (06) 7726951; fax (06) 77590009; e-mail info@embangola.com; internet www.ambasciatangolana.com; Ambassador FLORÊNCIO MARIANO DA CONCEIÇÃO DE ALMEIDA.

Argentina: Piazza dell'Esquilino 2, 00185 Roma; tel. (06) 48073300; fax (06) 48073331; e-mail eital@mrecic.gov.ar; internet www.ambasciatargentina.it; Ambassador TORCUATO SALVADOR DI TELLA.

Armenia: Via XX Settembre 98E, scala A, 00187 Roma; tel. (06) 3296638; fax (06) 3297763; e-mail info@ambasciataarmena.it; Ambassador SARGIS GHAZARYAN.

Australia: Via A. Bosio 5, 00161 Roma; tel. (06) 852721; fax (06) 85272300; e-mail info-rome@dfat.gov.au; internet www.italy.embassy.gov.au; Ambassador MIKE RANN.

Austria: Via G. B. Pergolesi 3, 00198 Roma; tel. (06) 8440141; fax (06) 8543286; e-mail rom-ob@bmeia.gv.at; Chargé d'affaires a.i. GERDA VOGL.

Azerbaijan: Via Regina Margherita 1, II piano, 00198 Roma; tel. (06) 85305557; fax (06) 85231448; e-mail rome@mission.mfa.gov.az; internet www.azembassy.it; Ambassador VAGIF SADIQOV.

Bangladesh: Via Antonio Bertoloni 14, 00197 Roma; tel. (06) 8078541; fax (06) 8084853; e-mail embangrm@mclink.it; Ambassador SHAHDAT HOSSAIN.

Belarus: Via delle Alpi Apuane 16, 00141 Roma; tel. (06) 8208141; fax (06) 82084099; e-mail italy@mfa.gov.by; internet italy.mfa.gov.by; Ambassador YEVGENII A. SHESTAKOV.

Belgium: Via dei Monti Parioli 49, 00197 Roma; tel. (06) 3609511; fax (06) 3610197; e-mail rome@diplobel.fed.be; internet www.diplomatie.be/romeit; Ambassador VINCENT MERTENS DE WILMARS.

Benin: Via dei Settemetri 11E, int. 6, 00118 Roma; tel. (06) 79846567; fax (06) 79810197; e-mail ambr201@tiscalinet.it; Ambassador MARIE ROSEMONDE YAKOUBOU.

Bolivia: Via Brenta 2A, int. 18, 00198 Roma; tel. (06) 8841001; fax (06) 8840740; e-mail infobolit@yahoo.it; internet www.embajadabolivia.it; Ambassador ANTOLIN AYAVIRI GÓMEZ.

Bosnia and Herzegovina: Piazzale Clodio 12, int. 17/18, 00195 Roma; tel. (06) 39742817; fax (06) 39030567; e-mail ambasciata@ambih.191.it; Ambassador NERKEZ ARIFHODZIC.

Brazil: Palazzo Pamphili, Piazza Navona 14, 00186 Roma; tel. (06) 683981; fax (06) 6867858; e-mail info@ambrasile.it; Ambassador RICARDO NEIVA TAVARES.

Bulgaria: Via Pietro Paolo Rubens 21, 00197 Roma; tel. (06) 3224643; fax (06) 3226122, e-mail embassy@bulemb.it; internet www.mfa.bg/en/107; Ambassador MARIN RAYKOV.

Burkina Faso: Via XX Settembre 86, 00187 Roma; tel. (06) 42010611; fax (06) 42016701; e-mail ambabf.roma@tin.it; Ambassador RAYMOND BALIMA.

Burundi: Via Enrico Accinni 63, scala B, int. 10, 00195 Roma; tel. (06) 36381786; fax (06) 36381171; e-mail ambaburoma@yahoo.fr; Ambassador JUSTINE NISUBIRE.

Cabo Verde: Via Giosuè Carducci 4, 1°, 00187 Roma; tel. (06) 4744678; fax (06) 4744643; Ambassador MANUEL AMANTE DA ROSA.

Cameroon: Via Siracusa 4–6, 00161 Roma; tel. (06) 44291285; fax (06) 44291323; e-mail segreteriaambcam@virgilio.it; internet www.cameroonembassy.it; Ambassador DOMINIQUE AWONO ESSAMA.

Canada: Via Salaria 243, 00199 Roma; tel. (06) 854441; fax (06) 854443911; e-mail rome@international.gc.ca; internet www.canadainternational.gc.ca/italy-italie; Ambassador PETER McGOVERN.

Chile: Via Po 23, 00198 Roma; tel. (06) 844091; fax (06) 8841452; e-mail embajada@chileit.it; internet www.chileit.it; Ambassador LUIS FERNANDO AYALA GONZALVEZ.

China, People's Republic: Via Bruxelles 56, 00198 Roma; tel. (06) 96524200; fax (06) 96524200; e-mail segreteria.china@gmail.com; internet it.china-embassy.org; Ambassador LI RUIYU.

Colombia: Via Giuseppe Pisanelli 4, 00196 Roma; tel. (06) 3612131; fax (06) 3225798; e-mail eitalia@cancilleria.gov.co; internet www.emcolombia.it; Ambassador JUAN SEBASTIÁN BETANCUR ESCOBAR.

Congo, Democratic Republic: Via Barberini 3, 00187 Roma; tel. and fax (06) 42010779; Ambassador ALBERT TSHISELEKA FELHA.

Congo, Republic: Via Ombrone 8–10, 00198 Roma; tel. and fax (06) 8417422; e-mail ambacorome@gmail.com; internet www.ambasciatadelcongobrazzaville.it; Ambassador MAMADOU KAMARA DEKAMO.

Costa Rica: Viale Liegi 2, int. 8, 00198 Roma; tel. (06) 84242853; fax (06) 85355956; e-mail embcr.italia@gmail.com; Chargé d'affaires a.i. ILEANA ORDOÑEZ CHACÓN.

Côte d'Ivoire: Via Guglielmo Saliceto 6–10, 00161 Roma; tel. (06) 44231129; fax (06) 44292531; e-mail ambassadecotedivoire61@rocketmail.com; Ambassador JANINE ADELE TAGLIANTE-SARACINO.

Croatia: Via Luigi Bodio 74–76, 00191 Roma; tel. (06) 36307650; fax (06) 36303405; e-mail vhrim@mvpei.hr; internet it.mfa.hr; Ambassador DAMIR GRUBIŠA.

Cuba: Via Licinia 7, 00153 Roma; tel. (06) 5717241; fax (06) 5745445; e-mail embajada@ecuitalia.it; Ambassador ALBA BEATRIZ SOTO PIMENTEL.

Cyprus: Via Ludovisi 35, V piano, scala A, int. 10, 00187 Roma; tel. (06) 8088365; fax (06) 8088338; e-mail cancelleria@ambasciatacipro.it; Ambassador TASOS TZIONIS.

Czech Republic: Via dei Gracchi 322, 00192 Roma; tel. (06) 36309571; fax (06) 3244466; e-mail rome@embassy.mzv.cz; internet www.mzv.cz/rome; Ambassador PETR BURIÁNEK.

Denmark: Via dei Monti Parioli 50, 00197 Roma; tel. (06) 9774831; fax (06) 97748399; e-mail romamb@um.dk; internet www.italien.um.dk; Ambassador BIRGER RIIS-JØRGENSEN.

Dominican Republic: Via Giuseppe Pisanelli 1, int. 8, 00196 Roma; tel. (06) 45434789; fax (06) 45448452; e-mail embajadadominicana@tiscali.it; internet www.embajadadominicanaitalia.org; Chargé d'affaires a.i GINA D'ALESSANDRO RICART.

Ecuador: Via Antonio Bertoloni 8, 00197 Roma; tel. (06) 89672820; fax (06) 8076271; e-mail mecuroma@flashnet.it; Ambassador JUAN FERNANDO HOLGUÍN FLORES.

Egypt: Villa Savoia, Via Salaria 267, 00199 Roma; tel. (06) 84401921; fax (06) 8554424; e-mail ambegitto@yahoo.com; Ambassador AMR MOSTAFA KAMAL HELMY.

El Salvador: Via G. Castellini 13, 00197 Roma; tel. (06) 8076605; fax (06) 8079726; e-mail embasalvaroma@tiscali.it; internet www.embasalvaroma.com; Ambassador AIDA LUZ SANTOS DE ESCOBAR.

Equatorial Guinea: Via Bruxelles 59A, 00198 Roma; tel. (06) 8555428; fax (06) 85305685; Ambassador CECILIA OBONO NDONG.

Eritrea: Via Boncompagni 16B, int. 6, 00187 Roma; tel. (06) 42741293; fax (06) 42086806; e-mail segretaria@embassyoferitrea.it; Ambassador PIETROS FESSEHAZION.

Estonia: Viale Liegi 28, int. 5, 00198 Roma; tel. (06) 84407510; fax (06) 84407519; e-mail embassy.rome@mfa.ee; internet www.estemb.it; Ambassador CELIA KUNINGAS-SAAGPAKK.

Ethiopia: Via Andrea Vesalio 16, 00161 Roma; tel. (06) 4416161; fax (06) 4403676; e-mail embethrm@rdn.it; Ambassador MULUGETA ALEMSEGED GESSESE.

Finland: Via Lisbona 3, 00198 Roma; tel. (06) 852231; fax (06) 8540362; e-mail sanomat.roo@formin.fi; internet www.finlandia.it; Ambassador PETRI TUOMAS TUOMI-NIKULA.

France: Piazza Farnese 67, 00186 Roma; tel. (06) 686011; fax (06) 68601360; internet www.ambafrance-it.org; Ambassador CATHERINE COLONNA.

Gabon: Via San Marino 36A, 00198 Roma; tel. (06) 85358970; fax (06) 8417278; e-mail cab.cdm@ambagabonrome.it; Ambassador CHARLES ESSONGHE.

Georgia: Corso Vittorio Emanuele II 21, scala A, 00186 Roma; tel. (06) 69925809; fax (06) 69941942; e-mail amgeorgia@libero.it; internet www.italy.mfa.gov.ge; Ambassador KARLO SIKHARULIDZE.

Germany: Via San Martino della Battaglia 4, 00185 Roma; tel. (06) 492131; fax (06) 4452672; e-mail info@rom.diplo.de; internet www.rom.diplo.de; Ambassador REINHARD SCHÄFERS.

Ghana: Via Ostriana 4, 00199 Roma; tel. (06) 86217191; fax (06) 86325762; e-mail info@ghanaembassy.it; internet www.ghanaembassy.it; Ambassador MOLLY ANIM ADDO.

Greece: Viale G. Rossini 4, 00198 Roma; tel. (06) 8537551; fax (06) 8415927; e-mail gremb.rom@mfa.gr; Ambassador THEMISTOKLIS DEMIRIS.

Guatemala: Via dei Colli della Farnesina 128, 00194 Roma; tel. (06) 36381143; fax (06) 3291639; e-mail embitalia@minex.gob.gt; Ambassador STEPHANIE HOCHSTETTER SKINNER-KLÉE DE TOWARA.

Guinea: Via Adelaide Ristori, 9B 13, 00197 Roma; tel. (06) 8078989; fax (06) 8077588; e-mail ambaguineerome1@virgilio.it; Chargé d'affaires a.i. ABDOULAYE TRAORÉ.

Haiti: Via di Villa Patrizi 7/7A, 00161 Roma; tel. (06) 44254106; fax (06) 44254208; e-mail segreteria@ambhaiti.it; Chargé d'affaires a.i. EMMANUEL CHARLES.

Holy See: Via Po 27A–29, 00198 Roma; tel. (06) 8546287; fax (06) 8549725; e-mail nunzio@nunziatura.it; Apostolic Nuncio Most Rev. ADRIANO BERNARDINI (Titular Archbishop of Falerii).

Honduras: Via Giambattista Vico 40, int. 8, 00196 Roma; tel. (06) 3207236; fax (06) 3207973; e-mail honduras@embajada.it; Ambassador CARMELO RIZZO.

Hungary: Via dei Villini 12–16, 00161 Roma; tel. (06) 4402032; fax (06) 4403270; e-mail mission.rom@kum.hu; internet www.huembit .it; Ambassador PÉTER SZENTMIHÁLYI SZABÓ.

India: Via XX Settembre 5, 00187 Roma; tel. (06) 4884642; fax (06) 4819539; e-mail gen.email@indianembassy.it; internet www .indianembassy.it; Ambassador BASANT K. GUPTA.

Indonesia: Via Campania 55, 00187 Roma; tel. (06) 4200911; fax (06) 4880280; e-mail indorom@indonesianembassy.it; internet www .kemlu.go.id/rome; Ambassador AUGUST PARENGKUAN.

Iran: Via Nomentana 361–363, 00162 Roma; tel. (06) 86328485; fax (06) 86328492; Ambassador JAHANBAKHSH MOZAFFARI.

Iraq: Via della Camilluccia, 355, 00135 Roma; tel. (06) 3014508; fax (06) 3014445; e-mail iraqembroma@yahoo.com; Ambassador SAYWAN SABIR MUSTAFA BARZANI.

Ireland: Via Giacomo Medici 1, 00153 Roma; tel. (06) 5852381; fax (06) 5813336; e-mail romeembassy@dfa.ie; internet www .embassyofireland.it; Ambassador BOBBY MCDONAGH.

Israel: Via Michele Mercati 14, 00197 Roma; tel. (06) 36198500; fax (06) 36198555; e-mail caoassist@roma.mfa.gov.il; internet embassies .gov.il/rome; Ambassador NAOR GILON.

Japan: Via Quintino Sella 60, 00187 Roma; tel. (06) 487991; fax (06) 4873316; e-mail giappone@ro.mofa.go.jp; internet www.it .emb-japan.go.jp; Ambassador KAZUYOSHI UMEMOTO.

Jordan: Via Giuseppe Marchi 1B, 00161 Roma; tel. (06) 86205303; fax (06) 8606122; e-mail embroma@jordanembassy.it; Ambassador ZAID MUFLEH FALEH AL-LOZI.

Kazakhstan: Via Cassia 471, 00189 Roma; tel. (06) 36301130; fax (06) 36292675; e-mail roma@mfa.kz; internet www.embkaz.it; Ambassador ANDRIAN YELEMESSOV.

Kenya: Via Luca Gaurico 205, 00143 Roma; tel. (06) 8082717; fax (06) 8082707; e-mail kenroma@rdn.it; internet www .embassyofkenya.it; Ambassador JOSEPHINE WANGARI GAITA.

Korea, Democratic People's Republic: Via dell'Esperanto 26, 00144 Roma; tel. (06) 54220749; fax (06) 54210090; e-mail permerepun@hotmail.com; Ambassador KIM CHUN GUK.

Korea, Republic: Via Barnaba Oriani 30, 00197 Roma; tel. (06) 802461; fax (06) 802462259; e-mail consul-it@mofat.go.kr; internet ita.mofat.go.kr; Ambassador JAE-HYUN BAE.

Kosovo: Via Tolmino 12, 00198 Roma; tel. (06) 85355316; fax (06) 8552212; e-mail embassy.italy@ks-gov.net; Ambassador BUKURIJE GJONBALAJ.

Kuwait: Via Archimede 124, 00197 Roma; tel. (06) 8078415; fax (06) 8076651; e-mail kwembrome@hotmail.com; Ambassador JABER DUAJI AL-SABAH.

Latvia: Via Giovanni Battista Martini 13, 00198 Roma; tel. (06) 8841227; fax (06) 8841239; e-mail embassy.italy@mfa.gov.lv; internet www.mfa.gov.lv/rome; Ambassador ARTIS BERTULIS.

Lebanon: Via Giacomo Carissimi 38, 00198 Roma; tel. (06) 8537211; fax (06) 8411794; e-mail ambalibano@hotmail.com; internet www .liban.it; Chargé d'affaires a.i. KARIM KHALIL.

Lesotho: Via Serchio 8, 00198 Roma; tel. (06) 8542496; fax (06) 8542527; e-mail secretary@lesothoembassyrome.com; internet www .lesothoembassyrome.com; Ambassador JOSEPH SEMPE LEJAHA.

Liberia: Piazza delle Medaglie d'Oro 7, scala A, int. 5, 00136 Roma; tel. (06) 35453399; fax (06) 35344729; e-mail liberiaembassy@ hotmail.com; Chargé d'affaires a.i. MOHAMMED S. L. SHERIFF.

Libya: Via Nomentana 365, 00162 Roma; tel. (06) 86320951; fax (06) 86205473; e-mail ambasciatadilibia@libero.it; Ambassador AHMED ELMABROUK SAFAR.

Lithuania: Viale di Villa Grazioli 9, 00198 Roma; tel. (06) 8559052; fax (06) 8559053; e-mail amb.it@urm.lt; internet it.mfa.lt; Ambassador JOLANTA BALČIŪNIENE.

Luxembourg: Via Santa Croce in Gerusalemme 90, 00185 Roma; tel. (06) 77201177; fax (06) 77201055; e-mail rome.amb@mae.etat.lu; internet rome.mae.lu; Ambassador JANINE FINCK.

Macedonia, former Yugoslav republic: Viale Bruxelles 73–75, 00198 Roma; tel. (06) 84241109; fax (06) 84241131; e-mail rome@mfa .gov.mk; Ambassador OLIVER SHAMBEVSKI.

Madagascar: Via Riccardo Zandonai 84A, 00194 Roma; tel. (06) 66620089; fax (06) 66621905; e-mail ambamad@hotmail.com; Chargé d'affaires a.i. JOSIANE RAVOLONDRIAK RATSIMBAZFY.

Malaysia: Via Nomentana 297, 00162 Roma; tel. (06) 8415764; fax (06) 8555040; e-mail mw.rome@flashnet.it; Ambassador Datin Paduka HALIMAH ABDULLAH.

Mali: Via Antonio Bosio 2, 00161 Roma; tel. (06) 44254068; fax (06) 44254029; e-mail amb.malirome@tiscalinet.it; Ambassador BRUNO MAÏGA.

Malta: Lungotevere Marzio 12, 00186 Roma; tel. (06) 6879990; fax (06) 6892687; e-mail maltaembassy.rome@gov.mt; Ambassador VANESSA FRAZIER.

Mauritania: Via Giovanni Paisiello 26, 00198 Roma; tel. (06) 85351530; fax (06) 85351441; Ambassador MARIÈM AOUFFA.

Mexico: Via Lazzaro Spallanzani 16, 00161 Roma; tel. (06) 4416061; fax (06) 44292703; e-mail correo@emexitalia.it; internet www.sre .gob.mx/italia; Ambassador MIGUEL RUÍZ-CABAÑAS IZQUIERDO.

Moldova: Via Montebello 8, 00185 Roma; tel. (06) 4740210; fax (06) 47881092; e-mail roma@mfa.md; internet www.italia.mfa.md; Ambassador STELA STINGACI.

Monaco: Via Antonio Bertoloni 36, 00197 Roma; tel. (06) 8083361; fax (06) 8077692; e-mail monaco@ambasciatadimonaco.it; internet www.ambasciatadimonaco.it; Ambassador ROBERT FILLON.

Mongolia: Via Vincenzo Bellini 4, 00198 Roma; tel. and fax (06) 8540536; e-mail italy@mfa.gov.mn; internet www.italy.mfa.gov.mn; Ambassador SHIJEEKHUU ODONBAATAR.

Montenegro: Via Antonio Gramsci 9, 00197 Roma; tel. (06) 88857745; fax (06) 88857743; e-mail montenegro-roma@libero.it; Ambassador ANTUN SBUTEGA.

Morocco: Via Lazzaro Spallanzani 8–10, 00161 Roma; tel. (06) 4402524; fax (06) 44004458; e-mail sifamaroma@ ambaciatadelmarocco.it; internet www.ambasciatadelmarocco.it; Ambassador HASSAN ABOUYOUB.

Mozambique: Via Filippo Corridoni 14, 00195 Roma; tel. (06) 37514675; fax (06) 37514699; e-mail sec@ambasciatamozambico.it; Ambassador CARLA ELISA LUIS MUCAVI.

Myanmar: Viale di Villa Grazioli 29, 00198 Roma; tel. (06) 36303753; fax (06) 36298566; e-mail merome2010@gmail.com; Ambassador U MYINT NAUNG.

Netherlands: Via Michele Mercati 8, 00197 Roma; tel. (06) 32286001; fax (06) 32286256; e-mail rom@minbuza.nl; internet italy.nlembassy.org; Ambassador DEN HOND.

New Zealand: Via Clitunno 44, 00198 Roma; tel. (06) 8537501; fax (06) 4402984; e-mail rome@nzembassy.it; internet www.nzembassy .com/italy; Ambassador PATRICK JOHN RATA.

Nicaragua: Via Ruffini 2A, 00195 Roma; tel. (06) 32110020; fax (06) 3203041; e-mail embanicitalia@cancilleria.gob.ni; Chargé d'affaires a.i. MARTHA IRENE ZUNIGA GUTIERREZ.

Niger: Via Antonio Baiamonti 10, 00195 Roma; tel. (06) 3720164; fax (06) 3729013; e-mail ambasciatadelniger@virgilio.it; Ambassador TOURÉ AMADOU.

Nigeria: Via Orazio 14–18, 00193 Roma; tel. (06) 683931; fax (06) 68393264; e-mail chancery@nigerianrome.org; internet www .nigerianrome.org; Ambassador ERIC TONYE AWORABHI.

Norway: Via delle Terme Deciane 7, 00153 Roma; tel. (06) 45238100; fax (06) 45238199; e-mail emb.rome@mfa.no; internet www .amb-norvegia.it; Ambassador BJØRN TRYGVE GRYDELAND.

Oman: Via della Camilluccia 625, 00135 Roma; tel. (06) 36300517; fax (06) 3296802; e-mail embassyoman@virgilio.it; Ambassador Dr AHMED BIN SALIM BA OMAR.

Pakistan: Via della Camilluccia 682, 00135 Roma; tel. (06) 36301775; fax (06) 36301936; e-mail pareprome1@tiscali.it; Ambassador TEHMINA JANJUA.

Panama: Largo di Torre Argentina 11, 00186 Roma; tel. (06) 44252173; fax (06) 44252237; e-mail embajadapanamaroma@ embajadadepanama.it; Ambassador FERNANDO BERGUIDO GUIZADO.

Paraguay: Via Firenze 43, scala A, 00184 Roma; tel. (06) 4741715; fax (06) 4745473; e-mail embaparoma@virgilio.it; Chargé d'affaires a.i. MIRKO SOTO SAPRIZA.

Peru: Via Francesco Siacci 2B, 00197 Roma; tel. (06) 80691510; fax (06) 80691777; e-mail embperu@ambasciatapperu.it; tel. www.am-basciatapperu.it; Chargé d'affaires a.i. PEDRO ROBERTO REÁTEGUI GAMARRA.

Philippines: Viale delle Medaglie d'Oro 112–114, 00136 Roma; tel. (06) 39746621; fax (06) 39740872; e-mail rome.pe@dfa.gov.ph; internet romepe.dfa.gov.ph; Ambassador VIRGILIO A. REYES, Jr.

Poland: Via Pietro Paolo Rubens 20, 00197 Roma; tel. (06) 36204200; fax (06) 3217895; e-mail roma.ufficio.stampa@msz.gov.pl; internet www.rzym.polemb.net; Chargé d'affaires a.i. MARTA ZIELIŃSKA-SLIWKA.

Portugal: Via Guido d'Arezzo 5, 00198 Roma; tel. (06) 844801; fax (06) 36309827; e-mail emb@embportroma.it; internet www .embportroma.it; Ambassador MANUEL LOBO ANTUNES.

Qatar: Via Antonio Bosio 14, 00161 Roma; tel. (06) 44249450; fax (06) 44245273; e-mail qatar.embassy@gmail.com; internet www .qatarembassy.it; Ambassador ABDULAZIZ AHMED AL-MALKI AL-JEHANI.

Romania: Via Nicolò Tartaglia 36, 00197 Roma; tel. (06) 8084529; fax (06) 8084995; e-mail amdiroma@roembit.org; internet roma.mae .ro; Ambassador DANA-MANUELA CONSTANTINESCU.

Russian Federation: Via Gaeta 5, 00185 Roma; tel. (06) 4941680; fax (06) 491031; e-mail rusembassy@libero.it; internet www .ambrussia.com; Ambassador SERGEY RAZOV.

San Marino: Via Eleonora Duse 35, 00197 Roma; tel. (06) 8072511; fax (06) 8070072; e-mail asmarino@ambrsm.it; Ambassador DANIELA ROTONDARO.

Saudi Arabia: Via G. B. Pergolesi 9, 00198 Roma; tel. (06) 844851; fax (06) 8551781; e-mail segretaria@arabia-saudita.it; internet www .arabia-saudita.it; Ambassador RAYED KHALID A. KRIMLY.

Senegal: Via Bruxelles 61/63, 00198 Roma; tel. (06) 6872381; fax (06) 68219294; e-mail ambasenequiri@tiscali.it; Ambassador SEYNABOU BADIANE.

Serbia: Via dei Monti Parioli 20, 00197 Roma; tel. (06) 3211950; fax (06) 3200868; e-mail info@ambroma.com; internet www.roma.mfa .gov.rs; Ambassador ANA HRUSTANOVIĆ.

Slovakia: Via dei Colli della Farnesina 144, 00135 Roma; tel. (06) 36715200; fax (06) 36715265; e-mail emb.roma@mzv.sk; internet www.mzv.sk/rim; Ambassador MÁRIA KRASNOHORSKÁ.

Slovenia: Via Leonardo Pisano 10, 00197 Roma; tel. (06) 80914310; fax (06) 8081471; e-mail vri@gov.si; internet rim.veleposlanistvo.si; Ambassador IZTOK MIROŠIČ.

Somalia: Via dei Gracchi 305, 00192 Roma; tel. (06) 3200898; fax (06) 32541832; e-mail somalrep@gmail.com; Ambassador MUSSA HASSAN ABDULLE.

South Africa: Via Tanaro 14, 00198 Roma; tel. (06) 852541; fax (06) 85254300; e-mail sae@sudafrica.it; internet www.sudafrica.it; Ambassador NOMATEMBA TAMBO.

Spain: Palazzo Borghese, Largo della Fontanella di Borghese 19, 00186 Roma; tel. (06) 6840401; fax (06) 6872256; e-mail emb.roma@ maec.es; internet www.maec.es/embajadas/roma; Ambassador FRANCISCO JAVIER ELORZA CAVENGT.

Sri Lanka: Via Adige 2, 00198 Roma; tel. (06) 8554560; fax (06) 84241670; e-mail embassy@srilankaembassyrome.org; internet www.srilankaembassyrome.org; Chargé d'affaires a.i. POSHITHA PERERA.

Sudan: Via Panama 48, 00198 Roma; tel. (06) 33222138; fax (06) 3340841; e-mail info@sudanembassy.it; Ambassador AMIRA DAOUD HASSAN GORNASS.

Sweden: Piazza Rio de Janeiro 3, 00161 Roma; tel. (06) 441941; fax (06) 44194760; e-mail ambassaden.rom@gov.se; internet www .swedenabroad.com/rom; Ambassador RUTH EVELYN JACOBY.

Switzerland: Via Barnaba Oriani 61, 00197 Roma; tel. (06) 809571; fax (06) 8088510; e-mail rom.vertretung@eda.admin.ch; internet www.eda.admin.ch/roma; Ambassador GIANCARLO KESSLER.

Syria: Piazza dell'Ara Coeli, 00186 Roma; tel. (06) 6749801; fax (06) 6794989; e-mail uffstampasyem@hotmail.it; Chargé d'affaires a.i. DIMA HARIRI.

Tanzania: Viale Cortina d'Ampezzo 185, 00135 Roma; tel. (06) 33485801; fax (06) 33485828; e-mail info@tanzania-gov.it; internet www.tanzania-gov.it; Ambassador JAMES ALEX MSEKELA.

Thailand: Via Nomentana 132, 00162 Roma; tel. (06) 86220524; fax (06) 86220555; e-mail thai.em.rome@wind.it.net; internet www .thaiembassy.org/rome; Ambassador SURAPIT KIRTIPUTRA.

Tunisia: Via Asmara 7, 00199 Roma; tel. (06) 8603060; fax (06) 86218204; e-mail at.roma@tiscali.it; Ambassador NACEUR MESTIRI.

Turkey: Palazzo Gamberini, Via Palestro 28, 00185 Roma; tel. (06) 445941; fax (06) 4941526; e-mail roma.be@libero.it; internet www .roma.be.mfa.gov.tr; Ambassador AYDIN ADNAN SEZGIN.

Uganda: Viale Giulio Cesare 71, II piano, scala A–B, 00192 Roma; tel. (06) 3225220; fax (06) 3213688; e-mail ugandaembassyrome@ hotmail.com; internet www.ugandaembassy.it; Ambassador DINAH GRACE AKELLO.

Ukraine: Via Guido d'Arezzo 9, 00198 Roma; tel. (06) 8412630; fax (06) 8547539; e-mail emb_it@mfa.gov.ua; internet www.mfa.gov.ua/ italy; Ambassador YEVHEN PERELYGIN.

United Arab Emirates: Via della Camilluccia 492, 00135 Roma; tel. (06) 36306100; fax (06) 36306155; e-mail uaeroma@tin.it; internet uae-embassy.ae/Embassies/it; Ambassador SAQER NASSER AHMED ABDULLAH ALRAISI.

United Kingdom: Via XX Settembre 80A, 00187 Roma; tel. (06) 42202431; fax (06) 42202333; e-mail romepoliticalsection@fco.gov .uk; internet www.ukinitaly.fco.gov.uk; Ambassador CHRISTOPHER PRENTICE.

USA: Palazzo Margherita, Via Vittorio Veneto 121, 00187 Roma; tel. (06) 46741; fax (06) 46742217; internet rome.usembassy.gov; Ambassador JOHN R. PHILLIPS.

Uruguay: Via Vittorio Veneto 183, 00187 Roma; tel. (06) 4821776; fax (06) 4823695; e-mail uruit@ambasciatauruguay.it; Chargé d'affaires a.i. MARIA GABRIELA CHIFFLET BIDE.

Uzbekistan: Via Pompeo Magno 1, 00192 Roma; tel. (06) 87860310; fax (06) 87860309; e-mail ambasciata@uzbekistanitalia.org; internet www.uzbekistanitalia.org; Ambassador RAVSHAN USMANOV.

Venezuela: Via Nicolò Tartaglia 11, 00197 Roma; tel. (06) 3216578; fax (06) 3208028; e-mail conve.roita@mppre.gob.ve; internet italia .embajada.gob.ve; Ambassador JULIÁN ISAÍAS RODRÍGUEZ DÍAZ.

Viet Nam: Via di Bravetta 156, 00164 Roma; tel. (06) 66160726; fax (06) 66157520; e-mail vnemb.it@mofa.gov.vn; internet www .vnembassy.it; Ambassador NGUYEN HOANG LONG.

Yemen: Via Antonio Bosio 10, 00161 Roma; tel. (06) 44231679; fax (06) 44234763; e-mail info@yemenembassy.it; internet www .yemenembassy.it; Chargé d'affaires a.i. HAYTHAM ABDULMOMEN HASSAN SHOJA'AADIN.

Zambia: Via Ennio Quirino Visconti 8, VI piano, 00193 Roma; tel. (06) 36002590; fax (06) 97613035; e-mail info@zambianembassy.it; internet www.zambianembassy.it; Ambassador FRANK MUTUBILA.

Zimbabwe: Via Virgilio 8, 00193 Roma; tel. (06) 68308282; fax (06) 68308324; e-mail zimrome-wolit@tiscali.it; Ambassador GODFREY MAGWENZI.

Judicial System

The Constitutional Court was established in 1956 and is an autonomous constitutional body, standing apart from the judicial system. Its most important function is to pronounce on the constitutionality of legislation both subsequent and prior to the present Constitution of 1948. It also judges accusations brought against the President of the Republic or ministers.

At the base of the system of penal jurisdiction are the District Courts (Preture), where offences carrying a sentence of up to four years' imprisonment are tried. Above the Preture are the Tribunali (Tribunals) and the Assize Courts attached to the Tribunals, Corti di Assise presso i Tribunali, where graver offences are dealt with. From these courts appeal lies to the Corti d'Appello (Courts of Appeal) and the parallel Corti di Assise d'Appello (Assize Courts of Appeal). Final appeal may be made, on juridical grounds only, to the Corte Suprema di Cassazione (Supreme Court of Cassation).

Civil cases may be taken in the first instance to Justices of the Peace (Giudici Conciliatori), Preture or Tribunali, according to the economic value of the case. Appeal from the Giudici Conciliatori lies to the Preture, from the Preture to the Tribunali, from the Tribunali to the Corti d'Appello, and finally, as in penal justice, to the Corte Suprema di Cassazione on juridical grounds only.

Special divisions for cases concerning labour relations are attached to civil courts. Cases concerned with the public service and its employees are tried by Tribunali Amministrativi Regionali and the Consiglio di Stato. Juvenile courts have criminal and civil jurisdiction.

A new penal code was introduced in late 1989.

CONSTITUTIONAL COURT

Corte Costituzionale: Palazzo della Consulta, Piazza del Quirinale 41, 00187 Roma; tel. (06) 46981; fax (06) 4698916; e-mail ccost@ cortecostituzionale.it; internet www.cortecostituzionale.it; consists of 15 judges, one-third appointed by the President of the Republic, one-third elected by Parliament in joint session, and one-third by the ordinary and administrative supreme courts; Pres. GAETANO SILVESTRI.

ADMINISTRATIVE COURTS

Consiglio di Stato: Palazzo Spada, Piazza Capo di Ferro 13, 00186 Roma; tel. (06) 68271; fax (06) 68272282; e-mail urp.cds@ giustizia-amministrativa.it; internet www.giustizia -amministrativa.it; established in accordance with Article 10 of the Constitution; has both consultative and judicial functions; Pres. Dott. GIORGIO GIOVANNINI.

Corte dei Conti: Via Giuseppe Mazzini 105, 00195 Roma; tel. (06) 38761; fax (06) 38763477; e-mail urp@corteconti.it; internet www .corteconti.it; functions as the court of public auditors for the state; Pres. RAFFAELE SQUITIERI.

SUPREME COURT OF CASSATION

Corte Suprema di Cassazione: Palazzo di Giustizia, Piazza Cavour, 00193 Roma; tel. (06) 68831; fax (06) 6883423; e-mail cortedicassazione@giustizia.it; internet www.cortedicassazione.it; supreme court of civil and criminal appeal; First Pres. Dott. GIORGIO SANTACROCE.

SUPERVISORY BODY

Consiglio Superiore della Magistratura (CSM): Piazza Indipendenza 6, 00185 Roma; tel. (06) 444911; fax (06) 4457175; e-mail protocollo.csm@giustiziacert.it; internet www.csm.it; f. 1958; 27

mems; Pres. GIORGIO NAPOLITANO (President of the Republic); Vice-Pres. MICHELE VIETTI.

Religion

More than 90% of the population of Italy are adherents of the Roman Catholic Church. Under the terms of the Concordat formally ratified in June 1985, Roman Catholicism was no longer to be the state religion, compulsory religious instruction in schools was abolished and state financial contributions reduced. The Vatican City's sovereign rights as an independent state, under the terms of the Lateran Treaty of 1929, were not affected.

Several Protestant churches also exist in Italy, with a total membership of about 65,000. There is a small Jewish community, and in 1987 an agreement recognized certain rights for the Jewish community, including the right to observe religious festivals on Saturdays by not attending school or work. There is also a substantial Islamic population.

CHRISTIANITY

The Roman Catholic Church

For ecclesiastical purposes, Italy comprises the Papal See of Rome, the Patriarchate of Venice, 60 archdioceses (including three directly responsible to the Holy See), two eparchies, 153 dioceses (including seven within the jurisdiction of the Pope, as Archbishop of the Roman Province, and 11 directly responsible to the Holy See), two territorial prelatures and seven territorial abbacies (including four directly responsible to the Holy See). Almost all adherents follow the Latin rite, but there are two dioceses and one abbacy (all directly responsible to the Holy See) for Catholics of the Italo-Albanian (Byzantine) rite.

Bishops' Conference: Conferenza Episcopale Italiana, Circonvallazione Aurelia 50, 00165 Roma; tel. (06) 663981; fax (06) 6623037; e-mail segrgen@chiesacattolica.it; internet www.chiesacattolica.it; f. 1965; Pres. Cardinal ANGELO BAGNASCO (Archbishop of Genova); Sec.-Gen. Bishop NUNZIO GALANTINO.

Primate of Italy, Archbishop and Metropolitan of the Roman Province and Bishop of Rome: His Holiness Pope FRANCIS.

Patriarch of Venice: FRANCESCO MORAGLIA.

Archbishops

Acerenza: Most Rev. GIOVANNI RICCHIUTI.

Agrigento: Cardinal FRANCESCO MONTENEGRO.

Amalfi-Cava de' Tirreni: Most Rev. ORAZIO SORICELLI.

Ancona-Osimo: Cardinal EDOARDO MENICHELLI.

L'Aquila: Most Rev. GIUSEPPE PETROCCHI.

Bari-Bitonto: Most Rev. FRANCESCO CACUCCI.

Benevento: Most Rev. ANDREA MUGIONE.

Bologna: Cardinal CARLO CAFFARRA.

Brindisi-Otsuni: Most Rev. DOMENICO CALIANDRO.

Cagliari: Most Rev. ARRIGO MIGLIO.

Camerino-San Severino Marche: Most Rev. FRANCESCO GIOVANNI BRUGNARO.

Campobasso-Boiano: Most Rev. GIANCARLO MARIA BREGANTINI.

Capua: Most Rev. SALVATORE VISCO.

Catania: Most Rev. SALVATORE GRISTINA.

Catanzaro-Squillace: Most Rev. VINCENZO BERTOLONE.

Chieti-Vasto: Most Rev. BRUNO FORTE.

Cosenza-Bisignano: Most Rev. SALVATORE NUNNARI.

Crotone-Santa Severina: Most Rev. DOMENICO GRAZIANI.

Fermo: Most Rev. LUIGI CONTI.

Ferrara-Comacchio: Most Rev. LUIGI NEGRI.

Firenze (Florence): Most Rev. GIUSEPPE BETORI.

Foggia-Bovino: Most Rev. VINCENZO PELVI.

Gaeta: Most Rev. FABIO BERNARDO D'ONORIO.

Genova (Genoa): Cardinal ANGELO BAGNASCO.

Gorizia: Most Rev. CARLO ROBERTO MARIA REDAELLI.

Lanciano-Ortona: Most Rev. EMIDIO CIPOLLONE.

Lecce: Most Rev. DOMENICO UMBERTO D'AMBROSIO.

Lucca: Most Rev. BENVENUTO ITALO CASTELLANI.

Manfredonia-Vieste-San Giovanni Rotondo: Most Rev. MICHELE CASTORO.

Matera-Irsina: Most Rev. SALVATORE LIGORIO.

Messina-Lipari-Santa Lucia del Mela: Most Rev. CALOGERO LA PIANA.

Milano (Milan): Cardinal ANGELO SCOLA.

Modena-Nonantola: (vacant).

Monreale: Most Rev. MICHELE PENNISI.

Napoli (Naples): Cardinal CRESCENZIO SEPE.

Oristano: Most Rev. IGNAZIO SANNA.

Otranto: Most Rev. DONATO NEGRO.

Palermo: Cardinal PAOLO ROMEO.

Perugia-Città della Pieve: Cardinal GUALTIERO BASSETTI.

Pesaro: Most Rev. PIERO COCCIA.

Pescara-Penne: Most Rev. TOMMASO VALENTINETTI.

Pisa: Most Rev. GIOVANNI PAOLO BENOTTO.

Potenza-Muro Lucano-Marsico Nuovo: Most Rev. AGOSTINO SUPERBO.

Ravenna-Cervia: Most Rev. LORENZO GHIZZONI.

Reggio Calabria-Bova: Most Rev. GIUSEPPE FIORINI MOROSINI.

Rossano-Cariati: Cardinal GIUSEPPE SATRIANO.

Salerno-Campagna-Acerno: Most Rev. LUIGI MORETTI.

Sant'Angelo dei Lombardi-Conza-Nusco-Bisaccia: Most Rev. PASQUALE CASCIO.

Sassari: Most Rev. PAOLO MARIO VIRGILIO ATZEI.

Siena-Colle di Val d'Elsa-Montalcino: Most Rev. ANTONIO BUONCRISTIANI.

Siracusa (Syracuse): Most Rev. SALVATORE PAPPALARDO.

Sorrento-Castellamare di Stabia: Most Rev. FRANCESCO ALFANO.

Spoleto-Norcia: Most Rev. RENATO BOCCARDO.

Taranto: Most Rev. FILIPPO SANTORO.

Torino (Turin): Most Rev. CESARE NOSIGLIA.

Trani-Barletta-Bisceglie: Most Rev. GIOVANNI BATTISTA PICHIERRI.

Trento: Most Rev. LUIGI BRESSAN.

Udine: Most Rev. ANDREA BRUNO MAZZOCATO.

Urbino-Urbania-Sant'Angelo in Vado: Most Rev. GIOVANNI TANI.

Vercelli: Most Rev. MARCO ARNOLFO.

Protestant Churches

Federazione delle Chiese Evangeliche in Italia (Federation of the Protestant Churches in Italy): Via Firenze 38, 00184 Roma; tel. (06) 4825120; fax (06) 4828728; internet www.fcei.it; f. 1967; total mems c. 65,000; Pres. MASSIMO AQUILANTE; 9 mem. churches, incl. the following:

    Chiesa Evangelica Luterana in Italia (Lutheran Church): Via Aurelia Antica 391, 00165 Roma; tel. (06) 66030104; fax (06) 66017993; e-mail decanato@chiesaluterana.it; internet www.chiesaluterana.it; Pres. CHRISTIANE GROEBEN; 7,000 mems.

    Chiesa Evangelica Valdese (Unione delle Chiese Metodiste e Valdesi) (Waldensian Evangelical Church): Via Firenze 38, 00184 Roma; tel. (06) 4743695; fax (06) 47885308; e-mail info@chiesavaldese.org; internet www.chiesavaldese.org; in 2002 the Tavola Valdese merged with the Chiese Evangeliche Metodiste in Italia (Methodists); Moderator MARIA BONAFEDE; 27,465 mems.

ISLAM

Associazione Musulmani Italiani (AMI) (Italian Muslim Association): CP 7167, Roma; tel. and fax (06) 44360619; e-mail info@amimuslims.org; internet www.amimuslims.org; f. 1982; Pres. Prince BARZANGI AHMED ABUCAR SULDAN.

Unione delle Comunità Islamiche d'Italia (UCOII): Via delle 4, Fontane, Roma; tel. (0183) 48939934; fax (0183) 764735; e-mail alessandro.paolantoni@ucoii.org; internet www.ucoii.org; f. 1990; Pres. IZZEDDIN ELZIR; Sec. AHMED ALESSANDRO PAOLANTONI.

JUDAISM

Unione delle Comunità Ebraiche Italiane (UCEI) (Union of Italian Jewish Communities): Lungotevere Sanzio 9, 00153 Roma; tel. (06) 45542200; fax (06) 5899569; e-mail info@ucei.it; internet www.ucei.it; f. 1930; represents 21 Jewish communities in Italy; Pres. RENZO GATTEGNA; Gen. Sec. Dott. GLORIA ARBIB.

The Press

Relative to the size of Italy's population, the number of daily newspapers is rather small. Rome and Milan are the main press centres. The most important national dailies are *Corriere della Sera* in Milan and *La Repubblica* in Rome, followed by Turin's *La Stampa* and Milan's *Il Sole 24 Ore*, the economic and financial newspaper with the highest circulation in Europe. Among the most widely read newspapers are *La Gazzetta dello Sport* and *Il Corriere dello Sport—Stadio*, both of which exclusively cover sports news.

PRINCIPAL DAILIES
(Average net circulation figures, for January–December 2011, unless otherwise stated.)

Ancona

Il Corriere Adriatico: Via Berti 20, 60126 Ancona; tel. (071) 4581; fax (071) 42980; e-mail info@corriereadriaticonline.it; internet www .corriereadriatico.it; f. 1860; Editorial Dir PAOLO TRAINI; circ. 23,549.

Bari

La Gazzetta del Mezzogiorno: Viale Scipione l'Africano 264, 70124 Bari; tel. (080) 5470200; fax (080) 5502130; e-mail direzione .politica@gazzettamezzogiorno.it; internet www.lagazzetta delmezzogiorno.it; f. 1887; independent; Editor MICHELE PARTIPILO; circ. 46,804.

Il Quotidiano di Bari: Piazza Aldo Moro 31, 70121 Bari; tel. (080) 5240473; fax (080) 5245486; e-mail redazione@quotidianodibari.it; internet www.quotidianodibari.it; Dir MATTEO TATARELLA.

Bergamo

L'Eco di Bergamo: Viale Papa Giovanni XXIII 118, 24121 Bergamo; tel. (035) 386111; fax (035) 386217; e-mail redazione@eco.bg.it; internet www.ecodibergamo.it; f. 1880; Catholic; Dir GIORGIO GANDOLA; circ. 57,986.

Bologna

Il Resto del Carlino: Via Enrico Mattei 106, 40138 Bologna; tel. (051) 6006111; fax (051) 536111; e-mail segreteria.redazione .bologna@monrif.net; internet www.ilrestodelcarlino.it; f. 1885; publr Poligrafici Editoriale, SpA; Dir GIOVANNI MORANDI; circ. 180,914.

Bolzano/Bozen

Alto Adige: Via Volta 10, 39100 Bozen; tel. (0471) 904111; fax (0471) 904263; e-mail bolzano@altoadige.it; internet www.altoadige.it; f. 1945; publr Gruppo Editoriale L'Espresso, SpA; Dir ALBERTO FAUSTINI; circ. 36,951.

Dolomiten: Weinbergweg 7, 39100 Bozen; tel. (0471) 925111; fax (0471) 925440; e-mail dolomiten@athesia.it; internet www.stol.it/ dolomiten; f. 1882; independent; German language; Dir Dott. TONI EBNER; circ. 55,654.

Brescia

Il Giornale di Brescia: Via Solferino 22, 25121 Brescia; tel. (030) 37901; fax (030) 3790289; e-mail info@giornaledibrescia.it; internet www.giornaledibrescia.it; f. 1947; Dir GIACOMO SCANZI; circ. 54,624.

Cagliari

L'Unione Sarda: Viale Regina Elena 12, 9100 Cagliari; tel. (070) 60131; fax (070) 6013306; e-mail unione@unionesarda.it; internet www.unionesarda.it; f. 1889; independent; Editor-in-Chief PAOLO FIGUS; circ. 70,699.

Catania

La Sicilia: Viale Odorico da Pordenone 50, 95126 Catania; tel. (095) 330544; fax (095) 336466; e-mail segreteria@lasicilia.it; internet www.lasicilia.it; f. 1945; independent; Man. Dott. MARIO CIANCIO SANFILIPPO; circ. 63,255.

Como

La Provincia di Como: Via Pasquale Paoli 21, 22100 Como; tel. (031) 582311; fax (031) 505003; e-mail laprovincia@laprovincia.it; internet www.laprovinciadicomo.it; f. 1892; independent; Dir DIEGO MINONZIO; circ. 56,000 (2003).

Firenze
(Florence)

La Nazione: Viale Giovine Italia 17, 50121 Firenze; tel. (055) 249511; fax (055) 2478207; e-mail segreteria@lanazione.it; internet www.lanazione.it; f 1859; publr Poligrafici Editoriale, SpA; Dir JOSEPH MASCAMBRUNO; circ. 149,393.

Foggia

Quotidiano di Foggia: Via Gramsci 73A, 71100 Foggia; tel. (0881) 686967; fax (0881) 632247; e-mail redazione@quotidianodifoggia.it; internet www.quotidianodifoggia.it; Dir MATTEO TATTARELLA; circ. 25,000 (2007).

Genova
(Genoa)

Il Secolo XIX: Piazza Piccapietra 21, 16121 Genova; tel. (010) 53881; fax (010) 5388426; e-mail redazione@ilsecoloxix.it; internet www .ilsecoloxix.it; f. 1886; independent; Dir CARLO PERRONE; circ. 96,419.

Lecce

Nuovo Quotidiano di Puglia: Via dei Mocenigo 29, 73100 Lecce; tel. (0832) 3382000; fax (0832) 338244; e-mail redazioneweb@ quotidianodipuglia.it; internet www.quotidianodipuglia.it; f. 1979 as *Il Quotidiano di Lecce*; 3 local edns covering Lecce, Brindisi and Taranto; Dir CLAUDIO SCAMARDELLA; circ. 24,109.

Livorno
(Leghorn)

Il Tirreno: Viale Alfieri 9, 57124 Livorno; tel. (0586) 220111; fax (0586) 402066; e-mail redazione.li@iltirreno.it; internet iltirreno .repubblica.it; f. 1978; publr Gruppo Editoriale L'Espresso, SpA; Dir ROBERTO BERNABÒ; circ. 93,939.

Mantova
(Mantua)

Gazzetta di Mantova: Piazza Cesare Mozzarelli 7, 46100 Mantova; tel. (0376) 3031; fax (0376) 303263; e-mail redazione.mn@ gazzettadimantova.it; internet www.gazzettadimantova.it; f. 1664; publr Gruppo Editoriale L'Espresso, SpA; Dir ANDREA FILIPPI; circ. 34,114.

Messina

Gazzetta del Sud: Uberto Bonino 15C, 98124 Messina; tel. (090) 2261; fax (090) 2936359; e-mail amministrazione@gazzettadelsud.it; internet www.gazzettadelsud.it; f. 1952; independent; Dir NINO CALARCO; circ. 59,227.

Milano
(Milan)

Avvenire: Piazza Carbonari 3, 20125 Milano; tel. (02) 67801; fax (02) 6780208; e-mail lettere@avvenire.it; internet www.avvenire.it; f. 1968; Catholic; organ of the Italian Bishops' Conference; Dir MARCO TARQUINIO; circ. 145,754.

Corriere della Sera: Via Solferino 28, 20121 Milano; tel. (02) 6339, fax (02) 29009668; internet www.corriere.it; f. 1876; independent; contains weekly supplement, *Sette*; Dir FERRUCIO DE BORTOLI; circ. 622,070.

Il Foglio Quotidiano: Via Carroccio 12, 20123 Milano; tel. (02) 7712951; fax (02) 782511; e-mail lettere@ilfoglio.it; internet www .ilfoglio.it; Dir GIULIANO FERRARA.

La Gazzetta dello Sport: Via Rizzoli 8, 20132 Milano; tel. (02) 62821; fax (02) 62827917; e-mail segretgaz@rcs.it; internet www .gazzetta.it; f. 1896; sport; Dir ANDREA MONTI; circ. 427,933.

Il Giornale: Via Gaetano Negri 4, 20123 Milano; tel. (02) 85661; fax (02) 72023880; e-mail segreteria@ilgiornale.it; internet www .ilgiornale.it; f. 1974; Editor ALESSANDRO SALLUSTI; circ. 258,941.

Il Giorno: Via Stradivari 4, 20123 Milano; tel. (02) 277991; fax (02) 27799537; e-mail ilgiorno@ilgiorno.it; internet www.ilgiorno.it; f. 1956; publr Poligrafici Editoriale, SpA; Dir GIOVANNI MORANDI; circ. 87,479.

Italia Oggi: Class Editori, Via M. Burigozzo 5, 20122 Milano; tel. (02) 58219256; e-mail italiaoggi@class.it; internet www.italiaoggi.it; f. 1991; economic daily; Dir PIERLUIGI MAGNASCHI; circ. 133,024.

Libero: Viale L. Majno 42, 20129 Milano; tel. (02) 99966300; fax (02) 99966305; internet www.liberoquotidiano.it; f. 2000; Dir EGREGIO MAURIZIO BELPIETRO; circ. 194,818.

MF (Milano Finanza): Class Editori, Via M. Burigozzo 5, 20122 Milano; tel. (02) 582191; internet www.milanofinanza.it; f. 1989; economic daily; Dir ENRICO ROMAGNA MANOJA.

Il Sole 24 Ore: Via Monte Rosa 91, 20149 Milano; tel. (02) 30221; fax (02) 312055; internet www.ilsole24ore.com; f. 1865; financial, political, economic; Dir ROBERTO NAPOLETANO; circ. 334,519.

Napoli
(Naples)

Corriere del Mezzogiorno: Vico II San Nicola alla Dogana 9, 80133 Napoli; tel. (081) 7602001; fax (081) 5802779; e-mail m.demarco@ corrieredelmezzogiorno.it; internet www.corrieredelmezzogiorno.it; f. 1997; publr RCS MediaGroup; Dir MARCO DEMARCO.

Il Denaro: Via Kennedy 54, 800125 Napoli; tel. (081) 421900; fax (081) 422212; e-mail denaro@denaro.it; internet www.denaro.it; economic daily; Dir ALFONSO RUFFO.

Il Mattino: Via Chiatamone 65, 80121 Napoli; tel. (081) 7947111; fax (081) 7947288; e-mail redazioneinternet@ilmattino.it; internet www .ilmattino.it; f. 1892; reformed 1950; independent; Dir-Gen. MASSIMO GARZILLI; Editor VIRMAN CUSENZA; circ. 99,776.

Padova
(Padua)

Il Mattino di Padova: Via N. Tommaseo, 65B, 35131 Padova; tel. (049) 8083411; fax (049) 8070067; e-mail mattino@mattinopadova.it; internet www.mattinopadova.it; f. 1978; publr Gruppo Editoriale L'Espresso, SpA; Dir ANTONIO RAMENGHI; circ. 34,282.

Palermo

Giornale di Sicilia: Via Lincoln 21, 90122 Palermo; tel. (091) 6627111; fax (091) 6627280; e-mail gds@gestelnet.it; internet www .gds.it; f. 1860; independent; Dir ANTONIO ARDIZZONE; circ. 73,269.

Parma

Gazzetta di Parma: Via Mantova 68, 43100 Parma; tel. (0521) 2251; fax (0521) 225522; e-mail gazzetta@gazzettadiparma.net; internet www.gazzettadiparma.it; f. 1735; Dir GIULIANO MOLOSSI; circ. 47,186.

Perugia

Corriere dell'Umbria: Via Pievaiola 166F, 06132 Perugia; tel. (075) 52731; fax (075) 5273400; e-mail info@corrieredellumbria.it; f. 1983; independent; Editor ANNA MOSSUTO; circ. 30,097.

Pescara

Il Centro: Via Tiburtina 91, 65129 Pescara; tel. (085) 20521; fax (085) 4318050; e-mail lettere@ilcentro.it; internet www.ilcentro.it; f. 1986; publr Gruppo Editoriale L'Espresso, SpA; Dir SERGIO BARALDI; circ. 29,063.

Piacenza

Libertà: Via Benedettine 68, 29100 Piacenza; tel. (0523) 393939; fax (0523) 321723; e-mail info@liberta.it; internet www.liberta.it; f. 1883; Dir RIZZUTO GAETANO; circ. 33,690.

Rimini

Corriere di Romagna: Piazza Tre Martiri 43A, 47900 Rimini; tel. (0541) 354111; fax (0541) 351499; e-mail lega@corriereromagna.it; internet www.corriereromagna.it; also distributed in San Marino; Dir MARIA PATRIZIA LANZETTI.

Roma
(Rome)

Conquiste del Lavoro: Via Po 22, 00198 Roma; tel. (06) 8473430; fax (06) 85412333; e-mail conquiste_lavoro@cisl.it; internet www .conquistedellavoro.it; owned by Confederazione Italiana Sindacati Lavoratori (CISL); Dir RAFFAELE BONANNI; circ. 90,000 (2008).

Il Corriere dello Sport—Stadio: Piazza Indipendenza 11B, 00185 Roma; tel. (06) 49921; fax (06) 4992275; e-mail segrdirgen@corsport .it; internet www.corsport.it; f. 1924; Editor ALESSANDRO VOCALELLI; circ. 314,576.

Il Manifesto: Via Tomacelli 146, 00186 Roma; tel. (06) 687191; fax (06) 68719573; e-mail redazione@ilmanifesto.it; internet www .ilmanifesto.it; f. 1971; splinter communist; Dir NORMA RANGERI; circ. 69,152.

Il Messaggero: Via del Tritone 152, 00187 Roma; tel. (06) 47201; fax (06) 4720300; e-mail posta@ilmessaggero.it; internet www .ilmessaggero.it; f. 1878; independent; Pres. FRANCO G. CALTAGIRONE; Editor NORMA RANGERI; circ. 265,063.

La Repubblica: Via Cristoforo Colombo 149, 00147 Roma; tel. (06) 49821; fax (06) 49822923; e-mail larepubblica@repubblica.it; internet www.repubblica.it; f. 1976; left-wing; publr Gruppo Editoriale L'Espresso, SpA; Dir EZIO MAURO; circ. 576,216.

Il Riformista: Via Trinità dei Pellegrini 12, 00186 Roma; tel. (06) 427481; fax (06) 42748215; e-mail redazione@ilriformista.it; internet www.ilriformista.it; political; Dir EMANUELE MACALUSO.

Il Tempo: Piazza Colonna 366, 00187 Roma; tel. (06) 675881; fax (06) 6758869; internet www.iltempo.it; f. 1944; independent; right-wing; Editor MARIO SECHI; circ. 57,922.

L'Unità: Via Ostiense 131L, 00154 Roma; tel. (06) 585571; fax (06) 58557219; e-mail unitaonline@unita.it; internet www.unita.it; f. 1924; Dir LUCA LANDÒ; circ. 118,662.

Salerno

La Città: Via San Leonardo 51, 84131 Salerno; tel. (089) 2783111; fax (089) 2783236; e-mail redazione@lacittadisalerno.it; internet www.lacittadisalerno.it; Dir ANGELO DI MARINO.

Sassari

La Nuova Sardegna: Strada 30–31, Predda Niedda, 07100 Sassari; tel. (079) 222400; fax (079) 2674086; e-mail lanuovasardegna.gelocal .it; internet lanuovasardegna.repubblica.it; f. 1891; publr Gruppo Editoriale L'Espresso, SpA; Dir ANDREA FILIPPI; circ. 163,175.

Torino
(Turin)

La Stampa: Via Marenco 32, 10126 Torino; tel. (011) 656811; fax (011) 655306; e-mail lettere@lastampa.it; internet www.lastampa.it; f. 1867; independent; Dir MARIO CALABRESI; circ. 381,423.

Trento

L'Adige: Via Missioni Africane 17, 38100 Trento; tel. (0461) 886111; fax (0461) 886264; e-mail p.giovanetti@ladige.it; internet www .ladige.it; f. 1946; independent; Dir Dott. PIERANGELO GIOVANETTI; circ. 30,646.

Trieste

Il Piccolo: Via Guido Reni 1, 34123 Trieste; tel. (040) 3733111; fax (040) 3733262; e-mail ufficio.centrale@ilpiccolo.it; internet ilpiccolo .repubblica.it; f. 1881; publr Gruppo Editoriale L'Espresso, SpA; Dir PAOLO POSSAMAI; circ. 41,999.

Primorski Dnevnik: Via dei Montecchi 6, 34137 Trieste; tel. (040) 7786300; fax (040) 7786339; e-mail redakcija@primorski.eu; internet www.primorski.eu; f. 1945; Slovene; Editor-in-Chief DUŠAN UDOVIČ; circ. 11,282 (2010).

Udine

Il Messaggero Veneto: Viale Palmanova 290, 33100 Udine; tel. (0432) 5271; fax (0432) 523072; e-mail ufficio.centrale@ messaggeroveneto.it; internet www.messaggeroveneto.it; f. 1946; publr Gruppo Editoriale L'Espresso, SpA; Dir ANDREA FILIPPI; circ. 56,496.

Varese

La Prealpina: Viale Tamagno 13, 21100 Varese; tel. (0332) 275700; fax (0332) 275701; e-mail direttore@prealpina.it; internet www .prealpina.it; f. 1888; Dir PAOLO PROVENZI; circ. 40,000 (2007).

Venezia
(Venice)

Il Gazzettino: Via Torino 110, 30172 Venezia-Mestre; tel. (041) 665111; fax (041) 665413; e-mail segredazione@gazzettino.it; internet www.gazzettino.it; f. 1887; independent; Dir ROBERTO PAPETTI; circ. 103,797.

Verona

L'Arena: Corso Porta Nuova 67, 37122 Verona; tel. (045) 9600111; fax (045) 597966; e-mail redazione@larena.it; internet www.larena .it; f. 1866; independent; Editor-in-Chief MAURIZIO CATTANEO; Man. Dir Ing. ALESSANDRO ZELGER; circ. 54,411.

Vicenza

Il Giornale di Vicenza: Via Enrico Fermi 205, 36100 Vicenza; tel. (0444) 396311; fax (0444) 396333; internet www.ilgiornaledivicenza .it; f. 1945; Dir ARIO GERVASUTTI; circ. 48,276.

SELECTED PERIODICALS
Art, Architecture and Design

Abitare: Via Angelo Rizzoli 8, 20132 Milano; tel. (02) 25841; e-mail mario.piazza@rcs.it; internet www.abitare.it; f. 1962; monthly; architecture and design; in Italian and English; publr RCS MediaGroup; Editor-in-Chief MARIO PIAZZA.

Casabella: Arnoldo Mondadori Editore, SpA, Via Mondadori 1, 20090 Segrate, Milano; tel. (02) 75421; fax (02) 75422706; e-mail casabella@mondadori.it; internet casabellaweb.eu; f. 1928; 11 a year; architecture and interior design; publr Mondadori Editore, SpA; Editor FRANCESCO DAL CO; circ. 40,000 (2014).

Domus: Via Gianni Mazzocchi 1/3, 20089 Rozzano, Milano; tel. (02) 824721; fax (02) 82472386; e-mail editorialedomus@edidomus.it; internet www.domusweb.it; f. 1928; 11 a year; architecture, interior design and art; Editor NICOLA DI BATTISTA; circ. 53,000.

Interni: Via D. Trentacoste 7, 20134 Milano; tel. (02) 215631; fax (02) 26410847; e-mail interni@mondadori.it; internet www

.internimagazine.it; monthly; interior decoration and design; Editor GILDA BOJARDI; circ. 50,000 (2013).

Lotus International: Via Santa Marta 19A, 20123 Milano; tel. (02) 45475745; fax (02) 45475746; e-mail lotus@editorialelotus.it; internet www.editorialelotus.it; f. 1963; quarterly; architecture, town planning; Editor PIERLUIGI NICOLIN.

Storia dell'Arte: CAM Editrice, Srl, Via Capodiferro 4, 00186 Roma; tel. and fax (06) 68300889; e-mail info@cameditrice.com; internet www.storiadellarterivista.it; f. 1968; quarterly; art history; Dir MAURIZIO CALVESI; circ. 2,500.

Education

Il Maestro: Clivo di Monte del Gallo 48, 00165 Roma; tel. (06) 634651; fax (06) 39375903; e-mail aimc@aimc.it; internet www.aimc.it; f. 1945; monthly; Catholic teachers' magazine; Dir GIUSEPPE DESIDERI; circ. 40,000.

Scuola e Didattica: Via Antonio Gramsci 26, 25121 Brescia; tel. (030) 29931; fax (030) 2993299; e-mail sdid@lascuola.it; internet www.lascuola.it; f. 1904; 18 a year; education; Editor PIERPAOLO TRIANI; circ. 40,000.

General, Political and Economic

Economy: Arnoldo Mondadori Editore, SpA, Via Mondadori 1, 20090 Segrate, Milano; tel. (02) 75421; fax (02) 75422302; e-mail economy@mondadori.it; f. 2003; weekly; economics and finance; Dir SERGIO LUCIANO; circ. 85,000.

L'Espresso: Via Cristoforo Colombo 90, 00147 Roma; tel. (06) 84781; fax (06) 84787220; e-mail espresso@espressoedit.it; internet espresso.repubblica.it; weekly; independent left; political; Editor BRUNO MANFELLOTTO; circ. 244,545 (2013).

Famiglia Cristiana: Piazza San Paolo 14, 12051 Alba; tel. (02) 48072777; fax (02) 48072778; e-mail famigliacristiana@stpauls.it; internet www.famigliacristiana.it; f. 1931; weekly; Catholic; illustrated; Dir ANTONIO SCIORTINO; circ. 392,645 (2013).

Gente: Via Roberto Bracco 6, 20159 Milano; tel. (02) 66191; e-mail abbonamenti@hearst.it; internet www.abbonationline.it; f. 1957; weekly; illustrated current events and general interest; Dir MONICA MOSCA; circ. 269,382 (2013).

Il Mulino: Strada Maggiore 37, 40125 Bologna; tel. (051) 256011; fax (051) 6486014; e-mail rivistailmulino@mulino.it; internet www.rivistailmulino.it; f. 1951; every 2 months; culture and politics; Dir MICHELE SALVATI.

Oggi: Via Angelo Rizzoli 8, 20132 Milano; tel. (02) 25841; fax (02) 27201485; internet www.oggi.it; f. 1945; weekly; current affairs, culture, family life; illustrated; publr RCS MediaGroup; Dir UMBERTO BRINDANI; circ. 353,681 (2013).

Panorama: Arnoldo Mondadori Editore, SpA, Via Mondadori 1, 20090 Segrate, Milano; tel. (02) 75421; fax (02) 75422302; e-mail info@panorama.it; internet www.panorama.it; f. 1962; weekly; current affairs; Dir GIORGIO MULÈ; circ. 300,240 (2013).

Visto: Via Angelo Rizzoli 8, 20132 Milano; tel. (02) 25841; f. 1989; weekly; entertainment, celebrities, current events; Dir FRANCO BONERA; circ. 69,368 (2013).

Zett—Die Zeitung am Sonntag: Weinbergweg 7, 39100 Bozen; tel. (0471) 925500; fax (0471) 200462; e-mail zett@athesia.it; internet www.stol.it/athesia/medien/zett; f. 1989; Sun; German language; Dir KLAUS INNERHOFER; circ. 34,000.

History, Literature and Music

Giornale della Libreria: Corso di Porta Romana 108, 20122 Milano; tel. (02) 89280802; fax (02) 89280862; e-mail redazione@giornaledellalibreria.it; internet www.giornaledellalibreria.it; f. 1888; monthly; organ of the Associazione Italiana Editori; bibliographical; Editor MARCO POLILLO; circ. 5,000.

Lettere Italiane: Via Beato Pellegrino 1, 35137 Padova; tel. (049) 8274861; e-mail pizzamig@unive.it; internet www.olschki.it/riviste/lettital.htm; f. 1949; quarterly; literary; Dirs CARLO OSSOLA, CARLO DELCORNO.

Il Pensiero Politico: Via Pascoli, 33, 06123 Perugia; tel. (075) 5855440; e-mail penspol@unipg.it; internet www.olschki.it/riviste/penspol.htm; f. 1968; every 4 months; political and social history; Dirs VITTOR IVO COMPARATO, CARLO CARINI.

Rivista di Storia della Filosofia: Via De Togni 7, 20123 Milano; tel. (02) 28371433; fax (02) 2613268; e-mail redazioni@francoangeli.it; internet www.francoangeli.it/riviste/sommario.asp?idrivista=45; f. 1946; quarterly; philosophy; Editor ENRICO I. RAMBALDI.

Leisure and Sport

Ciak: Arnoldo Mondadori Editore, SpA, Via Mondadori 1, 20090 Segrate, Milano; tel. (02) 75421; fax (02) 75422302; e-mail ciak@mondadori.it; f. 1985; monthly; cinema; Dir PIERA DETASSIS; circ. 36,571 (2013).

Cucina Moderna: Arnoldo Mondadori Editore SpA, Via Mondadori 1, 20090 Segrate, Milano; tel. (02) 75421; fax (02) 75422302; e-mail cucinamoderna@mondadori.it; f. 1996; monthly; cookery; Dir LAURA MARAGLIANO; circ. 309,547 (2013).

Dove: Via Angelo Rizzoli 8, 20132 Milano; tel. (02) 50951; e-mail marina.poggi@rcs.it; internet doveviaggi.corriere.it; f. 1991; monthly; lifestyle and travel; publr RCS MediaGroup; Dir CARLO MONTANARO; circ. 80,000 (2013).

Gambero Rosso: GRH, SpA, Via E. Fermi 161, 00146 Roma; tel. (06) 551121; fax (06) 55112260; e-mail gambero@gamberorosso.it; internet www.gamberorosso.it; f. 1987; monthly; food and wine; Dir LUIGI SALERNO.

Max: Via Solferino 28, 20121 Milano; tel. (02) 62821; fax (02) 62827917; e-mail max@rcs.it; internet max.corriere.it; f. 1985; monthly; men's lifestyle; Dir ANDREA ROSSI; circ. 132,412.

OK: Via Angelo Rizzoli 8, 20132 Milano; tel. (02) 62291; e-mail redazione@ok.rcs.it; internet ok.corriere.it; f. 2005; monthly; health; publr RCS MediaGroup; Editor SIMONA TEDESCO; circ. 277,931.

Quattroruote: Via Gianni Mazzocchi 1/3, 20089 Rozzano, Milano; tel. (02) 824721; fax (02) 57500416; e-mail redazione@quattroruote.it; internet www.quattroruote.it; f. 1956; motoring; monthly; Editor CARLO CAVICCHI; circ. 226,344 (2013).

Starbene: Arnoldo Mondadori Editore SpA, Via Mondadori 1, 20090 Segrate, Milano; tel. (02) 75421; fax (02) 75422302; e-mail starbene@mondadori.it; internet www.starbene.it; f. 1978; monthly; health and beauty; Dir CRISTINA MERLINO; circ. 165,592 (2013).

Telesette: Corso di Porta Nuova 3A, 20121 Milano; tel. (02) 63675415; fax (02) 63675524; e-mail segreteria@casaeditriceuniverso.com; f. 1978; weekly; television; Editor NICOLA DE FEO; circ. 551,601.

TV Sorrisi e Canzoni: Arnoldo Mondadori Editore, SpA, Via Mondadori 1, 20090 Segrate, Milano; tel. (02) 75421; fax (02) 75422302; e-mail sorrisi@mondadori.it; internet www.sorrisi.com; f. 1952; weekly; television, entertainment; Dir ALDO VITALI; circ. 682,033.

Vita in Campagna: Via Bencivenga/Biondani 16, 37133 Verona; tel. (045) 8057511; fax (045) 8009240; e-mail vitaincampagna@vitaincampagna.it; internet www.vitaincampagna.it; publr Editoriale L'Informatore Agrario, SpA; f. 1983; 11 a year; horticulture and smallholding; Dir GIORGIO VINCENZI; circ. 110,553 (2013).

Religion

La Civiltà Cattolica: Via di Porta Pinciana 1, 00187 Roma; tel. (06) 6979201; fax (06) 69792022; e-mail info@laciviltacattolica.it; internet www.laciviltacattolica.it; f. 1850; fortnightly; Catholic; Editor DOMENICO RONCHITELLI; circ. 17,000.

Humanitas: Via Gabriele Rosa 71, 25121 Brescia; tel. (030) 46451; fax (030) 2400605; e-mail redazione@morcelliana.it; internet www.morcelliana.it; f. 1946; every 2 months; religion, philosophy, science, politics, history, sociology, literature, etc.; Dir ILARIO BERTOLETTI.

Protestantesimo: Via Pietro Cossa 42, 00193 Roma; tel. (06) 3207055; fax (06) 3201040; e-mail protestantesimo@facoltavaldese.org; internet www.facoltavaldese.org; f. 1946; quarterly; Waldensian review; Dir Prof. FULVIO FERRARIO.

Rivista di Storia della Chiesa in Italia: Via Merulana 124A, 00185 Roma; e-mail maria.lupi@uniroma3.it; internet www.vitaepensiero.it; f. 1947; 2 a year; Editor AGOSTINO PARAVICINI BAGLIANI.

Science, Technology and Medicine

Alberi e Territorio: Via Goito 13, 40126 Bologna; tel. (051) 65751; e-mail redazione.edagricole@ilsole24ore.com; internet www.edagricole.it; f. 2004 as successor to *Monti e Boschi* (f. 1949); 6 a year; ecology and forestry; Editor ELIA ZAMBONI; circ. 4,500.

Focus: Via Battistotti Sassi 11A, 20133 Segrate, Milano; tel. (02) 762101; fax (02) 76013379; e-mail redazione@focus.it; internet www.focus.it; f. 1992; monthly; popular science and sociology; publr Gruner+Jahr/Mondadori; Editor-in-Chief FRANCESCA FOLDA; circ. 296,668.

Il Nuovo Medico d'Italia: Via Valpolicella 19, 00141 Roma; tel. and fax (06) 86398937; e-mail redazione@numedionline.it; internet www.numedionline.it; monthly; medical science; Dir Dott. MARIO BERNARDINI.

Newton: Corso Venezia 6, 20121 Milano; e-mail info@ridoservizieditoriali.it; internet newton.corriere.it; f. 1997; monthly; popular science; circ. 91,124.

Rivista Geografica Italiana: Via S. Gallo 10, 50129 Firenze; tel. and fax (055) 2757956; fax (055) 2725956; e-mail redazione@rivistageograficaitaliana.it; internet www.rivistageograficaitaliana

.it; f. 1894; quarterly; geographical review; owned by Società di Studi Geografici; Dir BRUNO VECCHIO.

Women's Interest

A—Anna: Via San Marco 21, 20121 Milano; tel. (02) 25843213; f. 1933; weekly; Editor MARIA LATELLA; circ. 125,495 (2013).

Amica: Via Angelo Rizzoli 2, 20132 Milano; tel. (02) 25841; f. 1962; monthly; Dir DANIELA BIANCHINI; circ. 188,905 (2013).

Chi: Arnoldo Mondadori Editore, SpA, Via Mondadori 1, 20090 Segrate, Milano; tel. (02) 75421; fax (02) 75422302; e-mail chiposta@mondadori.it; f. 1995; weekly; celebrities, fashion; Dir ALFONSO SIGNORINI; circ. 286,068.

Confidenze: Arnoldo Mondadori Editore, SpA, Via Mondadori 1, 20090 Segrate, Milano; tel. (02) 75421; fax (02) 75422302; e-mail braccif@mondadori.it; f. 1946; weekly; Dir ANNALISA MONFREDA; circ. 93,339 (2013).

Cosmopolitan: Via Roberto Bracco, 6, 20159 Milano; tel. (02) 66191; internet www.cosmopolitan.it; f. 2000; monthly; Dir ANNALISA MONFREDA; circ. 124,419.

Donna Moderna: Arnoldo Mondadori Editore, SpA, Via Mondadori 1, 20090 Segrate, Milano; e-mail donnamoderna@mondadori.it; internet www.donnamoderna.com; f. 1988; weekly; Dir ANNALISA MONFREDA; circ. 277,600 (2013).

Gioia: Via Roberto Bracco, 6, 20159 Milano; tel. (02) 66191; f. 1937; weekly; Dir VERA MONTANARI; circ. 116,566 (2013).

Grazia: Arnoldo Mondadori Editore, SpA, Via Mondadori 1, 20090 Segrate, Milano; tel. (02) 75421; fax (02) 75422302; e-mail graziamagazine@mondadori.it; internet www.graziamagazine.it; f. 1938; weekly; Dir SILVIA GRILLI; circ. 160,254 (2013).

Intimità: Piazza Aspromonte 13, 20131 Milano; tel. (02) 70642307; fax (02) 70642306; e-mail intimita@quadratum.it; internet www .quadratum.it; f. 1946; weekly; Dir ANNA GIUSTI; circ. 210,363 (2013).

Vanity Fair: Condé Nast S.p.A., Piazza Castello 27, 20121 Milano; e-mail abbonati@condenast.it; internet www.vanityfair.it; f. 2003; monthly; fashion, women's interest; Editor-in-Chief ROBERTO DELERA; circ. 243,406 (2013).

Vogue Italia: Piazza Castello 27, 20121 Milano; tel. (02) 85611; fax (02) 8055716; internet www.vogue.it; monthly; Editor FRANCA SOZZANI; circ. 84,863 (2013).

NEWS AGENCIES

AdnKronos: Palazzo dell'Informazione, Piazza Mastai 9, 00153 Roma; tel. (06) 58017; fax (06) 5807807; e-mail comunicazione@ adnkronos.com; internet www.adnkronos.it; Dir-Gen. MASSIMO CICATIELLO.

Agenzia Giornalistica Italia (AGI): Via Ostiense 72, 00154 Roma; tel. (06) 519961; fax (06) 51996362; e-mail info@agi.it; internet www .agi.it; f. 1950; Pres. MASSIMO MONDAZZI.

Agenzia Nazionale Stampa Associata (ANSA): Via della Dataria 94, 00187 Roma; tel. (06) 67741; fax (06) 67746383; e-mail redazione .internet@ansa.it; internet www.ansa.it; f. 1945; co-operative, owned by 34 Italian newspapers; 22 regional offices in Italy and 79 brs internationally; service in Italian, Spanish, French, English; Pres. GIULIO ANSELMI; Dir-Gen. GIUSEPPE CERBONE.

Asca (Agenzia Stampa Quotidiana Nazionale): Via Ennio Quirino Visconti 8, 00193 Roma; tel. (06) 361484; e-mail agenzia@asca.it; internet www.asca.it; f. 1969; Dir CLAUDIO SONZOGNO.

Documentazioni Informazioni Resoconti (Dire): Via Giuseppe Marchi 4, 00161 Roma; tel. (06) 45499500; fax (06) 45499509; e-mail segr.direzione@dire.it; internet www.dire.it; Dir NICOLA PERRONE.

Inter Press Service International Association (IPS): Viale delle Terme di Caracalla, 00153 Roma; tel. (06) 57050053; fax (06) 57050052; e-mail headquarters@ips.org; internet www.ips.org; f. 1964; non-profit asscn; international daily news agency; Dir-Gen. RAMESH JAURA.

TM News: Via di Santa Maria 6, 00187 Roma; tel. (06) 695391; fax (06) 69539522; e-mail rcc@tmnews.it; internet www.tmnews.it; f. 2009; 60% owned by Gruppo Abete and 40% by Telecom Italia Media; Pres. BRUNETTO TINI.

PRESS ASSOCIATIONS

Associazione della Stampa Estera in Italia: Via della Umiltà 83C, 00187 Roma; tel. (06) 675911; fax (06) 67591262; e-mail segreteria@stampa-estera.it; internet www.stampa-estera.it; foreign correspondents' asscn; Pres. MAARTEN VAN AALDEREN; Sec. CONSTANZE REUSCHER.

Federazione Italiana Editori Giornali (FIEG): Via Piemonte 64, 00187 Roma; tel. (06) 46201401; fax (06) 4871109; e-mail fieg@fieg.it; internet www.fieg.it; f. 1950; fedn of newspaper and magazine publrs; Pres. MAURIZIO COSTA; 123 mems.

Federazione Nazionale della Stampa Italiana (FNSI): Corso Vittorio Emanuele II 349, 00186 Roma; tel. (06) 680081; fax (06) 6871444; e-mail segreteria.fnsi@fnsi.it; internet www.fnsi.it; f. 1908; 19 affiliated unions; Pres. GIOVANNI ROSSI; Sec.-Gen. FRANCESCO ANGELO SIDDI; 16,000 mems.

Unione Stampa Periodica Italiana (USPI): Viale Bardanzellu 95, 00155 Roma; tel. (06) 4071388; fax (06) 4066859; e-mail uspi@uspi .it; internet www.uspi.it; Pres. ANTONIO BARBIERATO; Gen. Sec. FRANCESCO SAVERIO VETERE; 4,500 mems.

Publishers

There are more than 300 major publishing houses and many smaller ones.

Adelphi Edizioni, SpA: Via S. Giovanni sul Muro 14, 20121 Milano; tel. (02) 725731; fax (02) 89010337; e-mail info@adelphi.it; internet www.adelphi.it; f. 1962; classics, philosophy, biography, music, art, psychology, religion and fiction; Pres. ROBERTO CALASSO.

Franco Angeli Editore Srl: Viale Monza 106, 20127 Milano; tel. (02) 2613268; fax (02) 26144793; e-mail redazione@francoangeli.it; internet www.francoangeli.it; f. 1955; academic and general non-fiction.

Armando Editore: Viale Trastevere 236, 00153 Roma; tel. (06) 5894525; fax (06) 5818564; e-mail info@armando.it; internet www .armando.it; f. 1950; philosophy, psychology, social sciences, languages, ecology, education; Man. Dir ENRICO IACOMETTI.

Bollati Boringhieri Editore: Corso Vittorio Emanuele II 86, 10121 Torino; tel. (011) 5591711; fax (011) 543024; e-mail info@ bollatiboringhieri.it; internet www.bollatiboringhieri.it; f. 1957; owned by Gruppo Editoriale Mauri Spagnol; history, economics, natural sciences, psychology, social and human sciences, fiction and literary criticism; Chair. ROMILDA BOLLATI; Editorial Dir RENZO GUIDIERI.

Bulzoni Editore: Via dei Liburni 14, 00185 Roma; tel. (06) 4455207; fax (06) 4450355; e-mail bulzoni@bulzoni.it; internet www.bulzoni.it; science, arts, fiction, textbooks; Man. Dir IVANA BULZONI.

Caltagirone Editore, SpA: Via Barberini 28, 00187 Roma; tel. (06) 45412200; fax (06) 45412299; e-mail invrel@caltagironegroup.it; internet www.caltagironeeditore.com; f. 1999; news publisher; Pres. FRANCESCO GAETANO CALTAGIRONE.

Cappelli Editore: Via Farini 14, 40124 Bologna; tel. (051) 239060; fax (051) 239286; f. 1880; medical science, history, politics, literature, textbooks; Chair. and Man. Dir MARIO MUSSO.

Casa Editrice Bonechi: Via dei Cairoli 18B, 50131 Firenze; tel. (055) 576841; fax (055) 5000766; e-mail info@bonechi.it; internet www.bonechi.com; f. 1973; art, travel, cooking; Pres. GIAMPAOLO BONECHI.

Casa Editrice Clueb Scarl (Cooperativa Libraria Universitaria Editrice Bologna): Via Marsala 31, 40126 Bologna; tel. (051) 220736; fax (051) 237758; e-mail vendite@clueb.it; internet www.clueb.com; f. 1959; university education, arts, business, history, literature; Man. Dir LUIGI GUARDIGLI.

Casa Editrice Idelson Gnocchi Srl: Via Michele Pietravalle 85, 80131 Napoli; tel. (081) 5464991; fax (081) 5453443; e-mail info@ idelson-gnocchi.com; internet www.idelson-gnocchi.com; f. 1908; medical and scientific; CEO GUIDO GNOCCHI.

Casa Editrice Leo S. Olschki: Via del Pozzetto 8, 50126 Firenze; tel. (055) 6530684; fax (055) 6530214; e-mail info@olschki.it; internet www.olschki.it; f. 1886; reference, periodicals, textbooks, humanities; Editorial Dir DANIELE OLSCHKI.

Casa Editrice Luigi Trevisini Srl: Via Tito Livio 12, 20137 Milano; tel. (02) 5450704; fax (02) 55195782; e-mail trevisini@ trevisini.it; internet www.trevisini.it; f. 1859; school textbooks; Dirs LUIGI TREVISINI, GIUSEPPINA TREVISINI.

Casa Editrice Marietti, SpA: Via Donizetti 41, 20122 Milano; tel. (02) 778899; fax (02) 76003491; e-mail mariettieditore@ mariettieditore.it; internet www.mariettieditore.it; f. 1820; religion, liturgy, theology, fiction, history, literature, philosophy, poetry, art; Editor GIOVANNI UNGARELLI.

Casa Ricordi, SpA: Via Benigno Crespi 19, 20159 Milano; tel. (02) 80282811; fax (02) 80282882; e-mail promozione.ricordi.Italy@ umusic.com; internet www.ricordi.it; f. 1808; music; Chair. CRISTIANO OSTINELLI.

CEDAM, SpA: Via Jappelli 5/6, 35121 Padova; tel. (049) 8239111; fax (049) 8752900; e-mail info@cedam.com; internet www.cedam .com; f. 1903; law, economics, political and social sciences, engineering, science, medicine, literature, philosophy, textbooks; Dir ANTONIO MILANI.

De Agostini Editore: Via Giovanni da Verrazano 15, 28100 Novara; tel. (0321) 4241; fax (0321) 471286; internet www.deagostini.it; f. 1901; geography, maps, encyclopaedias, dictionaries, art, literature, textbooks, science; Pres. PIETRO BOROLI; CEO LORENZO PELLICIOLI.

Editori Laterza: Via di Villa Sacchetti 17, 00197 Roma; tel. (06) 45465311; fax (06) 3223853; e-mail glaterza@laterza.it; internet www.laterza.it; f. 1885; belles-lettres, biography, reference, religion, art, classics, history, economics, philosophy, social sciences; Editorial Dirs ALESSANDRO LATERZA, GIUSEPPE LATERZA.

Editrice Àncora: Via G. B. Niccolini 8, 20154 Milano; tel. (02) 3456081; fax (02) 34560866; e-mail editrice@ancoralibri.it; internet www.ancoralibri.it; f. 1934; religious, educational; Dir GILBERTO ZINI.

Editrice Ave (Anonima Veritas Editrice): Via Aurelia 481, 00165 Roma; tel. (06) 661321; fax (06) 6620207; e-mail info@editriceave.it; internet www.editriceave.it; f. 1935; theology, sociology, pedagogy, psychology, essays, learned journals, religious textbooks; Pres. ARMANDO OBERTI.

Editrice Ciranna: Via G. Besio 143, 90145 Palermo; tel. (091) 224499; fax (091) 311064; e-mail info@ciranna.it; internet www.ciranna.it; f. 1950; school textbooks; Editorial Dir LUCA POMARA.

Editrice La Scuola, SpA: Via Antonio Gramsci 26, 25121 Brescia; tel. (030) 29931; fax (030) 2993299; e-mail redazione@lascuola.it; internet www.lascuola.it; f. 1904; educational magazines, educational textbooks, audiovisual aids and toys; Chair. Dott. Ing. ELIA ZAMBONI.

Edizioni Borla Srl: Via delle Fornaci 50, 00165 Roma; tel. (06) 39375379; fax (06) 39376620; e-mail borla@edizioni-borla.it; internet www.edizioni-borla.it; f. 1853; religion, philosophy, psychoanalysis, ethnology, literature; Man. Dir JESSICA D'AGOSTINO.

Edizioni Lavoro: Via G. M. Lancisi 25, 00161 Roma; tel. (06) 44251174; fax (06) 44251177; e-mail info@edizionilavoro.it; internet www.edizionilavoro.it; f. 1982; history, politics, political philosophy, sociology, religion, Islamic, African, Arab and Caribbean literature; Chair. ANTONIO LOMBARDI.

Edizioni Mediterranee Srl: Via Flaminia 109, 00196 Roma; tel. (06) 32235433; fax (06) 3236277; e-mail info@edizionimediterranee.net; internet www.edizionimediterranee.it; f. 1953; alchemy, astrology, esoterism, meditation, natural medicine, parapsychology, hobbies, martial arts, zen.

Edizioni Rosminiane Sodalitas Sas: Corso Umberto I 15, 28838 Stresa; tel. (0323) 30091, fax (0323) 31623; e-mail edizioni.rosminiane@rosmini.it; internet www.rosmini.it; f. 1925; philosophy, theology, *Rivista Rosminiana* (quarterly); Dir Prof. PIER PAOLO OTTONELLO.

Edizioni San Paolo: Piazza Soncino 5, 20092 Cinisello Balsamo—Milano; tel. (02) 660751; fax (02) 66075211; e-mail sanpaoloedizioni@stpauls.it; internet www.edizionisanpaolo.it; f. 1914; Catholic; Gen. Man. VINCENZO SANTARCANGELO.

Edizioni Scientifiche Italiane, SpA (ESI): Via Chiatamone 7, 80121 Napoli; tel. (081) 7645443; fax (081) 7646477; e-mail info@edizioniesi.it; internet www.edizioniesi.it; f. 1945; law, economics, literature, arts, history, science; Pres. PIETRO PERLINGIERI.

Edizioni Studium: Via Crescenzio 25, 00193 Roma; tel. (06) 6865846; fax (06) 6875456; e-mail info@edizionistudium.it; internet www.edizionistudium.it; f. 1927; philosophy, literature, sociology, pedagogy, religion, economics, law, science, history, psychology; Pres. VINCENZO CAPPELLATTI.

Giulio Einaudi Editore, SpA: Via Umberto Biancamano 2, 10121 Torino; tel. (011) 56561; fax (011) 542903; e-mail einaudi@einaudi.it; internet www.einaudi.it; f. 1933; fiction, classics, general; CEO ENRICO SELVA CODDÈ.

Giangiacomo Feltrinelli Editore, Srl: Via Andegari 6, 20121 Milano; tel. (02) 725721; fax (02) 72572500; e-mail ufficio.stampa@feltrinelli.it; internet www.feltrinellieditore.it; f. 1954; fiction, juvenile, science, technology, history, literature, political science, philosophy; Chair. CARLO FELTRINELLI.

Garzanti Libri, SpA: Via Giuseppe Parini, 14 20121 Milano; tel. (02) 00623201; fax (02) 00623260; e-mail info@garzantilibri.it; internet www.garzantilibri.it; f. 1938; owned by Gruppo Editoriale Mauri Spagnol; literature, poetry, science, art, history, politics, encyclopaedias; Chair. GHERARDO COLOMBO; CEO STEFANO MAURI.

Ghisetti e Corvi Editori: Corso Concordia 7, 20129 Milano; tel. (02) 76006232; fax (02) 76009468; e-mail redazione@ghisetticorvi.it; internet www.ghisetticorvi.it; f. 1936; educational textbooks.

G. Giappichelli Editore Srl: Via Po 21, 10124 Torino; tel. (011) 8153511; fax (011) 8125100; e-mail contabilit@giappichelli.it; internet www.giappichelli.it; f. 1921; university publications on law, economics, politics and sociology.

Giunti Editore, SpA: Via Bolognese 165, 50139 Firenze; tel. (055) 50621; fax (055) 2985062; e-mail info@giunti.it; internet www.giunti.it; f. 1841; art, psychology, literature, science, law; CEO MARTINO MONTANARINI.

Gruppo Editoriale Mauri Spagnol, SpA: Via Gherardini 10, 20145 Milano; internet www.maurispagnol.it; f. 2005; owns Bollati Boringhieri Editore, La Cocinella, Casa Editrice Corbaccio, Garzanti Libri, Guanda, Longanesi, Editrice Nord, Ponte alle Grazie, Adriano Salani Editore, TEA (Tascabili degli Editori Associati), Antonio Vallardi Editore, and 50% of SuperPocket; Pres. STEFANO MAURI; CEO LUIGI SPAGNOL.

Gruppo Editoriale il Saggiatore: Via Melzo 9, 20129 Milano; tel. (02) 201301; fax (02) 29513061; e-mail commerciale@saggiatore.it; internet www.saggiatore.it; f. 1958; art, fiction, social sciences, history, travel, current affairs, popular science; Pres. LUCA FORMENTON.

Gruppo Ugo Mursia Editore, SpA: Via Melchiorre Gioia 45, 20124 Milano; tel. (02) 84251100; fax (02) 84251137; e-mail info@mursia.com; internet www.mursia.com; f. 1955; general fiction and non-fiction, reference, art, history, nautical books, philosophy, biography, sports, children's books; Gen. Man. FIORENZA MURSIA.

Guida Monaci, SpA: Via Salaria 1319, 00138 Roma; tel. (06) 8887777; fax (06) 8889996; e-mail infoitaly@italybygm.it; internet www.italybygm.it; f. 1870; commercial and industrial, financial, administrative and medical directories; Dir Ing. GIANCARLO ZAPPONINI.

Hearst Magazines Italia: Via Roberto Bracco 6, 20159 Milano; tel. (02) 66191; e-mail abbonamenti@hachette.it; internet www.hearst.it; f. 1969 as Rusconi Libri Srl; magazines; Pres. DIDIER QUILLOT.

S. Lattes e C. Editori, SpA: Via Confienza 6, 10121 Torino; tel. (011) 5625335; fax (011) 5625070; e-mail info@latteseditori.it; internet www.latteseditori.it; f. 1893; technical, textbooks; Pres. CATERINA BOTTARI LATTES; Man. Dir RENATA LATTES.

Levrotto e Bella, Libreria Editrice Universitaria: Via Pigafetta Antonio 2E, 10129 Torino; tel. (011) 5097367; fax (011) 504025; e-mail ammin@levrotto-bella.net; internet www.levrotto-bella.net; f. 1911; university textbooks; Man. Dir Dott. ELISABETTA GUALINI.

Liguori Editore Srl: Via Posillipo 394, 80123 Napoli; tel. (081) 5751272; fax (081) 5751231; e-mail info@liguori.it; internet www.liguori.it; f. 1949; linguistics, mathematics, engineering, economics, law, history, philosophy, sociology; Man. Dir Dott. GUIDO LIGUORI.

Loescher Editore: Via Vittorio Amedeo II 18, 10121 Torino; tel. (011) 5654111; fax (011) 5625822; e-mail mail@loescher.it; internet www.loescher.it; f. 1861; school textbooks, general literature, academic books, Chair. LORENZO ENRIQUES.

Longanesi e C., SpA: Via Gherardini 10, 20145 Milano; tel. (02) 34597620; fax (02) 34597212; e-mail info@longanesi.it; internet www.longanesi.it; f. 1946; owned by Gruppo Editoriale Mauri Spagnol; art, archaeology, culture, history, philosophy, fiction; Man. Dir STEFANO MAURI.

Arnoldo Mondadori Editore, SpA: Via Mondadori 1, 20090 Segrate, Milano; tel. (02) 75421; fax (02) 75422302; e-mail redazione.internet@mondadori.it; internet www.mondadori.it; f. 1907; books, magazines, printing, radio, advertising; CEO ERNESTO MAURI.

Neri Pozza Editore, SpA: Via E. Fermi 205, 36100 Vicenza; tel. (0444) 396323; fax (0444) 396325; e-mail info@neripozza.it; internet www.neripozza.it; f. 1946; art, fiction, history, politics; Pres. VITTORIO MINCATO; Dir ALESSANDRO ZELGER.

Palombi & Partner Srl: Via Gregorio VII 224, 00165 Roma; tel. (06) 636970; fax (06) 635746; e-mail info@palombieditori.it; internet www.palombieditori.it; f. 1914; history, art, etc. of Rome; Man. Dir Dott. FRANCESCO PALOMBI.

Pearson Italia, SpA: Via Archimede 10/23/51, 20129 Milano; tel. (02) 748231; fax (02) 74823278; internet www.pearson.it; f. 1946; school and university textbooks.

Petrini Editore: Strada del Portone 179, 10095 Grugliasco, Torino; tel. (011) 2098741; fax (011) 2098765; e-mail redazione@petrini.it; internet www.petrini.it; f. 1872; school textbooks.

Piccin Nuova Libraria, SpA: Via Altinate 107, 35121 Padova; tel. (049) 655566; fax (049) 8750693; e-mail info@piccinonline.com; internet www.piccinonline.com; f. 1952; scientific and medical textbooks and journals; Man. Dir Dott. MASSIMO PICCIN.

RCS Libri, SpA: Via San Marco 21, 20121 Milano; tel. (02) 25841; fax (02) 50952647; internet www.rcslibri.it; f. 1947; imprints include Rosellina Archinto Editore, Bompiani, BUR (Biblioteca Universale Rizzoli), Etas Srl, Fabbri, Marsilio Editore, La Nuova Editrice, SpA, Rizzoli, Sansoni, Sonzogno; fiction, children's books, education, textbooks, reference, literature, art books; Chair. ANGELO PROVASOLI.

Rosenberg & Sellier: Via Andrea Doria 14, 10123 Torino; tel. (011) 8127820; fax (011) 8127808; e-mail info@rosenbergesellier.it; internet www.rosenbergesellier.it; f. 1883; economics, history, gender studies, social sciences, philosophy, linguistics, Latin, dictionaries, scientific journals; Chair. and Man. Dir UGO GIANNI ROSENBERG.

Adriano Salani Editore Srl: Via Gherardini 10, 20145 Milano; tel. (02) 34597624; fax (02) 34597206; e-mail info@salani.it; internet www.salani.it; f. 1988; fiction, children's books; Editor LUIGI SPAGNOL.

Skira Editore: Palazzo Casati Stampa, Via Torino 61, 20123 Milano; tel. (02) 724441; fax (02) 72444211; e-mail skira@skira .net; internet www.skira.net; f. 1928; arts and literature; Pres. MASSIMO VITTA ZELMAN.

Società Editrice Dante Alighieri Srl: Via Somalia 5, 00199 Roma; tel. (06) 3725870; fax (06) 37514807; e-mail nuovarivistastorica@ dantealighierisrl.191.it; internet www.nuovarivistastorica.it; f. 1917; school textbooks, science and general culture; Dir GIGLIOLA SOLDI RONDININI.

Società Editrice Internazionale, SpA (SEI): Corso Regina Margherita 176, 10152 Torino; tel. (011) 52271; fax (011) 5211320; e-mail editoriale@seieditrice.com; internet www.seieditrice.com; f. 1908; textbooks, religion, history, education, multimedia; Head of Editorial Dept ULISSE JACOMUZZI.

Società Editrice Il Mulino: Strada Maggiore 37, 40125 Bologna; tel. (051) 256011; fax (051) 6486014; e-mail info@mulino.it; internet www.mulino.it; f. 1954; politics, history, philosophy, social sciences, linguistics, literary criticism, law, psychology, economics, journals; Pres. ALESSANDRO CAVALLI.

Il Sole 24 Ore Edagricole: Via Goito 13, 40126 Bologna; tel. (051) 65751; fax (051) 6575800; e-mail redazione.edagricole@ilsole24ore .com; internet www.edagricole.it; group includes Calderini (f. 1960; art, sport, electronics, mechanics, university and school textbooks, travel guides, nursing, architecture) and Edagricole (f. 1935; agriculture, veterinary science, gardening, biology, textbooks); Pres. Prof. GIANCARLO CERUTTI; Man. Dir DONATELLA TREU.

Sugarco Edizioni Srl: Via don Gnocchi 4, 20148 Milano; tel. (02) 4078370; fax (02) 4078493; e-mail info@sugarcoedizioni.it; internet www.sugarcoedizioni.it; f. 1957; fiction, biography, history, philosophy, Italian classics, Catholic apologetics; Gen. Man. ATTILIO TRENTINI.

Ulrico Hoepli Casa Editrice Libraria, SpA: Via Hoepli 5, 20121 Milano; tel. (02) 864871; fax (02) 864322; e-mail libreria@hoepli.it; internet www.hoepli.it; f. 1870; grammars, art, technical, scientific and school books, encyclopaedias; Chair. Dott. CARLO HOEPLI; Man. Dir GIOVANNI ENRICO HOEPLI.

UTET, SpA (Unione Tipografico-Editrice Torinese): Lungo Dora Colletta 67, 10153 Torino; tel. (011) 2099111; fax (011) 2099394; e-mail assistenza@utet.it; internet www.utet.it; f. 1791; part of Gruppo De Agostini; university and specialized editions on history, geography, art, literature, economics, sciences, encyclopaedias, dictionaries, etc.; Pres. ANTONIO BELLONI.

Vallecchi Editore, Srl: Via Ponte All'Asse 7, 50144 Firenze; tel. (055) 324761; fax (055) 3980561; e-mail ufficiostampa@vallecchi.it; internet www.vallecchi.it; f. 1903; art, fiction, literature, essays, media; Pres. FERNANDO CORONA.

Vita e Pensiero: Largo A. Gemelli 1, 20123 Milano; tel. (02) 72342335; fax (02) 72342260; e-mail editrice.vp@unicatt.it; internet www.vitaepensiero.it; f. 1918; publisher of the Catholic University of the Sacred Heart, Milan; philosophy, literature, social sciences, theology, history; Dir AURELIO MOTTOLA.

GOVERNMENT PUBLISHING HOUSE

Istituto Poligrafico e Zecca dello Stato (IPZS): Via Salaria 1027, 00138 Roma; tel. (06) 85081; fax (06) 85082517; e-mail informazioni@ ipzs.it; internet www.ipzs.it; f. 1928; art, literary, scientific, technical books and reproductions; Pres. and CEO Dott. MAURIZIO PRATO.

PUBLISHERS' ASSOCIATION

Associazione Italiana Editori (AIE): Corso di Porta Romana 108, 20122 Milano; tel. (02) 89280800; fax (02) 89280860; e-mail aie@aie .it; internet www.aie.it; f. 1869; Dir ALFIERI LORENZON; 420 mems.

Broadcasting and Communications

REGULATORY AUTHORITY

Autorità per le Garanzie nelle Comunicazioni (AGCOM): Centro Direzionale, Isola B5, Torre Francesco, 80143 Napoli; tel. (081) 7507111; fax (081) 7507616; e-mail info@agcom.it; internet www.agcom.it; f. 1997; regulatory authority with responsibility for telecommunications, broadcasting and publishing; Pres. ANGELO M. CARDANI; Sec.-Gen. FRANCESCO SCLAFANI.

TELECOMMUNICATIONS

3 Italia: Via Leonardo da Vinci 1, 20090 Trezzano sul Naviglio, Milano; tel. (02) 44581; fax (02) 445812713; internet www.tre.it; f. 2003; owned by Hutchison Whampoa Ltd (Hong Kong); mobile cellular telecommunications; CEO VINCENZO NOVARI.

FASTWEB: Via Caracciolo 51, 20155 Milano; tel. (02) 45451; fax (02) 45454811; internet www.fastweb.it; f. 2004 by merger of FastWeb and e.Biscom; offers fixed-line and mobile cellular telecommunications services, digital television and broadband internet services; owned by Swisscom AG; Chair. URS SCHAEPPI; Dir-Gen. ALBERTO CALCAGNO.

Telecom Italia: Piazza Affari 2, 20123 Milano; tel. (02) 85951; e-mail investitori.individuali@telecomitalia.it; internet www .telecomitalia.it; Italy's leading telecommunications operator; controlling stake owned by Telco, a consortium of Telefónica (Spain) and 4 Italian cos; Pres. GIUSEPPE RECCHI; CEO MARCO PATUANO.

TeleTu: Via Cassanese 210, 20090 Segrate, Milano; e-mail ufficio-stampa.tele2@tele2.it; internet www.teletu.it; f. 1999; fixed-line telecommunications and broadband internet services; owned by Vodafone Italia; Chair. SAVERIO TRIDICO; CEO MARCO BRAGADIN.

TIM (Telecom Italia Mobile): Via Luigi Rizzo 22, 00136 Roma; tel. (06) 39001; internet www.tim.it; f. 1995; owned by Telecom Italia; mobile cellular telecommunications.

Tiscali Italia: Loc. Sa Illetta, SS 195 Km 2300, 09123 Cagliari; tel. (070) 46011; fax (070) 4601296; e-mail info@tiscali.com; internet www.tiscali.it; f. 1998; internet service provider; Pres. and CEO RENATO SORU; Dir-Gen. LUCA SCANO.

Vodafone Italia: Via Caboto 15, 20094 Corsico, Milano; tel. (02) 41431; internet www.vodafone.it; f. 1995; mobile cellular telecommunications; Pres. ALEX ZANARDI; CEO ALDO BISIO.

WIND Telecomunicazioni, SpA: Via Cesare Giulio Viola 48, 00148 Roma; tel. (06) 831111; internet www.windgroup.it; f. 1997; brands include WIND (mobile cellular telecommunications services) and Infostrada (fixed-line telecommunications and broadband internet services); Pres. JO OLAV LUNDER; CEO MAXIMO IBARRA.

BROADCASTING

Radio

Rai—Radiotelevisione Italiana: Viale Mazzini 14, 00195 Roma; tel. (06) 38781; fax (06) 3725680; e-mail radio@rai.it; internet www .radio.rai.it; f. 1924; a public share capital co; programmes comprise Radio Uno (general), Radio Due (recreational), Radio Tre (cultural); there are also regional programmes in Italian and in the languages of minority ethnic groups, and a foreign service, Rai International; Pres. ANNA MARIA TARANTOLA; Dir-Gen. LUIGI GUBITOSI.

Independent Stations

Radio Deejay: CP 314, Milano; tel. (02) 342522; e-mail diretta@ deejay.it; internet www.deejay.it; f. 1982; propr Gruppo Editoriale L'Espresso, SpA; popular music; Dir GUIDO QUINTINO MARIOTTI.

Radio Italia Solo Musica Italiana: Viale Europa 49, 20093 Cologno Monzese, Milano; tel. (02) 254441; e-mail diretta@ radioitalia.it; internet www.radioitalia.it; f. 1982.

Radio Maria: Via Milano 12, 22036 Erba, Como; tel. (031) 610600; e-mail info.ita@radiomaria.org; internet www.radiomaria.it; f. 1987; Roman Catholic; founder mem. of World Family of Radio Maria, comprising 40 national asscns; Dir Fr LIVIO FANZAGA.

RDS Radio Dimensione Suono: Via Pier Ruggiero Piccio 55, 20122 Roma; tel. (06) 377041; e-mail customercare@rds.it; internet www.rds.it; f. 1978.

RTL 102.5: Via Scotti 11, 24122 Bergamo; tel. (02) 251515; fax (02) 25096201; e-mail ufficiostampa@rtl.it; internet www.rtl.it; f. 1975; Pres. LORENZO SURACI.

Rundfunk Anstalt Südtirol (RAS): Europaallee 164A, 39100 Bozen; tel. (0471) 546666; fax (0471) 200378; e-mail info@ras.bz.it; internet www.ras.bz.it; f. 1975; relays television and radio broadcasts from Germany, Austria and Switzerland to the population of South Tyrol; Pres. RUDI GAMPER; Dir GEORG PLATTNER.

Television

There are two main national television channels: the state-owned Rai—Radiotelevisione Italiana and the Gruppo Mediaset. The process to switch from analogue to digital broadcasting was completed in 2012.

Rai—Radiotelevisione Italiana: Viale Mazzini 14, 00195 Roma; tel. (06) 38781; fax (06) 3725680; e-mail rai-tv@rai.it; internet www .rai.it; f. 1924; operates 3 terrestrial channels, Rai 1, Rai 2 and Rai 3; satellite and digital channels include RaiNews24, Rai Sport and Rai Gulp (children's programmes); also broadcasts local programmes in Italian and in German for the South Tyrol; Pres. ANNA MARIA TARANTOLA; Dir-Gen. LUIGI GUBITOSI.

Independent Television Companies

Gruppo Mediaset: Piazza SS Giovanni e Paolo 8, 00184 Roma; tel. (06) 77081; e-mail mediaset@mediaset.it; internet www .gruppomediaset.it; f. 1993; operates Canale 5, Italia 1 and Rete 4; 41.3% stake owned by Fininvest; Pres. FEDELE CONFALONIERI; Vice-Pres. PIER SILVIO BERLUSCONI; Man. Dir GIULIANO ADREANI.

Rundfunk Anstalt Südtirol (RAS): see Radio.

Sky Italia: CP 13057, 20141 Milano; tel. (02) 70027300; e-mail info@ sky.it; internet www.sky.it; f. 2003; owned by 21st Century Fox (USA); broadcasts digital satellite channels; Chief Exec. ANDREA ZAPPIA.

Telecom Italia Media: Via della Pineta Sacchetti 229, 00168 Roma; tel. (06) 355841; e-mail carlo.demartino@telecomitalia.it; internet www.telecomitaliamedia.it; subsidiary of Telecom Italia, SpA; digital terrestrial broadcaster; operates 2 channels, La7 and MTV Italia; Pres. SEVERINO SALVEMINI; Man. Dir MARCO PATUANO.

Finance

(cap. = capital; res = reserves; dep. = deposits; m. = million; amounts in euros; brs = branches)

In 2011, of the 740 banks in existence, 214 were private banks, 411 were banche di credit cooperativo (co-operative banks), 37 were banche popolar (a form of savings bank) and 72 were branches of foreign banks.

BANKING

Central Bank

Banca d'Italia: Via Nazionale 91, 00184 Roma; tel. (06) 47921; fax (06) 47922983; e-mail email@bancaditalia.it; internet www .bancaditalia.it; f. 1893; cap. 0.2m., res 20,078.7m., dep. 64,061.9m. (Dec. 2009); Gov. IGNAZIO VISCO; Dir-Gen. FABRIZIO SACCOMANNI; 74 brs.

Major Banks

Banca Carige, SpA (Cassa di Risparmio di Genova e Imperia): Via Cassa di Risparmio 15, 16123 Genova; tel. (010) 5791; fax (010) 5794000; e-mail carige@carige.it; internet www.gruppocarige.it; f. 1846; name changed as above in 1991; cap. 2,177.2m., res 1,510.7m., dep. 21,357.3m. (Dec. 2012); Chair. Dott. GIOVANNI BERNESCHI; Gen. Man. ENNIO LA MONICA.

Banca Carime, SpA: Viale Crati, 87100 Cosenza; tel. (0984) 8011; fax (0984) 806988; internet www.carime.it; f. 1998 as a result of merger of Carical, Carisal and Caripuglia savings banks; 92.8% owned by Gruppo Unione di Banche Italiane (UBI Banca); cap. 1,468.2m., res 75.7m., dep. 5,275.9m. (Dec. 2012); Chair. ANDREA PISANI MASSAMORMILE; Gen. Man. RAFFAELE AVANTAGGIATO; 255 brs.

Banca CR Firenze, SpA: Via Carlo Magno 7, 50127 Firenze; tel. (055) 26121; fax (055) 2613872; e-mail estero@bancacrfirenze.it; internet www.bancacrfirenze.it; f. 1829; name changed as above in 2003; 89.7% stake owned by Intesa Sanpaolo, SpA; cap. 831.4m., res 581.8m., dep. 19,244.7m. (Dec. 2012); Chair. and Pres. AURELIANO BENEDETTI; Gen. Man. and CEO LUCIANO NEBBIA; 367 brs and agencies.

Banca Fideuram, SpA: Piazzale Giulio Douhet 31, 00143 Milano; tel. (06) 59021; fax (06) 59022634; internet www.bancafideuram.it; f. 1913; name changed as above in 1992; owned by Intesa Sanpaolo, SpA; cap. 186.3m., res 536.2m., dep. 7,239.9m. (Dec. 2012); Pres. SALVATORE MACCARONE; Gen. Man. MATTEO COLAFRANCESCO; 53 brs.

Banca IMI: Piazza Giordano dell'Amore 3, 20121 Milano; tel. (02) 72611; fax (02) 77512030; e-mail info@bancaimi.it; internet www .bancaimi.it; f. 2007 by merger of Banca d'Intermediazione Mobiliare, SpA and Banca Caboto, SpA; owned by Intesa Sanpaolo, SpA; cap. 962.5m., res 1,872.2m., dep. 10,883.9m. (Dec. 2012); Chair. EMILIO OTTOLENGHI; Man. Dir ANDREA MUNARI.

Banca delle Marche, SpA: Via Alessandro Ghislieri 6, 60035 Jesi; tel. (0731) 5391; fax (0731) 539695; e-mail info@bancamarche.it; internet www.bancamarche.it; f. 1994; cap. 662.7m., res 822.9m., dep. 14,078m. (Dec. 2012); Chair. MICHELE AMBROSINI; Gen. Man. MASSIMO BIANCONI; 293 brs.

Banca del Mezzogiorno–MedioCredito Centrale: Via Piemonte 51, 00187 Roma; tel. (06) 47911; fax (06) 47913130; e-mail mcc@mcc .it; internet www.mcc.it; f. 1952, renamed as above following demerger with Unicredit, SpA in 2011; cap. 132.5m., res 5.9m., dep. 117.3m. (Dec. 2012); Chair. MASSIMO SARMI; Man. Dir PIETRO D'ANZI.

Banca Monte dei Paschi di Siena, SpA (Mps): Piazza Salimbeni 3, 53100 Siena; tel. (0577) 294111; fax (0577) 294313; e-mail info@ banca.mps.it; internet www.mps.it; f. 1472; jt-stock co; part of Gruppo Montepaschi, which also includes Banca Antonveneta and Biverbanca (Cassa di Risparmio di Biella e Vercelli); cap. 7,484.5m.,

res 2,137.6m., dep. 104,941m. (Dec. 2012); Chair. ALESSANDRO PROFUMO; CEO FABRIZIO VIOLA; 2,744 brs.

Banca Nazionale del Lavoro, SpA: Via Vittorio Veneto 119, 00187 Roma; tel. (06) 47021; fax (06) 47027336; e-mail redazionebnl@ bnlmail.com; internet www.bnl.it; f. 1913; owned by BNP Paribas (France); cap. 2,076.9m., res 3,280.1m., dep. 50,289.5m. (Dec. 2012); Chair. Dott. LUIGI ABETE; Gen. Man. FABIO GALLIA; 864 brs.

Banca Popolare di Bergamo: Piazza Vittorio Veneto 8, 24122 Bergamo; tel. (035) 392111; fax (035) 392910; e-mail info@bpb.it; internet www.bpb.it; f. 1869; co-operative bank; name changed as above in 2003 following merger; 93% owned by Unione di Banche Italiane (UBI Banca); cap. 1,350.5m., res 812.6m., dep. 13,429.6m. (Dec. 2012); Chair. EMILIO ZANETTI; Man. Dir GIUSEPPE MASNAGA; 357 brs.

Banca Popolare Commercio e Industria, SpA: CP 10167, Via della Moscova 33, 20121 Milano; tel. (02) 62755; fax (02) 62755640; e-mail intbkg@bpci.it; internet www.bpci.it; f. 1888; 64.4% stake owned by Unione di Banche Italiane (UBI Banca); cap. 934.2m., res 226.3m., dep. 6,102.7m. (Dec. 2012); Chair. MARIO CERA; Gen. Man. FRANCESCO IORIO; 234 brs.

Banca Popolare dell'Emilia Romagna Società Cooperativa: Via San Carlo 8/20, 41121 Modena; tel. (059) 2021111; fax (059) 220537; e-mail relest@bper.it; internet www.bper.it; f. 1867; cap. 998.2m., res 3,075.8m., dep. 38,557.4m. (Dec. 2012); Chair. ETTORE CASELLI; Gen. Man. FABRIZIO TOGNI; 323 brs.

Banca Popolare di Milano Scarl: Piazza F. Meda 4, 20121 Milano; tel. (02) 77001; fax (02) 77002993; e-mail bipiemme@bpm.it; internet www.bpm.it; f. 1865; cap. 2,865.7m., res 1,579.1m., dep. 28,641.3m. (Dec. 2012); Pres., Supervisory Bd DINO PIERO GIARDA; Pres., Management Bd MARIO ANOLLI; 495 brs.

Banca Popolare di Sondrio Società Cooperativa per Azioni: Piazza Garibaldi 16, 23100 Sondrio; tel. (0342) 528111; fax (0342) 528204; e-mail info@popso.it; internet www.popso.it; f. 1871; cap. 924.4m., res 911.2m., dep. 25,579.5m. (Dec. 2012); Chair. and CEO PIERO MELAZZINI; Gen. Man. MARIO ALBERTO PEDRANZINI; 282 brs.

Banca Popolare di Vicenza: Via Battaglione Framarin 18, 36100 Vicenza; tel. (0444) 339111; fax (0444) 907125; e-mail intdep@popvi .it; internet www.popolarevicenza.it; f. 1866; cap. 296.9m., res 2,393.4m., dep. 23,323.5m. (Dec. 2012); Chair. GIOVANNI ZONIN; Gen. Man. SAMUELE SORATO; 544 brs.

Banca Regionale Europea, SpA: Via Monte di Pietà 7, 20121 Milano; tel. (02) 721211; fax (02) 865413; internet www.brebanca.it; f. 1995 by merger of Cassa di Risparmio di Cuneo and Banca del Monto di Lombardia; 56.5% stake owned by Unione di Banche Italiane (UBI Banca); cap. 587.9m., res 763.6m., dep. 5,662.2m. (Dec. 2012); Chair. LUIGI ROSSI DI MONTELERA; Gen. Man. ROBERTO TONIZZO; 229 brs.

Banco di Brescia San Paolo Cab, SpA (Banco di Brescia): Corso Martiri della Libertà 13, 25171 Brescia; tel. (030) 29921; fax (030) 2992470; e-mail info@bancodibrescia.com; internet www .bancodibrescia.com; f. 1999; 96.4% owned by Unione di Banche Italiane (UBI Banca); cap. 615.6m., res 775.1m., dep. 8,215.2m. (Dec. 2012); Chair. FRANCO POLOTTI; Dir-Gen. ELVIO SONNINO; 322 brs.

Banco di Sardegna, SpA: Viale Umberto 36, 07100 Sassari; tel. (079) 226000; fax (079) 226015; e-mail privacy@bancosardegna.it; internet www.bancosardegna.it; f. 1953; cap. 155.2m., res 1,021.5m., dep. 8,042.1m. (Dec. 2012); Chair. Prof. FRANCO ANTONIO FARINA; Gen. Man. Dott. ALESSANDRO VANDELLI; 392 brs.

Banco Popolare Società Cooperativa: Piazza Nogara 2, 37121 Verona; tel. (45) 8675111; e-mail ufficio.stampa@bancopopolare.it; internet www.bancopopolare.it; f. 2007 by merger of Banca Popolare Italiana and Banco Popolare di Verona e Novara; cap. 4,294.2m., res 3,414.3m., dep. 56,427.9m. (Dec. 2012); Chair., Supervisory Bd CARLO FRATTA PASINI; Chair., Management Bd VITTORIO CODA.

Cassa di Risparmio in Bologna, SpA (CARISBO): Via Farini 22, 40124 Bologna; tel. (051) 6454111; fax (051) 6454366; internet www .carisbo.it; f. 1837; owned by Intesa Sanpaolo, SpA; cap. 696.7m., res 191.2m., dep. 8,413.8m. (Dec. 2011); Pres. and Chair. FILIPPO CAVAZUTTI; Gen. Man. GIUSEPPE FELIZIANI; 201 brs.

Cassa di Risparmio di Parma e Piacenza, SpA (Cariparma): Via Università 1, 43100 Parma; tel. (0521) 912111; fax (0521) 912976; e-mail crprpc@cariparma.it; internet www.cariparma.it; f. 1860; name changed as above in 1993; 75% stake owned by Crédit Agricole SA (France); cap. 876.8m., res 3,346.3m., dep. 26,395.2m. (Dec. 2012); CEO GIAMPIERO MAIOLI; 537 brs.

Cassa di Risparmio di Venezia, SpA: San Marco 4216, Venezia 30124; tel. (041) 5291111; fax (041) 5292336; internet www.carive.it; f. 1822; owned by Intesa Sanpaolo, SpA; cap. 284.5m., res 84.8m., dep. 3,673.1m. (Dec. 2011); Chair. GIOVANNI SAMMARTINI; Gen. Man. MASSIMO MAZZEGA.

Credito Bergamasco, SpA: Largo Porta Nuova 2, 24122 Bergamo; tel. (035) 393111; fax (035) 393144; e-mail ufficio.estero@creberg.it; internet www.creberg.it; f. 1891 as Banca Piccolo Credito

Bergamasco; name changed as above in 1969; 88.9% owned by Banco Popolare Società Cooperativa; cap. 185.2m., res 1,209.2m., dep. 8,309.5m. (Dec. 2012); Pres. CESARE ZONCA; 245 brs.

Credito Emiliano, SpA (CREDEM): Via Emilia S. Pietro 4, 42100 Reggio-Emilia; tel. (0522) 582111; fax (0522) 433969; internet www .credem.it; f. 1910; cap. 332.4m., res 1,531.1m., dep. 18,539.1m. (Dec. 2012); Pres. GIORGIO FERRARI; CEO ADOLFO BIZZOCCHI; 563 brs.

Credito Valtellinese Società Cooperativa: Piazza Quadrivio 8, 23100 Sondrio; tel. (0342) 522111; fax (0342) 522700; e-mail creval@ creval.it; internet www.creval.it; f. 1908; present name adopted 2005; cap. 1,516.7m., res 787.6m., dep. 19,083.9m. (Dec. 2012); Chair. GIOVANNI DE CENSI; Man. Dir MIRO FIORDI; 107 brs.

Intesa Sanpaolo, SpA: Piazza San Carlo 156, 10121 Torino; tel. (011) 5551; fax (011) 5552989; e-mail investor.relations@ intesasanpaolo.com; internet www.group.intesasanpaolo.com; f. 2007 by merger of Sanpaolo IMI, SpA with Banca Intesa, SpA; cap. 8,546m., res 39,462m., dep. 285,343m. (Dec. 2012); CEO CARLO MESSINA.

UniCredit, SpA: Piazza Cordusio, 20123 Milano; tel. (02) 88621; fax (02) 88623034; e-mail info@unicreditgroup.eu; internet www .unicreditgroup.eu; f. 2007 by merger of Capitalia, SpA and Unicredito Italiano, SpA; present name adopted 2008; cap. 19,647.9m., res 42,271.2m., dep. 442,029.8m. (Dec. 2012); Chair. GIUSEPPE VITA; CEO FEDERICO GHIZZONI; 3 brs.

Unione di Banche Italiane Scpa (UBI Banca): Piazza Vittorio Veneto 8, 24122 Bergamo; tel. (035) 392111; fax (02) 392390; internet www.ubibanca.it; f. 2003 as Banche Popolari Unite; present name adopted 2007, following merger with Banca Lombarda e Piemontese; cap. 2,254.4, res 4,141.4m., dep. 64,256.4m. (Dec. 2012); Chair. EMILIO ZANETTI; Gen. Man. GRAZIANO CALDIANI.

FINANCIAL INSTITUTIONS

Dexia Crediop, SpA: Via Venti Settembre 30, 00187 Roma; tel. (06) 47711; fax (06) 47715952; e-mail cm@dexia-crediop.it; internet www .dexia-crediop.it; f. 1919; incorporated 1996 as CREDIOP; name changed as above in 2001; cap. 450.2m., res 668.7m., dep. 18,425.6m. (Dec. 2012); Dir JEAN BOURRELLY; Man. Dir JEAN LE NAOUR.

GE Capital Interbanca, SpA: Corso Venezia 56, 20121 Milano; tel. (02) 77311; fax (02) 76014913; e-mail marketing@interbanca.it; internet www.gecapitalinterbanca.it; f. 1961; acquired by GE Capital (UK) in Jan. 2009; name changed as above in 2012; cap. 217.3m., res 636.9m., dep. 270.8m. (Dec. 2012); Chair. FRANCESCO CARRI; 11 brs.

ICCREA Banca (Istituto Centrale del Credito Cooperativo): Via Lucrezia Romana 41, 00178 Roma; tel. (06) 72071; fax (06) 72077706; e-mail info@iccrea.bcc.it; internet www.iccrea.it; f. 1963; cap. 216.9m., res 237.6m., dep. 22,173.3m. (Dec. 2012); Chair. VITO LORENZO AUGUSTO DELL'ERBA; Gen. Man. LUCIANO GIORGIO GORNATI; 6 brs.

Mediobanca—Banca di Credito Finanziario, SpA: Piazzetta Enrico Cuccia 1, 20121 Milano; tel. (02) 88291; fax (02) 8829367; e-mail info@mediobanca.it; internet www.mediobanca.it; f. 1946; cap. 430.6m., res 6,589.9m., dep. 25,673.6m. (June 2013); Chair. RENATO PAGLIARO; Gen. Man. ALBERTO NAGEL; 1 br.

BANKERS' ORGANIZATION

Associazione Bancaria Italiana: Palazzo Altieri, Piazza del Gesù 49, 00186 Roma; tel. (06) 67671; fax (06) 6767457; e-mail abi@abi.it; internet www.abi.it; f. 1919; advocates the common interests of the banking industry; Pres. ANTONIO PATUELLI; Dir-Gen. Dott. GIOVANNI SABATINI; membership (1,003 mems) is composed of the following institutions: banks authorized to gather savings from the general public and exercise credit business as well as to perform other financial activities; brs and representative offices of foreign banks; asscns of banks or financial intermediaries; financial intermediaries engaging in one or more of the activities subject to mutual recognition under the Second Banking Directive or other financial activities subject to public prudential supervision.

STOCK EXCHANGES

Commissione Nazionale per le Società e la Borsa (CONSOB) (Commission for Companies and the Stock Exchange): Via G. B. Martini 3, 00198 Roma; tel. (06) 84771; fax (06) 8417707; e-mail consob@consob.it; internet www.consob.it; f. 1974; regulatory control over cos quoted on stock exchanges, convertible bonds, unlisted securities, insider trading, all forms of public saving except bank deposits and mutual funds; Dir-Gen. ANTONIO ROSATI.

Borsa Italiana (Italian Stock Exchange): Piazza degli Affari 6, 20123 Milano; tel. (02) 724261; fax (02) 72004333; e-mail media .relations@borsaitaliana.it; internet www.borsaitalia.it; merged with London Stock Exchange in 2007; Chair. ANGELO TANTAZZI; Pres. and CEO MASSIMO CAPUANO; 331 listed cos (Feb. 2010).

INSURANCE

In December 2013 there were 233 insurance and reinsurance companies operating in Italy, of which 131 were Italian.

Alleanza Toro, SpA: Via Mazzini 53, 10123 Torino; tel. (011) 0029111; fax (011) 837554; internet www.alleanzatoro.it; f. 2009 by the merger of Alleanza Assicurazioni, SpA and Toro Assicurazioni, SpA; life and non-life; Pres. LUIGI DE PUPPI.

Allianz, SpA: Largo Ugo Irneri 1, 34123 Trieste; tel. (40) 7781111; fax (40) 7781311; e-mail info@allianz.it; internet www.allianz.it; f. 1838; cap. 403m. (2008); Chair. CARLO SALVATORI; CEO GEORGE SARTOREL.

Assicurazioni Generali, SpA: Piazza Duca degli Abruzzi 2, 34132 Trieste; tel. (040) 671111; fax (040) 671127; e-mail press@generali .com; internet www.generali.com; f. 1831; life and non-life; Chair. GABRIELE GALATERI DI GENOLA; Group CEO MARIO GRECO.

Atradius Credit Insurance, NV, Rappresentanza Generale per l'Italia: Via Crescenzio 12, 00193 Roma; tel. (06) 688121; fax (06) 6874418; e-mail info.it@atradius.com; internet www.atradius.com; Chair., Supervisory Bd IGNACIO ÁLVAREZ; CEO ISIDORO UNDA.

Axa Assicurazioni: Corso Como 17, 20154 Milano; tel. (02) 480841; fax (02) 48084331; e-mail infodanni@axa.it; internet www.axa.it; f. 1956; Group CEO HENRI DE CASTRIES.

AXA MPS Assicurazioni Vita, SpA: Via Aldo Fabrizi 9, 00128 Roma; tel. (06) 508701; fax (06) 50870295; e-mail info@axa-mpsvita .it; internet www.axa-mps.it; f. 1974; Chair. PAOLO MANZATO; CEO FRÉDÉRIC MARIE DE COURTOIS D'ARCOLLIÈRES.

Carige Assicurazioni: Viale Certosa 222, 20156 Milano; tel. (02) 30761; fax (02) 3086125; e-mail info@carigeassicurazioni.it; internet www.carigeassicurazioni.it; f. 1920; part of Banca Carige group; Pres. PIERO GUIDO.

Creditras Vita, SpA: Corso d'Italia 23, 20122 Milano; tel. (02) 72161; fax (02) 72164032; e-mail info@creditrasvita.it; internet www .creditrasvita.it; f. 1995; part of Allianz, SpA; life; Pres. PIERO BOTTO.

FATA Assicurazioni, SpA (Fondo Assicurativo Tra Agricoltori): Via Urbana 169A, 00184 Roma; tel. (06) 47651; fax (06) 4871187; e-mail info@fata-assicurazioni.it; internet www.fata-assicurazioni .it; f. 1927; subsidiary of Gruppo Generali; CEO GIORGIO CAGNETTI.

Fondiaria—Sai, SpA: Corso Galileo Galilei 12, 10126 Torino; tel. (055) 6657111; fax (055) 6657685; e-mail fondiaria-sai@fondiaria-sai .it; internet www.fondiaria-sai.it; f. 1879; owned by Unipol Gruppo Finanziario; non-life; Pres. FABIO CERCHIAI; Dir-Gen. CARLO CIMBRI.

Groupama Assicurazioni, SpA: Via Cesare Pavese 385, 00144 Roma; tel. (06) 30181; fax (06) 80210831; e-mail info@groupama.it; internet www.groupama.it; f. 1929; fmrly known as Nuova Tirrena, SpA; name changed as above in 2009; part of Groupama; Pres. FRANÇOIS SCHMITT; Dir-Gen. and CEO CHRISTOPHE BUSO.

HDI Assicurazioni, SpA: Via Abruzzi 10, 00187 Roma; tel. (06) 421031; fax (06) 42103500; e-mail hdi.assicurazioni@hdia.it; internet www.hdia.it; f. 2001.

INA Assitalia, SpA: Via Leonida Bissolati 23, 00187 Roma; tel. (06) 84831; fax (06) 84833898; e-mail info@inaassitalia.it; internet www .inaassitalia.it; f. 1912; subsidiary of Gruppo Generali; Pres. SERGIO BALBINOT; Man. Dir FABIO BUSCARINI.

Intesa Sanpaolo Vita, SpA: Viale Stelvio 55–57, 20159 Milano; tel. (02) 30511; fax (02) 30518188; internet www.intesasanpaolovita.it; f. 2012; life insurance; Pres. Prof. SALVATORE MACCARONE; CEO Dr GIANEMILIO OSCULATI.

Italiana Assicurazioni, SpA: Via Traiano 18, 20149 Milano; tel. (02) 397161; fax (02) 3271270; internet www.italiana.it; f. 1889; part of Gruppo Reale Mutua; fmrly Cooperativa Italiana Incendio; name changed to current in 1995; Pres. ITI MIHALICH; Dir-Gen. LUIGI LANA.

Mediolanum Vita, SpA: Palazzo Meucci, Via Francesco Sforza 15, 20080 Basiglio, Milano; tel. (02) 90491; e-mail info@mediolanum.it; internet www.mediolanumvita.it; f. 1972; life insurance; Pres. DANILO PELLEGRINO; CEO LUIGI DEL FABBRO, EDOARDO LOMBARDI.

Milano Assicurazioni (Compagnia di Assicurazioni di Milano, SpA): Via Senigallia 18/2, 20161 Milano; tel. (02) 64021; fax (02) 64025389; e-mail milass@milass.it; internet www.milass.it; f. 1825; owned by Gruppo Unipol; Pres. FABIO CERCHIAI; CEO CARLO CIMBRI.

Poste Vita: Piazzale Konrad Adenauer 3, 00144 Roma; tel. (06) 549241; internet www.postevita.it; f. 2000; subsidiary of Gruppo Poste Italiane; life; Pres. ROBERTO COLOMBO.

SARA Assicurazioni, SpA: Via Po 20, 00198 Roma; tel. (06) 84751; fax (06) 8475223; internet www.sara.it; f. 1924; Chair. ROSARIO ALESSI; Gen. Man. Dr ALESSANDRO SANTOLIQUIDO.

Società Cattolica di Assicurazione—Società Cooperativa: Lungadige Cangrande 16, 37126 Verona; tel. (045) 8391111; fax (045) 8391112; e-mail cattolica@cattolicaassicurazioni.it; internet www.cattolicaassicurazioni.it; f. 1896; CEO Dott. GIOVANNI BATTISTA MAZZUCCHELLI.

Società Reale Mutua di Assicurazioni: Via Corte d'Appello 11, 10122 Torino; tel. (011) 4311111; fax (011) 4350966; e-mail buongiornoreale@realmutua.it; internet www.realemutua.it; f. 1828; net profit 15.71m. (2012); Chair. Dott. ITI MIHALICH; Gen. Man. LUIGI LANA.

Swiss Re Italia, SpA: Via dei Giuochi Istmici 40, 00194 Roma; tel. (06) 323931; fax (06) 3296572; e-mail srit-communicazione@swissre.com; internet www.swissre.com; f. 1922; Chair. WALTER B. KIELHOLZ; Man. Dir MAURIZIO VALSECCHI.

Unipol Assicurazioni, SpA: Via Stalingrado 45, 40128 Bologna; tel. (051) 5077111; fax (051) 375349; internet www.unipolassicurazioni.it; f. 1963; present name adopted in 2011; part of Grupo Unipol; non-life; Pres. VANES GALANTI; CEO CARLO CIMBRI.

Vittoria Assicurazioni, SpA: Via Ignazio Gardella 2, 20149 Milano; tel. (02) 482191; fax (02) 48203693; internet www.vittoriaassicurazioni.com; f. 1921; cap. 3,277.1m. (July 2008); Chair. Dott. GIORGIO ROBERTO COSTA; CEO ROBERTO GUARENA.

Zurich Insurance PLC: Via Benigno Crespi 23, 20159 Milano; tel. (02) 59661; fax (02) 59662603; e-mail informazioni@zurich.it; internet www.zurich.it; f. 1872; fmrly known as l'Unione delle assicurazioni; CEO CAMILLO CANDIA.

Regulatory Authority

Istituto per la Vigilanza sulle Assicurazioni (IVASS): Via del Quirinale 21, 00187 Roma; tel. (06) 421331; fax (06) 42133206; e-mail scrivi@ivass.it; internet www.ivass.it; f. 2013; supervises insurance cos; Pres. and Dir-Gen. SALVATORE ROSSI.

Insurance Association

Associazione Nazionale fra le Imprese Assicuratrici (ANIA): Via della Frezza 70, 00186 Roma; tel. (06) 326881; fax (06) 3227135; e-mail info@ania.it; internet www.ania.it; f. 1944; Pres. Dott. ALDO MINUCCI; Dir-Gen. Prof. DARIO FOCARELLI; 230 mems.

Trade and Industry

GOVERNMENT AGENCIES

Agenzia per la promozione all'estero e l'internazionalizzaizone delle imprese italiane (ICE) (Italian Trade Agency): Via Liszt 21, 00144 Roma; tel. (06) 59921; fax (06) 89280312; e-mail assistenza.export@ice.it; internet www.ice.gov.it; f. 1926; govt agency for the promotion of foreign trade; Pres. RICCARDO M. MONTI; Dir-Gen. ROBERTO LUONGO.

Autorità Garante della Concorrenza e del Mercato (AGCM) (Italian Competition Authority). Piazza G. Verdi 6A, 00198 Roma; tel. (06) 858211; fax (06) 85821256; e-mail antitrust@agcm.it; internet www.agcm.it; f. 1990; Chair. GIOVANNI PITRUZZELLA; Sec.-Gen. ROBERTO CHIEPPA.

Cassa depositi e prestiti SpA (CDP): Via Goito 4, 00185 Roma; tel. (06) 42211; fax (06) 42214026; internet www.cassaddpp.it; f. 1850; provides loans to public bodies and local govt; 80% owned by Ministry of the Economy and Finance, 18.4% by banking foundations, 1.5% by CDP (treasury shares); Chair. FRANCO BASSANINI; CEO GIOVANNI GORNO TEMPINI.

Società Italiana per le Imprese All'Estero, SpA (SIMEST) (Italian Company for Businesses Abroad): Corso Vittorio Emanuele II 323, 00186 Roma; tel. (06) 686351; fax (06) 68635220; e-mail info@simest.it; internet www.simest.it; f. 1990; 76% owned by Cassa depositi e prestiti (CDP); Pres. GIANCARLO LANNA.

CHAMBER OF COMMERCE

Unioncamere (Union of Chambers of Commerce, Industry, Crafts and Agriculture): Piazza Sallustio 21, 00187 Roma; tel. (06) 47041; fax (06) 4704240; e-mail segretaria.generale@unioncamere.it; internet www.unioncamere.it; f. 1901; fmrly Unione Italiana delle Camere di Commercio, Industria, Artigianato e Agricoltura (Italian Union of Chambers of Commerce, Industry, Crafts and Agriculture); Pres. FERRUCCIO DARDANELLO; Sec.-Gen. CLAUDIO GAGLIARDI.

INDUSTRIAL AND TRADE ASSOCIATIONS

Confederazione Generale dell'Industria Italiana (Confindustria) (General Confederation of Italian Industry): Viale dell'Astronomia 30, 00144 Roma; tel. (06) 59031; fax (06) 5919615; e-mail piei@confindustria.it; internet www.confindustria.it; f. 1910; re-established 1944; mems: 99 local asscns, 100 trade asscns, 15 regional confeds, 25 sectoral feds and 265 associated orgs, totalling 147,650 firms and 5.42m. employees; Pres. GIORGIO SQUINZI; Dir-Gen. MARCELLA PANUCCI.

Principal Organizations Affiliated to Confindustria

Associazione delle Imprese del Farmaco (FARMINDUSTRIA) (Pharmaceutical Industry): Largo del Nazareno 3/8, 00187 Roma; tel. (06) 675801; fax (06) 6786494; e-mail farmindustria@farmindustria.it; internet www.farmindustria.it; f. 1978; Pres. Dott. MASSIMO SCACCABAROZZI; 200 mem. firms.

Associazione delle Industrie del Dolce della Pasta Italiane (AIDEPI) (Pasta, Breakfast Cereals, Chocolate and Cocoa-based Products, Ice Creams, Sugar Confectionery and Biscuit Manufacturers): Via del Poggio Fiorito 61, 00144 Roma; tel. (06) 8091071; fax (06) 8073186; e-mail aidepi@aidepi.it; internet www.aidepi.it; Pres. PAOLO BARILLA; Dir-Gen. MARIO PICCIALUTI.

Associazione Industrie per l'Aerospazio, i Sistemi e la Difesa (AIAD) (Aerospace, Defence and Security): Via Nazionale 54, 00184 Roma; tel. (06) 4880247; fax (06) 4827476; e-mail aiad@aiad.it; internet www.aiad.it; f. 1947; Pres. REMO PERTICA; Sec.-Gen. CARLO FESTUCCI.

Associazione Italiana Tecnico Economica del Cemento (AITEC) (Cement): Piazza G. Marconi 25, 00144 Roma; tel. (06) 54210237; fax (06) 5915408; e-mail info@aitecweb.com; internet www.aitecweb.com; f. 1959; Pres. GIACOMO MARAZZI; Man. Dir Dott. GIUSEPPE SCHLITZER.

Associazione Mineraria Italiana (ASSOMINERARIA) (Oil and Mining Industry): Via delle Tre Madonne 20, 00197 Roma; tel. (06) 8073045; fax (06) 8073385; e-mail info@assomineraria.org; internet www.assomineraria.org; f. 1917; Pres. Dott. GIUSEPPE TANNOIA; Dir-Gen. Dott. ANDREA KETOFF; 150 mems.

Associazione Nazionale Costruttori Edili (ANCE) (Construction): Via Guattani 16, 00161 Roma; tel. (06) 845671; fax (06) 84567550; e-mail info@ance.it; internet www.ance.it; f. 1946; Pres. PAOLO BUZZETTI; Dir-Gen. CARLO FERRONI; mems: 20,000 firms in 102 provincial and 20 regional asscns.

Associazione Nazionale delle Imprese Elettriche (ASSO-ELETTRICA) (Electricity Generators and Distributors): Via Benozzo Gozzoli 24, 00142 Roma; tel. (06) 8537281; fax (06) 85356431; e-mail info@assoelettrica.it; internet www.assoelettrica.it; f. 2002; Pres. and Dir-Gen. CHICCO TESTA; 120 mem. cos.

Associazione Nazionale Filiera Industria Automobilistica (ANFIA) (Motor Vehicle Industries): Corso Galileo Ferraris 61, 10128 Torino; tel. (011) 5546505; fax (011) 545986; e-mail anfia@anfia.it; internet www.anfia.it; f. 1912; Pres. ROBERTO VAVASSORI; 245 mems.

Associazione Nazionale Italiana Industrie Grafiche, Cartotecniche e Trasformatrici (ASSOGRAFICI) (Printing and Paper-Processing Industries): Piazza Castello 28, 20121 Milano; tel. (02) 4981051; fax (02) 4816947; e-mail assografici@assografici.it; internet www.assografici.it; f. 1946; Pres. GIOVANNI COLOMBO; Gen. Dir Dott. CLAUDIO COVINI; 1,200 mems.

Confindustria Servizi Innovativi e Tecnologici (FITA) (Online Media, Market Research, Information Technology, etc.): Via Barbarini 11, 00187 Roma; tel. (06) 421401; fax (06) 92933019; internet www.confindustriasi.it; Pres. ENNIO LUCARELLI; 51 associ ated orgs and 62 regional sections.

Federazione delle Associazioni Nazionali di Categorie Industriali Varie (FEDERVARIE) (Miscellaneous Industries): Via Petitti 16, 20149 Milano; tel. (02) 32672222; fax (02) 32672299; e-mail info@confindustriafedervarie.it; internet www.confindustriafedervarie.it; f. 1945; Pres. Dott. DINO FENZI; 24 mem. asscns.

Federazione delle Associazioni Nazionali dell'Industria Meccanica Varia ed Affine (ANIMA) (Mechanical and Engineering Industries): Via Scarsellini 13, 20161 Milano; tel. (02) 45418500; fax (02) 45418545; e-mail anima@anima-it.com; internet www.anima-it.com; f. 1914; Pres. ALBERTO CAPRARI; Dir-Gen. ANDREA ORLANDO; 1,500 mems.

Federazione delle Imprese delle Comunicazioni e dell'Informatica (FEDERCOMIN) (Information and Communications Technologies): Via Barberini 11, 00187 Roma; tel. (06) 421401; fax (06) 42140444; e-mail info@federcomin.it; Pres. ALBERTO TRIPI; Dir-Gen. PIETRO VARALDO.

Federazione Italiana dell'Accessorio Moda e Persona (FIAMP) (Personal and Fashion Accessories): Via Monte Rosa 211, 20149 Milano; tel. (02) 438291; fax (02) 48005833; e-mail segreteria@fiamp.it; internet www.fiamp.it; f. 2004; Pres. CLETO SAGRIPANTI.

Federazione Italiana dell'Industria Alimentare (FEDERALIMENTARE) (Food Industry): Viale Pasteur 10, 00144 Roma; tel. (06) 5903380; fax (06) 5903342; e-mail direzione@federalimentare.it; internet www.federalimentare.it; Pres. FILIPPO FERRUA MAGLIANI; 16 mem. asscns.

Federazione Italiana delle Industrie del Legno, del Sughero, del Mobile e dell'Arredamento (FEDERLEGNO-ARREDO) (Wood, Cork, Furniture and Interior Design): Foro Bonaparte 65,

20121 Milano; tel. (02) 806041; fax (02) 80604392; e-mail flaroma@ federlegno.it; internet www.federlegno.it; f. 1945; Pres. ROBERTO SNAIDERO; Dir-Gen. GIOVANNI DE PONTI; 2,400 mems.

Federazione Italiana Industriali Produttori Esportatori e Importatori di Vini, Acquaviti, Liquori, Sciroppi, Aceti e Affini (FEDERVINI) (Producers, Importers and Exporters of Wines, Brandies, Liqueurs, Syrups, Vinegars, etc.): Via Mentana 2B, 00185 Roma; tel. (06) 4941630; fax (06) 4941566; e-mail federvini@federvini.it; internet www.federvini.it; f. 1917; Pres. SANDRO BOSCAINI; Dir-Gen. OTTAVIO CAGIANO DE AZEVEDO.

Federazione Nazionale delle Associazioni dei Produttori di Beni Strumentali destinati allo Svolgimento di Processi Manifatturieri dell'Industria e dell'Artigianato (FEDER-MACCHINE) (Machine manufacture): Viale Fulvio Testi 128, 20092 Cinisello Balsamo; tel. (02) 26255201; fax (02) 26255881; e-mail federmacchine@federmacchine.it; internet www .federmacchine.it; Pres. GIANCARLO LOSMA; Sec.-Gen. Dott. ALFREDO MARIOTTI.

Federazione Nazionale Fonderie (ASSOFOND) (Foundries): Via Copernico 54, 20090 Trezzano Sul Naviglio (Milano); tel. (02) 48400967; fax (02) 48401267; e-mail info@assofond.it; internet www .assofond.it; f. 1948; Pres. ROBERTO ARIOTTI; Dir-Gen. SILVANO SQUARATTI.

Federazione Nazionale Imprese Elettrotecniche ed Elettroniche (ANIE) (Electric and Electronic Sectors): Via Lancetti 43, 20158 Milano; tel. (02) 32641; fax (02) 3264395; e-mail info@anie .it; internet www.anie.it; Pres. CLAUDIO ANDREA GEMME; Gen. Dir MARIA ANTONIETTA PORTALURI.

Federazione Nazionale dell'Industria Chimica (FEDER-CHIMICA) (Chemical Industry): Via Giovanni da Procida 11, 20149 Milano; tel. (02) 345651; fax (02) 34565310; e-mail federchimica@federchimica.it; internet www.federchimica.it; f. 1945 as Aschimici; renamed as above in 1984; Pres. CESARE PUCCIONI; Dir-Gen. Dott. CLAUDIO BENEDETTI; 1,400 mem. cos.

Federazione Nazionale Industria dei Viaggi e del Turismo (FEDERTURISMO) (Tourism and Travel): Viale Pasteur 10, 00144 Roma; tel. (06) 5903351; fax (06) 5910390; e-mail federturismo@ federturismo.it; internet www.federturismo.it; f. 1993; Pres. RENZO IORIO; Dir-Gen. ANTONIO BARRECA; 21 sectoral asscns, 32 local asscns.

Federazione Nazionale dei Sistemi e delle Modalità di Trasporto e delle Attività Connesse (FEDERTRASPORTO): Viale Pasteur 10, 00144 Roma; tel. (06) 5903972; fax (06) 5903987; e-mail federtrasporto@federtrasporto.it; internet www.federtrasporto.it; f. 1993; Pres. ALBERTO BRANDANI; Dir VALERIA BATTAGLIA; 11 mem. asscns.

Federazione Sindacale dell'Industria Metalmeccanica Italiana (FEDERMECCANICA) (Metalworking): Piazzale B. Juarez 14, 00144 Roma; tel. (06) 5925446; fax (06) 5911913; e-mail mail .roma@federmeccanica.it; internet www.federmeccanica.it; f. 1971; Pres. FABIO STORCHI; Dir-Gen. Dott. STEFANO FRANCHI; 103 mem. asscns.

Unione Nazionale dei Cantieri e delle Industrie Nautiche e Affini (UCINA) (Marine Industry): Piazzale Kennedy 1, 16129 Genova; tel. (010) 5769811; fax (010) 5531104; e-mail ucina@ucina .it; internet www.ucina.it; Pres. MASSIMO PEROTTI; Dir-Gen. MARINA STELLA.

Unione Petrolifera (Petroleum Industries): Piazzale Luigi Sturzo 31, 00144 Roma; tel. (06) 5423651; fax (06) 59602925; e-mail info@ unionepetrolifera.it; internet www.unionepetrolifera.it; f. 1948; Pres. ALESSANDRO GILOTTI; Dir-Gen. Dott. PIETRO DE SIMONE; 33 mem. cos.

Other Industrial and Trade Organizations

Associazione fra le Società Italiane per Azioni (ASSONIME) (Limited Cos): Piazza Venezia 11, 00187 Roma; tel. (06) 695291; fax (06) 6790487; e-mail assonime@assonime.it; internet www.assonime .it; f. 1910; Pres. MAURIZIO SELLA; Dir-Gen. Prof. STEFANO MICOSSI.

Confederazione Generale della Agricoltura Italiana (CON-FAGRICOLTURA) (Agriculture): Corso Vittorio Emanuele II 101, 00186 Roma; tel. (06) 68521; fax (06) 6861726; e-mail info@ confagricoltura.it; internet www.confagricoltura.it; f. 1945; Pres. MARIO GUIDI.

Confederazione Generale Italiana del Commercio, del Turismo, dei Servizi e delle Piccole e Medie Industrie (PMI) (CONFCOMMERCIO) (Commerce, Tourism, Services and Small and Medium-sized Industries): Piazza G. G. Belli 2, 00153 Roma; tel. (06) 58661; fax (06) 5809425; e-mail confcommercio@confcommercio .it; internet www.confcommercio.it; f. 1945; Pres. Dott. CARLO SANGALLI; Dir-Gen. FRANCESCO RIVOLTA; 770,000 mems.

Confederazione Italiana della Piccola e Media Industria Privata (CONFAPI) (Small and Medium-sized Private Industries): Via del Plebiscito 117, 00186 Roma; tel. (06) 690151; fax (06) 6791488; e-mail mail@confapi.org; internet www.apiservizivarese.it/confapi;

f. 1947; Pres. MAURIZIO CASASCO; Dir-Gen. Dott. ARMANDO OCCHI-PINTI; 120,000 mems.

Confederazione Italiana della Proprietà Edilizia (CON-FEDILIZIA) (Real Estate): Via Borgognona 47, 00187 Roma; tel. (06) 6793489; fax (06) 6793447; e-mail roma@confedilizia.it; internet www.confedilizia.it; f. 1945; Pres. CORRADO SFORZA FOGLIANI; Sec.-Gen. GIORGIO SPAZIANI TESTA.

Federazione delle Associazioni Italiane Alberghi e Turismo (FEDERALBERGHI) (Hotels and Tourism): Via Toscana 1, 00187 Roma; tel. (06) 42034610; fax (06) 42034690; e-mail info@ federalberghi.it; internet www.federalberghi.it; f. 1950; Pres. BERNABO BOCCA; Dir-Gen. ALESSANDRO MASSIMO NUCARA; 30,000 mems.

Federazione Industrie Prodotti Impianti e Servizi per le Costruzioni (FINCO) (Construction Services and Systems): Via Brenta 13, 00198 Roma; tel. (06) 8555203; fax (06) 8559860; e-mail finco@fincoweb.org; internet www.fincoweb.org; f. 1994; Pres. CARLA TOMASI; Dir-Gen. Dott. ANGELO ARTALE.

UTILITIES

Autorità per l'Energia Elettrica e il Gas (AEEG) (Electric Energy and Gas Authority): Piazza Cavour 5, 20121 Milano; tel. (02) 655651; fax (02) 65565266; e-mail info@autorita.energia.it; internet www.autorita.energia.it; regulatory authority; f. 1996; Pres. GUIDO PIER PAOLO BORTONI.

Electricity

A2A, SpA: Via Lamarmora 230, 25124 Brescia; tel. (030) 35531; fax (030) 3553204; e-mail infobs@a2a.eu; internet www.a2a.eu; f. 2008 by merger of AEM, AMSA and ASM; electricity and gas manufacture and distribution; Chair. GIOVANNI VALOTTI.

Acea, SpA: Piazzale Ostiense 2, 00154 Roma; tel. (06) 57991; fax (06) 5758095; e-mail info@aceaspa.it; internet www.aceaspa.it; f. 1909; produces and distributes electricity in Rome area; also engaged in water provision; 51% stake owned by Rome City Council; Chair. CATIA TOMASETTI; CEO ALBERTO IRACE.

Edison, SpA: Foro Bonaparte 31, 20121 Milano; tel. (02) 62221; fax (02) 62227456; e-mail infoweb@edison.it; internet www.edison.it; f. 1884 as Società Generale Italiana di Elettricità Sistema Edison; electricity and natural gas; 99.48% owned by Transalpina di Energia Srl; Chair. HENRY PROGLIO; CEO BRUNO LESCOEUR.

Enel, SpA: Via le Regina Margherita 137, 00198 Roma; tel. (06) 85091; fax (06) 85092162; internet www.enel.it; f. 1962; 31.23% owned by the Ministry of the Economy and Finance; partially privatized; generates and distributes electricity and gas; Chair. MARIA PATRIZIA GRIECO; CEO FRANCESCO STARACE.

Gestore dei Servizi Energitici (GSE): Viale Maresciallo Pilsudski 92, 00197 Roma; tel. (06) 80111; fax (06) 80114392; e-mail info@gse.it; internet www.gse.it; f. 2000 as Gestore del Sistema Eletrico, SpA; name changed to present in 2009; owned by the Ministry of the Economy and Finance; manages electricity transmission and co-ordinates the power network; Chair. and Man. Dir NANDO PASQUALI.

Terna, SpA—Rete Elettrica Nazionale: Via Egidio Galbani 70, 00156 Roma; tel. (06) 83138111; e-mail info@terna.it; internet www .terna.it; f. 1999; electricity transmission co; owns nearly 100% of electricity transmission grid; Pres. CATIA BASTIOLI; CEO MATTEO DEL FANTE.

Gas

See the section on Electricity for companies that are involved in the supply of both gas and electricity.

Eni, SpA: Piazzale Enrico Mattei 1, 00144 Roma; tel. (06) 59821; fax (06) 59822141; e-mail segreteriasocietaria.azionisti@eni.com; internet www.eni.it; f. 1953; fmrly Ente Nazionale Idrocarburi; natural gas exploration, oil and gas power; 30% owned by the Ministry of Economy and Finance; Chair. EMMA MARCEGAGLIA; CEO CLAUDIO DESCALZI.

Eni Power: Piazza Vanoni 1, 20097 San Donato Milanese; tel. (02) 5201; fax (02) 5203180; internet www.enipower.eni.it; f. 1999; owned by Eni, SpA (q.v.); power generation and sale; Pres. and CEO DANIELE DE GIOVANNI.

Gruppo Hera, SpA: Viale C. Berti Pichat 2–4, 40127 Bologna; tel. (051) 287111; fax (051) 287525; internet www.gruppohera.it; f. 2002; distributes gas; also engaged in water provision; Chair. TOMASO TOMMASI DI VIGNANO; Man. Dir ROBERTO BARILLI.

Italgas, SpA: Largo Regio Parco 9, 10153 Torino; tel. (01) 123941; fax (01) 12394499; internet www.italgas.it; gas distribution; Pres. MARCO REGGIANI; CEO LUCA SCHIEPPATI.

Linde Gas Italia Srl: Via Guido Rossa 3, 20010 Arluno, Milano; tel. (02) 903731; fax (02) 90373599; e-mail lgi@it.linde-gas.com; internet www.linde-gas.it; f. 1991; CEO GIOVANNI PAVESI.

Plurigas: Corso di Porta Vittoria 4, 20122 Milano; tel. (02) 77203033; fax (02) 77203255; e-mail info@plurigas.it; internet www.plurigas.it; f. 2001; gas distribution; 70% owned by A2A, SpA; Chair. VALTER PALLANO; CEO ANNAMARIA ARCUDI.

Snam Rete Gas: Piazza Santa Barbara 7, 20097 San Donato Milanese; tel. (02) 37031; fax (02) 37039227; e-mail postmaster@ snamretegas.it; internet www.snamretegas.it; f. 1941 as Società Nazionale Metanodotti (Snam); adopted current name 2001; transports natural gas; Chair. CARLO MALACARNE; CEO PAOLO MOSA.

Water

Municipal administrations are responsible for water supply in Italy. Legislation promulgated in 1994 provided for the consolidation of water supply into 'single territorial units'. Since the mid-1990s many municipalities have formed limited companies to manage water supply, for example the supplier for Rome (Acea, SpA—see the section on Electricity) and the supplier for Milan (Amiaque, SpA). A small number of municipalities have contracted private companies to manage water supply.

TRADE UNIONS

The three main trade union federations are the Confederazione Generale Italiana del Lavoro (CGIL), the Confederazione Italiana Sindacati Lavoratori (CISL) and the Unione Italiana del Lavoro (UIL).

National Federations

Confederazione Autonoma Italiana del Lavoro (CONFAIL): Viale Abruzzi 38, 20131 Milano; tel. (02) 29404554; fax (02) 29525692; e-mail info@confail.org; internet www.confail.org; Gen. Sec. EVANGELISTA ZACCARIA.

Confederazione Autonoma Sindacati Artigiani (CASARTI-GIANI): Via Flaminio Ponzio 2, 00153 Roma; tel. (06) 57300241; fax (06) 5755036; e-mail casartigiani@tiscali.it; internet www .casartigiani.org; f. 1958; fed. of artisans' unions and regional and provincial asscns; Pres. GIACOMO BASSO.

Confederazione Generale Italiana dell'Artigianato (CONF-ARTIGIANATO) (Artisans): Via di S. Giovanni in Laterano 152, 00184 Roma; tel. (06) 703741; fax (06) 70452188; e-mail confartigianato@confartigianato.it; internet www.confartigianato .it; f. 1946; independent; 20 regional feds, 120 provincial asscns; 700,000 associate enterprises; Pres. GIORGIO MERLETTI; Sec.-Gen. CESARE FUMAGALLI.

Confederazione Generale Italiana del Lavoro (CGIL) (Italian General Confederation of Labour): Corso d'Italia 25, 00198 Roma; tel. (06) 84761; fax (06) 8845683; e-mail info@mail.cgil.it; internet www .cgil.it; f. 1906 as Confederazione Generale del Lavoro; refounded 1944; confederation of 13 feds; Sec.-Gen. SUSANNA CAMUSSO; 6m. mems.

Confederazione Generale dei Sindacati Autonomi dei Lavoratori (CONFSAL): Viale Trasevere 60, 00153 Roma; tel. (06) 5852071; fax (06) 5818218; e-mail info@confsal.it; internet www .confsal.it; f. 1979; Sec.-Gen. Prof. MARCO PAOLO NIGI.

Confederazione Italiana Dirigenti e Alte Professionalità—Manager e Alte Professionalità per l'italia (CIDA—MAPI): Via Barberini 36, 00187 Roma; tel. (06) 97605111; fax (06) 97605109; e-mail info@cida.it; internet www.cida.it; fed. of 10 managers' unions; Pres. Dott. SILVESTRE BERTOLINI; Dir Dott. ALBERTO SARTONI.

Confederazione Italiana Sindacati Addetti ai Servizi (CISAS): Piazza Roosevelt 3, 70027 Bari; tel. (080) 3813224; fax (080) 9911552; e-mail info@cisas.it; internet www.cisas.it.

Confederazione Italiana Sindacati Lavoratori (CISL): Via Po 21, 00198 Roma; tel. (06) 84731; fax (06) 8546076; e-mail cisl@cisl.it; internet www.cisl.it; f. 1950; affiliated to the International Trade Union Confederation (ITUC) and ETUC; fed. of 19 unions; publishes *Conquiste del Lavoro* (see Press); Sec.-Gen. RAFFAELE BONANNI; 4.5m. mems.

Confederazione Nazionale dell'Artigianato e delle Piccole e Media Imprese (CNA) (National Confederation of Italian SMEs and Handicrafts): Piazza M. Armellini 9A, 00162 Roma; tel. (06) 441881; fax (06) 44249511; e-mail cna@cna.it; internet www.cna.it; f. 1946; 108 provincial asscns; Pres. DANIELE VACCARINO; Gen. Sec. Dott. SERGIO SILVESTRINI.

Confederazione Unitaria Quadri (CUQ): Via Assarotti 9, 10122 Torino; tel. (011) 5612042; fax (011) 5630987; e-mail confquadri@tin .it; f. 1995; Pres. MARIO VIGNA.

Sindacato Nazionale dei Funzionari Direttivi, Dirigenti e delle Alte Professionalità della Pubblica Amministrazione (DIRSTAT): Piazza Risorgimento 59, 00192 Roma; tel. (06) 3222097; fax (06) 3212690; e-mail dirstat@dirstat.it; internet www.dirstat.it; f. 1948; fed. of 33 unions and asscns of civil service executives and officers; Pres. FIORILLO ALESSIO; Sec.-Gen. Dott. ARCANGELO D'AMBROSIO.

Unione Generale del Lavoro (UGL): Via Margutta 19, 00187 Roma; tel. (06) 324821; fax (06) 324820; e-mail segreteriaugl@ugl.it; internet www.ugl.it; f. 1950 as CISNAL; name changed as above 1995; upholds traditions of national syndicalism; fed. of 64 unions, 77 provincial unions; Gen. Sec. GEREMIA MANCINI; 2,137,979 mems.

Unione Italiana del Lavoro (UIL): Via Lucullo 6, 00187 Roma; tel. (06) 47531; fax (06) 4753208; e-mail info@uil.it; internet www.uil.it; f. 1950; socialist, social democrat and republican; affiliated to the International Confederation of Free Trade Unions and European Trade Union Confederation; 18 nat. trade union feds and 108 provincial union councils; Gen. Sec. LUIGI ANGELETTI; 1,758,729 mems.

Co-operative Unions

Associazione Generale delle Cooperative Italiane (AGCI): Via A. Bargoni 78, 00153 Roma; tel. (06) 583271; fax (06) 58327210; e-mail info@agci.it; internet www.agci.it; f. 1952; Pres. ROSARIO ALTIERI.

Confederazione Cooperative Italiane (CONFCOOPERA-TIVE): Borgo S. Spirito 78, 00193 Roma; tel. (06) 680001; fax (06) 68134236; e-mail confcooperative@confcooperative.it; internet www .confcooperative.it; f. 1919; confederation of co-operative unions; Pres. MAURIZIO GARDINI; Sec.-Gen. VINCENZO MANNINO.

Lega Nazionale delle Cooperative e Mutue (National League of Co-operative and Friendly Societies): Via Guattani 9, 00161 Roma; tel. (06) 84439391; fax (06) 84439406; e-mail info@legacoop.coop; internet www.legacoop.it; f. 1886; 10 affiliated unions; Pres. MAURO LUSETTI.

Unione Nazionale Cooperative Italiane (UNCI): Via San Sotero 32, 00165 Roma; tel. (06) 39366729; fax (06) 39375080; e-mail info@ unci.eu; internet www.unci.eu; f. 1971; Pres. Dott. PASQUALE AMICO.

Transport

RAILWAYS

The majority of Italian lines are controlled by an independent state-owned corporation, Ferrovie dello Stato, SpA. Its subsidiary Trenitalia operates a large number of train services in the country, and offers links to Spain, Slovenia, Hungary, Austria, Belgium and France. In 2011 the total length of the network was 16,726 km, of which 11,925 were electrified. Apart from the state railway system there are 24 local and municipal railway companies, many of whose lines are narrow gauge. A 182-km high-speed link connecting Bologna and Milan opened in 2008; an extension of the line, to Rome via Florence, and further extensions to Turin in the northwest, and to Naples and Salerno in the south, were completed in 2009. Work on a high-speed link to Lyon, France, from Turin, including a 58-km tunnel of which 12 km will be in Italy, was expected to be completed by 2023. There are metro systems in Rome, Catania, Genoa, Milan, Naples and Turin.

Ferrovie dello Stato, SpA (FS): Piazza della Croce Rossa 1, 00161 Roma; tel. (06) 44101; e-mail info_ferservizi@ferservizi.it; internet www.fsitaliane.it; controls 9 subsidiaries; Pres. MARCELLO MESSORI; CEO MICHELE MARIO ELIA.

ROADS

In 2009 there were 6,661 km of motorway, 19,375 km of major roads and 154,513 km of secondary roads in Italy. The length of the total road network was an estimated 487,700 km in 2005. All the autostrade (motorways) are toll roads except for that between Salerno and Reggio Calabria and those in Sicily. In 2009 the Government announced that plans to construct a 3.3-km road and rail bridge over the Straits of Messina, between Calabria and Sicily were to be revived. The project was, however, cancelled in February 2013.

ANAS, SpA: Via Monzambano 10, 00185 Roma; tel. (06) 44461; fax (06) 4456224; e-mail 841148@stradeanas.it; internet www .stradeanas.it; f. 1928 as Azienda Autonoma Statale della Strada (AASS); jt-stock co in partnership with the Ministry of the Economy and Finance; responsible for the construction and administration of state roads and their improvement and extension; Dir Dott. PIETRO CIUCCI.

Autostrade per l'Italia, SpA: Via Alberto Bergamini 50, 00159 Roma; tel. (06) 43631; fax (06) 43634090; e-mail info@autostrade.it; internet www.autostrade.it; maintenance and management of motorway network; Pres. Dott. FABIO CERCHIAAI; CEO GIOVANNI CASTELLUCCI.

SHIPPING

In 2014 the Italian flag registered fleet (2,162 vessels) had a total displacement of 16.8m. grt, including 252 tankers, 222 passenger ships and 76 general cargo ships.

Genova
(Genoa)

Costa Crociere, SpA: Piazza Piccapietra 48, 16121 Genova; tel. (010) 54831; fax (010) 5483290; e-mail corporate@costa.it; internet www.costacrociere.it; f. 1854; passenger and cargo service; Mediterranean, Northern Europe, Central and South America; Caribbean cruises; Chair. PIER LUIGI FOSCHI; CEO MICHAEL THAMM.

Fratelli Cosulich, SpA: Ponte Morosini 41, 16126 Genova; tel. (010) 27151; fax (010) 2715390; e-mail info@cosulich.it; internet www.cosulich.it; f. 1854; shipowners and shipping agents; domestic network and cargo to Near East, Red Sea, Hong Kong, Singapore, New York and Zürich; office network in main ports worldwide; Man. Dir AUGUSTO COSULICH.

Grandi Navi Veloci, SpA: Via Fieschi 17, 16121 Genova; tel. (010) 55091; fax (010) 5509333; internet www.gnv.it; f. 1991; passenger, cargo, containers and tramp to Europe; Pres. ROBERTO MARTINOLI; Dir-Gen. ARIODANTE VALERI.

Ignazio Messina & C., SpA: Via G. d'Annunzio 91, 16121 Genova; tel. (010) 53961; fax (010) 5396264; e-mail info@messinaline.it; internet www.messinaline.it; services to Arabian Gulf, India, Pakistan, Nigeria, North, East, South and West Africa, Libya and Near East, Red Sea, Malta, Europe; Chair. GIANFRANCO MESSINA.

Napoli
(Naples)

Tirrenia di Navigazione, SpA: Palazzo Sirignano, Rione Sirignano 2, 80121 Napoli; tel. (081) 7201111; fax (081) 7201441; internet www.tirrenia.it; f. 1963; ferry services to Sardinia, Sicily, North Africa; part of Gruppo Tirrenia di Navigazione.

Palermo

Compagnia Delle Isole SpA (SIREMAR): Calata Marinai d'Italia, Porto di Palermo, 90139 Palermo; tel. (091) 7493111; fax (091) 7493366; e-mail info@siremar.it; internet www.siremar.it; f. 1976; owned by Gruppo Tirrenia di Navigazione; ferry services; Pres. Dott. SALVATORE LAURO.

Grimaldi Compagnia di Navigazione: Via Emerico Amari 8, Palermo; internet www.grimaldi.napoli.it; cargo; Italy to North Europe, South, Central, North America, West Africa; Chair. GIANLUCA GRIMALDI; Man. Dirs EMANUELE GRIMALDI, DIEGO PACELLA.

Roma
(Rome)

Fratelli D'Amico Armatori, SpA: Via Liguria 36, 00187 Roma; tel. (06) 46711; fax (06) 4871914; e-mail damiship@damicofratelli.it; internet www.damicofratelli.it; dry cargo and tankers; Pres. GIUSEPPE D'AMICO; Gen. Man. CARLO CAMELI.

Trieste

Italia Marittima, SpA: Palazzo della Marineria, Passeggio S. Andrea 4, 34123 Trieste; tel. (040) 3180111; fax (040) 3180388; e-mail headoffice@ts.lloydtriestino.it; internet www.lloydtriestino.it; f. 1836; cargo services by container to South Africa, Australasia and Far East, plus trans-Pacific and -Atlantic services; privatized 1998; renamed as above in 2006; Pres. PIER LUIGI MANESCHI; Vice-Pres. and Man. Dir REN-GUNG SHYU; Dir-Gen. MAURIZIO SALCE.

Navigazione Montanari, SpA: Via S. Ceccarini 36, 61032 Fano; tel. (0721) 8801; fax (0721) 830430; e-mail info@navmont.com; internet www.navmont.com; f. 1889; cargo services to Mediterranean, Northern Europe, USA and Far East.

Venezia
(Venice)

Adriatica di Navigazione, SpA: Zattere 1411, CP 705, 30123 Venezia; tel. (041) 781861; fax (041) 781818; e-mail adrnav@interbusiness.it; internet www.adriatica.it; f. 1937; owned by Gruppo Tirrenia di Navigazione; passenger services from Italy, Albania, Croatia and Montenegro; Pres. GIORGIO GROSSO; Man. Dir ANTONIO CACUCCI.

Shipping Association

Confederazione Italiana Armatori (CONFITARMA): Piazza SS. Apostoli 66, 00187 Roma; tel. (06) 674811; fax (06) 69783730; e-mail confitarma@confitarma.it; internet www.confitarma.it; f. 1901; shipowners' asscn; Pres. PAOLO D'AMICO; Dir-Gen. GENNARO FIORE; 230 mems.

CIVIL AVIATION

In 2012 there were 39 commercial airports in Italy.

Civil Aviation Authority

Ente Nazionale per l'Aviazione Civile (ENAC) (Italian Civil Aviation Authority): Viale del Castro Pretorio 118, 00185 Roma; tel. (06) 445961; fax (06) 44596493; e-mail comunicazione@enac.gov.it; internet www.enac.gov.it; f. 1997; Pres. VITO RIGGIO; Dir-Gen. ALESSIO QUARANTA.

Airlines

Air Dolomiti: Via Paolo Bembo 70, 37062 Frazione di Dossobuono; tel. (045) 8605211; fax (045) 8605229; e-mail customer-relations@airdolomiti.it; internet www.airdolomiti.it; f. 1989; operates domestic flights and services between Italy and Austria, France and Germany; subsidiary of Deutsche Lufthansa AG; Pres. and CEO MICHAEL KRAUS.

Air One: Piazza Almerico da Schio, Palazzo RPU, 00054 Fiumicino; internet www.flyairone.it; f. 1983 as Aliadriatica; present name adopted 1995; acquired by Compagnia Aerea Italiana (CAI) 2009 and merged with Alitalia; Air One brand relaunched as a low-cost carrier 2010; domestic and international flights to destinations in Europe and North Africa.

Alitalia—Compagnia Aerea Italiana, SpA: Piazza Almerico da Schio, Palazzo RPU, 00054 Fiumicino; tel. (06) 65631; fax (06) 7093065; e-mail ufficio.stampa@alitalia.it; internet www.alitalia.com; f. 2008 as successor to the defunct, state-owned Alitalia, SpA (f. 1946); majority shareholding owned by Compagnia Aerea Italiana (CAI); 25% stake owned by Air France-KLM; in Aug. 2014 Etihad Airways signed an agreement to take a 49% share; merged with Air One 2009; domestic and international services throughout Europe and to Africa, North and South America, the Middle East, the Far East and Australia; Chair. LUCA CORDERO DI MONTEZEMOLO; CEO SILVANO CASSANO.

Livingston, SpA: Via Giovanni XXIII 206, 21010 Cardano al Campo; tel. (331) 267321; fax (331) 267421; e-mail info@lauda.it; internet www.lauda.it; f. 2003; acquired routes and fleet of Lauda Air Italia in 2005; operates charter and scheduled flights to destinations worldwide; owned by 4 Fly, SpA; Chair. GORDON MCDOUGALL; CEO PELLEGRINO D'AQUINO.

Meridiana Fly, SpA: Aeroporto Costa Smeralda, Olbia, 07026 Sardinia; tel. (0789) 52600; fax (0789) 645177; e-mail info.olbia@meridiana.it; internet www.meridiana.it; f. 1963 as Alisarda, renamed 2010 following merger with Eurofly; scheduled and charter services throughout Italy and Europe, and on a limited number of intercontinental services; Chair. MARCO RIGOTTI; CEO ROBERTO SCARAMELLA.

Tourism

A great number of tourists are attracted to Italy by its Alpine and Mediterranean scenery, sunny climate, Roman archaeological remains, medieval and Baroque churches, Renaissance towns and palaces, paintings and sculpture and famous opera houses. Each of the 95 provinces has a Board of Tourism; there are also about 300 Aziende Autonome di Cura, Soggiorno e Turismo, with information about tourist accommodation and health treatment, and about 2,000 Pro Loco Associations concerned with local amenities. In 2011 there were 47 UNESCO World Heritage Sites in Italy. There were some 50.3m. tourist arrivals in Italy in 2013; tourism receipts totalled US $43,835m. in that year.

Dipartimento per lo Sviluppo e la Competitività del Turismo: Via della Ferratella in Laterano 51, 00184 Roma; tel. (06) 455325955; fax (06) 70497131; e-mail cittadino@governo.it; part of the Office of the Prime Minister; Head of Dept CATERINA CITTADINO.

Ente Nazionale Italiano per il Turismo (ENIT) (Italian State Tourist Board): Via Marghera 2, 00185 Roma; tel. (06) 49711; fax (06) 4463379; e-mail sedecentrale@enit.it; internet www.enit.it; f. 1919; Chair. PIER LUIGI CELLI; Dir-Gen. ANDREA BABBI.

Defence

Italy has been a member of the North Atlantic Treaty Organization (NATO) since 1949. As assessed at November 2014, it maintained armed forces totalling 176,000, comprising an army of 103,100, a navy of 31,000 and an air force of 41,900. There were also reserves of 18,300 and paramilitary forces numbering 184,250 (including 104,950 military police—Carabinieri). Conscription was phased out by December 2004, under legislation that was approved in 2000 and which also provided for the recruitment of women soldiers. In November 2004 the European Union (EU) ministers responsible for defence agreed to create a number of 'battlegroups' (each comprising about 1,500 men), which could be deployed at short notice to crisis areas around the world. The EU battlegroups, two of which were to be ready for deployment at any one time, following a rotational schedule, reached full operational capacity from 1 January 2007.

Defence Expenditure: Budget estimated at €17,000m. in 2015.

General Chief of Defence Staff: Gen. CLAUDIO GRAZIANO.

Army Chief of Staff: Gen. DANILO ERRICO.

Navy Chief of Staff: Adm. GIUSEPPE DE GIORI.

Air Force Chief of Staff: Gen. PASQUALE PREZIOSA.

Chief Commander of the Carabinieri: Gen. TULLIO DEL SETTE.

Education

Compulsory education is free for students between the ages of six and 16 years, comprising six years of primary education, four years of lower secondary education and two years of higher secondary education. Pre-primary education is free and non-compulsory for pupils between the ages of three and six years. The curricula of all Italian schools are standardized by the Ministry of Education, Universities and Research. After primary school (scuola primaria), for children aged six to 11 years, the pupil enters the first level of secondary school (scuola media inferiore). An examination at the end of three years leads to a lower secondary school certificate (Diploma di Licenza della Scuola Media), which gives access to higher secondary school (scuola media superiore), of which only the first year is compulsory. Pupils wishing to enter a classical lycée (liceo classico) must also pass an examination in Latin.

Higher secondary education is provided by classical, artistic, linguistic and scientific lycées, training schools for elementary teachers, and technical and vocational institutes (industrial, commercial, nautical, etc.). After five years at a lycée, the student sits an examination for the higher secondary school certificate (Diploma di Esame di Stato), which allows automatic entry into any university or non-university institute of higher education. Special four-year courses are provided at the teachers' training schools and the diploma obtained permits entry to a special university faculty of education, the magistero, and a number of other faculties. The technical institutes provide practical courses that prepare students for a specialized university faculty.

In 2011/12 enrolment at primary schools included 97% of all children in the relevant age-group, while the comparable ratio for secondary enrolment was 92%.

In 2011/12 there were 1.8m. students enrolled in higher education in Italy; the largest universities are La Sapienza in Rome and the University of Bologna. In 2007/08 there were 74 institutes of higher education. Following the introduction of university reforms, courses last for a three-year cycle, followed by a two-year specialized cycle. Study allowances are awarded to students according to their means and merit; however, most parents pay fees. In 2010 government expenditure on education was €69,321m. In 2012 expenditure on education was equivalent to 3.9% of gross domestic product.

JAMAICA

Introductory Survey

LOCATION, CLIMATE, LANGUAGE, RELIGION, FLAG, CAPITAL

Jamaica is the third largest island in the Caribbean Sea, lying 145 km (90 miles) to the south of Cuba and 160 km (100 miles) to the south-west of Haiti. The climate varies with altitude, being tropical at sea-level and temperate in the mountain areas. The average annual temperature is 27°C (80°F) and mean annual rainfall is 198 cm (78 ins). The official language is English, although a local patois is widely spoken. The majority of the population belong to Christian denominations, the Church of God being the most numerous. The national flag (proportions 1 by 2) consists of a diagonal yellow cross on a background of black (hoist and fly) and green (above and below). The capital is Kingston.

CONTEMPORARY POLITICAL HISTORY

Historical Context

Jamaica, a British colony from 1655, was granted internal self-government in 1959, and full independence, within the Commonwealth, was achieved on 6 August 1962. Jamaica formed part of the West Indies Federation between 1958 and 1961, when it seceded, following a referendum. The Federation was dissolved in 1962. The two dominant political figures after the Second World War were Sir Alexander Bustamante, leader of the Jamaica Labour Party (JLP), who retired as Prime Minister in 1967, and Norman Manley, a former Premier and leader of the People's National Party (PNP), who died in 1969. The JLP won the elections of 1962 and 1967 but, under the premiership of Hugh Shearer, it lost the 1972 elections to the PNP, led by Michael Manley, the son of Norman. Manley advocated democratic socialism and his Government put great emphasis on social reform and economic independence.

Domestic Political Affairs

The early 1970s were marked by escalating violence and crime, with gang warfare rife in the deprived areas of Kingston. More than 160 people were killed in the first half of 1976, and in June the Government declared a state of emergency. Despite the unrest, high unemployment and severe economic stagnation, the PNP was returned to power in December with an increased majority. By January 1979, however, there was again widespread political unrest, and violent demonstrations signalled growing discontent with the Manley administration. In 1980, in the context of a worsening economic crisis, Manley rejected the stipulation of the IMF, as a condition of its making further loans to Jamaica, that economic austerity measures be undertaken. He called a general election to seek support for his economic policies and his decision to end dependence on the IMF. The electoral campaign was one of the most violent in Jamaica's history. In the October election the JLP won 51 of the 60 seats in the House of Representatives. Edward Seaga, the leader of the JLP, became Prime Minister; he supported closer political and economic links with the USA and the promotion of free enterprise. Negotiations on IMF assistance were resumed.

In November 1983 Seaga announced that an election would take place in December. Only four days were allowed for the nomination of candidates, and the PNP refused to participate, declaring the elections void. The JLP, opposed in only six constituencies (by independent candidates), won all 60 seats in the House of Representatives and formed a one-party legislature.

Devaluations of the Jamaican dollar and the withdrawal of food subsidies provoked demonstrations and sporadic violence in 1984. Despite government attempts to offset the effects of these economic austerity measures, imposed at the instigation of the IMF, unemployment, together with illicit trading in drugs, contributed to a rise in the incidence of crime and violence, especially in Kingston. In 1985 another increase in fuel prices precipitated further violent demonstrations in the capital and industrial unrest.

After a brief, and relatively peaceful, campaign, a general election took place in February 1989, in which the PNP secured an absolute majority of legislative seats. Manley, who had developed a more moderate image during his years in opposition, again became Prime Minister. The Government conceded the necessity for a devaluation of the Jamaican dollar in October. The two main parties achieved a limited consensus on the pursuit of an economic policy of austerity, despite its unpopularity and there was also agreement that further action should be taken against the drugs trade.

Patterson in power

In December 1991 controversy surrounding the waiving of taxes worth some US $30m. owed to Jamaica by an international company, Shell, resulted in the resignation of Horace Clarke, the Minister of Mining and Energy, and Percival J. Patterson, the Deputy Prime Minister, amid allegations of corruption. In March 1992 Manley resigned. Patterson was appointed Prime Minister at the end of the month.

At a general election in March 1993 Patterson's PNP secured 52 of the 60 seats in the House of Representatives. The scale of the PNP victory was widely attributed to Patterson's populism, and a perceived shift in political influence away from the capital, traditionally a power base of the JLP. In April Patterson announced plans to reform the electoral system. However, allegations of electoral malpractice and demands by the JLP for an official inquiry into suspected procedural abuses were rejected by the PNP. By February 1994 attempts at electoral reform had been undermined by the resignation of the Chairman of the Electoral Advisory Committee (EAC), and by the failure of the EAC to appoint a new Director of Elections. Demands for constitutional and electoral reform continued. An electronic voter registration system was installed in 1996 and new electoral rolls were finally completed in late 1997.

A general election was held in December 1997, at which the PNP won a majority of seats in the House of Representatives. Patterson, who was subsequently sworn in again as Prime Minister, announced plans for Jamaica to become a republic within five years.

In 1998 and 1999 public protests against a deepening economic crisis and police actions resulted in several riots. There was further unrest in April 1999 following the announcement of a proposed significant increase in the price of diesel. The JLP and National Democratic Movement (formed in 1995 by Bruce Golding), while initially helping to organize the protests, dissociated themselves from the subsequent violence. In July the authorities announced that army personnel were to be deployed on patrols in greater Kingston in an attempt to combat the high incidence of crime, the majority of which was reportedly related to drugs-trafficking. In October the British Government announced that it would grant £2.9m. in assistance towards the reform and modernization of the Jamaican police force. In the same month an investigation was begun into widespread allegations of police corruption.

Confrontations between the police and various sectors of the community continued in 2001. The human rights organization Amnesty International claimed that the Jamaican police force had one of the highest records for the execution of its own citizens. In 2000 the police had shot dead 140 suspected criminals. Furthermore, in July conflict broke out between police and rival PNP and JLP factions in Kingston. Following three days of fighting, in which 25 people were reported to have been killed, units of the Jamaica Defence Force were deployed to restore order.

A Commission of Inquiry into the July disturbances opened in September 2001, but the JLP refused to co-operate with the investigation. Meanwhile, sporadic outbreaks of violence in Kingston continued: in October the Government was forced to deploy army, air and coastguard units to suppress unrest. In January 2002 seven people were shot dead in a suburb known to be a traditional stronghold of the PNP, leading to accusations that the killings were politically motivated. In July the Commission of Inquiry cleared the security forces of the use of excessive brutality.

The PNP's fourth successive term

In a general election held in October 2002, the PNP was re-elected for a fourth consecutive term, albeit with a reduced majority. At his inauguration, Patterson became the first Jamaican Prime Minister to swear allegiance to the people and Constitution of Jamaica, rather than to the British monarch, in accordance with new legislation introduced in August. His new Cabinet retained most of the members of the previous administration.

In December 2002 the armed forces and police began a joint offensive on crime. The Government also revived a previously debated proposal to extend capital punishment to drugs-related crimes and to replace the Privy Council in London, United Kingdom, with a Caribbean Court of Justice (CCJ, see below) as the final court of appeal, thereby removing the Privy Council's ability to commute death sentences to life imprisonment. More than 1,000 murders were reported in 2002, and extended use of capital punishment gained increasing popular support. However, the Crime Management Unit (CMU), established in 2000, had been repeatedly criticized for its excessive use of force. In 2003 the CMU was disbanded and replaced by an Organised Crime Investigation Division. In October the police force was further criticized after two elderly men were accidentally shot during a confrontation between police and an armed gang. The killings prompted a 2,000-strong protest against alleged police and army tactics. In the same month a report was published by the UN Special Rapporteur, which condemned the Government and state security forces for the misuse of force and for failing properly to investigate those accused of extrajudicial executions. In mid-2004 the Prime Minister announced the launch of a National Investigative Authority to pursue allegations against the police. In 2004 the number of murders reached a record 1,445, largely attributed to gang-related conflicts.

In July 2004 the Privy Council abolished Jamaica's mandatory death sentence for convicted murderers. Legislative amendments to this effect were approved by the Senate in November. However, at the same time, amendments were also passed increasing the minimum period a convicted murderer must serve before being granted parole from seven to 20 years. In October the armed forces and the police launched Operation Kingfish, intended to reduce the ever-rising crime rate. The initiative was particularly targeted at dismantling the estimated 13 major criminal networks on the island. By October 2007 567 arrests had been made.

In February 2006 Patterson was succeeded as leader of the PNP by Portia Simpson Miller. Upon assuming office as Prime Minister in the following month, Simpson Miller pledged to eradicate violent crime, protect human rights and create employment.

In January 2007 the Attorney-General, Arnold J. Nicholson, proposed several constitutional reforms that would transform Jamaica into a republic, with a Jamaican President replacing the British monarch as Head of State. This post would not be vested with legislative or executive powers, but would be designated an independent arbiter of selected state appointments. Furthermore, a new Charter of Rights, the subject of extensive deliberations, was to be instituted, and all constitutional amendments would be ratified through an act of the Jamaican legislature, subject to approval in a plebiscite.

Meanwhile, in November 2006 the Government commissioned a comprehensive review of the country's judicial system, with the assistance of representatives from the Canadian Bar Association. The final report was presented in May 2007. The main problems identified were delays in the justice system, poor infrastructure, underfunding, and a lack of consistency in the enforcement of laws.

The return of the JLP

The general election of 2007, originally scheduled for 27 August, was postponed until 3 September owing to the widespread disruption caused by Hurricane Dean, in which three people were killed and much of the country's infrastructure damaged. The JLP won a narrow victory, securing 32 legislative seats, while the PNP won the remaining 28 seats. Some 60.5% of the registered electorate participated in the ballot. According to reports, at least 17 people were killed in political violence during the election campaign, in which the JLP focused on the high levels of crime in the country and the large fiscal deficit. The JLP leader, Bruce Golding (who had rejoined the party in 2001), was sworn in as Prime Minister on 11 September. Included in the new Cabinet was Dorothy Lightbourne, who became the country's first female Attorney-General.

Golding stated that anti-corruption measures and justice system reform would be priorities of the new Government. In November 2007 the Cabinet approved the drafting of legislation to create an Office of the Special Prosecutor, which would investigate high-level acts of corruption, and an independent commission to examine allegations of excessive use of force and of abuse by members of the security forces. (By June 2013 more than 400 members of the police force had been dismissed.) Lightbourne announced in February 2008 that the recommendations of the judicial system review would be incorporated into a national development plan, Vision 2030, which would include the building of new courthouses and the creation of a court agency service, in which the Chief Justice would be responsible for the administration of the courts.

The Government, struggling with a liquidity crisis, imposed an unpopular fuel tax in April 2009, precipitating protests throughout the island. Further taxes were announced in December, including a new levy on staple food items, which resulted in a more vociferous response from the opposition and the public, forcing the Government to rescind the food duty and replace it with a luxury goods tax and an increase in income tax for high earners.

A series of legal challenges launched by the PNP during 2008–11 against JLP members of Parliament accused of holding dual citizenship, which had in some cases led to deputies losing their seats and by-elections being staged, prompted demands for constitutional reform. The Constitution prohibited Jamaican nationals who also possessed citizenship of a non-Commonwealth country from being elected to the legislature, a stipulation that Golding, in January 2011, described as 'an absurdity'. In March Parliament approved the introduction of the long-awaited Charter of Rights, which would protect the rights and freedoms of Jamaicans; the constitutional amendment was approved by the Governor-General in April.

In May 2011 the Minister of Energy and Mining, James Robertson, resigned. His departure from the Cabinet came after his visa was revoked by the USA following allegations of corrupt practices made by a Jamaican national seeking asylum in the USA. In June the Prime Minister executed a reallocation of cabinet portfolios. Lightbourne was among those dismissed from Government. She had been criticized over her handling of the Dudus affair in 2010 (see below). Among the proposals made by the Commission of Inquiry into the affair was the separation of the posts of justice minister and the Attorney-General. To this end, Delroy Chuck, hitherto Speaker of the House of Representatives, was appointed Minister of Justice, while the Attorney-General post remained vacant.

Prime Minister Golding announced his intention in September 2011 to stand down as premier and leader of the JLP by November. He cited the criticism he had received over his involvement in the Dudus affair as one of the main reasons for his resignation. An election for his successor was scheduled to be held at the JLP's party conference in November; however, by mid-October Andrew Holness, the Minister of Education, had emerged as the clear frontrunner. Following Golding's formal resignation as head of government on 23 October, Holness was installed as his successor. His new Cabinet, installed two days later, contained many members of the previous administration. Although elections were not constitutionally due until December 2012, Holness indicated that a ballot would be held by the end of the year. The PNP criticized the handover of power, insisting that a general election should have been called as soon as Golding announced his intention to resign.

The Dudus affair

In 2009 the USA appealed for the extradition of Christopher 'Dudus' Coke, the alleged head of a major criminal gang operating from Tivoli Gardens (a slum area of Kingston), accusing him of drugs-smuggling and arms-trading. The Government initially rejected this petition on the grounds that evidence against Coke had been acquired through illegal wire-tapping. However, it was suspected that Coke was a political ally of Prime Minister Golding (Coke had allegedly mobilized the residents of Tivoli Gardens—Golding's constituency—to vote for the JLP during elections). Evidence to support this theory emerged in March 2010, when it was revealed that Golding apparently had procured the services of a law firm in the USA to lobby the US Administration to abandon its extradition request. Under domestic and US pressure, the Jamaican authorities finally issued a warrant for the arrest of Coke in May. However, this decision provoked Coke's supporters to erect barricades in Tivoli Gardens, and several police stations in the capital were attacked, prompting Golding to declare a state of emergency in the Kingston area on 23 May. Military troops were deployed to bolster the police operation to capture Coke, which involved some 2,000 members of the security forces. Violent clashes ensued in Tivoli Gardens, resulting in approximately 4,000 arrests and the deaths of 76 people, the vast majority of whom were civilians. On 1 June Golding's Government narrowly survived a vote of no confidence in the House of Representatives, proposed by the PNP in protest against the administration's perceived mishandling of the affair. Finally, on 22 June Coke surrendered to the authorities; he was extradited to the USA on 24 June. A Commission of Inquiry concluded in June 2011 that the Prime Minister had acted 'inappropriately', but not 'criminally', in his involvement in the extradition request. Coke was sentenced to 23 years' imprisonment in June 2012. In May 2013, following the release of an interim report into the conduct of security forces during the state of emergency, the Government agreed to appoint a further Commission of Inquiry to investigate alleged human rights abuses.

Recent developments: the PNP in power

As expected, a general election was held on 29 December 2011. The PNP won an overwhelming victory, gaining 42 of the 63 seats in the House of Representatives. The JLP's legislative representation was reduced to 21 seats. The resounding defeat of the JLP was largely attributed to continuing public dissatisfaction with the Government's handling of the Dudus extradition. The PNP leader, Portia Simpson Miller, was sworn into office on 5 January 2012. Her Cabinet contained a mixture of experience and youth. Arnold J. Nicholson was appointed Minister of Foreign Affairs and Foreign Trade, while responsibility for finance and planning was given to Peter Phillips, who had been in charge of the PNP's successful electoral campaign. Another senior PNP figure, Peter Bunting, was designated Minister of National Security and thus assumed responsibility for addressing the country's spiralling violent crime rate. The new Government made clear its intention to adopt the Caribbean Court of Justice (CCJ, see *Regional Relations*) as its final appellate court in place of the Privy Council.

However, the new Government's most pressing concern on taking office was the resumption of negotiations with the IMF towards a new funding facility. An earlier stand-by arrangement had been halted in early 2011 after the previous administration had failed to keep its promises on fiscal austerity (see *Economic Affairs*). The suspension of disbursements also meant Jamaica was unable to access much-needed aid from other multilateral agencies. Phillips, in February 2012, announced a J $21,600m. reduction in the budget. As well as the lack of international funding, Phillips blamed the cut on the JLP administration's decision to increase public sector wages by 7% in 2011, contrary to IMF recommendations. However, in the following month, the House of Representatives approved an $11,200m. increase in budgetary expenditure. In September it was announced that some 3,000 public sector workers were to be made redundant; a further 4,000 posts were to be cut in 2013–14. In May 2013 the IMF approved a new four-year Extended Fund Facility, which would result in a disbursement to Jamaica of US $510m. from both the World Bank and the Inter-American Development Bank (IDB), in return for the Government's commitment to a series of fiscal reforms (see *Economic Affairs*).

Jamaica celebrated 50 years of independence from the United Kingdom in August 2012. The annual Throne Speech, delivered by the Governor-General on 10 May, included the proposal that Jamaica become a republic with an elected President. Simpson Miller reiterated that her Government would also advance moves to end the jurisdiction of the Privy Council, in consultation with the opposition. Although the JLP supported the proposal, the party insisted that both matters should be put to a referendum. In November Minister of Justice Mark Golding reiterated that support by a two-thirds' majority in both houses of Parliament would be sufficient for the CCJ proposal to become law. While the PNP enjoyed such a majority in the House of Representatives, it could count on the support of only 13 of the 21 senators. A PNP attempt to debate the issue in Parliament in November 2014 was unsuccessful. It was announced in January 2015 that a vote on the CCJ proposal would take place in late April, although the JLP announced that it would vote against the proposal and recommended a final appeal court based in Jamaica, rather than the pan-national CCJ, which was based in Port-of-Spain, Trinidad and Tobago.

In September 2013 former finance minister Audley Shaw announced that he would challenge Andrew Holness as leader of the JLP, citing disunity within the party; at the election in November, however, Holness comfortably retained his leadership. In September Richard Azan, a Minister of State in the Ministry of Transport, Works and Housing resigned following a report by the Contractor-General of alleged improprieties in the awarding of a government construction contract. The House of Representatives passed a new Defamation Act in November, which, in addition to abolishing criminal libel, was to end the distinction between libel and slander and establish 'defamation' as a cause of action.

In May 2014 the IDB withdrew funding from a project to build a new power plant in Jamaica, for which Hong Kong-based Energy World International (EWI) had won the tender, citing criticism of the bidding process. The Government—which was seeking to reduce reliance on imported power, estimated to comprise one-third of total imports in 2013—revoked EWI's licence in July and established a committee to oversee the bidding process for a new contractor. In July the Minister of Finance, Horace Dalley, reported that the Casino Gaming Commission was preparing for the eventual introduction of casino gambling in Jamaica, and the Government was reviewing bids placed by luxury resort developments to integrate casinos into their operations, which was likely to lead to an expansion of the tourism sector. The Minister of Agriculture, Roger Clarke, died suddenly in August. Derrick Kellier, the Minister of Labour and Social Security, added the agriculture portfolio to his ministerial remit in October. In the same month the Minister of Trade and Industry, Anthony Hylton, announced proposals to establish special economic zones on the island in 2016, which would benefit from reduced trade tariffs, in order to attract foreign investment.

In September 2014 the Ministry of Justice introduced for debate draft proposals which would decriminalize the possession of small amounts of marijuana for personal or medical use, as well as for religious use by members of the Rastafarian sect. Following approval of an amended bill in the Senate earlier in the month, in February 2015 the House of Representatives endorsed changes to the law. A Cannabis Licensing Authority was to be established to oversee the changes, which came into effect in April, and to regulate the medical use of marijuana.

Violent crime

The high level of violent crime continued to be a significant matter of concern. In November 2008 the House of Representatives voted in favour of retaining the death penalty, a decision later approved by the Senate, while in mid-2009 the Government announced plans to enhance the professionalism and accountability of the police force. The Golding administration also revealed that the judicial system would be reformed and additional judges would be appointed to expedite the trials of violent criminals. The Commissioner of Police, Hardley Lewin, resigned in November, after the Prime Minister indicated that he had 'lost confidence' in him. Police patrols were expanded in 2010, and a programme to address corruption was introduced in January, with 149 officers dismissed throughout the year as a result. In June legislative approval was secured for a series of security measures, which included the extension of certain police powers, new restrictions on bail and parole, and additional controls on firearms. The Government's anti-crime strategy appeared to be having a positive effect: the number of murders declined from 1,683 in 2009 to 1,087 in 2012, a nine-year low. Despite this, the murder rate remained the highest in the Caribbean and the third highest worldwide (after El Salvador and Honduras). The new PNP Government (see above) adopted further anti-crime initiatives in 2012, which, *inter alia*, aimed to reduce the average murder rate from three per day to less than one by 2017. However, the murder rate rose in 2013, to some 1,200 in total. The US Government's International Narcotics Control Strategy Report in 2014 claimed that Jamaica was making 'slow but steady' progress in combating drugs-trafficking and organized crime. In March 2014 the Criminal Justice Bill was enacted, which provided for the disruption and suppression of criminal organizations. In the same month the Government approved plans to merge the Jamaica Constabulary Force and the Island Special Constabulary Force in order to reduce the rate of crime. The Commissioner of Police, Owen Ellington, reported in May that the murder rate had fallen by 44% since 2010. However, he resigned in June, citing the wish to separate himself from the leadership of the police force before the commencement of the Commission of Inquiry into the Dudus affair, over which he had presided. He was replaced by Carl Williams in September.

Foreign Affairs

Regional relations

In 1998 Jamaica withdrew from a UN treaty that allowed prisoners sentenced to death to appeal for a review by the UN Commission on Human Rights; later that year it also withdrew from the Inter-American Court of Human Rights (see p. 393) of the Organization of American States. In 2001 Jamaica was one of 11 Caribbean nations to establish a Caribbean Court of Justice (CCJ), to be based in Trinidad and Tobago. The Court was to replace the Privy Council in the United Kingdom as the final court of appeal, and would allow for the executions of convicted criminals. (The Privy Council generally commuted death sentences to life imprisonment on appeal.) Despite opposition from the JLP and from the Jamaica Bar Association, in 2004 Parliament approved legislation replacing the Privy Council with the CCJ. Opposition groupings appealed to the Privy Council itself that the legislation should be annulled because it had been passed without the approval of the electorate in a referendum. In February 2005 the Privy Council upheld the appeal. In total, the Privy Council annulled three such bills to confer trading and appellate jurisdiction on to the CCJ. Nevertheless, in April the House of Representatives ratified membership of the CCJ, but only as a court of original jurisdiction on trade matters. A further parliamentary vote on the matter was scheduled for late April 2014.

In 2005 Jamaica became one of 13 Caribbean nations to sign the Petrocaribe accord, under which the country would be allowed to purchase petroleum from Venezuela at reduced prices. In September 2013 Jamaica received a commitment from Venezuela not to change the terms of the accord at least until the expiry of its four-year Extended Fund Facility with the IMF in 2017. Jamaica made its first shipment of clinker under the trade compensation mechanism option of the accord in December 2013 and further shipments were made in 2014.

Other external relations

Relations between Jamaica and the USA have been hampered by persistent demands by the USA for the eradication of Jamaica's marijuana crop and deteriorated further in 2010 after the JLP Government appeared to attempt to prevent the extradition to the USA of alleged drugs-trafficker Christopher 'Dudus' Coke (see above). The cancellation by US authorities of the Minister of Energy and Mining's visa in May 2011 placed further strain on bilateral links.

Jamaica has enjoyed good diplomatic relations with the People's Republic of China, which have been strengthened by numerous trade and investment agreements. In April 2013 it was announced that the China Harbour Engineering Company (CHEC) was to invest in the development of a port in Jamaica comprising transshipment facilities, a manufacturing zone and an electricity generation plant. In September CHEC indicated that its preferred option was the Goat Islands. The terms of an initial framework agreement for the investment, worth some US $2,000m., were passed in the House of Representatives in February 2014. In August 2013, during a visit to China by Simpson Miller, a $16m. grant was pledged for development projects in Jamaica, as well as a loan of $300m. to the country's Major Infrastructure Development Programme. Meanwhile, in early 2014 the Jamaican Government and CHEC signed a Memorandum of Understanding to study the feasibility of damming at the Bog Walk Gorge in St Catherine, in order to store and increase the supply of potable water.

In September 2014 the National Reparations Commission advised the Government to consider writing off debt from countries that had benefited from the trans-Atlantic trade in slavery, including the United Kingdom and Spain, and recommended that it seek initial reparations of US $37.7m.—equivalent to the sum paid to slave-owners as compensation for the emancipation of their slaves in the 19th century. The Commission calculated that the total amount due in reparations from the United Kingdom to Jamaica—its largest and most profitable former colony in which the slave trade existed—was around US $3,500,000m.

CONSTITUTION AND GOVERNMENT

The Constitution came into force at Jamaica's independence in August 1962. The Head of State is the British monarch, who is represented locally by the Governor-General, appointed on the recommendation of the Prime Minister in consultation with the Leader of the Opposition. The Governor-General acts, in almost all matters, on the advice of the Cabinet.

Legislative power is vested in the bicameral Parliament: the Senate, with 21 appointed members, and the House of Representatives, with 63 elected members. Thirteen members of the Senate are appointed by the Governor-General on the advice of the Prime Minister and eight on the advice of the Leader of the Opposition. Members of the House are elected by universal adult suffrage for five years (subject to dissolution). Executive power lies with the Cabinet. The Prime Minister is appointed from the House of Representatives by the Governor-General, and is the leader of the party that holds the majority of seats in the House of Representatives. The Cabinet is responsible to Parliament. Jamaica is divided into 14 parishes.

REGIONAL AND INTERNATIONAL CO-OPERATION

Jamaica is a founding member of the Caribbean Community and Common Market (CARICOM, see p. 222) and of the Inter-American Development Bank (IDB, see p. 328). Jamaica was also one of the six founder members of CARICOM's Caribbean Single Market and Economy (CSME), inaugurated in 2006. The CSME was intended to facilitate the free movement of goods, services and labour throughout the CARICOM region, although owing to repeated delays this regional initiative had still not been realized by early 2015. The country is a member of the Association of Caribbean States (see p. 444), and of the Community of Latin American and Caribbean States (see p. 460), which was formally inaugurated in December 2011.

Jamaica became a member of the UN upon independence in 1962. The country acceded to the World Trade Organization (see p. 431) in 1995. Jamaica joined the Commonwealth (see p. 234) upon independence. Jamaica is a signatory of the Cotonou Agreement (see p. 321) with the European Union (see p. 271).

ECONOMIC AFFAIRS

In 2013, according to estimates by the World Bank, Jamaica's gross national income (GNI), measured at average 2011–13 prices, was US $14,163m., equivalent to US $5,220 per head. During 2004–13, it was estimated, the population increased at an average rate of 0.3% per year, while gross domestic product (GDP) per head increased at an average annual rate of 0.4% during 2002–11. According to official figures, overall GDP decreased, in real terms, at an average annual rate of 0.7% in 2007–13; the economy contracted by 0.6% in 2012, but expanded by 0.6% in 2013.

Agriculture (including forestry and fishing) contributed 6.8% of GDP in 2013 and engaged 18.4% of the economically active population in mid-2014. The principal cash crops are sugar cane (sugar accounted for an estimated 3.5% of total export earnings in 2013), coffee, citrus fruit, pimento and cocoa. Agricultural GDP increased at an annual average rate of 2.2% in 2004–13; the sector's GDP increased by 2.3% in 2012, but declined by 0.7% in 2013.

Industry (including mining, manufacturing, public utilities and construction) contributed 20.3% of GDP in 2013 and engaged 15.0% of the economically active population in mid-2014. Industrial GDP decreased at an average rate of 2.0% during 2004–13; the sector declined by 3.1% in 2012, but increased by 0.4% in 2013.

Mining and quarrying contributed an estimated 1.2% of GDP in 2013, and engaged only 0.5% of the active labour force in mid-2014. Mining is the principal productive sector of the economy, and in 2013 bauxite and its derivative, alumina (aluminium oxide), accounted for an estimated 58.2% of total export earnings. Bauxite, of which Jamaica is one of the world's leading producers, is the major mineral mined, but there are also reserves of marble, gypsum, limestone, silica and clay.

Manufacturing contributed an estimated 9.0% of GDP in 2013 and engaged some 6.3% of the active labour force in mid-2014. Much of the activity in the sector is dependent upon the processing of sugar and bauxite. Manufacturing GDP decreased at an average annual rate of 1.5% during 2004–13; the sector decreased by 0.5% in 2013.

Construction contributed an estimated 7.0% of GDP in 2013 and engaged some 7.4% of the active labour force in mid-2014. Construction GDP decreased at an average annual rate of 1.3% during 2004–13; the sector declined by 4.4% in 2012, but increased by 1.9% in 2013.

Energy is derived almost entirely from imported petroleum (91.8% in 2011). In 2013 imports of mineral fuels and lubricants accounted for 35.3% of the total value of merchandise imports. A project to build a 360 MW natural gas-fired plant in order to reduce reliance on imported power was stalled in mid-2014 after the contractor's licence was revoked (see *Recent developments*). Construction of a wind farm in St Elizabeth was under way in 2015.

The services sector contributed an estimated 72.8% of GDP in 2013 and engaged some 66.6% of the active labour force in mid-2014. Tourism is the principal source of foreign exchange earnings. In 2013 the World Travel and Tourism Council estimated that tourism contributed (directly and indirectly) 25.6% of GDP. Visitor arrivals stood at 2.0m. in 2013. The largest proportion of tourists is from the USA (63.3% in 2013). In addition, there were a further 1.3m. cruise ship arrivals in 2013. Tourism revenue totalled US $2,074m. in 2013. The GDP of the services sector increased at an average annual rate of 0.4% in 2004–13; the sector decreased by 0.1% in 2012, but increased by 0.2% in 2013.

In 2013 Jamaica recorded a visible merchandise trade deficit of US $3,797.0m., and there was a deficit of US $1,311.7m. on the current account of the balance of payments. In 2013 the principal source of imports (34.1%) was the USA. Other major suppliers were Venezuela and Trinidad and Tobago. In the same year the USA was also the principal market for exports (49.1%). Canada, the Netherlands and the United Kingdom were among other important purchasers. The principal exports in 2013 were crude materials, foodstuffs (including sugar and bananas), chemicals, mineral fuels and lubricants, and beverages and tobacco. The principal imports in 2013 were mineral fuels and lubricants, foodstuffs, machinery and transport equipment, chemicals, and manufactured goods.

In the financial year ending 31 March 2014 Jamaica recorded an estimated budget surplus of J $1,757.5m. Jamaica's general government gross debt was $2,067,630m. in 2013, equivalent to 141.6% of GDP. Total external debt at the end of 2012 was US $14,333.0m., of which US $7,383.0m. was public and publicly guaranteed debt. In that year, the cost of servicing long-term public and publicly guaranteed debt and repayments to the IMF was equivalent to 38.2% of the value of exports of goods, services and income (excluding workers' remittances). The average annual rate of inflation was 11.1% in 2004–13; consumer prices increased by an annual average of 9.4% in 2013. Some 13.8% of the labour force were unemployed in mid-2014.

The People's National Party administration, which took office in 2012, inherited a widening current account deficit and falling export revenues, as well as declining tourism receipts. The Government was quick to reopen negotiations with the IMF, disbursements on a US $1,270m. stand-by arrangement having been suspended in 2011 owing to the slow pace of economic and public sector reform. In May 2013 it secured an agreement on a new $932.3m. four-year Extended Fund Facility, a deal which would also release $510m. from both the World Bank and the Inter-American Development Bank. Among the conditions of the IMF loan were a reduction in the public sector wage bill from 11% to 9% of GDP by 2016 and an acceleration of the privatization programme. Wide-ranging fiscal reform was also to be implemented. Trade unions warned that the measures would lead to business closures and an increase in the already high rate of unemployment; however, the Government asserted that the agreement was necessary to reduce the unsustainable debt burden and bring about economic stability. In February 2014 the IMF announced that Jamaica's economic activity had been positive, although there were some shortfalls in tax revenues. The Ministry of Finance in early 2014 set out fiscal prudence, a fall in energy costs, and crime reduction as its priorities, while in April, upon presenting its budget, the Government announced its intention to create 21,000 jobs in 2014–15; a controversial proposal for a financial transaction tax was withdrawn. In May the European Union signed an agreement with the Government to provide some $75m. in development assistance during 2016–19. The IMF forecast economic growth of 1.0% in 2014 and of 1.8% in 2015, owing, in part, to a recovery in the agricultural sector since Hurricane Sandy in 2012. The Managing Director of the IMF, Christine Lagarde, visited Jamaica in June 2014 and commended the Government's economic reforms, while urging greater efforts in the collection of tax, and public sector reform; the Fund disbursed $67m. to Jamaica in December. The World Bank agreed loans worth $105m. to Jamaica in September, to promote youth employment and economic growth.

PUBLIC HOLIDAYS

2016: 1 January (New Year's Day), 10 February (Ash Wednesday), 25 March (Good Friday), 28 March (Easter Monday), 23 May (Labour Day), 1 August (Emancipation Day), 6 August (Independence Day), 17 October (National Heroes' Day), 25 December (Christmas Day), 26 December (Boxing Day).

Statistical Survey

Sources (unless otherwise stated): Statistical Institute of Jamaica, 7 Cecelio Ave, Kingston 10; tel. 926-5311; fax 926-1138; e-mail info@statinja.gov.jm; internet www.statinja.gov.jm; Jamaica Information Service, 58A Half Way Tree Rd, POB 2222, Kingston 10; tel. 926-3740; fax 926-6715; e-mail jis@jis.gov.jm; internet www.jis.gov.jm; Bank of Jamaica, Nethersole Pl., POB 621, Kingston; tel. 922-0750; fax 922-0854; e-mail info@boj.org.jm; internet www.boj.org.jm.

Area and Population

AREA, POPULATION AND DENSITY

Area (sq km)	10,991*
Population (census results)	
10 September 2001	2,607,632
5 April 2011	
Males	1,334,533
Females	1,363,450
Total	2,697,983
Population (UN estimates at mid-year)†	
2013	2,783,890
2014	2,798,835
2015	2,813,276
Density (per sq km) at mid-2015	256.0

* 4,243.6 sq miles.
† Source: UN, *World Population Prospects: The 2012 Revision*.

POPULATION BY AGE AND SEX
(UN estimates at mid–2015)

	Males	Females	Total
0–14 years	372,198	359,926	732,124
15–64 years	908,651	944,740	1,853,391
65 years and over	104,442	123,319	227,761
Total	**1,385,291**	**1,427,985**	**2,813,276**

Source: UN, *World Population Prospects: The 2012 Revision*.

PARISHES
(population at 2011 census)

	Area (sq km)	Population	Density (per sq km)
Clarendon	1,196	245,103	204.9
Hanover	450	69,533	154.5
Kingston and St Andrew . . .	453*	662,426	1,462.3
Manchester	830	189,797	228.7
Portland	814	81,744	100.4
St Ann	1,213	172,362	142.1
St Catherine	1,192	516,218	433.1
St Elizabeth	1,212	150,205	123.9
St James	595	183,811	308.9
St Mary	611	113,615	185.9
St Thomas	743	93,902	126.4
Trelawny	875	75,164	85.9
Westmoreland	807	144,103	178.6
Total	10,991	2,697,983	245.5

* Kingston 22 sq km, St Andrew 431 sq km.

PRINCIPAL TOWNS
(population at 2011 census)

Kingston (capital) .	584,627	Montego Bay . .	110,115
Portmore	182,153	May Pen	61,548
Spanish Town . .	147,152	Mandeville . . .	49,695

Mid-2014 (incl. suburbs, UN estimate): Kingston 587,702 (Source: UN, *World Urbanization Prospects: The 2014 Revision*).

BIRTHS, MARRIAGES AND DEATHS*

	Registered live births		Registered marriages		Registered deaths	
	Number	Rate (per 1,000)	Number	Rate (per 1,000)	Number	Rate (per 1,000)
2006	43,243	16.3	18,960	7.2	23,181	8.7
2007	43,385	16.3	20,550	7.7	20,250	7.6
2008	43,112	16.1	19,966	7.5	22,152	8.3
2009	42,782	16.0	18,855	7.0	21,692	8.1
2010	40,508	15.1	21,503	8.0	20,910	7.8
2011	39,673	14.7	16,926	6.3	20,685	7.6
2012	39,553	14.5	16,998	6.3	16,998	6.3
2013† . . .	36,746	13.5	18,835	9.9	15,427	5.7

* Data are tabulated by year of registration rather than by year of occurrence.
† Provisional.

Life expectancy (years at birth): 73.3 (males 70.8; females 75.9) in 2012 (Source: World Bank, World Development Indicators database).

ECONOMICALLY ACTIVE POPULATION
('000 persons aged 14 years and over, July 2014)

	Males	Females	Total
Agriculture, forestry and fishing .	167.6	38.7	206.3
Mining and quarrying	4.8	0.6	5.4
Manufacturing	48.6	21.7	70.3
Electricity, gas and water . . .	6.7	2.0	8.7
Construction	80.9	2.5	83.4
Wholesale and retail, repair of motor vehicles and equipment .	97.1	119.3	216.4
Hotels and restaurants . . .	32.2	50.5	82.7
Transport, storage and communications	58.4	18.1	76.5
Financial intermediation . . .	8.4	16.6	25.0
Real estate, renting and business activities	39.4	25.1	64.5

—continued	Males	Females	Total
Public administration and defence; compulsory social security . .	31.4	26.0	57.4
Education	17.0	56.0	73.0
Health and social work . . .	9.1	24.3	33.4
Community, social and personal services	29.8	33.9	63.7
Private households with employed persons	8.4	45.8	54.2
Sub-total	639.8	481.1	1,120.9
Activities not adequately defined .	0.8	2.9	3.7
Total employed	640.6	484.0	1,124.6
Unemployed	70.5	108.9	179.4
Total labour force	711.1	592.9	1,304.0

Health and Welfare

KEY INDICATORS

Total fertility rate (children per woman, 2012)	2.3
Under-5 mortality rate (per 1,000 live births, 2012) . . .	17
HIV/AIDS (% of persons aged 15–49, 2013)	1.8
Physicians (per 1,000 head, 2008)	0.4
Hospital beds (per 1,000 head, 2010)	1.9
Health expenditure (2011): US $ per head (PPP)	395
Health expenditure (2011): % of GDP	5.2
Health expenditure (2011): public (% of total)	53.6
Access to water (% of persons, 2012)	93
Access to sanitation (% of persons, 2012) . .	80
Total carbon dioxide emissions ('000 metric tons, 2010) . .	7,158.0
Carbon dioxide emissions per head (metric tons, 2010) . .	2.6
Human Development Index (2013): ranking	96
Human Development Index (2013): value	0.715

For sources and definitions, see explanatory note on p. vi.

Agriculture

PRINCIPAL CROPS
('000 metric tons)

	2011	2012	2013
Sweet potatoes	42	42	44
Yams	135	145	139
Sugar cane	1,518	1,475	1,403
Coconuts	290*	315†	310†
Cabbages and other brassicas .	33	33	35
Tomatoes	27	27	29
Pumpkins, squash and gourds .	49	52	52
Carrots and turnips	32	30	33
Bananas	47	47	37
Plantains	35	36	31
Oranges	100	92	83
Lemons and limes†	26	27	27
Grapefruit and pomelos† . . .	45	44	45
Pineapples	18	20	19

* Unofficial figure.
† FAO estimate(s).

Aggregate production ('000 metric tons, may include official, semi-official or estimated data): Total cereals 3.0 in 2011, 3.1 in 2012, 3.0 in 2013; Total roots and tubers 240.5 in 2011, 248.3 in 2012, 243.2 in 2013; Total vegetables (incl. melons) 267.7 in 2011, 273.5 in 2012, 287.2 in 2013; Total fruits (excl. melons) 324.2 in 2011, 320.7 in 2012, 297.2 in 2013.

Source: FAO.

LIVESTOCK

('000 head, year ending September, FAO estimates)

	2011	2012	2013
Horses	4	4	4
Mules	10	10	10
Asses	23	23	23
Cattle	170	170	170
Pigs	200	205	210
Sheep	1.4	1.4	1.4
Goats	500	520	520
Poultry	13,000	13,500	13,500

Source: FAO.

LIVESTOCK PRODUCTS

('000 metric tons)

	2011	2012	2013
Cattle meat	5.6	5.8	5.6
Goat meat	1.3	1.1	1.1
Pig meat	7.1	9.5	9.6
Chicken meat	101.5	102.2	103.8
Cows' milk	12.4	12.8	12.5
Hen eggs*	7.6	9.4	9.5
Honey*	0.8	0.8	0.8

* FAO estimates.

Source: FAO.

Forestry

ROUNDWOOD REMOVALS

('000 cubic metres, excl. bark, FAO estimates)

	2011	2012	2013
Sawlogs, veneer logs and logs for sleepers	1	1	1
Other industrial wood	151	151	152
Fuel wood	541	537	533
Total	693	689	686

Source: FAO.

SAWNWOOD PRODUCTION

('000 cubic metres, incl. railway sleepers, FAO estimates)

	2011	2012	2013
Coniferous (softwood)	3	3	3
Broadleaved (hardwood)	63	63	63
Total	66	66	66

Note: Annual production assumed to be unchanged from 1998.
Source: FAO.

Fishing

('000 metric tons, live weight)

	2010	2011*	2012
Capture	15.4	15.1	15.0*
Marine fishes	11.4	11.4	11.3*
Freshwater fishes	0.4	0.4	0.4*
Aquaculture*	4.1	1.2	0.6
Nile tilapia	3.9	1.1	0.6
Total catch*	19.5	16.3	15.6

* FAO estimate(s).
Source: FAO.

Mining

('000 metric tons)

	2010	2011	2012
Bauxite*	8,540	10,190	9,339
Alumina	1,591	1,960	1,758
Crude gypsum	230	96	100†
Lime	300†	300	n.a.
Salt	19.0†	n.a.	n.a.

* Dried equivalent of crude ore.
† Estimated figure.
Source: US Geological Survey.

Industry

SELECTED PRODUCTS

	2011	2012	2013
Sugar ('000 metric tons)	143.2	136.2	121.1
Rum ('000 litres)	17,627	24,508	31,259
Diesel and fuel oil (million litres)	987.8	982.8	937.1
Motor spirit (petrol, million litres)	194.3	181.2	167.1
Kerosene, turbo and jet fuel (million litres)	114.8	122.8	121.3
Cement ('000 metric tons)	717.3	760.3	824.9

Electrical energy (million kWh): 5,195 in 2009; 5,040 in 2010; 5,098 in 2011 (Source: UN Industrial Commodity Statistics Database).

Finance

CURRENCY AND EXCHANGE RATES

Monetary Units
100 cents = 1 Jamaican dollar (J$).

Sterling, US Dollar and Euro Equivalents (31 December 2014)
£1 sterling = J$178.540;
US$1 = J$114.390;
€1 = J$138.881;
J$1,000 = £5.60 = US$8.74 = €7.20.

Average Exchange Rate (J$ per US$)
2012   88.751
2013   100.241
2014   110.935

GOVERNMENT FINANCE

(budgetary central government, non-cash basis, J$ million, year ending 31 March)

Summary of Balances

	2010	2011*	2012*
Revenue	309,231	308,468	346,164
Less Expense	375,703	387,215	402,867
Gross operating balance	−66,472	−78,746	−56,703
Less Net acquisition of non-financial assets	26,752	24,149	25,040
Net lending/borrowing	−93,224	−102,895	−81,743

Revenue

	2010	2011*	2012*
Tax revenue	274,493	286,196	321,672
Taxes on income, profits and capital gains	116,954	121,427	138,513
Taxes on goods and services	124,799	129,990	142,744
Grants	9,669	3,347	1,123
Other revenue	25,069	18,925	23,370
Total	309,231	308,468	346,164

Expense/Outlays

Expense by economic type	2010	2011*	2012*
Compensation of employees . .	59,231	66,115	66,062
Use of goods and services . .	20,312	21,734	22,339
Interest	128,355	120,704	136,534
Social benefits	16,762	21,796	24,141
Other expense	151,043	156,866	153,792
Total	375,703	387,215	402,867

Outlays by functions of government†	2010	2011*	2012*
General public services . . .	173,781	183,238	193,256
Defence	10,138	11,926	12,312
Public order and safety . . .	34,805	40,060	42,959
Economic affairs	61,976	49,437	37,984
Environmental protection . .	712	937	1,103
Housing and community amenities	7,112	8,326	8,590
Health	34,627	37,384	36,365
Recreation, culture and religion .	3,441	3,810	4,623
Education	71,288	76,601	82,080
Social protection	7,071	7,259	7,285
Statistical discrepancy . . .	−2,496	−7,614	1,350
Total	402,455	411,364	427,907

* Preliminary.
† Including net acquisition of non-financial assets.

Source: IMF, *Government Finance Statistics Yearbook*.

2012/13 (central government operations, J $ million): *Revenue:* Tax revenue 319,764.9; Non-tax revenue 18,765.1; Other revenue 1,163.7; Capital revenue 1,015.8; Grants 3,968.3; Total 344,677.7. *Expenditure:* Current expenditure 361,521.0 (Programmes 87,201.5, Wages and salaries 147,381.8, Interest 126,937.7); Capital expenditure (incl. net lending) 37,757.9; Total 399,278.9 (Source: Ministry of Finance and Planning, Kingston).

2013/14 (central government operations, J $ million, estimates): *Revenue:* Tax revenue 343,836.1; Non-tax revenue 41,047.1; Other revenue 1,009.5; Capital revenue 658.1; Grants 10,627.4; Total 397,178.2. *Expenditure:* Current expenditure 360,248.9 (Programmes 93,967.7, Wages and salaries 156,361.7, Interest 109,919.5); Capital expenditure (incl. net lending) 35,171.8; Total 395,420.7 (Source: Ministry of Finance and Planning, Kingston).

2014/15 (central government operations, J $ million, projections): *Revenue:* Tax revenue 384,286.0; Non-tax revenue 34,186.4; Other revenue 17.9; Capital revenue 753.3; Grants 8,644.9; Total 427,888.5. *Expenditure:* Current expenditure 404,654.5 (Programmes 110,281.1, Wages and salaries 161,704.3, Interest 132,669.1); Capital expenditure (incl. net lending) 34,628.1; Total 439,282.6 (Source: Ministry of Finance and Planning, Kingston).

INTERNATIONAL RESERVES
(excl. gold, US $ million at 31 December)

	2011	2012	2013
IMF special drawing rights .	315.9	306.5	296.1
Foreign exchange	1,966.1	1,674.3	1,522.3
Total	2,281.9	1,980.8	1,818.4

Source: IMF, *International Financial Statistics*.

MONEY SUPPLY
(J $ million at 31 December)

	2011	2012	2013
Currency outside depository corporations	51,505	53,502	57,038
Transferable deposits	117,908	105,951	145,006
Other deposits	391,282	418,009	480,061
Securities other than shares . .	70,567	40,837	42,328
Broad money	631,262	618,299	724,433

Source: IMF, *International Financial Statistics*.

COST OF LIVING
(Consumer Price Index; base: December 2006 = 100)

	2011	2012	2013
Food (incl. non-alcoholic beverages)	190.7	211.3	237.8
Clothing and footwear . . .	166.1	183.3	204.0
Housing, utilities and fuel . .	190.4	201.6	218.9
All items (incl. others) . . .	172.8	184.7	202.0

NATIONAL ACCOUNTS
(J $ million at current prices)

Expenditure on the Gross Domestic Product

	2011	2012	2013
Government final consumption expenditure	196,315	215,230	225,253
Private final consumption expenditure	1,065,800	1,123,518	1,228,942
Increase in stocks . . .	5,535	3,069	4,732
Gross fixed capital formation .	259,834	258,093	300,553
Total domestic expenditure .	1,527,484	1,599,910	1,759,481
Exports of goods and services	376,784	397,813	428,713
Less Imports of goods and services	663,195	681,970	757,771
GDP in purchasers' values .	1,241,072	1,315,754	1,430,423

Gross Domestic Product by Economic Activity

	2011	2012	2013
Agriculture, forestry and fishing .	70,861	76,448	86,258
Mining and quarrying	15,487	14,811	15,525
Manufacturing	97,278	105,174	113,349
Electricity and water	36,288	36,496	40,049
Construction	77,921	80,330	87,987
Wholesale and retail trade; repairs and installation of machinery .	201,491	213,059	233,935
Hotels and restaurants . . .	45,481	48,175	53,222
Transport, storage and communication	104,137	101,214	105,551
Finance and insurance services .	111,869	117,250	123,411
Real estate, renting and business services	130,771	138,419	145,784
Producers of government services .	152,651	107,393	176,446
Other services	69,803	75,052	81,104
Sub-total	1,114,038	1,173,821	1,262,621
Less Financial intermediation services indirectly measured .	45,755	47,792	49,579
Gross value added in basic prices	1,068,282	1,126,030	1,213,041
Taxes, less subsidies, on products .	172,790	189,725	217,382
GDP in market prices . . .	1,241,072	1,315,754	1,430,423

BALANCE OF PAYMENTS
(US $ million)

	2011	2012	2013
Exports of goods	1,666.1	1,728.5	1,634.2
Imports of goods	−5,881.4	−5,632.4	−5,431.3
Balance on goods	−4,215.3	−3,903.9	−3,797.0
Exports of services	2,620.2	2,694.3	2,665.4
Imports of services	−1,946.0	−2,176.2	−2,067.0
Balance on goods and services	−3,541.2	−3,385.8	−3,198.6
Primary income received . . .	221.5	404.4	334.4
Primary income paid	−739.9	−629.2	−668.0
Balance on goods, services and primary income	−4,059.6	−3,610.7	−3,532.3
Secondary income received . .	2,284.0	2,381.9	2,463.7
Secondary income paid . . .	−287.6	−270.7	−243.2
Current balance	−2,063.2	−1,499.4	−1,311.7

—*continued*	2011	2012	2013
Capital account (net) . . .	−9.1	5.9	18.9
Direct investment assets . .	−29.1	−2.8	86.9
Direct investment liabilities . .	172.8	473.4	626.8
Portfolio investment assets .	−70.8	−109.8	−157.4
Portfolio investment liabilities .	240.5	−146.9	231.1
Financial derivatives and employee stock options (net)	—	8.7	−26.2
Other investment assets . . .	−274.4	−306.2	−80.5
Other investment liabilities .	1,270.8	188.8	461.4
Net errors and omissions . . .	494.9	565.1	−28.6
Reserves and related items .	−267.8	−823.2	−179.4

Source: IMF, *International Financial Statistics*.

External Trade

PRINCIPAL COMMODITIES
(US $ million)

Imports c.i.f.	2011	2012	2013
Foods	938.7	948.3	961.5
Beverages and tobacco	77.4	79.5	77.0
Crude materials (excl. fuels) . .	62.8	46.7	55.8
Mineral fuels and lubricants . .	2,310.9	2,218.0	2,177.6
Animal and vegetable oils and fats	58.6	51.5	42.8
Chemicals	873.4	895.6	724.1
Manufactured goods . . .	645.7	616.4	599.7
Machinery and transport equipment	932.1	902.4	897.4
Miscellaneous manufactured articles	471.5	454.4	443.0
Total (incl. others)	6,517.5	6,406.4	6,172.0

Exports f.o.b.	2011	2012	2013
Foods	232.3	273.8	241.0
Beverages and tobacco . . .	113.2	104.3	85.3
Crude materials (excl. fuels) . .	767.9	665.4	655.0
Mineral fuels and lubricants . .	186.6	200.8	186.6
Chemicals	46.8	228.5	199.1
Machinery and transport equipment	50.4	22.8	38.5
Miscellaneous manufactured articles	19.1	18.4	23.7
Total (incl. others)	1,623.7	1,728.5	1,634.2

PRINCIPAL TRADING PARTNERS
(US $ million)

Imports c.i.f.	2011	2012	2013
Barbados	38.3	26.2	63.0
Belgium	65.6	53.5	52.2
Brazil	323.7	241.9	165.5
Canada	117.7	101.3	100.5
China, People's Republic . . .	282.3	310.5	332.8
Colombia	70.5	54.6	48.1
Dominican Republic . . .	66.5	47.7	47.1
Germany	64.1	70.5	77.7
Japan	148.7	208.4	179.8
Mexico	242.6	264.1	272.1
Trinidad and Tobago . . .	831.3	699.0	764.5
United Kingdom	85.1	83.7	66.6
USA	2,163.3	2,349.2	2,122.7
Venezuela	958.8	1,013.9	928.5
Total (incl. others)	6,436.6	6,580.4	6,216.2

Exports f.o.b.	2011	2012	2013
Bahamas	2.1	21.8	2.5
Barbados	9.2	23.8	9.3
Bulgaria	0.0	18.3	0.0
Canada	263.7	121.6	225.1
China, People's Republic . . .	21.4	11.4	15.0
France	7.0	16.5	15.8
Georgia	9.1	36.2	41.5
Iceland	7.8	27.2	37.6
Italy	1.2	37.9	2.0
Japan	13.7	10.6	12.3
Latvia	0.0	59.9	0.0
Netherlands	91.4	70.6	108.5
Norway	41.8	0.1	0.1
Poland	0.0	18.6	0.0
Russia	10.7	59.2	25.2
Slovenia	51.5	71.4	63.4
Trinidad and Tobago . . .	21.0	18.3	16.4
United Arab Emirates . . .	1.7	69.2	9.5
United Kingdom	111.6	44.9	81.2
USA	839.3	823.5	770.8
Total (incl. others)	1,622.9	1,711.8	1,569.1

Source: Trade Map-Trade Competitiveness Map, International Trade Centre, www.intracen.org/marketanalysis.

Transport

ROAD TRAFFIC
(motor vehicles in use at 31 December)

	2005	2006	2008*
Passenger cars	357,810	373,742	224,520
Motorcycles	27,038	29,061	6,249

* Data for 2007 were not available.

2012: Passenger cars 382,096; Buses 14,659; Lorries 85,041; Motorcycles 11,777.

Source: IRF, *World Road Statistics*.

SHIPPING

Flag Registered Fleet
(at 31 December)

	2012	2013	2014
Number of vessels	27	40	55
Total displacement ('000 grt) . .	123.1	168.4	184.0

Source: Lloyd's List Intelligence (www.lloydslistintelligence.com).

International Seaborne Freight Traffic
('000 metric tons, estimates)

	2011	2012	2013
Goods loaded	16,570	12,951	12,514
Goods unloaded	13,844	11,013	9,911

Source: Port Authority of Jamaica.

CIVIL AVIATION
(traffic on scheduled services)

	2007	2008	2009
Kilometres flown (million) . .	57	27	26
Passengers carried ('000) . . .	1,618	1,500	1,380
Passenger-km (million) . . .	3,959	3,027	2,839
Total ton-km (million) . . .	380	315	295

Source: UN, *Statistical Yearbook*.

2010: Passengers carried ('000) 978 (Source: World Bank, World Development Indicators database).

Tourism

VISITOR ARRIVALS BY COUNTRY OF ORIGIN

	2011	2012	2013
Canada	378,938	403,200	399,331
USA	1,225,565	1,257,669	1,271,262
Total (incl. others)	1,951,752	1,986,082	2,008,409

Tourism revenue (US $ million): 2,012.5 in 2011; 2,046.3 in 2012; 2,073.9 in 2013.

Communications Media

	2011	2012	2013
Telephones ('000 main lines in use)	272.1	264.5	247.9
Mobile cellular telephones ('000 subscribers)	2,974.7	2,665.7	2,795.7
Broadband subscribers ('000) . .	106.5	119.7	132.5

Source: International Telecommunication Union.

Education

(2012/13 unless otherwise indicated)

	Institutions	Teachers	Students
Pre-primary	2,936	10,269	138,124
Primary	933	11,704	264,862
Secondary	387	13,914	236,002
Special schools	30	425	3,748
Tertiary	15	1,162	16,171
University*	2	1,049	26,295

* Figures for 2011/12.

Source: Ministry of Education, Kingston.

Pupil-teacher ratio (primary education, UNESCO estimate): 22.9 in 2011/12 (Source: UNESCO Institute for Statistics).

Adult literacy rate (UNESCO estimates): 87.5% (males 82.6%; females 92.1%) in 2012 (Source: UNESCO Institute for Statistics).

Directory

The Government

HEAD OF STATE

Queen: HM Queen ELIZABETH II.

Governor-General: Sir PATRICK LINTON ALLEN (took office 26 February 2009).

CABINET
(April 2015)

The Government is formed by the People's National Party.

Prime Minister and Minister of Defence, Development, Information and Sports: PORTIA SIMPSON MILLER.

Minister of Foreign Affairs and Foreign Trade: ARNOLD NICHOLSON.

Minister of Finance and Planning: Dr PETER PHILLIPS.

Minister of National Security: PETER BUNTING.

Minister of Education: Rev. RONALD THWAITES.

Minister of Water, Land, Environment and Climate Change: ROBERT PICKERSGILL.

Minister of Tourism and Entertainment: Dr KENNETH WYKEHAM MCNEIL.

Minister of Justice: MARK GOLDING.

Minister of Industry, Commerce and Investment: ANTHONY HYLTON.

Minister of Local Government and Community Development: NOEL ASCOTT.

Minister of Labour and Social Security, Agriculture and Fisheries: DERRICK KELLIER.

Minister of Health: Dr FENTON FERGUSON.

Minister of Youth and Culture: LISA HANNAH.

Minister of Transport, Works and Housing: Dr OMAR DAVIES.

Minister of Science, Technology, Energy and Mining: PHILLIP PAULWELL.

Minister without Portfolio in the Office of the Prime Minister with responsibility for Information: SANDREA FALCONER.

Minister without Portfolio in the Ministry of Finance and Planning with responsibility for the Public Service: HORACE DALLEY.

Minister without Portfolio in the Ministry of Transport, Works and Housing with responsibility for Housing: Dr MORAIS GUY.

Minister without Portfolio in the Office of the Prime Minister with responsibility for Sports: NATALIE NEITA-HEADLEY.

There are also eight Ministers of State.

MINISTRIES

Office of the Governor-General: King's House, Hope Rd, Kingston 6; tel. 927-6424; fax 927-4561; e-mail kingshouse@kingshouse.gov.jm; internet www.kingshousejamaica.gov.jm.

Office of the Prime Minister: Jamaica House, 1 Devon Rd, POB 272, Kingston 6; tel. 927-9941; fax 968-8229; e-mail pmo@opm.gov.jm; internet www.opm.gov.jm.

Ministry of Agriculture and Fisheries: Hope Gardens, POB 480, Kingston 6; tel. 927-1731; fax 927-1904; e-mail webmaster@moa.gov.jm; internet www.moaf.gov.jm.

Ministry of Education: 2 National Heroes Circle, Kingston 4; tel. 922-1400; fax 967-1837; e-mail webmaster@moec.gov.jm; internet www.moec.gov.jm.

Ministry of Finance and Planning: 30 National Heroes Circle, Kingston 4; tel. 922-8600; fax 922-7097; e-mail info@mof.gov.jm; internet www.mof.gov.jm.

Ministry of Foreign Affairs and Foreign Trade: 21 Dominica Dr., POB 624, Kingston 5; tel. 926-4220; fax 929-5112; e-mail mfaftjam@cwjamaica.com; internet www.mfaft.gov.jm.

Ministry of Health: RKA Bldg, 24–26 Grenada Cres., New Kingston, Kingston 5; tel. 967-1100; fax 967-1643; e-mail webmaster@moh.gov.jm; internet www.moh.gov.jm.

Ministry of Industry, Commerce and Investment (MITEC): 4 St Lucia Ave, Kingston 5; tel. 968-7116; fax 960-7422; e-mail communications@miic.gov.jm; internet www.miic.gov.jm.

Ministry of Justice: Mutual Life Bldg, NCB South Tower, 2 Oxford Rd, Kingston 5; tel. 906-4923; fax 906-1712; e-mail customerservice@moj.gov.jm; internet www.moj.gov.jm.

Ministry of Labour and Social Security: 1F North St, POB 10, Kingston; tel. 922-9500; fax 922-6902; e-mail mlss_perm_sect@yahoo.com; internet www.mlss.gov.jm.

Ministry of Local Government and Community Development: 85 Hagley Park Rd, Kingston 11; tel. 754-0992; fax 754-1000; e-mail communications@mlge.gov.jm; internet www.localgovjamaica.gov.jm.

Ministry of National Security: NCB North Tower, 2 Oxford Rd, Kingston 5; tel. 906-4908; fax 754-3601; e-mail information@mns.gov.jm; internet www.mns.gov.jm.

Ministry of Science, Technology, Energy and Mining: PCJ Bldg, 36 Trafalgar Rd, Kingston 10; tel. 929-8990; fax 960-1623; e-mail info@mem.gov.jm; internet www.mem.gov.jm.

Ministry of Tourism and Entertainment: 64 Knutsford Blvd, Kingston 5; tel. 929-9200; fax 929-9375; e-mail info@visitjamaica.com; internet www.tourismja.com.

Ministry of Transport, Works and Housing: 138H Maxfield Ave, Kingston 10; tel. 754-1900; fax 960-2886; e-mail ps@mtw.gov.jm; internet www.mtw.gov.jm.

Ministry of Water, Land, Environment and Climate Change: 25 Dominica Dr., Kingston 5; tel. 926-1690; fax 926-0543; e-mail info@mwh.gov.jm; internet www.mwh.gov.jm.

Ministry of Youth and Culture: 4–6 Trafalgar Rd, Kingston 5; tel. 978-7654; fax 968-4511; e-mail info@micys.gov.jm; internet www.micys.gov.jm.

Legislature

PARLIAMENT

Houses of Parliament: Gordon House, 81 Duke St, POB 636, Kingston; tel. 922-0202; fax 967-1708; e-mail clerk@japarliament.gov.jm; internet www.japarliament.gov.jm.

Senate

President: FLOYD MORRIS.

The Senate has a total of 21 members, including the President; 13 members are appointed on the advice of the Prime Minister and eight on the recommendation of the Leader of the Opposition.

House of Representatives

Speaker: MICHAEL PEART.

General Election, 29 December 2011

	Seats
People's National Party (PNP)	42
Jamaica Labour Party (JLP)	21
Total	63

Election Commission

Electoral Office of Jamaica (EOJ): 43 Duke St, Kingston; tel. 922-0425; fax 967-4058; e-mail eojinfo@eoj.com.jm; internet www.ecj.com.jm; f. 1943; Dir ORRETTE FISHER.

Political Organizations

Jamaica Alliance Movement (JAM): Flamingo Beach, Falmouth, Trelawny, Kingston; tel. 861-5233; e-mail nowjam@gmail.com; internet www.nowjam.org; f. 2001; Rastafarian; Pres. ASTOR BLACK.

Jamaica Labour Party (JLP): 20 Belmont Rd, Kingston 5; tel. 929-1183; e-mail join@jamaicalabourparty.com; internet www.jamaicalabourparty.com; f. 1943; supports free enterprise in a mixed economy and close co-operation with the USA; Leader ANDREW HOLNESS; Gen. Sec. HORACE CHANG.

National Democratic Movement (NDM): The Trade Centre, Unit 9, 30-32 Red Hills Rd, Kingston 10; tel. 906-8485; fax 922-7874; e-mail ndmjamaica@yahoo.com; internet www.ndmjamaica.com; f. 1995; advocates a clear separation of powers between the central executive and elected representatives; supports private investment and a market economy; mem. of the New Jamaica Alliance; Pres. PETER TOWNSEND; Chair. MICHAEL WILLIAMS.

People's National Party (PNP): 89 Old Hope Rd, Kingston 6; tel. 978-1337; fax 927-4389; e-mail information@pnpjamaica.com; internet www.pnpjamaica.com; f. 1938; socialist principles; affiliated with the National Workers' Union; Pres. PORTIA SIMPSON MILLER; Chair. ROBERT PICKERSGILL; Gen. Sec. PETER BUNTING.

Diplomatic Representation

EMBASSIES AND HIGH COMMISSIONS IN JAMAICA

Argentina: Dyoll Life Bldg, 6th Floor, 40 Knutsford Blvd, Kingston 5; tel. 926-5588; fax 926-0580; e-mail embargen@cwjamaica.com; Ambassador ARIEL FERNÁNDEZ.

Belgium: 6 St Lucia Ave, Kingston 5; tel. 754-7903; fax 906-5943; e-mail kingston@diplobel.fed.be; internet www.diplomatie.be/kingston; Ambassador GODELIEVE VAN DEN BERGH.

Brazil: 23 Millsborough Crescent, Kingston 6; tel. 946-9812; fax 927-5897; e-mail brasemb.kingston@itamaraty.gov.br; internet kingston.itamaraty.gov.br; Ambassador ANTÔNIO FRANCISCO DA COSTA E SILVA NETO.

Canada: 3 West Kings House Rd, POB 1500, Kingston 10; tel. 926-1500; fax 511-3493; e-mail kngtn@international.gc.ca; internet www.canadainternational.gc.ca/jamaica-jamaique; High Commissioner ROBERT READY.

Chile: Courtleigh Corporate Centre, 5th Floor, South Sixth St, Lucia Ave, Kingston 5; tel. 968-0260; fax 968-0265; e-mail echile.jamaica@minrel.gov.cl; internet chileabroad.gov.cl/jamaica; Ambassador EDUARDO BONILLA MENCHACA.

China, People's Republic: 8 Seaview Ave, POB 232, Kingston 10; tel. 927-3871; fax 927-6920; e-mail chinaemb_jm@mfa.gov.cn; internet jm.china-embassy.org; Ambassador DONG XIAOJUN.

Colombia: Victoria Mutual Bldg, 4th Floor, 53 Knutsford Blvd, Kingston 5; tel. 929-1701; fax 968-0577; e-mail ekingston@cancilleria.gov.co; internet www.embajadaenjamaica.gov.co; Ambassador LUÍS GUILLERMO MARTÍNEZ FERNÁNDEZ.

Costa Rica: 58 Hope Rd, Kingston 6; tel. 978-5210; e-mail embacostaricajamaica@gmail.com; Chargé d'affaires a.i. TANISHIA ELOÍSA ELLIS HAYLES.

Cuba: 9 Trafalgar Rd, Kingston 5; tel. 978-0931; fax 978-5372; e-mail embacubajam@cwjamaica.com; internet www.cubadiplomatica.cu/jamaica; Ambassador BERNARDO GUANCHE HERNÁNDEZ.

Dominican Republic: Townhouse, 12 Norbrook Views, 13 Norbrook Cres., Kingston 8; tel. 931-0044; fax 925-1057; e-mail domemb@cwjamaica.com; Ambassador Dr JOSÉ TOMÁS ARES GERMÁN.

France: 13 Hillcrest Ave, POB 93, Kingston 6; tel. 946-4000; fax 946-4020; e-mail frenchembassyjamaica@gmail.com; Ambassador GINETTE DE MATHA.

Germany: 10 Waterloo Rd, POB 444, Kingston 10; tel. 926-6728; fax 620-5457; e-mail germanembassa.kingston@gmail.com; internet www.kingston.diplo.de; Ambassador JOSEF BECK.

Haiti: 2 Munroe Rd, Kingston 6; tel. 927-7595; fax 978-7638; Chargé d'affaires a.i. MAX ALCE.

India: 27 Seymour Ave, POB 446, Kingston 6; tel. 927-4270; fax 978-2801; e-mail hicomindkin@cwjamaica.com; internet www.hcikingston.com; High Commissioner PRATAP SINGH.

Japan: NCB Towers, North Tower, 6th Floor, 2 Oxford Rd, POB 8104, Kingston 5; tel. 929-3338; fax 968-1373; internet www.jamaica.emb-japan.go.jp; Ambassador YASUO TAKASE.

Korea, Republic: 5 Oakridge, Kingston 8; tel. 924-2731; fax 924-7325; e-mail jamaica@mofat.go.kr; internet jam.mofat.go.kr; Chargé d'affaires a.i. JONG SEON LIM.

Mexico: PCJ Bldg, 36 Trafalgar Rd, Kingston 10; tel. 926-4242; fax 929-7995; e-mail embamexj@cwjamaica.com; internet embamex.sre.gob.mx/jamaica; Ambassador GERARDO LOZANO ARREDONDO.

Nicaragua: 2 Ottawa Ave, Kingston 6; tel. 285-9200; fax 631-7357; e-mail rhooker@cancilleria.gob.ni; Ambassador DAVID SIDNEY MCFIELD.

Nigeria: 5 Waterloo Rd, POB 94, Kingston 10; tel. 968-3732; fax 968-7371; e-mail nhckingston@mail.infochan.com; High Commissioner OLATOKUNBO KAMSON.

Panama: 34 Annette Cres., Suite 103, Kingston 10; tel. 924-5235; fax 924-3428; e-mail panaemba@hotmail.com; Chargé d'affaires a.i. ERICK CAJAR GRIMAS.

Peru: 23 Barbados Ave, POB 1818, Kingston 5; tel. 920-5027; fax 920-4360; e-mail embaperu-kingston@rree.gob.pe; Ambassador LUIS SÁNDIGA CABRERA.

Russian Federation: 22 Norbrook Dr., Kingston 8; tel. 924-1048; fax 925-8290; e-mail rusembja@colis.com; internet en.rejamaica.ru; Ambassador VLADIMIR POLENOV.

Saint Christopher and Nevis: 11A Opal Ave, Golden Acres, Red Hills, St Andrew; tel. 944-3861; e-mail clrharper@yahoo.com; fax 945-0105; High Commissioner CEDRIC HARPER.

Senegal: Courtleigh Corporate Centre, 6–8 St Lucia Ave, Kingston 5; tel. 906-2919; fax 622-5758; e-mail senegalembassyjamaica@gmail.com; Ambassador Dr NAFISSATOU DIAGNE.

South Africa: 15 Hillcrest Ave, Kingston 6; tel. 620-4840; fax 978-0339; e-mail jamaicak@dirco.gov.za; High Commissioner MATHU JOYINI.

Spain: Courtleigh Corporate Centre, 6th Floor, 6–8 St Lucia Ave, Kingston 5; tel. 929-5555; fax 929-8965; e-mail emb.kingston@mae.es; Ambassador ANÍBAL JULIO JIMÉNEZ.

Trinidad and Tobago: 25 Windsor Ave, Kingston 5; tel. 926-5730; fax 926-5801; e-mail kgnhctt@cwjamaica.com; internet www.kgnhctt.org; High Commissioner Dr IVA CAMILLE GLOUDON.

United Kingdom: 28 Trafalgar Rd, POB 575, Kingston 10; tel. 936-0700; fax 936-0737; e-mail PPA.Kingston@fco.gov.uk; internet www.gov.uk/government/world/jamaica; High Commissioner DAVID FITTON.

USA: 142 Old Hope Rd, Kingston 6; tel. 702-6000; e-mail kingstonirc@state.gov; internet kingston.usembassy.gov; Ambassador LUIS G. MORENO.

Venezuela: PCJ Bldg, 3rd Floor, 36 Trafalgar Rd, POB 26, Kingston 10; tel. 926-5510; fax 926-7442; e-mail embavene@n5.com.jm; Ambassador MARÍA JACQUELINE MENDOZA ORTEGA.

Judicial System

The judicial system is based on English common law and practice. Final appeal is to the Judicial Committee of the Privy Council in the United Kingdom.

Justice is administered by the Privy Council, Court of Appeal, Supreme Court, Resident Magistrates' Court (which includes the Traffic Court), two Family Courts and the Courts of Petty Sessions. The Caribbean Court of Justice, based in Trinidad and Tobago, is the court with jurisdiction for trade disputes.

Judicial Service Commission: Office of the Services Commissions, 30 National Heroes Circle, Kingston 4; tel. 922-8600; fax 924-9764; e-mail communications@osc.gov.jm; internet www.osc.gov.jm; advises the Governor-General on judicial appointments, etc.; Chief Justice ZAILA ROWENA MCCALLA.

Supreme Court: Public Bldg E, 134 Tower St, POB 491, Kingston; tel. 922-8300; fax 967-0669; e-mail webmaster@sc.gov.jm; internet supremecourt.gov.jm; Chief Justice ZAILA MCCALLA.

Court of Appeal: Public Bldg West, King St, POB 629, Kingston; tel. 665-2100; fax 967-1843; e-mail info@courtofappeal.gov.jm; internet www.courtofappeal.gov.jm; Pres. SEYMOUR PANTON.

Attorney-General: PATRICK ATKINSON.

Religion

CHRISTIANITY

Jamaica Council of Churches: 14 South Ave, Kingston 10; tel. and fax 926-0974; e-mail jchurch@cwjamaica.com; internet jamaicacouncilofchurches.yolasite.com; f. 1941; 10 mem. churches and 3 agencies; Gen. Sec. GARY HARRIOT.

The Anglican Communion

Anglicans in Jamaica are adherents of the Church in the Province of the West Indies, comprising eight dioceses. The Archbishop of the Province is the Bishop of Barbados. The Bishop of Jamaica and the Cayman Islands is assisted by three suffragan Bishops (of Kingston, Mandeville and Montego Bay). According to the 2001 census, some 4% of the population are Anglicans.

Bishop of Jamaica and the Cayman Islands: Rt Rev. HOWARD KINGSLEY AINSWORTH GREGORY, Church House, 2 Caledonia Ave, Kingston 5; tel. 926-8925; fax 968-0618; e-mail info@anglicandiocese.com; internet anglicandiocese.dthost.com.

The Roman Catholic Church

Jamaica comprises the archdiocese of Kingston in Jamaica (which also includes the Cayman Islands), and the dioceses of Montego Bay and Mandeville. Some 3% of the population are Roman Catholics. The Archbishop and Bishops participate in the Antilles Episcopal Conference (currently based in Port of Spain, Trinidad and Tobago).

Archbishop of Kingston in Jamaica: Most Rev. CHARLES HENRY DUFOUR, Archbishop's Residence, 21 Hopefield Ave, POB 43, Kingston 6; tel. 927-9915; fax 927-4487; e-mail rcabkgn@cwjamaica.com; internet www.archdioceseofkingston.org.

Other Christian Churches

According to the 2001 census, the largest religious bodies are the Church of God (whose members represent 24% of the population), Seventh-day Adventists (11% of the population), Pentecostalists (10%) and Baptists (7%). Other denominations include Jehovah's Witnesses, the Methodist and Congregational Churches, United Church, the Church of the Brethren, the Ethiopian Orthodox Church, the Disciples of Christ, the Moravian Church, the Church of Latter-Day Saints (Mormons), the Salvation Army and the Religious Society of Friends (Quakers).

Jamaica Baptist Union: 2B Washington Blvd, Kingston 20; tel. 969-2223; fax 924-6296; e-mail info@jbu.org.jm; internet www.jbu .org.jm; f. 1849; 40,000 mems in 332 churches; Pres. Rev. MICHAEL SHIM-HUE; Gen. Sec. Rev. KARL JOHNSON.

Jamaica Union Conference of Seventh-day Adventists (JUCSDA): 125 Manchester Rd, Mandeville; tel. 962-2284; fax 962-3417; e-mail info@wiunion.org; internet jmunion.org; f. 1903; Communications Dir NIGEL COKE; 205,000 mems.

Methodist Church (Jamaica District): 143 Constant Spring Rd, POB 892, Kingston 8; tel. 925-6768; fax 924-2560; e-mail jamaicamethodist@cwjamaica.com; internet www

.jamaicamethodist.org; f. 1789; 15,820 mems; District Pres. Rev. EVERALD GALBRAITH.

Moravian Church in Jamaica and the Cayman Islands: 3 Hector St, POB 8369, Kingston 5; tel. 619-1148; e-mail moravianchurch@cwjamaica.com; internet www.jamaicamoravian .com; f. 1754; 30,000 mems.

United Church in Jamaica and the Cayman Islands: 12 Carlton Cres., POB 359, Kingston 10; tel. 926-6059; fax 929-0826; e-mail synod@ucjci.com; internet www.ucjci.com; f. 1965 by merger of the Congregational Union of Jamaica (f. 1877) and the Presbyterian Church of Jamaica and Grand Cayman to become United Church of Jamaica and Grand Cayman; merged with Disciples of Christ in Jamaica in 1992 when name changed as above; 20,000 mems; Moderator Rt. Rev. J. OLIVER DALEY; Gen. Sec. Rev. NORBERT STEPHENS.

RASTAFARIANISM

Rastafarianism is an important influence in Jamaican culture. The cult is derived from Christianity and a belief in the divinity of Ras (Prince) Tafari Makonnen (later Emperor Haile Selassie) of Ethiopia. It advocates racial equality and non-violence, but causes controversy in its use of 'ganja' (marijuana) as a sacrament. According to the 2001 census, 1% of the population are Rastafarians. Although the religion is largely unorganized, there are some denominations.

Haile Selassie Jahrastafari Royal Ethiopian Judah Coptic Church: 11 Welcome Ave, Kingston 11; tel. 461-2721; fax 639-4173; e-mail royalethiopian@gmail.com; internet www .nationofjahrastafari.org; f. 1966; not officially incorporated; Head Pres. Dr MATT O'NEIL MYRIE HAILE SELASSIE I.

BAHÁ'Í FAITH

National Spiritual Assembly: 208 Mountain View Ave, Kingston 6; tel. 927-7051; fax 978-2344; internet www.jm.bahai.org; incorporated in 1970.

ISLAM

According to the 2001 census, there are an estimated 5,000 Muslims (less than 1% of the population).

JUDAISM

According to the 2001 census, there are some 350 Jews (less than 1% of the population).

United Congregation of Israelites: K. K. Shaare Shalom Synagogue, 92 Duke St, Kingston 6; tel. and fax 922-5931; e-mail info@ ucija.org; internet www.ucija.org; f. 1655; 250 mems; Rabbi DANA EVAN KAPLAN.

The Press

DAILIES

The Gleaner: 7 North St, POB 40, Kingston; tel. 922-3400; fax 922-6223; e-mail feedback@jamaica-gleaner.com; internet www .jamaica-gleaner.com; f. 1834; morning; independent; Chair. and Man. Dir CHRISTOPHER BARNES; Editor-in-Chief GARFIELD GRANDISON; circ. 50,000.

Jamaica Observer: 40–42 1/2 Beechwood Ave, Kingston 5; tel. 920-8136; fax 926-7655; e-mail editorial@jamaicaobserver.com; internet www.jamaicaobserver.com; f. 1993; Chair. GORDON 'BUTCH' STEWART.

The Jamaica Star: 7 North St, POB 40, Kingston; tel. 922-3400; fax 922-6223; e-mail star@gleanerjm.com; internet jamaica-star.com; f. 1951; evening; Editor-in-Chief GARFIELD GRANDISON; Editor DWAYNE GORDON; circ. 45,000.

PERIODICALS

All Woman: 40-42 1/2 Beechwood Ave, Kingston 5; tel. 920-8136; e-mail editorial@jamaicaobserver.com; internet www .jamaicaobserver.com/magazines/allwoman; beauty, health and wellness; published by the Jamaica Observer Ltd; other publs include *Sunday Observer* and *Western News*; Editor NOVIA MCDONALD-WHYTE.

The Anglican: 2 Caledonia Ave, Cross Roads, Kingston 5; tel. 920-2714; fax 968-0618; e-mail info@anglicandiocese.com; internet www .anglicandiocesejamaica.com; f. 2004 following cessation of *Jamaica Churchman*; quarterly; circ. 9,000.

Catholic Opinion: Roman Catholic Chancery Office, 21 Hopefield Ave, POB 43, Kingston 6; tel. 927-9915; fax 927-4487; e-mail rcabkgn@cwjamaica.com; internet www.archdioceseofkingston.org; 6 a year; religious; circulated in the *Sunday Gleaner*; Editor Mgr MICHAEL LEWIS; circ. 100,000.

Children's Own: 7 North St, POB 40, Kingston; tel. 922-3400; fax 922-6223; e-mail feedback@jamaica-gleaner.com; internet www .jamaica-gleaner.com; weekly during term-time; publ. by The Gleaner Co; other publs include *Sunday Gleaner* and *Weekend Star*; Editor-in-Chief GARFIELD GRANDISON; circ. 120,000.

HHG Magazine: 5–7 Dunrobin Ave, Kingston 10; tel. 924-4306; fax 924-4985; e-mail hhgmagazine@cwjamaica.com; internet www .hhgmagazine.com; f. 2001; published by Health, Home & Garden Promotions; 3 a year; Editor-in-Chief FAY WINT-SMITH.

Jamaica Journal: 10–16 East St, Kingston; tel. 922-0620; fax 922-1147; e-mail jamaicajournal@instituteofjamaica.org.jm; internet jj .instituteofjamaica.org.jm/ioj_wp; f. 1967; 2 a year; literary, historical and cultural review; publ. by Institute of Jamaica; Chair. of Editorial Cttee Dr KIM ROBINSON.

The Jamaican Magazine: POB 24, Kingston 7; tel. 977-3779; e-mail deeksdesigns@gmail.com; internet www .thejamaicanmagazine.com; f. 1986; art, culture and design; Editor LORRAINE MURRAY.

Mandeville Weekly: 29 Ward Ave, Mandeville, Manchester; tel. 961-0118; fax 961-0119; e-mail mandevilleweekly@flowja.com; internet www.mandevilleweekly.com; f. 1993; Chair. and Editor-in-Chief ANTHONY FRECKLETON; Man. Dir WENDY FRECKLETON.

North Coast Times: 130 Main St, Ocho Rios; tel. and fax 974-9306; e-mail sales@northcoasttimesja.com; internet www .northcoasttimesja.com; f. 1995; weekly; Publr FRANKLIN McKNIGHT.

Panache Jamaica: 22B Old Hope Rd, Kingston; e-mail editor@ panachejamagazine.com; internet www.panachejamagazine.com; f. 2008; fashion and lifestyle; Editorial Dir TRICIA WILLIAMSON.

Tallawah: Kingston; e-mail tyronesreid@gmail.com; internet www .tallawahmagazine.com; celebrity and lifestyle; monthly; Editor TYRONE S. REID.

West Indian Medical Journal: Faculty of Medical Sciences, University of the West Indies, Mona, Kingston 7; tel. 927-1214; fax 927-1846; e-mail wimj@uwimona.edu.jm; internet myspot.mona.uwi .edu/fms/wimj; f. 1951; monthly; Editor-in-Chief EVERARD N. BARTON; circ. 2,000.

PRESS ASSOCIATION

The Press Association of Jamaica (PAJ): 5 East Ave, Kingston 8; tel. and fax 631-6390; internet pressassociationjamaica.org; f. 1943; Pres. JACKSON MILLER; Sec. INGRID BROWN.

Publishers

Jamaica Publishing House Ltd: 97B Church St, Kingston; tel. 967-3866; fax 922-5412; e-mail jph@cwjamaica.com; f. 1969; subsidiary of Jamaica Teachers' Asscn; English language and literature, mathematics, history, geography, social sciences, music; Chair. WOODBURN MILLER; Man. ELAINE R. STENNETT.

LMH Publishing Ltd: 7 Norman Rd, Suite 10–11, Sagicor Industrial Park, POB 8296, Kingston CSO; tel. 938-0005; fax 759-8752; e-mail lmhbookpublishing@cwjamaica.com; internet www .lmhpublishing.com; f. 1970; educational textbooks, general, travel, fiction; Chair. L. MICHAEL HENRY; Man. Dir DAWN CHAMBERS-HENRY.

Ian Randle Publishers (IRP): 11 Cunningham Ave, POB 686, Kingston 6; tel. 978-0745; fax 978-1156; e-mail clp@ ianrandlepublishers.com; internet www.ianrandlepublishers.com; f. 1991; history, biography, politics, sociology, law, cooking and music; Chair. IAN RANDLE; Man. Dir CHRISTINE RANDLE.

University of the West Indies Press (UWI Press): 7A Gibraltar Hall Rd, Mona, Kingston 7; tel. 977-2659; fax 977-2660; internet www.uwipress.com; f. 1992; Caribbean history, culture and literature, gender studies, education and political science; Man. Editor LINDA SPETH.

Western Publishers Ltd: 4 Cottage Rd, POB 1258, Montego Bay; tel. 952-5253; fax 952-6513; e-mail westernmirror@mail.infochan .com; internet westernmirror.com; f. 1980; CEO and Editor-in-Chief LLOYD B. SMITH.

GOVERNMENT PUBLISHING HOUSE

Jamaica Printing Services: 77 1/2 Duke St, Kingston; tel. 967-2250; fax 967-2225; e-mail jps_1992@yahoo.com; internet jps1992 .org; Gen. Man. BLONDELL WYNDHAM.

ASSOCIATION

Caribbean Publishers' Network (CAPNET): 11 Cunningham Ave, Kingston 6; e-mail info@capnetonline.net; internet www .capnetonline.net; non-profit regional asscn; Pres. NEYSHA SOODEEN.

Broadcasting and Communications
TELECOMMUNICATIONS

Anbell Telecommunications Ltd: 51 Knutsford Blvd, Kingston 5; tel. 906-8479; fax 906-8487; e-mail support@anbell.net; internet anbell.net/telecom.htm; internet service provider; Man. GARFIELD BOLT.

Digicel Jamaica: 14 Ocean Blvd, Kingston 5; tel. 619-5000; fax 920-0948; e-mail customercare@digicelgroup.com; internet www .digiceljamaica.com; f. 2001; mobile cellular telephone operator; owned by Irish consortium, Mossel (Jamaica) Ltd; absorbed all operations and subscribers of Claro Jamaica in 2012; Chair. DENIS O'BRIEN; CEO (Jamaica) BARRY O'BRIEN.

Flow: 6–8 St Lucia Ave, Kingston 5; tel. 620-3000; e-mail mediainquiries@flowjamaica.com; internet discoverflow.co/jamaica; f. 2006; fmrly owned by Columbus Communications Jamaica Ltd, bought by Cable & Wireless (UK) in 2015; cable, internet and telephone service provider; Man. Dir GRANT HUME (acting).

LIME: 7 Cecilio Ave, Kingston 10; tel. 926-9700; fax 929-9530; e-mail customer.services@lime.com; internet www.lime.com/jm; f. 1989; name changed as above in 2008; 79% owned by Cable & Wireless (UK); landline, internet and mobile services; CEO PHIL BENTLEY; CEO (Jamaica) GARFIELD SINCLAIR; Chair. (LIME Jamaica) CHRIS DEHRING.

Noble Wi-Fi: Montego; tel. 410-8532; e-mail Sales-WiFi@noblecoms .com; internet noblecoms.com; f. 2014; internet service provider in north Jamaica; Dir RYAN FERNANDEZ.

Regulatory Authority
The sector is regulated by the Office of Utilities Regulation (see Utilities).

BROADCASTING
Radio

Abeng 88.7 FM: Accompong Town, St Elizabeth; f. 2014; aimed at the Maroon community.

Independent Radio: 6 Bradley Ave, Kingston 10; tel. 968-4880; fax 968-9165; commercial; broadcasts 24 hrs a day on FM; Man. Dir NEWTON JAMES.

Power 106: 6 Bradley Ave, Kingston 10; tel. 968-4880; fax 968-9165; e-mail power106@cwjamaica.com; internet www.go-jamaica .com/power; f. 1992; talk and sports programmes.

IRIE FM: 1B Coconut Grove, Ocho Rios, St Ann; tel. 968-5023; fax 968-8332; e-mail customerservice@iriefm.net; internet www.iriefm .net; f. 1990; owned by Grove Broadcasting Co; reggae music; Man. BRIAN SCHMIDT.

KLAS Sports FM 89: 17 Haining Rd, Kingston 5; tel. 929-1344; fax 960-0572; e-mail admin@klassportsradio.com; internet www .klassportsradio.com; f. 1991; sports broadcasting.

Kool 97 FM: 1 Braemar Ave, Kingston 10; tel. 978-4037; fax 978-3346; e-mail contact@kool97fm.com; internet www.kool97fm.com; f. 2001; music, news and tourism information.

Linkz 96 FM: 8 Beckford St, Savanna La Mar, Westmoreland; tel. 955-3686; fax 955-9523; e-mail linkz96fm@yahoo.com; internet www .linkzfm.com; f. 2004; Chair. ROGER ALLEN.

Love FM: 81 Hagley Park Rd, Kingston 10; tel. 968-9596; e-mail webmaster@love101.org; internet love101.org; f. 1993; commercial radio station, religious programming on FM; owned by National Religious Media Ltd; Gen. Man. Rt Rev. HERRO BLAIR.

Radio Jamaica Ltd (RJR): Broadcasting House, 32 Lyndhurst Rd, POB 23, Kingston 5; tel. 926-1100; fax 929-7467; e-mail rjr@ radiojamaica.com; internet www.radiojamaica.com; f. 1947; commercial, public service; 3 channels; Man. Dir GARY ALLEN.

FAME 95 FM: 32 Lyndhurst Rd, Kingston 5; tel. 18763567406 (mobile); internet www.fame95fm.com; e-mail famefm@rjrgroup .com; f. 1984; broadcasts on FM, island-wide 24 hrs a day.

Hitz 92 FM: internet www.radiohitz92fm.com; broadcasts on FM, island-wide 24 hrs a day; youth station.

RJR 94 FM: internet rjr94fm.com; broadcasts on AM and FM, island-wide 24 hrs a day; Exec. Producer NORMA BROWN-BELL.

Roots FM: Mustard Seed Communities, POB 267, Kingston 10; tel. 923-2165; fax 923-6000; e-mail roots.fm@mustardseed.com; internet www.mustardseed.com; Chair. TREVOR GORDON-SOMERS.

TBC FM: 51 Molynes Rd, Kingston 10; tel. 754-5120; fax 968-9159; e-mail gcallam@tbcradio.org; internet www.tbcradio.org; Gen. Man. GARY CALLAM.

ZIP 103 FM: 1B Courtney Walsh Dr., Kingston 10, Jamaica; tel. 929-6233; fax 929-4691; e-mail zip103fm@cwjamaica.com; internet www .zipfm.net; f. 2002; commercial radio station; Dir D'ADRA WILLIAMS.

104.9 FM: Shop 10, R.T. Plaza, Off Port Henderson Rd, Portmore, St Catherine; tel. 740-5087; e-mail motherincrisis@yahoo.com; internet www.suncityradio.fm; CEO DOREEN BILLINGS.

Television

Creative TV (CTV): Caenwood Campus, 37 Arnold Rd, Kingston 5; tel. 967-4482; fax 924-9432; internet www.creativetvjamaica.com; operated by Creative Production & Training Centre Ltd (CPTC); local cable channel; regional cultural, educational and historical programming; CEO Dr HOPETON DUNN.

CVM Television: 69 Constant Sprint Rd, Kingston 10; tel. 931-9400; fax 931-9417; e-mail contact@cvmtv.com; internet www.cvmtv.com; Pres. and CEO DAVID MCBEAN.

Television Jamaica Limited (TVJ): 32 Lyndhurst Rd, Kingston 5; tel. 926-1100; fax 929-1029; e-mail tvjadmin@cwjamaica.com; internet www.televisionjamaica.com; f. 1959 as Jamaica Broadcasting Corpn; privatized and adopted current name in 1997; subsidiary of RJR Communications Group; island-wide VHF transmission 24 hrs a day; Chair. MILTON SAMUDA; Gen. Man. GARY ALLEN.

Regulatory Authorities

Broadcasting Commission of Jamaica: 5th Floor, Victoria Mutual Bldg, 53 Knutsford Blvd, Kingston 5; tel. 929-1998; fax 929-1997; e-mail info@broadcom.org; internet www.broadcastingcommission.org; f. 1986; Chair. Prof. HOPETON DUNN.

Spectrum Management Authority: 13–19 Harbour St, Kingston; tel. 967-7948; fax 922-4093; e-mail info@sma.gov.jm; internet www.sma.gov.jm; f. 2000; national regulator for radio frequency spectrum; govt-run; Chair. CHRISTOPHER HONEYWELL.

Finance

(cap. = capital; res = reserves; dep. = deposits; m. = million; brs = branches; amounts in Jamaican dollars)

REGULATORY AUTHORITY

Jamaica International Financial Services Authority: Kingston; f. 2011 following an Act of Parliament; Chair. ERIC CRAWFORD.

BANKING

Central Bank

Bank of Jamaica: Nethersole Pl., POB 621, Kingston; tel. 922-0750; fax 922-0854; e-mail info@boj.org.jm; internet www.boj.org.jm; f. 1960; cap. 4.0m., res 8,831.2m., dep. 198,440.4m. (Dec. 2009); Gov. and Chair. BRIAN HECTOR WYNTER.

Commercial Banks

CIBC FirstCaribbean International Bank: CIBC Centre, 23-27 Knutsford Blvd, Kingston 5; tel. 929-9310; fax 926-7751; internet www.firstcaribbeanbank.com; FirstCaribbean f. in 2002 following merger of Caribbean operations of CIBC and Barclays Bank PLC; Barclays relinquished its stake in 2006, present name adopted in 2011; cap. 1,396.7m., res 5,671m., dep. 42,595.3m. (Oct. 2011); CEO RIK PARKHILL; Man. Dir NIGEL HOLNESS; 13 brs.

Citibank, NA: 19 Hillcrest Ave, Kingston 6; tel. 926-3270; fax 978-8889; e-mail peter.moses@citi.com; internet www.citibank.com/jamaica; owned by Citifinance Ltd; cap. 25.7m., res 128.4m., dep. 87.2m. (Dec. 2003); Man. Dir PETER MOSES.

National Commercial Bank Jamaica Ltd: 'The Atrium', 32 Trafalgar Rd, POB 88, Kingston 10; tel. 929-9050; fax 929-8399; tel. ncbinfo@jncb.com; internet www.jncb.com; f. 1837; merged with Mutual Security Bank in 1996; cap. 6,465.7m., res 32,191.8m., dep. 180,628.2m. (Sept. 2013); Chair. MICHAEL LEE-CHIN; Man. Dir PATRICK HYLTON; 37 brs.

Sagicor Bank Jamaica Ltd: Kingston 5; tel. 724-4267; internet www.sagicorjamaica.com; f. 1993 as Jamaica Citizens Bank Ltd; acquired by Royal Bank of Trinidad and Tobago in 2001 and name changed to RBTT Bank Jamaica Ltd; became RBC Royal Bank (Jamaica) Ltd in 2011; sold to Sagicor Ltd in 2014 and present name adopted; cap. 8,167.8m., res 2,764.5m., dep. 40,986m. (Dec. 2010); Chair. DODRIDGE D. MILLER.

Scotiabank Jamaica Ltd (Canada): Scotiabank Centre Bldg, cnr Duke and Port Royal Sts, POB 709, Kingston; tel. 922-1000; fax 924-9294; e-mail customercare-jam@scotiabank.com; internet www.scotiabank.com.jm; f. 1967; subsidiary of Bank of Nova Scotia (Canada); cap. 2,927.2m., res 18,264.3m., dep. 151,668.4m. (Oct. 2010); Chair. SYLVIA CHROMINSKA; Pres. and CEO JACQUELINE SHARP; 35 brs.

Development Banks

Development Bank of Jamaica Ltd: 11A–15 Oxford Rd, POB 466, Kingston 5; tel. 929-4000; fax 929-6055; e-mail mail@dbankjm.com; internet www.dbankjm.com; f. 2000 following merger of Agricultural Credit Bank of Jamaica and the National Devt Bank of Jamaica; provides funds for medium- and long-term devt-orientated projects; Chair. JOSEPH M. MATALON; Man. Dir MILVERTON REYNOLDS.

Jamaica Mortgage Bank: 33 Tobago Ave, POB 950, Kingston 5; tel. 929-6350; fax 968-5428; e-mail info@jmb.gov.jm; internet www.jmb.gov.jm; f. 1971 by the Jamaican Govt and the US Agency for Int. Devt; govt-owned statutory org. since 1973; functions primarily as a secondary market facility for home mortgages and to mobilize long-term funds for housing devts in Jamaica; also insures home mortgage loans made by approved financial institutions, thus transferring risk of default on a loan to the Govt; Chair. HOWARD MOLLISON; Gen. Man. PATRICK THELWALL.

Other Banks

National Export-Import Bank of Jamaica Ltd: 11 Oxford Rd, Kingston 5; tel. 960-9690; fax 960-9115; e-mail info@eximbankja.com; internet www.eximbankja.com; f. 1986; govt-owned; replaced Jamaica Export Credit Insurance Corpn; finances import and export of goods and services; Chair. WILLIAM CLARKE; Man. Dir LISA BELL.

Sagicor Investments Jamaica Ltd: 60 Knutsford Blvd, Kingston 5; tel. 929-5583; fax 926-4385; e-mail options@sagicor.com; internet www.sagicor.com; fmrly Trafalgar Devt Bank, name changed to Pan Caribbean Financial Services in 2002; present name adopted in 2012; investment bank; Chair. DODRIDGE D. MILLER; CEO ROHAN MILLER.

Banking Association

Jamaica Bankers' Association: PSOJ Bldg, 39 Hope Rd, POB 1079, Kingston 10; tel. 927-6238; fax 927-5137; e-mail jbainfo@jba.org.jm; internet www.jba.org.jm; f. 1973; Pres. BRUCE BOWEN.

STOCK EXCHANGE

Jamaica Stock Exchange Ltd: 40 Harbour St, POB 1084, Kingston; tel. 967-3271; fax 967-3277; internet www.jamstockex.com; f. 1968; Chair. DONOVAN H. PERKINS; Gen. Man. MARLENE STREET-FORREST.

INSURANCE

Financial Services Commission: 39–43 Barbados Ave, Kingston 5; tel. 906 3010; fax 906-3018; e-mail inquiry@fscjamaica.org; internet www.fscjamaica.org; f. 2001; succeeded the Office of the Superintendent of Insurance; regulatory body; Chair. COLIN BULLOCK; Exec. Dir JANICE P. HOLNESS.

Principal Companies

Advantage General Insurance Co Ltd: 4-6 Trafalgar Rd, Kingston 5; tel. 978-3690; fax 978-3718; internet www.advantagegeneral.com; f. 1964; general; Chair. DENNIS G. COHEN; Pres. and CEO MARK THOMPSON.

British Caribbean Insurance Co Ltd (BCIC): 36 Duke St, POB 170, Kingston; tel. 922-1260; fax 922-4475; e-mail dsales@bcic-jm.com; internet www.bciconline.com; f. 1962; affiliate of Victoria Mutual Insurance Co; general; Chair. JOSEPH M. MATALON; Man. Dir PETER LEVY.

General Accident Insurance Co Jamaica Ltd: 58 Half Way Tree Rd, Kingston 10; tel. 929-8451; fax 929-1074; e-mail info@genac.com; internet www.genac.com; f. 1981; general; Chair. PAUL B. SCOTT; Man. Dir SHARON DONALDSON.

Globe Insurance Co of Jamaica Ltd: 19 Dominica Dr., POB 401, Kingston 5; tel. 926-3720; fax 929-2727; e-mail info@globeins.com; internet www.globeins.com; f. 1963; fmr subsidiary of Lascelles deMercado, bought by Guardian Holdings Ltd in Sept. 2012; general; Man. Dir EVAN THWAITES.

Guardian General Insurance Jamaica Ltd: 19 Dominica Dr., Kingston 5; tel. 929-8080; fax 929-2727; e-mail insure@wia.com.jm; internet www.guardiangroup.com; f. 1969; subsidiary of Guardian Holdings Ltd (Trinidad and Tobago); general; Pres. KAREN BHOOR-ASINGH.

Guardian Life: 12 Trafalgar Rd, Kingston 5; tel. 978-8815; fax 978-4225; e-mail guardian@glil.com.jm; internet www.myguardiangroup.com; subsidiary of Guardian Holdings Ltd (Trinidad and Tobago); pension and life policies; Pres. ERIC HOSIN.

Insurance Co of the West Indies Ltd (ICWI): 2 St Lucia Ave, POB 306, Kingston 5; tel. 926-9040; fax 929-6641; e-mail direct@icwi.com; internet icwi.com/jamaica; general; Chair. and CEO DENNIS LALOR.

Jamaica General Insurance Co Ltd: 19–21 Knutsford Blvd, New Kingston; tel. 926-3204; fax 968-1920; e-mail info@jiiconline.com; internet www.jiiconline.com; f. 1981; subsidiary of GraceKennedy

Ltd; general; Chair. PETER MOSS-SOLOMON; Man. Dir GRACE BURNETT.

JN General Insurance Company Ltd (JNGI): NEM House, 9 King St, Kingston; tel. 922-1460; fax 922-4045; e-mail info@nemjam .com; internet www.nemjam.com; f. 1934; fmrly NEM Insurance, present name adopted 2012; subsidiary of Jamaica National Bldg Soc; general; Chair. OLIVER CLARKE; Gen. Man. CHRISTOPHER HIND.

NCB Insurance Co Ltd (NCBIC): 32 Trafalgar Rd, Kingston 10; tel. 935-2730; fax 929-7301; e-mail ncbic@jncb.com; internet www .ncbinsurance.com; f. 1989; fmrly OMNI Insurance Services Ltd; life; Chair. WAYNE CHEN; Gen. Man. VERNON JAMES.

Sagicor Life Jamaica Ltd: 28–48 Barbados Ave, Kingston 5; tel. 960-8920; fax 960-1927; internet www.sagicorjamaica.com; f. 1970; owned by Sagicor Group Jamaica; fmrly Life of Jamaica Ltd; life; Chair. R. DANNY WILLIAMS.

Scotia Jamaica Life Insurance Co Ltd (SJLIC): Duke and Port Royal Sts, Kingston; tel. 922-3765; e-mail sjlic.service@scotiabank .com; internet www.scotiabank.com; f. 1995; life; Pres. HUGH REID.

Association

Insurance Association of Jamaica (IAJ): 3–3A Richmond Ave, Kingston 10; tel. 929-8404; fax 906-1804; e-mail iaj@cwjamaica.com; internet www.iaj-online.com; f. 2005 by merger of the Jamaica Asscn of General Insurance Cos (JAGIC) and the Life Insurance Cos Asscn of Jamaica (LICA); Pres. HUGH REID; Exec. Dir ORVILLE JOHNSON.

Trade and Industry

GOVERNMENT AGENCY

Jamaica Information Service (JIS): 58A Half Way Tree Rd, POB 2222, Kingston 10; tel. 926-3740; fax 926-6715; e-mail jis@jis.gov.jm; internet www.jis.gov.jm; f. 1963; govt agency; CEO DONNA-MARIE ROWE.

DEVELOPMENT ORGANIZATIONS

Agro-Investment Corpn: Ministry of Agriculture and Fisheries, 188 Spanish Town Rd, Kingston 11; tel. 764-8071; fax 758-7160; e-mail agricultural@cwjamaica.com; internet www.assp.gov.jm; f. 2009; following the merger of Agricultural Devt Corp (ADC) and Agricultural Support Services Productive Projects Fund Ltd (ASSPPFL); agricultural devt, investment facilitation, promotion and management; Chair. DAVID LOWE; CEO HERSHELL BROWN.

JAMPRO Trade and Invest, Jamaica (JAMPRO): 18 Trafalgar Rd, Kingston 10; tel. 978-7755; fax 946-0090; e-mail info@jamprocorp .com; internet www.jamaicatradeandinvest.org; f. 1988 by merger of Jamaica Industrial Development Corpn, Jamaica National Export Corpn and Jamaica Investment Promotion Ltd; trade and investment promotion agency; Chair. MILTON SAMUDA; Pres. DIANE EDWARDS.

Planning Institute of Jamaica: 16 Oxford Rd, Kingston 5; tel. 960-9339; fax 906-5011; e-mail info@pioj.gov.jm; internet www.pioj.gov .jm; f. 1955 as the Central Planning Unit; adopted current name in 1984; formulates policy on and monitors performance in the fields of the economy and social, environmental and trade issues; publishing and analysis of social and economic performance data; Chair. and Dir-Gen. Dr GLADSTONE HUTCHINSON.

Urban Development Corpn: The Office Centre, 8th Floor, 12 Ocean Blvd, Kingston; tel. 922-8310; fax 922-9326; e-mail info@ udcja.com; internet www.udcja.com; f. 1968; responsibility for urban renewal and devt within designated areas; Chair. WAYNE CHEN; Gen. Man. DESMOND YOUNG.

CHAMBERS OF COMMERCE

American Chamber of Commerce of Jamaica: The Jamaica Pegasus, 81 Knutsford Blvd, Kingston 5; tel. 929-7866; fax 929-8597; e-mail amcham.ja@gmail.com; internet www.amchamjamaica.org; f. 1986; affiliated to the Chamber of Commerce of the USA; Pres. DERRICK NEMBHARD; Exec. Dir BECKY STOCKHAUSEN.

Jamaica Chamber of Commerce: UDC Office Centre, Suites 13–15, 12 Ocean Blvd, Kingston 10; tel. 922-0150; fax 924-9056; e-mail info@jamaicachamber.org.jm; internet www.jamaicachamber.org .jm; f. 1779; Pres. WARREN ALBERT MCDONALD; Gen. Man. PATRICIA PEART; 450 mems.

INDUSTRIAL AND TRADE ASSOCIATIONS

Cocoa Industry Board: Marcus Garvey Dr., POB 1039, Kingston 15; tel. 923-6411; fax 923-5837; e-mail cocoajam@cwjamaica.com; f. 1957; has statutory powers to regulate and develop the industry;

owns and operates 4 central fermentaries; Chair. FRANK PHIPPS; Man. and Sec. STEVE WATSON.

Coconut Industry Board: 18 Waterloo Rd, Kingston 10; tel. 926-1770; fax 968-1360; e-mail info@coconutindustryboard.org.jm; internet www.coconutindustryboard.org.jm; f. 1945; 9 mems; Chair. RICHARD A. JONES; Gen. Man. YVONNE BURNS.

Coffee Industry Board: 1 Willie Henry Dr., POB 508, Kingston 13; tel. 758-1259; fax 758-3907; e-mail datacoordinator@ciboj.org; internet www.ciboj.org; f. 1950; 9 mems; has wide statutory powers to regulate and develop the industry; Chair. HOWARD MITCHELL; Dir-Gen. CHRISTOPHER GENTLES.

Jamaica Bauxite Institute: Hope Gardens, POB 355, Kingston 6; tel. 927-2073; fax 927-1159; f. 1975; adviser to the Govt in the negotiation of agreements, consultancy services to clients in the bauxite/alumina and related industries, laboratory services for mineral and soil-related services, pilot plant services for materials and equipment-testing, research and devt; Chair. GARY PEART; Exec. Dir PARRIS LYEW-AYEE.

Jamaica Exporters' Association (JEA): 1 Winchester Rd, Kingston 10; tel. 960-4908; fax 960-9869; e-mail info@exportja.org; internet www.exportjamaica.org; f. 1966; promotes devt of export sector; Pres. VITUS EVANS; Gen. Man. JEAN SMITH.

Jamaica Manufacturers' Association Ltd (JMA): 85A Duke St, Kingston; tel. 922-8880; fax 922-9205; e-mail jma@cwjamaica.com; internet www.jma.com.jm; f. 1947; 340 mems; Pres. BRIAN PENGELLEY.

Sugar Industry Authority: 5 Trevennion Park Rd, POB 127, Kingston 5; tel. 926-5930; fax 926-6149; e-mail sia@cwjamaica .com; internet www.jamaicasugar.org; f. 1970; statutory body under portfolio of Min. of Agriculture and Fisheries; responsible for regulation and control of sugar industry and sugar-marketing; conducts research through Sugar Industry Research Institute; Exec. Chair. DERICK HEAVEN.

Trade Board Ltd: Air Jamaica Bldg, 10th Floor, 72 Harbour St, Kingston; tel. 967-0507; fax 948-5441; e-mail info@tradeboard.gov .jm; internet www.tradeboard.gov.jm; Trade Admin. DOUGLAS WEBSTER.

EMPLOYERS' ORGANIZATIONS

All-Island Banana Growers' Association Ltd: Banana Industry Bldg, 10 South Ave, Kingston 4; tel. 922-5497; fax 922-5497; e-mail aibga@cwjamaica.com; f. 1946; 1,500 mems (1997); Chair. GRETEL SESSING; Sec. I. CHANG.

Citrus Growers' Association Ltd: Bog Walk, St Catherine; tel. 708-2150; fax 708-2538; internet www.jcgja.com; f. 1944; 13,000 mems; Chair. JOHN THOMPSON; Gen. Man. DENNIS BOOTH.

Jamaica Association of Sugar Technologists: c/o Sugar Industry Research Institute, Kendal Rd, Mandeville; tel. 962-2241; fax 962-1288; e-mail jast@jamaicasugar.org; f. 1936; 275 mems; Chair. EARLE ROBERTS; Pres. IAN MAXWELL.

Jamaica Gasoline Retailers' Association (JGRA): Kings Plaza, POB 156, Kingston 10; tel. 929-2998; fax 929-8281; e-mail jgra@ cwjamaica.com; internet jgrajm.org; f. 1951; Pres. DERRICK THOMPSON.

Jamaica Livestock Association: Newport East, POB 36, Kingston; tel. 922-7130; fax 922-8934; internet www.jlaltd.com; f. 1941; 7,584 mems; Man. Dir and CEO HENRY J. RAINFORD.

Jamaica Sugar Cane Growers' Association (JSCGA): 4 North Ave, Kingston Gardens, Kingston 4; tel. 922-3010; fax 922-2077; e-mail allcane@cwjamaica.com; f. 1941; registered cane farmers; 27,000 mems; fmrly All-Island Cane Farmers' Asscn; name changed as above in 2008; Pres. ALLAN RICKARDS; Gen. Man. KARL JAMES.

Private Sector Organization of Jamaica (PSOJ): The Carlton Alexander Bldg, 39 Hope Rd, POB 236, Kingston 10; tel. 927-6957; fax 927-5137; e-mail psojinfo@psoj.org; internet www.psoj.org; f. 1976; federative body of private business individuals, cos and asscns; Pres. CHRISTOPHER ZACCA; CEO SANDRA GLASGOW.

Small Businesses' Association of Jamaica (SBAJ): 2 Trafalgar Rd, Kingston 5; tel. 978-0168; fax 927-7071; e-mail info@sbaj.org.jm; internet sbaj.org.jm; f. 1974; Pres. HUGH JOHNSON.

Sugar Manufacturing Corpn of Jamaica Ltd: 5 Trevennion Park Rd, Kingston 5; tel. 925-3650; fax 926-6746; est. to represent sugar mfrs in Jamaica; deals with all aspects of the sugar industry and its by-products; provides liaison between the Govt, the Sugar Industry Authority and the Jamaica Sugar Cane Growers' Asscn; 9 mems; Gen. Man. DERYCK T. BROWN.

UTILITIES
Regulatory Authority

Office of Utilities Regulation (OUR): PCJ Resource Centre, 3rd Floor, 36 Trafalgar Rd, Kingston 10; tel. 968-6053; fax 929-3635;

e-mail consumer@our.org.jm; internet www.our.org.jm; f. 1997; regulates provision of services in the following sectors: water and sewerage, electricity, telecommunications, public passenger transportation; Dir-Gen. ALBERT GORDON.

Electricity

Jamaica Energy Partners (JEP): Wikip Pl., Marcus Garvey Dr., Kingston 5; tel. 937-7915; fax 937-7937; e-mail info@jamenergy.com; internet jamenergy.com; f. 1995; owned by Conduit Capital Partners (USA); owns and operates 2 power barges at Old Harbour Bay, St Catherine; sells electricity to JPSCo; Gen. Man. and CEO WAYNE McKENZIE.

Jamaica Public Service Co (JPSCo): Dominion Life Bldg, 6 Knutsford Blvd, POB 54, Kingston 5; tel. 926-3190; fax 968-5341; e-mail calljps@jpsco.com; internet www.myjpsco.com; responsible for the generation and supply of electricity to the island; the JPSCo operating licence due to expire in 2027; Pres. and CEO KELLY TOMBLIN.

South Jamaica Power Co (SJPC): Kingston; jtly owned by Japan's Marubeni Corpn (40%), East West Power Korea (40%) and JPSCo (20%); Man. Dir VALENTINE FAGAN.

Water

National Water Commission: LOJ Centre, 5th Floor, 28–48 Barbados Ave, Kingston 5; tel. 929-5430; fax 926-1329; e-mail pr@nwc.com.jm; internet www.nwcjamaica.com; f. 1980; statutory body; provides potable water and waste water services; Chair. Dr LEARY MYERS.

Water Resources Authority: Hope Gardens, POB 91, Kingston 7; tel. 927-0077; fax 977-0179; e-mail info@wra.gov.jm; internet www.wra.gov.jm; f. 1996; manages, protects and controls allocation and use of water supplies; Man. Dir BASIL FERNANDEZ.

TRADE UNIONS

Caribbean Union of Teachers: 97 Church St, Kingston; tel. 922-1385; fax 922-3257; e-mail infor@caribbeanteachers.com; internet www.caribbeanteachers.com; f. 1935; umbrella org.; affiliates in 21 Caribbean countries; Pres. MARVIN ANDALL; Gen. Sec. Dr ADOLPH CAMERON.

Jamaica Confederation of Trade Unions (JCTU): 1A Hope Blvd, Kingston 6; tel. 927-2468; fax 977-4575; e-mail jctu@cwjamaica.com; Pres. LLOYD GOODLEIGH.

National Workers' Union of Jamaica (NWU): 130–132 East St, POB 344, Kingston 16; tel. 922-1150; fax 922-6608; e-mail nwyou@cwjamaica.com; f. 1952; affiliated to the International Trade Union Confederation; Pres. VINCENT MORRISON; Vice. Pres. HOWARD DUNCAN; 10,000 mems.

Transport

RAILWAYS

There are about 339 km of railway, all standard gauge, in Jamaica. Passenger services ceased in 1992.

Jamaica Railway Corpn (JRC): 142 Barry St, POB 489, Kingston; tel. 922-6443; fax 922-4539; e-mail odcrooks@cwjamaica.com; internet www.mtw.gov.jm/dep_agencies/ja_rail.aspx; f. 1845 as Jamaica Railway Co, the earliest British colonial railway; transferred to JRC in 1960; govt-owned; autonomous, statutory corpn until 1990, when it was partly leased to Alcan Jamaica Co Ltd (subsequently West Indies Alumina Co); planned privatization announced 2012; 215 km of railway; Chair. JOSEPH A. MATALON; Gen. Man. OWEN CROOKS.

ROADS

Jamaica has a good network of tar-surfaced and metalled motoring roads. In 2010 there were 22,121 km of roads in Jamaica. A five-year project to rehabilitate more than 570 km of roads across the island was undertaken in 2004–09, funded by a US $340m. loan from the Export-Import Bank of China. Development of a 66-km highway, the North–South Link, began in 2013. Work on the US $610m. project by the China Harbour Engineering Company was expected to be completed by December 2015.

Jamaica Urban Transit Company (JUTC): 1 Michael Manley Dr., Twickenham Park, Spanish Town, St Catherine; tel. 749-3192; fax 924-8158; e-mail marketing@jutc.com.jm; internet www.jutc.com; f. 1999; operates public transport in Kingston metropolitan region; Chair. Rev. GARNETT ROPER; Man. Dir Rear-Adm. HARDLEY LEWIN.

Transport Authority: 119 Maxfield Ave, Kingston 10; tel. 926-8912; fax 929-4178; e-mail customerservice@ta.org.jm; internet www.ta.org.jm; regulatory body; administers the licensing of public and commercial vehicles; Chair. NORTON HINDS; Man. Dir DANIEL DAWES.

SHIPPING

The principal ports are Kingston, Montego Bay and Port Antonio. The port at Kingston is a major transshipment terminal for the Caribbean area. In 2008 the fifth phase of an expansion project in Kingston was completed, doubling the port's handling capacity. Further plans for the expansion of Jamaica's port facilities, to include the construction of three additional berths and a second terminal at Montego Bay, were under way. A new cruise ship pier at Falmouth opened in 2011. At December 2014 the flag registered fleet comprised 55 vessels, totalling 184,003 grt.

Port Authority of Jamaica: 15–17 Duke St, Kingston; tel. 922-0290; fax 948-3575; e-mail paj@portjam.com; internet www.portjam.com; f. 1966; Govt's principal maritime agency; responsible for monitoring and regulating the navigation of all vessels berthing at Jamaican ports, for regulating the tariffs on public wharves, and for the devt of industrial free zones in Jamaica; Pres. and Chair. GORDON V. SHIRLEY.

Kingston Free Zone Co Ltd: 27 Shannon Dr., POB 1025, Kingston 15; tel. 923-6021; fax 923-6023; e-mail blee@portjam.com; internet www.pajfz.com; f. 1976; subsidiary of Port Authority of Jamaica; management and promotion of an export-orientated industrial free trade zone for cos from various countries; Gen. Man. KARLA HUIE.

Montego Bay Free Zone: POB 1377, Montego Bay; tel. 979-8696; fax 979-8088; e-mail gchenry@portjam.com; internet www.mbfz-jamaica.com; Vice-Pres. GLORIA HENRY.

Shipping Association of Jamaica: 4 Fourth Ave, Newport West, POB 1050, Kingston 13; tel. 923-3491; fax 923-3421; e-mail saj@jamports.com; internet www.jamports.com; f. 1939; 78 mems; regulates the supply and management of stevedoring labour in Kingston; represents mems in negotiations with govt and trade bodies; Pres. KIM CLARKE; Gen. Man. TREVOR RILEY.

Principal Shipping Company

Jamaica Freight and Shipping Co Ltd (JFS): 80–82 Second St, Newport West, Kingston 12; tel. 656-8629; fax 923-4091; e-mail jfs@jashipco.com; internet www.jashipco.com; f. 1976; liner and port agents, stevedoring services; Exec. Chair. CHARLES JOHNSTON.

CIVIL AVIATION

There are three international airports linking Jamaica with North America, Europe, and other Caribbean islands. The Norman Manley International Airport is situated 22.5 km outside Kingston. Sangster International Airport is 5 km from Montego Bay. A J $800m. programme to expand and improve the latter was completed in 2009. The Ian Fleming International Airport at Boscobel, 10 km from Ocho Rios, opened in 2011.

Airports Authority of Jamaica: Norman Manley International Airport, Palisadoes; tel. 924-8452; fax 924-8419; e-mail aaj@aaj.com.jm; internet www.airportsauthorityjamaica.aero; Chair. MARK HART; Pres. EARL ANTHONY RICHARDS.

Civil Aviation Authority: 4 Winchester Rd, POB 8998, Kingston 10; tel. 960-3948; fax 920-0194; e-mail info@jcaa.gov.jm; internet www.jcaa.gov.jm; f. 1996; Dir-Gen. Lt Col OSCAR DERBY.

Air Jamaica Ltd: 72–76 Harbour St, Kingston; tel. 922-3460; fax 967-3125; internet www.airjamaica.com; f. 1968; privatized in 1994, reacquired by Govt in 2004; sold to Caribbean Airlines (Trinidad and Tobago) in 2011; Govt of Jamaica retained 16% share; services within the Caribbean and to Canada (in asscn with Air Canada), the USA and the United Kingdom; Chair. GEORGE M. NICHOLAS, III; CEO ROBERT CORBIE (acting).

Exec Direct Aviation (EDA): Bldg II, Suite 11, 1 Ripon Rd, Kingston 5; tel. 618-5884; fax 618-5888; internet www.flyexecdirect.com; f. 2011; cargo services to Caribbean, Central and South American destinations; COO KAMAL CLARKE.

Fly Jamaica Airways: 2 Holborn Rd, Kingston 10; tel. 656-9832; fax 908-3069; e-mail info@fly-jamaica.com; internet www.fly-jamaica.com; f. 2013; Chair. and CEO Capt. PAUL RONALD REECE; Sec. Capt. LLOYD TAI.

Jamaica Air Shuttle: Tinson Pen Aerodrome, Marcus Garvey Dr., Kingston 11; tel. 923-0371; fax 506-9071; e-mail reservations@jamaicaairshuttle.com; internet www.jamaicaairshuttle.com; f. 2005; domestic and regional charter services to the Cayman Islands, Cuba, Dominican Republic and Haiti; Chair. CHRISTOPHER READ.

TimAir Ltd: Sangster International Airport, Montego Bay; tel. 952-2516; fax 979-1113; e-mail timair@usa.net; internet www.timair.com; f. 1983; charter services; Pres. FRASER MCCONNELL; Man. COLLEEN MCCONNELL.

Tourism

Tourists, mainly from the USA, visit Jamaica for its beaches, mountains, historic buildings and cultural heritage. In 2013 there were 2,008,409 visitor arrivals. Tourism receipts totalled US $2,073.9m. in that year.

Jamaica Hotel and Tourist Association (JHTA): 2 Ardenne Rd, Kingston 10; tel. 926-3635-6; fax 929-1054; e-mail info@jhta.org; internet www.jhta.org; f. 1961; trade asscn for hoteliers and other cos involved in Jamaican tourism; Pres. NICOLA MADDEN-GREIG; Exec. Dir CAMILLE NEEDHAM.

Jamaica Tourist Board (JTB): 64 Knutsford Blvd, Kingston 5; tel. 929-9200; fax 929-9375; e-mail info@visitjamaica.com; internet www.visitjamaica.com; f. 1955; a statutory body set up by the Govt to promote all aspects of the tourism industry; Chair. DENNIS MORRISON; Dir of Tourism PAUL PENNICOOK.

Defence

As assessed at November 2014, the total strength of the Jamaica Defence Force was 2,830. This included an army of 2,500, a coast-guard of 190 and an air wing of 140 members on active service. There were some 980 reservists.

Defence Budget: an estimated J $13,400m. (US $120m.) in 2014.

Chief of Defence Staff: Maj.-Gen. ANTONY BERTRAM ANDERSON.

Education

Primary education is compulsory in certain districts, and free education is ensured. The education system consists of a primary cycle of six years, followed by two secondary cycles of three and four years, respectively. In 2009/10 enrolment at primary schools included 82% of children in the relevant age-group. In the same year enrolment at secondary schools included 84% of children in the relevant age-group. Higher education was provided by four institutions, including the University of the West Indies, which has two campuses, at Mona and Montego Bay. Government spending on education in 2012/13 was budgeted at some J $73,829m.

JAPAN

Introductory Survey

LOCATION, CLIMATE, LANGUAGE, RELIGION, FLAG, CAPITAL

Japan lies in eastern Asia and comprises a curved chain of more than 3,000 islands. Four large islands, named (from north to south) Hokkaido, Honshu, Shikoku and Kyushu, account for about 98% of the land area. Hokkaido lies just to the south of Sakhalin, a large Russian island, and about 1,300 km (800 miles) east of Russia's mainland port of Vladivostok. Southern Japan is about 150 km (93 miles) east of the Republic of Korea (South Korea). Although summers are temperate everywhere, the climate in winter varies sharply from cold in the north to mild in the south. Temperatures in Tokyo range from −6°C (21°F) to 30°C (86°F). Typhoons and heavy rains are common in summer. The official language is Japanese. A small minority of indigenous Ainu speak a distinct language. The major religions are Shintoism and Buddhism, and there is a Christian minority. The national flag (proportions 7 by 10) is white, with a red disc (a sun without rays) in the centre. The capital is Tokyo.

CONTEMPORARY POLITICAL HISTORY

Historical Context

Following Japan's defeat in the Second World War, Japanese forces surrendered in August 1945. Japan signed an armistice in September, and the country was placed under US military occupation. A new democratic Constitution, which took effect in May 1947, renounced war and abandoned the doctrine of the Emperor's divinity. Following the peace treaty of September 1951, Japan regained its independence on 28 April 1952, although it was not until 1972 that the last of the US-administered outer islands, the remaining Ryukyu Islands (including Okinawa), were returned to Japanese sovereignty. The conservative Shigeru Yoshida served as Prime Minister in 1946–47 and again between 1948 and 1954, when he was succeeded by Ichiro Hatoyama.

Domestic Political Affairs

Liberal Democratic Party dominance, 1955–93

In November 1955 rival conservative groups merged to form the Liberal Democratic Party (LDP). Nobusuke Kishi, who became Prime Minister in February 1957, was succeeded by Hayato Ikeda in July 1960, and in November 1964 Ikeda was replaced by Eisaku Sato. Sato remained in office until July 1972, when he was succeeded by Kakuei Tanaka. Tanaka's premiership was beset by problems, leading to his replacement by Takeo Miki in December 1974. Tanaka was subsequently accused of accepting bribes from the Marubeni Corporation, and he was arrested in July 1976. The LDP lost its overall majority in the House of Representatives (the lower house of the Kokkai or Diet) at legislative elections held in December 1976. Miki resigned and was succeeded by Takeo Fukuda. However, Masayoshi Ohira defeated Fukuda in the LDP presidential election of November 1978, and replaced him as Prime Minister in December. Ohira failed to win a majority in the lower house at elections in October 1979. In May 1980 the Government was defeated in a motion of no confidence, forcing the dissolution of the lower house. Ohira died before the elections in June, when the LDP won 284 of the 511 seats. In July Zenko Suzuki was elected President of the LDP, and subsequently appointed Prime Minister. The growing factionalism of the LDP and the worsening economic crisis prompted Suzuki's resignation as Prime Minister and LDP President in October 1982. He was succeeded by Yasuhiro Nakasone.

At elections in June 1983 for one-half of the seats in the House of Councillors (the upper house of the Diet), a new electoral system was used. Of the 126 contested seats, 50 were filled on the basis of proportional representation. Two small parties thus entered the House of Councillors for the first time. The LDP increased its strength from 134 to 137 members in the 252-seat chamber. This result was seen as an endorsement of Nakasone's policies of increased expenditure on defence, closer relations with the USA and Japan's heightened presence in international affairs.

In October 1983 former Prime Minister Tanaka was found guilty of having accepted bribes. However, Tanaka's refusal to relinquish his parliamentary seat prompted an opposition-led boycott of the Diet, forcing Nakasone to call premature legislative elections in December. The Komeito (Clean Government Party), the Democratic Socialist Party (DSP) and the Japan Socialist Party (JSP) gained seats, at the expense of the Japanese Communist Party (JCP) and the New Liberal Club (NLC). The LDP, which had performed badly in the elections, formed a coalition with the NLC (which had split from the LDP over the Tanaka affair in 1976) and several independents. Nakasone again called early elections, held in July 1986, at which the LDP won 304 of the 512 seats. The record majority enabled the LDP to dispense with its coalition partner, the NLC (which disbanded in August and rejoined the LDP). In September the leaders of the LDP agreed to alter by-laws to allow party presidents one-year extensions beyond the normal limit of two terms of two years each. Nakasone was thus able to retain the posts of President of the LDP and Prime Minister until October 1987.

In July 1987 the Secretary-General of the LDP, Noboru Takeshita, left the Tanaka faction, with 113 other members, and announced the formation of a major new grouping within the ruling party. In the same month Tanaka's position was further weakened when the Tokyo High Court upheld his 1983 conviction for accepting bribes. In October 1987 Nakasone nominated Takeshita as his successor. The Diet was convened and Takeshita was formally elected as Prime Minister in November. In the new Cabinet Takeshita maintained a balance among the five major factions of the LDP, retaining only two members of Nakasone's previous Cabinet, but appointing four members of the Nakasone faction to senior ministerial posts (including Nakasone's ally, Sosuke Uno, as Minister of Foreign Affairs).

In January 1989 Emperor Hirohito, who had reigned since 1926, died after a long illness, thus ending the Showa era. He was succeeded by his son, Akihito, and the new era was named Heisei ('achievement of universal peace').

The Prime Minister and the LDP suffered a serious setback in June 1988 when several senior party members, including Nakasone, Kiichi Miyazawa and Takeshita himself, were alleged to have been indirectly involved in share-trading irregularities with the Recruit Cosmos Company; three cabinet ministers and the Chairman of the DSP were subsequently forced to resign, owing to their alleged involvement in the affair. In April 1989, as the allegations against politicians widened to include charges of bribery and malpractice, Takeshita announced his resignation. He was subsequently found to have accepted donations worth more than 150m. yen from the Recruit organization. Takeshita's nominee, Sosuke Uno, was elected as the new Prime Minister by the Diet in June. Notably, Uno was the first Japanese premier since the foundation of the LDP not to command his own political faction. Meanwhile, in May, following an investigation into the Recruit affair undertaken by an LDP special committee, public prosecutors indicted 13 people. Nakasone resigned from the LDP, assuming responsibility for the scandal, but did not relinquish his seat in the Diet.

Within days of Uno's assumption of office, a Japanese magazine published allegations of sexual impropriety involving the Prime Minister. As a result of a subsequent considerable increase in support for the JSP, led by Chairwoman Takako Doi, in July 1989 the LDP lost its majority in the upper house for the first time in the party's history. Uno's offer to resign was accepted by the LDP, which in August chose the relatively unknown Toshiki Kaifu, a former Minister of Education, to be the party's President and the new Prime Minister. Although the House of Councillors' ballot rejected Kaifu as the new Prime Minister in favour of Takako Doi, the decision of the lower house was adopted, in accordance with the Constitution.

At legislative elections held in February 1990, the LDP was returned to power with an unexpectedly large measure of support, securing 275 of the 512 seats in the House of Representatives. In January 1991 the JSP changed its English name to the Social Democratic Party of Japan (SDPJ) and Makato Tanabe later replaced Takako Doi as party Chairman. In September senior LDP officials forced Kaifu to abandon proposals for electoral reform, and the Takeshita faction of the LDP subsequently withdrew its support for the Prime Minister. With the backing of this faction, former Minister of Finance Kiichi Miyazawa was elected President of the LDP in October, and in November the Diet endorsed his appointment as Prime Minister. However, his position was undermined by new allegations of involvement in the Recruit affair, publicized by the SDPJ in December.

In early 1992 public disgust at official corruption was registered at two prefectural by-elections to the upper house, when the LDP lost seats that had previously been considered secure to Rengo-no-kai (the political arm of RENGO, the trade union confederation). The successful passage through the Diet in June—despite opposition from the SDPJ—of legislation authorizing the participation of Japan's armed forces, the Self-Defence Forces (SDF) in UN peacekeeping operations improved the Government's standing, and in elections to the upper house in July the LDP won 69 of the 127 seats contested. The SDPJ, by contrast, lost 25 of its 46 seats; the Komeito increased its total strength from 20 to 24 seats, and Rengo-no-kai failed to win any seats. The Japan New Party (JNP), founded by LDP dissidents only two months prior to the elections, secured four seats. A formal split within the Takeshita faction took place in December. The new faction was led nominally by Tsutomu Hata, the Minister of Finance, although it was widely recognized that Ichiro Ozawa, the former LDP Secretary-General, held effective power in the grouping.

Electoral reform was a major political issue in the first half of 1993. While the LDP favoured a single-member constituency system, the opposition parties proposed various forms of proportional representation. In June the lower house adopted a motion of no confidence against the Government, after the LDP refused to modify its reform proposals to meet opposition demands. Numerous LDP members opposed the Government or abstained from the vote. The Ozawa-Hata group, comprising 44 former LDP members, immediately established a new party, the Shinseito (Japan Renewal Party, JRP), in order to contest the forthcoming legislative elections. Another new party, the New Party Sakigake, was also formed by LDP Diet members. In the elections to the House of Representatives, held in July, the LDP won 223 of the 511 seats, thus falling 33 seats short of a majority. Miyazawa resigned as Prime Minister and a seven-party coalition Government was formed, excluding the LDP, which consequently became an opposition party for the first time since its foundation. In August Morihiro Hosokawa, the leader of the JNP, was elected Prime Minister, defeating the new President of the LDP, Chief Cabinet Secretary Yohei Kono.

In August 1993, following the release of a report that found that during the Second World War the Japanese military had been complicit in allowing large numbers of women from occupied territories to be forced into sexual slavery, the Chief Cabinet Secretary issued the so-called Kono Statement, acknowledging the use of coercion on many so-called 'comfort women'—a fact previously denied by the Government.

Successive Governments, 1994–2001

Hosokawa resigned as Prime Minister in April 1994. He was subsequently replaced by Tsutomu Hata, at the head of a minority Government which excluded the SDPJ and the New Party Sakigake. Hata was obliged to resign in June, however, owing to his continued failure to command a viable majority in the Diet, and a new coalition, composed of the SDPJ, the LDP and the New Party Sakigake, took office. The LDP thus ended its brief period in opposition. Tomiichi Murayama, the leader of the SDPJ, became Prime Minister, and Kono was appointed Deputy Prime Minister and Minister of Foreign Affairs.

In July 1994 Murayama recognized the right under Japan's pacifist Constitution to the existence of the SDF, which had been disputed within the SDPJ. In December nine opposition parties, including the JNP, the JRP, the DSP and the Komeito, amalgamated to form the Shinshinto (New Frontier Party, NFP). A faction of the Komeito remained outside the new party and was renamed Komei. Kaifu was elected leader of the NFP; Ozawa was appointed Secretary-General. The creation of the NFP was widely perceived to be a response to the approval by the Diet in November 1994 of the electoral reform bills first proposed in 1993, which appeared to favour larger political parties. Under the terms of the new law, the House of Representatives was to be reduced to 500 seats, comprising 300 single-seat constituencies and 200 seats determined by proportional representation; the proportional-representation base was to be divided into 11

regions, and a party would qualify for a proportional-representation seat if it received a minimum of 2% of the vote.

In January 1995 a massive earthquake in the Kobe region caused thousands of deaths and serious infrastructural damage. The Government was severely criticized for the poor co-ordination of the relief operation. In March the poisonous gas sarin was released into the Tokyo underground railway system, killing 12 people and injuring more than 5,000. A religious sect, Aum Shinrikyo, was accused of perpetrating the attack. Following a further gas attack, in Yokohama in April, a number of sect members were detained by the authorities. In June Shoko Asahara, the leader of Aum Shinrikyo, was indicted on a charge of murder; his trial continued until February 2004, when he was sentenced to death for his role in the Tokyo attack. (However, at February 2015, owing to various procedural delays, Asahara had not yet been executed.)

At the elections to one-half of the seats in the House of Councillors held in July 1995, of the 126 seats contested, the LDP won only 49 seats, the SDPJ 16 and the New Party Sakigake three, whereas the NFP, benefiting from the support of the Soka Gakkai religious organization, secured 40 seats. In September Ryutaro Hashimoto, the Minister of International Trade and Industry, replaced Kono as leader of the LDP.

In December 1995 Kaifu was succeeded by Ozawa as leader of the NFP. In January 1996 Murayama resigned as Prime Minister; however, he was re-elected Chairman of the SDPJ. The LDP leader, Ryutaro Hashimoto, was elected Prime Minister, and a coalition Cabinet, largely dominated by the LDP, was formed. In August Shoichi Ide and Hiroyuki Sonoda were elected Leader and Secretary-General, respectively, of the New Party Sakigake, following the resignations of Masayoshi Takemura and Yukio Hatoyama. The latter left the party and founded the Democratic Party of Japan (DPJ), with other dissident members of the New Party Sakigake and individual members of the SDPJ and NFP.

At legislative elections held in October 1996 the LDP won 239 of the 500 seats in the House of Representatives, while the NFP secured 156, the DPJ 52, the JCP 26, the SDPJ 15 and the New Party Sakigake two. In November Hashimoto was re-elected Prime Minister, and formed the first single-party Cabinet since 1993. Soon after the elections several government ministers and party leaders were implicated in various corruption scandals. In December 1996 former Prime Minister Hata left the NFP and established a new party, Taiyoto (Sun Party), together with 12 other dissident NFP members. Later that month Takako Doi was formally appointed Chairwoman of the SDPJ.

By September 1997 the LDP had regained its majority in the House of Representatives, following a series of defections by members of the NFP. In December a much-reduced NFP was dissolved. Six new parties were founded by former NFP members—Ozawa and his supporters forming the Liberal Party (LP)—and a significant political realignment thus took place. In January 1998 six opposition parties, including the DPJ, formed a parliamentary group, Minyuren, which constituted the largest opposition bloc in the Diet. In March the parties comprising Minyuren agreed on their integration into the DPJ, formally establishing a new DPJ, with Naoto Kan as its President, in the following month.

Meanwhile, from 1997 various circumstances contributed to the development of an economic crisis. Accordingly, the Hashimoto administration implemented a series of measures designed to encourage economic growth, including, in a major reversal of policy, the use of public funds to support the increasingly fragile banking system; the government response, however, was widely criticized for lacking speed and efficacy, and in 1998 the economy entered recession. In January and March 1998, respectively, the Minister of Finance, Hiroshi Mitsuzuka, and the Governor of the Bank of Japan (the central bank) resigned, as a far-reaching corruption scandal emerged that implicated several senior officials within the Government and the central bank and around 30 executives of other banks and financial institutions. Trials of those implicated in the bribery scandal took place during 1998–99.

In June 1998 the SDPJ and the New Party Sakigake withdrew from their alliance with the ruling LDP. The LDP performed poorly in elections for one-half of the seats in the House of Councillors in the following month, retaining only 44 of its 61 seats contested, while the DPJ won 27 seats, increasing its representation to 47 seats, and the JCP became the third largest party in the upper house, taking 15 seats. Hashimoto resigned as Prime Minister and President of the LDP and was succeeded in both posts by Keizo Obuchi, hitherto Minister of Foreign Affairs. Kiichi Miyazawa, the former Prime Minister, was appointed Minister of Finance in the so-called 'economic reconstruction' Cabinet. Obuchi announced the establishment of an Economic Strategy Council and promised substantial tax reductions. The issue of banking reform dominated the following months, and in October the Diet approved banking legislation that included provisions for the nationalization of failing banks, as demanded by the opposition.

Komei merged with another party, Shinto Heiwa, in November 1998 to form New Komeito, which thus became the second largest opposition party. Also in that month Fukushiro Nukaga, the Director-General of the Defence Agency, resigned from the Government to assume responsibility for a procurement scandal. In mid-November the LDP and the LP reached a basic accord on the formation of a coalition, although this would still lack a majority in the upper house. The Government was reorganized in January 1999 to include the LP.

In April 1999 the election to the governorship of Tokyo of Shintaro Ishihara, an outspoken nationalist writer and former Minister of Transport under the LDP (although now unaffiliated), was regarded as an embarrassment for the ruling party. In August the Diet voted to grant official legal status to the de facto national flag (*Hinomaru*) and anthem (*Kimigayo*), despite considerable opposition owing to their association with Japan's militaristic past. Meanwhile, in July New Komeito joined the ruling LDP-LP coalition, giving the Government a majority in the upper house and expanding its control in the lower house to more than 70% of the seats. Achieving consensus within the coalition on policy initiatives, however, proved challenging. Obuchi was re-elected President of the LDP in September, while Naoto Kan was replaced as President of the DPJ by Yukio Hatoyama, hitherto Secretary-General of the party. A new Cabinet was appointed in October, in which the LP and New Komeito each received one post. A basic accord on coalition policy included an agreement (initially opposed by New Komeito) to seek a reduction in the number of seats in the House of Representatives, first by 20 and subsequently by a further 30. The reduction in seats was endorsed by the Diet in February 2000, despite strong opposition protest, including a boycott of legislative proceedings. Meanwhile, multi-party committees were established in both Houses of the Diet in January with a mandate to review the Constitution.

In April 2000 the LP withdrew from the coalition Government; 26 party members defected at that time and formed the New Conservative Party—NCP (Hoshuto). In the same month Prime Minister Obuchi became incapacitated by ill health. (He died in May.) The LDP elected Secretary-General Yoshiro Mori as its new President. Mori was subsequently elected Prime Minister by both Houses of the Diet; he immediately affirmed his commitment to the reform initiatives of his predecessor, and established a coalition with New Komeito and the NCP. All ministers from the Obuchi administration were retained.

At the legislative elections held in June 2000 the number of seats in the House of Representatives was reduced from 500 to 480. The LDP won the largest number of seats, although its representation was reduced to 233. The DPJ increased its tally to 127 seats, New Komeito won 31 seats, the LP 22, the NCP 20 and the SDPJ 19. Despite numerous political gaffes and public errors of protocol (including a number of controversial public statements expressing imperialist views, for which he was forced publicly to apologize), Mori was returned as Prime Minister and appointed a new Cabinet in July.

Various revelations of corruption and misconduct emerged during 2000, resulting in several resignations, and further undermining Mori's premiership. In October Hidenao Nakagawa, Minister of State, Chief Cabinet Secretary, Director-General of the Okinawa Development Agency and Minister in Charge of Information Technology, resigned after it was alleged, *inter alia*, that he had lied regarding his links to a right-wing activist. In January 2001 Fukushiro Nukaga, the Minister of State for Economy, Industry and Information Technology, stood down, having been implicated in a 'cash for questions' scandal that came to light in November 2000.

Meanwhile, in November 2000 Fusako Shigenobu, the founder of the extremist left-wing Japanese Red Army, which had been responsible for a number of attacks during the 1970s, was arrested in Osaka. She was detained on suspicion of the seizure of the French embassy in the Netherlands in 1974 and subsequently indicted on various related charges. A number of other members of the group had been repatriated from several countries since 1995 to be tried for terrorism. (Shigenobu was sentenced to 20 years' imprisonment in February 2006 for her involvement in the seizure of the embassy.)

A major government reorganization was announced in December 2000. The number of ministries was reduced from 23 to 13, mainly through mergers, and various state agencies were absorbed into the newly created Cabinet Office. Despite the publication in late 2000 of photographs apparently showing the Prime Minister in the company of an alleged gangster and convicted murderer, and denying allegations that some years previously he had been arrested for violation of an anti-prostitution law (Mori sued for defamation on both counts), Mori won another vote of confidence in March 2001. In early April, however, he announced his intention to resign.

The administration of Junichiro Koizumi

In late April 2001 Junichiro Koizumi, a former Minister of Health and Welfare, unexpectedly defeated Ryutaro Hashimoto, the leader of the largest LDP faction, and one other candidate to secure the presidency of the ruling LDP and thus the premiership. Koizumi's victory was attributed to a change in party election rules that allowed a greater influence of local and ordinary party members in selecting the President. He subsequently reorganized the Cabinet, largely disregarding LDP factional politics, and appointed a number of reformists, including Makiko Tanaka, daughter of former Prime Minister Kakuei Tanaka, as Japan's first female Minister of Foreign Affairs, and Heizo Takenaka, an economics professor, as Minister of State for Economy, Industry and Information Technology. Koizumi also reorganized the LDP's senior leadership, appointing his ally Taku Yamasaki as Secretary-General, and Taro Aso as Chairman of the Policy Research Council. In addition to according priority to economic reform, Koizumi also sought to introduce direct elections for the post of prime minister and to upgrade the status of the SDF into that of a full army, which would involve an amendment to Article 9 of the Constitution, whereby Japan renounced the use of war.

In June 2001 the Government finally announced an economic reform programme, which included the privatization of special public institutions and a review of regulatory economic laws. However, veteran members of the LDP, particularly the Hashimoto faction, remained opposed to Koizumi's reforms. The Prime Minister's personal popularity was a major factor in the LDP's gains in elections to the House of Councillors held in July. Koizumi aroused controversy later in that month when he made an official visit to honour Japan's war dead at the Shinto Yasukuni Shrine, which controversially includes memorials to officers who were convicted of serious war crimes. Koizumi made five further visits to the shrine during his term of office, incurring both domestic and international criticism.

In September 2001 the terrorist attacks against targets on the US mainland again raised the subject of the role of Japan's military; Koizumi appeared to invoke the USA's subsequent war against the Taliban regime in Afghanistan as an argument to expand the role of the SDF. In October the Diet approved new legislation for the overseas deployment of the SDF in a non-combat support role, and in the following month Japan dispatched warships to the Indian Ocean, in the biggest such deployment since the Second World War (see *Foreign Affairs*). The Japanese people strongly supported logistical assistance to the USA, but there remained considerable public opposition to any amendment to Article 9 of the Constitution.

In December 2001 the Government agreed to abolish 17 public corporations and transfer 45 others (of a total of 163) to the private sector. However, Koizumi's major proposed reform, the privatization of the Postal Services Agency, was further delayed. Meanwhile, the opposition DPJ itself experienced divisions, between those who favoured co-operation with Koizumi and his reforms (including the party's President, Yukio Hatoyama) and those who favoured greater co-operation with other opposition parties. At the end of January 2002 Koizumi dismissed his Minister of Foreign Affairs, Makiko Tanaka, following months of disputes over reform within the ministry. The dismissal of the popular Tanaka was regarded as a victory for LDP veterans and as a setback for reform. The session of the Diet was extended until July in order to enable Koizumi to draft legislation for reforms to the postal services, as well as to the health service and defence and security sectors. These reforms were opposed by considerable elements within the LDP.

In September 2002 Koizumi implemented a long-expected cabinet reorganization, notably dismissing the Minister of State for the Financial Services Agency, Hakuo Yanagisawa, and appointing the Minister of State for Economic and Fiscal Policy, Heizo Takenaka, concurrently to hold that post. Plans to reform the banking sector created tensions between the LDP and its two coalition partners, New Komeito and the NCP. In October a tripartite committee of the ruling coalition published a banking reform plan that was far less radical than that sought by Takenaka, who had urged the nationalization of major banks to prevent their failure.

In December 2002 the DPJ elected Naoto Kan as its President, replacing Yukio Hatoyama, who had been forced to resign from the post after the failure of secret attempts to merge the party with the LP. Kan had previously headed the DPJ during 1997–99. Four DPJ members of the Diet, led by former party Vice-President Hiroshi Kumagai, resigned from the party in December 2002 and joined the NCP; the President of that party, Takeshi Noda, stood down in favour of Kumagai.

In March 2003 the Governor of Tokyo, Shintaro Ishihara, announced that he would seek re-election, ending months of speculation that he might form a new political party in order to challenge Koizumi. At the local elections in April Ishihara was overwhelmingly re-elected, and pledged to use his position to campaign for reform in the country as a whole.

In April 2003 the LDP announced its intention to amend the Constitution explicitly to state the legitimacy of the SDF and to expand its role in international peacekeeping and collective self-defence. In May the House of Representatives approved new legislation granting the Government and the SDF greater powers to act in the event of an attack on Japan; the bill, which was supported by the DPJ as well as by the ruling coalition, was approved the following month by the House of Councillors. In July, despite vehement opposition, the House of Councillors approved proposals, recently endorsed by the lower chamber, to send peacekeeping forces to Iraq, thereby allowing the largest deployment of Japanese troops abroad since the Second World War. Although troops were to engage in humanitarian work only, critics argued that the deployment would violate the Constitution, as, in practice, troops would be unable to avoid conflict areas.

In September 2003 Koizumi was re-elected leader of the LDP, defeating three rival candidates. Koizumi then announced a new Cabinet, which included the reappointment of Heizo Takenaka as Minister of State responsible for the Financial Services Agency, despite criticism of his banking reform policies (see above). Also in September, a merger agreement between the DPJ and the LP was signed, with the aim of creating an opposition movement capable of presenting a strong challenge to the LDP at the forthcoming legislative elections.

At the elections, held in November 2003, the LDP lost control of 10 of its previous 247 seats in the House of Representatives. The party's strength increased to 245 following the recruitment of four independent candidates and the absorption of the NCP, one of the LDP's two coalition partners, which had won four seats. The LDP's other coalition partner, New Komeito, secured 34 seats. The DPJ (incorporating the former LP) won 177 seats, thereby increasing its representation by 40.

Plans for the SDF deployment to Iraq, following the approval of the requisite legislation in July 2003 (see above), were strongly criticized by the President of the DPJ, Naoto Kan. Popular protests against the Iraq mission took place, and opposition within Japan to the deployment was strengthened by the deaths of two Japanese diplomats in Iraq in November. None the less, in January 2004 the first Japanese troops departed for Iraq.

In May 2004 a scandal over pension contributions prompted resignations by senior officials of the LDP and the opposition DPJ. The Chief Cabinet Secretary, Yasuo Fukuda of the LDP, resigned after admitting that he had not made the required payments to the compulsory state pension scheme. Naoto Kan resigned from the presidency of the DPJ shortly afterwards on similar grounds. Kan was replaced by Katsuya Okada, hitherto the party's Secretary-General. In the same month a government proposal for pension reform, involving increased premiums and reduced benefits, was approved by the House of Representatives. The reform plan was approved by the House of Councillors in June, despite strong opposition from the DPJ. In July nationwide voting took place to elect one-half of the members of the House of Councillors. Of the 121 seats contested, the LDP won 49, while the DPJ secured 50 (thus increasing its overall representation in the chamber from 60 seats to 82). Although the LDP and its coalition partner New Komeito, with a combined total of 139 seats, retained a majority in the 242-member House, the outcome was generally interpreted as reflecting a decline in the popular-

ity of Koizumi's administration. In September Koizumi effected a major reorganization of cabinet portfolios. Among notable new appointments was that of Nobutaka Machimura as Minister of Foreign Affairs. From October there were renewed protests against Japanese support for military operations in Iraq following the beheading of a Japanese tourist who had been taken hostage by a militant group there. Nevertheless, in December the LDP announced that the term of the SDF mission in Iraq was to be extended by one year.

In August 2005 Koizumi's postal reform bill, which had been narrowly approved by the House of Representatives in the previous month, was defeated in the House of Councillors. A total of 37 LDP members from both houses rebelled against the party leadership and voted against the proposed legislation. Koizumi responded to the defeat by dissolving the House of Representatives and calling elections for 11 September. Prohibited from standing as party members, several LDP 'rebels' formed separate parties, including the People's New Party (Kokumin Shinto—PNP), led by Tamisuke Watanuki, and the New Party Nippon (Shinto Nippon), led by Yasuo Tanaka. Other dissidents chose to stand as independent candidates. In the event, the elections resulted in unequivocal victory for Koizumi and, by implication, an endorsement of his reform programme by the electorate. The LDP increased its representation in the House of Representatives to 296 of the 480 seats (its first overall majority since 1990 and the largest number of seats won by a single party since the end of the Second World War), thereby creating, with its ally New Komeito, a ruling coalition bloc of 327 seats and securing more than two-thirds of the chamber. The DPJ's share of seats, meanwhile, was reduced by 64 to 113, prompting the resignation of its President, Katsuya Okada. The subsequent DPJ leadership election was won by Seiji Maehara. In October Koizumi reorganized his Cabinet. Shinzo Abe was appointed Chief Cabinet Secretary, Taro Aso became Minister of Foreign Affairs and Sadakazu Tanigaki was retained as Minister of Finance. The postal reform bill was resubmitted to the legislature, and in mid-October was approved by both houses of the Diet.

In September 2006 Chief Cabinet Secretary Shinzo Abe, with the clear support of the Prime Minister, was elected to succeed Koizumi as LDP President. Having secured the support of both houses of the Diet, at the end of the month Abe formally took office as Prime Minister. Only one incumbent minister of the Koizumi administration, namely the Minister of Foreign Affairs, Taro Aso, retained his position in the new Cabinet.

The Governments of Abe, Fukuda and Aso

On assuming the premiership, Shinzo Abe swiftly arranged discussions with the People's Republic of China and South Korea, relations with both of which had been strained by his predecessor's well-publicized visits to the Yasukuni Shrine (see *Foreign Affairs*). Abe envisaged the pursuit of an assertive foreign policy, stating that Japan should continue to seek a permanent seat on the UN Security Council and making clear his commitment to an uncompromising stance against the Democratic People's Republic of Korea (North Korea). More controversially, he undertook to revise Article 9 of the country's pacifist Constitution to permit the Japanese military to perform a wider role abroad. In terms of economic strategy, Abe pledged to pursue the reformist policies of his predecessor.

In December 2006 an official investigation found that under the Koizumi administration (when Abe held the post of Chief Cabinet Secretary) members of the public had been paid to ask specific questions of ministers at local meetings and that government officials had masqueraded as ordinary citizens. In the same month legislation to upgrade the Defence Agency was adopted by the Diet (the Defence Agency was officially elevated to a full ministry in January 2007). In late 2007, despite objections from four groupings, including the DPJ, controversial amendments to Japan's hitherto pacifist 1947 'Fundamental Law on Education' were also adopted, requiring schools to foster traditional and patriotic values.

In April 2007 the DPJ performed well in local elections, while Governor Ishihara was re-elected in Tokyo for a third consecutive term, with the (unsolicited) support of the ruling coalition. Also in April the House of Representatives approved legislation setting out procedures for national referendums on constitutional reform, including provision for the participation of all citizens over the age of 18 (compared with a minimum voting age of 20 for elections), although failing to impose a minimum participation rate for the validity of the referendum. The House of Councillors adopted the legislation in May 2007.

It emerged in May 2007 that, in an apparent compromise designed to appease both his more nationalistic supporters and neighbouring countries, the Prime Minister had sent an offering to the Yasukuni Shrine in the previous month, but had refrained from visiting the shrine himself. Similarly, Abe chose not to visit the shrine on the anniversary of Japan's surrender in the Second World War in August, instead attending a commemoration ceremony in Tokyo.

The Minister of Agriculture, Forestry and Fisheries, Toshikatsu Matsuoka, who was under investigation for alleged financial impropriety, committed suicide in May 2007. By June public support for Abe had declined significantly, amid widespread anger over the loss of some 50m. pension records by the Social Insurance Agency. The Government suffered a further reverse in July when the Minister of Defence, Fumio Kyuma, resigned, having provoked widespread offence by suggesting that the US nuclear attacks on the Japanese cities of Hiroshima and Nagasaki in 1945, towards the end of the Second World War, had been inevitable. Yuriko Koike, hitherto Abe's special adviser on national security affairs, was appointed to replace Kyuma, becoming Japan's first female Minister of Defence.

The ruling LDP-New Komeito coalition lost its overall majority in the House of Councillors in the partial elections that were held in July 2007. By contrast, the DPJ made significant gains, winning overall control of the house. The DPJ's Satsuki Eda subsequently became the first opposition politician to be elected Speaker of the upper house. Despite the ruling coalition's defeat in the elections, Abe remained in office, although Hidenao Nakagawa relinquished the post of Secretary-General of the LDP. At the beginning of August Norihiko Akagi, Matsuoka's successor as Minister of Agriculture, Forestry and Fisheries, having similarly been accused of financial impropriety, was forced to resign from the Government. The Minister of Justice, Jinen Nagase, was also at that time accused of improper financial conduct.

The Prime Minister reorganized the Cabinet in late August 2007 in an attempt to restore confidence in his administration. Several veteran members of the LDP were appointed to the Government, including faction leaders Nobutaka Machimura and Masahiko Koumura as Minister of Foreign Affairs and Minister of Defence, respectively, and Fukushiro Nukaga as Minister of Finance. Taro Aso became Secretary-General of the LDP. Only a week later, however, the new Minister of Agriculture, Forestry and Fisheries, Takehiko Endo, resigned, causing further embarrassment for Abe, after admitting that a private farming group of which he was Chairman had misappropriated state funds. In mid-September Abe himself stood down as Prime Minister and President of the LDP, acknowledging that he had lost the support and trust of the public.

Yasuo Fukuda, the son of a former Prime Minister and a moderate politician, who had served as Chief Cabinet Secretary under Koizumi, was elected as LDP President in late September 2007, and subsequently took office as Prime Minister, having secured the approval of a majority in the House of Representatives. Fukuda retained most of the ministers from his predecessor's Cabinet. Koumura, who became Minister of Foreign Affairs, was replaced at the Ministry of Defence by one of the few new appointees, Shigeru Ishiba (who had also held the defence portfolio in Koizumi's Government), while Machimura was appointed Chief Cabinet Secretary and Minister of State for the Abduction Issue. Aso was replaced as LDP Secretary-General by Bunmei Ibuki.

Fukuda advocated closer relations with neighbouring Asian countries (pledging not to visit the controversial Yasukuni Shrine), while maintaining a strong alliance with the USA, and promised to continue to pursue economic structural reforms. The new Prime Minister's first challenge was to secure approval for the extension of legislation enabling the Maritime Self-Defence Force to provide logistical support in the Indian Ocean to ships involved in US-led counter-terrorism operations in Afghanistan. The renewal of the legislation, which had first been adopted in 2001 and which was scheduled to expire at the beginning of November 2007, was opposed by the DPJ on the grounds that the US-led operations had not been sanctioned by the UN and that Japan's involvement violated its pacifist Constitution. Following the failure of efforts to reach a political consensus, in mid-October the Cabinet approved draft legislation that would extend the mission but, in a concession to its critics, would limit its role to supplying fuel and water to ships on anti-terrorism patrols rather than those involved in military operations. Yearly renewal of the proposed legislation would also

be required. However, the Diet remained in deadlock over the issue at the end of October, leading to the temporary suspension of the support mission.

In mid-November 2007 the House of Representatives approved the legislation to renew Japan's naval deployment in the Indian Ocean, shortly before Fukuda was due to visit the USA, which had been exerting strong pressure on Japan to resume its support for US counter-terrorism activities. The House of Councillors began debating the proposed resumption of the deployment in early December 2007, but the DPJ continued to refuse to approve the necessary legislation. In mid-January 2008 the Government forced through the passage of the bill, using its majority in the House of Representatives to supersede another vote against it by the House of Councillors (the first time this power had been used since 1951). Two Japanese vessels were dispatched to assist US forces in the Indian Ocean later that month.

In June 2008 the House of Representatives approved a resolution that for the first time formally recognized the minority Ainu as 'an indigenous people with a distinct language, religion and culture'. The resolution urged the establishment of a special panel to formulate government policy towards the Ainu people, who had long felt disadvantaged in the ethnically homogenous society of Japan and whose separate identity had been officially acknowledged only in 1997.

In August 2008 the Prime Minister effected an extensive cabinet reorganization, in which Bunmei Ibuki was appointed as Minister of Finance and Kaoru Yosano as Minister of State for Economic and Fiscal Policy. On the same day Taro Aso was appointed to replace Ibuki as Secretary-General of the LDP. In early September, however, the Prime Minister announced his resignation, citing the difficulties in reaching a consensus with the DPJ on the implementation of his legislative agenda. Shortly afterwards the latest Minister of Agriculture, Seiichi Ota, was also compelled to resign owing to the revelation of a scandal involving the import and distribution of contaminated rice.

Taro Aso was elected as the next President of the LDP, and in late September 2008 he was duly confirmed as Prime Minister by the House of Representatives. He immediately formed a new Cabinet, appointing Shoichi Nakagawa as Minister of Finance, Hirofume Nakasone as Minister of Foreign Affairs and Yasukazu Hamada as Minister of Defence. Aso had been widely expected to call early elections for the House of Representatives, but he ultimately decided against this, preferring to focus immediately on economic policy in view of the emerging global financial crisis.

In January 2009 Yoshimi Watanabe, a former Minister of State for Financial Services and Administrative Reform, who was opposed to the Government's fiscal stimulus programme and the additional budgetary expenditure involved, announced his departure from the LDP. (In August Watanabe formed a new political party, known as Your Party.) In February former Prime Minister Koizumi similarly criticized the Government's expenditure under the financial stimulus plans. Aso's plight worsened when the Minister of Finance, Shoichi Nakagawa, resigned, having apparently been intoxicated at a press conference held during a meeting of the Group of Seven (G7) leading industrialized nations in Italy.

In March 2009 the arrest of Takanori Okubo, the political secretary of Ichiro Ozawa, on suspicion of accepting illegal donations and falsifying party accounts, led to pressure on the leader of the opposition DPJ to resign. Okubo was formally indicted later in the month, and Ozawa, although denying any wrongdoing on his part, eventually responded to public opinion in May by resigning as President of the DPJ. He was replaced by the party's Deputy President, Yukio Hatoyama, who had been one of the original DPJ's founders in 1996 and had held the post of party President between 1999 and 2002.

The DPJ in power: 2009–12

In July 2009 diminishing support for the LDP was demonstrated when it was defeated by the DPJ in an election to the Tokyo Metropolitan Assembly (which the LDP had dominated for more than 40 years). As was widely predicted, at the legislative elections in August the DPJ was overwhelmingly successful, securing 308 of the 480 seats in the House of Representatives, while the LDP won 119 seats and New Komeito 21. The LDP was thus removed from government for only the second time since 1955 (the first having been the 11-month period during which it had been out of office in 1993–94). Despite having secured an overall majority, the DPJ negotiated with the SDPJ and the PNP (which had won seven and three seats, respectively, in the House of Representatives) to form a coalition, in order to widen the Government's support, particularly in the House of Councillors, where the DPJ lacked an overall majority. Hatoyama took office as Prime Minister in mid-September 2009. He appointed Naoto Kan, a former President of the DPJ, as Deputy Prime Minister and Minister of State for National Policy, Economic and Fiscal Policy, and Science and Technology Policy: Kan was to preside over a new National Strategy Bureau, which was to formulate policy and supervise budgetary allocations, thereby reducing what was perceived by the DPJ as the excessive power of the civil service. Katsuya Okada, hitherto Secretary-General of the DPJ, became Minister of Foreign Affairs, and the new Minister of Finance was Hirohisa Fujii, who had held the same position during the period of non-LDP rule in 1993–94. The Chairman of the SDPJ, Mizuho Fukushima, and the leader of the PNP, Shizuka Kamei, both received ministerial posts.

In September 2009 Ozawa was appointed Secretary-General of the DPJ, despite the allegations of irregular funding that had prompted his resignation as the party's President earlier in the year. Changes also took place within the parties that had been defeated in the August elections: Aso resigned as President of the LDP in early September and was succeeded by Sadakazu Tanigaki, the former Minister of Finance. The President of New Komeito, Akihiro Ota, and the party's Secretary-General, Kazuo Kitagawa, both of whom had lost their parliamentary seats in the elections, also resigned in early September. Ota was replaced by Natsuo Yamaguchi, hitherto the Chairman of the party's Policy Research Council.

Hatoyama's new Government, which announced its intention to impose stricter controls on government expenditure, was confronted by considerable obstacles to economic recovery, in particular the very high level of government debt, the strength of the yen against the US dollar and the problem of persistent deflation. In January 2010, following the resignation of the Minister of Finance, Hirohisa Fujii, owing to ill health, Deputy Prime Minister Kan assumed additional responsibility for the finance portfolio.

In April 2010 two new political parties were established, composed mainly of dissatisfied former members of the LDP. The Sunrise Party of Japan was led by Takeo Hiranuma, an independent member of the House of Representatives and a former Minister of Economy, Trade and Industry; he was joined by some erstwhile senior members of the LDP, including Kaoru Yosano, the former Minister of Finance. The New Renaissance Party was established by Yoichi Masuzoe, hitherto an LDP member of the House of Councillors and a former Minister of Health, Labour and Welfare.

In May 2010 Hatoyama admitted that his party's electoral pledge to remove an unpopular US military air base from the southern island of Okinawa (see *Foreign Affairs*) could not realistically be fulfilled, and he proposed, instead, adhering to an agreement made with the USA in 2006, whereby the base would be transferred to an alternative site on the island. Later in May 2010 he dismissed the leader of the SDPJ, Mizuho Fukushima, from her ministerial post after she criticized the decision; the SDPJ then elected to leave the ruling coalition. Hatoyama also incurred criticism from within his own party, the DPJ, for his apparent vacillation over the Okinawa base. The controversy over Okinawa, together with the conviction in April of Hatoyama's former secretary for falsifying political funding reports, persistent allegations of financial irregularities on the part of Ozawa and the widespread perception that he wielded undue influence in policy-making all combined to reduce the popularity of the ruling party.

On 2 June 2010 Hatoyama announced his own resignation as Prime Minister and President of the DPJ, and that of Ozawa as Secretary-General of the party. The DPJ then elected Naoto Kan as its President, and he became Prime Minister (Japan's fifth in four years) on 8 June. Kan retained most of the principal ministers appointed by his predecessor: his own previous post as Minister of Finance was allocated to Yoshihiko Noda (hitherto the deputy minister), and Yoshito Sengoku was appointed Chief Cabinet Secretary. Yukio Edano was appointed Secretary-General of the DPJ. Kan declared that he would uphold the controversial policy on Okinawa that Hatoyama had been obliged to adopt, and identified the reduction of government debt as the most pressing problem confronting his administration. The PNP agreed to remain in coalition with the DPJ, and the PNP's leader, Kamei, initially retained his ministerial responsibility for postal reform and financial services, but he resigned within a few days, after the DPJ refused to extend the current session of the Diet in order to debate legislation, supported by Kamei, on reversing the 2007 privatization of Japan Post (as the Postal Services Agency had become in 2003). However, the PNP remained within the coalition, and Kamei's ministerial portfolio was assumed by Shozaburo Jimi, the party's Secretary-General.

At elections for one-half of the seats in the House of Councillors held in July 2010, the DPJ lost the small majority that it had commanded (with its coalition partners) in the upper house, winning 44 of the 121 seats contested, so that its total representation was reduced to 106 of the 242 seats. The LDP won 51 of the contested seats, bringing its total to 84, while the DPJ's coalition partner, the PNP, failed to win any seats. The DPJ's loss of support was widely attributed to Kan's emphasis, during the election campaign, on a possible increase in consumption tax.

Kan was re-elected as DPJ President in September 2010 (his election in June had been only for the remainder of Hatoyama's allotted term of office). Kan reappointed Katsuya Okada, hitherto Minister of Foreign Affairs, as Secretary-General of the DPJ; in the ensuing partial reorganization of the Cabinet, the foreign affairs portfolio was allocated to Seiji Maehara, hitherto responsible for land, infrastructure and transport, while Banri Kaieda was appointed Minister of State for Economic and Fiscal Policy.

In December 2010 discussions took place on the possible establishment of a coalition between the DPJ and the Sunrise Party, but the latter refused to accept such an arrangement; however, one of the Sunrise Party's founding members, Kaoru Yosano, subsequently left the party, and in January 2011 he accepted the post of Minister of State for Economic and Fiscal Policy (a post that he had previously held, as a member of the LDP, in 2008–09). This appointment formed part of a cabinet reorganization, in which Yukio Edano replaced Yoshito Sengoku as Chief Cabinet Secretary, Akihiro Ohata replaced Sumio Mabuchi as Minister of Land, Infrastructure, Transport and Tourism, and Banri Kaieda replaced Ohata as Minister of Economy, Trade and Industry.

In January 2011 Ozawa was indicted for conspiring in the false reporting of political funds used in a purchase of land in 2004; three of his aides had been charged with the offence in February 2010. Ozawa denied the charge, claiming that he had no knowledge of his aides' actions, and refusing to relinquish his seat in the legislature or to accede to Kan's request that he temporarily leave the DPJ. The party's executive voted in February 2011 to suspend Ozawa's membership. The three former aides were convicted in September, while Owaza was acquitted in April 2012. In March 2011, meanwhile, Maehara resigned as Minister of Foreign Affairs, following revelations that he had illegally accepted a political donation from a foreign national.

On 11 March 2011 Japan was struck by a very severe earthquake, which had its epicentre in the Pacific Ocean off the northeast coast of Honshu island. The earthquake measured 9.0 in magnitude and caused a tsunami that devastated the adjoining coastal region, killing many thousands of people. Several nuclear power stations automatically shut down when the earthquake occurred, but one, at Fukushima, was seriously damaged, and its cooling systems were disabled. An evacuation was ordered within 20 km of the plant, while efforts were made to cool the nuclear reactors in order to prevent radioactive contamination. At the end of March the power station's operator, the Tokyo Electric Power Company (TEPCO), announced that four of the six nuclear reactors at Fukushima were to be decommissioned. As the critical situation at Fukushima continued, in April Japan's Nuclear and Industrial Safety Agency raised its evaluation of the crisis from Level 5 to Level 7, the highest level on the International Nuclear Event Scale, while confirmation emerged in early June that three of the reactors had experienced full meltdowns. Other nuclear power stations in Japan were closed down for safety inspections, while Kan began publicly to advocate the reduction of Japan's dependency on nuclear power and the investigation of renewable energy alternatives. In December the Government announced that the Fukushima plant had reached a state of 'cold shutdown', but estimated that full decommissioning of the damaged reactors could take between 30 and 40 years. According to figures published by Japan's National Police Agency in March 2012, 15,848 people were known to have died in the disaster and 3,305 were unaccounted for; around 350,000 reportedly remained homeless. The Japanese economy was severely affected by the earthquake and its aftermath.

Sustained domestic and international criticism was directed at both the Government of Japan and TEPCO for their management of the Fukushima crisis, and the reliability of information regarding developments at the power plant was questioned. In particular, Kan came under personal attack for his handling of the tsunami and subsequent nuclear crisis. Critics argued that his decision to fly over the Fukushima site on the day after the earthquake delayed the operation to cool the reactors, and condemned his reluctance to extend the evacuation zone around the plant from 20 km to 30 km in radius. When a number of DPJ legislators, including Hatoyama and Ozawa, threatened to support a vote of no confidence initiated by the opposition in early June 2011, Kan pledged to resign once he had prepared a second emergency budget to finance reconstruction (the first such emergency budget having been approved in May), and subsequently survived the vote. In late June Kan stated that his resignation would be conditional on the adoption of this second emergency budget, along with legislation concerning deficit bond issuance and the increased use of renewable energy. Kan also conducted a minor cabinet reshuffle in late June, appointing Goshi Hosono as Minister for the Restoration from and Prevention of Nuclear Accident, while Ryu Matsumoto became Minister for Reconstruction Measures from the Great East Japan Earthquake. However, Matsumoto resigned from his post in early July, in the wake of controversial comments made by him to regional governors in areas affected by the tsunami; he was replaced by Tatsuo Hirano. In early August it was announced that three senior government officials involved in nuclear policy were to be dismissed, and a new nuclear safety watchdog was to be created under the auspices of the Ministry of the Environment. Both developments were widely interpreted as an attempt by the Government to distance itself from accusations of its overly close relationship with the nuclear industry.

On 26 August 2011, following the successful passage into law of the aforementioned legislative bills, Kan announced his resignation from the presidency of the DPJ and, consequently, from the post of Prime Minister. After a first round of voting in the DPJ's subsequent leadership election proved inconclusive, the second round was won on 29 August by Yoshihiko Noda, hitherto Minister of Finance, defeating Banri Kaieda. Noda was elected Prime Minister by the Diet on the following day, and then appointed a reordered Cabinet, in which Jun Azumi succeeded him as Minister of Finance, while Osamu Fujimura became Chief Cabinet Secretary and Koichiro Gemba assumed the foreign affairs portfolio. Yasuo Ichikawa was appointed Minister of Defence, while Hosono, in addition to his existing nuclear accident portfolio, took on the post of Minister of the Environment. Yoshio Hachiro succeeded Kaieda as Minister of Economy, Trade and Industry, but resigned in early September after remarks he made on a visit to Fukushima were deemed offensive. He was replaced by Yukio Edano, who had served as Chief Cabinet Secretary in Kan's administration.

Noda, widely regarded as a fiscal conservative, sought to prioritize control of public debt and the rapidly appreciating yen. A third emergency reconstruction budget was approved in November 2011, and in the following month Noda instructed Azumi to draw up a fourth emergency budget to address reconstruction, a move unprecedented since the immediate post-war era. Meanwhile, a key proposal to increase sales tax met with hostility from some DPJ members (notably Ozawa) as well as from the opposition and the public. A cabinet reorganization in January 2012 was widely interpreted as an attempt to facilitate agreement on tax reform. The new post of Deputy Prime Minister was created and five cabinet ministers were replaced, including Minister of Defence Ichikawa (whose successor was Naoki Tanaka) and Minister for Consumer Affairs Kenji Yamaoka. Opposition parties had indicated that they would boycott further debates on tax reform unless Ichikawa and Yamaoka, who had both recently earned considerable opprobrium as a result of making what were considered to be highly inappropriate remarks in public, were dismissed. Katsuya Okada was appointed to the newly created post of Deputy Prime Minister, with responsibility for tax and social security reform. The Government submitted the necessary legislation for increasing sales tax to the Diet in March. Prime Minister Noda carried out another cabinet reorganization in early June in a renewed attempt to win opposition support for the proposed sales tax bill; among the changes was the replacement of Naoki Tanaka as Minister of Defence by Satoshi Morimoto. The approval of the sales tax legislation by the lower house later that month (and by the upper house in August) prompted the resignation of Ozawa and 48

other DPJ Diet members from the ruling party in July. The dissidents then formed a new party, the People's Life First, under the leadership of Ozawa (the party merged into the newly formed Tomorrow Party of Japan in November). In mid-September Noda's Government suffered a further setback following the suspected suicide of the Minister of Postal Reform and Minister of State for Financial Services, Tadahiro Matsushita. Despite his recent political troubles (including the DPJ's apparent vacillation over the future of Japan's nuclear power sector), Noda was re-elected to the presidency of the DPJ later that month. A few days later former Prime Minister Shinzo Abe was elected to replace Sadakazu Tanigaki as President of the LDP. In an apparent attempt to revitalize his Government, public support for which was noticeably waning, Prime Minister Noda made a number of ministerial changes at the beginning of October, including the replacement of Azumi as Minister of Finance by Koriki Jojima. Three weeks later, however, the newly appointed Minister of Justice, Keishu Tanaka, resigned from his post on the grounds of ill health, amid allegations over irregular political funding and his connections with members of an organized crime group; he was replaced by Makoto Taki (who had held the justice portfolio prior to Tanaka's assumption of the role on 1 October). In late October the popular Governor of Tokyo, Shintaro Ishihara, stood down from his long-held post to form a new national political party, the Japan Restoration Party, which absorbed the Sunrise Party on its foundation the following month.

The LDP is returned to power

The loss of support for the DPJ was vividly illustrated by its resounding defeat at the hands of Shinzo Abe's LDP in the legislative elections held on 16 December 2012. In the poll, which attracted a turnout of only 59.3% of the electorate, the LDP secured an outright majority in the House of Representatives, taking 294 of the 480 seats, while the DPJ's representation plummeted from 230 seats to 57 seats. Ishihara's Japan Restoration Party came in third place with 54 seats, New Komeito obtained 31 and Watanabe's Your Party won 18. With the support of its ally New Komeito, the LDP accordingly controlled a two-thirds' majority in the lower house. Following this party's overwhelming defeat, Noda resigned as President of the DPJ and was replaced by Banri Kaieda. Abe, whose electoral campaign had focused on restoring economic growth, reinstating nuclear energy and introducing a more assertive approach to foreign policy, assumed the premiership on 26 December at the head of a new Cabinet, which was almost exclusively composed of LDP members and which included former Prime Minister Taro Aso as Deputy Prime Minister and Minister of Finance, and Sadakazu Tanigaki as Minister of Justice. A few days later increasing tensions within the Tomorrow Party of Japan, which had performed poorly in the legislative elections, winning only nine seats in the House of Representatives, led to the defection from the party of Ozawa and most of its other Diet members to form the People's Life Party. Legislation was adopted in July 2013 reducing the number of seats in the House of Representatives by five, to 475, with effect from the next general election.

On 21 July 2013 the LDP and New Komeito regained control of the House of Councillors; the LDP increased its representation to 113 of the 242 seats (compared with 84 following the 2010 elections) and New Komeito secured 20 seats (up from 19). Your Party, the JCP and the Japan Restoration Party also made modest gains. The standing of the DPJ (and its allies) in the upper house, however, deteriorated markedly, declining from 106 seats in 2010 to just 59. The rate of participation by the electorate was relatively low, at 52.6%. Goshi Hosono resigned as DPJ Secretary-General in the wake of the party's poor electoral showing; he was succeeded by Akihiro Ohata. In August 2013 Kenji Eda was replaced as Secretary-General of Your Party by Keiichiro Asao. Eda, along with several other Your Party dissidents, established the Unity Party in December.

Controversial state secrecy legislation, prescribing lengthy gaol terms for those convicted of publicly divulging (or endeavouring to acquire) material that the authorities deemed a threat to national security, was passed by the Diet in December 2013. The new law attracted domestic and international criticism due to the apparent dearth of independent oversight, as well as concerns about the potential impact upon fundamental civil rights such as freedom of speech and freedom of the press. Further controversy was generated in November when the Government, in an apparent attempt to exert control over the nation's public broadcasting network, NHK, orchestrated the replacement of several members of its governing board with allies of the Prime Minister. In December the reconstituted board appointed a new President, Katsuto Momii, who intimated in the following month that the network would assume a pro-Government stance in its programming, prompting disquiet about the erosion of the broadcaster's independence.

In early December 2013 Abe established a National Security Council to oversee key security issues. Later in the month the Cabinet adopted the country's first National Security Strategy focusing on diplomatic and defence policy and providing for an increase in defence expenditure over the following five years. The document referred specifically to the expansion of China's maritime and air activities in relation to disputed territory with Japan and also to the threat posed by nuclear and missile development in North Korea. The strategy outlined Japan's plan to make a more 'proactive contribution to peace' ('proactive pacifism'), notably with regard to the issue of collective self-defence as part of the Japan-US alliance, in line with Abe's stated aim to broaden the activities undertaken by the SDF, which remained limited by the pacifist post-war Constitution. In accordance with the National Security Strategy, restrictions on arms exports were relaxed at the beginning of April 2014, allowing for exports in cases where such an action was held to promote peace and international co-operation or Japan's security. In early July the Cabinet approved a draft revision of Article 9 of the Constitution which aimed to expand the definition of the right to national self-defence to include collective self-defence against armed attacks on countries 'with close ties' to Japan, in a range of situations deemed to endanger the survival and security of Japan or its citizens. Under the proposed amendments the SDF would not, however, be permitted to exceed the minimum level of action required to protect national security.

Yoichi Masuzoe—the President of the New Renaissance Party and a minister in Abe's first administration—was elected as Governor of Tokyo in February 2014, comfortably defeating his main rivals, including former Prime Minister Hosokawa, who was supported by the DPJ. In the same month the Government appointed a panel to review the evidence on which Japan had, in the Kono Statement of 1993, acknowledged the forced exploitation of women as sex slaves during the Second World War, as well as the context in which the Statement had been made. However, Abe announced in the following month that the Kono Statement would not be withdrawn. The review panel issued a report in June which claimed that the 1993 findings were based on unverified testimonies alleging forced recruitment, and that the Statement had been drafted with South Korean participation. In July an independent legal panel made a recommendation that three former TEPCO executives should be indicted on criminal charges relating to their role in the 2011 Fukishima crisis.

Recent developments: Abe's renewed mandate

In early September 2014 Abe carried out a cabinet reorganization; of especial note was the significant increase in the number of women to be allocated ministerial portfolios, from two to five. The new female appointments included Midori Matsushima a former journalist, as Minister of Justice, replacing Sadakazu Tanigaki, and Yuko Obuchi, the daughter of former Prime Minister Keizo Obuchi, as Minister of Economy, Trade and Industry. However, the initial positive impact of this progressive reorganization was not sustained, as Matsushima and Obuchi resigned their posts in October, having both been accused of financial improprieties.

The Unity Party and the Japan Restoration Party merged in September 2014 to form the Japan Innovation Party. In November Abe announced that legislative elections would take place in December, two years ahead of schedule, with a view to winning a mandate to continue his Government's ongoing programme of far-reaching reforms (referred to as 'Abenomics') which aimed to revive the faltering economy, which had just re-entered recession, as well as to further the progress of the recently drafted constitutional amendments regarding collective self-defence. A reported internal rift relating to a proposed merger with the DPJ, in advance of the forthcoming elections, apparently prompted the disbandment of Your Party in November. At the elections, held on 14 December, the incumbent coalition retained an absolute majority in the slightly smaller House of Representatives: the LDP won 290 of the now 475 seats, while its partner in government, New Komeito, took 35. The DPJ performed slightly better than in 2012, winning 73 seats, while the new Japan Innovation Party accrued 41 seats and the JCP 21. The elections attracted a record low turnout, of only 52.4% of the electorate. Shortly afterwards the Cabinet was reappointed, unchanged other than the replacement of the Minister of Defence, Akinori

Eto—who had been accused of misappropriating political funding by Gen Nakatani, a former Director-General of the Defence Agency. In January 2015 former Prime Minister Katsuya Okada was elected as the President of the DPJ (a role that he had previously held in 2004–05).

In January 2015 the terrorist grouping Islamic State (known previously as Islamic State in Iraq and the Levant—ISIL), which declared an Islamist caliphate in parts of Iraq and Syria in mid-2014, beheaded two Japanese citizens whom it had been holding hostage. The executions followed a failure to extract from the Japanese Government a ransom fee of US \$200m. (representing the same amount pledged by Japan as non-military aid to support Middle Eastern states in combating the Islamist insurgency—the show of support having been cited by Islamic State as the reason for the hostage taking), or to exchange one of the hostages for the release of an Islamist terrorist imprisoned in Jordan. In February 2015 Abe announced that Japan would double the amount of funding (to be distributed through international organizations) that it had earlier pledged towards curbing terrorism in the Middle East and Africa, and proposed that the constitutional restrictions preventing the SDF from evacuating Japanese citizens endangered abroad should be withdrawn. However, Abe's departure from Japan's post-war non-interventionist approach to international security matters came under increasing scrutiny among the Japanese public at this time, as it was deemed by some to be, in fact, placing Japanese citizens at increased risk. In January the Government approved Japan's largest ever defence budget, which, within the framework of 'proactive pacifism', was to include the planned purchase of new military aircraft and amphibious vehicles to strengthen patrolling capabilities in the national maritime exclusive economic zone. The partial elections to the House of Councillors scheduled to take place in July 2016 were regarded as decisive for the future of Abe's proposed amendments to Article 9 of the Constitution, since, to enter into effect, they would require endorsement by two-thirds of the votes in both Houses of the Diet, as well as by more than one-half of voters in a national referendum.

Foreign Affairs

In the second half of the 20th century Japan, having renounced military activity in accordance with its 1947 Constitution, nevertheless gained international influence through its rapid economic growth: during the 1970s it became the world's second largest economy (after the USA) and retained this position until it was surpassed by China at the end of the first decade of the 21st century. Japan also became a major provider of overseas aid and investment. However, as a legacy of Japan's aggressive foreign policy during the first half of the 20th century, neighbouring countries remained suspicious of any sign of nationalist tendencies. Although Japan sought to increase its regional influence, its alliance with the USA remained the principal tenet of its foreign policy in the early 21st century.

Relations with the USA

Japan's bilateral security arrangements with the USA, concluded by treaty in 1951, granted the use of military bases in Japan to the USA, in return for a US commitment to provide military support to Japan in the event of external aggression. In May 1999 legislation was enacted on revised Guidelines for Japan-US Defense Co-operation (first compiled in 1978). These envisaged enhanced military co-operation between the USA and Japan, not only on Japanese territory but also in situations in unspecified areas around Japan, prompting criticism from China and Russia. The principal location for US bases in Japan was the island of Okinawa, in the far south of the country, which was returned from US administration to Japanese sovereignty only in 1972. The large US military presence caused resentment among many residents of Okinawa; in particular, the rape of a local schoolgirl by three US servicemen in 1995 led to considerable civil unrest on the island. Protracted negotiations with the US Government resulted in an agreement, concluded in May 2006, on the relocation of the principal US air base from Futenma, in a densely populated area of Okinawa, to a less populous area near the city of Nago, in the north of the island, while about one-third of the US military personnel stationed on Okinawa were to be relocated to the US Pacific Territory of Guam. However, many residents of the proposed site for the new air base opposed its construction. The agreement was signed in February 2009 by US Secretary of State Hillary Clinton; however, after taking office in September of that year, the Japanese Government of Yukio Hatoyama (whose DPJ had denounced the proposals while in opposition) undertook to review the decision during 2010. In April 2010 about 100,000 residents of Okinawa attended a rally, demanding that the Futenma air base be removed from the island altogether. In May Hatoyama (reportedly after pressure from the US Government) declared that the complete removal of the base was not a feasible option, and stated that the Government would, after all, implement the 2006 agreement to relocate the air base within Okinawa. At the end of April 2012, prior to a visit to the USA by Prime Minister Yoshihiko Noda, agreement was reached on the transfer of 9,000 US marines from Okinawa to Guam and other US bases in the Pacific. In April 2013 Japan and the USA concluded a plan outlining the return of certain facilities and land on Okinawa to Japan and the relocation of the Futenma base after 2021. The Okinawa authorities formally sanctioned the Futenma relocation plan in December 2013, although local opposition—particularly in Nago—remained widespread. In November 2014 the recently elected Governor of Okinawa, Takeshi Onaga, who had campaigned from a platform of opposition to the relocation plan, announced that he would visit Tokyo and Washington, DC, to further his case. The Japanese Government and the USA, however, reaffirmed their commitment to the joint decision.

In September 2001, following the attacks on the USA by Islamist militants attributed to al-Qa'ida, Japan immediately pledged co-operation in the USA's 'war on terror', including military support within the limits imposed by Japan's Constitution. Prime Minister Junichiro Koizumi announced that Japan would assist in the gathering of intelligence, and in the delivery of supplies and of medical and humanitarian relief. The requisite legislation was approved by the Diet, and in November Japan deployed several warships and 1,500 personnel to the Indian Ocean in this capacity, to support US military action in Afghanistan. Koizumi, despite strong opposition from the Japanese public, gave US President George W. Bush his full support for the USA's military offensive against Iraq, which commenced in March 2003. However, Japan refused to close the Iraqi embassy in Tokyo. Following the approval of legislation to permit the dispatch of Japanese troops to Iraq in a peacekeeping capacity, in early 2004 the first Japanese soldiers were deployed, numbering about 550 troops by April of that year. In December it was announced that the term of SDF involvement in Iraq would be extended by one year to aid the reconstruction of the country; however, following a further extension announced in December 2005, Japanese troops were withdrawn from Iraq in June and July 2006, with the exception of a small air support contingent.

In November 2007 the USA expressed disappointment at the withdrawal of Japan's Maritime Self-Defence Force from the Indian Ocean, where it had been supporting US-led counter-terrorism operations in Afghanistan since 2001 (see above), following the failure to secure approval for an extension of the mission in the Japanese Diet. Japan resumed its naval mission in support of US forces in the Indian Ocean in January 2008, after the Government forced the necessary legislation through the Diet. In October the House of Representatives voted to renew the naval mission. However, the DPJ administration that took office in September 2009 indicated that it would not support an extension of the mission in 2010, but would increase Japanese assistance for reconstruction in Afghanistan (see *Other external relations*). Accordingly, in January 2010 the Japanese naval mission was withdrawn from the Indian Ocean, despite US requests for its renewal.

Meanwhile, during the early 2000s disagreement persisted between Japan and the USA over President Bush's description of North Korea as part of an 'axis of evil'. Japan pursued a policy of engagement with North Korea (see below), while the USA adopted a more sceptical attitude to that country, particularly after North Korea allegedly admitted in October 2002 to pursuing a covert nuclear weapons programme. In December Japan and the USA held a meeting of ministers of defence and foreign affairs in Tokyo to address outstanding security issues. As well as seeking an early resolution of the crisis over the North Korean nuclear weapons programme, the two countries moved closer to agreement on the deployment of a joint missile shield. In February 2003 the Japanese Government stated that the two countries would conduct joint training in ballistic missile interception off the coast of Hawaii for a period of two years, beginning in 2004, and in December 2003 the Japanese Government announced that it was to develop an anti-ballistic missile defence system in co-operation with the USA. The ship-based system was successfully tested for the first time in December 2007. In a bid to counter the perceived growing ballistic missile threat from North

Korea, in September 2012 Japan and the USA agreed in principle to deploy a second joint missile defence system on Japanese territory.

Following talks in the USA in February 2013, Prime Minister Shinzo Abe and US President Barack Obama pledged to take a resolute stance on North Korea, which had recently conducted a nuclear test, and generally reaffirmed the Japanese-US security alliance. In early October, in view of Abe's agenda to reinterpret Japan's Constitution to permit the SDF to participate in collective self-defence, the two countries agreed to revise and broaden the Guidelines for Japan-US Defense Co-operation, with the aim of giving Japan a greater role in protecting its own sovereignty. (The deadline for completing the revisions was subsequently extended from the end of 2014 to mid-2015.) The two sides also agreed to boost bilateral regional military surveillance, including the installation of a second missile defence radar in Japan and the positioning of surveillance drones there for the first time. In April 2014 Obama confirmed that a group of uninhabited islands in the East China Sea, which were the focus of a territorial dispute with China (see below), were covered by Japan's mutual security treaty with the USA, although he emphasized that the dispute should be resolved peacefully. In late December Japan, the USA and South Korea concluded a Memorandum of Understanding (MOU) on intelligence-sharing with regard to North Korea.

Relations with China

Despite Japan's signing of a treaty of peace and friendship with the People's Republic of China in 1978, the historic enmity between the two countries continued to cause intermittent tension. Relations deteriorated in the late 1980s after China expressed concern at Japan's increased defence expenditure and at what China perceived as a more assertive military stance. Japanese aid to China was suspended in June 1989, following the Tiananmen Square massacre in the Chinese capital, Beijing, and was not resumed until November 1990. Relations between the two countries were strengthened by the visits to China by Emperor Akihito in October 1992, the first Japanese imperial visit to China, and by Prime Minister Hosokawa in March 1994. However, in August of that year Japan announced the suspension of economic aid to China, following renewed nuclear testing by the Chinese Government. The provision of economic aid was resumed in early 1997, following the declaration of a moratorium on Chinese nuclear testing.

In September 1997 China expressed concern at the revision of US-Japanese security arrangements (see *Relations with the USA*), following a statement by a senior Japanese minister that the area around Taiwan might be covered under the new guidelines. In November 1998, during a state visit by President Jiang Zemin, Prime Minister Obuchi and Jiang issued (but declined to sign) a joint declaration on friendship and co-operation, in which Japan expressed deep remorse for past aggression against China. However, China was reported to be displeased by the lack of a written apology. A subsequent US-Japanese agreement to initiate joint technical research on the development of a theatre missile defence system, followed by the Japanese Diet's approval, in May 1999, of legislation on the implementation of the revised US-Japanese defence guidelines, provoked severe criticism from China, despite Japan's insistence that military co-operation with the USA was purely defensive.

In April 2005 violent anti-Japanese protests took place across China, following Japan's approval of school textbooks that reportedly omitted any references to Japanese war crimes in China. The subsequent attacks on Japanese embassies and boycotts of Japanese products and companies were also thought to be partially motivated by Japan's ongoing campaign to acquire a permanent seat on the UN Security Council (see below), an ambition that China, a long-standing permanent member, vehemently opposed. In July the Chinese Government protested against the Japanese granting of drilling rights in disputed waters in the East China Sea to Teikoku Oil Co, and in October Japanese officials asserted that their reconnaissance information showed that Chinese platforms were operating in a contested region.

A periodic source of tension between the two countries is the Yasukuni Shrine (commemorating Japan's war dead, including those convicted of war crimes). In August 2001 China criticized the first visit to the Yasukuni Shrine by Japanese Prime Minister Junichiro Koizumi and urged Japan to renounce its militaristic past. During a visit to China in October Koizumi apologized for Japan's past crimes in the country. However, he continued to arouse anger in China by making several more visits to the Yasukuni Shrine.

Shinzo Abe's visit to Beijing in October 2006 (his first official overseas visit following his appointment in September as Prime Minister) represented the first meeting between Chinese and Japanese leaders for five years, and was described by Chinese President Hu Jintao as a turning point in Sino-Japanese relations. During the visit the two nations pledged to expand relations in the areas of trade, investment and technology. Furthermore, Abe acknowledged that Japan had inflicted suffering on Asian people in the past, and, with regard to the issue of Taiwan, he confirmed that the Japanese Government would adhere firmly to its 'one China' policy. During a reciprocal visit by the Chinese Prime Minister, Wen Jiabao, in April 2007, he became the first ever Chinese premier to address the Japanese Diet.

Meanwhile, however, in March 2007 Abe's questioning of the degree of compulsion used by Japan in engaging women for sexual purposes during the Second World War (see *Relations with South Korea*) had provoked much criticism in China and elsewhere, following which the Prime Minister was obliged to issue an apology for his remarks. In April the Japanese Supreme Court dismissed two appeals for compensation by Chinese nationals over their treatment by the Japanese during the war on the grounds that China had renounced all claims for reparation from Japan in a communiqué signed by the two countries in 1972. Subsequent similar appeals to the Court were also rejected.

It was anticipated that the improvement in Sino-Japanese relations experienced under Abe's premiership would continue under Yasuo Fukuda, who, upon taking office as Prime Minister in September 2007, expressed his intention to develop closer links with China and other neighbouring Asian countries. Fukuda and Wen held amicable talks in November while attending the annual summit meeting of the Association of Southeast Asian Nations (ASEAN, see p. 210), with both leaders emphasizing their commitment to strengthening bilateral relations. To this end, they agreed to accelerate efforts to resolve the ongoing dispute over exploration for hydrocarbons in the East China Sea. A goodwill visit to Japan by a Chinese warship later in that month (the first since 1934) was a further sign of improving relations, as was the first senior-level dialogue on closer economic co-operation, which was held in Beijing in December. In June China and Japan agreed to establish a joint exploration project for natural gas in the East China Sea. In May 2012 Japanese Prime Minister Yoshihiko Noda attended a meeting in Beijing with President Hu Jintao and the South Korean President, Lee Myung-Bak, during which the three leaders agreed to initiate negotiations on the establishment of a trilateral free trade pact. (The negotiations duly commenced in March 2013, and by January 2015 had entered a sixth round.) Later in May 2012 the promotion of trade between Japan and China was given a major boost when it was announced that from June China would permit direct trading of the Chinese yuan and the Japanese yen rather than using the US dollar as an intermediary currency.

The Senkaku Islands (or Diaoyu Islands in Chinese), a group of uninhabited islands situated in the East China Sea, have proved a periodic source of conflict between Japan and China. The islands—of strategic importance in that they are near to significant reserves of hydrocarbons, rich fishing grounds, and shipping lanes—are controlled by Japan, but are also claimed by China and Taiwan. In April 2012 the populist Governor of Tokyo, Shintaro Ishihara, announced a plan for the Tokyo metropolitan government to buy the Senkaku Islands from their private Japanese owners. The proposal was condemned by the Chinese Government, which reasserted China's claim to sovereignty over the islands. Tension escalated in September as a result of the purchase of three of the islands from their private Japanese owner by the central Japanese Government (in order to avoid the potentially much more provocative purchase and development of the islands by the nationalistic Ishihara), and there was an intensification in violent incidents against Japanese citizens and businesses in China. The Chinese Government described Japan's purchase of three of the islands as 'completely illegal and invalid'. The subsequent dispatch by China and Taiwan of several marine surveillance vessels to patrol the area around the islands prompted Japan to lodge an official protest against territorial encroachment. In December Japan lodged a further protest against the alleged violation of its airspace near the disputed islands by a Chinese government aircraft; this was

reportedly the first such intrusion by a Chinese aircraft since 1958. In February 2013 Japan again made a formal protest, accusing a Chinese naval frigate of directing weapon-targeting radar at a Japanese vessel and helicopter near the Senkaku Islands in the previous month; the Chinese Ministry of Defence rejected the allegations. China expressed opposition to an agreement signed by Japan and Taiwan in April, allowing vessels from Taiwan to fish within 19 km of the islands. Later that month Japanese Prime Minister Shinzo Abe warned China that he would authorize the use of military action if an attempt were made to seize the contested islands.

Bilateral relations deteriorated dramatically in November 2013 after China announced the establishment of an air defence identification zone encompassing large swathes of the East China Sea, including the waters surrounding the Senkaku Islands and certain expanses that Japan had previously declared to be within its own defence zone. Japan refused to recognize this edict and formally protested to the Chinese authorities. Later that month, in an apparent act of defiance, Japanese, South Korean and US military aircraft flew through the Chinese zone unannounced, although in December US Vice-President Joseph Biden toured the region in an effort to defuse the situation. Japan announced a number of security measures during December, including an increase in the defence budget, the adoption of a new, more expansive, military doctrine, the formation of a national security council, and the enactment of state secrecy legislation. China criticized Japan's new National Security Strategy, claiming it would increase regional tensions. The authorization by the Abe administration of new educational guidelines advocating that Japanese sovereignty over the Senkakus and other contested islands be emphasized in the school curriculum was not received well by China or South Korea. In October 2014, with a view to preventing an escalation of tensions in the Senkaku Islands area, Japanese and Chinese officials met to consider a long-standing proposal to establish a joint maritime crisis consultative mechanism, and a so-called military hotline between the countries' respective defence agencies.

Japan and China have also long disputed the status of the Okinotori Shima coral reef chain, in the Pacific Ocean to the south of Japan: Japan claims that the chain constitutes islands and thus, under international maritime law, Japanese sovereignty over them gives it the right to an exclusive economic zone in the surrounding waters; China, on the other hand insists that Okinotori Shima constitutes merely 'rocks', lacking the sustainable economic activity required to engender an exclusive zone. In recent years Japan has placed concrete fortifications on Okinotori Shima and planted additional coral to reinforce the land mass.

In June 2014 China rejected the findings of a panel appointed by the Abe administration to investigate the background to the Japanese Government's 1993 Kono Statement on the coercion of women into wartime sexual slavery (see *The LDP is returned to power*).

Relations with North Korea

Negotiations aimed at the normalization of diplomatic relations between Japan and North Korea were initiated in January 1991; these, however, soon reached an impasse, owing to Japan's dismissal of North Korean demands for financial reparations for the Japanese colonization of the country during 1910–45, North Korea's failure to address Japanese concerns over alleged past abductions by the North Korean security services of a number of Japanese citizens (reportedly for the purpose of training North Korean spies in Japanese customs and language), as well as the North Korean regime's refusal to allow inspectors from the International Atomic Energy Agency access to its nuclear facilities. From 1995 Japan contributed emergency food aid to combat the impact of severe famine in North Korea; this was, however, intermittently suspended, including in mid-1996, when concerns arose that the North Korean regime had developed a long-range missile capable of reaching Japanese territory, and again in mid-1998, following the apparent testing over Japan of such a missile. From late 1997 Japanese nationals resident in North Korea (then numbering around 1,800) were permitted to visit relatives in Japan. Tensions between Japan and North Korea were exacerbated in March 1999, when two suspected North Korean spy ships, which had infiltrated Japanese waters, were pursued and fired on by Japanese naval forces. Relations improved somewhat following North Korea's agreement with the USA, in September, to suspend its reported plans to test a new long-range missile. Several rounds of negotiations on the normalization of diplomatic relations were held in 2000, with Japan reiterating in September that normal bilateral relations could not be instituted until the issue of the alleged North Korean abductions of Japanese citizens had been resolved. In December 2001 the Japanese coastguard sank a suspected North Korean spy vessel after it had been expelled from Japan's exclusive economic zone.

In an unexpected diplomatic initiative, in September 2002 Junichiro Koizumi became the first incumbent Japanese Prime Minister to visit the North Korean capital, Pyongyang. During the visit the 'Supreme Leader', Kim Jong Il, acknowledged that North Korean agents had indeed abducted 13 Japanese citizens in the 1970s and 1980s, of whom five were still alive. Kim apologized for the abductions, but attributed them to rogue elements within the security services. The admission led to a hardening of attitudes against North Korea among the Japanese public, with some sources indicating that the total number of Japanese abductees might be as high as several hundred. The surviving known captives returned to Japan in October, and were refused permission by the Japanese authorities to return to North Korea. During that month, in view of allegations by the USA that North Korea was covertly developing a uranium enrichment programme (potentially the basis for pursuing a nuclear weapons agenda), and amid continuing uncertainty over the abductions issue, Koizumi suspended economic co-operation with North Korea. The North Korean Government, meanwhile, warned Japan that it would abandon its moratorium on testing long-range missiles if the normalization talks process failed to make progress. From August 2003 Japan (with North Korea, South Korea, China, the USA and Russia) participated in a new 'six party talks' format established to address North Korea's nuclear programme, in view of that country's disconcerting withdrawal, in January, from the Nuclear Non-Proliferation Treaty.

In January 2004 the House of Representatives approved legislation allowing Japan to impose economic sanctions on North Korea. In April the House of Councillors passed legislation requiring all ships entering Japanese ports from March 2005 to be insured against oil damage (effectively amounting to a ban on entry by most North Korean vessels). Following a further visit by Koizumi to Pyongyang in May 2004, the return of five children of the abductees who had repatriated to Japan in 2002 was secured in return for pledges of food aid and medical supplies. The Government of North Korea joined South Korea and China in condemning the approval in 2005 of a controversial history textbook for use in Japanese schools, as well as Prime Minister Koizumi's repeated visits to the controversial Yasukuni Shrine. The first round of diplomatic normalization talks between Japan and North Korea since 2002 was held in Beijing in February 2006.

The issue of abducted Japanese citizens came to the fore again in June 2006, when the Diet approved the North Korean Human Rights Act, which warned that economic sanctions would be imposed on North Korea unless it worked to resolve human rights issues, including the question of the abductees. Relations deteriorated further in the following month when North Korea conducted missile tests over the Sea of Japan, including the test of an intercontinental ballistic missile. Japan reacted immediately by banning a North Korean trading ferry from its ports and by imposing a moratorium on charter flights from Pyongyang. In September the Japanese Government announced the unilateral imposition of more comprehensive sanctions, which included freezing the assets of North Korean officials suspected of having links to their country's nuclear weapons programme.

In September 2006 Prime Minister Shinzo Abe appointed a special adviser on the abductions issue, and established a cabinet panel to deal with the affair. North Korea's announcement in October that it had tested a nuclear device greatly increased tensions. Clearly alarmed by the possibility of a nuclear power within the immediate region, Japan not only gave strong support to the UN Security Council's sanctions but also imposed its own additional restrictions, including a formal ban on the entry of North Korean ships into Japanese waters and on all North Korean imports.

In February 2007 the six-party talks on the North Korean nuclear programme resulted in an agreement aimed at curbing nuclear activities in that country, beginning with the closure of the Yongbyon nuclear site in return for substantial amounts of fuel aid from the other five participating countries. However, Japan insisted that it would only provide aid once progress had been made on the question of the abducted Japanese nationals. As a result of the agreement, in March Japan and North Korea

held their first diplomatic normalization talks for more than a year, although no apparent progress was made. After Yongbyon was officially declared closed in July, North Korea accused Japan of attempting to obstruct the normalization talks and to disrupt the six-party process with its refusal to provide energy aid and its insistence on the resolution of the abduction issue, which North Korea claimed had already been settled. A second round of bilateral negotiations was held in September. In October Japan announced that it would not resume aid to North Korea and extended sanctions for a further six months, despite the latter's recent commitment to disabling fully its Yongbyon facilities and declaring details of all its nuclear programmes by the end of the year (a deadline that, in the event, was missed), citing a continued lack of progress in the dispute over the abductees. The sanctions were again renewed in April 2008.

In March 2009, following North Korea's announcement of its imminent launch of what was declared to be a communications satellite, Japan prepared its missile interceptors, in the country's first deployment of this advanced technology. The Japanese Government reiterated its warning that it would attempt to destroy any missile or debris that threatened Japanese territory. In April, in response to the launch of the North Korean rocket, the Japanese Government renewed its sanctions against North Korea for a further year, but decided against a ban on exports to the country. In May 2010, following the sinking of a South Korean naval vessel, apparently by a North Korean torpedo, the Japanese Government extended its sanctions against North Korea.

Japan condemned the failed launch by North Korea in April 2012 of a rocket-mounted satellite, which was widely believed to be the testing of a long-range missile. In August Japan and North Korea held their first direct official talks (in Beijing) for four years. Hopes of any amelioration in relations under the new 'Great Leader' Kim Jong Un were dashed, however, by an announcement by the North Korean state media in February 2013 that North Korea had conducted an underground nuclear weapons test (its third such test in seven years). In response, Prime Minister Shinzo Abe called an urgent meeting of the UN Security Council, at which North Korea's provocative action met with unanimous condemnation. Following a series of threats made by North Korea against South Korea, Japan and US bases in the region, in April Japan dispatched two warships to the Sea of Japan and deployed missile defence systems in three locations in Tokyo to protect against a potential missile launch from North Korea. Informal talks between Japanese and North Korean officials were conducted in China in March 2014, when the two sides agreed to resume official dialogue (suspended since December 2012 when North Korea launched a long-range rocket over Japan). North Korea launched two medium-range ballistic missiles into the sea in March 2014 to coincide with a trilateral meeting of the South Korean, Japanese and US leaders in The Hague, Netherlands, provoking a protest from Japan. However, the first formal negotiations between North Korea and Japan since Abe took office proceeded as planned at the end of the month in Beijing. Talks focused on the issues of North Korean abductions of Japanese citizens and nuclear weapons and missile programmes. In May North Korea announced its decision to initiate a new investigation into the abductions, in exchange for a relaxation of Japan's unilateral punitive sanctions (this came into effect in July). In October Japanese and North Korean officials met in Pyongyang to discuss the progress of the investigation.

Relations with South Korea

Japan's relations with South Korea have intermittently been affected by the sensitive issue of Japanese colonial rule in 1910–45, and by territorial and fishing disputes. In February 1995 Prime Minister Tomiichi Murayama publicly acknowledged that Japan was responsible, in part, for the post-war division of the Korean peninsula. However, he was forced to retract the statement, following bitter controversy in the Diet. During a state visit by the South Korean President, Kim Dae-Jung, to Japan in October 1998, a joint declaration was signed, in which Japan apologized for the suffering inflicted on the Korean people during Japanese colonial rule. Japan also pledged substantial aid to South Korea to stimulate economic recovery. In August 1999 Japan and South Korea held their first joint military exercises since the Second World War, in the Tsushima Straits. In October 2000 Prime Minister Junichiro Koizumi visited Seoul and also apologized for past crimes and suffering under Japanese rule. In November Japan and South Korea, along with China, agreed to establish regular contacts between their ministers of finance and foreign affairs. Relations were adversely affected in 2001 and 2005 by the approval by the Japanese authorities of textbooks considered misleading with regard to Japan's wartime aggression. Furthermore, repeated visits to the controversial Yasukuni Shrine by Koizumi during his premiership were strongly condemned by South Korea. In March 2007 Prime Minister Shinzo Abe provoked considerable anger, particularly in South Korea and China, following his claims that there was no evidence that coercion had been used to recruit 'comfort women' (a group of whom had been denied official compensation by a Japanese court in 2000). Abe apologized for his remarks before the Japanese House of Councillors later in March. In August 2010, the month of the centenary of Japan's annexation of the Korean peninsula, a further apology was issued, by Prime Minister Naoto Kan, for the suffering caused by colonial rule.

A long-standing dispute between Japan and South Korea concerns sovereignty over a group of islands, called Takeshima in Japanese or Dokdo in Korean, situated in the Sea of Japan. The South Korean Government claims that the islands are historically part of Korea, while the Japanese Government maintains that they were incorporated into Japan at the beginning of the 20th century. In May 2006 the South Korean Government provoked fury in Japan by announcing a five-year plan for the disputed islands, which included the development of island facilities and the exploration of marine and mineral resources. Following Japan's renewal of its claim to the Takeshima islands in July 2008, when they were defined as Japanese territory in new teaching materials, the South Korean ambassador was recalled from Tokyo. In June 2011 a Korean Air test flight flew over the islands, in response to which the Japanese Government banned its officials from travelling with that airline.

In January 2011 the Japanese and South Korean defence ministers drew up agreements on the sharing of information and equipment, the first such military accords between the two countries since the end of Japanese imperial rule in 1945. In October 2011 Japanese Prime Minister Yoshihiko Noda, visited Seoul for a meeting with the South Korean President Lee Myung-Bak, which focused on economic co-operation. In a reciprocal visit to Japan in December, Lee raised once more the issue of compensation for Korean 'comfort women'. In June 2012, in response to persistent anti-Japanese sentiment, the South Korean Government postponed the official signing of the historic military pacts that had been agreed with Japan the previous year. Furthermore, Japan temporarily withdrew its ambassador from Seoul in August following a surprise visit to the disputed Takeshima islands by Lee Myung-Bak, the first by a South Korean President. None the less, negotiations on a trilateral free trade agreement, between Japan, South Korea and China, went ahead as planned in March 2013. However, in April South Korea cancelled a planned high-level meeting with Japan as a mark of protest against Deputy Prime Minister Taro Aso's visit to the Yasukuni Shrine earlier that month. Japan's relations with its neighbours were further undermined in May after Toru Hashimoto, the mayor of Osaka, publicly defended the recruitment of 'comfort women' during the Second World War. In December, moreover, Prime Minister Abe also made a trip to the Yasukuni Shrine, thereby provoking censure in South Korea and China; later that month the South Korean Government suspended a number of defence co-operation initiatives with Japan. In a bid to ease tension between Japan and South Korea, the USA organized a trilateral meeting between Obama, Abe and South Korean President Park Geun-Hye, on the sidelines of a nuclear security summit in The Hague, Netherlands, in March 2014; Abe and Park agreed at that time to resume dialogue between the two countries. Japan, South Korea and the USA signed an MOU in December aimed at enhancing intelligence-sharing on North Korea's military activities.

In June 2014 South Korea summoned the Japanese ambassador in Seoul to make a formal protest over the recent findings of a panel that had been appointed by the Abe administration to review the evidence on which Japan had, in the Kono Statement of 1993, formally acknowledged the forced wartime exploitation of 'comfort women'.

Other regional relations

During the 1990s and 2000s Japan sought to strengthen economic and security relations with the member countries of ASEAN. Japan's influence in South-East Asia largely depended on its aid and investment programmes. In November 2002 Japan signed an agreement to develop a comprehensive economic partnership with ASEAN members within 10 years—including the possible formation of a Japan-ASEAN free trade area. As one of the 'ASEAN + 3' countries (the member nations of ASEAN, plus China, Japan and South Korea), Japan has participated since 2005 in successive East Asia Summit meetings.

In May 2000 Singapore agreed to allow Japan to use its military bases for evacuating its citizens from crisis locations, and for regional peacekeeping missions, the first agreement of its kind between Japan and another country, and in October 2001 Japan reached a comprehensive free trade agreement with Singapore (which took effect in November 2002). In July 2006 a free trade agreement between Japan and Malaysia took effect, and a similar agreement with the Philippines was approved by the Japanese legislature in December. During 2007 free trade agreements were also concluded with Thailand and Brunei, and with Indonesia, which was to provide Japan with a stable supply of liquefied natural gas (LNG). Negotiations on a comprehensive free trade agreement between Japan and ASEAN were concluded in November. In January 2008 Prime Minister Yasuo Fukuda held a meeting in Tokyo with the ministers responsible for foreign affairs of Cambodia, Laos, Myanmar, Thailand and Viet Nam, offering increased economic aid to the five countries, while encouraging them to make more progress on human rights issues and democratization. Japan had provided substantial aid to Myanmar, but this was suspended in 2003 in protest against the detention of the country's opposition leader, Aung San Suu Kyi, although Japan continued to provide emergency and humanitarian assistance.

As Japan continued its efforts to improve relations with South-East Asia, in March 2009 the Japanese Ministry of Defence hosted a meeting of senior security officials from member countries of ASEAN, the first such meeting ever held in Japan. In October 2010, against the backdrop of renewed diplomatic tension between Japan and China (see above), Japan and Viet Nam concluded an agreement on increasing the supply of rare earth minerals from Viet Nam (thus reducing Japan's dependence on imports of these minerals from China), and on co-operation in the development of nuclear power plants in Viet Nam. At a meeting held in Tokyo in April 2012 between President Thein Sein of Myanmar and Prime Minister Noda, the latter agreed to resume development aid to Myanmar and to write off more than US $3,700m. of that country's debt. As part of his policy to strengthen ties with South-East Asia (apparently to counter the growing dominance of China), the newly appointed Japanese Prime Minister, Shinzo Abe, visited all 10 ASEAN member states during 2013, and also, in December, hosted a Japan-ASEAN summit meeting.

In March 2007 the Australian Prime Minister, John Howard, visited Tokyo for discussions with his Japanese counterpart. The two heads of government signed a new security agreement, to encompass peacekeeping and counter-terrorism operations, as well as issues of maritime and aviation security. The conclusion of this agreement, the first such bilateral accord since Japan's signing of the security treaty with the USA in 1951, was viewed as a clear manifestation of Japan's changing position with regard to international affairs. In April 2007 Japan and Australia commenced negotiations on a bilateral free trade agreement; this was signed in July 2014 and entered into force in January 2015. Also in July 2014, Japan and Australia concluded an accord governing the transfer of defence equipment and technologies.

Relations with Russia

Japan's relations with Russia have been dominated by the issue of the Northern Territories, known in Russia as the Southern Kurile (Kuril) Islands. These four small islands, situated close to Hokkaido, were annexed in 1945 by the USSR, and thousands of Japanese residents were subsequently deported. Both countries claimed sovereignty over the islands, and as a result no formal peace treaty ending the Second World War was concluded between them. After 1956, when Japan and the USSR resumed diplomatic relations, little progress was made with regard to resolving the dispute. A number of discussions took place during the 1990s, although relations between the two countries deteriorated following the disposal of nuclear waste in Japanese waters by Russian ships in November 1993, and Russia's decision, in August 1994, to open fire on Japanese vessels that were alleged to have been fishing in Russian waters. In November 1996 Japan indicated that it was prepared to resume the disbursement of aid, withheld since 1991, and in May 1997 the Japanese Government abandoned its opposition to Russia's proposed joining of the G7. Russian plans for joint development of the mineral and fishing resources of the disputed territory were followed, in July, by an outline agreement on the jurisdiction of the islands. Negotiations resulted in the conclusion of a framework fisheries agreement in December. Agreement was reached in November 1998 on the establishment of subcommissions to examine issues of border delimitation and joint economic activity on the disputed islands and in September 1999 on improved access to the disputed islands for former Japanese inhabitants. Despite the repudiation of Japan's claim to any of the islands by the Russian President, Vladimir Putin, during his first official visit to Tokyo in September, Russia subsequently offered to abide by a 1956 declaration that it would relinquish two of the islands after the signature of a peace treaty; however, Japan initially rejected this partial solution.

Tensions over the disputed islands were exacerbated in August 2006 when, in the first such incident for 50 years, a Japanese fisherman was shot dead by a Russian patrol boat near the Northern Territories; three other fishermen were temporarily detained. While the Russian coastguard insisted that the fishing vessel had defied orders to halt, the Japanese Government disputed this claim, accusing Russia of acting with excessive force. After the incident, Russia was reported to have intensified its patrols in the area, and in 2007 two more Japanese boats were seized.

In November 2010 the Russian President, Dmitrii Medvedev, paid a visit to one of the Northern Territories islands, the first Russian head of state to do so, and undertook to increase investment in the islands. The Japanese Prime Minister, Naoto Kan, initially described the visit as regrettable, and a formal protest was delivered to the Russian Government. In February 2011 the Russian Minister of Defence also visited the islands, and in the same month, addressing a rally on Japan's annual Northern Territories Day, Kan responded to nationalist sentiment by describing Medvedev's earlier visit as an 'unforgivable outrage'. The Russian Government then ordered a strengthening of the defences on the disputed islands. Later in February the Japanese Minister of Foreign Affairs visited Moscow to discuss the dispute, but no progress was reported. Japan was further angered by a second visit to the Northern Territories by Medvedev, in July 2012, and by the alleged violation of Japanese airspace by Russian military aircraft over the disputed islands in February 2013. Nevertheless, the new Japanese premier, Shinzo Abe, visited Russia in April and held productive discussions with President Putin. Both leaders agreed that negotiations on the territorial dispute would be resumed, while steps to enhance security and economic co-operation were to be taken. Talks on the islands recommenced in August.

In November 2013 the Japanese defence and foreign affairs ministers and their Russian counterparts, meeting in Tokyo, conducted 'two plus two' discussions on mutual security issues. As a result of these ground-breaking negotiations (the first of their kind), the two countries agreed that their armed forces would co-operate in their fight against terrorism and piracy, and that bilateral, high-level talks on security and defence matters, including cyber security, would be undertaken more frequently. However, relations cooled significantly following Japan's imposition in March 2014 of (relatively light) punitive sanctions against Russia, as part of an international protest at that country's destabilizing activities in Ukraine; in immediate response Russia imposed sanctions against Japan. Prime Minister Abe protested strongly to the Putin Government over the staging in August of Russian military manoeuvres on two of the four disputed Northern Territories islands (the first such drills to be undertaken there since 2010); these were believed to have been authorized as a further reprisal for Japan's imposition of sanctions. In September 2014 Abe announced the postponement of a planned state visit by Putin to Japan, which was to have taken place later that year.

In February 2010 Japan began to receive crude petroleum from a new East Siberian Pipeline, which, in its first phase, transported petroleum from Angarsk, in Siberia, to Skorovodino in Amur oblast, from where it was transported by rail to Nakhodka, on Russia's Pacific coast, and delivered by ship to Japan. The construction of the second phase of the pipeline, linking Skovorodino to Nakhodka, was initiated in December 2012. It was envisaged that the scheme would significantly reduce Japan's dependency on Middle Eastern supplies. In late 2014 it was reported that the construction of an oil pipeline linking the Russian island of Sakhalin, in the North Pacific, and the Japanese island of Hokkaido was under consideration.

Other external relations

In September 1990 Japan contributed financially to the international effort to force an unconditional Iraqi withdrawal from Kuwait. A controversial LDP-sponsored Peace Co-operation Bill, which provided for the dispatch to the Persian (Arabian) Gulf area of some 2,000 non-combatant personnel, was withdrawn in November after it encountered substantial domestic political opposition. In January 1991, following repeated US demands for a greater financial commitment to the resolution of the Gulf crisis, the Japanese Government announced plans substantially to increase its contribution and to provide aircraft for the transport of refugees in the region. Opposition to the proposal was again vociferous. The Government secured the support of several centrist parties, by pledging that any financial aid from Japan would be employed in a 'non-lethal' capacity, and legislation to approve the new contribution was adopted by the Diet in March. In June 1992 controversial legislation to permit the SDF to participate in UN peacekeeping operations was approved. However, their role was to be confined to logistical and humanitarian tasks, unless a special dispensation from the Diet were granted. Legislation was approved in November 1994 to enable Japanese forces to be deployed overseas if the Government believed the lives of Japanese citizens to be at risk.

In recent decades Japan has reiterated its desire to be a permanent member of the UN Security Council, particularly in view of its status as one of the world's largest donors of development aid and (in 2015) the second largest contributor—after the USA—to the UN budget. In a speech to the UN General Assembly in September 2004 Prime Minister Koizumi stated that Japan's role in supporting reconstruction in Afghanistan and Iraq, as well as the Japanese contributions to negotiations with North Korea on its nuclear programme, entitled Japan to a permanent seat. Japan's bid was believed to have the support of the USA. However, the prospect of Japan gaining permanent representation in the UN's highest forum has provoked strong objections from China and South Korea, as victims of past Japanese military aggression.

Following the commencement of US military action in Iraq in March 2003, the House of Councillors approved legislation to allow SDF forces to be dispatched to Iraq in a peacekeeping capacity. By mid-April 2004 there were some 550 Japanese troops stationed in Iraq. The withdrawal of these troops commenced at the end of June 2006 and was completed in July. A small contingent from the Japanese Air Self-Defence Force remained in a minor support role, transporting materials and personnel between Iraq and Kuwait; this mission was terminated in December 2008.

The Japanese Government criticized India and Pakistan for conducting nuclear tests in mid-1998 and suspended grants of non-humanitarian aid and loans to both countries. A series of missile tests carried out by India and Pakistan in April 1999 again provoked criticism from Japan. Following a visit to India by the Japanese Prime Minister in August 2000, differences over nuclear testing were set aside in favour of enhanced security, defence and research co-operation between Japan and India, which continued during 2001. The Indian Prime Minister, Atal Bihari Vajpayee, visited Japan in December, the first such visit since 1992. In addition to security issues, the two countries discussed closer co-operation in their software and computer industries. In December 2006 the two countries agreed to commence negotiations on a bilateral economic partnership agreement. In October 2008 the Japanese Government approved a low-interest loan for the construction of a new railway to carry freight between the Indian capital, New Delhi, and Mumbai; at US $4,500m., this was the largest loan ever extended by Japan to an overseas project; subsequent Japanese loan provision included a $2,100m. loan made in October 2013 for the development of India's first fully underground metro network, in Mumbai. In October 2010 Indian Prime Minister Manmohan Singh and the Japanese Prime Minister, Naoto Kan, announced the completion of negotiations on the economic partnership agreement, which was to include a gradual elimination of most trade tariffs over a 10-year period. Kan's successor, Yoshihiko Noda, visited India in December 2011, when talks with Singh resulted in pledges of increased co-operation in maritime security, a development widely interpreted as a response to China's growing maritime assertiveness. Accordingly, Japan and India conducted their first joint naval exercise, off the coast of Tokyo, in June 2012. In September 2014, meeting in Tokyo, Prime Minister Shinto Abe and his Indian counterpart, Narendra Modi, signed an agreement on pursuing a 'special strategic, global partnership', which included provisions on upgrading bilateral military and security ties. Significant further investment by Japan in India's infrastructure was pledged at that time, as well as a commitment to accelerate ongoing negotiations aimed at the conclusion of a civilian nuclear co-operation accord.

The whaling controversy

Japan has a long tradition of whale-hunting by small fishing communities, but whaling only became a large-scale commercial activity after the Second World War. Concern over the increasing rarity of many whale species throughout the world, as well as unease at inhumane methods of killing, led to a moratorium on commercial whaling being adopted in 1982 by the International Whaling Commission (IWC, established in 1946 to conserve and regulate whale stocks: Japan became a member in 1951). The ban took effect in 1986, but Japan submitted a legal objection (as did Norway, Peru and the USSR), and continued commercial whaling until 1988, when it withdrew its objection to the ban (after the USA threatened to reduce the quota of fish catches allocated to Japan in US waters if it did not do so). However, by exploiting a provision of the IWC's founding convention, whereby governments might issue special permits to allow whaling for the purposes of scientific research, Japan continued to hunt whales, and whale meat remained legally on sale in Japan as a by-product of research. In 1994 the IWC banned whaling in the Southern Ocean, declaring the area a sanctuary for whales. Japan again submitted a legal objection to the ban, asserting that whale stocks in the area were sustainable, and continued to hunt whales in the Southern Ocean, still claiming to be doing so for the purposes of scientific research.

In recent years a number of conservation organizations have attempted to disrupt whaling in the Southern Ocean. In January 2010 a vessel of the US-based Sea Shepherd Conservation Society sank after colliding with a Japanese whaling ship, while in February a New Zealand activist, belonging to Sea Shepherd, was arrested by the Japanese coastguard after boarding a Japanese whaling vessel. In June the Australian Government initiated legal action against Japan at the ICJ, stating that Japan had breached its obligations under international law by continuing to hunt whales in the Southern Ocean sanctuary. In February 2011 Japan announced an early close to its Antarctic whaling season, after Sea Shepherd activists had obstructed whaling vessels, and requested that the Australian and New Zealand Governments take action to prevent environmental groups from obstructing whaling ships. At the annual IWC conference in July, Japan and 22 other countries walked out of discussions on the formation of a South Atlantic whale sanctuary, disabling a vote on the proposal (which was, in the event, defeated at the annual conference in 2012). Although a resolution on 'Safety at Sea' tabled by Japan and directed primarily at Sea Shepherd was adopted at the 2011 conference, Sea Shepherd's activities were thought partially responsible for a reported catch of less than one-third of expected levels during Japan's Antarctic whaling season in early 2012. In February 2013 Australia made an official protest to Japan following the reported incursion of a Japanese whaling vessel into Australia's exclusive economic zone in the Southern Ocean, and in February 2014 New Zealand also issued a formal protest to Japan after a similar incident occurred in New Zealand's exclusive economic zone.

In March 2014 the ICJ delivered a non-binding ruling that Japan should halt its whaling programme in the Antarctic as it had not sufficiently justified that the quotas it set were necessary for the purposes of scientific research. Japan temporarily suspended its Antarctic whaling activities, but, in November, announced a new 12-year programme, with reduced quotas, which was to be implemented from 2015. Meanwhile, in April 2014 Japan proceeded with a planned whale hunt in the Pacific Ocean, but significantly reduced the quota of whales to be caught.

CONSTITUTION AND GOVERNMENT

Under the Constitution of 1947, the Emperor is head of state but has no governing power. Legislative power is vested in the bicameral Diet, comprising the House of Representatives (lower house), whose members are elected for a four-year term, and the House of Councillors (upper house), members of which are elected for six years, one-half being elected every three years. The House of Representatives comprises 475 seats—295 single-seat constituencies and 180 determined by proportional representation—and there are 242 seats in the House of Councillors. There is universal suffrage for all adults from 20 years of age. Executive power is vested in the Cabinet, which is responsible to the Diet. The Emperor appoints the Prime Minister (on desig-

nation by the Diet), who appoints the other Ministers in the Cabinet.

Japan has 47 prefectures, each administered by an elected Governor, legislature and administrative bureaucracy.

REGIONAL AND INTERNATIONAL CO-OPERATION

Japan is a member of the Asia-Pacific Economic Cooperation (APEC, see p. 200) forum, the Asian Development Bank (ADB, see p. 206), the UN's Economic and Social Commission for Asia and the Pacific (ESCAP, see p. 30) and the Colombo Plan (see p. 445). Japan is also an observer member of the South Asian Association for Regional Co-operation (SAARC, see p. 417) and the Arctic Council (see p. 444).

Japan became a member of the UN in 1956. As a contracting party to the General Agreement on Tariffs and Trade, Japan acceded to the World Trade Organization (WTO, see p. 431) upon its establishment in 1995. Japan is also a member of the Organisation for Economic Co-operation and Development (OECD, see p. 377). The country participates in the Group of Seven (G7, see p. 460) informal gathering of major industrialized nations, and also takes part in the Group of 20 (G20, see p. 451) major industrialized and systemically important emerging market nations.

ECONOMIC AFFAIRS

In 2013, according to estimates by the World Bank, Japan's gross national income (GNI), measured at average 2011–13 prices, was US $5,875,019m., equivalent to $46,140 per head (or $37,630 per head on an international purchasing-power parity basis). During 2004–13, it was estimated, the population remained stagnant, while gross domestic product (GDP) per head increased, in real terms, by an average of 0.6% per year. Overall GDP increased, in real terms, at an average annual rate of 0.6% in 2004–13; real GDP grew by 1.5% in 2013.

Agriculture (including forestry and fishing) contributed 1.2% of GDP in 2012 and engaged 3.7% of the employed labour force in 2013. The principal crops are rice, sugar beets, cabbages, potatoes and citrus fruits. During 2004–14, according to official sources, agricultural GDP declined, in real terms, at an average rate of 0.8% annually; sectoral GDP increased by 0.4% in 2012.

Industry (including mining, manufacturing, construction and utilities) contributed 25.6% of GDP in 2012 and engaged 25.3% of the employed labour force in 2013. During 2004–12, according to official sources, industrial GDP increased at an average annual rate of 0.3%; the sector's GDP grew by 15.2% in 2010, but decreased by 2.7% and 2.4% in 2011 and 2012, respectively.

Mining and quarrying contributed a mere 0.1% of GDP in 2012 and engaged less than 0.1% of the employed labour force in 2013. While the domestic output of limestone and sulphur is sufficient to meet domestic demand, all of Japan's requirements of bauxite, crude petroleum and iron ore, and a high percentage of its requirements of copper ore and coking coal, are met by imports. During 2004–12, according to official sources, mining GDP declined at an average annual rate of 6.6%; however, the sector grew by 4.3% in 2011 and by 0.9% in 2012.

Manufacturing contributed 18.2% of GDP in 2012 and engaged 16.7% of the employed labour force in 2013. The most important branches of manufacturing are machinery and transport equipment, electrical and electronic equipment, and iron and steel. Manufacturing GDP increased by an average of 1.2% per year in 2004–12, according to official figures; sectoral GDP increased by 20.8% in 2010, but decreased by 2.7% and 2.3% in 2011 and 2012, respectively.

Construction contributed 5.7% of GDP in 2012 and engaged 8.0% of the employed labour force in 2013. Construction GDP decreased by an average of 2.3% per year in 2004–12, according to official figures; the GDP of the sector expanded by 1.1% in 2012.

Japan imports most of its energy requirements, with imports of crude and partly refined petroleum comprising 17.5% of the value of total imports in 2013, according to official figures. Natural gas accounted for 41.5% of electricity output in 2012, coal for 28.4%, petroleum for 11.5%, hydropower for 7.6% and nuclear power for only 1.1% (compared with 26.9% in 2010). By May 2012, in response to the accident at Fukushima nuclear power plant in March 2011, all Japanese nuclear reactors were offline, pending routine maintenance work and safety evaluations. Initial plans to phase out nuclear power in response to the accident were reversed by the Government of Shinzo Abe. In April 2014 the Cabinet approved a national energy policy, the Basic Energy Plan, which confirmed that nuclear power was to feature in the country's future energy composition, while the production of power by renewable sources was also to be promoted. The plan provided for the eventual reactivation of nuclear reactors that complied with stringent regulatory standards.

The services sector contributed 73.2% of GDP in 2012 and engaged 71.0% of the employed labour force in 2013. The GDP of the services sector increased by an average of 0.5% annually in 2004–12; sectoral GDP expanded by 2.1% in 2012. Tourism receipts, totalling US $14,934m. in 2013, according to provisional figures, are a significant source of revenue. The number of tourist arrivals decreased by 27.8% in 2011, to 6.2m, but recovered in 2012, rising by 34.6%, to 8.4m; arrivals further increased, by 24.0%, in 2013 to reach 10.4m.

In 2013, according to IMF figures, Japan recorded a visible merchandise trade deficit of US $89,648m., while there was a surplus of $34,068m. on the current account of the balance of payments. In 2013 the USA and the People's Republic of China were the principal markets for Japanese exports, purchasing 18.5% and 18.1% of the total, respectively; other leading purchasers were the the Republic of Korea, Taiwan, Hong Kong and Thailand. The principal source of imports in that year was China (which supplied 21.7% of imports); other major suppliers were the USA, Australia, Saudi Arabia and the United Arab Emirates. The principal exports in 2013 were machinery and transport equipment, manufactured goods and chemicals. The principal imports were mineral fuels and lubricants, electrical machinery, food and live animals, chemicals, and manufactured goods.

The budget for the financial year ending March 2014 projected expenditure of 95,882,000m. yen. The allocation for social security remained the largest single category of government expenditure. With tax revenue expected to reach 50,001,000m. yen in that year, the Government planned to issue bonds totalling 41,250,000m. yen. Japan's general government gross debt was 1,124,488,600m. yen in 2012, equivalent to 237.3% of GDP. Japan's external debt was estimated at the equivalent of 59.6% of GNI in 2013. The annual rate of deflation averaged 0.1% in 2004–13. Consumer prices remained constant in 2012, but increased by 0.3% in 2013. The average rate of unemployment was 4.0% in 2013.

In terms of GDP the technologically advanced Japanese economy was the world's second largest (after the USA) for four decades until 2010 when it was surpassed by China. In recent years economic performance has been constrained by the strength of the Japanese currency and by the recurrent problem of deflation, which in turn has had a negative effect on consumer demand. Japan also faces the long-term demographic challenge of a shrinking and ageing population. The tsunami that struck Japan in March 2011, and the subsequent crisis at the Fukushima nuclear power plant, had a serious impact on the economy. Following the disaster, the Bank of Japan (BoJ) released large amounts of money into the banking system in an attempt to stabilize the Japanese financial markets. During 2011 and early 2012 the Diet approved four emergency budgets, providing a total of some 20,000,000m. yen for post-crisis reconstruction. The already strong yen rose to its highest point since 1945 in relation to the US dollar in the aftermath of the tsunami. The resultant decline in exports (exacerbated by the financial crisis in the eurozone), together with a significant increase in fuel imports, following the closure of nuclear power stations in the wake of the Fukushima disaster, contributed to Japan's first trade deficit in over 30 years being recorded in 2011. In 2012 the Government and the BoJ implemented various stimulus measures. None the less, the economy technically entered recession at the end of September, before stabilizing in the final quarter; overall, growth in that year remained stagnant. The raised cost of fuel imports (as a result of the continuing nuclear shutdown) contributed to a record high trade deficit in 2012. On assuming power in December, Prime Minister Shinzo Abe pledged to revive the ailing economy and, over the long term, reduce Japan's record levels of gross government debt (which reached around 227% of GDP in 2014, the highest in the industrialized world), by increasing public expenditure, weakening the value of the yen and transforming deflation into inflation. In January 2013 the Government approved a US $116,000m. stimulus package, which focused on infrastructure spending, job creation and investment, and the BoJ extended its asset purchase programme, with further expansions of the programme, and additional smaller stimulus measures introduced subsequently. The Abe administration's economic policies (referred to as 'Abenomics') appeared to have a positive (albeit moderate) impact on the economy during 2013. According to World Bank figures, the fiscal stimulus supported real GDP growth of 1.5% in that year, while consumer prices finally began to increase from mid-2013 due to the depreciation of the yen. A decline in unemployment was also reported. However, investment levels remained subdued and the trade deficit widened further (despite an upturn in exports). Following the implementation in April 2014 of the first incremental rise (from 5% to 8%) in a proposed doubling of the national sales tax, the economy contracted sharply (this was attributed to more austere consumer spending patterns), and in the third quarter it re-entered recession, temporarily. Abe consequently postponed the planned second and final sales tax increase to 10%, which was to have been effected by 2015, to April 2017. Having won a new mandate from the electorate to continue to pursue the 'Abenomics' approach in December 2014, Abe announced that further structural economic reforms would be implemented 'in a firm and dramatic manner'. With a view to offsetting the impact on living costs of the sales tax increase and the weak yen, Abe also in December urged businesses to raise employees' salaries in 2015, and introduced a small economic stimulus package at the end of 2014. In January 2015 the Government proposed a budget for 2015/16 with a focus on higher social, as well as defence expenditure, and on reduced borrowing, enabled by increased revenues from taxation. As the third highest net importer of petroleum globally (in 2013), the sharp decline in global oil prices from late 2014 reduced Japan's fuel import costs, thereby narrowing the trade deficit, but also, at the same time, in some measure reversing the desired inflationary impact of the depreciation of the yen. The BoJ hoped, through monetary easing, to effect an increase in the average rate of inflation to 2% in 2015. Following GDP growth of an estimated 0.9% in 2014, the IMF predicted further moderate growth, of 0.8%, in 2015.

PUBLIC HOLIDAYS

2016: 1 January (New Year's Day), 11 January (Coming of Age Day), 11 February (National Foundation Day), 21 March (for Vernal Equinox Day), 29 April (Showa Day), 3 May (Constitution Memorial Day), 4 May (Greenery Day), 5 May (Children's Day), 18 July (Marine Day), 19 September (Respect for the Aged Day), 22 September (Autumnal Equinox), 10 October (Sports Day), 3 November (Culture Day), 23 November (Labour Thanksgiving Day), 23 December (Emperor's Birthday),

Statistical Survey

Source (unless otherwise stated): Statistics Bureau and Statistics Center, 2-1-2, Kasumigaseki, Chiyoda-ku, Tokyo 100-8926; tel. (3) 5253-5111; fax (3) 3504-0265; e-mail webmaster@stat.go.jp; internet www.stat.go.jp.

Area and Population

AREA, POPULATION AND DENSITY

Area (sq km)	377,944*
Hokkaido district	83,457
Honshu district	231,112
Shikoku district	18,792
Kyushu district	42,190
Okinawa district	2,276
Population (census results)†	
1 October 2005	127,767,994
1 October 2010	
Males	62,327,737
Females	65,729,615
Total	128,057,352
Population (official estimates at 1 October)	
2011	127,799,000
2012	127,515,000
2013	127,298,000
Density (per sq km) at 1 October 2013	336.8

* 145,925 sq miles; total includes 118 sq km (45.6 sq miles) within Honshu and Shikoku districts yet to be demarcated fully.
† Excluding foreign military and diplomatic personnel and their dependants.

POPULATION BY AGE AND SEX
('000 persons, official estimates at 1 October 2013)

	Males	Females	Total
0–14 years	8,394	7,996	16,389
15–64 years	39,812	39,197	79,010
65 years and over	13,703	18,195	31,899
Total	61,909	65,388	127,298

Note: Totals may not be equal to the sum of components, owing to rounding.

PREFECTURES
(official population estimates at 1 October 2013)

Prefecture	Area (sq km)	Population ('000)	Density (per sq km)
Aichi	5,165	7,443	1,441.0
Akita	11,612	1,050	90.4
Aomori	9,607	1,335	139.0
Chiba	5,157	6,192	1,200.7
Ehime	5,678	1,405	247.4
Fukui	4,190	795	189.7
Fukuoka	4,977	5,090	1,022.7
Fukushima	13,783	1,946	141.2
Gifu	10,621	2,051	193.1
Gumma	6,363	1,984	311.8
Hiroshima	8,479	2,840	334.9
Hokkaido	83,457	5,431	65.1
Hyogo	8,396	5,558	662.0
Ibaraki	6,096	2,931	480.8
Ishikawa	4,186	1,159	276.9
Iwate	15,279	1,295	84.8
Kagawa	1,877	985	524.8
Kagoshima	9,189	1,680	182.8
Kanagawa	2,416	9,079	3,757.9
Kochi	7,105	745	104.9
Kumamoto	7,406	1,801	243.2
Kyoto	4,613	2,617	567.3
Mie	5,777	1,833	317.3
Miyagi	7,286	2,328	319.5
Miyazaki	7,735	1,120	144.8
Nagano	13,562	2,122	156.5
Nagasaki	4,104	1,397	340.4
Nara	3,691	1,383	374.7
Niigata	12,583	2,330	185.2
Oita	6,340	1,178	185.8
Okayama	7,113	1,930	271.3
Okinawa	2,276	1,415	621.7
Osaka	1,898	8,849	4,662.3
Saga	2,440	840	344.3

Prefecture—*continued*	Area (sq km)	Population ('000)	Density (per sq km)
Saitama	3,797	7,222	1,902.0
Shiga	4,017	1,416	352.5
Shimane	6,708	702	104.7
Shizuoka	7,780	3,723	478.5
Tochigi	6,408	1,986	309.9
Tokushima	4,147	770	185.7
Tokyo-to	2,188	13,300	6,078.6
Tottori	3,507	578	164.8
Toyama	4,248	1,076	253.3
Wakayama	4,726	979	207.2
Yamagata	9,323	1,141	122.4
Yamaguchi	6,114	1,420	232.3
Yamanashi	4,465	847	189.7
Total	377,944*	127,298	336.8

* Total includes 59 sq km of area straddling more than one prefecture or not fully demarcated.

Note: Totals may not be equal to the sum of components, owing to rounding.

PRINCIPAL CITIES
(census results at 1 October 2010)*

Tokyo (capital)†	8,945,695		Utsunomiya	467,666
Yokohama	3,688,773		Kanazawa	462,361
Osaka	2,665,314		Fukuyama	461,357
Nagoya	2,263,894		Amagasaki	453,748
Sapporo	1,913,545		Nagasaki	443,766
Kobe	1,544,200		Machida	426,987
Kyoto	1,474,015		Toyama	421,953
Fukuoka	1,463,743		Toyota	421,487
Kawasaki	1,425,512		Takamatsu	419,429
Saitama	1,222,434		Yokosuka	418,325
Hiroshima	1,173,843		Fujisawa	409,657
Sendai	1,045,986		Hirakata	407,978
Kitakyushu‡	976,846		Kashiwa	404,012
Chiba	961,749		Gifu	399,745
Sakai	841,966		Toyonaka	389,341
Niigata	811,901		Nagano	381,511
Hamamatsu	800,866		Toyohashi	376,665
Sagamihara	717,544		Wakayama	370,364
Shizuoka	716,197		Nara	366,591
Okayama	709,584		Okazaki	363,743
Kumamoto	676,103		Takatsuki	357,359
Funabashi	609,040		Suita	355,798
Kagoshima	605,846		Asahikawa	347,095
Hachioji	580,053		Kochi	343,393
Matsuyama	517,231		Kawagoe	342,670
Higashiosaka	509,533		Iwaki	342,249
Kawaguchi	500,598		Tokorozawa	341,924
Himeji	485,992		Maebashi	340,291
Matsudo	484,457		Koriyama	338,712
Nishinomiyai	482,640		Koshigaya	326,313
Kurashiki	475,513		Akita	323,600
Oita	474,094		Naha	315,954
Ichikawa	473,919		Aomori	299,520

* With the exception of Tokyo, the data for each city refer to an urban county (*shi*), an administrative division that may include some scattered or rural population as well as an urban centre.
† The figure refers to the 23 wards (*ku*) of the old city. The population of Tokyo-to (Tokyo Prefecture) was 13,159,388 at the census of 1 October 2010.
‡ Including Kokura, Moji, Tobata, Wakamatsu and Yahata (Yawata).

BIRTHS, MARRIAGES AND DEATHS*

	Registered live births		Registered marriages†		Registered deaths	
	Number	Rate (per 1,000)	Number	Rate (per 1,000)	Number	Rate (per 1,000)
2005 . .	1,062,530	8.4	714,265	5.7	1,083,796	8.6
2006 . .	1,092,674	8.7	730,971	5.8	1,084,450	8.6
2007 . .	1,089,818	8.6	719,822	5.7	1,108,334	8.8
2008 . .	1,091,156	8.7	726,106	5.8	1,142,407	9.1
2009 . .	1,070,035	8.5	707,734	5.6	1,141,865	9.1
2010 . .	1,071,304	8.5	700,214	5.5	1,197,012	9.5
2011 . .	1,050,806	8.3	661,895	5.2	1,253,066	9.9
2012 . .	1,037,231	8.2	668,869	5.3	1,256,359	10.0

* Figures relate only to Japanese nationals in Japan.
† Data are tabulated by year of registration rather than by year of occurrence.

Source: Ministry of Health, Labour and Welfare, Tokyo.

Life expectancy (years at birth): 83.1 (males 79.9; females 86.4) in 2012 (Source: World Bank, World Development Indicators database).

ECONOMICALLY ACTIVE POPULATION*
(annual averages, '000 persons aged 15 years and over)

	2011	2012	2013
Agriculture and forestry . . .	2,070	2,240	2,170
Fishing and aquaculture . . .	160	160	160
Mining and quarrying	30	30	30
Manufacturing	9,970	10,320	10,390
Electricity, gas and water . . .	290	310	300
Construction	4,730	5,030	4,990
Wholesale and retail trade . .	10,060	10,420	10,570
Restaurants and hotels . .	3,650	3,760	3,840
Transport, information and communications	5,190	5,280	5,320
Financing, insurance, real estate and business services . .	2,630	2,750	2,750
Health and welfare	6,480	7,060	7,350
Education	2,800	2,950	2,990
Government	2,100	2,240	2,280
Other services and activities not elsewhere classified . . .	9,050	9,530	9,050
Sub-total	59,210	62,060	62,190
Activities not adequately defined .	560	640	920
Total employed	59,770	62,700	63,110
Unemployed	2,840	2,850	2,650
Total labour force	62,610	65,550	65,770
Males	36,290	37,890	37,730
Females	26,320	27,660	28,040

* Figures are rounded to the nearest 10,000 persons, and therefore totals may not be equal to the sum of components.

Health and Welfare

KEY INDICATORS

Total fertility rate (children per woman, 2012) . . .	1.4
Under-5 mortality rate (per 1,000 live births, 2012) . .	3.0
HIV/AIDS (% of persons aged 15–49, 2011)	<0.1
Physicians (per 1,000 head, 2010)	2.3
Hospital beds (per 1,000 head, 2009)	13.7
Health expenditure (2011): US $ per head (PPP) . . .	3,415
Health expenditure (2011): % of GDP	10.0
Health expenditure (2011): public (% of total) . . .	82.1
Total carbon dioxide emissions ('000 metric tons, 2010) .	1,170,715.4
Carbon dioxide emissions per head (metric tons, 2010) . .	9.2
Human Development Index (2013): ranking	17
Human Development Index (2013): value	0.890

For sources and definitions, see explanatory note on p. vi.

Agriculture

PRINCIPAL CROPS
('000 metric tons)

	2011	2012	2013
Wheat	746.3	857.8	811.7
Rice, paddy	10,500.0	10,654.0	10,758.0
Barley	171.5	172.4	182.8
Potatoes	2,349.0	2,500.0	2,600.0
Sweet potatoes	885.9	875.9	942.3
Taro (Cocoyam)	171.3	172.5	175.0*
Yams	165.9	166.1	170.0*
Sugar cane	1,000.0	1,108.0	1,191.0
Sugar beet	3,547.0	3,758.0	3,435.0
Beans, dry	69.9	86.2	83.3
Soybeans (Soya beans) . .	218.8	235.9	199.9
Cabbages and other brassicas .	2,272.4	2,363.7	2,356.9*
Lettuce and chicory . . .	542.4	566.1	565.4*
Spinach	263.5	263.5	258.4*
Tomatoes	703.0	722.4	748.3
Cauliflowers and broccoli . .	152.4	159.3	162.0*
Pumpkins, squash and gourds .	209.2	227.1	227.3*
Cucumbers and gherkins . .	584.6	586.5	574.9
Aubergines (Eggplants) . .	322.4	327.4	321.2
Chillies and peppers, green . .	141.8	145.0	145.1
Onions and shallots, green . .	549.5	544.1	545.6*
Onions, dry	1,070.0	1,098.0	1,070.0
Carrots and turnips . . .	617.3	613.2	600.5*
Maize, green	240.3	255.3	254.8*
Mushrooms and truffles* . . .	60.2	61.5	61.5
Watermelons	362.5	370.3	356.1*
Cantaloupes and other melons .	180.4	176.3	165.8*
Grapes	172.6	198.3	189.7
Apples	655.3	793.8	741.7
Pears	312.8	299.0	294.4
Peaches and nectarines . .	139.8	135.2	124.7
Plums and sloes	22.5	22.3	21.8
Oranges*	54.1	53.0	47.6
Tangerines, mandarins, clementines and satsumas . .	928.2	846.3	895.9
Persimmons	207.5	253.8	214.7
Strawberries	177.3	163.2	160.2*
Tea	82.1	85.9	84.8
Tobacco, unmanufactured . .	23.6	19.7	19.7*

* FAO estimate(s).

Aggregate production ('000 metric tons, may include official, semi-official or estimated data): Total cereals 11,450.4 in 2011, 11,729.5 in 2012, 11,786.6 in 2013; Total roots and tubers 3,668.5 in 2011, 3,777.0 in 2012, 3,950.3 in 2013; Total vegetables (incl. melons) 11,176.3 in 2011, 11,413.4 in 2012, 11,314.6 in 2013; Total fruits (excl. melons) 2,950.5 in 2011, 3,034.6 in 2012, 2,984.8 in 2013.

Source: FAO.

LIVESTOCK
('000 head at 30 September)

	2011	2012	2013
Horses*	16	16	16
Cattle	4,230	4,172	4,065
Pigs	9,768	9,735	9,685
Sheep*	13	13	13
Goats*	16	16	17
Chickens	178,546	177,607	306,408

* FAO estimates.

Source: FAO.

LIVESTOCK PRODUCTS
('000 metric tons)

	2011	2012	2013
Cattle meat	500.4	518.7	508.0
Pig meat	1,267.3	1,296.9	1,309.1
Chicken meat	1,378.0	1,444.6*	1,450.0*
Cows' milk	7,474.3	7,630.4	7,508.3
Hen eggs	2,482.6	2,506.8	2,522.0

* Unofficial figure.

Source: FAO.

Forestry

ROUNDWOOD REMOVALS
('000 cubic metres, excl. bark)

	2011	2012	2013
Sawlogs, veneer logs and logs for sleepers	14,016	13,923	13,923*
Pulpwood	4,274	4,556	4,556*
Fuel wood*	84	80	76
Total*	18,374	18,559	18,555

* FAO estimate(s).

Source: FAO.

SAWNWOOD PRODUCTION
('000 cubic metres, incl. railway sleepers)

	2011	2012*	2013*
Coniferous (softwood)	9,294	8,267	8,713
Broadleaved (hardwood)	140	105	111
Total	9,434	8,372	8,824

* Unofficial figures.

Source: FAO.

Fishing

('000 metric tons, live weight)

	2010	2011	2012
Capture	4,065.9	3,775.5	3,644.3*
Chum salmon (Keta or Dog salmon)	173.5	143.6	13.1
Alaska (Walleye) pollock	251.2	238.9	229.8
Pacific saury (Skipper)	207.5	215.4	221.5
Japanese jack mackerel	159.4	168.4	133.9
Japanese anchovy	355.6	265.7	249.2
Skipjack tuna (Oceanic skipjack)	317.3	257.9	263.4
Chub mackerel	491.8	392.5	443.8
Yesso scallop	327.1	302.9	315.4
Japanese flying squid	199.8	242.3	169.1
Aquaculture*	718.3	556.8	633.0
Japanese amberjack	138.9	146.2	160.2
Pacific cupped oyster	200.3	165.9	161.1
Yesso scallop	219.6	118.4	184.3
Total catch*	4,784.1	4,332.3	4,277.4

* FAO estimate(s).

Note: Figures exclude aquatic plants ('000 metric tons): 530.0 (capture 97.2, aquaculture 432.8) in 2010; 437.5 (capture 87.8, aquaculture 349.7) in 2011; 539.3 (capture 98.5, aquaculture 440.8) in 2012 (FAO estimates). Also excluded are aquatic mammals (generally recorded by number rather than by weight), pearls, corals and sponges. The number of whales caught was: 1,022 in 2010; 771 in 2011; 1,136 in 2012. The number of dolphins and porpoises caught was: 6,467 in 2010; 3,082 in 2011; 1,342 in 2012. The catch of other aquatic mammals ('000 metric tons) was: 0.9 in 2010; 0.6 in 2011; 0.5 in 2012. For the remaining categories, catches (in metric tons) were: pearls 21.3 in 2010; 20.0 in 2011; 20.1 in 2012, and corals 5.0 in 2010; 5.2 in 2011; 5.3 in 2012.

Source: FAO.

Mining

('000 metric tons unless otherwise indicated)

	2010	2011	2012
Hard coal*	1,000	900	700
Quartzite stone	9,159	9,543	9,306
Limestone	133,974	134,176	140,038
Gold ore (kg)†	8,544	7,922	7,233
Crude petroleum ('000 barrels)	5,491	5,235	4,995
Natural gas (million cu m)‡	3,396	3,298	3,276

* Estimates.
† Figures refer to the metal content of ores.
‡ Includes output from gas wells and coal mines.

Source: US Geological Survey.

Industry

SELECTED PRODUCTS
('000 metric tons unless otherwise indicated)

	2011	2012	2013
Cotton yarn—pure and mixed*	43	38	37
Woven cotton fabrics—pure and mixed (million sq m)	128	124	128
Woven silk fabrics—pure and mixed (million sq m)	3.2	2.9	2.9
Wool yarn—pure and mixed	10	10	10
Woven woollen fabrics—pure and mixed (million sq m)	30	28	28
Woven fabrics of cellulosic fibres—pure and mixed (million sq m)†	98	84	86
Woven fabrics of non-cellulosic fibres (million sq m)	867	839	818
Leather footwear ('000 pairs)	16,629	16,212	15,456
Newsprint	3,211	3,254	3,219
Other printing and writing paper	8,765	8,420	8,576
Paperboard	11,163	10,890	11,059
Rubber products	1,470	1,415	1,396
Road motor vehicle tyres (million)	167	160	160
Sulphuric acid—100%	6,416	6,711	6,429
Caustic soda—Sodium hydroxide	3,960	3,566	3,636
Ammonia	1,211	1,055	1,007
Cement	51,291	54,737	57,962
Pig iron	81,028	81,405	83,849
Ferro-alloys‡	834	908	938
Crude steel	107,601	107,232	110,595
Aluminium—unwrought§	1,057	1,067	1,099
Refined copper—unwrought	1,328	1,516	1,468
Electrolytic, distilled and rectified zinc—unwrought	545	571	587
Air-conditioning machines ('000)	18,547	17,836	18,579
Video cameras ('000)	1,905	1,200	470
Digital cameras ('000)	19,545	17,994	9,716
DVD players ('000)	1,135	315	—
Cellular telephones ('000)	19,794	17,235	8,762
Personal computers ('000)	6,156	6,655	7,217
Passenger motor cars ('000)	7,159	8,556	8,189
Lorries and trucks ('000)	1,136	1,266	1,308
Motorcycles, scooters and mopeds ('000)	639	595	563
Bicycles ('000)	1,102	1,012	966
Watches	391,015	357,706	327,307
Construction: new dwellings started ('000)	834	883	n.a.
Electric energy (million kWh)	1,107,829	1,093,950	n.a.

* Including condenser cotton yarn.
† Fabrics of continuous and discontinuous rayon and acetate fibres, including pile and chenille fabrics at loom stage.
‡ Including silico-chromium.
§ Including alloys.

2011 ('000 metric tons): Liquefied petroleum gas 3,935; Naphthas 13,822; Motor spirit—gasoline 40,102; Kerosene 15,615; Jet fuel 10,036; Distillate fuel oil 46,081; Petroleum bitumen—Asphalt 3,939; Coke-oven coke 39,008 (Source: UN Industrial Commodity Statistics Database).

Finance

CURRENCY AND EXCHANGE RATES

Monetary Units
100 sen = 1 yen.

Sterling, Dollar and Euro Equivalents (31 December 2014)
£1 sterling = 188.295 yen;
US $1 = 120.640 yen;
€1 = 146.469 yen;
1,000 yen = £5.31 = $8.29 = €6.83.

Average Exchange Rate (yen per US $)
2012   79.790
2013   97.596
2014   105.945

BUDGET
('000 million yen, year ending 31 March)*

Revenue	2011/12	2012/13†	2013/14‡
Tax and stamp revenues . . .	42,346	43,096	50,001
Government bond issues . . .	44,244	42,851	41,250
Total (incl. others)	90,334	92,612	95,882

Expenditure	2011/12	2012/13†	2013/14‡
Defence	4,714	4,754	4,885
Social security	26,390	29,122	30,518
Public works	4,573	5,285	5,969
Servicing of national debt§ . .	21,944	22,242	23,270
Transfer of local allocation tax to local governments . . .	16,594	16,393	16,142
Total (incl. others)	90,334	92,612	95,882

* Figures refer only to the operations of the General Account budget. Data exclude transactions of other accounts controlled by the central Government: two mutual aid associations and four special accounts (including other social security funds).
† Initial forecasts.
‡ Budget figures.
§ Including the repayment of debt principal and administrative costs.

Source: Ministry of Finance, Tokyo.

INTERNATIONAL RESERVES
(US $ million at 31 December)

	2011	2012	2013
Gold (national valuation) . . .	37,666	40,939	29,560
IMF special drawing rights . .	19,745	19,910	20,130
Reserve position in IMF . .	17,178	13,659	14,164
Foreign exchange	1,221,249	1,193,578	1,202,924
Total	1,295,838	1,268,086	1,266,778

Source: IMF, *International Financial Statistics*.

MONEY SUPPLY
('000 million yen at 31 December)

	2011	2012	2013
Currency outside depository corporations	79,971	83,067	85,276
Transferable deposits	461,743	477,797	506,206
Other deposits	582,057	586,276	598,210
Broad money	1,123,770	1,147,139	1,189,693

Source: IMF, *International Financial Statistics*.

COST OF LIVING
(Consumer Price Index; base: 2010 = 100)

	2011	2012	2013
Food (incl. beverages)	99.6	99.7	99.6
Housing	99.8	99.5	99.1
Rent	99.8	99.4	99.0
Fuel, light and water charges .	103.3	107.3	112.3
Clothing and footwear	99.7	99.7	100.1
All items (incl. others) . . .	99.7	99.7	100.0

NATIONAL ACCOUNTS
('000 million yen at current prices, year ending 31 December)

National Income and Product

	2010	2011	2012
Compensation of employees . .	243,474.3	245,070.4	245,758.5
Operating surplus and mixed income	97,020.1	87,813.1	90,650.8
Domestic primary incomes	340,494.4	332,883.5	336,409.3
Consumption of fixed capital . .	103,779.0	101,796.3	100,589.6
Statistical discrepancy	1,356.3	−594.0	−631.9
Gross domestic product (GDP) at factor cost	445,629.7	434,085.8	436,367.0
Indirect taxes	39,864.4	40,219.8	40,314.9
Less Subsidies	3,109.7	2,994.8	2,904.7
GDP in purchasers' values .	482,384.4	471,310.8	473,777.2
Primary incomes received from abroad	18,238.4	20,382.1	21,213.7
Less Primary incomes paid abroad	5,264.1	5,707.0	6,168.9
Gross national income (GNI) .	495,358.7	485,985.9	488,822.0

Expenditure on the Gross Domestic Product

	2011	2012	2013
Government final consumption expenditure	96,116.6	96,940.4	98,608.3
Private final consumption expenditure	284,244.3	287,696.8	292,755.5
Changes in stocks	−1,883.1	−1,546.0	−3,138.7
Gross fixed capital formation . .	97,107.0	100,067.7	103,702.8
Total domestic expenditure .	475,584.8	483,158.9	491,927.9
Exports of goods and services . .	71,297.8	69,774.8	77,540.5
Less Imports of goods and services	75,571.8	79,156.5	91,100.2
GDP in purchasers' values .	471,310.8	473,777.2	478,368.2
GDP at constant 2005 prices .	527,883.9	527,851.2	n.a.

Gross Domestic Product by Economic Activity

	2010	2011	2012
Agriculture, hunting, forestry and fishing	5,655.6	5,425.7	5,730.1
Mining and quarrying	301.0	303.5	306.2
Manufacturing	94,333.1	87,283.9	85,637.3
Electricity, gas and water . . .	11,007.8	8,550.9	8,083.8
Construction	26,197.7	26,461.1	26,653.1
Wholesale and retail trade . .	65,980.5	67,131.0	68,122.2
Transport, storage and communications	49,443.5	48,729.1	49,970.7
Finance and insurance . . .	23,766.0	22,430.0	21,559.1
Real estate*	56,890.0	56,725.7	56,871.4
Public administration	29,566.1	29,665.6	29,464.9
Other government services . .	14,357.8	14,376.0	14,032.3
Other business, community, social and personal services . . .	91,266.4	91,183.0	93,789.1
Private non-profit services to households	10,009.2	10,698.7	11,133.8
Sub-total	478,774.6	468,964.2	471,354.1
Import duties	4,846.5	5,550.2	5,702.5
Less Consumption taxes for gross capital formation	2,593.0	2,609.5	2,647.6
Statistical discrepancy	1,356.3	−594.0	−631.9
GDP in purchasers' values .	482,384.4	471,310.8	473,777.2

* Including imputed rents of owner-occupied dwellings.

Source: Economic and Social Research Institute, Tokyo.

BALANCE OF PAYMENTS
(US $ million)*

	2011	2012	2013
Exports of goods	789,951	776,640	694,940
Imports of goods	−794,425	−830,124	−784,588
Balance on goods	−4,474	−53,484	−89,648
Exports of services	137,349	134,186	135,398
Imports of services	−175,780	−184,689	−170,878
Balance on goods and services	−42,905	−103,986	−125,128
Primary income received . . .	227,312	235,363	222,300
Primary income paid	−51,518	−56,173	−52,985
Balance on goods, services and primary income	132,889	75,204	44,187
Secondary income received . .	13,115	14,896	15,905
Secondary income paid . . .	−26,940	−29,240	−26,024
Current balance	119,064	60,859	34,068
Capital account (net)	497	−1,017	−7,681
Direct investment assets . . .	−110,593	−123,141	−136,441
Direct investment liabilities . .	79	2,525	3,715
Portfolio investment assets . .	−103,051	−151,333	78,703
Portfolio investment liabilities .	264,101	109,394	185,033
Financial derivatives and employee stock options assets . .	407,490	235,656	208,451
Financial derivatives and employee stock options liabilities . . .	−390,411	−242,793	−266,676
Other investment assets . . .	−92,678	−118,717	−174,164
Other investment liabilities . .	43,868	186,218	156,702
Net errors and omissions . .	38,258	4,087	−42,935
Reserves and related items .	176,624	−38,261	38,776

* Figures are rounded to the nearest US $10m., and totals may not, therefore, be equal to the sum of components.

Source: IMF, *International Financial Statistics*.

JAPANESE DEVELOPMENT ASSISTANCE
(net disbursement basis, US $ million)

	2010	2011	2012
Official flows	14,683	13,736	15,998
Bilateral assistance	7,337	6,943	6,402
Grants	6,943	8,567	6,759
Grant assistance . . .	3,464	5,033	3,117
Technical assistance . .	3,478	3,534	3,641
Loans	395	−1,624	−356
Contributions to multilateral institutions	3,684	3,888	4,202
Other official flows	3,662	2,905	5,393
Export credits	−1,039	−622	−623
Direct investment finance, etc.	4,217	3,889	6,829
Transfers to multilateral institutions	485	−362	−813
Private flows	32,837	47,594	32,493
Export credits	2,767	1,853	−3,951
Direct investment and others .	21,650	40,315	31,215
Bilateral investment in securities, etc.	7,428	5,844	6,470
Transfers to multilateral institutions	992	−419	−1,241
Grants from private voluntary agencies	692	497	487
Total	48,213	61,828	48,977

External Trade

PRINCIPAL COMMODITIES
('000 million yen)

Imports c.i.f.	2011	2012	2013
Food and live animals . . .	5,854	5,852	6,473
Fish and fish preparations* . .	1,350	1,400	1,466
Crude materials (inedible) except fuels	5,270	4,768	5,358
Mineral fuels, lubricants, etc. .	21,816	24,088	27,444
Crude and partly refined petroleum	11,415	12,247	14,245
Petroleum products	2,226	2,462	2,705
Liquefied natural gas . . .	4,787	6,004	7,059
Coal	2,459	2,321	2,307
Chemicals	6,098	5,926	6,464
Manufactured goods	6,069	5,508	6,245
Non-electrical machinery . .	4,970	5,004	5,969
Electrical machinery . . .	7,989	8,438	10,309
Semi-conductors, etc. . . .	1,762	1,779	2,445
Telephonic and telegraphic equipment	1,576	2,149	2,679
Transport equipment	1,738	2,312	2,788
Other	8,307	8,793	10,192
Clothing and clothing accessories .	2,598	2,680	3,248
Total (incl. others)†	68,111	70,689	81,243

Exports f.o.b.	2011	2012	2013
Chemicals	6,798	6,365	7,507
Manufactured goods . . .	8,786	8,442	9,177
Iron and steel	3,709	3,496	3,793
Machinery and transport equipment	39,436	39,243	41,743
Non-electrical machinery . . .	13,803	12,843	13,359
Power-generating machinery .	2,317	2,261	2,520
Electrical machinery, apparatus, etc.	11,600	11,405	12,052
Thermionic valves, tubes, etc. .	3,565	3,339	3,553
Transport equipment	14,033	14,995	16,332
Road motor vehicles	8,204	9,225	10,413
Road motor vehicle parts . .	2,997	3,205	3,476
Other	7,948	7,258	8,172
Scientific instruments and optical equipment	2,109	2,084	2,223
Total (incl. others)‡	65,546	63,748	69,774

* Including crustacea and molluscs.
† Including re-imports not classified according to kind.
‡ Including re-exports not classified according to kind.

PRINCIPAL TRADING PARTNERS
('000 million yen)*

Imports c.i.f.	2011	2012	2013
Australia	4,514	4,504	4,977
Brazil	1,009	952	1,070
Canada	1,032	1,012	1,170
Chile	782	744	776
China, People's Republic . . .	14,642	15,039	17,660
France	944	1,024	1,138
Germany	1,856	1,972	2,325
Indonesia	2,716	2,576	2,813
Iran	1,027	634	676
Italy	691	765	931
Korea, Republic	3,170	3,234	3,493
Kuwait	1,044	1,218	1,312
Malaysia	2,426	2,621	2,901
Philippines	712	745	901

Imports c.i.f.—*continued*	2011	2012	2013
Qatar	2,395	n.a.	n.a.
Russia	1,514	1,660	2,308
Saudi Arabia	4,026	4,376	4,863
Singapore	691	700	727
Taiwan	1,852	1,921	2,315
Thailand	1,953	1,886	2,150
United Arab Emirates	3,413	3,510	4,148
USA	5,931	6,082	6,815
Viet Nam	920	1,203	1,389
Total (incl. others)	68,111	70,689	81,243

Exports f.o.b.	2011	2012	2013
Australia	1,418	1,471	1,656
Belgium	542	500	517
Canada	709	819	848
China, People's Republic	12,902	11,509	12,625
Germany	1,871	1,660	1,850
Hong Kong	3,420	3,276	3,651
India	882	845	839
Indonesia	1,412	1,619	1,662
Korea, Republic	5,269	4,911	5,512
Malaysia	1,496	1,413	1,487
Mexico	815	844	946
Netherlands	1,429	1,290	1,357
Panama	1,190	n.a.	n.a.
Philippines	894	946	944
Russia	941	1,005	1,069
Saudi Arabia	517	657	668
Singapore	2,170	1,859	2,047
Taiwan	4,058	3,673	4,061
Thailand	2,989	3,489	3,507
United Arab Emirates	592	716	830
United Kingdom	1,304	1,065	1,084
USA	10,018	11,188	12,928
Viet Nam	764	857	1,029
Total (incl. others)	65,546	63,748	69,774

* Imports by country of production; exports by country of last consignment.

Transport

RAILWAYS
(traffic, year ending 31 March)

	2009/10	2010/11	2011/12
Japan Railways Group:			
Passengers (million)	8,818	8,837	8,963
Passenger-km (million)	244,593	246,937	253,788
Freight ('000 tons)	30,790	n.a.	n.a.
Freight ton-km (million)	20,228	n.a.	n.a.
Other private railways:			
Passengers (million)	13,851	13,795	14,079
Passenger-km (million)	148,874	148,130	150,606
Freight ('000 tons)	12,857	n.a.	n.a.
Freight ton-km (million)	171	n.a.	n.a.
Total:			
Passengers (million)	22,669	22,632	23,042
Passenger-km (million)	393,466	395,067	404,394
Freight ('000 tons)	43,647	39,886	42,340
Freight ton-km (million)	20,399	19,998	20,471

ROAD TRAFFIC
('000 motor vehicles owned, year ending 31 March)

	2011	2012	2013
Passenger cars	40,143	40,009	39,821
Buses and coaches	226	226	227
Trucks, incl. trailers	6,136	6,068	6,041
Special use vehicles	1,495	1,501	1,514
Light two-wheeled vehicles	1,543	1,566	1,595
Light motor vehicles	29,569	30,254	31,075
Total	79,113	79,625	80,273

SHIPPING

Flag Registered Fleet
(at 31 December)

	2012	2013	2014
Number of vessels	3,564	3,561	3,581
Total displacement ('000 grt)	18,554	19,921	21,158

Source: Lloyd's List Intelligence (www.lloydslistintelligence.com).

International Seaborne Traffic
('000 metric tons)

	2010	2011	2012
Exports	44,758	51,863	50,414
Imports	465,898	535,977	530,855
Cross transport	308,419	378,857	419,861
Total	819,075	966,697	1,001,130

CIVIL AVIATION
(traffic on scheduled services)

	2010	2011	2012
Kilometres flown (million)	945	938	1,024
Passengers carried (million)	98,932	89,747	98,936
Passenger-km (million)	139,111	122,731	138,126
Total ton-km (million)	7,661	6,565	7,052

Tourism

FOREIGN VISITOR ARRIVALS
(excl. Japanese nationals resident abroad)

Country of nationality	2011	2012	2013*
Australia	162,578	206,404	244,600
China, People's Republic	1,043,246	1,425,100	1,314,500
Hong Kong	364,865	481,665	745,800
Korea, Republic	1,658,073	2,042,775	2,456,100
Singapore	111,354	142,201	189,200
Taiwan	993,974	1,465,753	2,210,800
Thailand	144,969	260,640	453,600
United Kingdom	140,099	173,994	191,900
USA	565,887	716,709	799,200
Total (incl. others)	6,218,752	8,358,105	10,363,900

* Figures for 2013 are preliminary and are rounded to the nearest 100 persons.

Source: mainly Japan National Tourist Organization.

Receipts from tourism (US $ million, excl. passenger transport): 11,000 in 2011; 14,581 in 2012; 15,093 in 2013 (Source: World Tourism Organization).

Communications Media

	2011	2012	2013
Telephones ('000 main lines in use)	64,669	64,273	64,062
Mobile telephones ('000 subscribers)	132,761	138,363	146,455
Broadband subscribers ('000)	34,864	36,108	36,665
Book production:			
titles	78,863	82,200	n.a.
copies (million)	700	n.a.	n.a.
Daily newspapers:			
number of titles	119	118	117
circulation ('000 copies)	48,345	47,778	46,999

Sources: The Japan Newspaper Publishers and Editors Association; Foreign Press Center, *Facts and Figures of Japan*; International Telecommunication Union.

Education

(2013)

	Institutions	Teachers*	Students
Kindergartens	13,043	111,111	1,583,610
Elementary schools	21,131	417,553	6,676,920
Lower secondary schools	10,628	254,235	3,536,182
Upper secondary schools	4,981	235,062	3,319,640
Schools for special needs	1,080	77,663	132,570
Colleges of technology	57	4,336	58,226
Junior colleges	359	8,631	138,260
Universities	782	178,669	2,868,872
Special training schools	3,216	40,380	660,078
Miscellaneous vocational schools	1,330	8,845	122,890

* Figures refer to full-time teachers only.

Pupil-teacher ratio (primary education, UNESCO estimate): 17.1 in 2011/12 (Source: UNESCO Institute for Statistics).

Directory

The Government

HEAD OF STATE

His Imperial Majesty AKIHITO, Emperor of Japan (succeeded to the throne 7 January 1989).

THE CABINET
(April 2015)

The Government comprises a coalition of the Liberal Democratic Party (LDP) and New Komeito.

Prime Minister: SHINZO ABE (LDP).

Deputy Prime Minister, Minister of Finance, Minister in charge of Overcoming Deflation, and Minister of State for Financial Services: TARO ASO (LDP).

Minister for Internal Affairs and Communications: SANAE TAKAICHI (LDP).

Minister of Justice: YOKO KAMIKAWA (LDP).

Minister for Foreign Affairs: FUMIO KISHIDA (LDP).

Minister of Education, Culture, Sports, Science and Technology, and Minister in charge of Rebuilding Education, and of the Tokyo Olympic and Paralympic Games: HAKUBUN SHIMOMURA (LDP).

Minister of Health, Labour and Welfare: YASUHISA SHIOZAKI (LDP).

Minister of Agriculture, Forestry and Fisheries: YOSHIMASA HAYASHI.

Minister of Economy, Trade and Industry, Minister in charge of the Response to the Economic Impact caused by the Nuclear Accident and of Industrial Competitiveness, and Minister of State for Nuclear Damage Compensation and the Decommissioning Facilitation Corporation: YOICHI MIYAZAWA (LDP).

Minister of Land, Infrastructure, Transport and Tourism, and Minister in charge of Water Cycle Policy: AKIHIRO OTA (New Komeito).

Minister of the Environment and Minister of State for Nuclear Emergency Preparedness: YOSHIO MOCHIZUKI (LDP).

Minister of Defence and Minister in charge of Security Legislation: Gen. NAKATANI (LDP).

Chief Cabinet Secretary and Minister in charge of Alleviating the Burden of the Bases in Okinawa: YOSHIHIDE SUGA (LDP).

Minister for Reconstruction and Minister in charge of Comprehensive Policy Co-ordination for Revival from the Nuclear Accident at Fukushima: WATARU TAKESHITA (LDP).

Chairman of the National Public Safety Commission, Minister of State for Disaster Management, and Minister in charge of the Abduction Issue, of Ocean Policy and Territorial Issues, and of Building National Resilience: ERIKO YAMATANI (LDP).

Minister of State for Okinawa and Northern Territories' Affairs, for Science and Technology Policy and for Space Policy, and Minister in charge of Information Technology

Policy, of the 'Challenge Again' Initiative, and of the 'Cool Japan' Strategy: SHUNICHI YAMAGUCHI (LDP).

Minister in charge of Women's Empowerment, of Administrative Reform and of Civil Service Reform, and Minister of State for Consumer Affairs and Food Safety, for Regulatory Reform, for Measures for Declining Birthrate and for Gender Equality: HARUKO ARIMURA (LDP).

Minister in charge of Economic Revitalization and of Total Reform of Social Security and Tax, and Minister of State for Economic and Fiscal Policy: AKIRA AMARI (LDP).

Minister in charge of Overcoming Population Decline and Vitalizing Local Economy in Japan, and Minister of State for the National Strategic Special Zones: SHIGERU ISHIBA (LDP).

MINISTRIES

Imperial Household Agency: 1-1, Chiyoda, Chiyoda-ku, Tokyo 100-8111; tel. (3) 3213-1111; fax (3) 3282-1407; e-mail information@kunaicho.go.jp; internet www.kunaicho.go.jp.

Prime Minister's Office: 1-6-1, Nagata-cho, Chiyoda-ku, Tokyo 100-8968; tel. (3) 3581-2361; fax (3) 3581-1910; internet www.kantei.go.jp.

Cabinet Office: 1-6-1, Nagata-cho, Chiyoda-ku, Tokyo 100-8968; tel. (3) 5253-2111; internet www.cao.go.jp.

Ministry of Agriculture, Forestry and Fisheries: 1-2-1, Kasumigaseki, Chiyoda-ku, Tokyo 100-8950; tel. (3) 3502-5517; fax (3) 3592-7697; internet www.maff.go.jp.

Ministry of Defence: 5-1, Ichigaya, Honmura-cho, Shinjuku-ku, Tokyo 162-8801; tel. (3) 3268-3111; fax (3) 5261-8018; e-mail infomod@mod.go.jp; internet www.mod.go.jp.

Ministry of Economy, Trade and Industry: 1-3-1, Kasumigaseki, Chiyoda-ku, Tokyo 100-8901; tel. (3) 3501-1511; fax (3) 3501-6942; e-mail webmail@meti.go.jp; internet www.meti.go.jp.

Ministry of Education, Culture, Sports, Science and Technology: 3-2-2, Kasumigaseki, Chiyoda-ku, Tokyo 100-8959; tel. (3) 5253-4111; fax (3) 3595-2017; internet www.mext.go.jp.

Ministry of the Environment: 5 Godochosha, 1-2-2, Kasumigaseki, Chiyoda-ku, Tokyo 100-8975; tel. (3) 3581-3351; fax (3) 3502-0308; internet www.env.go.jp.

Ministry of Finance: 3-1-1, Kasumigaseki, Chiyoda-ku, Tokyo 100-8940; tel. (3) 3581-4111; fax (3) 5251-2667; e-mail info@mof.go.jp; internet www.mof.go.jp.

Ministry of Foreign Affairs: 2-2-1, Kasumigaseki, Chiyoda-ku, Tokyo 100-8919; tel. (3) 3580-3311; fax (3) 3581-2667; e-mail webmaster@mofa.go.jp; internet www.mofa.go.jp.

Ministry of Health, Labour and Welfare: 1-2-2, Kasumigaseki, Chiyoda-ku, Tokyo 100-8916; tel. (3) 5253-1111; fax (3) 3501-2532; e-mail www-admin@mhlw.go.jp; internet www.mhlw.go.jp.

Ministry of Internal Affairs and Communications: 2-1-2, Kasumigaseki, Chiyoda-ku, Tokyo 100-8926; tel. (3) 5253-5111; fax (3) 3504-0265; internet www.soumu.go.jp.

Ministry of Justice: 1-1-1, Kasumigaseki, Chiyoda-ku, Tokyo 100-8977; tel. (3) 3580-4111; fax (3) 3592-7011; e-mail webmaster@moj.go.jp; internet www.moj.go.jp.

Ministry of Land, Infrastructure, Transport and Tourism: 2-1-3, Kasumigaseki, Chiyoda-ku, Tokyo 100-8918; tel. (3) 5253-8111; fax (3) 3580-7982; e-mail webmaster@mlit.go.jp; internet www.mlit.go.jp.

Financial Services Agency: 3-2-1, Kasumigaseki, Chiyoda-ku, Tokyo 100-8967; tel. (3) 3506-6000; internet www.fsa.go.jp.

National Public Safety Commission: 2-1-2, Kasumigaseki, Chiyoda-ku, Tokyo 100-8974; tel. (3) 3581-0141; internet www.npsc.go.jp.

Legislature

DIET
(Kokkai)

The Diet consists of two chambers: the House of Councillors (upper house) and the House of Representatives (lower house). The members of the House of Representatives are elected for a period of four years (subject to dissolution). The House of Representatives has 475 members (reduced in 2014 from 480 members: 295 single-seat constituencies and 180 seats determined by proportional representation. The 242 members of the House of Councillors serve a six-year term of office, with elections for one-half of the members (including 48 chosen by proportional representation) being held every three years.

House of Councillors

House of Councillors: 1-7-1 Nagatacho, Chiyoda-ku, Tokyo 100-0014; tel. (3) 3581-3111; e-mail webmaster@sangiin.go.jp; internet www.sangiin.go.jp.

Speaker: MASAAKI YAMAZAKI.

Party	Seats after elections*	
	11 July 2010	21 July 2013
Liberal Democratic Party . . .	84	113
Democratic Party of Japan and the Shin-Ryokufukai	106	59
New Komeito	19	20
Your Party	11	18
Japanese Communist Party . . .	6	11
Japanese Restoration Party† . .	—	9
Social Democratic Party of Japan .	4	3
People's New Party	3	—
Sunrise Party of Japan . . .	3	1
New Renaissance Party . . .	2	1
New Party Nippon	1	—
People's Life Party	—	2
Independents and others . . .	3	4
Total	**242**	**242‡**

* One-half of the seats are renewable every three years.
† The Japanese Restoration Party merged with the Unity Party in September 2014 to form the Japan Innovation Party.
‡ Including one vacancy.

House of Representatives

House of Representatives: 1-7-1 Nagatacho, Chiyoda-ku, Tokyo 100-0014; tel. (3) 3581-3111; e-mail webmaster@shugiin.go.jp; internet www.shugiin.go.jp/internet/index.nsf/html/index_e.htm.

Speaker: NOBUTAKA MACHIMURA.

Election, 14 December 2014

Party	Seats
Liberal Democratic Party	291
Democratic Party of Japan	73
Japan Innovation Party	41
New Komeito	35
Japanese Communist Party	21
Party for Future Generations	2
Social Democratic Party of Japan	2
People's Life Party	2
Independents	8
Total	**475**

Election Commission

Central Election Management Council: 2nd Bldg of Central Common Government Office, 2-1-2, Kasumigaseki, Chiyoda-ku, Tokyo 100-8926; tel. (3) 5253-5111; fax (3) 5253-5575; mems nominated by Diet and approved by Cabinet; regulates proportional representation electoral elements for both legislative chambers; single-constituency elections for both chambers are supervised by an Election Control Cttee est. by each prefectural govt; Chair. AKIRA ISHIHARA.

Political Organizations

The Political Funds Regulation Law provides that any organization wishing to support a candidate for an elective public office must be registered as a political party. There are more than 10,000 registered parties in the country, mostly of local or regional significance.

Ainu Party: 80-27, Nibutani Biratori, Saru-gun, Hokkaido 055-0101; tel. (145) 74-6033; fax (145) 74-6035; e-mail info@ainu-org.jp; f. 2012; advocates equal rights for indigenous people; Pres. SHIRO KAYANO; Gen. Sec. HIROYUKI NOMOTO.

Democratic Party of Japan (DPJ): 1-11-1, Nagata-cho, Chiyoda-ku, Tokyo 100-0014; tel. (3) 3595-9988; fax (3) 3595-7318; e-mail dpjenews@dpj.or.jp; internet www.dpj.or.jp; f. 1998; est. by the integration into the original DPJ (f. 1996) of the Democratic Reform League, Minseito and Shinto Yuai; advocates a cabinet formed and controlled by the people; absorbed Party Sakigake in 2001; absorbed Liberal Party in 2003; Pres. KATSUYA OKADA; Sec.-Gen. AKIHIRO OHATA.

Japan Innovation Party (Ishin no To): 2-9-6 Nagata-cho, Chiyoda-ku, Tokyo 100-0014; internet ishinnotoh.jp; f. 2014; merger between the Japanese Restoration Party and the Unity Party; Leader KENJI EDA; Sec.-Gen YORIHISA MATSUNO.

Japanese Communist Party (JCP): 4-26-7, Sendagaya, Shibuya-ku, Tokyo 151-8586; tel. (3) 3403-6111; fax (3) 5474-8358; e-mail info@jcp.or.jp; internet www.jcp.or.jp; f. 1922; 305,000 mems (2015); Chair. of Exec. Cttee KAZUO SHII; Sec.-Gen. YOSHIKI YAMASHITA.

Liberal Democratic Party (LDP) (Jiyu-Minshuto): 1 11-23, Nagata-cho, Chiyoda-ku, Tokyo 100-8910; tel. (3) 3581-6211; fax (3) 5511-8855; e-mail koho@ldp.jimin.or.jp; internet www.jimin.jp; f. 1955; advocates establishment of a welfare state, promotion of industrial devt, improvement of educational and cultural facilities, and constitutional reform as needed; absorbed New Conservative Party in 2003; Pres. SHINZO ABE; Sec.-Gen. SADAKAZU TANIGAKI.

New Komeito: 17, Minami-Motomachi, Shinjuku-ku, Tokyo 160-0012; tel. (3) 3353-0111; fax (3) 3225-0207; internet www.komei.or.jp; f. 1964; est. as Komeito; renamed Komei in 1994 following defection of some mems to the New Frontier Party (Shinshinto, dissolved in 1997); absorbed Reimei Club in 1998; renamed as above in 1998 following merger of Komei and Shinto Heiwa; advocates political moderation, humanism and globalism; 400,000 mems (2003); Pres. NATSUO YAMAGUCHI; Sec.-Gen. YOSHIHISA INOUE.

New Party Daichi (Shinto Daichi): 2-9-6 Nagata-cho, Chiyoda-ku, Tokyo 100-0014; tel. (3) 3593-0171; fax (11) 3593-0276; internet www.muneo.gr.jp; f. 2005; regional grouping based in Hokkaido; Leader MUNEO SUZUKI.

New Party Nippon (Shinto Nippon): 1-7-11, Hirakawa-cho, Chiyoda-ku, Tokyo 102-0093; tel. (3) 5213-0333; fax (3) 5213-0888; e-mail goiken@nippon-dream.com; internet www.nippon-dream.com; f. 2005; founding mems included LDP rebels opposed to postal reform proposals of Prime Minister Koizumi; Leader YASUO TANAKA.

New Renaissance Party (Shinto Kaikaku): 2-8-15, Akasaka, Minato-ku, Tokyo; tel. (3) 6277-8105; fax (3) 6277-8115; internet shintokaikaku.jp; f. 2010; conservative grouping; Pres. YOICHI MASUZOE; Sec.-Gen. HIROYUKI ARAI.

New Socialist Party: Miyako Sakura Kosan Bldg, 3/F, 7-9, Nihon-bashi Tomizawa-cho, Chuo-ku, Tokyo; tel. (3) 5643-6002; fax (3) 3639-0150; e-mail honbu@sinsyakai.or.jp; internet www.sinsyakai.or.jp; f. 1996; est. by left-wing defectors from SDPJ; opposed to US military bases on Okinawa and introduction in 1996 of new electoral system; seeks to establish an ecological socio-economic system; Pres. MATSUEDA YOSHIHIRO; Sec.-Gen. OSANAMI HIROKUNI.

Party for Future Generations (PFG): 1 Chome II 28, Nagatacho, Chiyoda-ku, Tokyo; tel. (3) 3595-3555; fax (3) 3595-3357; internet jisedai.jp; f. 2014; grouping led by Shintaro Ishihara split from the former Japan Restoration Party prior to its merger with the Unity Party to form the Japan Innovation Party; Pres. TAKEO HIRANUMA; Sec.-Gen. NARIAKI NAKAYAMA.

People's Life Party (Seikatsu No To): SR Bldg, 3/F, 2-12-8, Nagata-cho, Chiyoda-ku, Tokyo 100-0014; tel. (3) 5501-2200; fax (3) 5501-2202; internet www.seikatsu1.jp; f. 2012 following a split in the Tomorrow Party of Japan; Leader ICHIRO OZAWA; Sec.-Gen. KATSUMASA SUZUKI.

Social Democratic Party of Japan (SDPJ) (Shakai Minshuto): 2-4-3, Nagata-cho, Chiyoda-ku, Tokyo 100-0014; tel. (3) 3580-1171; fax (3) 3580-0691; e-mail kokusai@sdp.or.jp; internet www.sdp.or.jp; f. 1945; est. as Japan Socialist Party (JSP); adopted present name in

1996; seeks the establishment of collective non-aggression and a mutual security system incl. Japan, the USA, the People's Republic of China and the Commonwealth of Independent States; Chair. YOSHIDA TADASHI SATOSHI; Sec.-Gen. SEIJI MATAICHI.

Tomorrow Party of Japan (Nippon Mirai No To): SR Bldg, 3/F, 2-12-8 Nagata-cho, Chiyoda-ku, Tokyo; fax (3) 6701-7018; e-mail info@nippon-mirai.jp; internet www.nippon-mirai.jp; f. 2012; advocates a 10-year plan for the complete elimination of nuclear power; Pres. TOMOKO ABE; Sec.-Gen. TETSUNARI IIDA.

Diplomatic Representation

EMBASSIES IN JAPAN

Afghanistan: 2-2-1, Azabudai, Minato-ku, Tokyo 106-0041; tel. (3) 5574-7611; fax (3) 5574-0195; e-mail public.relations@afghanembassyjp.org; internet www.afghanembassyjp.org; Ambassador SAYED M. AMIN FATIMIE.

Albania: Hokkoku Shimbun Bldg, 4/F, 6-4-8, Tsukiji, Chuo-ku, Tokyo 104-0045; tel. (3) 3543-6861; fax (3) 3543-6862; e-mail embassy.tokyo@mfa.gov.al; internet www.ambasadat.gov.al/japan; Ambassador BUJAR DIDA.

Algeria: 2-10-67, Mita, Meguro-ku, Tokyo 153-0062; tel. (3) 3711-2661; fax (3) 3710-6534; internet www.algerianembassy-japan.jp; Ambassador SID ALI KETRANDJI.

Angola: 2-10-24, Daizawa, Setagaya-ku, Tokyo 155-0032; tel. (3) 5430-7879; fax (3) 5712-7482; e-mail md-japan@angola.or.jp; internet www.angola.or.jp; Ambassador JOÃO MIGUEL VAHEKENI.

Argentina: 2-14-14, Moto-Azabu, Minato-ku, Tokyo 106-0046; tel. (3) 5420-7101; fax (3) 5420-7109; e-mail ejapo@mrecic.gov.ar; internet www.ejapo.mrecic.gov.ar; Ambassador RAÚL GUILLERMO DEJEAN RODRÍGUEZ.

Australia: 2-1-14, Mita, Minato-ku, Tokyo 108-8361; tel. (3) 5232-4111; fax (3) 5232-4149; internet www.australia.or.jp; Ambassador BRUCE MILLER.

Austria: 1-1-20, Moto-Azabu, Minato-ku, Tokyo 106-0046; tel. (3) 3451-8281; fax (3) 3451-8283; e-mail tokio-ob@bmeia.gv.at; internet www.bmeia.gv.at/tokio; Ambassador Dr BERNHARD ZIMBURG.

Azerbaijan: 1-19-15, Higashi-Gaoka, Meguro-ku, Tokyo 152-0021; tel. (3) 5486-4744; fax (3) 5486-7374; e-mail info@azembassy.jp; internet www.azembassy.jp; Ambassador GURSEL ISMAYILZADA.

Bahrain: Residence Viscountess 720 & 520, 1-11-36, Akasaka, Minato-ku, Tokyo 107-0052; tel. (3) 3584-8001; fax (3) 3584-8004; e-mail general@bahrain-embassy.or.jp; internet www.bahrain-embassy.or.jp; Ambassador Dr KHALIL HASSAN.

Bangladesh: 4-15-15, Meguro, Meguro-ku, Tokyo 153-0063; tel. (3) 5704-0216; fax (3) 5704-1696; e-mail bdembjp@yahoo.com; internet www.bdembassy.jp; Ambassador MASUD BIN MOMEN.

Belarus: Shirogane K House, 4-14-12, Shirogane, Minato-ku, Tokyo 108-0072; tel. (3) 3448-1623; fax (3) 3448-1624; e-mail japan@mfa.gov.by; internet japan.mfa.gov.by; Ambassador SYARHEY RAKHMANOV KIMOVICH.

Belgium: 5-4, Niban-cho, Chiyoda-ku, Tokyo 102-0084; tel. (3) 3262-0191; fax (3) 3262-0651; e-mail tokyo@diplobel.fed.be; internet countries.diplomatie.belgium.be/en/japan; Ambassador LUC LIEBAUT.

Benin: Asahi Bldg, 4/F, 1-2-2, Hirakawa-cho, Chiyoda-ku, Tokyo 102-0093; tel. (3) 5229-7232; fax (3) 5229-2838; e-mail abenintyo@beninembassy.jp; internet www.beninembassy.jp; Ambassador RUFIN ZOMAHOUN.

Bolivia: No. 38 Kowa Bldg, Rm 804, 4-12-24, Nishi-Azabu, Minato-ku, Tokyo 106-0031; tel. (3) 3499-5441; fax (3) 3499-5443; e-mail emboltk1@ad.il24.net; Ambassador ERICK M. SAAVEDRA.

Bosnia and Herzegovina: 2–3/F, 5-3-29, Minami-Azabu, Minato-ku, Tokyo 106-0047; tel. (3) 5422-8231; fax (3) 5422-8232; e-mail bih8emb@gol.com; Ambassador ANESA KUNDUROVIĆ.

Botswana: Kearny Place, 6/F, 4-5-10, Shiba, Minato-ku, Tokyo 108-0014; tel. (3) 5440-5676; fax (3) 5765-7581; e-mail botjap@sepia.ocn.ne.jp; internet www.botswanaembassy.or.jp; Ambassador JACOB DICKIE NKATE.

Brazil: 2-11-12, Kita-Aoyama, Minato-ku, Tokyo 107-8633; tel. (3) 3404-5211; fax (3) 3405-5846; e-mail webmaster@brasemb.or.jp; internet www.brasemb.or.jp; Ambassador ANDRÉ CORRÊA DO LAGO.

Brunei: 6-5-2, Kita-Shinagawa, Shinagawa-ku, Tokyo 141-0001; tel. (3) 3447-7997; fax (3) 3447-9260; e-mail contact@bruemb.jp; internet www.bruemb.jp; Ambassador Haji MAHAMUD Haji AHMAD.

Bulgaria: 5-36-3, Yoyogi, Shibuya-ku, Tokyo 151-0053; tel. (3) 3465-1021; fax (3) 3465-1031; e-mail embassy.tokyo@mfa.bg; internet www.mfa.bg/embassies/japan; Ambassador GEORGI VASSILEV.

Burkina Faso: 2-14-34, Moto Azabu, Minato-ku, Tokyo 106-0046; tel. (3) 3444-2660; fax (3) 3444-2661; e-mail faso-amb@khaki.plala.or.jp; Ambassador FRANÇOIS OUBIDA.

Cambodia: 8-6-9, Akasaka, Minato-ku, Tokyo 107-0052; tel. (3) 5412-8521; fax (3) 5412-8526; e-mail camembassyjp@gmail.com; internet www.cambodianembassy.jp; Ambassador HOR MONIRATH.

Cameroon: 3-27-16, Nozawa, Setagaya-ku, Tokyo 154-0003; tel. (3) 5430-4985; fax (3) 5430-6489; e-mail ambacamtokyo@gol.com; Ambassador Dr PIERRE NDZENGUE.

Canada: 7-3-38, Akasaka, Minato-ku, Tokyo 107-8503; tel. (3) 5412-6200; fax (3) 5412-6249; e-mail tokyo.admin@international.gc.ca; internet www.canadainternational.gc.ca/japan-japon; Ambassador MACKENZIE CLUGSTON.

Chile: Nihon Seimei Akabanebashi Bldg, 8/F, 3-1-14, Shiba, Minato-ku, Tokyo 105-0014; tel. (3) 3452-7561; fax (3) 3452-4457; e-mail echile.japon@minrel.gov.cl; internet chileabroad.gov.cl/japon; Ambassador PATRICIO TORRES.

China, People's Republic: 3-4-33, Moto-Azabu, Minato-ku, Tokyo 106-0046; tel. (3) 3403-3380; fax (3) 3403-3345; e-mail info@china-embassy.or.jp; internet www.china-embassy.or.jp; Ambassador CHENG YONGHUA.

Colombia: 3-10-53, Kami Osaki, Shinagawa-ku, Tokyo 141-0021; tel. (3) 3440-6451; fax (3) 3440-6724; e-mail embajada@emcoltokyo.or.jp; internet www.embassyin.jp/colombia; Ambassador ROBERTO VELEZ VALLEJO.

Congo, Democratic Republic: 1–2/F, 5-8-5, Asakusabashi, Taito-ku, Tokyo 111-0053; tel. (3) 5820-1580; fax (3) 3423-3984; e-mail drctokyo@ambardcongo.com; Chargé d'affaires a.i. RAPHAEL MWENDA BAMBINGANILA.

Costa Rica: No. 38 Kowa Bldg, Rm 901, 4-12-24, Nishi-Azabu, Minato-ku, Tokyo 106-0031; tel. (3) 3486-1812; fax (3) 3486-1813; Chargé d'affaires a.i. LILLIAM RODRIGUEZ JIMENEZ.

Côte d'Ivoire: 2-19-12, Uehara, Shibuya-ku, Tokyo 151-0064; tel. (3) 5454-1401; fax (3) 5454-1405; e-mail ambacijn@yahoo.fr; internet www.ahibo.com/ambaci-jp; Ambassador JÉRÔME KLÔH WEYA.

Croatia: 3-3-10, Hiroo, Shibuya-ku, Tokyo 150-0012; tel. (3) 5469-3014; fax (3) 5469-3015; e-mail croemb.tokyo@mvep.hr; Ambassador MIRA MARTINEC.

Cuba: 1-28-4, Higashi-Azabu, Minato-ku, Tokyo 106-0044; tel. (3) 5570-3182; fax (3) 5570-8566; e-mail embajada@ecujapon.jp; internet www.cubadiplomatica.cu/japon/EN/Mission/Embassy.aspx; Ambassador MARCOS RODRÍGUEZ COSTA.

Czech Republic: 2-16-14, Hiroo, Shibuya-ku, Tokyo 150-0012; tel. (3) 3400-8122; fax (3) 3400-8124; e-mail tokyo@embassy.mzv.cz; internet www.mzv.cz/tokyo; Ambassador TOMÁŠ DUB.

Denmark: 29-6, Sarugaku-cho, Shibuya-ku, Tokyo 150-0033; tel. (3) 3496-3001; fax (3) 3496-3440; e-mail tyoamb@um.dk; internet japan.um.dk; Ambassador A. CARSTEN DAMSGAARD.

Djibouti: 5-18-10, Shimo Meguro, Meguro-ku, Tokyo 153-0064; tel. (3) 5704-0682; fax (3) 5725-8305; e-mail djibouti@fine.ocn.jp; internet www.djiboutiembassy.jp; Ambassador AHMED ARAITA ALI.

Dominican Republic: No. 38 Kowa Bldg, Rm 904, 4-12-24, Nishi-Azabu, Minato-ku, Tokyo 106-0031; tel. (3) 3499-6020; fax (3) 3499-2627; Ambassador HECTOR PAULINO DOMINGUEZ RODRIGUEZ.

Ecuador: No. 38 Kowa Bldg, Rm 806, 4-12-24, Nishi-Azabu, Minato-ku, Tokyo 106-0031; tel. (3) 3499-2800; fax (3) 3499-4400; e-mail info@ecuador-embassy.or.jp; internet www.ecuador-embassy.or.jp; Ambassador LEONARDO CARRIÓN EGUIGUREN.

Egypt: 1-5-4, Aobadai, Meguro-ku, Tokyo 153-0042; tel. (3) 3770-8022; fax (3) 3770-8021; e-mail egyptemb@leaf.ocn.ne.jp; internet www.mfa.gov.eg/Tokyo_Emb; Ambassador ISMAIL KHAIRAT.

El Salvador: No. 38 Kowa Bldg, 8/F, 4-12-24, Nishi-Azabu, Minato-ku, Tokyo 106-0031; tel. (3) 3499-4461; fax (3) 3486-7022; e-mail embesaltokio@gol.com; Ambassador MARTHA LIDIA ZELAYANDÍA CISNEROS.

Eritrea: Shirokanedai ST Bldg, Rm 401, 4-7-4, Shirokanedai, Minato-ku, Tokyo, 108-0071; tel. (3) 5791-1815; fax (3) 5791-1816; e-mail info@eritreaembassy-japan.org; internet www.eritreaembassy-japan.org; Ambassador ESTIFANOS AFEWORKI.

Estonia: 2-6-15, Jingu-mae, Shibuya-ku, Tokyo 150-0001; tel. (3) 5412-7281; fax (3) 5412-7282; e-mail embassy.tokyo@mfa.ee; internet www.estemb.or.jp; Ambassador JAAK LENSMENT.

Ethiopia: Takanawa Kaisei Bldg, 2/F, 3-4-1, Takanawa, Minato-ku, Tokyo 108-0074; tel. (3) 5420-6860; fax (3) 5420-6866; e-mail info@ethiopia-emb.or.jp; internet www.ethiopia-emb.or.jp; Ambassador MARKOS TEKLE RIKE.

Fiji: Noa Bldg, 14/F, 2-3-5, Azabudai, Minato-ku, Tokyo 106-0041; tel. (3) 3587-2038; fax (3) 3587-2563; e-mail info@fijiembassy.jp; internet www.fijiembassy.jp; Ambassador ISIKELI MATAITOGA.

Finland: 3-5-39, Minami-Azabu, Minato-ku, Tokyo 106-8561; tel. (3) 5447-6000; fax (3) 5447-6042; e-mail sanomat.tok@formin.fi; internet www.finland.or.jp; Ambassador MANU VIRTAMO.

France: 4-11-44, Minami-Azabu, Minato-ku, Tokyo 106-8514; tel. (3) 5798-6000; fax (3) 5798-6328; e-mail ambafrance.tokyo@diplomatie.fr; internet www.ambafrance-jp.org; Ambassador THIERRY DANA.

Gabon: 1-34-11, Higashi-Gaoka, Meguro-ku, Tokyo 152-0021; tel. (3) 5430-9171; fax (3) 5430-9175; e-mail info@gabonembassyjapan.org; internet www.gabonembassyjapan.org; Ambassador FRANÇOIS PENDJET BOMBILA.

Georgia: Residence Viscountess 220, 1-11-36, Akasaka, Minato-ku, Tokyo 107-0052; tel. (3) 5575-6091; fax (3) 5575-9133; e-mail tokio.emb@mfa.gov.ge; internet japan.mfa.gov.ge; Ambassador LEVAN TSINTSADZE.

Germany: 4-5-10, Minami-Azabu, Minato-ku, Tokyo 106-0047; tel. (3) 5791-7700; fax (3) 5791-7773; e-mail info@tokyo.diplo.de; internet www.tokyo.diplo.de; Ambassador Dr HANS CARL VON WERTHERN.

Ghana: 1-5-21, Nishi-Azabu, Minato-ku, Tokyo 106-0031; tel. (3) 5410-8631; fax (3) 5410-8635; e-mail mission@ghanaembassy.or.jp; internet www.ghanaembassy.or.jp; Ambassador SYLVESTER PARKER-ALOTTEY.

Greece: 3-16-30, Nishi-Azabu, Minato-ku, Tokyo 106-0031; tel. (3) 3403-0871; fax (3) 3402-4642; e-mail gremb.tok@mfa.gr; internet www.mfa.gr/tokyo; Ambassador LOUKAS KARATSOLIS.

Guatemala: No. 38 Kowa Bldg, Rm 905, 4-12-24, Nishi-Azabu, Minato-ku, Tokyo 106-0031; tel. (3) 3400-1830; fax (3) 3400-1820; e-mail embguate@minex.gob.gt; internet www.embassy-avenue.jp/guatemala; Ambassador BYRON RENE ESCOBEDO MENÉNDEZ.

Guinea: 12-9, Hachiyama-cho, Shibuya-ku, Tokyo 150-0035; tel. (3) 3770-4640; fax (3) 3770-4643; e-mail ambagui-tokyo@gol.com; Ambassador SENKOUN SYLLA.

Haiti: No. 38 Kowa Bldg, Rm 906, 4-12-24, Nishi-Azabu, Minato-ku, Tokyo 106-0031; tel. (3) 3486-7096; fax (3) 3486-7070; e-mail amb.japon@diplomatie.ht; Chargé d'affaires a.i. JUDITH EXAVIER.

Holy See: Apostolic Nunciature, 9-2, Sanban-cho, Chiyoda-ku, Tokyo 102-0075; tel. (3) 3263-6851; fax (3) 3263-6060; Apostolic Nuncio Most Rev. JOSEPH CHENNOTH (Titular Archbishop of Milevum).

Honduras: No. 38 Kowa Bldg, Rm 802, 4-12-24, Nishi-Azabu, Minato-ku, Tokyo 106-0031; tel. (3) 3409-1150; fax (3) 3409-0305; e-mail honduras@interlink.or.jp, Ambassador MARLENE VILLELA.

Hungary: 2-17-14, Mita, Minato-ku, Tokyo 108-0073; tel. (3) 3798-8801; fax (3) 3798-8812; e-mail mission.tio@mfa.gov.hu; internet www.mfa.gov.hu/kulkepviselet/JP/HU; Ambassador Dr ISTVÁN SZERDAHELYI.

Iceland: 4-18-26, Takanawa, Minato-ku, Tokyo 108-0074; tel. (3) 3447-1944; fax (3) 3447-1945; e-mail icemb.tokyo@utn.stjr.is; internet www.iceland.is/jp; Ambassador HANNES HEIMISSON.

India: 2-2-11, Kudan-Minami, Chiyoda-ku, Tokyo 102-0074; tel. (3) 3262-2391; fax (3) 3234-4866; e-mail embassy@indembjp.org; internet www.embassyofindiajapan.org; Ambassador DEEPA GOPALAN WADHWA.

Indonesia: 5-2-9, Higashi-Gotanda, Shinagawa-ku, Tokyo 141-0022; tel. (3) 3441-4201; fax (3) 3447-1697; e-mail info@indonesianembassy.jp; internet kbritokyo.jp; Ambassador YUSRON IHZA MAHENDRA.

Iran: 3-13-9, Minami-Azabu, Minato-ku, Tokyo 106-0047; tel. (3) 3446-8011; fax (3) 3446-9002; e-mail info@iranembassyjp.org; internet www.tokyo.mfa.ir; Ambassador Dr REZA NAZARAHARI.

Iraq: 14-6 Kamiyama-cho, Shibuya-ku, Tokyo 150-0047; tel. (3) 5790-5311; fax (3) 5790-5315; e-mail embassy@iraqi-japan.com; internet www.iraqi-japan.com; Ambassador ALAA ABDUL MAJID AL-HASHIMY.

Ireland: Ireland House, 2-10-7, Kojimachi, Chiyoda-ku, Tokyo 102-0083; tel. (3) 3263-0695; fax (3) 3265-2275; e-mail tokyoembassy@dfa.ie; internet www.irishembassy.jp; Ambassador ANNE BARRINGTON.

Israel: 3, Niban-cho, Chiyoda-ku, Tokyo 102-0084; tel. (3) 3264-0911; fax (3) 3264-0791; e-mail consular@tokyo.mfa.gov.il; internet tokyo.mfa.gov.il; Ambassador RUTH KAHANOFF.

Italy: 2-5-4, Mita, Minato-ku, Tokyo 108-8302; tel. (3) 3453-5291; fax (3) 3456-2319; e-mail ambasciata.tokyo@esteri.it; internet www.ambtokyo.esteri.it/ambasciata_tokyo; Ambassador DOMENICO GIORGI.

Jamaica: Toranomon Yatsuka Bldg, 2/F, 1-1-11, Atago, Minato-ku, Tokyo 105-0002; tel. (3) 3435-1861; fax (3) 3435-1864; e-mail mail@jamaicaemb.jp; internet www.jamaicaemb.jp; Ambassador RICARDO ALLICOCK.

Jordan: 39-8, Kamiyama-cho, Shibuya-ku, Tokyo 100-0014; tel. (3) 5478-7177; fax (3) 5478-0032; e-mail jor-emb@bird.ocn.ne.jp; Ambassador DEMIYE ZUHER HADDAD.

Kazakhstan: 1-8-14, Azabudai, Minato-ku, Tokyo 106-0041; tel. (3) 3589-1821; fax (3) 3589-1822; e-mail japan@mfa.kz; internet www.embkazjp.org; Ambassador AKYLBEK KAMALDINOV.

Kenya: 3-24-3, Yakumo, Meguro-ku, Tokyo 152-0023; tel. (3) 3723-4006; fax (3) 3723-4488; e-mail general@kenyarep-jp.com; internet www.kenyarep-jp.com; Ambassador SOLOMON KARANJA MAINA.

Korea, Republic: 1-2-5, Minami-Azabu, Minato-ku, Tokyo 106-0047; tel. (3) 3452-7611; fax (3) 5232-6911; e-mail information_jp@mofat.go.kr; internet jpn-tokyo.mofat.go.kr; Ambassador YOO HEUNG SOO.

Kosovo: M.G. Atago Bldg, 10/F, 3-13-7, Nishi-Shinbashi, Minato-ku, Tokyo 105-0003; tel. (3) 6809-2577; fax (3) 6809-2579; e-mail embassy.japan@rks-gov.net; internet www.ambasada-ks.net/jp; Ambassador AHMET SHALA.

Kuwait: 4-13-12, Mita, Minato-ku, Tokyo 108-0073; tel. (3) 3455-0361; fax (3) 3456-6290; e-mail consular@kuwait-embassy.or.jp; internet kuwait-embassy.or.jp; Ambassador Sheikh ABDUL RAHMAN AL-OTAIBI.

Kyrgyzstan: 5-6-16, Shimomeguro, Meguro-ku, Tokyo 153-0064; tel. (3) 3719-0828; fax (3) 3719-0868; e-mail office@kyrgyzemb.jp; Ambassador RYSBEK MOLDOGAZIEV.

Laos: 3-3-22, Nishi-Azabu, Minato-ku, Tokyo 106-0031; tel. (3) 5411-2291; fax (3) 5411-2293; Ambassador KHENTHONG NUANTHASING.

Latvia: 37-11, Kamiyama-cho, Shibuya-ku, Tokyo 150-0047; tel. (3) 3467-6888; fax (3) 3467-6897; e-mail embassy.japan@mfa.gov.lv; Ambassador NORMANS PENKE.

Lebanon: Residence Viscountess 410, 1-11-36, Akasaka, Minato-ku, Tokyo 107-0052; tel. (3) 5114-9950; fax (3) 5114-9952; e-mail ambaliba@cropos.ocp.ne.jp; Chargé d'affaires a.i. IMAN YOUNES.

Lesotho: U & M Akasaka Bldg, 3/F, 7-5-47, Akasaka, Minato-ku, Tokyo 107-0052; tel. (3) 3584-7455; fax (3) 3584-7456; e-mail bochabela@lesothotokyo.org; internet www.lesothotokyo.org; Ambassador RICHARD RAMOELETSI.

Liberia: Moto-Azabu Kokusai Mansion 201, 3-2-13, Moto-Azabu, Minato-ku, Tokyo 106-0046; tel. (3) 3479-9882; fax (3) 3479-9883; e-mail embassyofliberia@heart.ocn.ne.jp; internet www.liberianembassyjp.org; Ambassador YOUNGOR SEVELEE TELEWODA.

Libya: 10-14, Daikanyama-cho, Shibuya-ku, Tokyo 150-0034; tel. (3) 3477-0701; fax (3) 3464-0420; internet www.lytokyo.org; Ambassador AHMED ABDEL KARIM SALEM OWN.

Lithuania: 3-7-18, Moto-Azabu, Minato-ku, Tokyo 106-0046; tel. (3) 3408-5091; fax (3) 3408-5092; e-mail amb.jp@mfa.lt; internet jp.mfa.lt; Ambassador EGIDIJUS MEILUNAS.

Luxembourg: Luxembourg House, 1/F, 8–9, Yonban-cho, Chiyoda-ku, 102-0081; tel. (3) 3265-9621; fax (3) 3265-9624; e-mail infotokyo.amb@mae.etat.lu; internet tokyo.mae.lu; Ambassador BÉATRICE KIRSCH.

Madagascar: 2-3-23, Moto-Azabu, Minato-ku, Tokyo 106-0046; tel. (3) 3446-7252; fax (3) 3446-7078; e-mail ambtyo@r5.dion.ne.jp; internet www.madagascar-embassy.jp; Chargé d'affaires a.i. EUGÈNE MAHAONISON.

Malawi: Takanawa-Kaisei Bldg, 7/F, 3-4-1, Takanawa, Minato-ku, Tokyo 108-0074; tel. (3) 3449-3010; fax (3) 3449-3220; e-mail malawi@luck.ocn.ne.jp; internet www.malawiembassy.org; Ambassador RUEBEN NGWENYA.

Malaysia: 20-16, Nanpeidai-cho, Shibuya-ku, Tokyo 150-0036; tel. (3) 3476-3840; fax (3) 3476-4971; e-mail maltokyo@kln.gov.my; internet www.kln.gov.my/web/jpn_tokyo; Ambassador Datuk AHMAD IZLAN IDRIS.

Maldives: Iikura IT Bldg, 8/F, 1-9-10, Azabudai, Minato-ku, Tokyo 106-0041; tel. (3) 6234-4315; fax (3) 6234-4316; e-mail info@maldivesembassy.jp; internet www.maldivesembassy.jp; Ambassador AHMED KHALEEL.

Mali: 3-12-9, Kami-Osaki, Shinagawa-ku, Tokyo 141-0021; tel. (3) 5447-6881; fax (3) 5447-6882; e-mail info@ambamali-jp.org; internet www.ambamali-jp.org; Ambassador MAHAMANE BANIA TOURÉ.

Marshall Islands: Meiji Park Heights, 1/F, Rm 101, 9-9, Minami-Motomachi, Shinjuku-ku, Tokyo 106-0012; tel. (3) 5379-1701; fax (3) 5379-1810; e-mail alfred@rmiembassyjp.org; Ambassador TOM D. KIJINER.

Mauritania: 5-17-5, Kita-Shinagawa, Shinagawa-ku, Tokyo 141-0001; tel. (3) 3449-3810; fax (3) 3449-3822; e-mail ambarim@seagreen.ocn.ne.jp; internet www.amba-mauritania.jp; Ambassador YAHYA NGAM.

Mexico: 2-15-1, Nagata-cho, Chiyoda-ku, Tokyo 100-0014; tel. (3) 3581-1131; fax (3) 3581-4058; e-mail infojpn@sre.gob.mx; internet embamex.sre.gob.mx/japon; Chargé d'affaires a.i. ARMANDO ARRIAGA OCHOATEGUI.

Micronesia, Federated States: Reinanzaka Bldg, 2/F, 1-14-2, Akasaka, Minato-ku, Tokyo 107-0052; tel. (3) 3585-5456; fax (3) 3585-5348; e-mail fsmemb@fsmemb.or.jp; Ambassador JOHN FRITZ.

Mongolia: Pine Crest Mansion, 21-4, Kamiyama-cho, Shibuya-ku, Tokyo 150-0047; tel. (3) 3469-2088; fax (3) 3469-2216; e-mail embmong@gol.com; Ambassador SODOVJAMTSYN KHÜRELBAATAR.

Morocco: 5-4-30, Minami-Aoyama, Minato-ku, Tokyo 107-0062; tel. (3) 5485-7171; fax (3) 5485-7173; e-mail sifamato@circus.ocn.ne.jp; internet www.morocco-emba.jp; Ambassador Dr SAMIR ARROUR.

Mozambique: Shiba Amerex Bldg, 6/F, 3-12-17 Mita, Minato-ku, Tokyo 108-0073; tel. (3) 5419-0973; fax (3) 5442-0556; e-mail moz.tokyo@embamoc.jp; internet www.embamoc.jp; Ambassador BELMIRO JOSÉ MALATE.

Myanmar: 4-8-26, Kita-Shinagawa, Shinagawa-ku, Tokyo 140-0001; tel. (3) 3441-9291; fax (3) 3447-7394; e-mail contact@myanmar-embassy-tokyo.net; internet www.myanmar-embassy-tokyo.net; Ambassador KHIN MAUNG TING.

Namibia: AMEREX Bldg, 3-5-7, Azabudai, Minato-ku, Tokyo 106-0041; tel. (3) 6426-5460; fax (3) 6426-5461; e-mail embassy@namibiatokyo.or.jp; Ambassador SOPHIA NANGOMBE.

Nepal: Fukukawa House B, 6-20-28, Shimomeguro, Meguro-ku, Tokyo.153-0064; tel. (3) 3713-6241; e-mail nepembjp@big.or.jp; internet www.nepal-embassy.org; Ambassador Dr MADAN KUMAR BHATTARAI.

Netherlands: 3-6-3, Shiba Koen, Minato-ku, Tokyo 105-0011; tel. (3) 5776-5400; fax (3) 5776-5535; e-mail osa@minbuza.nl; internet japan.nlambassade.org; Ambassador RADINCK JAN VAN VOLLENHOVEN.

New Zealand: 20-40, Kamiyama-cho, Shibuya-ku, Tokyo 150-0047; tel. (3) 3467-2271; fax (3) 3467-2278; e-mail tky@mfat.govt.nz; internet www.nzembassy.com/japan; Ambassador MARK SINCLAIR.

Nicaragua: No. 38 Kowa Bldg, Rm 903, 4-12-24, Nishi-Azabu, Minato-ku, Tokyo 106-0031; tel. (3) 3499-0400; fax (3) 3710-2028; e-mail nicjapan@gol.com; Ambassador SAÚL ARANA CASTELLÓN.

Nigeria: 3-6-1 Toranomon, Minato-ku, Tokyo 105-0001; tel. (3) 5425-8011; fax (3) 5425-8016; e-mail info@nigeriaembassy.jp; internet www.nigeriaembassy.jp; Ambassador GODWIN NSUDE AGBO.

Norway: 5-12-2, Minami-Azabu, Minato-ku, Tokyo 106-0047; tel. (3) 6408-8100; fax (3) 6408-8199; e-mail emb.tokyo@mfa.no; internet www.norway.or.jp; Ambassador ERLING RIMESTAD.

Oman: 4-2-17, Hiroo, Shibuya-ku, Tokyo 150-0012; tel. (3) 5468-1088; e-mail info@omanembassy.jp; internet omanembassy.jp; Ambassador KHALID BIN HASHIL BIN MOHAMMED AL-MUSLAHI.

Pakistan: 4-6-17, Minami-Azabu, Minato-ku, Tokyo 106-0047; tel. (3) 5421-7741; fax (3) 5421-3610; e-mail info@pakistanembassyjapan.com; internet www.pakistanembassyjapan.com; Ambassador FARRUKH AMIL.

Palau: 1-2–201, Katamachi, Shinjuku-ku, Tokyo 160-0001; tel. (3) 3354-5353; fax (3) 3354–5200; fax tyopalau@maple.ocn.ne.jp; Ambassador FRANCIS MATSUTARO.

Panama: No. 38 Kowa Bldg, Rm 902, 4-12-24, Nishi-Azabu, Minato-ku, Tokyo 106-0031; tel. (3) 3499-3741; fax (3) 5485-3548; e-mail panaemb@gol.com; internet www.embassyofpanamainjapan.org; Ambassador RITTER NOBEL DIAZ GOMEZ.

Papua New Guinea: 5-32-20, Shimo Meguro, Meguro-ku, Tokyo 153-0064; tel. (3) 3454-7801; fax (3) 3454-7275; e-mail png-tyo@nifty.ne.jp; Ambassador GABRIEL DUSAVA.

Paraguay: Ichibancho TG Bldg 2, 7/F, 2-2, Ichiban-cho, Chiyoda-ku, Tokyo 102-0082; tel. (3) 3265-5271; fax (3) 3265-5273; e-mail embajada-consulado@embapar.jp; internet www.embapar.jp; Ambassador NAOYUKI TOYOTOSHI.

Peru: 2-3-1, Hiroo, Shibuya-ku, Tokyo 150-0012; tel. (3) 3406-4243; fax (3) 3409-7589; e-mail embperutokyo@embperujapan.org; internet www.embajadadelperuenjapon.org; Ambassador ELARD ALBERTO ESCALA SÁNCHEZ-BARRETO.

Philippines: 5-15-5, Roppongi, Minato-ku, Tokyo 106-8537; tel. (3) 5562-1600; fax (3) 5562-1603; e-mail info@philembassy.net; internet tokyo.philembassy.net; Ambassador MANUEL M. LOPEZ.

Poland: 2-13-5, Mita, Meguro-ku, Tokyo 153-0062; tel. (3) 5794-7020; fax (3) 5794-7024; e-mail tokio.amb.sekretariat@msz.gov.pl; internet www.tokio.polemb.net; Ambassador CYRYL KOZACZEWSKI.

Portugal: Kamiura-Kojimachi Bldg, 5/F, 3-10-3, Kojimachi, Chiyoda-ku, Tokyo 102-0083; tel. (3) 5212-7322; fax (3) 5226-0616; e-mail portugal@embportjp.org; internet www.embaixadade portugal.jp; Ambassador FRANCISCO XAVIER ESTEVES.

Qatar: 2-3-28, Moto-Azabu, Minato-ku, Tokyo 106-0046; tel. (3) 5475-0611; fax (3) 5475-0617; e-mail tokyo@mofa.gov.qa; Ambassador YOUSUF MOHAMED BILAL.

Romania: 3-16-19, Nishi-Azabu, Minato-ku, Tokyo 106-0031; tel. (3) 3479-0311; fax (3) 3479-0312; e-mail office@ambrom.jp; internet tokyo.mae.ro; Ambassador RADU SERBAN.

Russian Federation: 2-1-1, Azabudai, Minato-ku, Tokyo 106-0041; tel. (3) 3583-4224; fax (3) 3505-0593; e-mail embassy@u01.gate01.com; internet www.russia-emb.jp; Ambassador EVGENY VLADIMIROVICH AFANASIEV.

Rwanda: Annex Fukazawa, 1-17-17, Fukazawa, Setagaya-ku, Tokyo 158-0081; tel. (3) 5752-4255; fax (3) 3703-0342; internet www.japan.embassy.gov.rw; Ambassador CHARLES MURIGANDE.

Samoa: Seiko Bldg, 3/F, 2-7-4, Irifune, Chuo-ku, Tokyo 104-0042; tel. (3) 6228-3692; fax (3) 6228–3693; e-mail samoa_tokyo@samoaembassy.jp; internet www.samoaembassy.jp; Ambassador Leiataua Tuitolova'a Dr KILIFOTI ETEUATI.

San Marino: 3-5-1, Moto-Azabu, Minato-ku, Tokyo 106-0046; tel. (3) 5414-7745; fax (3) 3405-6789; e-mail sanmarinoemb@tiscali.it; Ambassador MANLIO CADELO.

Saudi Arabia: 1-8-4, Roppongi, Minato-ku, Tokyo 106-0032; tel. (3) 3589-5241; fax (3) 3589-5200; e-mail info@saudiembassy.or.jp; internet www.saudiembassy.or.jp; Ambassador ABDULAZIZ TURKISTANI.

Senegal: 1-3-4, Aobadai, Meguro-ku, Tokyo 153-0042; tel. (3) 3464-8451; fax (3) 3464-8452; e-mail senegal@senegal.jp; Ambassador CHEIKH NIANG.

Serbia: 4-7-24, Kita-Shinagawa, Shinagawa-ku, Tokyo 140-0001; tel. (3) 3447-3571; fax (3) 3447-3573; e-mail embassy@serbianembassy.jp; internet www.tokyo.mfa.gov.rs; Ambassador NENAD GLIŠIĆ.

Singapore: 5-12-3, Roppongi, Minato-ku, Tokyo 106-0032; tel. (3) 3586-9111; fax (3) 3582-1085; e-mail singemb_tyo@sgmfa.gov.sg; internet www.mfa.gov.sg/tokyo; Ambassador CHIN SIAT YOON.

Slovakia: 2-11-33, Moto-Azabu, Minato-ku, Tokyo 106-0046; tel. (3) 3451-2200; fax (3) 3451-2244; e-mail emb.tokyo@mzv.sk; internet www.tokyo.mfa.sk; Ambassador MICHAL KOTTMAN.

Slovenia: 7-14-12, Minami-Aoyama, Minato-ku, Tokyo 107-0062; tel. (3) 5468-6275; fax (3) 5468-1182; e-mail vto@gov.si; internet tokyo.embassy.si; Ambassador HELENA DRNOVŠEK ZORKO.

South Africa: Hanzoman First Bldg, 4/F, 1-4 Kozimachi, Chiyoda-ku, Tokyo 102-0083; tel. (3) 3265-3366; fax (3) 3265-3573; e-mail cronjet@dfa.gov.za; internet www.sajapan.org; Ambassador MOHAU N. PHEKO.

Spain: 1-3-29, Roppongi, Minato-ku, Tokyo 106-0032; tel. (3) 3583-8531; fax (3) 3582-8627; e-mail emb.tokio@maec.es; internet www.exteriores.gob.es/embajadas/tokio/en; Ambassador GONZALO DE BENITO.

Sri Lanka: 2-1-54, Takanawa, Minato-ku, Tokyo 108-0074; tel. (3) 3440-6911; fax (3) 3440-6914; e-mail tokyojp@lankaembassy.jp; internet www.lankaembassy.jp; Chargé d'affaires a.i. SAJEEWA AGAMPODI UMANGA MENDIS.

Sudan: 4-7-1, Yakumo, Meguro-ku, Tokyo 152-0023; tel. (3) 5729-6170; fax (3) 5729-6171; e-mail info@sudanembassy.jp; internet www.sudanembassy.jp; Ambassador ABDELWAHAB MOHAMED AL-HIJAZI.

Sweden: 1-10-3-100, Roppongi, Minato-ku, Tokyo 106-0032; tel. (3) 5562-5050; fax (3) 5562-9095; e-mail ambassaden.tokyo@foreign.ministry.se; internet www.sweden.or.jp; Ambassador MAGNUS ROBACH.

Switzerland: 5-9-12, Minami-Azabu, Minato-ku, Tokyo 106-8589; tel. (3) 5449-8400; fax (3) 3473-6090; e-mail tok.vertretung@eda.admin.ch; internet www.eda.admin.ch/tokyo; Ambassador URS BUCHER.

Syria: Homat Jade, 6-19-45, Akasaka, Minato-ku, Tokyo 107-0052; tel. (3) 3586-8977; fax (3) 3586-8979; Chargé d'affaires a.i. WARIF HALABI.

Tajikistan: 3-5-22, Hiroo, Shibuya-ku, Tokyo 150-0012; tel. (3) 6427-2625; fax (3) 6427-2623; e-mail tajembjapan@yahoo.com; internet www.tajikistan.jp; Ambassador BOBOZODA GULOMJON JURA.

Tanzania: 4-21-9, Kami Yoga, Setagaya-ku, Tokyo 158-0098; tel. (3) 3425-4531; fax (3) 3425-7844; e-mail tzrepjp@tanzaniaembassy.or.jp; internet www.tanzaniaembassy.or.jp; Ambassador SALOME THADDAUS SIJAONA.

Thailand: 3-14-6, Kami-Osaki, Shinagawa-ku, Tokyo.141-0021; tel. (3) 5789-2433; fax (3) 3719-7507; e-mail infosect@thaiembassy.jp; internet www.thaiembassy.jp; Ambassador SIHASAK PHUANGKETKEOW (designate).

Timor-Leste: 8-9, Fujimi 1-chome, Chiyoda-ku, Tokyo 102-0071; tel. (3) 3238-0210; fax (3) 3238–0201; e-mail timor-leste77@yahoo.co.jp; Ambassador ISILIO ANTONIO DE FATIMA COELHO DA SILVA.

Tunisia: 3-6-6, Kudan-Minami, Chiyoda-ku, Tokyo 102-0074; tel. (3) 3511-6622; fax (3) 3511-6600; e-mail mailbox@tunisia.or.jp; internet www.tunisia.or.jp; Ambassador FARHAD KHLIF.

Turkey: 2-33-6, Jingumae, Shibuya-ku, Tokyo 150-0001; tel. (3) 6439-5700; fax (3) 3470-5136; e-mail embassy.tokyo@mfa.gov.tr; internet tokyo.be.mfa.gov.tr; Ambassador AHMET BÜLENT MERIÇ.

Turkmenistan: 2-6-14, Higashi, Shibuya-ku, Tokyo 150-0011; tel. (3) 5766-1150; fax (3) 5766-1151; e-mail turkmenistan.jp@gmail.com; Ambassador GURBANMAMET ELIASOV.

Uganda: 9-23, Hachiyama-cho, Shibuya-ku, Tokyo 150-0035; tel. (3) 3462-7107; fax (3) 3462-7108; e-mail ugabassy@tokyo.email.ne.jp; internet www.uganda-embassy.jp; Ambassador BETTY GRACE AKECH OKULLO.

Ukraine: 3-15-31, Nishi-Azabu, Minato-ku, Tokyo 106-0031; tel. (3) 5474-9770; fax (3) 5474-9772; e-mail ukrcn@rose.ocn.ne.jp; internet japan.mfa.gov.ua; Ambassador IHOR KHARCHENKO.

United Arab Emirates: 9-10, Nanpeidai-cho, Shibuya-ku, Tokyo 150-0036; tel. (3) 5489-0804; fax (3) 5489-0813; internet uae-embassy .ae/embassies/jp; Chargé d'affaires a.i. MUTAZ ABDULLA ABDULJALEEL MOHAMED AL-FAHEEM.

United Kingdom: 1, Ichiban-cho, Chiyoda-ku, Tokyo 102-8381; tel. (3) 5211-1100; fax (3) 5275-3164; e-mail consular.tokyo@fco.gov.uk; internet ukinjapan.fco.gov.uk; Ambassador TIMOTHY HITCHENS.

USA: 1-10-5, Akasaka, Minato-ku, Tokyo 107-8420; tel. (3) 3224-5000; fax (3) 3505-1862; internet tokyo.usembassy.gov; Ambassador CAROLINE KENNEDY.

Uruguay: No. 38 Kowa Bldg, Rm 908, 4-12-24, Nishi-Azabu, Minato-ku, Tokyo 106-0031; tel. (3) 3486-1888; fax (3) 3486-9872; e-mail urujap@luck.ocn.ne.jp; Ambassador EDUARDO BOUZOUT VIGNOLI.

Uzbekistan: 2-1-52, Takanawa, Minato-ku, Tokyo 108-0074; tel. (3) 6277-2166; fax (3) 3760-5950; Ambassador FARRUKH ISLOMDJONOVICH TURSUNOV.

Venezuela: No. 38 Kowa Bldg, Rm 703, 4-12-24, Nishi-Azabu, Minato-ku, Tokyo 106-0031; tel. (3) 3409-1501; fax (3) 3409-1505; e-mail embavene@interlink.or.jp; Ambassador SEIKO LUIS ISHIKAWA KOBAYASHI.

Viet Nam: 50-11, Moto-Yoyogi-cho, Shibuya-ku, Tokyo 151-0062; tel. (3) 3466-3313; fax (3) 3466-3391; e-mail vnembasy@blue.ocn.ne .jp; internet www.vietnamembassy-japan.org; Ambassador DOAN XUAN HUNG.

Yemen: No. 38 Kowa Bldg, Rm 807, 4-12-24, Nishi-Azabu, Minato-ku, Tokyo 106-0031; tel. (3) 3499-7151; fax (3) 3499-4577; e-mail info@yemen.jp; internet www.yemen.jp; Chargé d'affaires a.i. SAMIR MOHAMED KHAMIS.

Zambia: 1-10-2, Ebara, Shinagawa-ku, Tokyo 142-0063; tel. (3) 3491-0121; fax (3) 3491-0123; e-mail infoemb@zambia.or.jp; internet www.zambia.or.jp; Ambassador NG'ONA MWELWA CHIBESA-KUNDA.

Zimbabwe: 5-9-10, Shiroganedai, Minato-ku, Tokyo 108-0071; tel. (3) 3280-0331; fax (3) 3280-0466; e-mail zimtokyo@chive.ocn.ne.jp; Chargé d'affaires a.i. LLOYD P. SITHOLE.

Judicial System

The basic principles of the legal system are set forth in the Constitution, which lays down that judicial power is vested in the Supreme Court and in such inferior courts as are established by law, and enunciates the principle that no organ or agency of the Executive shall be given final judicial power. Judges are to be independent in the exercise of their conscience, and may not be removed except by public impeachment, unless judicially declared mentally or physically incompetent to perform official duties. The justices of the Supreme Court are appointed by the Cabinet, the sole exception being the Chief Justice, who is appointed by the Emperor after designation by the Cabinet.

The Court Organization Law, which came into force on 3 May 1947, decreed the constitution of the Supreme Court and the establishment of four types of lower court—High, District, Family (established 1 January 1949) and Summary Courts. The system of trial by jury, suspended since 1943, was reinstated in 2009. Jurors are selected at random from the electoral register.

SUPREME COURT

This court is the highest legal authority in the land, and consists of a Chief Justice and 14 associate justices. It has jurisdiction over Jokoku (Jokoku appeals) and Kokoku (Kokoku appeals), prescribed in codes of procedure. It conducts its hearings and renders decisions through a Grand Bench or three Petty Benches. Both are collegiate bodies, the former consisting of all justices of the Court, and the latter of five justices. A Supreme Court Rule prescribes which cases are to be handled by the respective Benches. It is, however, laid down by law that the Petty Bench cannot make decisions as to the constitutionality of a statute, ordinance, regulation, or disposition, or as to cases in which an opinion concerning the interpretation and application of the Constitution, or of any laws or ordinances, is at variance with a previous decision of the Supreme Court.

Supreme Court: 4-2, Hayabusa-cho, Chiyoda-ku, Tokyo 102-8651; tel. (3) 3264-8111; fax (3) 3221-8975; internet www.courts.go.jp; Chief Justice ITSURO TERADA.

LOWER COURTS

High Court

There are High Courts in Tokyo, Osaka, Nagoya, Hiroshima, Fukuoka, Sendai, Sapporo and Takamatsu, with six branch offices. A High Court conducts its hearings and renders decisions through a collegiate body, consisting of three judges, though for cases of insurrection the number of judges must be five. The Court has jurisdiction over: Koso appeals from judgments in the first instance rendered by District Courts, from judgments rendered by Family Courts, and from judgments concerning criminal cases rendered by Summary Courts; and Kokoku appeals against rulings and orders rendered by District Courts and Family Courts, and against rulings and orders concerning criminal cases rendered by Summary Courts, except those coming within the jurisdiction of the Supreme Court. It also deals with Jokoku appeals from judgments in the second instance rendered by District Courts and from judgments rendered by Summary Courts, except those concerning criminal cases, and actions in the first instance relating to cases of insurrection.

District Court

A District Court is generally the court of first instance, except for matters specifically coming under the exclusive original jurisdiction of other types of court. It also has appellate jurisdiction over appeals in civil cases lodged against judgments of summary courts. The Court conducts hearings and renders decisions through a single judge or, for certain types of cases, through a collegiate body of three judges. Japan has 50 district courts, with 203 branches.

Family Court

A Family Court handles cases through a single judge in case of rendering judgments or decisions. However, in accordance with the provisions of other statutes, it conducts its hearings and renders decisions through a collegiate body of three judges. A conciliation is effected through a collegiate body consisting of a judge and two or more members of the conciliation committee selected from among citizens. Japan has 50 family courts, with 203 branches and 77 local offices.

The Court adjudicates on cases relating to family, juvenile and adult criminal cases according to the Law for Adjudgment of Domestic Relations, Juvenile Law and Labour Standard Law, respectively, and in accordance with other laws especially enacted for the protection of juveniles.

Summary Court

A Summary Court handles cases through a single judge, and has jurisdiction in the first instance over the following matters: claims where the value of the subject matter does not exceed 1.4m. yen; criminal cases of offences liable to a fine or lesser penalty; offences liable to a fine as an optional penalty; and certain specified offences such as theft and embezzlement. There are 438 summary courts in Japan.

A Summary Court cannot impose imprisonment or a graver penalty. When it deems proper the imposition of a sentence of imprisonment or a graver penalty, it must transfer such cases to a District Court, but it can impose imprisonment with labour not exceeding three years for certain specified offences.

Religion

The traditional religions of Japan are Shintoism and Buddhism. Neither is exclusive, and many Japanese subscribe at least nominally to both.

SHINTOISM

Shintoism is an indigenous religious system embracing the worship of ancestors and of nature. It is divided into two cults: national Shintoism, which is represented by the shrines; and sectarian Shintoism, which developed during the second half of the 19th century. In 1868 Shinto was designated a national religion and all Shinto shrines acquired the privileged status of a national institution. Complete freedom of religion was introduced in 1947.

BUDDHISM

World Buddhist Fellowship: Hozenji Buddhist Temple, 3-24-2, Akabane-dai, Kita-ku, Tokyo; Head Rev. FUJI NAKAYAMA.

CHRISTIANITY

National Christian Council in Japan: Japan Christian Center, 2-3-18-24, Nishi-Waseda, Shinjuku-ku, Tokyo 169-0051; tel. (3) 3203-0372; fax (3) 3204-9495; e-mail general@ncc-j.org; internet ncc-j.org; f. 1923; 14 mems (churches and other bodies), 18 assoc. mems; Chair. KOUICHI KOBASHI; Gen. Sec. SHOUKO AMINAKA.

The Anglican Communion

Anglican Church in Japan (Nippon Sei Ko Kai): 65, Yarai-cho, Shinjuku-ku, Tokyo 162-0805; tel. (3) 5228-3171; fax (3) 5228-3175; e-mail general-sec.po@nskk.org; internet www.nskk.org; f. 1887; 11 dioceses; Primate of Japan Most Rev. NATHANIEL MAKOTO UEMATSU (Bishop of Hokkaido); Gen. Sec. JOHN MAKITO AIZAWA; 54,898 mems (2007).

The Orthodox Church

Japanese Orthodox Church (Nippon Haristosu Seikyoukai): Holy Resurrection Cathedral (Nicolai-Do), 4-1-3, Kanda Surugadai, Chiyoda-ku, Tokyo 101; tel. (3) 3291-1885; fax (3) 3291-1886; e-mail info@orthodoxjapan.jp; internet www.orthodoxjapan.jp; 3 dioceses; Archbishop of Tokyo, Primate and Metropolitan of All Japan Most Rev. DANIEL NUSHIRO; 24,821 mems.

Protestant Church

United Church of Christ in Japan (Nihon Kirisuto Kyodan): 2-3-18, Nishi-Shinjuku, Shinjuku-ku, Tokyo 169-0051; tel. (3) 3202-0541; fax (3) 3207-3918; e-mail ecumeni-c@uccj.org; internet www.uccj.or.jp; f. 1941; union of 34 Congregational, Methodist, Presbyterian, Reformed and other Protestant denominations; Moderator Rev. HIDEO ISHIBASHI; Gen. Sec. Rev. AOBORA TAEMAE; 196,044 mems (2007).

The Roman Catholic Church

Japan comprises three archdioceses and 13 dioceses. There were an estimated 554,447 adherents at 31 December 2007.

Catholic Bishops' Conference of Japan (Chuo Kyogikai): 2-10-10, Shiomi, Koto-ku, Tokyo 135-8585; tel. (3) 5632-4411; fax (3) 5632-4453; e-mail info@cbcj.catholic.jp; internet www.cbcj.catholic.jp; Pres. Most Rev. LEO JUN IKENAGA (Bishop of Osaka).

Archbishop of Nagasaki: Most Rev. JOSEPH MITSUAKI TAKAMI, Catholic Centre, 10-34, Uenomachi, Nagasaki-shi 852-8113; tel. (95) 846-4246; fax (95) 848-8310; internet www.nagasaki.catholic.jp.

Archbishop of Osaka: Most Rev. THOMAS AQUINO MANYO MAEDA, Archbishop's House, 2-24-22, Tamatsukuri, Chuo-ku, Osaka 540-0004; tel. (6) 6941-9700; fax (6) 6946-1345; internet www.osaka .catholic.jp.

Archbishop of Tokyo: Most Rev. PETER TAKEO OKADA, Archbishop's House, 3-16-15, Sekiguchi, Bunkyo-ku, Tokyo 112-0014; tel. (3) 3943-2301; fax (3) 3944-8511; e-mail diocese@tokyo.catholic .jp; internet www.tokyo.catholic.jp.

Other Christian Churches

Japan Baptist Convention: 1-2-4, Minami-Urawa, Minami-ku, Saitama-shi, Saitama 336-0017; tel. (48) 883-1091; fax (48) 883-1092; internet www.bapren.jp; f. 1947; Gen. Sec. Rev. MAKOTO KATO; 33,734 mems (March 2003).

Japan Baptist Union: 2-3-18, Nishi-Waseda, Shinjuku-ku, Tokyo 169-0051; tel. (3) 3202-0053; fax (3) 3202-0054; e-mail gs@jbu.or.jp; internet www.jbu.or.jp; f. 1958; Moderator TOMIJI YAMAMOTO; Gen. Sec. KAZUO OHYA; 3,900 mems.

Japan Evangelical Lutheran Church: 1-1, Sadohara-cho, Ichigaya-shi, Shinjuku-ku, Tokyo 162-0842; tel. (3) 3260-8631; fax (3) 3260-8641; e-mail contact@jelc.or.jp; internet www.jelc.or.jp; f. 1893; Pres. Rev. SUMIYUKI WATANABE; Exec. Dir Rev. YASUHIRO TATENO; 21,990 mems (2010).

Korean Christian Church in Japan: Japan Christian Center, Rm 52, 2-3-18, Nishi-Waseda, Shinjuku-ku, Tokyo 169-0051; tel. (3) 3202-5398; fax (3) 3202-4977; e-mail info@kccj.jp; internet kccj.jp; f. 1908; Moderator CHO JUNG LAE; Gen. Sec. KIM BYUNGHO; 4,800 mems.

West Japan Evangelical Lutheran Church: 2-2-11 Nakajima-dori, Chuo-Ku, Kobe 651-0052; tel. (78) 242-0887; fax (78) 242-4166; e-mail office@wjelc.or.jp; internet www.wjelc.or.jp; 3,887 mems (2010).

Among other denominations active in Japan are the Christian Catholic Church, the German Evangelical Church and the Tokyo Union Church.

OTHER COMMUNITIES

Bahá'í Faith

The National Spiritual Assembly of the Bahá'ís of Japan: 7-2-13, Shinjuku, Shinjuku-ku, Tokyo 160-0022; tel. (3) 3209-7521; fax (3) 3204-0773; e-mail info@bahaijp.org; internet www.bahaijp.org; f. 1955; Mem. DARYOUSH YAZDANI.

Judaism

Jewish Community of Japan: 3-8-8, Hiroo, Shibuya-ku, Tokyo 150-0012; tel. (3) 3400-2559; fax (3) 3400-1827; e-mail office@jccjapan .or.jp; internet www.jccjapan.or.jp; f. 1953; Pres. JEROME ROSENBERG; Leader Rabbi ANTONIO DI GESÙ.

Islam

Islam has been active in Japan since the late 19th century. There is a small Muslim community, maintaining several mosques, including those at Kobe, Nagoya, Chiba and Isesaki, the Arabic Islamic Institute and the Islamic Center in Tokyo. The construction of Tokyo Central Mosque was completed in 2000.

Islamic Center, Japan: 1-16-11, Ohara, Setagaya-ku, Tokyo 156-0041; tel. (3) 3460-6169; fax (3) 3460-6105; e-mail info@islamcenter .or.jp; internet www.islamcenter.or.jp; f. 1965; Chair. Dr SALIH AL-SAMARRAI.

The New Religions

Many new religions (Shinko Shukyo) emerged in Japan after 1945, based on a fusion of Shinto, Buddhist, Daoist, Confucian and Christian beliefs. Among the most important of these are Tenrikyo, Omotokyo, Soka Gakkai, Rissho Kosei-kai, Kofuku-no-Kagaku and Agonshu.

Kofuku-no-Kagaku (Institute for Research in Human Happiness): 1-6-7, Shinagawa-ku, Tokyo 142-0041; tel. (3) 6384-3777; fax (3) 6384-3778; e-mail info@irhpress.co.jp; internet www.irhpress.co.jp; f. 1986; believes its founder to be reincarnation of Buddha; 8.25m. mems; Leader RYUHO OKAWA.

Rissho Kosei-kai: 5/F, Fumon Hall, 2-6-1, Wada, Suginami-ku, Tokyo 166-8537; tel. and fax (3) 5341-1124; e-mail info@rk-world.org; internet www.rk-world.org; f. 1938; Buddhist lay org. based on the teaching of the Lotus Sutra, active inter-faith co-operation towards peace; Pres. Rev. Dr NICHIKO NIWANO; 2.05m. mem. households with 245 brs worldwide (2009).

Soka Gakkai: 32, Shinano-machi, Shinjuku-ku, Tokyo 160-8583; tel. (3) 5360-9830; fax (3) 5360-9885; e-mail contact@sgi.org; internet www.sgi.org; f. 1930; society of lay practitioners of the Buddhism of Nichiren; membership of 8.27m. households (2005); group promotes activities in education, international cultural exchange and consensus-building towards peace, based on the humanist world view of Buddhism; Hon. Pres. DAISAKU IKEDA; Pres. MINORU HARADA.

The Press

In 2013 there were 117 daily newspapers in Japan. Their average circulation (around 47m.) was among the highest in the world. The large number of weekly news journals is a notable feature of the Japanese press.

NATIONAL DAILIES

Asahi Shimbun: 5-3-2, Tsukiji, Chuo-ku, Tokyo 104-8011; tel. (3) 3545-0131; fax (3) 3545-0358; internet www.asahi.com; f. 1879; also publ. by Osaka, Seibu and Nagoya head offices and Hokkaido branch office; Editor-in-Chief TOSHIAKI MIURA; circ. morning 8.1m., evening 3.7m.

Mainichi Shimbun: 1-1-1, Hitotsubashi, Chiyoda-ku, Tokyo 100-8051; tel. (3) 3212-0321; fax (3) 3211-3598; internet www.mainichi.co .jp; f. 1882; also publ. by Osaka, Seibu and Chubu head offices, and Hokkaido branch office; Pres. MASATO KITAMURA; Editor-in-Chief TOSHIFUMI KAWANO; circ. morning 3.4m., evening 1.3m.

Nihon Keizai Shimbun: 1-3-7, Otemachi, Chiyoda-ku, Tokyo 1008066; tel. (3) 3270-0251; fax (3) 5255-2661; e-mail ecntct@ nikkei.co.jp; internet www.nikkei.co.jp; f. 1876; also publ. by Osaka head office and Sapporo, Nagoya and Seibu branch offices; Pres. KEN KOYANAGI; Editor-in-Chief YUICHI TAKAHASHI; circ. morning 3.3m., evening 1.6m.

Sankei Shimbun: 1-7-2, Otemachi, Chiyoda-ku, Tokyo 100-8077; tel. (3) 3231-7111; internet sankei.jp; f. 1933; also publ. by Osaka head office; Pres. and CEO NAGAYOSHI SUMIDA; Editor-in-Chief MASAFUMI KATAYAMA; circ. morning 2.0m., evening 636,649.

Yomiuri Shimbun: 1-7-1, Otemachi, Chiyoda-ku, Tokyo 100-8055; tel. (3) 3242-1111; e-mail webmaster@yomiuri.co.jp; internet www .yomiuri.co.jp; f. 1874; also publ. by Osaka, Seibu and Chubu head offices, and Hokkaido and Hokuriku branch offices; Chair. and Editor-in-Chief TSUNEO WATANABE; circ. morning 10.0m., evening 4.0m.

PRINCIPAL LOCAL DAILIES

Tokyo

Daily Sports: 1-5-7, Hyogo Higashikawasaki-cho, Chuo-ku, Tokyo 650-0044; tel. (3) 5434-1752; e-mail dsmaster@daily.co.jp; internet www.daily.co.jp; f. 1948; morning; Pres. NOBUHIKO NUMATA; circ. 400,254.

The Daily Yomiuri: 1-7-1, Otemachi, Chiyoda-ku, Tokyo 100-8055; tel. (3) 3242-1111; internet www.yomiuri.co.jp; f. 1955; morning; English; Man. Editor SHIGEYUKI OKADA; circ. 33,743.

Dempa Shimbun: 1-11-15, Higashi-Gotanda, Shinagawa-ku, Tokyo 141-8790; tel. (3) 3445-6111; fax (3) 3444-7515; e-mail multim@dempa.co.jp; internet www.dempa.co.jp; f. 1950; morning; Pres. TETSUO HIRAYAMA; circ. 300,000.

The Japan Times: 4-5-4, Shibaura, Minato-ku, Tokyo 108-8071; tel. (3) 3453-5312; internet www.japantimes.co.jp; f. 1897; morning; English; Chair. and Publr TOSHIAKI OGASAWARA; Dir and Pres. TAKEHARU TSUTSUMI; circ. 105,000.

The Mainichi Daily News: 1-1-1, Hitotsubashi, Chiyoda-ku, Tokyo 100-8051; tel. (3) 3212-0321; internet mdn.mainichi.jp; f. 1922; morning; English; also publ. from Osaka; Man. Editor YUTAKA ASAHINA; combined circ. 55,000.

Nihon Kaiji Shimbun (Japan Maritime Daily): Mori Bldg, 5-19-2, Shimbashi, Minato-ku, Tokyo 105-0004; tel. (3) 3436-3221; fax (3) 3436-3247; e-mail webmaster@jmd.co.jp; internet www.jmd.co.jp; f. 1942; morning; Man. Editor OSAMI ENDO; circ. 55,000.

Nihon Nogyo Shimbun (Agriculture): 2-3, Akihabara, Taito-ku, Tokyo 110-8722; tel. (3) 5295-7411; fax (3) 3253-0980; internet www.agrinews.co.jp; f. 1928; morning; Man. Editor YASUNORI INOUE; circ. 423,840.

Nihon Sen-i Shimbun (Textiles and Fashion): 1-6-5, Nihonbashi Kobuna-cho, Chuo-ku, Tokyo 103-0012; tel. (3) 5649-8711; fax (3) 5469-8717; internet www.nissenmedia.com; f. 1943; morning; Man. Editor KIYOSHIGE SEIRYU; circ. 116,000.

Nikkan Kogyo Shimbun (Industrial Daily News): 14-1, Nihonbashi Koami-cho, Chuo-ku, Tokyo 103-8548; tel. (3) 5644-7000; fax (3) 5644-7100; internet www.nikkan.co.jp; f. 1915; morning; Pres. HARUHIRO IMIZU; circ. 533,145.

Nikkan Sports News: 3-5-10, Tsukiji, Chuo-ku, Tokyo 104-8055; tel. (3) 5550-8888; fax (3) 5550-8901; e-mail webmast@nikkansports.co.jp; internet www.nikkansports.com; f. 1946; morning; Pres. YOSHITAKA SUZUKI; circ. 1,965,000.

Sankei Sports: 1-7-2, Otemachi, Chiyoda-ku, Tokyo 100 8077; tel. (3) 3231-7111; internet www.sanspo.com; f. 1963; morning; Man. Editor YUKIO INADA; circ. 809,245.

Shipping and Trade News: Tokyo News Service Ltd, 1-1-2, Uchisaiwai-cho, Chiyoda-ku, Tokyo 100-0011; tel. (3) 5510-8961; fax (3) 3504-6039; e-mail editorial.a@tokyonews.co.jp; internet www.tokyonews.co.jp/marine; f. 1949; English; Man. Editor TAKASHI TAKEDA; circ. 15,000.

Sports Hochi: 4-6-49, Kohnan, Minato-ku, Tokyo 108-8485; tel. (3) 5479-1111; e-mail webmaster@hochi.yomiuri.co.jp; internet hochi.yomiuri.co.jp; f. 1872; fmrly *Hochi Shimbun*; morning; Pres. TADASHI HAYAKAWA; circ. 755,670.

Sports Nippon: 2-1-30, Etchujima, Koto-ku, Tokyo 135-8735; tel. (3) 3820-0700; e-mail customer@sponichi.co.jp; internet www.sponichi.co.jp; f. 1949; morning; Pres. MORITO YUKIO; circ. 929,421.

Suisan Keizai Shimbun (Fisheries): 6-8-19, Roppongi, Minato-ku, Tokyo 106-0032; tel. (3) 3404-6531; fax (3) 3404-0863; internet www.suikei.co.jp; f. 1948; morning; Man. Editor NAGIKO YASUNARI; circ. 61,000.

Tokyo Chunichi Sports: 1-4, Uchisaiwai-cho, Chiyoda-ku, Tokyo 100-8505; tel. (3) 6910-2211; internet www.chunichi.co.jp/chuspo; f. 1956; evening; Pres. OOSHIMA TORAO; circ. 676,972.

Tokyo Shimbun: 1-4, Uchisaiwai-cho, Chiyoda-ku, Tokyo 100-8505; tel. (3) 6910-2211; internet www.chunichi.co.jp; f. 1942; Pres. OOSHIMA TORAO; circ. morning 605,096, evening 336,010.

Tokyo Sports: 2-1-30, Etchujima, Koto-ku, Tokyo 135-8721; tel. (3) 3820-0801; internet www.tokyo-sports.co.jp; f. 1959; evening; Pres. TSUNEO TACHIKAWA; circ. 1,560,000.

Yukan Fuji: 1-7-2, Otemachi, Chiyoda-ku, Tokyo 100-8077; tel. (3) 3231-7111; fax (3) 3246-0377; e-mail desk@zakzak.co.jp; internet www.zakzak.co.jp; f. 1969; evening; Man. Editor MASAMI KATO; circ. 268,984.

Osaka District

The Mainichi Daily News: 3-4-5, Umeda, Kita-ku, Osaka 530-8251; tel. (6) 6345-1551; internet www.mainichi.co.jp; f. 1922; morning; English; Pres. YUTAKA ASAHINA.

Nikkan Sports: 3-14-24, Hanshin, Fukushima Ward, Osaka; tel. (6) 6229-7005; internet www.nikkansports.com; f. 1950; morning; Man. Editor SUSUMU MATSUMOTO; circ. 513,498.

Sankei Kansai: 2-1-57, Minato-cho, Naniwa-ku, Osaka 556-8660; tel. (6) 6633-1221; fax (6) 6633-9738; e-mail osaka-soukyoku@sankei.co.jp; internet www.sankei-kansai.com; f. 1922; evening; fmrly *Osaka Shimbun*, name changed as above 2004; Pres. SUMIDA NAGAYOSHI; circ. 88,887.

Sankei Sports: 2-1-57, Minato-cho, Naniwa-ku, Osaka 556-8660; tel. (3) 3231-7111; fax (3) 3275-8994; f. 1955; morning; Pres. SUMIDA NAGAYOSHI; circ. 552,519.

Sports Nippon: 3-4-5, Umeda, Kita-ku, Osaka 530-8278; tel. (6) 6346-8500; f. 1949; morning; Man. Editor HIDETOSHI ISHIHARA; circ. 477,300.

Kanto District

Chiba Nippo (Chiba Daily News): 4-14-10, Chuo, Chuo-ku, Chiba 260-0013; tel. (43) 222-9211; internet www.chibanippo.co.jp; f. 1957; morning; Man. Editor YASUHIDE AKADA; circ. 200,000.

Ibaraki Shimbun: 2-15, Kitami-cho, Mito 310-8686; tel. (29) 248-5500; fax (29) 248-7745; e-mail i-net@ibaraki-np.co.jp; internet www.ibaraki-np.co.jp; f. 1891; morning; Pres. TAKASHI KOTABE; circ. 117,240.

Jomo Shimbun: 1-50-21, Furuichi-machi, Maebashi 371-8666; tel. (27) 254-9911; internet www.raijin.com; f. 1887; morning; Man. Dir WATANABE SACHIO; circ. 311,534.

Joyo Shimbun: 2-7-6, Manabe, Tsuchiura 300-0051; tel. (29)821-1780; e-mail info-02@joyo-net.com; internet www.joyo-net.com; f. 1948; morning; Pres. MINEO IWANAMI; Man. Editor AKIRA SAITO; circ. 88,700.

Kanagawa Shimbun: 2-23, Ota-cho, Kanagawa, Naka-ku, Yokohama 231-8445; tel. (45) 227-1111; e-mail soumu@kanagawa-np.co.jp; internet www.kanagawa-shimbun.jp; f. 1890; morning; Pres. JUNICHI SAITO; Man. Dir REN KATO; circ. 210,000.

Saitama Shimbun: 2-282-3, Yoshino, Kita-ku, Saitama; tel. (48) 795-9930; fax (48) 653-9020; e-mail desk@saitama-np.co.jp; internet www.saitama-np.co.jp; f. 1944; morning; Pres. HIDEKI OGAWA; circ. 162,071.

Shimotsuke Shimbun: 1-8-11, Showa, Utsunomiya 320-8686; tel. (28)625-1111; internet www.shimotsuke.co.jp; f. 1884; morning; Pres. YOSHINORI KANDO; circ. 316,847.

Tohoku District
(North-east Honshu)

Akita Sakigake Shimpo: 1-1, San-no-rinkai-machi, Akita 010-8601; tel. (18) 888-1800; fax (18) 866-9285; internet www.sakigake.co.jp; f. 1874; Man. Editor NAOKI OGASAWARA; circ. 230,000.

Daily Tohoku: 1-3-12, Shiroshita, Hachinohe 031-8601; tel. (178) 44-5111; internet www.daily-tohoku.co.jp; f. 1945; morning; Pres. KIYOSHI ARASE; circ. 106,410.

Fukushima Minyu: 4-29, Yanagi-machi, Fukushima 960-8648; tel. (24) 523-1191; fax (24) 523-2605; internet www.minyu-net.com; f. 1895; Man. Editor SHUNSUKE KANDA; circ. morning 250,000, evening 7,000.

Hokuu Shimpo: 3-2, Nishi-Dori-machi, Noshiro 016-0891; tel. (185) 54-3150; internet www.hokuu.co.jp; f. 1895; morning; Chair. KOICHI YAMAKI; circ. 31,490.

Iwate Nichi-nichi Shimbun: 60, Minami-Shinmachi, Ichinoseki 021-8686; tel. (191) 26-5114; e-mail iwanichi@iwanichi.co.jp; internet www.iwanichi.co.jp; f. 1923; morning; Pres. MANABU YAMAGISHI; circ. 59,850.

Iwate Nippo: 3-7, Uchimaru, Morioka 020-8622; tel. (19) 653-4111; fax (19) 626-1882; e-mail center@iwate-np.co.jp; internet www.iwate-np.co.jp; f. 1876; Pres. MIURA HIROSHI; circ. morning 267,890, evening 225,678.

Kahoku Shimpo: 1-2-28, Itsutsubashi, Aoba-ku, Sendai 980-8660; tel. (22) 211-1127; fax (22) 211-1448; e-mail houdou@po.kahoku.co.jp; internet www.kahoku.co.jp; f. 1897; Exec. Dir and Man. Editor MASAHIKO ICHIRIKI; circ. morning 503,318, evening 133,855.

Mutsu Shimpo: 2-1, Shimo-shirogane-cho, Hirosaki 036-8356; tel. (172) 34-3111; fax (172) 32-3138; e-mail box@mutusinpou.co.jp; internet www.mutusinpou.co.jp; f. 1946; morning; Man. Editor YUJI SATO; circ. 53,500.

Shonai Nippo: 8-29, Baba-cho, Tsuruoka 997-8691; tel. (235) 22-1480; fax (235) 22-1427; internet www.shonai-nippo.co.jp; f. 1946; morning; Pres. and CEO MASAYUKI HASHIMOTO; circ. 20,000.

To-o Nippo: 3-1-89, Dainitonya-machi, Aomori 030-0180; tel. (17) 739-1111; fax (17) 739-1141; internet www.toonippo.co.jp; f. 1888; Exec. Dir YOSHIO WAJIMA; Man. Editor TAKAO SHIOKOSHI; circ. morning 262,532, evening 258,590.

Yamagata Shimbun: 2-5-12, Hatagomachi, Yamagata 990-8550; tel. (23) 622-5271; e-mail info@yamagata-np.jp; internet yamagata-np.jp; f. 1876; Exec. Chair. YOSUKE KUROSAWA; Pres. and CEO SAGAE KOJI; circ. morning 213,057, evening 213,008.

Yonezawa Shimbun: 3-3-7, Monto-cho, Yonezawa 992-0039; tel. (238) 22-4411; fax (238) 24-5554; e-mail info@www.yoneshin.com; internet www.yoneshin.com; f. 1879; morning; Man. Dir and Editor-in-Chief MASAO HOKARI; circ. 13,750.

Chubu District
(Central Honshu)

Chubu Keizai Shimbun: 4-4-38, Meieki, Nakamura-ku, Nagoya 450-8561; tel. (52) 561-5215; fax (52) 561-5229; internet www .chukei-news.co.jp; f. 1946; morning; Pres. and CEO NAGAI SEITAIRA; circ. 87,000.

Chunichi Shimbun: 1-6-1, San-no-maru, Naka-ku, Nagoya 460-8511; tel. (52) 201-8811; internet www.chunichi.co.jp; f. 1942; Chair. BUNGO SHIRAI; Pres. KOIDE NORIAKI; circ. 4.2m.

Chunichi Sports: 1-6-1, San-no-maru, Naka-ku, Nagoya 460-8511; tel. (52) 201-8811; internet www.chunichi.co.jp/chuspo; f. 1954; evening; Pres. OOSHIMA TARAO; circ. 4.2m.

Gifu Shimbun: 10, Imako-machi, Gifu 500-8577; tel. (58) 264-1151; internet www.gifu-np.co.jp; f. 1881; Exec. Dir and Man. Editor TADASHI TANAKA; circ. morning 170,176, evening 31,775.

Higashi-Aichi Shimbun: 62, Torinawate, Shinsakae-machi, Toyohashi 441-8666; tel. (532) 32-3111; fax (532) 32-3737; e-mail hensyu@ higashiaichi.co.jp; internet www.higashiaichi.co.jp; f. 1957; morning; Pres. MASATO FUJIMURA; circ. 55,000.

Nagano Nippo: 3-1323-1, Takashima, Suwa 392-8611; tel. (266) 52-2000; fax (266) 58-8895; e-mail info@nagano-np.co.jp; internet www .nagano-np.co.jp; f. 1901; morning; Man. Editor HIDDYUKI SAKYIU; circ. 73,000.

Shinano Mainichi Shimbun: 657, Minami-Agatamachi, Nagano 380-8546; tel. (26) 236-3000; fax (26) 236-3098; internet www .shinmai.co.jp; f. 1873; Man. Editor SOTARO KOSAKA; circ. morning 500,000, evening 50,876.

Shizuoka Shimbun: 3-1-1, Toro, Suruga-ku, Shizuoka 422-8670; tel. (54) 284-8900; fax (54) 284-8994; e-mail webmaster@ shizuokaonline.com; internet www.shizuokaonline.com; f. 1941; Man. Editor JUN MATSUI; circ. morning 730,746, evening 730,782.

Yamanashi Nichi-Nichi Shimbun: 2-6-10, Kita-Guchi, Kofu 400-8515; tel. (552) 31-3199; fax (552) 31-3161; e-mail info@sannichi.co .jp; internet www.sannichi.co.jp; f. 1872; morning; Man. Editor NOGUCHI EIICHI; circ. 200,000.

Hokuriku District
(North Coastal Honshu)

Fukui Shimbun: 56, Owada-cho, Fukui 910-8552; tel. (776) 57-5111; internet www.fukuishimbun.co.jp; f. 1899; morning; Man. Editor YOSHIDA MASATO; circ. 207,000.

Hokkoku Shimbun: 2-5-1, Korinbo, Kanazawa 920-8588; tel. (762) 60-3402; fax (762) 60-3403; e-mail admin@hokkoku.co.jp; internet www.hokkoku.co.jp; f. 1893; Pres. and Man. Editor HIDEKAZU TOBITA; circ. morning 335,826, evening 93,021.

Hokuriku Chunichi Shimbun: 2-12-30, Korinbo, Kanazawa 920-8573; tel. (76) 261-3111; internet www.chunichi.co.jp/hokuriku; f. 1960; Pres. OOSHIMA TORAO; circ. 4.2m.

Kita-Nippon Shimbun: 2-14, Azumi-cho, Toyama 930-8680; tel. (764) 45-3300; internet www.kitanippon.co.jp; f. 1884; Dir and Man. Editor HITOSHI ITAKURA; circ. morning 240,000.

Niigata Nippo: 772-2, Nishi-ku, Niigata 950-1189; tel. (25) 378-9111; internet www.niigata-nippo.co.jp; f. 1942; Dir and Man. Editor MICHIEI TAKAHASHI; circ. morning 499,545, evening 63,790.

Kinki District
(West Central Honshu)

Daily Sports: 1-5-7, Higashi-Kawasaki-cho, Chuo-ku, Kobe 650-0044; tel. (78) 362-7100; e-mail dsmaster@daily.co.jp; internet www .daily.co.jp; morning; Man. Editor TAKASHI HIRAI; circ. 584,448.

Ise Shimbun: 34-6, Honmachi, Tsu 514-0831; tel. (59) 224-0003; fax (59) 226-3554; internet www.isenp.co.jp; f. 1878; morning; Man. Editor SENZO KOBAYASHI; circ. 108,630.

Kii Minpo: 100, Akizu-cho, Tanabe 646-8660; tel. (739) 22-7171; fax (739) 26-0077; internet www.agara.co.jp; f. 1911; evening; Man. Editor YOHACHIRO KOYAMA; circ. 45,342.

Kobe Shimbun: 1-5-7, Higashi-Kawasaki-cho, Chuo-ku, Kobe 650-8571; tel. (78) 362-7100; fax (78) 360-5501; internet www.kobe-np.co .jp; f. 1898; Pres. MIZUO HASHIDA; circ. morning 563,717, evening 239,604.

Kyoto Shimbun: 239, Shoshoi-machi, Ebisugawa-agaru, Karasuma-dori, Nakagyo-ku, Kyoto 604-8577; tel. (75) 241-5430; fax (75) 252-5454; e-mail kpdesk@mb.kyoto-np.co.jp; internet www .kyoto-np.co.jp; f. 1879; Man. Editor SYOZO MASUDA; circ. morning 504,304, evening 319,015.

Nara Shimbun: 2-4, Sanjo-machi, Nara 630-8686; tel. (742) 32-1000; fax (742) 32-2770; e-mail info@nara-np.co.jp; internet www .nara-np.co.jp; f. 1946; morning; Dir and Man. Editor HARUO AMARI; circ. 120,000.

Chugoku District
(Western Honshu)

Chugoku Shimbun: 7-1, Dobashi-cho, Naka-ku, Hiroshima 730-8677; tel. (82) 236-2111; fax (82) 236-2456; e-mail denshi@ hiroshima-cdas.or.jp; internet www.chugoku-np.co.jp; f. 1892; Pres. KAZUYUKI KAWAMOTO; circ. morning 723,981, evening 75,248.

Nihonkai Shimbun: 2-137, Tomiyasu, Tottori 680-8688; tel. (857) 21-2888; fax (857) 21-2891; e-mail info@nnn.co.jp; internet www.nnn .co.jp; f. 1976; morning; Pres. YOSHIOKA RIKATA; circ. 171,120.

San-In Chuo Shimpo: 383, Tono-machi, Matsue 690-8668; tel. (852) 32-3440; e-mail sanin@sanin-chuo.co.jp; internet www .sanin-chuo.co.jp; f. 1882; morning; Pres. TETSUO MORIWAKI; circ. 181,000.

Sanyo Shimbun: 2-1-1, Yanagi-machi, Okayama 700-8634; tel. (86) 803-8008; internet www.sanyo.oni.co.jp; f. 1879; Man. Dir and Man. Editor KOSHIMUNE TAKAMASA; circ. morning 500,000, evening 58,097.

Ube Jiho: 3-6-1, Kotobuki-cho, Ube 755-8557; tel. (836) 31-1511; internet www.ubenippo.co.jp; f. 1912; evening; Exec. Dir and Man. Editor KAZUYA WAKI; circ. 52,300.

Shikoku Island

Ehime Shimbun: 1-12-1, Otemachi, Matsuyama 790-8511; tel. (89) 935-2111; fax (89) 941-8108; e-mail webmaster@ehime-np.co.jp; internet www.ehime-np.co.jp; f. 1876; morning; Man. Editor HIDEO DOI; circ. 49,810,029.

Kochi Shimbun: 3-2-15, Honmachi, Kochi 780-8572; tel. (88) 822-2111; e-mail master@kochinews.co.jp; internet www.kochinews.co .jp; f. 1904; Pres. HAYAO MIYATA; circ. 230,000.

Tokushima Shimbun: 2-5-2, Naka-Tokushima-cho, Tokushima 770-8572; tel. (88) 655-7373; fax (86) 654-0165; e-mail jouhou@ topics.or.jp; internet www.topics.or.jp; f. 1944; Dir and Man. Editor HIROSHI MATSUMURA; circ. 250,000.

Hokkaido Island

Doshin Sports: 3-6, Nishi-Odori, Chuo-ku, Sapporo 060-8711; tel. (11) 210-5573; fax (11) 210-5575; e-mail koe@hokkaido-np.co.jp; internet www.hokkaido-np.co.jp; f. 1982; morning; Pres. TOSHIKAZU MASTUDA; circ. 146,390.

Hokkaido Shimbun: 3-6, Nishi-Odori, Chuo-ku, Sapporo 060-8711; tel. (11) 210-5573; fax (11) 210-5575; internet www .hokkaido-np.co.jp; f. 1942; Man. Editor MASATOSHI MURATA; circ. morning 1.2m., evening 701,934.

Kushiro Shimbun: 7-3, Kurogane-cho, Kushiro 085-8650; tel. (154) 22-1111; fax (154) 22-0050; internet www.news-kushiro.jp; f. 1946; morning; Pres. and CEO KASUGAI SHIGERU; circ. 80,000.

Muroran Mimpo: 1-3-16, Hon-cho, Muroran 051-8550; tel. (143) 22-5121; fax (143) 24-1337; e-mail honsya@muromin.mnw.jp; internet www.muromin.mnw.jp; f. 1945; Man. Editor TSUTOMO KUDO; circ. morning 63,300, evening 52,630.

Nikkan Sports: 3-1-30, Higashi, Kita-3 jo, Chuo-ku, Sapporo 060-8521; tel. (11) 242-3900; fax (11) 272-1754; internet www .nikkansports.com; f. 1962; morning; Pres. YOSHITAKA SUZUKI; circ. 142,330.

Tokachi Mainichi Shimbun: 8-2, Minami, Higashi-Ichijo, Obihiro 080-8688; tel. (155) 22-2121; fax (155) 25-2700; e-mail info@kachimai .co.jp; internet www.tokachi.co.jp; f. 1919; evening; Editor-in-Chief MITSUSHIGE HAYASHI; circ. 85,160.

Tomakomai Mimpo: 3-1-8, Wakakusa-cho, Tomakomai 053-8611; tel. (144) 32-5311; fax (144) 32-6386; e-mail henshu@tomamin.co.jp; internet www.tomamin.co.jp; f. 1950; evening; Dir and Man. Editor RYUICHI KUDO; circ. 60,676.

Yomiuri Shimbun: 4-1, Nishi, Kita-4 jo, Chuo-ku, Sapporo 060-8656; tel. (11) 242-3111; internet www.yomiuri.co.jp; f. 1959; Chair. and Editor-in-Chief WATANABE TSUNEO; circ. morning 261,747, evening 81,283.

Kyushu Island

Kumamoto Nichi-Nichi Shimbun: 172, Yoyasu-machi, Kumamoto 860-8506; tel. (96) 361-3082; internet www.kumanichi.com; f. 1942; Man. Editor EIICHI IZU; circ. morning 385,784, evening 99,049.

Kyushu Sports: Fukuoka Tenjin Center Bldg, 2-14-8, Tenjin-cho, Chuo-ku, Fukuoka 810-0001; tel. (92) 781-7401; f. 1966; morning; Head Officer HIROSHI MITOMI; circ. 449,850.

Minami-Nippon Shimbun: 1-9-33, Yojirou, Kagoshima 890-8603; tel. (99) 813-5001; fax (99) 813-5016; e-mail webmaster@373news .com; internet www.373news.com; f. 1881; Man. Editor NAOSUMI SAKASEGAWA; circ. morning 405,795.

Miyazaki Nichi-Nichi Shimbun: 1-1-33, Takachihodori, Miyazaki 880-8570; tel. (985) 26-9315; fax (985) 20-7254; e-mail info@

the-miyanichi.co.jp; internet www.the-miyanichi.co.jp; f. 1940; morning; Pres. YASUHISA MACHIKAWA; circ. 235,759.

Nagasaki Shimbun: 3-1, Mori-machi, Nagasaki 852-8601; tel. (95) 844-2111; e-mail houdou@nagasaki-np.co.jp; internet www .nagasaki-np.co.jp; f. 1889; Dir and Man. Editor TAKAHIRO MOTO-MURA; circ. morning 200,000.

Nankai Nichi-Nichi Shimbun: 10-3, Nagahama-cho, Naze 894-8601; tel. (997) 53-2121; fax (997) 52-2354; e-mail nankainn@po .synapse.ne.jp; internet www.nankainn.com; f. 1946; morning; Man. Editor MICHIO MURAYAMA; circ. 20,345.

Nishi-Nippon Shimbun: 1-4-1, Tenjin, Chuo-ku, Fukuoka 810-8721; tel. (92) 711-5555; internet www.nishinippon.co.jp; f. 1877; Pres. TAKAO KAWASAKI; Man. Dir KOGA YASUSHI; circ. morning 850,779, evening 148,750.

Oita Godo Shimbun: 3-9-15, Funai-machi, Oita 870-8605; tel. (975) 36-2121; internet www.oita-press.co.jp; f. 1886; Dir and Man. Editor KEN NAGANO; circ. morning 250,300, evening 250,264.

Okinawa Times: 1-3-31, Omoro-machi, Naha 900-8678; tel. (98) 860-3000; fax (98) 860-3664; internet www.okinawatimes.co.jp; f. 1948; Pres. TOYOHIRA YOSHITAKA; circ. morning 205,624.

Ryukyu Shimpo: 905, Naha 900-8525; tel. (98) 865-5111; fax (98) 861-6444; internet www.ryukyushimpo.co.jp; f. 1893; Man. Editor TATSUHIRO HIGA; circ. 203,470.

Saga Shimbun: 3-2-23, Tenjin, Saga 840-8585; tel. (952) 28-2121; fax (952) 29-5760; internet www.saga-s.co.jp; f. 1884; morning; Man. Editor SEIICHIRO NAKAO; circ. 150,768.

Yaeyama Mainichi Shimbun: 614, Tonoshiro, Ishigaki 907-0004; tel. (9808) 2-2121; internet www.y-mainichi.co.jp; f. 1950; morning; Exec. Dir and Man. Editor KIYOTAKA NAKAMA; circ. 18,000.

WEEKLIES

An-An: Magazine House, 3-13-10, Ginza, Chuo-ku, Tokyo 104-8003; tel. (3) 3545-7050; fax (3) 3546-0034; internet magazineworld.jp/anan; f. 1970; fashion; Editor ISHI YAMAZAKI MENG; circ. 650,000.

Diamond Weekly: Diamond Bldg, 6-12-17, Jingumae, Shibuya-ku, Tokyo 150-8409; tel. (3) 5778-7200; e-mail info@diamond.co.jp; internet www.diamond.co.jp; f. 1913; economics; Editor LUGU FUMIAKI; Man. Dir KUME ISAO; circ. 81,000.

Hanako: Magazine House, 3-13-10, Ginza, Chuo-ku, Tokyo 104-8003; tel. (3) 3545-7070; fax (3) 3545-7281; internet magazineworld .jp/hanako; f. 1988; consumer guide; Editor ISHI YAMAZAKI MENG; circ. 350,000.

Nikkei Business: Nikkei Business Publications Inc, 1-17-3, Shirokane, Minato-ku, Tokyo 108-8646; tel. (3) 6811-8101; fax (3) 5421-9117; internet www.nikkeibp.co.jp; f. 1969; Pres. TAIRA HIROSHI NAGATA; circ. 330,000.

Shukan Bunshun: Bungei-Shunju Ltd, 3-23, Kioi-cho, Chiyoda-ku, Tokyo 102-8008; tel. (3) 3288-6123; fax (3) 3234-3964; e-mail kawabe@bunshun.co.jp; internet www.bunshun.co.jp; f. 1959; general interest; Editor MANABU SHINTANI; circ. 800,000.

Shukan Gendai: Kodan-Sha Co Ltd, 2-12-21, Otowa, Bunkyo-ku, Tokyo 112; tel. (3) 5395-3438; fax (3) 3943-7815; f. 1959; general; Editor-in-Chief TETSU SUZUKI; circ. 500,000.

Shukan Josei: Shufu-To-Seikatsu Sha Ltd, 3-5-7, Kyobashi, Chuo-ku, Tokyo 104; tel. (3) 3563-5130; fax (3) 3563-2073; f. 1957; women's interest; Editor HIDEO KIKUCHI; circ. 638,000.

Shukan Post: Shogakukan Publishing Co Ltd, 2-3-1, Hitotsubashi, Chiyoda-ku, Tokyo 101-01; tel. (3) 3230-5951; internet www .weeklypost.com; f. 1969; general; Editor NORIMICHI OKANARI; circ. 696,000.

Shukan SPA: Fuso-Sha Co, 1-15-1, Kaigan, Minato-ku, Tokyo 105; tel. (3) 5403-8875; f. 1952; general interest; Editor-in-Chief TOSHI-HIKO SATO; circ. 400,000.

Shukan ST: Japan Times Ltd, 4-5-4, Shibaura, Minato-ku, Tokyo 108-8071; tel. (3) 3452-4077; fax (3) 3452-3303; e-mail shukanst@ japantimes.co.jp; internet www.japantimes.co.jp/shukan-st; f. 1951; English and Japanese; Editor MITSURU TANAKA; circ. 150,000.

Sunday Mainichi: Mainichi Newspapers Publishing Dept, 1-1-1, Hitotsubashi, Chiyoda-ku, Tokyo 100-51; tel. (3) 3212-0321; fax (3) 3212-7580; f. 1922; general interest; Editor HIDEHIRO SATO; circ. 237,000.

Tenji Mainichi: Mainichi Newspapers Publishing Dept, 3-4-5, Umeda, Osaka; tel. (6) 6346-8386; fax (6) 6346-8385; f. 1922; in Japanese braille; Editor YUTAKA ASAHINA; circ. 14,000.

Weekly Economist: Mainichi Newspapers Publishing Dept, 1-1-1, Hitotsubashi, Chiyoda-ku, Tokyo 100-51; tel. (3) 3212-0321; f. 1923; Editorial Chief NOBUHIRO SHUDO; circ. 120,000.

Weekly Toyo Keizai: Toyo Keizai Inc, 1-2-1, Hongoku-cho, Nihonbashi, Chuo-ku, Tokyo 103-8345; tel. (3) 3246-5551; fax (3) 3270-0332; e-mail sub@toyokeizai.co.jp; internet www.toyokeizai.net;

f. 1895; business, economics, finance, and corporate information; Editor TAKAHASHI HIROSHI; circ. 80,000.

PERIODICALS

Brutus: Magazine House, 3-13-10, Ginza, Chuo-ku, Tokyo 104-8003; tel. (3) 3545-7000; fax (3) 3546-0034; internet magazineworld.jp/brutus; f. 1980; every 2 weeks; men's interest; Pres. ISHIZAKI TAKESHI; circ. 250,000.

Bungei-Shunju: Bungei-Shunju Ltd, 3-23, Kioi-cho, Chiyoda-ku, Tokyo 102-8008; tel. (3) 3265-1211; fax (3) 3221-6623; internet www .bunshun.co.jp; f. 1923; monthly; general; Pres. HIRAO TAKAHIRO; circ. 647,000.

Business Tokyo: Keizaikai Bldg, 2-13-18, Minami-Aoyama, Minato-ku, Tokyo 105; tel. (3) 3423-8500; fax (3) 3423-8505; f. 1987; Dir TAKUO IDA; Editor ANTHONY PAUL; circ. 125,000.

Chuokoron: Chuokoron-Shinsha Inc, 2-8-7, Kyobashi, Chuo-ku, Tokyo 104-8320; tel. (3) 3563-1866; fax (3) 3561-5929; e-mail hanbai@ chuko.co.jp; internet www.chuko.co.jp; f. 1887; monthly; general interest; Chief Editor HIROSHI KOIZUMI; circ. 90,000.

Croissant: Magazine House, 3-13-10, Ginza, Chuo-ku, Tokyo 104-03; tel. (3) 3545-7111; fax (3) 3546-0034; f. 1977; every 2 weeks; home; Editor MASAAKI TAKEUCHI; circ. 600,000.

Fujinkoron: Chuokoron-Sha Inc, 2-8-7, Kyobashi, Chuo-ku, Tokyo 104; tel. (3) 3563-1866; fax (3) 3561-5920; internet www.fujinkoron .jp; f. 1916; monthly; women's literature; Editor YUKIKO YUKAWA; circ. 185,341.

Geijutsu Shincho: Shincho-Sha, 71, Yarai-cho, Shinjuku-ku, Tokyo 162-8711; tel. (3) 3266-5211; fax (3) 3266-5235; e-mail geishin@shinchosha.co.jp; f. 1950; monthly; fine arts, music, architecture, films, drama and design; Editor ICHIRO MOTOHASHI; circ. 50,000.

Ginza: Magazine House, 3-13-10, Ginza, Chuo-ku, Tokyo 104-8003; tel. (3) 3545-7040; fax (3) 3545-2133; internet magazineworld.jp/ginza; f. 1997; monthly; women's interest; Pres. ISHI YAMAZAKI MENG; circ. 250,000.

Ie-no-Hikari (Light of Home): Ie-no-Hikari Asscn, 11, Ichigaya Funagawaramachi, Shinjuku-ku, Tokyo 162-8448; tel. (3) 3266-9038; fax (3) 3266-9337; e-mail zugakon@ienohikari.or.jp; internet www.ienohikari.net; f. 1925; monthly; rural and general interest; Pres. SHUZO SUZUKI; circ. 928,000.

Japan Company Handbook: Toyo Keizai Inc, 1-2-1, Nihonbashi Hongoku-cho, Chuo-ku, Tokyo 103-8345; tel. (3) 3246-5551; fax (3) 3279-0332; e-mail info@toyokeizai.co.jp; internet www.toyokeizai.co .jp; f. 1974; quarterly; English; Editor EIICH FURUSHO; total circ. 16,000.

Junon: Shufu-To-Seikatsu Sha Ltd, 3-5-7, Kyobashi, Chuo-ku, Tokyo 104-8357; tel. (3) 3563-5120; fax (3) 5250-7081; e-mail webmaster@mb.shufu.co.jp; internet www.shufu.co.jp/junon; f. 1973; monthly; television and entertainment; circ. 560,000; Pres. KATSUTOSHI.

Keizaijin: Kansai Economic Federation, Nakanoshima Center Bldg, 6-2-27, Nakanoshima, Kita-ku, Osaka 530-6691; tel. (6) 6441-0104; fax (6) 6443-0443; e-mail kef_60_eng@kankeiren.or.jp; internet www.kankeiren.or.jp; f. 1947; monthly; economics; Editor M. YASUTAKE; circ. 2,600.

Lettuce Club: Toranomon Corpn, 2-2-5, Minatu-ku, Tokyo 105-8455; tel. (3) 5860-9820; fax (3) 5860-9829; e-mail info@sscom.co.jp; internet www.lettuceclub.net; f. 1987; every 2 weeks; cookery; Man. HIDEKI TAKAGAWA; circ. 800,000.

Money Japan: Toranomon Corpn, 2-2-5, Minato-ku, Tokyo 105-8455; tel. (3) 3560-8700; e-mail info@sscom.co.jp; internet www .moneyjapan-web.com; f. 1985; monthly; finance; Editor TOSHIO KOBAYASHI; circ. 500,000.

Popeye: Magazine House, 3-13-10, Ginza, Chuo-ku, Tokyo 104-8003; tel. (3) 3545-7160; fax (3) 3545-9026; internet magazineworld .jp/popeye; f. 1976; every 2 weeks; fashion, youth interest; Editor-in-Chief TAKAHIRO KINOSHITA; circ. 320,000.

President: President Inc, Hirakawacho Mori Tower, 13/F, 2-16-1, Hirakawa-cho, Chiyoda-ku, Tokyo 102-8641; tel. (3) 3237-3711; fax (3) 3237-3748; internet www.president.co.jp; f. 1963; monthly; business; Pres. YOSHIAKI NAGASAKA; circ. 263,308.

Ray: Shufunotomo Co Ltd, 2-9, Kanda Surugadai, Chiyoda-ku, Tokyo 101; tel. (3) 3294-1163; fax (3) 3291-5093; f. 1988; monthly; women's interest; Editor TATSURO NAKANISHI; circ. 244,000.

Ryoko Yomiuri: Yomiuri Travel Publishing Co Inc, 18-3, Nihonbashi, Chuo-ku, Tokyo 103-8545; tel. (3) 5847-8271; fax (3) 5847-8270; e-mail ad@ryokoyomiuri.co.jp; internet www.ryokoyomiuri.co.jp; f. 1966; monthly; travel; Pres. OGASAWARA SHINOBU; circ. 470,000.

Sekai: Iwanami Shoten Publishers, 2-5-5, Hitotsubashi, Chiyoda-ku, Tokyo 101-8002; tel. (3) 5210-4141; fax (3) 5210-4144; e-mail sekai@iwanami.co.jp; internet www.iwanami.co.jp/sekai; f. 1946;

monthly; review of world and domestic affairs; Editor ATSUSHI OKAMOTO; circ. 120,000.

Shinkenchiku: Shinkenchiku-Sha Co Ltd, Kasumigaseki Bldg, 17/F, 3-2-5, Kasumigaseki, Chiyoda-ku, Tokyo 100-6017; tel. (3) 6205-4380; fax (3) 6205-4386; e-mail ja-business@japan-architect.co.jp; internet www.japlusu.com; f. 1925; monthly; architecture; Editor NOBUYUKI YOSHIDA; circ. 87,000.

Shiso (Thought): Iwanami Shoten Publishers, 2-5-5, Hitotsubashi, Chiyoda-ku, Tokyo 101-8002; tel. (3) 5210-4055; fax (3) 5210-4037; e-mail shiso@iwanami.co.jp; internet www.iwanami.co.jp/shiso; f. 1921; monthly; philosophy, social sciences and humanities; Editor TATSUO HAYASHI; circ. 20,000.

Shosetsu Shincho: Shincho-Sha, 71, Yarai-cho, Shinjuku-ku, Tokyo 162-8711; tel. (3) 3266-5241; fax (3) 3266-5412; f. 1947; monthly; literature; Editor-in-Chief TOSHIMASA FUKE; circ. 80,000.

Shufunotomo: Shufunotomo Co Ltd, 2-9, Kanda Surugadai, Chiyoda-ku, Tokyo 101; tel. (3) 5280-7531; fax (3) 5280-7431; e-mail international-info@shufunotomo.co.jp; internet www.shufunotomo.co.jp; f. 1917; monthly; home and lifestyle; Editor YOSHIYUKI OGINO; circ. 450,000.

Shukan Gendai: Kodan-Sha Ltd, 2-12-21, Otowa, Bunkyo-ku, Tokyo 112-8001; tel. (3) 5395-3637; fax (3) 5395-5791; f. 1966; monthly; cultural and political; Editor NOBUHIRO NAGASAKI.

So-en: Bunka Publishing Bureau, c/o Bunka Fashion College, 3-22-7, Yoyogi, Shibuya-ku, Tokyo 151-8524; tel. (3) 3299-2531; fax (3) 3370-3712; e-mail info-bpb@bunka.ac.jp; internet books.bunka.ac.jp; f. 1936; monthly; fashion; Editor KEIKO SASAKI; circ. 270,000.

NEWS AGENCIES

Jiji Tsushin (Jiji Press Ltd): 5-15-8, Ginza, Chuo-ku, Tokyo 104-8178; tel. (3) 6800-1111; e-mail info@jiji.co.jp; internet www.jiji.com; f. 1945; Pres. YUTAKA NISHIZAWA.

Kyodo Tsushin (Kyodo News): Shiodome Media Tower, 1-7-1, Higashi-Shimbashi, Minato-ku, Tokyo 105-7201; tel. (3) 6252-8301; fax (3) 6252-8795; e-mail kokusai@kyodonews.jp; internet www.english.kyodonews.jp; f. 1945; Pres. MASAKI FUKUYAMA; Man. Editor FUMIKZAU YOSHIDA.

Radiopress Inc: R-Bldg Shinjuku, 5F, 33-8, Wakamatsu-cho, Shinjuku-ku, Tokyo 162-0056; tel. (3) 5273-2171; fax (3) 5273-2180; e-mail rptokyo@oak.ocn.ne.jp; f. 1945; provides news from the People's Repub. of China, the former USSR, Democratic People's Repub. of Korea, Viet Nam and elsewhere to the press and govt offices; Pres. AKIO IJUIN.

PRESS ASSOCIATIONS

Foreign Correspondents' Club of Japan: Yaruku-cho Denki Kita Bldg, 20/F, 1-7-1, Yuraku-cho, Chiyoda-ku, Tokyo 100-0006; tel. (3) 3211-3161; fax (3) 3211-3168; e-mail nakamura@fccj.or.jp; internet www.fccj.or.jp; f. 1945; 193 cos; Pres. LUCY BIRMINGHAM; Sec. MICHAEL PENN.

Foreign Press Center: Nippon Press Center Bldg, 6/F, 2-2-1, Uchisaiwai-cho, Chiyoda-ku, Tokyo 100-0011; tel. (3) 3501-3401; fax (3) 3501-3622; e-mail rr@fpcjpn.or.jp; internet www.fpcj.jp; f. 1976; est. by The Japan Newspaper Publishers and Editors Asscn and the Japan Fed. of Economic Orgs; provides services to the foreign press; Pres. KIYOTAKA AKASAKA.

Nihon Shinbun Kyokai (The Japan Newspaper Publishers and Editors Asscn): Nippon Press Center Bldg, 2-2-1, Uchisaiwai-cho, Chiyoda-ku, Tokyo 100-8543; tel. (3) 3591-3462; fax (3) 3591-6149; e-mail nsk-intl@pressnet.or.jp; internet www.pressnet.or.jp; f. 1946; mems include 130 cos (104 daily newspapers, 4 news agencies and 22 radio and TV cos); Pres. KOJIRO SHIRAISHI; Man. Dir AKIRA KAWASHIMA.

Nihon Zasshi Kyokai (Japan Magazine Publishers Asscn): 1-7, Kanda Surugadai, Chiyoda-ku, Tokyo 101-0062; tel. (3) 3291-0775; fax (3) 3293-6239; f. 1956; 85 mems; Pres. HARUHIKO ISHIKAWA; Sec. GENYA INUI.

Publishers

Akane Shobo Co Ltd: 3-2-1, Nishi-Kanda, Chiyoda-ku, Tokyo 101-0065; tel. (3) 3263-0641; fax (3) 3263-5440; e-mail mitsuharu02@akaneshobo.co.jp; internet www.akaneshobo.co.jp; f. 1949; juvenile; Pres. MASAHARU OKAMOTO.

Akita Publishing Co Ltd: 2-10-8, Iidabashi, Chiyoda-ku, Tokyo 102-8101; tel. (3) 3264-7011; fax (3) 3265-5906; e-mail media@akitashoten.co.jp; internet www.akitashoten.co.jp; f. 1948; social sciences, history, juvenile; Pres. SADAMI AKITA.

ALC Press Inc: 2-54-12, Eifuku, Suginami-ku, Tokyo 168-8611; tel. (3) 3323-1101; fax (3) 3327-1022; e-mail info@alc.co.jp; internet www

.alc.co.jp; f. 1969; linguistics, educational materials, dictionaries, juvenile; Pres. NODA TORU; Chair. TERUMARO HIRAMOTO.

Asahi Shimbun Publications Division: 5-3-2, Tsukiji, Chuo-ku, Tokyo 104-8011; tel. (3) 5541-8757; fax (3) 3545-0311; e-mail doors@asahi.com; internet publications.asahi.com; f. 1879; general; Pres. TADAKAZU KIMURA.

Asakura Publishing Co Ltd: 6-29, Shin Ogawa-machi, Shinjuku-ku, Tokyo 162-8707; tel. (3) 3260-7631; fax (3) 3260-0180; e-mail morikawa@asakura.co.jp; internet www.asakura.co.jp; f. 1929; natural sciences, medicine, social sciences; Pres. KUNIZO ASAKURA.

Asuka Publishing Inc: 2-11-5, Suido, Bunkyo-ku, Tokyo 112-0005; tel. (3) 5395-7650; fax (3) 5395-7654; e-mail askaweb@asuka-g.co.jp; internet www.asuka-g.co.jp; f. 1973; sociology, law, economics, languages; Pres. EIICHI ISHINO.

Baifukan Co Ltd: 4-3-12, Kudan-Minami, Chiyoda-ku, Tokyo 102-0074; tel. (3) 3262-5256; fax (3) 3262-5276; e-mail bfkeigyo@mx7.mesh.ne.jp; internet www.baifukan.co.jp; f. 1924; engineering, mathematics, natural and social sciences, psychology; Pres. ITARU YAMAMOTO.

Baseball Magazine-Sha: 3-10-10, Misaki-cho, Chiyoda-ku, Tokyo 101-8381; tel. (3) 3238-0081; fax (3) 3238-0106; internet www.bbm-japan.com; f. 1946; sports, physical education, recreation, travel; Pres. TETSUO IKEDA.

Bensey Publishing Inc: 2-20-6, Kanda Jimbo-cho, Chiyoda-ku, Tokyo 101-0051; tel. (3) 5215-9021; fax (3) 5215-9025; e-mail bensey@bensey.co.jp; internet www.bensey.co.jp; f. 1967; philosophy, religion, history, art, languages, literature; Pres. RINTARO OKADA.

Bijutsu Shuppan-Sha Ltd: Jinbo-cho Place, 9/F, 3-2-3, Kanda Jinbo-cho, Chiyoda-ku, Tokyo 101-8417; tel. (3) 3234-0942; fax (3) 3234-9451; e-mail info@bijutsu.co.jp; internet www.bijutsu.co.jp; f. 1905; fine arts, graphic design; Pres. KENTARO OSHITA.

Bonjinsha Co Ltd: 1-3-13, Hirakawa-cho, Chiyoda-ku, Tokyo 102-0093; tel. (3) 3263-3959; fax (3) 3263-3116; e-mail info@bonjinsha.com; internet www.bonjinsha.com; f. 1973; Japanese language teaching materials; Pres. HISAMITSU TANAKA.

Bun-eido Publishing Co Inc: 28, Kamitoba, Daimotsu-cho, Minami-ku, Kyoto 601-8691; tel. (75) 671-3161; fax (75) 671-3165; e-mail fujita@bun-eido.co.jp; internet www.bun-eido.co.jp; f. 1921; reference books, dictionaries, textbooks, juvenile, history; Pres. HIDEO-HIRO MASUI.

Bungei Shunju Ltd: 3-23, Kioi-cho, Chiyoda-ku, Tokyo 102-8008; tel. (3) 3265-1211; fax (3) 3265-1363; e-mail nishiyama@bunshun.co.jp; internet www.bunshun.co.jp; f. 1923; fiction, general literature, recreation, economics, sociology; Dir TAKAHIRO HIRAO.

Bunri Co Ltd: 1-1-5, Sekiguchi, Bunkyo-ku, Tokyo 112-0014; tel. (3) 3268-4113; fax (3) 3260-1717; e-mail webmaster@bnet.bunri.co.jp; internet www.bunri.co.jp; f. 1950; Pres. SHIRO HATA.

Chikuma Shobo: Chikumashobo Bldg, 2-5-3, Kuramae, Taito-ku, Tokyo 111-8755; tel. (3) 5687-2671; fax (3) 5687-1585; e-mail henshuinfo@chikumashobo.co.jp; internet www.chikumashobo.co.jp; f. 1940; general literature, fiction, history, juvenile, fine arts; Pres. TOSHIYUKI KUMAZAWA.

Child-Honsha Co Ltd: 5-24-21, Koishikawa, Bunkyo-ku, Tokyo 112-8512; tel. (3) 3813-3781; fax (3) 3813-3778; e-mail ehon@childbook.co.jp; internet www.childbook.co.jp; f. 1930; juvenile; Pres. SHUNJI ASAKA.

Chuo Hoki Publishing Co Ltd: 2-27-4, Yoyogi, Shibuya-ku, Tokyo 151-0053; tel. (3) 3379-3899; fax (3) 5371-7769; e-mail info@chuohoki.co.jp; internet www.chuohoki.co.jp; f. 1947; law, social sciences; Pres. AKIHIKO SHOMURA.

Chuo University Press: 742-1, Higashi-Nakano, Hachioji-shi, Tokyo 192-0393; tel. (426) 74-2351; fax (426) 74-2354; internet www2.chuo-u.ac.jp/up/; f. 1948; law, history, sociology, economics, science, literature; Pres. RYOJI YOSHIDA.

Chuokoron-Shinsha Inc: 2-8-7, Kyobashi, Chuo-ku, Tokyo 104-8320; tel. (3) 3563-1261; fax (3) 3561-5920; e-mail m-akashi@chuko.co.jp; internet www.chuko.co.jp; f. 1886; philosophy, history, sociology, general literature; Pres. YUKIKAZU KOBAYASHI.

Corona Publishing Co Ltd: 4-46-10, Sengoku, Bunkyo-ku, Tokyo 112-0011; tel. (3) 3941-3131; fax (3) 3941-3137; e-mail info@coronasha.co.jp; internet www.coronasha.co.jp; f. 1927; electronics, medical books, mechanical engineering, computer science; Pres. MASAYA GORAI.

Dempa Publications Inc: 1-11-15, Higashi-Gotanda, Shinagawa-ku, Tokyo 141-8715; tel. (3) 3445-6111; fax (3) 3444-7515; f. 1950; electronics, personal computer software, juvenile, trade newspapers, English and Japanese language publications; Pres. TETSUO HIRA-YAMA.

Diamond Inc: 6-12-17, Jingumae, Shibuya-ku, Tokyo 150-8409; tel. (3) 5778-7233; fax (3) 5778-6618; e-mail rights@diamond.co.jp; internet www.diamond.co.jp; f. 1913; business, management, economics, financial; Pres. FUMIAKI SHIKATANI.

Dohosha Ltd: TAS Bldg, 2-5-2, Nishi-Kanda, Chiyoda-ku, Tokyo 101-0065; tel. (3) 5276-0831; fax (3) 5276-0840; e-mail intl@dohosha.co.jp; f. 1997; general works, architecture, art, Buddhism, business, children's education, cooking, flower-arranging, gardening, medicine.

East Press Co Ltd: 1-19, Kanda Jimbo-cho, Chiyoda-ku, Tokyo 101-0051; tel. (3) 5259-7707; fax (3) 5259-7708; e-mail webmaster@eastpress.co.jp; internet www.eastpress.co.jp; f. 2005; literature, comics, business, self-help, parenting, health, sports, music; Chair. SHINGERU KOBAYASHI; Pres. OSAMU ASOSHINA.

Froebel-Kan Co Ltd: 6-14-9, Honkomagome, Bunkyo-ku, Tokyo 113-8611; tel. (3) 5395-6614; fax (3) 5395-6643; e-mail hirose-k@froebel-kan.co.jp; internet www.froebel-kan.co.jp; f. 1907; juvenile, educational; Pres. HIDEO MUTO.

Fukuinkan Shoten Publishers Inc: 6-6-3, Honkomagome, Bunkyo-ku, Tokyo 113-8686; tel. (3) 3942-0032; fax (3) 3942-1401; e-mail international-rights@fukuinkan.co.jp; internet www.fukuinkan.co.jp; f. 1952; juvenile; Pres. NOBORU OGURA; Chair. KATSUMI SATO.

Fusosha Publishing Inc: 1-15-1, Kaigan, Minato-ku, Tokyo 105-8070; tel. (3) 5403-8851; fax (3) 3578-3078; e-mail s_ishii@fusosha.co.jp; internet www.fusosha.co.jp; f. 1984; social sciences, business, mystery, magazines, textbooks; Pres. EIICHI KUBOTA.

Futabasha Publishers Ltd: 3-28, Higashi-Goken-cho, Shinjuku-ku, Tokyo 162-8540; tel. (3) 5261-4832; fax (3) 5261-3480; e-mail general@futabasha.co.jp; internet www.futabasha.co.jp; f. 1948; fiction, non-fiction, comics, guide books; Pres. MOTOHISA TOTSUKA.

Gakken Co Ltd: 2-11-8, Nishi-Gotanda, Shinagawa-ku, Tokyo 141-8415; tel. (3) 6431-1208; fax (3) 6431-1679; e-mail inq@gakken.co.jp; internet www.gakken.co.jp; f. 1946; juvenile, educational, art, encyclopaedias, dictionaries; Pres. HIROAKI MIYAHARA.

Graphic-sha Publishing Co Ltd: 1-14-17 Kudan-Kita, Chiyoda-ku, Tokyo 102-0073; tel. (3) 3263-4318; fax (3) 3263-5297; e-mail contact@graphicsha.co.jp; internet www.graphicsha.co.jp; f. 1962; art, design, architecture, manga techniques, hobbies; Pres. KUZE TOSHIRO.

Gyosei Corpn: 1-18-11, Shinkiba, Koto-ku, Tokyo 136-8575; tel. (3) 6892-6666; fax (3) 6892-6925; e-mail business@gyosei.co.jp; internet www.gyosei.co.jp; f. 1893; law, education, science, politics, business, art, language, literature, juvenile; Pres. YUJIRO SAWADA.

Hakusui-Sha Co Ltd: 3-24, Kanda Ogawa-machi, Chiyoda-ku, Tokyo 101-0052; tel. (3) 3291-7821; fax (3) 3291-7810; e-mail hpmaster@hakusuisha.co.jp; internet www.hakusuisha.co.jp; f. 1915; general literature, science and languages; Pres. NAOSHI OIKAWA.

Hayakawa Publishing Inc: 2-2, Kanda-Tacho, Chiyoda-ku, Tokyo 101-0046; tel. (3) 3252-3111; fax (3) 3254-1550; internet www.hayakawa-online.co.jp; f. 1945; wine books, children's books, coffee-table books, drama, comic books, monthly magazines; Pres. HIROSHI HAYAKAWA.

Heibonsha Ltd: 3-29, Kanda-Jimbocho, Chiyoda-ku, Tokyo 101-0051; tel. (3) 3230-6570; fax (3) 3230-6586; e-mail rights@heibonsha.co.jp; internet www.heibonsha.co.jp; f. 1914; encyclopaedias, art, history, geography, literature, science; Pres. NAOTO SHIMONAKA.

Hirokawa Publishing Co: 3-27-14, Hongo, Bunkyo-ku, Tokyo 113-0033; tel. (3) 3815-3651; fax (3) 5684-7030; f. 1925; natural sciences, medicine, pharmacy, nursing, chemistry; Pres. SETSUO HIROKAWA.

Hoikusha Publishing Co: 18-24, Hiroshi-bacho, Suita-shi, Osaka 564-0052; tel. (6) 6330-5680; fax (6) 6330-5681; e-mail matsui@hoikusha.co.jp; internet www.hoikusha.co.jp; f. 1947; natural sciences, juvenile, fine arts, geography; Pres. TAKAHIKO MATSUI.

Hokkaido University Press: Kita-9, Nishi-8, Kita-ku, Sapporo 060-0809; tel. (11) 747-2308; fax (11) 736-8605; e-mail hupress_2@hup.gr.jp; internet www.hup.gr.jp; f. 1970; social and natural sciences, technology, humanities; Pres. KATSUMI YOSHIDA.

Hokuryukan Co Ltd: 3-8-14, Takanawa, Minato-ku, Tokyo 108-0074; tel. (3) 5449-4591; fax (3) 5449-4950; e-mail hk-ns@hokuryukan-ns.co.jp; internet www.hokuryukan-ns.co.jp; f. 1891; natural sciences, medical science, juvenile, dictionaries; Pres. HISAKO FUKUDA.

The Hokuseido Press: Hayashi Bldg, 1-21-9, Sugamo, Toshima-ku, Tokyo 170-0002; tel. (3) 5940-0511; fax (3) 5940-0512; e-mail info@hokuseido.com; internet www.hokuseido.com; f. 1914; regional non-fiction, dictionaries, textbooks; Pres. KEISUKE YAMAMOTO.

Horitsubunka-sha: 7, Iwagakakiuchi-cho, Kamigamo, Kita-ku, Kyoto 603-8053; tel. (75) 791-7131; fax (75) 721-8400; e-mail eigyo@hou-bun.co.jp; internet www.hou-bun.co.jp; f. 1948; law, politics, economics, sociology, philosophy; Pres. JUNKO TANABIKI.

Hosei University Press: 3-2-7, Kudan-Kita, Chiyoda-ku, Tokyo 102-0073; tel. (3) 5214-5540; fax (3) 5214-5542; e-mail mail@h-up.com; internet www.h-up.com; f. 1948; philosophy, history, economics, sociology, natural sciences, literature; Pres. TOSHIO MASUDA.

Ie-No-Hikari Association: 11, Funagawara-cho, Ichigaya, Shinjuku-ku, Tokyo 162-8448; tel. (3) 3266-9000; fax (3) 3266-9048; e-mail hikari@mxd.mesh.ne.jp; internet www.ienohikari.net; f. 1925; social sciences, agriculture, cooking; Pres. TOSHIHIRO SONODA.

Igaku-Shoin Ltd: 1-28-23, Hongo, Bunkyo-ku, Tokyo 113-8719; tel. (3) 3817-5600; fax (3) 3815-4114; e-mail pa@igaku-shoin.co.jp; internet www.igaku-shoin.co.jp; f. 1944; medicine, nursing; Pres. YU KANEHARA.

Ikubundo Publishing Co Ltd: 5-30-21, Hongo, Bunkyo-ku, Tokyo 113-0033; tel. (3) 3814-5571; fax (3) 3814-5576; e-mail webmaster@ikubundo.com; internet www.ikubundo.com; f. 1899; languages, dictionaries; Pres. TOSHIYUKI OI.

Institute for Financial Affairs Inc (KINZAI): 19, Minami-Motomachi, Shinjuku-ku, Tokyo 160-8519; tel. (3) 3358-1161; fax (3) 3359-7947; e-mail JDI04072@nifty.ne.jp; internet www.kinzai.or.jp; f. 1950; finance and economics, banking laws and regulations, accounting; Pres. MASATERU YOSHIDA.

Ishiyaku Publishers Inc: 1-7-10, Honkomagome, Bunkyo-ku, Tokyo 113-8612; tel. (3) 5395-7600; fax (3) 5395-7606; e-mail webmaster@ishiyaku.co.jp; internet www.ishiyaku.co.jp; f. 1921; medicine, dentistry, rehabilitation, nursing, nutrition and pharmaceutics; Pres. HIDEHO OHATA.

Iwanami Shoten, Publishers: 2-5-5, Hitotsubashi, Chiyoda-ku, Tokyo 101-8002; tel. (3) 5210-4000; fax (3) 5210-4039; e-mail rights@iwanami.co.jp; internet www.iwanami.co.jp; f. 1913; natural and social sciences, humanities, literature, fine arts, juvenile, dictionaries; Pres. AKIO YAMAGUCHI.

Iwasaki Publishing Co Ltd: 1-9-2, Suido, Bunkyo-ku, Tokyo 112-0005; tel. (3) 3812-0151; fax (3) 3812-1381; e-mail ask@iwasakishoten.co.jp; internet www.iwasakishoten.co.jp; f. 1934; juvenile; Pres. HIROAKI IWASAKI.

Japan Broadcast Publishing Co Ltd: 41-1, Udagawa-cho, Shibuya-ku, Tokyo 150-8081; tel. (3) 3464-7311; fax (3) 3780-3394; e-mail kikaka@nhk-book.co.jp; internet www.nhk-book.co.jp; f. 1931; foreign language textbooks, gardening, home economics, sociology, education, art, juvenile; Pres. AKIHIDE MIZOGUCHI.

Japan External Trade Organization (JETRO): Ark Mori Bldg, 6/F, 1-12-32, Akasaka, Minato-ku, Tokyo 107-6006; tel. (3) 3582-5511; fax (3) 3587-2485; internet www.jetro.go.jp; f. 1958; trade, economics, investment; Chair. HIROYUKI ISHIGE.

Japan Publications Trading Co Ltd: 1-2-1, Sarugaku-cho, Chiyoda-ku, Tokyo 101-0064; tel. (3) 3292-3751; fax (3) 3292-0410; e-mail jpt@jptco.co.jp; internet www.jptco.co.jp; f. 1942; general works, art, health, sports; Pres. AYAMORI TOYOHIKO.

The Japan Times Ltd: 4-5-4, Shibaura, Minato-ku, Tokyo 108-0023; tel. (3) 3453-2013; fax (3) 3453-8023; e-mail jt-books@kt.rim.or.jp; internet bookclub.japantimes.co.jp; f. 1897; linguistics, culture, business; Pres. TOSHIAKI OGASAWARA.

Jikkyo Shuppan Co Ltd: 5, Goban-cho, Chiyoda-ku, Tokyo 102-8377; tel. (3) 3238-7700; fax (3) 3238-7719; e-mail sato.a@jikkyo.co.jp; internet www.jikkyo.co.jp; f. 1941; textbooks; Pres. YOJI TOTSUKA.

Jimbun Shoin: 9, Nishi-Uchihata-cho, Takeda, Fushimi-ku, Kyoto 612-8447; tel. (75) 603-1344; fax (75) 603-1814; e-mail jmsb@jimbunshoin.co.jp; internet www.jimbunshoin.co.jp; f. 1927; general literature, philosophy, fiction, social sciences, religion, fine arts; Pres. HIROSHI WATANABE.

Jitsugyo No Nihonsha Ltd: 3-7-5, Kyobashi, Chuo-ku, Tokyo 104-8233; tel. (3) 3562-1021; fax (3) 3562-2662; e-mail soumu@j-n.co.jp; internet www.j-n.co.jp; f. 1897; general, social sciences, juvenile, travel, business, comics; Pres. HIDEO MURAYAMA.

JTB Publishing (Japan Travel Bureau): Urban-net Ichigaya Bldg, 25-5, Haraikatamachi, Shinjuku-ku, Tokyo 162-8446; tel. (3) 6888-7811; fax (3) 6888-7809; e-mail jtbpublishing@rurubu.ne.jp; internet www.jtbpublishing.com; f. 2004; travel, geography, history, fine arts, languages; Pres. YUJI YOKOYAMA.

Kadokawa Group Publishing Inc: 2-13-3, Fujimi, Chiyoda-ku, Tokyo 102-8177; tel. (3) 3238-8715; fax (3) 3262-7734; e-mail k-master@kadokawa.co.jp; internet www.kadokawa.co.jp; f. 1945; literature, history, dictionaries, religion, fine arts, books on tape, compact discs, CD-ROMs, comics, animation, video cassettes, computer games; Pres. MATSUBARA MAKOTO TATSUKI.

Kaibundo Publishing Co Ltd: 2-5-4, Suido, Bunkyo-ku, Tokyo 112-0005; tel. (3) 3815-3291; fax (3) 3815-3052; e-mail soumu@kaibundo.jp; internet www.kaibundo.jp; f. 1914; marine affairs, natural sciences, engineering, industry; Pres. SETSUO OKADA.

Kaiseisha Publishing Co Ltd: 3-5, Ichigaya Sadohara-cho, Shinjuku-ku, Tokyo 162-8450; tel. (3) 3260-3229; fax (3) 3260-3540; e-mail foreign@kaiseisha.co.jp; internet www.kaiseisha.net; f. 1936; juvenile; Pres. MASAKI IMAMURA.

Kanehara & Co Ltd: 2-31-14, Yushima, Bunkyo-ku, Tokyo 113-8687; tel. (3) 3811-7185; fax (3) 3813-0288; e-mail kanehara@abox5

.so-net.ne.jp; internet www.kanehara-shuppan.co.jp; f. 1875; medical, agricultural, engineering and scientific; Pres. :SUMIO FURUYA.

Keiso Shobo Publishing Co Ltd: 2-1-1, Suido, Bunkyo-ku, Tokyo 112-0005; tel. (3) 3814-6861; fax (3) 3814-6968; e-mail h-imura@ keisoshobo.co.jp; internet www.keisoshobo.co.jp; f. 1948; law, economics, politics, literature, psychology, philosophy, sociology; Pres. HISATO IMURA.

Kenkyusha Ltd: 2-11-3, Fujimi, Chiyoda-ku, Tokyo 102-8152; tel. (3) 3288-7777; fax (3) 3288-7799; e-mail hanbai@kenkyusha.co.jp; internet www.kenkyusha.co.jp; f. 1907; bilingual dictionaries, books on languages; Pres. YUSUKE KOSAKAI.

Kinokuniya Co Ltd: 3-7-10, Shimomeguro, Meguro-ku, Tokyo 153-8504; tel. (3) 6910-0508; fax (3) 6420-1354; e-mail publish@ kinokuniya.co.jp; internet www.kinokuniya.co.jp; f. 1927; humanities, social and natural sciences; Pres. MASASHI TAKAI.

KK Best Sellers Co Ltd: 2-29-7, Minami-Otsuka, Toshima-ku, Tokyo 170-8457; tel. (3) 5976-9121; fax (3) 5976-9240; e-mail tatuya@ bestsellers.co.jp; internet www.kk-bestsellers.com; f. 1967; nonfiction, general literature; Pres. SHIGERU SUGAWARA.

Kodansha Ltd: 2-12-21, Otowa, Bunkyo-ku, Tokyo 112-8001; tel. (3) 3946-6201; fax (3) 3944-9915; e-mail foreignrights@kodansha.co.jp; internet www.kodansha.co.jp; f. 1909; fine arts, fiction, literature, juvenile, comics, dictionaries; Pres. YOSHINOBU NOMA.

Kosei Publishing Co Ltd: 2-7-1, Wada, Suginami-ku, Tokyo 166-8535; tel. (3) 5385-2319; fax (3) 5385-2331; e-mail kspub@ kosei-shuppan.co.jp; internet www.kosei-shuppan.co.jp; f. 1966; general works, philosophy, religion, history, pedagogy, social science, art, juvenile; Pres. MORIYASU OKABE.

Kumon Publishing Co Ltd: Gobancho Grand Bldg, 3-1, Gobancho, Chiyoda-ku, Tokyo 102-8180; tel. (3) 3234-4004; fax (3) 3234-4483; e-mail international@kumonshuppan.com; internet www .kumonshuppan.com; f. 1988; juvenile, dictionaries, education; Pres. NAOTO SHIMURA.

Kwansei Gakuin University Press: 1-155, Uegahara Ichiban-cho, Nishi-Nomiya-shi, Hyogo 662-0891; tel. (798) 53-7002; fax (798) 53-9592; internet www.kwansei.ac.jp/press; f. 1997; natural and social sciences, philosophy, literature; Pres. KIKUYO TANAKA.

Kyoritsu Shuppan Co Ltd: 4-6-19, Kohinata, Bunkyo-ku, Tokyo 112-8700; tel. (3) 3947-2511; fax (3) 3947-2539; e-mail nanjo@ kyoritsu-pub.co.jp; internet www.kyoritsu-pub.co.jp; f. 1926; scientific and technical; Pres. MITSUAKI NANJO.

Kyoto University Press: Kyodai-Yoshida-Minami, 69, Yoshidakonoe-cho, Sakyo-ku, Kyoto 606-8315; tel. (75) 761-6182; fax (75) 761-6190; e-mail sales@kyoto-up.or.jp; internet www.kyoto-up.or.jp; f. 1989; history, literature, philology, anthropology, sociology, economics, area studies, ecology, architecture, psychology, philosophy, space physics, earth and planetary science; Rep. Prof. TAMEJIRO HIYAMA.

Kyushu University Press: 7-1-146, Hakozaki, Higashi-ku, Fukuoka 812-0053; tel. (92) 641-0515; fax (92) 641-0172; e-mail kup@kup.or.jp; internet www.kup.or.jp/en; f. 1975; history, political science, law, economics, technology, linguistics, literature, psychology, medicine, agriculture; Chief Dir NAOYUKI ISOGAWA.

Maruzen Publishing Co Ltd: Kanda-Jimbocho, 6F, 2-17, Kanda-Jimbocho, Chiyoda-ku, Tokyo 101-0051; tel. (3) 3512-3263; fax (3) 3512-3272; e-mail s_yasu@maruzen.co.jp; internet pub.maruzen.co .jp; f. 1869; general works; Pres. KAZUHIRO IKEDA.

Meisei University Press: 2-1-1, Hodokubo, Hino-shi, Tokyo 191-8506; tel. (42) 591-9979; fax (42) 593-0192; f. 1975; humanities, education, social and natural sciences; Pres. TETSUO OGAWA.

Minerva Shobo: 1, Tsutsumidani-cho, Hinooka, Yamashina-ku, Kyoto 607-8494; tel. (75) 581-5191; fax (75) 581-8379; e-mail info@ minervashobo.co.jp; internet www.minervashobo.co.jp; f. 1948; general non-fiction and reference; Pres. KEIZO SUGITA.

Misuzu Shobo Ltd: 5-32-21, Hongo, Bunkyo-ku, Tokyo 113-0033; tel. (3) 3815-9181; fax (3) 3818-8497; e-mail nakagawa@msz.co.jp; internet www.msz.co.jp; f. 1946; general, philosophy, history, psychiatry, literature, science, art; Pres. HISAO MOCHITANI.

Morikita Shuppan Co Ltd: 1-4-11, Fujimi, Chiyoda-ku, Tokyo 102-0071; tel. (3) 3265-8341; fax (3) 3261-1349; e-mail hiro@morikita.co .jp; internet www.morikita.co.jp; f. 1950; natural sciences, engineering; Pres. HIROSHI MORIKITA.

Nagaoka Shoten Co Ltd: 1-7-14, Toyotama-Kami, Nerima-ku, Tokyo 176-8518; tel. (3) 3992-5155; fax (3) 3948-9161; e-mail info@ nagaokashoten.co.jp; internet www.nagaokashoten.co.jp; f. 1963; dictionaries, home economics, sports, recreation, law; Pres. SHUICHI NAGAOKA.

Nakayama-Shoten Co Ltd: 1-25-14, Hakusan, Bunkyo-ku, Tokyo 113-8666; tel. (3) 3813-1100; fax (3) 3816-1015; e-mail kojima@ nakayamashoten.co.jp; internet www.nakayamashoten.co.jp; f. 1948; medicine, biology, zoology; Pres. TADASHI HIRATA.

Nanzando Co Ltd: 4-1-11, Yushima, Bunkyo-ku, Tokyo; tel. (3) 5689-7868; fax (3) 5689-7869; e-mail nanzando-soumubu@nanzando .com; internet www.nanzando.com; f. 1901; medical reference, paperbacks; Pres. HAJIME SUZUKI.

Nigensha Publishing Co Ltd: 6-2-1, Honkomagome, Bunkyo-gu, Tokyo, 113-0021; tel. (3) 5395-2041; fax (3) 5395-2045; e-mail intl@ nigensha.co.jp; internet www.nigensha.co.jp; f. 1955; calligraphy, fine arts, art reproductions, cars, watches; Chair. TAKAO WATANABE.

Nihon Vogue Co Ltd: 3-23, Ichigaya Honmura-cho, Shinjuku-ku, Tokyo 162-8705; tel. (3) 5261-5081; fax (3) 3269-8760; e-mail wada-t@ tezukuritown.com; internet www.tezukuritown.com; f. 1954; quilting, needlecraft, handicrafts, knitting, decorative painting, pressed flowers; Pres. NOBUAKI SETO.

Nihonbungeisha Co Ltd: 1-7, Kanda Jimbo-cho, Chiyoda-ku, Tokyo 101-0051; tel. (3) 3294-7771; fax (3) 3294-7780; e-mail mmac@nihonbungeisha.co.jp; internet www.nihonbungeisha.co.jp; f. 1959; home economics, sociology, fiction, technical books; Pres. MITSURU TOMODA.

Nikkei Publishing Inc: Shin-Otemachi Bldg, 2-2-1, Otemachi, Chiyoda-ku, Tokyo 100-0004; tel. (3) 5255-2800; fax (3) 5255-2864; internet www.nikkeibook.com; f. 1876; economics, business, politics, fine arts, video cassettes, CD-ROMs; Pres. HISAO SAIDA.

Nippon Hyoronsha: 3-12-4, Minami-Otsuka, Toshima-ku, Tokyo 170-8474; tel. (3) 3987-8611; fax (3) 3987-8593; e-mail tkuroda@ nippyo.co.jp; internet www.nippyo.co.jp; f. 1918; jurisprudence, economics, science, mathematics, medicine, psychology, business; Pres. HIROSHI KUSHIZAKI.

Nippon Jitsugyo Publishing Co Ltd: 3-2-12, Hongo, Bunkyo-ku, Tokyo 113-0033; tel. (3) 3814-5651; fax (3) 3818-2723; e-mail yasumura@njg.co.jp; internet www.njg.co.jp; f. 1950; business, management, finance and accounting, sales and marketing; Pres. JUN-ICHI SUGIMOTO.

Nosan Gyoson Bunka Kyokai (Rural Culture Association): 7-6-1, Akasaka, Minato-ku, Tokyo 107-8668; tel. (3) 3585-1141; fax (3) 3589-1387; e-mail rural@mail.ruralnet.or.jp; internet www.ruralnet .or.jp; f. 1940; agriculture, food and health, education, economics, philosophy; Pres. YOSHIHIRO HAMAGUCHI.

NTT Publishing Co Ltd: JR Tokyu Meguro Bldg, 7/F, 3-1-1, Kami-Osaki, Shinagawa-ku, Tokyo 141-8654; tel. (3) 5434-1011; fax (3) 5434-1008; e-mail hiroshi.kamino@nttpub.co.jp; internet www .nttpub.co.jp; f. 1987; essays, biography, philosophy, sociology, history, management, economics, technology, telecommunications, picture books, computer game guides; Pres. SHINJI JIKUYA.

Obunsha Co Ltd: 55, Yokodera-cho, Shinjuku-ku, Tokyo 162-8680; tel. (3) 3266-6429; fax (3) 3266-6412; e-mail masao.takahashi@ obunsha.co.jp; internet www.obunsha.co.jp; f. 1931; textbooks, reference, general science and fiction, magazines, encyclopaedias, dictionaries; software; audio-visual aids; CEO DAIICHI IKOMA.

Ohmsha Ltd: 3-1, Kanda Nishiki-cho, Chiyoda-ku, Tokyo 101-8460; tel. (3) 3233-0641; fax (3) 3233-2426; e-mail kaigaika@ohmsha.co.jp; internet www.ohmsha.co.jp; f. 1914; engineering, technical and scientific; Pres. OSAMI TAKEO.

Ongaku No Tomo Sha Corpn (ONT): 6-30, Kagurazaka, Shinjuku-ku, Tokyo 162-8716; tel. (3) 3235-2111; fax (3) 3235-2110; e-mail home_ontomo@ongakunotomo.co.jp; internet www .ongakunotomo.co.jp; f. 1941; compact discs, videograms, music magazines, music books, music data, music textbooks; Pres. KUMIO HORIUCHI.

Osaka University of Economics and Law: 6-10, Gakuonji, Yao-shi, Osaka 581-8511; tel. (729) 41-8211; fax (729) 41-9979; e-mail kondo-t@keiho-u.ac.jp; internet www.keiho-u.ac.jp/research/ syuppan/index.html; f. 1987; economics, law, philosophy, history, natural science, languages, politics; Pres. SHUNKUO KANAZAWA.

Osaka University Press: 2-7, Yamadaoka, Suita-shi, Osaka 565-0871; tel. and fax (6) 6877-1614; fax (6) 6877-1617; e-mail info@ osaka-up.or.jp; internet www.osaka-up.or.jp; f. 1993; economics, history, literature, medicine, philosophy, politics, science, sociology, technology; Pres. KENJI MITSUNARI.

PHP Institute Inc: 11, Kita-Nouchi-cho, Nishi-Kujo, Minami-ku, Kyoto 601-8411; tel. (75) 681-4433; fax (75) 681-9921; internet www .php.co.jp; f. 1946; social sciences; Pres. TAKATOSHI SHIMIZU.

Poplar Publishing Co Ltd: 22-1, Daikyo-cho, Shinjuku-ku, Tokyo 160-8565; tel. (3) 3357-2232; fax (3) 3359-2801; e-mail saegusa@ poplar.co.jp; internet www.poplar.co.jp; f. 1947; general, children's, comics; CEO HIROYUKI SAKAI.

Sanrio Co Ltd: 1-11-1, Osaki, Shinagawa-ku, Tokyo 141-8603; tel. (3) 3779-8101; fax (3) 3779-8702; internet www.sanrio.co.jp; f. 1960; juvenile; Pres. SHINTARO TSUJI.

Sanseido Co Ltd: 2-22-14, Misaki-cho, Chiyoda-ku, Tokyo 101-8371; tel. (3) 3230-9411; fax (3) 3230-9547; e-mail ssd-s@ sanseido-publ.co.jp; internet www.sanseido.co.jp; f. 1881; dictionaries, educational, languages, social and natural sciences; Pres. KATSUHIKO KITAGUCHI.

Sanshusha Publishing Co Ltd: Aoyama Kumano Jinja Bldg, 2-2-22, Jingu-mae, Shibuya-ku, Tokyo 150-0001; tel. (3) 3405-4511; fax (3) 3405-4522; e-mail webmaster@sanshusha.co.jp; internet www.sanshusha.co.jp; f. 1938; languages, dictionaries, philosophy, sociology, electronic publishing (CD-ROM); Pres. TOSHIHIDE MAEDA.

Seibido Shuppan Co Ltd: 1-7, Shinogawamachi, Shinjuku-ku, Tokyo 162-8445; tel. (3) 5206-8151; fax (3) 5206-8159; internet www.seibidoshuppan.co.jp; f. 1969; sports, recreation, travel guides, music, motor sports, cooking, novels, computer, childcare, picture books; Pres. KENJI KAZAHAYA.

Seibundo-Shinkosha Co Ltd: 3-3-11, Hongo, Bunkyo-ku, Tokyo 113-0033; tel. (3) 5800-5775; fax (3) 5800-5773; internet www.seibundo-shinkosha.net; f. 1912; scientific, gardening, electronics, graphic design; Pres. YUICHI OGAWA.

Seishun Publishing Co Ltd: 12-1, Wakamatsu-cho, Shinjuku-ku, Tokyo 162-0056; tel. (3) 3203-5121; fax (3) 3207-0982; e-mail information@seishun.co.jp; internet www.seishun.co.jp; f. 1955; science, education, history, sociology, philosophy, economics, literature; Pres. GENTARO OZAWA.

Seitoku University Press: 550, Iwase, Matsudo-shi, Chiba 271-8755; tel. (47) 365-1111; fax (47) 363-1401; e-mail shuppan@seitoku.ac.jp; f. 2002; human science, medicine, art; Pres. HIROZUMI KAWANAMI.

Seizando Shoten Publishing Co Ltd: 4-51, Minami-Motomachi, Shinjuku-ku, Tokyo 160-0012; tel. (3) 3357-5861; fax (3) 3357-5867; e-mail publisher@seizando.co.jp; internet www.seizando.co.jp; f. 1954; maritime affairs, aviation, engineering; Pres. NORIKO OGAWA.

Sekai Bunka Publishing Inc: 4-2-29, Kudan-Kita, Chiyoda-ku, Tokyo 102-8187; tel. (3) 3262-5111; fax (3) 3262-5750; e-mail y-muta@sekaibunka.co.jp; internet www.sekaibunka.com; f. 1946; history, natural sciences, geography, education, art, literature, juvenile; Pres. MINAKO SUZUKI.

Shincho-Sha Co Ltd: 71, Yarai-cho, Shinjuku-ku, Tokyo 162-8711; tel. (3) 3266-5250; fax (3) 3266-5432; e-mail takimoto@shinchosha.co.jp; internet www.shinchosha.co.jp; f. 1896; general literature, fiction, non-fiction, fine arts, philosophy; Pres. TAKANOBU SATO.

Shinkenchiku-Sha Co Ltd: 2-31-2, Yushima, Bunkyo-ku, Tokyo 113-8501; tel. (3) 3811-7101; fax (3) 3812-8229; e-mail ja-business@japan-architect.co.jp; internet www.japan-architect.co.jp; f. 1925; architecture; Pres. AKIHIKO OMORI.

Shinsei Publishing Co Ltd: 4-7-6, Taito, Taito-ku, Tokyo 110-0016; tel. (3) 3831-0743; fax (3) 3831-0758; internet www.shin-sei.co.jp; f. 1944; guidebooks, state examinations, personal computers; Pres. YASUHIRO TOMINAGA.

Shogakukan Inc: 2-3-1, Hitotsubashi, Chiyoda-ku, Tokyo 101-8001; tel. (3) 3230-5658; fax (3) 3230-9750; e-mail bunsho88@mail.shogakukan.co.jp; internet www.shogakukan.co.jp; f. 1922; juvenile, education, geography, history, encyclopaedias, dictionaries; Pres. MASAHIRO OHGA.

Shokabo Publishing Co Ltd: 8-1, Yomban-cho, Chiyoda-ku, Tokyo 102-0081; tel. (3) 3262-9166; fax (3) 3262-7257; e-mail c-right@shokabo.co.jp; internet www.shokabo.co.jp; f. 1716; natural sciences, engineering; Pres. KAZUHIRO YOSHINO.

Shokokusha Publishing Co Ltd: 8-21, Tomihisa-cho, Shinjuku-ku, Tokyo 162-0067; tel. (3) 3359-3231; fax (3) 3357-3961; e-mail tomishige@shokokusha.co.jp; internet www.shokokusha.co.jp; f. 1932; architectural, technical and fine arts; Pres. TAKESHI GOTO.

Shueisha Inc: 2-5-10, Hitotsubashi, Chiyoda-ku, Tokyo 101-8050; tel. (3) 3230-6111; fax (3) 3262-1309; e-mail oyoshi@shueisha.co.jp; internet www.shueisha.co.jp; f. 1926; literature, fine arts, language, juvenile, comics; Pres. MARUE HORIUCHI.

Shufunotomo Co Ltd: 2-9, Kanda Surugadai, Chiyoda-ku, Tokyo 101-8911; tel. (3) 5280-7567; fax (3) 5280-7568; e-mail kohashi@shufunotomo.co.jp; internet www.shufunotomo.co.jp; f. 1916; domestic science, fine arts, gardening, handicraft, cookery and magazines; Pres. YOSHIYUKI OGINO.

Shufu-To-Seikatsusha Ltd: 3-5-7, Kyobashi, Chuo-ku, Tokyo 104-8357; tel. (3) 3563-5120; fax (3) 3563-2073; e-mail houmu@mb.shufu.co.jp; internet www.shufu.co.jp; f. 1935; home economics, recreation, fiction, medicine, comics, cooking, interiors, handicraft, fishing, fashion; Pres. KATSUHISA TAKANOU.

Shunju-Sha: 2-18-6, Soto-Kanda, Chiyoda-ku, Tokyo 101-0021; tel. (3) 3255-9611; fax (3) 3253-1384; e-mail main@shunjusha.co.jp; internet www.shunjusha.co.jp; f. 1918; philosophy, religion, literature, economics, music; Pres. YOSHIKAZU SAWAHATA.

Sony Magazines Inc: Banchokaikan, 12-1, Goban-cho, Chiyoda-ku, Tokyo 102-8679; tel. (3) 3234-5811; fax (3) 3234-5842; internet www.sonymagazines.jp; f. 1979; music books, general literature; Pres. SHIGERU MURATA.

Taishukan Publishing Co Ltd: 2-1-1, Yushima, Bunkyo-ku, Tokyo 113-8541; tel. (3) 3868-2211; fax (3) 3868-2641; e-mail kaneko@taishhukan.co.jp; internet www.taishukan.co.jp; f. 1918; reference, Japanese and foreign languages, sports, dictionaries, audio-visual aids; Pres. KAZUYUKI SUZUKI.

Takahashi Shoten Co Ltd: 1-26-1, Otowa, Bunkyo-ku, Tokyo 112-0013; tel. (3) 3943-4525; fax (3) 3943-4288; e-mail ta_contact@takahashishoten.co.jp; internet www.takahashishoten.co.jp; f. 1954; business, food and drink, sport, dictionaries, education, juvenile; Pres. HIDEO TAKAHASHI.

Tamagawa University Press: 6-1-1, Tamagawa-Gakuen, Machida-shi, Tokyo 194-8610; tel. (42) 739-8935; fax (42) 739-8940; e-mail tup@tamagawa.ac.jp; internet www.tamagawa.jp/introduction/press; f. 1929; education, philosophy, religion, arts, juvenile, area studies; Pres. YOSHIAKI OBARA.

Tankosha Publishing Co Ltd: 19-1, Miyanishi-cho Murasakino, Kita-ku, Kyoto 603-8691; tel. (75) 432-5151; fax (75) 432-5152; e-mail sec@tankosha.co.jp; internet www.tankosha.co.jp; f. 1949; tea ceremony, fine arts, history; Pres. and CEO YOSHITO NAYA.

Teikoku-Shoin Co Ltd: 3-29, Kanda Jimbo-cho, Chiyoda-ku, Tokyo 101-0051; tel. (3) 3262-0834; fax (3) 3262-7770; e-mail kenkyu@teikokushoin.co.jp; internet www.teikokushoin.co.jp; f. 1926; geography, atlases, maps, textbooks, history, civil studies; Pres. MASAYOSHI SAITO.

Tohoku University Press, Sendai: 2-1-1, Katahira, Aoba-ku, Sendai 980-8577; tel. (22) 214-2777; fax (22) 214-2778; e-mail info@tups.jp; internet www.tups.jp; f. 1996; natural and social sciences, humanities, history, literature, psychology, philosophy, art, language; Chair. SHIGERU HISAMICHI.

Tokai University Press: 3-10-35, Minami-Yana, Hadano-shi, Kanagawa 257-0003; tel. (463) 79-3921; fax (463) 69-5087; e-mail trem@tsc.u-tokai.ac.jp; internet www.press.tokai.ac.jp; f. 1962; social sciences, cultural science, natural sciences, engineering, art; Pres. TATSURO MATSUMAE.

Tokuma Shoten Publishing Co Ltd: 2-2-1, Shiba-Daimon, Minato-ku, Tokyo 105-8055; tel. (3) 5403-4300; fax (3) 5403-4375; e-mail takeuti@shoten.tokuma.com; internet www.tokuma.jp; f. 1954; Japanese classics, history, fiction, juvenile; Pres. TORU IWABUCHI.

Tokyo News Service Ltd: Hamarikyu Park Side Place Bldg, 7-16-3, Tsukiji, Chuo-ku, Tokyo 104-8415; tel. (3) 6367-8000; fax (3) 3545-3628; internet www.tokyonews.co.jp; f. 1947; shipping, trade and television guides; Pres. TAKASHI OKUYAMA.

Tokyo Shoseki Co Ltd: 2-17-1, Horifune, Kita-ku, Tokyo 114-8524; tel. (3) 5390-7513; fax (3) 5390-7409; e-mail shoseki@tokyo-shoseki.co.jp; internet www.tokyo-shoseki.co.jp; f. 1909; textbooks, reference books, cultural and educational books; Pres. and CEO YASUNORI KAWABATA.

Tokyo Sogen-Sha Co Ltd: 1-5, Shin-Ogawa-machi, Shinjuku-ku, Tokyo 162-0814; tel. (3) 3268-8201; fax (3) 3268-8230; internet www.tsogen.co.jp; f. 1954; mystery and detective stories, science fiction, literature; Pres. SHINICHI HASEGAWA.

Toyo Keizai Inc: 1-2-1, Nihonbashi Hongoku-cho, Chuoku, Tokyo 103-8345; tel. (3) 3246-5551; fax (3) 3279-0332; e-mail info@toyokeizai.co.jp; internet toyokeizai.net; f. 1895; periodicals, economics, business, finance, corporation information; Pres. YUICHIRO YAMAGATA.

Tuttle Publishing Co Inc: Yaekari Bldg, 3/F, 5-4-12, Osaki Shinagawa-ku, Tokyo; tel. (3) 5437-0171; fax (3) 5437-0755; e-mail customer@tuttle.co.jp; internet www.tuttle.co.jp; f. 1948; Japanese and Asian religion, history, social sciences, arts, languages, literature, juvenile, cookery; Pres. ERIC OEY.

United Nations University Press: 5-53-70, Jingumae, Shibuya-ku, Tokyo 150-8925; tel. (3) 5467-1212; fax (3) 3499-2828; e-mail sales@hq.unu.edu; internet www.unu.edu; f. 1975; social sciences, humanities, pure and applied natural sciences; Head KONRAD OSTERWALDER.

University of Nagoya Press: 1, Furocho, Chikusa-ku, Nagoya 464-0814; tel. (52) 781-5027; fax (52) 781-0697; e-mail sogo@unp.nagoya-u.ac.jp; internet www.unp.or.jp; f. 1982; social sciences, humanities, natural sciences, medicine; Chair. MITSUKI ISHII.

University of Tokyo Press: 7-3-1, Hongo, Bunkyo-ku, Tokyo 113-8654; tel. (3) 3811-0964; fax (3) 3815-1426; e-mail info@utp.or.jp; internet www.utp.or.jp; f. 1951; natural and social sciences, humanities; Japanese and English; Chair. HIROSHI WATANABE.

Waseda University Press: 1-1-7, Nishiwaseda, Shinjuku-ku, Tokyo 169-0051; tel. (3) 3203-1551; fax (3) 3207-0406; e-mail shuppanbu@list.waseda.jp; internet www.waseda-up.co.jp; f. 1886; politics, economics, law, sociology, philosophy, literature, education, business, drama, journalism; Pres. YOICHI SHIMADA.

Yama-Kei Publishers Co Ltd: 3-2-11, Sumitomo Kudankita, Chiyoda-ku, Tokyo 102-0075; tel. (3) 6744-1900; fax (3) 6234-1628; e-mail info@yamakei.co.jp; internet www.yamakei.co.jp; f. 1930;

natural sciences, geography, mountaineering, outdoor activities; Pres. AKIO SEKIMOTO.

Yoshikawa Kobunkan: 7-2-8, Hongo, Bunkyo-ku, Tokyo 113-0033; tel. (3) 3813-9151; fax (3) 3812-3544; e-mail hongo@yoshikawa-k.co.jp; internet www.yoshikawa-k.co.jp; f. 1857; history, biography, art, languages, religion; Pres. MOTOYASU MAEDA.

Yuhikaku Publishing Co Ltd: 2-17, Kanda Jimbo-cho, Chiyoda-ku, Tokyo 101-0051; tel. (3) 3264-1312; fax (3) 3264-5030; e-mail nishino@yuhikaku.co.jp; internet www.yuhikaku.co.jp; f. 1877; social sciences, law, economics; Pres. SADAHARU EGUSA.

Yuki Shobo: 3-7-9, Kudan-Minami, Chiyoda-ku, Tokyo 102-0074; tel. (3) 5275-8088; fax (3) 5275-8099; e-mail takeshi.nanri@yukishobo.co.jp; internet www.yukishobo.co.jp; f. 1957; home economics, juvenile, recreation, sociology, sports; Pres. MASAO OKAJIMA.

Yuzankaku Shuppan: 2-6-9, Fujimi, Chiyoda-ku, Tokyo 102-0071; tel. (3) 3262-3231; fax (3) 3262-6938; e-mail info@yuzankaku.co.jp; internet www.yuzankaku.co.jp; f. 1916; history, fine arts, religion, archaeology; Pres. TETSUO MIYATA.

Zen-on Music Co Ltd: 2-13-3, Kami-Ochiai, Shinjuku-ku, Tokyo 161-0034; tel. (3) 3227-6283; fax (3) 3227-6288; e-mail web-info@zen-on.co.jp; internet www.zen-on.co.jp; f. 1931; classics, pop, books on music; Pres. KASAI TSUNEAKI.

Zoshindo Juken Kenkyusha Co Ltd: 2-19-15, Shinmachi, Nishi-ku, Osaka 550-0013; tel. (6) 6532-1581; fax (6) 6532-1588; e-mail y.okamoto@zoshindo.co.jp; internet www.zoshindo.co.jp; f. 1890; educational, juvenile; Pres. AKITAKA OKAMATO.

GOVERNMENT PUBLISHING HOUSE

Government Publications' Service Centre: 1-2-1, Kasumigaseki, Chiyoda-ku, Tokyo 100-0013; tel. (3) 3504-3885; fax (3) 3504-3889.

PUBLISHERS' ASSOCIATIONS

Japan Book Publishers Association: 6, Fukuro-machi, Shinjuku-ku, Tokyo 162-0828; tel. (3) 3268-1302; fax (3) 3268-1196; e-mail rd@jbpa.or.jp; internet www.jbpa.or.jp; f. 1957; 438 mems (2013); Pres. MASAHIRO OGA; Exec. Dir TADASHI YAMASHITA.

Publishers' Association for Cultural Exchange, Japan: 1-2-1, Sarugaku-cho, Chiyoda-ku, Tokyo 101-0064; tel. (3) 3291-5685; fax (3) 3233-3645; e-mail culturalexchange@pace.or.jp; internet www.pace.or.jp; f. 1953; 72 mems (2012); Pres. TADATAKA EGUSA; Man. Dir HARUHIKO ISHIKAWA.

Broadcasting and Communications

Telecommunications and broadcasting are regulated by the Ministry of Internal Affairs and Communications.

TELECOMMUNICATIONS

BIGLOBE Inc.: 4-12-4, Shinagawa Seaside Park Tower, Shinagawa-ku, Tokyo 140-0002; internet www.biglobe.co.jp; f. 2006; provides internet and other information services; CEO KATSUHIRO NAKAGAWA.

KDDI Corpn: Garden Air Tower, 3-10-10, Iidabashi, Chiyoda-ku, Tokyo 102-8460; tel. (3) 3347-0077; fax (3) 6678-0305; internet www.kddi.com; f. 1984; est. by merger of DDI Corpn, Kokusai Denshin Denwa Corpn (KDD) and Nippon Idou Tsuhin Corpn (IDO); major international telecommunications carrier; Pres. TAKASHI TANAKA.

Nippon Telegraph and Telephone Corpn (NTT): TT Hibiya Bldg, 1-1-6 Uchisaiwai-cho, Chiyoda-ku, Tokyo 100-8019; tel. (3) 5293-9450; fax (3) 5205-5589; internet www.ntt.co.jp; f. 1985; operates local, long-distance and international services; largest telecommunications co in Japan; holding co for NTT East, NTT West, NTT Communications, NTT Data Corpn and NTT DOCOMO; Pres. and CEO HIROO UNOURA.

NTT DOCOMO: 2-11-1, Nagatacho, Chiyoda-ku, Tokyo 100-6150; tel. (3) 5156-1111; fax (3) 5156-0271; internet www.nttdocomo.co.jp; f. 1991; operates mobile telephone network; Pres. and CEO KAORU KATO.

SoftBank Telecom Corpn: 1-9-1, Higashi-Shimbashi, Minato-ku, Tokyo 105-7316; tel. 0088-41; e-mail tcsc@tm.softbank.co.jp; internet www.softbanktelecom.co.jp; fmrly Japan Telecom; fixed-line business acquired by Ripplewood Holdings in 2003; acquired by SoftBank Corpn in 2004; merged with International Digital Communications (IDC) in 2005; name changed as above in 2006; Chair. and CEO MASAYOSHI SON.

Ymobile Corporation: 1-9-2, Higashi-Shimbashi, Minato-ku, Tokyo; tel. (3) 3588-7682; fax (3) 3588-7201; internet www.ymobile.jp; f. 1999 as eAccess Ltd; name changed to present in 2014; mobile voice, data services and mobile broadband services; Pres. and CEO ERIC GAN.

BROADCASTING

NHK (Japan Broadcasting Corporation): 2-2-1, Jinnan, Shibuya-ku, Tokyo 150-8001; tel. (3) 3465-1111; fax (3) 3469-8110; e-mail webmaster@nhk.or.jp; internet www.nhk.or.jp; f. 1925; fmrly Nippon Hoso Kyokai (NHK—Japan Broadcasting Corpn); Japan's sole public broadcaster; operates 4 TV channels (incl. 2 terrestrial services—general TV and educational TV, and 2 satellite services—BS-1 and BS Premium), 3 radio channels, Radio 1, Radio 2, and FM Radio, and 3 worldwide services, NHK World TV, NHK World Premium and NHK World Radio Japan; headquarters in Tokyo, regional headquarters in Osaka, Nagoya, Hiroshima, Fukuoka, Sendai, Sapporo and Matsuyama; Pres. KATSUTO MOMII; Exec. Dir-Gen. of Broadcasting YUJI ITANO.

Japan Commercial Broadcasters Association (JBA): 3-23, Kioi-cho, Chiyoda-ku, Tokyo 102-8577; tel. (3) 5213-7711; fax (3) 5213-7730; e-mail webmaster@nab.or.jp; internet www.j-ba.or.jp; f. 1951; includes 205 cos (incl. terrestrial broadcasting cos, radio and TV stations); fmrly National Association of Commercial Broadcasters in Japan; Pres. INOUE HIROSHI; Exec. Dir AOKI TAKAFUMI.

Some of the most important companies are:

Asahi Hoso—Asahi Broadcasting Corpn: 1-1-30, Fukushima, Fukushima-ku, Osaka 553-8503; tel. (6) 6458-5321; internet www.asahi.co.jp; f. 1951; Pres. and CEO SATOSHI WAKISAKA.

Chubu-Nippon Broadcasting Co Ltd: 1-2-8, Shinsakae, Naka-ku, Nagoya 460-8405; tel. (052) 241-8111; internet cbc-global.jp; f. 1950; Pres. MASAKI SUGIURA.

Fuji Television Network, Inc: 2-4-8, Daiba, Minato-ku, Tokyo 137-8088; tel. (3) 5500-8888; fax (3) 5500-8027; internet www.fujitv.co.jp; f. 1959; owned by Fuji Media Holding Inc; Chair. and CEO HISASHI HIEDA; Pres. CHIHIRO KAMEYAMA.

Kansai TV Hoso (KTV)—Kansai Telecasting Corpn: 2-1-7, Ogimachi, Kita-ku, Osaka 530-8408; tel. (6) 6314-8888; internet www.ktv.co.jp; f. 1958; Pres. SUMIO FUKUI.

Mainichi Hoso (MBS)—Mainichi Broadcasting System, Inc: 17-1, Chayamachi, Kita-ku, Osaka 530-8304; tel. (6) 6359-1123; fax (6) 6359-3503; internet www.mbs.jp; f. 1950; Pres. KAZUTOMO KAWAUCHI.

Nippon Cultural Broadcasting, Inc: 1-31, Hamamatsu-cho, Minato-ku, Tokyo 105-8002; tel. (3) 5403-1111; internet www.joqr.co.jp; f. 1952; Pres. AKIHIRO MIKI.

Nippon Hoso—Nippon Broadcasting System, Inc: 1-9-3, Yurakucho Itchome, Chiyoda, Tokyo; tel. (3) 5500-1234; fax (3) 5500-3902; e-mail saiyo2013@jolf.jp; internet www.jolf.co.jp; f. 1954; 49.8% controlling stake acquired by Livedoor Co Ltd in 2005, but subsequently purchased by Fuji TV Network, Inc; Pres. AKINOBU KAMEBUCHI.

Nippon TV Hoso-MO (NTV)—Nippon Television Network Corpn: 1-6-1, Higashi-Shimbashi, Minato-ku, Tokyo 105-7444; tel. (3) 6215-1111; fax (3) 6215-3157; internet www.ntv.co.jp; f. 1953; Pres. YOSHIO OKUBO.

Okinawa TV Hoso (OTV)—Okinawa Television Broadcasting Co Ltd: 1-2-20, Kumoji Hisashi, Naha 900-8588; tel. (988) 63-2111; fax (988) 61-0193; e-mail otvweb@otv.co.jp; internet www.otv.co.jp; f. 1959; Pres. HIROSHI MACHIDA.

Radio Nikkei: 1-2-8 Toranomon, Minato-ku, Tokyo 105-8565; tel. (3) 6205-7810; fax (3) 3583-9062; internet www.radionikkei.jp; f. 1954; Pres. KENJI SUZUKI.

Ryukyu Hoso (RBC)—Ryukyu Broadcasting Co: 2-3-1, Kumoji, Naha 900-8711; tel. (98) 867-2151; fax (98) 864-5732; e-mail info@rbc.co.jp; internet www.rbc.co.jp; f. 1954.

Tokyo Hoso (TBS)—Tokyo Broadcasting System Holdings Inc: 5-3-6, Akasaka, Minato-ku, Tokyo 107-8006; tel. (3) 3746-1111; fax (3) 3588-6378; internet www.tbs.co.jp; f. 1951 as Radio Tokyo, Inc.; name changed to present 1959; Chair. HIROSHI INOUE; Pres. TOSHICHIKA ISHIHARA.

TV Asahi Corpn: 6-9-1, Roppongi, Minato-ku, Tokyo 106-8001; tel. (3) 6406-1111; fax (3) 3405-3714; internet www.tv-asahi.co.jp; f. 1957; Pres. and CEO HIROSHI HAYAKAWA.

TV Osaka (TVO)—Television Osaka, Inc: 1-2-18, Otemae, Chuo-ku, Osaka 540-8519; tel. (6) 6947-7777; fax (6) 6946-9796; e-mail takoru@tv-osaka.co.jp; internet www.tv-osaka.co.jp; f. 1981; Pres. FUMIO TATEISHI.

TV Tokyo Corpn: 4-3-12, Toranomon, Minato-ku, Tokyo 105-8012; tel. (3) 5470-7777; fax (3) 5473-6393; internet www.tv-tokyo.co.jp; f. 1964; Pres. and CEO YUICHI TAKAHASHI.

Yomiuri TV Hoso (YTV)—Yomiuri Telecasting Corpn: 2-2-33, Shiromi, Chuo-ku, Osaka 540-8510; tel. (6) 6947-2111; e-mail licensing@ytv.co.jp; internet www.ytv.co.jp; f. 1958; 20 hrs broadcasting daily; Pres. NORIO MOCHIZUKI.

Satellite, Cable and Digital Television

In addition to the two broadcast satellite services that NHK introduced in 1989, a number of commercial satellite stations are in operation. Cable television is available in urban areas. Satellite digital television services first became available in 1996.

SKY Perfect JSAT Corpn: 1-4-14, Akasaka, Minato-ku, Tokyo 107-0052; tel. (3) 5571-7800; internet www.sptvjsat.com; f. 1994 as DMC Planning Inc.; renamed as present in 2007 following merger of SKY Perfect Comm. Inc.and JSAT Corpn; Chair. SHIGEKI NISHIYAMA; Pres. SHINJI TAKADA.

Finance

(cap. = capital; p.u. = paid up; res = reserves; dep. = deposits;
m. = million; brs = branches; amounts in yen)

BANKING

Japan's central bank and bank of issue is the Bank of Japan. At July 2013 there were 198 banks (not including the central bank) in the country, including four major commercial banks, four trust banks, 57 foreign banks and 64 regional banks.

An important financial role is played by co-operatives and by the many small enterprise institutions. There are also two types of private financial institutions for small business. At April 2008 there were 164 credit co-operatives, and at March 2010 there were 271 Shinkin banks (credit associations), which lend only to members. The latter also receive deposits.

The most popular form of savings is through the post office network. In October 2005 legislation was approved to permit the privatization of Japan Post. Following its transfer to a holding company, Japan Post was divided into four units (savings, insurance and postal services, along with personnel and property management). Having been established in September 2006, the Japan Post Bank (JPB) commenced operations in October 2007. The JPB thus became the world's largest financial institution in terms of deposits; it is also the largest provider of life insurance.

Central Bank

Nippon Ginko (Bank of Japan): 2-1-1, Motoishi-cho, Nihonbashi, Chuo-ku, Tokyo 103-0021; tel. (3) 3279-1111; fax (3) 5200-2256; e-mail prdmail@boj.or.jp; internet www.boj.or.jp; f. 1882; cap. 100m., res 2,660,006m., dep. 38,168,703m. (March 2010); Gov. HARUHIKO KURODA; Dep. Govs HIROSHI NAKASO, KIKUO OWATA; 32 brs.

Principal Commercial Banks

Asahi Shinkin Bank: 2-1-2, Higashi-Kanda, Chiyoda-ku, Tokyo 101-0031; tel. (3) 3862-0321; fax (3) 5687-6867; internet www.asahi-shinkin.co.jp; f. 1923; est. as Shinyo Kumiai Tomin Kinko; name changed as above after merger in 2002; cap. 22,048m., res 32,805m., dep. 1,692,300m. (March 2012); Chair. KUNITAKE MORIWAKI; Pres. KAZUO KOBAYASHI; 62 brs.

Ashikaga Bank Ltd: 4-1-25, Sakura, Utsunomiya, Tochigi 320-8610; tel. (28) 622-0111; e-mail ashigin@ssctnet.or.jp; internet www.ashikagabank.co.jp; f. 1895; nationalized Nov. 2003 owing to insolvency; cap. 135,000m., res 13,067m., dep. 4,807,955m. (March 2012); CEO SATOSHI FUJISAWA; 150 brs.

Bank of Fukuoka Ltd: 2-13-1, Tenjin, Chuo-ku, Fukuoka 810-8727; tel. (92) 723-2442; fax (92) 711-1371; internet www.fukuokabank.co.jp; f. 1945; cap. 82,329m., res 137,125m., dep. 7,991,413m. (March 2011); Chair. and Pres. MASAAKI TANI; 166 brs.

Bank of Tokyo-Mitsubishi UFJ Ltd: 2-7-1, Marunouchi, Chiyoda-ku, Tokyo 100-8388; tel. (3) 3240-1111; fax (3) 3240-4197; internet www.bk.mufg.jp; f. 2006; est. through merger of Bank of Tokyo-Mitsubishi Ltd and UFJ Bank Ltd; specializes in international banking and financial business; subsidiary of Mitsubishi UFJ Financial Group (f. 2005 through merger of Mitsubishi Tokyo Financial Group and UFJ Holdings); cap. 1,711,958m., res 4,369,110m., dep. 116,239,242m. (March 2012); Pres. NOBUYUKI HIRANO; 841 brs (767 domestic, 74 overseas).

Bank of Yokohama Ltd: 3-1-1, Minatomirai, Nishi-ku, Yokohama, Kanagawa 220-8611; tel. (45) 225-1111; fax (45) 225-1160; e-mail iroffice@hamagin.co.jp; internet www.boy.co.jp; f. 1920; cap. 215,628m., res 227,524m., dep. 11,089,041m. (March 2012); Chair. TADASHI OGAWA; Pres. TATSUMARO TERAZAWA; 197 brs (196 domestic, 1 overseas).

Chiba Bank Ltd: 1-2, Chiba-minato, Chuo-ku, Chiba 260-8720; tel. (43) 245-1111; fax (43) 242-9121; e-mail int@chibabank.co.jp; internet www.chibabank.co.jp; f. 1943; cap. 145,069m., res 136,457m., dep. 9,639,615m. (March 2012); Pres. HIDETOSHI SAKUMA; 156 domestic brs, 3 overseas brs.

Chiba Kogyo Bank Ltd: 2-1-2, Saiwa-cho, Mihama-ku, Chiba; tel. (43) 243-2111; fax (43) 244-9203; internet www.chibakogyo-bank.co

.jp; f. 1952; cap. 57,941m., res 33,400m., dep. 2,116,586m. (March 2012); Pres. and CEO SHUNICHI AOYAGI; 71 brs.

Hachijuni Bank: 178-8, Okada, Nagano-shi, Nagano 380-8682; tel. (26) 227-1182; fax (26) 226-5077; internet www.82bank.co.jp; f. 1931; cap. 52,243m., res 90,889m., dep. 5,725,089m. (March 2012); Chair. YOSHIYUKI YAMAURA; Pres. SHOICHI YUMOTO; 156 brs (155 domestic, 1 overseas).

Hokkaido Bank Ltd: 4-1, Nishi-Odori, Chuo-ku, Sapporo 060-8678, Hokkaido; tel. (11) 233-1093; fax (11) 231-3133; internet www.hokkaidobank.co.jp; f. 1951; cap. 93,524m., res 27,223m., dep. 4,155,748m. (March 2012); Pres. YOSHIHIRO SEKIHACHI; 139 brs.

Hokkoku Bank Ltd: 1 Shimotsutsumi-cho, Kanazawa 920-8670, Ishikawa; tel. (76) 263-1111; fax (76) 223-3362; internet www.hokkokubank.co.jp; f. 1943; cap. 26,673m., res 42,552m., dep. 3,096,757m. (March 2012); Pres. TATEKI ATAKA; 112 brs.

Hokuetsu Bank Ltd: 2-2-14, Otedori, Nagaoka 940-8650, Niigata; tel. (258) 353-111; fax (258) 375-113; internet www.hokuetsubank.co.jp; f. 1942; cap. 24,538m., res 29,329m., dep. 2,157,929m. (March 2012); Pres. SATORU ARAKI; 89 brs.

Hokuriku Bank Ltd: 1-2-26, Tsutsumichodori, Toyama 930-8637; tel. (76) 423-7111; fax (76) 491-5908; e-mail info@hokuhoku-fg.co.jp; internet www.hokugin.co.jp; f. 1877; cap. 140,409m., res 45,333m., dep. 5,545,101m. (March 2012); Pres. EISHIN IHORI; 188 brs.

Hokuto Bank Ltd: 3-1-41, Nakadori, Akita 010-0001; tel. (18) 833-4211; fax (18) 832-1942; e-mail hokutobank@hokutobank.co.jp; internet www.hokutobank.co.jp; f. 1895; est. as Masuda Bank Ltd, name changed as above after merger with Akita Akebono Bank in 1993; cap. 11,000m., res 23,085m., dep. 1,115,137m. (March 2012); Pres. TAKEO KAGAYA; 84 brs.

Japan Net Bank: 2-1-1, Nishi-Shinjuku, Shinjuku-ku, Tokyo 163-0406; tel. (3) 6739-5000; internet www.japannetbank.co.jp; f. 2000; Japan's first internet-only bank; cap. 37,250m., res 4,393m., dep. 494,419m. (March 2012); Pres. YOSHIYUKI MIYAI.

Joyo Bank Ltd: 2-5-5, Minami-Machi, Mito-shi, Ibaraki 310-0021; tel. (29) 231-2151; fax (29) 255-6522; e-mail joyointl@po.net-ibaraki.ne.jp; internet www.joyobank.co.jp; f. 1935; cap. 85,113m., res 83,703m., dep. 7,277,708m. (March 2012); Chair. KUNIO ONIZAWA; Pres. KAZUYOSHI TERAKADO; 172 brs.

Juroku Bank Ltd: 8-26, Kandamachi, Gifu 500-8516; tel. (582) 652-111; fax (582) 661-698; internet www.juroku.co.jp; f. 1877; cap. 36,839m., res 65,418m., dep. 4,889,423m. (March 2012); Pres. HAKUMI HORIE; 149 brs.

Kansai Urban Banking Corpn: 1-2-4, Nishi-Shinbashi, Chuo-ku, Osaka; tel. (6) 6834 4581, internet www.kansaiurban.co.jp; f. 1922; cap. 470,039m., res 64,400m., dep. 3,945,438m. (March 2012); Chair. and CEO AKIRA KITAMURA; Pres. KOJI KITA; 147 brs.

Kumamoto Family Bank Ltd: 6-29-20, Suizenji, Kumamoto 862-8601; tel. (96) 385-1111; fax (96) 385-4272; internet www.kf-bank.jp; f. 1992; cap. 33,847m., res 35,097m., dep. 1,095,663m. (March 2011); Pres. KENJI HAYASHI.

Miyazaki Bank Ltd: 4-3-5, Tachibanadori-Higashi, Miyazaki 880-0805; tel. (985) 273-131; fax (985) 225-952; e-mail kokusai@miyagin.co.jp; internet www.miyagin.co.jp; f. 1932; cap. 14,697m., res 20,238m., dep. 1,914,863m. (March 2012); Pres. KOICHI KOIKE; 97 brs.

Mizuho Bank Ltd: 1-3-3, Marunouchi, Chiyoda-ku, Tokyo 100-8210; tel. (3) 3596-1111; fax (3) 3596-2179; internet www.mizuhobank.co.jp; f. 1971 as Dai-Ichi Kangyo Bank; merged with Fuji Bank and Industrial Bank of Japan in 2002; merged with Mizuho Corporate Bank Ltd in July 2013; cap. 1,404,065m., res 1,225,839m., dep. 29,608,085m. (March 2012); Pres. and CEO YASUHIRO SATO; 334 domestic brs, 17 overseas brs.

North Pacific Bank (Hokuyo Bank): 3-7, Nishi-Odori, Chuo-ku, Sapporo 060-8661; tel. (11) 261-1416; fax (11) 232-6921; internet www.hokuyobank.co.jp; f. 1917; est. as Hokuyo Sogo Bank Ltd; adopted present name 1989; cap. 121,101m., res 131,934m., dep. 7,128,750m. (March 2012); Chair. RYUZO YOKOUCHI; Pres. JUNJI ISHII.

Resona Bank Ltd: 2-2-1, Bingo-machi, Chuo-ku, Osaka 540-8610; tel. (6) 6271-1221; internet www.resona-gr.co.jp; f. 1918; merged with Asahi Bank in 2002 and changed name as above; cap. 279,928m., res 633,189m., dep. 22,909,218m. (March 2013); Pres. KAZUHIRO HIGASHI; 339 brs.

Saitama Resona Bank Ltd: 7-4-1, Tokiwa, Urawa-ku, Saitama 330-9088; tel. (48) 824-2411; internet www.resona-gr.co.jp/saitamaresona; f. 2002; cap. 70,000m., res 129,350m., dep. 10,642,545m. (March 2012); Pres. MASAHITO KAMIJO.

San-in Godo Bank Ltd: 10, Uomachi, Matsue, Shimane 690-0062; tel. (852) 551-000; fax (852) 273-398; e-mail soki@gogin.co.jp; internet www.gogin.co.jp; f. 1941; cap. 20,705m., res 54,422m., dep. 3,585,898m. (March 2012); Pres. ICHIRO KUBOTA; Chair. MAKOTO FURUSE; 145 brs.

The Senshu Ikeda Bank Ltd: 18-14, Kita-ku, Osaka Chayamachi; tel. (6) 6375-1005; internet www.sihd-bk.jp; cap. 50,710m., res

82,038m., dep. 4,424,910m. (March 2012); Chair. KAZUYUKI KATAOKA; Pres. HIROHISA FUJITA.

Shiga Bank Ltd: 1-38, Hamamachi, Otsu 520-8686, Shiga; tel. (77) 521-2360; fax (77) 521-2892; internet www.shigagin.com; f. 1933; cap. 33,076m., res 77,403m., dep. 4,089,983m. (March 2012); Chair. KOICHI TAKATA; Pres. YOSHIO DAIDO; 134 domestic brs, 1 overseas.

Shikoku Bank Ltd: 1–1–1, Minami-Harimaya-cho, Kochi 780-8605; tel. (88) 823-2111; fax (88) 873-0322; internet www .shikokubank.co.jp; f. 1873; cap. 25,000m., res 26,178m., dep. 2,401,728m. (March 2012); Chair. AKIHIRO AOKI; Pres. TADASHI NOMURA; 112 brs.

Shimizu Bank: 2-1, Fujimi-cho, Shimizu-ku, Shozuoka-shi, Shizuoka 424-0941; tel. (543) 535-151; fax (543) 636-776; internet www .shimizubank.co.jp; f. 1928; cap. 8,670m., res 6,605m., dep. 1,305,199m. (March 2012); Chair. NORIJI YAMADA; Pres. KATSUICHIRO TOYOSHIMA; 77 brs.

Shizuoka Bank Ltd: 1-10, Gofuku-cho, Aoi-ku, Shizuoka 420-8761; tel. (54) 345-5700; fax (54) 349-5501; internet www.shizuokabank.co .jp; f. 1943; cap. 90,845m., res 116,717m., dep. 8,080,087m. (March 2012); Chair. SEIYA ITO; Pres. and CEO KATSUNORI NAKANISHI; 168 domestic brs, 3 overseas brs.

Toho Bank Ltd: 3-25, Ohmachi, Fukushima 960-8633; tel. (24) 523-3131; fax (24) 524-1583; internet www.tohobank.co.jp; f. 1941; cap. 23,519m., res 19,584m., dep. 4,033,235m. (March 2012); Chair. TOSHIO SEYA; Pres. SEISHI KITAMURA; 113 brs.

Tokyo Star Bank: 2-3-5 Akasaka, Minato-ku, Tokyo; tel. (3) 3586-3111; fax (3) 3586-5137; internet www.tokyostarbank.co.jp; f. 2001; est. as Nippon Finance Investment Ltd, name changed as above in May 2001; cap. 26,000m., res 27,570m., dep. 2,069,960m. (March 2012); Chair. YASUMINE SATAKE; Pres. MASARU IRIE; 31 brs.

Tokyo Tomin Bank Ltd: 2-3-11, Roppongi, Minato-ku, Tokyo 106-8525; tel. (3) 3582-8251; fax (3) 3582-1979; e-mail jdu02670@nifty.ne .jp; internet www.tominbank.co.jp; f. 1951; cap. 48,120m., res 17,805m., dep. 2,355,069m. (March 2013); Chair. TETSUYA SHIINA; Pres. ISAO KOBAYASHI; 72 brs.

Tomato Bank Ltd: 2-3-4, Bancho, Okayama 700-0811, Ehime; tel. (86) 221-1010; fax (86) 221-1040; internet www.tomatobank.co.jp; f. 1931; est. as Sanyo Sogo Bank; became a commercial bank in 1989, when present name was assumed; cap. 14,310m., res 14,389m., dep. 892,003m. (March 2012); Pres. TAKANOBU NAKAGAWA; 60 brs.

Tsukuba Bank Ltd: 2-11-7, Chuo-ku, Tsuchiura, Ibaraki 305-0032; tel. (29) 859-8111; internet www.tsukubabank.co.jp; f. 1952; cap. 48,868m., res 28,615m., dep. 2,001,931m. (March 2012); Chair. KOZO KIMURA; 147 brs.

Principal Trust Banks

Mitsubishi UFJ Trust and Banking Corporation: 1-4-5, Marunouchi, Chiyoda-ku, Tokyo 100-8212; tel. (3) 3212-1211; fax (3) 3514-6660; internet www.tr.mufg.jp; f. 2005; est. upon merger of Mitsubishi Tokyo Financial Group and UFJ Holdings to form Mitsubishi UFJ Financial Group, of which it is a subsidiary; cap. 324,279m., res 886,157m., dep. 17,243,293m. (March 2012); Chair. KINYA OKAUCHI; Pres. TATSUO WAKABAYASHI; 62 domestic brs, 5 overseas brs.

Mizuho Trust and Banking Co Ltd: 1-2-1, Yaesu, Chuo-ku, Tokyo 103-8670; tel. (3) 3278-8111; fax (3) 3274-4670; internet www .mizuho-tb.co.jp; f. 1925; fmrly Yasuda Trust and Banking Co Ltd; cap. 247,303m., res 30,403m., dep. 3,372,235m. (March 2011); Pres. and CEO TAKASHI NONAKA; 36 brs.

Sumitomo Mitsui Trust Bank Ltd: 1-4-1, Marunouchi, Chiyoda-ku, Tokyo 100-8233; internet www.smtb.jp; f. 1925; present name adopted following merger with Sakura Bank Ltd in 2001; wholly owned subsidiary of Sumitomo Mitsui Financial Group (SMFG—f. 2002); cap. 342,037m., res 300,102m., dep. 16,350,030m. (March 2012); Chair. KUNITARO KITAMURA; Pres. HITOSHI TSUNEKAGE; 118 domestic brs, 4 overseas brs.

Long-term Credit Banks

Aozora Bank: 1-3-1, Kudan-Minami, Chiyoda-ku, Tokyo 102-8660; tel. (3) 3263-1111; fax (3) 3265-7024; e-mail sora@aozora.co.jp; internet www.aozorabank.co.jp; f. 1957; nationalized Dec. 1998, sold to consortium led by Softbank Corpn in Aug. 2000; fmrly The Nippon Credit Bank, name changed as above 2001; 62% owned by Cerberus Group; cap. 419,780m., res 13,505m., dep. 3,062,459m. (March 2012); Pres. and CEO SHINSUKE BABA; Chair. BRIAN PRINCE; 19 brs.

Shinsei Bank Ltd: 2-4-3, Nihonbashi-muromachi, Chuo-ku, Tokyo 103-8303; tel. (3) 6680-7000; internet www.shinseibank.com; f. 1952; est. as The Long-Term Credit Bank of Japan; nationalized Oct. 1998, sold to Ripplewood Holdings (USA), renamed as above June 2000; cap. 512,204m., res −5,287m., dep. 5,475,513m. (March 2012); Pres. and CEO SHIGEKI TOMA; 29 domestic brs, 1 overseas br.

Co-operative Bank

Shinkin Central Bank: 1-3-7, Yaesu, Chuo-ku, Tokyo 103-0028; tel. (3) 5202-7700; fax (3) 3278-7033; e-mail s1000551@facetoface.ne .jp; internet www.shinkin-central-bank.jp; f. 1950; cap. 490,998m., res 182,305m., dep. 22,592,928m. (March 2012); Chair. KOJI OMAE; Pres. and CEO MITSUO TANABE; 14 domestic brs, 4 overseas brs.

Principal Government Institutions

Development Bank of Japan: 1-9-6, Otemachi, Chiyoda-ku, Tokyo 100-8178; tel. (3) 3270-3211; fax (3) 3245-1938; e-mail safukas@dbj.go.jp; internet www.dbj.jp; f. 1951; est. as Japan Devt Bank; renamed Oct. 1999 following consolidation with Hokkaido and Tohoku Devt Finance Public Corpn; provides long-term loans; subscribes for corporate bonds; guarantees corporate obligations; invests in specific projects; borrows funds from Govt and abroad; issues external bonds and notes; provides market information and consulting services for prospective entrants to Japanese market; legislation providing for the bank's privatization (by 2015) approved in 2008; cap. 1,187,788m., res 1,107,342m., dep. 1,856,894m. (March 2012); Pres. and CEO TORU HASHIMOTO; 10 domestic brs, 6 overseas brs.

Japan Bank for International Cooperation (JBIC): 1-4-1, Otemachi, Chiyoda-ku, Tokyo 100-8144; tel. (3) 5218-3100; fax (3) 5218-3955; e-mail ir@jbic.go.jp; internet www.jbic.go.jp; f. 1999; est. by merger of the Export-Import Bank of Japan (f. 1950) and the Overseas Economic Co-operation Fund (f. 1961); governmental financial institution, responsible for Japan's external economic policy and co-operation activities; cap. 1,291,000m., res 951,272m. (March 2012); Gov. HIROSHI OKUDA.

Japan Finance Corporation (JFC): 1-9-3, Otemachi, Chiyoda-ku, Tokyo 100-0004; internet www.jfc.go.jp; f. 2008; govt financial institution formed from merger of National Life Finance Corpn (NLFC), Agriculture, Forestry and Fisheries Finance Corpn (AFC), Japan Finance Corpn for Small and Medium Enterprise (JASME) and International Finance Operations (IFOs) of Japan Bank for International Cooperation (JBIC); cap. 3,075,700m., res 2,236,200m. (March 2012); Gov. and CEO SHOSAKU YASUI; 152 brs.

Japan Post Bank Co Ltd (JPB): 1-3-2, Kasumigaseki, Chiyoda-ku, Tokyo 100-8798; tel. (3) 3504-4436; internet www.jp-bank .japanpost.jp; f. 2006; wholly owned by Japan Post Holdings Co Ltd; cap. 3,500,000m., res 5,167,567m., dep. 175,635,370m. (March 2012); Chair. SEIJIROU ADACHI; Pres. YOSHIYUKI IZAWA.

Norinchukin Bank (Central Co-operative Bank for Agriculture, Forestry and Fisheries): 1-13-2, Yuraku-cho, Chiyoda-ku, Tokyo 100-8420; tel. (3) 3279-0111; fax (3) 3218-5125; internet www.nochubank .or.jp; f. 1923; main banker to agricultural, forestry and fisheries co-operatives; receives deposits from individual co-operatives, federations and agricultural enterprises; extends loans to these and to local govt authorities and public corpns; adjusts excess and shortage of funds within co-operative system; issues debentures, invests funds and engages in other regular banking business; cap. 3,425,909m., res 382,150m., dep. 51,065,358m. (March 2012); Pres. and CEO YOSHIO KONO; 25 domestic brs, 5 overseas brs.

Shoko Chukin Bank (Central Co-operative Bank for Commerce and Industry): 2-10-17, Yaesu, Chuo-ku, Tokyo 104-0028; tel. (3) 3272-6111; fax (3) 3272-6169; e-mail JDK06560@nifty.ne.jp; internet www.shokochukin.co.jp; f. 1936; provides general banking services to facilitate finance for smaller enterprise co-operatives and other organizations formed mainly by small and medium-sized enterprises; issues debentures; began process of privatization in 2008; cap. 218,653m., res 559,102m., dep. 3,862,948m. (March 2012); Pres. TETSUO SEKI; 92 domestic brs, 1 overseas br.

Other government financial institutions include the Japan Finance Corpn for Municipal Enterprises, the Small Business Credit Insurance Corpn and the Okinawa Development Finance Corpn.

Bankers' Associations

Japanese Bankers Association: 1-3-1, Marunouchi, Chiyoda-ku, Tokyo 100-8216; tel. (3) 3216-3761; fax (3) 3201-5608; internet www .zenginkyo.or.jp; f. 1945; fmrly Fed. of Bankers Asscns of Japan; merged into Tokyo Bankers Asscn in 2011, new entity renamed as above; 122 full mems, 64 assoc. mems, 59 special mems, 3 bank holding co mems (April 2012); Chair. YASUHIRO SATO.

National Association of Labour Banks: 2-5-15, Kanda Surugadai, Chiyoda-ku, Tokyo 101-0062; tel. (3) 3295-6721; fax (3) 3295-6751; e-mail kikaku@ho.rokinbank.or.jp; internet all.rokin.or.jp; f. 1951; Pres. YASUHIKO OKADA.

Regional Banks Association of Japan: 3-1-2, Uchikanda, Chiyoda-ku, Tokyo 101-8509; tel. (3) 3252-5171; fax (3) 3254-8664; internet www.chiginkyo.or.jp; f. 1936; 64 mem. banks; Chair. HIDETOSHI SAKUMA.

Second Association of Regional Banks: 5, Sanban-cho, Chiyoda-ku, Tokyo 102-8356; tel. (3) 3262-2181; fax (3) 3262-

2339; e-mail hp-master@dainichiginkyo.or.jp; internet www
.dainichiginkyo.or.jp; f. 1989; fmrly Nat. Asscn of Sogo Banks; 42
commercial banks; Chair. NOBUO KOJIMA.

STOCK EXCHANGES

Nagoya Stock Exchange: 3-8-20, Sakae, Naka-ku, Nagoya 460-
0008; tel. (52) 262-3172; fax (52) 241-1527; e-mail kikaku@nse.or.jp;
internet www.nse.or.jp; f. 1949; Pres. NOBORU KUROYANAGI; Exec.
Vice-Pres. MASAKI TAKEDA.

Osaka Securities Exchange (OSE): 1-8-16, Kitahama, Chuo-ku,
Osaka 541-0041; tel. (6) 4706-0875; fax (6) 6231-2639; e-mail koho@
ose.or.jp; internet www.ose.or.jp; f. 1949; 83 regular transaction
partners, 5 transaction partners in futures and options trading, 2
IPO transaction partners; Pres. and CEO MICHIO YONEDA.

Jasdaq: 1-5-8, Nihonbashi Kayaba-cho, Chuo-ku, Tokyo 103-
0025; tel. (3) 3669-5410; internet www.ose.or.jp/e/jasdaq; f. 1963;
became wholly owned subsidiary of Osaka Securities Exchange
2009; resumed operations following merger of smaller markets,
Jasdaq, Hercules and NEO in 2010; over 1,400 listed cos.

Sapporo Securities Exchange: 5-14-1, Nishi, Minami 1-jo, Chuo-
ku, Sapporo 060-0061; tel. (11) 241-6171; fax (11) 251-0840; e-mail
info@sse.or.jp; internet www.sse.or.jp; 75 listed cos; Pres. YOSHIRO
ITOH.

SBI Japannext Co Ltd: 1-1-1, Hirakawacho Court, Hirakawacho,
Chiyoda-ku, Tokyo, 102-0093; tel. (3) 4577-4040; fax (3) 3261-1702;
e-mail ptsbiz@japannext.co.jp; internet en.japannext.co.jp; Co-CEOs
CHUCK CHON, MASAMI HATAKEYAMA.

Tokyo Stock Exchange, Inc: 2-1, Nihonbashi Kabuto-cho, Chuo-
ku, Tokyo 103-8224; tel. (3) 3665-1881; fax (3) 3662-0547; internet
www.tse.or.jp; f. 1949; 97 general trading participants, 56 bond
futures trading participants, 2 stock index futures trading participants; cap. 11,500m., issued shares 2,300,000 (June 2010); Chair.
TAIZO NISHIMURO; Pres. and CEO ATSUSHI SAITO.

Supervisory Body

Securities and Exchange Surveillance Commission: 3-2-1,
Kasumigaseki, Chiyoda-ku, Tokyo 100-8922; tel. (3) 3581-7868;
fax (3) 5251-2151; internet www.fsa.go.jp/sesc; f. 1992; est. for the
surveillance of securities and financial futures transactions; Chair.
KENICHI SADO.

INSURANCE

Principal Life Companies

AIG Edison Life Insurance Co: Olinas Tower, 4-1-3, Sumida-ku,
Tokyo 130-8625; tel. (3) 6658-6000; internet www.aigedison.co.jp;
fmrly GE Edison Life Insurance Co, itself fmrly Toho Mutual Life
Insurance Co; became subsidiary of Gibraltar Life Insurance in Feb.
2011; Pres. TORU MATSUZAWA.

AIG Star Life Insurance Co Ltd: 4-1-3, Sumida-ku, Tokyo 130-
8625; internet www.aigstar-life.co.jp; fmrly Chiyoda Mutual Life
Insurance Co, acquired by American International Group, Inc (AIG)
in 2001; became subsidiary of Gibraltar Life Insurance in Feb. 2011;
Pres. and CEO NORIO TOMONO.

Aioi Life Insurance Co Ltd: 3-1-6, Nihonbashi, Chuo-ku, Tokyo
103-0027; tel. (3) 3273-0101; internet www.ioi-life.co.jp; Pres.
YOSHIHISA ISHII.

**American Family Life Assurance Co of Columbus (AFLAC
Japan):** Shinjuku Mitsui Bldg, 12/F, 2-1-1, Nishi-Shinjuku, Shinjuku-ku, Tokyo 163-0456; tel. (3) 3344-2701; fax (3) 0424-3001;
internet www.aflac.co.jp; f. 1974; Chair. CHARLES D. LAKE, II; Pres.
TOHRU TONOIKE.

American Life Insurance Co (Japan): 4-1-3, Sumida-ku, Tokyo;
tel. (3) 3284-4111; fax (3) 3284-3874; internet www.alico.co.jp;
f. 1972; Pres. SASHIN N. SHAH.

Asahi Mutual Life Insurance Co: 1-23, Tsurumaki, Tama-shi,
Tokyo 206-8611; tel. (42) 338-3111; internet www.asahi-life.co.jp;
f. 1888; Pres. MIKI SATO.

AXA Japan Holding Co Ltd: NBF Platinum Tower, 1-17-3,
Minato-ku, Tokyo 150-8020; tel. (3) 3407-6210; internet www.axa
.co.jp; Pres. and CEO FUJII YASUYUKI.

Cardif Assurance Vie: Infoss Tower, 9/F, 20-1, Sakuragaoka-cho,
Shibuya-ku, Tokyo 150-0031; tel. (3) 6415-8275; internet www.cardif
.co.jp/vie; f. 2000; Pres. ATSUSHI SAKAUCHI.

Dai-ichi Mutual Life Insurance Co: 1-13-1, Yuraku-cho,
Chiyoda-ku, Tokyo 100-8411; tel. (3) 3216-1211; fax (3) 5221-3340;
internet www.dai-ichi-life.co.jp; f. 1902; acquired 100% ownership of
Neo First Life Insurance Co. Ltd. (formerly known as Sompo Japan
DIY Life Insurance); Chair. KATSUTOSHI SAITO; Pres. KOICHIRO
WATANABE.

Neo First Life Insurance Co. Ltd.: Osaki Wiz Tower, 11-1-2,
Osaki, Shinagawa-ku, Tokyo; internet www.neofirst.co.jp; f. 1999;
part of Dai-ichi Life Insurance Co; Pres. HIROSHI TOKUOKA.

Fuji Life Insurance Co Ltd: 1-18-17, Minami-Senba, Chuo-ku,
Osaka-shi 542-0081; tel. (6) 6261-0284; fax (6) 6261-0113; internet
www.fujiseimei.co.jp; f. 1996; Pres. YOSHIAKI YONEMURA.

Fukoku Mutual Life Insurance Co: 2-2-2, Uchisaiwai-cho,
Chiyoda-ku, Tokyo 100-0011; tel. (3) 3508-1101; fax (3) 3591-6446;
internet www.fukoku-life.co.jp; f. 1923; Chair. TOMOFUMI AKIYAMA;
Pres. YOSHITERU YONEYAMA.

Gibraltar Life Insurance Co Ltd: 2-13-10, Tamati Hisashi, Tokyo
100-8953; tel. (3) 5501-6001; internet www.gib-life.co.jp; f. 1947;
fmrly Kyoei Life Insurance Co Ltd, declared bankrupt Oct. 2000;
resumed operations in 2001 as mem. of Prudential Financial, USA;
Pres. KEI SATO.

Hartford Life Insurance K. K.: Shiodome Bldg, 15/F, 1-2-20,
Kaigan, Minato-ku, Tokyo 105-0022; tel. (3) 6219-3784; internet
www.hartfordlife.co.jp; f. 2000; Pres. NAKAMURA HIROSHI.

ING Life Insurance Co Ltd: New Otani Garden Court, 26/F, 4-1,
Kioi-cho, Chiyoda-ku, Tokyo 102-0094; tel. (3) 5210-0300; fax (3)
5210-0430; internet www.ing-life.co.jp; f. 1985; Pres. SATISH
BAPATTO.

Japan Post Insurance: 1-3-2, Kasumigaseki, Chiyoda-ku, Tokyo
100-8798; tel. (3) 3504-4411; internet www.jp-life.japanpost.jp;
f. 2006; wholly owned by Japan Post Holdings Co Ltd; Pres. and
CEO MASAMI ISHII.

Kyoei Kasai Shinrai Life Insurance Co Ltd: 1-18-6, Shimbashi,
Minato-ku, Tokyo 105-8604; tel. (3) 3504-0131; fax (3) 5372-7701;
internet www.kyoeikasai.co.jp; f. 1996; Pres. KENZI SUGIYAMA.

Manulife Life Insurance Co: 4-34-1, Kokuryo-cho, Chofu-shi,
Tokyo 182-8621; tel. (3) 2442-7120; fax (3) 2442-7977; e-mail
craig_bromley@manulife.com; internet www.manulife.co.jp; f. 1999;
fmrly Manulife Century Life Insurance Co; absorbed bankrupt
Daihyaku Mutual Life Insurance Co in 2001; Pres. and CEO GAVIN
ROBINSON.

MassMutual Life Insurance Co: 1-5-7, Ariake, Koto-ku, Tokyo
135-0063; internet www.massmutual.co.jp; Pres. and CEO MITSURU
IMOTO.

Meiji Yasuda Life Insurance Co: 2-1-1, Marunouchi, Chiyoda-ku,
Tokyo 100-0005; tel. (3) 3283-8293; fax (3) 3215-8123; internet www
.meijiyasuda.co.jp; f. 2004; est. by merger of Meiji Life Insurance Co
(f. 1881) and Yasuda Mutual Life Insurance Co (f. 1880); Chair.
NOBUYA SUZUKI; Pres. AKIO NEGISHI.

Mitsui Life Insurance Co Ltd: 2-1-1, Otemachi, Chiyoda-ku,
Tokyo 100-8123; tel. (3) 6831-8000; internet www.mitsui-seimei.co
.jp; f. 1927; Chair. ENDO OSAMU; Pres. and CEO ARISUE SHINYA.

Nippon Life Insurance Co (Nissay): 3-5-12, Imabashi, Chuo-ku,
Osaka 541-8501; tel. (6) 6209-4500; e-mail hosokawa15560@nissay
.co.jp; internet www.nissay.co.jp; f. 1889; Chair. KUNIE OKAMOTO;
Pres. YOSHINOBU TSUTSUI.

ORIX Life Insurance Corpn: Mita NN Bldg, 4-1-23, Shiba,
Minato-ku, Tokyo 108-0014; tel. (3) 5419-5102; fax (3) 5419-5901;
e-mail koho@orix.co.jp; internet www.orix.co.jp; f. 1991; Chair.
YOSHIHIKO MIYAUCHI; Pres. and CEO MAKOTO INOUE.

Prudential Life Insurance Co Ltd: Prudential Tower, 2-13-10,
Nagata-cho, Chiyoda-ku, Tokyo 100-0014; tel. (3) 5501-5500; fax (3)
3221-2305; internet www.prudential.co.jp; f. 1987; Chair. MITSUO
KURASHIGE; Pres. and CEO ICHITANI SHOICHIRO.

Sompo Japan Nipponkoa Insurance Inc.: 26-1, Nishi-Shinjuku
1-chome, Shinjuku-ku, Tokyo 160-8338; internet www.sjnk.co.jp;
f. 2014; formed by merger of Sompo Japan Insurance Inc. and
Nipponkoa Insurance Co. Ltd; Pres. MASAYA FUTAMIYA.

Sony Life Insurance Co Ltd: Shin-Aoyama Bldg, 3/F, 1-1-1,
Minami-Aoyama, Minato-ku, Tokyo 107-8585; tel. (3) 3475-8811;
fax (3) 3475-8914; internet www.sonylife.co.jp; f. 1979; Chair.
KUNIKITA ANDO; Pres. and CEO KATSUMI IHARA.

Sumitomo Life Insurance Co: 7-18-24, Tsukiji, Chuo-ku, Tokyo
104-8430; tel. (3) 5550-1100; fax (3) 5550-1160; internet www
.sumitomolife.co.jp; f. 1907; Pres. and CEO MASAHIRO HASHIMOTO;
Chair. YOSHIO SATO.

T & D Holdings Inc: Shiodome Shiba-Rikyu Bldg, 1-2-3, Kaigan,
Minato-ku, Tokyo 105-0022; tel. (3) 3434-0111; fax (3) 3434-9055;
internet www.td-holdings.co.jp; f. 1895; fmrly Tokyo Mutual Life
Insurance Co; T & D Financial Life Insurance Co Holdings company
formed in April 2004 through merger of T & D Financial Life
Insurance Co, Taiyo Mutual Life Insurance Co and Daido Life
Insurance Co; Pres. KENJI NAKAGOME.

Tokio Marine & Nichido Life Insurance Co Ltd: 1-2-1, Marunouchi, Chiyoda-ku, Tokyo 100-0005; tel. (3) 5223-2111; fax (3)
5223-2165; internet www.tmn-anshin.co.jp; Pres. SUKEAKI OHTA.

Yamato Mutual Life Insurance Co: 1-1-7, Uchisaiwai-cho, Chiyoda-ku, Tokyo 100-0011; tel. (3) 3508-3111; fax (3) 3508-3118; internet www.yamato-life.co.jp; f. 1911; Pres. TAKEO NAKAZONO.

Zurich Life Insurance Co Ltd: Shinanomachi Rengakan, 35, Shinanomachi, Shinjuku-ku, Tokyo 160-0016; tel. (3) 5361-2700; fax (3) 5361-2705; internet www.zurichlife.co.jp; f. 1996; Pres. NAGANO TOSHIYUKI.

Principal Non-life Companies

ACE Insurance: 6-7-29, Kita-Shinagawa, Shinagawa-ku, Tokyo 141-8679; tel. (3) 6364-7000; fax (3) 5740-0608; internet www .ace-insurance.co.jp; f. 1999; Chair.and CEO EVAN G. GREENBERG.

Aioi Nissay Dowa Insurance Co Ltd: 1-28-1, Ebisu, Shibuya-ku, Tokyo 150-8488; tel. (3) 5424-0101; internet www.aioinissaydowa.co .jp; est. by merger of Aioi Insurance Co Ltd and Nissay Dowa General Insurance Co Ltd in 2010; member of MS&AD Insurance Group Holdings, Inc; Chair. HISAHITO SUZUKI; Pres. and CEO YASUYOSHI KARASAWA.

Allianz Fire and Marine Insurance Japan Ltd: Anzen Bldg, 1-6-6, Moto-Akasaka, Minato-ku, Tokyo 107-0051; tel. (3) 4558-7500; e-mail netadmin@allianz.co.jp; internet www.allianz.co.jp; f. 1990; Chair. AXEL THEIS; Pres. KEN MOTODA.

Asahi Fire and Marine Insurance Co Ltd: 2-6-2, Kaji-cho, Chiyoda-ku, Tokyo 101-8655; tel. (3) 3294-2111; fax (3) 3348 -4561; e-mail asahifmi@blue.ocn.ne.jp; internet www.asahikasai.co.jp; f. 1951; Pres. SOEDA TOMONORI.

AXA Japan Holding Co Ltd: NBF Platinum Tower, 1-17-3, Minato-ku, Tokyo 150-8020; tel. (3) 3407-6210; internet www.axa .co.jp; f. 1998; Pres. and CEO FUJII YASUYUKI.

Daido Fire and Marine Insurance Co Ltd: 1-12-1, Kumoji, Naha-shi, Okinawa 900-8586; tel. (98) 867-1161; fax (98) 862-8362; internet www.daidokasai.co.jp; f. 1971; Pres. NAOTO MIRAYA.

Fuji Fire and Marine Insurance Co Ltd: 1-18-11, Minami-Senba, Chuo-ku, Osaka 542-8567; tel. (6) 6271-2741; fax (6) 6266-7115; internet www.fujikasai.co.jp; f. 1918; Pres. and CEO TAKAYOSHI YOKOYAMA.

Japan Earthquake Reinsurance Co Ltd: Fuji Plaza, 4/F, 8-1, Nihonbashi Kobuna-cho, Chuo-ku, Tokyo 103-0024; tel. (3) 3664-6074; fax (3) 3664-6169; e-mail kanri@nihonjishin.co.jp; internet www.nihonjishin.co.jp; f. 1966; Man. Dir TADASHI BABA.

JI Accident & Fire Insurance Co Ltd: A1 Bldg, 20-5, Ichiban-cho, Chiyoda-ku, Tokyo 102-0082; tel. (3) 3237-2111; fax (3) 3237-2240; internet www.jihoken.co.jp; f. 1989; Pres. HIROHIKO TAKAGI.

Kyoei Mutual Fire and Marine Insurance Co: 1-18-6, Shimba-shi, Minato-ku, Tokyo 105-8604; tel. (3) 3504-0131; fax (3) 3508-7680; e-mail reins.intl@kyoeikasai.co.jp; internet www.kyoeikasai.co.jp; f. 1942; Pres. HIROFUMI SUGINAKA.

Meiji Yasuda General Insurance Co Ltd: 2-11-1, Kanda Tsu-kasa-cho, Chiyoda-ku, Tokyo 101-0048; tel. (3) 3257-3111; fax (3) 3257-3295; internet www.meijiyasuda-sonpo.co.jp; f. 1996; Pres. ENDO HIROSHITOSHI.

Mitsui Direct General Insurance Co Ltd: 1-5-3, Koraku, Bun-kyou-ku, Tokyo 112-0004; tel. (3) 5804-7711; internet www .mitsui-direct.co.jp; f. 1996; Pres. FUNAKI RYUHEI.

Mitsui Sumitomo Insurance Co Ltd: 27-2-2, Shinkawa, Chuo-ku, Tokyo 104-8252; tel. (3) 3297-1111; internet www.ms-ins.com; f. 2001; formed by merger of Mitsui Marine and Fire Insurance and Sumitomo Marine and Fire Insurance; Chair. TOSHIAKI EGASHIRA; Pres. YASUYOSHI KARASAWA.

Nipponkoa Insurance Co Ltd: 3-7-3, Kasumigaseki, Chiyoda-ku, Tokyo 100-8965; tel. (3) 3593-3111; fax (3) 3593-5388; internet www .nipponkoa.co.jp; f. 1892; fmrly The Nippon Fire and Marine Insurance Co Ltd before merging with The Koa Fire and Marine Insurance Co Ltd; acquired Taiyo Fire and Marine Insurance Co Ltd in 2002; Pres. and CEO MAKOTO HYODO.

Nisshin Fire and Marine Insurance Co Ltd: 2-3, Kanda Sur-ugadai, Chiyoda-ku, Tokyo 100-8329; tel. (3) 3292-8000; fax (3) 5282-5582; e-mail nisshin@mb.infoweb.ne.jp; internet www.nisshinfire.co .jp; f. 1908; Pres. MASATO MURASHIMA.

Saison Automobile and Fire Insurance Co Ltd: Sunshine 60 Bldg, 3-1-1, Higashi-Ikebukuro, Toshima-ku, Tokyo 170-6068; tel. (3) 3988-2711; fax (3) 3980-7367; internet www.ins-saison.co.jp; f. 1982; Pres. and CEO NISHIWAKI YOSHIKAZU.

Secom General Insurance Co Ltd: 2-6-2, Hirakawa-cho, Chiyoda-ku, Tokyo 102-8645; tel. (3) 5216-6129; fax (3) 5216-6149; internet www.secom-sonpo.co.jp; f. 1950; Pres. ITIRO OJEKI.

Sompo Japan Insurance Inc: 26-1-1, Nishi-Shinjuku, Shinjuku-ku, Tokyo 160-8338; tel. (3) 3349-3111; fax (3) 3349-4697; internet www.sompo-japan.co.jp; f. 2002; est. by merger of Yasuda Fire and Marine Insurance (f. 1888) and Nissan Fire and Marine Insurance (f. 1911); Pres. MATATOSHI SATO.

Sonpo 24 Insurance Co Ltd: Sunshine 60 Bldg, 44/F, 3-1-1, Higashi-Ikebukuro, Toshima-ku, Tokyo 170-6044; tel. (3) 5957-0111; internet www.sonpo24.co.jp; Pres. ATSUSHI KUMANOMIDO.

Sony Assurance Inc: Aroma Sq., 11/F, 5-37-1, Kamata, Ota-ku, Tokyo 144-8721; tel. (3) 5744-0300; fax (3) 5744-0480; internet www .sonysonpo.co.jp; f. 1999; Pres. and CEO NIWA ATSUO.

Toa Reinsurance Co Ltd: 3-6, Kanda Surugadai, Chiyoda-ku, Tokyo 101-8703; tel. (3) 3253-3171; fax (3) 3253-1208; internet www .toare.co.jp; f. 1940; Pres. and CEO TOMOATSU NOGUCHI.

Tokio Marine & Nichido Fire Insurance Co Ltd: 1-2-1, Mar-unouchi, Chiyoda-ku, Tokyo 100-8050; tel. (3) 3212-6211; internet www.tokiomarine-nichido.co.jp; f. 2004; Pres. TSUYOSHI NAGANO.

Insurance Associations

General Insurance Association of Japan (Nihon Songai Hoken Kyokai): General Insurance Bldg, 2-9, Kanda Awaji-cho, Chiyoda-ku, Tokyo 101-8335; tel. (3) 3255-1439; fax (3) 3255-1234; e-mail kokusai@sonpo.or.jp; internet www.sonpo.or.jp; f. 1946; 26 mems (Sept. 2014); Chair. KENGO SAKURADA; Exec. Dir MASAYOSHI HORI.

General Insurance Rating Organization of Japan: 3-7-1, Nishi-Shinjuku, Shinjuku-ku, Tokyo 163-1029; e-mail service@nliro.or.jp; internet www.giroj.or.jp; f. 2002; 39 mems (Dec 2014); Chair. AKIO MORISHIMA; Exec. Dir HIROSHI AMEMIYA.

Life Insurance Association of Japan (Seimei Hoken Kyokai): Shin-Kokusai Bldg, 3/F, 3-4-1, Marunouchi, Chiyoda-ku, Tokyo 100-0005; tel. (3) 3286-2652; fax (3) 3286-2630; e-mail kokusai@seiho.or .jp; internet www.seiho.or.jp; f. 1908; 43 mem. cos (Jan. 2014); Chair. KOICHIRO WATANABE.

Nippon Export and Investment Insurance: Chiyoda First Bldg, East Wing, 3/F, 3-8-1, Kanda Nishi, Chiyoda-ku, Tokyo; tel. (3)3512-7650; fax (3)3512-7660; internet www.nexi.go.jp; f. 2001; Chair. and CEO KAZUHIKO BANDO.

Trade and Industry

CHAMBERS OF COMMERCE AND INDUSTRY

Japan Chamber of Commerce and Industry (Nihon Shoko Kaigi-sho): 3-2-2, Marunouchi, Chiyoda-ku, Tokyo 100-0005; tel. (3) 3283-7523; fax (3) 3216-6497; e-mail info@jcci.or.jp; internet www.jcci.or.jp; f. 1922; the central org. of all chambers of commerce and industry in Japan; mems: 514 local chambers of commerce and industry; Chair. TADASHI OKAMURA; Pres. TOSHIO NAKAMURA.

Principal chambers include:

Kobe Chamber of Commerce and Industry: 6-1, Minatojima-nakamachi, Chuo-ku, Kobe 650-8543; tel. (78) 303-5806; fax (78) 306-2348; e-mail kokusai-info@kobe-cci.or.jp; internet kobe-cci.weebly .com; f. 1878; 11,000 mems; Chair. TADAHARU OHASHI; Pres. YASUO MURATA.

Kyoto Chamber of Commerce and Industry: 240, Shoshoi-cho, Ebisugawa-agaru, Karasumadori, Nakakyo-ku, Kyoto 604-0862; tel. (75) 212-6420; fax (75) 251-0743; e-mail kokusai@kyo.or.jp; internet www.kyo.or.jp/kyoto; f. 1882; 11,500 mems; Chair. YOSHIO TATEISI; Pres. TUNEOKI OKUHARA.

Nagoya Chamber of Commerce and Industry: 2-10-19, Sakae, Naka-ku, Nagoya, Aichi 460-8422; tel. (52) 223-5722; fax (52) 232-5751; e-mail info@nagoya-cci.or.jp; internet www.nagoya-cci.or.jp; f. 1881; 17,000 mems; Chair. JIRO TAKAHASHI.

Naha Chamber of Commerce and Industry: 2-2-10, Kume Naha, Okinawa; tel. (98) 868-3758; fax (98) 866-9834; e-mail cci-naha@ nahacci.or.jp; internet www.nahacci.or.jp; f. 1927; 4,874 mems; Chair. AKIRA SAKIMA; Pres. KOSEI YONEMURA.

Osaka Chamber of Commerce and Industry: 2-8, Hommachi-bashi, Chuo-ku, Osaka 540-0029; tel. (6) 6944-6400; fax (6) 6944-6293; e-mail intl@osaka.cci.or.jp; internet www.osaka.cci.or.jp; f. 1878; 28,845 mems; Chair. SHIGETAKA SATO; Pres. NADAMOTO MASAHIRO.

Tokyo Chamber of Commerce and Industry: 3-2-2, Marunou-chi, Chiyoda-ku, Tokyo 100-0005; tel. (3) 3283-7523; fax (3) 3216-6497; e-mail kokusai@tokyo-cci.or.jp; internet www.tokyo-cci.or.jp; f. 1878; 77,247 mems (April 2010); Chair. TADASHI OKAMURA; Pres. TOSHIO NAKAMURA.

Yokohama Chamber of Commerce and Industry: Sangyo Boueki Center Bldg, 8/F, Yamashita-cho, Naka-ku, Yokohama 231-8524; tel. (45) 671-7400; fax (45) 671-7410; e-mail soumu@ yokohama-cci.or.jp; internet www.yokohama-cci.or.jp; f. 1880; 14,965 mems; Chair. KENJI SASAKI; Pres. NAMIO OBA.

INDUSTRIAL AND TRADE ASSOCIATIONS

General

Association for the Promotion of International Trade, Japan (JAPIT): 1-9-13, Chiyoda-ku, Tokyo 101-0047; tel. (3) 6740-8261; fax (3) 6740-6160; internet www.japitcn.com; f. 1954 to promote trade with the People's Repub. of China; 700 mems; Chair. YOHEI KONO.

Industry Club of Japan: 1-4-6, Marunouchi, Chiyoda-ku, Tokyo; tel. (3) 3281-1711; fax (3) 3281-1797; e-mail soumu@kogyoclub.or.jp; internet www.kogyoclub.or.jp; f. 1917; est. to develop closer relations between industrialists at home and abroad and promote expansion of Japanese business activities; c. 1,600 mems; Pres. IMAI TAKASHI; Exec. Dir KOUICHIROU SHINNO.

Japan Commercial Arbitration Association: Hirose Bldg, 3/F, 3-17, Kanda Nishiki-cho, Chiyoda-ku, Tokyo 101-0054; tel. (3) 5280-5200; fax (3) 5280-5170; e-mail arbitration@jcaa.or.jp; internet www.jcaa.or.jp; f. 1950; 700 mems; provides facilities for mediation, conciliation and arbitration in international trade disputes; Pres. TADASHI OKAMURA.

Japan External Trade Organization (JETRO): Ark Mori Bldg, 6/F, 1-12-32, Akasaka-cho, Minato-ku, Tokyo 107-6006; tel. (3) 3582-5511; fax (3) 3582-5662; e-mail seh@jetro.go.jp; internet www.jetro.go.jp; f. 1958; information on international trade, investment, import promotion, exhibitions of foreign products; Chair. and CEO YASUO HAYASHI; Pres. TADASHI IZAWA.

Japan Federation of Smaller Enterprise Organizations (JFSEO) (Nippon Chusokigyo Dantai Renmei): 2-8-4, Nihonbashi, Kayaba-cho, Chuo-ku, Tokyo 103-0025; tel. (3) 3669-6862; f. 1948; 18 mems and c. 1,000 co-operative socs; Pres. MASATAKA TOYODA; Chair. of Int. Affairs SEIICHI ONO.

Japan General Merchandise Exporters' Association: 2-4-1, Hamamatsu-cho, Minato-ku, Tokyo; tel. (3) 3435-3471; fax (3) 3434-6739; f. 1953; 40 mems; Pres. TADAYOSHI NAKAZAWA.

Japan Productivity Center (JPC): 3-1-1, Shibuya, Shibuya-ku, Tokyo 150-8307; tel. (3) 3409-1112; fax (3) 3409-1986; internet www.jpc-net.jp; f. 1994; est. by merger between Japan Productivity Center and Social Economic Congress of Japan; fmrly Japan Productivity Center for Socio-Economic Development, renamed as above 2009; 10,000 mems; concerned with management problems and research into productivity; Chair. JIRO USHIO; Pres. TSUNEAKI TANIGUCHI.

Keizai Doyukai (Japan Association of Corporate Executives): 1-4-6, Marunouchi, Chiyoda-ku, Tokyo 100-0005; tel. (3) 3211-1271; fax (3) 3213-2946; e-mail kdcontact205@doyukai.or.jp; internet www.doyukai.or.jp; f. 1946; c.1,400 mems; corporate executives concerned with national and international economic and social policies; Chair. MASAMITSU SAKURAI.

Nihon Boeki-Kai (Japan Foreign Trade Council, Inc): World Trade Center Bldg, 6/F, 2-4-1, Hamamatsu-cho, Minato-ku, Tokyo 105-6106; tel. (3) 3435-5959; fax (3) 3435-5979; e-mail mail@jftc.or.jp; internet www.jftc.or.jp; f. 1947; 192 mems; Chair. SHOEI UTSUDA; Exec. Man. Dir MASAYOSHI AMANO.

Chemicals

Japan Chemical Industry Association: Sumitomo Fudosan Rokko Bldg, 1-4-1, Shinkawa, Chuo-ku, Tokyo 104-0033; tel. (3) 3297-2550; fax (3) 3297-2610; e-mail chemical@jcia-net.or.jp; internet www.nikkakyo.org; f. 1948; 266 mems; Chair. HIROMASA YONEKURA.

Japan Cosmetic Industry Association: 45 MT Bldg, 6/F, 5-1-5, Toranomon, Minato-ku, Tokyo 105-0001; tel. (3) 5472-2530; fax (3) 5472-2536; e-mail info@jcia.org; internet www.jcia.org; f. 1959; 687 mem. cos; Chair. REIJIRO KOBAYASHI.

Japan Perfumery and Flavouring Association: Saeki No. 3 Bldg, 3/F, 37, Kandakonya-cho, Chiyoda-ku, Tokyo 101-0035; tel. and fax (3) 3526-7855; f. 1947; Chair. YONEJIRO KORAYASHI.

Japan Pharmaceutical Manufacturers' Association: Torii Nihonbashi Bldg, 3-4-1, Nihonbashi Hon-cho, Chuo-ku, Tokyo 103-0023; tel. (3) 3241-0326; fax (3) 3242-1767; internet www.jpma.or.jp; 67 mems; Pres. YASUCHIKA HASEGAWA.

Photo-Sensitized Materials Manufacturers' Association: JCII Bldg, 25, Ichiban-cho, Chiyoda-ku, Tokyo 102-0082; tel. (3) 5276-3561; fax (3) 5276-3563; internet pmma.a.la9.jp; f. 1948; Pres. SHIGETAKA KOMORI.

Fishing and Pearl Cultivation

Japan Fisheries Association (Dainippon Suisankai): Sankaido Bldg, 1-9-13, Akasaka, Minato-ku, Tokyo 107-0052; tel. (3) 3585-6681; fax (3) 3582-2337; e-mail japan@suisankai.or.jp; internet www.suisankai.or.jp; Pres. TOSHIRO SHIRASU.

Japan Pearl Export and Processing Co-operative Association: 3-6-15, Kyobashi, Chuo-ko, Tokyo 104-0031; tel. (3) 3562-5011; f. 1951; 130 mems.

Japan Pearl Exporters' Association: 122, Higashi-Machi, Chuo-ku, Kobe 650-0031; tel. (78) 331-4031; fax (78) 331-4345; e-mail jpeakobe@lime.ocn.ne.jp; internet www.japan-pearl.com; f. 1954; 56 mems; Pres. YOSHIHIRO SHIMIZU.

Machinery and Precision Equipment

Camera and Imaging Products Association (CIPA) (Camera Eizo Kiki Kogyo-kai): JCII Bldg, 25, Ichiban-cho, Chiyoda-ku, Tokyo 102-0082; tel. (3) 5276-3891; fax (3) 5276-3893; internet www.cipa.jp; f. 1954; fmrly Japan Camera Industry Asscn, renamed as above 2002; 54 mems; Pres. TSUYOSHI KIKUKAWA.

Japan Clock and Watch Association: Kudan Sky Bldg, 1-12-11, Kudan-Kita, Chiyoda-ku, Tokyo 102-0073; tel. (3) 5276-3411; fax (3) 5276-3414; internet www.jcwa.or.jp; Chair. SHINJI HATTORI.

Japan Electric Association: Denki Bldg, 4/F, 1-7-1, Yuraku-cho, Chiyoda-ku, Tokyo 100-0006; tel. (3) 3216-0551; fax (3) 3214-6005; internet www.denki.or.jp; f. 1921; 4,610 mems; Pres. TATSUO KAWAI.

Japan Electric Measuring Instruments Manufacturers' Association (JEMIMA): Keisoku Kaikan Bldg, 2-15-12, Nihonbashi-Kakigara-cho, Chuo-ku, Tokyo 103-0014; tel. (3) 3662-8181; fax (3) 3662-8180; e-mail katsuta@jemima.or.jp; internet www.jemima.or.jp; 79 mems; Chair. SEIJI ONOKI.

Japan Electrical Manufacturers' Association: 17-4, Ichiban-cho, Chiyoda-ku, Tokyo 102-0082; tel. (3) 3556-5881; fax (3) 3556-5889; internet www.jema-net.or.jp; f. 1948; 262 mems; Chair. MICHIHIRO KITAZAWA; Pres. TOSHIMI HAYANO.

Japan Electronics and Information Technology Industries Association (JEITA): Ote Center Bldg, 1-1-3, Otemachi, Chiyoda-ku, Tokyo 100-0004; tel. (3) 5218-1050; fax (3) 5218-1070; internet www.jeita.or.jp; promotes manufacturing, international trade and consumption of electronics products and components; Chair. RYOJI CHUBACHI; Pres. TSUTOMU HANDA.

Japan Energy Association: Kawate Bldg, 1-5-8, Nishi-Shimbashi, Minato-ku, Tokyo 105-0003; tel. (3) 3502-1261; fax (3) 3502-2760; e-mail info@jea-wec.or.jp; internet www.jea-wec.or.jp; f. 1950; 133 mems; Chair. TERUAKI MASUMOTO; Exec. Dir HAJIME MURATA.

Japan Machine Tool Builders' Association: Kikai Shinko Bldg, 3-5-8, Shiba Koen, Minato-ku, Tokyo 105-0011; tel. (3) 3434-3961; fax (3) 3434-3763; e-mail intl@jmtba.or.jp, internet www.jmtba.or.jp; f. 1951; 112 mems; Chair. KENICHI NAKAMURA; Pres. TOSHIONI SHONO.

Japan Machine Tools Importers' Association: Toranomon Kogyo Bldg, 1-2-18, Toranomon, Minato-ku, Tokyo 105-0001; tel. (3) 3501-5030; fax (3) 3501-5040; e-mail info@jmtia.gr.jp, internet www.jmtia.gr.jp; f. 1955; 42 mems; Chair. YUZO CHIBA.

Japan Machinery Center for Trade and Investment (JMC): Kikai Shinko Bldg, 4/F, 3-5-8, Shiba Koen, Minato-ku, Tokyo 105-0011; tel. (3) 3431-9507; fax (3) 3436-6455; e-mail info@jmcti.or.jp; internet www.jmcti.org; f. 1952; 290 mem. cos; Pres. KENJI MIYAHARA.

The Japan Machinery Federation: Kikai Shinko Bldg, 3-5-8, Shiba Koen, Minato-ku, Tokyo 105-0011; tel. (3) 3434-5381; fax (3) 3434-2666; e-mail koho@jmf.or.jp; internet www.jmf.or.jp; f. 1952; Pres. MOTOTSUGU ITO; Exec. Dir KYOSHI ISHIZAKA.

Japan Microscope Manufacturers' Association: Kikai Shinko Bldg, 5-8-3, Shiba Koen, Minato-ku, Tokyo 105-0011; tel. (3) 3432-5100; fax (3) 3432-5611; e-mail jmma@microscope.jp; internet www.microscope.jp; f. 1954; 27 mems; Chair. HIROYUKI SASA.

Japan Motion Picture Equipment Industrial Association: Kikai Shinko Bldg, 3-5-8, Shiba Koen, Minato-ku, Tokyo 105-0011; tel. (3) 3434-3911; fax (3) 3434-3912; Pres. MASAO SHIKATA; Gen. Sec. TERUHIRO KATO.

Japan Optical Industry Association: Kikai Shinko Bldg, 3-5-8, Shiba Koen, Minato-ku, Tokyo 105-0011; tel. (3) 3431-7073; f. 1946; 7 mems; Chair. MICHIO KARIYA; Exec. Sec. SHIRO IWAHASHI.

Japan Society of Industrial Machinery Manufacturers: Kikai Shinko Bldg, 3-5-8, Shiba Koen, Minato-ku, Tokyo 105-0011; tel. (3) 3434-6821; fax (3) 3434-4767; e-mail obd@jsim.or.jp; internet www.jsim.or.jp; f. 1948; 170 mems; Pres. YOSHIO HINOU.

Japan Textile Machinery Association: Kikai Shinko Bldg, Rm 101, 5-22, Shiba Koen, Minato-ku, Tokyo 105-0011; tel. (3) 3434-3821; fax (3) 3434-3043; e-mail am-jtma@jtma.or.jp; internet www.jtma.or.jp; f. 1951; Pres. TETSURO TOYODA.

Metals

Japan Aluminium Association (JAA): Tsukamoto-Sozan Bldg, 4-2-15, Ginza, Chuo-ku, Tokyo 104-0061; tel. (3) 3538-0221; fax (3) 3538-0233; internet www.aluminum.or.jp; f. 1999; est. by merger of Japan Aluminium Federation and Japan Light Metal Association; 146 mems; Chair. ISHIYAMA TAKASHI.

Japan Copper and Brass Association: Usagiya Bldg, 5/F, 1-10-10, Ueno, Taito-ku, Tokyo 110-0005; tel. (3) 3836-8801; fax (3) 3836-8808; e-mail jbmajwcc@copper-brass.gr.jp; internet www

.copper-brass.gr.jp; f. 1948; 62 mems; Chair. Takao Hashida; Sec.-Gen. Toshinobu Hidaka.

The Japan Iron and Steel Federation: Tekko Kaikan Bldg, 3-2-10, Nihonbashi Kayaba-cho, Chuo-ku, Tokyo 103-0025; tel. (3) 3669-4811; fax (3) 3664-1457; internet www.jisf.or.jp; f. 1948; mems: 61 mfrs, 61 dealers, 6 orgs; Chair. Eiji Hayashida.

Japan Stainless Steel Association: TMM Bldg, 3/F, 1-10-5, Iwamoto-cho, Chiyoda-ku, Tokyo; tel. (3) 5687-7831; fax (3) 5687-8551; e-mail yabe@jssa.gr.jp; internet www.jssa.gr.jp; f. 1959; 80 mems; Chair. Hiroshi Kinoshita.

Steel Castings and Forgings Association of Japan (JSCFA): Shikoku Bldg Bekkan, 8/F, 1-14-4, Uchikannda, Chiyoda-ku, Tokyo 101-0047; tel. (3) 5283-1611; fax (3) 5283-1613; e-mail cf@jscfa.gr.jp; internet www.jscfa.gr.jp; f. 1972; mems: 48 cos, 44 plants; Pres. Yamaguchi Ikuhiro.

Mining and Petroleum

Japan Coal Energy Center (JCOAL): Meiji Yasuda Seimei Mita Bldg, 9/F, 3-14-10, Mita, Minato-ku, Tokyo 108-0073; tel. (3) 6400-5191; fax (3) 6400-5206; e-mail jcoal-qa@jcoal.or.jp; internet www.jcoal.or.jp; f. 1997; est. by merger of Japan Coal Asscn, Coal Mining Research Centre, and the Japan Technical Cooperation Center for Coal Resources Devt; 111 mems; Pres. Yoshihiko Nagasaki.

Japan Mining Industry Association: c/o Eiha Bldg, 17-11-3, Kanda Nishiki-cho, Chiyoda-ku, Tokyo 101-0054; tel. (3) 5280-2321; fax (3) 5280-7128; internet www.kogyo-kyokai.gr.jp; f. 1948; 52 mem. cos; Chair. Sadao Senda; Pres. Shinichi Ozeki.

Japan Petrochemical Industry Association: 1-4-1, Shinkawa, Chuo-ku, Tokyo 104-0033; tel. (3) 3297-2011; fax (3) 3297-2017; e-mail inquiries_hp@jpca.or.jp; internet www.jpca.or.jp; Chair. Kyohei Takahashi.

Japan Petroleum Development Association: Keidanren Bldg, 17/F, 1-3-2, Otemachi, Chiyoda-ku, Tokyo 100-0004; tel. (3) 3214-1701; fax (3) 3214-1703; e-mail jpda-sekkoren@sekkoren.jp; internet www.sekkoren.jp; f. 1961; Chair. Naoki Kuroda.

Paper and Printing

Japan Federation of Printing Industries: 1-16-8, Shintomi, Chuo-ku, Tokyo 104-0041; tel. (3) 3553-6051; fax (3) 3553-6079; internet www.jfpi.or.jp; f. 1985; 10 mems; Chair. Satoshi Sawatari.

Japan Paper Association: Kami Parupu Bldg, 3-9-11, Ginza, Chuo-ku, Tokyo 104-8139; tel. (3) 3248-4801; fax (3) 3248-4826; internet www.jpa.gr.jp; f. 1946; 54 mems; Chair. Kazuhisa Shinoda; Pres. Masataka Hayama.

Japan Paper Exporters' Association: Kami Parupu Bldg, 3-9-11, Ginza, Chuo-ku, Tokyo 104-8139; tel. (3) 3248-4831; fax (3) 3248-4834; e-mail info@jpeta.or.jp; internet www.jpeta.or.jp; f. 1952; 32 mems; Chair. Shinichi Sato.

Japan Paper Importers' Association: Kami Parupu Bldg, 3-9-11, Ginza, Chuo-ku, Tokyo 104-8139; tel. (3) 3248-4831; fax (3) 3248-4834; e-mail info@jpeta.or.jp; internet jpeta.or.jp; f. 1981; 21 mems; Chair. Yasuyuki Amakusa.

Japan Paper Products Manufacturers' Association: 4-2-6, Kotobuki, Taito-ku, Tokyo; tel. (3) 3543-2411; f. 1949; Exec. Dir Kiyoshi Satoh.

Textiles

Central Raw Silk Association of Japan: 1-9-4, Yuraku-cho, Chiyoda-ku, Tokyo; tel. (3) 3214-5777; fax (3) 3214-5778.

Japan Chemical Fibers Association: Seni Kaikan, 7/F, 3-1-11, Nihonbashi-Honcho, Chuo-ku, Tokyo 103-0023; tel. (3) 3241-2311; fax (3) 3246-0823; internet www.jcfa.gr.jp; f. 1948; 17 mems, 1 assoc. mem, 20 supporting mems; Pres. Akihiro Nikkaku; Dir-Gen. Tsunehiro Ogara.

Japan Cotton and Staple Fibre Weavers' Association: 1-8-7, Nishi-Azabu, Minato-ku, Tokyo; tel. (3) 3403-9671; internet www.jcwa-net.jp; 28 mems; Pres. Osamu Makoto.

Japan Silk Spinners' Association: Hasegawa Bldg 3F, 2-4-5, Horidome-cho, Nihonbashi, Chuo-ku, Tokyo 103-0012; tel. (3) 3661-0235; fax (3) 3661-0596; f. 1948; 95 mem. cos; Chair. Ichiji Ohtani.

Japan Spinners' Association: Mengyo Kaikan Bldg, 6/F, 2-5-8, Bingomachi, Chuo-ku, Osaka 541-0051; tel. (6) 6231-8431; fax (6) 6229-1590; e-mail spinas@cotton.or.jp; internet www.jsa-jp.org; f. 1948; 16 mems; Head Kojiro Abe.

Transport Machinery

Japan Association of Rolling Stock Industries: Awajicho Suny Bldg, 7/F, 1-2, Kanda Suda-cho, Chiyoda-ku, Tokyo 101-0041; tel. (3) 3257-1901; e-mail info@tetsushako.or.jp; internet www.tetsushako.or.jp; Chair. Hirai Masaharu.

Japan Auto Parts Industries Association: Jidosha Buhin Bldg, 5/F, 1-16-15, Takanawa, Minato-ku, Tokyo 108-0074; tel. (3) 3445-4211; fax (3) 3447-5372; e-mail info@japia.or.jp; internet www.japia.or.jp; f. 1948; 530 mem. cos; Chair. Hisataka Nobumoto; Exec. Dir K. Shibasaki.

Japan Automobile Manufacturers Association, Inc (JAMA): Jidosha Kaikan, 1-1-30, Shiba Daimon, Minato-ku, Tokyo 105-0012; tel. (3) 5405-6126; fax (3) 5405-6136; e-mail kaigai_tky@mta.jama.or.jp; internet www.jama.or.jp; f. 1967; 14 mem. cos; Chair. Fumihiko Ike; Pres. Seiichi Nagatsuka.

Japan Bicycle Manufacturers' Association: 1-9-3, Akasaka, Minato-ku, Tokyo 107; tel. (3) 3583-3123; fax (3) 3589-3125; f. 1955.

Japan Ship Exporters' Association: Toranomon 30 Mori Bldg, 5/F, 3-2-2, Toranomon, Minato-ku, Tokyo 105-0001; tel. (3) 5425-9671; fax (3) 5425-9674; e-mail postmaster@jsea.or.jp; internet www.jsea.or.jp; 32 mems; Pres. Masamoto Tazaki.

Japanese Marine Equipment Association: Kaiyo Senpaku Bldg, 15-16, Toranomon, Minato-ku, Tokyo 105-0001; tel. (3) 3502-2041; fax (3) 3591-2206; e-mail info@jsmea.or.jp; internet www.jsmea.or.jp; f. 1956; 219 mems; Chair. Zenshichi Asasaka.

Japanese Shipowners' Association: Kaiun Bldg, 2-6-4, Hiraka-wa-cho, Chiyoda-ku, Tokyo 102-8603; tel. (3) 3264-7171; fax (3) 3262-4760; internet www.jsanet.or.jp; Pres. Koji Miyahara.

Shipbuilders' Association of Japan: 30 Mori Bldg, 5/F, 3-2-2, Toranomon, Minato-ku, Tokyo 105-0001; tel. (3) 5425-9527; fax (3) 5425-9533; internet www.sajn.or.jp; f. 1947; 21 mems; Chair. Takao Motoyama.

Society of Japanese Aerospace Companies (SJAC): Toshin-Tameike Bldg, 2/F, 1-1-14, Akasaka, Minato-ku, Tokyo 107-0052; tel. (3) 3585-0511; fax (3) 3585-0541; e-mail itahara-hiroharu@sjac.or.jp; internet www.sjac.or.jp; f. 1952; reorg. 1974; 117 mems, 41 assoc. mems; Chair. Kazuo Tsukuda; Pres. Kosuke Imashimizu.

Miscellaneous

Communications Industry Association of Japan (CIA-J): Shuwa Dai-ichi Hamamatsucho Bldg, 3/F, 2-2-12, Hamamatsu-cho, Minato-ku, Tokyo 105-0013; tel. (3) 5403-9363; fax (3) 5463-9360; e-mail admin@ciaj.or.jp; internet www.ciaj.or.jp; f. 1948; non-profit org. of telecommunications equipment mfrs; 236 mems; Chair. Kawamura Takashi; Pres. Yoshiyuki Sukemune.

Japan Canners' Association: Tokyo; tel. (3) 5256-4801; fax (3) 5256-4805; internet www.jca-can.or.jp; Pres. Keinosuke Hisai.

Japan Cement Association: Daiwa Nihonbashi-Honcho Bldg, 7/F, 1-9-4, Chuo-ku, Tokyo 103-0023; tel. (3) 5200-5057; fax (3) 5200-5062; e-mail international@jcassoc.or.jp; internet www.jcassoc.or.jp; f. 1948; 18 mem. cos; Chair. Keiji Tokuue.

Japan Lumber Importers' Association: Yushi Kogyo Bldg, 3-13-11, Nihonbashi, Chuo-ku, Tokyo 103-0027; tel. (3) 3271-0926; fax (3) 3271-0928; f. 1950; 130 mems; Pres. Tamba Tosikhito.

Japan Plastics Industry Federation: 3-5-2 Nihonbashi-Kayabacho, Chuo-ku, Tokyo 103-0025; tel. (3) 6661-6811; fax (3) 6661-6810; e-mail info@jpif.gr.jp; internet www.jpif.gr.jp; f. 1950; 102 mems; Exec. Dir Yasuhiko Mizuno.

Japan Plywood Manufacturers' Association: Meisan Bldg, 1-18-17, Nishi-Shimbashi, Minato-ku, Tokyo 105; tel. (3) 3591-9246; fax (3) 3591-9240; f. 1965; 92 mems; Pres. Koichi Mataga.

Japan Pottery Manufacturers' Federation: Toto Bldg, 1-1-28, Toranomon, Minato-ku, Tokyo; tel. (3) 3503-6761.

Japan Rubber Manufacturers' Association: Tobu Bldg, 2/F, 1-5-26, Moto-Akasaka, Minato-ku, Tokyo 107-0051; tel. (3) 3408-7101; fax (3) 3408-7106; e-mail soumu@jrma.or.jp; internet www.jrma.gr.jp; f. 1950; 126 mems; Pres. Mitsuaki Asai.

Japan Spirits and Liquors Makers' Association: Koura Dai-ichi Bldg, 7/F, 1-1-6, Nihonbashi-Kayaba-cho, Chuo-ku, Tokyo 103; tel. (3) 3668-4621.

Japan Sugar Refiners' Association: 5-7, Sanban-cho, Chiyoda-ku, Tokyo 102; tel. (3) 3288-1151; fax (3) 3288-3399; internet www.sugar.or.jp; f. 1949; 17 mems; Senior Man. Dir Katsuyuki Suzuki.

Japan Tea Exporters' Association: 17, Kitaban-cho, Aoiku, Shizuoka Prefecture 420-0005; tel. (54) 271-3428; fax (54) 271-2177; e-mail japantea1953@yahoo.co.jp; f. 1953; 75 mems; Pres. Toshiaki Kirishima.

Japan Toy Association: 4-22-4, Higashi-Komagata, Sumida-ku, Tokyo 130; tel. (3) 3829-2513; fax (3) 3829-2510; e-mail otoiawase2009@toys.or.jp; internet www.toys.or.jp; 228 mems; Chair. Takeo Takasu.

Motion Picture Producers' Association of Japan, Inc: Nihonbashi Bldg, 2/F, 1-17-12, Nihonbashi, Chuo-ku, Tokyo 103-0027; tel. (3) 3243-9100; fax (3) 3243-9101; e-mail info@eiren.org; internet www.eiren.org; f. 1945; Pres. Nobuyoshi Otani.

EMPLOYERS' ORGANIZATION

Japan Business Federation (JBF) (Nippon Keidanren): Keidanren Kaikan, 1-3-2, Otemachi, Chiyoda-ku, Tokyo 100-8188; tel. (3) 6741-0171; fax (3) 6741-0301; e-mail webmaster@keidanren.or.jp; internet www.keidanren.or.jp; f. 2002; est. by merger of Keidanren (f. 1946) and Nikkeiren (f. 1948); 1,601 mems (June 2010); Chair. HIROMASA YONEKURA; Dir-Gen. YOSHIO NAKAMURA.

UTILITIES

Electricity

Chubu Electric Power Co Inc: 1, Higashi-Shin-cho, Higashi-ku, Nagoya 461-8680; tel. (52) 951-8211; fax (52) 962-4624; internet www .chuden.co.jp; f. 1951; Chair. TOSHIO MITA; Pres. and CEO AKIHISA MIZUNO.

Chugoku Electric Power Co Inc: 4-33, Komachi, Naka-ku, Hiroshima 730-8701; tel. (82) 241-0211; fax (82) 523-6185; e-mail angel@ inet.energia.co.jp; internet www.energia.co.jp; f. 1951; Chair. TAKASHI YAMASHITA; Pres. TOMOHIDE KARITA.

Electric Power Development Co Ltd (J-Power): 6-15-1, Ginza, Chuo-ku, Tokyo 104-8165; tel. (3) 3546-2211; fax (3) 3546-9532; e-mail webmaster@jpower.co.jp; internet www.jpower.co.jp; f. 1952; Chair. KIYOSHI SAWABE; Pres. MASAYOSHI KITAMURA.

Hokkaido Electric Power Co Inc: 1-2, Higashi-Odori, Chuo-ku, Sapporo, Hokkaido 060-8677; tel. (11) 251-1111; internet www.hepco .co.jp; f. 1951; Chair. YOSHITAKA SATO; Pres. KATSUHIKO KAWAI.

Hokuriku Electric Power Co Inc: 15-1, Ushijima-cho, Toyamashi, Toyama 930-8686; e-mail pub-mast@rikuden.co.jp; internet www.rikuden.co.jp; f. 1951; Chair. ISAO NAGAHARA; Pres. SUSUMU KYUWA.

Kansai Electric Power Co Inc: 3-6-16, Nakanoshima, Kita-ku, Osaka 530-8270; tel. (6) 6441-8821; fax (6) 6441-8598; e-mail postmaster@kepco.co.jp; internet www.kepco.co.jp; Pres. MAKOTO YAGI.

Kyushu Electric Power Co Inc: 2-1-82, Watanabe-dori, Chuo-ku, Fukuoka 810-8726; tel. (92) 761-3031; fax (92) 731-8719; internet www.kyuden.co.jp; Chair. SHINGO MATSUO; Pres. TOSHIO MANABE.

Okinawa Electric Power Co Inc: 5-2-1, Makiminato, Urasoe, Okinawa 901-2602; tel. (98) 877-2341; fax (98) 877-6017; e-mail ir@ okiden.co.jp; internet www.okiden.co.jp; f. 1972; Chair. TSUGIYOSHI TOMA; Pres. DENICHIRO ISHIMINE.

Shikoku Electric Power Co Inc: 2-5, Marunouchi, Takamatsu 760-8573; tel. (878) 21-5061; fax (878) 26-1250; e-mail postmaster@ yonden.co.jp; internet www.yonden.co.jp; f. 1951; Chair. MOMOKI TOKIWA; Pres. AKIRA CHIBA.

Tohoku Electric Power Co Inc: 1-7-1, Hon-cho, Aoba-ku, Sendai 980-8550; tel. (22) 225-2111; fax (22) 225-2550; e-mail webmaster@ tohoku-epco.co.jp; internet www.tohoku-epco.co.jp; Chair. HIROAKI TAKAHASHI; Pres. MAKOTO KAIWA.

Tokyo Electric Power Co Inc: 1-2-2, Yuraku-cho, Chiyoda-ku, Tokyo 100-8560; tel. (3) 6373-1111; fax (3) 3596-8508; internet www .tepco.co.jp; Chair. KAZUHIKO SHIMOKOBE; Pres. TOSHIO NISHIZAWA.

Federation

Federation of Electric Power Companies of Japan (FEPC JAPAN): 1-3-2, Keidanren Kaikan, Ohte-machi, Chiyoda-ku, Tokyo 100-8118; tel. (3) 5221-1440; fax (3) 6361-9024; e-mail webadmin2@ fepc.or.jp; internet www.fepc.or.jp; f. 1952; Chair. MAKOTO YAGI.

Gas

Hokkaido Gas Co Ltd: 7-3-1, Nishi-Odori, Chuo-ku, Sapporo; tel. (11) 231-9511; internet www.hokkaido-gas.co.jp; Chair. SHIGERO KUSANO; CEO HIROSHI OHTSUKI.

Keiyo Gas Co Ltd: 2-8-8, Ichikawa-Minami, Ichikawa, Chiba 272-8580; tel. (47) 361-0211; fax (47) 325-1049; internet www.keiyogas.co .jp; f. 1927; Chair. TOMO KIKUCHI; Pres. HIDEKIYO GATAYAMA.

Osaka Gas Co Ltd: 4-1-2, Hiranomachi, Chuo-ku, Osaka 541-0046; tel. (6) 6205-4715; fax (6) 6222-5831; e-mail keiri@osakagas.co.jp; internet www.osakagas.co.jp; f. 1905; Pres. HIROSHI OZAKI.

Saibu Gas Co: 1-17-1, Chiyo, Hakata-ku, Fukuoka; tel. (92) 633-2345; internet www.saibugas.co.jp; f. 1930; Chair. HIROKI OGAWA; Pres. YUUJI TANAKA.

Toho Gas Co Ltd: 19-18, Sakurada-cho, Atsuta-ko, Nagoya 456-8511; tel. (52) 871-3511; internet www.tohogas.co.jp; f. 1922; Chair. TAKASHI SAEKI; Pres. KOICHI YASUI.

Tokyo Gas Co Inc: 1-5-20, Kaigan, Minato-ku, Tokyo 105; tel. (3) 3433-2111; fax (3) 5472-5385; internet www.tokyo-gas.co.jp; f. 1885; Chair. NORIO ICHINO; Pres. TSUYOSHI OKAMOTO.

Association

Japan Gas Association: 1-1-3, Nishi-Shinbashi, Minato-ku, Tokyo 105-0003; tel. (3) 3502-0116; fax (3) 3502-3676; internet www.gas.or .jp; f. 1947; comprises 209 city gas utilities and 275 assoc. mems; Chair. MITSUNORI TORIHARA.

Water

Nagoya City Waterworks & Sewerage Bureau: 3-1-1, Sannomaru, Naka-ku, Nagoya 460-8508; tel. (52) 972-3608; fax (52) 972-3710; e-mail mail@water.city.nagoya.jp; internet www.water.city .nagoya.jp.

Osaka City Waterworks Bureau: 2-1-10, Nanko-Kita, Suminoe-ku, Osaka 559-8558; tel. (6) 6458-1132; fax (6) 6458-2100; internet www.city.osaka.lg.jp.

Sapporo City Waterworks Bureau: 2-11, Higashi-Odori, Chuo-ku, Sapporo 060-0041; tel. (11) 211-7007; fax (11) 232-1740; e-mail su .somu@suido.city.sapporo.jp; internet www.city.sapporo.jp/suido.

Tokyo Bureau of Waterworks: Yotsuya Kumin Center, 3/F, 87 Naito-cho, Shinjuku-ku, Tokyo 160-8587; tel. (3) 5368-3055; fax (3) 3358-5900; internet www.waterworks.metro.tokyo.jp.

Yokohama Waterworks Bureau: 1-1, Minato-cho, Naka-ku, Yokohama; tel. (45) 671-3055; fax (45) 664-6774; e-mail su-somu@ city.yokohama.jp; internet www.city.yokohama.jp/suidou.

Association

Japan Water Works Association (JWWA): 4-8-9, Kudan-Minami, Chiyoda-ku, Tokyo 102-0074; tel. (3) 3264-2281; fax (3) 3262-2244; e-mail kokusai@jwwa.or.jp; internet www.jwwa.or.jp; f. 1932; Exec. Dir MASARU OZAKU.

TRADE UNIONS

A feature of Japan's trade union movement is that the unions are usually based on single enterprises, embracing workers of different occupations in that enterprise. In June 2012 there were 54,773 unions; union membership stood at 9.89m. workers in that year.

Japanese Trade Union Confederation (JTUC–RENGO): 3-2-11, Kanda Surugadai, Chiyoda-ku, Tokyo 101-0062; tel. (3) 5295-0526; fax (3) 5295-0548; e-mail jtuc-kokusai@sv.rengo-net.or.jp; internet www.jtuc-rengo.org; f. 1989; 6.8m. mems; Pres. NOBUAKI KOGA.

Transport

RAILWAYS

Operated by the Japan Railways Group (see below), the high-speed Shinkansen rail network links major cities in Japan. The network consists of the Tokaido line from Tokyo to Shin-Osaka (515.4 km), the Sanyo line from Shin-Osaka to Hakata (553.7 km), the Tohoku line from Tokyo to Shin–Aomori (674.9 km), the Joetsu line from Omiya to Niigata (269.5 km), the Nagano (Hokuriku) line from Takasaki to Nagano (117.4 km) and the Kyushu line from Hakata to Kagoshima-Chuo (256.8 km). The Yamagata line from Fukushima to Shinjo (148.6 km) is operated as a branch of the Tohoku line with through trains from Tokyo. The Tohoku line also has another branch line, the Akita line, which runs from Morioka to Akita (127.3 km). The Shinkansen network had a total route length of 2,387.7 km in 2014.

Japan Railways (JR) Group: 1-6-5, Marunouchi, Chiyoda-ku, Tokyo 100-0005; tel. (3) 3215-9649; fax (3) 3213-5291; fmrly the state-controlled Japanese National Railways (JNR); reorg. and transferred to private sector in 1987.

   Central Japan Railway Co: JR Central Towers, 1-1-4, Meieki, Nakamura-ku, Nagoya 450-6101; tel. (3) 3274-9727; fax (3) 5255-6780; internet www.jr-central.co.jp; f. 1987; also operates travel agency services, etc.; Chair. YOSHIYUKI KASAI; Pres. YOSHIOMI YAMADA.

   East Japan Railway Co: 2-2-2, Yoyogi, Shibuya-ku, Tokyo 151-8578; tel. (3) 5334-1151; fax (3) 5334-1110; internet www.jreast.co .jp; privatized in 1987; Chair. SATOSHI SEINO; Pres. and CEO TETSURO TOMITA.

   Hokkaido Railway Co: 15-1-1, Kita-11-jo, Chuo-ku, Sapporo 060-8644; tel. (11) 700-5717; fax (11) 700-5719; e-mail keieki@ jrhokkaido.co.jp; internet www.jrhokkaido.co.jp; Chair. HIROHIKO KAKINUMA; Pres. KOIKO AKIO.

   Japan Freight Railway Co: 5-33-8, Sendagaya, Shibuya-ku, Tokyo 151-0051; internet www.jrfreight.co.jp; f. 1987; Chair. MASAAKI KOBAYASHI; Pres. SHUJI TAMURA.

   Kyushu Railway Co: 3-25-21, Hakataekimae, Hakata-ku, Fukuoka 812-8566; tel. (92) 474-2501; fax (92) 474-9745; internet www.jrkyushu.co.jp; f. 1987; Chair. KOJI KARAIKE; Pres. SUSUMU ISHIHARA.

Shikoku Railway Co: 8-33, Hamano-cho, Takamatsu, Kagawa 760-8580; tel. (87) 825-1626; fax (87) 825-1623; internet www.jr-shikoku.co.jp; Chair. HIROSHI MATSUDA KIYOSHI; Pres. and CEO MASAFUMI IZUMI.

West Japan Railway Co: 2-4-24, Shibata, Kita-ku, Osaka 530-8341; tel. (6) 6375-8981; fax (6) 6375-8919; e-mail wjr01020@mxy.meshnet.or.jp; internet www.westjr.co.jp; fully privatized in 2004; Chair. TAKAYUKI SASAKI; Pres. SEIJI MANABE.

Other Principal Private Companies

Hankyu Hanshin Holdings Inc: 1-16-1, Shibata, Kita-ku, Osaka 530-0012; tel. (6) 6373-5001; fax (6) 6373-5042; e-mail web-info@hankyu-hanshin.co.jp; internet www.hankyu-hanshin.co.jp; f. 1907; links Osaka, Kyoto, Kobe and Takarazuka; Pres. KAZUO SUMI.

Keihan Electric Railway Co Ltd: 1-7-31, Otemae, Chuo-ku, Osaka; tel. (6) 6944-2521; fax (6) 6944-2501; internet www.keihan.co.jp; f. 1906; Chair. SHIGETAKA SATO; Pres. YOSHIFUMI KATO.

Keihin Express Electric Railway Co Ltd (Keikyu): 2-20-20, Takanawa, Minato-ku, Tokyo 108-8625; tel. (3) 3280-9120; fax (3) 3280-9199; internet www.keikyu.co.jp; f. 1899; Chair. AKIRA KOTANI; Pres. TSUNEO ISHIWATA.

Keio Electric Railway Co Ltd: 1-9-1, Sekido, Tama-shi, Tokyo 206-8052; tel. (42) 337-3106; fax (42) 374-9322; internet www.keio.co.jp; f. 1913; Chair. KAN KATO; Pres. TADASHI NAGATA.

Keisei Electric Railway Co Ltd: 1-10-3, Oshiage, Sumida-ku, Tokyo 131; tel. (3) 3621-2242; fax (3) 3621-2233; internet www.keisei.co.jp; f. 1909; Pres. NORIO SAIGUSA.

Kinki Nippon Railway Co Ltd (Kintetsu): 6-1-55, Uehommachi, Tennoji-ku, Osaka 543-8585; tel. (6) 6775-3444; fax (6) 6775-3468; internet www.kintetsu.co.jp; f. 1910; Chair. MASANORI YAMAGUCHI; Pres. TETSUYA KOBAYASHI.

Nagoya Railroad Co Ltd: 1-2-4, Meieki, Nakamura-ku, Nagoya-shi 450-8501; tel. (52) 588-0813; fax (52) 588-0815; e-mail info@meitetsu.co.jp; internet www.meitetsu.co.jp; Chair. HIDEO KONO; Pres. ADO YAMAMOTO.

Nankai Electric Railway Co Ltd: 5-1-60, Namba, Chuo-ku, Osaka 542; tel. (6) 6644-7121; internet www.nankai.co.jp; f. 1925; Chair. MAKOTO YAMANAKA; Pres. SHINJI WATARI.

Nishi-Nippon Railroad Co Ltd: 1-11-17, Tenjin-cho, Chuo-ku, Fukuoka 810; tel. (92) 761-6631; fax (92) 722-1405; e-mail www-admin@nnr.co.jp; internet www.nnr.co.jp; serves northern Kyushu; Chair. TSUGUO NAGAO; Pres. KAZUYUKI TAKESHIMA.

Odakyu Electric Railway Co Ltd: 1-8-3, Nishi-Shinjuku, Shinjuku-ku, Tokyo 160-8309; tel. (3) 3349-2526; fax (3) 3346-1899; e-mail ir@odakyu-dentetsu.co.jp; internet www.odakyu.jp; f. 1948; Chair. YORIHIKO OSUGA; Exec. Pres. TOSHIMITSU YAMAKI.

Sanyo Electric Railway Co Ltd: 3-1-1, Oyashiki-dori, Nagata-ku, Kobe 653; tel. (78) 653-0843; internet www.sanyo-railway.co.jp; Chair. FUMIHIKO AMANO; Pres. KAZUHIRO UEKADO.

Seibu Railway Co Ltd: 1-11-1, Kasunokidai, Tokorozawa-shi, Saitama 359; tel. (429) 26-2035; fax (429) 26-2237; internet www.seibu-group.co.jp/railways; f. 1894; Pres. TAKASHI GOTO.

Tobu Railway Co Ltd: 1-1-2, Oshiage, Sumida-ku, Tokyo 131-8522; tel. (3) 3621-5057; internet www.tobu.co.jp; f. 1897; Pres. YOSHIZUMI NEZU.

Tokyo Express Electric Railway (Tokyu) Co Ltd: 5-6, Nanpeidai-cho, Shibuya-ku, Tokyo 150-8511; tel. (3) 3477-0109; fax (3) 3477-6109; e-mail public@tokyu.co.jp; internet www.tokyu.co.jp; f. 1922; Chair. TOSHIAKI KOSHIMURA; Pres. HIROFUMI NOMOTO.

Principal Subways, Monorails and Tunnels

Subway services operate in Tokyo, Osaka, Kobe, Nagoya, Sapporo, Yokohama, Kyoto, Sendai and Fukuoka. A subway was planned to begin operations in Kawasaki in 2018. Most subway lines operate reciprocal through-services with existing private railway lines that connect the cities with suburban areas.

The first commercial monorail system was introduced in 1964 with straddle-type cars between central Tokyo and Tokyo International Airport, a distance of 13 km. Monorails also operate in other cities, including Urayasu, Naha, Osaka and Kitakyushu.

In 1985 the 54-km Seikan Tunnel (the world's longest undersea tunnel), linking the islands of Honshu and Hokkaido, was completed. Electric rail services through the tunnel began operating in 1988.

Fukuoka City Subway: Fukuoka Municipal Transportation Bureau, 2-5-31, Daimyo, Chuo-ku, Fukuoka 810-0041; tel. (92) 732-4202; fax (92) 721-0754; internet subway.city.fukuoka.jp; 3 lines, of a combined 29.8 km open; Dir KENNICHIROU NISHI.

Kobe Rapid Transit Railway Co Ltd: 3-3-9 Tamondoori, Chuo-ku, Kobe; tel. (78) 351-0881; fax (78) 351-1607; internet www.kobe-kousoku.jp; 22.7 km open; Pres. and CEO KEIJI SHIMA.

Nagoya Subway: Transportation Bureau City of Nagoya, Nagoya City Hall, 3-1-1, Sannomaru, Naka-ku, Nagoya 460-8508; tel. (52) 972-3824; fax (52) 972-3938; e-mail goiken@tbcn.city.nagoya.lg.jp; internet www.kotsu.city.nagoya.jp; 87 km open; Dir-Gen. NOBUO YOSHII.

Osaka Monorail: 1-1-5, Higashi-Machi, Shin-Senri, Toyonakashi, Osaka 560-0082; tel. (6) 6871-8281; fax (6) 6871-8284; internet www.osaka-monorail.co.jp; 113.5 km open; Pres. AKIRA INOUE.

Osaka Underground Railway: Osaka Municipal Transportation Bureau, 1-12-62, Kujo-Minami, Nishi-ku, Osaka 550-8552; tel. (6) 6585-1400; fax (6) 6585-6466; internet www.kotsu.city.osaka.jp; f. 1933; 129.9 km; the 7.9 km computer-controlled 'New Tram' service began between Suminoekoen and Nakafuto in 1981; seventh line between Kyobashi and Tsurumi-ryokuchi opened in 1990; eighth line between Itakano and Imazato opened in 2006; Gen. Man. YOSHIHIDE KUSUMOTO.

Sapporo Transportation Bureau: 2-4-1, Oyachi-Higashi, Atsu-betsu-ku, Sapporo 004-8555; tel. (11) 896-2708; fax (11) 232-2277; internet www.city.sapporo.jp/st; f. 1971; 3 lines of 48 km; Dir T. IKEGAMI.

Sendai City Subway: Sendai City Transportation Bureau, 1-4-15, Kimachidori, Aoba-ku, Sendai-shi, Miyagi-ken 980-0801; tel. (22) 224-5111; fax (22) 224-6839; internet www.kotsu.city.sendai.jp; 15.4 km open; Dir T. IWAMA.

Tokyo Metro Co Ltd: 3-19-6, Higashi-Ueno, Taito-ku, Tokyo 110-8614; tel. (3) 3837-7046; fax (3) 3837-7219; internet www.tokyometro.jp; f. 2004; operates 8 lines; 195.1 km open (2010); Pres. YOSHIMITSU OKU.

Tokyo Metropolitan Government (TOEI) Underground Railway: Bureau of Transportation, Tokyo Metropolitan Government, 2-8-1, Nishi-Shinjuku, Tokyo 163-8001; tel. (3) 5320-6026; internet www.kotsu.metro.tokyo.jp; operates 4 underground lines, totalling 105 km.

Yokohama Municipal Subway: Transportation Bureau, 6-145, Hanasaki-cho, Nishi-ku, Yokohama 220-0022; tel. (45) 664-2525; fax (45) 664-2828; internet www.city.yokohama.jp/me/koutuu; 40.4 km open; Dir-Gen. MICHINORI KISHIDA.

ROADS

In 2010 Japan's road network extended to an estimated 1,269,000 km, including approximately 55,000 km of highways, and in 2012 Japan had 8,325 km of motorways. In 1999 work was completed on a 29-year project to construct three routes, consisting of a total of 19 bridges, between the islands of Honshu and Shikoku across the Seto inland sea. There is a national bus service, 60 publicly operated bus services and 298 privately operated bus services.

In 2005 the major state-owned road authorities were transferred to the private sector. The Japan Highway Public Corpn was privatized and divided into three separate regional expressway companies, servicing central, eastern and western zones. The others were Metropolitan Expressway Public Corpn, Hanshin Expressway Public Corpn and Honshu-Shikoku Bridge Authority.

Central Nippon Expressway Co Ltd: Nagoya Sumimoto Bldg, 8/F, 2-18-19, Nishiki Naka-ku, Nagoya 460-0003; tel. (52) 222-1620; internet www.c-nexco.co.jp; f. 2005; Pres. and CEO TAKEKAZU KANEKO.

East Nippon Expressway Co Ltd: Kasumigaseki Bldg, 15/F, 3-2 Kasumigaseki, Chiyoda-ku, Tokyo 100-8979; tel. (3) 3506-0111; internet www.e-nexco.co.jp; f. 2005; Pres. and CEO HIROSHI HIROSE.

West Nippon Expressway Co Ltd: 1-6-20, Dojima, Kita-ku, Osaka; tel. (6) 6344-4000; internet corp.w-nexco.co.jp; f. 2005; Pres. YOSHINARI ISHIZUKA.

SHIPPING

At 31 December 2014 the Japanese flag registered fleet comprised 3,581 vessels, with a total displacement of 21.2m. grt. The main ports are Tokyo, Yokohama, Nagoya and Osaka.

Principal Companies

Daiichi Chuo Kisen Kaisha: 2-14-4, Shintomi-cho, Chuo-ku, Tokyo 104-8544; tel. (3) 5540-1997; fax (3) 3523-8987; internet www.firstship.co.jp; f. 1960; liner and tramp services; Pres. MASAKAZU YAKUSHIJI.

Iino Kaiun Kaisha Ltd: Iino Bldg, 2-10-1, Uchisaiwai-cho, Chiyoda-ku, Tokyo 100-0011; tel. (3) 5408-0356; e-mail ikk_soumu2@ex.iino.co.jp; internet www.iino.co.jp; f. 1899; cargo and tanker services; Pres. TOMOYUKI SEKINE.

Kawasaki Kisen Kaisha Ltd (K Line): Iino Bldg, 2-1-1, Uchisai-wai-cho, Chiyoda-ku, Tokyo 100-8540; tel. (3) 3595-5000; fax (3) 3595-5001; e-mail otaki@email.kline.co.jp; internet www.kline.co.jp; f. 1919; containers, cars, LNG, LPG and oil tankers, bulk carriers; Chair. of Bd HIROYUKI MAEKAWA; Pres. JIRO ASAKURA.

Mitsui OSK Lines Ltd: Shosen Mitsui Bldg, 2-1-1, Toranomon, Minato-ku, Tokyo 105-8688; tel. (3) 3587-7092; fax (3) 3587-7734;

internet www.mol.co.jp; f. 1942; merged with Navix Line Ltd in 1999; worldwide container, liner, tramp, and specialized carrier and tanker services; Chair. AKIMITSU ASHIDA; Pres. KOICHI MUTO.

Nippon Yusen Kaisha (NYK) Line: 2-3-2, Marunouchi, Chiyoda-ku, Tokyo 100-0005; tel. (3) 3284-5151; fax (3) 3284-6361; internet www.nyk.com; f. 1885; merged with Showa Line Ltd in 1998; worldwide container, cargo, pure car and truck carriers, tanker and bulk carrying services; Chair. KOJI MIYAHARA; Pres. YASUMI KUDO.

Nissho Shipping Co Ltd: Mori Bldg, 7/F, Rm 33, 3-8-21, Tora-nomon, Minato-ku, Tokyo 105-0001; tel. (3) 3438-3511; fax (3) 3438-3566; f. 1943; Pres. KENICHI YAMAGUCHI.

Ryukyu Kaiun KK: 1-24-11, Nishi-Machi, Naha, Okinawa 900-0036; tel. (98) 868-8161; fax (98) 868-8561; internet www.rkkline.co.jp; f. 1950; cargo and passenger services on domestic routes; Pres. YAMASHIRO HIROMI.

Taiheiyo Kaiun Co Ltd: Mitakokusai Bldg, 23/F, 1-4-28, Minato-ku, Tokyo 108-0073; tel. (3) 5445-5800; fax (3) 5445-5801; internet www.taiheiyokk.co.jp; f. 1951; cargo and tanker services; Pres. TAKESHI MATSUNAGA.

CIVIL AVIATION

Three international airports serve Tokyo: Narita, located in Chiba prefecture; Haneda; and Ibaraki (previously Hyakuri Airfield), which commenced civil aviation operations in 2010. In 1994 the world's first offshore international airport (Kansai International Airport) was opened in Osaka Bay, and a second runway was completed in 2007. Another offshore international airport, Chubu Centrair International Airport, located in Ise Bay and serving Nagoya, commenced operations in 2005. Some 95 other airports handle regional and some international flights.

Air Do Co Ltd: 1-2-9, Kita Sanjo Nishi, Chuo-ku, Sapporo; tel. (11) 252-5533; fax (11) 252-5580; e-mail postbear@airdo.co.jp; internet www.airdo.co.jp; f. 1996, fmrly Hokkaido International Airlines Co Ltd, adopted trading name as above in 2012; domestic service between Tokyo and Sapporo; Pres. SAITO SADAO.

All Nippon Airways (ANA): Shiodome City Center, 1-5-2, Higashi-Shimbashi, Minato-ku, Tokyo 105-7133; tel. (3) 6735-1000; fax (3) 6735-1005; internet www.ana.co.jp; f. 1952; operates domestic passenger and freight services; scheduled international services to the Far East, the USA and Europe; charter services worldwide; Chair. YOJI OHASHI; Pres. and CEO SHINCHIRO ITO.

ANA Wings: 3-3-2, Haneda Airport, Ota-ku, Tokyo 144-8515; internet www.anawings.co.jp; f. 2010 from the merger of All Nippon Network, Air Next and Air Central; wholly owned subsidiary of All Nippon Airways; regional and domestic services; Pres. and CEO AKIHIKO HASEGAWA.

Hokkaido Air System: New Chitose Airport, Bibi Chitose City, Hokkaido 066-0055; tel. (123) 46-5533; fax (123) 46-5534; internet www.hac-air.co.jp; f. 1997; domestic services on Hokkaido; Pres. CHIHIRO TAMURA.

Ibex Airlines: 1-2-3, Shinsuna, Koto-ku, Tokyo 136-8640; internet www.ibexair.co.jp; f. 1999; operates domestic flights from Osaka and Narita International Airports; Chair. TAKAO ASAI; Pres. HATTORI HIROYUKI.

Japan Air Commuter: 787-4, Mizobe Humototyou, Kirishima, Kagoshima Prefecture; tel. (995) 582-151; fax (995) 582-673; e-mail info@jac.co.jp; internet www.jac.co.jp; f. 1983; subsidiary of JAL; domestic services; Chair. YOSHITOMI ONO; Pres. ARATA YASUJIMA.

Japan Airlines (JAL): 2-4-11, Higashi-Shinagawa, Shinagawa-ku, Tokyo 140-8605; tel. (3) 5769-6476; internet www.jal.com; f. 2002; Chair. KAZUO INAMORI; Pres. YOSHIHARU UEKI.

Japan Transocean Air Co Ltd: 3-24, Yamashita-cho, Naha-shi, Okinawa 900-0027; tel. (98) 857-2112; fax (98) 857-9396; internet www.jal.co.jp/jta; f. 1967; adopted present name 1993; subsidiary of JAL; domestic passenger services; Pres. MANABU SATO.

Skymark Airlines: 3-5-7, Haneda Airport, Ota-ku, Tokyo 144-0041; tel. (3) 5402-6767; fax (3) 5402-6770; e-mail info@skymark.co.jp; internet www.skymark.co.jp; f. 1997; domestic services; Chair. TAKASHI IDE; Pres. and CEO MASAKAZU ARIMORI.

Tourism

The ancient capital of Kyoto, pagodas and temples, forests and mountains, traditional festivals and the classical Kabuki theatre are some of the many tourist attractions of Japan. Receipts from tourism (excluding passenger transport) in 2013 totalled an estimated US $15,093m. International arrivals declined by 27.8% in 2011, to 6.2m. This decrease, reportedly the largest since records began in 1950, was attributed to the impact of the earthquake, tsunami and nuclear disaster that occurred in March that year, as well as to the strength of the yen. However, the number of arrivals subsequently recovered, rising by 34.6%, to 8.4m., in 2012 and by a further 24.0%, to an estimated 10.4m., in 2013. The Republic of Korea, Taiwan and the People's Republic of China are the leading sources of visitors.

Japan National Tourism Organization (JNTO): Tokyo Kotsu Kaikan Bldg, 2-10-1, Yuraku-cho, Chiyoda-ku, Tokyo 100-0006; tel. (3) 3201-3331; fax (3) 3216-1846; internet www.jnto.go.jp; f. 1964; Pres. RYOICHI MATSUYAMA.

Japan Tourism Agency (JTA): General Affairs Division, National and Regional Planning Bureau, 2-1-3, Kasumigaseki, Chiyoda-ku, Tokyo 100-8918; tel. (3) 5253-8111; fax (3) 3580-7982; e-mail webmaster@mlit.go.jp; internet www.mlit.go.jp/kankocho; f. 2008; aims to promote Japan as a tourist destination and, in conjunction with JNTO, to achieve govt objectives; Commr NORIFUMI IDEE.

Defence

As assessed at November 2014, the total strength of the Japanese Self-Defence Forces was some 247,150: ground self-defence 151,050, maritime self-defence 45,500, air self-defence 47,100 and central staff 3,500. Paramilitary forces numbered 12,650, and reserve forces comprised an additional 56,100 personnel. Military service is voluntary. At November 2013 US forces stationed in Japan comprised 2,300 army, 12,400 air force and 19,600 navy personnel, together with 15,700 members of the US Marine Corps.

Defence Budget: 4,980,100m. yen for the financial year ending 31 March 2016.

Chief of Staff of the Joint Staff Council: Adm. KATSUTOSHI KAWANO.

Chief of Staff of Ground Self-Defence Force: Gen. EIJI KIMIZUKA.

Chief of Staff of Maritime Self-Defence Force: Adm. TOMOHISA TAKEI.

Chief of Staff of Air Self-Defence Force: Gen. HARUKAZU SAITO.

Education

Education is compulsory between the ages of six and 15. A kindergarten (*yochien*) system provides education for children aged between three and five years of age, although the majority of kindergartens are privately controlled. In 2013 there were 13,043 kindergartens, which were attended by 1.6m. children. All children between six and 15 are required to attend six-year elementary schools (*shogakko*) and three-year lower secondary schools (or middle schools—*chugakko*). In 2009/10 enrolment at pre-primary school included 88% of pupils in the relevant age-group, while enrolment at primary level in 2010/11 included 100% of pupils in the relevant age-group. Enrolment at secondary level included 99% of students in the relevant age-group in the same year. In 2013 there were 21,131 elementary schools, at which 6.7m. pupils were enrolled, and 10,628 lower secondary schools, at which 3.5m. pupils were enrolled. Upper secondary schools (or high schools— *kotogakko*) provide a three-year course in general topics, or a vocational course in subjects such as agriculture, commerce, fine art and technical studies. In 2013 there were 4,981 upper secondary schools, at which 3.3m. pupils were enrolled.

There are four types of institution for higher education. Universities (*daigaku*) offer degree and postgraduate courses. In 2013 there were 782 universities and graduate schools, at which 2.9m. students were enrolled. Junior colleges (*tanki-daigaku*) provide less specialized two- to three-year courses, credits for which can count towards a first degree. In 2013 there were 359 junior colleges in Japan. Both universities and junior colleges offer facilities for teacher training. Colleges of technology (*koto-senmon-gakko*), of which there were 57 in 2013, offer a five-year specialized training course. Since 1991 colleges of technology have been able to offer short-term advanced courses. A combined total of 196,486 students were enrolled at junior colleges and colleges of technology in 2013. Special training colleges (*senshu-gakko*) offer advanced courses in technical and vocational subjects, lasting for at least one year. In 2013 there were 3,216 special training colleges in Japan. The budget for the financial year ending 31 March 2016 allocated 5,361,300m. yen to education and science (equivalent to 5.6% of projected expenditure).

JORDAN

Introductory Survey

LOCATION, CLIMATE, LANGUAGE, RELIGION, FLAG, CAPITAL

The Hashemite Kingdom of Jordan is an almost landlocked state in western Asia. It is bordered by Israel and the Palestinian Territories to the west, by Syria to the north, by Iraq to the east and by Saudi Arabia to the south. The port of Aqaba, in the far south, gives Jordan a narrow outlet to the Red Sea. The climate is hot and dry. The average annual temperature is about 15°C (60°F), but there are wide diurnal variations. Temperatures in Amman are generally between −1°C (30°F) and 32°C (90°F). More extreme conditions are found in the valley of the River Jordan and on the shores of the Dead Sea (a lake on the Israeli–Jordanian frontier), where the temperature may exceed 50°C (122°F) in summer. The official language is Arabic. More than 90% of the population are Sunni Muslims, while there are small communities of Christians and Shi'a Muslims. The national flag (proportions 1 by 2) has three equal horizontal stripes, of black, white and green, with a red triangle, containing a seven-pointed white star, at the hoist. The capital is Amman.

CONTEMPORARY POLITICAL HISTORY

Historical Context

Palestine (including the present-day West Bank territory) and Transjordan (the East Bank) were formerly parts of Turkey's Ottoman Empire. During the First World War (1914–18), when Turkey was allied with Germany, the Arabs under Ottoman rule rebelled. British forces, with Arab support, occupied Palestine and Transjordan in 1917–18, when the Turks withdrew. British occupation continued after the war, when the Ottoman Empire was dissolved. In 1920 Palestine and Transjordan were formally placed under British administration by a League of Nations mandate. In 1921 Abdullah ibn Hussein, a member of the Hashimi (Hashemite) dynasty of Arabia, was proclaimed Amir (Emir) of Transjordan.

Under the British mandate Transjordan (formally separated from Palestine in 1923) gained increasing autonomy, and in 1928 the United Kingdom acknowledged its nominal independence, while retaining certain financial and military powers. Amir Abdullah followed a generally pro-British policy and supported the Allied cause in the Second World War (1939–45). The mandate was terminated on 22 March 1946, when Transjordan attained full independence. On 25 May Abdullah was proclaimed King, and a new Constitution took effect.

When the British Government terminated its mandate in Palestine in May 1948, Jewish leaders there proclaimed the State of Israel. Palestinian Arabs, however, with military support from Arab states, opposed Israeli claims, and hostilities continued until July. Transjordan's forces occupied about 5,900 sq km of Palestine, including East Jerusalem, and this was confirmed by the armistice with Israel in April 1949. In June the country was renamed Jordan, and in April 1950, following a referendum, King Abdullah formally annexed the West Bank territory, which contained many Arab refugees from Israeli-held areas.

Domestic Political Affairs

In July 1951 King Abdullah was assassinated in Jerusalem by a Palestinian belonging to an extremist Islamist organization. Abdullah was succeeded by his eldest son, Talal ibn Abdullah, hitherto Crown Prince. However, in August 1952, because of Talal's mental incapacity, the crown passed to his son, Hussein ibn Talal, then 16 years of age. King Hussein formally came to power in May 1953.

In March 1956, responding to Arab nationalist sentiment, King Hussein dismissed the British army officer who had been Chief of Staff of the British-equipped and -financed Arab Legion (the Jordanian armed forces) since 1939. Jordan's treaty relationship with the United Kingdom was ended in March 1957, and British troops completed their withdrawal from Jordan in July.

The refugee camps in the West Bank became the centre of Palestinian resistance to Israel, and during the 1950s there were numerous attacks on Israeli territory by groups of Palestinian

fedayeen ('martyrs'). In September 1963 the creation of a unified 'Palestinian entity' was approved by the Council of the League of Arab States (the Arab League, see p. 359), and the first Palestinian congress was held in the Jordanian sector of Jerusalem in May–June 1964, at which it was agreed to form the Palestine Liberation Organization (PLO), which would be financed by the Arab League and would recruit military units to form a Palestine Liberation Army (PLA). The principal Palestinian guerrilla organization within the PLO was the Palestine National Liberation Movement, known as Fatah ('Conquest'), led from 1968 by Yasser Arafat. However, King Hussein regarded the establishment of the PLO as a threat to Jordanian sovereignty, and from the outset refused to allow the PLA to train in Jordan or the PLO to levy taxes from Palestinian refugees residing in his country.

In April 1965 Hussein nominated his brother Hassan ibn Talal to be Crown Prince. During the Six-Day War of June 1967 Israel made substantial military gains, including possession of the whole of Jerusalem (which was incorporated into Israel) and the West Bank; the latter became an Israeli 'administered territory'. The influx of Palestinian refugees into the East Bank bolstered the strength of the PLO, whose continued armed raids on the Israeli-administered territories challenged the personal authority of King Hussein and the sovereignty of the Jordanian Government. King Hussein responded by expelling the guerrilla groups, after a civil war that lasted from September 1970 to July 1971. Aid to Jordan from Kuwait and other wealthy Arab states, suspended after the expulsion of the Palestinian fighters, was restored only following Jordan's military support for Syria during the Arab–Israeli War of October 1973. At an Arab summit meeting in Rabat, Morocco, in October 1974 King Hussein supported a unanimous resolution recognizing the PLO as the 'sole legitimate representative of the Palestinian people' and granting the organization the right to establish an independent national authority on any piece of Palestinian land to be liberated.

In response to this resolution, in November 1974 both chambers of the Jordanian National Assembly (which had equal representation for the East and West Banks) approved constitutional amendments that empowered the King to dissolve the Assembly and to postpone elections for up to 12 months. The Assembly was dissolved later that month, although it was briefly reconvened in February 1976, when it approved a constitutional amendment giving the King power to postpone elections indefinitely and to convene the Assembly as required. A royal decree of April 1978 provided for the creation of a National Consultative Council, with 60 members appointed for a two-year term by the King, on the Prime Minister's recommendation, to debate proposed legislation.

Joint Palestinian-Jordanian peace initiatives

A proposal put forward by US President Ronald Reagan in September 1982 for an autonomous Palestinian authority on the West Bank, in association with Jordan, was rejected by Yasser Arafat following talks with King Hussein. In January 1984, however, the King responded by dissolving the National Consultative Council and recalling the National Assembly for the first time since 1967—in effect creating the kind of Palestinian forum envisaged by the Reagan initiative. Israel allowed the surviving West Bank deputies to attend the Assembly, which approved constitutional amendments enabling elections to be held in the East Bank, while West Bank deputies would be chosen by the Assembly itself. After discussions with the PLO leader in January 1984 on a joint Palestinian-Jordanian peace initiative, King Hussein's proposals for negotiations, based on UN Security Council Resolution 242 (the resolution, adopted in November 1967, sought to return the region's territorial boundaries to the pre-Six-Day War status, but incorporated implicit recognition of an Israeli state), met with a non-committal response from the Palestine National Council (PNC), which convened in Amman in November 1984. In February 1985 King Hussein and Yasser Arafat announced the terms of a Jordanian-Palestinian agreement, proposing a confederated state of Jordan and Palestine.

In July 1985 Israel rejected a list of seven Palestinians, five of whom were members of the PLO or had links with the PNC, whom King Hussein had presented to the USA as candidates for a joint Jordanian-Palestinian delegation to preliminary peace talks. Further progress was hindered by a series of terrorist incidents in which the PLO was implicated, and King Hussein came under increasing pressure to advance the peace process, if necessary without PLO participation. In September President Reagan revived his 1984 plan to sell military equipment to the value of some US $1,900m. to Jordan. The proposal was approved by the US Congress on the condition that Jordan enter into direct talks with Israel by March 1986. However, such talks were obstructed by a gradual rapprochement between Jordan and Syria.

Frustrated by the lack of co-operation from Yasser Arafat in advancing the aims of the Jordanian-PLO peace initiative, King Hussein publicly severed political links with the PLO on 19 February 1986. Arafat was subsequently ordered to close his main PLO offices in Jordan by 1 April. A number of Fatah officers loyal to Arafat were expelled, and in July the Jordanian authorities closed all 25 Fatah offices in Amman; only 12 bureaux belonging to the PLO remained.

Despite the termination of political co-ordination with the PLO, Jordan continued to reject Israeli requests for direct peace talks that excluded a form of PLO representation. However, Jordan's subsequent efforts to strengthen its influence in the Israeli-occupied territories (Occupied Territories), and to foster a Palestinian constituency there independent of Arafat's PLO, coincided with Israeli measures to grant limited autonomy to Palestinians in the West Bank. In March 1986 the Jordanian House of Representatives approved a draft law increasing the number of seats in the House from 60 to 142 (71 seats each for the East and West Banks), thereby providing for greater representation for West Bank Palestinians in the National Assembly. In August, with Israeli support, Jordan announced a five-year development plan, valued at US $1,300m., for the West Bank and Gaza Strip.

In May 1987, following secret meetings with King Hussein, the Israeli Minister of Foreign Affairs, Shimon Peres, claimed to have made significant progress on the crucial issue of Palestinian representation at a Middle East peace conference. He reportedly had the consent of Egypt, Jordan and the USA to convene a conference involving the five permanent members of the UN Security Council and a delegation of Palestinians—including the PLO—who rejected terrorism and accepted Security Council Resolutions 242 and 338 (the latter defined the terms of immediate peace following the 1973 Arab–Israeli War) as the basis for negotiations. However, Israel's Prime Minister, Itzhak Shamir, reiterated his alternative proposal of direct regional talks excluding the PLO, and Peres failed to secure the support of a majority of the Israeli Cabinet for his proposals.

At the first full meeting of the Arab League for eight years, convened in Amman in November 1987, King Hussein pursued an agenda of greater Arab unity in support of Iraq in its war with Iran. Prior to the summit, Jordan restored full diplomatic relations with Libya (severed in 1984), which had modified its support for Iran. However, King Hussein's appeal for Egypt to be restored to membership of the League (suspended following the peace treaty with Israel in 1979) was resisted by Libya and Syria, although 11 Arab states subsequently re-established diplomatic relations. Jordan also announced the resumption of co-operation with the PLO.

These achievements were soon overshadowed by the Palestinian *intifada* (uprising), which erupted in the West Bank and Gaza Strip in December 1987, in protest against the continued Israeli occupation and the seemingly indifferent attitude of Arab League states to the Palestinians' plight. At an extraordinary meeting of the Arab League held in the Algerian capital, Algiers, in June 1988, King Hussein gave the *intifada* his unconditional support and insisted that the PLO must represent the Palestinians at any future peace conference. Furthermore, in accordance with agreements reached at the meeting, on 31 July Jordan cancelled the West Bank development plan and severed its legal and administrative links with the territory.

On 15 November 1988 the PNC, meeting in Algiers, proclaimed the establishment of an independent State of Palestine and, for the first time, endorsed UN Security Council Resolution 242 as a basis for a Middle East peace settlement, thus implicitly recognizing Israel. Jordan and 60 other countries recognized the new state. Addressing a special session of the UN General Assembly in Geneva, Switzerland, in December, Arafat renounced violence on behalf of the PLO. The USA subsequently opened a dialogue with the organization.

In April 1989 there was rioting in several cities, after the Jordanian Government imposed sizeable price increases on basic goods and services. The riots led to the resignation of the Prime Minister, Zaid Rifai, and his Cabinet. Field Marshal Sharif Zaid ibn Shaker, a former Commander-in-Chief of the Jordanian Armed Forces, was appointed to head a new Government. King Hussein subsequently announced that a general election would be held for the first time since 1967. The election to the 80-seat House of Representatives, which proceeded in November 1989, was contested by 647 candidates, mostly independents, as the ban on political parties (in force since 1963) remained. However, the Muslim Brotherhood was able to present candidates for election, owing to its legal status as a charity; it won 20 seats, while as many as 14 seats were won by independent Islamist candidates who supported the Brotherhood. In December King Hussein appointed former premier Mudar Badran as Prime Minister. In January 1990 Badran pledged to abolish martial law (which had been suspended in December 1989) within four to six months, and to liberalize the judicial system; he also announced the abolition of the anti-communism law (in force since 1954). In April King Hussein appointed a 60-member commission to devise a national charter that would legalize political parties. The draft national charter was approved by the King in January 1991. Also in January the Cabinet was reorganized to include five members of the Muslim Brotherhood.

Iraq's invasion of Kuwait in August 1990, and the consequent imposition of economic sanctions by the UN against Iraq, had a profound effect on Jordan: Iraq was its principal trading partner, and Jordan relied on supplies of Iraqi petroleum. Although King Hussein condemned the Iraqi invasion, he was slow to do so, and advocated an 'Arab solution' to the crisis. There was considerable support for the Iraqi President, Saddam Hussain, among the Jordanian population, particularly among Palestinians. King Hussein was critical of the US-led deployment of multinational military forces in Saudi Arabia and the Persian (Arabian) Gulf, and in late 1990 he visited numerous Middle East and other capitals in an attempt to avert a war. Jordan's response to the Gulf crisis prompted the USA to review its military and economic assistance to the kingdom and led to a deterioration in Jordan's relations with Egypt and Saudi Arabia, both of which contributed to the US-led force. However, diplomatic relations between Jordan and Iran were re-established (having been severed in 1981).

Meanwhile, Jordan secured the approval of the USA by agreeing to join with a Palestinian delegation at the Middle East peace conference, which opened in Madrid, Spain, in October 1991. Subsequent talks in Washington, DC, USA, and Moscow, Russia, between the Israeli and the joint Jordanian-Palestinian delegations remained deadlocked with regard to substantive issues until September 1993, when Israel and the PLO agreed to a declaration of principles regarding Palestinian self-rule in the Occupied Territories. On the signing of the Declaration of Principles, which King Hussein welcomed, the Jordanian-Palestinian delegation was disbanded, and Jordan and Israel concluded an agreement that defined the agenda for subsequent bilateral negotiations within the context of the Middle East peace conference. The talks were to address the following issues: refugees and displaced persons; security; water resources; the demarcation of the border between Jordan and Israel; and future bilateral co-operation.

In 1991 Jordan and the PLO had agreed on the principle of confederation between Jordan and whatever Palestinian entity ultimately emerged from the Middle East peace process, and in July 1993 they undertook to form six committees to discuss relations between Jordan and the Occupied Territories during a period of transitional Palestinian self-rule. Jordan was formally excluded from discussion of some of the issues, however, following the signing of the Declaration of Principles. In January 1994 the PLO agreed to sign a comprehensive economic co-operation agreement and a draft security accord with Jordan.

King Hussein concludes a peace treaty with Israel

On 25 July 1994 King Hussein and the Israeli Prime Minister, Itzhak Rabin, meeting in the US capital, signed the Washington Declaration, which formally ended the state of war that had existed between Jordan and Israel since 1948. In October 1994 the two countries signed a full peace treaty providing, *inter alia*, for the establishment of diplomatic relations and for talks on economic and security co-operation. The official normalization of relations between Jordan and Israel had been completed by

18 January 1996. In Jordan the peace treaty was opposed by Islamist militants, and it was also criticized by Syria. The PLO leadership complained that the treaty undermined Palestinian claims to sovereignty over Jerusalem. None the less, in January 1995 the PLO and Jordan signed an agreement regulating relations between Jordan and the Palestinian territories with regard to economic and social affairs. At the same time, the PLO acknowledged Jordan's custodianship of the Muslim holy places in Jerusalem for as long as Jordan recognized and supported Palestinian claims to sovereignty over East Jerusalem.

Meanwhile, in June 1991 Taher al-Masri was appointed to replace Badran as Prime Minister. However, it became clear that al-Masri could not command majority support in the legislature; he was forced to resign in November, whereupon Sharif Zaid ibn Shaker again assumed the premiership. In July 1992 the House of Representatives adopted legislation whereby, subject to certain conditions, political parties were formally legalized. In May 1993 King Hussein appointed Abd al-Salam al-Majali, the head of the Jordanian delegation to the Middle East peace conference, to the premiership.

In August 1993 King Hussein unexpectedly dissolved the House of Representatives. Some 68% of the electorate were reported to have participated in Jordan's first multi-party general election, held on 8 November. By far the largest number of deputies returned to the House of Representatives were independent centrists loyal to the King. The Islamic Action Front (IAF, the political wing of the Muslim Brotherhood) emerged as the second largest party in the legislature. A new Senate (House of Notables) was appointed by the King on 18 November, and a new Cabinet, led by al-Majali, was announced in December. Al-Majali was dismissed in January 1995, whereupon ibn Shaker once again assumed the premiership.

King Hussein implemented a further extensive cabinet reorganization in February 1996, appointing Abd al-Karim al-Kabariti, the Minister of Foreign Affairs (a post he retained), as Prime Minister and Minister of Defence. In August rioting erupted in southern Jordan after the Government imposed a sharp increase on the price of bread. The unrest quickly spread to other parts of the country. King Hussein responded by suspending the legislature and deploying the army in order to suppress the worst disturbances. Prime Minister al-Kabariti was unexpectedly dismissed by Hussein in March 1997, reportedly as a result of disagreement over issues relating to Jordan's policies towards Israel. Al-Majali again assumed the premiership.

In July 1997 the IAF announced its intention to boycott the forthcoming parliamentary elections, in protest at what it regarded as the Government's excessively concessionary policies towards Israel and at recent restrictive amendments to press legislation. Several other parties also boycotted the polls. At the general election, which took place on 4 November, 62 of the 80 seats in the new House of Representatives were won by pro-Government candidates; 10 seats were secured by nationalist and left-wing candidates, and eight by independent Islamists. A new Senate was appointed by the King on 22 November. In August 1998 Fayez al-Tarawneh was appointed Prime Minister, and a new Cabinet was subsequently named.

The accession of King Abdullah

Meanwhile, in July 1998 King Hussein began to undergo treatment for cancer in the USA. In August he issued a royal decree transferring responsibility for certain executive duties to his brother, Crown Prince Hassan. On King Hussein's return to Jordan in January 1999, he prompted renewed speculation about the royal succession by appointing Hassan as his 'deputy'. On 24 January King Hussein issued a royal decree naming his eldest son, Abdullah, as Crown Prince of Jordan. Although Hassan had been regent since 1965, King Hussein was said to have been dissatisfied with his brother's handling of Jordanian affairs during his absence, in particular his attempts to intervene in military matters. Two days later the King left Jordan for emergency treatment in the USA, following a rapid deterioration in his health. King Hussein returned to Amman on 5 February 1999 and was pronounced dead on 7 February. The Crown Prince was sworn in, as King Abdullah ibn al-Hussein, on the same day. Prince Hamzeh ibn al-Hussein, the late King's youngest son, became the new Crown Prince.

In March 1999 King Abdullah announced the formation of a new Cabinet, in which several ministers regarded as loyal to Prince Hassan were replaced. Abd al-Raouf al-Rawabdeh replaced al-Tarawneh as Prime Minister and Minister of Defence. King Abdullah charged al-Rawabdeh with implementing 'fundamental reforms', including a strengthening of the rule of law and further democratization, as well as economic reforms to address the serious problems of poverty and unemployment. Opposition groups expressed cautious loyalty to the new monarch. Although in March 1999 King Abdullah had, under a recent amnesty law, released almost 500 prisoners, in April the Arab Human Rights Organization in Jordan criticized the Government for an increase in human rights violations, including arrests of journalists and harsh treatment of prisoners held in detention centres. Nevertheless, in June the Government agreed to amend part of the controversial Press and Publications Law in order to ease certain restrictions on journalists. In June King Abdullah dismissed Prime Minister al-Rawabdeh, appointing Ali Abu al-Ragheb in his place; a new Cabinet was duly appointed.

In April 2001 King Abdullah extended the current term of the House of Representatives by two years. On 16 June the King ordered the dissolution of the House and effected a cabinet reorganization. On 22 July he approved new electoral legislation, which provided for the redrawing of electoral boundaries (the number of constituencies was to rise from 21 to 44) in order to increase the number of seats in the House of Representatives from 80 to 104. The Muslim Brotherhood threatened to boycott the forthcoming elections, in view of the Government's failure to meet its demand for the reintroduction of an 'electoral list' system. Shortly afterwards it was reported that the November elections were to be postponed until late 2002 for technical reasons. In August 2001 legislation was enacted imposing a ban on public gatherings and demonstrations. In October, following the suicide attacks on the USA (see *Foreign Affairs*), King Abdullah issued a royal decree amending Jordan's penal code in order to strengthen counter-terrorism measures. In November the King appointed a new 40-member Senate upon the expiry of its term.

In January 2002 Prime Minister al-Ragheb submitted the resignation of his Government, but was asked by King Abdullah to form a new administration capable of initiating economic and social reforms prior to parliamentary elections. A new Cabinet was named shortly afterwards. In late January violent clashes, in which a policeman died, erupted between protesters and security forces in Ma'an, following the death of a local youth in police custody, who demonstrators alleged had been the victim of police brutality. In November security forces in Ma'an carried out a large-scale operation aimed at detaining a local Islamist cleric, Muhammad Shalabi, and his supporters, who the Government claimed had played an important role in the unrest. Many observers believed that the security operation was linked to the recent assassination of a US diplomat (see *Foreign Affairs*). At least three civilians and two police officers were reportedly killed during the week-long campaign; however, Shalabi apparently evaded capture. Meanwhile, King Abdullah announced in August 2002 that legislative elections would be postponed until 2003, owing to the continuing instability in the region. In February of that year he approved amendments to draft electoral legislation that would—from the next general election—increase the number of seats in the House of Representatives from 104 to 110, in order to provide a quota of six seats for female legislators.

The 2003 legislative elections

At parliamentary elections held on 17 June 2003 tribal representatives and Hashemite loyalists won 80 of the 110 seats in the House of Representatives, while the IAF, the largest opposition party, won 17 seats. In July a new Cabinet led by al-Ragheb was announced. However, the Prime Minister resigned in October, following criticism of the Government over the slow pace of reform and accusations of corruption. Shortly thereafter, King Abdullah inaugurated a new Cabinet under the premiership of Faisal al-Fayez, who was also named as Minister of Defence. The appointment of three female ministers preceded that of an expanded 55-member Senate in November.

It was revealed in April 2004 that Jordanian security forces had made a number of arrests that had possibly averted a major terrorist attack in the kingdom. It was alleged that militant Islamists closely linked to the al-Qa'ida network had planted huge quantities of explosives in trucks, which they had planned to detonate against a number of targets, including the Prime Ministry and the Ministry of the Interior. One of the arrested militants reportedly confessed that the instigator of the plot was Abu Musab al-Zarqawi, the Jordanian national whom US officials believed was directing attacks against the US-led coalition and civilian targets in Iraq. In February 2006 a military court sentenced to death nine men, including al-Zarqawi (who, together with three other defendants, was charged *in absentia*), for their role in the terrorist plot.

In November 2004 King Abdullah removed the title of Crown Prince from his half-brother, Hamzeh ibn al-Hussein, citing the wish to give him more freedom to undertake tasks that this 'symbolic' position did not permit. The King accepted the resignation of al-Fayez's Government in April 2005 and appointed Adnan Badran as Prime Minister; two days later a new Government was sworn in.

In November 2005 three Iraqi citizens carried out suicide bomb attacks in three hotels frequented by Western businessmen and diplomats in Amman, killing up to 60 people. Al-Zarqawi announced that he had instigated the blasts—the victims of which were mostly Jordanian—as retaliation for the Government's support for the USA and other Western countries. Within two days over 120 people had been arrested in connection with the attacks, and thousands of people joined protests against the bombings. Following Badran's resignation from the premiership later in the month, King Abdullah invited Marouf al-Bakhit, who had served as Jordan's ambassador to Israel until his appointment as national security adviser in the aftermath of the bombings, to form a new government. Abdullah appealed to al-Bakhit to increase security and combat the fundamentalist ideologies behind militant Islamism. The King inaugurated the new Cabinet in late November: al-Bakhit assumed additional responsibility for defence.

Details were published in January 2006 of a 10-year National Agenda, the principal objectives of which were 'the creation of income-generating opportunities, the improvement of standards of living and the guarantee of social welfare'. However, by 2015 the majority of the measures outlined in the plan had yet to be introduced.

In mid-2006 seven people were convicted (including six *in absentia*) and sentenced to death for their part in the November 2005 bombings in Amman. Meanwhile, in June 2006 al-Zarqawi was killed in a US air raid near the Iraqi town of Baquba.

The Prevention of Terrorism Act passed into law in November 2006, provoking censure from human rights organizations, which alleged that the new legislation could potentially be abused in order to suppress non-violent opponents of the Government. In June Amnesty International had claimed that the General Intelligence Department (GID)—the state agency responsible for internal security—routinely used torture as a tool with which to extract false confessions from political detainees, strongly implying that it did so on behalf of the US Administration. Furthermore, Jordan's State Security Court was accused of accepting confessions obtained by torture as admissible evidence.

The 2007 legislative elections

In early November 2007 one of the men convicted and sentenced to death *in absentia* for the 2002 murder of the US diplomat Laurence Foley (see *Foreign Affairs*) was also convicted of helping to plan the 2003 attack on the Jordanian embassy in Baghdad. Muammar al-Jaghbeer, who had been captured in Iraq and extradited to Jordan in 2005, was deemed to have acted on the orders of al-Zarqawi and was given a second death sentence. In late November 2007 al-Jaghbeer's death sentence for the murder of Foley was commuted to a 10-year term of imprisonment. In May 2008 the Supreme Court suspended al-Jaghbeer's 10-year sentence and ordered a new trial to take place at the State Security Court. Following the retrial, in July 2009 al-Jaghbeer was again convicted and sentenced to death for his role in Foley's murder. However, following an appeal hearing in November, this sentence was commuted to 15 years' imprisonment, with hard labour.

At legislative elections held on 20 November 2007 independents and tribal representatives loyal to King Abdullah secured 104 of the 110 seats in the House of Representatives. The IAF won the remaining six seats, down from 17 in the 2003 poll. The party subsequently accused the Government of electoral fraud, pointing to its apparent failure to win a single seat in the two traditional IAF strongholds of Irbid and Zarqa, an impoverished city to the north-east of Amman. The Government insisted that, aside from a few isolated incidents of vote-buying, the polls had been conducted in a free and fair manner. On 22 November King Abdullah appointed Nader al-Dahabi as the new Prime Minister, in place of al-Bakhit. Al-Dahabi's new Cabinet was formally inaugurated on 25 November.

In April 2008 24 out of Jordan's 36 registered political parties were dissolved after their failure to comply with the terms of a new political parties law, which came into force in April 2007

with the provision of a one-year deadline. The new law stipulated that parties must have a minimum of 500 founding members drawn from at least five different governorates, and compelled parties to grant the Government access to their accounts. Twelve parties, including the IAF, successfully validated their status. Meanwhile, a report released by the US-based organization Human Rights Watch alleged that the US Central Intelligence Agency (CIA) had transferred at least 14 suspected terrorists to Jordan for interrogation and torture between September 2001 and 2004. The allegations were denied by the Jordanian Government.

A royal decree issued in July named Prince Hussein ibn al-Abdullah, the King's eldest son, as Crown Prince. The position had been vacant since King Abdullah relieved his half-brother, Prince Hamzeh, of the title in 2004.

The 2010 legislative elections

In late November 2009 King Abdullah issued decrees dissolving the House of Representatives, two years before the expiry of its term, and ordering the holding of early legislative elections. The dissolution was believed to be in response to widespread dissatisfaction with the parliament. According to the Constitution, a new parliament was required to be formed within four months of dissolution. However, in a decree issued in early December, the King postponed legislative elections indefinitely pending the formulation of new electoral legislation. Following this development, Prime Minister al-Dahabi submitted the resignation of his Government, and King Abdullah appointed Samir Rifai as Prime Minister-designate. The King approved the formation of a new Cabinet led by Prime Minister Rifai in mid-December 2009. Shortly afterwards the King appointed a new Senate.

Following a significant rise in reports of inter-tribal violence and clashes between various tribes and the security forces, in early May 2010 the Government appointed a new Director of the Public Security Directorate (PSD), Maj.-Gen. Hussein Hazaa Majali, a former Commander of the Royal Guard. The Cabinet subsequently announced the establishment of a panel of inquiry to investigate the causes of the recent violence.

The revised electoral law, which was finally approved by royal decree in mid-May 2010, expanded the number of seats in the House of Representatives from 110 to 120; other changes included an increase in the number of seats reserved for female candidates from six to 12. However, the amended law retained the controversial 'one person, one vote' electoral system (in place since 1993), which was viewed by opposition groups as favouring tribal, rather than party, politics. Opponents of the legislation complained that it would increase representation from rural, tribal areas traditionally supportive of King Abdullah while lowering the number of seats from urban constituencies, where there was a higher proportion of Jordanians of Palestinian origin (who were considered more likely to vote for opposition Islamist candidates). In July 2010 the IAF declared that it was to boycott the legislative elections, stating that the authorities could not guarantee that they would be 'fair and transparent'.

At elections to the House of Representatives held on 9 November 2010, independents and tribal representatives loyal to the Hashemite monarchy secured all 120 of the seats in the newly enlarged legislature. A reported 17 of the elected independents were aligned with opposition groups, including one member of the IAF who had refused to join his party's boycott. According to the terms of the revised electoral law, 12 seats were allocated to the female candidates receiving the greatest number of votes. (A 13th woman was elected in Amman, independently of the quota system.) Voter turnout was officially recorded at around 53%; however, the IAF claimed that the figure was in fact closer to 30%. During the polls, it was reported that one person had died in a series of violent clashes between opposing political factions; riots were also reported after the final results were announced.

On 24 November 2010 King Abdullah issued a decree endorsing a new Cabinet under the continued premiership of Rifai. On the following day the King appointed a new Senate, the membership of which had been expanded from 55 to 60.

King Abdullah accelerates reforms after 2011 protests

During January 2011 anti-Government protests took place in cities across the country, including in Amman, by thousands of demonstrators angered by the high levels of unemployment and poverty, rapidly increasing prices for basic foodstuffs and perceived corruption among government officials. Many of the protesters, who included trade unionists, Islamists and leftist groups, demanded the resignation of the Prime Minister and a change in Jordan's political system to allow future Prime

Ministers to be elected, rather than appointed by the King. Having first implemented new economic measures (see *Economic Affairs*), on 1 February King Abdullah dismissed Rifai and his administration, and designated Marouf al-Bakhit (premier during 2005–07) as Prime Minister. A new Government, which the King charged with swiftly implementing the necessary political reforms to modernize the kingdom, was formed in early February 2011. The change of government appeared to be an attempt by the monarch to prevent a repeat of the large-scale street protests which in Tunisia and Egypt had recently led to the removal from office of both countries' Presidents. On 3 March al-Bakhit's new Government narrowly won a vote of confidence.

At the request of King Abdullah, on 14 March 2011 the Government established a National Dialogue Committee, which would enter into discussions with political parties and trade unions, as well as youth and elders' representatives concerning key legislation, particularly the electoral and political parties laws. However, calls by members of the opposition for a dissolution of parliament and fresh elections were rejected by the King. The Secretary-General of the IAF, Hamza Mansour, was said to have turned down an invitation for his movement to join the Government, and he declared that the IAF would not be involved in the work of the new committee owing to its composition and modest aims.

Meanwhile, small and largely peaceful demonstrations were staged by pro-democracy protesters in the kingdom throughout March 2011. The first fatality as a result of the protests was reported on 25 March, after a pro-reform rally in Amman turned into violent clashes between pro- and anti-Government protesters, leading to the intervention of the security forces. There were reports that the demonstration had been instigated by Jordanians of Palestinian origin and thus posed a threat to the monarchy. On 27 March the lower chamber rejected opposition demands immediately to reduce King Abdullah's constitutional powers. On 7 April a man was seriously wounded by setting fire to himself in front of the Prime Minister's office in Amman. Violence occurred again on 15 April, when a group of hardline Salafist Islamists who were demanding the release of Islamist prisoners allegedly attacked members of the police force in Zarqa; their assault apparently followed attacks on the Salafists by pro-regime supporters. Dozens of Islamists were detained by the authorities, although many were subsequently released.

On 26 April 2011 King Abdullah established the Royal Committee on Constitutional Review, which was to examine the recommendations of the National Dialogue Committee regarding possible amendments to the Constitution concerning political parties and the electoral system. On 4 June al-Masri presented the National Dialogue Committee's final report to the Prime Minister. However, opposition parties, including the IAF, expressed anger at what they considered to be the limited nature of the proposed reforms, particularly since they included the retention of the 'one person, one vote' system in the majority of parliamentary seats. During a televised speech on 12 June, the King announced that he would henceforth allow cabinets to be formed on the basis of parliamentary majority and thus permit the Prime Minister to be appointed by parliament rather than by the monarch; however, the exact time-frame for the reform was unclear. Abdullah also outlined proposals to strengthen political parties and stated that municipal elections would take place by the end of 2011.

In June 2011 the Minister of State for Media Affairs and Communications, Taher Odwan, resigned in protest against what he deemed to be overly restrictive new legislation concerned with press and publications, the penal system and the fight against corruption. In a government reorganization effected by King Abdullah on 2 July, al-Bakhit retained the premiership. Notably, Mazen al-Saket replaced the unpopular Saad Hayel Srour as Minister of the Interior. (Srour had been accused of taking an excessively firm stance against those involved in the recent protests.)

The Royal Committee on Constitutional Review presented its findings to King Abdullah on 14 August 2011. Most notable among the 42 suggested amendments to the Constitution were the formation of an independent constitutional court in place of the Higher Council for the Interpretation of the Constitution; the establishment of an independent commission to monitor legislative and municipal elections; a reduction in the powers of the State Security Court; and new provisions that would improve freedom of the press and of expression. Although the proposed amendments were welcomed by many sections of Jordanian society, the IAF insisted that future Prime Ministers should

be elected and demanded a further reduction in the powers of the intelligence services. Both the House of Representatives and the Senate approved a total of 41 constitutional amendments during September. One crucial change had been the decision of parliament to retain the State Security Court, but to restrict its responsibilities to dealing with cases of terrorism, treason and espionage. The official endorsement of the constitutional amendments by King Abdullah at the end of September prompted further protests by opposition activists, who again demanded al-Bakhit's resignation. The Muslim Brotherhood urged more extensive reforms, such as dissolving the State Security Court and introducing an elected upper house. Despite the introduction of the revised legislation, which stated that the municipal elections should be held by September 2012, the polls did not in fact take place until August 2013 (see *Recent developments*).

Street demonstrations, albeit smaller in scale, were held throughout mid-2011 by protesters still frustrated by the lack of progress on political and economic reforms. By September the demonstrators were increasingly focusing their attention on the Cabinet and parliament's perceived failure to reduce the high levels of corruption. On 16 October a reported 70 of the 120 deputies in the House of Representatives had asked the King to dismiss al-Bakhit owing to their dissatisfaction with the Prime Minister's performance. After al-Bakhit had been requested by King Abdullah to resign on 17 October, the King named Awn al-Khasawneh—a judge at the International Court of Justice who had previously served as chief of the royal court—as premier, and asked him to lead the country through an intense period of political reform. A new Cabinet was inaugurated under Prime Minister al-Khasawneh on 24 October. The IAF Secretary-General, Hamza Mansour, again declined an invitation to join the new administration. On 25 October a new Senate was appointed

A draft electoral law was approved by the Cabinet in early April 2012. Among the changes proposed by the Government included the replacement of the 'one person, one vote' system with one under which voters would cast two ballots in favour of individual candidates for a particular governorate and a separate ballot for a national party. The number of seats in the House of Representatives would be increased from 120 to 138, some 15 of which would be allocated to national political groups on a proportional basis. The quota for female legislators would also be increased from 12 to 15. The proposals were rejected by some opposition groups, notably the IAF. In late April al-Khasawneh tendered his resignation as Prime Minister, along with that of his Cabinet. Reports suggested that al-Khasawneh's Government was deemed to have been too slow in carrying out the requisite political reforms. Fayez al-Tarawneh (Prime Minister in 1998–99) was subsequently instructed by King Abdullah to form a new Government, which duly took office in May 2012. The new Cabinet was asked by the King to administer the country for a 'limited transitional period' in order to adopt the necessary legislation to enable early parliamentary elections to be held in late 2012. However, street protests continued, as many demonstrators expressed frustration at King Abdullah's decision to install new ministers rather than implement the more far-reaching reforms being demanded by opposition groups. Nevertheless, a significant reform proposed by the Royal Committee on Constitutional Review was instituted later in May, when the members of the new Independent Election Commission (IEC) were sworn into office.

In mid-June 2012 the House of Representatives approved the new electoral law, which had been amended so that the number of seats in the legislature would be increased from 120 to 140, with 17 seats allocated to national political groups on a proportional basis. The legislation was endorsed by the Senate in late June and by King Abdullah in late July. In its final form, after an intervention by the monarch in a stated effort to encourage the participation of all political groups in the election process, the 2012 Elections Law raised the number of parliamentary seats set aside for political parties to 27; the House of Representatives would thus henceforth constitute 150 members. Even after the introduction of a larger number of party-allocated seats, the political leadership of the Muslim Brotherhood voted in mid-July to boycott the forthcoming legislative polls. In September King Abdullah also angered many journalists by approving controversial amendments to the Press and Publications Law that would require news websites to obtain a licence from the authorities and therefore render their content subject to official censorship. Government sources claimed to have prevented access to at least 300 such websites by June 2013.

Recent developments: the 2013 legislative and municipal elections

On 4 October 2012 King Abdullah issued a decree dissolving the House of Representatives in order to allow for fresh parliamentary elections to be held; it was subsequently announced by the IEC that the polls would take place on 23 January 2013. Meanwhile, on 10 October 2012 the King appointed Abdullah Ensour, a reformist member of the Senate, as Prime Minister-designate. On the following day a new Cabinet under Ensour was inaugurated. During October the IAF repeated its pledge to boycott the next parliamentary elections. One of the largest demonstrations held by Islamist opposition activists since the start of the protests in early 2011 was staged in Amman on 5 October 2012, when up to 20,000 protesters demanded that the new electoral legislation be repealed.

Further rallies were held in Amman and other cities in November 2012 by Islamists, trade unionists and youth movements following the Government's decision to withdraw certain fuel subsidies. There were widespread calls for the Government under Prime Minister Ensour to resign, while some protesters were reported to have openly demanded an end to the Jordanian monarchy. Government officials insisted that the subsidies had been removed in an effort to resolve the country's 'very critical' financial situation (see *Economic Affairs*). Three people were reported to have died and more than 70 others were wounded as several of the nationwide protests turned into violent clashes between demonstrators and the security forces.

At the elections to the newly expanded, 150-member House of Representatives, which took place on 23 January 2013, independents and tribal representatives loyal to King Abdullah were reported to have secured around 75% of the seats, with moderate Islamist and other opposition candidates winning the remaining 25%; 37 of the newly elected deputies were said to come from the opposition. According to the IEC, voter turnout was 56.5%; however, the IAF dismissed this figure as being excessively high, and alleged that electoral fraud had occurred. The IEC Chairman, Abdelilah al-Khatib, admitted that instances of 'minor irregularities' had taken place, but affirmed that these had not affected the election's final outcome. Observers from the European Union also described the election process as 'transparent and credible', while also acknowledging that there had been instances of vote-buying. On 27 January Ensour submitted the resignation of his Cabinet to the King. On 5 March Ensour won a vote of confidence in the House of Representatives and four days later was asked by the King to remain as Prime Minister. On 30 March a new Cabinet was duly sworn into office.

Anti-Government protests continued in several cities in the aftermath of the poll, with some demonstrators increasingly demanding an end to King Abdullah's reign. During mid-2013 there was also a notable increase in the number of violent incidents being reported in southern Jordan, where tribal youths protested against their poor living standards and the apparent failure of the Government to improve their prospects of employment. Four people died, and up to 30 were injured, after violence erupted at a university in Ma'an in April, and two others were killed following clashes at a university in Kerak in April and July. Many opposition activists accused the security forces of responding to the unrest with excessive force.

King Hussein effected an extensive reorganization of the Cabinet under Prime Minister Ensour in August 2013, in advance of municipal elections that were due to be held that month. The new Government—in which the number of ministers was increased from 19 to 27—included many technocrats, and was asked by the King to effect the necessary economic reforms, as required by the IMF, in order to reduce Jordan's huge budget deficit and stimulate growth.

At the municipal elections held on 27 August 2013, overall voter turnout was officially reported at 30% (compared with around 50% in 2007). The polls were again boycotted by the IAF and certain left-wing groups. Thus, the elections represented a success for tribal representatives loyal to the monarchy. There were several reports of election violations and some violent incidents occurred at polling stations.

In April 2014 unrest was reported in the southern city of Ma'an when gunmen reportedly opened fire at police officers guarding a courthouse in the city, seriously wounding one of them. The security forces' efforts to apprehend those responsible—reported to be Islamist militants—prompted unrest in the city, during which a man was killed during clashes between demonstrators and police officers. By the end of the month more than 150 suspects had been arrested in Ma'an, while a number were still

being pursued. In May the state security court sentenced 11 men to prison terms of between four and 20 years after they were found guilty of affiliation to al-Qa'ida and of planning attacks against diplomatic and commercial targets in Amman. In June Abu Qatada, a Salafist cleric who had been sentenced in Amman *in absentia* in 1999 to life imprisonment on charges of planning attacks in Amman in 1998, and to 25 years in prison for plotting to attack US and Israeli citizens in the capital in 2000 (although the attacks never took place), and subsequently arrested in the United Kingdom in 2001 on charges of terrorism, and deported in 2013, was cleared of the charge relating to an attack in Amman in 1998; in September he was cleared of charges relating to the later offence and released from gaol. In December 2014 some 11 prisoners were executed after the Jordanian authorities ended a moratorium on the death penalty, which had been in place since 2006. The Minister of the Interior, Hussein Hazaa Majali, claimed that the measure was intended as a deterrent to rising crime, although human rights groups criticized the executions and encouraged the regime to address the political and economic causes of serious criminality. In February 2015 two of those convicted of perpetrating the November 2005 bombings in Amman were executed, ostensibly in response to the killing in Syria of a Jordanian air force pilot by militants belonging to Islamic State (see *Foreign Affairs*).

A government reorganization took place in March 2015. The Minister of Education, Muhammad Thneibet, and the Minister of Foreign and Expatriates Affairs, Nasser Judeh, were both appointed as deputy premiers, in addition to their existing responsibilities. The number of female ministers increased to five with the appointment of Maha Ali as Minister of Industry, Trade and Supply, and of Majd Shweikeh as Minister of Information and Communications Technology. The labour and tourism portfolios were divided: Nidal Katamine retained responsibility for labour, but Nayef al-Fayez joined the Government as Minister of Tourism and Antiquities. New Ministers of Energy and Mineral Resources, Planning and International Co-operation, and Higher Education and Scientific Research were also appointed.

Foreign Affairs

Regional relations

Relations with Israel were severely undermined in September 1997 when the head of the political bureau of the Palestinian Islamic Resistance Movement (Hamas), Khalid Meshaal, survived an assassination attempt in Amman by agents of the Israeli intelligence service, Mossad. Intensive negotiations involving Crown Prince Hassan, Israeli Prime Minister Binyamin Netanyahu and US officials resulted in an agreement in October whereby Israel freed the Hamas spiritual leader, Sheikh Ahmad Yassin, in return for Jordan's release of two Mossad agents arrested in connection with the attack on Meshaal. Israel and Jordan signed several bilateral trade agreements in March 1998, and in October King Hussein's mediation at the US-brokered peace summit held between Israel and the Palestinian (National) Authority (PA) was crucial to the signing of the Wye Memorandum. In December Israel agreed to open its airspace to foreign airlines en route for Jordan.

Upon his accession in February 1999 King Abdullah assured Israel that he would pursue his father's commitment to the Middle East peace process. The King welcomed the reactivation of the stalled Wye Memorandum by the signing (to which he was a witness) of the Sharm el-Sheikh Memorandum (Wye Two—see the chapter on Israel) by the Israeli Prime Minister, Ehud Barak, and Yasser Arafat in September.

There was considerable speculation at the time of the Wye Two agreement that recent efforts to bring an end to Hamas's political activities in Jordan had been motivated by a consensus among the Jordanian, Palestinian, Israeli and US authorities on the need to contain potential Islamist opposition to a revival of the peace process. In August 1999 the Jordanian security forces closed down Hamas offices in Amman, on the grounds that these were being used by foreign groups for illegal political activities. The home of Khalid Meshaal was also raided, and in the following months numerous Hamas officials were arrested on various charges including involvement in illicit political activities and the illegal possession of firearms. In November it was reported that Hamas had rejected an offer by the Jordanian Government to release the detained activists provided that they agreed to cease all political activity and that their leaders left the country. Later in the month the Jordanian authorities released some 24 Hamas officials, including four leaders (among them Meshaal and spokesman Ibrahim Ghosheh) who were immediately flown to Qatar. The Jordanian authorities granted permission for Ghosheh to enter the country in June 2001, after he had agreed to end his involvement with Hamas.

In advance of the Israeli-Palestinian peace talks held at the US presidential retreat at Camp David, Maryland, in July 2000, the Jordanian Government stated that it would not accept any more Palestinian refugees and that it supported their right of return to their homeland. In June 2000 there were 1,570,192 Palestinian refugees in Jordan registered with the UN Relief and Works Agency for Palestine Refugees in the Near East (UNRWA, see p. 103). By July 2014 this figure had risen to 2,097,338. Meanwhile, in August 2000 King Abdullah reiterated that Jordan would not accept Israeli or international sovereignty over the Islamic holy sites in East Jerusalem, an issue that had been a major obstacle to progress at Camp David.

In October 2000 King Abdullah attended a US-brokered summit meeting between Barak and Arafat in Sharm el-Sheikh, Egypt. As violence between Palestinians and Israeli security forces escalated, Jordan came under growing pressure from other Arab states to sever diplomatic ties with Israel, while large-scale public demonstrations against Israeli and US policies towards the new Palestinian uprising (often termed the al-Aqsa *intifada*) were held in Amman and at Jordan's refugee camps. One 'anti-normalization' protest held in early October resulted in violent confrontations between protesters and police; the Government subsequently issued a ban on public demonstrations. Meanwhile, Jordan delayed the dispatch of its new ambassador to Israel, in response to the deteriorating situation in the West Bank and Gaza. In November the Israeli Vice-Consul in Amman was injured in a gun attack by militant Islamists; another Israeli diplomat was wounded in a similar attack in December.

The convening of a summit meeting of Arab League heads of state in Amman in March 2001 reflected Jordan's prominent role in diplomatic efforts to resolve the Israeli–Palestinian conflict. At the summit Arab leaders pledged to transfer funds to the PA as part of a US $1,000m. fund established in late 2000. Jordan and Egypt both refused to return their ambassadors to Israel in protest against Israeli military actions against the Palestinians, although they did not proceed to a formal suspension of diplomatic relations. The summit's final communiqué—the so-called Amman Declaration—repeated demands for Israel to withdraw its armed forces from all occupied territory. Further mass demonstrations were held in Jordanian cities and Palestinian refugee camps in March–April 2002, after Israel had reoccupied Palestinian-controlled towns in the West Bank.

On 4 June 2003 King Abdullah hosted a summit meeting between US President George W. Bush, Israeli premier Ariel Sharon and the newly appointed Palestinian Prime Minister, Mahmud Abbas. The aim of the summit was to begin the implementation of the 'roadmap' peace plan, an initiative that had been drawn up in late 2002 by the Quartet group (comprising the USA, the UN, Russia and the EU) and announced by President Bush in April 2003, following the US-led invasion of Iraq and the removal from power of Saddam Hussain.

In February 2004 a Jordanian delegation travelled to the International Court of Justice (ICJ) in The Hague, Netherlands, to present a document condemning Israel's construction of a 'security fence' in the West Bank (see the chapters on Israel and the Palestinian Territories). The ICJ had been asked by the UN General Assembly to rule on the legality of the barrier, and Jordan was one of 14 countries to present evidence against its construction. It was reported in March that King Abdullah and Ariel Sharon had held secret talks in southern Israel regarding the controversial barrier. In May Israel and Jordan agreed to upgrade their bilateral trade agreement, which had been signed months after the 1994 peace treaty. In February 2005 King Abdullah attended the summit meeting, held in Sharm el-Sheikh, between Sharon and Mahmud Abbas—recently elected as Executive President of the PA following the death of Arafat in November 2004—at which the two leaders issued verbal declarations that Israel and the PA would cease all acts of violence against each other. Later that month Jordan returned an ambassador to Israel. However, at an Arab League summit in Algiers in March, King Abdullah failed to secure approval for a proposal for peace with Israel that would not oblige Israel to relinquish all the territories it had occupied in 1967.

Following the victory of Hamas in the Palestinian legislative elections of January 2006, King Abdullah argued that the election results should not prevent further peace negotiations from taking place between Israel and the PA. None the less, Jordan

appeared increasingly supportive of US efforts to coerce the Hamas Cabinet into recognizing Israel through a process of isolation. In April Jordan cancelled a planned official visit by Palestinian Minister of Foreign Affairs Mahmud Khalid al-Zahhar, after the apparent discovery of an arms cache which had allegedly been smuggled into Jordan by Hamas from Syria; Hamas officials denied the claim. In May Jordanian authorities announced that 20 Hamas members had been arrested on suspicion of plotting terrorist attacks in Jordan.

In May 2007 the ministers responsible for foreign affairs of Jordan, Israel and Egypt convened in the Egyptian capital, Cairo, to discuss an Arab League initiative for peace in the Middle East; the Arab proposal offered Israel peace and normalized relations with all Arab countries, in exchange for an Israeli withdrawal from those lands seized in 1967. However, the complete blockade of the Hamas-controlled Gaza Strip, imposed by the Israeli Government in January 2008, prompted forceful condemnation from King Abdullah, who insisted that meaningful peace negotiations could not be held while Israel persisted with such measures against the Palestinian people. Nevertheless, in April Israeli Prime Minister Ehud Olmert visited Amman for talks with the King, which largely focused on ways of advancing the objectives of the Annapolis Conference, the peace summit hosted by the USA in November 2007.

Israel's military offensive against Hamas targets in the Gaza Strip, launched on 27 December 2008, provoked a wave of protests throughout Jordan, with demonstrators demanding the severance of diplomatic ties with Israel. Two days later the same demand was made in a petition signed by 29 parliamentary deputies. The two countries' respective ambassadors were temporarily withdrawn from Amman and Tel-Aviv; however, no formal severance of diplomatic relations was announced. Throughout the crisis Jordan provided a vitally important route for humanitarian aid into the Gaza Strip. Following the Israeli declaration of a unilateral ceasefire on 18 January, King Abdullah attended a summit meeting on that day in Sharm el-Sheikh, jointly hosted by the Egyptian and French Presidents, Hosni Mubarak and Nicolas Sarkozy, which aimed to forge a unified European and Arab response to the crisis in Gaza. The Sharm el-Sheikh summit, which was also attended by PA President Abbas and the Secretaries-General of the UN and the Arab League, represented those parties committed to seeking solutions through the framework of the existing Middle East peace process.

In May 2009 Binyamin Netanyahu, who had been appointed Prime Minister of Israel in March, attended a summit in Jordan, during which the King reiterated the conditions of the Arab peace initiative. However, during the latter part of 2009 Jordan was critical of Israel's ongoing settlement construction in East Jerusalem, and tensions were exacerbated by allegations of Israeli encroachment on holy sites in Jerusalem, which led to sporadic outbreaks of civil unrest from September. By early 2010 it was reported that relations between King Abdullah and the Israeli premier were frozen. However, at the end of January the King held discussions on the stalled peace process with Israeli President Shimon Peres during the World Economic Forum in Davos, Switzerland. In late February the King strongly condemned Israel's decision to include two sites venerated by Jews, Muslims and Christians—Rachel's Tomb in Bethlehem and the Cave of the Patriarchs in Hebron—on a list of Israeli national heritage sites. In April King Abdullah travelled to Washington, DC, where he urged the US President, Barack Obama, to use his influence to persuade the Israeli Government to impose a permanent ban on Jewish settlement construction in the West Bank. Jordan chose not to replace its ambassador to Tel-Aviv when, in July 2010, its current envoy was appointed to a ministerial post in Amman.

Direct negotiations between Netanyahu and Abbas—the first to take place between the leaders of Israel and the PA since December 2008—finally commenced in Washington, DC, in September 2010, chaired by US Secretary of State Hillary Clinton. They followed meetings held on the previous day between President Obama and both Israeli and Palestinian leaders, as well as with King Abdullah of Jordan and Egypt's President Mubarak. However, the discussions ended without any substantial progress. In late November 2011 the King visited the West Bank for talks with President Abbas, to demonstrate Jordan's continuing pursuit of a Middle East peace settlement and its solidarity with the Palestinians in their quest for statehood. (In September 2011 the PA leadership had submitted a formal application to the UN for full Palestinian membership.)

Further direct negotiations finally took place between Israeli and Palestinian officials in Amman on 4 January 2012. However, after five 'exploratory' meetings in the period up to 25 January, once again no breakthrough was reported. The PA continued to demand the complete cessation of Israeli settlement activity on the West Bank and an agreement from Israel to discuss the pre-1967 borders of a Palestinian state before agreeing to new peace talks. Both King Abdullah and the Minister of Foreign Affairs, Nasser Judeh, had participated in the meetings. In October 2012—more than two years after Jordan had chosen not to replace its envoy to Israel—a new ambassador to Tel-Aviv formally assumed his post. In December King Abdullah visited the West Bank town of Ramallah to hold talks with President Abbas, after the UN had, in the previous month, agreed to upgrade the status of the Palestinian territories to that of a 'non-member observer state'.

After several weeks of intensive diplomatic efforts by regional leaders, including King Abdullah, and the US Secretary of State, John F. Kerry, preliminary discussions regarding a final status agreement between Israel and the PA were held in Washington, DC, on 29–30 July 2013. Formal peace negotiations between the two sides began in Jerusalem on 14 August. However, the proposed deadline for a preliminary accord to be signed passed without any significant progress.

In late February 2014 the Prime Minister and Minister of Defence, Abdullah Ensour, indicated that the Jordanian Government might reconsider its 1994 peace treaty with Israel, after members of the Knesset (parliament) debated legislation concerning an Israeli declaration of sovereignty over the Temple Mount/Haram al-Sharif compound in East Jerusalem, which is currently administered by Jordan. In response to the Knesset debate, Jordanian deputies in the House of Representatives voted unanimously to expel the Israeli ambassador from Amman and to recall Jordan's envoy to Tel-Aviv. However, the Ensour Government awaited the outcome of the Israeli debate before taking any possible action. Bilateral relations deteriorated further in March 2014, after the reported shooting dead by Israeli soldiers of a Jordanian judge of Palestinian origin, Raed Zuaiter, on the West Bank side of the border. The two countries subsequently agreed to hold a joint investigation into the affair, and the Israeli Government apologized for the judge's death following considerable pressure from Jordan. In November Jordan withdrew its ambassador from Israel for consultations after violent clashes between Palestinian protesters and Israeli security forces at the Temple Mount/Haram al-Sharif compound and reportedly inside the al-Aqsa mosque. Jordan claimed that the Israeli authorities had violated the terms of the 1994 peace treaty. The clashes occurred after right-wing Jewish activists had proposed that Jews should be permitted to worship at the compound, a practice which had been de facto prohibited since 1967. The ambassador returned to his post in February 2015.

After August 1995, when Jordan granted political asylum to the two sons-in-law of the Iraqi President, Saddam Hussein, and their wives, King Hussein became more openly critical of the Iraqi regime; however, Jordan continued to provide Iraq with a crucial external economic link. In December 1997 Jordan recalled its chargé d'affaires from Baghdad and expelled a number of Iraqi diplomats from Jordan, in protest at the execution of four Jordanians by the Iraqi authorities. Later that month, however, the two countries signed an agreement whereby Iraq was to supply 4.8m. metric tons of crude petroleum and refined petroleum products to Jordan in 1998. In January of that year more than 50 Jordanian detainees were released by Iraq.

In response to critical confrontations between Iraq and the UN during 1998 over the issue of weapons inspections, Jordan indicated that it would not allow its territory or airspace to be used for air strikes against Iraq. King Hussein consistently advocated a diplomatic resolution of the crises, while urging Iraq to comply with all pertinent UN resolutions. This position allowed Jordan to improve its relations with some Arab states, notably Egypt. Jordan strongly condemned the air strikes carried out against Iraq by US and British forces in December, and in early 1999 the Jordanian National Assembly voted in favour of an end to the UN embargo against Iraq.

King Abdullah made attempts to improve Jordan's relations with Iraq following his accession in February 1999. In November 2000 Prime Minister al-Ragheb undertook an official visit to Iraq and the two states agreed to increase the value of their trade agreement from US $300m. in 2000 to $450m. in 2001. By mid-2001 Jordan was increasingly concerned that the proposed imposition by the UN of sanctions against Iraq would result in the loss of its oil supply from Iraq, in addition to its main regional export market. At discussions held in Amman in January 2002, Iraq and Jordan renewed their oil protocol and also agreed to the creation of a free trade zone.

Following the ousting of Saddam Hussein's regime by the US-led coalition in April 2003, the establishment was announced in June of a joint Jordanian-Iraqi business council to facilitate relations between the two countries and to aid the recovery of the Iraqi economy. In January 2005 Amman hosted a meeting of five of the six countries neighbouring Iraq to discuss the elections to a transitional Iraqi legislature scheduled to be held later that month. Iran boycotted the meeting after Jordanian officials accused Iran of seeking to influence Iraqi voting in order to encourage the formation of a Shi'a-dominated government in the country. Following reports that a suicide bombing in the Iraqi town of Hillah in February (in which some 125 people died) had been perpetrated by a Jordanian militant, bilateral relations deteriorated and large anti-Jordanian protests took place in Baghdad. The Iraqi authorities alleged that Jordan was failing to prevent insurgents from crossing the border into Iraq, and in March both countries temporarily withdrew diplomatic envoys from their respective capitals.

In September 2007 the UN High Commissioner for Refugees (UNHCR) estimated the number of displaced Iraqis living in Jordan at between 500,000 and 750,000 (some of whom had been displaced prior to the conflict in Iraq from 2003). In an attempt to stem the influx of refugees, Jordan had introduced new legislation in February 2007, rendering mandatory for all Iraqi refugees a recently introduced type of passport, issued only in Baghdad. Later that year the border with Iraq was effectively closed to all but exceptional cases. Despite the fact that Jordan, along with Syria, had absorbed more Iraqi refugees than any other countries, the kingdom was not a signatory to the Refugee Convention of 1951 and refused to accord the Iraqis official refugee status, preferring to describe them as 'temporary visitors'. In March 2008 the Government requested all Iraqi visitors to provide appropriate documents proving their entitlement to stay in Jordan, such as work contracts. Those without the relevant qualifications (estimated to be some 80% of the total Iraqi population) were instructed either to leave Jordan, or to pay one-half of their overstay fines and rectify their status. However, the authorities stopped short of forceful deportations and concentrated on a policy of encouraging Iraqis to return home. By October it was reported that hundreds were returning to Iraq under an Iraqi government-sponsored scheme that gave financial assistance to families returning voluntarily. At December 2012 the Government estimated the number of Iraqi refugees living in Jordan at 450,500.

The official visit to Amman of Iraqi Prime Minister Nuri al-Maliki in June 2008 heralded new progress in bilateral relations, and in August King Abdullah made a surprise visit to Baghdad for further talks with al-Maliki. This was the first visit to Baghdad by an Arab head of state since the fall of the previous Iraqi regime in 2003. In September 2008 a new deal was announced governing the supply of subsidized Iraqi oil to Jordan. In October Jordan's new ambassador to Iraq took up his post—the first such appointment since the withdrawal of the previous ambassador following the bombing of the Jordanian embassy in August 2003. In January 2009 King Abdullah directed the Government to ease the restrictions on Iraqis entering and residing in the kingdom. Meanwhile, the volume of trade between the neighbouring countries had doubled in 2008 compared with the preceding year, and the signing of a free trade agreement in September 2009 led to a further increase in bilateral trade. At the same time, the Iraqi authorities expressed their intention to double the volume of crude oil exports to Jordan, although this was dependent on the completion of repairs on the Kirkuk–Banias oil pipeline. In September 2011 a joint Iraqi-Jordanian committee pledged to implement additional measures to increase the level of cross-border trade.

King Abdullah decided not to attend the historic summit meeting of the Arab League held in Baghdad in March 2012, with Jordan instead being represented by Prime Minister Awn al-Khasawneh. Many Arab governments, notably those of the Gulf monarchies, had chosen to send lower-level delegations to the meeting in protest at the Iraqi Government's close relations with Iran and its apparently 'neutral' position on the Syrian crisis. Nevertheless, in March 2013 the Iraqi and Jordanian authorities confirmed the launch of a joint project involving the construction of a pipeline to transport crude petroleum and natural gas from Iraq's southern city of Basra to Aqaba. The project was expected to cost around US $18,000m. and to be completed in 2017.

President Hafiz al-Assad of Syria led a Syrian delegation at King Hussein's funeral in February 1999, following which Jordan's relations with Syria improved significantly. In August the first senior Syrian delegation for almost a decade visited Amman for a session of the Jordanian-Syrian Higher Committee; the meeting resulted in an accord that officials hoped might double the volume of bilateral trade. King Abdullah attended the funeral of President Assad in June 2000, and acted swiftly to forge close relations with the new Syrian President, Bashar al-Assad. In November Syria confirmed that it had upgraded its diplomatic representation in Amman to ambassadorial status. The Syrian authorities declared in January 2001 that all Jordanian prisoners held in Syria would soon be released; in November Jordanian officials claimed that there were still hundreds of Jordanian nationals being held in Syrian prisons. In August 2002 the two countries signed an agreement under which Syria was to provide Jordan with water to ease the latter's water shortages. Under the terms of a deal concluded between King Abdullah and President Assad in November 2006, 18 Jordanian detainees were released by Syria. A multilateral free trade accord was signed by officials from Jordan, Syria, Lebanon and Turkey in August 2010, and in December the four countries established what was termed the Levant Business Forum, to facilitate the further integration of their economies.

However, relations between Jordan and Syria have been damaged by the military campaign being carried out by Syrian government forces in the wake of the protests which began in that country in March 2011. Although the Jordanian authorities were initially anxious about the consequences for their own country's stability should the Syrian regime be ousted, in November King Abdullah became the first Arab leader to issue a public demand for President Assad to resign. His statement was followed by an attack on the Jordanian embassy in Damascus by supporters of Assad. In December some 3,000 Jordanians took part in a sit-in at the Syrian embassy in Amman against the Syrian Government's violent crackdown on protesters and other civilians, and demanded the expulsion of Syria's ambassador to Jordan.

In early 2013, after hopes of a swift resolution to the conflict had diminished, the number of Syrians entering Jordan increased rapidly, adding further to the country's already grave economic problems and placing a severe strain on the Government's ability to provide basic services. King Abdullah requested urgent international assistance for those nations hosting Syrian refugees, in particular Jordan, Turkey and Lebanon. Some clashes were also reported in Amman between a minority of Jordanians who continued to support the Assad regime and those, including members of the IAF, who backed the Syrian opposition. Moreover, some defecting members of the Syrian regime had sought refuge in Jordan, and there were growing fears that the kingdom could eventually be drawn into the conflict. By July 2013, according to the UN, at least 100,000 Syrians had died in the violence and more than 4m. had been displaced.

A Syrian national was shot dead by Jordanian police officers and around 30 were injured in April 2014 in the Zaatari refugee camp near Mafraq during unrest following the alleged detention of refugees by the Jordanian authorities for attempting to leave the camp illegally. Later that month the Jordanian air force carried out a bombing raid on a convoy of vehicles entering Jordan from Syria; it was reported that the convoy was involved in the illegal trafficking of military equipment across the border. At the end of the month 10 members of the jihadi Salafist movement were sentenced by the State Security Court to five years in prison with hard labour for having attempted to join Islamist militias in Syria in August 2013, although the court immediately reduced the sentences to two-and-a-half years. The verdicts raised to 50 the total number of Jordanians imprisoned for their support for Syrian jihadist groups since December 2013. In December 2014 UNHCR estimated the number of Syrian refugees resident in Jordan to be 640,000, although the Jordanian Government claimed that the true total was more than double that number, and emphasized the strain on its society, in terms of access to clean water and education, and high youth unemployment. While the Jordanian Government insisted its border remained open in late 2014, UNHCR recorded 6,000 new refugee arrivals in September and only 250 in November. Human rights group Amnesty International claimed in August

that Jordan had banned entry to Palestinian refugees from Syria, as well as forcibly deporting those who managed to enter Jordan, and UNHCR reported that during October a majority of refugees from Syria had been turned back from the Rabaa al-Sarhan transit centre in Jordan without being able to register with the organization, and that some 4,000 to 5,000 refugees from Syria had been stranded between the Syrian and Jordanian borders. UNHCR reported in December that Jordan had effectively closed its border to Syria once again.

Jordan's motivation for securing its borders was the rise in Syria of the fundamentalist militia group, the Islamic State in Iraq and the Levant (ISIL; renamed Islamic State in June 2014). ISIL prompted concern in Jordan in January 2014 when it captured the Iraqi city of Fallujah in Anbar province, which borders Jordan. The Jordanian Government responded immediately by deploying troops to reinforce its eastern border. The situation escalated in June after the sudden assault by Islamic State on multiple targets in Iraq, when it captured Mosul, as well as Tikrit, Ramadi and Rutba—around only 100 km from the Iraqi border with Jordan. While Jordan reassured itself that its own military was better trained and more disciplined than that of Iraq, Islamic State posed an ideological threat as a rallying point for the increasing number of jihadists and Salafists in Jordan. In mid-2014 Islamic State had released footage on the internet of Jordanian nationals in Ma'an destroying their passports and issuing threats to carry out suicide bombings in Jordan. Soon after the capture of Mosul by Islamic State, the Jordanian authorities discovered a plot by sympathizers of the group in Ma'an to raise the Islamic State flag over the city. By mid-2014 some 2,200 Jordanians were reported to be fighting alongside the al-Nusra Front and Islamic State in Syria. Moreover, as the border with Iraq was effectively closed in order to prevent infiltration by Islamic State forces, trade with Iraq and Turkey was severely disrupted, and in mid-2014 Jordan was confronted by a shortage of essential goods and a sharp increase in prices.

While the Jordanian Government was concerned by the rise of Islamic State, it initially refrained from contributing formally to the US-led military coalition created in early August 2014 to carry out air strikes on Islamic State forces in Iraq. Later that month around 40 Islamist militants were arrested in Jordan, ostensibly as a precautionary measure. However, in late September Jordanian forces participated in air strikes against targets in northern Syria. It was reported that the USA had urged Arab governments to take an active role in military operations before agreeing to extend the campaign from Iraq to Islamic State-held territory in Syria. In late December a Jordanian military jet was shot down while flying over Syria and the pilot was captured by Islamic State forces, who offered in January to exchange him for two Islamist militants held in gaol in Amman. In negotiations between the Jordanian Government and Islamic State later that month, Jordan demanded 'proof of life' before proceeding to the exchange. In early February Islamic State released via the internet footage of the captured pilot being burned to death; the killing had reportedly taken place several weeks before the footage was made public. King Abdullah vowed immediate retaliation and the Government proceeded to authorize the execution of the two prisoners who were subject to Islamic State's demands; air strikes by the Jordanian air force against Islamic State forces in Mosul, Iraq, commenced on the same day. The following day the Jordanian air force also attacked targets in the Syrian city of Raqqa.

Upon his accession, King Abdullah sought to strengthen relations with other Arab states. His first major foreign visit, in March 1999, was for talks with President Mubarak in Egypt (with which Jordan had signed an agreement in December 1998 providing for the future establishment of a free trade zone). Meanwhile, following the restoration of full diplomatic relations with Kuwait (which had been severed at the start of the Gulf crisis in 1990), in March 1999 Jordan reopened its embassy in Kuwait City; in October Kuwait returned an ambassador to Amman. In September 1999 King Abdullah visited Lebanon and held discussions with senior officials regarding the Middle East peace process and bilateral issues. However, despite signing an agreement on free trade and economic co-operation in October 2002, the two countries failed to ratify the agreement.

Pan-Arab relations were strained as a result of the US-led military campaign in Iraq in early 2003. Nevertheless, Jordan arranged to import oil from Saudi Arabia, Kuwait and the United Arab Emirates, reportedly at no cost, to circumvent shortages induced by the conflict in Iraq. In November Minister of Foreign Affairs Marwan al-Muasher visited Iran, primarily to discuss the status of some 1,000 members of the dissident Iranian militant group, the Mujahidin-e-Khalq, who were formerly based in Iraq but who were now being held under Jordanian supervision in the border area between Iraq and Jordan.

In February 2004 Jordan signed a free trade agreement with Egypt, Morocco and Tunisia, which committed each party to removing trade tariffs between them; the so-called Agadir Agreement entered into force in 2007. Meanwhile, in January 2007 King Abdullah urged Iran to exercise its influence over its neighbours in a positive manner, imploring the Iranian Government to refrain from adding to existing regional instability, particularly within Iraq, the Palestinian territories and Lebanon. Relations between Jordan and Saudi Arabia have improved in recent years, and in December 2007 officials from the two countries signed a border pact on the demarcation of their shared marine border in the Gulf of Aqaba.

Turkish President Abdullah Gül made a three-day state visit to Jordan in December 2009. During the visit, representatives of the two countries signed an agreement on the establishment of a free trade zone, which, it was hoped, would provide Jordanian businesses with improved access to European markets. The free trade agreement entered into effect in March 2011. During a visit to the Turkish capital, Ankara, in March 2013, King Abdullah and President Gül held further discussions concerning bilateral trade and investment, as well as the conflict in Syria and the Middle East peace process.

King Abdullah declared his support for the ouster of Egyptian President Muhammad Mursi by the Egyptian armed forces in July 2013. In October Saudi Arabia declined its non-permanent seat on the UN Security Council, apparently in protest against the perceived inaction on the part of the UN against the Assad Government in Syria, and in resolving the Israeli-Palestinian conflict; Jordan was subsequently elected to the Security Council in December, to serve a two-year term from January 2014. In April Jordanian officials reported that a military alliance had been proposed between the Co-operation Council of the Arab States of the Gulf (Gulf Co-operation Council), Jordan and Morocco. However, despite its close ties with Saudi Arabia, Jordan sought accommodation with states opposed to Saudi interests. It restored diplomatic relations with Iran in February, and in March King Abdullah received the Amir of Qatar, Sheikh Tamim bin Hamad Al Thani, during a visit to Amman. Meanwhile, the Jordanian ambassador to Libya was abducted in the capital, Tripoli, in April, by assailants demanding the release of an Islamist captive imprisoned in 2007 in Amman for attempting to detonate an explosive device at the Queen Alia international airport. The ambassador was released the following month, in exchange for the prisoner.

Other external relations

Jordan's relations with the USA in the early 1990s were frequently strained by US allegations of Jordanian assistance to Iraq in circumventing the UN trade embargo, as well as Jordan's vocal criticism of US-led policies towards Iraq. However, in September 1993 US President Bill Clinton announced that some US $30m. in economic and military aid to Jordan was to be released in recognition of the country's enforcement of sanctions against Iraq and of its role in the Middle East peace process. In early 1994 renewed tensions emerged with the USA over the Jerusalem issue and the US-led naval blockade of Jordan's only port at Aqaba, imposed to enforce sanctions against Iraq. Following a sharp deterioration in Jordanian-Iraqi relations in August 1995, when King Hussein granted political asylum to four senior members of the Iraqi regime, Clinton promised to support Jordan in the event of any threat to its security; however, the USA failed to persuade Jordan to sever all economic links with Iraq. In January 1996 the USA offered Jordan $300m. in military assistance, and an expansion of bilateral military co-operation was announced in March. In June 1997 the USA pledged $100m. in economic aid to Jordan, reportedly in recognition of Jordan's contributions to the regional peace process. In the same month Jordan signed a debt-rescheduling agreement with the USA, in accordance with a deal reached in May by members of the 'Paris Club' of Western official creditors to reschedule approximately $400m. of Jordanian debt.

In May 1999 King Abdullah began a three-week tour of the USA and several European capitals. Prior to the visit, the King had announced that he would be seeking US support for an agreement by Western countries to write off as much as 50% of Jordan's debt. He achieved some success when the 'Paris Club' agreed, in late May, to reschedule about US $800m. of Jordanian debt. During a visit by King Abdullah to Washington, DC, in

October 2000, Jordan and the USA signed a free trade agreement involving the reciprocal removal of all customs duties by 2010. The deal was implemented in December 2001.

King Abdullah strongly condemned the September 2001 suicide attacks against New York and Washington, DC, for which the USA held Osama bin Laden's al-Qa'ida network principally responsible, and the King swiftly affirmed Jordan's commitment to the proposed US-led 'war on terror'. Jordanian armed forces joined US and European forces when, from October, they launched military strikes against al-Qa'ida bases and the Sunni fundamentalist Taliban regime in Afghanistan (which was believed to be harbouring bin Laden). However, Abdullah emphasized that the international community must simultaneously renew efforts to resolve the Israeli-Palestinian conflict. He also warned that any extension of the US-led military action to target any Arab country, such as Iraq, would undermine the international campaign. In July 2002 King Abdullah asserted that Jordan would not allow its territory to be used by US troops to launch a military attack aimed at ousting the Iraqi regime of Saddam Hussain. In October the USA was said to have pledged US $85m. to Jordan, apparently in an effort to secure the country's support during a possible US-led military campaign in Iraq and to enable the Jordanian economy to withstand the consequences of a war.

In October 2002 a senior US diplomat, Laurence Foley, was assassinated in Jordan. The Jordanian security forces detained a large number of suspected Islamist militants following the assassination, and in December two alleged members of al-Qa'ida—one Jordanian and the other Libyan—were arrested on suspicion of involvement in Foley's murder. The trial of 11 suspects charged with involvement in the murder began in July 2003, with six of the defendants, including Abu Musab al-Zarqawi, being tried *in absentia*. At the conclusion of the trial in April 2004, all but one of the defendants were convicted: al-Zarqawi and seven others were sentenced to death, and the remaining two were given terms of imprisonment. In February 2003, meanwhile, Jordanian officials confirmed that the USA was to provide the kingdom with an anti-missile defence system in the event of a conflict in Iraq; Jordan had received six F-16 fighter aircraft from the US military in January. King Abdullah visited the USA in April 2004, but a meeting with President Bush was cancelled in protest at US support for Israel. The rescheduled meeting took place in May. In November 2006 the King hosted President Bush and Iraqi Prime Minister Nuri al-Maliki in Amman for talks on the need to impose stability and security within Iraq; thousands of protesters amassed in the streets of Amman, rallying against US foreign policy, and three Jordanian men were arrested on suspicion of plotting to assassinate the US President.

In April 2009 King Abdullah was the first Arab head of state to visit the USA after the inauguration of President Barack Obama in January. The visit indicated that the King was likely to be a key intermediary in US-brokered efforts to forge a Middle East peace settlement. In March 2013 Obama made an official visit to Jordan, where he held talks with King Abdullah over the ongoing crisis in Syria and the process of political reforms in the kingdom. In June it was revealed that 900 military personnel from the USA had been sent to Jordan to assist the Government in protecting its citizens from possible security risks arising from the Syrian civil war. The Obama Administration was also to send a consignment of F-16 fighter planes and *Patriot* missile-defence systems to the Jordanian authorities. King Abdullah made an official visit to the USA in February 2014 and confirmed the terms of loan guarantees worth US $1,000m. to finance expenses arising from the influx of refugees into Jordan from Syria. In September Jordan became the first Arab nation to carry out air strikes, over Syria, as part of the US-led coalition which had been formed in August to combat Islamic State in northern Iraq and Syria (see *Regional relations*).

CONSTITUTION AND GOVERNMENT

A revised Constitution for the Hashemite Kingdom of Jordan was ratified in January 1952 by King Talal I. Two amendments were adopted in November 1974 giving the King the right to dissolve the Senate or to take away membership from any of its members, and to postpone general elections for a period not to exceed a year, if there are circumstances in which the Cabinet feels that it is impossible to hold elections. A further amendment in February 1976 enabled the King to postpone elections indefinitely. In January 1984 two amendments were adopted, allowing elections 'in any part of the country where it is possible to hold them' (effectively, only the East Bank) and empowering the National Assembly to elect deputies from the Israeli-held West Bank. (However, in July 1988 King Hussein dissolved the legislature, renouncing Jordan's administrative and legal ties to the West Bank.) Under the terms of a revised electoral law approved in July 2012, the number of seats in the House of Representatives reserved for women was increased from 12 to 15, while a further 27 seats were allocated to candidates from political parties.

Jordan is a constitutional monarchy. Legislative power is vested in a bicameral National Assembly: the Senate has 60 members, appointed by the King for eight years (one-half of the members retiring every four years), while the House of Representatives has 150 members, elected by universal adult suffrage for four years. Executive power is vested in the King, who governs with the assistance of an appointed Cabinet, responsible to the Assembly. There are 12 administrative provinces.

REGIONAL AND INTERNATIONAL CO-OPERATION

Jordan was a founder member of the League of Arab States (the Arab League, see p. 359), and also participates in the Council of Arab Economic Unity (see p. 366) and the Arab Monetary Fund (see p. 366).

Jordan became a member of the UN in 1955, and joined the World Trade Organization (WTO, see p. 431) in 2000. The country is also a member of the Organization of Islamic Cooperation (OIC, see p. 401).

ECONOMIC AFFAIRS

In 2013, according to estimates by the World Bank, Jordan's gross national income (GNI), measured at average 2011–13 prices, was US $31,973m., equivalent to $4,950 per head (or $11,660 per head on an international purchasing-power parity basis). During 2004–13, it was estimated, the population increased at an average annual rate of 2.2%, while Jordan's gross domestic product (GDP) per head increased, in real terms, by an average of 2.9% per year. Overall GDP increased, in real terms, at an average annual rate of 5.2% in 2004–13; According to preliminary official figures, growth of 2.8% was recorded in 2013.

Agriculture (including hunting, forestry and fishing) contributed about 3.2% of Jordan's GDP in 2013, according to preliminary figures, and accounted for about 5.1% of the country's economically active population at mid-2015, according to FAO estimates. The principal cash crops are tomatoes, aubergines (eggplants), and olives production is also important; vegetable products accounted for 9.0% of export earnings in 2013. In December 2013 Jordan, Israel and the Palestinian (National) Authority signed a water-sharing agreement whereby a 180-km pipeline would be constructed to transfer water from a desalination plant on the Gulf of Aqaba, which extends north from the Red Sea, to the Dead Sea, thereby reversing the latter's rapid loss of water supply as well as providing drinking water for the three territories. According to the World Bank, the sector's GDP increased at an average annual rate of 3.5% during 2004–13. According to preliminary official figures, GDP decreased by an estimated 9.4% in 2012 and further decreased by 3.5% in 2013.

Industry (including mining, manufacturing, construction and power) provided 28.1% of GDP in 2013, according to preliminary figures; about 25.4% of the country's active labour force were employed in the sector in 2012. According to the World Bank, during 2004–13 industrial GDP increased by an average of 4.6% per year. According to preliminary official figures, the sector's GDP increased by 2.3% in 2013.

Mining and quarrying contributed 2.5% of GDP in 2013, according to preliminary figures, and accounted for about 0.8% of the employed labour force in 2012. Mineral exports—of which phosphates and potash were the principal components—accounted for around 5.8% of total export earnings in 2013. In 2009 parliamentary approval was granted for an agreement with Royal Dutch Shell of the Netherlands/United Kingdom to develop the kingdom's large reserves of oil-bearing shale. A concession agreement was signed with the Estonian company Eesti Energia in 2010, and a similar agreement with the Saudi Arabian Corporation for Oil Shale was approved by the Government in 2013. Meanwhile, the authorities concluded a deal with British Petroleum in October 2009 encompassing exploration rights and production at the Risha gasfield, near the border with Iraq. Preliminary official figures suggested that mining GDP decreased by an average rate of 0.6% per year during 2003–12;

the sector's GDP decreased by 17.1% in 2012 and again by 11.0% in 2013.

Manufacturing provided 18.4% of GDP in 2013, according to preliminary figures, and engaged 18.4% of the employed labour force in 2012. The most important branches of manufacturing, measured by gross value of output, are food, beverages and tobacco, pharmaceutical and other chemical products, non-metallic mineral products, wearing apparel, refined petroleum products and metal products. According to the World Bank, manufacturing GDP increased by an average of 5.0% per year in 2004–13. According to preliminary official figures, the sector recorded growth of 1.9% in 2013.

The construction sector contributed 4.8% of GDP in 2013, according to preliminary figures; about 4.7% of the country's active labour force were employed in the sector in 2012. According to preliminary official figures, during 2003–12 construction GDP increased by an average of 5.4% per year; the sector's GDP decreased by 0.9% in 2012, but increased by 8.7% in 2013.

Energy has traditionally been derived principally from imported petroleum, but attempts are being made to develop alternative sources of power, including wind, solar and nuclear power. In 2003 petroleum provided 90.0% of total electricity production, but by 2009 this had declined to just 8.5%, increasing again to 72.5% in 2011; conversely, natural gas accounted for only 9.3% of total electricity production in 2003, but this increased to 91.0% in 2009, and decreased to 27.0% in 2011. This renewed reliance on petroleum as a source of power was largely attributed to the loss of supply from Egypt owing to increased political instability in that country. Imports of mineral products comprised 25.9% of the total value of imports in 2013. Following the discovery of substantial reserves of uranium, the Government has instigated plans for the development of a nuclear power industry; several civil nuclear co-operation accords have been signed with other countries since 2008. In February 2012 the Jordan Atomic Energy Commission (JAEC) revealed that al-Mafraq governorate was its preferred location for the construction of the country's first nuclear power plant. In October 2013 the JAEC awarded a contract for the construction of two reactors to the Russian firm Rosatom; the plant was expected to begin production in 2021. In addition to boosting Jordan's domestic energy capacity, it is envisaged that the nuclear programme will facilitate the implementation of much-needed water desalination projects.

Services accounted for some 68.7% of Jordan's GDP in 2013, according to preliminary figures, and engaged an estimated 74.6% of the employed labour force in 2012. The tourism industry has suffered considerably since 2011 as a result of the ongoing political instability in neighbouring countries; the number of tourist arrivals declined from 6.8m. in 2011 to 6.3m. in 2012 and, according to preliminary figures, to just 5.4m. in 2013. During 2004–13, according to the World Bank, the GDP of the sector increased by an average of 5.0% per year. According to preliminary official figures, sectoral growth increased by 3.6% in 2013.

In 2013 Jordan recorded a visible merchandise trade deficit of US $11,469.8m., and there was a deficit of $3,358.8m. on the current account of the balance of payments. In 2013 Saudi Arabia was the main source of imports (with 18.2% of the total); other major suppliers were the People's Republic of China, the USA and India. In that year Iraq was the principal market for exports (with 17.6% of the total); other significant purchasers were the USA, Saudi Arabia and India. The principal exports in 2013 were chemicals and related products, textiles, vegetable products, machinery and mechanical appliances, mineral products, base metals and articles, and prepared foodstuffs, beverages, spirits and tobacco products while the principal imports were mineral fuels, oils and distillation products, machinery and mechanical appliances, base metals and articles, chemicals and related products, vegetable products, textiles, vehicles, aircraft and transport equipment, and prepared foodstuffs, beverages, spirits and tobacco products.

In 2014, according to budgeted official figures, a budget deficit of JD 1,547.1m. was envisaged (including external aid payments and revenues from the sale of land). Jordan's general government gross debt was JD 20,603m. in 2013, equivalent to 85.8% of GDP. Jordan's external debt totalled US $18,632m. at the end of 2012, of which $6,302m. was public and publicly guaranteed debt. In that year, the cost of servicing long-term public and publicly guaranteed debt and repayments to the IMF was equivalent to 6.9% of the value of exports of goods, services and income (excluding workers' remittances). According to official figures, the annual rate of inflation averaged 5.3% in

2006–13; consumer prices increased by an average of 5.6% in 2013. In the same year some 12.6% of the economically active population was unemployed.

By early 2015 the National Agenda, published by the Government in January 2006, had still not been effectively implemented by the authorities. This was an ambitious 10-year plan to improve the quality and effectiveness of public administration through the reduction of poverty and unemployment (by creating 600,000 jobs) and the achievement of annual real GDP growth of 7.2%. Austerity measures, including the withdrawal of some fuel subsidies, were introduced in 2012 following a worsening of the country's fiscal situation. The profound instability arising from anti-government uprisings in many countries across the region in the previous year had led to a decline in exports, foreign direct investment, tourism receipts and remittances from abroad, as well as higher energy costs. Moreover, the rapid influx of refugees fleeing the conflict in neighbouring Syria from 2012 added considerably to the burden on Jordan's state finances. In August 2013 the IMF agreed a 36-month stand-by arrangement—worth an estimated US $2,000m.—with the Government to assist it in achieving its fiscal and growth targets under the national economic programme for 2012–15. The Government projected GDP

growth to reach 3.1% in 2014 and 3.8% in 2015, aided by the substantially reduced cost of importing oil. However, in March 2014 the IMF had assessed that Jordan required an annual growth rate of at least 7% in order to create a sufficient number of jobs for the country's increasing population and to reduce poverty. Inflation declined to 2.4% at the end of that year, from around 6% at the end of 2013. The fiscal deficit was estimated at around 8% by the end of 2014, despite the Government announcing its intention to reduce it by 2013. However, foreign exchange reserves increased from 2013, largely owing to substantial inflows of aid from the Gulf Co-operation Council and the IMF arrangement.

PUBLIC HOLIDAYS

2016: 1 May (Labour Day), 4 May* (Leilat al-Meiraj, Ascension of Muhammad), 25 May (Independence Day), 6 July* (Id al-Fitr, end of Ramadan), 11 September* (Id al-Adha, Feast of the Sacrifice), 2 October* (Muharram, Islamic New Year), 11 December* (Mouloud, Birth of Muhammad).

*These holidays are dependent on the Islamic lunar calendar and may vary by one or two days from the dates given.

Statistical Survey

Source: Department of Statistics, POB 2015, Amman 11181; tel. (6) 5300700; fax (6) 5300710; e-mail stat@dos.gov.jo; internet www.dos.gov.jo.

Area and Population

AREA, POPULATION AND DENSITY

Area (sq km)	88,794*
Population (census results)	
10 December 1994	4,139,458
1 October 2004	
Males	2,620,287
Females	2,477,352
Total	5,103,639
Population (official estimates at 31 December)†	
2011	6,249,000
2012	6,388,000
2013	6,530,000
Density (per sq km) at 31 December 2013	73.5

* 34,284 sq miles.

† Figures exclude the refugee population, which, according to UNHCR estimates, totalled almost 650,000 at the end of 2013 (including more than 50,000 from Iraq and almost 600,000 from Syria).

POPULATION BY AGE AND SEX
(estimated population at 31 December 2012)

	Males	Females	Total
0–14 years	1,223,055	1,159,270	2,382,325
15–64 years	1,962,900	1,831,475	3,794,375
65 years and over	107,045	104,255	211,300
Total	3,293,000	3,095,000	6,388,000

Note: Figures are rounded to nearest five persons.

GOVERNORATES
(estimated population at 31 December 2012)

	Area (sq km)	Population	Density (per sq km)
Amman	7,579	2,473,400	326.3
Irbid	1,572	1,137,100	723.3
Al-Zarqa (Zarqa)	4,761	951,800	199.9
Al-Balqa	1,120	428,000	382.1
Al-Mafraq	26,551	300,300	11.3
Al-Karak (Kerak)	3,495	249,100	71.3
Jarash (Jerash)	410	191,700	467.6
Madaba	940	159,700	169.9
Ajloun	420	146,900	349.8
Al-Aqabah (Aqaba)	6,905	139,200	20.2
Ma'an	32,832	121,400	3.7
Al-Tafilah	2,209	89,400	40.5
Total	88,794	6,388,000	71.9

Note: Population figures are rounded to nearest 100 persons.

PRINCIPAL TOWNS
(population at 2004 census)

Amman (capital) .	1,036,330		Wadi al-Sir . . .	122,032
			Tila' al-Ali (Tla' El-	
Al-Zarqa (Zarqa) .	395,227		Ali)	113,197
			Khuraybat as-Suq	
Irbid	250,645		(Khraibet Essoq) .	84,975
Al-Rusayfah				
(Russeifa) .	227,735		Al-Aqabah (Aqaba) .	80,059
Al-Quwaysimah .	135,500			

Mid-2014 (incl. suburbs, UN estimate): Amman 1,147,700 (Source: UN, *World Urbanization Prospects: The 2014 Revision*).

BIRTHS, MARRIAGES AND DEATHS*

	Registered live births		Registered marriages		Registered deaths	
	Number	Rate (per 1,000)	Number	Rate (per 1,000)	Number	Rate (per 1,000)
2005 . .	152,276	27.8	56,418	10.3	17,883	3.3
2006 . .	162,972	29.1	59,335	10.6	20,397	3.6
2007 . .	185,011	32.3	60,548	10.6	20,924	3.7
2008 . .	181,328	31.0	60,922	10.4	19,403	3.3
2009 . .	179,872	30.1	63,389	10.6	20,251	3.4
2010 . .	183,948	30.1	62,107	10.2	21,550	3.5
2011 . .	178,435	28.6	64,665	10.3	21,730	3.5
2012 . .	177,695	28.1	70,621	11.2	22,785	3.6

* Data are tabulated by year of registration rather than by year of occurrence. Registration of births and marriages is reported to be complete, but death registration is incomplete. Figures exclude foreigners, but include registered Palestinian refugees.

Life expectancy (years at birth): 73.7 (males 72.1; females 75.4) in 2012 (Source: World Bank, World Development Indicators database).

EMPLOYMENT
(economic survey at October, public and private sectors, excl. armed forces)

	2010	2011	2012
Mining and quarrying	8,520	8,600	8,731
Manufacturing	188,015	186,517	191,386
Electricity, gas and water . . .	15,878	14,255	15,745
Construction	46,105	50,130	48,799
Wholesale and retail trade; repair of motor vehicles and motorcycles and personal and household goods	210,318	214,079	219,091
Hotels and restaurants . .	40,908	44,917	46,856
Transport, storage and communications	36,354	38,069	39,372
Financial intermediation . . .	29,041	31,282	31,450
Real estate, renting and business activities	46,641	49,464	53,980
Public administration and compulsory social security . .	104,431	107,142	106,163
Education	170,384	181,940	189,287
Health and social work . .	57,879	59,647	61,535
Other community, social and personal service activities . .	23,241	26,055	28,844
Total employed	977,714	1,012,096	1,041,239
Males	752,121	779,466	796,123
Females	225,593	232,630	245,116

Note: Figures include foreign nationals employed in Jordan, numbering 121,726 in 2010, 111,721 in 2011 and 109,007 in 2012. Figures are assumed to exclude data for those engaged in agriculture and fishing—according to FAO estimates some 116,000 of a total economically active population of 2,256,000 were engaged in the sector at mid-2015.

Health and Welfare

KEY INDICATORS

Total fertility rate (children per woman, 2012)	3.3
Under-5 mortality rate (per 1,000 live births, 2012) . . .	19
HIV/AIDS (% of persons aged 15–49, 2007)	<0.2
Physicians (per 1,000 head, 2010)	2.6
Hospital beds (per 1,000 head, 2010)	1.8
Health expenditure (2011): US $ per head (PPP)	494
Health expenditure (2011): % of GDP	8.8
Health expenditure (2011): Public (% of total)	65.5
Access to water (% of persons, 2012)	96
Access to sanitation (% of persons, 2012)	98
Total carbon dioxide emissions ('000 metric tons, 2010) . .	20,821.2
Carbon dioxide emissions per head (metric tons, 2010) . .	3.4
Human Development Index (2013): ranking	77
Human Development Index (2013): value	0.745

For sources and definitions, see explanatory note on p. vi.

Agriculture

PRINCIPAL CROPS
('000 metric tons)

	2011	2012	2013
Wheat	19.8	19.2	29.5
Barley	29.3	32.1	40.9
Maize	16.5	14.4	14.2
Potatoes	216.5	141.6	103.2
Olives	131.8	155.6	128.2
Cabbages and other brassicas .	22.1	39.5	29.0
Lettuce and chicory	40.4	39.5	63.6
Tomatoes	777.8	616.4	869.1
Cauliflowers and broccoli . .	62.5	35.7	68.4
Pumpkins, squash and gourds .	93.1	69.0	87.1
Cucumbers and gherkins . .	227.6	155.9	172.3
Aubergines (Eggplants) . .	117.0	177.7	109.4
Chillies and peppers, green . .	63.7	70.5	60.9
Onions and shallots, green . .	1.1	3.0	2.9*
Onions, dry	40.8	26.5	13.0
Beans, green	8.5	11.6	14.0
Okra	8.6	5.9	8.8
Watermelons	121.8	108.7	87.7
Cantaloupes and other melons .	38.6	42.0	48.7
Bananas	48.3	38.9	42.0
Grapefruit and pomelos . .	7.6	8.1	6.8
Oranges	38.7	40.9	40.0
Tangerines, mandarins, clementines and satsumas . .	34.1	35.8	22.7
Lemons and limes	26.4	26.5	26.8
Apples	39.7	36.4	40.6
Peaches and nectarines . .	26.9	39.8	42.0
Grapes	38.4	35.7	35.2

* FAO estimate.

Aggregate production ('000 metric tons, may include official, semi-official or estimated data): Total cereals 83.0 in 2011, 84.0 in 2012, 103.1 in 2013; Total roots and tubers 216.5 in 2011, 141.6 in 2012, 103.2 in 2013; Total vegetables (incl. melons) 1,749.6 in 2011, 1,518.3 in 2012, 1,765.3 in 2013; Total fruits (excl. melons) 319.7 in 2011, 321.5 in 2012, 320.6 in 2013.

Source: FAO.

LIVESTOCK
('000 head, year ending September)

	2011	2012	2013*
Horses	2	2	2
Asses*	9	9	9
Mules*	1.2	1.2	1.2
Cattle	67.6	68.5	69.0
Camels	13	13*	14
Sheep	2,264.6	2,234.0	2,250.0
Goats	752.2	792.0	795.0
Chickens*	26,000	26,500	27,000

* FAO estimate(s).

Source: FAO.

LIVESTOCK PRODUCTS
('000 metric tons)

	2011	2012	2013
Cattle meat	17.8	19.6	19.8*
Sheep meat	12.1	17.6	18.0*
Goat meat	5.1	7.1	7.2*
Chicken meat	190.5	190.3	190.6*
Cows' milk	238.6	240.7	236.8
Sheep's milk	57.9	59.8	62.6†
Goats' milk	10.5	9.9	7.7†
Hen eggs	69.3	43.3	41.8
Wool, greasy*	2.8	2.9	2.9

* FAO estimate(s).
† Unofficial figure.

Source: FAO.

Forestry

ROUNDWOOD REMOVALS
('000 cu m, excluding bark, FAO estimates)

	2011	2012	2013
Industrial wood	4	4	4
Fuel wood	310	318	326
Total	314	322	330

Source: FAO.

Fishing

(metric tons, live weight)

	2010	2011	2012*
Capture	486	500	500
Freshwater fishes	350	350	350
Tunas	93	102	102
Aquaculture (Tilapias) . . .	541	575	580
Common carp	259	404	400
Total catch	1,027	1,075	1,080

* FAO estimates.

Source: FAO.

Mining

('000 metric tons unless otherwise indicated)

	2010	2011	2012
Crude petroleum ('000 barrels) .	8.9	7.2	8.8
Phosphate rock	6,529	7,594	6,383
Potash salts*	2,141	2,259	1,824
Bromine	329	148	136
Gypsum	292	255	857

* Figures refer to the K$_2$O content.

Source: US Geological Survey.

Industry

SELECTED PRODUCTS
(42-gallon barrels unless otherwise indicated)

	2010	2011	2012
Asphalt	914	648	n.a.
Phosphatic fertilizers ('000 metric tons)	812	824	640
Cement ('000 metric tons) . .	3,043	2,816	5,588
Liquefied petroleum gas . .	1,971	1,971	2,008
Motor spirit (petrol) . . .	5,986	5,950	6,022
Jet fuel and kerosene . . .	4,526	4,453	4,453
Distillate fuel oils	11,388	11,498	11,461
Electric energy (million kWh) .	14,777	14,647	16,595

Sources: mainly US Geological Survey.

Finance

CURRENCY AND EXCHANGE RATES

Monetary Units
1,000 fils = 1 Jordanian dinar (JD).

Sterling, Dollar and Euro Equivalents (31 December 2014)
£1 sterling = JD 1.108;
US $1 = 710 fils;
€1 = JD 0.862;
JD 10 = £9.02 = $14.08 = €11.61.

Exchange Rate: An official mid-point rate of US $1 = 709 fils (JD1 = $1.4104) has been maintained since October 1995.

BUDGET
(JD million)*

Revenue†	2012	2013	2014‡
Taxation	3,351.4	3,652.4	4,077.0
Taxes on income and profits .	688.3	681.9	765.0
Corporations	556.5	550.0	612.8
Individuals	64.4	59.8	72.3
Taxes on domestic transactions	2,274.7	2,532.9	2,840.0
General sales tax	2,274.7	2,532.9	2,840.0
Taxes on foreign trade . . .	285.6	324.9	340.0
Other revenue	1,351.2	1,445.3	1,730.0
Fees	682.4	792.2	977.3
Interest and profits	304.5	264.2	285.2
Repayment	28.6	24.2	42.0
Pensions	24.3	22.1	24.0
Total	4,726.9	5,119.8	5,831.0

Expenditure	2012	2013	2014‡
Current	6,202.8	6,056.1	6,827.8
Wages and salaries	1,109.0	1,183.8	1,283.4
Purchases of goods and services	235.5	270.5	332.4
Interest payments	582.9	736.5	1,100.0
Domestic	483.1	634.7	885.0
Foreign	99.9	101.8	215.0
Food and oil subsidies . . .	892.7	260.2	225.0
Pensions	982.4	1,046.5	1,115.0
Defence and security	1,756.8	1,778.7	1,908.5
Capital	675.4	1,021.0	1,268.6
Total	6,878.2	7,077.1	8,096.4

* Figures represent a consolidation of the Current, Capital and Development Plan Budgets of the central Government. The data exclude the operations of the Health Security Fund and of other government agencies with individual budgets.
† Excluding foreign grants received (JD million): 401.7 in 2012; 639.1 in 2013; 718.3 in 2014 (budget figure).
‡ Budget figures.

Source: Ministry of Finance, Amman.

INTERNATIONAL RESERVES
(US $ million at 31 December)

	2011	2012	2013
Gold (national valuation) . .	637.7	739.9	600.3
IMF special drawing rights . .	224.8	220.3	213.5
Reserve position in the IMF . .	0.5	0.5	0.5
Foreign exchange	11,241.9	7,868.7	13,009.7
Total	12,105.0	8,829.4	13,824.1

Source: IMF, *International Financial Statistics*.

MONEY SUPPLY
(JD million at 31 December)

	2011	2012	2013
Currency outside banks . . .	3,019.3	3,215.0	3,606.6
Demand deposits at commercial banks	4,206.3	3,934.5	4,711.3
Total money (incl. others) . .	7,228.0	7,152.1	8,320.5

Source: IMF, *International Financial Statistics*.

COST OF LIVING
(Consumer Price Index; base: 2006 = 100)

	2011	2012	2013
Food (incl. beverages) . . .	143.4	150.0	155.6
Clothing (incl. footwear) . . .	130.5	136.7	144.5
Housing	123.1	127.4	140.0
All items (incl. others) . . .	130.0	136.0	143.6

NATIONAL ACCOUNTS
(JD million at current prices)

Expenditure on the Gross Domestic Product

	2011	2012	2013
Government final consumption expenditure	3,916.2	4,192.5	4,402.1
Private final consumption expenditure	17,597.2	18,837.8	19,292.5
Changes in stocks	322.3	346.4	367.5
Gross fixed capital formation . .	4,430.6	4,743.1	5,032.7
Total domestic expenditure .	26,266.3	28,119.8	29,094.8
Exports of goods and services . .	9,334.1	10,158.3	10,857.5
Less Imports of goods and services	15,123.8	16,312.6	16,664.9
Statistical discrepancy . . .	—	—	564.2
GDP in purchasers' values .	20,476.6	21,965.5	23,851.6

Source: UN National Accounts Main Aggregates Database.

GDP in constant 1994 prices (preliminary estimates): 10,243.8 in 2011; 10,515.3 in 2012; 10,812.8 in 2013.

Gross Domestic Product by Economic Activity
(preliminary estimates)

	2011	2012	2013
Agriculture, hunting, forestry and fishing	598.3	604.5	713.7
Mining and quarrying	803.5	723.5	563.9
Manufacturing	3,485.3	3,633.4	4,074.4
Electricity and water	417.5	482.8	531.0
Construction	888.0	961.7	1,060.6
Wholesale and retail trade, restaurants and hotels . . .	1,845.3	2,055.8	2,279.9
Transport, storage and communications	2,426.1	2,637.4	2,889.2
Finance, insurance, real estate and business services	3,483.9	3,838.4	4,205.2
Public administration, defence, and social security	4,121.3	4,485.6	4,831.6
Other services	854.3	951.8	1,044.7
Sub-total	18,923.5	20,375.0	22,194.2
Less Imputed bank service charge.	935.8	1,076.9	1,212.8
GDP in basic prices	17,987.7	19,298.2	20,981.4
Taxes on products (net) . . .	2,488.9	2,667.3	2,870.2
GDP in purchasers' values .	20,476.6	21,965.5	23,851.6

BALANCE OF PAYMENTS
(US $ million)

	2011	2012	2013
Exports of goods	8,006.3	7,886.6	7,910.8
Imports of goods	−16,825.6	−18,430.9	−19,380.7
Balance on goods	−8,819.3	−10,544.3	−11,469.8
Exports of services	5,737.5	6,420.8	6,357.7
Imports of services	−4,475.5	−4,544.4	−4,575.1
Balance on goods and services	−7,557.4	−8,667.7	−9,687.2
Primary income received . .	710.4	689.5	793.5
Primary income paid . . .	−974.9	−1,078.1	−1,132.3
Balance on goods, services and primary income	−7,821.8	−9,056.3	−10,026.0
Secondary income received . .	5,365.5	4,977.6	7,149.3
Secondary income paid . . .	−499.7	−632.7	−482.1

—*continued*	2011	2012	2013
Current balance	−2,956.0	−4,711.4	−3,358.8
Capital account (net)	—	2.5	2.4
Direct investment assets . . .	−30.8	−5.4	−15.7
Direct investment liabilities . .	1,473.5	1,497.3	1,798.5
Portfolio investment assets . .	282.5	221.8	−19.6
Portfolio investment liabilities .	11.1	69.2	1,616.2
Other investment assets . .	−496.5	−1,006.6	861.8
Other investment liabilities . .	390.0	766.9	3,233.1
Net errors and omissions . . .	−326.4	−488.0	466.5
Reserves and related items .	−1,652.6	−3,653.7	4,584.4

Source: IMF, *International Financial Statistics*.

External Trade

PRINCIPAL COMMODITIES
(distribution by HS, JD million)

Imports c.i.f.	2011	2012	2013
Live animals and animal products	496.1	599.0	677.7
Vegetable products	986.2	1,025.0	1,087.9
Cereals	604.5	621.7	624.9
Prepared foodstuffs; beverages, spirits and vinegar; tobacco and manufactured tobacco substitutes	738.5	815.8	848.9
Mineral products	3,979.3	4,571.2	4,053.0
Mineral fuels, oils, distillation products, etc.	3,921.4	4,538.1	4,022.3
Crude petroleum oils . .	1,856.3	1,958.2	1,828.2
Non-crude petroleum oils . .	1,588.5	2,278.3	1,867.4
Petroleum gases	253.0	301.7	326.6
Chemicals and related products	1,049.7	1,089.1	1,111.0
Plastics, rubbers, and articles thereof	536.5	617.7	658.5
Plastics and articles thereof . .	465.1	528.3	573.9
Textiles and textile articles .	701.3	758.0	901.6
Base metals and articles thereof	1,037.9	1,093.4	1,313.2
Iron and steel	405.0	552.0	527.0
Machinery and mechanical appliances	1,624.0	1,565.9	1,873.2
Machinery, boilers, etc. . . .	997.8	973.3	956.4
Electrical, electronic equipment .	626.2	592.6	916.8
Vehicles, aircraft, vessels and associated transport equipment	795.2	850.8	964.4
Vehicles other than railway, tramway	708.1	748.4	896.0
Motor cars and other passenger vehicles	446.6	461.8	n.a.
Total (incl. others)	13,440.2	14,733.7	15,668.0

Exports f.o.b.	2011	2012	2013
Live animals and animal products	168.8	158.8	221.1
Vegetable products	455.4	488.8	506.8
Edible vegetables, roots and tubers	340.3	334.5	338.0
Prepared foodstuffs; beverages, spirits and vinegar; tobacco and manufactured tobacco substitutes	257.1	272.7	313.9
Mineral products	512.1	470.3	326.2
Salt, sulphur, earth, stone, plaster, lime and cement	496.8	453.1	309.7
Natural calcium and aluminium phosphates, phosphatic chalk.	446.1	426.0	n.a.
Chemicals and related products	1,765.4	1,679.7	1,711.9
Inorganic chemicals	252.5	299.9	211.6
Pharmaceutical products . . .	414.3	447.5	511.8
Medicaments put in doses . .	321.6	306.2	n.a.
Fertilizers	889.9	723.0	n.a.
Nitrogenous mineral or chemical fertilizers	256.1	204.1	n.a.
Potassic mineral or chemical fertilizers	600.9	483.8	n.a.
Plastics, rubbers, and articles thereof	171.9	229.1	252.7
Plastics and articles thereof . .	166.0	219.3	246.7
Textiles and textile articles .	764.4	813.8	896.0
Articles of apparel and clothing accessories, knitted or crocheted	656.1	693.9	775.6
Pearls; precious or semi-precious stones; precious metals	273.0	182.3	88.9
Gold, unwrought, semi-manufactured or powdered . .	186.7	101.4	n.a.
Base metals and articles thereof	363.2	287.3	321.4
Machinery and mechanical appliances	451.1	409.0	404.6
Machinery, boilers, etc. . . .	203.4	185.6	190.0
Electrical, electronic equipment .	247.7	223.4	214.6
Vehicles, aircraft, vessels and associated transport equipment	123.8	113.8	145.2
Total (incl. others)	5,684.6	5,599.5	5,618.0

PRINCIPAL TRADING PARTNERS
(countries of consignment, JD million)

Imports c.i.f.	2011	2012	2013
Argentina	173.7	233.3	215.4
Australia	118.8	147.2	171.1
Belgium	91.2	78.6	276.8
Brazil	147.3	180.4	245.7
China, People's Republic . . .	1,317.4	1,416.4	1,620.1
Egypt	535.0	560.5	500.2
Finland	56.3	38.1	221.9
France	264.2	265.7	270.8
Germany	607.5	575.2	598.1
India	360.2	506.8	789.9
Iraq	220.0	230.8	252.9
Italy	688.5	658.6	735.9
Japan	259.0	277.5	341.6
Korea, Republic	435.9	406.3	257.8
Romania	136.3	119.1	206.3
Russia	513.1	450.3	235.4
Saudi Arabia	2,968.7	3,469.7	2,850.4

Imports c.i.f.—*continued*	2011	2012	2013
Spain	163.5	137.0	164.8
Switzerland	118.6	110.7	366.8
Syria	268.4	171.3	184.4
Taiwan	178.5	194.4	257.8
Turkey	393.5	568.9	538.5
Ukraine	146.2	356.8	230.3
United Arab Emirates	504.9	418.8	520.2
United Kingdom	212.9	183.2	195.6
USA	861.4	977.5	969.3
Total (incl. others)	13,440.2	14,733.7	15,668.0

Exports f.o.b.	2011	2012	2013
Algeria	90.1	93.5	99.1
China, People's Republic . . .	144.5	134.1	75.1
Egypt	89.2	93.6	94.8
Ethiopia	69.0	22.5	32.3
India	649.0	515.3	352.0
Indonesia	157.1	192.7	161.7
Iraq	862.2	868.3	987.1
Israel	80.5	89.0	80.2
Kuwait	102.0	74.9	98.6
Lebanon	238.3	208.6	109.4
Malaysia	80.0	46.7	67.4
Qatar	66.3	82.8	95.1
Saudi Arabia	482.9	547.9	684.3
Sudan	59.4	45.9	58.6
Switzerland	57.2	21.0	7.3
Syria	203.6	156.1	108.2
Turkey	69.7	93.9	73.3
United Arab Emirates	205.6	224.0	225.3
USA	738.7	799.0	856.1
Total (incl. others)	5,684.6	5,599.5	5,618.0

Transport

RAILWAYS
(traffic, million)

	2009	2010	2012*
Passenger-km	0.9	1.3	1.0
Freight ton-km	439	344	216

* Data for 2011 were not available.

Source: IRF, *World Road Statistics*.

ROAD TRAFFIC
(motor vehicles in use at 31 December)

	2008	2009	2010
Passenger cars	601,312	673,125	742,149
Buses	17,521	18,143	18,902
Lorries and vans	240,869	227,582	236,526
Motorcycles	3,845	3,489	4,079

2012 (motor vehicles in use at 31 December): Passenger cars 860,352; Buses 19,953; Lorries and vans 249,769; Motorcycles 5,847; *Total* 1,135,921.

Source: IRF, *World Road Statistics*.

SHIPPING

Flag Registered Fleet
(at 31 December)

	2012	2013	2014
Number of vessels	23	27	29
Displacement ('000 grt) . . .	79.8	68.2	102.3

Source: Lloyd's List Intelligence (www.lloydslistintelligence.com).

International Seaborne Freight Traffic
('000 metric tons)

	2010	2011	2012
Goods loaded	9,631	10,862	9,215
Goods unloaded	8,796	10,208	11,944

CIVIL AVIATION
(traffic on scheduled services)

	2010	2011
Kilometres flown (million)	69	72
Passengers carried ('000)	2,972	3,155
Passenger-km (million)	7,805	8,316
Total ton-km (million)	908	950

Source: UN, *Statistical Yearbook*.

2013 ('000): Passengers carried 3,471 (Source: World Bank, World Development Indicators database).

Tourism

ARRIVALS BY NATIONALITY
('000)*

	2011	2012	2013†
Egypt	326.5	353.8	263.0
Iraq	292.1	373.1	325.3
Israel	211.9	203.7	184.6
Lebanon	108.6	65.9	58.8
Palestinian Territories . . .	441.6	470.2	474.3
Saudi Arabia	1,074.2	1,144.1	1,079.4
Syria	1,903.7	1,190.2	548.7
Turkey	156.0	46.1	20.0
USA	156.6	159.4	150.8
Total (incl. others)	6,812.4	6,314.3	5,388.9

* Including pilgrims and excursionists (same-day visitors).
† Preliminary.

Source: Ministry of Tourism and Antiquities, Amman.

Tourism receipts (US$ million, excl. passenger transport): 3,425 in 2011; 4,061 in 2012; 4,117 in 2013 (provisional) (Source: World Tourism Organisation).

Communications Media

	2011	2012	2013
Telephones ('000 main lines in use)	465.4	434.4	378.4
Mobile cellular telephones ('000 subscribers)	7,482.6	8,984.3	10,314.0
Internet subscribers ('000) . .	208.1	n.a.	n.a.
Broadband subscribers ('000) . .	199.9	193.6	205.5

Source: International Telecommunication Union.

Education

(2011/12 unless otherwise indicated)

	Schools	Teachers	Pupils
Pre-primary	1,248*	6,111†	110,165
Primary	2,877*	39,441‡	849,390
Secondary: general	1,002*	30,426‡	694,344†
Secondary: vocational	40*	2,759§	25,076†
Higher	22*	10,024‖	306,630
of which universities&para .	20	3,982	89,010

* 2003/04 figure.
† 2010/11 figure.
‡ 2002/03 figure.
§ 2007/08 figure.
‖ 2009/10 figure.
&para 1996/97 figures.
Source: partly UNESCO Institute for Statistics.

Pupil-teacher ratio (primary education, UNESCO estimate): 19.9 in 2002/03 (Source: UNESCO Institute for Statistics).

Adult literacy rate (UNESCO estimates): 97.9% (males 98.4%; females 97.4%) in 2012 (Source: UNESCO Institute for Statistics).

Directory

The Government

HEAD OF STATE

King: King ABDULLAH IBN AL-HUSSEIN (succeeded to the throne on 7 February 1999).

CABINET
(April 2015)

Prime Minister and Minister of Defence: ABDULLAH ENSOUR.
Deputy Prime Minister and Minister of Education: Dr MUHAMMAD THNEIBAT.
Deputy Prime Minister and Minister of Foreign and Expatriates Affairs: NASSER JUDEH.
Minister of the Interior: HUSSEIN HAZAA MAJALI.
Minister of Water and Irrigation: Dr HAZEM AL-NASSER.
Minister of Agriculture: Dr AKIF AL-ZU'BI.
Minister of the Environment: TAHER AL-SHAKHSHIR.
Minister of Finance: Dr UMAYYA TOUQAN.
Minister of Public Sector Development: Dr KHLEIF AL-KHAWALDEH.
Minister of Planning and International Co-operation: IMAD FAKHOURI.
Minister of Tourism and Antiquities: NAYEF AL-FAYEZ.
Minister of Labour: NIDAL KATAMINE.

Minister of State for Prime Ministry Affairs: Dr AHMAD ZEYADAT.
Minister of Municipal Affairs: WALID AL-MASRI.
Minister of State for Media Affairs and Communications: Dr MUHAMMAD HUSSEIN MOMANI.
Minister of Social Development: REEM MAMDOUH ABU HASSAN.
Minister of Energy and Mineral Resources: IBRAHIM SAIF.
Minister of Public Works and Housing: SAMI HALASEH.
Minister of Justice: Dr BASSAM SAMIR AL-TALHOUNI.
Minister of Health: Dr ALI AL-NAHLEH HIASAT.
Minister of State: SALAMEH AL-NEIMAT.
Minister of Awqaf (Religious Endowments) and Islamic Affairs: Dr HAYEL ABD AL-HAFIZ DAWOOD.
Minister of Political and Parliamentary Affairs: KHALID AL-KALALDEH.
Minister of Culture: Dr LANA MAMKEGH.
Minister of Transport: Dr LINA SHABIB.
Minister of Industry, Trade and Supply: MAHA ALI.
Minister of Higher Education and Scientific Research: Dr LABIB KHADRA.
Minister of Information and Communications Technology: MAJD SHWEIKEH.
Note: The Head of Intelligence and the Governor of the Central Bank also have full ministerial status.

MINISTRIES

The Prime Ministry of Jordan: POB 80, Amman 11180; tel. (6) 4641211; fax (6) 4642520; e-mail info@pm.gov.jo; internet www.pm.gov.jo.

Ministry of Agriculture: POB 2099, Amman; tel. (6) 5686151; fax (6) 5686310; e-mail moa.mail@moa.gov.jo; internet www.moa.gov.jo.

Ministry of Awqaf (Religious Endowments) and Islamic Affairs: POB 659, Amman; tel. (6) 5666141; fax (6) 5602254; e-mail awqaf@awqaf.gov.jo; internet www.awqaf.gov.jo.

Ministry of Culture: POB 6140, Amman; tel. (6) 5696218; fax (6) 5691640; e-mail info@culture.gov.jo; internet www.culture.gov.jo.

Ministry of Defence: POB 80, Amman; tel. (6) 4641211; fax (6) 4642520; e-mail info@jaf.mil.jo; internet www.jaf.mil.jo.

Ministry of Education: POB 1646, Amman 11118; tel. (6) 5607331; fax (6) 5666019; e-mail moe@moe.gov.jo; internet www.moe.gov.jo.

Ministry of Energy and Mineral Resources: POB 2310, Amman; tel. (6) 5803060; fax (6) 5865714; e-mail memr@memr.gov.jo; internet www.memr.gov.jo.

Ministry of the Environment: Amman; tel. (6) 5560113; fax (6) 5560288; e-mail info@moenv.gov.jo; internet www.moenv.gov.jo.

Ministry of Finance: POB 85, King Hussein St, Amman 11118; tel. (6) 4636321; fax (6) 4618527; e-mail info@mof.gov.jo; internet www.mof.gov.jo.

Ministry of Foreign and Expatriates Affairs: POB 35217, Amman 11180; tel. (6) 5735150; fax (6) 5735163; e-mail inquiry@mfa.gov.jo; internet www.mfa.gov.jo.

Ministry of Health: POB 86, Amman 11118; tel. (6) 5200230; fax (6) 5689177; e-mail info@moh.gov.jo; internet www.moh.gov.jo.

Ministry of Higher Education and Scientific Research: POB 35262, Amman 11180; tel. (6) 5347671; fax (6) 5349079; e-mail mohe@mohe.gov.jo; internet www.mohe.gov.jo.

Ministry of Industry, Trade and Supply: POB 2019, 11181 Amman; tel. (6) 5629030; fax (6) 5684692; e-mail info@mit.gov.jo; internet www.mit.gov.jo.

Ministry of Information and Communications Technology: POB 9903, Amman 11191; tel. (6) 5805700; fax (6) 5861059; e-mail moict@moict.gov.jo; internet www.moict.gov.jo.

Ministry of the Interior: POB 100, Amman; tel. (6) 5691141; fax (6) 5606908; e-mail info@moi.gov.jo; internet www.moi.gov.jo.

Ministry of Justice: POB 6040, Amman 11118; tel. (6) 4603630; fax (6) 4643197; e-mail feedback@moj.gov.jo; internet www.moj.gov.jo.

Ministry of Labour: POB 8160, Amman 11118; tel. (6) 5802666; fax (6) 5855072; e-mail info@mol.gov.jo; internet www.mol.gov.jo.

Ministry of Municipal Affairs: POB 1799, Amman 11118; tel. (6) 4641393; fax (6) 4640404; e-mail mma3@nic.net.jo; internet www.mma.gov.jo.

Ministry of Planning and International Co-operation: POB 555, Amman 11118; tel. (6) 4644466; fax (6) 4642247; e-mail mop@mop.gov.jo; internet www.mop.gov.jo.

Ministry of Political and Parliamentary Affairs: POB 841367, Amman 11180; tel. (6) 5695216; fax (6) 5686582; e-mail info@mopd.gov.jo; internet www.mopd.gov.jo.

Ministry of Public Sector Development: POB 3575, Amman 11821; tel. (6) 5695216; fax (6) 5686282; e-mail info@mopsd.gov.jo; internet www.mopsd.gov.jo.

Ministry of Public Works and Housing: POB 1220, Amman 11118; tel. (6) 5803838; fax (6) 5857590; e-mail mpwh@mpwh.gov.jo; internet www.mpwh.gov.jo.

Ministry of Social Development: POB 6720, Amman 11118; tel. (6) 5679327; fax (6) 5679961; e-mail contact@mosd.gov.jo; internet www.mosd.gov.jo.

Ministry of Tourism and Antiquities: POB 224, Amman 11118; tel. (6) 4603360; fax (6) 4648465; e-mail contacts@mota.gov.jo; internet www.mota.gov.jo.

Ministry of Transport: POB 35214, Amman 11180; tel. (6) 5518111; fax (6) 5527233; e-mail info@mot.gov.jo; internet www.mot.gov.jo.

Ministry of Water and Irrigation: POB 2412, Amman 11181; tel. (6) 5652265; fax (6) 5652287; e-mail admin@mwi.gov.jo; internet www.mwi.gov.jo.

Legislature

HOUSE OF REPRESENTATIVES

House of Representatives: POB 72, Amman 11118; tel. (6) 5635200; fax (6) 5685970; e-mail info@representatives.jo; internet www.representatives.jo.

Speaker: ATIF YOUSUF TARAWNEH.

General Election, 23 January 2013

Party/Group	Seats
Independents and tribal representatives	108
Islamic Centrist Party	3
Nation Party	2
National Current Party	2
National Union	2
Stronger Jordan	1
Other parties	17
Total	**150***

* In accordance with the terms of electoral legislation approved in July 2012, 27 seats were allocated to political parties, while a further 15 seats were reserved for female candidates.

SENATE

The Senate (House of Notables) consists of 60 members, appointed by the King. The current Senate was appointed on 25 October 2011.

Senate: POB 72, Amman 11101; tel. (6) 5664121; fax (6) 5689313; e-mail info@senate.jo; internet www.senate.jo.

Speaker: ABD AL-RAOUF RAWABDEH.

Election Commission

Independent Election Commission: POB 375, Tlaa al-Ali Area, Musa Saket Rd, Next to Chief Justice Bldg, Jordan 11953; tel. (6) 5607406; fax (6) 5607423; e-mail info@entikhabat.jo; internet www.entikhabat.jo; f. 2012; comprises Board of Commissioners and Executive apparatus; Chair. RIYAD ADEL MUHAMMAD AL-SHAK'AH.

Political Organizations

With the exception of the officially sanctioned Jordanian National Union (1971–76), political parties were effectively banned for most of the reign of King Hussein. However, in June 1991 a National Charter, one feature of which was the legalization of political parties, was formally endorsed. In August 1992 legislation allowing the formation of political parties was approved by royal decree, and by March 1993 nine parties had received official recognition. New amendments to the political parties law, approved by parliament in March 2007, required parties to have 500 founding members drawn from five different governorates with equal representation, and compelled parties to grant the Government access to their accounts; the reform also provided for public funding for political parties. Parties were given a period of one year to meet the new requirements or face dissolution. By April 2008 12 out of the 36 existing political parties had rectified their status; all other parties were dissolved, while two new parties were licensed. A number of parties were expected to launch lawsuits contesting their dissolution.

Arab Islamic Democratic Party (Dua'a): POB 104, Amman 11941; tel. and fax (6) 5514443; e-mail info@duaa-jo.com; f. 1993; moderate Islamist party; Founder YOUSUF ABU BAKR.

Higher Co-ordination Committee for Opposition Parties: Amman; opposition bloc currently consisting of 7 leftist, pan-Arab and Islamist parties: Baath Arab Progressive Party, Jordanian Arab Socialist Baath Party, Islamic Action Front, Jordanian Communist Party, Jordan People's Democratic Party (HASHD), National Movement for Direct Democracy and Jordanian Democratic Popular Unity Party (leftist).

Hizb-ut-Tahrir al-Islami (Party of Islamic Liberation): e-mail info@hizb-ut-tahrir.org; internet www.hizb-ut-tahrir.org; f. 1953; transnational org. prohibited in Jordan and many other countries; aims to establish Islamic caliphate throughout the world; denies claims that it is a militant group; Leader in Jordan RAMZI SAWALHAH.

Islamic Action Front (Jabhat al-Amal al-Islami—IAF): POB 925310, Abdali, Amman 11110; tel. (6) 5696985; fax (6) 5696987; e-mail info@jabha.net; internet www.jabha.net; f. 1992; seeks implementation of *Shari'a* (Islamic law) and preservation of the *Umma* (Islamic community); mem. of Higher Co-ordination Committee for Opposition Parties; Sec.-Gen. MUHAMMAD AWAD AL-ZYOUD.

Islamic Centrist Party (Hizb al-Wasat al-Islami): POB 2149, Haswa Bldg, 3rd Floor, Amman 11941; tel. and fax (6) 5353966; e-mail alwasaat2001@gmail.com; internet www.wasatparty.org; f. 2001 by fmr mems of Islamic Action Front and Muslim Brotherhood; Sec.-Gen. MADALLAH AL-TARAWNEH.

Jordan People's Democratic Party (Hizb al-Shaab al-Dimuqrati—HASHD): POB 9966, Amman 11191; tel. (6) 5691451; fax (6) 5686857; e-mail ahali@go.com.jo; internet www.hashd-ahali.org.jo;

f. 1989; leftist party, which seeks to establish legal and institutional processes to protect the people, instigate economic, social, democratic and agricultural reform, and organize, unify and protect the working classes; supports the Palestinian cause; mem. of Higher Co-ordination Cttee for Opposition Parties; Sec.-Gen. ABLA ABU ULBAH.

Jordanian Arab Socialist Baath Party (Hizb al-Baath al-Arabi al-Ishtiraki al-Urduni): POB 8383, Amman; tel. (6) 4658618; fax (6) 4658617; f. 1993; promotes pan-Arabism; mem. of Higher Co-ordination Cttee for Opposition Parties; Sec.-Gen. AKRAM AL-HOMSI.

Jordanian Communist Party: POB 2349, Amman; tel. and fax (6) 4624939; e-mail jcp@nets.com.jo; internet www.jocp.org; f. 1951; merged with Communist Workers Party of Jordan 2008; Sec.-Gen. Dr MUNIR HAMARNEH.

Jordanian Democratic Popular Unity Party: POB 922110, Amman; tel. (6) 5692301; fax (6) 5692302; e-mail wihdaparty@gmail.com; internet www.wihda.org; f. 1990; publishes *Nida'a al-Watan* newspaper; Sec.-Gen. SAEED THIYAB.

National Constitutional Party (Al-Hizb al-Watani al-Dusturi—NCP): POB 1825237, Amman 11118; tel. (6) 5696256; fax (6) 5686248; f. 1997 by merger of 9 parties; Pres. ABD AL-HADI AL-MAJALI; Sec.-Gen. AHMAD SHUNNAQ.

National Current Party: Amman; f. 2009; seeks to promote the cause of national unity through the reform of political institutions; pro-monarchy; Sec.-Gen. SALEH IRSHEIDAT.

National Movement for Direct Democracy: POB 922478, Amman 11192; tel. (6) 5652125; fax (6) 5639925; f. 1997; Sec.-Gen. MUHAMMAD AL-QAQ.

Stronger Jordan (Urdun Aqwa): Amman; f. 2013; list formed to contest Jan. 2013 parliamentary elections; Leader ROLA AL-FARRA HROUB.

Other licensed parties include: Baath Arab Progressive Party, Al-Hayat, Jordan National Party, Mission Party (Hizb al-Risala) and the Unified Jordanian Front.

Diplomatic Representation

EMBASSIES IN JORDAN

Algeria: POB 830375, Amman 11183; tel. (6) 4641271; fax (6) 4616552; e-mail ambalg@go.com.jo; Ambassador MUHAMMAD BOUROUBA.

Australia: POB 35201, 41 Kayed al-Armouti St, Abdoun, Amman 11180; tel. (6) 5807000; fax (6) 5807001; e-mail amman.austremb@dfat.gov.au; internet www.jordan.embassy.gov.au; Ambassador HEIDI VENAMORE.

Austria: POB 830795, Jabal Amman, Amman 11183; tel. (6) 4601101; fax (6) 4612725; e-mail amman-ob@bmeia.gv.at; internet www.bmeia.gv.at/en/embassy/amman.html; Ambassador ASTRID HARZ.

Azerbaijan: POB 851894, 13 al-Awabed St, al-Kursi, Amman 11185; tel. (6) 5935525; fax (6) 5932826; e-mail amman@mission.mfa.gov.az; internet www.azembassyjo.org; Ambassador SABIR AGHABAYOV.

Bahrain: POB 5220, Faris al-Khoury St, Shmeisani, Amman 11183; tel. (6) 5664148; fax (6) 5664190; e-mail bahemb@maktoob.com; internet www.mofa.gov.bh/amman; Ambassador NASSER RASHID AL-KAABI.

Bangladesh: POB 5685, 10 Muzdalifa St, al-Rabieh, Amman 11183; tel. (6) 5529192; fax (6) 5529194; e-mail info@bdembassyjordan.com; internet www.bdembassyjordan.com; Ambassador MUHAMMAD ENAYET HUSSAIN.

Belgium: POB 942, 17 Sa'ad Jumah St, Jabal Amman, Amman 11118; tel. (6) 4655730; fax (6) 4655740; e-mail amman@diplobel.fed.be; internet www.diplomatie.be/amman; Ambassador THOMAS BAEKELANDT.

Bosnia and Herzegovina: POB 850836, 67 Said al-Mufti St, Amman 11185; tel. (6) 5856921; fax (6) 5856923; e-mail embjoamm@wanadoo.jo; Ambassador DARKO ZELENIKA.

Brazil: POB 5497, Amman 11183; tel. (6) 5923941; fax (6) 5931098; e-mail jorbrem@wanadoo.jo; Ambassador RENATE STILLE.

Brunei: POB 851752, Amman 11185; tel. (6) 5928021; fax (6) 5928024; e-mail amman.jordan@mfa.gov.bn; Ambassador NOORADIN BIN Haji YA'AKOB.

Bulgaria: POB 950578, 7 al-Mousel St, Amman 11195; tel. (6) 5529392; fax (6) 5539393; e-mail embassy.amman@mfa.bg; internet www.mfa.bg/embassies/jordan; Ambassador VENELIN LAZAROV.

Canada: POB 815403, Amman 11180; tel. (6) 5901500; fax (6) 5901501; e-mail amman@international.gc.ca; internet www.canadainternational.gc.ca/jordan-jordanie; Ambassador BRUNO SACCOMANI.

Chile: POB 830663, 28 Hussein Abu Ragheb St, Abdoun, Amman 11183; tel. (6) 5923360; fax (6) 5924263; e-mail echile@orange.jo; internet chileabroad.gov.cl/jordania; Ambassador EDUARDO ESCOBAR MARÍN.

China, People's Republic: POB 7365, 9 Jakarta St, Amman 11118; tel. (6) 5516136; fax (6) 5518713; e-mail chinaemb_jo@hotmail.com; internet jo.china-embassy.org; Ambassador GAO YUSHENG.

Cyprus: POB 5525, Bldg 233, Wadi Sakra St, Amman 11183; tel. (6) 5657143; fax (6) 5657895; e-mail info@cyprusembassyamman.org; Ambassador CHARALAMBOS HADJISAVVAS.

Czech Republic: POB 2213, 34 Halab St, Abdoun, Amman 11181; tel. (6) 5927051; fax (6) 5927053; e-mail amman@embassy.mzv.cz; internet www.mzv.cz/amman; Ambassador PETR HLADÍK.

Egypt: POB 35178, 14 Riyad el-Mefleh St, Amman 11180; tel. (6) 5605202; fax (6) 5604082; e-mail eg.emb_amman@mfa.gov.eg; Ambassador KHALED THARWAT.

France: POB 5348, Amman 11183; tel. (6) 4641273; fax (6) 4659606; e-mail cad.amman-amba@diplomatie.fr; internet www.ambafrance-jo.org; Ambassador CAROLINE DUMAS.

Georgia: POB 851903, 31 Odeh Abu Tayeh, Shmeisani, Amman 11185; tel. (6) 5926433; fax (6) 5923374; e-mail geoemb@orange.jo; internet www.jordan.mfa.gov.ge; Ambassador GREGORY TABATADZE.

Germany: POB 183, 25 Benghazi St, Jabal Amman 11118; tel. (6) 5901170; fax (6) 5901282; e-mail info@amman.diplo.de; internet www.amman.diplo.de; Ambassador RALPH TARRAF.

Greece: POB 35069, 7 Suleiman Youssef Sukkar St, Amman 11180; tel. (6) 5922724; fax (6) 5927622; e-mail gremb.amn@mfa.gr; internet www.mfa.gr/amman; Ambassador MARIA LUIZA MARINAKI.

Holy See: POB 142916, 14 Anton al-Naber St, Amman 11814; tel. (6) 5929934; fax (6) 5929931; e-mail nuntiusjordan@gmail.com; Apostolic Nuncio Most Rev. Archbishop GIORGIO LINGUA.

Hungary: POB 3441, 23 Yaqoub Ammari St, Abdoun, Amman 11181; tel. (6) 5925614; fax (6) 5930836; e-mail mission.amm@kum.hu; internet www.mfa.gov.hu/emb/amman; Ambassador CSABA CZIBERE.

India: POB 2168, Amr bin Masadah St, Jabal Amman, 1st Circle, Amman 11181; tel. (6) 4622098; fax (6) 4659540; e-mail amb.amman@mea.gov.in; internet indembassy-amman.org; Ambassador ANIL TRIGUNAYAT.

Indonesia: POB 811784, 13 Ali Seedo al-Kurdi St, Sweifieh, Amman 11181; tel. (6) 5926908; fax (6) 5926796; e-mail amman96@go.com.jo; internet www.kemlu.go.id/amman; Ambassador TEGUH WARDOYO.

Iran: POB 173, Amman 11118; tel. (6) 4641281; fax (6) 4641383; e-mail pub-rel@iranembassyjordan.org; Ambassador MOJTABA FERDOSIPOUR.

Iraq: POB 2025, Amman; tel. (6) 4623175; fax (6) 4619172; e-mail amaemb@mofaml.gov.iq; internet www.mofamission.gov.iq/amn; Ambassador Dr JAWAD HADI ABBAS.

Israel: POB 95866, 47 Maysaloon St, Dahiat al-Rabieh, Amman 11195; tel. (6) 5503500; fax (6) 5503579; e-mail embassy@amman.mfa.gov.il; internet amman.mfa.gov.il; Ambassador DANNY NEVO.

Italy: POB 9800, Jabal al-Weibdeh, 5 Hafiz Ibrahim St, Amman 11191; tel. (6) 4638185; fax (6) 4659730; e-mail info.amman@esteri.it; internet www.ambamman.esteri.it; Ambassador PATRIZIO FONDI.

Japan: POB 2835, Fa'eq Halazon St, Zahran, Abdun Shamali, Amman 11181; tel. (6) 5932005; fax (6) 5931006; e-mail mail@embjapan.org.jo; internet www.jordan.emb-japan.go.jp; Ambassador SHUICHI SAKURAI.

Kazakhstan: Abu Bakir al-Banany St, Amman; tel. (6) 5927953; fax (6) 5927952; e-mail amman@mfa.kz; internet www.kazakhstan.org.jo; Ambassador AZMAT BERDIBAY.

Korea, Democratic People's Republic: POB 799, Amman; tel. (6) 4417614; fax (6) 4424735; e-mail dprk-embv@scs-net.org; Ambassador RI SI HONG.

Korea, Republic: POB 3060, Bahjat Homsi St, Amman 11181; tel. (6) 5930745; fax (6) 5930280; e-mail jordan@mofa.go.kr; internet jor.mofa.go.kr; Ambassador CHOI HONG-GHI.

Kuwait: POB 2107, Amman 11181; tel. (6) 5675135; fax (6) 5681971; e-mail q8@kuwaitembassyamman.org; Ambassador Dr HAMAD SALEH DUAIJ.

Lebanon: POB 811779, Amman 11181; tel. and fax (6) 5929111; Ambassador MICHELIN PAZ.

Libya: POB 2987, Amman; tel. (6) 5693101; fax (6) 5693404; Ambassador (vacant).

Malaysia: POB 5351, Tayseer Na'na'ah St, off Umawiyyeen St, Abdoun, Amman 11183; tel. (6) 5902400; fax (6) 5934343; e-mail mwamman@kln.gov.my; internet www.kln.gov.my/web/jor_amman; Ambassador ZAKRI JAAFAR.

Mauritania: POB 851594, Saleh Zakee St, Villa 19, Sweifiyeh, Amman 11185; tel. (6) 5855146; fax (6) 5855148; e-mail muritanyaembassy_amman1@hotmail.com; Ambassador ELY OULD AHMEDOU.

Morocco: POB 2175, Amman 11183; tel. (6) 5680591; fax (6) 5680253; e-mail ambmaroc@batelco.jo; Ambassador HASSAN ABD AL-KHALIQ.

Netherlands: POB 941361, 3 Abu Bakr Siraj al-Din St, Amman 11194; tel. (6) 5902200; fax (6) 5930161; e-mail amm-info@minbuza .nl; internet jordan.nlembassy.org; Ambassador PAUL VAN DEN IJSSEL.

Norway: POB 830510, 25 Damascus St, Amman 11183; tel. (6) 5902450; fax (6) 5902479; e-mail emb.amman@mfa.no; internet www .norway.jo; Ambassador SISSEL BREIE.

Oman: POB 20192, Amman 11118; tel. (6) 5686155; fax (6) 5698871; e-mail amman@mofa.gov.om; Ambassador KHAMIS BIN MUHAMMAD BIN ABDULLAH AL-FARSI.

Pakistan: POB 1232, al-Akhtal St, Jabal al-Weibdeh, Amman 11118; tel. (6) 4622787; fax (6) 4611633; e-mail parepamman@ gmail.com; internet www.embassyofpakistanjordan.com; Ambassador Lt-Gen. AHSAN AZHAR HAYAT.

Philippines: POB 925207, 5 Salem al-Batarseh St, Amman 11190; tel. (6) 5923748; fax (6) 5923744; e-mail amman.pe@dfa.gov.ph; internet www.philembassy-amman.net; Ambassador OLIVIA V. PALALA.

Poland: POB 942050, Amman 11194; tel. (6) 5512593; fax (6) 5512595; e-mail amman.wk.dyzurny@msz.gov.pl; internet amman .msz.gov.pl; Ambassador KRZYSZTOF BOJKO.

Qatar: POB 5098, Bldg 38, Hajj Hassan St, Amman 11183; tel. (6) 5902300; fax (6) 5902301; e-mail amman@mofa.gov.qa; internet www.qatarembassy-jo.net; Ambassador ZAYED BIN SAEED AL-KHAYARIN.

Romania: POB 2869, 35 Madina Munawwara St, Amman 11181; tel. (6) 5813423; fax (6) 5812521; e-mail roemb@orange.jo; internet amman.mae.ro; Ambassador BOGDAN FILIP.

Russian Federation: POB 2187, 22 Zahran St, 3rd Circle, Amman 11181; tel. (6) 4641158; fax (6) 4647448; e-mail rusembjo@mail.ru; internet www.jordan.mid.ru; Ambassador BORIS F. BOLOTIN.

Saudi Arabia: POB 2133, Zahrat al-Talhoni Bldg, Jabal Amman, Amman 11183; tel. (6) 5924154; fax (6) 5921154; e-mail joemb@mofa .gov.sa; Ambassador SAMI IBN ABDULLAH AL-SALIH.

South Africa: POB 851508, Sweifiyeh, Amman 11185; tel. (6) 5921194; fax (6) 5920080; e-mail saembjor@index.com.jo; Ambassador JOHN DAVIES.

Spain: Zahran St, POB 454, Jabal Amman, Amman 11118; tel. (6) 4614166; fax (6) 4614173; e-mail emb.amman@maec.es; internet www.exteriores.gob.es/embajadas/amman; Ambassador SANTIAGO CABANAS ANSORENA.

Sri Lanka: POB 830731, al-Madina al-Munawara St, Amman 11183; tel. (6) 5820611; fax (6) 5820615; e-mail lankaembjo@ orange.jo; Ambassador GAMINI RAJAPAKSE.

Sudan: POB 3305, Bayader Wadi al-Seer, 7th Circle, Musa Irsheed al-Taib St, Amman 11181; tel. (6) 5854500; fax (6) 5854501; e-mail sudani@nets.com.jo; Ambassador MUHAMMAD OSMAN MUHAMMAD SAEED.

Sweden: POB 830536, 20 Abd al-Majid al-Adwan St, Abdoun, Amman 11183; tel. (6) 5901300; fax (6) 5930179; e-mail ambassaden.amman@gov.se; internet www.swedenabroad.com/ amman; Ambassador HELENA RIETZ.

Switzerland: POB 5341, 19 Ibrahim Ayoub St, 4th Circle, Amman 11183; tel. (6) 5931416; fax (6) 5930685; e-mail amm.vertretung@eda .admin.ch; internet www.eda.admin.ch/amman; Ambassador MICHAEL WINZAP.

Syria: POB 1733, Amman 11118; tel. (6) 5920684; fax (6) 5920635; Ambassador (vacant).

Thailand: POB 144329, 33 al-Hashemeen St, Dirghabar-Abdoun, Amman 11814; tel. (6) 5903888; fax (6) 5903899; e-mail thaiamm@ mfa.go.th; internet www.thaiembassy.org/amman; Ambassador APICHART PHETCHARATANA.

Tunisia: POB 17185, Amman 11195; tel. (6) 5922743; fax (6) 5922769; e-mail atamman@go.com.jo; Ambassador AFIFAH MALLAH.

Turkey: POB 2062, 31 Abbas Mahmoud al-Aqqad St, Amman 11181; tel. (6) 5002325; fax (6) 4612353; e-mail embassy.amman@mfa.gov .tr; internet amman.emb.mfa.gov.tr; Ambassador SEDAT ÖNAL.

Ukraine: POB 5244, 6 al-Umouma St, al-Sahl, Amman; tel. (6) 5922402; fax (6) 5922408; e-mail emb_jo@mfa.gov.ua; internet www .mfa.gov.ua/jordan; Ambassador SERGIY PASKO.

United Arab Emirates: POB 2623, Bldg 65, 5th Circle, Boumedienne St, Amman 11181; tel. (6) 5934780; fax (6) 5932666; e-mail amman@mofa.gov.ae; internet www.uae-embassy.ae/embassies/jo; Ambassador Dr ABDULLAH NASIR SULTAN AL-AMERI.

United Kingdom: POB 87, Abdoun, Amman 11118; tel. (6) 5909200; fax (6) 5909279; e-mail amman.enquiries@fco.gov.uk; internet ukinjordan.fco.gov.uk; Ambassador PETER MILLETT.

USA: POB 354, Umawiyyeen St, Abdoun, Amman 11118; tel. (6) 5906000; fax (6) 5920133; e-mail webmasterjordan@state.gov; internet jordan.usembassy.gov; Ambassador ALICE G. WELLS.

Yemen: POB 3085, Prince Hashem bin Al-Hussain St, Amman 11181; tel. (6) 5923771; fax (6) 5923773; Ambassador SHAYA MOHSIN ZINDANI.

Judicial System

With the exception of matters of purely personal nature concerning members of non-Muslim communities, the law of Jordan was based on Islamic Law for both civil and criminal matters. During the days of the Ottoman Empire certain aspects of Continental law, especially French commercial law and civil and criminal procedure, were introduced. Owing to British occupation of Palestine and Transjordan from 1917 to 1948, the Palestine territory has adopted, either by statute or case law, much of the English common law. Since the annexation of the non-occupied part of Palestine and the formation of the Hashemite Kingdom of Jordan, there has been a continuous effort to unify the law. A Constitutional Court was formally inaugurated on 7 October 2012, to replace the Higher Council for the Interpretation of the Constitution.

Constitutional Court: f. 2012; The Constitutional Court, established by royal decree in October 2012, retains the authority to decide 'the constitutionality of laws and regulations in force and issue its judgements in the name of the King'. It also 'has the right to interpret the provisions of the Constitution if requested, either by virtue of a decision of the Council of Ministers or by a resolution taken by the Senate or the Chamber of Deputies passed by an absolute majority.' The court comprised nine members, including the President, appointed by the King; Pres. TAHER HIKMAT.

Court of Cassation (Supreme Court): The Court of Cassation consists of seven judges, who sit in full panel for exceptionally important cases. In most appeals, however, only five members sit to hear the case. All cases involving amounts of more than JD 100 may be reviewed by this Court, as well as cases involving lesser amounts and those that cannot be monetarily valued. However, for the latter types of cases, review is available only by leave of the Court of Appeal, or, upon refusal by the Court of Appeal, by leave of the President of the Court of Cassation. In addition to these functions as final and Supreme Court of Appeal, the Court of Cassation also sits as High Court of Justice to hear applications in the nature of habeas corpus, mandamus and certiorari dealing with complaints of a citizen against abuse of governmental authority; Pres. HISHAM TAL.

Courts of Appeal: There are three Courts of Appeal, each of which is composed of three judges, whether for hearing of appeals or for dealing with Magistrates Courts' judgments in chambers. Jurisdiction of the three Courts is geographical, with one each in Amman, Irbid and Ma'an. Appellate review of the Courts of Appeal extends to judgments rendered in the Courts of First Instance, the Magistrates' Courts and Religious Courts.

Courts of First Instance: The Courts of First Instance are courts of general jurisdiction in all matters civil and criminal except those specifically allocated to the Magistrates' Courts. Three judges sit in all felony trials, while only two judges sit for misdemeanour and civil cases. Each of the 11 Courts of First Instance also exercises appellate jurisdiction in cases involving judgments of less than JD 20 and fines of less than JD 10, rendered by the Magistrates' Courts.

Magistrates' Courts: There are 17 Magistrates' Courts, which exercise jurisdiction in civil cases involving no more than JD 250 and in criminal cases involving maximum fines of JD 100 or maximum imprisonment of one year.

Religious Courts: There are two types of religious court: the *Shari'a* Courts (Muslims); and the Ecclesiastical Courts (Eastern Orthodox, Greek Melkite, Roman Catholic and Protestant). Jurisdiction extends to personal (family) matters, such as marriage, divorce, alimony, inheritance, guardianship, wills, interdiction and, for the Muslim community, the constitution of *Awqaf* (Religious Endowments). When a dispute involves persons of different religious communities, the Civil Courts have jurisdiction in the matter unless the parties agree to submit to the jurisdiction of one or the other of the Religious Courts involved; Each *Shari'a* (Muslim) Court consists of one judge (*Qadi*), while most of the Ecclesiastical (Christian) Courts are normally composed of three judges, who are usually clerics. *Shari'a* Courts apply the doctrines of Islamic Law, based on the Koran and the *Hadith* (Precepts of Muhammad), while the Ecclesiastical Courts base their law on various aspects of Canon Law. In the event of conflict between any two Religious Courts or between a Religious Court and a Civil Court, a Special Tribunal of three judges is appointed by the President of the Court of Cassation, to decide which court shall have jurisdiction. Upon the advice of experts on the law of the various communities, this Special Tribunal decides on the venue for the case at hand; Chief of Islamic Justice AHMAD HILAYEL; Dir of *Shari'a* Courts Sheikh ISSAM ABD AL-RAZZAQ ARABIYYAT.

Religion

Over 90% of the population are Sunni Muslims, and the King can trace unbroken descent from the Prophet Muhammad. There is a Christian minority, living mainly in the towns, and there are smaller numbers of non-Sunni Muslims.

ISLAM

Chief of Islamic Justice and Imam of the Royal Court: AHMAD HILAYEL.

Grand Mufti of the Hashemite Kingdom of Jordan: Sheikh ABD AL-KARIM KHASAWNEH.

CHRISTIANITY

The Roman Catholic Church

Chaldean Rite

The Chaldean Patriarch of Babylon is resident in Baghdad, Iraq.

Chaldean Patriarchal Vicariate in Jordan: Jabal al-Wabdeh, POB 910833, Amman 11191; tel. and fax (6) 4629061; e-mail raymovicariate66@hotmail.com; internet www.chaldeanjordan.org; f. 2002; Patriarchal Exarch Rev. RAYMOND MOUSSALLI.

Latin Rite

Jordan forms part of the Patriarchate of Jerusalem (see the chapter on Israel).

Vicar-General for Transjordan: Most Rev. SELIM SAYEGH (Titular Bishop of Aquae in Proconsulari), Latin Vicariate, POB 851379, Sweifiyeh, Amman 11185; tel. (6) 5929546; fax (6) 5920548; e-mail regina-pacis2000@yahoo.com.

Maronite Rite

The Maronite community in Jordan is under the jurisdiction of the Maronite Patriarch of Antioch (resident in Lebanon).

Patriarchal Exarchate of Jordan: Mgr PAUL NABIL SAYAH, St Charbel's Parish, Amman; tel. (6) 4202558; fax (6) 4202559; e-mail stcharbelparish@yahoo.com.

Melkite Rite

Jordan forms part of the Greek-Melkite archdiocese of Petra (Wadi Musa) and Philadelphia (Amman).

Archbishop of Petra and Philadelphia: Most Rev. YASSER AYYACH, Archevêché Grec-Melkite Catholique, POB 2435, Jabal Amman 11181; tel. and fax (6) 5866673; e-mail fryaser@yahoo.com.

Syrian Rite

The Syrian Catholic Patriarch of Antioch is resident in Beirut, Lebanon.

Patriarchal Exarchate of Jerusalem (Palestine and Jordan): Mont Achrafieh, POB 510393, Rue Barto, Amman; e-mail st_thomas@bezeqint.net; Exarch Patriarchal Mgr GRÉGOIRE PIERRE MELKI (Titular Bishop of Batne of the Syrians).

The Anglican Communion

Within the Episcopal Church in Jerusalem and the Middle East, Jordan forms part of the diocese of Jerusalem. The President Bishop of the Church is the Bishop in Cyprus and the Gulf (see the chapter on Cyprus).

Other Christian Churches

The Coptic Orthodox Church, the Greek Orthodox Church (Patriarchate of Jerusalem) and the Evangelical Lutheran Church in Jordan are also active.

The Press

DAILIES

Al-Anbat: POB 962556, Amman 11192; tel. (6) 5200100; fax (6) 5200113; e-mail info@alanbat.net; internet www.alanbat.net; f. 2005; independent; Arabic; political; Man. Editor FARIS SHARAAN.

Al-Arab al-Yawm (Arabs Today): POB 962198, Queen Rania St, Amman 11196; tel. (6) 5683333; fax (6) 5620552; e-mail mail@alarabalyawm.net; internet www.alarabalyawm.net; f. 1997; Arabic; Chief Editor MUHAMMAD KAAOUSH.

Al-Diyar (The Homeland): Al-Fanar Complex, Queen Rania Al-Abdullah St, Amman; tel. (6) 5166588; f. 2004; Arabic; Chair. of Bd MAHMOUD KHARABSHEH.

Ad-Dustour (The Constitution): POB 591, Amman 11118; tel. (6) 5608000; fax (6) 5667170; e-mail dustour@addustour.com.jo; internet www.addustour.com; f. 1967; Arabic; publ. by the Jordan Press and Publishing Co Ltd; owns commercial printing facilities; Chair. KAMEL AL-SHARIF; Chief Editor MUHAMMAD HASSAN TAL; circ. 70,000.

Al-Ghad (Tomorrow): POB 3535, Amman 11821; tel. (6) 5544000; fax (6) 5544055; e-mail editorial@alghad.jo; internet www.alghad.jo; f. 2004; independent; Arabic; Editor-in-Chief JUMANA GHNEIMAT.

The Jordan Times: POB 6710, Queen Rania Al-Abdullah St, Amman 11118; tel. (6) 5600800; fax (6) 5696183; e-mail editor@jordantimes.com; internet www.jordantimes.com; f. 1975; English; publ. by Jordan Press Foundation; Editor-in-Chief SAMIR BARHOUM; circ. 15,000.

Al-Rai (Opinion): POB 6710, Queen Rania Al-Abdullah St, Amman 11118; tel. (6) 5667171; fax (6) 5676581; e-mail info@jpf.com.jo; internet www.alrai.com; f. 1971; morning; independent; Arabic; publ. by Jordan Press Foundation; Editor-in-Chief SAMIR HIYARI; circ. 90,000.

Al-Sabeel (The Path): POB 213545, Amman 11121; tel. (6) 5692852; fax (6) 5692854; e-mail info@assabeel.net; internet www.assabeel.net; f. 1993; fmrly weekly; became daily publ. 2009; Arabic; Islamist; Editor-in-Chief ATEF GOLANI.

WEEKLIES

Al-Ahali (The People): POB 9966, Amman 11191; tel. (6) 5691451; fax (6) 5686857; e-mail ahali@go.com.jo; internet www.hashd-ahali.org.jo; f. 1990; Arabic; publ. by the Jordan People's Democratic Party; Editor-in-Chief SALEM NAHHAS; circ. 5,000.

Akhbar al-Usbou (News of the Week): POB 605, Amman; tel. (6) 5677881; fax (6) 5677882; f. 1959; Arabic; economic, social, political; Chief Editor and Publr ABD AL-HAFIZ MUHAMMAD; circ. 50,000.

Al-Hadath: POB 961167, Amman 11196; tel. (6) 5160824; fax (6) 5160810; e-mail info@alhadathnews.net; internet www.alhadathnews.net; Arabic; general news; Man. Editor FATEH MANSOUR.

Al-Haqeqa al-Duwalia (Fact International): POB 712678, Amman 11171; tel. (6) 5828292; fax (6) 5816646; e-mail info@factjo.com; internet www.factjo.com; f. 1996; independent; Arabic and English; aims to promote moderate image of Islam and to counter conflicts within the faith; Editor-in-Chief HILMI AL-ASMAR.

Al-Liwa' (The Standard): POB 3067, 2nd Circle, Jabal Amman 11181; tel. (6) 5642770; fax (6) 5656324; e-mail info@al-liwa.com; internet www.aliwaa.com; f. 1972; Arabic; Editor-in-Chief HASSAN AL-TAL; circ. 15,000.

Al-Majd (The Glory): POB 926856, Amman 11190; tel. (6) 5530553; fax (6) 5530352; e-mail almajd@almajd.net; internet www.almajd.net; f. 1994; Arabic; political; Editor-in-Chief FAHID NIMER; circ. 8,000.

Shihan: POB 96-654, Amman; tel. (6) 5603585; fax (6) 5696183; Arabic; Editor-in-Chief (vacant); circ. 60,000.

The Star: POB 591, Queen Rania St, Amman 11118; tel. (6) 5653325; fax (6) 5697415; e-mail star@addustour.com.jo; internet www.star.com.jo; f. 1966; English; political, economic, social and cultural; publ. by the Jordan Press and Publishing Co; Editor-in-Chief MAHA AL-SHARIF; circ. 12,430.

PERIODICALS

Anty Magazine: POB 3024, Amman 11181; tel. (6) 5820058; fax (6) 5855892; e-mail chiefeditor@anty.jo; internet www.anty.jo; monthly; Arabic; publ. by Front Row Publishing and Media Services; fashion, culture and current affairs from a professional woman's perspective; Chief Editor SAHAR ALOUL; circ. 20,000.

Huda El-Islam (The Right Way of Islam): POB 659, Amman; tel. (6) 5666141; f. 1956; monthly; Arabic; scientific and literary; publ. by the Ministry of Awqaf (Religious Endowments) and Islamic Affairs; Editor Dr AHMAD MUHAMMAD HULAYYEL.

Jordan: POB 224, Amman; e-mail webmaster@jordanembassyus.org; internet www.jordanembassyus.org/new/newsletter.shtml; f. 1969; quarterly; publ. by Jordan Information Bureau, Embassy of Jordan, Washington, DC, USA; 3 a year; Editor-in-Chief MERISSA KHURMA; circ. 100,000.

Jordan Business: POB 3024, Amman 11181; tel. (6) 5820058; fax (6) 5855892; e-mail jordanbusinessonline@jordan-business.net; internet www.jordan-business.net; monthly; English; publ. by Front Row Publishing and Media Services; circ. 10,000.

Jordan Today: Media Services International, POB 9313, Amman 11191; tel. (6) 652380; fax (6) 648298; e-mail star@arabia.com; internet www.jordantoday.com.jo; f. 1995; monthly; English;

tourism, culture and entertainment; Editor-in-Chief ZEID NASSER; circ. 10,000.

Military Magazine: Army Headquarters, Amman; f. 1955; quarterly; dealing with military and literary subjects; publ. by Armed Forces.

Royal Wings: POB 3024, Amman 11181; tel. (6) 5820058; fax (6) 5855892; e-mail royalwings@frontrow.jo; internet www.frontrow.jo; bi-monthly; Arabic and English; magazine for Royal Jordanian Airline; publ. by Front Row Publishing and Media Services; Man. Dir USAMA FARAJ; circ. 40,000.

Skin: POB 940166, ICCB Centre, Queen Rania Abdullah St, Amman 11194; tel. (6) 5163357; fax (6) 5163257; e-mail amer@neareastmedia.com; internet www.skin-online.com; f. 2006; quarterly; English; publ. by Near East Media Iraq; art, design, fashion, photography, film and music; Editor-in-Chief TARIQ AL-BITAR.

NEWS AGENCY

Jordan News Agency (PETRA): POB 6845, Amman 11118; tel. (6) 5609700; fax (6) 5682478; e-mail petra@petra.gov.jo; internet www.petra.gov.jo; f. 1965; independent entity since 2004; previously controlled by Ministry of Information prior to its disbandment in 2001; Chair. Dr MUHAMMAD HUSSEIN MOMANI (Minister of State for Media Affairs and Communications); Dir-Gen. RAMADAN AL-RAWASHDEH.

PRESS ASSOCIATION

Jordan Press Association (JPA): POB 8876, Abbas Mahmoud al-Aqqad St, Jabal Amman, 2nd Circle, Amman 18888; tel. (6) 5372005; fax (6) 5372003; e-mail info@jpa.jo; internet www.jpa.jo; f. 1953; Pres. TAREQ MOMANI.

Publishers

Alfaris Publishing and Distribution Co: POB 9157, Amman 11191; tel. (6) 5605432; fax (6) 5685501; e-mail mkayyali@airpbooks.com; internet www.airpbooks.com; f. 1989; Dir MAHER SAID KAYYALI.

Aram Studies Publishing and Distribution House: POB 997, Amman 11941; tel. (6) 835015; fax (6) 835079; art, finance, health, management, science, business; Gen. Dir SALEH ABOUSBA.

Dar al-Manhal Publishers and Distributors: POB 926428, Amman 11190; tel. (6) 5698308; fax (6) 5639185; e-mail info@dmanhal.com; internet www.dmanhal.com; f. 1990; children's and educational publs; Exec. Man. KHALED BILBEISI.

Dar al-Nafa'es: POB 927511, al-Abdali, Amman 11190; tel. (6) 5693940; fax (6) 5693941; e-mail alnafaes@hotmail.com; internet www.al-nafaes.com; f. 1990; education, Islamic; CEO SUFYAN OMAR AL-ASHQR.

Dar al-Thaqafa: Amman 11118; tel. (6) 4646361; fax (6) 4610291; e-mail info@daralthaqafa.com; internet www.daralthaqafa.com; f. 1984; academic publr, specializes in law; Man. Editor KHALID MAHMOUD GABR.

Al Faridah for Specialized Publications: POB 1223, Amman 11821; tel. (6) 5630430; fax (6) 5630440; e-mail hakam@alfaridah.com.jo; internet www.alfaridah.com.jo; f. 2003; publr of magazines incl. *Layalina*, *Ahlan!*, *JO*, *Viva*, *Venture*; Editors-in-Chief RANIA OMEISH, SHIRENE RIFAI; Man. Dir QAIS ELIAS.

Front Row Publishing and Media Services: POB 3024, Muhammad Baseem Khammash St, Villa 3, Amman 11181; tel. (6) 5820058; fax (6) 5855892; e-mail info@frontrow.jo; internet www.frontrow.jo; f. 1997; publr of magazines incl. *Jordan Business*, *Living Well*, *Home*, *Royal Wings*; CEO IYAD SHEHADEH.

Jordan Book Centre Co Ltd: POB 301, al-Jubeiha, Amman 11941; tel. (6) 5151882; fax (6) 5152016; e-mail jbc@go.com.jo; internet www.JBC.com.jo; f. 1982; fiction, business, economics, computer science, medicine, engineering, general non-fiction; Man. Dir J. J. SHARBAIN.

Jordan Distribution Agency: POB 3371, Amman 11181; tel. (6) 5358855; fax (6) 5337733; e-mail jda@aramex.com; f. 1951; history; subsidiary of Aramex; Chair. FADI GHANDOUR; Gen. Man. WADIE SAYEGH.

Jordan House for Publication: POB 1121, Basman St, Amman; tel. (6) 24224; fax (6) 51062; f. 1952; medicine, nursing, dentistry; Man. Dir MURSI AL-ASHKAR.

Jordan Press and Publishing Co Ltd: POB 591, Amman 11118; tel. (6) 5608000; fax (6) 5667170; e-mail info@addustour.com.jo; internet www.addustour.com; f. 1967 by *Al-Manar* and *Falastin* dailies; publishes *Ad-Dustour* (daily), *Ad-Dustour Sport* (weekly) and *The Star* (English weekly); Chair. AMIN MASHAQBEH; Gen. Man. SAMER RAJOUB.

Jordan Press Foundation: POB 6710, Amman 11118; tel. (6) 5667171; fax (6) 5661242; e-mail info@jpf.com.jo; internet www.alrai.com; f. 1971; publishes *Al-Rai* (daily), *The Jordan Times* (daily) and *Hatem* (monthly); Chair. ALI AYED; Editor SAMIR HIYARI.

Al-Tanwir al-Ilmi (Scientific Enlightenment Publishing House): POB 4237, al-Mahatta, Amman 11131; tel. and fax (6) 4899619; e-mail taisir@yahoo.com; internet www.icieparis.net; f. 1990; affiliated with the Int. Centre for Innovation in Education; education, engineering, philosophy, science, sociology; Gen. Dir Prof. Dr TAISIR SUBHI YAMIN.

Broadcasting and Communications

TELECOMMUNICATIONS

Jordan Mobile Telephone Services Co (Zain Jordan): POB 940821, 8th Circle, King Abdullah II St, Amman 11194; tel. (7) 97900900 (mobile); fax (6) 5828200; e-mail info@jo.zain.com; internet www.jo.zain.com; f. 1994 as Jordan Mobile Telephone Services Co (JMTS—Fastlink); merged with Mobile Telecommunications Co (MTC—Kuwait) 2003, corpn renamed Zain Group 2007; Zain Jordan merged with PalTel (Palestinian Territories) in 2009; private co; has operated Jordan's first mobile telecommunications network since 1995; CEO, Levant Region and CEO, Jordan AHMAD AL-HANANDEH.

Jordan Telecom Group (Orange Jordan): POB 1689, Amman 11118; tel. (6) 5630090; fax (6) 5630098; e-mail webmaster@orange-jtg.jo; internet www.orange.jo; f. 1971; fmrly Jordan Telecommunications Corpn, Jordan Telecommunications Co and Jordan Telecom; current name adopted in Feb. 2006 following integration of the following cos' operations into a single management structure: Jordan Telecom, MobileCom (mobile cellular telecommunications services), Wanadoo (internet services) and e-Dimension (information technology); in 2007 Jordan Telecom, MobileCom and Wanadoo were all rebranded as Orange Jordan; 30.5% govt-owned, 69.5% privately owned: France Télécom SA, France, 51.0%; Social Security Corpn 12.4%; 6.1% of shares listed on Amman Stock Exchange; assets JD 664.8m., revenue JD 397.9m. (2007); CEO JEAN-FRANCOIS THOMAS.

Petra Jordanian Mobile Telecommunications: POB 941477, Amman 11194; tel. (6) 5630090; fax (6) 5630098; e-mail business@orange.jo; internet www.orange.jo; subsidiary of Jordan Telecom Group; CEO JEAN-FRANÇOIS THOMAS.

Umniah Mobile Company: POB 942481, Amman 11194; tel. (6) 5005000; fax (6) 5622772; e-mail contact@umniah.com; internet www.umniah.com; awarded contract for Jordan's third GSM licence in 2004; commenced operations in June 2005; first provider of wireless broadband internet services in Jordan; subsidiary of Alghanim Group (Kuwait); 96% owned by Bahrain Telecommunications Co (Batelco); 3m. mobile subscribers (2013); CEO IHAB HINNAWI.

Regulatory Authority

Telecommunications Regulatory Commission (TRC): POB 850967, Amman 11185; tel. (6) 5501120; fax (6) 5690830; e-mail trc@trc.gov.jo; internet www.trc.gov.jo; f. 1995; Chair. and CEO MUHAMMAD AL-TAANI.

BROADCASTING

A new Audio Visual Media Law, enacted in 2002, allowed for the establishment of private broadcasters in Jordan for the first time. By 2007 16 new radio licences had been awarded. Jordan's first licensed independent television channel, Al-Ghad TV (ATV), was officially launched in August 2007; however, the channel was taken off-air before it began broadcasting, owing to a dispute over the terms of its licence. In 2008 ATV was purchased by Arab Telemedia Group and plans were announced for the launch of a two-channel network. By late 2014 ATV had yet to begin broadcasting.

Regulatory Authority

Audio Visual Commission (AVC): POB 142515, Amman 11814; tel. (6) 5560378; fax (6) 5535093; e-mail avc.dg@nic.net.jo; internet www.avc.gov.jo; f. 2002; Dir-Gen. AMJAD AL-QADI.

Radio and Television

Jordan Radio and Television Corporation (JRTV): POB 1041, Amman; tel. (6) 773111; fax (6) 751503; e-mail general@jrtv.gov.jo; internet www.jrtv.jo; f. 1968; state broadcaster; operates 4 TV channels and 6 radio channels broadcasting programmes in Arabic, English and French; advertising accepted; Chair. Dr MUHAMMAD HUSSEIN MOMANI (Minister of State for Media Affairs and Communications); Dir-Gen. RAMADAN AL-RAWASHDEH; Dir of Radio Administration MAZEN AL-MAJALI; Dir of Television Administration AREF AL-FAYEZ.

Radio Al-Balad: POB 20513, Amman 11118; tel. (6) 4645486; fax (6) 4630238; e-mail info@ammannet.net; internet www.ammannet.net; f. 2000 as internet radio station AmmanNet; began broadcasting as an FM radio station 2005, renamed as above 2008; news, politics and community broadcasts; Gen. Man. DAOUD KUTTAB.

Sawt al-Madina (SAM): POB 1171, Amman 1953; tel. (6) 5500006; fax (6) 5500009; e-mail fateen@al-baddad.com; internet www .al-baddad.com; f. 2006; owned by Al-Baddad Media and Communications; radio station broadcasting news and politics programmes; Group Gen. Man. FATEEN H. AL-BADDAD.

Other independent radio stations include Mazaj FM, Amin FM, Al-Hayat FM, Rotana FM Jordan and Radio Fann FM.

Finance

(cap. = capital; p.u. = paid up; dep. = deposits; m. = million; res = reserves; br.(s) = branch(es); amounts in Jordanian dinars unless otherwise indicated)

BANKING

Central Bank

Central Bank of Jordan: POB 37, King Hussein St, Amman 11118; tel. (6) 4630301; fax (6) 4638889; e-mail redp@cbj.gov.jo; internet www.cbj.gov.jo; f. 1964; cap. 48.0m., res 742m., dep. 7,362m. (Dec. 2013); Gov. and Chair. ZIAD FARIZ; 2 brs.

National Banks

Arab Bank PLC: POB 950545, Shmeisani, Amman 11195; tel. (6) 5607231; fax (6) 5606793; e-mail corpcomm@arabbank.com.jo; internet www.arabbank.com; f. 1930; cap. US $776m., res $6,506m., dep. $36,722m. (Dec. 2012); Chair. SABIH AL-MASRI; CEO NEMEH SABBAGH; 84 brs in Jordan, 99 brs abroad.

Bank of Jordan PLC: POB 2140, Shmeisani, Amman 11181; tel. (6) 5696277; fax (6) 5696291; e-mail boj@bankofjordan.com.jo; internet www.bankofjordan.com; f. 1960; cap. 155m., res 77m., dep. 1,672m. (Dec. 2012); Chair. and Gen. Man. TAWFIK SHAKER FAKHOURI; 77 brs and offices.

Cairo Amman Bank: POB 950661, Cairo Amman Bank Bldg, Wadi Saqra St, Amman 11195; tel. (6) 5006000; fax (6) 5007100; e-mail info@cab.jo; internet www.cab.jo; f. 1960; cap. 100m., res 61m., dep. 1,541m. (Dec. 2012); Chair. YAZID ADNAN AL-MUFTI; Gen. Man. KAMAL GHARIB AL-BAKRI; 63 brs in Jordan, 18 brs in the West Bank.

Capital Bank of Jordan: POB 941283, Issam Ajlouni St, Amman 11194; tel. (6) 5100200; fax (6) 5692062; e-mail info@capitalbank.jo; internet www.capitalbank.jo; f. 1996 as Export and Finance Bank; name changed as above 2006; cap. 150m., res 25m., dep. 1,069m. (Dec. 2011); Chair. BASSEM KHALIL SALEM AL-SALEM; Gen. Man. HAYTHAM KAMHIYAH.

Jordan Ahli Bank: POB 3103, Queen Noor St, Shmeisani, Amman 11181; tel. (6) 5608730; fax (6) 5699867; e-mail info@ahlibank.com.jo; internet www.ahli.com; f. 1955 as Jordan Nat. Bank; name changed as above 2006; cap. 150m., res 91m., dep. 2,260m. (Dec. 2012); Chair. RAJAI MUASHER; CEO and Gen. Man. MARWAN AWAD; 46 brs in Jordan, 6 brs abroad.

Jordan Commercial Bank: POB 9989, Yakoub Sarrouf St, Shmeisani, Amman 11191; tel. (6) 5603931; fax (6) 5664110; e-mail jcb@jcbank.com.jo; internet www.jcbank.com.jo; f. 1977 as Jordan Gulf Bank; name changed as above 2004; cap. 93m., res 8m., dep. 714m. (Dec. 2012); Chair. MICHAEL FAIQ IBRAHIM AL-SAYEGH; CEO and Gen. Man. ABDUL MAHDI ALAWI; 23 brs in Jordan, 3 brs in West Bank.

Jordan Islamic Bank: POB 926225, Shmeisani, Amman 11190; tel. (6) 5677377; fax (6) 5666326; e-mail jib@islamicbank.com.jo; internet www.jordanislamicbank.com; f. 1978; fmrly Jordan Islamic Bank for Finance and Investment; current name adopted Oct. 2009; cap. 125m., res 56m., dep. 2,726. (Dec. 2012); Chair. ADNAN AHMAD YOUSUF; Vice-Chair. and Gen. Man. MUSA ABD AL-AZIZ SHIHADEH; 59 brs.

Jordan Kuwait Bank: POB 9776, Abdali, Amman 11191; tel. (6) 5629400; fax (6) 5695604; e-mail info@jkbank.com.jo; internet www .jordan-kuwait-bank.com; f. 1976; cap. US $141m., res $252m., dep. $2,728m. (Dec. 2012); Chair. and CEO ABD AL-KARIM AL-KABARITI; Dir-Gen. MUHAMMAD YASSER M. AL-ASMAR; 43 brs.

Société Générale de Banque-Jordanie: POB 560, 30 Prince Shaker bin Zeid St, Shmeisani, Amman 11118; tel. (6) 500300; fax (6) 5693410; e-mail sgbj.webmaster@socgen.com; internet www.sgbj .com.jo; f. 1965 as Middle East Investment Bank; became part of the Société Générale Group (France) 2000; name changed as above 2003; cap. 100m., res 818,896, dep. 357m. (Dec. 2012); Chair. HASSAN MANGO; Gen. Man. NADIM ABAOUAT; 16 brs.

Specialized Credit Institutions

Agricultural Credit Corporation: POB 77, Amman 11118; tel. (6) 5661105; fax (6) 5668365; e-mail acc@go.com.jo; internet www.acc .gov.jo; f. 1959; cap. 24m., res 12.4m., total assets 125.1m. (Dec. 2000); Chair. Dr AKIF AL-ZU'BI (Minister of Agriculture); Vice-Chair. and Dir-Gen. MUHAMMAD AL-HAERI; 22 brs.

Arab Jordan Investment Bank: POB 8797, Arab Jordan Investment Bank Bldg, Shmeisani, Amman 11121; tel. (6) 5607126; fax (6) 5681482; e-mail info@ajib.com; internet www.ajib.com; f. 1978; cap. 100m., res 19m., dep. 859m. (Dec. 2012); Chair. ABD AL-KADER AL-QADI; CEO HANI AL-QADI; 8 brs in Jordan, 2 brs abroad.

Bank al Etihad: POB 35104, Prince Shaker Ben Zeid St, Shmeisani, Amman 11180; tel. (6) 5607011; fax (6) 5666149; e-mail info@bankaletihad.com; internet www.bankaletihad.com; f. 1978 as Arab Finance Corpn; name changed to Union Bank for Savings and Investment 1991; name changed as above 2011; cap. 100m., res 111m., dep. 1,493m. (Dec. 2012); Chair. ISAM SALFITI; Gen. Man. NADIA AL-SAEED; 22 brs.

Cities and Villages Development Bank (CVDB): POB 1572, Amman 11118; tel. (6) 5682691; fax (6) 5668153; e-mail cvdb100@hotmail.com; internet www.cvdb.gov.jo; f. 1979; 30% state-owned; cap. 50m. (Dec. 2002); Chair. ALI GHAZAWI; Gen. Man. WALID AL-MASRI; 10 brs.

Housing Bank for Trade and Finance (HBTF): POB 7693, Parliament St, Amman 11118; tel. (6) 5005555; fax (6) 5690207; e-mail info@hbtf.com.jo; internet www.hbtf.com; f. 1973; cap. 355m., res 1,476m., dep. 6,667m. (Dec. 2012); Chair. Dr MICHEL MARTO; Gen. Man. OMAR MALHAS; 116 brs.

INVESTBANK: Issam Ajlouni St, Shmeisani, Amman; tel. (6) 5001500; fax (6) 5681410; e-mail info@investbank.jo; internet www.investbank.jo; f. 1982 as Jordan Investment and Finance Corpn; name changed 2009; cap. 100m., res 20m., dep. 525m. (Dec. 2012); Chair. BISHER M. JARDANEH; CEO MUNTASER DAWWAS; 9 brs.

Jordan Dubai Islamic Bank: POB 1982, al-Kuliah al-Elmiah, Amman 11118; tel. (6) 4602200; fax (6) 4647821; e-mail idb@indevbank.com.jo; internet www.jdib.jo; f. 1965 as Industrial Devt Bank; current name adopted Jan. 2010; cap. 100m., res 21m., dep. 334m. (Dec. 2012); Chair. ISMAIL TAHBOUB; CEO SAMI HUSSAM AL-AFGHANI; 7 brs.

STOCK EXCHANGE

Amman Stock Exchange (ASE): POB 212466, Arjan, nr Ministry of the Interior, Amman 11121; tel. (6) 5664109; fax (6) 5664071; e-mail info@ase.com.jo; internet www.exchange.jo; f. 1978 as Amman Financial Market; name changed as above 1999; 236 listed cos (2014); Chair. MARWAN BATAYNEH; CEO NADER AZAR.

INSURANCE

At the end of 2008 there were 29 companies operating in the insurance sector in Jordan.

Jordan Insurance Co Ltd (JIC): POB 279, Company's Bldg, 3rd Circle, Jabal Amman, Amman 11118; tel. (6) 4634161; fax (6) 4637905; e-mail allinsure@jicjo.com; internet www.jicjo.com; f. 1951; cap. 30m. (Dec. 2006); Chair. OTHMAN BDEIR; Man. Dir IMAD ABD AL-KHALEQ; 7 brs (3 in Jordan, 3 in the United Arab Emirates and 1 in Kuwait).

Middle East Insurance Co Ltd (MEICO): POB 1802, al-Kindi St, Um Uthanina, 5th Circle, Jabal Amman, Amman 11118; tel. (6) 5527100; fax (6) 5527801; e-mail info@meico.com.jo; internet www .meico.com.jo; f. 1962; cap. p.u. 18.0m., total assets 66,285.0m. (Dec. 2007); Chair. SAMIR KAWAR; Gen. Man. Dr RAJAI SWEIS; 13 brs.

National Insurance Co: POB 6156-2938, Sayed Qotub St, Shmeisani, Amman 11118; tel. (6) 5671169; fax (6) 5684900; e-mail natinsur@go.com.jo; f. 1965 as above; name changed to National Ahlia Insurance Co in 1986, following merger with Ahlia Insurance Co (f. 1975); reverted to original name July 2007; cap. 2m.; Chair. MUSTAFA ABU GOURA; Gen. Man. GHALEB ABU-GOURA.

Social Security Corporation: POB 926031, Amman 11110; tel. (6) 5501880; fax (6) 5501888; e-mail webmaster@ssc.gov.jo; internet www.ssc.gov.jo; f. 1978; regulates and implements a social security system, incl. the provision of health insurance, life insurance and unemployment benefit, funded by both voluntary and employer contributions; Dir-Gen. Dr MAEN NSOUR.

United Insurance Co Ltd: POB 7521, United Insurance Bldg, King Hussein St, Amman; tel. (6) 4648513; fax (6) 4629417; e-mail uic@united.com.jo; internet www.united.com.jo; f. 1972; all types of insurance; cap. p.u. 8m.; Chair. RAOUF ABU JABER; Gen. Man. IMAD AL-HAJI.

Insurance Federation

Jordan Insurance Federation (JOIF): POB 1990, Amman 11118; tel. (6) 5689266; fax (6) 5689510; internet www.joif.org; f. 1989 to replace the Jordan Assen for Insurance Cos (f. 1956); regulatory and management authority; Chair. JAWAD HADID; Sec.-Gen. MAHER AL-HUSAIN.

Trade and Industry

GOVERNMENT AGENCIES

Jordan Atomic Energy Commission: POB 70, Amman 11934; tel. (6) 5230978; fax (6) 5231017; internet www.jaec.gov.jo; f. 2007; devt of civil nuclear energy programme; Chair. Dr KHALED TOUKAN.

Natural Resources Authority: POB 7, Amman 11118; tel. (6) 5504390; fax (6) 5811866; e-mail dirgen@nra.gov.jo; internet www.nra.gov.jo; f. 1965; supervision and devt of mineral and non-nuclear energy resources; Dir-Gen. Dr MAHER HIJAZIN.

DEVELOPMENT ORGANIZATIONS

Aqaba Development Corporation (ADC): POB 2680, Chamber of Commerce Bldg, Aqaba 77110; tel. (3) 2039100; fax (3) 2039110; e-mail info@adc.jo; internet www.adc.jo; f. 2004 by Aqaba Special Economic Zone Authority and Govt of Jordan; devt and strategic management of infrastructure, industry, trade, transport, real estate, tourism and education within Aqaba Special Economic Zone; CEO MUHAMMAD SALEM TURK.

Development Zones Commission (DZC): POB 141277, Amman 11814; tel. (6) 3001300; e-mail info@dzc.jo; internet www.dzc.jo; f. 2008; responsible for creating, developing and monitoring the 3 development zones within Jordan; Chief Commr BILAL BASHIR.

Jordan Enterprise Development Corporation (JEDCO): POB 7704, Amman 11118; tel. (6) 5603507; fax (6) 5684568; e-mail jedco@jedco.gov.jo; internet www.jedco.gov.jo; f. 2003 to replace Jordan Export Devt and Commercial Centres Corpn; devt and promotion of industry, trade and exports; Chair. MAHA ALI (Minister of Industry, Trade and Supply); CEO YARUB AL-QUDAH.

Jordan Investment Board (JIB): POB 893, Amman 11821; tel. (6) 5608400; fax (6) 5608416; e-mail info@jib.com.jo; internet www.jordaninvestment.com; f. 1995; CEO Dr MAEN NSOUR.

Jordan Valley Authority (JVA): POB 2769, Amman 11183; tel. (6) 5689400; fax (6) 5689916; e-mail jva_complain@mwi.gov.jo; internet www.jva.gov.jo; f. 1973 as Jordan Valley Comm.; renamed as above 1977; govt org. responsible for the integrated social and economic devt of the Jordan Valley, with particular emphasis on the utilization and management of water resources; responsible for construction of several major irrigation, hydroelectric and municipal water projects; other projects include housing, schools and rural roads, and the devt of tourism infrastructure; Sec.-Gen. MUSA AL-JAMA'ANI.

CHAMBERS OF COMMERCE AND INDUSTRY

Amman Chamber of Commerce: POB 287, Amman 11118; tel. (6) 5666151; fax 5666155; e-mail info@ammanchamber.org.jo; internet www.ammanchamber.org.jo; f. 1923; more than 45,000 regd mems (2013); Chair. ISSA MURAD; Dir-Gen. MUHANNAD ATTAR.

Amman Chamber of Industry: POB 1800, Amman 11118; tel. (6) 5643001; fax (6) 5647852; e-mail aci@aci.org.jo; internet www.aci.org.jo; f. 1962; approx. 7,500 regd industrial cos (2007); Chair. Dr HATEM H. HALAWANI.

Aqaba Chamber of Commerce: POB 12, Aqaba 77110; tel. (3) 2012229; fax (3) 2013070; e-mail info@aqabacc.com; internet www.aqabacc.com; f. 1965; Chair. NAEL AL-KABARITI; Sec.-Gen. MAHMOUD FRAIH.

Jordan Chamber of Commerce: POB 7029, Amman 11118; tel. (6) 5902040; fax (6) 5902051; e-mail info@jocc.org.jo; internet www.jocc.org.jo; f. 1955 as Fed. of the Jordanian Chambers of Commerce; renamed as above in 2003; intended to promote co-operation between the various chambers of commerce in Jordan, and to consolidate and co-ordinate the capabilities of each; Chair. NAEL AL-KABARITI; Sec.-Gen. SAEED SALEM BAZBAZ.

Jordan Chamber of Industry: POB 811986, Amman 11181; tel. (6) 4642649; fax (6) 4643719; e-mail jci@jci.org.jo; internet www.jci.org.jo; promotes competitiveness in the industrial sector and co-operation between the various chambers of industry in Jordan; Chair. Dr HATEM H. HALAWANI; Dir-Gen. ZAKI M. AYOUBI.

Professional Associations Council (PAC): Professional Associations Complex, Amman; rep. body for 14 professional asscns; Pres. TAHER SHAKHSHIR.

PETROLEUM AND GAS

Jordan Oil Shale Co: c/o Royal Dutch Shell plc, Carel van Bylandtlaan 30, 2596 HR The Hague, The Netherlands; e-mail webmaster@josco.jo; internet www.josco.jo; f. 2009; wholly owned

subsidiary of Royal Dutch Shell plc (Netherlands/United Kingdom); exploration and exploitation of oil shale deposits.

Jordan Oil Shale Energy Co: POB 962497, Amman 11196; tel. (6) 5157064; fax (6) 5157046; e-mail info@joseco.com.jo; internet www.joseco.com.jo; f. 2007; state-owned; promotion and devt of oil shale projects; Chair. ABDALLAH SHAWABKEH.

National Petroleum Co PLC: POB 3503, Amman 11821; tel. (6) 5548888; fax (6) 5536912; e-mail management@npc.com.jo; internet www.npc.com.jo; f. 1995; petroleum and natural gas exploration and production; signed partnership agreement with BP (United Kingdom) for devt of Risha gasfield 2009; Chair. Dr ABD AL-RAZZAQ AL NUSUR.

UTILITIES

Electricity

Electricity Regulatory Commission: POB 1865, Amman 11821; tel. (6) 5805000; fax (6) 5805003; e-mail abedalraheem.akayle@erc.gov.jo; internet www.erc.gov.jo; f. 2001; regulatory authority; Chief Commr and CEO IBRAHIM SAIF (Minister of Energy and Mineral Resources).

Central Electricity Generating Company (CEGCO): POB 2564, Amman 11953; tel. (6) 5340008; fax (6) 5340800; e-mail cegco@cegco.com.jo; internet www.cegco.com.jo; part-privatized in Sept. 2007; 51% owned by ENARA Energy Arabia, 40% by Govt and 9% by Social Security Corpn; electricity generation; Chair. MUHAMMAD ABDULLAH RASHID ABUNAYYAN.

Electricity Distribution Company (EDCO): POB 2310, Orthodox St, 7th Circle, Jabal Amman, Amman; tel. (6) 5331330; fax (6) 5818336; e-mail info@edco.jo; internet www.edco.jo; f. 1999; privatized in Nov. 2007; wholly owned by Kingdom Electricity, a jt venture between Jordan, Kuwait and the United Arab Emirates; electricity distribution for southern, eastern and Jordan Valley regions; Dir-Gen. AHMAD ZINAT.

Irbid District Electricity Company (IDECO): POB 46, Amman; tel. (6) 7201500; fax (6) 7245495; e-mail ideco@ideco.com.jo; internet www.ideco.com.jo; f. 1957; 55.4% stake acquired by Kingdom Electricity (see EDCO) in Nov. 2007; electricity generation, transmission and distribution for northern regions; Chair. FAYEZ KHASAWNEH; Gen. Man. Eng. AHMAD THAINAT.

Jordanian Electric Power Company (JEPCO): POB 618, Amman 11118; tel. (6) 5503600; fax (6) 5503619; e-mail jepco@go.com.jo; internet www.jepco.com.jo; f. 1938; privately owned; electricity distribution for Amman, al-Salt, al-Zarqa and Madaba; Chair. ISSAM BDEIR; Gen. Man. MARWAN BUSHNAQ.

National Electric Power Company (NEPCO): POB 2310, Amman 11118; tel. (6) 5858615; fax (6) 5818336; e-mail info@nepco.com.jo; internet www.nepco.com.jo; f. 1996; fmrly Jordan Electricity Authority; electricity transmission; govt-owned; Chair. Eng. KHALDOUN QUTISHAT; Dir-Gen. Dr GHALEB AL-MAABRAH.

Samra Electric Power Co (SEPCO): POB 1885, Um Al-Sumaq, Zaal Abu Tayeh St, Amman 11821; tel. (6) 5506510; fax (6) 5506520; e-mail samra@sepco.com.jo; internet www.sepco.com.jo; f. 2004; electricity generation, gas turbines supply and installation and plant construction; Chair. Dr MAHIR MADADHAH; Dir-Gen. Eng. AMJAD AL-RAWASHDEH.

Water

Aqaba Water: POB 252, Aqaba 77110; tel. (3) 2014390; fax (3) 2015982; e-mail info@aw.jo; internet www.aqabawater.com; f. 2004; successor to the Water Authority in Aqaba; water supply and wastewater services; Pres. Eng. SAAD ABU HAMMOUR; CEO Eng. NAEM SALEH.

Jordan Water Company (Miyahuna): POB 922918, Amman 11192; tel. (6) 5666111; fax (6) 5682642; internet www.miyahuna.com.jo; f. 2007; owned by Water Authority of Jordan; operates as an independent commercial entity; management of water and sewage services in Amman; CEO Eng. MUNIR OWIES; Chair. Eng. ABD AL-RAHMAN AL-KHATIB.

Water Authority of Jordan (WAJ): POB 2412, Amman 11183; tel. (6) 5680100; fax (6) 5679143; e-mail info_waj@mwi.gov.jo; internet www.waj.gov.jo; f. 1984; govt-owned; scheduled for privatization; Sec.-Gen. Eng. TAWFIQ HABASHNEH.

TRADE UNION

The General Federation of Jordanian Trade Unions: POB 1065, Amman; tel. (6) 5675533; fax (6) 5687911; e-mail khyasat@rja.com.jo; f. 1954; 17 affiliated unions; 200,000 mems; mem. of Arab Trade Unions Confed; Pres. MAZEN MA'AYTEH.

Transport

RAILWAYS

The Hedjaz–Jordan Railway crosses the Syrian border and enters Jordanian territory south of Dar'a. It runs for approximately 366 km to Naqb Ishtar, passing through Zarqa, Amman, Qatrana and Ma'an. An express rail link between Amman and Damascus was inaugurated in 1999. In 2008 a feasibility study concerning the upgrade and revival of the entire Hedjaz Railway was launched by the Governments of Jordan, Saudi Arabia and Syria. Formerly a division of the Hedjaz–Jordan Railway, the Aqaba Railway was established as a separate entity in 1972; it retains close links with the Hedjaz, but there is no regular through traffic between Aqaba and Amman. It comprises 292 km of 1,050-mm gauge track and is used solely for the transportation of minerals from three phosphate mines to Aqaba port.

In 2012 the Ministry of Transport announced its intention to proceed with the construction of a national railway network. Upon completion, anticipated for 2020, a north–south line of more than 500 km will link the Red Sea port of Aqaba with Amman, Zarqa and Irbid in the north, while two smaller branches will extend from Zarqa to the borders with Iraq and Saudi Arabia, eventually linking with rail networks being developed in those countries. In 2010 the total length of Jordanian railways was 294 route-km.

Aqaba Railways Corporation (ARC): POB 50, Ma'an; tel. (3) 2132114; fax (3) 2131861; e-mail arc@orange.jo; internet www.arc.gov.jo; f. 1975; length of track 292 km (1,050-mm gauge); privately owned; Dir-Gen. HUSSEIN KRISHAN.

Jordan Hedjaz Railways: POB 4448, Amman 11131; tel. (6) 4895414; fax (6) 4894117; e-mail mkhazaleh@jh-railway.com; internet www.jh-railway.com; f. 1952 as Hedjaz–Jordan Railway; administered by the Ministry of Transport; length of track 496 km (1,050-mm gauge); Chair. Dr LINA SHABIB (Minister of Transport); Dir-Gen. SALAH AL-LAWZI.

ROADS

Amman is linked by road with all parts of the kingdom and with neighbouring countries. All cities and most towns are connected by a two-lane, paved road system. In addition, several thousand kilometres of tracks make all villages accessible to motor transport. In 2012 there was a total road network of 7,234 km, of which 2,878 km were highways, main or national roads, 1,749 km were secondary or regional roads and 2,602 km were rural roads.

Jordanian-Syrian Land Transport Co: POB 20686, Amman 11118; tel. (6) 4711545; fax (6) 4711517; e-mail josyco@josyco.com.jo; f. 1975; jt venture between Govts of Jordan and Syria; transports goods between ports in Jordan and Syria; operates 210 heavy-duty trailers; underwent restructuring in 2010; Dir-Gen. JAMIL ALI MUJAHID.

SHIPPING

The port of Aqaba, Jordan's only outlet to the sea, consists of a main port, container port (540 m in length) and industrial port, with 25 modern and specialized berths. It has 761,300 sq m of open and contained storage area. There is a ferry link between Aqaba and the Egyptian port of Nuweibeh. In 2008 the Government initiated a tendering process for a US $700m. project to relocate Aqaba's main port to the southern industrial zone. The new development, to be supervised by the Aqaba Development Corporation, was significantly to increase overall capacity, comprising a general cargo terminal with roll-on roll-off (ro-ro) facilities, a dedicated grain terminal and a new ferry terminal. Once vacated, the existing port site was to be redeveloped as a major new commercial, residential and tourism centre.

At 31 December 2014 Jordan's flag registered fleet totalled 29 vessels, with an aggregate displacement of 102,347 grt, of which four were general cargo ships.

Port Authorities

Aqaba Container Terminal (ACT): POB 1944, King Hussein bin Talal St, Aqaba 77110; tel. (3) 2091111; fax (3) 2039133; e-mail customerservice@act.com.jo; internet www.act.com.jo; CEO JEPPE NYMANN JENSEN.

Aqaba Ports Corporation: POB 115, Aqaba 77110; tel. (3) 2014031; fax (3) 2016204; e-mail info@aqabaports.com.jo; internet www.aqabaports.com; f. 1952 as Aqaba Port Authority; name changed as above 1978; Dir-Gen. MUHAMMAD AL-MUBAIDEN.

Principal Shipping Companies

Amman Shipping & Trading Co Ltd (ASTCO): POB 213083, 5th Floor, Blk A, Aqqad Bldg, Gardens St, Amman 11121; tel. (6) 5514620; fax (6) 5532324; e-mail sts@albitar.com; internet www.1stjordan.net/astco/index.html; f. 1990.

Arab Bridge Maritime Co: POB 989, Aqaba; tel. (3) 2092000; fax (3) 2092001; e-mail info@abmaritime.com.jo; internet www.abmaritime.com.jo; f. 1985; jt venture by Egypt, Iraq and Jordan; commercial shipping of passengers, vehicles and cargo between Aqaba and the Egyptian port of Nuweibeh; Man. Dir HUSSEIN AL-SOUOB.

T. Gargour & Fils (TGF): POB 419, 1st Floor, Bldg No. 233, Arar St, Wadi Saqra, Amman 11118; tel. (6) 4626611; fax (6) 4622425; e-mail info@oma-jo.com; internet www.tgf.com.jo; f. 1928; shipping agents and owners; CEO Dr DUREID MAHASNEH.

Jordan National Shipping Lines Co Ltd (JNSL): POB 5406, Bldg No. 51, Wadi Saqra St, Amman 11183; POB 557, Aqaba; tel. (6) 5511500; fax (6) 5511501; e-mail jnslamman@jnslgroup.com; internet www.jnslgroup.com; f. 1976; 75% govt-owned; service from Antwerp (Netherlands), Bremen (Germany) and Tilbury (United Kingdom) to Aqaba; daily passenger ferry service to Egypt; land transportation to various regional destinations; Chair. AHMAD ARMOUSH.

Amin Kawar & Sons Co WLL: POB 222, 24 Abd al-Hamid Sharaf St, Shmeisani, Amman 11118; tel. (6) 5609500; fax (6) 5698322; e-mail kawar@kawar.com.jo; internet www.kawar.com; chartering, forwarding and shipping line agents; Chair. TAWFIQ KAWAR; CEO RUDAIN T. KAWAR; Pres. KARIM KAWAR.

Naouri Group: Um Uthaina, Saad Bin Abi Waqqas St, Bldg No. 30, Amman 11118; tel. (6) 5777900; fax (6) 5777911; e-mail kareem.naouri@naouri.com; internet www.naouri.com; f. 1994; operates several cos in shipping sector incl. Ammon Shipping and Transport, Salam Shipping and Forwarding, Kareem Logistics; Chair. IBRAHIM NAOURI.

Orient Shipping Co Ltd: Jordan Insurance Bldg, Bldg (A), 3rd Floor, POB 207, Amman 11118; tel. (6) 4641695; fax (6) 4651567; e-mail orship@orientshipping.jo; internet www.orientshipping.jo; f. 1965; shipping agency.

Petra Navigation and International Trading Co Ltd: POB 942502, Amman 11194; tel. (6) 5607021; fax (6) 5601362; e-mail info@petra.jo; internet www.petra.jo; f. 1977; general cargo, ro-ro and passenger ferries; Chair. AHMAD ARMOUSH; Man. Dir ANWAR SBEIH.

Red Sea Shipping Agency Co: POB 1248, 24 Sharif Abd al-Hamid Sharaf St, Shmeisani, Amman 11118; tel. (6) 5609501; fax (6) 5688241; e-mail rss@rssa.com.jo; internet www.redseashipping.com.jo; f. 1955.

Salam International Transport and Trading Co: POB 212955, Salam Trading Center, Arar St, Wadi Saqra, 11121; tel. (6) 5654510; fax (6) 5697014; e-mail tdajani@aagroup.jo; internet www.sittcogroup.com; f. 1996; publicly listed; diversified shipping, logistics, and oil and gas group; CEO TAREK DAJANI.

PIPELINES

Two oil pipelines cross Jordan. The former Iraq Petroleum Co pipeline, carrying petroleum from the oilfields in Iraq to Israel's Mediterranean port of Haifa, has not operated since 1967. The 1,717-km (1,067-mile) Trans-Arabian Pipeline (Tapline) carries petroleum from the oilfields of Dhahran in Saudi Arabia to Sidon on the Mediterranean seaboard in Lebanon. Tapline traverses Jordan for a distance of 177 km (110 miles) and has frequently been cut by hostile action. Confronted with the challenge of meeting rising oil demands, the Jordanian Government has been considering plans to rehabilitate disused sections of Tapline, at an estimated cost of US $200m.–$300m., since early 2005. In April 2013 the Governments of Jordan and Iraq signed an agreement for the construction of a US $18,000m., 1,700-km double pipeline to transport oil and natural gas from Basra province in Iraq to Aqaba.

CIVIL AVIATION

There are three international airports, two serving Amman and one in Aqaba. A 25-year concession to expand and operate Queen Alia International Airport at Zizya, 40 km south of Amman, including the construction of a new terminal building, was awarded to an international consortium, Airport International Group, in May 2007. The new terminal was officially opened in March 2013, increasing the airport's potential annual capacity to approximately 9m. passengers. The second phase of the expansion project, which was intended to increase annual capacity to 12m. passengers, commenced in January 2014. Completion of the US $100m. project was expected by 2017.

Jordan Civil Aviation Regulatory Commission (CARC): POB 7547, Amman 11110; tel. (6) 4892282; fax (6) 4891653; e-mail info@carc.gov.jo; internet www.carc.jo; f. 2007, to replace Civil Aviation Authority (f. 1950); Chief Commr and CEO Capt. GABRIEL SIVZATTIAN.

Aqaba Airports Co: POB 2662, King Hussein International Airport, Special Economic Zone, Aqaba 77110; tel. (3) 2034010; fax (3) 2034011; e-mail info@aac.jo; internet www.aac.jo; f. 2007; Dir MUNIR ASAD.

Jordan Aviation (JATE): POB 922358, Amman 11192; tel. (6) 5501760; fax (6) 5538746; e-mail info@jordanaviation.jo; internet www.jordanaviation.jo; f. 2000; first privately owned airline in Jordan; operates regional and international charter and scheduled flights; Chair. and CEO Capt. MUHAMMAD AL-KHASHMAN.

Royal Jordanian Airline: POB 302, Housing Bank Commercial Centre, Queen Noor St, Amman 11118; tel. (6) 5202000; fax (6) 5672527; e-mail AMMDDRJ@rj.com; internet www.rj.com; f. 1963; privatized in 2007; regional and international scheduled and charter services; Chair., Pres. and CEO NASSER A. LOZI.

Royal Wings Co Ltd: POB 314018, Amman 11134; tel. (6) 5803340; fax (6) 5803344; e-mail info@royalwings.com.jo; internet www.royalwings.com.jo; f. 1996; subsidiary of Royal Jordanian Airline; operates regional and domestic scheduled and charter services; Man. Dir ABD AL-QADER KAILANI.

Tourism

The ancient cities of Jarash (Jerash) and Petra, and Jordan's proximity to biblical sites, have encouraged tourism. The development of Jordan's Dead Sea coast is currently under way; owing to the Sea's mineral-rich waters, the growth of curative tourism is anticipated. The Red Sea port of Aqaba is also undergoing a major programme of development, with a view to becoming a centre for water sports, diving and beach holidays. Since the creation of the Wadi Rum Protected Area in 1998 tourism in this desert region is promoted on the basis of its unique ecosystem, landscape and the traditional culture of its Bedouin inhabitants. The National Tourism Strategy (NTS) 2004–10 set out ambitious targets that included doubling the figures for foreign visitors and tourism-related income and jobs. (By 2008 the sector appeared already to have achieved the goal of doubling income.) However, political turmoil in the Middle East and North Africa contributed to a decline in visitors and revenue from 2011. According to data from the Ministry of Tourism and Antiquities, the number of foreign visitors to Jordan declined to 6.3m., in 2012, although receipts increased to a provisional US $4,117m. in 2013.

Ministry of Tourism and Antiquities: see Ministries; Sec.-Gen. FAROUK AL-HADIDI.

Jordan Tourism Board (JTB): POB 830688, Amman 11183; tel. (6) 5678444; fax (6) 5678295; e-mail lana@visitjordan.com; internet www.visitjordan.com; f. 1997; Man. Dir Dr ABED AL-RAZZAQ ISSAM ARABIYAT.

Defence

Supreme Commander of the Armed Forces: King ABDULLAH IBN AL-HUSSEIN.

Chairman of the Joint Chiefs of Staff: Lt-Gen. MESHAAL MUHAMMAD AL-ZABIN.

Commander of the Royal Jordanian Navy: Brig.-Gen. QASEM FADEEL NAHAR TANASHAT.

Commander of the Royal Jordanian Air Force: Maj.-Gen. MANSOUR AL-JABOUR.

Defence Budget (2014): JD 899m.

Total Armed Forces (as assessed at November 2014): 100,500: army 74,000; navy est. 500; special operations 14,000; air force 12,000. Reserves 65,000 (army 60,000, joint 5,000).

Paramilitary Forces (as assessed at November 2014): 15,000.

Education

Primary education, beginning at six years of age, is free and compulsory. This 10-year preparatory cycle is followed by a two-year secondary cycle. The UN Relief and Works Agency (UNRWA) provides educational facilities and services for Palestinian refugees. According to UNESCO estimates, in 2011 primary enrolment included 98% of children in the relevant age-group; in the same year secondary enrolment included 88% of children in the relevant age-group. There were 306,630 students in higher education in 2011/12. Education in Jordan was provided at 5,167 schools and 22 institutions of higher education in 2003/04. The budget for central Government spending in 2012 allocated JD 738.5m. (11.1% of total current expenditure) to education.

KAZAKHSTAN

Introductory Survey

LOCATION, CLIMATE, LANGUAGE, RELIGION, FLAG, CAPITAL

The Republic of Kazakhstan extends 1,900 km (1,200 miles) from the Volga river in the west to the Altai mountains in the east, and about 1,300 km (800 miles) from the Siberian plain in the north to the Central Asian deserts in the south. To the south it borders Turkmenistan, Uzbekistan and Kyrgyzstan. To the east the border is with the People's Republic of China. There is a long border in the north with Russia and a coastline of 2,320 km (1,400 miles) on the Caspian Sea in the south-west. The climate is of a strongly continental type, but there are wide variations throughout the territory. Average temperatures in January range from −18°C (0°F) in the north to −3°C (27°F) in the south. In July average temperatures are 19°C (66°F) in the north and 28°C–30°C (82°F–86°F) in the south. Average annual rainfall in mountainous regions reaches 1,600 mm (63 ins), whereas in the central desert areas it is less than 100 mm (4 ins). The state language is Kazakh; however, Russian is employed officially in state and local government bodies. The predominant religion is Islam, most ethnic Kazakhs being Sunni Muslims of the Hanafi school. Other ethnic groups have their own religious communities, notably the (Christian) Russian Orthodox Church, which is attended mainly by Slavs. The national flag (proportions 1 by 2) consists of a light blue field, at the centre of which is a yellow sun (a disc surrounded by 32 rays), framed by the wings of a flying eagle, also in yellow, with a vertical stripe of national ornamentation in yellow near the hoist. In November 1997 the capital was moved from Almatı to Aqmola (formerly Tselinograd); the city was renamed Astana in 1998.

CONTEMPORARY POLITICAL HISTORY

Historical Context

After the February Revolution and the Bolshevik coup in Russia in 1917, there was civil war throughout Kazakhstan, which had come under Russian control in the first half of the 18th century. In 1920, following the victory of Bolshevik forces, the Kyrgyz Autonomous Soviet Socialist Republic (ASSR) was created within the Russian Soviet Federative Socialist Republic (the Russian Federation): the Kazakhs were known to the Russians as Kyrgyz, to distinguish them from the unrelated Cossacks. In 1925 the Kyrgyz ASSR was renamed the Kazakh ASSR; the Karakalpak region (Qoraqalpog'iston) was detached in 1930, and became an autonomous republic within the Uzbek Soviet Socialist Republic (SSR) in 1936. In December 1936 the Kazakh ASSR became a full Union Republic of the USSR, as the Kazakh SSR.

Under Soviet rule, parts of Kazakhstan were heavily industrialized. More than 1m. people were estimated to have died as a result of the starvation that accompanied the campaign in the early 1930s to collectivize agriculture and settle nomadic peoples. Many of those deported from elsewhere in the USSR during the Second World War were sent to the Republic. During Nikita Khrushchev's period in office as Soviet leader (1953–64) large areas of previously uncultivated land in Kazakhstan were transformed into arable land. This, along with Intensive industrialization, and the development of nuclear-testing sites and the Baikonur space centre brought large numbers of ethnic Russians to Kazakhstan. This dismissal, in December 1986, by Soviet leader Mikhail Gorbachev of Dinmuhamed Konaev, First Secretary of the Kazakhstan Kommunistik Partiyasi (KKP—Communist Party of Kazakhstan) precipitated demonstrations and unrest, which continued for three days, in several major cities.

In June 1989 Nursultan Nazarbaev, Chairman of the republican Council of Ministers since March 1984, was appointed First Secretary of the KKP. As part of political changes instituted in September 1989, a permanent Supreme Kenges (Supreme Council or Supreme Soviet—legislature) was to be established, and multi-candidate elections conducted. The state duties hitherto held by the First Secretary of the KKP were transferred to the Chairman of the Supreme Kenges, to which post Nazarbaev was elected in February 1990. Many candidates stood unopposed at elections to the chamber in March, and the system of reserved seats for KKP-affiliated organizations was retained, resulting in a substantial communist majority. In April the body elected Nazarbaev the first President of Kazakhstan. On 25 October the Supreme Kenges declared its sovereignty.

In the referendum on the future of the USSR conducted in nine Soviet republics in March 1991, almost 90% of the electorate voted in Kazakhstan, of whom 94% endorsed the proposal to preserve a 'union of sovereign states'. In June the Supreme Kenges voted, in principle, to adopt a draft union treaty. Kazakhstan was to sign the treaty in August, but this was forestalled by an attempted coup by conservative communists, in Moscow, the Soviet and Russian capital. As the coup attempt collapsed, Nazarbaev resigned from the Politburo and Central Committee of the Communist Party of the Soviet Union (KPSS). The KKP was ordered to cease activities in state and government organs, and in September the party withdrew from the KPSS; elements from the party went on to form the Kazakstan Sotsialistik Partiyasy (KSP—Socialist Party of Kazakhstan).

On 1 December 1991 Nazarbaev was elected unopposed as President of Kazakhstan in direct popular elections. On 8 December the leaders of Russia, Ukraine and Belarus signed an agreement establishing the Commonwealth of Independent States (CIS, see p. 241). On 16 December Kazakhstan became the last of the republics to declare independence from the USSR. The country became a co-founder of the CIS on 21 December, when the leaders of 11 former Soviet republics met in Almatı.

Domestic Political Affairs

In June 1992 some 5,000 people demonstrated in Almatı against continued communist predominance. A new Constitution, which denoted Kazakh as the state language, was adopted in January 1993. The Union of National Unity of Kazakhstan was established in the following month, with the declared aim of countering radical nationalism. Nazarbaev became Chairman of the Union, which was reorganized as a political party, the National Unity Party, later that year.

After independence

In December 1993 the Supreme Kenges voted to dissolve itself and to grant Nazarbaev the power to rule by decree pending elections to a new legislature. Kazakhstan's first multi-party elections were duly held on 7 March 1994, with the participation of 74% of the electorate; international observers reported a number of irregularities. The National Unity Party obtained 33 seats, which, when combined with the 42 seats won by candidates from the so-called 'President's List', emerged as the strongest force in the 177-member assembly. The Kazakstan Respublikasynyn Kesipodktar Federatsiyasy (KRKF—Federation of Trade Unions of the Republic of Kazakhstan) won 11 seats, the Kazakstan Kalyk Kongresi (KKK—People's Congress of Kazakhstan) nine and the KSP eight. The KKP was granted legal status in March. In that month the KRKF, the KSP and the KKK formed an opposition bloc in the Supreme Kenges.

In May 1994 some 96 members of the Supreme Kenges endorsed a motion expressing no confidence in the Government's economic, social and legal policies, and in June Nazarbaev announced a major government reorganization. The Government of Sergei Tereshchenko (premier since 1991) resigned in October 1994. Akejan Kajegeldin, an economist and First Deputy Prime Minister in the outgoing Council of Ministers, was appointed Premier.

In February 1995 the Constitutional Court declared the results of the 1994 general election to be invalid, owing to procedural irregularities. Nazarbaev was thereby effectively empowered to rule by decree pending further legislative elections. At a referendum on 29 April 1995 more than 95% of voters endorsed the extension of Nazarbaev's five-year mandate until December 2000. In May 1995 Nazarbaev ordered the establishment of a special council to prepare a new constitution. The final draft, which was approved by 89.1% of the electorate in a referendum on 30 August, preserved the President's extensive executive powers. The Supreme Kenges was replaced by a bicameral Parliament, comprising a 47-member Senat (Senate), 40 members of which were to be elected by regional administrations and seven appointed by the President, and a directly elected

67-member Majlis (Assembly). The Constitutional Court was replaced by a Constitutional Council, the rulings of which were to be subject to a presidential right of veto. Indirect elections to the Senate took place on 5 December. Some 80.7% of the electorate participated in direct elections to the Majlis on 9 December; further rounds of voting took place later in the month and in February 1996.

Popular dissatisfaction with the Government's economic and social policies became more pronounced in 1996. In April a new opposition movement, Citizen (Azamat), was established. Prolonged delays in payments of wages in state-owned enterprises were a principal cause of strikes and unauthorized demonstrations throughout 1997 and early 1998, as was the ongoing reform of pensions legislation. Meanwhile, in November 1997 Nazarbaev officially inaugurated the new capital city of Aqmola, in the north of the country; the city was renamed Astana (meaning 'capital city') at a further ceremony in June 1998.

In March 1997 Nazarbaev undertook a major reorganization and rationalization of the state apparatus, under which the Ministry of Petroleum and Natural Gas was abolished and replaced by a new state company, KazakhOil, while seven government institutions and ministries were directly subordinated to the President, and the structure of regional government was reorganized. In October Kajegeldin resigned as premier, after a Russian newspaper published an admission by him of his previous involvement with the Soviet state security service (KGB). Nazarbaev appointed Nurlan Balgymbaev, hitherto head of KazakhOil, as his successor.

In September 1998 Nazarbaev outlined proposals for political reforms, including amendments to electoral procedures and enhanced legislative powers. In October, however, Parliament rejected Nazarbaev's proposed constitutional reforms, and instead voted to schedule a presidential election before the expiry of Nazarbaev's extended mandate in 2000 and to decrease the quota of the votes required by parties in order to secure representation in the legislature from 10% to 7%.

During November 1998 the Central Electoral Commission (CEC) deemed several opposition figures, including Kajegeldin, ineligible to contest the presidency, in accordance with a presidential decree that prevented those convicted of an administrative offence in the 12 months prior to an election from registering as a candidate. Several opposition parties were formed, although some were prevented from registering. Among those to be accorded official status was the pro-presidential Otan (Fatherland) party.

The conduct of the presidential election, contested by four candidates on 10 January 1999, prompted criticism from the Organization for Security and Co-operation in Europe (OSCE, see p. 385) and other international bodies. Nazarbaev was elected to a further term, with 81.0% of the votes cast by 88.3% of the registered electorate. A new Government, headed by Balgymbaev, was appointed later in the month. In August the Minister of Defence, Gen. Muxtar Altynbaev, and the Chairman of the National Security Committee (KNB), Nurtai Abykaev, were dismissed, after admitting responsibility for the attempted illegal sale of military aircraft to the Democratic People's Republic of Korea (North Korea). In September Kajegeldin, who had been charged with tax evasion in April, was arrested at an airport in Moscow; he was released following criticism of his detention by the OSCE. Kajegeldin was barred from registering as a candidate for the parliamentary elections in October, and further charges were brought against him in February 2000.

In early October 1999 Balgymbaev resigned as premier and resumed his former position as President of KazakhOil. He was succeeded by Kasym-Jomart Tokaev. Elections to the Majlis were held in two rounds on 10 and 24 October. Otan was the largest political grouping, with 23 seats; the Kazakhstan Azamattyk Partiyasy (KAzP—Civic Party of Kazakhstan) held 13 seats and the KRKF 11. Three other parties obtained representation, and 23 independent candidates were elected.

In June 2000 a law was approved awarding Nazarbaev certain lifetime guarantees and rights. In September 2001 Kajegeldin was sentenced *in absentia* to 10 years' imprisonment, having been found guilty of abuse of power, tax evasion and the illegal possession of weapons. In November Nazarbaev approved the resignation of Rahat Aliev (the husband of his daughter, Darigha Nazarbaeva) as Deputy Chairman of the KNB, amid accusations that he had abused his powers. Persistent reports that Aliev and Nazarbaeva controlled the majority of Kazakhstan's media outlets and influenced their output prompted the Akim (Governor) of Pavlodar Oblast (region), Galymjan Jakiyanov, and a number

of other prominent political and business figures, including the Deputy Prime Minister, Oraz Jandosov, to form a new political movement, the Kazakstannyn Demokratiyalyk Tandauy (KDT—Democratic Choice of Kazakhstan). Tokaev subsequently announced that two attempts to assassinate the President had been averted, and threatened to resign as Prime Minister unless the President dismissed ministers involved in the formation of the KDT. Jandosov and Alixan Baymenov (the Minister of Labour and Social Security) resigned shortly afterwards; Nazarbaev dismissed Jakiyanov on the same day.

In January 2002 amendments to media legislation came into effect, which required 50% of all radio and television programmes to be broadcast in Kazakh, and imposed restrictions on the rebroadcast of foreign television programmes and on internet media. Later in the month Tokaev resigned, but was appointed State Secretary and Minister of Foreign Affairs in a new Government formed on 31 January and led by Imangali Tasmagambetov, a former Deputy Prime Minister. Meanwhile, divisions emerged within the KDT, and several of its founding members, including Jandosov and Jakiyanov, formed a new party, the Kazakstannyn Ak Jol Demokratiyalyk Partiyasy (Ak Jol—Bright Road Democratic Party of Kazakhstan). Jakiyanov, however, was subsequently arrested, and sentenced in August to a seven-year gaol term on charges of abuse of power during his tenure as Akim of Pavlodar Oblast.

In July 2002 Nazarbaev signed into effect new legislation requiring political parties to have a minimum of 50,000 members (rather than the previous 3,000). In the same month a former Minister of Energy, Industry and Trade and founding member of the KDT, Muxtar Ablyazov, was sentenced to six years' imprisonment, having been found guilty of abuse of office.

In January 2003 it was reported that Jandosov had been appointed as a presidential aide. Also in January the Ministry of Justice annulled the KDT's registration. By the end of the re-registration period in April, only seven parties had satisfied the requisite criteria. Meanwhile, in January Sergei Duvanov, an independent journalist, was sentenced to three-and-a-half years' imprisonment on charges of rape. In February the European Parliament adopted a resolution condemning the sentences imposed on Duvanov, Ablyazov and Jakiyanov, and demanding that an independent investigation into their trials be carried out. Ablyazov was pardoned in May, and subsequently announced his withdrawal from politics. (Duvanov was released in August 2004, and Jakiyanov was released on parole in January 2006.)

However, on 9 June 2003 Tasmagambetov tendered his resignation, after it emerged that the results of an unsuccessful no confidence vote, conducted in the legislature in May, had been falsified. A new, substantially unchanged Government, led by Danïal Axmetov, a former Akim of Pavlodar Oblast, was appointed in June.

Nazarbayev further consolidates power

Although newly emerged political parties continued to be refused registration, in October 2003 a new organization led by Darigha Nazarbaeva, Asar (Mutual Help), was officially registered, as were the Kazakstan Kommunistik Halyk Partiyasy (KKHP—Communist People's Party of Kazakhstan) and the Kazakstan Demokratiyalyk Partiyasy (KDP—Democratic Party of Kazakhstan) in June 2004. On 19 September and 3 October 2003 elections took place to the Majlis. Otan obtained 42 seats. An electoral coalition formed by the Kazakstan Agrarlyk Partiyasy (KAgP—Agrarian Party of Kazakhstan) and the KAzP won 11 seats, while Asar obtained four seats. Ak Jol and the KDP each obtained one seat, and 18 non-partisan candidates were elected. Monitors from the OSCE criticized the conduct of the polls and electoral coverage by the media. Baymenov, now a member of Ak Jol, and who was effectively the only opposition representative elected to the new legislature, subsequently announced that he would not take up his seat in the Majlis, alleging that the results of the elections had been falsified. The Chairman of the outgoing legislature, Jarmakhan Tuyakbay, resigned from Otan to protest against the conduct of the elections.

In January 2005, following a declaration by the KDT in the previous month that it regarded the Kazakhstani Government to be illegitimate, and urging non-violent civil disobedience, a court ordered that the party be dissolved. Later in the month the KDT, Ak Jol and the KKP (which had established an alliance) organized an unsanctioned rally to protest against the court ruling. In February the three parties announced that they were to establish a new movement, to be known as Ediletti Kazakstan Ushin (EKU—For a Just Kazakhstan). In March former members of the KDT announced the establishment of a new grouping, Alga

(Forward), led by Asylbek Kojaxmetov (which was subsequently refused registration). In April another new party, Naghyz Ak Jol (NAJ—Real Bright Road), held its founding congress, following divisions within Ak Jol.

Meanwhile, in December 2004 President Nazarbaev issued a decree allowing the election of village akims (who had hitherto been appointed), as well as the 'experimental' election of several oblast akims. Elections were held in villages and in four oblasts during 2005. In the elections to the oblast posts, all the incumbent candidates were returned to office, and all candidates had been nominated by the local authorities.

In April 2005 legislation was introduced to prohibit public demonstrations both during and immediately after elections. The EKU coalition, led by Tuyakbay, and now including the KKP, Alga and NAJ, was granted official registration in August. In the presidential ballot, conducted on 4 December, one year earlier than had been anticipated, Nazarbaev was re-elected President, with 91.2% of the votes cast, according to official results. Of the four other candidates, his closest rival was Tuyakbay, with 6.6%. The rate of participation was 76.8%. Monitors from the OSCE declared that the conduct of the election had not satisfied democratic standards. On 18 January 2006 both legislative chambers unanimously approved Nazarbaev's nomination of Axmetov as Prime Minister.

In February 2006 Altynbek Sarsenbaev, one of the leaders of NAJ and a prominent supporter of Tuyakbay's presidential campaign, was shot dead in Almatı. Those detained on suspicion of involvement in the case included five KNB officials and the head of the administration of the Senat, Erjan Utembaev. The head of the KNB, Nartai Dutbaev, subsequently resigned as a result of the investigation. In March NAJ was granted official registration. The conviction, in August, of 10 people (including Utembaev) charged with involvement in the killing of Sarsenbaev attracted international criticism; a former security officer received the death sentence, and Utembaev was sentenced to 20 years' imprisonment. (In February 2014 his sentence was reduced to 13 years.) In July Otan merged with Asar, thereby consolidating parliamentary support for Nazarbaev. In December the KAgP and the KAzP also merged with Otan; the new party, known as Nur Otan (Light of the Fatherland) thereby controlled 57 seats in the Majlis.

On 8 January 2007 Axmetov resigned as Prime Minister; he had been subject to repeated presidential criticism for poor organization and budget-planning. On 10 January the Majlis voted to approve Nazarbaev's nomination of Karim Mäsımov as premier. Aslan Musin was appointed as Deputy Prime Minister (retaining his existing portfolio as Minister of the Economy and Budgetary Planning), while Axmetov became Minister of Defence. Tokaev became Chairman of the Senat. In May Parliament approved extensive constitutional amendments, proposed by President Nazarbaev, strengthening the powers of an expanded Majlis, which was henceforth to approve prime ministerial appointments. The presidential term of office was to be reduced from seven to five years with effect from 2012, while the restriction on the incumbent President to two terms in office was to be removed.

In June 2007 Rahat Aliev, by then the Kazakhstani ambassador to Austria, was arrested in that country, after Kazakhstan had issued an arrest warrant against him for his alleged involvement in the kidnapping of two banking associates; Kazakhstan officially requested his extradition. (In January 2008 a district court in Almatı imposed *in absentia* a 20-year sentence of imprisonment on Aliev, who had claimed asylum in Austria, for his involvement in the creation of an organized criminal group and the abductions of the banking officials. In March, at a second trial *in absentia*, a military court sentenced Aliev to another 20 years' imprisonment for illegal possession of armaments and ammunition, misappropriation of property and planning a coup.)

In mid-June 2007 Nazarbaev dissolved the Majlis and announced legislative elections were to be held on 18 August (two years earlier than scheduled). At the elections Nur Otan won 88.4% of the votes cast, securing all 98 contested seats in the enlarged 107-member Majlis. None of the other six parties participating in the poll achieved the 7% minimum of votes required to gain representation in the chamber; the newly established Jalpyulttyk Sotsial Demokratiyalyk Partiyasy (JSDP—National Social Democratic Party) received 4.5% and Ak Jol 3.1%. The leaders of the JSDP, Ak Jol and the KKHP refused to acknowledge the results and demanded that the poll be repeated. In accordance with the amended Constitution, the

Assembly of the Nations of Kazakhstan (representing minority ethnic groups, and which was later renamed the Assembly of the Nation of Kazakhstan) elected the remaining nine deputies to the Majlis on 20 August. A reorganized Government was approved on 2 September; Ómirzaq Şökeev, hitherto Akim of Southern Kazakhstan Oblast, became the new Deputy Prime Minister, succeeding Musin, who was elected Chairman of the Majlis. In February 2008, during a party congress, NAJ was renamed Azat (Freedom).

In early 2009 Ablyazov fled to the United Kingdom (UK), where he claimed political asylum, after the Kazakhstani authorities issued an arrest warrant against him for embezzlement in his previous post as Chairman of BTA Bank. (In July 2011 Ablyazov was granted asylum by the UK, where BTA Bank initiated a court case against him on allegations of fraud. In February 2012 he left the UK, after he was sentenced to 22 months' imprisonment for failing to disclose his assets. In July 2013 Ablyazov was arrested in France, on a warrant issued at the request of Ukraine, and in January 2014 a French court ruled that he could be extradited, to either Russia or Ukraine, to face trial on charges of fraud. Earlier in 2013, Ablyazov's wife and daughter had been deported from Italy to Kazakhstan, but were allowed to return to Italy in December.)

In March 2009 a number of significant appointments of government ministers and other public officials were effected. Şökeev received the post of First Deputy Prime Minister, while Serik Axmetov, hitherto Minister of Transport, became a Deputy Prime Minister. The removal of Danïal Axmetov as Minister of Defence in June was believed to be connected to a contract he had agreed with an Israeli company in 2007, which had resulted in a substantial loss of government funds and had prompted the arrest of various senior officials on charges of corruption. Adilbek Jaqsıbekov, hitherto ambassador to Russia, was appointed as the new Minister of Defence. In September Qanatbek Sawdabaev was appointed as Minister of Foreign Affairs to succeed Marat Täjïn, who became a presidential aide.

In June 2009 Parliament adopted legislative amendments, designating all online resources as mass media, thereby allowing any websites deemed to be in violation of existing media regulations to be blocked and their owners prosecuted. In September a sentence of four years' imprisonment imposed on human rights activist Yevgeny Jovtis, after he had been convicted of manslaughter resulting from a car accident, prompted protests from human rights groups and the OSCE. (Jovtis was freed under amnesty in February 2012.) Later that month the deputy leader of Nur Oran urged the adoption of legislation that would permit Nazarbaev to remain as President indefinitely. At a unification congress in October Azat and the JSDP agreed to form a single party, to be known as the Azat JSDP, which was to be headed jointly by the leaders of the two constituent parties.

In March 2010 a substantial reorganization of the Government and other state agencies was implemented. In May both parliamentary chambers approved legislation awarding Nazarbaev the title 'Leader of the Nation', while also granting him and his relatives immunity from prosecution, and making it a criminal offence to utter or publish insulting remarks about the President. Although Nazarbaev formally refused to sign the legislation into law, it automatically entered into force on 15 June.

Opposition unrest

On 29 December 2010 both chambers of the Parliament adopted a motion in favour of extending Nazarbaev's term in office until 2020, subject to approval at a national referendum. On 6 January 2011, however, Nazarbaev issued a decree vetoing the proposal. On 14 January both parliamentary chambers voted unanimously to amend the Constitution to permit the referendum, following the submission of a petition of 5m. signatures in its support. However, Nazarbaev subsequently refused to sign the constitutional amendments into force, instead referring them to the Constitutional Court, which, on 31 January, ruled against the organization of a referendum on the proposals. Nazarbaev announced his acceptance of the Court's decision and proposed that an early presidential election be conducted.

Nazarbaev was returned to office at the presidential election on 3 April 2011, securing 95.6% of the votes cast, according to official results; voter turnout of 89.9% was recorded. The three other candidates who secured registration themselves expressed support for Nazarbaev, while the Azat JSDP boycotted the poll. Nazarbaev was inaugurated for a further five-year term on 8 April. In response to the international criticism of the electoral process, he issued pledges to increase anti-corruption efforts and institutional reforms (including commitments that political parties other than Nur Otan be represented in the Majlis). On the same day the Majlis approved the reappointment of Mäsımov as premiers. Nazarbaev subsequently reorganized the Government, notably replacing Sawdabaev as Minister of Foreign Affairs with a former ambassador to the UN, Erjan Qazıxanov, and appointing Qayrat Kelimbetov as Minister of Economic Development and Trade. A new Minister of Internal Affairs, Qalmuxanbet Qasımov was also appointed, while a new ministerial position, of Economic Integration, was created. Meanwhile, on 15 April Kayrat Mami, hitherto Prosecutor-General, was elected Chairman of the Senat, after he had been appointed to the chamber by Nazarbaev. A new Prosecutor-General was appointed on the same day, and one day later Nazarbaev dismissed six judges of the Supreme Court, who were under investigation for corrupt activity.

In April 2011 a man blew himself up in the north-western city of Aqtöbe, injuring at least two people, in what was reported to be Kazakhstan's first suicide bombing. (Twelve men were imprisoned in December in connection with the incident.) Violent confrontations in Aqtöbe Oblast between Islamist militants and security forces in June and July reportedly resulted in the deaths of nine militants and three police officers, while the detonation of a bomb in Aqtöbe in July resulted in three deaths. (In February 2012 five men were sentenced to prison terms for their involvement in the attack.) Meanwhile, in June 2011 two bodies, found in Almatı during the previous month, were identified as being those of the former banking associates of Rahat Aliev who had been kidnapped in 2007. Aliev was charged *in absentia* with involvement in their deaths, but the Austrian Government rejected an extradition request. (In February 2015 Aliev died while in custody in Austria.)

In June 2011 the First Secretary of the KKP, Gaziz Aldamjarov, and the leader of Alga, Vladimir Kozlov, together with representatives of several non-governmental organizations, announced the formation of a Popular Front. Meanwhile, in May 2011 petroleum sector workers in western Kazakhstan commenced strike action in support of wage increases and rights for trade unions. Several activists were arrested and prosecuted, including a lawyer representing the workers, Nataliya Sokolova, who received a six-year prison sentence in August. (She was released on probation in March 2012.) Also in August 2011 Jaqsılıq Dosqaliev, who had been dismissed as Minister of Health the previous October, was sentenced to seven years' imprisonment after he was found guilty of corruption.

On 19 August 2011 Nur Otan secured all 16 contested seats in partial elections in the Senat. In October Valerii Proskuryakov, a prominent member of Nur Oran, was shot dead in the eastern city of Öskemen. In October Nazarbaev signed into law legislation that imposed further restrictions on religious activity, and requiring all religious organizations to re-register with the authorities. the legislation was widely considered to be directed against the influence of fundamentalist Islam. Also in October the KKP's operations were suspended for six months by a court order, on the grounds that the formation of the Popular Front had violated the law on public organizations. Aldamjarov claimed that the court's ruling was politically motivated, in light of the Popular Front's support for the strike action by petroleum industry workers, and in April 2012 the suspension was extended by a further six months.

In late October 2011 two explosions occurred in the western city of Atiraw, reportedly killing one person. A militant Islamist group based in the territories on the borders of Afghanistan and Pakistan, Jund al-Khilafah (Soldiers of the Caliphate), claimed responsibility for the bombings, and voiced its opposition to the recently introduced religious legislation. (In April 2012 some 47 people were sentenced to between five and 15 years' imprisonment on terrorism charges in connection with the Atiraw bombings.) In November, seven people were shot dead in the southern city of Taraz by an Islamist militant who subsequently blew himself up. (Five men charged with involvement in the incident were sentenced to imprisonment in April 2012.) Jund al-Khilafah also claimed that five men killed in a security operation near Almatı were members of its organization.

In November 2011, in response to a petition from members of the Majlis, President Nazarbaev dissolved the lower house and scheduled pre-term elections for January 2012, seven months before the expiry of the mandate of the chamber. On 16 December, Independence Day, at least 17 people were killed in violent confrontations between striking petroleum workers and security forces in the western town of Jañaözen, in Mañğıstaw Oblast.

Nazarbaev declared a state of emergency and curfew in Jañaözen; this was subsequently extended to the end of January 2012.

At legislative elections held on 15 January 2012, three parties secured representation in the Majlis: Nur Otan won 81.0% of the votes cast, according to the CEC, obtaining 83 of the 98 directly elected seats, ahead of Ak Jol, which won 7.5% of the vote and eight seats, and the KKHP, with 7.2% of the vote and seven seats. Nine further deputies were appointed by the Assembly of the Nation of Kazakhstan. Participation was recorded at 75.4% of registered voters. Observers from the OSCE criticized the poll, citing in particular the denial of registration to the candidates of certain parties—including the entire list of candidates proposed by the Ruhniyat Partiyasy (Spirituality Party)—and the ongoing suspension of the KKP. The new Majlis was formally inaugurated on 20 January. It reconfirmed Mäsımov as Prime Minister, and appointed Nurlan Nigmatulin as its Chairman.

Following the elections, in January 2012 the authorities began to arrest large numbers of opposition figures and journalists in connection with the unrest in Jañaözen. The offices of Alga were raided by police, and Kozlov was arrested. The Government alleged that Ablyazov had been involved in instigating the unrest from exile, and that earlier in the year a series of terrorist attacks planned by individuals connected to Alga and to Ablyazov had been averted. In May five police officers were sentenced to prison terms of between five and seven years for abusing their authority during the suppression of the protests in Jañaözen. Following a separate trial in June, 34 people were convicted on charges of organizing or participating in the violence, of whom 13 received custodial sentences. In August the trial commenced in Aktaw of Kozlov, together with two other opposition activists, on charges that included inciting social unrest and seeking to overthrow the constitutional order during the strike in Jañaözen. In September Orak Sarbopeev, a former Akim of Jañaözen, was found guilty of preparing criminal activity and sentenced to 10 years' imprisonment. In October Kozlov was sentenced to seven-and-a-half-years' imprisonment, and the other two activists received suspended sentences. Meanwhile, in September further bomb attacks were staged in Atiraw, including an explosion near a mosque in which one person was killed, and one at interior ministry offices in which two policemen were injured.

On 24 September 2012 President Nazarbaev appointed Serik Axmetov (First Deputy Prime Minister since January) as Prime Minister, replacing Mäsımov, who became presidential Chief of Staff. Qırımbek Köşerbaev, who had resigned as Akim of Mañğıstaw Oblast following the violence in Jañaözen, became First Deputy Prime Minister, Minister of Regional Development, while other government changes included the appointment of Erlan Idırısov, hitherto ambassador to the USA, as Minister of Foreign Affairs.

Following Kozlov's conviction, in November 2012 prosecutors demanded a ban on the activities of Alga and the Popular Front, together with the closure of the main independent media outlets, on the grounds that they had incited the overthrow of the Government prior to the violence in Jañaözen. The authorities claimed that Alga and several opposition organs were financed by Ablyazov, who in the same month was ordered to pay the equivalent of more than US $1,630m., after a British court upheld the charges brought by BTA Bank against him and froze his remaining assets. Also in November a court in the southern town of Qızılorda sentenced former Deputy Akim of Mañğıstaw, Amangeldy Aitkulov, to 12 years' imprisonment for abuse of office and corrupt practices. Following the suspension of their activities, in December an Almatı court upheld the ban on the two opposition movements and the media outlets, which were declared extremist. In the same month a prominent human rights lawyer, Vadim Kuramshin, was imprisoned for 12 years for attempting to extort a bribe (after having been cleared of the charges earlier in the year). Opposition supporters staged demonstrations in several towns to mark the anniversary on 16 January of the killing in Jañaözen. In December Nazarbaev announced a programme in accordance with which the Kazakh language would be written solely in the Latin script (rather than principally in Cyrillic, as had been the case since 1940) by 2025.

Administrative reorganizations

In January 2013 the President appointed Bakıtjan Sagıntaev, hitherto Deputy Chairman of Nur Oran and a former economy minister, to replace Köşerbaev as First Deputy Prime Minister, Minister of Regional Development (for which portfolio a new ministry was created); Köşerbaev became Akim of Qızılorda Oblast. As part of an extensive reorganization of the government administrative structure, the Ministry of Economic

Development and Trade was reconstituted as the Ministry of the Economy and Budgetary Planning. Local media speculated in March 2013 that Nazarbayev, who took temporary leave of absence from office on 13 March, had been treated for prostate cancer in Israel (earlier reports had suggested that he had received treatment in Germany). Two small opposition political parties—Adilet (Justice), and Ruxniyat—announced their merger into a new party, Birlik (Unity), in April, led by Serik Sultangali. In June reports emerged of an unsuccessful plot by Islamist militants to blow up public buildings in Astana and attack senior Government officials. Nazarbaev subsequently released in October a draft State Programme on Counteracting Religious Extremism and Terrorism for 2013–17, which would extend the existing restrictions on religious activity, as well as the monitoring of religious groups. Later in October 2013 Kasym-Jomart Tokaev, a senior UN official who had formerly served as Prime Minister, was appointed Chairman of the Senat, a post he had held during 2007–11. On 2 April 2014 Serik Axmetov resigned as Prime Minister; he was succeeded on the same day by his immediate predecessor, Mäsımov; Nigmatulin replaced Mäsımov as presidential Chief of Staff, and was himself succeeded as Chairman of the Assembly, on 3 April, by Kabibulla Jakupov. Axmetov was appointed Minister of Defence in Mäsımov's Government.

In April 2014 Nazarbaev announced a new criminal code, which, following parliamentary approval, he signed into law on 3 July; human rights groups criticized the changes, in particular an increase in the number of crimes punishable by the death penalty to include war crimes and acts of terrorism, the introduction of penalties for participation in unregistered religious or social organizations, further restrictions on the freedom of assembly and the criminalization of expressing separatist sentiments and disseminating rumours. Meanwhile, following the signature of a treaty creating a Eurasian Economic Union (EEU, see p. 446) on 29 May (see *Regional relations*), protests were staged in Astana and a number of demonstrators were arrested. Concerns at the activities of extremist elements in the country increased; in July five people were convicted in Almatı for participation in the prohibited Islamist organization Hizb ut-Tahrir-al-Islami (Hizb ut-Tahrir—Party of Islamic Liberation), after attending the group's meetings where the creation of an caliphate in Kazakhstan was discussed. On 3 November Nazarbaev signed more stringent anti-extremist measures into law, under which the authorities were enabled immediately to dissolve any group designated as extremist or terrorist and to confiscate its property. (Critics of the Government maintained that opposition and independent media outlets had been subject to further restriction under anti-extremist legislation.)

Amid increasing economic difficulties, on 6 August 2014 Nazarbaev announced an extensive rationalization of government and public administration, in which the number of ministries was reduced from 17 to 12, and the number of deputy premierships from three to two; new appointments included that of Vladimir Shkolnik, formerly President of the Kazakhstani National Atomic Industry Co, to the newly created post of Minister of Energy. In October Axmetov resigned his post as Minister of Defence, following allegations that he had attempted to influence the legal case of the Akim of Qarağandi Oblast, who, together with several other public officials of the region, had been detained on charges of corruption earlier that month. (A former mayor of Astana, Imangali Tasmagambetov, was subsequently appointed as Minister of Defence.) Axmetov was charged with embezzlement and placed under house arrest in November. On 11 November Gulshara Abdykhalikova was replaced as Deputy Prime Minister by Berdibek Saparbayev, formerly Akim of Eastern Kazakhstan, and appointed as a Secretary of State. Nurali Aliev, a grandson of Nazarbaev, was appointed deputy mayor of Astana in December.

Recent developments: early presidential election

Clashes erupted between the Kazakh and Tajik communities in the village of Bostandyk in southern Kazakhstan in early February 2015, following the killing of a Kazakh in a residential dispute. Following a proposal by the Assembly of the Nation of Kazakhstan, on 19 February the Senate approved the organization of an early presidential election (which had been due to take place in December 2016), and affirmed its support for President Nazarbaev to seek a further term in office. On 11 March 2015 Nazarbaev announced that a presidential election would be conducted on 26 April, stating that his Government required a new mandate to implement an economic stimulus programme and to strengthen internal stability. On the same day he accepted the nomination of Nur Otan to be the party's presidential candidate in the forthcoming election. The election was contested by three candidates. According to the official results published by the Central Election Commission, 95.2% of the electorate participated in voting, and Nazarbaev was overwhelmingly re-elected, being attributed 97.75% of the votes cast.

Foreign Affairs

Regional relations

The question of the legal status of the Caspian Sea—and the division of the mineral resources located in the seabed—has been a source of tension between the five littoral states: Azerbaijan, Iran, Kazakhstan, Russia and Turkmenistan. In 1998 President Nazarbaev and his Russian counterpart, Boris Yeltsin, signed a bilateral agreement on the delineation of their countries' respective boundaries of the seabed, by which Russia for the first time formally recognized Kazakhstan's claim to its offshore petroleum resources. Iran, however, asserted that partitioning of the seabed required the consensus of all five littoral states. In 2000 Nazarbaev and the President of Russia, Vladimir Putin, signed an additional agreement, on the definition of the legal status of the Caspian Sea. The 1998 agreement was further augmented in May 2002, when an accord was signed on the equal division of three oil fields in the northern Caspian. Russia and Kazakhstan have also signed a Treaty of Eternal Friendship and Co-operation, which provides for mutual military assistance in the event of aggression by a third party. In November 2001 Kazakhstan concluded a bilateral agreement with Azerbaijan on the two countries' respective mineral rights in the Caspian Sea, prompting further protests from Iran. In May 2003 Azerbaijan, Kazakhstan and Russia signed a trilateral agreement. In January 2005 Nazarbaev and Putin signed a treaty in Moscow defining the land border between their two countries. Meeting in the Azerbaijani capital, Baku (Bakı), in November 2010, the Heads of State of Azerbaijan, Iran, Kazakhstan, Russia and Turkmenistan signed an agreement on security co-operation. Iranian President Hassan Rouhani made his first official visit to Kazakhstan in September 2014, when, following the relaxation of Western sanctions against Iran, the resumption of bilateral co-operation arrangements was under discussion.

In the early 1990s the question of the formerly Soviet, subsequently Russian-controlled, nuclear warheads deployed in Kazakhstan was the focus of international concern. By April 1995 all nuclear warheads had been transferred to Russia, and in September 1996 Russia and Kazakhstan signed a final protocol governing the withdrawal of military units linked to the Russian nuclear weapons facilities in Kazakhstan.

In May 2001 the signatories of the CIS Collective Security Treaty (Armenia, Belarus, Kazakhstan, Kyrgyzstan, Russia and Tajikistan) agreed to form a Collective Rapid Response Force, based in Bishkek, Kyrgyzstan, to combat Islamist militancy in Central Asia. An anti-terrorism centre became operational in Bishkek in August 2001. In April 2003 the signatories of the Treaty formally inaugurated the Collective Security Treaty Organization (CSTO, see p. 460), to which Uzbekistan subsequently acceded. Kazakhstan ratified an agreement to join the Collective Rapid Response Force in February 2010.

In 1992 Kazakhstan joined the Economic Co-operation Organization (ECO, see p. 264), founded by Iran, Pakistan and Turkey. In 1994 Kazakhstan, Kyrgyzstan and Uzbekistan formed a trilateral economic area, and in February 1995 an Interstate Council was established to supervise its implementation. In 1997 Tajikistan joined the alliance, which became the Central Asian Co-operation Organization (CACO) in 2002. Meanwhile, Kazakhstan signed a treaty with Russia, Belarus and Kyrgyzstan in 1996, which envisaged a common market and a customs union between the four countries; Tajikistan signed the agreement in April 1998. In October 2000 a new economic body, the Eurasian Economic Community (EurAsEC), was established, and this organization merged with CACO in January 2006. In June 2009, at a trilateral meeting of Heads of State, it was announced that Russia, Kazakhstan and Belarus were to establish a Customs Union. Russia, Kazakhstan and Belarus introduced unified customs tariffs on 1 January 2010, and the Customs Union officially entered into force in July. In December 2011 the three countries' Presidents signed an agreement to establish an Eurasian Economic Commission, which was envisioned as the next stage towards the ultimate creation of an Eurasian Economic Union (EEU, see p. 446). In January 2013 the Kazakhstani and Russian Ministers of Defence, meeting in Astana, signed an agreement providing for the establishment of a joint regional air defence system. In 2014 Russia agreed to allow Kazakhstan to extend its administrative legislation to Kazakhstani citizens in Baikonur, and to permit the establishment of Kazakhstani curricula in schools in the city, which, as the base of the Baikonur space centre, was leased to Russia and was otherwise under Russian jurisdiction. The agreement to create a unified air defence system with Russia, to be headed by officials appointed by the Presidents of both countries, was ratified by Nazarbaev on 26 May, following parliamentary approval. An accord formally creating the EEU was signed by Kazakhstan with Russia and Belarus on 29 May. Nazarbaev signed legislation ratifying the treaty on 14 October (following endorsement by the Presidents of Russia and Belarus). The Union, in which Armenia and Kyrgyzstan were also to participate, formally entered into effect on 1 January 2015.

Meanwhile, the Kazakhstani Government recognized as legitimate the results of referendums (unrecognized by the Ukrainian authorities) in Ukraine's Crimean peninsula, then under de facto Russian control, on 16 March 2014, which provided for Russia's annexation of the territory (see the chapter on Ukraine). It was also critical of Western sanctions subsequently introduced against Russia, but, amid continuing negotiations with the EU (see *Other external relations*), in August announced that it would not participate in retaliatory sanctions imposed by Russia on imports from EU states. Presidents Nazarbaev and Putin met on the occasion of an inter-regional co-operation forum in Atiraw in September, when agreement was reached on the proposed joint construction of a nuclear power plant in Kazakhstan. In early December French President François Hollande visited Astana, and later that month Nazarbaev for the first time met Ukrainian President Petro Poroshenko in the Ukrainian capital, Kyiv, after which he confirmed his willingness for Kazakhstan to host negotiations on the continuing conflict in the Donetsk and Luhansk oblasts of eastern Ukraine. Nazarbaev subsequently undertook mediation efforts, although a summit meeting in Astana planned for mid-January 2015 was cancelled.

Bilateral relations between Kazakhstan and the People's Republic of China were strengthened by two accords concluded in 1997, which granted China permission to exploit two of the largest oil fields in Kazakhstan, and provided for the construction of a petroleum pipeline (completed in 2005) connecting the two countries. In November 1998 Nazarbaev made a state visit to China, which resulted in the signature of a communiqué on the full settlement of outstanding border issues. In July 2005 Nazarbaev and Chinese President Hu Jintao signed an agreement on the establishment of a strategic partnership. China and Kazakhstan belonged to the so-called Shanghai Five (also comprising Kyrgyzstan, Russia and Tajikistan), which aimed to promote economic co-operation and regional co-ordination on border and security issues. Members of the alliance, which became the Shanghai Co-operation Organization (SCO, see p. 463) upon the accession of Uzbekistan in 2001, signed the Shanghai Convention on Combating Terrorism, Separatism and Extremism in June 2001. Several bilateral co-operation agreements were signed during a Chinese official visit to Kazakhstan in November 2007. A second section of the petroleum pipeline system linking Kazakhstan with China entered into operation in July 2009. During an official visit to China in February 2011, Nazarbaev signed a number of major economic and energy agreements with Hu, including a memorandum of understanding to support the construction of a modernized rail link between Astana and Almatı. A further meeting between the two Presidents in Astana in June resulted in the conclusion of a strategic partnership agreement. Nazarbaev made a state visit to China in May 2014, when a further 16 bilateral co-operation agreements were signed.

Other external relations

Following the suicide attacks on the USA on 11 September 2001, President Nazarbaev expressed his support for US-led military action against the al-Qa'ida militant Islamist organization and the regime of its hosts, the Taliban, in Afghanistan. Kazakhstan offered the USA the use of airports, airspace and military bases. Nazarbaev's links with US petroleum companies were subject to legal scrutiny from March 2003, when James H. Giffen, a US businessman and former adviser to Nazarbaev, was indicted in the USA on charges of offering bribes to prominent Kazakhstani politicians, including Nazarbaev, in return for securing valuable contracts for US petroleum companies. In April 2004 a US federal court indicted Giffen and an executive of the petroleum company, ExxonMobil, on charges of corrupt business practices. In September 2006 Nazarbaev met US President George W.

Bush during an official visit to Washington, DC, USA. A Strategic Partnership Dialogue between Kazakhstan and the USA officially began in April 2012, following an agreement in January. The Minister of Foreign Affairs, Erlan Idırısov (a former ambassador to the USA), met US Secretary of State Hillary Clinton for discussions in the US capital in October. Idırısov met US Secretary of State John Kerry in New York in September 2014, and in Washington, DC, in December, to discuss, under an existing Strategic Partnership Dialogue, increased co-operation on counter-terrorism in view of an ongoing withdrawal of US and NATO forces from Afghanistan.

Despite criticism by the OSCE of the conduct of elections held in August 2007, and continuing international concerns over human rights abuses in the country, on 1 January 2010 Kazakhstan assumed the OSCE rotating chairmanship for the period of one year. Amid considerable publicity, the authorities convened an OSCE summit meeting in Astana in December. In March 2011 Kazakhstan submitted an application for membership of the UN Human Rights Council, which, despite continuing criticism by human rights groups of the country's record, was approved in November 2012. Following the initiation of negotiations in late 2013, President Nazarbaev on 9 October 2014 signed an Enhanced Partnership and Cooperation Agreement with the European Union (see p. 271) in Brussels, Belgium, becoming the first country in Central Asia to have secured such an accord.

CONSTITUTION AND GOVERNMENT

Under the terms of the 1995 Constitution (as subsequently amended), the President of the Republic is Head of State and commander-in-chief of the armed forces, and holds broad executive powers. The President is directly elected by universal adult suffrage. Under constitutional amendments approved in 2007, the presidential term was reduced from seven to five years, with effect from 2012. The Government, headed by the Prime Minister, is responsible to the President. The supreme legislative organ is the bicameral Parliament, comprising the Senat (Senate, upper chamber) and the Majlis (Assembly, lower chamber). The Senat comprises 47 members, of whom 32 are elected by regional assemblies, while the remaining 15 deputies are appointed by the President. The Majlis comprises 107 deputies, of whom 98 are directly elected; the remaining nine deputies are elected by the Assembly of the Nation of Kazakhstan (a 350-member body representing the country's minority ethnic groups). The Senat's term is six years, and that of the Majlis is five years. One-half of the elected deputies in the Senat are subject to election every three years. Judicial power is exercised by local courts and the Supreme Court. For administrative purposes, Kazakhstan is divided into 16 units (14 regions and the cities of Almatı and Astana). The city of Baikonur, which serves the Baikonur space centre was transferred to Russian jurisdiction in August 1995. In January 2004 President Nazarbaev and the Russian President, Vladimir Putin, signed an agreement permitting Russia's continued use of the Baikonur space centre until 2050.

REGIONAL AND INTERNATIONAL CO-OPERATION

Kazakhstan is a founder member of the Commonwealth of Independent States (CIS, see p. 241) and participates in the Collective Security Treaty Organization (CSTO, see p. 460), the Conference on Interaction and Confidence-Building Measures in Asia (CICA) and in the Customs Union of Belarus, Russia and Kazakhstan, which entered into effect in July 2010. It is also a member of the Organization for Security and Co-operation in Europe (OSCE, see p. 385). Kazakhstan is a member of the Economic Cooperation Organization (ECO, see p. 264), the Eurasian Economic Union (EEU, see p. 446), the Shanghai Co-operation Organization (SCO, see p. 463) and the Organization of Islamic Cooperation (see p. 401). Kazakhstan joined the UN in 1992.

ECONOMIC AFFAIRS

In 2013, according to estimates by the World Bank, Kazakhstan's gross national income (GNI), measured at average 2011–13 prices, was US $193,810m., equivalent to $11,380 per head (or $20,570 per head on an international purchasing-power parity basis). During 2004–13, it was estimated, the population increased at an average annual rate of 1.4%, while gross domestic product (GDP) per head increased, in real terms, by an average annual rate of 5.1%. Overall GDP increased, in real terms, at an average annual rate of 6.6% in 2004–13. Real GDP increased by 6.0% in 2013, according to the Asian Development Bank (ADB).

Agriculture (including forestry and fishing) contributed 4.9% of GDP and provided 24.2% of total employment in 2013. There are large areas of land suitable for agriculture, and Kazakhstan is a major producer and exporter of agricultural products. The principal crops include wheat, potatoes, barley, watermelons and aubergines. Livestock-breeding is also important, and Kazakhstan is a significant producer of karakul and astrakhan wools. According to the World Bank, the GDP of the agricultural sector increased, in real terms, by an average of 2.5% per year in 2004–12. Agricultural GDP decreased by 17.4% in 2012, but increased by 10.6% in 2013, according to the ADB.

Industry (including mining, manufacturing, construction and power) contributed 36.9% of GDP and provided 19.8% of total employment in 2013. The principal branches of industry include the fuel industry and metal-processing. According to World Bank figures, industrial GDP increased, in real terms, at an average annual rate of 6.0% in 2004–12. The GDP of the sector increased by 2.7% in 2013, according to the ADB.

Mining and quarrying contributed 16.7% of GDP and provided 2.9% of employment in 2013. Kazakhstan possesses immense mineral wealth, and large-scale mining and processing industries have been developed. There are major coalfields, as well as substantial deposits of iron ore, lead, zinc ore, titanium, magnesium, chromium, tungsten, molybdenum, gold, silver, copper and manganese. Petroleum is extracted, and Kazakhstan possesses substantial reserves of natural gas. In 2004 the state-owned hydrocarbons company KazMunaiGaz awarded the Russian energy company LUKoil a 50% stake in a 40-year production-sharing contract for the development of the Tyub-Karagan field in the Caspian Sea, which has petroleum reserves of an estimated 100m. metric tons. In 2005 the Kazakhstani and Russian Presidents signed an agreement confirming the equal rights of both countries to the Imashevskoye natural gas field, the second largest natural gas field in Kazakhstan, which was to be developed jointly by KazMunaiGaz and the Russian energy company Gazprom. Also in 2005 a subsidiary of KazMunaiGaz signed a production-sharing agreement with the Russian state-owned petroleum companies Zarubezhneft and Rosneft to develop the offshore Kurmanagazy oil field, estimated to contain recoverable reserves of petroleum of between 900m. and 1,000m. metric tons. At the end of 2013 Kazakhstan's proven total reserves (on shore and off shore) of petroleum and natural gas were estimated at 30,000m. barrels and 1,525,430m. cu m, respectively.

Manufacturing contributed 11.6% of GDP and provided 6.4% of employment in 2013. The GDP of the manufacturing sector increased at an average annual rate of 5.0% in 2004–12, according to the World Bank. The sector's GDP increased by 3.0% in 2012.

The construction sector contributed 6.5% of GDP and engaged 7.7% of the employed labour force in 2013. During 2004–13, according to UN estimates, the GDP of the sector increased at an average annual rate of 10.8%. Construction GDP increased by 3.0% in 2013.

In 2011 coal-fired thermal power stations provided around 81.1% of annual domestic electricity production, while natural gas accounted for 9.2% of production, and hydroelectric power stations for a further 9.1%. In 2013 mineral products accounted for 12.4% of total imports.

The services sector contributed some 58.2% of GDP and provided 56.0% of employment in 2013. According to the World Bank, the GDP of the services sector increased, in real terms, at an average annual rate of 7.8% during 2004–12. Services GDP increased by 7.1% in 2013, according to the ADB.

In 2013 Kazakhstan recorded a visible merchandise trade surplus of US $33,691.5m. while there was a deficit of $117.8m. on the current account of the balance of payments. In 2013 the principal source of imports was Russia, which accounted for 36.2% of total imports. Other major suppliers were the People's Republic of China and Germany. The principal market for exports in that year was Italy, which accounted for 18.5% of total exports. Other major purchasers of exports were the People's Republic of China, the Netherlands, Russia, France and Switzerland. The principal imports in 2013 were machinery and mechanical appliances, vehicles, base metals, mineral products, and chemical products. The main exports in that year were mineral products and base metals.

In 2014 Kazakhstan recorded a budgetary deficit of some 1,000,256.6m. tenge. Kazakhstan's general government gross debt was 4,536,780m. tenge in 2013, equivalent to 12.9% of GDP. At the end of 2012 Kazakhstan's total external debt amounted to US $137,014m. of which $7,375m. was public and publicly guaranteed. In that year, the cost of servicing long-term public and publicly guaranteed debt and repayments to the IMF was equivalent to 23.5% of the value of exports of goods, services and income (excluding workers' remittances). The annual average rate of inflation was 9.5% during 2005–2014, according to official data. According to official figures, consumer prices increased by 5.8% in 2013. In 2013 some 5.2% of the labour force were unemployed.

In July 2013 the World Trade Organization (see p. 431) indicated that Kazakhstan was not yet eligible to be admitted (following its application for membership in 1996), owing to contradictions in membership of the organization and Kazakhstan's commitments to the Russian-led Customs Union (also including Belarus), which had been established in 2010. In February 2014 the National Bank of Kazakhstan devalued the tenge by almost one-fifth against the US dollar. The measure was intended to ensure that exports to Russia remained affordable, following a weakening in the value of that country's currency. The Kazakhstani Government subsequently promised US $5,400m. increases in public sector salaries, pensions and welfare payments, from April, to offset the negative effects of the devaluation. Meanwhile, a large number of privatizations were scheduled during 2014–15 under an ongoing reorganization of the Samruk-Kazyna sovereign wealth funded (founded in 2008), which by then controlled some 600 state companies and was believed to be hampered by corruption and bureaucratic inefficiency. On 29 May 2014 Kazakhstan signed a treaty with Russia and Belarus that formally created the Eurasian Economic Union, to succeed the Customs Union. (The Union, in which Armenia and Kyrgyzstan were also to participate, formally entered into effect on 1 January 2015.) In October 2014 the Government also signed an Enhanced Partnership and Cooperation Agreement with the European Union (see p. 271). However, Kazakhstan's export revenue was severely affected by a Russian economic crisis that had followed the imposition of EU and US sanctions against Russia in response to Russia's annexation of Ukraine's Crimean peninsula in March. In November a new economic strategy was announced, under which the National Fund of oil reserves was to finance $9,000m. in stimulus spending, principally on infrastructure projects, over three years. As a result of a halt in production at Kazakhstan's Kashagan offshore oil field in October 2013 (following the discovery of gas leaks in the pipeline network), the sharp decline in the international price of petroleum from late 2014 and the regional impact of continued conflict in Ukraine, growth (which had slowed to an estimated 4.1% in 2014) was expected to be further depressed in 2015.

PUBLIC HOLIDAYS

2016: 1–2 January (New Year), 7 January (Russian Orthodox Christmas), 8 March (International Women's Day), 21–23 March (Nauryz Meyramy, Spring Holiday), 1 May (Day of Unity of the Peoples of Kazakhstan), 9 May (Victory Day, Day of Remembrance), 6 July (Day of the Capital City), 30 August (Constitution Day), 12 September* (Kurban Bayram, Id al-Adha or Feast of the Sacrifice), 1 December (Day of the First President of Kazakhstan), 16–18 December (Independence Day).

* This holiday is dependent on the Islamic lunar calendar and may vary by one or two days from the date given.

Statistical Survey

Source (unless otherwise stated): Agency of Statistics of the Republic of Kazakhstan, 010000 Astana, Orynbor kosh. 8, Ministrilkter uyi, 4 kireberis; tel. (7172) 74-90-16; fax (7172) 74-94-94; e-mail statistika@stat.kz; internet www.stat.gov.kz.

Area and Population

AREA, POPULATION AND DENSITY

Area (sq km)	2,724,900*
Population (census results)	
25 February–4 March 1999	14,953,126
25 February–6 March 2009	
Males	7,712,200
Females	8,297,400
Total	16,009,600
Population (official estimates at 1 January)	
2013	16,909,776
2014	17,160,774
2015	17,417,447
Density (per sq km) at 1 January 2015	6.4

* 1,049,150 sq miles.

POPULATION BY AGE AND SEX
('000 persons, official estimates at 1 January 2014)

	Males	Females	Total
0–14 years	2,289.4	2,169.0	4,458.4
15–64 years	5,589.2	5,964.8	11,554.0
65 years and over	406.2	742.2	1,148.4
Total	**8,284.8**	**8,876.0**	**17,160.8**

POPULATION BY ETHNIC GROUP
(official estimates at 1 January 2014)

	Number ('000)	%
Kazakh	11,244.5	65.5
Russian	3,685.0	21.5
Uzbek	521.3	3.0
Ukrainian	301.3	1.8
Uygur (Uighur)	246.8	1.4
Tatar	203.1	1.2
German	181.9	1.1
Others	776.8	4.5
Total	**17,160.8**	**100.0**

Note: Classification of ethnicity reflects national methodology.

ADMINISTRATIVE DIVISIONS
(official population estimates at 1 January 2014)

	Area (sq km)	Population	Density (per sq km)	Capital city
Oblasts				
Almatı . . .	224,000	1,984,518	8.86	Taldykorgan
Aqmola . . .	146,200	735,566	5.03	Köksetaw
Aqtöbe . . .	300,600	808,932	2.69	Aqtöbe
Atiraw . . .	118,600	567,861	4.79	Atiraw
Eastern Kazakhstan .	283,200	1,394,018	4.92	Öskemen
Jambıl . . .	144,300	1,084,482	7.52	Taraz
Mañğıstaw . .	165,600	587,419	3.55	Aktaw
Northern Kazakhstan .	98,000	575,766	5.88	Petropavl
Pavlodar . . .	124,800	752,793	6.03	Pavlodar
Qarağandi . .	428,000	1,369,667	3.20	Qarağandi
Qızılorda . .	226,000	739,776	3.27	Qızılorda
Qostanay . .	196,000	880,776	4.49	Qostanay
Southern Kazakhstan .	117,300	2,733,279	23.30	Chimkent
Western Kazakhstan .	151,300	623,977	4.12	Oral

—continued	Area (sq km)	Population	Density (per sq km)	Capital city
Cities				
Almatı . . .	700	1,507,509	2,153.58	—
Astana (capital) .	300	814,435	2,714.78	—
Total . . .	**2,724,900**	**17,160,774**	**6.30**	**—**

PRINCIPAL TOWNS
(official population estimates at 1 January 2014)

Almatı	1,475,429	Qızılorda	. . .	232,714
Astana (capital) .	778,198	Qostanay	. . .	219,224
Chimkent . . .	662,330	Atiraw	. . .	213,481
Qarağandi . . .	479,214	Petropavl	. . .	205,015
Aqtöbe	420,567	Temirtaw	. . .	180,970
Pavlodar . . .	345,759	Aktaw	. . .	180,705
Taraz	343,275	Köksetaw	. . .	141,415
Semey	313,508	Ekibastuz	. . .	137,795
Öskemen . . .	309,510	Rudniy	. . . .	127,726
Oral	269,389			

IMMIGRATION AND EMIGRATION

	2011	2012	2013
Immigrants	402,654	366,137	361,372
Emigrants	397,558	367,563	361,651

BIRTHS, MARRIAGES AND DEATHS

	Registered live births		Registered marriages		Registered deaths	
	Number	Rate (per 1,000)	Number	Rate (per 1,000)	Number	Rate (per 1,000)
2006 . .	301,756	19.7	137,204	9.0	157,210	10.3
2007 . .	321,963	20.8	146,379	9.5	158,297	10.2
2008 . .	356,555	22.8	135,280	8.6	152,706	9.7
2009 . .	357,552	22.0	140,785	8.0	142,780	8.0
2010 . .	367,752	22.5	146,443	9.0	145,875	8.9
2011 . .	372,208	22.6	160,494	9.8	144,616	8.8
2012 . .	381,005	22.7	164,681	9.8	142,880	8.5
2013 . .	387,227	22.7	168,447	9.9	135,950	8.0

Life expectancy (official estimates, years at birth, 2013): 70.5 (males 65.8; females 75.1).

ECONOMICALLY ACTIVE POPULATION
(labour force survey, annual averages, '000 persons)

	2011	2012	2013
Agriculture, forestry and fishing	2,196.1	2,172.7	2,073.6
Mining and quarrying	206.8	225.1	249.3
Manufacturing	542.2	543.5	548.0
Electricity, gas and water supply	211.3	235.8	241.8
Construction	614.0	644.5	660.0
Wholesale and retail trade; repair of motor vehicles, motor cycles and personal and household goods	1,233.7	1,200.7	1,256.5
Hotels and restaurants	122.5	129.0	139.0
Transport, storage and communications	672.0	705.1	702.0
Financial intermediation	119.2	138.8	138.3
Real estate, renting and business activities	485.4	468.0	461.9
Public administration and defence; compulsory social security	391.9	385.8	402.4
Education	851.5	892.1	923.2
Health and social work	392.4	413.8	424.8
Community, social and personal services	238.6	332.8	334.8
Households with employed persons	23.9	19.0	14.6
Extraterritorial organizations and bodies	0.1	0.5	0.4
Total employed	8,301.6	8,507.1	8,570.6
Unemployed	473.0	474.8	470.7
Total labour force	8,774.6	8,981.9	9,041.3

Health and Welfare

KEY INDICATORS

Total fertility rate (children per woman, 2012)	2.5
Under-5 mortality rate (per 1,000 live births, 2012)	19
HIV/AIDS (% of persons aged 15–49, 2011)	0.2
Physicians (per 1,000 head, 2012)	3.6
Hospital beds (per 1,000 head, 2009)	7.6
Health expenditure (2011): US $ per head (PPP)	534
Health expenditure (2011): % of GDP	3.9
Health expenditure (2011): public (% of total)	57.9
Access to water (% of persons, 2012)	93
Access to sanitation (% of persons, 2012)	97
Total carbon dioxide emissions ('000 metric tons, 2010)	248,728.9
Carbon dioxide emissions per head (metric tons, 2010)	15.2
Human Development Index (2013): ranking	70
Human Development Index (2013): value	0.757

For sources and definitions, see explanatory note on p. vi.

Agriculture

PRINCIPAL CROPS
('000 metric tons)

	2011	2012	2013
Wheat	22,732.0	9,841.1	13,940.8
Rice, paddy	346.8	350.8	344.3
Barley	2,593.1	1,490.6	2,539.0
Maize	482.0	520.4	569.3
Rye	28.4	28.6	43.4
Oats	258.3	147.2	304.8
Millet	43.4	22.6	54.5
Buckwheat	37.4	48.0	68.0*
Potatoes	3,076.1	3,126.4	3,343.6
Sugar beet	200.4	151.6	646.1
Beans, dry	0.4	0.5	0.5
Peas, dry	97.9	51.5	42.8
Soybeans	133.1	169.8	203.3
Sunflower seed	409.1	400.3	572.7
Safflower seed	151.2	127.2	174.9
Seed cotton	336.1	397.7	396.7
Cabbages and other brassicas	465.4	442.3	494.4
Tomatoes	609.4	650.6	653.7

—continued	2011	2012	2013
Cucumbers and gherkins	331.6	362.8	356.9
Aubergines (Eggplants)	605.2	703.7	756.5
Chillies and peppers, green	131.5	148.2	162.8
Onions, dry	545.4	573.4	573.6
Carrots and turnips	404.2	445.8	488.8
Watermelons	785.8	817.9	938.8
Apples	114.7	129.7	143.9
Pears	10.9	13.7	14.2
Cherries	10.9	11.5	11.0
Plums and sloes	5.5	5.9	4.9
Grapes	57.1	71.7	68.1
Tobacco, unmanufactured	2.8	3.0†	3.0†

* Unofficial figure.
† FAO estimate.

Aggregate production ('000 metric tons, may include official, semi-official or estimated data): Total cereals 26,641.5 in 2011, 12,788.6 in 2012, 18,141.3 in 2013; Total roots and tubers 3,076.1 in 2011, 3,126.4 in 2012, 3,343.6 in 2013; Total vegetables (incl. melons) 4,126.3 in 2011, 4,711.3 in 2012, 4,955.0 in 2013; Total fruits (excl. melons) 233.3 in 2011, 283.0 in 2012, 287.3 in 2013.

Source: FAO.

LIVESTOCK
('000 head, year ending September)

	2011	2012	2013
Horses	1,607.5	1,686.2	1,784.5
Asses*	30	30	30
Cattle	5,702.4	5,690.0	5,851.2
Buffaloes*	10.0	10.0	10.0
Camels	173.2	164.8	160.9
Pigs	1,204.3	1,031.6	922.3
Sheep	15,439.4	15,137.2	15,197.8
Goats	2,652.4	2,496.1	2,362.8
Chickens†	32,500	32,600	33,200
Turkeys†	280	270	300

* FAO estimates.
† Unofficial figures.

Source: FAO.

LIVESTOCK PRODUCTS
('000 metric tons)

	2011	2012	2013
Cattle meat	392.8	373.5	383.5
Sheep meat	129.6	133.0	135.4
Goat meat	19.9	20.8	21.0
Horse meat	75.6	85.1	89.4
Pig meat	213.6	103.3	99.9
Chicken meat	102.0	123.1	135.8
Cows' milk	5,197.8	4,815.7	4,890.7
Sheeps' milk*	32.3	34.0	37.7
Goats' milk	2.4	1.9	1.9
Hen eggs*	207.2	204.8	217.2
Wool, greasy	38.5	38.4	37.6

* Unofficial figures.

Source: FAO.

Forestry

ROUNDWOOD REMOVALS
(cubic metres, excl. bark)

	2011	2012	2013
Industrial roundwood	73,000	42,000	106,000
Fuel wood	272,000*	244,000†	215,000†
Total	345,000	286,000	321,000

* FAO estimate.
† Unofficial figure.

Source: FAO.

SAWNWOOD PRODUCTION
(cubic metres, incl. railway sleepers)

	2010*	2012	2013†
Coniferous (softwood)	97,823	590,300	832,295
Broadleaved (hardwood) . . .	9,977	32,000	43,805
Total	107,800	622,300	876,100

* FAO estimates.
† Unofficial figures.

Source: FAO.

Fishing

('000 metric tons, live weight)

	2009	2010	2011*
Capture	35.0	43.0	43.0
Freshwater bream	17.1	22.1	22.1
Common carp	0.2	0.1	0.1
Crucian carp	2.3	2.7	2.7
Roaches	4.2	5.0	5.0
Asp	1.4	1.6	1.6
Northern pike . . .	1.3	1.4	1.4
Wels (Som) catfish	2.5	2.4	2.5
Pike-perch	4.1	5.5	5.6
Aquaculture	0.3	0.2	0.3
Total catch	35.3	43.2	43.3

* FAO estimates.
2012: Production assumed to be unchanged from 2011 (FAO estimates).

Source: FAO.

Mining

('000 metric tons, unless otherwise indicated)

	2011	2012	2013
Hard coal			
Brown coal (incl. lignite) . .	116,449	120,528	119,574
Crude petroleum*	80,061	79,225	81,786
Natural gas (million cu m) . .	35,531	40,299	42,405
Iron ore (gross weight) . . .	24,736	25,889	25,228
Bauxite	5,495	5,170	5,192
Lead ore (metal content) . .	39	38	40
Zinc ore (metal content) . .	377	370	362
Manganese ore	2,963	2,975	2,851
Chromite	5,059	5,233	5,255
Uranium (metric tons)† . . .	19,450	21,317	22,548
Silver ore (metal content, metric tons)	650,649	963,182	963,829
Gold (metal content, kg) . .	53,518	39,903	42,552
Asbestos	223	241	243

* Including gas condensate.
† Uranium content of ores. (Source: World Nuclear Association).

Industry

SELECTED PRODUCTS
('000 metric tons unless otherwise indicated)

	2011	2012	2013
Wheat flour	3,847	4,009	3,881
Raw sugar	272	173	357
Wine ('000 hl)	158	153	67
Beer ('000 hl)	4,258	4,811	4,606
Cigarettes (million)	25,222	27,056	25,682
Motor spirit (petrol) . . .	2,775	2,877	2,745
Kerosene	387	421	409
Gas-diesel (distillate fuel) oils .	4,665	4,714	5,141
Residual fuel oils (Mazout) . .	4,277	3,936	3,734
Cement	5,619	6,412	7,072
Copper (unrefined, metric tons) .	338,524	367,161	352,061
Woven cotton fabrics . . .	19,192	24,013	25,783
Electric energy (million kWh) .	86,586	90,614	92,616

Crude steel ('000 metric tons): 3,477 in 2013.

Finance

CURRENCY AND EXCHANGE RATES

Monetary Units
100 tein = 1 tenge.

Sterling, Dollar and Euro Equivalents (31 December 2014)
£1 sterling = 284.612 tenge;
US $1 = 182.350 tenge;
€1 = 221.391 tenge;
1,000 tenge = £3.51 = $5.48 = €4.52.

Average Exchange Rate (tenge per US $)
2012   149.113
2013   152.129
2014   179.192

STATE BUDGET
(million tenge)

Revenue*	2012	2013	2014
Tax revenue	4,095,366.3	4,779,004.4	5,115,743.5
Other current revenue . . .	285,144.1	141,716.8	179,487.8
Capital revenue	52,493.1	56,131.7	71,045.4
Official transfers	1,380,000.0	1,405,500.0	1,955,000.0
Total	5,813,003.5	6,382,352.9	7,321,276.7

Expenditure†	2012	2013	2014
General public services . . .	326,128.6	382,136.4	483,662.9
Defence	341,103.7	396,512.3	431,664.4
Public order and security . . .	558,217.6	608,345.5	601,047.9
Education	1,210,115.4	1,237,421.4	1,358,669.2
Health care	730,819.9	795,092.4	856,221.6
Social security and social assistance	1,239,018.4	1,359,663.8	1,548,637.6
Housing and communal services .	438,585.7	472,369.3	554,696.0
Recreation and cultural activities .	223,065.3	258,431.4	297,795.3
Agriculture, forestry, water management, fishing and environmental protection . .	292,572.9	258,838.9	349,079.5
Transport and communications .	482,059.8	511,365.9	614,202.1
Other expenditure	427,284.7	572,534.0	696,191.0
Total	6,268,972.0	6,852,711.3	7,791,867.5

* Excluding grants received (million tenge): 28,588.0 in 2012; 25,804.2 in 2013; 43,206.9 in 2014.
† Excluding net expenditure minus repayments (million tenge): 405,752.2 in 2012; 204,765.1 in 2013; 572,872.7 in 2014.

Source: Ministry of Finance, Astana.

INTERNATIONAL RESERVES
(US $ million at 31 December)

	2012	2013	2014
Gold	6,148.4	5,551.2	7,394.7
IMF special drawing rights	531.2	536.4	504.6
Reserve position in IMF	0.0	0.0	0.0
Foreign exchange	21,600.3	18,590.2	21,019.9
Total	28,279.9	24,677.8	28,919.2

Source: IMF, *International Financial Statistics.*

MONEY SUPPLY
(million tenge at 31 December)

	2011	2012	2013
Currency outside depository corporations	1,365,698	1,527,995	1,512,261
Transferable deposits	3,324,220	3,059,550	2,857,373
Other deposits	5,062,317	5,934,915	7,228,485
Broad money	9,752,236	10,522,460	11,598,118

Source: IMF, *International Financial Statistics.*

COST OF LIVING
(Consumer Price Index; base: previous year = 100)

	2011	2012	2013
Food and beverages	111.9	104.5	104.3
All items (incl. others)	108.3	105.1	105.8

Source: Asian Development Bank.

NATIONAL ACCOUNTS

Expenditure on the Gross Domestic Product
(million tenge at current prices)

	2011	2012	2013
Final consumption expenditure	14,733,828	17,444,451	21,515,524
Households	11,568,531	13,622,640	17,535,469
Non-profit institutions serving households	223,332	278,011	345,697
General government	2,941,965	3,543,801	3,634,359
Gross capital formation	6,204,641	7,514,031	8,440,297
Gross fixed capital formation. Acquisitions, less disposals of valuables	5,771,550	6,761,447	7,472,853
Changes in inventories	433,091	752,585	967,444
Total domestic expenditure	20,938,469	24,958,483	29,955,821
Exports of goods and services	13,123,054	13,680,508	13,492,592
Less Imports of goods and services	7,527,613	9,246,628	9,417,048
Statistical discrepancy	1,037,978	954,596	1,243,788
GDP in market prices	27,571,889	30,346,958	35,275,153

Gross Domestic Product by Economic Activity

	2011	2012	2013
Agriculture, hunting, forestry and fishing	1,409,003	1,330,025	1,621,195
Mining and quarrying	5,003,253	5,288,741	5,477,694
Manufacturing	3,131,187	3,436,731	3,828,487
Electricity, gas and water supply	574,003	618,225	679,816
Construction	1,816,612	1,915,692	2,145,249
Wholesale and retail trade; repair of motor vehicles, motorcycles and personal and household goods	3,819,299	4,624,795	5,415,975
Hotels and restaurants	239,580	277,329	311,180
Transport, storage and communications	2,635,934	3,105,475	3,682,700
Financial intermediation	550,693	655,343	986,544
Real estate, renting and business activities	4,151,804	4,595,207	5,186,519
Public administration and defence; compulsory social security	551,535	608,373	711,440
Education	886,296	949,216	1,029,843
Health and social work	482,062	516,548	577,127
Other community, social and personal services	495,374	585,899	1,231,174
Gross value added in basic prices	25,746,635	28,507,597	32,884,941
Taxes, less subsidies, on products	1,825,254	1,839,361	2,390,213
GDP in market prices	27,571,889	30,346,958	35,275,153

BALANCE OF PAYMENTS
(US $ million)

	2011	2012	2013
Exports of goods	85,193.9	86,931.1	83,406.9
Imports of goods	−40,349.8	−48,785.8	−49,715.4
Balance on goods	44,844.1	38,145.2	33,691.5
Exports of services	4,337.7	4,828.2	5,271.4
Imports of services	−10,972.9	−12,776.2	−12,147.0
Balance on goods and services	38,208.8	30,197.3	26,815.9
Primary income received	2,232.0	2,086.0	2,320.0
Primary income paid	−29,978.5	−30,193.7	−27,665.2
Balance on goods, services and primary income	10,462.4	2,089.6	1,470.7
Secondary income received	2,745.9	2,613.4	2,691.2
Secondary income paid	−3,011.1	−3,623.9	−4,279.8
Current balance	10,197.2	1,079.1	−117.8
Capital account (net)	31.8	15.4	−6.4
Direct investment assets	−5,177.6	−1,959.5	−1,948.1
Direct investment liabilities	13,760.3	13,784.8	9,738.5
Portfolio investment assets	−13,590.3	−15,068.2	−8,503.1
Portfolio investment liabilities	722.1	−2,319.7	2,540.9
Financial derivatives and employee stock options (net)	126.7	−108.9	−104.0
Other investment assets	−3,569.8	−2,421.1	−4,695.8
Other investment liabilities	1,708.7	7,160.4	6,509.8
Net errors and omissions	−3,908.7	−4,468.8	−5,825.8
Reserves and related items	300.4	−4,306.5	−2,411.8

Source: IMF, *International Financial Statistics.*

External Trade

PRINCIPAL COMMODITIES
(distribution by HS, US $ million)

Imports c.i.f.	2011	2012	2013
Prepared foodstuffs; beverages, spirits, vinegars; tobacco and articles thereof	2,075.0	2,180.3	2,323.7
Mineral products	5,245.6	5,637.6	6,053.4
Mineral fuels, oils, distillation products, etc.	4,878.6	4,814.0	5,435.9
Crude petroleum oils	2,502.4	2,198.9	2,839.9
Petroleum oils, not crude	1,379.5	1,455.0	1,573.0
Chemicals and related products	3,117.5	3,645.2	4,110.6
Pharmaceutical products	985.0	1,298.4	1,603.3
Plastics, rubber, and articles thereof	1,851.6	2,105.2	2,289.6
Plastics and articles thereof	1,245.6	1,397.4	1,565.8
Iron and steel; other base metals and articles of base metal	3,763.7	5,479.7	6,192.1
Articles of iron or steel	2,005.1	3,514.2	4,256.4
Tubes and pipes	239.0	997.6	1,719.8
Machinery and mechanical appliances; electrical equipment; parts thereof	9,376.8	10,747.2	11,168.8
Machinery, boilers, etc.	5,561.6	6,806.7	7,258.1
Electrical, electronic equipment	3,815.2	3,940.5	3,910.8
Vehicles, aircraft, vessels and associated transport equipment	4,245.9	6,174.1	6,495.4
Railway, tramway locomotives, rolling stock, equipment	1,476.0	2,370.0	1,228.6
Railway or tramway goods vans and wagons, not self-propelled	949.1	1,642.2	318.6
Vehicles other than railway, tramway	1,871.7	3,309.1	4,424.8
Cars (incl. station wagons)	654.4	1,384.1	2,137.5
Optical, medical apparatus, etc.; clocks and watches; musical instruments; parts thereof	1,993.2	1,087.8	1,239.2
Optical, photo, technical, medical, etc. apparatus	1,972.3	1,066.4	1,207.6
Miscellaneous manufactured articles	934.4	1,087.7	1,126.0
Total (incl. others)	38,010.2	44,538.1	48,871.9

Exports f.o.b.	2011	2012	2013
Mineral products	68,595.6	69,222.0	65,816.4
Ores, slag and ash	4,428.1	3,994.0	2,725.0
Mineral fuels, oils, distillation products, etc.	63,456.3	64,485.7	62,571.8
Crude petroleum oils	55,174.4	56,442.4	55,221.4
Petroleum oils, not crude	2,433.4	3,226.8	3,144.3
Petroleum gases	3,820.8	3,620.0	3,385.3
Chemicals and related products	3,194.5	3,737.8	3,334.0
Inorganic chemicals, precious metal compound, isotopes	3,011.9	3,533.9	3,136.3
Iron and steel; other base metals and articles of base metal	11,592.6	12,067.1	7,722.1
Iron and steel	6,122.3	5,890.4	3,238.4
Ferro-alloys	3,370.6	3,893.0	1,715.7
Copper and articles thereof	3,294.4	3,770.4	2,887.1
Refined copper and copper alloys, unwrought	2,874.7	3,427.9	2,678.0
Total (incl. others)	88,107.9	92,281.5	82,510.0

Source: Trade Map-Trade Competitiveness Map, International Trade Centre, www.intracen.org/marketanalysis.

PRINCIPAL TRADING PARTNERS
(US $ million)

Imports c.i.f.	2011	2012	2013
Austria	220.7	268.2	741.9
Belarus	623.4	675.5	681.7
China, People's Republic	5,021.1	7,497.7	8,192.7
France (incl. Monaco)	687.7	584.3	924.7
Germany	2,082.0	2,270.5	2,805.8
Italy	1,145.0	960.4	995.5
Japan	645.1	904.8	1,059.4
Korea, Republic	622.5	956.7	1,250.3
Poland	391.3	470.4	491.8
Russia	16,269.1	17,110.5	17,685.6
Spain	149.5	228.2	503.7
Turkey	729.3	786.1	900.6
Ukraine	1,734.4	2,923.0	2,248.5
United Kingdom	526.0	579.0	606.7
USA	1,716.1	2,119.8	2,392.1
Uzbekistan	770.6	817.2	962.6
Total (incl. others)	38,010.2	44,538.1	48,871.9

Exports f.o.b.	2011	2012	2013
Austria	3,876.5	4,955.9	3,613.3
Canada	2,629.3	3,080.1	2,636.6
China, People's Republic	16,291.5	16,484.4	14,334.3
France (incl. Monaco)	5,414.7	5,633.0	5,262.1
Germany	1,610.2	1,838.1	426.7
Iran	1,077.0	626.9	538.9
Israel	1,418.5	1,535.7	818.3
Italy	15,045.3	15,465.7	15,223.1
Japan	1,043.9	1,146.4	624.8
Netherlands	6,637.1	7,479.4	9,729.3
Poland	1,305.4	1,632.0	679.6
Portugal	1,137.8	1,019.5	933.4
Romania	2,265.8	3,033.8	2,263.9
Russia	7,514.5	6,747.2	5,806.5
Spain	1,135.4	768.2	1,844.3
Switzerland-Liechtenstein	4,952.8	4,965.2	4,258.5
Turkey	2,574.4	3,229.0	2,595.1
Ukraine	2,670.5	2,549.0	2,035.5
United Kingdom	1,619.2	1,694.6	1,502.4
USA	1,028.9	441.9	394.4
Uzbekistan	1,179.5	1,343.7	1,126.6
Total (incl. others)	88,107.9	92,281.5	82,510.0

Source: Trade Map-Trade Competitiveness Map, International Trade Centre, www.intracen.org/marketanalysis.

Transport

RAILWAYS
(estimated traffic)

	2012	2013	2014
Paying passengers (million journeys)	24.1	28.5	34.4
Passenger-km (million)	19,081	20,619	23,751
Freight carried ('000 metric tons)	290,874	289,350	273,400
Freight net ton-km (million)	232,940	229,142	214,111

ROAD TRAFFIC
('000 motor vehicles in use at 31 December)

	2011	2012	2013
Passenger cars	3,553.8	3,642.8	3,678.3
Lorries and vans	414.0	428.9	n.a.
Buses and coaches	98.4	97.3	101.0

SHIPPING

Flag Registered Fleet
(at 31 December)

	2012	2013	2014
Number of vessels	167	182	175
Total displacement (grt) . . .	183,229	232,106	231,951

Source: Lloyd's List Intelligence (www.lloydslistintelligence.com).

CIVIL AVIATION
(traffic on scheduled services)

	2012	2013	2014
Passengers carried (million) . .	4.6	5.0	5.4
Passenger-km (million) . . .	8,795.8	9,704.6	10,588.9
Total ton-km (million)	54.9	63.2	49.2

Tourism

FOREIGN TOURIST ARRIVALS

Country of residence	2011	2012	2013
China, People's Republic . . .	128,312	154,226	205,066
Kyrgyzstan	1,539,885	1,454,124	1,382,706
Russia	1,346,594	1,371,306	1,780,574
Tajikistan	187,956	176,212	186,214
Uzbekistan	1,932,298	2,288,617	2,494,568
Total (incl. others)	5,685,132	6,163,204	6,841,085

Tourism receipts (US $ million, excl. passenger transport): 1,208.5 in 2011; 1,346.8 in 2012; 1,459.5 in 2013.

Communications Media

	2011	2012	2013
Telephones ('000 main lines in use)	4,265.8	4,361.4	4,384.4
Mobile cellular telephones ('000 subscribers)	25,240.8	30,235.4	29,675.6
Internet subscribers ('000) . .	1,261.5	n.a.	n.a.
Broadband subscribers ('000) . .	1,193.4	1,592.1	1,907.3

Source: International Telecommunication Union.

Education

(state educational institutions, 2012/13 unless otherwise indicated)

	Institutions	Teachers	Students ('000)
Pre-primary	7,661*	63,304	634.5*
Primary *and* Secondary: general*†	7,561	310,847	2,581.6
Secondary: vocational . . .	610	34,416	520.4
Professional-technical schools .	184	4,669	64.8
Higher	128*	41,224	527.2*

* 2013/14.
† Excluding secondary-general evening schools.

Note: There were, additionally: 155 independent primary and secondary-general schools, with 20,000 students; 179 independent secondary-vocational schools, with 88,700 students; and 134 non-governmental higher education institutes, with 297,900 students, in 2003/04.

Pupil-teacher ratio (primary education, UNESCO estimate): 16.5 in 2012/13 (Source: UNESCO Institute for Statistics).

Adult literacy rate (UNESCO estimates): 99.7% (males 99.8%; females 99.6%) in 2010 (Source: UNESCO Institute for Statistics).

Directory

The Government

HEAD OF STATE

President: NURSULTAN A. NAZARBAEV (elected indirectly 24 April 1990; elected unopposed 1 December 1991; term extended by referendum 29 April 1995; re-elected 10 January 1999, 4 December 2005, 3 April 2011 and 26 April 2015; inaugurated 29 April 2015).

GOVERNMENT
(May 2015)

Prime Minister: KARIM Q. MÄSIMOV.

First Deputy Prime Minister: BAKITJAN Ä. SAGINTAEV.

Deputy Prime Minister: BERDIBEK M. SAPARBAEV.

Minister of Foreign Affairs: ERLAN Ä. IDIRISOV.

Minister of Defence: IMANGALI N. TASMAGAMBETOV.

Minister of Internal Affairs: QALMUXANBET N. QASIMOV.

Minister of Justice: BERIK M. İMAŞEV.

Minister of Agriculture: ASILJAN S. MAMITBEKOV.

Minister of Education and Science: ASLAN B. SÄRÏNJÏPOV.

Minister of Finance: BAKYT T. SULTANOV.

Minister of Investment and Development: ÄSET Ö. ÏSEKEŞEV.

Minister of Health and Social Development: TAMARA B. DÜYSENOVA.

Minister of Culture and Sports: ARYSTANBEK MUXAMEDIULY.

Minister of Energy: VLADIMIR S. SHKOLNIK.

Minister of the National Economy: ERBOLAT A. DOSAEV.

Minister of Economic Integration: JANAR S. AYTJANOVA.

MINISTRIES

Office of the President: 010000 Astana, Beibitshilik kosh. 11; tel. (7172) 32-13-99; fax (7172) 32-61-72; e-mail egov@nitec.kz; internet www.akorda.kz.

Office of the Prime Minister: 010000 Astana, Beibitshilik kosh. 11; tel. (7172) 74-54-00; fax (7172) 32-40-89; internet www.government.kz.

Ministry of Agriculture: 010000 Astana, Kenesary kosh. 36; tel. (7172) 55-59-95; e-mail ministr@minagri.gov.kz; internet www.minagri.kz.

Ministry of Culture and Sport: 010000 Astana, Orynbor kosh. 8; tel. (7172) 74-04-29; fax (7172) 74-04-54; e-mail mki@mki.gov.kz; internet www.mki.gov.kz.

Ministry of Defence: 010000 Astana, Soljagaw, AEA, 2-ui Barlyk kukyktar korgalgan; tel. (7172) 72-13-84; fax (7172) 72-12-40; e-mail mod@mod.gov.kz; internet www.mod.gov.kz.

Ministry of Education and Science: 010000 Astana, Orynbor kosh. 8; tel. (7172) 74-24-28; fax (7172) 74-24-16; e-mail info@edu.gov.kz; internet www.edu.gov.kz.

Ministry of Energy: 010000 Astana, Kabanbai batyr kosh. 19; tel. (7172) 97-68-90; e-mail bogdanova@mgm.gov.kz; internet mgm.gov.kz.

Ministry of Finance: 010000 Astana, Zhenis d-ly 11; tel. (7172) 71-77-64; fax (7172) 71-77-85; e-mail administrator@minfin.kz; internet www.minfin.gov.kz.

Ministry of Foreign Affairs: 010000 Astana, D. Kunaev kosh. 31; tel. (7172) 72-05-18; fax (7172) 72-05-16; e-mail astana@mfa.kz; internet www.mfa.kz.

Ministry of Health and Social Development: 010000 Astana, Orynbor kosh. 8, Ministrilkter uyi, 6 kireberis; tel. (7172) 74-37-23; e-mail mintrud@enbek.kz; internet www.enbek.gov.kz.

Ministry of Internal Affairs: 010000 Astana, Tauelsizdik d-ly 1; tel. (7172) 71-32-30; e-mail kense@mvd.kz; internet www.mvd.kz.

Ministry of Investment and Development: 010000 Astana, Kabanbai batyr d-ly 32/1, 'Transport Tauer'; tel. (3172) 24-04-75; e-mail mint@mint.gov.kz; internet www.mint.gov.kz.

Ministry of Justice: 010000 Astana, Soljagaw, Orynbor kosh. 8, Ministrilkter uyi, 13 kireberis; tel. (7172) 74-06-37; e-mail kanc@minjust.kz; internet www.adilet.gov.kz.

Ministry of the National Economy: 010000 Astana, Orynbor kosh. 8; tel. (7172) 74-28-09; fax (7172) 74-31-48; e-mail info@minplan.kz; internet www.minplan.kz.

President

Presidential Election, 26 April 2015

Candidates							Votes	%
Nursultan A. Nazarbaev	.	.	.	.	.	.	8,833,250	97.75
Turgun I. Syzdykov	.	.	.	.	.	.	145,756	1.61
Abelgazi K. Kusainov	.	.	.	.	.	.	57,718	0.64
Total	.	.	.	.	.	.	**9,036,724**	**100.00**

Legislature

Parliament is a bicameral legislative body, comprising the Senat (Senate) and the Majlis (Assembly).

Assembly
(Majlis)

010000 Astana, Parliament House; tel. (7172) 74-63-01; e-mail smimazh@parlam.kz; internet www.parlam.kz.

Chairman: KABIBULLA K. JAKUPOV.

General Election, 15 January 2012

Parties						Votes	%	Seats
Nur Otan	.	.	.	.	.	5,621,436	80.99	83
Ak Jol	.	.	.	.	.	518,405	7.47	8
KKHP	.	.	.	.	.	498,788	7.19	7
Azat JSDP	.	.	.	.	.	116,534	1.68	—
Auyl	.	.	.	.	.	82,623	1.19	—
KPP	.	.	.	.	.	57,732	0.83	—
Adilet (Justice)	.	.	.	.	.	45,702	0.66	—
Total	.	.	.	.	.	**6,941,220**	**100.00**	**107***

* Including nine deputies elected by the Assembly of the Nation of Kazakhstan (a body representing the country's minority ethnic groups) on 16 January 2012.

Senate
(Senat)

010000 Astana, Abay d-ly 33, Parliament House; tel. (7172) 74-72-39; fax (7172) 24-26-19; internet www.parlam.kz.

Chairman: KASYM-JOMART K. TOKAEV.

The 47-member Senate is the upper chamber of Parliament. Elections are held every three years for one-half of the 32 seats elected by special colleges (comprising members of local councils) in Kazakhstan's 14 regions and two cities; the term of office for members of the Senate is six years. Under constitutional amendments adopted on 18 May 2007, the number of deputies appointed by the President increased from seven to 15; the additional eight members were officially appointed to the Senat by presidential decree in August. The most recent partial elections to the Senate were conducted on 19 August 2011 and 1 October 2014.

Election Commission

Ortalyk Sailau Komissiyasy (Central Election Commission): 010000 Astana, Beibitshilik kosh. 4; tel. (7172) 75-21-21; fax (7172) 33-33-88; e-mail info@election.kz; internet www.election.kz; Chair. KUANDYK T. TURGANKULOV.

Political Organizations

A new law was introduced in July 2002, which required all parties to have a minimum of 50,000 members from among all the country's regions in order to qualify for official registration. In 2014 the following nine parties were registered:

Auyl Kazakstandyk Sotsial-Demokratiyalyk Partiyasy (Auyl) (Village Kazakhstani Social Democratic Party): 010000 Astana, Beibitshilik kosh. 46/109; tel. and fax (7172) 31-71-57; e-mail kaliev@parlam.kz; registered in 2002; seeks to strengthen government support for the agricultural sector; Chair. GANI A. KALIEV; 61,043 mems (2007).

Azat Jalpyulttyk Sotsial Demokratiyalyk Partiyasy (Azat JSDP) (Freedom National Social Democratic Party): 050000 Almatı, Kajymukan kosh. 70; tel. (727) 296-52-22; e-mail ocdp@mail.ru; f. 2009 by merger of Azat (Freedom) and Jalpyulttyk Sotsial Demokratiyalyk Partiyasy (National Social Democratic Party); supports construction of a democratic, secular, social government and the rule of law, and an open society; Chair. JARMAKHAN A. TUYAKBAY; 400,000 mems (2009).

Birlik (Unity): Almatı; f. 2013 by merger of Adilet (Justice) and Ruhniyat (Spirituality); Chair. SERIK SULTANGALI; 140,000 mems.

Kazakstannyn Ak Jol Demokratiyalyk Partiyasy (Ak Jol) (Bright Road Democratic Party of Kazakhstan): 010000 Astana, Saraishyk kosh. 11; tel. (7172) 50-70-01; fax (7172) 50-70-20; e-mail akzholpress@mail.ru; internet www.akzhol.kz; f. 2002 by former mems of the Kazakstannyn Demokratiyalyk Tandauy (Democratic Choice of Kazakhstan); merged with Justice Democratic Party (Adilet) in 2007; Chair. AZAT PERUASHEV; 220,000 mems (2008).

Kazakstan Kommunistik Halyk Partiyasy (KKHP) (Communist People's Party of Kazakhstan): 010000 Astana, Karasai batyr 14/7; tel. and fax (7172) 29-39-90; e-mail zenterknpk@mail.ru; internet www.knpk.kz; f. 2004 by fmr mems of the Kazakstan Kommunistik Partiyasy; Sec. of Central Cttee JAMBYL A. AHMETBEKOV, TURGUN I. SYZDYKOV, DMITRY M. LEGKIY; 100,000 mems (2014).

Kazakstan Kommunistik Partiyasy (CPK) (Communist Party of Kazakhstan): 010000 Astana, Beibitshilik kosh. 27/49; tel. and fax (7172) 21-32-97; e-mail pravdakz@list.ru; f. 1937; suspended Aug. 1991, re-registered Aug. 1998 and March 2003; mem. of For a Just Kazakhstan opposition bloc formed in 2005; suspended from participation in political activities for a period of six months from Oct. 2011 by court ruling (this period was extended by a further six months in April 2012); Chair. SERIKBOLSYN A. ABDILDIN; First Sec. GALIZ ALDAMJAROV; 54,246 mems (2007).

Kazakstan Patriottary Partiyasy (KPP) (Party of Patriots of Kazakhstan): 050000 Almatı, Jibek-joly kosh. 76/318; tel. and fax (7172) 22-98-34; f. 2000; Chair. GANI E. KASYMOV; 172,000 mems (2007).

Kazakstannyn Ak Jol Demokratiyalyk Partiyasy (Ak Jol) (Bright Road Democratic Party of Kazakhstan): 010000 Astana, Saraishyk kosh. 11; tel. (7172) 50-70-01; fax (7172) 50-70-20; e-mail akzholpress@mail.ru; internet www.akzhol.kz; f. 2002 by former mems of the Kazakstannyn Demokratiyalyk Tandauy (Democratic Choice of Kazakhstan); merged with Justice Democratic Party (Adilet) in 2007; Chair. AZAT PERUASHEV; 220,000 mems (2008).

Nur Otan Khalyktyk Demokratiyalyk Partiyasy (Nur Otan) (Light of the Fatherland People's Democratic Party): 010000 Astana, Kunaev kosh. 12/1; tel. (7172) 55-55-62; fax (727) 279-40-66; e-mail partyotan@nursat.kz, internet nurotan.kz; f. 2006; supports administration of President Nazarbaev; Chair. NURSULTAN A. NAZARBAEV; Sec. ERLAN T. KARIN; 607,557 mems (2007).

Note: of unregistered or proscribed political organizations, **Alga (Forward)**, led by VLADIMIR KOZLOV (who was sentenced to seven-and-a-half years' imprisonment in October 2012) is among the most prominent.

Diplomatic Representation

EMBASSIES IN KAZAKHSTAN

Afghanistan: 010000 Astana, Karaotel kosh. 3; tel. (7172) 57-14-42; fax (7172) 24-04-54; e-mail embassy@afghanembassy.kz; internet www.afghanembassy.kz; Ambassador FAROOQ BARAKI.

Armenia: 101990 Astana, Komsomolskii Jibek kosh. 19; tel. (7172) 40-20-15; fax (7172) 40-19-70; e-mail armkazakhstanembassy@mfa.am; internet kazakhstan.mfa.am; Ambassador ARA SAHAKYAN.

Austria: 010000 Astana, Kosmonavtov kosh. 62; tel. (7172) 97-78-69; fax (7172) 97-78-50; e-mail astana-ob@bmeia.gv.at; internet www.bmeia.gv.at/botschaft/astana.html; Ambassador Dr WOLFGANG BÁNYAI.

Azerbaijan: 010000 Astana, Diplomatiyalyk kalashyk B-6; tel. (7172) 24-15-81; fax (7172) 24-15-32; e-mail astana@azembassy.kz; internet www.azembassy.kz; Ambassador ZAKIR HASHIMOV.

Belarus: 010000 Astana, Kenesary kosh. 35; tel. and fax (7172) 32-48-29; e-mail kazakhstan@mfa.gov.by; internet www.kazakhstan.mfa.gov.by; Ambassador ANATOLY NICHKASOV.

Belgium: 010000 Astana, Kosmonavtov kosh. 62; tel. (7172) 97-44-85; fax (7172) 97-78-49; e-mail embassy.astana@diplobel.fed.be; internet www.diplomatie.be/astana; Ambassador MICHAEL PEETERMANS.

Brazil: 010000 Astana, Kabanbai batyr kosh. 6/1, Kaskad Business Centre; tel. (7172) 24-46-84; fax (7172) 24-47-43; e-mail brasemb.astana@itamaraty.gov.br; internet www.brasembastana.kz; Ambassador DEMETRIO BUENO CARVALHO.

Bulgaria: 010000 Astana, Imanov kosh. 11; tel. (7172) 90-15-15; fax (7172) 90-18-19; e-mail embassy.astana@mfa.bg; internet www.mfa .bg/embassies/kazakhstan; Ambassador VASSIL PETKOV.

Canada: 010000 Almatı, Karasai batyr kosh. 13/1; tel. (727) 47-55-77; fax (727) 47-55-87; e-mail astnag@international.gc.ca; internet www.canadainternational.gc.ca/kazakhstan; Ambassador SEAN PERRY STYLE.

China, People's Republic: 010000 Astana, Kabanbai batyr d-ly 37; tel. (3172) 79-35-61; fax (7172) 79-35-65; e-mail chinaemb_kz@mfa .gov.cn; internet kz.china-embassy.org; Ambassador ZHANG HANHUI.

Cuba: 010000 Astana, Kabanbai batyr d-ly 18/2; tel. (7172) 24-24-67; fax (7172) 24-26-38; e-mail natembacu@mail.online.kz; internet www.cubadiplomatica.cu/kazajstan; Ambassador CARLOS ENRIQUE VALDES DE LA CONCEPCIÓN.

Czech Republic: 010000 Astana, Orynbor kosh. 4, Biznes-Tsentr Altyn, 11th Floor; tel. (7172) 66-04-72; fax (7172) 66-01-42; e-mail astana@embassy.mzv.cz; internet www.mzv.cz/astana; Ambassador ELISKA ZHIGOVA.

Egypt: 010000 Astana, Saraishyk kosh. 30; tel. (7172) 28-60-67; fax (7172) 28-60-50; e-mail embassy.astana@mfa.gov.eg; Ambassador NABILA IBRAHIM SALAMA FARHANA.

Estonia: 010000 Astana, Kabanbai batyr kosh. 28; tel. (7172) 24-02-80; fax (7172) 24-02-81; e-mail embassy.astana@mfa.ee; internet www.astana.vm.ee; Ambassador JAAN REINHOLD.

France: 010000 Astana, Kosmonavtov kosh. 62, 4th Floor; tel. (7172) 79-51-00; fax (7172) 79-51-01; e-mail admin-francais.astana-amba@ diplomatie.gouv.fr; internet ambafrance-kz.org; Ambassador FRANCIS ETIENNE.

Georgia: 010000 Astana, Diplomatiyalyk kalashyk C-4; tel. (7172) 24-32-58; fax (7172) 24-34-26; e-mail astana.emb@mfa.gov.ge; internet www.kazakhstan.mfa.gov.ge; Ambassador ZURAB PATRADZE.

Germany: 010000 Astana, Kosmonavtov kosh. 62; tel. (7172) 79-12-00; fax (7172) 79-12-13; internet www.astana.diplo.de; Ambassador Dr GUIDO HERZ.

Greece: 010000 Astana, Karaotkel sh-a 2, 109; tel. (7172) 56-37-14; fax (7172) 56-38-26; e-mail gremb.ast@mfa.gr; Ambassador EFTHYMIOS PANTZOPOULOS.

Holy See: 010000 Astana, Jekebatyr kosh. 20; tel. (7172) 24-12-69; fax (7172) 24-16-04; e-mail nuntius_kazakhstan@lycos.com; Apostolic Nuncio Most Rev. MIGUEL MAURY BUENDÍA (Titular Archbishop of Italica).

Hungary: 010000 Astana, Kosmonavtov kosh. 62; tel. (7172) 55-03-23; fax (7172) 55-03-24; e-mail mission.ast@mfa.gov.hu; internet www.mfa.gov.hu/emb/astana; Ambassador IMRE LASZLÓCZKI.

India: 010000 Astana, Kabanbai batyr kosh. 6/1, Kaskad Business Centre, 5th Floor; tel. (7172) 92-57-00; fax (7172) 92-57-15; e-mail hoc .astana@mea.gov.in; internet indembastana.in; Ambassador ASHOK KUMAR SHARMA.

Indonesia: 010000 Astana, Saraishyk kosh. 26/1; tel. (7172) 79-06-70; fax (7172) 79-06-73; e-mail embassy@kbri-astana.kz; internet www.kbri-astana.kz; Ambassador FOSTER GULTOM.

Iran: 010000 Astana, Daraboz kosh. 23, Akbulak 3 Mikroraion; tel. (7172) 26-53-61; fax (7172) 26-53-60; e-mail iranemb.tse@mfa.gov.ir; internet astana.mfa.ir; Ambassador MOJTABA DAMIRCHILU.

Iraq: 010000 Astana, Konaev kosh. 19; tel. (7127) 28-60-92; fax (7172)-28-60-96; e-mail astemb@iraqmfamail.com; Ambassador RAGEH SABER AL-MOUSSAWI ABBOUD.

Israel: 010000 Astana, Auezov kosh. 8; tel. (7172) 68-87-39; fax (7172) 68-87-35; e-mail info@astana.mfa.gov.il; internet embassies .gov.il/astana; Ambassador ELI TASMAN.

Italy: 010000 Astana, Shuba sh-a, Kosmonavtov kosh. 62; tel. (7172) 24-38-68; fax (7172) 24-36-86; e-mail ambasciata.astana@esteri.it; internet www.ambastana.esteri.it; Ambassador ALBERTO PIERI.

Japan: 010000 Astana, Chubar sh-a, Kosmonavtov kosh. 62, 5th Floor; tel. (7172) 97-78-43; fax (7172) 97-78-42; e-mail info@aq.mofa .go.jp; internet www.kz.emb-japan.go.jp; Ambassador MASAYOSHI KAMOHARA.

Jordan: 010000 Astana, Novostroitel kosh. 8/2; tel. (7172) 24-52-54; fax (7172) 24-52-53; e-mail astana@fm.gov.jo; Ambassador SLAIMAN ARABIAT.

Korea, Republic: 010000 Astana, Kabanbai batyr d-ly 6/1/91–93, Kaskad Business Centre; tel. (7172) 92-55-91; fax (7172) 92-55-96; e-mail koreaemb-kz@mofat.go.kr; internet kaz.mofat.go.kr; Ambassador BAIK JOO-HWEON.

Kuwait: 010000 Astana; Ambassador TAREQ ABDULLAH AL-FARAJ.

Kyrgyzstan: 010000 Astana, Diplomatiyalyk kalashyk B-5; tel. (7172) 24-20-24; fax (7172) 24-24-14; e-mail kz@mail.online.kz; Ambassador ESENGUL OMURALIYEV.

Latvia: 010000 Astana, Kabanbai batyr d-ly 6/1/122, Kaskad Business Centre; tel. (7172) 92-53-16; fax (7172) 92-53-19; e-mail embassy .kazakhstan@mfa.gov.lv; internet www.latvia.kz; Ambassador JURIS MAKLAKOVS.

Lebanon: 010000 Astana, Kunayev kosh. 2, 13th Floor; tel. (7172) 79-35-15; fax (7172) 79-35-16; e-mail embassylebanon-kz@hotmail .com; Ambassador VAZKEN KAVLAKIAN.

Libya: 010000 Astana, Karaokel sh-a, 36-8 kosh. 6; tel. (7172) 56-37-65; fax (7172) 24-27-57; e-mail lpb_ast@yahoo.com; Ambassador ABAD AL-RAHMAN AL-SALIM SUEYTI.

Lithuania: 010000 Astana, Kabanbai batyr kosh. 6/1, Kaskad Business Centre 10A; tel. (7172) 92-58-50; fax (7172) 92-58-53; e-mail amb.kz@urm.lt; internet kz.mfa.lt; Ambassador VYTAUTAS NAUDUZAS.

Malaysia: 010000 Astana, Saraishyk kosh. 26; tel. (7272) 79-06-90; fax (7272) 79-06-92; e-mail mwastana@kln.gov.my; internet www .kln.gov.my/web/kaz_astana/home; Ambassador HIDAYAT BIN ABDUL HAMID.

Mongolia: 050000 Almatı, Musabaev kosh. 1; tel. (727) 269-35-70; fax (727) 229-37-90; e-mail info@mongemb.kz; Ambassador JAGIRYN SÜKHEE.

Netherlands: 010000 Astana, Kosmonavtov kosh. 62; tel. (7172) 55-54-50; fax (7172) 55-54-74; e-mail ast@minbuza.nl; internet www .netherlands-embassy.kz; Ambassador HANS DRIESSER.

Oman: 010000 Astana, Chubar sh-a, Novostroitel kosh. 1; tel. (7172) 52-85-70; fax (7172) 52-86-75; e-mail astana@mofa.gov.om; Ambassador Dr SAID BIN MUHAMMAD BIN ALI AL-BARAMI.

Pakistan: 010000 Astana, Syganak kosh. 27, Biznes-Tsentr, 15th Floor; tel. (7172) 79-93-74; fax (7172) 79-93-98; e-mail parepastana@ mofa.gov.pk; internet www.mofa.gov.pk/kazakhstan; Ambassador ABDUL SALIK KHAN.

Poland: 010000 Astana, Saryarka kosh. 15, Biznes-Tsentr Isker; tel. (7172) 94-44-00; fax (7172) 94-44-01; e-mail astana.sekretariat@msz .gov.pl; internet astana.msz.gov.pl; Ambassador JACEK KLUCZKOWSKI.

Qatar: 010000 Astana, Saraishyk kosh. 20A; tel. (7172) 28-61-23; fax (7172) 28-61-33; Ambassador ABDULLAH AHMAD YOUSEF AHMAD AL-MUTAWA.

Romania: 010000 Astana, Saraishyk kosh. 28; tel. (7172) 28-62-01; fax (7172) 28-62-03; e-mail amb@romania.kz; internet astana.mae .ro; Ambassador NICOLAE URECHE.

Russian Federation: 010000 Astana, Baraev kosh. 4; tel. (7172) 44-07-83; fax (7172) 44-08-07; e-mail rfekz@yandex.ru; internet www .rfembassy.kz; Ambassador MIKHAIL N. BOCHARNIKOV.

Saudi Arabia: 010000 Astana, Akyn Sary kosh. 19; tel. (7172) 92-57-52; fax (7172) 92-57-62; e-mail kzemb@mofa.gov.sa; Ambassador GHURM IBN SAEED AL-MILHAN.

Serbia: 010000 Astana, Saraishyk kosh. 6; tel. (7172) 99-00-27; fax (7172) 99-00-26; e-mail ambasadarsastana@mail.ru; internet astana .mfa.gov.rs; Ambassador VLADIMIR MIRKOVIĆ.

Slovakia: 010000 Astana, Dipgorodok, A. Kunaev kosh. 1; tel. (7172) 79-06-88; fax (7172) 79-06-89; e-mail emb.astana@mzv.sk; internet www.mzv.sk/astana; Ambassador PETER JUZA.

South Africa: 010000 Astana, Kabanbai batyr d-ly 6/1, Biznes-Tsentr Kaskad, 17th Floor; tel. (7172) 92-53-26; fax (7172) 92-53-29; e-mail astana.consular@dirco.gov.za; internet www.dirco.gov.za/ astana; Ambassador SHIRISH M. SONI.

Spain: 010000 Astana, Kenesary kosh. 47/25; tel. (7172) 20-15-35; fax (7172) 20-03-17; e-mail emb.astana@maec.es; internet www .exteriores.gob.es/embajadas/astana; Ambassador MANUEL LARROTCHA PARADA.

Switzerland: 010000 Astana, Kosmonavtov kosh. 62; tel. (7172) 97-98-92; fax (7172) 97-98-94; e-mail ast.vertretung@eda.admin.ch; internet www.eda.admin.ch/astana; Ambassador MAURO REINA.

Tajikistan: 010000 Astana, Chubar sh-a, Marsovaya kosh. 15; tel. and fax (7172) 24-09-29; e-mail embassy_tajic@mbox.kz; Ambassador NAZIRMAD ALIZODA.

Turkey: 010000 Astana, Tashenov kosh. 3; tel. (7172) 70-47-04; fax (7172) 20-45-31; e-mail embassy.astana@mfa.gov.tr; internet astana .be.mfa.gov.tr; Ambassador ÖMER BURHAN TÜZEL.

Turkmenistan: 010000 Astana, Otyrar kosh. 8/1; tel. and fax (7172) 21-08-82; fax (7172) 21-08-23; e-mail tm_emb@astanatelecom.kz; Ambassador MAGTYMGULY AKMYRADOV.

Ukraine: 010000 Astana, Kenesary kosh. 41; tel. (7172) 32-60-42; fax (7172) 32-68-11; e-mail emb_kz@mfa.gov.ua; internet www.mfa .gov.ua/kazakhstan; Chargé d'affaires YURIY S. LAZEBNYK.

United Arab Emirates: 010000 Astana, Diplomatiyalyk kalashyk C-15; tel. (7172) 24-36-75; fax (7172) 24-36-76; e-mail astana@mofa .gov.ae; Ambassador SUHAIL MATTAR AL-KETBI.

United Kingdom: 010000 Astana, Shubar sh-a, Kosmonavtov kosh. 62; tel. (7172) 55-62-00; fax (7172) 55-62-11; e-mail ukinkz@fco.gov .uk; internet www.gov.uk/world/kazakhstan; Ambassador Dr CAROLYN BROWNE.

USA: 010010 Astana, Rahymjan Qoshqarbaev d-ly 3; tel. (7172) 70-21-00; fax (7172) 54-09-14; e-mail astanainfo@state.gov; internet kazakhstan.usembassy.gov; Ambassador GEORGE KROL.

Uzbekistan: 050010 Almatı, Beribaev kosh. 36; tel. (727) 291-78-86; fax (727) 291-10-55; e-mail emb-uzbekistan@mail.ru; Ambassador ALISHER A. SALAXITDINOV.

Viet Nam: 010000 Astana, Saryarka kosh. 6, Biznes-Tsentr Arman; tel. (7172) 66-03-75; fax (7172) 66-03-79; e-mail vnemb.kz@mofa.gov.vn; internet www.mofa.gov.vn/vnemb.kz; Ambassador NGUYEN VAN HOA.

Judicial System

Supreme Court of the Republic of Kazakhstan (Kazakstan Respublikasynyn Zhogargy Soty): 010000 Astana, D. Kunaev kosh. 39; tel. (7172) 74-75-85; internet sud.gov.kz; Chair. KAYRAT A. MAMI.

Constitutional Council of the Republic of Kazakhstan (Kazakstan Respublikasy Konstitutsiyalyk Keneci): 010000 Astana, Soljagaw, Tauelsizdik kosh. 39; tel. (7172) 74-79-60; fax (7172) 74-76-51; e-mail ksrk@constcouncil.kz; internet www.constcouncil.kz; f. 1995; seven mems; Chair. IGOR I. ROGOV.

Prosecutor-General: ASKAT K. DAUYLBAEV, 010000 Astana, Orynbor kosh. 8; tel. (7172) 71-28-68; fax (7172) 50-25-34; e-mail gp-rk@mail.online.kz; internet www.procuror.kz.

Religion

The major religion of the Kazakhs is Islam. They are almost exclusively Sunni Muslims of the Hanafi school. The Russian Orthodox Church is the dominant Christian denomination; it is attended mainly by Slavs. There are also Protestant Churches (mainly Baptists), as well as a Roman Catholic presence and a Jewish community. In mid-2005 legislation was introduced, which required all religious organizations and communities to register with the state authorities.

ISLAM

The Kazakhs were converted to Islam only in the early 19th century, and for many years elements of animist practices remained. Over the period 1985–90 the number of mosques in Kazakhstan increased from 25 to 60. By 1991 there were an estimated 230 Muslim religious communities functioning in Kazakhstan and an Islamic institute had been opened in Almatı. The Islamic revival intensified following Kazakhstan's independence from the USSR, and during 1991–94 some 4,000 mosques were reported to have been opened.

Religious Administration of Muslims of Kazakhstan (Kazakstan musylmandary dini baskarmasy): 050000 Almatı; tel. (727) 230-63-65; fax (727) 297-94-23; e-mail susaev@bk.ru; internet www.muftyat.kz; Chair. Chief Mufti Haji ERJAN MAYAMEROV.

CHRISTIANITY

The Roman Catholic Church

The organization of the Roman Catholic Church in Kazakhstan comprises one archdiocese, two dioceses and one apostolic administration. Most Catholics in Kazakhstan are enrolled in the Latin Rite, and there are also a number of Byzantine Rite communities. There were an estimated 250,000 adherents at April 2008. A newly constructed cathedral at Qaraǧandi was consecrated in September 2012.

Catholic Bishops' Conference of Kazakhstan: 010010 Astana, Tashenov kosh. 3, POB 622; tel. (7172) 37-25-53; e-mail bishops-conf.kz@mail.ru; internet www.catholic-kazakhstan.org; f. 2003; Pres. Rt Rev. TOMASZ PETA (Archbishop of the Archdiocese of the Most Holy Virgin Mary at Astana).

Archbishop of the Archdiocese of the Most Holy Virgin Mary at Astana: Rt Rev. TOMASZ PETA, 010010 Astana, Tashenov kosh. 3, POB 622; tel. (7172) 37-29-35; fax (7172) 37-29-27; e-mail catholic_astana@mail.ru; internet www.catholic-kazakhstan.org.

Apostolic Administrator of Atiraw: Most Rev. JANUSZ KALETA (Titular Bishop of Phelbes), 060009 Atiraw, Avangard 3/34 A; tel. (7122) 28-16-86; fax (7122) 28-16-84; e-mail catholic.atyrau@gmail.com.

The Russian Orthodox Church

The Russian Orthodox Church of the Moscow Patriarchate in Kazakhstan is represented by a Metropolitan District, established in 2003, comprising three dioceses. In 2009 there were 112 parishes.

Metropolitan District of Kazakhstan: 010000 Astana, pl. Respubliki 12; tel. (7172) 28-60-49; fax (7172) 28-69-84; e-mail cross@orthodox.kz; internet www.mitropolia.kz; f. 2003; three dioceses (of Astana and Almatı, Chimkent and Aqmola, and Oral and Guriyev—

Atiraw) Metropolitan of Astana and Kazakhstan ALEKSANDR (MOGILEV).

JUDAISM

Mitsva Association of Kazakhstan: Almatı; tel. (727) 273-54-49; fax (727) 258-34-59; e-mail contact@mitsva.kz; internet www.mitsva.kz; f. 1992; unites Jewish communities across Kazakhstan; Pres. ALEKSANDR BARON.

Rabbi of Almatı: Rabbi MENACHEM GERSHOVICH.

The Press

PRINCIPAL DAILY NEWSPAPERS

Aikyn/Liter (Travel Warrant): 050029 Almatı, Mukanova kosh. 223B; tel. (727) 295-24-52; fax (727) 315-24-57; e-mail info@liter.kz; internet www.aikyn.kz; internet www.liter.kz; f. 2004; five a week; Kazakh and Russian edns; weekly arts and information supplement, *Aikyn apta/Liter nedelya* (Thurs); Editor-in-Chief LEV TARAKOV; circ. 39,300 (Kazakh edn, *Aikyn*), 33,600 (Russian edn, *Liter*).

Almaty Herald: 050000 Almatı, Rozybakiev kosh. 37; tel. (727) 241-45-69; fax (727) 241-40-78; e-mail herald@nursat.kz; Editor-in-Chief OLESSYA IVANOVA.

Anyz Adam (Legendary Person): 050012 Almatı, Masanchi kesheı 78; tel. (727) 295-46-42; internet www.anyzadam.kz; monthly; Editor-in-Chief JARYLKAP KALYBAI; circ. 25,000 (2014).

Egemen Kazakhstan (Sovereign Kazakhstan): Astana, Egemen Kazakhstan kosh. 5/13; tel. (7172) 37-65-27; e-mail egemenkz@mail.online.kz; internet www.egemen.kz; f. 1919; 6 a week; organ of the Govt; in Kazakh; Pres. SAUYTBEK ABDRAXMANOV; Editor-in-Chief JANBOLAT AUPBAEV.

Ekspress–K: 010000 Almatı, Kabanbai batyr kosh. 30A; tel. (727) 259-24-27; fax (727) 259-24-02; e-mail daily@express-k.kz; internet www.express-k.kz; f. 1920; 5 a week; in Russian; Editor-in-Chief TLEPBERGEN BEKMAGANBETOV; circ. 19,500.

Kazakhstanskaya Pravda (Kazakhstani Truth): 010000 Astana, Jenis kosh. 18A; tel. (727) 232-17-29; fax (727) 250-18-73; e-mail kpam@kaznet.kz; internet www.kazpravda.kz; f. 1920; 5 a week; publ. by the Govt; in Russian; Editor-in-Chief TATIANA V. KOSTINA; circ. 100,000 (2010).

Vechernii Almaty (Evening Almatı): 050016 Almatı, Abylai-xan d-ly 2; tel. and fax (727) 279-28-90; e-mail info@vecher.kz; internet www.vecher.kz; f. 1968; in Russian; Editor-in-Chief NIKOLAI N. ZHOROV.

Vremya (Time): 050000 Almatı, Raiymbek d-ly 115; tel. (727) 259-71-96; e-mail info@time.kz; internet www.time.kz; f. 1999; in Russian; general; Editor-in-Chief VADIM N. BOREIKO; circ. 250,000 (2004).

OTHER PUBLICATIONS

Akikat (Justice): 050044 Almatı, Gogol kosh. 39; tel. (727) 273-84-03; f. 1921; monthly; social and political.

Ana Tili (Native Language): 050044 Almatı, Dostyk d-ly 7; tel. (727) 233-22-21; fax (727) 233-34-73; f. 1990; weekly; in Kazakh; Editor-in-Chief J. BEISENBAY-ULI; circ. 11,073.

Dala Men Qala: 050029 Almatı, Abilaijan kosh. 79; tel. (727) 315-06-86; fax (727) 315-06-89; e-mail dalamenkala@mail.ru; internet dmk.kz; f. 2003; weekly; politics, society; Editor-in-Chief SAPARBAY PARMANKULOV.

Delovaya Nedelya (Business Week): 050044 Almatı, Jibek-joly d-ly 64; tel. (727) 250-62-72; fax (727) 273-91-48; e-mail info@dn.kz; internet www.dn.kz; f. 1992; weekly; business, politics, finance of Kazakhstan and Central Asia; in Russian; Editor-in-Chief S. A. KORJUMBAEV; circ. 15,000.

Delovoi Kazakhstan (Business Kazakhstan): 050013 Almatı, pl. Respubliki 15/553, POB 388; tel. (727) 250-72-68; fax (727) 295-23-02; e-mail dk@intelsoft.kz; internet www.dknews.kz; in Russian; weekly; f. 2006; Chief Editor SERIK KORJUMBAEV; circ. 15,000 (2009).

Druzhnye Rebyata (Friendly Chaps): 050009 Almatı, Abay d-ly 143/508; tel. (727) 242-77-89; e-mail jorken@mail.ru; f. 1933 as *Pioner Kazakhstana* (Kazakhstani Pioneer); present name adopted 1956; weekly; in Russian; for children.

Ekologicheskii Kuryer int (Ecological Courier International): 050000 Almatı, Panfilov kosh. 106A; tel. (727) 261-12-23; fax (727) 261-12-10; e-mail ecocourier@nursat.kz; every two weeks; in Russian; environmental concerns; Editor EDUARD MATSKEVICH; circ. 3,000.

Ekspert Kazakhstan: 050000 Almatı, Furmanov kosh. 122; tel. (727) 272-73-69; fax (727) 295-28-33; e-mail skir@expert.ru; internet www.expert.ru/printissues/kazakhstan; f. 2003; weekly; business and economics; in Russian; Chief Editor Yurii Dorokhov; circ. 10,000 (2011).

Jas Alash (Young Generation): 050002 Almatı, Jibek-joly kosh. 50; tel. (727) 273-75-59; fax (727) 273-87-55; e-mail zhasalash2010@mail.ru; internet www.zhasalash.kz; f. 1921; publ. by the Kazakhstan Youth Union; two a week; in Kazakh; Editor-in-Chief Rysbek Sarsenbay.

Karavan (Caravan): 050000 Almatı, pl. Respubliki 13; tel. (727) 258-36-24; fax (727) 258-36-25; e-mail kaztag@caravan.kz; internet www.caravan.kz; f. 1991; weekly; in Russian; Editor-in-Chief Larisa Uvalieva; circ. 250,000.

Kazak Adebiety (Kazakh Literature): 050000 Almatı, Ablai-xan kosh. 105; tel. and fax (727) 269-54-62; f. 1934; weekly; organ of the Union of Writers of Kazakhstan; in Kazakh; Editor-in-Chief A. Jaksybaev; circ. 7,874.

Kazakhstan: 050044 Almatı, Jibek-joly d-ly 50; tel. (727) 233-13-56; f. 1992; weekly; analytical publication on the extractive industry intended for an audience of international investors; in Russian and English; Editor-in-Chief N. Orazbekov.

Kazakstan Aielderi (Women of Kazakhstan): 050044 Almatı, Jibek-joly d-ly 50; tel. (727) 233-06-23; fax (727) 246-15-53; f. 1925; monthly; culture and housekeeping; in Kazakh; Editor-in-Chief Altynshash K. Jaganova; circ. 15,200.

Kazakstan Mektebi (Kazakhstani School): 050004 Almatı, Ablai-xan d-ly 34; tel. (727) 239-76-65; f. 1925; monthly; publ. by the Ministry of Education and Science; in Kazakh; Editor-in-Chief S. Abisheva; circ. 10,000.

Kazakstan Zaman (Kazakh Time): 050002 Almatı, Dostyk d-ly 106g; tel. (727) 265-07-39; e-mail info@kazakzaman.kz; internet www.kazakzaman.kz; f. 1992; in Kazakh and Turkish; weekly; Gen. Dir Ertay Aigalyevich; circ. 15,000.

Kazakstannyn zher resurstary/Zemelnye Resursy Kazakhstana (Land Resources of Kazakhstan): 010000 Astana, 8 Orynbor kosh., 12 kireberis, 5th Floor; tel. and fax (7172) 74-16-52; e-mail info@auzr.kz; internet www.auzr.kz; every two months; Kazakh and Russian edns; publication of Republican Agency for the Management of Land Resources; Chair. of Editorial Bd Aljanbay Shayahmetov.

Kontinent (Continent): 050000 Almatı, POB 271; tel. (727) 250-10-39; fax (727) 250-10-41; e-mail bzchyt@kaznet.kz; f. 1999; every two weeks; policy and society journal; Editor-in-Chief Andrei Kukushkin; circ. 10,000.

Korye Ilbo (Korean News): 050044 Almatı, Jibek-joly d-ly 50; tel. (727) 233-90-10; fax (727) 263-25-46; f. 1923; weekly; in Korean and Russian; Editor-in-Chief Yan Won Sik.

Kredo (Credo): 100029 Qarağandi, Oktyabrskaya 25; tel. (721) 222-38-40; e-mail credogazeta@gmail.com; internet www.catholic-kazakhstan.org/credo; f. 1995; monthly; Catholic; in Russian; Chief Editor N. Mamaev.

Megapolis (Megalopolis): 050060 Almatı, P. Tajibaevoy kosh. 155; tel. and fax (727) 315-09-87; e-mail info@megapolis.kz; internet www.megapolis.kz; f. 2000; general; weekly; CEO Rinat Askarov; Editor-in-Chief Igor Shaxnovich.

Novoye Pokoleniye (New Generation): 050091 Almatı, Bogenbai batyr kosh. 156A/505; tel. (727) 334-09-11; fax (727) 250-95-46; e-mail np@np.kz; internet www.np.kz; f. 1998; weekly; economic and political affairs of Kazakhstan and the CIS, with supplement on the arts; in Russian; Editor-in-Chief Sergei Aparin; circ. 40,000.

Panorama: 050013 Almatı, pl. Respubliki 15/647; tel. (727) 291-50-46; fax (727) 291-50-36; e-mail panorama@intelsoft.kz; internet www.panorama.kz; f. 1992; weekly; analytical coverage of politics, economics, business and international relations; in Russian; Dir Aleksandr Nesukannyi; Editor-in-Chief Lera Tsoy; circ. 20,000.

Petroleum of Kazakhstan: 050000 Almatı, Nauryzbai batyr kosh. 58; tel. (727) 258-28-38; fax (727) 250-50-82; e-mail office@petroleumjournal.kz; internet www.petroleumjournal.kz; every two months; in Russian and English; Editor-in-Chief Oleg C. Chervinsky; circ. 1,000.

Pro Sport Kazakhstan: 050008 Almatı, Bogenbai batyr kosh. 34A/87A; tel. and fax (727) 250-90-30; two a week; in Russian; sport.

Rukh-Miras (Heritage Movement): 050013 Almatı, Abay d-ly 14; tel. (727) 267-28-83; e-mail ieshua@front.ru; internet www.nlrk.kz; f. 2004; quarterly; literature, fine arts; in Kazakh and Russian; Chair. of Editorial Bd Murat Auezov; Chief Editor Talasbek Asemkulov.

Russkii Yazyk i Literatura v Kazakhskoye Shkole (Russian Language and Literature in the Kazakh School): 050091 Almatı, Abylai-xan kosh. 34; tel. (727) 239-76-68; f. 1962; every two months; in Russian; Editor-in-Chief B. S. Mukanov.

Strana i Mir (The Country and The World): 050029 Almatı, Abylai-xan kosh. 79; tel. (727) 315-06-85; fax (727) 315-06-89; e-mail reklamanyr@liter.kz; internet sim.kz; politics; weekly; in Russian; f. 2003; Editor-in-Chief Rashid Garipov.

Turkistan: 050009 Almatı, Abay kosh. 143; tel. (727) 394-42-51; fax (727) 394-41-80; e-mail turkestan_gazeta@mail.ru; internet www.turkystan.kz; f. 1994; weekly; political analysis; in Kazakh; Editor-in-chief Shamshidin A. Patteev; circ. 10,000.

Uigur Avazi (Uigur Voice): 050044 Almatı, Jibek-joly d-ly 50; tel. (727) 233-84-59; f. 1957; two a week; publ. by the Govt; socio-political; in Uighur; Editor-in-Chief I. Azamatov; circ. 9,000.

Ulan (Man Alive): 050044 Almatı, Jibek-joly d-ly 50; tel. (727) 233-80-03; f. 1930; weekly; in Kazakh; for children and teenagers; Editor-in-Chief S. Kaliev; circ. 183,014.

Zerde (Intellect): 050044 Almatı, Jibek-joly d-ly 50; tel. (727) 233-83-81; f. 1960; monthly; popular, scientific, technical; in Kazakh; Editor-in-Chief E. Raushan-uly; circ. 68,600.

NEWS AGENCY

National Information Agency 'Kazinform': 010000 Astana, Beibitshilik kosh. 10; tel. and fax (7172) 32-75-67; e-mail product@inform.kz; internet www.inform.kz; f. 1997; 100% state-owned open jt-stock co; provides information on govt activities in Kazakhstan and abroad; Chair. of Bd Dauren Diyarov.

Publishers

Almatıkitap: 050012 Almatı, Jambıl 111; tel. (727) 250-29-58; fax (727) 292-81-10; e-mail alkitap@intelsoft.kz; internet almatykitap.kz; art, educational and children's books; Chair. Eleanora N. Batalova.

Civil Engineering & Architecture Publishing House: 050043 Almatı, Ryskulbekov kosh. 28; tel. (727) 309-63-49; fax (727) 309-61-53; e-mail esengalieva_b@email.ru; f. 2002; publr of KazGASA Kazakh Chief Architectural-Construction Academy; Dir Batima Esengalieva.

Gylym (Science): 050010 Almatı, Pushkin kosh. 111–113; tel. (727) 291-18-77; fax (727) 261-88-45; f. 1946; books on natural sciences, humanities and scientific research journals; Dir S. G. Baimenov.

Kainar (Spring): 050009 Almatı, Abay d-ly 143; tel. (727) 242-27-96; e-mail kainar_baspasy@mail.ru; f. 1962; agriculture, history, culture, religion; Dir Orazbek S. Sarsenbaev.

Kazakhskaya Entsiklopediya (Kazakh Encyclopedia): 050000 Almatı; tel. (727) 262-55-66; f. 1968; Editor-in-Chief Baurzhan Jakyp.

Kazakhstan Publishing House: 050000 Almatı, Abay d-ly 143; tel. and fax (727) 242-29-29; f. 1920; political science, economics, medicine, general and social sciences; Dir E.X. Syzdykov; Editors-in-Chief M. D. Sitko, M. A. Rashev.

Mektep: 050009 Almatı, Abay d-ly 143; tel. (727) 394-42-34; fax (727) 394-37-58; e-mail mektep@mail.ru; internet www.mektep.kz; f. 1947; mainly literature for educational institutions; dictionaries, phrase books, children's textbooks, teaching materials, reference books; publishes books in Kazakh, Russian, Uighur and Uzbek; Gen. Dir Erlan Satybaldiev.

Oner (Art): 050000 Almatı, Abay d-ly 143; tel. (727) 242-08-88; f. 1980; Dir S. S. Orazalinov; Editor-in-Chief A. A. Askarov.

Zhazushy (Writer): 050000 Almatı, Abay d-ly 143; tel. (727) 242-28-49; e-mail zhazushi@mail.ru; internet www.adai@mail.ru; f. 1934; literature, literary criticism, essays, poetry, textbooks; Dir Yessengali Raushanov.

Broadcasting and Communications
GOVERNMENT AGENCY

Republican Agency for Information and Communications: 010000 Astana, Ministry Bldg, Soljagaw, Ishim; tel. (7172) 74-01-35; fax (7172) 74-10-03; e-mail press@aic.gov.kz; Chair. Askar Jumagaliev.

TELECOMMUNICATIONS

The fixed-line telecommunications market is dominated by the state-owned company, Kazakhtelekom, while the mobile telecommunications sector has three main operators. In 2013 there were 3.3m. main telephone lines in use, and 29.7m. subscriptions to mobile cellular telecommunications services in Kazakhstan.

Altel: 050020 Almatı, Dostyk kosh. 248b; tel. (727) 259-81-20; fax (727) 259-81-21; internet www.altel.kz; f. 1994; provides mobile cellular communications and wireless internet services in Kazakhstan (under the brand names City, Dalacom, Jet and PAThWORD); Chair. Maksut Sauranbekov.

GSM Kazakhstan (Kcell): 050013 Almatı, Timiriyazev kosh. 2g; tel. (727) 258-83-00; fax (727) 258-89-10; e-mail info@kcell.kz;

internet www.kcell.kz; f. 1998; 51% owned by TeliaSonera (Sweden), 49% by Kazakhtelekom; provides mobile cellular telecommunications services (as Kcell and Activ) in 1,449 settlements across Kazakhstan; provides internet services; 7.5m. subscribers (May 2009); Chief Exec. ALI AGAN.

KaR-tel (Beeline): 050000 Almatı, Tole bi 55; tel. (727) 266-23-33; fax (727) 250-16-11; e-mail info@beeline.kz; internet www.beeline.kz; f. 1999; wholly-owned subsidiary of VympelKom-Bilain (Russia); provides mobile cellular telecommunications services (as K-Mobile, Excess and Beeline) in more than 100 settlements and along principal roads across Kazakhstan; Gen. Man. TARAS PARHOMENKO.

Kazakhtelekom: 010000 Astana, Sauran kosh. 12; tel. (717) 258-06-59; fax (717) 258-77-24; internet www.telecom.kz; f. 1994; internet and telecommunications services; public limited co; Chair. KUANYSHBEK YESEKEEV.

KazTransCom: 050009 Almatı, Radostovets kosh. 69/204A; tel. (727) 237-73-10; fax (727) 237-73-18; e-mail info@kaztranscom.kz; internet www.kaztranscom.kz; f. 2001 as a result of merger of CaspiMunayBailanys, Aktjubneftesviaz and Bailanys; jt-stock co; provides telecommunications services to the petroleum and natural gas sectors, and long-distance and international telephone calls; Gen. Dir ANDREI V. XAN.

BROADCASTING

Private radio and television stations began operating in Kazakhstan in the 1990s.

Kazakh State Television and Radio Broadcasting Corpn: 050013 Almatı, Jeltoksan kosh. 175A; tel. (727) 263-37-16; f. 1920; Pres. YERMEK TURSUNOV.

Radio

Kazakh Radio: 050013 Almatı, Konaev kosh. 4; tel. (727) 255-33-37; fax (727) 265-03-87; internet kazradio@kazradio.kz; f. 1921; broadcasts in Kazakh, Russian, Uighur, German and other minority languages; Gen. Dir TOREXAN DANIYAR.

Radio 31: 050060 Almatı, Tajibaevoi kosh. 155; tel. (727) 315-31-31; e-mail tv_31@31.kz; internet www.31.kz; f. 1994; news and music; Dir BAGDAT KOJAHMETOV.

Television

Khabar News Agency: 050013 Almatı, Jeltosan kosh. 185; tel. (727) 270-10-01; fax (727) 270-10-40; e-mail khabar@khabar.kz; internet www.khabar.kz; f. 1959; international broadcasts in Kazakh, Uighur, Russian and German; five television channels; Chair. of the Bd of Dirs DAUREN A. ABAEV; Dir AJDOS UKIBAEV.

KTK (Kazakh Commercial Television): 050013 Almatı, pl. Respubliki 13; tel. and fax (727) 258-36-55; e-mail ktk@ktk-tv.kz; internet www.ktk-tv.kz; f. 1990; independent; Gen. Dir ARMAN SHURAEV.

NTK (Association of TV and Radio Broadcasters of Kazakhstan): 050013 Almatı, pl. Respubliki 13, 6th Floor; tel. (727) 270-01-83; fax (727) 270-01-85; e-mail kaztvradio@nursat.kz; f. 2000; privately owned; Pres. AIDAR JUMABAEV.

STV: 050010 Almatı, Karasai batyr kosh. 88; tel. (727) 292-98-37; e-mail info@rakhattv.kz; internet stv-online.kz; f. 1994; privately owned; fmrly Rakhat-TV, present name adopted 2009; information and entertainment broadcasts to Aktaw, Almatı, Astana, Atiraw, Pavlodar, Petropavl and Toldykorgan, also available on cable networks and satellite.

Finance

(cap. = capital; res = reserves; dep. = deposits; m. = million; brs = branches; amounts in tenge, unless otherwise indicated)

BANKING

Central Bank

National Bank of Kazakhstan (NBK): 050040 Almatı, Koktem-3 21; tel. (727) 270-45-91; fax (727) 270-47-03; e-mail hq@nationalbank .kz; internet www.nationalbank.kz; f. 1990; cap. 20,000.0m.; Gov. QAYRAT N. KELIMBETOV; 17 brs.

Major Commercial Banks

Alliance Bank: 050000 Almatı, Furmanov kosh. 50; tel. (727) 258-40-40; fax (727) 259-80-71; e-mail ir@alb.kz; internet www.alb.kz; f. 1993; cap. 273,090m., res –12,200m., dep. 347,524m. (Dec. 2012); Chair. MAXAT KABASHEV.

ATFBank: 050000 Almatı, Furmanov kosh. 100; tel. (727) 250-30-40; fax (727) 250-19-95; e-mail info@atfbank.kz; internet www .atfbank.kz; f. 1995; present name adopted 2002; cap. 167,878.5m., res 16,543.9m., dep. 553,660.2m. (Dec. 2012); Chair. TIMUR ISSATAEV; 10 brs.

Bank Centercredit: 050000 Almatı, Panfilov kosh. 98; tel. (727) 259-85-98; fax (727) 258-45-10; e-mail info@centercredit.kz; internet www.centercredit.kz; f. 1988; present name adopted 1996; 30.5% owned by Kookmin Bank (Rep. of Korea); cap. 69,798m., res 3,729m., dep. 790,913m. (Dec. 2012); Chair. of Bd BAKYTBEK R. BAYSEITOV; 19 brs.

BTA Bank: 050051 Almatı, Samal 2, Joldasbekov kosh. 97; tel. (727) 250-40-70; fax (727) 250-02-24; e-mail post@bta.kz; internet www .bta.kz; f. 1997 as Bank TuranAlem; name changed as above 2008; 75.1% state-owned; cap. 1,366,771m., res 109,835m., dep. 541,018m. (Dec. 2012); Chair. of Bd KENES RAKISHEV; Chair. of Managing Bd KADYRJAN DAMITOV; 23 brs.

Development Bank of Kazakhstan: 010000 Astana, pl. Respublika 32; tel. (7172) 58-02-60; fax (7172) 58-02-76; e-mail info@kdb .kz; internet www.kdb.kz; f. 2001; wholly state-owned; cap. 258,667.5m., res 43,621.3m., dep. 4,056.5m. (Dec. 2012); Chair. of Bd NURLAN KUSSAINOV.

Eurasian Bank (Yevraziiskii Bank): 050002 Almatı, Kunaev kosh. 56; tel. (727) 250-77-05; fax (727) 250-86-50; e-mail info@ eurasian-bank.kz; internet www.eurasian-bank.kz; f. 1994; cap. 30,110.2m., res 6,553.9m., dep. 335,948.9m. (Dec. 2012); Chair. MICHAEL EGGLETON; 18 brs.

Eurasian Development Bank: 050000 Almatı, Panfilov kosh. 98; tel. (727) 244-40-44; fax (727) 244-65-70; e-mail info@eabr.org; internet www.eabr.org; f. 2006; cap. US $1,515.7m., res $98.1m., dep. $564.1m. (Dec. 2013); Chair. IGOR FINOGENOV.

Halyk Bank: 050046 Almatı, Rozybakiev kosh. 97; tel. (727) 259-00-00; fax (727) 259-02-71; e-mail halykbank@halykbank.kz; internet www.halykbank.kz; f. 1936 as br. of Savings Bank of USSR; fully privatized in Nov. 2001; cap. 143,695m., res –59,919m., dep. 1,777,887m. (Dec. 2013); Chair. and Chief Exec. UMUT SHAYAKHMETOVA.

HSBC Bank Kazakhstan: 050010 Almatı, Dostyk d-ly 43; tel. (727) 259-69-00; fax (727) 259-69-02; e-mail info@hsbc.kz; internet www .hsbc.kz; f. 1998; 100% owned by HSBC Bank PLC (United Kingdom); cap. 7,050.0m., res 2,422.5m., dep. 147,898.6m. (Dec. 2012); Chair. of Bd DEREK P. LUNT.

Kaspi Bank: 050012 Almatı, Adi Sharipov kosh. 90; tel. (727) 250-18-00; fax (727) 250-95-96; e-mail office@bankcaspian.kz; internet www.bc.kz; 96% owned by Caspian Group (Netherlands); fmrly Caspian Bank; present name adopted 2008; cap. 16,049.9m., res 2,655.7m., dep. 442,585.7m. (Dec. 2012); Chair. MIXEIL LOMTADZE; 17 brs.

KazInvestBank: 050051 Almatı, Dostyk d-ly 176; tel. (727) 261-90-60; fax (727) 259-86-58; e-mail info@kib.kz; internet www.kib.kz; f. 1993; open jt-stock co; cap. 13,644.1m., res 1,684.7m., dep. 99,617.9m. (Dec. 2012); Chair. ADNAN ALLY AGHA; 3 brs.

Kazkommertsbank (KKB): 050060 Almatı, Gagarin kosh. 135; tel. (727) 258-53-01; fax (727) 258-51-61; e-mail mailbox@kkb.kz; internet www.kkb.kz; f. 1991; cap. 9,044m., res 200,350m., dep. 1,715,936m. (Dec. 2013); Chair. NURJAN S. SUBXANBERDIN; Man. Dir ANDREI I. TIMCHENKO; 23 brs.

Nurbank: 050010 Almatı, Dostyk d-ly 38; tel. (727) 259-97-10; fax (727) 250-16-09; e-mail bank@nurbank.kz; internet www.nurbank .kz; f. 1992; cap. 127,611.2m., res 389.3m., dep. 149,757.8m. (Dec. 2012); Chair. NURMUXAMED BEKTEMISOV; 56 brs.

Tsesnabank: 010000 Astana, Jengis d-ly 29; tel. (7172) 77-07-70; fax (7172) 77-01-95; e-mail info@tsb.kz; internet www.tsb.kz; f. 1992; cap. 32,409.8m., res 7,001.6m., dep. 518,469.4m. (Dec. 2012); Chair. YERKEGALI YEDENBAEV; 22 brs.

Islamic Bank

Al Hilal Bank Kazakhstan: 050059 Almatı, Al Farabi kosh. 36, Bldg B, 6th Floor; tel. (727) 233-00-00; internet www.alhilalbank.kz; f. 2010; owned by Al Hilal Bank Abu Dhabi (United Arab Emirates); Chair. AHMED ATEEQ AL-MAZROUEI; Gen. Man. PRASAD JOSE ABRAHAM.

Bankers' Organization

Bank Association of Kazakhstan: 010000 Almatı, Panfilov kosh. 98; tel. (727) 273-16-89; fax (727) 273-90-85; Pres. BAXYTBEK BAISEITOV.

STOCK EXCHANGES

Kazakhstan Stock Exchange (KASE): 050040 Almatı, Baizakov kosh. 280; tel. (727) 237-53-00; fax (727) 296-64-02; e-mail info@kase .kz; internet www.kase.kz; f. 1993; Pres. KADYRZHAN DAMITOV.

Regional Financial Centre of Almatı City: 050059 Almatı, Al-Farabi kosh. 17/1, Biznes-Tsentr 'Nurly-Taw' 4B, 9th Floor; tel. (727) 311-09-31; fax (727) 311-09-42; e-mail info@rfca.kz; internet www .rfca.gov.kz; f. 2007; Chair. of Bd DAUREN B. UTKELBAEV.

INSURANCE

Almatı International Insurance Group: 050000 Almatı, Kabanbai batyr kosh. 112; tel. and fax (727) 250-12-31; f. 1994; Chair. SUREN AMBARTSUMIAN.

Centras Insurance: 050008 Almatı, Shevchenko kosh. 157в; tel. (727) 260-06-02; fax (727) 259-77-66; e-mail insurance@centras.kz; internet www.cic.kz; f. 1997; non-life insurance and reinsurance; Chair. BEIBIT TURYSBEKOV.

Dynasty Life Insurance Co: 050000 Almatı, Seifullin kosh. 410; tel. (727) 250-73-95; e-mail dynasty@bta.nursat.kz; Chair. SERIK TEMIRGALEEV.

Industrial Insurance Group (IIG): 050046 Almatı, Nauryzbai batyr kosh. 65–69; tel. (727) 250-96-95; fax (727) 250-96-98; e-mail iig@kaznet.kz; f. 1998; Pres. IVAN MIXAILOV.

Interteach Kazakhstani Health and Medical Insurance Corpn: 050059 Almatı, Furmanov kosh. 275D; tel. and fax (727) 320-02-06; e-mail interteach@interteach.kz; internet www.interteach.kz; f. 1989; medical and travel insurance, health care, accident and employee liability insurance; 290 employees; 48 brs; Gen. Dir ERNST M. KURLEUTOV.

KazAgroPolits Insurance Co: 050000 Almatı, Nauryzbai batyr kosh. 49–61; tel. (727) 232-13-24; fax (727) 232-13-26; e-mail kazagropolise@mail.banknet.kz; Chair. YERMEK USPANOV.

Kazakhinstrakh (Kazakh International Insurance Co): 050044 Almatı, Abai kosh. 109; tel. (727) 259-98-48; fax (727) 244-81-82; e-mail info@kis.com.kz; internet www.kazakhinstrakh.kz; f. 1995; owned by Halyk Bank (Kazakhstan); non-life insurance and reinsurance; Chair., Supervisory Bd DAUREN S. KARABAEV; Chair., Management Bd MARAT S. SATUBALDIN.

Kazkommerts-Polis: 050013 Almatı, Satpaev kosh. 24; tel. (727) 258-48-08; fax (727) 292-73-97; e-mail info@kkp.kz; internet www .kkp.kz; f. 1996; non-life; Chair. SERGEY D. MOKROUSOV; Dir BERIK ABUOV.

Trade and Industry

GOVERNMENT AGENCY

Republican Agency for the Regulation of Natural Monopolies: 010000 Astana, Bukei-xan kosh. 14; tel. (7172) 59-16-77; fax (7172) 21-54-73; e-mail info@arem.kz; internet www.regulator.kz; Chair. NURLAN SH. ALDABERGENOV.

CHAMBERS OF COMMERCE

Union of Chambers of Commerce and Industry of Kazakhstan: 050000 Almatı, Masanchi kosh. 26; tel. (727) 292-00-52; fax (727) 250-70-29; e-mail tpprkaz@online.ru; internet www.ccikaz.kz; f. 1959; Chair. ABLAI MYRZAXMETOV.

Almatı City Chamber of Commerce and Industry: 050000 Almatı, Tole bi 45; tel. (727) 262-03-01; e-mail alcci@nursat.kz; internet www.atpp.marketcenter.ru; Chair. ABLAI MYRZAXMETOV.

Astana City Chamber of Commerce and Industry: 010000 Astana, Auezov kosh. 66, POB 1966; tel. (7172) 32-38-33; e-mail akmcci@dan.kz; internet www.chamber.kz; Chair. TATYANA I. KONONOVA.

Jambıl Oblast Chamber of Commerce and Industry: 080012 Jambıl obl., Taraz, Karaxan kosh. 2; tel. (7262) 43-05-98; Chair. ADILXAN JAPARBEKOV.

Qarağandi Oblast Chamber of Commerce and Industry: 100008 Qarağandi, bulv. Mira 31; tel. (7212) 30-06-84; fax (7212) 30-05-05; e-mail karcci@karcci.kz; internet www.karcci.kz; f. 1959; Chair. of Presidium NESSIP SEITOVA.

Southern Kazakhstan Oblast Chamber of Commerce and Industry: 160000 Southern Kazakhstan obl., Chimkent, Taukexan kosh. 31; tel. (7252) 21-14-05; Chair. SYRLYBAJ ORDABEKOV.

EMPLOYERS' ORGANIZATIONS

Confederation of Employers of the Republic of Kazakhstan (KRRK): 050060 Almatı, Radostovets kosh. 212; tel. (727) 390-17-14; fax (727) 395-66-58; e-mail krrk@krrk.kz; internet www.krrk.kz; Pres. KADYR BAYIKENOV.

Kazakhstan Petroleum Association: 050010 Almatı, Zenkov 59; tel. (727) 311-67-05; fax (727) 311-67-04; e-mail kpa@arna.kz; internet www.kpakz.kz; f. 1998; Chair. RZABEK ARTYGALIEV; 40 mem. cos.

UTILITIES

Electricity

KEGOS—Kazakhstan Electricity Grid Operating Co (Elektr jelilerin baskaru janindegi Kazakstan kompaniyasy): 050000 Almatı, Kozybaev kosh. 23; tel. (727) 271-93-59; internet www .kegoc.kz; f. 1997; technical electricity network operator; Pres. BAKYTJAN KAJIEV.

Water

Almatı Vodokanal: 050057 Almatı, Jarokov kosh. 196; tel. (727) 274-84-02; fax (727) 274-98-41; e-mail vk.prm@itte.kz; f. 1936; state-owned; responsible for water supply and sewerage in Almatı and surrounding villages; Gen. Dir VLADISLAV GALIEV.

STATE HYDROCARBONS COMPANIES

KazMunaiGaz: 010000 Astana, Kabanbai batyr kosh. 22; tel. (7172) 97-60-00; fax (7172) 97-60-01; e-mail info@kmg.kz; internet www .kmg.kz; f. 2002 by merger of KazakhOil and Transneftegas; national jt-stock co; subsidiaries include petroleum transportation co KazTransOil, and gas transportation co KazTransGas; Dir-Gen. DANIAR TIYESOV.

Munaigaz: 010000 Astana, Jeltoksan kosh. 7/1; tel. and fax (7172) 39-03-11; e-mail info@munaygas.com; internet www.munaygas .com; f. 2004; prospecting for, and production of, petroleum and gas; Pres. JENISHBEK JUMASHEV (acting).

Olzha: 050009 Almatı, Bogenbai batyr kosh. 303; tel. (727) 374-34-90; fax (727) 374-35-72; e-mail info@olzha.com; internet olzha.com; f. 1995; transportation, storage and sale of petroleum products; Gen. Dir BOLAT E. DYUYSEKIN.

TRADE UNIONS

Confederation of Free Trade Unions of Coal and Mining Industries: 050000 Almatı; Chair. V. GAIPOV.

Confederation of Free Trade Unions of Kazakhstan: 160006 Shymkent; tel. and fax (7252) 47-90-72; e-mail larisa_harkova@mail .ru; f. 1991; fmrly Independent Trade Union Centre of Kazakhstan; 5 regional brs with 2,200 mems; Chair. LARISA N. HARKOVA.

Federation of Trade Unions of Kazakhstan (FPRK/KRKF) (Federatsiya Profsoyuzov Respubliki Kazakhstan/Kazakstan Respublikasynyn Kesipodktar Federatsiyasy): 010000 Astana, pr. Abay 38; tel. (7172) 21-61-68; fax (7172) 21-68-35; e-mail interdep@ fprk.kz; internet www.fprk.kz; 24 affiliated unions with 2,047,185 mems (2009); Chair. ABELGAZI K. KUSAINOV.

Transport

RAILWAYS

In 2010 the total length of rail track in use was 14,184 km (4,054 km of which were electrified). Much of the rail network is in the north of the country, where it joins the rail lines of Russia. There are also connections with Kyrgyzstan, Uzbekistan and the People's Republic of China. Two new railway lines, amounting to 1,200 km, opened in August 2014, connecting Jezkazgan, in central Kazakhstan, with Beyneu, in the south-west of the country, and Arqalıq with Shubarkol, both in the north of Kazakhstan.

An underground railway in Almatı opened to passengers in December 2011. In Astana the construction of a rapid transit system was planned.

Kazakstan Temir Joly (Kazakhstan Railways): 010000 Astana, Konaev kosh. 6; tel. (7172) 93-01-13; e-mail temirzhol@railways.kz; internet www.railways.kz; f. 1997; Pres. ASKAR U. MAMIN.

ROADS

In 2011 Kazakhstan's total road network was 97,155 km, including 23,494 km of main roads. Some 88.7% of the total network was hard-surfaced.

INLAND WATERWAYS

Kazakhstan has an inland waterway network extending over some 4,000 km. The main navigable river is the Ertis (Irtysh).

Committee of Transport and Railways (Ministry of Transport and Communications): 010000 Astana, Kabanbai batyr kosh. 32/ 1; tel. (7172) 24-10-79; fax (7172) 24-12-98; e-mail ktps_info@mtc.gov .kz; internet www.ktps.gov.kz; f. 2008; Chair. NURDAULET I. KILYBAY.

SHIPPING

A ferry port was inaugurated on the Caspian Sea at Aktaw in 2001, with services operating to Azerbaijan, Iran and Russia. At 31 December 2014 Kazakhstan's flag registered fleet comprised 175 vessels, with a combined displacement of 231,951 grt.

Aktau (Aktaw) International Commercial Sea Port: 130000 Mañğıstaw obl., Aktaw akimat, Ömırzaq; tel. (7292) 51-45-49; fax (7292) 44-51-01; e-mail aktauport@aktauport.kz; internet www .portaktau.kz; f. 1963; Dir MIHAIL J. JALBACHEV; 609 employees.

CIVIL AVIATION

There are 18 domestic airports, and four airports with international services, located at Aktaw, Almatı, Astana and Atiraw.

Department of Aviation (Ministry of Transport and Communications): 010000 Astana, Kabanbai batyr kosh. 32/1; tel. (7172) 24-26-05; fax (7172) 24-31-65; e-mail kga_info@mtc.gov.kz; internet www.caa.gov.kz; Chair. RADILBEK ADIMOLDA.

Air Astana: 050039 Almatı, Zakarpatska kosh. 4A; tel. (7172) 58-41-35; fax (7172) 59-87-01; internet www.airastana.com; f. 2001 jointly by the Samruk-Kazyna National Welfare Fund (51%) and BAE Systems (United Kingdom—49%); domestic and international flights; Chair. NURJAN BAIDAULETOV; Pres. PETER FOSTER.

Tourism

Tourism is not widely developed in Kazakhstan. In 2013 there were 6.8m. tourist arrivals in Kazakhstan, while receipts from tourism (excluding passenger transport) amounted to US $1,460m.

Kazakhstan Tourist Association (KTA): 050022 Almatı, Abay d-ly 42/44/302; tel. (727) 292-53-31; fax (727) 292-48-53; e-mail kta@mail.kz; f. 1999.

Defence

Kazakhstan was one of the four former Union Republics to become a nuclear power in succession to the USSR, but dismantled its final nuclear-testing capabilities at Semey (Semipalatinsk) in July 2000. In mid-1992 Kazakhstan signed a Collective Security Treaty with five other members of the Commonwealth of Independent States (CIS); in May 2001 it was announced that the signatory countries were to form a Collective Rapid Reaction Force to combat Islamist militancy in Central Asia. In April 2003 the Collective Security Treaty Organization (CSTO) was inaugurated as the successor to the CIS collective security system, comprising Armenia, Belarus, Kazakhstan, Kyrgyzstan, Russia and Tajikistan. Kazakhstan participates, with Russia and Azerbaijan, in the operation of the Caspian Sea Flotilla, based at Astrakhan, Russia, and established its own navy in 2003. In May 1994 Kazakhstan joined the North Atlantic Treaty Organization's (NATO) 'Partnership for Peace' programme of military co-operation. As assessed at November 2014, the country's total armed forces numbered some 39,000, with an army of 20,000, an air force of 12,000, a navy of 3,000 and 4,000 joint troops answerable to the Ministry of Defence. There were also 31,500 paramilitary troops, including 20,000 internal security troops under the command of the Ministry of Internal Affairs, a 2,000-strong Presidential Guard, a 500-member Government Guard, and 9,000 state border protection forces answerable to the Ministry of Internal Affairs. Conscripts serve for a period of 12 months.

Chairman of Joint Chiefs of Staff: Gen.-Col SAKEN A. JASUZAKOV.

Defence Expenditure: Budgeted at 377,000m. tenge in 2015.

Education

General education (pre-primary, primary and secondary) is compulsory, and is fully funded by the state. Since 2010 primary education, which begins at seven years of age and lasts for four years, has been preceded by one year of pre-primary education, while secondary education continues for a further seven years. In 2013/14 total enrolment at primary schools included 86% of children in the relevant age-group, while the comparable ratio for secondary enrolment in 2012/13 was 86%. In 2013/14 there were 7,561 state general schools. After completing general education, pupils may continue their studies at vocational secondary schools; there were 610 such schools in the state sector in 2012/13. In addition, there were 184 professional-technical schools.

In 2013/43 there were 128 state higher schools (including universities), attended by 527,200 students. There were also numerous independent institutes of higher education. Government expenditure on education in 2014 was 1,358,669.2m. tenge (17.4% of total spending).

KENYA

Introductory Survey

LOCATION, CLIMATE, LANGUAGE, RELIGION, FLAG, CAPITAL

The Republic of Kenya lies astride the equator on the east coast of Africa, with Somalia to the north-east, Ethiopia and South Sudan to the north, Uganda to the west and Tanzania to the south. The climate varies with altitude: the coastal region is hot and humid, with temperatures averaging between 20°C and 32°C (69°F–90°F), while inland, at more than 1,500 m (5,000 ft) above sea-level, temperatures average 7°C–27°C (45°F–80°F). The highlands and western areas receive ample rainfall (an annual average of 1,000 mm–1,250 mm) but most of northern Kenya is very dry (about 250 mm). Kiswahili and English are the country's two official languages, while 22% and 13% of the population, respectively, speak Kikuyu and Luo as their mother tongue. Most of the country's inhabitants follow traditional beliefs. There is a sizeable Christian community, while Muslims form a smaller proportion of the population. The national flag (proportions 2 by 3) has three broad horizontal stripes, of black, red and green, separated by two narrow white stripes. Superimposed in the centre is a red shield, with black and white markings, upon crossed white spears. The capital is Nairobi.

CONTEMPORARY POLITICAL HISTORY

Historical Context

Formerly a British colony (inland) and protectorate (along the coast), Kenya became independent, within the Commonwealth, on 12 December 1963, and a republic exactly one year later. Jomo Kenyatta, a Kikuyu, and leader of the Kenya African National Union (KANU), was appointed Prime Minister in June 1963 and became the country's first President in December 1964. (He was subsequently re-elected to the presidency, unopposed, in 1969 and 1974.)

Kenyatta died in August 1978; the Vice-President, Daniel arap Moi, was proclaimed President in October, and was the sole candidate at a presidential election held (concurrently with a KANU-only general election) in November 1979. In June 1982 the National Assembly officially declared Kenya a one-party state. Moi was returned unopposed in presidential elections in 1983 and 1988.

Domestic Political Affairs

By the early 1990s pressure for political reform had grown and in November 1991 several members of the Forum for the Restoration of Democracy (FORD), an outlawed political movement, were arrested prior to a planned pro-democracy rally in Nairobi, which was suppressed by the security forces. The Kenyan authorities were condemned internationally and bilateral and multilateral creditors suspended aid to Kenya indefinitely, pending the acceleration of both economic and political reforms. In December a special conference of KANU delegates acceded to the demands for reform, resolving to introduce a multi-party political system. The National Assembly subsequently endorsed appropriate amendments to the Constitution. Former Vice-President Mwai Kibaki resigned as Minister of Health later in the month, in protest against alleged electoral malpractice by KANU, and founded the Democratic Party (DP).

During the first half of 1992 some 2,000 people were reportedly killed in tribal clashes in western Kenya. In March the Government banned all political rallies, and restrictions were placed on the activities of the press. Following a general strike in April, organized by FORD, the Government ended the ban on political rallies. In August FORD split into two opposing factions, which were registered in October as separate political parties, FORD—Asili and FORD—Kenya, respectively led by Kenneth Matiba and Oginga Odinga.

At multi-party presidential and legislative elections held in December 1992 Moi was elected for a fourth term of office as President, winning 36.3% of the votes cast, ahead of Matiba (26.0%), Kibaki (19.5%) and Odinga (17.5%). Of the 188 elective seats in the National Assembly, KANU won 100 (including 16 uncontested); FORD—Asili and FORD—Kenya secured 31 seats each, and the DP took 23. Votes were cast predominantly in accordance with ethnic affiliations, with the two largest tribes, the Kikuyu and Luo, overwhelmingly rejecting KANU. In 1993 the international donor community agreed to resume the provision of aid to Kenya, in response to the Government's progress in implementing political and economic reforms.

During the mid-1990s Kenya's human rights record came under intense domestic and international scrutiny. In response to its critics, the Moi administration provisionally withdrew controversial draft legislation in January 1996 that would have severely restricted the freedom of the press and, in July, inaugurated a human rights committee to investigate alleged humanitarian abuses (including the torture of criminal suspects and opposition activists by security forces).

Divisions within opposition parties continued to undermine efforts to present a cohesive challenge to Moi and KANU prior to the 1997 elections. A renewed attempt to establish a coalition of opposition organizations, initiated in November 1995, was short-lived. Meanwhile, following an unsuccessful attempt to assume the leadership of FORD—Kenya, Raila Odinga (the son of Oginga Odinga, who died in January 1994, and a prominent opposition activist) left that party and subsequently became leader of the National Development Party (NDP). In October 1997 Matiba's faction of FORD—Asili registered as an independent party, the Forum for the Restoration of Democracy for the People (FORD—People). During the mid-1990s several opposition deputies, disaffected by these internal rivalries, defected to KANU.

In August 1997 the IMF suspended assistance to Kenya, pending the implementation of decisive action to eliminate official corruption and to improve the system of revenue collection; the Government consequently announced the inauguration of an anti-corruption body. In the following month the National Assembly approved legislation that amended the Constitution with the stated aim of ensuring free and fair democratic elections. All political parties were granted equal access to the media, and detention without trial was prohibited. In addition, the new legislation enabled the opposition to participate in selecting the 12 nominated members of the National Assembly and 10 of the 12 members of the supervisory Electoral Commission.

The presidential and legislative elections, which took place concurrently on 29 December 1997, were undermined by allegations of widespread fraud, as well as by logistical difficulties. Moi was re-elected President, winning 40.6% of the valid votes cast, while Kibaki came second, with 31.5% of the votes. KANU secured 107 of the 210 elected seats in the enlarged National Assembly, and the remainder were divided between nine opposition parties, with the DP taking 39 seats, the NDP 21, FORD—Kenya 17 and the Social Democratic Party 15. Moi was inaugurated for a fifth (and final) term as President in January 1998.

In August 1998 a car bomb exploded at the US embassy in central Nairobi, concurrently with a similar attack on the US mission in Dar es Salaam, Tanzania. Some 254 people were killed in Nairobi, and more than 5,000 suffered injuries. The attacks were believed to have been co-ordinated by international Islamist terrorists, and the USA retaliated by launching air strikes against targets in Afghanistan and Sudan. Four men were convicted of involvement in the bombings by a court in New York, USA, in May 2001 and were later sentenced to life imprisonment.

Meanwhile, during late 2000 a parliamentary anti-graft committee sought the adoption by the National Assembly of a report in which the alleged perpetrators of corruption were named, and also proposed legislation that would allow the anti-corruption authority significant powers of prosecution. In January 2001, however, the IMF and the World Bank expressed concern over delays in the implementation of the reforms, particularly the failure to approve legislation on public service ethics and economic crimes. In August the National Assembly again refused to approve anti-corruption legislation, and the IMF suspended aid to Kenya indefinitely.

In January 2001 Odinga, on behalf of the Luo-dominated NDP, signed a memorandum of understanding with KANU, which allowed Moi to appoint ministers from the NDP. In June Moi reorganized the Cabinet and appointed Odinga as Minister of Energy, thereby creating the first coalition Government in Kenya's history. Moi reshuffled the Cabinet again in November, introducing younger KANU ministers in an apparent attempt to provide suitable candidates for his succession; most notably Uhuru Kenyatta (son of the late President Jomo Kenyatta) was appointed as Minister for Local Government.

The NDP was dissolved and absorbed into KANU in mid-March 2002, despite opposition from elements within both parties; Moi was elected as party Chairman, while Odinga became Secretary-General. In July some 12 opposition parties, including the DP, FORD—Kenya and the National Party of Kenya, formed an electoral alliance, the National Alliance Party of Kenya (NAK).

The 2002 elections

In August 2002 Moi publicly announced that he favoured Uhuru Kenyatta as KANU's presidential candidate. However, several senior KANU members, including the Vice-President, Prof. George Saitoti, and Odinga, subsequently announced their intention to seek the party's presidential nomination and formed the Rainbow Alliance (RA) to campaign within KANU for a democratic vote to select its candidate. Moi responded by dismissing Saitoti. In October, in protest against Moi's attempts to impose his preferred successor, members of the RA resigned from their posts in the Government and from KANU, together with some 30 KANU deputies. The RA boycotted the KANU conference, at which Kenyatta's presidential candidacy was endorsed, and established a new party, the Liberal Democratic Party (LDP), which joined with the NAK to form the National Rainbow Coalition (NARC), with Kibaki as its presidential candidate.

At the presidential and legislative elections, held concurrently on 27 December 2002, the opposition secured a decisive victory, with Kibaki winning 62.3% of the votes cast in the presidential election, and the NARC securing 125 of the 210 elected seats in the National Assembly, while Kenyatta received 31.2% of the votes cast for the presidency, and KANU won 64 seats in the legislature. The NARC was allocated a further seven appointed seats, increasing its representation to 132, and KANU a further four seats, bringing its total to 68.

Following his inauguration as President on 30 December 2002, Kibaki promised reforms, including the adoption of a new constitution, under which certain powers would be transferred from the President to the legislature, and the adoption of anti-corruption legislation. In January 2003 Kibaki appointed a new Cabinet; however, divisions within the ruling coalition soon became apparent, as a group of 25 LDP deputies accused Kibaki of breaching a power-sharing agreement signed by the constituent parties of the NARC prior to the elections. In May the Anti-Corruption and Economic Crimes Act, which provided for the establishment of the Kenya AntiCorruption Commission (KACC), and the Public Service (Code of Conduct and Ethics) Act, requiring elected officials and senior civil servants to declare their wealth, came into effect.

In February 2003 Kibaki appointed a commission of inquiry into a financial scandal, in which public funds had been paid to the company Goldenberg International as subsidies for non-existent exports of gold and diamonds during 1990–93. The illicit payments to Goldenberg were estimated at some US $600m., although it was indicated that the total amount misappropriated could reach $4,000m. The commission's findings were reported to Kibaki in February 2005; however, the Government stated that further investigations were necessary before any charges could be brought.

Meanwhile, a constitutional review conference opened in April 2003, but divisions persisted between the LDP and Kibaki's supporters over the proposed post of Prime Minister. In March 2004 the constitutional review conference voted to reduce the powers vested in the presidency and to create the post of Prime Minister following the next elections, which were scheduled to be held in December 2007. Under the recommendations adopted by the conference, greater power was to be accorded to the National Assembly. The Government withdrew from the conference in protest; however, the draft constitution was successfully presented to the Attorney-General, after which it was to be considered by the National Assembly. The High Court subsequently ruled that the document required the endorsement of a simple majority at a referendum. The draft constitution, which retained the executive functions of the President, was approved by the National Assembly in July 2005.

Several months of campaigning, punctuated by a number of violent demonstrations, ensued. Seven ministers announced

their opposition to the proposed new constitution, including, most notably, Raila Odinga, whose LDP split from the NARC coalition and joined with KANU to form the Orange Democratic Movement (ODM). At the referendum, held on 21 November 2005, the draft constitution was rejected by 58.1% of voters. Kibaki conceded defeat, but dismissed the entire Cabinet, and in early December announced a new administration, from which those ministers who had opposed the draft constitution were removed. Those NARC members who maintained their support for Kibaki subsequently formed a new coalition party, the National Rainbow Coalition—Kenya (NARC—Kenya), to contest the 2007 elections.

Corruption

Meanwhile, during 2004 evidence emerged of continuing endemic corruption in Kenya, despite the NARC Government's pledge to take measures to combat it. In July the British High Commissioner, Sir Edward Clay, claimed that corruption had cost Kenya some Ks. 15,000m. since Kibaki took office and warned that it could lead to a reduction in donor assistance; later that month the European Union (see p. 271) withheld substantial aid. Clay subsequently produced a dossier of some 20 allegedly dubious contracts involving corruption in four ministries.

Amid increasing public resentment, in February 2005 the Permanent Secretary for Governance and Ethics in the Office of the President, John Githongo, resigned. Kibaki did not appoint a replacement for Githongo, and in November disbanded the Office of Governance and Ethics. Following Githongo's resignation, the USA and Germany announced that they would withhold anti-corruption aid, and the United Kingdom imposed travel restrictions on government ministers and others implicated in corruption. Following demands from within the Government for the resignations of corrupt ministers, Kibaki reorganized the Cabinet, dismissing several high-ranking civil servants and transferring the hitherto Minister of State for Provincial Administration and National Security in the Office of the President, Christopher Murungaru, to the Ministry of Transport. Meanwhile, in February the Kenya Law Society announced that it was to prosecute senior figures on corruption charges, including Vice-President Arthur Moody Awori, the Attorney-General, Amos Wako, and the Minister of Finance, David Mwiraria. However, Wako invoked a provision in the Constitution granting him the power to take over private prosecutions initiated by individuals or institutions, and terminated the case.

In November 2005 Githongo presented Kibaki with a dossier detailing his investigations into corruption in Kenya and death threats made against him. Awori, Mwiraria, Murungaru and Kiraitu Murungi (the Minister of Energy) were implicated by Githongo in the intended embezzlement of some US $700m. through false military and security contracts. The four accused were subsequently summoned to appear before the KACC; they all denied the allegations. In January 2006 Githongo (who had fled to the United Kingdom) released a copy of his dossier to the British media. In early February Mwiraria resigned from the Cabinet. Pressure increased on the Government and later that month Kibaki announced the resignations of Murungi and Saitoti, the Minister of Education. In March Saitoti was questioned by the police about his role in the Goldenberg affair, but the High Court of Kenya later rejected recommendations that he be charged. In a cabinet reorganization in November he was readmitted to the Government as Minister of Education, alongside Murungi, who resumed responsibility for the energy portfolio.

Division among the main parties intending to contest the forthcoming presidential and legislative elections emerged during 2007. In June NARC—Kenya indicated that Kibaki was to be named as its presidential candidate. In November, however, when primary elections were held, Kibaki defected from the ruling NARC—Kenya and chose to contest the elections under his newly established Party of National Unity (PNU). Odinga was named the presidential candidate for the ODM.

Post-election violence

At the legislative elections, held on 27 December 2007, the ODM secured 99 of the 210 seats in the National Assembly, the PNU won 43, the ODM—Kenya, which had broken away from the main party in August, 16 and KANU 14. Results in three constituencies were not released. The presidential election was held concurrently and the Electoral Commission of Kenya (ECK) announced that Kibaki had narrowly been re-elected to the presidency with 4,584,721 votes; Odinga was reported to have secured 4,352,993 votes. Odinga and other opposition candidates vehemently denounced the results, while independent international observers expressed scepticism regarding the credibility of the election, which had taken place amid allegations of widespread procedural violations. The results led to an upsurge in violence: by the end of December some 120 people had been killed in clashes between Kibaki's Kikuyu and Odinga's Luo supporters, and police. Nevertheless, on 30 December Kibaki was sworn in for a second term.

On 8 January 2008 Kibaki announced the partial composition of his new Cabinet; despite the ODM having secured the largest number of seats in the legislature, no representatives from that party were included in the new Government. Proposed African Union (AU, see p. 188) mediation was rejected by the Kenyan Government, and on 16 January the ODM, defying a ban on public demonstrations, commenced nationwide protests. These were violently dispersed by the security forces, resulting in additional fatalities. Meanwhile, in January clashes and reprisal killings between the Kalenjin, Luo and Kikuyu ethnic groups escalated rapidly, particularly in the Rift Valley.

On 29 January 2008 the former UN Secretary-General, Kofi Annan, formally launched negotiations. Discussions were temporarily suspended, after two senior ODM officials were killed in continuing ethnic fighting; in early February, however, the establishment of a power-sharing transitional government was proposed. On 28 February Kibaki and Odinga signed an agreement on the division of power and the creation of the posts of Prime Minister and two Deputy Prime Ministers, pending a full constitutional review to be carried out within 12 months. Odinga conceded the presidency to Kibaki and accepted the role of Prime Minister. The National Accord and Reconciliation Act, which endorsed the power-sharing agreement and allowed a new coalition government to begin to implement a recovery programme, was ratified by the National Assembly in late March. (By that time over 1,000 people had been killed and some 600,000 displaced as a result of the violence.)

In April 2008 Kibaki named a new coalition Government, comprising members of the PNU, the ODM and ODM—Kenya, including Kenyatta as Deputy Prime Minister and Minister of Trade and Wycliffe Musalia Mudavadi as Deputy Prime Minister and Minister of Local Government; Stephen Kalonzo Musyoka, who had been appointed as Vice-President and Minister of Home Affairs in January, and Moses Wetangula, who assumed responsibility for the foreign affairs portfolio at the same time, retained their positions in the new Cabinet. The establishment of a commission of inquiry, chaired by Appellate Judge Philip Waki, to investigate the causes and perpetrators of the post-election violence was agreed. However, divisions soon emerged within the Cabinet as Odinga and ministers allied to the ODM sought an amnesty for all those arrested in the violence, which was ultimately rejected. Waki's report, published in October, recommended the establishment of a Special Tribunal for Kenya to 'seek accountability against persons bearing the greatest responsibility for crimes, particularly crimes against humanity' relating to the 2007 elections. It also recommended that a comprehensive reform of the Kenya Police Service be undertaken. Kibaki and Odinga agreed to the establishment of the Special Tribunal in December 2008 and the following month legislation providing for its creation was introduced before the National Assembly.

Election inquiry

On 11 June 2008 by-elections were held for five seats in the National Assembly: the killings of two ODM deputies and the failure to announce the results in two Rift Valley constituencies during the unrest that followed the 2007 elections had left four seats vacant (while the other seat had previously been occupied by the newly elected speaker of the National Assembly). The by-elections were conducted peacefully, despite fears of further unrest, with the ODM winning three of the seats and the PNU securing two, taking their total representations in the legislature to 102 and 45 seats, respectively.

The issue of corruption remained significant for the Government during 2008. In July Amos Kimunya resigned from his position as Minister of Finance, owing to allegations that he had given false information regarding the sale of a hotel to Libyan investors, although a government inquiry later cleared him of any wrongdoing. In January 2009 Kimunya was named as Minister of Trade in a minor government reorganization. At the same time Kenyatta was appointed as the new Minister of Finance (retaining the deputy premiership).

In September 2008 a report was published by the independent commission of inquiry, chaired by Johann Kriegler, a South African judge and the former Chairperson of that country's Independent Electoral Commission, set up to investigate the disputed elections in December 2007. It concluded that the conduct of the elections made it impossible to verify results reliably, and recommended that the ECK should undergo major reforms or be replaced by a new body. In December 2008 the ECK was disbanded and provision was made for its replacement by a new nine-member body, the Interim Independent Electoral Commission.

In February 2009 the UN Special Rapporteur on Extrajudicial, Summary or Arbitrary Executions, Philip Alston, issued a report in which he accused Kenya's security forces of widespread extrajudicial killings, and demanded the removal of Kenya's Police Commissioner, Hussein Ali, and Attorney-General Wako. The report concluded that death squads had been formed on the orders of senior police officials to exterminate members of the Mungiki (an illegal religious sect allegedly responsible for a number of murders and involved in extortion), although the Kenyan Government rejected the findings. In early March two leading members of the Oscar Foundation, a civil rights advocacy group which had been accused by the Government of having links with the Mungiki, were killed by unidentified gunmen. Prior to the murders, the Oscar Foundation had led demonstrations in the capital, expressing anger at government corruption and accusing the Kenyan police of brutality and widespread extrajudicial killings and arrests, especially of suspected Mungiki members. The deaths of the two activists precipitated further demonstrations in which one student was shot dead, and on 10 March violent protests were staged in Nairobi. The Government suffered a further reverse later in March when Minister of Justice, National Cohesion and Constitutional Affairs Martha Karua announced her resignation, citing Kibaki's appointment of judges without her knowledge as the main reason for her departure.

In July 2009 the Kenya National Commission on Human Rights (KNCHR) named 219 people suspected of involvement in the violence that took place after the 2007 elections; these included Deputy Prime Minister and Minister of Finance Uhuru Kenyatta and a number of other government ministers. In the same month former UN Secretary-General Kofi Annan submitted a list of 10 suspects to be investigated by the International Criminal Court (ICC) with regard to their involvement in the post-election violence. The Kenyan authorities were divided on whether suspects would be tried at a local tribunal or at the ICC, in The Hague, Netherlands. Also in July President Kibaki announced the formation of a nine-member Kenya Truth, Justice, and Reconciliation Commission to investigate a number of 'injustices' including land allocation and regional imbalances.

It was reported that five people had been killed during violent demonstrations in the mainly Somali Nairobi suburb of Eastleigh against the detention of a radical, Jamaican-born Muslim cleric, Sheikh Abdullah al-Faisal, in mid-January 2010. Al-Faisal, who had entered Kenya with the stated intention of carrying out a preaching tour, had been arrested in early January after the Kenyan Government declared that he was a threat to national security. Some 328 people were reported to have been arrested in the days following the protests, including a number of citizens with alleged links to a Somali militant Islamist group, al-Shabaab ('The Youth'), and Al-Amin Kimathi, the Chairman of Kenya's Muslim Human Rights Forum. Kimathi was among eight of those charged with incitement to violence later in January. Al-Faisal was deported to Jamaica on 22 January.

In February 2010 President Kibaki suspended a number of senior officials from the agriculture, education and special programmes ministries, after inquiries into the work of a subsidized maize scheme and Kenya's free primary education programme revealed corrupt practices. Shortly afterwards Prime Minister Odinga announced the suspension of Minister of Agriculture William Ruto (who had also featured on the KNCHR list of those suspected of major involvement in the post-election violence) and Minister of Education Samson Ongeri to allow independent investigations into the corruption allegations to proceed. However, Kibaki overturned Odinga's decision, maintaining that he did not have the constitutional powers to suspend the two ministers. (In April Ruto was removed as Minister of Agriculture and appointed Minister of Higher Education.)

In early March 2010 the Chief Prosecutor of the ICC, Luis Moreno-Ocampo, presented evidence relating to the potential prosecution of 20 people for their role in the post-election violence in which an estimated 1,100 people had been killed, stating that senior political and business leaders from both the ODM and the PNU had organized and financed post-election attacks against civilians in 2008. At the end of March the ICC's pre-trial chamber announced that it was to initiate an investigation into the alleged crimes against humanity.

New Constitution

On 1 April 2010 the National Assembly unanimously approved the text of a draft constitution. In a referendum held on 4 August the new Constitution was endorsed by 66.9% of votes cast. In Central and Nyanza provinces, dominated by the Kikuyu and Luo, respectively, an overwhelming majority voted in favour of the new Constitution, which had been supported by Odinga and Kenyatta; however, in Rift Valley, dominated by the Kalenjin, a significant majority had voted against it, following a campaign led by former President Moi and Ruto. The new Constitution notably provided for the abolition of the post of Prime Minister and creation of a deputy presidency, and the devolution of some powers to 47 new counties, which were to be represented by a second legislative chamber, the Senate. On 17 August the Government established a committee, to be chaired by Kibaki and Odinga, which was to supervise the implementation of the constitutional reforms. The new Constitution was officially signed into law by President Kibaki on 27 August.

In October 2010 Ruto was suspended as Minister of Higher Education, following a court ruling that he be tried on charges of illegally selling forest land during his tenure of the agriculture portfolio. (He was cleared of the charges in April 2011.) Later that month Wetangula submitted his resignation as Minister of Foreign Affairs, after being implicated in allegedly irregular property agreements conducted by Kenyan embassies overseas. In November Kiplagat was obliged to resign as Chairman of the Kenya Truth, Justice, and Reconciliation Commission, after he was accused of being implicated in a 1984 massacre by security forces. In December Moreno-Ocampo issued indictment requests formally naming six principal suspects accused of organizing the post-election violence, the most notable being Deputy Prime Minister and Minister of Finance Kenyatta. The other accused were: the Cabinet Secretary and close associate of Kibaki, Francis Muthaura; Ruto, who had travelled to the ICC in The Hague shortly beforehand in an effort to reach a compromise agreement; Henry Kosgey, the Chairman of the ODM and Minister of Industrialization; a former police commissioner, Mohammed Hussein Ali; and a radio broadcaster, Joshua Arap Sang. The announcement of the high-level suspects (all of whom denied the charges) prompted public controversy and later in December, following a motion submitted by Ruto, the National Assembly voted overwhelmingly for Kenya to withdraw from the jurisdiction of the ICC. The Minister of Justice and 13 foreign envoys subsequently urged Kibaki and Odinga to ignore the parliamentary resolution. In early 2011 Kosgey resigned from the post of Minister of Industrialization, following allegations of corruption against him. On 8 March the ICC issued summonses for the six accused to appear before the Court; hearings to confirm the charges against them were conducted in September.

In May 2011 the Government of the British Crown Dependency island of Jersey issued arrest warrants for a former head of Kenya Power and Lighting, Samuel Gichuru, and a former Minister of Energy, Chris Okemo, for corruption, alleging they had both received bribes from European engineering companies and a US communications company. However, the Kenyan Government refused to extradite either suspect. In August Ruto was dismissed in a government reorganization, in which Wetangula was reinstated as Minister of Foreign Affairs. In October one person was killed and a further 23 injured in two grenade attacks in Nairobi; later that month a Kenyan national, who confessed to being a member of al-Shabaab, was sentenced to life imprisonment, after pleading guilty to involvement in one of the incidents.

ICC announcement and terrorist attacks

On 23 January 2012 the ICC officially announced that Ruto was to stand trial, together with Arap Sang, for crimes against humanity perpetrated against supporters of Kibaki, while Kenyatta was to be tried with Muthaura for crimes against humanity directed at Odinga supporters; the charges against Kosgey and Ali were not confirmed. On 26 January Kenyatta and Muthaura both resigned their government posts; President Kibaki accepted Kenyatta's resignation as Minister of Finance, but announced that he was to retain the post of Deputy Prime Minister in accordance with the Constitution. Minister of Nairobi Metropolitan Development Benjamin Githae subsequently assumed additional responsibilities as acting Minister of Finance. On 24 May the ICC rejected an appeal by the accused challenging its jurisdiction.

In March 2012 six people were killed and 69 injured in a grenade attack in central Nairobi, which was widely attributed to al-Shabaab (following several attacks in border regions in late 2011 that were regarded as retaliation for Kenyan involvement in Somalia—see *Foreign Affairs*). An increasing number of similar incidents took place in the capital and other principal towns in the following months, including two simultaneous attacks on churches in the north-eastern city of Garissa in July, in which 17 people were killed and 40 injured.

Meanwhile, in early May 2012 Mudavadi tendered his resignation as Deputy Prime Minister and Minister of Local Government, announcing that he was to leave the ODM to join the United Democratic Forum Party (UDFP), which had been formed in the previous month by supporters of Kibaki. Kenyatta also established a new political organization, The National Alliance (TNA), later that month, in preparation for the forthcoming presidential and legislative elections. In June the Minister of Provincial Administration and Internal Security, Saitoti, and five others were killed when a police helicopter crashed in the outskirts of Nairobi. (Katoo Ole Metito was appointed to replace Saitoti as part of a government reorganization in September.) After the withdrawal of the corruption charges against Kosgey in July, in early August Kibaki reappointed him as Minister of Industrialization.

In August 2012 a radical Muslim cleric, who had been arrested in January for possession of armaments and subsequently also charged with membership of al-Shabaab, was shot dead by unknown assailants in Mombasa, prompting violent rioting and attacks against police in the town, in which five people were killed. (In early September Muslim cleric Abubaker Sharif was charged with inciting the violence.) It was reported in September that two suspects, who were arrested with a cache of armaments in Nairobi, had confessed that they were part of a terrorist group affiliated to al-Shabaab that had planned to attack the parliamentary building and assassinate senior politicians. In October a meeting addressed by the Minister of Fisheries Development, Amason Jeffah Kingi, in the coastal town of Kilifi was attacked by suspected members of the Muslim separatist Mombasa Republican Council (MRC), who killed three people and injured Kingi. Later that month the MRC leader, Omar Mwamnuadzi, and a number of his supporters were arrested in the nearby town of Kwale, following an exchange of fire in which two people were killed. Mwamnuadzi was later charged with possession of armaments and incitement to violence. In December at least six people were killed in a grenade attack outside a mosque in Nairobi, which was followed by violent protests by youths. In January 2013 five people were shot dead in a further terrorist attack against a hotel in Garissa.

The 2013 elections

In February 2013 the High Court ruled that Kenyatta, together with his running mate, Ruto, were entitled to contest the presidential election, despite the ICC indictments against them. Presidential and legislative elections, together with the country's first gubernatorial polls, were held peacefully on 4 March, although some 18 people were killed in attacks in Mombasa, Kilifi and Kwale shortly beforehand. The MRC (which had opposed the organization of the elections) denied accusations by the authorities that its members were responsible for the violence. According to official results, the ODM won 78 of the 290 directly elected constituency seats in the expanded National Assembly, while the TNA received 72 seats, and the United Republican Party (URP), newly established by Ruto, 62. (Of 47 additional women members elected from the newly created counties, 15 represented the ODM, 14 the TNA and 10 the URP.) Under the terms of the 2010 Constitution, elections were also held for a new Senate, at which the ODM and the TNA both obtained 11 of the 47 directly elected seats, and the URP nine. Overall, following the additional nomination of deputies, the Jubilee Coalition, an alliance including both the TNA and the URP, had secured 167 of the total 349 seats in the National Assembly, and 30 of the 67 seats in the Senate, while the ODM-led Coalition for Reforms and Democracy (CORD) had taken 141 seats in the lower and 28 in the upper chamber. CORD elected 23 and the Jubilee Coalition 18 of the 47 governors. The results of the presidential election indicated a victory for Kenyatta, with about 50.5% of the votes cast, followed by Odinga, with 43.7%, and Mudavadi, with 4.0%. Turnout was about 86%.

In response to an appeal by Odinga, who alleged malpractice following delays and technical malfunctions in the vote-counting, on 25 March 2013 the Supreme Court ordered a partial recount of the votes. However, on 30 March the Supreme Court issued a ruling upholding Kenyatta's victory; two people were killed when police violently suppressed ensuing protests. Meanwhile, on 11 March the ICC announced that the charges against Muthaura had been withdrawn, owing to lack of witness evidence; the trial of Ruto and Arap Sang had been postponed until 28 May, and that of Kenyatta to 9 July, following defence applications. (In June the trial of Ruto and Arap Sang was further deferred to 10 September, and that of Kenyatta to 12 November.)

Kenyatta was sworn in as President on 9 April 2013, and later that month he announced a major restructuring of the Government, reducing the number of ministries from 44 to 18. The new Government, which was approved in May, notably included several women, among them Amina Mohamed as Secretary for Foreign Affairs. In May the Truth, Justice, and Reconciliation Commission presented a report that implicated Kenyatta and Ruto in organizing the post-election violence of 2007–08, and listed a number of other suspects, including the Secretary for Mining, Najib Balala, and a former Chairman of the Commission, Bethuel Kiplagat. In June 2013 15 people were injured in two grenade attacks in Nairobi and Mombasa, while al-Shabaab claimed responsibility for the abduction of two police officers in north-eastern Kenya the previous month. Meanwhile, on 6 June the British Government (while officially denying legal liability) agreed to a compensation payment of £13.9m. to be shared between 5,228 victims of torture in detention camps during the Mau Mau insurgency against British colonial authority in the 1950s.

During August 2013 further clashes between security forces and al-Shabaab militants took place in the region of Garissa. On 5 September the National Assembly approved a motion for Kenya to withdraw from membership of the ICC, which was accused of pursuing politically motivated persecutions. Nevertheless, the trial of Ruto and Arap Sang on three counts of crimes against humanity began on 10 September in The Hague.

Recent developments: deteriorating security situation

On 21 September 2013 groups of al-Shabaab militants staged an attack on the Westgate retail complex in Nairobi during which at least 67 people, including 18 foreign nationals and six members of the Kenyan security forces, were killed. A large number of hostages were held within the complex and heavy exchanges of fire continued for nearly four days, as security forces attempted to regain control of the complex. The Government declared that the siege had ended on 24 September, and stated that four terrorists had been killed during operations to release the hostages, while 11 people suspected of involvement with the assault had been taken into custody. At the end of September the Kenyan authorities announced an investigation into the country's security system, following media reports that security services had been warned of a possible large-scale terrorist attack in Nairobi. As part of anti-terrorism operations carried out by the police following the attack, some 300 people were arrested in Nairobi in early November on suspicion of being illegal immigrants. Kenyatta's trial was further postponed, until February 2014, to enable him to address its impact, although in mid-November 2013 the UN Security Council rejected a proposal by Rwanda for a suspension in the proceedings against him and Ruto.

On 7 December 2013 the National Assembly approved a decision by Kenyatta to send troops to four counties in northern Kenya, owing to intensifying inter-communal conflict in the border Moyale region of Marsabit County, in which some 100 people had been killed and at least 72,000 displaced since the beginning of the year. In the same month some 15 people were killed in al-Shabaab attacks, including six in an explosion on a Nairobi bus. Following a parliamentary inquiry into the Westgate attack, a report issued in February 2014 urged the establishment of a new Directorate of National Security, which would co-ordinate between intelligence and security agencies in an effort to avert further such incidents. Suspected al-Shabaab gunmen murdered six people during a raid on a church in Likoni in March, and later that month a further six people were killed in a grenade attack at a restaurant in the capital. A series of bombings in Nairobi and Mombasa during April and May left a further 24 people dead. Moreover, a group of around 50 al-Shabaab militants orchestrated a major attack in mid-June on the town of Mpeketoni, in Lamu County, killing approximately 60 people and kidnapping another 12. Neighbouring villages also

came under assault shortly thereafter, and a further 26 fatalities were reported. Two more villages, situated in Lamu and Gamba, respectively, were targeted by al-Shabaab in early July, resulting in at least 29 additional deaths. The Government appeared reluctant to attribute these latest atrocities to al-Shabaab (which had repeatedly affirmed its culpability) and intimated that CORD or the MRC may have been involved in fomenting the violence—allegations that were firmly rejected by Odinga and MRC Secretary-General Randu Nzai Ruwa. It was estimated that 12 people were killed later in July in separate attacks in Wajir, Lamu and Mombasa; further outbreaks of deadly violence were reported in the following month in Mandera and Lamu. MRC leader Omar Mwamnuadzi was detained in mid-October, while in early November the authorities declared the separatist group responsible for raids on security installations in Nyali and Malindi. (Mwamnuadzi was subsequently charged with plotting to stage future attacks.) Also in that month, 20 police officers operating in the Kapedo region were ambushed and murdered.

In mid-November 2014 four mosques in Mombasa, which had allegedly been used to promote extremism, were stormed by the security forces, and some 360 people were arrested. The operation left one person dead and precipitated violence in the city that led to four more deaths being recorded. Later that month, in retaliation for the Mombasa raids, heavily armed al-Shabaab fighters hijacked a public bus travelling between Mandera and Nairobi and killed 28 non-Muslim passengers. The Government responded by authorizing air strikes against al-Shabaab targets in Somalia; officials claimed that over 100 militants were killed in the strikes, although al-Shabaab disputed this number. Further increasing inter-communal tensions during November was the assassination in Likoni of prominent Muslim cleric Sheikh Salim Bakari Mwarangi, the latest in a series of similar shootings. In early December members of al-Shabaab killed at least 36 non-Muslim workers at a quarry in Mandera. In the immediate aftermath of this new atrocity, Kenyatta reorganized his senior domestic security team, appointing Maj.-Gen. (retd) Joseph Nkaissery as Secretary for the Interior and Co-ordination of National Government and Joseph Kipchirchir Boinett as Inspector-General of Police. Moreover, in mid-December the Government ordered the deregistration of 15 non-governmental organizations accused of financing militant activity. Shortly thereafter, controversial counter-terrorism legislation, which, *inter alia*, granted additional powers to the security forces, provided for the detention of suspects without charge for up to 360 days, and imposed restrictions on the media and the right to assemble freely, was adopted by the National Assembly amid violent clashes between Jubilee Coalition and opposition deputies. CORD denounced the new security proposals as unconstitutional and submitted an appeal to the High Court, while Western nations and international human rights organizations also expressed concern about the extent of the measures. In early 2015 the High Court abrogated some of the most contentious elements of the security legislation, including the limitations on press freedom.

Meanwhile, in February 2014 Kenyatta's trial was again deferred after another of a series of principal witnesses withdrew from the case. In March the ICC declared that Kenyatta's trial would begin on 7 October, but in September legal proceedings were suspended again due to delays arising from the Kenyan Government's lack of co-operation with the Court. Kenyatta was questioned in person at a pre-trial hearing at the ICC in October, while later that month the Court censured the Government for repeatedly releasing classified legal information into the public sphere. In December it was revealed that the charges against Kenyatta had been retracted owing to ongoing Kenyan obstructionism and the consequent difficulty of conducting a comprehensive investigation into the alleged crimes and gathering sufficient evidence to support the prosecution's case. In January 2015 the members of the ruling Jubilee Coalition agreed to merge into a new party—the Jubilee National Alliance.

In March 2015 the Ethics and Anti-Corruption Commission submitted a report to Kenyatta, which listed more than 100 senior government officials, as well as several heads of parastatal organizations, who were believed to have been implicated in corrupt dealings. Kenyatta requested that all those named step down from their positions pending further investigations, and five members of the Cabinet duly tendered their resignations.

In early April 2015 some 148 people were killed and a further 79 were injured when Al-Shabaab fighters attacked a university campus in Garissa in eastern Kenya. Five militants suspected of involvement in the incident were subsequently detained, while

Kenya carried out a number of airstrikes against suspected al-Shabaab camps in Somalia.

Foreign Affairs

Following an improvement in relations between Kenya and Uganda from the late 1980s, in November 1994 President Moi, Ugandan President Yoweri Museveni and Tanzanian President Ali Hassan Mwinyi met in Arusha, Tanzania, and established a commission for co-operation. In March 1996 the Secretariat of the Permanent Tripartite Commission for East African Co-operation was formally inaugurated, with a view to reviving the East African Community (EAC), which had been dissolved in 1977. A treaty for the re-establishment of the EAC, providing for the promotion of free trade between the member states, the development of the region's infrastructure and economy and the creation of a regional legislative assembly and court, was ratified by the Kenyan, Tanzanian and Ugandan Heads of State in November 1999. The new EAC (see p. 446) was officially inaugurated in Arusha in January 2001. Talks on integrating the economies of the three EAC members followed, and in March 2004 President Mwai Kibaki, Museveni and President Benjamin Mkapa of Tanzania signed a protocol on the creation of a customs union, eliminating most duties on goods traded within the Community, which took effect from January 2005. In November 2009 the Heads of State of Tanzania, Kenya, Uganda, Rwanda and Burundi signed a common market protocol in Arusha (Rwanda and Burundi having joined the EAC in 2007), allowing the free movement of goods, services, people and capital within the EAC. The common market protocol entered into force in July 2010.

In 2011 tensions increased between Kenya and Uganda over two small disputed islands in Lake Victoria; Kenyan security forces were dispatched to Migingo Island in August, following appeals from Kenyan fishermen for protection. It was agreed later that month that joint policing of the islands by Kenya and Uganda would be undertaken, while a joint border committee would conduct a survey in an effort to resolve the issue of the islands' sovereignty. In mid-2013, however, Ugandan police clashed with, and injured, three Kenyan police officers on Migingo Island. At bilateral discussions in Kisumu in November, Kenyan officials urged that the survey committee complete its review process (which had become delayed). In February 2014 further arrests of Kenyan fishermen by Ugandan security personnel in the region were reported.

In 1989 Sudan renewed a long-standing dispute with Kenya over the sovereignty of territory on the Kenyan side of the two countries' common border, known as the 'Elemi triangle'. During the late 1990s Kenya hosted a series of peace talks between the Sudanese Government and opposition leaders, under the auspices of the Intergovernmental Authority on Development (IGAD, see p. 331), in an attempt to resolve the conflict in southern Sudan. In July 2002 the Sudanese Government and the opposition Sudan People's Liberation Movement (SPLM) signed an accord in Machakos, Kenya, which provided for the holding of a referendum on self-determination for southern Sudan after a transitional period. In September 2003 Kenya and Sudan agreed to form a joint border committee. After further negotiations conducted in Kenya throughout 2003 and 2004, in January 2005 the Sudanese Government and the SPLM signed a peace accord in Nairobi (see the chapter on Sudan). Following South Sudan's secession in July 2011, its links with Kenya strengthened (although its claim to the 'Elemi triangle' remained unresolved), while Kenya's relations with Sudan consequently became strained; amid a protracted oil transit dispute between the authorities of South Sudan and Sudan, in January 2012 an agreement was reached for the construction of a pipeline linking oil fields in South Sudan to Kenya's Lamu port. An eruption of inter-ethnic violence in South Sudan in December 2013 resulted in an influx of refugees to Kenya, with numbers totalling 97,780 at January 2015, according to the office of the UN High Commissioner for Refugees (UNHCR).

Following an increased incidence of cross-border attacks in 1997, a number of communiqués were signed by the Kenyan and Ethiopian Governments, agreeing to reinforce border security, and to take measures to prevent the smuggling of arms and drugs. Bilateral relations became strained in late 2000, after it was reported that some 50 Kenyans had been killed, allegedly by Ethiopian militia forces, in cross-border clashes. In January 2001 representatives from both countries met in Nairobi and agreed to initiate measures aimed at ending border disputes. In April 2006 Kenya closed part of its border with Ethiopia when militia forces allegedly entered Kenyan territory and fighting

ensued. In May 2011 more than 50 people were reported to have been killed in the border area, following a cross-border raid by militia from the Ethiopia-based Merille tribe. In May 2012 it was reported that Kenya and Ethiopia had agreed to renegotiate the demarcation of their international boundary, in response to further incidents.

After President Moi agreed to mediate between an interim Government and opposing rebel factions in Somalia, an IGAD-sponsored Somali reconciliation conference opened in Eldoret in October 2002 and was moved to Nairobi in February 2003. In January 2004 the conference reached agreement on the establishment of a new Somali parliament, which was based in Nairobi until mid-2005. In October 2011 Kenya dispatched troops into southern Somalia in pursuit of insurgents of the al-Shabaab militant Islamist group, who were held responsible for a number of abductions of Western tourists and aid workers from Kenyan territory following a marked increase in Somali banditry and piracy. Al-Shabaab subsequently conducted a large number of violent reprisal attacks in Kenya. In early 2012 Kenyan ground troops and fighter aircraft staged attacks against al-Shabaab bases in southern Somalia, in which large numbers of insurgents were reportedly killed. In February a UN Security Council resolution endorsed an AU request that Kenyan troops reinforce an expanded African Union Mission in Somalia (AMISOM), which had been established to counter the al-Shabaab insurgency in the country. A total of 4,664 Kenyan personnel deployed in Somalia were officially integrated into AMISOM in July. In December the new Somali President, Abdi Farah Shirdon Saaid, made an official visit to Kenya, where he and Kibaki pledged continued co-operation in operations against al-Shabaab, and finalized a border security agreement. In August 2014 Somalia submitted a long-standing dispute over the delimitation of the Kenyan–Somali offshore boundary to the International Court of Justice; hearings commenced in the following month.

The conflict in Somalia resulted in large influxes of refugees to Kenya. In late 2010 UNHCR urged the Kenyan authorities, which claimed that the Somali refugees placed an intolerable burden on the country's resources, to halt their forced repatriation. In 2011 further arrivals from Somalia to north-eastern Kenya resulted in severe overcrowding at three refugee camps in Dadaab which also affected the surrounding area, obliging the Kenyan Government to allocate additional land to settle refugees. In January 2013 UNHCR expressed concern at a government directive for all refugees to be relocated from Nairobi and other urban centres to refugee camps, which, following an application by refugee rights groups, was temporarily suspended by the High Court. In May representatives from the Kenyan and Somali Governments met in Nairobi to discuss the repatriation of Somali refugees, who at that time were believed to number about 1m. (of whom 600,000 were officially registered). In March 2014 the Kenyan Government again ordered urban refugees to relocate to the country's refugee camps, and in the following month the authorities detained approximately 4,000 Somalis in an operation to identify illegal immigrants and al-Shabaab supporters. UNHCR and civil liberties groups criticized these measures owing to concerns about human rights abuses and discrimination against the Somali community. Somalia briefly withdrew its ambassador from Kenya in April in protest against the detention of a Somali diplomat during the Kenyan crackdown. Controversial security legislation adopted by the Kenyan National Assembly in December included a stipulation that limited the number of refugees permitted in the country to no more than 150,000, prompting expressions of disapproval from UNHCR and human rights organizations. However, a successful legal appeal in early 2015 resulted in the revocation of this clause. According to UNHCR, Somali refugees in Kenya totalled 462,970 at January 2015.

CONSTITUTION AND GOVERNMENT

Under the terms of the Constitution that was approved at a national referendum on 4 August 2010 and entered into force on 27 August, legislative power is vested in and exercised by Parliament, which consists of the National Assembly and the Senate. Members of Parliament serve concurrent five-year terms. The National Assembly consists of 290 members, each elected by the registered voters of single member constituencies; 47 women members (one elected in each county); 12 members nominated by parliamentary political parties according to their proportion of members of the National Assembly to represent special interests including the youth, persons with disabilities and workers; and the Speaker, who is an ex officio member. The Senate consists of 47 members each elected by the registered voters of the counties, each county constituting a single-member constituency; 16 women members who shall be nominated by political parties according to their proportion of members of the Senate; two members representing the youth; two members representing persons with disabilities; and the Speaker, who is an ex officio member. The President is the Head of State and Government and exercises the executive authority of the Republic, with the assistance of the Deputy President and Cabinet Secretaries. The Cabinet consists of the President, the Deputy President, the Attorney-General and not fewer than 14 and not more than 22 Cabinet Secretaries. Each of the 47 counties has an elected governor.

REGIONAL AND INTERNATIONAL CO-OPERATION

Kenya is a member of the Common Market for Eastern and Southern Africa (see p. 232) and, with Burundi, Rwanda, Tanzania and Uganda, of the East African Community (see p. 446).

Kenya became a member of the UN in 1963. As a contracting party to the General Agreement on Tariffs and Trade, Kenya joined the World Trade Organization (WTO, see p. 431) on its establishment in 1995.

ECONOMIC AFFAIRS

In 2013, according to estimates by the World Bank, Kenya's gross national income (GNI), measured at average 2011–13 prices, was US $41,220m., equivalent to $930 per head (or $2,250 per head on an international purchasing-power parity basis). During 2004–13, it was estimated, the population increased at an average annual rate of 2.7%, while gross domestic product (GDP) per head grew, in real terms, by an average of 2.0% per year. Overall GDP increased, in real terms, at an average annual rate of 4.8% in 2004–13. Real GDP rose by 4.7% in 2013.

Agriculture (including forestry and fishing) contributed 28.6% of GDP and accounted for 15.3% of workers engaged in paid employment in the formal sector in 2013, according to provisional official figures. (According to FAO, some 67.9% of the labour force were employed in the agriculture sector in mid-2015). The principal cash crops are tea (which contributed 20.1% of total export earnings in 2011) and coffee. Horticultural produce (Kenya is the world's fourth largest exporter of cut flowers), pyrethrum, sisal, sugar cane and cotton are also important. Maize is the principal subsistence crop. There is a significant dairy industry for domestic consumption and export. During 2004–12, according to the World Bank, agricultural GDP increased at an average annual rate of 2.3%. According to provisional official figures, agricultural GDP increased by 3.0% in 2013.

Industry (including mining, manufacturing, construction and power) contributed 17.0% of GDP and employed an estimated 19.6% of workers engaged in paid employment in the formal sector in 2013, according to provisional official figures. During 2004–12, according to the World Bank, industrial GDP increased at an average annual rate of 4.6%. Industrial GDP grew by 5.2% in 2013, according to provisional official figures.

Mining contributed 0.7% of GDP and employed an estimated 0.4% of those in paid formal-sector employment in 2013, according to provisional official figures. Soda ash is the principal mineral export. Fluorspar, iron ore, salt, limestone, gold, gemstones (including rubies and sapphires), vermiculite and lead are also mined. Kenya has substantial reserves of titanium. According to official figures, the GDP of the mining sector increased at an average annual rate of 7.1% during 2009–13. According to provisional official figures, sectoral GDP increased by 7.4% in 2013.

Manufacturing contributed 9.9% of GDP and employed an estimated 12.4% of workers engaged in paid employment in the formal sector in 2013, according to provisional official figures. During 2004–12, according to the World Bank, manufacturing GDP increased at an average annual rate of 4.1%. According to provisional official figures, manufacturing GDP grew by 4.8% in 2013.

Construction contributed 4.9% of GDP and employed an estimated 5.8% of workers engaged in paid employment in the formal sector in 2013, according to provisional official figures. The GDP of the construction sector grew at an average annual rate of 4.8% during 2009–13. According to provisional official figures, sectoral GDP increased by an estimated 5.5% in 2013.

Hydroelectric power accounted for 44.0% of total electricity generated in 2011. It had accounted for an average of 81.9% of annual electricity generated during 1990–98, whereafter recurrent droughts began to affect hydroelectric production. This shortfall was taken up by petroleum, which accounted for 32.7% in 2011 (as opposed to an average of 9.2% per year during 1990–98). Kenya does not produce electricity from coal, natural gas or nuclear power. Energy for domestic use is derived principally from fuel wood and charcoal. In February 2004 it was announced that the Kenyan and Tanzanian national grids were to be connected to that of Zambia under a cross-border energy project; the first phase of the project, which was to cost some US $300m., was commissioned in 2007, followed by a second phase in 2012. In 2011 imports of mineral fuels and lubricants (including crude petroleum intended for refining) comprised 27.8% of the value of total imports.

The services sector contributed 54.4% of GDP and employed an estimated 65.1% of workers engaged in paid employment in the formal sector in 2012, according to provisional official figures. Tourism makes an important contribution to Kenya's economy and has been the country's principal source of foreign exchange since 1987. Following terrorist attacks in 2001, however, and subsequent warnings against travel to Kenya by the United Kingdom and the USA, the tourism industry experienced difficulties for several years. The industry was also adversely affected by the violence that followed the 2007 elections. By 2013, however, tourist arrivals had recovered to reach some 1,520,000 (in 2012 receipts from tourism—excluding passenger transport—amounted to an estimated US $935m.). The GDP of the services sector increased at an average annual rate of 5.3% in 2004–12, according to the World Bank. Services GDP increased by an estimated 5.5% in 2013, according to provisional official figures.

In 2012 Kenya recorded a visible merchandise trade deficit of US $9,307.8m. and there was a deficit of $4,252.5m. on the current account of the balance of payments. In 2013 the principal source of imports was India (which supplied 18.3% of total imports in that year); other major suppliers were the People's Republic of China, Japan and South Africa. Uganda was the principal market for Kenya's exports (purchasing 13.0%) in 2013; other important purchasers were Tanzania, the United Kingdom, the USA and the UAE. The principal exports in 2011 were coffee and tea; while other major exports were vegetables and vegetable products, prepared foodstuffs, beverages, spirits, vinegar and tobacco, chemicals and related products, mineral products, iron and steel, and textiles articles. The principal imports in that year were mineral products, machinery and mechanical appliances, chemicals and related products, vehicles, aircraft and associated transport equipment, iron and steel, vegetables and vegetable products, and plastics and rubber.

In the financial year ending 30 June 2014 there was an estimated budgetary deficit of Ks. 286,800m. Kenya's general government gross debt was Ks. 1,943,540m. in 2013, equivalent to 41.0% of GDP. The country's external debt was US $11,569m. at the end of 2012, of which $8,834m. was public and publicly guaranteed debt. In that year the cost of servicing long-term public and publicly guaranteed debt and repayments to the IMF was equivalent to 5.1% of the value of exports of goods, services and income (excluding workers' remittances). According to the IMF, the annual rate of inflation averaged 14.8% in 2004–13. According to official figures, consumer prices increased by 9.3% in 2012 and by 5.7% in 2013. Some 23% of the labour force were estimated to be unemployed in late 2000.

Kenya's economy is reasonably diversified, although the country is highly vulnerable to fluctuations in international prices for its cash crops, most notably tea and coffee. Poverty is widespread, and the revelation in the mid-2000s of large-scale state corruption adversely affected investment and led international donors to withhold aid. Following a slowdown resulting from the 2008–09 global economic crisis, GDP growth continued to strengthen, principally generated by foreign investment in oil and natural gas exploitation, and large infrastructure projects. However, an increase in abductions of tourists from Kenyan territory by Somali bandits and pirates from 2011, and numerous terrorist attacks in principal towns attributed to the al-Shabaab militant Islamist group (see *Foreign Affairs*) presented a significant obstacle to investment and to the country's tourism industry. In January 2011 the IMF approved a three-year Extended Credit Facility (ECF) arrangement to support the Government's implementation of economic reforms. Following the election of President Uhuru Kenyatta in March 2013, his Government strengthened revenue with the adoption of a value-added tax, in accordance with IMF recommendations, and the introduction of a new levy on imports. In December the IMF issued a final review of economic progress under the ECF-supported programme, and approved a credit of about US $110.2m., bringing total disbursements under the arrangement to about $748.4m.; the Board commended the Kenyan authorities' commitment to fiscal reform. Although the tourism sector was further undermined in 2014 by frequent al-Shabaab attacks, real GDP growth increased to an estimated 5.3% (up from 4.6% in 2012 and 2013), supported by robust levels of investment and the expansion of the construction and manufacturing industries. Agricultural performance was poor, however, owing to adverse weather conditions. In late 2014 Kenya achieved lower middle income status following a rebasing of GDP data. Meanwhile, in March the African Development Bank approved funding of $930m. to support infrastructure development and job creation for 2014–18, and in June the World Bank pledged financial support of $4,000m. over a five-year period. Later that year the Government also generated revenue of $2,750m. through successive bond issues. In February 2015, moreover, the IMF authorized a $497.1m. Stand-By Arrangement and a $191.2m. Stand-By Credit Facility to 'provide a policy anchor for continued macroeconomic and institutional reforms'. The Fund projected that real GDP would increase by 6.2% in 2015.

PUBLIC HOLIDAYS

2016: 1 January (New Year's Day), 25–28 March (Easter), 1 May (Labour Day), 1 June (Madaraka Day, anniversary of self-government), 6 July* (Id al Fitr, end of Ramadan), 20 October (Mashujaa Day), 12 December (Jamhuri Day), 25–26 December (Christmas).

* This holiday is determined by the Islamic lunar calendar and may vary by one or two days from the date given.

Statistical Survey

Source (unless otherwise stated): Kenya National Bureau of Statistics, POB 30266, Nairobi; tel. (20) 317583; fax (20) 315977; e-mail director@knbs.go.ke; internet www.knbs.or.ke.

Area and Population

AREA, POPULATION AND DENSITY

Area (sq km)	
Land area	580,609
Inland water	11,362
Total	591,971*
Population (census results)†	
24 August 1999	28,686,607
24 August 2009	
Males	19,192,378
Females	19,417,719
Total	38,610,097
Population (UN estimates at mid-year)‡	
2013	44,353,690
2014	45,545,979
2015	46,748,617
Density (per sq km) at mid-2015§	80.5

* 228,561 sq miles.
† Excluding adjustment for under-enumeration.
‡ Source: UN, *World Population Prospects: The 2012 Revision*.
§ Land area only.

POPULATION BY AGE AND SEX
(UN estimates at mid-2015)

	Males	Females	Total
0–14 years	9,826,708	9,714,343	19,541,051
15–64 years	12,904,652	13,012,815	25,917,467
65 years and over	587,275	702,824	1,290,099
Total	23,318,635	23,429,982	46,748,617

Source: UN, *World Population Prospects: The 2012 Revision*.

PRINCIPAL ETHNIC GROUPS
(population at 2009 census)

African	38,445,941	European . . .	32,338
Arab	40,760	Other	9,267
Asian	81,791	**Total**	38,610,097

PROVINCES*
(2010, projected population estimates)

	Area (sq km)†	Population	Density (per sq km)
Central	13,174	3,908,907	296.7
Coast	82,787	3,205,175	38.7
Eastern	154,311	5,587,781	36.2
Nairobi	707	3,240,155	4,583.0
North-Eastern . . .	126,226	1,489,363	11.8
Nyanza	12,646	5,201,996	411.4
Rift Valley	182,453	9,101,524	49.9
Western	8,305	4,552,522	548.2
Total	580,609	36,287,423	62.5

* A new Constitution, promulgated in 2010, established 47 administrative counties to replace the old system of provinces.
† Land area only.

Note: Population projections not adjusted to take account of 2009 census results.

PRINCIPAL TOWNS
(at census of August 2009)

Nairobi (capital) .	3,133,518	Machakos . . .	150,041
Mombasa . . .	938,131	Mavoko	137,211
Kisumu	388,311	Thika	136,917
Nakuru	307,990	Nyeri	119,353
Eldoret	289,380	Vihiga	118,696
Ruiru	238,858	Malindi	118,265
Kikuyu	233,231	Kitui	109,568
Naivasha . . .	169,142	Kitale	106,187

Mid-2014 (incl. suburbs, UN estimate): Nairobi (capital) 3,767,650 (Source: UN, *World Urbanization Prospects: The 2014 Revision*).

BIRTHS AND DEATHS
(annual averages, UN estimates)

	2000–05	2005–10	2010–15
Birth rate (per 1,000)	38.9	37.9	35.1
Death rate (per 1,000)	12.2	10.2	8.3

Source: UN, *World Population Prospects: The 2012 Revision*.

Life expectancy (years at birth): 61.1 (males 59.3; females 62.9) in 2012 (Source: World Bank, World Development Indicators database).

EMPLOYMENT
(labour force survey, selected urban and rural settlements, '000s)*

	2011	2012	2013†
Agriculture and forestry . . .	330.4	337.7	346.7
Mining and quarrying	8.7	9.0	9.4
Manufacturing	270.2	271.0	280.3
Electricity and water	19.0	22.8	24.2
Construction	106.1	116.1	130.3
Wholesale and retail trade; repair of motor vehicles, motorcycles and personal and household goods	190.4	198.0	212.4
Hotels and restaurants . . .	65.6	68.9	73.7
Transport, storage and communications	153.4	160.9	169.1
Financial intermediation . . .	58.1	61.6	67.0
Real estate, renting and business activities	69.1	70.9	74.0
Public administration and defence; compulsory social security . .	206.0	207.4	217.8
Education	370.0	384.8	400.8
Health and social work . . .	97.9	104.7	112.8
Community, social and personal services	33.4	34.6	36.5
Private households with employed persons	104.8	106.3	109.7
Extraterritorial organizations and bodies	1.0	1.0	1.1
Total	**2,084.1**	**2,155.8**	**2,265.7**

* Data are for salaried employees in the formal sector only, and therefore exclude self-employed and unpaid family workers and a vast number of workers in the informal sector (9,272.1 in 2011, according to official estimates). According to the ILO, the 1999 census recorded an employed population of 14,474,200.
† Provisional figures.

Note: Totals may not be equal to the sum of components, owing to rounding.

Health and Welfare

KEY INDICATORS

Total fertility rate (children per woman, 2012)	4.5
Under-5 mortality rate (per 1,000 live births, 2012) . . .	73
HIV/AIDS (% of persons aged 15–49, 2013)	6.0
Physicians (per 1,000 head, 2011)	0.2
Hospital beds (per 1,000 head, 2010)	1.4
Health expenditure (2011): US $ per head (PPP)	73
Health expenditure (2011): % of GDP	4.4
Health expenditure (2011): public (% of total)	39.4
Access to water (% of persons, 2012)	62
Access to sanitation (% of persons, 2012)	30
Total carbon dioxide emissions ('000 metric tons, 2010) . .	12,427.5
Carbon dioxide emissions per head (metric tons, 2010) . .	0.3
Human Development Index (2013): ranking	147
Human Development Index (2013): value	0.535

For sources and definitions, see explanatory note on p. vi.

Agriculture

PRINCIPAL CROPS
('000 metric tons)

	2011	2012	2013
Wheat	268.5	441.8	485.8
Barley	65.2	72.9	77.4
Maize	3,376.9	3,600.0	3,390.9
Millet	73.4	74.9	64.1
Sorghum	159.9	166.6	138.5
Potatoes	2,365.3	2,915.1	2,500.0*
Sweet potatoes	759.5	859.6	1,153.4
Cassava (Manioc)	679.2	893.1	1,112.4
Sugar cane	5,338.6	5,822.6	5,900.0*
Beans, dry	577.7	613.9	529.3
Cow peas, dry	81.5	114.0	122.7
Pigeon peas	84.3	89.4	73.2

—continued	2011	2012	2013
Cashew nuts	20.9	29.0	30.0*
Coconuts	87.5	120.1	125.0*
Seed cotton	22.1	11.7	13.0
Cottonseed*	14.4	7.6	7.8
Cabbages and other brassicas .	599.6	684.0	800.8
Tomatoes	407.4	397.0	503.2
Onions, dry	112.0	85.8	87.0*
Carrots and turnips . . .	61.3	95.0	90*
Bananas	1,198.0	1,394.4	1,398.1
Plantains*	31.0	30.0	31.0
Guavas, mangoes and mangosteens	4,548.7	5,221.3	5,829.1
Avocados	201.5	186.3	191.5
Pineapples	123.5	129.6	128.9
Papayas	18.4	117.9	120.0*
Coffee, green	36.3	46.0	39.8
Tea (made)	377.9	369.4	432.4
Tobacco, unmanufactured* . .	14.0	15.0	15.0
Sisal	27.6	27.9	28.0*

* FAO estimate(s).

Aggregate production ('000 metric tons, may include official, semi-official or estimated data): Total cereals 4,057.8 in 2011, 4,482.7 in 2012, 4,307.5 in 2013; Total roots and tubers 3,831.5 in 2011, 4,695.4 in 2012, 4,791.7 in 2013; Total vegetables (incl. melons) 2,030.6 in 2011, 2,298.5 in 2012, 2,857.4 in 2013; Total fruits (excl. melons) 2,549.1 in 2011, 2,773.3 in 2012, 2,389.8 in 2013.

Source: FAO.

LIVESTOCK
('000 head, year ending September)

	2011	2012	2013*
Cattle	18,174	19,130	19,500
Sheep	17,822	18,171	18,500
Goats	28,861	29,409	30,000
Pigs	344	355	360
Camels	3,091	3,065	3,100
Chickens	33,011	32,865	32,500

* FAO estimates.

Source: FAO.

LIVESTOCK PRODUCTS
('000 metric tons)

	2011	2012	2013*
Cattle meat	458.0	410.6	425.0
Sheep meat	41.4	40.2	42.0
Goats' meat	45.7	40.5	42.0
Pig meat	12.8	13.0	15.4
Chicken meat	25.5	23.7	20.9
Game meat*	26.0	26.0	27.5
Camel meat*	64.5	64.5	65.1
Cows' milk	3,711.4	3,733.0	3,750.0
Sheep's milk*	32.0	33.0	33.6
Goats' milk	262.9	267.9	223.5
Camels' milk	912.5	933.6	937.0
Hen eggs	94.4	96.1	98.0
Honey	9.8	11.7	12.0

* FAO estimates.

Source: FAO.

Forestry

ROUNDWOOD REMOVALS
('000 cubic metres, excluding bark, FAO estimates)

	2010	2011	2012
Sawlogs, veneer logs and logs for sleepers	494	512	514
Pulpwood	450	450	450
Other industrial wood	189	189	189
Fuel wood	26,400	26,400	26,400
Total	27,533	27,551	27,553

2013: Production assumed to be unchanged from 2012 (FAO estimates).

Source: FAO.

SAWNWOOD PRODUCTION
('000 cubic metres, including railway sleepers)

	2011	2012	2013
Coniferous (softwood) . . .	129	140	266
Broadleaved (hardwood) . . .	30	30*	30*
Total	159	170*	296*

* FAO estimate.

Source: FAO.

Fishing

('000 metric tons, live weight)

	2010	2011	2012
Capture	140.2	181.4	156.9
Silver cyprinid	47.7	72.3	52.9
Nile tilapia	24.6	38.2	25.3
Nile perch	39.0	46.6	53.1
Aquaculture	12.2	22.1	21.5
Total catch	152.4	203.6	178.3

Note: Figures exclude crocodiles, recorded by number rather than by weight. The number of Nile crocodiles caught was: 5,259 in 2010; 4,180 in 2011; 6,403 in 2012.

Source: FAO.

Mining

('000 metric tons)

	2010	2011	2012
Soda ash	473.7	499.1	440.0*
Fluorspar	44.5	117.4	110.0
Salt	6.2	24.6	25.0*
Limestone flux*	47.0	50.0	50.0

* Estimate(s).

Source: US Geological Survey.

Industry

SELECTED PRODUCTS
('000 metric tons unless otherwise indicated)

	2009	2010	2011
Wheat flour	497.4	513.9	515.1
Raw sugar	548.0	523.7	490.2
Soft drinks ('000 litres) . .	359.1	365.9	371.4
Beer ('000 hectolitres)	3,968.2	3,986.2	4,537.9
Cigarettes (million)	11,012.8	11,443.7	12,801.3
Cement	3,320.3	3,709.8	4,478.0
Jet fuel	217	200	275
Motor gasoline (petrol)	157	181	178
Gas-diesel oils	372	347	429
Residual fuel oils	498	450	520
Electric energy (million kWh) .	6,450	6,867	7,848

2012: Raw sugar 493.9; Soft drinks ('000 litres) 370.5.

2013: Raw sugar 600.2 (provisional).

Source: mainly UN Industrial Commodity Statistics Database.

Finance

CURRENCY AND EXCHANGE RATES

Monetary Units
100 cents = 1 Kenya shilling (Ks.).
Ks. 20 = 1 Kenya pound (K£).

Sterling, Dollar and Euro Equivalents (31 December 2014)
£1 sterling = Ks. 141.41;
US $1 = Ks. 90.60;
€1 = Ks. 109.99;
Ks. 1,000 = £7.07 sterling = $11.04 = €9.09.

Average Exchange Rate (Ks. per US $)
2011   88.811
2012   84.530
2013   86.123

Note: The foregoing information refers to the Central Bank's mid-point exchange rate. However, with the introduction of a foreign exchange bearer certificate (FEBC) scheme in October 1991, a dual exchange rate system is in effect. In May 1994 foreign exchange transactions were liberalized and the Kenya shilling became fully convertible against other currencies.

BUDGET
(Ks. '000 million, year ending 30 June)

Revenue*	2012/13	2013/14†	2014/15‡
Tax revenue	701.2	851.8	1,006.5
Taxes on income and profits .	373.4	449.6	541.9
Taxes on goods and services .	270.1	334.6	386.9
Value-added tax	184.6	232.6	267.1
Excise duties	85.5	102.0	119.8
Taxes on international trade .	57.7	67.6	77.7
Import duties	57.7	67.6	77.7
Non-tax revenue	146.0	117.4	169.0
Total	847.2	969.2	1,175.5

Expenditure§	2012/13	2013/14†	2014/15‡
Recurrent expenditure . . .	808.3	965.9	1,054.8
Current transfers to counties .	0.0	169.4	178.7
Wages and benefits	274.4	288.5	303.3
Defence	91.2	89.9	90.7
Interest payments	121.2	134.1	142.1
Internal	110.2	119.2	122.9
External	11.1	14.9	19.2
Other expenditure	321.5	284.0	340.0
Development expenditure . .	296.5	313.0	493.3
Domestically financed . .	201.8	214.6	336.0
Foreign financed	94.7	98.4	157.3
Total (incl. others)	1,114.6	1,278.9	1,556.5

* Excluding grants received (Ks. '000 million): 21.0 in 2012/13; 25.2 in 2013/14 (estimate); 29.3 in 2014/15 (programmed figure).
† Estimates.
‡ Programmed figures.
§ Excluding net lending (Ks. '000 million): 2.4 in 2012/13; 2.3 in 2013/14 (estimate); 2.9 in 2014/15 (programmed figure).

Source: IMF, *Kenya: 2014 Article IV Consultation—Staff Report; Press Release; and Statement by the Executive Director for Kenya* (October 2014).

INTERNATIONAL RESERVES
(excl. gold, US $ million at 31 December)

	2011	2012	2013
IMF special drawing rights . .	16.9	9.1	30.4
Reserve position in IMF . . .	20.0	20.0	20.5
Foreign exchange	4,227.5	5,681.9	6,547.3
Total	4,264.4	5,711.0	6,598.2

Source: IMF, *International Financial Statistics.*

MONEY SUPPLY
(Ks. million at 31 December)

	2011	2012	2013
Currency depository corporations .	136,983	147,753	163,180
Transferable deposits	621,196	706,679	804,639
Other deposits	764,029	886,752	996,984
Securities other than shares . .	—	105	106
Broad money	1,522,208	1,741,289	1,964,909

Source: IMF, *International Financial Statistics.*

COST OF LIVING
(Consumer Price Index; base: February 2009 = 100)

	2011	2012	2013
Food and non-alcoholic beverages .	131.8	144.9	155.4
Clothing and footwear	112.4	123.2	129.7
Housing and utilities	117.1	128.0	133.8
All items (incl. others) . . .	121.2	132.5	140.1

NATIONAL ACCOUNTS
(Ks. million at current prices)

Expenditure on the Gross Domestic Product

	2011	2012	2013*
Government final consumption expenditure	498,881	584,840	744,915
Private final consumption expenditure	2,350,742	2,657,187	2,846,328
Changes in inventories . .	16,228	−6,967	−46,020
Gross fixed capital formation .	609,255	702,223	735,352
Total domestic expenditure .	3,475,106	3,937,283	4,280,575
Exports of goods and services .	879,542	956,357	957,346
Less Imports of goods and services	1,374,101	1,520,748	1,540,636
Statistical discrepancy . .	67,146	30,642	100,703
GDP at market prices . . .	3,047,392	3,403,534	3,797,988
GDP at constant 2001 prices .	1,540,520	1,610,653	1,686,149

Gross Domestic Product by Economic Activity

	2011	2012	2013*
Agriculture, forestry and fishing .	740,115	853,738	979,046
Mining and quarrying	21,153	23,610	22,480
Manufacturing	292,401	321,723	338,378
Electricity, gas and water . .	31,849	47,803	53,193
Construction	125,132	142,261	166,906
Wholesale and retail trade, restaurants and hotels . . .	371,434	413,887	444,272
Transport, storage and communications	305,092	328,152	345,616
Finance, insurance, real estate and business services	327,777	323,895	340,134
Public administration and defence	152,445	186,339	256,025
Other services	360,614	412,643	476,076
Sub-total	2,728,012	3,054,051	3,422,126
Less Financial intermediation services indirectly measured	31,787	27,758	36,818
Indirect taxes, less subsidies . .	351,167	377,242	412,680
GDP in market prices . . .	3,047,392	3,403,534	3,797,988

* Provisional figures.

BALANCE OF PAYMENTS
(US $ million)

	2010	2011	2012
Exports of goods	5,210.9	5,791.8	6,164.7
Imports of goods	−11,442.2	−14,162.1	−15,472.4
Balance on goods	−6,231.3	−8,370.3	−9,307.8
Exports of services	3,772.2	4,114.5	4,861.0
Imports of services	−2,089.1	−2,186.5	−2,447.3
Balance on goods and services	−4,548.3	−6,442.2	−6,894.1
Primary income received . . .	144.2	223.2	179.8
Secondary income paid . . .	−291.9	−282.5	−350.4
Balance on goods, services and primary income	−4,695.9	−6,501.5	−7,064.7
Secondary income received . .	2,370.4	2,717.6	2,851.8
Secondary income paid . . .	−43.2	−46.4	−39.7
Current balance	−2,368.7	−3,830.4	−4,252.5
Capital account	240.2	234.9	235.3
Direct investment assets . .	−1.6	−9.4	−16.1
Direct investment liabilities . .	178.1	335.2	258.6
Portfolio investment assets . .	−51.2	−81.2	−40.8
Portfolio investment liabilities .	22.2	23.8	27.2
Other investment assets . .	94.7	−668.5	348.3
Other investment liabilities . .	1,886.0	2,767.4	4,137.6
Net errors and omissions . .	141.9	16.4	521.3
Reserves and related items .	141.6	−1,211.7	1,219.0

Source: IMF, *International Financial Statistics.*

External Trade

PRINCIPAL COMMODITIES
(distribution by HS, US $ million)

Imports c.i.f.	2009	2010	2011
Vegetables and vegetable products	919.5	536.1	845.4
Cereals	749.2	396.7	646.5
Maize (corn)	439.6	689.7	1,247.3
Animal or vegetable fats and oils, and products thereof .	369.1	484.7	643.7
Palm oil and its fraction . . .	332.6	452.0	589.8
Prepared foodstuffs; beverages, spirits, vinegar; tobacco and articles thereof .	286.4	426.5	432.2
Mineral products	2,284.5	2,790.4	4,273.1
Mineral fuels, oils, distillation products, etc.	2,223.5	2,699.8	4,178.4
Crude petroleum oils . . .	705.8	915.2	1,423.7
Refined petroleum products .	1,399.2	1,646.3	2,563.3
Chemicals and related products	1,001.8	1,178.5	1,467.0

Imports c.i.f.—*continued*	2009	2010	2011
Plastics, rubber, and articles thereof	495.9	635.7	784.7
Plastics and articles thereof . .	371.6	492.3	615.3
Pulp of wood, paper and paperboard, and articles thereof	283.0	368.4	412.2
Textiles and textiles articles .	324.9	466.4	558.6
Iron and steel, other base metals and articles of base metal	722.9	861.1	1,187.2
Iron and steel	397.8	489.1	672.0
Machinery and mechanical appliances; electrical equipment; parts thereof .	1,940.0	2,408.1	2,522.8
Machinery and boilers, etc. . .	966.6	1,215.8	1,475.1
Electrical and electronic equipment	973.4	1,192.3	1,047.6
Electrical appliances for line telephony	342.1	520.0	431.5
Vehicles, aircraft, vessels and associated transport equipment	1,169.8	1,441.3	1,269.7
Vehicles other than railway and tramway	815.9	898.7	986.7
Aircraft, spacecraft, and parts thereof	349.5	517.7	267.7
Aircraft and spacecraft	305.4	453.2	199.8
Total (incl. others)	10,202.0	12,092.9	15,027.5

Exports f.o.b.	2009	2010	2011
Vegetables and vegetable products	1,963.8	2,284.3	2,372.4
Live trees, plants and cut flowers, etc.	479.4	454.5	512.0
Cut flowers and flower buds .	421.5	396.2	454.3
Edible vegetables, certain roots and tubers	224.8	270.5	246.3
Vegetables, fresh or chilled . .	175.4	150.3	576.5
Coffee, tea, mate and spices . .	1,104.6	1,380.6	1,411.0
Coffee	201.2	207.5	223.5
Tea	894.0	1,163.6	1,176.3
Animal or vegetable fats and oils, and products thereof .	109.0	150.2	198.0
Prepared foodstuffs; beverages, spirits, vinegar; tobacco and articles thereof .	387.9	445.4	551.6
Tobacco and manufactured tobacco substitutes	136.2	135.8	215.9
Mineral products . . .	331.5	358.4	470.2
Salt, sulphur, and cement, etc. .	141.1	137.7	200.4
Mineral fuels, oils, distillation products, etc.	189.0	218.0	258.4
Refined petroleum products .	177.9	205.2	239.0
Chemicals and related products	402.5	407.1	533.5
Inorganic chemicals and precious metal compounds	135.3	124.5	176.9

Exports f.o.b.—*continued*	2009	2010	2011
Plastics, rubber, and articles thereof	131.2	156.0	185.9
Textiles and textiles articles .	243.6	279.5	347.8
Iron and steel, other base metals and articles of base metal	256.0	298.2	362.7
Iron and steel	104.5	130.6	181.9
Machinery and mechanical appliances; electrical equipment; parts thereof .	139.9	179.6	183.4
Total (incl. others)	4,463.4	5,169.1	5,853.3

Source: Trade Map-Trade Competitiveness Map, International Trade Centre, www.intracen.org/marketanalysis.

2012 (Ks. million): *Imports:* Animal and vegetable fats and oils 54,876; Petroleum products 237,557; Medicinal and pharmaceutical products 41,307; Plastic goods 47,650; Iron and steel 56,667; Industrial machinery 194,666; Road motor vehicles 73,768; Total imports (incl. others) 1,374,586.9. *Exports:* Total exports 517,846.9.

2013 (Ks. million): *Imports* (provisional): Animal and vegetable fats and oils 48,371; Petroleum products 252,673; Plastic goods 47,650; Iron and steel 55,182; Industrial machinery 231,440; Road motor vehicles 83,330; Total imports (incl. others) 1,413,316.0. *Exports* (provisional): Total exports 502,287.0.

PRINCIPAL TRADING PARTNERS
(US $ million)

Imports c.i.f.	2009	2010	2011
Bahrain	97.9	57.9	219.0
Brazil	65.2	60.6	225.6
China, People's Republic . .	965.2	1,522.5	1,638.3
Egypt	124.3	232.1	204.8
Finland	55.7	178.6	55.9
France (incl. Monaco) . . .	206.8	235.8	228.1
Germany	294.4	332.6	365.5
India	1,078.1	1,301.6	1,714.5
Indonesia	243.1	339.8	516.3
Italy	179.9	151.1	165.5
Japan	632.7	734.6	660.2
Korea, Republic	38.6	248.7	332.8
Netherlands	225.9	232.7	258.7
Pakistan	100.4	103.6	198.2
Russia	63.3	122.1	257.7
Saudi Arabia	356.4	406.8	598.0
Singapore	342.2	400.1	372.9
South Africa	913.8	754.2	818.4
Switzerland-Liechtenstein . .	69.8	143.0	173.8
Tanzania	101.1	133.0	180.8
Turkey	44.4	63.1	191.9
Ukraine	131.9	110.4	44.8
United Arab Emirates . . .	1,161.8	1,462.9	2,280.6
United Kingdom	473.2	626.3	492.1
USA	649.1	496.0	508.0
Total (incl. others)	10,202.0	12,092.0	15,027.5

Exports f.o.b.	2009	2010	2011
Afghanistan	98.9	150.5	157.7
Belgium	43.9	52.5	51.2
Burundi	59.5	68.8	67.4
Congo, Democratic Republic . .	146.5	161.4	200.0
Egypt	153.8	228.5	267.1
Ethiopia	55.9	55.3	55.0
France (incl. Monaco) . . .	56.1	65.5	66.1
Germany	95.1	97.3	86.9
India	66.5	106.9	107.5
Italy	31.5	41.1	75.7
Malawi	40.7	53.8	66.4
Netherlands	340.7	338.9	377.2
Pakistan	196.3	227.9	241.4
Russia	46.8	57.0	66.0
Rwanda	123.4	132.9	155.0
Somalia	145.1	164.7	187.7
South Africa	46.3	30.8	32.4

Exports f.o.b.—*continued*		2009	2010	2011
Sudan	. .	165.1	237.5	254.1
Switzerland-Liechtenstein	. .	13.6	21.6	94.3
Tanzania	. .	389.3	420.2	476.1
Uganda	.	598.3	657.3	872.6
United Arab Emirates	. . .	138.7	237.8	229.3
United Kingdom	. . . .	498.1	507.2	536.0
USA	.	226.1	284.9	293.1
Yemen	.	42.9	57.0	53.0
Zambia	.	62.5	59.1	70.1
Total (incl. others)		4,463.4	5,169.1	5,853.3

Source: Trade Map-Trade Competitiveness Map, International Trade Centre, www.intracen.org/marketanalysis.

2012 (Ks. million): *Imports c.i.f.:* Bahrain 22,915.0; China, People's Republic 167,206.3; Egypt 29,844.3; France 27,080.5; Germany 41,474.2; India 195,230.1; Japan 63,134.8; Kuwait 16,882.5; Netherlands 17,634.8; Pakistan 12,880.9; Russia 15,211.7; Saudi Arabia 66,841.2; South Africa 61,953.8; Switzerland 6,464.4; Tanzania 14,401.6; Turkey 11,406.3; Uganda 15,322.8; United Kingdom 43,848.6; USA 65,966.4; Total imports (incl. others) 1,374,586.9; *Exports f.o.b.:* Burundi 5,308.8; China, People's Republic 5,383.9; Congo, Democratic Republic 18,427.4; Egypt 21,464.4; India 7,528.3; Pakistan 23,888.8; Rwanda 16,151.4; Somalia 19,236.8; Sudan 6,633.3; Tanzania 46,036.2; Uganda 67,450.1; United Arab Emirates 28,607.6; United Kingdom 40,630.3; USA 26,404.8; Zambia 6,666.6; Total exports (incl. others) 517,846.9.

2013 (Ks. million, provisional): *Imports c.i.f.:* Bahrain 34,977.3; China, People's Republic 182,355.6; Egypt 25,602.9; France 20,666.3; Germany 37,487.6; India 258,229.7; Japan 83,720.5; Kuwait 2,733.9; Netherlands 24,787.9; Pakistan 15,646.5; Russia 23,181.9; Saudi Arabia 41,422.9; South Africa 70,724.1; Switzerland 7,261.9; Tanzania 11,666.4; Turkey 14,062.1; Uganda 16,085.8; United Kingdom 49,019.6; USA 57,412.1; Total imports (incl. others) 1,413,316.0; *Exports f.o.b.:* Burundi 5,599.0; China, People's Republic 4,199.2; Congo, Democratic Republic 18,436.9; Egypt 17,001.5; India 9,475.0; Pakistan 24,130.1; Rwanda 13,499.7; Somalia 16,940.5; South Sudan 16,680.4; Sudan 6,424.5; Tanzania 40,496.5; Uganda 67,361.9; United Arab Emirates 25,143.7; United Kingdom 37,612.5; USA 29,936.1; Zambia 6,287.7; Total exports (incl. others) 502,287.0.

Transport

RAILWAYS
(traffic)

	2011	2012	2013*
Passengers carried ('000)	6,004	4,077	4,016
Passenger-km (million) . . .	283	221	183
Freight carried ('000 metric tons).	1,596	1,394	1,214
Freight ton-km (million) . . .	1,135	995	848

* Provisional figures.

ROAD TRAFFIC
(motor vehicles in use)

	2011	2012	2013*
Motor cars	591,958	644,805	709,812
Light vans	234,427	242,372	252,188
Lorries, trucks and heavy vans .	100,180	108,001	117,570
Buses and mini-buses	91,627	93,343	95,644
Motorcycles and autocycles . .	514,241	610,056	738,219
Other motor vehicles	52,310	55,449	58,803

* Provisional figures.

SHIPPING
Flag Registered Fleet
(at 31 December)

	2012	2013	2014
Number of vessels	32	33	34
Total displacement (grt) . . .	15,949	16,574	18,329

Source: Lloyd's List Intelligence (www.lloydslistintelligence.com).

International Seaborne Freight Traffic
('000 metric tons at Kenyan ports)

	2011	2012	2013*
Goods handled	19,953	21,920	22,307

* Provisional figures.

CIVIL AVIATION
(traffic on scheduled services)

	2010	2011
Kilometres flown (million)	114	118
Passengers carried ('000)	4,040	4,509
Passenger-km (million)	9,236	9,998
Total ton-km (million)	1,214	1,289

Source: UN, *Statistical Yearbook.*

Passengers carried ('000): 4,653 in 2012; 4,473 in 2013 (Source: World Bank, World Development Indicators database).

Tourism

FOREIGN TOURIST ARRIVALS
('000 overnight stays at accommodation establishments)

	2011	2012	2013
France	239.5	160.0	113.9
Germany	677.0	748.9	751.1
India	110.1	110.3	101.1
Italy	495.3	415.5	234.8
Switzerland	95.8	98.2	96.9
Tanzania	68.5	69.2	64.5
Uganda	76.2	81.8	110.2
United Kingdom	765.9	521.6	498.3
USA	283.8	291.5	294.6
Total (incl. others)	4,353.4	4,027.0	3,840.1

Tourism receipts (US $ million, excl. passenger transport): 800 in 2010; 926 in 2011; 935 in 2012.

Source: World Tourism Organization.

Communications Media

	2011	2012	2013
Telephones ('000 main lines in use)	284	252	206
Mobile cellular telephones ('000 subscribers)	28,081	30,732	31,309
Broadband subscribers ('000) . .	42.4	42.9	57.0

Internet subscribers ('000): 12.2 in 2010.

Source: International Telecommunication Union.

Education

(2012/13, provisional)

	Institutions	Teachers	Pupils
Primary	30,122	199,686	10,182,555
Secondary	8,848	65,494	2,104,262
Teacher training colleges . . .	257*	2,143	37,068
Higher education institutions† .	800	2,323	148,009

* Includes private and public institutions for pre-primary, primary and secondary (diploma) training.
† Includes universities, national polytechnics, institutes of technology and youth polytechnics.

Source: Ministry of Education, Nairobi.

Pupil-teacher ratio (primary education, UNESCO estimate): 46.8 in 2008/09 (Source: UNESCO Institute for Statistics).

Adult literacy rate (UNESCO estimates): 87.4% (males 90.6%; females 84.2%) in 2010 (Source: UNESCO Institute for Statistics).

Directory

The Government

HEAD OF STATE

President: UHURU KENYATTA (inaugurated 9 April 2013).

Deputy President: WILLIAM SAMOEI RUTO.

CABINET
(May 2015)

President: UHURU KENYATTA.

Deputy President: WILLIAM SAMOEI RUTO.

Secretary for Information, Communication and Technology and Acting Secretary for Land, Housing and Urban Development: Dr FRED OKENGO MATIANG'I.

Secretary for the National Treasury and Acting Secretary for Energy and Petroleum: HENRY K. ROTICH.

Secretary for Health and Acting Secretary for Transport and Infrastructure: JAMES WAINAINA MACHARIA.

Secretary for Foreign Affairs: AMINA MOHAMED.

Secretary for Industrialization and Enterprise Development and Acting Secretary for Agriculture, Livestock and Fisheries: ADAN ABDULLA MOHAMED.

Secretary for Devolution and Planning: ANNE WAIGURU.

Secretary for Defence and Acting Secretary for Labour: RAYCHELLE OMAMO.

Secretary for Sports, Culture and the Arts: Dr HASSAN WARIO ARERO.

Secretary for Education, Science and Technology: Prof. JACOB KAIMENYI.

Secretary for East African Affairs, Commerce and Tourism: PHYLLIS JEPKOSGEI KIPKINGOR-KANDIE.

Secretary for the Environment, Water and Natural Resources: JUDI WANGALWA WAKHUNGU.

Secretary for Mining: NAJIB BALALA.

Secretary for the Interior and Co-ordination of National Government: Maj-Gen. (retd) JOSEPH NKAISSERY.

Secretary for Water and Irrigation: EUGENE WAMALWA.

MINISTRIES

Office of the President: State House, Statehouse Rd, POB 40530, 00100 Nairobi; tel. (20) 2227436; e-mail president@statehousekenya .go.ke; internet www.president.go.ke.

Office of the Deputy President: POB 74434, 00200 Nairobi; tel. (20) 3247000; e-mail dp@deputypresident.go.ke; internet www .deputypresident.go.ke.

Ministry of Agriculture, Livestock and Fisheries: Kilimo House, off Cathedral Rd, POB 34188, 00100 Nairobi; tel. (20) 2718870; e-mail info@kilimo.go.ke; internet www.kilimo.go.ke.

Ministry of Defence: Ulinzi House, Lenana Rd, POB 40668, 00100 Nairobi; tel. (20) 2721100; fax (20) 2737322; e-mail info@mod.go.ke; internet www.mod.go.ke.

Ministry of Devolution and Planning: POB 30005, 00100 Nairobi; tel. (20) 2252299; fax (20) 2218475; e-mail info@ devolutionplanning.go.ke; internet www.devolutionplanning.go.ke.

Ministry of East African Affairs, Commerce and Tourism: Co-operative House, 16th Floor, Haile Selassie Ave, POB 8846, 00200 Nairobi; tel. (20) 2245741; fax (20) 2229650; e-mail ps@meac.go.ke; internet www.meac.go.ke.

Ministry of Education, Science and Technology: Jogoo House 'B', Harambee Ave, POB 30040, 00100 Nairobi; tel. (20) 318581; fax (20) 214287; e-mail info@education.go.ke; internet www.education .go.ke.

Ministry of Energy and Petroleum: Nyayo House, 23rd Floor, Kenyatta Ave, POB 30582, 00100 Nairobi; tel. (20) 310112; fax (20) 228314; e-mail info@energy.go.ke; internet www.energy.go.ke.

Ministry of the Environment, Water and Natural Resources: NHIF Bldg, Ragati Rd, POB 30126, 00100 Nairobi; tel. (20) 2730808; fax (20) 2725707; internet www.environment.go.ke.

Ministry of Foreign Affairs: Old Treasury Bldg, Harambee Ave, POB 30551, 00100 Nairobi; tel. (20) 318888; fax (20) 240066; e-mail press@mfa.go.ke; internet www.mfa.go.ke.

Ministry of Health: Medical HQ, Afya House, Cathedral Rd, POB 30016, 00100 Nairobi; tel. (20) 2717077; fax (20) 2713234; e-mail ps@ health.go.ke; internet www.health.go.ke.

Ministry of Industrialization and Enterprise Development: Social Security House, Block A, 17th and 23rd Floors, POB 30418, 00100 Nairobi; tel. (20) 2731531; fax (22) 2731511; e-mail ps@ industrialization.go.ke; internet www.industrialization.go.ke.

Ministry of Information, Communication and Technology: Teleposta Towers, Kenyatta Ave, POB 30025, 00100 Nairobi; tel. (20) 4920000; fax (20) 315147; e-mail info@information.go.ke; internet www.information.go.ke.

Ministry of the Interior and Co-ordination of National Government: POB 350100, 00100 Nairobi; tel. (20) 2227411; e-mail ps .interior@kenya.go.ke; internet www.interior.go.ke.

Ministry of Labour, Social Security and Services: Social NSSF Bldg, Block 'C', Bishop Rd, POB 40326, 00100 Nairobi; tel. (20) 2729800; fax (20) 2726497; e-mail info@labour.go.ke; internet www .labour.go.ke.

Ministry of Land, Housing and Urban Development: Ardhi House, 1st Ngong Ave, POB 30450, 00100 Nairobi; tel. (20) 2718050; fax (20) 2721248; e-mail complaints@ardhi.go.ke; internet www .ardhi.go.ke.

Ministry of Mining: POB 30009, 00100 Nairobi; tel. (20) 2723101; fax (20) 2714398; e-mail info@mining.go.ke; internet www.mining.go .ke.

Ministry of Transport and Infrastructure: Transcom House, Ngong Rd, POB 52692, 00200 Nairobi; tel. (20) 2729200; fax (20) 2730330; e-mail ps@transport.go.ke; internet www.transport.go.ke.

Ministry of Sports, Culture and the Arts: Kencom House, 3rd Floor, Moi Ave, POB 49849, 00100 Nairobi; tel. (20) 2251164; e-mail psoffice@minspoca.go.ke; internet www.minspoca.go.ke.

National Treasury: Treasury Bldg, Harambee Ave, POB 30007, Nairobi; tel. (20) 2252299; e-mail ps@treasury.go.ke; internet www .treasury.go.ke.

President

Election, 4 March 2013

Candidate	Votes	% of valid votes
Uhuru Kenyatta (TNA)	6,173,433	50.51
Raila Amollo Odinga (ODM) . . .	5,340,546	43.70
Wycliffe Musalia Mudavadi (UDF) .	483,981	3.96
Peter Kenneth (KNC) . . .	72,786	0.60
Mohamed Abduba Dida (ARK) . . .	52,848	0.40
Martha Wangari Karua (NARC—Kenya)	43,881	0.36
James Legilisho Kiyiapi (RBK) . .	40,998	0.34
Paul Kibugi Muite (Safina) . . .	12,580	0.10
Total	12,221,053*	100.00

* In addition, there were 108,975 invalid votes.

Legislature

NATIONAL ASSEMBLY

National Assembly: Parliament Bldgs, POB 41842, 00100 Nairobi; tel. (20) 2221291; fax (20) 2243694; e-mail clerk@parliament.go.ke; internet www.parliament.go.ke.

Speaker: JUSTIN MUTURI.

General Election, 4 March 2013

Party	Constituency seats	Women members	Total seats
ODM	78	15	93
TNA	72	14	86
URP	62	10	72
WDM—Kenya . .	19	6	25
UDFP	11	—	11
FRD—Kenya . .	9	—	9
KANU	6	—	6
New FORD—Kenya .	4	2	6
APK	5	—	5
FORD—People . .	3	—	3
FPK	3	—	3
NRC	3	—	3
CCU	2	—	2

Party—continued	Constituency seats	Women members	Total seats
KNC	2	—	2
FORD—Kenya	1	—	1
KADU—Asili	1	—	1
IP	1	—	1
MDP	1	—	1
MP	1	—	1
NARC—Kenya	1	—	1
PDP	1	—	1
Independents	4	—	4
Total	**290**	**47**	**337***

* In addition to the 290 directly elected constituency seats and 47 women members elected in each of the counties, 12 members (three each from the ODM, the TNA and the URP, and one each from FORD—Kenya, the UDFP and the WDM—Kenya) were nominated by parliamentary political parties according to their respective proportion of members of the National Assembly to represent special interests, including the country's youth, persons with disabilities and workers. The Speaker is also, ex officio, a member of the National Assembly.

SENATE

Senate: KICC Bldg, 1st Floor, POB 41842, 00100 Nairobi; tel. (20) 3261304; e-mail csenate@parliament.go.ke; internet www .parliament.go.ke.

Speaker: EKWEE DAVID ETHURO.

General Election, 4 March 2013

Party	Seats
ODM	11
TNA	11
URP	9
FORD—Kenya	4
WDM—Kenya	4
APK	2
KANU	2
UDFP	2
FPK	1
NARC	1
Total	**47***

* In addition, 16 women members were nominated by political parties according to their proportion of members of the Senate (four each from the ODM and the TNA, three from the URP, and one each from the APK, FORD—Kenya, KANU, the UDFP and the WDM—Kenya). A further two members represent the country's youth (one each from the ODM and the TNA) and two members (also one each from the ODM and the TNA) represent persons with disabilities. The Speaker is also, ex officio, a member of the Senate.

Election Commission

Independent Electoral and Boundaries Commission (IEBC): Anniversary Towers, 6th Floor, University Way, POB 45371, 00100 Nairobi; tel. (20) 2769000; e-mail info@iebc.or.ke; internet www.iebc .or.ke; f. 2011 to replace Electoral Commission of Kenya, which was disbanded following disputed elections in 2007; Chair. AHMED ISSACK HASSAN; Sec. and CEO EZRA CHILOBA SIMIYU.

Political Organizations

In 2013 there were 59 political parties registered with the Office of the Registrar of Political Parties. At the March 2013 elections the TNA, NARC and the URP were members of the Jubilee Alliance, while the ODM, the WDM—Kenya and FORD—Kenya were part of the Coalition for Reforms and Democracy.

Alliance Party of Kenya (APK): El-Molo Dr., Lavington, POB 21398, 00100 Nairobi; tel. (20) 2094424; e-mail info@ alliancepartyofkenya.net; Sec.-Gen. BEATRICE ELACHI.

Alliance for Real Change (ARK): Gilfillan House, 2nd Floor, Kenyatta Ave, Suite No. 203, POB 1462, 00100 Nairobi; tel. (20) 2496334; e-mail info@allianceforrealchange.com; internet www .allianceforrealchange.com; f. 2010; Leader MOHAMED ABDUBA DIDA; Sec.-Gen. AMINA GUYO.

Chama Cha Uzalendo (CCU): Danpark Apartment, off Airport, Embakasi, Nairobi; tel. 738836701 (mobile); e-mail

chamachauzalendokenya@gmail.com; Chair. MAUR ABDALLAH BWANAMAKA.

Democratic Party of Kenya (DP): Gitanga Rd, POB 53695, 00200 Nairobi; tel. (20) 2625977; e-mail info@democraticpartyofkenya.co .ke; internet democraticpartyofkenya.org; f. 1991; Leader JOSEPH MUNYAO; rival faction led by NGENGI MUIGAI.

Federal Party of Kenya (FPK): POB 25091, Nairobi; tel. 722302368 (mobile); e-mail info@federalpartykenya.org; Chair. CALEB BURUDI; Sec.-Gen. KENNEDY OKELLO OLUOCH.

Forum for the Restoration of Democracy—Asili (FORD—Asili): 58 Duplex Apt, Upper Hill, Matumbato Rd, POB 69564, 00400 Nairobi; e-mail fordasili@gmail.com; tel. 722779005 (mobile); f. 1992; Chair. ISSAC ONEKA MUNANAIRI.

Forum for the Restoration of Democracy—Kenya (FORD—Kenya): Simba House, Gatundu Cres., Kileleshwa, off Gatundu Rd, POB 43591, 00100 Nairobi; tel. (20) 3869338; e-mail fordkenya@ yahoo.com; internet www.fordkenya.or.ke; f. 1992; predominantly Luo support; Leader MOSES WETANGULA; Sec.-Gen. Dr DAVID ESELI SIMIYU.

Forum for the Restoration of Democracy for the People (FORD—People): Muchai Dr., off Ngong Rd, POB 5938, 00200 Nairobi; tel. (20) 2737015; f. 1997 by fmr mems of FORD—Asili; Nat. Chair. REUBEN OYONDI.

The Independent Party (TIP): Karesh Complex Inn, Mlolongo, POB 6854, 00200 Nairobi; tel. 722352009 (mobile); e-mail tiptipamanikenya@yahoo.com; Leader KALEMBE NDILE; Sec.-Gen. JANE WILLY.

Kenya African Democratic Union—Asili (KADU—Asili): Door 1, Dockworkers Union Bldg, Makuli Fagia, Kenyatta Ave, 2nd Floor, POB 83229, Mombasa; Sec.-Gen. PATIENCE M. CHOME.

Kenya African National Union (KANU): Yaya Center, Chania Rd, POB 72394, 00200 Nairobi; tel. (20) 245791; e-mail info@ kanuparty.com; internet www.kanuparty.com; f. 1960; sole legal party 1982–91; absorbed the National Development Party (f. 1994) in 2002; Chair. UHURU KENYATTA; Sec.-Gen. NICK SALAT.

Kenya National Congress (KNC): Mbabane Rd, POB 1498, 00100 Nairobi; tel. (20) 2604013; e-mail info@kenyanationalcongress.com; internet www.kenyanationalcongress.com; f. 1992; Chair. HERBERT MWACHIRO.

Maendeleo Democratic Party (MDP): Mwalimu Centre, 2nd Floor, Room No. 207, Muril Rd, POB 1980, 50100 Kakamega; tel. 729706770 (mobile); e-mail mdpparty@yahoo.com; f. 2007; Sec.-Gen. ALEX AMASAKHA.

Mazingira Greens Party of Kenya (MPK): POB 14832, Nairobi; tel. 737444901 (mobile); e-mail info@greenspartyofkenya.com; internet www.greenspartyofkenya.com; f. 2007; campaigns for the equitable sharing of wealth, sustainable use of natural resources, women's rights and the defence of Kenyan cultural values; Leader WANGARI MAATHAI.

Muungano Party (MP): Nyahururu House, Kilome Rd, POB 19080, 00100 Nairobi; tel. and fax (20) 8059439; e-mail muunganodevelopmentparty@yahoo.com; internet muunganoparty .or.ke.

The National Alliance (TNA): Promiso Plaza, Jogoo Rd, POB 13913, 00800 Nairobi; e-mail info@tna.co.ke; internet tna.co.ke; Chair. JOHNSON SAKAJA; Sec.-Gen. ONYANGO OLOO.

National Party of Kenya (NPK): Ole Shapara Rd, POB 2013, 00200 Nairobi; internet nationalpartyofkenya.org; f. 1992; Chair. CHARITY KALUKI NGILU; Sec.-Gen. FIDELIS MWEKE.

National Rainbow Coalition (NARC): Othaya Road, House No. 18, POB 51498–00200, Nairobi; tel. (20) 2022617; f. 2002; Chair. CHARITY KALUKI NGILU; Sec.-Gen. FIDELLIS NGULLI.

National Rainbow Coalition—Kenya (NARC—Kenya): Woodlands Rd, off Lenana Rd, Kilimani, POB 34200, 00100 Nairobi; tel. (20) 2726783; fax (20) 2726784; e-mail narckenya06@yahoo.com; internet www.narckenya.org; f. 2006 by former mems of NARC; Chair. MARTHA W. KARUA.

New FORD—Kenya: Magumo Rd, House No. 33, POB 49416, 00100 Nairobi; tel. 721399626 (mobile); e-mail newfordkenya@gmail.com; f. 2007; Chair. SOITA SHITANDA.

Orange Democratic Movement (ODM): Orange House, Menelik Rd, Kilimani, POB 2478, 00202 Nairobi; tel. (20) 2053481; f. 2005; Leader RAILA AMOLO ODINGA.

Peoples Democratic Party (PDP): Cannon Annex, Parliament Lane, POB 10734, 00400 Nairobi; tel. 7212019203 (mobile); e-mail info@peoples-democratic-party.com; internet peoples-democratic-party.com; Leader JAMES OMINGO MAGARA; Sec.-Gen. ERIC MBIU.

Restore and Build Kenya (RBK): Juma House, Makasembo St, POB 2670, 30100 Eldoret; tel. 720661812 (mobile); Leader JAMES LEGILISHO KIYIAPI.

Safina ('Noah's Ark'): Amboseli Rd, off Gitanga Rd, Lavington, POB 14746-00100 Nairobi; tel. (20) 5202211; fax (20) 3864242; e-mail info@safinaparty.org; internet www.safinaparty.org; f. 1995; aims to combat corruption and human rights abuses and to introduce proportional representation; Chair. PAUL KIBUGI MUITE.

Social Democratic Party of Kenya (SDP): Tena Estate, House No. 574, Manyanja Rd, POB 4403, 00100 Nairobi; tel. 729497009 (mobile); e-mail info@sdpkenya.org; internet www.sdpkenya.org; f. 1992; Chair. MWANDAWIRO MGHANGA; Sec.-Gen. BENEDICT WACHIRA.

United Democratic Forum Party (UDFP): POB 50905, 00100 Nairobi; tel. (20) 8020819; e-mail info@udfparty.org; internet udfparty.org; Chair. HASSAN A. OSMAN; Sec.-Gen. ABRAHAM K. LIMO.

United Democratic Movement (UDM): Matambato Rd, Upperhill, POB 44820, Nairobi; tel. 722752156 (mobile); e-mail uniteddemocraticmovement@yahoo.com; internet www.uniteddemocraticmovement.com; Chair. Rev. PAUL CHEBOI; Sec.-Gen. STANLEY K. ROTICH.

United Republican Party (URP): POB 2169, 00200 Nairobi; tel. (20) 2166885; e-mail info@urp.co.ke; Leader WILLIAM KIPCHIRCHIR SAMOEI RUTO; Sec.-Gen. DAVID KIMUTAI CHIRCHIR.

Wiper Democratic Movement—Kenya (WDM—Kenya): Wiper House, 408 Othaya Rd, POB 403-00100, Nairobi; tel. (20) 2663336; fax (20) 3864498; e-mail wiper@wipermovement.com; internet www.wipermovement.com; f. 2007 following split in the ODM; Leader STEPHEN KALONZO MUSYOKA.

Diplomatic Representation

EMBASSIES AND HIGH COMMISSIONS IN KENYA

Algeria: Mobil Plaza, POB 64140, 00620 Nairobi; tel. (20) 3755559; fax (20) 3755560; e-mail algerianembassy@wananchi.com; Ambassador ALI BENZERGA.

Angola: Nairobi; Ambassador VIRGÍLIO DE FARIA.

Argentina: Kitisuru Rd, POB 30283, 00100 Nairobi; tel. (20) 4183119; fax (20) 4183054; e-mail ekeny@mrecic.gov.ar; internet www.ekeny.mrecic.gob.ar; Chargé d'affaires a.i. FERNANDO ROLANDELLI.

Australia: ICIPE House, Riverside Dr., off Chiromo Rd, POB 39341, 00623 Nairobi; tel. (20) 4277100; fax (20) 4277139; e-mail australian.hc.kenya@dfat.gov.au; internet www.kenya.embassy.gov.au; High Commissioner JOHN FEAKES.

Austria: 536 Limuru Rd, Muthaiga, POB 30560, 00100 Nairobi; tel. (20) 4060022; fax (20) 4060025; e-mail nairobi-ob@bmeia.gv.at; internet www.bmeia.gv.at/botschaft/nairobi; Ambassador HARALD GÜNTHER.

Bangladesh: Ole Odume Rd, off Argwings Khodek Rd, Kilimani, POB 41645, Nairobi; tel. (20) 3870467; fax (20) 3874133; e-mail bdhc@bdootnairobi.com; internet www.bdootnairobi.com; High Commissioner WAHIDUR RAHMAN.

Belgium: Muthaiga, Limuru Rd, POB 30461, 00100 Nairobi; tel. (20) 7122011; fax (20) 7123050; e-mail nairobi@diplobel.fed.be; internet www.diplomatie.be/nairobi; Ambassador ROXANE DE BILDERLING.

Botswana: LR Block 91/238, Gigiri Dr., off United Nations Ave, Nairobi; tel. (20) 7123412; fax (20) 7123418; e-mail botkena@gov.bw; internet botswanamission.or.ke; High Commissioner JOHN MORETI.

Brazil: Tanar Center, UN Crescent Rd, UN Close, Gigiri, POB 30754, 00100 Nairobi; tel. (20) 7125765; fax (20) 7125767; e-mail brasemb.nairobi@itamaraty.gov.br; internet nairobi.itamaraty.gov.br; Ambassador MARCELA MARIA NICODEMOS.

Burundi: International Life House, 1st Floor, Mama Ngina St, POB 61165, 00200 Nairobi; tel. (20) 310826; fax (20) 310827; e-mail embunai@yahoo.fr; Ambassador FULGENCE NDAYISHIMIYE.

Canada: Limuru Rd, Gigiri, POB 1013, 00621 Nairobi; tel. (20) 3663000; fax (20) 3663900; e-mail nrobi@international.gc.ca; internet www.canadainternational.gc.ca/kenya; High Commissioner DAVID ANGELL.

Chile: Riverside Dr. 66, Riverside, POB 45554, 00100 Nairobi; tel. (20) 4452950; fax (20) 4443209; e-mail echile@echile.co.ke; Ambassador KONRAD PAULSEN.

China, People's Republic: Woodlands Rd, Kilimani, POB 30508, Nairobi; tel. (20) 2722559; fax (20) 2726402; e-mail chinaemb_ke@mfa.gov.cn; internet ke.china-embassy.org; Ambassador LIU XIANFA.

Colombia: UN Crescent, House No 91/244, POB 48494, 00100 Nairobi; tel. (20) 7120850; fax (20) 7120304; e-mail enairobi@cancilleria.gov.co; Ambassador MARIA EUGENIA CORREA OLARTE.

Congo, Democratic Republic: Electricity House, 12th Floor, Harambee Ave, POB 48106, 00100 Nairobi; tel. (20) 2229772; fax (20) 3754253; e-mail ambardckenyal@yahoo.com; Ambassador TADUMI ON'OKOKO.

Cuba: International House, Mama Ngina St, 13th Floor, POB 41931, 00606 Nairobi; tel. (20) 2241003; fax (20) 2241023; e-mail consulado@ke.embacuba.cu; internet www.cubadiplomatica.cu/kenya; Ambassador PAUL RODRIGUEZ RAMOS.

Cyprus: Eagle House, 5th Floor, Kimathi St, POB 30739, 00100 Nairobi; tel. (20) 2220881; fax (20) 312202; e-mail ckapsos@mfa.gov.cy; High Commissioner CHARALAMBOS KAPSOS.

Denmark: 13 Runda Dr., Runda, POB 40412, 00100 Nairobi; tel. (20) 4253000; fax (20) 4253299; e-mail nboamb@um.dk; internet kenya.um.dk; Ambassador GEERT AAGAARD ANDERSEN.

Djibouti: Comcraft House, 2nd Floor, Haile Selassie Ave, POB 59528, Nairobi; tel. (20) 339640; Ambassador ADEN MARIAM AHMED GOUMEH.

Egypt: Othaya Rd, Kileleshwa, POB 30285, 00100 Nairobi; tel. (20) 3870360; fax (20) 3870383; Ambassador MAHMOUD ALI TALAAT MAHMOUD.

Eritrea: New Rehema House, 2nd Floor, Westlands, POB 38651, Nairobi; tel. (20) 4443164; fax (20) 4443165; Ambassador BEYENE RUSSOM.

Ethiopia: State House Ave, POB 45198, 00100 Nairobi; tel. (20) 2732052; fax (20) 2732054; e-mail ethiopian22embassy@yahoo.com; Ambassador DINA MUFTI.

Finland: Eden Sq., Blk 3, 6th Floor, Greenway Rd, off Westlands Rd, POB 30379, 00100 Nairobi; tel. (20) 3750721; fax (20) 3750714; e-mail sanomat.nai@formin.fi; internet www.finland.or.ke; Ambassador ANNA BRITA SOFIE FROM-EMMESBERGER.

France: Barclays Plaza, 9th Floor, Loita St, POB 41784, 00100 Nairobi; tel. (20) 2778000; fax (20) 2778180; e-mail ambafrance.nairobi@diplomatie.gouv.fr; internet www.ambafrance-ke.org; Ambassador RÉMI MARÉCHAUX.

Germany: Ludwig Krapf House, Riverside Dr. 113, POB 30180, Nairobi; tel. (20) 4262100; fax (20) 4262129; e-mail info@nairobi.diplo.de; internet www.nairobi.diplo.de; Ambassador ANDREAS PESCHKE.

Greece: Nation Centre, 13th Floor, Kimathi St, POB 30543, 00100 Nairobi; tel. (20) 340722; fax (20) 2216044; e-mail gremb.nai@mfa.gr; Ambassador ELEFTHERIOS KOVARITAKIS.

Holy See: 151 Manyani Rd West, Waiyaki Way, POB 14326, 00800 Nairobi; tel. (20) 2148971; fax (20) 2631120; e-mail nunciokenya@nunciokenya.org; Apostolic Nuncio Most Rev. CHARLES DANIEL BALVO (Titular Archbishop of Castello).

Hungary: Kabarsiran Ave, off James Gichuru Rd, Lavington, POB 61146, Nairobi; tel. 738150391 (mobile); fax (20) 4442101; e-mail mission.nai@kum.hu; internet www.mfa.gov.hu/kulkepviselet/ke; Chargé d'affaires LÁSZLÓ PAPP.

India: Jeevan Bharati Bldg, 2nd Floor, Harambee Ave, POB 30074, Nairobi; tel. (20) 2225104; fax (20) 316242; e-mail hcindia@kenyaweb.com; internet www.hcinairobi.co.ke; High Commissioner YOGESHWAR VARMA.

Indonesia: Menengai Rd, Upper Hill, POB 48868, Nairobi; tel. (20) 2714197; fax (20) 2713475; e-mail indonbi@indonesia.or.ke; internet www.kemlu.go.id/nairobi; Ambassador SUNU MAHADI SOEMARNO.

Iran: Dennis Pritt Rd, POB 49170, Nairobi; tel. (20) 711257; fax (20) 339936; Ambassador MALEK HOSSEIN GIVZAD.

Ireland: Eden Sq. Complex Block 1, 7th Floor, Chiromo Rd, PO Box 30659-00100, Nairobi; tel. (20) 3673353; fax 703041353 (mobile); Ambassador Dr VINCENT O'NEILL.

Israel: Bishop's Rd, POB 30354, 00100 Nairobi; tel. (20) 4927500; fax (20) 2715966; e-mail info@nairobi.mfa.gov.il; internet nairobi.mfa.gov.il; Ambassador SHALOM COHEN.

Italy: Int. House, 9th Floor, Mama Ngina St, POB 30107, 00100 Nairobi; tel. (20) 2247750; fax (20) 2247086; e-mail ambasciata.nairobi@esteri.it; internet www.ambnairobi.esteri.it; Ambassador MAURO MASSONI.

Japan: Mara Rd, Upper Hill, POB 60202, 00200 Nairobi; tel. (20) 2898000; fax (20) 2898531; e-mail jinfocul@eojkenya.org; internet www.ke.emb-japan.go.jp; Ambassador TATSUSHI TERADA.

Korea, Republic: Misha Tower, 1st and 2nd Floors, Westlands Rd, POB 30455, 00100 Nairobi; tel. (20) 3749931; fax (20) 3741337; e-mail emb-k@mofat.go.kr; internet ken.mofat.go.kr; Ambassador CHOI DONG-GYOU.

Kuwait: Muthaiga Rd, POB 42353, Nairobi; tel. (20) 761614; fax (20) 762837; Ambassador YAQOUB YOUSEF EID AL-SANAD.

Libya: Jamahiriya House, Loita St, POB 47190, Nairobi; tel. (20) 250380; fax (20) 243730; e-mail jamahiriyanbi@wananchi.com; Chargé d'affaires HESHAM ALI SHARIF.

Malawi: Sports Rd, POB 30453, Nairobi; tel. (20) 4440569; fax (20) 440568; Deputy High Commissioner Brig.-Gen. MARCEL CHIRWA.

Malaysia: Block 91/404, Gigiri Grove, Gigiri, POB 42286, 00200 Nairobi; tel. (20) 7123374; fax (20) 7123371; e-mail mwnairobi@kln

.gov.my; internet www.kln.gov.my/web/ken_nairobi; High Commissioner ISMAIL SALAM.

Mexico: Kibagare Way, off Loresho Ridge, POB 14145, 00800 Nairobi; tel. 728389813 (mobile); e-mail inforken@sre.gob.mx; internet embamex.sre.gob.mx/kenia; Ambassador (vacant).

Morocco: UN Ave, Gigiri, POB 617, 00621 Nairobi; tel. (20) 7120765; fax (20) 7120817; e-mail sifmanbi@clubinternetk.com; Ambassador ABDELILAH BENRYANE.

Mozambique: Bruce House, 3rd Floor, Standard St, POB 66923, Nairobi; tel. (20) 221979; fax (20) 222446; e-mail embamoc.quenia@minec.gov.mz; High Commissioner DANIEL ANTÓNIO.

Netherlands: Riverside Lane, off Riverside Dr., POB 41537, 00100 Nairobi; tel. (20) 4288000; fax (20) 4288264; e-mail nlgovnai@africaonline.co.ke; internet kenia.nlembassy.org; Ambassador FRANS A. MAKKEN (designate).

Nigeria: Lenana Rd, Hurlingham, POB 30516, Nairobi; tel. (20) 3864116; fax (20) 3875871; e-mail info@nhc.org; High Commissioner SOLOMON OYATERU.

Norway: 58 Red Hill Rd, Gigiri, POB 2472-00621, 00100 Nairobi; tel. (20) 4251000; fax (20) 4451517; e-mail emb.nairobi@mfa.no; internet www.norway.or.ke; Ambassador VICTOR CONRAD RØNNEBERG.

Oman: Nairobi; tel. (20) 4248348; fax (20) 4248331; e-mail trifoil@nbnet.co.ke; Ambassador SALEH BIN SULIMAN BIN AHMED AL HARTHY.

Pakistan: St Michel Rd, Westlands Ave, POB 30045, 00100 Nairobi; tel. (20) 4443911; fax (20) 4446507; e-mail parepnairobi@iwayafrica.com; internet www.pakhc.or.ke; High Commissioner RAFUZZAMAN SIDDIQUI.

Poland: 58 Red Hill Rd, POB 30086, 00100 Nairobi; tel. (20) 7120019; fax (20) 7120106; e-mail nairobi.secretary@msz.gov.pl; internet www.nairobi.msz.gov.pl/en; Ambassador MAREK ZIÓŁKOWSKI.

Qatar: Gigiri Court Rd, off UN Crescent Rd, Block 91–98, GIGIRI/UN Close, POB 2697-00621, Nairobi; tel. (20) 7121300; fax (20) 7121301; e-mail nairobi@mofa.gov.qa; Ambassador IBRAHIM BIN MOHAMMED ABDULRAHMAN AL-ABDULLAH.

Romania: Eliud Mathu St, Runda, POB 63240, 00619 Nairobi; tel. (20) 721214073; e-mail secretariat@romanianembassy.co.ke; Ambassador JULIA PATAKI.

Russian Federation: Lenana Rd, POB 30049, Nairobi; tel. (20) 2728700; fax (20) 2721888; e-mail russembkenya@mail.ru; Ambassador ALEXANDER MAKARENKO.

Rwanda: International House, 12th Floor, Mama Ngina St, POB 48579, Nairobi; tel. (20) 560178; fax (20) 561932; internet kenya.embassy.gov.rw; High Commissioner YAMINA KARITANYI.

Saudi Arabia: Muthaiga Rd, POB 58297, Nairobi; tel. (20) 762781; fax (20) 760939; e-mail keemb@mofa.gov.sa; internet embassies.mofa.gov.sa/sites/kenya; Ambassador GHORM SAID MALHAN.

Senegal: Andrew Xagoritis Rd 873, Runda Estate, Nairobi; Ambassador MOMAR GUEYE.

Serbia: State House Ave, POB 30504, 00100 Nairobi; tel. (20) 2710076; fax (20) 2714126; e-mail nairobi@embassyofserbia.or.ke; internet www.embassyofserbia.or.ke; Ambassador IVAN ZIVKOVIĆ.

Slovakia: Milimani Rd, POB 30204, Nairobi; tel. (20) 2721896; fax (20) 2717291; e-mail emb.nairobi@mzv.sk; internet www.mzv.sk/nairobi; Ambassador MICHAEL MLYNÁR.

Somalia: POB 30769, Nairobi; tel. (20) 580165; fax (20) 581683; internet www.kenya.somaligov.net; Ambassador MOHAMMED ALI NUR.

South Africa: Roshanmaer Place, Lenana Rd, POB 42441, 00100 Nairobi; tel. (20) 2827100; fax (20) 2827236; e-mail nairobi@foreign.gov.za; High Commissioner RATUBATSI SUPER MOLOI.

South Sudan: Bishops Gate, 6th Floor, 5 Ngong Ave, cnr Bishop Rd, POB 73699, 00200 Nairobi; tel. (20) 4349107; fax (20) 4349109; Ambassador MAJOK GUANDON THIEP.

Spain: CBA Bldg, Mara and Ragati Rds, Upper Hill, POB 45503, 00100 Nairobi; tel. (20) 2720222; fax (20) 2720226; e-mail emb.nairobi@maec.es; internet www.exteriores.gob.es/Embajadas/Nairobi; Ambassador JOSÉ JAVIER NAGORE SAN MARTÍN.

Sri Lanka: Lenana Rd, POB 48145, Nairobi; tel. (20) 3872627; fax (20) 3872141; e-mail slhckeny@africaonline.co.ke; internet www.slhcnairobi.net; High Commissioner THAMBIRAJAH RAVEENTHIRAN.

Sudan: Kabarnet Rd, off Ngong Rd, POB 48784, 00100 Nairobi; tel. (20) 3875159; fax (20) 3878187; e-mail embassy@sudanebassyke.org; Ambassador (vacant).

Sweden: United Nations Cres., Gigiri, POB 30600, 00100 Nairobi; tel. (20) 4234000; fax (20) 4234339; e-mail embassy.nairobi@gov.se; internet www.swedenabroad.com/nairobi; Ambassador JOHAN BORGSTAM.

Switzerland: General Mathenge Dr. 89, POB 2600, 00100 Nairobi; tel. (20) 2673282; fax (20) 2673535; e-mail nai.vertretung@eda.admin.ch; internet www.eda.admin.ch/nairobi; Ambassador HARALD GÜNTHER.

Tanzania: Re-Insurance Plaza, 9th Floor, Taifa Rd, POB 47790, 0100 Nairobi; tel. (20) 312027; fax (20) 2218269; e-mail nairobi@foreign.go.tz; internet www.tanzaniahc.or.ke; High Commissioner Dr BATILDA BURIAN.

Thailand: Rose Ave, off Denis Pritt Rd, POB 58349, 00200 Nairobi; tel. (20) 2715243; fax (20) 2715801; e-mail thainbi@thainbi.or.ke; internet www.thaiembassy.org/nairobi; Ambassador (vacant).

Turkey: 30 Gigiri Rd, off Limuru Rd, POB 64748, 00620 Nairobi; tel. and fax (20) 7126929; fax (20) 7126931; e-mail embassy.nairobi@mfa.gov.tr; internet www.nairobi.emb.mfa.gov.tr; Ambassador DENIZ EKE (designate).

Uganda: Uganda House, 1st Floor, Kenyatta Ave, POB 60853, 00200 Nairobi; tel. (20) 4449096; fax (20) 4443772; e-mail info@ugahicom.co.ke; internet www.ugahicom.co.ke; High Commissioner ANGELINA WAPAKHABULO.

Ukraine: Limuru Rd 674, Muthaiga, POB 63566, 00619 Nairobi; tel. and fax (20) 5224545; e-mail emb_ke@mfa.gov.ua; internet kenya.mfa.gov.ua/ua; Ambassador VOLODYMIR BUTYAGA.

United Kingdom: Upper Hill Rd, POB 30465, 00100 Nairobi; tel. (20) 2844000; fax (20) 2844088; e-mail nairobi.enquiries@fco.gov.uk; internet www.gov.uk/world/kenya; High Commissioner Dr CHRISTIAN TURNER.

USA: UN Ave, Village Market, POB 606, 00621 Nairobi; tel. (20) 3636000; fax (20) 3633410; internet nairobi.usembassy.gov; Ambassador ROBERT F. GODEC.

Venezuela: Int. House, 3rd Floor, Mama Ngina St, POB 34477, 00100 Nairobi; tel. (20) 340134; fax (20) 248105; e-mail embavene@swiftkenya.com; Ambassador JHONY FREDY BALZA ARISMENDI.

Yemen: cnr Ngong and Kabarnet Rds, POB 44642, Nairobi; tel. (20) 564379; fax (20) 564394; Ambassador AHMAD MAYSARI.

Zambia: Nyerere Rd, POB 48741, Nairobi; tel. (20) 2593059; e-mail zambiacom@swiftkenya.com; High Commissioner JOSEPHINE CHILUFYA MUMBI PHIRI.

Zimbabwe: 2 Westlands Close, Westlands, POB 30806, 00100 Nairobi; tel. (20) 3744052; fax (20) 3748079; e-mail zimna@africaonline.co.ke; Ambassador KELEBERT NKOMANI.

Judicial System

The superior courts are the Supreme Court, the Court of Appeal and the High Court, the Employment and Labour Relations Court and any court established to hear matters concerning the environment, and the use of, occupation of and title to land.

Chief Justice: Dr WILLY MUNYWOKI MUTUNGA.

Supreme Court: Supreme Court Bldg, City Hall Way, POB 30041, Nairobi; e-mail info@judiciary.go.ke; internet www.judiciary.go.ke; comprises the Chief Justice, who acts as the president of the court, the Deputy Chief Justice and five other judges; has jurisdiction to hear and determine disputes relating to the elections to the office of President and appellate jurisdiction to hear and determine appeals from the Court of Appeal and any other court or tribunal as prescribed by national legislation.

Court of Appeal: POB 30187, Nairobi; tel. 730181000 (mobile); e-mail courtofappeal@judiciary.go.ke; comprises not fewer than 12 judges; the final court of appeal for Kenya in civil and criminal process; sits at Nairobi, Mombasa, Kisumu, Nakuru and Nyeri; Pres. PAUL KIHARA KARIUKI.

High Court: between Taifa Rd and City Hall Way, POB 30041, Nairobi; tel. (20) 221221; e-mail hck-lib@nbnet.co.ke; has unlimited criminal and civil jurisdiction at first instance; jurisdiction to determine the question whether a right or fundamental freedom in the Bill of Rights has been denied, violated, infringed or threatened; jurisdiction to hear an appeal from a decision of a tribunal appointed under the Constitution to consider the removal of a person from office; and jurisdiction to hear any question respecting the interpretation of the Constitution; Principal Judge RICHARD MWONGO.

The subordinate courts are the Magistrates' courts, the Kadhis' courts, the Courts Martial and any other court or local tribunal as may be established by an Act of Parliament.

Resident Magistrates' Courts: have countrywide jurisdiction, with powers of punishment by imprisonment for up to five years or by fines of up to Ks. 500. If presided over by a chief magistrate or senior resident magistrate, the court is empowered to pass any sentence authorized by law. For certain offences, a resident magistrate may pass minimum sentences authorized by law.

District Magistrates' Courts: of first, second and third class; have jurisdiction within districts and powers of punishment by imprisonment for up to five years, or by fines of up to Ks. 500.

Kadhis' Courts: have jurisdiction within districts, to determine questions of Islamic law; comprise a Chief Kadhi and no fewer than three other Kadhis.

Religion

According to the 2009 census, Protestants, the largest religious group, represent some 48% of the population. Approximately 24% of the population is Roman Catholic, 11% of the population practises Islam, 0.1% practises Hinduism and the remainder follow various traditional indigenous religions or offshoots of Christian religions. There are very few atheists. Muslim groups dispute government estimates; most often they claim to represent 15% to 20% of the population, sometimes higher. Members of most religious groups are active throughout the country, although certain religions dominate particular regions. Muslims dominate North-Eastern Province, where the population is chiefly Somali. Muslims also dominate Coast Province, except for the western areas of the Province, which are predominantly Christian. Eastern Province is approximately 50% Muslim (mostly in the north) and 50% Christian (mostly in the south). The rest of the country is largely Christian. Many foreign missionary groups operate in the country, the largest of which are the African Inland Mission (Evangelical Protestant), the Southern Baptist Church, the Pentecostal Assembly of Kenya, and the Church Missionary Society of Britain (Anglican). The Government has generally permitted these missionary groups to assist the poor and to operate schools and hospitals. The missionaries openly promote their religious beliefs and have encountered little resistance.

CHRISTIANITY

National Council of Churches of Kenya: Jumuia Pl., Lenana Rd, POB 45009, 00100 Nairobi; tel. (20) 2721249; fax (20) 2724183; e-mail communications@ncck.org; internet www.ncck.org; f. 1943 as Christian Council of Kenya; 27 mem. churches and 17 Christian orgs; Chair. Rev. Canon ROSEMARY MBOGO; Sec.-Gen. Rev. Canon PETER KARANJA MWANGI.

The Anglican Communion

Anglicans are adherents of the Church of the Province of Kenya, which was established in 1970. It comprises 30 dioceses, and has about 2.5m. members.

Primate and Archbishop of All Kenya: Most Rev. Dr ELIUD WABUKALA, POB 40502, Nairobi; tel. (20) 2714755; fax (20) 2718442; e-mail archoffice@swiftkenya.com.

Greek Orthodox Church

Archbishop of East Africa: NICADEMUS OF IRINOUPOULIS, Nairobi; jurisdiction covers Kenya, Tanzania and Uganda.

The Roman Catholic Church

Kenya comprises four archdioceses, 20 dioceses, one Apostolic Vicariate and one military ordinariate. Some 24% of the total population are adherents of the Roman Catholic Church.

Kenya Episcopal Conference: Kenya Catholic Secretariat, Waumini House, 4th Floor, Westlands, POB 13475, Nairobi; tel. (20) 443133; fax (20) 442910; e-mail csk@users.africaonline.co.ke; internet www.catholicchurch.or.ke; f. 1976; Pres. Cardinal JOHN NJUE (Archbishop of Nairobi); Sec.-Gen. Rev. Fr VINCENT WAMBUGU.

Archbishop of Kisumu: Most Rev. ZACCHAEUS OKOTH, POB 1728, 40100 Kisumu; tel. (57) 2020725; fax (57) 2022203; e-mail archdiocese-kisumu@africaonline.co.ke.

Archbishop of Mombasa: Most Rev. MARTIN KIVUVA MUSONDE, Catholic Secretariat, Nyerere Ave, POB 84425, Mombasa; tel. (41) 2311801; fax (41) 2228217; e-mail catholicsecretariat@msarchdiocese.org.

Archbishop of Nairobi: Cardinal JOHN NJUE, Archbishop's House, POB 14231, 00800 Nairobi; tel. (20) 241391; fax (20) 4447027; e-mail arch-nbo@wananchi.com.

Archbishop of Nyeri: Most Rev. PETER J. KAIRO, POB 288, 10100 Nyeri; tel. (61) 2030446; fax (61) 2030435; e-mail adn@wananchi.com.

Other Christian Churches

Africa Gospel Church: POB 458, Kericho 20200; tel. (52) 20123; e-mail agc@agckenya.org; internet www.agckenya.org; Admin. Sec. JOSEPH TONUI.

African Christian Church and Schools: POB 1365, Thika; e-mail accsheadoffice@yahoo.com; f. 1948; Moderator Rt Rev. JOHN NJUNGUNA; Gen. Sec. Rev. SAMUEL MWANGI; 50,000 mems.

African Israel Nineveh Church: Nineveh HQ, POB 701, Kisumu; f. 1942; High Priest Rt Rev. JOHN KIVULI, II; Gen. Sec. Rev. JOHN ARAP TONUI; 350,000 mems.

Baptist Convention of Kenya: Jogoo Rd, POB 14907, Nairobi; tel. (20) 2494462; e-mail admin@baptistconventionofkenya.com; internet baptistconventionofkenya.com; f. 1972; Moderator Rev. ELIJA WANJE (acting); Gen. Sec. THOMAS OPIYO (acting).

Church of God in East Africa: Pres. Rev. Dr BYRUM MAKOKHA.

Evangelical Alliance of Kenya (EAK): Valley Rd, POB 20571, 00100 Nairobi; tel. (20) 2721269; e-mail secretariat@eakenya.org; internet eakenya.org; Co-ordinator Rt Rev. Bishop Dr BONIFES ADOYO; Sec.-Gen. Rev. Dr WELLINGTON MUTISO.

Evangelical Lutheran Church in Kenya (ELCK): POB 44685, 00100 Nairobi; tel. and fax 716194811; e-mail bishopobarewa@yahoo.com; internet elckenya.com; f. 1948; Archbishop Most Rev. Dr WALTER OBARE OMWANZA; Gen. Sec. Rev. BENJAMIN LEMOSI; 120,000 mems (2014).

Kenya African Church of the Holy Spirit: POB 183, Kakamega; internet kenyaafricanchurchoftheholyspirit.org; f. 1927; 20,000 mems.

Kenya Evangelical Lutheran Church: POB 54128, 00200 City Sq., Jogoo Rd, off Nile Rd, Nairobi; tel. and fax (20) 780454; e-mail info@kelc.or.ke; internet www.kelc.or.ke; Bishop ZACHARIAH W. KAHUTHU; 44,000 mems (2010).

Methodist Church in Kenya: POB 47633, 00100 Nairobi; tel. (20) 2403437; fax (20) 2729790; e-mail mckconf@insightkenya.com; internet www.methodistchurchkenya.org; f. 1862; autonomous since 1967; Presiding Bishop Rev. Dr JOSEPH NTOMBURA MWAINE; 900,000 mems (2005).

Presbyterian Church of East Africa: Jitegemea House, Muhoho Ave, South C, POB 27573, 00506 Nairobi; tel. (20) 6008848; fax (20) 6009102; e-mail info@pcea.or.ke; internet pceaheadoffice.org; f. 1891; Moderator Rt Rev. Dr DAVID RIITHO GATHANJU; Sec.-Gen. Rev. FESTUS KABURU GITONGA.

Other denominations active in Kenya include the African Brotherhood Church, the African Independent Pentecostal Church, the Africa Inland Church in Kenya, the African Interior Church, the Episcopal Church of Kenya, the Free Pentecostal Fellowship of Kenya, the Full Gospel Churches of Kenya, the National Independent Church of Africa, the Pentecostal Assemblies of God, the Pentecostal Evangelistic Fellowship of God and the Reformed Church of East Africa.

BAHÁ'Í FAITH

National Spiritual Assembly: POB 47562, Nairobi; tel. (20) 725447; e-mail nsakenya@yahoo.com; mems resident in 9,654 localities.

ISLAM

Supreme Council of Kenyan Muslims (SUPKEM): Islamia House, 2nd and 3rd Floors, Njugu Lane, POB 415163, 00100 Nairobi; tel. and fax (20) 243109; e-mail admin@supkem.com; internet supkem.com; Nat. Chair. Prof. ABD AL-GHAFUR AL-BUSAIDY; Sec.-Gen. ADAN WACHU.

Chief Kadhi: SHEIKH AHMED MUHDHAR.

The Press

PRINCIPAL DAILIES

Business Daily: Nation Center, 2nd Floor, Kimathi St, POB 49010, 00100 Nairobi; tel. (20) 3288104; fax (20) 211130; e-mail bdfeedback@ke.nationmedia.com; internet www.businessdailyafrica.com; Editorial Dir JOSEPH ODINDO; Man. Editor OCHIENG RAPURO.

Daily Nation: Nation Centre, Kimathi St, POB 49010, 00100 Nairobi; tel. (20) 3288000; fax (20) 2337710; e-mail newsdesk@nation.co.ke; internet www.nation.co.ke; f. 1960; English; owned by Nation Media Group; Man. Editor MUTUMA MATHIU; circ. 195,000.

The People: POB 10296, 00100 Nairobi; tel. (20) 2249686; fax (20) 2228503; e-mail info@people.co.ke; internet www.people.co.ke; f. 1993; Man. Editor MUGO THEURI; circ. 40,000.

The Standard: Mombasa Rd, POB 30080, 00100 Nairobi; tel. (20) 3222111; fax (20) 214467; e-mail ads@standardmedia.co.ke; internet www.standardmedia.co.ke; f. 1902 as African Standard; renamed East African Standard before adopting present name in 2004; Editor OKETCH KENDO; circ. 59,000.

The Star: Lion Place, Waiyaki Way, POB 74497-0200, Nairobi; tel. (20) 4244000; fax (20) 4447410; e-mail webmaster@the-star.co.ke; internet www.the-star.co.ke; Editor CATHERINE GICHERU.

Taifa Leo: POB 49010, Nairobi 00100; tel. (20) 3288419; e-mail taifa@ke.nationmedia.com; f. 1960; daily and weekly edns;

Kiswahili; owned by Nation Media Group; Man. Editor NICHOLAS MUEMA; circ. 15,000.

Kenya also has a thriving vernacular press, but titles are often short-lived.

SELECTED PERIODICALS
Weeklies and Fortnightlies

Coastweek: Oriental Bldg, 2nd Floor, Nkrumah Rd, POB 87270, Mombasa; tel. (41) 2230125; fax (41) 2225003; e-mail coastwk@africaonline.co.ke; internet www.coastweek.com; f. 1978; English, with German section; Friday; Editor ADRIAN GRIMWOOD; Man. Dir SHIRAZ D. ALIBHAI; circ. 54,000.

Diplomat East Africa: Vision Plaza, Ground Floor, Suite 37, Mombasa Rd, POB 23399, Nairobi; tel. (20) 2525253; e-mail editor@diplomateastafrica.com; internet www.diplomateastafrica.com.

The East African: POB 49010, 00506 Nairobi; tel. (20) 3288000; fax (20) 2213946; e-mail newsdesk@nation.co.ke; internet www.theeastafrican.co.ke; f. 1994; weekly; English; owned by Nation Media Group; Editor-in-Chief JOE ODINDO; Man. Editor MBATAU WA NGAI.

Kenya Gazette: POB 30746, Nairobi; tel. (20) 334075; e-mail info@kenyalaw.org; internet kenyalaw.org/KenyaGazette; f. 1898; official notices; weekly; circ. 8,000.

Kenya Today: c/o Office of Public Communications, KICC Bldg, 3rd Floor, POB 45617, 00100 Nairobi; e-mail comms@comms.go.ke; f. 2009; govt-owned; weekly; Dir JERRY OKUNGU.

Sunday Nation: POB 49010, Nairobi; f. 1960; English; owned by Nation Media Group; Man. Editor BERNARD NDERITU; circ. 170,000.

Sunday Standard: POB 30080, Nairobi; tel. (20) 552510; fax (20) 553939; English; Man. Editor DAVID MAKALI; circ. 90,000.

Taifa Jumapili: POB 49010, Nairobi; tel. (20) 3288419; e-mail taifa@ke.nationmedia.com; f. 1987; Kiswahili; owned by Nation Media Group; Man. Editor NICHOLAS MUEMA; circ. 15,000.

Other Periodicals

African Ecclesiastical Review: POB 4002, 30100 Eldoret; tel. (53) 2061218; fax (53) 2062570; e-mail gabapubs@africaonline.co.ke; internet www.gabapublications.org; f. 1969; scripture, religion and devt; 4 a year; Editor and Dir Sister JUSTINE C. NABUSHAWO; circ. 2,500.

Azania: POB 30710, 00100 Nairobi; tel. (20) 4343190; fax (20) 4343365; f. 1966; annual (Dec.); English and French; history, archaeology, ethnography and linguistics of East African region; circ. 650.

Defender: AMREF, POB 30125, Nairobi; tel. (20) 201301; f. 1968; quarterly; English; health and fitness; Editor WILLIAM OKEDI; circ. 100,000.

Kenya Statistical Digest: POB 30007, Nairobi; tel. (20) 338111; fax (20) 330426; govt publ; quarterly.

Safari: Norwich Bldg, 4th Floor, Mama Ngina St, POB 30339, Nairobi; tel. (20) 2246612; fax (20) 2215127; 6 a year; English.

NEWS AGENCY

Kenya News Agency (KNA): Information House, POB 8053, Nairobi; tel. (20) 223201; internet www.kenyanewsagency.go.ke; f. 1963; Dir S. MUSANDU.

Publishers

Academy Science Publishers: POB 24916, Nairobi; tel. (20) 884401; fax (20) 884406; e-mail asp@africaonline.co.ke; f. 1989; part of the African Academy of Sciences; Editor-in-Chief Prof. KETO E. MSHIGENI.

AMECEA Gaba Publications: Amecea Pastoral Institute, POB 4002, 30100 Eldoret; tel. (53) 2061218; fax (53) 2062570; e-mail gabapubs@africaonline.co.ke; f. 1958; anthropology, religious; owned by AMECEA Bishops; Editor and Dir Sister JUSTINE C. NABUSHAWO.

Camerapix Publishers International: ABC Place, 3rd Floor, Waiyaki Way, POB 45048, 00100 Nairobi; tel. (20) 4448923; fax (20) 4448818; e-mail camerapixuk@btinternet.co.uk; internet www.camerapix.com; f. 1960; travel, topography, natural history; Man. Dir RUKHSANA HAQ.

East African Educational Publishers: cnr Mpaka Rd and Woodvale Grove, Westlands, POB 45314, 00100 Nairobi; tel. (20) 4444700; fax (20) 2324761; e-mail eaep@eastafricanpublishers.com; internet www.eastafricanpublishers.com; f. 1965 as Heinemann Kenya Ltd; present name adopted 1992; academic, educational, creative writing;

some books in Kenyan languages; Chair. Dr HENRY CHAKAVA; Man. Dir S. S. NGIGI.

Evangel Publishing House: Lumumba Drive, off Kamiti Rd, Thika Rd, Private Bag 28963, 00200 Nairobi; tel. (20) 2320565; fax (20) 8562050; e-mail info@evangelpublishing.org; internet www.evangelpublishing.org; f. 1952; Christian literature; current backlist of over 300 titles; marriage and family, leadership, Theological Education by Extension (TEE); Gen. Man. LUCY NDUTA (acting).

Jomo Kenyatta Foundation: Industrial Area, Enterprise Rd, POB 30533, 00100 Nairobi; tel. (20) 6531965; fax (20) 6531966; e-mail info@jkf.co.ke; internet www.jkf.co.ke; f. 1966; primary, secondary, university textbooks; Man. Dir ROSEMARY K. A. BARASA.

Kenya Literature Bureau: Bellevue Area, Popo Rd, off Mombasa Rd, POB 30022, 00100 Nairobi; tel. (20) 600839; fax (20) 601474; e-mail info@klb.com; f. 1947 as East African Literature Bureau; name changed as above in 1980; educational and general books; CEO E. A. OBARA.

Longman Kenya Ltd: Kijabe St, next to Simlaw Seeds, POB 10679, 00100 Nairobi; tel. (20) 2119177; fax (20) 2219176; e-mail kkarani@longmankenya.com; internet www.longmanafrica.co.za/kenya.

Moran (EA) Publishers Ltd: Judda Complex, Forest Rd, POB 30797, 00100 Nairobi; tel. (20) 2013580; fax (20) 2013583; e-mail info@moranpublishers.co.ke; internet www.moranpublishers.com; f. 1970; as Macmillan Kenya Publishers Ltd; sole distributor of Macmillan Education and Palgrave titles in Eastern Africa; renamed as above in 2010; atlases, children's educational, guide books, literature; Man. Dir DAVID MUITA.

Oxford University Press (Eastern Africa): Elgon Rd, Upper Hill, The Oxford Place, POB 72532, Nairobi; tel. (20) 2732047; fax (20) 2732011; e-mail enq@oxford.co.ke; internet www.oxford.co.ke; f. 1954; children's, educational and general; Regional Man. MURIUKI NJERU.

Paulines Publications Africa: POB 49026, 00100 Nairobi; tel. (20) 447202; fax (20) 442097; e-mail publications@paulinesafrica.org; internet www.paulinesafrica.org; f. 1985; African bible, theology, children's, educational, religious, psychology, audio CDs, tapes, videos; Pres. Sister MARIA KIMANI; Dir Sister TERESA MARCAZZAN.

Phoenix Publishers: Kijabe St, POB 18650, 00500 Nairobi; tel. (20) 2609087; fax (20) 2675538; e-mail info@phoenixpublish.com; internet www.phoenixpublishers.co.ke; Man. Dir JOHN MWAZEMBA.

Spotlight Publishers (E.A.) Ltd: Devan Plaza, 2nd Floor, Chiromo Rd, Westlands, POB 13433, 00800 Nairobi; tel. (20) 4441345; fax (20) 4441622; e-mail ssossion@spotlightpublishers.co.ke; internet www.spotlightpublishers.co.ke; f. 2008; Man. Dir SIMON SOSSION.

Storymoja Publishers: Njamba House, Shanzu Rd, off Lower Kabete Rd, Westlands, POB 264, 00606 Nairobi; tel. (20) 208959; e-mail info@storymojaafrica.co.ke; internet www.storymojaafrica.co.ke; Gen. Man. MARTIN NJAGA.

University of Nairobi Press: Jomo Kenyatta Memorial Library Bldg, 3rd Floor, University of Nairobi, University Way, POB 30197, 00100 Nairobi; tel. (20) 2318262; e-mail nup@uonbi.ac.ke; internet press.uonbi.ac.ke.

WordAlive Publishers: Unit 5, Korosho Rd, Hendred Ave, Valley Arcade, POB 4547, 00100 Nairobi; tel. (20) 3572380; fax (20) 3572382; e-mail info@wordalivepublishers.com; internet wordalivepublishers.com; Man. Dir DAVID WAWERU.

GOVERNMENT PUBLISHING HOUSE

Government Press: POB 30128, Nairobi; tel. (20) 31740; internet www.governmentpress.go.ke; f. 1895; Govt Printer A. G. RUKARIA.

PUBLISHERS' ORGANIZATION

Kenya Publishers' Association: Occidental Plaza, Westlands, 2nd Floor, POB 42767, 00100 Nairobi; tel. (20) 3752344; fax (20) 3754076; internet www.kenyapublishers.org; f. 1971; organizes Nairobi International Book Fair each Sept; Chair. LAWRENCE NJAGI; 37 mems.

Broadcasting and Communications

TELECOMMUNICATIONS

In 2013 there were four providers of mobile telephone services in Kenya, one of which, Telkom Kenya Ltd, was also the sole provider of fixed-line services. In 2013, according to the International Telecommunication Union, there were 206,000 fixed-line telephones in use and 31.3m. subscribers to mobile telephone services.

Airtel Kenya: Parkside Towers, Mombasa Rd, Nairobi; tel. (20) 6910000; e-mail info.africa@airtel.com; internet africa.airtel.com/kenya; f. 2004; mobile cellular telephone network provider; fmrly

Celtel; name changed as above in 2010; Man. Dir ADIL EL YOUSSEFI; 5.5m. subscribers (2013).

Essar Telecom Kenya Ltd: Brookside Grove, Muguga Green Lane, Westlands, POB 45742, 00100 Nairobi; tel. 750049003 (mobile); e-mail communications@yu.co.ke; internet www.yu.co.ke; f. 2008; owner of yuMobile brand; Country Man. MADHUR TANEJA.

Safaricom Ltd: Safaricom House, Waiyaki Way, Westlands, POB 66827, 00800 Nairobi; tel. (20) 4273272; e-mail info@safaricom.co.ke; internet www.safaricom.co.ke; f. 1999; owned by Telkom Kenya Ltd and Vodafone Airtouch (UK); operates a national mobile cellular telephone network; Chair. NICHOLAS NG'ANG'A; CEO ROBERT WILLIAM COLLYMORE; 20.8m. subscribers (2013).

Telkom Kenya Ltd: Telkom Plaza, Ralph Bunche Rd, POB 30301, Nairobi; tel. (20) 2221000; e-mail customercare@orange-tkl.co.ke; internet www.telkom.co.ke; f. 1999; 51% owned by France Telecom; provides both fixed-line and mobile telephone services; Chair. EDDY NJOROGE; CEO VINCENT LOBRY.

Regulatory Authority

Communications Authority of Kenya (CA): Waiyaki Way, POB 14448, Westlands, 00800 Nairobi; tel. (20) 4242000; fax (20) 4451866; e-mail info@ca.go.ke; internet ca.go.ke; f. 1999 as Communications Commission of Kenya; name changed as above in 2013; Chair. BEDAN N. GITUKU; Dir-Gen. FRANCIS W. WANGUSI.

BROADCASTING

Radio

Kenya Broadcasting Corpn (KBC): Broadcasting House, Harry Thuku Rd, POB 30456, Nairobi; tel. (20) 2223757; fax (20) 2220675; e-mail md@kbc.co.ke; internet www.kbc.co.ke; f. 1989; state corpn responsible for radio and television services; Chair. EDWARD MUSEBE; Man. Dir WAITHAKA WAIHENYA.

Radio: National service (Kiswahili); General service (English); Vernacular services (Borana, Burji, Hindustani, Kalenjin, Kikamba, Kikuyu, Kimasai, Kimeru, Kisii, Kuria, Luo, Luhya, Rendile, Somali, Suba, Teso and Turkana).

Capital FM: Lonrho House, 19th Floor, City Sq., POB 74933, Nairobi; tel. (20) 2210020; fax (20) 340621; e-mail info@capitalfm.co.ke; internet www.capitalfm.co.ke; f. 1999; commercial station broadcasting to Nairobi and environs.

Easy FM: Nation Centre, Kimathi St, POB 49010, Nairobi; tel. (20) 32088801; fax (20) 241892; e-mail info@nation.co.ke; internet www.nationmedia.com; f. 1999; commercial radio station broadcasting in English and Kiswahili; fmrly Nation FM; owned by Nation Media Group; Man. Dir IAN FERNANDES.

IQRA Broadcasting Network: Kilimani Rd, off Elgeyo Marakwet Rd, POB 21186, 00505 Nairobi; tel. (20) 3861542; fax (20) 4443978; e-mail iqrafm@swiftkenya.com; Islamic radio station broadcasting religious programmes in Nairobi; Man. Dir SHARIF HUSSEIN OMAR.

Kameme FM: Longonot Pl., Kijabe St, POB 49640, 00100 Nairobi; tel. (20) 2217963; fax (20) 2249781; e-mail info@kamemefm.com; internet www.kameme.co.ke; commercial radio station broadcasting in Kikuyu in Nairobi and its environs; Man. Dir ROSE KIMOTHO.

Kitambo Communications Ltd: Bishop's Tower, 4th Floor, Bishop's Rd, POB 56155, Nairobi; tel. (20) 4244000; commercial radio and television station broadcasting Christian programmes in Mombasa and Nairobi; Man. Dir Dr R. AYAH.

Radio Africa Ltd (KISS FM): 2nd Floor, Lion Pl., Waiyaki Way, POB 74497, 00200 Nairobi; tel. (20) 4244000; Man. Dir KIPRONO KITTONY.

Radio Citizen: Communication Centre, Maalim Juma Rd, off Dennis Pritt Rd, POB 7468, Nairobi; tel. (20) 2721415; fax (20) 2724220; e-mail citizen@royalmedia.co.ke; internet radiocitizen.co.ke; commercial radio station broadcasting in Nairobi and its environs; owned by Royal Media Services Ltd; Chair. SAMUEL KAMAU MACHARIA.

Sauti ya Rehema RTV Network: Gulab Lochab Bldg, Oginga Odinga St, POB 4139, Eldoret; tel. (20) 2045239; e-mail elirop2003@gmail.com; f. 1999; Christian, broadcasts in Eldoret and its environs; Man. Dir Rev. ELI ROP.

Television

Kenya Broadcasting Corpn (KBC): see Radio

Television: KBC–TV; services in Kiswahili and English; operates three channels—KBC1, KBC2 and Metro TV.

Citizen TV: Communication Centre, Maalim Juma Rd, off Dennis Pritt Rd, POB 7468, Nairobi; tel. (20) 2721415; fax (20) 2724220; e-mail citizen@royalmedia.co.ke; internet www.citizentv.co.ke; f. 1999, relaunched 2006; commercial station broadcasting in Nairobi and its environs; Chair. SAMUEL KAMAU MACHARIA.

Family Media: Dik Dik Gardens, off Gatundu Rd, Kileleshwa, POB 2330, Nairobi; tel. (20) 4200000; fax (20) 4200100; e-mail admin@familymedia.tv; internet www.familymedia.tv; f. 1999; Gen. Man. KEN MASIOLO.

Kenya Television Network (KTN–TV): Nyayo House, 22nd Floor, POB 56985, Nairobi; tel. (20) 3222111; fax (20) 215400; e-mail news@ktnkenya.com; internet www.ktnkenya.tv; f. 1990; commercial station operating in Nairobi and Mombasa; Man. Dir D. J. DAVIES.

NTV: POB 49010, Nairobi; e-mail ntv@nation.co.ke; internet www.nationmedia.com/ntv; f. 1999 as Nation TV; commercial station; owned by Nation Media Group; Man. Dir IAN FERNANDES.

Stellagraphics TV (STV): NSSF Bldg, 22nd Floor, POB 42271, Nairobi; tel. (20) 218043; fax (20) 222555; f. 1998; commercial station broadcasting in Nairobi; Gen. Man. KANJA WARURU.

Finance

(cap. = capital; res = reserves; dep. = deposits; m. = million; brs = branches; amounts in Kenya shillings)

BANKING

At the end of 2012 there were 43 licensed commercial banks and one mortgage finance company operating in Kenya, of which 31 were locally owned and 13 were foreign owned.

Central Bank

Central Bank of Kenya (Banki Kuu Ya Kenya): City Sq., Haile Selassie Ave, POB 60000, 00200 Nairobi; tel. (20) 22863000; fax (20) 2250783; e-mail info@centralbank.go.ke; internet www.centralbank.go.ke; f. 1966; bank of issue; cap. 5,000m., res 34,005m., dep. 125,637m. (June 2009); Gov. (vacant).

Commercial Banks

African Banking Corpn Ltd: ABC-Bank House, Mezzanine Floor, Koinange St, POB 46452, Nairobi; tel. (20) 2223922; fax (20) 2222437; e-mail headoffice@abcthebank.com; internet www.abcthebank.com; f. 1984 as Consolidated Finance Co; converted to commercial bank and adopted present name 1995; cap. 1,050m., res 135.5m., dep. 16,839.8m. (Dec. 2013); Chair. RICHARD OMWELA; CEO SHAMAZ SAVANI; 11 brs.

Bank of Africa—Kenya: Re-Insurance Plaza, Taifa Rd, POB 69562, 00400 Nairobi; tel. (20) 3275000; fax (20) 2214166; e-mail customerservice@boakenya.com; internet www.boakenya.com; f. 2004; cap. 4,167.6m., res 1,318.4m., dep. 47,207.7m. (Dec. 2013); Chair. DENNIS AWORI; Man. Dir KWAME AHADZI; 5 brs.

Barclays Bank of Kenya Ltd: West End Bldg, Level 6, off Waiyaki Way, POB 30120, 00100 Nairobi; tel. (20) 4254000; fax (20) 2213915; e-mail barclays.kenya@barclays.com; internet www.barclays.com/africa/kenya; f. 1916; cap. 2,716m., res 3,288m., dep. 158,371m. (Dec. 2013); Chair. FRANCIS OKOMO-OKELLO; Man. Dir JEREMY AWORI; 119 brs.

CFC Stanbic Bank Ltd: CFC Centre, Chiromo Rd, Westlands, POB 30550, 00100 Nairobi; tel. (20) 3268000; fax (20) 3752905; e-mail customercare@stanbic.com; internet www.cfcstanbicbank.co.ke; formed by merger of CFC Bank Ltd and Stanbic Bank Kenya Ltd in June 2008; 100% owned by CFC Stanbic Holdings Ltd; cap. 3,411.5m., res 4,582.9m., dep. 131,266.5m. (Dec. 2013); Man. Dir GREG BRACKENRIDGE; 24 brs.

Chase Bank (Kenya) Ltd: Riverside Mews, Ring Rd Riverside and Riverside Westlane, POB 66015, 00800 Nairobi; tel. (20) 2774000; fax (20) 4454816; e-mail info@chasebank.co.ke; internet www.chasebankkenya.co.ke; cap. 4,500.0m., res 344.2m., dep. 40,298.7m. (Dec. 2012); Chair. OSMAN MURGIAN; Group Man. Dir MOHAMED ZAFRULLAH KHAN; 21 brs.

Commercial Bank of Africa Ltd: Commercial Bank Bldg, Upper Hill, cnr Mara and Ragati Rds, POB 30437, Nairobi; tel. (20) 2884000; fax (20) 335827; e-mail cba@cba.co.ke; internet www.cbagroup.com/ke; f. 1962; cap. 4,915.4m., res 4,097.1m., dep. 129,048.8m. (Dec. 2013); Chair. DESTERIO A. OYATSI; Group Man. Dir ISAAC O. AWUONDO; 22 brs.

Consolidated Bank of Kenya Ltd: Consolidated Bank House, 6th Floor, 23 Koinange St, POB 51133, 00200 Nairobi; tel. (20) 3215000; fax (20) 340836; e-mail tellus@consolidated-bank.com; internet www.consolidated-bank.com; f. 1989; cap. 1,119.5m., res 398.3m., dep. 12,977.3m. (Dec. 2013); Chair. Dr BENSON ATENG; CEO JAPHETH KISILU (acting); 17 brs.

Dubai Bank Kenya Ltd: ICEA Bldg, Kenyatta Ave, POB 11129-00400, Nairobi; tel. (20) 311109; fax (20) 2245242; e-mail info@dubaibank.co.ke; internet www.dubaibank.co.ke; 20% owned by World of Marble and Granite, Dubai (United Arab Emirates), 22.4% owned by Abdul Hassan Ahmed, 16% owned by Hassan Bin Hassan Trading Co LLC, Dubai (United Arab Emirates), 17.6% owned by

Ahmed Mohamed; cap. 967.4m., res 38.1m., dep. 1,584.8m. (Dec. 2013); Chair. HASSAN AHMED ZUBEIDI; Man. Dir BINAY DUTTA; 5 brs.

Ecobank Kenya Ltd: Ecobank Towers, 5th Floor, Muindi Mbingu St, POB 49584, 00100 Nairobi; tel. (20) 22883000; fax (20) 22883304; e-mail kenya@ecobank.com; internet www.ecobank.com; f. 1972 as Akiba Bank Ltd, present name adopted 2008; cap. 7,869.0m., res −2,335.3m., dep. 30,209.3m. (Dec. 2013); Chair. PETER TIRAS KANYAGO; Man. Dir EHOUMAN KASSI; 25 brs.

Equatorial Commercial Bank Ltd: Waiyaki Way, POB 52467, Nairobi; tel. (20) 4981000; fax (20) 2719625; e-mail ecbcustomerservice@ecb.co.ke; internet www.equatorialbank.co.ke; f. 1983; cap. 2,316.7m., res 155.7m., dep. 13,856.4m. (Dec. 2013); Chair. DAN AMEYO; Man. Dir SAMMY A. S. ITEMERE.

Equity Bank: Equity Centre, 9th Floor, Hospital Rd, Upper Hill, POB 75104, 00200 Nairobi; tel. (20) 2262000; fax (20) 2737276; e-mail info@equitybank.co.ke; internet www.equitybank.co.ke; f. 1984; cap. 1,851m., res 17,042m., dep. 195,153m. (Dec. 2013); Chair. PETER MUNGA; CEO JAMES MWANGI; 145 brs.

Family Bank: Family Bank Tower, Muindi Mbingu St, POB 74145, 00200 Nairobi; tel. (20) 2240601; fax (20) 318174; e-mail info@familybank.co.ke; internet www.familybank.co.ke; f. 1984; Chair. WILFRED DAVID KIBORO; CEO PETER MUNYIRI.

Fidelity Commercial Bank Ltd: IPS Bldg, 7th Floor, Kimathi St, POB 34886, Nairobi; tel. (20) 2242348; fax (20) 2243389; e-mail customerservice@fidelitybankkenya.com; internet www.fidelitybank.co.ke; f. 1993 as Fidelity Finance; present name adopted 1996; cap. 999.2m., res 71.0m., dep. 10,528.6m. (Dec. 2012); Exec. Dir SULTAN KHIMJI; Man. Dir RANA SENGUPTA; 11 brs.

First Community Bank: Prudential Assurance Bldg, 1st Floor, Wing A, Wabera St, POB 26219, 00100 Nairobi; tel. (20) 2843000; e-mail info@fcb.co.ke; internet www.firstcommunitybank.co.ke; f. 2007; Islamic banking; Chair. HASSAN VARVANI; Gen. Man. OMAR SHEIKH.

Giro Commercial Bank Ltd: Giro House, Kimathi St, POB 46739, 00100 Nairobi; tel. (20) 4229000; fax (20) 4229300; e-mail info@girobankltd.com; internet www.girobankltd.com; f. 1992 as Giro Bank Ltd; name changed as above in 1999 after merging with Commerce Bank Ltd; 21.76% owned by Blandford Investments Ltd, Nairobi; cap. 803.0m., res 81.2m., dep. 11,461.6m. (Dec. 2013); Chair. CHANDAN JETHANAND GIDOOMAL; Man. Dir SANJAY GIDOOMAL; 8 brs.

Guaranty Trust Bank Ltd: Fina House, Kimathi St, POB 20613, 00200 Nairobi; tel. (20) 3284000; fax (20) 2247164; e-mail banking@gtbank.com; internet gtbank.co.ke; f. 1986 as The Finance Institute of Africa Ltd; subsequently became a commercial bank in 1996 (Fina Bank Ltd); name changed as above in 2014; cap. 1,212.1m., res 3,611.4m., dep. 29,357.2m. (Dec. 2013); Chair. DHANJI HANSRAJ CHANDARIA; Man. Dir ADEKUNLE SONOLA; 13 brs.

Gulf African Bank (GAB): Geminia Insurance Plaza, Kilimanjaro Ave, Upper Hill, POB 43683, Nairobi; tel. (20) 2740000; fax (20) 2715655; e-mail info@gulfafricanbank.com; internet www.gulfafricanbank.com; f. 2007; 20% owned by Bank Muscat International (BMI), 10% owned by the International Finance Corpn (IFC); cap. 358.4m., res 2,248.6m., dep. 13,022.2m. (Dec. 2013); Chair. JAMAL ALI AL-HAZEEM; CEO ABDALLA ABDULKHALIK; 13 brs.

Imperial Bank Ltd: Westlands Rd, Westlands, POB 44905, 00100 Nairobi; tel. (20) 2874000; fax (20) 22719498; e-mail info@imperialbank.co.ke; internet www.imperialbank.co.ke; f. 1992 as Imperial Finance and Securities Company; converted to a bank and name changed as above in 1995; 100% owned by Kenyan shareholders; cap. 1,248.4m., res 145.0m., dep. 31,764.8m. (Dec. 2012); Chair. ALNASHIR POPAT; Man. Dir ABDULMALEK JANMOHAMED; 23 brs.

Kenya Commercial Bank Ltd: Kencom House, Moi Ave, POB 48400, 00100 Nairobi; tel. (20) 3270000; fax (20) 2216405; e-mail kcbhq@kcb.co.ke; internet www.kcb.co.ke; f. 1970; 23.1% state-owned; cap. 2,984.2m., res 23,771.9m., dep. 312,310.1m. (Dec. 2013); Chair. NGENY BIWOTT; Man. Dir JOSHUA NYAMWEYA OIGARA; 166 brs and sub-brs.

Middle East Bank Kenya Ltd: Mebank Tower, Milimani Rd, POB 47387, 00100 Nairobi; tel. (20) 2723120; fax (20) 343776; e-mail ho@mebkenya.com; internet www.mebkenya.com; f. 1981; 25% owned by Banque Belgolaise SA (Belgium), 75% owned by Kenyan shareholders; cap. 506.8m., res 36.8m., dep. 4,111.6m. (Dec. 2013); Chair. A. A. K. ESMAIL; Man. Dir DHIRENDRA RANA; 3 brs.

National Bank of Kenya Ltd (Banki ya Taifa La Kenya Ltd): National Bank Bldg, Harambee Ave, POB 72866, Nairobi; tel. (20) 2828000; fax (20) 311444; e-mail info@nationalbank.co.ke; internet www.nationalbank.co.ke; f. 1968; 42% owned by National Social Security Fund, 22.5% state-owned; cap. 7,075.0m., res 1,535.8m., dep. 78,817.6m. (Dec. 2013); Chair. MOHAMED ABDIRAHMAN HASSAN; Man. Dir MUNIR S. AHMED; 58 brs.

Oriental Commercial Bank Ltd: Apollo Centre, 2nd Floor, Ring Rd, POB 14357, 00800 Nairobi; tel. (20) 3743289; fax (20) 3743270; e-mail info@orientalbank.co.ke; internet www.orientalbank.co.ke;

f. 1991; name changed as above in 2003; cap. 1,645.5m., res 217.8m., dep. 5,442.0m. (Dec. 2013); Chair. SHANTI SHAH; Man. Dir and CEO R. B. SINGH; 6 brs.

Paramount Universal Bank Ltd: Sound Plaza, 4th Floor, Woodvale Grove, Westlands, POB 14001, 00800 Nairobi; tel. (20) 44492668; fax (20) 4449265; e-mail info@paramountbank.co.ke; internet www.paramountbank.co.ke; f. 1993 as Combined Finance Ltd; name changed as above in 2000; 25% owned by Tormount Holdings Ltd, St Helier, 25% owned by Anwarali Merali, 25% owned by Tasneem Padamshi; cap. 500.0m., res 17.3m., dep. 3,562.3m. (Dec. 2010); Chair. ANWARALI MERALI; Man. Dir AYAZ MERALI; 4 brs.

Standard Chartered Bank Kenya Ltd: Stanbank House, 48 Westlands Rd, POB 30003, Nairobi; tel. (20) 32093000; fax (20) 2214086; e-mail mds.office@ke.standardchartered.com; internet www.standardchartered.com/ke; f. 1987; 74.5% owned by Standard Chartered Holdings (Africa) BV (Netherlands); cap. 1,825.7m., res 16,261.3m., dep. 163,310.8m. (Dec. 2013); Chair. ANNE MUTAHI; CEO LAMIN MANJANG; 37 brs.

Trans-National Bank Ltd: Transnational Plaza, 2nd Floor, City Hall Way, POB 34353, 00100 Nairobi; tel. (20) 2224235; fax (20) 2222522; e-mail info@tnbl.co.ke; internet www.tnbl.co.ke; f. 1985; cap. 1,000.0m., res 104.5m., dep. 7,428.2m. (Dec. 2013); Chair. MICHAEL K. CHERWON; CEO SAMMY LANGAT; 16 brs.

Merchant Banks

Diamond Trust Bank Ltd: Nation Centre, 8th Floor, Kimathi St, POB 61711, 00200 Nairobi; tel. (20) 2849000; fax (20) 2245495; e-mail info@dtbkenya.co.ke; internet www.dtbafrica.com; f. 1945; cap. 880.4m., res 4,592.8m., dep. 133,506.7m. (Dec. 2013); Chair. ABDUL SAMJI; Man. Dir NASIM MOHAMED DEVJI; 45 brs.

National Industrial Credit Bank Ltd (NIC): NIC House, Masaba Rd, POB 44599, 00100 Nairobi; tel. (20) 2888000; fax (20) 2888505; e-mail info@nic-bank.com; internet www.nic-bank.com; Chair. J. P. M. NDEGWA; cap. 2,714.9m., res 1,476.4m., dep. 97,461.3m. (Dec. 2013); Man. Dir ALAN DODD; 21 brs.

Co-operative Bank

Co-operative Bank of Kenya Ltd: Co-operative Bank House, Haile Selassie Ave, POB 48231, Nairobi; tel. (20) 3276000; fax (20) 2219831; e-mail customerservice@co-opbank.co.ke; internet www.co-opbank.co.ke; f. 1968; cap. 4,190.8m., res 5,589.2m., dep. 180,887.4m., total assets 231,215.3m. (Dec. 2013); Chair. STANLEY C. MUCHIRI; Man. Dir GIDEON MURIUKI; 123 brs.

Development Banks

Development Bank of Kenya Ltd: Finance House, 16th Floor, Loita St, POB 30483, 00100 Nairobi; tel. (20) 340426; fax (20) 2250399; e-mail dbk@devbank.com; internet www.devbank.com; f. 1963 as Development Finance Co of Kenya; current name adopted 1996; owned by Industrial and Commercial Devt Corpn (89.3%), the Commonwealth Development Corpn (10.7%); cap. 347.5m., res 269.1m., dep. 11,046.4m. (Dec. 2013); Chair. Prof. HAROUN NGENY KIPKEMBOI MENGECH; CEO VICTOR J. O. KIDIWA.

East African Development Bank: Rahimtulla Tower, 2nd Floor, Upper Hill Rd, POB 47685, Nairobi; tel. (20) 340642; fax (20) 2731590; e-mail cok@eadb.org; internet www.eadb.org; Resident Man. BERNARD MBOHA.

IDB Capital Ltd: National Bank Bldg, 18th Floor, Harambee Ave, POB 44036, Nairobi; tel. (20) 247142; fax (20) 318929; e-mail bizcare@idbkenya.com; internet www.idbkenya.com; f. 1973 as Industrial Development Bank Ltd; adopted present name in 2005; 49% state-owned; Chair. PETERSON MWAI MUNENE; Man. Dir JAMES KARANJA.

STOCK EXCHANGE

Nairobi Securities Exchange (NSE): 55 Westlands Rd, POB 43633, 00100 Nairobi; tel. (20) 2831000; fax (20) 2224200; e-mail info@nse.co.ke; internet www.nse.co.ke; f. 1954; Chair. EDWARD NJOROGE; CEO PETER MWANGI.

INSURANCE

In 2013 there were 49 insurance companies registered in Kenya.

Insurance Regulatory Authority: Zep-Re Place, off Mara Road, Upper Hill, POB 43505, 00100 Nairobi; tel. (20) 4996000; fax (20) 2710126; internet www.ira.go.ke; f. 2006; Chair. STEVE O. MAINDA; CEO SAMMY MUTUA MAKOVE.

Africa Merchant Assurance Co Ltd: Transnational Plaza, 2nd Floor, Mama Ngina St, POB 61599, 00200 Nairobi; tel. (20) 2204000; fax (20) 340022; e-mail info@amaco.co.ke; internet www.amaco.co.ke; f. 2000; Chair. SILAS SIMATWO; Man. Dir JONAH TOMNO.

AIG Kenya Co Ltd: Eden Sq. Complex, Chiromo Rd, POB 49460, 00100 Nairobi; tel. (20) 3676000; fax (20) 3676001; e-mail aigkenya@aig.com; internet www.aig.co.ke; Man. Dir JAPH OLENDE.

APA Insurance Ltd: 7 Ring Rd, Parklands, Westlands, POB 30065, 00100 Nairobi; tel. (20) 2862000; fax (20) 2862200; e-mail info@apainsurance.org; internet www.apainsurance.org; f. 2003; Chair. JOHN P. N. SIMBA; COO SURESH KUMAR.

Apollo Life Assurance Ltd: Apollo Centre, 3rd Floor, Ring Rd Parklands, Westlands, POB 30389, 00100 Nairobi; tel. (20) 3641000; fax (20) 3641100; e-mail insurance@apollo.co.ke; internet www.apollo.co.ke; f. 1977; life and general; Chair. BUDHICHAND M. SHAH; CEO PIYUSH SHAH.

British-American Insurance Co: Mara and Ragati Rds Junction, Upper Hill, POB 30375, 00100 Nairobi; tel. (20) 2710927; fax (20) 2714927; e-mail insurance@british-american.co.ke; internet www.british-american.co.ke; f. 1965; Man. Dir STEPHEN WANDERA; 298 employees.

Cannon Assurance (Kenya) Ltd: Gateway Business Park, Mombasa Rd, Block D, POB 30216, Nairobi; tel. (20) 3966000; fax (20) 829075; e-mail info@cannonassurance.com; internet www.cannonassurance.com; f. 1964; life and general; Man. Dir MAINA MUKOMA.

CfC Life Assurance Co Ltd: CfC House, Mamlaka Rd, POB 30364, 00100 Nairobi; tel. (20) 2866000; fax (20) 2718365; e-mail cfclife@cfclife.co.ke; internet www.cfclife-kenya.com; f. 1964; life and general; Man. Dir ABEL MUNDA.

CIC Insurance Group Ltd: Mara Rd, Upper Hill, POB 59485, 00200 Nairobi; tel. (20) 2823000; fax (20) 2823333; e-mail cic@cic.co.ke; internet www.cic.co.ke; f. 1968; fmrly The Co-operative Insurance Co of Kenya Ltd, name changed as above in 2010; later demerged into CIC Life Assurance, CIC General Insurance Ltd and CIC Asset Management Ltd; Chair. JAPHETH ANAVILA MAGOMERE; Group CEO NELSON CHEGE KURIA.

East Africa Reinsurance Co Ltd: EARe House, 98 Riverside Dr., POB 20196, 00200 Nairobi; tel. (20) 4443588; fax (20) 4455391; e-mail info@eastafricare.com; internet www.eastafricare.com; Chair. J. P. M. NDEGWA; CEO PETER K. MAINA.

Fidelity Shield Insurance Ltd: 4th Floor, Rank Xerox House, Parklands Rd, Westlands, POB 47435, 00100 Nairobi; tel. (20) 4443063; fax (20) 4445699; e-mail info@fidelityshield.com; internet www.fidelityshield.com; Man. Dir SHEHNAZ SUMAR.

First Assurance Co Ltd: Gitanga Rd, Lavington, POB 30064, 00100 Nairobi; tel. (20) 2900000; fax (20) 2692290; f. 1979 as Prudential Assurance Co. of Kenya Ltd; present name adopted 1991; life and general; Chair. M. H. DA GAMA ROSE; Man. Dir STEPHEN GITHIGA.

GA Insurance Ltd: GA Insurance House, 4th Floor, Ralph Bunche Rd, POB 42166, 00100 Nairobi; tel. (20) 2711633; fax (20) 2714542; e-mail insure@gakenya.com; internet www.gakenya.com; general; Chair. SURESH B. R. SHAH; CEO VIJAY SRIVASTAVA.

Heritage Insurance Co Ltd: CFC House, Mamlaka Rd, POB 30390, 00100 Nairobi; tel. (20) 2783000; fax (20) 2727800; e-mail info@heriaii.com; internet www.heritageinsurance.co.ke; f. 1976; general; Chair. P. N. GETHI; Man. Dir JOHN H. D. MILNE.

Jubilee Insurance Co Ltd: Jubilee Insurance House, 5th Floor, Wabera St, POB 30376, 00100 Nairobi; tel. (20) 3281000; fax (20) 3281150; e-mail info@jubileekenya.com; internet www.jubileeafrica.com; f. 1937; long term (life and pensions) and short term (general and medical) insurance; Chair. NIZAR JUMA; Gen. Man. PATRICK TUMBO NYAMEMBA.

Kenindia Assurance Co Ltd: Kenindia House, 11th Floor, Loita St, POB 40512, Nairobi; tel. (20) 3316099; fax (20) 2218380; e-mail kenindia@kenindia.com; internet www.kenindia.com; f. 1978; life and general; Chair. M. N. MEHTA; Man. Dir VINOD BHARATAN.

Kenya Reinsurance Corpn Ltd (KenyaRe): Reinsurance Plaza, Taifa Rd, POB 30271, Nairobi; tel. (20) 2240188; fax (20) 2252106; e-mail kenyare@kenyare.co.ke; internet www.kenyare.co.ke; f. 1970; Chair. NELIUS KARIUKI; Man. Dir JADIAH MWARANIA.

Madison Insurance Co Kenya Ltd: Upper Hill Rd, POB 47382, 00100 Nairobi; tel. (20) 2864000; e-mail madison@madison.co.ke; internet www.madison.co.ke; life and general; Chair. SAMUEL G. NGARUIYA; Man. Dir JAMES NGUNJIRI; 21 brs.

Mercantile Insurance Co Ltd: Ecobank Towers, 16th Floor, Muindi Mbingu St, POB 20680, Nairobi; tel. (20) 2219486; fax (20) 215528; e-mail mercantile@mercantile.co.ke; internet www.mercantile.co.ke; Chair. N. P. G. WARREN; Man. Dir SUPRIYO SEN.

Monarch Insurance Co Ltd: Monarch House 664, Olenguruone Ave, off James Gichuru Rd, Lavington, POB 44003, Nairobi; tel. (20) 4292000; fax (20) 4292100; e-mail info@monarchinsurance.co.ke; internet www.monarchinsurance.co.ke; f. 1975; life and general; Man. Dir DAVID MARANGA.

Pan Africa Life Assurance Ltd: Pan Africa House, Kenyatta Ave, POB 44041, 00100 Nairobi; tel. (20) 247600; fax (20) 217675; e-mail insure@pan-africa.com; internet www.panafrica.co.ke; f. 1946; life and general; Chair. JOHN SIMBA; CEO TOM GITOGO.

Phoenix of East Africa Assurance Co Ltd: Ambank House, 17th and 18th Floors, University Way, POB 30129, 00100 Nairobi; tel. (20) 2251350; fax (20) 2211848; e-mail general@phoenix.co.ke; general; Gen. Man. KAUSHAL KUMAR.

PTA Reinsurance Co (ZEP-RE): Zep-Re Pl., Longonot Rd, Upper Hill, POB 42769, Nairobi; tel. (20) 2738221; fax (20) 2738444; e-mail mail@zep-re.com; internet www.zep-re.com; f. 1992; Chair. MICHAEL GONDWE; Man. Dir RAJNI VARIA.

REAL Insurance Co: Royal Ngao House, Hospital Rd, POB 40001, 00100 Nairobi; tel. (20) 2712620; fax (20) 2713831; e-mail general@realinsurance.co.ke; internet www.realinsurance.co.ke; f. 1979; general; Chair. S. K. KAMAU; CEO JOSEPH W. KIUNA.

Shield Assurance Co Ltd: Offices Suite, 7th Floor, 5th Ave, off Ngong Rd, POB 25093, 00100 Nairobi; tel. (20) 2712591; fax (20) 2712597; e-mail info@shieldassurance.co.ke; internet www.shieldassurance.co.ke; f. 2009 following demerger from Blue Shield Insurance; life.

UAP Insurance Co Ltd: Bishop Garden Towers, Bishops Rd, POB 43013, 00100 Nairobi; tel. (20) 2850000; fax (20) 2719030; e-mail uapinsurance@uapkenya.com; internet www.uapkenya.com; f. 1980; general and health insurance; UAP Life Assurance Ltd is also part of the UAP group; Chair. J. B. WANJUI; Man. Dir JAMES WAMBUGU.

Insurance Association

Association of Kenya Insurers (AKI): AKI Centre, Mimosa Rd, Muchai Dr., off Ngong Rd, POB 45338, 00100 Nairobi; tel. (20) 2731330; fax (20) 2731339; e-mail info@akinsure.com; internet www.akinsure.or.ke; Chair. MARK OBUYA.

Trade and Industry

GOVERNMENT AGENCIES

Export Processing Zones Authority: Administration Bldg, Viwanda Rd, Athi River Export Processing Zone, off Nairobi-Namanga Highway, Athi River, POB 50563, Nairobi; tel. (45) 26421; fax (45) 26427; e-mail info@epzakenya.com; internet www.epzakenya.com; est. by the Govt to promote investment in Export Processing Zones; Chair. MATHENGE WANDERI; Chief Exec. CYRILLE NABUTOLA.

Export Promotion Council: Anniversary Towers, 1st and 16th Floors, University Way, POB 40247, Nairobi; tel. (20) 2228534; fax (20) 2218013; e-mail chiefexe@epc.or.ke; internet www.epckenya.org; f. 1992; Chair. HUDSON ALUVANZE; CEO RUTH MWANIKI.

Kenya Investment Authority: Railways HQ, Block D, 3rd Floor, Workshops Rd, off Haile Selassie Ave, POB 55704, 00200 Nairobi; tel. (20) 2221401; fax (20) 2243862; e-mail info@investmentkenya.com; internet www.investmentkenya.com; f. 1986; promotes and facilitates local and foreign investment; Chair. ANNE WANGARI KIRIMA-MUCHOKI; Man. Dir Dr MOSES IKIARA.

Kenya National Trading Corpn Ltd: Yarrow Rd, off Nanyuki Rd, POB 30587, Nairobi; tel. (20) 2430861; fax (20) 556331; e-mail customercare@kntcl.com; internet www.kntcl.com; f. 1965; promotes wholesale and retail trade; Chair. MOHAMMED HASSAN; Man. Dir GLADYS MAINA.

DEVELOPMENT ORGANIZATIONS

Agricultural Development Corpn: Development House, 10th Floor, Moi Ave, POB 47101, Nairobi; tel. (20) 250695; fax (20) 243571; e-mail info@adc.co.ke; internet www.adc.co.ke; f. 1965 to promote agricultural devt and reconstruction; Chair. JAMES KAPAITO TOIYANGA; CEO Dr ANDREW TUIMUR (acting).

Agricultural Finance Corpn: Development House, Moi Ave, POB 30367, Nairobi; tel. (20) 317199; fax (20) 219390; e-mail info@agrifinance.org; internet www.agrifinance.org; a statutory organization providing agricultural loans; Man. Dir OMUREMBE IYADI.

Horticultural Crops Development Authority: Nairobi Horticultural Centre, Airport Rd, opp. JKIA, POB 42601, Nairobi; tel. (20) 2088469; fax (20) 3235898; e-mail md@hcda.or.ke; internet www.hcda.or.ke; f. 1968; invests in production, dehydration, processing and freezing of fruit and vegetables; exports of fresh fruit and vegetables; Chair. JOSEPH G. KIBE; Man. Dir ALFRED SEREM.

Housing Finance Co of Kenya Ltd: Rehani House, cnr Kenyatta Ave and Koinange St, POB 30088, 00100 Nairobi; tel. (20) 317474; fax (20) 340299; e-mail housing@housing.co.ke; internet www.housing.co.ke; f. 1965; Chair. STEVE MAINDA; Man. Dir FRANK M. IRERI.

Industrial and Commercial Development Corpn: Uchumi House, 17th Floor, Aga Khan Walk, POB 45519, Nairobi; tel. (20) 2229213; fax (20) 317456; e-mail info@icdc.co.ke; internet www.icdc .co.ke; f. 1954; govt-financed; assists industrial and commercial devt; Chair. MARTIN KARIUKI MURAGU; Exec. Dir PETER KIMURWA.

Kenya Industrial Estates Ltd: Nairobi Industrial Estate, Likoni Rd, POB 78029, Nairobi; tel. (20) 651348; fax (20) 651355; e-mail admin@kie.co.ke; internet www.kie.co.ke; f. 1967 to finance and develop small-scale industries; Chair. AHMED MOHAMMED; Man. Dir WACHIRA MAHIHU.

Kenya Industrial Research and Development Institute: South C Campus, Popo Rd, off Mombasa Rd, POB 30650, Nairobi; tel. (20) 6003842; fax (20) 6007023; e-mail info@kirdi.go.ke; internet www .kirdi.go.ke; f. 1942; reorg. 1979; restructured 1995; research and devt in industrial and allied technologies, including engineering, agro-industrial, mining and environmental technologies; Chair. Eng. Dr SIPHILA MUMENYA; Dir Dr CHARLES M. Z. MOTURI.

Kenya Tea Development Agency: Moi Ave, POB 30213, Nairobi; tel. (20) 3227000; fax (20) 2221441; e-mail info@ktdateas.com; internet www.ktdateas.com; f. 1964 as Kenya Tea Development Authority to develop tea growing, manufacturing and marketing among African smallholders; operates 65 tea factories and 6 subsidiaries; privatized in 2000; Chair. PETER KANYAGO; CEO LERIONKA TIAMPATI.

CHAMBER OF COMMERCE

Kenya National Chamber of Commerce and Industry: Ufanisi House, Haile Selassie Ave, POB 47024, Nairobi; tel. (20) 2402833; fax (20) 318740; internet www.kenyachamber.or.ke; f. 1965; 69 brs; Nat. Chair. KIPRONO KITTONY; Chief Exec. TITUS G. RUHIU.

INDUSTRIAL AND TRADE ASSOCIATIONS

Coffee Board of Kenya: Coffee Plaza, 10th Floor, Exchange Lane, off Haile Selassie Ave, POB 30566, Nairobi; tel. and fax (20) 315754; fax (20) 311079; e-mail info@coffeeboard.co.ke; internet www .coffeeboardkenya.co.ke; f. 1947; Chair. KIMAMO KURIA; Man. Dir LOISE W. NJERU.

East African Tea Trade Association (EATTA): Tea Trade Centre, Nyerere Ave, POB 85174, 80100 Mombasa; tel. (41) 2220093; fax (41) 2225823; e-mail info@eatta.co.ke; internet www .eatta.com; f. 1957; organizes Mombasa weekly tea auctions; Chair. PETER KIMANGA; Man. Dir EDWARD MUDIBO; 178 mems in 9 countries.

Fresh Produce Exporters' Association of Kenya (FPEAK): New Rehema House, 4th Floor, Rhapta Rd, Westlands, POB 40312, 00100 Nairobi; tel. (20) 4451488; fax (20) 445189; e-mail info@fpeak.org; internet www.fpeak.org; Chair. RICHARD COLLINS; CEO Dr STEPHEN MBITHI MWIKYA.

Kenya Association of Manufacturers (KAM): 86 Riverside Lane, off Riverside Dr., next to Netherlands Embassy, Riverside, POB 30225, Nairobi; tel. (20) 2324817; fax (20) 2166658; e-mail info@kam .co.ke; internet www.kam.co.ke; Chair. POLYCARP K. IGATHE; CEO BETTY MAINA; 200 mems.

Kenya Dairy Board: NSSF Bldg, 10th and 11th Floors, Bishops Rd, POB 30406, Nairobi; tel. (20) 310559; fax (20) 244064; e-mail info@ kdb.co.ke; internet www.kdb.co.ke; f. 1958; Chair. MARTHA MULWA; Man. Dir MACHIRA GICHOHI.

Kenya Fish Processors' and Exporters' Association: 5th Floor, New Rehema House, Raphta Rd, Westlands, POB 345, 00606 Nairobi; tel. and fax (20) 4440858; e-mail info@afipek.org; internet www.afipek.org; f. 2000; Chair. KALIM HASSANALI; CEO BETH WAGUDE.

Kenya Flower Council: Green House Bldg, 4th Floor, Suite 12, Adams Arcade, Ngong Rd, POB 56325, 00200 Nairobi; tel. and fax (20) 2679268; e-mail info@kenyaflowercouncil.org; internet www .kenyaflowercouncil.org; regulates production of cut flowers; CEO JANE NGIGE.

Kenya Meat Commission: POB 30414, Nairobi; tel. (45) 6626041; fax (45) 6626520; e-mail info@kenyameat.co.ke; internet www .kenyameat.co.ke; state-owned; f. 1953; purchasing, processing and marketing of beef livestock; Chair. JOSIAH TARAIYA OLE KORES.

Kenya Sisal Board: Mutual Bldg, Kimathi St, POB 41179, Nairobi; tel. (20) 2245556; fax (20) 240091; e-mail kensisal@sisalboardkenya .go.ke; internet www.sisalboardkenya.go.ke; f. 1946; Man. Dir NAOMI NJERI KAMAU.

Kenya Sugar Board: Sukari Plaza, off Waiyaki Way, POB 51500, Nairobi; tel. 722203128 (mobile); fax (20) 593273; e-mail info@ kenyasugar.co.ke; internet www.kenyasugar.co.ke; f. 2002 to succeed the Kenya Sugar Authority; Chair. KIPTORUS ARAP KIRIOR; CEO ROSEMARY MKOK.

National Cereals and Produce Board (NCPB): POB 30586, Nairobi; tel. (20) 536028; fax (20) 557622; e-mail info@ncpb.co.ke; internet www.ncpb.co.ke; f. 1985; grain marketing and handling,

provides drying, weighing, storage and fumigation services to farmers and traders, stores and manages strategic national food reserves, distributes famine relief; Chair. Prof. WILFRED MWANGI; Man. Dir CORNELIUS NGELECHEI (acting).

Pyrethrum Board of Kenya (PBK): POB 420, Nakuru; tel. (51) 2211567; fax (51) 2210466; e-mail pbk@pyrethrum.co.ke; internet www.kenya-pyrethrum.com; f. 1935; 14 mems; Chair. SOLOMON BOIT; Man. Dir ALFRED BUSOLO TABU.

Tea Board of Kenya: Naivasha Rd, off Ngong Rd, POB 20064, 00200 Nairobi; tel. (20) 3874446; fax (20) 3862120; e-mail info@ teaboard.or.ke; internet www.teaboard.or.ke; f. 1950; regulates tea industry on all matters of policy, licenses tea processing, carries out research on tea through **Tea Research Foundation of Kenya**, monitors tea planting and trade through registration, promotes Kenyan tea internationally; Chair. TITUS GODFREY KIPYAB; Man. Dir ELIZABETH KIMENYI (acting).

EMPLOYERS' ORGANIZATIONS

Federation of Kenya Employers (FKE): Waajiri House, Argwings Kodhek Rd, POB 48311, Nairobi; tel. (20) 2721929; fax (20) 2721990; e-mail fkehq@fke-kenya.org; internet fke-kenya.org; Chair. PATRICK OBATH; Exec. Dir JACQUELINE MUGO.

Association of Local Government Employers (ALGAE): POB 52, Muranga; Chair. SAMUEL NYANGESO.

Kenya Association of Hotelkeepers and Caterers: Heidelberg House, 2nd Floor, Mombasa Rd, POB 9977, 00100 Nairobi; tel. (20) 6004419; fax (20) 6002539; e-mail info@kahc.co.ke; internet www.kahc.co.ke; f. 1944; Chair. JAIDEEP S. VOHRA; CEO MIKE MACHARIA.

Kenya Bankers' Association: International Life House, 13th Floor, Mama Ngina St, POB 73100, 00200 Nairobi; tel. (20) 2221704; fax (20) 2221792; e-mail info@kba.co.ke; internet www .kba.co.ke; f. 1962; Chair. JOSHUA OIGARA; CEO HABIL O. OLAKA; 43 mem. orgs.

Kenya Coffee Producers' Association (KCPA): Wakulima House, 4th Floor, Room 408, Haile Selassie Ave, Ronald Ngala, POB 8100, 00300 Nairobi; tel. (20) 311235; e-mail info@kcpa.or.ke; internet www.kcpa.or.ke; f. 2009; Chair. JAMES K. GITAO.

Kenya Vehicle Manufacturers' Association: Garissa Rd, POB 1436, Thika; tel. (20) 350309; fax (67) 31434; e-mail kvm@kvm.co .ke; internet www.kvm.co.ke; f. 1974; name changed as above in 1989; Chair. KENNETH KEBAARA.

UTILITIES

Electricity

Energy Regulatory Commission (ERC): Eagle Africa Centre, Longonot Rd, Upperhill, POB 42681, 00100 Nairobi; tel. (20) 2717627; fax (20) 2717603; e-mail info@erc.go.ke; internet www .erc.go.ke; f. 1997 as Energy Regulatory Board; present name adopted in 2007; govt-owned; regulates the generation, distribution, supply and use of electric power; Chair. Eng. EMMA KIILU; Dir-Gen. JOSEPH NGANGA.

Kenya Electricity Generating Co Ltd (KenGen): Stima Plaza, Phase 3, Kolobot Rd, Parklands, POB 47936, Nairobi; tel. (20) 3666000; fax (20) 248848; e-mail comms@kengen.co.ke; internet www.kengen.co.ke; f. 1997 as Kenya Power Co; present name adopted 1998; generates 82% of Kenya's electricity requirements; partially privatized in 2006; Chair. TITUS KITILI MBATHI; CEO ALBERT MUGO.

Kenya Power and Lighting Co (KPLC): Electricity House, Harambee Ave, POB 301779, Nairobi; tel. (20) 221251; fax (20) 337351; e-mail custcare@kplc.co.ke; internet www.kplc.co.ke; partially privatized in 2006; 4% owned by Transcentury Group; coordinates electricity transmission and distribution; Man. Dir and CEO Dr BEN CHUMO.

WATER

Nairobi City Water and Sewerage Co (NWSC): Kampala Rd, off Enterprise Rd, POB 30656, 00100 Nairobi; tel. (20) 3988000; internet www.nairobiwater.co.ke; f. 2002; Chair. RAPHAEL NZOMO; Man. Dir PHILIP GICHUKI.

TRADE UNIONS

Central Organization of Trade Unions (Kenya) (COTU): Solidarity Bldg, Digo Rd, POB 13000, Nairobi; tel. (20) 6761375; fax (20) 6762695; e-mail info@cotu-kenya.org; internet www.cotu-kenya.org; f. 1965 as the sole trade union fed.; Chair. RAJABU W. MWONDI; Sec.-Gen. FRANCIS ATWOLI.

Transport

RAILWAYS

In 2004 there were some 1,920 km of track open for traffic. In 2006 the Rift Valley Railways consortium assumed management of the Kenya Railways Corpn. In 2010 a new railway project was proposed to connect Jomo Kenyatta International Airport (JKIA) with Embakasi and the Nairobi city centre to relieve congestion on the road system; construction of the long-awaited rail link was expected to be completed in 2015. In 2011 plans were announced to construct a railway line linking the proposed port of Lamu with oil fields in South Sudan and eventually with Ethiopia. Construction work on the project began in 2012. In mid-2013 the Government revived plans (first proposed in 2009, but subsequently shelved owing to financial constraints and procurement controversies) to construct a railway line connecting Mombasa with Malaba (on the Ugandan border), with a branch line to Kisumu. It was projected that the project would cost some US $5,200m. and would be completed in 2017.

Kenya Railways Corpn: POB 30121, Nairobi; tel. (20) 221211; fax (20) 224156; internet www.krc.co.ke; f. 1977; management of operations assumed by Rift Valley Railways consortium in Nov. 2006; Chair. Gen. (retd) JEREMIAH KIANGA; Man. Dir ATANAS MAINA.

ROADS

In 2012 there were an estimated 160,886 km of classified roads, of which 14,092 km were main roads and 10,725 km were secondary roads. Only an estimated 14.3% of road surfaces were paved. An all-weather road links Nairobi to Addis Ababa, in Ethiopia, and there is a 590-km road link between Kitale (Kenya) and Juba (South Sudan).

Akamba Public Road Services: Industrial Area, POB 40322, Nairobi; tel. (20) 556062; fax (20) 559885; e-mail info@akambabus.com; internet www.akambabus.com; operates bus services from Nairobi to all major towns in Kenya and to some major towns in Uganda and Tanzania.

East African Road Services Ltd: Nairobi; tel. (20) 764622; f. 1947; operates bus services from Nairobi to all major towns in Kenya; Chair. S. H. NATHOO.

Kenya Bus Service Management Ltd: Utali Lane, View Park Towers, 10th Floor, Rm 1010, POB 41001, 00100 Nairobi; tel. (20) 2223235; fax (20) 2223110; e-mail info@kenyabus.net; internet kenyabus.net; promotes and develops transport enterprises; Man. Dir EDWINS MUKABANAH.

Kenya National Highways Authority (KeNHA): Blue Shield Towers, Hospital Rd, Upper Hill, POB 49712, 00100 Nairobi; tel. (20) 8013842; e-mail info@kenha.co.ke; internet www.kenha.co.ke; Chair. HANNAH W. MURIITHI; Dir-Gen. Eng. M. O. KIDENDA.

Kenya Roads Board: Kenya Re Towers, 3rd Floor, Ragati Rd, Upper Hill, POB 73718, Nairobi; tel. (20) 722865; internet www.krb.go.ke; f. 2000 to co-ordinate maintenance, rehabilitation and devt of the road network; Chair. JOEL WANYOIKE; Exec. Dir JACOB RUWA.

Kenya Rural Roads Authority: Blue Shield Towers, 6th Floor, Hospital Rd, Upper Hill, POB 48151, 00100 Nairobi; tel. (20) 2710464; e-mail kerra@roadsnet.go.ke; internet www.kerra.go.ke; Dir-Gen. Eng. MWANGI MAINGI.

Kenya Urban Roads Authority: 2nd Floor, IKM Place, 5th Ngong Ave, POB 41727, 00100 Nairobi; tel. (20) 8013844; e-mail info@kura.go.ke; internet www.kura.go.ke; Chair. Prof. Eng. SIXTUS K. MWEA; Dir-Gen. Eng. JOSEPH NKADAYO.

SHIPPING

The major international seaport of Mombasa has 16 deep-water berths, with a total length of 3,044 m, and facilities for the off-loading of bulk carriers, tankers and container vessels. Kenyan ports handled an estimated 22.3m. metric tons of cargo in 2013. In December 2014 the Kenyan flag registered fleet comprised 34 vessels with a total displacement of 18,329 grt. In 2011 plans were announced for the construction of a second international port, at Lamu.

Kenya Maritime Authority: White House, Moi Ave, Mombasa; tel. (41) 2318398; fax (41) 2318397; e-mail info@kma.go.ke; internet www.kma.go.ke; f. 2004; regulates, co-ordinates and oversees maritime affairs; Chair. MWALIMU DIGORE KITAMBI; Dir-Gen. NANCY W. KARIGITH.

Kenya Ports Authority: POB 95009, Mombasa; tel. (41) 2112999; fax (41) 2311867; e-mail customerfeedback@kpa.co.ke; internet www.kpa.co.ke; f. 1978; sole operator of coastal port facilities; also operates two inland container depots at Nairobi and Kisumu; Chair. DANSON MUNGTANA; Man. Dir GICHURI NDUA.

Inchcape Shipping Services Kenya Ltd: Inchcape House, Archbishop Makarios Cl., off Moi Ave, POB 90194, 80100 Mombasa; tel. (41) 2221885; fax (41) 2314662; e-mail mail@iss-shipping.com; internet www.iss-shipping.com; covers all ports in Kenya, Tanzania, Uganda, South Africa, Namibia, Nigeria, Ghana and Mauritius; Vice-Pres. (Africa Operations) DAVID MACKAY.

Mitchell Cotts Kenya Ltd: Voi St, Shimanzi, POB 42485, 80100 Mombasa; tel. (20) 2315780; fax (20) 2226181; e-mail sales@mitchellcotts.co.ke; internet www.mitchellcottskenya.com; f. 1926; transport and shipping agents; freight handling and distribution; warehousing; Man. Dir DANIEL TANUI.

Motaku Shipping Agencies Ltd: Motaku House, Tangana Rd, POB 80419, 80100 Mombasa; tel. (41) 2229065; fax (41) 2220777; e-mail motaku@motakushipping.com; internet motakushipping.googlepages.com/home; f. 1977; ship managers and shipping agents, freight broker and charter; Man. Dir KARIM KUDRATI.

PIL (Kenya) Ltd: Liberty Plaza, Mombasa Rd, POB 40109, Nairobi; tel. (20) 825082; fax (20) 821086; e-mail admin@nbo.pilship.com; internet www.pilship.com.

Shipmarc Ltd: POB 99553, Mombasa; tel. (41) 229241; fax (41) 221390; e-mail info@shipmarckenya.com.

CIVIL AVIATION

Kenya has four major international airports: Jomo Kenyatta International Airport (JKIA), in south-eastern Nairobi, Moi International Airport, at Mombasa, Eldoret International Airport and Kisumu International Airport. Wilson Airport, in south-western Nairobi, and the airport at Malindi handle internal flights. Kenya also has about 250 smaller airfields. Kenya's airports handled a total of 4.5m. passengers in 2013.

Kenya Airports Authority: Jomo Kenyatta International Airport, POB 19001, Nairobi; tel. (20) 825400; fax (20) 822300; e-mail info@kenyaairports.co.ke; internet www.kenyaairports.co.ke; f. 1991; state-owned; responsible for the provision, management and operation of all airports and private airstrips; Man. Dir YATICH KANGUGO (acting).

Aero Kenya: Shelter Afrique House, Mamlaka Rd, Nairobi; tel. (20) 2719091; fax (20) 2719264; e-mail info@aerokenya.com; f. 1997; operates domestic charter and schedule services; Man. Dir Capt. CHARLES K. MUTHAMA.

African Express Airways: Airport North Rd, Jomo Kenyatta International Airport, POB 19202, 00501 Nairobi; tel. (20) 2014746; fax (20) 2049888; e-mail afex@africanexpress.co.ke; internet www.africanexpress.co.ke.

Airkenya Express Ltd: Wilson Airport, POB 30357, 00100 Nairobi; tel. (20) 3916000; fax (20) 6003129; e-mail info@airkenya.com; internet www.airkenya.com; f. 1985; operates internal scheduled and charter passenger services; Gen. Man. DINO BISLETI.

Astral Aviation: 1st Floor, Mechanised Freight Terminal, Specialised Freight Rd, 1st Ave, Jomo Kenyatta International Airport, POB 594, 00606 Nairobi; tel. (20) 827222; fax (20) 827243; e-mail info@astral-aviation.com; internet www.astral-aviation.com; f. 2001; cargo services; CEO SANJEEV S. GADHIA.

Blue Bird Aviation Ltd: Wilson Airport, Langata Rd, POB 52382, Nairobi; tel. (20) 602338; fax (20) 602337.

Eagle Aviation (African Eagle): POB 93926, Mombasa; tel. (11) 434502; fax (11) 434249; e-mail eaglemsa@africaonline.co.ke; f. 1986; scheduled regional and domestic passenger and cargo services; Chair. RAJA TANUJ; CEO Capt. KIRAN PATEL.

Five Forty Aviation Ltd (fly540.com): ABC Pl. Westlands, POB 10293, Nairobi; tel. (20) 4453252; fax (20) 4453257; e-mail info@fly540.com; internet www.fly540.com; f. 2006; low-cost airline operating domestic and regional flights; COO NEIL STEFFEN.

Jetlink Express: Unit 3, Jomo Kenyatta International Airport, Nairobi; tel. (20) 827915; e-mail customercare@jetlink.co.ke; internet www.jetlink.co.ke; f. 2006; provides internal services and also operates flights to Juba (South Sudan), Goma (DRC) and Kigali (Rwanda); Man. Dir and CEO Capt. ELLY ALUVALE.

Kenya Airways Ltd (KQ): Airport North Road, Jomo Kenyatta International Airport, POB 19142, Nairobi; tel. (20) 6422000; fax (20) 823488; e-mail contact@kenya-airways.com; internet www.kenya-airways.com; f. 1977; in private sector ownership since 1996; passenger services to Africa, Asia, Europe and Middle East; freight services to Europe; internal services from Nairobi to Kisumu, Mombasa and Malindi; also operates a freight subsidiary; Chair. EVANSON MWANIKI; Man. Dir and CEO MBUVI NGUNZE.

CIVIL AVIATION AUTHORITY

Kenya Civil Aviation Authority: Jomo Kenyatta International Airport, POB 30163, 00100 Nairobi; tel. (20) 827470; fax (20) 822300; e-mail info@kcaa.or.ke; internet www.kcaa.or.ke; f. 2002; regulatory and advisory services for air navigation; Chair. SAMUEL POGHISIO; Dir-Gen. JOSEPH KITPOO CHEBUNGEI (acting).

Tourism

Kenya's main attractions for visitors are its wildlife, with 25 National Parks and 23 game reserves, the Indian Ocean coast and an equable year-round climate. In 2013 there were an estimated 3.8m. foreign visitors. Earnings from the sector totalled US $935m. (excluding passenger transport) in 2012.

Kenya Tourism Board: Kenya-Re Towers, Ragati Rd, POB 30630, 00100 Nairobi; tel. (20) 2711262; fax (20) 2719925; e-mail info@kenyatourism.org; internet www.magicalkenya.com; f. 1997; promotes Kenya as a tourist destination, monitors the standard of tourist facilities; Chair. KITILI MBATHI; Man. Dir MURIITHI NDEGWA.

Kenya Tourist Development Corpn: Utalii House, 11th Floor, Uhuru Highway, POB 42013, Nairobi; tel. (20) 2229751; fax (20) 2227817; e-mail info@ktdc.co.ke; internet www.ktdc.co.ke; f. 1965; Chair. MOHAMMED SHAIYA; Man. Dir MARIANNE NDEGWA-JORDAN.

Defence

As assessed at November 2014, Kenya's armed forces numbered 24,120, comprising an army of 20,000, an air force of 2,500 and a navy of 1,620. Military service is voluntary. The paramilitary police general service unit was 5,000 strong. In 2013 a total of 45,019 troops were stationed abroad, of whom 22 were observers.

Defence Expenditure: Budgeted at Ks. 90,700m. for 2015.

Commander-in-Chief of the Armed Forces: Pres. UHURU KENYATTA.

Chief of Defence Forces: Lt.-Gen. SAMSON J. MWATHETHE (designate).

Army Commander: Lt-Gen. JOSEPH KIPTOO KASAON.

Air Force Commander: Maj.-Gen. SAMUEL NG'ANG'A THUITA.

Navy Commander: Maj.-Gen. NGEWA MUKALA.

Education

The Government provides, or assists in the provision of, schools. In 2007/08 enrolment at pre-primary level was 26% (26% of boys; 26% of girls). Primary education, which is compulsory, is provided free of charge. The education system involves eight years of primary education (beginning at six years of age), four years at secondary school and four years of university education. According to UNESCO estimates, in 2009 enrolment at primary schools included 82% of pupils in the relevant age-group (males 81%; females 82%), while enrolment at secondary schools included 50% of children in the relevant age-group (males 52%; females 48%). Tertiary enrolment in 2009 was equivalent to 4% of those in the relevant age-group, according to UNESCO estimates. There are six state universities and seven private universities. In 2011/12 an estimated total of 127,691 students were enrolled in higher education. In 2010 spending on education represented 17.2% of total budgetary expenditure.

KIRIBATI

Introductory Survey

LOCATION, CLIMATE, LANGUAGE, RELIGION, FLAG, CAPITAL

The Republic of Kiribati (pronounced 'Kir-i-bas') comprises 32 atolls, in three principal groups, scattered within an area of about 5m. sq km (2m. sq miles) in the mid-Pacific Ocean, and the island of Banaba (formerly Ocean Island). The country extends about 3,870 km (2,400 miles) from east to west and about 2,050 km (1,275 miles) from north to south. Its nearest neighbours are Nauru, to the west, and Tuvalu and Tokelau, to the south. The climate varies between maritime equatorial in the central islands and tropical in the north and south, with daytime temperatures varying between 26°C (79°F) and 32°C (90°F). There is a season of north-westerly trade winds from March to October and a season of rains and gales from October to March. However, average annual rainfall varies greatly, from 3,000 mm (118 in) in the northern islands to 1,500 mm (59 in) in Tarawa and 700 mm (28 in) in the Line Islands. Droughts often occur in the central and southern islands. The principal languages are I-Kiribati (Gilbertese) and English, and the islands' inhabitants are mostly Christians. The national flag (proportions 1 by 2) depicts a golden frigate bird in flight, on a red background, above a rising sun and six alternating wavy horizontal lines of blue and white, representing the sea. The capital is the island of Bairiki, in Tarawa Atoll.

CONTEMPORARY POLITICAL HISTORY

Historical Context

In 1892 the United Kingdom established a protectorate over the 16 atolls of the Gilbert Islands and the nine Ellice Islands (now Tuvalu). The two groups were administered together by the Western Pacific High Commission (WPHC), which was based in Fiji until its removal to the British Solomon Islands (now Solomon Islands) in 1953. The phosphate-rich Ocean Island (now Banaba), west of the Gilberts, was annexed by the UK in 1900. The Gilbert and Ellice Islands were annexed in 1915, effective from January 1916, when the protectorate became a colony. The local representative of the WPHC was the Resident Commissioner, based on Tarawa Atoll in the Gilbert group. Later in 1916 the new Gilbert and Ellice Islands Colony (GEIC) was extended to include Ocean Island and two of the Line Islands, far to the east. Christmas Island (now Kiritimati), another of the Line Islands, was added in 1919, and the eight Phoenix Islands (then uninhabited) in 1937. The Line and Phoenix Islands, south of Hawaii, were also claimed by the USA. A joint British-US administration for two of the Phoenix group, Canton (now Kanton) and Enderbury, was agreed in April 1939. During the Second World War the GEIC was invaded by Japanese forces, who occupied the Gilbert Islands in 1942–43. Tarawa Atoll was the scene of some of the fiercest fighting in the Pacific between Japan and the USA.

In 1963, to prepare the GEIC for self-government, the first of a series of legislative and executive bodies was established. In 1972 a Governor of the GEIC was appointed to assume almost all the functions previously exercised in the colony by the High Commissioner. The five uninhabited Central and Southern Line Islands, previously administered directly by the High Commissioner, became part of the GEIC at this time. In 1974 the Legislative Council was replaced by a House of Assembly, with 28 elected members and three official members. The House elected Naboua Ratieta as Chief Minister.

In October 1975 the Ellice Islands were allowed to secede from the GEIC to form a separate territory, Tuvalu (q.v.). The remainder of the GEIC was renamed the Gilbert Islands, and the House of Assembly's membership was reduced. The Gilbert Islands obtained internal self-government on 1 January 1977. Later in that year the number of elected members in the House of Assembly was increased to 36, and provision was subsequently made for a member appointed by the Rabi Council of Leaders. Following a general election in 1978, Ieremia Tabai, Leader of the Opposition in the previous House, was elected Chief Minister. On 12 July 1979 the Gilbert Islands became an independent republic within the Commonwealth, under the name of Kiribati.

The House of Assembly was renamed the Maneaba ni Maungatabu, and Ieremia Tabai became the country's first President (Beretitenti). In September Kiribati signed a treaty of friendship with the USA, which relinquished its claim to the Line and Phoenix Islands, including Kanton and Enderbury. Kiribati did not become a member of the UN until September 1999, although it had previously joined some of the organization's agencies.

In 1975, meanwhile, the UK refused to recognize as legitimate a demand for independence by the people of Ocean Island (Banaba), who had been in litigation with the British Government since 1971 over revenues derived from exports of phosphate. Opencast mining had adversely affected the island's environment to such an extent that most Banabans had been resettled on Rabi Island, 2,600 km (1,600 miles) away in Fiji. The Banabans rejected the British Government's argument that phosphate revenues should be distributed over the whole territory of the Gilbert Islands. In 1976 the High Court in London dismissed the Banabans' claim for unpaid royalties but upheld that for damages. An offer made by the British Government in 1977 of an *ex gratia* payment of $A10m., without admission of liability and on condition that no further judicial appeal would be made, was rejected. In 1981, however, the Banaban community on Rabi decided to accept the British Government's *ex gratia* offer of compensation, although it continued to seek self-government. The 1979 Constitution provided for the establishment of an independent commission of inquiry to review the political status of the Banabans three years after Kiribati had achieved independence; however, the inquiry was not commissioned until 1985. (In 2009 it was reported that rehabilitation work was being undertaken on Banaba. The work was expected to cost $A50m. and take 20 years to complete, whereupon the Banaban community hoped to return to the island. In 2010 Banabans appealed to Australia, New Zealand, Japan and the UK for additional funding for the project.)

As part of the UK's programme to develop its own nuclear weapons, the first test of a British hydrogen bomb was conducted near Christmas Island in May 1957. Two further thermonuclear tests in the same vicinity followed later in the year. Serious concerns with regard to the monitoring of radioactivity levels in the area were subsequently raised. In addition to the potential effects on the health of both islanders and service personnel, millions of birds were reported to have died as a direct result of the high-altitude tests. The USA also operated a test programme, conducting 26 nuclear experiments in the vicinity of Christmas Island in 1962. The UK announced its withdrawal from the Christmas Island base in 1964. Despite various 'clean-up' operations, including one financed by the British Government in 2005–06, concerns arising from the environmental impact of the testing programmes persisted.

Domestic Political Affairs

The first general election since independence took place in March–April 1982. The members of the new Maneaba all sat as independents. In accordance with the 1979 Constitution, the legislature nominated from among its members candidates for the country's first presidential election, to be held on the basis of direct popular vote. The incumbent President, Ieremia Tabai, was confirmed in office at the election in May. The Government resigned in December, after the Maneaba had twice rejected proposals to increase the salaries of civil servants. A fresh general election took place in January 1983, and the formation of the new Maneaba necessitated a further presidential election in February, at which Tabai was re-elected for a third term of office. He was elected to a fourth term in May 1987 (following a general election in March). After the May 1991 legislative elections former Vice-President Teatao Teannaki narrowly defeated Roniti Teiwaki to replace Tabai, who had served the maximum number of presidential terms permitted by the Constitution.

In May 1994 the Government was defeated on a motion of confidence, following opposition allegations that cabinet ministers had misused travel allowances. At the ensuing legislative elections in July five ministers lost their seats. Of the newly elected members, 13 were supporters of the Maneaban Te Mauri

(Protect the Maneaba), while only eight were known to support the previously dominant National Progressive Party grouping. At the presidential election in September, Teburoro Tito, of the Maneaban Te Mauri, was elected, receiving 51.1% of the votes cast.

In 1995 a committee was created with the aim of assessing public opinion regarding possible amendments to the Constitution. Its recommendations were considered in March 1998 at a Constitutional Review Convention in Bairiki. These included equalizing the status of men and women with regard to the citizenship rights of foreigners marrying I-Kiribati and changes to the structure of the Council of State (comprising the Chairman of the Public Services Commission, the Chief Justice and the Speaker of the House of Assembly).

At the general election held in September 1998, which was contested by a record 191 candidates, the Government and opposition each lost seven seats. Tito was re-elected as President in November, defeating Harry Tong with 52.3% of the votes cast.

The Government was accused of attempting to stifle freedom of expression in late 1999, when a New Zealand journalist working for Agence France-Presse was banned from entering Kiribati. The Government had claimed that articles by the correspondent, published in a regional magazine and unfavourable to Kiribati, were biased and sensationalist. Moreover, in December former President Ieremia Tabai and a former member of the Maneaba, Atiera Tetoa, were fined for importing telecommunications equipment without a permit. They had launched Newair FM, an independent commercial radio station, 12 months previously, but it had been immediately suspended. Tabai subsequently established Kiribati's first private newspaper, the *Kiribati Newstar*, in an attempt to reduce government control over the media in the islands. The radio station was eventually granted a licence to broadcast, in December 2002.

Campaigning for the general election during late 2002 was characterized by numerous allegations of improper conduct. Observers noted that officials from the Chinese embassy in Tarawa, accompanied by government candidates, had been donating gifts to the local community in the weeks preceding the election. (The Government had recently amended the Elections Act to allow gifts to be distributed to the public by candidates during their electoral campaigns, a practice that had been banned hitherto.) Moreover, under the newly amended Newspaper Registration Act, President Tito ordered police to seize opposition election pamphlets in November.

A total of 176 candidates contested the election in November 2002, at which the Government suffered significant losses, with 14 of its supporters (including seven ministers) failing to retain their seats. At the presidential election in February 2003, Tito narrowly defeated opposition candidate Taberannang Timeon to secure a third term. However, in the following month Tito was ousted in a motion of no confidence and his Government was replaced by the Council of State, acting in an interim capacity. At a further general election, held in May, supporters of Tito secured a majority of seats. Opposition candidate Anote Tong defeated his brother, Harry Tong, by a slim margin, at the presidential election in July. Anote Tong's electoral campaign, which had focused on his pledge to review the lease of the Chinese satellite-tracking station on South Tarawa (opened in 1997), had been characterized by a series of personal criticisms of his brother.

In November 2003 several hundred people staged a protest in Tarawa against the Government's decision to establish diplomatic relations with Taiwan, in place of the People's Republic of China, claiming that it had been made in return for Taiwanese funding of Anote Tong's election campaign. The President strongly denied this allegation, but did confirm that Taiwan had offered extensive development funds to Kiribati for adopting such a position regarding diplomatic ties (see *Regional Affairs*).

The 2007 general election

Legislative elections, contested by a total of 146 candidates, were held in August 2007. The ruling Boutokan Te Koaua (Pillars of Truth) grouping of Anote Tong secured 18 of the 44 elective seats in the newly enlarged legislature, defeating the Maneaban Te Mauri, which won seven. The remainder were secured by independents. Anote Tong was re-elected President in October, receiving almost twice as many votes as his nearest rival, Nabuti Mwemwenikarawa.

In August 2009 there was an outbreak of violence on the island of Maiana between the two ruling bodies, Te Bau Ni Maiana (the traditional elders' association) and the democratically elected council. The mayor and the council refused to comply with an

order from Te Bau Ni Maiana to vacate their seats so that a fresh election could take place. Following a High Court ruling in favour of the council, the mayor's house was destroyed in an arson attack. The council subsequently acceded to Te Bau Ni Maiana's demands. The Minister of Environment, Lands and Agricultural Development, Tetabo Nakara, resigned in response to criticism of the Government's handling of the issue.

A report on domestic abuse by the Social Welfare Division of the Ministry of Internal and Social Affairs was published in December 2009. According to its findings, nearly 70% of women in Kiribati had experienced abuse by their husbands, close relatives or others. Human rights organizations responded to the report by urging the Government to take action.

The 2011 general election

The general election held on 21 and 28 October 2011 was contested by 138 candidates, of whom only 12 were women. A total of 30 members, including seven government ministers, retained their seats in the Maneaba, with Anote Tong's Boutokan Te Koaua grouping securing 15 seats and Tetaua Taitai's Karikirakean Tei-Kiribati (United Coalition Party, which had been formed in 2010 by the merger of the Maneaban Te Mauri and the Kiribati Tabomoa party) taking 10 seats. The Maurin Kiribati Party secured three seats, with the remainder won by independents. During the campaign period Tong had alleged that Chinese interests had provided funding for opposition candidates, in the hope that a new government would switch recognition from Taiwan back to the People's Republic of China. The claims were denied by the opposition. At the presidential election held on 13 January 2012, Anote Tong was re-elected, receiving 42.2% of the valid votes, compared with 35.0% for Tetaua Taitai and 22.8% for Rimeta Beniamina (of the Maurin Kiribati Party).

The issue of press freedom resurfaced in June 2012, when a fortnightly newspaper, the *Kiribati Independent*, which had begun publication in December 2011, was ordered to cease operating on the grounds that it had not been registered. The editor, Taberannang Korauaba, stated that the newspaper's application to register, lodged in late 2011, had been ignored by the authorities. In defiance of the ban, the newspaper resumed publication in January 2013. Kiribati's sole television station, state-owned Kiribati Television, was suspended by the Government in March owing to financial difficulties and a lack of expertise in programming and production.

Recent developments: the Family Peace Bill and re-emergence of concerns over media freedom

In August 2012 the Government proposed a constitutional revision providing for the creation of a Ministry of Women and Youth with the aim of addressing Kiribati's very high rate of violence against women. However, the draft amendment did not receive the requisite approval of a two-thirds' majority in the Maneaba. The decision of the opposition not to support the proposal, leading to its defeat in the legislature, was condemned by human rights and women's groups. Following the successful adoption of a similar amendment in April 2013, however, a Ministry of Women and Youth was established. Tangariki Reete was given charge of the new portfolio. The issue of domestic violence in Kiribati had, in recent years, attracted regional and international attention. Ongoing efforts to tackle the problem continued during 2013 with a campaign by the Government, in partnership with the Pacific Community, which aimed to increase awareness of the issue, expand support services for victims and help perpetrators understand the criminality of their actions. Furthermore, draft legislation known as the 'Family Peace Bill', which included measures to help eliminate domestic violence against women and children, was approved by the Maneaba in April 2014. In February of that year the Minister of Labour and Human Resource Development, Boutu Bateriki, resigned from his post a week after his appearance in court on charges of beating his former wife; he was replaced by Martin Moreti. The revelation in June that six women had been murdered by their partners during the first half of the year, despite the efforts of campaigners against gender-based violence, led to calls for harsher punishments for the perpetrators of such crimes. In September a draft amendment to the penal code was presented to the Maneaba which proposed the introduction of the death penalty in certain cases of murder. A commission of inquiry was subsequently established to conduct a public consultation, with the possibility of a future referendum on the issue.

Meanwhile, in September 2013 nine members of the Maneaba petitioned President Tong to dismiss two ministers accused of misconduct in relation to allegedly excessive allowance payments. Taberannang Timeon, Minister of Communications, Transport and Tourism Development, and Kirabuke Teiaua, Minister of Public Works and Utilities, resigned in October, and were replaced by Rimeta Beniamina and Waysang Kumkee, respectively. In response to the case, a new law aimed at making the system of legislators' allowances more equitable was approved in December.

The country's state-controlled media once again attracted criticism in June 2014 when a journalist at Radio Kiribati was suspended for broadcasting a response by an opposition member of the Maneaba to allegations made against him in a state newspaper. The regional media organization Pacific Freedom Forum demanded the journalist's immediate reinstatement. In December an opposition-drafted amendment to the Broadcasting and Publications Authority Act, proposing the granting of greater freedoms to reporters within the state-owned media, was rejected.

Climate Change and Other Environmental Concerns

In addition to the legacies of phosphate-mining operations and of the testing of hydrogen bombs, by the end of the 20th century the impact of climate change on the islands had begun to assume major significance. In 1989 a UN report on the greenhouse effect (the heating of the earth's atmosphere, and a resultant rise in sea level, as a consequence of pollution) listed Kiribati as one of the countries that would completely disappear beneath the sea in the 21st century, unless drastic action were taken. None of the land on the islands was more than 3 m above sea level, making the country extremely vulnerable to the potential effects of climate change. Rising sea levels were expected not only to cause flooding but also to upset the balance between sea and fresh water (below the coral sands), rendering water supplies undrinkable. A report by the World Bank in 2000 listed the flooding and loss of low-lying areas, more intense cyclones and droughts, the failure of subsistence crops and coastal fisheries, the death of coral reefs and the spread of mosquito-borne diseases such as malaria and dengue fever as consequences of climate change on Pacific island nations. In 1999 Kiribati experienced one of the worst droughts ever recorded, and in that year two of the country's uninhabited coral reefs were submerged as a result of rising sea levels. During the early 2000s the causeways linking villages on Tarawa atoll were flooded by high tides, and shortages of drinking water, which had become common, were reported to be approaching critical levels by 2009. Assistance from the UN Development Programme (UNDP, see p. 56) included projects to drill boreholes on Tarawa atoll to measure the extent of the underground fresh water supply and attempt to prevent contamination by salt water, and the planting of more than 37,000 mangroves to alleviate coastal erosion.

Kiribati continued to urge the UN to work towards a co-ordinated response to the challenge of global warming. President Anote Tong addressed the UN Climate Change Conference in Copenhagen, Denmark, in December 2009, expressing profound disappointment when it failed to reach consensus on a legally binding agreement to reduce carbon emissions. In November 2010 Kiribati hosted a conference on climate change, at which the 19 countries and numerous organizations represented drew up a declaration urging the adoption of definite measures to prevent disastrous levels of global warming and emphasizing the need for funding to combat its effects on vulnerable developing countries.

Government policy regarding climate change has increasingly focused on mitigation and on developing ways to ensure the future of the I-Kiribati population. In March 2012 it was reported that the Government of Kiribati was seeking to purchase a 23 sq km plot of land on Vanua Levu in Fiji, at a cost of US $9.6m. The land was to be used primarily to afford Kiribati a degree of food security as its own territory became unusable for farming, although President Anote Tong stated that it could also be used for the relocation of I-Kiribati residents when their islands were rendered uninhabitable by climate change. Purchase of the land was completed in mid-2014. Tong also emphasized the increasing importance of education for citizens of Kiribati, claiming that their future would be more secure as skilled migrants than as poorly educated refugees.

During 2014 President Tong continued to campaign for international action on climate change, which he described as 'the greatest moral challenge of our times'. In May a delegation from Kiribati joined others from Papua New Guinea and Tuvalu at a meeting in the Australian capital of Canberra, where they urged the Australian Government to provide greater assistance to island nations suffering from the effects of climate change. Tong condemned Australian Prime Minister Tony Abbott's efforts to create an international alliance of conservative governments to resist carbon trading and other initiatives aimed at reducing global carbon emissions. At a meeting of the Coalition of Atoll Nations on Climate Change in July Tong stated that, although it was too late to save Kiribati, the islands' fate should serve as an early warning system for the rest of the world regarding the impact of climate change and the need to take urgent action. Furthermore, in September he addressed the UN Climate Summit in New York where he demanded stronger international leadership in addressing climate change. In November Fiji's Prime Minister Frank Bainimarama nominated Tong for a Nobel Peace Prize for his campaigning work on the issue of climate change.

Kiribati's high rate of population growth and, in particular, the overpopulation of South Tarawa has prompted various efforts to resettle inhabitants on outlying atolls, mainly in the Line Islands. In mid-2014 representatives of the UN Population Fund travelled to Kiribati to discuss ways of curbing the country's rapidly expanding population, which was causing increasing stress to the local environment. It was estimated that there were more than 2,000 births every year (some 2,400—a birth rate of 23.3 per 1,000 live births—were registered in 2013), compared with an average of around 400 deaths (with a death rate of 6.0 per 1,000 people in 2013). South Tarawa's water supply and sanitation provision were unable to meet the needs of the growing population, and in 2014 the Asian Development Bank (ADB) estimated that the associated health care and social costs of the situation were equivalent to some 4% of Kiribati's annual gross domestic product.

Sea Launch, an international consortium led by the US Boeing Commercial Space Company, began a rocket-launching operation near the islands in 1999. Kiribati, which did not benefit financially from the project as the consortium had sought to carry out its activities in international waters near the outer limits of the islands' exclusive economic zone (EEZ), had, together with the South Pacific Regional Environment Programme (see p. 457), expressed concerns regarding the adverse environmental impact of the site (particularly the dumping of large quantities of waste fuel in the islands' waters).

In 2006 President Anote Tong announced that a large marine reserve was to be established in Kiribati. From 1 January 2015 all commercial fishing was banned in the Phoenix Islands Protected Area (PIPA), which at 408,250 sq km constituted the largest marine protected area in the world. The area had been designated by UNESCO as a World Heritage site in 2010. The Pacific Oceanscape initiative, modelled on Kiribati's PIPA, outlined plans in 2012 to establish a protected area of 38m. sq km, covering all the Pacific islands' EEZs and the areas between these boundaries. The initiative, which had been endorsed by all the leaders of the Pacific Islands Forum (see p. 413) member nations, proposed the establishment of a framework to manage the EEZs in an integrated way and to respond more effectively to the impact of climate change on the marine environment.

Regional Affairs

Following its accession to independence in 1979, Kiribati maintained good relations with other island nations of the Pacific region, as well as with Australia and New Zealand, both of which continued to provide significant development assistance. Through the Pacific Patrol Boat Program, for example, Australia supported Kiribati in the area of maritime surveillance. During 2009 Australia announced a programme to provide training for I-Kiribati nursing students and signed a partnership development agreement with Kiribati and Solomon Islands to assist in improving education, workforce skills and economic management.

In June 2008, during an I-Kiribati state visit to New Zealand, President Anote Tong and Prime Minister Helen Clark signed a declaration aimed at increasing political and economic links, including the provision by New Zealand of financial assistance of $NZ15m. over a five-year period to address the issue of rapid urbanization in Kiribati, particularly on South Tarawa. In 2010 the Government of New Zealand announced a doubling of annual aid to Kiribati, emphasizing the need to improve the islands' water supplies and sanitation.

In November 2003 President Anote Tong announced the establishment of diplomatic relations with Taiwan. The Government's decision to transfer its recognition from the People's

Republic of China to Taiwan caused considerable controversy. The satellite-tracking station opened on South Tarawa in 1997, which had played an important role in China's first manned space flight, was promptly dismantled. After unsuccessful attempts by the Chinese authorities to persuade Kiribati to reconsider its decision (attempts which many observers believed were motivated by the islands' strategic importance), China suspended its diplomatic relations with Kiribati. Following Kiribati's transfer of diplomatic allegiance, a Taiwanese embassy was opened in Tarawa in January 2004, and in May 2005 President Chen Shui-bian of Taiwan became the first foreign head of state to visit Kiribati in an official capacity. However, relations between the two countries were strained when in October 2014 the Taiwanese ambassador asked the authorities in Kiribati to account for some US $1.5m. of Taiwanese aid, intended to finance a vessel to service the outer islands. A police investigation was subsequently launched into the apparent disappearance of the funds.

Relations with Japan have been tested by various issues. In 1992 the legislature approved an opposition motion urging the Government to seek compensation from Japan for damage caused to the islands during the Second World War. As a result of discussions held at the Pacific Islands Forum summit meeting in Kiribati in 2000, Japan announced its willingness to negotiate compensation claims. Furthermore, a visit by President Teburoro Tito to Japan in the following year resulted in a number of informal agreements aimed at enhancing relations between the two countries, particularly regarding the contentious issues of tuna fishing, whaling and nuclear fuel shipments. In June 2010 the Government of Kiribati denied allegations that it had accepted financial assistance from Japan in return for voting, at that month's annual meeting of the International Whaling Commission, in favour of an end to the moratorium on commercial whaling.

In 2003 the UN Children's Fund (UNICEF) established a field office in Kiribati as part of a wider strategy to increase the UN's presence in the region. In 2007 the efforts of a team of Cuban doctors were reported to have resulted in an 80% decrease in infant mortality rates, and there was a subsequent agreement for the training of I-Kiribati medical students by Cuban doctors in Kiribati. In 2013, however, child mortality rates (of those under 5 years of age) in Kiribati remained the highest in the region, at 58.0 per 1,000 live births, according to UNICEF.

In 2013 the Government of Kiribati joined other human rights groups in the region in urging the authorities in Australia and New Zealand to amend their respective immigration policies to respond to the problems confronting the inhabitants of low-lying Pacific islands. The situation came to prominence in late 2013 when an I-Kiribati citizen, whose home was threatened by rising sea levels, sought unsuccessfully to claim refugee status in New Zealand. During a state visit to Kiribati in early 2014 Fiji's President Ratu Epeli Nailatikau formally stated that all I-Kiribati nationals would be welcome to resettle in Fiji when climate change rendered their islands inhabitable.

In September 2013 Kiribati and the USA signed a maritime boundary treaty formalizing the 1,260-nautical mile boundary between the US territories of Palmyra Atoll, Kingman Reef, Jarvis and Baker Islands and Kiribati's Line and Phoenix Islands. In November 2014 the two countries signed a co-operation agreement to support joint efforts to conserve and protect the marine environment around their territories.

CONSTITUTION AND GOVERNMENT

Under the Constitution of 1979, legislative power is vested in the unicameral Maneaba ni Maungatabu (House of Assembly). It has 44 members elected by universal adult suffrage for four years (subject to dissolution), one nominated representative of the Banaban community and, if he/she is not an elected member, the Attorney-General as an ex officio member. The head of state is the Beretitenti (President), who is also head of government. The President is elected by direct popular vote. The President governs with the assistance of the Vice-President and Cabinet, whom he appoints from among members of the Maneaba. Executive authority is vested in the Cabinet, which is responsible to the Maneaba.

REGIONAL AND INTERNATIONAL CO-OPERATION

Kiribati is a member of the Pacific Community (see p. 410), the Pacific Islands Forum (see p. 413) and the Asian Development Bank (ADB, see p. 206). The country is an associate member of the UN's Economic and Social Commission for Asia and the Pacific (ESCAP, see p. 30). In September 2013 Kiribati was formally accepted as a member of the G77 group.

Kiribati became a member of the UN in 1999. It is a signatory to the Lomé Conventions and successor Cotonou Agreement (see p. 321) with the European Union.

ECONOMIC AFFAIRS

In 2013, according to estimates by the World Bank, Kiribati's gross national income (GNI), measured at average 2011–13 prices, was US $268m., equivalent to $2,620 per head (or $2,780 on an international purchasing-power parity basis). During 2004–13, it was estimated, the population increased at an average annual rate of 1.6%, while gross domestic product (GDP) per head declined, in real terms, by an estimated average of 0.2% per year. Overall GDP increased, in real terms, at an average annual rate of 1.4% in 2004–13; growth in 2013 was 3.0%. According to the Asian Development Bank (ADB), real GDP grew by 3.0% in 2014.

Agriculture and fishing contributed 25.7% of GDP in 2013, according to UN estimates. The sector engaged 22.1% of the economically active population in 2010, according to census figures for that year. FAO projected that 20.8% of the population would be engaged in agriculture at mid-2015. The principal cash crop is coconut, yielding copra as well as coconut oil. In 2010 exports of crude coconut oil accounted for 43.5% of the country's total receipts from exports and re-exports. Export revenue from copra and copra cake declined from $A1.8m. in 2008, accounting for 21.0% of the total, to $A681,000 in 2009 (8.5%). Bananas, taro, screw-pine (*Pandanus*), breadfruit and papaya are cultivated as food crops. The cultivation of seaweed began in the mid-1980s. In 2010 seaweed provided 1.1% of total export earnings. Sea cucumbers (*bêches-de-mer*) have become an increasingly important source of export revenue, accounting for 10.6% of the total in 2010. Pigs and chickens are kept. The sale of fishing licences to foreign fleets (notably from the Republic of Korea, Japan, the People's Republic of China, Taiwan and the USA) has provided an important source of income. Revenue from the sale of fishing licences reached a record $A52m. in 2001, but declined over the next few years. Receipts from fishing licences rose from $A25.4m. in 2007 to $A32.2m. in 2008, before decreasing to $A29.5m. in 2009, when they accounted for 42.4% of total government revenue. However, income from licence fees increased by 41.4% in 2010, to $A41.7m. (51.5% of total revenue), mainly owing to the introduction in September of that year of an auction scheme for fishing rights, which was intended to replace bilateral access agreements. Kiribati and the European Union (EU) drew up a new Fisheries Partnership Agreement in 2012, which was to cover the period 2012–15, during which time the EU's annual financial contribution was to total €1.3m. The agreement permitted EU vessels (from Spain, France and Portugal) to fish for tuna in Kiribati waters. According to UN estimates, the GDP of the agricultural sector increased at an average annual rate of 1.1% in 2004–13. Agricultural GDP increased by 3.4% in 2012, but decreased by 0.1% in 2013.

Industry (including manufacturing, construction and utilities) contributed 9.6% of GDP in 2012, according to UN estimates. According to 2010 census figures, the sector engaged 16.1% of the economically active population in that year. According to UN estimates, industrial GDP expanded by an average of 1.3% per year in 2004–13. Sectoral growth was 5.3% in 2013.

Mining of phosphate rock on the island of Banaba, which ceased in 1979, formerly provided some 80% of export earnings. Interest from a phosphate reserve fund, the Revenue Equalization Reserve Fund (RERF, which was established in 1956), became an important source of income (see below). The production of solar-evaporated salt for export to other islands of the Pacific (for use on fishing vessels with brine refrigeration systems) began on Kiritimati in 1985.

Manufacturing, which contributed 5.3% of GDP in 2012, according to UN estimates, is confined to the small-scale production of coconut-based products, soap, foods, handicrafts, furniture, leather goods and garments. According to UN estimates, manufacturing GDP increased by an average of 1.7% per year in 2004–13. The GDP of the manufacturing sector increased by 6.3% in 2013.

The construction sector contributed 3.1% of GDP in 2013, according to UN estimates. The sector engaged 2.0% of the economically active population in 2010, according to census figures for that year. According to UN estimates, construction GDP increased at an average annual rate of 0.9% in 2004–13. The GDP of the construction sector expanded by 4.3% in 2013.

Production of electrical energy increased from 15m. kWh in 2000 to 24m. kWh in 2011. Mineral fuels accounted for 16.5% of total import costs in 2012. The use of solar energy is of increasing significance.

The services sector provided 64.2% of GDP in 2013, according to UN estimates. Services engaged 61.8% of the economically active population in 2010, according to census figures for that year. Although impeded by factors such as the high costs of transport to Kiribati, the tourism sector makes a significant contribution to the economy. Receipts from tourism totalled US $3.2m. in 2012. Details of a five-year plan to revitalize the country's tourism sector, which aimed to increase the annual number of visitors to 10,000 by 2015, were announced in December 2009, and a new promotional campaign was launched in April 2010. International visitor arrivals increased from some 5,000 in 2012 to an estimated 6,000 in 2013. According to UN estimates, the GDP of the services sector increased at an average annual rate of 2.1% in 2004–13. Sectoral growth was 3.8% in 2013.

In 2012, according to the ADB, Kiribati recorded a visible merchandise trade deficit of $A85.9m., and there was a deficit of $A20.8m. on the current account of the balance of payments. Kiribati depends on imports for almost all essential commodities, and import duties are a major source of government revenue. In 2012 the principal source of imports was Australia (24.4% of the total); other major suppliers were Japan, Singapore, Fiji and New Zealand. The principal recipient of exports in that year was Morocco (47.0%); other major purchasers were Taiwan, Hong Kong, Viet Nam and Fiji. The major imports in 2012 were mineral fuels, oils and distillation products; prepared foodstuffs, beverages, spirits, vinegar, and tobacco and articles thereof; vehicles, aircraft, vessels and associated transport equipment; iron and steel, other base metals and articles of base metal; and vegetables and vegetable products. The major exports in 2012 included animal or vegetable fats and oils, and products thereof; live animals and animal products; and prepared foodstuffs, beverages, spirits, vinegar, and tobacco and articles thereof.

Following annual budgetary deficits since 1998, according to official figures, the central government budget returned to surplus, of $A21.2m. (equivalent to 11.3% of GDP), in 2013. Budgetary deficits continued to be financed by drawdowns from the RERF. It was feared that the Government's repeated recourse to such drawdowns, estimated at $A37.5m. in 2012 (above the Government's target limit of $A15m.), would be unsustainable in the longer term (see below). However, the budgetary surplus achieved in 2013 enabled the Government to deposit $A17.7m. in the RERF. The country is reliant on foreign assistance for its development budget. Australia is a major provider of development assistance, with emphasis on the management of human resources, training, governance, health, education and improved customs procedures, within the framework of a new co-operation strategy. In 2014/15 aid from Australia was budgeted at $A26.9m. Aid from New Zealand was budgeted at $NZ12m. for 2013/14 and $NZ10m. for 2014/15. Through the ADB, Taiwan has provided aid to finance various development projects, as has Japan. Kiribati's total external debt was estimated by the ADB to total US $19m. in 2013. The cost of debt-servicing was estimated to be the equivalent of 2.6% of the value of exports of goods and services in that year. The annual rate of inflation averaged 0.2% in 2004–13, according to ADB figures. Consumer prices declined by 3.0% in 2012 and by a further 1.5% in 2013, before increasing

by 2.6% in 2014 (largely as a result of higher project-related expenditure). According to the 2010 census, about 30.6% of the labour force were unemployed in that year. Opportunities for formal employment are limited, the majority of jobs available being in the public sector.

With its isolated location and extremely limited export base, Kiribati is one of the world's least developed nations. Its economy is further challenged by a widely dispersed population, overcrowding in urban areas, a vulnerability to economic shocks and, most significantly, by the impact of climate change. Remittances from Kiribati's emigrant workers, the majority of whom have traditionally been seafarers employed on foreign ships, are a vital source of income for many families, but have been decreasing in recent years. Seamen's remittances totalled $A5.6m. in 2014, compared with a peak of $A12.5m. in 2002. The Government aimed to limit the annual drawdown to a maximum of $A15m. in 2011–15. In 2013 the IMF predicted that the real per-head balance of the RERF (estimated at $A4,110 in that year) would be depleted to almost one-half of its 2014 value by 2030, in view of the substantial drawdowns of recent years, as well as losses on investments, such as those in failed Icelandic banks (which cost the country the equivalent of 25% of its annual GDP in 2009). The value of the RERF was reported to have increased slightly to $A668m. in 2013 (equivalent to 381% of GDP), largely as a result of deposits to the Fund made possible by higher fishing licence revenues during 2012–13. The introduction of a value-added tax (VAT) from April 2014 was intended further to improve the fiscal position and therefore mitigate the need for unsustainable drawdowns from the RERF. Substantial offshore assets are also held through the Kiribati Provident Fund. According to the IMF, GDP grew by 2.8% in 2013, driven by infrastructure projects, particularly road building, water and sanitation works, and airport reconstruction, financed by development partners. According to the ADB, the economy expanded by 3.0% in 2014, helped by continuing high levels of revenue from fishing licence fees and by the newly introduced VAT. However, the rate of growth was forecast to decelerate to around 1.5% in 2015 as the various development projects were completed. Following his re-election in 2012, President Anote Tong reiterated his intention to develop the skills of the islands' young people, many of whom would need to seek employment overseas, through the Marine Training Centre and the Technical Institute. A five-year fisheries training programme was introduced in 2013, with assistance from New Zealand, to help achieve this goal. As part of an ongoing attempt to diversify its sources of revenue, the Kiribati Government announced in January 2015 that state-owned company Marawa Research and Exploration Ltd had been granted a 15-year contract by the International Seabed Authority to conduct exploration for deep-sea polymetallic nodules in international waters.

PUBLIC HOLIDAYS

2016: 1 January (New Year), 7 March (for International Women's Day), 25 March (Good Friday), 28 March (Easter Monday), 7 April (National Health Day), 11 July (National Church Day), 15–16 July (National Day Celebrations), 7 August (for Youth Day), 9 December (for Human Rights and Peace Day), 25 December (Christmas), 26 December (Boxing Day).

Statistical Survey

Source (unless otherwise stated): Statistics Office, Ministry of Finance and Economic Development, POB 67, Bairiki, Tarawa; tel. 21082; fax 21307; e-mail statistics@mfep.gov.ki; internet www.spc.int/prism/kiribati.

AREA AND POPULATION

Area: 810.5 sq km (312.9 sq miles). *Principal Atolls* (sq km): Banaba (island) 6.3, Tarawa 31.0 (North 15.3, South 15.8), Abemama 27.4, Tabiteuea 37.6 (North 25.8, South 11.9), Total Gilbert group (incl. others) 285.5; Kanton (Phoenix Is) 9.2, Tabuaeran (Fanning—Line Is) 33.7, Kiritimati (Christmas—Line Is) 388.4, Total Line and Phoenix group (incl. others) 525.0 (Line Is 496.6, Phoenix Is 28.5).

Population: 92,533 at census of 7 November 2005; 103,058 (males 50,796, females 52,262) at census of 7 November 2010. *Principal Atolls* (2010): Banaba (island) 295; Abaiang 5,502; Tarawa 56,284 (North 6,102, South 50,182); Tabiteuea 4,979 (North 3,689, South

1,290); Total Gilbert group (incl. others) 93,791; Kanton (Phoenix Is) 31; Kiritimati 5,586; Total Line and Phoenix Group (incl. others) 9,267. *Mid-2015* (Secretariat of the Pacific Community estimate): 113,438 (Source: Pacific Regional Information System).

Density (mid-2015): 140.0 per sq km.

Population by Age and Sex (Secretariat of the Pacific Community estimates at mid-2015): *0–14 years:* 39,934 (males 20,374, females 19,560); *15–64 years:* 69,511 (males 33,926, females 35,585); *65 years and over:* 3,993 (males 1,540, females 2,453); *Total* 113,438 (males 55,840, females 57,598) (Source: Pacific Regional Information System)

Population by Ethnic Group (2000 census): Micronesians 83,452; Polynesians 641; Europeans 154; Others 247; *Total* 84,494. Note: Classification of ethnicity reflects national census methodology.

Principal Villages (population at 2010 census): Betio 15,755; Bikenibeu 6,568; Teaoraereke 4,171; Bairiki (capital) 3,524; Eita 3,061; Temwaiku 3,135; Bonriki 2,355. Note: All of the listed villages are in South Tarawa atoll.

Births, Marriages and Deaths (Secretariat of the Pacific Community estimates, 2010, unless otherwise indicated): Registered live births 2,774 (birth rate 27.8 per 1,000); Marriages (registrations, 1988) 352 (marriage rate 5.2 per 1,000); Registered deaths 827 (death rate 8.3 per 1,000) (Source: mainly Pacific Regional Information System).

Life Expectancy (years at birth): 68.5 (males 65.8; females 71.4) in 2012. Source: World Bank, World Development Indicators database.

Economically Active Population (persons aged 15 years and over, 2010 census): Agriculture, hunting, forestry and fishing 5,983; Manufacturing 3,563; Electricity, gas and water 271; Construction 535; Trade, restaurants and hotels 4,980; Transport, storage and communications 1,729; Financing, insurance, real estate and business services 805; Public administration 2,021; Education, health and social work 1,298; Other community, social and personal service activities 5,699; Private households with employed persons 64; Extraterritorial organizations and bodies 148; *Total employed* 27,096 (males 15,333, females 11,763); Unemployed 11,938 (males 5,853, females 6,085); *Total labour force* 39,034 (males 21,186, females 17,848). *Mid-2015:* Agriculture, etc. 11,000; Total labour force 53,000 (Source: FAO).

HEALTH AND WELFARE

Key Indicators

Total Fertility Rate (children per woman, 2012): 3.0.

Under-5 Mortality Rate (per 1,000 live births, 2012): 60.

Physicians (per 1,000 head, 2010): 0.4.

Hospital Beds (per 1,000 head, 2010): 1.4.

Health Expenditure (2011): US $ per head (PPP): 257.

Health Expenditure (2011): % of GDP: 10.8.

Health Expenditure (2011): public (% of total): 82.0.

Access to Water (% of persons, 2012): 67.

Access to Sanitation (% of persons, 2012): 40.

Total Carbon Dioxide Emissions ('000 metric tons, 2010): 62.3.

Total Carbon Dioxide Emissions Per Head (metric tons, 2010): 0.6.

Human Development Index (2013): ranking: 133.

Human Development Index (2013): value: 0.607.

For sources and definitions, see explanatory note on p. vi.

AGRICULTURE, ETC.

Principal Crops ('000 metric tons, 2013, FAO estimates): Taro (Cocoyam) 2.0; Other roots and tubers 9.2; Coconuts 170.0; Vegetables 6.3; Bananas 7.0.

Livestock ('000 head, year ending September 2013, FAO estimates): Pigs 14.0; Chickens 610.

Livestock Products (metric tons, 2013, FAO estimates): Pig meat 920; Poultry meat 765; Hen eggs 350.

Fishing (metric tons, live weight, 2012): Capture 82,541* (Emperors 135; Mullets 345; Snappers and jobfishes 505; Jacks and crevalles 431; Skipjack tuna 56,809; Yellowfin tuna 15,232; Other marine fishes 854; Marine molluscs 2,605*); Aquaculture 11; *Total catch* 82,552*. Figures exclude aquatic plants (metric tons): 8,280 (all aquaculture).
* FAO estimate.

Source: FAO.

INDUSTRY

Copra Production (processed, metric tons): 9,686 in 2006; 8,808 in 2007; 9,135 in 2008.

Electric Energy (million kWh): 22 in 2009; 24 in 2010; 24 in 2011.

Sources: Asian Development Bank; UN Industrial Commodity Statistics Database.

FINANCE

Currency and Exchange Rates: Australian currency: 100 cents = 1 Australian dollar ($A). *Sterling, US Dollar and Euro Equivalents*

(31 December 2014): £1 sterling = $A1.903; US $1 = $A1.219; €1 = $A1.480; $A100 = £52.55 = US $82.02 = €67.56. *Average Exchange Rate* (Australian dollars per US $): 0.9658 in 2012, 1.0358 in 2013, 1.1094 in 2014.

Budget (central government operations, $A '000, year ending 31 December 2012): *Revenue:* Current 128,807 (Tax 27,343, Non-tax 101,464); Capital receipts 36; Total 128,843. *Current Expenditure:* General public services 12,651; Public order and safety 9,039; Education 18,964; Health 14,053; Welfare and environment 2,584; Community and culture 2,913; Agriculture, etc. 1,959; Industry 2,350; Transport and communications 2,627; Other 40,180; Total 107,320. Source: Asian Development Bank.

Cost of Living (Consumer Price Index; base: 2000 = 100): All items 108.3 in 2006; 112.9 in 2007; 125.3 in 2008. Source: ILO.

Gross Domestic Product ($A '000 at constant 2006 prices): 152,479 in 2009; 151,719 in 2010; 156,681 in 2011.

Expenditure on the Gross Domestic Product ($A million at current prices, 2013): Government final consumption expenditure 71.2; Private final consumption expenditure 185.2; Gross fixed capital formation 79.9; Change in stocks 0.5; *Total domestic expenditure* 336.8; Exports of goods and services 20.3; *Less* Imports of goods and services 176.3; *GDP in purchasers' values* 180.8. Source: UN National Accounts Main Aggregates Database.

Gross Domestic Product by Economic Activity ($A million at current prices, 2013): Agriculture, hunting, forestry and fishing 46.4; Mining 2.1; Manufacturing 9.6; Construction 5.6; Wholesale and retail trade, hotels and restaurants 14.2; Transport and communications 17.5; Other activities 84.4; *Gross value added* 179.9; Net taxes on products 0.9 (figure obtained as a residual); *GDP in purchasers' values* 180.8. Source: UN National Accounts Main Aggregates Database.

Balance of Payments ($A '000, 2012): Exports of goods 9,841.6; Imports of goods –95,758.9; *Trade balance* –85,917.4.; Exports of services and income 110,683.7; Imports of services and income –83,141.6; *Balance on goods, services and income* –58,375.2; Current transfers received 44,590.8; Current transfers paid –7,062.9; *Current balance* –20,847.3; Capital account (net) 18,131.0; Financial account (net) 5,905.8; Net errors and omissions –4,441.1; *Overall balance* –1,251.5. Source: Asian Development Bank.

EXTERNAL TRADE

Principal Commodities (distribution by HS, US $ '000, 2012): *Imports:* Live animals and animal products 4,029; Vegetables and vegetable products 14,029 (Cereals 8,385); Prepared foodstuffs; beverages, spirits, vinegar; tobacco and articles thereof 17,979 (Tobacco and manufactured tobacco substitutes 5,445); Mineral products 19,533 (Mineral fuels, oils, distillation products, etc. 17,892); Chemicals and related products 3,847; Iron and steel, other base metals and articles of base metal 13,853 (Iron and steel 8,908; Articles of iron or steel 3,830); Machinery and mechanical appliances; electrical equipment; parts thereof 8,666 (Machinery, boilers, etc. 6,053); Vehicles, aircraft, vessels and associated transport equipment 14,218 (Vehicles other than railway, tramway 6,138; Ships, boats and other floating structures 8,043); Total (incl. others) 108,558. *Exports:* Live animals and animal products 946 (Fish, crustaceans, molluscs, aquatic invertebrates, etc. 946); Animal or vegetable fats and oils, and products thereof 3,776; Prepared foodstuffs; beverages, spirits, vinegars; tobacco and articles thereof 353 (Residues, wastes of food industry, animal fodder 194); Machinery and mechanical appliances; electrical equipment; parts thereof 192 (Machinery, oilers, etc. 192); Optical, photo, technical, medical, etc. apparatus 237; Total (incl. others) 5,816. Source: Trade Map-Trade Competitiveness Map, International Trade Centre (www.intracen.org/marketanalysis).

Principal Trading Partners (US $ '000, 2012): *Imports:* Australia 26,443; China, People's Republic 5,336; Fiji 15,126; Hong Kong 1,258; Japan 22,890; New Zealand 7,150; Singapore 16,721; Timor-Leste 1,118; USA 4,295; Total (incl. others) 108,558. *Exports:* Australia 272; Fiji 340; Hong Kong 621; Morocco 2,736; Nauru 100; New Zealand 104; Taiwan 1,186; Viet Nam 362; Total (incl. others) 5,816. Source: Trade Map-Trade Competitiveness Map, International Trade Centre (www.intracen.org/marketanalysis).

TRANSPORT

Road Traffic (vehicles in use, 2008): Passenger cars 9,600; Buses 160; Trucks 4,320; Motorcycles 2,080. Source: IRF, *World Road Statistics*.

Shipping: *Flag Registered Fleet* (at 31 December 2014): Number of vessels 203; Total displacement 581,558 grt. Source: Lloyd's List Intelligence (www.lloydslistintelligence.com).

TOURISM

Foreign Tourist Arrivals: 5,000 in 2011; 5,000 in 2012; 6,000 in 2013 (provisional).

Tourist Arrivals by Country of Residence (2013): Australia 1,060; Germany 62; Japan 216; New Zealand 598; United Kingdom 142; USA 1,335; Total (incl. others) 5,868.

Tourism Receipts (US $ million, excl. passenger transport): 3.2 in 2012.

Source: World Tourism Organization.

COMMUNICATIONS MEDIA

Telephones (main lines in use, 2013): 9,000.

Mobile Cellular Telephones (subscribers, 2013): 17,000.

Broadband Subscribers (2013): 1,100.

Source: International Telecommunication Union.

EDUCATION

Primary (2011): 94 schools; 15,458 students (males 7,735, females 7,723); 628 teachers (males 118, females 510).

Secondary (2011 unless otherwise indicated): 41 schools (2008); 11,514 students (males 5,189, females 6,325); 647 teachers (males 302, females 345).

Teacher-training (2001): 198 students; 22 teachers.

Vocational (2001): 1,303 students; 17 teachers.

Pupil-teacher Ratio (primary education, UNESCO estimate): 25.0 in 2007/08. Source: UNESCO Institute for Statistics.

Adult Literacy Rate (UNESCO estimates): 92.5% (males 93%; females 92%) in 2001. Source: UNESCO, _Assessment of Resources, Best Practices and Gaps in Gender, Science and Technology in Kiribati._

Directory

The Government

HEAD OF STATE

President (Beretitenti): ANOTE TONG (elected 4 July 2003; re-elected 17 October 2007; re-elected 13 January 2012).

Vice-President (Kauoman-ni-Beretitenti): TEIMA ONORIO.

CABINET
(May 2015)

President and Minister of Foreign Affairs and Immigration: ANOTE TONG.

Vice-President and Minister of Internal and Social Affairs: TEIMA ONORIO.

Minister of Public Works and Utilities: WAYSANG KUM KEE.

Minister of Education: MAERE TEKANENE.

Minister of Communications, Transport and Tourism Development: RIMETA BENIAMINA.

Minister of Health and Medical Services: Dr KAUTU TENAUA.

Minister of Environment, Lands and Agricultural Development: TIARITE KWONG.

Minister of Commerce, Industry and Co-operatives: PINTO KATIA.

Minister of Finance and Economic Development: TOM MURDOCH.

Minister of Fisheries and Marine Resource Development: TINIAN REIHER.

Minister of the Line and Phoenix Islands: TAWITA TEMOKU.

Minister of Labour and Human Resource Development: MARTIN MORETI.

Minister of Women, Youth and Social Affairs: TANGARIKI REETE.

Attorney-General: TITABU TABANE.

MINISTRIES

Office of the Attorney-General: POB 62, Bairiki, Tarawa; tel. 21242; fax 21025.

Office of the President (Beretitenti): POB 68, Bairiki, Tarawa; tel. 21183; fax 21145; e-mail info@ob.gov.ki; internet www.president.gov.ki.

Ministry of Commerce, Industry and Co-operatives: POB 510, Betio, Tarawa; tel. 26158; fax 26233; e-mail enquiry@mcic.gov.ki; internet www.mcic.gov.ki.

Ministry of Communications, Transport and Tourism Development: POB 487, Betio, Tarawa; tel. 26003; fax 26193.

Ministry of Education: POB 263, Bikenibeu, Tarawa; tel. 28091; fax 28222; internet www.moe.gov.ki.

Ministry of Environment, Lands and Agricultural Development: POB 234, Bikenibeu, Tarawa; tel. 28211; fax 28334.

Ministry of Finance and Economic Development: POB 67, Bairiki, Tarawa; tel. 21801; fax 21307; e-mail account@mfep.gov.ki; internet www.mfed.gov.ki.

Ministry of Fisheries and Marine Resource Development: POB 64, Bairiki, Tarawa; tel. 21099; fax 21120.

Ministry of Foreign Affairs and Immigration: POB 68, Bairiki, Tarawa; tel. 21342; fax 21466; e-mail mfa@tskl.net.ki.

Ministry of Health and Medical Services: POB 268, Bikenibeu, Tarawa; tel. 28100; fax 28152; e-mail inquiry@health.gov.ki; internet www.health.gov.ki.

Ministry of Internal and Social Affairs: POB 75, Bairiki, Tarawa; tel. 21092; fax 21133; e-mail homeaffairs@tskl.net.ki.

Ministry of Labour and Human Resource Development: POB 69, Bairiki, Tarawa; tel. 21097; fax 21452; internet www.labour.gov.ki.

Ministry of the Line and Phoenix Islands: POB 164, Bairiki, Tarawa; tel. 81211; fax 81278.

Ministry of Public Works and Utilities: POB 498, Betio, Tarawa; tel. 26192; fax 26172.

Ministry of Women, Youth and Social Affairs: POB 267, Bairiki, Tarawa; tel. 22120.

President and Legislature

PRESIDENT

Election, 13 January 2012

Candidate	Votes	% of votes
Anote Tong	14,315	42.20
Tetaua Taitai	11,866	34.98
Rimeta Beniamina	7,738	22.81
Total	33,919	100.00

HOUSE OF ASSEMBLY
(Maneaba Ni Maungatabu)

This is a unicameral body comprising 44 elected members (most of whom formally present themselves for election as independent candidates), and one nominated representative of the Banaban community, along with the Attorney-General in an ex officio capacity (if the latter is not elected). An election was held on 21 October 2011, with a second round of voting being conducted on 28 October. A total of 30 members of the outgoing House of Assembly were re-elected in 2011. Boutokan Te Koaua (Pillars of Truth) secured 15 of the 44 elective seats, while Karikirakean Tei-Kiribati (United Coalition Party) won 10 and the Maurin Kiribati Party three, with the remainder obtained by independents.

Speaker: TAOMATI IUTA.

Election Commission

Election Commission: Tarawa; Electoral Commr RINE UEARA.

Political Organizations

Political organizations in Kiribati are not conventional organized bodies but loose groupings of individuals supporting similar policies. In addition to the groupings listed below, also in existence are the National Progressive Party, led by Teatao Teannaki, and the Liberal Party, led by Tewareka Tentoa.

Boutokan Te Koaua (Pillars of Truth): c/o Maneaba Ni Maungatabu, Tarawa; tel. 21880; fax 21278; mems affiliated to Anote Tong.

Karikirakean Tei-Kiribati (United Coalition Party): c/o Maneaba Ni Maungatabu, Tawara; tel. 21880; fax 21278; f. 2010; est. by merger of Maneaban Te Mauri and Kiribati Tabomoa groupings.

Maurin Kiribati Party: c/o Maneaba Ni Maungatabu, Tawara; Sec. NABUTI MWEMWENIKARAWA.

Diplomatic Representation

EMBASSY AND HIGH COMMISSIONS IN KIRIBATI

Australia: POB 77, Bairiki, Tarawa; tel. 21184; fax 21904; e-mail ahc.tarawa@dfat.gov.au; internet www.kiribati.embassy.gov.au; High Commissioner GEORGE FRASER.

New Zealand: POB 53, Bairiki, Tarawa; tel. 21400; fax 21402; e-mail nzhctarawa@mfat.govt.nz; High Commissioner DONALD JAMES HIGGINS.

Taiwan (Republic of China): POB 104, Bairiki, Tarawa; tel. 22557; fax 22535; e-mail kir@mofa.gov.tw; internet www.taiwanembassy.org/KI; Ambassador ABRAHAM CHU.

Judicial System

There are 24 Magistrates' Courts (each consisting of one presiding magistrate and up to eight other magistrates) hearing civil, criminal and land cases. When hearing civil or criminal cases, the presiding magistrate sits with two other magistrates, and when hearing land cases, with four other magistrates. A single magistrate has national jurisdiction in civil and criminal matters. Appeal from the Magistrates' Courts lies, in civil and criminal matters, to a single judge of the High Court, and, in matters concerning land, divorce and inheritance, to the High Court's Land Division, which consists of a judge and two Land Appeal Magistrates.

The High Court of Kiribati is a superior court of record and has unlimited jurisdiction. It consists of the Chief Justice and a Puisne Judge. Appeal from a single judge of the High Court, both as a Court of the First Instance and in its appellate capacity, lies to the Kiribati Court of Appeal, which is also a court of record and consists of a panel of three judges.

Judicial appointments are made by the Beretitenti (President).

High Court: POB 501, Betio, Tarawa; tel. 26007; fax 26149; Chief Justice Sir JOHN BAPTIST MURIA.

Religion

CHRISTIANITY

Most of the population are Christians: 55.8% Roman Catholic and 33.6% members of the Kiribati Protestant Church, according to the 2010 census.

The Roman Catholic Church

Kiribati forms part of the diocese of Tarawa and Nauru, suffragan to the archdiocese of Suva (Fiji). At 31 December 2007 the diocese contained an estimated 60,686 adherents. The Bishop participates in the Catholic Bishops' Conference of the Pacific, based in Suva (Fiji).

Bishop of Tarawa and Nauru: Most Rev. PAUL EUSEBIUS MEA KAIUEA, Bishop's House, POB 79, Bairiki, Tarawa; tel. 21279; fax 21401; e-mail diocesetarawa@tskl.net.ki.

The Anglican Communion

Kiribati is within the diocese of Polynesia, part of the Anglican Church in Aotearoa, New Zealand and Polynesia. The Bishop in Polynesia is resident in Fiji.

Protestant Church

Kiribati Protestant Church: POB 80, Bairiki, Tarawa; tel. 21195; fax 21453; e-mail kpc@tskl.net.ki; f. 1988; Moderator Rev. BAITEKE NABETARI; Gen. Sec. Rev. MAREWEIA RITETI; over 30,000 mems

Other Churches

Seventh-day Adventist, Church of God and Assembly of God communities are also represented, as is the Church of Jesus Christ of Latter-day Saints (Mormon).

BAHÁ'Í FAITH

National Spiritual Assembly: POB 269, Bikenibeu, Tarawa; tel. and fax 28074; e-mail natbahaikiribati@gmail.com; 2,322 mems, according to 2010 census.

The Press

Butim'aea Manin te Euangkerio: POB 80, Bairiki, Tarawa; tel. 21195; e-mail kpc@tskl.net.ki; f. 1913; Protestant Church newspaper; weekly; a monthly publication *Te Kaotan te Ota* is also produced; Editor Rev. TOOM TOAKAI.

Kiribati Business Link: Bairiki, Tarawa; English.

Kiribati Independent: Tarawa; f. 2011; fortnightly; Editor TABERANNANG KORAUABA; circ. 1,000.

Kiribati Newstar: POB 10, Bairiki, Tarawa; tel. 21652; fax 21671; f. 2000; independent; weekly; English and I-Kiribati; Editor-in-Chief NGAUEA UATIOA.

Te Itoi ni Kiribati: POB 231, Bikenibeu, Tarawa; tel. 28138; fax 21341; f. 1914; Roman Catholic Church newsletter; monthly; circ. 2,300.

Te Mauri: Protestant Church newspaper; Editor BATIRI BATAUA.

Te Uekera: Broadcasting and Publications Authority, POB 78, Bairiki, Tarawa; tel. 21162; fax 21096; e-mail bpa_admin@tskl.net.ki; f. 1945; bi-weekly; English and I-Kiribati; Editor ROOTI TERUBEA; circ. 6,000.

Broadcasting and Communications

TELECOMMUNICATIONS

Telecom Kiribati Ltd: Bairiki, Tarawa; govt-owned; Gen. Man. ENOTA INGINTAU.

Telecom Services Kiribati Ltd: POB 72, Bairiki, Tarawa; tel. 20700; fax 21424; e-mail admin@tskl.net.ki; internet www.tskl.net.ki; f. 1990; Chair. ELLIOT ALI; CEO BARANIKO TONGANIBEIA.

BROADCASTING

Regulatory Authority

Broadcasting and Publications Authority: POB 78, Bairiki, Tarawa; tel. 21187; fax 21096; Gen. Man. BETARIM RIMON.

Radio

Radio Kiribati: Broadcasting and Publications Authority, POB 78, Bairiki, Tarawa; tel. 21187; fax 21096; f. 1954; statutory body; station Radio Kiribati broadcasting on SW and MW transmitters; programmes in I-Kiribati (90%) and English (10%); some advertising; Gen. Man. TANIERI TEIBUAKO.

Television

Television Kiribati Ltd: Betio, Tarawa; tel. 26036; fax 26045; f. 1987; suspended by the Govt in March 2013 owing to financial difficulties; a review to decide whether the closure should be permanent was subsequently initiated; CEO TAOM KAITARA.

Finance

(auth. = authorized; cap. = capital; brs = branches)

BANKING

ANZ Bank (Kiribati) Ltd: POB 66, Bairiki, Tarawa; tel. 21095; fax 21200; e-mail anzkiribati@anz.com; internet www.anz.com/kiribati; f. 1984; fmrly The Bank of Kiribati Ltd, name changed as above 2009; 75% owned by ANZ Bank, 25% by Govt of Kiribati; CEO RUFUS PINTO; 3 brs.

Development Bank of Kiribati: POB 33, Bairiki, Tarawa; tel. 21345; fax 21297; e-mail dbk@tskl.net.ki; internet www.dbk.com.ki; f. 1986; took over the assets of the National Loans Board; identifies, promotes and finances small-scale projects; auth. cap. $A5m.; Gen. Man. KIETAU TABWEBWEITI; 5 brs.

A network of lending entities known as 'village banks' operates throughout the islands, as do a number of credit unions under the management of the Credit Union League.

INSURANCE

Kiribati Insurance Corpn: POB 509, Betio, Tarawa; tel. 253367; fax 25338; e-mail enquire@kic.org.ki; internet www.kic.org.ki; f. 1981; govt-owned; sole insurance co; reinsures overseas; Gen. Man. TONY VAIA.

Trade and Industry

GOVERNMENT AGENCIES

Kiribati Copra Mill Co Ltd: POB 607, Betio, Tarawa; tel. 26831; fax 26635; e-mail kcmc@tskl.net.ki; internet www.kcmcl.ki; f. 2001.

Kiribati Housing Corporation: Bairiki, Tarawa; tel. 21092; operates the Housing Loan and Advice Centre; Chair. TOKOREAUA KAIRORO.

Kiribati Provident Fund: POB 76, Bairiki, Tarawa; tel. 21153; fax 21300; internet www.kpf.com.ki; f. 1977; Chair. TEKIERA ABERA.

CHAMBER OF COMMERCE AND INDUSTRIES

Kiribati Chamber of Commerce and Industries: POB 550, Betio, Tarawa; tel. 26351; fax 26332; e-mail kiribatichamber@gmail.com; internet www.kcci.org.ki; Pres. MARTIN TOFINGA.

UTILITIES

Public Utilities Board: POB 443, Betio, Tarawa; tel. 26292; fax 26106; e-mail ceo.pub@tskl.net.ki; f. 1977; govt-owned; provides electricity, water and sewerage services in Tarawa; CEO TABOIA METUTERA.

Solar Energy Company (SEC): POB 493 Betio, Tarawa; tel. 26058; fax 26210; e-mail sec@tskl.net.ki; a co-operative administering and implementing solar-generated electricity projects in North Tarawa and the outer islands.

CO-OPERATIVE SOCIETIES

Co-operative societies dominate trading in Tarawa and enjoy a virtual monopoly outside the capital, except for Banaba and Kiritimati.

Bobotin Kiribati Ltd (BKL): POB 485, Betio, Tarawa; tel. 26092; fax 26224; replaced Kiribati Co-operative Wholesale Society; govt-owned; Gen. Man. AKAU TIARE.

The Kiribati Copra Co-operative Society Ltd: POB 489, Betio, Tarawa; tel. 26534; fax 26391; e-mail kccs@tskl.net.ki; f. 1976; the sole exporter of copra; 7 cttee mems; 29 mem. socs; Chair. RAIMON TAAKE; CEO RUTIANO BENETITO.

TRADE UNIONS

Kiribati Trades Union Congress (KTUC): POB 166, Bairiki, Tarawa; tel. 28157; fax 28712; e-mail ktc@tskl.net.ki; f. 1982; unions and asscns affiliated to the KTUC include: Fishermen's Union, Co-operative Workers' Union, Seamen's Union, Teachers' Union, Nurses' Asscn, Public Employees' Asscn, Bankers' Union, Butaritari Rural Workers' Union, Christmas Island Union of Federated Workers, Pre-school Teachers' Asscn, Makim Island Rural Workers' Org., Nanolelei Retailers' Union, Plantation Workers' Union of Fanning Island and Overseas Fishermen's Union; 2,500 mems; Pres. TATOA KAITEIE; Gen. Sec. TAMARETI TAAU.

Transport

ROADS

Wherever practicable, roads are built on all atolls, and connecting causeways between islets are also being constructed as funds and labour permit. Kiribati has about 670 km of roads that are suitable for motor vehicles; all-weather roads exist in Tarawa and Kiritimati. In March 2011 it was announced that, with a loan of US $12m. from the Asian Development Bank, the road network in South Tarawa was to be upgraded.

SHIPPING

A major project to rehabilitate the port terminal and facilities at Betio, with finance totalling some US $22m. from Japan, was completed in 2000. There are other port facilities at Banaba, Kanton and English Harbour.

Kiribati Shipping Services Ltd (KSSL): POB 495, Betio, Tarawa; tel. 26195; fax 26204; e-mail kssl@tskl.net.ki; govt-owned; operates 3 passenger/freight vessels on inter-island services connecting Kiribati, Nauru, Tuvalu, the Wallis and Futuna Islands, and Suva (Fiji), and 1 landing craft and multi-purpose cargo vessels between Fiji, Tuvalu, Nauru and Marshall Islands; Gen. Man. Capt. ITIBWINNANG AIAIMOA.

Nikoraoi Shipping: Betio, Tarawa; tel. 26536; fax 26367.

CIVIL AVIATION

There are five international airports (Bonriki on South Tarawa, Cassidy on Kiritimati, Antekana on Butaritari, as well as two others, on Kanton and Tabuaeran) and several other airfields in Kiribati. Air Pacific, the Fijian carrier, operates services to Tarawa and Kiritimati, with links to Nadi (Fiji) and Honolulu (Hawaii, USA).

Air Kiribati Ltd: POB 274, Bonriki, Tarawa; tel. 28533; fax 29716; e-mail admin@airkiribati.net; internet www.airkiribati.net; f. 1977; fmrly Air Tungaru; national airline; operates scheduled services to outer islands; CEO Capt. IOSABATA NAMAKIN.

Tourism

Kiribati's attractions include fishing and bird-watching opportunities, as well as the sites of Second World War battles. In 1997 Caroline Island, situated close to the recently realigned International Date Line, was renamed Millennium Island, in an attempt to maximize its potential for attracting visitors. The Phoenix Islands Protected Area (PIPA), a 408,250-sq km expanse of marine and terrestrial habitats, was inscribed by UNESCO on its World Heritage List in 2010. PIPA contains about 800 species of fauna, including 200 coral species, 500 fish species, 18 marine mammals and 44 bird species. The objectives of the 2010–15 plan for the development of the tourism sector included an increase in the annual number of visitors to 10,000 by the end of the plan period. A campaign to attract more visitors was launched in April 2010. International visitor arrivals increased significantly thereafter, reaching an estimated 6,000 in 2013, largely supported by the Australian, US and New Zealand markets. Tourism receipts totalled US $3.2m. in 2012.

Kiribati National Tourism Office: Ministry of Communications, Transport and Tourism Development, POB 487, Betio, Tarawa; tel. 25573; fax 26193; e-mail info@kiribatitourism.gov.ki; internet www.visit-kiribati.com; Senior Tourist Officer IATAAKE KING.

Defence

Kiribati has no professional defence forces. Assistance is provided by Australia and New Zealand. In 2011 expenditure by Kiribati on the islands' defence totalled $A9.1m. (equivalent to 9.1% of total government spending).

Education

Education is compulsory for children between six and 15 years of age. This generally involves six years at a primary school and at least three years at a secondary school. Every atoll is provided with at least one primary school. In 2011 there were 94 primary schools, with an enrolment of 15,458 students. There were 41 secondary schools in 2008; a total of 11,514 students attended secondary school in 2011. Teaching staff at primary level numbered 628 in 2011; in that year there were 647 secondary school teachers. In 2001/02 enrolment at primary schools reached 97% of pupils in the relevant age-group, according to UNESCO estimates. In 2004/05 enrolment at secondary schools included 69% of students in the relevant age-group, according to UNESCO estimates. The tertiary sector is based on Tarawa, except for one of the two private colleges, which is located on Abemama. The Government administers a technical college and training colleges for teachers, nurses and seafarers (the last, the Marine Training Centre, trains about 200 students each year for employment by overseas shipping companies). There were 198 students enrolled in teacher-training and 1,303 in other vocational training in 2001. An extra-mural centre of the University of the South Pacific (based in Fiji) is also located on South Tarawa. In 2012 government expenditure on education totalled $A19.0m. (equivalent to 17.7% of total expenditure).

THE DEMOCRATIC PEOPLE'S REPUBLIC OF KOREA

Introductory Survey

LOCATION, CLIMATE, LANGUAGE, RELIGION, FLAG, CAPITAL

The Democratic People's Republic of Korea (North Korea) occupies the northern part of the Korean peninsula, bordered to the north by the People's Republic of China and, for a very short section to the north-east, by the Russian Federation, and to the south by the Republic of Korea (South Korea). The climate is continental, with cold, dry winters and hot, humid summers; temperatures range from −6°C to 25°C (21°F to 77°F). The language is Korean. Buddhism, Christianity and Chundo Kyo are officially cited as the principal religions. The national flag (proportions 33 by 65) is red, with blue stripes on the upper and lower edges, each separated from the red by a narrow white stripe. Left of centre is a white disc containing a five-pointed red star. The capital is Pyongyang.

CONTEMPORARY POLITICAL HISTORY

Historical Context

Korea was formerly an independent monarchy. It was occupied by Japanese forces in 1905 and annexed by Japan in 1910, when the Emperor was deposed. Following Japan's surrender in August 1945, ending the Second World War, Korea was divided at latitude 38°N into military occupation zones, with Soviet forces in the North and US forces in the South. A Provisional People's Committee, led by Kim Il Sung of the Korean Communist Party (KCP), was established in the North in February 1946 and accorded government status by the Soviet occupation forces. In July the KCP merged with another group to form the North Korean Workers' Party. In 1947 a legislative body, the Choe Ko In Min Hoe Ui (Supreme People's Assembly—SPA), was established, and Kim Il Sung became Premier. A new Assembly was elected in August 1948, and the Democratic People's Republic of Korea (North Korea) was proclaimed on 9 September. In the same year the Republic of Korea (South Korea) was proclaimed in the South. Initially, North Korea was recognized only by the USSR and other communist countries. Soviet forces withdrew from North Korea in December 1948. In the following year, as a result of a merger between communists in the North and South, the Korean Workers' Party (KWP) was formed, under the leadership of Kim Il Sung. The KWP continued to hold power in North Korea in the second decade of the 21st century.

The two republics each claimed to have legitimate jurisdiction over the whole Korean peninsula. North Korean forces crossed the 38th parallel in June 1950, precipitating a three-year war between North and South. The UN mounted a collective defence action in support of South Korea, and the invasion was repelled. North Korean forces were supported by the People's Republic of China from October 1950. The heavy bombardment of the North resulted in a high number of civilian casualties. Peace talks began in July 1951 and an armistice agreement was concluded in July 1953. The ceasefire line, which approximately followed the 38th parallel, became the frontier between North and South Korea, with a demilitarized zone (DMZ), supervised by UN forces, separating the two countries. No final peace agreement was concluded, and North and South Korea remained technically at war.

Domestic Political Affairs

Through the 'personality cult' of Kim Il Sung (the 'Great Leader') and of his son Kim Jong Il (the 'Dear Leader'), and a policy of strict surveillance of the entire population, overt opposition to the KWP was effectively eliminated. The only organized opposition to the regime (albeit in exile) appeared to be the Salvation Front for the Democratic Unification of Chosun, established by former military and other officials of North Korea in the early 1990s, with branches in Russia, Japan and China. International human rights organizations indicated that they believed there to be a number of concentration camps in North Korea, in which many thousands of political prisoners were being held (see *Humanitarian Issues*).

A new Constitution, adopted in December 1972, created the office of President, and Kim Il Sung was duly elected to the post. Kim Jong Il was appointed to several key positions within the KWP in 1980. In July 1984 Radio Pyongyang referred to Kim Jong Il, for the first time, as the 'sole successor' to his father, but there were reports of opposition to the President's heir, particularly among older members of the KWP.

Following elections to the eighth SPA, in November 1986 (when the 655 members were returned unopposed), Kim Il Sung was re-elected President, and a new Administration Council (cabinet) was formed. In March 1990 Kim Il Sung was returned to the post of President, and Kim Jong Il was appointed to his first state (as distinct from party) post, as First Vice-Chairman of the National Defence Commission. In February 1991 it was rumoured that there had been an unsuccessful military coup against Kim Jong Il. In December he was appointed Supreme Commander of the Korean People's Army (KPA), in place of his father, and in January 1992 he was reported to have been given control of foreign policy. In April Kim Jong Il was appointed to the rank of Marshal, while his father assumed the title of Grand Marshal.

In what was interpreted as a partial attempt to adapt to the change in international conditions following the collapse of communist regimes worldwide, the SPA (according to South Korean reports) made several amendments to North Korea's Constitution in April 1992. Principal among these were the deletion of all references to Marxism-Leninism, and the promotion of 'economic openness' to allow limited foreign investment in North Korea (although the KWP's guiding principle of *Juche*, or self-reliance, was strongly emphasized). In September measures to address the deteriorating economic situation included a drastic devaluation of the national currency. At the fifth session of the ninth SPA in April 1993 Kim Jong Il was elected Chairman of the National Defence Commission. In July Kim Il Sung's younger brother, Kim Yong Ju, unexpectedly returned to political life after a 17-year absence, and was subsequently elevated to the position of Vice-President and to membership of the Central Committee of the KWP's Political Bureau (Politburo).

The death of Kim Il Sung and rise of Kim Jong Il

Kim Il Sung died of heart failure on 8 July 1994. One hundred days of national mourning were observed, but, contrary to expectations, Kim Jong Il was not appointed to the leading post of President of North Korea. Kim Jong Il did not appear in public during this period, reviving earlier speculation that he was either in poor health or that a struggle for power was taking place. It was thought that Kim Song Ae, the widow of Kim Il Sung and stepmother of Kim Jong Il, favoured her eldest son, Kim Pyong Il, for the presidency. In February 1995 the Minister of the People's Armed Forces, Marshal O Jin U, died; O had been a significant supporter within the military of Kim Jong Il's succession. Scheduled elections to the SPA did not take place in April 1995, and no session of the Assembly was convened in 1996.

Meanwhile, from the mid-1990s, the influence of the KPA expanded significantly, as Kim Jong Il increasingly relied upon the military to maintain his hold on power, and the policy of *Songun* ('military first') was emphasized as the regime's central doctrine. The 50th anniversary of the establishment of the KWP in October 1995 was dominated by the military rather than the party, and several generals were promoted. However, Kim Jong Il did not assume any new posts. In February 1996 Sung Hye Rim, a former consort of Kim Jong Il and mother of his eldest son, Kim Jong Nam, defected to Western Europe. In February 1997 Premier Kang Song San, who had made no public appearance since early 1996, was dismissed, and replaced on an acting basis by Hong Song Nam. Deepening social unrest was indicated by an increase in the rate of defections. In February 1997 Hwang Jang Yop, a close adviser to Kim Jong Il, sought political asylum in the

South Korean embassy in China while returning from an official visit to Japan, and warned that North Korea was preparing to launch a military assault on South Korea. Hwang's defection appeared to precipitate significant changes in the KWP and military high command, as did the deaths of the Minister of the People's Armed Forces, Marshal Choe Kwang, and of his deputy, Kim Kwang Jin. Many senior officials were replaced, and some 123 generals, including many allies of Kim Jong Il, were promoted in rank in April. In August two senior North Korean diplomats, including the ambassador to Egypt, defected to the USA. There were also rumours of unrest and coup attempts, and several senior officials disappeared from public view without explanation. The official mourning period for Kim Il Sung was formally declared to be at an end in July 1997, on the third anniversary of his death. It was announced that, henceforth, the country was to use the *Juche* calendar, with 1912, the year of Kim Il Sung's birth, designated the first year of the new calendar. On 8 October 1997 Kim Jong Il was elected General Secretary of the KWP.

Elections to the SPA finally took place in July 1998, at which the single list of candidates received 100% of the votes cast. Some two-thirds of the 687 deputies were newcomers to the Assembly, while the military reportedly doubled its representation. The first session of the 10th SPA was convened in September. However, the anticipated appointment of Kim Jong Il as President of North Korea did not occur, as the post was effectively abolished under major amendments to the Constitution that extensively revised the structure of government. The deceased Kim Il Sung was designated 'Eternal President', thus remaining *de jure* head of state, while Kim Jong Il, who had been re-elected Chairman of the National Defence Commission (now apparently the highest office in the state hierarchy), was reported to have assumed the role of de facto head of state. Vice-Marshal Jo Myong Rok, the Director of the General Political Bureau of the KPA, was appointed First Vice-Chairman of the National Defence Commission, becoming the de facto second-ranking official in North Korea. The Cabinet, as the Administration Council was redesignated, assumed many of the functions of the Central People's Committee, which was abolished. A new Presidium of the SPA was established, the President of which was to represent the state in diplomatic affairs; Kim Yong Nam, hitherto Minister of Foreign Affairs, was appointed to this position. Hong Song Nam was formally appointed Premier of the new Cabinet. Jo Chang Dok and Kwak Pom Gi were appointed as Vice-Premiers.

In October 2000 the Minister of Finance, Rim Kyong Suk, and the President of the Central Bank of North Korea, Jong Song Thaek, were dismissed. They were replaced, respectively, by Mun Il Bong and Kim Wan Su. The replacement of the Minister of Foreign Trade in December was similarly unexplained. The Minister of Agriculture was replaced in March 2001.

In January 2001 the Government urged a 'new way of thinking' to address the country's economic problems and to complement the *Kangsong Taeguk* ('prosperous and powerful nation') philosophy. Meanwhile, the number of people defecting from the North to the South continued to increase, bringing the total to 650 since 1996. At the fifth session of the 10th SPA held in March 2002, a new land planning law was adopted. Premier Hong Song Nam also urged improved trade and economic co-operation, including joint ventures with other countries. In April Kim Jong Il promoted some 55 military leaders, including Jang Song U, the elder brother of Kim's brother-in-law, Jang Song Thaek.

The question of the succession of the next generation of leadership became increasingly important following Kim Jong Il's 60th birthday in February 2002. Kim was initially believed to have been preparing his eldest son, Kim Jong Nam, who had served in the Ministry of Public Security and as head of the country's information technology industry since the late 1990s; however, in May 2001 he was detained in Tokyo, Japan, on charges of entering that country with a false passport, and subsequently deported to China. Thenceforth it was reported that Kim Jong Il was preparing for leadership Kim Jong Chol, the elder son of Ko Yong Hui, described as Kim Jong Il's unofficial wife.

In September 2002 the Government designated the city of Sinuiju, close to the Chinese border and connected by road and rail bridge to the Chinese city of Dandong, a 'Special Administrative Region' designed to attract foreign investment. However, by 2004 plans to develop Sinuiju as an experiment in market economy appeared to have been largely abandoned. In late 2002 the Government also established a special industrial zone in Kaesong, with South Korean investment, and a special tourist zone in the region of Mount Kumgang, although these did not have the same special status as Sinuiju. A meeting of senior law enforcement officials was held in Pyongyang in December during which Premier Hong urged the elimination of 'non-socialist elements'. In early 2003 it was reported that travel restrictions within the country had been reintroduced.

Kim Jong Il did not attend the sixth session of the 10th SPA, held in March 2003. Having reportedly disappeared from public view for 50 days, Kim reappeared in April. Celebrations took place in July to commemorate the 50th anniversary of the Korean War truce (celebrated as a triumph for North Korea by the country's media). In August elections were held to form the 11th SPA. Voter turnout was reported to be have been 99.9%, and all 687 candidates were elected unopposed. At the first session of the 11th SPA in September, Kim Jong Il was re-elected as Chairman of the National Defence Commission. The appointment of Pak Pong Ju, hitherto Minister of Chemical Industry, as Premier was endorsed.

In July 2004 Ju Sang Song was appointed as Minister of People's Security, replacing Choe Ryong Su. Choe had been removed from his post only one year after being appointed, and the reason for his removal was unclear. There were tentative suggestions throughout 2004 that a power struggle was taking place in Pyongyang. It was believed that in April Kim had removed his brother-in-law, Jang Song Thaek, from his position as vice-director of the KWP Central Committee and placed him under house arrest. Later in the year Jang's wife, Kim Jong Il's sister Kim Kyong Hui, was injured in a traffic incident, which was believed to have been a deliberate attack. Meanwhile, in April Kim Jong Il's eldest son, Kim Jong Nam, reportedly survived an assassination attempt in Austria.

In May 2005 South Korean media reported that the North Korean Minister of Post and Telecommunications, Ri Kum Bom, had been dismissed, apparently as a result of his failure to control the revelation of information earlier in the year disclosing that North Korea was in the process of combating outbreaks of avian influenza ('bird flu'). In October the 60th anniversary of the KWP was celebrated with a national meeting in Pyongyang, at which the primacy of the *Songun* policy was reaffirmed, as was the need for economic development in order to achieve the objective of *Kangsong Taeguk*. In January 2006 Jang Song Thaek made his first public appearance since 2003, prompting speculation that he had been rehabilitated following his apparent removal from favour in 2004.

At the fifth session of the 11th SPA in April 2007, Premier Pak Pong Ju was replaced by Kim Yong Il, hitherto Minister of Land and Marine Transport. Although no official explanation was given, observers later suggested that Pak had unsuccessfully attempted to introduce economic reforms, including allowing greater autonomy for state enterprises. At the same time Vice-Marshal Kim Yong Chun, hitherto Chief of General Staff of the KPA, was appointed as a Vice-Chairman of the National Defence Commission, filling the vacancy left by the death of Yon Hyong Muk in October 2005. Gen. Kim Kyok Sik became the new KPA Chief of General Staff. The permanent staff of the National Defence Commission was expanded as part of a further reorganization of senior military officials in May 2007, with the appointment of Gen. Ri Myong Su, the former operations director of the KPA, as a standing member. The changes at the National Defence Commission were generally interpreted as an attempt to enhance its role and powers. Rumours suggesting that Kim Jong Il's health was deteriorating prompted renewed speculation regarding his successor, which intensified in August following reports that Kim's eldest son, Kim Jong Nam, had returned from exile to work in the organization and guidance bureau of the KWP. In November it was reported that Jang Song Thaek had been promoted from the position of vice-director within the KWP to the directorship of the party's department responsible for state internal security, while Kim Jong Il's second eldest son, Kim Jong Chol, had been appointed as a vice-director of another department of the KWP.

The future leadership question

Several government changes were reported to have been implemented at senior level in 2008–09. Meanwhile, elections to the new SPA, originally due to be held in August 2008, were postponed, thereby further increasing speculation about the health of Kim Jong Il, who failed to attend a parade commemorating the country's 60th anniversary in September and was not seen in public for three months subsequently. Although he had resumed his public duties by the beginning of 2009, Kim Jong Il did not appear to be in robust health, and it was widely concluded that he had suffered a stroke.

In January 2009 it was announced that the elections for the 12th SPA would take place on 8 March. A total of 687 candidates were duly elected unopposed; 316 deputies were reported to be entering the SPA for the first time, fewer than the number of new members elected in 2003. The level of voter participation was declared to have been 99.98%. Observers noted that the list of incoming deputies included none of Kim Jong Il's three sons, the youngest of whom, Kim Jong Un (the younger son of Ko Yong Hui), had become the subject of much speculation with regard to the succession issue. In February 2009 Gen. Ri Yong Ho replaced Kim Kyok Sik as KPA Chief of General Staff. Various changes to the leadership were effected at the first session of the SPA, which opened on 9 April. Notable appointments were those of Kim Wan Su as Minister of Finance and Ri Kwang Gon as President of the Central Bank, who exchanged responsibilities. Ro Tu Chol remained as a Vice-Premier, in addition being appointed as Chairman of the State Planning Commission. O Su Yong relinquished the electronics industry portfolio upon his appointment as a Vice-Premier, in place of Jon Sung Hun. Kim Jong Il's influential brother-in-law, Jang Song Thaek, became a member of the National Defence Commission, of which Vice-Marshal O Kuk Ryol (a former Chief of General Staff of the KPA) was appointed a Vice-Chairman, as was the Minister of the People's Armed Forces, Vice-Marshal Kim Yong Chun. Also joining the National Defence Commission were Gen. U Tong Chuk Chuk (the deputy director of the State Security Agency) and Ju Kyu Chang, a senior party official and aide of Kim Jong Il.

Also in April 2009 the SPA adopted the text of a revised Constitution (although this was not published until the end of September): for the first time, the charter gave official recognition to the Chairman of the National Defence Commission (the post held by Kim Jong Il) as the 'supreme leader' of the nation, and added a reference to *Songun* alongside *Juche* as guiding principles. In June South Korean media quoted intelligence reports that Kim Jong Un had formally been declared his father's successor; however, this was not confirmed in the North Korean state media, and it appeared possible that Kim Jong Un's youth (he was believed to be only 27 or 28 years of age) would be an obstacle to his acceptance by the political establishment.

In December 2009 the Government announced a revaluation of the currency, obliging North Koreans to exchange existing banknotes for new notes worth 1% of the old currency. A limit on the amount per family that could be exchanged meant that savings above a modest level became worthless. The aim of the revaluation was apparently to reduce inflation and to eliminate profiteering by unofficial traders; however, it resulted in price rises, disruption to the distribution of goods, and food shortages. Furthermore, there were reports of considerable public resentment. In February 2010 it was reported that the official responsible for the revaluation, Pak Nam Gi (the director of the KWP's department for planning and finance), had been dismissed, and in March he was reported to have been executed.

In May 2010 the Government condemned as a 'fabrication' a report by international experts that concluded that the sinking of a South Korean naval vessel in March had been caused by a North Korean torpedo (see *Inter-Korean Relations*), leading to speculation by observers that the attack might have been perpetrated by officers who had not been duly authorized, or alternatively that the attack had been deliberately ordered by the Government in an attempt to associate the possible future leader, Kim Jong Un, with a successful military action.

In an unusual development, after its regular meeting in April 2010 the SPA convened for a second session in June, when the appointment of Choe Yong Rim (hitherto chief secretary of the KWP's Pyongyang city committee) as Premier was announced, replacing Kim Yong Il, possibly because the latter had presided over the unsuccessful currency revaluation at the end of the previous year. Six new Vice-Premiers were appointed and three recalled; several cabinet portfolios were reallocated. The appointments as Vice-Premier included that of Jo Pyong Ju, retaining his previous post as Minister of Machine-building Industries, and Han Kwang Bok, retaining her previous post as Minister of the Electronics Industry; the four other new Vice-Premiers were Kang Nung Su (hitherto chairman of the State Film Commission), Kim Rak Hui, Ri Tae Nam and Jon Ha Chol (senior KWP officials reportedly specializing in agricultural management, steel production and financial planning, respectively). Other appointments were to the ministries responsible for light industry (An Song Ju), the foodstuff and daily necessities

industry (Jo Yong Chol), and physical culture and sports (Pak Myong Chol). The promotion of Jang Song Thaek, Kim Jong Il's brother-in-law, to the powerful position of a Vice-Chairman of the National Defence Commission was also announced. Both Jang and Choe Yong Rim were reported to be supporters of Kim Jong Un as a successor to his father.

In August 2010 former Premier Pak Pong Ju was described as a First Deputy Director of the KWP Central Committee, having apparently been reinstated after his demotion in 2007; Pak was believed to be a close ally of Jang Song Thaek. In September 2010 Kang Sok Ju, a cousin of Kim Jong Il and hitherto the Vice-Minister of Foreign Affairs, was promoted to Vice-Premier, while two senior negotiators in the six-nation talks on North Korea's nuclear policy, Kim Kye Gwan and Ri Yong Ho (as distinct from Gen. Ri, the Chief of General Staff of the armed forces), became Vice-Ministers of Foreign Affairs. Later in September a delegates' conference of the KWP was convened, the first such meeting since 1980. Widespread speculation that the conference would be the setting for the official appearance of Kim Jong Un as Kim Jong Il's heir appeared to be confirmed when, shortly beforehand, Kim Jong Un (who had no record of military service) was awarded the rank of general. The same rank was conferred on Kim Kyong Hui (the sister of Kim Jong Il and wife of Jang Song Thaek), and on two other civilians: Choe Ryong Hae (whose father, Choe Hyon, had been a close colleague of Kim Il Sung), and Kim Kyong Ok (deputy director of the KWP's organization and guidance department).

At the conference itself, Kim Jong Il was re-elected General Secretary of the KWP. Kim Jong Un was appointed a Vice-Chairman of the KWP's Central Military Commission (a newly created post), and a member of the party's Central Committee; however, he was not given membership of the Politburo or the National Defence Commission. The KPA Chief of General Staff, Gen. Ri Yong Ho, was promoted to the rank of Vice-Marshal and became a member of the Presidium of the Politburo, and was also, alongside Kim Jong Un, appointed a Vice-Chairman of the KWP's Central Military Commission. Jang Song Thaek was elected an alternate member of the Politburo and a member of the KWP's Central Military Commission, while his wife, Kim Kyong Hui, was also elected to the KWP's Politburo. Reports and photographs of Kim Jong Un published after the conference were believed to represent the first time that he had been mentioned by name in the North Korean media.

The 'Young General', as Kim Jong Un was now often called, appeared with Kim Jong Il at a large military parade held in Pyongyang in October 2010 to celebrate the 65th anniversary of the KWP, and was subsequently reported to be accompanying his father on various official visits. In November Kim Jong Un was reported to be in charge of an investigation into corrupt officials. In the same month Vice-Marshal Jo Myong Rok, the Director of the KPA General Political Bureau and First Vice-Chairman of the National Defence Commission, died, and there was speculation that Kim Jong Un might shortly be appointed to the latter post. Observing the year's events, analysts generally concluded that, in the event of Kim Jong Il's death or incapacity, while Kim Jong Un might be his nominal successor, the latter's youth and inexperience would mean that real power would be exercised collectively by older party members, in particular Jang Song Thaek, Kim Kyong Hui, and Vice-Marshal Ri Yong Ho.

In January 2011 Yi Kyong Sik replaced Kim Chang Sik as Minister of Agriculture, a post Yi was reported to have held previously between 2003 and 2008. Following a meeting of the SPA in April 2011 there were, contrary to expectations, no announcements of any new appointment for Kim Jong Un. A Vice-Premier, Ri Tae Nam, left his post for reasons of health. Ri Myong Su was appointed as Minister of People's Security, a position vacated in March by Ju Sang Song, also reportedly owing to ill health. Pak To Chun, an alternate member of the KWP Politburo, joined the membership of the National Defence Commission, replacing Jon Pyong Ho who was transferred to another post. In September Kim Sok Jun was reported to have replaced Pae Tae Jun as Minister of Land Development and Construction Affairs.

Recent developments: the succession of Kim Jong Un

Kim Jong Il died suddenly of heart failure on 17 December 2011. His death was followed by widespread public demonstrations of grief. Kim Jong Un was immediately described as the 'great successor' by the official media, and at his father's funeral ceremonies he was described as 'supreme leader of the party, the armed forces and the people' by the titular head of state, Kim Yong Nam. Kim Jong Un's uncle by marriage, Jang Song Thaek, was observed to be in close attendance during the ceremonies (unprecedentedly wearing military uniform, with insignia indicating that he had been awarded the rank of general). A meeting of the Politburo in late December was reported to have confirmed Kim Jong Un as Supreme Commander of the KPA. Official pronouncements during the early weeks of Kim Jong Un's leadership emphasized continuity and the maintenance of the *Songun* policy. In March 2012, however, South Korean media reported that, in an apparent purge, some senior North Korean military officers had been executed.

A KWP conference was convened in April 2012, at which Kim Jong Un was appointed to the newly created post of First Secretary of the party, while his deceased father, Kim Jong Il, was designated Eternal General Secretary. Kim Jong Un was also appointed Chairman of the party's Central Military Commission and elected to the Presidium of the Politburo. Choe Ryong Hae, of late promoted to the rank of Vice-Marshal, and reported as having recently been appointed (although he was a civilian) to the influential position of Director of the KPA General Political Bureau in succession to the late Jo Myong Rok, now became a Vice-Chairman of the KWP's Central Military Commission, and was also elected to the Presidium of the Politburo. (Besides Kim Jong Un and Choe Ryong Hae, the Presidium's other three members were Kim Yong Nam, Choe Yong Rim, the Premier, and Vice-Marshal Ri Yong Ho.) Two days later the transfer of power to Kim Jong Un was consolidated when a session of the SPA appointed him First Chairman of the National Defence Commission, in practice regarded as the highest office in the state hierarchy (with the late Kim Jong Il being designated Eternal Chairman); Choe Ryong Hae became a member of the National Defence Commission, as did Ri Myong Su, the Minister of People's Security. Also in April, as part of the celebrations to mark the 100th anniversary of the birth of Kim Il Sung, North Korea defied international protests and launched a long-range rocket, ostensibly with the intention of putting a satellite into orbit. It was widely suspected (as on previous occasions) that the operation was in fact intended to test long-range missile technology. The launch was promoted in North Korea as a symbol of the country's technological advances, but in the event the rocket was reported by US and South Korean agencies to have broken up shortly after take off and fallen into the sea. In an unusual admission of failure, the North Korean authorities confirmed that the satellite had indeed failed to go into orbit. The Government reacted indignantly to international condemnation of the launch, and throughout 2012 it maintained its traditionally belligerent attitude towards South Korea and the USA (see *Inter-Korean Relations* and *Foreign Affairs*).

During 2012 the official North Korean media encouraged public adulation of Kim Jong Un similar to that directed at his father and grandfather, although he appeared to be cultivating a more informal and affable image, sometimes appearing in the company of his wife, Ri Sol Ju. In July the sudden removal of Vice-Marshal Ri Yong Ho from all his political and military posts, officially due to illness, gave rise to speculation that Ri Yong Ho had objected to the increasing prominence of Choe Ryong Hae, and that Kim Jong Un (who assumed the rank of Marshal shortly afterwards) was attempting to exert his own authority over the armed forces. A little-known army general, Hyon Yong Chol, replaced Ri as Chief of General Staff of the KPA. In November Vice-Marshal Kim Jong Gak, who had replaced Vice-Marshal Kim Yong Chun as Minister of the People's Armed Forces in April, was reported to have been replaced in his turn by Gen. Kim Kyok Sik, hitherto First Vice-Minister in the same department and reputed to favour a confrontational attitude to South Korea. It was observed that the state media gave greater prominence to economic affairs during 2012, and in August it was reported that a number of reforms had been announced, including permitting farmers to keep and sell 30% of their output and allowing manufacturers to set their own prices; however, it was not clear whether these changes were already being implemented.

The North Korean Government again defied international opinion by launching another long-range rocket, ostensibly bearing a satellite (this time with apparent success) in December 2012 and by conducting a third test of a nuclear device in February 2013, encouraging public celebrations of both events. The Government's extremely bellicose reaction to joint military exercises by South Korean and US forces in March and April also appeared to have the aim of increasing domestic support in the face of supposed external threats: mass rallies were held in Pyongyang and other cities, denouncing the exercises and the UN Security Council's recent intensification of sanctions against North Korea (see *Fluctuating tensions on the Korean peninsula*). In February, meanwhile, the Minister of People's Security, Gen. Ri Myong Su, was removed from office and subsequently from the Politburo and the National Defence Commission: his ministerial position was assigned to Gen. Choe Pu Il (formerly director of the operations bureau of the KPA General Staff). In April the Premier, Choe Yong Rim, was replaced by Pak Pong Ju (who had held the office in 2003–07), among other ministerial changes unspecified at the time; in the same month a new Ministry of the Atomic Energy Industry was created.

In May 2013 there were yet more changes in senior military positions: another new Minister of the People's Armed Forces took office, when the reputedly bellicose Gen. Kim Kyok Sik was replaced by a little-known general, Jang Jong Nam. Gen. Kim Kyok Sik replaced Hyon Yong Chol as Chief of General Staff of the KPA in the same month (a post which he had previously held in 2007–09), but in August he himself was replaced by Gen. Ri Yong Gil (who had succeeded Gen. Choe Pu Il at the head of the KPA General Staff operations bureau). By the end of 2013, according to South Korean sources, Kim Jong Un had replaced some 44% of the DPRK's 218 most senior military and administrative officials since assuming power. The most dramatic dismissal occurred in December, when Jang Song Thaek was arrested, summarily tried for treason, and executed. The state media published unusually detailed accounts of Jang's alleged crimes: he was accused of corruption and 'factionalism' and of having planned to seize power with the help of senior military officers. Jang had been regarded as favouring economic reforms similar to those undertaken by China, thus observers speculated that his downfall had been linked to competition between the armed forces and Jang's associates for control of lucrative enterprises, particularly fisheries and coal exports. In the accompanying purge, members of Jang's family were reportedly killed, although it was not clear what had happened to his (possibly estranged) wife, Kim Jong Un's aunt, Kim Kyong Hui; numerous officials associated with the enterprises that Jang had supervised, particularly in the country's special economic zones (see *Economic Affairs*), were also reported to have been removed from their posts. Gen. O Kuk Ryol (one of the Vice-Chairmen of the National Defence Commission) was reported to have assumed control of many of Jang's economic responsibilities. New ministers of the coal industry and of the metal industry were mentioned in the media, having apparently been appointed after Jang's execution.

An election to the SPA took place on 9 March 2014: 99.97% of the registered electorate were reported to have participated, and, as before, 687 deputies were elected unopposed: they included Kim Jong Un in the constituency of Mount Paektu. Those listed as having been elected included (contrary to expectations) several senior figures previously regarded as close associates of Jang. However, a number of veteran military personnel were no longer on the list. The first session of the 13th SPA was convened on 9 April, when changes in the National Defence Commission and the Cabinet were disclosed. The strong political standing of Vice-Marshal Choe Ryong Hae, who was regarded as having replaced Jang as the de facto second most powerful member of the Government, was reinforced by his appointment as a Vice-Chairman of the National Defence Commission. The Assembly approved the appointment of Ri Su Yong (a former ambassador to Switzerland) as Minister of Foreign Affairs, and of a number of other apparently recently nominated ministers, including those responsible for electric power, transport, machine-building, posts and telecommunications, education and culture; the number of Vice-Premiers listed was reduced from nine to four. It was noted at this time that Kim Jong Un's younger sister, Kim Yo Jong, had reappeared in the leader's entourage; her role was described as that of a 'senior official' within the ruling party, and her position was confirmed in November as vice-director in the propaganda and agitation department of the KWP. (Furthermore, in January 2015 it was reported that Kim Yo Jong had strengthened her political status through marrying one of Choe Ryong Hae's sons.) In late April 2014 Choe Ryong Hae was succeeded as Director of the KPA's General Political Bureau by Hwang Pyong So, the vice-director of the organization and guidance department of the KWP (at the same time Hwang was also reportedly promoted to the rank of Vice-Marshal). Choe's departure in the same month from his position as a Vice-Chairman of the KWP's Central Military Commission and his replacement as a Vice-Chairman of the National Defence Commission by Hwang after only five months in the post prompted speculation that Hwang had supplanted Choe (who had also apparently been demoted to the rank of General) as the regime's second-in-command. However, this speculation appeared to be refuted in November when the official news agency announced that Choe was to visit Russia as a special envoy of Kim Jong Un. Meanwhile, in June state media reported that former Chief of General Staff Hyon Yong Chol had replaced Jang Jong Nam as Minister of the People's Armed Forces. Diplomatic activity intensified in the second half of 2014, with Kang Sok Ju, the secretary and director of the KWP's international affairs department, heading a delegation to Germany, Belgium, Switzerland and Italy, and Minister of Foreign Affairs Ri Su Yong visiting Iran and the UN General Assembly in New York, USA. Speculation about Kim Jong Un's health arose as a result of his absence from public events for a six-week period in September and October. (South Korean news sources subsequently claimed that he had been unable to carry out his public duties owing to a leg injury.) At the end of October all foreign tourism to North Korea was suspended until March 2015, and quarantine arrangements for foreign nationals put in place, over fears of the spread of the Ebola Virus Disease.

In December 2014 it was announced that the Government had imposed a ban on North Korean citizens sharing the name of Kim Jong Un (as had been the case with the names of his father and grandfather). In the same month, North Korea marked the official end of a three-year period of mourning for former leader Kim Jong Il. International pressure on the regime continued to mount in December, with North Korea being accused of launching cyber-attacks on the US company Sony Pictures Entertainment (see *Foreign Affairs*) and on the South Korean nuclear power operator (see *Inter-Korean Relations*). In the same month the UN General Assembly approved a non-binding resolution urging the UN Security Council to refer North Korea to the International Criminal Court for alleged human rights violations (see *Humanitarian Issues*). In December 2014 and January 2015, amid reports that since May 2014 a second round of purges of associates of Jang Song Thaek had been carried out, with an estimated 50 people being expelled from Pyongyang or executed, a number of new military appointments were announced, including the replacement in December of Col-Gen. Ri Pyong Chol as commander of the KPA's air and anti-air forces by SPA member Lt-Gen. Choe Yong Ho; Ri, who had been elected to the National Defence Commission in September, was widely expected to be given a high-ranking post in the Central Committee of the KWP. In early April 2015 Hwang Pyong So's status as the regime's second most powerful official appeared to be confirmed by his promotion to become the fourth member of the Presidium of the Politburo of the KWP. Although Choe Ryong Hae remained an important political figure in his capacity as a member of the Presidium of the Politburo and of the secretariat of the KWP, his recent departure from several high-ranking military posts (two of which were subsequently filled by Hwang) appeared to confirm his declining influence.

Humanitarian Issues

During the 1990s intermittent severe flooding interspersed with drought exacerbated food shortages in North Korea. Humanitarian assistance was provided by China, the USA, South Korea and Japan. (Subsequent provision of aid fluctuated in accordance with political developments: see *Inter-Korean Relations* and *Foreign Affairs*). In 1997 and 1998 the UN's World Food Programme (WFP, see p. 108) issued appeals for food and medical supplies. UN representatives sent to North Korea to assess the extent of the crisis confirmed that chronic malnutrition was widespread, and that the medical system was no longer able to provide even basic health care. In 1998 agreement was reached with North Korea whereby additional UN staff were to be permitted to enter the country in order to monitor the distribution of aid, following allegations that previous supplies had been diverted to the army.

From 2000 intermittent severe weather conditions, including both drought and flooding, exacerbated the situation. A survey conducted by WFP in 2004 concluded that 37% of North Korean children aged six years and under were chronically malnourished. In September 2005, however, the North Korean Government announced that, following a successful harvest, it had asked humanitarian aid agencies operating in North Korea to terminate food aid programmes and withdraw the majority of their foreign staff, and expressed a desire to progress from humanitarian to developmental aid. (Analysts speculated that the Government of North Korea preferred to rely on food aid from China and South Korea, as the distribution of aid from these countries was monitored less closely and the political

implications of allowing Westerners access to the country were thereby avoided.)

Severe flooding in July 2006 prompted the North Korean Government to seek further humanitarian aid, but donor nations (including South Korea) expressed reluctance to give aid to North Korea following its missile tests in July and October. After further flooding in August 2007 the UN and the Red Cross launched international appeals for funding. South Korea resumed deliveries of fertilizer to the North in March and of food aid in June. In April 2008 WFP warned of a humanitarian crisis, the food deficit for the coming year having been revised upwards to 1.66m. metric tons, more than double that of the previous year: in March 2009, however, it was revealed that WFP operations in the country had been substantially scaled down, owing to serious funding difficulties, and that aid had reached only 15% of the extent originally planned. The revaluation of the currency in December led to further hardship, with widespread food shortages being reported.

In August and September 2010 heavy flooding, followed by typhoon damage, was reported. South Korea suspended aid to the North following the attacks by North Korea on South Korean targets in 2010 (see *Inter-Korean Relations*). In March 2011 the UN reported that more than 6m. North Koreans were in urgent need of food aid. Following further flooding in North Korea in mid-2011, South Korea resumed humanitarian assistance through the Red Cross and UN agencies. In March 2012, after North Korea had agreed to suspend its nuclear activities (see *The Inception of North Korea's Nuclear Programme*) the USA planned to provide 240,000 metric tons of food aid; however, the deal was suspended when North Korea announced the forthcoming launch of a long-range rocket, which took place (unsuccessfully) in April. In late 2013 the UN Food and Agriculture Organization (FAO) reported that recent more successful harvests had reduced the food deficit to about 100,000 tons in 2012/13 (of which China provided about two-thirds and WFP one-third), but that many households still suffered chronic food shortages, and that pupils in nurseries and schools, which most North Korean children attended from a very young age, were often not receiving a diet nutritious enough for their healthy development.

In May 2011 the human rights organization Amnesty International reported that, according to satellite photographs, labour camps for political prisoners in remote areas of North Korea had expanded in size over the previous decade: the number of detainees was estimated to be as many as 200,000. Former inmates reported extremely harsh and inhumane conditions. The existence of the camps was denied by the North Korean Government. In 2012 it was reported by South Korean human rights groups that harsher penalties had recently been announced in the North for defectors and their families. The South Korean authorities reported a decline in the number of refugees from North Korea arriving in 2012, to just over 1,500, compared with some 2,700 in 2011. (See *Inter-Korean Relations* and *Relations with China* concerning policy with regard to defectors in previous years.) In March 2013 the UN Human Rights Council resolved to establish a commission of inquiry into abuses of human rights in North Korea, particularly in prison camps. North Korea refused to allow access by investigators, and the inquiry's report, published in February 2014, was therefore based largely on the testimony of more than 300 North Koreans who had escaped from the country. It described the 'disappearance' of alleged political offenders to prison camps where deliberate starvation, forced labour, summary executions, torture and rape were commonplace; the denial of the right to freedom of thought, conscience and religion, and of access to independent information; discrimination (including limits on access to food and health care) practised through the *songbun* system of social and political classification; abductions of persons from other countries; and violations of freedom of movement and residence. The commission recommended that North Korea's leaders should be prosecuted by the International Criminal Court (ICC) for crimes against humanity. The findings were angrily rejected by the North Korean Government. In November the UN General Assembly's special committee on human rights approved, by an overwhelming margin of 111 votes to 19, a non-binding resolution urging the UN Security Council to refer the case to the ICC. The North Korean Government organized a mass rally in protest, accusing the USA of initiating the resolution, and threatened to conduct a nuclear test. Following the UN General Assembly's approval of the resolution (by 116 votes to 20), in late December the UN Security Council convened its first ever hearing on the issue of human rights in North Korea, despite China and Russia voting against the inclusion of the issue on the Council's permanent agenda. Although these discussions represented an historic step forward in the campaign against North Korea's alleged human rights violations, it was considered highly probable that, in the event, China and Russia would ultimately veto the UN Security Council referring North Korea to the ICC.

Inter-Korean Relations

After the consolidation of power in the North by Kim Il Sung, North Korea's relations with South Korea remained tense. In 1971 discussions took place for the first time between the Red Cross Societies of North and South Korea. However, negotiations were prorogued in 1973, and hopes for better relations were undermined by a series of clashes between North and South Korean vessels in disputed waters during 1974. Propaganda campaigns, suspended by agreement in 1972, were resumed by both sides. In October 1978 the UN Command (UNC—under which troops were stationed in South Korea) accused North Korea of threatening the 1953 truce, after the discovery of an underground tunnel (the third since 1974) beneath the DMZ. During the 1980s the increasing prominence of Kim Jong Il, who advocated an uncompromising policy towards the South, appeared to aggravate the situation. In 1983 some 17 South Koreans, including four government ministers, were killed in a bomb explosion in Burma (now Myanmar), in what appeared to be an assassination attempt on the South Korean President, Chun Doo-Hwan. North Korea was held responsible for the attack, and Burma severed relations with the country. In January 1984, none the less, North Korea suggested tripartite discussions on reunification, involving North and South Korea and the USA, but the proposal was rejected by South Korea, which favoured bilateral talks. North Korea's propaganda campaign was moderated, and in September North Korea provided emergency relief to flood-stricken areas of the South. In November the first discussions, on possible economic co-operation, were held, and negotiations continued in 1985. However, in February 1986, during the annual South Korean-US 'Team Spirit' military manoeuvres, North Korea suspended all negotiations with the South. North Korea denied accusations of involvement in the explosion of a South Korean airliner over Burma in November 1987, despite the subsequent confession of an alleged North Korean agent. In August 1988 three sessions of talks were held at the 'peace village' of Panmunjom (in the DMZ) between delegates of the legislatures of North and South Korea, although the discussions (the first formal contact between the two countries since 1986) produced no conclusive results. Further negotiations in 1989 were suspended by North Korea.

Inter-Korean discussions resumed in mid-1990, and in September the North Korean Premier visited the South Korean capital, Seoul, for discussions with his counterpart: this was the most senior-level bilateral contact since the end of the Korean War. Subsequent discussions culminated in the signing of an 'Agreement on Reconciliation, Non-aggression and Exchanges and Co-operation between the South and the North', in Seoul in December 1991. Both states pledged, *inter alia*, to desist from mutual slander, vilification and sabotage; to promote economic and other co-operation; to facilitate the reunion of families separated by the war; and to work towards a full peace treaty to replace the 1953 armistice agreement. In November 1992, however, North Korea threatened a complete suspension of contacts with the South, in protest against the latter's decision to resume the 'Team Spirit' military exercises in March 1993. (The 1992 exercises had been cancelled, owing to the improvement in relations between the two states.) Relations had also been seriously impaired by the South's announcement, in October 1992, that an extensive North Korean espionage network had been discovered in South Korea, and by the North's repeated refusals to agree to simultaneous nuclear inspections in both countries.

While the controversy surrounding North Korea's suspected nuclear programme continued, inter-Korean relations were strained by North Korea's withdrawal in May 1994 of its mission to the Military Armistice Commission (the Panmunjom-based body overseeing the maintenance of the 1953 truce). Following discussions between Kim Il Sung and former US President Jimmy Carter, who visited North Korea in June 1994, it was announced that the first summit meeting at presidential level between the two Korean states would be held in Pyongyang in July. However, the death of Kim Il Sung led to the indefinite postponement of the meeting. The signature of the US-North Korean nuclear accord in October caused South Korea to make renewed efforts to resume the inter-Korean negotiations, and in February 1995 the South announced the cancellation of the annual 'Team Spirit' manoeuvres (for the second consecutive year).

Tension increased markedly in April 1996, when North Korea announced its decision to abandon the 1953 armistice. North Korean troops subsequently made a number of incursions into the DMZ, thereby violating the provisions of the agreement. Later in the month, in an attempt to revitalize the peace process and replace the armistice agreement with a formal peace treaty, President Bill Clinton of the USA and President Kim Young-Sam of South Korea proposed four-way talks, involving the two Koreas, the USA and China. China responded positively, but North Korea declared its willingness to hold discussions only with the USA. In September 1996 a submarine from North Korea was discovered abandoned in South Korean waters. One of the two surviving crew members claimed that this was the fourth such mission by armed North Koreans. South Korea suspended all contact with North Korea; the UN Security Council expressed 'serious concern' at the incident. Following mediation by the USA, an unprecedented apology was broadcast in South Korea by the official North Korean news agency.

After exploratory talks in March 1997 involving delegates from North Korea, South Korea and the USA, North Korea announced that its participation in full quadripartite negotiations was conditional upon the receipt of substantial food aid. In May representatives of the Red Cross organizations of North and South Korea reached agreement on the provision of grain to North Korea. Negotiations were concluded in October to allow foreign airlines, including those from South Korea, to use North Korean airspace. Full quadripartite negotiations, aimed at concluding a peace treaty between North and South Korea, finally opened in Geneva, Switzerland, in December, but North Korea continued to insist on the inclusion on the agenda of the withdrawal of US troops from the Korean peninsula.

Following the inauguration of the new South Korean President, Kim Dae-Jung, in February 1998, North Korea urged 'dialogue and negotiation' with the South Korean administration. In April, as part of Kim Dae-Jung's 'sunshine' policy of co-operation with North Korea, the South Korean Government announced measures to encourage inter-Korean economic contacts. During 1998 the North Korean authorities permitted several visits by Chung Ju-Yung, the founder of the South Korean conglomerate Hyundai, to deliver gifts of cattle to his home district, and in November some 800 tourists from South Korea participated in the first tour to Mount Kumgang. In December a proposal for the construction by Hyundai of an industrial complex at Haeju was approved. Also in December, however, South Korean naval forces sank a suspected North Korean spy boat, after pursuing it into international waters.

In June 1999 a week-long confrontation between North and South Korean naval forces in the Yellow Sea resulted in a brief gun battle, during which one North Korean torpedo boat was sunk. Two rounds of bilateral discussions in Beijing in June and July ended in failure. In September North Korea declared invalid the Northern Limit Line (the maritime border that had separated the territorial waters of the two Koreas since 1953), in protest against the UNC's refusal to renegotiate its demarcation. In August 2000 Hyundai agreed to establish a technologically advanced industrial compound in Kaesong, and agreements with two other major South Korean companies on joint industrial projects followed.

The summit meeting of 2000 and subsequent events

In June 2000 an historic summit meeting took place between Kim Jong Il and Kim Dae-Jung in Pyongyang, following which detailed agreements were signed pledging the promotion of economic co-operation, the building of mutual trust and the resolution of reunification issues. In July ministerial-level delegations from both countries met in Seoul. This was the first visit to the South by North Korean officials since 1991. A joint communiqué was issued allowing for, *inter alia*, the reopening of liaison offices at Panmunjom, which had been closed in 1996, and the reconnection of the inter-Korean Kyongui railway line. In September 2000 Kim Dae-Jung formally inaugurated the project to remove thousands of land-mines and rebuild the railway line and an adjacent highway. Meanwhile, in August 100 North Korean families travelled to Seoul and 100 South Korean families visited Pyongyang simultaneously to meet with relatives from whom they had been separated by the Korean War.

In a symbolic display of unity, in September 2000 the two countries marched under the same flag in the opening ceremony of the Olympic Games in Sydney, Australia. In late September North Korea's Minister of the People's Armed Forces, Vice-Marshal Kim Il Chol, visited the South and met his counterpart, Cho Seong-Tae, the first such ministerial meeting ever held. In October Kim Dae-Jung was awarded the Nobel Peace Prize in recognition of his reunification efforts. Further sessions of inter-ministerial, military and economic talks took place during 2000 and early 2001, and further family reunions were arranged by the North and South Korean Red Cross organizations. However, in its annual defence policy document published in December 2000, South Korea described the North as its main enemy and alleged that North Korea had expanded its military capacity along the DMZ. The North Korean Government was also displeased by the approval of a resolution in the South Korean legislature to demand the repatriation of prisoners of war who, it alleged, remained in detention in the North.

The uncompromising attitude towards North Korea displayed by the new US Administration of President George W. Bush, inaugurated in 2001, threatened to undermine the reconciliation process. However, in April 2002 Kim Jong Il received Kim Dae-Jung's special envoy, Lim Dong-Won, and the two sides agreed to further reunions for separated families and to continuing discussions on economic co-operation. North Korea also agreed to Lim's request that it renew dialogue with the USA and Japan. In May the increasing number of defectors from the North received international attention as several groups sought asylum at Canadian, Japanese and South Korean diplomatic buildings in China. They were eventually allowed to travel to the South, via the Philippines. At the end of June a gun battle between North and South Korean vessels in the Yellow Sea resulted in the sinking of a Southern patrol boat and the deaths of six of its crew members, while an estimated 30 North Korean crewmen were also killed in the confrontation. In July South Korea suspended rice shipments to the North and economic co-operation projects, reflecting widespread public anger at the incident. None the less, Kim Dae-Jung maintained his 'sunshine' policy towards the North. In August North and South Korea held a seventh round of ministerial discussions in Seoul, focusing on future family reunions, railway links and cultural exchanges. In September the first inter-Korean military 'hotline' was inaugurated to allow for improved communications in circumstances of potential tension.

The eighth round of ministerial talks was held in Pyongyang in October 2002 and focused mainly on economic co-operation issues, despite the fact that the USA had earlier revealed the existence of a secret nuclear weapons programme in the North. At the end of that month a North Korean economic delegation began a nine-day tour of the South, including several major industrial facilities in the itinerary. At the end of December the South Korean Ministry of National Defence published a 'white paper', which, for the first time, excluded any reference to the North as its main enemy.

The election in December 2002 of Roh Moo-Hyun, the candidate of Kim Dae-Jung's party, as President of South Korea heralded a continuation of Kim's 'sunshine' policy. In February 2003 the first road reconnecting the North with the South was completed, on the eastern coast of the Korean peninsula. However, in May 2003 North Korea announced that it no longer recognized a Joint Declaration of the Denuclearization of the Korean Peninsula, signed with the South in 1992. North Korea warned that the South would risk 'unspeakable disaster' if it became too confrontational in co-operating with the USA on the nuclear issue (the threat followed a summit meeting between Roh and US President George W. Bush). Attempts to develop inter-Korean relations were also complicated by confirmation in June 2003 by South Korean investigators that former President Kim Dae-Jung had arranged for the Korea Development Bank to give a Hyundai affiliate substantial funds to transfer to the North in order to finance the historic inter-Korean summit meeting of 2000. South Korea took part in the six-party talks on North Korea's nuclear programme which began in August 2003 (see *Relations with the USA and multilateral talks*).

In May 2004 senior-level military discussions took place between the two sides, at which the establishment of a radio communication line between the North and South Korean navies was agreed, ostensibly to reduce naval conflicts between the two sides. In July more than 450 North Korean defectors arrived in Seoul. North Korea subsequently accused South Korean officials of kidnapping its citizens and suspended bilateral dialogue. By the end of 2004 the number of North Koreans who had defected to South Korea had reportedly exceeded 6,000.

In July 2005 the 15th ministerial discussions between North and South Korea, held in Seoul, concluded with a 12-point joint statement in which the two sides pledged, *inter alia*, to reopen military talks, continue reunions for separated families and hold North-South Red Cross discussions on the question of South Korean soldiers and civilians allegedly abducted to North Korea during and after the 1950–53 war, more than 1,000 of whom, according to the South Korean Government, remained in detention in the North. In November it was announced that North and South Korea would present joint teams at the 2006 Asian Games in Doha, Qatar, and at the 2008 Olympic Games in Beijing, China. In March 2006 military negotiations were held between the two Koreas in the DMZ, following a hiatus of some two years; these were reportedly the most senior-level military talks between the two sides since the 1953 armistice. However, the North Korean Government postponed the scheduled 18th round of ministerial discussions between the two sides in protest against the South's conduct of joint military exercises with the USA.

The testing of North Korea's intercontinental *Taepodong-2* missile in July 2006 prompted South Korea to announce an indefinite suspension of food aid; however, it insisted that business co-operation, notably at Kaesong and Mount Kumgang, would not be affected. In response, North Korea suspended family reunions. Aid was resumed after North Korea suffered severe flooding later in that month, with the South Korean Government granting US $10.5m. to the North via non-governmental organizations (NGOs) in August, followed by supplies of rice and equipment. However, following the testing of a nuclear device by the North in October the South Korean Government announced a suspension of humanitarian aid, although again pledging to continue its economic co-operation in Kaesong and Mount Kumgang (despite express US pleas for these links to be severed). Although the South Korean Minister of Foreign Affairs, Ban Ki-Moon, reportedly stated that North Korea deserved sanctions under the UN Security Council Resolution, he also urged a resumption of dialogue. The South Korean Government refused to join the US-led Proliferation Security Initiative, which provided for the stopping and searching of North Korean ships that were suspected of carrying materials for use in nuclear, chemical or biological weapons. None the less, in a reversal of previous policy, in mid-November South Korea supported a UN resolution condemning North Korea's human rights record (in previous votes it had been absent or abstained). Furthermore, a South Korean defence policy document published at the end of December described North Korea as a 'serious threat' to the South—the most strongly worded assessment since the inception of the latter's policy of engagement in 2000. It was reported in February 2007 that the number of defectors from North to South Korea since 1953 had reached 10,000.

Following the progress made in mid-February 2007 at six-party talks on North Korea's nuclear programme (see below), North and South Korea held ministerial discussions later in that month and family reunions were resumed in May. Inter-Korean talks on economic co-operation were held in Pyongyang in April, shortly after North Korea had failed to meet a deadline agreed in February for the closure of its nuclear reactor at Yongbyon. South Korea agreed to revive its food aid programme to the North, with the provision of 400,000 metric tons of rice, but only on condition that North Korea demonstrate some progress in complying with its commitments under the February six-party accord. Following senior-level military talks at Panmunjom, in May cross-border rail links were finally completed when, for the first time in more than 50 years, passengers were conveyed on trains travelling in each direction. Agreement was also reached in principle, on the creation of a joint fishing zone in the disputed Yellow Sea, where naval clashes had previously occurred. However, ministerial discussions in Seoul in late May and early June ended without progress, as South Korea continued to refuse to dispatch any rice to the North while the latter's pledge to shut down the Yongbyon reactor remained unfulfilled. In late June, as inspectors of the International Atomic Energy Agency (IAEA, see p. 118) were permitted to enter North Korea for the first time since December 2002, South Korea announced the resumption of food aid to the North with a first shipment of rice, and the first instalment of heavy fuel oil followed in July. None the less, senior-level military talks ended in late July 2007 without agreement on the disputed maritime boundary, the Northern Limit Line, which North Korea refused to recognize, and in

August North and South Korean soldiers exchanged gunfire across the DMZ.

In October 2007, in only the second meeting between the two countries' leaders since the Korean War, Kim Jong Il welcomed President Roh to Pyongyang for a three-day summit. Kim and Roh, who was approaching the end of his term of office, issued a declaration, in which they committed North and South Korea, *inter alia*, to working towards the replacement of the 1953 armistice agreement with a peace treaty; to making joint efforts for the smooth implementation of the six-party nuclear agreements; to creating a special 'peace zone' around Haeju; to establishing the planned joint fishing zone in the Yellow Sea; and to expanding co-operation on economic and humanitarian projects. It was also decided to resume a cross-border freight rail service. In November 2007, during the first bilateral prime ministerial discussions since 1992, Premier Kim Yong Il and the South Korean Prime Minister, Han Duck-Soo, agreed on a timetable for resuming cross-border freight rail services and on the establishment of a joint committee to advance the creation of the 'peace zone' at Haeju. A daily freight service, connecting the South with Kaesong, was duly launched in December, although North Korea continued to oppose the introduction of regular passenger services.

Fluctuating tensions on the Korean peninsula

The conservative Lee Myung-Bak, who was elected President of South Korea in December 2007, advocated the adoption of a more uncompromising approach towards North Korea than that pursued over the preceding 10 years by Presidents Kim Dae-Jung and Roh Moo-Hyun: specifically he demanded increased progress on denuclearization in return for the continuation of economic co-operation. In January 2008 President Lee announced plans to review the agreements reached at the inter-Korean summit in the previous October, and the Ministry of Unification was reduced in importance. In March North Korea expelled South Korean officials from Kaesong and test-fired missiles in the Yellow Sea. The North Korean Government was reportedly dissatisfied with Lee's association of humanitarian assistance with preconditions on nuclear disarmament and human rights. Tensions rose further in July, when a South Korean tourist was shot dead by a North Korean soldier at Mount Kumgang, having allegedly crossed into a restricted area. In response, the South Korean Government halted tours to the area, while the North refused to participate in a joint investigation into the death, warning that it would expel all 'unnecessary' South Korean nationals from the resort. (In August 2011 the North Korean Government announced that it was seizing South Korean assets at the site, considering them to have been abandoned, and expelling the remaining South Korean staff: as of early 2015 South Korean tourist visits to the resort had still to resume, although some visitors from other countries (including China) had been allowed access to the site.) In November 2007 South Korea acted as the co-sponsor of a UN resolution criticizing human rights violations in North Korea. Later in that month the North announced the suspension of non-military telephone connections with the South, as well as the closure of the border. The rail service between the two sides was discontinued by the North in November 2008. In early March 2009, in their first, albeit brief, meeting since 2002, North Korean officials and UNC representatives had discussions at Panmunjom, in an attempt to reduce tensions.

Also in early March 2009 the North Korean Government again temporarily closed the border, in response to the holding of joint US-South Korean military exercises. In April the South Korean Government condemned the launch by North Korea of a rocket-mounted satellite, which was believed to be, in reality, a pretext for testing a long-range missile. In May, following North Korea's testing of a nuclear device, South Korea undertook to join the Proliferation Security Initiative, whereupon North Korea declared that it no longer considered itself bound by the armistice agreement with the South, and would respond with military action if any of its vessels were seized and searched. In August, however, following a meeting between Kim Jong Il and the chairwoman of the Hyundai group, the North Korean Government announced that it would reopen the border and permit tourism and family reunions to resume. The first family reunions since 2007 duly took place in September 2009.

In November 2009 North and South Korean naval vessels exchanged fire across the disputed maritime boundary (the first such incident for seven years), and in January 2010 there was a further exchange of land-based artillery fire across the maritime boundary. In March a South Korean naval vessel, the *Cheonan*, exploded and sank near the boundary, with the loss of 46 lives. The South Korean Government did not immediately accuse North Korea of deliberately causing the disaster, but in May a multinational team of experts concluded that the only plausible explanation for the explosion was that it had been caused by a torpedo from a North Korean submarine. This was vehemently denied by the North Korean Government, which threatened to respond aggressively to any retaliation. Joint naval exercises undertaken by South Korea and the USA in July were described as an 'intolerable provocation' by North Korea. In September, following severe flooding in the North, South Korea offered food aid, although the amount was criticized as inadequate by the Government of North Korea. In the same month North Korea suggested the organizing of further family reunions (which took place in late October). Also in September, discussions took place at Panmunjom between senior military officers, for the first time in two years, but they ended without agreement, reportedly after the South Korean representatives urged the North to apologize for the sinking of the *Cheonan* and to punish those responsible.

In November 2010 North Korea fired artillery shells at the South Korean island of Yeonpyeong, where South Korean forces had been conducting a military exercise. The bombardment killed four people, including two civilians, injured several more and caused widespread damage. In the same month South Korea and the USA conducted further (previously planned) naval exercises in the Yellow Sea. South Korea announced the suspension of the aid that it had promised to North Korea in September, but after further flooding in North Korea in mid-2011, South Korea offered to resume humanitarian aid. In August the South Korean Minister for Unification, Hyun In-Taek, was replaced by Yu Woo-Ik; although the South Korean Government denied that the replacement indicated a change in policy, Yu was believed to favour a less confrontational attitude to the North than that of his predecessor. Following the death of Kim Jong Il in December, the bellicose language used by his successor, Kim Jong Un, in February 2012, when denouncing forthcoming joint South Korean and US military exercises, and in March, when visiting Panmunjom, suggested that no immediate change in North Korean policy was likely. The South Korean Government described as a 'grave provocation' North Korea's announcement in March that it was to launch a rocket-mounted satellite in the following month, suspecting that the event would actually be a long-range missile test (as had been generally assumed in similar circumstances in April 2009). South Korea condemned the launch in April, which proved unsuccessful, as a breach of the UN resolution prohibiting the use of ballistic missile technology, and later in April announced that it had deployed new cruise missiles with a range of 1,000 km, which could reach any North Korean nuclear or missile site.

During the South Korean presidential election campaign in the second half of 2012 both the principal candidates undertook to improve inter-Korean relations; the North Korean state media, which had routinely denounced the incumbent President Lee and his Saenuri Party as 'traitors', urged South Koreans to support the opposition. Tensions were increased by North Korea's successful launch of another long-range rocket in December, a few days before the election. Following the electoral victory of the Saenuri Party candidate, Park Geun-Hye, however, it was observed that the North Korean media desisted from vilifying her. President-elect Park promised to conduct 'trust-based diplomacy' with the North and offered economic co-operation if progress were made in denuclearization. Kim Jong Un's new year message for 2013 urged an end to confrontation between north and south, but later in January, after the UN Security Council voted to extend sanctions against North Korea as a result of the recent rocket launch, the North Korean Government reacted defiantly, declaring its intention to proceed with a third nuclear test, which it duly conducted in February. President-elect Park described the test as undermining efforts for peace, but following her inauguration in late February she undertook to continue the 'trust-building process', urging the North to stop wasting its resources on the development of nuclear missiles. However, the North Korean authorities described as a 'war of aggression' the forthcoming annual joint military exercises to be held by US and South Korean forces in March and April, and after a new UN Security Council resolution in March, which further extended sanctions, the North's belligerent rhetoric intensified: it announced an end to the 1953 armistice and all non-aggression agreements with the South, the closure of the 'hot-line' military telephone link and the closure of the border crossing-point at Panmunjom in the DMZ.

In March 2013 the North Korean authorities alleged that state internet servers had been subject to a cyber-attack by 'hostile forces', and shortly afterwards the computer systems of several South Korean broadcasters and financial institutions were temporarily shut down by the implantation of malicious codes from an unknown source. At the end of March, following the inclusion of US B-52 bomber aircraft and 'stealth' bomber and fighter aircraft in the joint military exercises with South Korea, a North Korean Government statement declared that North–South relations were now in a 'state of war'. Operations at the joint Kaesong industrial complex (which in 2015 employed some 53,000 North Koreans working for 124 South Korean companies, providing a major source of hard-currency income for the North) were suspended by North Korea in April 2013 for the first time since the establishment of the complex. After the conclusion of the US and South Korean military exercises, however, North Korea's threatening attitude was moderated: in August the Government called for the reopening to South Korean visitors of the tourist resort at Kumgang. By October normal production operations had been resumed at Kaesong, while the North-South military telephone link was re-established in September. Also in October, it was announced that a new hi-tech industrial park was to be built adjacent to the existing Kaesong complex, with collaboration from a multinational consortium. In August, meanwhile, President Park urged the resumption of family reunions (suspended since 2010); a reunion for several hundred people was arranged by Red Cross officials for late September 2013, but was postponed by the North Korean authorities, finally taking place in February 2014. In the same month government-level bilateral talks were held at Panmunjom for the first time in almost seven years, but without a closing communiqué being issued.

In January 2014 an open letter was sent to the South Korean Government by the North Korean National Defence Commission, urging an end to 'hostile military acts'. During the Panmunjom talks in February, North Korean officials requested postponement of South Korea's regular joint military exercises with the USA, due to begin in the same month; the request was declined, and the exercises began as planned. Apparently in response, during late February and March North Korea launched more than 70 short-range ballistic missiles and two medium-range missiles into the sea. In late March there was an exchange of shell fire by the respective sides across the disputed western maritime border. In the same month the North Korean media denounced President Park as a 'servant and stooge' of the USA, after she warned that an accident at the Yongbyon nuclear plant (see below) could have disastrous consequences and that the North's nuclear material could fall into the hands of terrorists.

It was claimed by the South Korean Ministry of National Defence in early April 2014 that two unmanned drones had penetrated South Korean airspace in late March before failing and crashing south of the border; the drones were thought to have been launched from North Korea and concerns were raised about a technological shift in methods of intelligence-gathering. North Korean state media denied any involvement, accusing South Korea of 'fabricating' a 'fiction' in order to divert public attention away from the *Sewol* ferry disaster (see South Korea). In July North Korea again fired short-range rockets into the sea, apparently in protest against a five-day US-South Korean naval exercise which involved the presence of a US aircraft carrier in the South Korean port of Busan. In October a delegation led by Hwang Pyong So, the Director of the KPA's General Political Bureau (and also including his predecessor in that post, Choe Ryong Hae), unexpectedly attended the closing ceremony of the Asian Games in Incheon, South Korea. However, tensions resurfaced a few days later when shots were fired by both countries across marine and land borders, reportedly following the dropping of anti-North Korea leaflets from balloons launched by South Korean activists. In an unprecedented move, in mid-December South Korea's constitutional court issued a ban on the activities of the pro-North Unified Progressive Party, ordering its immediate disbandment. Later that month South Korea's nuclear power operator alleged that non-critical data had been stolen in an apparent cyber-attack on its headquarters, in which the hacker reportedly demanded the shutdown of three reactors; in March 2015 it was claimed that there was strong evidence that the attack had originated from computers based in North Korea.

Meanwhile, in December 2014 South Korea's Minister of Unification, Ryoo Kihl-Jae, called for the renewal of high-level bilateral talks. Early in the following month both Kim Jong Un and President Park expressed their willingness to hold talks on unification, with Park stating there should be no preconditions. However, in response to the holding in March 2015 of the annual US-South Korean military exercises, North Korea fired two short-range ballistic missiles and seven ground-to-air missiles into the sea, and issued a statement claiming that the opportunity for improving North-South dialogue had now passed.

In February 2015 South Korea's Ministry of Unification described as 'unacceptable' a unilateral decision by Pyongyang to abandon a 5% ceiling on the annual increase in the monthly remuneration paid (in US dollars) per employee at the Kaesong industrial complex by participating South Korean companies to the North Korean Government, raising the minimum monthly remuneration per employee to US $74. (It was speculated that this action had been taken to compensate for the absence of a 5% increase during the period of closure of the complex between April and September 2013.) Following the failure of talks in March between North Korean officials and a delegation of South Korean industrialists visiting the complex, South Korea's Ministry of Unification announced in early April that it would urge individual employers not to raise remuneration as demanded by Pyongyang. According to South Korea's Ministry of Unification, output at the Kaesong complex was valued at $470m. in both 2012 and 2014; the temporary closure in 2013 reduced revenue from production by more than half in that year, to $224m.

The Inception of North Korea's Nuclear Programme

In the early 1990s there was growing international concern that North Korea had intensified its clandestine nuclear programme at Yongbyon, north of Pyongyang (believed to have been operational since 1986), and would soon be capable of manufacturing a nuclear weapon. During 1991 pressure was applied, by the USA and Japan in particular, for North Korea to sign the Nuclear Safeguards Agreement (NSA) with the IAEA. This was required by North Korea's signature, in 1985, of the Treaty on the Non-Proliferation of Nuclear Weapons (the Non-Proliferation Treaty—NPT), in order that IAEA representatives might be permitted to inspect the country's nuclear facilities. However, North Korea consistently refused to allow such inspections to take place unless there was to be a simultaneous inspection (or withdrawal) of US nuclear weapons sited in South Korea. Tension was eased considerably by the USA's decision, in October 1991, to remove all its tactical nuclear weapons from South Korea, and by South Korea's subsequent declaration that it would not manufacture, deploy or use nuclear, chemical or biological weapons. In December the South Korean Government stated that all US nuclear weapons had been withdrawn, and proposed that simultaneous inspections of military bases in the South and nuclear facilities in the North be conducted. Later in the month the two Korean states concluded an agreement 'to create a non-nuclear Korean peninsula', and in January 1992 North Korea signed the NSA. In March delegates of North and South, meeting at Panmunjom, agreed to form a Joint Nuclear Control Commission (JNCC) to permit inter-Korean nuclear inspections.

In 1992 IAEA inspectors were allowed to make several visits to North Korean nuclear facilities. Despite the findings of the inspectors (who concluded that the Yongbyon plant was 'primitive' and far from completion, although potentially capable of producing plutonium), suspicions persisted regarding North Korean nuclear ambitions. Moreover, North Korea repeatedly failed to agree to separate nuclear inspections by the JNCC, finally announcing in January 1993 its intention to boycott all future inter-Korean nuclear talks (in protest against the imminent resumption of the joint US-South Korean 'Team Spirit' military manoeuvres). In March it announced that it was to withdraw from the NPT. In May the UN Security Council adopted a resolution urging North Korea to reconsider its decision to withdraw from the NPT and to allow an inspection by the IAEA of the country's nuclear facilities. Following negotiations with the USA, North Korea agreed to suspend its withdrawal from the NPT; in return, the USA agreed to assist North Korea in the development of its non-military nuclear programme. International concern regarding the North Korean weapons programme was further heightened by the successful testing of a medium-range missile in May.

In February 1994, following further discussions between North Korea and the USA, an agreement was reached whereby the IAEA would be allowed to visit all the country's declared nuclear facilities. In March it was discovered that seals placed on nuclear materials by IAEA representatives during previous visits had been broken, leading the IAEA to conclude that North Korea had probably produced more plutonium than had been admitted. In August the USA and North Korea reached an agreement on the replacement of the latter's existing nuclear reactors by two light-water reactors, which were considered to be less easily adapted to the production of nuclear weaponry. Under an agreement concluded in October the USA undertook to establish an international consortium to finance and supply the light-water reactors, while North Korea agreed to suspend operation of its existing reactors and halt construction at two further sites. To compensate for North Korea's consequent shortfall in energy production until the new reactors were fully operational, the USA agreed to donate to North Korea 500,000 metric tons annually of heavy fuel oil. IAEA inspectors travelled to Pyongyang to oversee the suspension of the country's nuclear programme.

In March 1995 several countries, led by the USA, South Korea and Japan, created the Korean Peninsula Energy Development Organization (KEDO). In December North Korea and KEDO reached agreement on the details of implementing the October 1994 accord. In January 1996 North Korea announced its willingness to permit routine inspections of its nuclear installations by the IAEA. In March the Korea Electric Power Corporation (KEPCO) was commissioned by KEDO as the principal contractor for the construction of the light-water reactors. Discussions between KEDO and North Korea to negotiate the terms of repayment by the latter of the construction costs of the light-water reactors were successfully concluded in April 1997.

Meanwhile, US energy experts began the sealing of spent fuel rods at North Korea's nuclear facilities. However, North Korea's continued refusal to grant IAEA inspectors access to several suspect laboratories again provoked concern that North Korea was developing its nuclear programme. Preparation of the nuclear-reactor site at Sinpo formally began in August 1997. Negotiations held in early 1998 between the participants in KEDO (which the European Union—EU—had joined in mid-1997) concerning the financing of the light-water reactors (estimated at US $5,170m.) proved difficult, and were further complicated by South Korea's financial problems, raising fears that progress on the project would be hindered. In June 1998 the North Korean Government admitted to having sold nuclear missiles abroad, claiming that such exports were necessary, given ongoing US economic sanctions against North Korea.

Talks held during mid-1999 between the USA and North Korea culminated in September in a decision by the USA to ease several long-standing economic sanctions against North Korea. In return, North Korea agreed to suspend missile test-firing for the duration of negotiations with the USA. After several months of delays caused by disputes over the division of the costs of the project, in December KEDO and KEPCO finally signed the contract for the construction of the two light-water reactors. In November 2000 North Korea, frustrated by delays in the construction of the reactors, threatened to restart missile testing unless the building programme was accelerated. North Korea denied the IAEA's claim that delays were due to the former's refusal to allow nuclear inspections.

In June 2000 the North Korean Government confirmed its moratorium on test flights of ballistic missiles. In the following month the USA rejected North Korea's demand for annual payments from the USA of US $1,000m. in return for the curtailment of weapons exports. In early 2001 the new US Administration of George W. Bush adopted a less conciliatory stance towards North Korea, refusing to grant economic aid unless transparency in North Korea's missile production and export were assured and verified. Since the late 1990s elements in Bush's Republican Party had been strongly arguing in favour of a planned 'national missile defence' (NMD) system to protect the USA from long-range missile attack, and had frequently cited North Korea as a developer and exporter of such missiles; it was feared that North Korea had developed an intercontinental ballistic missile, the *Taepodong-2*, capable of striking the west coast of the USA. Bush's commitment to develop NMD was denounced by North Korea, which responded by threatening to abandon the 1994 framework, and to resume ballistic missile testing. In June 2001 President Bush sought to broaden discussions with North Korea about its missile programme to include nuclear technology and a reduction of the country's conventional forces. The North responded that discussions on the latter would take place only following the withdrawal of the 37,000 US troops from the South, and that it was also seeking financial compensation for the delay in building KEDO's two light-water reactors, which were now not expected to be completed until 2008 at the earliest. In October 2001 the North rejected suggestions by the

head of the IAEA and later by US officials that inspections of its nuclear facilities were necessary; however, in December it agreed to limited international access to certain laboratories. (See *Foreign Affairs* for subsequent developments.)

Foreign Affairs

North Korea's international relations have been dominated by its hostility to the USA and to perceived US influence in South Korea, resulting in belligerent official rhetoric and actions, despite the country's chronic need for economic assistance. China, North Korea's principal ally and economic partner, has played an important role in persuading North Korea to take part in international negotiations. North Korea's unilateral application for UN membership, first announced in May 1991, represented a radical departure from its earlier insistence that the two Koreas should occupy a single UN seat. This development was welcomed by South Korea, and both countries were admitted separately to the UN in September of that year.

Relations with China

North Korea's relations with the People's Republic of China have remained a focus of North Korean foreign policy. During the years of the so-called Sino-Soviet dispute North Korea fluctuated in its allegiance to each of its powerful northern neighbours, China and the USSR. Kim Il Sung made several official visits to China in the late 1980s, which were interpreted by some Western observers as an attempt to establish closer relations in view of the erosion of communist power in many Eastern European countries. However, North Korea was aggrieved at China's establishment of full diplomatic relations with South Korea in 1992. China appeared largely conciliatory with regard to North Korea's nuclear programme, and during 1993 and the first months of 1994 indicated that it would veto any attempt by the UN Security Council to impose economic sanctions on North Korea. In 1997 China agreed to provide substantial food aid to North Korea to alleviate the effects of flooding. Later in that year China accepted US and South Korean proposals for quadripartite negotiations with North Korea to conclude a new peace agreement with the South, and between December 1997 and August 1999 it participated in all six rounds of these negotiations.

In late 1999 international attention was focused on the uncertain situation of the large number of North Koreans (estimated at some 30,000 by South Korean sources and at 200,000 by the voluntary organization Médecins Sans Frontières) who had crossed the border into China in recent years. In early 2000 it was reported that China had returned some 10,000 escapees to North Korea during 1999. The number of migrants was thought to fluctuate, according to the season.

In February 2000 China permitted North Korea to open a consulate-general in Hong Kong. In May Kim Jong Il visited China, his first official trip abroad for 17 years, followed by a second visit in January 2001, when Kim had extensive discussions with Chinese leaders in Beijing, and also toured the new business zones of Shanghai and Shenzhen. In September the Chinese President, Jiang Zemin, undertook an official visit to North Korea, the first such visit since 1990. Jiang promised additional food aid and fuel to alleviate North Korea's economic crisis.

During 2002 North Korea and China continued to seek the reconnection of the inter-Korean railway lines and their subsequent linking to China's own railway system. In May, however, China's forcible removal of North Korean refugees from South Korean embassy premises in the People's Republic again brought the issue of the refugees to international attention. Several groups of North Korean refugees had, in 2002, fled to Western, Japanese and South Korean diplomatic offices in China, embarrassing the latter, since the Chinese Government had signed a treaty with North Korea providing for the repatriation of refugees. In June China allowed 24 North Korean refugees who had been concealed in the embassy of South Korea to leave for that country. After that incident, China began an operation against South Korean activists and missionaries who had been helping North Koreans to flee via China. It was estimated that as many as 300,000 North Korean refugees were already residing in China, with US sources stating that as many as 50,000 had fled to China in 2001 alone.

In February 2003 the President of North Korea's SPA Presidium, Kim Yong Nam, visited Beijing and pledged to maintain strong bilateral relations. In April China hosted and participated in senior-level meetings between North Korea and the USA over the North Korean nuclear weapons programme. Immediately prior to the discussions, Vice-Marshal Jo Myong Rok, North Korea's second highest ranking official, led a military delegation to China, and held meetings with President Hu Jintao and senior military leaders. Chinese diplomatic efforts played a major role in ensuring North Korean participation in the first round of six-party talks on the nuclear issue that were held in Beijing in August (as well as in subsequent rounds—see below). In April 2004 Kim Jong Il made a covert visit to China, where he held talks with President Hu and other officials. Topics under discussion included economic matters and the nuclear issue, with China reportedly urging North Korea to modify its stance. During 2004 repeated instances of defectors from North Korea seeking refuge in foreign embassies in Beijing posed a dilemma for China, which as an official ally of North Korea continued to refuse to grant refugee status to such persons. Many defectors were none the less able to travel to Seoul via a third country. In November, however, China forcibly repatriated a group of 70 North Korean nationals. It was believed that they would be imprisoned and possibly executed upon their return to North Korea. Chinese diplomacy received considerable credit for the achievement of the joint draft agreement at the end of the fourth round of six-party talks in September 2005. In October President Hu made his first official visit to Pyongyang, in advance of the fifth round of discussions in November. In January 2006 Kim Jong Il again visited the special economic zone of Shenzhen, to observe China's economic modernization.

The North Korean nuclear weapon test in October 2006 embarrassed the Chinese Government, which had repeatedly urged North Korea to forgo its plans. Somewhat unexpectedly, China agreed to UN sanctions against the country, while ensuring that they did not contain a threat of military action. Moreover, the Chinese Government indicated that North Korean refugees being sheltered in a US consulate in north-eastern China would be allowed to travel to South Korea or the USA (a transfer that China had originally opposed), and stated that it would no longer object to Japan raising the issue of the abduction of Japanese citizens by North Korea at the six-party talks. China helped to broker another diplomatic advance at the end of October, when North Korea indicated that it was willing to rejoin the six-way nuclear talks. In September 2007 China provided North Korea with 50,000 metric tons of fuel oil, in accordance with the agreement reached in February at the six-party talks, which China continued to host. Following North Korea's failure to meet the deadline for the disablement of its nuclear facilities and disclosure of its nuclear activities, in late January 2008 the head of the Chinese Communist Party's international liaison department visited Pyongyang to urge Kim Jong Il to comply with his commitments under the six-party agreement. During a visit to Beijing in February US Secretary of State Condoleezza Rice exhorted the Chinese Government to use its influence to persuade North Korea to implement the agreement fully. The newly appointed Chinese Vice-President, Xi Jinping, who was already widely viewed as a potential successor to President Hu Jintao, chose North Korea as the destination for his first official visit, meeting with Kim Jong Il and other senior officials in June.

Following North Korea's launch of a long-range ballistic missile, purporting to be a satellite, in April 2009, China joined the UN Security Council's unanimous condemnation of the launch, but expressed opposition to any new sanctions that might exacerbate the situation. After North Korea tested its second nuclear device in May, China stated that it was resolutely opposed to the test, urged North Korea to return to negotiations, and concurred with the UN Security Council's resolution on stricter sanctions, agreed in June. In October Chinese Premier Wen Jiabao visited North Korea, and it was reportedly his influence that led Kim Jong Il to announce, during the visit, that North Korea was ready to return to the six-party negotiations on its nuclear programme. In May 2010 Kim Jong Il embarked upon a visit to China, holding discussions with both the Chinese President and Prime Minister: it was reported that the North Korean leader had declared his commitment to ending the country's nuclear programme and expressed his intention to create conditions favourable to the resumption of the six-party talks. Kim Jong Il paid another visit to China in August, reportedly accompanied by his son, Kim Jong Un, and in November the Premier of North Korea, Choe Yong Rim, spent eight days touring various industrial sites in China, particularly in Jilin Province, adjoining North Korea. Meanwhile, despite the conclusion by international investigators in May that the sinking of a South Korean naval vessel in March had been caused by a

North Korean torpedo (see *Inter-Korean Relations*), China had refused to support a UN Security Council resolution condemning the action: China merely referred to the incident as unfortunate, and described subsequent joint South Korean and US naval exercises as unnecessarily confrontational. Following the bombardment of the South Korean island of Yeonpyeong by North Korea in November, China expressed concern and urged both countries to display restraint.

Kim Jong Il paid further official visits to China in May and August 2011, visiting industrial sites. Following his death in December, the Chinese Government promptly endorsed Kim Jong Un as his successor. In March 2012 China expressed concern when North Korea announced plans to launch a rocket-mounted satellite in the following month: it was widely suspected that in reality the operation would be the testing of a long-range missile. After the failed launch of the rocket in April, China urged South Korea, the USA and Japan not to aggravate regional tensions by overreacting, and later in the month President Hu pledged to strengthen China's relations with North Korea. In August a large North Korean delegation, led by Jang Song Thaek, toured the neighbouring Chinese provinces of Jilin and Liaoning, and an agreement was signed on the joint development of two special economic zones. The Chinese Government expressed 'regret' after North Korea's successful launch of another long-range rocket in December, and agreed to approve a UN Security Council resolution condemning the launch and extending the scope of sanctions against North Korean institutions and individuals.

In early 2013 the Chinese authorities urged North Korea not to proceed with its threat to conduct a third nuclear test, and expressed 'firm opposition' once the test had taken place in February, again supporting a UN Security Council resolution that condemned the test and further expanded sanctions. Unprecedented financial pressure from China was applied from May when the Bank of China suspended transactions with North Korea's Foreign Trade Bank. Later in May Vice-Marshal Choe Ryong Hae (the influential Director of the KPA's General Political Bureau) visited Beijing and held discussions with President Xi Jinping, who urged the resumption of the six-party talks on denuclearization of the Korean peninsula: Chinese state media reported that Choe had expressed willingness to resume the talks. In September China announced a ban on certain exports to North Korea that could be used in developing nuclear weapons. After the execution in December of Jang Song Thaek, who had played a leading role in fostering relations between the two countries, the Chinese Government urged North Korea to 'maintain stability' and issued a pressing invitation to Kim Jong Un to visit Beijing. Following the report issued by a UN commission in February 2014, describing North Korean human rights violations (see above), the official Chinese reaction was that the evidence had not been verified and that the inquiry would not help to resolve the human rights situation in North Korea; in December China (together with Russia) voted against the inclusion of the issue on the permanent agenda of the UN Security Council. Over the course of 2014 Chinese Minister of Foreign Affairs Wang Yi asserted on a number of occasions that it was essential that North and South Korea agreed to resume six-party talks as soon as possible to 'firmly uphold peace and stability on the peninsula'. Xi Jinping's visit to South Korea in July was significant in that it marked the first time that a newly appointed Chinese President had visited the South without first visiting North Korea. Meanwhile, it was estimated that the number of North Koreans working in China had increased from 54,000 in 2010 to 93,000 in late 2014. Relations between China and North Korea were further strained in early April 2015 following China's rejection of an application by North Korea to join the newly established, Beijing-based Asian Infrastructure Investment Bank on the grounds that the country's financial sector was not sufficiently developed or transparent.

Relations with Japan

North Korea's relations with Japan have been characterized by continuing hostility towards the latter as a result of the atrocities committed in Korea during the Japanese occupation of 1910–45. The North Korean Government had demanded thousands of millions of dollars in compensation from Japan, before normal relations could be restored. In the 1980s, following the testimony of defectors, Japan began to suspect that North Korean agents had kidnapped a number of Japanese citizens during the late 1970s and early 1980s. Japan imposed sanctions on North Korea after North Korean agents were accused of attempting to assassinate the South Korean President in Burma in 1983. Following the destruction (by a concealed bomb) of a South Korean aircraft in 1987, allegedly by North Korean agents posing as Japanese citizens, Japan reimposed sanctions during 1988; North Korea then severed diplomatic contacts with Japan, although mutual trade continued. From late 1990 there was a significant rapprochement between North Korea and Japan, and in January 1991 a Japanese government delegation visited Pyongyang for discussions concerning the possible normalization of diplomatic relations. The Japanese delegation offered apologies, on behalf of its Government, for Japanese colonial aggression on the Korean peninsula between 1910 and 1945. Moreover, the Japanese Government expressed its willingness to make reparations for Japanese abuses of human rights in Korea during this period. However, subsequent negotiations in 1991 foundered, owing to North Korea's demand for reparations for damage inflicted after 1945 (which the Japanese Government denied) and to Japan's insistence that North Korea's nuclear installations be opened to outside inspection; normalization talks collapsed in November 1992, when the North Korean delegation abandoned the proceedings. Relations with Japan were further strained after North Korea's testing of the *Rodong-1* missile in the Sea of Japan (also known as the East Sea) in May 1993. The missile, according to US intelligence reports, would be capable of reaching most of Japan's major cities (and potentially of carrying either a conventional or a nuclear warhead). None the less, Japan, like South Korea, opposed the possible imposition of international economic sanctions on North Korea in response to North Korea's refusal to allow inspections of its nuclear facilities. During 1995–96 Japan provided emergency rice aid and fuel oil to alleviate North Korea's energy shortfall.

Relations were complicated in 1997 by renewed Japanese allegations that North Korea had abducted several Japanese citizens during the 1970s. However, in August 1997, for the first time since 1992, negotiations opened on the restoration of normal bilateral relations. An agreement was signed whereby some 1,800 Japanese women married to North Koreans, who had never been permitted to leave North Korea, were to be allowed to visit their relatives in Japan for short periods; the first such visits took place in November 1997 and January 1998. Moreover, in October 1997 the Japanese Government resumed the provision of aid to North Korea, suspended since mid-1996, donating food and medical supplies in response to the renewed appeals issued by the UN. In mid-1998, however, the North Korean Government cancelled a third visit of the Japanese women to their homeland, following Japan's rejection of a North Korean investigation into the alleged abduction of Japanese nationals. Japan broke off normalization talks, suspended food aid and postponed its contribution to the KEDO project following the testing by North Korea of a multi-stage *Taepodong* long-range missile in August; the rocket was believed to have flown over Japan and landed in the Pacific Ocean, exceeding North Korea's known capability.

In March 1999 Japanese naval forces pursued and opened fire on suspected North Korean spy ships that had infiltrated Japanese waters. However, relations improved following North Korea's agreement with the USA, in September, to suspend its reported plans further to test its new long-range missile. In December, after a successful visit to North Korea by a group of Japanese parliamentarians, Japan announced an end to its ban on food aid. Later in that month intergovernmental preparatory discussions on re-establishing diplomatic relations were held in Beijing. Progress was achieved by the Japanese and North Korean Red Cross Societies at a meeting in March 2000. It was reported that North Korea had agreed to co-operate in a further investigation into the fate of some 10 missing Japanese nationals, while Japan had agreed to a search for Korean citizens who had disappeared prior to 1945. In addition, visits to their homeland by Japanese women married to North Koreans were to resume, and Japan was to provide some 100,000 metric tons of rice to North Korea through WFP. In April 2000 Japanese charter flights to North Korea resumed. In the same month, following informal contacts between the North Korean and Japanese Governments, full normalization talks commenced; further rounds of discussions took place during the year.

In September 2000 the long-delayed third visits home by the Japanese wives of North Korean men took place. In October Japan decided, on humanitarian grounds, to provide 500,000 metric tons of rice to North Korea. None the less, in December North Korea reiterated that normal relations with Japan could be restored only after the latter delivered an apology and compensation for its earlier colonial rule. In May 2001 Japan deported Kim Jong Nam, the eldest son of Kim Jong Il, for

entering the country on a false passport. In December a suspected North Korean spy vessel was sunk by Japanese coastguard forces after it had been expelled from Japan's exclusive economic zone. North Korea condemned the incident, accusing Japan of seeking to mislead world opinion. In February 2002 North Korea released a Japanese journalist who had been detained on spying charges since December 1999.

Junichiro Koizumi visited Pyongyang in September 2002, becoming the first incumbent Japanese Prime Minister to do so. During his visit Koizumi held discussions with Kim Jong Il, who admitted that North Korean agents had abducted 12 Japanese citizens in the 1970s and 1980s, of whom five were still alive. Kim apologized for the incidents, attributing them to rogue elements within the security services. The surviving captives were temporarily allowed to return to Japan in October 2002, although they had to leave behind any spouses or children. The Japanese authorities then refused to allow the abductees to return to North Korea.

In October 2002 the alleged admission by North Korean officials to their visiting US counterparts that North Korea was pursuing a secret nuclear weapons programme greatly alarmed Japan. In separate incidents in February and March 2003, North Korea test-launched two short-range ground-to-ship missiles in the Sea of Japan, and in April tested a third missile in the Yellow Sea. However, it refrained from testing longer-range ballistic missiles, which Japan considered a threat to its security. In March the North Korean Government condemned Japan's launching of two spy satellites, believed to be part of a programme of intelligence-gathering on North Korea initiated following the suspected testing of the North Korean *Taepodong* missile over Japan in 1998. Japan was a participant in the six-party talks on North Korea's nuclear programme, beginning in August 2003 (see *Relations with the USA and multilateral talks*).

In January 2004 the Japanese House of Representatives approved legislation to permit the imposition of economic sanctions on North Korea. In April legislation was passed requiring all ships entering Japanese ports from March 2005 to be insured against oil damage. This in practice amounted to a ban on entry of all but 16 of an estimated 100 North Korean ships that were involved in trade with Japan. Following a second visit by Japanese Prime Minister Koizumi to Pyongyang in May 2004, five children of the abductees who had returned to Japan in 2002 (see above) were permitted to fly to Tokyo. Their release had been secured in return for pledges of food aid and medical supplies. However, suspicions remained over the fate of other missing Japanese nationals.

Japan remained reluctant to impose direct economic sanctions on North Korea, not wishing to jeopardize negotiations on the nuclear weapons programme. The six-party agreement of September 2005 contained a clause whereby the two countries undertook to 'take steps to normalize their relations'. In June 2006 the Japanese legislature enacted the North Korean Human Rights Act, which expressly linked the imposition of sanctions to issues of human rights in North Korea. The Act stated that economic sanctions would be imposed unless North Korea worked to resolve human rights issues, including the abduction of Japanese nationals. When North Korea conducted missile tests in July, Japan was one of its most vehement critics, announcing unilateral sanctions against North Korea in September: these included the suspension of transfers of funds to North Korea by groups suspected of having links to the country's nuclear weapons or missiles programmes.

When Shinzo Abe became Japanese Prime Minister in September 2006, he adopted a more robust stance on North Korea. Following the North Korean nuclear test in October, Japan not only supported sanctions under the UN Security Council, but also imposed firm measures of its own, banning all North Korean imports and prohibiting North Korean ships from entering Japanese waters, and banning the export of luxury goods to North Korea. However, the restoration of normal relations between North Korea and Japan was one of the tenets of the agreement reached during six-party talks in February 2007, and a working group was established to conduct negotiations. Bilateral discussions were held in Viet Nam in March, but they broke down over the issue of the Japanese abductees. In July the North Korean Government accused Japan of attempting to obstruct the talks on the normalization of bilateral relations and to disrupt the six-party process with its refusal to provide energy aid and its insistence on the resolution of the abduction issue, which North Korea claimed had already been settled. In October Japan announced that it would not resume aid to North Korea and extended its sanctions for a further six months, renewing them again in April 2008. In June North Korea and Japan attended bilateral talks in Beijing, with the former agreeing to carry out another investigation into the abduction issue in exchange for the withdrawal of certain Japanese sanctions, including restrictions on port visits by North Korean vessels carrying humanitarian cargo. In October, with little progress having been made on the abduction issue, Japan sought to withhold aid for North Korea under the six-party agreement.

In March 2009, following the revelation that North Korea was shortly to launch a satellite (widely believed to represent, in reality, a test of long-range missile technology), Japan mobilized its missile interceptors, in the country's first deployment of this technology. The Japanese Government reiterated its warning that it would attempt to destroy any North Korean missile or debris that threatened Japanese territory. In June, after North Korea's testing of a nuclear device in the previous month, Japan banned all exports to North Korea. In May 2010, following the conclusion by multinational investigators that North Korea had been responsible for the sinking of a South Korean naval vessel in March (see *Inter-Korean Relations*), the Japanese Government stated that it would consider imposing additional sanctions on North Korea.

In March 2012 the Japanese Government urged North Korea not to proceed with its announced intention to launch another rocket-mounted 'satellite' in the following month, and stated that the country's missile defence systems would be deployed if the rocket passed over Japanese territory. Although the launch in April failed as the rocket broke up over the sea, Japan condemned it as a threat to its security and a violation of UN resolutions. In August discussions between diplomatic representatives of Japan and North Korea—the first for four years—took place in China, followed by discussions at a more senior level in Mongolia in November, covering the habitual topics of reparations and abduction as obstacles to establishing normal diplomatic relations. In September it was announced that the US and Japanese Governments had agreed to establish a second missile defence system in Japan, in order to counter the threat of North Korean ballistic missiles. Japan strongly protested at North Korea's successful launch of a long-range rocket in December and condemned, as a 'grave threat' to Japan and the region, the testing of a nuclear device that ensued in February 2013. In April Japan deployed missile defence systems to protect against a potential missile launch from North Korea. In March 2014 the two countries resumed senior-level discussions on humanitarian matters, in Beijing, after a hiatus of some 16 months: the first such contact since Shinzo Abe took office as Prime Minister of Japan for a second time, in December 2012. In July 2014 the Japanese Government lifted a number of unilateral sanctions after North Korea agreed to reopen investigations into the issue of Japanese abductees; however, in early April 2015 Japan announced that the sanctions would be reimposed for two years, citing the absence of any progress in the investigations.

Other regional relations

In April 2000 North Korea formally applied to join the Association of Southeast Asian Nations (ASEAN, see p. 210). Following North Korea's admittance to the ASEAN Regional Forum (ARF), a meeting in Thailand in July was attended for the first time by the North Korean Minister of Foreign Affairs, who held unprecedented meetings with his South Korean, Japanese and US counterparts; North Korea was regularly represented at the ARF thereafter, and the meetings provided an important opportunity for informal regional contacts. In November the Asia-Pacific Economic Co-operation (APEC, see p. 200) forum supported North Korea's guest status in that organization.

In May 2000 Australia restored diplomatic links with North Korea. Diplomatic relations were established with the Philippines in 2000, with New Zealand in 2001 and with Timor-Leste in 2002. In 2003 there were reports that military relations with Myanmar were being developed; diplomatic relations were reestablished (after a hiatus of 25 years) in April 2007. A UN report released in November 2010 stated that North Korea was supplying nuclear-related technology to Myanmar, but this was denied by the Myanma Government: in September 2012, following progress towards democratic reform in Myanmar, the US Government urged the Myanma Government to reduce its links with North Korea. In June 2009, meanwhile, ASEAN leaders, attending a summit meeting in Seoul, condemned North Korea's recent testing of a nuclear device, urging the elimination of nuclear weapons on the Korean peninsula and North Korea's

return to the six-party negotiations; ASEAN member governments again expressed serious concern at North Korea's long-range rocket launches in April and December 2012 and at its testing of a third nuclear device in February 2013.

Relations with the USA and multilateral talks

From the time of the Korean War, North Korea persistently depicted the USA as its main enemy and repeatedly accused South Korea of being a US 'puppet' state. Relations deteriorated after North Korea seized a US naval vessel, the *USS Pueblo*, in 1968 and detained its crew for several months. In 1969 North Korea shot down a US reconnaissance aircraft, which had apparently violated North Korean airspace, resulting in the deaths of 31 US servicemen. In 1987, in response to alleged North Korean involvement in the bombing of a South Korean airliner, the USA placed North Korea on its list of countries supporting terrorism, and restricted contacts between US and North Korean diplomats. From the 1990s relations with the USA were largely dominated by North Korea's nuclear ambitions. In December 1994 it was announced that agreement had been reached to establish liaison offices in Washington, DC, and Pyongyang in 1995, in preparation for an eventual resumption of full diplomatic relations. However, the USA insisted that normal relations would be restored only when North Korea ceased to export ballistic missiles and withdrew its troops from the border with South Korea; North Korea, in turn, stated that liaison offices could only be opened when, in accordance with the October 1994 agreement between North Korea and the USA, light-water nuclear reactors had been supplied. In January 1995 North Korea opened its ports to US commercial shipping and removed restrictions on the import of goods from the USA. Following severe flooding in North Korea in 1995 and 1996, the USA provided relief aid.

The issue of four-way talks dominated relations between the USA and North Korea in 1996, but parallel negotiations were conducted concerning the estimated 8,100 US soldiers who were listed as 'missing in action' following the Korean War. The USA agreed to provide funds to assist in locating the remains. In early 1997 the USA responded to a renewed appeal issued by the UN for food aid and humanitarian assistance for North Korea, as a result of which North Korea announced its intention to take part in exploratory discussions about the proposed quadripartite talks. Bilateral discussions with the USA focused on the establishment of liaison offices, missile non-proliferation and procedures for the exhumation of the US servicemen listed as 'missing in action'. In August, however, the defection to the USA of two North Korean diplomats (the most senior officials yet to seek asylum in North America) resulted in the suspension of the third round of missile non-proliferation talks. North Korea was unsuccessful in attempting to make its participation in full quadripartite talks conditional upon the withdrawal of US forces from the Korean peninsula and upon the provision of food aid. The exhumation of US soldiers listed as 'missing in action' proceeded, with the remains of more than 40 soldiers being returned in 1998–2000.

Relations between North Korea and the USA deteriorated during 2001 following the inauguration of George W. Bush as US President. Bush adopted a more hostile position towards North Korea than that of his predecessor, and this also adversely affected inter-Korean relations. North Korea condemned the joint US-South Korean military exercises held in April. In June Bush stated that he was willing to resume negotiations with North Korea, albeit linking these to a reduction in North Korea's missile programme and military deployments—terms rejected by the North. Despite signing two UN treaties against terrorism in November, North Korea remained on the USA's list of states sponsoring terrorism, and in January 2002 President Bush referred to North Korea as forming an 'axis of evil' with Iran and Iraq. Bush's comments were believed to reflect concern that North Korea was exporting weapons technology to countries the USA considered to be 'rogue states'. (During the 1990s North Korea had exported missiles and related technology to Egypt, Iran, Libya, Pakistan and Syria, allegedly earning up to US $1,000m. a year.) In April the North accepted a South Korean request to reopen dialogue with the USA. At the same time the USA announced that it would release $95m. to North Korea in order to accelerate the building of replacement nuclear reactors—construction of which finally began in August 2002.

In October 2002 the USA revealed that senior North Korean officials had confirmed US intelligence reports that North Korea was pursuing a secret nuclear weapons programme; the USA declared the agreement concluded in October 1994 to be null and void and placed renewed pressure on North Korea to halt its nuclear activities. North Korea responded by stating that it would consider halting its nuclear programme if the USA were to sign a non-aggression treaty guaranteeing it sovereignty, a demand rejected by the USA. In November 2002 the USA finally halted petroleum shipments to North Korea, citing the latter's violation of the 1994 framework. It was widely reported that Pakistan had provided the technical expertise for North Korea's nuclear programme in exchange for ballistic missiles.

In December 2002 North Korea announced that it would restart its nuclear reactor at Yongbyon and removed the IAEA's monitoring and surveillance equipment from the facility. Security analysts, meanwhile, concluded that North Korea already possessed between two and five nuclear devices. The IAEA reported that North Korean technicians had transferred 1,000 fuel rods (of the 8,000 necessary to reactivate it) to the Yongbyon reactor, ostensibly for the production of electricity, but probably for the production of plutonium required to manufacture nuclear devices. North Korea expelled the two remaining IAEA inspectors at the end of the year.

In January 2003 the North Korean Government announced its withdrawal from the NPT, and in February it stated that the Yongbyon reactor was operating normally. In March the USA and South Korea began their annual joint military exercises, as usual incurring condemnation by the North, which announced at the end of the month that it was severing military contacts with the USA at the liaison office in the DMZ. Between late February and the beginning of April North Korea test-fired three short-range missiles, although it refrained from testing its longer-range ballistic missiles. By early April the USA had imposed new sanctions on North Korea's Government and its Changgwang Sinyong Corporation, for exporting ballistic missiles to Pakistan. However, the sanctions were largely symbolic, since the USA had minimal economic links with North Korea. Also in April, the seizure by Australian authorities of a North Korean ship carrying large amounts of heroin confirmed US claims that North Korea was involved in drugs-trafficking.

Following the holding in April 2003 of the UN Security Council's first discussions on the North Korean crisis, in June North Korea for the first time publicly defended its nuclear weapons strategy, declaring that the development of nuclear weapons was a 'deterrent'. In July there were new indications from US and Asian intelligence sources that North Korea was operating a second secret nuclear facility, in addition to the plant at Yongbyon. At the end of July it was announced that North Korea had agreed to take part in multilateral talks on its nuclear weapons programme with the USA, South Korea, Japan, China and Russia. The six-party talks duly took place in Beijing in August, but little progress was achieved, the USA insisting that North Korea unconditionally abandon its nuclear weapons programme, while North Korea reiterated that it would continue to develop its nuclear capacity unless the USA provided a guarantee of non-aggression. In September the US Government indicated that verifiable progress on dismantling might be sufficient to elicit concessions, but that a bilateral non-aggression treaty, as desired by North Korea, was not a possibility, and that any guarantee would involve China, Russia, South Korea and Japan, as well as the USA. In October the North Korean state news agency claimed that North Korea had successfully generated sufficient plutonium to build a nuclear bomb. In November the Central Intelligence Agency (CIA) reported to the US Congress that it believed North Korea had the technology to turn its nuclear fuel into functioning weapons. In December KEDO (the international consortium established in 1995, following the 1994 agreement with the USA on assistance for energy development in North Korea in return for nuclear non-proliferation) announced that it would be suspending for one year its construction in North Korea of two non-military nuclear reactors. Also in December, the USA rejected an offer from North Korea to freeze its nuclear programme in return for concessions on security and energy aid.

In January 2004 there was speculation about the existence of a second nuclear programme for enriching uranium (in addition to the plutonium-reprocessing activities at Yongbyon). In February and June further six-party talks took place, but no significant resolutions were reached, with North Korea continuing to deny the existence of a uranium enrichment programme. In August it was reported that North Korea was developing a new sea-based long-range missile system, which would possibly be capable of targeting the USA. A fourth round of six-party talks scheduled for September 2004 was suspended when North Korea refused to

attend, citing US hostility. In November KEDO declared that it would continue its suspension of the construction of non-military nuclear reactors.

In a state radio broadcast in February 2005 North Korea for the first time explicitly stated that it possessed nuclear weapons, and that it intended to postpone indefinitely its participation in six-party negotiations. Subsequent suggestions by North Korea for bilateral discussions with the USA were rejected by the latter. In May North Korea test-fired a ballistic missile into the Sea of Japan. An apparent improvement in relations in June included a US pledge of 50,000 metric tons of food aid, and the fourth round of six-party talks began in Beijing in July. Meanwhile, the USA continued to insist that the restoration of normal relations, removal of sanctions and guarantees of security could only follow the 'complete, verifiable and irreversible dismantling' of North Korea's nuclear weapons programme, while the latter reiterated that only after the normalization of relations, including the signing of a peace treaty ending the Korean War, and the removal of US nuclear weapons from South Korea (the presence of which the US side denied) would the North agree to abandon its military nuclear aspirations.

In September 2005 a draft joint agreement was signed by all sides in the six-party negotiations, in which North Korea committed itself to dismantling its nuclear weapons programme, returning to the NPT and permitting IAEA inspectors to visit its nuclear facilities. In return, the USA declared that it maintained no nuclear weapons on the Korean peninsula and had no intention of attacking North Korea. North Korea's right to peaceful nuclear energy was acknowledged, and it was envisaged that the provision of a civilian light-water nuclear reactor to North Korea would be discussed 'at an appropriate time'. The other five parties also undertook to provide North Korea with energy assistance. Although significant, the agreement was compromised almost immediately when the North Korean Government insisted that it would take no steps towards dismantling its nuclear weapons programme until provided with a light-water reactor as specified in the agreement. The USA insisted that concessions such as the provision of the reactor could be expected to come into force only after North Korea had fulfilled its dismantlement obligations. The fifth round of talks, which began in Beijing in November, ended without agreement. Later in November KEDO announced that it was considering the termination of its light-water reactor construction project in North Korea, which had been suspended since 2003. (All workers were withdrawn from KEDO's construction site in Kumho, North Korea, in January 2006, and in December KEDO's executive board signed an agreement to terminate the project.)

Meanwhile, the resumption of the six-party nuclear negotiations appeared to be jeopardized by US allegations of financial crimes on the part of North Korea. In September 2005 the US Government had ordered that all transactions with Banco Delta Asia in the Chinese Special Administrative Region of Macao be terminated, in relation to suspected money-laundering activities conducted with the bank by the North Korean Government, and had also frozen the assets of eight North Korean companies, which it accused of proliferating weapons of mass destruction. In October the US Department of Justice accused North Korea of having forged millions of US dollars' worth of counterfeit banknotes since 1989, and in December 2005 the US ambassador to South Korea publicly described North Korea as a 'criminal regime'. Although the US Administration insisted that the sanctions were purely a legal matter and had no political connection to the nuclear issue, the North Korean Government declared that no further six-party negotiations could be held until sanctions against it were removed.

By mid-2006 speculation was rife that North Korea was soon to test-launch an intercontinental ballistic missile, thus breaking the moratorium on tests imposed in 1999. The US Government warned that a test would be regarded as a provocative act, while Japan threatened stern action should a test missile be launched. However, North Korea continued to insist that it might be prepared to halt the planned test should the USA agree to direct bilateral talks, a request that the US Government once again rejected. Instead, the USA announced that it would deploy advanced *Patriot* missiles (capable of intercepting North Korean ballistic missiles, as well as cruise missiles and aircraft) on Japanese soil for the first time. North Korea's decision to test seven missiles in early July 2006 was regarded as a deliberate attempt to provoke the USA. Of the missiles tested, at least one was a *Taepodong-2* missile, thought to be capable of reaching Alaska; although the US Department of State claimed that the

Taepodong-2 failed shortly after take-off, the North Korean Government hailed the tests as a success, announcing that more test launches were planned.

While the international community broadly condemned the tests, harsh criticism from the USA and Japan was tempered by the more cautious stance adopted by China, Russia and South Korea. The USA and Japan urged the UN Security Council to adopt sanctions against North Korea, while Russia and China, which as permanent members of the Council held the power of veto, emphasized the importance of the resumption of dialogue. The UN Security Council adopted a resolution in mid-July 2006, requiring member states to ban the import and export of missile-related material to and from North Korea. In September the USA attempted once more to revive the six-party talks, but reiterated that its position had not changed.

In defiance of international opinion North Korea conducted a nuclear test in October 2006, reportedly from a test site near Kimchaek city in North Hamgyong Province. The South Korean Minister for Unification denounced the test as a clear challenge to world peace and stability. Although the size of the device tested was thought to be very small, the detection of airborne radiation by US analysts confirmed that the device was nuclear in nature. The test prompted an emergency meeting of the UN Security Council in New York, USA, amid strong condemnation from many governments. The Security Council approved a unanimous resolution imposing sanctions on North Korea, with Russia and China unexpectedly agreeing to a range of sanctions, albeit measures that were purely economic and commercial, rather than military, in nature. The resolution urged North Korea to suspend immediately its ballistic weapons programme and further nuclear tests and to return to the six-party talks without precondition. Sanctions included provision for the inspection of cargo entering and leaving North Korean ports, a ban on weapons-related imports, a travel ban on North Korean officials thought to be involved in the weapons programme and a freezing of their assets, and also a ban on the import of luxury goods. At the end of October, following discussions among Chinese, US and North Korean officials, North Korea indicated that it would return to the six-party talks. While North Korea set no conditions for its return to the discussions, it expressed the hope that one of the topics would be the removal of financial sanctions and the release of North Korean assets.

Intense diplomatic activity resulted in the resumption of the six-party talks in December 2006. However, North Korea stated that it would consider halting its nuclear programme only if the US and UN sanctions were removed. The country also reiterated demands for a nuclear reactor to generate electricity. The US negotiators, meanwhile, were reported by South Korean sources to have offered a fresh programme of incentives, which would give North Korea aid and security guarantees if it agreed to declare all its nuclear-related programmes and place them under permanent external inspection. In February 2007 North Korea agreed to permit IAEA inspections and to shut down its nuclear reactor at Yongbyon within 60 days in exchange for the equivalent of 50,000 metric tons of heavy fuel oil and the assurance of negotiations on the restoration of normal relations with Japan and the USA, with the latter notably agreeing to begin the process of ending the designation of North Korea as a state sponsoring terrorism. Five working groups were to be established to address North Korean relations with both Japan and the USA, economic and energy co-operation, denuclearization of the Korean peninsula, and the establishment of a North-East Asia peace and security mechanism. North Korea was given an incentive of a further 950,000 tons of heavy fuel oil for immobilizing its nuclear facilities and providing a complete declaration of all its nuclear programmes as part of the next phase of the agreement. Although the formal accord did not directly mention the North Korean funds in the Banco Delta Asia in Macao that had been frozen by the USA in 2005, this issue was covered by a reference to 'resolving pending bilateral issues', and the USA subsequently agreed to return the funds. In March 2007 a further round of six-party talks faltered over delays to the release of the North Korean funds in Macao, and North Korea missed the 14 April closure deadline for the Yongbyon reactor. As progress on the implementation of the February agreement remained stalled, with commercial banks reportedly unwilling to transfer the Banco Delta Asia funds, North Korea test-fired three short-range missiles in late May and early June.

US Assistant Secretary of State Christopher Hill visited Pyongyang for the first time in late June 2007. Shortly afterwards North Korea confirmed that it had received the Banco Delta Asia funds, which amounted to US \$25m. and had been transferred via a Russian bank, and on the following day IAEA inspectors arrived on their first visit to North Korea since their expulsion in December 2002. In mid-July 2007 North Korea announced that it had shut down Yongbyon, and this was subsequently verified by the IAEA. Participants in the six-party talks met in Beijing a few days later, but failed to agree upon a timetable for the second phase of the February accord, i.e. the disclosure and disablement of all North Korea's nuclear facilities. Following the discussions, North Korea renewed its demands for a light-water reactor in exchange for immobilizing its Yongbyon nuclear reactor. Working groups established by the six nations involved in the talks on ending North Korea's nuclear weapons programme held meetings in Panmunjom in August to discuss the technical details of the next stage of the process. Following talks between North Korea and the USA on improving their bilateral relations, which were held in Geneva in early September, Hill announced that North Korea had agreed to declare and disable all its nuclear facilities by the end of the year.

A new round of six-party talks, which was held in Beijing in late September 2007, resulted in formal agreement on a deadline of 31 December for the completion of the second phase of the February accord, under which North Korea would receive a further 900,000 metric tons of heavy fuel oil (100,000 tons having already been supplied by South Korea and China). In October a US team of government officials and nuclear experts spent a week in North Korea discussing detailed plans for disablement. Work on immobilizing the Yongbyon reactor, which was to entail the removal of 8,000 fuel rods, commenced in November under US supervision. However, North Korea failed to meet the deadline to disclose details of its nuclear activities. The disablement of the country's nuclear facilities had also not been completed by the end of 2007, although this was attributed to technical difficulties.

At discussions between US and North Korean negotiators, held in February 2008, disagreement remained over North Korea's continued denial of US claims of the existence of a covert North Korean nuclear programme for enriching uranium; this was followed in April by the USA's contention that North Korea had passed sensitive nuclear information to Syria. In May North Korea accepted the USA's offer of substantial amounts of food aid, the bulk of which was to be delivered by WFP. Official documentation on North Korea's nuclear programme and assets, delivered in late June to the Chinese Government, prompted President Bush to announce that North Korea would be removed from the USA's list of state sponsors of terrorism and that US trade sanctions would be withdrawn. Soon afterwards, the cooling tower of the Yongbyon reactor was destroyed by the North Korean authorities. However, further movement on the terms of the agreement was slow, owing to disputes over the method of authentication of the North Korean progress reports and delays to North Korea's official redesignation as a non-terrorist nation. These disagreements resulted in an announcement by North Korea in August that it would stop dismantling its Yongbyon reactor; it further announced, in September, that the reactor was to be restarted. The impasse appeared to have been resolved in the following month, when the USA implemented the redesignation of North Korea in return for the latter's assurance of compliance with nuclear inspections, albeit with conditions. However, the issue of the verification procedure continued to impede progress when the six-party talks resumed in Beijing in December.

After Barack Obama had taken office as President of the USA in January 2009, his Secretary of State, Hillary Clinton, declared that if North Korea were to eliminate its nuclear weapons programme 'genuinely and verifiably' the new Administration would be prepared to establish normal diplomatic relations and provide economic assistance. In March, however, following the closure of the border in response to South Korea's participation in its regular joint military exercises with the USA, and as speculation mounted with regard to the precise nature of an imminent satellite launch announced by North Korea, the North Korean Government refused to accept any further supplies of US food aid and instructed five US aid groups to leave the country by the end of the month.

North Korea's announcement of its forthcoming launch of a communications satellite aroused much concern. The US, South Korean and Japanese Governments suspected that the operation might prove to be a long-range ballistic missile test. In April 2009 North Korea proceeded to launch its rocket, in defiance of international warnings, and announced that the launch had enabled the placement of a communications satellite into orbit; however, this was contested by the US military, which asserted that the rocket's payload had landed in the Pacific Ocean. At the request of the Japanese Government, the UN Security Council convened an emergency session, at which Chinese and Russian envoys urged restraint, while the USA and Japan advocated a reinforcement of sanctions against North Korea. However, later in April the Security Council released a statement condemning the rocket launch and the violation of the ban on missile tests by North Korea. In response, North Korea expelled all UN nuclear inspectors and announced its withdrawal from the six-party talks and the resumption of its nuclear programme.

In late May 2009 North Korea exploded an underground nuclear device, believed to be larger than the one tested in October 2006. On the same day three short-range ballistic missiles were also fired, followed by several more over the ensuing days. The nuclear test was condemned by the USA, China, Russia and numerous other countries, and in June 2009 the UN Security Council unanimously approved a resolution condemning the test 'in the strongest terms', demanding that North Korea not conduct any further nuclear test or any launch using ballistic missile technology, urging the country to reverse its withdrawal from the NPT and strengthening the sanctions that had been imposed on North Korea in 2006. The resolution prohibited the export of all weapons from North Korea and the import of all except minor weapons, and urged member states to inspect North Korean cargo ships and aircraft for materials related to the production of nuclear weapons. North Korea responded by firing several short-range and medium-range ballistic missiles in early July 2009. Later in July the Security Council's committee on sanctions nominated five companies and five individuals to be subject to a freeze of financial assets and a ban on foreign travel, including North Korea's General Bureau of Atomic Energy and its director, and three trading companies.

In June 2009 two US journalists who had been detained in North Korea in March were tried, convicted of illegal entry into the country and 'hostile acts', and sentenced to 12 years' labour. In August, however, former US President Bill Clinton travelled to Pyongyang (reportedly at the indirect invitation of the North Korean Government) and secured the release of the two women: his visit, although unofficial, included a meeting with Kim Jong Il. In October, during a visit to Pyongyang by the Chinese Premier, Wen Jiabao, Kim Jong Il expressed readiness to resume multilateral talks on the nuclear programme, depending on the outcome of bilateral discussions with the USA. The Obama Administration, for its part, stated that bilateral dialogue was acceptable, provided that it led to a resumption of the six-party talks, and in November it was announced that a special US envoy to North Korea, Stephen Bosworth, had been appointed. During a visit to South Korea in that month, President Obama offered economic assistance to North Korea if it demonstrated an irreversible halt to its development of nuclear weapons.

In April 2010 North Korea's principal negotiator on nuclear affairs, Kim Kye Gwan, was reported to have been refused entry to the USA for bilateral discussions, since no North Korean undertaking to resume the six-party talks had been made. In May, following the conclusion by expert investigators that North Korea had been responsible for the sinking of the South Korean naval vessel *Cheonan* in March (see *Inter-Korean Relations*), the US Government condemned the incident as an unacceptable provocation. In the same month a preliminary report by a group of experts, commissioned by the UN, reported that North Korea had been exporting nuclear technology to Iran, Myanmar and Syria, in defiance of sanctions imposed by the UN Security Council. In June President Obama announced an extension of US sanctions against North Korea. In July North Korea reacted with outrage to four days of large-scale joint naval exercises by South Korea and the USA, in international waters off North Korea. During a visit to North Korea in August by former US President Jimmy Carter, the veteran statesman was successful in securing the freedom of a US citizen who had been imprisoned after entering the country illegally in January. Although the visit was private, Carter met Kim Kye Gwan and Kim Yong Nam (a senior member of the KWP and the country's titular head of state), and the latter was reported by the North Korean media to have expressed willingness to resume the six-party negotiations. Later in August the US Government imposed new sanctions and travel bans on North Korean organizations and individuals, including a clandestine branch of the KWP, known as Office 39, which was alleged to have been dealing in illicit drugs, and the Green Pine Corporation, which was believed to export weapons.

In November a senior US nuclear scientist visited North Korea and reported that he had been shown an advanced uranium enrichment facility, which was much more extensive and up-to-date than expected; the facility was intended to supply a new light-water reactor that was under construction at Yongbyon, ostensibly for the peaceful production of electricity. Later in November, after North Korea's bombardment of the South Korean island of Yeonpyeong, President Obama reaffirmed the USA's commitment to South Korea's defence, and the two countries again undertook joint naval exercises in the Yellow Sea.

In July 2011 discussions took place in New York between the representatives of North Korea and the USA, Kim Kye Gwan and Bosworth, after which the North Korean Government announced that it was willing to resume the six-party talks from which it had withdrawn in April 2009. In August 2011 the USA agreed to provide emergency aid for flood victims in North Korea, while North Korea agreed to resume negotiations on repatriating the remains of US soldiers: repatriations had been halted in 2005. In October a new US special envoy, Glyn Davies, was appointed to replace Bosworth. In February 2012, after a third session of bilateral talks, held in Beijing, the North Korean Government announced that it would suspend its uranium enrichment activities, long-range missile tests and the testing of nuclear weapons, and allow IAEA inspectors to return to the country. In response, the US Government announced the provision of 240,000 metric tons of food aid. In March, however, the USA unilaterally cancelled the agreement after North Korea's announcement that in the following month it was to launch another rocket-mounted satellite (an operation again generally suspected to be, in reality, the testing of a long-range missile). Despite international protests, the launch took place in April, although the rocket failed shortly after take-off. The US Government condemned the launch and reaffirmed its commitment to the security of its allies in the area. The North Korean Government subsequently announced that it was no longer bound by the moratorium on missile and nuclear tests agreed with the US Government in February, accusing the latter of violating the accord. In May the UN Security Council imposed sanctions on three North Korean state-owned companies (reportedly involved in weapons trading) in response to the failed rocket launch.

In December 2012 the North Korean authorities announced that another satellite was to be launched for peaceful purposes, using a long-range rocket, and this time the attempt was apparently successful. As on previous occasions, it was widely suspected that the launch represented a test of long-range missile technology, and it was described by the US Government as a 'highly provocative act'. In January 2013 the UN Security Council unanimously condemned the launch and extended sanctions against North Korea to include more individuals and state-owned trading companies, a bank and the national space agency. The North Korean Government promptly announced that it was proceeding with plans to test a third nuclear device, which it duly did in February. The test, which as on previous occasions took place underground, involved a 'miniaturized' device which could possibly be mounted on a long-range rocket and was believed to be twice as powerful as that used in the 2009 test. In March 2013 a new UN Security Council resolution (the fifth since 2006) further expanded sanctions on financial transactions and strengthened the authority of the member states to inspect North Korean ships and aircraft suspected of carrying weapons-related cargoes.

Meanwhile, in anticipation of the annual joint military exercises to be undertaken by South Korean and US forces in March and April 2013, there was a marked increase in anti-US rhetoric on the part of the North Korean authorities, which threatened 'pre-emptive nuclear strikes' and declared that artillery units were ready to target US bases in South Korea and the Pacific region. The US deployment of B-52 bomber aircraft and 'stealth' bombers and fighter jets (for the first time) over South Korea, as part of the exercises, was viewed as particularly provocative. In early April North Korea announced that it was recommencing activities (officially suspended since 2007) at the Yongbyon nuclear plant, the source for plutonium for the country's nuclear programme; in September 2014 the IAEA announced that it believed the Yongbyon facility to be operational again, based on analysis of satellite imagery. Also in early April 2013 the US Government announced that it was to move an advanced missile defence system to the US Pacific territory of Guam in response to North Korean threats, but at the same time postponed planned tests of its own long-range ballistic missile, for fear of exacerbating the crisis. In May two North Korean medium-range missiles that had been moved to a coastal launch site in April were reportedly removed in an apparent effort to reduce tension prior to a meeting between the South Korean and US Presidents. Also in May a US citizen, Kenneth Bae, was sentenced to 15 years' hard labour in North Korea, on charges of attempting to overthrow the Government. In September another US citizen, Matthew Miller, was sentenced to six years' hard labour by the Supreme Court in Pyongyang on charges of 'hostile acts'; Miller had intentionally damaged his tourist visa while travelling to Pyongyang by air, and had refused to comply with requests to leave the country. In November, following an unprecedented visit to North Korea by the US director of national intelligence, Bae and Miller were released from custody and returned to the USA. The annual joint military exercises conducted by the USA and South Korea in February–March 2014 provoked a less belligerent reaction in North Korea, in terms of rhetoric, than in the previous year, but during this period North Korea fired numerous short-range ballistic missiles into the sea, followed by two medium-range missiles in late March, in defiance of UN resolutions; this action was condemned by the UN Security Council. Also in March President Obama held a meeting with President Park and the Japanese Prime Minister, Shinzo Abe, at which the three leaders discussed how to resume the six-party talks on denuclearization and Obama affirmed the US Government's commitment to protecting South Korea and Japan from the nuclear threat posed by the North. In July North Korea's UN ambassador made an official complaint to the UN Secretary-General that the production and distribution of a forthcoming US satirical film, the subject of which involved an assassination plot against Kim Jong Un, promoted terrorism against the country and constituted 'an act of war'. In November computer systems at Sony Pictures Entertainment, the parent company of the film's distributor Columbia Pictures, were hacked in what was described as a highly sophisticated cyber-attack; details concerning several forthcoming productions were leaked and employees' sensitive data was published on the Internet. Responsibility for the attack was claimed by a group calling itself the 'Guardians of Peace', which subsequently threatened terrorist attacks against cinemas that screened the film. US investigators claimed direct North Korean involvement in the hacking; this was explicitly denied by the North Korean Government, which opined that the attack could have been 'a righteous deed of supporters and sympathizers'. In late December, following US President Obama's warning of a 'proportionate' US response to the cyber-attack, North Korea offered to launch a joint inquiry into the incident with the USA, threatening 'grave consequences' if its offer were rejected. In January 2015, in an effort further to isolate North Korea's defence industry, the USA announced new sanctions on three organizations and 10 individuals in North Korea; the sanctions were angrily denounced by the North Korean authorities, which in February issued a statement threatening the use of 'smaller, precision and diversified nuclear striking' in a retaliatory campaign against the USA. In March 2015 North Korea responded to the onset of the annual US-South Korean military manoeuvres with the launch—once again—of missiles (including two medium-range missiles) into the sea.

Other external relations

In the mid-1980s North Korea placed increased emphasis on its relations with the USSR. North Korea's diplomatic isolation became more pronounced in the early 1990s, as former communist bloc countries attempted to foster relations with South Korea. Furthermore, the USSR announced that, from January 1991, its barter trading system with North Korea would be abolished in favour of trade in convertible currencies at world market prices. However, an agreement was reported to have been signed in May 1993 by North Korea and the Russian Federation (which, following the dissolution of the USSR, had assumed responsibility for many of the USSR's international undertakings) on technological and scientific co-operation. In February 2000 the two countries concluded a new bilateral treaty of friendship, good neighbourliness and co-operation (to replace a 1961 bilateral treaty). In July President Vladimir Putin became the first Russian (or Soviet) leader to visit North Korea. Following Putin's visit, co-operation between Russia and North Korea placed a strong emphasis on connecting the latter's rail system to the Trans-Siberian railway, and in March 2001 the two countries signed a railway co-operation agreement. In August Kim Jong Il undertook a 24-day visit across Russia to the capital, Moscow, where he and President Putin signed a new declaration of co-operation in politics, the economy, military matters, science and technology, and culture. However, at the same time Russia also urged North Korea to settle its outstanding bilateral debt.

As the diplomatic crisis over North Korea's nuclear weapons programme intensified in January 2003, Russia sought to defuse the situation by urging a three-stage formula whereby the international community would accept a nuclear-free Korean peninsula, guarantees for the regime's security, and a resumption of aid. North Korea reiterated that the crisis could be resolved only through discussions with the USA. From August Russia participated in the six-party talks on North Korea's nuclear programme (see *Relations with the USA and multilateral talks*).

In July 2006, following the North's missile tests, Russia and China ensured that attempts by the UN Security Council to impose sanctions on North Korea were obstructed. However, Russia modified its staunch anti-sanctions policy following the nuclear test conducted by North Korea in October, while—like China—using its power of veto to ensure that the subsequent UN Security Council resolution did not include the threat of military action. The Russian authorities assisted in the process of transferring previously frozen North Korean funds from the Banco Delta Asia in Macao to North Korea via a Russian bank in June 2007, thus removing the main obstacle to the implementation of the February agreement on North Korea's nuclear programme (see *Relations with the USA and multilateral talks*). In January 2008 Russia provided North Korea with 50,000 metric tons of fuel oil as part of its commitment under the six-party agreement on the dismantling of North Korea's nuclear facilities. In April Russia and North Korea signed an agreement to restore an existing railway line between Khasan on the Russian border and Rajin in North Korea. Russia condemned North Korea's launch of a long-range missile in April 2009, but opposed the imposition of stricter sanctions; however, after North Korea conducted a nuclear test in the following month, Russia agreed to accept the new sanctions imposed by the UN Security Council. Following the conclusion by an expert inquiry in May 2010 that the sinking of a South Korean naval vessel in March had been caused by a torpedo fired by a North Korean submarine, the Russian Government undertook to 'closely consult' South Korea, and urged restraint on both sides.

In August 2011 Kim Jong Il paid a visit to Russia (his first since 2002) during which he held discussions with President Dmitrii Medvedev concerning North Korea's outstanding debt, the resumption of the six-party talks on North Korean nuclear facilities, and the possible construction of a pipeline supplying Russian gas to South Korea via North Korea. In September 2012 the Russian Government agreed to cancel 90% of the total of some US $11,000m. owed to it by North Korea, and to reinvest the remaining 10% as 'debt-for-aid' in the fields of energy, health and education. In April, meanwhile, Russia condemned the failed launch by North Korea of a long-range rocket, accusing North Korea of defying the UN Security Council. Russia likewise expressed 'regret' when North Korea launched another rocket, this time successfully, in December; following the testing of a North Korean nuclear device in February 2013 the Russian Government urged North Korea to 'cease its unlawful acts'. Russia gave its support to the respective UN Security Council resolutions that followed both events. During the marked increase in tension in March and April between North Korea on the one side and South Korea and the USA on the other, Russia urged all parties to prevent the situation from escalating. In March 2014 a Russian government delegation visited North Korea, concluding an agreement on using the Russian rouble for transactions between the two countries, with the aim of increasing bilateral trade to around US $1,000m. per year by 2020 (from some $105m. in 2013); in October it was reported that the two countries had signed a $25,000m. deal to modernize 3,500 km of North Korea's rail network. In November Choe Ryong Hae, the former Director of the KPA's General Political Bureau, visited Russia as a special envoy of Kim Jong Un, meeting with Russian President Putin and Minister of Foreign Affairs Sergei Lavrov. Following the visit, Lavrov announced that North Korea was prepared to resume the six-party denuclearization talks without preconditions. At the beginning of 2015 Kim Jong Un had still not undertaken any official foreign visits since his accession to power in 2011. In late January 2015 Russia announced that 'the North Korean leader' would be visiting Moscow in early May to attend the 70th anniversary celebrations of the Soviet victory over Nazi Germany in the Second World War; however, in late April a

Russian spokesman announced that Kim Jong Un would not be making the trip, owing to internal North Korean affairs.

North Korea has maintained close relations with a number of Middle Eastern countries, including Egypt, Libya, Syria and Iran, and with many African nations. In May 2004 it was reported that an IAEA investigation of uranium delivered to the USA by Libya in late 2003 had revealed that the material had been supplied to Libya by North Korea through an illicit nuclear technology procurement network operated by a Pakistani nuclear scientist. Further evidence concerning the transfer of nuclear material from North Korea to Libya emerged in early 2005. In January 2007 North Korea was reported to have agreed to share its data from the October 2006 nuclear test with scientists from Iran, but denied the allegations. In September 2007 North Korea similarly rejected claims that it was assisting Syria to develop a nuclear weapons programme. In March 2008 a visit by Kim Yong Nam and senior ministers to Namibia prompted speculation regarding North Korea's interest in that country's uranium resources. In September 2012 an agreement on scientific co-operation was concluded between North Korea and Iran, arousing suspicions that the co-operation was likely to include nuclear technology. During a visit to Syria by Minister of Foreign Affairs Ri Su Yong in June 2014, the two sides discussed bilateral co-operation, economic development and reconstruction.

North Korea maintains cordial relations with Cuba. In July 2013 the authorities in Panama seized a North Korean-registered ship, en route from Cuba, containing undeclared military items concealed under a cargo of sugar; the North Korean Government stated that it had a legitimate contract to repair the obsolete weaponry, but UN inspectors upheld the Panamanian view that the captain of the vessel was violating the embargo on supplying weapons to North Korea. Against the background of a growing rapprochement between the USA and Cuba, in March 2015 Minister of Foreign Affairs Ri Su Yong headed a delegation of North Korean officials on a state visit to the Cuban capital of Havana.

In January 2000 Italy became the first member of the Group of Seven (G7) Western industrialized nations (and the sixth member of the EU) to establish diplomatic relations with North Korea. Diplomatic relations were established with the United Kingdom in December 2000. During 2001 North Korea further expanded its range of diplomatic partners, opening relations with the EU itself and several other European countries, including Germany and Spain, as well as with Canada, Brazil and Turkey. The EU and individual member states strongly condemned North Korea's tests of nuclear devices in 2006, 2009 and 2013, urging the North Korean Government to resume negotiations on nuclear non-proliferation.

CONSTITUTION AND GOVERNMENT

Under the Constitution of 1972, the highest organ of state power is the unicameral Supreme People's Assembly (SPA), with 687 members, elected (unopposed) for five years by universal adult suffrage. The SPA elects, for its duration, the Chairman (First Chairman, since April 2012) of the National Defence Commission, who, since the effective abolition of the presidency in September 1998, holds the most senior accessible office of state. This position was designated as that of 'supreme leader' in 2009. The SPA elects the Premier and, on the latter's recommendation, appoints other Ministers to form the Cabinet. The President of the SPA Presidium, the members of which are elected by the SPA, represents the state in its relations with foreign countries.

Political power is held by the communist Korean Workers' Party (KWP), which is the most influential party in the Democratic Front for the Reunification of the Fatherland (comprising the KWP and two minor parties). The Front presents an approved list of candidates for elections to representative bodies. The KWP's highest authority is the Party Congress, which elects a Central Committee to supervise party work. The Committee elects a Political Bureau (Politburo) to direct policy. The Presidium of the Politburo is the KWP's most powerful policy-making body.

North Korea comprises nine provinces and two cities, each with an elected Local People's Assembly.

REGIONAL AND INTERNATIONAL CO-OPERATION

North Korea formally applied to join the Association of Southeast Asian Nations (ASEAN, see p. 210) in 2000, and the country was subsequently admitted to the ASEAN Regional Forum (ARF). The country has guest status in the Asia-Pacific Economic Co-operation (APEC, see p. 200) forum. North Korea is a member of the UN's Economic and Social Commission for Asia and the Pacific (ESCAP, see p. 30), having been admitted to the UN in 1991.

ECONOMIC AFFAIRS

In 2013, according to the Bank of Korea (the South Korean central bank), the gross national income (GNI) of North Korea was estimated to total 33,844.0m. won, equivalent to about 1.379m. won per head. According to UN estimates (based on a different method of calculation), North Korea's GNI per head decreased from US \$583 in 2012 to \$495 in 2013. During 2003–12, according to estimates by the World Bank, the population increased by an annual average of 0.6%. In 2004–13, according to UN estimates, gross domestic product (GDP) increased at an average annual rate of 0.7%; GDP growth in 2013 was an estimated 0.8%.

Agriculture (including hunting, forestry and fishing) contributed 22.4% of GDP in 2013, according to UN estimates. According to FAO, some 20.3% of the active labour force were estimated to be employed in the agricultural sector at mid-2015. The principal crops are maize, potatoes and rice. North Korea is not self-sufficient in food, and imports substantial amounts of wheat, rice and maize annually. Intermittent food shortages became a serious problem from the mid-1990s, and considerable support has been provided by the World Food Programme (WFP—see *Contemporary Political History*). Total estimated cereal production saw a moderate increase from 5.20m. metric tons in 2012 to 5.23m. tons in 2013. Potato production was 1.8m. tons in 2013, compared with 1.5m. metric tons in 2012, according to estimates. The raising of livestock (principally cattle and pigs), forestry and fishing are important. During 2004–13, according to UN estimates, agricultural GDP decreased by an average of 2.9% per year; according to the Bank of Korea, the sector's GDP was estimated to have increased by 6.9% in 2012, before declining by 7.9% in 2013.

In 2013, according to UN estimates, industry (including mining, manufacturing, construction and utilities) contributed 47.7% of GDP, and 34.3% of the employed population were engaged in the sector at the time of the 2008 census, according to official figures. During 2004–13, according to estimates from the UN, industrial GDP increased at an average annual rate of 0.7%. Industrial GDP increased by 4.5% in 2012, but decreased by 3.0% in 2013.

Mining contributed 17.8% of GDP in 2013, according to South Korean estimates. At the time of the 2008 census 5.9% of the employed population were engaged in the sector, according to official estimates. North Korea possesses considerable mineral wealth, with large deposits of coal, iron, lead, copper, zinc, tin, silver and gold. Output of hard coal totalled an estimated 41.0m. metric tons in 2012. There are unexploited offshore deposits of petroleum and natural gas, although the extent of these deposits has not yet been ascertained. South Korean sources estimated that the output of the mining sector increased by 2.1% in 2013.

In 2013, according to UN estimates, the manufacturing sector contributed 21.9% of GDP, and 23.7% of the employed population were engaged in the sector at the time of the 2008 census, according to official figures. Industrial development is concentrated on heavy industry (metallurgy—notably steel production, machine-building, cement and chemicals). The textiles industry has provided significant exports. According to UN estimates, the GDP of the manufacturing sector increased at an average annual rate of 0.9% in 2004–13. Manufacturing GDP expanded by 5.2% in 2012, but declined by 3.9% in 2013.

Construction, according to UN estimates, contributed 7.9% of GDP in 2013. The sector engaged 3.0% of the employed population at the time of the 2008 census, according to official figures. The GDP of the construction sector was estimated to have decreased at an average annual rate of 2.7% in 2004–13. The sector's GDP increased by 3.6% in 2012, before decreasing by 2.4% in 2013.

In 2011 it was estimated that 61.0% of North Korea's energy supply was derived from hydroelectricity, followed in importance by coal (36.3%) and petroleum (2.7%). A 30-MW nuclear reactor was believed to have been inaugurated at Yongbyon in 1987. From the 1990s North Korea experienced increasing power shortages, as generation declined and transmission infrastructure deteriorated. By late 2013 it was reported that the country's electricity generation was meeting less than 20% of its needs. Furthermore, the production of hydroelectric power was adversely affected by intermittent drought. In 2011 North Korea's electricity production totalled 21,630m. kWh, compared with 23,206m. kWh in 2008. Fuel oil shipments to North Korea have been intermittently suspended owing to international concerns regarding the country's nuclear programme.

According to UN estimates, the services sector contributed 29.9% of GDP in 2013, and the sector engaged 29.6% of the employed population at the time of the 2008 census, according to official figures. The GDP of the services sector was estimated to have decreased at an average annual rate of 1.8% in 2004–13; services GDP increased by 5.7% in 2012, but decreased by 2.4% in 2013.

According to South Korean sources, in 2013 total exports, excluding trade with South Korea, reached US $3,220m. and imports totalled $4,130m. Reportedly, North Korea's principal source of imports in 2011 was the People's Republic of China, which accounted for 90.6% of total imports. China was also North Korea's principal market for exports in that year, purchasing 87.9% of goods. Other trading partners in that year were Russia, Germany, India and Bangladesh. The principal exports in 2011 were coal (accounting for 41.8% of the total value of exports), minerals (14.3%) and textiles (13.9%). The principal imports in 2011 were petroleum and other fuels (23.1% of the value of total imports), machinery (8.6%) and electronic items (7.7%). According to data from the Bank of Korea, inter-Korean trade decreased from $1,971.1m. in 2012 to $1,135.9m. in 2013.

The Government planned an increase in overall budgetary spending in 2010 of 8.3%, while revenue was projected to rise by 6.3%. The 2011 budget, endorsed in April of that year, provided for expenditure of 567,000m. won. By 2008, according to one source, North Korea's total external debt was estimated to have reached US $18,000m. Following the introduction of market-orientated reforms in 2002, the inflation rate was believed to have reached 4,000% in that year. Between mid-2007 and mid-2008 the prices of staple foods reportedly increased by 100% in Pyongyang. The revaluation of the currency in December 2009 had major repercussions, and prices of basic commodities were reported to have risen substantially in 2010.

North Korea is one of the poorest countries in Asia, in contrast with South Korea, where income per head was estimated to be about 19 times that of the North in 2013. To date, North Korea's centrally planned economy has not overcome the difficulties caused by high external debt, lack of investment, international economic sanctions and disproportionate military spending, while agricultural production has often been affected by recurrent drought and flooding. Since the 1990s the country has intermittently depended on food and fertilizer aid (especially from China) to avert famine. In 2002 limited reforms allowed private agricultural production and marketing; at the same time, 'unofficial' private enterprise and trading began to proliferate in many sectors of the economy. The establishment of a special industrial zone at Kaesong from 2002 provided an important source of revenue for North Korea (see *Inter-Korean Relations*). A revaluation of the currency in December 2009 (apparently aimed at reducing inflation and currency hoarding by unofficial traders) eliminated many citizens' savings and, coupled with adverse weather affecting agricultural production, resulted in food shortages. By late 2010, the price of rice had soared to 40 times its pre-revaluation level. According to the South Korean Bank of Korea, GDP contracted in 2009 and 2010 before returning to positive growth, of 0.8%, in 2011. In January 2011 the State Strategy Plan for Economic Development, a new 10-year plan encompassing the period to 2020, was announced: covering 12 separate areas of development, it envisaged projects in the agricultural, petroleum and energy sectors, as well as improvements in the transport network. In June 2011 the North Korean

and Chinese Governments announced the expansion of an underdeveloped special economic zone (SEZ) at Rajin-Sonbong (Rason). The SEZ is linked to Russia by a 54-km railway and to China by road, in both cases funded by those countries, and has been accessible from North Korea since early 2014. In November 2013 the Government announced plans for the establishment of 13 new SEZs, across all provinces. Three were designated for industrial development, two for agriculture, two for export processing, and two for tourism. In March 2015 detailed proposals were announced for the development of a 430-sq km tourist region which would link the seaside resort of Wonsan with the Mount Kumgang area. (Despite government efforts to encourage foreign investment in the SEZs, it was reported in late 2014 that participation from countries other than Russia and China remained very low.) During 2012 there were reports (not officially confirmed) of significant policy changes, namely that the North Korean authorities were to allow manufacturers to set their own prices, and that farmers were to be permitted to keep 30% of their output to consume or sell, thus having an incentive to produce more food. According to UN estimates, North Korea recorded economic growth of 1.3% in 2012 and 0.8% in 2013. Electricity output was boosted from early 2012 by the completion of two power stations at Huichon, in Chagang Province, with an estimated joint generating capacity of 300 MW. In April 2013 agriculture, light industry and the modernization of the steel industry were identified as priority sectors for development in a budget speech by the outgoing Premier, Choe Yong Rim. According to South Korean research, total trade between North and South Korea was reported to have recovered in 2014 to reach some $2,300m. (following a year-on-year decrease of more than 42% to $1,135.9m. in 2013 largely as a result of the protracted closure of the Kaesong joint industrial complex); total trade with China declined by some 2% to $6,400m. in 2014, following an increase of more than 10% in 2013. Although an FAO-WFP food security assessment published in November 2013 indicated a cereals deficit of some 40,000 metric tons in 2013/14, it was reported in October 2014 that food exports to China had increased by 35% in 2013. Evidence of a growing unregulated private economy in North Korea was indicated by the introduction, in the second half of 2014, of measures permitting the selective application of free-market principles to the state economy. State factory managers were reportedly able to purchase raw materials and sell a portion of production on the open market, as well as recruiting and setting salary levels for their own staff. Family-based farming appeared to have been reinstated on an experimental basis, with farmers entitled to retain an increased quota, of 60%, of their own harvest.

PUBLIC HOLIDAYS

The *Juche* calendar was introduced in North Korea in 1997; AD1912, the year of the late Kim Il Sung's birth, was designated the first year of the new calendar.

2016: 1 January (New Year), 8 February (Seollal), 16–17 February (Day of the Shining Star, Kim Jong Il's Birthday), 4 April (Chungmyung Day), 15–16 April (Day of the Sun, Kim Il Sung's Birthday), 25 April (Army Day), 1 May (May Day), 27 July (Fatherland Liberation War Day), 15 August (Anniversary of Liberation), 9 September (Independence Day), 15 September (Chuseok), 10 October (Anniversary of the Foundation of the Korean Workers' Party), 27 December (Anniversary of the Constitution).

Statistical Survey

Area and Population

AREA, POPULATION AND DENSITY*

Area (sq km)	122,762†
Population (census results)	
31 December 1993	21,213,378
1 October 2008	
Males	11,721,838
Females	12,330,393
Total	24,052,231
Population (UN estimates at mid-year)‡	
2013	24,895,481
2014	25,026,590
2015	25,155,326
Density (per sq km) at mid-2015	204.9

* Excluding the demilitarized zone between North and South Korea, with an area of 1,262 sq km (487 sq miles).

† 47,399 sq miles.

‡ Source: UN, *World Population Prospects: The 2012 Revision.*

POPULATION BY AGE AND SEX
(UN estimates at mid-2015)

	Males	Females	Total
0–14 years	2,605,256	2,719,477	5,324,733
15–64 years	8,698,040	8,732,868	17,430,908
65 years and over	1,552,263	847,422	2,399,685
Total	12,855,559	12,300,767	25,155,326

Source: UN, *World Population Prospects: The 2012 Revision.*

ADMINISTRATIVE DIVISIONS
(population at 2008 census)

	Area (sq km)	Population ('000)	Density (per sq km)
Chagang Province	16,968	1,299,830	76.6
Hamgyong North Province* . .	17,570	2,327,362	132.5
Hamgyong South Province . .	18,970	3,066,013	161.6
Hwanghae North Province . .	9,262	2,113,672	228.2
Hwanghae South Province . .	8,002	2,310,485	288.7
Kangwon Province	11,152	1,477,582	132.5
Pyongan North Province . .	12,191	2,728,662	223.8
Pyongan South Province . .	12,330	4,051,696	328.6
Yanggang (Ryanggang) Province .	14,317	719,269	50.2
Pyongyang City	2,000	3,255,288	1,627.6
Total	122,762	24,052,231†	195.9

* Includes Najin-Sonbong, which enjoys the administrative status of Special City.

† Total includes population living in military camps.

Source: partly Thomas Brinkhoff, *City Population* (www.citypopulation.de).

PRINCIPAL TOWNS
(population at 2008 census)*

Pyongyang (capital).	2,581,076	Sariwon	271,434
Hamhung . . .	703,610	Kaechon	262,389
Chongjin . . .	614,892	Kanggye . . .	251,971
Sinuiju . . .	334,031	Sunchon . . .	250,738
Wonsan	328,467	Haeju	241,599
Nampo	310,531	Tanchon	240,873

* Population for urban areas of cities, as enumerated at census.

Mid-2014 (incl. suburbs, UN estimate): Pyongyang 2,856,050 (Source: UN, *World Urbanization Prospects: The 2014 Revision*).

BIRTHS AND DEATHS
(annual averages, UN estimates)

	2000–05	2005–10	2010–15
Birth rate (per 1,000)	16.7	14.7	14.4
Death rate (per 1,000)	8.4	9.0	9.2

Source: UN, *World Population Prospects: The 2012 Revision.*

2008 census (12 months ending 1 October 2008): Live births 345,630; deaths 216,616.

Life expectancy (years at birth): 69.5 (males 66.1; females 73.1) in 2012 (Source: World Bank, World Development Indicators database).

EMPLOYMENT
(persons aged 16 years and over at 2008 census)

	Males	Females	Total
Agriculture, forestry and fishing .	2,082,297	2,304,598	4,386,895
Mining and quarrying	458,484	259,711	718,195
Manufacturing	1,507,014	1,375,968	2,882,982
Electricity, gas and water . . .	161,098	55,184	216,282
Construction	285,941	81,709	367,650
Wholesale and retail trade; repair of motor vehicles	173,962	383,393	557,355
Transport, storage and communications	337,983	144,175	482,158
Hotels and restaurants . . .	26,591	114,614	141,205
Finance and insurance activities .	12,374	13,854	26,228
Professional, scientific and technical activities	80,574	37,558	118,132
Administrative and support service activities	287,951	163,385	451,336
Public administration and defence; compulsory social security . .	439,586	284,592	724,178
Education	263,635	284,497	548,132
Health and social welfare . . .	134,306	196,396	330,702
Arts, entertainment and recreation	72,290	58,292	130,582
Other services	35,852	66,856	102,708
Total employed	6,359,938	5,824,782	12,184,720

Note: Of the remaining total population aged 16 years and over, 940,886 were studying, 155,093 were disabled, 3,147,553 were retired, 921,191 were engaged in housework and 17,326 were described as 'other'.

Mid-2015 (estimates in '000): Agriculture, etc. 2,893; Total labour force 14,258 (Source: FAO).

Health and Welfare

KEY INDICATORS

Total fertility rate (children per woman, 2012)	2.0
Under-5 mortality rate (per 1,000 live births, 2012) . . .	29
HIV/AIDS (% of persons aged 15–49, 1994)	<0.01
Physicians (per 1,000 head, 2003)	3.3
Hospital beds (per 1,000 head, 2002)	13.2
Health expenditure (2006): US $ per head (PPP)	1
Health expenditure (2006): % of GDP	3.5
Health expenditure (2006): public (% of total)	85.6
Access to water (% of persons, 2012)	98
Access to sanitation (% of persons, 2012)	82
Total carbon dioxide emissions ('000 metric tons, 2010) . .	71,623.8
Carbon dioxide emissions per head (metric tons, 2010) . .	2.9

For sources and definitions, see explanatory note on p. vi.

Agriculture

PRINCIPAL CROPS
('000 metric tons)

	2011	2012	2013
Wheat*	127	74	75
Rice, paddy	2,479	2,861	2,901
Barley*	55	29	30
Maize	1,857	2,040	2,002
Rye†	70	74	82
Oats†	18	20	21
Millet	70*	70†	82†
Sorghum†	35	38	40
Potatoes	1,756	1,520	1,804
Sweet potatoes	439	380	451
Beans, dry†	340	305	310
Soybeans (Soya beans)* . . .	350	350	340
Cabbages and other brassicas† .	616	700	700
Tomatoes†	64	66	66
Pumpkins, squash and gourds† .	75	76	76
Cucumbers and gherkins . . .	66†	68†	68*
Aubergines (Eggplants)† . . .	47	48	48
Chillies and peppers, green† . .	47	50	50
Onions and shallots, green† . .	88	90	90
Onions, dry†	83	86	86
Garlic†	77	80	80
Apples†	752	785	780
Pears†	143	147	145
Peaches and nectarines† . . .	116	119	118
Watermelons†	86	90	90
Cantaloupes and other melons† .	88	88	88
Tobacco, unmanufactured† . .	79	80	80

* Unofficial figure(s).
† FAO estimate(s).

Aggregate production ('000 metric tons, may include official, semi-official or estimated data): Total cereals 4,711 in 2011, 5,202 in 2012, 5,233 in 2013; Total roots and tubers 2,195 in 2011, 1,900 in 2012, 2,255 in 2013; Total vegetables (incl. melons) 3,381 in 2011, 3,498 in 2012, 3,498 in 2013; Total fruits (excl. melons) 1,559 in 2011, 1,586 in 2012, 1,578 in 2013.

Source: FAO.

LIVESTOCK
('000 head)

	2010	2011	2012*
Horses	48*	48*	48
Cattle	577	577	590
Pigs	2,248	2,269	2,256
Sheep	166	168	170
Goats	3,556	3,657	3,600
Chickens	16,569	17,500	18000
Ducks	5,936	6,000*	6,500

* FAO estimate(s).

2013: Figures assumed to be unchanged from 2012 (FAO estimates).
Source: FAO.

LIVESTOCK PRODUCTS
('000 metric tons, FAO estimates)

	2010	2011	2012
Cattle meat	21.8	21.8	22.0
Goat meat	14.6	15.0	14.7
Pig meat	110.0	110.0	112.5
Chicken meat	31.9	31.9	33.0
Cows' milk	95.4	96.0	98.0
Hen eggs	114.0	120.0	125.0

2013: Figures assumed to be unchanged from 2012 (FAO estimates).
Source: FAO.

Forestry

ROUNDWOOD REMOVALS
('000 cubic metres, excl. bark, FAO estimates)

	2011	2012	2013
Sawlogs, veneer logs and logs for sleepers	1,000	1,000	1,000
Other industrial wood	500	500	500
Fuel wood	6,027	6,047	6,076
Total	7,527	7,547	7,576

Sawnwood production ('000 cubic metres, incl. railway sleepers): 280 (coniferous 185, broadleaved 95) per year in 1970–2013 (FAO estimates).

Source: FAO.

Fishing

('000 metric tons, live weight, FAO estimates)

	2010	2011	2012
Capture	200.0	207.0	212.0
Freshwater fishes	4.9	5.1	5.2
Alaska pollock	58.5	60.6	62.0
Other marine fishes	105.0	108.6	111.4
Marine crustaceans	15.6	16.2	16.5
Squids	9.3	9.6	9.8
Aquaculture	64.1	64.1	64.1
Molluscs	60.0	60.0	60.0
Total catch	264.1	271.1	276.1

Note: Figures exclude aquatic plants (FAO estimates, '000 metric tons, aquaculture only): 444.3 in 2007–12.

Source: FAO.

Mining

('000 metric tons, unless otherwise indicated, estimates)

	2008	2009	2010
Hard coal	25,060	36,000	41,000
Iron ore: gross weight	5,316	5,300	5,300
Iron ore: metal content . . .	1,488	1,500	1,500
Copper ore*	12	12	12
Lead ore*	13	13	13
Zinc ore*	70	70	70
Tungsten concentrates (metric tons)*	270	100	100
Silver (metric tons)*	20	20	20
Gold (kg)*	2,000	2,000	2,000
Magnesite (crude)	150,000	150,000	150,000
Phosphate rock†	300	300	300
Fluorspar‡	13	13	13
Salt (unrefined)	500	500	500
Graphite (natural)	30	30	30
Talc, soapstone and pyrophyllite .	50	50	50

* Figures refer to the metal content of ores and concentrates.
† Figures refer to gross weight.
‡ Metallurgical grade.

Note: No recent data were available for the production of molybdenum ore and asbestos.

2011–12: Production assumed to be unchanged from 2010.

Source: US Geological Survey.

Industry

SELECTED PRODUCTS
('000 metric tons unless otherwise indicated)

	2010	2011	2012
Motor spirit (petrol)	177	176	n.a.
Kerosene	36	36	n.a.
Gas-diesel (distillate fuel) oils .	189	188	n.a.
Residual fuel oils	108	108	n.a.
Cement*	6,400	6,400	6,400
Pig-iron*	900	900	900
Crude steel*	1,300	1,300	1,300
Refined copper (primary and secondary metal)*	15	15	15
Refined lead (primary and secondary metal)*	9	9	9
Zinc (primary and secondary metal)	75	75	75
Electric energy (million kWh) .	21,665	21,630	n.a.

* US Geological Survey estimates.

Source: mostly UN Industrial Commodity Statistics Database.

Finance

CURRENCY AND EXCHANGE RATES

Monetary Units
100 chon (jun) = 1 won.

Sterling, Dollar and Euro Equivalents (31 December 2014)
£1 sterling = 160.684 won;
US $1 = 102.950 won;
€1 = 124.992 won;
1,000 won = £6.22 = $9.71 = €8.00.

Note: In August 2002 it was reported that a currency reform had been introduced, whereby the exchange rate was adjusted from US $1 = 2.15 won to $1 = 150 won: a devaluation of 98.6%. In November 2009 reports of further currency reform emerged; a 'currency exchange' was believed to have been implemented in December, whereby denominations of the former currency were exchanged for new currency at a rate of 100 old won for 1 new won, resulting in an official exchange rate of some US $1 = 35 won. Despite reports in January 2010 that an exchange rate of US $1 = 96.9 won had been established by some financial institutions, prevailing market exchange rates were believed to be in the order of US $1 = 8,000 won by mid-2015, by which time international currencies including the US dollar, the euro and the renminbi were reported to be increasingly favoured for a majority of transactions.

BUDGET
(million won, reported)

	2004	2005	2006
Revenue	337,546	n.a.	n.a.
Expenditure	348,807	419,700	388,950

2007 (million won, reported, estimate): Total expenditure 440,200 (Defence 69,200).

2008 (million won, reported): Total expenditure 451,500 (Defence 71,300).

2009 (million won, reported): Total expenditure 482,600 (Defence 76,300).

2013 (percentage of total expenditure): Economic consolidation (incl. agriculture and construction) 45.2; Social projects (incl. education, health, arts and sports) 38.8; Defence 16.

NATIONAL ACCOUNTS
(million won, UN estimates)

Expenditure on the Gross Domestic Product

	2011	2012	2013
Total domestic expenditure . .	1,593,027.2	1,679,069.0	1,611,887.9
Exports of goods and services . .	88,851.2	93,626.0	89,994.9
Less Imports of goods and services	168,634.3	177,758.4	170,588.9
GDP in purchasers' values	1,513,244.1	1,594,936.6	1,531,293.9
GDP in constant 2005 prices	1,805,740.3	1,829,367.3	1,843,353.9

Gross Domestic Product by Economic Activity

	2011	2012	2013
Agriculture, hunting, forestry and fishing	348,849.3	372,831.7	343,332.0
Mining, manufacturing and utilities	600,404.0	628,631.3	608,863.1
Manufacturing	332,100.6	349,492.5	335,724.1
Construction	119,602.8	123,870.6	120,904.1
Services	444,392.6	469,598.1	458,196.5
Sub-total	1,513,248.8	1,594,931.8	1,531,295.6
Indirect taxes (net)*	−4.7	4.8	−1.7
GDP in purchasers' values .	1,513,244.1	1,594,936.6	1,531,293.9

* Figures obtained as a residual.

Source: UN National Accounts Main Aggregates Database.

External Trade

PRINCIPAL COMMODITIES
(US $ million)*

Imports	2000	2001	2002
Live animals and animal products	20.3	73.9	103.4
Vegetable products	159.0	221.0	118.4
Animal or vegetable fats and oils; prepared edible fats; animal or vegetable waxes			
Prepared foodstuffs; beverages, spirits and vinegar; tobacco and manufactured substitutes . .	89.1	89.9	72.3
Mineral products	171.2	231.1	235.9
Products of chemical or allied industries	108.4	123.4	122.1
Plastics, rubber and articles thereof	67.5	66.0	66.0
Textiles and textile articles . .	171.9	203.9	158.5
Base metals and articles thereof	85.2	100.4	88.2
Machinery and mechanical appliances; electrical equipment; sound and television apparatus . . .	205.1	243.8	234.7
Vehicles, aircraft, vessels and associated transport equipment	146.2	88.4	76.1
Total (incl. others)	1,406.5	1,620.3	1,525.4

Exports	2000	2001	2002
Live animals and animal products	97.9	158.4	261.1
Vegetable products	30.3	42.0	27.5
Mineral products	43.2	50.5	69.8
Products of chemical or allied industries	44.9	44.6	42.4
Plastics, rubber and articles thereof			
Wood, cork and articles thereof; wood charcoal; manufactures of straw, esparto, etc. . . .	10.9	5.6	10.2
Textiles and textile articles .	140.0	140.5	123.1
Natural or cultured pearls, precious or semi-precious stones, precious metals and articles thereof; imitation jewellery; coin	9.8	14.1	14.6

Exports—*continued*	2000	2001	2002
Base metals and articles thereof	43.9	60.2	57.4
Machinery and mechanical appliances; electrical equipment, sound and television apparatus . . .	105.2	97.9	85.6
Total (incl. others)	565.8	650.2	735.0

* Excluding trade with the Republic of Korea (US $ million): *Imports:* 272.8 in 2000; 226.8 in 2001; 370.2 in 2002. *Exports:* 152.4 in 2000; 176.2 in 2001; 271.6 in 2002.

Source: Korea Trade-Investment Promotion Agency (KOTRA), Republic of Korea.

2010 (US $ million, unofficial estimates): *Excluding Republic of Korea:* Total imports 2,660; Total exports 1,510. *Republic of Korea only:* Total imports 868; Total exports 1,044 (Source: Bank of Korea, Republic of Korea).

2011 (US $ million, unofficial estimates): *Excluding Republic of Korea:* Total imports 3,570; Total exports 2,790. *Republic of Korea only:* Total imports 800; Total exports 914 (Source: Bank of Korea, Republic of Korea).

2012 (US $ million, unofficial estimates): *Excluding Republic of Korea:* Total imports 3,930; Total exports 2,880. *Republic of Korea only:* Total imports 897; Total exports 1,074 (Source: Bank of Korea, Republic of Korea).

PRINCIPAL TRADING PARTNERS
(US $ million)*

Imports	2001	2002	2003
China, People's Republic . . .	570.7	467.3	627.6
Germany	82.1	140.4	n.a.
Hong Kong	42.6	29.2	n.a.
India	154.8	186.6	157.9
Japan	249.1	135.1	91.5
Netherlands	9.1	27.6	n.a.
Russia	63.8	77.0	115.6
Singapore	112.3	83.0	n.a.
Spain	31.6	n.a.	n.a.
Thailand	106.0	172.0	203.6
United Kingdom	40.7	n.a.	n.a.
Total (incl. others)	1,620.3	1,525.4	1,614.4

Exports	2001	2002	2003
Bangladesh	38.0	32.3	n.a.
China, People's Republic . . .	166.8	270.9	395.3
Germany	22.8	27.8	n.a.
Hong Kong	38.0	21.9	n.a.
India	3.1	4.8	1.6
Japan	225.6	234.4	173.8
Netherlands	10.4	6.4	n.a.
Russia	4.5	3.6	2.8
Spain	12.6	n.a.	n.a.
Thailand	24.9	44.6	50.7
Total (incl. others)	650.2	735.0	777.0

* Excluding trade with the Republic of Korea (US $ million): *Imports:* 226.8 in 2001; 370.2 in 2002; 435.0 in 2003. *Exports:* 176.2 in 2001; 271.6 in 2002; 289.3 in 2003.

Source: Korea Trade-Investment Promotion Agency (KOTRA), Republic of Korea.

2004 (US $ million): *Imports:* China, People's Republic 800; Japan 89; Korea, Republic 439; Total (incl. others) 2,280. *Exports:* China, People's Republic 586; Japan 163; Korea, Republic 258; Total (incl. others) 1,280 (Source: Ministry of Unification, Republic of Korea).

Trade with Republic of Korea (US $ million, unofficial estimates): *Total imports:* 800.2 in 2011; 897.2 in 2012; 520.6 in 2013. *Total exports:* 913.7 in 2011; 1,074.0 in 2012; 615.2 in 2013 (Source: Bank of Korea, Republic of Korea).

Transport

SHIPPING
Flag Registered Fleet
(at 31 December)

	2012	2013	2014
Number of vessels	316	301	300
Total displacement ('000 grt) . .	879.7	742.8	702.3

Source: Lloyd's List Intelligence (www.lloydslistintelligence.com).

CIVIL AVIATION
(traffic on scheduled services)

	2007	2008	2009
Kilometres flown (million) . .	1	1	1
Passengers carried ('000) . . .	111	109	101
Passenger-km (million) . . .	45	44	41
Total ton-km (million)	7	7	6

Source: UN, *Statistical Yearbook*.

Passengers carried ('000): 78.6 in 2011; 100.1 in 2012; 107.7 in 2013 (Source: World Bank, World Development Indicators database).

Tourism

	1996	1997	1998
Tourist arrivals ('000)	127	128	130

Source: World Tourism Organization.

Communications Media

	2011	2012	2013
Telephones ('000 main lines in use)	1,180	1,180	1,180
Mobile cellular telephones ('000 subscribers)	1,000.0	1,700.0	2,420.0

Source: International Telecommunication Union.

Education

(2000)

	Institutions	Students
Kindergartens	14,167	748,416
Primary	4,886	1,609,865
Senior middle schools	4,772	2,181,524

Source: mainly Government of the Democratic People's Republic of Korea, *UNESCO Education for All Assessment Report 2000*.

Universities and Colleges: The *UNESCO Education for All Assessment Report 2000* identified more than 300 universities and colleges, with 1.89m. students and academics.

Teachers (1987/88, UNESCO estimates): Pre-primary 35,000, Primary 59,000, Secondary 111,000, Universities and colleges 23,000, Other tertiary 4,000 (Source: UNESCO, *Statistical Yearbook*).

Directory

The Government

HEAD OF STATE

Following the death of the General Secretary of the Korean Workers' Party and the Chairman of the National Defence Commission, Kim Jong Il, who had ruled the country since the death of his father Kim Il Sung in 1994, his third son, Kim Jong Un, was declared the Supreme Leader on 29 December 2011, by the Titular Head of State, Kim Yong Nam. The following day Kim Jong Un was formally confirmed as Supreme Commander of the Korean People's Army and was referred to by the state media as the Great Leader. He was appointed First Chairman of the National Defence Commission on 14 April 2012, while Kim Jong Il was named Eternal Chairman.

Eternal President: President KIM IL SUNG died on 8 July 1994 and was declared Eternal President in September 1998.

Eternal Chairman of the National Defence Commission: KIM JONG IL died on 17 December 2011 and was declared Eternal Chairman on 13 April 2012.

First Chairman of the National Defence Commission: Marshal KIM JONG UN.

Titular Head of State: KIM YONG NAM.

CABINET
(May 2015)

The Government is formed by the Korean Workers' Party (KWP).

Premier: PAK PONG JU.

Vice-Premier: KIM YONG JIN.

Vice-Premier and Chairman of the State Planning Commission: RO TU CHOL.

Vice-Premier and Minister of Chemical Industry: RI MU YONG.

Vice-Premier and Minister of Agriculture: RI CHOL MAN.

Minister of Foreign Affairs: RI SU YONG.

Minister of the People's Armed Forces: (vacant).

Minister of State Security: Gen. KIM WON HONG.

Minister of People's Security: Gen. CHOE PU IL.

Minister of Electric Power Industry: KIM MAN SU.

Minister of Machine-building Industries: RI JONG GUK.

Minister of the Electronics Industry: KIM JAE SONG.

Minister of the Coal Industry: MUN MYONG HAK.

Minister of the Mining Industry: RI HAK CHOL.

Minister of the Oil Industry: PAE HAK YI.

Minister of the Metal Industry: KIM YONG KWANG.

Minister of National Resource Development: RI CHUN SAM.

Minister of Construction and Building Materials Industries: TONG JONG HO.

Minister of Railways: JON KIL SU.

Minister of Land and Marine Transport: KANG JONG GWAN.

Minister of Light Industry: AN JONG SU.

Minister of Foreign Trade: RI RYONG NAM.

Minister of Atomic Energy Industry: RI JE SON.

Minister of Forestry: HAN RYONG GUK.

Minister of Fisheries: RI HYUK.

Minister of Urban Management: KANG YONG SU.

Minister of State Construction Control: KWON SONG HO.

Minister of Land and Environmental Protection: KIM KYUNG JUN.

Minister of Commerce: KIM KYONG NAM.

Minister of Food Procurement and Administration: MUN UNG JO.

Minister of Education: KIM SUNG DU.

Minister of Higher Education: THAE HYONG CHOL.

Minister of Post and Telecommunications: SIM CHOL HO.

Minister of Culture: PAK CHUN NAM.

Minister of Labour: JONG YONG SU.

Minister of Public Health: KANG HA-GUK.

Minister of State Inspection: KIM UI SUN.

Minister of Finance: CHOE KWANG JIN.

Minister of the Foodstuff and Daily Necessities Industry: JO YONG CHOL.

Minister of Physical Culture and Sports: RI JONG MU.

President of the State Academy of Sciences: JANG CHOL.

President of the Central Bank: KIM CHON GYUN.

Chairman of the State Science and Technology Commission: CHOE SANG GON.

Director of the Central Statistics Bureau: RI SUNG HO.

Secretary-General of the Cabinet: KIM YONG HO.

MINISTRIES

All Ministries and Commissions are in Pyongyang.

Legislature

SUPREME PEOPLE'S ASSEMBLY
(Choe Ko In Min Hoe Ui)

The 687 members of the 13th Supreme People's Assembly (SPA) were elected unopposed for a five-year term on 9 March 2014. The SPA's permanent body is the Presidium.

Chairman: CHOE TAE BOK.

President of the Presidium: KIM YONG NAM.

Vice-Presidents of the Presidium: YANG HYONG SOP, KIM YONG DAE.

Secretary-General of the Presidium: HONG SON OK.

Political Organizations

Democratic Front for the Reunification of the Fatherland: Pyongyang; f. 1946; vanguard org. comprising political parties and mass working people's orgs seeking the unification of North and South Korea; Dir KIM YANG GON.

The component parties are:

Chondoist Chongu Party: Pyongyang; tel. (2) 334241; f. 1946; follows the guiding principle of *Innaechon* (the realization of 'heaven on earth'); satellite party of the KWP; Chair. RYU MI YONG.

Korean Social Democratic Party (KSDP) (Joson Sahoeminju-dang): Pyongyang; tel. (2) 5591323; fax (2) 3814410; f. 1945; advocates national independence and a democratic socialist society; satellite party of the KWP; Chair. KIM YONG DAE.

Korean Workers' Party (KWP): Pyongyang; internet www.rodong.rep.kp; f. 1945; merged with South Korean Workers' Party in 1949; follows the guiding principle of *Juche*, based on the concept that man is the master and arbiter of all things; most significant political entity in the DPRK; Central Cttee of 124 full mems and 105 alternate mems; 3m. mems; First Sec. Marshal KIM JONG UN.

SEVENTH CENTRAL COMMITTEE OF THE KWP

Eternal General Secretary: Generalissimo KIM JONG IL.

POLITICAL BUREAU (POLITBURO) OF THE KWP

Presidium: Marshal KIM JONG UN, KIM YONG NAM, Gen. CHOE RYONG HAE, Vice-Marshal HWANG PYONG SO.

Full Members: KIM KI NAM, CHOE THAE BOK, YANG HYONG SOP, KANG SOK JU, Vice-Marshal RI YONG MU, KIM KYONG HUI, PAK TO CHUN, PAK PONG JU, Gen. KIM WON HONG, Gen. O KUK RYOL.

Alternate Members: KIM YANG GON, O SU YONG, Gen. CHOE PU IL, THAE JONG SU, KIM PYONG HAE, Gen. RI YONG GIL, Gen. HYON YONG CHOL, KWAK POM GI, RO TU CHOL, JO YON JUN, CHOE YONG RIM.

Secretariat: Marshal KIM JONG UN, KIM KI NAM, CHOE THAE BOK, CHOE RYONG HAE, MUN KYONG DOK, PAK TO CHUN, KIM YONG IL, KIM YANG GOK, TAE JONG SU, KIM PYONG HAE, KIM KYONG HUI, KWAK POM GI.

The component mass working people's organizations (see under Trade Unions) are:

General Federation of Trade Unions of Korea (GFTUK).

Kim Il Sung Socialist Youth League.

Korean Democratic Women's Union (KDWU).

Union of Agricultural Working People of Korea.

Diplomatic Representation

EMBASSIES IN THE DEMOCRATIC PEOPLE'S REPUBLIC OF KOREA

Brazil: 3 Munsudong, Taedongkang District, Pyongyang; tel. (2) 3817955; fax (2) 3817699; Ambassador ARNALDO CARRILHO.

Bulgaria: Munsudong, Taedongkang District, Pyongyang; tel. (2) 3817343; fax (2) 3817342; e-mail embassy.pyongyang@mfa.bg; internet www.mfa.bg/embassies/nordkorea; Chargé d'affaires VENTZISLAV IVANOV.

Cambodia: Munsudong, Taedongkang District, Pyongyang; tel. (2) 3817283; fax (2) 3817625; e-mail recpyongyang@gmail.com; Ambassador OP SISAWADA.

China, People's Republic: Kinmauldong, Moranbong District, Pyongyang; tel. (2) 3813116; fax (2) 3813425; e-mail chinaemb_kp@mfa.gov.cn; internet kp.china-embassy.org; Ambassador LI JINJUN.

Cuba: Munsudong, Taedongkang District, POB 5, Pyongyang; tel. (2) 3817370; fax (2) 3817703; e-mail embajada@rpdc.cubaminrex.cu; Ambassador GERMÁN HERMÍN FERRAS ALVAREZ.

Czech Republic: Taedongkang Guyok 38, Taehakgori, Puksudong, Pyongyang; tel. (2) 3817021; fax (2) 3817022; e-mail pyongyang@embassy.mzv.cz; internet www.mzv.cz/pyongyang; Ambassador MILAN HUPCEJ.

Egypt: 39 Munsudong, Taedongkang District, Pyongyang; tel. (2) 3817414; fax (2) 3817410; e-mail embassy.pyongyang@mfa.gov.eg; internet www.mfa.gov.eg/english/embassies/egyptian_embassy_north_korea; Ambassador EMAN MUSTAFA.

Ethiopia: Munsudong, Taedongkang District, POB 55, Pyongyang; tel. (2) 3827554; fax (2) 3827550; Chargé d'affaires a.i. FEKADE S. G. MESKEL.

Germany: Munsudong, Pyongyang; tel. (2) 3817385; fax (2) 3817397; e-mail info@pjoengjang.diplo.de; Ambassador Dr THOMAS SCHÄFER.

India: 6 Taehak St, Munsudong, Taedongkang District, Pyongyang; tel. (2) 3817274; fax (2) 3817619; e-mail amb.pyongyang@mea.gov.in; Ambassador AJAY K. SHARMA.

Indonesia: 5 Foreigners' Bldg, Munsudong, Taedongkang District, Pyongyang; tel. (2) 3827439; fax (2) 3817620; e-mail kompyg2@public2.bta.net.cn; Ambassador BAMBANG HIENDRASTO.

Iran: Munhungdong, Monsu St, Taedongkang District, Pyongyang; tel. (2) 3817214; fax (2) 3817612; e-mail embpyong@mfa.gov.ir; Ambassador MANSOUR CHAVOSHI.

Laos: Munhungdong, Taedongkang District, Pyongyang; tel. (2) 3827363; fax (2) 3817722; Ambassador KIETTISAK KEOBANHDITH.

Malaysia: Munhungdong, Taedongkang District, Pyongyang; tel. (2) 3817125; fax (2) 3817845; e-mail mwpyongyang@kln.gov.my; Ambassador (vacant).

Mongolia: 17 Taehak St, Munsudong, Taedongkang District, Pyongyang; tel. (2) 3827322; fax (2) 3817616; e-mail mon-emb@kcckp.net; Ambassador MANIBADRAKHYN GANBOLD.

Nigeria: Munsudong, Taedongkang District, POB 535, Pyongyang; tel. (2) 3827558; fax (2) 3817293; e-mail empngrdprk@yahoo.com; Ambassador ALEXANDER NWOFE.

Pakistan: 23, Blk 66, Munsudong, Taedongkang District, Pyongyang; tel. (2) 3827479; fax (2) 3817622; e-mail parep.pyongyang@gmail.com; internet www.mofa.gov.pk/northkorea; Ambassador SYED HASAN HABIB.

Poland: Munsudong, Taedongkang District, Pyongyang; tel. (2) 3817325; fax (2) 3817634; e-mail pjongjang.amb.sekretariat@msz.gov.pl; internet www.pjongjang.polemb.net; Ambassador KRZYSZTOF CIEBIEŃ.

Romania: Munhungdong, Taedongkang District, Pyongyang; tel. (2) 3827336; fax (2) 3817336; e-mail romania.dprk@yahoo.com; Chargé d'affaires a.i. ANDY AVRAM.

Russian Federation: Sinyangdong, Central District, Pyongyang; tel. (2) 3813101; fax (2) 3813427; e-mail embassy@rusembdprk.ru; internet www.dprk.mid.ru; Ambassador ALEXANDR IVANOVICH MATSEGORA.

Sweden: Munsudong, Taedongkang District, Pyongyang; tel. (2) 3817485; fax (2) 3817663; e-mail ambassaden.pyongyang@foreign.ministry.se; Ambassador KARL-OLOF ANDERSSON.

Syria: Munsudong, Taedongkang District, Pyongyang; tel. (2) 3827473; fax (2) 3817635; Ambassador TAMMAM AHMAD SULEIMAN.

United Kingdom: Munsudong, Taedongkang District, Pyongyang; tel. (2) 3817980; fax (2) 3817985; e-mail postmaster.pyonx@fco.gov.uk; internet ukindprk.fco.gov.uk/en; Ambassador MICHAEL JOHN GIFFORD.

Viet Nam: 7 Munsudong, Taedongkang District, Pyongyang; tel. (2) 3817358; fax (2) 3817649; e-mail vnembassydprk@mofa.gov.vn; internet www.vietnamembassy-pyongyang.org; Ambassador PHAM VIET HUNG.

Judicial System

Central Court (Supreme Court): Pyongyang; the highest judicial organ, which supervises the work of all courts (the Court of the Province—or city under central authority—and the People's Court, each constituted by judges and people's assessors; Pres. (vacant).

Central Procurator's Office: Pyongyang; supervises the work of procurator's offices in provinces, counties and cities; procurators examine the ordinances and regulations of all ministries and the decisions and directives of local organs of state power to ensure that they conform to the Constitution, laws and decrees, as well as to the decisions and other measures of the Cabinet; procurators can bring suits against criminals in the name of the state, and participate in civil cases to protect the interests of the state and citizens; Procurator-General RI KIL SONG.

Religion

The religions that are officially reported to be practised in North Korea are Buddhism, Christianity and Chundo Kyo, a religion peculiar to Korea combining elements of Buddhism and Christianity. Religious co-ordinating bodies are believed to be under strict state control. The exact number of religious believers is unknown.

Korean Religious Believers' Council: Pyongyang; f. 1989; brings together members of religious organizations in North Korea; Chair. JANG JAE ON.

BUDDHISM

In 2002 it was reported that there were an estimated 300 Buddhist temples in North Korea; the number of believers was estimated at about 10,000 in 2003.

Korean Buddhists' Federation: POB 77, Pyongyang; tel. (2) 43698; fax (2) 3812100; f. 1945; Chair. Cen. Cttee SHIM SANG JIN; Sec. JONG SO JONG.

CHRISTIANITY

In 2003 it was reported that there were approximately 13,000 Protestants and 3,000 Roman Catholics in the country, many of whom worshipped in house churches (of which there were said to be about 500 in 2002). The construction of North Korea's first Russian Orthodox church was completed in 2006.

Korean Christians' Federation: Pyongyang; f. 1946; Chair. Cen. Cttee KANG YONG SOP; Sec. O KYONG U.

The Roman Catholic Church

For ecclesiastical purposes, North and South Korea are nominally under a unified jurisdiction. North Korea contains two dioceses (Hamhung and Pyongyang), both suffragan to the archdiocese of Seoul (in South Korea), and the territorial abbacy of Tokwon (Tokugen), directly responsible to the Holy See.

Diocese of Hamhung: Catholic Mission, Hamhung; 134-1 Waekwan-dong Kwan Eub, Chil kok kun, Gyeongbuk 718-800, Republic of Korea; tel. (545) 970-2000; Bishop (vacant); Apostolic Administrator of Hamhung and of the Abbacy of Tokwon Fr PLACIDUS DONG-HO RI.

Diocese of Pyongyang: Catholic Mission, Pyongyang; Bishop Rt Rev. FRANCIS HONG YONG HO (absent); Apostolic Administrator Most Rev. NICHOLAS CHEONG JIN-SUK (Archbishop of Seoul, South Korea).

Korean Catholics' Association: Changchung 1-dong, Songyo District, Pyongyang; tel. (2) 23492; f. 1988; Chair. Cen. Cttee JANG JAE ON; Vice-Chair. MUN CHANG HAK.

CHUNDO KYO

According to officials quoted in 2002, there were approximately 40,000 practitioners of Chundo Kyo in North Korea.

Korean Chundoists' Association: Pyongyang; tel. (2) 334241; f. 1946; Chair. of Central Guidance Cttee RYU MI YONG.

The Press

PRINCIPAL NEWSPAPERS

Choldo Sinmun: Pyongyang; f. 1947; every two days.

Joson Inmingun (Korean People's Army Daily): Pyongyang; f. 1948; daily; Editor-in-Chief RI TAE BONG.

Kyowon Sinmun: Pyongyang; f. 1948; publ. by the Education Commission; weekly.

Minju Choson (Democratic Korea): Pyongyang; f. 1946; govt organ; 6 a week; Exec. Editor JONG RI JONG; circ. 200,000.

Nongup Kunroja: Pyongyang; publ. of Cen. Cttee of the Union of Agricultural Working People of Korea.

Pyongyang Sinmun: Pyongyang; f. 1957; general news; 6 a week; Editor-in-Chief SONG RAK GYUN.

Rodong Chongnyon (Working Youth): Pyongyang; f. 1946; organ of the Cen. Cttee of the Kim Il Sung Socialist Youth League; 6 a week; Editor-in-Chief RI JONG GI.

Rodong Sinmun (Labour Daily): Pyongyang; internet www.kcna .co.jp/today-rodong/rodong.htm; f. 1946; organ of the Cen. Cttee of the Korean Workers' Party; daily; Exec. Editor RI YONG SIK; circ. 1.5m.

Rodongja Sinmun (Workers' Newspaper): Pyongyang; f. 1945; organ of the Gen. Fed. of Trade Unions of Korea; Editor-in-Chief RI SONG JU.

Saenal (New Day): Pyongyang; f. 1971; publ. by the Kim Il Sung Socialist Youth League; 2 a week; Deputy Editor CHOE SANG IN.

Sonyon Sinmun: Pyongyang; f. 1946; publ. by the Kim Il Sung Socialist Youth League; 2 a week; circ. 120,000.

Tongil Sinbo: Kangan 1-dong, Youth Ave, Songyo District, Pyongyang; f. 1972; non-affiliated; weekly; Chief Editor PAK JIN SIK; circ. 300,000.

PRINCIPAL PERIODICALS

Chollima: Pyongyang; popular magazine; monthly.

Choson (Korea): Pyongyang; social, economic, political and cultural; bi-monthly.

Choson Minju Juuiinmin Gonghwaguk Palmyonggongbo (Official Report of Inventions in the DPRK): Pyongyang; 6 a year.

Choson Munhak (Korean Literature): Pyongyang; organ of the Cen. Cttee of the Korean Writers' Union; monthly.

Choson Yesul (Korean Arts): Pyongyang; organ of the Cen. Cttee of the Gen. Fed. of Unions of Literature and Arts of Korea; monthly.

Economics: POB 73, Pyongyang; fax (2) 3814410; quarterly.

History: POB 73, Pyongyang; fax (2) 3814410; quarterly.

Hwahakgwa Hwahakgoneop: Pyongyang; organ of the Hamhung br. of the Korean Acad. of Sciences; chemistry and chemical engineering; 6 a year.

Jokook Tongil: Kangan 1-dong, Youth Ave, Songyo District, Pyongyang; organ of the Cttee for the Peaceful Unification of Korea; f. 1961; monthly; Chief Editor LI MYONG GYU; circ. 70,000.

Korean Medicine: POB 73, Pyongyang; fax (2) 3814410; quarterly.

Kunroja (Workers): 1 Munshindong, Tongdaewon, Pyongyang; f. 1946; organ of the Cen. Cttee of the Korean Workers' Party; monthly; Editor-in-Chief RYANG KYONG BOK; circ. 300,000.

Kwahakwon Tongbo (Bulletins of the Academy of Science): POB 73, Pyongyang; fax (2) 3814410; organ of the Standing Cttee of the Korean Acad. of Sciences; 6 a year.

Mulri (Physics): POB 73, Pyongyang; fax (2) 3814410; quarterly.

Munhwao Haksup (Study of Korean Language): POB 73, Pyongyang; fax (2) 3814410; publ. by the Publishing House of the Acad. of Social Sciences; quarterly.

Philosophy: POB 73, Pyongyang; fax (2) 3814410; quarterly.

Punsok Hwahak (Analysis): POB 73, Pyongyang; fax (2) 3814410; organ of the Cen. Analytical Inst. of the Korean Acad. of Sciences; quarterly.

Ryoksagwahak (Historical Science): Pyongyang; publ. by the Acad. of Social Sciences; quarterly.

Saengmulhak (Biology): Pyongyang; fax (2) 3814410; publ. by the Korea Science and Encyclopedia Publishing House; quarterly.

Sahoekwahak (Social Science): Pyongyang; publ. by the Acad. of Social Sciences; 6 a year.

Suhakkwa Mulli: Pyongyang; organ of the Physics and Mathematics Cttee of the Korean Acad. of Sciences; quarterly.

FOREIGN LANGUAGE PUBLICATIONS

The Democratic People's Republic of Korea: Korea Pictorial, Pyongyang; f. 1956; illustrated news; Korean, Russian, Chinese, English, French, Arabic and Spanish edns; monthly; Editor-in-Chief HAN POM CHIK.

Foreign Trade of the DPRK: Foreign Trade Publishing House, Potonggang District, Pyongyang; economic developments and export promotion; English, French, Japanese, Russian and Spanish edns; monthly.

Korea: Pyongyang; f. 1956; illustrated; Korean, Arabic, Chinese, English, French, Spanish and Russian edns; monthly.

Korea Today: Foreign Languages Publishing House, Pyongyang; current affairs; Chinese, English, French, Russian and Spanish edns; monthly; Vice-Dir and Editor-in-Chief HAN PONG CHAN.

Korean Women: Pyongyang; English and French edns; quarterly.

Korean Youth and Students: Pyongyang; English and French edns; monthly.

The Pyongyang Times: Sochondong, Sosong District, Pyongyang; tel. (2) 51951; English, Spanish and French edns; weekly.

NEWS AGENCY

Korean Central News Agency (KCNA): Potonggangdong 1, Potonggang District, Pyongyang; e-mail eng-info@kcna.co.jp; internet www.kcna.co.jp; f. 1946; sole distributing agency for news in the DPRK; publs daily bulletins in English, Russian, French and Spanish; Dir-Gen. KIM PYONG HO.

PRESS ASSOCIATION

Korean Journalists' Union: Pyongyang; tel. (2) 36897; f. 1946; assists in the ideological work of the Korean Workers' Party; Chair. Cen. Cttee KIM SONG GUK.

Publishers

Academy of Sciences Publishing House: Nammundong, Central District, Pyongyang; tel. (2) 51956; f. 1953.

Academy of Social Sciences Publishing House: Pyongyang; Dir CHOE KWAN SHIK.

Agricultural Press: Pyongyang; labour, industrial relations; Pres. HO KYONG PIL.

Central Science and Technology Information Agency: Pyongyang; f. 1963; Dir JU SONG RYONG.

Education Publishing House: Pyongyang; f. 1945; Pres. KIM CHANG SON.

Foreign Language Press Group: Sochondong, Sosong District, Pyongyang; tel. (2) 841342; fax (2) 812100; f. 1949; Dir CHOE KYONG GUK.

Foreign Language Publishing House: Oesong District, Pyongyang; Dir KIM YONG MU.

Higher Educational Books Publishing House: Pyongyang; f. 1960; Pres. PAK KUN SONG.

Kim Il Sung University Publishing House: Pyongyang; f. 1965.

Korea Science and Encyclopedia Publishing House: POB 73, Pyongyang; tel. (2) 18111; fax (2) 3814410; publishes numerous periodicals and monographs; f. 1952; Dir-Gen. KIM JUNG HYOP; Dir of International Co-operation JEAN BAHNG.

Korean People's Army Publishing House: Pyongyang; Pres. YUN MYONG DO.

Korean Social Democratic Party Publishing House: Pyongyang; tel. (2) 5591709; fax (2) 3814410; f. 1946; publishes quarterly journal *Joson Sahoemingjudang* (in Korean) and *KSDP Says* (in English); Dir RI KANG SIK.

Korean Workers' Party Publishing House: Pyongyang; f. 1945; fiction, politics; Exec. Editor and Dir RI YONG CHOL.

Kumsong Youth Publishing House: Pyongyang; f. 1946; Dir HAN JONG SOP.

Literature and Art Publishing House: Pyongyang; f. by merger of Mass Culture Publishing House and Publishing House of the Gen. Fed. of Literary and Art Unions; Dir-Gen. RI PHYO U.

Transportation Publishing House: Namgyodong, Hyongjaesan District, Pyongyang; f. 1952; travel; Editor PAEK JONG HAN.

Working People's Organizations Publishing House: Pyongyang; f. 1946; fiction, government, political science; Dir MIN SANG HYON.

WRITERS' UNION

Korean Writers' Union: Pyongyang; Chair. Cen. Cttee KIM PYONG HUN.

Broadcasting and Communications

Information flow within North Korea is still mainly conducted via a closed intranet system (Kwangmyong), which was opened in 2000, with access to the global internet severely limited. In October 2001 North Korea launched its first e-mail service provider in co-operation with the China-based company Silibank, which can be used by registered users for business and trade purposes. Although a mobile telephone network was established in 2002, the use of mobile telephones was banned in 2004. However, the ban was subsequently removed, and Orascom Telecom Holding, a provider based in Egypt, was permitted to establish a 3G mobile service, Koryolink, as a joint venture with the state-owned Korea Post and Telecommunications Corporation in 2008. There were reported to be over 2m. subscribers to Koryolink by mid-2013. In January 2013 a previous policy was reversed and foreign visitors were permitted to bring mobile telephones into North Korea and purchase a SIM card for the local network; in February Koryolink launched a mobile internet service for foreign visitors. As of April 2015 North Korean citizens were not permitted to call overseas and were also unable to call numbers owned by foreign residents. Foreign residents were usually allowed to call overseas, but were unable to call the numbers of ordinary North Koreans.

TELECOMMUNICATIONS

Korea Post and Telecommunications Co: Pyongyang.

BROADCASTING

Regulatory Authority

Central Broadcasting Committee of the DPRK: Jonsungdong, Moranbong District, Pyongyang; tel. (2) 3816035; fax (2) 3812100; Chair. HWANG YONG BO.

Radio

There are 17 AM radio stations, 14 FM stations and 11 short-wave stations.

Korean Central Broadcasting Station: Pyongyang; programmes relayed nationally with local programmes supplied by local radio cttees; loudspeakers are installed in factories and in open spaces in all towns; home broadcasting 22 hours daily; foreign broadcasts in Russian, Chinese, English, French, German, Japanese, Spanish and Arabic.

Television

There are four television stations in operation.

General Bureau of Television: Gen. Dir CHA SUNG SU.

DPRK Radio and Television Broadcasting Committee: see Radio.

Kaesong Television: Kaesong; broadcasts five hours on weekdays, 11 hours at weekends.

Korean Central Television Station: Ministry of Post and Telecommunications, Pyongyang; broadcasts five hours daily; satellite broadcasts commenced Oct. 1999.

Mansudae Television Station: Mansudae, Pyongyang; f. 1983; broadcasts nine hours of cultural programmes, music and dance, foreign films and news reports at weekends.

Finance

(cap. = capital; res = reserves; dep. = deposits; m. = million; br(s) = branch(es); amounts in won)

BANKING

A total of 18 banks were reported to be in operation in mid-2011.

Central Bank

Central Bank of the DPRK: Munsudong, Seungri St 58-1, Central District, Pyongyang; tel. (2) 3338196; fax (2) 3814624; e-mail kcb_idkb@co.chesin.com; f. 1946; bank of issue; supervisory and control bank; Pres. PAEK RYONG CHON; 13 brs.

State Banks

Credit Bank of Korea: Chongryu 1-dong, Munsu St, Otandong, Central District, Pyongyang; tel. (2) 3818285; fax (2) 3817806; f. 1986; est. as International Credit Bank, name changed 1989; Pres. LI SUN BOK; Vice-Pres. SON YONG SUN.

Foreign Trade Bank of the DPRK: FTB Bldg, Jungsongdong, Seungri St, Central District, Pyongyang; tel. (2) 3815270; fax (2) 3814467; e-mail ftb@co.chesin.com; f. 1959; deals in international settlements and all banking business; Pres. and Chair. O KWANG CHOL; 12 brs.

International Industrial Development Bank: Jongpyong-dong, Pyongchon District, Pyongyang; tel. (2) 3818610; fax (2) 3814427; f. 2001; Pres. SHIN DOK SONG.

Korea Daesong Bank: Segoridong, Gyongheung St, Potonggang District, Pyongyang; tel. (2) 3818221; fax (2) 3814576; e-mail kdb@co .chesin.com; f. 1978; cap. 158,205.8m., res 25,917.6m., dep. 1,990,582.5m. (Dec. 2006); Pres. RI GYONG HA.

Koryo Bank: Ponghwadong, Potonggang District, Pyongyang; tel. (2) 18333; fax (2) 3814410; e-mail krbankpy@co.chesin.com; f. 1989; est. as Koryo Finance Joint Venture Co, name changed 1994; co-operative, devt, regional, savings and universal bank; Pres. PAK YONG CHIL.

Kumgang Bank: Jungsongdong, Central District, Pyongyang; tel. (2) 3818532; fax (2) 3814467; f. 1979; Chair. KIM JANG HO.

State Development Bank: Pyongyang; f. 2010; Dir-Gen. JEON IL CHUN.

Private Banks

Bank of East Land: BEL Bldg, Jonseung-dong, Moranbong District, POB 32, Pyongyang; tel. (2) 3818923; fax (2) 3814410; e-mail bel@co.chesin.com; f. 2001; commercial, investment, merchant, private and retail banking; Pres. PAK HYONG GIL.

Tanchon Commercial Bank: Saemaeul 1-dong, Pyongchon District, Pyongyang; tel. (2) 18111999; fax (2) 3814793; e-mail cbktm828@co.chesin.com; f. 1983; fmrly Changgwang Credit Bank, merged with Samchon-ri Bank and named as above Nov. 2003; cap. 50,043.9m., res 93,817.9m., dep. 875,021.9m. (Dec. 2003); Chair. KIM CHOL HWAN; Pres. KYE CHANG HO.

Joint-venture Banks

Korea Joint Bank (KJB): Ryugyongdong, Potonggang District, Pyongyang; tel. (2) 3818151; fax (2) 3814410; e-mail kjb@silibank .com; f. 1989; est. with co-operation of Fed. of Korean Traders and Industrialists in Japan; 50% owned by Korea Int. General Jt Venture Co, 50% owned by Gen. Asscn of Koreans in Japan; Gen. Man. O HO RYOL; 6 domestic brs, 1 br. in Tokyo.

Korea Joint Financial Co: f. 1988; jt venture with Koreans resident in the USA.

Korea Nagwon Joint Financial Co: f. 1987; est. by Nagwon Trade Co and a Japanese co.

Korea Rakwon Joint Banking Co: Pyongyang; Man. Dir HO POK DOK.

Korea United Development Bank: KUDB Bldg, Ryugyong, Jongpyong-dong, Potonggang District, Pyongyang; tel. (2) 3814165; fax (2) 3814483; e-mail kudb888@yahoo.com; f. 1991; 51% owned by Zhongce Investment Corpn (Hong Kong), 49% owned by Osandok Gen. Bureau; Pres. KIM SE HO.

Koryo Commercial Bank: Raknang 1-dong Thong Il St, Raknang District, Pyongyang; tel. (2) 3812060; fax (2) 3814441; f. 1988; jt venture with Koreans resident in the USA.

Foreign Investment Banks

Daedong Credit Bank: Potonggang Hotel, 401 Ansan-dong, Pyongchon District, Pyongyang; tel. (2) 3814866; fax (2) 3814723; internet www.daedongcreditbank.com; f. 1996; est. as Peregrine-Daesong Devt Bank; jt venture between Oriental Commercial Holdings Ltd (Hong Kong) and Korea Daesong Bank; Gen. Man. and CEO NIGEL COWIE.

Golden Triangle Bank: Rason (Rajin-Sonbong) Special Economic Zone; f. 1995.

INSURANCE

State Insurance Bureau: Central District, Pyongyang; tel. (2) 38196; handles all life, fire, accident, marine, hull insurance and reinsurance.

Korea Foreign Insurance Co (Chosunbohom): Central District, Pyongyang; tel. (2) 3818024; fax (2) 3814464; f. 1974; conducts marine, motor, aviation and fire insurance, reinsurance of all classes, and all foreign insurance; brs in Chongjin, Hungnam and Nampo, and agencies in foreign ports; overseas representative offices in Chile, France, Germany, Pakistan, Singapore; Pres. RI JANG SU.

Korea International Insurance Co: Pyongyang; Dir PAEK MYONG RON.

Korea National Insurance Corpn: Central District, Pyongyang; tel. (2) 18111222; fax (2) 3814410; e-mail knic.re.dept@silibank.net .kp; internet www.knic.com.k; Chair. SO TONG MYONG.

Trade and Industry

GOVERNMENT AGENCIES

DPRK Committee for the Promotion of External Economic Co-operation: Jungsongdong, Central District, Pyongyang; tel. (2) 333974; fax (2) 3814498; Chair. PAEK HONG BONG.

DPRK Committee for the Promotion of International Trade: Central District, Pyongyang; Pres. RI SONG ROK; Chair. KIM YONG JAE.

Economic Co-operation Management Bureau: Ministry of Foreign Trade, Pyongyang; f. 1998; Dir KIM YONG SUL.

Korea International Joint Venture Promotion Committee: Pyongyang; Chair. CHAE HUI JONG.

Korean Association for the Promotion of Asian Trade: Pyongyang; Pres. RI SONG ROK.

Korean International General Joint Venture Co: Pyongyang; f. 1986; promotes jt economic ventures with foreign countries; Man. Dir RO TU CHOL.

CHAMBER OF COMMERCE

DPRK Chamber of Commerce: Jungsongdong, Central District, POB 89, Pyongyang; tel. (2) 3815926; fax (2) 3815827; e-mail micom@co.chesin.com.

INDUSTRIAL AND TRADE ASSOCIATIONS

Korea Building Materials Trading Co: Tongdaewon District, Pyongyang; tel. (2) 18111-3818085; fax (2) 3814555; chemical building materials, woods, timbers, cement, sheet glass, etc.; Dir SHIN TONG BOM.

Korea Cereals Export and Import Corpn: Jungsongdong, Central District, Pyongyang; tel. (2) 18111-3818278; fax (2) 3813451; high-quality vegetable starches, etc.

Korea Chemicals Export and Import Corpn: Central District, Pyongyang; petroleum and petroleum products, raw materials for the chemical industry, rubber and rubber products, fertilizers, etc.

Korea Daesong General Trading Corpn: Pulgungori 1-dong, Potonggang District, Pyongyang; tel. (2) 18111; fax (2) 3814432; e-mail Daesong@silibank.com; Gen. Dir CHOE JONG SON.

Korea Daesong Jei Trading Corpn: Pulgungori 1-dong, Potonggang District, Pyongyang; tel. (2) 18111-3818213; fax (2) 3814431; machinery and equipment, chemical products, textiles, agricultural products, etc.

Korea Daesong Jesam Trading Corpn: Pulgungori 1-dong, Potonggang District, Pyongyang; tel. (2) 18111-3818562; fax (2) 3814431; remedies for diabetes, tonics, etc.

Korea Ferrous Metals Export and Import Corpn: Potonggang 2-dong, Potonggang District, Pyongyang; tel. (2) 18111-3818078; fax (2) 3814581; steel products.

Korea Film Export and Import Corpn: Taedongmundong, Central District, POB 113, Pyongyang; tel. (2) 180008034; fax (2) 3814410; f. 1956; feature films, cartoons, scientific and documentary films; Dir-Gen. CHOE HYOK U.

Korea First Equipment Export and Import Co: Central District, Pyongyang; tel. (2) 334825; f. 1960; export and import of ferrous and non-ferrous metallurgical plant, geological exploration and mining equipment, communication equipment, machine-building plant, etc.; construction of public facilities such as airports, hotels, tourist facilities, etc.; jt-venture business in similar projects; Pres. CHAE WON CHOL.

Korea Foodstuffs Export and Import Corpn: Kangan 2-dong, Songyo District, Pyongyang; tel. (2) 18111-3818289; fax (2) 3814417; cereals, wines, meat, canned foods, fruits, cigarettes, etc.

Korea Fruit and Vegetables Export Corpn: Central District, Pyongyang; tel. (2) 35117; vegetables, fruit and their products.

Korea General Corpn for External Construction (GENCO): Sungri St 25, Jungsongdong, Central District, Pyongyang; tel. (2) 18111-3818090; fax (2) 3814611; e-mail gen122@co.chesin.com; f. 1961; construction of dwelling houses, public establishments, factories, hydroelectric and thermal power stations, irrigation systems, ports, bridges, transport services, technical services; Gen. Dir CHOE BONG SU.

Korea General Machine Co: Tongsin 3-dong, Tongdaewon, Pyongyang; tel. (2) 18555-3818102; fax (2) 3814495; Dir RA IN GYUN.

Korea Hyopdong Trading Corpn: Othan-dong, Kangan St, Central District, Pyongyang; tel. (2) 18111-3818011; fax (2) 3814454; fabrics, glass products, ceramics, chemical goods, building materials, foodstuffs, machinery, etc.

Korea Industrial Technology Co: Jungsongdong, Central District, Pyongyang; tel. (2) 18111-3818025; fax (2) 3814537; Pres. KWON YONG SON.

Korea International Chemical Joint Venture Co: Pyongyang; Chair. RYO SONG GUN.

Korea Jangsu Trading Co: Kyogudong, Central District, Pyongyang; tel. (2) 18111-3818834; fax (2) 3814410; medicinal products and clinical equipment.

Korea Jeil Equipment Export and Import Corpn: Jungsongdong, Central District, Pyongyang; tel. (2) 334825; f. 1960; ferrous and non-ferrous metallurgical plant, geological exploration and mining equipment, power plant, communications and broadcasting equipment, machine-building equipment, railway equipment, construction of public facilities; Pres. CHO JANG DOK.

Korea Koryo Trading Corpn: Jongpyongdong, Pyongchon District, Pyongyang; tel. (2) 18111-3818104; fax (2) 3814646; Dir KIM HUI DUK.

Korea Kwangmyong Trading Corpn: Jungsongdong, Central District, Pyongyang; tel. (2) 18111-3818111; fax (2) 3814410; dried herbs, dried and pickled vegetables; Dir CHOE JONG HUN.

Korea Light Industry Import-Export Co: Juchetab St, Tongdaewon District, Pyongyang; tel. (2) 37661; exports silk, cigarettes, canned goods, drinking glasses, ceramics, handbags, pens, plastic flowers, musical instruments, etc.; imports chemicals, dyestuffs, machinery, etc.; Dir CHOE PYONG HYON.

Korea Machine Tool Trading Corpn: Tongdaewon District, Pyongyang; tel. (2) 18555-381810; fax (2) 3814495; Dir KIM KWANG RYOP.

Korea Machinery and Equipment Export and Import Corpn: Potonggang District, Pyongyang; tel. (2) 333449; f. 1948; metallurgical machinery and equipment, electric machines, building machinery, farm machinery, diesel engines, etc.

Korea Mansu Trading Corpn: Chollima St, Central District, POB 250, Pyongyang; tel. (2) 43075; fax (2) 812100; f. 1974; antibiotics, pharmaceuticals, vitamin compounds, drugs, medicinal herbs; Dir KIM JANG HUN.

Korea Marine Products Export and Import Corpn: Central District, Pyongyang; canned, frozen, dried, salted and smoked fish, fishing equipment and supplies.

Korea Minerals Export and Import Corpn: Central District, Pyongyang; minerals, solid fuel, graphite, precious stones, etc.

Korea Namheung Trading Co: Sinri-dong, Tongdaewon District, Pyongyang; tel. (2) 18111-3818974; fax (2) 3814623; high-purity reagents, synthetic resins, vinyl films, essential oils, menthol and peppermint oil.

Korea Non-ferrous Metals Export and Import Corpn: Potonggang 2-dong, Potonggang District, Pyongyang; tel. (2) 18111-3818247; fax (2) 3814569.

Korea Okyru Trading Corpn: Kansongdong, Pyongchon District, Pyongyang; tel. (2) 18111-3818110; fax (2) 3814618; agricultural and marine products, household goods, clothing, chemical and light industrial products.

Korea Ponghwa Contractual Joint Venture Co: Pyongyang; Dir MUN YONG OK.

Korea Ponghwa General Trading Corpn: Jungsongdong, Central District, Pyongyang; tel. (2) 18111-3818023; fax (2) 3814444; machinery, metal products, minerals and chemicals.

Korea Publications Export and Import Corpn: Yokjondong, Yonggwang St, Central District, Pyongyang; tel. (2) 3818536; fax (2) 3814404; f. 1948; export of books, periodicals, postcards, paintings, cassettes, videos, CDs, CD-ROMs, postage stamps and records; import of books; Pres. RI YONG.

Korea Rungra Co: Sinwondong, Potonggang District, Pyongyang; tel. (2) 18111-3818112; fax (2) 3814608; Dir CHOE HENG UNG.

Korea Rungrado Trading Corpn: Segori-dong, Potonggang District, Pyongyang; tel. (2) 18111-3818022; fax (2) 3814507; food and animal products; Gen. Dir PAK KYU HONG.

Korea Ryongaksan General Trading Corpn: Pyongyang; Gen. Dir HAN YU RO.

Korea Samcholli General Corpn: Pyongyang; Dir JONG UN OP.

Korea Technology Corpn: Jungsongdong, Central District, Pyongyang; tel. (2) 18111-3818090; fax (2) 3814410; scientific and technical co-operation.

Korea Unha Trading Corpn: Rungra 1-dong, Taedongkang District, Pyongyang; tel. (2) 18111-3818236; fax (2) 3814506; clothing and fibres.

Korea Yonghung Trading Co: Tongan-dong, Central District, Pyongyang; tel. (2) 18111-3818223; fax (2) 3814527; e-mail greenlam@co.chesin.com; f. 1979; export of freight cars, vehicle parts, marine products, electronic goods; import of steel, chemical products; Pres. CHOE YONG DOK.

Pyongsu JV Co Ltd: Pyongyang; f. 2004; pharmaceutical mfr, medical products, incl. analgesics; jt venture with Interpacific/Zuellig Pharma (Switzerland).

TRADE UNIONS

General Federation of Trade Unions of Korea (GFTUK): Dongmun-dong, Taedongkang District, POB 333, Pyongyang; fax (2) 3814427; f. 1945; 1.6m. mems (2003); seven affiliated unions (2003); Pres. RYOM SUN GIL.

Transport

RAILWAYS

In 2009 the total length of track was estimated at 5,242 km, of which at least 70% was electrified. There are international train services to Moscow (Russia) and Beijing (People's Republic of China).

There is an underground railway system in Pyongyang, with two public lines serving 17 stations.

ROADS

In 2010 the road network was estimated at 25,554 km, of which most were unpaved. As part of the Government's current 10-year plan, an additional 3,000 km of expressways were to be constructed by 2020.

INLAND WATERWAYS

In 2005 the total length of inland waterways was estimated at 2,253 km, most of which was navigable only by small craft. The Yalu (Amnok-gang), Taedong, Tumen and Ryesong are the most important commercial rivers. Regular passenger and freight services: Nampo–Chosan–Supung; Chungsu–Sinuiju–Dasado; Nampo –Jeudo; Pyongyang–Nampo.

SHIPPING

The principal ports are Nampo, Wonsan, Chongjin, Rajin, Hungnam, Songnim and Haeju. At 31 December 2014 North Korea's flag registered fleet comprised 300 vessels, with a combined displacement of 702,337 grt.

Bochon Shipping Co: Pyongchon District, Pyongyang.

Chon Song Shipping Co Ltd: Sochang-dong, Potonggang District, Pyongyang.

Korea Ansan Shipping Co: Nampo.

Korea Chartering Corpn: Central District, Pyongyang; arranges cargo transport and chartering.

Korea Daehung Shipping Co: Ansan 1-dong, Pyongchon District, Pyongyang; tel. (2) 18111, ext. 8695; fax (2) 3814508; f. 1994; owns 6 reefers, 3 oil tankers, 1 cargo ship.

Korea East Sea Shipping Co: Pyongyang; Dir RI TUK HYON.

Korea Foreign Transportation Corpn: Central District, Pyongyang; arranges transport of cargoes for export and import (transit goods and charters).

Korea Myohyang Shipping Co: Ryonhwadong Changgoan St, Chung District, Pyongyang; tel. (3) 8160590; fax (3) 8146420.

Korea Myongsang Shipping Co: Chongpyong-dong, Pyongchon District, Pyongyang; tel. (2) 3815842; fax (2) 3815942.

Korea Tonghae Shipping Co: Changgwang St, Central District, POB 120, Pyongyang; tel. (2) 345805; fax (2) 3814583; arranges transport by Korean vessels.

Korea Undok Shipping Co Ltd: Nampo.

Korean-Polish Shipping Co Ltd: Moranbong District, Pyongyang; tel. (2) 3814384; fax (2) 3814607; f. 1967; maritime trade mainly with Polish and Far East ports.

Ocean Maritime Management Co Ltd: Tonghungdong, Central District, Pyongyang.

Ocean Shipping Agency of the DPRK: Moranbong District, POB 21, Pyongyang; tel. (2) 3818100; fax (2) 3814531; Pres. O JONG HO.

CIVIL AVIATION

In 2012 there were 81 airports in North Korea, 39 of which possessed paved runways. The international airport is at Sunan, 22 km north-west of the centre of Pyongyang. The airport has two runways, and a new terminal building opened in 2011.

Chosonminhang/General Civil Aviation Bureau of the DPRK: Sunan Airport, Sunan District, Pyongyang; tel. (2) 37917; fax (2) 3814625; f. 1954; internal services and external flights by Air Koryo to Beijing and Shenyang (People's Republic of China), Bangkok (Thailand), Macao, Nagoya (Japan), Kuala Lumpur (Malaysia), Moscow, Khabarovsk and Vladivostok (Russia), Sofia (Bulgaria) and Berlin (Germany); charter services are operated to Asia, Africa and Europe; Pres. KIM YO UNG.

Tourism

Tourism is permitted only in officially accompanied parties. Mount Kumgang has been developed as a tourist attraction, as part of a joint venture between North Korea and Hyundai, the South Korean conglomerate. In early 2015 proposals were announced for the development of a 430-sq km tourist region which would link the seaside resort of Wonsan with the Mount Kumgang area. Mount Paekdu, Korea's highest mountain, is another tourist attraction. In 2012 it was estimated that around 4,000 Western tourists visited North Korea. It was estimated that more than 101,700 South Koreans visited the North in 2006 (of whom about 88,000 were business travellers to Kaesong), excluding visitors to Mount Kumgang.

Korea International Tourist Bureau: Central District, Pyongyang; tel. (2) 3817201; fax (2) 3817607; Pres. HAN PYONG UN.

Korean International Youth Tourist Co: Mankyongdae District, Pyongyang; tel. (2) 73406; f. 1985; Dir HWANG CHUN YONG.

Kumgangsan International Tourist Co: Central District, Pyongyang; tel. (2) 31562; fax (2) 3812100; f. 1988.

Ryohaengsa (Korea International Travel Company): Central District, Pyongyang; tel. (2) 3817201; fax (2) 3817607; f. 1953; has relations with more than 200 tourist companies throughout the world; Pres. CHO SONG HUN.

State General Bureau of Tourism: Mangyongdae District, Pyongyang; e-mail kitc_1@silibank.com; Pres. KIM DO JUN.

Defence

The estimated total strength of the armed forces, as assessed at November 2014, was 1,190,000: army 1,020,000, air force 110,000 and navy 60,000. Security and border troops numbered 189,000, and there was a workers' and peasants' militia ('Red Guards') numbering about 5.7m. Military service is selective: army for five to 12 years; navy for five to 10 years; and air force for three to four years. Reserve forces were estimated to total 600,000 in 2014.

Defence Expenditure: total expenditure was estimated at 76,300m. won in 2009.

Supreme Commander of the Korean People's Army and First Chairman of the National Defence Commission: Marshal KIM JONG UN.

Vice-Chairmen of the National Defence Commission: Vice-Marshal RI YONG MU, Vice-Marshal KIM YONG CHUN, Vice-Marshal O KUK RYOL, Vice-Marshal HWANG PYONG SO.

Chief of General Staff of the Korean People's Army: Gen. RI YONG GIL.

Commander of the Air Force: Lt-Gen. CHOE YONG HO.

Commander of the Navy: Vice-Adm. KIM MYONG SIK.

Education

Universal, compulsory primary and secondary education were introduced in 1956 and 1958, respectively, and are provided at state expense. Free and compulsory 11-year education in state schools was introduced in 1975, and was extended by one more year in 2012. Children enter kindergarten at five years of age, and primary school at the age of six. After four years, they advance to senior middle school for six years, which was proposed in 2012 to be divided into two three-year curricula. English is compulsory as a second language from the age of 14. A report submitted to UNESCO by the North Korean Government in 2000 stated that there were 27,017 nurseries for 1,575,000 pupils, 14,167 kindergartens for 748,416 pupils, 4,886 primary schools for 1,609,865 pupils, 4,772 senior middle schools for 2,181,524 pupils, and more than 300 universities and colleges with a combined total of 1.89m. students and academics. The adult literacy rate was reported to be 100% in 2008. In June 2010 it was reported that the Ministry of Education had reorganized as the Education Commission, comprising the Ministry of Higher Education and the Ministry of Common Education. The Pyongyang University of Science and Technology, established in October 2010 in co-operation with a South Korean education foundation, was the first private university in the country. The University initially offered courses in information science and technology and planned to include management courses. In 2013 it was reported that the University planned to open schools in public health care and construction engineering.

THE REPUBLIC OF KOREA

Introductory Survey

LOCATION, CLIMATE, LANGUAGE, RELIGION, FLAG, CAPITAL

The Republic of Korea (South Korea) forms the southern part of the Korean peninsula, in eastern Asia. To the north, separated by a frontier that roughly follows the 38th parallel, is the country's only neighbour, the Democratic People's Republic of Korea (North Korea). To the west is the Yellow Sea, to the south is the East China Sea, and to the east is the Sea of Japan. The climate is marked by cold, dry winters, with an average temperature of −6°C (21°F), and hot, humid summers, with an average temperature of 25°C (77°F). The language is Korean. Confucianism, Mahayana Buddhism, and Chundo Kyo are the principal traditional religions. Chundo Kyo is peculiar to Korea, and combines elements of Shaman, Buddhist and Christian doctrines. There were an estimated 13.7m. Christians in South Korea in 2008, of whom about 8.6m. were Protestants and 5.1m. Roman Catholics. The national flag (proportions 2 by 3) comprises, in the centre of a white field, a disc divided horizontally by an S-shaped line, red above and blue below, surrounded by four configurations of parallel, broken and unbroken black bars. The capital is Seoul; by late 2015, as part of an administrative decentralization process, at least 36 government agencies were expected to have relocated to Sejong City, some 120 km south of the capital.

CONTEMPORARY POLITICAL HISTORY

Historical Context

(For more details of the history of Korea up to 1953, including the Korean War, and subsequent bilateral relations see the Democratic People's Republic of Korea—North Korea.)

UN-supervised elections to a new legislature, the National Assembly (Kuk Hoe), took place in May 1948. The Assembly adopted a democratic Constitution, and South Korea became the independent Republic of Korea on 15 August 1948, with Dr Syngman Rhee, leader of the Liberal Party, as the country's first President. He remained in the post until his resignation in April 1960. Elections in July were won by the Democratic Party, led by Chang Myon, but his Government was deposed in May 1961 by a military coup, led by Gen. Park Chung-Hee. Power was assumed by the Supreme Council for National Reconstruction, which dissolved the National Assembly, suspended the Constitution and disbanded all existing political parties. In January 1963 the military leadership formed the Democratic Republican Party (DRP). Under a new Constitution, Gen. Park became President of the Third Republic in December.

Domestic Political Affairs

Opposition to Park's regime led to the imposition of martial law in October 1972. A Constitution for the Fourth Republic, giving the President greatly increased powers, was approved by national referendum in November. A new body, the National Conference for Unification (NCU), was elected in December. The NCU re-elected President Park for a six-year term, and the DRP obtained a decisive majority in elections to the new National Assembly. In May 1975 opposition to the Government was effectively banned, and political trials followed. Elections to the NCU were held in May 1978, and the President was re-elected for a further six-year term in July. In October 1979 serious rioting erupted when Kim Young-Sam, the leader of the opposition New Democratic Party (NDP), was accused of subversive activities and expelled from the National Assembly. On 26 October Park was assassinated in an alleged coup attempt, led by the head of the Korean Central Intelligence Agency. Martial law was reintroduced, and on 6 December the Prime Minister, Choi Kyu-Hah, was elected President by the NCU. A military coup on 12 December was led by the head of the Defence Security Command, Lt-Gen. Chun Doo-Hwan, who arrested the Army Chief of Staff and effectively took power. Nevertheless, President Choi was inaugurated on 21 December to complete his predecessor's term of office (to 1984).

Choi promised liberalizing reforms, but in May 1980 demonstrations by students and confrontation with the army led to the arrest of about 30 political leaders, including Kim Dae-Jung, former head of the NDP. Martial law was extended throughout the country, the National Assembly was suspended, and all political activity was banned. Almost 200 people were killed when troops stormed the southern city of Gwangju, which had been occupied by students and dissidents. In August Choi resigned, and Gen. Chun was elected President. Acting Prime Minister Nam Duck-Woo formed a new State Council (cabinet) in September. In the same month the sentencing to death of Kim Dae-Jung for plotting rebellion was condemned internationally. (The sentence was subsequently suspended.) In October a new Constitution was overwhelmingly approved by referendum.

Martial law was ended in January 1981, and new political parties were formed. In the following month President Chun was re-elected: the start of his new term, in March, inaugurated the Fifth Republic. Chun's Democratic Justice Party (DJP) became the majority party in the new National Assembly, which was elected shortly afterwards. Amid opposition demands for liberalization, Chun pledged that he would retire at the end of his term in 1988, thus becoming the country's first head of state to transfer power constitutionally.

During 1984, following an escalation in student unrest, the Government adopted a more flexible attitude towards dissidents. Several thousand prisoners were released, and the political 'blacklist' was finally abolished in March 1985. In January 1985 the New Korea Democratic Party (NKDP) was established by supporters of Kim Young-Sam and Kim Dae-Jung. At the general election to the National Assembly held in February, the DJP retained its majority, but the NKDP emerged as the major opposition force, boosted by the return from exile of Kim Dae-Jung. The new party secured 67 of the Assembly's 276 seats, while the DJP won 148 seats. Chun appointed a new State Council, with Lho Shin-Yong as Prime Minister. Before the opening session of the new National Assembly many deputies defected to the NKDP.

In April 1987 internal divisions within the NKDP led to the formation of a new opposition party, the Reunification Democratic Party (RDP); Kim Young-Sam was elected to its presidency in May. In April Chun unexpectedly announced the suspension of the process of reform until after the Olympic Games (due to be held in Seoul in September 1988). While confirming that he would leave office in February 1988, Chun indicated that his successor would be elected by the existing electoral college system, precipitating violent clashes between anti-Government demonstrators and riot police.

In June 1987 Roh Tae-Woo was nominated as the DJP's presidential candidate. However, Roh subsequently informed Chun that he would relinquish both the DJP chairmanship and his presidential candidature if the principal demands of the opposition for constitutional and electoral reform were not satisfied. Under international pressure, Chun acceded, and negotiations on constitutional amendments were announced. In August the DJP and the RDP announced that a bipartisan committee had agreed a draft constitution. Among its provisions were the reintroduction of direct presidential elections by universal suffrage, and the restriction of the presidential mandate to a single five-year term; the President's emergency powers were also to be reduced, and serving military officers were to be prohibited from taking government office. Having been approved by the National Assembly, the amendments were endorsed in a national referendum in October, and the amended Constitution was promulgated shortly thereafter.

Kim Dae-Jung joined the RDP in August 1987; however, in November he became President of a new Peace and Democracy Party (PDP), and declared himself a rival presidential candidate. At the presidential election, in December, Roh Tae-Woo won some 36% of the votes, while Kim Dae-Jung and Kim Young-Sam each received about 27%. Roh Tae-Woo was inaugurated as President on 25 February 1988, whereupon the Sixth Republic was established. At the general election to the National Assembly, in April, the DJP failed to achieve an overall majority, securing 125 of the 299 seats. The PDP won 70 seats, thus becoming the main opposition party; the remainder went to the

RDP and the New Democratic Republican Party (NDRP—the revived and renamed DRP), led by Kim Jong-Pil.

In February 1990 the DJP merged with the RDP and the NDRP to form the Democratic Liberal Party (DLP). Roh was subsequently elected President of the DLP, while Kim Young-Sam and Kim Jong-Pil were elected as two of the party's three Chairmen. The DLP thus controlled more than two-thirds of the seats in the National Assembly. The PDP, effectively isolated as the sole opposition party, condemned the merger and demanded new elections. In March a new opposition group, the Democratic Party (DP), was formed, largely comprising members of the RDP who had opposed the merger.

In July 1990 a large rally was held in Seoul to denounce the adoption by the National Assembly of several items of controversial legislation, including proposals to restructure the military leadership and to reorganize the broadcasting media. In protest, all the opposition members of the National Assembly tendered their resignations. Although the Assembly's Speaker refused to accept the resignations, the PDP deputies returned to the National Assembly only in November, following an agreement with the DLP that local council elections would take place in the first half of 1991, to be followed by gubernatorial and mayoral elections in 1992. The DLP also agreed to abandon plans for the transfer, by constitutional amendment, of executive powers to the State Council. The first local elections to be held in the Republic of Korea (South Korea) for 30 years took place in March and June 1991, and resulted in a decisive victory for the DLP.

Meanwhile, in April 1991 the PDP merged with the smaller opposition Party for New Democratic Alliance to form the New Democratic Party (NDP). In September the NDP and the DP agreed to merge (under the latter's name) to form a stronger opposition front. A further opposition group, the Unification National Party (UNP), was established in January 1992 by Chung Ju-Yung, the founder and Honorary Chairman of the powerful Hyundai industrial conglomerate.

At elections to the National Assembly in March 1992, the DLP unexpectedly failed to secure an absolute majority, obtaining a total of 149 of the 299 seats. The remainder of the seats were won by the DP (97), the UNP (31), the New Political Reform Party (NPRP—one) and independent candidates (21). In May Kim Young-Sam was chosen as the DLP's candidate for the presidential election, scheduled for December, and in August he replaced Roh as the party's President; divisions within the DLP led to defections from the party by opponents of Kim Young-Sam.

The presidency of Kim Young-Sam

The presidential election of December 1992 was won by Kim Young-Sam, with some 42% of the votes cast. Kim (who was inaugurated in February 1993) was the first South Korean President since 1960 without military connections. In February 1993 Chung Ju-Yung resigned as President of the United People's Party (UPP—as the UNP had been renamed), following allegations that he had embezzled Hyundai finances to fund his election campaign; he was given a three-year suspended sentence in November. Kim Young-Sam appointed Hwang In-Sung as Prime Minister, and a new State Council was formed.

Kim Young-Sam acted swiftly to honour his campaign pledge to eliminate corruption in business and politics; in all, during 1993, Kim's anti-corruption measures were reported to have resulted in the dismissal of, or disciplinary action against, some 3,000 business, government and military officials, and new regulations to restrict the activities of the country's industrial conglomerates (*chaebol*) were announced.

Hwang In-Sung resigned as Prime Minister in December 1993 and was succeeded by Lee Hoi-Chang, hitherto Chairman of the Board of Audit and Inspection (BAI). However, he too resigned, in April 1994, and was replaced by Lee Yung-Duk, latterly the Deputy Prime Minister responsible for national unification.

In July 1994 the UPP and the NPRP merged to form the New People's Party (NPP). In October the Government announced that its inquiry into the role played by former Presidents Chun and Roh in the 1979 coup had found that both had participated in a 'premeditated military rebellion'. In December 1994 Lee Hong-Koo (hitherto the Deputy Prime Minister responsible for national unification) was appointed Prime Minister, as part of a major restructuring of the State Council.

The DLP fared badly at local elections in May 1995, in contrast to the success of a new party, the United Liberal Democrats (ULD), established in March by defectors from the DLP and led by Kim Jong-Pil (who had resigned as DLP Chairman earlier in the year). In September Kim Dae-Jung returned to politics, establishing his own party, the National Congress for New Politics (NCNP). The DP was severely undermined when many of its members left to join the NCNP.

A major scandal erupted in October 1995, when Roh Tae-Woo admitted in a televised address that he had amassed a vast sum of money during his term of office. He was arrested in the following month; at his trial, which opened in December, Roh confessed to having received donations from South Korean businesses, but denied that these constituted bribes. Many senior politicians and business leaders were also detained and interrogated in connection with the affair. Kim Dae-Jung, meanwhile, unexpectedly admitted that his campaign for the 1992 presidential election had been supported by a donation of money from Roh's 'slush fund'. Kim Young-Sam denied opposition allegations that he too had benefited from a similar donation. In December 1995, in an effort to distance his party from the deepening scandal, Kim Young-Sam changed the DLP's name to the New Korea Party (NKP). A major reorganization of the State Council was effected, in which Lee Hong-Koo was replaced as Prime Minister by Lee Soo-Sung, the President of Seoul National University.

In late 1995 it was announced that Roh Tae-Woo and Chun Doo-Hwan were to be prosecuted for their involvement in the 1979 coup and the 1980 Gwangju massacre. Chun was arrested in December 1995, and in the following month he was additionally accused of accumulating political funds through bribe-taking. Legal proceedings in connection with the events of 1979 and 1980 opened in March 1996: Chun was charged with mutiny for his organization of the 1979 coup, and with sedition in connection with the Gwangju massacre, while Roh was charged with aiding Chun. Roh and Chun were convicted as charged in August 1996, receiving lengthy prison sentences; each was heavily fined in the corruption cases.

Contrary to widespread predictions, at the elections to the National Assembly in April 1996 the NKP only narrowly failed to retain its parliamentary majority, winning a total of 139 of the 299 seats. Recent incursions into the demilitarized zone (DMZ, separating North and South Korea) by North Korean troops had apparently caused many voters to favour the ruling party out of concern for national security. The NCNP took 79 seats, and the party's leader, Kim Dae-Jung, failed to win a seat. By the time the National Assembly convened in June, the NKP had secured a working majority with the support of several opposition and independent members.

The revision of the country's labour laws, to introduce greater flexibility into the employment market (a condition of South Korea's impending membership of the Organisation for Economic Co-operation and Development—OECD, see p. 377), was initiated in May 1996. However, the reforms proposed by the Government in early December were severely criticized by trade unions and opposition parties. Many thousands of factory workers, as well as public sector employees, participated in a strike called by the country's principal workers' confederation, the Federation of Korean Trade Unions (FKTU), after the Government convened a dawn session of the National Assembly, which approved the labour reform bill in the absence of opposition deputies. Anti-Government demonstrators in Seoul and other major cities repeatedly clashed with riot police, and warrants were issued for the arrest of several leaders of the Korean Confederation of Trade Unions (KCTU), which, according to the newly introduced reforms, would not be officially recognized until 2002. By mid-January 1997 support for the strikes was abating; the KCTU suggested that it might accept a modification of the labour law, having previously insisted on its complete annulment. In a significant concession, President Kim agreed to meet the leaders of the opposition parties to discuss amendments to the law; warrants for the arrest of union leaders were also suspended. In March the National Assembly approved a revised version of the legislation, whereby the implementation of certain proposals was delayed for two years, while the KCTU was granted immediate official recognition.

Meanwhile, bribery scandals persisted, prompting several government resignations during 1996. The infiltration of a North Korean submarine into South Korean waters in September resulted in the dismissal of the Minister of Defence, Lee Yang-Ho. He was subsequently charged with divulging classified information and with receiving bribes in connection with the procurement of helicopters for the army, and in December was sentenced to four years' imprisonment.

In January 1997 a further major scandal erupted when Hanbo, one of the country's largest steel and construction conglomerates, was declared bankrupt. Allegations were made that Hanbo had bribed the Government to exert pressure on banks to provide substantial loans to the conglomerate. The chief executives of several large Korean banks were arrested on charges of receiving bribes, and in February the Minister of Home Affairs, Kim Woo-Suk, resigned following allegations that he too had accepted payments from the company. President Kim issued an official apology for the loan scandal, and in March Lee Soo-Sung resigned as Prime Minister in a gesture of contrition. He was replaced by Goh Kun, hitherto President of Myongju University. The repercussions of the Hanbo affair widened further, implicating, among others, Kim Soo-Han, the Speaker of the National Assembly, and President Kim himself, whose 1992 election campaign was alleged to have been funded partially by the conglomerate. In June 1997 the former Chairman of Hanbo and several senior banking officials and politicians, including Kim Woo-Suk, were convicted on charges relating to the scandal.

In July 1997 Lee Hoi-Chang, former Prime Minister and Chairman of the NKP, was nominated as the ruling party's candidate for the presidential election, scheduled for December. However, Lee's candidacy was severely affected by various scandals surrounding the NKP and his family. In September Lee was elected President of the NKP, replacing Kim Young-Sam, who subsequently resigned from the party in order to ensure his neutrality in the forthcoming election. In October the NCNP and the ULD established an informal electoral alliance, uniting behind the NCNP presidential nominee, Kim Dae-Jung. In November the NKP announced its merger with the DP, to form the Grand National Party (GNP).

However, internal party politics were overshadowed by the crisis experienced by the Korean economy in the latter half of 1997 and the revelation that many of the *chaebol* had amassed huge debts. Following the rejection by the legislature of the Government's financial liberalization measures, President Kim dismissed Kang Kyung-Shik, the Deputy Prime Minister and Minister of Finance and the Economy, in November, replacing him with Lim Chang-Yul, latterly Minister of Trade, Industry and Energy. An economic stabilization programme failed to curb the depreciation of the national currency, and the Government was forced to request the assistance of the IMF. In December the IMF agreed to allocate substantial funds to prevent South Korea from defaulting on its repayments of external debt, subject to the implementation of a programme of extensive reforms.

The presidency of Kim Dae-Jung

The presidential election of mid-December 1997 was narrowly won by Kim Dae-Jung, representing the first peaceful transfer of power to an opposition politician in South Korea's history. Six other candidates contested the election. In a gesture to promote a sense of national unity, former Presidents Chun Doo-Hwan and Roh Tae-Woo were granted a presidential pardon and released from prison.

Legislation for financial reforms, to comply with the terms of the IMF agreement, was approved by the National Assembly in late December 1997. Discussions with South Korea's overseas creditors to renegotiate the terms of the country's debt repayments were successfully concluded at the end of January 1998. Compulsory reform of the *chaebol*, which had been widely criticized for contributing to the debt-repayment crisis through their extensive borrowing, and legislation to allow foreign investors to acquire majority shareholdings in South Korean companies, were among reform measures promulgated in early 1998.

Kim Dae-Jung was formally inaugurated as President in late February 1998. Despite resistance from the opposition, Kim Dae-Jung designated Kim Jong-Pil, the leader of the ULD, as acting Prime Minister, and a new State Council was formed in early March, with the ministries divided equally between the NCNP and the ULD. Tens of thousands participated in strikes in May and July to protest against rising unemployment, the Government's privatization proposals and plans by Hyundai Motor and Daewoo Motor for mass redundancies.

In August 1998 the National Assembly formally confirmed Kim Jong-Pil as Prime Minister, following months of legislative inactivity, during which the GNP had refused to support his nomination. However, the GNP boycotted parliamentary sessions throughout the latter part of the year, further delaying the consideration of urgent economic reforms, in protest against government anti-corruption measures which, it claimed, were partisan, aimed at dividing the opposition and involved

surveillance of opposition deputies. In early January 1999, as the boycott continued, the ruling parties unilaterally endorsed 130 bills without debate, including legislation on banking reform and a controversial fishing agreement with Japan. In mid-January, however, the ruling and opposition parties agreed that all issues relating to the anti-corruption investigations be referred to the National Assembly's steering committee. In May a major reorganization of the State Council was effected. However, in June corruption scandals led to the replacement of the newly appointed Ministers of Justice and of the Environment.

As the next legislative elections approached, in January 2000 Kim Jong-Pil resigned as Prime Minister to chair the ULD, nominating Park Tae-Joon, the founder of Pohang Iron and Steel Company, as his successor. Lee Hun-Jai, hitherto the Chairman of the Financial Supervisory Commission, was appointed as Minister of Finance and the Economy. Kim Dae-Jung established a new party, the Millennium Democratic Party (MDP), to succeed the ruling NCNP, having reportedly failed in attempts to effect a merger with the ULD. In February the National Assembly approved revisions to the election law, which reduced the number of legislative seats from 299 to 273 (227 directly elected and 46 allocated by proportional representation), and reversed a ban on civic groups campaigning against candidates. Lee Han-Dong, recently elected as President of the ULD, subsequently announced the party's withdrawal from the ruling coalition, claiming that the MDP had failed to fulfil its electoral pledges, although Prime Minister Park was to remain in the Government.

At the elections to the National Assembly held in April 2000 the GNP, which won 133 of the 273 seats, retained its position as the party with the largest representation in the legislature, but fell four seats short of a majority. The ruling MDP secured 115 seats, while the ULD suffered a serious reverse, taking only 17 seats (compared with 50 in the 1996 elections). Two seats were won by the Democratic People's Party (DPP), which had been formed in February by defectors from the GNP. In mid-May Park resigned as Prime Minister, amid increasing controversy over allegations of tax evasion. The designation of Lee Han-Dong as Park's successor indicated a restoration of MDP-ULD co-operation. Amid criticism that reform of the *chaebol* was proceeding too slowly, President Kim Dae-Jung effected a major government reorganization in August, which primarily affected the economic portfolios.

President Kim enjoyed increasing respect within the international community, in October 2000 being awarded the Nobel Peace Prize for his contribution to democracy and human rights (and particularly for his successful attempts at reconciliation with North Korea). However, his pursuit of reunification was criticized domestically by those who felt that, given the country's own economic problems, South Korea could ill afford assistance to North Korea.

During 2000 and early 2001 dissatisfaction with the Government manifested itself on numerous occasions in the form of industrial and agricultural unrest. In November 2000 farmers held a strike to demand that their debts be cancelled and that the Government intervene on their behalf at the World Trade Organization (WTO, see p. 431), and other workers protested against government-led corporate restructuring, which it was feared would result in large-scale retrenchment.

A major cabinet reorganization in March 2001 included the replacement of Lee Joung-Binn as Minister of Foreign Affairs and Trade by Han Seung-Soo of the minor opposition DPP, replaced. In the following month the DPP joined the ruling MDP-led coalition, despite protests from within the MDP. By May Kim Dae-Jung's popularity had declined sharply, as voters grew disillusioned by his failure to implement political reforms. In September the Minister of Unification, Lim Dong-Won, was forced to resign after the National Assembly approved a motion of no confidence in him, organized by the GNP and supported by the MDP's coalition partner, the ULD. The latter's actions effectively dissolved the ruling coalition, and President Kim appointed four new ministers. In addition, Lim was immediately appointed presidential adviser on reunification, national security and foreign affairs.

In October 2001 the GNP won three by-elections, increasing its representation in the National Assembly to 136 seats—just one short of a majority. The opposition victories created new rifts within the ruling MDP between younger reformers and party veterans, and President Kim resigned from the party presidency in November, ostensibly in order to administer state affairs without being involved in party disputes. He was succeeded, on an interim basis, by Han Kwang-Ok.

In late January 2002 President Kim again reorganized the State Council, dismissing the recently appointed Minister of Unification, Hong Soon-Young, and reallocating seven other posts, as well as the positions of six of the eight senior presidential secretaries and his presidential chief of staff. Within days, the Minister of Foreign Affairs and Trade, Han Seung-Soo, was also dismissed, owing to the country's strained relations with the USA.

A power struggle within the opposition GNP resulted in the departure of the party's Vice-President, Park Geun-Hye (daughter of former President Park Chung-Hee). In May 2002 Park established a new party, the Korean Coalition for the Future (KCF); however, the KCF merged with the GNP in November.

President Kim and six of his ministers resigned from the MDP in May 2002, in order to focus on state affairs during the final months of Kim's presidency. Kim had become increasingly embarrassed by corruption scandals involving two of his sons. The scandals adversely affected the MDP's performance in local elections held in June.

In mid-July 2002 President Kim announced a cabinet reorganization, including the nomination of Chang Sang, hitherto President of Ewha Woman's University, as the country's first female Prime Minister. However, at the end of the month the National Assembly rejected Chang's appointment on the grounds of dubious property dealings and the fact that her son had adopted US citizenship. In her place, President Kim nominated Chang Dae-Whan, a former newspaper proprietor, but he too was rejected by the National Assembly in late August on the grounds of questionable financial practices. A third nominee, Kim Suk-Soo, a former Supreme Court judge and previously Head of the National Election Commission, was finally accepted by the National Assembly in October, thus ending several months of political paralysis.

The MDP suffered further setbacks in by-elections held in August 2002 when the GNP won 11 out of 13 seats contested, giving it an overall majority in the National Assembly. In September Chung Mong-Joon (the sixth son of Hyundai founder Chung Ju-Yung), who was President of the Korean Football Association, announced that he was standing for the country's presidency. Chung's popularity had risen sharply following South Korea's successful co-hosting of the 2002 football World Cup. In November Chung formally established his 'National Unity 21' party, receiving support from a broad political spectrum. However, later in that month Chung and Roh Moo-Hyun, a lawyer and human rights activist who had secured the presidential nomination of the MDP earlier in the year, agreed to present a joint candidate for the presidency, namely Roh, in order to prevent the election of the GNP's candidate, Lee Hoi-Chang, as President in December. Meanwhile, in October it emerged that President Kim and Chung Mong-Joon had arranged for a Hyundai subsidiary to transfer a substantial sum of money to North Korea via the (South Korean) state-owned Korea Development Bank prior to the historic inter-Korean summit of June 2000, effectively 'buying' the meeting (see below).

The presidency of Roh Moo-Hyun

The presidential election of December 2002, which attracted a turnout of 70.8%, was narrowly won by Roh Moo-Hyun, who received 48.9% of the votes cast, against 46.6% for the sole other candidate, Lee Hoi-Chang. Roh's victory, despite the late withdrawal of Chung Mong-Joon's support, was generally attributed to his uncompromising stance in favour of a foreign policy more independent from the USA, whereas Lee was widely seen as having very close relations with the US Government.

In January 2003 Goh Kun, hitherto the president of Transparency International Korea, an anti-corruption agency, and himself a former Prime Minister, was reappointed to that post by President-elect Roh, while Moon Hee-Sang, an MDP legislator, was appointed presidential chief of staff, and concurrently Chairman of the Civil Service Commission. Roh was inaugurated in late February and promptly appointed a new cabinet. President Roh also reorganized the military and intelligence services, appointing Gen. Kim Jong-Hwan as Chairman of the Joint Chiefs of Staff and Ko Young-Koo, a human rights lawyer, as director of the National Intelligence Service (NIS). The latter appointment reflected Roh's determination to depoliticize the agency, which had been responsible for surveillance of political figures even after the transition to democracy.

In April 2003 the GNP won two out of three seats in by-elections to the National Assembly, raising its total representation to 153 seats. However, the victory in the other seat of a reformist ally of the MDP, Rhyu Si-Min, was welcomed by the Government as an indication of support for the reform process. Also in April, despite widespread public opposition, the National Assembly voted in favour of the dispatch of South Korean troops to support US military action in Iraq in a non-combat capacity.

In June 2003 two aides of former President Kim Dae-Jung, former Minister of Unification Lim Dong-Won and former Minister of Culture and Tourism Park Jie-Won, were charged in connection with illegal payments made through the Hyundai group to North Korea to arrange the 2000 presidential summit meeting (later in the year Lim received an 18-month prison sentence and Park a 12-year sentence). Also implicated in the scandal was Hyundai heir Chung Mong-Hun (the fifth son of company founder Chung Ju-Yung), who committed suicide in August.

In September 2003 a faction of the MDP announced its intention to form a new party, owing to internal divisions over corruption and other issues. President Roh subsequently relinquished his membership of the MDP, although he did not commit himself to joining the new organization, which was named the Uri (meaning 'our') Party in October. A large number of MDP legislators, including MDP Chairman Chyung Dai-Chul, joined the Uri Party, thus leaving the MDP with only 62 seats in the National Assembly. The Uri Party was officially inaugurated in November; Chung Dong-Young was elected Chairman of the new party in early 2004). Another development in September 2003, meanwhile, was the resignation of the Minister of Home Affairs, Kim Doo-Kwan, following an incident in which protesters had infiltrated a US base in Pocheon.

President Roh's declining popularity was further eroded in October 2003 by the arrest of his former aide Choi Do-Sul, on charges of receiving illegal funds from a major *chaebol* following the 2002 presidential election. In an attempt to restore his popularity, Roh announced proposals for a referendum to be held on the issue of his presidency later in the year. However, the proposed referendum prompted further political instability, with Prime Minister Goh Kun and other government ministers tendering their resignations (which were rejected by President Roh). Both the GNP and the MDP dismissed the referendum proposal as unconstitutional.

Official investigations into illegal campaign funding from leading *chaebol* during the 2002 presidential election, involving both the MDP and the GNP, were instigated in October 2003. At the end of November President Roh vetoed a bill, already approved by the National Assembly, which urged an independent investigation into the funding allegations. In December the National Assembly voted to rescind the veto (in the first reversal of a presidential decision since 1954), and an independent investigator was subsequently appointed. In the same month President Roh announced that he would step down if the MDP were found by the investigation to have received one-10th of the illegal funding taken by the GNP. Also in December 2003, the GNP's Lee Hoi-Chang, Roh's rival in the 2002 election, publicly admitted that his party had accepted US $42m. in illegal donations.

In January 2004 the Minister of Foreign Affairs and Trade, Yoon Young-Kwan, resigned, reportedly following a dispute related to President Roh's policy on independence from the USA over issues such as the North Korean nuclear weapons programme. Yoon was replaced by Ban Ki-Moon. There were further government changes in February, following the resignation of Kim Jin-Pyo, the Deputy Prime Minister for Finance and the Economy, in order to stand as a Uri Party candidate in the legislative elections scheduled for April. Kim was replaced as Deputy Prime Minister by Lee Hun-Jai.

Meanwhile, investigations into political corruption continued in early 2004, and both the former MDP Chairman, Chyung Dai-Chul (now of the Uri Party), and the former Secretary-General of the GNP, Kim Young-Iel, were arrested. In February there was also speculation that Park Geun-Hye had received undeclared funds from the GNP for the purposes of a merger with her KCF. In March it was reported that President Roh's MDP election campaign had received 12,500m. won in illicit funds, amounting to one-seventh of the 84,000m. won allegedly received by the GNP and thus to more than the proportion of one-10th that Roh had previously stated would prompt his resignation. At the end of March it was confirmed that Roh's former aide Choi Do-Sul had received US $530,000 in illegal funding.

In March 2004 President Roh was impeached over the issue of his publicly expressing support for the pro-Government Uri Party, thus violating electoral law. A total of 193 legislators, mostly from the GNP and Roh's former party, the MDP, voted in favour of the impeachment. Following the vote there were vehement protests from the President's supporters in the National Assembly and from members of the public, with opinion polls indicating that around 70% of the population did not support the impeachment. It was announced that President Roh's position was to be reviewed by the Constitutional Court within six months, with Prime Minister Goh Kun becoming acting head of state for this period.

At elections to the National Assembly in April 2004, the Uri Party won a narrow majority, securing 152 seats of the total of 299 in the newly expanded chamber (243 of which were determined by direct election and the remainder by proportional representation). The GNP, now under the leadership of Park Geun-Hye, secured 121 seats. Roh's former party, the MDP, won only nine seats. The success of the Uri Party was regarded as a victory for Roh and an expression of public disapproval of his impeachment. In May Roh was reinstated as President following the decision of the Constitutional Court to dismiss the case for impeachment. He became a formal member of the Uri Party in the same month.

Following Roh's reinstatement to the presidency, Prime Minister Goh Kun resigned from his post; Lee Hae-Chan, a former education minister, was approved by the National Assembly as Prime Minister in June 2004. Three new ministerial appointments were then made, including that of former Uri Party Chairman Chung Dong-Young as Minister of Unification. Also in June, the Government announced that the deployment of 3,000 South Korean troops to Iraq, originally approved by the National Assembly in February, would take place in August. Public opposition to this decision increased dramatically a few days later when a South Korean translator, Kim Sun-Il, who had been taken hostage in Iraq, was beheaded by his captors. In July the Minister of National Defence, Cho Young-Kil, resigned, taking responsibility for an incident in which a South Korean ship had fired warning shots at a North Korean vessel believed to be intruding in South Korean waters, with naval staff reportedly having failed to report radio communication with the North Korean ship. Cho was replaced by Yoon Kwang-Woong. In August President Roh announced that investigations were to be held into the past conduct of politicians during the period of Japanese rule and of dictatorial governments extending into the 1980s. Shin Ki-Nam, who had replaced Chung Dong Young as leader of the Uri Party in May 2004, was forced to resign after it was found that his father had committed human rights abuses as a police officer during the period of Japanese colonization. Shin was replaced by Lee Bu-Young. In September controversy arose over the anti-communist national security law, which dated back to the country's pre-democratic era. Human rights groups, supported by President Roh, claimed that the law was outdated and subject to abuse. However, proposals to abolish the law were rejected by the Supreme Court. In November there was labour unrest in protest against government plans to reform labour legislation to prohibit strikes by public sector workers and to allow employers to hire staff on a temporary basis. In December the National Assembly approved a proposal for South Korean troops in Iraq to remain there until the end of 2005, despite continuing strong public opposition to the deployment.

In January 2005 Lee Bu-Young resigned from the leadership of the Uri Party, citing his party's failure to realize its reform aims such as the abolition of the anti-communist national security law. Moon Hee-Sang was elected party leader in April. Meanwhile, in March the Deputy Prime Minister for Finance and the Economy, Lee Hun-Jai, resigned as a result of controversy over his wife's real estate investments. He was replaced by Han Duck-Soo, hitherto the Minister of Government Policy Co-ordination. At by-elections held in late April for six seats vacated by Uri Party deputies who had been convicted of electoral malpractice in the elections of April 2004, the Uri Party lost all six seats (and thus its parliamentary majority), with the opposition GNP taking five seats, and the sixth being won by an independent candidate. In May 2005 it was announced that the MDP was changing its name to the Democratic Party (DP). Another round of by-elections (again occasioned by the incumbents' convictions for electoral malpractice in 2004) was held in October; the GNP won all four contested seats, thereby further reducing the Uri Party's parliamentary representation to 144 and prompting the resignation of the party's senior leadership, including Chairman Moon. Chung Sye-Kyun was appointed acting Chairman pending a leadership election. Former party Chairman Chung Dong-Young resigned as Minister of

Unification in December 2005 in order to stand in the leadership election, as did Kim Geun-Tae, the Minister of Health and Welfare. In the event, at the Uri Party's national convention in February 2006, Chung Dong-Young was elected to the post of Chairman for a second time.

A scandal developed in March 2006 regarding the conduct of Prime Minister Lee Hae-Chan, after he chose to play golf rather than oversee the Government's reaction to the first day of a national strike. Furthermore, his golfing partners on that day reportedly included a businessman with a criminal record for the manipulation of share prices. Lee resigned in mid-March. Roh's nomination of Han Myeong-Sook as Lee's successor was approved by a vote in the National Assembly in mid-April, and she was thus appointed as the country's first female Prime Minister.

Local elections held at the end of May 2006 resulted in victory for the GNP, which garnered 54.5% of the votes cast nationwide, compared with just 21.2% received by the Uri Party. Significantly, of the 16 provincial governor and city mayoral positions, the Uri Party took only one against the GNP's 12. In June, taking responsibility for the party's disastrous election performance, Chairman Chung Dong-Young resigned and was replaced by Kim Kun-Tae. Legislative by-elections held in July further emphasized the Uri Party's declining popularity: the GNP won three of the four seats contested, while the DP took the fourth.

Following the North Korean nuclear test on 9 October 2006 (see below), both the Minister of Unification, Lee Jong-Seok, and the Minister of National Defence, Yoon Kwang-Woong, resigned amid both domestic and international criticism of the South Korean Government's continuing policy of engagement with the North. The new Minister of Unification was Lee Jae-Joung, a former Uri Party legislator, while the Army Chief of Staff, Kim Jang-Soo, took the defence portfolio. Another new appointment was that of Song Min-Soon, who was assigned the post of Minister of Foreign Affairs and Trade (a position vacated by Ban Ki-Moon, following his appointment as UN Secretary-General). Parliamentary by-elections and local elections held that month resulted in defeat, once again, for the Uri Party's candidates.

In addition to the issue of engagement with North Korea, public dissatisfaction with President Roh's handling of the economy also increased; house prices had risen rapidly and the education system had undergone a controversial restructuring. Many South Koreans were also deeply suspicious of the Government's plans to sign a free trade agreement (FTA) with the USA, and in November 2006 thousands took to the streets to protest against the proposed deal, leading to violent clashes with the police (see *Relations with the USA*).

In January 2007 the Uri Party formally announced that it would disband and establish a new party. Initial reports suggested that the party would seek an alliance with the DP (defectors from which had originally formed the Uri Party in 2003), and that a number of Uri Party legislators had already switched their party allegiance to the DP. However, in early February 2007, before these plans could be implemented, 23 legislators announced their defection from the Uri Party, joining six others who had resigned in the previous fortnight. Following this mass defection, the GNP held 127 seats and the Uri Party 110 in the National Assembly. President Roh announced his departure from the Uri Party in late February.

In March 2007, after only 10 months in office, Prime Minister Han Myeong-Sook resigned and was succeeded by Han Duck-Soo, a former Deputy Prime Minister for Finance and the Economy. The GNP suffered a reverse in by-elections held in April, securing only one of the three seats contested; voter participation in the polls was only 27.7%. Moreover, the GNP lost five of six mayoral and gubernatorial posts being contested concurrently. The poor performance of the GNP prompted the resignation of several senior party leaders, although Chairman Kang Jae-Seop remained in his post. The party was also damaged by antagonism between its two rival presidential contenders for the election due to be held in December: Park Geun-Hye, the former GNP Chairwoman, believed to be popular among conservative voters, and Lee Myung-Bak, the Chief Executive of Hyundai Engineering and Construction Company and former mayor of Seoul. The GNP elected Lee as its presidential candidate by a narrow margin in August.

Meanwhile, the disintegration of the Uri Party continued, with a series of further defections in mid-2007, including that of former Chairman Chung Dong-Young, which left the party with only 58 seats in the National Assembly. In early August Chung and 79 other former legislators of the Uri Party joined with five defectors from the DP to form the United New Democratic Party (UNDP). Later that month the Uri Party finally disbanded and was absorbed into the UNDP, thus making the new party the largest in the National Assembly, with 143 seats. Chung was elected as the UNDP's presidential candidate in October. In November, in a development that threatened to split the conservative vote, former Prime Minister Lee Hoi-Chang unexpectedly announced that he was leaving the GNP to stand as an independent candidate, in a third attempt to secure the country's presidency.

In the mean time, a major corruption scandal at Samsung arose in October 2007, when the former head of its legal department claimed that senior executives at the *chaebol* had regularly bribed politicians, government officials and prosecutors. In the following month the National Assembly approved legislation authorizing an independent investigation into the allegations, which Samsung vigorously denied. Also to be examined were claims that the conglomerate had made improper payments to candidates in the 2002 presidential election. (The investigation commenced in January 2008. In April, having been charged with tax evasion and breach of trust, the Chairman of Samsung, Lee Kun-Hee, resigned, and in July he was convicted on the former charge and given a three-year suspended prison sentence. He was pardoned by President Lee Myung-Bak in December 2009.) Meanwhile, the head of the National Tax Service and two of Roh's former presidential aides were also arrested on various corruption charges. These developments proved embarrassing for Roh, who had pledged to reduce corruption.

The presidency of Lee Myung-Bak

At the presidential election of December 2007 the GNP's Lee Myung-Bak achieved a decisive victory, securing 48.7% of the votes cast, despite corruption allegations overshadowing the latter stages of the electoral campaign. Of the nine other candidates, his nearest rivals were Chung Dong-Young, with 26.1% of the votes, and Lee Hoi-Chang, with 15.1%. However, the level of voter participation, at 62.9%, was relatively low. Lee's win (by the largest margin since the reintroduction of direct elections in 1987) was attributed to the electorate's dissatisfaction with the achievements of the incumbent centre-left administration, and its attraction to the President-elect's focus during the election campaign on improving the economy.

Shortly after his exoneration by an independent counsel re-examining accusations of financial impropriety against him, Lee Myung-Bak was inaugurated as President in late February 2008. The National Assembly subsequently approved Lee's nomination of Han Seung-Soo, an experienced politician and diplomat, for the post of Prime Minister. Other notable appointments to the State Council included Kang Man-Soo as Minister of Strategy and Finance, Kim Ha-Joong as Minister of Unification, and Yu Myung-Hwan as Minister of Foreign Affairs and Trade. The position of Deputy Prime Minister was terminated. Meanwhile, there was some realignment of political parties in early 2008 in advance of the forthcoming legislative elections. Lee Hoi-Chang created the Liberty Forward Party, which later absorbed the People First Party (founded in 2005), and the UNDP and the DP merged to form the United Democratic Party (UDP).

At the legislative elections conducted in April 2008, the GNP secured a narrow majority, winning 153 of the 299 seats in the National Assembly. The UDP won 81 seats and the Liberty Forward Party 18 seats, while the pro-Park coalition (comprising former GNP members allied to the party's defeated presidential nominee, Park Geun-Hye) took 14 seats. A total of 245 candidates were directly elected, with the remaining seats being determined by proportional representation. The electoral turnout, at some 46%, was the lowest ever recorded at a general election. The GNP's lack of a strong majority was expected to curtail the new President's programme of economic reform, while the presence of more than 50 supporters of Park Geun-Hye within the GNP contingent, as well as the pro-Park coalition and independents, was another possible constraint on Lee's ambitions.

One of President Lee's first challenges emerged in April 2008, when he agreed to rescind the country's ban on beef imports from the USA (imposed in 2003), reportedly to improve bilateral relations and expedite the FTA process. Amid widespread public fear of bovine spongiform encephalopathy (BSE) contamination, daily demonstrations were attended by thousands of South Koreans; although initially peaceful, the protests subsequently escalated into violence. As the protests continued, the issue became symbolic of wider public dissatisfaction with major government initiatives, including Lee's ambitious plans to construct a 540-km transnational canal system (which was subsequently reported to have been abandoned) and the privatization of several state-owned businesses. At local elections in June the GNP secured only 10 of 52 positions (in comparison with the 22 won by the UDP, now known as the Democratic Party—DP). With the BSE affair rapidly becoming a national crisis, the members of the State Council offered to resign. In July President Lee responded by effecting a cabinet reorganization, replacing the Minister of Food, Agriculture, Forestry and Fisheries, Chung Woon-Chun, with Jang Tae-Pyoung.

President Lee implemented another cabinet reorganization in January 2009, appointing Hyun In-Taek to succeed Kim Ha-Joong as Minister of Unification and dismissing Kang Man-Soo as Minister of Strategy and Finance, to be replaced by Yoon Jeung-Hyun. By-elections for five seats in the National Assembly were held in April. In a rebuke to the ruling GNP, voters elected three independents (including former UNDP presidential candidate Chung Dong-Young) and one DP member to the Assembly, while the New Progressive Party, which had been founded in the previous year by a breakaway faction of the Democratic Labour Party, secured its first seat in the legislature.

Former President Roh Moo-Hyun became embroiled in a corruption scandal in April 2009, when he was questioned by prosecutors in connection with allegations that he and members of his family had accepted US $6m. in bribes from a businessman. With the former President's indictment believed to be imminent and his reputation severely damaged (combating corruption had been a central tenet of his presidency), Roh committed suicide in May. In August two former senior aides to Roh were sentenced to prison terms after being convicted on bribery charges. In December former Prime Minister Han Myeong-Sook, appointed by Roh in 2006, was arrested on charges of accepting bribes. She was acquitted in April 2010, describing her trial as having been politically motivated. She was indicted in July on further charges of accepting bribes, but was acquitted of the separate offences in October 2011 and January 2012.

President Lee announced a major reorganization of the State Council in September 2009, which included the appointment of a new Prime Minister, Chun Un-Chan, hitherto president of Seoul National University. Gen. Kim Tae-Young, the former Chairman of the Joint Chiefs of Staff, was appointed as Minister of National Defence, Lee Kwi-Nam was allocated the justice portfolio, and Joo Ho-Young became the Minister for Special Affairs, a new position created to enhance cross-party co-operation. In October Chung Mong-Joon assumed the chairmanship of the GNP, replacing Park Hee-Tae, who had resigned in order to contest a seat at legislative by-elections later that month.

The 2010 budget was approved unilaterally in December 2009, following a boycott of the National Assembly by the DP. Controversially, the budget incorporated significant funding for the President's plan to rehabilitate South Korea's four main rivers. Critics had expressed concern about the cost of the scheme and potential environmental damage, while many believed that Lee's ultimate objective was to revive his scheme for a national canal network.

Resignation of Chun Un-Chan as Prime Minister and appointment of Kim Hwang-Sik

The GNP performed poorly in local elections held in June 2010, despite predictions that the party would benefit from President Lee's firm attitude to North Korea following the sinking of the *Cheonan* warship in March (see North Korea). In response to the defeats, Chung Mong-Joon resigned as GNP Chairman along with the party's entire Supreme Council; Ahn Sang-Soo was elected to replace Chung in July. In the same month, in spite of a better performance by the GNP in further by-elections to the National Assembly, on the day after the polling Chun Un-Chan announced his resignation as Prime Minister, claiming responsibility for a series of reverses suffered by the Government during his 10 months in office: in particular, he cited his failure to secure legislative approval for the Government's revised development plan for Sejong City, a new town under construction in the Chungcheong region. President Roh Moo-Hyun had originally proposed establishing the city as a new capital, before modifying the plan to entail transferring a limited number of ministries and government agencies from Seoul; the Lee administration had proposed abandoning Roh's plan and instead turning Sejong City into an industrial and scientific centre. Following the National Assembly's defeat of Lee's proposal in June, in mid-July the Government announced that the relocation of some 36 state agencies to Sejong City would commence in mid-2012; the relocation process was expected to be completed in 2015.

In early August 2010 President Lee nominated Kim Tae-Ho for the premiership, also naming seven other ministers (although the principal portfolios remained unchanged) and other senior officials. However, during August Kim and several of the other nominees were subjected to fierce criticism from opposition legislators at their confirmation hearings before the National Assembly, amid allegations of impropriety. At the end of the month Kim resigned as Prime Minister-designate, having failed to refute claims that he had accepted bribes from Park Yeon-Cha while Governor of South Gyeongsang province in 2004–09; Kim was one of several leading politicians, in addition to former President Roh, who had been implicated in the corruption scandal surrounding Park. Two other ministers-designate also resigned after admitting unethical conduct. In mid-September Lee nominated Kim Hwang-Sik, the Chairman of the BIA, for the post of Prime Minister, and his nomination was finally confirmed by the National Assembly in early October. Shortly afterwards Kim Sung-Hwan was appointed Minister of Foreign Affairs and Trade, filling a vacancy left in early September by Yu Myung-Hwan, who had resigned owing to allegations of nepotism.

Sohn Hak-Kyu was elected Chairman of the DP at the party's convention in October 2010, defeating Chung Dong-Young, the former UNDP presidential candidate, and Chung Sye-Kyun, the outgoing Chairman, who had resigned following the DP's poor performance at the by-elections in July.

The Government was severely criticized by both opposition and GNP politicians for its hesitant response to the fatal shelling of Yeonpyeong island by North Korean artillery in November 2010 (see North Korea), and for the armed forces' apparent lack of preparedness. The incident prompted the resignation as Minister of National Defence of Kim Tae-Young, whose earlier offer to resign in March over the sinking of the *Cheonan* had been refused by the President; he was replaced by Kim Kwan-Jin, a former Chairman of the Joint Chiefs of Staff.

At by-elections in April 2011 the GNP secured only one of the three contested National Assembly seats. In May Lee replaced five ministers, and further ministerial changes in August included the replacement of Hyun In-Taek as Minister of Unification by Yu Woo-Ik, the erstwhile ambassador to China and regarded as likely to favour a less confrontational attitude to North Korea than his predecessor. Public concern over stagnating property prices and high levels of household indebtedness was exacerbated during 2011 by reports that officials of the financial supervisory service had accepted bribes in return for not reporting financial problems (particularly loss-making property developments) and corruption in a number of savings banks; by September the Government had suspended the operations of 16 of the country's savings banks, including the largest, the Busan Savings Bank. In November the Government encountered vociferous opposition within the legislature, as well as public protests outside, when it finally succeeded in gaining ratification of the long-delayed FTA with the USA (see *Relations with the USA*).

Party reorganizations and the 2012 elections

Both the principal political parties carried out major changes during 2011, in anticipation of the general election scheduled for April 2012 and the presidential election due to take place in December 2012. The GNP Chairman, Ahn Sang-Soo, and other members of the ruling party's leadership resigned after the by-election defeats in April 2011, and a new Chairman, Hong Joon-Pyo, and Supreme Council were elected in July. In October an independent candidate, Park Won-Soon, was victorious in the election to the influential post of mayor of Seoul, unexpectedly defeating the GNP candidate. In December Hong Joon-Pyo responded to critics within the GNP by resigning as Chairman, and Park Geun-Hye assumed the chair in an 'emergency' capacity, undertaking to introduce reforms. In February 2012 the Speaker of the National Assembly, Park Hee-Tae, resigned after being accused of offering bribes while contesting the GNP leadership election in 2008; he was later convicted of the offence. Also in February 2012 the GNP absorbed the small Future Hope Alliance, and later in the month the party's 'emergency committee' announced that the party was to be 'reborn' as the Saenuri Party (variously translated as the New Frontier or New World Party). The same month saw the formation of a new conservative party, the Korea Vision Party, led by Park Se-Il.

In December 2011, meanwhile, the main opposition party, the DP, merged with the small Civil Unity Party, with the support of the FKTU, to form the Democratic United Party (DUP); Sohn

Hak-Kyu, who had supported the merger, then retired from the party chair. In January 2012 (following her acquittal earlier in that month, and in the previous October, on separate charges of accepting bribes) the former Prime Minister, Han Myeong-Sook, was elected as Chairwoman of the DUP. In the same month she reached an agreement with Park Geun-Hye on adopting a revision of party electoral rules to allow an 'open primary system', whereby members of the public would be allowed to nominate DUP candidates for election to the National Assembly. In February Park Won-Soon, the mayor of Seoul (elected in the previous October as an independent candidate) announced that he was joining the DUP. In March the Unified Progressive Party (UPP, which had been formed in the previous December by a merger of three smaller groupings—the People's Participation Party, the Democratic Labour Party and a faction of the New Progressive Party) agreed to form an electoral alliance with the DUP and the remainder of the New Progressive Party: joint candidates for the general election were nominated by 'primary' voting in over 70 constituencies.

A general election to the National Assembly (enlarged to 300 seats, of which 246 were for directly elected candidates and 54 for candidates chosen by proportional representation) was held on 11 April 2012, attracting a turnout of 54.3%. Despite losing control of 13 seats, the Saenuri Party retained a narrow majority, winning 152 seats, while the DUP secured 127, the UPP 13, the Liberty Forward Party (which subsequently changed its name to the Advancement and Unification Party) five and independents the remaining three. Han Myeong-Sook subsequently announced her resignation from the chair of the DUP, taking responsibility for the party's defeat; she was replaced in June by Lee Hae-Chan, Prime Minister during 2004–06.

During 2012 the problem of corruption in public life remained pronounced. In July President Lee made an apology to the nation when his brother, Lee Sang-Deuk, a former legislator, was implicated in the savings banks scandal (see above): Lee Sang-Deuk had been arrested for having allegedly received bribes from officials of two savings banks (and was convicted of the offence in January 2013). In August 2012 the Chairman of Hanwha, one of South Korea's largest *chaebol*, was convicted of embezzlement (but the verdict was overturned by the Supreme Court in September 2013). In November 2012 the Chief Prosecutor, Han Sang-Dae, resigned after the revelation of corruption scandals within the prosecution service, although not implicated himself. In January 2013, shortly before the end of his term of office, President Lee controversially issued a pardon for more than 50 associates who had been convicted of corruption or malpractice, including the former Speaker of the National Assembly, Park Tee-Hae. In February the Chairman of another major *chaebol*, SK Group, was sentenced to a prison term for misuse of funds.

In August 2012, meanwhile, Park Geun-Hye was officially nominated as the Saenuri Party's presidential candidate, while in September the DUP selected as its candidate Moon Jae-In, who had been presidential chief of staff of former President Roh Moo-Hyun. Prominent among several independent presidential candidates was Ahn Cheol-Soo, a wealthy businessman and academic who advocated reform of the political system. In November the Chairman of the DUP, Lee Hae-Chan, and other senior party members resigned, apparently in response to criticism by Ahn. Later in November Ahn relinquished his candidacy so as not to split the liberal vote, encouraging his supporters to vote for Moon. At the election, on 19 December, Park Geun-Hye won 51.6% of the votes against Moon Jae-In's 48.0%; voter participation was 75.8%. In January 2013 the DUP chose Moon Hee-Sang, a long-standing member of the National Assembly, as its 'emergency' Chairman.

Recent developments: the presidency of Park Geun-Hye

Park Geun-Hye, South Korea's first female head of state, took office as President on 25 February 2013. She promised to undertake a 'trust-building process' with North Korea, but almost immediately had to confront an extreme intensification in hostile utterances from the North, denouncing the routine military exercises conducted by South Korea jointly with the USA in March and April (see North Korea). Park also encountered difficulties in her attempts to form a new administration. She was accused of failing to observe adequate vetting procedures when her original nominees for the posts of Prime Minister and Minister of National Defence, Kim Yong-Joon and Kim Byung-Kwan, respectively, were obliged to decline their nominations following various allegations of past misconduct. Park then appointed Chung Hong-Won, a prominent lawyer, as Prime Minister and retained the incumbent Minister of National

Defence, Kim Kwan-Jin, in his post. The new Minister of Foreign Affairs was Yun Byung-Se, a former diplomat, and the new Minister of Strategy and Finance, Hyun Oh-Seok, the erstwhile President of the Korea Development Institute, was given the additional, revived post of Deputy Prime Minister. Two new ministries were created—one for science, ICT (information and communications technology) and future planning, and the other for trade, industry and energy—and a ministry covering maritime affairs, the Ministry of Oceans and Fisheries, was re-established. In addition, a new Office of National Security was established within the presidential office. In April Park's Government proposed a supplementary budget, which included additional defence expenditure, amid continued heightened tensions with North Korea, and announced further measures to stimulate the economy. In May the DUP elected Kim Han-Gil as its new Chairman and voted to revert to its previous name, the Democratic Party (DP).

In June 2013 a scandal emerged involving the former director of the NIS, Won Sei-Hoon, who was charged with attempting to influence the result of the 2012 presidential election by instructing his agents to post online comments favourable to Park, using hundreds of false identities. In January 2014 Won was found guilty on a separate charge of receiving bribes from the head of a construction company in 2009–10; in September 2014, following his release from jail, Won was found guilty of the political charges and was given another custodial sentence, which was subsequently suspended. However, in February 2015 the suspension was overturned by the Seoul High Court and Won was again taken into custody, to serve three years' imprisonment for violating electoral law. Meanwhile, in March 2014 opposition politicians demanded the resignation of the incumbent head of the NIS, Nam Jae-Joon, after the organization was accused of submitting forged documents to a court that was trying an alleged North Korean defector accused of espionage.

In August 2013, meanwhile, a UPP legislator, Lee Seok-Ki, was arrested on charges of sympathizing with North Korea (in violation of the National Security Law of 1948) and of planning, together with some 130 supporters, an armed revolt against the Government. Lee was found guilty in February 2014 and sentenced to 12 years' imprisonment (later reduced to nine years). At the Government's behest, in December the Constitutional Court ruled that the UPP should be dissolved.

In September 2013 the Minister of Health and Welfare, Chin Young, resigned after disagreeing with the President's decision to provide basic old-age pensions for only the least wealthy 70% of senior citizens, instead of for all those aged 65 years and over, as Park had promised in her electoral campaign. Moon Hyung-Pyo, the Vice-President of the Korea Development Institute, was appointed to replace Chin in November. Park also attracted criticism for failing (in the budget for 2014) to fulfil other pre-election commitments to increase spending on higher education, social welfare and health care, while her efforts to reform heavily indebted public sector enterprises were strongly opposed by the trade unions. More than 8,000 employees of Korea Railway Corporation (Korail) took part in a 22-day strike (the longest in the company's history) in December 2013 to protest against restructuring plans which were claimed to be paving the way for the company's privatization.

In March 2014 Lee Ju-Young assumed responsibility for the Ministry of Oceans and Fisheries after the incumbent, Yoon Jin-Sook, was dismissed for responding inadequately to a coastal oil spillage. In the same month a new political party, the New Politics Alliance for Democracy (NPAD), was formed by the DP in alliance with Ahn Cheol-Soo, the popular independent candidate in the 2012 presidential election. Ahn had been elected to the legislature as an independent candidate in a by-election in April 2013; he had subsequently been expected to establish (and had taken steps toward founding) his own political party, so the merger with the DP in 2014 surprised many observers and reportedly disappointed many of Ahn's supporters, who had hoped to challenge the dominance of the two main parties. The NPAD, which commanded 130 seats in the National Assembly, was initially led jointly by Kim Han-Gil and Ahn. It aimed to challenge the ruling Saenuri Party in the local elections scheduled to be held in June 2014.

The sinking of South Korea's largest passenger ferry, the MV *Sewol* (owned by the Chonghaejin Marine Co), on 16 April 2014 en route from the northern city of Incheon to Jeju Island off the country's south-west coast, with the resultant loss of more than 300 lives (the majority of whom were teenage children from a single secondary school) had major political repercussions.

Following widespread public criticism of the flagrant breach of safety regulations by the *Sewol*'s owners, in having carried out illegal modifications to the vessel, and the disorganized rescue operation, on 27 April Prime Minister Chung Hong-Won accepted full responsibility for the disaster and tendered his resignation. (In the event, at President Park's request Chung remained in office, albeit with diminished authority, until January 2015, firstly while the full inquiry into the disaster was undertaken and then while two successive nominees for his replacement —Ahn Dai-Hee, an erstwhile Supreme Court justice, and Moon Chang-Keuk, a one-time newspaper editor—were obliged to withdraw their nominations following media criticism of the former's wealth and remarks made in public by the latter on the subject of Japanese colonial rule in Korea.) Chung's resignation was swiftly followed, in early May 2014, by those of Nam Jae-Joon, Director of the NIS, and Kim Jang-Soo, head of the National Security Office. In mid-May, amid continuing widespread anger among the South Korean populace, the President publicly apologized for the authorities' initially mishandled response to the disaster in an emotional televised speech and pledged to dismantle the national coast guard. In mid-November the *Sewol*'s captain, Lee Joon-Seok, was imprisoned for 36 years on charges of gross negligence, being found to have abandoned the sinking vessel with hundreds of passengers on board. The chief engineer, Park Gi-Ho, received a 30-year sentence for homicide, while 13 other crew members were jailed for between five and 20 years each on various charges including criminal negligence and accidental homicide. Later that month the head of Chonghaejin Marine Co, Kim Han-Sik, was sentenced to 10 years' imprisonment for failing to prevent improper storage and the overloading of cargo on the ferry. Four other officials of the company were sentenced to between three and six years in prison on similar charges. A nationwide manhunt for Yoo Byung-Un, the wealthy head of the family that owned Chonghaejin Marine Co, ended in late July when it was established that his body had been found.

In June 2014, in the aftermath of the ferry disaster, extensive government changes were effected. Among the most notable of these was the replacement of Minister of Defence Kim Kwan-Jin by Gen. Han Min-Koo, a former Chairman of the Joint Chiefs of Staff; the appointment of Choi Kyoung-Hwan as Deputy Prime Minister and Minister of Strategy and Finance; and the appointment of Chong Jong-Sup as Minister of Government Administration and Home Affairs, despite his failing to obtain the endorsement of the National Assembly owing to allegations of historical misconduct.

In mid-2014 the electorate had two separate opportunities to pass judgement on the Government's handling of the crisis—at the local elections held in June and at parliamentary by-elections in July. Campaigning was dominated by issues concerning public safety. Among the main posts contested at the local elections were nine provincial gubernatorial seats and eight mayorships. Of these 17 polls, the NPAD won nine (including the key mayorship of Seoul), while the Saenuri Party won eight, in a better performance than had been anticipated. In the July by-elections the ruling party secured 11 of the 15 contested National Assembly seats; in the face of this comfortable victory by the Saenuri Party, the NPAD's joint leaders, Kim Han-Gil and Ahn Cheol-Soo, resigned with immediate effect.

In mid-November 2014, shortly after the search and rescue operations at the *Sewol* accident site were finally terminated, the Government dismantled the Korea Coast Guard and the National Emergency Management Agency. Two new institutions were established within the office of the Prime Minister: a Ministry of Personnel Management and a new disaster control agency, the Ministry of Public Safety and Security. The creation of the latter body meant that responsibility for disaster management was taken away from the Ministry of Security and Public Administration, which now became the Ministry of Government Administration and Home Affairs. In late January 2015, with her popularity reportedly having dwindled to its lowest level since the 2012 election, partly as a result of the protracted process of reorganizing government posts, President Park nominated Lee Wan-Koo as the new Prime Minister. Prior to his confirmation, numerous allegations surfaced against him, including accusations that he had speculated in property, plagiarized his doctoral thesis and that his son had avoided mandatory military service. In addition, NPAD, which had initially supported his nomination, released a recording of Lee boasting about his ability to influence both the coverage and personnel decisions of media organizations. Despite these serious allegations, Lee was finally confirmed in the post in February receiving parliamentary approval by 148 votes to 128. After his confirmation, Lee initiated a new anti-corruption campaign. Three further cabinet appointments were announced in February, including that of Hong Young-Pyo as the new Minister of Unification. Also in February, the NPAD party convention elected former DUP presidential candidate Moon Jae-In as the new Chairman of the NPAD.

In early March 2015, following years of debate which had gathered pace in the wake of the *Sewol* disaster, the National Assembly approved more stringent anti-corruption legislation under which it would no longer legally be necessary to prove a direct link between the receipt of a gift or money by a public official (or their family members) and a favour rendered in return. Those found guilty of such acts of bribery could face a maximum penalty of three years' imprisonment. The legislation was expected to come into effect in late 2016. Meanwhile, in February 2015, in a case that attracted much attention in the international media, Cho Hyun-Ah, daughter of the Chairman of Korean Air and herself a former executive within the airline, received a one-year jail sentence on charges of having obstructed aviation safety after she forced a passenger aircraft to abandon take-off at an airport in New York, USA, so that she could discipline a crew member regarding a service standards issue. The case reignited much public debate about the economic and social privileges enjoyed by the family members of the *chaebol*. In early April, following a reported cyber-attack on Korea Hydro and Nuclear Power Co (KHNP) in December 2014, President Park announced the creation of a new secretariat for cyber-security within the presidential office.

In mid-April 2015 Lee Wan-Koo offered his resignation as Prime Minister, following allegations of involvement in a bribery scandal, which he denied. A business executive named Sung Wan-Jong, who was facing arrest on corruption charges, committed suicide in early April, leaving a note naming officials who had received cash bribes from him, including the Prime Minister. In addition, he accused the Prime Minister of corruption in a radio broadcast shortly before his death. Lee was alleged to have received 30m. won in secret campaign funds from Sung in 2013, when Lee was contesting a parliamentary seat. Other allies of President Park in the Saenuri Party were also implicated. At the end of April 2015 the President accepted Lee Wan-Koo's resignation and he stepped down from office.

Relations with North Korea

For details of relations between North and South Korea, see the Democratic People's Republic of Korea (North Korea), *Inter-Korean Relations*.

Foreign Affairs

The foreign policy of the Republic of Korea (South Korea) has been dominated by its relations with the major powers of Japan, the People's Republic of China, the USA and Russia, owing to its geographical position, and by the quest for stability on the Korean peninsula. Since 2010 South Korea has been involved in negotiations with Australia, Brunei, Canada, Chile, Japan, Malaysia, Mexico, New Zealand, Peru, Singapore, the USA and Viet Nam to create a trade zone, the Trans-Pacific Partnership, which would create a trading bloc responsible for an estimated 40% of the world's output; however, negotiations on the US-led initiative were repeatedly stalled during 2014 as the USA and Japan debated tariffs for agricultural products and vehicles.

Relations with Japan

Relations between South Korea and Japan, which had long been strained, were eased by President Chun's official visit to Japan in September 1984 (the first such visit undertaken by a South Korean head of state), during which Emperor Hirohito and Prime Minister Yasuhiro Nakasone formally expressed their regret for Japanese aggression in Korea in the past. In May 1990, during a visit to Japan by President Roh, Emperor Akihito offered official apologies for the cruelties of Japanese colonial rule in Korea. In January 1992 the Japanese Prime Minister, Kiichi Miyazawa, visited South Korea, where he publicly expressed regret at the enslavement during the Second World War of an estimated 100,000 Korean women, who were used by the Japanese military for sexual purposes ('comfort women'). In August 1993, following an inquiry, a statement made by Japan's Chief Cabinet Secretary, Yohei Kono, officially acknowledged the role of the Japanese military in coercing women into brothels and expressed 'sincere apologies and remorse' on the part of the Government. In late 1994 the Japanese Government announced

that it would not make compensation payments directly to individuals, but would finance a programme to construct vocational training centres for the women concerned. In August 1995, on the 50th anniversary of the end of the Second World War, the Japanese Prime Minister, Tomiichi Murayama, issued a statement expressing 'deep reflection and sincere apologies' for Japanese colonial aggression, while in June 1996 his successor, Ryutaro Hashimoto, issued a public apology to the 'comfort women'. However, the South Korean Government regarded Japanese proposals to provide compensation through private sources of funding, rather than government money, as tantamount to a denial of moral responsibility. The conclusion of new defence co-operation guidelines between Japan and the USA in September 1997 was of concern for South Korea, which feared an expansion in Japanese military capability. Negotiations for a new fisheries agreement, under way since mid-1996, were unilaterally terminated by Japan in January 1998, as a result of continuing disagreement regarding sovereignty of the Dokdo islands (or Takeshima in Japanese, located between South Korea and Japan in the East Sea—also known as the Sea of Japan), to which both countries laid claim. In April the South Korean Government announced its intention to make payments itself to surviving 'comfort women'.

In October 1998, during a visit to Tokyo, Japan, by President Kim Dae-Jung, a joint declaration was signed, in which Japan apologized for the suffering inflicted on the Korean people during Japanese colonial rule. In addition, South Korea agreed to revoke a ban on the import of various Japanese goods, while Japan promised substantial financial aid to South Korea in support of its efforts to stimulate economic recovery. In November the two countries concluded negotiations on the renewal of their bilateral fisheries agreement, which came into effect in January 1999, despite the objections of the main South Korean opposition party, which protested that it failed positively to affirm South Korea's claim to sovereignty over the disputed Dokdo/Takeshima islands. In early 1999 protests by South Korean fishermen, who were apparently suffering heavy losses because of the revised agreement, forced the resignation of the Minister of Maritime Affairs and Fisheries.

During 2001 relations with Japan deteriorated owing to the publication in February of new Japanese history textbooks, which sought to justify Japan's aggression towards its Asian neighbours during the Second World War, and neglected to mention the forced prostitution of Asian (mainly Korean) 'comfort women' by the Japanese army and the forcible transfer and use of Koreans as slave labour in Japan. Large-scale protests were held in Seoul, and bilateral military co-operation was suspended. In August South Korean opinion was further outraged by the visit of the Japanese Prime Minister, Junichiro Koizumi, to the controversial Yasukuni Shrine in Tokyo honouring Japan's war dead (including some who were regarded as war criminals). Amid popular protests, Koizumi visited Seoul in October and delivered an apology for the suffering of Koreans under Japanese rule.

Along with China and North Korea, South Korea condemned Koizumi's return visits to the Yasukuni Shrine in April 2002 and January 2003. However, in March 2002 Koizumi and Kim Dae-Jung agreed to begin discussions on a possible bilateral FTA, and mutual hostility between the two countries was superseded by the need for co-operation in engaging with the North. In June 2003 Roh made his first state visit to Japan and held discussions with Koizumi on the issue of North Korea's nuclear weapons programme. Although both leaders opposed any development of nuclear weapons in North Korea, Roh urged dialogue with that country, whereas Koizumi favoured stricter measures.

In March 2005 the local legislature of Japan's Shimane Prefecture, which claimed the Dokdo/Takeshima islands as part of its territory, voted to establish a 'Takeshima Day'. In response, the South Korean Minister of Foreign Affairs and Trade, Ban Ki-Moon, cancelled a scheduled visit to Japan, while protests were held outside the Japanese embassy in Seoul. Further public demonstrations took place in April in reaction to the approval for use in Japanese schools of history textbooks—including one first published in 2001 (see above)—which were regarded by Koreans (and Chinese) as failing to address the true nature of Japanese wartime conduct. Another visit to the Yasukuni Shrine by Prime Minister Koizumi in October 2005 prompted President Roh to cancel a scheduled visit to Japan in December. South Korea antagonized the Japanese authorities in July 2006 when it conducted a survey of the waters around the Dokdo/Takeshima islands, against the express wishes of Japan (which, in turn, had announced its intention to conduct a similar survey in April, prompting the South Korean Government to declare plans to develop facilities on the islands and to explore the area's marine and mineral resources).

Yasuo Fukuda, who became Japanese Prime Minister in September 2007, identified strengthening relations with South Korea as a priority, notably pledging not to visit the controversial Yasukuni Shrine. Fukuda attended Lee Myung-Bak's inauguration as South Korean President in February 2008, following which the two leaders agreed to undertake regular reciprocal visits and to promote the resumption of negotiations on the establishment of an FTA (which had stalled in late 2004). In July 2008, however, the dispute over the Dokdo/Takeshima islands re-emerged when the Japanese Government announced that the islands would be described as Japanese in teachers' materials; the publication in September of an official defence document reiterating this stance by Japan placed a further strain on relations.

In August 2010, in a statement made in advance of the centenary of Japan's annexation of the peninsula, the new Japanese Prime Minister, Naoto Kan, expressed 'deep remorse' for the period of colonial rule and announced the repatriation to South Korea of a number of cultural artefacts seized during the occupation. However, a number of new Japanese textbooks and government documents published over the course of the year once again reiterated Japan's claim to the Dokdo/Takeshima islands, prompting protests by South Korea.

In March 2012 South Korea, Japan and China completed negotiations on the terms of a trilateral agreement on investment, which was signed in May in the Chinese capital of Beijing. In November the three countries agreed to begin negotiations on a trilateral FTA; the seventh round of talks took place in Seoul in April 2015. Meanwhile, in August 2012 Japan strongly criticized a visit by President Lee to the Dokdo/Takeshima islands (the first such visit by a South Korean head of state). In the same month the South Korean Government declined a Japanese offer to submit the dispute over the islands to the International Court of Justice in The Hague, Netherlands. Renewed visits to the Yasukuni Shrine during October by Japanese politicians, including the leader of the main opposition party, Shinzo Abe, again offended South Korean opinion, and there was apprehension that tension would be increased further after Abe became Prime Minister (for the second time) in December. After taking office in February 2013 President Park Geun-Hye announced no plans to visit Japan, stating in November that there was no point in holding a summit meeting, given Japan's attitude to its wartime conduct. In April South Korea's Minister of Foreign Affairs cancelled a visit to Tokyo, after senior Japanese government ministers visited the Yasukuni Shrine, and a visit to the shrine by Abe himself in December was described as 'deplorable' by the South Korean authorities. Moreover, in July the bilateral currency swap agreement between the two countries, which had been in place for eight years, was allowed to expire.

In March 2014 Park and Abe held discussions in their official capacity for the first time, at a meeting convened by the US President, Barack Obama, during a conference on nuclear security in the Netherlands: Obama declared the USA's commitment to both South Korea and Japan in view of the threat posed by North Korea's nuclear activities, and both Park and Abe referred to the need for close co-operation in responding to North Korean actions. Notably, in the latter half of the year Abe twice sent offerings to the Yasukuni Shrine in lieu of a personal visit. Meanwhile, in April, however, the Dokdo/Takeshima dispute intensified following the approval of new Japanese elementary school textbooks reinforcing claims to the islands (compounded in April 2015 by the approval of new middle school textbooks). In December, following cyber-attacks alleged to have been perpetrated by North Korean agents on Sony Pictures Entertainment in the USA and on the South Korean nuclear power operator KHNP, South Korea, Japan and the USA signed a pact providing for the sharing of military intelligence on North Korea; the pact had first been mooted in mid-2012 but signing had been postponed by South Korea in the wake of popular protests. In April 2015 South Korea and Japan held their first high-level security talks since 2009 when the two countries' respective defence and foreign affairs ministers convened in Seoul for a 'two plus two' meeting.

Other regional relations

Full diplomatic relations with the People's Republic of China were established in 1992 (a development that was denounced by North Korea, of which China had been the principal ally

hitherto). Relations with China were strengthened by numerous subsequent reciprocal ministerial visits. In October 2000 agreement was reached on the resumption of the quadripartite conference, incorporating the two Koreas, China and the USA, with the aim of establishing a peace mechanism for the Korean Peninsula (see North Korea). Later in the month, following strong opposition from China, South Korea refused to grant a visa to the Dalai Lama, Tibet's spiritual leader, on the grounds that it would be 'inappropriate'.

In November 2001 the ministers of economics, finance and foreign affairs from China, South Korea and Japan agreed to hold regular meetings to foster closer co-operation. In mid-2002 the Chinese authorities sought to prevent North Korean refugees from seeking asylum in various diplomatic buildings in China, including the South Korean embassy in Beijing.

The growing diplomatic crisis over North Korea's nuclear programme from late 2002 led South Korea to seek China's assistance in persuading the North to work towards a peaceful solution. Chinese diplomatic efforts subsequently played a major role (see North Korea). In August 2004, however, relations between South Korea and China were damaged by controversy over which country had a more legitimate claim to the historical kingdom of Koguryo, which had covered the area of modern North Korea and part of South Korea, as well as areas of northern China.

China's continuing policy of forcibly repatriating North Korean defectors who had been apprehended in China (regarding them as illegal migrants) attracted criticism in South Korea and was condemned by human rights organizations, including Amnesty International and the office of the UN High Commissioner for Refugees, particularly in early 2012 after the new North Korean leadership was reported to have increased the severity of punishments for captured defectors. In February and March there were protests in South Korea concerning the fate of some 30 North Korean defectors who were facing repatriation from China, and the South Korean Government urged China to fulfil its obligations as a signatory to international treaties on the status of refugees.

A further cause of tension was illegal fishing by Chinese vessels in South Korean territorial waters, particularly after the killing of a South Korean coastguard by the captain of a Chinese fishing boat in December 2011: more than 400 Chinese fishing boats had been seized by the Korean authorities in that year. The matter was raised by President Lee on a state visit to China in January 2012. Nevertheless, the strengthening of economic ties with China (South Korea's principal export market) remained a priority, and during the visit the two Governments agreed to prepare for formal negotiations on a bilateral FTA, for which feasibility studies had been initiated in 2007. A trilateral agreement with China and Japan on investment was signed in May 2012; negotiations on a trilateral FTA commenced in March 2013 and had reached their seventh round by April 2015. Meanwhile, in November the South Korean Government announced that it would not recognize China's establishment in that month of an air defence identification zone (ADIZ) in the East China Sea, in support of China's claim to the Diaoyu/Senkaku islands, also claimed by Japan: the ADIZ also included an area of submerged rocks (Ieodo or Suyan) claimed by South Korea. In December the South Korean Government declared that it had expanded its own air defence zone to overlap that of China and include the Ieodo rocks. In the same month the South Korean authorities announced that they would repatriate the remains of more than 400 Chinese soldiers who had been killed during the Korean War; the repatriations began in March 2014, with a second transfer scheduled for early 2015. In November 2014, at their fifth summit meeting since coming to power, President Park and her Chinese counterpart, Xi Jinping, concluded discussions on a bilateral FTA; the agreement, which was initialled in February 2015 and scheduled to come into force after 2016, provided for the reduction of tariffs within 20 years on 90% of traded items between the two countries.) From October 2014 China joined Russia in expressing strong opposition to the possible deployment of a US Terminal High-Altitude Area Defense (THAAD) missile defence system in South Korea, claiming that such a deployment would endanger burgeoning relations between the two countries.

In November 2000, after eight years' suspension, the 25th Joint Conference of Korea-Taiwan Business Councils took place in Seoul. It was agreed that henceforth annual conferences would be held alternately in the respective capitals of Seoul and Taipei. In the same month a Korean passenger aircraft flew from Seoul to Taipei for the first time since 1992, when diplomatic relations had been severed. South Korea also maintained close relations with South-East Asian countries, and an agreement on free trade in merchandise goods was reached between South Korea and nine of the 10 members of the Association of Southeast Asian Nations (ASEAN, see p. 210) in August 2006. Under the agreement, which took effect in June 2007, 97% of South Korean products exported to the nine ASEAN countries were exempt from tariffs or would carry tariffs of less than 5% by 2010. Although more commonly known as the South Korea-ASEAN FTA, the arrangement did not include Thailand, which refused to participate in protest against South Korea's insistence on the exclusion of rice from the agreement. However, several rounds of free trade negotiations were held between the two countries during 2007, and in January 2008 it was reported that an agreement had been reached whereby Thailand would be allowed more flexibility in reducing or waiving its tariffs compared with the other ASEAN nations. Meanwhile, in November 2007 South Korea and all 10 members of ASEAN signed an agreement on free trade in services; a further accord, covering investment, was concluded in 2009. In October 2011 the first official meeting of the ministers of foreign affairs of South Korea and the Mekong River nations (Cambodia, Laos, Myanmar, Thailand and Viet Nam) discussed South Korean development co-operation and investment in the region, and in November the South Korean and Vietnamese Governments agreed to conduct a joint study on the building of nuclear power plants by South Korea in Viet Nam. A bilateral FTA with Viet Nam was signed in December 2014; under the agreement, import tariffs were to be removed on more than 90% of traded items (although rice was, again, excluded from the agreement).

In 2006 trade negotiations commenced between South Korea and India, and in August 2009 a Comprehensive Economic Partnership Agreement was signed by the two countries, entering into effect in January 2010. In July 2011 an agreement was concluded on the export of South Korean nuclear technology to India. President Park Geun-Hye paid a visit to India in January 2014, when agreements were signed on co-operation in cyber-technology, space technology, defence and trade, and it was announced that work on a major steel plant in the state of Odisha (for which the South Korean steel company POSCO had agreed in 2005 to provide investment of US $12,000m., the largest foreign direct investment project ever undertaken in India) was soon to begin, despite local opposition and international controversy. However, at April 2015 work on the steel plant had not yet commenced.

Relations with the USA

Relations between South Korea and the USA were frequently strained from the late 1970s, in particular by the proposal to withdraw US ground troops from South Korea (which was abandoned in 1979) and by the trial of Kim Dae-Jung (see *Domestic Political Affairs*). Disputes between South Korea and the USA in the late 1980s over trade issues had subsided by mid-1991. US President George Bush visited the country in January 1992, when the two sides agreed to cancel that year's 'Team Spirit' joint military exercises. In December 1991 it had been announced that all US nuclear weapons had been withdrawn from South Korean territory. The 'Team Spirit' exercises were resumed in 1993, and in January 1994 it was announced that the USA was to deploy air-defence missiles on South Korean territory. In April 1996, during a visit to Seoul, President Bill Clinton issued a joint US-South Korean proposal for quadripartite negotiations with North Korea and the People's Republic of China (see above). In late 1997 the USA pledged financial support for South Korea, following the latter's conclusion of an agreement with the IMF.

President Kim Dae-Jung was warmly received on a state visit to the USA in June 1998, during which he outlined his 'sunshine' policy of engagement with North Korea. In March 1999 the South Korean Government welcomed a major advance in negotiations between North Korea and the USA on US access to a suspected nuclear site in North Korea. In October the US and South Korean Governments began investigations into the alleged massacre of as many as 300 Korean refugees by US troops near Nogun-ri, in the South Korean province of North Chungcheong, shortly after the beginning of the Korean War. Revelations of the use of defoliants in the DMZ in the late 1960s created further controversy in November 1999. The herbicides, which had apparently been provided by the USA but applied by South Korean troops, included Agent Orange, which had later been found to be highly toxic. The South Korean Government announced that it was

prepared to compensate both soldiers and civilians adversely affected by the defoliants, but the USA reportedly refused to accept any liability. In December a lawsuit was filed against seven US chemical companies by a group of Koreans demanding compensation for damage they claimed to have suffered as a consequence of the herbicides. (In January 2006, in the first such ruling, a South Korean court ordered the US manufacturers to pay 68,000m. won in compensation to 6,800 individuals.)

In May 2000 violent protests took place after a US aircraft accidentally released several bombs close to a village south-west of Seoul, causing minor injuries and damage to property. In response, opposition politicians demanded a review of the Status of Forces Agreement (SOFA), which governed the 37,000 US troops stationed in South Korea. Following the successful conclusion of negotiations, a revised agreement was signed in January 2001. However, South Korean civic groups protested that the partnership between the two countries remained biased in favour of the USA. Also in January outgoing US President Bill Clinton made an unprecedented statement of regret for the massacre near Nogun-ri, but many South Koreans were angry that no apology was forthcoming.

In November 2001 the USA and South Korea agreed to a major 'land swap' whereby existing US bases would relocate to other areas within the country, allowing a consolidation of bases and training facilities over the next 10 years. In the following month the National Assembly endorsed the deployment of non-combat troops to assist the US-led campaign in Afghanistan, mainly in a logistical capacity.

In November 2002 two US soldiers, whose vehicle had accidentally struck and killed two South Korean girls in June, were acquitted of negligent homicide by a US military court, leading to a significant increase in anti-US sentiment among the public. Although President George W. Bush apologized for the incident, in December hundreds of thousands of people attended anti-US rallies in Seoul and across the country. The rallies became a forum of protest against the country's perceived dependency on the USA and that country's policy towards North Korea. Meanwhile, in October a new joint base pact came into force whereby the US military would reduce the number of its bases from 41 to 23 and return 50% of the land it used to South Korea. However, there had yet to be changes to the SOFA that governed the conduct of US troops in Korea—amendments to which had long been demanded by South Koreans.

Before his election as President, Roh Moo-Hyun had campaigned for a foreign policy more independent of the USA. However, in January 2003 he indicated a more conciliatory stance, but nevertheless warned the USA against attacking North Korea, instead urging the resumption of US-North Korean dialogue. Despite domestic protests, in April the National Assembly approved the dispatch of 700 non-combatant troops to Iraq in support of the US-led military operation. In June plans were confirmed to withdraw US troops to locations 120 km south of the DMZ, as part of a wider reorganization of US forces in South Korea. In October 2004 an agreement for the planned withdrawal of one-third of all US troops in South Korea was reached, to take place in three phases extending to 2008. In November 2004 South Korean forces assumed responsibility for patrolling the DMZ.

Meanwhile, the deployment of 3,000 South Korean troops to Iraq at the request of the USA, which had been approved by the National Assembly in February 2004, went ahead in August, despite public outrage at the beheading of a South Korean hostage in that country in June. In December 2004, following a vote in the National Assembly, it was announced that South Korean troops in Iraq (now numbering around 3,600) would remain there throughout 2005. In December 2005 the National Assembly voted to reduce the number of South Korean troops in Iraq to 2,300 and to extend their deployment until the end of 2006.

In February 2007, following a review of their 1953 Mutual Defense Treaty, the two Governments agreed that in April 2012 operational control of South Korean military forces in the event of war would be transferred from the USA to South Korea and that at the same time the Combined Forces Command would be disbanded (three years later than the USA had proposed). A new 'supporting-supported command relationship' was to be established, under which the United States Forces Korea would continue to support the South Korean military and South Korea would remain dependent on the USA for military intelligence. The two Governments also reaffirmed earlier agreements on the relocation of US forces from Seoul to the Osan-Pyeongtaek and

Daegu-Busan regions and on a reduction in the number of US troops stationed in South Korea from around 30,000 to 25,000 by 2008. Following his election as South Korean President in December 2007, Lee Myung-Bak pledged to forge closer relations with the USA, asserting that South Korea continued to require US protection. The National Assembly voted to extend the deployment of South Korean troops in Iraq until the end of 2008, but to reduce their number from around 1,250 to 650. The South Korean Government had come under pressure from the Bush Administration to maintain its military presence in Iraq, despite continued domestic public opposition to the deployment. In December 2008 South Korea withdrew its remaining soldiers from Iraq.

Meanwhile, in February 2006 it was announced that discussions had commenced with regard to the drawing up of an FTA between South Korea and the USA. However, as negotiations proceeded in July an estimated 30,000 demonstrators took to the streets of Seoul to protest against what they described as 'economic subjugation'. South Korean farmers, in particular, were concerned that the proposed FTA might prove detrimental to their livelihoods. Major corporations expressed reservations with regard to US demands that trade-related legislation, including fair trade laws, be applied to the South Korean *chaebol*. A further obstacle was the USA's insistence that goods produced in the North Korean industrial complex of Kaesong should be exempt from the trade pact. In November at least 65,000 people joined protests across South Korea, as part of a general strike organized by the KCTU, to demonstrate their disapproval of the proposed FTA.

In April 2007 South Korea and the USA finally reached a compromise on the terms of the FTA. The principal elements of the agreement included wider access to the US market for South Korean car manufacturers, a reduction of taxes payable by television and mobile telephone manufacturers and the cessation of duties levied on beef imports; the agreement did not encompass rice imports, as South Korea objected to the liberalization of that particular market. Many argued that increased US imports would render local businesses uncompetitive, thus threatening numerous livelihoods. Several amendments to the FTA, incorporating stricter labour and environmental provisions (mainly to facilitate ratification in the US Congress), were agreed before it was formally signed at the end of June. In April 2008, prior to a visit to the USA by the newly elected President Lee Myung-Bak, the South Korean Government agreed to relax restrictions on imports of US beef (imposed in 2003). The decision prompted large-scale public protests in mid-2008 and, along with other factors, was responsible for a sharp decline in support for Lee (see *The presidency of Lee Myung-Bak*). Ratification of the FTA was delayed in both the South Korean National Assembly and the US Congress (which had expressed concern that the FTA would negatively affect the troubled US car industry). In December 2010, following talks between Lee and US President Barack Obama in the previous month, the two countries signed a revised version of the FTA that sought to address some of the concerns raised by both legislatures, in particular by delaying the elimination of tariffs on vehicle imports. The agreement was finally ratified by the US legislature in October 2011, and by the South Korean National Assembly (accompanied by violent protests both within and outside the legislature) in November. It entered into effect in March 2012: tariffs on 80% of goods traded between the two countries were immediately abolished, and the proportion was to rise to 95% within five years.

In November 2009, meanwhile, President Obama travelled to South Korea and held discussions with Lee on the resumption of the six-party talks to address the issue of North Korea's nuclear programme. In June 2010 Lee reached an agreement with the US Government to delay the transfer of war-time operational control of South Korean forces (see above) until the end of 2015. In September 2012 an agreement with the USA was announced whereby South Korea was to increase the range of its ballistic missile system to 800 km, to counteract threats of military action by North Korea (the previous agreement, concluded in 2001, had limited the range to 300 km).

After North Korea reacted with an unusual degree of belligerence (including the conduct of a third nuclear test) to the beginning of annual joint military exercises conducted by South Korea and the USA in March 2013, the USA and South Korea concluded an agreement allowing a joint response to possible limited-scale attacks by the North. In early April it was announced that South Korea and the USA were to begin negotiations on revising a bilateral agreement (dating from 1974) that limited South Korea's civilian nuclear activities (in particular, by banning the reprocessing of spent fuel, a potential source of plutonium for military use). US Secretary of State John Kerry visited Seoul in mid-April, holding talks with President Park Geun-Hye on tensions with North Korea and reaffirming the USA's commitment to protect South Korea. The US Government made repeated diplomatic efforts to reconcile South Korea and Japan in view of their continuing disagreements (see *Relations with Japan*). In October, during a visit to South Korea by the US Secretary of Defense, Chuck Hagel, the two countries concluded a new agreement on a bilateral strategy for 'tailored deterrence' of the use of nuclear or chemical weapons by North Korea. The issue of the eventual transfer to South Korea of operational control over South Korean troops in the event of war, currently held by the USA but due to be assumed by South Korea at the end of 2015, was discussed at high-level meetings in June and October 2014; citing the 'intensifying threat' posed by North Korea, the two sides decided that the transfer would be postponed indefinitely and would be dependent on a change in conditions. Meanwhile, from late 2014 the potential deployment of the US-developed THAAD high-altitude missile defence system in South Korea attracted criticism from Russia and China (see *Relations with China*). In March 2015 the US ambassador to South Korea was hospitalized following a public knife attack by a nationalist South Korean activist, who was subsequently charged with attempted murder. In April the potential installation of the THAAD system in South Korea was not on the agenda at bilateral talks in Seoul between the South Korean defence minister and his US counterpart; instead, the two sides used the talks to explore ways of improving joint capabilities and reinforcing deterrence against North Korea's nuclear weaponry.

Other external relations

South Korea established full diplomatic relations with the USSR in 1990. In 1991 South Korea extended a substantial loan to the USSR; this debt was subsequently transferred to the Russian Federation (Russia) following the disintegration of the USSR later in that year. In September 1993 it was announced that South Korea and Russia were to participate in joint naval exercises, and in 1994 it was reported that Russia was to supply 'defensive missiles' in order to repay a part of its debt to South Korea. Further arrangements were made concerning the settlement of Russia's debt, through the provision of commodities, in 1997. President Vladimir Putin of Russia paid a state visit to South Korea in February 2001, when he agreed to proceed with a tripartite framework of co-operation between Russia and both Koreas. Arrangements were made for Russia to supply weapons to South Korea, which were to be partially paid for by the cancellation of some Soviet-era debt. South Korea and Russia also issued a joint statement supporting the 1972 Anti-Ballistic Missile treaty; however, US displeasure with this led to the resignation of the Minister of Foreign Affairs and Trade, Lee Joung-Binn. In December 2002 the South Korean Government agreed to accept military equipment worth US $534m. from Russia as further debt repayment.

There were indications that Roh Moo-Hyun would seek to improve relations with Russia during his presidency, as part of a broader policy of reducing dependency on the USA. In March 2003 Roh revived the idea of building a 4,000-km pipeline that would provide North Korea with Russian natural gas from Sakhalin in exchange for North Korea abandoning its nuclear weapons programme. A significant agreement between state-owned oil companies of the two countries (Korean National Oil Corporation—KNOC—and Russia's Rosneft) was signed in September 2004. In April 2005 the two sides' respective defence ministers, at a meeting in Russia, discussed the provision of Russian 'advanced weapons technology' by way of further repaying the Russian debt to South Korea. In November 2011, during a visit to Russia by President Lee Myung-Bak, the two Governments agreed to undertake studies on the construction of a pipeline to bring Russian natural gas to South Korea (via North Korea), instead of transporting it by sea as was currently the case; they also agreed to encourage the resumption of the six-party talks on North Korea's nuclear programme (see above). President Putin visited South Korea in November 2013 to discuss a proposed extension of the trans-Siberian railway via North Korea to the South Korean port of Busan, forming the so-called 'Iron Silk Road' to link eastern Asia with Europe.

From late 2001 South Korean forces participated in the International Security Assistance Force (ISAF) in Afghanistan. The withdrawal from Afghanistan of South Korea's 210-strong ISAF contingent (comprising military medical and engineering personnel) was completed by mid-December 2007. None the less, in February 2010 the GNP-dominated National Assembly approved the deployment of some 350 troops to Afghanistan to protect the South Korean Provincial Reconstruction Team, despite an opposition boycott of the parliamentary vote and the staging of demonstrations outside the National Assembly building. The troops began operating in Afghanistan in July and all of them had been withdrawn by mid-2014.

As the country continued to sign various bilateral accords providing for free trade, in May 2007 South Korea and the European Union (EU) commenced negotiations on the establishment of an FTA; the final agreement was signed in October 2009. Despite the opposition of the EU's vehicle-manufacturing industry and South Korean farmers, the FTA was ratified by the European Parliament in February 2011 and by the South Korean National Assembly in May; it entered into force in July.

In March 2009 President Lee Myung-Bak embarked upon a state visit to Australia, where he and Prime Minister Kevin Rudd signed a pact pledging closer co-operation in the area of security, including counter-terrorism strategies and the combating of transnational crime. The commencement of formal negotiations on an FTA between the two countries was also announced, and an agreement was finally signed in April 2014 (followed by an FTA between South Korea and New Zealand in March 2015).

CONSTITUTION AND GOVERNMENT

Under the Constitution of the Sixth Republic (adopted in October 1987), executive power is held by the President, who is directly elected for one term of five years by universal suffrage. The President appoints and governs with the assistance of the State Council (cabinet), led by the Prime Minister. Legislative power is vested in the unicameral National Assembly (Kuk Hoe), popularly elected for a four-year term. The Assembly has 300 members; in the general election of April 2012 246 were directly elected and 54 were chosen by proportional representation.

REGIONAL AND INTERNATIONAL CO-OPERATION

The Republic of Korea (South Korea) is a member of the Asian Development Bank (ADB, see p. 206), Asia-Pacific Economic Co-operation (APEC, see p. 200), the Colombo Plan (see p. 445) and the UN's Economic and Social Commission for Asia and the Pacific (ESCAP, see p. 30). In 1991 South Korea was accepted as a dialogue partner of the Association of Southeast Asian Nations (ASEAN, see p. 210), subsequently becoming one of the three additional partners of ASEAN + 3.

South Korea joined the UN in 1991, and held a two-year mandate as a non-permanent member of the UN Security Council in 2013-15. As a contracting party to the General Agreement on Tariffs and Trade (GATT), the country joined the World Trade Organization (WTO, see p. 431) upon its establishment in 1995. South Korea is also a member of the Organisation for Economic Co-operation and Development (OECD, see p. 377).

ECONOMIC AFFAIRS

In 2013, according to estimates by the World Bank, the gross national income (GNI) of the Republic of Korea (South Korea), measured at average 2011-13 prices, was US $1,301,575m., equivalent to $25,920 per head (or $33,440 per head on an international purchasing-power parity basis). During 2004-13, it was estimated, the population increased at an average annual rate of 0.5%, while gross domestic product (GDP) per head increased, in real terms, by an average of 3.2% per year. Overall GDP increased, in real terms, at an average annual rate of 3.7% in 2004-13; GDP rose by 3.0% in 2013.

Agriculture (including forestry and fishing) contributed 2.3% of GDP in 2013, and engaged 5.7% of the employed labour force in 2014. The principal crop is rice, but potatoes, sweet potatoes, maize, chestnuts and barley are also important, as is the raising of livestock (principally poultry, pigs and cattle). Fishing provides food for domestic consumption, as well as a substantial surplus for export. South Korea is one of the world's leading ocean-fishing nations. During 2004-13, according to figures from the World Bank, the GDP of the agricultural sector increased by an average of 1.6% per year; agricultural GDP declined by 0.9% in 2012, but increased by 5.8% in 2013.

Industry (including mining and quarrying, manufacturing, utilities and construction) contributed 38.6% of GDP in 2013, and engaged 24.3% of the employed labour force in 2014. Industry is dominated by large conglomerate companies (*chaebol*), with greatly diversified interests, especially in construction and manufacturing. According to figures from the World Bank, during 2004-13 industrial GDP increased at an average annual rate of 4.5%; the sector's GDP expanded by 3.2% in 2013.

South Korea is not richly endowed with natural resources. Mining and quarrying contributed only 0.2% of GDP in 2013, and employed a negligible percentage of the labour force in 2014. There are deposits of coal (mainly anthracite). Other minerals include iron ore, lead, zinc, silver, gold and limestone. Substantial offshore reserves of natural gas have been discovered. According to official chain-linked data, the sector's GDP declined by 0.3% in 2012, but increased by 7.6% in 2013.

Manufacturing contributed 31.1% of GDP in 2013, and engaged 16.9% of the employed labour force in 2014. The most important branches of manufacturing include electrical machinery, transport equipment (mainly road motor vehicles and shipbuilding), non-electrical machinery, chemicals, food products, iron and steel, and textiles. During 2004-13 manufacturing GDP increased by an average of 5.6% per year, according to figures from the World Bank. The sector's GDP expanded by 3.3% in 2013.

Construction contributed 5.0% of GDP in 2013, and engaged 7.0% of the employed labour force in 2014. According to official chain-linked data, construction GDP declined by 1.8% in 2012, but increased by 3.6% in 2013.

Energy is derived principally from nuclear power and coal. In 2012 42.2% of total electricity output was generated from coal and 29.3% by nuclear power. In March 2015 there were 24 nuclear units in operation in the country. South Korea also produces liquefied natural gas for domestic and industrial consumption. Imports of petroleum and its products comprised 35.0% of the value of merchandise imports in 2013.

The services sector contributed 59.1% of GDP in 2013, and engaged 70.0% of the employed labour force in 2014. Receipts from tourism are significant, totalling US $14,272m. in 2013, according to provisional figures. The number of visitor arrivals rose by 9.3% in 2013, to reach 12.2m. During 2004-13, according to figures from the World Bank, the GDP of the services sector increased at an average annual rate of 3.5%; the GDP of the services sector increased by 2.9% in 2013.

In 2013 South Korea recorded a visible merchandise trade surplus of US $80,569m. and there was a surplus of $79,884m. on the current account of the balance of payments. The People's Republic of China (accounting for 16.1%) was the principal source of imports in 2013; other important suppliers were Japan, the USA, Saudi Arabia and Qatar. China was the principal market for exports in that year (purchasing 26.1%). Other important markets included the USA, Japan and Hong Kong. The main exports in 2013 were electrical machinery and equipment, nuclear reactors, boilers, etc., vehicles other than railway and tramway, ships, boats and floating structures, mineral fuels, oils and distillation products, iron and steel and other base metals and their articles, plastics and articles thereof, chemical products, and optical, photographic and cinematographic apparatus, etc. The principal imports in that year were mineral fuels, oils and distillation products, electrical machinery and equipment, nuclear reactors, boilers, etc., base metals and articles of base metals, and chemical products.

South Korea recorded a budget surplus of 30,600,000m. won, equivalent to 2.1% of GDP in 2013. The general government gross debt was 445,133,000m. won in 2012, equivalent to 32.3% of GDP. At the end of 2013, according to the Asian Development Bank (ADB), the total external debt reached US $416,595m. In that year the cost of debt-servicing was equivalent to 7.5% of the value of exports of goods and services. According to official figures, the average annual rate of inflation was 3.0% in 2004-13; consumer prices increased by 1.3% in 2013. The rate of unemployment was 3.5% in 2014.

Strong growth in both domestic consumption and private investment prevailed until the deterioration in global economic conditions from mid-2008. The diversification of the South Korean manufacturing sector in the preceding years afforded some resilience amid changing global conditions, as did the continuing demand from China, South Korea's leading export market. A robust recovery ensued in 2010, with expansion of 6.5% in GDP (compared with 0.7% in 2009), as investment and domestic consumption rebounded. GDP growth of 3.7% in 2011 was slower than anticipated, as high levels of personal and household debt, together with stagnating property prices, curbed domestic demand, while exports to the European Union (EU), South Korea's second largest export market, were adversely affected by the debt crisis in the eurozone. The conclusion of free trade agreements (FTAs) with the EU, the USA and other partners during the early 2010s was expected eventually to yield major benefits to the South Korean economy. Growth in GDP slowed to 2.3% in 2012, however, as industrial production faltered and exports continued to be adversely affected by global problems, while the weakness of the Japanese currency made that country's exports more competitive, at the expense of rival South Korean enterprises. The Bank of Korea, the central bank, reduced interest rates twice during 2012, to 2.75% at the end of the year, with a further reduction to 2.5% in May 2013. The Government of President Park Geun-Hye, who came to power in February 2013, identified as its economic priorities job creation, supporting the development of small and medium-sized enterprises in the face of the dominance of the *chaebol*, and the reduction of household debt (which was equivalent to 164% of household disposable income in 2012). South Korea's GDP increased by 2.9% in 2013, reflecting upward trends in exports, public and consumer spending, and construction activity. In 2014 the Government further increased expenditure on public construction and social welfare. In February it announced a three-year 'economic innovation' plan, including measures to assist new businesses, create jobs, increase the competitiveness of public corporations, deregulate the services sector, and reform public sector pensions, while continuing to encourage trade through FTAs, especially those with China and Japan. However, consumer spending declined significantly following the *Sewol* ferry disaster in April. In July a US $40,000m.

stimulus package was launched to boost consumption and revitalize the housing market. In addition, the central bank reduced the interest rate three times, in August and October 2014 and again in March 2015, to a record low of 1.75%, despite increasing concern about the levels of household debt. GDP growth in 2014 was lower than forecast, at 3.3%, partly owing to a fall in China's demand for exports; meanwhile, inflation remained stagnant in 2014 at around 1.3%. In an attempt to encourage economic growth, the Government planned to increase public spending by a further 5.7% in 2015, with particular focus on social welfare, and safety and support for technology-based start-ups. The rise in expenditure was forecast to result in the budget deficit expanding from the equivalent of 1.7% of GDP in 2014 to 2.1% of GDP in 2015. The ADB predicted GDP growth of 3.5% in 2015 and 3.7% in 2016, with inflation remaining below the central bank's target range of 2.5%–3.5%, at 1.3% in 2015 and 2.1% in 2016.

PUBLIC HOLIDAYS

2016: 1 January (New Year's Day), 8 February–10 February (Seollal, Lunar New Year), 1 March (Sam Il Jol, Independence Movement Day), 5 May (Children's Day), 14 May (Buddha's Birthday), 6 June (Memorial Day), 15 August (Liberation Day), 14–16 September (Juseok, Korean Thanksgiving Day), 3 October (National Foundation Day), 9 October (Hangeul, Korean Alphabet Day), 25 December (Christmas).

Statistical Survey

Source (unless otherwise stated): Statistics Korea, Bldg III, Government Complex-Daejeon 920, Dunsan-dong, Seo-gu, Daejeon 302-701; tel. (42) 481-2120; fax (42) 481-2460; internet kostat.go.kr.

Area and Population

AREA, POPULATION AND DENSITY*

Area (sq km)	99,646†
Population (census results)	
1 November 2005	47,041,434
1 November 2010	
Males	24,167,098
Females	24,413,195
Total	48,580,293
Population (official estimates at mid-year)	
2013	50,219,669
2014	50,423,955
2015	50,617,045
Density (per sq km) at mid-2015	508.0

* Excluding the demilitarized zone between North and South Korea, with an area of 1,262 sq km (487 sq miles).
† 38,474 sq miles. The figure indicates territory under the jurisdiction of the Republic of Korea, surveyed on the basis of land register in 2005.

POPULATION BY AGE AND SEX
(official estimates at mid-2015)

	Males	Females	Total
0–14 years	3,638,831	3,400,763	7,039,594
15–64 years	18,896,526	18,056,805	36,953,331
65 years and over	2,767,163	3,856,957	6,624,120
Total	25,302,520	25,314,525	50,617,045

ADMINISTRATIVE DIVISIONS
(official estimates at mid-2015)

Province	Area (sq km)	Population	Density (per sq km)
Busan	764.4	3,400,069	4,448.0
Chungcheongbuk-do . .	7,431.4	1,560,784	210.0
Chungcheongnam-do . .	8,600.5	2,089,470	242.9
Daegu	884.5	2,454,733	2,775.3
Daejeon	539.8	1,535,639	2,844.8
Gangwon-do	16,613.5	1,506,142	90.7
Gwangju	501.4	1,516,527	3,024.6
Gyeonggi-do	10,130.9	12,397,902	1,223.8
Gyeongsangbuk-do . .	19,026.0	2,641,879	138.9
Gyeongsangnam-do . .	10,520.8	3,285,260	312.3
Incheon	994.1	2,886,172	2,903.3
Jeju-do	1,848.3	587,217	317.7
Jeollabuk-do	8,054.6	1,798,234	223.3
Jeollanam-do	12,073.5	1,756,831	145.5
Seoul	605.4	9,860,372	16,287.4
Ulsan	1,057.1	1,142,469	1,080.8
Total	99,646.2	50,617,045	508.0

PRINCIPAL TOWNS
(population at 1995 census)

Seoul (capital) .	10,231,217		Jeonju (Chonju) .	563,153
Busan (Pusan) . .	3,814,325		Jeongju (Chongju) .	531,376
Daegu (Taegu) . .	2,449,420		Masan	441,242
Incheon (Inchon) .	2,308,188		Jinju (Chinju) . .	329,886
Daejeon (Taejon) .	1,272,121		Kunsan	266,559
Gwangju (Kwangju) .	1,257,636		Jeju (Cheju) . .	258,511
Ulsan	967,429		Mokpo	247,452
Seongnam			Chuncheon	
(Songnam) . .	869,094		(Chunchon) . .	234,528
Suwon	755,550			

2000 census: Seoul 9,853,972; Busan 3,655,437; Daegu 2,473,990; Incheon 2,466,338; Daejeon 1,365,961; Gwangju 1,350,948; Ulsan 1,012,110.

Mid-2014 (incl. suburbs, UN estimate): Seoul 9,775,380 (Source: UN, *World Urbanization Prospects: The 2014 Revision*).

BIRTHS, MARRIAGES AND DEATHS*

	Registered live births		Registered marriages		Registered deaths	
	Number	Rate (per 1,000)	Number	Rate (per 1,000)	Number	Rate (per 1,000)
2006	448,153	9.2	330,634	6.8	242,266	5.0
2007	493,189	10.0	343,559	7.0	244,874	5.0
2008	465,892	9.4	327,715	6.6	246,113	5.0
2009	444,849	9.0	309,759	6.2	246,942	5.0
2010	470,171	9.4	326,104	6.5	255,405	5.1
2011	471,265	9.4	329,087	6.6	257,396	5.1
2012	484,550	9.6	327,073	6.5	267,221	5.3
2013	436,455	8.6	322,807	6.4	266,257	5.2

* Owing to late registration, figures are subject to continuous revision.

Life expectancy (official figures, years at birth): 81.4 (males 78.0; females 84.6) in 2012.

ECONOMICALLY ACTIVE POPULATION*

(labour force survey, '000 persons aged 15 years and over)

	2012	2013	2014
Agriculture, forestry and fishing .	1,528	1,520	1,452
Mining and quarrying	15	16	13
Manufacturing	4,105	4,184	4,330
Electricity, gas and water . . .	76	90	83
Construction	1,773	1,754	1,796
Wholesale and retail trade, repair of motor vehicles and personal and household goods . . .	3,689	3,660	3,792
Restaurants and hotels . . .	1,906	1,971	2,098
Transport, storage and communications	2,079	2,105	2,121
Financial intermediation . . .	842	864	837
Real estate, renting and business activities	2,630	2,680	2,713
Public administration and defence; compulsory social security . .	951	966	957
Education	1,744	1,748	1,807
Health and social work . . .	1,399	1,554	1,693
Other community, social and personal service activities . .	1,768	1,777	1,780
Households with employed persons	166	172	116
Extraterritorial organizations and bodies	9	7	14
Total employed	24,681	25,066	25,599
Unemployed	820	807	937
Total labour force	25,501	25,873	26,536
Males	14,891	15,071	15,387
Females	10,609	10,802	11,149

* Excluding armed forces.

Note: Totals may not be equal to the sum of components, owing to rounding.

Health and Welfare

KEY INDICATORS

Total fertility rate (children per woman, 2012)	1.3
Under-5 mortality rate (per 1,000 live births, 2012) . . .	4
HIV/AIDS (% of persons aged 15–49, 2011)	<0.1
Physicians (per 1,000 head, 2012)	2.1
Hospital beds (per 1,000 head, 2009)	10.3
Health expenditure (2011): US $ per head (PPP)	2,198
Health expenditure (2011): % of GDP	7.4
Health expenditure (2011): public (% of total)	55.3
Access to water (% of persons, 2012)	98
Total carbon dioxide emissions ('000 metric tons, 2010) . .	567,567.3
Carbon dioxide emissions per head (metric tons, 2010) . .	11.5
Human Development Index (2013): ranking	15
Human Development Index (2013): value	0.891

For sources and definitions, see explanatory note on p. vi.

Agriculture

PRINCIPAL CROPS
('000 metric tons)

	2011	2012	2013
Rice, paddy	6,304.0	5,934.0	5,631.7
Barley	75.5	59.8	60.5
Maize	73.6	83.2	80.5
Potatoes	622.2	607.5	727.4
Sweet potatoes	255.3	342.7	329.5
Beans, dry	5.5	6.4	10.0
Chestnuts	64.6	70.0*	67.9*
Soybeans (Soya beans) . . .	129.4	122.5	154.1
Sesame seed	9.5	9.7	12.4
Cabbages and other brassicas .	3,049.3	2,118.9	2,434.4
Lettuce and chicory	116.8	112.0	96.7*
Spinach	104.5	96.2	91.1
Tomatoes	368.2	432.7	388.5
Pumpkins, squash and gourds .	300.4	325.1	323.4
Cucumbers and gherkins . .	303.8	288.1	254.6
Chillies and peppers, green . .	262.3	302.0	298.9
Onions and shallots, green . .	482.1	356.7	430.6
Onions, dry	1,520.0	1,195.7	1,294.0
Garlic	295.0	339.1	412.3
Carrots and turnips	93.7	64.0	79.8
Mushrooms	24.8	26.0	25.5
Watermelons	609.0	642.9	672.9
Cantaloupes and other melons .	180.0	186.7	176.6
Tangerines, mandarins, clementines and satsumas . .	680.5	692.2	682.8
Apples	379.5	394.6	493.7
Pears	290.5	172.6	282.2
Peaches and nectarines . . .	185.1	172.6	193.2
Plums and sloes	57.4	52.2	56.1
Strawberries	171.5	192.1	216.8
Grapes	269.2	277.9	260.3
Persimmons	390.8	401.0	352.0
Tobacco, unmanufactured* . .	35.0	36.0	36.0

* FAO estimate(s).

Aggregate production ('000 metric tons, may include official, semi-official or estimated data): Total cereals 6,243 in 2011, 6,135 in 2012, 5,818 in 2013; Total roots and tubers 878 in 2011, 950 in 2012, 1,057 in 2013; Total vegetables (incl. melons) 11,176 in 2011, 9,927 in 2012, 10,435 in 2013; Total fruits (excl. melons) 2,642 in 2011, 2,767 in 2012, 2,752 in 2013.

Source: FAO.

LIVESTOCK
('000 head)

	2011	2012	2013
Cattle	3,353	3,479	3,342
Pigs	8,171	9,916	9,912
Goats	248	257	260*
Chickens	149,511	146,836	151,337

* FAO estimate.

Source: FAO.

LIVESTOCK PRODUCTS
('000 metric tons)

	2011	2012	2013
Cattle meat	280.0	312.0	336.0
Pig meat	837.0*	982.0†	1,007.0†
Chicken meat	617.0*	598.0†	616.0†
Duck meat	69.0*	70.0†	70.0†
Cows' milk	1,869.0	2,111.0	2,093.0
Goats' milk†	4.1	3.9	3.9
Hen eggs†	595.0	600.0	615.0
Other poultry eggs†	31.5	32.0	32.0
Honey†	21.4	25.0	25.0

* Unofficial figure.
† FAO estimate(s).

Source: FAO.

Forestry

ROUNDWOOD REMOVALS
('000 cubic metres, excl. bark)

	2010	2011	2012
Sawlogs, veneer logs and logs for sleepers	458	537	533
Pulpwood	2,503	2,666	2,598
Other industrial wood	505	471	727
Fuel wood*	2,477	2,479	2,480
Total*	5,943	6,153	6,338

* FAO estimates.

2013: Production assumed to be unchanged from 2012 (FAO estimates).

Source: FAO.

SAWNWOOD PRODUCTION
('000 cubic metres, incl. sleepers, unofficial figures)

	2010	2011	2012
Coniferous (softwood)	3,500	3,654	3,000
Broadleaved (hardwood)	122	102	113
Total	3,622	3,756	3,113

2013: Production assumed to be unchanged from 2011.

Source: FAO.

Fishing

('000 metric tons, live weight)

	2010	2011	2012
Capture	1,733.3	1,748.2	1,670.4
Alaska pollock	46.8	48.8	39.0
Yellow croaker	31.9	59.2	36.8
Japanese anchovy	249.6	292.7	222.0
Skipjack tuna	216.7	173.3	211.6
Chub mackerel	94.4	138.8	125.4
Largehead hairtail	59.2	33.1	32.5
Argentine shortfin squid	25.0	40.0	57.4
Japanese flying squid	159.1	171.6	181.4
Aquaculture	475.6	507.1	484.4
Pacific cupped oyster	267.8	281.0	284.9
Total catch	2,208.9	2,255.2	2,154.8

Note: Figures exclude aquatic plants ('000 metric tons): 914.7 (capture 13.0, aquaculture 901.7) in 2010; 1,007.1 (capture 14.8, aquaculture 992.3) in 2011; 1,032.4 (capture 10.1, aquaculture 1,022.3) in 2012. Also excluded are aquatic mammals, recorded by number rather than by weight; the number of dolphins and whales caught was: 577 in 2010; 644 in 2011; 2,637 in 2012.

Source: FAO.

Mining

('000 metric tons unless otherwise indicated)

	2010	2011	2012
Hard coal (Anthracite)	2,084	2,084	2,000*
Iron ore: gross weight	513	542	593
Iron ore: metal content	287	303	332
Lead ore (metric tons)†	1,168	2,577	3,879
Zinc ore (metric tons)†	710	1,486	2,868
Kaolin	764	799	515
Feldspar	496.5	384.2	360.4
Salt (unrefined)	222.5	372.2	308.8
Mica (metric tons)	36,486	31,260	25,594
Talc (metric tons)	5,729	15,608	21,625
Pyrophyllite	673.9	510.7	483.1

* Estimate.
† Figures refer to the metal content of ores.

Source: US Geological Survey.

Industry

SELECTED PRODUCTS
('000 metric tons unless otherwise indicated)

	2009	2010	2011
Wheat flour	1,808	1,916	1,918
Beer (million litres)	18,831	19,401	n.a.
Cigarettes (million)	129,070	124,633	n.a.
Cotton yarn—pure and mixed	210	221	227
Plywood ('000 cu m)	493	438	455
Newsprint	1,497	1,591	1,566
Caustic soda	1,572	1,799	1,861
Liquefied petroleum gas	3,026	2,973	1,579
Naphtha	19,034	20,167	22,953
Kerosene	4,642	4,931	4,632
Gas-diesel (distillate fuel oil)	35,519	36,441	39,604
Residual fuel oil	18,470	19,002	18,496
Cement	53,826	50,695	52,004
Pig-iron†	27,475	31,228	42,213
Crude steel	48,434	57,907	68,519
Electric energy (million kWh)	454,504	499,508	523,286
Carbon black*†	500.0	500.0	500.0
Products of petroleum refineries ('000 barrels)*†	750,000	750,000	750,000

* Estimate.
† Source: US Geological Survey.

Rubber tyres ('000): 68,771 in 2007.

Source: mostly UN Industrial Commodity Statistics Database.

2012 ('000 metric tons unless otherwise indicated): Crude steel 69,073; Carbon black 500.0 (estimate); Products of petroleum refineries ('000 barrels) 750,000 (estimate) (Source: US Geological Survey).

Finance

CURRENCY AND EXCHANGE RATES

Monetary Units
100 chun (jeon) = 10 hwan = 1 won.

Sterling, Dollar and Euro Equivalents (31 December 2014)
£1 sterling = 1,715.63 won;
US $1 = 1,099.20 won;
€1 = 1,334.54 won;
10,000 won = £5.83 = $9.10 = €7.49.

Average Exchange Rate (won per US $)
2012	1,126.47
2013	1,094.93
2014	1,053.02

BUDGET
('000 million won)

Revenue	2011	2012	2013
Current revenue	289,797	307,754	311,136
Tax revenue	192,381	203,015	201,906
Non-tax revenue	97,415	104,739	109,230
Capital revenue	2,527	3,702	3,302
Total	292,324	311,456	314,438

Expenditure	2011	2012	2013
General public services . . .	27,844	31,210	33,752
Defence	30,134	30,765	32,370
Education	40,988	45,093	48,263
Health	2,641	2,617	3,057
Social security and welfare . .	60,107	66,114	72,806
Housing and community amenities	12,758	15,844	12,705
Economic services	48,546	48,803	48,909
Transport and communications .	15,497	15,659	16,563
Others	47,638	48,638	44,696
Total	270,655	289,084	296,557

Source: Asian Development Bank.

2014 ('000 million won, budget forecasts): Total revenue 370,700 (Taxes 218,500); Total expenditure 357,700 (Source: Ministry of Strategy and Finance, Sejong City).

2015 ('000 million won, budget figures): Total revenue 382,700; Total expenditure 376,000 (Source: Ministry of Strategy and Finance, Sejong City).

INTERNATIONAL RESERVES
(US $ million at 31 December)

	2011	2012	2013
Gold (national valuation) . . .	2,166.6	3,761.4	4,794.5
IMF special drawing rights . .	3,457.7	3,525.7	3,489.9
Reserve position in IMF . . .	2,564.3	2,783.7	2,512.3
Foreign exchange	298,232.9	316,897.7	335,647.5
Total	306,421.5	326,968.5	346,444.2

Source: IMF, *International Financial Statistics.*

MONEY SUPPLY
('000 million won at 31 December)

	2011	2012	2013
Currency outside depository corporations	39,609	44,174	53,316
Transferable deposits	402,468	425,837	462,327
Other deposits	1,213,119	1,276,591	1,305,671
Securities other than shares . .	96,262	89,041	99,481
Broad money	1,751,458	1,835,642	1,920,795

Source: IMF, *International Financial Statistics.*

COST OF LIVING
(Consumer Price Index; base: 2010 = 100)

	2012	2013	2014
Food and non-alcoholic beverages .	112.4	113.4	113.7
Housing, water and fuels . . .	109.3	113.2	116.5
Clothing and footwear . . .	108.3	111.4	115.9
All items (incl. others) . . .	106.3	107.7	109.0

Source: Bank of Korea.

NATIONAL ACCOUNTS
('000 million won at current prices)

National Income and Product

	2011	2012	2013
Compensation of employees . .	570,366.6	599,308.5	624,341.6
Operating surplus	372,684.6	369,525.0	378,383.0
Domestic factor incomes . .	943,051.2	968,833.5	1,002,724.6
Consumption of fixed capital . .	252,381.9	267,390.0	285,649.1
Gross domestic product (GDP) at factor cost . .	1,195,433.1	1,236,223.5	1,288,373.7
Indirect taxes, *less* subsidies . .	137,248.0	141,233.3	139,920.9
GDP in purchasers' values . .	1,332,681.0	1,377,456.7	1,428,294.6
Net factor income from abroad .	7,848.8	14,138.8	12,768.9
Gross national income . . .	1,340,529.8	1,391,595.5	1,441,063.5
Less Consumption of fixed capital .	252,381.9	267,390.0	285,649.1
National income in market prices	1,088,147.9	1,124,205.5	1,155,414.4

Expenditure on the Gross Domestic Product

	2011	2012	2013
Final consumption expenditure .	873,522.7	911,938.2	942,109.1
Households (incl. non-profit institutions serving households)	679,141.5	707,614.0	728,910.1
General government	194,381.2	204,324.2	213,199.0
Gross capital formation . . .	439,236.1	427,028.5	414,042.6
Gross fixed capital formation .	403,045.3	407,306.9	423,582.0
Changes in inventories . . .	36,190.8	19,721.6	−9,539.4
Total domestic expenditure .	1,312,758.8	1,338,966.7	1,356,151.7
Exports of goods and services .	742,936.0	776,062.4	770,202.6
Less Imports of goods and services	723,013.8	737,572.4	697,888.7
Statistical discrepancy	—	—	−171.0
GDP in market prices . . .	1,332,681.0	1,377,456.7	1,428,294.6

Gross Domestic Product by Economic Activity

	2011	2012	2013
Agriculture, forestry and fishing .	30,454.0	30,775.1	30,563.3
Mining and quarrying	2,287.0	2,278.5	2,465.3
Manufacturing	379,521.0	388,010.1	405,526.5
Electricity, gas and water . . .	23,994.1	26,178.2	30,037.2
Construction	58,587.3	59,959.4	64,644.4
Wholesale and retail trade, restaurants and hotels . . .	140,705.3	146,807.7	150,275.0
Transport, storage and communications	89,285.6	92,344.9	97,061.7
Financial intermediation . . .	77,872.6	75,808.5	71,374.0
Real estate, renting and business activities	177,993.4	187,751.7	198,464.5
Public administration and defence, compulsory social security . .	83,290.8	88,654.6	93,562.9
Education	66,559.6	68,546.3	71,029.1
Health and social work . . .	46,656.1	50,031.3	53,494.6
Other service activities . . .	32,749.4	34,309.0	35,436.5
Gross value added at basic prices	1,209,956.2	1,251,455.3	1,303,935.0
Taxes, less subsidies, on products .	122,724.8	126,001.4	124,359.7
GDP in market prices . . .	1,332,681.0	1,377,456.7	1,428,294.6

Source: Bank of Korea.

BALANCE OF PAYMENTS
(US $ million)

	2011	2012	2013
Exports of goods	587,100	603,509	617,128
Imports of goods	−558,010	−554,103	−536,559
Balance on goods	29,090	49,406	80,569
Exports of services	90,900	103,533	101,507
Imports of services	−103,179	−108,747	−109,435
Balance on goods and services	16,811	44,192	72,641
Primary income received . . .	27,436	30,161	31,207
Primary income paid	−20,876	−18,044	−19,782
Balance on goods, services and primary income	23,371	56,309	84,066
Secondary income received . .	8,432	8,558	9,084
Secondary income paid . . .	−13,148	−14,032	−13,267
Current balance	18,656	50,835	79,884
Capital account (net)	−112	−42	−28
Direct investment assets . . .	−29,705	−30,632	−29,172
Direct investment liabilities . .	9,773	9,496	12,221
Portfolio investment assets . .	−4,138	−26,080	−26,848
Portfolio investment liabilities .	17,281	32,827	18,561
Financial derivatives and employee stock options (net)	−1,031	2,628	3,840
Other investment assets . . .	−22,166	−8,600	−36,164
Other investment liabilities . .	19,624	−18,037	−4,839
Net errors and omissions . . .	5,843	758	−2,997
Reserves and related items .	14,024	13,154	14,456

Source: IMF, *International Financial Statistics.*

External Trade

PRINCIPAL COMMODITIES
(distribution by HS, US $ million)*

Imports c.i.f.	2011	2012	2013
Mineral products	196,108.4	206,057.2	197,933.9
Ores, slag and ash	21,387.6	18,915.1	16,618.1
Mineral fuels, oils, distillation products, etc.	173,675.0	186,191.1	180,432.8
Chemicals and related products	40,111.3	39,243.9	39,072.3
Iron and steel, other base metals and articles of base metals	55,069.9	48,518.2	45,508.5
Iron and steel	28,438.2	23,822.0	20,369.7
Machinery and mechanical appliances; electrical equipment; parts thereof	119,076.8	113,289.2	119,723.2
Boilers, machinery, etc. . . .	49,328.6	46,424.2	47,449.5
Electrical machinery and equipment	69,748.2	66,865.0	72,273.7
Optical, medical apparatus etc.; clocks and watches; musical instruments; parts thereof	17,783.7	19,388.3	18,064.0
Optical, photographic, cinematographic, precision, medical or surgical instruments and apparatus	17,048.8	18,608.3	17,235.3
Total (incl. others)	524,413.1	519,584.5	515,585.5

Exports f.o.b.	2011	2012	2013
Mineral products	53,896.8	58,248.8	54,786.9
Mineral fuels, oils, distillation products, etc.	53,088.4	57,492.6	54,112.8
Chemicals and related products	35,876.5	36,063.4	38,392.4
Organic chemicals	22,468.8	23,284.7	24,856.0
Plastics, rubber, and articles thereof	36,933.0	37,721.4	39,493.9
Plastics and articles thereof . .	27,719.4	28,381.2	31,172.5
Iron and steel, other base metals and articles of base metals	51,875.6	49,984.8	46,057.4
Iron and steel	27,581.1	25,375.0	22,269.9
Machinery and mechanical appliances; electrical equipment; parts thereof .	178,201.5	178,064.3	194,815.5
Boilers, machinery, etc. . . .	59,658.7	58,979.9	59,318.4
Electrical machinery and equipment	118,542.9	119,084.4	135,497.1
Vehicles, aircraft, vessels and associated transport equipment	122,980.7	109,934.3	110,868.4
Vehicles other than railway, tramway	67,097.0	70,074.1	72,771.8
Ships, boats and floating structures	54,133.1	37,828.4	35,869.8
Optical, medical apparatus etc.; clocks and watches; musical instruments; parts thereof	36,736.4	37,853.6	36,169.9
Optical, photographic, cinematographic, precision, medical or surgical instruments and apparatus	36,499.2	37,611.6	35,943.2
Total (incl. others)	555,213.7	547,869.8	559,632.4

* Excluding trade with the Democratic People's Republic of Korea.

Source: Korea International Trade Association.

PRINCIPAL TRADING PARTNERS
(US $ million)*

Imports c.i.f.	2011	2012	2013
Australia	26,316.3	22,987.9	20,784.6
Brazil	6,342.9	6,085.4	5,573.1
Canada	6,611.9	5,247.4	4,717.3
China, People's Republic . .	86,432.2	80,784.6	83,052.9
France	6,314.9	4,924.0	6,012.9
Germany	16,962.6	17,645.4	19,336.0
India	7,893.6	6,920.8	6,180.2
Indonesia	17,216.4	15,676.3	13,190.0
Iran	11,358.4	8,544.4	5,564.4
Iraq	9,137.8	10,227.1	9,260.7
Italy	4,373.9	4,828.2	5,383.5
Japan	68,320.2	64,363.1	60,029.4
Kuwait	16,959.6	18,297.1	18,725.1
Malaysia	10,467.8	9,796.4	11,095.8
Oman	5,362.8	5,305.7	4,783.3
Qatar	20,749.4	25,504.7	25,873.8
Russia	10,852.2	11,354.3	11,495.5
Saudi Arabia	36,972.6	39,707.1	37,665.2
Singapore	8,966.7	9,676.4	10,369.4
Taiwan	14,693.6	14,012.0	14,632.6
Thailand	5,413.4	5,353.2	5,231.0
United Arab Emirates . . .	14,759.4	15,115.3	18,122.9
United Kingdom	3,818.1	6,366.8	6,193.7
USA	44,569.0	43,341.0	41,511.9
Total (incl. others)	524,413.1	519,584.5	515,585.5

Exports f.o.b.	2011	2012	2013
Australia	8,163.8	9,250.5	9,563.1
Brazil	11,821.4	10,286.1	9,688.2
China, People's Republic . .	134,185.0	134,322.6	145,869.5
France	5,707.4	2,598.8	3,488.0
Germany	9,500.9	7,509.7	7,907.9
Hong Kong	30,968.4	32,606.2	27,756.3
India	12,654.1	11,922.0	11,375.8
Indonesia	13,564.5	13,955.0	11,568.2
Iran	6,068.3	6,256.5	4,480.9
Japan	39,679.7	38,796.1	34,662.3
Liberia	7,389.3	3,803.7	3,512.9
Malaysia	6,275.1	7,723.5	8,587.8
Mexico	9,729.1	9,042.4	9,727.4
Philippines	7,338.9	8,210.7	8,783.4
Russia	10,304.9	11,097.1	11,149.1
Saudi Arabia	6,964.3	9,112.0	8,827.7
Singapore	20,839.0	22,887.9	22,289.0
Taiwan	18,206.0	14,814.9	15,699.1
Thailand	8,459.0	8,221.1	8,071.7
Turkey	5,071.0	4,551.6	5,657.8
United Arab Emirates . . .	7,267.8	6,861.7	5,737.7
USA	56,207.7	58,524.6	62,052.5
Viet Nam	13,464.9	15,946.0	21,087.6
Total (incl. others)	555,213.7	547,869.8	559,632.4

* Excluding trade with the Democratic People's Republic of Korea.

Source: Korea International Trade Association.

Trade with the Democratic People's Republic of Korea (US $ million, unofficial estimates): *Total imports:* 913.7 in 2011; 1,074.0 in 2012; 615.2 in 2013. *Total exports:* 800.2 in 2011; 897.2 in 2012; 520.6 in 2013 (Source: Bank of Korea).

Transport

RAILWAYS
(traffic)

	2011	2012	2013
Passengers carried ('000) . . .	1,118,622	1,151,523	1,224,820
Passenger-km (million) . . .	41,909	42,493	38,531
Freight ('000 metric tons) . . .	40,012	40,309	39,822
Freight ton-km (million) . . .	9,997	10,271	10,459

ROAD TRAFFIC
(motor vehicles in use at 31 December)

	2009	2010	2012*
Passenger cars	13,023,819	13,631,769	14,577,193
Goods vehicles	3,220,704	3,259,862	3,306,507
Buses and coaches	1,080,687	1,049,725	986,833
Motorcycles and mopeds . . .	1,820,729	1,825,474	n.a.

* Data for 2011 were not available.

Source: IRF, *World Road Statistics*.

SHIPPING

Flag Registered Fleet
(at 31 December)

	2012	2013	2014
Number of vessels	2,029	2,134	2,146
Total displacement ('000 grt) . .	11,913.0	12,604.9	12,966.5

Source: Lloyd's List Intelligence (www.lloydslistintelligence.com).

CIVIL AVIATION
(scheduled services)

	2010	2011
Kilometres flown (million)	601	628
Passengers carried ('000)	36,988	39,912
Passenger-km (million)	87,457	95,487
Total ton-km (million)	21,029	21,425

Source: UN, *Statistical Yearbook*.

Passengers carried ('000): 39,970 in 2012; 41,083 in 2013 (Source: World Bank, World Development Indicators database).

Tourism

FOREIGN VISITOR ARRIVALS*

Country of residence	2011	2012	2013
China, People's Republic . . .	2,220,196	2,836,881	4,326,869
Hong Kong	280,849	360,027	400,435
Japan	3,289,051	3,518,792	2,747,750
Philippines	337,268	331,346	400,686
Russia	154,835	166,721	175,360
Taiwan	428,208	548,233	544,662
Thailand	309,413	387,441	372,878
USA	661,503	697,866	722,315
Total (incl. others)	9,794,796	11,140,017	12,175,550

* Including same-day visitors (excursionists) and crew members from ships; also including Korean nationals resident abroad.

Receipts from tourism (US $ million, excl. passenger transport): 12,476 in 2011; 13,429 in 2012; 14,272 in 2013 (provisional) (Source: World Tourism Organization).

Communications Media

	2011	2012	2013
Telephones ('000 main lines in use)	29,468.5	30,099.2	30,333.1
Mobile cellular telephones ('000 subscribers)	52,506.8	53,624.4	54,680.8
Internet subscribers ('000)* . .	17,859.0	n.a.	n.a.
Broadband subscribers ('000) . .	17,859.0	18,252.2	18,737.1

* Estimates based on percentage.

Source: International Telecommunication Union.

Education

(2010)

	Institutions	Teachers	Pupils
Kindergarten	8,388	36,461	538,587
Primary schools	5,855	176,756	3,299,133
Middle schools	3,144	109,059	1,979,656
General high schools . . .	1,561	90,735	1,496,277
Vocational high schools . . .	692	35,688	466,129
Junior colleges	149	12,573	772,509
Teachers' colleges	10	813	21,618
Universities and colleges . .	179	55,972	2,028,841
Graduate schools	1,098	5,124	309,559

Source: Ministry of Education, Seoul.

2013: *Kindergarten:* Institutions 8,678; Teachers 46,126; Pupils 658,188. *Primary schools:* Institutions 5,913; Teachers 181,585; Pupils 3,220,621. *Middle schools:* Institutions 3,173; Teachers 112,690; Pupils 2,415,087.

Pupil-teacher ratio (primary education, UNESCO estimate): 17.9 in 2011/12 (Source: UNESCO Institute for Statistics).

Adult literacy rate (UNESCO estimates): 97.9% (males 99.2%; females 96.6%) in 2001 (Source: UN Development Programme, *Human Development Report*).

Directory

The Government

HEAD OF STATE

President: PARK GEUN-HYE (took office 25 February 2013).

STATE COUNCIL
(May 2015)

The Government is formed by the Saenuri Party (New Frontier Party).

Prime Minister: (vacant).

Deputy Prime Minister and Minister of Strategy and Finance: CHOI KYOUNG-HWAN.

Deputy Prime Minister and Minister of Education: HWANG WOO-YEA.

Minister of Foreign Affairs: YUN BYUNG-SE.

Minister of Unification: HONG YOUNG-PYO.

Minister of Culture, Sports and Tourism: KIM JONG-DEOK.

Minister of Government Administration and Home Affairs: CHONG JONG-SUP.

Minister of Justice: HWANG KYO-AHN.

Minister of Trade, Industry and Energy: YOON SANG-JICK.

Minister of Environment: YOON SEONG-KYU.

Minister of Agriculture, Food and Rural Affairs: LEE DONG-PIL.

Minister of Employment and Labour: LEE KI-KWEON.

Minister of Gender Equality and Family: KIM HEE-JUNNG.

Minister of Land, Infrastructure and Transport: YOO IL-HO.

Minister of National Defence: Gen. HAN MIN-KOO.

Minister of Science, ICT and Future Planning: CHOI YANG-HEE.

Minister of Health and Welfare: MOON HYUNG-PYO.

Minister of Oceans and Fisheries: YOO KI-JUNE.

Minister of Public Safety and Security: PARK IN-YONG.

Minister of Personnel Management: LEE GEUN-MYEON.

MINISTRIES

Office of the President: Chong Wa Dae (The Blue House), 1, Sejong-no, Jongno-gu, Seoul; tel. (2) 730-5800; e-mail foreign@president.go.kr; internet www.president.go.kr.

Prime Minister's Office: 55, Sejong-no, Jongno-gu, Seoul 110-760; tel. (2) 2100-2114; fax (2) 739-5830; e-mail webmaster@pmo.go.kr; internet www.pmo.go.kr.

Ministry of Agriculture, Food and Rural Affairs: Govt Complex, 94 Euhjin-dong, Sejong City 339-012; tel. (2) 1577-1020; fax (44) 868-0846; e-mail webmaster@mafra.go.kr; internet www.mafra.go.kr.

Ministry of Culture, Sports and Tourism: 215, Changggyeong-gung-ro, Jongno-gu, Seoul 110-630; tel. (2) 3704-9114; fax (2) 3704-9154; e-mail webadmin@www.mct.go.kr; internet www.mcst.go.kr.

Ministry of Education: 77-6, Sejong-no, Jongno-gu, Seoul 110-760; tel. (2) 6222-6060; fax (2) 2100-6133; e-mail webmaster@moe.go.kr; internet www.moe.go.kr.

Ministry of Employment and Labour: Govt Complex, 2, 47 Gwanmun-ro, Gwacheon City, Gyeonggi-do 427-718; tel. (2) 2110-7497; fax (2) 503-6623; internet www.moel.go.kr.

Ministry of Environment: Govt Complex, 11, Doum 6-ro, Sejong City 339-012; tel. (44) 201-6568; e-mail webmaster@me.go.kr; internet www.me.go.kr.

Ministry of Foreign Affairs: 37, Sejong-no, Seoul 110-787; tel. (2) 2100-2114; fax (2) 2100-7999; e-mail web@mofa.go.kr; internet www.mofa.go.kr.

Ministry of Gender Equality and Family: Premiere Place Bldg, 96, Mugyo-dong, Jung-gu, Seoul 100-777; tel. (2) 2075-4500; fax (2) 2075-4780; e-mail webadmin@mogef.go.kr; internet www.mogef.go.kr.

Ministry of Government Administration and Home Affairs: 209, Sejong-no, Jongno-gu, Seoul 110-760; tel. (2) 2100-3399; internet www.mogaha.go.kr.

Ministry for Health and Welfare: 75, Yulgong-ro, Jongno-gu, Seoul 110-793; internet www.mohw.go.kr.

Ministry of Justice: Bldg 5, 1, Jungang-dong, Gwacheon City, Gyeonggi Prov. 427-720; tel. (2) 2110-3009; fax (2) 503-7113; e-mail webmaster@moj.go.kr; internet www.moj.go.kr.

Ministry of Land, Infrastructure and Transport: Govt Complex, 11, Doum 6-ro, Sejong City 339-012; tel. (44) 201-4672; fax (44) 860-9500; e-mail webmaster@molit.go.kr; internet www.molit.go.kr.

Ministry of National Defence: 1, 3-ga, Yeongsan-dong, Yeongsan-gu, Seoul 140-701; tel. (2) 795-0071; fax (2) 703-3109; e-mail cyber@mnd.go.kr; internet www.mnd.go.kr.

Ministry of Oceans and Fisheries: 94 Govt Complex, 5-dong, Sejong City 339-012; tel. (44) 200-5555; internet www.mof.go.kr.

Ministry of Personnel Management: 209, Sejong-no, Jongno-gu, Seoul 110-760; internet www.mpm.go.kr.

Ministry of Public Safety and Security: 209, Sejong-no, Jongno-gu, Seoul 110-760; tel. (2) 2100-2114; internet www.mpss.go.kr.

Ministry of Science, ICT and Future Planning: Govt Complex, Gwacheon City, Gyeonggi Prov. 427-700; internet www.msip.go.kr.

Ministry of Strategy and Finance: Govt Complex, 477, Galmae-ro, Sejong City 339-012; tel. (44) 215-2114; fax (44) 215-4000; e-mail forumnet@mosf.go.kr; internet www.mosf.go.kr.

Ministry of Trade, Industry and Energy: 47, Gwanmunro, Gwacheon City, Gyeonggi Prov. 427-723; tel. (2) 1577-0900; e-mail webmke@mke.go.kr; internet www.motie.go.kr.

Ministry of Unification: Govt Complex, 77-6, Sejong-no, Jongno-gu, Seoul 110-760; tel. (2) 2100-5722; fax (2) 2100-5799; e-mail hanabyun@unikorea.go.kr; internet www.unikorea.go.kr.

President and Legislature

PRESIDENT

Election, 19 December 2012

Candidate	Votes	% of total
Park Geun-Hye (Saenuri Party) . .	15,773,128	51.55
Moon Jae-In (Democratic United Party*)	14,692,632	48.02
Kang Ji-Won (Independent) . . .	53,303	0.17
Kim Soon-Ja (Independent) . . .	46,017	0.15
Kim So-Yeon (Independent) . . .	16,687	0.05
Park Jong-Sun (Independent) . . .	12,854	0.04
Total (incl. others)	**30,721,459**	**100.00**

* In May 2013 the Democratic United Party changed its name to the Democratic Party and in March 2014 merged to become part of the New Politics Alliance for Democracy.

LEGISLATURE

National Assembly
(Kuk Hoe)

1 Yeouido-dong, Yeongdeungpo-gu, Seoul 150-701; tel. (2) 788-2001; fax (2) 788-3375; e-mail webmaster@assembly.go.kr; internet www.assembly.go.kr.

Speaker: KANG CHANG-HEE.

General Election, 11 April 2012

Party	Representatives		
	Elected	Proportional	Total
Saenuri Party	127	25	152
Democratic United Party* . .	106	21	127
Unified Progressive Party . .	7	6	13
Liberty Forward Party† . .	3	2	5
Independents	3	—	3
Total	**246**	**54**	**300**

* In May 2013 the Democratic United Party changed its name to the Democratic Party and in March 2014 merged to become part of the New Politics Alliance for Democracy.

† In May 2012 the Liberty Forward Party changed its name to the Advancement and Unification Party.

Election Commission

National Election Commission: 2-3 Junggang-dong, Gwacheon-si, Gyeonggi-do 427-727; tel. (2) 503-1114; e-mail nec@nec.go.kr; internet www.nec.go.kr; Chair. LEE IN-BOK.

Political Organizations

Advancement and Unification Party (AUP): Yeongsan Bldg, 3rd Floor, 14-14, Yeouido-dong, Yeoungdeungpo-gu, Seoul; tel. (2) 780-3988; fax (2) 780-3983; e-mail webmaster@jayou.or.kr; internet www.aup.or.kr; conservative; merged with People First Union Sept. 2011; fmrly Liberty Forward Party; renamed as above May 2012; Leader RHEE IN-JE.

New Politics Alliance for Democracy (NPAD): 133-6, Young-deungpo-dong, Youngdeungpo-gu, Seoul 150-036; fax (2) 2630-0145; internet www.minjoo.kr; f. 2014; merger between the Democratic Party and the independent Ahn Cheol-Soo's prospective New Political Vision Party; Chair. of the Emergency Measures Committee PARK YOUNG-SUN.

New Progressive Party (NPP): 371-12, Seogyo-dong, Mapo-gu, Seoul 121-893; tel. (2) 6004-2000; fax (2) 6004-2001; e-mail newjinbo@gmail.com; internet www.newjinbo.org; f. 2008; left-wing; est. by splinter group of DLP; absorbed the Korea Socialist Party in 2012; Pres. HONG SEHWA.

Saenuri Party (New Frontier Party): 14-31, Yeouido-dong, Yeong-deungpo-gu, Seoul 156-768; tel. (2) 3786-3000; fax (2) 3786-3610; internet www.saenuriparty.kr; f. 1997; est. as Grand National Party by merger of the original Democratic Party (f. 1990) and New Korea Party; renamed as above in 2012; Chair. KIM MOO-SUNG; Sec.-Gen. HONG MOON-JONG.

Civic groups play an increasingly significant role in South Korean politics. These include: the People's Solidarity for Participatory Democracy (Dir JANG HASUNG); the Citizens' Coalition for Economic Justice (Sec.-Gen. PARK BYEONG-OK); and the Citizens' Alliance for Political Reform (Leader KIM SOK-SU).

Diplomatic Representation

EMBASSIES IN THE REPUBLIC OF KOREA

Afghanistan: 27-2, Hannam-dong, Yeongsan-gu, Seoul 140-210; tel. (2) 793-3535; fax (2) 795-2662; e-mail info@afghanistanembassy.or.kr; internet www.afghanistanembassy.or.kr; Ambassador MOHAMMAD SALEEM SAYEB.

Algeria: 2-6, Itaewon 2-dong, Yeongsan-gu, Seoul 140-857; tel. (2) 794-5034; fax (2) 794-5040; e-mail sifdja01@kornet.net; internet www.algerianemb.or.kr; Ambassador HOCINE SAHRAOUI.

Angola: 1-398, Hannam 2-dong, Yeongsan-gu, Seoul 140-884; tel. (2) 792-8463; fax (2) 792-8467; e-mail embassy@angolaembassy.or.kr; internet www.angolaembassy.or.kr; Ambassador ALBINO MALUNGO.

Argentina: Chun Woo Bldg, 5th Floor, 534, Itaewon-dong, Yeongsan-gu, Seoul 140-861; tel. (2) 797-0636; fax (2) 792-5820; e-mail ecore@cancilleria.gob.ar; internet ecore.cancilleria.gov.ar; Ambassador JORGE JOSÉ ALBERTO ROBALLO.

Australia: Kyobo Bldg, 19th Floor, 1, Jongno 1-ga, Jongno-gu, Seoul 110-714; tel. (2) 2003-0100; fax (2) 2003-0196; e-mail seoul-inform@dfat.gov.au; internet www.southkorea.embassy.gov.au; Ambassador WILLIAM PATERSON.

Austria: Kyobo Bldg, 21st Floor, 1-1, Jongno 1-ga, Jongno-gu, Seoul 110-714; tel. (2) 732-9071; fax (2) 732-9486; e-mail seoul-ob@bmeia .gv.at; internet www.bmeia.gv.at/seoul; Ambassador Dr ELISABETH BERTAGNOLI.

Azerbaijan: Hannam Tower, Annex Bldg, 1st Floor, 730, Hannam-dong, Yeongsan-gu, Seoul 140-893; tel. (2) 797-1765; fax (2) 797-1767; e-mail info@azembassy.co.kr; internet www.azembassy.co.kr; Ambassador RAMZI TEYMUROV.

Bangladesh: 310-22, Dongbinggo-dong, Yeongsan-gu, Seoul; tel. (2) 796-4056; fax (2) 790-5313; e-mail bdootseoul@kornet.net; internet www.bdembseoul.org; Ambassador ZULFIQUR RAHMAN.

Belarus: 432-1636, Sindang 2-dong, Jung-gu, Seoul 100-835; tel. (2) 2237-8171; fax (2) 2237-8174; e-mail korea@mfa.gov.by; internet korea.mfa.gov.by; Ambassador NATALLIA ZHYLEVICH.

Belgium: Itaewon-ro 45-gil 23, Yeongsan-gu, Seoul 140-893; tel. (2) 749-0381; fax (2) 797-1688; e-mail seoul@diplobel.fed.be; internet www.diplomatie.belgium.be/seoul; Ambassador FRANÇOIS BONTEMPS.

Bolivia: Jung-gu, Seoul 110-191; tel. (2) 318-1767; fax (2) 3789-2757; e-mail embolseul@gmail.com; Ambassador GUADALUPE PALOMEQUE DE TABOADA.

Brazil: Ihn Gallery Bldg, 4th and 5th Floors, 141, Palpan-dong, Jongno-gu, Seoul; tel. (2) 738-4970; fax (2) 738-4974; e-mail braseul@kornet.net; internet seul.itamaraty.gov.br; Ambassador EDMUNDO SUSSUMU FUJITA.

Brunei: 39-1, Cheongun-dong, Jongno-gu, Seoul 110-030; tel. (2) 790-1078; fax (2) 790-1084; e-mail kbnbd_seoul@yahoo.com; Ambassador Dato' Paduka Haji HARUN BIN Haji ISMAIL.

Bulgaria: 723-42, Hannam 2-dong, Yeongsan-gu, Seoul 140-894; tel. (2) 794-8626; fax (2) 794-8627; e-mail embassy.seoul@mfa.bg; internet www.mfa.bg/embassies/korea; Ambassador PETAR ANDONOV.

Cambodia: 653-110, Hannam-dong, Yeongsan-gu, Seoul 140-887; tel. (2) 3785-1041; fax (2) 3785-1040; e-mail camboemb@korea.com; Ambassador DINA SUTH.

Canada: 16-1, Jeong-dong, Jung-gu, CPOB 6299, Seoul 100-662; tel. (2) 3783-6000; fax (2) 3783-6239; e-mail seoul@international.gc.ca; internet www.canadainternational.gc.ca/korea-coree; Ambassador ERIC WALSH.

Chile: Coryo Daeyungak Tower, Unit 1801, 25-5, Chungmoro 1-ga, Jung-gu, Seoul 100-706; tel. (2) 779-2610; fax (2) 779-2615; e-mail echilekr@yahoo.co.kr; internet www.coreachile.org; Ambassador HERNÁN BRANTES.

China, People's Republic: 54, Hyoja-dong, Jongno-gu, Seoul 110-033; tel. (2) 738-1038; fax (2) 738-1046; e-mail chinaemb_kr@mfa.gov .cn; internet www.chinaemb.or.kr; Ambassador QIU GUOHONG.

Colombia: Kyobo Bldg, 11th Floor, Jongno 1-ga, Jongno-gu, Seoul 110-714; tel. (2) 720-1369; fax (2) 725-6959; e-mail cseul@cancilleria .gov.co; Ambassador TITO SAUL PINILLA.

Congo, Democratic Republic: Daewoo Complex Bldg, Unit 702, 167, Naesu-dong, Jongno-gu, Seoul 110-070; tel. (2) 722-7958; fax (2) 722-7998; e-mail congokoreaembassy@yahoo.com; Ambassador NDAMBO CHRISTOPHE NGWEY.

Costa Rica: Iljin Bldg, Unit 8, 50-1, Dohwa-dong, Mapo-gu, Seoul 121-040; tel. (2) 707-9249; fax (2) 707-9255; e-mail embajadacr@ecostarica.or.kr; internet www.ecostarica.or.kr; Ambassador JAIRO LÓPEZ.

Côte d'Ivoire: Chungam Bldg, 2nd Floor, 794-4, Hannam-dong, Yeongsan-gu, Seoul 140-894; tel. (2) 3785-0561; fax (2) 3785-0564; e-mail ambaciseoul@gmail.com; internet cotedivoireembassy.or.kr; Ambassador SYLVESTRE KOUASSI BILE.

Czech Republic: 17, Gyeonghuigung 1-gil, Jongno-gu, Seoul 110-062; tel. (2) 725-6765; fax (2) 734-6452; e-mail seoul@embassy.mzv .cz; internet www.mzv.cz/seoul; Ambassador TOMÁŠ HUSÁK.

Denmark: Namsong Bldg, 5th Floor, 260-199, Itaewon-dong, Yeongsan-gu, Seoul 140-200; tel. (2) 795-4187; fax (2) 796-0986; e-mail selamb@um.dk; internet sydkorea.um.dk; Ambassador THOMAS LEHMANN.

Dominican Republic: Taepyeong-no Bldg, 19th Floor, 310, Taepyeong-no 2-ga, Jung-gu, Seoul; tel. (2) 756-3513; fax (2) 756-3514; e-mail embadom@kornet.net; internet embadomcorea@gmail.com; Ambassador GRECIA FIORDALICIA PICHARDO POLANCO.

Ecuador: SC First Bank Bldg, 19th Floor, 100, Gongpyeong-dong, Jongno-gu, Seoul 110-702; tel. (2) 739-2401; fax (2) 739-2355; e-mail ecuadorkoreaembassy@gmail.com; internet ecuadorkorea.org; Ambassador OSCAR GUSTAVO HERRERA GILBERT.

Egypt: 46-1, Hannam-dong, Yeongsan-gu, Seoul 140-210; tel. (2) 749-0787; fax (2) 795-2588; e-mail embassyegyptkorea@yahoo.com; internet www.mfa.gov.eg/Seoul_Emb; Ambassador HANY SELIM LABIB.

El Salvador: Samsung Life Insurance Bldg, 20th Floor, 150, Taepyeong-no 2-ga, Jung-gu, Seoul 100-716; tel. (2) 753-3432; fax (2) 753-3456; e-mail koresal@kornet.net; Chargé d'affaires a.i. JASON MANUEL CASTRO OLIVARES.

Ethiopia: 258–6, Itaewon-dong, Yeongsan-gu, Seoul 140–856; tel. (2) 790-9766; fax (2) 790-0156; e-mail embassy@seoulethioembassy .or.kr; internet seoulethioembassy.or.kr; Ambassador DIBABA ABDETTA.

Fiji: 210-69, Itaewon-dong, Yeongsan-gu, Seoul; tel. (2) 792–6396; fax (2) 792–6397; Ambassador FILIMONE KAU.

Finland: Kyobo Bldg, 18th Floor, Jongno 1, Jongno-gu, Seoul 110-714; tel. (2) 732-6737; fax (2) 723-4969; e-mail sanomat.seo@formin .fi; internet www.finland.or.kr; Ambassador MATTI HEIMONEN.

France: 30, Hap-dong, Seodaemun-gu, Seoul 120-030; tel. (2) 3149-4300; fax (2) 3149-4310; e-mail ambafrance@hanafos.com; internet www.ambafrance-kr.org; Ambassador JÉRÔME PASQUIER.

Gabon: Yoosung Bldg, 4th Floor, 738-20, Hannam-dong, Yeongsan-gu, Seoul; tel. (2) 793-9575; fax (2) 793-9574; e-mail amgabsel@unitel .co.kr; Ambassador CARLOS VICTOR BOUNGOU.

Germany: 32, Jangmun-ro, Jongno-gu, Seoul 140-816; tel. (2) 748-4114; fax (2) 748-4161; e-mail info@seoul.diplo.de; internet www .seoul.diplo.de; Ambassador ROLF MAFAEL.

Ghana: 5-4, Hannam-dong, Yeongsan-gu, CPOB 3887, Seoul 140-884; tel. (2) 3785-1427; fax (2) 3785-1428; e-mail ghana3@kornet.net; internet www.ghanaembassy.or.kr; Ambassador ELIZABETH NICOL.

Greece: Hanwha Bldg, 27th Floor, 1, Janggyo-dong, Jung-gu, Seoul 100-797; tel. (2) 729-1401; fax (2) 729-1402; e-mail greekemb@kornet .net; Ambassador DIONISIOS SOURVANOS.

Guatemala: 614, Lotte Hotel, 1, Sogong-dong, Jung-gu, Seoul 100-635; tel. (2) 771-7582; fax (2) 771-7584; e-mail embcorea@minex.gob .gt; Ambassador GUSTAVO ADOLFO LÓPEZ CALDERON.

Holy See: 2, Gungjeong-dong, Jongno-gu, Seoul 110-031 (Apostolic Nunciature); tel. (2) 736-5725; fax (2) 739-5738; e-mail apnunkr@yahoo.com; Apostolic Nuncio Most Rev. OSVALDO PADILLA (Titular Archbishop of Voli).

Honduras: Jongno Tower Bldg, 22nd Floor, 6, Jongno 2-ga, Jongno-gu, Seoul 110-160; tel. (2) 738-8402; fax (2) 738-8403; e-mail hondurasembassy@hotmail.com; Ambassador MICHEL IDIAQUEZ BARADAT.

Hungary: 58, Jangmun-ro, Dongbinggo-dong, Yeongsan-gu, Seoul 140-809; tel. (2) 792-2105; fax (2) 792-2109; e-mail mission.sel@mfa .gov.hu; internet www.mfa.gov.hu/emb/seoul; Ambassador GÁBOR CSABA.

India: 37-3, Hannam-dong, Yeongsan-gu, CPOB 3466, Seoul 140-210; tel. (2) 798-4257; fax (2) 796-9534; e-mail eoiseoul@sinbiro.com; internet www.indembassy.or.kr; Ambassador VISHNU PRAKASH.

Indonesia: 55, Yeouido-dong, Yeongdeungpo-gu, Seoul 150-010; tel. (2) 783-5675; fax (2) 780-4280; e-mail kbriseoul@kornet.net; internet www.kemlu.go.id/seoul; Ambassador JOHN A. PRASETIO.

Iran: 1-93, Dongbinggo-dong, Yeongsan-gu, Seoul 140-809; tel. (2) 793-7751; fax (2) 792-7052; e-mail iranssy@chol.com; Ambassador HASSAN TAHERIAN.

Iraq: 1-94, Dongbinggo-dong, Yeongsan-gu, Seoul 140-811; tel. (2) 790-4202; fax (2) 790-4206; e-mail sulemb@iraqmfamail.com; internet www.mofamission.gov.iq/kor; Ambassador KHALIL AL-MOSAWI.

Ireland: Leema Bldg, 13th Floor, 146-1, Susong-dong, Jongno-gu, Seoul 110-755; tel. (2) 721-7200; fax (2) 774-6458; e-mail seoulembassy@dfa.ie; internet www.embassyofireland.or.kr; Ambassador AINGEAL O'DONOGHUE.

Israel: Cheonggye 11 Bldg, 18th Floor, 149, Seorin-dong, Jongno-gu, Seoul 110-726; tel. (2) 3210-8500; fax (2) 3210-8555; e-mail info@seoul.mfa.gov.il; internet seoul.mfa.gov.il; Ambassador URI GUTMAN.

Italy: Ilshin Bldg, 3rd Floor, 714, Hannam-dong, Yongsan-gu, Seoul 140-894; tel. (2) 796-0491; fax (2) 797-5560; e-mail embassy.seoul@esteri.it; internet www.ambseoul.esteri.it; Ambassador SERGIO MERCURI.

Japan: 18 11, Junghak-dong, Jongno-gu, Seoul 110-150; tel. (2) 2170-5200; fax (2) 734-4528; e-mail info@so.mofa.go.jp; internet www.kr.emb-japan.go.jp; Ambassador KORO BESSHO.

Jordan: Twin-Tree Tower, Bldg B, 6th Floor, 14 Joonghak-dong, Jongno-gu, Seoul 110-792; tel. (2) 318-2897; fax (2) 318-3644; e-mail jdembassy@gmail.com; internet www.jordankorea.gov.jo; Ambassador OMAR AL-NAHAR.

Kazakhstan: 53, Jangmun-ro, Yeongsan-gu, Seoul 140-809; tel. (2) 379-9714; fax (2) 395-9766; e-mail seoul@mfa.kz; internet www .kazembassy.org; Ambassador DULAT BAKISHEV.

Kenya: 243-36, Itaewon-dong, Yeongsan-gu, Seoul 140-200; tel. (2) 3785-2903; fax (2) 3785-2905; e-mail info@kenya-embassy.or.kr; internet www.kenya-embassy.or.kr; Ambassador MOHAMED ABDI GELLO.

Kuwait: 309-15, Dongbinggo-dong, Yeongsan-gu, Seoul; tel. (2) 749-3688; fax (2) 749-3687; e-mail kuwaitembassy@kornet.net; Ambassador JASEM MOHAMMAD AL-BUDAIWI.

Kyrgyzstan: Namsong Bldg, Unit 403, 260-199, Itaewon-dong, Yeongsan-gu, Seoul 140-200; tel. (2) 379-0951; fax (2) 379-0953; e-mail seoulembassykg@gmail.com; internet www.kyrgyzembkorea .com; Ambassador DUISHONKUL CHOTONOV.

Laos: 657-9, Hannam-dong, Yeongsan-gu, Seoul 140-887; tel. (2) 796-1713; fax (2) 796-1771; e-mail amphayk@ hotmail.com; Ambassador KHAMLA SAYACHAK.

Lebanon: 310-49, Dongbinggo-dong, Yeongsan-gu, Seoul 140-230; tel. (2) 794-6482; fax (2) 794-6485; e-mail emleb@lebanonembassy .net; internet www.lebanonembassy.net; Chargé d'affaires a.i. ELIAS NICOLAS.

Libya: 4-5, Hannam-dong, Yeongsan-gu, Seoul; tel. (2) 797-6001; fax (2) 797-6007; e-mail libyaemb@kornet.net; Ambassador OTMAN S. SAAD AHBARA.

Malaysia: 4-1, Hannam-dong, Yeongsan-gu, Seoul 140-884; tel. (2) 2077-8600; fax (2) 794-5480; e-mail malseoul@kln.gov.my; internet www.malaysia.or.kr; Ambassador Datuk ROHANA RAMLI.

Mexico: 33-6, Hannam 1-dong, Yeongsan-gu, Seoul 140-885; tel. (2) 798-1694; fax (2) 790-0939; e-mail embajada@embamexcor.org; internet embamex.sre.gob.mx/corea; Ambassador JOSÉ LUIS BERNAL RODRÍGUEZ.

Mongolia: 33-5, Hannam-dong, Yeongsan-gu, Seoul 140-885; tel. (2) 794-1350; fax (2) 794-7605; e-mail mongol6@kornet.net; internet www.mongolembassy.com; Ambassador BAASANJAVYN GANBOLD.

Morocco: Hannam Tower, Annex Bldg, 4th Floor, 730, Hannam-dong, Yeongsan-gu, Seoul; tel. (2) 793-6249; fax (2) 792-8178; e-mail sifamase@kornet.net; Ambassador MOHAMED CHRAÏBI.

Myanmar: 724-1, Hannam-dong, Yeongsan-gu, Seoul 140-210; tel. (2) 790-3814; fax (2) 790-3817; e-mail myanmar@kotis.net; internet www.meseoul.org; Ambassador SOE LWIN.

Nepal: 37-24, Sungbuk-dong, Yeongsan-gu, Seoul; tel. (2) 3789-9770; fax (2) 736-8848; e-mail info@nepembseoul.gov.np; internet www.nepembseoul.gov.np; Ambassador KAMAN SINGH LAMA.

Netherlands: Jeongdong Bldg, 10/F, 15-5 Jeong-dong, Jung-gu, Seoul; tel. (2) 311-8600; fax (2) 311-8650; e-mail seo@minbuza.nl; internet southkorea.nlembassy.org; Ambassador LODY EMBRECHTS.

New Zealand: Jeong-dong Bldg, 8th Floor, Jeong-dong, Jung-gu, Seoul 100-784; tel. (2) 3701-7700; fax (2) 3701-7701; e-mail nzembsel@kornet.net; internet www.nzembassy.com/korea; Ambassador PATRICK RATA.

Nicaragua: Danam Tower, 23rd Floor, 10, Sowol-ro, Jung-gu, Seoul; tel. (2) 6272–1670; fax (2) 6272–1671; e-mail embanickorea@ cancilleria.gob.ni; Ambassador JORGE RAMÓN ARNESTO ALM.

Nigeria: 13, Jangmun-ro, Yeongsan-gu, Seoul 140-817; tel. (2) 797-2370; fax (2) 796-1848; e-mail chancery@nigerianembassy.or.kr; internet www.nigerianembassy.or.kr; Ambassador DESMOND AKAWOR.

Norway: Jeong-dong Bldg, 13th Floor, 15-5 Jeong-dong, Jung-gu, Seoul 100-784; tel. (2) 727-7100; fax (2) 727-7199; e-mail emb.seoul@ mfa.no; internet www.norway.or.kr; Ambassador TORBJØRN HOLTHE.

Oman: 58-1, Shinmoon-ro 1-ga, Jongno-gu, Seoul 110-700; tel. (2) 790-2431; fax (2) 790-2430; e-mail omanembs@kornet.net; Ambassador MOHAMED SALIM AL-HARTHY.

Pakistan: 124-13, Itaewon-dong, Yeongsan-gu, Seoul 140-200; tel. (2) 796-8252; fax (2) 796-0313; e-mail consular@pkembassy.or.kr; internet www.pkembassy.or.kr; Ambassador ZAHID NASRULLAH KHAN.

Panama: 407, Somerset Palace, Soosong-dong, Jongno-gu, Seoul 110-885; tel. (2) 734-8610; fax (2) 734-8613; e-mail panaemba@kornet .net; Ambassador RUBÉN AROSEMENA VALDÉS.

Papua New Guinea: Doosan We've Pavilion Bldg, Unit 210, 58, Soosong-dong, Jongno-gu, Seoul 110-858; tel. (2) 2198-5771; fax (2) 2198-5779; e-mail ambassador@kunduseoul.kr; internet www .papuanewguineaembassy.kr; Ambassador BILL VERI.

Paraguay: 302, Hannam Tower, Annex Bldg, 3rd Floor, 730, Hannam-dong, Yeongsan-gu, Seoul; tel. (2) 792-8335; fax (2) 792-8334; e-mail pyemc2@kornet.net; internet www.embaparcorea.org; Ambassador CEFERINO ADRIÁN VALDEZ PERALTA.

Peru: Daeyungak Bldg, Unit 2002, 25-5, Jungmu-no 1-ga, Jung-gu, Seoul 100-706; tel. (2) 757-1735; fax (2) 757-1738; e-mail embaperuencorea@gmail.com; internet www.embassyperu.or.kr; Ambassador JAIME POMAREDA MONTENEGRO.

Philippines: 5-1, Itaewon 2-dong, Yeongsan-gu, Seoul; tel. (2) 796-7387; fax (2) 796-0827; e-mail seoulpe@philembassy-seoul.com; internet www.philembassy-seoul.com; Ambassador RAUL HERNANDEZ.

Poland: Samcheong-ro 20-1 Jongno-Gu, Seoul 110-190; tel. (2) 723-9681; fax (2) 723-9680; e-mail seul.amb.sekretariat@msz.gov.pl; internet seul.msz.gov.pl; Ambassador KRZYSZTOF MAJKA.

Portugal: Wonseo Bldg, 2nd Floor, 171, Wonseo-dong, Jongno-gu, Seoul 110-280; tel. (2) 3675-2251; fax (2) 3675-2250; e-mail embport@ chol.com; internet www.portugalseoul.com; Ambassador ANTÓNIO QUINTEIRO NOBRE.

Qatar: 309-5, Dongbinggo-dong, Yeongsan-gu, Seoul 140-817; tel. (2) 798-2444; fax (2) 790-1027; e-mail qatarembassy@koreamail.com; Ambassador MOHAMMED ABDULLAH AL-DUHAIMI.

Romania: 50, Jangmun-ro, Yongsan-gu, Seoul 140-809; tel. (2) 797-4924; fax (2) 794-3114; e-mail embassy@romania.ollehoffice.com; internet seoul.mae.ro; Ambassador CĂLIN FABIAN.

Russian Federation: 34-16, Jeong-dong, Jung-gu, Seoul 100-120; tel. (2) 318-2116; fax (2) 754-0417; e-mail russemb@gmail.com; internet www.russian-embassy.org; Ambassador ALEKSANDR ANDREEVICH TIMONIN.

Rwanda: Sooyong Bldg, Unit 503, 64-1, Hannam-dong, Yeongsan-gu, Seoul 140-889; tel. (2) 798-1052; fax (2) 798-1054; e-mail info@ rwanda-embassy.or.kr; internet rwanda-embassy.or.kr; Ambassador EMMA FRANÇOISE ISUMBINGABO.

Saudi Arabia: 36-37, Itaewon 1-dong, Yeongsan-gu, Seoul 140-201; tel. (2) 739-0631; fax (2) 739-0041; e-mail embassysaudi@yahoo.co .kr; Ambassador AHMED BIN YUNUS AL-BARRAK.

Senegal: Coryo Daeyungak Tower, 13th Floor, Unit 1302, 25-5, Chungmuro 1-ga, Jung-gu, Seoul 100-706; tel. (2) 745-5554; fax (2) 745-5524; e-mail ambassenseoul@hotmail.com; Ambassador MAMADOU NDIAYE.

Serbia: 730, Hannam-dong, Yeongsan-gu, Seoul; tel. (2) 797-5109; fax (2) 790-6109; e-mail emserbseul@yahoo.com; internet www .embserb.or.kr; Ambassador ZORAN KAZAZOVIĆ.

Singapore: Seoul Finance Bldg, 28th Floor, 84, Taepyeong-no 1-ga, Jung-gu, Seoul 100-101; tel. (2) 774-2464; fax (2) 773-2463; e-mail singemb_seo@sgmfa.gov.sg; internet www.mfa.gov.sg/seoul; Ambassador YIP WEI KIAT.

Sierra Leone: 1-111 Seongbuk-dong, Seongbuk-gu, Seoul 136–822; tel. (2) 741-0083; fax (2) 741-0084; e-mail info@slembassyseoul.or.kr; Ambassador OMRIE MICHAEL GOLLEY.

Slovakia: 389-1, Hannam-dong, Yeongsan-gu, Seoul 140-210; tel. (2) 794-3981; fax (2) 794-3982; e-mail emb.seoul@mzv.sk; internet www.mzv.sk/seoul; Ambassador MILAN LAJCIAK.

South Africa: 1-37, Hannam-dong, Yeongsan-gu, Seoul 140-885; tel. (2) 792-4855; fax (2) 792-4856; e-mail general@ southafrica-embassy.or.kr; internet www.southafrica-embassy.or .kr; Ambassador HILTON ANTHONY DENNIS.

Spain: 726-52, Hannam-dong, Yeongsan-gu, Seoul 140-894; tel. (2) 794-3581; fax (2) 796-8207; e-mail emb.seoul@maec.es; internet www .maec.es/subwebs/Embajadas/Seul; Ambassador GONZALO ORTIZ.

Sri Lanka: 347-359, Shindang-dong, Jung-gu, Seoul 100-450; tel. (2) 735-2966; fax (2) 737-9577; e-mail lankaemb@kornet.net; internet www.slembassykorea.org; Ambassador W. W. T. WIJERATNE.

Sudan: Vivien Bldg, 3rd Floor, 4-52, Seobinggo-dong, Yeongsan-gu, Seoul 140-240; tel. (2) 793-8692; fax (2) 793-8693; e-mail sudanembassykorea@gmail.com; internet www.sudanembassy.co .kr; Ambassador MOHAMED ABDUL-AL HAROUN.

Sweden: Danam Bldg, 8th Floor, 10, Sowol-ro, Jung-gu, CPOB 3577, Seoul 100-704; tel. (2) 3703-3700; fax (2) 3703-3701; e-mail embassy@ swedemb.or.kr; internet www.swedenabroad.com/seoul; Ambassador LARS DANIELSSON.

Switzerland: 32-10, Songwol-dong, Jongno-gu, CPOB 2900, Seoul 110-101; tel. (2) 739-9511; fax (2) 737-9392; e-mail seo.vertretung@ eda.admin.ch; internet www.eda.admin.ch/seoul; Ambassador JÖRG ALOIS REDING.

Thailand: 653-7, Hannam-dong, Yeongsan-gu, Seoul 140-210; tel. (2) 795-3098; fax (2) 798-3448; e-mail rteseoul@kornet.net; internet www.thaiembassy.or.kr; Ambassador KUMUT SINGHARA NA AYUDHYA.

Timor-Leste: Hannam Tower Bldg II, Unit 405, 725-23, Hannam-dong, Yeongsan-gu, Seoul 140-894; tel. (2) 797-6151; fax (2) 797-6152; e-mail tlembseoul@gmail.com; Ambassador HERNANI F. COELHO DA SILVA.

Tunisia: 1-17, Dongbinggo-dong, Yeongsan-gu, Seoul 140-809; tel. (2) 790-4334; fax (2) 790-4333; e-mail ambtnkor@kornet.net; Ambassador MOHAMED ALI NAFTI.

Turkey: Vivien Corpn Bldg, 4th Floor, 4-52, Seobinggo-dong, Yeongsan-gu, Seoul 140-240; tel. (2) 794-0255; fax (2) 797-8546; e-mail turkemb.seoul@hotmail.com; internet www.seul.be.mfa.gov .tr; Ambassador ARSLAN HAKAN OKÇAL.

Turkmenistan: Yongsan-gu, Seoul 31-45; tel. 796-9975; fax 796-9976; e-mail tmembassy.skr@gmail.com; Ambassador MYRAT MAMMETALIYEV.

Ukraine: 51, Jangmun-ro, Yeongsan-gu, Seoul; tel. (2) 790-5696; fax (2) 790-5697; e-mail emb_kr@mfa.gov.ua; internet www.mfa.gov.ua/ korea; Ambassador VASYL MARMAZOV.

United Arab Emirates: 5-5, Hannam-dong, Yeongsan-gu, Seoul 140-884; tel. (2) 790-3235; fax (2) 790-3238; e-mail uaeemb@kornet .net; Ambassador ABDULLA KHALFAN MATAR AL-ROMAITHI.

United Kingdom: 19-gil 24, Sejong-no, Jung-gu, Seoul 100-120; tel. (2) 3210-5500; fax (2) 725-1738; e-mail enquiry.seoul@fco.gov.uk; internet www.ukinkorea.fco.gov.uk; Ambassador CHARLES HAY.

USA: 188, Sejong-no, Jongno-gu, Seoul 110-710; tel. (2) 397-4114; fax (2) 397-4080; e-mail embassyseoulpa@state.gov; internet seoul .usembassy.gov; Ambassador MARK LIPPERT.

Uruguay: 653-30, Hannam 1-dong, Yeongsan-gu, Seoul 140-887; tel. (2) 6245-3179; fax (2) 6245-3181; e-mail uruseul@embrou.or.kr; internet www.embrou.or.kr; Ambassador ALBA ROSA FLORIO LEGNANI.

Uzbekistan: Diplomatic Center, Unit 701, 1376-1, Seocho 2-dong, Seocho-gu, Seoul; tel. (2) 574-6554; fax (2) 578-0576; internet www .uzbekistan.or.kr; Ambassador BOTIRZHON ASADOV.

Venezuela: SC First Bank Bldg, 16th Floor, 100, Gongpyeong-dong, Jongno-gu, CPOB 10043, Seoul 110-702; tel. (2) 732-1546; fax (2) 732-1548; e-mail emvesel@soback.kornet.net; internet www .venezuelaemb.or.kr; Chargé d'affaires a.i. YADIRA HIDALGO DE ORTIZ.

Viet Nam: 28-58, Samcheong-dong, Jongno-gu, Seoul 140-210; tel. (2) 738-2318; fax (2) 739-2064; e-mail vndsq@yahoo.com; internet www.vietnamembassy-seoul.org; Ambassador PHAM HUU CHI.

Zambia: 708–33, Yeoksam-dong, Gangnamgu, Seoul; tel. (2) 557-3240; fax (2) 557-3241; e-mail asilumesi@yahoo.com; Ambassador MUMBA KAPUMPA.

Judicial System

Supreme Court: 219 Seocho-dong, Seocho-gu, Seoul; tel. (2) 533-2824; fax (2) 533-1911; e-mail webmaster@scourt.go.kr; internet www.scourt.go.kr; the Supreme Court is empowered to receive and decide on appeals against decisions of the High Courts, the Patent Court, and the appellate panels of the District Courts or the Family Court in civil, criminal, administrative, patent and domestic relations cases; the Court is also authorized to act as the final tribunal to review decisions of courts-martial and to consider cases arising from presidential and parliamentary elections; consists of 13 Justices, including the Chief Justice, who are appointed for six years by the President, subject to the consent of the National Assembly; other sitting judges are appointed on the recommendation of the Chief Justice; Chief Justice YANG SUNG-TAE.

Constitutional Court: 15 Gahoero, Jongno-gu, Seoul 110-250; tel. (2) 708-3629; fax (2) 708-3566; e-mail interdiv@ccourt.go.kr; internet www.ccourt.go.kr; adjudicates the following matters: constitutionality of a law (when requested by the other courts); impeachment; dissolution of a political party; disputes between state agencies, or between state agencies and local governments; and petitions relating to the Constitution; composed of nine adjudicators appointed by the President, of whom three are chosen from among persons selected by the National Assembly and three from persons nominated by the Chief Justice; Pres. PARK HAN-CHUL.

High Courts: there are five High Courts, situated in Seoul, Daegu, Busan, Gwangju and Daejeon, with five chief, 78 presiding and 145 other judges; the courts have appellate jurisdiction in civil and criminal cases and can also pass judgment on administrative litigation against government decisions.

Patent Court: 45 Cheongsodong-ro, Seo-gu, Daejeon 302-784; tel. (42) 480-1400; established in March 1998 to deal with cases in which the decisions of the Intellectual Property Tribunal are challenged; cases are conducted by a judge, with the assistance of technical examiners.

District Courts: there are 13 District Courts, with 13 chief, 241 presiding and 966 other judges; they exercise jurisdiction over all civil and criminal cases in the first instance.

Municipal Courts: there are 103 Municipal Courts within the District Court system, dealing with small claims, minor criminal offences, and settlement cases.

Family Court: there is one Family Court, in Seoul, with a chief judge, four presiding judges and 16 other judges; the court has jurisdiction in domestic matters and cases of juvenile delinquency.

Administrative Court: established in Seoul in March 1998 to deal with cases that are specified in the Administrative Litigation Act; the Court has jurisdiction over cities and counties adjacent to Seoul, and deals with administrative matters, including taxes, expropriations of land, labour and other general administrative matters.

Courts-Martial: exercise jurisdiction over all offences committed by armed forces personnel and civilian employees and are also authorized to try civilians accused of military espionage or interference with the execution of military duties.

Religion

BUDDHISM

Korean Mahayana Buddhism has about 80 denominations. The Chogye-jong is the largest Buddhist order in Korea, having been introduced from China in AD 372. The Chogye Order accounts for almost two-thirds of all Korean Buddhists. Won Buddhism combines elements of Buddhism and Confucianism.

Korean United Buddhist Association (KUBA): 46-19, Soosong-dong, Jongno-gu, Seoul 110-140; tel. (2) 732-4885; 28 mem. Buddhist orders; Pres. SONG WOL-JOO.

CHRISTIANITY

National Council of Churches in Korea: Christian Bldg, Rm 706, 136-46, Yeonchi-dong, Jongno-gu, Seoul 110-736; tel. (2) 744-8981; fax (2) 744-6189; e-mail kncc@kncc.or.kr; internet www.kncc.or.kr; f. 1924; est. as National Christian Council; present name adopted 1946; eight mem. churches; Pres. Rev. LEE YOUNG-HOON; Gen. Sec. Rev. KIM YOUNG-JU.

The Anglican Communion

South Korea has three Anglican dioceses, collectively forming the Anglican Church of Korea (founded as a separate province in April 1993), under its own Primate, the Bishop of Seoul.

Archbishop of Korea and Bishop of Seoul: Most Rev. PAUL KIM KEUN-SANG, 3, Jeong-dong, Jung-gu, Seoul 100-120; tel. (2) 738-6597; fax (2) 738-3982; e-mail skhseoul@skhseoul.or.kr; internet www .skhseoul.or.kr.

Bishop of Pusan (Busan): Rt Rev. SOLOMON JONG-MO YOON, 18, 2-ga, Daechung-dong, Jung-gu, Busan 600-600; tel. (51) 463-5742; fax (51) 463-5957; e-mail adpusan@hanmail.net; internet skhpusan .onmam.com.

Bishop of Taejon (Daejeon): Rt Rev. MICHAEL KWON HI-YEON, POB 22, Daejeon 300-600; tel. (42) 256-9988; fax (42) 255-8918; e-mail djdio@djdio.or.kr; internet www.djdio.or.kr.

The Roman Catholic Church

For ecclesiastical purposes, North and South Korea are nominally under a unified jurisdiction. South Korea comprises three archdioceses, 12 dioceses and one military ordinate. At 31 December 2007 some 4,821,020 people were adherents of the Roman Catholic Church.

Bishops' Conference: Catholic Bishops' Conference of Korea, 643-1, Junggok-dong, Gwangjin-gu, Seoul 143-912; tel. (2) 460-7500; fax (2) 460-7505; e-mail cbck@cbck.or.kr; internet www.cbck.or.kr; f. 1857; Pres. Most Rev. PETER KANG (Bishop of Cheju—Jeju).

Archbishop of Kwangju (Gwangju): Most Rev. HYGINUS KIM HEE-JONG, Archdiocesan Office, 997-1, Sangmu 2-dong, Gwangju 502-855; tel. (62) 380-2801; fax (62) 380-2806; e-mail biseo1@kjcatholic.or .kr; internet www.kjcatholic.or.kr.

Archbishop of Seoul: Cardinal ANDREW YEOM SOO-JUNG, Archdiocesan Office, 1, 2-ga, Myeong-dong, Jung-gu, Seoul 100-022; tel. (2) 727-2114; fax (2) 773-1947; e-mail ao@seoul.catholic.or.kr; internet www.catholic.or.kr.

Archbishop of Daegu (Taegu): Most Rev. THADDEUS CHO HWAN-KIL, Archdiocesan Office, 225-1, Namsan 3-dong, Jung-gu, Daegu 700-804; tel. (53) 253-7011; fax (53) 253-9441; e-mail taegu@ tgcatholic.or.kr; internet www.tgcatholic.or.kr.

Protestant Churches

Korean Methodist Church: 64-8, 1-ga, Taepyeong-no, Jung-gu, Seoul 100-101; KPO Box 285, Seoul 110-602; tel. (2) 399-4300; fax (2) 399-4307; e-mail bishop@kmcweb.or.kr; internet www.kmcweb.or .kr; f. 1885; 1,534,504 mems (2007); Bishop KANG HEUNG-BOK.

Presbyterian Church in the Republic of Korea (PROK): Academy House, San 76, Suyu 6-dong, Kangbuk-ku, Seoul 142-714; tel. (2) 3499-7600; fax (2) 3499-7630; e-mail prok3000@chol.com; internet www.prok.org; f. 1953; 337,570 mems (2007); Gen. Sec. Rev. BAE TAE-JIN.

Presbyterian Church of Korea (PCK): The Korean Church Centennial Memorial Bldg, 135, Yunji-dong, Jongno-gu, Seoul 110-470; tel. (2) 741-4350; fax (2) 766-2427; e-mail thepck@pck.or .kr; internet www.pck.or.kr; 2,395,323 mems (Dec. 2003); Moderator Rev. JUNG SUH-KIM; Gen. Sec. Rev. SEONGI CHO.

There are some 160 other Protestant denominations in the country, including the Korea Baptist Convention and the Korea Evangelical Church.

OTHER RELIGIONS

Chundo Kyo, a religion indigenous and unique to Korea, combines elements of Shamanistic, Buddhist, and Christian doctrines. Confucianism also has a significant number of followers. Taejong Gyo is Korea's oldest religion, dating back 4,000 years, and comprising beliefs in the national foundation myth, and the triune god, Hanul. By the 15th century the religion had largely disappeared, but a revival began in the late 19th century.

The Press

NATIONAL DAILIES
(In Korean, unless otherwise indicated)

Chosun Ilbo: 61, 1-ga, Taepyeong-no, Jung-gu, Seoul 100-756; tel. (2) 724-5114; fax (2) 724-5059; e-mail englishnews@chosun.com; internet www.chosun.com; f. 1920; morning, weekly and children's edns; independent; Korean, English, Chinese and Japanese; Exec. Editor KIM CHAN; circ. 2,470,000.

Daily Sports Seoul: 25, 1-ga, Taepyeong-no, Jung-gu, Seoul; tel. (2) 721-5114; fax (2) 721-5396; internet www.seoul.co.kr; f. 1985; morning; sports and leisure; Pres. LEE HAN-SOO; Man. Editor LEE CHOL-HWI.

Dong-A Ilbo: 139-1, 3-ga, Sejong-no, Jongno-gu, Seoul 100-715; tel. (2) 2020-0114; fax (2) 2020-1239; e-mail newsroom@donga.com; internet www.donga.com; f. 1920; morning; independent; Publr and CEO KIM JAE-HO; Editor-in-Chief LEE HYUN-NAK; circ. 2,150,000.

Han-Joong Daily News: 91-1, 2-ga, Myeong-dong, Jung-gu, Seoul; tel. (2) 776-2801; fax (2) 778-2803; Chinese.

Hankook Ilbo: 14, Junghak-dong, Jongno-gu, Seoul; tel. (2) 724-2114; fax (2) 724-2244; internet www.hankooki.com; f. 1954; morning; independent; Pres. PARK JIN-YEOL; Editor-in-Chief HA JONG-OH; circ. 2,000,000.

Hankuk Kyungje Shinmun (The Korea Economic Daily): 441, Junglim-dong, Jung-gu, Seoul 100-791; tel. (2) 360-4114; fax (2) 779-4447; e-mail hkinfo@hankyung.com; internet www.hankyung.com; f. 1964; morning; Pres. and CEO KIM KI-WOONG; Man. Dir and Editor-in-Chief LEE HAK-YOUNG.

Hankyoreh (One Nation): 116-25, Gongdeok-dong, Mapo-gu, Seoul 121-750; tel. (2) 1566-9595; internet www.hani.co.kr; f. 1988; centre-left; Korean, English; CEO and Publr YANG SANG-WOO; Editor-in-Chief PARK CHAN-SU; circ. 500,000.

JoongAng Ilbo (JoongAng Daily News): 7, Soonhwa-dong, Jung-gu, 100-759 Seoul; tel. (2) 751-9215; fax (2) 751-9219; e-mail iht@joongang.co.kr; internet joongangdaily.joins.com; f. 1965; morning; Korean and English; Publr LHO CHOL-SOO; Exec. Dir RYU KWON-HA; circ. 2,300,000.

Kookmin Ilbo: Kookmin Ilbo Bldg, 5/F, 12, Yeouido-dong, Yeongdeungpo-gu, Seoul; tel. (2) 781-9114; fax (2) 781-9781; e-mail kimyh@kmib.co.kr; internet www.kukminilbo.co.kr; Pres. RO SEUNG-SOOK; Editorial Dir KIM Y. H.

Korea Daily News: 25, 1-ga, Taepyeong-no, Jung-gu, Seoul; tel. (2) 2000-9000; fax (2) 2000-9659; e-mail webmaster@seoul.co.kr; internet www.kdaily.com; f. 1945; morning; independent; Publr and Pres. SON CHU-HWAN; Man. Editor LEE DONG-HWA; circ. 700,000.

Korea Herald: 1-17, Jeong-dong, Jung-gu, Seoul; tel. (2) 727-0205; fax (2) 727-0670; e-mail editor@heraldcorp.com; internet www .koreaherald.co.kr; f. 1953; morning; English; independent; Pres. WOOK HONG-JUNG; CEO LEE YOUNG-MAN; circ. 150,000.

Korea Times: 81, Tongilro, Seodaemun-gu, Seoul 120-705; tel. (2) 724-2859; fax (2) 736-4061; e-mail webmaster@koreatimes.co.kr; internet www.koreatimes.co.kr; f. 1950; morning; English; independent; Pres. PARK MOO-JONG; Man. Editor OH YOUNG-JIN; circ. 100,000.

Kyung-hyang Shinmun: 22, Jeong-dong, Jung-gu, Seoul; tel. (2) 3701-1114; fax (2) 737-6362; internet www.khan.co.kr; f. 1946; evening; independent; Pres. HONG SUNG-MAN; Exec. Editor KIM JI-YOUNG; circ. 350,000.

Maeil Business Newspaper: 30-1, 1-ga, Bil-dong, Jung-gu, Seoul 100-728; tel. (2) 2000-2114; fax (2) 2269-6200; internet www.mk.co .kr; f. 1966; evening; economics and business; Korean, English; Pres. CHANG DAE-WHAN; Chief Editor JANG YONG-SUNG; circ. 235,000.

Munhwa Ilbo: 68, 1-ga, Chungjeong-no, Jung-gu, Seoul 110-170; tel. (2) 3701-5114; fax (2) 3701-5566; internet www.munhwa.co.kr; f. 1991; evening; Pres. and Publr LEE BYUN-KYU; Editor-in-Chief KANG SIN-KU.

Naeway Economic Daily: 1-12, 3-ga, Hoehyon-dong, Jung-gu, Seoul 100; tel. (2) 727-0114; fax (2) 727-0661; f. 1973; morning; Pres. KIM CHIN-OUK; Man. Editor HAN DONG-HEE; circ. 300,000.

Segye Times: 550-15, Gasan-dong, Seoul; tel. (2) 2000-1160; fax (2) 2000-1349; e-mail webmaster@segye.com; internet www.segyetimes .co.kr; f. 1989; morning; Pres. SA KWANG-KEE; Editor MOK JUNG-GYUM.

Seoul Kyungje Shinmun (Seoul Economic Daily): 14, Junghak-dong, Jongno-gu, Seoul; tel. (2) 724-2114; fax (2) 732-2140; e-mail webmaster@hanooki.com; internet economy.hankooki.com; f. 1960; morning; Pres. LIM KONG-JON; Man. Editor LEE JONG-WHAN; circ. 500,000.

Sports Chosun: 61, 1-ga, Taepyeong-no, Jung-gu, Seoul; tel. (2) 3219-8114; fax (2) 724-6979; e-mail readers@sportschosun.com; internet www.sportschosun.com; f. 1964; Publr BANG SANG-HOON; circ. 400,000.

LOCAL DAILIES

Chungcheong Daily News: 304, Sachang-dong, Hungduk-gu, Cheongju, N. Chungcheong Prov.; tel. (43) 279-5000; fax (43) 279-5050; e-mail webmaster@ccilbo.com; internet www.ccilbo.com; f. 1946; morning; Pres. SEO JEONG-OK; Editor IM BAIK-SOO.

Daegu Ilbo: 177-10, Sincheon 2-dong, Dong-gu, Daegu; tel. (53) 757-5700; fax (53) 757-5757; internet www.idaegu.com; f. 1953; morning; Pres. LEE TAE-YEUL; Editor KIM KYUNG-PAL.

Daejon Ilbo: 1-135, Munhwa 1-dong, Jung-gu, Daejeon; tel. (42) 251-3311; fax (42) 253-3320; f. 1950; evening; Pres. CHO JOON-HO; Editor KWAK DAE-YEON.

Halla Ilbo: 568-1, Samdo 1-dong, Jeju; tel. (64) 750-2114; fax (64) 750-2520; e-mail webmaster@ihalla.com; internet www.ihalla.com; f. 1989; evening; Chair. KANG YONG-SOK; Man. Editor HONG SONG-MOK.

Incheon Ilbo: 18-1, 4-ga, Hang-dong, Jung-gu, Incheon; tel. (32) 763-8811; fax (32) 763-7711; e-mail webmaster@itimes.co.kr; internet www.itimes.co.kr; f. 1988; evening; Chair. MUN PYONG-HA; Man. Editor LEE JAE-HO.

Jeju Daily News: 2324-6, Yeon-dong, Jeju; tel. (64) 740-6114; fax (64) 740-6500; e-mail webmaster@jejunews.com; internet www .jejunews.com; f. 1945; evening; Pres. and Publr WU RONGZHU.

Jeonbuk Domin Ilbo: 417-62, 2-ga, Deokjin-dong, Deokjin-gu, Jeonju, N. Jeolla Prov.; tel. (63) 251-7113; fax (63) 251-7127; internet www.domin.co.kr; f. 1988; morning; Pres. LIM BYOUNG-CHAN; Man. Editor YANG CHAE-SUK.

Jeonbuk Ilbo: 710-5, Kumam-dong, Deokjin-gu, Jeonju, N. Jeolla Prov.; tel. (63) 250-5500; fax (63) 250-5550; f. 1950; evening; Chair. SUH CHANG-HOON; Man. Editor LEE KON-WOONG.

Jeonju Ilbo: 568-132, Sonosong-dong, Deokjin-gu, Jeonju, N. Jeolla Prov.; tel. (63) 285-0114; fax (63) 285-2060; f. 1991; morning; Chair. KANG DAE-SOON; Man. Editor SO CHAE-CHOL.

Joongdo Ilbo: 274-7, Galma-dong, Seo-gu, Daejeon; tel. (42) 530-4114; fax (42) 535-5334; internet joongdoilbo.co.kr; f. 1951; morning; CEO KIM WOK-SIK; Man. Editor SONG HYOUNG-SOP.

Kangwon Ilbo: 23, Jungang-no, Chuncheon, Gangwon Prov.; tel. (33) 258-1000; fax (33) 258-1114; internet www.kwnews.co.kr; f. 1945; evening; Pres. CHOI SEUNG-IK; Editor-in-Chief KIM SUNG-KEE.

Kookje Daily News: 76-2, Goje-dong, Yeonje-gu, Busan 611-702; tel. (51) 500-5114; fax (51) 500-4274; e-mail jahwang@ms.kookje.co .kr; internet www.kookje.co.kr; f. 1947; morning; Pres. ROH KI-TAE; Editor-in-Chief JEONG WON-YOUNG.

Kwangju Ilbo: 20-2, Geumnam-no, Dong-gu, Gwangju; tel. (62) 222-8111; fax (62) 227-9500; e-mail kwangju@kwangju.co.kr; internet www.kwangju.co.kr; f. 1952; evening; Chair. KIM CHONG-TAE; Man. Editor CHO DONG-SU.

Kyeonggi Ilbo: 452-1, Songjuk-dong, Changan-gu, Suwon, Gyeonggi Prov.; tel. (31) 250-3333; fax (31) 250-3306; e-mail webmaster@kyeonggi.com; internet www.kgib.co.kr; f. 1988; evening; Pres. SHIN CHANG-GI; Man. Editor LEE CHIN-YONG.

Kyeongin Ilbo: 1276, Maetan-dong, Yeongtong-gu, Suwon, Gyeonggi-do; tel. (31) 231-5114; fax (31) 232-1231; e-mail webmaster@kyeongin.com; internet www.kyeongin.com; f. 1960; evening; Pres. WOO JE-CHAN; Man. Editor KIM HWA-YANG.

Kyungnam Shinmun: 100-5, Sinwol-dong, Changwon, S. Gyeongsang Prov.; tel. (55) 283-2211; fax (55) 210-6048; internet www .knnews.co.kr; f. 1946; evening; Pres. KIM DONG-KYU; Editor PARK SUNG-KWAN.

Maeil Shinmun: 71, 2-ga, Gyesan-dong, Jung-gu, Daegu; tel. (53) 255-5001; fax (53) 255-8902; e-mail imaeil@msnet.co.kr; internet www.imaeil.com; f. 1946; evening; Pres. Cho Hwan-Kil; Editor Lee Yong-Keun; circ. 300,000.

Pusan Daily News: 1-10, Sujeong-dong, Dong-gu, Busan 601-738; tel. (51) 461-4114; fax (51) 463-8880; internet www.pusanilbo.co.kr; f. 1946; Pres. Jeong Han-Sang; Man. Editor Ahn Ki-Ho; circ. 427,000.

Yeongnam Ilbo: 111, Sincheon-dong, Dong-gu, Daegu; tel. (53) 756-8001; fax (53) 756-9011; internet www.yeongnam.co.kr; f. 1945; morning; Chair. Park Chang-Ho; Man. Editor Kim Sang-Tae.

SELECTED PERIODICALS

Eumak Dong-A: 139, Sejong-no, Jongno-gu, Seoul 110-715; tel. (2) 781-0640; fax (2) 705-4547; f. 1984; monthly; music; Publr Kim Byung-Kwan; Editor Kwon O-Kie; circ. 85,000.

Han Kuk No Chong (FKTU News): 35, Yeouido-dong, Yeong-deungpo-gu, Seoul 150-885; tel. (2) 6277-0026; fax (2) 6277-0068; internet www.fktu.or.kr; f. 1961; labour news; circ. 20,000.

Hyundae Munhak: Seoul; tel. (2) 516-3770; fax (2) 516-5433; e-mail webmaster@hdmh.co.kr; internet www.hdmh.co.kr; f. 1955; literature; circ. 200,000.

Korea Business World: Yeouido, POB 720, Seoul 150-607; tel. (2) 532-1364; fax (2) 594-7663; f. 1985; monthly; English; Publr and Pres. Lee Kie-Hong; circ. 40,200.

Korea Buyers Guide: Rm 2301, Korea World Trade Center, 159, Samseong-dong, Gangnam-gu, Seoul; tel. (2) 551-2376; fax (2) 551-2377; e-mail info@buyersguide.co.kr; internet www.buykorea21.com; f. 1973; monthly, consumer goods; quarterly, hardware; circ. 360,000.

Korea Journal: Korean National Commission for UNESCO, CPOB 64, Seoul 100-600; tel. (2) 6958-4110; e-mail kj@unesco.or.kr; internet www.ekoreajournal.net; f. 1961; quarterly; organ of the Korean National Commission for UNESCO; focus on Korean Studies; Editor Hahm Seong-Deuk; Publr Min Dong-Seok.

Korea Newsreview: 1-12, 3-ga, Hoehyeon-dong, Jung gu, Seoul 100-771; tel. (2) 756-7711; weekly; English; Publr and Editor Park Chung-Woong.

Korea and World Affairs: Rm 1723, Daewoo Center Bldg, 5-541, Namdaemun-no, Jung-gu, Seoul 100-714; tel. (2) 777-2628; fax (2) 319-9591; organ of the Research Center for Peace and Unification of Korea; Pres. Chang Dong-Hoon.

Korean Business Review: FKI Bldg, 28-1, Yeouido-dong, Yeong-deungpo-gu, Seoul 150-756; tel. (2) 3771-0114; fax (2) 3771-0138; monthly; publ. by Fed. of Korean Industries; Publr Kim Kak-Choong; Editor Sohn Byung-Doo.

Monthly Travel: Cross Bldg, 2nd Floor, 46-6, 2-ga, Namsan-dong, Jung-gu, Seoul 100-042; tel. (2) 757 6161; fax (2) 757-6089; e-mail kotfa@unitel.co.kr; Pres. Shin Joong-Mok; circ. 50,000.

News Maker: 22, Jung-dong, Jung-gu, Seoul 110-702; tel. (2) 3701-1114; fax (2) 739-6190; e-mail hudy@kyunghyang.com; internet www.kyunghyang.com/newsmaker; f. 1992; Pres. Jang Jun-Bong; Editor Park Myung-Hun.

Reader's Digest: 295-15, Deoksan 1-dong, Geumcheon-gu, Seoul 153-011; tel. (2) 3670-5497; fax (2) 3670-5001; internet www.readersdigest.co.kr; f. 1978; monthly; general; Pres. Yang Sung-Mo; Editor Park Soon-Hwang; circ. 115,000.

Shin Dong-A (New East Asia): 139, Chungjeong-no, Seodaemun-gu, Seoul 120-715; tel. (2) 361-0974; fax (2) 361-0988; e-mail hans@donga.com; internet shindonga.donga.com; f. 1931; monthly; general; Publr Kim Jae-Ho; Editor Lee Hyung-Sam; circ. 150,000.

Taekwondo: Joyang Bldg 113, 4/F, Samseong-dong, Gangnam-gu, Seoul; tel. (2) 566-2505; fax (2) 553-4728; e-mail wtf@wtf.org; internet www.wtf.org; f. 1973; annual; organ of the World Taekwondo Federation; Pres. Dr Choue Chung-Won.

Vantage Point: 85-1, Susong-dong, Jongno-gu, Seoul, 110-140; tel. (2) 398-3114; fax (2) 398-3539; e-mail master@yna.co.kr; internet www.yonhapnews.co.kr; f. 1978; monthly; developments in North Korea; Editor Kwak Seung-Ji.

Weekly Chosun: 61, Taepyong-no 1, Jung-gu, Seoul; tel. (2) 724-5114; fax (2) 724-6899; e-mail weekly@chosun.com; internet weekly.chosun.com; Publr Kim Chang-Ki; Editor Choi Joon-Suk; circ. 350,000.

The Weekly Hankook: 14, Junghak-dong, Jongno-gu, Seoul; tel. (2) 732-4151; fax (2) 724-2444; internet weekly.hankooki.com; f. 1964; Publr Chang Chae-Kuk; circ. 400,000.

NEWS AGENCY

Yonhap News Agency: 85-1, Susong-dong, Jongno-gu, Seoul; tel. (2) 398-3114; fax (2) 398-3567; e-mail ldm@yna.co.kr; internet www.yonhapnews.co.kr; f. 1980; Pres. Kim Kun.

PRESS ASSOCIATIONS

Journalists Association of Korea (JAK): Korea Press Center Bldg, 25 1-ga, Taepyeong-no, Jung-gu, Seoul; tel. (2) 737-2483; fax (2) 738-1003; e-mail jakmaster@journalist.or.kr; internet www.journalist.or.kr; Pres. Jang Kyung-Woo.

Korean Association of Newspapers: Korea Press Center, 13th Floor, 25, 1-ga, Taepyeong-no, Jung-gu, Seoul 100-745; tel. (2) 733-2251; fax (2) 720-3291; e-mail iwelcome@presskorea.or.kr; internet www.presskorea.or.kr; f. 1962; 48 mems; Pres. Jae-Ho; Sec.-Gen. Moon Han-Kwon.

Korean Newspaper Editors' Association: Korea Press Center, 13th Floor, 25, 1-ga, Taepyeong-no, Jung-gu, Seoul; tel. (2) 732-1726; fax (2) 739-1985; f. 1957; 416 mems; Pres. Seong Byong-Wuk.

Seoul Foreign Correspondents' Club: Korea Press Center, 18/F, 1-ga, Taepyeong-no, Jung-gu, Seoul; tel. (2) 734-3272; fax (2) 734-7712; e-mail master@sfcc.or.kr; internet www.sfcc.or.kr; f. 1956; Pres. Ryoji Ito.

Publishers

Ahn Graphics Ltd: 48-6, Sangamsan-ro, Mapo-gu, Seoul 121-904; tel. (2) 743-8065; fax (2) 744-3251; e-mail agmaster@ag.co.kr; internet www.ag.co.kr; f. 1985; art, literature, computer graphics; Pres. Kim Ok-Chul.

BIR Publishing Co Ltd: 4/F, Gangnam Publishing Culture Center, 506 Sinsa-dong, Gangnam-Gu, Seoul 135-887; tel. (2) 515-2000; fax (2) 3442-4661; e-mail bir@bir.co.kr; internet www.bir.co.kr; f. 1994; children's books; Pres. Park Sang-Hee.

Bobmun Sa Publishing Co: 526-3, Munbal-ri, Gyoha-eup, Paju-si, Gyeonggi-do 413-756; tel. (31) 955-6500; fax (31) 955-6525; e-mail bms@bobmunsa.co.kr; internet www.bobmunsa.co.kr; f. 1954; law, politics, philosophy, history; Pres. Bae Hyo-Seon.

Bookhouse Publishing Co Ltd: 6/F, Dongsomun Bldg, Seoul 136-034; tel. (2) 3144-3123; e-mail editor@bookhouse.co.kr; internet www.bookhouse.co.kr; business, foreign novels, health; CEO Kim Jeong-Sun.

Bumwoo Publishing Co: 525-2, Paju Book City, Munbal-ri, Gyoha-eup, Paju-si, Gyeonggi-do; tel. (31) 955-6900; fax (31) 955-6905; e-mail bumwoosa@chol.com; internet www.bumwoosa.co.kr; f. 1966; philosophy, religion, social science, technology, art, literature, history; Pres. Yoon Hyung-Doo.

Chaeksesang Publishing Co (Book World): 68-7, Sinsu-dong, Mapu-gu, Seoul 121-854; tel. (2) 704-1251; fax (2) 719-1258; e-mail webmaster@bkworld.co.kr; internet www.bkworld.co.kr; f. 1975; art, literature, religion, science and technology; Pres. Kim Jik-Seung.

Changhae Publishing: 336-10, Ahyun 2-dong, Seoul 121-012; tel. (2) 313-3200; fax (2) 313-3204.

Cheong Moon Gak Publishing Co Ltd: 486-9, Kirum 3-dong, Seongbuk-gu, Seoul 136-800; tel. (2) 985-1451; fax (2) 988-1456; e-mail cmgbook@cmgbook.co.kr; internet www.cmgbook.co.kr; f. 1974; science, technology, business; subsidiaries HanSeung Publishers, Lux Media; Pres. Kim Hong-Seok; Man. Dir Hans Kim.

Crayon House Co Ltd: 5/F, Crayon House Bldg, Seoul; tel. (2) 3436-1711; fax (2) 3436-1410; e-mail crayong@korea.com; internet www.crayonhouse.co.kr; f. 1996; children's books.

Dai Won Publishing Co: 40-456, Hangangno 3-ga, Yeongsan-gu, Seoul 140-880; tel. (2) 2071-2000; fax (2) 793-8994; e-mail webmaster@dwci.co.kr; internet www.dwci.co.kr; f. 1990; comics.

Design House Publishing Co: Taekwang Bldg, 162-1, Jangchung-dong, 2-ga, Jung-gu, Seoul 100-855; tel. (2) 2275-6151; fax (2) 2267-6158; e-mail yhlee@design.co.kr; internet www.design.co.kr; f. 1987; social science, art, literature, languages, children's periodicals; Pres. Lee Young-Hee.

Dongmoonsun Publishing Co: 21 Insa-dong-gil, Jongno-gu, Seoul 110-300; tel. (2) 737-2795; fax (2) 723-4518; e-mail dmspub@hanmail.net; humanities; Pres. Sin Sung-dae.

Doosan Corporation Publishing BG: 14-34, Yeouido-dong, Yeongdeungpo-gu, Seoul; tel. (2) 2167-0601; fax (2) 2167-0668; e-mail dudvkf@doosan.com; internet www.bookdonga.com; f. 1951; general works, school reference, social science, periodicals; Pres. Choi Tae-Kyung.

E*Public Co: 923-11, Mok 1-dong, Yangcheon-gu, Seoul 158-051; tel. (2) 2653-5131; fax (2) 2653-2454; e-mail webmaster@epublic.co.kr; internet www.epublic.co.kr; f. 1955; social science, pure science, technology, medicine, linguistics; Pres. and CEO Liu Sung-Kwon.

Eulyoo Publishing Co Ltd: 46-1, Susong-dong, Jongno-gu, Seoul 110-603; tel. (2) 733-8151; fax (2) 732-9154; e-mail eulyoo1945@gmail.com; internet www.eulyoo.co.kr; f. 1945; linguistics, literature, social science, history, philosophy; Pres. Chung Jee-Young.

Gilbut Publishing Co Ltd: 467-9, Seogyo-dong, Mapo-gu, Seoul 121-842; tel. (2) 332-0931; fax (2) 323-0586; e-mail gilbut@gilbut.co.kr; internet www.gilbut.co.kr; f. 1991.

Gimm-Young Publishers Inc: 515-1, Munbal-ri, Gyoha-eup, Paju-si, Gyeonggi-do 413-756; tel. (31) 3668-3203; fax (31) 745-4827; e-mail jinhee@gimmyoung.com; internet en.gimmyoung.com; f. 1979; current affairs, humanities, history, religion, children's books; Pres. GIMM GHANG-YU.

Hainaim Publishing Co Ltd: 5/F, Hainaim Bldg, 368-4, Seogyo-dong, Mapo-gu, Seoul; tel. (2) 326-1600; fax (2) 326-1624; e-mail jwlee@hainaim.com; internet www.hainaim.com; f. 1983; philosophy, literature, children's; Pres. SONG YOUNG-SUK.

Haksan Publishing Co: Haksan Bldg, 777-1, Sangdo-dong, Dong-jak-gu, Seoul 156-830; tel. (2) 828-8988; fax (2) 828-8890; internet www.haksanpub.co.kr; f. 1995; children's books, comics, magazines.

Hangilsa Corpn: 520-11, Paju Book City, Munbal-ri, Gyoha-eup, Paju-si, Gyeonggi-do; tel. (31) 955-2000; fax (31) 955-2005; e-mail hangilsaone@hangilsa.co.kr; internet www.hangilsa.co.kr; f. 1976; social science, history, literature; Pres. KIM EOUN-HO.

Hanul Publishing Company: 3/F Seoul Bldg, 105-90 Gongdeok-dong, Mapo-gu, Seoul 121-801; tel. (2) 336-6183; fax (2) 333-7543; e-mail hanul@hanulbooks.co.kr; internet www.hanulbooks.co.kr; f. 1980; general, philosophy, university books, periodicals; Pres. KIM CHONG-SU.

Hollym Corporation: 13-13, Gwancheol-dong, Jongno-gu, Seoul 110-111; tel. (2) 735-7551; fax (2) 730-5149; e-mail info@hollym.co.kr; internet www.hollym.co.kr; f. 1963; academic and general books on Korea in English; Pres. SANGBEK RHIMM.

Hyang Mun Sa Publishing Co: 3/F, Burim Bldg, 1668-14, Seocho 1-dong, Seocho-gu, Seoul 137-881; tel. (2) 584-5671; fax (2) 584-5673; f. 1950; science, agriculture, history, engineering, home economics; Pres. NAH JOONG-RYOL.

Hyeonam Publishing Co Ltd: 481-12, Seogyo-dong, Mapo-gu, Seoul 121-841; tel. (2) 365-5051; fax (2) 365-2729; e-mail ks@hyeonamsa.com; internet www.hyeonamsa.com; f. 1951; general, children's, literature, periodicals; Pres. CHO KEUN-TAE.

Hyungseul Publishing Co: 7-33, Tongeui-dong, Jongno-gu, Seoul; tel. (2) 738-6052; fax (2) 736-7134; e-mail hs@hyungseul.co.kr; internet www.hyungseul.co.kr; social science, university books.

Il Jin Sa Publishing Co: Iljin Bldg, 3rd Floor, 5-104, Hyochang-dong, Yeongsan-gu, Seoul; tel. (2) 704-1616; fax (2) 715-3536; e-mail webmaster@iljinsa.com; internet www.iljinsa.com; f. 1979; vocational, science and technology, social sciences, fine arts; CEO LEE JUNG-IL.

Ilchokak Publishing Co Ltd: 1-335, Sinmunno 2-ga, Jongno-gu, Seoul 110-062; tel. (2) 733-5430; fax (2) 738-5857; e-mail ilchokak@hanmail.net; internet www.ilchokak.co.kr; f. 1953; history, literature, sociology, linguistics, medicine, law, engineering; Pres. KIM SI-YEON.

Jigyungsa Publishers Ltd: 790-14, Yeoksam-dong, Gangnam-gu, Seoul 135-080; tel. (2) 557-6351; fax (2) 557-6352; e-mail jigyung@uriel.net; internet www.jigyung.co.kr; f. 1979; children's, periodicals; Pres. KIM BYUNG-JOON.

Jihak Publishing Co Ltd: 180-20, Dongkyo-dong, Mapo-gu, Seoul 121-200; tel. (2) 330-5200; fax (2) 325-4488; e-mail webmaster@jihak.co.kr; internet www.jihak.co.kr; f. 1965; philosophy, language, literature; Pres. KWON BYONG-IL.

Jimoondang: 95, Waryon-dong, Jongno-gu, Seoul 110-360; tel. (2) 743-0227; fax (2) 742-4657; e-mail sale@jimoon.co.kr; internet www.jimoon.co.kr; f. 1970; scholarly books on Korean history, society, language, literature, religion, art, folklore, politics and economy; Pres. LIM SAM-KYU.

Jisik Sanup Publications Co Ltd: 35-18, Dongui-dong, Jongno-gu, Seoul 110-040; tel. (2) 734-1978; fax (2) 720-7900; e-mail jsp@jisik.co.kr; internet www.jisik.co.kr; f. 1969; religion, social science, art, literature, history, children's; Pres. KIM KYUNG-HEE.

Kemongsa Publishing Co Ltd: 772, Yeoksam-dong, Gangnam-gu, Seoul 135-080; tel. (2) 531-5335; fax (2) 531-5520; e-mail kmcc@kemongsa.co.kr; internet www.kemongsa.co.kr; f. 1946; picture books, juvenile, encyclopaedias, history, fiction; Pres. RHU SEUNG-HEE.

Kookminbooks Co Ltd: 514-4, Paju Book City, Munbal-ri, Gyoha-eup, Paju-si, Gyeonggi-do; tel. (31) 955-7851; fax (31) 955-7855; internet www.kmbooks.co.kr; f. 1961; children's books.

Korea Britannica Corpn: 117, 1-ga, Jungchung-dong, Seoul 100-391; tel. (2) 272-2151; fax (2) 278-9983; e-mail webmaster@britannica.co.kr; internet www.britannica.co.kr; f. 1968; encyclopaedias, dictionaries; Pres JANG HO-SANG, SUJAN ELEN TAPANI.

Korea University Press: 1-2, Anam-dong, 5-ga, Seongbuk-gu, Seoul 136-701; tel. (2) 3290-4232; fax (2) 923-6311; e-mail kupress@korea.ac.kr; internet www.kupress.com; f. 1956; philosophy, history, language, literature, Korean studies, education, psychology, social science, natural science, engineering, agriculture, medicine; Pres. LEE KI-SU.

Kum Sung Publishing Co: 242-63, Gongdeok-dong, Mapo-gu, Seoul 121-022; tel. (2) 713-9651; fax (2) 701-9345; e-mail webmaster@kumsungpub.co.kr; internet www.kumsung.co.kr; f. 1965; literature, juvenile, social sciences, history, fine arts; Pres. KIM NAK-JOON.

Kyohak-sa Publishing Co Ltd: 105-67, Gongdeok-dong, Mapo-gu, Seoul 121-020; tel. (2) 707-5100; fax (2) 707-5184; e-mail webmaster@kyohak.co.kr; internet www.kyohak.co.kr; f. 1952; dictionaries, educational, children's; Pres. YANG CHEOL-WOO.

Kyung Hee University Press: 1, Hoeki-dong, Dongdaemun-gu, Seoul 130-701; tel. (2) 961-0106; fax (2) 962-8840; f. 1960; general, social science, technology, language, literature; Pres. CHOE YOUNG-SEEK.

Kyungnam University Press: 28-7, Samchung-dong, Jongno-gu, Seoul 110-230; tel. and fax (2) 3700-0700; fax (2) 3700-0707; e-mail ifes@kyungnam.ac.kr; internet ifes.kyungnam.ac.kr; Pres. PARK JAE-KYU.

Minumsa Publishing Co Ltd: 5/F Kangnam Publishing Culture Centre, 506, Sinsa-dong, Gangnam-gu, Seoul 135-120; tel. (2) 515-2000; fax (2) 514-3249; e-mail webmaster@minumsa.com; internet www.minumsa.com; f. 1966; literature, philosophy, linguistics, pure science; Pres. PARK SANG-JUN.

Munhakdongne Publishing Co Ltd: 210, Hoedong-gil, Paju-si, Gyeonggi-do, 413-120; tel. (31) 955-8888; fax (31) 955-8855; e-mail editor@munhak.com; internet www.munhak.com; f. 1993; art, literature, science, philosophy, non-fiction, children's, periodicals; Pres. KANG BYUNG-SUN.

Sakyejul Publishing Ltd: 513-3, Paju Book City, Munbal-ri, Gyoha-eup, Paju-si, Gyeonggi-do; tel. (31) 955-8558; fax (31) 955-8595; e-mail skj@sakyejul.co.kr; internet www.sakyejul.co.kr; f. 1982; social sciences, art, literature, history, children's; Pres. KANG MAR-XILL.

Sam Joong Dang Publishing Co: 261-23, Soke-dong, Yeongsan-gu, Seoul 140-140; tel. (2) 704-6816; fax (2) 704-6819; f. 1931; literature, history, philosophy, social sciences, dictionaries; Pres. LEE MIN-CHUL.

Sam Seong Dang Publishing Co: 101-14, Non Hyun-dong, Gangnam-gu, Seoul 135-010; tel. (2) 3442-6767; fax (2) 3442-6768; e-mail kyk@ssdp.co.kr; f. 1968; literature, fine arts, history, philosophy; Pres. KANG MYUNG-CHAE.

Samseongdang Publishing Co Ltd: 9/F, Samsungdang Bldg, 101-14, Nonhyeon-dong, Gangnam-gu, Seoul 135-820; tel. (2) 3443-2681; fax (2) 3443-2683; internet www.ssdp.co.kr; children's; Pres. KANG JEAN-KYUN.

Samsung Publishing Co Ltd: Samsung Publishing Bldg, 1516-2, Seocho 3-dong, Seocho-gu 137-871; tel. (2) 3470-6800; fax (2) 525-5057; e-mail jykim@samsungbooks.com; internet www.samsungbooks.com; children's books, comics, cooking, parenting, health, travel; f. 1951; Pres. KIM JIN-YONG.

Segyesa Publishing Co Ltd: 529-2, Munbal-ri, Gyoha-eup, Paju-si, Gyeonggi-do 413-756; tel. (31) 955-8080; fax (31) 955-8070; e-mail info@segyesa.co.kr; internet www.segyesa.co.kr; f. 1988; general, philosophy, literature, periodicals; Pres. CHOI SUN-HO.

Se-Kwang Music Publishing Co: 232-32, Seogye-dong, Yeongsan-gu, Seoul 140-140; tel. (2) 719-2652; fax (2) 719-2191; e-mail sekwang@sekwang.co.kr; internet www.sekwang.co.kr; f. 1953; music, art; Pres. PARK SEI-WON; Chair. PARK SHIN-JOON.

Seong An Dang Publishing Co: 4579, Singil-6-dong, Yeong-deungpo-gu, Seoul 150-056; tel. (2) 3142-4151; fax (2) 323-5324; f. 1972; technology, text books, university books, periodicals; Pres. LEE JONG-CHOON.

Seoul National University Press: 599, Gwanak-ro, Gwanak-gu, Seoul 151-742; tel. (2) 889-0785; fax (2) 888-4148; e-mail snubook@snu.ac.kr; internet www.snupress.com; f. 1961; philosophy, engineering, social science, art, literature; Dir KIM CHONG-SUH.

Si-sa-young-o-sa, Inc: 55-1, 2-ga, Jongno, Jongno-gu, Seoul 110-122; tel. (2) 274-0509; fax (2) 271-3980; internet www.ybmsisa.co.kr; f. 1959; language, literature; Pres. CHUNG YOUNG-SAM.

Sogang University Press: Rm 332, Kim Daegon Hall, 35 Baekbeom-ro, Mapo-gu, Seoul 121-742; tel. (2) 705-8212; fax (2) 705-8612; e-mail kje@sogang.ac.kr; internet sgpress.sogang.ac.kr; f. 1978; philosophy, religion, science, art, history; Pres. LEE JONG-WOOK.

Sookmyung Women's University Press: 53-12, 2-ga, Jongpa-dong, Yeongsan-gu, Seoul 140-742; tel. (2) 710-9162; fax (2) 710-9090; f. 1968; general; Pres. LEE KYUNG-SOOK.

Sungkyunkwan University Press: 53, Myeongnyun-dong 3-ga, Jongno-gu, Seoul; tel. (2) 760-1252; fax (2) 762-7452; internet www.skku.edu.

Sungshin Women's University Press: 249-1, Dongsun-dong 3-ga, Seongbuk-gu, Seoul; tel. (2) 920-7327; fax (2) 920-7326; internet www.sungshin.ac.kr/press.

Tam Gu Dang Publishing Co: 158, 1-ga, Hanggangno, Yeongsan-gu, Seoul 140-011; tel. (2) 3785-2211; fax (2) 3785-2272; e-mail tamgudang@tamgudang.co.kr; internet www.tamgudang.co.kr; f. 1950; linguistics, literature, social sciences, history, fine arts; Pres. HONG YOUNG-SOO.

Woongjin Think Big Co Ltd: Kukdong Bldg, 24th Floor, Chungmuro 3-ga, Jung-gu, Seoul; tel. (2) 3670-1832; fax (2) 766-2722; e-mail webmaster@wjholdings.co.kr; internet www.woongjin.com; children's; Pres. YOON SEOK-KEUM.

Yearimdang Publishing Co Ltd: Yearim Bldg, 153-3, Samseong-dong, Gangnam-gu, Seoul 135-090; tel. (2) 566-1004; fax (2) 567-9660; e-mail yearim@yearim.co.kr; internet www.yearim.kr; f. 1973; children's; Pres. NA CHOON-HO.

Yonsei University Press: 134, Sincheon-dong, Seodaemun-gu, Seoul 120-749; tel. (2) 2123-3380; fax (2) 2123-6673; e-mail dykim@yonsei.ac.kr; internet www.yonsei.ac.kr/press; f. 1955; philosophy, religion, literature, history, art, social science, pure science; Pres. KIM BYUNG-SOO.

Youl Hwa Dang: Paju Book City, 520-10, Munbal-ri, Gyoha-eup, Paju-si, Gyeonggi-do 413-832; tel. (31) 955-7000; fax (31) 955-7010; e-mail yhdp@youlhwadang.co.kr; internet www.youlhwadang.co.kr; f. 1971; art; Pres. YI KI-UNG.

Younglim Cardinal Inc: Hyecheon Bldg, 831, Yeoksam-dong, Gangnam-gu, Seoul 135-792; tel. (2) 553-8516; fax (2) 552-0436; e-mail edit@ylc21.co.kr; internet www.ylc21.co.kr; f. 1987.

PUBLISHERS' ASSOCIATION

Korean Publishers' Association: 105-2, Sagan-dong, Jongno-gu, Seoul 110-190; tel. (2) 735-2702; fax (2) 738-5414; e-mail kpa@kpa21.or.kr; internet www.kpa21.or.kr; f. 1947; Pres. BAEK SOK-GHEE; Sec.-Gen. KO HUNG-SIK.

Broadcasting and Communications

TELECOMMUNICATIONS

Korea Telecom: 206, Jungja-dong, Bundang-gu, Seongnam-si, Gyeonggi Prov. 463-711; tel. (2) 727-0114; fax (2) 750-3994; internet www.kt.co.kr; domestic and international telecommunications services and broadband internet services; privatized in June 2002; CEO HWANG CHANG-GYU.

LG UPlus: 827, Namdaemunno 5-ga, Jung-gu, Seoul 100-095; tel. (70) 4080-1114; e-mail ir@lguplus.co.kr; internet www.uplus.co.kr; subsidiary of LG Corpn; mobile telecommunications and wireless internet services; CEO SANG CHUL-LEE.

Onse Telecom: 192-2, Gumi-dong, Bundang-gu, Seongnam-si, Gyeonggi Prov. 463-500; tel. and fax (31) 738-6000; internet www.onse.net; domestic and international telecommunications services; Chair. and CEO KIM HYEONG JIN.

SK Telecom Co Ltd: 11, Euljiro, 2-ga, Jung-gu, Seoul 100-999; tel. (2) 6100-2114; fax (2) 2121-3999; e-mail webmaster@sktelecom.com; internet www.sktelecom.com; cellular mobile telecommunications and wireless internet services; merged with Shinsegi Telecom in Jan. 2002; Pres. and CEO CHO DAE-SIK.

BROADCASTING

Regulatory Authority

Broadcasting and Communications Commission: KBS Bldg, 923-5, Mok-dong, Yangcheon-gu, Seoul 158-715; tel. (2) 3219-5117; fax (2) 3219-5371; e-mail admin@kbc.go.kr; internet www.kbc.go.kr; Chair. CHOI SUNG-JOON.

Radio

Korean Broadcasting System (KBS): 18, Yeouido-dong, Yeongdeungpo-gu, Seoul 150-790; tel. (2) 781-1000; fax (2) 781-4179; internet www.kbs.co.kr; f. 1926; publicly owned corpn with 26 local broadcasting and 855 relay stations; overseas service in Korean, English, German, Indonesian, Chinese, Japanese, French, Spanish, Russian and Arabic; Pres. and CEO CHO DAE-HYUN.

Buddhist Broadcasting System (BBS): 140, Mapo-dong, Mapo-gu, Seoul 121-050; tel. (2) 705-5114; fax (2) 705-5229; e-mail webmaster@bbsfm.co.kr; internet www.bbsfm.co.kr; f. 1990; Pres. CHO HAE-HYONG.

Christian Broadcasting System (CBS): 917-1, Mok-dong, Yangcheon-gu, Seoul 158-701; tel. (2) 650-0500; fax (2) 654-0505; e-mail help@cbs.co.kr; internet www.cbs.co.kr; f. 1954; independent religious network with 14 network stations, incl. Seoul, Daegu, Busan

and Gwangju; also satellite, cable and digital media broadcasting; programmes in Korean; Pres. LEE JEONG-SIK.

Educational Broadcasting System (EBS): 463-2, Dogok-dong, Gangnam-gu, Seoul 135-854; tel. (2) 526-2000; fax (2) 526-2179; e-mail hotline@ebs.co.kr; internet www.ebs.co.kr; f. 1990; Pres. Dr YONGSUP SHIN.

Far East Broadcasting Co (FEBC): 89, Sangsu-dong, Mapo-gu, Seoul 121-707; tel. (2) 320-0114; fax (2) 320-0229; e-mail febcadm@febc.net; internet www.febc.net; Christian programmes; 11 local stations; Chair. Dr BILLY KIM.

> **Radio Station HLAZ:** MPO Box 88, Seoul 121-707; tel. (2) 320-0114; fax (2) 320-0129; e-mail febcadm@febc.net; internet www.febc.net; f. 1973; religious, educational service operated by Far East Broadcasting Co; programmes in Korean, Chinese, Russian and Japanese; Chair. Dr BILLY KIM.

> **Radio Station HLKX:** MPO Box 88, Seoul 121-707; tel. (2) 320-0114; fax (2) 320-0129; e-mail febcadm@febc.net; internet www.febc.net; f. 1956; religious, educational service operated by Far East Broadcasting Co; programmes in Korean, Chinese and English; Chair. Dr BILLY KIM.

Munhwa Broadcasting Corpn (MBC): 31, Yeouido-dong, Yeongdeungpo-gu, Seoul 150-728; tel. (2) 784-2000; fax (2) 784-0880; e-mail mbcir@mbc.com; internet www.imbc.com; f. 1961; public; CEO AHN GWANG-HAN.

Pyong Hwa Broadcasting Corpn (PBC): 2-3, 1-ga, Jeo-dong, Jung-gu, Seoul 100-031; tel. (2) 270-2114; fax (2) 270-2210; internet www.pbc.co.kr; f. 1990; religious and educational programmes; Pres. OH JI-YEONG.

Seoul Broadcasting System (SBS): SBS Broadcasting Center, 920-1, Mok-dong, Yangcheon-gu, Seoul 158-051; tel. (2) 786-0792; fax (2) 780-2530; e-mail webmaster@sbs.co.kr; internet www.sbs.co.kr; f. 1991; Pres. WOO WONGIL.

US Forces Network Korea (AFN Korea): Seoul; tel. (2) 7914-6495; fax (2) 7914-5870; e-mail info@afnkorea.net; internet www.afnkorea.net; f. 1950; six originating stations and 19 relay stations; 24 hours a day.

Television

There are numerous large national and regional television broadcasting companies. The switch to digital services was completed by the end of 2012.

Educational Broadcasting System (EBS): see Radio.

Jeonju Television Corpn (JTV): 656-3, Sonosong-dong, Deokjin-gu, Jeonju, Jeollabuk-do; tel. (63) 250-5200; fax (63) 250-5249; e-mail jtv@jtv.co.kr; internet www.jtv.co.kr; f. 1997; Pres. KIM TAEK-GON.

Korean Broadcasting System (KBS): 18, Yeouido-dong, Yeongdeungpo-gu, Seoul 150-790; tel. (2) 781-1000; fax (2) 781-4179; e-mail webmaster@kbs.co.kr; internet www.kbs.co.kr; f. 1961; publicly owned corpn with 25 local broadcasting and 770 relay stations; Pres. CHO DAE-HYUN.

Munhwa Broadcasting Corpn (MBC-R/TV): 31, Yeouido-dong, Yeongdeungpo-gu, Seoul 150-728; tel. (2) 789-2851; fax (2) 782 3094; e-mail song@mbc.co.kr; internet www.imbc.com; f. 1961; public; owned by the Foundation for Broadcast Culture (70%) and the Chung-Soo Scholarship Foundation (30%); includes terrestrial, cable and satellite TV stations, regional stations and radio stations; Pres. and CEO KIM JAE-CHEOL.

Seoul Broadcasting System (SBS): see Radio.

Finance

(cap. = capital; res = reserves; dep. = deposits; m. = million; brs = branches; amounts in won)

REGULATORY AUTHORITIES

Financial Services Commission: 38, Yeoui-daero, Yeongdeungpo-gu, Seoul 150-743; tel. (2) 2156-8000; fax (2) 2156-9538; e-mail aykim@korea.kr; internet www.fsc.go.kr; f. 1998; deliberates on and resolves financial supervision issues; oversees Financial Supervisory Service; Chair. SHIN JE-YOON.

Financial Supervisory Service: 38, Yeoui-daero, Yeongdeungpo-gu, Seoul 150-743; tel. (2) 3145-5114; fax (2) 785-3475; e-mail fssintl@fss.or.kr; internet www.fss.or.kr; f. 1999; examines and supervises financial institutions; Gov. CHOI SOO-HYUN.

BANKING

At August 2012 there were 58 commercial banks in South Korea, comprising six specialized banks and 39 branches of foreign banks. The Financial Supervisory Service oversees the operations of commercial banks and the financial services sector.

Central Bank

Bank of Korea: 110, 3-ga, Namdaemun-no, Jung-gu, Seoul 100-794; tel. (2) 759-4114; fax (2) 759-4060; e-mail bokdplp@bok.or.kr; internet www.bok.or.kr; f. 1950; bank of issue; res 3,342m., dep. 283,785m. (Dec. 2009); Gov. LEE JU-YEOL; Sr Dep. Gov. JANG BYUNG-HWA; 16 domestic brs, 6 overseas offices.

Commercial Banks

Citibank Korea Inc: 39, Da-dong, Jung-gu, Seoul 100-180; tel. (2) 3455-2114; fax (2) 3455-2969; internet www.citibank.co.kr; f. 1983; fmrly KorAm Bank, name changed as above 2004; acquired by Citigroup in 2004; cap. 1,518,322m., res 1,963,247m., dep. 34,458,803m. (Dec. 2010); CEO and Chair. HA YUNG-KU; 215 brs.

Hana Bank: 101-1, 1-ga, Ulchi-no, Jung-gu, Seoul 100-191; tel. (2) 2002-1111; fax (2) 775-7472; e-mail webmaster@hanabank.co.kr; internet www.hanabank.co.kr; f. 1991; merged with Boram Bank in Jan. 1999; merged with Seoulbank in Dec. 2002; cap. 1,147,404m., res 2,958,344m., dep. 106,424,262m. (Dec. 2011); Chair. and CEO KIM JONG-JUN; 604 brs.

Kookmin Bank: 9-1, 2-ga, Namdaemun-no, Jung-gu, Seoul 100-703; tel. (2) 1644-9999; fax (2) 2073-3296; e-mail corres@kookminbank.com; internet www.kookminbank.com; f. 1963; est. as Citizen's National Bank, renamed 1995; re-est. Jan. 1999, following merger with Korea Long Term Credit Bank; merged with H & CB in Nov. 2001; cap. 2,481,896m., res 7,912,460m., dep. 185,504,184m. (Dec. 2010); Chair. EUH YOON-DAE; Pres. and CEO MIN BYUNG-DUK; 1,122 domestic brs, 6 overseas brs.

Korea Exchange Bank: 181, 2-ga, Ulchi-no, Jung-gu, Seoul 100-793; tel. (2) 729-0114; fax (2) 775-2565; internet www.keb.co.kr; f. 1967; merged with Korea International Merchant Bank in Jan. 1999; acquired by Hana Financial Group in 2012; cap. 3,224,534m., res 1,112,486m., dep. 68,781,556m. (Dec. 2010); Pres. and CEO RO YUN-YONG; 345 domestic brs, 19 overseas brs.

Shinhan Bank: 120, 2-ga, Taepyeong-no, Jung-gu, Seoul 100-102; tel. (2) 6360-3000; fax (2) 6360-3082; e-mail irshy@shinhan.com; internet www.shinhan.com; f. 1982; merged with Chohung Bank in April 2006; cap. 7,928,078m., res 8,653,091m., dep. 162,996,416m. (Dec. 2011); Pres. and CEO SUH JIN-WON; 957 domestic brs, 12 overseas brs.

Standard Chartered Bank Korea Limited: 100, Gongpyeong-dong, Jongno-gu, Seoul 110702; tel. (2) 3702-3114; fax (2) 3702-4934; e-mail scbk.webmaster@sc.com; internet www.scfirstbank.com; f. 1929; acquired by Standard Chartered Bank in Jan. 2005; name changed from Standard Chartered First Bank Korea Limited to above in Jan. 2012; cap. 1,313,043m., res 1,032,407m., dep. 46,535,388m. (Dec. 2011); Chair. ROBERT T. BARNUM; CEO RICHARD HILL; 414 brs.

Woori Bank: 203, 1-ga, Hoehyeon-dong, Jung-gu, Seoul; tel. (2) 2002-3000; fax (2) 2002-5687; internet www.wooribank.com; f. 2002; est. by merger of Hanvit Bank and Peace Bank of Korea; 78% govt-owned; privatization plans deferred in 2008; cap. 3,829,783m., res 3,032,208., dep. 164,092,476m. (Dec. 2011); Pres. and CEO LEE SOON-WOO; 712 domestic brs.

Development Banks

Export-Import Bank of Korea: 16-1, Yeouido-dong, Yeong-deungpo-gu, Seoul 150-996; tel. (2) 3779-6114; fax (2) 784-1030; e-mail iro@koreaexim.go.kr; internet www.koreaexim.go.kr; f. 1976; cap. 6,258,755m., res −50,307m., dep. 2,103,275m. (Dec. 2011); Chair. and Pres. KIM YONG-HWAN; 10 brs.

Korea Development Bank: 16-3, Yeouido-dong, Yeongdeungpo-gu, Seoul 150-973; tel. (2) 787-6934; fax (2) 787-6991; e-mail KDBir@kdb.co.kr; internet www.kdb.co.kr; f. 1954; cap. 9,251,861m., res 617,033m., dep. 33,116,805m. (June 2012); Chair. and CEO HONG KY-TTACK; 69 domestic brs, 16 overseas brs.

Specialized Banks

Industrial Bank of Korea: 50, 2-ga, Ulchi-no, Jung-gu, Seoul 100-758; tel. (2) 729-6114; fax (2) 729-6402; e-mail ifd@ibk.co.kr; internet www.ibk.co.kr; f. 1961; est. as the Small and Medium Industry Bank; 85.5% govt-owned; cap. 3,219,869m., res 7,048,604m., dep. 66,919,658m. (Dec. 2011); Chair. and CEO YOON YONG-RO; 417 domestic brs, 5 overseas brs.

Meritz Investment Bank: Seoul Financial Center, 5th Floor, 84, Taepyeong-no 1-ga, Jung-gu, Seoul 100-768; tel. (2) 777-7711; fax (2) 318-7060; internet home.imeritz.com; f. 1977; fmrly Korean-French Banking Corpn (SogeKo).

Provincial Banks

Daegu Bank Ltd: 118, 2-ga, Susong-dong, Susong-gu, Daegu 706-712; tel. (53) 756-2001; fax (53) 756-2095; internet www.daegubank

.co.kr; f. 1967; cap. 660,625m., res 53,303m., dep. 19,094,668m. (Dec. 2010); Chair. and CEO HA CHUN-SOO; 209 brs.

Jeju Bank: 1349, Ido-1-dong, Jeju 690-021, Jeju Prov.; tel. (64) 720-0200; fax (64) 753-4132; internet www.e-jejubank.com; f. 1969; cap. 110,644m., dep. 2,442,222m. (Dec. 2011); merged with Central Banking Co in 2000, joined the Shinhan Financial Group in 2002; CEO HEO CHANG-GI; 34 brs.

Jeonbuk Bank Ltd: 669-2, Geumam-dong, Deokjin-gu, Jeonju 561-711, N. Jeolla Prov.; tel. (63) 250-7114; fax (63) 250-7078; internet www.jbbank.co.kr; f. 1969; cap. 277,539m., res 17,998m., dep. 6,797,837m. (2010); Chair. and Pres. HONG SUNG-JOO; 74 brs.

Kwangju Bank Ltd: 7-12, Daein-dong, Dong-gu, Gwangju 501-719; tel. (62) 239-5000; fax (62) 239-5199; e-mail kbjint1@nuri.net; internet www.kjbank.com; f. 1968; cap. 247,069m., res 98,899m., dep. 11,424,534m. (Dec. 2010); Pres. and CEO SONG KI-JIN; 124 brs.

Kyongnam Bank: 315 Main St, Masan, Hoiwon-gu, Changwon-si, Gyeongsangnam-do 630-807; tel. (551) 290-8000; fax (551) 294-9426; internet www.knbank.co.kr; f. 1970; est. as Gyeongnam Bank Ltd, name changed 1987; cap. 290,250m., res 120,770m., dep. 16,486,459m. (Dec. 2010); Chair. and CEO PARK YOUNG-BEEN; 155 brs.

Banking Association

Korea Federation of Banks: 19, 1-ga, Myeong-dong, Jung-gu, Seoul 100-021; tel. (2) 3705-5000; fax (2) 3705-5337; e-mail webmaster@kfb.or.kr; internet www.kfb.or.kr; f. 1928; 61 mems; Chair. BAHK BYONG-WON; Vice-Chair. KIM KONG-JIN.

STOCK EXCHANGE

Korea Exchange (KRX): Nulwon Bldg, 825-3, Beomil-dong, Dong-gu, Busan 601-720; tel. (51) 662-2000; fax (51) 662-2478; internet www.krx.co.kr; f. 2005; formed by merger of Korea Stock Exchange, Korea Futures Exchange, Kosdaq Stock Market, Korea Securities Dealers Association; Chair. and CEO KIM BONG-SOO.

INSURANCE

Principal Life Companies

Allianz Life Insurance Co Ltd: Allianz Tower, 45-21, Yeouido-dong, Yeongdeungpo-gu, Seoul 150-978; tel. (2) 3787-7000; e-mail webadmin@allianzlife.co.kr; internet www.allianzlife.co.kr; fmrly Allianz Jeil Life Insurance; formed in 2000 following acquisition of Jeil (First Life) by Allianz Group; renamed as above in 2002; Pres. and CEO MANUEL BAUER.

American International Assurance Korea: Shinil Bldg, 5/F, 64-5, 2-ga, Chungmu-ro, Jung-gu, Seoul; tel. (2) 3707-4800; fax (67) 725-0783; e-mail kr.webmaster@aia.com; internet www.aia.co.kr; f. 1977; Regional Rep. DANIEL LEE COSTELLO.

Dongbu Life Insurance Co Ltd: Dongbu Bldg, 7th Floor, 891-10, Daechi-dong, Gangnam-gu, Seoul 135-820; tel. (2) 1588-3131; fax (2) 3011-4100; internet www.dongbulife.co.kr; f. 1989; CEO LEE TAE-UN.

Hana HSBC Life Insurance Ltd: Hana Bank HQ Bldg, 17/F, 101-1 Ulchiro-1ga, Jung-gu, Seoul 100-191; tel. (2) 3709-7300; fax (2) 755-0668; internet www.hanahsbclife.co.kr; jt venture between HSBC Insurance (Asia-Pacific) Holdings Ltd and Hana Financial Group; CEO DAVID YOON.

Hungkuk Life Insurance Co Ltd: 226, Sinmun-no 1-ga, Jongno-gu, Seoul 100-061; tel. (2) 2002-7000; fax (2) 2002-7804; e-mail webmaster@hungkuk.co.kr; internet www.hungkuk.co.kr; f. 1958; CEO JIN HUN-JIN.

ING Life Insurance Co Korea Ltd: ING Center, 53 Sunhwa-dong, Jung-gu, Seoul 100-130; tel. (2) 3703-9500; fax (2) 734-3309; e-mail webmaster@inglife.co.kr; internet www.inglife.co.kr; f. 1991; Pres. and CEO JOHN WYLIE.

KB Life Insurance Co Ltd: 2–5/F, 16-49, Hangangro-3 ga, Yong-san-gu, Seoul; tel. (2) 398-6800; fax (2) 398-6843; e-mail webmaster@kbli.co.kr; internet www.kbli.co.kr.

Korea Life Insurance Co Ltd: 60, Yeouido-dong, Yeongdeungpo-gu, Seoul 150-603; tel. (2) 789-5114; fax (2) 789-8173; internet www.korealife.com; f. 1946; cap. 3,550,000m. (2002); CEO SHIN EUN-CHUL.

Korean Reinsurance Company: 80, Susong-dong, Jongno-gu, Seoul 110-733; tel. (2) 3702-6000; fax (2) 739-3754; internet www.koreanre.co.kr; f. 1963; cap. 57,000m. (2010); Pres. PARK JONG-WON.

Kumho Life Insurance Co Ltd: 57, 1-ga, Sinmun-no, Jongno-gu, Seoul 110-061; tel. (2) 1588-4040; fax (2) 771-7561; internet www.kumholife.co.kr; f. 1988; acquired Dong-Ah Life Insurance in 2000; cap. 211,249m. (2002); Pres. CHOI BYEONG-GIL.

Kyobo Life Insurance Co Ltd: 1, 1-ga, Jongno, Jongno-gu, Seoul 110-714; tel. (2) 721-2121; fax (2) 737-9970; internet www.kyobo.co

.kr; f. 1958; cap. 102,500m.; Chair. and CEO SHIN CHANG-JAE; 84 main brs.

Life Insurance Association of North America: Seoul City Tower, 14/F, 581, Namdaemunro-5-ga, Jung-gu, Seoul; tel. (2) 3781-1000; fax (2) 792-6063; internet www.lina.co.kr; f. 1987; CEO BENJAMIN HONG.

MetLife Insurance Co of Korea Ltd: Sungwon Bldg, 8/F, 141, Samseong-dong, Gangnam-gu, Seoul 135-716; tel. (2) 3469-9600; fax (2) 3469-9700; internet www.metlifekorea.co.kr; f. 1989; CEO DAMIEN GREEN.

Mirae Asset Life Insurance: Times Sq. Bldg A, 442, 4-ga, Yeongdeungpo-dong, Seoul 150-034; tel. (2) 3271-4114; fax (2) 3271-4400; e-mail msp@miraeasset.com; internet www.miraeassetlife.com; f. 2005; CEO PARK HYEON-JOO.

PCA Life Insurance Co Ltd: PCA Life Tower, 706, Yeoksam-dong, Gangnam-gu, Seoul; tel. (2) 6960-1700; fax (2) 6960-1606; internet www.pcakorea.co.kr; f. 1990; Pres. MIKE BISHOP.

Prudential Life Insurance Co of Korea Ltd: Prudential Bldg, Yeoksam-dong, Gangnam-gu, Seoul; tel. (2) 2144-2000; fax (2) 2144-2100; internet www.prudential.co.kr; f. 1989; cap. 26,400m.; Pres. HWANG OU-JIN.

Samsung Life Insurance Co Ltd: 150, 2-ga, Taepyeong-no, Jung-gu, Seoul 100-716; tel. (2) 751-8000; fax (2) 751-8100; e-mail samsunglife.ir@samsung.com; www.samsunglife.com; f. 1957; cap. 100,000m. (2002); Pres. LEE SOO-CHANG; 1,300 brs.

Shinhan Life Insurance Co Ltd: 120, 2-ga, Taepyeong-no, Jung-gu, Seoul 100-102; tel. (2) 3455-4000; fax (2) 775-3286; internet www.shinhanlife.co.kr; f. 1990; CEO GWEON JEUM-JOO.

Tong Yang Life Insurance Co Ltd: 185, Ulchi-no 2-ga, Jung-gu, Seoul 100-192; tel. (2) 728-9114; fax (2) 728-9563; internet www.myangel.co.kr; f. 1989; Pres. KU JA-HONG.

Woori Aviva Life Insurance Co Ltd: Woori Aviva Life Insurance Bldg, Sujung 3-dong, Dong-gu, Busan 601-716; tel. (2) 2087-9337; fax (2) 2087-93258; internet www.wooriaviva.com; f. 1988; fmrly LIG Life Insurance Co Ltd; name changed as above after joint acquisition by Woori Finance Holdings Co Ltd and Aviva Life Insurance Co; CEO KIM YONG-BOK.

Non-Life Companies

Dongbu Insurance Co Ltd: Dongbu Financial Center, 12/F, 891-10, Daechi-dong, Gangnam-gu, Seoul 135-840; tel. (2) 2262-3450; fax (2) 3001-3159; e-mail dongbu@dongbuinsurance.co.kr; internet www.idongbu.com; f. 1962; cap. 30,000m.; Pres. KIM JING-NAM.

First Fire and Marine Insurance Co Ltd: 12-1, Seosomun-dong, Jung-gu, CPOB 530, Seoul 100-110; tel. (2) 316-8114; fax (2) 771-7319; f. 1949; Pres. KIM WOO-HOANG.

Green Non-Life Insurance Co Ltd: Green Non-Life Insurance Co Bldg, 705-19, Yeoksam-dong, Gangnam-gu, Seoul; tel. (2) 3788-2000; fax (2) 774-8368; internet www.greenfire.co.kr; CEO LEE YOUNG DOO.

Heungkuk Fire and Marine Insurance Co Ltd: 226, Sinmun-no, 1-ga, Jongno-gu, Seoul; tel. (2) 724-9000; fax (2) 774-8368; e-mail sfmi@ssy.insurance.co.kr; internet www.insurance.co.kr; f. 1948; fmrly Ssangyong Fire and Marine Insurance Co; cap. 239,900m.; Pres. KIM YONG-GWON.

Hyundai Marine and Fire Insurance Co Ltd: 178, Sejongno, Jongno-gu, Seoul 110-731; tel. (2) 732-1212; fax (2) 732-5687; e-mail webpd@hdinsurance.co.kr; internet www.hi.co.kr; f. 1955; cap. 30,000m.; Pres. and CEO SEO TAI-CHANG.

Korean Reinsurance Co: 80, Susong-dong, Jongno-gu, Seoul 100-733; tel. (2) 3702-6000; fax (2) 739-3754; e-mail service@koreanre.co.kr; internet www.koreanre.co.kr; f. 1963; cap. 59,100m.; CEO WON JONG-GYU.

Kyobo AXA General Insurance Co Ltd: 395-70, Sindaebang-dong, Dongjak-gu, Seoul; tel. (2) 3479-4900; fax (2) 3479-4800; internet www.kyobodirect.com; fmrly Kyobo Auto Insurance Co Ltd, name changed as above in 2007; Pres. GUY MARCILLAT.

LIG Insurance Co Ltd: 649-11, Yeoksam-dong, Gangnam-gu, Seoul; tel. (2) 310-2391; fax (2) 753-1002; e-mail webmaster@lginsure.com; internet www.lig.co.kr; f. 1959; fmrly LG Insurance Co; CEO KIM BYUNG-HUN.

Lotte Insurance Co Ltd: 51-1, Namchang-dong, Jung-gu, Seoul 100-778; tel. (2) 1588-3344; fax (2) 754-5220; internet www.lotteins.co.kr; f. 1946; cap. 19,500m.; fmrly Dachan Fire and Marine Insurance Co Ltd, name changed as above in 2008; CEO KIM HYUN-SOO.

Meritz Fire and Marine Insurance Co Ltd: 825-2, Yeoksam-dong, Gangnam-gu, Seoul 135-080; tel. (2) 3786-1910; fax (2) 3786-1940; e-mail ir@meritzfire.com; internet www.meritzfire.com; f. 1922; CEO NAM JAE-HO.

Samsung Fire and Marine Insurance Co Ltd: Samsung Insurance Bldg, 87, 1-ga, Ulchi-no, Jung-gu, Seoul 100-191; tel. (2) 758-7948; fax (2) 758-7831; internet www.samsungfire.com; f. 1952; cap. 14,260m.; Pres. AHN MIN-SU.

Seoul Guarantee Insurance Co: 136-74, Yeonchi-dong, Jongno-gu, Seoul 110-470; tel. (2) 3671-7459; fax (2) 3671-7480; internet www.sgic.co.kr; f. 1969; Pres. and CEO KIM OK-CHAN.

Insurance Associations

General Insurance Association of Korea: KRIC Bldg, 6th Floor, 80, Susong-dong, Jongno-gu, Seoul; tel. (2) 3702-8539; fax (2) 3702-8549; e-mail jhero@knia.or.kr; internet www.knia.or.kr; f. 1946; 16 corporate mems; fmrly Korea Non-Life Insurance Asscn; Chair. CHANG NAM-SIK.

Korea Life Insurance Association: Kukdong Bldg, 16th Floor, 60-1, 3-ga, Jungmu-no, Jung-gu, Seoul 100-705; tel. (2) 2262-6685; fax (2) 2262-6580; e-mail info@klia.or.kr; internet www.klia.or.kr; f. 1950; Chair and CEO. LEE SOO-CHANG.

Trade and Industry

GOVERNMENT AGENCIES

Fair Trade Commission: 217, Banpo-dong, Seocho-gu, Seoul; tel. (2) 2023-4248; fax (2) 2023-4241; e-mail kftc@korea.kr; internet www.ftc.go.kr; Chair. KIM DONG-SOO; Sec.-Gen. LEE DONG-KYU.

Federation of Korean Industries: FKI Bldg, 14/F, 28-2, Yeouido-dong, Yeongdeungpo-gu, Seoul 150-756; tel. (2) 3771-0354; fax (2) 3771-0110; e-mail webmaster@fki.or.kr; internet www.fki.or.kr; f. 1961; conducts research and survey work on domestic and overseas economic conditions and trends; advises the Govt and other interested parties on economic matters; exchanges economic and trade missions with other countries; sponsors business conferences; 366 corporate mems and 63 business asscns; Chair. HUH CHANG-SOO.

Korea Appraisal Board: 171-2, Samseong-dong, Gangnam-gu, Seoul; tel. (2) 2189-8000; fax (2) 561-6133; internet www.kab.co.kr; Chair. KWAN JIN-BONG.

Korea Asset Management Corpn (KAMCO): 450, Gangnam-daero, Gangnam-gu, Seoul; tel. (2) 3420-5000; fax (2) 3420-5030; e-mail irkamco@kamco.or.kr; internet www.kamco.or.kr; f. 1963; collection and foreclosure agency; appointed following Asian financial crisis as sole institution to manage and dispose of non-performing loans for financial institutions; Chair. and CEO CHANG YONG-CHUL.

Korea Export Industrial Corpn: 33, Seorin-dong, Jongno-gu, Seoul; tel. (2) 853-5573; f. 1964; encourages industrial exports, provides assistance and operating capital, conducts market surveys; Pres. KIM KI-BAE.

Korea Industrial Research Institutes: FKI Bldg, 28-1, Yeouido-dong, Yeongdeungpo-gu, Seoul; tel. (2) 780-7601; fax (2) 785-5771; f. 1979; analyses industrial and technological information from abroad; Pres. KIM CHAE-KYUM.

Korea Institute for Industrial Economics and Trade (KIET): 66 Hoegi-ro, Dongdaemun-gu, Seoul; tel. (2) 3299-3114; fax (2) 963-8540; e-mail webmaster@kiet.re.kr; internet www.kiet.re.kr; f. 1976; economic and industrial research; Pres. SONG BYOUNG-JUN.

Korea Land and Housing Corpn: 217, Jeongja-dong, Seongnam-shi, Gyeonggi-do; tel. (31) 738-7114; fax (31) 717-5431; internet www.lh.or.kr; f. 1975; land development; est. by merging Korea Land Corpn and Korea National Housing Corpn; CEO LEE JI-SONG.

Korea Resources Corpn (KORES): 606, Siheung-daero, Dongjak-gu, Seoul; tel. (2) 840-5600; e-mail csmaster@kores.or.kr; internet www.kores.or.kr; f. 1967; provides technical and financial support for the national mining industry; Pres. KIM SHIN-JONG.

Korea Trade Insurance Corpn: Seoul Central Bldg, 2/F, 136, Seorin-dong, Jongno-gu, Seoul 110-729; tel. (2) 399-6800; fax (2) 399-7439; internet www.ksure.or.kr; f. 1992; financial support services for traders; fmrly Korea Export Insurance Corpn; Chair. and Pres. RYU CHANG-MOO.

Korea Trade-Investment Promotion Agency (KOTRA): 300-9, Yeomgok-dong, Seocho-gu, Seoul; tel. (2) 3460-7114; fax (2) 3460-7777; e-mail digitalkotra@kotra.or.kr; internet www.kotra.or.kr; f. 1962; various trade promotion activities, market research, cross-border investment promotion, etc.; 102 overseas brs; Pres. OH YOUNG-HO.

Korean Intellectual Property Office: Government Complex-Daejeon Bldg 4, 189, Cheongsa-ro, Seo-gu, Daejeon; tel. (42) 481-5071; fax (42) 472-9314; e-mail kipoicd@kipo.go.kr; internet www.kipo.go.kr; Commissioner LEE SOO-WON.

CHAMBER OF COMMERCE

Korea Chamber of Commerce and Industry: 45, 4-ga, Namdaemun-no, Jung-gu, Seoul 100-743; tel. (2) 6050-3114; fax (2) 6050-3400; e-mail webmaster@korcham.net; internet www.korcham.net; f. 1884; over 47,000 mems; 70 local chambers; promotes development of the economy and of international economic co-operation; Chair. SOHN KYUNG-SHIK.

INDUSTRIAL AND TRADE ASSOCIATIONS

Construction Association of Korea: Construction Bldg, 8th Floor, 71-2, Nonhyon-dong, Gangnam-gu, Seoul 135-701; tel. (2) 3485-0200; fax (2) 542-6264; internet www.cak.or.kr; f. 1947; national licensed contractors' asscn; 6,823 mem. firms (2006); Pres. KWON HONG-SA.

Korea Agro-Fisheries Trade Corpn (aT): aT Center, 232 Yangjae-dong, Seocho-gu, Seoul; tel. (2) 6300-1114; fax (2) 6300-1600; internet www.at.or.kr; f. 1967; fmrly Agricultural and Fishery Marketing Corpn; integrated devt for secondary processing and marketing distribution for agricultural products and fisheries products; Pres. JANG BAE-YOO; Exec. Vice-Pres. KIM JIN-KYU.

Korea Automobile Manufacturers Association (KAMA): 1461-15, Seocho 3-dong, Seocho-gu, Seoul 137-720; tel. (2) 3660-1854; fax (2) 3660-1900; e-mail webmaster@kama.or.kr; internet www.kama.or.kr/index.jsp; f. 1988; Chair. YOUN YEO-CHUL.

Korea Electronics Association: Digital Innovation Center, 11–12/F, 1599, Sangnam-dong, Mapo-gu, Seoul; tel. (2) 6388-6000; fax (2) 6388-6009; e-mail webmaster@gokea.org; internet www.gokea.org; f. 1976; 328 mems; Chair. YUN JONG-YONG.

Korea Federation of Textile Industries: Textile Center, 16/F, 944-31, Daechi 3-dong, Gangnam-gu, Seoul 135-713; tel. (2) 528-4052; fax (2) 528-4069; e-mail kofoti@kofoti.or.kr; internet www.kofoti.or.kr; f. 1980; 50 corporate mems; Chair. CHAN RO-HEE.

Korea Foods Industry Association: 1002-6, Bangbae-dong, Seocho-gu, Seoul; tel. (2) 3470-8100; fax (2) 3471-3492; internet www.kfia.or.kr; f. 1969; 104 corporate mems; Pres. CHUN MYUNG-KE.

Korea Importers Association (KOIMA): 218, Hangang-no, 2-ga, Yeongsan-gu, Seoul 140-875; tel. (2) 792-1581; fax (2) 785-4373; e-mail koima@koima.or.kr; internet www.koima.or.kr; f. 1970; 6,804 mems; Chair. Dr LEE JU-TAE.

Korea International Trade Association: 159-1, Samseong-dong, Gangnam-gu, Seoul; tel. (2) 6000-5114; fax (2) 6000-5115; e-mail kitainfo@kita.net; internet www.kita.org; f. 1946; private, non-profit making business org. representing all licensed traders in South Korea; provides foreign businesses with information, contacts and advice; 80,000 corporate mems; Chair. and CEO HAN DUCK-SOO.

Korea Iron and Steel Association: Posteel Tower, 19th Floor, 735-3, Yeoksam-dong, Gangnam-gu, Seoul; tel. (2) 559-3500; fax (2) 559-3508; internet www.kosa.or.kr; f. 1975; 39 corporate mems; Chair. YOO SANG-BOO.

Korea Oil Association: 28-1, Yeouido-dong, Yeongdeungpo-gu, Seoul; tel. (2) 555-8322; fax (2) 555-7825; e-mail oilassn@yahoo.co.kr; internet www.koreaoil.or.kr; f. 1980; Pres. CHOI DOO-HWAN.

Korea Productivity Center: 122-1, Jeokseon-dong, Jongno-gu, Seoul 110-751; tel. (2) 724-1114; fax (2) 736-0322; internet www.kpc.or.kr; f. 1957; services to increase productivity of industries, consulting services, education and training of specialized personnel; Chair. and CEO CHOI DONG-KYU.

Korea Sericultural Association: 17-9, Yeouido-dong, Yeongdeungpo-gu, Seoul; tel. (2) 783-6072; fax (2) 780-0706; e-mail jamsa@silktopia.or.kr; internet ksa.silktopia.or.kr; f. 1946; improvement and promotion of silk production; 50,227 corporate mems; Pres. PARK DONGCHUI.

Korea Shipbuilders' Association: Landmark Tower, 18/F, 837-36, Yeoksam-dong, Gangnam-gu, Seoul 135-937; tel. (2) 2112-8181; fax (2) 2112-8182; internet www.koshipa.or.kr; f. 1977; 9 mems; Chair. NAM SANG-TAE.

Korea Textiles Trade Association: Textile Center, 16/F, 944-31, Daechi 3-dong, Gangnam-gu, Seoul 135-713; tel. (2) 528-5158; fax (2) 528-5188; e-mail keat@kotis.net; internet www.textra.or.kr; f. 1981; 947 corporate mems; Pres. KANG TAE-SEUNG.

Korean Apparel Industry Association: Textile Center, 16/F, 944-31, Daechi 3-dong, Gangnam-gu, Seoul 135-713; tel. (2) 528-0114; fax (2) 528-0120; internet www.kaia.or.kr; f. 1993; 741 corporate mems; Chair. LEE IN-SUNG.

Mining Association of Korea: 35-24, Dongui-dong, Jongno-gu, Seoul 110; tel. (2) 737-7748; fax (2) 720-5592; f. 1918; 128 corporate mems; Pres. KIM SANG-BONG.

Spinners and Weavers Association of Korea: 43-8, Gwancheol-dong, Jongno-gu, Seoul 110; tel. (2) 735-5741; fax (2) 735-5749; internet www.swak.org; f. 1947; 20 corporate mems; Chair. KIM HYONG-SANG.

EMPLOYERS' ORGANIZATION

Korea Employers' Federation: KEF Bldg, 276-1, Daeheung-dong, Mapo-gu, Seoul 121-726; tel. (2) 3270-7310; fax (2) 3270-7431; e-mail admin@kef.or.kr; internet www.kef.or.kr; f. 1970; advocates employers' interests with regard to labour and social affairs; 13 regional employers' asscns, 20 economic and trade asscns, and 4,000 major enterprises; Dir LEE HYUNG-JOON.

UTILITIES

Electricity

Korea Electric Power Corpn (KEPCO): 167, Samseong-dong, Gangnam-gu, Seoul; tel. (2) 3456-3114; fax (2) 3456-3699; internet www.kepco.co.kr; f. 1961; transmission and distribution of electric power, and development of electric power sources; six power generation subsidiaries formed in 2001; Pres. and CEO CHO HWAN-IK.

Oil and Gas

Daegu City Gas Co Ltd: 2268-1, Namsan 4-dong, Jung-gu, Daegu; tel. (53) 606-1000; fax (53) 606-1004; e-mail kej@taegugas.co.kr; internet www.taegugas.co.kr; f. 1983; Pres. and CEO LEE CHONG-MOO.

Daehan City Gas: 27-1, Daechi-dong, Kangnam-gu, Seoul; tel. (2) 3410-8000; internet www.daehancitygas.com; f. 1978; supplies liquefied natural gas (LNG) to customers in Seoul and Gyeonggi Province; Co-CEOs NAH SEONG-HWA, KIM BOK-HWAN.

GS Caltex: GS Tower, 679 Yeoksam-dong, Gangnam-gu, Seoul; tel. (2) 2005-1114; internet www.gscaltex.com; subsidiary of GS Holdings Corpn; fmrly LG Caltex Oil, renamed as above March 2005; Chair. and CEO HUR DONG-SOO.

Hanjin City Gas: 711, Sanggye 6-dong, Nowon-gu, Seoul; tel. (2) 950-5000; fax (2) 950-5001; e-mail webmaster@daeryunens.com; internet www.daeryunens.com; f. 1985; supplies natural gas to Seoul and Gyeonggi; CEO LEE SEUNG-CHIL.

Incheon City Gas Corpn: 178-24, Gajoa-dong, Seo-gu, Incheon; tel. (32) 1600-0002; fax (32) 576-2710; internet www.icgas.co.kr; f. 1983; CEO PARK DAE-YONG.

Jungbu City Gas Co Ltd: Asan, Chungcheongnam-do; fax (41) 530-1800; f. 1992; Pres. YOO TAE-PEO.

Korea Gas Corpn: 215, Jeongja-dong, Bundang-gu, Seongnam, Gyeonggi-do; tel. (31) 710-0114; fax (31) 710-0117; e-mail kogasmaster@kogas.or.kr; internet www.kogas.or.kr; f. 1983; state-owned; privatization pending; Pres. and CEO CHOO KANG-SOO.

Korea National Oil Corpn (KNOC): 57, Gwanpyeong-ro, 212 Beon-gil, Anyang-S Dongan-gu, Gyeonggi-do; tel. (31) 380-2114; fax (31) 387-9321; e-mail webmaster@knoc.co.kr; internet www.knoc.co.kr; CEO SUH MOON-KYU.

KyungDong City Gas Co: 939, Jinjang-dong, Book-gu, Ulsan; tel. (52) 219-5300; internet www.kdgas.co.kr; distributes liquefied natural gas (LNG) to residential, commercial and industrial customers in Ulsan and Yangsan; CEO SONG JAE-HO.

Kyungnam Energy Co Ltd: 55-5, Ungnam-dong, Changwon, Gyeongsangnam-do 641-290; tel. (55) 260-4432; fax (55) 285-9861; e-mail admin@knenegy.co.kr; internet www.knenergy.co.kr; f. 1972; supplies natural gas to Changwon and the surrounding area; Pres. and CEO CHUNG YEUN-WOOK.

Samchully Co Ltd: 35-6, Yeouido-dong, Yeongdeungpo-gu, Seoul; tel. (2) 368-3300; fax (2) 783-1206; e-mail webmaster@samchully.co.kr; internet www.samchully.co.kr; f. 1966; gas supply co for Seoul metropolitan area and Gyeonggi Prov; Pres. and CEO SHIN MAN-JOONG.

Seoul City Gas Co: 281, Yeomchang-dong, Gangseo-gu, Seoul 157-864; tel. (2) 810-8000; fax (2) 828-6740; internet www.seoulgas.co.kr; f. 1983; distributes gas in Seoul and Gyeonggi Province; Chair. and CEO KIM YOUNG-MIN.

SK E & S: 99, Seorin-dong, Jongno-gu, Seoul; tel. (2) 2121-3114; fax (2) 2121-3198; internet www.skens.net; f. 1999; jt venture between SK Corpn and Enron Corpn (USA); supplies natural gas through various cos, incl.: Chongju City Gas, Chonnam City Gas, Chungnam City Gas, Iksan City Gas, Iksan Energy, Kangwon City Gas, Kumi City Gas and Pusan City Gas; Pres. and CEO MOON DUK-KYU.

Yesco Co Ltd: 249-8, Yongdap-dong, Sungdong-gu, Seoul; tel. (2) 1644-0303; fax (2) 3390-3117; e-mail webmaster@lsyesco.com; internet www.gaspia.com; f. 1981; fmrly Kukdong City Gas Co; part of the LS Group; supplies liquefied natural gas (LNG) to the Seoul metropolitan area; Pres. and CEO CHOI KYUNG-HOON.

Water

Korea Water Resources Corpn: 6-2, Yeonchuk-dong, Daedeok-gu, Daejeon; tel. (42) 629-3114; fax (42) 623-0963; e-mail limetree@kwater.or.kr; internet www.kowaco.or.kr; CEO KIM JUNG-YUN.

Office of Waterworks, Seoul Metropolitan Govt: 27-1 Hap-dong, Seodaemun-gu, Seoul; tel. (2) 390-7332; fax (2) 362-3653; internet arisu.seoul.go.kr; f. 1908; responsible for water supply in Seoul; Head CHOI DONG-YON.

Ulsan City Water and Sewerage Board: 646-4, Sin-Jung 1-dong, Nam-gu, Ulsan; tel. (52) 743-020; fax (52) 746-928; f. 1979; respon-sible for water supply and sewerage in Ulsan; Dir HO KUN-SONG.

CO-OPERATIVES

Korea Auto Industries Co-operative Association: 1638-3, Seo-cho-dong, Seocho-gu, Seoul 137-070; tel. (2) 587-0014; fax (2) 583-7340; e-mail kaica@kaica.or.kr; internet www.kaica.or.kr; f. 1962; Chair. SHIN DAL-CHUK.

Korea Computers Co-operative: 14-8, Yeouido-dong, Yeong-deungpo-gu, Seoul; tel. (2) 780-0511; fax (2) 780-7509; f. 1981; Pres. MIN KYUNG-HYUN.

Korea Federation of Knitting Industry Co-operatives: 586-1, Sinsa-dong, Gangnam-gu, Seoul; tel. (2) 548-2131; fax (2) 3444-9929; e-mail kts01@korea.com; internet www.knit.or.kr; f. 1962; Chair. JOUNG MAN-SUB.

Korea Federation of Non-ferrous Metal Industry Co-operatives: Backsang Bldg, Rm 715, 35-2, Yeouido-dong, Yeong-deungpo-gu, Seoul; tel. (2) 780-8551; fax (2) 784-9473; f. 1962; Chair. PARK WON-SIK.

Korea Federation of Plastic Industry Co-operatives: 146-2, Ssangrim-dong, Jung-gu, Seoul; tel. (2) 2280-8200; fax (2) 2277-3915; internet www.koreaplastic.or.kr; f. 1973.

Korea Federation of Small and Medium Business (Kbiz): 16-2, Yeouido-dong, Yeongdeungpo-gu, Seoul 150-740; tel. (2) 2124-3114; fax (2) 3775-1981; e-mail webmaster@kbiz.or.kr; internet www.kbiz.or.kr; f. 1962; Chair. KIM KI-MUN.

Korea Federation of Weaving Industry Co-operatives: tel. (2) 752-8097; fax (2) 755-6994; e-mail weaving3@hanmail.net; internet www.weaving.or.kr; f. 1964.

Korea Information and Communication Industry Co-operative: tel. (2) 711-2266; fax (2) 7111-2272; e-mail webmaster@kicic.or.kr; internet www.kicic.or.kr; f. 1962; CEO JOO DAE-CHULL.

Korea Metal Industry Co-operative: tel. (2) 780-4411; fax (2) 785-5067; e-mail master@koreametal.or.kr; internet www.koreametal.or.kr; f. 1962.

Korea Mining Industry Co-operative: 35-24, Dongui-dong, Jong-no-gu, Seoul; tel. (2) 735-3490; fax (2) 735-4658; f. 1966; Chair. JEON HYANG-SIK.

Korea Steel Industry Co-operative: 915-14, Bangbae-dong, Seocho-gu, Seoul; tel. (2) 587-3121; fax (2) 588-3671; internet www.kosic.or.kr; f. 1962; Pres. KIM DUK-NAM.

National Agricultural Co-operative Federation (NACF): Saemunangil 91, Jung-gu, Seoul; tel. (2) 2080-5114; fax (2) 1544-2100; internet www.nonghyup.com; f. 1961; international banking, marketing, co-operative trade, utilization and processing, supply, co-operative insurance, banking and credit services, education and research; Chair. CHOI WUN-BYUNG.

National Federation of Fisheries Co-operatives: 11-6, Sincheon-dong, Songpa-gu, Seoul; tel. (2) 2240-2114; fax (2) 2240-3024; e-mail webmaster@suhyup.co.kr; internet www.suhyup.co.kr; f. 1962; CEO LEE JONG-KOO.

TRADE UNIONS

Federation of Korean Trade Unions (FKTU): 35, Yeouido-dong, Yeongdeungpo-gu, Seoul 150-885; tel. (2) 6277-0026; fax (2) 6277-0068; e-mail fktu@fktu.or.kr; internet www.fktu.or.kr; f. 1941; Pres. LEE YONG-DEUK; affiliated to ITUC; 26 affiliated union federations.

Korean Confederation of Trade Unions: 5th Daeyoung Bldg, 139, 2-ga, Yeouido-dong, Yeongdeungpo-gu, Seoul 150-032; tel. (2) 2670-9234; fax (2) 2635-1134; internet www.kctu.org; f. 1995; legalized 1999; Chair. KIM YOUNG-HOON; 600,000 mems.

Transport

RAILWAYS

In 2010 there were 3,379 km of railways in operation. The first phase of construction of a new high-speed rail system connecting Seoul to Busan (412 km) via Cheonan, Daejeon, Daegu and Gyungju was completed in early 2004. The second phase, Daejeon–Busan, became operational in November 2010.

Korean National Railroad (Korail): 293-74 Soje-dong, Dong-gu, Daejeon 300-720; tel. (42) 472-3014; fax (42) 259-2197; e-mail admin@korail.com; internet www.korail.com; f. 1963; operates all railways under the supervision of the Ministry of Land, Infrastructure and Transport; Pres. and CEO CHING CHANG-YOUNG.

City Underground Railways

Busan Subway: Gyotonggongsa 1-ro, Busanjin-gu, Busan 614-722; tel. (51) 640-7186; fax (51) 640-7010; e-mail ipsubway@buta.or.kr; internet www.subway.busan.kr; f. 1988; length of 71.6 km (2 lines, with a further line under construction); Pres. BAE TAE-SOO.

Daegu Metropolitan Transit Corpn: 1500, Sangin 1-dong, Dal-seo-gu, Daegu 704-808; tel. (53) 643-2114; fax (53) 640-2189; e-mail webmaster@daegusubway.co.kr; internet www.dtro.or.kr; length of 57.3 km (two lines, with further routes totalling 125.4 km planned or under construction); CEO BAE SANG-MIN.

Daejeon Metropolitan Express Transit Corpn: tel. (42) 539-3114; fax (42) 539-3119; e-mail qnsdlqkr@hanmail.net; internet www.djet.co.kr; f. 2006; operates one line, with a further four lines planned.

Gwangju Metropolitan Rapid Transit Corpn: 165-27 Mareuk-dong, Seo-gu, Gwangju 502-750; tel. (62) 604-8000; fax (62) 604-8069; internet www.gwangjusubway.co.kr; f. 2004; one line, with a further line planned; Pres. LEE HO-JOON.

Incheon Rapid Transit Corpn: 67-2, Gansok-dong, Namdong-gu, Incheon 405-233; tel. (32) 451-2114; fax (32) 451-2200; e-mail webmaster@ictr.or.kr; internet www.ictr.or.kr; length of 31.1 km (29 stations, 1 line), with two further lines planned; Pres. LEE KWANG-YUONG.

Seoul Metropolitan Rapid Transit Corporation: 133-783, Seongdong-gu, Yongdap-dong 223-3, Seoul; tel. (2) 6311-2200; internet www.smrt.co.kr; operates lines 5–8; Pres. KIM KI-CHUN.

Seoul Metropolitan Subway Corpn: 447-7, Bangbae-dong, Seo-cho-gu, Seoul; tel. (2) 520-5020; fax (2) 520-5039; internet www.seoulsubway.co.kr; f. 1981; length of 134.9 km (115 stations, lines 1–4); Pres. KIM IK-HWAN.

ROADS

In 2012 there were 105,703 km of roads, of which 13,766 km were highways, while 18,162 km were regional roads. A network of motorways (approximately 4,044 km) links all the principal towns, the most important being the 428-km Gyeongbu (Seoul–Busan) motorway. Improvements in relations with North Korea resulted in the commencement of work on a highway to link Seoul and the North Korean capital, Pyongyang, in September 2000. In February 2003 a road link between the two countries was completed.

Korea Expressway Corpn: 293-1, Kumto-dong, Sujong-gu, Seong-nam, Gyeonggi-do 461-703; tel. (822) 2230-4114; fax (822) 2230-4308; internet www.ex.co.kr; f. 1969; responsible for construction, maintenance and management of toll roads; CEO CHANG SEOK-HYO.

SHIPPING

In December 2014 South Korea's flag registered fleet (2,146 vessels) had a total displacement of 12.9m. grt, and included 388 general cargo ships, 305 tankers, 162 bulk carriers, 66 gas tankers and 456 fishing vessels. Major ports include Busan, Incheon, Donghae, Masan, Yeosu, Gunsan, Mokpo, Pohang, Ulsan, Jeju and Gwangyang.

Busan Port Authority: 79-9, Jungangdong 4-ga, Junggu, Busan 600-817; tel. (2) 999-3000; fax (2) 988-8878; e-mail bpmaster@busanpa.com; internet www.busanpa.com; f. 2004; Pres. LIM KI-TACK.

Korea Shipowners' Association: Sejong Bldg, 10th Floor, 100, Dangju-dong, Jongro-gu, Seoul 110-071; tel. (2) 739-1551; fax (2) 739-1558; e-mail korea@shipowners.or.kr; internet www.shipowners.or.kr; f. 1960; 181 shipping co mems (March 2011); Chair. LEE JONG-CHUL.

Korea Shipping Association: 660-10, Dungchon 3-dong, Gangseo-gu, Seoul 157-033; tel. (2) 6096-2000; fax (2) 6096-2029; e-mail kimny@haewoon.co.kr; internet www.haewoon.co.kr; f. 1962; management consulting and investigation, mutual insurance; 1,189 mems; CEO LEE IN-SOO.

Principal Companies

DooYang Line Co Ltd: 170-8, Samseong-dong, Gangnam-gu, Seoul 135-091; tel. (2) 569-7722; fax (2) 550-1777; f. 1984; worldwide tramping and conventional liner trade; Pres. CHO DONG-HYUN.

Hanjin Shipping Ltd: 25-11, Yeouido-dong, Yeongdeungpo-gu, Seoul; tel. (2) 3770-6114; fax (2) 3770-6748; e-mail micaela@hanjin.com; internet www.hanjin.com; f. 1977; marine transport, harbour service, warehousing, shipping and repair, vessel sales, harbour department and cargo service; Chair. and CEO CHOI EUN-YOUNG.

Hyundai Merchant Marine Co Ltd: 1-7, Yeonje-dong, Jongno-gu, Seoul 110-052; tel. (2) 3706-5114; fax (2) 778-4341; internet www.hmm.co.kr; f. 1976; Pres. and CEO LEE SUK-HUI.

Korea Line Corpn: 135-878 KLC Bldg, 145-9, Samseong-dong, Gangnam-gu, Seoul; tel. (2) 3701-0114; fax (2) 733-1610; internet www.korealines.co.kr; f. 1968; worldwide transport service and shipping agency service; Pres. KIM CHANG-SHIK.

STX Pan Ocean Co Ltd: STX Namsan Tower, 631 Namdaemunno 5-ga, Jung-nu, Seoul; tel. (2) 316-5114; fax (2) 316-5209; internet www.stxpanocean.co.kr; f. 1966; transport of passenger cars and trucks, chemical and petroleum products, dry bulk cargo; STX Shipbuilding Co Ltd became the majority shareholder in 2004; CEO PAE SEON-RYUNG.

CIVIL AVIATION

There are international airports at Incheon (Seoul), Gimpo (Seoul), Busan, Jeongju, Daegu, Gwangju, Jeju and Yangyang. The main gateway into Seoul is Incheon International Airport, located 52 km from Seoul, which opened for service in 2001. The second phase of construction was completed in 2008.

Asiana Airlines Inc: 47, Osae-dong, Gangseo-gu, Seoul; tel. (2) 2669-8000; fax (2) 2669-8180; internet flyasiana.com; f. 1988; serves 12 domestic cities and 67 destinations in 20 countries; fmrly Seoul Air International; CEO YOON YOUNG-DOO.

Jeju Air: Jeju; tel. (64) 746-7003; fax (64) 746-7011; internet www .jejuair.net; f. 2005; 25% owned by Jeju provincial govt, 75% by the Aekyung Group; operates low-cost domestic and international services; CEO CHOI KYU-NAM.

Jin Air Co Ltd: 653-25 Deungchon-dong, Gangseo-gu, Seoul; internet www.jinair.com; f. 2008; low-cost subsidiary of Korean Air; CEO KIM JAE-KUN.

Korean Air: 1370, Gonghang-dong, Gangseo-gu, Seoul 157-712; tel. (2) 2656-7857; fax (2) 656-7289; internet www.koreanair.com; f. 1962; est. by the Govt, privately owned since 1969; fmrly Korean Air Lines (KAL); operates domestic and regional services and routes in Asia and to the Americas, Europe, the Far East and the Middle East; Chair. and CEO CHO YANG-HO.

T'way Airlines: 18/F, Tomato Tower, Yeoksam-dong, Gangnam-gu, Seoul; tel. (43) 1599-1090; fax (43) 210-0520; internet www.twayair .com; f. 2004 as Hansung Airlines, relaunched in 2010 under above name; operates low-cost flights between Jeongju and Jeju City; CEO SHIN DONG-CHUN.

Tourism

South Korea's mountain scenery and historic sites are the principal attractions for tourists. Jeju Island, located some 100 km off the southern coast, is a popular resort. In 2011 the city of Pyeongchang was selected to host the 2018 Winter Olympics. The number of visitor arrivals increased by 9.3% in 2013, to some 12.2m. Japan and the People's Republic of China are the leading sources of visitors. Receipts from tourism totalled an estimated US \$14,272m. in 2013.

Korea Tourism Association: KTO Bldg, 8th Floor, 40, Cheonggyecheon-ro, Jung-gu, Seoul 100-180; tel. (2) 757-7485; fax (2) 757-7489; internet www.koreatravel.or.kr; f. 1963; Chair. SHIN JOONG-MOK.

Korea Tourism Organization: KTO Bldg, 40, Cheonggyecheon-ro, Jung-gu, Seoul 100-180; tel. (2) 729-9600; fax (2) 757-5997; e-mail webmaster@mail.knto.or.kr; internet kto.visitkorea.or.kr; f. 1962; est. as International Tourism Corpn; name changed to Korea National Tourism Corpn in 1982 and to Korea National Tourism Organization in 1996, before present name was adopted; Chair. and CEO LEE CHARM.

Defence

As assessed at November 2014, the strength of the active armed forces was 655,000: army 522,000, navy 68,000, air force 65,000. Paramilitary forces included a 3m.-strong civilian defence corps. Military service is compulsory and lasts for 26 months. In November 2014 US forces stationed in South Korea comprised 19,200 army personnel, 250 navy, 8,800 air force and 250 marines.

Defence Expenditure: Budgeted at 35,700,000m. won for 2014.

Chairman of the Joint Chiefs of Staff: Adm. CHOI YUN-HEE.

Chief of Staff (Army): Gen. KIM YO-HWAN.

Chief of Staff (Air Force): Gen. CHOI CHA-GYU.

Chief of Naval Operations: Adm. JUNG HO-SUB.

Education

Education, available free of charge, is compulsory for nine years between the ages of six and 15 years. Enrolment in pre-primary education was 89% in 2011. Primary education begins at six years of age and lasts for six years. In 2012 enrolment at primary schools included 99% of children in the appropriate age-group. Secondary education begins at 12 years of age and lasts for up to six years, comprising two cycles of three years each. Enrolment at secondary schools in 2012 included 96% of children in the relevant age-group. A five-day school week was introduced in 2012. (From 2006 school pupils had been granted two Saturdays off school every month; previously, they had attended school six days every week.) In 2010 there were 179 colleges and universities and 1,098 graduate schools. In 2001, according to UNESCO estimates, the rate of adult literacy averaged 97.9% (males 99.2%, females 96.6%). Budgetary expenditure on education by the central Government in 2013 was 48,263,000m. won, representing 16.3% of total spending.

KOSOVO

Introductory Survey

LOCATION, CLIMATE, LANGUAGE, RELIGION, FLAG, CAPITAL

The Republic of Kosovo (Kosova), formerly the province officially named Kosovo and Metohija within the Republic of Serbia, is situated in the central Balkan peninsula in south-eastern Europe. There are borders with Serbia in the north-west and north-east, the former Yugoslav republic of Macedonia in the south, Albania in the south-west, and Montenegro to the west. The climate is continental. Under a new Constitution, approved in April 2008, the official languages of Kosovo are Albanian and Serbian, while the Turkish, Bosnian and Roma languages are also accorded official status at municipal level. The principal religion in Kosovo is Islam. Serbs are principally adherents of Orthodox Christianity, as represented by the Serbian Orthodox Church. The state flag (proportions 2 by 3) is blue, with an arc of six white stars above a golden map of Kosovo. The capital is Prishtina (Prishtinë—Priština).

CONTEMPORARY POLITICAL HISTORY

Historical Context

Kosovo was part of the Serbian state established by the Nemanja dynasty in 1166. The Serbian Orthodox Patriarchate was established in Kosovo in the 13th century, and the territory was the location of the defeat of the Serbs by the Turkish Ottoman Empire at Fushë Kosovë (Kosovo Polje—'the Field of Blackbirds') in 1389. After continued Albanian resistance to Ottoman rule, the League of Prizren political organization was established in 1878. Kosovo remained under Ottoman rule until its annexation by Serbia during the First Balkan War in 1912. During the Second World War (1939–45) Kosovo was annexed by Albania (in personal union with the Italian Crown). Following the establishment of the Federative People's Republic of Yugoslavia, the 1946 Constitution provided for the establishment of Kosovo and Metohija (as the region was renamed) and the northern territory of Vojvodina as autonomous units within Serbia. In 1963 the autonomous region of Kosovo and Metohija was formally upgraded in status to that of an autonomous province, a status that was confirmed by the 1974 Constitution, which also renamed the territory as Kosovo and increased the powers of the two autonomous provinces at the federal level of the state.

From the mid-1980s increasing Serb nationalism, and the rise to power of Slobodan Milošević (President of Serbia in 1989–97), exacerbated tensions in the province. A new Serbian Constitution, adopted in 1990, revoked the autonomy of Kosovo and Vojvodina; this was confirmed by the April 1992 Constitution that created the Federal Republic of Yugoslavia (FRY). A republic-wide referendum, largely boycotted by the ethnic Albanians, was conducted on 2 July 1990, when a majority of Serbs approved the new Constitution. It was formally promulgated on 28 September, whereupon the designation of Kosovo reverted to that of Kosovo and Metohija. Following the constitutional referendum, 114 of 180 deputies in the Kuvendi i Kosovës/Skupština Kosova (Kosovo Assembly) met and declared Kosovo independent of Serbia. On 5 July the Serbian authorities dissolved the provincial Assembly and Government. The Kosovo presidency resigned in protest, and Serbia introduced a special administration. On 7 September members of the former representative body declared the Kosovo Assembly to have been reconvened and subsequently proclaimed a basic law of a 'Republic of Kosovo'. Meanwhile, elections, declared illegal by the Serbian authorities, were held in the province on 24 May. The Lidhja Demokratike e Kosovës (LDK—Democratic League of Kosovo) secured the most seats in the 130-member Assembly, and the LDK leader, Ibrahim Rugova, was elected President of the self-proclaimed 'Republic of Kosovo'.

Domestic Political Affairs

Throughout the mid-1990s there were reports of harassment of Kosovo Albanians by Serbian police. In early 1996 an ethnic Albanian militant organization, the Ushtria Çlirimtare e Kosovës (UÇK—Kosovo Liberation Army), announced its intention to achieve independence for Kosovo through armed resistance against the Serbian authorities, and began attacks against security forces. Special Serbian security units undertook reprisals.

Negotiations regarding the implementation of a ceasefire in Kosovo and the withdrawal of Serbian forces were conducted throughout 1998. In October, following a North Atlantic Treaty Organization (NATO, see p. 367) ultimatum, Milošević, President of the FRY (Serbia and Montenegro) since the previous year, agreed to the presence in Kosovo of an Organization for Security and Co-operation in Europe (OSCE, see p. 385) mission, which began deployment in early November. Nevertheless, armed clashes between Serbian forces and the UÇK increased. In January 1999 the bodies of 45 Albanians were discovered in the village of Reçak (Račak), increasing international concerns of a humanitarian crisis. In February a peace conference in Rambouillet, France, attended by Serbian and ethnic Albanian delegations, including UÇK representatives, commenced. Although the Albanian delegation signed a peace agreement on 18 March, the Serbian delegation continued to present objections to the plan. On 23 March the Serbian legislature adopted a resolution condemning aggression against its country and opposing the deployment of NATO forces in Kosovo.

On 24 March 1999 a NATO-led aerial bombardment of military and civilian installations in the FRY commenced. Serbian security forces in Kosovo subsequently conducted mass expulsions and large-scale massacres of the Albanian civilian population. According to the Office of the UN High Commissioner for Refugees (UNHCR), a total of 848,100 Albanians fled or were expelled from Kosovo. On 3 June a peace agreement providing for the withdrawal of Serbian forces from Kosovo and the deployment of a joint NATO-Russian peacekeeping force was approved by the Serbian legislature. On 10 June, following a Military Technical Agreement between NATO and the Federal Government, the withdrawal of Serbian forces from Kosovo commenced, and NATO officially suspended its air operations. On the same day a UN Security Council resolution was approved, authorizing the deployment of international civil and security presences in Kosovo, and providing for the establishment of the UN Interim Administration Mission in Kosovo (UNMIK) as the supreme legal and executive authority in the region. On 12 June both Russian and NATO troops entered Kosovo. By 20 June the Serb withdrawal had been completed and the multinational NATO-led Kosovo Force (KFOR), which had an authorized strength of up to 50,000 personnel, was established. Some three weeks after the end of the conflict, an estimated 600,000 Albanians had returned to Kosovo. Over the same period some 180,000 Serbs and Roma fled the province.

Kosovo under UN administration

In February 2000 Rugova announced the dissolution of the 'Republic of Kosovo'. In local government elections, held in Kosovo on 28 October, Rugova's reconstituted LDK secured 58% of the votes cast to 30 municipal councils, while the Partia Demokratike e Kosovës (PDK—Democratic Party of Kosovo), led by a former UÇK commander, Hashim Thaçi, won 27% of the votes. Elections to 100 seats of the 120-member Kosovo Assembly were conducted on 17 November 2001, under a UNMIK programme for establishing partial and provisional self-government in the province. (The remaining 20 seats were reserved for representatives of Serbs and other minority ethnic groups.) The LDK secured 47 seats, while the PDK won 26 seats and a coalition of Serb parties 22 seats. On 4 March 2002, following protracted inter-party discussions, Rugova was elected President of Kosovo. Under a coalition agreement, a member of the PDK, Bajram Rexhepi, became Prime Minister, and a Government was subsequently established. In April the Serb coalition agreed to join the administration.

In March 2004 the deaths of three Albanian boys, who had allegedly been pursued by a group of Serbs into the Ibar River, precipitated rioting in Mitrovicë (Kosovska Mitrovica), escalating into several days of clashes between the Serbian and Albanian communities throughout Kosovo. Some 2,000 KFOR reinforcements were dispatched to quell the violence, in which 11

Albanians and eight Serbs were killed. At elections to the Kosovo Assembly on 23 October, the LDK secured 45.4% of the votes cast, retaining 47 seats in the 120-member legislature. The PDK won 28.9% of the votes, increasing its representation to 30 seats, while the Aleanca për Ardhmërinë e Kosovës (AAK—Alliance for the Future of Kosovo) obtained 8.4% of the votes and nine seats. The LDK negotiated a coalition agreement, whereby the leader of the AAK, Ramush Haradinaj, became the new Prime Minister on 3 December. The election of Haradinaj, a former senior UÇK leader who had been under investigation by the International Criminal Tribunal for the former Yugoslavia (ICTY, see p. 22) for alleged war crimes in Kosovo, was strongly criticized by Serb parties. Although an overall participation rate of 53.6% of the registered electorate was recorded, only about 0.3% of the Serb community voted. (Serbs retained an allocation of 10 seats in the Assembly, but continued to boycott the provisional institutions.) On 8 March 2005 Haradinaj, indicted by the ICTY on a total of 37 charges, resigned as Prime Minister and surrendered to the Tribunal, amid widespread protests. On 23 March a new Government, led by Bajram Kosumi, also of the AAK, was established. (In April 2008 the ICTY acquitted Haradinaj.)

The resolution of Kosovo's future status became an increasingly pressing issue. On 4 October 2005 a UN Special Envoy submitted a review to the Secretary-General of the organization, stating that the Kosovo Government had made significant progress towards establishing executive, legislative and judicial institutions. On 24 October the UN Security Council endorsed the initiation of final status negotiations on Kosovo. In November the Serbian Government adopted a resolution rejecting the independence of Kosovo, while the Kosovo Assembly approved a motion stating that it would accept only independence as the final status of the territory. Later that month former Finnish President Martti Ahtisaari, who had been appointed UN Special Envoy for the Future Status Process for Kosovo, commenced separate discussions with Serbian and Kosovo leaders. Following Rugova's death on 21 January 2006, on 10 February Fatmir Sejdiu of the LDK was elected unopposed as the new President by the Kosovo Assembly. On 1 March Kosumi resigned as Prime Minister. Nine days later, the Kosovo Assembly approved Agim Çeku, a former UÇK chief of staff, as his successor. Meanwhile, final status negotiations between Kosovo and Serbian government delegations commenced in Vienna, Austria, on 20–21 February. The Presidents and Prime Ministers of Serbia and Kosovo attended the discussions in Vienna for the first time in July; the Kosovo delegation reiterated demands for full independence for the province, while the Serbian leaders maintained that Serbia would not accept a loss of territory.

On 2 February 2007 Ahtisaari presented his recommendations for the future status of Kosovo. After discussions on the draft in Vienna ended without success in March, Ahtisaari concluded that there was no prospect of achieving a negotiated agreement. On 26 March Ahtisaari submitted to the UN Security Council the finalized Comprehensive Proposal for the Kosovo Status Settlement, which recommended independence for the province, initially under international military and civilian supervision. Kosovo was to adopt a constitution, flag and anthem, and be granted rights to membership of international organizations; the rights of minority groups living in the province were to be protected. An International Civilian Representative, operating under a UN and European Union (EU, see p. 271) mandate, would be appointed to supervise the implementation of the Settlement, and would be empowered to veto legislation and dismiss local officials. KFOR would continue to provide security in the province, while the EU would deploy a police mission to assist in the development of institutions of law enforcement. On 3 April the Serbian premier announced to the UN Security Council that Serbia rejected the Proposal. On 5 April Ahtisaari's Proposal was approved by 100 of the 101 votes cast in the Kosovo Assembly. A series of negotiations between the Serbian and Kosovo delegations from August failed to resolve the impasse. On 10 December the UN Secretary-General was informed that no agreement could be reached.

Meanwhile, legislative elections were conducted in Kosovo on 17 November 2007. According to official results, the PDK secured the highest number of votes cast, with 34.3% of the total, taking 37 seats in the Assembly, while the LDK received some 22.6% of the votes and 25 seats. With a boycott of the elections by Serb parties, a participation rate of about 43% of the electorate was recorded. Following a coalition agreement between the PDK and the LDK, on 9 January 2008 a Government headed by Thaçi, and comprising eight members of the PDK, six members of the LDK,

two representatives of Serb groups and one representative of the ethnic Turkish community, was approved by the Assembly. With both main ruling parties in favour of independence, Thaçi confirmed to the Assembly that a declaration of independence was imminent. On the same day Sejdiu was re-elected President in a third round of voting in the Assembly for a term that was extended to five years. Jakup Krasniqi of the PDK was elected President of the Assembly.

Declaration of independence

On 17 February 2008 the Assembly of Kosovo endorsed a declaration establishing the province as the Republic of Kosovo (Kosova), a sovereign state independent from Serbia, the resolution adopted being based on Ahtisaari's Comprehensive Proposal for the Kosovo Status Settlement and in accordance with UN Security Council Resolution 1244 (of 1999). Serbia immediately protested that the declaration of independence contravened international law and demanded that it be annulled. An emergency meeting of the UN Security Council failed to agree on a new resolution, with Russia, in continued support of Serbia, and the People's Republic of China opposing Kosovo's sovereignty. Several countries, including Albania, France, the USA and the United Kingdom, extended recognition to Kosovo on 18 February, and were rapidly followed by a number of other states. On 28 February the International Steering Group for Kosovo appointed a Dutch diplomat, Pieter Feith, already the EU Special Representative, as an International Civilian Representative, to supervise the implementation of the Settlement. An EU Rule of Law Mission in Kosovo (EULEX), comprising some 1,900 foreign personnel, was to be deployed in Kosovo to support the authorities in maintaining public order. In March a member of UNMIK was killed in fierce clashes between Serb protesters and UNMIK and KFOR troops in Mitrovica. Also in March Serbia announced that it intended to submit a legal challenge against Kosovo's declaration of independence at the International Court of Justice (ICJ, see p. 25) in The Hague, Netherlands. A new Constitution, which had been drafted by a Constitutional Commission in accordance with the principles of the Settlement, was adopted by the Assembly on 9 April, after being approved by Feith. The Constitution, which declared Kosovo to be an independent and sovereign state, was to enter into effect on 15 June, when UNMIK was officially to transfer its functions to the Kosovo authorities. However, it became increasingly evident that the deployment of EULEX would not proceed as envisaged, owing to the refusal of Kosovo Serbs and the Serbian Government to accept an EU mission. A report by the UN Secretary-General, published in April, stated that UNMIK's mandate would remain in force under Resolution 1244, pending a further decision by the UN Security Council.

The new Constitution entered into effect on 15 June 2008, as scheduled. The NATO Secretary-General announced that the remaining KFOR contingent was to organize the dissolution of the Kosovo Protection Corps (KPC—formed in 1999 largely on the basis of the UÇK) and the establishment of a 2,500-member multi-ethnic Kosovo Security Force. Following polls conducted among Kosovo Serbs on 11 May 2008, without the recognition of the Kosovo Government, but supported by Serbia, on 28 June a parallel legislature comprising representatives of the Serb community from 26 municipalities, the 'Assembly of the Community of Municipalities of the Autonomous Province of Kosovo and Metohija', was convened in Mitrovica. In September it was announced that Kosovo had appointed its first 10 envoys to countries that had recognized its statehood, while a number of diplomatic missions in Prishtina had become embassies. In October the UN General Assembly, in support of Serbia, voted in favour of referring to the ICJ the issue of whether Kosovo's unilateral declaration of independence from Serbia was in accordance with international law.

Following the continued refusal of Kosovo Serbs to accept the deployment of EULEX, on 26 November 2008 the UN Security Council endorsed an amended plan presented by the UN Secretary-General on the reconfiguration of the international presence in Kosovo, under which officials in the Serb-majority areas would receive directives from a reduced UNMIK contingent, while those in Albanian-majority areas would be the responsibility of EULEX. On 9 December EULEX began deployment throughout the country, including in Mitrovica; it was later confirmed that a reduced UNMIK presence was to remain in the country indefinitely under Resolution 1244. In January 2009 the KPC was dissolved and replaced by the Kosovo Security Force. On the first anniversary of Kosovo's declaration of independence, 80 opposition deputies of the Serbian legislature joined the

Kosovo Serb 'Assembly' in approving a declaration affirming the constitutional status of Kosovo within Serbia and rejecting the activities of the Kosovo institutions.

In June 2009 former Prime Minister Agim Çeku was arrested in Bulgaria, under an international warrant issued by Serbia for alleged war crimes committed while he was a UÇK military commander; however, a Bulgarian court rejected the request for Çeku's extradition and he returned to Kosovo.

The first elections since independence to elect councils and mayors in Kosovo's 36 municipalities (including six new municipalities) took place on 15 November 2009. Voter turnout was 45.4%, after a Serb boycott urged by the Serbian Government was only partially observed. A mission from the European Network of Election Monitoring Organizations concluded that the elections had generally met international standards. A second round of voting was conducted on 13 December. According to the Central Election Commission (CEC), the PDK secured the largest number of municipalities, with 16. Voting was repeated in two municipalities on 31 January 2010, and in a further constituency on 14 March, after allegations of irregularities were upheld.

In March 2010 the PDK and the LDK agreed to the replacement of three ministers from each party in a government reorganization; notably, former Prime Minister Bajram Rexhepi was appointed as the new Minister of Internal Affairs. On 30 May unauthorized elections were organized to the Serb 'Assembly' in Mitrovica. In July one protester was killed when two bombs were thrown into a crowd of Kosovo Serbs who were demonstrating against the Government's plan to open an office in Mitrovica. Later that month the appeals chamber of the ICTY overturned the acquittal of Haradinaj and an associate in April 2008, on the grounds that witnesses had been intimidated, and ordered their retrial.

On 22 July 2010 the ICJ issued a non-binding, advisory opinion that Kosovo's declaration of independence had breached neither international law nor UN Security Council Resolution 1244; nevertheless, Serbia reaffirmed its intention to continue to withhold recognition of the independence of Kosovo. In early September the UN General Assembly adopted a resolution, supported by Serbia and the 27 EU member states, urging a direct dialogue between Serbia and Kosovo on ensuing issues. On 27 September Sejdiu tendered his resignation as President of Kosovo, following a ruling by the Constitutional Council that holding the office was incompatible with his chairmanship of the LDK. In October Sejdiu withdrew the LDK from the coalition Government, which consequently lost its majority in the Assembly. In November the Assembly adopted a motion of no confidence in the Government, after Thaçi urged PDK deputies to support it and thereby bring an end to the institutional crisis; early legislative elections were subsequently scheduled for 12 December. On 7 November the mayor of Prishtina, Isa Mustafa, was elected Chairman of the LDK, replacing Sejdiu.

In December 2010 Swiss senator and Council of Europe rapporteur Dick Marty presented a report (adopted by the Parliamentary Assembly of the Council of Europe) containing allegations of war crimes and organized crime during and after the 1999 conflict in Kosovo. An EU Special Investigative Task Force (SITF) was established in September 2011 to conduct an independent investigation.

Early legislative elections

The legislative elections on 12 December 2010 were monitored by officials from embassies in Kosovo, together with local observers; Serb voters again boycotted the elections. Following allegations by all parties of voter intimidation and major electoral irregularities, complaints were upheld in five municipalities, where polls were repeated on 9 January and (in the case of Mitrovica) on 23 January 2011. The final election results were released by the CEC on 7 February: the PDK, with 32.1% of the votes cast, secured 34 seats, while the LDK won 24.7% of the votes and 27 seats; an ethnic Albanian nationalist party, Vetëvendosje! (VV—Self-Determination!), was placed third, with 12.7% of the votes and 14 seats, followed by the AAK, with 11.0% and 12 seats, and a coalition led by the Aleanca Kosova e Re (AKR—New Kosovo Alliance), with 7.3% and eight seats. A voter turnout of about 45% was recorded. On 22 February, under a coalition agreement reached between the PDK and the AKR, a construction industry magnate and President of the AKR, Behgjet Pacolli, was elected unopposed as the President of Kosovo in a third round of voting in the new Assembly (with opposition parties boycotting the session). On the same day Thaçi was re-elected as Prime Minister and the appointment of a new coalition Government was

approved. The five Deputy Prime Ministers in the new administration included for the first time a Kosovo Serb, the Chairman of the Samostalna Liberalna Stranka (SLS—Independent Liberal Party), Slobodan Petrović. In March Kosovo and Serbian delegations began an EU-supported dialogue in Brussels, Belgium, which was subsequently endorsed by a resolution in the Kosovo Assembly. Following a challenge by the LDK, on 28 March the Constitutional Court ruled the election of Pacolli to be illegitimate, owing to the absence of the requisite parliamentary quorum; Pacolli resigned from the presidency on 30 March. Following an unprecedented agreement between the PDK, the LDK and the AKR on a consensus candidate, on 7 April the deputy director of the Kosovo police, Maj.-Gen. Atifete Jahjaga, was elected President with 80 of 100 votes cast in the Assembly, becoming the country's first female head of state. The Government announced that Jahjaga would serve in an interim capacity (pending constitutional reforms that would allow the direct election of a President). Pacolli was subsequently appointed as First Deputy Prime Minister.

In July 2011 a Kosovo special police officer was killed by Kosovo Serbs, who resisted an attempt by the police to assume control of two crossing-points at the border with Serbia, which were supervised by KFOR and EULEX. Kosovo Serbs continued to obstruct government efforts to establish authority throughout the state; in September EULEX units were deployed to take control of two border posts after local Serbs erected road blocks. In November some 30 members of KFOR were injured in clashes with Serbs, following an attempt by the troops to dismantle a road block preventing Kosovo police and customs officers from gaining access to border crossing-points. Serbian President Boris Tadić (who aspired to secure EU candidate status for Serbia) subsequently urged Serb protesters to remove the barricades. On 2 December the ongoing discussions in Brussels resulted in an agreement that would allow Kosovo officials to establish control of the border crossing-points, although most of the road blocks subsequently remained in place. In January 2012 the Serbian Government urged Kosovo Serbs in four northern municipalities to abandon a planned referendum; nevertheless, the non-binding plebiscite took place on 14–15 February, with 99.7% of those participating in the municipalities rejecting the authority of Kosovo state institutions. On 15 February the Kosovo Assembly adopted a resolution declaring the referendum to be illegal.

On 18 February 2012 the Kosovo Government signed a Status of Forces Agreement with the USA. The barricades at the border with Serbia were removed on 23 February, following an agreement between the Serb authorities in northern Kosovo and EULEX, which allowed the mission free movement in the region. Also in February it was announced that the negotiations in Brussels had resulted in a significant compromise that Kosovo be represented in regional meetings under the name 'Kosovo', rather than 'Kosovo-UNMIK' (with an explanatory addendum). Following his election to the Serbian presidency in May, nationalist Tomislav Nikolić indicated that he would make no concessions regarding Serbia's perceived claim to Kosovo. In early June the Kosovo Government announced that the discussions in Brussels had effectively been suspended, owing to the failure to implement the measures already agreed.

Unsupervised independence

Following an official visit to Kosovo by UN Secretary-General Ban Ki-Moon on 24 June 2012, the International Steering Group announced on 2 July that Kosovo's period of supervised independence would end in September, three months earlier than anticipated. On 11 July Thaçi submitted an application for membership of NATO's 'Partnership for Peace' (see p. 371) programme. Also in July the Constitutional Court ruled that the parliamentary resolution of April 2011, which had elected Jahjaga as President on an interim basis, had been illegitimate (thereby entitling her to remain in office until 2016).

On 7 September 2012 the Assembly adopted a number of constitutional amendments required in order to permit the end of supervised independence. Kosovo officially attained full independence on 10 September, with the closure of the International Civilian Office; however, under an agreement reached between the Kosovo Government and the EU on 1 August, the mandate of EULEX had been renewed until June 2014, while KFOR troops and a small UNMIK contingent also remained in the country. Following EU and US pressure, in October 2012 dialogue on the normalization of relations between Kosovo and Serbia formally resumed in Brussels, with a meeting between Thaçi and the new Serbian Prime Minister, Ivica Dačić. VV organized a further protest against the negotiations in Prishtina. A border management agreement between Kosovo and Serbia, providing for the opening of crossing-points, was reached in November. Meanwhile, on 29 November Haradinaj was acquitted following his retrial at the ICTY. In the same month, however, public protests followed a Kosovo Supreme Court order for the retrial of PDK Deputy Chairman Fatmir Limaj and a further three former members of the UÇK, who had been acquitted earlier that year following charges of committing war crimes during 1997–99.

In January 2013 the EU-mediated discussions resulted in Kosovo's appointment of a liaison officer to Serbia, the hitherto ambassador to Sweden, Lulzim Peci; the Serbian Government subsequently appointed a counterpart, Dejan Pavićević. In the same month, however, Kosovo Serbs in the north erected further road blocks, and continued attacks were staged on Kosovo government targets in Prishtina, in protest against the negotiations in Brussels. In February Jahjaga and Nikolić met for the first time, with EU mediation, in Brussels; both Presidents pledged commitment to continued dialogue, which subsequently gained momentum, as the Serbian Government sought to secure the opening of EU accession negotiations. The EU High Representative for Foreign Affairs and Security Policy, Catherine Ashton, visited Prishtina in March, and subsequently declared that the two sides were close to agreement on the dismantling of the Serb 'Assembly', financed by Serbia, in northern Kosovo, and the operation of a legitimate 'Association of Serbian Municipalities'.

Agreement with Serbia

On 19 April 2013 Thaçi and Dačić initialled an accord in Brussels, which confirmed that ethnic Serb-dominated northern Kosovo was to be administered by the central authorities, while retaining autonomy in a number of areas, including powers to appoint a police commander for the region, and to establish a separate court of appeal; the agreement also allowed both Kosovo and Serbia to seek EU accession without obstruction. On 16 May the hitherto Minister of Economic Development, Besim Beqaj, was appointed Minister of Finance, following the resignation in January of Bedri Hamza (who was subsequently appointed Governor of the Central Bank); Beqaj was succeeded in his former post by Fadil Ismajli. On 22 May Dačić and Thaçi signed an agreement in Brussels on implementation of the EU-mediated accord, under which all members of Serb security bodies in Kosovo would be integrated into the state structures. In June Kosovo and Serbia formally exchanged the envoys appointed earlier that year, Peci and Pavićević, who were based at EU offices in the respective capitals. Amid protests organized by VV (which opposed perceived concessions made to the Serb population), on 27 June the Assembly ratified the accord with Serbia, with 84 votes cast in favour (and three against). On the following day the EU Council authorized the opening of negotiations on a Stabilization and Association Agreement (SAA). As part of reconciliation efforts, on 11 July the Assembly adopted legislation granting amnesty from prosecution for various crimes, including armed rebellion, that had not resulted in death or injury. Following a challenge by VV, on 3 September the Constitutional Court ruled that both the agreement with Serbia and the amnesty legislation were in accordance with the Constitution. Later that month a EULEX customs officer was shot dead in northern Kosovo.

Local government elections on 3 November and 1 December 2013 were contested for the first time by representatives of the Serb population in the north, which had formed the Građanska Inicijativa Srbija (GIS—Civic Initiative of Serbia). Voting was disrupted by violence in North Mitrovicë and in the predominantly Serb municipality of Partesh, where polls were repeated. According to the CEC, the PDK won a majority in 11 municipalities, the LDK in nine and the GIS in eight, although VV secured control of Prishtina (previously held by the LDK). Meanwhile, protests were staged in November by former UÇK supporters in Prishtina, after EULEX indicted 15 former UÇK combatants, including a mayor and the ambassador to Albania, for war crimes. Further discussions between Thaçi and Dačić in Brussels in December resulted in agreement on a number of issues, including the recruitment of Serbs to the Kosovo police force. However, in March the Serbian Government expressed objections to plans by the Kosovo authorities for the Kosovo Security Force to be reconstituted as regular armed forces by 2019, subject to approval by the Assembly. According to the OSCE, 34.4% of eligible voters in Kosovo participated in Serbia's legislative elections on 16 March 2014. In April the Assembly adopted legislation providing for the establishment of a special court to investigate allegations of war crimes by former members of the UÇK; it also voted in favour of extending EULEX's

mandate until June 2016. After Serb deputies boycotted a parliamentary vote on the creation of the national armed forces, the main political leaders decided that early legislative elections would be held, and on 7 May 2014 the Assembly was dissolved, in advance of elections in June.

Recent developments: early elections and political unrest

Elections to the Assembly were conducted on 8 June 2014. According to the official results, Thaçi's PDK received 37 of the 120 seats and 30.4% of the votes (in coalition with four smaller parties). The LDK was placed second, with 30 seats and 25.2%, and Vetëvendosje! third, with 16 seats and 13.6%. The AAK obtained 11 seats and 9.5%, and the Srpska Lista (Serb List) obtained 5.2% and nine seats. The Nisma për Kosovën (NISMA—Initiative for Kosovo), established at the end of February by former members of the PDK, obtained 5.2% and six seats. Thaçi's PDK had failed to secure a parliamentary majority, and its constitutional right to form a new government was challenged by an alliance that was formed after the elections by the LDK, the AAK and the NISMA, with the support of Vetëvendosje!, and headed by Haradinaj; the appointment of LDK Chairman Mustafa as President of the Kosovo Assembly, with the support of deputies from the newly allied parties, was overruled by the Constitutional Court, which confirmed that a member of the PDK (as the party with the most seats in the Assembly according to the results of the general election) should fill the post. Following five months of negotiations, in mid-November President Jahjaga mediated a compromise agreement between Thaçi and Mustafa, which allowed for a new coalition government to be formed. On 8 December Kadri Veseli of the PDK was elected as President of the Kosovo Assembly, and on the following day a new Government, led by Mustafa, was approved in the Assembly; Thaçi was allocated the post of Deputy Prime Minister and Minister of Foreign Affairs, and representatives of, respectively, the LDK and the Srpska Lista also received deputy premierships.

Unrest was prompted by controversy over the loss-making Trepça mining complex in Mitrovica in January 2015: government plans to transfer it to state control were contested by Serbia, which claimed ownership of 75% of the complex and threatened that the measure would damage the ongoing EU-mediated discussions. Consequently, at a parliamentary session on 19 January the Government revoked draft legislation, under which Trepça would have been transformed into a public enterprise. Some 350 miners at Trepça subsequently staged strike action in protest against the decision. Vetëvendosje! announced a series of protests to demand that the nationalization of Trepça proceed and that the ethnic Serb Minister of Communities and Resettlement, Aleksandër Jabllanoviq, resign, after he referred disparagingly to Albanian protesters who had prevented Serbs from entering an Orthodox church in the western town of Gjakova. On 27 January opposition rallies in central Prishtina degenerated into violence (considered to be the worst since 2008), in which some 170 people were injured. The Government attributed responsibility for the violence to opposition leaders, accusing them of attempting to seize power. On 3 February Mustafa announced that Jabllanoviq had been removed from the Government. Jabllanoviq's Srpska Lista party subsequently threatened to withdraw from the ruling coalition, and commenced a boycott of the Assembly. In early February normalization discussions between the Kosovo and Serbian delegations resumed in Brussels, with EU mediation, for the first time since March 2014, at which agreement was reached on the integration of courts in the north into the central judiciary. However, the Kosovo authorities subsequently announced the intention to initiate a lawsuit against Serbia for genocide and damages caused during 1998–99; a resolution to that effect, drafted by the PDK, was submitted to the Assembly in March 2015. On 8 April the ministers responsible for foreign affairs in Croatia and Kosovo met in the Croatian capital, Zagreb, where a European partnership agreement was signed. On 24 April Mustafa appointed Dalibor Jevtić of Srpska Lista as the new Minister of Communities and Resettlement. Three days later the Srpska Lista ended its boycott of the Assembly. At the end of April the European Commission adopted the SAA with Kosovo, which had been initialled in July 2014.

CONSTITUTION AND GOVERNMENT

A new Constitution entered into effect in Kosovo on 15 June 2008, after the Kuvendi i Kosovës/Skupština Kosova (Kosovo

Assembly) adopted a declaration of independence on 17 February. This declaration was based on the Comprehensive Proposal for the Kosovo Status Settlement drawn up by the UN Special Envoy of the Secretary-General for the Future Status Process for Kosovo, Martti Ahtisaari, and in accordance with UN Security Council Resolution 1244 (of 1999). An European Union (EU, see p. 271) Rule of Law Mission in Kosovo (EULEX), which became operational under the overall authority of the UN in December, was deployed in Kosovo to maintain public order and security, and to assist in the development of judicial institutions. A reduced UN Interim Administration Mission in Kosovo (UNMIK) remained in the country under Resolution 1244. Kosovo's period of supervised independence officially ended on 10 September 2012, with the closure of the International Civilian Office.

Under the Constitution, the Kosovo Assembly comprises 120 deputies, of whom 100 are directly elected (the remaining 20 seats are reserved for the elected representatives of specified minority ethnic communities, including eight allocated to Serbs). The Assembly has a nine-member Presidency. The President of Kosovo is elected by the Assembly for a five-year term (renewable only once). The President nominates a Prime Minister, who proposes a Government, for approval by the Assembly. Kosovo comprises seven regions, which are divided into 38 municipalities.

REGIONAL AND INTERNATIONAL CO-OPERATION

Following Kosovo's unilateral declaration of independence on 17 February 2008, a total of 110 UN member states, including 22 of the 27 member states of the European Union (EU, see p. 271), recognized Kosovo as an independent sovereign state at April 2015. Kosovo joined the Central European Free Trade Agreement (CEFTA, see p. 445) in July 2007, and the European Bank for Reconstruction and Development (EBRD, see p. 266) in December 2012.

ECONOMIC AFFAIRS

In 2013, according to estimates by the World Bank, the gross national income (GNI) of Kosovo, measured at average 2011–13 prices, was US $7,101m., equivalent to $3,890 per head. During 2004–13, it was estimated, the population increased at an average annual rate of 0.8%. During 2004–13 gross domestic product (GDP) per head increased, in real terms, at an average annual rate of 3.8%. Overall GDP grew, in real terms, at an average annual rate of 4.6% in 2004–13; growth was 3.0% in 2013.

Agriculture contributed some 14.4% of GDP in 2013, and the sector (including hunting, forestry and fishing) engaged 5.9% of the total employed labour force in the same year. The principal crops are wheat, potatoes, maize and peppers. According to UN figures, agricultural production increased at an average annual rate of 1.6% in 2004–13; the sector's GDP decreased by 17.4% in 2012, but increased by 23.7% in 2013.

Industry contributed some 28.2% of GDP in 2013, and the sector (including mining, manufacturing, construction and power) engaged around 28.1% of the employed labour force. Industrial production increased at an average annual rate of 3.7% in 2004–13, according to UN figures. Output decreased by 3.8% in 2012, but increased by 8.3% in 2013.

The mining sector contributed some 2.7% of GDP in 2013, and mining and quarrying engaged around 1.3% of the employed labour force in that year. One of the principal minerals extracted is halloysite, a clay mineral used in the production of porcelain and bone china. More significantly, Kosovo has some 14.7m. metric tons of proven lignite reserves. Lead, zinc, chromium and bauxite are also mined. According to UN figures, the GDP of mining and utilities together increased at an average annual rate of 18.0% in 2004–13; growth declined by 12.8% in 2012, but expanded by 11.5% in 2013.

Manufacturing contributed 13.2% of GDP in 2013. The manufacturing sector employed about 12.6% of the population in 2013. Manufacturing decreased at an average annual rate of 1.8% in 2004–13, according to UN figures; sectoral GDP increased by 45.7% in 2012, but decreased by 14.4% in 2013.

The construction sector contributed some 7.9% of GDP in 2013, and engaged around 11.4% of the employed labour force in the same year. According to UN figures, the GDP of the sector declined at an average annual rate of 4.8% in 2004–13. Sectoral GDP decreased by 24.6% in 2012, but increased by 39.2% in 2013.

Energy in Kosovo is derived principally from coal (which contributed, on average, 97.8% of total electricity generated in 2011). Imports of mineral fuels accounted for some 16.8% of the value of total imports to Kosovo in 2013.

Services contributed some 57.4% of GDP in 2013, and engaged around 65.9% of the employed labour force in 2013. Important areas of the services sector include wholesale and retail trade, education and administration. According to UN estimates, GDP in the services sector increased at an average annual rate of 4.1% in 2004–13; sectoral GDP rose by 4.0% in 2013.

In 2013 Kosovo recorded a visible merchandise trade deficit of €2,652m. and there was a deficit of €451m. on the current account of the balance of payments. In 2013 the principal source of imports to Kosovo was Serbia, accounting for 11.7% of the total; other major sources were Germany, Italy, Turkey, the former Yugoslav republic of Macedonia (FYRM), the People's Republic of China and Greece. The principal market for exports in that year was Italy (taking 25.3% of total exports); other important purchasers were Albania, India, the FYRM and Montenegro. The main exports in 2013 were base metals (accounting for 49.0% of export trade), in particular iron and steel. Exports of mineral products, prepared foodstuffs, beverages, spirits, vinegar, and tobacco, plastics and rubber articles, and vegetables and vegetable products were also significant. The principal imports in that year were mineral products (which accounted for 19.7% of imports), prepared foodstuffs, beverages, spirits, vinegar, and tobacco, machinery and mechanical products, electrical equipment, base metals, chemicals and related products, plastics and rubber, vehicles and transport equipment, and vegetables and vegetable products.

In 2013 the overall budgetary deficit for Kosovo was estimated to be €153m., equivalent to 2.9% of GDP. In 2004–14 the rate of inflation in Kosovo increased at an average annual rate of 2.8%. Consumer prices increased by 0.5% in 2014. The rate of unemployment in Kosovo was 30.0% in 2013, according to official estimates.

Following its declaration of independence in 2008, Kosovo remained one of the poorest territories in Europe, with one of the highest unemployment rates, and was highly reliant upon remittances from abroad. The inability of the Kosovo institutions to exert authority in northern Serb-dominated areas obstructed economic development. The IMF approved a 20-month stand-by credit arrangement for Kosovo in April 2012. In October the Government signed an agreement on the sale of the Kosovo Energy Corporation for €26.3m. to a private Turkish consortium. Meanwhile, in October the European Commission emphasized that the failure of five European Union (EU, see p. 271) member states to extend recognition to Kosovo presented a major impediment to the signature of a Stabilization and Association Agreement (SAA) with Kosovo. Nevertheless, after an accord was reached between the Governments of Kosovo and Serbia in April 2013, the European Commission recommended the opening of SAA negotiations with Kosovo, which officially commenced in October. The IMF completed the final review of performance supported by the stand-by arrangement (under which a total of €87.9m. had been disbursed) in December, commending progress in structural reforms. In late July 2014 the EU initialled the SAA with Kosovo; its signature, conditional on further reforms, was envisaged for 2015. A new coalition Government was installed in December 2014, following a lengthy impasse following early legislative elections in June. However, in January 2015 plans by the new administration to nationalize the loss-making Trepča mining complex (which prior to the 1989 conflict had accounted for around 70% of the then province's GDP) were cancelled owing to strong objections from Serbia, prompting large-scale political violence (see *Domestic Political Affairs*). The Kosovo Privatization Agency was to be allowed a further three years to restructure the Trepča complex, although the Government announced that it would re-evaluate its decision in response to the public pressure. After severe regional flooding (in addition to the political unrest), GDP growth fell, to an estimated 2.5%, in 2014.

PUBLIC HOLIDAYS

2016: 1–2 January (New Year's Day), 7 January (Orthodox Christmas), 17 February (Independence Day), 28 March (Catholic Easter Monday), 9 April (Constitution Day), 1 May (Labour Day), 9 May (Europe Day), 6 July* (Small Bayram, end of Ramadan), 12 September* (Great Bayram, Feast of the Sacrifice), 25 December (Catholic Christmas).

* These holidays are dependent on the Islamic lunar calendar and may vary by one or two days from the dates given.

Statistical Survey

Source (unless otherwise indicated): Statistical Office of Kosovo, 10000 Prishtina, Rruga Zenel Salihu 4; e-mail eskinfo@ks-gov.net; internet esk.rks-gov.net.

Area and Population

AREA, POPULATION AND DENSITY

Area (sq km)	10,908*
Population (census results)	
31 March 1991†	1,956,196
1–15 April 2011‡	
Males	875,900
Females	863,925
Total	1,739,825
Population (official estimates at 31 December)	
2011	1,798,645
2012	1,815,606
2013	1,837,012
Density (per sq km) at 31 December 2013	168.4

* 4,212 sq miles.

† Assessment of the Office of Statistics of the Socialist Federal Republic of Yugoslavia.

‡ Enumerated population, excluding data for municipalities of Leposaviq, Zubin Potok, Zveçan and North Mitrovicë where no census was conducted; a consolidated total census population of 1,780,021 (including estimates for these municipalities) was published in 2013.

POPULATION BY AGE AND SEX
(at 2011 census)

	Males	Females	Total
0–14 years	252,405	235,172	487,577
15–64 years	568,903	566,560	1,135,463
65 years and over	54,592	62,193	116,785
Total	875,900	863,925	1,739,825

POPULATION BY ETHNIC GROUP
(at 2011 census*)

	Population	%
Albanian	1,616,869	92.9
Bosniak	27,533	1.6
Serb	25,532	1.5
Turk	18,738	1.1
Ashkali	15,436	0.9
Egyptian	11,524	0.7
Goran	10,265	0.5
Roma	8,824	0.5
Others†	5,104	0.3
Total	1,739,825	100.0

* Excluding data for the (principally Serb-inhabited) municipalities of Leposaviq, Zubin Potok, Zveçan and North Mitrovicë where no census was conducted.

† Including other groups, non-declared persons and those of unknown ethnicity.

Note: Classification of ethnic groups reflects national census methodology.

MUNICIPALITIES
(official population estimates at 31 December 2013)

Municipality*	Area (sq km)	Population	Density (per sq km)
Deçan/Dečani	294	40,954	139.3
Dragash/Dragaš	434	34,775	80.1
Ferizaj/Uroševac	345	112,657	326.5
Fushë Kosovë/Kosovo Polje . .	84	37,514	446.6
Gjakovë/Đakovica	587	97,127	165.5
Gjilan/Gnjilane	392	92,369	235.6
Gllogovc/Glogovac	276	60,687	219.9
Graçanicë/Gračanica	131	11,178	85.3
Hani i Elezit/Đeneral Jankovič .	83	9,696	116.8
Istog/Istok	454	40,388	89.0
Junik	78	6,262	80.3
Kaçanik/Kačanik	211	34,293	162.5
Kamenicë/Kamenica . . .	405	35,931	88.7

Municipality*—*continued*	Area (sq km)	Population	Density (per sq km)
Klinë/Klina	309	39,943	129.3
Kllokot/Klokot	29	2,629	90.7
Leposaviq/Leposavić . . .	540	13,617	25.2
Lipjan/Lipljan	338	59,773	176.8
Malishevë/Mališevo	306	57,136	186.7
Mamushë/Mamuša	11	5,737	521.5
Mitrovicë/Mitrovica† . . .	336	86,373	257.1
Novobërdë/Novo Brdo . . .	204	6,905	33.8
Obiliq/Obilić	105	22,309	212.5
Partesh/Parteš	23	1,745	75.9
Pejë/Peć	603	98,603	163.5
Podujevë/Podujevo	633	90,568	143.1
Prishtina (Prishtinë)/Priština	514	208,230	405.1
Prizren	627	183,810	293.2
Rahovec/Orahovac	276	58,259	211.1
Ranillug/Ranilug	89	3,821	42.9
Shtërpcë/Štrpce	248	6,972	28.1
Shtime/Štimlje	134	28,369	211.7
Skënderaj/Srbica	374	52,175	139.5
Suharekë/Suva Reka . . .	361	61,976	171.7
Viti/Vitina	270	48,288	178.8
Vushtrri/Vučitrn	345	71,977	208.6
Zubin Potok	338	6,572	19.4
Zveçan/Zvečan	123	7,394	60.1
Total	10,908	1,837,012	168.4

* The Serbian names are given after the Albanian names, where they differ.

† Including Mitrovica e Veriut/Severna Kosovska Mitrovica (North Mitrovicë), with an estimated population of 12,250.

BIRTHS, MARRIAGES AND DEATHS

	Registered live births		Registered marriages		Registered deaths	
	Number	Rate (per 1,000)	Number	Rate (per 1,000)	Number	Rate (per 1,000)
2006 . .	34,187	16.3	15,825	7.5	7,479	3.6
2007 . .	33,112	15.6	16,824	7.9	6,681	3.1
2008 . .	34,399	16.0	17,950	8.3	6,852	3.2
2009 . .	34,240	15.7	20,209	9.3	7,030	3.2
2010 . .	33,751	15.3	18,289	8.3	7,234	3.3
2011 . .	34,262	19.7	17,343	10.0	7,556	4.3
2012 . .	27,743	15.3	17,169	9.5	7,317	4.0
2013 . .	29,459	16.0	15,436	8.4	7,681	4.2

Life expectancy (years at birth): 70.5 (males 68.4; females 72.7) in 2012 (Source: World Bank, World Development Indicators database).

EMPLOYMENT
(labour force survey, '000 persons, 2013)

	Male	Female	**Total**
Agriculture, hunting, forestry and fishing	14.4	5.9	20.3
Mining and quarrying	3.9	0.4	4.3
Manufacturing	38.2	4.9	43.1
Electricity, gas and water supply .	9.0	0.9	9.9
Construction	38.2	0.8	39.0
Wholesale and retail trade; repair of motor vehicles, motorcycles and personal and household goods	33.6	10.0	43.6
Hotels and restaurants . . .	15.5	2.5	18.0
Transport, storage and communications	18.0	2.8	20.8
Financial intermediation . . .	5.8	1.8	7.6
Real estate, renting and business activities	5.8	1.8	7.6
Administrative and support service activities	10.3	2.8	13.1

—*continued*	Male	Female	**Total**
Public administration and defence; compulsory social security . .	12.9	3.7	16.7
Education	22.5	15.6	38.1
Health and social work . . .	12.9	14.9	27.8
Arts, entertainment and recreation	4.7	1.3	6.0
Other community, social and personal service activities . .	8.8	3.7	12.5
Activities of households as employers	4.4	3.0	7.4
Activities of extraterritorial organizations and bodies . .	4.3	2.0	6.3
Total employed	263.2	78.8	342.1

Note: Reliable estimates of the number of employed people were not available. According to the results of an official agricultural household survey conducted at the end of 2005, some 500,000 farm residents of working age were engaged in some level of farming activity (of which 135,000 were employed in this activity on a full-time basis). An official statistical overview of some 54,000 registered private sector businesses at the end of 2002 recorded 186,000 employees, while the number of people engaged in public administration at the end of 2005 totalled 74,081.

Registered unemployed (at 31 December): 325,261 in 2011; 259,341 in 2012; 268,104 in 2013. Note: According to official estimates, some 30.0% of the total labour force were unemployed in 2013.

Agriculture

PRINCIPAL CROPS
('000 metric tons)

	2005	2007	2008
Wheat	273.4	207.2	293.1
Barley	11.3	3.7	6.4
Oats	9.8	7.8	8.9
Maize (incl. mixed crops) . . .	79.9	37.5	58.5
Potatoes	87.4	95.1	104.0
Tomatoes	15.0	14.7	20.6
Peppers	55.0	36.0	51.3
Pumpkins (incl. mixed crops) . .	8.3	5.0	11.6
Cabbages	18.9	15.4	19.0
Onions	11.0	10.9	16.0
Beans (incl. mixed crops) . . .	7.5	2.5	6.2
Cucumbers	6.1	7.1	9.0
Watermelons	13.5	15.0	24.7
Apples	7.1	6.3	12.6
Pears	2.8	1.8	2.9
Plums	12.0	8.0	10.9
Vine grapes	2.2	2.8	1.9
Other grapes	3.5	3.5	8.6

Note: Data exclude second crops and autumn crops; production from state-owned enterprises is also excluded. Data for 2006 are not available.

2012: Wheat 345.0; Barley 1.8; Oats 4.9; Maize (incl. mixed crops) 30.0; Potatoes 33.4; Tomatoes 13.7; Peppers 50.7; Pumpkins (incl. mixed crops) 8.7; Cabbages 14.0; Onions 8.6; Beans (incl. mixed crops) 3.5; Cucumbers 5.2; Watermelons 17.1; Apples 8.1; Pears 1.6; Plums 17.5; Vine grapes 7.2; Other grapes 8.7.

2013: Wheat 391.7; Barley and barley beer 4.4; Oats 6.8; Maize (incl. mixed crops) 82.1; Potatoes 50.8; Tomatoes 17.3; Peppers 72.9; Pumpkins (incl. mixed crops) 7.8; Cabbages 21.9; Onions 15.3; Beans (incl. mixed crops) 1.1; Cucumbers 9.0; Watermelons 17.6; Apples 16.8; Pears 4.3; Plums 24.4; Vine grapes .2; Other grapes 2.6.

LIVESTOCK
('000 head, October–December)

	2006	2007	2008
Horses	6.7	6.1	5.0
Cattle	382.0	321.6	341.6
Pigs	68.2	39.6	26.8
Sheep	100.8	139.2	124.1
Goats	12.1	12.6	8.9
Chickens	2,337.1	2,058.8	2,046.9
Other poultry	187.4	219.4	166.5

2012: Horses 2.1; Cattle 313.8; Pigs 55.8; Sheep 93.9; Goats 12.1; Chickens 2,250; Other poultry 67.6.

2013: Horses 2.9; Cattle 321.4; Pigs 49.2; Sheep 108.0; Goats 12.1; Chickens 2,108; Other poultry 136.4.

Note: Data exclude livestock belonging to state-owned enterprises.

LIVESTOCK PRODUCTS
(total value of products sold, € '000)

	2007	2008
Meat	2,955.5	2,331.4
Milk	15,266.4	20,995.6
Fat	85.8	343.9
Other dairy products	463.6	1,480.3
Eggs	616.6	1,389.7
Honey	871.6	958.7
Total (incl. others)	24,135.2	33,139.7

2012: Meat 4,368.8; Milk 22,889.6; Fat 474.0; Other dairy products 1,170.6; Eggs 1,876.9; Honey 659.0; Total (incl. others) 40,284.6.

2013: Meat 5,248.8; Milk 34,311.5; Fat 582.2; Other dairy products 1,245.9; Eggs 2,313.2; Honey 1,062.5; Total (incl. others) 54,530.5.

Note: Data exclude production by state-owned enterprises.

Forestry

FORESTRY REMOVALS
('000 cubic metres)

	2007	2008
Fuel wood	468.9	451.7
Total (incl. others)	482.9	456.0

2012: Fuel wood 464.9; Total (incl. others) 503.6.

2013: Fuel wood 412.0; Total (incl. others) 415.6.

Note: Data exclude removals by state-owned enterprises.

Mining

('000 metric tons)

	2011	2012	2013
Coal	8,212.1	8,028.4	8,072.6

Industry

(million kWh)

	2011	2012	2013
Electric energy	5,712	5,912	6,385

Finance

CURRENCY AND EXCHANGE RATES

Monetary Units
100 cents = 1 euro (€).

Sterling, Dollar and Euro Equivalents (31 December 2014)
£1 sterling = 1.286 euros;
US $1 = 0.824 euros;
€10 = £7.78 = $12.14.

Average Exchange Rate (euros per US $)
2012   0.7783
2013   0.7532
2014   0.7537

BUDGET
(consolidated accounts, € million)

Revenue	2013	2014*	2015*
Tax revenue	1,105	1,264	1,350
Non-tax revenue	168	193	195
Dividends	43	—	30
Total (incl. others)	1,316	1,458	1,576

Expenditure	2013	2014*	2015*
Current expenditure . . .	946	1,050	1,205
Wages and salaries . . .	417	483	549
Goods and services	216	252	218
Subsidies and transfers . .	313	314	438
Capital expenditure and net lending	523	531	471
Total (incl. others)	1,469	1,589	1,682

*Budget figures.

2016 (projections): *Revenue:* Tax revenue 1,342; Non-tax revenue 200; Dividends 30; Total 1,573. *Expenditure:* Current expenditure 1,208 (Wages and salaries 552, Goods and services 216, Subsidies and transfers 441); Capital expenditure and net lending 445; Total (incl. others) 1,664.

Source: Ministry of Finance, Prishtina.

COST OF LIVING
(Consumer Price Index; base: May 2002 = 100)

	2012	2013	2014
All items	124.8	127.0	127.6

NATIONAL ACCOUNTS
(€ million at current prices)

Expenditure on the Gross Domestic Product

	2011	2012	2013
Government final consumption expenditure	802.1	842.1	863.9
Private final consumption expenditure	4,173.4	4,478.3	4,675.4
Gross fixed capital formation . .	1,475.9	1,316.8	1,322.6
Changes in inventories . . .	156.5	148.3	148.3
Total domestic expenditure .	6,607.9	6,785.5	7,010.2
Exports of goods and services . .	943.4	922.1	927.1
Less Imports of goods and services	2,736.7	2,648.8	2,610.7
GDP at market prices . . .	4,814.5	5,058.8	5,326.6

Note: Data include contributions from UN Interim Mission in Kosovo operations.

Gross Domestic Product by Economic Activity

	2011	2012	2013
Agriculture, hunting, forestry and fishing	614.3	617.6	638.7
Mining	124.1	114.0	118.3
Manufacturing	493.9	549.3	584.8
Construction	361.9	341.2	352.2
Electricity and water supply . .	157.7	164.9	196.9
Wholesale and retail trade; repair of motor vehicles, motorcycles and personal and household goods	535.2	611.6	655.4
Hotels and restaurants . . .	34.8	39.1	49.8
Transport, storage and communications	228.7	242.1	287.0
Financial intermediation . . .	173.5	192.6	213.3
Real estate, renting and business activities	416.9	437.2	475.5
Administrative and support service activities	81.7	94.5	96.2
Public administration and defence; compulsory social security . .	477.0	497.8	495.5
Other community, social and personal service activities . .	245.1	265.2	272.0
Gross value added in basic prices	3,944.9	4,167.0	4,435.5
Taxes, *less* subsidies, on products .	869.7	891.8	891.1
GDP at market prices . . .	4,814.5	5,058.8	5,326.6

Note: Totals may not be equal to the sum of components, owing to rounding.

BALANCE OF PAYMENTS
(€ million)

	2011	2012	2013
Exports of goods	441.2	362.1	386.9
Imports of goods	−3,289.1	−2,990.3	−3,038.5
Balance on goods	−2,847.9	−2,628.2	−2,651.6
Exports of services	893.1	818.6	830.6
Imports of services	−535.6	−407.0	−417.3
Balance on goods and services	−2,490.4	−2,216.6	−2,238.4
Primary income received . . .	336.1	296.4	302.5
Primary income paid	−193.7	−97.5	−140.4
Balance on goods, services and primary income	−2,348.0	−2,017.7	−2,076.2
Secondary income received . .	1,476.2	1,664.8	1,733.2
Secondary income paid . . .	−156.5	−131.5	−108.3
Current balance	−1,028.2	−484.5	−451.4
Capital account (net)	29.4	16.8	46.3
Direct investment assets . . .	−6.9	−20.2	−23.8
Direct investment liabilities . .	546.2	293.2	343.2
Portfolio investment assets . .	−83.2	−234.9	−170.7
Portfolio investment liabilities .	—	0.9	−1.3
Other investment assets . . .	−132.8	186.8	−102.0
Other investment liabilities . .	243.2	173.2	111.1
Net errors and omissions . . .	350.2	284.2	219.0
Reserves and related items .	−82.2	215.6	−29.6

Source: IMF, *International Financial Statistics*.

External Trade

PRINCIPAL COMMODITIES
(distribution by HS, € '000)

Imports c.i.f.	2011	2012	2013
Live animals and animal products	98,433	101,299	105,769
Vegetable and vegetable products	136,877	136,504	124,349
Prepared foodstuffs; beverages, spirits, vinegar; tobacco and articles thereof	304,095	310,987	327,916
Beverages, spirits and vinegar	57,900	57,688	59,555
Tobacco and manufactured tobacco substitutes	57,067	59,539	60,117
Mineral products	539,579	550,075	481,288
Mineral fuels, mineral oils and products of their distillation	452,779	458,131	412,591
Chemicals and related products	181,179	185,599	190,264
Pharmaceutical products	50,757	49,994	51,687
Plastics, rubber and articles thereof	137,563	140,251	148,148
Plastics and articles thereof	114,430	116,259	123,746
Wood, wood charcoal, cork, and articles thereof	53,885	51,496	52,809
Wood and articles of wood, wood charcoal	53,674	51,371	52,608
Pulp of wood, paper and paperboard, and articles thereof	46,669	38,666	38,752
Paper and paperboard, articles of paper pulp	40,131	33,735	32,305
Textiles and textile articles	88,598	83,236	87,616
Articles of stone, plaster, cement, asbestos; ceramics and glass products	91,174	95,257	96,772
Ceramic products	57,083	58,211	57,762
Base metals and articles thereof	228,156	248,466	247,173
Iron and steel	119,302	136,456	135,363
Machinery and mechanical appliances; electrical equipment; parts thereof	273,047	268,893	256,816
Boilers, machinery and mechanical equipment and parts	155,099	159,417	149,711
Electrical machinery and equipment and parts thereof, sound recorders and producers and signal recorders	117,949	109,477	107,105
Vehicles, aircraft, vessels and associated transport equipment	155,650	150,624	135,482
Transport equipment	153,649	150,113	133,627
Miscellaneous manufactured articles	61,955	61,403	70,312
Total (incl. others)	2,492,348	2,507,609	2,449,064

Exports f.o.b.	2011	2012	2013
Vegetables and vegetable products	12,766	14,359	15,408
Malt products of the milling industry	7,256	8,316	8,448
Prepared foodstuffs; beverages, spirits, vinegar; tobacco and articles thereof	12,937	16,051	19,337
Beverages, spirits and vinegars	8,106	10,195	13,300
Mineral products	40,575	36,485	48,352
Ores, slag and ash	20,104	20,528	21,540
Mineral fuels, mineral oils and products of their distillation	17,758	14,888	23,937
Plastics, rubber and articles thereof	12,429	14,003	18,205
Raw hides and skins, leather, furskins, etc., and articles thereof	9,406	10,418	11,691
Raw hides and skins (other than fur)	9,399	10,406	11,534
Base metals and articles thereof	193,143	145,813	143,911
Iron and steel	162,038	112,725	112,212
Articles of iron and steel	7,766	9,857	12,712
Copper and articles thereof	14,461	11,962	10,157
Aluminium and articles thereof	7,561	8,519	6,537
Machinery and mechanical appliances; electrical equipment; parts thereof	15,276	16,659	12,590
Boilers, machinery and mechanical equipment and parts	13,005	13,439	7,594
Total (incl. others)	319,165	276,100	293,842

PRINCIPAL TRADING PARTNERS
(€ '000)

Imports c.i.f.	2011	2012	2013
Albania	96,400	110,528	110,597
Austria	38,669	34,073	36,858
Bosnia and Herzegovina	79,835	85,309	83,531
Brazil	40,925	41,791	45,756
Bulgaria	50,541	39,125	44,515
China, People's Republic	170,285	159,651	179,554
Croatia	64,063	72,012	73,331
France	34,755	24,077	26,846
Germany	293,441	304,195	252,594
Greece	103,179	109,188	145,546
Hungary	35,020	27,665	28,236
Italy	159,444	213,469	228,519
Macedonia, FYR	365,961	287,739	185,020
Netherlands	18,195	21,261	38,831
Poland	32,963	30,970	36,595
Serbia	254,917	278,388	285,356
Slovenia	71,614	68,385	61,314
Switzerland	22,194	22,664	21,020
Turkey	184,452	199,881	204,922
United Kingdom	17,084	13,630	13,209
USA	42,847	46,916	52,152
Total (incl. others)	2,492,348	2,507,609	2,449,064

Exports f.o.b.	2011	2012	2013
Albania	34,566	40,180	43,774
Austria	5,711	4,425	6,327
Belgium	5,085	473	807
China, People's Republic	28,268	3,266	1,290
Croatia	2,794	2,359	2,594
Germany	24,144	14,995	10,985
India	15,482	22,889	28,953
Italy	83,924	71,351	74,363
Macedonia, FYR	30,949	26,376	26,139
Montenegro	6,988	16,759	17,310
Poland	650	737	3,870
Serbia	7,198	14,968	14,463
Slovakia	2,405	3,175	2,037
Slovenia	6,001	1,417	1,434
Switzerland	17,611	15,133	7,155
Turkey	7,831	11,380	7,393
Total (incl. others)	319,165	276,100	293,842

Transport

RAILWAYS

	2011	2012	2013
Passengers carried ('000)	358	367	369
Freight carried ('000 metric tons)	1,001	826	904
Freight ton-km (million)	56	49	43

ROAD TRAFFIC
(vehicles registered at 31 December)

	2004	2005	2006
Passenger cars	137,981	145,546	146,744
Buses, coaches, lorries and vans	22,707	27,644	20,850
Heavy goods vehicles	7,213	4,769	6,457
Total (incl. others)	169,072	200,000	178,185

2012 (vehicles in use at 31 December): Passenger cars 205,630; Buses and coaches 1,203; Vans and lorries 18,656; Motorcycles and mopeds 240,035 (Source: IRF, *World Road Statistics*).

CIVIL AVIATION
(traffic at Prishtina International Airport)

	2011	2012	2013
Aircraft movements	6,738	6,947	7,305
Passengers arrivals	696,033	746,824	794,179
Passenger departures	716,269	780,310	834,499

Education

(2012/13)

	Institutions	Pupils	Teachers
Kindergarten	66	26,431	1,450
Primary	1,034	286,677	17,663
Secondary	140	107,303	6,142
Special	50*	915	191*
Primary	46*	782	155*
Secondary	4*	133	36*
University level	n.a.	65,315	2,929

* 2010/11.

Directory

The Government

HEAD OF STATE

President: ATIFETE JAHJAGA (inaugurated 7 April 2011).

GOVERNMENT
(May 2015)

A coalition of the Partia Demokratike e Kosovës (PDK—Democratic Party of Kosovo), Lidhja Demokratike e Kosovës (LDK—Democratic League of Kosovo), Srpska Lista (Serb List), Koalicija Vakat (Vakat Coalition) and Kosova Demokratik Türk Partisi (KDTP—Turkish Democratic Party of Kosovo).

Prime Minister: ISA MUSTAFA (LDK).

Deputy Prime Minister and Minister of Foreign Affairs: HASHIM THAÇI (PDK).

Deputy Prime Minister and Minister of Culture: KUJTIM SHALA (LDK).

Deputy Prime Minister: BRANIMIR STOJANOVIĆ (Srpska Lista).

Minister of Public Administration: MAHIR YAĞCILAR (KDTP).

Minister of Local Self-Governance: LUBOMIR MARIQ (Srpska Lista).

Minister of Education, Science and Technology: ARSIM BAJRAMI (PDK).

Minister of the Diaspora: VALON MURATI (PDK).

Minister of Justice: HAJREDIN KUÇI (PDK).

Minister of Finance: ABDULLAH HOTI (LDK).

Minister of Economic Development: BLERAND STAVILECI (PDK).

Minister of European Integration: BEKIM ÇOLLAKU (PDK).

Minister of the Kosovo Security Force: HAKI DEMOLLI (LDK).

Minister of the Environment and Spatial Planning: FERID AGANI (PDK).

Minister of Labour and Social Welfare: ARBAN ABRASHI (LDK).

Minister of Agriculture: MEMLI KRASNIKI (PDK).

Minister of Internal Affairs: SKENDER HYSENI (LDK).

Minister of Communities and Resettlement: DALIBOR JEVTIĆ (Srpska Lista).

Minister of Health: IMET RRAHMANI (LDK).

Minister of Trade and Industry: HIKMETE BAJRAMI (LDK).

Minister of Infrastructure: LUTFI ZHARKU (LDK).

Minister without portfolio: EDITA TAHIRI (PDK).

Minister without portfolio: RASIM DEMIRI (Koalicija Vakat).

MINISTRIES

Office of the President: 10000 Prishtina, Rruga Nënë Terezë; tel. (38) 213222; fax (38) 211651; e-mail protocol@president-ksgov.net; internet www.president-ksgov.net.

Office of the Prime Minister: 10000 Prishtina, Rruga Nënë Terezë; tel. (38) 200211202; e-mail izkp.zkm@rks-gov.net; internet www.kryeministri-ks.net.

Ministry of Agriculture: 10000 Prishtina, Rruga Nënë Terezë; tel. (38) 211821; e-mail jusuf.salihu@ks-gov.net; internet www.mbpzhr-ks.net.

Ministry of Communities and Resettlement: 12000 Fushë Kosovë, Sheshi Nënë Terezë; tel. (38) 552045; e-mail natasa.popovic@rks-gov.net; internet www.mkk-ks.org.

Ministry of Culture: 10000 Prishtina, Sheshi Nënë Terezë; tel. (38) 211637; fax (38) 211440; e-mail info@mkrs-ks.org; internet www.mkrs-ks.org.

Ministry of the Diaspora: 10000 Prishtina, Nënë Terezë; tel. (38) 20017001; e-mail ministriaediaspores@ks-gov.net; internet med.rks-gov.net.

Ministry of Economic Development: 10000 Prishtina, Sheshi Nënë Terezë; tel. (38) 200215; e-mail mzhe.informimi@gmail.com; internet mzhe.rks-gov.net.

Ministry of Education, Science and Technology: 10000 Prishtina, Rruga Agim Ramadani; tel. (38) 213327; e-mail masht@ks-gov.net; internet www.masht-gov.net.

Ministry of the Environment and Spatial Planning: 10000 Prishtina, Ish Pallati i Mediave, Kati 14-17; tel. (38) 20032517; fax

(38) 20032041; e-mail webmaster.mmph@ks-gov.net; internet mmph
.rks-gov.net.

Ministry of European Integration: 10000 Prishtina, Rruga Nënë
Terezë, Ndërtesa e Qeverisë, Kati 9; tel. (38) 20027001; e-mail bardha
.ajvazi@rks-gov.net; internet www.mei-ks.net.

Ministry of Finance: 10000 Prishtina, Sheshi Nënë Terezë; tel. (38)
20034101; fax (38) 213113; e-mail adea.muharremi@mf-rks.org;
internet mf.rks-gov.net.

Ministry of Foreign Affairs: 10000 Prishtina, Ndërtesa e Qeverisë, Rruga Nënë Terezë; tel. (38) 20011087; fax (38) 213985; e-mail
mfa@rks-gov.net; internet www.mfa-ks.net.

Ministry of Health: 10000 Prishtina, Rruga Zagrebi; tel. (38)
213886; e-mail faik.hoti@ks-gov.net; internet www.msh-ks.org.

Ministry of Infrastructure: 10000 Prishtina, Ndërtesa e Kuvendit
të Kosovës, Aneksi i Ri, Rruga Nënë Terezë; tel. (38) 211022; e-mail
mi.info@rks-gov.net; internet mi-ks.net.

Ministry of Internal Affairs: 10000 Prishtina, Rruga Luan Haradinaj; tel. (38) 20019545; fax (38) 20019640; e-mail zip-mpb@
rks-gov.net; internet www.mpb-ks.org.

Ministry of Justice: 10000 Prishtina, Ndërtesa e ish Rilindjes, Kati
VIII, Zyra 817/A; tel. (38) 20018018; e-mail zkp.md@rks-gov.net;
internet www.md-ks.org.

Ministry of the Kosovo Security Force: 10000 Prishtina, Lagjja
Emshiri-1; tel. (38) 551437; e-mail violeta.reka@ks-gov.net; internet
mksf-ks.org.

Ministry of Labour and Social Welfare: 10000 Prishtina, Rruga
UÇK-së 1; tel. and fax (38) 20026049; e-mail behxhet.gaxhiqi@ks-gov
.net; internet mpms.rks-gov.net.

Ministry of Local Self-Governance: 10000 Prishtina, Ndërtesa e
ish Rilindjes, Katet 10–13; tel. (38) 20035630; e-mail eranda.bobaj@
rks-gov.net; internet mapl.rks-gov.net.

Ministry of Public Administration: 10000 Prishtina, Kati V, Zyra
534, Ndërtesa e ish Rilindjes; tel. (38) 20030660; fax (38) 20030008;
e-mail mahir.yagcilar@rks-gov.net; internet map.rks-gov.net.

Ministry of Trade and Industry: 10000 Prishtina, Lagjja e
Spitalit, Rruga Muharrem Fejza; tel. (38) 512059; fax (38) 512798;
e-mail zkp.mti@rks-gov.net; internet www.mti-ks.org.

INTERNATIONAL REPRESENTATIVE

**Special Representative of the Secretary-General of the UN,
Head of the UN Interim Administration Mission in Kosovo
(UNMIK):** FARID ZARIF.

Legislature

Kosovo Assembly
(Kuvendi i Kosovës/Skupština Kosova)

10000 Prishtina, Rruga Nënë Terezë; tel. (38) 211169; fax (38)
211188; e-mail info@assembly-kosova.org; internet www
.assembly-kosova.org.

President: KADRI VESELI.

Election, 8 June 2014*

Parties and Coalitions	Votes	% of votes	Seats
Partia Demokratike e Kosovës (PDK)†	222,181	30.38	37
Lidhja Demokratike e Kosovës (LDK)	184,596	25.24	30
Vetëvendosje!	99,397	13.59	16
Aleanca për Ardhmërinë e Kosovës (AAK)	69,793	9.54	11
Srpska Lista	38,199	5.22	9
Nisma për Kosovën	37,681	5.15	6
Kosova Demokratik Türk Partisi (KDTP)	7,424	1.02	2
Koalicija Vakat	6,476	0.89	2
Others	65,504	8.97	7‡
Total	731,251	100.00	120

* The figures shown in this table incorporate the results of voting to
the 20 seats reserved for representatives of designated minority
ethnic groups (10 seats are elected by Serbs, four by a constituency
comprising Roma, Ashkali and 'Egyptian' Roma, three by Bosniaks,
two by Turks and one by Gorani).

† In coalition with the Partia e Drejtësise (PD), the Lëvizja për
Bashkim (LB), the Partia Shqiptare Demokristane e Kosovës
(PSHDK), and the Partia Konservatore e Kosovës (PK).

‡ The other parties to obtain representation (one seat apiece) were
the Koalicija Za Gora (KZG), the Kosovaki Nevi Romani Partia
(KNRP), the Nova Demokratska Stranka (NDS), the Partia Demokratike e Ashkanlive të Kosovës (PDAK), the Partia e Ashkalinjeve
për Integrim (PAI), the Partia Liberale Egjiptiane (PLE) and the
Progresivna Demokratska Stranka (PDS).

Election Commission

Central Election Commission (Komisioni Qendror i Zgjedhjeve):
10000 Prishtina, Rruga Migjeni p.n.; tel. (38) 211337; fax (38)
246602; e-mail kqz.sekretariati@kqz-ks.org; internet www.kqz-ks
.org; f. 2004; Chair. VALDETE DAKA.

Political Organizations

Aleanca Kosova e Re (AKR) (New Kosovo Alliance): 10000 Prishtina, Rruga UÇK 55; tel. (38) 224021; fax (38) 247988; e-mail info@
akr-ks.com; internet akr-ks.com; f. 2006; Pres. BEHGJET PACOLLI.

Aleanca për Ardhmërinë e Kosovës (AAK) (Alliance for the
Future of Kosovo): 10000 Prishtina, Bulevardi i Dëshmorëve 49; tel.
(38) 550171; e-mail info@aak-ks.com; internet www.aak-ks.net;
f. 2001; Chair. RAMUSH HARADINAJ.

Koalicija Vakat (Vakat Coalition): Dragaš; f. 2004; coalition of
representatives of the Demokratska stranka Bošnjačka (Bosniak
Democratic Party), the Demokratska stranka Vatan (Fatherland
Democratic Party) and the Bošnjačka stranka Kosova (Bosniak
Party of Kosovo); Leader SADIK IDRIZI.

Kosova Demokratik Türk Partisi (KDTP) (Turkish Democratic
Party of Kosovo): 20000 Prizren, Sheshi e Lidhjes Cad. 47; tel. (29)
242534; fax (38) 20030008; e-mail info@kdtp.org; internet www.kdtp
.org; f. 1990; Chair. MAHIR YAĞCILAR.

Lidhja Demokratike e Dardanisë (LDD) (Democratic League of
Dardania): 10000 Prishtina, Rruga Rrustem Statovci 50; tel. (45)
277755; e-mail info@ldd-kosova.org; f. Jan. 2007 by fmr mems of
Lidhja Demokratike e Kosovës; Leader NEXHAT DAÇI.

Lidhja Demokratike e Kosovës (LDK) (Democratic League of
Kosovo): 10000 Prishtina, Kompleksi Qafa; tel. (38) 242242; fax (38)
245305; e-mail info@ldk-ks.eu; internet www.ldk-ks.eu; f. 1989;
Chair. ISA MUSTAFA.

Nisma për Kosovën (NISMA) (Initiative for Kosovo): 24000 Mal-
ishevë; internet www.facebook.com/NismaPerKosoven; f. 2014;
Chair. FATMIR LIMAJ.

Partia Demokratike e Kosovës (PDK) (Democratic Party of
Kosovo): 10000 Prishtina, Rruga Nënë Terezë 20; tel. (44) 183445;
e-mail separikosova@pdk49.com; internet www.pdk49.com; f. 1999;
present name adopted 2000; Chair. HASHIM THAÇI.

Partia e Drejtësisë (PD) (Justice Party): 10000 Prishtina, Vel-
lusha, Rruga Bajram Kelmendi 22; tel. and fax (44) 248920; internet
www.drejtesia.org; f. 2000; contested 2014 legislative elections in
coalition with Partia Demokratike e Kosovës (q.v.) and three other
parties; Chair. FERID AGANI.

Partia Liberale e Kosovës (PLK) (Liberal Party of Kosovo): 10000
Prishtina, Goleshi St 10/2; tel. and fax (38) 244780; e-mail info@
plk-kosova.org; Chair. Prof. GJERGJ DEDAJ.

Partia Shqiptare Demokristane e Kosovës (PSHDK) (Albanian
Christian Democratic Party of Kosovo): 10000 Prishtina, Dëshmorët
e Kombit 7B/5; tel. (44) 393793; e-mail info@pshdk.com; internet
www.pshdk.com; f. 2000; contested 2014 legislative elections in
coalition with the Partia Demokratike e Kosovës (q.v.) and three
other parties; Chair. UKË BERISHA.

Partia Social Demokrate (PSD) (Social Democratic Party): 10000
Prishtina, Rruga Gustav Meyer 1; tel. (38) 225645; e-mail info@
psd-ks.org; internet www.psd-ks.org; Pres. MAJLINDA NUSHI.

Partia Socialiste e Kosovës (Socialist Party of Kosovo): 10000
Prishtina, Rruga Thimi Mitko 6; tel. (44) 131832; e-mail info@ps-ks
.org; internet www.ps-ks.org; f. 1982; Chair. ILAZ KADOLLI.

Samostalna Liberalna Stranka (SLS) (Independent Liberal
Party): Gračanica, Poslovni centar 'Lazic'; tel. (44) 682452; e-mail
predsednik@sls-ks.org; internet www.sls-ks.org; f. 2006; represents
Serb interests; Chair. SLOBODAN PETROVIĆ.

Srpska Lista (Serb List): Mitrovica; coalition of representatives of
local brs of Serb groups, incl. Srpski Pokret Obnove and the Socijaldemokratska Partija Srbije; fmrly Srpska Lista za Kosovo i
Metohiju (Serb List for Kosovo and Metohija); Leader OLIVER
IVANOVIĆ.

Vetëvendosje! (Self-Determination!): 10000 Prishtina, Qyteza Pejton, Rruga Bajram Kelmendi 10; tel. (44) 411174; e-mail info@
vetevendosje.org; internet www.vetevendosje.org; f. 2005; ethnic
Albanian nationalist movement; Pres. ALBIN KURTI.

Other political parties include: the **Građanska Inicijativa Gore**
(Civic Initiative of Gora); **Građanska Inicijativa Srbija** (Civic
Initiative of Serbia); **Iniciativa e re Demokrarike e Kosovës**
(New Democratic Initiative of Kosovo), representing the 'Egyptian'
Roma; **Partia Demokratike e Ashkanlive të Kosovës** (Demo-
cratic Ashkali Party of Kosovo); **Partia Rome e Bashkuar e
Kosovës** (United Roma Party of Kosovo); **Savez Nezavisnih
Socijaldemokrata Kosova i Metohije** (Union of Independent

Social Democrats of Kosovo and Metohija), led by NEBOJŠA ŽIVIĆ; **Srpska Demokratska Stranka Kosova i Metohije** (Serb Democratic Party of Kosovo and Metohija), led by SLAVIŠA PETKOVIĆ; **Srpska Kosovsko-Metohijka Stranka** (Serb Kosovo and Metohija Party), led by DRAGIŠA MIRIĆ; **Srpska Narodna Stranka** (Serb People's Party), led by MIHAJL ŠĆEPANOVIĆ; and **Stranka Demokratske Akcije** (Party of Democratic Action).

Diplomatic Representation

EMBASSIES IN KOSOVO

By April 2015 110 countries were reported to have officially recognized Kosovo.

Albania: 10000 Prishtina, Qyteza Pejton, Rruga Mujo Ulqinaku 18; tel. (38) 248208; fax (38) 248209; e-mail embassy.pristina@mfa.gov.al; Ambassador QEMAL MINXHOZI.

Austria: 10000 Prishtina, Fan Noli 22, Arbëri 1; tel. (38) 249284; fax (38) 249285; e-mail pristina-as@bmeia.gv.at; Ambassador JOHANN BRIEGER.

Bulgaria: 10000 Prishtina, Arbëri 1, Rruga Ismail Qemali 12; tel. (38) 245540; fax (38) 245543; e-mail embassy.pristina@mfa.government.bg; internet www.mfa.bg/embassies/kosovo; Ambassador NEDIALTCHO DANTCHEV.

Croatia: 10000 Prishtina, Fehmi Agani 69A; tel. (38) 223320; fax (38) 223979; e-mail croemb.pristina@mvpei.hr; Ambassador ZORAN VODOPIJA.

Czech Republic: 10000 Prishtina, Dragodan, Rruga Ismail Qemali 31; tel. (38) 246676; fax (38) 248782; e-mail pristina@embassy.mzv.cz; Chargé d'affaires a.i. JIŘÍ DOLEŽEL.

Finland: 10000 Prishtina, Lagja Payton, Perandori Justinian 19; tel. (43) 737000; fax (43) 732863; e-mail sanomat.pri@formin.fi; internet www.finlandkosovo.org; Chargé d'affaires a.i. ANNE MESKANEN.

France: 10000 Prishtina, Dragodan, Rruga Ismail Qemali 67; tel. (38) 22458800; fax (38) 22458801; e-mail admin-etrangers.pristina-amba@diplomatie.gouv.fr; internet www.ambafrance-kosovo.org; Ambassador MARYSE DAVIET.

Germany: 10000 Prishtina, Arbëri, Rruga Azem Jashanica 17; tel. (38) 254500; fax (38) 254536; e-mail info@pristina.diplo.de; internet www.pristina.diplo.de; Ambassador ANGELIKA VIETS.

Hungary: 10000 Prishtina, Arbëri, 24 Maj 23; tel. (38) 247763; fax (38) 247764; e-mail mission.prs@mfa.gov.hu; internet www.mfa.gov.hu/pristina; Ambassador LÓRÁNT BALLA.

Italy: 10000 Prishtina, Dragodan, Rruga Azem Jashanica 5; tel. (38) 244925; fax (38) 244929; e-mail pubblico.pristina@esteri.it; Ambassador ANDREAS FERRARESE.

Macedonia, former Yugoslav republic: 10000 Prishtina, Rruga 24 Maji 121; tel. (38) 247462; fax (38) 247463; e-mail macedonialiaison@mail.net.mk; Ambassador ILIJA STRASHEVSKI.

Montenegro: 10000 Prishtina, Rruga Nënë Terezë 28/3; tel. (38) 222048; fax (38) 222054; e-mail kosovo@mfa.gov.me; Chargé d'affaires RADOVAN MILJANIĆ.

Netherlands: 10000 Prishtina, Velania, Xhemajl Berisha 12; tel. (38) 516101; fax (38) 516103; e-mail pri@minbuza.nl; internet kosovo.nlambassade.org; Ambassador ROBERT BOSCH.

Norway: 10000 Prishtina, Pejton, Sejdi Kryeziu 6; tel. (38) 23211100; fax (38) 23211122; e-mail embpri@mfa.no; internet www.norway-kosovo.no; Ambassador JAN BRAATHU.

Slovenia: 10000 Prishtina, Anton Ceta 6; tel. (38) 246255; fax (38) 246256; e-mail mpi@gov.si; Ambassador MILJAN MAJHEN.

Sweden: 10000 Prishtina, Pejton, Perandori Justian 19; tel. (38) 245795; fax (38) 245791; e-mail ambassaden.pristina@foreign.ministry.se; Chargé d'affaires a.i. HENRIK NILSSON.

Switzerland: 10060 Prishtina, Adrian Krasniqi 11; tel. (38) 261261; fax (38) 26126190; e-mail pri.vertretung@eda.admin.ch; internet www.eda.admin.ch/pristina; Ambassador KRYSTYNA MARTY LANG.

Turkey: 10000 Prishtina, Arbëri, Rruga Ismail Qemali 59; tel. (38) 226044; fax (38) 226031; e-mail embassy.prishtina@mfa.gov.tr; internet www.prishtina.emb.mfa.gov.tr; Ambassador SONGÜL OZAN BÜYÜKELÇI.

United Kingdom: 10000 Prishtina, Arbëri, Rruga Ismail Qemali 6; tel. (38) 254700; fax (38) 243062; e-mail britishoffice.pristina@fco.gov.uk; internet www.gov.uk/government/world/kosovo; Ambassador IAN CAMERON CLIFF.

USA: 10000 Prishtina, Arbëri, Nazim Hikmet 30; tel. (38) 593000; fax (38) 549890; e-mail papristina@state.gov; internet pristina.usembassy.gov; Ambassador TRACEY ANN JACOBSON.

Judicial System

The court system comprises a Supreme Court, Constitutional Court, district courts, municipal courts and minor offences courts.

Supreme Court: 10000 Prishtina; tel. (38) 243348; fax (38) 245219; e-mail ajna.gashi@rks-gov.net; internet www.gjykatasupreme-ks.org; Pres. FEJZULLAH HASANI.

Constitutional Court: 10000 Prishtina, Rruga Perandori Justinian; tel. (38) 220103; e-mail gjykata.kushtetuese@gjk-ks.org; fax (38) 220112; internet www.gjk-ks.org; f. 2009; Chair. Prof. ENVER HASANI; Dep. Chair. Prof. Dr IVAN ČUKALOVIĆ.

Religion

Most of the inhabitants of Kosovo are adherents of Islam, although most Serbs are Orthodox Christians, and several sites of historic importance to Serbian Orthodoxy are located within Kosovo. A significant minority of the Kosovo Albanian population are Roman Catholics.

ISLAM

Islamic Community: 10000 Prishtina; tel. and fax (38) 245700; internet www.bislame.net; f. 1951; Pres. of the Islamic Community NAIM TERNAVA.

CHRISTIANITY

The Eastern Orthodox Church

The Patriarchate of the Serbian Orthodox Church is located at Pej (Peć), in central Kosovo.

The Roman Catholic Church

There are an estimated 65,000 Roman Catholics within the Apostolic Administration of Prizren. In the early 2010s a Catholic co-cathedral was under construction in Prishtina.

Apostolic Administrator of Prizren: GJERGJU DODË, 20000 Prizren, Rruga I. L. Ribar 7; tel. (29) 41933; fax (29) 41232; e-mail ipeshkvia_pz@yahoo.com.

The Press

PRINCIPAL DAILIES

Bota Sot (The World Today): 10000 Prishtina, Rruga Jakove Xoxa 18; tel. and fax (38) 226881; e-mail info@botasot.info; internet www.botasot.info; in Albanian; Editor IDRIZ MORINA.

Epoka e Re (The New Age): 10000 Prishtina, Rruga Nënë Terezë; tel. (44) 127434; e-mail epoka_mm@yahoo.com; internet www.epokaere.com; f. 2000; Editor MAL QORRAJ.

Express: 10000 Prishtina, Dardania 1/1; tel. (38) 767676; fax (38) 767678; e-mail info@gazetaexpress.com; internet www.gazetaexpress.com; f. 2005; in Albanian; Chief Editor LEONARD KERQUKI.

Koha Ditore: 10000 Prishtina, Rruga Nënë Terezë, POB 202; tel. (38) 249104; fax (38) 249106; e-mail info@koha.net; internet www.kohaditore.com; f. 1990; in Albanian; Editor-in-Chief AGRON BAJRAMI.

Kosova Sot (Kosovo Today): 10000 Prishtina, Zona Industriale; tel. (38) 601007; fax (38) 601010; e-mail redaksia@kosova-sot.info; internet www.kosova-sot.info; f. 1998; in Albanian; Editor-in-Chief MARGARITA KADRIU.

Lajm (The News): 10000 Prishtina, UÇK 58; tel. (44) 215791; fax (38) 243009; e-mail lajmonline@gmail.com; internet www.gazetalajm.info; f. 2004; in Albanian; supports Aleanca Kosova e Re; Chief Exec. BEHGJET PACOLLI.

Prishtina Post: 10000 Prishtina, Bulevardi Bil Klinton; tel. and fax (38) 555566; e-mail redaksia@prishtinapost.info; in Albanian; Editor FATON ABDULLAHU.

Tribuna: 10000 Prishtina; tel. (38) 223204; e-mail gazeta@tribunashqiptare.info; internet www.gazetatribuna.com.

PERIODICALS

Alem: 1000 Prishtina, Rruga Hajdar Dushi 1A; tel. (44) 185099; fax (38) 243800; e-mail info@alemnet.info; f. 2001; weekly; in Bosnian; Editor-in-Chief NADIRA A. VLASSI.

Fokus Kosova/Fokus Kosovo/Focus Kosovo: 10000 Prishtina, UNMIK Administrative HQ; e-mail focuskosovo@un.org; f. 2001; publ. by UNMIK; Albanian, Serbian and English edns; seven a year; Publr ALEXANDER IVANKO; Editors MYRIAM DESSABLES (Albanian and Serbian edns), RICARDO Z. DUNN.

Gradanski Glasnik (The Civil Herald): 10000 Prishtina, Tringe Ismaili 34A; tel. (44) 431106; e-mail gg@gradjanskiglasnik.com; every two weeks; in Serbian; Editor-in-Chief JELENA BJELICA.

Official Gazette of the Republic of Kosovo (Gazeta Zyrtare e Republikës së Kosovës/Sluzbeni list Republike Kosova/Kosova Cumhuriyeti Resmi Gazetesi/Sluzbeni Novine Republike Kosova): 10000 Prishtina, Ndërtesa e re e Qeverisë; tel. (38) 20114039; fax (38) 20114180; e-mail info-gzk@ks-gov.net; internet www.ks-gov.net/GazetaZyrtare; f. 2005; monthly; publishes official text of laws adopted by the Kosovo Assembly as promulgated by the Special Representative of the Secretary-General, resolutions adopted by the Kosovo Assembly, secondary and other legislation issued by the Government and ministries of Kosovo, international agreements, etc.; edns in Albanian, Serbian, English, Turkish and Bosnian; administered by the Office of the Prime Minister; Editorial Dir NASER CANOLLI.

Yeni Dönem (New Era): Prizren, Rruga Ceraviqa 13A; tel. (29) 630230; fax (29) 44788; e-mail yenidonem@hotmail.com; in Turkish; weekly.

Zëri (The Voice): 10000 Prishtina, Media House Annex II; tel. (38) 249071; fax (38) 222451; e-mail redaksia@zeri.info; internet www.zeri.info; f. 1945; in Albanian; weekly; Editor-in-Chief ASTRIT GASHI.

NEWS AGENCIES

Infosot: Prishtina; tel. (44) 383333; e-mail info@infosot.com; f. 2007; Exec. Dir FATLUM RRAHMANI.

KosovaLive: 1000 Prishtina, Aneksi të Pallati i Shtypit, Kati II; tel. (38) 248276; fax (38) 248277; e-mail editor@kosovalive.com; internet www.kosovalive360.com; f. 2000; Editor-in-Chief KELMEND HAPÇIU.

Kosovapress: 10000 Prishtina, Rruga Hamez Jashari 28/22A; tel. and fax (38) 248721; e-mail info@kosovapress.com; internet www.kosovapress.com; f. 1999; Dir and Editor SKENDER KRASNIQI.

Press Association

Press Council of Kosovo: 10000 Prishtina, Rruga Hajdar Dushi 7; tel. (44) 291810; e-mail presscouncil.kosovo@gmail.com; internet www.presscouncil-ks.org; self-regulatory body of the print media; Chair. of Bd Dr IBRAHIM BERISHA; Dir NEHAT ISLAMI.

Publishers

Dukagjini Publishing House: 10000 Pejë, Rruga Fehmi Agani 16; tel. (39) 432025; fax (39) 434281; internet books.dukagjinigroup.com; literature and contemporary philosophy; titles publ. in three series: Rozafa, Ballkan and Fryma; owned by Dukagjini Group; Pres. RAMADAN MEHMETI.

Gjon Buzuku Publishing House: 10000 Prishtina, Rruga Brigadat e Kosovës; tel. and fax (38) 530873; e-mail buzuku@prishtina .com; f. 1990; Pres. HANA ZENELI.

Panorama: 10000 Prishtina; f. 1994; publishes newspapers and journals in Serbian, Albanian and Turkish; Dir JORDAN RISTIĆ.

Rilindja Publishing House: 10000 Prishtina, Pallati i mediave, Dom štampe pa nr; tel. (38) 549675; popular science, literature, children's fiction, travel books, textbooks in Albanian; Dir DAUT DEMAKU.

Broadcasting and Communications

TELECOMMUNICATIONS

Kosovo's telecommunications industry has been liberalized, with one licensed fixed-line telecommunication service provider and two licensed mobile operators in 2010. As Kosovo's independence is not recognized by the International Telecommunication Union, it has been unable to obtain an international dialling code of its own, and network operators in Kosovo at present use one of the country codes of Monaco, Slovenia or Serbia.

iPKO: 10000 Prishtina, Rruga Zija Shemsiu, Lagjja Ulpiana; tel. (38) 643700700; e-mail info@ipko.com; internet www.ipko.com; f. 1999; subsidiary of Telekom Slovenije (Slovenia); mobile cellular telecommunications services, and provider of internet and digital cable television.

PTK (Post and Telecommunications of Kosovo): 10100 Prishtina, Dardania pa nr, Kati VIII, Zyra 808; tel. (38) 500555; e-mail info@valamobile.com; internet www.ptkonline.com; f. 1959; became jt-stock co in 2005; provides postal and telecommunications services; CEO EJUP QERIMI.

Vala: 10000 Prishtina, Dardania; tel. (38) 535353; e-mail info@valamobile.com; internet www.valamobile.com; f. 2000; mobile cellular telecommunications services; Dir VALON ZHUNIQI.

Regulatory Authority

Telecommunications Regulatory Authority (Kosovo) (ART) (Autoriteti Rregullator i Telekomunikacionit): 10000 Prishtina, Qyteza Pejton, Rruga Pashko Vasa 12; tel. (38) 212345; e-mail info@art-ks.org; internet www.art-ks.org; f. 2004; Chair. EKREM HOXHA.

BROADCASTING

In 2010 there were three national television channels and four national radio stations.

Radio Televizioni i Kosovës (RTK) (Radio-Television Kosovo): 10000 Prishtina, Rruga Xhemajl 12; tel. (38) 230102; fax (38) 235336; e-mail post@rtklive.com; internet www.rtklive.com; subsidiaries include Radio Kosova and Radio Blue Sky; Chair. RRAHMAN PAÇARIZI; Dir-Gen. MENTOR SHALA; Editor-in-Chief MUFAIL LIMANI.

RadioTelevizioni21 (RTV21): 10000 Prishtina, Pallati i Mediave, Aneks II; tel. and fax (38) 241522; e-mail lajmet@rtv21.tv; internet www.rtv21.tv; radio and television broadcaster.

Finance

(cap. = capital; res = reserves; dep. = deposits; m. = million; amounts in euros; brs = branches)

BANKING

Regulatory Authority

Central Bank of the Republic of Kosovo (Banka Qendrore Republikës së Kosovës): 10000 Prishtina, Rruga Garibaldi 33; tel. (38) 222055; fax (38) 243763; e-mail info@bqk-kos.org; internet www.bqk-kos.org; f. 1999 as the Banking and Payments Authority of Kosovo; became Central Banking Authority of Kosovo in 2006; total assets 1,113.2m. (Dec. 2008); Gov. and Chair. BEDRI HAMZA.

Registered Banks

There are nine registered commercial banks operating in Kosovo, of which seven are foreign owned.

Banka Kombëtare Tregtare: 10000 Prishtina, Qyteza Pejton, Rruga Kosta Novakoviç 9; tel. (38) 666666; fax (38) 222906; e-mail infobktkosova@bkt.com; internet www.bkt.com.al; f. 1993; total assets 18.3m. (Dec. 2008), Chair. of Bd MEHMET USTA; CEO SEYHAN PENCABLIGIL.

Banka për Biznes (Bank for Business—BpB): Prishtina, Rruga UÇK 41; tel. (38) 620620; fax (38) 243656; e-mail informata@bpbbank .com; internet www.bpbbank.com; f. 2001; CEO RICHARD BEASLEY.

Economic Bank: 10000 Prishtina, Rruga Migjeni 1; tel. (38) 225353; fax (38) 225454; e-mail info@bekonomike.com; internet www.bekonomike.com; f. 2001; total assets 86.1m. (Dec. 2008); Chair. VALENTIN TOÇI; Dir-Gen. MERITA PEJA (acting).

Komercijalna Banka a.d. Beograd: 40000 Mitrovica, Rruga Kralja Petra Prvog 33; tel. (28) 3028582; fax (28) 3346810; e-mail posta@kombank.com; internet www.kombank.com; f. 1970; Chair. SINIŠA MALI; CEO IVICA SMOLIĆ.

NLB Prishtina: 10000 Prishtina, Rruga Kosta Novakoviq; tel. (38) 234111; fax (38) 246189; e-mail info@nlbprishtina-kos.com; internet www.nlbprishtina-kos.com; f. Jan. 2008 by merger of NLB Kasabank and NLB New Bank of Kosova; 80.4% owned by NLB d.d; cap. 20.5m., res 0.2m., dep. 367.4m. (Dec. 2012); Gen. Man. ALBERT LUMEZI.

ProCredit Bank Kosova: 10000 Prishtina, Nënë Terezë 16; tel. (38) 555555; fax (38) 248777; e-mail info@procreditbank-kos.com; internet www.procreditbank-kos.com; f. 2000 as Micro Enterprise Bank; present name adopted 2003; cap. 51.3m., res 4.5m., dep. 676.0m. (Dec. 2012); CEO ILIR I. ALIU.

Raiffeisen Bank Kosovo: Rruga UÇK 51; tel. (38) 222222; e-mail info@raiffeisen-kosovo.com; internet 7www.raiffeisen-kosovo.com; fmrly American Bank of Kosovo; acquired by Raiffeisen International (Austria) and name changed in 2003; cap. 58.0m., res 0.3m., dep. 548.6m. (Dec. 2009); Chair. and CEO ROBERT WRIGHT; 43 brs.

TEB sh. a.: 10000 Prishtina, Rruga Agim Ramadani 15; tel. (38) 230123; fax (38) 224699; e-mail info@teb-kos.com; internet www.teb-kos.com; f. Jan. 2008; joint venture of TEB (Turkey) and BNP Paribas (France); cap. 23.0m., dep. 270.4m., total assets 300.2m. (Dec. 2012); Dir MUSA ERDEN; Exec. Dir AYHAN ALBEYOGLU.

INSURANCE

In 2009 there were 14 registered insurance companies operating in Kosovo.

Croatia Sigurimi-Kosovo: 10000 Prishtina, Rruga Luan Haradinaj 5A; tel. (38) 246956; fax (38) 426957; e-mail ivopcro@yahoo.com; owned by Croatia Sigurimi (Croatia); Dir IVICA PEZO.

Dardania Kompania e Sigurimeve (Dardania Insurance Co JSC): 10000 Prishtina, Rruga Sylejman Vokshi 4; tel. (38) 244080;

fax (38) 244081; e-mail info@dardaniainsurance.com; internet www
.dardaniainsurance.com; f. 2002; Gen. Dir KORAB LLUKA.

Elsig: 10000 Prishtina, Rruga e Trepçës 15; tel. (38) 221112; fax (38)
221115; e-mail office@kselsig.com; internet www.kselsig.com;
f. 2008; non-life; Dir REXHEP IDRIZAJ.

Illyria Insurance Co: 10000 Prishtina, Nënë Terezë 33; tel. (38)
225386; fax (38) 225384; e-mail info@illyriainsurance.com; internet
www.illyriainsurance.com; Dir GIANNI SOKOLIČ.

Insig Kosovo: 10000 Prishtina, Mujo Ulqinaku, Pejton 6; tel. (38)
249900; fax (38) 249901; e-mail shberisha@insig-ks.com; Dir ILDA
KEKEZI.

Kompania e Sigurimeve Illyria (Illyria Insurance Co): 10000
Prishtina, Sheshi Nënë Terezë 33; tel. (38) 225385; fax (38) 225384;
e-mail info@illyriainsurance.com; internet www.illyriainsurance
.com; f. 2002; 100% owned by Sava Re (Slovenia); Chair. of Bd
PRIMOŽ MOCIVNIK; Gen. Dir GIANNI SOKOLIČ.

Kosova e Re Insurance Co (New Kosova Insurance Co): 10000
Prishtina, Lagja Kalabria 5/1B; tel. (38) 770777; fax (38) 770888;
e-mail info@kosovaere.com; internet www.kosovaere.com; f. 2002;
owned by Kürüm Holding; Gen. Man. MUHAMED XHYRXHEHALO.

Sigal Kosovë: 10000 Prishtina, Rruga Vaso Pasha; tel. and fax (38)
240241; e-mail info@sigal-ks.com; internet www.sigal-ks.com;
f. 2003; owned by Uniqa Group Austria; five main brs in Prishtina,
Prizren, Peja, Ferizaj and Gjilan; two sub-brs in Gjakova and
Mitrovica; more than 50 agencies throughout Kosovo; Dir SOFO
LIMAJ.

Sigkos: 10000 Prishtina, Rruga Sylejman Vokshi, Pallati i Kuq; tel.
(38) 240022; fax (38) 240222; e-mail info@sigkos.com; internet www
.sigkos.com; f. 2006; Dir IBRAHIM KASTRATI.

Sigma Kosovo: 10000 Prishtina, Qyteza Pejton, Rruga Pashko
Vasa; tel. (38) 246301; fax (38) 246302; e-mail info@sigma-ks.net;
internet www.sigma-ks.net; f. 2004; part of Vienna Insurance Gp;
Dir ROLAND KACANI.

Siguria: 10000 Prishtina, Rruga Luan Haradinaj; tel. (38) 248848;
fax (38) 248850; e-mail info@ks-siguria.com; internet www
.ks-siguria.com; f. 2000; Dir RRAHIM PACOLLI.

Trade and Industry

GOVERNMENT AGENCIES

Investment Promotion Agency of Kosovo (IPAK): 10000 Prishtina, Rruga Muharrem Fejza; tel. (38) 20036527; fax (38) 212807;
e-mail info@invest-ks.org; internet www.invest-ks.org; CEO VAL-
DRIN LLUKA.

Privatization Agency of Kosovo: 10000 Prishtina, Rruga Ilir
Konushevci 8; tel. (38) 500400; e-mail info@pak-ks.org; internet www
.pak-ks.org; fmrly Kosovo Trust Agency, supervised by UNMIK;
restructured as above in June 2008; Vice-Chair. and Dir HAXHI ARIFI.

CHAMBERS OF COMMERCE

American Chamber of Commerce: 10000 Prishtina, Fehmi Agani
36/3; tel. (38) 246012; fax (38) 248012; e-mail info@amchamksv.org;
internet www.amchamksv.org; f. 2004; Exec. Dir VISAR BAJRA; 90
mem. cos.

Kosovo Chamber of Commerce (Oda Ekonomike e Kosovës):
10000 Prishtina, Rruga Nënë Terezë 20; tel. and fax (38) 224299;
e-mail info@oek-kcc.org; internet www.oek-kcc.org; Pres. SAFET
GËRXHALIU; Sec.-Gen. BERAT RUKIQI.

UTILITIES

Kosovo Energy Corpn (Korporata Energetike e Kosovës/Ener-
getska Korporacija Kosova—KEK): 10000 Prishtina; e-mail
komunikime@kek-energy.com; internet www.kek-energy.com; generation and distribution of electricity; Chair. FADIL ÇITAKU.

Prishtina Regional Water Company (Kompania Ujësjellësi Rajo-
nal 'Prishtina'): 10000 Prishtina, Rruga Tahir Zajmi; tel. (38) 551010;
e-mail info@kur-prishtina.com; internet www.kur-prishtina.com;

f. 2007; offers services in central Kosovo, 550,000 customers (est.);
Dir SKENDER BUBLAKU.

TRADE UNIONS

Union of Independent Trade Unions of Kosovo (BSPK) (Bashkimi i Sindikatave të Pavarura të Kosovës): 10000 Prishtina, Rruga
Nënë Terezë 35; tel. and fax (38) 222859; e-mail info@bspk.org;
internet www.bspk.org; 120,000 mems in 18 federations (2006);
Chair. HAXHI ARIFI.

Transport

RAILWAYS

In 2013 there were 430 km of railways and 33 railway stations in
operation in Kosovo.

Hekurudhat e Kosovës/Kosovske Železnice (Kosovo Railways):
Fushë Kosovë, Sheshi i lirisë pn; tel. (38) 536355; fax (38) 536307;
e-mail info@kosovorailway.com; f. 2005 to replace UNMIK Railway;
jt-stock co; operates railway services within Kosovo and international services to Skopje, former Yugoslav republic of Macedonia;
Man. Dir XHEVAT RAMOSAJ.

ROADS

Kosovo's road network totalled 6,955 km in 2010, including 38 km of
motorways; 26.02% of roads were paved.

CIVIL AVIATION

There is an international airport at Prishtina.

Defence

Under an agreement between the North Atlantic Treaty Organization (NATO) and the Federal Government, reached in June 1999, and
a subsequent UN resolution, the NATO-led Kosovo Force (KFOR—
with a maximum authorized strength of 50,000 personnel) was
deployed in the province of Kosovo, and the UN Interim Administration Mission in Kosovo (UNMIK) was installed. In September,
following the disarmament of the Kosovo Liberation Army paramilitary organization, the movement was reconstituted as a 5,000-
member civil emergency security force, the Kosovo Protection Corps.
After Kosovo's declaration of independence in February 2008, an EU
Rule of Law Mission (EULEX Kosovo), comprising some 1,900 foreign personnel and 1,100 local staff, became operational under the
overall authority of the UN in December. In April 2014 the mandate
of EULEX was extended until mid-2016. In January 2009 the Kosovo
Protection Corps was dissolved and a new, multi-ethnic, Kosovo
Security Force was launched, with 2,500 active members, plus 800
reserves. A reduced UNMIK presence was to continue in the country
indefinitely under UN Resolution 1244. By February 2015 UNMIK
comprised just 15 uniformed personnel (eight military liaison officers
and seven police officers). At that time 4,651 multi-national KFOR
troops, led by NATO, continued to maintain security in support of
Kosovo's institutions.

Commander of KFOR: Maj.-Gen. FRANCESCO PAOLO FIGLIUOLO.

Education

Responsibility for education was transferred to the Ministry of
Education, Science and Technology in 2002. The system of compulsory education was extended from eight to nine years in 2003/04. The
education system comprises a five-year period of primary education,
beginning at seven years, and two cycles of secondary education,
lasting four years and three years, respectively. The higher education system operates through two state universities, the University
of Prishtina, and the University of Mitrovica; a total of 65,315
students were enrolled in higher education in 2012/13.

KUWAIT

Introductory Survey

LOCATION, CLIMATE, LANGUAGE, RELIGION, FLAG, CAPITAL

The State of Kuwait lies at the north-west extreme of the Persian (Arabian) Gulf, bordered to the north-west by Iraq and to the south by Saudi Arabia. The state comprises a mainland region and nine small islands, of which the largest is Bubiyan and the most populous is Failaka. Immediately to the south of Kuwait, along the Gulf, lies a Neutral (Partitioned) Zone of 5,700 sq km, which is shared between Kuwait and Saudi Arabia. Much of Kuwait is arid desert, and the climate is generally hot and humid. Temperatures in July and August often exceed 45°C (113°F), and in the winter months are frequently above 20°C (68°F)—although there is often frost at night. Average annual rainfall is only 111 mm. The official language is Arabic, which is spoken by the majority of Kuwaiti nationals (estimated to have comprised 30.8% of Kuwait's population in mid-2013) and by many of the country's non-Kuwaiti residents. Apart from other Arabs, the non-Kuwaitis are mainly Iranians, Indians and Pakistanis. The majority of Kuwaitis are Muslims, around 70% of whom are thought to belong to the Sunni sect. The national flag (proportions 1 by 2) has three equal horizontal stripes, of green, white and red, with a superimposed black trapezoid at the hoist. The capital is Kuwait City.

CONTEMPORARY POLITICAL HISTORY

Historical Context

Kuwait became part of Turkey's Ottoman Empire in the 16th century. During the later years of Ottoman rule Kuwait became a semi-autonomous Arab monarchy, with local administration controlled by a Sheikh of the al-Sabah family, which is still the ruling dynasty. In 1899, fearing an extension of Turkish control, the ruler of Kuwait made a treaty with the United Kingdom, accepting British protection while surrendering control over external relations. Nominal Turkish suzerainty over Kuwait ended in 1918, with the dissolution of the Ottoman Empire.

Petroleum was first discovered in Kuwait in 1938, but exploration was interrupted by the Second World War (1939–45). After 1945 drilling resumed on a large scale, and extensive deposits of petroleum were found. Sheikh Ahmad (ruler since 1921) was succeeded in 1950 by his cousin, Sheikh Abdullah al-Salim al-Sabah, who inaugurated a programme of public works and educational development, funded by petroleum revenues, which transformed Kuwait's infrastructure and introduced a comprehensive system of welfare services.

Domestic Political Affairs

Kuwait became fully independent on 19 June 1961, when the United Kingdom and Kuwait agreed to terminate the 1899 treaty. The ruler took the title of Amir and assumed full executive power. Kuwait was admitted to the League of Arab States (the Arab League, see p. 359) despite opposition from Iraq, which claimed that Kuwait was historically part of Iraqi territory. Kuwait's first election took place in December 1961, when voters chose 20 members of a Constituent Assembly (the other members being government ministers appointed by the Amir). The Assembly drafted a new Constitution, which was adopted in December 1962. A 50-member Majlis al-Umma (National Assembly) was elected, under a limited franchise, in January 1963. In the absence of formal political parties (which remain illegal), candidates contested the poll as independents, although some known opponents of the Government were elected. In the same month the Amir appointed his brother, Sheikh Sabah al-Salim al-Sabah (the heir apparent), to be Prime Minister. Iraq renounced its claim to Kuwait in October, and diplomatic relations between the two countries were established.

In January 1965, following conflict between the paternalistic ruling family and the democratically inclined National Assembly, the powers of the Council of Ministers were strengthened. The Amir died in November 1965, and Sheikh Sabah succeeded to the throne. He was replaced as Prime Minister by his cousin, Sheikh Jaber al-Ahmad al-Sabah, who was named heir apparent in May 1966. The Neutral (Partitioned) Zone between Kuwait and Saudi Arabia was formally divided between the two countries in 1969: revenues from oil production in the area are shared equally.

As Kuwait's petroleum sector expanded during the 1960s, the country became increasingly wealthy. The Government effected an extensive redistribution of income, through public expenditure and a land compensation scheme, but there was some popular discontent concerning corruption, and official manipulation of the media and the National Assembly. A more representative legislature was elected in January 1971 (again under a limited franchise). A further general election took place in January 1975, but in August 1976 the Amir dissolved the assembly, on the grounds that it was acting against the best interests of the state. Sheikh Sabah died in December 1977 and was succeeded by Crown Prince Jaber. In January 1978 the new Amir appointed Sheikh Saad al-Abdullah al-Salim al-Sabah to be his heir apparent. The new Crown Prince, hitherto Minister of Defence and the Interior, became Prime Minister in the following month. In accordance with an Amiri decree of August 1980, a new National Assembly was elected in February 1981, although only one-half of the eligible 6% of the population registered to vote.

The collapse of Kuwait's unofficial stock exchange, the Souk al-Manakh, in September 1982 caused a prolonged financial crisis, and eventually led to the resignations of the Ministers of Finance (in 1983) and of Justice (in 1985). The National Assembly subsequently opposed several government measures, including proposed price increases for public services, educational reforms and legislation to restrict the press, and questioned the competence of certain ministers. In July 1986 the Council of Ministers submitted its resignation to the Amir, who then dissolved the assembly and suspended some articles of the Constitution, declaring his intention to rule by decree. The Crown Prince was immediately reappointed Prime Minister. An Amiri decree accorded the Council of Ministers greater powers of press censorship.

In late 1989 the Amir refused to accept a petition, signed by more than 20,000 Kuwaiti citizens, seeking the restoration of the National Assembly. In January 1990 police dispersed two pro-democracy demonstrations, although later in the month the Government agreed to relax press censorship. In June 62% of eligible voters participated in a general election for 50 members of a 'provisional' National Council; a further 25 members were appointed by the Amir. The election was boycotted by pro-democracy activists, who continued to demand the full restoration of the National Assembly.

Relations between Kuwait and Iraq were stable until 1973, when Iraqi troops occupied a Kuwaiti outpost on their joint border. Kuwait none the less supplied aid to Iraq from the outbreak of the Iran–Iraq War in 1980. As a result, Kuwaiti petroleum installations and shipping in the Persian (Arabian) Gulf were targeted intermittently by Iranian forces, and by pro-Iranian groups within Kuwait, for much of the 1980s. A large number of Iranians were among 27,000 expatriates deported in 1985–86, and in 1987 the Government initiated a five-year plan to reduce the number of expatriates in the Kuwaiti workforce. Kuwait resumed diplomatic relations with Iran following the 1988 ceasefire between Iran and Iraq.

Iraqi invasion of Kuwait

In July 1990 the Iraqi Government implicitly criticized Kuwait (among other states) for disregarding the petroleum production quotas stipulated by the Organization of the Petroleum Exporting Countries (OPEC, see p. 406). It also declared that Kuwait should cancel Iraq's war debt and compensate it for losses of revenue incurred during the war with Iran, and as a result of Kuwait's overproduction of petroleum—to which Iraq attributed a decline in international oil prices. In addition, Iraq alleged that Kuwait had established military posts and drilled oil wells on Iraqi territory. Despite regional mediation efforts, Iraq began to deploy armed forces on the Kuwait–Iraq border. Direct negotiations in Jeddah, Saudi Arabia, at the end of the month between Kuwaiti and Iraqi officials collapsed, and on 2 August some

100,000 Iraqi troops invaded Kuwait (the total military strength of which was about 20,000): Iraq stated that it had entered at the invitation of insurgents who had overthrown the Kuwaiti Government. The Amir and other government members fled to Saudi Arabia, where they established a 'Government-in-exile', while Iraq declared that a provisional Government had been formed in Kuwait comprising Iraqi-sponsored Kuwaiti dissidents. The UN Security Council immediately adopted a series of resolutions, of which the first (Resolution 660) condemned the invasion, demanded the immediate and unconditional withdrawal of Iraqi forces from Kuwait, and appealed for a negotiated settlement of the conflict. A trade embargo was then imposed on Iraq and Kuwait. Meanwhile, the USA and member states of the European Community (now European Union—EU, see p. 271) froze all Kuwait's overseas assets to prevent their repatriation. Five days after the invasion US troops and aircraft were deployed in Saudi Arabia, with the stated aim of securing that country's borders with Kuwait in the event of further Iraqi territorial expansion. A number of European governments, together with some Arab League states, agreed to provide military support for the US forces. The Iraqi Government subsequently announced the formal annexation of Kuwait, and ordered the closure of foreign diplomatic missions there. At the end of August most of Kuwait was officially declared to be the 19th Governorate of Iraq, while a northern strip was incorporated into the Basra Governorate.

In the months following the invasion apparent attempts at demographic manipulation—by settling Iraqis and Palestinians in Kuwait and by forcing Kuwaitis to assume Iraqi citizenship—were documented. The population was estimated to have decreased from approximately 2m. prior to the invasion to some 700,000, of whom Kuwaitis constituted about 300,000, Palestinians 200,000, and the remainder comprised other Arab and Asian expatriates. Many Kuwaitis, and Arab and Asian expatriates, had fled Iraq and Kuwait into Jordan, while most European and US expatriates were temporarily detained as hostages.

UN Security Council Resolution 678, adopted in November 1990, authorized the multinational force by now stationed in Saudi Arabia and the Gulf region to use 'all necessary means' to liberate Kuwait. It was implied that should Iraq not begin, by 15 January 1991, to implement the terms of 10 resolutions hitherto adopted regarding the invasion, military action would ensue. Renewed international diplomatic attempts failed to avert a military confrontation. On the night of 16–17 January the US-led multinational force launched an intensive aerial bombardment of Iraq. Ground forces entered Kuwait during the night of 23–24 February, encountering relatively little effective Iraqi opposition. Within three days the Iraqi Government had agreed to comply with the terms of all Security Council resolutions concerning Kuwait, and on 28 February the USA suspended military operations. Resolutions 686 and 687, adopted by the UN Security Council in March and April, respectively, dictated the terms to Iraq for a permanent ceasefire: Iraq was required to release all allied prisoners of war and Kuwaitis detained as hostages, repeal all laws and decrees concerning the annexation of Kuwait, and recognize the inviolability of the Iraq–Kuwait border. Iraq promptly announced its compliance with both resolutions. Resolution 689, adopted in April, provided for the establishment of a demilitarized zone, to be supervised by a UN Iraq-Kuwait Observation Mission (UNIKOM).

Meanwhile, in October 1990, at a conference in Jeddah of some 1,000 prominent Kuwaitis, the exiled Crown Prince Saad pledged to restore the country's Constitution and legislature and to organize free elections after Kuwait's eventual liberation. In February 1991, however, the Government-in-exile excluded the possibility of early elections, maintaining that the need to rebuild and repopulate the country took precedence over that for political reform. Immediately following liberation an Amiri decree imposed martial law in Kuwait, and in March the formation of a state security committee was announced: its objectives included the investigation of individuals suspected of collaboration with the Iraqi authorities in Kuwait and the prevention of unofficial acts of reprisal. Palestinians in Kuwait were a particular target of reprisals, and it was alleged by several human rights organizations that they were subject to torture by Kuwaiti security forces. Kuwait's Palestinian population, which had totalled around 400,000 prior to the Iraqi invasion, was estimated to have declined to less than 50,000 by early 1992.

The Amir, the Prime Minister and other members of the exiled regime returned to Kuwait in March 1991. The Council of Ministers resigned later that month, apparently in response to public discontent at the Government's failure to restore essential services. Although several specialists were appointed to strategic posts within the new Government named by Sheikh Saad in April (most notably to the finance, planning and oil portfolios), other important positions (including the foreign affairs, interior and defence ministries) were allocated to members of the al-Sabah family.

In May 1991 it was revealed that some 900 people were under investigation in Kuwait in connection with crimes committed during the Iraqi occupation; about 200 of these were accused of collaboration. The Government undertook to investigate alleged abuses documented by the human rights organization Amnesty International, which claimed that trials were being conducted without the provision of adequate defence counsel and that in some cases torture had been used to extract confessions. Martial law was ended in June, and 29 death sentences hitherto imposed on convicted collaborators were commuted to custodial terms. In August a tribunal, said to guarantee defendants the right to greater legal protection, was established to replace the martial law courts.

It was announced in August 1991 that the USA would maintain 1,500 troops in Kuwait for several more months, after little progress had been achieved in negotiations for the establishment of a regional defence force. In September the US and Kuwaiti Governments signed a 10-year defence co-operation agreement, permitting the storage of US supplies in Kuwait, and providing for joint military training and exercises. (The agreement was renewed for a further 10 years in February 2001, then from 2011 remained in force for an indefinite period.) Defence accords were signed with both the United Kingdom and France in 1992.

In June 1993 the State Security Court was reported to have issued death sentences against 17 people who had been found guilty of collaborating with Iraq in 1990–91; Alaa Hussein Ali, the leader of the provisional Government installed by Iraq in August 1990, was convicted *in absentia*. Human rights organizations welcomed the endorsement by the National Assembly, in August 1995, of government proposals to abolish the State Security Court, which they had criticized for convicting some 120 alleged collaborators by trials that failed to satisfy international standards.

Political developments following the Gulf War

Elections to the new National Assembly, in October 1992, were contested by some 280 candidates, many of whom (although nominally independent) were affiliated to one of several quasi-political organizations; the franchise was again restricted. Anti-Government candidates, notably those representing Islamist groups, were unexpectedly successful, securing 31 of the chamber's 50 seats. The Prime Minister subsequently formed a new Government, including six parliamentarians; members of the ruling family retained control of foreign affairs, the interior and defence.

In December 1992 the National Assembly established a commission of inquiry into the circumstances surrounding the 1990 invasion. The commission's report, published in May 1995, revealed profound negligence on the part of government and military officials, who had apparently ignored warnings of an imminent invasion. The report also claimed that the immediate flight of members of the royal family and the Council of Ministers had deprived the country of political leadership and military organization.

Meanwhile, in June 1994 the National Assembly approved legislation extending the franchise to sons of naturalized Kuwaitis. In July 1996 the Ministry of the Interior announced that an electorate of just over 107,000 men was entitled to vote in the forthcoming elections to the assembly, scheduled for 7 October. Pro-Government candidates were the most successful, securing the majority of the 50 seats, and Sheikh Saad was reappointed Prime Minister.

However, Sheikh Saad submitted his Government's resignation in March 1998, after members of parliament proposed a motion of no confidence in the Minister of Information, Sheikh Sa'ud Nasir al-Sa'ud al-Sabah, who had allowed what were deemed 'un-Islamic' publications to be exhibited at a book fair in Kuwait. The Amir immediately reappointed the Crown Prince as Prime Minister, and a new Government was named at the end of the month.

In May 1999 the Amir dissolved the National Assembly and ordered fresh elections. At the election, which took place on 3 July, pro-Government candidates took just 12 seats; Islamist candidates won 20 seats and liberals 14, with the remaining four seats going to independents. Sheikh Saad was again reappointed

Prime Minister, and the ruling family retained control of the strategic foreign affairs, oil, interior and defence portfolios, although a number of liberal deputies joined the Government.

Alaa Hussein Ali, who had been in self-imposed exile since Kuwait's liberation, returned to Kuwait in January 2000 in order to appeal against the death sentence pronounced in June 1993. The Court of Appeal upheld the ruling in July 2001, but in March 2001 commuted Hussein's death sentence to one of life imprisonment.

In July 2000 unrest was reported in the Al-Jahra region, where a community of *bidoun* ('stateless' Arabs) form the majority of the population. (About 100,000 *bidoun* reside in Kuwait, but the authorities refuse to recognize their claims to Kuwaiti nationality.) The unrest followed the approval, in May, of a draft amendment to the Citizenship Law that would grant only a small number of *bidoun* the right to Kuwaiti citizenship. Some 1,000 *bidoun* obtained citizenship in early 2001, leading to protests by those whose applications had been refused.

Sheikh Saad tendered his Government's resignation in January 2001. The Crown Prince denied that this constituted an attempt to prevent parliamentary scrutiny of the Minister of Justice and of Awqaf and Islamic Affairs, Saad Jasem Yousuf al-Hashil, relating to allegations of inefficiency and corruption in his ministry. The Amir immediately reappointed Sheikh Saad as Prime Minister, and a new Government was named in February.

In January 2002 Adil Khalid al-Sabih resigned as Minister of Oil, following an explosion at the Raudhatain oilfield in which four people were killed. Several members of the increasingly assertive National Assembly, however, demanded the resignation of the entire Government, alleging that the explosion was the result of state corruption and mismanagement.

After a campaign that was overshadowed by the US-led military intervention in Iraq (which was largely conducted from Kuwaiti territory), parliamentary elections were held, as scheduled, in early July 2003. Islamist candidates secured 21 of the 50 seats available, while pro-Government candidates won 14 seats, independents (regarded as being aligned with the Government) 12 and liberals three. Later that month the ailing Crown Prince relinquished the position of Prime Minister. The appointment of Sheikh Sabah al-Ahmad al-Sabah as his replacement represented an unprecedented separation between the post of Prime Minister and the position of Crown Prince, and provided encouragement to reformists after their heavy electoral losses. A new Council of Ministers was announced in mid-July.

In June 2005 the Prime Minister appointed Massouma Saleh al-Mubarak as Minister of Planning and Minister of State for Administrative Development Affairs, making her Kuwait's first female member of the Council of Ministers. In a further significant improvement of women's rights, in May 2005 the National Assembly approved legislation that would permit women to vote in and contest future municipal and parliamentary elections.

The accession of Sheikh Sabah

On 15 January 2006 the death of the Amir, Sheikh Jaber, was announced. He was automatically succeeded by the Crown Prince, Sheikh Saad. However, in an unprecedented development, on 24 January Sheikh Saad, who had yet to take the oath of office, was removed from the position of Amir on health grounds, following a formal request from the Council of Ministers that the National Assembly debate the issue. The parliamentary vote in favour of replacing Sheikh Saad was unanimous. In the absence of a nominated Crown Prince, the Prime Minister, Sheikh Sabah, who was in any case regarded as the de facto ruler of the emirate, temporarily assumed the powers of the Amir. After his nomination as a permanent head of state by the Council of Ministers had been unanimously approved by the assembly, Sheikh Sabah was sworn in as Amir on 29 January. The sole controversy attached to Sheikh Sabah's accession was that, like the late Sheikh Jaber, he belonged to the al-Jaber branch of the ruling al-Sabah family, which, by tradition, alternated the position of Amir with the al-Salim branch of the family, of which Sheikh Saad was a member.

The new Amir accepted the resignation of the Council of Ministers in January 2006. In February Sheikh Sabah appointed his nephew, Sheikh Nasser al-Muhammad al-Ahmad al-Sabah, as the new Prime Minister, and his brother, Sheikh Nawwaf al-Ahmad al-Jaber al-Sabah, as Crown Prince. The appointments emphasized the channelling of power towards the al-Jaber branch of the ruling family. Later that month the Amir approved Sheikh Nasser's first Council of Ministers.

A long-running campaign for electoral reform, which sought to reduce the number of electoral constituencies in Kuwait, began to attract popular support from May 2006. A proposal by the Government to reduce the number of constituencies from 25 to 10 was rejected by the opposition, which advocated a reduction to just five constituencies. The Amir subsequently dissolved parliament and called for elections to be held in late June. A loose alliance of 29 pro-reform members of the outgoing legislature was formed to contest the elections. Reformists made significant gains at the polls, winning 34 of the 50 seats contested. The remaining 16 seats were won by independents and pro-Government candidates. A reform bill drafted by the new assembly proposing the introduction of a five-constituency electoral system was passed into law in July. Also in that month a new Council of Ministers was named under Prime Minister Sheikh Nasser.

In December 2006 the Minister of Information, Muhammad Nasser al-Sanousi, resigned following a request by the increasingly confrontational parliament to question him over allegations that he had curbed media freedom during the recent election campaign. In February 2007 deputies cross-examined the Minister of Health, Sheikh Ahmad Abdullah al-Ahmad al-Sabah, on charges related to the deteriorating state of the health service. However, in early March, one day before the National Assembly was due to debate a motion of no confidence in the minister, the entire Council of Ministers resigned. Sheikh Ahmad was excluded from the new, largely unchanged Government that was approved by the Amir in late March. In June Sheikh Ali al-Jarrah al-Sabah resigned as Minister of Oil; the assembly had been scheduled to debate a motion of no confidence in the minister after having questioned him over allegations of corruption. In October Prime Minister Sheikh Nasser instigated an extensive reorganization of the Council of Ministers.

In March 2008 the Council of Ministers resigned, stating that the assembly was obstructing ministers' attempts to carry out their duties effectively. The immediate cause of the crisis involved a dispute concerning salary increases for state employees, with deputies asserting that the proposed pay rise was too low. Sheikh Sabah ordered the dissolution of parliament in order for fresh elections to take place in May.

Meanwhile, in February 2008 tensions increased between Kuwait's majority Sunni and minority Shi'a communities after several hundred Shi'a had held a rally to commemorate the death of a senior commander of the militant Shi'a organization Hezbollah in Lebanon. Imad Mughniyeh, who had been killed earlier that month in a bomb attack in the Syrian capital, Damascus, was described by the Kuwaiti Government as a 'terrorist'. It was claimed that Mughniyeh had been responsible for the hijacking of a Kuwait Airways plane in 1988, in which two Kuwaiti passengers were killed. A number of prominent Shi'a politicians and clerics were questioned by the authorities over their involvement in the rally, and many arrests were reported. In October 2008 it was reported that two prominent Shi'a members of parliament were among seven people acquitted by a court in Kuwait for their alleged membership of an illegal opposition group, Hezbollah Kuwait.

Escalating tension between the National Assembly and the Government following the election of May 2008

At the legislative election held on 17 May 2008, Islamist candidates performed strongly, with Sunni Islamists winning 21 of the 50 seats in the National Assembly and Shi'a Islamists (including the Popular Action Bloc) nine; independents garnered 13 seats, and liberals seven. The Amir subsequently reappointed Sheikh Nasser to the post of Prime Minister. In late May Sheikh Nasser appointed a new Council of Ministers, which included two women.

In July 2008 hundreds of Bangladeshi workers protested about low wages and poor working conditions. The demonstration turned violent, and the police reportedly arrested and later deported some 1,000 of the protesters. The incident renewed international discussion of Kuwait's human rights record. The Council of Ministers subsequently announced that it would introduce a minimum monthly wage of KD 40 (US \$150) for workers employed by companies contracted by the Government. In October the Government announced its intention to draft legislation abolishing its much-criticized employee sponsorship system (which stipulates that foreign workers must be sponsored by a Kuwaiti employer); however, labour market reforms aimed at improving the conditions of expatriate workers approved by the National Assembly in December did not address this system. Although the Government pledged in December 2010 to terminate the system during 2011, it remained in place in 2015.

Meanwhile, parliamentarians continued to express disquiet over the Prime Minister's handling of the Government and his alleged mismanagement of public funds. In early November 2008 three Sunni Islamist members of the National Assembly submitted a request to question Sheikh Nasser over the decision to allow the controversial Iranian Shi'a cleric, Muhammad Baqer al-Fali, to visit Kuwait (al-Fali had been banned from entering Kuwait after being convicted of religious slurs against Sunni Muslims and of 'threatening national unity'). To avert parliamentary questioning of the Prime Minister, on 25 November the entire Council of Ministers resigned. The Amir accepted its resignation on 1 December, and on 12 January 2009 approved the formation of a new, largely unchanged Government under Sheikh Nasser.

In March 2009 several Islamist members of the legislature sought to question the Prime Minister about allegations of misuse of public funds and the failure to adapt economic policy to the worsening global financial climate. The continued refusal by Sheikh Nasser to submit to scrutiny precipitated the resignation of the entire Council of Ministers in mid-March, as a result of which the Amir ordered the dissolution of parliament; fresh elections were subsequently called for May. Meanwhile, in April the Government's programme of economic stimulus, envisaging expenditure of up to US $5,200m. to support Kuwait's beleaguered financial markets, entered into effect.

An estimated 59% of eligible voters participated in the parliamentary elections held on 16 May 2009: Sunni Islamists retained only 11 seats in the 50-member National Assembly, losing out to Shi'a Islamists (who won nine seats) and liberals (eight seats), with the balance gained by tribal-based independents. For the first time since women were allowed to participate in electoral politics in 2005, four female candidates were successful. Sheikh Nasser was reappointed Prime Minister and a new Council of Ministers was named in late May 2009.

Political events after the 2009 elections

At the inaugural session of the new legislature in late May 2009, the Amir stressed the need for co-operation at all levels of government in order to safeguard national unity and promote economic development. However, the session was boycotted by 14 Islamist and tribal deputies in protest at the composition of the new Council of Ministers. Several Islamist deputies also lodged objections against two female members of parliament, who declined to wear the *hijab* (Islamic headscarf) during the opening session, accusing them of violating legislation requiring women to adhere to *Shari'a* (Islamic) law.

In an unprecedented move, on 8 December 2009 Prime Minister Sheikh Nasser agreed to submit himself to formal scrutiny by members of parliament, concerning allegations of misuse of public funds; similar motions were lodged against three other senior government ministers. Following the interrogation of the Prime Minister and the Ministers of Defence, the Interior, and Public Works and Municipal Affairs in a closed parliamentary session on 9 December, 10 deputies proposed a motion of non-co-operation against Sheikh Nasser. The Prime Minister comfortably survived the vote against him a week later.

Despite the ongoing tensions between the executive and the legislature, a four-year economic development plan proposed by the Government received parliamentary support in February 2010, and was implemented in April. In May parliament approved legislation allowing the privatization of certain state assets—excluding the production of petroleum and natural gas, oil refineries and the health and education sectors.

In July 2010 the Prime Minister and Minister of Information declared that public criticism of the Amir, Prime Minister, government ministers and countries with which Kuwait enjoyed close relations constituted a threat to national unity, and announced that the Government intended to amend the press and publications law accordingly. In November a prominent Kuwaiti journalist, Muhammad Abd al-Qader al-Jassem, was convicted on a charge of defaming the Prime Minister and was sentenced to one year's imprisonment; in the following month this was reduced to three months. Although al-Jassem was released in January 2011, after the Supreme Court again overturned his original conviction, a new series of similar charges was levelled against the writer at the end of that month. In October 2012 the Ministry of Foreign Affairs threatened to take legal action against al-Jassem (who was acting as the lawyer of former parliamentarian Musallam al-Barrak—see *Recent developments*), after he was accused of damaging the close diplomatic relations between Kuwait and both Saudi Arabia and the United

Arab Emirates (UAE) by comments he had made concerning their 'unacceptable interference' in Kuwait's domestic affairs.

In mid-December 2010 the Government shut down the local offices of the Qatar-based broadcaster Al Jazeera. A few days previously Al Jazeera had broadcast video footage that purported to show Kuwaiti security forces using excessive force to disperse people attending an opposition rally earlier that month. In late December a motion of non-co-operation was filed against Sheikh Nasser by members of an opposition grouping in the National Assembly, which blamed the Prime Minister for the violence. Sheikh Nasser narrowly survived the motion, which was conducted in January 2011.

Opposition members pledged to continue to fight for the removal from office of the Prime Minister and Government. In February 2011 the Deputy Prime Minister and Minister of the Interior, Sheikh Jaber, was replaced by Sheikh Ahmad Homoud al-Jaber al-Sabah; Sheikh Jaber had resigned in January before parliamentary questioning over allegations of the use of torture by the police. In early March a number of youth opposition groups began protests in the capital demanding the resignation of Sheikh Nasser and reform of the political system; the pro-democracy rallies mirrored similar ones taking place across much of the Arab world, having begun in Tunisia at the end of 2010. Later in March 2011 parliamentarians filed requests to interrogate the Prime Minister and a number of his ministers, all of whom were members of the ruling family, relating to allegations including corruption and financial mismanagement.

On 1 April 2011 the Amir accepted the resignation of the Council of Ministers, which had been announced the previous day by the Prime Minister. However, on 5 April Sheikh Nasser was reappointed as Prime Minister and instructed to form a government. The new Council of Ministers took office in May 2011; members of the ruling family retained the foreign affairs, interior and defence portfolios.

Meanwhile, in February 2011 Kuwaiti security forces had acted forcefully to bring to an end anti-Government protests being held by groups of *bidoun* in Al-Jahra and elsewhere against their continued failure to secure certain basic rights, principally the right to gain Kuwaiti citizenship; a number of the demonstrators were detained by the authorities. Further unrest occurred in Al-Jahra in March, after it was revealed that the passage through the National Assembly of draft legislation that would grant basic entitlements to the *bidoun*, such as free provision of medical and educational services, had been blocked by the Government. In early December legal proceedings began against 52 demonstrators, the charges against whom included holding illegal public gatherings and attacking security forces. Renewed protests were held by stateless Arabs in Al-Jahra in that month, leading to further arrests. Nevertheless, in late December the Government pledged to consider granting citizenship to around 34,000 of the stateless provided that they fulfilled certain eligibility criteria. A bill allowing up to 4,000 foreigners to gain Kuwaiti citizenship during 2013, adopted by parliament in March of that year, was widely expected to be used to naturalize a further group of stateless Arabs. However, it was reported in January 2014 that no *bidoun* had been naturalized in 2013, with discussions ongoing between the Council of Ministers and National Assembly about how to proceed with the naturalization of up to 4,000 stateless residents by the end of 2014.

In early May 2011 Prime Minister Sheikh Nasser was again questioned by opposition members of the National Assembly relating to his management of Kuwait's four-year economic development plan and his alleged involvement in corrupt practices. However, in mid-May parliament agreed to allow a postponement of Sheikh Nasser's interrogation until May 2012, while the Constitutional Court examined the Prime Minister's case. Opposition activists continued to demand the resignation of the Prime Minister and his administration. On 13 June 2011 the Deputy Prime Minister and Minister for Housing Affairs, Sheikh Ahmad Fahad al-Sabah, resigned from the Government, stating that a request for a group of parliamentarians to question him over claims of corruption and mismanagement was unconstitutional.

On 14 June 2011 Sheikh Nasser was questioned by two Sunni Islamist deputies and one independent legislator about his Government's close relationship with Iran. This was, they claimed, to the detriment of Kuwait's relations with other Cooperation Council for the Arab States of the Gulf (Gulf Cooperation Council—GCC) member states and thus to the emirate's security. The request to interrogate the Prime Minister was made after Kuwait had been slow to respond to calls from the

Bahraini Government for military support to quell the Shi'a-led pro-democracy protests that were taking place there, and after a controversial visit by the Iranian Minister of Foreign Affairs, Ali Akbar Salehi, to Kuwait in May. (Kuwait did eventually send a small naval force to Bahrain in May 2011 to assist the GCC 'Peninsula Shield' forces that had arrived in March.) There was evidence of an increase in tensions between Kuwait's Sunni and Shi'a communities as a result of the 'Arab spring' protests erupting across the Middle East and North Africa, and particularly the situation in Bahrain: Shi'a and moderate Kuwaitis strongly opposed the Bahraini authorities' harsh crackdown on the anti-Government protests. On 23 June Sheikh Nasser survived another no-confidence motion.

Early election in 2012 and annulment of result

Sheikh Muhammad, the long-serving Deputy Prime Minister and Minister of Foreign Affairs, resigned on 17 October 2011. He had been implicated in a judicial investigation into allegations of official corruption, which reportedly involved the transfer of US $350m. of public funds as bribes to some 16 pro-Government deputies, in exchange for securing the deputies' support in parliamentary votes. On 23 October Sheikh Sabah al-Khaled al-Hamad al-Sabah was appointed to succeed Sheikh Muhammad in both his former roles. Following a recurrence of pro-democracy demonstrations and strikes in November, to which the security forces again responded forcefully, on 16 November pro-reform campaigners and opposition deputies forced entry into the National Assembly building and demanded the resignation of the Prime Minister. Their action came after a further demand to interrogate Sheikh Nasser by opposition parliamentarians, relating to the same corruption scandal, was defeated by pro-Government deputies. Many of the protesters were arrested, and trial proceedings were subsequently launched against 24 opposition activists.

On 28 November 2011 the Prime Minister and Council of Ministers resigned, and on 30 November Sheikh Sabah asked Sheikh Jaber Mubarak al-Hamad al-Sabah, the outgoing First Deputy Prime Minister and Minister of Defence, to serve as premier at the head of a transitional government. Sheikh Jaber was sworn in on 4 December, and, in an attempt to resolve the dispute between the Government and parliament over corruption allegations and amid increasing anti-Government protests, on 6 December the Amir dissolved the National Assembly and ordered new parliamentary elections to be held more than one year ahead of schedule. A new Council of Ministers to take charge in the lead-up to the polls was inaugurated on 14 December.

Elections to the National Assembly were held on 2 February 2012, in which voter turnout was estimated at 60%. For the first time, foreign and local election monitors were officially permitted to observe the conduct of the polls. Sunni Islamists opposed to the Government made significant progress by winning 23 seats; liberals secured nine; Shi'a Islamists took seven; and the remaining seats were won by independent candidates. Unlike in 2009 (when four female candidates were successful), no women were elected to the assembly. The Prime Minister tendered his resignation on 5 February, but on the following day was asked by the Amir to lead a new government. A new Council of Ministers was sworn in on 14 February; there was a notable absence of any female or Islamist cabinet members. There was also only one elected deputy in the new Government (the minimum number required according to the Constitution). On 15 February, in an apparent concession to the opposition, Ahmad al-Saadoun, the leader of the Shi'a Popular Action Bloc, which had won five parliamentary seats, was elected as Speaker of the National Assembly.

On 17 May 2012 Sheikh Sabah rejected a proposal by a parliamentary faction called the Islamic Justice Bloc to amend the Constitution in order to change the reference to Islam as a 'major source' of legislation to the 'only source' of legislation. The campaign to render all Kuwaiti laws subject to *Shari'a* law had reportedly been endorsed by 31 of the 50 newly elected deputies. The Amir also, on 6 June, refused to endorse a bill recently adopted by the National Assembly that proposed introducing the death penalty for those convicted of blasphemy. Meanwhile, on 28 May 2012 the resignation was accepted of the Deputy Prime Minister and Minister of Finance, Mustafa al-Shamali; he had been interrogated by opposition legislators about a range of alleged financial irregularities, including squandering public funds and having links with Iran and its Lebanese ally Hezbollah. On 10 June former Prime Minister Sheikh Nasser refused for a second time to appear before a parliamentary committee concerning the corruption scandal revealed in late 2011

(although he had recently been cleared of wrongdoing by a special judicial tribunal set up to look into the matter, owing to a lack of evidence). On 11 June 2012 the Minister of Social Affairs and Labour, Ahmad Abd al-Latif al-Rujeib, also resigned, after the Assembly had sought to question him regarding the issuing of work permits.

On 20 June 2012 the Constitutional Court annulled the results of the legislative elections held in February, having ruled that the dissolution of the previous legislature had been unconstitutional. The ruling prompted the effective restoration of the more pro-Government Assembly elected in 2009; however, more than one-half of its members immediately resigned their seats in protest against the decision, citing the fact that the previous assembly had been implicated in several cases of corruption. The Government under Sheikh Jaber resigned on 25 June 2012; its resignation was accepted by the Amir on 1 July. Meanwhile, a reported 30,000 Islamist and other demonstrators took part in a protest rally held in Kuwait City on 29 June 2012, at which they demanded the restoration of parliament and introduction of a constitutional monarchy with full democratic rights for Kuwaiti citizens. On 5 July Sheikh Sabah asked Sheikh Jaber to lead an interim administration. The new Council of Ministers was approved by the Amir on 19 July. The scheduled inauguration of the Council of Ministers before a session of the recently reinstated Assembly on 31 July was delayed by the fact that so many deputies had chosen not to take up their seats.

The restored National Assembly was itself dissolved by Amiri decree on 7 October 2012, and early elections were subsequently scheduled for December. Leading opposition groups declared that they would boycott the poll in protest against amendments to the electoral law, announced in another decree signed by Sheikh Sabah on 19 October, which reintroduced a system of one vote (rather than four) for each constituency. On 25 September the Constitutional Court had rejected draft legislation put forward by the Council of Ministers which involved a redrawing of the country's electoral boundaries (from the five-constituency system created in 2006). Large-scale protests were held during October 2012, as opposition activists sought to persuade the Council of Ministers not to approve amendments that would favour pro-Government candidates at the forthcoming polls by making it harder for opposition groups, including Islamists, to form coalitions. Around 20,000 demonstrators reportedly engaged in violent clashes with security forces in front of the Assembly building on 21 October. The authorities responded to the upsurge in demonstrations by banning groups of more than 20 people from holding public gatherings and launching trial proceedings against those deemed to be involved in anti-Government dissent—including opposition deputies and journalists. The former parliamentary deputy Musallam al-Barrak was arrested on 29 October, having been accused of 'undermining the status of the Amir' by criticizing Sheikh Sabah's 'autocratic' rule during a rally held on 15 October; however, he was freed on bail on 1 November. A number of opposition activists were charged with offences such as insulting the Amir. By mid-2013 several of the activists had been given substantial prison sentences, and the Kuwaiti authorities received widespread criticism from international human rights organizations for their ongoing crackdown on freedom of speech.

At the elections held on 1 December 2012, Shi'a Islamist candidates secured 17 seats, while Sunni Islamists won just four. As a result of the electoral boycott by Islamist, liberal and nationalist opposition movements, the new National Assembly was reported to be largely pro-Government. According to the Ministry of Information, voter turnout was recorded at 38.8%. On 3 December Sheikh Sabah accepted the resignation of Sheikh Jaber and his interim Council of Ministers, before asking the incumbent Prime Minister to form a new administration. A Government led by Sheikh Jaber was sworn into office by the Amir on 12 December. Meanwhile, significant anti-Government rallies continued into early 2013, with many protesters urging the authorities to annul the results of the recent poll.

Recent developments: electoral law amended and early election held in 2013

On 8 January 2013 the newly elected National Assembly voted to adopt the amendment to the electoral law decreed by the Amir in October 2012, which had prompted the opposition's electoral boycott. On 5 February 2013 three former parliamentarians were given three-year prison terms, having been convicted of the charges of insulting Sheikh Sabah during an anti-Government rally against the proposed electoral law changes on 10 October

2012. However, on 10 February 2013 an appeals court over-turned the verdict and the three politicians were subsequently released on bail pending further court hearings. Meanwhile, during February several deputies sought to interrogate government ministers who were alleged to have committed a range of legal violations. Some opposition politicians alleged that the deputies' actions represented an attempt to force the dissolution of parliament before a scheduled ruling by the Constitutional Court on the recent changes to Kuwait's electoral law. In March Musallam al-Barrak announced the formation of the Opposition Coalition, which included a range of Islamist, nationalist, leftist, trade union and youth groups, in the hope that a stronger anti-Government alliance would be able to persuade the authorities to dissolve the current parliament, reverse the recent electoral amendment and ultimately transform Kuwait into a genuine parliamentary democracy. In April al-Barrak received a five-year prison term, having been convicted of the charge of 'under-mining' Sheikh Sabah; however, his sentence was overturned by an appeals court in May.

The assembly continued its campaign against government ministers deemed either to have engaged in corrupt practices or to have been ineffective in their posts, and in May 2013 some ministers chose to resign in order to avoid being questioned by parliamentarians. These included Hani Hussein, who tendered his resignation as the Minister of Oil, having been criticized for his role in a large compensation payment made, in 2012, by Kuwait's state-owned Petrochemical Industries Co to a US chemicals firm with which a joint venture had been terminated.

After opposition groups had lodged an appeal against the amendments to the electoral law first decreed by the Amir in October 2012 (which introduced the system of one vote for each constituency), on 16 June 2013 the Constitutional Court ruled in favour of the Government's amendments. In a similar action to that taken in June 2012, the Court therefore annulled the results of the polls of December 2012 and ordered the dissolution of the National Assembly for procedural reasons. The Council of Ministers held an emergency meeting on 20 June and announced that fresh elections would be held in late July. A number of opposition groups, including Islamists and some liberals, declared that they would boycott the polls in protest against the revisions to Kuwait's electoral legislation; however, some pro-reform groups chose to end their boycott of the electoral process.

At the elections which took place on 27 July 2013, candidates representing tribal areas secured 24 of the 50 seats in the National Assembly. Shi'a Islamist candidates won just eight seats, while Sunni Islamists took seven seats. Liberals were reported to have won five seats, while the remainder went to independent candidates, some of whom represented the *bidoun*. Voter turnout at the polls was recorded at 52.5%; two female candidates were among those elected. Many commentators noted that the Opposition Coalition had been considerably weakened. A new Council of Ministers was sworn in by the Amir on 4 August 2013, with Sheikh Jaber remaining as Prime Minister.

Sheikh Jaber and the Council of Ministers resigned on 23 December 2013. The Prime Minister's decision to resign was believed to be an attempt to provide a response to the ongoing criticism of the Government by opposition members of the National Assembly, with legislators continuing to file requests to question ministers about policies and alleged mis-demeanours. Earlier on 23 December the Constitutional Court had rejected two petitions calling for the results of July's elections to be annulled and the assembly dissolved. Sheikh Sabah ordered a reorganization of the Council of Ministers on 6 January 2014. The new Council of Ministers contained more Islamists than the previous one but only one Shi'a representative.

In late April 2014 publication of two independent newspapers, *Al-Watan* and *Al-Alam Al-Yawm*, was suspended over articles regarding an alleged plot to overthrow the Government, in contravention of a ban on publication being imposed. The Prime Minister, Sheikh Jaber, told the National Assembly that video footage purporting to depict a senior member of the royal family and other officials plotting a coup had been falsified, but opposition deputies claimed that the footage was genuine and provided evidence of an internal struggle for power between members of the ruling al-Sabah family. The public prosecutor's office had questioned Sheikh Ahmad Fahad al-Sabah, a former Deputy Prime Minister, about the video on 7 April, although he was not charged with any offence. The National Assembly rejected a proposal to form an investigative panel into the allegations and

the royal court appealed to the public to allow the public prosecutor to continue his investigations without debate. Also in that month the Government introduced legislation prohibiting the police from deporting expatriates without the prior approval of the Ministry of the Interior. In May the Minister of Justice, Nayif al-Ajmi, resigned after being accused by the US Treasury's Under-Secretary for Terrorism and Financial Intelligence, David Cohen, of involvement in funding militant groups operating in Syria. Al-Ajmi, who admitted having participated in fundraising activities for Syria, but for humanitarian rather than military purposes, had tendered his resignation in the previous month, but it was rejected by the Amir. He was replaced in an acting capacity by the Minister of State for Cabinet Affairs, Sheikh Muhammad Abdullah al-Mubarak al-Sabah, who also retained his existing portfolio.

In May 2014 the National Assembly approved the so-called Unified Media Law. The legislation envisaged the establishment of a Commission for Mass Communications and Information Technology to oversee all technical matters pertaining to mobile telephone and internet service providers. Human rights activists criticized the law for suppressing freedom of expression and claimed that it would allow the authorities to suspend websites and mobile telephone lines for security reasons, to imprison individuals for harming the reputation of others, and to issue warrants to search houses without a prior legal order. For its part, the Ministry of Communications stated that the legislation was of a regulatory nature and that no intervention would take place without authorization from the public prosecutor.

A large-scale 'anti-corruption' demonstration was held in Kuwait City in June 2014; the demonstration had been instigated by the former opposition deputy, Musallam al-Barrak, who revealed the names of officials, including judges, whom he accused of accepting bribes. Al-Barrak was subsequently arrested on 2 July on charges of insulting the judiciary. Demonstrations demanding the release of al-Barrak took place in the following days; participants also demanded greater transparency and accountability in government and for ordinary citizens to contest the office of Prime Minister, rather than it being reserved for members of the ruling family. Al-Barrak was released from custody on 7 July, although violent clashes ensued between police officers and demonstrators appealing for the release of some 40 of their number who had been arrested. Also in that month the Government revoked the nationality of Ahmad al-Jaber al-Shemmeri, a naturalized Kuwaiti and the owner of the *Al-Alam Al-Yawm* newspaper, and his family, as well as that of an Islamist former deputy, Abdallah al-Barghash, and his three siblings, on charges of 'jeopardizing state security'. A further 10 citizens had their Kuwaiti nationality revoked in August, including a spokesman for the Popular Action Bloc. Human Rights Watch condemned the Kuwaiti Government in October for revoking the citizenship of some 33 Kuwaitis in 2014, many of whom it claimed the Government had targeted in order to suppress dissent. The Government claimed that in most cases citizenship had been revoked due to fake documentation or the holding of dual nationality, which is not recognized in Kuwait. In a related development emphasizing the sensitive nature of Kuwaiti citizenship, in November the Government proposed to offer some 34,000 stateless *bidoun*—most of whom are considered to be of Iraqi ancestry—the citizenship of the African island nation of the Comoros, which would enable them to legal residency in Kuwait and access to free provision of health and education, as well as legal employment. However, the Kuwaiti Government stated that it would not offer this option to around 75,000 other stateless people who had either emigrated to Kuwait or were the descendants of emigrants.

In December 2014 Kuwait imprisoned three men for allegiance to Islamic State (formerly Islamic State in Iraq and the Levant), including a Kuwaiti citizen who received a 10-year sentence in gaol for urging support for the jihadist organization and for insulting the Amir, and a Jordanian and an Egyptian who received four-year sentences for distributing pro-Islamic State material.

It was announced in March 2015 that the Minister of Electricity and Water and Minister of Public Works, Abd al-Aziz al-Ibrahim, had resigned from office. The resignation followed his questioning by members of the National Assembly regarding a nationwide power cut that had occurred in mid-February, and a subsequent controversy over his remarks about the motives of some deputies. Ahmad Khalid Ahmad al-Jassar replaced al-Ibrahim later in March.

Regional relations

The continued friction between Kuwait and Iraq following the Gulf War was exacerbated by the issue of the demarcation of their joint border. The UN commission with responsibility for delineating the frontier formalized the land border as it had been defined by British administrators in 1932 (and officially agreed by Kuwait and Iraq in 1963). The boundary, the validity of which was now rejected by Iraq, was established some 570 m north of its pre-war position, dividing the Iraqi port of Umm Qasr, with the effect that Iraq retained the town and much of the harbour, while Kuwait was awarded hinterland that included an abandoned Iraqi naval base; the border also situated several Iraqi oil wells on Kuwaiti territory. In January 1993 the USA led air attacks on Iraq, and more than 1,000 US troops were dispatched to Kuwait, in response to a series of incursions by Iraqi forces into Kuwaiti territory in the days immediately preceding the designated entry into force of the new border; its formal delineation was completed in March. Allegations made by Kuwait of Iraqi violations of the border intensified during the second half of 1993, and there were sporadic reports of exchanges of fire in the border region. In November an armed UNIKOM reinforcement was deployed in northern Kuwait, with authorization to use its weapons to assist the unarmed force already in the demilitarized zone.

In October 1994 Iraq deployed some 70,000 troops and 700 tanks near the border with Kuwait, in an apparent attempt to force an easing of UN economic sanctions. Kuwait immediately mobilized some 20,000 troops to the border region. The USA committed almost 40,000 forces to the region; France and the United Kingdom deployed naval vessels, and the United Kingdom dispatched about 1,200 troops. In mid-October the UN Security Council adopted a resolution (No. 949) requiring Iraq's unconditional recognition of Kuwait's sovereignty and borders and restricting the movement of Iraqi troops in the border area. In November Iraq officially recognized Kuwait's sovereignty and territorial integrity, as well as its UN-defined borders. Most of the US and British reinforcements deployed in the region in October had been withdrawn by December.

Kuwait's relations with Iraq deteriorated sharply in September 1996, after the Kuwaiti Government agreed to the deployment in Kuwait of US military aircraft and troops in support of a US operation to force the withdrawal of Iraqi armed forces from the Kurdish 'safe haven' in northern Iraq. In December the USA announced that some 4,200 US troops deployed in Kuwait during 1996 would be withdrawn by the end of the year, although the deployment of US fighter aircraft was to be extended.

As the crisis involving weapons inspections in Iraq by the UN Special Commission deepened in February 1998, fears were expressed for Kuwait's security—in particular that an attack on Iraq might result in retaliation against Kuwait. By the end of the month, when the UN Secretary-General and the Iraqi Government reached a compromise agreement regarding weapons inspections, some 6,000 US ground troops—supported by the British military—had been dispatched to Kuwait. Iraq accused Kuwait of collaborating in a series of air strikes against targets in Iraq by US and British forces from December, and frequently reiterated claims to Kuwaiti territory. In December 1999 the Kuwaiti Government welcomed UN Security Council Resolution 1284 (establishing a new weapons inspectorate for Iraq), which incorporated demands for the repatriation of Kuwaiti and other prisoners from Iraq and the return of Kuwaiti property seized during the occupation.

In September 2000 Iraq renewed its accusation that Kuwait was drilling oil wells on Iraqi territory, and accused Kuwait and Saudi Arabia of inflicting suffering on the Iraqi population through the maintenance of UN sanctions. In November 2001 Kuwait issued a formal complaint to the UN, following an alleged violation of its territory by Iraq. In January 2002 the Kuwaiti leadership was reported to have rejected attempts by the Arab League to persuade it to accept Iraqi proposals aimed at improving bilateral relations. However, at the Arab League summit held in Beirut, Lebanon, in March, it was announced that Kuwait and Iraq had reached agreement on the resolution of outstanding differences.

Relations with Iraq were profoundly affected by the political repercussions of the suicide attacks against New York and Washington, DC, USA, in September 2001. Kuwait thereafter assumed an important role in persuading other Gulf states to join the US-led 'coalition against terror'. US bases in Kuwait were subsequently used to provide logistical support to the US-led campaign against al-Qa'ida (held by the USA to be principally responsible for the suicide attacks) and its Taliban hosts in Afghanistan during late 2001. Meanwhile, in October the Kuwaiti authorities revoked the citizenship of the official spokesperson of al-Qa'ida, Sulayman Abu Ghaith, after remarks that he had made via Al Jazeera.

During 2002 increased speculation that the US Administration of George W. Bush intended to extend the 'war on terror' to target the regime of Saddam Hussein in Iraq threatened to exacerbate an increasingly tense political situation in Kuwait. The entire northern half of Kuwait was designated a closed military zone from February 2003. At the outset of military action, which commenced in March, US-led troops in Kuwait, the base for the main ground assault on Iraq, numbered some 140,000. Iraqi armed forces launched several missiles at Kuwaiti territory, although little damage was caused in the emirate during the course of the conflict. In the aftermath of the most intense period of fighting, which President Bush declared to have ended by May, Kuwait renewed its financial demands against Iraq, while a number of Kuwaiti firms entered into agreements with the US-led occupying powers. In October the demilitarized zone between Iraq and Kuwait was ended and, having fulfilled its mandate, UNIKOM's operations were terminated.

The resumption of diplomatic relations between Iraq and Kuwait was announced in mid-2004. In 2005 Kuwait began the construction of a 200-km steel barrier along the border with Iraq, parts of which were destroyed by Iraqi militants who claimed that it was encroaching upon their land; however, in November 2006 Iraq agreed to allow the fence to be completed. In October 2008 the first Kuwaiti ambassador since the Iraqi invasion of 1990 took up his post in the Iraqi capital, Baghdad. Iraq had earlier reopened its embassy in Kuwait, which was initially headed by a chargé d'affaires; Iraq's first ambassador to Kuwait was subsequently appointed in April 2010.

In June 2009 Iraq's Permanent Representative to the UN, Hamid al-Bayati, lodged an official request with the Security Council requesting a reduction in the reparation payments owed to Kuwait. In July the issue of reparations was the primary topic in talks between Iraqi Prime Minister Nuri al-Maliki and UN Secretary-General Ban Ki-Moon. However, later that month Kuwait stated that Iraqi 'violations' of their common border continued to represent a serious threat to regional security and bilateral relations, and urged Iraq to respect all existing UN resolutions relating to the Gulf War. Bilateral negotiations aimed at resolving all outstanding differences between Kuwait and Iraq, under UN auspices, continued throughout 2009–10. In January 2011 Prime Minister Sheikh Nasser paid an official visit to Baghdad, the first visit to Iraq by a Kuwaiti premier since the Gulf War. In February the Kuwaiti authorities approved the construction of a large seaport, the Mubarak al-Kabir Port, on Bubiyan Island, which the Iraqi Government claimed violated international maritime border legislation and would severely restrict its vessels' access to international shipping lanes in the Gulf. Iraq initially demanded an end to construction of the port, which began in April (with an expected completion date of 2016).

An improvement in relations between Kuwait and Iraq was assisted by the completion of the US military withdrawal from Iraq in December 2011. In April 2012, following a visit by the Amir to Iraq, the Kuwaiti and Iraqi Governments reached a settlement concerning their land and maritime border dispute. Nevertheless, the bilateral dispute over construction of the Mubarak al-Kabir Port remained a source of tension. In July it was reported that the Kuwaiti authorities had agreed to reduce the number of shipping berths under construction. However, Iraq continued to insist that the project would hinder its access to international shipping lanes. In February 2013 an Iraqi Airways plane became the first Iraqi aircraft to land in Kuwait since the 1990–91 Gulf crisis, after the two countries had agreed to the resumption of direct flights in April 2012. In June 2013 Prime Minister Sheikh Jaber undertook an official visit to Baghdad during which he and his Iraqi counterpart, al-Maliki, signed various co-operation accords. (For further details on bilateral relations, see the chapter on Iraq.)

Meanwhile, in May 1994 the governing body of the UN Compensation Commission (UNCC), responsible for considering claims for compensation arising from the 1990–91 Gulf crisis, approved the first disbursements, totalling US $2.7m. By late 1996 payments amounting to $3,000m. (to be financed partly by Iraqi petroleum revenues) had been endorsed by the UN, which had yet to consider claims for a further $190,000m. In December international arbitrators recommended that a payment of $610m. should be made to the Kuwait Oil Company (KOC), in compensation for the cost of extinguishing oil wells set alight by retreating Iraqi troops in early 1991. In March 1997 the Kuwaiti general committee responsible for evaluating war damages stated that it was to begin compensation payments, initially to some 4,500 citizens who had incurred losses valued at less than $100,000. The disbursement of a further $84m. to some 33,800 individuals was authorized by the UN in February 1999. In September 2000 the UN Security Council approved the payment to the Kuwait Petroleum Corporation (which controls the KOC) of $15,900m. in compensation for lost petroleum revenues arising from the Iraqi occupation. However, the Security Council decided at the same time to reduce the share of Iraqi petroleum revenues to be paid into the compensation fund from 30% to 25%.

By mid-2003 the majority of individual claimants (Kuwaitis and expatriates in Kuwait and Iraq during the Gulf War) had received compensation, with total disbursements being valued at some US $17,600m. In May UN Security Council Resolution 1483 reduced the share of Iraqi petroleum revenue to be used for compensation payments from 25% to 5%, which was expected to result in outstanding compensation payments believed to total more than $30,000m. remaining unpaid for several decades. In June the UNCC authorized the payment of only $1,500m. of a claim of $86,000m. by the Kuwait Investment Agency, principally in recompense for lost earnings during the conflict. Following similar announcements by the Governments of the UAE and Qatar in January 2004, Sheikh Sabah stated that Kuwait was prepared to waive a 'significant proportion' of the estimated $16,000m. owed by Iraq. This did not, however, include any war reparations still claimed by the Government. In 2005 the UN panel overseeing payments to victims of the Gulf crisis approved disbursements of $632m. to families of those who had died in Iraqi detention. The claims assessment process was concluded thereafter, and payments to individuals ceased in 2007. In 2010 payments worth a total of $1,240m. were made by the UNCC, principally to Kuwaiti state-owned and private companies and government agencies for losses incurred as a result of the Iraqi invasion and occupation. A further $3,657m. was disbursed in 2011, while some $4,430m. was paid out during 2012 and $4,740m. during 2013. Following further compensation payments of $1,030m. in January 2014 and $990m. in April, the total value of payments issued by the UNCC since 1994 reached around $45,500m. According to the UNCC, some $6,900m. remained owing to Kuwait, although the Iraqi Government anticipated that this would be received by 2015. In December the UNCC accepted the Iraqi Government's request to postpone payment of the remaining funds owed to Kuwait until January 2016, owing to a projected increase in Iraq's budget deficit, which was prompted in part by the cost of military operations against Islamic State, and by the falling price of oil.

In July 2000 Kuwait and Saudi Arabia signed an agreement finalizing the delineation of their maritime borders. Kuwait subsequently began negotiations with Iran on the demarcation of respective rights to the continental shelf, following complaints by the Kuwaiti and Saudi authorities over Iran's decision to begin drilling for gas in the disputed Arash/Dorra offshore field. Iraq asserted that, as a concerned party, it should be included in the Kuwaiti-Iranian discussions. Iran suspended drilling pending the conclusion of the dispute. Despite issuing remarks in early 2012 threatening to recommence drilling without Kuwaiti permission, by mid-2012 the managing director of the National Iranian Offshore Oil Co indicated that the Islamic Republic was keen to reach an agreement with the Kuwaiti authorities for the joint development of the gas field; the dispute remained unresolved in early 2015. At an extraordinary GCC summit in Riyadh, Saudi Arabia in April, Sheikh Sabah helped to broker an agreement between the Governments of Saudi Arabia, Bahrain and the UAE, and that of Qatar. The former three countries had severed diplomatic relations with Qatar in March over its alleged interference in their internal affairs, and continued support for the Muslim Brotherhood and its regional affiliates, but relations were restored after the summit. In August it was announced that Kuwait and Saudi Arabia had decided to postpone their joint development of the Dorra offshore field for an indefinite period, following disagreement between the two Governments about how to share any gas originating from the field. Meanwhile, in December 2000 a defence agreement was signed by the six member states of the GCC. In July 2007 the US Administration unveiled a US $20,000m. package of military assistance and weapons sales to Kuwait and the other GCC member states, in an attempt to bolster security in the Gulf region and to encourage the GCC to support the USA in its dispute with the Iranian regime regarding the latter's nuclear

programme. However, Kuwait remained opposed to military action against Iran over its persuit of a nuclear energy programme.

Prime Minister Sheikh Nasser made an official visit to Tehran, Iran, in November 2009, the first such visit by a Kuwaiti premier since the foundation of the Islamic Republic in 1979. Discussions on the possible construction of a sub-marine gas pipeline connecting Kuwait with Iran's gas network were also conducted. In April 2010 several bilateral co-operation agreements were concluded. However, relations were threatened by the discovery in May of an allegedly Iranian-led network of spies in Kuwait; seven people (four Iranians, one Syrian, one Kuwaiti soldier and one *bidoun*), were arrested on suspicion of belonging to the network. Iran denied any involvement in espionage in Kuwait. The seven detainees were charged in early August with, *inter alia*, passing confidential military information relating to both Kuwaiti and US forces to Iran's Islamic Revolutionary Guards Corps, and their trial, *in camera*, commenced later that month. Despite the defendants initially confessing, their lawyer subsequently claimed that these confessions had been extracted under duress.

In March 2011, having been found guilty of involvement in the espionage network, two of the Iranian defendants and the Kuwaiti were given death sentences, while the Syrian and the *bidoun* received terms of life imprisonment; the two other Iranians were both acquitted. Iran reacted strongly to the announcement of the verdicts, and the case was subsequently referred to Kuwait's Court of Appeal. In its ruling issued in May 2012, the Court commuted the three death sentences to ones of life imprisonment, confirmed the life sentence given to the *bidoun*, but acquitted the Syrian defendant. A further appeal against the verdicts was brought before the Court of Cassation but resulted, in May 2013, in the four life terms being upheld; the three other alleged spies were all acquitted. Meanwhile, in March 2011 Kuwait withdrew its ambassador from Tehran and ordered three Iranian diplomats to leave the country. The Iranian authorities responded in April by expelling a similar number of Kuwaiti diplomats from Tehran. After high-level bilateral discussions aimed at resolving the dispute, by May both ambassadors had been returned to their respective capitals. However, at the same time the Kuwaiti Government alleged that another spy network, linked both to Iran and the Lebanese Hezbollah, was operating within Kuwait and plotting terrorist acts against civilians. In June 2013 the Government welcomed the election to the Iranian presidency of Hassan Rouhani, who was widely believed to be more conciliatory than his predecessor, Mahmoud Ahmadinejad.

CONSTITUTION AND GOVERNMENT

Under the 1962 Constitution, executive power is vested in the Amir, the head of state (who is chosen by and from members of the ruling family), and is exercised through the Council of Ministers. The Amir appoints the Prime Minister and, on the latter's recommendation, other ministers. Legislative power is vested in the unicameral National Assembly (Majlis al-Umma), with 50 elected members who serve for four years (subject to dissolution), along with some 15 government ministers who sit as ex officio members. In May 2005 legislation was approved allowing women to vote in legislative and municipal elections for the first time. The country is divided administratively into six governorates.

REGIONAL AND INTERNATIONAL CO-OPERATION

Kuwait is a member of the Cooperation Council for the Arab States of the Gulf (Gulf Cooperation Council—GCC, see p. 245); the six GCC states established a unified regional customs tariff in January 2003, and agreed to create a single market and currency. The economic convergence criteria for the monetary union were agreed at a GCC summit in Abu Dhabi, the UAE, in December 2005, and in January 2008 the GCC launched its common market. Kuwait also participates in the League of Arab States (the Arab League, see p. 359) and the Organization of Arab Petroleum Exporting Countries (OAPEC, see p. 398).

Kuwait became a member of the UN in May 1963 and, as a contracting party to the General Agreement on Tariffs and Trade, joined the World Trade Organization (WTO, see p. 431) upon its establishment in 1995. The country is also a participant in the Organization of the Petroleum Exporting Countries (OPEC, see p. 406) and the Organization of Islamic Cooperation (OIC, see p. 401).

ECONOMIC AFFAIRS

In 2011, according to estimates by the World Bank, Kuwait's gross national income (GNI), measured at average 2009–11 prices, was US $140,425m., equivalent to $44,940 per head (or $88,170 on an international purchasing-power parity basis). During 2004–13, it was estimated, the population increased at an average annual rate of 4.9%, while in 2004–12 gross domestic product (GDP) per head decreased, in real terms, by an average of 1.5% per year. According to the World Bank, overall GDP was estimated to have increased, in real terms, at an average annual rate of 3.5% in 2004–12. Real GDP rose by 6.6% in 2012 and by a provisional 1.5% in 2013, according to official figures.

Agriculture (including hunting, forestry and fishing) contributed a provisional 0.3% of GDP in 2013. The sector engaged 2.2% of the classified labour force in mid-2011. The principal crops are tomatoes, cucumbers, potatoes, dates and aubergines. Owing to scarcity of water, little grain is produced, and the bulk of food requirements is imported. (Imports of live animals and vegetable products together accounted for 9.4% of merchandise imports in 2013.) Livestock, poultry and fishing are also important. According to the Central Bank of Kuwait (CBK), agricultural GDP increased, in real terms, by an average annual rate of 1.5% in 2002–11. The agricultural sector declined by 1.3% in 2012, but, according to provisional figures, expanded by 0.7% in 2013.

Industry (including mining, manufacturing, construction and power) provided 65.0% of GDP in 2013, according to provisional figures, and employed 17.1% of the classified labour force in mid-2011. During 2002–11 industrial GDP increased, in real terms, at an average annual rate of 4.4%, according to the CBK. The GDP of the sector decreased by a provisional 1.0% in 2013.

Mining and quarrying contributed a provisional 55.9% of GDP in 2013, although the sector engaged only 0.4% of the classified labour force in mid-2011. The production of petroleum and its derivatives is the most important industry in Kuwait, providing an estimated 94.3% of export revenue in 2013. At the end of 2013 the country's proven recoverable reserves of petroleum were 101,500m. barrels, representing about 6.1% of world reserves. Kuwait's petroleum production averaged 3.12m. barrels per day (b/d) in 2013; the Government aimed to increase its production capacity to 4.0m. b/d by 2020. As a member of the Organization of the Petroleum Exporting Countries (OPEC, see p. 406), Kuwait is subject to production quotas agreed by the Organization's Conference. There are significant reserves of natural gas (1,784,000m. cu m at the end of 2013) associated with the petroleum deposits. Output was 15,590m. cu m in that year. However, although in March 2006 a major discovery of non-associated gas in the north of the country was announced, Kuwait remains a net importer of natural gas. According to the CBK, during 2002–11 the GDP of the mining sector increased, in real terms, at an average rate of 4.7% per year. The sector's GDP increased by 9.9% in 2012, but declined by a provisional 0.7% in 2013.

Manufacturing provided 6.0% of GDP in 2013, according to provisional figures, and employed 6.3% of the classified labour force in mid-2011. Petroleum refineries accounted for a provisional 73.1% of manufacturing activity, measured by gross value of output, in 2013. Of the other branches of manufacturing, the most important are the production of building materials (and related activities such as aluminium extrusion), fertilizer production, food-processing and the extraction of salt and chlorine. During 2002–11 manufacturing GDP increased, in real terms, at an average annual rate of 3.1%, according to the CBK. The sector's GDP expanded by a provisional 13.9% in 2013.

Construction contributed a provisional 1.5% of GDP in 2013, and engaged 9.6% of the classified labour force in mid-2011. According to the CBK, during 2002–11 construction GDP increased, in real terms, at an average annual rate of 2.9%. The GDP of the sector increased by 2.0% in 2013, according to provisional figures.

Electrical energy is derived from Kuwait's own resources of petroleum (providing 62.0% of total electricity production in 2011) and both local and imported natural gas (38.0%).

Services contributed 34.7% of GDP in 2013, according to provisional figures, and employed 80.8% of the classified labour force in mid-2011. Kuwait's second most important source of revenue is investment abroad, both in petroleum-related ventures and in other industries, chiefly in the USA, Western Europe and Japan; many such investments are held by the Future Generations Fund (to which 25% of petroleum revenues must by law be contributed each year, and which is intended to provide an income after hydrocarbon resources have been exhausted) and managed by the Kuwait Investment Authority. As part of its efforts to diversify the economy, the Government plans to develop the islands of Bubiyan and Failaka into major tourist resorts. The combined GDP of the service sectors increased, in real terms, at an average rate of 6.8% per year during 2002–11, according to the CBK. The services sector expanded by a provisional 4.1% in 2013.

In 2013 Kuwait recorded a visible merchandise trade surplus of US $89,992.1m., and there was a surplus of $69,782.9m. on the current account of the balance of payments. In 2013 the principal source of imports was the People's Republic of China (13.4%); other important suppliers in that year were the USA, the UAE, Japan and Germany. Details concerning the destinations of Kuwait's petroleum exports are not available for recent years; however, the major markets for non-petroleum exports in 2013 included China (15.8%), the UAE, India, Saudi Arabia and Iraq. In 2013 the principal imports were machinery, mechanical appliances and electrical equipment, vehicles, aircraft, and transport equipment, base metals and articles of base metal, chemicals and related products, and prepared foodstuffs, beverages, and tobacco. The principal non-petroleum exports in that year were chemicals and related products, plastic goods, vehicles, aircraft, and transport equipment, base metals and articles of base metal, and machinery, mechanical appliances and electrical equipment.

A budget surplus of KD 12,701m. was recorded for the financial year ending 30 June 2013. Kuwait's general government gross debt was KD 3,068m. in 2013, equivalent to 6.2% of GDP. The average annual rate of inflation in 2007–13 was 4.4%; consumer prices increased by an estimated average of 2.7% in 2013. The rate of unemployment among Kuwaiti nationals was estimated at 3.4% in 2011; however, underemployment was unofficially reported to be up to 50% in June 2009.

Despite its significant, oil-based wealth, Kuwait has a number of fundamental weaknesses in its economic structure: instability in its relations with Iraq have necessitated a high level of defence expenditure; reliance on petroleum revenues has impeded diversification into other industries; and its constitutional commitment to provide employment for all Kuwaitis has resulted in a heavy burden on government spending. The budget for 2011/12 envisaged a significant increase in government expenditure, much of which was to be allocated to social spending, in response to a series of anti-Government protests taking place from early 2011. However, following lower-than-anticipated spending levels and significantly higher revenues, a record budget surplus of around US $47,000m. was achieved. The escalating tensions between the Government and the legislature during 2012 meant that the adoption of important financial legislation and the progress of several major capital projects was postponed. In October the value of shares on the Kuwait Stock Exchange declined by the highest daily rate since July 2009, amid an intensification of opposition protests over planned amendments to electoral legislation (for subsequent developments, see *Contemporary Political History*). In February 2013 the Government allocated KD 5,400m. to the 2013/14 tranche of its four-year development plan in order to improve infrastructure in the utilities, transport, education and health sectors. In October 2014 the Government approved the 2014/15 budget, which forecast a significant surplus of $45,000m. The IMF forecast GDP growth of 1.3% in 2014 and 1.7% in 2015. However, OPEC's decision in November 2014 to maintain a high level of oil production despite the rapidly declining price in international markets cast doubt over the validity of Kuwaiti Government forecasts in 2015. The IMF reported in December that, for a balanced budget to be achieved, Kuwait required the price per barrel of oil to reach $75. By March 2015 the cost of a barrel had fallen to around $60. In January, meanwhile, the Minister for Finance, Anas al-Salih, insisted that the decline in oil prices and anticipated fall in revenue would not affect capital and infrastructure expenditure; al-Salih announced that the removal of subsidies from petrol, water and electricity was to be postponed.

PUBLIC HOLIDAYS

2016: 1 January (New Year's Day), 25 February (Kuwaiti National Day), 26 February (Liberation Day), 4 May* (Leilat al-Meiraj, Ascension of the Prophet), 6 July* (Id al-Fitr, end of Ramadan), 12 September* (Id al-Adha, Feast of the Sacrifice), 2 October (Muharram, Islamic New Year), 11 December* (Mouloud, Birth of the Prophet).

* These holidays are dependent on the Islamic lunar calendar and may vary by one or two days from the dates given.

Statistical Survey

Sources (unless otherwise stated): Economic Research Department, Central Bank of Kuwait, POB 526, 13006 Safat, Kuwait City; tel. 22403257; fax 22440887; e-mail cbk@cbk.gov.kw; internet www.cbk.gov.kw; Central Statistical Bureau, Arabian Gulf St, Sharq, Kuwait City; tel. 22428200; fax 22437048; e-mail csb@csb .gov.kw; internet www.csb.gov.kw.

Area and Population

AREA, POPULATION AND DENSITY

Area (sq km)	17,818*
Population (census results)†	
20 April 2005‡	2,193,651
21 April 2011	
Males	1,738,372
Females	1,327,478
Total	3,065,850§
Population (official estimates at 31 December)‖	
2012	3,823,728
2013	3,965,144
Density (per sq km) at 31 December 2013	222.5

* 6,880 sq miles.
† Figures include Kuwaiti nationals abroad.
‡ Excluding adjustment for underenumeration; the total population at the 2005 census comprised 860,324 Kuwaiti nationals and 1,333,327 non-Kuwaitis.
§ Comprising 1,089,969 Kuwaitis and 1,975,881 non-Kuwaitis.
‖ Source: Public Authority for Civil Information.

POPULATION BY AGE AND SEX
(UN estimates at mid-2015)

	Males	Females	Total
0–14 years	448,994	430,933	879,927
15–64 years	1,641,385	974,999	2,616,384
65 years and over	49,240	37,848	87,088
Total	2,139,619	1,443,780	3,583,399

Source: UN, *World Population Prospects: The 2012 Revision.*

GOVERNORATES
(official population estimates at 31 December 2013)

Governorate	Area (sq km)*	Population	Density (per sq km)
Capital	199.8	528,094	2,643.1
Hawalli	} 368.4	874,812	} 5,864.3
Mubarak al-Kabir .		229,301	
Farwaniya . . .		1,056,298	
Al-Jahra	11,230.2	484,502	43.1
Al-Ahmadi . . .	5,119.6	787,037	153.7
Total	16,918.0	3,960,044†	234.1

* Excluding the islands of Bubiyan and Warba (combined area 900 sq km).
† Excluding population of areas not officially demarcated (estimated at 5,100 persons).

PRINCIPAL TOWNS
(official population estimates at 31 December 2013)

Jaleeb al-Shuyukh .	294,926	Fahaheel . . .	93,386
Salmiya	280,087	Sabah al-Salim . .	83,081
Farwaniya . . .	236,932	Salwa	80,999
Hawalli	194,834	Sabahiya . . .	79,762
Khitan	146,621	Saad al-Abdulla .	76,566
Munkaf	115,222	Jabriya	75,645
Mahbula . . .	103,342		

BIRTHS AND DEATHS
(annual averages, UN estimates)

	2000–05	2005–10	2010–15
Crude birth rate (per 1,000) . .	21.2	21.7	18.8
Crude death rate (per 1,000) . .	3.1	3.1	2.9

Source: UN, *World Population Prospects: The 2012 Revision.*

Births: 58,198 in 2011; 59,753 in 2012; 58,540 in 2013.

Marriages: 13,993 in 2010; 19,860 in 2011; 14,320 in 2012.

Deaths: 5,339 in 2011; 5,950 in 2012; 5,677 in 2013.

Life expectancy (years at birth): 74.4 (males 73.4; females 75.4) in 2012 (Source: World Bank, World Development Indicators database).

ECONOMICALLY ACTIVE POPULATION
('000 persons aged 15 years and over, mid-2011)

	Kuwaitis	Non-Kuwaitis	Total
Agriculture, hunting and fishing .	0.4	41.4	41.8
Mining and quarrying . . .	4.9	2.1	7.1
Manufacturing	9.0	112.7	121.6
Electricity, gas and water . .	13.1	2.0	15.1
Construction	10.9	175.8	186.8
Wholesale and retail trade . .	14.5	331.2	345.7
Transport, storage and communications	9.3	59.9	69.1
Finance, insurance, real estate and business services . . .	19.3	95.7	114.9
Public administration	270.6	764.0	1,034.6
Sub-total	352.0	1,584.9	1,936.7
Activities not adequately defined	37.9	252.8	290.7
Total labour force	389.7	1,837.7	2,227.4

Note: Totals may not be equal to the sum of components, owing to rounding.

Source: IMF, *Kuwait: Selected Issues and Statistical Appendix* (June 2012).

Employment (official estimates, 2012): Government sector 331,333 (Kuwaitis 240,170, Non-Kuwaitis 91,163); Private sector 1,221,877 (Kuwaitis 61,890, Non-Kuwaitis 1,159,987).

Health and Welfare

KEY INDICATORS

Total fertility rate (children per woman, 2012)	2.6
Under-5 mortality rate (per 1,000 live births, 2012) . .	11
HIV/AIDS (% of persons aged 15–49, 1994)	<0.2
Physicians (per 1,000 head, 2009)	1.8
Hospital beds (per 1,000 head, 2009)	2.0
Health expenditure (2011): US $ per head (PPP)	1,190
Health expenditure (2011): % of GDP	2.6
Health expenditure (2011): public (% of total)	82.4
Access to water (% of persons, 2012)	99
Total carbon dioxide emissions ('000 metric tons, 2010) . .	93,695.5
Carbon dioxide emissions per head (metric tons, 2010) . .	31.3
Human Development Index (2013): ranking	46
Human Development Index (2013): value	0.814

For sources and definitions, see explanatory note on p. vi.

Agriculture

PRINCIPAL CROPS
('000 metric tons, FAO estimates)

	2011	2012	2013
Potatoes	45.0	45.6	46.8
Cabbages and other brassicas .	13.7	14.0	14.4
Lettuce	12.3	13.5	14.1
Tomatoes	71.3	73.0	74.4
Cauliflowers and broccoli . . .	22.1	25.0	26.9
Pumpkins, squash and gourds .	12.5	13.0	13.5
Cucumbers and gherkins . .	53.1	54.0	55.9
Aubergines (Eggplants) . .	25.0	25.0	26.1
Chillies and peppers, green . .	16.3	17.5	18.3
Onions, dry	19.7	20.5	21.8
Dates	33.6	34.6	37.0

Aggregate production ('000 metric tons, may include official, semi-official or estimated data): Total cereals 21.4 in 2011, 22.5 in 2012, 23.8 in 2013; Total roots and tubers 45.0 in 2011, 45.6 in 2012, 46.8 in 2013; Total vegetables (incl. melons) 304.6 in 2011, 316.1 in 2012, 327.1 in 2013; Total fruits (excl. melons) 36.5 in 2011, 37.6 in 2012, 40.0 in 2013.

Source: FAO.

LIVESTOCK
('000 head, year ending September, FAO estimates)

	2011	2012	2013
Cattle	35.0	35.5	36.0
Camels	11.0	11.5	12.0
Sheep	470	475	477
Goats	178.7	175.0	174.0
Chickens	32,000	32,500	33,000

Source: FAO.

LIVESTOCK PRODUCTS
('000 metric tons, FAO estimates)

	2011	2012	2013
Cattle meat	2.6	2.7	2.7
Sheep meat	35.7	37.0	37.0
Chicken meat	39.0	40.0	40.5
Cows' milk	58.0	60.0	62.0
Goats' milk	4.2	4.5	4.6
Hen eggs	42.0	42.5	43.0

Source: FAO.

Fishing

(metric tons, live weight)

	2008	2009	2010*
Capture	3,979	4,707	4,500
Hilsa shad	84	110	110
Mullets	22	53	50
Groupers	140	147	150
Grunts and sweetlips . . .	119	121	130
Croakers and drums . . .	54	57	60
Yellowfin seabream . . .	299	382	350
Indo-Pacific king mackerel . .	57	120	100
Carangids	39	54	60
Natantian decapods	1,807	1,754	1,700
Silver pomfret	115	268	220
Aquaculture*	310	310	310
Nile tilapia*	300	300	300
Total catch*	4,289	5,017	4,810

* FAO estimates.

2011–12: Figures assumed to be unchanged from 2010 (FAO estimates).

Source: FAO.

Mining

	2011	2012	2013
Crude petroleum ('000 metric tons)	139,672	152,494	151,253
Natural gas (million cu m) . .	13,530	14,540	15,590

Source: BP, *Statistical Review of World Energy*.

Industry

SELECTED PRODUCTS
('000 metric tons unless otherwise stated)

	2011	2012	2013
Bran and flour	355.1	370.8	n.a.
Sulphur (by-product)*	830	800	820
Chlorine	21.4	21.0	n.a.
Caustic soda (Sodium hydroxide) .	40.2	44.0	n.a.
Salt*	15.0	15.0	15.0
Nitrogenous fertilizers*† . . .	460	405	420
Motor spirit (petrol) (million barrels)*‡	76	79	80
Kerosene (million barrels)*‡ . .	62	67	68
Gas-diesel (distillate fuel) oils (million barrels)*‡	88	96	97
Residual fuel oils (mazout—million barrels)*‡	64	73	74
Quicklime*	50	50	50
Cement*	2,250	2,250	2,250
Electric energy (million kWh)‡ .	57,457	61,119	n.a.

* Source: US Geological Survey; estimates.

† Production in terms of nitrogen.

‡ Including an equal share of production with Saudi Arabia from the Neutral (Partitioned) Zone.

Finance

CURRENCY AND EXCHANGE RATES

Monetary Units
1,000 fils = 10 dirhams = 1 Kuwaiti dinar (KD).

Sterling, Dollar and Euro Equivalents (31 December 2014)
£1 sterling = 457.00 fils;
US $1 = 292.80 fils;
€1 = 355.49 fils;
10 Kuwaiti dinars = £21.88 = $34.15 = €28.13.

Average Exchange Rate (fils per US $)
2012   279.9
2013   283.6
2014   284.6

From 1 January 2003 the official exchange rate was fixed within the range of US $1 = 289 fils to $1 = 310 fils (KD 1 = $3.2258 to KD 1 = $3.4602), but this 'peg' to the US dollar was abandoned in May 2007 in favour of a basket of currencies including the pound sterling, the euro and the yen.

GENERAL BUDGET
(KD million, year ending 30 June)

Revenue	2010/11	2011/12	2012/13
Tax revenue	320.1	326.1	350.7
International trade and transactions	218.4	222.9	259.0
Non-tax revenue	21,181.9	29,910.0	31,657.8
Oil revenue	19,947.4	28,569.6	29,969.7
Total operating revenue of government enterprises . .	566.6	576.7	706.7
Total	21,502.0	30,236.1	32,008.5

Expenditure	2010/11	2011/12	2012/13
Current expenditure	11,329.2	11,097.4	13,089.4
Land acquisitions	3.6	21.0	135.4
Capital expenditure	152.9	147.0	158.7
Construction expenditure . . .	1,684.5	1,631.0	1,516.4
Other expenditure	3,050.8	4,111.1	4,407.6
Total	16,221.0	17,007.4	19,307.6

INTERNATIONAL RESERVES
(US $ million at 31 December)

	2011	2012	2013
Gold (national valuation) . . .	113.9	112.8	112.5
IMF special drawing rights . .	2,219.0	2,222.4	2,227.5
Reserve position in IMF . . .	654.7	699.2	777.0
Foreign exchange	22,921.4	25,964.1	29,179.9
Total	25,909.0	28,998.5	32,296.9

Source: IMF, *International Financial Statistics*.

MONEY SUPPLY
(KD million at 31 December)

	2011	2012	2013
Currency outside depository corporations	1,019.2	1,120.7	1,172.7
Transferable deposits	5,839.0	6,889.2	7,911.6
Other deposits	20,888.5	21,530.8	23,339.5
Broad money	27,746.6	29,540.7	32,423.7

Source: IMF, *International Financial Statistics*.

COST OF LIVING
(Consumer Price Index; base: 2007 = 100)

	2011	2012	2013
Food and non-alcoholic beverages .	130.2	136.4	141.9
Clothing and footwear	121.8	127.0	126.9
Housing	120.1	122.9	127.7
All items	121.9	125.8	129.2

NATIONAL ACCOUNTS
(KD million at current prices)

Expenditure on the Gross Domestic Product

	2011	2012	2013*
Government final consumption expenditure	6,326.6	7,337.4	8,386.9
Private final consumption expenditure	10,309.5	11,524.3	12,122.7
Increase in stocks . . . . } Gross fixed capital formation . }	5,759.5	6,253.5	6,908.0
Total domestic expenditure.	22,395.6	25,115.2	27,417.6
Exports of goods and services .	31,126.0	36,411.0	35,682.3
Less Imports of goods and services	11,010.0	12,804.0	13,237.3
GDP in purchasers' values .	42,511.6	48,722.2	49,862.6
GDP at constant 2010 prices	36,264.1	38,667.1	39,239.0

Gross Domestic Product by Economic Activity

	2011	2012	2013*
Agriculture, hunting, forestry and fishing	186.6	175.3	175.3
Mining and quarrying	26,984.8	31,848.9	31,384.7
Manufacturing	2,386.2	2,906.0	3,374.4
Electricity, gas and water . .	772.6	862.5	900.4
Construction	772.9	832.7	860.4
Trade	1,400.8	1,449.0	1,643.3
Restaurants and hotels . .	288.9	309.7	332.0
Transport, storage and communications	2,282.8	2,455.8	2,613.0
Finance, insurance, real estate and business services	5,985.9	6,164.3	6,494.8
Community, social and personal services	6,548.7	7,541.5	8,394.1
Sub-total	47,610.2	54,545.8	56,172.5
Indirect taxes (net)	−3,338.5	−4,040.5	−4,492.2
Less Imputed bank service charges	1,760.1	1,783.1	1,817.7
GDP in purchasers' values .	42,511.6	48,722.2	49,862.6

* Provisional figures.

BALANCE OF PAYMENTS
(US $ million)

	2011	2012	2013
Exports of goods f.o.b.	102,854.7	119,642.9	115,854.1
Imports of goods f.o.b.	−22,597.2	−24,241.4	−25,861.9
Balance on goods	80,257.5	95,401.3	89,992.1
Exports of services	10,097.0	8,836.5	5,864.1
Imports of services	−19,013.2	−21,097.2	−21,618.9
Balance on goods and services	71,341.4	83,140.6	74,237.3
Primary income received . . .	10,602.9	13,999.0	13,781.6
Primary income paid	−1,422.5	−1,303.6	−1,616.4
Balance on goods, services and primary income	80,521.8	95,836.0	86,402.6
Secondary income received . .	2.3	1.9	2.0
Secondary income paid . . .	−14,786.6	−17,130.2	−16,621.7
Current balance	65,737.5	78,707.7	69,782.9
Capital account (net)	3,409.6	4,243.0	4,471.2
Direct investment assets . .	−10,772.9	−24,509.2	−9,670.6
Direct investment liabilities . .	3,259.1	2,872.6	1,843.4
Portfolio investment assets . .	−8,448.7	−7,657.2	−28,476.8
Portfolio investment liabilities .	786.1	1,507.3	215.3
Financial derivatives and employee stock options (net)	623.7	63.8	−39.9
Other investment assets . . .	−47,737.5	−47,179.7	−35,181.9
Other investment liabilities . .	2,223.0	−5,814.9	2,379.6
Net errors and omissions . . .	−4,608.0	1,124.5	−1,967.5
Reserves and related items .	4,471.8	3,357.8	3,355.6

Source: IMF, *International Financial Statistics*.

External Trade

PRINCIPAL COMMODITIES
(distribution by HS, KD million)

Imports c.i.f.	2011	2012	2013
Live animals and animal products	354.2	356.1	385.7
Vegetables and vegetable products	389.5	383.4	398.0
Prepared foodstuffs; beverages, spirits, vinegar; tobacco and articles thereof .	375.2	386.6	419.2
Chemicals and related products	620.3	650.2	722.9
Pharmaceutical products . . .	234.6	245.3	271.9
Plastics, rubber, and articles thereof	252.4	262.7	271.4
Textiles and textile articles .	340.9	386.0	411.2
Pearls, precious or semi-precious stones, precious metals, and articles thereof .	212.5	232.1	399.6
Iron and steel, other base metals and articles of base metal	392.4	810.0	841.3
Articles of iron or steel . . .	828.0	403.1	404.3
Machinery and mechanical appliances; electrical equipment and parts thereof	1,635.8	1,748.7	1,807.1
Machinery and mechanical appliances	889.0	973.7	914.7
Electrical machinery and equipment and parts thereof .	746.8	775.0	892.4
Vehicles, aircraft, vessels and associated transport equipment	980.9	1,346.8	1,452.2
Road vehicles	971.1	1,338.7	1,438.0
Optical, medical apparatus, etc.; clocks and watches; musical instruments and parts thereof	188.6	209.9	266.0
Total (incl. others)	6,938.1	7,631.7	8,312.9

Exports f.o.b.*	2011	2012	2013
Prepared foodstuffs; beverages, spirits, vinegar; tobacco and articles thereof .	40.5	40.2	65.1
Chemicals and related products	907.0	543.8	579.2
Organic chemicals	394.7	375.9	423.8
Fertilizers	122.6	118.3	114.2
Plastics, rubber, and articles thereof	510.8	491.2	457.0
Plastics and articles thereof . .	505.3	486.5	453.3
Pearls, precious or semi-precious stones, precious metals, and articles thereof .	39.8	50.5	83.0
Iron and steel, other base metals and articles of base metal	126.6	107.5	121.3
Machinery and mechanical appliances; electrical equipment; parts thereof .	105.7	106.5	99.4
Vehicles, aircraft, vessels and associated transport equipment	110.3	194.7	233.8
Road vehicles	110.0	194.3	232.6
Total (incl. others)	1,471.1	1,674.7	1,854.3

*Excluding petroleum exports (KD million): 26,868.8 in 2011; 30,376.5 in 2012; 30,505.4 in 2013.

PRINCIPAL TRADING PARTNERS
(KD million)*

Imports c.i.f.	2011	2012	2013
Australia	183.5	160.0	162.3
Brazil	101.0	102.2	113.8
Canada	72.3	82.2	96.1
China, People's Republic . . .	1,024.2	1,007.9	1,114.5
Egypt	73.9	83.4	97.9
France (incl. Monaco)	153.5	178.5	207.1
Germany	457.6	488.0	561.2
India	413.3	364.7	332.1
Italy	266.3	363.0	344.3
Japan	457.3	599.0	630.7
Korea, Republic	263.5	342.8	323.7
Netherlands	92.1	96.6	125.8
Oman	83.9	63.4	142.8
Saudi Arabia	398.1	401.5	399.1
Spain	63.9	76.9	87.5
Switzerland-Liechtenstein . .	109.7	127.2	165.6
Thailand	109.3	133.5	130.5
Turkey	115.6	109.1	130.7
United Arab Emirates	442.4	554.3	743.4
United Kingdom	186.4	235.7	233.4
USA	741.5	762.8	823.2
Total (incl. others)	6,938.1	7,631.7	8,312.9

Exports f.o.b.†	2011	2012	2013
Bahrain	22.9	31.6	27.5
Belgium-Luxembourg . . .	14.8	4.5	23.2
China, People's Republic . .	229.1	235.0	293.5
Hong Kong	25.2	28.7	23.4
India	176.3	182.2	203.3
Indonesia	35.2	94.3	52.5
Iran	22.7	25.0	20.8
Iraq	15.8	24.7	159.0
Jordan	31.5	33.6	34.1
Malaysia	29.4	28.6	28.4
Oman	22.8	52.9	36.5
Pakistan	68.2	63.7	63.0
Qatar	39.3	47.0	45.8
Saudi Arabia	190.0	197.4	199.0
Taiwan	1.2	63.1	54.6
Turkey	62.9	67.7	84.2
United Arab Emirates	189.3	204.8	237.4
USA	51.8	80.9	56.8
Total (incl. others)	1,171.1	1,674.7	1,854.3

* Imports by country of production; exports by country of last consignment.
† Excluding petroleum exports.

Transport

ROAD TRAFFIC
(motor vehicles in use at 31 December)

	2011	2012	2013
Passenger cars	1,265,655	1,331,703	1,411,372
Buses and coaches	26,099	26,860	30,212
Motorcycles and mopeds . . .	10,306	12,055	14,591

SHIPPING

Flag Registered Fleet
(at 31 December)

	2012	2013	2014
Number of vessels	155	157	168
Displacement ('000 grt) . . .	2,479.5	2,332.7	3,136.6

Source: Lloyd's List Intelligence (www.lloydslistintelligence.com).

CIVIL AVIATION
(traffic on scheduled services)

	2010	2011
Kilometres flown (million)	74	58
Passengers carried ('000)	4,563	3,723
Passenger-km (million)	10,219	9,058
Total ton-km (million)	1,298	1,112

Source: UN, *Statistical Yearbook*.

Passengers carried ('000): 3,581 in 2012; 3,180 in 2013 (Source: World Bank, World Development Indicators database).

Tourism

VISITOR ARRIVALS BY COUNTRY OF ORIGIN
(incl. excursionists)

	2011	2012	2013
Bahrain	121,482	163,783	230,269
Bangladesh	107,817	105,983	108,788
Egypt	594,099	646,093	710,415
India	789,694	826,526	917,539
Lebanon	104,739	108,277	111,408
Pakistan	215,194	200,037	215,742
Philippines	139,988	154,389	56,952
Saudi Arabia	2,063,815	2,160,291	2,365,262
Sri Lanka	100,782	90,260	92,066
Syria	269,013	227,429	199,456
USA	178,517	140,124	129,448
Total (incl. others)	5,574,302	5,728,697	6,216,936

Tourism receipts (US $ million, excl. passenger transport): 320 in 2011; 426 in 2012; 297 in 2013.

Source: World Tourism Organization.

Communications Media

	2011	2012	2013
Telephones ('000 main lines in use)	514.7	510.0	508.0
Mobile cellular telephones ('000 subscribers)	4,934.2	5,100.0	6,410.0
Broadband subscribers ('000) . .	47	47	47

Source: International Telecommunication Union.

Education

(state-controlled schools, 2013/14)

	Schools	Teachers	Students		
			Males	Females	Total
Kindergarten . .	199	6,332	20,930	22,190	43,120
Primary . . .	259	22,742	68,848	74,925	143,773
Intermediate . .	206	18,554	51,419	55,244	106,663
Secondary . .	139	13,274	28,712	38,577	67,289
Religious institutes . .	9	668	1,719	1,082	2,801
Special training institutes* . .	29	1,369	1,051	696	1,747

* 2012/13 figures.

Private education (2013/14): 107 kindergarten schools (2,086 teachers, 39,497 students); 134 primary schools (5,815 teachers, 107,002 students); 135 intermediate schools (3,247 teachers, 61,334 students); 113 secondary schools (3,192 teachers, 41,330 students).

Pupil-teacher ratio (primary education, UNESCO estimate): 8.6 in 2011/12 (Source: UNESCO Institute for Statistics).

Adult literacy rate (UNESCO estimates): 95.5% (males 95.8%; females 95.0%) in 2012 (Source: UNESCO Institute for Statistics).

Directory

The Government

HEAD OF STATE

Amir of Kuwait: His Highness Sheikh SABAH AL-AHMAD AL-JABER AL-SABAH (acceded 29 January 2006).

COUNCIL OF MINISTERS
(May 2015)

Prime Minister: Sheikh JABER MUBARAK AL-HAMAD AL-SABAH.

Deputy Prime Minister and Minister of Foreign Affairs: Sheikh SABAH AL-KHALID AL-HAMAD AL-SABAH.

Deputy Prime Minister and Minister of the Interior: Sheikh MUHAMMAD KHALID AL-AHMAD AL-SABAH.

Deputy Prime Minister and Minister of Defence: Lt-Gen. Sheikh KHALID AL-JARRAH AL-SABAH.

Minister of Education and Higher Education: Dr BADER HAMAD AL-ESSA.

Minister of Social Affairs and Labour and Minister of State for Planning and Development: HIND SABEEH AL-SABEEH.

Minister of Oil and Minister of State for National Assembly Affairs: ALI SALIH AL-OMAIR.

Minister of Finance: ANAS KHALID AL-SALIH.

Minister of State for Housing Affairs: YASSER ABUL.

Minister of Information and Minister of State for Youth Affairs: Sheikh SALMAN SABAH SALIM AL-HUMOUD AL-SABAH.

Minister of Electricity and Water and Minister of Public Works: AHMAD KHALID AHMAD AL-JASSAR.

Minister of State for Municipal Affairs and Minister of Communications: ISSA AHMAD AL-KANDARI.

Minister of State for Cabinet Affairs and Minister of Commerce and Industry: Sheikh MUHAMMAD ABDULLAH AL-MUBARAK AL-SABAH.

Minister of Health: Dr ALI AL-OBAIDI.

Minister of Justice and Minister of Awqaf and Islamic Affairs: Dr YACOUB ABD AL-MOHSEN AL-SANEA.

MINISTRIES

Diwan of the Prime Minister: POB 2, 15015 Kuwait City; tel. 22000000; fax 22223048; e-mail contact@pm.gov.kw; internet www .pm.gov.kw.

Ministry of Awqaf (Religious Endowments) and Islamic Affairs: POB 13, 13001 Safat, Kuwait City; tel. 22487225; fax 22427754; e-mail contact_us@islam.gov.kw; internet www.islam .gov.kw.

Ministry of Commerce and Industry: POB 2944, 13030 Safat, Kuwait City; tel. 2248000; fax 22424411; e-mail office@moci.gov.kw; internet www.moci.gov.kw.

Ministry of Communications: POB 15, 13001 Safat, Kuwait City; tel. 24819033; fax 24814448; internet www.moc.kw.

Ministry of Defence: POB 1170, 13012 Safat, Kuwait City; tel. 24848300; fax 24846059; e-mail mod_info@mod.gov.kw; internet www.mod.gov.kw.

Ministry of Education: POB 7, 13001 Safat, Hilali St, Kuwait City; tel. 24754271; fax 24754274; e-mail webmaster@moe.edu.kw; internet www.moe.edu.kw.

Ministry of Electricity and Water: POB 12, South al-Sourra St, Ministries Area, Al Assimah, 13001 Safat, Kuwait City; tel. 25371000; fax 25371420; internet www.mew.gov.kw.

Ministry of Finance: POB 9, 13001 Safat, al-Morkab St, Ministries Complex, Kuwait City; tel. 22480000; fax 22404025; e-mail wqanaie@mof.gov.kw; internet www.mof.gov.kw.

Ministry of Foreign Affairs: POB 3, 13001 Safat, Gulf St, Kuwait City; tel. 22225555; fax 22224444; e-mail mofa.site@mofa.gov.kw; internet www.mofa.gov.kw.

Ministry of Health: POB 5, 13001 Safat, Arabian Gulf St, Kuwait City; tel. 24863840; fax 24863485; e-mail health@moh.gov.kw; internet www.moh.gov.kw.

Ministry of Higher Education: tel. 24925177; fax 24925260; internet www.mohe.edu.kw.

Ministry of Information: POB 193, 13002 Safat, al-Sour St, Kuwait City; tel. 22415301; fax 22418605; e-mail info@moinfo.gov .kw; internet www.media.gov.kw.

Ministry of the Interior: POB 11, 13001 Safat, Kuwait City; tel. 22430500; fax 22435487; e-mail contact@moi.gov.kw; internet www .moi.gov.kw.

Ministry of Justice: POB 6, 13001 Safat, al-Morkab St, Ministries Complex, Kuwait City; tel. 22486261; fax 22442257; e-mail info@moj .gov.kw; internet www.moj.gov.kw.

Ministry of Oil: POB 5077, 13051 Safat, Kuwait City; tel. 22406990; e-mail alnaft@moo.gov.kw; internet www.moo.gov.kw.

Ministry of Planning and Development Affairs: POB 15, 13001 Safat, Kuwait City; tel. 22428200; fax 22430403; e-mail info@mop .gov.kw.

Ministry of Public Works: POB 8, 13001 Safat, Kuwait City; tel. 25385520; fax 25380829; e-mail undersecretary@mpw.gov.kw; internet www.mpw.gov.kw.

Ministry of Social Affairs and Labour: POB 563, 13006 Safat, Kuwait City; tel. 22480000; fax 22419877; internet www.mosal.gov .kw.

Legislature

Elections to the 50-seat National Assembly took place more than one year early on 2 February 2012, following the dissolution of the legislature by Sheikh Sabah in December 2011 (precipitated by a dispute between the Government and parliament over allegations of corruption and public protests against the Government). Sunni Islamists opposed to the Government won 23 seats; liberals and their allies secured nine; Shi'a Islamists took seven; and the remaining seats were won by independent candidates. On 20 June 2012 the National Assembly was dissolved and the Assembly members elected in 2009 reinstated, following a ruling by the Constitutional Court that declared the results of the February 2012 elections to be null and void. However, more than one-half of those reinstated members immediately resigned their seats in protest against the decision. The restored Assembly was itself dissolved by Amiri decree on 7 October, and early elections were subsequently scheduled for 1 December. Despite a boycott organized by leading opponents of the Government and ongoing anti-Government protests, the election took place as scheduled. Shi'a Islamist candidates secured 17 seats (compared with just seven at the February 2012 election), while Sunni Islamists won four seats (compared with 23 in February).

The Assembly was again dissolved in mid-June 2013, after the Constitutional Court upheld changes to the electoral law decreed by the Amir in October 2012. Early elections were scheduled for 25 July 2013, but were subsequently postponed by two days. According to the final results of the elections, which were held on 27 July, candidates representing tribal areas secured 24 of the Assembly's 50 seats. Shi'a Islamist candidates won just eight seats, while Sunni Islamists took seven. Liberals and their allies were reported to have won five seats, while the remainder went to independent candidates, some of whom represented the *bidoun*. Voter turnout was recorded at 52.5%. The new Assembly was inaugurated on 6 August.

National Assembly: POB 716, 13008 Safat, Kuwait City; tel. 22436336; fax 22436331; e-mail kwt-ipu-grp@majlesalommah.net; internet www.kna.kw.

Speaker: MARZOUQ AL-GHANIM.

Political Organizations

Political parties are not permitted in Kuwait. However, several quasi-political organizations are in existence. Among those that have been represented in the Majlis since 1992 are:

Islamic Constitutional Movement (Hadas): internet www.icmkw .org; f. 1991; Sunni Muslim; political arm of the Muslim Brotherhood; Sec.-Gen. NASSER AL-SANE.

Islamic Salafi Alliance: Sunni Muslim; Sec.-Gen. ALI AL-OMAIR (acting).

Justice and Peace Alliance: Shi'a Muslim; Leader HASSAN NASIR.

Kuwait Democratic Forum: internet www.alminbarkw.org; f. 1991; loose asscn of secular, liberal and Arab nationalist groups; campaigned for the extension of voting rights to women; Sec.-Gen. BANDAR AL-KHAIRAN.

National Action Bloc: liberal, nationalist.

National Democratic Alliance (NDA): f. 1997; secular, liberal; Sec.-Gen. KHALED AL-KHALED.

National Islamic Alliance: Shi'a Muslim; Leader HUSSAIN AL-MATOUQ.

Popular Action Bloc: loose asscn of nationalists and Shi'a Muslims; Leader AHMAD AL-SAADOUN.

Diplomatic Representation

EMBASSIES IN KUWAIT

Afghanistan: POB 33186, 73452 Rawdah, Block 6, Surra St, Across Surra Co-op Society, House 16, Kuwait City; tel. 25328156; fax 25326274; e-mail afg_emb_kuw@hotmail.com; Ambassador Dr ASADULLAH HANIF BALKHI.

Algeria: POB 578, 13006 Safat, Istiqlal St, Kuwait City; tel. 22519984; fax 22519497; e-mail ambalg.kw@gmail.com; internet www.algerianembassy-kuwait.com; Ambassador KHAMISI ARIF.

Argentina: POB 3788, 40188 Mishref, Kuwait City; tel. 25379211; fax 25379212; e-mail ekuwa@mrecic.gov.ar; internet ekuwa .cancilleria.gov.ar; Ambassador JORGE OMAR ANTONIO BIGA.

Armenia: Jabriya District, Blk 8, St 3, Villa 8, Kuwait City; tel. 25322175; fax 25314656; e-mail embassy.kuwait@mfa.am; internet kuwait.mfa.am; Ambassador FADEY CHARCHOGHLYAN.

Australia: Dar al-Awadi Bldg (Level 12), Ahmad al-Jaber St, Sharq, Kuwait City; tel. 22322422; fax 22322430; e-mail austemb.kuwait@ dfat.gov.au; internet www.kuwait.embassy.gov.au; Ambassador WARREN HAUCK.

Austria: POB 15013, Daiyah, Ahmed Shawki St, House 10, 35451 Kuwait City; tel. 22552532; fax 22563052; e-mail kuwait-ob@bmeia .gv.at; internet www.bmeia.gv.at/botschaft/kuwait; Ambassador ULRICH FRANK.

Azerbaijan: al-Yarmouk, Block 2, Villa 15, Kuwait City; tel. 25355247; fax 25355246; e-mail embazerbaijan@yahoo.com; internet www.azerembassy-kuwait.org; Ambassador TURAL RZAYEV.

Bahrain: POB 196, al-Surrah, Plot 5, al-Surrah Rd, Villa 27, Kuwait City; tel. 25318530; fax 25330882; e-mail Kuwait.mission@mofa.gov .bh; internet www.mofa.gov.bh/kuwait; Ambassador Sheikh KHALIFA BIN HAMAD AL KHALIFA.

Bangladesh: House 11, St 29, Blk 2, Khaldiya, Kuwait City; tel. 24913219; fax 24913205; e-mail ambassador.kuwait@mofa.gov.bd; Ambassador Maj.-Gen. MUHAMMAD ASHAB UDDIN.

Belgium: POB 3280, Bayan, Blk 13, St 4, Villa 8, Safat, 13033 Kuwait City; tel. 25384582; fax 25384583; e-mail kuwait@diplobel .fed.be; internet www.diplomatie.be/kuwait; Ambassador ANDY DETAILLE.

Bhutan: POB 1510, 13016 Safat, Adailiya-Block 3, Issa Abd al-Rahman al-Assoussi St, Jadda 32, Villa 7, Kuwait City; tel. 22516640; fax 22516550; e-mail bhutankuwait@gmail.com; Ambassador Dasho TASHI PHUNTSOG.

Bosnia and Herzegovina: Bayan, Blk 5, Rd 2, St 5, Villa 18, Kuwait City; tel. 25392637; fax 25392106; Ambassador (vacant).

Brazil: POB 39761, 73058 Nuzha, Blk 1, St 116, House 47, Kuwait City; tel. 25378561; fax 25378560; e-mail embassy@brazil.org.kw; internet www.brazil.org.kw; Ambassador ANTONIO CARLOS DO NASCIMENTO PEDRO.

Bulgaria: POB 12090, 71651 Shamiya, Jabriya, Area 11, St 107 and St 1, Kuwait City; tel. 25314458; fax 25321453; e-mail Embassy .Kuwait@mfa.bg; internet www.mfa.bg/embassies/kuwait; Ambassador ALEXANDAR OLSHEVSKI.

Canada: POB 25281, 13113 Safat, Daiyah, Blk 4, al-Mutawakkel St, Villa 24, Kuwait City; tel. 22563025; fax 22560173; e-mail kwait@ international.gc.ca; internet www.canadainternational.gc.ca/ kuwait-koweit; Ambassador MARTINE MOREAU.

China, People's Republic: POB 2346, 13024 Safat, Yarmouk, Sheikh Ahmad al-Jaber Bldgs 4 & 5, St 1, Villa 82, Kuwait City; tel. 25333340; fax 25333341; e-mail chinaemb_kw@mfa.gov.cn; internet kw.chineseembassy.org; Ambassador CUI JIANCHUN.

Cuba: Block 3, Abu Hayyan Al-Tawhidi St, House 74, Rawda, POB 1604, Kuwait City; tel. 22549361; fax 22549360; e-mail cubaemba@ qualitynet.net; internet www.cubadiplomatica.cu/kuwait; Ambassador ANDRÉS GONZÁLEZ GARRIDO.

Czech Republic: Nuzha, Blk 3, St 34, House 13, Kuwait City; tel. 22529018; fax 22529021; e-mail kuwait@embassy.mzv.cz; internet www.mzv.cz/kuwait; Ambassador MARTIN VÍTEK.

Djibouti: Kuwait City; Ambassador MUHAMMAD ALI MUMIN.

Egypt: POB 11252, 35153 Dasmah, Istiqlal St, Kuwait City; tel. 22519955; fax 22563877; e-mail embassy.kuwait@mfa.gov.eg; Ambassador ABD AL-KARIM SULEIMAN.

Eritrea: POB 53016, 73015 Nuzha, Jabriya, Block 9, St 21, House 9, Kuwait City; tel. 25317427; fax 26631304; Ambassador MOHAMMED OMAR MAHMOUD.

Ethiopia: POB 939, 45710 Safat, Jabriya, Blk 10, St 107, Villa 30, Kuwait City; tel. 25330128; fax 25331179; e-mail ethiokwt@ qualitynet.net; Ambassador MUHAMMAD GUDETA.

France: POB 1037, 13011 Safat, Mansouriah, Blk 1, St 13, Villa 24, Kuwait City; tel. 22582020; fax 22571058; e-mail cad.koweit-amba@ diplomatie.gouv.fr; internet www.ambafrance-kw.org; Ambassador CHRISTIAN NAKHLÉ.

Georgia: Qurtoba, Blk 2, Area 1, Ave 3, Villa 6, Kuwait City; tel. 25352909; fax 25354707; e-mail kuwait.emb@mfa.gov.ge; internet kuwait.mfa.gov.ge; Ambassador ROLAND BERIDZE.

Germany: POB 805, 13009 Safat, Dahiya Abdullah al-Salem, Area 1, Ave 14, Branch of al-Yousef St, Villa 13, Kuwait City; tel. 22520827; fax 22520763; e-mail info@kuwa.diplo.de; internet www .kuwait.diplo.de; Ambassador EUGEN WOLLFARTH.

Greece: POB 23812, 13099 Safat, Khaldiya, Block 4, St 44, House 4, Kuwait City; tel. 24817100; fax 24817103; e-mail gremb.kuw@mfa .gr; internet www.mfa.gr/kuwait; Ambassador Dr THEODOROS THEODOROU.

Holy See: POB 29724, 13158 Safat, Kuwait City; tel. 25337767; fax 25327776; e-mail nuntiuskuwait@gmail.com; Apostolic Nuncio Most Rev. Archbishop PETAR RAJIC (Titular Archbishop of Sarsenterum).

Hungary: POB 23955, 13100 Safat, Bayan, Blk 13, St 30, Villa 381, Kuwait City; tel. 25379351; fax 25379350; e-mail mission.kwi@mfa .gov.hu; internet www.mfa.gov.hu/emb/kuwait; Ambassador MIHÁLY BAYER.

India: POB 1450, 13015 Safat, Diplomatic Enclave, Arabian Gulf St, Kuwait City; tel. 22530600; fax 22546958; e-mail contact@ indembkwt.org; internet www.indembkwt.org; Ambassador SUNIL JAIN.

Indonesia: POB 21560, 13076 Safat, Kaifan, Blk 6, al-Andalus St, House 29, Kuwait City; tel. 24839927; fax 24819250; e-mail unitkom@kbrikuwait.org; internet kuwaitcity.kemlu.go.id; Ambassador TATANG BUDIE UTAMA RAZAK.

Iran: POB 4686, 13047 Safat, Daiyah, Embassies Area, Block B, Kuwait City; tel. 22560694; fax 22529868; e-mail iranembassy@ hotmail.com; Ambassador ALI REZA ENAYATI.

Iraq: Kuwait City; e-mail kuwemb@iraqmfamail.com; Ambassador MUHAMMAD HUSSAIN BAHR AL-ULUM.

Italy: POB 4453, 13045 Safat, Jabriya, Blk 9, St 1, Villa 84, Kuwait City; tel. 25356010; fax 25356030; e-mail ambasciata.alkuwait@ esteri.it; internet www.ambalkuwait.esteri.it; Ambassador FABRIZIO NICOLETTI.

Japan: POB 2304, 13024 Safat, Plot 57, Blk 7A, Diplomatic Zone, Mishref, Kuwait City; tel. 25309400; fax 25309401; e-mail info@ embjp-kw.org; internet www.kw.emb-japan.go.jp; Ambassador TOSHIHIRO TSUJIHARA.

Jordan: POB 39891, 73059 Kuwait City; tel. 22533261; fax 22533270; e-mail kujor@qualitynet.net; Ambassador MUHAMMAD AL-KAYED.

Korea, Republic: POB 4272, 13043 Safat, Plot 6, Blk 7A, Diplomatic Zone 2, Mishref, Kuwait City; tel. 25378621; fax 25378628; e-mail kuwait@mofa.go.kr; internet kwt.mofa.go.kr; Ambassador SHIN BOONAM.

Lebanon: POB 253, 13003 Safat, Da'Yiah Diplomatic Area, Plot 6, Kuwait City; tel. 22562103; fax 22571682; e-mail lebembassy@ lebanonembassy.org.kw; internet www.lebanonembassy.org.kw; Ambassador Dr KHADIR HILWE.

Libya: POB 21460, 13075 Safat, 27 Istiqlal St, Kuwait City; tel. 22575183; fax 22575182; Ambassador Dr MUHAMMAD SALEM EMAISH.

Malaysia: POB 4105, 13042 Safat, Daiya, Diplomatic Enclave, Area 5, Yemen St, Plot 5, Kuwait City; tel. 22550394; fax 22550384; e-mail malkuwait@kln.com.my; internet www.kln.gov.my/perwakilan/ kuwait; Ambassador (vacant).

Mongolia: Block 8, St 806, Villa 161, al-Zahra Area, Kuwait City; tel. 25216551; fax 25216557; e-mail kuwait@mfat.gov.mn; Ambassador SODNOMYN ENKHBAT.

Morocco: Yarmouk, Blk 2, St 2, Villa 14, Kuwait City; tel. 25312980; fax 25317423; e-mail ambkow@yahoo.fr; Ambassador YAHYA BANANI.

Nepal: Blk 8, St 13, Villa 514, Jabriya, Kuwait City; tel. 25321603; fax 25321628; e-mail info@nepembku.org; internet www.kuwait .mofa.gov.np; Ambassador YAGYA BAHADUR HAMAL.

Netherlands: Blk 6, St 11, House 7, Jabriya, Kuwait City; tel. 25312650; fax 25326334; e-mail kwe@minbuza.nl; internet www .netherlandsembassy.gov.kw; Ambassador NICOLAAS BEETS.

Niger: POB 44451, 32059 Hawalli, Salwa Block 12, St 6, Villa 183, Kuwait City; tel. 25652943; fax 25640478; Ambassador ABDOUL-KARIMOU SEINI.

Nigeria: POB 6432, 32039 Hawalli, Surra, Area 1, St 14, House 24, Kuwait City; tel. 18278813; fax 18278896; Ambassador HARUNA GARBA.

Oman: POB 21975, 13080 Safat, al-Odeilia Block 3, St 3, Villa 25, Kuwait City; tel. 22561956; fax 22561963; e-mail kuwait@mofa.gov .om; Ambassador HAMID BIN SAID BIN SALIM AL-IBRAHIM.

Pakistan: POB 988, 13010 Safat, Jabriya, Police Station Rd, St 101, Plot 5, Blk 11, Villa 46, Kuwait City; tel. 25327649; fax 25327648; e-mail parepkuwait@mofa.gov.pk; internet www.mofa.gov.pk/ kuwait; Ambassador MUHAMMAD ASLAM KHAN.

Philippines: POB 26288, 13123 Safat, Blk 6, Villa 153, Nouman Bin Basher St, corner Damascus St, Faiha, Kuwait City; tel. 22528422; fax 22511805; e-mail kuwaitpe@philembassykuwait.gov.kw; internet www.philembassykuwait.gov.kw; Ambassador LAMBERTO V. MONSANTO.

Poland: POB 5066, 13051 Safat, Jabriya, Blk 7, St 3, Villa 20, Kuwait City; tel. 25311571; fax 25311576; e-mail kuwejt.amb .sekretariat@msz.gov.pl; internet kuwejt.msz.gov.pl; Ambassador GRZEGORZ OLSZAK.

Qatar: POB 1825, 13019 Safat, Diiyah, Istiqlal St, Kuwait City; tel. 22523107; fax 22513604; e-mail kuwait@mofa.gov.qa; Ambassador HAMAD ALI JABER AL-HENZAB.

Romania: POB 13574, 35152 Dasmah, Keifan, Area 4, Moona St, House 34, Kuwait City; tel. 24845079; fax 24848929; e-mail ambsa@ kems.net; Ambassador VASILE SOFINETI.

Russian Federation: POB 1765, Safat, Daya Diplomatic Area, Plot 17, Blk 5, Kuwait City; tel. 22560427; fax 22524969; e-mail rusposkuw@mail.ru; internet www.kuwait.mid.ru; Ambassador ALEKSEJ V. SOLOMATIN.

Saudi Arabia: POB 20498, 13065 Safat, Istiqlal St, Kuwait City; tel. 22550021; fax 22551858; e-mail kwemb@mofa.gov.sa; internet embassies.mofa.gov.sa/sites/kuwait; Ambassador ABD AL-AZIZ AL-FAYEZ.

Senegal: POB 23892, 13099 Safat, Rawdah, Block 3, St 35, Villa 9, Kuwait City; tel. 22573477; fax 22542044; e-mail senegal_embassy@ yahoo.com; Ambassador ABDOU LAHAD MBACKE.

Serbia: POB 20511, 13066 Safat, Surra, Blk 5, St 1, Villa 71, Kuwait City; tel. 25327548; fax 25327568; e-mail embrskw@qualitynet.net; internet kuwait.mfa.gov.rs; Ambassador VLADIMIR KOHUT.

Sierra Leone: POB 176, Blk 8, St 807, Bldg 8, Surra, Kuwait City; tel. 25243234; fax 25243238; e-mail info@salembassykuwait.org; internet www.salembassykuwait.org; Ambassador IBRAHIM BAKARR KAMARA.

Slovakia: Blk 2, St 16, Villa 22, Area 13123, Surra, Kuwait City; tel. 25353893; fax 25353894; e-mail emb.kuwait@mzv.sk; internet www .mzv.sk/kuvajt; Ambassador PAVOL SVETÍK.

Somalia: POB 22766, 13088 Safat, Bayan, St 1, Block 7, Villa 25, Kuwait City; tel. 25394795; fax 25394829; e-mail webmaster@ somaligov.net; internet www.kuwait.somaligov.net; Ambassador Dr ABDUL KHADIR AMIN SHEIKH ABUBAKER.

South Africa: POB 2262, 40173 Mishref, Salwa Block 10, St 1, Villa 91, Unit 3, Kuwait City; tel. 25617988; fax 25617917; e-mail kuwait .political@dirco.gov.za; Ambassador DELAREY VAN TONDER.

Spain: POB 22207, 13083 Safat, Surra, Block 3, St 14, Bldg 19, Kuwait City; tel. 25325827; fax 25357439; e-mail emb.kuwait@maec .es; internet www.exteriores.gob.es/embajadas/kuwait; Ambassador CARLOS SÁENZ DE TEJADA.

Sri Lanka: POB 44650, Jabriya, Blk 10, St 107, Bldg 1, Kuwait City; tel. 25339140; fax 25339154; e-mail lankemb@qualitynet.net; internet www.slembkwt.org; Chargé d'affaires N. M. M. ANAS.

Swaziland: POB 632, Block 7, St 101, Villa 69, Jabriya 46307; tel. 25313306; fax 23513307; e-mail swazikuwait@gmail.com; Ambassador MLONDI DLAMINI.

Switzerland: POB 23954, 13100 Safat, Qortuba, Blk 2, St 1, House 122, Kuwait City; tel. 25340172; fax 25340176; e-mail kow .vertretung@eda.admin.ch; internet www.eda.admin.ch/kuwait; Ambassador ETIENNE THÉVOZ.

Thailand: POB 66647, 43757 Bayan, Blk 6, St 8, Villa 1, Jabriya, Kuwait City; tel. 25317530; fax 25317532; e-mail thaiemkw@kems .net; internet www.thaiembassy.org/kuwait; Ambassador SURASAK CHUASUKONTHIP.

Tunisia: POB 5976, 13060 Safat, Nuzha, Plot 2, Nuzha St, Villa 45, Kuwait City; tel. 2542144; fax 2528995; e-mail tunemrku@ncc.moc .kw; Ambassador NOUREDDINE EL-RAI.

Turkey: POB 20627, 13067 Safat, Blk 5, Plot 16, Istiqlal St, Kuwait City; tel. 22277400; fax 22560403; e-mail embassy.kuwait@mfa.gov .tr; internet kuwait.emb.mfa.gov.tr; Ambassador MURAT TAMER.

Ukraine: POB 7588, 32096 Hawalli, Jabriya, Blk 10, St 6, House 5, Kuwait City; tel. 25318507; fax 25318508; e-mail emb_kw@mfa.gov .ua; internet www.mfa.gov.ua/kuwait; Ambassador VOLODYMYR TOLKACH.

United Arab Emirates: POB 1828, 13019 Safat, Blk 5, Yemen St, Bldg 7, Kuwait City; tel. 22528544; fax 22526382; e-mail kuwait@ mofa.gov.ae; internet uae-embassy.ae/Embassies/kw; Ambassador RAHMA HUSSAIN AL-ZA'ABI.

United Kingdom: POB 2, 13001 Safat, Arabian Gulf St, Kuwait City; tel. 22594320; fax 22594339; e-mail kuwait.generalenquiries@ fco.gov.uk; internet www.gov.uk/government/world/kuwait; Ambassador MATTHEW LODGE.

USA: POB 77, 13001 Safat, Bayan, al-Masjed al-Aqsa St, Plot 14, Block 14, Kuwait City; tel. 22591001; fax 25380282; e-mail paskuwaitm@state.gov; internet kuwait.usembassy.gov; Ambassador DOUGLAS A. SILLIMAN.

Uzbekistan: Mishref, Blk 2, St 5, Villa 18A, Kuwait City; Ambassador ABDURAFIK A. HOSHIMOV.

Venezuela: POB 24440, 13105 Safat, Block 5, St 7, Area 356, Surra, Kuwait City; tel. 25324367; fax 25324368; e-mail embavene@ qualitynet.net; Ambassador ELOY FERNÁNDEZ AZUAJE.

Yemen: POB 7182, al-Jabriya St, Kuwait City; tel. 25349416; fax 25349415; Chargé d'affaires a.i. MUHAMMAD SALIH AL-BERRI.

Zimbabwe: POB 36484, 24755 Salmiya, Kuwait City; tel. 25620845; fax 25621491; e-mail zimkuwait@hotmail.com; Ambassador MARK GREY MARONGWE.

Judicial System

Constitutional Court: Comprises five judges. Interprets the provisions of the Constitution; considers disputes regarding the constitutionality of legislation, decrees and rules; has jurisdiction in challenges relating to the election of members, or eligibility for election, to the Majlis al-Umma.

Court of Cassation: Comprises five judges. Is competent to consider the legality of verdicts of the Court of Appeal and State Security Court; Chief Justice FAISAL AL-MOURSHID.

Court of Appeal: Comprises three judges. Considers verdicts of the Court of First Instance; Chief Justice RASHED AL-HAMMAD.

Court of First Instance: Comprises the following divisions: Civil and Commercial (one judge), Personal Status Affairs (one judge), Lease (three judges), Labour (one judge), Crime (three judges), Administrative Disputes (three judges), Appeal (three judges), Challenged Misdemeanours (three judges); Chief Justice MUHAMMAD AL-SAKHOBY.

Summary Courts: Each governorate has a Summary Court, comprising one or more divisions. The courts have jurisdiction in the following areas: Civil and Commercial, Urgent Cases, Lease, Misdemeanours. The verdict in each case is delivered by one judge.

There is also a Traffic Court, with one presiding judge.

Prosecutor-General: DHARAR AL-AS'OUSI.

Religion

ISLAM

The majority of Kuwaitis are Muslims of the Sunni or Shi'a sects. The Shi'a community comprises about 30% of the total.

CHRISTIANITY

The Roman Catholic Church

Latin Rite

For ecclesiastical purposes, Kuwait forms part of the Apostolic Vicariate of Northern Arabia.

Vicar Apostolic: CAMILLO BALLIN (Titular Bishop of Arna), Bishop's House, POB 25362, Rd 4603, House 137/125, Blk 946, Awali, Bahrain; tel. (+973) 39504488; fax 22420297; e-mail mail@ camilloballin.com; internet www.avona.org.

Melkite Rite

Exarch Patriarchal: Rev. BOUTROS GHARIB, Vicariat Patriarchal Greek-Melkite, POB 1205, Salwa Block 12, St 6, House 58, 22013 Salmiya, Kuwait City, tel. and fax 25652802; e-mail greekcatholickuwait@yahoo.com.

Syrian Rite

The Syrian Catholic Patriarch of Antioch is resident in Beirut, Lebanon. The Patriarchal Exarchate of Basra and the Gulf is based in Basra, Iraq.

The Anglican Communion

Within the Episcopal Church in Jerusalem and the Middle East, Kuwait forms part of the diocese of Cyprus and the Gulf. The Anglican congregation in Kuwait is entirely expatriate. The Bishop in Cyprus and the Gulf is resident in Cyprus, while the Archdeacon in the Gulf is resident in Bahrain.

Other Christian Churches

National Evangelical Church in Kuwait: POB 80, 13001 Safat, Kuwait City; tel. 22407195; fax 22431087; e-mail elc@ncc.moc.kw; Rev. NABIL ATTALLAH (pastor of the Arabic-language congregation), Rev. JERRY A. ZANDSTRA (senior pastor of the English-speaking congregation); an independent Protestant Church founded by the Reformed Church in America; services in Arabic, English, Korean, Malayalam and other Indian languages; combined weekly congregation of some 20,000.

The Armenian, Greek, Coptic and Syrian Orthodox Churches are also represented in Kuwait.

The Press

Freedom of the press and publishing is guaranteed in the Constitution, although press censorship was in force between mid-1986 and early 1992 (when journalists adopted a voluntary code of practice). In February 1995 a ruling by the Constitutional Court effectively endorsed the Government's right to suspend publication of newspapers; however, legislation passed in 2006 rendered this illegal without a court order. The Government provides financial support to newspapers and magazines.

DAILIES

Al-Anbaa (The News): POB 23915, 13100 Safat, Kuwait City; tel. 22272727; fax 24832647; e-mail editorial@alanba.com.kw; internet www.alanba.com.kw; f. 1976; Arabic; general; Editor-in-Chief YOUSEF KHALED AL-MARZOOQ; circ. 85,000.

Arab Times: POB 2270, Airport Road, Shuwaikh, 13023 Safat, Kuwait City; tel. 24849144; fax 24818267; e-mail arabtimes@ arabtimesonline.com; internet www.arabtimesonline.com; f. 1977; English; political and financial; no Fri. edn; Editor-in-Chief AHMAD ABD AL-AZIZ AL-JARALLAH; Man. Editor MISHAL AL-JARALLAH; circ. 41,922.

Al-Jarida (The Newspaper): POB 29846, 13159 Safat, Kuwait City; tel. 22257036; fax 22257035; e-mail info@aljarida.com; internet www .aljarida.com; f. 2007; Arabic; affiliated with the Nat. Democratic Alliance; Editor-in-Chief KHALID HILAL AL-MUTAIRI.

Kuwait Times: POB 1301, 13014 Safat, Kuwait City; tel. 24833199; fax 24835621; e-mail info@kuwaittimes.net; internet www .kuwaittimes.net; f. 1961; English, Malayalam and Urdu; political; Editor-in-Chief ABD AL RAHMAN ALYAN; circ. 32,000.

Al-Qabas (Firebrand): POB 21800, 13078 Safat, Kuwait City; tel. 24812822; fax 24834355; e-mail info@alqabas.com.kw; internet www .alqabas.com.kw; f. 1972; Arabic; independent; Gen. Man. FOUZAN AL-FARES; Editor-in-Chief WALEED ABD-LATIF AL-NISF; circ. 60,000.

Al-Ra'i al-'Aam (Public Opinion): POB 761, 13008 Safat, Kuwait City; tel. 24953100; fax 24815921; e-mail editor@alraialaam.com; internet www.alraialaam.com; f. 1961; Arabic; political, social and cultural; Editor-in-Chief YOUSUF AL-JALAHMA; circ. 101,500.

Al-Seyassah (Policy): POB 2270, Shuwaikh, Kuwait City; tel. 24813566; fax 24818267; internet www.al-seyassah.com; f. 1965; Arabic; political and financial; Editor-in-Chief AHMAD ABD AL-AZIZ AL-JARALLAH; circ. 70,000.

Al-Watan (The Homeland): POB 1142, 13012 Safat, Kuwait City; tel. 24840950; fax 24818481; e-mail alwatan@alwatan.com.kw; internet www.alwatan.com.kw; f. 1962; Arabic; political; Editor-in-Chief Sheikh KHALIFA ALI AL-KHALIFA AL-SABAH; Gen. Man. DINA AL-MALLAK; circ. 91,726.

WEEKLIES AND PERIODICALS

Al-Balagh (Communiqué): POB 4558, 13046 Safat, Kuwait City; tel. 24818820; fax 24812735; e-mail albalagh5@yahoo.com; internet www.al-balagh.com; f. 1969; weekly; Arabic; general, political and Islamic affairs; Editor-in-Chief ABD AL-RAHMAN RASHID AL-WALAYATI; circ. 29,000.

Byzance: Kuwait City; f. 2007; bi-monthly; Arabic and French; lifestyle magazine, incl. features on fashion, jewellery, furniture and art; Man. Editor JEAN-PIERRE GUEIRARD; Exec. Editor-in-Chief ANTOINE DAHER.

Al-Dakhiliya (The Interior): POB 71655, 12500 Shamiah, Kuwait City; tel. 22410091; fax 22410609; e-mail moipr@qualitynet.net; monthly; Arabic; official reports, transactions and proceedings; publ.

by Public Relations Dept, Ministry of the Interior; Editor-in-Chief Lt-Col AHMAD A. AL-SHARQAWI.

Dalal Magazine: POB 6000, 13060 Safat, Kuwait City; tel. 24832098; fax 24832039; internet www.dalal-kw.com; f. 1997; monthly; Arabic; family affairs, beauty, fashion; Editor-in-Chief AHMAD YOUSUF BEHBEHANI.

Friday Times: POB 1301, 13014 Safat, Kuwait City; tel. 24833199; fax 24835627; e-mail info@kuwaittimes.net; internet www .kuwaittimes.net; f. 2005; weekend edn of *Kuwait Times*.

Al-Hadaf (The Objective): POB 2270, 13023 Safat, Kuwait City; tel. 24813566; fax 24816042; internet www.al-seyassah.com/alhadaf; f. 1964; weekly; Arabic; social and cultural; Editor-in-Chief AHMAD ABD AL-AZIZ AL-JARALLAH; circ. 268,904.

Al-Iqtisadi al-Kuwaiti (Kuwaiti Economist): POB 775, 13008 Safat, Kuwait City; tel. 1805580; fax 22300074; e-mail kcci@kcci .org.kw; internet www.kcci.org.kw; f. 1960; monthly; Arabic; commerce, trade and economics; publ. by Kuwait Chamber of Commerce and Industry; Editor MAJED B. JAMALUDDIN; circ. 6,000.

Journal of the Gulf and Arabian Peninsula Studies: POB 17073, 72451 Khaldiya, Kuwait University, Kuwait City; tel. 24833215; fax 24833705; e-mail jotgaaps@kuc01.kuniv.edu.kw; internet pubcouncil.kuniv.edu.kw/jgaps; f. 1975; quarterly; Arabic and English; publ. by Academic Publication Council of Kuwait Univ; Editor-in-Chief Prof. BADER AL-OMAR.

Al-Khaleej Business Magazine: POB 25725, 13118 Safat, Kuwait City; tel. 22433765; e-mail aljabriya@gulfweb.com; Editor-in-Chief AHMAD ISMAIL BEHBEHANI.

Kuwait Medical Journal (KMJ): POB 1202, 13013 Safat, Kuwait City; tel. 25316023; fax 25317972; e-mail kmj@kma.org.kw; internet www.kma.org.kw/KMJ; f. 1967; quarterly; English; publ. by the Kuwait Medical Asscn; original articles, review articles, case reports, short communications, letters to the editor and book reviews; Editor-in-Chief Prof. FOUAD ABDULLAH M. HASSAN; circ. 5,000.

Kuwait al-Youm (Kuwait Today): POB 193, 13002 Safat, Kuwait City; tel. 24842167; fax 24831044; e-mail info@ipd.gov.kw; internet www.ipd.gov.kw; f. 1954; weekly; Arabic; statistics, Amiri decrees, laws, govt announcements, decisions, invitations for tenders, etc.; publ. by the Ministry of Information; circ. 5,000.

Al-Kuwaiti (The Kuwaiti): Information Dept, POB 9758, 61008 Ahmadi, Kuwait City; tel. 23981076; fax 23983661; e-mail kocinfo@ kockw.com; f. 1961; monthly journal of the Kuwait Oil Co; Arabic; Editor-in-Chief KHALED AL-KHAMEES; circ. 6,500.

The Kuwaiti Digest: Information Dept, POB 9758, 61008 Ahmadi, Kuwait City; tel. 23981076; fax 23983661; e-mail kocinfo@kockw .com; f. 1972; quarterly journal of the Kuwait Oil Co; English; Editor-in-Chief KHALED AL-KHAMEES; circ. 7,000.

Al-Majaless (Meetings): POB 5605, 13057 Safat, Kuwait City; tel. 24841178; fax 24847126; e-mail qasem@almajaless.com; weekly; Arabic; current affairs; Editor-in-Chief QASIM ABD AL-QADIR; circ. 60,206.

Mejallat al-Kuwait (Kuwait Magazine): POB 193, 13002 Safat, Kuwait City; tel. 22415300; fax 22419642; f. 1961; monthly; Arabic; illustrated magazine; science, arts and literature; publ. by the Ministry of Information.

Mirat al-Umma (Mirror of the Nation): POB 1142, 13012 Safat, Kuwait City; tel. 24837212; fax 24838671; weekly; Arabic; Editor-in-Chief MUHAMMAD AL-JASSEM; circ. 79,500.

Al-Nahdha (The Renaissance): POB 695, 13007 Safat, Kuwait City; tel. 24813133; fax 24849298; f. 1967; weekly; Arabic; social and political; Editor-in-Chief THAMER AL-SALAH; circ. 170,000.

Osrati (My Family): POB 2995, 13030 Safat, Kuwait City; tel. 24813233; fax 24838933; e-mail info@osratimag.com; f. 1964; weekly; Arabic; women's magazine; publ. by Fahad al-Marzouk Establishment; Editor GHANIMA F. AL-MARZOUK; circ. 10,500.

Al-Talia (The Ascendant): POB 1082, 13011 Safat, Kuwait City; tel. 24831200; fax 24840471; f. 1962; weekly; Arabic; politics and literature; Editor AHMAD YOUSUF AL-NAFISI; circ. 10,000.

Al-Yaqza (The Awakening): POB 6000, 13060 Safat, Kuwait City; tel. 24831318; fax 24832039; internet www.alyaqza.com; f. 1966; weekly; Arabic; political, economic, social and general; Editor-in-Chief AHMAD YOUSUF BEHBEHANI; circ. 91,340.

NEWS AGENCY

Kuwait News Agency (KUNA): POB 24063, 13101 Safat, Kuwait City; tel. 24834546; fax 24813424; e-mail feedback@kuna.net.kw; internet www.kuna.net.kw; f. 1979; public corporate body; independent; also publishes research digests on topics of common and special interest; Chair. and Dir-Gen. Sheikh MUBARAK AL-DUAIJ AL-SABAH.

PRESS ASSOCIATION

Kuwait Journalists Association: POB 5454, 13055 Safat, Kuwait City; tel. 24843351; fax 24842874; e-mail kja@kja-kw.com; internet www.kja-kw.com; Chair. AHMAD YOUSUF BEHBEHANI.

Publishers

Al-Abraj Translation and Publishing Co WLL: POB 26177, 13122 Safat, Kuwait City; tel. 22442310; fax 22407024; Man. Dir Dr TARIQ ABDULLAH.

Dar al-Seyassah Publishing, Printing and Distribution Co: POB 2270, 13023 Safat, Kuwait City; tel. 24813566; fax 24833628; internet www.dar-al-seyassah.com; publ. *Arab Times*, *Al-Seyassah* and *Al-Hadaf*.

Gulf Centre Publishing and Publicity: POB 2722, 13028 Safat, Kuwait City; tel. 22402760; fax 22458833; Propr HAMZA ISMAIL ESSLAH.

Kuwait National Advertising and Publishing Co (KNAPCO): POB 2268, 13023 Safat, Kuwait City; tel. 25745770; fax 25745779; e-mail support@knapco.com; internet www.knapco.com; f. 1995; publ. annual commercial business directory, *Teledymag*; Founder NAWAF ABD AL-RAZAK.

Kuwait Publishing House Co: POB 1446, 13015 Safat, Kuwait City; tel. 22449686; fax 22436956; e-mail info@kuwaitpocketguide .com; f. 1970; Dir ESAM AS'AD ABU AL-FARAJ.

Kuwait United Co for Advertising, Publishing and Distribution WLL: POB 29359, 13153 Safat, Kuwait City; tel. 24817111; fax 24817797.

Al-Talia Printing and Publishing Co: POB 1082, Airport Rd, Shuwaikh, 13011 Safat, Kuwait City; tel. 24840470; fax 24815611; Man. AHMAD YOUSUF AL-NAFISI.

GOVERNMENT PUBLISHING HOUSE

Ministry of Information: see Ministries

Broadcasting and Communications

TELECOMMUNICATIONS

National Mobile Telecommunications Co KSC (Wataniya Telecom): POB 613, 13007 Safat, Kuwait City; tel. 65805555; fax 22423369; e-mail info@wataniya.com; internet www.wataniya.com; f. 1999; Qatar Telecommunications Corpn (Q-Tel) acquired 51% stake 2007; Chair. and Man. Dir Sheikh ABDULLAH BIN MUHAMMAD BIN SAUD AL THANI; CEO and Gen. Man. ABD AL-AZIZ IBRAHIM FAKHROO.

VIVA: POB 181, Salmiya 22002, Kuwait City; tel. 55670000; fax 55676666; e-mail info@viva.com.kw; internet www.viva.com.kw; f. 2008; mobile cellular communications; commercial brand of Kuwait Telecom Co; Chair. ADEL MUHAMMAD AL-ROUMI; CEO Eng. SALMAN BIN ABD AL-AZIZ AL-BADRAN.

Zain Kuwait: POB 22244, 13083 Safat, Kuwait City; tel. 24644444; fax 24641111; e-mail info.kw@zain.com; internet www.kw.zain.com; f. 1983 as Mobile Telecommunications Co; in Sept. 2007 began operating under new global brand, Zain; group operates in 24 countries in the Middle East and Africa; 1.8m. subscribers in Kuwait, 69.5m. total group subscribers (30 June 2009); CEO OMAR AL-OMAR.

BROADCASTING

Radio

Radio of the State of Kuwait: POB 397, 13004 Safat, Kuwait City; tel. 22423774; fax 22456660; e-mail info@moinfo.gov.kw; internet www.moinfo.gov.kw; f. 1951; broadcasts daily in Arabic, Farsi, English and Urdu, some in stereo; Dir of Radio Dr ABD AL-AZIZ ALI MANSOUR; Dir of Radio Programmes ABD AL-RAHMAN HADI.

Television

Kuwait Television: POB 193, 13002 Safat, Kuwait City; tel. 22451288; fax 22438403; e-mail info@moinfo.gov.kw; internet www.moinfo.gov.kw; f. 1961; transmission began privately in Kuwait in 1957; transmits in Arabic; colour television service began in 1973; has a total of eight channels; Head of News Broadcasting MUHAMMAD AL-KAHTANI.

Al-Rai: Kuwait City; tel. 24817777; fax 24953002; e-mail alraitv@ alrai.tv; internet www.alrai.tv; f. 2004; first private satellite television station in Kuwait; admin. offices in Kuwait and transmission facilities in Dubai (United Arab Emirates); owned by Al-Rai Media Group.

Finance

(cap. = capital; res = reserves; dep. = deposits; m. = million;
br(s) = branch(es); amounts in Kuwaiti dinars unless otherwise
stated)

BANKING

Central Bank

Central Bank of Kuwait: POB 526, 13006 Safat, Abdullah al-Salem St, Kuwait City; tel. 22449200; fax 22464887; e-mail cbk@cbk.gov.kw; internet www.cbk.gov.kw; f. 1969; cap. 5m., res 562m., dep. 3,369m. (March 2010); Governor Dr MUHAMMAD AL-HASHEL.

National Banks

Al-Ahli Bank of Kuwait KSC (ABK): POB 1387, 13014 Safat, Ahmad al-Jaber St, Kuwait City; tel. 22400900; fax 22424557; e-mail marketing@abkuwait.com; internet www.eahli.com/abk; f. 1967; wholly owned by private Kuwaiti interests; cap. 151m., res 280m., dep. 2,396m. (Dec. 2012); Chair. AHMAD YOUSUF BEHBEHANI; Dep. Chair. and Man. Dir ALI HILAL AL-MUTAIRI; 25 domestic brs and 2 foreign brs.

Ahli United Bank KSC (BKME): POB 71, 13001 Safat, Joint Banking Centre, East Tower, Darwazat Abd al-Razzak, Kuwait City; tel. 22459771; fax 22461430; e-mail hayakom@bkme.com.kw; internet www.ahliunited.com.kw; f. 1971; fmrly Bank of Kuwait and the Middle East KSC; current name adopted in April 2010 after acquiring Kuwait brs of British Bank of the Middle East; 75% owned by Ahli United Bank (Bahrain); cap. 118m., res 70m., dep. 2,296m. (Dec. 2012); Chair. and Man. Dir HAMAD ABD AL-MOHSEN AL-MARZOUQ; 26 brs.

BBK: POB 24396, 13104 Safat, Ahmad al-Jaber St, Kuwait City; tel. 22417140; fax 22440937; e-mail bbkp@batelco.com.bh; internet www.bbkonline.com; f. 1971 as Bank of Bahrain and Kuwait BSC; name changed as above in 2005; cap. 85m., res 154m., dep. BD 1,756.4m. (Dec. 2012); Chair. MURAD ALI MURAD; Chief Exec. ABD AL-KARIM AHMAD BUCHEERI.

Boubyan Bank KSC: POB 25507, 13116 Safat, Kuwait City; tel. 22325000; fax 22454263; e-mail info@bankboubyan.com; internet www.bankboubyan.com; f. 2004; cap. 183m., res 77m., dep. 1,896m. (Dec. 2012); Chair. MAHMOUD Y. AL-FULAIJ; CEO ADEL ABD AL-WAHAB AL-MAJID.

Burgan Bank SAK: POB 5389, 12170 Safat, Abd al-Haih al-Ahmad St, Kuwait City; tel. 22439000; fax 22461148; e-mail info@burgan.com; internet www.burgan.com; f. 1975; 33.9% owned by Kuwait Projects Co (Holding), Safat; cap. 162m., res 226m., dep. 6,089m. (Dec. 2013); Chair. MAJID EISA AL-AJEEL; CEO EDUARDO EGUREN LINSEN; 20 brs.

Commercial Bank of Kuwait SAK: POB 2861, 13029 Safat, Mubarak al-Kabir St, Kuwait City; tel. 22411001; fax 22464870; e-mail cbkinq@cbk.com; internet www.cbk.com; f. 1960 by Amiri decree; cap. 127m., res 309m., dep. 3,074m. (Dec. 2012); Chair. and Man. Dir ALI MOUSA M. AL-MOUSA; CEO ELHAM YOUSRY MAHFOUZ (acting); 51 brs.

Gulf Bank KSC: POB 3200, 13032 Safat, Mubarak al-Kabir St, Kuwait City; tel. 22449501; fax 22445212; e-mail customerservice@gulfbank.com.kw; internet www.e-gulfbank.com; f. 1960; cap. 276m., res 169m., dep. 4,393m. (Dec. 2013); Chair. OMAR KUTAYBA AL-GHANIM; CEO and Chief Gen. Man. MICHEL ACCAD; 52 brs.

Industrial Bank of Kuwait KSC (IBK): POB 3146, 13032 Safat, Joint Banking Centre, Darwazzat Abd al-Razaq, Commercial Area 9, Kuwait City; tel. 22337000; fax 22406595; e-mail ibk@ibkuwt.com; internet www.ibkuwt.com; 31.4% state-owned; f. 1973; cap. 20m., res 173m., dep. 147m. (Dec. 2012); Chair. and Man. Dir ABD AL-MOHSEN YOUSUF AL-HANIF; Gen. Man. ALI ABD AL-NABI KHAJA.

Kuwait Finance House KSC (KFH): POB 24989, 13110 Safat, Abdullah al-Mubarak St, Kuwait City; tel. 22445050; fax 22963962; e-mail kfh@kfh.com; internet www.kfh.com; f. 1977; 45% state-owned; Islamic banking and investment co; cap. 290m., res 950m., dep. 9,506m. (Dec. 2012); Chair. MUHAMMAD ALI AL-KHUDAIRI; Chief Exec. MUHAMMAD SULAYMAN AL-OMAR; 44 brs.

Kuwait International Bank (KIB): POB 22822, 13089 Safat, West Tower, Joint Banking Centre, Mubarak al-Kabir St, Kuwait City; tel. 22458177; fax 22462516; e-mail contact@kib.com.kw; internet www.kib.com.kw; f. 1973 as Kuwait Real Estate Bank KSC; name changed as above upon conversion into an Islamic bank in 2007; wholly owned by private Kuwaiti interests; cap. 103m., res 86m., dep. 787m. (Dec. 2012); Chair. MUHAMMAD JARRAH AL-SABAH; CEO LOAI MAQAMIS; 11 brs.

National Bank of Kuwait SAK (NBK): POB 95, 13001 Safat, Abdullah al-Ahmad St, Kuwait City; tel. 22422011; fax 22431888; e-mail webmaster@nbk.com; internet www.nbk.com; f. 1952; cap. 457m., res 1,117m., dep. 15,663m. (Dec. 2013); Chair. NASSER

MUSAED AL-SAYER; CEO IBRAHIM S. DABDOUB; 66 brs in Kuwait, 44 brs abroad.

INSURANCE

Al-Ahleia Insurance Co SAK: POB 1602, Ahmad al-Jaber St, 13017 Safat, Kuwait City; tel. 1888444; fax 22416495; e-mail aic@alahleia.com; internet www.alahleia.com; f. 1962; all forms of insurance; cap. 15.6m. (July 2007); Chair. and Man. Dir SULAYMAN HAMAD MUHAMMAD AL-DALALI.

Arab Commercial Enterprises WLL (Kuwait): POB 2474, 13025 Safat, Kuwait City; tel. 22413854; fax 22409450; e-mail acekwt@ace-ins.com; f. 1952; Man. SALIM ABOU HAIDAR.

First Takaful Insurance Co (FTIC): Abdullah al-Mubarak St, Alenma'a Tower, POB 5713, 13058 Safat, Kuwait City; tel. 21880055; fax 22444599; e-mail info@firsttakaful.com; internet www.firsttakaful.com; f. 2000; Islamic insurance; Chair. and Man. Dir KHALIL IBRAHIM MUHAMMAD AL-SHAMI; 5 brs.

Gulf Insurance Group KSCP: POB 1040, 13011 Safat, Ahmad al-Jaber St, Kuwait City; tel. 1802080; fax 22961998; e-mail contacts@gig.com.kw; internet www.gulfins.com.kw; f. 1962 as Gulf Insurance Co KSC; cap. 18.7m. (2013); all forms of insurance; Chair. FARKAD ABDULLAH AL-SANEA; Group CEO KHALED SAOUD AL-HASSAN.

Al-Ittihad al-Watani Insurance Co for the Near East SAL: 4th Floor, Bahman Bldg, Ahmad al-Jaber St, POB 781, 13008 Safat, Kuwait City; tel. 22420390; fax 22420366; e-mail webmaster@alittihadalwatani.com.lb; Man. JOSEPH ZACCOUR.

Kuwait Insurance Co SAK (KIC): POB 769, 13008 Safat, Abdullah al-Salem St, Kuwait City; tel. 1884433; fax 22428530; e-mail info@kic-kw.com; internet www.kic-kw.com; f. 1960; cap. US $64.6m.; all life and non-life insurance; Chair. MUHAMMAD SALEH BEHBEHANI; Gen. Man. Dr ALI HAMAD AL-BAHAR.

Kuwait Reinsurance Co KSCC: POB 21929, 13080 Safat, Kuwait City; tel. 22432011; fax 22427823; e-mail kuwaitre@kuwaitre.com; internet www.kuwaitre.com; f. 1972; cap. 10.0m., total assets 59.3m. (2006); Chair. FAHAD AL-IBRAHIM; CEO AMIR AL-MUHANNA.

Mohd Saleh Behbehani & Co: POB 341, 13004 Safat, Kuwait City; tel. 24721670; fax 24760070; e-mail msrybco@qualitynet.net; f. 1963; Pres. MUHAMMAD SALEH YOUSUF BEHBEHANI.

New India Assurance Co: 19th Floor, Behbehani Bldg, Jaber al-Mubarak St, Sharq, POB 370, 13004 Safat, Kuwait City; tel. 22404258; fax 22412089; e-mail newindia@qualitynet.net; f. 1919; Man. Dr G. VENKATAIAH.

The Oriental Insurance Co Ltd: Burj Jassim, 9th floor, Al Soor St, Kuwait City; tel. 22960500; fax 22960499; e-mail insurance@almullagroup.com; internet www.orientalinsurance.org.in; f. 1947; Man. ANIL KUMAR PARASHER.

Sumitomo Marine & Fire Insurance Co (Kuwait Agency): POB 3458, 13035 Safat, Kuwait City; tel. 22433087; fax 22430853; Contact ABDULLAH BOUDROS.

Warba Insurance Co SAK: POB 24282, 13103 Safat, Kuwait City; tel. 22445140; fax 22466131; e-mail warba@warbaonline.com; internet www.warbaonline.com; f. 1976; cap. 7.7m. (2002), total assets 80.1m. (Dec. 2005); all forms of insurance; Chair. ANWAR JAWAD KHAMSEEN; Man. Dir TAWFIK SHAMLAN AL-BAHAR; 3 brs.

Wethaq Takaful Insurance Co: Khaled bin al-Waleed St, City Tower, Kuwait City; tel. 21866662; fax 22491280; f. 2000; Islamic insurance; Chair. ABDULLAH YOUSUF AL-SAIF; Gen. Man. MAJID Y. AL-ALI.

STOCK EXCHANGE

Kuwait Stock Exchange (KSE): POB 22235, 13083 Safat, Mubarak al-Kabir St, Kuwait City; tel. 22992000; fax 22420779; e-mail webmaster@kuwaitse.com; internet www.kuwaitse.com; f. 1983; 226 cos and one mutual fund listed (Aug. 2009); Dir-Gen. SALEH MUBARAK AL-FALAH.

Markets Association

Kuwait Financial Markets Association (KFMA): 6th Floor, Deema Bldg, POB 25228, 13113 Safat, Block 3, St 64, Kuwait City; tel. 22498560; fax 22498561; e-mail kfma@kfma.org.kw; internet www.kfma.org.kw; f. 1977; represents treasury, financial and capital markets and their mems; Pres. AQEEL NASSER HABIB; Sec.-Gen. AHMAD AL-SUMAIT.

Trade and Industry

GOVERNMENT AGENCY

Kuwait Investment Authority (KIA): POB 64, 13001 Safat, Kuwait City; tel. 22485600; fax 22454059; e-mail information@kia.gov.kw; internet www.kia.gov.kw; oversees the Kuwait Investment

Office (London, United Kingdom); sovereign wealth fund; responsible for the Kuwaiti General Reserve; Chair. ANAS KHALID AL-SALIH (Minister of Finance); Man. Dir BADER MUHAMMAD AL-SAAD.

DEVELOPMENT ORGANIZATIONS

Arab Planning Institute (API): POB 5834, 13059 Safat, Kuwait City; tel. 24843130; fax 24842935; e-mail api@api.org.kw; internet www.arab-api.org; f. 1966; 15 Arab mem. states; publishes *Journal of Development and Economic Policies* (twice-yearly) and proceedings of seminars and discussion group meetings, offers research, training programmes and advisory services; Dir-Gen. BADER MALALLAH.

Industrial and Financial Investments Co (IFIC): POB 26019, 13121 Safat, Joint Banking Complex, 8th Floor, Industrial Bank Bldg, Derwaza Abd al-Razak, Kuwait City; tel. 22429073; fax 22448850; e-mail ific@ific.net; internet www.ific.net; f. 1983; privatized in 1996; invests directly in industry; Chair. and Man. Dir Dr TALEB AHMAD ALI.

Kuwait Fund for Arab Economic Development (KFAED): POB 2921, 13030 Safat, cnr Mubarak al-Kabir St and al-Hilali St, Kuwait City; tel. 22999000; fax 22999000; e-mail info@kuwait-fund.org; internet www.kuwait-fund.org; f. 1961; cap. KD 2,000m.; state-owned; provides and administers financial and technical assistance to developing countries; Chair. Sheikh SABAH AL-KHALID AL-HAMAD AL-SABAH (Deputy Prime Minister and Minister of Foreign Affairs); Dir-Gen. ABD AL-WAHAB A. AL-BADER.

Kuwait International Investment Co SAK (KIIC): POB 22792, 13088 Safat, al-Salhiya Commercial Complex, Kuwait City; tel. 22438273; fax 22454931; 30% state-owned; domestic real estate and share markets; Chair. and Man. Dir JASEM MUHAMMAD AL-BAHAR.

Kuwait Investment Co SAK (KIC): POB 1005, 13011 Safat, 5th Floor, al-Manakh Bldg, Mubarak al-Kabir St, Kuwait City; tel. 65888852; fax 22444896; e-mail info@kic.com.kw; internet www.kic.com.kw; f. 1981; 88% state-owned, 12% owned by private Kuwaiti interests; cap. KD 50.0m. (2002); international banking and investment; Chair. and Man. Dir BADER NASSER AL-SUBAIEE.

Kuwait Planning Board: POB 15, 13001 Safat, Kuwait City; tel. 22428200; fax 22414734; f. 1962; supervises long-term devt plans; through its Central Statistical Office publishes information on Kuwait's economic activity; Dir-Gen. AHMAD ALI AL-DUAIJ.

Mega Projects Agency (MPA): c/o Ministry of Public Works, POB 8, 13001 Safat, Kuwait City; tel. 25385520; fax 25385234; e-mail hmansour@mpa.gov.kw; f. 2005; supervises the progress of Failaka and Bubiyan island devts; Chair. BADER AL-HUMAIDI.

Public Authority for Industry (PAI): POB 4690, 13047 Safat, Kuwait City; POB 10033, Shuaiba; tel. 25302222; fax 25302190; internet www.pai.gov.kw; f. 1997; successor to Shuaiba Area Authority (f. 1964); develops, promotes and supervises industry in Kuwait; CEO Dr ABD AL-MOHSIN AL-MADAJ (Deputy Prime Minister and Minister of Commerce and Industry); Gen. Man. ALI FAHAD AL-MUDHAF.

CHAMBER OF COMMERCE

Kuwait Chamber of Commerce and Industry: POB 775, 13008 Safat, Commercial Area 9, al-Shuhadaa St, Kuwait City; tel. 1805580; fax 22404110; e-mail kcci@kcci.org.kw; internet www.kuwaitchamber.org.kw; f. 1959; 36,000 mems; Chair. ALI MUHAMMAD THUNAYAN AL-GHANIM; Dir-Gen. RABAH AL-RABAH.

STATE HYDROCARBONS COMPANIES

Supreme Petroleum Council (SPC): Kuwait City; f. 1974; highest energy decision-making body, responsible for national oil policy; Chair. Sheikh JABER MUBARAK AL-HAMAD AL-SABAH (Prime Minister).

Kuwait Petroleum Corpn (KPC): POB 26565, 13126 Safat, al-Salhiya Commercial Complex, Fahed al-Salem St, Kuwait City; tel. 22455455; fax 22467159; e-mail info@kpc.com.kw; internet www.kpc.com.kw; f. 1980; co-ordinating org. to manage the petroleum industry; Chair. ALI SALIH AL-OMAIR (Minister of Oil and Minister of State for National Assembly Affairs); CEO NIZAR AL-ADASANI; subsidiaries include:

Kuwait Aviation Fuelling Co KSC (KAFCO): POB 1654, 13017 Safat, Kuwait City; tel. 23828000; fax 23828505; e-mail airfuel@kafco.com; internet www.kafco.com; f. 1963; Gen. Man. AHMAD SULAYMAN AL-MUDHAF; 200 employees.

Kuwait Foreign Petroleum Exploration Co KSC (KUFPEC): POB 5291, 13053 Safat, Kuwait City; tel. 1836000; fax 24921818; internet www.kufpec.com; f. 1981; state-owned; overseas oil and gas exploration and devt; Chair. SANAD AL-SANAD; Man. Dir Sheikh NAWAF SAUD AL-SABAH; 169 employees.

Kuwait Gulf Oil Co KSC (KGOC): POB 9919, Ahmadi 61010; tel. 25454254; e-mail info@kgoc.com; internet www.kgoc.com; f. 2002 to take over Kuwait's interest in the Neutral (Partitioned) Zone's offshore operator, Khafji Joint Operations, and all of Kuwait's other offshore exploration and production activities;

Chair. MUHAMMAD SAYYID ABD AL-WAHAB; Man. Dir ALI AL-SHEMMERI.

Kuwait National Petroleum Co KSC (KNPC): POB 70, 13001 Safat, Ali al-Salem St, Kuwait City; tel. 23989900; fax 23986188; internet www.knpc.com.kw; f. 1960; oil refining, production of liquefied petroleum gas, and domestic marketing and distribution of petroleum by-products; Chair. ASSAD AL-SAAD; Man. Dir MUHAMMAD AL-MUTAIRI; 5,611 employees.

Kuwait Oil Co KSC (KOC): POB 9758, 61008 Ahmadi; tel. 23983661; fax 23984971; e-mail kocinfo@kockw.com; internet www.kockw.com; f. 1934; state-owned; Chair. NABIL BOURESLI; Man. Dir HASHIM HASHIM; 4,815 employees.

Kuwait Petroleum International (Q8): POB 1819, 13019 Safat, Kuwait City; tel. 22332800; fax 22332776; e-mail info-kuwait@q8.com; internet www.q8.com; marketing division of KPC; controls 4,000 petrol retail stations in Europe, and European refineries with capacity of 235,000 b/d; Man. Dir BAKHIT AL-RASHIDI.

UTILITIES

The Government planned to create regulatory bodies for each of Kuwait's utilities, with a view to facilitating their privatization.

Ministry of Electricity and Water: see Ministries; provides subsidized services throughout Kuwait.

TRADE UNIONS

Kuwait Trade Union Federation (KTUF): POB 5185, 13052 Safat, Kuwait City; tel. 25636389; fax 25627159; e-mail ktuf@hotmail.com; internet www.ktuf.org; f. 1967; central authority to which all trade unions are affiliated; Pres. FAIEZ ALI AL-MUTAIRI; Gen. Sec. BADR SALIM AL-SAWAGH.

Transport

RAILWAYS

There are currently no railways in Kuwait. However, plans for a 518-km national rail network, which would be linked to a regional rail network, connecting Kuwait with member countries of the Cooperation Council for the Arab States of the Gulf (or Gulf Cooperation Council—GCC), were announced in 2008. A four-line, 171-km metro system in Kuwait City was at the planning stage in 2014. The project, the total cost of which was estimated at US $7,000m., was scheduled to commence operations by 2020.

ROADS

In 2012 the total road network was estimated at 7,180 km. Roads in the towns are metalled, and the most important are motorways or dual carriageways. There are metalled roads linking Kuwait City to Ahmadi, Mina al-Ahmadi and other centres of population in Kuwait, and to the Iraqi and Saudi Arabian borders. In late 2012 a US $3,700m. design-and-build contract for a causeway linking Kuwait City with Madinat al-Hareer (Silk City—a new development under construction in Subiya) was awarded to Hyundai Engineering and Construction Co of the Republic of Korea (South Korea).

Kuwait Public Transport Co SAK (KPTC): POB 375, 13004 Safat, Murghab, Safat Sq., Kuwait City; tel. 22328501; fax 22328870; e-mail info@kptc.com.kw; internet www.kptc.com.kw; f. 1962; state-owned; provides internal bus service; regular service to Mecca, Saudi Arabia; Chair. and Man. Dir EISSA ABDULLAH AL-HUBAIL.

SHIPPING

Kuwait has three commercial seaports. The largest, Shuwaikh, situated about 3 km from Kuwait City, comprises 21 deep-water berths, with a total length of 4 km, three shallow-water berths and three basins for small craft, each with a depth of 3.35 m. Shuaiba Commercial Port, 56 km south of Kuwait City, comprises 20 berths with a total length of 4 km. Since 2003 this has been used by the US Army as a base for supplying its troops in Iraq. Expansion plans were announced in 2009. Doha, the smallest port, has 20 small berths, each 100 m long. An oil port at Mina al-Ahmadi, 40 km south of Kuwait City, comprises 12 tanker berths, one bitumen-carrier berth, two LPG export berths and bunkering facilities, and is able to load more than 2m. barrels of oil per day.

Plans for the privatization of Kuwait's ports were under development in the late 2000s. In 2010 a contract for the construction of a new US $1,200m. international port at Bubiyan island was awarded to Hyundai Engineering and Construction Co. The Mubarak al-Kabir port was expected to commence operations in 2016.

At 31 December 2014 Kuwait's flag registered fleet numbered 168 vessels, with a total displacement of 3.1m. grt, of which one was a fish carrier, four were gas tankers and two were general cargo ships.

Port Authority

Kuwait Ports Authority: POB 3874, 13039 Safat, Kuwait City; tel. 24812622; fax 24819714; e-mail info@kpa.gov.kw; internet www.kpa.gov.kw; f. 1977; Dir-Gen. Dr SABER JABER AL-ALI AL-SABAH.

Principal Shipping Companies

Arab Maritime Petroleum Transport Co (AMPTC): POB 22525, 13086 Safat, Kuwait City; tel. 24959400; fax 24842996; e-mail amptc.kuwait@amptc.net; internet www.amptc.net; f. 1973; six crude petroleum tankers, four LPG carriers and one product carrier; owned by Algeria, Bahrain, Egypt, Iraq, Kuwait, Libya, Qatar, Saudi Arabia and the UAE; Gen. Man. SULAYMAN I. AL-BASSAM.

Heavy Engineering Industries and Shipbuilding Co (Heisco): POB 21998, 13080 Safat, Kuwait City; tel. 24835488; fax 24830291; e-mail heisco@heisco.com; internet www.heisco.com; f. 1974 as Kuwait Shipbuilding and Repairyard Co; name changed as above in 2003; ship repairs and engineering services, underwater services, maintenance of refineries, power stations and storage tanks; maintains floating dock for vessels up to 35,000 dwt; synchrolift for vessels up to 5,000 dwt with transfer yard; seven repair jetties up to 550 m in length and floating workshop for vessels lying at anchor; Chair. JUHAIL MUHAMMAD AL-JUHAIL.

KGL Ports Int. Co (KGL PI): POB 42438, Shuwaikh 70655; tel. 22245155; fax 22245166; e-mail info@kglpi.com; internet www.kglpi.com; f. 2004; subsidiary of Kuwait and Gulf Link Transport Co; port management and stevedoring; operates Shuaiba Commercial Port Container Terminal; also operations and management contracts with ports in United Arab Emirates and Saudi Arabia; Chair. and Man. Dir FADHEL AL-BAGHLI.

Kuwait Maritime Transport Co KSC (KMTC): POB 22595, 13086 Safat, Nafisi and Khatrash Bldg, Jaber al-Mubarak St, Kuwait City; tel. 22449974; fax 22420513; f. 1981; Chair. YOUSUF AL-MAJID.

Kuwait Oil Tanker Co SAK (KOTC): POB 810, 13009 Safat, Shuwaikh Administrative Sector (P), Camal Abdel Nasser St, Kuwait City; tel. 24625050; fax 24913597; e-mail nakilat@kotc.com.kw; internet www.kotc.com.kw; f. 1957; state-owned; operates eight crude oil tankers, 11 product tankers and five LPG vessels; sole tanker agents for Mina al-Ahmadi, Shuaiba and Mina al-Abdullah and agents for other ports; LPG filling and distribution; Chair. and Man. Dir HASHIM SAYED HASHIM.

United Arab Shipping Co SAG (UASC): POB 20722, 13068 Safat, UASC Bldg, Old Airport Rd, Beside Zain Bldg, Kuwait City; tel. 24943300; fax 24943088; e-mail gencom.uasackwt@uasc.net; internet www.uasc.net; f. 1976; nat shipping co of six Arabian Gulf countries; services between Europe, Far East, Mediterranean ports, Japan and east coast of USA and South America, and ports of participant states on Persian (Arabian) Gulf and Red Sea; operates 42 vessels; subsidiary cos include: United Arab Shipping Agencies Co (Kuwait), Arab Transport Co (Aratrans), United Arab Chartering Ltd (United Kingdom), Middle East Container Repair Co (UAE), Arabian Chemicals Carriers (Saudi Arabia), United Arab Agencies Inc (USA) and United Arab Shipping Agencies Co (Saudi Arabia); Chair. SALEM ALI AL-ZAABI; Pres. and CEO JØRN HINGE.

CIVIL AVIATION

Kuwait International Airport opened in 1980, and by 2011 handled 8.5m. passengers, compared with 3.8m. in 2001. The airport is undergoing a major programme of expansion: the first phase of the project was to expand the airport's annual capacity to 20m. passengers and to modernize facilities, with a further final phase of development intended to achieve passenger capacity of 55m.

Directorate-General of Civil Aviation (DGCA): POB 17, 13001 Safat, Kuwait City; tel. 24744256; fax 24744396; e-mail president@dgca.gov.kw; internet www.dgca.gov.kw; Pres. FAWAZ AL-FARAH; Dir-Gen. Eng. YOUSIF AL-FOUZAN.

Jazeera Airways: POB 29288, 13153 Safat, Kuwait City; e-mail helpdesk@jazeeraairways.com; internet www.jazeeraairways.com; f. 2005; low-cost airline owned by Boodai Group; serves 26 destinations in the Middle East, North Africa, Europe and Asia; Chair. MARWAN BOODAI.

Kuwait Airways Corpn (KAC): POB 394, Kuwait International Airport, 13004 Safat, Kuwait City; tel. 22434560; fax 22441304, e-mail web@kuwaitairways.com; internet www.kuwaitairways.com; f. 1954; scheduled and charter passenger and cargo services to the Arabian peninsula, Asia, Africa, the USA and Europe; scheduled for privatization; Chair. and Man. Dir RASHA A. AL-ROUMI.

Tourism

Attractions for visitors include the Kuwait Towers leisure and reservoir complex, the Entertainment City theme park, the Kuwait Zoological Garden in Omariya and the Khiran Resort tourist village near the border with Saudi Arabia, as well as extensive facilities for sailing and other water sports. In 2013 foreign tourist arrivals totalled some 6.2m. According to provisional data, tourism receipts (excluding passenger transport) of US $298m. were recorded in 2013.

Department of Tourism: Ministry of Information, Tourism Affairs, POB 193, 13002 Safat, al-Sour St, Kuwait City; tel. 22457591; fax 22401540.

Kuwait Tourism Services Co: POB 21774, 13078 Safat, Kuwait City; tel. 2451734; fax 2451731; e-mail kts@kts-kuwait-tourism.com; internet www.kts-kuwait-tourism.com; f. 1997; Chair. KHALID AL-DUWAISAN.

Touristic Enterprises Co (TEC): POB 23310, 13094 Safat, Kuwait City; tel. 24965555; fax 24965055; e-mail info@tec.com.kw; internet www.kuwaittourism.com; f. 1976; 92% state-owned; manages 23 tourist facilities; Chair. BADER AL-BAHAR; Vice-Chair. SHAKER AL-OTHMAN.

Defence

Supreme Commander of the Armed Forces: HH Sheikh SABAH AL-AHMAD AL-JABER AL-SABAH.

Chief of Staff of Armed Forces: Lt-Gen. MUHAMMAD KHALID AL-KHODER.

Commander of the Air Force: Maj.-Gen. KHAMIS SULTAN AL-FARHAN.

Commander of the Navy: Rear Adm. JASSIM MUHAMMAD AL-ANSARI.

Defence Budget (2014): KD 1,370m.

Military Service: voluntary.

Total Armed Forces (as assessed at November 2014): 15,500: army 11,000; navy est. 2,000 (including 500 coast guards); air force 2,500. Reserves 23,700.

Paramilitary Forces (as assessed at November 2014): est. 7,100 (national guard est. 6,600; coast guard 500).

Education

Compulsory education for children between six and 14 years of age was introduced in 1966–67. However, many children spend two years prior to this in a kindergarten, and go on to complete their general education at the age of 18 years. It is government policy to provide free education to all Kuwaiti children from kindergarten stage to university. In 2012/13 a total of 358,475 pupils attended 797 government schools (198 kindergarten, 258 primary, 204 intermediate and 137 secondary). In 2011/12 a total of 235,739 pupils attended 488 private schools (107 kindergarten, 132 primary, 137 intermediate and 112 secondary).

Primary education lasts for five years between the ages of six and 10, after which the pupils move on to an intermediate school for another four years. Secondary education, which is optional and lasts between the ages of 14 and 18, is given mainly in general schools. There are also commercial institutes, a Faculty of Technological Studies, a health institute, religious institutes (with intermediate and secondary stages) and 11 institutes for handicapped children. In 2008/09 enrolment at primary schools was equivalent to 95% of children in the relevant age-group, while at secondary schools the rate was equivalent to 90% of children in the relevant age-group.

Scholarships are granted to students to pursue courses not offered by Kuwait University. Such scholarships are mainly used to study in Egypt, Lebanon, the United Kingdom and the USA. There are also pupils from Arab, African and Asian states studying in Kuwait schools on scholarships provided by the Kuwaiti Government. Kuwait University had about 20,000 students in 2006, and also provides scholarships for a number of Arab, Asian and African students. In May 1996 the National Assembly approved a draft law to regulate students' behaviour, dress and activities, with regard to observance of the teachings of *Shari'a* (Islamic) law, and to eradicate co-educational classes at Kuwait University over a five-year period. A KD 1,000m. project to build a new university campus and to gather the institution's dispersed facilities onto one site was expected to be completed by 2025. In 2008/09 an estimated 61,920 students were enrolled in tertiary education. Expenditure on education by the central Government in 2010/11 totalled KD 1,441m. (12.0% of total expenditure).

KYRGYZSTAN

Introductory Survey

LOCATION, CLIMATE, LANGUAGE, RELIGION, FLAG, CAPITAL

The Kyrgyz Republic is a small, landlocked state situated in eastern Central Asia. It borders Kazakhstan to the north, Uzbekistan to the west, Tajikistan to the south and west, and the People's Republic of China to the east. There are distinct variations in climate between low-lying and high-altitude areas. In the valleys the mean July temperature is 28°C (82°F), falling to an average of −18°C (−0.5°F) in January. Annual rainfall ranges from 180 mm (7 ins) in the eastern Tien Shan mountains to 750 mm–1,000 mm (30 ins–39 ins) in the Farg'ona (Fergana) mountain range. In the settled valleys the annual average varies between 100 mm and 500 mm (4 ins–20 ins). The state language is Kyrgyz; in addition, Russian has the status of an official language. The main religion is Islam, with the majority of ethnic Kyrgyz being Sunni Muslims of the Hanafi school. The national flag (proportions 3 by 5) consists of a red field, at the centre of which is a yellow sun, with 40 counter-clockwise rays surrounding a red-bordered yellow disc, on which are superimposed two intersecting sets of three red, curved, narrow bands. The capital is Bishkek.

CONTEMPORARY POLITICAL HISTORY

Historical Context

Following the October Revolution of 1917 in Russia, Kyrgyzstan (which had been formally incorporated into the Russian Empire in 1876) experienced civil war, with the Russian White Army and local armed groups (*basmachi*), fighting against the Bolshevik Red Army. In 1918 the Turkestan Autonomous Soviet Socialist Republic (ASSR) was established within the Russian Soviet Federative Socialist Republic, and Soviet power was established in the region by 1919. In 1924 the Kara-Kyrgyz Autonomous Oblast (Region) was created. In 1925 the region was renamed the Kyrgyz Autonomous Oblast, and became the Kyrgyz ASSR in 1926.

Land reforms undertaken in the 1920s resulted in the settlement of many of the nomadic Kyrgyz. An agricultural collectivization programme implemented in the early 1930s was strongly opposed, and many 'national communists' were expelled from the Kyrgyzstan Kommunisttik Partiyasy (KKP—Kyrgyz Communist Party) and imprisoned or exiled. In 1936 the Kyrgyz Soviet Socialist Republic (SSR) was established as a full union republic of the USSR.

The introduction of the policies of perestroika (restructuring) and glasnost (openness) under the Soviet leader Mikhail Gorbachev from 1985, led to the resignation of Turdakan Usubaliyev as First Secretary of the KKP. The republic's Supreme Soviet (Jogorku Kenesh or Supreme Council—legislature) adopted Kyrgyz as the official language, retaining Russian as a 'language of inter-ethnic communication'. A notable group influential at this time was Osh Aymaghi, based in the southern Osh Oblast (region), which attempted to obtain land and housing provision for Kyrgyz in the Uzbek-dominated region, where demands for the establishment of an Uzbek autonomous region were also being voiced. In 1990 land disputes developed into violent inter-ethnic confrontations, in which more than 300 people died. A state of emergency and a curfew were introduced, the former remaining in force until 1995.

At elections to the Kyrgyzstani Supreme Soviet held in February 1990 KKP candidates won most seats unopposed, and in April Absamat Masaliyev, the party's First Secretary, was elected Chairman of the Supreme Soviet. In October an extraordinary session of the Supreme Soviet was convened to elect the President. The growth in support for the opposition Kyrgyzstan Demokratiyalyk Kyimyly (Democratic Movement of Kyrgyzstan), combined with the discrediting of Masaliyev as a consequence of the conflict in Osh, meant that Masaliyev failed to be elected in the first round of voting. In a further round of voting a compromise candidate, Askar Akayev, the President of the Kyrgyz Academy of Sciences, was elected President. In December Masaliyev resigned as Chairman of the Supreme Soviet, and was replaced by Medetkan Sherimkulov. In January 1991

Akayev replaced the Council of Ministers with a smaller, largely reformist, cabinet. In February the capital, Frunze, reverted to its pre-1926 name of Bishkek. In a referendum held in nine Soviet Union Republics in March, 87.7% of eligible voters in Kyrgyzstan approved the proposal to retain the USSR as a 'renewed federation'.

Domestic Political Affairs

In August 1991, when conservative communist putschists announced that they had assumed power in the Russian and Soviet capital, Moscow, there was an attempt to depose Akayev in Kyrgyzstan. Akayev dismissed the Chairman of the republican Committee of State Security (KGB) and ordered interior ministry troops to guard strategic buildings in Bishkek. Akayev publicly denounced the coup and issued a decree prohibiting activity by any political party in government or state bodies. After the coup had collapsed in Moscow, on 31 August the Kyrgyzstani Supreme Soviet voted to declare independence from the USSR. Akayev (the sole candidate) was re-elected republican President by direct popular vote on 12 October, receiving 95% of the votes cast. In October Akayev signed, with representatives of seven other republics, a treaty to establish a new economic community. On 21 December Kyrgyzstan was among the 11 signatories to the Almatı Declaration, which formally established the Commonwealth of Independent States (CIS, see p. 241)

After independence

A new Constitution, promulgated on 5 May 1993, provided for a parliamentary system of government. Legislative power was to be vested in a 105-member Supreme Council. The country's official name was changed from the Republic of Kyrgyzstan to the less ethnically neutral Kyrgyz Republic. In July Akayev's attempts to encourage non-Kyrgyz to remain in the republic suffered a serious reverse when German Kuznetsov, the First Deputy Prime Minister, announced his decision to return to his native Russia. By mid-1993 some 145,000 Russians were estimated to have left the republic since 1989. Akayev's presidency was destabilized during 1993 by a series of corruption scandals. Two commissions of inquiry were established to investigate the business dealings of Vice-President Feliks Kulov and to examine allegations that senior politicians, including Prime Minister Tursunbek Chyngyshev, had been involved in unauthorized gold exports. In December Kulov resigned. Although a legislative vote of confidence in the Government failed to secure the required two-thirds' majority, Akayev none the less dismissed the entire cabinet. A new Government, headed by Apas Jumagulov, was approved later in the month. A referendum of confidence in President Akayev, held in January 1994, overwhelmingly endorsed his leadership. In June, in an attempt to curb the rate of emigration, Akayev issued a decree promoting the use of Russian and simplifying the procedure of application for dual citizenship.

In September 1994 more than 180 deputies demanded the dissolution of the legislature and the holding of fresh elections, in protest at the continuing obstruction of economic reforms. The Government resigned, and Akayev called new parliamentary elections, re-instating the Government. A constitutional referendum, held in October, endorsed the formation of a bicameral Supreme Council, comprising a 70-member El Okuldor Palatasy (People's Assembly) to represent regional interests at twice-yearly sessions and a permanent 35-member Myizam Chygaru Palatasy (Legislative Assembly). Elections to the two legislative chambers were held in February 1995. The two chambers of the Supreme Council held their inaugural sessions on 28 March. A new Government, again led by Jumagulov, was appointed in April. In September the Legislative Assembly vetoed a proposal to hold a referendum on extending the President's term of office until 2000. On 24 December 1995 Akayev received 71.6% of the votes cast in a direct presidential election; Masaliyev (who had recently been reinstated as the leader of the revived KKP, now called the Kyrgyzstan Kommunistterinin Partiyasy—Party of Communists of Kyrgyzstan) won 24.4% of the votes. Some 82% of the electorate participated. Akayev was inaugurated on

30 December. Following a decree issued by Akayev, a referendum was held on 10 February 1996, at which the majority of the electorate endorsed amendments to the Constitution increasing presidential powers and decreasing those of the legislature.

In March 1998, after Jumagulov announced his retirement, the Supreme Council endorsed Kuvachbek Jumaliyev as Prime Minister. A referendum held on 17 October overwhelmingly approved constitutional amendments, including an increase in the number of deputies in the Legislative Assembly to 60, a concomitant reduction in the membership of the People's Assembly to 45, the introduction of restrictions on parliamentary immunity, the legalization of private land ownership, and the prohibition of the adoption of any legislation restricting freedom of speech or of the press. The Supreme Council and the majority of political parties declared their opposition to the constitutional changes and, in particular, to the introduction of private land ownership. In December the President dissolved the Government. Jumabek Ibraimov was appointed Prime Minister and a new, substantially unchanged, Government was formed. Akayev strengthened the Prime Minister's mandate, empowering him to appoint and dismiss ministers and heads of departments (hitherto the prerogative of the President). Ibraimov died in April 1999, and Amangeldy Muraliyev was appointed as his successor.

A new electoral law was introduced in May 1999. Henceforth, 15 seats in the Legislative Assembly were to be allocated on a proportional basis for those parties that secured a minimum of 5% of the votes. In June legislation came into effect banning political organizations deemed a threat to Kyrgyzstan's stability and ethnic harmony. In July two new opposition parties were established, including the Ar-Namys Partiyasy (Ar-Namys—Dignity Political Party), led by Kulov (by this time Mayor of Bishkek).

Two rounds of elections were held to both chambers of the Supreme Council on 20 February and 12 March 2000. In the first round, six parties surpassed the 5% threshold required to secure party-list seats in the Legislative Assembly. The Organization for Security and Co-operation in Europe (OSCE, see p. 385) recorded a number of electoral violations. Overall, nominally independent candidates took 73 of the 105 seats in the two chambers, while the Union of Democratic Forces bloc (a three-party alliance led by the Kyrgyzstandyn Sotsial-Demokratiyalyk Partiyasy—KSDP—Social Democratic Party of Kyrgyzstan) achieved the greatest representation of any group, securing a total of 12 seats, compared with the KKP's six. Ar-Namys was prohibited from participating in the elections, and Kulov, contesting the poll as an independent, failed to win a seat.

At the presidential election held on 29 October 2000 Akayev was re-elected, securing 74.5% of the votes cast. His closest rival was Omurbek Tekebayev, the leader of the Ata Meken Partiyasy (Ata Meken—Fatherland Socialist Political Party), with 13.9%, while Almazbek Atambayev, the leader of the KSDP, obtained 6.0% of the ballot. According to official figures, 74% of the electorate participated. Although the Chairman of the Central Commission for Elections and Referendums conceded that electoral violations had occurred, the Constitutional Court formally endorsed the results.

Akayev was inaugurated for a third term on 9 December 2000 and on 21 December Kurmanbek Bakiyev, hitherto the Governor of Chui Oblast, was appointed Prime Minister; a new Government was announced in January 2001. In the same month Kulov was sentenced to seven years' imprisonment, having been found guilty of abuse of office as Minister of National Security in 1997–98. Kulov's appeal was rejected in March, and in May 2002 he was found guilty, additionally, of embezzlement. Meanwhile, in November 2001 opposition parties including Ar-Namys and Ata Meken announced the formation of a new People's Congress, and elected the imprisoned Kulov its Chairman. In December Akayev signed into law a constitutional amendment granting Russian the status of official language, alongside Kyrgyz.

In January 2002 the arrest of Azimbek Beknazarov, an opposition deputy, was denounced as politically motivated. In March security forces shot dead six demonstrators in the village of Aksy, in the southern Jalal-Abad region, where Beknazarov's trial was being held; the trial was subsequently suspended. In May the Legislative Assembly ratified a controversial Sino-Kyrgyzstani border treaty (which transferred territory from Kyrgyzstan to the People's Republic of China) signed in 1999, prompting two weeks of anti-Government demonstrations, hunger strikes and civil disobedience. Protesters demanded that the Government accept responsibility for the violence of March 2002, rescind the ratification of the border treaty, and close the criminal case against Beknazarov. The People's Assembly ratified the treaty later in May, and it was signed into law by the President. As controversy continued about his alleged responsibility for ordering the killings by the security forces, in May Prime Minister Bakiyev tendered his resignation. The First Deputy Prime Minister, Nikolai Tanayev, was appointed Prime Minister, and a new Government was formed. In the same month Beknazarov received a one-year suspended prison sentence. Following an appeal and further large-scale demonstrations, his sentence was annulled (although the initial guilty verdict was upheld), enabling him to retain his parliamentary seat. In June the Legislative Assembly approved an amnesty, proposed by Tanayev for both protesters and law enforcement officials involved in the disturbances of March.

A referendum on several constitutional amendments was held on 2 February 2003. The amendments, which provided for the introduction of a unicameral legislature, in which all deputies were to be elected in single-member constituencies, were approved by 76.6% of the electorate, while 78.7% of voters supported Akayev's remaining in office until 2005; the reported rate of participation was 86.7%.

A major government reorganization took place in February 2004. In April the President introduced a new law designating Kyrgyz the state language, and stipulating measures for its promotion, although Russian was to remain an official language. Meanwhile, in advance of legislative elections, an opposition electoral bloc led by Bakiyev was formed in September.

'The tulip revolution'

During February 2005 several demonstrations demanding free and fair parliamentary elections, or the impeachment of Akayev, occurred. Notably, in January, the leader of the recently formed Ata-Jurt Partiyasy (Ata-Jurt—Homeland Idealistic Democratic Party), Roza Otunbayeva, had been denied permission to register as a candidate, on the grounds that, as a former ambassador, she had not been resident in Kyrgyzstan for the previous five years. In the first round of voting on 27 February, at which 31 candidates (each of whom had received an absolute majority of votes cast in their respective electoral districts) were elected to the restructured, unicameral, 75-member Supreme Council, the rate of participation by the electorate was reported as 60%. Most of those elected were nominally independent candidates. The Alga, Kyrgyzstan (Forward, Kyrgyzstan) party, founded in 2003 and regarded as generally sympathetic to Akayev's administration, became the largest party faction to achieve representation, with 10 deputies. OSCE monitors concluded that the elections had not fully complied with democratic standards, while opposition and independent observers asserted that large-scale electoral fraud had taken place. Protests to dispute polling results took place in various regions before the second round of elections, held on 13 March, while media outlets critical of the authorities were suppressed. Following the second round of voting, a further 37 candidates were elected (with a participation rate of 55%); only six opposition candidates obtained representation in the new legislature. Dissatisfaction at the conduct of the elections resulted in large-scale protests in a number of cities, particularly in the south. The Central Commission for Elections and Referendums declared that the results of voting for 69 of the 75 seats were valid; investigations into the conduct of voting in the remaining six districts were to continue. The Supreme Court, however revoked the mandate of the newly elected Supreme Council, asserting that the previous bicameral legislature continued to hold authority. Akayev dismissed the Minister of Internal Affairs, Bakirdin Subanbekov, who had declared that he would not use force to end the protests, and the Prosecutor-General.

By 24 March 2005 demonstrations had spread to Bishkek, where protesters stormed the presidential palace and government buildings. Akayev fled the country, while maintaining that he remained Head of State, and Tanayev resigned as Prime Minister. Protesters freed Kulov from gaol. On the same day, at an emergency session, the lower chamber of the legislature elected in 2000 named Bakiyev acting Prime Minister (he automatically became acting President in Akayev's absence) and Kulov was given responsibility for overseeing the country's law enforcement agencies and armed forces. After the election commission announced that the powers of the bicameral legislature elected in 2000 were terminated, the lower and upper chambers dissolved themselves on 28 and 29 March, respectively, thereby effectively confirming the legitimacy of the recently elected legislature. Meanwhile, on 28 March the new Supreme Council voted to confirm Bakiyev as interim Prime Minister, and to elect

Tekebayev as legislative Chairman. (In late April Tekebayev was also appointed as Chairman of the Constitutional Court.) On 30 March Kulov resigned, reportedly owing to disagreement with Bakiyev.

On 4 April 2005 Akayev, speaking at the Kyrgyzstani embassy in Moscow, announced his resignation as President (the Supreme Council approved this decision on 11 April). On 8 April the Supreme Council voted to remove immunity from prosecution from members of Akayev's family; it subsequently scheduled a presidential election for 10 July. From mid-April protests were staged outside the Supreme Court against the conduct of the legislative elections, demanding the resignation of the Court's Chairman. Although the Chairman submitted his resignation later in the month, Bakiyev rejected it. Meanwhile, the Court overturned Kulov's convictions. In May Bakiyev reached an agreement with Kulov, the latter agreeing to withdraw his candidacy in the presidential election (in which he had been regarded as Bakiyev's principal rival) in return for a guarantee that he would be appointed Prime Minister in the event that Bakiyev was elected President.

On 10 July 2005 Bakiyev won 88.7% of the votes cast in the presidential election, defeating five other candidates. The OSCE reported some irregularities in vote-counting. Bakiyev was inaugurated as President on 14 August, and on 1 September the Supreme Council confirmed Kulov's appointment as Prime Minister. In late September the Supreme Council approved 10 of the 16 ministers proposed by Bakiyev. Many ministers in the outgoing interim administration retained their portfolios. In October the Office of the Prosecutor-General charged Tanayev, who was under house arrest in Bishkek, with abuse of power as Prime Minister. (The case against him was closed in 2006.) The Supreme Council rejected Bakiyev's nomination of Daniyar Usenov, an opponent of Kulov, as First Deputy Prime Minister, instead approving the appointment, in November 2005, of Medetbek Kerimkulov, whose Government was sworn in on 20 December. Meanwhile, in October a parliamentary deputy, Tynychbek Akmatbayev, was killed by inmates during an official visit to a gaol; two other deputies had been murdered since July. Large rallies, led by Akmatbayev's brother, Ryspek, a prominent and controversial figure alleged to be involved in organized crime, subsequently took place to demand the dismissal of Kulov, whom the protesters accused of having collaborated to organize the killing of Akmatbayev.

In January 2006 Bakiyev (who had pledged to increase the powers of the legislature) decreed that measures be taken to organize a referendum on the division of powers between the President and parliament. Later in the month Kulov demanded reform of the judicial and law enforcement systems, and accused the Chairman of the National Security Service of having allowed criminal elements to infiltrate the organization. In February Bakiyev removed the deputy head of the National Security Service, and accepted the resignation of the Deputy Secretary of the Security Council. In the same month Bakiyev accused the legislature of fomenting political instability and exceeding its mandate, in response to which Tekebayev resigned as parliamentary chairman.

Parliamentary by-elections, scheduled to take place in three districts in April 2006, generated considerable controversy owing to the candidacy of Rysbek Akmatbayev. Akmatbayev, who had previously been twice convicted for assault and robbery and who was regarded as the most prominent organized criminal in the country, had recently been tried and acquitted for the murder of a police officer; however, his acquittal was in the process of being appealed, thus rendering his candidacy constitutionally illegitimate. In protest, thousands of demonstrators amassed in Bishkek, urging the Government to adopt a tougher stance against organized crime. The by-elections proceeded as planned on 9 April 2006, and Akmatbayev secured a comfortable victory in his constituency. In May, however, Akmatbayev was shot dead. Meanwhile, in late April the Supreme Council voted to evaluate the performance of individual members of the Government: only Kulov, two ministers and the head of a state committee were given positive appraisals, and 14 ministers resigned in early May. Although President Bakiyev rejected their resignations and the ministers subsequently agreed to remain in their posts, Bakiyev effected a cabinet reorganization in mid-May, which included the appointment of Usenov as First Deputy Prime Minister.

Constitutional disputes

In November 2006 mass protests gathered to demand constitutional reform and Bakiyev's resignation. On 8 November the Supreme Council approved a new Constitution, which diminished the powers of the President and augmented those of the legislature, the capacity of which was to be enlarged to 90 members; the membership of governments was henceforth to be determined by the Supreme Council, rather than the President. Bakiyev signed the new Constitution into effect on 9 November. In mid-December Kulov tendered his resignation (together with that of his Government), with the stated aim of forcing early parliamentary elections. In late December the legislature voted to adopt a number of amendments to the new Constitution, including the retraction of the legislature's power to appoint the Government, which was henceforth to be appointed by the President at the suggestion of the Prime Minister, without the need for legislative approval. These amendments were signed into law on 17 January 2007.

In late January 2007 the Supreme Council formally approved Bakiyev's nomination of Azim Isabekov as Prime Minister, having twice rejected the nomination of Kulov. In February Isabekov formed a new Government, in which the majority of key posts were allocated to close associates of President Bakiyev, including Usenov, who was re-appointed First Deputy Prime Minister. In the same month Kulov added his voice to opposition demands for the President's resignation. On 29 March Isabekov resigned as premier, after Bakiyev reversed his decision to dismiss five government ministers. One day later the Supreme Council approved the appointment of Atambayev as Prime Minister; Usenov was dismissed in an ensuing governmental reorganization. In April security forces dispersed demonstrations in Bishkek organized by a recently established opposition grouping led by Kulov, the United Front For A Worthy Future For Kyrgyzstan; some 100 demonstrators were arrested and two prominent opposition leaders were detained on charges of inciting unrest.

In September 2007 the Constitutional Court ruled that the adoption of the two Constitutions of November 2006 and January 2007 had been illegal, since the drafts had not been submitted to a national referendum; consequently the Constitution in place prior to November 2006 again entered into force. Bakiyev subsequently announced that a further new constitutional text was to be proposed. In October Bakiyev established a political party, the Ak Jol Partiyasy (Ak Jol—Bright Road Party). The Constitution proposed at the national referendum on 21 October was endorsed by 76.1% of the electorate (with a voter turnout of 81.6%); henceforth, the number of parliamentary deputies was to increase from 75 to 90, all of whom were to be elected from party lists. One day later Bakiyev dissolved the Supreme Council; early legislative elections were scheduled for 16 December. The Government submitted its resignation on 24 October.

On 29 November 2007 Bakiyev dismissed Atambayev as premier; on the same day he appointed Iskenderbek Aidaraliyev First Deputy Prime Minister and also assigned him the role of acting Prime Minister. At the elections, held on 16 December, Ak Jol won 47.0% of votes cast, securing 71 legislative seats, ahead of the KSDP, with 5.1% of the votes cast and 11 seats, and the KPP, with 5.1% of the votes cast and eight seats. Ata Meken, despite gaining 8.3% of votes overall, narrowly failed to qualify for representation, owing to a new electoral requirement that each party obtain at least 0.5% of the votes cast in each of the country's seven oblasts and two largest cities. This stipulation was particularly criticized by OSCE observers, who stated that the conduct of the elections failed to meet democratic standards. On 24 December Igor Chudinov was appointed Prime Minister, while Adahan Madumarov (of Ak Jol) was elected legislative Chairman. A new Government, which retained the principal ministers of the former administration, was approved in the Supreme Council on 27 December.

On 29 May 2008 Madumarov resigned as legislative Chairman, after he was found to have contravened regulations concerning expenditure relating to the redecoration of the parliamentary chamber; he was replaced by a close ally of President Bakiyev, Aitibai Tagayev. In September Bakiyev dismissed the Minister of Justice, Marat Kaiyypov, and the head of the penal service, following an investigation into a prison riot, in which two officers had been killed. Later that month, the Chairman of the electoral commission, Klara Kabilova, fled the country, subsequently accusing Maksim Bakiyev, the son of the President and a prominent businessman, of issuing threats against her. In local elections, held on 5 October, observers from local non-governmental organizations (NGOs) alleged that numerous irregularities had enabled pro-Government candidates to win most seats in municipal councils. In November the Government imposed restrictions on the operation of religious organizations, stating that the legislation had been introduced in response to a growth in support for extremist Islamist groups, particularly in the south of the country. In late December an alliance of the major opposition parties, the United People's Movement, was established to demand the resignation of Bakiyev and to oppose the proposed privatization of various important facilities. Aidaraliyev was replaced as First Deputy Prime Minister by Omurbek Babanov.

In February 2009 Bakiyev indicated that he intended to seek a second term in office; several opposition leaders had appealed to the Constitutional Court to bring forward the next poll (due to take place in October 2010). Opposition parties threatened to begin a campaign of protests to demand that the Government end repressive measures against opposition leaders and activists. In March 2009, shortly after Bakiyev had agreed to negotiate with opposition leaders, a prominent supporter of Tekebayev and member of the opposition For Justice Movement, Alikbek Jekshenkulov, was arrested on suspicion of involvement in the killing of a Turkish businessman in 2007. He was also charged with abuse of office while serving as Minister of Foreign Affairs in 2005–07. Jekshenkulov was given a five years' suspended sentence, including a three-year period during which he was prohibited from seeking public office in March 2010. Also in March 2009 Medet Sadyrkulov, who recently had been replaced as head of the presidential administration, was killed in an allegedly suspicious automobile collision. On 19 March the Constitutional Court ruled that the next presidential election must take place no later than 25 October. In late March an opposition alliance, led by Beknazarov, staged large anti-Government demonstrations in Bishkek and other major towns; in April the alliance announced that it had selected Atambayev as its presidential candidate. By that month five parliamentarians had been assassinated since Bakiyev became President. In early May Ak Jol confirmed its endorsement of Bakiyev as its presidential candidate. In July Almaz Tashiyev, a journalist who had often criticized the Government for its social policies, died, having been severely beaten by several police officers.

On 23 July 2009 Bakiyev was re-elected President, obtaining 76.4% of the votes cast, according to official results. Shortly after polling began, Atambayev announced his withdrawal from the election on the grounds that extensive fraud was being perpetrated. Some 79.1% of the electorate were recorded to have participated. Observers from the OSCE described the election as falling short of full democratic standards, and around 20 opposition supporters were reported to have been detained by the police on polling day. On 29 July clashes broke out in Bishkek between demonstrators, protesting at the conduct of the election, and police, precipitating the imposition of a ban of mass gatherings.

In September 2009, in an address to the Supreme Council, Bakiyev proposed a series of administrative reforms. Chudinov opposed these proposals, consequently resigning as Prime Minister on 21 October. Many members of the outgoing administration were reappointed to the new Government led by Usenov, formed one day later, and in which, notably, responsibility for foreign affairs was transferred to the Office of the President. In late December a prominent Kyrgyzstani journalist critical of Bakiyev and who had been involved with negotiations with Atambayev on the establishment of an online news site, Gennadii Pavlyuk (also known as Ibragim Rustamek), died after he was thrown to the ground from a high-rise building in Almatı, Kazakhstan. The Kazakhstani police stated that they regarded Pavlyuk's death as murder, prompting speculation that his killing was politically motivated. The European Union (EU, see p. 271) subsequently demanded that a full investigation into Pavlyuk's killing be conducted; two people were arrested in Almatı in October 2010 in connection with the killing, while a third, the prime suspect, was apprehended two months later. In March 2010 the Government ordered the closure of two opposition newspapers, and prohibited the rebroadcasting on local radio stations of the Kyrgyz programming of the US-funded Radio Free Europe/Radio Liberty, while blocking access to two prominent independent news websites. In April a Bishkek court ordered another newspaper to cease publication, after it had allegedly called for the overthrow by force of the Government.

The 2010 uprising and ethnic unrest

On 3 April 2010 a visit by UN Secretary-General Ban Ki-Moon to Kyrgyzstan was a focus for protests in Bishkek, led by members of civil rights organizations. On 6 April, following the arrest of opposition leader Bolotbek Sherniyazov, several thousand protesters demanding the resignation of President Bakiyev stormed the regional government offices in the north-western town of Talas, holding the regional governor hostage, while rioting ensued throughout the town. A further cause of discontent was the recent appointment of relatives of the President to senior positions in the security services, and of Maksim Bakiyev as Chairman of a state committee responsible for the control of all financial flows into the country and several major companies. On the same day Atambayev was arrested and accused of inciting the unrest in Talas, while other prominent opposition leaders, including Tekebayev, were detained in Bishkek.

On 7 April 2010 demonstrations in Bishkek attended by an estimated 5,000 people demanding the resignation of Bakiyev, and expressing opposition to increases in fuel tariffs and the arrest of opposition leaders, rapidly degenerated into violent disorder, as unruly crowds undertook extensive looting of commercial and government premises. Opposition supporters gained control of the state TV channel. The First Deputy Prime Minister, Akylbek Japarov, was taken hostage, and the Minister of the Interior, Moldomusa Kongantiyev, was severely beaten. Anti-Bakiyev protesters also seized control of government and police buildings in two provincial capitals, Naryn and Tokmok. In Bishkek, police officers opened fire on demonstrators during an attempt to storm the main government building. In the ensuing violence around 80 people were killed and more than 1,000 others injured. By the end of 7 April the Government had effectively lost control, and President Bakiyev, having been forced to leave Bishkek, flew to Osh, from where he announced his refusal to resign from office. Meanwhile, Otunbayeva, now the leader of the parliamentary faction of the KSDP, declared herself to be the leader of a transitional administration, the Interim Government of National Trust (later simply the Interim Government), which would hold office for a period of six months prior to the organization of a presidential election. Other senior members of this administration included Temir Sarayev, the leader of the Ak Shumkar Partiyasy (Al Shumkar—White Falcon Political Party), Atambayev, Tekebayev and Beknazarov. On 11 April the transitional administration dissolved the Supreme Council and temporarily assumed all legislative functions.

On 15 April 2010 officials of the Interim Government announced that Bakiyev had resigned as President. Following negotiations (mediated by the OSCE) between the transitional administration and the leaders of Kazakhstan, Russia and the USA, Bakiyev was granted safe passage to Kazakhstan, from where he denied that he had resigned. Meanwhile, the Minister of Defence in the Bakiyev administration, Bakytbek Kalyyev, was arrested on charges related to the use of force against unarmed civilians in Bishkek during the uprising. On 22 April Tekebayev announced that a referendum on a new Constitution, which would reduce presidential powers, would be held on 27 June. Meanwhile, the Belarusian President, Alyaksandr Lukashenka, announced that he had granted asylum to Bakiyev, who stated that his letter of resignation had been written against his will, following a telephone conversation with the Chairman of the Russian Government, Vladimir Putin. On 4 May Otunbayeva signed an agreement seeking Bakiyev's extradition, ordering the opening of a criminal investigation against him in connection with the violent suppression of protests in April. However, Lukashenka stated that he would not permit Bakiyev's extradition from Belarus. Violent clashes erupted on 19 May between Kyrgyz and Uzbek groups in Jalal-Abad and Osh, in which two people died and more than 70 were injured; a state of emergency was declared in Jalal-Abad. Also on 19 May the Interim Government announced that Otunbayeva was to serve additionally as interim President until the end of 2011, and that she would be prohibited from contesting the next presidential election (to be held in October 2011 and not, as previously announced, in 2010). On 21 May the Interim Government published a new draft Constitution, which provided for a parliamentary system of government. The scheduling of parliamentary elections for 10 October 2010 was confirmed.

On 9–10 June 2010 renewed ethnic violence erupted in Osh. A series of attacks against Kyrgyz resulted in reprisals against the city's Uzbek population, prompting the dispatch of troops to the region and the declaration of a state of emergency. Unrest subsequently spread to other cities, including Jalal-Abad, and tens of thousands of Uzbeks attempted to flee to Uzbekistan. The Interim Government appealed to Russia for help in restoring peace. On 14 June Uzbekistan closed its borders with Kyrgyzstan. The UN stated that it had identified evidence that the violence was 'orchestrated, targeted and well-planned'.

Although the Interim Government accused supporters of Bakiyev of inciting the unrest, a subsequent report by the international organization Human Rights Watch stated that the Kyrgyzstani military had played a role in facilitating the attacks against the Uzbek population. At least 400 people were officially reported to have died in the conflict, which lasted just four days, and 400,000 people were displaced, of whom at least 100,000 had crossed into Uzbekistan. On 17 June the Russian-led Collective Security Treaty Organization (CSTO) announced that it would not deploy a peacekeeping mission to Kyrgyzstan. On 25 June it was reported that Sanjarbek Bakiyev, a nephew of the ousted president, had been detained on charges of organizing the ethnic unrest in Jalal-Abad in May. (He was found guilty and sentenced to 10 years in gaol in November, but was released in November 2014 after the Supreme Court reduced his sentence.)

Despite the unrest, the Kyrgyzstani authorities proceeded with the constitutional referendum on 27 June 2010, the conduct of which the OSCE described as 'largely transparent'. Some 90.6% of votes cast supported the Constitution, and voter participation was estimated at 72%. The Constitution came into force on 2 July; one day later Otunbayeva was sworn in as interim President, while remaining Prime Minister. Subsequently, several prominent members of the Interim Government, including deputy premiers Atambayev, Tekebayev and Sarayev resigned in order to participate in the forthcoming legislative elections. On 14 July several new senior ministers were appointed to the Interim Government. The Interim Government announced that it would establish a national commission to investigate the events of the previous month. Later in July the OSCE approved the deployment of a 52-member police force to Osh and Jalal-Abad. The move was met with protests, led by the Mayor of Osh, Melisbek Myrzakmatov. (Having postponed the deployment of the police force owing to security threats, in November the OSCE announced that the mission would be reduced to around 30 personnel.) Meanwhile, On 15 September 2010 a prominent Uzbek activist, Azimjan Askarov, and seven other Uzbeks were found guilty of the murder of a Kyrgyz policemen during the conflict in June. Askarov and four of his co-defendants were sentenced to life imprisonment.

Legislative and presidential elections

Some 29 political parties contested the elections to the new 120-seat legislature, held on 10 October 2010. The announcement of the final results was delayed until 1 November 2010, owing to allegations of procedural irregularities and confusion over the number of voters. Five parties won the requisite number of votes (5% of the total registered electorate) for representation in the Supreme Council: Ata-Jurt won 15.3% of the votes cast (equivalent to 8.5% of the registered electorate), and obtained 28 seats; the KSDP won 14.2% (26 seats); Ar-Namys 13.7% (25 seats); the Respublika Sayasiy Partiyasy (Respublika—Republic Political Party), a new party led by Babanov, 12.5% (23 seats); and Tekebayev's Ata Meken won 9.9% (18 seats). Some 55.3% of the registered electorate participated in the ballot. Supporters of the Butun Kyrgyzstan Sayasiy Partiyasy (United Kyrgyzstan Political Party), which failed to obtain legislative representation, despite winning 8.3% of the votes cast, staged protests in Bishkek and Osh, and submitted a legal challenge to the results. In addition, on 24 October, following claims by Tashiyev that he had been the target of an assassination attempt by state security forces, hundreds of his supporters held a rally in Bishkek.

The first session of the new Supreme Council was held on 10 November 2010, when some 150 activists from the Meken Sheyitteri (Martyrs of the Fatherland) movement, comprising relatives of those killed during the clashes between protesters and security forces on 7 April, attempted to prevent the delegates from entering the parliament building.

On 7 November 2010 some 500 Kyrgyz activists illegally occupied land in two Uzbek-populated villages in Osh Oblast, with the intention of dividing it into plots. The following day at least 20 Kyrgyz were arrested after several hundred activists joined the protesters. On 9 November the regional governor promised representatives of the group, whose homes had been destroyed during the ethnic violence in June, that they would be allocated land. On 17 November the trial, *in absentia*, of ousted President Bakiyev and 27 of his aides opened in Bishkek, on charges of ordering special forces troops to open fire on civilians during the protests on 7 April. The hearing was immediately adjourned after relatives of those killed in the violence disrupted proceedings. On 30 November a bomb exploded outside the stadium in which the trial was being held, injuring at least three people. One day earlier four people alleged to have connections

with the O'zbekiston Islomiy Harakati (OIH—Islamic Movement of Uzbekistan) had been killed by security forces in Osh, while interior ministry officials announced that nine people suspected of planning to carry out terrorist attacks had been arrested.

On 30 November 2010 the KSDP formed a legislative coalition with Respublika and Ata Meken. Atambayev was nominated Prime Minister, with Babanov as his deputy; Tekebayev was to become Chairman of the Supreme Council. On 2 December, however, Tekebayev's nomination narrowly failed to obtain a majority in the Supreme Council, and the coalition subsequently collapsed. On 4 December Otunbayeva instructed Babanov to form a government. On 15 December it was announced that Respublika was to join a new coalition with the KSDP and Ata-Jurt. On the same day the trial began of Akmat Bakiyev, brother of the ousted President, on charges relating to ethnic violence. Also in December the NGO Amnesty International claimed that by early November 271 people had been detained in investigations relating to the June unrest, and that the 'overwhelming majority' of those brought to trial had been Uzbeks, notwithstanding the fact that Uzbek casualties during the violence had far exceeded those of ethnic Kyrgyz.

On 20 December 2010 the Supreme Council endorsed the nominations of Atambayev as Prime Minister and of Akhmatbek Keldibekov as legislative Chairman. A new Government was formed, including Babanov as First Deputy Prime Minister. A ministerial position for the reconstruction and development of Osh and Jalal-Abad was created. Later in December a vehicle packed with explosives was discovered outside Bishkek's main police headquarters, in connection with which nine people were later arrested. In early January 2011 three policemen were killed while carrying out identity checks in Bishkek; two suspects were killed and a third was detained by security forces the following day. The Minister of Internal Affairs subsequently announced that the men had been responsible for the recent bombing in Bishkek and the attempted car bomb, and had been planning further terrorist attacks.

On 11 January 2011 the national commission appointed to investigate the violence of June 2010 published its findings, concluding that a combination of Uzbek leaders in southern Kyrgyzstan, relatives of ousted President Bakiyev, drugs dealers, Islamist extremists and 'outside forces' were responsible for the violence. The commission's report criticized several high-ranking officials serving in the Interim Government at the time of the crisis, including Sherniyazov, as well as the head of the National Security Committee and the Prosecutor-General, for having failed to act with sufficient rapidity to curb the violence. Maksim Bakiyev and a prominent Uzbek businessman, Kadyrjon Batyrov, both of whom had left the country, were among those found to be implicated in initiating the violence, while the elder brother of the former President, Janysh Bakiyev, was accused of having financed the unrest. Also on 11 January 2011 the National Security Committee announced the arrest of a local leader of the transnational, Islamist Hizb-ut-Tahrir al-Islami (Party of Islamic Liberation) in Jalal-Abad Oblast. At least four other members of the organization were apprehended in southern Kyrgyzstan in that month. In April Urmat Baryktabasov, the leader of a Kyrgyz nationalist group, Meken Tuu (Flag of the Fatherland), was sentenced to four years' imprisonment, after he and 14 associates were convicted of possession of armaments and attempting to seize power. (In August, however, Baryktabasov was released under an amnesty.) In August Akmat Bakiyev was sentenced to seven and a half years' imprisonment. (In March 2012 it was reported that he had escaped from detention, after having sought medical treatment.)

In mid-April 2011 Atambayev agreed to First Deputy Prime Minister Babanov's request that he resign from office, for the period of one month, while investigations of corruption in relation to Megacom, a major mobile telecommunications service provider, be investigated; Babanov also requested that the Supreme Council form a special commission to investigate the accusations against him. In September some 15 of the 25 parliamentary deputies representing Ar-Namys voted to remove Kulov as the leader of their parliamentary faction and party, electing Kamila Taliyeva as their leader. However, Kulov refused to accept this decision, stating that such a measure could be effected only by the entire party membership, and he retained effective control of the party.

On 25 September 2011 Atambayev resigned as Prime Minister in order to contest the forthcoming presidential election. Consequently, Babanov became acting premier. A total of 16 candidates (of a reported 86 who had applied for registration) contested the presidential election on 30 October. Atambayev was decisively elected as President, securing 62.5% of the votes cast; Madumarov, representing Butun Kyrgyzstan, was placed second, with 14.8%; and Tashiyev, the leader of Ata-Jurt, attained third place, with 14.3%. A rate of participation of 61.3% was recorded. OSCE observers reported that the voting process had been peaceful, but subject to significant violations, while noting that the pre-election campaign had largely met democratic standards. Atambayev was officially inaugurated on 1 December. On 16 December the KSDP formed a new parliamentary coalition with Respublika, Ata Meken and Ar-Namys, which together held 92 parliamentary seats. The Supreme Council confirmed Babanov's appointment as Prime Minister on 23 December; the opposition criticized the inclusion of several members of previous administrations in the new Government. The balance of power was again perceived to favour northern interests over those in the south.

Unstable coalition administrations

On 22 August 2012, following ongoing allegations of corruption against Babanov, Ata Meken and Ar-Namys both withdrew from the Government. Ata Meken had accused the premier earlier in the month of having accepted a bribe from a Turkish businessman in exchange for a construction contract relating to facilities at the US airbase at Manas. On 12 September a new Government was sworn in, comprising members of the KSDP, Ata Meken and Ar-Namys; the coalition parties between them held a slim parliamentary majority, with 67 of the 120 seats. Respublika and Ata-Jurt, which had recently formed a new alliance, were excluded from the coalition. President Atambayev nominated the non-partisan Jantoro Satybaldiyev, hitherto presidential Chief of Staff and a former Governor of Osh Oblast, as Prime Minister; the Supreme Council overwhelmingly endorsed his appointment on 5 September. Other ministerial appointees included Djoomart Otorbayev as First Deputy Prime Minister and Erlan Abdyldayev as Minister of Foreign Affairs. Also in September a Judicial Selection Council completed its selection of 25 judges for a new Constitutional Chamber under the Supreme Court, which was established to uphold the constitution and protect civil and constitutional rights.

On 3 October 2012 Tashiyev and two other senior members of Ata-Jurt were detained and charged with inciting unrest during a protest rally in Bishkek. The rally, attended by around 1,000 people, had been called to demand the renationalization of the Kumtor gold mine, partly as a result of concerns about the social and environmental costs of the project. On 5 October further demonstrations took place around the country after a court in Bishkek extended the pre-trial detention of Tashiyev and his associates to two months. Also in October Maksim Bakiyev (who was, in addition, subject to charges of money-laundering and corruption in Kyrgyzstan) was arrested in London, United Kingdom at the request of the US Department of Justice, on charges of fraud and conspiracy to pervert the course of justice in the USA in 2010–12, in connection with the supply of fuel to the US airbase at Manas. (In May 2013 the extradition request was retracted.)

The trial of Tashiyev and his associates began on 10 January 2013. In the following month the cabinet of ministers was reorganized. In March around 1,000 protesters gathered in Jalal-Abad to demand the immediate release of Tashiyev and his associates but on 29 March all three were convicted and sentenced to terms of up to 18 months' imprisonment on charges of having attempted to seize power; as a result, they were obliged to relinquish their seats in the legislature. More rioting ensued in their support, and in June they were acquitted by an appeals court. However, the Supreme Court on 6 August reversed the acquittal and the politicians were again stripped of their Supreme Council mandates, although they were not obliged to return to gaol.

Meanwhile, in February 2013 former President Bakiyev was sentenced *in absentia* to 24 years' imprisonment for abuse of power. His brother Janysh (who was also in exile in Belarus) was sentenced *in absentia* to life in prison, having been found guilty of the murder of Sadyrkulov in March 2009; in November 2013 he also received an 18-year sentence from Suzak district court on charges relating to the organization of a bank robbery in 2005, during the unrest that brought his brother to power. In March 2013 Maksim Bakiyev was also sentenced *in absentia* to 25 years' imprisonment for illegal land purchases and corrupt share dealing. In an unrelated but also politically connected case, a court in Bishkek on 22 November ordered that Keldibekov be

held in pre-trial detention for two months, pending an investigation into suspected abuse of office and corruption in the early 2000s, when he managed the State Social Fund and the State Tax Service. Protest rallies took place in central Bishkek and in Osh, where supporters also blockaded the road to the border with China; the start of his trial was subsequently postponed on numerous occasions (with several further protests and roadblocks being organized by his supporters in the Osh region), and in August 2014 he left Kyrgyzstan to receive medical treatment abroad.

On 25 January 2013 the legislature adopted the recommendations of a commission that aspects of a deal reached in 2009 with a foreign operator regarding one of the country's primary sources of income, the Kumtor gold mine, should be restructured. The Government subsequently commenced negotiations with the Canada-based operator, Centerra Gold, to reach a new operating agreement. In late May 2013 protesters blocked the road to the mine and cut off electricity supplies. The Government imposed a local state of emergency until 10 June. Meanwhile, in Jalal-Abad hundreds of people laid siege to the Governor's office on 31 May in support of the Kumtor protesters. Protests broke out again in October, with a major road being blocked and the regional governor briefly being held hostage. The Supreme Council voted on 23 October to reject a memorandum of understanding between the Government and Centerra Gold concluded in the previous month. The deal would have made the state an equal partner in Kumtor, a significant increase on its existing 33% stake. Legislators demanded that the Government increase its stake to 67% or nationalize the mine, imposing a deadline of 23 December. However, on 6 February 2014 the Supreme Council endorsed a resolution approving a restructuring plan agreed on 24 December 2013 for the mine that would entail state-owned gold entity Kyrgyzaltyn exchanging its 37% stake in Centerra Gold for a 50% stake in a new joint venture company that would own and operate Kumtor. The state had the option of increasing its stake to 67% in the future. Centerra Gold warned that aspects of the parliamentary resolution ran counter to its agreement with the Government.

The central authorities in December 2013 dismissed Myrzakmatov as Mayor of Osh, after he appeared to support an anti-Government protest. On 15 January 2014 Myrzakmatov lost in indirect mayoral elections to Government-backed candidate Aitmamat Kadyrbayev. Several thousand people took to the streets to protest against the result, and attempted to storm the municipal administration building in Osh, before dispersing. A new Minister of Agriculture and Land Reclamation was appointed in early February.

On 19 March 2014 President Atambayev accepted the resignation of the coalition Government, one day after Ata Meken, its smallest constituent faction, had withdrawn from the ruling coalition. Tekebayev cited abuse of office by Satybaldiyev and the misappropriation of state funds allocated to help stabilize the country's southern regions since the unrest in 2010. He also declared the party's opposition to the new proposed ownership structure of the Kumtor mine. However, after the premiership (to which position he was confirmed by the Supreme Council on 3 April) was offered to Otorbayev, a member of Ata Meken, the ruling coalition was restored, and the majority of appointees in the outgoing Government returned to their posts, although Taiyrbek Sarpashev succeeded Otorbayev as First Deputy Prime Minister, while other new appointments included that of Abibilla Kudaiberdiyev as Minister of Defence.

In late July 2014 former President Bakiyev was sentenced, *in absentia*, to a further term of life imprisonment for his role in the killing of protesters during the 2010 uprising; his brother Janysh and former Prime Minister Usenov also obtained life sentences *in absentia*, while 25 other defendants were awarded custodial sentences of between six and 25 years.

In mid-September 2014 Melis Tuganbayev was appointed acting Minister of Internal Affairs, succeeding Abdulda Suranchiyev (who had also held in the post in an acting capacity). Also in mid-September a new trial commenced, *in absentia*, of Maksim Bakiyev; the brother of the former President and two of his associates were charged with fraud and financial malpractice; in the following month Kyrgyzstan made a new formal request to the United Kingdom for his extradition. In mid-October Kubanychbek Turdubayev was appointed as Minister of Energy and Industry, initially in an acting capacity, succeeding Osmonbek Artykbayev; a new Minister of Culture, Information and Tourism had been appointed earlier in the month, and a new Minister of Health was appointed in early November. Also in early

November Altynbek Muraliyev, a senior official in the Ministry of Foreign Affairs and the son of former Prime Minister Amangeldy Muraliyev, was arrested on charges of espionage for an unnamed country. In mid-December Aliasbek Alymkulov was dismissed as Minister of Education and Science, following a dispute over allocation of student places at a university in Bishkek; he was succeeded by Elvira Sariyeva, a member of the KSDP and hitherto one of the three deputy prime ministers in the Government; Damira Niyazaliyeva, a legislative deputy of the party, became a deputy premier in her place; the Minister of Labour, Migration and Youth was also replaced.

Recent developments: resignation of Otorbayev

Concerns about proposals that would have the effect of limiting the activities of NGOs were increasingly expressed from late 2014. In December President Atambayev stated that the activities of certain NGOs could endanger national security; meanwhile, two bills that would place new restrictions on certain areas of civil society activity, seemingly based on similar legislation that had entered into force in Russia in recent years, were under parliamentary discussion. One of these bills would require NGOs that received funding from outside Kyrgyzstan to register as 'foreign agents', while the second would proscribe the 'promotion of non-traditional sexual relationships' and forbid the operation of NGOs concerned with issues pertaining to sexual minorities. On 23 December, shortly before the organization's formation, President Atambayev signed an agreement providing for Kyrgyzstan's accession to the Eurasian Economic Union (EEU, see p. 446) Economic Union (see *Regional relations*), although this was not expected to enter formally into effect until May 2015.

In mid-January 2015 the Prosecutor-General, Aida Salyanova, resigned, after it was reported that her husband was suspected of fraud in his role as an assistant to the Minister of Justice, Almambet Shykmamatov. Shykmamatov was himself dismissed in early February, being succeeded by his erstwhile deputy, Jyldyz Mambetaliyeva, later in the month. In late February Atambayev made a speech in which he strongly urged Belarus to extradite Kurmanbek and Janysh Bakiyev, and demonstrations were staged in support of these demands outside the Belarusian embassy in Bishkek.

Increasing concern was also expressed about the quantity of Kyrgyzstani citizens who (in defiance of national law) had joined combat with militant Islamist groups of the Islamic State (IS) organization in Syria; by January 2015 the Government estimated that between 200 and 500 Kyrgyzstani citizens (the majority of whom were believed to be ethnic Uzbeks from the south of the country) were fighting for IS, although unofficial estimates of the number of Kyrgyzstani fighters were substantially higher. At the end of that month five men (four of whom had undertaken military training in Syria) were arrested in Osh, on suspicion of planning attacks in both Kyrgyzstan and Uzbekistan. Shortly afterwards five members of Hizb-ut-Tahrir were detained in Naryn, in central Kyrgyzstan. In mid-February the Ministry of Internal Affairs announced that fighters returning to Kyrgyzstan from Syria would be prosecuted as mercenaries. In mid-March IS was formally categorized as a terrorist organization by the Government, and it, along with three other militant Islamist groups, was proscribed in Kyrgyzstan. (Other Kyrgyzstani citizens were reported to be fighting for militant Islamist groups in Afghanistan and Pakistan.) Further members of Hizb-ut-Tahrir were detained near Jalal-Abad in late March; also in late March a US citizen, Umar Farooq, who had reportedly been conducting interviews on inter-ethnic violence, was detained in Osh, and accused with possessing material of a 'religious extremist and terrorist' nature.

In mid-April 2015 Olga Lavrova of Ar-Namys resigned as Minister of Finance. Later in the month Kalykbek Sultanov of Ata Mekan was dismissed as Minister of Transport and Communications. Shortly afterwards, on 23 April, after further disagreement over the future ownership of the Kumtor gold mine, notably as the result of a proposal by Otorbayev that the Government increase its representation on the board of directors of Centerra, in preference to the establishment of a joint venture, the Government resigned. On 1 May Temir Sarayev, the hitherto Minister of the Economy, and an independent since the dissolution of Ak Shumkar, was confirmed as Prime Minister; he was succeeded in his former position by Oleg Pankratov; the remainder of the ministers in the outgoing Government were reappointed, and new appointments were made to the two vacant posts.

Foreign Affairs
Regional relations

Kyrgyzstan was a member of the Eurasian Economic Community (EurAsEC) formed in 2000 as the successor to a 'community of integrated states' comprising Kyrgyzstan, Belarus, Kazakhstan and Russia, and which absorbed the Central Asian Co-operation Organization (CACO) in 2002, which had also included Kyrgyzstan among its members. Kyrgyzstan sought to accede to a Customs Union between Belarus, Kazakhstan and Russia that entered into effect in 2010, which it was itself succeeded by the Eurasian Economic Union (EEU, see p. 446—with Armenia also joining) in January 2015. Although Kyrgyzstan participated in the activities of the Union from its formation, its formal membership was not expected to commence before late May of that year. Kyrgyzstan is also a member of the Collective Security Treaty Organization (CSTO, see p. 460) that was inaugurated in 2003 as the successor of the CIS Collective Security Treaty, which had agreed to form a Collective Rapid Reaction Force in Bishkek to combat Islamist militancy in Central Asia.

Kyrgyzstan's campaign against Islamist extremism—particularly against the clandestine, transnational, Islamist Hizb-ut-Tahrir organization—intensified in 1999, after a number of kidnappings and hostage-taking incidents perpetrated by Islamist groups believed to be based in Uzbekistan and Tajikistan, including the O'zbekiston Islomiy Harakati (OIH—Islamic Movement of Uzbekistan). Islamist militants made a further series of incursions from Tajikistan in mid-2000, leading to armed conflict with government forces. Relations with Uzbekistan were further strained in mid-2005, when the Government refused to return a large number of refugees who had fled Uzbekistan after violence broke out in Andijon in May (see Uzbekistan). In January 2013 hundreds of residents of Uzbekistan's Sokh district (which forms one of four exclaves of the country, surrounded by Kyrgyzstani territory) clashed with Kyrgyzstani border guards who were installing power lines on disputed territory. According to reports, at least three Uzbekistani citizens were shot, while one Kyrgyzstani policeman was severely beaten. On the following day, residents of Sokh took hostage 30 Kyrgyzstani from a nearby village, although they were subsequently released. On 23 July an exchange of gunfire between Kyrgyzstani and Uzbekistani border guards in Aksy district resulted in the death of an Uzbekistani border guard. In April 2014 Uzbekistan suspended natural gas deliveries to Kyrgyzstan, shortly after the Russian state-controlled Gazprom corporation obtained control of the formerly state-owned Kyrgyzgaz for the symbolic sum of US $1. In November a Kyrgyzstani citizen was shot dead by Uzbekistani border guards in a disputed region near Jalal-Abad; Uzbekistan did not restore gas supplies until the end of the year.

Meanwhile, although just over one-half of the 600-mile (1,000km) border with Tajikistan has been demarcated, the fact that 450 km of the border with Tajikistan remain undemarcated has contributed to regular low-level clashes over access to water and agricultural land. Following a number of protests in 2013, the two sides at the end of the year agreed to resume bilateral talks on border demarcation. Further clashes and killings occurred at the border on three occasions in July–August 2014, as a result of which at least two people were killed and at least 11 injured. In January 2015 it was announced that Soviet-era archives would be used in the ongoing process of delimiting the border.

In October 2003 a Russian airbase (the first Russian military installation established outside Russia since the dissolution of the USSR) became operational at Kant. Russia harshly criticized the decision of President Bakiyev, announced in June 2009, to reverse the proposed closure of the US airbase at Manas, 30 km from Kant, and which was used by the US-led coalition fighting in Afghanistan. In August 2009 a summit meeting of the CSTO took place in Cholpon-Ata, in northern Kyrgyzstan, when Presidents Bakiyev and Medvedev signed a preliminary memorandum of understanding on the opening of a second Russian military base in Kyrgyzstan. The base, which was to operate under the auspices of the CSTO, was to be leased to Russia for a period of up to 49 years, extensible for subsequent 25-year periods, and all Russian personnel at the base were to be granted diplomatic immunity. Although final agreement on the base was to have been reached by 1 November, negotiations subsequently stalled, owing to opposition from Uzbekistan.

Following the ethnic unrest in southern Kyrgyzstan in June 2010, the Russian Government was reluctant to accept that the proposed new parliamentary system of government in

Kyrgyzstan would be the most effective at achieving stability. During the campaign for the October legislative elections, several party leaders visited Moscow; of these Kulov was seen to be most closely allied with the Russian administration, particularly after he signed a co-operation agreement with the de facto ruling party of Russia, United Russia, on behalf of his party, Ar-Namys. The new President, Almazbek Atambayev, made an official visit to Moscow in February 2012, during which he reportedly pledged commitment to Russia's stated aim of greater economic integration between post-Soviet states. Tensions subsequently emerged, after Atambayev criticized Russia, and demanded that it pay US $15m. in rent arrears for the use of the airbase at Kant. Nevertheless, in September 2012 President Vladimir Putin of Russia visited Bishkek and reached an agreement whereby, in exchange for cancellation of Kyrgyzstan's debt, Russia would be granted a further 15-year lease on military facilities that it had been due to vacate in 2017. In July 2013 it was announced that Russia would provide Kyrgyzstan with around $1,000m. of military hardware. In October, following the US's definitive decision to close its airbase at Manas, Russia announced an increase in the number of its aircraft that would be stationed at the Kant airbase. Meanwhile, in July 2013 the energy ministers of Russia and Kyrgyzstan, meeting in Moscow, signed an intergovernmental agreement relating to co-operation on the transport, distribution and sale of natural gas in Kyrgyzstan. The 25-year agreement entailed the sale of all assets belonging to state entity Kyrgyzgaz (including pipelines, underground storage facilities and other infrastructure) to Russian company Gazprom for the nominal sum of $1. In December the Kyrgyzstani legislature ratified the agreement. In May 2014 President Atambayev and his counterparts from Belarus, Kazakhstan and Russia signed a 'road map' on Kyrgyzstan's eventual accession to the Customs Union in which the three states participated. Russia was to provide substantial financial assistance to Kyrgyzstan in order to facilitate its membership. Despite the signature of an accession agreement on 23 December 2014, Kyrgyzstan was not initially granted the status of a member of the Eurasian Economic Union (EEU, see p. 446), which succeeded the Customs Union with effect from January 2015 (and to the membership of which Armenia also acceded). Nonetheless, it participated in the activities of the Union prior to its full membership, which was expected to enter in effect in late May.

Other external relations

Following the suicide attacks on the US cities of New York and Washington, DC, on 11 September 2001, Kyrgyzstan announced that it would permit US military aircraft access to Kyrgyzstani airspace for the aerial bombardment of militants of the Islamist al-Qa'ida organization (which co-ordinated the attacks) and its Taliban hosts in Afghanistan. In November the US-led coalition was also granted access to the country's military bases and, later, the airbase at Manas airport. Kyrgyzstani and US troops undertook joint exercises in February 2002. In early 2006 Kyrgyzstan presented the USA with new conditions for the use of the Manas airbase, proposing to increase the rent payable by the USA from US $2m. to $200m. In July an agreement was signed allowing the continued US use of the airbase in exchange for a payment of $150m. In February 2009 Bakiyev announced that the airbase was to be closed; this followed a visit to Moscow during which Russia had offered Kyrgyzstan assistance and loans equivalent to more than $2,000m. On 19 February the Supreme Council approved the closure of the airbase, without setting a date for this. However, in June Kyrgyzstan and the USA concluded an agreement to reverse the decision on the closure of the airbase, although the new agreement stipulated that the USA would use the site as a transit centre, rather than as a full military facility, while the rent charged was to be increased more than three-fold, to an annual rate of $60m. The five-year agreement was signed into law in July following legislative approval.

Following the overthrow of President Bakiyev in April 2010, the new interim leader, Otunbayeva stated that Kyrgyzstan wished to maintain co-operative relations with the USA. After his election in October 2011, President Atambayev announced that the lease on the US transit centre at Manas airbase would not be renewed after the expiry of the existing agreement in July 2014. On 21 May 2013 the Government adopted a draft law to close the transit centre at Manas. In October the USA indicated that it had taken a definitive decision to withdraw from the base, and in June 2014 control of the base was handed back to the Kyrgyzstani authorities.

CONSTITUTION AND GOVERNMENT

Under the Constitution adopted on 2 July 2010, following a national referendum, presidential powers in Kyrgyzstan were substantially reduced. Legislative power is vested in the 120-seat Jogorku Kenesh (Supreme Council), elected by universal adult suffrage for a term of five years. Executive power is vested in the President, who is directly elected for only one term of six years. The President appoints the members of the Government, including the Prime Minister. Judicial power is exercised by the Supreme Court and regional courts. For administrative purposes, Kyrgyzstan is divided into seven oblasts (regions) and the municipality of Bishkek (the capital).

REGIONAL AND INTERNATIONAL CO-OPERATION

Kyrgyzstan is a member of the Commonwealth of Independent States (CIS, see p. 241), and has also joined the Collective Security Treaty Organization (CSTO, see p. 460), the Shanghai Cooperation Organization (SCO, see p. 463) and the Organization of Islamic Cooperation (see p. 401). Kyrgyzstan participated in the activities of the Eurasian Economic Union (EEU, see p. 446), from its formation in January 2015; it expected to accede to membership of the Union in May of that year.

Kyrgyzstan joined the UN in 1992 and became a member of the World Trade Organization (WTO, see p. 431) in 1998.

ECONOMIC AFFAIRS

In 2013, according to estimates by the World Bank, Kyrgyzstan's gross national income (GNI), measured at average 2011–13 prices, was US $6,881m., equivalent to $1,200 per head (or $3,070 per head on an international purchasing-power parity basis). During 2004–13 it was estimated that the population increased by an annual average of 1.3%, while gross domestic product (GDP) per head increased, in real terms, at an average annual rate of 2.9%. According to the World Bank, overall GDP increased, in real terms, at an estimated average annual rate of 4.2% in 2004–13. Real GDP decreased by 0.1% in 2012, but increased by 10.5% in 2013, according to the Asian Development Bank (ADB, see p. 206).

Agriculture (including forestry and fishing) contributed an estimated 17.1% of GDP, according to the ADB, and engaged 31.7% of the employed labour force, according to official figures, in 2013. By tradition, the Kyrgyz are a pastoral nomadic people, and the majority of the population (some 63.3% in 2010, according to UN estimates) reside in rural areas. Livestock-rearing, once the mainstay of agricultural activity, is declining in importance. Only about 7% of the country's land area is arable; of this, some 70% depends on irrigation. The principal crops are potatoes, maize, wheat and barley. According to UN estimates, the GDP of the agricultural sector decreased, in real terms, by an average annual rate of 1.1% per year in 2004–13. Agricultural GDP grew by 2.9% in 2013, according to the ADB.

Industry (comprising manufacturing, mining, utilities and construction) contributed 25.7% of GDP, according to the ADB, and provided 20.2% of employment, according to official figures, in 2013. According to UN estimates, real industrial GDP remained constant, on average, during 2004–13. According to the ADB, industrial GDP decreased by 11.7% in 2012, but increased by 28.0% in 2013.

The mining and quarrying sector provided 0.8% of GDP, according to the ADB, and engaged 0.4% of the employed workforce, according to official figures, in 2013. Kyrgyzstan has considerable mineral deposits, including coal, gold, tin, mercury, antimony, zinc, tungsten and uranium. Production of gold from the Kumtor mine, which is believed to contain the eighth largest deposit of gold in the world (over 200 metric tons), began in January 1997. he As a result, by 2001 Kyrgyzstan had become the 10th largest extractor and seller of gold worldwide, although the operation and ownership of the mine has been a frequent cause of political controversy. Production of gold from the Jeruy deposit commenced in 2002. In April 2006 an agreement was signed with a Kazakhstani company on the development of the Taldy Bulak Levoberezhny gold deposit. Gold production totalled 19.7 tons in 2011 and 11.3 tons in 2012.

Manufacturing contributed 15.0% of GDP, according to the ADB, and engaged 6.9% of the employed labour force, according to official figures, in 2013. Real manufacturing GDP increased by 0.4% in 2004–13, according to UN estimates; the GDP of the sector decreased by 27.6% in 2012, but increased by 45.4% in 2013.

Kyrgyzstan's principal source of domestic energy production (and a major export) is hydroelectricity (generated by the country's mountain rivers), which provided 93.3% of the country's total energy requirements in 2011. Kyrgyzstan has insufficient petroleum and natural gas to meet its needs, and substantial imports of hydrocarbons are thus required; Kyrgyzstan exports electricity to Kazakhstan and Uzbekistan in return for coal and natural gas, respectively. Imports of mineral products comprised 22.7% of the value of total recorded imports in 2013.

The construction sector contributed 7.6% of GDP in 2013, according to the ADB, and engaged 10.8% of the employed labour force, according to official figures, in 2013. During 2004–13, according to UN figures, the GDP of the sector increased at an average annual rate of 13.2%. Construction GDP increased by 12.4% in 2013.

In 2013 the services sector contributed 57.2% of GDP, according to the ADB, and engaged 48.1% of the employed labour force, according to official figures, in 2013. In 2004–13, according to UN estimates, the GDP of the sector increased, in real terms, by an average of 7.4% per year. Services GDP increased by 5.1% in 2013, according to the ADB.

In 2013 Kyrgyzstan recorded a visible merchandise trade deficit of US $3,565.2m., and there was a deficit of $1,684.2m. on the current account of the balance of payments. In 2013 the principal source of imports (accounting for 33.6% of the total) was Russia; other major suppliers were the People's Republic of China and Kazakhstan. The main market for exports in that year was Switzerland (which accounted for 25.4% of all exports); other principal export markets were Kazakhstan, the United Arab Emirates, Uzbekistan and Russia. The main exports in 2013 were precious and semi-precious stones, mineral products, vegetable products, and textiles and fabrics. The principal imports in that year were mineral products, vehicles and transport equipment, machinery and electrical equipment, metals, chemicals, prepared foodstuffs, and textiles and fabrics.

In 2013 Kyrgyzstan recorded an overall budgetary deficit of 8,216.0m. soms, equivalent to 2.3% of GDP. Kyrgyzstan's general government gross debt was 167,052m. soms in 2013, equivalent to 47.7% of GDP. Kyrgyzstan's total external debt was US $6,026m. at the end of 2012, of which $2,840m. was public and publicly guaranteed debt. In that year, the cost of servicing long-term public and publicly guaranteed debt and repayments to the IMF was equivalent to 10.9% of the value of exports of goods, services and income (excluding workers' remittances). According to the ADB, the annual rate of inflation averaged 9.3% in 2004–13; consumer prices increased by 6.7% in 2013. The average rate of unemployment was 8.3% in 2013.

Kyrgyzstan's economy depends substantially upon gold, agriculture and remittances. A steep increase in consumer tariffs for electricity, fuel and water, which exacerbated economic hardship, was a significant factor in precipitating the protests that led to the overthrow of President Kurmanbek Bakiyev in April 2010. Shortly after it assumed power, the Interim Government reversed the increase in energy tariffs, although energy supplies remained a topic of great national importance. In 2014 the Russian state-controlled Gazprom corporation acquired the state utility company Kyrgyzgaz and pledged to invest substantially in the country's gas infrastructure, including the construction of a new pipeline connecting northern and southern regions; seemingly in response, Uzbekistan suspended gas supplies to Kyrgyzstan. Later in the year Gazprom announced that it would supply gas to Kyrgyzstan at the rate of US $165 per 1,000 cu m, a substantially cheaper rate than that at which Kyrgyzstan had previously purchased gas from Uzbekistan or Kazakhstan, apparently guaranteeing security of supplies. Meanwhile, arrangements for electricity to be imported from Kazakhstan were made for the winter of 2014/15, as a result of an energy deficit resulting from the low water levels in Kyrgyzstan's reservoirs that feed its hydropower plants. President Almazbek Atambayev, who was elected in October 2011, pledged commitment to Kyrgyzstan's membership of a Russian-led Customs Union, although accession was subsequently delayed because of dissatisfaction with the terms on offer. In 2014, however, the country drew up a 'road map' for admission to the successor organization to the Customs Union founded in January 2015, the Eurasian Economic Union (EEU, see p. 446), to which it signed a treaty of accession in December 2014; Kyrgyzstani membership of the Union (which included Armenia as well as the founding states of Russia, Belarus and Kazakhstan) was expected to take effect from May 2015, although the country effectively became involved in the Union's activities from its formation. In April the IMF approved a three-year Extended Credit Facility worth around $92.4m. for Kyrgyzstan, subject to regular reviews. The IMF estimated GDP growth of 3.6% in 2014 and forecast growth of 1.7% in 2015, the downturn in growth in part resulting from the economic contraction in one of Kyrgyzstan's principal partners and source of remittances, Russia.

PUBLIC HOLIDAYS

2016: 1 January (New Year's Day), 7 January (Christmas), 8 March (International Women's Day), 21 March (Nooruz, Spring Holiday), 1 May (International Labour Day), 5 May (Constitution Day), 9 May (Victory Day), 8 July* (Orozo Ait, Id al-Fitr, end of Ramadan), 31 August (Independence Day), 12 September* (Kurban Ait, Id al-Adha, Feast of the Sacrifice).

* These holidays are dependent on the Islamic lunar calendar and may vary by one or two days from the dates given.

Statistical Survey

Source (unless otherwise stated): National Statistical Committee, 720033 Bishkek, Frunze 374; tel. (312) 22-63-63; fax (312) 22-07-59; e-mail zkudabaev@nsc.bishkek.su; internet www.stat.kg.

Area and Population

AREA, POPULATION AND DENSITY

Area (sq km)	199,900*
Population (census results)†	
24 March 1999	4,822,938
24 March 2009	
Males	2,645,921
Females	2,716,872
Total	5,362,793
Population (official estimates at 1 January)	
2012	5,551,888
2013	5,663,133
2014	5,776,570
Density (per sq km) at 1 January 2014	28.9

* 77,182 sq miles.

† Figures refer to *de jure* population. The *de facto* total was 4,850,700 at the 1999 census and 5,107,640 in 2009.

POPULATION BY AGE AND SEX
(official estimates at 1 January 2014)

	Males	Females	Total
0–14 years	914,659	876,454	1,791,113
15–64 years	1,844,760	1,893,424	3,738,184
65 years and over	97,126	150,147	247,273
Total	2,856,545	2,920,025	5,776,570

POPULATION BY ETHNIC GROUP
(official estimates at 1 January 2014)

	Number	%
Kyrgyz	4,193,850	72.6
Uzbek	836,065	14.5
Russian	369,939	6.4
Dungan	64,565	1.1
Uigur	52,456	0.9
Tajik	50,174	0.9
Turk	40,953	0.7
Kazakh	33,701	0.6
Tatar	28,059	0.5
Ukrainian	14,485	0.3
Others	92,323	1.5
Total	5,776,570	100.0

Note: Classification of ethnicity reflects national methodology.

ADMINISTRATIVE DIVISIONS
(official estimates at 1 January 2014)

	Area (sq km)	Population ('000)	Density (per sq km)	Principal city
Oblasts (regions) .				
Batken	17,000	469.7	27.6	Batken
Chui	20,200	853.7	42.3	Tokmok
Jalal-Abad . .	33,700	1,099.2	32.6	Jalal-Abad
Naryn	45,200	271.3	6.0	Naryn
Osh	29,200	1,465.1	50.2	Osh*
Talas	11,400	243.4	21.4	Talas
Yssyk-Kul . .	43,100	458.5	10.6	Karakol
City				
Bishkek . . .	100	915.7	9,157.0	—
Total	199,900	5,776.6	28.9	

* The city of Osh also constitutes a separate administrative area, with a population numbering 265,200 at 1 January 2014.

PRINCIPAL TOWNS
(official estimates at 1 January 2014)

Bishkek (capital) .	901,700	Karakol	69,300
Osh	265,200	Tokmok	57,400
Jalal-Abad . . .	105,300	Uzgen	53,400

BIRTHS, MARRIAGES AND DEATHS

	Registered live births		Registered marriages		Registered deaths	
	Number	Rate (per 1,000)	Number	Rate (per 1,000)	Number	Rate (per 1,000)
2006 . .	120,737	23.3	43,760	8.4	38,566	7.4
2007 . .	123,251	23.5	44,392	8.5	38,180	7.3
2008 . .	127,332	23.9	44,258	8.3	37,710	7.1
2009 . .	135,494	25.2	47,567	8.8	35,898	6.7
2010 . .	146,123	26.8	50,362	9.2	36,174	6.6
2011 . .	149,612	27.1	56,509	10.2	35,941	6.5
2012 . .	154,918	27.6	55,176	9.8	36,186	6.5
2013 . .	155,520	27.2	53,578	9.4	34,880	6.1

Life expectancy (years at birth, official estimates): 70.2 (males 66.3; females 74.3) in 2013.

IMMIGRATION AND EMIGRATION

	2011	2012	2013
Immigrants	6,337	5,532	4,349
Emigrants	45,740	13,019	11,552

ECONOMICALLY ACTIVE POPULATION
(annual averages, '000 persons)

	2011	2012	2013
Agriculture, hunting forestry and fishing	700.3	688.2	716.7
Mining and quarrying	16.7	13.0	9.8
Manufacturing	173.1	173.4	156.9
Electricity, gas and water supply .	38.7	50.7	45.7
Construction	249.1	259.0	244.9
Wholesale and retail trade; repair of motor vehicles, motor cycles and personal and household goods	345.9	346.3	359.9
Hotels and restaurants . . .	86.5	84.3	79.8
Transport, storage and communications	147.2	164.5	167.9
Financial intermediation . . .	17.7	23.1	22.4
Real estate, renting and business activities	56.0	43.9	40.5
Public administration and defence; compulsory social security . .	102.6	109.3	95.8
Education	177.1	180.4	174.9
Health and social work . . .	78.5	84.1	80.2
Other services	88.3	66.2	67.7
Total employed	2,277.7	2,286.4	2,263.0
Unemployed	212.4	210.4	205.7
Total labour force	2,490.1	2,496.8	2,468.7
Males	1,448.6	1,463.5	1,471.6
Females	1,041.5	1,033.3	997.1

Health and Welfare

KEY INDICATORS

Total fertility rate (children per woman, 2012)	3.1
Under-5 mortality rate (per 1,000 live births, 2012) . . .	27
HIV/AIDS (% of persons aged 15–49, 2013)	0.2
Physicians (per 1,000 head, 2012)	2.0
Hospital beds (per 1,000 head, 2007)	5.1
Health expenditure (2011): US $ per head (PPP)	152
Health expenditure (2011): % of GDP	6.2
Health expenditure (2011): public (% of total)	59.9
Access to water (% of persons, 2012)	88
Access to sanitation (% of persons, 2012)	92
Total carbon dioxide emissions ('000 metric tons, 2010) . .	6,398.9
Carbon dioxide emissions per head (metric tons, 2010) . .	1.2
Human Development Index (2013): ranking	125
Human Development Index (2013): value	0.628

For sources and definitions, see explanatory note on p. vi.

Agriculture

PRINCIPAL CROPS
('000 metric tons)

	2011	2012	2013
Wheat	799.8	540.5	819.4
Rice, paddy	19.4	23.1	27.2
Barley	233.8	212.7	309.9
Maize	446.4	578.3	568.2
Potatoes	1,379.2	1,312.7	1,332.0
Sugar beet	158.8	102.0	195.4
Sunflower seed	45.6	45.9	42.5
Cabbages and other brassicas .	127.8	103.1	109.4
Tomatoes	176.7	191.7	195.1
Cucumbers and gherkins . .	79.9	90.8	87.5

—*continued*	2011	2012	2013
Onions, dry	138.0	151.0	152.1
Garlic	30.6	37.1	36.2
Carrots and turnips	152.2	128.9	136.7
Apples*	127.0	137.0	143.0
Apricots*	22.0	22.0	23.0
Peaches and nectarines* . . .	12.5	17.8	18.5
Grapes	6.7	7.8	8.1
Watermelons	151.6	193.3	195.8
Seed cotton	101.3	84.7	68.6
Tobacco, unmanufactured . . .	9.9	7.4	6.5

* Unofficial figures.

Aggregate production ('000 metric tons, may include official, semi-official or estimated data): Total cereals 1,504.7 in 2011, 1,357.0 in 2012, 1,728.3 in 2013; Total roots and tubers 1,379.2 in 2011, 1,312.7 in 2012, 1,332.0 in 2013; Total vegetables (incl. melons) 972.7 in 2011, 1,015.6 in 2012, 1,077.5 in 2013; Total fruits (excl. melons) 221.8 in 2011, 230.5 in 2012, 241.8 in 2013.

Source: FAO.

LIVESTOCK
('000 head at 1 January)

	2011	2012	2013
Horses	389.0	398.8	407.4
Asses	71	73	77
Cattle	1,338.6	1,367.5	1,404.1
Pigs	59.2	55.9	51.8
Sheep	4,314.7	4,490.1	4,680.8
Goats	973.4	933.7	960.4
Chickens	4,490	3,665	3,793
Turkeys	166	175	188

Source: FAO.

LIVESTOCK PRODUCTS
('000 metric tons)

	2011	2012	2013
Cattle meat	98.7	97.1	98.6
Sheep meat	41.1	43.1*	43.8*
Goat meat	9.0	8.0*	8.1*
Pig meat	16.3	16.1	16.3
Horse meat	18.8	21.6	21.8
Chicken meat	6.1	6.1	6.2
Cows' milk	1,321.7	1,350.1	1,374.1
Hen eggs*	21.9	23.0	23.6
Honey	1.2	1.7	1.6
Wool, greasy	11.1	10.8	11.6

* Unofficial figure(s).
Source: FAO.

Forestry

ROUNDWOOD REMOVALS
('000 cubic metres, excl. bark, FAO estimates)

	2008	2009	2010
Sawlogs, veneer logs and logs for sleepers	4.7	4.7	4.7
Other industrial wood	4.7	4.7	4.7
Fuel wood	18.0	28.5	36.6
Total	27.4	37.9	46.0

2011–13: Figures assumed to be unchanged from 2010 (FAO estimates).
Source: FAO.

SAWNWOOD PRODUCTION
('000 cubic metres, incl. railway sleepers, unofficial figures)

	2011	2012	2013
Coniferous (softwood) . . .	42.9	96.0	86.0
Broadleaved (hardwood) . . .	42.9	2.0	2.0
Total	85.8	98.0	88.0

Source: FAO.

Fishing

(metric tons, live weight)

	2010	2011	2012
Capture	27	27	27
Common carp	15	15	15
Silver carp	3	3	3
Goldfish	3	3	3
Aquaculture	352*	395*	297
Common carp	132*	245	144
Grass carp	12	40	46
Silver carp	40*	82	79
Rainbow trout	168*	11	11
Total catch	379*	422*	324

* FAO estimate.
Source: FAO.

Mining

('000 metric tons unless otherwise indicated)

	2011	2012	2013
Coal	830.7	1,106.7	1,424.6
Crude petroleum	89.9	78.9	83.7
Natural gas (million cu m) . .	26.6	28.5	32.5

Gold (metric tons): 19.7 in 2011; 11.3 in 2012; 20.2 in 2013 (Source: Thomson Reuters GFMS, *Gold Survey 2014*).

Industry

SELECTED PRODUCTS
('000 metric tons unless otherwise indicated)

	2011	2012	2013
Vegetable oil	15.1	14.0	27.8
Refined sugar	17.0	13.3	25.2
Vodka ('000 hl)	15.6	15.7	16.0
Beer ('000 hl)	21.2	21.9	23.9
Cigarettes (million)	2,446.6	1,688.2	935.4
Textile fabrics ('000 sq m) . .	727.9	704.5	337.2
Footwear	5,024.0	2,599.1	2,051.9
Motor spirit (petrol)	15.0	10.5	9.0
Gas-diesel (distillate fuel) oil . .	28.4	30.5	27.2
Residual fuel oils (mazout) . .	43.7	39.5	41.4
Cement	1,016.6	1,238.7	1,682.7
Electric energy (million kWh) .	15,158.0	15,166.4	14,011.0

Finance

CURRENCY AND EXCHANGE RATES

Monetary Units
100 tiyiyns = 1 som.

Sterling, Dollar and Euro Equivalents (31 December 2014)
£1 sterling = 91.910 soms;
US $1 = 58.887 soms;
€1 = 71.494 soms;
1,000 soms = £10.88 = $16.98 = €13.99.

Average Exchange Rate (soms per US $)
2012   47.004
2013   48.438
2014   53.654

BUDGET
(million soms)*

Revenue†	2011	2012	2013
Taxation	53,017.4	63,911.4	72,842.4
Corporate income taxes . . .	2,652.8	2,761.0	1,840.7
Personal income taxes . .	8,402.6	11,232.4	11,812.6
Value-added tax	20,352.9	25,769.3	30,083.2
Excise taxes	2,187.0	2,826.7	4,089.7
Taxes on international trade and transactions	7,146.8	9,429.5	11,886.2
Other current revenue	15,654.8	17,248.7	19,754.8
Capital revenue	456.1	236.0	136.3
Total	69,128.3	81,396.2	92,733.5

Expenditure‡	2011	2012	2013
Current expenditure	82,393.8	100,019.0	86,600.7
General public services . . .	10,121.0	10,906.6	10,775.5
Defence and public security .	9,719.0	9,957.6	11,355.9
Economic affairs	15,370.3	22,228.8	3,842.1
Environmental protection . .	562.0	507.4	506.8
Education	18,231.3	21,685.5	21,701.9
Health care	9,079.9	11,369.0	11,828.6
Social insurance and security .	14,182.5	17,490.1	20,356.5
Housing and public utilities .	2,893.3	3,441.9	3,547.4
Cultural and religious activity .	2,234.5	2,432.1	2,685.9
Capital expenditure	8,944.5	7,217.5	17,668.1
Total	91,338.3	107,236.5	104,268.8

* Figures represent a consolidation of the budgetary transactions of the central Government and local governments. The operations of extra-budgetary accounts, including the Social Fund (formed in 1994 by an amalgamation of the Pension Fund, the Unemployment Fund and the Social Insurance Fund), are excluded.
† Excluding grants received (million soms): 8,672.3 in 2011; 5,608.3 in 2012; 9,189.2 in 2013.
‡ Excluding lending minus repayments (million soms): 15,960.8 in 2011; 17,323.8 in 2012; 5,869.9 in 2013.

Source: National Bank of the Kyrgyz Republic.

INTERNATIONAL RESERVES
(US $ million at 31 December)

	2012	2013	2014
Gold	162.9	139.8	152.7
IMF special drawing rights . .	185.8	198.0	180.8
Foreign exchange	1,717.3	1,900.6	1,623.9
Total	2,066.0	2,238.4	1,957.4

Source: IMF, *International Financial Statistics*.

MONEY SUPPLY
(million soms at 31 December)

	2005	2006	2007
Currency outside banks . . .	13,065	19,410	26,675
Demand deposits at banking institutions	2,123	3,655	5,669
Total money	15,188	23,065	32,343

Source: IMF, *International Financial Statistics*.

COST OF LIVING
(Consumer Price Index; base: 1995 = 100)

	2011	2012	2013
Food and non-alcoholic drinks .	800.2	784.0	825.6
Non-food products	399.1	439.5	471.9
All items (incl. others) . . .	691.5	710.6	757.9

Source: Asian Development Bank.

NATIONAL ACCOUNTS
(million soms at current prices)

Expenditure on the Gross Domestic Product

	2011	2012	2013
Government final consumption expenditure	52,128.5	60,687.8	63,272.5
Private final consumption expenditure	238,522.0	295,115.7	331,119.4
Changes in inventories . . .	4,214.7	12,726.7	13,101.2
Gross fixed capital formation .	68,635.2	85,790.8	106,920.5
Total domestic expenditure	363,500.4	454,321.0	514,413.6
Exports of goods and services .	155,974.1	150,532.6	165,100.8
Less Imports of goods and services	233,485.4	303,428.5	335,738.6
Statistical discrepancy	—	2,925.0	6,252.6
GDP in market prices . . .	285,989.1	304,350.1	350,028.4

Gross Domestic Product by Economic Activity

	2011	2012	2013
Agriculture, forestry and fishing .	47,361.0	53,166.2	53,125.3
Mining	2,169.5	4,085.5	2,437.4
Manufacturing	52,454.6	37,940.0	46,736.2
Electricity, gas and water supply .	9,684.1	9,154.9	7,150.0
Construction	14,078.3	17,234.2	23,644.5
Wholesale and retail trade; repair of motor vehicles, motorcycles and personal and household goods	43,368.5	49,193.4	56,455.9
Transport and communication .	23,278.7	26,140.1	33,273.5
Financial intermediation . . .	9,956.0	11,581.0	12,516.4
Public administration and defence; compulsory social security . .	14,543.7	15,494.5	17,740.2
Others*	45,871.7	49,116.1	57,536.3
Sub-total	262,766.1	273,105.9	310,615.7
Less Financial intermediation services indirectly measured .	8,344.6	9,614.0	10,824.2
Gross value added in basic prices	254,421.5	263,491.9	299,791.5
Taxes, less subsidies, on products .	31,567.6	40,858.2	50,236.9
GDP in market prices . . .	285,989.1	304,350.1	350,028.4

* Including hotels and restaurants; real estate, renting and business activities; education; health and social work; and other community, social and personal services.

Source: Asian Development Bank.

BALANCE OF PAYMENTS
(US $ million)

	2011	2012	2013
Exports of goods	2,267.0	1,954.4	2,048.4
Imports of goods	−3,935.9	−5165.1	−5,613.6
Balance on goods	−1,669.0	−3,210.7	−3,565.2
Exports of services	860.2	966.6	1,042.7
Imports of services	−963.9	−1,323.1	−1,109.2
Balance on goods and services	−1,772.6	−3,567.2	−3,631.7
Primary income received . . .	31.6	29.7	40.1
Primary income paid	−690.8	−199.0	−330.6
Balance on goods, services and primary income	−2,431.7	−3,736.6	−3,922.2
Secondary income received . .	2,044.1	2,339.2	2,610.7
Secondary income paid . . .	−205.4	−277.7	−372.7
Current balance	−593.0	−1,675.1	−1,684.2

—*continued*	2011	2012	2013
Capital account (net) . . .	64.1	166.1	280.3
Direct investment assets . .	0.1	−0.3	—
Direct investment liabilities . .	693.5	292.7	757.6
Portfolio investment assets .	−5.8	5.6	6.2
Portfolio investment liabilities .	5.5	0.1	−1.4
Financial derivatives and employee stock options (net)	—	−0.4	−0.1
Other investment assets . . .	−232.1	138.1	−113.0
Other investment liabilities . .	399.2	433.0	289.0
Net errors and omissions . . .	−224.1	831.9	731.1
Reserves and related items .	107.3	191.7	265.5

Source: IMF, *International Financial Statistics*.

External Trade

PRINCIPAL COMMODITIES
(distribution by HS, US $ million)

Imports c.i.f.	2011	2012	2013
Vegetable products	166.3	190.7	214.5
Prepared foodstuffs, beverages and tobacco	376.3	590.4	447.4
Mineral products	1,002.2	1,237.4	1,378.9
Products of chemical or allied industries	405.1	478.8	523.8
Plastics, rubber and articles thereof	172.2	215.0	274.7
Textiles and fabrics . . .	296.0	375.3	370.7
Metals and articles thereof . .	284.9	424.4	556.4
Machinery, electrical equipment and parts	485.8	642.9	713.1
Vehicles and transport equipment	482.0	709.9	782.9
Total (incl. others)	4,261.2	5,576.3	6,069.8

Exports f.o.b.	2011	2012	2013
Live animals and animal products	38.5	33.9	30.7
Vegetable products	138.5	147.6	170.0
Prepared foodstuffs, beverages and tobacco	46.3	42.9	43.7
Mineral products	216.5	240.7	206.9
Products of chemical or allied industries	49.1	57.7	48.2
Raw hides and skins, leather, fur, travel articles and bags . . .	12.0	10.7	11.6
Textiles and fabrics	189.0	204.6	140.5
Natural and cultured pearls, precious and semi-precious stones, precious metals and products, and coins	1,017.1	569.0	742.7
Metals and articles thereof . .	70.6	74.7	83.5
Machinery, electrical equipment and parts	55.7	71.0	78.8
Vehicles and transport equipment	69.4	140.2	100.0
Total (incl. others)	2,242.2	1,927.6	2,019.6

PRINCIPAL TRADING PARTNERS
(US $ million)

Imports c.i.f.	2011	2012	2013
Belarus	109.5	151.8	116.7
Canada	22.4	28.1	17.0
China, People's Republic (incl. Hong Kong)	923.5	1,214.9	1,452.8
Germany	144.6	197.8	232.9
Japan	164.5	216.1	245.0
Kazakhstan	411.4	698.6	569.9
Korea, Republic	63.2	86.2	104.6
Netherlands	40.9	60.1	57.0
Russia	1,429.6	1,816.6	2,040.3
Turkey	117.1	175.6	211.1
Ukraine	124.9	141.2	158.1
USA	210.3	251.4	222.9
Uzbekistan	84.3	67.5	96.9
Total (incl. others)	4,261.2	5,576.3	6,069.8

Exports f.o.b.	2011	2012	2013
Afghanistan	23.5	25.8	12.5
China, People's Republic (incl. Hong Kong)	42.0	61.4	35.9
Kazakhstan	289.7	394.7	395.6
Russia	284.4	219.1	153.5
Switzerland	873.6	547.9	513.2
Tajikistan	36.3	39.7	51.7
Turkey	54.5	50.2	85.8
United Arab Emirates	150.0	16.1	222.0
USA	0.6	3.0	4.0
Uzbekistan	124.4	190.1	163.5
Total (incl. others)	2,242.2	1,927.6	2,019.6

Transport

RAILWAYS
(traffic)

	2011	2012	2013
Paying passengers ('000 journeys).	596.9	549.2	407.0
Passenger-km (million) . . .	82.8	75.8	55.5
Freight carried ('000 metric tons) .	1,033.7	1,119.3	1,360.6
Freight net ton-km (million) . .	798.3	922.7	1,001.7

ROAD TRAFFIC
(vehicles in use at 31 December)

	2005	2006	2007
Passenger cars	201,430	218,718	229,735
Motorcycles and mopeds . . .	10,059	9,948	9,099

2010: Passenger cars 342,439; Motorcycles and mopeds 6,443.

Source: IRF, *World Road Statistics*.

CIVIL AVIATION
(traffic on scheduled services)

	2011	2012	2013
Passengers carried ('000) . . .	707.9	823.9	1,050.2
Passenger-km (million) . . .	1,400.4	1,601.6	2,099.4
Freight carried (metric tons) . .	1,300	700	500
Total ton-km (million)	111.0	99.2	109.9

Tourism

FOREIGN VISITOR ARRIVALS
('000 persons, selected countries)

Country of residence	2011	2012	2013
China, People's Republic . . .	25.3	24.1	30.1
Germany	8.6	11.7	9.2
Kazakhstan	865.0	1,675.6	2,156.0
Korea, Republic	3.7	5.7	3.7
Russia	1,020.6	364.6	448.9
Turkey	15.7	18.4	25.4
Uzbekistan	212.2	158.6	190.5
Total (incl. others)	2,277.5	2,406.0	3,076.0

Tourism receipts (US $ million, excl. passenger transport): 284 in 2010; 640 in 2011; 435 in 2012 (Source: World Tourism Organization).

Communications Media

	2011	2012	2013
Telephones (main lines in use) .	502,020	488,853	461,277
Mobile cellular telephones ('000			
subscribers)	6,277.1	6,797.9	6,737.5
Internet subscribers ('000) . .	115.1	n.a.	n.a.
Broadband subscribers . . .	36,960	48,114	53,346
Book production (incl. brochures):			
titles	1,070	1,080	1,149
copies ('000)	1,705.1	2,207.2	2,362.1
Newspapers (incl. periodicals):			
titles	195	181	185
copies ('000)	37,900	34,100	30,600
Magazines:			
titles	48	44	45
copies ('000)	463.7	219.9	207.4

Source: partly International Telecommunication Union.

Education

(2013)

	Institutions	Teachers	Students
Pre-primary	927	4,492	132,481
Primary and Secondary: general .	2,207	74,407	1,027,123
Secondary: vocational . . .	241	10,635	121,016
Higher (all institutions) . . .	55	14,059	223,241

Pupil-teacher ratio (primary education, UNESCO estimate): 23.9 in 2011/12 (Source: UNESCO Institute for Statistics).

Adult literacy rate (UNESCO estimates): 99.2% (males 99.5%; females 99.0%) in 2009 (Source: UNESCO Institute for Statistics).

Directory

The Government

HEAD OF STATE

President: ALMAZBEK ATAMBAYEV (elected 30 October 2011, inaugurated 1 December).

THE GOVERNMENT
(May 2015)

The Government comprises independents, and members of the following parties: the Ata Meken Partiyasy (Ata Meken); the Ar-Namys Partiyasy (Ar-Namys); the Kyrgyzstandyn Sotsial-Demokratiyalyk Partiyasy (KSDP); and the Respublika Sayasiy Partiyasy (Respublika).

Prime Minister: TEMIR SARIYEV (Independent).

First Deputy Prime Minister: TAIYRBEK SARPASHEV (Independent).

Deputy Prime Minister: ABDYRAKHMAN MAMATALIYEV (Ar-Namys).

Deputy Prime Minister: VALERIY DIL (Ar-Namys).

Deputy Prime Minister: DAMIRA NIYAZALIYEVA (KSDP).

Minister, Head of the Government Staff: NURKHANBEK MOMUNALIYEV (Independent).

Minister of Foreign Affairs: ERLAN ABDYLDAYEV (Independent).

Minister of Defence: ABIBILLA KUDAIBERDIYEV (Independent).

Minister of Internal Affairs: MELIS TURGANBAYEV (acting) (Independent).

Minister of Justice: JYLDYZ MAMBETALIYEVA (Independent).

Minister of Finance: ADYLBEK KASYMALIYEV (Independent).

Minister of the Economy: OLEG PANKRATOV (Independent).

Minister of Agriculture and Land Reclamation: TAALAIBEK AIDARALIYEV (Ar-Namys).

Minister of Transport and Communications: ARGYNBEK MALABAYEV (Independent).

Minister of Emergency Situations: KUBATBEK BORONOV (Respublika).

Minister of Energy and Industry: KUBANYCHBEK TURDUBAYEV (KSDP).

Minister of Education and Science: ELVIRA SARIYEVA (KSDP).

Minister of Health: TALANTBEK BATYRALIYEV (Independent).

Minister of Culture, Information and Tourism: ALTYNBEK MAKSUTOV (Independent).

Minister of Social Development: KUDAIBERGEN BAZARBAYEV (Ata Meken).

Minister of Labour, Migration and Youth: AYBEK AZYRANKULOV (KSDP).

Chairman of the State Committee for National Security: BUSURMANKUL TABALDIYEV (Independent).

MINISTRIES

Office of the President: 720003 Bishkek, pr. Chui 205; tel. (312) 63-89-20; e-mail psp@adm.gov.kg; internet www.president.kg.

Office of the Government: 720003 Bishkek, Dom Pravitelstva; tel. (312) 66-49-23; e-mail ps@mail.gov.kg; internet www.gov.kg.

Ministry of Agriculture and Land Reclamation: 720040 Bishkek, Kiyevskaya 96A; tel. (312) 62-36-16; fax (312) 62-36-22; e-mail agroprod@agroprod.kg; internet www.agroprod.kg.

Ministry of Culture, Information and Tourism: 720026 Bishkek, Pushkina 78; tel. (312) 62-04-82; fax (312) 62-35-89; e-mail info@mincultinfo.kg; internet www.minculture.gov.kg.

Ministry of Defence: 720001 Bishkek, Logvinenko 26; tel. (312) 66-18-04; fax (312) 66-19-04; e-mail udmo@list.ru; internet www.mil.kg.

Ministry of the Economy: 720002 Bishkek, pr. Chui 106; tel. (312) 62-52-41; fax (312) 66-18-37; e-mail mail@mineconom.kg; internet www.mineconom.kg.

Ministry of Education and Science: 720040 Bishkek, Tynystanova 257; tel. (312) 62-24-42; e-mail minedukg@gmail.com; internet edu.gov.kg.

Ministry of Emergency Situations: 720055 Bishkek, Toktonaliyeva 2/1; tel. (312) 54-79-86; fax (3222) 5-60-77; e-mail mchs@elcat .kg; internet mes.kg.

Ministry of Energy and Industry: 720055 Bishkek, Akhunbayeva 119; tel. (312) 56-18-22; fax (312) 56-20-28; internet energo.gov.kg.

Ministry of Finance: 720040 Bishkek, bul. Erkindik 58; tel. (312) 66-12-27; fax (312) 66-16-45; e-mail minfin@mf.gov.kg; internet www .minfin.kg.

Ministry of Foreign Affairs: 720040 Bishkek, bul. Erkindik 57; tel. (312) 62-05-45; fax (312) 66-05-01; e-mail gendep@mfa.gov.kg; internet www.mfa.kg.

Ministry of Health: 720040 Bishkek, Moskovskaya 148; tel. (312) 62-26-80; fax (312) 66-07-17; e-mail mz@med.kg; internet www.med .kg.

Ministry of Internal Affairs: 720000 Bishkek, Frunze 469; tel. (312) 66-24-50; fax (312) 26-62-80; e-mail pressa@mvd.kg; internet www.mvd.kg.

Ministry of Justice: 720010 Bishkek, M. Gandi 32; tel. (312) 65-64-90; fax (312) 65-65-02; e-mail minjust.ep@mail.ru; internet www .minjust.gov.kg.

Ministry of Labour, Migration and Youth: 720000 Bishkek, Razzakova 8/1; tel. (312) 30-02-32; e-mail manas-ordo.kg@mail.ru; internet www.mz.kg.

Ministry of Social Development: 720000 Bishkek, ul. Tynystanova 215; tel. (312) 66-34-00; fax (312) 66-57-24; e-mail mlsp@mlsp .kg; internet www.mlsp.kg.

Ministry of Transport and Communications: 720017 Bishkek, Isanova 42; tel. (312) 31-43-85; fax (312) 31-28-11; e-mail mtk@mtk .gov.kg; internet mtc.gov.kg.

President

Presidential Election, 30 October 2011

Candidates	Votes	%
Almazbek Atambayev	1,161,929	62.52
Adahan Madumarov	274,639	14.78
Kamchibek Tashiyev	266,189	14.32
Others	104,311	5.61
Against all candidates	13,419	0.72
Total*	1,858,632	100.00

* Including 38,145 invalid votes (2.05% of the total).

Legislature

**Supreme Council
(Jogorku Kenesh)**

720053 Bishkek, Abdymomunov 207; tel. (312) 61-16-04; fax (312) 62-50-12; e-mail zs@kenesh.gov.kg; internet www.kenesh.kg.

Chairman: ASILBEK JEENBEKOV.

General Election, 10 October 2010

Parties	Votes	%*	Seats
Ata-Jurt Partiyasy	257,100	15.31	28
Kyrgyzstandyn Sotsial-Demokratiyalyk Partiyasy	237,634	14.15	26
Ar-Namys Partiyasy	229,916	13.69	25
Respublika Sayasiy Partiyasy	210,594	12.54	23
Ata Meken Partiyasy	166,714	9.93	18
Butun Kyrgyzstan Sayasiy Partiyasy	139,548	8.31	—
Others	427,365	25.44	—
Against all	10,839	0.65	—
Total valid votes	1,679,710	100.00	120

* Parties were required to obtain the support of at least 5% of the total registered electorate (3,036,703 persons) in order to be eligible for legislative representation. (Some 44.69% of the registered electorate either did not participate or cast invalid votes.) The results announced by the Central Commission for Elections and Referendums presented the share of the vote received by each party as a proportion of the total electorate, rather than of the valid votes cast. The five parties that obtained legislative representation received the support of the following share of the total electorate: Ata-Jurt 8.47%; KSDP 7.83%; Ar-Namys 7.57%; Respublika 6.93%; Ata Meken 5.49%.

Election Commission

Central Commission for Elections and Referendums (Shailoo Jana Referendum Otkoruu Boyuncha Borborduk Komissiyasy): 720040 Bishkek, ul. Razzakova 59; tel. (312) 62-68-25; fax (312) 66-58-60; e-mail cec@shailoo.gov.kg; internet www.shailoo.gov.kg; independent govt organ; one-third of mems nominated by President; Chair. TUIGUNAALY ABDRAIMOV.

Political Organizations

A total of 29 parties contested the legislative elections held in October 2010. The following were among the most important operating in early 2015.

Ar-Namys Partiyasy (Ar-Namys) (Dignity Political Party): 720000 Bishkek, Pushkin 135; tel. (312) 61-04-07; internet www .ar-namys.org; f. 1999; Chair. FELIKS KULOV; c. 11,000 mems.

Ata-Jurt Partiyasy (Ata-Jurt) (Homeland Idealistic Democratic Political Party): 720000 Bishkek, Chygysh-5 33/3; tel. (312) 89-01-50; e-mail iyikatajurt@gmail.com; internet atajurt.org; f. 2004; nationalist; Chair. KAMCHYBEK TASHIYEV (imprisoned).

Ata Meken Partiyasy (Ata Meken) (Fatherland Socialist Political Party): 720040 Bishkek, Ibraimova 108; tel. (312) 89-55-12; fax (312) 66-46-38; e-mail pr@atameken.kg; f. 1992; nationalist, socialist; supports state control of the economy and parliamentary system of govt; Chair. OMURBEK TEKEBAYEV; more than 2,000 mems.

Butun Kyrgyzstan Sayasiy Partiyasy (Butun Kyrgyzstan) (United Kyrgyzstan Political Party): 720000 Bishkek, Turusbekov 109/1; tel. (312) 39-40-48; fax (312) 39-40-70; e-mail pressa@bytyn .kg; internet bytyn.kg; f. 2010; supportive of former President Bakiyev; Chair. ADAHAN MADUMAROV.

Kyrgyzstan Kommunistterinin Partiyasy (KKP) (Party of Communists of Kyrgyzstan): 720001 Bishkek, pr. Chui 114/206; tel. (312) 62-49-99; fax (312) 67-02-55; disbanded 1991, re-established 1992, re-registered 2007; successor to the Communist Party of Kyrgyz SSR; Chair. KLARA AJIBEKOVA; 20,000 mems.

Kyrgyzstandyn Sotsial-Demokratiyalyk Partiyasy (KSDP) (Social Democratic Party of Kyrgyzstan): 720000 Bishkek, Shabdan Batyr 46D; tel. (312) 53-16-84; fax (312) 53-16-87; e-mail sdpkkenesh@gmail.com; internet www.sdpk.kg; f. 1993; supports parliamentary system of govt; Chair. ALMAZBEK ATAMBAYEV.

Meken Yntymagy Sayasiy Partiyasy (Meken Yntymagy) (Harmonious Fatherland Party): Bishkek; f. 2010; represents interests of Kyrgyz diaspora; Leader TEMIRBEK ASANBEKOV.

Onuguu–Progress Sayasiy Partiyasy (Onuguu—Progress) (Progress Political Party): 722040, Bishkek, Razzakova 100; tel. (312) 66-38-48; internet www.onuguu.kg; f. 2013; represents interests of southern regions of Kyrgyzstan; Leader BAKYT TOROBAYEV.

Respublika Sayasiy Partiyasy (Respublika) (Republic Political Party): 720000 Bishkek, Toktogula 126; tel. (312) 66-31-21; e-mail pr@republic.kg; internet www.republic.kg; f. 2010; supportive of fmr Pres. Bakiyev; Leader OMURBEK BABANOV.

Uluttar Birimdigi Eldik Partiyasy (Uluttar Birimdigi) (Unity of Ethnicities People's Party): Osh; represents interests of southern regions of Kyrgyzstan; Leader MELISBEK MYRZAKMATOV.

Zamadash Sayasiy Partiyasy (Zamandash-Sovremennik) (Contemporary Political Party): 720001 Bishkek, Turusbekov 118; tel. (312) 34-02-08; fax (312) 34-01-88; e-mail partiya.zamandash@ gmail.com; internet zamandash.kg; f. 2010; represents interests of Kyrgyz diaspora; Co-Chair. EMILBEK OMURAKUNOV, SHER-NIYAZ SADYK.

Diplomatic Representation

EMBASSIES IN KYRGYZSTAN

Azerbaijan: 720040 Bishkek, Shurukova 41; tel. (312) 51-07-70; fax (312) 51-31-72; e-mail bishkek@mission.mfa.az; Ambassador HIDAYAT HUDUSH ORUJOV.

Belarus: 720040 Bishkek, Moskovskaya 210; tel. (312) 35-28-35; fax (312) 35-34-33; e-mail kyrgyzstan@mfa.gov.by; internet www .kyrgyzstan.mfa.gov.by; Ambassador VIKTAR DZYANISENKA.

China, People's Republic: 720016 Bishkek, pr. Mira 299/7; tel. (312) 59-74-86; fax (312) 59-74-84; e-mail chinaemb_kg@mfa.gov.cn; internet kg.chineseembassy.org; Ambassador QI DAYU.

Germany: 720040 Bishkek, Razzakova 28; tel. (312) 90-50-00; fax (312) 30-07-43; internet www.bischkek.diplo.de; Ambassador GUDRUN SRÄGA.

India: 720010 Bishkek, Mahatma Gandkhi 100A; tel. (312) 97-92-56; fax (312) 97-92-55; e-mail cons.bishkek@mea.gov.in; internet www .embassyofindia.kg; Ambassador JAYANT KHOBRAGADE.

Iran: 720026 Bishkek, Razzakova 36; tel. (312) 62-12-81; fax (312) 66-02-09; e-mail embiran@mail.kg; internet bishkek.mfa.ir; Ambassador ALI NADJAFI.

Japan: 720040 Bishkek, Razzakova 16; tel. (312) 30-00-50; fax (312) 30-00-52; internet www.kg.emb-japan.go.jp; Ambassador TAKAYUKI KOIKE.

Kazakhstan: 720044 Bishkek, pr. Mira 95 A; tel. (312) 69-20-98; fax (312) 69-20-94; e-mail kaz_emb@elcat.kg; internet www.kaz-emb.kg; Ambassador AIYMDOS BOZHIGITOV.

Korea, Republic: 720005 Bishkek, Akhunbaeva 35; tel. (312) 57-97-71; fax (312) 57-97-74; e-mail korea.kg@gmail.com; internet kgz .mofat.go.kr; Ambassador (vacant).

Qatar: 720011 Bishkek, Isanova 123–125; tel. (312)32-35-55; fax (312) 32-39-00; e-mail ashawi@mofa.gov.qa; Ambassador MUHAMMAD BIN ARAR AL-NUAIMI.

Pakistan: 720033 Bishkek, Serova 37; tel. (312) 37-39-01; fax (312) 37-39-05; internet www.mofa.gov.pk/kyrgyzstan; Ambassador ABDUL MATIN HAN.

Russian Federation: 720001 Bishkek, Manas 55; tel. (312) 61-09-05; fax (312) 90-33-84; e-mail rusemb@infotel.kg; internet www .kyrgyz.mid.ru; Ambassador ANDREI A. KRUTKO.

Saudi Arabia: 720040 Bishkek, Frunze 503; tel. (312) 32-56-08; fax (312) 32-48-79; Ambassador ABD AL-RAHMAN AL-JUMAH.

Switzerland: 720040 Bishkek, bul. Erkindik 21; tel. (312) 30-10-36; fax (312) 30-36-77; e-mail bik.vertretung@eda.admin.ch; internet www.eda.admin.ch/bishkek; Ambassador RENÉ HOLENSTEIN.

Tajikistan: 720031 Bishkek, Karadarynskaya 36; tel. (312) 51-23-43; e-mail tjemb@ktnet.kg; internet www.tajikemb.kg; Ambassador OLIM S. RAHIMOV.

Turkey: 720040 Bishkek, Moskovskaya 89; tel. (312) 90-59-00; fax (312) 90-99-13; e-mail embassy.bishkek@mfa.gov.tr; internet bishkek.emb.mfa.gov.tr; Ambassador METIN KILIÇ.

Turkmenistan: Bishkek; Ambassador BATYR G. NIYAZLIYEV.

Ukraine: 720040 Bishkek, bul. Akhunbayeva 201; tel. (312) 25-17-67; fax (312) 25-17-80; e-mail emb@mfa.gov.ua; internet kirgizia .mfa.gov.ua; Chargé d'affaires a.i. MYKOLA A. YAREMCHUK.

United Kingdom: 720040 Bishkek, bul. Erkindik 21/404; tel. (312) 30-36-37; e-mail ukin.kyrgyzrepublic@fco.gov.uk; Ambassador JUDITH MARGARET FARNWORTH.

USA: 720016 Bishkek, pr. Mira 171; tel. (312) 55-12-41; fax (312) 55-12-64; internet bishkek.usembassy.gov; Chargé d'affaires a.i. RICHARD M. MILES.

Uzbekistan: 720040 Bishkek, Tynystanova 213; tel. (312) 66-20-65; fax (312) 66-44-03; e-mail uzbembish@infotel.kg; internet www .uzbekistan.kg; Ambassador KOMIL K. RASHIDOV.

Judicial System

Supreme Court: 720000 Bishkek, Orozbekova 37; tel. (312) 66-33-18; fax (312) 66-29-46; e-mail scourt@bishkek.gov.kg; incl. Constitutional Chamber; Chair. FERUZA DJAMASHEVA.

Office of the Prosecutor-General: 720040 Bishkek; Prosecutor-General INDIRA JOLDUBAEVA.

Religion

ISLAM

The majority of Kyrgyz are Sunni Muslims (Hanafi school), as are the Uzbeks and Tajiks living in Kazakhstan.

Chief Mufti of the Muslims of Kyrgyzstan: MAKSATBEK TOKTOMUSHEV, 720000 Bishkek.

International Islamic Centre of Kyrgyzstan: 714018 Osh; Pres. Haji SADYKJAN KAMALUDDIN.

CHRISTIANITY

Roman Catholic Church

The Church is represented in Kyrgyzstan by an Apostolic Administration, established in March 2006. There were an estimated 500 adherents in the country at 31 December 2007.

Apostolic Administrator of Kyrgyzstan: Most Rev. NIKOLAUS MESSMER (Titular Bishop of Carmeiano), 720040 Bishkek, Mayakovskogo 25; tel. (312) 28-50-03; fax (312) 67-03-92; e-mail nikmessmer@hotmail.com; internet www.catholic-kyrgyzstan.org.

Russian Orthodox Church (Moscow Patriarchate)

The Russian Orthodox Church (Moscow Patriarchate) in Kyrgyzstan comes under the jurisdiction of the Eparchy of Tashkent and Central Asia, based in Uzbekistan.

The Press

In 2012 there were 181 newspapers, with an average circulation of 34,100, and 44 magazines, with an average circulation of 194,300.

PRINCIPAL NEWSPAPERS

Bishkek Observer: 720001 Bishkek, Ibraimova 105; tel. (312) 28-95-96; fax (312) 29-28-21; e-mail dssuri@elcat.kg; f. 2000; weekly; independent; in English; Editor AVTAR SINGH.

Bishkek Taims (Bishkek Times): 720040 Bishkek, Pushkina 70; tel. (312) 62-15-70; fax (312) 62-15-68; e-mail b-times@yandex.ru; internet www.presskg.com/bt; Editor-in-Chief NURALY KAPAROV.

Delo N°... (Case Number...): 720000 Bishkek, Frunze 282A; tel. (312) 43-11-21; fax (312) 43-11-25; e-mail delonom@ktnet.kg; internet delo.kg; f. 1991; weekly; in Russian; independent; politics, crime; Editor S. KRASILNIKOVA; circ. 40,000.

Erkin Too (Free Mountain): 720040 Bishkek, Ibraimova 24; tel. (312) 59-15-30; fax (312) 59-16-31; f. 1991; 2 a week; organ of the Govt; publishes laws, presidential, parliamentary and govt decrees, and other legal documents; in Kyrgyz; Chief Editor ABDUVAKHAB MONIYEV; circ. 10,000.

Gazeta.kg: 720000 Bishkek; e-mail info@gazeta.kg; internet gazeta .kg; online only, in Russian and English; independent; politics and analysis of current affairs; culture; regional news; f. 2003; Chief Editor ANTON NOSIK.

Kyrgyz Madaniyaty (Kyrgyz Culture): 720301 Bishkek, Bokonbayeva 99; tel. (312) 26-14-58; f. 1967; weekly; organ of the Union of Writers; Editor NURALY KAPAROV; circ. 15,940.

Kyrgyz Rukhu: 720040 Bishkek, Abdymomunova 193; tel. (312) 62-76-60; fax (312) 66-11-60; f. 1991; weekly; in Kyrgyz; Editor-in-Chief BAKBYRBEK ALENOV; circ. 7,000.

Kyrgyz Tuusu (Flag of Kyrgyzstan): 720040 Bishkek, Abdymomunova 193; tel. (312) 62-20-29; fax (312) 62-20-25; e-mail tuusu@infotel .kg; f. 1924; fmrly *Sovettik Kyrgyzstan*; daily; organ of the Govt; in Kyrgyz; Chief Editor KYAZ MOLDOKASYMOV; circ. 20,000.

Limon (Lemon): 720040 Bishkek, Moskovskaya 189; tel. (312) 45-66-72; fax (312) 65-02-04; e-mail limon@akipress.org; internet www .limon.kg; f. 1994; in Russian; youth newspaper; Editor-in-Chief VENERA JAMONA KULOVA.

MSN—Moya Stolitsa—Novosti (My Capital City—News): 720001 Bishkek, Turusbekova 47; tel. (312) 48-62-15; fax (312) 48-61-24; e-mail city@infotel.kg; internet www.msn.kg; f. 2001; independent; 3 a week; in Russian; Editor-in-Chief ALEXANDER KIM; circ. 5,000 (Tues. and Thurs.), 50,000 (Fri.).

Slovo Kyrgyzstana (Word of Kyrgyzstan): 720004 Bishkek, Abdymomunova 193; tel. (312) 66-60-88; fax (312) 66-59-28; e-mail slovo@ infotel.kg; f. 1925; daily; organ of the Govt; in Russian; Chief Editor TAMARA SLASHCHEVA.

The Times of Central Asia: 720000 Bishkek, Abdrahmanova 175A; tel. (312) 66-17-37; fax (312) 66-01-67; e-mail edittimes@timesca .com; internet www.timesca.com; f. 1999; weekly; in English; also distributed in Kazakhstan, Turkmenistan, Tajikistan and Uzbekistan, and internationally; Publr GIORGIO FIACCONI.

Vechernii Bishkek (Bishkek Evening News): 720021 Bishkek, Usenbayeva 2; tel. (312) 48-65-65; fax (312) 68-02-68; e-mail webmaster@vb.kg; internet www.vb.kg; f. 1974; daily; independent; in Russian; Editor-in-Chief GENNADII A. KUZMIN; circ. 700,000.

Zaman Kyrgyzstan (Herald of Kyrgyzstan): 720040 Bishkek, Ibraimova 24; tel. (312) 61-46-42; fax (312) 61-46-20; e-mail zamantur@hotmail.com; f. 1992; weekly; independent; in Kyrgyz, Turkish and English; Editor-in-Chief MUSTAFA BASHKURT; circ. 7,500.

PRINCIPAL PERIODICALS

AKIpress: 720010 Bishkek, Moskovskaya 189; tel. and fax (312) 45-54-38; e-mail admin@akipress.org; internet www.akipress.org; f. 1993; monthly; in Russian; independent; analysis of political and economic affairs; Editor-in-Chief SAMAGAN AITYMBETOV; circ. 1,000.

Kut Bilim (Good Knowledge): 720001 Bishkek, Tynystanova 257; tel. (312) 62-04-86; e-mail kutbilim@elcat.kg; internet kb.host.net .kg; f. 1953 as *Mugalimder Gazetasy*; current name adopted 1993; organ of the Ministry of Education and Science; weekly; in Kyrgyz; Editor-in-Chief KUBATBEK CHEKIROV; circ. 6,000.

Literaturnyi Kyrgyzstan (Literary Kyrgyzstan): 720301 Bishkek, Pushkina 70; tel. (312) 626-16-01; e-mail literary_kyrgyzstan@

rambler.ru; f. 1955; journal of the Union of Writers; fiction, literary criticism, journalism; monthly; in Russian; Editor-in-Chief A. I. IVANOV; circ. 3,000.

Zhany Agym (Current): 720021 Bishkek, Usenbayeva 2; tel. (312) 38-67-73; fax (312) 48-61-24; e-mail agym@vb.kg; internet presskg .com/agym; f. 1992 as Agym; renamed as above in 2010; 2 a week; in Kyrgyz; political; Editor-in-Chief ASKER SAKYBAEVA.

NEWS AGENCY

Kabar Kyrgyz News Agency: 720011 Bishkek, Abdrahmanova 175; tel. (312) 62-05-74; fax (312) 66-11-68; e-mail kabar@kabar.kg; internet www.kabar.kg; f. 1937; Dir KUBANYCHBEK A. TAABALDIEV.

Publishers

Ilim (Science): 720071 Bishkek, pr. Chui 265A; tel. (312) 39-20-70; e-mail ilimph@mail.ru; f. 1954; state-owned; scientific and science fiction; Dir L. V. TARASOVA.

Kyrgyz-Russian Slavic University Publishing House (Izdatelstvo Kyrgyzsko-Rossiiskogo slavyanskogo universiteta): 720000 Bishkek, Kiyevskaya 44; tel. (312) 25-53-60; internet www.krsu.edu .kg/Rus/EduIzd.htm; f. 1995; academic works of university staff; textbooks; Dir LARISA V. TARASOVA.

Broadcasting and Communications

National Communications Agency of the Kyrgyz Republic: 720005 Bishkek, Baytik Baatyra 7B; tel. (312) 54-41-03; fax (312) 54-41-05; e-mail nta@infotel.kg; internet www.nas.kg; f. 1997; Dir Gen. SULTAN JUMAGULOV (acting).

TELECOMMUNICATIONS

Kyrgyzstan's telecommunications sector was liberalized in 1998, and competition across all segments of the market has been permitted since 2007. In 2013 there were 461,277 main telephone lines in use, and 6.7m. subscriptions to mobile cellular telephone services.

BiMoKom (Megacom): 720011 Bishkek, ul. Suyumbayeva 123; tel. (312) 90-52-21; fax (312) 90-52-40; e-mail pr@megacom.kg; internet www.megacom.kg; f. 2006; mobile cellular telecommunications services; Dir ANDREI G. SILICH; c. 2.7m. subscribers.

Kyrgyztelekom AO: 720000 Bishkek, pr. Chui 96; tel. (312) 68-16-16; fax (312) 66-24-24; e-mail info@kt.kg; internet www.kt.kg; f. 1993, transformed into joint stock co in 1997; 77.8% state-owned; provides mobile and fixed telephone and internet services; Chair. TALAIBEK S. OROZOV.

Sky Mobile (Beeline Kyrgyzstan): 720011 Bishkek, pr. Chui 121; tel. (775) 58-80-00; fax (312) 90-09-16; e-mail answer@beeline.kg; internet beeline.kg; f. 1997; mobile cellular telecommunications services; 50.1% owned by VympelKom-BiLain (Russia); Dir-Gen. OLEG KLOCHKO; 2.66m. subscribers (Dec. 2013).

BROADCASTING

Radio and Television

Public Broadcasting Corporation of the Kyrgyz Republic (KTRK): 720010 Bishkek, bul. Molodoi Gvardii 59; tel. (312) 39-20-59; fax (312) 39-24-04; e-mail public@ktrk.kg; internet ktrk.kg; f. 1958; fmrly National TV and Radio Broadcasting Corporation of the Kyrgyz Republic; name changed as above in 2010; includes Musyka, Kultura, Balastan channels; Dir-Gen. ILIM M. KARYPBEKOV; 30 mems.

Channel Five: 720031 Bishkek, Ibraimova 24; tel. (312) 54-77-27; fax (312) 54-77-15; e-mail office@koort.kg; f. 1997; fmrly Kyrgyz Public Educational Radio and Television; renamed as above in 2007; broadcasts in Kyrgyz and Russian; educational programmes and entertainment; Gen. Dir AZIMA ABDIMAMINOVA; 103 employees.

Radio

Public Broadcasting Corporation of the Kyrgyz Republic: 720010 Bishkek, bul. Molodoi Gvardii 59; tel. (312) 65-98-18; fax (312) 65-10-64; f. 1931; broadcasts in Kyrgyz, Russian, English, German, Ukrainian, Uzbek, Dungan and Uigur; includes Kyrgyz Radiosu, Birinchi Radio, Min Kyal FM and Dostuk Radio; Dir-Gen. ILIM M. KARYPBEKOV.

Radio Azattyk: 720000 Bishkek; tel. (312) 31-61-53; fax (312) 31-60-80; e-mail djumataevav@rferl.org; internet www.azattyk.org; Kyrgyz language news broadcasts by Radio Free Europe/Radio Liberty (USA—based in the Czech Republic); Dir VENERA JUMATAEVA; Bureau Chief SULTAN KANAZAROV.

Radio Television Pyramid: 720300 Bishkek, Jantosheva 70; tel. and fax (312) 51-15-50; e-mail pyramid@tom.kg; f. 1992; privately

owned; broadcasts to Bishkek and neighbouring regions; Pres. MIRBEK OROZOV.

There are several other private radio stations operating in Kyrgyzstan.

Television

In addition to two state-owned television stations, there are four major private national and six major private regional television stations in Kyrgyzstan.

Kyrgyz Television: 720300 Bishkek, Molodoi Gvardii 63; tel. (312) 25-79-36; fax (312) 25-79-30; subsidiary of Public Broadcasting Corporation of the Kyrgyz Republic (q.v.); Pres. KYYAS MOLDOKASYMOV.

TV Pyramid: 720005 Bishkek, Jantosheva 70; tel. (312) 51-15-50; fax (312) 51-00-12; e-mail pyramid@ss5-22.kyrnet.kg; f. 1991; privately owned; broadcasts to Bishkek and neighbouring regions; Pres. ADYLBEK T. BIINAZAROV.

Finance

(cap. = capital; res = reserves; dep. = deposits; m. = million; br(s). = branch(es); amounts in soms, unless otherwise indicated)

BANKING

Central Bank

National Bank of the Kyrgyz Republic (Kyrgyz Respublikasynyn Uluttuk Banky): 720040 Bishkek, Umetaliyeva 101; tel. (312) 66-90-08; fax (312) 61-07-30; e-mail mail@nbkr.kg; internet www.nbkr .kg; f. 1991, name changed in 1992, and as above in 1993; cap. 300.0m., res 10,331.5m., dep. 27,047.0m. (Dec. 2009); Gov. ZINA ASANKOJOYEVA.

Other Banks

Bank Bakai: 720001 Bishkek, Isanov 77; tel. (312) 61-02-42; fax (312) 61-02-43; e-mail bank@bakai.kg; internet www.bakai.kg; f. 1998; cap. 339.9m., dep. 1,974.7m., total assets 2,525.1m. (Dec. 2013); Chair. AALY B. UMANKULOV; Pres. SERGEI IBRAGIMOV; 5 brs.

BTA Bank: 720040 Bishkek, Moskovskaya 118; tel. (312) 90-50-50; fax (312) 62-45-65; e-mail info@ineximbank.com; internet www.bta .kg; f. 1996; name changed as above 2008; cap. 1,000.0m., res 118.8m., dep. 1,917.9m. (Dec. 2012); Chair. of Bd MURAT KUNAKUNOV; 4 brs.

Commercial Bank Kyrgyzstan: 720001 Bishkek, Togolok Moldo 54A; tel. (312) 21-95-98; fax (312) 61-02-20; e-mail akb@bankkg.kg; internet www.bankkg.kg; f. 1991; name changed as above in 2006; cap. 521.1m., res 0.02m., dep. 3,814.2m. (Dec. 2012); Chair. ABIROV NURBEK; 29 brs.

Demir Kyrgyz International Bank (DKIB): 720001 Bishkek, pr. Chui 245; tel. (312) 61-04-44; fax (312) 66-64-44; e-mail demir@ demirbank.kg; internet www.demirbank.kg; f. 1997; cap. 132.5m., res 4.3m., dep. 8,365.4m. (Dec. 2012); Gen. Man. L. SEVKI SARILAR; 5 brs.

Kyrgyz Investment and Credit Bank: 720001 Bishkek, Ibraimova 115A, Dordoi Plaza Business Centre; tel. (312) 69-05-55; fax (312) 69-05-60; e-mail kicb@kicb.net; internet www.kicb.net; f. 2001; 21% owned by Aga Khan Fund for Economic Development, 18% by Habib Bank (Pakistan), 17% by Deutsche Investitions und Entwicklungsgesellschaft GmbH (Germany), 17% by European Bank for Reconstruction and Development (United Kingdom), 17% by International Finance Corpn; cap. US $17.5m., res $0.5m., dep. $162.5m. (Dec. 2012); Chief Exec. KUANG YOUNG CHOI; 8 brs.

Optima Bank OJSC: 720070 Bishkek, Jibek Jolu 493; tel. and fax (312) 90-59-59; e-mail contact-center@optimabank.kg; internet www .optimabank.kg; f. 1992; fmrly ATFBank–Kyrgyzstan, present name adopted 2010; cap. 700.0m., res 2.2m., dep. 8,376.8m. (Dec. 2012); Chair. of Bd of Dirs BEIBUT KAPYSHEV; 14 brs.

Russian Investment Bank: 720021 Bishkek, Moskovskaya 80/1; tel. (312) 55-44-44; e-mail call-center@rib.kg; internet www.rib.kg; f. 2010 as Zalkar Bank; present name adopted 2013; owned by Russian Investment and Trade Business Holding OJSC (Russia); cap. 40.9m., res 444.2m., dep. 2,659.6m. (Dec. 2012); 66 brs and sub-brs; Chair. of Board of Dirs ANDREI V. ASTAKHOV; Chair. of Management ULAN K. SARBANOV.

Tolubay Bank: 720040 Bishkek, Umetaliyeva 105; tel. (312) 65-88-88; fax (312) 25-63-14; e-mail tolubay@infotel.kg; internet www .tolubaybank.kg; f. 1996; cap. 63.0m., res 12.5m., dep. 293.1m. (Dec. 2006); Chair. JENISHBEK S. BAIGUTTIYEV; 1 br.

COMMODITY EXCHANGE

Kyrgyzstan Commodity and Raw Materials Exchange: 720001 Bishkek, Belinskaya 40; tel. (312) 22-13-75; fax (312) 22-27-44; f. 1990; Gen. Dir TEMIR SARIYEV.

STOCK EXCHANGE

Kyrgyz Stock Exchange (Kyrgyz Fonduluk Birjasy/ Kyrgyzskaya Fondovaya Birzha): 720010 Bishkek, Moskovskaya 172; tel. (312) 31-14-84; fax (312) 31-14-83; e-mail kse@kse.kg; internet www.kse.kg; f. 1994; privately owned; Pres. AIBEK TOLUBAEV.

INSURANCE

At July 2011 there were 19 registered insurance companies in Kyrgyzstan.

Anglo-Kyrgyz Insurance Co: 720000 Bishkek, ul. Akhunbaeva 100; tel. (312) 54-90-23; fax (312) 54-90-49; e-mail anglokgz@elcat.kg; life and non-life.

ATN Polis: 720000 Bishkek, ul. Isanova 42/1; tel. (312) 93-79-37; fax (312) 90-32-52; e-mail info@atnpolis.kg; internet www.atnpolis.kg; f. 2001; life and non-life.

Insurance Group of Central Asia: 720000 Bishkek, Baitik Baatyra 191, Hyatt Hotel, room 103; tel. (312) 68-12-21.

Kyrgyzinstrakh: 720001 Bishkek, pr. Chui 219; tel. (312) 61-45-88; fax (312) 61-46-45; e-mail kinstrakh@ingo.kg; internet www.ingo.kg; f. 1996 by the Russian joint stock insurance company Investstrakh and the Kyrgyz Government to insure foreign investors; brs in Karakol and Osh; insurance and reinsurance; Chair. of Bd E. M. SEIDAKHMETOVA.

Kyrgyzstan Insurance Co: 720000 Bishkek, Moskovskaya 76 B; tel. (312) 38-31-31; fax (312) 38-32-56; e-mail office@insurance.kg; internet www.insurance.kg; f. 1991; Dir MARIYA ADENOVA.

Trade and Industry

GOVERNMENT AGENCIES

Centre for Standardization and Metrology: 720040 Bishkek, Panfilova 197; tel. (312) 62-68-70; fax (312) 66-13-67; e-mail nism@nism.gov.kg; internet www.nism.gov.kg; f. 1927 as the Division of the Chamber of Measures and Weights; present name adopted 2010; certification, control and testing of products and services; Dir ALIMBEK KURMANBAEV.

State Agency for Geology and Mineral Resources: 720739 Bishkek, pr. Erkindik 2; tel. (312) 66-49-01; fax (312) 66-03-91; e-mail mail@geoagency.bishkek.gov.kg; f. 1938; Chair. SHEISHENALY MURZAGAZIYEV.

State Committee for Management of State Property: 720017 Bishkek, Moskovskaya 151; tel. (312) 61-51-87; fax (312) 66-02-36; e-mail goskomitet@ktnet.kg; f. 1991; responsible for the privatization of state-owned enterprises and dealing with bankruptcies; Dir MARAT AMANKULOV.

CHAMBER OF COMMERCE

Chamber of Commerce and Industry of the Kyrgyz Republic: 720001 Bishkek, Kiyevskaya 107; tel. (312) 61-38-72; fax (312) 61-38-75; e-mail info@cci.kg; internet www.cci.kg; f. 1959; supports foreign economic relations and the development of small and medium-sized enterprises; regional brs in Balykchy, Batken, Jalal-Abad, Karakol, Naryn, Osh, Talas and Tokmok; Pres. MARAT D. SHARSHEKEEV.

UTILITIES

Electricity

NES Kyrgyzstana (National Electric Grid of Kyrgyzstan) (NESK): 720070 Bishkek, pr. Jibek Jolu 326; tel. (312) 66-10-01; fax (312) 66-16-09; e-mail nesk@elcat.kg; internet www.energo.kg; f. 2001; comprises five companies, incl. three regional distribution companies, Oshelektro, Jalabadelektro, Vostokelektro and one heating company, Bishkekteploset; 80.5% owned by State Cttee for State Property, 13.2% owned by Social Fund of the Kyrgyz Republic; Gen. Dir MEDETBEK AITKULOV.

Severelektro: 722160 Chui obl., Lebedinovka, Chkalova 3; tel. (312) 33-33-94; fax (312) 33-33-93; e-mail severpiu@mail.ru; internet www.severelectro.kg; f. 2001; state-owned; distribution of electricity in northern regions of Kyrgyzstan, incl. Bishkek, Chui and Talas Oblasts; Gen. Dir ISKENDER KADYRKULOV.

Gas

Kyrgyzgaz: 720661 Bishkek, Gorkogo 22; tel. (312) 53-00-35; fax (312) 53-00-33; e-mail admin@kg.elcat.kg; internet www.kyrgyzgaz.kg; gas distribution co; 100% owned by Gazprom (Russia); Dir-Gen. TURGUNBEK N. KULMURZAYEV.

TRADE UNIONS

Trade Union Federation of Kyrgyzstan: 720032 Bishkek, Chui 207; tel. (312) 21-77-08; fax (312) 62-57-53; e-mail fpk.kg@mail.ru; f. 1925; affiliated with the General Confed. of Trade Unions; Chair. IMANKADYR RYSALIEV.

Transport

RAILWAYS

Kyrgyzstan's railway network consists of one main line (417 km) in northern Kyrgyzstan, which connects the country to Kazakhstan and Russia, and some local lines that connect Osh and Jalal-Abad with Uzbekistan.

Kyrgyz Railway Administration (Kyrgyz Temir Jolu): 720009 Bishkek, L. Tolstogo 83; tel. (312) 65-69-32; fax (312) 65-06-90; e-mail asoup@imfiko.bishkek.su; internet www.kjd.kg; f. 1992; Pres. (vacant).

ROADS

In 2007 Kyrgyzstan's road network totalled an estimated 34,000 km; in 1996 there were 3,200 km of main roads and 6,380 km of secondary roads.

CIVIL AVIATION

There are three international airports at Bishkek (Manas), Osh and Tamchy (in the Yssyk-Kul region).

Air Kyrgyzstan: 720017 Bishkek, pr. Manasa 12A; tel. (312) 31-30-26; fax (312) 31-27-42; internet www.air.kg; f. 2001 as Altyn Air; present name adopted 2006 after merger with Kyrgyzstan Airlines; state-owned; scheduled and charter passenger services between Kyrgyzstan and destinations in Uzbekistan and Russia; Pres. JOLDOSH T. BEKTURGANOV.

Tourism

In 2013 there were 3.1m. foreign tourist arrivals, compared with 398,078 in 2004. Tourism receipts (excluding passenger transport) amounted to US $435m. in 2012.

State Committee for Tourism, Sport and Youth Policy: 720033 Bishkek, Togolok Moldo 17; tel. (312) 62-24-99; fax (312) 21-28-45; e-mail gktsm@gks.gov.kg; Chair. TURUSBEK CH. MAMASHEV.

Defence

Military service is compulsory, and lasts for 18 months. As assessed at November 2014, Kyrgyzstan's total armed forces numbered 10,900, comprising an army of 8,500 and an air force of 2,400. There were 9,500 paramilitary forces (comprising 5,000 border guards—including both Kyrgyzstani conscripts and Russian officers, 3,500 troops attached to the Ministry of Internal Affairs and a national guard of 1,000). About 500 Russian troops were deployed at the Kant airbase (established by Russia in October 2003). In August 2009 a preliminary memorandum of understanding was signed on the establishment of a second Russian military base in Kyrgyzstan for a period of up to 49 years. The US military presence at Manas logistics centre (formerly an airbase), which had hosted some 1,000 US forces since 2001, ended in June 2014.

Defence Expenditure: Budgeted at 4,870m. soms in 2014.

Chief of the General Staff: Maj.-Gen. ASANBEK ALYMKOJOYEV.

Education

Compulsory education comprises four years of primary education (between the ages of seven and 10), followed by five years of lower secondary school (ages 11 to 15). Pupils may then attend upper secondary schools, specialized secondary schools or technical and vocational schools. In 2012/13 total enrolment at primary schools included 91% of children in the relevant age-group; enrolment at secondary schools in 2011/12 included 80% of the school-age population. In 2013 there were 55 institutes of higher education in Kyrgyzstan, attended by 223,241 students. Government budgetary expenditure on education in 2013 was 21,701.9m. soms (representing 20.8% of total spending).

LAOS

Introductory Survey

LOCATION, CLIMATE, LANGUAGE, RELIGION, FLAG, CAPITAL

The Lao People's Democratic Republic is a landlocked country in South-East Asia, bordered by the People's Republic of China to the north, by Viet Nam to the east, by Cambodia to the south, by Thailand to the west and by Myanmar (formerly Burma) to the north-west. The climate is tropical, with a rainy monsoon season lasting from May to September. The temperature in the capital ranges between 23°C and 38°C in the hottest month, April, and between 14°C and 28°C in the coolest month, January. Laos comprises 149 ethnic groups, with 47 main ethnicities. The official language, Lao or Laotian, is spoken by about two-thirds of the population. French is also spoken, and there are numerous tribal languages, including Meo. The principal religion is Buddhism. There are also some Christians and followers of animist beliefs. The national flag (proportions 2 by 3) has three horizontal stripes, of red, blue (half the total depth) and red, with a white disc in the centre. The capital is Vientiane (Viangchan).

CONTEMPORARY POLITICAL HISTORY

Historical Context

Laos was formerly a part of French Indo-China and comprised the three principalities of Luang Prabang, Vientiane and Champasak. These were merged in 1946, when France recognized Sisavang Vong, ruler of Luang Prabang since 1904, as King of Laos. In May 1947 the King promulgated a democratic constitution (although women were not allowed to vote until 1957). The Kingdom of Laos became independent, within the French Union, in July 1949, and full sovereignty was recognized by France in October 1953. The leading royalist politician was Prince Souvanna Phouma, who was Prime Minister in 1951–54, 1956–58, 1960 and in 1962–75. King Sisavang Vong died in October 1959, and was succeeded by his son, Savang Vatthana.

Domestic Political Affairs

From 1950 the Royal Government was opposed by the Neo Lao Haksat (Lao Patriotic Front—LPF), an insurgent movement established by a group of former anti-French activists. The LPF's Chairman was Prince Souphanouvong, a half-brother of Prince Souvanna Phouma, but its dominant element was the communist People's Party of Laos (PPL), led by Kaysone Phomvihane. During the 1950s the LPF's armed forces, the Pathet Lao, gradually secured control of the north-east of the country with the assistance of the Vietnamese communists, the Viet Minh, who were engaged in war with the French (until 1954). By 1965 the de facto partition of Laos was established, with the LPF refusing to participate in national elections and consolidating its power over the north-eastern provinces.

During the 1960s, as the 'Ho Chi Minh Trail' (the communist supply route to South Viet Nam) ran through Pathet Lao-controlled areas, Laos remained closely involved with the war between communist forces and anti-communist troops (supported by the USA) in Viet Nam. In 1973 the Viet Nam peace negotiations included provisions for a ceasefire in Laos. A new Government was formed in April 1974 under Prince Souvanna Phouma, with royalist, neutralist and LPF participation; Prince Souphanouvong was appointed Chairman of the Joint National Political Council. However, the LPF increased its power and eventually gained effective control of the country. This was confirmed by election victories in October and November 1975. In November King Savang Vatthana abdicated, and Prince Souvanna Phouma resigned as head of government.

In December 1975 the National Congress of People's Representatives (264 delegates elected by local authorities) abolished the monarchy and elected a 45-member legislative body, the Supreme People's Council. Souphanouvong was appointed President of the renamed Lao People's Democratic Republic and President of the Supreme People's Council. Kaysone Phomvihane, who had become Secretary-General of the Phak Pasason Pativat Lao (Lao People's Revolutionary Party—LPRP, a successor to the PPL), was appointed Chairman of the Council of Ministers. The former King, Savang Vatthana, was designated Supreme Counsellor to the President, but he refused to co-operate with the new regime and was arrested in March 1977. (He was subsequently reported to have died in a 're-education camp'.) The LPF was replaced in February 1979 by the Lao Front for National Construction (LFNC), under the leadership of the LPRP.

In October 1986 the ailing Souphanouvong announced his resignation from his duties as President of the Republic (while retaining the title) and of the Supreme People's Assembly (as the Supreme People's Council had been renamed). Phoumi Vongvichit, formerly a Vice-Chairman in the Council of Ministers, became acting President of the Republic, while Sisomphon Lovansai, a Vice-President of the Supreme People's Assembly and a member of the LPRP Political Bureau (Politburo), became acting President of the Assembly. In November Kaysone Phomvihane was re-elected Secretary-General of the LPRP. In September 1987 it was announced that Phoumi Vongvichit had also replaced Souphanouvong as Chairman of the LFNC.

In June 1988 elections (the first since the formation of the Lao People's Democratic Republic) took place to the district-level People's Councils, and provincial prefectural elections were held in November; all of the electoral candidates had been approved by the LFNC prior to polling. At the legislative elections of March 1989, 121 candidates contested 79 seats in the enlarged Supreme People's Assembly. At its inaugural session in May, Nouhak Phoumsavanh (a Vice-Chairman of the Council of Ministers) was elected President of the Assembly.

In March 1991, at the Fifth Congress of the LPRP, Souphanouvong stood down from all his party posts. Phoumi Vongvichit and Sisomphon Lovansai also retired, and the three were appointed to a newly created advisory board to the LPRP Central Committee. Kaysone Phomvihane's title was changed to President of the LPRP, and his power was slightly enhanced following the abolition of the party Secretariat. A new Politburo and (younger) Party Central Committee were elected. Gen. Sisavat Keobounphan, the military Chief of the General Staff, was not re-elected to the Politburo.

On 14 August 1991 the Supreme People's Assembly adopted a new Constitution, which provided for a National Assembly, confirmed the leading role of the LPRP, enshrined the right to private ownership and endowed the presidency with executive powers. Kaysone Phomvihane was appointed President of Laos. Gen. Khamtay Siphandone, a Vice-Chairman of the Council of Ministers, Minister of National Defence and Supreme Commander of the Lao People's Army, replaced Kaysone Phomvihane as Chairman of the Council of Ministers, the position being restyled Prime Minister.

Kaysone Phomvihane died in November 1992. He was replaced as President of the LPRP by Gen. Khamtay Siphandone, and the Supreme People's Assembly elected Nouhak Phoumsavanh as the country's President. At elections to the new National Assembly in December, 99.3% of the electorate participated in the polls, in which 154 LFNC-approved candidates contested 85 seats. In February 1993 the new National Assembly re-elected Nouhak Phoumsavanh as President, confirmed Khamtay Siphandone as Prime Minister, and implemented the most extensive reorganization of the Council of Ministers since the LPRP's accession to power in 1975. Phoumi Vongvichit died in January 1994, and Souphanouvong in January 1995.

Although the 20th anniversary of the beginning of communist rule was celebrated in 1995, the Lao Government was attempting gradually to replace communist ideology with Lao nationalism, as Laos developed a market economy with increasing foreign participation. In July senior Buddhist monks were assembled in Vientiane (as Buddhism was deemed central to Lao cultural identity) and were encouraged by the Government to lead a 'cultural renaissance'. Meanwhile, the Government urged the security forces to suppress social problems, particularly corruption and prostitution, perceived as arising from increasing external influences.

The country's progress towards a form of military-dominated authoritarian government was consolidated by the Sixth LPRP

Congress in March 1996. The armed forces gained a majority of seats on the new Politburo; Khamtay Siphandone was elected as its President (replacing Nouhak Phoumsavanh, who retired from this post), and the Minister of National Defence and Commander-in-Chief of the armed forces, Lt-Gen. Choummaly Sayasone, was promoted to third position, after the President of the National Assembly, Lt-Gen. Saman Vignaket. Lts-Gen. Choummaly Sayasone and Saman Vignaket were widely regarded to be opposed to rapid economic and political reform.

At the opening session of the National Assembly in April 1996 Nouhak Phoumsavanh was, despite his retirement from the Politburo, confirmed as head of state until the end of his term of office in February 1998. Sisavat Keobounphan (who had been restored to the Politburo at the elections in March 1996) was elected to the new office of Vice-President, in order to relieve Nouhak Phoumsavanh of a number of presidential duties. A new State Planning Committee was established, which assumed some of the responsibilities hitherto exercised by the State Committee for Planning and Co-operation.

At elections to the National Assembly in December 1997, when 159 LFNC-approved candidates contested 99 seats, the turnout was officially recorded as 99.4%; one of the four 'independent' candidates without affiliation to the LPRP was elected. The first session of the new National Assembly was held in February 1998, when Gen. Khamtay Siphandone was elected to succeed Phoumsavanh as President of Laos. The Assembly also endorsed the appointment of Sisavat Keobounphan as Prime Minister and of Oudom Khattigna in Sisavat's place as Vice-President, and re-elected Saman Vignaket as President of the National Assembly.

At the Seventh Congress of the LPRP, held in March 2001, Oudom was replaced as the country's Vice-President by Lt-Gen. Choummaly Sayasone, who had withdrawn his candidacy for the premiership owing to ill health. Prime Minister Sisavat Keobounphan was forced to resign, in order to take responsibility for the mismanagement of the economy following the Asian financial crisis of 1997/98. His successor, the former Deputy Prime Minister and Minister of Finance, Boungnang Volachit, provided a civilian balance to the entirely military executive branch. The appointment of Thongloun Sisolit to the post of Deputy Prime Minister further increased the civilian representation on the Council of Ministers.

In February 2002 elections took place from among 166 LFNC-approved candidates for the 109 contested seats in the National Assembly. Only one of the elected members was not affiliated to the LPRP. In April, at the opening session of the National Assembly, the existing Council of Ministers was almost wholly re-elected. The former Minister of the Interior, Maj.-Gen. Asang Laoli, became Deputy Prime Minister and Maj.-Gen. Soudchai Thammasith subsequently assumed the interior portfolio. In January 2003 a cabinet reorganization was announced in an apparent attempt to strengthen the national economy; among the changes was the appointment of Chansy Phosikham, the former Governor of the central bank, as Minister of Finance. In October Politburo member Bouasone Bouphavanh was appointed fourth Deputy Prime Minister, with responsibility for home affairs.

The 2006 legislative elections

In February 2006 it was announced that legislative elections would be held at the end of April, almost a year ahead of schedule, in order to enable the new Council of Ministers and the incoming legislature to commence their respective terms of office within close proximity of one another, so as to facilitate the forging of a strong working relationship. In March the LPRP held its Eighth Party Congress, during which Gen. Khamtay tendered his resignation from the Politburo; he was replaced as party leader by Vice-President Lt-Gen. Choummaly Sayasone. Two new members were elected to the Politburo, including Pany Yathotou (a Vice-President of the National Assembly), the only female member. Elections for a new Central Committee were also held, at which 55 members were selected. The party Secretariat, comprising seven members, was revived.

In the legislative elections held on 30 April 2006, two nominally independent candidates were elected, alongside 113 members of the LPRP; of the incoming deputies, 71 were newly elected. The new National Assembly was convened in June, electing Thongsing Thammavong, Politburo member and Mayor of Vientiane, as the chamber's President. Lt-Gen. Choummaly Sayasone was chosen to succeed Gen. Khamtay as President of Laos. Boungnang Volachit became Vice-President, and was replaced as Prime Minister by Bouasone Bouphavanh. Two women were among the new cabinet appointments; other notable

changes included the transfer of the foreign affairs portfolio from Somsavat Lengsavat to Thongloun Sisolit, both of whom remained as Deputy Prime Ministers, as did Maj.-Gen. Asong Laoli. Lt-Gen. Douangchai Phichit retained the defence portfolio and was promoted to the position of Deputy Prime Minister. The National Assembly approved several ministerial changes proposed by Prime Minister Bouasone in July 2007, including Chansy Phosikham's replacement as Minister of Finance by his deputy, Somdy Douangdy.

Recent developments: Thongsing Thammavong as Prime Minister

In December 2010 Bouasone Bouphavanh unexpectedly announced his resignation as Prime Minister three months prior to the expiry of his term of office, citing family issues. However, some observers speculated that the decision was more likely to have been due to a shift in the balance of power within the Politburo. Bouasone had been widely expected to be reappointed Prime Minister at the forthcoming LPRP Congress. Thongsing Thammavong was elected unanimously by the National Assembly as the new premier. Thongsing was replaced as President of the National Assembly by Pany Yathotou, the first woman to assume the role.

The Ninth Congress of the LPRP, which was convened in March 2011, was attended by 576 delegates. Following the appointment of a new, 61-member Central Committee, Choummaly Sayasone was re-elected as Secretary-General of the party for a further five-year term. Bouasone Bouphavanh was removed from both the Politburo and from the Central Committee, while another former Prime Minister, Sisavat Keobounphan, and Saman Vignaket retired from the Politburo. The incoming 11-member body thus incorporated three new members. A nine-member Secretariat was also appointed.

The legislative elections held on 30 April 2011 were contested by 190 candidates and attracted a reported turnout of 99.6%. Four of the 132 seats in the expanded National Assembly were won by nominally independent candidates; 33 seats were secured by female candidates. On 15 June the National Assembly re-elected Choummaly Sayasone as the country's President for a further five-year term. Thongsing Thammavong was similarly confirmed in the position of Prime Minister, and a new cabinet was formally approved by the National Assembly. The incoming Council of Ministers incorporated several new members, including Phouphet Khamphounvong, hitherto Governor of the central bank, who was appointed Minister of Finance in place of Somdy Douangdy, who was assigned the post of Minister of Planning and Investment. Four new ministries—with responsibility for home affairs, for science and technology, for natural resources and environment, and for post, telecommunication and communication—were established.

In May 2012 Dr Khampeuy Panmalaythong, a member of the LPRP Central Committee and Director of the Academy of Social Sciences, was dismissed from both posts, apparently in response to views expressed in the previous year. Addressing the National Assembly, Dr Khampeuy had questioned the relevance of Marxism-Leninism as the leading ideology in the Lao educational system, while in an article published in the journal of the Academy of Social Sciences—although not explicitly advocating the introduction of political pluralism in Laos—he had questioned the effectiveness of single-party political systems.

In March 2014, as part of a bid by the Government to strengthen financial discipline and manage the country's widening fiscal deficit, Phouphet Khamphounvong was replaced as Minister of Finance by Dr Lien Thikeo, the erstwhile Governor of Sayabouri province. In May five high-ranking officials, including Deputy Prime Minister and Minister of National Defence (and senior Politburo member) Lt-Gen. Douangchai Phichit, Minister of Public Security Thongbanh Sengaphone, and the Mayor of Vientiane, Sukhan Mahalad, were killed, along with 12 others, when the military aircraft on which they were travelling crashed in the province of Xiangkhouang. In the following month Gen. Sengnouane Sayalath, previously Douangchai's deputy, was chosen to replace him, while Brig.-Gen. Somkeo Silavong was appointed acting Minister of Public Security.

Dissidence and Civil Unrest

Armed opposition to the Government persisted during the 1980s, particularly among hill tribes. In December 1989 the right-wing United Lao National Liberation Front (ULNLF) proclaimed the 'Revolutionary Provisional Government' of Laos. The self-styled Government, which was headed by Outhong Souvannavong (the former President of the Royal Council of King Savang Vatthana), claimed to have used military force to 'liberate' one-third of Lao territory, although it was widely assumed that this was an exaggeration and that the ULNLF's proclamation was an attempt to elicit popular support. Responsibility for defence in the 'Revolutionary Provisional Government' was reportedly allocated to Gen. Vang Pao, a leader of the Hmong tribe who in the 1970s had been a commander of the Royalist army (and who had lived in exile in the USA since 1975). In October 1992 Gen. Vang Pao's brother, Vang Fung, and another Hmong rebel, Moua Yee Julan (who were allegedly preparing an incursion into Laos under Gen. Vang Pao's command), were arrested in Thailand; Vang Fung was subsequently deported to the USA. In September 1993 Thai troops launched an offensive against Gen. Vang Pao's forces, expelling 320 rebels from Thai territory.

From the mid-1990s uprisings against the Government became more frequent. In July 1995 an army unit based near Luang Prabang mutinied after its commander, a Hmong general, was passed over for promotion. Five members of the armed forces died in the rebellion, which was believed to be symptomatic of the resentment felt by hill tribes over the political and military dominance by the lowland Lao. About 2,000 troops were dispatched to Luang Prabang to restore order. In October a shipment of explosives, allegedly destined for Hmong insurgents, was intercepted on the Mekong River.

In October 1999 an anti-Government demonstration by students and teachers was held in Vientiane—an extremely rare overt demonstration of public dissatisfaction, which was reportedly swiftly dispersed by police. The Government subsequently denied that the demonstration had taken place; however, it was claimed that about 50 people suspected to have been involved in the protest had been arrested, and in March 2000 it was reported that the whereabouts of six of these alleged detainees—one professor and five students—remained unknown.

Civil unrest intensified from 2000, with at least 14 bomb explosions in 2000–01, including two separate attacks in Vientiane in May 2000, coinciding with the respective visits of the Thai Prime Minister and his Minister of Foreign Affairs and an attack prior to a summit meeting of the European Union (EU) and the Association of Southeast Asian Nations (ASEAN, see p. 210) in December 2000. In October 2003 a previously unknown group, the Free Democratic People's Government of Laos (FDPGL), comprising disaffected former members of the armed forces, claimed responsibility for the bombings. A further series of attacks across Laos in 2002–03 included three separate attacks on buses, which were believed to have been perpetrated by Hmong rebels and which claimed the lives of at least 30 people, including several foreign nationals, and three bombings in the capital in October 2003. Conflicting claims of responsibility for the bombings were issued by the FDPGL and a German-based organization, the Committee for Independence and Democracy in Laos, which also claimed responsibility for a number of attacks in 2004, including a bombing in February in the southern town of Savannakhet, where ASEAN tourism ministers had convened. Two minor bomb explosions occurred in a village near Vientiane in November, prompting a heightening of security in advance of the ASEAN summit meeting that was held in the capital at the end of the month.

Meanwhile, in October 2001 five European activists, including a Belgian member of the European Parliament, were arrested for distributing pro-democracy leaflets at a peaceful protest in Vientiane. The protest was held to commemorate the second anniversary of the disappearance of the five students who had participated in the demonstration of October 1999. In November 2001, following a swift trial, the detained activists were convicted of attempting to spread unrest and ordered to be deported.

In March 2004 some 700 Hmong, including five senior commanders, were reported to have recently surrendered to the authorities, having been offered amnesty. In September the human rights organization Amnesty International alleged that up to 40 government troops had murdered five Hmong children in the Xaysomboun special zone in northern Laos in May; the Government denied the accusations.

In June 2007 10 Hmong resident in the USA and a former officer of the California National Guard were arrested and charged in connection with an alleged plot to overthrow the Lao Government, which had been uncovered by US federal agents. Most of the 11 defendants, including Gen. Vang Pao, the purported leader of the group, were released on bail in July. The charges against all 11 defendants were withdrawn in 2009. (Gen. Vang Pao died in 2011.)

Foreign Affairs
Regional relations
Laos was formally admitted as a full member of ASEAN in 1997. Laos hosted the 10th summit meeting of the Association in November 2004 and the 38th Ministerial Meeting in July 2005, which did much to raise the international profile of Laos. In February 2008 Laos ratified the new ASEAN Charter, which codified the principles and purposes of the Association. Laos was the venue for the ninth summit of the Asia-Europe Meeting (ASEM), in Vientiane, in November 2012. It was hoped that Laos's successful hosting of the event, which constituted the largest international event ever to be held in the country, would help to boost foreign investment inflows.

Laos's closest regional partner for many years was Viet Nam. However, in recent years Vietnamese influence in Laos has begun to be eclipsed by that of the People's Republic of China. From 1975 Laos was dependent on Vietnamese economic and military assistance, permitting the stationing of Vietnamese troops (estimated in 1987 to number between 30,000 and 50,000) on its territory. In 1977 a 25-year treaty of friendship between the two countries was signed, and Laos supported the Vietnamese-led overthrow of the Khmer Rouge regime in Kampuchea (Cambodia) in January 1979. Following the outbreak of hostilities between Viet Nam and China in that year, Laos allied itself with the former. Viet Nam withdrew its military presence from Laos during 1988. The two countries signed a protocol governing military co-operation in March 1994. Subsequent senior-level reciprocal visits affirmed the strength of relations between the two countries.

In February 2006 a major border crossing was opened between Sekong province in Laos and Quang Nam province in Viet Nam; it was hoped that this would facilitate economic exchanges and help to control smuggling along the common border. Discussions held during an official visit to Laos by the Vietnamese President, Nguyen Minh Triet, in February 2007 also focused on the expansion of economic co-operation. Further high-level state visits included that of Prime Minister Bouasone Bouphavanh to Viet Nam in September 2010, and that of Nguyen Phu Trong, the General Secretary of the Communist Party of Viet Nam Central Committee, to Vientiane in June 2011, during which 2012 was declared as the 'Year of Viet Nam-Laos Friendship and Solidarity'. According to Lao government figures, during 1989–2012 Viet Nam was the largest overall foreign investor in Laos, closely followed by Thailand and China. In November 2012 Laos and Viet Nam signed an agreement to construct a 220-km high-speed rail link between the two countries (from Savannakhet province, on Laos' south-western border with Thailand, to the Vietnamese border town of Lao Bao). In April 2013 a Malaysian financial institution approved a loan of US $5,000m. to fund the project, of which Laos had sole ownership. Following protracted delays, the rail link's construction, to be undertaken by another Malaysian company, was scheduled to commence in 2015 and to be completed by 2019. This and other proposed new railway projects (see below) were expected to boost investment inflows in Laos, while also lowering the cost of exports into the landlocked country.

Full diplomatic relations between the LPRP and the Chinese Communist Party were restored in August 1989, following an assurance that Chinese support would be withdrawn from Lao resistance groups operating from within China. In October 1991 the Lao and Chinese Prime Ministers signed a treaty, which established a framework for meetings of a Lao-Chinese joint border committee, and in June 1992 an agreement on the delineation of the common border was signed. In November 1994 Laos and China signed a reciprocal agreement on the transport of passengers and goods on each other's sections of the Mekong River. In February 1996 the two countries opened a section of their border to highway traffic. The first ever visit by a Chinese head of state to Laos was undertaken by President Jiang Zemin in November 2000.

As the volume of bilateral trade continued to increase, Lao-Chinese relations were further strengthened by a series of high-level state visits including those of Chinese President Hu Jintao to Vientiane in November 2006, Lao Prime Minister Bouasone to China in August 2007 (during which six agreements on co-operation in a range of areas were signed) and Chinese Premier Wen Jiabao to Laos for discussions with Bouasone in March 2008. However, China's increasing involvement in the Laotian economy, mainly in infrastructural development projects, had begun to concern the Lao people. Many were perturbed by the influx of Chinese workers and business entrepreneurs, who, according to some estimates, totalled as many as 300,000 by 2008. Following a pilot programme launched in the capital in November 2013, in August 2014 the authorities announced that regulations governing the foreign workforce were to be enforced nationwide from August 2015; unregistered foreign workers would be able to apply for documentation allowing them to work legally in Laos, provided that their employer was willing to certify the application; those unable to meet the requirements would be deported. Regulations requiring foreign operators to register their businesses would also be enforced. In April 2010 Laos and China signed a memorandum of understanding (MOU) agreeing to co-operate as joint stakeholders in the development of a 420-km high-speed railway from China's Yunnan province to Vientiane, from where it would connect to the rail network in Thailand before ultimately extending to Singapore, via Malaysia. The planned railway, which was forecast to cost some US $7,200m. and was to be funded by a long-term loan from the Chinese Government, prompted consternation in Laos on account of the high number of Chinese workers expected to be involved (some 64,000, according to Lao officials). In October 2012 the participating Chinese construction company withdrew from the venture, reportedly owing to concerns about profitability; however, the Lao authorities, having been offered another loan by the China Exim Bank in November, decided to assume sole ownership of the project. Following official visits to the Chinese capital, Beijing, by President Choummaly Sayasone, in September 2013, and Prime Minister Thongsing Thammavong, in April 2014, the Laotian and Chinese Governments reaffirmed their joint commitment to the rail project, stating that the project was 'crucial' to boosting bilateral economic and trade co-operation. However, by early 2015 no date had been announced for the commencement of construction, and doubts remained as to the financial viability of the project, which, were it to proceed, would render Laos one of the world's most heavily indebted nations.

Meanwhile, some 18 bilateral co-operation agreements on trade and development, among other fields, were signed by Laos and China in June 2010, and a military co-operation agreement was concluded in July. A series of high-level bilateral visits was conducted in 2011, and in April of that year Lao and Chinese companies signed an agreement providing for the construction of a 25-ha urban development project (at a cost of some US $180m.) in Vientiane. In December 2012 another Chinese company reached an agreement with the Lao Government to develop an area of 365 ha around That Luang Lake into a commercial, residential and tourism complex; the project was forecast to cost around $1,600m. In January 2014, according to Chinese government figures, China overtook Thailand and Viet Nam as the largest foreign investor in Laos, with total cumulative investment since 1989 of around $5,100m. Seven bilateral co-operation agreements, including deals intended to strengthen co-operation in the fields of trade and hydropower, were signed in July 2014. Meanwhile, in December 2011, following the murder of 13 Chinese nationals on the Mekong, China deployed armed patrols in Laos (as well as in Thailand and Viet Nam) to provide security along the river.

Japan resumed the provision of official loans to Laos in 1996. In August 2000 a bridge over the Mekong, built with a grant from the Japanese Government, was officially opened in Paksé. In September 2001 Japan agreed a further loan to fund the construction of the second Mekong Friendship Bridge. During a visit to Japan by Bouasone Bouphavanh in May 2007, the Lao Prime Minister held a meeting with his Japanese counterpart, Shinzo Abe, who pledged to provide continued economic assistance to Laos. Furthermore, it was hoped that a bilateral agreement on investment, which was signed in January 2008, would encourage the participation of Japanese businesses in the Lao economy. Relations were strengthened yet more by further senior-level reciprocal visits in 2010–14, including a state visit to Vientiane in August 2014 by Abe, his first visit to Laos since his re-election as Japanese premier in December 2013. Numerous Japanese grants were extended to Laos during 2013–14, many of them within the health care and education sectors; other Lao beneficiaries of Japanese funding included a project to clear unexploded ordnance remaining from the Viet Nam War in Saravan and Champasack provinces, the completion of which was announced in July 2014.

In April 1995 in Chiang Rai, Thailand, representatives of Laos, Cambodia, Thailand and Viet Nam signed an agreement providing for the establishment of the Mekong River Commission (MRC, see p. 448), a facilitating and advisory body intended to ensure the effective management and sustainable development of the Mekong River. The second summit meeting of the MRC, the primary focus of which was the challenges posed by climate change to water, energy and food security in the Lower Mekong Basin, was convened in Ho Chi Minh City, Viet Nam, in April 2014.

Meanwhile, in August 2008 Laos, Cambodia and Viet Nam signed a border-crossing agreement that defined the intersection point of their borders and affirmed their resolve to complete works related to the demarcation of their land borders. In December 2010 Laos and Viet Nam signed an agreement pledging to enhance border security co-operation. In June 2011 the Lao, Cambodian and Vietnamese Governments signed an agreement providing for the establishment of a trilateral economic development zone, which called for an acceleration of the border demarcation process. The Lao-Vietnamese border demarcation process was completed in July 2013, while in August 2014 demarcation of Laos' border with Cambodia was reported to be 86% complete. During a state visit to Vientiane in February 2014 by Cambodian Prime Minister Hun Sen, seven bilateral agreements were signed, covering a number of fields, including culture, education, health care and public security, while an increase in annual bilateral trade, to US $20m. by 2015 (from $10m. in 2000), was targeted. Laos, Cambodia and Viet Nam pledged to expand defence co-operation during a trilateral meeting of the countries' respective military leaders in Hanoi, Viet Nam, in October 2014.

Meanwhile, tensions arose between the three countries owing to a controversial plan to build a 1,300-MW hydropower dam on the Mekong River at Sayabouri in northern Laos. In April 2012 a Thai company, CH. Karnchang, signed a contract with the Lao authorities to proceed with the construction of the dam, the project having previously been suspended, in December 2011, pending the completion of more environmental studies, amid claims that the project would adversely affect agriculture and fish stocks downstream. It was alleged that funding for the controversial project had been secured on the understanding that, once the dam was completed (at a projected cost of US $3,500m.), Thailand would purchase some 95% of the electricity produced. Despite vociferous opposition from Viet Nam and Cambodia and from environmentalists, in November 2012 the Lao Government formally approved the commencement of full construction work at the site, claiming that the requisite environmental studies had been completed; construction, which was due to be completed by the end of 2018, was reported to be 45% complete at November 2014. Meanwhile, the dispute broadened in October 2013, when the Lao Government announced that it was to construct another dam on the Mekong River, at Don Sahong, in southern Laos, close to the Cambodian border. Environmental groups claimed that the proposed 260-MW dam would result in increased water salinity and soil erosion, disrupt the movement of migratory fish and negatively impact local communities. The Cambodian and Vietnamese authorities argued that the MRC required any such project to be subject to a six-month prior consultation, while the Lao Government insisted that, because the dam was to be constructed on a tributary of the Mekong River, rather than on its mainstream, it was obliged merely to notify the other Commission members of its intention to proceed with the project. Although the Lao Government agreed in June 2014 to postpone construction of the dam to allow for a six-month consultation process, which took place between July 2014 and January 2015, related infrastructural work continued throughout this period and in mid-December 2014 the Government announced that construction was to begin soon after the consultation process.

Relations with Thailand from 1975 were characterized by mutual suspicion. Thailand intermittently closed its border to Lao imports and exports, causing considerable hardship. Disputed sovereignty claims in border areas were a cause of friction, and led to clashes between Lao and Thai troops in 1984. Further hostilities erupted in December 1987, resulting in hundreds of casualties. In February 1988 the two sides agreed to declare a ceasefire, to withdraw their troops from the combat area and to attempt to negotiate a peaceful solution. In March 1991 (following a military coup in Thailand) representatives of the two countries signed an agreement providing for the immediate withdrawal of troops from disputed areas. The Thai Government also undertook to suppress the activities of Lao insurgents operating from Thai territory. In December Thailand and Laos signed a border co-operation agreement.

The first bridge linking Laos and Thailand, the so-called 'Friendship Bridge', was opened in April 1994; the bridge (over the Mekong River) connected Vientiane and Nong Khai province in north-eastern Thailand. In September 1996 the countries' Joint Co-operation Commission agreed to establish a boundary commission, in an effort to resolve demarcation problems. Despite various diplomatic efforts to stimulate further co-operation between the two countries, the relationship was strained by a number of incidents, including the occupation of two islands in the Mekong River, and the eviction of 65 Thai farming families, by Lao troops in August 2000. Laos claimed that, under a treaty of 1926, it had sovereignty over all the islands in the Mekong, while Thailand requested the withdrawal of the troops.

In March 2004, for the first time, the Thai and Lao Governments held a joint cabinet meeting to discuss bilateral co-operation. A second Mekong Friendship Bridge (the third bridge over the river in total), connecting Savannakhet in Laos to the Thai province of Mukdahan, was officially opened in December 2006. In March 2009 the first rail link between Laos and Thailand was inaugurated, with the route between Vientiane and Nong Khai province in north-eastern Thailand. A fourth Mekong bridge (the third Friendship Bridge), between the Lao province of Khammouane and the Thai province of Nakhon Pathom, was inaugurated in November 2011. A fifth bridge over the Mekong, linking the Lao province of Bokeo and the northernmost Thai province, Chiang Rai, was inaugurated in December 2013. The new bridge (the fourth Friendship Bridge) constituted the first direct road link from the Chinese province of Yunnan, through Laos, to the Thai capital of Bangkok. The project was financed jointly by the Lao and Thai Governments, although the Chinese Government contributed US $20m. to the Lao share of the cost. In May 2010 it was announced that Laos had secured financing of some $50m. from the Chinese Government for a sixth bridge over the Mekong, which would connect the Lao province of Oudomxay with Thailand's Nan province. Following delays owing to a dispute between the Lao and Chinese Governments over the terms of the deal, construction of the bridge finally commenced in December 2012 and was expected to be completed by the end of 2015. Plans for the construction of two further Friendship Bridges—which would connect the Lao province of Bolikhamsai with Thailand's Bueng Karn province and link Saravan province in Laos with Ubon Ratchathani province in Thailand—were among the matters discussed during an official visit to Laos by the Thai Prime Minister, Gen. Prayuth Chan-ocha, in November 2014. Following the failure to meet several prior deadlines for the completion of the demarcation of their 735-km land border and their 1,100-km water border, in January 2015 Laos and Thailand agreed upon two new deadlines: 2016 for the land border and 2018 for the water border.

Also in January 2015, meeting on the sidelines of the Special ASEAN Senior Officials Meeting on Energy, which was being hosted by Vientiane, officials from Laos, Thailand, Malaysia and Singapore held discussions on a proposal to export Lao electricity to Singapore via existing transmission lines in Thailand and Malaysia. Further talks on the proposal were due to be held later in the year.

During the 1970s and 1980s thousands of Lao refugees fled to Thailand to escape from civil war and food shortages. The office of the UN High Commissioner for Refugees (UNHCR) began a programme of voluntary repatriation in 1980. In June 1991 UNHCR, Laos and Thailand signed an agreement guaranteeing the repatriation or resettlement in a third country of the remaining 60,000 Lao refugees in Thailand by the end of 1994; however, this deadline was subsequently revised on several occasions. By February 2000 more than 25,000 Lao refugees had returned to Laos under UNHCR's repatriation programme, and approximately 325,000 others had been resettled in third countries. In December 2003 the USA agreed to accept around 15,000 Lao Hmong refugees living in refugee camps in Thailand.

An agreement between the Thai and Lao Governments in December 2006 to repatriate the 8,000 or so Hmong living in refugee camps in Thailand's Phetchabun province, who were alleged to be economic migrants (and to whom UNHCR did not have access), prompted widespread international criticism. In January 2007 UNHCR urged the suspension of all deportations pending the introduction of procedures to allow a proper assessment of the needs and claims of the Hmong. None the less, the Thai authorities proceeded with the repatriation process, claiming to have received assurances from the Lao authorities that the Hmong would be treated well upon their return to Laos. Following a mass protest at the Ban Huay Nam Khao camp in

Phetchabun in June 2008, the Thai authorities promptly deported 837 Hmong refugees to Laos. However, some 1,300 refugees remained unaccounted for after the incident. Although the 837 repatriations were described by the Thai army as voluntary, concerns were raised by human rights organizations, including Amnesty International and Human Rights Watch. In December 2009 the Thai Government forcibly deported to Laos the final 4,000 or so Hmong remaining at the Ban Huay Nam Khao camp, as well as 158 UNHCR-recognized political refugees being held in an immigration detention centre, despite protests by UNHCR, the USA and other members of the international community. In July 2010 the USA urged the Lao Government to allow the group of 158 UNHCR-recognized political refugees to leave Laos for a third country. However, the Lao authorities claimed that the group wished to remain in Laos. Although foreign diplomats who had been allowed access to the refugees earlier in the year had stated that there was no evidence to suggest that the group had been mistreated, media reports indicated that the refugees' living conditions were extremely poor and that they were being kept under the constant supervision of armed guards. Little was known of their subsequent whereabouts.

Other external relations

During the Viet Nam War US aircraft completed almost 600,000 bombing missions over Laos, leaving large amounts of undetonated explosives, which continued to claim the lives of Laos in the early 21st century. The National Unexploded Ordnance Awareness and Clearance Programme was established in Laos in 1995, with support from the UN. Following the adoption by 107 countries in May 2008 of the Convention on Cluster Munitions, banning the use, production, stockpiling and transfer of cluster bombs, the treaty was opened for signature in December. The First Meeting of States Parties to the Convention on Cluster Munitions was held in Vientiane in November 2010. About 1,200 foreign delegates attended the meeting, during which the Convention adopted the Vientiane Declaration, which included a pledge by the signatories to foster greater international co-operation in order better to assist victims of cluster bombs and to accelerate efforts to destroy cluster munition stockpiles and clear buried remnants.

Meanwhile, bilateral operations to locate and repatriate the remains of US soldiers missing in Laos took place from the 1980s. In November 1991, in response to continued Lao co-operation and the implementation of limited political and economic reforms, the US Government announced that diplomatic relations with Laos were to be upgraded to ambassadorial level. In May 1995 the USA announced the ending of a 20-year embargo on aid to Laos. In December 2004, following its adoption by Congress, US President George W. Bush signed legislation according normal trade relations (NTR) status to Laos: this status had been suspended in 1975. The US Senate had separately adopted a resolution condemning Laos's human rights record, concerns over which had delayed the approval of NTR status. A bilateral trade agreement entered into force in February 2005; according to the US Department of State, trade between the two countries almost tripled between 2007 and 2010. A meeting in Washington, DC, USA, between Deputy Prime Minister and Minister of Foreign Affairs Thongloun Sisolit and US Secretary of State Hillary Clinton in July 2010 represented the first official visit to the USA by a Lao foreign affairs minister since the establishment of the Lao People's Democratic Republic in 1975. In July 2012, in the course of a major tour of Asia, Clinton made the first visit to Laos by a US Secretary of State since 1955. During her visit, Clinton held discussions with Prime Minister Thongsing Thammavong and other senior officials on a variety of topics, including economic ties, the legacies of the Viet Nam War (unexploded ordnance and missing personnel), the Sayabouri dam and Laos's pending entry into the World Trade Organization (see p. 431).

In November 2002 Indian Prime Minister Atal Bihari Vajpayee paid the first visit to Laos by an Indian head of government in more than 45 years. During his stay, bilateral agreements on defence co-operation and the control of drugs-trafficking were signed. Regular meetings of the Laos-India Joint Commission for Bilateral Co-operation subsequently took place, the seventh being held in Vientiane in September 2013, at which India pledged US $66.2m. to support irrigation and hydropower projects in Laos. A free trade agreement signed between India and ASEAN in August 2009 was implemented between India and Laos in January 2011.

The disappearance of a prominent human rights activist, Sombath Somphone, in December 2012, and the Lao authorities' ongoing reticence on the issue, attracted significant international censure. Footage from closed-circuit television (CCTV) cameras appeared to show Sombath being forced into another vehicle after his car had been stopped at a police checkpoint in Vientiane. Claims by the Lao authorities that they had had no involvement in Sombath's apparent abduction were widely dismissed by international rights organizations, including Amnesty International and Human Rights Watch, both of which enjoined the Lao Government to establish an independent commission to investigate the circumstances surrounding the activist's disappearance. Offers of technical assistance in analysing the CCTV footage were reportedly rejected by the Lao authorities. Some claimed that Sombath's disappearance was linked to the activist's opposition to the controversial Sayabouri dam project; others alleged that it was Sombath's key role in organizing the ninth Asia-Europe People's Forum—which was staged in Vientiane in October 2012, and which represented an unprecedented opportunity for the discussion of local, regional and global issues with activists from around the world—that had led to his disappearance.

CONSTITUTION AND GOVERNMENT

Under the terms of the 1991 Constitution, executive power is vested in the President of State, while legislative power resides with the National Assembly. The President is elected for five years by the National Assembly. Members of the National Assembly are elected for a period of five years by universal adult suffrage. The Lao People's Revolutionary Party remains the sole legal political party. With the approval of the National Assembly, the President appoints the Prime Minister and members of the Council of Ministers, who conduct the government of the country. The President also appoints provincial governors and mayors of municipalities, who are responsible for local administration.

REGIONAL AND INTERNATIONAL CO-OPERATION

Laos is a member of the Association of Southeast Asian Nations (ASEAN, see p. 210), the Asian Development Bank (ADB, see p. 206), the UN's Economic and Social Commission for Asia and the Pacific (ESCAP, see p. 30), the Colombo Plan (see p. 445), which promotes economic and social development in Asia and the Pacific, and the Mekong River Commission (see p. 448).

Laos became a member of the UN in 1955. In February 2013, following a 15-year bid for admission, the country was finally admitted as a full member of the World Trade Organization (WTO, see p. 431). Laos is a member of the International Labour Organization (ILO, see p. 139) and the Non-aligned Movement (see p. 462).

ECONOMIC AFFAIRS

In 2013, according to estimates by the World Bank, Laos's gross national income (GNI), measured at average 2011–13 prices, was US $9,880m., equivalent to $1,460 per head (or $4,570 per head on an international purchasing-power parity basis). During 2004–13, it was estimated, the population increased at an average annual rate of 1.9%, while gross domestic product (GDP) per head increased, in real terms, by an average of 5.9% per year. Overall GDP increased, in real terms, at an average annual rate of 8.0% in 2004–13. According to the Asian Development Bank (ADB), GDP expanded by 8.0% in 2013.

Agriculture (including forestry and fishing) contributed 24.1% of GDP in 2013, according to UN estimates. According to the ADB, an estimated 72.2% of the working population were employed in the sector in 2010; FAO estimated that 74.0% of the labour force were employed in the sector at mid-2015. Rice is the staple crop. Other crops include maize, cassava, sugar cane, bananas and watermelons. Coffee is grown for export. In 2012 natural forest covered about 42% of the country's total land area (compared with 70% in 1940). Although declining, timber remained a significant export commodity in 2008, accounting for an estimated 8.0% of total export revenue in that year (compared with 27.2% in 2003, prior to the growth of copper exports). The illicit cultivation of narcotic drugs has been widespread. Although the UN Office on Drugs and Crime (UNODC) estimated that the area under opium poppy cultivation in Laos had declined from 26,800 ha in 1998 to 1,500 ha in 2007, thereafter there were five successive years of increases, reaching 6,800 ha in 2012. UNODC's survey for 2014 recorded the area under cultivation at 6,200 ha. In early 2015 the Lao authorities announced that efforts to destroy areas under opium poppy cultivation had commenced in Phongsali province, which UNODC estimated to be responsible for 42% of total cultivation in 2014. During 2004–13 agricultural GDP increased at an average annual rate of 3.4%, according to the ADB; growth in the sector was estimated at 2.9% in 2013.

Industry (including mining, manufacturing, construction and utilities) contributed 34.1% of GDP in 2013, according to UN estimates. According to the ADB, the sector employed 8.1% of the working population in 2010. During 2004–13 industrial GDP increased at an average annual rate of 12.2%, according to the ADB; growth in the industrial sector was estimated at 8.9% in 2013.

Mining and utilities contributed 19.0% of GDP in 2013, according to UN estimates. Laos has considerable mineral resources: copper, gold, tin, coal, iron ore, gemstones and gypsum are among the minerals exploited. Other mineral deposits include zinc, nickel, potash, lead, limestone and silver. Copper production totalled 86,295 metric tons in 2012. Exports of copper decreased slightly from US $683.1m. in 2012 to an estimated $680.6m. in 2013. The value of gold exports (including re-exports) similarly saw a moderate fall, from $150.7m. in 2012 to an estimated $147.6m. in 2012. According to ADB figures, during 2004–13 the GDP of the mining sector increased by an average of 23.3% per year. The start of gold production in 2003 greatly enhanced the sector's output. Mining GDP increased by 8.1% in 2012 but by only 2.8% in 2013.

Manufacturing contributed 8.1% of GDP in 2013, according to UN estimates. The sector is mainly confined to the processing of raw materials (chiefly sawmilling) and agricultural produce, the production of garments (a significant export, accounting for an estimated 10.0% of total exports in 2013), and the manufacture of handicrafts and basic consumer goods for the domestic market. According to the ADB, manufacturing GDP increased at an average annual rate of 9.2% in 2004–13; manufacturing GDP grew by an estimated 7.7% in 2013.

Construction contributed 7.0% of GDP in 2013, according to UN estimates. In 2004–13 the GDP of the sector increased at an average annual rate of 11.9%, according to ADB figures; growth in the construction sector was 9.9% in 2013.

Electrical energy is principally derived from hydroelectric power. Electricity is exported to Thailand and Viet Nam, and is an important source of foreign exchange. Laos's total hydroelectric power potential is estimated at around 28,000 MW. Hydroelectricity production reached 12,802m. kWh in 2012. The 1,070-MW Nam Theun 2 hydroelectric project began commercial operations in March 2010. Initial operations at the 615-MW Nam Ngum 2 hydropower plant commenced in late 2010. At October 2014 there were 25 operational hydropower plants in Laos, with a total installed capacity of about 3,230 MW. As of March 2013, some 72 new hydropower projects were planned or under construction, including: the 440-MW Nam Ngum 3 hydro-power plant, which was expected to provide 2,072 GWh of clean energy annually for export to Thailand upon completion (scheduled by 2017), generating around $770m. for the Lao Government; the 290-MW Nam Ngiep 1 hydropower project (construction of which commenced in October 2014 and was expected to be completed by the end of 2018); and the controversial Sayabouri dam project (see *Contemporary Political History*). Laos is dependent on imports, mainly from Thailand, for supplies of mineral fuels. Petroleum accounted for 15.0% of total import costs in 2008.

The services sector contributed 41.7% of GDP in 2013, according to UN estimates. According to the ADB, the sector engaged 19.7% of the total labour force in 2010. According to official figures, tourist arrivals increased by 17.6% in 2013, to 3.7m. In 2013 receipts from tourism were estimated to have reached US $596m. The country's first stock exchange commenced trading in early 2011. According to the ADB, the GDP of the services sector increased at an average annual rate of 8.5% in 2004–13; sectoral growth in 2013 was an estimated 7.6%.

In 2013, according to the IMF, Laos recorded a visible merchandise trade deficit of US $755.7m. and there was a deficit of $376.2m. on the current account of the balance of payments. Remittances from relatives residing overseas are a significant source of income for many Lao. In 2013 Thailand was the principal source of imports, supplying an estimated 56.0% (including any goods in transit) of the total. The People's Republic of China was also an important source of imports in that year, along with Viet Nam. The principal destination of exports from Laos in 2013 was Thailand, which purchased an estimated 33.3%

(including any goods in transit) of the total. Other significant purchasers in that year were China and Viet Nam. The main export in 2013 was copper, followed by electricity, garments, agricultural products, gold and coffee. The principal imports were capital goods and consumption goods.

An overall budget deficit of 985,000m. new kips was recorded in 2011/12. Laos's general government gross debt was 49,183.1m. new kips in 2013, equivalent to 61.3% of GDP. According to the ADB, at the end of 2013 the country's public external debt totalled US $4,611m. In 2012 the cost of servicing long-term public and publicly guaranteed debt and repayments to the IMF was equivalent to 8.2% of the value of exports of goods, services and income (excluding workers' remittances). According to ILO, consumer prices increased by an average of 5.6% per year in 2004–13. Consumer prices rose by 6.4% in 2013, according to ADB figures. The unemployment rate was estimated by the ADB at 1.9% of the labour force in 2010.

Despite being a communist country, Laos implemented gradual economic reforms to liberalize its economy moderately in the 2000s. Although historically one of the world's poorer nations and still very much dependent on foreign aid, Laos's economy grew at an average annual rate of 7.9% over the period of its Sixth National Socio-economic Development Plan (2006–10), largely owing to the development of mining and hydropower projects. The Seventh National Socio-economic Development Plan (2011–15) targeted an annual economic growth rate of at least 8%, supporting the Government's objective to graduate from least developed country status by 2020. Considerable progress had already been made towards alleviating poverty, which remained a priority for the Government, as did the greater integration of Laos into the regional economy. To this end, the Lao Government signed two separate agreements, in 2010 and 2012, respectively, to build high-speed rail links connecting Laos to China and Viet Nam (see *Contemporary Political History*). The country intended to expand its hydropower production significantly—to 12,000 MW by 2020 (from 3,200 MW in 2014)—exploiting its abundant natural resources. In order to comply with the requirements of the World Trade Organization (WTO, see p. 431), which Laos joined in February 2013, the Government implemented numerous measures to improve trade and investment conditions. Membership of the WTO was expected to boost levels of foreign direct investment, which amounted to US $1,436m. in 2012, according to the ADB. With effect from February 2014, value-added tax—introduced, at a rate of 10%, in 2010—was abolished on certain materials and machinery that could not be produced locally, in a bid to promote investment in commercial production to meet domestic and external demand. The Lao Securities Exchange, which began operations with just two listed companies in January 2011, was boosted by the listing of two additional companies, in December 2013 and December 2014, respectively; it was hoped that this, together with the anticipated listing on the exchange of a further two companies during 2015, would significantly increase equity and bond sales on the exchange and help to attract increased levels of foreign investment. Laos's ranking in the World Bank's Ease of Doing Business index improved modestly from 155th out of the 189 economies surveyed in 2014 to 148th in 2015. Inflation increased from 4.3% in 2012 to 6.4% in 2013, mainly owing to rising food prices; a subsequent moderation in domestic demand eased inflationary pressures, resulting in inflation slowing to 4.8% in the first eight months of 2014. Following the robust GDP growth of 2010–13, the ADB envisaged a slight moderation in the pace of growth, to 7.3% and 7.4%, in 2014 and 2015, respectively, as the Government reined in investment spending and attempted to lower the widening fiscal deficit. The World Bank forecast that the fiscal deficit would decrease to 4.2% of GDP in 2014/15, from 5.6% of GDP in 2012/13, owing to increased revenues and lower wages and capital expenditure).

PUBLIC HOLIDAYS

2016: 1 January (New Year's Day), 6 January (Pathet Lao Day), 20 January (Army Day), 8 February (Chinese New Year), 8 March (International Women's Day), 22 March (People's Party Day), 13–15 April (Lao New Year), 1 May (Labour Day), 1 June (Children's Day), 13 August (Free Laos Day), 23 August (for Liberation Day), 12 October (Liberation from the French Day, Vientiane only), 2 December (Independence Day),

Statistical Survey

Source (unless otherwise stated): National Statistics Centre, rue Luang Prabang, Vientiane; tel. (21) 214740; fax (21) 219129; e-mail nscp@laotel.com; internet www.nsc.gov.la.

Area and Population

AREA, POPULATION AND DENSITY

Area (sq km)	236,800*
Population (census results)	
1 March 1995	4,581,258
1 March 2005	
Males	2,800,551
Females	2,821,431
Total	5,621,982
Population (UN estimates at mid-year)†	
2013	6,769,726
2014	6,894,098
2015	7,019,652
Density (per sq km) at mid-2015	29.6

* 91,400 sq miles.
† Source: UN, *World Population Prospects: The 2012 Revision.*

POPULATION BY AGE AND SEX
(UN estimates at mid-2015)

	Males	Females	Total
0–14 years	1,231,529	1,180,645	2,412,174
15–64 years	2,147,712	2,189,119	4,336,831
65 years and over	118,485	152,162	270,647
Total	**3,497,726**	**3,521,926**	**7,019,652**

Source: UN, *World Population Prospects: The 2012 Revision.*

PROVINCES
(official estimates, population at mid-2012)

	Area (sq km)	Population	Density (per sq km)
Attopu	10,320	133,545	12.9
Bokeo	6,196	173,962	28.1
Bolikhamsai	14,863	281,207	18.9
Champasak	15,415	670,122	43.5
Houaphanh	16,500	333,762	20.2
Khammouane	16,315	390,701	23.9
Luang Namtha	9,325	171,967	18.4
Luang Prabang	16,875	463,485	27.5
Oudomxay	15,370	314,269	20.4
Phongsali	16,270	179,822	11.1
Saravan	10,691	384,438	36.0
Savannakhet	21,774	937,907	43.1
Sayabouri	16,389	389,139	23.7
Sekong	7,665	103,326	13.5
Vientiane	22,554	506,881	22.5
Vientiane Municipality . . .	3,920	797,130	203.3
Xiangkhouang	16,358	282,769	17.3
Total	**236,800**	**6,514,432**	**27.5**

Note: In January 2014 the Government approved the redesignation of the former Xaysomboun district of Vientiane province as a new province in its own right.

Principal Town (incl. suburbs, population at mid-2014, UN estimate): Vientiane (Viangchan, capital) 945,715 (Source: UN, *World Urbanization Prospects: The 2014 Revision*).

BIRTHS AND DEATHS
(official estimates)

	2010	2011	2012
Birth rate (per 1,000) . . .	29.9	28.0	28.1
Death rate (per 1,000) . . .	8.0	7.7	7.4

Life expectancy (years at birth): 67.8 (males 66.5; females 69.2) in 2012 (Source: World Bank, World Development Indicators database).

ECONOMICALLY ACTIVE POPULATION
('000 persons in 2003)

	Total
Agriculture, etc.	2,085
Industry	235
Services	217
Total employed	2,537
Unemployed	136
Total labour force	2,673

2010 ('000 persons): Agriculture 1,461; Industry 164; Services 399; Total employed 2,023.

Source: Asian Development Bank.

Mid-2015 (estimates in '000): Agriculture, etc. 2,792; Total labour force 3,773 (Source: FAO).

Health and Welfare

KEY INDICATORS

Total fertility rate (children per woman, 2012)	3.1
Under-5 mortality rate (per 1,000 live births, 2012) . . .	72
HIV/AIDS (% of persons aged 15–49, 2013)	0.2
Physicians (per 1,000 head, 2012)	0.2
Hospital beds (per 1,000 head, 2010)	0.7
Health expenditure (2011): US $ per head (PPP)	75
Health expenditure (2011): % of GDP	2.8
Health expenditure (2011): public (% of total)	49.4
Access to adequate water (% of persons, 2012)	72
Access to adequate sanitation (% of persons, 2012) . . .	65
Total carbon dioxide emissions ('000 metric tons, 2010) . .	1,873.8
Carbon dioxide emissions per head (metric tons, 2010) . .	0.3
Human Development Index (2013): ranking	139
Human Development Index (2013): value	0.569

For sources and definitions, see explanatory note on p. vi.

Agriculture

PRINCIPAL CROPS
('000 metric tons)

	2011	2012	2013
Rice, paddy	3,066	3,489	3,415*
Maize	1,096	1,125	1,150*
Potatoes	29	33	34†
Sweet potatoes	134	81	85†
Cassava (Manioc)	743	1,061	1,120†
Sugar cane	1,222	1,056	1,180†
Watermelons	123	108	112†
Cantaloupes and other melons .	6	8	9†
Bananas	230*	365	402†
Oranges†	40	42	42
Tangerines, mandarins, clementines and satsumas† .	38	40	41
Pineapples	60	50	50†
Coffee, green	52	87	89†
Tobacco, unmanufactured . .	43*	41*	41†

* Unofficial figure.
† FAO estimate(s).

Aggregate production ('000 metric tons, may include official, semi-official or estimated data): Total cereals 4,162 in 2011, 4,615 in 2012, 4,565 in 2013; Total roots and tubers 906 in 2011, 1,175 in 2012, 1,239 in 2013; Total vegetables (incl. melons) 955 in 2011, 1,041 in 2012, 1,074 in 2013; Total fruits (excl. melons) 438 in 2011, 565 in 2012, 602 in 2013.

Source: FAO.

LIVESTOCK
('000 head, year ending September)

	2011	2012	2013*
Horses*	32	32	33
Cattle	1,538	1,692	1,700
Buffaloes	1,197	1,188	1,180
Pigs	2,650	2,794	2,280
Goats	431	444	450
Chickens	26,852	28,779	30,000
Ducks*	3,350	3,400	3,450

* FAO estimates.

Source: FAO.

LIVESTOCK PRODUCTS
('000 metric tons, FAO estimates)

	2011	2012	2013
Cattle meat	26.5	28.0	28.6
Buffalo meat	19.6	19.6	19.6
Pig meat	56.6	62.0	64.0
Chicken meat	20.4	20.8	20.8
Cows' milk	7.8	7.2	7.2
Hen eggs	15.5	16.0	16.5

Source: FAO.

Forestry

ROUNDWOOD REMOVALS
('000 cubic metres, excl. bark, FAO estimates)

	2011	2012	2013
Sawlogs, veneer logs and logs for sleepers	723	723	723
Other industrial wood	132	132	132
Fuel wood	5,935	5,922	5,911
Total	6,790	6,777	6,766

Source: FAO.

SAWNWOOD PRODUCTION
('000 cubic metres, incl. railway sleepers, unofficial figures)

	2009	2010	2011
Total (all broadleaved) . . .	151	170	183

2012–13: Production assumed to be unchanged from 2011 (FAO estimates).

Source: FAO.

Fishing

('000 metric tons, live weight)

	2010	2011*	2012*
Capture	30.9	34.0	34.1
Cyprinids	4.9	5.4	5.4
Other freshwater fishes . .	26.0	28.6	28.7
Aquaculture	82.1*	95.6	101.9
Common carp	6.1*	7.0	7.5
Roho labeo	5.6*	6.5	6.9
Mrigal carp	4.9*	5.7	6.0
Bighead carp	6.9*	8.0	8.5
Silver carp	8.4*	9.7	10.4
Nile tilapia	20.6*	24.0	25.5
Total catch	113.0*	129.6	136.0

Source: FAO.
* FAO estimate(s).

Mining

('000 metric tons unless otherwise indicated)

	2010	2011	2012
Coal (all grades)	501.6	511.7	578.1
Gemstones, sapphire ('000 carats)*	1,200.0	1,200.0	n.a.
Gold (kg)	5,061	3,984	6,415
Gypsum	553.3	686.1	578.5
Salt	13.4	23.4	12.0
Copper (metric tons)†	64,241	78,859	86,295
Tin (metric tons)†	925	674	762

* Estimates.
† Figures refer to metal content.
Source: US Geological Survey.

Industry

SELECTED PRODUCTS

	2010	2011	2012
Beer ('000 hectolitres)	2,391	2,726	4,407
Soft drinks ('000 hectolitres) . .	430	490	324
Cigarettes (million packs) . . .	212	227	151
Garments (million pieces) . . .	61	68	n.a.
Plastic products (metric tons) . .	11,271	11,722	12,864
Detergent (metric tons) . . .	2,112	2,218	2,021
Agricultural tools ('000 metric tons)	61,579	66,813	69,543
Nails (metric tons)	2,590	2,797	2,576
Bricks (million)	771	917	540
Hydroelectric energy (million kWh)	8,623	12,952	12,802
Tobacco (metric tons)	5,908	6,381	6,731
Plywood (million sheets) . . .	3,645	3,802	1,392

Source: Ministry of Industry and Commerce, Vientiane.

Finance

CURRENCY AND EXCHANGE RATES

Monetary Units
100 at (cents) = 1 new kip.

Sterling, Dollar and Euro Equivalents (29 August 2014)
£1 sterling = 13,351.5 new kips;
US $1 = 8,046.9 new kips;
€1 = 10,612.3 new kips;
100,000 new kips = £7.49 = $12.43 = €9.42.

Average Exchange Rate (new kips per US $)
2011   8,030.1
2012   8,007.8
2013   7,860.1

Note: In September 1995 a policy of 'floating' exchange rates was adopted, with commercial banks permitted to set their rates.

GENERAL BUDGET

('000 million new kips, year ending 30 September)*

Revenue†	2011/12	2012/13‡	2013/14‡
Tax revenue	10,915	12,490	15,313
Profits tax	2,196	2,123	2,879
Income tax	744	949	1,294
Turnover tax	2,827	3,201	3,663
Excise tax	2,344	2,554	2,965
Import duties	1,047	1,546	2,155
Timber royalties	884	946	1,024
Other taxes	872	1,172	1,332
Non-tax revenue	1,513	1,738	1,932
Total	12,428	14,228	17,245

Expenditure	2011/12	2012/13‡	2013/14‡
Current expenditure	9,065	13,725	15,220
Wages and salaries	3,560	8,000	8,800
Transfers	2,015	2,244	2,649
Interest	591	962	925
Other recurrent expenditure .	2,899	2,519	2,846
Net acquisition of non-financial assets	5,881	7,150	7,074
Domestically financed . .	2,876	4,150	4,250
Foreign-financed and net onlending	3,005	3,001	2,824
Total	14,945	20,875	22,294

* Since 1992 there has been a unified budget covering the operations of the central Government, provincial administrations and state enterprises.
† Excluding grants received ('000 million new kips): 1,532 in 2011/12; 1,438 in 2012/13 (budget forecasts); 1,542 in 2013/14 (budget forecasts).
‡ Budget forecasts.
Source: IMF, *Lao People's Democratic Republic: Staff Report for the 2013 Article IV Consultation* (December 2013).

INTERNATIONAL RESERVES
(US $ million at 31 December)

	2010	2011	2012
Gold (national valuation) . . .	9.99	16.00	19.05
IMF special drawing rights . .	78.65	78.41	78.50
Foreign exchange	624.70	662.80	720.59
Total	713.34	757.21	818.14

2013: IMF special drawing rights 78.65.

Source: IMF, *International Financial Statistics*.

MONEY SUPPLY
(million new kips at 31 December*)

	2008	2009	2010
Currency outside banks . . .	2,223,230	3,085,780	3,790,530
Demand deposits at commercial banks	1,491,680	1,704,000	2,555,300
Total (incl. others)	3,715,330	4,790,490	6,349,830

* Figures rounded to the nearest ten million.

Source: IMF, *International Financial Statistics*.

2013 ('000 million new kips at 31 December): Currency outside banks 6,055.8; Demand deposits at commercial banks 2,189.6; *Total* 8,245.3 (Source: Asian Development Bank).

COST OF LIVING
(Consumer Price Index; base: December 2010 = 100)

	2010	2011	2012
Food	98.74	108.8	114.8
Others	98.3	104.3	107.2
All items	98.5	106.0	110.5

2013 (base: December 2010 = 100): All items 117.5.

NATIONAL ACCOUNTS
('000 million new kips at current prices)

Expenditure on the Gross Domestic Product

	2011	2012	2013
Government final consumption expenditure	8,125.0	10,746.7	11,109.9
Private final consumption expenditure	38,918.3	43,476.1	50,524.9
Gross fixed capital formation . .	19,719.6	26,840.7	26,826.5
Changes in inventories . . .	−2,220.5	−3,022.4	−3,020.8
Total domestic expenditure .	64,542.4	78,041.1	85,440.5
Exports of goods and services . .	15,405.8	16,970.2	19,714.4
Less Imports of goods and services	17,344.0	22,028.0	22,690.4
Statistical discrepancy	2,122.9	2,267.9	2,107.5
GDP in purchasers' values .	64,727.1	75,251.2	84,572.0
GDP at constant 2005 prices .	45,911.7	49,538.0	53,485.2

Source: UN Statistics Division, National Accounts Main Aggregates Database.

Gross Domestic Product by Economic Activity

	2010	2011	2012*
Agriculture, hunting, forestry and fishing	16,056.0	17,628.8	18,929.4
Mining and quarrying	4,273.4	6,833.7	7,286.0
Manufacturing	5,231.7	6,246.1	7,456.4
Electricity, gas and water . .	2,238.9	2,851.8	3,048.9
Construction	2,913.2	3,849.6	4,886.0
Wholesale and retail trade . .	11,485.2	12,085.0	13,883.5
Transport, storage and communications	2,847.4	2,928.8	3,165.5
Finance	2,040.1	2,242.1	2,616.9
Government services	4,119.1	4,482.7	5,342.9
Other services	3,327.2	3,758.3	4,207.7
Sub-total	54,532.2	62,906.9	70,823.1
Less Financial intermediation services indirectly measured (FISIM)	1,592.1	1,925.9	2,224.1
GDP at factor cost	52,940.3	60,981.0	68,599.0
Taxes on imports	3,582.3	3,746.0	4,128.4
GDP in purchasers' values .	56,522.6	64,727.1	72,727.5

* Preliminary figures.

Gross Domestic Product by Economic Activity ('000 million new kips at current prices, 2013): Agriculture, hunting, forestry and fishing 19,848.8; Mining (incl. utilities) 15,628.8; Manufacturing 6,671.2; Construction 5,777.7; Wholesale and retail trade, hotels and restaurants 15,811.3; Transport and communications 3,024.9; Other activities 15,509.9; *Gross value added* 82,272.6; Net taxes on products (figure obtained as a residual) 2,299.4; *GDP in purchasers' values* 84,572.0. Source: UN National Accounts Main Aggregates Database.

BALANCE OF PAYMENTS
(US $ million)

	2011	2012	2013
Exports of goods	2,189.6	2,270.7	2,263.9
Imports of goods	−2,404.2	−3,055.1	−3,019.7
Balance on goods	−214.6	−784.5	−755.7
Services and primary income (net)	150.0	119.8	141.9
Balance on goods, services and primary income	−64.6	−664.7	−613.8
Secondary income (net) . . .	222.8	252.0	237.6
Current balance	158.2	−412.7	−376.2
Direct investment (net) . . .	466.9	294.4	426.7
Portfolio investment (net) . .	11.5	5.7	6.7
Other investments (net) . . .	161.4	321.7	252.9
Net errors and omissions . . .	-854.9	−147.6	−500.0
Reserves and related items .	−57.0	61.6	−189.9

Source: Asian Development Bank.

External Trade

PRINCIPAL COMMODITIES
(US $ million)

Imports c.i.f.	2011	2012	2013*
Capital goods	1,423.7	1,602.3	1,729.8
Consumption goods	867.6	1,352.7	1,187.1
Garments	14.0	18.8	21.6
Gold and silver	51.9	8.6	8.5
Electricity	40.9	63.4	67.8
Total (incl. others)	2,404.2	3,055.1	3,019.7

Exports f.o.b.	2011	2012	2013*
Agricultural products	152.2	220.8	194.7
Coffee	67.8	114.9	116.5
Garments	219.9	183.9	227.3
Copper	696.3	683.1	680.6
Gold	111.8	150.7	147.6
Electricity	327.2	502.2	589.8
Total (incl. others)	2,189.6	2,270.7	2,263.9

* Preliminary figures.

Source: Bank of the Lao People's Democratic Republic, Vientiane.

PRINCIPAL TRADING PARTNERS
(US $ million)

Imports	2011	2012	2013
Australia	26.8	40.7	42.1
Belgium	34.2	37.5	32.0
China, People's Republic . . .	519.3	1,027.7	1,892.6
France	146.7	19.4	14.6
Germany	37.9	158.8	46.2
Japan	85.9	151.1	133.6
Korea, Republic	169.9	181.5	205.8
Singapore	38.2	33.1	29.1
Thailand*	3,011.4	3,923.3	4,068.8
Viet Nam	301.5	463.5	488.1
Total (incl. others)	4,635.1	6,339.1	7,264.6

Exports	2011	2012	2013
Australia	6.2	45.8	50.9
China, People's Republic . . .	729.0	713.7	927.9
Germany	72.9	68.1	83.4
India	61.0	128.0	101.6
Japan	88.3	112.4	97.8
Netherlands	29.3	39.3	45.4
Thailand*	1,029.1	1,131.1	1,231.0
United Kingdom	95.1	95.5	71.6
USA	54.8	23.4	28.3
Viet Nam	418.2	404.3	425.7
Total (incl. others)	3,120.0	3,323.9	3,697.9

* Trade with Thailand may be overestimated, as it may include goods in transit to and from other countries.

Note: Data reflect the IMF's direction of trade methodology and, as a result, the totals may not be equal to those presented for trade in commodities.

Source: Asian Development Bank.

Transport

ROAD TRAFFIC
(motor vehicles in use at 31 December)

	2010	2011	2012
Passenger cars and jeeps . . .	24,040	44,890	52,667
Motorcycles and mopeds . . .	512,055	826,228	1,013,635
Buses and trucks	21,383	27,961	36,776
Vans and pick-ups	60,022	117,781	185,226

SHIPPING

Inland Waterways
(traffic)

	2010	2011	2012
Freight ('000 metric tons)	1,088.3	993.4	1,418.0
Freight ton-kilometres (million)	69.7	70.0	79.2
Passengers ('000)	2,026.0	1,899.0	2,652.0
Passenger-kilometres (million)	65.5	48.6	71.8

Source: Ministry of Communications, Transport, Post and Construction, Vientiane.

Flag Registered Fleet
(registered at 31 December)

	2012	2013	2014
Number of vessels	1	2	2
Total displacement ('000 grt)	1.1	15.7	15.7

Source: Lloyd's List Intelligence (www.lloydslistintelligence.com).

CIVIL AVIATION
(traffic on scheduled services)

	2010	2011	2012
Passengers carried ('000)	289	439	425
Passenger-kilometres (million)	83	171	159
Freight carried ('000 tons)	2.4	2.1	1.6
Freight net ton-km (million)	1.2	0.3	0.5

Passengers carried ('000): 1,151 in 2013 (Source: World Bank, World Development Indicators database).

Tourism

FOREIGN VISITOR ARRIVALS
(incl. excursionists)

Country of nationality	2010	2011	2012
Australia	30,538	31,874	33,878
China, People's Republic	161,854	150,791	199,857
France	44,844	44,399	46,903
Japan	34,076	37,883	42,026
Thailand	1,517,064	1,579,941	1,937,612
United Kingdom	37,272	35,622	35,694
USA	49,782	50,092	53,380
Viet Nam	431,011	561,586	705,596
Total (incl. others)	2,513,028	2,723,564	3,330,089

Tourism receipts (US $ million, excl. passenger transport): 382 in 2010; 406 in 2011; 451 in 2012 (Source: World Tourism Organization).

Communications Media

	2011	2012	2013
Telephones ('000 main lines in use)	107.6	450.0	678.7
Mobile cellular telephones ('000 subscribers)	5,480.9	4,300.0	4,481.4
Broadband subscribers ('000)	6.3	7.5	9.0

Internet subscribers ('000): 15.6 in 2009.

Sources: International Telecommunication Union.

Education

(2012/13 unless otherwise indicated)

	Institutions	Teachers	Students
Pre-primary	1,802	7,722	137,359
Primary	8,927	33,847	878,283
Secondary:			
lower	908	27,266†	385,552
upper	33	6,000†	157,737
vocational†	39	374	11,937
University level†	5	4,334	72,662
Other higher†	97	1,950	35,234

* 2011/12 figure(s).
† 2008/09 figure.

Source: Ministry of Education and Sports, Vientiane.

Pupil-teacher ratio (primary education, UNESCO estimate): 27.1 in 2011/12 (Source: UNESCO Institute for Statistics).

Adult literacy rate (UNESCO estimates): 73.2% (males 80.0%; females 66.6%) in 2007 (Source: UNESCO Institute for Statistics).

Directory

The Government

HEAD OF STATE

President of State: Lt-Gen. CHOUMMALY SAYASONE (elected 8 June 2006; re-elected 15 June 2011).

Vice-President: BOUNGNANG VOLACHIT.

COUNCIL OF MINISTERS
(May 2015)

The Council of Ministers comprises members of the Phak Pasason Pativat Lao (Lao People's Revolutionary Party—LPRP).

Prime Minister: THONGSING THAMMAVONG.

Deputy Prime Minister and Minister of Foreign Affairs: THONGLOUN SISOLIT.

Minister of National Defence: Lt-Gen. SENGNOUANE SAYALATH.

Deputy Prime Ministers: Maj.-Gen. ASANG LAOLI, SOMSAVAT LENGSAVAT.

Minister of Finance: Dr LIEN THIKEO.

Minister of Public Security: Brig.-Gen. SOMKEO SILAVONG (acting).

Minister of Justice: CHALEUN YIAPAOHEU.

Minister of Agriculture and Forestry: VILAYVANH PHOMKHE.

Minister of Post, Telecommunication and Communication: HIEM PHOMMACHANH.

Minister of Industry and Commerce: KHEMMANY PHOLSENA.

Minister of Information, Culture and Tourism: Dr BOSENGKHAM VONGDARA.

Minister of Labour and Social Welfare: ONECHANH THAMMAVONG.

Minister of Education and Sports: Dr PHANKHAM VIPHAVANH.

Minister of Public Health: Dr EKSAVANG VONGVICHIT.

Minister of Energy and Mines: SOULIVONG DALAVONG.

Minister of Planning and Investment: SOMDY DOUANGDY.

Minister of Home Affairs: XAYSI SANTIVONG.

Minister of Natural Resources and Environment: NOULIN SINBANDITH.

Minister of Public Works and Transport: Dr BOUNCHANH SINTHAVONG.

Minister of Science and Technology: Dr BOVIENGKHAM VONGDARA.

Minister to the Office of the President: PHONGSAVATH BOUPHA.

Ministers to the Office of the Prime Minister: SINLAVONG KHOUPHAYTHOUNE, Dr BOUNTIEM PHITSAMAY, BOUNPHENG MOUNPHOSAY, KHEMPHENG PHOLSENA, Dr DOUANGSAVAT SOUPHANAOUVONG, BOUNHEUANG DUANGPHACHANH.

Governor of the Central Bank: SOMPAO PHAYSITH.

MINISTRIES

Office of the President: ave Lane Xang, Vientiane; tel. (21) 214200; fax (21) 214208.

Office of the Prime Minister: Ban Sisavat, Vientiane; tel. (21) 213653; fax (21) 213560.

Ministry of Agriculture and Forestry: Ban Phonxay, Vientiane; tel. (21) 412359; fax (21) 412344; internet www.maf.gov.la.

Ministry of Education and Sports: 1 ave Lane Xang, BP 67, Vientiane; tel. (21) 216013; fax (21) 216006; e-mail esitc@moe.gov.la; internet www.moe.gov.la.

Ministry of Energy and Mines: rue Nongbone, Ban Hatsady, POB 11694, Vientiane; tel. (21) 414319; fax (21) 413013; e-mail admin@mem.ddns.net; internet www.mem.gov.la.

Ministry of Finance: 23 rue Singha, Ban Phonxay, BP 24, Vientiane; tel. and fax (21) 900943; e-mail ict@mof.gov.la; internet www.mof.gov.la.

Ministry of Foreign Affairs: 23 rue Singha, Ban Phonxay, Vientiane; tel. (21) 413148; fax (21) 414009; e-mail ict@mofa.gov.la; internet www.mofa.gov.la.

Ministry of Home Affairs: rue Samsenthai, Vientiane; tel. (21) 212545; internet www.moha.gov.la.

Ministry of Industry and Commerce: rue Phonxay, BP 4107, Vientiane; tel. (21) 911628; fax (21) 416140; e-mail moicpsi@yahoo.com; internet www.moic.gov.la.

Ministry of Information, Culture and Tourism: rue Setthathirath, Ban Xiengnyeun, Chanthaboury, BP 122, Vientiane; tel. (21) 212406; fax (21) 212408; e-mail email@mic.gov.la.

Ministry of Justice: ave Lane Xang, Vientiane; tel. (21) 414105; fax (21) 414102.

Ministry of Labour and Social Welfare: rue Pangkham, Ban Sisaket, BP 347, Vientiane; tel. (21) 213003; fax (21) 213287; e-mail molsw@hotmail.com.

Ministry of National Defence: ave Kaysone Phomvihane, Ban Phone Kheng, Vientiane; tel. (21) 911550; fax (21) 911118; e-mail kongthap@yahoo.com; internet www.kongthap.gov.la.

Ministry of Natural Resources and Environment: That Dam, Vientiane; tel. (21) 263799; fax (21) 263799; e-mail monre@monre.gov.la; internet www.monre.gov.la.

Ministry of Planning and Investment: rue Luang Prabang, Vientiane 01001; tel. (21) 217012; fax (21) 215491; e-mail ipd@investlaos.gov.la; internet www.investlaos.gov.la.

Ministry of Post, Telecommunication and Communication: ave Lane Xang, Vientiane; tel. (21) 218897; fax (21) 285259; e-mail info@mpt.gov.la; internet www.mpt.gov.la.

Ministry of Public Health: rue Samsenthai, Ban That Khao, Sisattanak, Vientiane; tel. (21) 214000; fax (21) 214003; e-mail contact@moh.gov.la.

Ministry of Public Security: rue Nongbone, Xaysettha, POB 7040, Vientiane; tel. (21) 951084.

Ministry of Public Works and Transport: rue Dongpalane, Ponesavanh, Sisattanak, Vientiane; tel. (21) 451943; fax (21) 412250; e-mail webmaster@mpwt.gov.la; internet www.mpwt.gov.la.

Ministry of Science and Technology: rue Tha Gnong, Ban Dontia, POB 2279, Vientiane; tel. (21) 213470; fax (21) 213472; e-mail most_info@most.gov.la; internet www.most.gov.la.

Legislature

The National Assembly was expanded from 115 to 132 members in 2011. At the election held on 30 April 128 candidates of the Lao People's Revolutionary Party (LPRP) and four independents were elected to the legislature. The next election was due in April 2016.

President of the National Assembly: PANY YATHOTOU.

Vice-Presidents: Dr XAYSOMPHONE PHOMVIHANE, SOMPHANH PHENGKHAMMY.

Political Organizations

COMMUNIST PARTY

Phak Pasason Pativat Lao (Lao People's Revolutionary Party—LPRP): Vientiane; f. 1955; est. as People's Party of Laos; reorg. under present name in 1972; 191,700 mems (2011); Cen. Cttee of 61 full mems elected at Ninth Party Congress in March 2011; Sec.-Gen. Lt-Gen. CHOUMMALY SAYASONE.

Political Bureau (Politburo)

Full members: Lt-Gen. CHOUMMALY SAYASONE, THONGSING THAMMAVONG, BOUNGNANG VOLACHIT, Maj.-Gen. ASANG LAOLI, THONGLOUN SISOLIT, SOMSAVAT LENGSAVAT, PANY YATHOTOU, Dr BOUNTHONG CHITMANY, Dr BOUNPONE BOUTTANAVONG, Dr PHANKHAM VIPHAVANH.

OTHER POLITICAL ORGANIZATIONS

Lao Front for National Construction (LFNC): Thanon Khouvieng, Ban Sisaket, Chanthaboury, Vientiane; tel. and fax (21) 213752; f. 1979; est. to replace Lao Liberal Front and Lao Patriotic Front; comprises representatives of various political and social groups, of which the LPRP is the dominant force; fosters national solidarity; 165-mem. cttee elected in July 2011; Chair. PHANDOUANGCHIT VONGSA; Vice-Chair. TONG YERTHOR.

Numerous factions are in armed opposition to the Government. The principal groups are:

Democratic Chao Fa Party of Laos: led by PA KAO HER until his death in Oct. 2002; Pres. SOUA HER; Vice-Pres. TENG TANG.

Free Democratic Lao National Salvation Force: based in Thailand.

United Front for the Liberation of Laos: Leader PHOUNGPHET PHANARETH.

United Front for the National Liberation of the Lao People: f. 1980; led by Gen. PHOUMI NOSAVAN until his death in 1985.

United Lao National Liberation Front: Sayabouri Province; comprises an est. 8,000 mems, mostly Hmong (Meo) tribesmen; Sec.-Gen. VANG SHUR.

Diplomatic Representation

EMBASSIES IN LAOS

Australia: rue Thadeua, Ban Wat Nak, Km 4, Sisattanak, Vientiane; tel. (21) 353800; fax (21) 353801; e-mail austemb.laos@dfat.gov.au; internet www.laos.embassy.gov.au; Ambassador JOHN WILLIAMS.

Brunei: rue Setthathirath, Ban Xieng Ngun, Chanthabouly District, Vientiane; tel. (21) 255231; fax (21) 255234; e-mail vientiane.laos@mfa.gov.bn; Ambassador Dr Haji EMRAN BIN BAHAR.

Cambodia: rue Thadeua, Km 2, BP 34, Vientiane; tel. (21) 314952; fax (21) 314951; e-mail camemb.lao@mfa.gov.kh; Ambassador DAN YI.

China, People's Republic: rue Wat Nak, Sisattanak, BP 898, Vientiane; tel. (21) 315100; fax (21) 315104; e-mail chinaemb_la@mfa.gov.cn; internet la.china-embassy.org/chn; Ambassador GUAN HUABING.

Cuba: rue Bourichanne 422, Xaysettha, Vientiane; tel. (21) 314902; fax (21) 314901; e-mail embacuba@etllao.com; internet www.cubadiplomatica.cu/laos; Ambassador WALDO REYES SARDIÑAS.

France: rue Setthathirath, BP 06, Vientiane; tel. (21) 267400; fax (21) 267439; e-mail contact@ambafrance-laos.org; internet www.ambafrance-laos.org; Ambassador YVES CARMONA.

Germany: rue Sok Paluang 26, Sisattanak, BP 314, Vientiane; tel. (21) 312111; fax (21) 351152; e-mail info@vientiane.diplo.de; internet www.vientiane.diplo.de; Ambassador MICHAEL GRAU.

India: 2 Ban Wat Nak, rue Thadeua, Km 3, Sisattanak, BP 225, Vientiane; tel. (21) 352301; fax (21) 352300; e-mail info@indianembassylaos.org; internet www.indianembassylaos.org; Ambassador (vacant).

Indonesia: ave Kaysone Phomvihane, BP 277, Vientiane; tel. (21) 413909; fax (21) 214828; e-mail kbrivte@laotel.com; internet www.kbrivientiane.la; Ambassador IRMAWAN EMIR WISNANDAR.

Japan: rue Sisangvone, Vientiane; tel. (21) 414401; fax (21) 414406; internet www.la.emb-japan.go.jp; Ambassador HIROYUKI KISHINO.

Korea, Democratic People's Republic: Ban Wat Nak, Vientiane; tel. (21) 315261; fax (21) 315260; Ambassador RI SANG CHUN.

Korea, Republic: Lao-Thai Friendship Rd, Ban Wat Nak, Sisattanak, BP 7567, Vientiane; tel. (21) 352031; fax (21) 352035; e-mail laos@mofa.go.kr; internet lao.mofa.go.kr; Ambassador KIM SOO-GWON.

Malaysia: 23 rue Singha, Ban Phonxay, BP 789, Vientiane; tel. (21) 414205; fax (21) 414201; e-mail mwvientiane@kln.gov.my; internet www.kln.gov.my/web/lao_vientiane; Ambassador Dato' THAN TAI HING.

Mongolia: Ban Wat Nak, Km 3, BP 370, Vientiane; tel. (21) 315220; fax (21) 315221; e-mail embmong@laotel.com; Ambassador LODOIDAMBA GALBADRAKH.

Myanmar: Lao-Thai Friendship Rd, Ban Wat Nak, Sisattanak, BP 11, Vientiane; tel. (21) 314910; fax (21) 314913; e-mail mmevte@laotel.com; internet www.mevientiane.org; Ambassador KYAW SOE WIN.

Philippines: Ban Saphanthong Kang, Sisattanak, BP 2415, Vientiane; tel. (21) 452490; fax (21) 4524932; e-mail pevientiane@yahoo.com; internet vientianepe.dfa.gov.ph; Ambassador MARIA LUMEN ISLETA.

Russian Federation: rue Thadeua, Ban Thaphalanxay, Km 4, BP 490, Vientiane; tel. (21) 312222; fax (21) 312210; e-mail embrus_lao@mail.ru; internet www.laos.mid.ru; Ambassador MIKHAIL V. BARANOV.

Singapore: Unit 4, rue Thadeua, Ban Wat Nak, Km 3, Sisattanak, Vientiane; tel. (21) 353939; fax (21) 353938; e-mail singemb_vte@sgmfa.gov.sg; internet www.mfa.gov.sg/vientiane; Ambassador DOMINIC GOH.

Thailand: ave Kaysone Phomvihane, Xaysettha, Vientiane; tel. (21) 214581; fax (21) 214580; e-mail thaivte@mfa.go.th; internet www.thaiembassy.org/vientiane; Ambassador PISANU CHANVITAN.

United Kingdom: rue Nehru, Phonexay, Xaysettha, Vientiane; e-mail BritishEmbassy.Vientiane@fco.gov.uk; internet www.gov.uk/government/world/laos; Ambassador PHILIP MALONE.

USA: 19 rue Bartholonie, That Dam, BP 114, Vientiane; tel. (21) 267000; fax (21) 267190; e-mail webmastervientiane@state.gov; internet laos.usembassy.gov; Ambassador DANIEL A. CLUNE.

Viet Nam: Unit 85, 23 rue Singha, Ban Phonxay, Xaysettha, Vientiane; tel. (21) 990986; fax (21) 416720; e-mail vnemba.la@gmail.com; internet www.mofa.gov.vn/vnemb.la; Ambassador NGUYEN MANH HUNG.

Judicial System

People's Supreme Court: the highest judiciary body in Laos; supervises decisions made by the People's Provincial and Municipal Courts and military courts; judges are elected by the National Assembly Standing Committee, with the President being elected by the National Assembly on the recommendation of the Standing Committee; Pres. KHAMPANH SITTHIDAMPHA.

Office of the Public Prosecutor: monitors the observance of laws by ministries, government organizations, local administrative bodies, state employees and citizens; supervises public prosecutors at the lower (province, prefecture, district) level and military prosecutors; the Public Prosecutor-General is appointed by the National Assembly on the recommendation of the Standing Committee; Public Prosecutor-General KHAMSANE SOUVONG.

Religion

The 1991 Constitution guarantees freedom of religious belief. The principal religion of Laos is Buddhism.

BUDDHISM

Lao Unified Buddhists' Association: Maha Kudy, Wat That Luang, Vientiane; f. 1964; Pres. (vacant); Sec.-Gen. Rev. SIHO SIHAVONG.

CHRISTIANITY

The Roman Catholic Church

For ecclesiastical purposes, Laos comprises four Apostolic Vicariates. At 31 December 2007 an estimated 0.6% of the population were adherents.

Episcopal Conference of Laos and Cambodia: c/o 787 Preah Monivong Blvd, Boeung Trabek, Chamkarmon, Phnom Penh,

Cambodia; f. 1971; Pres. Mgr LOUIS-MARIE LING MANGKHANEKHOUN (Vicar of Paksé).

Vicar Apostolic of Luang Prabang: Bishop LEONELLO BERTI, Evêché, BP 74, Luang Prabang.

Vicar Apostolic of Paksé: Mgr LOUIS-MARIE LING MANGKHANEKHOUN (Titular Bishop of Proconsulari), Centre Catholique, BP 77, Paksé, Champasak; tel. (31) 212879; fax (31) 251439.

Vicar Apostolic of Savannakhet: Fr JEAN MARIE PRIDA INTHIRATH (Titular Bishop of Lemfocta), Centre Catholique, BP 12, Thakhek, Khammouane; tel. (51) 212184; fax (51) 213070.

Vicar Apostolic of Vientiane: Mgr JEAN KHAMSÉ VITHAVONG (Titular Bishop of Moglaena), Centre Catholique, BP 113, Vientiane; tel. (21) 216593; fax (21) 215085.

The Anglican Communion

Laos is within the jurisdiction of the Anglican Bishop of Singapore.

The Protestant Church

Lao Evangelical Church: BP 4200, Vientiane; tel. (21) 169136; Exec. Pres. Rev. KHAMPHONE KOUTHAPANYA.

BAHÁ'Í FAITH

National Spiritual Assembly: BP 189, Vientiane; tel. and fax (21) 216996; e-mail usme@laotel.com; f. 1956; Sec. SUSADA SENCHANTHISAY.

The Press

Aloun Mai (New Dawn): rue That Luang, Ban Nongbone, Xaysettha, Vientiane; tel. (21) 413029; fax (21) 413037; f. 1985; quarterly; theoretical and political organ of the LPRP; Editor-in-Chief SISOUK PHILAVONG.

Finance: rue That Luang, Ban Phonxay, Vientiane; tel. (21) 412401; fax (21) 412415; organ of Ministry of Finance.

Heng Ngan: 87 ave Lane Xang, BP 780, Vientiane; tel. (21) 212756; fax (21) 219750; fortnightly; organ of the Federation of Lao Trade Unions; Editor CHANSING KOKKEOBOUNMA.

Khaokila (Sports Daily News): Ban Mixay, Chanthaboury, Vientiane; tel. (21) 252908; fax (21) 252909; e-mail khaokila@hotmail.com; f. 1999; Editor-in-Chief SUKSAKHONE SIPASEUT.

Lao Dong (Labour): 87 ave Lane Xang, Vientiane; f. 1986; fortnightly; organ of the Federation of Lao Trade Unions; circ. 46,000.

Laos: 80 rue Setthathirath, BP 3770, Vientiane; tel. (21) 21447; fax (21) 21445; quarterly; published in Lao and English; illustrated; Editor V. PHOMCHANHEUANG; English Editor O. PHRAKHAMSAY.

Meying Lao: rue Manthatoarath, BP 59, Vientiane; e-mail chansoda@hotmail.com; f. 1980; monthly; women's magazine; organ of the Lao Women's Union; Editor-in-Chief VATSADY KHUTNGOTHA; Editor CHANSODA PHONETHIP; circ. 7,000.

Noum Lao (Lao Youth): rue Phonthan, Ban Phonthan Neua, Xaysettha, Vientiane; tel. (21) 951067; fax (21) 416727; f. 1979; fortnightly; organ of the Lao People's Revolutionary Youth Union; Editor KHANKAB BUDARAT; circ. 1,500.

Pasason (The People): 80 rue Setthathirath, BP 110, Vientiane; tel. (21) 212466; fax (21) 212470; e-mail infonews@pasaxon.org.la; internet www.pasaxon.org.la; f. 1940; daily; Lao; organ of the Cen. Cttee of the LPRP; Editor-in-Chief BOUALAPHANH THANPHILOM; circ. 28,000.

Pathet Lao: 80 rue Setthathirath, Vientiane; tel. (21) 212447; f. 2001; daily; Lao and English; organ of the Lao News Agency, Khao San Pathet Lao (KPL); Editor KHEMTHONG SANOUBAN.

Sciences and Technics: Science, Technology and the Environment Agency (STEA), BP 2279, Vientiane; f. 1991; est. as Technical Science Magazine; quarterly; organ of the Ministry of Science and Technology; scientific research and development.

Siang Khong Gnaovason Song Thanva (Voice of the 2 December Youths): Vientiane; monthly; youth journal.

Sieng Khene Lao: Vientiane; monthly; organ of the Lao Writers' Association.

Suksa Mai: Vientiane; e-mail sm.touk1@gmail.com; monthly; organ of the Ministry of Education and Sports.

Valasan Khosana (Propaganda Journal): Vientiane; f. 1987; organ of the Cen. Cttee of the LPRP.

Vannasinh: Vientiane; monthly; literature magazine.

Vientiane Mai (New Vientiane): 36 rue Setthathirath, BP 989, Vientiane; tel. (21) 212623; fax (21) 215989; e-mail admin@vientianemai.net; internet www.vientianemai.net; f. 1975; morning daily; organ of the LPRP Cttee of Vientiane province and city; Editor SOMPHET INTHISARATH; circ. 2,500.

Vientiane Times: rue Pangkham, BP 5723, Vientiane; tel. (21) 216364; fax (21) 216365; e-mail info@vientianetimes.gov.la; internet www.vientianetimes.org.la; f. 1994; daily; English; Editor-in-Chief SAVANKHONE RAZMOUNTRY; circ. 3,000.

There is also a newspaper published by the Lao People's Army, and several provinces have their own newsletters.

NEWS AGENCY

Khao San Pathet Lao (Lao News Agency—KPL): 80 rue Set-thathirath, BP 3770, Vientiane; tel. (21) 215402; fax (21) 212446; e-mail kplnews@yahoo.com; internet www.kpl.net.la; f. 1968; dept of the Ministry of Information, Culture and Tourism; news service for press, radio and television broadcasting; daily bulletins in Lao, English and French; Gen. Dir SOUNTHONE KHANTHAVONG; English Editor TITONY SISOURATH.

PRESS ASSOCIATION

Lao Journalists' Association (LJA): BP 122, Vientiane; tel. (21) 212420; fax (21) 212408; Pres. Dr BOSENGKHAM VONGDARA; Vice-Pres. SOMSANOUK MIXAY.

Publishers

Khoualuang Kanphim: 2–6 Khoualuang Market, Vientiane.

Lao-phanit: Ministry of Education and Sports, Bureau des Manuels Scolaires, rue Lane Xang, Ban Sisavat, Vientiane; educational, cookery, art, music, fiction.

Pakpassak Kanphim: 9–11 quai Fa-Hguun, Vientiane.

Department of Publishing, Printing, Distribution and Libraries: Ministry of Information, Culture and Tourism, BP 122, Vientiane; tel. (21) 212421; fax (21) 212408; oversees the State Publishing and Book Distribution House and the State Printing Enterprise; Dir NOUPHAY KOUNLAVONG.

Broadcasting and Communications

TELECOMMUNICATIONS

Entreprise de Télécommunications de Laos (ETL): rue Saylom, Ban Saylom, Chanthaboury, Vientiane; tel. (21) 260015; fax (21) 260051; e-mail csd@etllao.com; internet www.etllao.com; state enterprise, telephone, mobile and Voice over Internet Protocol (VoIP) services; Dir-Gen. PADAPPHET SAYAKHOT.

Lao Télécommunications Co Ltd: ave Lane Xang, BP 5607, 01000 Vientiane; tel. (21) 244212; fax (21) 241638; e-mail ltc-webmaster@laotel.com; internet laotel.com; f. 1996; jt venture between a subsidiary of Shinawatra Group of Thailand and Entreprises des Postes et Télécommunications de Laos; awarded 25-year contract by Govt in 1996 to undertake all telecommunications projects in Laos; Dir-Gen. THONGSAY SANEXAYA.

SKY Telecom State Company: rue Saylom, Vientiane; tel. (21) 215353; internet www.skytel.com.la; internet provider; f. 2011; Dir KHAMKHITH SAYSONGKHAM.

Star Telecom Co Ltd (Unitel): rue Nongbone, Ban Phonxay, Xaysettha, Vientiane; tel. (21) 998888; fax (21) 988988; e-mail startelecom@unitel.com.la; internet www.unitel.com.la; f. 2009; jt venture between Viettel Global Joint Stock Co and Lao Asia Telecom (LAT); operates mobile, fixed-line and internet services; Chair. OULAHA THONGVANHTHA.

VimpelCom Lao Co. Ltd (Beeline): Lane Xang Business Center, 14 ave Lane Xang, Unit 4, Ban Hatsadi, Chanthaboury, BP 4693, Vientiane; tel. 77800700 (mobile); fax 77800701; e-mail customer.care@beeline.la; internet www.beeline.la; f. 2011; CEO ALEXANDER IZOSIMOV.

Regulatory Authority

National Authority of Posts and Telecommunications (NAPT): ave Lane Xang, Vientiane 01000; tel. (21) 219857; fax (21) 219858; e-mail depostel@laotel.com; Dir-Gen. SNITH XAPHAKDY.

BROADCASTING

Radio

Lao National Radio: rue Phangkham, Km 6, BP 310, Vientiane; tel. (21) 212468; fax (21) 212430; e-mail laonradio@lnr.org.la; f. 1960; state-owned; programmes in Lao, French, English, Thai, Khmer and Vietnamese; domestic and international services; Dir-Gen. VORA-SACK PRAVONGVIENGKHAM.

Television

A domestic television service was launched in 1983. In 2012 there were six television stations and 17 provincial stations.

Lao National Television (TVNL): rue Sivilay, BP 5635, Vientiane; tel. (21) 710067; fax (21) 710182; e-mail tnlinfo@tnl.gov.la; internet www.tnl.gov.la; f. 1983; colour television service; Dir-Gen. BOUNCHOM VONGPHET.

Laos Television 3: BP 860, Vientiane; tel. (21) 315449; fax (21) 215628; f. 1994; est. as IBC Channel 3; 30% govt-owned, 70% owned by Int. Broadcasting Corpn Co Ltd (Thailand); operated by latter; programmes in Lao.

Finance

(cap. = capital; res = reserves; dep. = deposits; brs = branches; m. = million)

BANKING

The banking system was reorganized in 1988–89, ending the state monopoly of banking. Some commercial banking functions were transferred from the central bank and the state commercial bank to a new network of autonomous banks. The establishment of joint ventures with foreign financial institutions was permitted.

Central Bank

Banque de la RDP Lao: rue Yonnet, BP 19, Vientiane; tel. (21) 213109; fax (21) 213108; e-mail bol@bol.gov.la; internet www.bol.gov.la; f. 1959; est. as the bank of issue; became Banque Pathetlao 1968; took over the operations of Banque Nationale du Laos 1975; known as Banque d'Etat de la RDP Lao from 1982 until adoption of present name; dep. 23,532,240m. kips (Dec. 2011); Gov. SOMPAO PHAYSITH.

Commercial Banks

Acleda Bank Lao: 372 cnr rues Dongpalane and Dongpaina, Unit 21, Ponesavanh, Sisattanak, Vientiane; tel. (21) 264994; fax (21) 264995; e-mail acledabank@acledabank.com.la; internet www.acledabank.com.la; f. 2008; cap. 220,000m. kips, res 3,809m. kips, dep. 243,297m. kips (Dec. 2011); Chair. CHEA SOK; CEO and Man. Dir PHON NARIN.

Agriculture Promotion Bank: 58 rue Hengboun, Ban Haysok, BP 5456, Vientiane, tel. (21) 241394; fax (21) 223714; e-mail apblao@laotel.com; internet www.apblao.com.la; Dir BOUANGEUN PHONGSAVATH.

ANZ Vientiane Commercial Bank Ltd: 33 ave Lane Xang, Ban Hatsady, Chanthaboury, Vientiane; tel. (21) 222700; fax (21) 213513; e-mail vccbank@laotel.com; internet www.anz.com/laos; f. 1993; renamed as above in 2007; private jt venture owned by Laotian, Thai, Taiwanese and Australian investors; Chair. JOHN MORSCHEL; CEO MICHAEL SMITH.

Banque pour le Commerce Extérieur Lao (BCEL): 1 rue Pangkham, Ban Xiengnheun, Chanthaboury, Vientiane; tel. (21) 213200; fax (21) 213202; e-mail bcelhqv@bcel.com.la; internet www.bcel.com.la; f. 1975; 100% state-owned; cap. 682,888m. kips, res 90,096m. kips, dep. 11,666,795m. kips (Dec. 2011); Chair. SALSAMONE SAYSOULIEN; Man. Dir VANKHAM VORAVONG.

Banque Franco-Lao: ave Lane Xang, Ban Hatsady, Chanthaboury, Vientiane; tel. (21) 285111; fax (21) 285222; e-mail commercial@bfl.la; internet www.banquefrancolao.com; f. 2010; Lao-French jt venture; Man. Dir GUILLAUME PERDON.

Indochina Bank: 116 Capital Tower, 23 rue Singha, BP 6029, Vientiane; tel. (21) 455000; fax (21) 455111; e-mail info@indochinabank.com; internet www.indochinabank.com; f. 2009; Lao-South Korean jt venture; Chair. OH SEI YOUNG; Man. Dir TAY HONG HENG.

International Commercial Bank: 127/07, rue Hatsady, Ban Hatsady Tai, Chanthaboury, Vientiane; tel. (21) 250388; fax (21) 250479; e-mail enquiry@icb-lao.com; internet www.icb-lao.com; f. 2008; Chair. TEE KIM CHAN; CEO ZULKIFLEE BIN ABDULLAH.

Joint Development Bank: 82 rue Lane Xang, Vientiane; tel. (21) 213531; fax (21) 213530; e-mail jdb@jdbbank.com; internet www.jdbbank.com; f. 1989; 100% owned by Phrom Suwan Silo and Drying Co Ltd; cap. US $5m.; Gen. Man. SAROGE SINGSOMBOON.

Lao Development Bank (LDB): 13 ave Souphanouvong, Ban Sihome, Chanthaboury, BP 2700, Vientiane; tel. (21) 213300; fax (21) 213304; e-mail ldbhovte@ldblao.com; internet www.ldblao.com; f. 1999; est. as Lao May Bank upon consolidation by the Govt of ParkTai Bank, Lao May Bank and Nakornluang Bank; merged with Lane Xang Bank Ltd in 2001; name changed as above in 2003; 100% govt-owned; lends mainly to SMEs; Man. Dir BOUALIANE PHOMMAVONGSA; 18 brs.

Lao-Viet Bank (LVB): 44 ave Lane Xang, Ban Hatsady, Chanthaboury, Vientiane; tel. (21) 216316; fax (21) 212197; e-mail lvbho@laotel.com; internet www.lao-vietbank.com; f. 1999; jt venture between BCEL and Bank for Investment and Devt of Vietnam; cap. US $15m.; Chair. PHANSANA KHOUNNOUVONG; Man. Dir NGUYEN VANHEING; 3 brs.

Nayoby Bank: ave Kaysone Phomvihane, Ban Phonphanao, Xaysettha, Vientiane; tel. (21) 264407; fax (21) 264408; e-mail nbb_ho@ nayobybank.org; internet www.nayobybank.org; f. 2007; 100% state-owned; Man. Dir BOUALONG XAYAVONG.

Phongsavanh Bank Ltd: Unit 1, ave Kaysone Phomvihane, Ban Phakhao, Xaythany, Vientiane; tel. (21) 711566; fax (21) 711556; e-mail info@phongsavanhbank.com; internet www.phongsavanh bank.com; f. 2007; Man. Dir SENGDAO BOUPHAKONEKHAM; cap. US $10m. (2007).

STOCK EXCHANGE

Lao Securities Exchange (LSX): Ban Phonethan Neue, rue T4, Xaysettha, Vientiane; internet www.lsx.com.la; f. 2010; establishment funded by the Banque de la RDP Lao (51% of capital) and Republic of Korea (49%); trading began in 2011; Chair. and CEO DETHPHOUVANG MOULARAT.

INSURANCE

Assurances Générales du Laos (AGL): Vientiane Commercial Bank Bldg, 33 ave Lane Xang, BP 4223, Vientiane; tel. (21) 215903; fax (21) 215904; e-mail agl@agl-allianz.com; internet www .agl-allianz.com; f. 1990; jt venture between Lao Govt (49%) and Assurances Générales de France (51%); Group Chair. Dr MICHAEL DIEKMANN; Man. Dir GUY APOVY.

Lane Xang Assurance Co (LAP): Vientiane; f. 2010; equal jt venture between Lao Development Bank and Post and Telecommunication Joint Venture Insurance Corpn; life and general.

Trade and Industry

GOVERNMENT AGENCY

National Economic Research Institute (NERI): ave Kaysone Phomvihane, Ban Sivilay, Xaythany, Vientiane; tel. and fax (21) 711181; e-mail nerilaos@yahoo.com; govt policy development unit; Dir SOUPHAN KEOMISAY.

DEVELOPMENT ORGANIZATIONS

Department of Domestic and Foreign Investment (DDFI): rue Luang Prabang, 01001 Vientiane; tel. (21) 222690; fax (21) 215491; e-mail fimc@laotel.com; internet invest.laopdr.org; fmrly Foreign Investment Management Committee (FIMC); provides information and assistance to existing and potential investors.

Department of Livestock and Fisheries: Ministry of Agriculture and Forestry, Ban Phonxay, BP 811, Vientiane; tel. (21) 416932; fax (21) 415674; e-mail eulaodlf@laotel.com; public enterprise; imports and markets agricultural commodities; produces and distributes feed and animals; Dir-Gen. BOUAPHAN KONEDAVONG.

National Agriculture and Forestry Research Institute (NAFRI): Nongviengkham, BP 7170, Vientiane; tel. (21) 770084; fax (21) 770047; e-mail bounthong@nafri.org.la; internet www.nafri .org.la; f. 1999; supports sectoral devt and formulation of strategies and programmes in accordance with govt policy; Dir-Gen. Dr BOUNTHONG BOUAHOM.

State Committee for State Planning: Office of the Prime Minister, Ban Sisavat, Vientiane; tel. (21) 213653; fax (21) 213560.

CHAMBER OF COMMERCE

Lao National Chamber of Commerce and Industry (LNCCI): ave Kaysone Phomvihane, Ban Phonphanao, Xaysettha, BP 4596, Vientiane; tel. (21) 452579; fax (21) 452580; e-mail lncci@laopdr.com; internet www.lncci.laotel.com; f. 1989; 800 mems; Pres. KISSANA VONGSAY; Sec.-Gen. KHAMPANH SENGTHONGKHAM.

TRADE ASSOCIATION

Société Lao Import-Export (SOLIMPEX): 43–47 ave Lane Xang, BP 2789, Vientiane; tel. (21) 213818; fax (21) 217054; Dir KANHKEO SAYCOCIE; Dep. Dir PHONGSAMOUTH VONGKOT.

UTILITIES

Electricity

Electricité du Laos (EDL): Lao-Thai Friendship Rd, BP 2392, Sisattanak, Vientiane; tel. (21) 312791; fax (21) 314236; e-mail eedlmdo@edl.com.la; internet www.edl.com.la; f. 1959; state-owned corpn; responsible for production and distribution of electricity;

shares in subsidiary EDL-Generation Co offered in 2011; Chair. and Man. Dir SISAVATH THIRAVONG.

Lao National Grid Co: Vientiane; responsible for Mekong hydro-electricity exports.

Water

Nam Papa Nakhoneluang (Laos Water Supply State Enterprise): ave Kaysone Phomvihane, Ban Thatluang, Xaysettha, Vientiane; tel. (21) 412880; fax (21) 414378; e-mail nampapalao@laotel.com; internet www.nampapa.com.la; f. 1962; Gen. Man. DAOPHET BOUAPHA.

Water Supply Authority (WASA): Dept of Housing and Urban Planning, Ministry of Public Works and Transport, ave Lane Xang, Vientiane; tel. and fax (21) 415764; fax (21) 451826; e-mail mctpcwwa@laotel.com; f. 1998; regulates the urban water industry; Dir NOUPHEUAK VIRABOUTH.

STATE ENTERPRISES

Agricultural Forestry Development Import-Export and General Service Co: trading co of the armed forces.

Bolisat Phatthana Khet Phoudoi Import-Export Co: rue Khoun Boulom, Vientiane; tel. (21) 216234; fax (21) 215046; f. 1984; trading co of the armed forces.

Dao-Heuang Import-Export Co: 242-7 Route 13 South, Ban Thaluang, Paksé, Champasak Province; tel. (31) 212250; fax (31) 212438; e-mail daoheuangcafe@laopdr.com; internet www .daoheuangcoffee.com; f. 1990; imports and distributes whisky, beer, mineral water, coffee and foodstuffs; Pres. LEUANG LITDANG.

Lao Commodities Export Co Ltd (Lacomex): Ban Wattuang, Paksé, Champasak Province; tel. (31) 212552; fax (31) 212553; e-mail sisanouk@laotel.com; f. 1994; exports coffee under the Paksong Cafe Lao brand; Man. Dir SISANOUK SISOMBAT.

Lao Houng Heuang Export-Import Co: rue Nongbone, Vientiane; tel. (21) 217344; fax (21) 212107.

Lao State Material Import-Export Co (Lasmac): 59 Ban Hatsady Tai, Chanthaboury, Vientiane; tel. (21) 216578; fax (21) 217149; e-mail lasmac@laotel.com; internet www.lasmac.laopdr.com; f. 1983; mfr of wood products and woven plastic; exports agricultural and wood products; imports construction materials.

Luen Fat Hong Lao Plywood Industry Co: BP 83, Vientiane; tel. (21) 314990; fax (21) 314992; e-mail lfhsdsj@laotel.com; internet www.luenfathongyada.laopdr.com; devt and management of forests, logging and timber production.

TRADE UNION ORGANIZATION

Federation of Lao Trade Unions: 87 ave Lane Xang, BP 780, Vientiane; tel. (21) 212754; e-mail kammabanlao@pan-laos.net.la; f. 1956; 21-mem. Cen. Cttee and 5 mem. Control Cttee; Pres. KHAMLA LORLONESY; 70,000 mems.

Transport

RAILWAYS

In November 2012 plans were announced for the construction of a 220-km high-speed rail link from Savannakhet province to the Vietnamese border town of Lao Bao; construction work was scheduled to commence in 2015 and to be completed by 2019. In early 2015 plans were also being discussed by the Lao and Chinese authorities to build a 420-km high-speed railway from the Chinese–Lao border to Vientiane.

ROADS

The Asian Development Bank has supported an extensive development programme for the road network in Laos. In 2012 there were an estimated 43,604 km of roads. The main routes link Vientiane and Luang Prabang with Ho Chi Minh City in southern Viet Nam and with northern Viet Nam and the Cambodian border, Vientiane with Savannakhet, Phongsali to the Chinese border, Vientiane with Luang Prabang and the port of Ha Tinh (northern Viet Nam), and Savannakhet with the port of Da Nang (Viet Nam). Laos, Thailand and China are linked by the Kunming–Bangkok Highway, 250 km of which traverse Laos. In 2004 construction of a 245-km national road (Route 9) was completed, linking Laos with Thailand and Viet Nam.

A number of bridges across the Mekong River link Laos to Thailand. The fourth bridge, linking Khammouane in Laos with the Thai province of Nakhon Pathom, was completed in November 2011. A fifth bridge, between the Lao province of Bokeo and the northernmost Thai province of Chiang Rai, was inaugurated in December 2013, with a further three bridges scheduled for completion in the latter half of the decade.

INLAND WATERWAYS

The Mekong River, which forms the western frontier of Laos for much of its length, is the country's greatest transport artery. However, the size of river vessels is limited by rapids, and traffic is seasonal. There are about 4,600 km of navigable waterways.

CIVIL AVIATION

Wattay airport, Vientiane, is the principal international airport. In 1998 Luang Prabang airport also gained formal approval to receive international flights. Construction of a new airport in Oudomxay province was completed in the late 1990s. Savannakhet Airport was to be developed into an international facility, as part of plans for the east–west economic corridor project, a proposed transport network linking Laos with Myanmar, Thailand and Viet Nam.

Lao Civil Aviation Department: BP 119, Vientiane; tel. (21) 512163; fax (21) 520237; e-mail laodca@laotel.com; internet www .dca.mpwt.gov.la; Dir-Gen. YAKUA LOPANGKAO.

Lao Air: rue Asiane, Ban Akat, Wattay Airport, BP 6618, Vientiane; tel. (21) 513022; fax (21) 512027; e-mail info@lao-air.com; internet www.lao-air.com; f. 2002; domestic flight services; Man. Dir BOUNMA CHANTHAVONGSA.

Lao Airlines: National Air Transport Co, 2 rue Pangkham, BP 6441, Vientiane; tel. (21) 212057; fax (21) 212065; e-mail laoairlines@ laoairlines.com; internet www.laoairlines.com; f. 1975; state airline, fmrly Lao Aviation; operates internal and international passenger and cargo transport services within South-East Asia; CEO SOMPHONE DOUANGDARA.

Lao Central Airlines: Vientiane; internet www.flylaocentral.com; f. 2012; 3 flights a week from Vientiane to Bangkok and Luang Prabang; CEO SAVANHPHONE PHONGSAVANH.

Tourism

Laos has spectacular scenery and ancient pagodas. Luang Prabang was approved by UNESCO as a World Heritage site in 1995, as was the Wat Phu temple complex in southern Laos in 2001. Foreign visitor arrivals were reported to have increased by 22.3% in 2012 to reach 3.3m., with the largest number of visitors coming from Thailand and Viet Nam. Receipts from tourism were estimated to have risen by 11.1% in 2012 to reach some US $451m.

National Tourism Administration of Lao PDR: ave Lane Xang, BP 3556, Hatsady, Chanthaboury, Vientiane; tel. (21) 212251; fax (21) 212769; e-mail tmpd_lnta@yahoo.com; internet www .tourismlaos.org; parastatal org.; promotes Laos as a tourist destination and regulates the tourism industry; 17 provincial offices; Chair. SOMPHONG MONGKHONVILAY.

Defence

As assessed at November 2014, the total strength of the armed forces was an estimated 29,100: army 25,600 (including an army marine section of an estimated 600); air force 3,500. Conscription lasts a minimum of 18 months. Paramilitary forces comprise militia self-defence forces numbering about 100,000 men.

Defence Expenditure: Budgeted for 2014: 197,000m. kips.

Supreme Commander of the Lao People's Army (Commander-in-Chief): Lt-Gen. CHOUMMALY SAYASONE.

Chief of the General Staff: Brig.-Gen. SOUVENE LEUANGBOUNMY.

Education

A comprehensive educational system is in force, and Lao is the language of instruction.

In 2012 enrolment in pre-primary education included 24% of pupils in the relevant age-group (males 23%; females 24%). In the same year enrolment in primary education, which begins at six years of age and lasts for five years, included 96% of children in the relevant age-group (males 97%; females 95%). Secondary education, beginning at the age of 11, lasts for six years, comprising two three-year cycles. In 2012 enrolment in secondary education included 41% of pupils in the relevant age-group (males 43%; females 40%).

In the 2012/13 academic year there were 1,802 pre-primary institutions, which were attended by 137,359 children, and 8,927 primary schools, attended by 878,283 pupils. The 980 secondary schools provided education for a total of 555,226 students (including 39 vocational schools at which 11,937 students were enrolled). There were 102 tertiary institutions, including five university-level establishments at which 72,662 students were enrolled, while 35,234 were studying at 97 other institutions of higher education. There are several regional technical colleges. The National University of Laos was founded in 1996. Government spending on education in 2010 was an estimated 13.2% of total budgetary expenditure.

LATVIA

Introductory Survey

LOCATION, CLIMATE, LANGUAGE, RELIGION, FLAG, CAPITAL

The Republic of Latvia is situated in north-eastern Europe, on the east coast of the Baltic Sea. The country is bounded by Estonia to the north and by Lithuania to the south and south-west. To the east it borders Russia, and to the south-east Belarus. Owing to the influence of maritime factors, the climate is relatively temperate, but changeable. Average temperatures in January range from −2.8°C (26.6°F) in the western coastal town of Liepāja to −6.6°C (20.1°F) in the inland town of Daugavpils. Mean temperatures for July range from 16.7°C (62.1°F) in Liepāja to 17.6°C (63.7°F) in Daugavpils. Average annual rainfall in Rīga is 617 mm (24 ins). The official language is Latvian. The major religion is Christianity: most ethnic Latvians are traditionally Lutherans or Latin-rite Catholics, whereas ethnic Russians are mainly adherents of the Russian Orthodox Church. The national flag (proportions 1 by 2) has a maroon background, with a narrow white horizontal stripe superimposed across the central part. The capital is Rīga (Riga).

CONTEMPORARY POLITICAL HISTORY

Historical Context

In November 1917 representatives of Latvian nationalist groups elected a provisional national council, which informed the Russian Government of its intention to establish an independent Latvian state. On 18 November 1918 the newly constituted Latvian National Council proclaimed the independent Republic of Latvia, with Jānis Cakste as President. Independence, under the Government of Kārlis Ulmanis, was fully achieved after the expulsion of the Bolsheviks from Rīga in May 1919, with the aid of German troops, and from the eastern province of Latgale, with Polish and Estonian assistance, in January 1920. A Latvian-Soviet peace treaty was signed in August. Latvia's first Constitution was adopted in 1922. An electoral system based on proportional representation permitted many small parties to be represented in the Saeima (Parliament), resulting in 18 changes of government in 1922–34. None the less, under the dominant party, the Latvijas Zemnieku Savienība (LZS—Latvian Farmers' Union), led by Ulmanis, agrarian reforms were successfully introduced. The worldwide economic decline of the early 1930s prompted a coup in May 1934, led by Ulmanis. Martial law was introduced, the Parliament was dissolved and all political parties, including the LZS, were banned. A Government of National Unity assumed the legislative functions of the Parliament, and Ulmanis (hitherto the Prime Minister) became President in 1936.

Under the Treaty of Non-Aggression signed by Germany and the USSR in August 1939, the incorporation of Latvia into the Soviet 'sphere of interests' was agreed by the two powers. A 'treaty of mutual aid' with the USSR allowed the establishment of Soviet military bases in Latvia, and in June 1940 Soviet forces occupied the country. A 'puppet' administration, under Augusts Kirhenšteins, was installed, and the election to the Parliament of Soviet-approved candidates took place in July. The new legislature proclaimed the Latvian Soviet Socialist Republic, which was formally incorporated into the USSR as a constituent union republic in August.

Following a period of German occupation from July 1941 during the Second World War, Soviet Latvia was re-established in 1944–45 and the process of 'sovietization' was resumed. There were further mass deportations of Latvians to Russia and Central Asia. Independent political activities were prohibited and the Latvijas Komunistiskā Partija (LKP—Communist Party of Latvia) exercised exclusive political power.

Anti-Soviet demonstrations staged from 1986 were frequently suppressed by police. In October 1988 representatives of the leading opposition movements established the Latvijas Tautas Fronte (LTF—Latvian Popular Front), which resolved to seek Latvian sovereignty within a renewed Soviet federation. Meanwhile, in September Jānis Vagris was appointed First Secretary of the LKP, and the new leadership of the party came increasingly under the influence of the LTF. Later that month Latvian

was designated the state language. In March 1989 LTF-supported candidates won 26 of the 34 contested seats representing Latvia in elections to the USSR's Congress of People's Deputies. On 28 July, following similar measures in Lithuania and Estonia, the Latvian Supreme Soviet (Supreme Council—legislature) adopted a declaration of sovereignty and economic independence. Meanwhile, there was growing support within the republic for full independence, as advocated by the Latvijas Nacionālās Neatkarības Kustība (LNNK—Latvian National Independence Movement), formed in 1988, particularly among ethnic Latvians—who, however, were outnumbered by Slavs (mostly Russians and Ukrainians) in Rīga and the other large cities in the republic. In December 1989 candidates supported by the LTF won some 75% of seats contested in local elections.

In January 1990 the Latvian Supreme Soviet voted to abolish the constitutional guarantees of the LKP's political predominance. In February the Supreme Soviet formally condemned the Latvian legislature's decision to request admission to the USSR in 1940, and restored to official use the state emblems of pre-1940 Latvia. At elections to the Supreme Soviet in March–April 1990, LTF-endorsed candidates won 131 of the 201 seats; the LKP and the anti-independence Interfront (dominated by members of the Russian-speaking population) together won 59 seats. The LKP subsequently split into two parties: the majority of delegates at an extraordinary congress elected Alfrēds Rubiks, an opponent of independence, as First Secretary.

The new Supreme Council, convened in May 1990, elected Anatolijs Gorbunovs of the LKP as its Chairman (de facto president of the Republic). On 4 May the Supreme Council announced the beginning of a transition towards full political and economic independence. Four articles of the 1922 Constitution, defining the Republic of Latvia as an independent democratic state and asserting the sovereignty of the Latvian people, were restored. Ivars Godmanis, the Deputy Chairman of the LTF, was elected Prime Minister in a new Government. Meanwhile, a rival body to the Supreme Soviet, the Congress of Latvia, had been elected in an unofficial poll, in which only citizens of the pre-1940 republic and their descendants had been entitled to vote. The LNNK-dominated Congress, convening at the end of April 1990, declared Latvia to be an occupied country and adopted resolutions on independence and the withdrawal of Soviet troops.

The Supreme Council's resolutions, although more cautious than the independence declarations adopted in Lithuania and Estonia, severely strained relations with the Soviet authorities. On 14 May 1990 the Soviet President, Mikhail Gorbachev, issued a decree annulling the Latvian declaration of independence. The declaration was also opposed within the republic by some Slavs, who organized protest strikes and demonstrations. In December the Latvian Government claimed that special OMON units of the Soviet Ministry of Internal Affairs had caused a series of explosions in Rīga, and in January 1991 OMON troops seized the Rīga Press House. Later in January a 'Committee of Public Salvation', headed by Rubiks, declared itself as a rival Government to the Godmanis administration; on the same day five people died when OMON troops attacked the Ministry of the Interior in Rīga.

Latvia refused to conduct the all-Union referendum on the future of the USSR on 17 March 1991 (although some 680,000 people, mostly Slavs, did participate, unofficially). Instead, a referendum on Latvian independence took place on 3 March. Of those eligible to vote, 87.6% participated, of whom, according to official results, 73.7% supported independence.

During the attempted overthrow by conservative communists of the Gorbachev administration in the Russian and Soviet capital, Moscow, in August 1991, an emergency session of the Latvian Supreme Council was convened and the full independence of the country proclaimed. As the coup collapsed, the Godmanis Government banned the LKP and detained Rubiks. (In July 1995 Rubiks was found guilty of involvement in the coup attempt. He was released in November 1997.) On 6 September 1991 the USSR State Council formally acknowledged Latvian independence; Latvia was admitted to the UN later that month. In late 1991 the Supreme Council adopted legislation guaranteeing the right of citizenship to all citizens of the pre-1940 republic and their descendants. Other residents of Latvia were to be required to apply for naturalization after final legislation governing citizenship had been determined.

Domestic Political Affairs

Around 90% of the electorate participated in legislative elections held in June 1993. (Around 27% of the adult population, mostly Slavs, were ineligible to participate). Eight groups secured representation in the 100-seat Parliament. Latvijas Ceļš (LC—Latvian Way), a broadly based movement, emerged as the largest party, with 32% of the votes cast and 36 seats. The more moderate nationalist parties obtained strong popular support, while socialist-orientated parties, including the successor of the LKP, the Latvijas Sociālistickā Partija (LSP—Latvian Socialist Party), failed to win representation. Only 11 of the elected deputies were not ethnically Latvian.

Restoration of the 1922 Constitution

The new Parliament voted to restore the 1922 Constitution, and undertook to elect the President of the Republic from among three prominent deputies. At a third round of voting on 7 July 1993 Guntis Ulmanis (great-nephew of Kārlis Ulmanis) of the revived LZS succeeded in winning a majority, with 53 votes. He was inaugurated as President the following day, when he appointed Valdis Birkavs of LC as Prime Minister. The Cabinet of Ministers represented a coalition agreement between LC (the majority partner) and the LZS.

The requirements for naturalization proposed by the Government's draft citizenship law included a minimum of 10 years' permanent residence in Latvia, a knowledge of Latvian to conversational level and an oath of loyalty to the republic. In July 1994 the Parliament amended the legislation on citizenship, thereby placating some international criticism. In the same month the LZS announced its withdrawal from the governing coalition, following disagreements with LC over economic and agricultural policy. A new Cabinet of Ministers, appointed in September, was dominated by LC members, including the Prime Minister, Māris Gailis; Birkavs became Deputy Prime Minister and Minister of Foreign Affairs. Latvia was admitted to the Council of Europe (see p. 250) in February 1995.

A general election was held on 30 September–1 October 1995. Nine parties and coalitions succeeded in obtaining the 5% of the votes required for legislative representation. LC's share of the 100 seats was reduced significantly, to 17, while the largest number of seats (18) was won by the newly established, leftist Demokrātiskā Partija 'Saimnieks' (DPS–'The Master' Democratic Party). The Tautas Kustība 'Latvijai'—Zīgerista partija ('TKL—People's Movement for Latvia—Zigerists' Party), an extreme nationalist party led by a German-Latvian, Joahims Zigerists, won 16 seats. In December the Parliament endorsed a Cabinet of Ministers led by an entrepreneur with no party affiliation, Andris Šķēle. The new Government was a coalition principally comprising the DPS, LC, the Tēvzemei un Brīvībai (TB—For Fatherland and Freedom Union), the LNNK and the LZS. On 18 June 1996 the Parliament re-elected Ulmanis for a second three-year term as President.

At the end of July 1997, following a series of corruption scandals, Šķēle's Government resigned. Ulmanis invited Guntars Krasts, the outgoing Minister of the Economy, to form a new administration. In August the Parliament approved Krasts's proposals for a five-party coalition, comprising his own party, the TB/LNNK (formed in the previous month by the merger of the TB and the LNNK), the DPS, LC, the LZS and the Kristīgi Demokrātiskā Savienība (Christian Democratic Union). In March 1998 Šķēle announced the formation of a new political party, later named the Tautas Partija (TP—People's Party).

In April 1998 the Minister of the Economy, Atis Sausnītis, was dismissed. Later that month the DPS withdrew from the ruling coalition, and the Government was reorganized. In June the Parliament approved amendments substantially liberalizing the procedures required to obtain citizenship, in accordance with recommendations made by the Organization for Security and Co-operation in Europe (OSCE, see p. 385). However, nationalist parliamentary factions successfully demanded the organization of a referendum on the reforms on 3 October, when they were narrowly endorsed, with the support of 52.5% of voters.

At the legislative elections of 3 October 1998, held concurrently with the referendum, the TP was the most successful party, taking 21.2% of the votes (and 24 of the 100 legislative seats), ahead of LC with 18.1% (21 seats) and the TB/LNNK with 14.7% (17 seats). Six parties secured the minimum 5% of the

votes necessary for representation in the Parliament. In November 1998 the Parliament approved a minority coalition Government, headed by Vilis Krištopans of LC, comprising representatives of LC, the TB/LNNK and the Jaunā Partija (New Party, which held eight legislative seats).

On 17 June 1999 Vaira Vīķe-Freiberga, a non-partisan figure who had been resident in Canada in 1954–98, was elected President at a seventh round of voting in the Parliament, with the support of 53 deputies. At her inauguration on 8 July 1999 Vīķe-Freiberga identified as priorities Latvia's entry into the European Union (EU, see p. 271) and the North Atlantic Treaty Organization (NATO, see p. 367). Meanwhile, on 5 July Krištopans announced his Government's resignation. After Vīķe-Freiberga invited Šķēle to form a new government, he headed a coalition administration comprising TP, the TB/LNNK (which two parties had recently signed a co-operation accord, precipitating the collapse of the outgoing Government), and LC. Later in July the Parliament adopted legislation requiring all business and state- and municipally-organized gatherings to be conducted in Latvian. Russia denounced the legislation, which was also condemned by the OSCE, the Council of Europe, the European Commission and, within Latvia, by groups representing Russophones. Revised legislation, which incorporated amendments urged by the OSCE, was approved in December and took effect in September 2000. Meanwhile, Šķēle resigned as premier in April 2000, after LC withdrew from the governing coalition. Vīķe-Freiberga asked Andris Bērziņš, hitherto the Mayor of Rīga, to form a new government; the Parliament approved an administration, principally comprising the TP, LC and the TB/LNNK, in May.

In legislative elections, held on 5 October 2002, Jaunais Laiks (JL—New Era), a rightist party founded in the previous year by Einars Repše, a former Governor of the Bank of Latvia, won 23.9% of the votes cast, obtaining 26 seats; the leftist, pro-Russian electoral bloc Par Cilvēka Tiesībām Vienotā Latvijā (PCTVL—For Human Rights in a United Latvia), including the Tautas Saskaņas Partija (TSP—National Harmony Party) and the LSP, obtained 18.9% of the votes (25 seats); and the TP received 16.7% (20 seats). Other groups to achieve representation in the Parliament were the Zaļo un Zemnieku Savienība (ZZS—Greens' and Farmers' Union)—an alliance of the Centriskā Partija (Centre Party), the LZS and the Latvijas Zaļā Partija (LZP—Latvian Green Party)—with 12 seats, the recently formed Christian Democratic Latvijas Pirmā Partija (LPP—Latvian First Party), with 10 seats, and the TB/LNNK (seven); LC failed to obtain parliamentary representation. The rate of participation by the electorate was some 72.5%. On 7 November Parliament endorsed a coalition Government headed by Repše and comprising members of JL, the LPP, the ZZS and the TB/LNNK. A new post of Deputy Prime Minister was established, to which Ainārs Šlesers of the LPP was appointed. In late November Atis Slakteris replaced Šķēle as Chairman of the TP.

In February 2003 the TSP withdrew from the PCTVL alliance, apparently in order to pursue more moderate policies. In June the LSP also announced its withdrawal; the remainder of PCTVL was officially reconstituted as a united organization later that year. On 20 June Vīķe-Freiberga was re-elected unopposed to serve a second term of office as President. In January 2004 Repše dismissed Šlesers as Deputy Prime Minister; Šlesers alleged that his removal had been prompted by a proposal to establish a special investigative committee to examine the premier's property dealings. The LPP subsequently withdrew from the Government and on 5 February Repše's administration resigned. On 20 February President Vīķe-Freiberga nominated the Co-Chairman of the LZP, Indulis Emsis, as premier. Emsis secured the support of the ZZS, the LPP and the TP, and on 9 March the Parliament approved a new coalition Government.

After accession to the European Union

Following Latvia's accession to the EU on 1 May 2004 (see *Other external relations*), elections to the European Parliament were conducted on 13 June; the opposition TB/LNNK won four of Latvia's nine seats, while its ally JL won two, and PCTVL, the LPP and LC each won one seat. Neither of the two major parties in the ruling coalition obtained representation. Rihards Piks resigned as Minister of Foreign Affairs in order to take his seat in the European Parliament; he was replaced by Artis Pabriks. On 28 October the Parliament voted to reject the draft budget, precipitating the collapse of the ruling coalition. Vīķe-Freiberga nominated Aigars Kalvītis of the TP (which had led opposition to the proposed budget) to form a new government. On 2 December the Parliament approved the formation of a Government comprising members of the TP, JL, the ZZS and the LPP. Several members of the outgoing administration were retained in the same posts, including Pabriks and Oskars Spurdziņš (both of the TP), as Minister of Foreign Affairs and Minister of Finance, respectively. A revised draft budget was approved in the Parliament on 20 December.

In July 2005 Jānis Jurkāns resigned as leader of the TSP, in protest at the party's decision, following electoral defeats at both European and local level, to form an alliance with Jaunais Centrs (JC—New Centre), a party that had been established by former members of the TSP. The new union, the Saskaņas Centrs (SC—Harmony Centre) alliance, was joined by the LSP in December. In November Jānis Urbanovičs was elected as leader of the TSP, while Nils Ušakovs, a journalist, became leader of the SC alliance.

In October 2005 the Minister of the Interior, Ēriks Jēkabsons, tendered his resignation, after attracting criticism for his performance; Dzintars Jaundzeikars of the LPP was appointed as his successor. In December Repše resigned as Minister of Defence, following the announcement of a criminal investigation into his property investments; he also resigned his parliamentary seat and withdrew from the leadership of JL. Linda Mūrniece succeeded him as Minister of Defence. In March 2006 Kalvītis dismissed Slesers as Minister of Transport, after evidence emerged implicating him in electoral malpractice in the 2005 municipal elections. In April 2006 the Ministry of the Interior launched an inquiry into allegations of financial misconduct by the JL Minister of the Economy, Krišjānis Kariņš. JL accused the LPP of misusing its control of the interior ministry and subsequently withdrew its seven representatives from the Government, after Kalvītis refused to remove the LPP from the governing coalition. On 8 April the Parliament approved a three-party minority Government, in which JL was not represented.

At elections to the Parliament on 7 October 2006 the TP won 19.6% of the votes cast and 23 seats, the ZZS alliance 16.7% (18 seats), JL 16.4% (18 seats), the SC alliance 14.4% (17 seats), the LPP, allied with LC, 8.6% (10 seats), the TB/LNNK 6.9% (eight seats) and PCTVL 6.0% (six seats). The outgoing governing coalition of the TP, the ZZS and the LPP thus secured a narrow parliamentary majority. Around 62.3% of the electorate participated in the elections. Kalvītis invited the TB/LNNK to join the governing coalition in order to strengthen its parliamentary majority; Parliament approved a new Government on 7 November.

On 31 May 2007 the Parliament elected Valdis Zatlers, the candidate proposed by the ruling coalition, as President, to succeed Vīķe-Freiberga. Zatlers (a medical doctor without political experience) was inaugurated on 8 July. In August the LPP merged with LC; the reconstituted LPP/LC was jointly chaired by Slesers and Godmanis.

In mid-September 2007 Jurijs Strods of the TB/LNNK resigned as Minister of the Economy. On 22 September the Chairman of the Parliament, Emsis, resigned, after the opening of a criminal investigation into allegations that he had given false testimony in a case related to corruption in the city of Ventspils. He was succeeded by Gundars Daudze, a close ally of the Mayor of Ventspils, Aivars Lembergs, who had been arrested for corruption and abuse of public office in March. In October Kalvītis dismissed the Minister of Regional Development and Local Government, who had voted against a government motion to remove the director of the Anti-Corruption Bureau, Aleksejs Loskutovs, who had been suspended from his post in connection with alleged accounting irregularities. Later in the month Pabriks resigned as Minister of Foreign Affairs (and subsequently from the TP), in protest at the action against Loskutovs, which opponents of Kalvītis claimed was motivated by the bureau's investigations into official corruption. Although the crisis precipitated a mass anti-Government demonstration in Rīga, a parliamentary motion of no confidence was defeated. At the end of October the Minister of Welfare resigned, following opposition to proposed pensions reforms. In early December Kalvītis tendered the resignation of his Government. Zatlers, after rejecting an attempt by the TP to propose a further candidate as Prime Minister, nominated Godmanis (who had hitherto held the interior portfolio) to the premiership. On 20 December the Parliament approved a new coalition Government, comprising representatives of the TP, the LPP/LC, the ZZS and the TB/LNNK.

In April 2008 a new, centre-right party, the Pilsoniskā Savienība (PS—Civic Union), was founded by two prominent politicians, Sandra Kalniete (formerly a member of JL) and Valdis

Kristovskis (formerly of the TB/LNNK). Also in April it was announced that at least 10% of the electorate had signed a petition in support of a constitutional amendment that would enable voters to dissolve the legislature by referendum, thereby requiring a national referendum to be held on the matter. In June the Parliament voted to dismiss Loskutovs (who remained under investigation). On 2 August the proposed constitutional amendment failed to secure sufficient support (a minimum of 50% of the registered electorate) at the referendum. However, Zatlers described the referendum result, which was equivalent to about 40.2% of the electorate voting in favour, as significant, and submitted a legal initiative to the Parliament for consideration of the amendment.

In January 2009, following the severe impact of the international financial crisis upon Latvia, around 10,000 people attended a demonstration in Rīga to protest against perceived economic mismanagement by the Government and in support of the holding of early legislative elections; after riots ensued, some 100 protesters were arrested. Zatlers issued an ultimatum threatening to dissolve the Parliament in the event that it (and the Government) had not, by the end of March, implemented certain political reforms (including the adoption of the constitutional amendment on the dissolution of the legislature by a national referendum initiated by voters). In February the Government survived a parliamentary motion of no confidence, initiated by JL. However, following protests by farmers about increasing hardship, the Minister of Agriculture resigned. After the Cabinet of Ministers failed to adopt proposed measures to reduce the number of existing government ministries, Zatlers declared that he had lost confidence in Godmanis as Prime Minister. On 20 February, after the TP and the ZZS threatened to withdraw from the governing coalition, Godmanis tendered his resignation.

The Governments of Valdis Dombrovskis

President Zatlers nominated Valdis Dombrovskis, a member of JL and a former Minister of Finance, as Prime Minister. Subsequently, JL invited all parties represented in the Parliament, except PCTVL, to enter into consultations on the formation of a new administration. On 12 March 2009 a new coalition Government, comprising representatives of JL, the TP, the ZZS alliance, the TB/LNNK and the PS and headed by Dombrovskis, was approved by the Parliament; new appointments included those of Repše as Minister of Finance and Artis Kampars of JL as Minister of the Economy. On the same day the Parliament appointed a new director of the Anti-Corruption Bureau (thereby fulfilling one of the political reforms stipulated by Zatlers). On 8 April the Parliament approved constitutional amendments to enter into effect following the next parliamentary elections, enabling voters to initiate a referendum on the dissolution of the legislature during the second and third years of its term.

On 6 June 2009 elections to the European Parliament took place. Of the eight seats allocated to Latvia, the PS and the SC alliance both won two, while PCTVL, the LPP/LC, the TB/LNNK and JL each won one. On the same day local elections were held, prior to the establishment, in July, of a new, single-tier structure of local government across the country. The SC performed strongly in the polls, securing just over one-third of the vote in Rīga. In mid-June the Minister of Health, Ivars Eglītis, resigned, in protest at spending reductions in the health sector, approved as part of efforts to satisfy conditions for the disbursement of EU funds. In February 2010 the TSP merged with the JC and another small party of the SC to form the Sociāldemokrātiskā Partija 'Saskaņa' (Saskaņa—Harmony Social Democratic Party), under the leadership of Urbanovics. In March the founding congress was held of a new conservative alliance, Vienotība (Unity), comprising JL, the PS and the Sabiedrība Citai Politikai (Society for a Different Politics). In mid-March the TP withdrew its five ministers (including the Minister of Foreign Affairs) from the governing coalition, after Dombrovskis refused to sign an economic agreement with the party. Dombrovskis henceforth led a minority Government. At the end of April Aivis Ronis, a former ambassador to the USA and to NATO, was appointed as Minister of Foreign Affairs. Meanwhile, another conservative electoral coalition, the Par Labu Latviju! (PLL—Alliance for A Good Latvia), headed by Ulmanis and comprising the TP and the LPP/LC, was established. In May the Constitutional Court reversed a government decision to reduce pensions substantially as part of its programme of austerity measures.

At the legislative elections held on 2 October 2010, the Vienotība coalition was the most successful group, securing 31.9% of the votes cast and a total of 33 seats. The SC electoral alliance (which was strongly opposed to recently introduced economic austerity measures) demonstrated an increase in support, receiving 26.6% of the vote and 29 seats. The ZZS alliance obtained 20.1% of the vote and 22 seats; both a coalition of the nationalist Visu Latvijai! (VL—All For Latvia) party and the TB/LNNK, and the PLL obtained 7.8% of the votes cast winning eight seats apiece. Dombrovskis formed a coalition Government comprising the parties of the Vienotība coalition and the ZZS alliance, although attempts to negotiate the inclusion of the TB/LNNK proved unsuccessful. None the less, the ruling coalition held 55 of the 100 seats in the Parliament. Among the principal appointments in the new Government were Ģirts Kristovskis of the PS as Minister of Foreign Affairs and Artis Kampars of JL as Minister of the Economy.

In February 2011 Mūrniece tendered her resignation as Minister of the Interior, after persistent concerns about corruption within the police and security forces were exacerbated by an incident, in late January, in which a group of police officers were discovered robbing a casino in Jekabpils; one of the officers dispatched to the casino to apprehend the criminals was shot dead, and two others were injured. At the request of Dombrovskis, Mūrniece remained in office until early June, when Minister of Justice Aigars Štokenbergs assumed the interior portfolio in an acting capacity.

An investigation was launched in May 2011 into charges of corruption brought against Lembergs, Šķēle and Šlesers. However, the Anti-Corruption Bureau was refused permission to search their residences, and there were allegations that the Parliament was obstructing the course of justice. Later that month President Zatlers announced that a referendum on the dissolution of the Parliament would be held. The referendum was conducted on 23 July, when 94.3% of voters supported the motion to dissolve the Parliament.

On 2 June 2011, in the first round of the presidential election in the Parliament, Zatlers obtained the support of only 43 deputies, while 50 voted for Andris Bērziņš (no relation to the former Prime Minister of the same name), a former banking and business executive, and the candidate of the ZZS. In a second ballot, which took place on the same day, Bērziņš secured the requisite majority of votes, with 53, to be elected President; he was inaugurated on 8 July. Zatlers's defeat was ascribed to his earlier decision to call the referendum on the dissolution of the Parliament. Zatlers later announced the establishment of a new party, the Zatlers Reformu Partija (ZRP—Zatlers's Reform Party), which would not co-operate with the ZZS, the LPP/LC and the TP. Meanwhile, a campaign led by the Nacionālā Apvienība (NA—National Alliance—recently formed by the TB/LNNK and VL) to gather support for the organization of a referendum on the compulsory use of Latvian as the sole language of instruction in state-funded schools failed to obtain the requisite number of signatures. However, Russophones subsequently began a petition for a referendum on the amendment of the Constitution to grant Russian the status of second official language.

Following the dissolution of the Parliament, legislative elections were conducted on 17 September 2011. The SC alliance secured 28.4% of the votes cast, taking 31 seats in the Parliament. The Reformu Partija (RP—as the ZRP had become) won 20.8% of the votes and 22 seats. Vienotība (which had been constituted as a single party) received 18.8% of the votes and 20 seats. The NA and the ZZS took 14 and 13 seats, respectively. On 25 October a new coalition Government, led by Dombrovskis was approved by 57 votes in the Parliament. Gaidis Bērziņš of the NA was appointed Minister of Justice; RP members Rihards Kozlovskis and Edgars Rinkēvičs became, respectively, Minister of the Interior and Minister of Foreign Affairs, Pabriks and Andris Vilks, both of Vienotība, continued as Ministers of Defence and of Finance, respectively.

Following the collection of sufficient signatures in support of a referendum on the constitutional status of the Russian language, in December 2011 the plebiscite was scheduled to take place on 18 February 2012. (In order to be approved, the proposals would require the approval of at least one-half of the registered electorate.) In the referendum, the proposals were overwhelmingly defeated, with some 74.8% of the votes cast being against the proposed amendments (71.1% of the electorate participated), although a majority of those who voted in some eastern regions were in support. However, some 290,000 Russophones, who continued to lack Latvian citizenship, were not entitled to vote. In August PCTVL succeeded in securing sufficient signatures to demand that a referendum be conducted on the granting of automatic citizenship to the Russophone population. In

November, however, the members of the Central Election Commission voted to ban the referendum, claiming that the proposed measure would contravene the Constitution and international law.

Although opinion polls indicated that a majority of Latvians continued to oppose introduction of the euro, legislation providing for its adoption in January 2014 was endorsed by the Parliament on 31 January 2013, and signed into effect by President Bērziņš on 15 February. On 4 March Latvia submitted a formal application to join the eurozone. On 5 June Dombrovskis announced that Latvia had met the various economic criteria required for the country to be admitted to the eurozone; on 9 July the EU ministers of finance granted final approval for Latvia to adopt the euro, and the country duly adopted the euro as its currency, as planned, on 1 January 2014.

Recent developments: the 2014 legislative elections

In November 2013 at least 54 people were killed when the roof of a supermarket in Rīga collapsed; a criminal investigation into the incident was announced, amid speculation that building standards had been violated. In response, on 27 November Dombrovskis tendered the resignation of his Government, stating that the formation of a new administration with strong parliamentary support was necessary. President Bērziņš nominated the erstwhile Minister of Agriculture, Laimdota Straujuma of Vienotība, as the new premier on 6 January 2014; the appointment of a new coalition Government, comprising members of Vienotība, the RP, the ZZS and the NA, and headed by Straujuma was approved by the Parliament on 22 January. In mid-March Straujuma dismissed Einārs Cilinskis of the NA as Minister of Environmental Protection and Regional Development, after he announced that he would participate in commemorations, to be held on 16 March, of Latvian soldiers in the Second World War who had fought in Nazi German *Waffen SS* units; he was succeeded later in the month by Romāns Naudiņš.

In elections to the European Parliament on 24 May 2014, Vienotība, led by former Prime Minister Dombrovskis, was the first-placed party, winning 46.2% of the votes and four seats. The ZZS, the NA, Saskaņa and the Latvijas Krievu Savienība (Latvian Russian Union—as the PCTVL had recently renamed itself) each secured one seat. The rate of participation was only 30.0% of the registered electorate.

In August 2014 NA Co-Chairman Gaidis Bērziņš was appointed Minister of Justice, following the resignation from the post of Baiba Broka in response to a decision by the Prosecutor-General not to allow her access to classified information. Legislative elections were scheduled for 4 October (the parliamentary term having been reduced to three years following early elections in 2011, in accordance with the Constitution). Saskaņa, contesting the elections independently of the LSP, and under the leadership of Mayor of Rīga Ušakovs (who had succeeded Urbanovičs as party Chairman the previous year), secured 23.0% of the votes cast and 24 seats in the Parliament. Vienotība, which had incorporated RP candidates under an electoral agreement, received 21.9% and 23 seats, the ZZS 19.5% and 21 seats, and the NA 16.6% and 17 seats. Two newly formed associations, the Latvijas Regionu Apvienība (Latvian Association of Regions) and No Sirds Latvijai (For Latvia From the Heart), also obtained representation, with, respectively, 6.7% of the votes and eight seats, and 6.9% and seven seats. Later that month Vienotība, the ZZS and the NA agreed to form a further coalition Government (which held an increased parliamentary majority of 61 seats), under the continued premiership of Straujuma. The new Government was formally approved by the Parliament on 5 November; many principal ministers of the former administration retained their portfolios, while Jānis Reirs of Vienotība was appointed as Minister of Finance, replacing Vilks, and Dana Reizniece-Ozola of the ZZS as Minister of the Economy.

Foreign Affairs

Regional relations

Latvia enjoys close relations with Estonia and Lithuania, and the three countries have established institutions to promote co-operation, including the interparliamentary Baltic Assembly and the Baltic Council of Ministers. In 1992 Latvia became a founder member of the Council of the Baltic Sea States, a principal aim of which was to assist the political and economic development of its former communist member states (including Russia). Agreement on the delimitation of the maritime border with Estonia was reached in 1996. A further agreement on fishing rights was concluded in 1997, in which year the demarcation of the land border between the two countries was completed. Negotiations between Latvia and Lithuania on their maritime border were complicated in 1996 by the Parliament's ratification of an agreement with two foreign petroleum companies to explore and develop offshore oilfields in disputed maritime areas. Although the two countries signed an agreement on the delimitation of their territorial waters in 1999, the Parliament refused to ratify the agreement. In 2000 a protocol was signed on the re-demarcation of the land border with Lithuania. In 2006 the leaders of the Baltic countries reached agreement on measures aimed at reducing Russian dominance in the supply of energy. Latvia, Estonia and Lithuania established a common Nordic-Baltic energy market in mid-2013, under the European Commission's 2009 Baltic Energy Market Interconnection Plan; the North-Western European power market coupling project, which covered 15 countries including the three Baltic states, and was designed to create an integrated European electricity market, was formally launched in February 2014.

A priority of Latvian foreign policy was attaining full membership of the EU. Latvia applied for membership in October 1995, and formal negotiations on accession commenced in February 2000. In December 2002 Latvia, together with nine other countries, was formally invited to become a full member of the EU in 2004. A referendum on EU membership was held on 20 September 2003. Of the 72.5% of the electorate who participated in the plebiscite, 66.8% voted in support of Latvia's accession to the EU, although in certain, predominantly Russian-speaking areas of the country a majority of votes were cast against EU membership. The country became a full member on 1 May 2004. In December 2007 Latvia, together with eight other countries, implemented the EU's Schengen Agreement, enabling its citizens to travel to and from other member states without border controls. On 8 May 2008 the Parliament voted to ratify the EU's Lisbon Treaty. Latvia assumed the rotating Presidency of the Council of the EU for a period of six months on 1 January 2015 and was to host an EU Eastern Partnership summit meeting in May.

Latvia's post-independence relations with Russia were troubled by two questions: the citizenship and linguistic rights of Latvia's large Russian-speaking community; and the withdrawal of the 100,000 former Soviet troops still stationed in Latvia (jurisdiction over whom had been transferred, following the dissolution of the USSR, to Russia). Following negotiations, withdrawal of the troops began in 1992. In April 1994 agreements were concluded on the complete withdrawal of the remaining 10,000 Russian troops by the end of August (although Russia was allowed use of its military radar station at Skrunda, in western Latvia, for a further four years), as well as on social guarantees for the estimated 22,000 Russian military pensioners residing in Latvia. Negotiations regarding the demarcation of the Latvian–Russian border, and Latvia's claim to 1,640 sq km of land transferred to Russia during the Soviet era, commenced in 1996. Full agreement on a border treaty was reached in October 1997, although it remained unratified. In January 2007 Latvia agreed to remove a declaration from the draft treaty, which Russia had interpreted as making a territorial claim over the land that had formerly constituted part of Latvia. The treaty was officially signed by Prime Minister Kalvītis and his Russian counterpart, Mikhail Fradkov, in Moscow on 27 March. The treaty was endorsed by Vīķe-Freiberga in May and by Russian President Vladimir Putin in October. In August 2008 Zatlers, together with the Presidents of Estonia, Lithuania and Poland, condemned a Russian military offensive in Georgia (see the chapter on Georgia).

Meanwhile, tensions arising from repeated Russian threats to impose economic sanctions against Latvia, should the Government not promptly address perceived infringements of minority rights, were exacerbated by Latvia's 1999 state language law. Russia also condemned amendments to legislation on education, which took effect from September 2004, in accordance with which 60% of lessons in minority schools were to be taught in the Latvian language. On 9 May 2005 President Vīķe-Freiberga travelled to Moscow to attend celebrations to commemorate the 60th anniversary of the end of the Second World War in Europe (her Estonian and Lithuanian counterparts declined to attend). Three days later the Parliament adopted a declaration denouncing the Soviet occupation of Latvia and urging Russia to accept moral, legal and financial responsibility for the losses incurred by the Latvian people under Soviet rule. In late May the Parliament ratified the Council of Europe's Framework Convention for the Protection of National Minorities; however, a declaration was appended, stipulating that only Latvian citizens would be regarded as members of a national minority. In August 2006 the Latvian authorities introduced a new citizenship law provision, stipulating that applicants who failed a Latvian language test three times would be disqualified permanently from obtaining citizenship. Proposals on granting Russian the status of a second official language in Latvia, were overwhelmingly rejected at a national referendum in February 2012, while later that year the Central Election Commission ruled against the organization of a further poll on the granting of automatic citizenship to the Russophone population (see *The Governments of Valdis Dombrovskis*). The new Latvian Government of Prime Minister Straujuma formed in January 2014 declared its intention to maintain good relations with Russia, despite its plans to introduce full liberalization of the gas market, which was then supplied solely by Russian state enterprise Gazprom.

However, Russia's annexation of the Crimean peninsula in March 2014 (see the chapter on Ukraine) was followed by a new crisis in Russia's relations with the EU, and heightened regional tensions. Amid concerns over broadcasts by Russian-language television stations deemed to be propagandist, in April the Latvian authorities suspended the re-broadcasting of the programmes of the Russian state-owned channel Telekanal 'Rossiya' for three months, under legislation banning 'incitement to war', and subsequently levied fines on the Pervyi Baltiiskii Kanal—Latviya channel for coverage deemed to be biased. In the same month the USA stationed 150 troops in Latvia (and in the other Baltic states) to begin land forces training. Following the return to government of the coalition led by Straujuma in October, she pledged to increase the combat readiness of the country's armed forces in response to concerns about increased intimidatory tactics by Russia, and to raise defence spending to 2% of GDP by 2020 (in accordance with NATO requirements). (According to Latvia's Ministry of Defence, during 2014 Russian warships had approached Latvian waters on around 50 occasions and Russian military aircraft had neared Latvian airspace some 200 times.) In February 2015 NATO announced plans to establish an expanded rapid reaction force, under which new NATO command centres were to be installed in Latvia and five other Eastern European states. As part of its stated commitment to collective security, the USA dispatched military equipment to Latvia in March, while some 3,000 US troops were to participate in training missions with the armed forces of the Baltic states over the following three months. Also in March Latvia's Minister of the Interior announced March that a new security system was to be established at the country's borders with Russia and Belarus.

CONSTITUTION AND GOVERNMENT

Under the terms of the 1922 Constitution, which was restored in July 1993 and subsequently amended, Latvia is an independent democratic parliamentary republic. The supreme legislative body is the Saeima (Parliament), the 100 members of which are elected by universal adult suffrage for a four-year term. The President of the Republic, who is Head of State, is elected by a secret ballot of the Parliament, also for a period of four years. The President, who is also Head of the Armed Forces, may not serve for more than two consecutive terms. Executive power is held by the Cabinet of Ministers, which is headed by the Prime Minister. The Prime Minister is appointed by the President; the remaining members of the Cabinet are nominated by the Prime Minister. Judges are independent, and their appointment is confirmed by the Parliament. For administrative purposes, Latvia is divided into nine cities (including the capital, Rīga) and 109 municipalities.

REGIONAL AND INTERNATIONAL CO-OPERATION

Latvia is a member of the European Bank for Reconstruction and Development (EBRD, see p. 266), the Council of the Baltic Sea States (see p. 249), the Baltic Council (see p. 459), the Council of Europe (see p. 250) and the Organization for Security and Co-operation in Europe (see p. 385). In 2004 it acceded to the European Union (see p. 271).

Latvia joined the UN in 1991, and was admitted to the World Trade Organization (see p. 431) in 1999. The country joined the North Atlantic Treaty Organization (see p. 367) in 2004.

ECONOMIC AFFAIRS

In 2013, according to estimates by the World Bank, Latvia's gross national income (GNI), measured at average 2011–13 prices, was

US $30,774m., equivalent to $15,280 per head (or $22,970 per head on an international purchasing-power parity basis). During 2004–13, it was estimated, the population decreased by an annual average of 1.3%, while gross domestic product (GDP) per head increased at an average annual rate of 3.7%, in real terms. Overall GDP increased, in real terms, at an average annual rate of 2.3% in 2004–13, according to World Bank estimates. According to chain-linking methodologies, real GDP increased by 4.2% in 2013.

Agriculture (including hunting, forestry and fishing) contributed 3.6% of GDP and provided 8.1% of employment in 2013. The principal sectors are dairy farming and pig-breeding. Cereals, potatoes and fodder crops are the main crops grown. As part of the process of land reform and privatization, the dissolution of collective and state farms was undertaken in the early 1990s. Fishing makes an important contribution to the economy (an estimated 70% of the total annual catch is exported). According to UN estimates, agricultural GDP increased, in real terms, by an average of 1.9% per year in 2004–13. According to chain-linking methodologies, the real GDP of the sector decreased by 0.4% in 2013.

Industry (comprising mining and quarrying, manufacturing, construction and utilities) contributed 23.3% of GDP and provided 23.9% of employment in 2013. According to UN estimates, industrial GDP increased, in real terms, at an average annual rate of 1.6% in 2004–13; GDP of the industrial sector increased, in real terms, by 1.3%, in 2013.

Mining and quarrying (along with utilities) contributed 4.4% of GDP in 2013, and employed 0.3% of workers in 2010. Latvia has limited mineral resources, the most important being peat, dolomite, limestone, gypsum, amber, gravel and sand. Offshore and onshore petroleum reserves have been located. According to chain-linking methodologies, the sector's GDP increased, in real terms, by 3.2% in 2013.

The manufacturing sector contributed 12.6% of GDP and (along with utilities) provided 16.4% of employment in 2013. According to UN estimates, real manufacturing GDP increased by an average of 2.2% per year in 2004–13. According to chain-linking methodologies, the GDP of the sector increased, in real terms, by 4.6% in 2012 with negligible growth in 2013.

The construction sector contributed 6.4% of GDP and provided 7.5% of employment in 2013. During 2004–13, according to UN estimates, the GDP of the sector increased at an average annual rate of 0.8%. According to chain-linking methodologies, construction GDP increased by 14.5% in 2012 and by 7.5% in 2013.

Latvia is highly dependent on imported fuels to provide energy. In 2013 mineral products represented 17.2% of the total value of Latvia's imports. Electric energy is supplied primarily by Estonia and Lithuania, and petroleum products are supplied by Russia and Lithuania. In 2011 natural gas provided some 49.5% of annual domestic electricity production in Latvia; 47.4% was derived from hydroelectric plants.

The services sector contributed 73.1% of GDP and accounted for 68.0% of employment in 2013. According to UN estimates, the GDP of the sector increased, in real terms, by an annual average of 2.9% in 2004–13; real services GDP increased by 5.1% in 2013.

In 2013 Latvia recorded a visible merchandise trade deficit of US $2,921.2m., and there was a deficit of $249.6m. on the current account of the balance of payments. The principal source of imports in 2013 was Lithuania, which accounted for 20.4% of total imports; other major sources were Germany, Poland, Russia and Estonia. The main market for exports in that year was also Lithuania, which accounted for 17.2% of the total; other

significant purchasers were Estonia, Russia, Germany, Poland and Sweden. The principal exports in 2013 were wood and wood articles, followed by machinery and electrical equipment, base metals and manufactures, prepared foodstuffs, beverages and tobacco, mineral products, chemicals, and vegetable products. The principal imports in that year were machinery and electrical equipment, mineral products, chemicals, base metals, vehicles and transport equipment, prepared foodstuffs, beverages and tobacco, and plastics and rubber.

In 2013 there was a budgetary deficit of €199.7m. (equivalent to 0.9% of GDP). Latvia's general government gross debt was €8,166m. in 2013, equivalent to 35.0% of GDP. At the end of 2011 Latvia's external debt totalled US $38,255m., of which $7,075m. was public and publicly guaranteed debt. In that year the cost of debt-servicing was equivalent to 47.0% of the value of exports of goods and services. Annual consumer-price inflation averaged 5.2% in 2004–13. Consumer prices increased by 2.2% in 2012, and remained constant in 2013. According to official statistics, some 11.9% of the population were unemployed in 2013.

Following a period of rapid economic growth after 1999, Latvia suffered a GDP contraction of 18% in 2009, as a consequence of the international financial crisis. The introduction of an IMF- and European Union (EU, see p. 271)-funded programme of austerity measures brought about an economic stabilization, and growth resumed in 2010. Following the successful issuance of an international bond, the Government announced in December 2012 that repayment of all its outstanding obligations to the IMF would take place earlier than scheduled. In March 2013 Latvia submitted a formal application to enter the eurozone on 1 January 2014 (having been admitted to the EU's exchange rate mechanism—ERM II—in 2005). The Government confirmed that it had fulfilled all the necessary fiscal criteria for the adoption of the euro as the national currency; legislation had been adopted in January to enforce the stipulations of the EU's 'fiscal compact' treaty that government debt remain below 60% and the general budget deficit below 3% of GDP. Following approval by the EU finance ministers in July 2013, Latvia duly adopted the euro on 1 January 2014. The new Government of Prime Minister Laimdota Straujuma established later in January secured the approval of legislation providing for a process of full liberalization of the country's natural gas market by 2017. Straujuma's coalition Government, which was returned to office in elections in October 2014, subsequently announced plans to separate the supply and distribution branches of state gas utility Latvijas gāze in 2016, in accordance with EU regulations and the priority of reducing reliance on Russian gas imports. Meanwhile, Latvian exports had been severely affected by the regional impact of continued conflict in eastern Ukraine during 2014, together with the imposition of EU sanctions against Russia in March, and Russia's retaliatory introduction of a ban on the import of foodstuffs from EU states in August; GDP growth in Latvia fell to an estimated 2.5% in 2014. Although the Government continued to pledge adherence to the austerity policies of the previous administration, expenditure grew in the 2015 budget, particularly on defence.

PUBLIC HOLIDAYS

2016: 1 January (New Year's Day), 25–28 March (Easter), 1 May (Labour Day), 4 May (Declaration of Independence Day), 23–24 June (Midsummer Festival), 18 November (National Day, proclamation of the Republic), 25–26 December (Christmas—Gregorian), 31 December (New Year's Eve).

Statistical Survey

Source (unless otherwise stated): Central Statistical Bureau of Latvia, Lāčplēša iela 1, Rīga 1301; tel. 6736-6850; fax 6783-0137; e-mail csb@csb.lv; internet www.csb.lv.

Area and Population

AREA, POPULATION AND DENSITY

Area (sq km)	64,559*
Population (census results)†	
31 March 2000	2,377,383
1 March 2011	
Males	946,102
Females	1,124,269
Total	2,070,371
Population (official estimates at 1 January, provisional)† .	
2012	2,044,813
2013	2,023,825
2014	2,001,468
Density (per sq km) at 1 January 2014	31.0

* 24,926 sq miles.
† Figures refer to the resident population.

POPULATION BY AGE AND SEX
(official estimates at 1 January 2014)

	Males	Females	Total
0–14 years	150,881	143,503	294,384
15–64 years	642,083	683,386	1,325,469
65 years and over	124,081	257,534	381,615
Total	**917,045**	**1,084,423**	**2,001,468**

POPULATION BY ETHNIC GROUP
(official estimates at 1 January 2014)

	Number	%
Latvian	1,229,067	61.4
Russian	520,136	26.0
Belarusian	68,695	3.4
Ukrainian	45,282	2.3
Polish	43,365	2.2
Lithuanian	25,025	1.3
Romanian	5,594	0.3
Jewish	5,402	0.3
German	2,886	0.1
Estonian	1,882	0.1
Other	54,134	2.7
Total	**2,001,468**	**100.0**

Note: Classification of ethnic groups reflects national methodology.

PRINCIPAL TOWNS
(official estimates 1 January 2014)

Rīga (Riga, capital) .	643,368	Jūrmala	49,750
Daugavpils . . .	87,403	Ventspils . . .	36,677
Liepāja	71,926	Rēzekne	29,948
Jelgava	57,332		

BIRTHS, MARRIAGES AND DEATHS

	Registered live births		Registered marriages		Registered deaths	
	Number	Rate (per 1,000)	Number	Rate (per 1,000)	Number	Rate (per 1,000)
2006 . .	22,264	9.7	14,616	6.4	33,098	14.5
2007 . .	23,273	10.2	15,486	6.8	33,042	14.5
2008 . .	23,948	10.6	12,946	5.7	31,006	13.7
2009 . .	21,677	9.6	9,925	4.4	29,897	13.3
2010 . .	19,219	8.6	9,290	4.1	30,040	13.4
2011 . .	18,586	9.0	10,760	5.2	28,519	13.8
2012 . .	19,897	9.8	11,244	5.5	29,025	14.3
2013 . .	20,596	10.3	11,436	5.7	28,691	14.3

Life expectancy (years at birth): males 69.5; females 79.0 in 2013.

IMMIGRATION AND EMIGRATION

	2011	2012	2013
Immigrants	10,234	13,303	8,299
Emigrants	30,311	25,163	22,561

ECONOMICALLY ACTIVE POPULATION
(annual averages, '000 persons aged 15–74 years)

	2011	2012	2013
Agriculture, forestry and fishing	76.6	73.3	71.9
Manufacturing; electricity, gas and water supply	136.5	143.1	146.3
Construction	60.9	62.3	67.3
Wholesale and retail trade; repair of motor vehicles, motorcycles and personal and household goods; hotels and restaurants .	161.4	155.6	159.9
Transport, storage and communications	98.5	96.6	101.7
Financial intermediation; real estate, renting and other business activities	91.1	100.5	102.7
Public administration and defence, compulsory social security . .	59.4	58.9	61.3
Education	88.8	92.1	94.6
Health and social work . . .	51.6	51.2	47.7
Other community, social and personal service activities . .	36.6	41.4	39.5
Sub-total	**861.4**	**875.0**	**892.9**
Activities not adequately defined .	0.2	0.6	1.0
Total employed	**861.6**	**875.6**	**893.9**
Males	416.2	428.2	440.6
Females	445.4	447.4	453.3
Unemployed	166.6	155.1	120.4
Total labour force	**1,028.2**	**1,030.7**	**1,014.2**

Health and Welfare

KEY INDICATORS

Total fertility rate (children per woman, 2012)	1.6
Under-5 mortality rate (per 1,000 live births, 2012) . . .	9
HIV/AIDS (% of persons aged 15–49, 2012)	1.1
Physicians (per 1,000 head, 2011)	2.9
Hospital beds (per 1,000 head, 2009)	6.4
Health expenditure (2011): US $ per head (PPP)	1,141
Health expenditure (2011): % of GDP	6.0
Health expenditure (2011): public (% of total)	57.1
Access to water (% of persons, 2012)	98
Access to sanitation (% of persons, 2008)	78
Total carbon dioxide emissions ('000 metric tons, 2010) . .	7,616.4
Carbon dioxide emissions per head (metric tons, 2010) . .	3.4
Human Development Index (2012): ranking	44
Human Development Index (2012): value	0.814

For sources and definitions, see explanatory note on p. vi.

Agriculture

PRINCIPAL CROPS
('000 metric tons)

	2011	2012	2013
Wheat	937.0	1,539.8	1,435.0
Barley	236.7	236.9	232.6
Rye	76.4	124.2	75.6
Oats	120.9	137.0	134.2
Triticale (wheat-rye hybrid) . .	21.4	48.8	36.6
Potatoes	499.0	539.0	226.8
Peas, dry	2.9	2.4	5.2
Rapeseed	219.1	303.5	296.6
Cabbages and other brassicas .	61.2	62.1	52.7
Cucumbers and gherkins . . .	9.8	9.7	9.4
Onions, dry	20.2	16.1	10.4
Carrots and turnips	38.6	28.1	32.0
Apples	7.5	9.4	14.8
Currants	0.4	0.6	0.5

Aggregate production ('000 metric tons, may include official, semi-official or estimated data): Total cereals 1,409.5 in 2011, 2,112.8 in 2012, 1,948.7 in 2013; Total roots and tubers 499.0 in 2011, 539.0 in 2012, 226.8 in 2013; Total vegetables (incl. melons) 168.6 in 2011, 161.7 in 2012, 140.8 in 2013; Total fruits (excl. melons) 11.7 in 2011, 13.9 in 2012, 20.0 in 2013.

Source: FAO.

LIVESTOCK
('000 head at 1 January)

	2011	2012	2013
Cattle	380	381	393
Pigs	390	375	355
Sheep	77	80	84
Goats	14	13	13
Horses	12	11	11
Chickens*	4,208	3,756	4,100
Turkeys*	741	662	811

* Unofficial figures.

Source: FAO.

LIVESTOCK PRODUCTS
('000 metric tons unless otherwise indicated)

	2011	2012	2013
Cattle meat	18.0	17.3	16.7
Pig meat	37.6	35.7	35.9
Chicken meat	23.0	24.6	26.8
Cows' milk	841.7	870.6	912.0
Hen eggs	41.9	42.3	39.7

Source: FAO.

Forestry

ROUNDWOOD REMOVALS
('000 cubic metres, excl. bark)

	2011	2012	2013
Sawlogs, veneer logs and logs for			
sleepers	7,652	6,995	6,636
Pulpwood	3,254	3,467	3,305
Other industrial wood	743	895	1,042
Fuel wood	1,184	1,173	1,258
Total	12,833	12,530	12,241

Source: FAO.

SAWNWOOD PRODUCTION
('000 cubic metres, incl. railway sleepers)

	2011	2012	2013
Coniferous (softwood)	2,870	2,714	2,788
Broadleaved (hardwood) . . .	562	602	579
Total	3,432	3,316	3,367

Source: FAO.

Fishing

('000 metric tons, live weight)

	2010	2011	2012
Capture	164.8	155.3	94.5
Atlantic cod	5.2	4.9	4.3
Jack and horse mackerels . .	40.2	26.9	7.6
Atlantic herring	21.4	22.8	20.1
Sardinellas	14.2	19.4	7.8
European sprat	45.9	33.4	30.7
Chub mackerel	8.1	11.7	5.8
Northern prawn	1.0	0.4	0.5
Aquaculture	0.5	0.5	0.6
Total catch	165.4	155.9	95.1

Source: FAO.

Mining

('000 metric tons)

	2010	2011	2012
Peat	1,119.4	1,378.7	1,378.0
Gypsum*	230.0	230.0	230.0
Cement*	1,100.0	1,100.0	1,200.0

* Estimates.

Source: US Geological Survey.

Industry

SELECTED PRODUCTS
('000 metric tons, unless otherwise indicated)

	2009	2010	2011
Sausages	37	34	33
Preserved fish	40	46	52
Yoghurt	66	67	64
Ice cream (million litres) . . .	8.3	10.2	10.4
Beer ('000 hectolitres)	1,283	1,475	1,472
Plywood ('000 cu metres) . . .	191	298	290
Electric energy (million kWh) .	5,569	6,627	6,094

Source: UN Industrial Commodity Statistics Database.

Finance

CURRENCY AND EXCHANGE RATES

Monetary Units
100 cents = 1 euro (€).

Sterling and Dollar Equivalents (31 December 2014)
£1 sterling = 1.286 euros;
US $1 = 0.824 euros;
€10 = £7.78 = $12.14.

Average Exchange Rate (euros per US $)
2012   0.7783
2013   0.7532
2014   0.7537

Note: From 2005 the lats was pegged to the euro at 0.702804 = 1 euro, and the euro was adopted as the sole legal currency of Latvia on 1 January 2014

GOVERNMENT FINANCE
(general government operations, million lats)

Summary of Balances

	2010	2011	2012
Revenue	4,592.1	5,071.4	5,734.1
Less Expense	5,012.6	4,936.8	5,132.1
Net operating balance	−420.5	134.6	602.0
Less Net acquisition of non-financial assets	377.5	572.1	575.1
Net lending/borrowing	−798.0	−437.5	26.9

Revenue

	2010	2011	2012
Tax revenue	2,346.5	2,649.0	2,970.4
Social contributions	1,093.2	1,229.6	1,324.0
Grants	600.0	663.6	846.0
Other revenue	552.3	529.3	593.7
Total	4,592.1	5,071.4	5,734.1

Expense/Outlays

Expense by economic type	2010	2011	2012
Compensation of employees	1,087.1	1,130.9	1,153.2
Use of goods and services	688.3	729.2	730.4
Interest	177.1	204.0	234.7
Subsidies	1,171.0	1,110.9	1,218.1
Social benefits	1,744.3	1,609.2	1,610.2
Other expense	144.7	152.6	185.5
Total	5,012.6	4,936.8	5,132.1

Outlays by function of government	2010	2011	2012
General public services	554.7	606.0	709.7
Defence	131.3	142.0	132.7
Public order and safety	253.8	269.9	277.3
Education	759.8	815.5	838.5
Health care	475.0	474.6	480.9
Social security and social welfare	1,800.3	1,690.2	1,707.3
Housing and community amenities	148.2	177.8	181.4
Recreation, sport, cultural and religious affairs	181.8	196.4	215.9
Economic affairs	973.5	1,043.8	1,062.6
Environmental protection	111.7	92.6	100.9
Total	5,390.1	5,508.9	5,707.2

Source: IMF, *Government Finance Statistics Yearbook*.

2013 (general government operations, € million): Total revenue 8,089.8; Total expenditure 8,289.5.

Central Government Consolidated Budget (million lats): *Revenue:* 6,847 (Taxes 5,170) in 2013; 7,044 (Taxes 5,391) in 2014 (forecasts); 7,448 (Taxes 5,625) in 2015 (forecasts); 7,060 (Taxes 5,810) in 2016 (forecasts). *Expenditure:* 6,835 in 2013; 7,187 in 2014 (forecast); 7,055 in 2015 (forecast); 7,298 in 2016 (forecast) (Source: Ministry of Finance, Rīga).

INTERNATIONAL RESERVES
(US $ million at 31 December)

	2011	2012	2013
Gold (Eurosystem valuation)	386.15	411.96	297.39
IMF special drawing rights	144.69	156.64	186.07
Reserve position in IMF	0.09	0.09	0.09
Foreign exchange	5,852.50	6,954.08	7,409.56
Total	6,383.43	7,522.77	7,893.11

Source: IMF, *International Financial Statistics*.

MONEY SUPPLY
(million lats at 31 December)

	2011	2012	2013
Currency outside depository corporations	1,040	1,082	470
Transferable deposits	3,317	3,751	4,756
Other deposits	2,105	1,875	1,606
Securities other than shares	199	139	202
Broad money	6,661	6,847	7,034

Source: IMF, *International Financial Statistics*.

COST OF LIVING
(Consumer Price Index; base: 2010 = 100)

	2011	2012	2013
Food and non-alcoholic beverages	108.4	111.0	112.4
Alcoholic beverages and tobacco	103.4	106.4	108.2
Clothing and footwear	101.9	100.1	99.9
Housing, water, electricity, gas and other fuels	107.6	114.9	114.9
Health	97.4	97.7	99.0
Education	100.2	98.7	98.0
Transport	107.8	111.1	108.2
Communication	98.0	95.2	89.8
Recreational and culture	99.2	98.8	98.4
Restaurant and hotels	101.4	103.7	104.7
Miscellaneous goods and services	100.6	101.9	103.8
All items	104.4	106.7	106.7

NATIONAL ACCOUNTS
(€ million at current prices)

Expenditure on the Gross Domestic Product

	2011	2012	2013
Government final consumption expenditure	3,700.9	3,795.9	4,078.5
Private final consumption expenditure	12,676.5	13,491.6	14,375.8
Gross fixed capital formation	4,494.5	5,548.2	5,401.1
Changes in inventories	436.2	180.4	103.0
Total domestic expenditure	21,308.1	23,016.1	23,958.4
Exports of goods and services	11,738.4	13,418.0	13,799.9
Less Imports of goods and services	12,749.0	14,391.2	14,536.4
GDP in market prices	20,297.4	22,043.0	23,221.9

Gross Domestic Product by Economic Activity

	2011	2012	2013
Agriculture, forestry and fishing .	697.7	714.0	734.9
Mining and quarrying; electricity, gas and water supply . . .	895.4	913.7	887.2
Manufacturing	2,329.0	2,487.4	2,537.8
Construction	958.2	1,171.5	1,284.0
Wholesale and retail trade; repair of motor vehicles, motorcycles and personal and household goods	2,607.1	2,719.7	2,865.1
Hotels and restaurants . . .	297.7	301.1	321.8
Transport, storage and communications	2,581.8	2,816.4	2,897.9
Financial intermediation . . .	725.1	804.9	846.3
Real estate, renting and business activities	3,408.5	3,803.5	4,192.6
Public administration and defence; compulsory social security . .	1,357.0	1,431.4	1,442.5
Education	895.8	926.4	956.7
Health and social work . . .	526.6	568.6	599.6
Other community, social and personal service activities . .	513.6	577.9	648.2
GDP at basic prices	17,793.6	19,236.5	20,214.6
Taxes *less* subsidies on products .	2,503.8	2,806.5	3,007.3
GDP in purchasers' values .	20,297.4	22,043.0	23,221.9

BALANCE OF PAYMENTS
(US $ million)

	2011	2012	2013
Exports of goods	11,498.8	12,346.0	13,058.6
Imports of goods	−14,740.1	−15,422.2	−15,979.8
Balance on goods	−3,241.3	−3,076.2	−2,921.2
Exports of services	4,616.8	4,675.2	5,063.6
Imports of services	−2,606.7	−2,618.2	−2,715.7
Balance on goods and services	−1,231.2	−1,019.2	−573.3
Primary income received . . .	1,251.3	1,257.4	1,265.2
Primary income paid	−1,516.7	−1,759.5	−1,703.5
Balance on goods, services and primary income	−1,496.6	−1,521.3	−1,011.6
Secondary income received . .	1,815.6	1,794.2	1,877.9
Secondary income paid . . .	−947.2	−974.9	−1,115.9
Current balance	−628.2	−702.0	−249.6
Capital account (net) . . .	606.7	822.8	758.9
Direct investment assets . .	−106.9	−161.5	−412.3
Direct investment liabilities . .	1,502.3	1,076.3	880.8
Portfolio investment assets .	−857.2	−953.2	−626.6
Portfolio investment liabilities .	236.8	2,260.6	353.5
Financial derivatives and employee stock options (net)	123.3	80.5	291.4
Other investment assets . . .	−404.0	−363.1	−87.3
Other investment liabilities . .	−1,556.7	410.1	−129.6
Net errors and omissions . .	−102.5	62.1	−254.3
Reserves and related items .	−1,186.4	2,532.6	524.9

Source: IMF, *International Financial Statistics*.

External Trade

PRINCIPAL COMMODITIES
(distribution by HS, € million)

Imports c.i.f.	2011	2012	2013
Live animals and animal products	378.3	430.4	486.3
Vegetables and vegetable products	448.6	511.8	462.5
Prepared foodstuffs; beverages, spirits and vinegar; tobacco and manufactured substitutes .	726.4	857.4	943.6
Mineral products	1,903.7	2,209.6	2,170.8
Mineral fuels, mineral oils and products of their distillation; bituminous substances; mineral waxes	1,860.0	2,149.4	2,105.0
Petroleum oils and oils obtained from bituminous minerals, other than crude	1,124.4	1,346.2	1,290.4
Petroleum gases and other gaseous hydrocarbons . .	450.8	558.1	568.8
Products of chemical or allied industries	1,048.4	1,109.8	1,187.9
Pharmaceutical products . .	465.4	416.1	482.9
Medicaments	341.3	324.5	364.4
Plastics, rubber and articles thereof	592.2	645.9	698.6
Plastics and articles thereof . .	424.9	457.5	492.8
Textiles and textile articles .	466.8	527.0	601.1
Base metals and articles thereof	1,200.4	1,303.6	1,093.5
Iron and steel	683.0	698.7	487.2
Machinery and mechanical appliances; electrical equipment; sound and television apparatus . . .	1,902.5	2,284.2	2,326.9
Machinery and mechanical appliances; parts thereof . .	1,054.8	1,244.5	1,119.7
Electrical machinery and equipment	847.8	1,039.7	1,207.2
Telephone sets, including telephones for cellular networks or for other wireless networks; other apparatus for the transmission or reception of voice, images or other data	175.4	258.0	409.2
Vehicles, aircraft, vessels and associated transport equipment	988.0	1,078.3	967.8
Vehicles other than rolling-stock, and parts and accessories thereof	879.5	881.7	873.2
Total (incl. others)	10,983.3	12,512.3	12,635.1

Exports f.o.b.	2011	2012	2013
Live animals and animal products	375.3	430.9	499.7
Vegetable products	366.4	721.4	574.7
Cereals	139.9	406.0	301.7
Wheat and meslin	102.3	358.0	256.0
Prepared foodstuffs; beverages, spirits and vinegar; tobacco and manufactured substitutes	628.5	841.0	937.8
Beverages, spirits and vinegar	322.9	462.0	499.1
Undenatured ethyl alcohol; spirits, liqueurs and other spirituous beverages	227.7	352.2	385.9
Mineral products	780.7	858.8	873.0
Mineral fuels, mineral oils and products of their distillation; bituminous substances; mineral waxes	719.6	793.5	810.5
Petroleum oils and oils obtained from bituminous minerals, other than crude	417.5	510.9	533.1
Products of chemical or allied industries	631.1	636.9	673.6
Pharmaceutical products	308.8	268.1	296.1
Plastics, rubber and articles thereof	265.4	299.6	303.7
Wood, cork and articles thereof; wood charcoal; manufactures of straw, esparto, etc.	1,437.2	1,466.8	1,594.0
Wood and articles of wood; wood charcoal	1,436.0	1,465.8	1,593.0
Wood sawn or chipped lengthwise, sliced or peeled	418.7	433.7	480.3
Textiles and textile articles	345.5	386.6	430.2
Base metals and articles thereof	1,235.1	1,381.0	1,051.7
Iron and steel	714.1	829.2	496.8
Other bars and rods of iron or non-alloy steel	309.6	423.4	140.6
Articles of iron and steel	270.9	312.1	312.4
Machinery and mechanical appliances; electrical equipment; sound and television apparatus	1,085.8	1,352.6	1,561.0
Machinery and mechanical appliances	472.7	530.5	542.8
Electrical machinery and equipment	613.1	822.1	1,018.2
Vehicles, aircraft, vessels and associated transport equipment	571.6	534.0	452.4
Vehicles other than rolling-stock, and parts and accessories thereof	506.6	461.6	380.6
Motor cars and other motor vehicles principally designed for the transport of persons	290.1	190.2	118.1
Total (incl. others)	8,535.1	9,871.1	10,021.3

PRINCIPAL TRADING PARTNERS
(€ million)*

Imports c.i.f.	2011	2012	2013
Austria	118.3	143.6	159.4
Belarus	485.6	447.3	310.3
Belgium	206.0	215.2	200.8
China, People's Republic	294.4	348.2	335.5
Czech Republic	162.0	184.4	174.5
Denmark	245.3	282.4	277.4
Estonia	818.0	969.3	1,031.5
Finland	506.0	569.0	585.5
France	260.2	230.1	250.9
Germany	1,331.1	1,444.7	1,463.4
Hungary	115.5	121.3	129.3
Italy	353.5	434.5	434.2

Imports c.i.f.—*continued*	2011	2012	2013
Lithuania	2,062.6	2,482.0	2,571.7
Netherlands	395.1	424.5	463.2
Poland	889.2	1,077.2	1,246.1
Russia	937.9	1,177.8	1,057.7
Spain	120.1	177.9	149.9
Sweden	420.7	421.7	437.9
Switzerland	138.9	87.7	84.3
Ukraine	138.1	174.5	129.5
United Kingdom	192.9	200.7	202.5
Total (incl. others)	10,983.3	12,512.3	12,635.1

Exports f.o.b.	2011	2012	2013
Afghanistan	131.2	136.2	14.7
Algeria	49.3	204.7	95.5
Belarus	152.9	180.8	186.9
Belgium	91.6	126.1	122.4
Czech Republic	66.0	80.3	111.3
Denmark	286.6	388.7	410.3
Estonia	1,164.3	1,285.6	1,275.6
Finland	262.2	268.4	264.6
France	123.5	139.8	150.4
Germany	706.3	782.6	742.2
Italy	130.5	110.7	127.4
Lithuania	1,546.3	1,575.6	1,724.3
Netherlands	194.8	269.0	221.9
Norway	203.3	259.9	265.8
Poland	500.7	593.5	672.7
Russia	901.5	1,125.8	1,163.1
Sweden	541.4	511.3	503.1
Turkey	107.0	144.1	130.5
United Kingdom	260.5	321.1	367.6
USA	101.7	109.5	118.1
Total (incl. others)	8,535.1	9,871.1	10,021.3

* Imports by country of origin; exports by country of destination.

Transport

RAILWAYS
(traffic)*

	2011	2012	2013
Passenger journeys (million)	20.5	19.8	19.8
Passenger-kilometres (million)	741	725	729
Freight transported (million metric tons)	59.4	60.6	55.8
Freight ton-kilometres (million)	21,410	21,867	19,532

* Data relating to passengers include railway personnel, and data on freight include passengers' baggage, parcel post and mail.

ROAD TRAFFIC
(motor vehicles in use at 31 December)

	2011	2012	2013
Passenger cars	612,321	618,274	634,603
Buses and coaches	5,186	5,044	4,989
Lorries and vans (incl. road tractors)	72,622	76,303	79,899

SHIPPING
Flag Registered Fleet
(at 31 December)

	2012	2013	2014
Number of vessels	153	160	173
Total displacement ('000 grt)	181.4	241.3	255.3

Source: Lloyd's List Intelligence (www.lloydslistintelligence.com).

International Seaborne Freight Traffic
('000 metric tons)

	2011	2012	2013
Goods loaded	61,028	66,130	62,350
Goods unloaded	7,793	9,063	8,130

CIVIL AVIATION
(traffic)

	2011	2012	2013
Passengers carried (million) . .	3.5	3.2	3.0
Passenger-kilometres (million) .	4,113	3,715	3,537
Cargo carried ('000 metric tons) .	13	19	14
Cargo ton-kilometres (million) .	13	13	11

Tourism

FOREIGN TOURIST ARRIVALS*

Country of residence	2011	2012	2013
Belarus	16,682	21,545	29,408
Estonia	81,979	87,026	105,558
Finland	90,991	74,172	63,515
Germany	113,064	120,447	122,737
Italy	37,963	33,205	31,826
Lithuania	100,561	93,270	109,118
Norway	72,309	67,643	66,160
Poland	35,309	32,103	39,785
Russia	174,343	232,552	310,266
Sweden	63,135	51,458	55,799
United Kingdom	43,959	37,960	39,994
USA	18,115	22,186	26,522
Total (incl. others)	1,063,294	1,096,274	1,249,814

* Figures refer to the number of visitors arriving at accommodation establishments.

Tourism receipts (US $ million, excl. passenger transport): 771 in 2011; 745 in 2012; 865 in 2013 (Source: World Tourism Organization).

Communications Media

	2011	2012	2013
Telephones ('000 main lines in use)*	516	501	480
Mobile cellular telephones ('000 subscribers)	2,309	2,310	2,800
Broadband subscribers ('000) . .	457.4	481.1	506.0
Book production: titles	2,128	2,083	2,223
Book production: copies ('000) .	3,500	3,500	3,200
Newspapers: number	208	251	242
Newspapers: average annual circulation (million copies) . .	111	100	85
Other periodicals: number . .	339	329	308
Other periodicals: average annual circulation (million copies) . .	39.1	39.2	37.9

* At 31 December.

Source: partly International Telecommunication Union.

Education

(2013/14 unless otherwise indicated)

	Institutions	Students
Pre-primary (children ages 3–6)	617	93,533
General schools*	807	197,863
Primary (Grades 1–4)	54	10,480
Basic (Grades 5–9)	334	39,019
Secondary (Grades 10–12)	358	141,276
Special	61	7,088
Vocational schools†	62	29,829
Higher education institutions‡	60	85,881

* Full-time education.
† 2014/15.

Teachers (2002 unless otherwise indicated): Pre-primary 7,996 (2004); Primary (including basic schools) 9,252; Secondary 16,495; Special schools 1,837; Vocational 5,639; Higher 4,917 (2012/13).

Pupil-teacher ratio (primary education, UNESCO estimate): 11.0 in 2011/12 (Source: UNESCO Institute for Statistics).

Adult literacy rate (UNESCO estimates): 99.9% (males 99.9%; females 99.9%) in 2011 (Source: UNESCO Institute for Statistics).

Directory

The Government

HEAD OF STATE

President: ANDRIS BĒRZIŅŠ (inaugurated 8 July 2011).

CABINET OF MINISTERS
(May 2015)

A coalition, comprising members of Vienotība, Reformu Partija (RP), Zaļo un Zemnieku Savienība (ZZS), Nacionālā Apvienība (NA), and independents.

Prime Minister: LAIMDOTA STRAUJUMA (Vienotība).
Minister of Foreign Affairs: EDGARS RINKĒVIČS (RP).
Minister of Finance: JĀNIS REIRS (Vienotība).
Minister of Defence: RAIMONDS VĒJONIS (ZZS).
Minister of Welfare: ULDIS AUGULIS (ZZS).
Minister of Agriculture: JĀNIS DŪKLAVS (ZZS).
Minister of Environmental Protection and Regional Development: KASPERS GERHARDS (NA).
Minister of Justice: DZINTARS RASNAČS (NA).
Minister of Transport: ANRIJS MATĪSS (Independent).
Minister of the Interior: RIHARDS KOZLOVSKIS (RP).
Minister of Culture: DACE MELBĀRDE (NA).
Minister of the Economy: DANA REIZNIECE-OZOLA (ZZS).
Minister of Education and Science: MĀRĪTE SEILE (Independent).

Minister of Health: GUNTIS BELĒVIČS (ZZS).

MINISTRIES

Chancery of the President: Pils lauk. 3, Rīga 1900; tel. 6709-2106; fax 6709-2157; e-mail prese@president.lv; internet www.president .lv.

Office of the Cabinet of Ministers: Brīvības bulv. 36, Rīga 1520; tel. 6708-2800; fax 6728-0469; e-mail vk@mk.gov.lv; internet www .mk.gov.lv.

Ministry of Agriculture: Republikas lauk. 2, Rīga 1981; tel. 6702-7010; fax 6702-7512; e-mail zm@zm.gov.lv; internet www.zm.gov.lv.

Ministry of Culture: K. Valdemāra iela 11A, Rīga 1364; tel. 6733-0200; fax 6733-0293; e-mail mail@km.gov.lv; internet www.km.gov .lv.

Ministry of Defence: K. Valdemāra iela 10–12, Rīga 1473; tel. 6733-5114; fax 6721-2307; e-mail kanceleja@mod.gov.lv; internet www.mod.gov.lv.

Ministry of the Economy: Brīvības iela 55, Rīga 1519; tel. 6701-3100; fax 6728-0882; e-mail pasts@em.gov.lv; internet www.em.gov .lv.

Ministry of Education and Science: Vaļņu iela 2, Rīga 1050; tel. 6722-6209; fax 6722-3905; e-mail info@izm.gov.lv; internet www.izm .gov.lv.

Ministry of Environmental Protection and Regional Development: Peldu iela 25, Rīga 1494; tel. 6702-6533; fax 6782-0442; e-mail pasts@varam.gov.lv; internet www.varam.gov.lv.

Ministry of Finance: Smilšu iela 1, Rīga 1919; tel. 6709-5405; fax 6709-5503; e-mail info@fm.gov.lv; internet www.fm.gov.lv.

Ministry of Foreign Affairs: K. Valdemāra iela 3, Rīga 1395; tel. 6701-6201; fax 6782-8121; e-mail mfa.cha@mfa.gov.lv; internet www .mfa.gov.lv.

Ministry of Health: Brīvības iela 72, Rīga 1011; tel. 6787-6000; fax 6787-6002; e-mail vm@vm.gov.lv; internet www.vm.gov.lv.

Ministry of the Interior: Čiekurkalna 1, līnija 1, korp. 2, Rīga 1026; tel. 6721-9263; fax 6782-9686; e-mail kanceleja@iem.gov.lv; internet www.iem.gov.lv.

Ministry of Justice: Brīvības bulv. 36, Rīga 1536; tel. 6703-6801; fax 6721-0823; e-mail tm.kanceleja@tm.gov.lv; internet www.tm.gov .lv.

Ministry of Transport: Gogoļa iela 3, Rīga 1743; tel. 6702-8205; fax 6782-0630; e-mail una.vitola@sam.gov.lv; internet www.sam.gov.lv.

Ministry of Welfare: Skolas iela 28, Rīga 1331; tel. 6702-1600; fax 6727-6445; e-mail lm@lm.gov.lv; internet www.lm.gov.lv.

President

In voting by members of Parliament, conducted on 2 June 2011, ANDRIS BĒRZIŅŠ was elected President. In a first round of voting (in which a successful candidate was required to obtain 51 votes) he obtained the support of 50 deputies, compared with the 43 who voted in favour of the incumbent, VALDIS ZATLERS. In a second round of voting, held on the same day, BĒRZIŅŠ was duly elected, receiving 53 votes, while ZATLERS obtained 41. BĒRZIŅŠ was inaugurated on 8 July.

Legislature

Parliament
(Saeima)

Jēkaba iela 11, Rīga 1811; tel. 6708-7321; fax 6708-7100; e-mail info@ saeima.lv; internet www.saeima.lv.

Chairman: INĀRA MŪRNIECE.

General Election, 4 October 2014

Parties/Coalitions	Votes	%	Seats
Saskaņa Sociāldemokrātiskā Partija .	209,887	23.00	24
Vienotība	199,535	21.87	23
Zaļo un Zemnieku Savienība* . . .	178,210	19.53	21
Nacionālā Apvienība . . .	151,567	16.61	17
Latvijas Regionu Apvienība . . .	60,812	6.66	8
No Sirds Latvijai	62,521	6.85	7
Others	44,006	5.48	—
Total†	906,538	100.00	100

* Comprising Latvijas Zaļā Partija and Centriskā Partija Latvijas Zemnieku Savienība.
† Excluding invalid votes.

Election Commission

Central Election Commission (Centrālā vēlēšanu komisija—CVK): Smilšu iela 4, Rīga 1050; tel. 6732-2688; fax 6732-5251; e-mail cvk@cvk.lv; internet www.cvk.lv; Chair. ARNIS CIMDARS.

Political Organizations

The following are among the most influential political parties in Latvia:

Centriskā Partija Latvijas Zemnieku Savienība (CP LZS) (Centre Party Latvian Farmers' Union): Republikas lauk. 2, Rīga 1010; tel. 6732-3628; fax 6702-7467; e-mail info@lzs.lv; internet www .lzs.lv; f. 1990; rural, centrist; forms part of the ZZS; Chair. AUGUSTS BRIGMANIS.

Latvijas Krievu Savienībā (LKS) (Latvian Russian Union): Rūpniecības iela 9, Rīga 1010; tel. and fax 6732-0290; e-mail pctvl.info@ gmail.com; internet www.pctvl.lv; f. 1998 as Par Cilvēka Tiesībām Vienotā Latvijā/Za Prava Cheloveka v Yedinoi Latvii (For Human Rights in a United Latvia) electoral alliance; became united party Nov. 2003; present name adopted 2014; represents interests of Russian-speaking communities in Latvia; opposed to Latvian membership of NATO; Leaders TATJANA ŽDANOKA, JAKOVS PLINERS, MIROSLAV MITROFANOV.

Latvijas Regionu Apvienība (LRA) (Latvian Association of Regions): Lāčplēša iela 24A, Rīga; tel. 2943-7397; e-mail birojs@ latvijasregionuapvieniba.lv; internet latvijasregionuapvieniba.lv; f. 2014; an alliance of Regionu Alianse and Vidzemes Partija; Chair. MĀRTIŅŠ BONDARS.

Latvijas Sociāl-demokrātiskā strādnieku Partija (LSDSP) (Latvian Social Democratic Workers' Party): Aldaru iela 8, Rīga 1050; tel. 6735-6585; fax 6735-6588; e-mail lsdsp@lis.lv; internet www.lsdsp.lv; f. 1904; Chair. AIVARS TIMOFEJEVS.

Latvijas Sociālistiskā Partija/Sotsialisticheskaya partiya Latvii (LSP) (Latvian Socialist Party): Citadeles iela 2, Rīga 1010; tel. and fax 6755-5535; e-mail latsocpartija@inbox.lv; internet www.latsocpartija.lv; f. 1994; joined the SC alliance in Dec. 2005, remained affiliated to SC at 2006 and 2010 legislative elections; Chair. ALFRĒDS RUBIKS.

Latvijas Zaļā Partija (LZP) (Latvian Green Party): Kalnciema iela 30, Rīga 1046; tel. and fax 6761-4272; e-mail birojs@zp.lv; internet www.zp.lv; f. 1990; forms part of the ZZS; Co-Chair. VIESTURS SILENIEKS, RAIMONDS VĒJONIS.

Nacionālā Apvienība (National Alliance): Kaļķu iela 11, Rīga 1050; tel. 2775-5997; e-mail info@nacionalaapvieniba.lv; internet www.nacionalaapvieniba.lv; f. 2011 by merger of Tēvzemei un Brīvībai/Latvijas Nacionālās Neatkarības Kustība (For Fatherland and Freedom Union) and Visu Latvijai! (All For Latvia!); Co-Chair. GAIDIS BĒRZIŅŠ, RAIVIS DZINTARS.

No Sirds Latvijai (For Latvia From the Heart): Aldaru iela 10–3, Rīga 1050; tel. 6713-1270; fax 6713-3075; e-mail nosirds@kustiba.lv; internet nosirdslatvijai.lv; f. 2014; Pres. INGUNA SUDRABA.

Reformu Partija (RP) (Reform Party): Vīlandes iela 14-1/6, Rīga 1050; tel. 6728-3908; e-mail birojs@reformupartija.lv; internet www .reformupartija.lv; f. 2011 by fmr President Valdis Zatlers; centre-right; contested 2014 legislative elections in pact with Vienotība (q.v.); Chair. VALDIS ZATLERS.

Saskaņa Sociāldemokrātiskā Partija (Harmony Social Democratic Party): 'Spīķeru kvartāls', Maskavas iela 4, Rīga 1050; tel. 2510-5016; internet www.saskana.info; supports closer relations with Russia, and concerned with the interests of the Russian-speaking population of Latvia; Chair. NILS UŠAKOVS.

Vienotība (Unity): K. Barona iela 3, Rīga 1050; tel. 6720-5472; e-mail birojs@vienotiba.lv; internet vienotiba.lv; f. 2010 as coalition of Pilsoniskā Savienība (PS—the Civic Union, f. 2008), Jaunais Laiks (New Era, f. 2002) and Sabiedrība Citai Politikai (Society for a Different Politics, f. 2008); constituted as a party 2011; Pres. SOLVITA ĀBOLTIŅA.

Zaļo un Zemnieku Savienība (ZZS) (Greens' and Farmers' Union): Republikas lauk. 2, Rīga 1010; e-mail info@zzs.lv; internet www.zzs.lv; f. 2002; alliance of the CP LZS and the LZP; Leader RAIMONDS VĒJONIS.

Diplomatic Representation

EMBASSIES IN LATVIA

Austria: Elizabetes iela 15, 4th Floor, Rīga 1010; tel. 6721-6125; fax 6721-6126; e-mail riga-ob@bmeia.gv.at; internet www.bmeia.gv.at/ riga; Ambassador ARAD BENKÖ.

Azerbaijan: Raiņa bulv. 2–5, Rīga 1050; tel. 6714-2889; fax 6714-2896; e-mail office@azembassy.lv; internet www.azembassy.lv; f. 2005; Ambassador ELMAN ZEYNALOV.

Belarus: Jēzusbaznīcas iela 12, Rīga 1050; tel. 6722-2560; fax 6732-2891; e-mail latvia@mfa.gov.by; internet www.latvia.mfa.gov.by; Ambassador MARINA DOLGOPOLOVA.

Belgium: Alberta iela 13, Rīga 1010; tel. 6711-4852; fax 6711-4855; e-mail riga@diplobel.fed.be; internet www.diplomatie.be/riga; Ambassador FRANK ARNAUTS.

Canada: Baznicas iela 20–22, Rīga 1010; tel. 6781-3945; fax 6781-3960; e-mail riga@international.gc.ca; internet latvia.gc.ca; Ambassador ALAIN HAUSSER.

China, People's Republic: Ganību dambis 5, Rīga 1045; tel. 6735-7023; fax 6735-7025; e-mail chinaemb_lv@mfa.gov.cn; internet lv .chineseembassy.org; Ambassador GUOQIANG YANG.

Czech Republic: Elizabetes iela 29A, Rīga 1010; tel. 6721-7814; fax 6721-7821; e-mail riga@embassy.mzv.cz; internet www.mfa.cz/riga; Ambassador PAVOL SEPEĽÁK.

Denmark: Pils iela 11, Rīga 1863; tel. 6722-6210; fax 6782-0234; e-mail rixamb@um.dk; internet letland.um.dk; Ambassador PER CARLSEN.

Estonia: Skolas iela 13, Rīga 1010; tel. 6781-2020; fax 6781-2029; e-mail embassy.riga@mfa.ee; internet www.estemb.lv; Ambassador TÕNIS NIRK.

Finland: Kalpaka bulv. 1, Rīga 1605; tel. 6707-8800; fax 6707-8814; e-mail sanomat.rii@formin.fi; internet www.finland.lv; Ambassador OLLI KANTANEN.

France: Raiņa bulv. 9, Rīga 1050; tel. 6703-6600; fax 6703-6616; e-mail webmastre.ambafrance-lv@diplomatie.gouv.fr; internet www .ambafrance-lv.org; Ambassador STÉPHANE VISCONTI.

Georgia: Raiņa bulv. 3/2, Rīga 1050; tel. and fax 6721-3136; e-mail riga.emb@mfa.gov.ge; internet www.latvia.mfa.gov.ge; Ambassador TEIMURAZ JANJALIA.

Germany: Raiņa bulv. 13, Rīga 1050; tel. 6708-5100; fax 6708-5149; e-mail info@riga.diplo.de; internet www.riga.diplo.de; Ambassador ANDREA WIKTORIN.

Greece: Ausekļa iela 1-5, 2nd Floor, Rīga 1010; tel. 6735-6345; fax 6735-6351; e-mail gremb.rig@mfa.gr; internet www.mfa.gr/riga; Ambassador GEORGIOS CHATZIMICHELAKIS.

Hungary: Baznicas iela 20/22, Rīga 1010; tel. 6721-7500; e-mail mission.rix@mfa.gov.hu; internet www.mfa.gov.hu/emb/riga; Ambassador GÁBOR DOBOKAY.

Ireland: Alberta iela 13, Rīga 1010; tel. 6703-9370; fax 6703-9371; internet www.embassyofireland.lv; Ambassador AIDAN KIRWAN.

Israel: Elizabetes iela 2, Rīga 1010; tel. 6763-5574; fax 6763-5555; e-mail press@riga.mfa.gov.il; internet embassies.gov.il/riga; Ambassador HAGIT BEN-YAAKOV.

Italy: Teātra iela 9, Rīga 1050; tel. 6721-6069; fax 6721-6084; e-mail ambitalia.riga@esteri.it; internet www.ambriga.esteri.it; Ambassador GIOVANNI POLIZZI.

Japan: Vesetas iela 7, Rīga 1013; tel. 6781-2001; fax 6781-2004; internet www.lv.emb-japan.go.jp; Ambassador TOSHIYUKI TAGA.

Lithuania: Rūpniecibas iela 24, Rīga 1010; tel. 6732-1519; fax 6732-1589; e-mail info@lv.mfa.lt; internet lv.mfa.lt; Ambassador RIČARDAS DEGUTIS.

Moldova: Zigfrīda Annas Meierovica bulv. 14, Rīga 1050; tel. 6735-9160; fax 6735-9165; e-mail riga@moldovaembassy.lv; internet www .letonia.mfa.md; Ambassador ALEKSEI CRACAN.

Netherlands: Torņa iela 4-1A, Jēkaba Kazarmas, Rīga 1050; tel. 6732-6147; e-mail rig@minbuza.nl; internet www .nctherlandsembassy.lv; Ambassador HENDRIK G. C. VAN DEN DOOL.

Norway: Kaļķu iela 15, POB 181, Rīga 1050; tel. 6781-4100; e-mail emb.riga@mfa.no; internet www.norvegija.lv; Ambassador STEINARS EGILS HÅGENS.

Poland: Mednieku iela 6B, Rīga 1010; tel. 6703-1512; fax 6703-1549; e-mail ryga.ambasada@msz.gov.pl; internet ryga.msz.gov.pl; Ambassador EWA DĘBSKA.

Russian Federation: Antonijas iela 2, Rīga 1010; tel. 6733-2151; fax 6783-0209; e-mail rusembas@delfi.lv; internet www.latvia.mid .ru; Ambassador ALEKSANDR A. VESHNYAKOV.

Slovakia: Smilšu iela 8, Rīga 1050; tel. 6781-4280; fax 6781-4290; e-mail emb.riga@mzv.sk; internet www.mzv.sk/riga; Ambassador PETER HATIAR.

Spain: Elizabetes iela 11, 3rd Floor, Rīga 1010; tel. 6732-0281; fax 6732-5005; e-mail emb.riga@maec.es; internet www.maec.es/ embajadas/riga; Ambassador PEDRO MIGUEL JIMÉNEZ NÁCHER.

Sweden: A. Pumpura iela 8, Rīga 1010; tel. 6768-6600; fax 6768-6601; e-mail ambassaden.riga@gov.se; internet www.swedenabroad .com; Ambassador HENRIK LANDERHOLM.

Switzerland: World Trade Centre, Elizabetes iela 2, Rīga 1340; tel. 6733-8351; fax 6733-8354; e-mail rig.vertretung@eda.admin.ch; internet www.eda.admin.ch/riga; Ambassador MARKUS DUTLY.

Turkey: A. Pumpura iela 2, Rīga 1010; tel. 6782-1600; fax 6732-0334; e-mail embassy.riga@mfa.gov.tr; internet riga.emb.mfa.gov .tr; Ambassador HAYRI HAYRET YALAV.

Ukraine: Kalpaka bulv. 3, Rīga 1010; tel. 6724-3082; fax 6732-5583; e-mail emb_lv@mfa.gov.ua; internet www.mfa.gov.ua/latvia; Ambassador ANATOLIY T. OLIYNYK.

United Kingdom: J. Alunāna iela 5, Rīga 1010; tel. 6777-4700; fax 6777-4707; e-mail britishembassy.riga@fco.gov.uk; internet www .gov.uk/world/latvia; Ambassador SARAH COWLEY.

USA: Samnera Velsa iela 1, Rīga 1510; tel. 6710-7000; fax 6710-7050; e-mail ambassador-riga@state.gov; internet riga.usembassy.gov; Ambassador MARK PEKALA.

Uzbekistan: Elizabetes iela 11/11, Rīga 1010; tel. 6732-2424; fax 6732-2306; e-mail posoluz@apollo.lv; internet www.uzbekistan.lv; Ambassador AFZAL ARTYKOV.

Judicial System

Constitutional Court (Latvijas Republikas Satversmes tiesa): J. Alunāna iela 1, Rīga 1010; tel. 6721-0274; fax 6783-0770; e-mail tiesa@satv.tiesa.gov.lv; internet www.satv.tiesa.gov.lv; f. 1996;

comprises seven judges, appointed by the Saeima for a term of 10 years; Chair. ALDIS LAVIŅŠ.

Supreme Court (Latvijas Republikas Augstākā tiesa): Brīvības bulv. 36, Rīga 1511; tel. 6702-0350; fax 6702-0351; e-mail at@at.gov .lv; internet www.at.gov.lv; Chair. IVARS BIČKOVIČS.

Office of the Prosecutor-General: Kalpaka bulv. 6, Rīga 1801; tel. 6704-4400; fax 6704-4449; e-mail gen@lrp.gov.lv; internet www.lrp .gov.lv; Prosecutor-General ĒRIKS KALNMEIERS.

Religion

From the 16th century the traditional religion of the Latvians was Lutheran Christianity, although there remained a substantial Roman Catholic population. Russian Orthodoxy is the religion of much of the Slavic population. During the period of Soviet rule many places of religious worship were closed. Following the restoration of independence in 1991, religious organizations regained their legal rights and property.

Board of Religious Affairs: Pils lauk. 4, Rīga 1050; tel. 6722-0585; e-mail zlp@zlp.gov.lv; f. 2000; govt agency, attached to the Ministry of Justice; Principal IRETA ROMANOVSKA.

CHRISTIANITY

Protestant Churches

Evangelical Lutheran Church of Latvia: Pils iela 4, Rīga 1050; tel. 6782-0041; fax 6722-5436; e-mail lelb@lelb.lv; internet www.lelb .lv; f. 1922; 708,000 mems; Archbishop JĀNIS VANAGS.

Latvian Conference of Seventh-day Adventists in Latvia: Baznīcas iela 12A, Rīga 1010; tel. and fax 6724-0013; e-mail viesturs@baznica.lv; internet www.adventistu.baznica.lv; f. 1920; Pres. of Council VIESTURS REĶIS.

Latvian Pentecostal Union: J. Asara iela 8, Jelgava 3001; tel. 6308-1401; fax 6308-1407; e-mail lvdaddf@hotmail.com; f. 1989; Bishop JĀNIS OZOLINKEVIČS.

Union of Baptist Churches in Latvia: Lāčplēša iela 37, Rīga 1011; tel. and fax 6722-3379; internet www.lbds.lv; e-mail kanceleja@lbds .lv; f. 1860; Bishop Dr PĒTERIS SPROĢIS.

United Methodist Church in Latvia: Klaipēdas iela 56, Liepāja 3401; tel. 6349-2161; fax 6346-9848; rc cat. 1001; Supt ĀRIJS VĪKSNA.

The Roman Catholic Church

Latvia comprises one archdiocese and three dioceses.

Bishops' Conference: M. Pils iela 2A, Rīga 1050; tel. 6722-7266; fax 6722-0775; Pres. Cardinal JĀNIS PUJATS (Archbishop of Rīga).

Archbishop of Rīga: Cardinal JĀNIS PUJATS, Pils iela 2A, Rīga 1050; tel. 6722-7266; fax 6722-0775; e-mail curia@e-apollo.lv; internet www.catholic.lv.

The Orthodox Church

Although the Latvian Orthodox Church has close ties with the Moscow Patriarchate, it has administrative independence.

Latvian Orthodox Church: Pils iela 14, Rīga 1050; tel. 6722-5855; fax 6722-4345; e-mail sinode@orthodoxy.lv; internet www .pareizticiba.lv; f. 1850; Metropolitan of Rīga and all Latvia ALEKSANDR (KUDRJASHOV).

Latvian Old Believer (Old Ritualist) Pomor Church: Krasta iela 73, Rīga 1003; tel. 6711-3083; fax 6714-4513; e-mail oldbel@junik .lv; f. 1760 in split from Moscow Patriarchate; Head of Central Council IVANS MIZOĻUBOVS.

JUDAISM

Jewish Religious Community of Rīga: Peitavas iela 6/8, Rīga 1050; tel. 6722-4549; f. 1764; Rabbi NATAN BARKAN.

The Press

In 2013 a total of 242 daily and non-daily newspapers and 308 other periodicals were published. The publications listed below are in Latvian, unless otherwise indicated.

DAILIES

Bizness & Baltiya (Business and the Baltics): K. Valdemāra iela 149, Rīga 1013; tel. 6703-3047; fax 6703-3040; e-mail bb@bb.lv; internet www.bb.lv; f. 1991; 5 a week; in Russian; Editor-in-Chief ALEKSEI SHERBAKOV; circ. 12,000 (2007).

Diena (Day): Mūkusalas iela 15, Rīga 1004; tel. 6706-3100; fax 6706-3190; e-mail info@dienasmediji.lv; internet www.diena.lv; f. 1990;

social and political issues; Editor-in-Chief GATIS MADŽIŅŠ; circ. 85,000 (2009).

Neatkarīgā Rīta Avīze (Independent Morning Paper): Cēsu iela 31/2, Rīga 1012; tel. 6788-6700; e-mail office@medijunams.lv; internet www.nra.lv; f. 1990; Editor-in-Chief ANITA DAUKŠTE; circ. 40,000.

Rīgas Balss (RB) (Voice of Rīga): Rīga; tel. 6706-2420; fax 6706-2400; e-mail balss@rb.lv; internet www.rigasbalss.lv; f. 1957; city evening newspaper; Editor-in-Chief IVETA MEDIŅA; circ. 18,100 (Mon.–Thur.), 42,700 (Fri.).

Vakara Ziņas (The Evening News): Cēsu iela 31/2, Rīga 1012; tel. 6788-6760; e-mail sandrisv@nra.lv; f. 1993; popular; Editor-in-Chief SANDRIS VANZOVIČS; circ. 53,000.

Vesti Segodnya (News Today): Mūkusalas iela 41, Rīga 1004; tel. 6706-8130; fax 6706-8131; e-mail info@ves.lv; internet www.ves.lv; f. 1945; in Russian; 6 a week; Editor-in-Chief ALEKSANDRS BĻINOVS; circ. 25,500.

OTHER NEWSPAPERS

The Baltic Times: Strēlnieku 11-4, Rīga 1010; tel. 6722-9978; fax 6722-6041; e-mail editor@baltictimes.com; internet www .baltictimes.com; f. 1996; news from Estonia, Latvia and Lithuania; in English; weekly; Man. Dir ERIK LISMANIS; Editor DORIAN ZIEDONIS; circ. 12,000 (2007).

Dienas Bizness (Daily Business): Mūkusalas iela 15, Rīga 1004; tel. 6706-3100; fax 6706-3190; e-mail redakcija@db.lv; internet www.db .lv; f. 1992; Editor-in-Chief JĀNIS OGSTS; circ. 17,000.

Ieva (Eve): Stabu iela 34, Rīga 1880; tel. 6700-6102; fax 6700-6111; e-mail ieva@santa.lv; internet www.ieva.lv; f. 1997; weekly; illustrated journal for women; Editor-in-Chief INITA SILA; circ. 73,650.

Izglitība un Kultūra (Education and Culture): Marijas iela 2, Rīga 1050; tel. 6735-7585; fax 6735-7584; e-mail redakcija@ izglitiba-kultura.lv; internet www.izglitiba-kultura.lv; f. 1948; Man. Editor DAIGA KĻANSKA.

Latvijas Avīze (Latvian Newspaper): Dzirnavu iela 21, Rīga 1010; tel. 6709-6600; fax 6709-6645; e-mail redakcija@la.lv; internet la.lv; f. 1987; fmrly *Lauku Avīze* (Country Newspaper); present name adopted 2004; 5 issues a week; popular; agriculture, politics and sport; Editor-in-Chief LINDA RASA; circ. 21,500.

Latvijas Vēstnesis (Latvian Herald): Bruņinieku iela 41, Rīga 1011; tel. 6731-0675; fax 6731-2190; e-mail info@lv.lv; internet www.vestnesis.lv; f. 1993; official newspaper; 5 a week; Editor-in-Chief INESE LUSTE.

Privātā Dzīve (Private Life): Stabu iela 34, Rīga 1011; tel. 6700-6104; fax 6700-6111; e-mail pdz@santa.lv; celebrity news, TV, radio, films; weekly; Man. Editor GUNDEGA BICEVSKA; circ. 56,000 (2010).

Rīgas Viļņi (Riga Waves): Kaļķu iela 15, Rīga 1050; tel. 6784-2577; fax 6784-2578; e-mail info@rigasvilni.lv; weekly.

PRINCIPAL PERIODICALS

Baltiskii Kurs/The Baltic Course: Brīvības iela 159/11, Rīga 1012; tel. 2926-9645; e-mail olga.pavuk@baltic-course.com; internet www.baltic-course.com; f. 1996; online; business; in Russian and English; Int. Editor EUGENE ETERIS; Editor-in-Chief OLGA PAVUK.

Karogs (Banner): Kuršu iela 24, Rīga 1006; tel. 6755-4128; fax 6755-4146; e-mail karogs@apollo.lv; internet www.ekarogs.lv; f. 1940; literary monthly; Editor-in-Chief IEVA KOLMANE; circ. 1,500.

Klubs (Club): Stabu iela 34, Rīga 1880; tel. 6700-6103; fax 6700-6111; e-mail klubs@santa.lv; internet www.klubs.lv; f. 1994; monthly; politics, business, fashion; Editor-in-Chief AIVARS PASTAL-NIEKS; circ. 17,000 (Jan. 2010).

Latvijas Ekonomists: Alūksnes iela 5, Rīga 1045; tel. 6779-0631; fax 6779-0619; e-mail birojs@ekonomists.lv; internet www .ekonomists.lv; f. 1992; monthly; in Latvian and Russian; Dir INESE LAPIŅA.

Māksla Plus (M+): Akadēmijas lauk. 1, a.k. 41, Rīga 1027; tel. 6722-0722; fax 6782-0608; e-mail makslaplus@inbox.lv; internet www .makslaplus.lv; f. 1997; cultural magazine (cinema, music, theatre, photography); Editor-in-Chief SANITA BUČINIECE.

Mans Mazais (My Little One): Stabu iela 34, Rīga 1880; tel. 6700-6105; fax 6700-6111; e-mail mansmazais@santa.lv; internet www .mansmazais.lv; f. 1994; monthly; illustrated journal for parents; Editor-in-Chief SINDIJA MELUŠKĀNE; circ. 20,000.

Mūsmājas (Our Home): Mūkusalas iela 15, Rīga 1004; tel. 6729-9105; fax 6729-2701; e-mail musmajas@musmajas.lv; internet www .musmajas.lv; f. 1993; monthly; home and family magazine; Editor-in-Chief ANIJA PELŪDE; circ. 50,000.

Mūzikas Saule (Musical Sun): K. Barona iela 37/5, Rīga 1011; tel. 2935-9688; fax 2678-9826; e-mail saule@muzikassaule.lv; internet www.muzikassaule.lv; music; Editor-in-Chief ORESTS SILABRIEDIS.

Rīgas Laiks (Rīga Times): Zaļā iela 5-1, Rīga 1010; tel. 6728-7922; e-mail pasts@rigaslaiks.lv; internet www.rigaslaiks.lv; f. 1993; monthly; Editor-in-Chief ULDIS TĪRONS; circ. 6,000.

Santa: Stabu iela 34, Rīga 1880; tel. 6700-6103; fax 6700-6111; e-mail santa@santa.lv; internet www.zurnalssanta.lv; f. 1991; monthly; illustrated journal for women; Editor-in-Chief SANTA DANSBERGA-ANČA; circ. 42,000.

Zinātnes Vēstnesis (Scientific Herald): Akadēmijas lauk. 1, Rīga 1050; tel. 6721-2706; fax 6782-1109; e-mail lza@lza.lv; internet www .lza.lv/zv00.htm; f. 1989; published by the Latvian Scientific Council, the Latvian Academy of Science and the Latvian Society of Scientists; two a month; Man. Editor JURIS EKMANIS.

NEWS AGENCIES

Baltic News Service: Berga Bazārs, Marijas iela 13/1, Rīga 1050; tel. 6708-8600; fax 6708-8601; e-mail bns@bns.lv; internet www.bns .lv; f. 1990; news from Latvia, Lithuania, Estonia and the CIS; in English, Russian and the Baltic languages; Dir SIGITA KIRILKA.

LETA Latvian News Agency: Marijas iela 2, Rīga 1050; tel. 6722-2509; fax 6722-3850; e-mail redaktori@leta.lv; internet www.leta.lv; independent; Chair. MĀRTIŅŠ BARKĀNS.

PRESS ASSOCIATION

Latvian Union of Journalists (Latvijas Žurnālistu savienība): K. Valdemāra iela 118–211, Rīga 1013; tel. and fax 6721-1433; e-mail zurnalistusavieniba@e-apollo.lv; internet www.zurnalistusavieniba .lv; f. 1992; 600 mems; Pres. JURIS PAIDERS.

Publishers

AGB: K. Barona iela 31, Rīga 1011; tel. 6728-0464; fax 6728-0356; e-mail info@izdevnieciba.com; internet www.izdevnieciba.com.

Avots (Spring): Puškina iela 1A, Rīga 1050; tel. 6721-1394; fax 6722-5824; e-mail avots@apollo.lv; f. 1980; non-fiction, dictionaries, crafts, hobbies, etc.; Pres. JĀNIS LEJA.

Elpa (Breath): Doma lauk. 1, Rīga 1050; tel. 6721-1776; fax 6722-6497; e-mail elpa@apollo.lv; f. 1990; books and newspapers; Pres. MAIRITA SOLIMA.

Jāņa sēta: Elizabetes iela 83–85, Rīga 1050; tel. 6709-2290; fax 6709-2292; e-mail janaseta@janaseta.lv; internet www.janaseta.lv; f. 1991; travel and culinary books; Dir AIVARS ZVIRBULIS.

Jumava: Dzirnavu iela 73, Rīga 1011; tel. and fax 6728-0314; e-mail jumava@parks.lv; internet www.jumava.lv; f. 1994; translations, dictionaries, fiction, etc.; Pres. JURIS VISOCKIS.

Kontinents: Elijas iela 17, Rīga 1050; tel. 6720-4130; fax 6720-4129; e-mail kontinent@ml.lv; internet www.kontinents.lv; f. 1991; translated fiction, non-fiction and colour children's books; Chair. of Bd OLEG MIHALEVICH.

Nordik: Daugavgrīvas 36–9, Rīga 1048; tel. 6760-2672; fax 6760-2818; e-mail nordik@nordik.lv; internet www.nordik.lv; f. 1992; sister Co, Tapals, at same address; Dir JĀNIS JUŠKA; Editor-in-Chief IEVA JANAITE.

Preses nams (Press House): Balasta dambis 3, Rīga 1081; tel. 6246-5732; internet www.presesnams.lv; f. 1990; newspapers, magazines, encyclopedias and scientific literature; controlling interest owned by Ventspils Nafta; Dir EGONS LAPIŅŠ.

Smaile (Peak): Rīga; tel. 6731-5137; f. 1999; fiction, poetry, fine arts; Dir ANDREJS BRIMERBERGS.

Zinātne Publishers: Akadēmijas lauk. 1, Rīga 1050; tel. 6721-2797; fax 6722-7825; e-mail zinatne@zinatne.com.lv; internet www .zinatnesgramatas.lv; f. 1951; non-fiction, textbooks, dictionaries, reference books; Dir INGRĪDA SEGLINA.

Zvaigzne ABC: K. Valdemāra iela 6, Rīga 1010; tel. 6750-8799; fax 6750-8798; e-mail info@zvaigzne.lv; internet www.zvaigzne.lv; f. 1966; privately owned; educational literature, textbooks, dictionaries, non-fiction for children and adults, fiction; Head of Bd VIJA KILBLOKA.

PUBLISHERS' ASSOCIATION

Latvian Publishers' Asscn (Latvijas Grāmatizdevēju asociācija): Rīga; tel. 6728-2392; fax 6728-0549; e-mail lga@gramatizdeveji.lv; internet www.gramatizdeveji.lv; f. 1993; 40 mems; Pres. JĀNIS LEJA.

Broadcasting and Communications

TELECOMMUNICATIONS

At the end of 2013 there were 480,000 main telephone lines in use and 2.8m. subscriptions to mobile telephone services.

Lattelecom SIA: Dzirnavu iela 105, Rīga 1011; tel. 6700-0177; fax 8000-8041; e-mail lattelecom@lattelecom.lv; internet www .lattelecom.lv; f. 1992; 51% state-owned, 49% by TeliaSonera AB (Sweden); telecommunications and internet service provider; CEO JURIS GULBIS; 3,000 employees.

Latvian Mobile Telephone Co (Latvijas Mobilais Telefons SIA— LMT): Ropažu iela 6, Rīga 1039; tel. 8076-8076; fax 6777-3707; e-mail info@lmt.lv; internet www.lmt.lv; f. 1992; 24.5% owned by Sonera Holding BV (Finland), 24.5% owned by TeliaSonera AB (Sweden), 23.0% owned by SIA Lattelekom, 23.0% owned by Digitālais Latvijas radio un televīzijas centrs; mobile telecommunications and internet service provider; Pres. JURIS BINDE.

SIA Bite Latvija: Uriekstes iela 2A, Rīga 1005; tel. 2585-0600; fax 2585-0610; e-mail info@bite.lv; internet www.bite.lv; f. 2005; mobile cellular telecommunications; CEO FRED HRENCHUK.

SIA Radiokoms: Elizabetes iela 45–47, Rīga 1010; tel. 6733-3355; fax 6782-0013; e-mail radiokoms@radiokoms.lv; internet www .radiokoms.lv; f. 1992; Dir PETERIS GRAZULS.

Tele2: Rīga; tel. 6706-0069; fax 6706-0176; e-mail tele2@tele2.lv; internet www.tele2.lv; f. 2000; owned by Tele2 AB (Sweden); fmrly Baltkom GSM; mobile telecommunications and internet service provider; Pres. VALDIS VANCOVI; 110 employees.

Regulatory Organizations

Dept of Communications (Ministry of Transport): Gogoļa iela 3, Rīga 1743; tel. 6702-8100; fax 6782-0636; e-mail edmunds.belskis@ sam.gov.lv; f. 1991; Dir EDMUNDS BELSKIS.

Public Utilities Commission (Sabiedrisko Pakalpojumu Regulē-šanas Komisija): see Trade and Industry (Utilities) section.

BROADCASTING
Regulatory Organization

National Electronic Mass Media Council (NEPLP) (Nacionālā elektronisko plašsaziņas līdzekļu Padome): Doma lauk. 8A, Rīga 1939; tel. 6722-1848; fax 6722-0448; e-mail neplpadome@ neplpadome.lv; internet www.neplpadome.lv; f. 1995; independent regulatory authority; Chair. AINĀRS DIMANTS.

Radio

Latvijas Radio (Radio Latvia): Doma lauk. 8, Rīga 1505; tel. 6720-6722; fax 6720-6709; e-mail radio@latvijasradio.lv; internet www .latvijasradio.lv; f. 1925; state-operated service; broadcasts in Latvian and Russian; CEO ALDIS PAULIŅŠ.

Alise Plus: Raiņa iela 28, Daugavpils 5403; tel. and fax 6542-2322; e-mail radio@aliseplus.lv; internet www.aliseplus.lv; 24-hour trans-missions in Russian and Latvian.

European Hit Radio: Elijas iela 17, Rīga 1050; tel. 6720-4404; fax 6720-4407; e-mail birojs@superfm.lv; internet www .europeanhitradio.com; f. 1992; 24-hour transmissions in Latvian and English; Pres. UĢIS POLIS; Dir RICHARD ZAKSS.

Latvijas Kristīgais Radio (Latvian Christian Radio): Lāčplēša iela 37, Rīga 1011; tel. 6721-3704; fax 6782-0633; e-mail lkr@lkr.lv; internet www.lkr.lv; f. 1993; 24-hour transmissions in Latvian and Russian.

Radio Imanta: Tērbatas iela 1, Valmiera 4201; tel. 422-4070; fax 6420-7350; e-mail radio.imanta@tl.lv; internet www.radioimanta.lv; f. 1993; 24-hour transmissions in Russian and Latvian; Chief Editor NILS INTERBERGS.

Radio Mix FM: Kr. Valdemāra iela 8, Rīga 1010; tel. 6700-1027; e-mail info@mixnews.lv; internet www.mixnews.lv; 24-hour trans-missions in Russian.

Radio SWH: Ganību dambis 24D, Rīga 1005; tel. 6737-0067; fax 6782-8283; e-mail radio@radioswh.lv; internet www.radioswh.lv; f. 1993; owned by Communicorp Group Ltd (Ireland); Chair. JĀNIS SIPKĒVICS.

Radio Zemgale: Elizabetes iela 55, Rīga 1010; tel. 6394-1981; e-mail rz@apollo.lv; f. 2000; 24-hour transmissions in Latvian; Dir DACE DUBKEVIČA.

Television

Latvia has one publicly owned television network and nine private stations. In 2010 satellite television reached approximately 10% of the population.

Latvijas Televīzija (Latvian Television—LTV): Zaķusalas krast-mala 3, Rīga 1509; tel. 6720-0316; fax 6720-0025; e-mail ltv@ltv.lv; internet www.ltv.lv; f. 1954; state-operated service; two channels in Latvian, LTV1 and LTV7 (LTV7 also includes programmes in Russian, English and French); Chair. IVARS BELTE.

Latvijas Neatkariga Televizija (Latvian Independent Televi-sion—LNT): Dzelzavas iela 120G, Rīga 1021; tel. 6707-0200; fax 6782-1128; e-mail lnt@lnt.lv; internet www.lnt.lv; f. 1996; owned by

Modern Times Group(MTG—Sweden); entertainment, news reports; Dir-Gen. EDGARS KOTS.

Pervyi Baltiiskii Kanal—Latviya (PBK—Latviya) (First Baltic Channel—Latvia): Gertudas iela 12-3, Rīga 1010; tel. 6718-6735; e-mail office@1tv.lv; internet www.1tv.lv; f. 2002; Russian-language programming; Exec. Dir ANTON BLINOV.

TV3 Latvia: Dzelzavas iela 120G, Rīga 1021; tel. 6747-9100; fax 6747-9299; e-mail tv3@tv3.lv; internet www.tv3.lv; f. 1998; owned by Modern Times Group–MTG (Sweden); affiliated with channel 3+, targeted at a Russian-speaking audience; Dir BAIBA ZŪZENA.

Finance

(cap. = capital; res = reserves; dep. = deposits; m. = million; brs = branches; amounts in lats)

BANKING
Central Bank

Bank of Latvia (Latvijas Banka): K. Valdemāra iela 2A, Rīga 1050; tel. 6702-2300; fax 6702-2420; e-mail info@bank.lv; internet www .bank.lv; f. 1990; cap. 25.0m., res 163.5m., dep. 2,135.9m. (Dec. 2008); Gov. and Chair. of Council ILMĀRS RIMŠĒVIČS.

Commercial Banks

ABLV Bank AS: Elizabetes iela 23, Rīga 1010; tel. 6777-5222; fax 6777-5200; e-mail bank@ab.lv; internet www.ab.lv; f. 1993; present name adopted 2011; cap. 21.1m., res 31.3m., dep. 1,955.5m. (Dec. 2013); Chair. of Bd ALEKSANDRS BERGMANIS.

Bank M2M Europe AS: 3 Antonijas iela, Rīga 1010; tel. 6708-0000; fax 6708-0001; e-mail info@bankm2m.com; internet www.bankm2m .com; f. 1992 as Latvijas Biznesa Banka; present name adopted 2013; Chair. ANDREJS VDOVINS; CEO ROBERTS IDELSONS.

Citadele banka: Republikas lauk. 2A, Rīga 1522; tel. 6701-0000; fax 6701-0001; e-mail info@citadele.lv; internet www.citadele.lv; f. 2010; founded on the basis of Parex banka; 75% state-owned; 25% owned by the European Bank for Reconstruction and Development; cap. 103.0m., res 0.1m., dep. 1,585.1m. (Dec. 2013); Pres. and Chair. of Bd NILS MELNGAILIS; 72 brs.

DNB Banka: Skanstes iela 12, Rīga 1013; tel. 6717-1880; fax 6732-3449; e-mail info@dnb.lv; internet www.dnb.lv; f. 1989; present name adopted 2011; 100% owned by Bank DnB A/S (Denmark); cap. 134.4m., res 206.6m., dep. 1,508.6m (Dec. 2013); Pres. and Chair. of Bd ANDRIS OZOLINS; 10 brs.

Expobank AS: Grēcinieku iela 22, Rīga 1050; tel. 6704-3510; fax 6704-3511; e-mail ltb@ltblv.com; internet www.expobank.eu; f. 1991; fmrly LTB Bank; present name adopted 2012; owned by MDM Bank (Russian Federation); cap. 8.2m., res 4.7m., dep. 227.7m. (Dec. 2013); Chair. ARMANDS STEINBERGS.

GE Capital Latvia: Aspazija bulv. 24, Rīga 1050; tel. 6700-1878; fax 6782-0319; e-mail capital.lv.info@ge.com; internet www.gecapital .lv; f. 2008; fmrly GE Money Bank; present name adopted 2013; cap. 26.4m., res 42.7m., dep. 65.1m. (Dec. 2012); Chair. ANDREW CHARLES BULL; CEO JURITA BRUNAVA.

Latvijas Attīstības Finanšu Institūcija Altum (Latvian Devel-opment Financial Institution Altum): Doma lauk. 4, Rīga 1977; tel. 6777-4010; fax 6782-0143; e-mail altum@altum.lv; internet www .hipo.lv; f. 1993; present name adopted in 2014; state-owned; cap. 216.6m., res 3.3m., dep. 182.7m. (Dec. 2012); Chair. of Bd ROLAND PAŅKOVALDES; 9 brs.

Norvik Banka: E. Birznieka-Upiša iela 21, Rīga 1011; tel. 6704-1100; fax 6704-1111; e-mail welcome@norvik.eu; internet www .norvik.eu; f. 1992; fmrly Lateko Bank; present name adopted 2006; cap. and res 48.7m., dep. 759.5m. (March 2014); Chair. of Bd OLIVER RONALD BRAMWELL; 15 brs.

PrivatBank: Terbatas iela 4, Rīga 1134; tel. 6704-1300; fax 6728-2981; e-mail info@privatbank.lv; internet www.privatbank.lv; f. 1992; fmrly Paritate Banka; present name adopted 2007; cap. 56.5m., res 3.8m., dep. 505.6m. (Dec. 2013); Chair. of Bd OLEKSANDR TRUBAKOV; 16 brs.

Rietumu Banka: Vesetas iela 7, Rīga 1013; tel. 6702-5555; fax 6702-5588; e-mail info@rietumu.lv; internet www.rietumu.lv; f. 1992; cap. 100.0m., res 14.6m., dep. 1,826.7m. (Dec. 2013); Pres. and Chair. of Exec. Bd ALEKSANDRS PANKOVS.

SEB Banka: SEB finanšu centrs, Meistaru iela 1, Valdlauci 1076; tel. 2777-8777; fax 6721-5335; e-mail info@seb.lv; internet www.seb .lv; f. 1993; fmrly SEB Latvijas Unibanka; present name adopted 2008; owned by SEB (Skandinaviska Enskilda Banken AB, Sweden); cap. 102.1m., res 7.9m., dep. 2,616.6m. (Dec. 2013); CEO AINĀRS OZOLS; 68 brs.

Swedbank Latvia: Balasta dambis 1A, Rīga 1048; tel. 6744-4444; fax 6744-4344; e-mail info@swedbank.lv; internet www.swedbank

.lv; f. 1992; present name adopted 2008, following merger between Hansabank and Swedbank; cap. 662.6m., res 0.3m., dep. 2,776.3m. (Dec. 2013); Pres. and CEO MARIS MANCINSKIS; 55 brs.

Trasta komercbanka—TKB (Trust Commercial Bank): Miesnieku iela 9, Rīga 1050; tel. 6702-7777; fax 6702-7700; e-mail info@tkb.lv; internet www.tkb.lv; f. 1989; present name adopted 1996; cap. 14.5m., res 4.7m., dep. 239.7m. (Dec. 2013); Pres. and Chair. GUNDARS GRIEZE.

UniCredit Finance: Elizabetes iela 63, Rīga 1050; tel. 6708-5500; fax 6708-5507; e-mail info@unicreditgroup.lv; internet www .unicreditbank.lv; f. 1997; fmrly Vereinsbank Rīga, and known as UniCredit Bank from 2005; present name adopted 2014; 100% owned by Bank Austria Creditanstalt AG (Austria); cap. 86.1m., res 0.2m., dep. 490.2m. (Dec. 2012); Chair. of Bd GINTERS FRĪDLS.

Regulatory Authority

Financial and Capital Market Commission (Finanšu un kapitāla tirgus komisija—FKTK): Kungu iela 1, Rīga 1050; tel. 6777-4800; fax 6722-5755; e-mail fktk@fktk.lv; internet www.fktk.lv; f. 2001; Chair. KRISTAPS ZAKULIS.

Banking Association

Association of Latvian Commercial Banks (Latvijas Komercbanku asociācija): Pērses iela 9–11, Rīga 1011; tel. 6728-4528; fax 6782-8170; e-mail asoc@bankasoc.lv; internet www.bankasoc.lv; f. 1992; 24 mems; Pres. MARTINS BICEVSKIS.

INSURANCE

At September 2004 there were 18 insurance companies in Latvia, of which six were involved in life insurance and 12 in non-life insurance operations.

Balta Insurance Co: Raunas iela 10/12, Rīga 1039; tel. 6708-2333; fax 6708-2345; e-mail balta@balta.lv; internet www.balta.lv; f. 1992; non-life; Chair. BOGDAN BENCZAK.

BTA Apdrošināšana: K. Valdemāra iela 63, Rīga 1142; tel. 2612-1212; fax 6702-5190; e-mail bta@bta.lv; internet www.bta.lv; f. 1993; non-life; Chair. of Bd JĀNIS LUCAUS.

Colemont FKB Latvia: Dārzauglu iela 1-50, Rīga 1012; tel. 6724-0066; fax 6720-1737; e-mail info@colemontfkb.lv; internet www .colemontfkb.lv; f. 2000; 60% owned by Colemont Insurance Brokers (USA); present name adopted 2013; Chair. of Bd ARVILS PŪPOLS.

ERGO Latvija: Cēsu iela 31, III korpuss, Rīga 1012; tel. 6735-6320; fax 6708-1715; e-mail riga@ergo.lv; internet www.ergo.lv; owned by Alte Leipziger (Germany); life and non-life; Chair. of Bd THOMAS HANS SCHIRMER.

Gjensidige Baltic: Brīvības iela 39, Rīga 1010; tel. 6711-2222; fax 6710-6444; e-mail info@gjensidige.lv; internet www.gjensidige.lv; subsidiary of Gjensidige Forsikring (Norway); non-life; Chair. of Bd KIM RUD-PETERSEN.

If P&C Insurance AS: Republikas lauk. 2A, Rīga 1010; fax 6709-4702; internet www.if.lv; f. 1999; non-life; owned by Sampo Abp (Finland); Chair. ANDRIS MOROZOVS; CEO TORBJÖRN MAGNUSSON.

SEB Dzīvības Apdrošināšana (SEB Life Insurance): Antonijas iela 9, Rīga 1010; tel. 6707-9800; fax 6707-9808; e-mail dziviba@seb .lv; internet www.seb.lv; f. 1940; present name adopted 2005; Chair. of Bd INTS KRASTS.

Seesam Latvia: Muitas iela 1, Rīga 1010; tel. 6706-1000; fax 6706-1022; e-mail seesam@seesam.lv; internet www.seesam.lv; f. 1993; owned by Pohjola Group Plc (Finland); non-life; Chair. of Supervisory Bd JOUKO PÖLÖNEN; Chair. of Management Bd TOOMAS ABNER.

Insurance Association

Latvijas Apdrošinātāju Asociācija (Latvian Insurers' Association—LAA): Lomonosova iela 9, Rīga 1019; tel. 6736-0898; fax 6736-0838; e-mail office@laa.lv; internet www.laa.lv; f. 1993; Pres. JĀNIS ABĀŠINS; Chair. UĢIS VORONS; 19 mem cos.

COMMODITY AND STOCK EXCHANGE

NASDAQ OMX Riga (NASDAQ OMX Riga AS): Valņu iela 1, Rīga 1050; tel. 6721-2431; fax 6722-9411; e-mail riga@nasdaqomx.com; internet www.nasdaqomxbaltic.com; f. 1993; owned by the NASDAQ OMX Group (USA); Chair. of Managing Bd DAIGA AUZIŅA-MELALKSNE.

Trade and Industry

GOVERNMENT AGENCIES

Bureau for the Prevention and Combat of Corruption (KNAB) (Korupcuas Novēršanas un Apkarošanas Birojs): Brīvības iela 104, blk 2, Rīga 1001; tel. 6735-6161; fax 6733-1150; e-mail

knab@knab.gov.lv; internet www.knab.gov.lv; f. 2002; ind. authority under government supervision; Dir JAROSLAVS STREĻČENOKS.

Latvian Privatization Agency (Latvijas Privatizācijas agentūra): K. Valdemāra iela 31, Rīga 1887; tel. 6702-1358; fax 6783-0363; e-mail lpa@mail.bkc.lv; internet www.lpa.bkc.lv; f. 1994; became state joint-stock Co in 2004; Dir-Gen. ARTIS KAMPARS.

DEVELOPMENT ORGANIZATION

Investment and Development Agency of Latvia (Latvijas Investīciju un Attības Agentūra—LIAA): Pērses iela 2, Rīga 1442; tel. 6703-9400; fax 6703-9401; e-mail liaa@liaa.gov.lv; internet www .liaa.gov.lv; f. 1993; promotion of business development in Latvia and foreign markets; Dir ANDRIS OZOLS.

CHAMBER OF COMMERCE

Latvian Chamber of Commerce and Industry (Latvijas Tirdzniecības un rūpniecības kamera): K. Valdemāra iela 35, Rīga 1010; tel. 6722-5595; fax 6782-0092; e-mail info@chamber.lv; internet www .chamber.lv; f. 1934; re-est. 1990; Pres. GUNDARS STRAUTMANIS; Chair. of Bd JĀNIS ENDZIŅŠ.

INDUSTRIAL AND TRADE ASSOCIATIONS

Employers' Confederation of Latvia: Baznicas iela 25-3, Rīga 1010; tel. 6722-5162; fax 6722-4469; e-mail lddk@lddk.lv; internet www.lddk.lv; f. 1993; Pres. VITĀLIJS GAVRILOVS.

Latvian Builders' Association (Latvijas Būvnieku Asociācija—LBA): Skolas iela 21-201, Rīga 1010; tel. 6722-8584; fax 6721-0023; e-mail lba@latnet.lv; internet latvijas-buvnieku-asociacija.lv; f. 1996; Pres. NORMUNDS GRINBERGS; 6 brs.

Latvian Electrical Engineering and Electronics Industry Association (LETERA): Dzirnavu iela 93, Rīga 1011; tel. 6728-8360; fax 6728-8390; e-mail letera@latnet.lv; internet www.letera.lv; f. 1995; 50 mems (enterprises and education institutions); Pres. NORMUNDS BERGS.

Latvian Fuel Traders' Association (Latvijas Degvielas Tirgotāju Asociācija): Citadeles iela 1A, Rīga 1010; tel. 6732-0229; fax 6732-0228; e-mail birojs@ldta.lv; internet www.ldta.lv; f. 1998; Chair. of Bd MĀRTIŅŠ STIRĀNS; Pres. OJĀRS KARČVSKIS.

Latvian Information Technology and Telecommunications Association (Latvijas Informācijas un Komunikācijas Tehnologijas Asociācija—LIKTA): Stabu iela 47-1, Rīga 1011; tel. 6731-1821; fax 6731-5567; e-mail office@likta.lv; internet www.likta.lv; f. 1998; Pres. SIGNE BĀLIŅA.

Latvian Timber Exporters' Association (LTEA) (Latvijas Kokmateriālu Eksportētāju Asociācija): Skaistkalnes iela 1, Rīga 1004; tel. 6706-7369; fax 6786-0268; e-mail office@latvianwood.lv; internet www.latvianwood.lv; f. 1998; Pres. JANIS APSITIS.

UTILITIES
Regulatory Authority

Public Utilities Commission (Sabiedrisko Pakalpojumu Regulēšanas Komisija): Ūnijas iela 45, Rīga 1039; tel. 6709-7200; fax 6709-7277; e-mail sprk@sprk.gov.lv; internet www.sprk.gov.lv; f. 2001; multi-sector regulator overseeing electricity, gas, electronic communications, post, water, district heating and railway sectors; Chair. VALDIS LOKENBAHS.

Electricity

Latvenergo: Pulkveža Brieža iela 12, Rīga 1230; tel. 6772-8222; fax 6772-8880; e-mail info@latvenergo.lv; internet www.latvenergo.lv; state-owned joint-stock co; generation and supply of electricity and thermal energy; provision of electricity distribution services and management of transmission system assets; five regional subsidiary cos and two associated cos; Chair. of Bd and CEO Dr ĀRIS ŽĪGURS.

Gas

Latvian Gas (Latvijas gāze): Vagonu iela 20, Rīga 1009; tel. 6704-1818; fax 6782-1604; e-mail latvijas_gaze@lg.lv; internet www.lg.lv; partially privatized in 2000–01; jt-stock co; 8% state-owned; Chair. ADRIAN DAVIS; 2,817 employees.

Water

Major suppliers include:

Aizkraukle Water Co (Aizkraukles ūdens): Torņu iela 1, Aizkraukle 5101; fax 6512-2150; e-mail udensall@inbox.lv.

Daugavpils Water Co (Daugavpils ūdens): Ūdensvada iela 3, Daugavpils 5401; tel. 6544-4608; fax 6542-5547; e-mail kontakti@ daugavpils.udens.lv; internet www.daugavpils.udens.lv; f. 1889.

Liepāja Water Co (Liepājas ūdens): K. Valdemāra iela 12, Liepāja 3401; tel. 6541-1416; fax 6541-0769; e-mail dmeu@dpu.lv.

Rīga Water Co (Rīgas ūdens): Zigfrīda Annas Meierovica bulv. 1, Rīga 1495; tel. 6708-8555; fax 6722-2660; e-mail office@rw.lv; internet www.rw.lv; water supply and sewage treatment.

TRADE UNIONS

Free Trade Union Confederation of Latvia (Latvijas Brīvo Arodbiedrību Savienība—LBAS): Bruņinieku iela 29–31, Rīga 1001; tel. 6727-0351; fax 6727-6649; e-mail lbas@lbas.lv; internet www.lbas.lv; f. 1990; 20 branch or professional affiliated unions; Pres. PETERIS KRIGERS; 110,602 mems (2009).

Transport

RAILWAYS

In 2011 the total length of railway lines in use was 1,865 km. In 2013 Latvian railways carried 19.8m. passengers and 55.8m. metric tons of freight.

Latvian Railways (Latvijas Dzelzceļš): Gogoļa iela 3, Rīga 1547; tel. 6723-1181; fax 6723-4327; e-mail info@ldz.lv; internet www.ldz.lv; f. 1993; state joint-stock co; Chair. of Bd UĢIS MAGONIS.

ROADS

In 2012 Latvia's total road network was 58,566 km, of which 1,670 km were main roads.

Latvian State Roads (Latvijas Valsts Ceļi): Gogoļa iela 3, Rīga 1050; tel. 6702-8169; fax 6702-8171; internet www.lvceli.lv; f. 2004 to replace Latvian Road Administration; state jt-stock co; manages state road network, administers State Road Fund; Chair. JĀNIS LANGE.

SHIPPING

At 31 December 2014 the Latvian flag registered fleet numbered 173 vessels, with a combined total displacement of 255,332 grt. In 2013 some 70.5m. metric tons of seaborne freight were transported through the country's three main ports (Ventspils, Rīga and Liepāja) and seven smaller ports.

Maritime Department (Ministry of Transport): Gogoļa icla 3, Rīga 1743; tel. 6702-8198; fax 6733-1406; e-mail laima.rituma@sam.gov.lv; internet www.sam.gov.lv; Dir LAIMA RITUMA.

Port Authorities and Ports

Freeport of Rīga Authority (Rīgas Brīvostas Pārvalde): Kalpaka bulv. 12, Rīga 1010; tel. 6703-0800; fax 6703-0835; e-mail info@rop.lv; internet www.rop.lv; f. 1994; CEO LEONĪDS LOGINOVS; Chair. of Bd ANDRIS AMERIKS.

Liepāja Port Authority: Liepāja Special Economic Zone, Feniksa iela 4, Liepāja 3401; tel. 6342-7605; fax 6348-0252; e-mail authority@lsez.lv; internet www.liepaja-sez.lv; Man. Dir GUNTARS KRIEVIŅŠ.

Rīga Commercial Port (Rīgas Tirdzniecības osta): Eksporta iela 15к–1, Rīga 1045; tel. 6732-9816; fax 6732-6501; e-mail info@rto.lv; internet www.rto.lv; f. 2005; Chair. RALFS KĻAVIŅŠ.

Ventspils Commercial Port (Ventspils Tirdzniecības Ostā): Dzintaru iela 22, Ventspils 3602; tel. 6366-8706; fax 6366-8860; e-mail vcp@vto.lv; internet www.vto.lv; Chair. of Bd VALERIJ PASHUTA.

Ventspils Free Port Authority (Ventspils brīvostas pārvalde): Jāņa iela 19, Ventspils 3601; tel. 6362-2586; fax 6362-1297; e-mail info@vbp.lv; internet portofventspils.lv; f. 1991; Chief Exec. IMANTS SARMULIS.

Shipping Company

Latvijas kuģniecība (LASCO) (Latvian Shipping Co): Elizabetes iela 1, Rīga 1807; tel. 6702-0111; fax 6782-8106; e-mail lsc@lscgroup.lv; internet www.lk.lv; f. 1991; tanker, reefer, liquid petroleum gas and dry-cargo transportation; 49.94% owned by Ventspils Nafta (q.v.); Chair. of Bd ALASTAIR JAMES MCKEE.

CIVIL AVIATION

There are three international airports, at Rīga, Liepāja and Ventspils.

airBaltic Corpn: Rīga Airport, Rīga 1053; tel. 6720-7069; fax 6720-7369; e-mail info@airbaltic.lv; internet www.airbaltic.com; f. 1995; 52.6% govt-owned; Pres. and Chief Exec. MARTINS GAUSS; Chair. of Bd VIGO LEGZDINS.

Civil Aviation Agency (Civilās Aviācijas Agentūra): Rīga Airport 10/1, Mārupes novads, Rīga 1053; tel. 6783-0936; fax 6783-0967; e-mail latcaa@latcaa.gov.lv; internet www.caa.lv; f. 2006 to replace Civil Aviation Administration; Dir MĀRIS GORODCOVS.

Tourism

Among Latvia's principal tourist attractions are the historic centre of Rīga, with its medieval and art nouveau buildings, the extensive beaches of the Baltic coastline, and Gauja National Park, which stretches east of the historic town of Sigulda for nearly 100 km. Revenue from tourism (excluding passenger transport) amounted to US $865m. in 2013, when foreign tourist arrivals at accommodation establishments numbered 1.2m.

Latvian Tourism Development Agency: Brīvības iela 55, Rīga 1519; tel. and fax 6722-9945; e-mail info@latvia.travel; internet www.latvia.travel; f. 1993; Dir ARMANDS SLOKENBERGS.

Defence

A Latvian Ministry of Defence was established in November 1991. In August 1994 the withdrawal from Latvia of all former Soviet forces was completed. As assessed at November 2014, Latvia's total armed forces numbered 5,310, comprising an army of 1,250, a navy of 550, an air force of 310, joint staff of 2,600, and a national guard of 600. Army volunteer reservists numbered 7,850. Conscription ended in 2006. Latvia joined the North Atlantic Treaty Organization's (NATO) 'Partnership for Peace' programme in February 1994, and became a full member of the Alliance on 29 March 2004. In February 2015 NATO announced plans to establish an expanded rapid reaction force, under which new NATO command centres were to be installed in Latvia and five other Eastern European states.

Defence Expenditure: Budgeted at 154m. lats for 2013.

Commander of the National Armed Forces: Lt-Gen. RAIMONDS GRAUBE.

Commander of the Air Force: Col AIVARS MEZRS.

Commander in Chief of the Navy: Capt. JURIS ROZE.

Education

Primary education begins at seven years of age and lasts for four years. Secondary education, beginning at the age of 11, comprises a first cycle of five years and a second of three years. Only the first nine years of education are officially compulsory. In 2011/12 enrolment at primary schools included 97% of pupils in the relevant age-group; in that year enrolment at secondary schools included 85% of pupils in the relevant age-group. In the 2004/05 academic year some 65% of school-age pupils were taught in Latvian-language schools and some 25% were taught in Russian-language schools; 10% were taught in schools offering instruction in both Latvian and Russian. In 2013/14 higher education was offered at 61 institutions and enrolment totalled 89,671 students. According to official figures, in 2012 consolidated central government expenditure on education amounted to 838.5m. lats (representing 14.7% of total expenditure).

LEBANON

Introductory Survey

LOCATION, CLIMATE, LANGUAGE, RELIGION, FLAG, CAPITAL

The Republic of Lebanon lies in western Asia, bordered by Syria to the north and east, and by Israel and the Palestinian Territories to the south. The country has a coastline of about 220 km (135 miles) on the eastern shore of the Mediterranean Sea. The climate varies widely with altitude. The coastal lowlands are hot and humid in summer, becoming mild (cool and damp) in winter. In the mountains, which occupy much of Lebanon, the weather is cool in summer, with heavy snowfalls in winter. Rainfall is generally abundant. The official language is Arabic, which is spoken by almost all of the population. French is widely used as a second language, while Kurdish and Armenian are spoken by small ethnic minorities. According to the UN Relief and Works Agency for Palestine Refugees in the Near East (UNRWA), at July 2014 there were 449,957 Palestinian refugees registered in Lebanon. The major religions are Islam and Christianity, and there is a very small Jewish community. In the early 1980s it was estimated that 57% of Lebanon's inhabitants were Muslims, with about 43% Christians; these figures were believed to have changed to 60% and 39%, respectively, by 2008. The principal Muslim sects are Shi'a and Sunni, and there is also a significant Druze community. Most Christians adhere to the Maronite rite of the Roman Catholic Church; there are also Armenian, Greek and Syrian sects (both Catholic and Eastern Orthodox) and small groups of Protestants. The national flag (proportions 2 by 3) has three horizontal stripes, of red, white (half the depth) and red, with a representation of a cedar tree (in green and brown) in the centre of the white stripe. The capital is Beirut.

CONTEMPORARY POLITICAL HISTORY

Historical Context

Lebanon, the homeland of the ancient Phoenicians, became part of the Turkish Ottoman Empire in the 16th century, and following the dissolution of the Ottoman Empire after the First World War (1914–18), a Greater Lebanese state was created by the Allied powers. The new state was formed in order to meet the nationalist aspirations of the area's predominantly Christian population, but it also included largely Muslim-populated territories traditionally considered to be part of Syria. Lebanon was administered by France, under a League of Nations mandate, from 1920 until independence was declared on 26 November 1941. A republic was established in 1943, and full autonomy was granted in January 1944.

Christians formed a slight majority of the population at independence, the largest single community (nearly 30% of the total) being the Maronites, who mostly inhabited the north of the country and the capital, Beirut. Other Christian groups included Greek Orthodox communities, Greek Catholics and Armenians. The Muslim groups were: the Sunnis, living mainly in the coastal towns of Sur (Tyre), Saida (Sidon) and Beirut; the Shi'a, a predominantly rural community in southern Lebanon and the northern Beqa'a valley; and, in much smaller numbers, the Druzes, an ancient community in central Lebanon. The relative size of the various communities provided the basis for the unwritten 'national pact' of 1943, whereby executive and legislative posts were to be shared in the ratio of six Christians to five Muslims, and seats in the Chamber of Deputies (renamed the National Assembly in March 1979) were distributed on a religious, rather than politico-ideological, basis. The convention according to this 'confessional' arrangement was that the President was a Maronite, the Prime Minister a Sunni, and the President of the National Assembly a Shi'a.

Lebanon's first President, Sheikh Bishara el-Khoury (1943–52), was succeeded by Camille Chamoun, whose reforms included the enfranchisement of women. Following elections to the Chamber of Deputies in 1957, there was considerable unrest, mainly among Muslims who mistrusted Chamoun's pro-Western foreign policy and advocated Lebanon's closer alignment with Syria and Egypt. Chamoun sought US military assistance in July 1958, and US forces remained in Beirut until October, by which time peace had been restored and Chamoun

had been persuaded not to seek a further presidential term. He was succeeded in September by Fouad Chehab, who adopted a non-aligned foreign policy and introduced state provision of health, education and other services. Chehab was succeeded in 1964 by Charles Hélou.

After the establishment of Israel in 1948, and during the subsequent Arab–Israeli wars, thousands of Palestinians fled to Lebanon, where most were housed in refugee camps in the south of the country. Following the creation of the Palestine Liberation Organization (PLO) in 1964, military training centres for Palestinian guerrilla fighters were established in the camps. From 1968 these self-styled *fedayeen* ('martyrs') began making raids into Israel, provoking retaliatory attacks by Israeli forces. In 1969 there were clashes between Lebanese security forces and the *fedayeen*. Many Christians, particularly the Maronites, advocated strict government control over the Palestinians, but the majority of Muslims strongly supported Palestinian operations against Israel.

Domestic Political Affairs

Hélou's successor as President, Sulayman Franjiya, took office in 1970. In 1971 a further influx of Palestinian fighters who had been expelled from Jordan led to fierce fighting between Israeli forces and Palestinians based in Lebanon, while Christian groups began their own armed campaign against the *fedayeen*. In 1974 Palestinian forces clashed with militia of the Phalangist Party (the Phalanges Libanaises or al-Kataeb, a militant right-wing Maronite group now also known as the Lebanese Social Democratic Party). From April 1975 the conflict between the Palestinians and Phalangists quickly descended into civil war between the left-wing Muslim Lebanese National Movement (LNM), led by Kamal Joumblatt of the mainly Druze Parti Socialiste Progressiste (PSP), and conservative Christian groups (principally the Phalangist militia). Constitutional matters overtook the status of Palestinians as the main divisive issue, with the LNM advocating an end to the 'confessional' system on the grounds that this unduly favoured Christians (who by now formed a minority of the population). Despite diplomatic efforts by Arab and Western countries, no durable ceasefire was achieved until October 1976, largely as a result of intervention in the conflict (in order to prevent an outright LNM victory) by Syrian forces. Under the terms of the ceasefire, a 30,000-strong Arab Deterrent Force (ADF), composed mainly of Syrian troops, entered Lebanon.

President Franjiya was succeeded by Elias Sarkis in September 1976. Legislative elections, due in April that year, were postponed for an initial period of 26 months. Although the constitutional status quo remained intact, more than 30,000 people had already died in the civil war, and the militias of the various warring factions controlled most of the country. East Beirut and much of northern Lebanon was controlled by Maronite militias now grouped in the Lebanese Forces (LF); west Beirut was controlled by Muslim groups; and Palestinians dominated much of south-west Lebanon.

In March 1978 Israeli forces advanced into southern Lebanon in a counter-attack against forces of Fatah (the Palestine National Liberation Movement), the main guerrilla faction within the PLO. UN Security Council Resolution 425, adopted on 17 March, demanded an Israeli withdrawal from Lebanon, and also established a UN Interim Force in Lebanon (UNIFIL, see p. 85), initially 4,000-strong. Israeli forces withdrew in June, but transferred control of a border strip to the pro-Israeli Christian militia that in 1980 became known as the South Lebanon Army (SLA). Meanwhile, in October 1978, following renewed fighting in Beirut between Syrian troops of the ADF and right-wing Christian militias, the ADF states agreed a peace plan (the Beiteddin Declaration), which aimed to restore the authority of the Lebanese Government and army. Attempts to implement the plan were unsuccessful, however, and Lebanon's fragmentation deepened.

Selim al-Hoss resigned as Prime Minister in June 1980, and was replaced in October by Chafiq al-Wazzan. In August 1982, in an election boycotted by most Muslim deputies, the renamed

National Assembly designated Bashir Gemayel (the younger son of the founder of the Phalangist Party and commander of the LF) to succeed President Sarkis. The President-elect was assassinated in September, and his brother, Amin, was elected in his place. Following the assassination, Phalangist forces (with the apparent complicity of occupying Israeli forces) entered the Palestinian refugee camps of Sabra and Chatila, in west Beirut, killing some 2,000 refugees. Israeli forces had re-entered Lebanon in 1982, with the declared aim of eliminating the PLO's military threat to Israel's northern border; they quickly defeated Palestinian forces in south-west Lebanon and surrounded the western sector of Beirut, trapping more than 6,000 Palestinian fighters. A US-led diplomatic initiative resulted in an agreement enabling the PLO fighters to disperse among several Arab states, and a multinational peacekeeping force (of some 5,800 mainly French, Italian and US personnel) was deployed in Beirut. In September 1983 intense fighting between rival factions of Fatah resulted in a truce agreement, brokered by Saudi Arabia and Syria, that led to a second evacuation of some 4,000 Palestinian fighters, among them the PLO Chairman, Yasser Arafat, who was exiled to Tunisia. In May, meanwhile, Lebanon and Israel agreed to end all hostilities—including the theoretical state of war that had existed between them since 1948—and to withdraw all foreign troops from Lebanon. However, Syria did not recognize the accord, and retained 40,000 of its own troops and 7,000 PLO fighters in the Beqa'a valley and northern Lebanon. Israel, for its part, redeployed a reduced force of 10,000 troops along the Awali river, south of Beirut. The SLA was to police southern areas as Israel's role lessened.

Meanwhile, the multinational force in Beirut came under frequent attack from Muslim militias who opposed what they regarded as its support for the Christian-led Government. The resumption of heavy fighting in February 1984 (which the reconstituted, US-trained Lebanese army was unable to suppress) led to the resignation of Prime Minister al-Wazzan, followed shortly afterwards by the withdrawal of the USA, Italy, France and the United Kingdom from the peacekeeping force. In March, by which time government forces had effective control only in mainly Christian-populated east Beirut, President Gemayel abrogated the previous year's agreement with Israel; and in April, with Syrian support, he formed a national unity Government under Rashid Karami (who been Prime Minister on several previous occasions). The Israeli Government formed by Shimon Peres in September pledged to withdraw Israeli forces from Lebanon. However, by the time the Israeli withdrawal was completed, in June 1985, Israel had ensured that a narrow security zone, policed by the SLA, was in place along the border. With the Israeli presence in Lebanon reduced to a token force, Syria withdrew about one-third of its troops from the Beqa'a valley in July, leaving some 25,000 in position.

In December 1985 the leaders of the three main Lebanese militias (the Druze forces, the Shi'a Amal and the LF) signed an accord in the Syrian capital, Damascus, providing for an immediate ceasefire and for the cessation of the civil war within a year. However, the militias of the Sunni Murabitoun and the Iranian-backed Shi'a Hezbollah were not parties to the agreement, which was also opposed by influential Christian elements. Elements of the LF were, moreover, opposed to the concessions made, and in January 1986 the group's leader, Elie Hobeika, was forced into exile and replaced as head of the LF by Samir Geagea.

During 1986 Palestinian guerrillas resumed rocket attacks on settlements in northern Israel, provoking retaliatory air attacks by Israel on targets in the Beqa'a valley and southern Lebanon. Meanwhile, Hezbollah escalated its attacks on SLA positions within the Israeli security zone and also clashed with UNIFIL. Following an escalation of fighting between Palestinian guerrillas and Amal militias for control of the refugee camps in south Beirut, a ceasefire was imposed around the camps in June, as part of a Syrian-sponsored peace plan for Muslim west Beirut. The activities of the Amal, Druze and Sunni militias in west Beirut were temporarily curtailed by the deployment of Lebanese and Syrian troops, but fighting across the so-called 'Green Line', which had effectively divided the area from Christian east Beirut since 1984, continued. By the time Amal and the PLO agreed, in September 1987, to end hostilities, more than 2,500 people had died in the 'war of the camps'. In January 1988 the Amal leader, Nabih Berri, announced an end to the siege of the Palestinian refugee camps in Beirut and southern Lebanon, avowedly as a gesture of support for the *intifada* (uprising) by Palestinians in the Israeli-occupied territories.

Al-Hoss was appointed acting Prime Minister after Karami was killed in a bomb explosion in June 1987. In 1988 there was a political crisis concerning the succession to President Gemayel. Franjiya was Syria's preferred candidate, but was notably opposed by Geagea, who apparently ensured that the National Assembly was inquorate when it convened to vote in August. Upon the expiry of his term of office, Gemayel appointed an interim military administration, comprising three Christians and three Muslims, with the Commander-in-Chief of the Lebanese army, Gen. Michel Aoun, as Prime Minister. However, the three nominated Muslim officers immediately refused to serve in the new administration. With two governments claiming legitimacy, the constitutional crisis deepened in November, when al-Hoss' Minister of Defence dismissed Aoun as army commander; none the less, since Aoun retained the loyalty of large sections of the military, he remained its de facto leader.

The Ta'if agreement

In September 1989, following six months of fighting in Beirut between Aoun's Lebanese army and Syrian forces, a Tripartite Arab Committee—comprising King Hassan of Morocco, King Fahd of Saudi Arabia and President Ben Djedid Chadli of Algeria—announced a peace plan whereby the Lebanese National Assembly would convene to discuss a draft charter of national reconciliation. A ceasefire took effect, and in October the Lebanese National Assembly, meeting in Ta'if, Saudi Arabia, agreed to endorse what became known as the Ta'if agreement. The charter provided for the transfer of executive power from the presidency to a cabinet, with portfolios to be divided equally between Christians and Muslims. The number of seats in the National Assembly was to be increased from 99 to 108, comprising equal numbers of Christian and Muslim deputies. Following the election of a President and the formation of a new government, all militias involved in the Lebanese conflict were to be disbanded within six months. Syrian armed forces would assist the new Government in implementing the security plan for a maximum of two years.

The Ta'if agreement was unanimously ratified by the National Assembly on 5 November 1989. At the same session deputies elected René Mouawad as state President. However, Gen. Aoun, who denounced the agreement as a betrayal of Lebanese sovereignty, proclaimed himself President, having declared the presidential election unconstitutional and its result null and void. Mouawad was assassinated on 22 November. Two days later the National Assembly elected Elias Hrawi as the new President, and voted to extend its own term until 1994. In August 1990 the National Assembly approved amendments to the Constitution as envisaged under the Ta'if Agreement. President Hrawi formally endorsed the amendments on 21 September, whereupon the Second Lebanese Republic was officially inaugurated.

Meanwhile, Geagea's refusal to reject the Ta'if agreement precipitated violent clashes between his LF and Aoun's forces in early 1990: by March more than 800 people had been killed in inter-Christian fighting. In October Aoun and his forces were expelled from east Beirut by Syrian forces and units of the Lebanese army loyal to Hrawi; Aoun subsequently sought refuge in the French embassy. The Lebanese army began to deploy in Beirut in December, by which time all militia forces had withdrawn from the city. In the same month al-Hoss submitted his Government's resignation, and Hrawi invited Omar Karami to form a government of national unity, as stipulated by the Ta'if agreement. By early 1991 the Lebanese army was established in most major towns in the south, and by September the militias had been largely disbanded (although Hezbollah maintained armaments in southern Lebanon and the Beqa'a valley). In May the National Assembly approved amendments to the electoral law, and in June the Cabinet appointed 40 deputies to fill the seats that had become vacant since the last election in 1972, as well as the nine new seats created under the Ta'if agreement. In August 1991 the National Assembly approved a general amnesty for crimes perpetrated during the civil war, although its terms excluded several specified crimes committed during 1975–90. Under a presidential pardon, Aoun departed for exile in France.

In May 1991 Lebanon and Syria signed a bilateral treaty establishing formal relations in political, military and economic affairs, and confirming the role of the Syrian army as guarantor of the security plans enshrined in the Ta'if agreement. Israel immediately condemned the treaty as a further step towards the formal transformation of Lebanon into a Syrian protectorate, while its opponents within Lebanon denounced it as a threat to the country's independence. In September Lebanon and Syria concluded a mutual security agreement. Syrian forces began to withdraw from Beirut in March 1992, in preparation for their scheduled withdrawal to eastern Lebanon by September. Israel, meanwhile, reasserted its intention of maintaining a military presence in the security zone, and its support for the SLA, by launching fierce attacks on Palestinian bases in southern Lebanon in June 1991. Lebanese forces began to take up positions in Sidon in July. Initial resistance from Palestinians loyal to Arafat was swiftly overcome, and an agreement was concluded with the PLO to allow the Lebanese army to assume control of the area. The conflict escalated further in February 1992, following the assassination by the Israeli air force of the Secretary-General of Hezbollah, Sheikh Abbas Moussawi.

The deteriorating economic situation, combined with allegations of government corruption and incompetence, and a series of general strikes, provoked the resignation of the Karami Government in May 1992. Subsequent talks in Damascus between President Hrawi and the Syrian leadership led to the appointment of Rashid Solh (premier in 1974–75) as Prime Minister. In July 1992 the National Assembly approved a new electoral law whereby the number of seats in the Assembly was again raised from 108 to 128, to be divided equally between Christian and Muslim deputies.

The 1992 and 1996 elections to the National Assembly

Lebanon's first legislative elections for 20 years took place (in three rounds, according to governorate) in August–September 1992. Turnout was low—especially in Maronite districts, where leaders had urged a boycott—with participation nationwide averaging 32%. Hezbollah, contesting the elections for the first time as a political party, enjoyed considerable success in the south. The Amal leader, Nabih Berri, was appointed President of the new National Assembly in October, and President Hrawi invited Rafiq Hariri, a Lebanese-born Saudi Arabian businessman, to form a new government. Hariri's Cabinet was dominated by technocrats, and the system of distributing portfolios on an entirely 'confessional' basis was somewhat diluted. In December the Lebanese army took up positions in southern Beirut for the first time in eight years, apparently meeting no resistance from Hezbollah, which had hitherto effectively controlled these areas.

In July 1993 Israeli armed forces launched their heaviest artillery and air attacks since 1982 on targets in southern Lebanon. The declared aim of 'Operation Accountability' was to eradicate the threat posed by Hezbollah and Palestinian guerrillas, and to create a flow of refugees so as to compel the Lebanese and Syrian authorities to take action against militant groups. According to Lebanese sources, the week-long offensive displaced some 300,000 civilians towards the north and resulted in 128 (mainly civilian) deaths. Despite a US-brokered ceasefire understanding, hostilities continued. In October 1994 an Israeli attack on the town of Nabatiyah, in which seven civilians died, was apparently provoked by the deaths of 22 people in a bomb attack, attributed to Palestinian militants of the Islamic Resistance Movement (Hamas), in the Israeli city of Tel-Aviv.

In March 1994 the National Assembly approved legislation instituting the death penalty for 'politically motivated' murders. The Maronite LF was proscribed shortly afterwards, on the grounds that it had sought the country's partition. In June 1995 Geagea was convicted of instigating the murder, in 1990, of his political rival Dany Chamoun, son of former President Camille Chamoun; Geagea was (together a co-defendant and seven others convicted *in absentia*) sentenced to death, although the sentences were immediately commuted to life imprisonment with hard labour. By mid-1997 Geagea had received two further (commuted) death sentences—one for ordering the murder of another Maronite rival in 1990, and one for the attempted assassination of the Minister of Defence, Michel Murr, in 1991. He received another life sentence for orchestrating the death of Prime Minister Karami in 1987.

In October 1995 the National Assembly voted to amend the Constitution to extend President Hrawi's mandate for a further three years. Prime Minister Hariri had sought an extension of the presidential term, in the stated interest of promoting stability in the economic reconstruction process.

In April 1996 Israel undertook a sustained military offensive ('Operation Grapes of Wrath') in southern Lebanon and suburbs to the south of Beirut, aimed at preventing rocket attacks by Hezbollah on settlements in northern Israel. A ceasefire understanding took effect in late April, after more than two weeks of hostilities. According to the Israeli authorities, the operation resulted in no Israeli deaths, while 170–200 Lebanese civilians and some 50 militants were killed. Hezbollah claimed to have sustained minimal casualties, and its military capacity appeared largely undiminished. In July Israel and Hezbollah reportedly exchanged prisoners and the bodies of members of their armed forces for the first time since 1991.

Elections to the National Assembly took place (in five rounds) in August–September 1996. Pro-Hariri candidates enjoyed considerable success in the rounds in Mount Lebanon, North Lebanon and Beirut governorates. In the South and Nabatiyah, and in the Beqa'a valley, an electoral alliance led by Amal and Hezbollah was reported to have won all but one of the 46 seats. Prior to this last round, Syria had effected the redeployment (delayed since 1992) of 12,000 of its estimated 30,000 troops in Lebanon to the eastern Beqa'a valley. The overall rate of voter participation averaged about 45%. Berri was re-elected President of the incoming legislature, and Hariri subsequently formed a new Government. Lebanon's first municipal elections since 1963 took place in May–June 1998, although municipal voting did not take place in southern Lebanon until September 2001, following the withdrawal of Israeli troops in 2000.

Emile Lahoud's accession to the presidency; Israeli withdrawal from southern Lebanon

As President Hrawi's mandate neared completion in 1998, the Commander-in-Chief of the Army, Gen. Emile Lahoud, emerged as a likely successor: his firm stance on corruption, and his success in having reconstructed the army following the civil war, were regarded as likely to further the process of political reform and economic regeneration. Moreover, despite his strong nationalist tendency, Lahoud was endorsed by Syria. Lahoud was duly elected President in October, with the approval of all National Assembly deputies present (although the vote was boycotted by the Druze leader, Walid Joumblatt, and his supporters), and took office in November. In December al-Hoss was designated Prime Minister, after Rafiq Hariri unexpectedly declined an invitation to form a new government. The new Cabinet's subsequently appointed Gen. Michel Suleiman to succeed Lahoud as head of the armed forces.

In April 1998 Israel's 'inner' Security Cabinet voted to adopt UN Security Council Resolution 425, with the stipulation that Lebanon must provide guarantees of the security of Israel's northern border. Clashes persisted in southern Lebanon, amid continuing protests of violations of the April 1996 ceasefire understanding. During the 1999 general election campaign in Israel, the eventual winner, Ehud Barak, pledged to withdraw Israeli forces from southern Lebanon by July 2000. In June 1999 the SLA completed a unilateral withdrawal from the enclave of Jezzine, in the north-east of the occupied zone. Later than month, in response to Hezbollah attacks on northern Israel, the outgoing administration of Binyamin Netanyahu ordered a series of air strikes against infrastructure targets in central and southern Lebanon—the heaviest aerial bombardment since Operation Grapes of Wrath in 1996. In December 1999 an 'understanding in principle' was reportedly reached between Israel and Syria to curb the fighting in southern Lebanon, although the informal ceasefire ended in January 2000 when a senior SLA commander was killed. In March the Barak Government voted unanimously to withdraw Israeli forces from southern Lebanon by July, regardless of progress on the Israeli-Syrian track of the Middle East peace process. In April Israel gave the UN official notification that it intended to withdraw its forces from southern Lebanon by 7 July. The Lebanese Government conceded that it would accept a UN peacekeeping force in southern Lebanon after the Israeli withdrawal.

In May 2000 Israel's Security Cabinet voted to accelerate the withdrawal of its remaining troops from Lebanon, after Hezbollah had taken control of about one-third of southern Lebanon following the evacuation by the SLA of outposts transferred to its control by the Israeli army. The rapid and chaotic withdrawal of Israeli forces from southern Lebanon was completed on 24 May, almost six weeks ahead of Barak's original deadline. In June the UN Security Council officially confirmed that the Israeli withdrawal had been completed. However, both the Lebanese Government and Hezbollah maintained that Israel was still required to depart from territory known as Shebaa Farms, and to release all Lebanese prisoners. (The UN maintains that Shebaa Farms is part of territory captured by Israel from Syria, and as such must be considered under the Israeli-Syrian track of the peace process.) UNIFIL assumed responsibility for the Lebanese border with Israel from July. In August a Joint Security Force of some 1,000 Lebanese troops and Internal Security Forces (ISF) personnel was reportedly deployed in southern Lebanon (other than in the border area), charged with the provision of general security there. By January 2001 more than 2,000 former SLA members were reported to have been convicted of having collaborated with Israel during its occupation of southern Lebanon.

The 2000 legislative elections; Rafiq Hariri reappointed Prime Minister

Elections to the National Assembly took place, in two rounds, in August–September 2000. Residents of the former Israeli-occupied zone of southern Lebanon participated in the elections for the first time since 1972. Former Prime Minister Rafiq Hariri's Al-Karamah (Dignity) list secured 18 of the 19 assembly seats in Beirut, while the incumbent al-Hoss lost his own seat. The Druze leader, Walid Joumblatt (one of former Prime Minister Rafiq Hariri's staunchest allies), notably secured an overwhelming victory in Mount Lebanon governorate. In the South, an alliance of Hezbollah and Amal candidates took all the governorate's 23 seats, while Hezbollah enjoyed similar successes in the Beqa'a valley. Overall, Hariri was reported to have the support of 92–106 of the 128 seats in the new legislature. In October President Lahoud formally appointed Rafiq Hariri as Prime Minister.

Pro- and anti-Syrian elements in Lebanon became increasingly polarized following Israel's withdrawal from southern Lebanon in May 2000 and the death of Syrian President Hafiz al-Assad in the following month. An unofficial visit to Beirut by Assad's successor, Bashar al-Assad, shortly before the legislative elections appeared to indicate that he intended to continue his late father's role as power broker in Lebanon. In December Syria freed 46 Lebanese political detainees (including many Christians who had been detained by Syrian troops during 1975–90), apparently as a goodwill gesture; previously, Syria had never confirmed that it was holding any Lebanese prisoners. In April 2001, following student protests demanding the withdrawal of Syrian troops, the Lebanese Government banned all unlicensed demonstrations against Syria.

With the renewed uprising in the Palestinian territories from September 2000, there was uncertainty in Lebanon as to the permanence of the Israeli withdrawal, particularly as Hezbollah renewed its campaign against the Israeli military. The killing of an Israeli soldier in Shebaa Farms in November prompted Israel to launch air strikes against suspected Hezbollah targets in southern Lebanon. Earlier that month the UN Security Council had urged the Lebanese Government to comply with international law by deploying its armed forces on the Israeli border with southern Lebanon (where Hezbollah still controlled the line of withdrawal, or 'Blue Line'), but Lebanon rejected such a deployment until such time as Israel signed a comprehensive peace treaty with both Lebanon and Syria.

In June 2001 Syria withdrew an estimated 6,000–10,000 troops from the largely Christian eastern and southern suburbs of Beirut and from Mount Lebanon, and redeployed the majority to the Beqa'a valley. None the less, Syria retained 15 military bases in strategic parts of Beirut. In August the Maronite patriarch, Cardinal Sfeir, and the Druze leader, Walid Joumblatt, held discussions intended to signify a new era of reconciliation between the two communities. Within days, however, the mainly pro-Syrian army intelligence service began mass arrests of Maronite Christians (mostly members of the banned LF and supporters of the exiled Michel Aoun) who continued to demand a complete Syrian withdrawal from Lebanon. Hariri's political standing was apparently weakened by the security forces' actions, as the National Assembly subsequently approved legislation granting increased powers to President Lahoud.

In July 2001 the UN Security Council voted to extend UNIFIL's mandate for a further six months; prior to the expiry of the mandate, the status of the peacekeeping force was adjusted to that of an observer mission. In January 2002 the Security Council expressed concern regarding recent Israeli violations of Lebanese airspace, and criticized Hezbollah for its frequent interference with UNIFIL's freedom of movement. The UN again urged the Lebanese Government to deploy its army along the Blue Line. The UNIFIL mandate was extended for further six-month periods in January and July, and at intervals thereafter.

In January 2002 former LF leader Elie Hobeika was killed in a car bombing in Beirut: he was reportedly the first prominent Lebanese politician to be assassinated since the end of the civil war in 1990. A previously unknown anti-Syrian group claimed responsibility for the attack. Israel strongly denied assertions made by some Lebanese sources that Israeli interests had instigated the killing, since Hobeika had declared his willingness to give evidence to an investigation being undertaken by a

Belgian court into alleged 'crimes against humanity' by the now Israeli Prime Minister, Ariel Sharon, related to the Sabra and Chatila refugee camp massacres in 1982. (In June 2002 a Belgian appeals court ruled the case against Sharon to be inadmissible.)

Amid rising tensions between Israel and Lebanon, in early 2002 Iran denied allegations made by Israeli officials that it was supplying Hezbollah with *Katyusha* rockets, and that it had sent members of its Revolutionary Guards Corps to Lebanon. In March and August Hezbollah initiated cross-border attacks against Israeli military targets in Shebaa Farms, asserting that these were in retaliation for Israeli violations of Lebanese airspace. Israel responded by shelling suspected militant bases in southern Lebanon. In April, meanwhile, the UN condemned Hezbollah for increasing instability along the Blue Line, and also for an incident in which five UNIFIL personnel allegedly came under attack by Hezbollah guerrillas near Shebaa Farms.

President Bashir al-Assad of Syria made an official visit to Beirut in March 2002. This was the first official visit by a Syrian leader since 1947, and was welcomed by many as a formal recognition by Syria of Lebanese sovereignty. It was subsequently reported that Syrian troops were soon to redeploy from central Lebanon to the Beqa'a valley, thus fulfilling one of the requirements of the 1989 Ta'if agreement; however, hundreds of Syrian intelligence officers were expected to remain in central Lebanon. In February 2003 Syria commenced the gradual redeployment of more than 4,000 troops stationed in northern Lebanon.

In April 2003, following weeks of disagreement between members of the Cabinet over economic and other domestic policies, Prime Minister Hariri tendered his resignation and that of his Government. Hariri, who retained the support of the National Assembly was asked by President Lahoud to form a new administration. The resultant Government, which contained no members of the Christian opposition, nor of Hezbollah, was widely considered to be the most pro-Syrian for more than a decade.

It was reported in May 2003 that Lebanese security forces had arrested suspected members of the militant Islamist al-Qa'ida organization in Sidon. Those detained were accused of plotting to attack the US embassy in Beirut and to kidnap members of the Lebanese Cabinet. In December some 27 Lebanese were convicted, and given varying prison sentences, on charges of carrying out recent bomb attacks against mostly US and British businesses in Lebanon; however, a military court in Beirut acquitted three defendants of plotting to assassinate the US ambassador to Lebanon.

Following mediation by Germany, Israel agreed in November 2003 to release more than 400 Palestinian, Lebanese (mostly Hezbollah) and other Arab prisoners in exchange for the remains of three soldiers kidnapped by Hezbollah in Shebaa Farms in 2000, as well as the return of an abducted Israeli businessman. In January 2004 the first 30 Lebanese and other Arab prisoners to be released by Israel were flown to Germany, where the exchange took place. The other Palestinian prisoners, and the remains of 59 Lebanese militants held by Israel, were later released at Israeli border posts.

Lahoud's mandate extended; Syrian influence under renewed scrutiny

In August 2004, in advance of the scheduled expiry, in November, of President Lahoud's six-year term of office, the Cabinet approved a proposed amendment to the Constitution to extend the current mandate by three years. Hariri had previously opposed to the amendment, but was apparently persuaded to support it after meeting with Syrian politicians, including President Assad. None the less, many Muslim and Christian politicians remained opposed to the amendment, and four cabinet ministers resigned after the National Assembly voted, in September, in favour of the amendment. The day before the vote, the UN Security Council had adopted Resolution 1559, demanding that: Lebanon's sovereignty be respected; a 'free and fair' presidential election be held; the Government assert its power throughout the whole country; all foreign forces leave Lebanon; and all militias in the country, both Lebanese and non-Lebanese, disband and disarm. (Neither Hezbollah nor Syria was specifically referred to.) The Security Council gave Lebanon 30 days to comply with the resolution, threatening to take measures against the country if it failed to meet its terms. Later that month Syria redeployed about 3,000 special forces from positions to the south of Beirut, although some 14,000 Syrian troops remained in Lebanon. (Further redeployments of Syrian troops followed in December.) In October, expressing concern at non-compliance with Resolution 1559, the Security Council requested that the UN Secretary General provide a report every six months detailing steps towards its fulfilment. Hariri dissolved his Cabinet the following day, declaring that he would not attempt to head the next government. He was replaced by Omar Karami, whose new Government was considered to be still more favourable than its predecessor to continued Syrian influence in Lebanese affairs.

In November 2004 some 3,000 university students and right-wing Christian activists defied a government ban to demonstrate in Beirut, on Independence Day, against Syria's influence in Lebanon. The Government subsequently endorsed a mass rally, reportedly involving more than 100,000 people, in support of Syria and rejecting UN Security Council Resolution 1559. In December a joint statement by organizations including the Christian opposition group the Qornet Shehwan Gathering, the mainly Druze-supported PSP and the proscribed Lebanese Forces Party (the political successor to the LF) demanded an end to foreign interference in Lebanon, and urged the release from detention of Geagea.

The assassination of Rafiq Hariri

Former Prime Minister Rafiq Hariri was killed, with 21 other people, by a car bomb in Beirut in February 2005. The attack was condemned by Syrian President Assad, but the USA none the less recalled its ambassador to Syria for consultations, and subsequently demanded that all Syrian troops and security forces withdraw from Lebanon. Karami dissolved his Cabinet and resigned as Prime Minister at the end of February, following a general strike and mass protests in Beirut to demand the complete withdrawal of Syrian troops and an end to Syrian influence in Lebanese politics. Presidents Assad and Lahoud agreed at a summit meeting to the withdrawal of Syrian troops to the Beqa'a valley by the end of March. Subsequently, Syria was reported to have withdrawn 4,000–6,000 of its soldiers and intelligence agents from Lebanon to Syria; 8,000–10,000 Syrian military personnel remained in the Beqa'a valley. In April the UN Security Council approved Resolution 1595, establishing an International Independent Investigation Commission (UNIIIC) to investigate Hariri's murder. After Syria declared that it had fulfilled its undertaking to withdraw all troops, military assets and intelligence apparatus, in May the UN verified the absence of Syrian military personnel in areas that it had inspected.

In March 2005, meanwhile, President Lahoud reappointed Karami as Prime Minister, but, having failed to form a new administration, Karami again tendered his resignation in April. Najib Miqati was named as caretaker Prime Minister; his Cabinet was to be responsible for the implementation of legislation facilitating a general election. Three senior Lebanese security officials with close ties to Syria announced their resignation in late April, and by mid-May a number of other pro-Syrian security officials had been dismissed.

Elections to the National Assembly followed, in four rounds, between 29 May and 19 June 2005. According to final results, the anti-Syrian Rafiq Hariri Martyr List—headed by the Future Movement of Rafiq Hariri's son, Saad Hariri, and including the PSP, the now-legalized Lebanese Forces Party, and the Qornet Shehwan Gathering—secured 72 of the National Assembly's 128 seats; the Resistance and Development Bloc—made up of the pro-Syrian Shi'a organizations Amal and Hezbollah and their allies—won 35 seats; and the Free Patriotic Movement (FPM) of Michel Aoun took 21. (Aoun, newly returned from exile, had declared prior to the election that he was no longer hostile to Syria since it had withdrawn its forces from Lebanon.) Turnout was lowest in Beirut, at 28%, and highest in Mount Lebanon governorate, at some 54%.

The incoming National Assembly re-elected Berri as its President in June 2005. President Lahoud subsequently appointed Fouad Siniora of the Future Movement (a close ally of the late Rafiq Hariri), as Prime Minister. Siniora's Cabinet, announced in July, included for the first time a representative of Hezbollah. In the same month Geagea, now head of the Lebanese Forces Party, was released from detention, under an amnesty approved by the National Assembly. (Geagea survived an assassination attempt outside his home in Beirut in April 2012, amid escalating sectarian tensions as a result of the unrest in Syria from early 2011 and subsequent civil conflict.)

The UNIIIC began work in June 2005. Its first report, issued in October, stated that there was evidence that senior Lebanese and Syrian intelligence and security officials were directly involved in Hariri's assassination. Both Lebanon and Syria denounced the findings as being politically motivated. The UN Security Council responded to the first UNIIIC report with Resolution 1636, adopted in October, establishing targeted sanctions against suspects in the assassination, including travel bans and asset freezes. The resolution urged Syria to co-operate fully with the UNIIIC and detain suspects identified by the inquiry, threatening unspecified further action should Syria fail to comply by 15 December.

Meanwhile, also in October 2005 a report by the UN Special Envoy, Terje Rød-Larsen, on the implementation of UN Security Council Resolution 1559 commended the withdrawal of Syrian troops from Lebanon, but noted that Lebanon had still not complied with the demands that all militias disarm and disband, and that government authority be extended throughout the country.

The second UNIIIC report, presented to the UN Security Council in December 2005, noted that Syria had presented five officials to the commission for interrogation, but reiterated that Syria was hindering the investigation. It stated that the UNIIIC had found further evidence that the Lebanese and Syrian intelligence and security services had been involved in the assassination of Rafiq Hariri, and revealed that the inquiry had identified 19 suspects, six of whom were Syrian (including the five currently being questioned). In January 2006 UNIIIC investigators declared that they wished to question Syrian President Assad and Minister of Foreign Affairs Farouk al-Shara' in relation to Hariri's murder. Syria announced that it would not permit the UNIIIC to interview Assad. Al-Shara' announced in March that he had reached an agreement with the UNIIIC that provided for full Syrian co-operation with the investigation, while preserving the country's 'sovereignty and dignity'.

The 2006 conflict with Israel

On 12 July 2006 Hezbollah soldiers conducted a cross-border raid in which three Israeli troops were killed and two were captured; five more Israeli soldiers were killed during an attempt to rescue the kidnapped men. Later that day Israel launched a series of air raids on a number of suspected Hezbollah positions across southern Lebanon. Further strikes during the night caused extensive damage to civilian infrastructure in the area. Hezbollah declared 'open war' on 14 July, firing barrages of rockets into northern Israel in response to Israeli air strikes. On the same day the UN Security Council held an emergency meeting, at which Lebanon accused Israel of instigating the violence.

Numerous strikes were exchanged between the two warring factions on a daily basis and many civilians were killed or injured in the conflict and thousands of homes were destroyed. Israel systematically targeted Lebanese infrastructure—roads and bridges were destroyed, seaports were blockaded and Beirut International Airport was bombed. An estimated 70% of civilians living in southern Lebanon fled to the north of the country to escape the worst of the violence. In late July 2006 at least 28 civilians, including 19 children, were reported to have been killed when a residential building in the Lebanese village of Qana was struck by missiles during an Israeli air raid. At a further emergency session of the UN Security Council, convened on the following day, UN Secretary-General Kofi Annan, while apportioning blame for the initial outbreak of the conflict to Hezbollah, denounced the scale of the Israeli response as excessive and unacceptable. Nevertheless, in early August the Israeli Cabinet approved a plan to send a large number of ground troops further into Lebanon, as far as the Litani river (approximately 30 km north of the Israeli–Lebanese border).

On 11 August 2006 the UN Security Council unanimously adopted Resolution 1701, calling for: an immediate and full cessation of hostilities; the extension of the Lebanese Government's authority over the whole country; and the delineation of Lebanese international boundaries, with particular regard to disputed sectors such as Shebaa Farms. The resolution also provided for an increase in the strength of UNIFIL from its then level of some 2,000 to a maximum of 15,000. Furthermore, the original UNIFIL mandate was substantively expanded to include, *inter alia*, monitoring the cessation of hostilities, and helping to ensure humanitarian access to civilian populations and the voluntary and safe return of displaced persons. Resolution 1701 was endorsed by the Lebanese Government on 12 August, and the Hezbollah leader, Sheikh Hasan Nasrallah, announced that Hezbollah would honour the call for a ceasefire; however, 24 Israeli soldiers were killed on that same day. Similarly, despite Israel's Cabinet approving the resolution on 13 August, on the following day Israeli troops launched an attack on a refugee camp in Sidon, killing an UNRWA staff member approximately one hour before the ceasefire was scheduled to take effect.

Nasrallah acknowledged in late August 2006 that Hezbollah's kidnapping of the two Israeli soldiers that had triggered the conflict had been deeply regrettable and that talks concerning their possible return, in exchange for Lebanese nationals detained by Israel, were ongoing. However, he remained defiant, claiming during a rally staged in Beirut in September that Hezbollah was stronger than it had been prior to the conflict and that the organization possessed in excess of 20,000 rockets in its arsenal. Earlier that month Israel had lifted its naval blockade of Lebanon and rescinded its restrictions on air travel to and from Lebanon, thereby formalizing the end of the conflict. However, much of southern Lebanon remained uninhabitable owing to the presence of unexploded cluster bombs. According to figures released by Lebanon's Higher Relief Council, an estimated 1,191 Lebanese civilians were killed during the conflict, and a further 4,410 were thought to have been injured. According to the Israeli Ministry of Foreign Affairs, 119 Israeli troops and 44 Israeli civilians had died in the fighting, and more than 530 Hezbollah members had also been killed. In November the findings of an official UN investigation into the conflict determined that Israel had fired artillery shells containing white phosphorus, an incendiary substance the use of which against civilians, or against legitimate military targets within residential areas, is banned under the terms of the Geneva Convention. However, the Israeli Government insisted that the shells had been aimed solely at military targets in open ground. Meanwhile, in September 2006 the human rights group Amnesty International accused Hezbollah of having committed war crimes by deliberately targeting Israeli civilians in its recent missile launches.

Increasing political and sectarian division

In October 2006 Sheikh Hasan Nasrallah requested that Hezbollah be allocated one-third of the seats in an expanded national unity government, prompting accusations that he was attempting to attain the right of veto in order to protect the Syrian Government from prosecution in the ongoing investigation into the assassination of Rafiq Hariri. Nasrallah's demands were disregarded, however, and in the following month five ministers—two members of Hezbollah and three from its ally, Amal—resigned from the Cabinet, thereby removing any Shi'a presence from the Government. A sixth resignation, that of a Christian pro-Syrian minister, followed soon afterwards. The assassination, in November, of Pierre Gemayel, the Minister of Industry since 2005, rendered the political situation even more unstable. Since the Lebanese Constitution decrees that any government in which one-third of the ministers have vacated their posts must automatically be dissolved and a new administration formed, Gemayel's assassination meant that the departure of one further minister would force the collapse of the Government.

In December 2006 thousands of demonstrators gathered in Beirut and erected tents in the capital's main square, besieging government buildings and proclaiming that the Cabinet was now constitutionally invalid and should therefore resign. When the protests had failed to achieve this result by late January 2007, the opposition intensified its efforts and called for a general strike; at least three people were killed during clashes between protesters and the authorities. Yet, despite the Government's refusal to submit to the wishes of the opposition, the presence of two separate Lebanese delegations at the annual summit meeting of the Arab League, held in Saudi Arabia in March, aptly symbolized the endemic divisions threatening the country's future stability.

Meanwhile, a disagreement between pro-Government Sunni and anti-Government Shi'a students at Beirut Arab University in January 2007 escalated into violent clashes; up to four people were killed and more than 150 injured. In an effort to prevent further violence, the Government imposed an overnight curfew in Beirut for the first time in a decade. In February two bombs were detonated on buses travelling through Ein Alaq, a village to the north-east of Beirut, killing three people. The attacks were thought to have been intended to deter people from travelling to Beirut to attend a large rally to mark the second anniversary of Rafiq Hariri's assassination. In March the Lebanese authorities announced that four Syrian members of Fatah al-Islam—a militant Islamist Palestinian group inspired by al-Qa'ida, and which they alleged to be supported by Syria—had been arrested on suspicion of involvement in the bus explosions.

The seventh UNIIIC report into the assassination of Rafiq Hariri, released in March 2007, stated that the Commission had identified some 250 individuals whom it wanted to question. In the same month UN Secretary-General Ban Ki-Moon issued his report on the implementation of UN Security Council Resolution 1701, in which he rebuked both Israel and Lebanon for failing to adhere to all of its terms. However, the Secretary-General praised both sides' overall commitment to maintaining the ceasefire, and proposed the establishment of an independent assessment mission to assist with the monitoring of the Israeli–Lebanese border.

In May 2007 the UN Security Council adopted Resolution 1757, authorizing the formation of a Special Tribunal for Lebanon (STL) to try the suspects in assassination of Rafiq Hariri. While the creation of the STL was welcomed by the Siniora Government, the Hezbollah-led opposition challenged its validity: Nasrallah insisted that any such tribunal not authorized by the Lebanese National Assembly was illegitimate.

Walid Eido, a member of the National Assembly for the Future Movement, was killed in a car bombing in Beirut in June 2007. Syrian officials vehemently denied allegations of the country's involvement. Following a request by Prime Minister Siniora, the UN Security Council announced that the UNIIIC was to assist with the investigation into Eido's assassination. The UNIIIC's eighth report, published in July, asserted that a number of persons of particular interest had now been identified who might have been involved in Hariri's assassination, and stated that Syria and other states had continued to provide a mostly positive response to the Commission's requests for co-operation and information. In the same month Lebanese investigators concluded that Fatah al-Islam had been responsible for the killing of Pierre Gemayel.

In September 2007 a 105-day siege of the Nahr al-Bared refugee camp in Tripoli was finally concluded when the Lebanese army seized control from Islamist militants. More than 300 people were believed to have been killed in fierce clashes between the army and militants in the camp, which forced an estimated 40,000 Palestinian refugees to flee the violence. The Syrian Government commended the efforts of the Lebanese army in ending the siege, and continued to deny claims that it supported the activities of Fatah al-Islam. In March 2008 Fatah al-Islam's leader, Shaker al-Abassi (who was reported to have gone missing), was charged with incitement to murder, in connection with the bus explosions at Ein Alaq in February 2007.

The 2007 constitutional crisis

With the scheduled expiry, in November 2007, of Lahoud's presidential term, the attention of the Government and the opposition in the preceding months came increasingly to focus on the election of his successor. The first session of the National Assembly to elect a new president was duly arranged for 25 September—the first time that the legislature was to have met since October 2006. In a conciliatory overture, the President of the Assembly, Nabih Berri, proposed an initiative whereby the opposition would relinquish its long-standing demand for a national unity government if the rival factions could agree on a presidential candidate, although the response from Siniora and his supporters to the proposal was muted. According to the Constitution, if a new president was not elected by 23 November 2007, then Siniora and his Cabinet would automatically assume executive control. However, the Constitution also authorized the President to decree the resignation of the Cabinet, allowing Lahoud, should he have chosen, to appoint a new, opposition cabinet, which would almost certainly have elected a pro-Syrian, anti-Government president. Since the Government and opposition were unwilling to co-operate in order to elect a new president, leading to an opposition boycott, the National Assembly failed to achieve the requisite two-thirds' quorum of members on 25 September; a second vote was thus scheduled for 23 October.

Hezbollah and Israel carried out a limited exchange of prisoners and bodies in October 2007. However, the two Israeli soldiers whose abduction by Hezbollah militants in July 2006 had apparently provoked the month-long conflict were not included in the arrangement. In early June 2008 Hezbollah handed over to Israel the remains of several Israeli soldiers killed during the conflict, while the Israeli authorities returned a Lebanese civilian who had served a six-year prison term for espionage. In late June the Israeli Cabinet controversially voted to exchange the bodies of the two soldiers abducted by Hezbollah in 2006 (who it now transpired were dead) for five Lebanese detainees; the exchange occurred in July 2008.

The second postponement of the scheduled ballot to elect a successor to President Lahoud was announced by Berri on 22 October 2007, the day before the vote was to take place; a new date of 12 November was declared. In early October US President George W. Bush had warned the Syrian Government not to interfere in Lebanon's internal affairs, since it was a boycott of the National Assembly by pro-Syrian opposition members that had rendered the parliament inquorate. Thus began a seven-month period during which no fewer than 17 further postponements of the presidential election were ordered. When the parliamentary session scheduled for 23 November—at the end of which Lahoud's term of office expired—was postponed until 30 November, the Constitution dictated that presidential duties would be assumed by the Siniora Government in an acting capacity. However, shortly before the expiry of his mandate, Lahoud had issued a statement asserting that, owing to conditions being present for a 'state of emergency', he would hand over responsibility for the country's security to the armed forces. (He and other representatives of the pro-Syrian opposition refused to recognize the legitimacy of the Government following the ministerial resignations of November 2006.) Lahoud's stance was firmly rejected by the Prime Minister, who insisted that no head of state could call a state of emergency without the approval of the Cabinet. This represented the first time that Lebanon had been without a president since the civil war ended in 1990.

Although the Commander-in-Chief of the Army, Gen. Michel Suleiman (a Maronite Christian), was chosen as a compromise candidate, towards the end of November 2007, disagreements remained as to how to amend the Constitution in order to permit Suleiman, as a serving senior state official, to assume the office of head of state. Finally, in January 2008, the ministers responsible for the foreign affairs of Arab League member states, meeting in Cairo, Egypt, approved details of a plan intended to bring to an end Lebanon's presidential vacuum. The three-phase proposals included the election of Suleiman as president, establishment of a Lebanese government of national unity (where Suleiman would have the deciding vote in any dispute) and approval of new electoral legislation. It was reported that the Arab League plan had received the support of both the Lebanese and Syrian administrations, but that Hezbollah and its principal allies continued to demand that they receive at least one-third of government portfolios in any new cabinet, thus granting them the right to veto important decisions. A National Assembly session to elect a president was postponed (for the 19th time) on 13 May. In April, meanwhile, Suleiman had announced his intention to retire from his military post in August, three months in advance of the scheduled date.

In December 2007 Brig.-Gen. François al-Hajj, the army's head of operations, was killed, along with three other people, in a car bomb attack in east Beirut. Al-Hajj had been widely expected to be promoted to Commander-in-Chief should Suleiman become President. It was, however, unclear which group had carried out the assassination, with Syria, Israel and Fatah al-Islam all being accused by various parties of responsibility for the blast. In January 2008 Capt. Wissam Eid, a senior member of the police team charged with investigating the recent bombings and assassinations, was killed in another car bomb attack in Beirut. In February Imad Mughniyeh, one of Hezbollah's most senior militants, was killed in a car bombing in the Syrian capital. Hezbollah representatives immediately blamed Israel for Mughniyeh's death; however, Israeli officials rejected such claims. Mughniyeh had been implicated in a number of high-profile kidnappings of Western journalists, military personnel and religious envoys in Lebanon during the 1980s, as well as in several bomb attacks against principally US interests in the 1980s and 1990s.

Lebanon's political situation deteriorated rapidly in early May 2008, when a decision taken by the Government to close both a private telecommunications network controlled by Hezbollah and Beirut International Airport (where Hezbollah was accused of using surveillance equipment to spy on pro-Government politicians) prompted fierce clashes between members of the Shi'a opposition group and government loyalists. Moreover, a general strike called by the opposition in protest against price increases and to demand higher salaries descended into violence. As Sheikh Hasan Nasrallah called the Government's actions against his organization a 'declaration of war', gunmen from Hezbollah and its allies besieged the Beirut offices of the media controlled by the Future Movement's Saad Hariri, while major roads were blocked. Observers noted that west Beirut was now effectively controlled by militants of the Hezbollah-led opposition. After several days of violent clashes, which spread to other cities such as Tripoli, at least 81 people had been killed, and up to 250 wounded, in Lebanon's worst period of unrest since the civil war. However, by mid-May the Government and army claimed to have regained control, and, following mediation by the Arab League, the Cabinet voted to revoke the measures that had provoked the recent violence—an outcome widely viewed as a demonstration of Hezbollah's growing military strength and influence.

The Doha Agreement

On 21 May 2008 some 18 months of conflict between the Lebanese Government and Hezbollah and its allies was apparently ended through the signing of the Doha Agreement, following mediation by the Qatari leadership under the auspices of the Arab League. The Agreement encompassed: the election of a new head of state; formation of a national unity government, which would involve power-sharing with Hezbollah; and introduction of a new electoral law. A few days after the signing of the unity accord, Siniora was chosen by the National Assembly to remain as Prime Minister. Suleiman was sworn in as President on 25 May. Prior to his election by the National Assembly, the President of the legislature, Berri, rejected demands by some deputies that the Constitution be amended formally to permit Suleiman, as a serving public officer, to become head of state: this occasion was deemed exceptional, since the presidency was in fact vacant. A new, 30-member national unity Cabinet was formed in July (made up of 16 ministers of the Western-supported majority coalition, 11 linked to Hezbollah and its allies, and three appointed by the President). Meanwhile, heavy fighting between supporters of the Government and pro-opposition activists was reported in the eastern Beqa'a valley and Tripoli. The new Siniora Government, which was to administer the country until fresh legislative elections were held in 2009, secured a parliamentary vote of confidence in August 2008. At the end of that month Gen. Jean Kahwaji became Commander-in-Chief of the Army, in succession to Suleiman.

A landmark agreement was reached between Lebanon and Syria in July 2008, when the two countries announced that they were for the first time to enter into diplomatic relations and open embassies in their respective capitals. It was also announced that the work of a committee to demarcate the Lebanese–Syrian border and to investigate the issue of missing persons since Lebanon's civil war would be resumed. President Suleiman undertook an official visit to Damascus in August for discussions with his Syria counterpart. Ambassadors were formally exchanged in March 2009. However, the deployment of some 10,000 Syrian special forces along the border with northern Lebanon in September 2008 (which the Syrian Government insisted was to prevent cross-border smuggling) made many Lebanese question Syria's long-term intentions towards their country.

In September 2008 the National Assembly adopted new electoral legislation involving the redrawing of electoral boundaries and the staging of elections on one day, rather than over several days, in preparation for the general election subsequently scheduled for 7 June 2009. In October 2008 Sheikh Hasan Nasrallah and Saad Hariri held their first meeting since 2006, in advance of a second round of discussions between Lebanon's rival political factions as part of the national dialogue that had begun on 16 September 2008. The talks were held in November and hosted by President Suleiman; however, the 14 participants (representing each of Lebanon's parliamentary blocs) failed to agree on a national defence strategy, largely owing to their lack of consensus on how to deal with Hezbollah's military arsenal. Further national reconciliation discussions were held during December 2008, and in January and March 2009.

Meanwhile UN Secretary-General Ban Ki-Moon announced in November 2008 that the STL, established to try those charged with the assassination of former Prime Minister Rafiq Hariri in February 2005, would be inaugurated in The Hague, Netherlands, on 1 March 2009. In the 11th (and final) UNIIIC report, issued in December 2008, the Commission asserted that it had discovered evidence of links between Hariri's assassination and other political attacks that had taken place in Lebanon. UNIIIC's mandate (which, on establishment in 2005, had been for an initial three-month period) formally concluded on 28 February 2009. The following day three of the seven suspects being detained on suspicion of withholding information and misleading the investigation of Hariri's murder were released on bail. Four pro-Syrian army generals, including Maj.-Gen. Jamil

Sayyed, former head of the General Security Directorate, remained in Lebanese custody, although they had not been formally charged. They were unexpectedly released from custody in April, after the newly installed STL ruled that there was insufficient evidence to charge them.

In March 2009 the National Assembly approved a bill which reduced the voter eligibility age in Lebanese parliamentary elections from 21 to 18; the new legislation would not, however, take effect until after the general election due to be held on 7 June as, under the terms of the Constitution, the Cabinet had four months during which to endorse it. The change in electoral law satisfied a long-standing demand of Hezbollah and its ally, Amal, since it would affect the eligibility to vote of a substantial number of young Shi'a voters.

The 2009 legislative elections

Despite the failure of the National Assembly to approve electoral reforms proposed by the Cabinet, legislative elections proceeded as scheduled on 7 June 2009. The March 14 Alliance of Saad Hariri—notably including Hariri's Future Movement, the PSP and the Lebanese Forces Party—retained its status as the largest group in the legislature, with 71 of the 128 seats in the National Assembly. The March 8 Alliance, which included Amal, the FPM and Hezbollah, secured 57 seats; voter turnout was recorded at 54%. The following day Hariri, as Prime Minister-designate, proposed a cabinet for the approval of President Suleiman; however, the proposal was denounced by the Hezbollah leader, Sheikh Hasan Nasrallah, who claimed that his party had not been consulted. Protracted negotiations between the constituent parties of the two main electoral alliances failed to secure an agreement. The process was further complicated in August when the leader of the PSP, Walid Joumblatt, announced his party's withdrawal from the March 14 Alliance. In early September Hariri resigned as Prime Minister-designate; however, the following week President Suleiman again instructed him to lead talks over the formation of a national unity coalition, and on 9 November a new, 30-member administration was sworn in by the President. In total, 12 cabinet portfolios were assigned to members of the March 14 Alliance, 10 to the March 8 Alliance and three to March 14-affiliated independents. In addition, five ministers were nominated by Suleiman. In December Prime Minister Hariri visited Damascus to meet with President Assad, and, in what appeared to be a further indication of waning anti-Syrian sentiment among the March 14 parties and its allies, in March 2010 Joumblatt also travelled to Damascus for talks with the Syrian President.

The issue of integrating Hezbollah's weapons and fighters into the Lebanese armed forces, under the terms of the 2008 Doha Agreement, remained a cause for concern among the international community, amid increasing tensions along the Israeli–Lebanese border. Following reports that Hezbollah had acquired *Scud* missiles capable of reaching targets across Israel, in April 2010 Israel accused Syria of supplying the weapons; both the Lebanese and Syrian Governments denied the allegations. In May UNIFIL declared southern Lebanon to be free of *Scud* missiles.

The collapse of the national unity Government

President Assad and King Abdullah of Saudi Arabia held a tripartite summit meeting with President Suleiman in Beirut in July 2010, in an effort to dissuade Lebanon's Sunni and Shi'a political factions from once again resorting to violence. The meeting was convened amid growing tensions in Lebanon over reports that an indictment by the STL was imminent, and that members of Hezbollah were likely to be named as suspects in the assassination of Rafiq Hariri.

An exchange of gunfire between Lebanese and Israeli forces across their joint border in August 2010 reportedly led to the deaths of at least two Lebanese soldiers and a journalist, and one Israeli commander. This constituted the most serious violence between the two sides since the conflict between Israel and Hezbollah in mid-2006. Israeli and Lebanese officials each blamed the other's military for having been first to violate the terms of UN Security Council Resolution 1701. The foreign affairs committee of the US House of Representatives declared in August 2010 that the US Administration had decided to suspend US $100m. of military assistance to Lebanon, and that this recent incident highlighted concerns among many in the USA that its weaponry might be employed by Lebanese troops, with the possible influence of Hezbollah, to attack Israeli targets. In November Israel announced that, in line with the terms of UN Security Council Resolution 1701, its military was

preparing to withdraw from the northern part of the disputed village of Ghajar, just north of the Blue Line and thus inside Lebanese territory. (At early 2015, however, the Israeli withdrawal had still not taken place.)

Meanwhile, in August 2010 the National Assembly approved legislation granting limited rights to Palestinian refugees resident in Lebanon, including the right to work legally in some areas of the private sector. The law was highly controversial and had required a number of amendments, since many of Lebanon's political factions (particularly Christian groups) were afraid of the consequences for the country's fragile sectarian balance of fully integrating Palestinian refugees into Lebanese society.

Prime Minister Saad Hariri stated in September 2010 that he had been mistaken in initially having accused the Syrian Government of involvement in his father's assassination.

As the country awaited the issuing of the first indictment by the STL, on 12 January 2011 the parties comprising the March 8 Alliance announced the withdrawal from the Cabinet of their 10 ministers, after Prime Minister Hariri refused to accede to Hezbollah demands that the Government end its co-operation with the STL; one of President Suleiman's five appointed ministers also resigned. The resignation of more than one-third of cabinet ministers (including the Minister of Foreign Affairs and Emigrants, Ali Shamy) thus prompted the collapse of the national unity Government after just 14 months in office. Having instructed ministers to remain in office pending the approval of a new cabinet, on 25 January Suleiman invited Najib Miqati—previously caretaker Prime Minister in 2005—to begin negotiations to form a new administration. The Prime Minister-designate had received support from the March 8 Alliance, but was widely viewed as a moderate politician, who claimed to be independent and who was acceptable to both the Saudi and Syrian leaderships. However, supporters of Hariri held large-scale protests in Beirut, Tripoli (Miqati's mainly Sunni home town), Sidon and other cities, amid widespread anger about Hezbollah's role in the collapse of the Government and Miqati's subsequent appointment. Meanwhile, on 17 January 2011 the STL Prosecutor, Daniel Bellemare, submitted the first sealed indictment in respect of Rafiq Hariri's assassination to the pre-trial judge; the latter was required to confirm the indictment before any arrest warrants could be issued. In February Saad Hariri announced formally that his March 14 Alliance would not join a cabinet led by Miqati.

New coalition agreement; intensified sectarian divisions heightened by the conflict in Syria

By May 2011 there were reports that Syria was exerting pressure on Lebanon to agree a new government without delay, particularly in light of the popular uprisings taking place in many countries of the Middle East and North Africa, which had already led to the overthrow of the Tunisian and Egyptian Presidents and had spread to Syria itself by April. (In Lebanon, too, there had been a series of mass rallies in recent months to demand reform and an end to sectarian politics.) Eventually, a coalition agreement was reached after almost five months of complex discussions, and the new Cabinet under Najib Miqati was sworn in by President Michel Suleiman in June. Hezbollah and its allies received a combined total of 17 of the 30 cabinet portfolios, with Hezbollah itself receiving two; Aoun's FPM and its allies held 10. Although the new administration won a parliamentary motion of confidence in July, deputies of the March 14 Alliance refused to participate in the vote, with Saad Hariri claiming that Miqati had formed a 'Hezbollah Government'. With regard to the STL Miqati undertook to support the work of the tribunal, on condition that it did not jeopardize Lebanon's stability.

In August 2011, a year after a bill was adopted to facilitate offshore exploration and drilling of potential oil and gas reserves, the National Assembly endorsed legislation outlining Lebanon's maritime boundaries with Israel and Cyprus. In the previous month Lebanese officials had rejected a border map drawn up by the Israeli Government for UN inspection, claiming that it included Lebanese sovereign territory.

At least six people were killed in clashes in June 2011 between rival pro- and anti-Syrian gunmen in Tripoli. The city's predominantly Sunni population was generally supportive of the uprising against the Alawite regime in Syria, and the fighting started after a rally was held in support of the anti-Assad movement. There was further violence in Tripoli in subsequent months. In October, as the conflict in Syria deepened, the Lebanese security forces held the Syrian regime responsible for the abduction of a number of Syrian dissidents who had fled to Beirut. Some Syrian opposition activists were reported to have been arrested and handed over to the Syrian authorities as soon as they arrived in Lebanon, prompting politicians from the March 14 Alliance to accuse the Miqati Government of acting on behalf of the Assad regime.

In late June 2011 the STL formally submitted to the Lebanese Prosecutor-General the indictments and arrest warrants in respect of the four accused in the case of Rafiq Hariri's assassination; international arrest warrants were issued in early July. In late July—after confidential details of the indictment were leaked to the Lebanese media, which identified the four suspects as members of Hezbollah—the STL ordered that the requirement for confidentiality could be removed in order to facilitate the arrest of the men. Accordingly, details of the indictments were published in August. It was alleged that Hezbollah's head of operations, Mustafa Amine Badreddine (the brother-in-law of Imad Mughniyeh), had been the most senior militant responsible for carrying out the assassination. In February 2012, by which time none of the four suspects had been handed over by the Hezbollah leadership nor arrested by Lebanese security forces, the STL declared that the accused would be tried *in absentia*.

Meanwhile, in October 2011, in a further report on the implementation of UN Security Council Resolution 1559, UN Secretary-General Ban Ki-Moon urged the Syrian Government to order an immediate halt to military incursions being carried out in parts of northern Lebanon close to the Syrian border (as a result of which at least three Syrians had been killed) and in disputed territory. As the crisis in Syria deepened, Hezbollah denied that it was providing military support to the Assad regime, its traditional ally. Following an upsurge in the fighting amid an intensification of Syrian government efforts to eradicate the opposition, particularly in the city of Homs, by March 2012 it was estimated that more than 7,000 Syrians had been displaced to Lebanon since April 2011. In February 2012 Lebanon joined 14 other member states in abstaining from a UN General Assembly vote on a resolution condemning the actions of the Syrian leadership and demanding that President Assad step down.

Sectarian tensions between members of the Sunni and Alawite communities in Tripoli escalated further in May 2012, after a leading Sunni cleric, Sheikh Ahmad Abd al-Wahid, who was known to be supportive of the Syrian opposition, was shot dead by Lebanese armed forces at a military checkpoint close to the city. Mass protests by Sunnis in Tripoli spread to areas of Beirut. The abduction, shortly afterwards, of a group of Lebanese Shi'a pilgrims (who were travelling home from Iran) by militants in the Syrian city of Aleppo further heightened tensions within Lebanon, and a number of Syrian workers were targeted in retaliatory attacks. Hezbollah denied suggestions that the pilgrims were members of the organization. (Two of the hostages were freed in subsequent months, following Turkish diplomatic efforts; and Qatar stated that its mediation resulted in the release of the nine remaining hostages in October 2013, in exchange for two Turkish pilots who had recently been kidnapped in Lebanon.) As clashes between rival pro- and anti-Syrian gunmen in Tripoli intensified throughout mid-2012, concerns rose that the country risked returning once again to the levels of violence of the 1975–90 civil war. In August 2012, in response to a series of retaliatory sectarian kidnappings, Bahrain, Kuwait, Qatar, Saudi Arabia and the United Arab Emirates all recommended that their citizens leave Lebanon.

Amid ongoing disagreements within the Lebanese Government concerning funding obligations to the STL, the tribunal's pre-trial judge, Daniel Fransen, announced in July 2012 that he had scheduled 25 March 2013 as a possible date for the start of trial proceedings. In February 2013, however, it was announced that the STL proceedings were to be postponed. The proceedings finally commenced in January 2014 (see *Recent developments*).

Meanwhile, in October 2012 the head of intelligence of the ISF, Brig.-Gen. Wissam al-Hassan, was killed, together with seven others, in a car bomb attack in east Beirut. Closely associated with Saad Hariri and the March 14 Alliance, al-Hassan had played a key role in investigations into the assassination of Rafiq Hariri in 2005. Mass protests in Beirut blamed the Syrian regime for the assassination, and, when the demonstrations turned violent, the Lebanese authorities deployed armed forces who used use tear gas to bring the situation under control. The armed forces also intervened in Tripoli, arranging a ceasefire (which failed to hold) after renewed sectarian clashes there. The Prime Minister was reported to have offered his resignation, but was asked by President Suleiman to remain in post in the national interest.

The upsurge in sectarian violence between more radical elements of the Sunni and Alawite communities of Tripoli and Beirut continued into 2013. From mid-2012, furthermore, there were clashes between Syrian armed forces and rebel fighters who had crossed the border and apparently established bases in Lebanon from which they were attempting to oust the Assad regime. Despite the official policy of dissociation adopted by President Suleiman, and the terms of the Baabda Declaration signed by political leaders in June, which aimed at preserving national stability through the country's neutrality, Lebanon was thus drawn further into the Syrian conflict. In March 2013 Syrian military aircraft fired four rockets into northern Lebanon, near the town of Arsal in the Beqa'a valley, following warnings by the Assad Government that it would target what it described as armed terrorist gangs across the border; Arsal was also home to many civilian refugees from the Syrian conflict. Both the USA and France condemned the attack as a violation of Lebanese sovereignty and a dangerous escalation of the conflict. Meanwhile, the numbers of Syrian refugees entering Lebanon increased at a rapid rate, not only further aggravating the country's widening sectarian divisions, but also putting severe strain on its economy and infrastructure: Lebanon—which, in contrast to other countries in the region, kept its borders open to refugees from Syria—notably allowed refugees access to its education and health systems. In April 2014 the UN announced that the number of Syrian refugees living in Lebanon had surpassed 1m.

The Miqati Government resigns

Attacks by Shi'a militants in two predominantly Shi'a districts of Beirut in mid-March 2013, in which three Sunni clerics were injured, provoked angry demonstrations in the capital. Both Hezbollah and Amal publicly condemned the incidents, and Prime Minister Miqati appealed for calm.

Miqati submitted his resignation, and that of his Government, in late March 2013, amid deep divisions in the Cabinet. Ministers representing the March 8 Alliance (particularly those from Hezbollah) were opposed to the proposed extension of the term of office of the head of the ISF, Gen. Achraf Rifi, whose five-year term was due to expire on 1 April. (As a Sunni, Rifi was considered to be an opponent of the Assad regime in Syria.) The March 8 Alliance, which was opposed to Lebanon's existing electoral law, also rejected the proposed appointment of members to a commission to monitor the forthcoming legislative elections, scheduled for June. The March 14 Alliance was also predominantly in favour of agreeing a new electoral law prior to the elections, while Miqati and the PSP leader, Joumblatt, supported the retention of the existing legislation. Miqati, whose administration was to remain in office pending the appointment of a Cabinet, urged the leaders of all political parties to work together in forming a national unity government in order to prevent a further deterioration in the country's already precarious situation. In early April President Suleiman asked Tammam Salam, a former Minister of Culture, to begin discussions on the formation of a new cabinet, after Salam's nomination had received almost unanimous support from the National Assembly. Salam declared his main priority on taking office to be presiding over elections and pledged that he would seek to form a cabinet of 'national interest'. Consultations began on 10 April, but were complicated by conflicting demands by the rival parliamentary blocs; while the March 8 Alliance favoured the formation of a national unity government, the March 14 Alliance advocated the appointment of a technocratic administration. Meanwhile, the National Assembly approved an amendment to the 1960 electoral law to suspend applications for candidacies until May, in order to allow legislators more time for the formulation of a new electoral law.

Political deadlock and increasing sectarian violence

Further Syrian rocket attacks were reported close to Arsal and other predominantly Shi'a border areas, including Hermel, between March and June 2013, prompting repeated demands by the USA for Syria to respect Lebanese sovereignty. In June President Suleiman issued a memo to the UN regarding territorial violations in Lebanon by the warring Syrian factions; Suleiman's move followed his repeated requests that Minister of Foreign Affairs Adnan Mansour file a similar complaint to the UN, which went unheeded.

In May 2013 renewed violence broke out in Tripoli between the rival neighbourhoods of Bab al-Tabbaneh and Jabal Mohsen (whose communities were predominantly Sunni and Alawite, respectively), despite a heavy military presence in the city. The violence came shortly after the Syrian army, with support from Hezbollah, attacked the rebel-held town of Qusair; it was subsequently reported that some 31 people had been killed in the ensuing clashes in Tripoli. An explosion near the Blue Line on Lebanon's southern border in early August, which injured several Israeli soldiers, was declared by Lebanon to be the result of an incursion by the Israeli military into its territory. Hezbollah subsequently claimed responsibility for planting the explosives in response to intelligence that the Israeli military were planning to cross into Lebanese territory. Later that month a rocket attack launched from Lebanon into Israel was condemned by the Lebanese authorities. While Israel subsequently carried out two days of flights by military and reconnaissance planes over Lebanon, two suspects were arrested over the attack. (In late August the UN Security Council adopted Resolution 2115, extending the mandate of UNIFIL for a further 12-month period. The military strength of the force at January 2014 was 10,389.)

Meanwhile, following the events in Qusair in May 2013, the US State Department demanded that Hezbollah cease its involvement in the conflict in Syria. A few days later Lebanese security sources reported that a clash had occurred east of Ba'albek between Hezbollah fighters and Syrian rebels in the first incident of its kind on Lebanese soil. Meanwhile, the eastern border town was the site of a clash in late May between unidentified gunmen and the Lebanese military, in which three soldiers were killed. This followed a similar incident in February. At a demonstration held outside the Iranian embassy in Beirut on 9 June to protest against Iran and Hezbollah's role in the Syrian conflict, one man was killed during clashes between pro- and anti-Hezbollah activists. In response to the incident, President Suleiman called on Hezbollah to adhere to Lebanon's official policy of 'disassociation' from the Syria conflict. The killing of three Lebanese Shi'a and a Turkish man in the Beqa'a valley the following week raised fears that sectarian violence would spread across Lebanon and the wider region. (In January 2014 14 people were sentenced to death, having been convicted of carrying out the explosion in which the four men were killed.)

Violence erupted in the southern city of Sidon in June 2013 between supporters of radical Sunni cleric Sheikh Ahmad Assir and a pro-Hezbollah group; one person was killed in the clashes. Renewed fighting broke out in Sidon after an attack by supporters of Assir on an army checkpoint, in which 10 soldiers were killed. The following day the Lebanese armed forces seized control of the complex where Assir's mosque was located. Assir was reported to have fled the complex; a warrant was issued for his arrest and that of 123 of his followers. In July a military prosecutor charged Assir and 36 others with, *inter alia*, undermining state authority, murder and possession of weapons. A total of 72 suspects were indicted in October, of whom 48 had been detained and 16 were at large, while the full identities of the remaining eight had not yet been determined. In February 2014 Assir and 56 others were formally charged by a military investigative judge on charges of murder and incitement to murder, in relation to the June 2013 clashes; the issuing judge recommended that any defendants found guilty should be sentenced to death. By early 2015 Assir had yet to be apprehended.

Meanwhile, Miqati's caretaker Government had agreed in May 2013 that legislative elections should be held on 16 June under the controversial 1960 electoral law, and approved the formation of an electoral committee to supervise the process. A total of 706 candidates had submitted their applications by the 27 May deadline. However, on 31 May the National Assembly voted to extend its mandate until November 2014, citing the unstable security situation in the country and the ongoing political disagreement over the formation of a permanent government and new electoral law. Aoun's FPM boycotted the parliamentary session, while President Suleiman also expressed his intention to challenge the extension. On 3 June 2013 the FPM submitted a formal challenge to the extension to the Constitutional Council. However, owing to a lack of quorum in the Constitutional Court on three occasions, the challenge to the extension had effectively failed, as the National Assembly's term was due to expire—prompting the extension to take effect—one day before the fourth scheduled meeting of the Council.

A decision by the President of the National Assembly, Nabih Berri, to convene a session of parliament in early July 2013 sparked controversy among political figures, including Miqati, who disputed the constitutionality of such a meeting. The first scheduled session of parliament's extended term failed to convene owing to a lack of quorum; in addition to Miqati, the Lebanese Forces, al-Kataeb and independent members of the March 14 Alliance boycotted the session. Meanwhile, the extension of Commander-in-Chief Gen. Kahwaji's term for two years was eventually approved by an administrative decree from Minister of National Defence Fayiz Ghosn, a move that Aoun declared unconstitutional. Immediately upon the extension of his term, Gen. Kahwaji announced internal reforms which included initiatives to reduce the influence of political parties over the military.

On the first day of the holy month of Ramadan, in early July 2013, a car bomb was exploded in a southern suburb of Beirut, traditionally a stronghold of Hezbollah, wounding more than 50 people. The following week an ambush on a road linking the Beqa'a valley to Syria killed one Hezbollah member and wounded three others. Meanwhile six men of Palestinian, Syrian and Lebanese nationality who were alleged members of Jabhat al-Nusra li-Ahl al-Sham (the Front for the Support of the People of Syria, commonly known as the al-Nusra Front), a radical Islamist group fighting against the Assad regime in Syria, were charged by the military with forming an armed gang in order to conduct terrorist acts in Lebanon. On 19 July Mansour issued a formal request to his European Union (EU) counterparts that Hezbollah not be included on that organization's list of terrorist organizations, describing the militant group as a 'principle component of Lebanese political life'. None the less, three days later it was announced that the armed wing of Hezbollah had been indeed been added to the list, in part owing to concerns over its involvement in Syria. At least 300 people were wounded and 24 killed in a further car bomb explosion in southern Beirut on 16 August, on the same day as it was announced that a Syrian had been arrested over alleged involvement in the bombing in July. In September security forces were deployed in the city's southern suburbs in place of Hezbollah checkpoints, a move that received much support among politicians and the general public. The following month three people—two Syrians and one Lebanese national—were arrested on charges of belonging to a terrorist network that was planning further bomb attacks in Lebanon, as well as political assassinations.

On 23 August 2013, the day after a Hezbollah activist and two others were killed in Tripoli, two car bombs were exploded outside mosques in the city, killing 47 people and wounding more than 400. Five people, including an alleged Syrian intelligence officer, were subsequently charged over the incident. Seven more suspects were charged in October, one of whom was reported to be affiliated with the pro-Assad Arab Democratic Party. Meanwhile, the security situation in the east of Lebanon deteriorated further, as sectarian tensions escalated between the mainly Sunni population of Arsal and the Shi'a of the Beqa'a valley. In mid-August the mayor of Arsal was injured and two members of his convoy killed in an ambush following a hostage swap of 16 residents of Arsal in return for a member of the Moqdad clan whose abduction was linked to the murder of four Shi'a in the region in June. The Brigade of the Four Martyrs, a group apparently named after the Shi'a who died, claimed responsibility for the attack. In November local officials in Arsal announced that the town was struggling to cope with a sudden influx of some 13,000 Syrian refugees as a result of heavy fighting in the Qalamoun region of Syria.

On 20 August 2013 the National Assembly failed to convene for a fourth time in succession, owing to lack of quorum. President Suleiman made an urgent appeal to political leaders, following the car bomb attacks in Tripoli, to end the political instability by forming a new Government and disassociating the country from regional conflicts. Berri, meanwhile, proposed all-party talks to resolve the impasse. In early September Hezbollah once again rejected a proposal for a Cabinet of 24 members comprised equally of members of the March 8 Alliance, the March 14 Alliance and centrists, reiterating its demand for a Government in which parties were represented in proportion to their representation in parliament. Three subsequent sessions of the National Assembly were postponed by Berri as the same parties, as well as Miqati, continued their boycott on grounds of unconstitutionality.

In late September 2013 the STL named a fifth suspect in the assassination of Rafiq Hariri, a supporter of Hezbollah. It was reported that an indictment and arrest warrant had been issued for the suspect the previous month, but his arrest had been impeded by the deterioration in the security situation in Beirut.

In late October 2013, after five days of clashes in Tripoli, which had erupted following an televised appearance by Syrian

President Assad, violence spread to the district of Zahrieh, where a number of businesses owned by members of the Christian and Alawite communities were attacked. A few days later tensions in the city were heightened when an arrest warrant was issued for an Alawite leader, Ali Eid, and his son Rifaat, in connection with the August bombings. On 12 November Ali Eid failed to attend a military tribunal to be charged with aiding the escape of a man suspected of involvement in the August bombings. On the same day a pro-Hezbollah Sunni cleric was shot and killed. An additional 500 members of the ISF were subsequently deployed in Tripoli in an attempt to contain the violence. In early December, following the deaths of some 12 people in the previous month, the Government requested that the army take direct control of security policy in the city for a period of six months.

Two suicide bombings occurred on 19 November 2013 near the Iranian embassy in Beirut, killing at least 25 people (including an Iranian diplomat) and wounding over 150. The Sunni militant group the Abdullah Azzam Brigades claimed responsibility for the attacks, which they declared to be a retaliation for Iran's involvement in the Syrian conflict. The bombers, a Lebanese national and a Palestinian from a south Lebanon refugee camp, were thought to have links with the fugitive radical cleric Sheikh Ahmad Assir. On 4 December a senior Hezbollah commander was assassinated outside his home in Beirut; the organization accused Israel of having carried out the attack.

In December 2013, following more than eight months of political deadlock, caretaker Prime Minister Miqati's attempts to convene a cabinet session to address the deteriorating security situation in Lebanon, were opposed by President Suleiman, who called for the formation of a new government in time to prepare for the presidential elections in 2014. In late December 2013, amid a disagreement between Miqati and the Minister of Finance, Muhammad Safadi, over delays in funding the STL, the Lebanese Government came under intense pressure from STL officials and the EU to pay its share for 2013, which at that time amounted to almost US $38m. The Audit Bureau approved a decree on the funding a few days later. Trial proceedings began at the STL on 16 January 2014; all of the four suspects were tried *in absentia*. On 12 February the trial of the fifth suspect, Hassan Habib Merhi, was officially linked to that of the four others. However, at the end of the month the proceedings were adjourned until mid-May.

An Israeli soldier was killed by a Lebanese soldier on the border between the two countries in mid-December 2013. Following an extraordinary tripartite meeting between senior military officials the Lebanese army and UNIFIL both stated that the soldier had acted alone. On the same day a Lebanese army officer and four militants were killed during two suicide attacks on army checkpoints in Sidon; the attackers were thought to have had links both to Sheikh Ahmad Assir and to the al-Nusra Front. Stricter security measures were subsequently imposed in and around Sidon by the Lebanese army. At least 32 gunmen from the al-Nusra Front and one member of Hezbollah were killed in an ambush on the Syrian border in late December. Meanwhile, a car bomb exploded in central Beirut on 27 December, killing former Minister of Finance Muhammad Shatah, a senior aide to Saad Hariri, as well as six others.

In early January 2014 the Lebanese army captured seven Syrian rebels on the outskirts of Tripoli who were affiliated with the Abdullah Azzam Brigades and the al-Nusra Front. Later that month four people were killed and 77 wounded when a car bomb exploded in southern Beirut. The death was subsequently announced of the Saudi-born leader of the Abdullah Azzam Brigades, Majid al-Majid, who was thought to have orchestrated the bomb attack near the Iranian embassy in November. Although it was not revealed how long al-Majid had been under arrest, it was reported that he had died of natural causes. Al-Majid's body was later returned to Saudi Arabia for burial. A commander in the Abdullah Azzam Brigades, Jamal Daftardar, who was thought to have assumed leadership of the group following the death of al-Majid, was arrested in the Beqa'a valley later that month. Daftardar and 12 others (including three Lebanese and nine Palestinians) were charged with planning terrorist attacks in Lebanon by a military prosecutor in late January. Naim Abbas, a leading Palestinian member of Abdullah Azzam Brigades, was arrested by the Lebanese army in mid-February, leading to the charging of 21 further suspects and the dismantling of a vehicle carrying explosives in Beirut. On 25 February Abbas was formally charged with involvement in the January attacks in the capital.

Bomb attacks and sectarian violence also affected other parts of the country throughout early 2014. On 16 January a car bomb attack in Hermel in north-east Lebanon killed five people and wounded 43; the al-Nusra Front claimed responsibility. The following day a rocket attack launched from Syria killed eight people, including six children, in Arsal. The latter incident prompted renewed sectarian violence in Tripoli, which continued for several days and resulted in the deaths of nine people, two of whom were Lebanese soldiers. A suspected suicide bombing in southern Beirut on 21 January killed four people and wounded 46 others, while the al-Nusra Front was alleged to have carried out two further car bombings in Hermel in February, in which a total of seven people died, including two soldiers. A further five fatalities were reported following two suicide bombings near a cultural centre in Beirut on 19 February, for which the Abdullah Azzam Brigades claimed responsibility. Violence, in the form of suicide bombings and rocket attacks launched from Syria, was also reported in the east of the country throughout March.

On 31 December 2013 an agreement was reached between President Suleiman and Prime Minister-designate Salam to attempt to form a 14-member, politically neutral Cabinet by 25 January 2014. The President also announced that Lebanon had accepted a grant of some US $3,000m. from Saudi Arabia for the purchase of military materiel for use by the Lebanese armed forces. In mid-January a deal appeared to be in place for the formation of a Cabinet comprised of eight members each from the March 8 and March 14 Alliances and a further eight members selected by the President, Salam and PSP leader Joumblatt. On 24 January Salam demanded publicly that the March 8 Alliance approve his latest proposal or accept the alternative of a *fait accompli* government. However, despite the March 8 Alliance's eventual compliance, further delays to the proceedings were caused by FPM leader Aoun's opposition to the rotation of ministers and his insistence that his son-in-law, Gebran Bassil, retain the energy portfolio.

Salam's Government 'of national interest' was finally announced on 15 February 2014. Notable among the appointees were Samir Moqbel (Deputy Prime Minister and Minister of National Defence), Nuhad Machnouq (Minister of the Interior and Municipalities) and Gebran Bassil (Minister of Foreign Affairs and Emigrants). Tensions were evident in the Cabinet as it attempted to draft its policy statement; while most parties agreed on the Baabda Declaration forming the basis of such a statement, Hezbollah insisted on a clause referring to 'resistance'. Following two days of debate in the National Assembly regarding Hezbollah's arsenal and its involvement in the Syrian conflict, the new Government received a vote of confidence. On 21 March President Suleiman called for a National Dialogue session to be convened at the end of that month to discuss the national defence strategy, specifically the issue of Hezbollah's armed wing. Meanwhile, Berri announced his intention to begin consultations with leading parliamentary figures in order to secure a quorum for the election of a new President in May. However, in April the first round of voting in the National Assembly was inconclusive, with both Hezbollah and the FPM in particular opposing the sole declared candidate, Samir Geagea, who received the support of just 48 of the 120 parliamentarians. A further two rounds of voting, in late April and early May, were boycotted by at least 45 deputies, rendering the Assembly inquorate and thereby forcing Speaker Berri to adjourn the parliamentary session. President Suleiman's term of office expired on 25 May, despite parliament's failure to elect a successor or to extend his term of office. Presidential powers were, therefore, transferred to the Cabinet on an interim basis, in accordance with the Constitution. The FPM stated that it would not attend the fifth round of voting on the presidency scheduled for the end of May, unless an agreement over a consensus candidate was in place; the Assembly was thus again rendered inquorate. A sixth round of voting on 9 June also failed after the FPM and Hezbollah maintained their boycott. The seventh attempt failed on 18 June after the major parties were unable to agree on a mechanism for exercising the Cabinet's authorities in the absence of a President, leading to the March 14 Alliance to boycott the parliamentary session. A further three attempts to convene the Assembly failed during July–August.

In August 2014 Saad Hariri unexpectedly returned to Lebanon from Saudi Arabia, where he had been living for the previous three years. Hariri's return was prompted by a US $1,000m. grant for the armed forces that had been offered to the Lebanese Government by Saudi Arabia on the condition that Hariri supervised its distribution. Four further rounds of voting over the presidency were, none the less, rendered inquorate in September–October. A 15th round of voting failed in November. Also in that month the Assembly voted by an overwhelming majority to extend its own mandate to June 2017. Hezbollah deputies claimed that the organization was too deeply involved in fighting Sunni rebels in Syria to campaign for re-election, while members of the March 14 Alliance justified deferring elections by claiming that the security forces would not agree to conduct an election amid the ongoing violence in the country. Protesters opposed to the extension tried to block access to the parliament building on the day of the passage of the law, while the Beirut office of Human Rights Watch condemned the decision and described the political leadership in Lebanon as 'oligarchical'. Parliament failed for a 16th time to elect a President in December owing to a lack of quorum as a result of a boycott by the 8 March alliance; several further attempts were postponed in January–April 2015. A 23rd attempt to convene the Assembly was scheduled to take place on 13 May.

The UN reported in April 2014 that the number of Syrian refugees in Lebanon had exceeded 1m.; Lebanon was thus hosting more refugees per head of population than any other country in the world. This inflow of refugees put severe pressure on Lebanon's infrastructure and public services, and some Lebanese, notably Christians, warned that the long-term presence of Syrian refugees in Lebanon would affect the country's fragile balance of power. Minister of Foreign Affairs and Emigrants Bassil appealed for the construction of camps on the Syrian side of the mutual border to cater for those displaced by the conflict in Syria. However, the Lebanese Government's policy of not formally engaging with the Syrian Government prevented such measures from being formally agreed.

Meanwhile, also in April 2014 the Lebanese Government began to implement a security plan to counter worsening sectarian violence in the Beqa'a valley, Tripoli and on the Syrian border. It established checkpoints and patrols in areas of sectarian tensions, raided the homes of members of Sunni militia groups and seized weapons. While the plan appeared to succeed in reducing the overall level of violence, sporadic attacks by Sunni factions continued. For its part, Sunni Muslims demonstrated against army deployments, claiming that Sunni communities had been disproportionately targeted by Shi'a and Alawite factions of the army. In May security forces arrested the Syrian Islamist militant leader Omar Bakri Muhammad, who had been sentenced to life imprisonment in Lebanon in 2010 on charges of terrorism, before being released after witnesses withdrew their evidence. In June 2014 a soldier was killed in Tripoli and two police officers were killed in suicide bombings in Beirut and the Beqa'a valley; the attacks were claimed by Sunni Islamist militants as a revenge attack against Hezbollah. In early July security officials announced the discovery of militant groups planning suicide attacks against Lebanese officials and civilians. Some 28 people were charged with belonging to the fundamentalist Islamist group Islamic State (previously Islamic State in Iraq and the Levant). It was reported that Islamic State and al-Qa'ida affiliate the al-Nusra Front, while fighting each other in Syria, had agreed a truce in the border region around Qalamoun in mid-2014 to confront more effectively the Lebanese army and Hezbollah.

In August 2014 Syrian jihadists, some of whom were reportedly linked to Islamic State, seized the predominantly Sunni town of Arsal near the border with Syria, apparently in response to the capture by the Lebanese authorities of Emad Gomaa, an al-Nusra Front commander. A large community of Syrian refugees and opposition groups had previously settled in Arsal, the loss of which led to fears of the possible expansion into Lebanon of Islamic State. However, control of the town was subsequently regained by the Lebanese army after a five-day operation. As part of a negotiated agreement, Islamic State militants withdrew from the town, with 31 soldiers and police officers whom they had abducted, to a mountainous region on the Lebanese–Syrian border. The March 14 alliance accused Hezbollah of provoking the jihadist incursion into Lebanon through its military involvement in Syria and expressed its support for the US-led military coalition which had been formed that month to curtail the expansion of Islamic State in Syria and northern Iraq. In September the militants who had withdrawn from Arsal executed three of the captured Lebanese soldiers, and demanded the release of Sunni Islamists imprisoned in Lebanon and the withdrawal of Hezbollah from Syria. The executions worsened sectarian tensions and provoked attacks by Lebanese Shi'a on Syrian refugees and a series of abductions between Sunni and Shi'a communities in the Beqa'a valley. Violence escalated further in late September after Hezbollah rejected the possibility of negotiations with Sunni militant groups: two soldiers were killed in a roadside bombing in Arsal on 19 September, while several people were reportedly killed on 22 September in Syrian Government air strikes targeting rebel groups near Arsal.

In October 2014 the al-Nusra Front attacked the Hezbollah stronghold of Britel in north-east Lebanon, reportedly killing dozens of Shi'a militants and civilians. Fighting was reported to have spread to towns in the Akkar and Dinniyeh regions and the army carried out raids and arrested dozens of alleged rebels in northern Lebanon and Beirut. The major political factions repeatedly declared support for the army, despite reports of an alleged indiscriminate crackdown on Syrian refugees and Sunni Islamists, and the destruction of residential areas. At the end of the month violence escalated between the army and Sunni militants in Tripoli after at least 11 soldiers and five civilians were killed in an army raid against a militant-held location. The Minister of Social Affairs, Rachid Derbas, warned in that month that the Government would soon adopt a policy of halting refugee inflows from Syria to stem the insecurity. In January 2015 the Government introduced the requirement for Syrians to obtain a visa prior to entering Lebanon, and claimed that the numbers entering the country would be dramatically reduced; Syrian nationals had previously been able to reside in Lebanon for six months without a visa. By that time some 1.1m. refugees were registered in the country, although the Lebanese Government claimed that the actual figure was closer to 1.6m.

In November 2014 Saudi Arabia and France finalized an agreement for the former to finance the purchase of US \$3,000m. worth of French weaponry by the Lebanese army. The agreement had been announced in December 2013, and was intended primarily to enhance the army's ability to suppress the activities of militant groups operating in Lebanon. Nevertheless, unidentified militants killed six soldiers near the Syrian border on 2 December 2014; the army responded by shelling militant positions in the area and arrested at least 10 people. On 5 December the al-Nusra Front executed a Lebanese police officer who had been held captive since the capture of Arsal in August, in response to the arrest by the army of the wife and children of an Islamic State commander; some 26 Lebanese servicemen remained in al-Nusra Front or Islamic State captivity at the end of 2014. The Government's failure to successfully resolve the hostage situation resulted in outbreaks of violence by civilians following the execution. Groups of Lebanese Shi'a blocked roads in the east of the country and encircled the town of Arsal, while a Syrian refugee camp was set alight. Three militants were reported to have been killed by the army near Arsal on 26 December, including a Syrian member of the al-Nusra Front.

Sunni–Alawite tensions increased in Tripoli in mid-January 2015. This followed two suicide bombings by the al-Nusra Front in a predominantly Alawite area of that city, which killed nine people. The army responded by raiding a prison in the city, the Islamist inmates of which were thought implicated in planning the attacks. Later that month eight soldiers and dozens of Islamist militants were reported to have been killed in clashes between the army and Islamist militants near the eastern border village of Ras Ba'albek.

CONSTITUTION AND GOVERNMENT

The Constitution was promulgated on 23 May 1926 and amended by the Constitutional Laws of 1927, 1929, 1943, 1947 and 1990. Legislative power is held by the National Assembly, with 128 members elected by universal adult suffrage for four years (subject to dissolution), on the basis of proportional representation. Seats are allocated on a religious or 'confessional' basis (divided equally between Christians and Muslims); according to convention, the President of the Assembly is usually a Shi'a Muslim. The President of the Republic (usually a Maronite Christian) is elected for six years by the National Assembly. The President, in consultation with deputies and the President of the National Assembly, appoints the Prime Minister (a Sunni Muslim) and other ministers to form the Cabinet, in which executive power is vested. The Ta'if agreement of October 1989 (see *Contemporary Political History*) stated that cabinet portfolios must be distributed equally between Christians and Muslims. Lebanon is divided into six administrative governorates.

REGIONAL AND INTERNATIONAL CO-OPERATION

Lebanon is a member of the League of Arab States (the Arab League, see p. 359). A Euro-Mediterranean Association Agreement was signed with the European Union (EU, see p. 271) in 2002. Lebanon joined the UN on 10 October 1966. The country also participates in the Organization of Islamic Cooperation (OIC, see p. 401). Lebanon has observer status at the World Trade Organization (WTO, see p. 431), membership of which was applied for in 1999.

ECONOMIC AFFAIRS

In 2013, according to estimates by the World Bank, Lebanon's gross national income (GNI), measured at average 2011–13 prices, was US $44,081m., equivalent to $9,870 per head (or $17,390 per head on an international purchasing-power parity basis). During 2004–13, it was estimated, the population increased at an average annual rate of 1.7%, while gross domestic product (GDP) per head grew, in real terms, by an average of 3.4% per year. Overall GDP increased, in real terms, at an average annual rate of 5.1% in 2004–13; GDP growth of 0.9% was recorded in 2013.

Agriculture (including hunting, forestry and fishing) contributed an estimated 4.2% of GDP in 2013. According to FAO estimates, the sector employed 1.3% of the total labour force in mid-2015. The principal crops are tomatoes, potatoes, cucumbers, wheat, apples, bananas and oranges. Viticulture is also significant. The cultivation of hashish is a notable, albeit illegal, activity in the Beqa'a valley, despite official efforts to eradicate crops and switch land to other production. According to World Bank estimates, the GDP of the agricultural sector increased at an average annual rate of 2.1% in 2004–13; agricultural GDP grew by 7.0% in 2013.

The industrial sector (including manufacturing, construction and power) contributed an estimated 18.8% of GDP in 2013. Lebanon's only mineral resources consist of small reserves of lignite and iron ore, and their contribution to GDP is insignificant. According to World Bank estimates, the GDP of the industrial sector increased by an average of 6.4% per year in 2004–13; industrial GDP expanded by 3.7% in 2013.

Manufacturing (including mining and quarrying) contributed an estimated 8.8% of GDP in 2013. The most important branches have traditionally been food processing, petroleum refining, textiles, and furniture and woodworking. According to World Bank estimates, manufacturing GDP increased at an average annual rate of 5.3% in 2004–13; the GDP of the sector grew by 3.7% in 2013.

Construction contributed an estimated 6.7% of GDP in 2013. According to the UN, the GDP of the construction sector increased at an average annual rate of 8.6% in 2004–13; real GDP expanded by 0.6% in 2012 and by a further 7.4% in 2013.

Energy is derived principally from thermal power stations, mainly using imported petroleum (which accounted for 95.1% of total electricity production in 2011). Generating capacity is inadequate to meet Lebanon's peak requirements, and interruptions to supply are frequent. Since 2009 Lebanon has been supplied with electricity from the regional power grid, and has imported natural gas from Egypt. In January 2010 Turkey also agreed to supply electricity and natural gas via Syria. In September 2011 the National Assembly ratified a new government strategy for the power sector, which aimed to improve infrastructure and to encourage the use of liquefied petroleum gas and renewable energy sources over a four-year period. Meanwhile, in August 2010 legislation was approved permitting the exploration and drilling of potential oil and gas reserves off Lebanon's Mediterranean coast. The new law increased tensions with Israel since no formal maritime border exists between the two states (see *Contemporary Political History*). In November 2012 a Petroleum Administration Board was established to oversee future licensing rounds for the exploration of these reserves. Imports of mineral fuels accounted for 23.6% of the value of total imports in 2013.

The services sector contributed an estimated 77.0% of GDP in 2013. Financial services, particularly banking, withstood many of the disruptions inflicted on the economy by the civil conflict during 1975–90 (although trading on the Beirut Stock Exchange was suspended in 1983–96). The revival of tourism, which was of considerable importance prior to the civil conflict, remains vulnerable to the political and security situation. Nevertheless, the sector contributed around 22% of GDP in 2011. Although tourism experienced strong growth in 2008–10, arrivals of foreign tourists decreased in subsequent years. This decline was attributed

both to domestic and regional instability. In February 2012 the Ministry of Tourism revealed a plan for the sector that aimed to increase the annual number of visitors to 4.0m. by 2015; however, the number of arrivals declined to just 1.3m. in 2013. According to World Bank estimates, the GDP of the services sector increased at an average annual rate of 5.7% in 2004–13; the sector's GDP expanded by 0.2% in 2013.

In 2012 Lebanon recorded a merchandise trade deficit of US $14,711.6m. and there was a deficit of $1,662.8m. on the current account of the balance of payments. The principal market for exports in 2013 was Syria (which took 13.3% of Lebanese exports); other significant purchasers included South Africa, Saudi Arabia, the United Arab Emirates and Iraq. In 2013 the principal supplier of imports was the People's Republic of China (10.8%); Italy, France, the USA, Germany and Turkey were also important suppliers. The principal exports in 2013 were pearls and precious or semi-precious stones, iron and steel, other base metals and articles of base metal, machinery and electrical equipment, food, beverages and tobacco, mineral products, chemical products, and vegetables and vegetable products. The principal imports in that year were mineral products, machinery and electrical equipment, chemical products, vehicles and transport equipment, iron and steel, other base metals and articles of base metal, food, beverages and tobacco, and pearls and precious or semi-precious stones. In 2013, according to official estimates, Lebanon recorded an overall budget deficit of £L6,362,000m. Lebanon's general government gross debt was £L95,692,000m. in 2013, equivalent to 141.0% of GDP. At the end of 2012 Lebanon's total external debt was US $28,950m., of which $23,990m. was public and publicly guaranteed debt. In that year, the cost of servicing long-term public and publicly guaranteed debt and repayments to the IMF was equivalent to 14.2% of the value of exports of goods, services and income (excluding workers' remittances). According to ILO, the annual rate of inflation averaged 4.4% in 2008–13. According to official figures, the annual rate of inflation was 5.6% in 2013. Some 6.4% of the adult labour force were unemployed in 2009.

The increase in sectarian tensions in Lebanon, which led to the collapse of the Hariri Government in January 2011 (see *Contemporary Political History*), had a negative impact on Lebanon's hitherto impressive rates of economic growth. Amid regional instability, GDP growth declined to 3.0% in 2011 from 7.0% in 2010. The five-month political stalemate prior to the formation of a new Government under Prime Minister Najib Miqati in June 2011, as well as regional unrest—particularly that in neighbouring Syria—led to a slowdown in the tourism, trade, real estate and banking sectors, which affected foreign investment. In May 2012 the IMF urged the Lebanese authorities to guarantee fiscal discipline in order to reduce further the debt-to-GDP ratio which, despite the Government's efforts, registered more than 135% in 2014—one of the highest rates in the world. The rate of youth unemployment—estimated by the World Bank to be as high as 35% in mid-2014—remained a major concern. Owing to the tense political and security situation in Lebanon, no government has managed to gain approval for a draft budget since 2005. The Ministry of Finance reported in 2014 that the budget deficit had exceeded 30% in 2013, while revenue increased by less than 1%. In June 2014 the IMF estimated GDP growth of just 1.5% for 2013, rising to 1.8 % in 2014 and 2.5% in 2015. However, the rapid influx of Syrian refugees into Lebanon (estimated to total at least 1.1m. in January 2015) and worsening sectarian divisions combined to prevent economic growth, and discourage foreign investment and badly-needed infrastructure improvement. Indeed, GDP growth failed to meet the IMF forecast, reaching just 0.9% in 2013. According to the Ministry of Finance, export revenues declined by 12% in that year, while the country continued to experience reductions in foreign investment and in tourist receipts, particularly from Gulf Arab states. In 2014 the IMF urged the Government to undertake revenue-enhancing measures, such as broadening the tax base and improving tax collection, and urged reform of the electricity sector by raising tariffs, which have remained at the same heavily subsidized level since 1996. The National Assembly was debating a proposal to increase public sector salaries in early 2015, which would increase still further the budget deficit.

PUBLIC HOLIDAYS

2016: 1 January (New Year's Day), 6 January (Christmas Day—Armenian Orthodox Church only), 9 February (Feast of St Maron), 25 March (Feast of the Annunciation), 1 May (Labour

Day), 1 May (Easter, Western and Greek Orthodox Churches), 2 May (Martyrs' Day), 4 May* (Leilat al-Meiraj, ascension of Muhammad), 9 June (Ascension Day, Western and Greek Orthodox Churches), 6 July* (Id al-Fitr, end of Ramadan), 15 August (Assumption), 12 September* (Id al-Adha, Feast of the Sacrifice), 2 October* (Muharram, Islamic New Year), 11 October*

(Ashoura), 1 November (All Saints' Day), 22 November (Independence Day), 11 December* (Mouloud/Yum al-Nabi, birth of Muhammad), 25 December (Christmas Day).

* These holidays are determined by the Islamic lunar calendar and may vary by one or two days from the dates given.

Statistical Survey

Sources (unless otherwise stated): Central Administration for Statistics, Beirut; tel. (1) 373169; internet www.cas.gov.lb; Direction Générale des Douanes, Beirut.

Area and Population

AREA, POPULATION AND DENSITY

Area (sq km)	10,452*
Population (official estimate)	
15 November 1970†	
Males	1,080,015
Females	1,046,310
Total	2,126,325
Population (UN estimates at mid-year)‡	
2013	4,821,970
2014	4,965,909
2015	5,053,624
Density (per sq km) at mid-2015	483.5

* 4,036 sq miles.

† Figures are based on the results of a sample survey, excluding Palestinian refugees in camps. According to UNRWA, the total number of registered Palestinian refugees in Lebanon was around 450,000 at mid-2014, although the actual resident number in refugee camps was estimated to be 247,000. In the first six months of 2013 UNHCR estimated that the number of refugees fleeing to Lebanon from the ongoing crisis in Syria increased by more than 400,000, to some 570,000; by mid-2014 there were 1.1m. Syrian refugees in Lebanon.

‡ Source: UN, *World Population Prospects: The 2012 Revision.*

2007 (official estimate): Total resident population 3,759,134 (males 1,857,659, females 1,901,475).

POPULATION BY AGE AND SEX
(UN estimates at mid-2015)

	Males	Females	Total
0–14 years	495,624	487,066	982,690
15–64 years	1,845,441	1,779,238	3,624,679
65 years and over	222,214	224,041	446,255
Total	2,563,279	2,490,345	5,053,624

Source: UN, *World Population Prospects: The 2012 Revision.*

PRINCIPAL TOWNS
(population in 2003)*

Beirut (capital) . .	1,171,000	Jounieh	79,800
Tarabulus (Tripoli) .	212,900	Zahle	76,600
Saida (Sidon) . .	149,000	Baabda	58,500
Sur (Tyre) . . .	117,100	Ba'albak (Ba'albek) .	29,800
Al-Nabatiyah al-			
Tahta (Nabatiyah)	89,400	Alayh	26,700

* Figures are rounded.

Source: Stefan Helders, *World Gazetteer.*

Mid-2014 (incl. suburbs, UN estimate): Beirut 2,178,830 (Source: UN, *World Urbanization Prospects: The 2014 Revision*).

BIRTHS, MARRIAGES AND DEATHS
(annual averages, UN estimates)

	2000–05	2005–10	2010–15
Birth rate (per 1,000)	16.3	12.7	13.5
Death rate (per 1,000)	5.2	4.5	4.4

Source: UN, *World Population Prospects: The 2012 Revision.*

Live births (numbers registered, official estimates): 98,569 in 2011; 79,283 in 2012; 95,246 in 2013.

Marriages (numbers registered, official estimates): 42,500 in 2011; 32,577 in 2012; 38,737 in 2013.

Deaths (numbers registered, official estimates): 26,070 in 2011; 19,549 in 2012; 24,013 in 2013.

Life expectancy (years at birth): 79.8 (males 77.8; females 82.0) in 2012 (Source: World Bank, World Development Indicators database).

ECONOMICALLY ACTIVE POPULATION
('000, FAO estimates at mid-year)

	2013	2014	2015
Agriculture, etc.	27	26	25
Total labour force (incl. others) .	1,832	1,894	1,905

2007 (household survey, persons aged 15 years and over): Total employed 1,033,572 (Agriculture and fishing 52,528, Unskilled 126,684, Skilled 188,168, Intermediate professions 108,051, Specialists 115,420, Office employees 84,269, Service sector workers and salespersons 131,950, General and corporate managers 132,761, Drivers 93,741). Note: Figures exclude members of the armed forces (84,224) and non-respondents (585) (Source: National Employment Office).

2009 (household survey, '000 persons aged 15 years and over): Total employed 1,118 (Public sector 176, Private sector 931, Other sectors 11); Unemployed 111; Total labour force 1,229 (Source: National Employment Office).

Health and Welfare

KEY INDICATORS

Total fertility rate (children per woman, 2012)	1.5
Under-5 mortality rate (per 1,000 live births, 2012) . . .	9
HIV/AIDS (% of persons aged 15–49, 2011)	0.1
Physicians (per 1,000 head, 2011)	3.2
Hospital beds (per 1,000 head, 2009)	3.5
Health expenditure (2011): US $ per head (PPP) . . .	1,003
Health expenditure (2011): % of GDP	7.4
Health expenditure (2011): public (% of total)	38.0
Access to sanitation (% of persons, 2012)	100
Total carbon dioxide emissions ('000 metric tons, 2010) . .	20,403.2
Carbon dioxide emissions per head (metric tons, 2010) . .	4.7
Human Development Index (2013): ranking	65
Human Development Index (2013): value	0.765

For sources and definitions, see explanatory note on p. vi.

Agriculture

PRINCIPAL CROPS
('000 metric tons)

	2011	2012	2013
Wheat*	125	150	140
Barley*	30	35	35
Potatoes†	390	405	412
Almonds, with shell†	27	27	25
Olives	88	70	97†
Cabbages and other brassicas†	46	47	45
Lettuce and chicory†	55	58	61
Tomatoes†	315	320	325
Cauliflowers and broccoli†	20	22	23
Pumpkins, squash and gourds†	25	26	25
Cucumbers and gherkins†	170	175	178
Aubergines (Eggplants)†	43	44	46
Onions, dry†	91	95	90
Garlic†	4	4	3
Beans, green†	25	27	26
Carrots and turnips†	4	4	4
Watermelons†	70	75	74
Cantaloupes and other melons†	22	22	20
Bananas†	120	125	130
Oranges†	125	130	124
Tangerines, mandarins, clementines and satsumas†	23	24	22
Lemons and limes†	80	82	78
Grapefruit and pomelos†	7	8	6
Apples†	150	155	153
Pears†	20	24	22
Apricots†	22	24	22
Sweet cherries†	21	23	20
Peaches and nectarines†	36	37	37
Plums and sloes†	23	24	23
Strawberries†	2	2	2
Grapes†	89	92	87
Figs†	9	10	10

* Unofficial figures.
† FAO estimate(s).

Aggregate production ('000 metric tons, may include official, semi-official or estimated data): Total cereals 159 in 2011, 189 in 2012, 179 in 2013; Total roots and tubers 391 in 2011, 406 in 2012, 413 in 2013; Total vegetables (incl. melons) 958 in 2011, 989 in 2012, 993 in 2013; Total fruits (excl. melons) 792 in 2011, 825 in 2012, 823 in 2013.

Source: FAO.

LIVESTOCK
('000 head, year ending September)

	2011	2012	2013*
Horses	3	4*	4
Asses*	15	15	15
Mules*	5	5	5
Cattle	70	78	80
Pigs*	8	8	8
Sheep	450	450	452
Goats	550	550	553
Chickens	58,692	63,648	65,000

* FAO estimate(s).
Source: FAO.

LIVESTOCK PRODUCTS
('000 metric tons)

	2011	2012	2013
Cattle meat	44.7	44.1	47.5
Sheep meat*	8.1	8.1	7.6
Goat meat*	3.9	3.9	3.5
Pig meat*	0.8	0.8	0.8
Chicken meat	95.0	100.0	85.0*
Cows' milk	301.1	301.1	367.5
Sheep's milk	4.0	4.0	8.1
Goats' milk	14.0	13.9	13.5
Hen eggs	19.4	18.9	23.7
Wool, greasy*	2.2	2.3	2.3

* FAO estimate(s).

Source: FAO.

Forestry

ROUNDWOOD REMOVALS
('000 cubic metres, excluding bark, FAO estimates)

	2009	2010	2011
Sawlogs, veneer logs and logs for sleepers*	7.2	7.2	7.2
Fuel wood	18.9	18.9	18.8
Total	26.1	26.0	26.0

* Assumed to be unchanged since 1992.

2012–13: Figures assumed to be unchanged from 2011 (FAO estimates).
Source: FAO.

SAWNWOOD PRODUCTION
('000 cubic metres, including railway sleepers, FAO estimates)

	2011	2012	2013
Total (all broadleaved)	9.1	9.1	9.1

Note: Figures assumed to be unchanged from 1993.
Source: FAO.

Fishing

(metric tons, live weight)

	2004	2005	2006
Capture	3,866	3,798	3,811
Groupers and seabasses	245	250	252
Porgies and seabreams	365	370	371
Surmullets (Red mullets)	200	190	190
Barracudas	250	240	240
Mullets	360	365	360
Scorpionfishes	125	110	115
Carangids	400	380	383
Clupeoids	600	580	580
Tuna-like fishes	400	385	389
Mackerel-like fishes	300	320	322
Marine crustaceans	60	55	57
Aquaculture	790	803	803
Rainbow trout	700	708	708
Total catch	4,656	4,601	4,614

2007–12: Capture assumed to be unchanged from 2006 (FAO estimates).

Aquaculture (FAO estimates): 1,180 (Rainbow trout 1,100) in 2010; 1,280 (Rainbow trout 1,200) in 2011; 1,280 (Rainbow trout 1,200) in 2013.

Total catch (FAO estimates): 4,991 in 2010; 5,091 in 2011; 5,091 in 2012.
Source: FAO.

Mining

('000 metric tons, estimates)

	2010	2011	2012
Gypsum	105	105	105
Salt (unrefined)	20	20	20
Phosphoric acid	60	60	60

Source: US Geological Survey.

Industry

SELECTED PRODUCTS
('000 metric tons unless otherwise indicated)

	2010	2011	2012
Cigarettes (metric tons) . . .	n.a.	454.0	n.a.
Cement	5,227	5,550	5,309
Wine*	14	15	15
Electric energy (million kWh) .	12,459	12,469	10,946

*FAO estimates (Source: FAO).

Flour and flour derivatives: 379 in 2007.

Bottled water and soda (million litres): 532 in 2008.

Electric energy (million kWh): 12,108 in 2013.

Finance

CURRENCY AND EXCHANGE RATES

Monetary Units:
100 piastres = 1 Lebanese pound (£L).

Sterling, Dollar and Euro Equivalents (31 December 2014):
£1 sterling = £L2,352.9;
US $1 = £L1,507.5;
€1 = £L1,830.3;
£L10,000 = £4.25 sterling = $6.63 = €5.46.

Exchange Rate: The official exchange rate has been maintained at US $1 = £L1,507.5 since September 1999.

BUDGET
(£L '000 million)

Revenue	2011	2012	2013
Tax revenue	9,885	10,187	10,116
Taxes on income, profits and			
capital gains	2,423	2,516	2,502
Taxes on property . . .	1,144	1,193	1,201
Domestic taxes on goods and			
services	3,685	3,749	3,782
Taxes on international trade .	2,179	2,251	2,158
Other taxes	454	478	473
Non-tax revenue	3,468	3,286	3,269
Income from public enterprises .	2,679	2,530	2,518
Administrative fees and charges	570	587	606
Fines and confiscations . . .	10	10	9
Other	208	159	136
Treasury revenue	718	691	816
Total	**14,070**	**14,164**	**14,201**

Expenditure	2011	2012	2013
Personnel costs	5,533	6,723	6,473
Salaries and wages . . .	3,818	4,409	4,276
Interest payments and financial			
charges	5,655	5,457	5,714
Foreign debt principal repayment .	379	295	287
Materials and supplies . . .	329	305	455
External services	135	122	153
Various transfers	3,278	4,256	4,173
Acquisitions of land, buildings, for			
the construction of roads, ports,			
airports and water networks .	1	18	12
Equipment	52	70	75
Construction in progress . . .	402	486	571
Maintenance	186	180	297
Other expenditures (including			
unclassified and statistical			
discrepancy)	1,650	2,169	2,353
Total	**17,600**	**20,081**	**20,563**

Source: Ministry of Finance, Beirut.

INTERNATIONAL RESERVES
(US $ million at 31 December)

	2011	2012	2013
Gold (national valuation) . . .	14,400.7	15,312.3	11,103.7
IMF special drawing rights . .	295.7	295.6	296.1
Reserve position in IMF . . .	53.2	53.3	53.4
Foreign exchange	33,391.6	36,836.6	36,398.5
Total	**48,141.2**	**52,497.8**	**47,851.7**

Source: IMF, *International Financial Statistics*.

MONEY SUPPLY
(£L '000 million at 31 December)

	2011	2012	2013
Currency outside banks . . .	2,891.0	3,213.2	3,407.5
Demand deposits at commercial			
banks	3,200.6	3,808.1	4,144.1
Total money (incl. others) . .	**6,138.4**	**7,103.6**	**7,620.4**

Source: IMF, *International Financial Statistics*.

COST OF LIVING
(Consumer Price Index for Beirut; base: December 2007 = 100)

	2011	2012	2013
Food and non-alcoholic beverages .	127.8	135.3	138.8
Clothing and footwear	116.2	120.9	119.5
Water, electricity and gas . . .	111.8	115.7	116.5
Housing	111.2	135.7	160.2
All items (incl. others) . . .	**116.0**	**123.6**	**130.5**

NATIONAL ACCOUNTS
(£L '000 million)

Expenditure on the Gross Domestic Product

	2011	2012	2013
Government final consumption			
expenditure	7,306	8,730	8,879
Private final consumption			
expenditure	53,384	60,788	62,534
Gross fixed capital formation . }	16,183	16,154	19,778
Changes in stocks . . . . }			
Total domestic expenditure .	**76,873**	**85,672**	**91,191**
Exports of goods and services .	22,318	21,250	20,095
Less Imports of goods and			
services	38,776	40,442	40,102
GDP in purchasers' values .	**60,414**	**66,481**	**71,185**

Gross Domestic Product by Economic Activity

	2011	2012	2013
Agriculture, hunting, forestry and fishing	2,290	2,469	2,793
Mining and quarrying	304	319	386
Manufacturing	4,562	4,844	5,444
Electricity, gas and water . . .	1,396	1,994	2,162
Construction	2,690	3,434	4,437
Wholesale and retail trade; repair of motor vehicles, motorcycles and personal and household goods	9,538	9,871	10,156
Hotels and restaurants . . .	1,685	1,722	1,890
Transport, storage and communications	3,466	3,658	4,159
Financial intermediation . . .	4,418	4,802	5,136
Real estate, renting and business activities	12,413	14,020	14,539
Government services	5,544	6,669	6,639
Education	3,645	4,164	4,596
Health	1,658	1,755	2,135
Personal and community services .	1,900	1,874	1,804
Gross value added in basic prices	**55,509**	**61,596**	**66,275**
Net taxes on products	4,905	4,884	4,909
GDP in market prices . . .	**60,414**	**66,481**	**71,185**

Note: Indirect taxes assumed to be distributed at origin.

BALANCE OF PAYMENTS
(US $ million)

	2010	2011	2012
Exports of goods	4,688.7	5,385.5	5,615.3
Imports of goods	−17,187.8	−19,304.4	−20,326.9
Balance on goods	**−12,499.0**	**−13,918.9**	**−14,711.6**
Exports of services	16,040.1	19,672.6	22,265.3
Imports of services	−13,034.0	−12,963.3	−12,274.5
Balance on goods and services	**−9,492.9**	**−7,209.6**	**−4,720.8**
Primary income received . . .	1,448.1	1,629.1	1,758.0
Primary income paid	−1,957.0	−1,803.4	−1,367.3
Balance on goods, services and primary income	**−10,001.8**	**−7,383.9**	**−4,330.1**
Secondary income received . .	7,956.6	7,859.9	8,528.7
Secondary income paid . . .	−5,506.8	−5,334.8	−5,861.3
Current balance	**−7,552.1**	**−4,858.8**	**−1,662.8**
Capital account (net)	267.9	164.7	178.2
Direct investment assets . . .	−486.7	−754.3	−569.8
Direct investment liabilities . .	4,279.9	3,490.2	3,678.0
Portfolio investment assets . .	−1,910.6	−444.6	594.5
Portfolio investment liabilities .	−724.7	−305.4	154.9
Other investment assets . . .	2,025.7	3,131.9	−595.1
Other investment liabilities . .	332.6	3,868.6	2,808.7
Net errors and omissions . . .	6,827.3	−1,998.0	−3,969.3
Reserves and related items .	**3,059.4**	**2,294.2**	**617.3**

Source: IMF, *International Financial Statistics*.

External Trade

PRINCIPAL COMMODITIES
(distribution by HS, £L '000 million)

Imports c.i.f.	2011	2012	2013
Live animals and animal products	1,307.6	1,243.0	1,344.5
Vegetables and vegetable products	1,281.2	1,308.4	1,391.6
Prepared foodstuffs; beverages, spirits and vinegar; tobacco and articles thereof	1,947.0	2,115.3	2,126.0
Mineral products	6,972.3	9,100.2	7,705.8
Mineral fuels, mineral oils and products thereof	6,739.1	8,885.5	7,539.3
Petroleum oils, not crude . .	6,267.1	8,317.6	7,032.1

Imports c.i.f.—*continued*	2011	2012	2013
Chemicals and related products	2,602.0	2,622.8	2,920.6
Pharmaceutical products. . . .	1,467.0	1,462.9	1,645.6
Medicament mixtures . . .	n.a.	1,253.3	1,410.5
Plastics, rubber and articles thereof	1,062.1	1,148.7	1,256.4
Plastics and articles thereof . .	857.9	911.6	1,031.1
Textiles and textile articles .	1,060.0	1,133.5	1,195.7
Pearls, precious or semi-precious stones, precious metals, and articles thereof .	3,229.2	2,390.4	1,712.6
Gold	2,541.7	1,788.9	1,284.6
Iron and steel, other base metals and articles of base metal	2,297.0	2,304.9	2,369.9
Iron and steel	1,348.4	1,336.0	1,299.0
Machinery and mechanical appliances; electrical equipment; parts thereof .	3,212.1	3,126.1	3,906.2
Boilers, machinery and mechanical appliances	1,963.7	1,772.6	2,004.6
Electrical machinery and equipment and parts there of .	1,248.4	1,353.5	1,901.6
Vehicles, aircraft, vessels and associated transport equipment	2,231.2	2,282.1	2,633.1
Vehicles other than railway . .	2,174.3	2,199.6	2,359.7
Motor vehicles	1,646.3	1,660.5	1,761.0
Total (incl. others)	**30,398.7**	**32,090.0**	**32,012.6**

Exports f.o.b.	2011	2012	2013
Vegetables and vegetable products	242.2	258.2	325.3
Prepared foodstuffs; beverages, spirits and vinegar; tobacco and articles thereof	572.8	591.4	682.6
Mineral products	52.3	198.7	537.8
Mineral fuels, mineral oils and products thereof	6.3	135.3	507.9
Petroleum oils, not crude . .	5.7	109.1	450.1
Chemicals and related products	578.6	516.5	496.3
Plastics, rubber and articles thereof	202.5	220.7	217.4
Plastics and articles thereof . .	185.1	205.2	206.1
Pulp of wood, paper and paperboard and articles thereof	326.6	274.8	264.2
Paper and paperboard, articles of paper pulp	227.2	139.0	132.7
Textiles and textile articles .	194.7	175.6	183.1
Pearls, precious or semi-precious stones, precious metals, and articles thereof .	2,250.3	2,600.5	1,160.7
Gold	1,762.4	2,104.6	842.2
Iron and steel, other base metals and articles of base metal	792.2	709.8	795.0
Iron and steel	373.3	224.8	244.9
Ferrous waste and scrap; remelting scrap ingots . .	349.8	201.7	221.7
Copper and articles thereof . .	158.9	243.0	288.6
Copper waste and scrap . . .	155.4	237.0	283.3

Exports f.o.b.—*continued*	2011	2012	2013
Machinery and mechanical appliances; electrical equipment; sound and parts thereof	782.9	721.3	763.9
Boilers, machinery and mechanical appliances	309.6	327.0	373.3
Electrical machinery and equipment and parts there of .	473.3	394.3	390.6
Electric generating sets and rotary converters.	264.3	217.1	205.7
Total (incl. others)	6,432.3	6,760.6	5,935.4

Source: Ministry of Finance, Lebanese Customs Administration, Beirut.

PRINCIPAL TRADING PARTNERS
(£L '000 million)

Imports c.i.f.	2011	2012	2013
Belgium	377.2	421.3	453.6
Brazil	459.3	455.5	553.5
Bulgaria	72.6	117.5	358.5
China, People's Republic . .	2,449.1	2,672.6	3,442.2
Egypt	1,421.1	1,267.7	971.7
France	2,277.1	2,323.6	2,314.2
Germany	1,719.1	1,812.2	1,872.8
Greece	457.6	1,343.2	916.0
India	534.4	525.5	615.0
Italy	2,816.6	2,759.1	2,698.4
Japan	609.1	548.4	563.7
Korea, Republic	396.2	463.3	511.7
Kuwait	456.3	950.6	680.6
Netherlands	519.8	613.3	466.5
Romania	314.9	293.9	360.2
Russia	775.5	637.9	1,358.3
Saudi Arabia	801.7	638.8	663.6
Spain	510.2	642.4	567.4
Switzerland	1,499.1	765.7	965.4
Syria	467.7	401.4	273.4
Thailand	306.3	358.1	393.0
Togo	229.7	220.2	337.8
Turkey	1,267.2	1,456.0	1,710.2
Ukraine	580.3	638.7	835.0
United Arab Emirates . . .	896.0	627.8	572.5
United Kingdom	786.0	782.0	953.1
USA	3,001.2	3,582.3	2,262.6
Total (incl. others)	30,398.7	32,090.0	32,012.6

Exports f.o.b.	2011	2012	2013
Angola	74.3	82.8	79.6
Belgium	196.7	168.2	68.9
Congo, Republic	62.4	67.1	76.1
Egypt	102.0	132.9	110.4
France	86.5	90.0	74.2
Germany	68.2	52.0	68.5
Iraq	297.9	318.7	410.6
Jordan	191.7	214.5	213.8
Korea, Republic	40.3	85.5	133.5
Kuwait	115.7	102.7	110.7
Nigeria	74.2	65.2	110.6
Qatar	120.4	128.9	141.5
Saudi Arabia	464.3	541.3	523.0
South Africa	1,015.0	1,303.5	600.1
Spain	73.8	66.3	48.2
Switzerland	776.2	825.4	263.5
Syria	324.0	443.8	789.7
Turkey	416.2	237.0	275.7
United Arab Emirates . . .	486.0	530.9	500.1
United Kingdom	92.2	67.3	56.5
USA	96.9	97.4	96.3
Total (incl. others)	6,432.3	6,760.6	5,935.4

Source: Ministry of Finance, Lebanese Customs Administration, Beirut.

Transport

SHIPPING

Flag Registered Fleet
(at 31 December)

	2012	2013	2014
Number of vessels	52	54	56
Total displacement ('000 grt) . .	151.8	180.6	210.3

Source: Lloyd's List Intelligence (www.lloydslistintelligence.com).

International Seaborne Freight Traffic
('000 metric tons)

	2008	2009	2010
Goods loaded	841	669	1,080
Goods unloaded	4,906	5,641	7,019

CIVIL AVIATION
(traffic on scheduled services)

	2010	2011
Kilometres flown (million)	38	37
Passengers carried ('000)	1,893	2,030
Passenger-km (million)	3,619	3,827
Total ton-km (million)	430	453

Source: UN, *Statistical Yearbook*.

Passengers carried ('000): 2,149 in 2012; 1,954 in 2013 (Source: World Bank, World Development Indicators database).

Tourism

FOREIGN TOURIST ARRIVALS
('000)*

Country of nationality	2011	2012	2013
Canada	80.0	75.8	71.8
Egypt	62.8	64.0	63.6
France	129.0	120.1	117.7
Germany	68.4	62.2	61.1
Iraq	129.3	127.0	142.0
Jordan	129.6	89.1	78.0
Saudi Arabia	111.7	72.7	41.0
United Kingdom	53.2	50.2	48.5
USA	110.2	110.5	103.5
Total (incl. others)	1,655.1	1,365.8	1,274.4

*Figures exclude arrivals of Syrian nationals, Palestinians and students.

Source: Ministry of Tourism, Beirut.

Tourism receipts (US $ million, excl. passenger transport): 7,659 in 2010; 6,146 in 2011; 5,787 in 2012 (Source: World Tourism Organization).

Communications Media

	2011	2012	2013
Telephones ('000 main lines in use)	855.0	867.0	870.0
Mobile cellular telephones ('000 subscribers)	3,456.7	3,755.2	3,884.8
Broadband subscribers ('000) . .	371.0	451.0	480.0

Internet subscribers ('000): 468.5 in 2011.

Source: International Telecommunication Union.

Education

(2011/12 unless otherwise indicated)

	Institutions	Teachers	Students
Pre-primary	1,938*	10,159	158,873
Primary	2,160*	31,816	456,206
Secondary:			
general	n.a.	32,728	328,684
vocational	275†	11,022‡	56,167
Higher	n.a.	28,462	212,467

* 1996/97 figure.
† 1994 figure.
‡ 2010/11 figure.

Sources: UNESCO Institute for Statistics; Banque du Liban, *Annual Report*.

Pupil-teacher ratio (primary education, UNESCO estimates): 14.3 in 2011/12 (Source: UNESCO Institute for Statistics).

Adult literacy rate (UNESCO estimates): 89.6% (males 93.4%; females 86.0%) in 2007 (Source: UNESCO Institute for Statistics).

Directory

The Government

HEAD OF STATE

The presidency became vacant on 24 May 2014 upon the expiry of Michel Suleiman's term of office. (Suleiman had been inaugurated as President on 25 May 2008.) This development was prompted by the failure of the National Assembly to elect a successor. In accordance with the Constitution, presidential powers were assumed by the Cabinet, pending the confirmation of a new President.

CABINET
(May 2015)

Prime Minister: TAMMAM SALAM.

Deputy Prime Minister and Minister of National Defence: SAMIR MOQBEL.

Minister of the Interior and Municipalities: NUHAD MACHNOUQ.

Minister of Foreign Affairs and Emigrants: GEBRAN BASSIL.

Minister of Justice: ACHRAF RIFI.

Minister of Industry: HUSSEIN HAJJ HASSAN.

Minister of Energy and Water: ARTHUR NAZARIAN.

Minister of Public Works and Transportation: GHAZI ZEAITER.

Minister of Economy and Trade: ALAIN HAKIM.

Minister of Education and Higher Education: ELIAS ABOU SAAD.

Minister of Culture: RONNIE ARAYJI.

Minister of Information: RAMZI JREIJ.

Minister of Tourism: MICHEL PHARAOUN.

Minister of Telecommunications: BOUTROS HARB.

Minister of Labour: SEJAAN AZZI.

Minister of Agriculture: AKRAM CHEHAYYEB.

Minister of the Environment: MUHAMMAD MACHNOUQ.

Minister of Public Health: WAËL ABOU FAOUR.

Minister of Social Affairs: RACHID DERBAS.

Minister of the Displaced: ALICE CHABTINI.

Minister of Youth and Sports: ABD AL-MUTALEB HENNAOUI.

Minister of State for Administrative Reform: NABIH DE FREIJ.

Minister of State for Finance: ALI HASSAN KHALIL.

Minister of State for Parliamentary Affairs: MUHAMMAD FNEISH.

MINISTRIES

Presidency of the Republic of Lebanon: Presidential Palace, Baabda, Beirut; tel. (5) 900900; fax (5) 900919; e-mail president_office@presidency.gov.lb; internet www.presidency.gov.lb.

Office of the President of the Council of Ministers: Grand Sérail, place Riad el-Solh, Beirut; tel. (1) 746800; fax (1) 746805; e-mail Conseilm@pcm.gov.lb; internet www.pcm.gov.lb.

Ministry of Agriculture: Embassies St, Bir Hassan, Beirut; tel. (1) 849600; fax (1) 849620; e-mail ealawiea@agriculture.gov.lb; internet www.agriculture.gov.lb.

Ministry of Culture: Immeuble Hatab, rue Madame Curie, Verdun, Beirut; tel. (1) 744250; fax (1) 756322; e-mail amalm@culture.gov.lb; internet www.culture.gov.lb.

Ministry of the Displaced: POB 9150, Minet el-Hosn, Starco Centre, Beirut; tel. (1) 366373; fax (1) 366087; e-mail modbeirut@hotmail.com; internet www.ministryofdisplaced.gov.lb.

Ministry of Economy and Trade: 5th Floor, Azarieh Bldg, rue Riad el-Solh, Hamra, Beirut; tel. (1) 982360; fax (1) 982293; e-mail Info@economy.gov.lb; internet www.economy.gov.lb.

Ministry of Education and Higher Education: Unesco Quarter, Habib Abi Chahla, Beirut; tel. (1) 772500; fax (1) 772529; e-mail info@higher-edu.gov.lb; internet www.higher-edu.gov.lb.

Ministry of Energy and Water: Beirut River Highway, Beirut; tel. (1) 565100; e-mail mew@terra.net.lb; internet www.energyandwater.gov.lb.

Ministry of the Environment: POB 11-2727, 7th and 8th Floors, Lazarieh Centre, Beirut; tel. (1) 976555; fax (1) 976530; e-mail webmaster@moe.gov.lb; internet www.moe.gov.lb.

Ministry of Finance: MOF Bldg, place Riad el-Solh, Beirut; tel. (1) 981001; fax (1) 981059; e-mail infocenter@finance.gov.lb; internet www.finance.gov.lb.

Ministry of Foreign Affairs and Emigrants: al-Sultana Bldg, al-Jnah, Sultan Ibrahim, Beirut; tel. (1) 840767; fax (1) 840924; e-mail director@emigrants.gov.lb; internet www.emigrants.gov.lb.

Ministry of Industry: Ministry of Industry and Petroleum Bldg, ave Sami Solh, Beirut; tel. (1) 423338; fax (1) 427112; e-mail ministry@industry.gov.lb; internet www.industry.gov.lb.

Ministry of Information: rue Hamra, Beirut; tel. (1) 351038; fax (1) 343370; e-mail dghassanf@nna-leb.gov.lb; internet www.ministryinfo.gov.lb.

Ministry of the Interior and Municipalities: Grand Sérail, place Riad el-Solh, Beirut; tel. (1) 754200; fax (1) 750084; e-mail info@moim.gov.lb; internet www.moim.gov.lb.

Ministry of Justice: rue Sami Solh, Beirut; tel. (1) 422112; fax (1) 427957; e-mail info@justice.gov.lb; internet www.justice.gov.lb.

Ministry of Labour: Shiah, Beirut; tel. (1) 556804; fax (1) 556806; e-mail ministry@labor.gov.lb; internet www.labor.gov.lb.

Ministry of National Defence: Yarze, Beirut; tel. (5) 420000; fax (5) 951014; e-mail cmd@army.gov.lb; internet www.lebarmy.gov.lb.

Ministry of Public Health: Hussein Mansour Bldg, Museum St, Beirut; tel. (1) 615030; fax (1) 615773; e-mail info@moph.gov.lb; internet www.moph.gov.lb.

Ministry of Public Works and Transportation: 3rd Floor, Starco Center, Georges Picot St, Beirut; tel. (1) 371644; fax (1) 371647; e-mail ministry@transportation.gov.lb; internet www.transportation.gov.lb.

Ministry of Social Affairs: rue Badro, Beirut; tel. (1) 611260; fax (1) 611245; e-mail info@socialaffairs.gov.lb; internet www.socialaffairs.gov.lb.

Ministry of State for Administrative Reform: 5th Floor, Immeuble Starco, rue Omar Daouk, place Minet el-Hosn 2020 3313, Beirut; tel. (1) 371510; fax (1) 371599; e-mail info@omsar.gov.lb; internet www.omsar.gov.lb.

Ministry of State for Parliamentary Affairs: Beirut.

Ministry of Telecommunications: Ministry of Telecom Bldg, 1st Floor, place Riad el-Solh, Beirut; tel. (1) 979319; fax (1) 979316; e-mail webmaster@mpt.gov.lb; internet www.mpt.gov.lb.

Ministry of Tourism: POB 11-5344, rue Banque du Liban 550, Beirut; tel. (1) 340940; fax (1) 340945; e-mail info@destinationlebanon.gov.lb; internet mot.gov.lb.

Ministry of Youth and Sports: rue Sami Solh, Beirut; tel. (1) 425770; fax (1) 424387; e-mail minijes@cyberia.net.lb.

Legislature

The equal distribution of seats among Christians and Muslims is determined by law, and the Cabinet must reflect the level of representation achieved by the various religious denominations within that principal division. Deputies of the same religious denomination do not necessarily share the same political or party allegiances. The distribution of seats is as follows: Maronite Catholics 34; Sunni Muslims 27; Shi'a Muslims 27; Greek Orthodox 14; Druzes 8; Greek-Melkite Catholics 8; Armenian Orthodox 5; Alawites 2; Armenian Catholics 1; Protestants 1; Others 1.

National Assembly: Place de l'Etoile, Beirut; tel. (1) 982047; fax (1) 982059; e-mail info@lp.gov.lb; internet www.lp.gov.lb.

President: NABIH BERRI.

General Election, 7 June 2009

Party list	Seats
March 14 Alliance*	71
March 8 Alliance†	57
Total	128

* Electoral list comprising the Future Movement, Parti Socialiste Progressiste, Lebanese Forces Party, Al-Kataeb, Democratic Left, Parti National Libéral, Ramgavar Party, Al-Jama'a al-Islamiya and independents.

† Electoral list comprising Amal, Hezbollah, the Free Patriotic Movement, Armenian Revolutionary Federation, Syrian Social Nationalist Party, Al-Baath, Islamic Action Front, El-Marada Movement, Lebanese Democratic Party and independents.

Political Organizations

Amal (Hope—Afwaj al-Muqawamah al-Lubnaniyyah—Lebanese Resistance Detachments): e-mail info@amal-movement.com; internet www.amal-movement.com; f. 1975 as a politico-military organization; Shi'a political party; contested 2009 legislative elections as part of March 8 Alliance; Leader NABIH BERRI.

Armenian Revolutionary Federation (ARF) (Tashnag): rue Spears, Beirut; internet www.arfd.am; f. 1890; principal Armenian party; historically the dominant nationalist party in the independent Armenian Republic of Yerevan of 1917–21, prior to its becoming part of the USSR; socialist ideology; contested 2009 legislative elections as part of March 8 Alliance; Leader HRANT MARKARIAN.

Al-Baath (Baath Arab Socialist Party): Beirut; f. 1948; local branch of secular pro-Syrian party with policy of Arab union; contested 2009 legislative elections as part of March 8 Alliance; Leader FAYEZ SHUKER.

Bloc National Libanais (Lebanese National Bloc): rue Pasteur, Gemmayze, Beirut; tel. (1) 584585; fax (1) 584591; e-mail ketleh@ketleh.org; internet www.ketleh.org; f. 1943; right-wing Lebanese party with policy of power-sharing between Christians and Muslims and the exclusion of the military from politics; Pres. CARLOS EDDÉ.

Free Patriotic Movement (FPM) (Tayar al-Watani al-Horr): Beirut; tel. (3) 122858; e-mail info@tayyar.org; internet www.tayyar.org; aims to recover sovereignty and complete independence for Lebanon; majority of leaders and supporters are from the Christian community, although party is officially secular; largest party in the Change and Reform parliamentary bloc; contested 2009 legislative elections as part of March 8 Alliance; Leader Gen. MICHEL AOUN.

Future Movement (Tayar al-Mustaqbal): POB 123, Koraytem, Hamra, Beirut; tel. (3) 375442; fax (1) 375442; e-mail info@almustaqbal.org; internet www.almustaqbal.org; opposed to Syrian influence in Lebanese affairs; contested 2009 legislative elections as largest party of the March 14 Alliance; Leader SAAD EL-DIN HARIRI.

Hezbollah (Party of God): Beirut; e-mail info@moqawama.org; internet www.moqawama.org; f. 1982 by Iranian Revolutionary Guards who were sent to Lebanon; militant Shi'a faction, which has become the leading organization of Lebanon's Shi'a community and a recognized political party; demands the withdrawal of Israeli forces from the occupied Shebaa Farms area of what it considers to be southern Lebanon (but which is designated by the UN as being part of Syria) and the release of all Lebanese prisoners from Israeli detention; contested 2009 legislative elections as part of March 8 Alliance; Chair. MUHAMMAD RA'D; Leader and Sec.-Gen. Sheikh HASAN NASRALLAH; Spiritual Leader Ayatollah MUHAMMAD HUSSAIN FADLALLAH.

Hizb-ut-Tahrir al-Islami (Party of Islamic Liberation): e-mail info@hizb-ut-tahrir.org; internet www.hizb-ut-tahrir.org; f. 1953; transnational org. granted a political parties licence in Lebanon in 2006; aims to establish Islamic caliphate throughout the world; denies claims that it is a militant group; Global Leader Sheikh ABU YASIN ATA IBN KHALIL ABU RASHTA, (Sheikh Ata Abu Rashta).

Al-Kataeb (Lebanese Social Democratic Party): POB 992, place Charles Hélou, Beirut; tel. (1) 584107; internet www.party.kataeb.org; f. 1936 as the Phalangist Party (Phalanges Libanaises); nationalist, reformist, democratic social party; largest Maronite party, although is officially secular; contested 2009 legislative elections as part of March 14 Alliance; 100,000 mems; Pres. AMIN GEMAYEL.

Lebanese Democratic Party (LDP): Beirut; e-mail webmaster@ldparty.org; internet www.ldparty.org; f. 2001; contested 2009 legislative elections as part of March 8 Alliance; Leader TALAL ARSLAN; Sec.-Gen. WALID BARAKAT.

Lebanese Forces Party: Beirut; tel. and fax (9) 212989; e-mail contact@lebanese-forces.com; internet www.lebanese-forces.com; political successor to the **Lebanese Forces** (f. 1976; coalition of Maronite Christian militias); launched as political party in 1989; proscribed by the Government in 1994; resumed activities as a legal party in 2005; contested 2009 legislative elections as part of March 14 Alliance, securing 5 seats; Leader SAMIR GEAGEA.

Lebanese Option Gathering: POB 45-489, Hazmieh, Mar Takla, La Diva Bldg, Beirut; tel. (5) 957257; fax (5) 957357; e-mail lebaneseoption@lebaneseoption.org; internet lebaneseoption.org; f. 2007; aims to contest Hezbollah's monopoly over Shi'a political representation in Lebanon, and to reform and develop the south of the country; Leader AHMAD AL-ASSAD.

El-Marada Movement: Zgharta; e-mail info@elmarada.org; internet elmarada.org; f. as the Marada Brigade, relaunched in 1996 as a political party; advocates Lebanese unity, sovereignty and independence; contested 2009 legislative elections as part of March 8 Alliance; Leader SULAYMAN FRANJIYA.

March 8 Alliance: contested 2009 legislative elections as an electoral bloc comprising Hezbollah, Amal, the Free Patriotic Movement, the Armenian Revolutionary Federation, the Syrian Social Nationalist Party, Al-Baath, the Islamic Action Front, the El-Marada Movement, the Lebanese Democratic Party and independents.

March 14 Alliance: contested 2009 legislative elections as an electoral bloc comprising Future Movement, Parti Socialiste Progressiste (PSP), the Lebanese Forces Party, Al-Kataeb and other smaller parties and independents; following disagreements over the formation of a new government, the PSP withdrew from the alliance in August 2009.

National Dialogue Party: POB 15-5060, Immeuble Marj el-Zouhour, 1st Floor, rue Donna Maria, Ras el-Nabeh, Beirut; tel. (1) 637000; fax (1) 6311234; e-mail info@alhiwar.com; internet www.alhiwar.com; f. 2004; advocates a comprehensive national dialogue to bring about political, social and judicial reforms; also seeks to target corruption and to ensure that the State has authority over the whole of Lebanon; Founder and Chair. FOUAD MUSTAFA MAKHZOUMI.

Parti Communiste Libanais (PCL) (Lebanese Communist Party): rue al-Bahatri, al-Watuat, Beirut; tel. and fax (1) 739615; e-mail lcparty@lcparty.org; internet www.lcparty.org; f. 1924; officially dissolved 1948–71; Marxist, with much support among intellectuals; Sec.-Gen. KHALID HADDADEH.

Parti National Libéral (PNL) (Al-Wataniyin al-Ahrar): POB 165576, rue du Liban, Beirut; tel. (1) 338000; fax (1) 200335; e-mail ahrar@ahrar.org.lb; internet www.ahrar.org.lb; f. 1958; liberal reformist secular party, although has traditionally had a predominantly Maronite Christian membership; contested 2009 legislative elections as part of March 14 Alliance; Pres. DORY CHAMOUN.

Parti Socialiste Progressiste (PSP) (Al-Takadumi al-Ishteraki): POB 11-2893, Beirut 1107 2120; tel. (1) 309123; fax (1) 318119; e-mail internationalrelation@psp.org.lb; internet www.psp.org.lb; f. 1949; progressive party, advocates constitutional road to socialism and democracy; over 25,000 mems; mainly Druze support; contested 2009 legislative elections as part of March 14 Alliance; Pres. WALID JOUMBLATT.

Syrian Social Nationalist Party (al-Hizb al-Suri al-Qawmi al-Ijtima'i): internet www.ssnp.net; f. 1932 in Beirut; banned 1962–69; seeks creation of a 'Greater Syrian' state, incl. Lebanon, Syria, Iraq, Jordan, the Palestinian territories, Kuwait, Cyprus and parts of Egypt, Iran and Turkey; advocates separation of church and State, the redistribution of wealth and a strong military; supports Syrian involvement in Lebanese affairs; contested 2009 legislative elections as part of March 8 Alliance; Leader ASSAD HARDANE.

Al-Wa'ad (National Secular Democratic Party—Pledge): Beirut; f. 1986 by the late Elie Hobeika; pro-Syrian splinter group of Lebanese Forces; officially secular, although most supporters are Maronite Christians; aligned with March 8 Alliance; did not achieve parliamentary representation in June 2009 legislative elections; Leader JOSEPH HOBEIKA.

Other parties include the **Independent Nasserite Movement** (Murabitoun; Sunni Muslim militia; Leader IBRAHIM QULAYAT) and the **Lebanese Popular Congress** (Pres. KAMAL SHATILA). The **Nasserite Popular Organization** and the **Arab Socialist Union** merged in January 1987, retaining the name of the former. The **Islamic Amal** is a breakaway group from Amal, based in Ba'albek (Leader HUSSEIN MOUSSAVI). **Islamic Jihad** is a pro-Iranian fundamentalist guerrilla group. The **Popular Liberation Army** (f. 1985 by the late MUSTAFA SAAD) is a Sunni Muslim faction, active in the south of Lebanon. **Tawhid Islami** (the Islamic Unification Movement; f. 1982; Sunni Muslim) and the **Arab Democratic Party** (or the Red Knights; Alawites; pro-Syrian; Leader ALI EID) are based in Tripoli.

Diplomatic Representation

EMBASSIES IN LEBANON

Algeria: POB 4794, face Hôtel Summerland, 1 rue Jnah, Sector 8, Beirut; tel. (1) 826712; fax (1) 826711; e-mail ambalbey@dm.nt.lb; Ambassador AHMED BOU ZAYYAN.

Argentina: Residence des Jardins, Immeuble Moutran, 2e étage, 161 rue Sursock, Achrafieh, Beirut; tel. (1) 210803; fax (1) 210802; e-mail elbno@mrecic.gov.ar; internet www.elbno.mrecic.gov.ar; Ambassador RICARDO SEGUNDO LARRIERA.

Armenia: rue Jasmin 28, Mtaileb, Beirut; tel. (4) 418860; fax (4) 402952; e-mail armlebanonembassy@mfa.am; internet lebanon.mfa.am; Ambassador ASHOT KOCHARIAN.

Australia: Embassy Complex, Sérail Hill, Beirut; tel. (1) 960600; fax (1) 960601; internet www.lebanon.embassy.gov.au; Ambassador GLENN MILES.

Austria: POB 11-3924, Immeuble Tabaris, 8e étage, 812 ave Charles Malek, Achrafieh, Beirut 2071 1606; tel. (1) 213017; fax (1) 217772; e-mail beirut-ob@bmeia.gv.at; internet www.bmeia.gv.at/en/embassy/beirut; Ambassador URSULA FAHRINGER.

Belgium: Bloc A, Immeuble Lazarie, 10e étage, rue Emir Béchir, Beirut; tel. (1) 976001; fax (1) 976007; e-mail beirut@diplobel.fed.be; internet www.diplomatie.be/beirut; Ambassador ALEX LENEARTS.

Brazil: POB 11-562, rue de l'Armée, Colline du Sérail, Beirut; tel. (1) 982161; fax (1) 982159; e-mail brasemb.beirute@itamaraty.gov.br; internet beirute.itamaraty.gov.br; Ambassador JORGE GERALDO KADRI.

Bulgaria: POB 11-6544, Sector 6, Mar-Takla, Hazmieh, Beirut; tel. (5) 452883; fax (5) 452892; e-mail embassy.beirut@mfa.bg; internet www.mfa.bg/embassies/lebanon; Chargé d'affaires PLAMEN TSOLOV.

Canada: POB 60163, Immeuble Coolrite, 1er et 2e étage, Autoroute Jal el-Dib 43, Beirut; tel. (4) 726700; fax (4) 710595; e-mail berut@international.gc.ca; internet www.lebanon.gc.ca; Ambassador HILARY CHILDS-ADAMS.

Chile: Nouvelle Naccache, Sector 2, rue 64, Immeuble Antoine Boukather, 1er étage, Beirut; tel. (4) 418670; fax (4) 418672; e-mail echilelb@dm.net.lb; internet chileabroad.gov.cl/libano; Ambassador JOSÉ MIGUEL MENCHACA.

China, People's Republic: POB 11-8227, 72 rue Nicolas Ibrahim Sursock, Ramlet el-Baida, Beirut 1107 2260; tel. (1) 856133; fax (1) 822492; e-mail chinaemb_lb@mfa.gov.cn; internet lb.china-embassy.org; Ambassador JIANG JIANG.

Colombia: Immeuble Sarkis Group, 8e étage, Zalka Highway, Amaret Chalhoub, Beirut; tel. (1) 895381; fax (1) 895380; e-mail ebeirut@cancilleria.gov.co; internet libano.embajada.gov.co; Ambassador GEORGINE KHALIL EL-CHAER.

Cuba: Center Farrania, 2e étage, rue Saïd Freiha, Mar-Takla, Hazmieh, Beirut 2901 6727; tel. (1) 459925; fax (1) 950070; e-mail libancub@cyberia.net.lb; internet www.cubadiplomatica.cu/libano; Ambassador RENÉ CEBALLO PRATS.

Cyprus: Hajal Bldg, 5e étage, Autoroute Jal el-Dib, Beirut; tel. (4) 718363; fax (4) 718365; e-mail info@cyprusembbeirut.org; internet www.cyprusembbeirut.org; Ambassador HOMER MAVROMMATIS.

Czech Republic: POB 40195, Baabda, Beirut; tel. (5) 929010; fax (5) 922120; e-mail beirut@embassy.mzv.cz; internet www.mzv.cz/beirut; Ambassador SVATOPLUK CUMBA.

Denmark: POB 11-5190, rue de l'Armée, Colline du Sérail, Beirut; tel. (1) 991001; fax (1) 991006; e-mail beyamb@um.dk; internet www.libanon.um.dk; Ambassador ROLF M. HAY PEREIRA HOLMBOE.

Egypt: POB 5037, rue Dr Mohamad el-Bezri, Bir Hassan, Beirut; tel. (1) 825566; fax (1) 859988; Ambassador MUHAMMAD BADREDDINE ZAYED.

France: rue de Damas, Beirut; tel. (1) 420000; fax (1) 420013; e-mail cad.beyrouth-amb@diplomatie.gouv.fr; internet www.ambafrance-lb.org; Ambassador PATRICE PAOLI.

Gabon: POB 11-1252, Riad el-Solh, Hadath, Beirut 1107 2080; tel. (5) 924649; fax (5) 924643; Ambassador SIMON NTOUTOUME EMANE.

Germany: POB 11-2820, Riad el-Solh, Beirut 1102 2110; tel. (4) 935000; fax (4) 935001; e-mail info@beirut.diplo.de; internet www.beirut.diplo.de; Ambassador CHRISTIAN CLAGES.

Greece: POB 11-0309, Immeuble Boukhater, rue des Ambassades, Nouvelle Naccache, Beirut; tel. (4) 521700; fax (4) 418774; e-mail gremb.bei@mfa.gr; internet www.mfa.gr/beirut; Ambassador AIKATERINI BOURA.

Holy See: POB 1061, Jounieh (Apostolic Nunciature); tel. (9) 263102; fax (9) 264488; e-mail naliban@terra.net.lb; Apostolic Nuncio Most Rev. GABRIELE GIORDANO CACCIA (Titular Archbishop of Sepino).

Hungary: POB 113-5259, Immeuble BAC, 9e étage, rue Justinien, Sanayeh, Beirut; tel. (1) 730083; fax (1) 741261; e-mail mission.bej@mfa.gov.hu; internet www.mfa.gov.hu/emb/beirut; Ambassador LÁSZLÓ VÁRADI.

India: POB 113-5240, 239 rue Ibrahim Abed el-Aal, Beirut; tel. (1) 741270; fax (1) 741283; e-mail amboffice.beirut@mea.gov.in; internet www.indianembassybeirut.org; Ambassador ANITA NAYAR.

Indonesia: POB 40007, ave Palais Presidential, rue 68, Secteur 3, Baabda, Beirut; tel. (5) 924682; fax (5) 924678; e-mail kbri@kbri-beirut.org; internet www.indonesianembassy.net; Ambassador AHMAD CHOZIN CHUMAIDI.

Iran: POB 5030, Bir Hassan, Beirut; tel. (1) 821224; fax (1) 821229; Ambassador MUHAMMAD FATHALI.

Iraq: Beirut; tel. (1) 453209; fax (1) 459850; e-mail brtemb@iraqmofamail.net; Ambassador RAAD AL-ALLOUSI.

Italy: POB 57, rue du Palais Présidentiel, Baabda, Beirut 2902 2633; tel. (5) 954955; fax (5) 959616; e-mail amba.beirut@esteri.it; internet www.ambbeirut.esteri.it; Ambassador GIUSEPPE MORABITO.

Japan: POB 11-3360, rue de l'Armée, Zkak al-Blat, Colline du Sérail, Beirut; tel. (1) 989751; fax (1) 989754; e-mail japanemb@japanemb.org.lb; internet www.lb.emb-japan.go.jp; Ambassador SEIICHI OTSUKA.

Jordan: POB 109, Beirut 5113; tel. (5) 922500; fax (5) 922502; e-mail joremb@dm.net.lb; Ambassador ZEID ZREIQAT.

Korea, Republic: POB 40-290, Diplomat Bldg 2F, Rue Palais Presidentiel, Baabda, Beirut; tel. (5) 953167; fax (5) 953170; e-mail lbkor@mofa.go.kr; internet lbn.mofa.go.kr; Ambassador CHOI JONG-IL.

Kuwait: POB 4580, Rond-point du Stade, Bir Hassan, Beirut; tel. (1) 756100; fax (1) 842220; e-mail info@kuwaitinfo.net; Ambassador ABD AL-AAL AL-QINAI.

Mexico: POB 70-1150, 1er étage, Immeuble Mansour 90, rue 53, Sector 2, New Naccache, Antélias, Beirut; tel. and fax (4) 418871; e-mail mail@embassyofmexicoinlebanon.org; internet embamex.sre.gob.mx/libano; Ambassador JAIME ENRIQUE GARCÍA AMARAL.

Morocco: Bir Hassan, Beirut; tel. (1) 859851; fax (1) 859839; e-mail sifmar@cyberia.net.lb; Ambassador ALI OUMLIL.

Netherlands: POB 167190, Netherlands Tower, ave Charles Malek, Achrafieh, Beirut 2073 0802; tel. (1) 211150; fax (1) 211173; e-mail bei@minbuza.nl; internet lebanon.nlembassy.org; Ambassador HESTER M.J. SOMSEN.

Norway: POB 113-7001, Immeuble Dimashki, rue Bliss, Ras Beirut, Hamra, Beirut 1103 2150; tel. (1) 960000; fax (1) 960099; e-mail emb.bey@mfa.no; internet www.norway-lebanon.org; Ambassador SVEIN AASS.

Pakistan: POB 135506, UNESCO Centre Crossroad, 8e étage, rue Saeb Salam, Immeuble 1, Verdun, Beirut; tel. (1) 790327; fax (1) 790471; e-mail pakemblb@gmail.com; internet www.mofa.gov.pk/lebanon; Ambassador G. R. MALIK.

Paraguay: Immeuble La Rosa, Rez-de-chaussée, rue Farid Zeidan, Hazmieh, Mar Takla, Beirut; tel. (5) 5458502; fax (5) 458503; e-mail embaparlibano@hotmail.com; internet www.embaparlebanon.com; Ambassador HASSAN KHALIL DAY.

Philippines: POB 136631, rue Mar Geries, Immeuble W, Hadath, Baabda, Beirut; tel. (5) 953522; fax (5) 953521; e-mail beirut.pe@dfa.gov.ph; Ambassador LEAH M. BASINANG-RUIZ.

Poland: POB 40-215, Immeuble Khalifa, ave Président Sulayman Franjiya 52, Baabda, Beirut; tel. (5) 924591; fax (5) 924882; e-mail beirut.embassy@msz.gov.pl; internet bejrut.msz.gov.pl; Ambassador WOJCIECH BOŻEK.

Qatar: POB 11-6717, Immeuble Deebs, 1er étage, Shouran, Beirut; tel. (1) 865271; fax (1) 810460; e-mail beirut@mofa.gov.qa; Ambassador ALI BIN HAMAD AL-MARRI.

Romania: route du Palais Présidentiel, Baabda, Beirut; tel. (5) 924848; fax (5) 924747; e-mail beirut@mae.ro; internet beirut.mae.ro; Ambassador VICTOR MIRCEA.

Russian Federation: POB 5220, rue Mar Elias el-Tineh, Wata Mseitbeh, Beirut; tel. (1) 300041; fax (1) 303837; internet www.lebanon.mid.ru; Ambassador ALEKSANDR ZASYPKIN.

Saudi Arabia: POB 136144, Kuraitem, Beirut; tel. (1) 762722; fax (1) 762706; e-mail lbemb@mofa.gov.sa; Ambassador ALI BIN AWADH ASSERI.

Spain: POB 11-3039, Palais Chehab, Hadath Antounie, Beirut; tel. (5) 464120; fax (5) 464030; e-mail emb.beirut@maec.es; internet www.exteriores.gob.es/embajadas/beirut; Ambassador MILAGROS HERNANDO ECHEVARRÍA.

Sri Lanka: POB 175, Hazmieh, Beirut; tel. (5) 956031; fax (5) 956033; e-mail slemblbn@cyberia.net.lb; Ambassador RANJITH GUNARATHNA.

Sudan: POB 2504, Hamra, Beirut; tel. (1) 350057; fax (1) 353271; Ambassador AHMED HASSAN.

Switzerland: POB 11-172, Immeuble Bourj al-Ghazal, ave Fouad Chehab, Achrafieh, Beirut 1107 2020; tel. (1) 324129; fax (1) 324167; e-mail bey.vertretung@eda.admin.ch; internet www.eda.admin.ch/beirut; Ambassador FRANÇOIS BARRAS.

Syria: rue Makdessi, Hamra, Beirut; Ambassador ALI ABD AL-KARIM ALI.

Tunisia: Mar-Takla, Hazmieh, Beirut; tel. (5) 457431; fax (5) 950434; Ambassador HATEM SAYEM.

Turkey: POB 70-666, zone II, rue 1, Rabieh, Beirut; tel. (4) 528061; fax (4) 407557; e-mail ambassade.beyrouth@mfa.gov.tr; internet beirut.emb.mfa.gov.tr; Ambassador SÜLEYMAN INAN OZYILDIZ.

Ukraine: POB 40268, rue Antoine El Rayes, Mount Lebanon, Casa Baabda, Beirut; tel. (5) 921975; fax (5) 921974; e-mail emb_lb@mfa.gov.ua; internet www.mfa.gov.ua/lebanon; Chargé d'affaires VITALIY BOROVKO.

United Arab Emirates: Ramla al-Bayda, Jnah, Beirut; tel. (1) 857000; fax (1) 857009; e-mail beirut@mofa.gov.ae; internet uae-embassy.ae/embassies/lb; Ambassador HAMAD SAEED SULTAN AL-SHAMSI.

United Kingdom: POB 11-471, Embassies Complex, rue de l'Armée, Colline du Sérail, Zkak al-Blat, Beirut; tel. (1) 960800; fax (1) 960855; e-mail chancery@cyberia.net.lb; internet ukinlebanon.fco.gov.uk; Ambassador TOM FLETCHER.

USA: POB 70-840, Antélias, Beirut; tel. (4) 542600; fax (4) 544136; e-mail beirutpd@state.gov; internet lebanon.usembassy.gov; Ambassador DAVID HALE.

Uruguay: POB 2051, Centre Stella Marris, 7e étage, rue Banque du Liban, Jounieh; tel. (9) 636529; fax (9) 636531; e-mail uruliban@dm.net.lb; internet www.embauruguaybeirut.org; Ambassador Dr MARTA INÉS PIZZANELLI.

Venezuela: POB 11-603, rue Amaret Chalhoub, Immeuble Baezevale House, 5e étage, Zalka, Beirut; tel. (4) 718612; fax (4) 718614; e-mail embajadora@embavenelibano.com; internet www.embavenelibano.com; Ambassador ZOED KARAM.

Yemen: Bir Hassan, Beirut; tel. (1) 852688; fax (1) 821610; Ambassador (vacant).

Judicial System

Law and justice in Lebanon are administered in accordance with the following codes, which are based upon modern theories of civil and criminal legislation:

Code de la Propriété (1930).

Code des Obligations et des Contrats (1932).

Code de Procédure Civile (1933).

Code Maritime (1947).

Code de Procédure Pénale (Code Ottoman Modifié).

Code Pénal (1943).

Code Pénal Militaire (1946).

Code d'Instruction Criminelle.

Courts of First Instance: 56 courts, each consisting of a single judge, and dealing in the first instance with both civil and criminal

cases; there are 17 such courts in Beirut and 7 in Tripoli; Pres. Dr FADI ELIAS.

Courts of Appeal: 11 courts, each consisting of three judges, including a President and a Public Prosecutor, and dealing with civil and criminal cases; there are 5 such courts in Beirut; First Pres. MAYSSAM NOUEIRI.

Courts of Cassation: 4 courts, 3 dealing with civil and commercial cases and the fourth with criminal cases. A Court of Cassation, to be properly constituted, must have at least 3 judges, 1 being the President and the other 2 Councillors. If the Court of Cassation reverses the judgment of a lower court, it does not refer the case back but retries it itself; General Prosecutor of Cassation HATEM MADI.

State Consultative Council: deals with administrative cases; Pres. SHUKRI SADER.

Court of Justice: a special court consisting of a President and 4 judges, deals with matters affecting the security of the State; there is no appeal against its verdicts.

Constitutional Council: considers matters pertaining to the constitutionality of legislation; Pres. ISSAM SULEIMAN.

Higher Judicial Council: considers matters involving members of the executive branch; Pres. JEAN FAHED.

Military Court: competent to try crimes and misdemeanours involving the armed and security forces; Chief of the Military Court Brig. KHALIL IBRAHIM.

In addition, Islamic (*Shari'a*), Christian and Jewish religious courts deal with affairs of personal status (marriage, death, inheritance, etc.).

Religion

Of all the countries of the Middle East, Lebanon probably presents the closest juxtaposition of sects and peoples within a small territory. In 1994 it was estimated that 29%–32% of the population of Lebanon were Shi'a Muslims, 25%–28% Maronites, 16%–20% Sunni Muslims and 3.5% Druzes. The Maronites, a uniate sect of the Roman Catholic Church, inhabited the old territory of Mount Lebanon, i.e. immediately east of Beirut. In the south, towards the Israeli frontier, Shi'a villages are most common, while between the Shi'a and the Maronites live the Druzes (divided between the Yazbakis and the Joumblatis). The Beqa'a valley has many Greek Christians (both Roman Catholic and Orthodox), while the Tripoli area is mainly Sunni Muslim.

CHRISTIANITY

The Roman Catholic Church

Armenian Rite

Patriarchate of Cilicia: Patriarcat Arménien Catholique, rue de l'Hôpital orthodoxe, Jeitawi, Beirut 2078 5605; tel. (1) 570555; fax (1) 570558; e-mail ncrbcd19@magnarama.com; internet www.armeniancatholic.org; f. 1742; est. in Beirut since 1929; includes patriarchal diocese of Beirut, with an estimated 12,000 adherents; Patriarch His Beatitude NERSES BEDROS XIX TARMOUNI.

Chaldean Rite

Diocese of Beirut: Evêché Chaldéen de Beyrouth, POB 373, Hazmieh, Beirut; tel. (5) 457732; fax (5) 457731; e-mail chaldepiscopus@hotmail.com; an estimated 10,000 adherents (31 December 2007); Bishop of Beirut MICHEL KASSARJI.

Latin Rite

Apostolic Vicariate of Beirut: Vicariat Apostolique, POB 11-4224, Riad el-Solh, Beirut 1107 2160; tel. (9) 236101; fax (9) 236102; e-mail vicariatlat@hotmail.com; an estimated 15,000 adherents (31 December 2007); Vicar Apostolic PAUL DAHDAH (Titular Archbishop of Arae in Numidia).

Maronite Rite

Patriarchate of Antioch and all the East: Patriarcat Maronite, Bkerké; tel. (9) 915441; fax (9) 938844; e-mail jtawk@bkerke.org.lb; includes patriarchal dioceses of Jounieh, Sarba and Jobbé; the Maronite Church in Lebanon comprises 4 archdioceses and 6 dioceses; Patriarch Cardinal BÉCHARA BOUTROS RAÏ.

Archbishop of Antélias: Most Rev. JOSEPH MOHSEN BÉCHARA, Archevêché Maronite, POB 70400, Antélias; tel. (4) 410020; fax (4) 415872.

Archbishop of Beirut: Most Rev. PAUL YOUSUF MATAR, Archevêché Maronite, 10 rue Collège de la Sagesse, Achrafieh, Beirut; tel. (1) 561980; fax (1) 561930; e-mail maronitebeyrouth@yahoo.fr; also representative of the Holy See for Roman Catholics of the Coptic Rite in Lebanon.

Archbishop of Tripoli: Most Rev. GEORGES BOU-JAOUDÉ, Archevêché Maronite, POB 104, rue al-Moutran, Karm Sada, Tripoli; tel. (6) 624324; fax (6) 629393; e-mail rahmat@inco.com.lb.

Archbishop of Tyre: Most Rev. CHUCRALLAH-NABIL HAGE, Archevêché Maronite, Tyre; tel. (7) 740059; fax (7) 344891; e-mail abounacharbel@cyberia.net.lb.

Melkite Rite

Patriarch of Antioch: Patriarcat Grec-Melkite Catholique, POB 22249, 12 ave al-Zeitoon, Bab Charki, Damascus, Syria; tel. (11) 5441030; fax (11) 5417900; e-mail pat.melk@scs-net.org; internet www.pgc-lb.org; f. 1724; the Melkite Church in Lebanon comprises 7 archdioceses, with an estimated 393,000 adherents (31 December 2009); Patriarch of Antioch and all the East, of Alexandria and of Jerusalem His Beatitude GREGORIOS III LAHAM.

Archbishop of Ba'albek: Most Rev. ELIAS RAHAL, Archevêché Grec-Catholique, Ba'albek; tel. (8) 370200; fax (8) 373986.

Archbishop of Baniyas: Most Rev. GEORGES NICOLAS HADDAD, Archevêché de Panéas, Jdeidet Marjeyoun; tel. and fax (3) 830007.

Archbishop of Beirut and Jbeil: CYRILLE SALIM BUSTROS, Archevêché Grec-Melkite-Catholique, POB 11-901, 655 rue de Damas, Beirut; tel. (1) 616104; fax (1) 616109; e-mail agmcb@terra.net.lb.

Archbishop of Saida (Sidon): Most Rev. ELIE BÉCHARA HADDAD, Archevêché Grec-Melkite-Catholique, POB 247, rue el-Moutran, Sidon; tel. (7) 720100; fax (7) 722055; e-mail mhaddad.saida@hotmail.com.

Archbishop of Tripoli: Most Rev. GEORGE RIASHI, Archevêché Grec-Catholique, POB 72, rue al-Kanaess, Tripoli; tel. (6) 431602; fax (6) 441716.

Archbishop of Tyre: Most Rev. GEORGES BAKOUNY, Archevêché Grec-Catholique, POB 257, Tyre; tel. (7) 740015; fax (7) 349180; e-mail pbacouni@yahoo.com.

Archbishop of Zahleh and Furzol: Most Rev. ISSAM JOHN DARWISH, Archevêché Grec-Melkite-Catholique, Saidat el-Najat, Zahleh; tel. (8) 800333; fax (8) 822406; e-mail info@catholiczahle.org; internet www.catholiczahle.org.

Syrian Rite

Patriarchate of Antioch: Patriarcat Syrien Catholique d'Antioche, POB 116–5087, rue de Damas, Beirut 1106 2010; tel. (1) 615892; fax (1) 616573; e-mail psc_lb@yahoo.com; jurisdiction over about 150,000 Syrian Catholics in the Middle East; Patriarch Most Rev. IGNACE JOSEPH III YOUNAN; Protosyncellus Mgr GEORGES MASRI.

The Anglican Communion

Within the Episcopal Church in Jerusalem and the Middle East, Lebanon forms part of the diocese of Jerusalem (see the chapter on Israel).

Other Christian Groups

Armenian Apostolic Orthodox Church: Armenian Catholicosate of Cilicia, POB 70317, Antélias; tel. (4) 410001; fax (4) 419724; e-mail info@armenianorthodoxchurch.org; internet www.armenianorthodoxchurch.org; f. 301 AD in Armenia, re-established in 1293 in Cilicia (now in Turkey), transferred to Antélias, Lebanon, 1930; Leader His Holiness ARAM KESHISHIAN I (Catholicos of Cilicia); jurisdiction over an estimated 3.5m. adherents in Lebanon, Syria, Cyprus, Kuwait, Greece, Iran, Qatar, the United Arab Emirates, South America, the USA and Canada.

National Evangelical Synod of Syria and Lebanon: POB 70890, Antélias; tel. (4) 525030; fax (4) 411184; e-mail nessl@synod-sl.org; internet www.synod-sl.org; f. 1959; 20,000 adherents (2010); Gen. Sec. Rev. FADI DAGHER.

Patriarchate of Antioch and all the East (Greek Orthodox): Patriarcat Grec-Orthodoxe, POB 9, Damascus, Syria; tel. (11) 5424400; fax (11) 5424404; e-mail info@antiochpat.org; internet www.antiochpat.org; Patriarch His Beatitude IGNATIUS (HAZIM) IV.

Patriarchate of Antioch and all the East (Syrian Orthodox): Patriarcat Syrien Orthodoxe, Bab Toma, POB 22260, Damascus, Syria; tel. (11) 5951870; fax (11) 5951880; internet www.syrian-orthodox.com; Patriarch IGNATIUS ZAKKA I IWAS.

Supreme Council of the Evangelical Community in Syria and Lebanon: POB 70/1065, rue Rabieh 34, Antélias; tel. (4) 525036; fax (4) 405490; e-mail suprcoun@minero.net; Pres. Rev. Dr SALIM SAHIOUNY.

Union of the Armenian Evangelical Churches in the Near East: POB 11-377, Beirut; tel. (1) 565628; fax (1) 565629; e-mail uaecne@cyberia.net.lb; f. 1846 in Turkey; comprises about 30 Armenian Evangelical Churches in Syria, Lebanon, Egypt, Cyprus, Greece, Iran, Turkey and Australia; Pres. Rev. MEGRDICH KARAGOEZIAN; Gen. Sec. SEBOUH TERZIAN.

ISLAM

Shi'a Muslims: Leader Imam Sheikh SAYED MOUSSA AL-SADR (went missing during visit to Libya in August 1978); Vice-Pres. of the Supreme Islamic Council of the Shi'a Community of Lebanon ABD AL-AMIR QABALAN; Beirut.

Sunni Muslims: Grand Mufti of Lebanon, Dar el-Fatwa, rue Ilewi Rushed, Beirut; tel. (1) 422340; Leader Sheikh Dr MUHAMMAD RASHID QABBANI.

Druzes: Supreme Spiritual Leader of the Druze Community, Beirut; tel. (1) 341116; Supreme Spiritual Leader Sheikh AL-AQL BAHJAT GHAITH; Political Leader WALID JOUMBLATT.

Alawites: a schism of Shi'a Islam; there are an estimated 50,000 Alawites in northern Lebanon, in and around Tripoli.

JUDAISM

A small Jewish community, thought to number less than 100 people, remains in Lebanon.

Jewish Community: Pres. ISAAC ARAZI (Beirut).

The Press

DAILIES

Al-Akhbar (The News): POB 5963-113, Concorde Centre, 6th Floor, rue Verdun, Beirut; tel. (1) 759500; fax (1) 759597; internet www.al-akhbar.com; f. 2006; Arabic; independent; Editor-in-Chief IBRAHIM AL-AMIN.

Al-Anwar (Lights): c/o Dar Assayad, POB 11-1038, Hazmieh, Beirut; tel. (5) 456374; fax (5) 452700; e-mail info@alanwar.com; internet www.alanwar.com; f. 1959; Arabic; independent; supplement, Sunday; cultural and social; publ. by Dar Assayad SAL; Editors-in-Chief MICHEL RAAD, RAFIK KHOURY; circ. 24,508.

Aztag: POB 80-860, Shaghzoyan Cultural Centre, Bourj Hammoud; tel. (1) 258526; fax (1) 258529; e-mail info@aztagdaily.com; internet www.aztagdaily.com; f. 1927; Armenian; Editor-in-Chief SHAHAN KANDAHARIAN; circ. 6,500.

Al-Balad: Beirut; tel. (1) 494694; fax (1) 494894; e-mail crm@albaladonline.com; internet albaladonline.com; Arabic; Chair. AHMAD BADRANI; Man. Editor GEORGE JABARA.

Al-Bayrak (The Standard): Immeuble Dimitri Trad, rue Issa Maalouf, Achrafieh, Beirut; tel. (1) 216393; fax (1) 338928; e-mail dalwl@dm.net.lb; f. 1913; Arabic; publ. by Dar Alf Leila wa Leila Publishing House; politics and society; Editor-in-Chief MELHEM KARAM; circ. 10,000.

Daily Star: Markaziah Centre, 3rd Floor, Umm Gelias St, Beirut Central District, Beirut; tel. (1) 587277; fax (1) 561333; e-mail editorial@dailystar.com.lb; internet www.dailystar.com.lb; f. 1952; English; Publr SALMA EL-BISSAR; Editor-in-Chief NADIM LADKI; circ. 10,550.

Al-Diyar (The Homeland): al-Nahda Bldg, Yarze, Beirut; tel. (5) 923830; fax (5) 923773; e-mail info@addiyaronline.com; internet www.aldiyaronline.com; f. 1987; Arabic; Propr and Editor-in-Chief CHARLES AYYUB.

Al-Hayat (Life): POB 11-1242, rue Maarad, place Riad el-Solh, Beirut; tel. (1) 987990; fax (1) 983921; e-mail information@alhayat.com; internet www.daralhayat.com; f. 1946; Arabic; independent; Editor-in-Chief GHASSAN CHARBEL; circ. 196,800.

Al-Liwaa (The Standard): POB 11-2402, Beirut; tel. (1) 735745; fax (1) 735749; e-mail events@aliwaa.com.lb; internet www.aliwaa.com; f. 1963; Arabic; Propr ABD AL-GHANI SALAM; Editor SALAH SALAM; circ. 26,000.

Al-Mustaqbal: POB 14-5426, Beirut; tel. (1) 746301; fax (1) 746312; e-mail rnakib@almustaqbal.com.lb; internet www.almustaqbal.com.lb; f. 1999; Dir RAFIQ NAKIB; Editor-in-Chief HANI HAMMOUD; circ. 20,000.

An-Nahar (The Day): Immeuble An-Nahar, place des Martyrs, Marfa', Beirut 2014 5401; tel. (1) 994888; fax (1) 996777; e-mail webmaster@annahar.com.lb; internet www.annahar.com; f. 1933; Arabic; independent; publ. by Editions Dar an-Nahar SAL; Editor-in-Chief NAYLA TUENI; circ. 50,000.

L'Orient-Le Jour: POB 11-2488, Route de Damas, montée Fiyaddiyé, 200m aprés station Total, Beirut; tel. (5) 956444; fax (5) 957444; e-mail administration@lorientlejour.com; internet www.lorientlejour.com; f. 1970; by merger of two newspapers, *L'Orient* and *Le Jour*; French; independent; Pres. and CEO MICHEL EDDÉ; Editor-in-Chief MICHEL TOUMA; circ. 23,000.

As-Safir: POB 113–5015, Immeuble as-Safir, rue Monimina, Hamra, Beirut 1103-2010; tel. and fax (1) 350001; e-mail mail@assafir.com; internet www.assafir.com; f. 1974; Arabic; political; Publr and Editor-in-Chief TALAL SALMAN; circ. 45,000.

Zartonk: POB 11-617, rue Nahr Ibrahim, Beirut; tel. and fax (1) 566709; e-mail info@zartonkdaily.com; internet www.zartonkdaily .com; f. 1937; Armenian, Arabic and English; official organ of Armenian Liberal Democratic Party; Man. Editor BAROUYR H. AGHBASHIAN.

WEEKLIES

Achabaka (The Net): c/o Dar Assayad SAL, POB 11-1038, Said Freiha St, Hazmieh, Beirut; tel. (5) 453673; fax (5) 452700; e-mail info@dar-assayad.com; internet www.achabaka.com; f. 1956; Arabic; society and features; Founder SAID FREIHA; Editor ELHAM FREIHA; circ. 139,775.

Al-Anwar Supplement: c/o Dar Assayad, POB 11-1038, Hazmieh, Beirut; tel. (5) 450406; fax (5) 452700; e-mail info@alanwar.com; internet www.alanwar.com; cultural and social; every Sun.; supplement to daily *Al-Anwar*; Editor ISSAM FREIHA; circ. 90,000.

Assayad (The Hunter): c/o Dar Assayad, POB 11-1038, Hazmieh, Beirut; tel. (5) 450933; fax (5) 452700; e-mail assayad@inco.com.lb; internet www.al-sayad.com; f. 1943; Arabic; political and social; Editor-in-Chief MOUNIR NAJJAR; circ. 76,192.

Attamaddon: POB 90, Aljimzzat St, Tripoli; tel. (6) 441164; fax (6) 435252; e-mail info@attamaddon.com; internet www.attamaddon .com; f. 1972; political.

Al-Bayan: 5th Floor, Karim Centre, Tripoli; tel. and fax (6) 425555; e-mail info@albayanlebanon.com; internet albayanlebanon.com; political.

Ad-Dabbour: place du Musée, Beirut; tel. and fax (1) 616771; e-mail addabbour@yahoo.com; f. 1922; Arabic; CEO JOSEPH RICHARD MOUKARZEL; circ. 12,000.

L'Hebdo Magazine: POB 11-1404, Immeuble Sayegh, rue Sursock, Beirut; tel. (1) 202070; fax (1) 202663; e-mail info@ediori.com.lb; internet www.magazine.com.lb; f. 1956; French; political, economic and social; publ. by Editions Orientales SAL; Pres. CHARLES ABOU ADAL; Editor-in-Chief PAUL KHALIFEH; circ. 18,000.

Al-Hiwar (Dialogue): rue Donna Maria, Beirut; tel. (1) 637000; fax (1) 631282; e-mail info@alhiwar.info; internet www.alhiwar.info; f. 2000; Arabic; publ. by the National Dialogue Party; Chair. FOUAD MAKHZOUMI; Editor-in-Chief SAM MOUNASSA.

Al-Hurriya (Freedom): Beirut; e-mail info@alhourriah.org; internet www.alhourriah.org; f. 1960; Arabic; organ of the Democratic Front for the Liberation of Palestine; Editor AHMAD M. SHIHABI; circ. 30,000.

Al-Intiqad: internet www.alintiqad.com; Arabic; political; organ of Hezbollah; Editor IBRAHIM MOUSSAWI.

Al-Kifah al-Arabi (The Arab Struggle): POB 5158-14, Immeuble Rouche-Shams, Beirut; tel. (1) 809300; fax (1) 808281; e-mail editor@ kifaharabi.com; internet www.kifaharabi.com; f. 1974; Arabic; political, socialist, pan-Arab; Publr WALID HUSSEINI.

Massis: Immeuble Eglise Ste Croix des Arméniens Catholiques, rue Zoghbi, Zalka, Beirut; tel. (4) 715263; e-mail hebdomassis@sodetel .net.lb; internet www.armeniancatholic.org; f. 1947; Armenian; Catholic; Editor-in-Chief SARKIS NADJARIAN; circ. 2,500.

Al-Moharrer (The Liberator): POB 136702, rue Hamra, Beirut; tel. (1) 750516; fax (1) 750515; e-mail almoharrer@almoharrer.net; f. 1962; Arabic; circ. 87,000; Gen. Man. WALID ABOU ZAHR.

Monday Morning: POB 165612, Immeuble Dimitri Trad, rue Issa Maalouf, Achrafieh, Beirut; tel. (1) 200961; fax (1) 335079; e-mail info@mmorning.com; f. 1971; political and social affairs; publ. by Dar Alf Leila wa Leila; circ. 15,000; Editor-in-Chief MELHEM KARAM.

Al-Nass (The People): POB 145583, ave Fouad Chehab, Beirut; tel. (3) 376185; fax (8) 376610; e-mail an-nass@live.com; f. 1959; Arabic; weekly news magazine; Editor-in-Chief HASSAN YAGHI; circ. 22,000.

Al-Ousbou' al-Arabi (Arab Week): POB 11-1404, Immeuble Sayegh, rue Sursock, Beirut; tel. (1) 202070; fax (1) 202663; e-mail info@arabweek.com.lb; internet www.arabweek.com.lb; f. 1959; Arabic; political and social; publ. by Editions Orientales SAL; Chair. and Editor-in-Chief CHARLES ABOU ADAL; circ. 88,407 (circulates throughout the Arab world).

La Revue du Liban (Lebanon Review): POB 165612, Immeuble Dimitri Trad, rue Issa Maalouf, Achrafieh, Beirut; tel. (1) 200961; fax (1) 338929; e-mail rdl@rdl.com.lb; internet www.rdl.com.lb; f. 1928; French; political, social, cultural; publ. by Dar Alf Leila wa Leila; Publr MELHEM KARAM; Gen. Man. MICHEL MISK; circ. 22,000.

Al-Shiraa (The Sail): POB 13-5250, Beirut; tel. (1) 703000; fax (1) 866050; e-mail alshiraa@alshiraa.com; internet www.alshiraa.com; Arabic; Chief Editor HASSAN SABRA; circ. 40,000.

OTHER SELECTED PERIODICALS

Alam Attijarat (Business World): Immeuble Strand, rue Hamra, Beirut; f. 1965; monthly; commercial; Editor (vacant); international circ. 17,500.

Al Computer, Communications and Electronics (ACCE): c/o Dar Assayad, POB 1038, Hazmieh, Beirut; tel. (5) 450935; fax (5) 452700; e-mail assayad@inco.com.lb; internet www.accemagazine .com; f. 1984; monthly; computer technology; publ. by Dar Assayad Int; Chief Editor ANTOINE BOUTROS; circ. 31,912 (Jan.–June 2006).

Arab Construction World: POB 13-5121, Chouran, Beirut 1102 2802; tel. and fax (1) 748333; e-mail info@acwmag.com; internet www.acwmag.com; f. 1983; monthly; English and Arabic; publ. by CPH World Media; Publr FATHI CHATILA; Pres. and CEO MUHAMMAD RABIH CHATILA; circ. 6,025.

Arab Defence Journal: c/o Dar Assayad, POB 11-1038, Hazmieh, Beirut; tel. (5) 456374; fax (5) 450609; e-mail info@dar-assayad.com; internet www.arabdefencejournal.com; f. 1976; monthly; military; publ. by Dar Assayad Int; Editor-in-Chief FAWZI ABOU FARHAT; circ. 24,831 (July–Dec. 2005).

Arab Water World: POB 13-5121, Chouran, Beirut 1102-2802; tel. (1) 748333; fax (1) 352419; e-mail editorial@awwmag.com; internet www.awwmag.com; f. 1977; monthly; English and Arabic; publ. by CPH World Media; Pres., Publr and Editor-in-Chief FATHI CHATILA; circ. 7,580.

The Arab World: POB 567, Jounieh; tel. and fax (9) 935096; e-mail info@naamanculture.com; internet www.naamanculture.com; f. 1985; 24 a yr; publ. by Dar Naamān lith-Thaqāfa (Maison Naaman pour la Culture); Editor NAJI NAAMAN.

BusinessWeek Al-Arabiya: POB 11-4355, Beirut; tel. (1) 739777; fax (1) 749090; f. 2005; monthly; Arabic edn of US weekly business publ; publ. by InfoPro SA; distributed across 22 countries; Regional Dir SYLVIE GYURAN.

Le Commerce du Levant: POB 45-332 Baabda, Route de Damas, Immeuble l'Orient-Le Jour, 3e étage, Hazmieh, Beirut; tel. (1) 952259; fax (1) 453644; e-mail redaction@lecommercedulevant .com; internet www.lecommercedulevant.com; f. 1929; monthly; French; commercial and financial; publ. by Société de la Presse Economique; Chief Editor SIBYLLE RIZK; circ. 15,000.

Déco: POB 11-1404, Immeuble Sayegh, rue Sursock, Beirut; tel. (1) 202070; fax (1) 202663; e-mail info@decomag.com.lb; internet www .decomag.com.lb; f. 2000; quarterly; French; architecture and interior design; publ. by Editions Orientales SAL; Pres. CHARLES ABOU ADAL; circ. 14,000.

Fairuz International: Dar Assayad, POB 11-1038, Hazmieh, Beirut; tel. (5) 456373; fax (5) 450609; e-mail assayad@inco.com.lb; internet www.fairuzmagazine.com; f. 1982; monthly; Arabic; for women; publ. by Dar Assayad Int; Chief Editor ELHAM FREIHA; circ. 93,892 (July–Dec. 2005).

Al-Fares: c/o Dar Assayad, POB 11-1038, Hazmieh, Beirut; tel. (5) 450406; fax (5) 450609; e-mail assayad@inco.com.lb; internet www .alfaresmagazine.com; f. 1991; monthly; Arabic; men's interest; publ. by Dar Assayad Int; Chief Editor ELHAM FREIHA; circ. 79,237 (July–Dec. 2005).

Al-Idari (The Manager): c/o Dar Assayad, POB 11-1038, Hazmieh, Beirut; tel. (5) 450406; fax (5) 450609; e-mail assayad@inco.com.lb; internet www.alidarimagazine.com; f. 1975; monthly; Arabic; business management, economics, finance and investment; publ. by Dar Assayad Int; Pres. BASSAM FREIHA; Gen. Man. ELHAM FREIHA; circ. 31,867.

Lebanese and Arab Economy: POB 11-1801, Sanayeh, Beirut; tel. (1) 744160; fax (1) 353395; e-mail information@ccib.org.lb; internet www.ccib.org.lb; f. 1951; monthly; Arabic, English and French; publ. by Chamber of Commerce, Industry and Agriculture of Beirut and Mount Lebanon.

Lebanon Opportunities: c/o InfoPro sal, POB 11-4355, 2nd Floor, rue Hamra, Piccadilly Center, Beirut; tel. (1) 739777; fax (1) 749090; e-mail infopro@infopro.com.lb; internet www.opportunities.com.lb; monthly; English; real estate, business and general finance and economy; publ. by InfoPro SA; Publr and Editor-in-Chief RAMZI EL-HAFEZ.

Al-Mar'a: POB 11-1404, Immeuble Sayegh, rue Sursock, Beirut; tel. (1) 202070; fax (1) 202663; e-mail info@almara.com.lb; internet www .almara.com.lb; f. 2000; monthly; Arabic; for women; publ. by Editions Orientales SAL; Dir MOUNA BÉCHARA; Chief Editor PAUL KHALIFEH; circ. 20,000.

MENA Health World: POB 13-5121, Chouran, Beirut 1102 2802; tel. (1) 748333; fax (1) 352419; e-mail editorial@mhwmag.net; internet www.mhwmag.net; f. 1986 as Arab Health World magazine, but publ. suspended in 1993; relaunched as above 2006; bi-monthly; English and Arabic; publ. by CPH World Media; Pres. and Publr FATHI CHATILA; Editor-in-Chief Dr RAJAA CHATILA ALAYLI.

Middle East Food: POB 13-5121, Chouran, Beirut 1102 2802; tel. and fax (1) 748333; fax (1) 352419; e-mail content@mefmag.com; internet www.mefmag.com; f. 1985; monthly; publ. by CPH World Media; Pres. and CEO MUHAMMAD RABIH CHATILA; Editor-in-Chief ROULA HAMDAN; circ. 6,863.

Siyassa was Strategia (Politics and Strategy): POB 567, Jounieh; tel. and fax (9) 935096; e-mail naamanculture@lynx.net.lb; internet www.naamanculture.com; f. 1981; 36 a year; Arabic; publ. by Dar Naamān lith-Thaqāfa (Maison Naaman pour la Culture); Editor NAJI NAAMAN.

Takarir Wa Khalfiyat (Background Reports): c/o Dar Assayad, POB 11-1038, Hazmieh, Beirut; tel. (5) 456374; fax (5) 452700; f. 1976; monthly; Arabic; political and economic bulletin; publ. by Dar Assayad SAL; Editor-in-Chief HASSAN EL-KHOURY.

Al-Tarik (The Road): Beirut; monthly; Arabic; cultural and theoretical; publ. by the Parti communiste libanais; circ. 5,000.

Travaux et Jours (Works and Days): Rectorat de l'Université Saint-Joseph, rue de Damas, Beirut; tel. (1) 421000; fax (1) 421005; e-mail travauxetjours@usj.edu.lb; internet www.usj.edu.lb; f. 1961; 2 a year; French; political, social and cultural; Editor MOUNIR CHAMOUN.

NEWS AGENCY

National News Agency (NNA): Hamra, Beirut; tel. (1) 754400; fax (1) 745776; e-mail news@nna-leb.gov.lb; internet www.nna-leb.gov.lb; state-owned; Dir LAURE SLEIMAN; Chief Editor ALI LAHHAM.

PRESS ASSOCIATION

Lebanese Press Order: POB 2039-5801, ave Saeb Salam, Beirut; tel. (1) 350800; fax (1) 519865; e-mail info@pressorderlebanon.com; internet pressorderlebanon.com; f. 1911; 18 mems; Pres. AOUNI AL-KAAKI; Sec. ABD AL-KARIM EL-KHALIL.

Publishers

Dar al-Adab: POB 4123, Beirut; tel. (1) 795135; fax (1) 861633; e-mail d_aladab@cyberia.net.lb; internet www.adabmag.com; f. 1953; dictionaries, literary and general; Man. AIDA MATRAJI IDRISS; Editor-in-Chief SAMAH IDRISS.

Arab Institute for Research and Publishing (Al-Mouasasah al-Arabiyah Lildirasat Walnashr): POB 11-5460, Beirut; tel. and fax (1) 751438; e-mail info@airpbooks.com; internet www.airpbooks.com; f. 1969; works in Arabic and English; Dir MAHER KAYYALI.

Arab Scientific Publishers BP: POB 13-5574, Immeuble Ein al-Tenah Reem, rue Sakiet al-Janzir, Beirut; tel. (1) 786233; fax (1) 786230; e-mail asp@asp.com.lb; internet www.asp.com.lb; computer science, biological sciences, cookery, travel, politics, fiction, children's; Pres. BASSAM CHEBARO.

Dar Assayad Group (SAL and International): POB 11-1038, Hazmieh, Beirut; tel. (5) 456376; fax (5) 452700; e-mail info@dar-assayad.com; internet www.dar-assayad.com; Dar Assayad SAL f. 1943; Dar Assayad Int. f. 1983 and provides publishing, advertising and distribution services; publishes in Arabic *Al-Anwar* (daily), *Assayad* (weekly), *Achabaka* (weekly), *Background Reports*, *Arab Defense Journal* (monthly), *Fairuz* (international monthly edition), *Al-Idari* (monthly), *Al Computer, Communications and Electronics* (monthly), *Al-Fares* (monthly); also publishes monthly background reports; has offices and correspondents in Arab countries and most parts of the world; Chair. ISSAM FREIHA; CEO BASSAM FREIHA; Man. Dir ELHAM FREIHA.

CPH World Media SARL: POB 13-5121, Chouran, Beirut 1102 2802; tel. (1) 352413; fax (1) 352419; e-mail marketing@cphworldmedia.com; internet www.cphworldmedia.com; f. 1977 as Chatila Publishing House; adopted present name 2008; magazine publishing, events and research; publishes *Arab Construction World* (monthly), *Arab Water World* (monthly), *MENA Health World* (monthly), *Middle East Food* (monthly); Pres. and Publr FATHI CHATILA; CEO MUHAMMAD RABIH CHATILA.

Edition Française pour le Monde Arabe (EDIFRAMO): POB 113-6140, Immeuble Elissar, rue Bliss, Beirut; tel. (1) 862437; Man. TAHSEEN S. KHAYAT.

Editions Orientales SAL: POB 11-1404, Immeuble Sayegh, rue Sursock, Beirut; tel. (1) 202070; fax (1) 202663; e-mail info@ediori.com.lb; internet www.ediori.com.lb; political and social newspapers and magazines; Pres. and Editor-in-Chief CHARLES ABOU ADAL.

GeoProjects SARL: POB 113-5294, Immeuble Barakat, 13 rue Jeanne d'Arc, Beirut; tel. (1) 344236; fax (1) 342217; e-mail info@geo-publishers.com; internet www.geo-publishers.com; f. 1978; cartographers, researchers, school textbook publrs; Dir-Gen. RIDA ISMAIL.

Dar el-Ilm Lilmalayin: POB 1085, Centre Metco, rue Mar Elias, Beirut 2045 8402; tel. (1) 306666; fax (1) 701657; e-mail info@malayin.com; internet www.malayin.com; f. 1945; dictionaries, encyclopedias, reference books, textbooks, Islamic cultural books; CEO TAREF OSMAN.

InfoPro SARL: POB 11-4355, Centre Piccadilly, rue Hamra, Beirut; tel. (1) 739777; fax (1) 749090; e-mail infopro@infopro.com.lb;

internet www.infopro.com.lb; f. 1997; information-based magazines, incl. *BusinessWeek Al-Arabiya* and *Lebanon Opportunities*, as well as reference books; Pres. RAMZI EL-HAFEZ.

Institute for Palestine Studies, Publishing and Research Organization (IPS): POB 11-7164, rue Anis Nsouli, Verdun, Beirut 1107 2230; tel. (1) 868387; fax (1) 814193; e-mail ipsbrt@palestine-studies.org; internet www.palestine-studies.org; f. 1963; independent non-profit Arab research org., which promotes better understanding of the Palestine problem and the Arab–Israeli conflict; publishes books, reprints, research papers, etc.; Chair. Dr TAREK MITRI; Gen. Dir MAHMOUD SOUEID.

The International Documentary Center of Arab Manuscripts: POB 2668, Immeuble Hanna, Ras Beirut, Beirut; e-mail alafaq@cyberia.net.lb; f. 1965; publishes and reproduces ancient and rare Arabic texts; Propr ZOUHAIR BAALBAKI.

Dar al-Kashaf: POB 11-2091, rue Assad Malhamee, Beirut; tel. (1) 249952; e-mail dakashaf4@yahoo.com; f. 1930; publrs of *Al-Kashaf* (Arab Youth Magazine), maps, atlases and business books; printers and distributors; Propr M. A. FATHALLAH.

Dar al-Kitab al-Lubnani: POB 11-8330, Beirut; tel. (1) 735731; fax (1) 351433; e-mail info@daralkitabalmasri.com; internet www.daralkitabalmasri.com; f. 1929; publr of books on Islamic studies, history, sciences and literature; Pres. and Gen. Dir Dr HASSAN EL-ZEIN.

Dar Alf Leila wa Leila: BP 165612, rue Issa Maalouf, Immeuble Dimitri Trad, Achrafieh, Beirut; tel. (1) 200961; fax (1) 338929; e-mail rdl@rdl.com.lb; internet www.rdl.com.lb; publishes *Al-Bayraq* (Arabic, daily), *Al-Hawadeth* (Arabic, weekly), *La Revue du Liban* (French, weekly), *Monday Morning* (English, weekly); Editor-in-Chief MELHEM KARAM.

Librairie du Liban Publishers: POB 11-9232, Beirut; tel. (9) 217944; fax (9) 217734; e-mail info@ldlp.com; internet www.ldlp.com; f. 1944; publr of children's books, dictionaries and reference books; distributor of books in English and French; Man. Dirs HABIB SAYEGH, PIERRE SAYEGH.

Dar al-Maaref Liban SARL: POB 2320, Riad el-Solh, Beirut; tel. (1) 931243; f. 1959; children's books and textbooks in Arabic; Man. Dir Dr FOUAD IBRAHIM; Gen. Man. JOSEPH NACHOU.

Dar al-Machreq SARL: POB 166778, Beirut 1100 2150; tel. (1) 202423; fax (1) 202424; e-mail info@darelmachreq.com; internet www.darelmachreq.com; f. 1848; religion, art, Arabic and Islamic literature, history, languages, science, philosophy, school books, dictionaries and periodicals; Man. Dir SALAH ABOUJAOUDE.

Dar Naamān lith-Thaqāfa (Maison Naaman pour la Culture): POB 567, Jounieh; tel. and fax (9) 935096; fax (9) 935096; e-mail info@najinaaman.org; f. 1979; publishes *Mawsou'atul 'Alamil 'Arabiyyil Mu'asser* (Encyclopedia of the Contemporary Arab World), *Mawsou'atul Waqa'e'il 'Arabiyya* (Encyclopedia of Arab Events), and *Qitāboul A'lamil A'rabi*; Propr NAJI NAAMAN; Exec. Man. MARCELLE AL-ASHKAR.

Editions Dar an-Nahar SAL: BP 11-226, Immeuble an-Nahar, rue Banque du Liban, Hamra, Beirut; tel. (1) 747620; fax (1) 747623; e-mail darannahar@darannahar.com; internet www.darannahar.com; f. 1967; pan-Arab publishing house; Pres. GHASSAN TUÉNI; Dir JANA TAMER.

Naufal Group SARL: POB 11-2161, Immeuble Naufal, rue Sourati, Beirut; tel. (1) 354898; fax (1) 354394; e-mail naufalgroup@terra.net.lb; f. 1970; encyclopaedias, fiction, children's books, history, law and literature; subsidiary cos: Macdonald Middle East Sarl, Les Editions Arabes; Man. Dir TONY NAUFAL.

Publitec Publications: POB 16-6142, Beirut; tel. (1) 495401; fax (1) 493330; e-mail info@whoswhointhearabworld.info; f. 1965; publishes *Who's Who in Lebanon* and *Who's Who in the Arab World* (both bi-annual); Pres. CHARLES GEDEON; Man. KRIKOR AYVAZIAN.

Rihani Printing and Publishing House: 13-5378, Beirut; tel. (1) 838281; fax (1) 868384; f. 1963; Propr ALBERT RIHANI; Man. DAOUD STEPHAN.

Sader Publishers: POB 55530, Immeuble Sader, Dekwaneh, Beirut; tel. (1) 488776; e-mail sader@saderpublishers.com; internet www.saderpublishers.com; f. 1863; legal publr; Chair. JOSEPH SADER.

Samir Éditeur: POB 175132, rue Gouraud Gemmayzé, Sin el-Fil, Beirut; tel. (1) 448181; fax (1) 482541; e-mail samir@samirediteur.com; internet www.samirediteur.com; children's books in Arabic, English and French.

World Book Publishing: POB 11-3176, rue al-Khansa, Rifai Bldg, Beirut; tel. and fax (1) 659894; e-mail info@wbpbooks.com; internet www.wbpbooks.com; f. 1926; literature, education, philosophy, current affairs, self-help, children's books; Chair. M. SAID EL-ZEIN; Man. Dir RAFIK EL-ZEIN.

Broadcasting and Communications

TELECOMMUNICATIONS

OGERO (Organisme de Gestion et d'Exploitation de l'ex Radio Orient): POB 11-1226, Bir Hassan, Beirut 1107 2070; tel. (1) 840000; fax (1) 826823; internet www.ogero.gov.lb; f. 1972; 100% state-owned; plans for the incorporation of OGERO and 2 depts of the Ministry of Telecommunications into a single operator, Liban Télécom, were announced in 2005; however, no progress has since been made; fixed-line operator.

In late 2008 it was announced that the planned privatization of Lebanon's two state-owned mobile telephone networks would be deferred until after the 2009 legislative elections. New management contracts to operate the Mobile Interim Company (MIC) networks until April 2010 were awarded with effect from February 2009 to Orascom Telecom Holding of Egypt (which was to operate the MIC1 network) and Zain Group of Kuwait (MIC2); those contracts have subsequently been extended on an annual basis.

Alfa: Palm Center, rond-point Chevrolet, Beirut; tel. (3) 391111; fax (3) 391109; e-mail alfa.customercareteam@alfamobile.com.lb; internet www.alfa.com.lb; managed by Orascom Telecom Holding (Egypt); operates the state-owned MIC1 mobile telephone network under licence; offers 4G LTE services; 1.85m. subscribers (2013); Chair. and CEO MARWAN HAYEK.

touch: POB 17-5051, Immeuble MTC Touch, ave Charles Helou, Beirut; tel. (3) 792000; e-mail info@mtc.com.lb; internet www.touch.com.lb; f. 2004 as MTC Touch; present name adopted 2012; managed by Zain Group (fmrly Mobile Telecommunications Co—Kuwait); operates the state-owned MIC2 mobile telephone network under licence; Gen. Man. WASSIM MANSOUR.

Regulatory Authority

Telecommunications Regulatory Authority (TRA): Marfaa Bldg 200, 2nd Floor, Beirut Central District, Beirut; tel. (1) 964300; fax (1) 964341; e-mail info@tra.gov.lb; internet www.tra.gov.lb; f. 2007; Chair. and CEO Dr IMAD HOBALLAH.

BROADCASTING

Radio

Al-Nour: POB 197/25, Beirut; tel. (1) 543555; fax (1) 450771; e-mail alnour@alnour.com.lb; internet www.alnour.com.lb; f. 1988; owned by Lebanese Communication Group; affiliated to Hezbollah; broadcasts on 91.7FM, 91.9FM and 92.2FM.

Radio Liban: rue Emile Edée, Sanayeh, Hamra, Beirut; tel. (1) 756185; fax (1) 347489; internet www.96-2.com; run by the Ministry of Information in conjunction with Radio France International; f. 1937; Arabic programmes broadcast on 98.1 FM and 98.5 FM; scheduled for privatization; Dir-Gen. FOUAD KABALAN HAMDAN; Dir of Programmes MICHÈLE DE FREIGE.

The Home Service broadcasts in Arabic on short wave, and the Foreign Service broadcasts in Portuguese, Armenian, Arabic, Spanish, French and English.

Television

Lebanese Broadcasting Corpn (LBC) Sat Ltd: POB 111, Zouk, Beirut 165853; tel. (9) 850850; fax (9) 850916; e-mail lbcsat@lbcsat.com.lb; internet www.lbcgroup.tv; f. 1985 as Lebanese Broadcasting Corpn Int. SAL; name changed 1996; operates satellite channel on Arabsat 2C, Arabsat 3A and Nilesat 102; programmes in Arabic, French and English; broadcasts to Lebanon, the Middle East, Europe, the USA and Australia; Chair. Sheikh PIERRE EL-DAHER.

Future Television (Al-Mustaqbal): POB 13-6052, White House, rue Spears, Sanayeh, Beirut; tel. (1) 355355; fax (1) 753434; e-mail future@future.com.lb; internet www.futuretvnetwork.com; f. 1993; privately owned; commercial; Gen. Man. NADIM AL-MONLA.

Al-Manar (Lighthouse): Bir Hassan, Beirut; tel. (1) 276000; fax (1) 555953; e-mail info@almanar.com.lb; internet www.almanar.com.lb; f. 1991; owned by Lebanese Communication Group; broadcasts to Arab and Muslim audiences worldwide; operates satellite channel since May 2000; affiliated to Hezbollah; Chair. of Bd IBRAHIM FARHAT.

Murr Television: Naccache, Beirut; internet www.mtv.com.lb; f. 1991; closed down in 2002 for contravening electoral laws; relaunched April 2009; privately owned; CEO MICHEL EL-MURR.

Finance

(cap. = capital; dep. = deposits; res = reserves; m. = million; br.(s) = branch(es); amounts in Lebanese pounds)

BANKING

Beirut was, for many years, the leading financial and commercial centre in the Middle East, but this role was destroyed by the civil conflict during 1975–90. To restore the city as a regional focus for investment banking has been a key element of the reconstruction plans of successive governments.

Central Bank

Banque du Liban: POB 11-5544, rue Masraf Loubnane, Beirut; tel. (1) 750000; fax (1) 747600; e-mail bdlfx@bdl.gov.lb; internet www.bdl.gov.lb; f. 1964 as successor in Lebanon to the Banque de Syrie et du Liban; cap. and res 3,342,331m., dep. 63,932,268m. (Dec. 2009); Gov. RIAD T. SALAMEH; 9 brs.

Principal Commercial Banks

Bank Audi SAL: POB 11-2560, Riad el-Solh, Beirut 1107 2808; tel. (1) 994000; fax (1) 990555; e-mail contactus@banqueaudi.com; internet www.banqueaudi.com; f. 1962 as Bank Audi; acquired Orient Credit Bank 1997 and Banque Nasr 1998; absorbed into Audi Saradar Group in 2004; cap. 457,710m., res 2,588,684m., dep. 41,066,828m. (Dec. 2012); Chair. and Gen. Man. RAYMOND W. AUDI; CEO SAMIR HANNA; 80 brs in Lebanon, 12 brs in Jordan.

Bank of Beirut SAL: POB 11-7354, Bank of Beirut SAL Bldg, Foch St, Beirut Central District, Beirut; tel. (1) 983999; fax (1) 972972; internet www.bankofbeirut.com.lb; f. 1973; acquired Transorient Bank 1999, Beirut Riyad Bank 2002; cap. 851,955m., res 468,760m., dep. 14,711,131m. (Dec. 2012); Chair. and Gen. Man. SALIM G. SFEIR; 46 brs.

BankMed SAL: POB 11-0348, Centre Groupe Méditerranée, 482 rue Clémenceau, Beirut 2022 9302; tel. (1) 373937; fax (1) 362706; internet www.bankmed.com.lb; f. 1944 as Banque Naaman et Soussou; name changed to Eastern Commercial Bank 1955, Banque de la Méditerranée SAL 1970 and as above 2006; acquired Allied Bank SAL in 2006; cap. 1,109,937m., res 124,091m., dep. 15,826,465m. (Dec. 2012); Chair. and Gen. Man. MUHAMMAD HARIRI; 51 brs.

Banque Bemo SAL: POB 16-6353, Immeuble Bemo, place Sassine, ave Elias Sarkis, Achrafieh, Beirut 1100 2120; tel. (1) 200505; fax (1) 217860; e-mail bemosal@dm.net.lb; internet www.bemobank.com; f. 1964 as Future Bank SAL; name changed to BEMO (Banque Européenne pour le Moyen-Orient) SAL 1994 and as above 2006; cap. 92,150m., res 92,150m., dep. 2,033,016m. (Dec. 2011); Chair. and Gen. Man. RIAD BECHARA OBEGI; Man. Dir and Gen. Man. SAMIH H. SAADEH; 9 brs in Lebanon, 1 br. in Cyprus.

Banque Libano-Française SAL: POB 11-0808, Tour Liberty, 5 rue de Rome, Beirut 1107 2804; tel. and fax (1) 791332; e-mail info@eblf.com; internet www.eblf.com; f. 1967; cap. 586,828m., res 425,888m., dep. 14,189,526m. (Dec. 2012); Chair. WALID RAPHAËL; 47 brs.

Banque Misr Liban SAL: rue Riad el-Solh, Beirut 2011 9301; tel. (1) 986666; fax (1) 964296; e-mail mail@bml.com.lb; internet www.bml.com.lb; f. 1929 as Banque Misr Syrie Liban; name changed as above 1958; cap. 100,000m., res 35,125m., dep. 1,452,435m. (Dec. 2012); Chair. MUHAMMAD KAMAL EL-DIN BARAKAT; Exec. Gen. Man. HADI NAFFI; 14 brs.

BBAC (Bank of Beirut and the Arab Countries) SAL: POB 11-1536, Immeuble de la Banque, 250 rue Clémenceau, Riad el-Solh, Beirut 1107 2080; tel. (1) 360460; fax (1) 365200; e-mail contactus@bbac.com.lb; internet www.bbacbank.com; f. 1956; cap. 269,616m., res 134,457m., dep. 6,650,600m. (Dec. 2012); Chair. and Gen. Man. GHASSAN T. ASSAF; 37 domestic brs and 1 foreign rep. office.

BLC Bank SAL: POB 11-1126, BLC Bldg, Adlieh Intersection, Beirut 2064 5809; tel. and fax (1) 429000; e-mail info@blcbank.com; internet www.blcbank.com; f. 1950; 74.8% owned by Fransabank SAL; cap. 153,650m., res 282,380m., dep. 6,482,114m. (Dec. 2012); Chair. and Gen. Man. MAURICE SEHNAOUI; 35 brs.

BLOM Bank SAL: POB 11-1912, Immeuble BLOM Bank, rue Rachid Karameh, Verdun, Beirut 1107 2807; tel. (1) 743300; fax (1) 738946; e-mail blommail@blom.com.lb; internet www.blom.com.lb; f. 1951 as Banque du Liban et d'Outre-Mer; name changed as above 2000; cap. 282,000m., res 1,666,333m., dep. 33,468,040m. (Dec. 2012); Chair. and Gen. Man. SAAD AZHARI; 62 domestic brs and 11 foreign brs.

Byblos Bank SAL: POB 11-5605, ave Elias Sarkis, Achrafieh, Beirut 1107 2811; tel. (1) 335200; fax (1) 339436; e-mail byblosbk@byblosbank.com.lb; internet www.byblosbank.com; f. 1959; merged with Banque Beyrouth pour le Commerce SAL 1997; acquired Byblos Bank Europe SA 1998, Wedge Bank Middle East SAL 2001 and ABN AMRO Bank Lebanon 2002; cap. 689,113m., res 1,362,047m., dep.

21,176,621m. (Dec. 2012); Chair. and Gen. Man. Dr FRANÇOIS S. BASSIL; 78 brs in Lebanon, 23 brs abroad.

Creditbank SAL: POB 16-5795, Immeuble Crédit Bancaire SAL, 680 blvd Bachir Gemayel, Achrafieh, Beirut 1100 2802; tel. (1) 501600; fax (1) 485245; e-mail info@creditbank.com.lb; internet www.creditbank.com.lb; f. 1981 as Crédit Bancaire SAL; name changed as above following merger with Crédit Lyonnais Liban SAL 2002; cap. 60,725m., res 162,438m., dep. 3,011,442m. (Dec. 2012); Chair. and Gen. Man. TAREK JOSEPH KHALIFÉ; 20 brs.

Crédit Libanais SAL: POB 16-6729, Centre Sofil, 5e étage, ave Charles Malek, Beirut 1100 2811; tel. (1) 200028; fax (1) 325713; e-mail info@creditlibanais.com.lb; internet www.creditlibanais.com.lb; f. 1961; cap. 268,400m., res 886,861m., dep. 10,790,958m. (Dec. 2013); Chair. and Gen. Man. Dr JOSEPH M. TORBEY; 67 brs in Lebanon, 4 brs abroad.

Fenicia Bank SAL: POB 113-6248, Immeuble Fenicia Bank, rue Foch, Beirut Central District, Beirut 1103 2110; tel. (1) 957857; e-mail info@feniciabank.com; internet www.bkawbank.com; f. 1959; as Bank of Kuwait and the Arab World SAL; name changed as above 2010; 74% owned by Achour Group, 15% by Maacaron Group, 10% by Merhi Group and 1% by Dr Cheaib; cap. 100,000m., res 56,405m., dep. 1,698,183m. (Dec. 2012); Chair. and Gen. Man. ABD AL-RAZZAK ACHOUR; 14 brs in Lebanon.

First National Bank SAL: POB 11-0435, Immeuble 147, rue Allenby, Riad el-Solh, Beirut 2012 6004; tel. (1) 963000; fax (1) 973090; e-mail info@fnb.com.lb; internet www.fnb.com.lb; f. 1996; acquired Société Bancaire du Liban SAL 2002; cap. 177,105m., res 59,598m., dep. 4,648,454m. (Dec. 2012); Chair. RAMI REFAAT EL-NIMER; Gen. Man. ELIAS SALIM BAZ; 21 brs.

Fransabank SAL: POB 11-0393, rue Hamra, Riad el-Solh, Beirut 1107 2803; tel. (1) 745761; fax (1) 354572; e-mail fsb@fransabank.com; internet www.fransabank.com; f. 1921; acquired Banque Tohmé SAL 1993, Universal Bank SAL 1999, United Bank of Saudi and Lebanon SAL 2001 and Banque de la Beka'a SAL 2003; Banque de la Beka'a was subsequently sold to Bank of Sharjah Ltd (United Arab Emirates) in July 2007; cap. 446,000m., res 659,375m., dep. 20,057,437m. (Dec. 2012); Chair. ADNAN KASSAR; 63 brs.

IBL Bank SAL: POB 11-5292, Immeuble Ittihadiah, ave Charles Malek, Beirut 1107 2190; tel. (1) 200350; fax (1) 204524; e-mail ibl@ibl.com.lb; internet www.ibl.com.lb; f. 1961 as Intercontinental Bank of Lebanon SAL; cap. 221,606m., res 56,940m., dep. 6,047,161m. (Dec. 2012); Chair. and Gen. Man. SALIM Y. HABIB; 17 brs.

Jammal Trust Bank SAL: POB 11-5640, Immeuble Jammal, rue Verdun, Beirut; tel. (1) 781999; fax (1) 800361; e-mail services@jammalbank.com.lb; internet www.jammalbank.com.lb/home.html; f. 1963 as Investment Bank SAL; cap. 70,000m., res 19,472m., dep. 905,663m. (Dec. 2012); Chair. and Gen. Man. ANWAR A. AL-JAMMAL; 22 brs in Lebanon, 3 rep. offices abroad.

Lebanese Swiss Bank SAL: POB 11-9552, Immeuble Hoss, 6e étage, rue Emile Eddé, place Hamra, Ras Beirut, Beirut; tel. (1) 354501; fax (1) 346242; e-mail lsb@lebaneseswissbank.com; internet www.lebaneseswissbank.com; f. 1962; cap. 70,000m., res 78,000m., dep. 2,045,000m. (Dec. 2013); Chair. and Gen. Man. Dr TANAL SABBAH; 17 brs.

Lebanon and Gulf Bank SAL: POB 11-3360, 124 Allenby St, Beirut Central District, Beirut; tel. (1) 965000; fax (1) 965199; e-mail info@lgb.com.lb; internet www.lgb.com.lb; f. 1963 as Banque de Crédit Agricole; name changed as above 1980; cap. 106,000m., res 123,367m., dep. 3,298,245m. (Dec. 2012); Chair. and Gen. Man. ABD AL-HAFIZ MAHMOUD ITANI; 13 domestic brs, 1 foreign br.

MEAB SAL: POB 14-5958, Immeuble Hejeij, ave Adnan al-Hakim, Beirut 1105 2080; tel. (1) 826740; fax (1) 841190; e-mail meab@meabank.com; internet www.meabank.com; f. 1991 as Middle East and Africa Bank SAL; name changed as above 2003; cap. 82,000m., res 10,977m., dep. 1,531,821m. (Dec. 2011); Chair. and Gen. Man. KASSEM HEJEIJ; 6 brs.

Société Nouvelle de la Banque de Syrie et du Liban SAL (BSL): POB 11-957, rue Riad el-Solh, Beirut; tel. (1) 980080; fax (1) 980991; e-mail info@bsl.com.lb; internet www.bsl.com.lb; f. 1963; cap. 46,920m., res 64,676m., dep. 1,084,953m. (Dec. 2010); Chair. RAMSAY A. EL-KHOURI; Gen. Man. SÉLIM STÉPHAN; 8 brs.

Syrian Lebanese Commercial Bank SAL: SLCB Bldg, Makdessi St, Beirut; tel. (1) 741666; fax (1) 738214; e-mail info@slcb.com.lb; internet www.slcb.com.lb; f. 1974; cap. 150,000m., res 26,116m., dep. 114,965m. (Dec. 2011); Chair. FIRAS SELMAN; 3 brs in Lebanon.

Development Bank

Audi Saradar Investment Bank SAL: POB 16-5110, Bank Audi Plaza, Omar al-Daouk St, Beirut; tel. (1) 994000; fax (1) 999406; e-mail contactus@asib.com; internet www.asib.com; f. 1974 as Investment and Finance Bank; name changed to Audi Investment Bank SAL 1996 and as above 2004; medium- and long-term loans, 100% from Lebanese sources; owned by Bank Audi SAL—Audi

Saradar Group; cap. 25,075m., res 147,851m., dep. 440,179m. (Dec. 2012); Chair. and Gen. Man. Dr MARWAN M. GHANDOUR; Gen. Man. RAMZI N. SALIBA.

Supervisory Body

Banking Control Commission of Lebanon: POB 11-5544, rue Masraf Loubnane, Beirut; tel. (1) 350167; fax (1) 750040; internet www.bccl.gov.lb; f. 1967; Chair. OSAMA MEKDASHI.

Banking Association

Association of Banks in Lebanon: POB 976, Gouraud St, Saifi, Beirut; tel. (1) 970500; e-mail abl@abl.org.lb; internet www.abl.org.lb; f. 1959; serves and promotes the interests of the banking community in Lebanon; mems: 64 banks and 7 foreign rep. offices; Chair. FRANÇOIS S. BASSIL.

STOCK EXCHANGE

Beirut Stock Exchange (BSE): POB 11-3552, Immeuble Azareih, 4e étage, Bloc O1, Beirut; tel. (1) 993555; fax (1) 993444; e-mail bse@bse.com.lb; internet www.bse.com.lb; f. 1920; recommenced trading in Jan. 1996; 10 cttee mems; Vice-Chair. GHALEB MAHMASSANI.

INSURANCE

About 80 insurance companies were registered in Lebanon in the late 1990s, although fewer than one-half of these were operational. An insurance law enacted in 1999 increased the required capital base for insurance firms and provided tax incentives for mergers within the sector.

Allianz SNA SAL: POB 16-6528, Immeuble Allianz SNA, Hazmieh, Beirut 1100 2130; tel. (1) 956600; fax (1) 956624; e-mail info@allianzsna.com; internet www.allianzsna.com; f. 1963 as Société Nationale d'Assurances SAL; renamed as above 2008; part of Allianz Group; cap. 13,264m. (2007); Chair. ANTOINE WAKIM; CEO XAVIER DENYS.

Arabia Insurance Co SAL: POB 11-2172, Arabia House, rue de Phénicie, Beirut; tel. (1) 363610; fax (1) 365139; e-mail arabia@arabia-ins.com.lb; internet www.arabiainsurance.com; f. 1944; cap. 51,000m.; Chair. WAHBÉ A. TAMARI; CEO FADY SHAMMAS.

Bankers Assurance SAL: POB 11-4293, 4th Floor, Immeuble Asseily, rue El Mir Bechir, Riad el-Solh Sq., Beirut; tel. (1) 962700; fax (1) 984004; e-mail mail@bankers-assurance.com; internet www.bankers-assurance.com; f. 1972; Chair. GINO NADER; Gen. Man. RAYMOND CHAM.

Commercial Insurance Co (Lebanon) SAL: POB 11-4351, Centre Starco, North Block, 9th Floor, Beirut; tel. (1) 373070; fax (1) 373071; e-mail comins@commercialinsurance.com.lb; internet www.commercialinsurance.com.lb; f. 1962; cap. 6,000m. (March 2006); Chair. MAX R. ZACCAR; 2 brs.

Compagnie Libanaise d'Assurances SAL: POB 3685, rue Riad el-Solh, Beirut; tel. (1) 868988; e-mail lebanese@sodetel.net.lb; internet www.lebaneseinsurance.com; f. 1951; cap. 22,500m.; Chair. PEDRO ABOUJAOUDÉ; Gen. Man. JIHAD SAKR.

Al-Ittihad al-Watani: POB 11-1270, Jisr al-Wati, Immeuble Al-Ittihad al-Watani, Beirut; tel. (1) 426480; fax (1) 426486; e-mail webmaster@alittihadalwatani.com.lb; internet www.alittihadalwatani.com.lb; f. 1947; cap. 20.6m. (2005); Chair. and Gen. Man. TANNOUS FEGHALI.

Libano-Suisse Insurance Co SAL: POB 11-3821, Immeuble Commerce and Finance, Beirut 1107 2150; tel. (1) 374900; fax (1) 368724; e-mail libano-suisse@libano-suisse.com; internet www.libano-suisse.com; f. 1959; Chair. MICHEL PIERRE PHARAON; Gen. Man. LUCIEN LETAYEF, Jr.

Al-Mashrek Insurance and Reinsurance SAL: POB 16-6154, Immeuble Al-Mashrek, Antélias Main Rd, Rabieh, Beirut 1100 2100; tel. (4) 408666; fax (4) 417688; e-mail almashrek@almashrek.com.lb; internet www.almashrek.com.lb; f. 1962; Chair. and CEO ALEX-ANDRE MATOSSIAN.

'La Phénicienne' SAL: POB 11-5652, Immeuble Hanna Haddad, rue Amine Gemayel, Sioufi, Beirut; tel. (1) 425484; fax (1) 424532; e-mail phenicienne@sodetel.net.lb; f. 1964; cap. 3,167m.; Chair. and Gen. Man. CAROLE FÉGHALI CHAMOUN.

Trade and Industry

DEVELOPMENT ORGANIZATIONS

Council for Development and Reconstruction (CDR): POB 116-5351, Tallet el-Serail, Beirut; tel. (1) 980096; fax (1) 981252; e-mail general@cdr.gov.lb; internet www.cdr.gov.lb; f. 1977; an autonomous public institution reporting to the Cabinet, the CDR is charged with the co-ordination, planning and execution of Lebanon's public reconstruction programme; it plays a major role in attracting foreign funds; Pres. NABIL ADNAN EL-JISR.

Investment Development Authority of Lebanon (IDAL): POB 113-7251, Azarieh Tower, 4th Floor, Emir Bechir St, Riad el-Solh, Beirut; tel. (1) 983306; fax (1) 983302; e-mail invest@idal.com.lb; internet www.idal.com.lb; f. 1994; state-owned; Chair. and Gen. Man. NABIL ITANI.

Société Libanaise pour le Développement et la Reconstruction de Beyrouth (Solidere): POB 11-9493, 149 rue Saad Zaghoul, Beirut 2012-7305; tel. (1) 980650; fax (1) 980662; e-mail solidere@solidere.com.lb; internet www.solidere.com.lb; f. 1994; real estate co responsible for reconstruction of Beirut Central District after the civil war; Chair. NASSER CHAMMAA; Gen. Man. MOUNIR DOUAIDY.

CHAMBERS OF COMMERCE AND INDUSTRY

Federation of the Chambers of Commerce, Industry and Agriculture in Lebanon: POB 11-1801, Immeuble CCIAB, rue Justinien, Sanayeh, Beirut; tel. (1) 744702; fax (1) 349614; e-mail fccial@cci-fed.org.lb; internet www.cci-fed.org.lb; f. 1996; Pres. MUHAMMAD CHOUCAIR.

Chamber of Commerce, Industry and Agriculture of Beirut and Mount Lebanon: POB 11-1801, 1 rue Justinian, Sanayeh, Beirut; tel. (1) 353390; fax (1) 353395; e-mail information@ccib.org.lb; internet www.ccib.org.lb; f. 1898; 16,000 mems; Pres. MUHAMMAD CHOUCAIR.

Chamber of Commerce, Industry and Agriculture in Sidon and South Lebanon: POB 41, rue Maarouf Saad, Sidon; tel. (7) 720123; fax (7) 722986; e-mail chamber@ccias.org.lb; internet www.ccias.org.lb; f. 1933; Pres. MUHAMMAD SALEH.

Chamber of Commerce, Industry and Agriculture of Tripoli and North Lebanon: POB 47, rue Bechara Khoury, Tripoli; tel. (6) 627162; fax (6) 442042; e-mail abdallahg@cciat.org.lb; internet www.cciat.org.lb; Chair. ABDALLAH GHANDOUR.

Chamber of Commerce, Industry and Agriculture of Zahleh and Beqa'a: POB 100, Zahleh; tel. (8) 802602; fax (8) 800050; e-mail info@cciaz.org.lb; internet www.cciaz.org.lb; f. 1939; 2,500 mems; Pres. EDMOND JREISSATI.

EMPLOYERS' ASSOCIATION

Association of Lebanese Industrialists: POB 11-1520, Chamber of Commerce and Industry Bldg, 5e étage, rue Justinien, Sanayeh, Beirut; tel. (1) 350280; fax (1) 351167; e-mail ali@ali.org.lb; internet www.ali.org.lb; Pres. FADY ABBOUD; Gen. Man. SAAD S. OUEINI.

UTILITIES

Electricity

Electricité du Liban (EDL): POB 131, Immeuble de l'Electricité du Liban, 22 rue du Fleuve, Beirut; tel. (1) 442720; fax (1) 443828; e-mail info@edl.gov.lb; internet www.edl.gov.lb; f. 1954; state-owned; Chair. and Dir Gen. KAMAL F. HAYEK.

Water

Legislation introduced in 2000 allowed for the merging of 21 water authorities into four new regional establishments for water exploitation—Beirut and the Mount of Lebanon; North Lebanon; South Lebanon; and the Beqa'a. Under the reorganization the new authorities were to operate under the supervision of the Ministry of Energy and Water.

The Water Establishment of Beirut and the Mount of Lebanon: Beirut; internet www.ebml.gov.lb; f. 2000.

The Water Establishment of the Beqa'a: Zahleh; f. 2000; Gen. Dir Eng. MAROUN MOUSSALLEM.

The Water Establishment of North Lebanon: Tripoli; f. 2000; Chair. JAMAL KRAYYEM.

The Water Establishment of South Lebanon: Sidon; f. 2000; Chair. and Dir-Gen. Eng. AHMAD HASSAN NIZAM.

Litani River Authority: rue Bechara el-Khoury, Beirut; tel. (1) 666662; fax (1) 660476; e-mail webmaster@litani.gov.lb; internet www.litani.gov.lb; f. 1954; responsible for water resources management, irrigation, and the devt of dams and hydroelectric facilities; Chair. Dr SALIM CATAFAGO; Dir-Gen. ADEL AL-HUMANI (acting).

TRADE UNION FEDERATION

Confédération Générale des Travailleurs du Liban (CGTL): POB 4381, Beirut; f. 1958; 300,000 mems; only national labour centre in Lebanon and sole rep. of working classes; comprises 18 affiliated feds, incl. all 150 unions in Lebanon; Pres. GHASSAN GHOSN.

Transport

RAILWAYS

Office des Chemins de Fer et des Transports en Commun (OCFTC): POB 11-109, Gare St Michel, Nahr, Beirut; tel. (1) 587211; fax (1) 447007; since 1961 all railways in Lebanon have been state-owned; the original network of some 412 km is no longer functioning; however, in 2004 work began on a project to reconstruct a section of the railway network between Tripoli and the Syrian border; Dir-Gen. and Pres. RADWAN BOU NASSER EL-DIN.

ROADS

In 2005 Lebanon had an estimated 6,970 km of roads, of which some 170 km were motorways and 6,800 km were other roads. The two international motorways are the north–south coastal road and the road connecting Beirut with Damascus in Syria. Among the major roads are those crossing the Beqa'a and continuing south to Bent-Jbail and the Shtaura–Ba'albek road. It was reported that up to 80% of Lebanon's major roads, and almost all of its bridges, were destroyed as a result of the Israeli military offensive in mid-2006.

SHIPPING

In the 1990s a two-phase programme to rehabilitate and expand the port of Beirut commenced, involving the construction of an industrial free zone, a fifth basin and a major container terminal, at an estimated cost of US $1,000m.; the container terminal became operational in February 2005. A further extension to the container terminal, increasing total capacity at the port to 1.5m. TEUs, opened in November 2013. Tripoli, the northern Mediterranean terminus of the oil pipeline from Iraq, is also a busy port, with good equipment and facilities. Jounieh, north of Beirut, is Lebanon's third most important port. A new deep-water sea port was to be constructed south of Sidon. The reconstructed port of al-Naqoura, in what was then the 'security zone' along the border with Israel, was inaugurated in June 1987. Several ports were bombed by Israeli forces during the conflict of mid-2006.

At 31 December 2014 Lebanon's flag registered fleet totalled 56 vessels, with an aggregate displacement of 210,326 grt, of which three were bulk carriers and 17 were general cargo ships.

Port Authorities

Gestion et Exploitation du Port de Beyrouth: POB 1490, Beirut; tel. (1) 580211; fax (1) 585835; e-mail gepb@portdebeyrouth.com; internet www.portdebeyrouth.com; Pres., Dir-Gen. and Man. Dir HASSAN KAMEL KRAYTEM; Harbour Master MAROUN KHOURY.

Service d'Exploitation du Port de Tripoli: rond point Tripoli, rue Mina, Tripoli; tel. (6) 600413; fax (6) 220180; e-mail tport@terra.net.lb; f. 1959; Harbour Master MARWAN BAROUDI.

Principal Shipping Companies

Ademar Shipping Lines: POB 175-231, rue Shafaka, al-Medawar, Beirut; tel. (1) 444100; fax (1) 444101; e-mail admin@adelmarservices.com; internet www.ademarlb.com; f. 1992.

Beirut Cargo Center: Kurban Bldg, Corniche al-Nahr, Beirut; tel. (1) 585582; fax (1) 585580; e-mail bcc@bcc.com.lb; internet www.bcc.com.lb; f. 1993; air, sea and land freight forwarder; CEO JOSEPH HARB.

Consolidated Bulk Inc (CBI): POB 70-152, Centre St Elie, blk A, 6e étage, Antélias, Beirut; tel. (4) 410724; fax (4) 402842; e-mail info@bulkgroup.com; internet www.bulkgroup.com; f. 1993; Gen. Man. SAMI P. ZACCA.

Continental Shipping Agencies SARL: POB 17-5039, Immeuble Medawar, 5e étage, rue Saifi-Pasteur, Beirut; tel. (1) 567130; fax (1) 567132; e-mail info@csa-continental.com; internet www.csa-continental.com; f. 1991; member of The Lebanese Shipping Agents Syndicates and The Lebanese Shipping Association.

O. D. Debbas & Sons: POB 3, blvd Corniche du Fleuve, Achrafieh, Beirut; tel. (1) 585253; fax (1) 587135; e-mail oddebbas@oddebbas.com; internet www.oddebbas.com; f. 1892; Man. Dir OIDIH ELIE DEBBAS.

Freight Leader SARL: POB 175530, Immeuble Medawar, 5th Floor, rue Pasteur, Saifi, Beirut; tel. (1) 581870; fax (1) 564387; e-mail info@freightleader.com; internet www.freightleader.com; f. 2001; transportation services and logistics; Exec. Man. MOUSSA SALAMOUN.

Gezairi Ltd (GEZACHART): POB 11-1402, Immeuble Oseili, place Riad Solh, Beirut 2034 0716; tel. (1) 783783; fax (1) 784784; e-mail gezairi@gezairi.com; internet www.gezairi.com; f. 1945; ship management, chartering, brokerage; Pres. and CEO MONA BOUAZZA BAWARSHI.

Gulf Agency Co (Lebanon) Ltd: Immeuble Modern, 7e étage, rue el Arz, Beirut; tel. (1) 446189; fax (1) 446097; e-mail lebanon@gac

.com; internet www.gac.com/lebanon; f. 1967; Man. Dir Simon G. Bejjani.

Lebanese Navigators Co SARL: POB 175179, Immeuble Pasteur 40, 1er étage, Achrafieh, Beirut; tel. (1) 570571; fax (1) 575730; e-mail navigators@navigators-lb.com; internet www.navigators-lb.com; Man. Dir Antoine Mouhayar.

Orient Shipping and Trading Co SARL: POB 11-2561, Immeuble Moumneh 72, rue Ain al-Mraisseh 54, Beirut; tel. (1) 364455; fax (1) 365570; e-mail ortship@inco.com.lb; internet orientgroup.net/lebanon.swf; Chair. Elie Zarouby.

Ets Paul Adem: Centre Moucarri, 6e étage, autostrade Dora, Bourj Hammoud, Beirut; tel. (1) 244610; fax (1) 244612; e-mail padco@inco.com.lb; f. 1971; ship owners, operators, maritime agents, brokers, consultants; Gen. Man. Paul Adem.

G. Sahyouni & Co SARL: POB 17-5452, Mar Mikhael, Beirut 1104 2040; tel. (1) 257046; fax (1) 241317; e-mail postmaster@georgesahyouni.com; internet www.georgesahyouni.com; f. 1989; agents for Baltic Control Lebanon Ltd, SARL, and Lloyds; Man. Dir George Sahyouni.

CIVIL AVIATION

In late 2001 a major expansion project at Beirut International Airport was completed, at an estimated cost of US $600m.; facilities included a new terminal building and two new runways, increasing handling capacity to 6m. passengers a year. In May 2005 the airport was renamed Beirut Rafiq Hariri International Airport in honour of the former Prime Minister who had been killed in February of that year. The airport was targeted by Israeli armed forces in 2006, and was closed to commercial flights during the conflict between Israel and Hezbollah. Following extensive repairs to damaged runways and other infrastructure, the airport reopened to commercial operations in August. In 2010 some 5.6m. passengers used the airport.

MEA (Middle East Airlines, Air Liban SAL): POB 11-206, blvd de l'Aéroport, Beirut 1107 2801; tel. (1) 628888; fax (1) 629260; e-mail mikaouir@mea.com.lb; internet www.mea.com.lb; f. 1945; acquired Lebanese Int. Airways in 1969; regular services throughout Europe, the Middle East, N. and W. Africa, and the Far East; Chair. and Dir-Gen. Muhammad A. el-Hout.

Trans-Mediterranean Airways SAL (TMA): POB 30-1001, Beirut Rafiq Hariri International Airport, Beirut; tel. (1) 629210; fax (1) 629219; e-mail cargo@tmacargo.com; internet www.tma.com.lb; f. 1953; cargo services covering Europe, the Middle East, Africa and the Far East; also provides handling, storage and maintenance services; CEO Capt. Riad Mikaoui.

Tourism

Since the end of the civil conflict in 1990 Lebanon's scenic beauty, sunny climate and historic sites have once again attracted foreign visitors. The Government has chosen to concentrate its efforts on the promotion of cultural as well as conference and exhibition-based tourism, while the country is also being promoted as an 'eco-tourism' destination. Excluding Syrian visitors, the annual total of tourist arrivals increased from 177,503 in 1992 to some 1.3m. in 2004. The Lebanese tourism industry experienced a significant downturn in the aftermath of the conflict between Israel and Hezbollah in 2006. However, there was a marked revival in the sector following the Doha Agreement of May 2008, and by 2010 annual foreign tourist arrivals reached some 2.2m. Receipts from tourism totalled US $5,787m. in 2012. Tourist arrivals had declined to 1.3m. by 2013, principally owing to the political instability in the region.

Ministry of Tourism: see section on The Government—Ministries.

Defence

Commander-in-Chief of the Army: Gen. Jean Kahwaji.

Chief of Staff of Armed Forces: Maj.-Gen. Walid Salman.

Commander of the Air Force: Brig.-Gen. Ghassan Chahine.

Commander of the Navy: Rear Adm. Nazih Joubeily.

Director-General of State Security Forces: Maj.-Gen. Georges Karaa.

Defence Budget (2013): £L1,839,150m.

Total armed forces (as assessed at November 2014): 60,000: army 56,600; navy 1,800; air force 1,600.

Paramilitary forces included an estimated 20,000 members of the Internal Security Force, attached to the Ministry of the Interior and Municipalities. Compulsory military service was formally abolished in February 2007. Hezbollah's active members numbered some 2,000, as assessed at November 2009.

Following conflict in Lebanon between Hezbollah and Israeli armed forces in July–August 2006, the UN Security Council unanimously adopted Resolution 1701, calling for a full cessation of hostilities, upon which Lebanon was to deploy government forces in southern Lebanon and the presence there of the UN Interim Force in Lebanon (UNIFIL) was to be expanded to a maximum authorized strength of 15,000 troops, while Israel was to commence the parallel withdrawal of all its forces from that region. A formal ceasefire entered into effect on 14 August. At the end of February 2015 there were 10,395 UNIFIL military personnel deployed in Lebanon.

Education

Education is compulsory for a period of nine years between six and 15 years of age. Primary education has been available free of charge in state schools since 1960, but private institutions still provide the main facilities for secondary and university education. Private schools enjoy almost complete autonomy, except for a certain number that receive government financial aid and are supervised by inspectors from the Ministry of Education and Higher Education. In the 2010 budget some £L1,293,000m. was allocated to the Ministry of Education and Higher Education (representing 5.9% of total budgetary expenditure).

Primary education begins at six years of age and lasts for six years, comprising two cycles of three years each. Secondary education, beginning at the age of 13, lasts for up to six years, comprising two cycles of three years each. Technical education is provided mainly at the National School of Arts and Crafts, which offers four-year courses in electronics, mechanics, architectural and industrial drawing, and other subjects. There are also public vocational schools providing courses for lower levels. In 2012 enrolment at primary schools included 93% of the relevant age-group, while the comparable rate for secondary schools was 68%. Higher education is provided by at least 14 institutions, including 12 universities, an arts academy and a school of theology. Some 212,467 students were enrolled in higher education institutes in 2011/12.

LESOTHO

Introductory Survey

LOCATION, CLIMATE, LANGUAGE, RELIGION, FLAG, CAPITAL

The Kingdom of Lesotho is a landlocked country, entirely surrounded by South Africa. The climate is generally mild, although cooler in the highlands: lowland temperatures range from a maximum of 32°C (90°F) in summer (October to April) to a minimum of −7°C (20°F) in winter. Rainfall averages about 725 mm (29 ins) per year, mostly falling in summer. The official languages are English and Sesotho; other languages spoken include Zulu and Xhosa. About 90% of the population are Christians. The largest denominations are the Roman Catholic, Lesotho Evangelical and Anglican Churches. The national flag (official proportions 2 by 3) has three horizontal stripes from top to bottom of blue, white and green, with a black traditional Basotho hat in the centre of the white stripe. The capital is Maseru.

CONTEMPORARY POLITICAL HISTORY

Historical Context

Lesotho was formerly Basutoland, which became a separate British colony in 1884 and was administered as one of the High Commission Territories in southern Africa (the others being the protectorates of Bechuanaland, now Botswana, and Swaziland). The British Act of Parliament that established the Union of South Africa in 1910 also provided for the possible inclusion in South Africa of the three High Commission Territories, subject to local consent: the native chiefs opposed requests by successive South African Governments for the transfer of the three territories.

Within Basutoland a revised Constitution, which established the colony's first Legislative Council, was introduced in 1956. A new document, granting limited powers of self-government, was adopted in September 1959. Basutoland's first general election, on the basis of universal adult suffrage, took place on 29 April 1965, and full internal self-government was achieved the following day. Moshoeshoe II, Paramount Chief since 1960, was recognized as King. The Basutoland National Party (BNP), a conservative group supporting limited co-operation with South Africa, narrowly won a majority of the seats in the new Legislative Assembly. The BNP's leader, Chief Leabua Jonathan, was appointed Prime Minister in July 1965. Basutoland became independent, as Lesotho, on 4 October 1966. The new Constitution provided for a bicameral legislature, comprising the 60-seat National Assembly and the 33-member Senate; executive power was vested in the Cabinet, which was presided over by the Prime Minister. The King was designated Head of State.

Domestic Political Affairs

The BNP, restyled the Basotho National Party, remained in power at independence. A general election was held in January 1970, at which the opposition Basotho Congress Party (BCP), a pan-Africanist group led by Dr Ntsu Mokhehle, appeared to have won a majority of seats in the National Assembly. Chief Jonathan declared a state of emergency, suspended the Constitution and arrested several BCP organizers. The election was annulled, and the legislature prorogued. King Moshoeshoe II was placed under house arrest and subsequently exiled, although he returned in December after accepting a government order banning him from participating in politics. The country was thus effectively under the Prime Minister's personal control. An interim National Assembly, comprising the former Senate (mainly chiefs) and 60 members nominated by the Cabinet, was inaugurated in April 1973 and the state of emergency was revoked in July. However, following a failed coup attempt in January 1974 by alleged supporters of the BCP, Chief Jonathan introduced stringent security laws. Mokhehle and other prominent members of the BCP went into exile abroad, and the party split into two factions, internal and external, the latter led by Mokhehle.

Although Lesotho was economically dependent on South Africa, and the Government's official policy during the 1970s was one of 'dialogue' with its neighbour, Chief Jonathan repeatedly criticized the apartheid regime, and supported the then banned African National Congress of South Africa (ANC). In December 1982 South African forces launched a major assault on the homes of ANC members in Maseru, killing more than 40 people. Lesotho's persistent refusal to sign a joint non-aggression pact led South Africa to impound consignments of armaments destined for Lesotho, and the imposition of a blockade on the common border from early 1986.

On 20 January 1986 Chief Jonathan's Government was overthrown in a coup led by Maj.-Gen. Justin Lekhanya, the head of the armed forces. A Military Council, chaired by Lekhanya, was established and executive and legislative powers were to be vested in King Moshoeshoe, assisted by the Military Council and a (mainly civilian) Council of Ministers. In March 1986 the Military Council suspended all formal political activity.

Although the South African Government denied having any part in the coup, the Lekhanya regime proved to be more amenable to South Africa's regional security policy. In March 1986 it was announced that the two countries had reached an informal agreement whereby neither would allow its territory to be used for attacks against the other. Moreover, the Lesotho Government did not join other African states in pressing for international economic sanctions against South Africa. In March 1988 Lesotho and South Africa reached final agreement on the Lesotho Highlands Water Project (LHWP), a major scheme to supply water to South Africa.

In May 1988 Mokhehle was allowed to return to Lesotho after 14 years of exile and by 1990 the two factions of the BCP had apparently reunited under Mokhehle's leadership.

In February 1990 Lekhanya dismissed three members of the Military Council and one member of the Council of Ministers, accusing them of 'insubordination'. When Moshoeshoe refused to approve new appointments to the Military Council, Lekhanya suspended the monarch's executive and legislative powers, which were assumed by the Military Council in March. Moshoeshoe (who remained Head of State) was exiled in the United Kingdom. Lekhanya announced that a general election would take place during 1992; however, party political activity remained outlawed. In June 1990 a National Constituent Assembly (including Lekhanya, members of the Council of Ministers, representatives of banned political parties, traditional chiefs and business leaders) was inaugurated to draft a new constitution. In October Lekhanya invited the King to return from exile. Moshoeshoe responded that his return would be conditional upon the ending of military rule and the establishment of an interim government, pending the readoption of the 1966 Constitution. On 6 November 1990 Lekhanya promulgated an order dethroning the King with immediate effect. Lesotho's 22 principal chiefs elected Moshoeshoe's elder son, Prince David Mohato Bereng Seeiso, as the new King; on 12 November he acceded to the throne, as King Letsie III, having undertaken to remain detached from politics.

On 30 April 1991 Lekhanya was deposed in a coup organized by disaffected army officers. Col (later Maj.-Gen.) Elias Phitsoane Ramaema succeeded Lekhanya as Chairman of the Military Council. Ramaema repealed the ban on party political activity, and by July the National Constituent Assembly had completed the draft Constitution. In May 1992 Lesotho and South Africa agreed to establish diplomatic relations at ambassadorial level. Following talks in the UK with Ramaema, former King Moshoeshoe returned from exile in July.

The general election was eventually held in March 1993. The BCP secured all 65 seats in the new National Assembly, winning 54% of the votes cast. In April Mokhehle was inaugurated as Prime Minister, and King Letsie swore allegiance to the new Constitution, under the terms of which he remained Head of State with no executive or legislative powers; executive authority was vested in the Cabinet.

Suspension of constitutional government

A mutiny by the Royal Lesotho Defence Force (RLDF) took place in November 1993 following which four senior army officers were reported to have resigned their posts. Skirmishes near Maseru in

January 1994 escalated into more serious fighting between some 600 rebel troops and a 150-strong contingent of forces loyal to the Government, reportedly resulting in the deaths of at least five soldiers and three civilians. Following mediation efforts involving representatives of Botswana, South Africa, Zimbabwe, the Commonwealth (see p. 234), the Organization of African Unity (OAU, now the African Union—AU, see p. 188) and the UN, a truce entered into force, and at the beginning of February the rival factions surrendered their weapons and returned to barracks. In April, however, the Deputy Prime Minister, Selometsi Baholo, was killed during an abduction attempt by disaffected troops.

On 17 August 1994 Letsie announced that he had dissolved the National Assembly, dismissed the Government and suspended sections of the Constitution, citing 'popular dissatisfaction' with the BCP administration. Although several thousand people gathered outside the royal palace in Maseru in support of the deposed Government, army and police support for Letsie's 'royal coup' was evident, and subsequent clashes between demonstrators and the security forces reportedly resulted in five deaths. A well-known human rights lawyer, Hae Phoofolo, was appointed Chairman of a transitional Council of Ministers. Phoofolo identified as a priority for his administration the amendment of the Constitution to facilitate the restoration of Moshoeshoe; in the mean time, King Letsie was to act as executive and legislative Head of State.

The suspension of constitutional government was widely condemned outside Lesotho. The Presidents of Botswana, South Africa and Zimbabwe led diplomatic efforts to restore the elected Government, supported by the OAU and the Commonwealth. The USA withdrew financial assistance, and several other countries threatened sanctions. Following negotiations in South Africa, in September 1994 King Letsie and Mokhehle signed an agreement, guaranteed by Botswana, South Africa and Zimbabwe, providing for the restoration of Moshoeshoe II as reigning monarch and for the restitution of the elected organs of government; all those involved in the 'royal coup' were to be immune from prosecution; the political neutrality of the armed forces and public service was to be guaranteed, and consultations were to be undertaken with the aim of broadening the democratic process. Moshoeshoe was restored to the throne on 25 January 1995, undertaking not to interfere in politics. Letsie took the title of Crown Prince.

King Moshoeshoe was killed in a motor accident on 15 January 1996. The College of Chiefs subsequently elected Crown Prince David to succeed his father, and the prince was restored to the throne, resuming the title King Letsie III, on 7 February. Letsie undertook not to involve the monarchy in any aspect of political life.

In June 1997, following a protracted struggle between rival factions for control of the party, Mokhehle resigned from the BCP and formed the Lesotho Congress for Democracy (LCD), to which he transferred executive power. Some 38 members of the National Assembly joined the LCD. At the first annual conference of the LCD, held in January 1998, Mokhehle resigned as leader, and was made Honorary Life President of the party. In February Deputy Prime Minister Bethuel Pakalitha Mosisili was elected to succeed him as party leader. (Mokhehle died in January 1999.)

Elections to an expanded National Assembly took place on 23 May 1998, at which the LCD won 78 of the Assembly's 80 seats; the BNP was the only other party to win representation. The Independent Electoral Commission (IEC) and observers representing the Southern African Development Community (SADC, see p. 420) concluded that the polls had been generally free and fair. Mosisili was elected Prime Minister by the National Assembly in late May, and a new Government was appointed in June.

In August 1998 opposition activists began a mass vigil outside the royal palace to protest against the outcome of the May elections. Tensions escalated as LCD militants blocked access roads to the capital, in a stated attempt to prevent supplies of weapons reaching the protesters. Following consultations involving the Lesotho Government and the main opposition parties, with mediation by the Government of South Africa, Mosisili announced the establishment of an independent commission, comprising representatives of the SADC 'troika' of Botswana, South Africa and Zimbabwe, to investigate the conduct and results of the May election.

SADC intervention

The commission's report, which was released on 17 September 1998, expressed serious concerns at apparent irregularities and discrepancies in the conduct of the May general election, but the commission was 'unable to state that the invalidity of the elections had been conclusively established'. On 22 September an SADC peacekeeping force, initially comprising 600 South African troops and 200 from Botswana, entered Lesotho. In response to criticism that he had not consulted King Letsie prior to requesting external military assistance, Mosisili stated that the monarch had, by harbouring opposition protesters in the palace grounds, contributed to the instability that had necessitated SADC intervention. Within Lesotho, there was widespread outrage at what was perceived as an effective 'invasion' by South Africa, and the SADC force encountered unexpectedly strong resistance. There was sustained fighting between the intervention force and rebel units of the Lesotho Defence Force (LDF, as the RLDF had been redesignated), while rioting in Maseru and other towns targeted, in particular, South African interests and caused widespread destruction.

Following meetings with representatives of the SADC 'troika', in October 1998 it was reported that the LCD and the main opposition parties had agreed in principle that fresh elections should be held within 15–18 months. In the mean time the IEC was to be restructured, and the electoral system was to be reviewed, with the aim of ensuring wider inclusion in political affairs (many parties felt that the simple majority voting system was incompatible with the nature of Lesotho's political evolution). Agreement was also reached on a transitional structure, designated the Interim Political Authority (IPA), to comprise representatives of 12 political parties, as well as government and parliamentary delegates, to oversee preparations for fresh elections.

The withdrawal of the SADC intervention force was completed in May 1999. This force was immediately succeeded by a new SADC mission, comprising some 300 military personnel from South Africa, Botswana and (subsequently) Zimbabwe, which remained until May 2000, assisting in the retraining and restructuring of the LDF.

Meanwhile, the 24-member IPA was inaugurated on 9 December 1998. After protracted consultations, it was announced that the number of seats in the National Assembly was to be increased by 50, to 130, effective from the elections scheduled for April 2000, with 80 seats to be allocated on the basis of simple majority in single-member constituencies, and 50 by proportional representation. In the mean time, the Presidents of South Africa, Botswana, Mozambique and Zimbabwe, together with the UN, the OAU and the Commonwealth Secretaries-General, were to act as guarantors to ensure the implementation of the accord. The elections were subsequently postponed due to delays in enacting legislation concerning voter registration and the electoral model.

In April 2000 the establishment of a commission of inquiry to investigate political events during July–November 1998 was announced. In August three LDF members were convicted by a court martial of participation in the mutiny of September 1998 and sentenced to a combined 29 years' imprisonment; a further 33 LDF members were convicted in November. The commission of inquiry, which submitted its report to Prime Minister Mosisili in October 2001, rejected demands for a general amnesty to be granted to perpetrators of violence during the period under review, recommending the indictment of a number of opposition politicians and members of the armed forces.

In January 2001 a congress of the LCD re-elected Mosisili as party leader. Deputy Prime Minister Kelebone Maope resigned from the Government in September and broke away from the LCD, together with Shakhane Mokhehle, to form a new opposition party, the Lesotho People's Congress (LPC), to prepare for forthcoming elections. By mid-October a total of 27 deputies had defected from the LCD to join the LPC.

In January 2002 Parliament finally approved amendments to the electoral legislation, providing for the expansion of the National Assembly to 120 members, with 80 to be elected on a constituency basis and 40 selected by proportional representation.

The LCD won a resounding victory at the general election, which took place on 25 May 2002, retaining 77 of the 78 contested constituency seats, with 54.9% of the valid votes cast. The BNP became the second largest legislative party, securing 21 of the 40 seats allocated by proportional representation (known as compensatory seats), with 22.4% of the votes cast; the LPC won one constituency seat and four compensatory seats. Voting in two constituencies was postponed, owing to the deaths of candidates. Of the remaining 15 compensatory seats, the National Independent Party (NIP) secured five, the Basutoland African Congress (BAC) and the BCP both won three, while four smaller parties each took one seat. Mosisili was re-elected Prime Minister by the National Assembly in early June and a new Cabinet was subsequently appointed.

Political realignments and a new ruling party

In late January 2006 Khauhelo Raditapole and Kelebone Maope, the leaders of the BAC and the LPC, respectively, announced that their parties would form an alliance, following appeals by the BCP for reconciliation between political parties. Legislative elections took place on 17 February 2007, at which the LCD retained its parliamentary majority, although the party's total number of seats in the National Assembly was reduced from 77 to 61. The NIP took 21 of the 40 compensatory seats, thus becoming the second largest legislative party, while the All Basotho Convention (ABC) secured 17 constituency seats and the Lesotho Workers' Party (LWP) 10 compensatory seats. The Alliance of Congress Parties and five other parties each secured one compensatory seat. Observers from SADC and the AU declared the elections to have been free and fair. It emerged that an alliance had formed between the LCD and the NIP and that the NIP had fielded candidates from the LCD at the elections, giving the coalition a total of 82 seats in the National Assembly; a similar arrangement was made between the ABC and the LWP, resulting in that alliance securing 27 seats in total. Mosisili was reappointed Prime Minister later that month and in early March a new Cabinet was sworn in.

In April 2009 Mosisili's residence was attacked by 16 gunmen in an apparent assassination attempt. Four of the attackers were reported to have been killed and a number of individuals suspected of involvement in the incident were detained in South Africa; the Prime Minister escaped unharmed. Makotoko Lerotholi, who was suspected of organizing the attack, died of an illness while in custody in South Africa.

In an attempt to resolve the long-standing dispute over the distribution of compensatory seats following the 2007 elections (opposition parties had argued that the allocation of these seats to the LCD-NIP alliance had been unfair), in February 2010 SADC requested that a 'road map' be drawn up to address the main points of disagreement among the country's political organizations and to examine the possibility of modifying the Constitution and the legislation governing elections. A further meeting was held by SADC in April 2011 to discuss the issue of allocation of seats. On this occasion an agreement to amend the electoral law was reached between the Government, political parties and the IEC.

Opposition threats to boycott the May 2010 local elections—in protest against, *inter alia*, proposed 'affirmative action' laws (which had been criticized for being too heavily weighted in favour of female candidates), constituency boundaries and the unreformed simple majority electoral system still employed in local ballots—led Parliament in April to postpone the vote until 2011. The decision to suspend the elections received cross-party support and was intended to facilitate the parliamentary approval of amendments to the existing legislation regulating local elections. The IEC implemented a restructuring of constituency boundaries in July 2010, although the leader of the ABC, Thomas Thabane, argued that the alterations would benefit the LCD. The local elections took place in late 2011, with the LCD gaining control of 691 of the 1,276 council seats and 79 of the 87 councils.

Meanwhile, Mosisili effected a cabinet reorganization in October 2010. The ministers responsible for trade, tourism, agriculture and employment—all of whom were believed to be members of an influential faction within the LCD reportedly led by Mothetjoa Metsing, the Minister of Communications, Science and Technology—were replaced by close associates of the Prime Minister. Following the reorganization, supporters of the dismissed ministers besieged the LCD's headquarters in protest and accused Monyane Moleleki, the Minister of Natural Resources and alleged leader of a rival wing of the LCD, of pressuring Mosisili to remove Metsing's allies from the Cabinet. The discord within the ruling party was confirmed in November, when Mosisili publicly criticized the 'hatred and divisions' afflicting the LCD. Infighting was also evident within the opposition parties during 2010. The fragile ABC-LWP alliance ended in July due to continued disagreements between the leaders of the respective parties, precipitating a dispute over control of the

compensatory seats allocated to the now-defunct coalition after the 2007 elections.

Following continued factional infighting and a series of disagreements with the national executive committee of the LCD, Mosisili left the ruling party in February 2012, but remained Prime Minister. The previous month he had dismissed Metsing, along with two junior members of the Government. Mosisili subsequently announced the formation of a new political party, the Democratic Congress (DC), which secured the support of 44 deputies, sufficient to give it a slight majority and move the LCD into opposition.

Coalition Government

In legislative elections held on 26 May 2012 the DC secured 39.6% of the votes cast and the largest number of seats in the National Assembly (of which 41 were constituency seats and seven compensatory seats). The ABC, under the leadership of Thabane, won 25.2% of the votes cast (26 constituency and 4 compensatory seats), while the LCD, under the leadership of Metsing, won 22.0% (12 constituency and 14 compensatory seats). The BNP, the Popular Front for Democracy (PFD) and the NIP secured five, three and two total seats, respectively. Despite the DC winning more votes and securing more seats than any other single party, the ABC and LCD formed a coalition Government (the first in Lesotho's history) following the DC's failure to win an absolute majority; erstwhile Prime Minister Mosisili accepted defeat after failing to form a coalition of his own. The BNP, PFD and the Marematlou Freedom Party (MFP) also joined the coalition. On 7 June King Letsie named Thabane as Prime Minister; Thabane also assumed the role of Minister of Defence, Police and National Security. Later that month Thabane named his new Cabinet, in which Metsing was appointed Deputy Prime Minister, while Dr Leketekete Victor Ketso (of the LCD) took over the finance portfolio and Tlali Khasu (of the ABC) was named Minister of Mining. BNP leader Thesele 'Maseribane, who had been at the forefront of anti-Government riots following Mosisili's election victory in 1998, was named Minister of Gender, Youth, Sports and Recreation.

Relations within the coalition appeared to be tense during 2013. A number of interparty disagreements had been made public, most notably concerning diplomatic appointments and the administration of the LHWP. Discord between the Government and the judiciary was also evident during that year. An acrimonious seniority dispute between Chief Justice Mahapela Lehohla and the President of the Court of Appeal, Mathealira Ramodibedi, prompted Thabane to request the resignation of both judges. While Lehohla agreed to relinquish his post, Ramodibedi refused, accusing the Prime Minister of acting in violation of the Constitution. Impeachment proceedings were instituted against Ramodibedi, who responded by lodging an appeal. However, the Court of Appeal ruled against Ramodibedi in April 2014, and he tendered his resignation later that month.

Thabane controversially prorogued Parliament for nine months in June 2014 in an apparent attempt to prevent a DC-led vote of no confidence in his premiership from being conducted. Shortly thereafter, Metsing declared that the LCD was planning to withdraw from the coalition Government owing to frustration within the party over Thabane's unilateral decision-making (including his decision to suspend Parliament). The LCD, furthermore, concluded a preliminary agreement with the DC on the formation of a new coalition administration, although the ABC claimed that such a move would not be possible while Parliament was prorogued. With the Government on the verge of collapse and rumours circulating in the capital of an imminent military coup, the ABC, the LCD and the BNP held a series of crisis talks in an effort to resolve their differences. In late July, following SADC mediation, the three parties signed the Windhoek Declaration in Namibia, reaffirming their commitment to the governing coalition. According to the terms of the accord, the LCD would abandon its agreement with the DC, while Thabane would move to end the prorogation of Parliament. However, the Prime Minister appeared reluctant to uphold this pledge, and by late August Parliament remained suspended, prompting criticism from the LCD and the opposition.

Recent developments: alleged coup attempt and early elections

On 29 August 2014 Thabane attempted to remove LDF Commander Lt-Gen. Tlali Kamoli from his post, replacing him with Lt-Gen. Maaparankoe Mahao. However, on the following day Thabane was forced to flee to South Africa after the LDF, allegedly at Kamoli's behest, seized control of police stations in Maseru and besieged the Prime Minister's official residence. Thabane denounced the military action as a coup, although the LDF rejected this assertion, claiming that it had acted in response to the machinations of rogue police officers who were conspiring to supply weapons to an unnamed political group. The Prime Minister accused Metsing and his allies in the military of organizing the unrest, a charge that was dismissed by the LCD. On 31 August Mahao's home came under attack during an apparent assassination attempt.

SADC brokered a reconciliation deal in early September 2014 that involved Thabane's return to Lesotho and the recall of Parliament; the regional body also agreed to deploy an observation mission in the kingdom. Thabane, under South African police protection, arrived back in Lesotho on 3 September. However, the Prime Minister again appeared reluctant to reconvene Parliament as it was expected to precipitate the adoption of a motion of no confidence and the dissolution of his Government. In an effort to end the political deadlock, in mid-September further SADC-mediated talks between the coalition leaders were held, which resulted in an agreement on the organization of early elections. (It was subsequently determined that the general election would be moved from 2017 to February 2015.) Also in mid-September 2014, the police force, which was believed to be aligned with Thabane, initiated an investigation into Kamoli and the alleged coup. Violent clashes between the armed forces and police officers were reported on several occasions during September.

Parliament was finally recalled on 17 October 2014 after parties had pledged to refrain from tabling a no-confidence motion. Moreover, under SADC pressure, Kamoli, Mahao and Police Commissioner Khothatso Tsooana (a Thabane loyalist) agreed to step down from their respective positions and to leave the country during the pre-election period in order to ease institutional tensions. The three men pledged to end hostilities between the military and the police. Nevertheless, the security situation remained unstable, and the subsequently appointed interim Commander of the LDF, Khoantle Motsomotso, repeatedly challenged Thabane's authority. Another alleged coup plot, purportedly involving the recruitment of West African mercenaries to assassinate Thabane, was uncovered in November. Meanwhile, in early February 2015 two of the Prime Minister's bodyguards were seriously wounded after exchanging gunfire with soldiers in the capital.

Military personnel were confined to their barracks during the run-up to the general election, and voting took place peacefully on 28 February 2015. Mosisili's DC won 37 of the 80 constituency seats in the National Assembly and 10 of the 40 compensatory seats, while the ABC secured 40 seats and six seats, respectively. The LCD gained control of 12 seats (including 10 compensatory seats) and the BNP garnered seven seats (six compensatory). The remaining eight compensatory seats were distributed among the BCP, the LPC, the MFP, the NIP, the PFD and the Reformed Congress of Lesotho. The results were endorsed by monitors from SADC, the AU and the Commonwealth.

To ensure a legislative majority, the DC agreed to form a coalition government with the LCD, the BCP, the LPC, the MFP, the NIP and the PFD. Mosisili was inaugurated as Prime Minister on 17 March 2015, and a new Cabinet was installed on 31 March. Metsing again became Deputy Prime Minister, despite being the subject of an ongoing corruption investigation. Lekhetho Rakuoane was designated as Minister of Home Affairs, Moeketse Malebo received the justice portfolio, 'Mamphono Khaketla was named Minister of Finance, and Tšeliso Mokhosi was given responsibility for defence and national security. Moleleki, who had been charged with multiple counts of corruption, was controversially appointed as Minister of Police and Public Safety.

Foreign Affairs

As exemplified by South Africa's prominent role in the resolution of the 1994 constitutional crisis and by its intervention in the political crises of September 1998 and August–September 2014, Lesotho's internal affairs continue to be strongly influenced by its larger neighbour. Long-standing problems of border security and, in particular, the issue of disputed land in South Africa's Free State (formerly Orange Free State) have periodically caused friction between the two countries. During a visit to Lesotho by President Thabo Mbeki of South Africa in April 2001, it was agreed to replace an intergovernmental liaison committee that had been established following SADC intervention in 1998 (see above) with a joint binational commission at ministerial level, with the aim of enhancing bilateral relations. Relations between Lesotho and South Africa were further enhanced in May 2002, when their respective ministers of foreign affairs signed the Joint Bilateral Commission of Co-operation programme, which aimed to raise Lesotho from its current status as a 'least developed country'.

CONSTITUTION AND GOVERNMENT

Lesotho is an hereditary monarchy. Under the terms of the Constitution, which came into effect following the March 1993 election, the King, who is Head of State, has no executive or legislative powers. The College of Chiefs is theoretically empowered, under traditional law, to elect and depose the King by a majority vote. Executive power is vested in the Cabinet, which is headed by the Prime Minister. Legislative power is exercised by the National Assembly, which is elected, at intervals of no more than five years, by universal adult suffrage in the context of a multi-party political system. A system of mixed-member proportional representation was introduced at the general election of May 2002, when the National Assembly was expanded to 120 members (80 elected by simple majority in single-member constituencies and 40 selected from party lists). The upper house, the Senate, comprises traditional chiefs and 11 nominated members. Lesotho comprises 10 administrative districts, each with an appointed district co-ordinator.

REGIONAL AND INTERNATIONAL CO-OPERATION

Lesotho is a member of the Common Monetary Area (with Namibia, South Africa and Swaziland), and a member of the Southern African Customs Union (SACU—with Botswana, Namibia, South Africa and Swaziland). Lesotho also belongs to the Southern African Development Community (SADC, see p. 420) and the African Union (see p. 188).

Lesotho became a member of the UN in 1966 and was admitted to the World Trade Organization (WTO, see p. 431) in 1995.

ECONOMIC AFFAIRS

In 2013, according to estimates by the World Bank, Lesotho's gross national income (GNI), measured at average 2011–13 prices, was US $3,211m., equivalent to $1,550 per head (or $3,320 per head on an international purchasing-power parity basis). During 2004–13, it was estimated, the population increased at an average annual rate of 0.9%, while gross domestic product (GDP) per head increased, in real terms, by an average of 3.8% per year. Overall GDP increased, in real terms, at an average annual rate of 4.8% in 2004–13; growth in 2013 was 5.9%.

Agriculture, forestry and fishing contributed 8.5% of GDP in 2013, according to official figures. The sector engaged some 37.4% of the labour force in mid-2015, according to FAO estimates. The principal agricultural export is tobacco. The main subsistence crops are maize, potatoes, sorghum and wheat. Lesotho remains a net importer of staple foodstuffs, largely owing to its vulnerability to adverse climatic conditions, especially drought. According to the World Food Programme, less than 10% of land is arable and there is no irrigation. It was reported in 2011 that the International Fund for Agriculture Development would provide US $10m. to farmers in four of Lesotho's districts in order to help increase agricultural production. Some 15,000 households were expected to benefit from the provision. According to official figures, during 2004–13 agricultural GDP increased at an average annual rate of 2.1%; the sector's GDP declined by 8.6% in 2012, but grew by 17.1% in 2013.

Industry (including mining, manufacturing, construction and power) provided 29.3% of GDP in 2013, according to official figures. The sector engaged 9.3% of the labour force in 1999. During 2004–13 industrial GDP increased by an average annual rate of 4.2% per year. Industrial GDP increased by 0.3% in 2013.

Mining contributed 4.8% of GDP in 2013, according to official figures. Lesotho has reserves of diamonds, which during the late 1970s provided more than 50% of visible export earnings, but large-scale exploitation of these ceased in 1982. The Lets'eng-la-Terae diamond mine reopened in April 2004, and by the time of its official inauguration in November, gems with an estimated value of US $28m. had been recovered. Industrial mining at other sites was also envisaged, including a second diamond mine at Liqhobong. Lesotho also possesses deposits of uranium, lead and iron ore, and is believed to have petroleum deposits. According to official figures, the GDP of the mining sector increased by an average of 28.2% per year in 2004–13; the GDP of the sector increased by 22.6% in 2012, but decreased by 5.3% in 2013.

Manufacturing contributed 10.7% of GDP in 2013, according to official figures. The sector employed 3.5% of the total labour force in 1999. During 2004–13 manufacturing GDP declined by an average of 2.3% per year; it decreased by 10.1% in 2013.

According to official figures, the construction sector contributed 9.4% of GDP in 2013. The sector engaged 4.8% of the employed labour force in 1999. During 2004–13 construction GDP increased by an average of 12.1% per year; the GDP of the sector increased by 21.5% in 2013.

The Lesotho Highlands Water Project (LHWP) provides hydroelectricity sufficient for all Lesotho's needs and for export to South Africa; phases 1A and 1B were inaugurated in 1998 and 2004, respectively. In late September 2005 an agreement was signed for a feasibility study concerning the location of the second phase of the project. The scheme was expected to be completed by about 2030. The R200m. (US $30m.) that Lesotho receives annually in royalties from South Africa for the LHWP represents the country's largest single source of foreign exchange. Prior to the LHWP more than 90% of Lesotho's energy requirements were imported from South Africa. Imports of mineral fuels and lubricants comprised 0.6% of the total value of imports in 2008. In October 2011 it was announced that the country would embark on a large-scale wind and hydroelectric power project—the largest in Africa—in the Maluti mountains, at a cost of some $15,000m. The Lesotho Highlands Power Project (LHPP), 80% of the cost of which was to be financed with loans from China, was expected to generate some 10,000 MW of energy on completion.

The services sector contributed 62.2% of GDP in 2013, according to official figures. Only 18.3% of the labour force was employed in the services sector in 1999. During 2004–13 the GDP of the services sector increased at an average annual rate of 5.0%; growth was 6.4% in 2013.

In 2013 Lesotho recorded a visible merchandise trade deficit of US $1,037.2m., and there was a deficit of $77.3m. on the current account of the balance of payments. In 2012 the principal source of imports (89.1%) was South Africa, which was also the largest market for exports (47.4%). The USA was also a major purchaser. The principal exports in 2012 were textiles, machinery and electrical equipment, and beverages and tobacco. The principal imports in 2012 were textiles, mineral products, machinery and electrical equipment food, beverages, and tobacco, chemicals, plastic products, vehicles, and vegetable products.

In the financial year ending 31 March 2014 there was an estimated budgetary surplus of M3,010m. Lesotho's general government gross debt was M9,639m. in 2013, equivalent to 42.7% of GDP. Lesotho's external debt totalled US $860m. at the end of 2012, of which $745m. was public and publicly guaranteed debt. In 2012, the cost of servicing long-term public and publicly

guaranteed debt and repayments to the IMF was equivalent to 2.3% of the value of exports of goods, services and income (excluding workers' remittances). According to ILO figures, the annual rate of inflation averaged 6.1% in 2004–13; consumer prices increased by 4.9% in 2013. In 1999 231,742 people were registered as unemployed, equivalent to 27.3% of the labour force. In 2006 51,595 Basotho were employed as miners in South Africa, compared with 129,000 in 1989. The number was expected to continue to decrease in the coming years. According to the Central Bank of Lesotho, in 2004 Basotho miners' remittances amounted to M1,795.0m. and accounted for more than 70% of total earnings during the period 1997–2004. South African officials estimated that around 300,000 Basotho were employed in South Africa at any given time.

Impediments to economic development in Lesotho include vulnerability to drought and serious land shortages, combined with the country's dependence on South Africa (the Lesotho currency, the loti, is fixed at par with the South African rand, exposing Lesotho to fluctuations within the South African economy). Political instability has also hindered growth. The textile industry benefited considerably from the USA's African Growth and Opportunities Act (AGOA), for which Lesotho was first declared eligible in April 2001. However, faced with increasing competition from producers in Asia and the global financial crisis in late 2008 and early 2009, the industry suffered through job losses, factory closures and reduced production levels. Declining SACU revenues, which provided up to 60% of the country's annual income, and a proposed restructuring of SACU tariffs presented additional challenges for the Lesotho authorities. None the less, real GDP growth has remained relatively robust as a result of increased mining investment (and strong demand internationally for diamonds in particular) and ongoing public infrastructure projects. Growth was estimated at 5.7% in 2013 and 4.3% in 2014, according to the IMF, and was forecast to reach 4.7% in 2015. The medium-term outlook appeared favourable, with the LHPP expected to provide a major stimulus for the economy. There remain concerns, however, regarding the high levels of unemployment and poverty, particularly in rural areas with the latter, while the country also continues to register poor health and social indicators.

PUBLIC HOLIDAYS

2016: 1 January (New Year's Day), 11 March (Moshoeshoe Day), 25–28 March (Easter), 1 May (Workers' Day), 5 May (Ascension Day), 25 May (Africa Day and Heroes' Day), 17 July (King's Birthday), 4 October (National Independence Day), 25 December (Christmas Day), 26 December (Boxing Day).

Statistical Survey

Sources (unless otherwise stated): Bureau of Statistics, POB 455, Maseru 100; tel. 22323852; fax 22310177; internet www.bos.gov.ls; Central Bank of Lesotho, POB 1184, Maseru 100; tel. 22314281; fax 22310051; e-mail cbl@centralbank.org.ls; internet www.centralbank.org.ls.

Area and Population

AREA, POPULATION AND DENSITY

Area (sq km)	30,355*
Population (*de jure* census results)	
14 April 1996	1,862,275
9 April 2006	
Males	912,798
Females	963,835
Total	1,876,633
Population (UN estimates at mid-year)†	
2013	2,074,466
2014	2,097,513
2015	2,120,116
Density (per sq km) at mid-2015	69.8

* 11,720 sq miles.
† Source: UN, *World Population Prospects: The 2012 Revision*.

2011 (*de jure* population, Lesotho Demographic Survey): 1,894,194 (males 934,357, females 959,837).

POPULATION BY AGE AND SEX
(UN estimates at mid-2015)

	Males	Females	Total
0–14 years	380,603	374,650	755,253
15–64 years	634,303	642,121	1,276,424
65 years and over	34,361	54,078	88,439
Total	1,049,267	1,070,849	2,120,116

Source: UN, *World Population Prospects: The 2012 Revision*.

DISTRICTS
(Lesotho Demographic Survey results, population at 2011)

District	Area (sq km)	Population	Density (per sq km)
Berea	2,222	273,832	123.2
Butha-Buthe	1,767	105,403	59.7
Leribe	2,828	331,117	117.1
Mafeteng	2,119	183,507	86.6
Maseru	4,279	389,627	91.1
Mohale's Hoek	3,530	181,196	51.3
Mokhotlong	4,075	105,538	25.9
Qacha's Nek	2,349	63,910	27.2
Quthing	2,916	129,533	44.4
Thaba-Tseka	4,270	130,532	30.6
Total	30,355	1,894,194	62.4

Principal Town (including suburbs, population at mid-2014, UN estimate): Maseru (the capital) 266,580 (Source: UN, *World Urbanization Prospects: The 2014 Revision*).

BIRTHS AND DEATHS
(annual averages, UN estimates)

	2000–05	2005–10	2010–15
Birth rate (per 1,000)	29.8	28.2	25.5
Death rate (per 1,000)	18.8	17.3	14.8

Source: UN, *World Population Prospects: The 2012 Revision*.

Life expectancy (years at birth): 48.8 (males 48.6; females 49.0) in 2012 (Source: World Bank, World Development Indicators database).

ECONOMICALLY ACTIVE POPULATION
(household survey, persons aged 10 years and over, 1999)

	Males	Females	Total
Agriculture	270,919	175,760	446,679
Fishing	125	—	125
Mining and quarrying	2,392	611	3,003
Manufacturing	7,957	13,839	21,795
Electricity, gas and water supply	1,722	1,541	3,263
Construction	18,947	10,548	29,495
Wholesale and retail trade; repair of motor vehicles, motorcycles and household goods	11,099	17,915	29,014
Hotels and restaurants	918	3,529	4,447
Transport, storage and communications	9,307	1,363	10,670
Financial intermediation	1,041	810	1,851
Real estate, renting and business activities	3,405	2,032	5,437
Public administration and defence; compulsory social security	5,181	2,395	7,576
Education	5,125	8,099	13,224
Health and social work	2,070	2,895	4,965
Other community, social and personal service activities	1,765	7,686	9,451
Households with employed persons	4,474	21,970	26,444
Extraterritorial organizations and bodies	126	—	126
Total employed	346,573	270,993	617,566
Unemployed	90,964	140,778	231,742
Total labour force	437,537	411,771	849,308

Source: ILO.

2008 (labour force survey, persons aged 15 years and over): Subsistence agriculture 247,258; Government and parastatals 43,762; Private sector 182,868; Private households 135,263; *Total employed* 609,152; Unemployed 179,390; *Total labour force* 788,541.

2011 (Lesotho Demographic Survey, persons aged 10 years and over): Total employed 536,529; Unemployed 49,757; *Total labour force* 586,286. Note: A further 895,366 persons aged 10 years and over were recorded as not economically active.

Mid-2015 (estimates in '000): Agriculture, etc. 350; Total labour force 935 (Source: FAO).

Health and Welfare

KEY INDICATORS

Total fertility rate (children per woman, 2012)	3.1
Under-5 mortality rate (per 1,000 live births, 2012)	100
HIV/AIDS (% of persons aged 15–49, 2013)	22.9
Physicians (per 1,000 head, 2003)	0.05
Hospital beds (per 1,000 head, 2006)	1.30
Health expenditure (2011): US $ per head (PPP)	219
Health expenditure (2011): % of GDP	11.7
Health expenditure (2011): public (% of total)	77.5
Access to water (% of persons, 2012)	81
Access to sanitation (% of persons, 2012)	30
Total carbon dioxide emissions ('000 metric tons, 2010)	18.3
Carbon dioxide emissions per head (metric tons, 2010)	<0.1
Human Development Index (2013): ranking	162
Human Development Index (2013): value	0.486

For sources and definitions, see explanatory note on p. vi.

Agriculture

PRINCIPAL CROPS
('000 metric tons)

	2011	2012	2013
Wheat	20.1	10.5	13.0*
Maize	73.4	16.8	86.0*
Sorghum	9.6	1.9	7.0*
Potatoes†	112.0	115.0	125.0
Beans, dry	7.1	8.0†	8.0†
Peas, dry	0.7	0.9†	1.0†
Vegetables†	30	29	29

* Unofficial figure.
† FAO estimate(s).
Source: FAO.

LIVESTOCK
('000 head, year ending September, FAO estimates)

	2011	2012	2013
Cattle	635	650	665
Sheep	1,215	1,220	1,230
Goats	845	835	850
Pigs	80	80	81
Horses	69	69	70
Asses	132	128	130
Chickens	485	500	500

Source: FAO.

LIVESTOCK PRODUCTS
('000 metric tons, FAO estimates)

	2011	2012	2013
Cattle meat	12.5	12.6	13.5
Cows' milk	39.2	39.3	39.3
Pig meat	3.6	3.7	3.7
Chicken meat	1.6	1.6	1.6
Game meat	5.2	5.2	5.2
Hen eggs	1.7	1.7	1.7
Wool, greasy	4.0	4.0	4.0

Source: FAO.

Forestry

ROUNDWOOD REMOVALS
('000 cubic metres, excluding bark, FAO estimates)

	2011	2012	2013
Total (all fuel wood)	2,099.7	2,107.6	2,115.6

Source: FAO.

Fishing

(metric tons, live weight)

	2010	2011	2012
Capture	45	45	50
Common carp	15	15	19
North African catfish . . .	5	5	6
Other freshwater fishes . . .	25	25	25
Aquaculture	300	300	400
Rainbow trout	300	300	400
Total catch	345	345	450

Source: FAO.

Mining

(cubic metres unless otherwise indicated)

	2010	2011	2012
Fire clay*	14,000	12,000	15,000
Diamond (carats)	100,000*	100,000*	478,926
Gravel and crushed rock* . . .	300,000	n.a.	n.a.

* Estimated production.

Source: US Geological Survey.

Finance

CURRENCY AND EXCHANGE RATES

Monetary Units
100 lisente (singular: sente) = 1 loti (plural: maloti).

Sterling, Dollar and Euro Equivalents (31 December 2014)
£1 sterling = 18.076 maloti;
US $1 = 11.581 maloti;
€1 = 14.060 maloti;
100 maloti = £5.53 = $8.63 = €7.11.

Average Exchange Rate (maloti per US $)
2012   8.2100
2013   9.6551
2014   10.8527

Note: The loti is fixed at par with the South African rand.

BUDGET
(million maloti, year ending 31 March)

Revenue*	2011/12	2012/13†	2013/14‡
Tax revenue	4,283	4,595	4,996
Taxes on net income and profits	2,395	2,349	2,680
Taxes on property	125	150	196
Taxes on goods and services .	1,590	1,819	1,882
Taxes on international trade .	151	277	235
Other taxes	22	—	3
Non-tax revenue	1,143	885	1,031
Property income	419	109	142
Sales of goods and services .	692	772	886
Other non-tax revenue . . .	32	4	2
SACU	2,753	5,966	6,055
Total	8,179	11,446	12,081

Expenditure and net lending	2011/12	2012/13†	2013/14‡
Compensation of employees . .	3,638	3,749	4,492
Wages and salaries	3,136	3,226	3,855
Goods and services	2,177	2,357	2,825
Subsidies	237	253	235
Interest payments	137	166	232
Grants	960	882	898
Social benefits	587	611	817
Other expenditures	943	747	771
Total	8,680	8,764	10,269

* Excluding grants received (million maloti): 1,437 in 2011/12; 1,703 in 2012/13 (estimate); 1,198 in 2013/14 (preliminary).
† Estimates.
‡ Preliminary.

Source: IMF, *2014 Article IV Consultation—Staff Report; Press Release; and Statement by the Executive Director for the Kingdom of Lesotho* (July 2014).

INTERNATIONAL RESERVES
(excl. gold, US $ million at 31 December)

	2011	2012	2013
IMF special drawing rights . .	54.22	58.25	73.18
Reserve position in IMF . . .	5.55	5.71	5.85
Foreign exchange	859.32	963.95	976.20
Total	919.09	1,027.91	1,055.24

Source: IMF, *International Financial Statistics*.

MONEY SUPPLY
(million maloti at 31 December)

	2011	2012	2013
Currency outside depository corporations	688.70	769.05	953.33
Transferable deposits	2,132.83	2,707.35	3,034.88
Other deposits	3,858.58	3,672.43	4,673.40
Broad money	6,680.10	7,148.83	8,661.61

Source: IMF, *International Financial Statistics*.

COST OF LIVING
(Consumer Price Index; base: 2000 = 100)

	2011	2012	2013
Food, beverages and tobacco . .	193.7	212.7	224.2
All items (incl. others) . . .	207.6	220.4	231.3

Source: ILO.

NATIONAL ACCOUNTS
(million maloti at current prices)

Expenditure on the Gross Domestic Product

	2011	2012	2013
Government final consumption expenditure	6,310	7,361	7,526
Private final consumption expenditure	18,128	19,390	20,288
Changes in inventories	−522	−610	−446
Gross fixed capital formation	4,331	5,937	7,538
Total domestic expenditure	28,248	32,078	34,905
Exports of goods and services	8,864	8,597	8,761
Less Imports of goods and services	18,960	20,192	21,615
Statistical discrepancy	−91	−910	−1,363
GDP in purchasers' values	18,061	19,572	20,688

Gross Domestic Product by Economic Activity

	2011	2012	2013
Agriculture	1,314	1,300	1,571
Mining and quarrying	1,684	1,291	893
Manufacturing	1,916	1,981	1,983
Electricity, gas and water	787	842	824
Construction	913	1,352	1,750
Wholesale and retail trade, restaurants and hotels	1,529	1,830	2,053
Transport and communication	1,085	1,194	1,318
Finance, insurance, real estate and business services	3,018	3,310	3,704
Public administration and defence	1,789	1,999	1,845
Other services	2,284	2,461	2,634
Sub-total	16,319	17,560	18,575
Less Imputed bank service charge	304	293	315
Indirect taxes, less subsidies	2,047	2,306	2,427
GDP in purchasers' prices	18,061	19,572	20,688

BALANCE OF PAYMENTS
(US $ million)

	2011	2012	2013
Exports of goods	1,174.8	972.4	847.1
Imports of goods	−2,155.4	−2,254.1	−1,884.2
Balance on goods	−980.6	−1,281.8	−1,037.2
Exports of services	50.8	72.9	60.3
Imports of services	−477.5	−452.0	−374.8
Balance on goods and services	−1,407.3	−1,660.9	−1,351.7
Primary income received	727.1	617.7	539.8
Primary income paid	−394.9	−127.9	−94.2
Balance on goods, services and primary income	−1,075.1	−1,171.1	−906.0
Secondary income received	635.6	886.1	849.0
Secondary income paid	−21.0	−20.9	−20.2
Current balance	−460.5	−305.9	−77.3
Capital account (net)	188.0	195.6	112.2
Direct investment assets	−3.6	−20.2	−17.2
Direct investment from liabilities	200.3	73.7	44.9
Portfolio investment assets	0.1	−2.0	−1.7
Portfolio investment liabilities	31.4	—	—
Other investment assets	−34.0	111.9	−67.4
Other investment liabilities	48.7	63.9	106.2
Net errors and omissions	95.3	−6.2	111.8
Reserves and related items	65.7	110.8	211.6

Source: IMF, *International Financial Statistics*.

External Trade

PRINCIPAL COMMODITIES
(distribution by HS, US $ million)

Imports	2010	2011	2012
Live animals and animal products	55.9	76.8	67.7
Meat and edible meat offal	34.7	47.3	37.8
Vegetables and vegetable products	83.6	98.5	115.4
Prepared foodstuffs; beverages, spirits, vinegar; tobacco and articles thereof	128.1	161.1	140.0
Mineral products	165.6	218.6	210.2
Mineral fuels, oils, distillation products,	156.4	207.8	198.5
Petroleum oils, not crude	71.9	160.0	153.2
Chemicals and related products	118.2	130.9	129.0
Plastics, rubber, and articles thereof	54.9	69.2	121.5
Plastics and articles	44.6	57.5	106.7
Pulp of wood, paper and paperboard, and articles thereof	41.4	48.3	46.0
Textiles and textile articles	177.0	145.2	234.3
Cotton	45.2	48.8	75.7
Knitted or crocheted fabric	25.2	17.0	55.6
Iron and steel, other base metals and articles of base metal	55.4	68.7	79.9
Machinery and mechanical appliances; electrical equipment; parts thereof	181.3	158.1	181.8
Machinery and boilers, etc.	55.0	81.0	91.1
Electrical, electronic equipment	126.2	77.1	90.7
Vehicles, aircraft, vessels and associated transport equipment	86.5	93.2	119.1
Road vehicles	84.3	92.0	118.0
Total (incl. others)	1,354.4	1,475.4	1,621.4

Exports	2010	2011	2012
Vegetables and vegetable products	18.5	32.6	23.8
Milling products, malt, and starches,	17.4	31.6	23.1
Prepared foodstuffs; beverages, spirits, vinegar; tobacco and articles thereof	65.7	76.4	74.0
Beverages, spirits and vinegar	61.5	68.0	65.4
Mineral and aerated waters	61.4	67.9	65.3
Textiles and textile articles	229.7	502.9	444.5
Wool and fabrics thereof	20.1	21.0	37.1
Wool, not carded or combed	16.4	18.0	36.3
Cotton	20.0	36.6	24.1
Articles of apparel, accessories, knit or crochet	96.3	221.7	218.2
Women's suits, and dresses, knit or crochet	29.7	65.6	78.3
Men's shirts, knitted or crocheted	13.0	37.2	44.2
Men's suits, jackets, trousers	52.0	142.3	111.8

Exports—*continued*	2010	2011	2012
Women's suits, jackets, and dresses	24.9	55.1	33.4
Articles of apparel, accessories, not knit or crochet	86.3	217.8	163.8
Footwear, headgear, umbrellas, walking sticks .	35.9	38.0	29.6
Pearls, precious or semi-precious stones, precious metals, and articles thereof .	14.4	24.6	23.1
Diamonds	13.3	24.3	23.0
Machinery and mechanical appliances; electrical equipment; parts thereof .	134.7	101.0	79.4
Electrical, electronic equipment .	134.7	100.8	79.4
Television receivers	83.9	38.4	15.1
Electrical equipment parts . .	40.5	41.1	35.2
Total (incl. others)	509.4	787.3	686.5

Source: Trade Map-Trade Competitiveness Map, International Trade Centre, www.intracen.org/marketanalysis.

2013 (million maloti, preliminary): *Imports* Total 18,121. *Exports* Food and Live animals 266; Beverages and tobacco 667 (Beverages 665); Crude materials 2,321 (Diamonds 2,296); Manufactured goods 247; Machinery and transport equipment 903; Miscellaneous manufactured goods 3,755; Total exports (incl. re-exports) 8,181.

PRINCIPAL TRADING PARTNERS
(US $ million)

Imports c.i.f.	2010	2011	2012
China, People's Republic . . .	29.4	5.5	44.9
India	16.3	8.5	7.9
South Africa	1,101.2	1,426.0	1,444.0
Taiwan	57.9	3.7	75.0
USA	26.3	8.5	7.9
Total (incl. others)	1,354.4	1,475.4	1,621.4

Exports f.o.b.	2010	2011	2012
Belgium	—	23.6	21.9
Canada	8.0	45.3	5.9
South Africa	383.3	353.4	325.2
United Arab Emirates	—	5.5	11.2
USA	107.3	319.5	300.8
Total (incl. others)	509.4	787.3	686.5

Source: Trade Map-Trade Competitiveness Map, International Trade Centre, www.intracen.org/marketanalysis.

Exports (incl. re-exports) (million maloti, preliminary): 8,181.3 (European Union 2,819.7; North America 2,275.3; South African Customs Union 2,919.8) in 2013.

Transport

ROAD TRAFFIC
(motor vehicles in use at 31 December, estimates)

	1994	1995	1996
Passenger cars	9,900	11,160	12,610
Lorries and vans	20,790	22,310	25,000

Source: IRF, *World Road Statistics*.

CIVIL AVIATION
(traffic on scheduled services)

	1997	1998	1999
Kilometres flown (million) . .	0	1	0
Passengers carried ('000) . . .	10	28	1
Passenger-km (million) . . .	3	9	0
Total ton-km (million)	0	1	0

Source: UN, *Statistical Yearbook*.

2008 (domestic and international traffic): Flights 2,769; Arriving passengers 22,206; Departing passengers 19,453.

Tourism

FOREIGN TOURIST ARRIVALS BY COUNTRY OF RESIDENCE

	2011	2012	2013
Botswana	1,419	1,752	2,200
Germany	3,927	3,746	4,727
Netherlands	2,890	3,594	4,870
South Africa	393,645	394,336	397,696
Swaziland	875	1,071	1,332
United Kingdom	2,585	1,811	2,380
USA	2,578	2,222	2,679
Zimbabwe	2,619	3,551	3,785
Total (incl. others)	398,149	422,597	432,966

Tourism receipts (US $ million, excl. passenger transport): 25 in 2010; 29 in 2011; 46 in 2012.

Source: World Tourism Organization.

Communications Media

	2011	2012	2013
Telephones ('000 main lines in use)	38.6	50.8	57.7
Mobile cellular telephones ('000 subscribers)	1,232.4	1,544.8	1,790.3
Broadband subscribers . . .	1,339	1,451	2,275

Internet subscribers: 980 in 2010.

Source: International Telecommunication Union.

Education
(2011/12 unless otherwise indicated)

	Institutions	Teachers	Students Males	Students Females	Students Total
Pre-primary* .	n.a.	2,159	n.a.	n.a.	52,646
Primary . . .	1,455†	11,200	194,849	186,841	381,690
Secondary:					
general . .	240†	5,094	54,756	73,096	127,852
technical and vocational .	8‡	200§	526*	1,990*	2,516*
teacher training .	1‡	108‖	n.a.	n.a.	2,335¶
University . .	1‡	638†	3,810†	4,690†	8,500†

* 2009/10.
† 2005/06.
‡ 2002/03.
§ 2006/07.
‖ 2001/02.
¶ 2004/05.

Source: partly UNESCO Institute for Statistics.

Pupil-teacher ratio (primary education, UNESCO estimate): 34.1 in 2011/12 (Source: UNESCO Institute for Statistics).

Adult literacy rate (UNESCO estimates): 89.6% (males 83.3%; females 95.6%) in 2010 (Source: UNESCO Institute for Statistics).

Directory

The Government

HEAD OF STATE

King: HM King LETSIE III (acceded to the throne 7 February 1996).

CABINET
(May 2015)

The Cabinet is a coalition formed by the Basutoland Congress Party (BCP), the Democratic Congress (DC), the Lesotho Congress for Democracy (LCD), the Lesotho People's Congress (LPC), the Marematlou Freedom Party (MFP), the National Independent Party (NIP) and the Popular Front for Democracy (PFD).

Prime Minister: Dr PAKALITHA BETHUEL MOSISILI (DC).

Deputy Prime Minister: MOTHETJOA METSING (LCD).

Minister of Home Affairs: LEKHETHO RAKUOANE (PFD).

Minister of Justice, Human Rights and Correctional Services: MOEKETSE MALEBO (MFP).

Minister of Labour and Employment: THULO MAHLAKENG (BCP).

Minister in the Prime Minister's Office: KIMETSO MATHABA (NIP).

Minister of Social Development: MOLAHLEHI LETLOTLO (LPC).

Minister of Police and Public Safety: MONYANE MOLELEKI (DC).

Minister of Finance: Dr ·MAMPHONO KHAKETLA (DC).

Minister of Local Government and Chieftainship Affairs: Dr PONTŠO SEKATLE (DC).

Minister of Water Affairs: RALECHATE ·MOKOSE (DC).

Minister of Forestry, Range and Soil Conservation: KABELO MAFURA (DC).

Minister of Energy: SELIBE MOCHOBOROANE (LCD).

Minister of Defence and National Security: TŠELISO MOKHOSI (LCD).

Minister of Public Works and Transport: TŠOEU MOKERETLA (DC).

Minister of Public Service: TSUKUTLANE AU (DC).

Minister of Development Planning: MOKOTO HLOAELE (DC).

Minister of Law and Constitutional Affairs: MOTLALENTOA LETSOSA (DC).

Minister of Communications, Science and Technology: KHOTSO LETSATSI (DC).

Minister of Tourism, Arts and Culture: LIKELELI TAMPANE (DC).

Minister of Gender, Youth and Sports: MATHIBELI MOKHOTHU (DC).

Minister of Foreign Affairs and International Relations: TLOHANG SEKHAMANE (DC).

Minister of Education and Training: Dr MAHALI PHAMOTSE (DC).

Minister of Small Business Development, Co-operatives and Marketing: THABISO LITSIBA (DC).

Minister of Agriculture and Food Security: ·MAPALESA MOTHOKHO (LCD).

Minister of Health: Dr ·MOLOTSI MONYAMANE (DC).

Minister of Trade and Industry: JOSHUA SETIPA (LCD).

Minister of Mining: LEBOHANG THOTANYANA (LCD).

In addition there were seven deputy ministers.

MINISTRIES

Office of the Prime Minister: Govt Office Complex, Phase 1, Qhobosheaneng, POB 527, Maseru 100; tel. 22326359; fax 22310444; internet www.gov.ls/pm.

Ministry of Agriculture and Food Security: POB 24, Maseru 100; tel. 22324651; fax 22310186; e-mail lereko.masupha@gov.ls; internet www.gov.ls/agric/.

Ministry of Communications, Science and Technology: Moposo House, 3rd Floor, POB 36, Maseru 100; tel. 22323864; fax 22310264; e-mail gposholi@gmail.com; internet www.gov.ls/comms.

Ministry of Defence and National Security: Kingsway, opp. National Library, Private Bag A166, Maseru 100; tel. 22326651; fax 22310444; e-mail pglerotholi@gmail.com; internet www.gov.ls/defence.

Ministry of Development Planning: POB 24, Maseru 100; tel. 22311100; fax 22310186; e-mail info.planning@gov.ls; internet www.planning.gov.ls.

Ministry of Education and Training: POB 47, Maseru 100; tel. 22313045; fax 22310562; e-mail theko.tlebere@gov.ls; internet www.gov.ls/education.

Ministry of Energy: POB 772, Maseru 100; tel. 22311741; fax 22310520; internet www.gov.ls/energy.

Ministry of Finance: Finance House, 3rd Floor, High Court Rd, POB 395, Maseru 100; tel. 22310826; fax 22310411; internet www.finance.gov.ls.

Ministry of Foreign Affairs and International Relations: Qhobosheaneng Govt Complex, Griffith Hill Rd, POB 1387, Maseru 100; tel. 22311150; fax 22310178; e-mail moeketsim@foreign.gov.ls; internet www.foreign.gov.ls.

Ministry of Forestry, Range and Soil Conservation: Industrial Site, opp. Lesotho Standard Bank, cnr Raboshabane and Senate Rds, POB 92, Maseru 100; tel. 22323600; fax 22310515; internet www.gov.ls/forestry.

Ministry of Gender, Youth and Sports: POB 729, Maseru 100; tel. 22314763; fax 22310506; internet www.gov.ls/gender.

Ministry of Health: POB 514, Maseru 100; tel. 22314404; internet www.gov.ls/health.

Ministry of Home Affairs: POB 174, Maseru 100; tel. 22327205; fax 22310013; e-mail hkoali@homeaffairs.gov.ls; internet www.gov.ls/safety.

Ministry of Justice, Human Rights and Correctional Services: POB 402, Maseru 100; tel. 22322683; fax 22310365; e-mail dps@justice.gov.ls; internet www.gov.ls/justice.

Ministry of Labour and Employment: Private Bag A1164, Maseru 100; tel. 22323565; fax 22325163; internet www.gov.ls/employment.

Ministry of Law and Constitutional Affairs: POB 33, Maseru 100; tel. 22315983; fax 22310929; internet www.gov.ls/law.

Ministry of Local Government and Chieftainship Affairs: Rorisang David Mahlo, POB 686, Maseru 100; tel. 22325331; fax 22327782; e-mail rorisang.mahlo@gmail.com; internet www.gov.ls/local.

Ministry of Mining: POB 750, Maseru 100; tel. 22322841; fax 22310498; e-mail mmpooa@yahoo.com; internet www.gov.ls/mining.

Ministry of Police and Public Safety: Private Bag A166, Maseru 100; tel. 22326651.

Ministry of Public Service: POB 228, Maseru 100; tel. 22311130; fax 22310883; e-mail mapoulo.maseela@gov.ls; internet www.mps.gov.ls.

Ministry of Public Works and Transport: POB 20, Maseru 100; tel. 22323624; fax 22310125; e-mail pssecretary@mopwt.gov.ls; internet www.gov.ls/works.

Ministry of Small Business Development, Co-operatives and Marketing: POB 747, Maseru 100; tel. 22325272.

Ministry of Social Development: Private Bag A222, Maseru 100; tel. 22226004; fax 58461527; e-mail makhethampho@yahoo.com; internet www.gov.ls/social.

Ministry of Tourism, Arts and Culture: POB 52, Maseru 100; tel. 22313034; fax 22310194; e-mail info.mtec@gov.ls; internet www.gov.ls/tourism.

Ministry of Trade and Industry: POB 747, Maseru 100; tel. 22325272; e-mail lihaelon@yahoo.com; internet www.gov.ls/trade.

Ministry of Water Affairs: POB 772, Maseru 100.

Legislature

NATIONAL ASSEMBLY

National Assembly: POB 190, Maseru; tel. 22323035; fax 22310023; internet www.parliament.ls/assembly.

Speaker: NTLHOI MOTSAMAI.

General Election, 28 February 2015

Party	Constituency seats	Compensatory seats*	Total seats
Democratic Congress . . .	37	10	47
All Basotho Convention . . .	40	6	46
Lesotho Congress for Democracy .	2	10	12
Basotho National Party . . .	1	6	7
Popular Front for Democracy .	—	2	2
Reformed Congress of Lesotho .	—	2	2
Basutoland Congress Party . .	—	1	1
Lesotho People's Congress . .	—	1	1
Marematlou Freedom Party . .	—	1	1
National Independent Party . .	—	1	1
Total	**80**	**40**	**120**

* Allocated by proportional representation.

SENATE

Senate: POB 553, Maseru 100; tel. 22315338; fax 22310023; internet www.parliament.ls/senate.

President: Chief SEEISO BERENG SEEISO.

The Senate is an advisory chamber, comprising 22 traditional chiefs and 11 members appointed by the monarch.

Election Commission

Independent Electoral Commission (IEC): Moposo House, 7th Floor, Kingsway, POB 12698, Maseru 100; tel. 22314991; fax 22310398; internet www.iec.org.ls; f. 1997 as successor to the Constituency Delimitation Commission; Chair. LIMAKATSO MOKHOTHU.

Political Organizations

In March 2015 a total of 24 parties were registered by the Independent Electoral Commission.

All Basotho Convention (ABC): Maseru; f. 2006 by fmr mems of the Lesotho Congress for Democracy; Pres. THOMAS MOTSOAHAE THABANE.

Basotho Batho Democratic Party (BBDP): f. 2006; Leader JEREMANE RAMATHEBANE.

Basotho Democratic National Party (BDNP): e-mail joangmolapo@hotmail.com; f. 2006; Leader THABANG NYEOE; Sec.-Gen. PELELE LETSOALA.

Basotho National Party (BNP): POB 124, Maseru 100; f. 1958; Leader THESELE MASERIBANE; Sec.-Gen. MOLETSANE JONATHAN; 280,000 mems.

Basutoland Congress Party (BCP): POB 111, Maseru 100; tel. 8737076; f. 1952; Leader THULO MAHLAKENG.

Democratic Congress: POB 12002, Maseru 100; tel. 22322944; e-mail ralehlathebonang@yahoo.com; internet www.dc.org.ls; f. 2012; Leader BETHUEL PAKALITHA MOSISILI.

Lesotho Congress for Democracy (LCD): POB 7, Mohole's Hoek; tel. 785207; f. 1997 as a result of divisions within the BCP; Chair. MOEKETSI MOLETSANE; Acting Sec.-Gen. TSELISO MOKHOSI; 200,000 mems.

Lesotho People's Congress (LPC): f. 2001 following split in the LCD; Leader KELEBONE ALBERT MAOPE; Sec.-Gen. SHAKHANE MOKHEHLE.

Lesotho Workers' Party (LWP): Maseru; f. 2001; Leader MACAEFA BILLY.

Marematlou Freedom Party (MFP): POB 0443, Maseru 105; tel. 22315804; f. 1962 following merger between the Marema Tlou Party and Basutoland Freedom Party; Leader MOEKETSE MALEBO; Dep. Leader THABO LEANYA.

National Independent Party (NIP): Maseru; f. 1984; Pres. ANTHONY CLOVIS MANYELI.

Popular Front for Democracy (PFD): Maseru; f. 1991; left-wing; Leader LEKHETHO RAKUOANE.

Reformed Congress of Lesotho (RCL): Maseru; Leader KEKETSO RANTSO; Sec.-Gen. MAMULULA NTABE.

Diplomatic Representation

EMBASSIES AND HIGH COMMISSIONS IN LESOTHO

China, People's Republic: POB 380, Maseru 100; tel. 22316521; fax 22310489; e-mail chinaemb_ls@mfa.gov.cn; internet ls .china-embassy.org; Ambassador HU DINGXIAN.

Ireland: Tona-Kholo Rd, Private Bag A67, Maseru 100; tel. 22314068; fax 22310028; e-mail maseruembassy@dfa.ie; internet www.embassyofireland.org.ls; Ambassador GERRY GERVIN.

Libya: 173 Tona-Kholo Rd, Maseru West, POB 432, Maseru 100; tel. 22320148; fax 22327750; Chargé d'affaires a.i. ABDUL-MOEINE GARGOUM.

South Africa: Lesotho Bank Tower, 10th Floor, Kingsway, Private Bag A266, Maseru 100; tel. 22315758; fax 22310128; e-mail madibam@dirco.gov.za; High Commissioner Rev. HARRIS MAJEKE.

USA: 254 Kingsway, POB 333, Maseru 100; tel. 22312666; fax 22310116; e-mail infomaseru@state.gov; internet maseru .usembassy.gov; Ambassador MATTHEW T. HARRINGTON.

Judicial System

The Constitution provides for an independent judicial system, consisting of a Court of Appeal, a High Court, Magistrates' Courts, and traditional courts that exist predominantly in rural areas. All but one of the Justices on the Court of Appeal are South African jurists.

Court of Appeal: POB 90, Maseru; tel. 22312188; Pres. KANANELO MOSITO.

High Court: POB 90, Maseru; tel. 22312188; the High Court is a superior court of record, and in addition to any other jurisdiction conferred by statute it is vested with unlimited original jurisdiction to determine any civil or criminal matter; it also has appellate jurisdiction to hear appeals and reviews from the subordinate courts; appeals may be made to the Court of Appeal; Chief Justice NTHOMENG MAJARA.

Subordinate Courts: each of the 10 districts possesses subordinate courts, presided over by magistrates; Chief Magistrate MOLEFI MAKARA.

Judicial Commissioners' Courts: these courts hear civil and criminal appeals from central and local courts; further appeal may be made to the High Court and finally to the Court of Appeal.

Central and Local Courts: there are 71 such courts (of which 58 are local courts and 13 are central courts), which also serve as courts of appeal from the local courts; they have limited civil and criminal jurisdiction.

Religion

About 90% of the population profess Christianity.

CHRISTIANITY

African Federal Church Council (AFCC): POB 70, Peka 340; f. 1927; co-ordinating org. for 48 African independent churches.

Christian Council of Lesotho (CCL): POB 547, Maseru 100; tel. 22313639; fax 22310310; f. 1833; 112 congregations; 261,350 mems (2003); Chair. Rev. PHILLIP MOKUKU; Sec. CATHERINE RAMOKHELE.

The Anglican Communion

Anglicans in Lesotho are adherents of the Anglican Church of Southern Africa (formerly the Church of the Province of Southern Africa). The Metropolitan of the Province is the Archbishop of Cape Town, South Africa. Lesotho forms a single diocese, with an estimated 200,000 members.

Bishop of Lesotho: MALLANE ADAM TAASO, Bishop's House, POB 87, Maseru 100; tel. 22311974; fax 22310161; e-mail diocese@ilcsotho .com.

The Roman Catholic Church

Lesotho comprises one archdiocese and three dioceses. Some 52% of the total population are Roman Catholics.

Lesotho Catholic Bishops' Conference: Catholic Secretariat, POB 200, Maseru 100; tel. 22312525; fax 22310294; f. 1972; Pres. Most Rev. GERARD TLALI LEROTHOLI.

Archbishop of Maseru: Most Rev. GERARD TLALI LEROTHOLI, Archbishop's House, 19 Orpen Rd, POB 267, Maseru 100; tel. 22312565; fax 22310425; e-mail archmase@lesoff.co.za.

Other Christian Churches

At mid-2000 there were an estimated 279,000 Protestants and 257,000 adherents professing other forms of Christianity in Lesotho.

African Methodist Episcopal Church: POB 223, Maseru 100; tel. 22311801; fax 22310548; e-mail bishopsarah@leo.co.ls; f. 1903; Presiding Prelate Rt Rev. SARAH F. DAVIS; 15,000 mems.

Lesotho Evangelical Church: POB 260, Maseru 100; tel. 22323942; f. 1833; independent since 1964; Pres. Rev. TSELISO MASEMENE; Exec. Sec. Rev. GILBERT RAMATLAPENG; 230,000 mems (2003).

Other denominations active in Lesotho include the Apostolic Faith Mission, the Assemblies of God, the Dutch Reformed Church in Africa, the Full Gospel Church of God, Methodist Church of Southern Africa and the Seventh-day Adventists. There are also numerous African independent churches.

BAHÁ'Í FAITH

National Spiritual Assembly of the Bahá'ís of Lesotho: POB 508, Maseru 100; tel. 22312346; e-mail bahailesotho@leo.co.ls.

The Press

Lesotho does not have a daily newspaper.

Informative: Suite 03, Metcash Complex, Kingsway Rd, Maseru; tel. 22327228; fax 22327234; e-mail editor@informativenews.co.ls; internet www.informativenews.co.ls; weekly; owned by BAM Media; Man. Editor BOITUMELO KOLOI.

Leseli ka Sepolesa (The Police Witness): Press Dept, Police Headquarters, Maseru CBD, POB 13, Maseru 100; tel. 22317262; fax 22310045; fortnightly; Sesotho; publ. by the Lesotho Mounted Police Services; Editor-in-Chief CLIFFORD MOLEFE.

Leselinyana la Lesotho (Light of Lesotho): Morija Printing Works, POB 7, Morija 190; tel. 22360244; fax 22360005; e-mail mpw@lesoff.co.ls; f. 1863; fortnightly; Sesotho, with occasional articles in English; publ. by the Lesotho Evangelical Church; Editor MABATSOENENG EMELY SIBOLLA; circ. 12,000.

Lesotho Times: Maseru; tel. 22315335; fax 22315352; e-mail editor@lestimes.co.ls; internet lestimes.com.

Moeletsi oa Basotho: Mazenod, Maseru, 180; tel. 28350466; fax 22350010; e-mail moeletsioabasotho@gmail.com; f. 1933; weekly; Sesotho; publ. by the Roman Catholic Church; Editor FRANCIS KHOARIPE; circ. 20,000.

Mohahlaula: Allied Bldg, 1st Floor, Manonyane Centre, POB 14430, Maseru 100; tel. 22312777; fax 22320941; weekly; Sesotho; publ. by Makaung Printers and Publrs; Editor WILLY MOLLUNGOA.

Mololi: Cooperatives Bldg, Main North 1 Rd, POB 9933, Maseru 100; tel. 22312287; fax 22327912; f. 1997; Sesotho; organ of the Lesotho Congress for Democracy; Editor (vacant).

Mopheme (The Survivor): Allied Bldg, 1st Floor, Manonyane Centre, POB 14184, Maseru; tel. and fax 22311670; e-mail mopheme@lesoff.co.za; weekly; English and Sesotho; publ. by Newsshare Foundation; Owner and Editor LAWRENCE KEKETSO; circ. 2,500.

Public Eye/Mosotho: House No. 14A3, Princess Margaret Rd, POB 14129, Old Europa, Maseru 100; tel. 22321414; fax 22310614; e-mail editor@publiceye.co.ls; internet www.publiceye.co.ls; f. 1997; weekly; 80% English, 20% Sesotho; publ. by Voice Multimedia; also publ. *Eye on Tourism* and *Family Mirror* magazines; Editor-in-Chief BETHUEL THAI; circ. 20,000 (Lesotho and South Africa).

PERIODICALS

Achiever: Metcash Complex, Kingsway Rd, POB 1803, Maseru 100; tel. 22328920; fax 222656333; e-mail editor@achievermagazine.co.ls; internet www.achievermagazine.co.ls; f. 2012; education and entertainment; Man. Editor MYRA NTLATLAPA.

Finite: Maseru; tel. 22328919; e-mail info@finitemagazine.co.ls; internet www.finitemagazine.co.ls; f. 2009; woman's magazine.

Justice and Peace: Catholic Bishops' Conference, Our Lady of Victories Cathedral Catholic Centre, POB 200, Maseru 100; tel. 22312750; fax 22312751; quarterly; publ. by the Roman Catholic Church.

Moqolotsi (The Journalist): House No. 1B, Happy Villa, POB 14139, Maseru 100; tel. and fax 22320941; e-mail medinles@lesoff.co.za; monthly newsletter; English; publ. by the Media Institute of Lesotho (MILES).

NGO Web: 544 Hoohlo Extension, Florida, Maseru 100; tel. 22325798; fax 22317205; e-mail lecongo@lecongo.org.ls; quarterly; English and Sesotho; publ. of the Lesotho Council of NGOs; circ. 2,000.

Shoeshoe: POB 36, Maseru 100; tel. 22323561; fax 22310003; quarterly; women's interest; publ. by Ministry of Communications, Science and Technology.

Other publications include *Mara LDF Airwing/Airsquadron* and *The Sun/Thebe*.

NEWS AGENCY

Lesotho News Agency (LENA): Lesotho News Agency Complex, Lerotholi St, opp. Royal Palace, POB 36, Maseru 100; tel. 22325317; fax 22324608; e-mail l_lenanews@hotmail.com; internet www.lena.gov.ls; f. 1985; Dir MOTHEPANE KOTELE; Editors MOROA MOPELI, LITEBOHO MAHULA.

Publishers

Longman Lesotho (Pty) Ltd: 104 Christie House, 1st Floor, Orpen Rd, Old Europa, POB 1174, Maseru 100; tel. 22314254; fax 22310118; e-mail puseletso@longles.co.ls; internet www.longmanafrica.co.za/lesotho; Man. Dir SEYMOUR R. KIKINE.

Macmillan Boleswa Publishers Lesotho (Pty) Ltd: 523 Sun Cabanas Hotel, POB 7545, Maseru 100; tel. 22317340; fax 22310047; e-mail macmillan@lesoff.co.ls; Man. Dir PAUL MOROLONG.

Mazenod Institute: POB 39, Mazenod 160; tel. 22350224; f. 1933; Roman Catholic; Man. Fr B. MOHLALISI.

Morija Sesuto Book Depot: POB 4, Morija 190; tel. and fax 22360204; f. 1862; owned by the Lesotho Evangelical Church; religious, educational and Sesotho language and literature.

St Michael's Mission: The Social Centre, POB 25, Roma; tel. 22316234; f. 1968; religious and educational; Man. Dir Fr M. FERRANGE.

GOVERNMENT PUBLISHING HOUSE

Government Printer: POB 268, Maseru; tel. 22313023.

Broadcasting and Communications

TELECOMMUNICATIONS

In 2014 there were two providers of mobile cellular telephone services and one provider of fixed-line telephone services.

Lesotho Communications Authority (LCA): Moposo House, 6th Floor, Kingsway Rd, POB 15896, Maseru 100; tel. 22224300; fax 22310984; e-mail lca@lca.org.ls; internet www.lca.org.ls; f. 2000; regulates telecommunications and broadcasting; Chief Exec. MONEHELA POSHOLI.

Econet Telecom Lesotho (ETL): Kingsway Rd, POB 1037, Maseru 100; tel. 22211000; fax 22310600; e-mail enquiries@telecom.co.ls; internet www.etl.co.ls; 70% holding acquired by the Econet Wireless Group in 2007; 30% state-owned; Chair. PAKO PETLANE; CEO NICO HEYNS.

Vodacom Lesotho (Pty) Ltd: Block B, 7th Floor, Development House, Kingsway Rd, POB 7387, Maseru 100; tel. 52212201; fax 22311079; internet www.vodacom.co.za; f. 1996; jt venture between Telecom Lesotho and Vodacom (Pty) Ltd; fmrly VCL Communications; mobile cellular telecommunications provider; CEO PIETER UYS.

BROADCASTING

RADIO

The first licences for private radio stations were issued in 1998. Licences are issued by the Lesotho Telecommunications Authority. Radio Lesotho is the only station to broadcast nationwide; all the other stations are restricted to urban areas and their peripheries.

Catholic Radio FM: Our Lady of Victories Cathedral, Catholic Centre POB 200, Maseru 100; tel. 22323247; fax 22310294; f. 1999.

Harvest FM: Carlton Centre, 3rd Floor, Room No. 312, POB 442, Maseru 100; tel. 22313168; fax 22268659; e-mail mlekhoaba@harvestfm.co.ls; internet www.harvestfm.co.ls; f. 2003; operated by Harvest FM; current affairs and Christian programmes; Man. Dir MALICHABA MOSHOESHOE-LEKHOABA.

Joy FM: Lesotho Sun Hotel, Suites 2204–2206, Private Bag A457, Maseru 100; tel. 22310920; fax 22310104; internet www.joyfm.co.ls; f. 2001; Sesotho and English; relays Voice of America broadcasts.

Khotso FM: Institute of Extramural Studies, National University of Lesotho POB 180, Roma; Private Bag A47, Maseru 100; tel. 22322038; fax 22340000; community radio station; sister station of DOPE FM (f. 2004).

MoAfrika FM: Carlton Centre, 2nd Floor, Kingsway, POB 7234, Maseru 100; tel. and fax 22321956; e-mail info@moafrika.co.ls; internet www.moafrikafm-online.com; Sesotho, Xhosa and Mandarin; news and entertainment; Man. and Editor-in-Chief Prof. SEBONONOLA R. K. RAMAINOANE.

People's Choice Radio (PCFM): LNDC Centre, Development House, Level 9, Block D, POB 8800, Maseru 100; tel. 22322122; fax 22310888; internet www.pcfm.co.ls; f. 1998; news and entertainment; Man. Dir MOTLATSI MAJARA.

Radio Lesotho: Lesotho News Agency Complex, Lerotholi St, opp. Royal Palace, POB 36, Maseru 100; tel. and fax 22322714; e-mail enquiries@africanextension.com; f. 1964; state-owned; part of Lesotho Nat. Broadcasting Services; Sesotho and English; Dir of Broadcasting LEBOHANG DADA MOQASA.

TELEVISION

Lesotho Television (LTV): Lesotho News Agency Complex, Lerotholi St, opp. Royal Palace, POB 36, Maseru 100; tel. 22324735; fax 22310149; e-mail mfalatsa@yahoo.com; f. 1988 in association with M-Net, South Africa; state-owned; part of Lesotho Nat. Broadcasting Services; Sesotho and English.

Finance

(cap. = capital; res = reserves; dep. = deposits; m. = million;
br(s) = branch(es); amounts in maloti)

BANKING

In 2014 there were four commercial banks in Lesotho.

Central Bank

Central Bank of Lesotho: cnr Airport and Moshoeshoe Rds, POB 1184, Maseru 100; tel. 22314281; fax 22310051; e-mail cbl@centralbank.org.ls; internet www.centralbank.org.ls; f. 1978 as the Lesotho Monetary Authority; present name adopted in 1982; bank of issue; cap. 25.0m., res 1,479.1m., dep. 5,093.2m. (Dec. 2009); Gov. and Chair. Dr RETŠELISITSOE MATLANYANE.

Commercial Banks

First National Bank Lesotho: cnr Kingsway and Parliament Rds, POB 11902, Maseru 100; tel. 22247100; fax 22317037; internet www.fnb.co.ls; f. 2004; CEO EMIL HEPPELL; 1 br.

Lesotho PostBank (LPB): Oblate House, Kingsway Rd, Private Bag A121, Maseru 100; tel. 22317842; fax 22313170; e-mail info@lpb.co.ls; internet www.lpb.co.ls; f. 2004; state-owned; Chair. TŠELISO MOKELA; CEO LEBAKENG TIGELI; 12 brs.

Nedbank (Lesotho) Ltd: 115–117 Griffith Hill, Kingsway St, POB 1001, Maseru 100; tel. 22312696; fax 22310025; e-mail georgego@nedcor.co.za; internet www.nedbank.co.ls; f. 1997; fmrly Standard Chartered Bank Lesotho Ltd; 100% owned by Nedbank Ltd (South Africa); cap. 20m., res 44m., dep. 2,325m. (Dec. 2010); Chair. SOPHIA MOHAPI; Man. Dir LAZARUS MURAHWA; 7 brs and 2 agencies.

Standard Lesotho Bank: Banking Bldg, 1st Floor, Kingsway Rd, Kingsway Town Centre, POB 1053, Maseru 100; tel. 22212000; fax 22460016; internet www.standardlesothobank.co.ls; f. 2006 following merger between Lesotho Bank (1999) Ltd (f. 1972) and Standard Bank Lesotho Ltd (fmrly Stanbic Bank Lesotho Ltd); cap. 20.6m., res 114.2m., dep. 4,326.0m. (Dec. 2012); Man. Dir MPHO VUMBUKANI; 11 brs.

INSURANCE

In 2013 there were five insurance companies in Lesotho.

Alliance Insurance Co Ltd: Alliance House, 4 Bowker Rd, POB 01118, Maseru West 105; tel. 22312357; fax 22310313; e-mail alliance@alliance.co.ls; internet www.alliance.co.ls; f. 1993; life and short-term insurance; Man. Dir ROB DUNCAN; Gen. Mans MOK'HAPHEK'HA LAZARO, THABISO MADIBA.

Lesotho National General Insurance Co Ltd (LNIG): Lesotho Insurance House, Kingsway, Private Bag A65, Maseru 100; tel. 22313031; fax 22310007; e-mail manager@lngic.com; f. 1977 as Lesotho National Insurance Group; 60% owned by Regent Insurance Co Ltd (South Africa), 20% state-owned, 20% owned by Molepe Investment Holdings (Pty) Ltd; part-privatized in 1995; incorporating subsidiaries specializing in life and short-term insurance; Chair. Dr TIMOTHY THAHANE; Man. Dir R. J. LETSOELA.

Metropolitan Lesotho Ltd: Metropolitan Bldg, Kingsway St, POB 645, Maseru; tel. 22222300; fax 22317278; internet www.metropolitan.co.ls; f. 2003; subsidiary of Metropolitan Holdings Ltd, South Africa; Man. Dir NKAU MATETE.

Trade and Industry

GOVERNMENT AGENCIES

Lesotho Revenue Authority (LRA): Ground Floor, Finance House Bldg, Government Office Complex, Kingsway Rd, Maseru; tel. 22313796; fax 22312091; internet www.lra.org.ls; f. 2003.

Privatisation Unit: Privatisation Project, Lesotho Utilities Sector Reform Project, Ministry of Finance and Development Planning, Lesotho Bank Mortgage Division Bldg, 2nd Floor, Kingsway St, Private Bag A249, Maseru 100; tel. 22317902; fax 22317551; e-mail mntsasa@privatisation.gov.ls; internet www.privatisation.gov.ls; CEO MOSITO KHETHISA.

DEVELOPMENT ORGANIZATIONS

Basotho Enterprises Development Corpn (BEDCO): House No. 201, Maseru West, along Tona-kholo Rd, POB 1216, Maseru 100; tel. 22312094; fax 22310455; e-mail info@bedco.org.ls; internet www.bedco.org.ls; f. 1980; promotes and assists in the establishment and devt of Basotho-owned enterprises, with emphasis on small- and medium-scale; Chair. MOHLOMI D. RANTEKOA; CEO TS'ELISO MOKHOSI.

Lesotho Council of Non-Governmental Organizations (LCN): House 544, Hoohlo Extension, Private Bag A445, Maseru 100; tel.

22317205; fax 22310412; e-mail admin@lcn.org.ls; internet www.lcn.org.ls; f. 1990; promotes sustainable management of natural resources, socio-economic devt and social justice; Exec. Dir SEABATA MOTSAMA.

Lesotho Highlands Development Authority (LHDA): Lesotho Bank Tower, 3rd Floor, Kingsway, POB 7332, Maseru 100; tel. 22311280; fax 22310665; e-mail lhwp@lhda.org.ls; internet www.lhda.org.ls; f. 1986 to implement the Lesotho Highlands Water Project, being undertaken jtly with South Africa; Chair. J. EAGAR; CEO PETER MAKUTA (acting).

Lesotho National Dairy Board: Maseru; f. 1991; prescribes standards of production, storage, packaging, processing and distribution of dairy products.

Lesotho National Development Corpn (LNDC): Development House, Block A, Kingsway, Private Bag A96, Maseru 100; tel. 22312012; fax 22310038; e-mail info@lndc.org.ls; internet www.lndc.org.ls; f. 1967; state-owned; total assets M477.5m. (March 2006); interests in manufacturing, mining, food-processing and leisure; Chair. MOHLOMI RANTEKOA; CEO JOSHUA SETIPA.

CHAMBER OF COMMERCE

Lesotho Chamber of Commerce and Industry: Kingsway Ave, POB 79, Maseru 100; tel. 22316937; fax 22322794; Pres. NTAOTE SEBOKA.

EMPLOYERS' ORGANIZATION

Association of Lesotho Employers: 18 Bowker Rd, POB 1509, Maseru 100; tel. 22315736; fax 22325384; e-mail makeka@leo.co.ls; f. 1961; represents mems in industrial relations and on govt bodies, and advises the Govt on employers' concerns; Pres. RADITAPOLE LETSOELA; Exec. Dir THABO MAKEKA.

UTILITIES

Lesotho Electricity Authority (LEA): Moposo House, 6th Floor, Kingsway, Private Bag A315, Maseru; tel. 22312479; fax 22315094; e-mail secretary@lea.org.ls; internet www.lea.org.ls; f. 2004; Chair. FRANCINA LIAKO MOLOI; Chief Exec. NTOI PAUL RAPAPA.

Lesotho Electricity Co (LEC): 53 Moshoeshoe Rd, POB 423, Maseru 100; tel. 22312236; fax 22310093; e-mail info@lec.co.ls; internet www.lec.co.ls; f. 1969; 100% state-owned; Chair. Dr K. LESOETSA; Man. Dir F. M. HLOAELE.

Lesotho Water and Sewerage Authority (WASA): POB 426, Maseru 100; tel. 22312449; fax 22312006; internet www.wasa.co.ls; Chair. REFILOE TLALI.

TRADE UNIONS

Congress of Lesotho Trade Unions (COLETU): POB 13282, Maseru 100; tel. 22320958; fax 22310081; f. 1998; Sec.-Gen. VUYANI TYHALI; 15,587 mems.

Lesotho Congress of Democratic Unions (LECODU): POB 15851, Maseru 100; tel. and fax 22323559; f. 2004; Sec.-Gen. DANIEL MARAISANE; 15,279 mems (2005).

Transport

RAILWAYS

Lesotho is linked with the South African railway system by a short line (2.6 km in length) from Maseru to Marseilles, on the Bloemfontein–Natal main line.

ROADS

In 2007 Lesotho's road network totalled 2,371 km, of which some 58% were paved. In March 2000 a major road network was opened, linking Maseru with the Mohale Dam.

Department of Traffic and Transport: Maseru.

Road Fund: Post Office Bldg, 4th Floor, Kingsway, POB 14644, Maseru 100; tel. 22321696; fax 22321698; e-mail roadfund@lesoff.org.ls; internet www.roadfund.org.ls; f. 1995; CEO N. M. MAKARA.

CIVIL AVIATION

King Moshoeshoe I International Airport is at Thota-Moli, some 20 km from Maseru. There are also 29 regional aerodromes and airstrips. International services between Maseru and Johannesburg, South Africa, are operated by South African Airlink. The national airline company, Lesotho Airways, was sold to a South African company in 1997 as part of the Government's ongoing privatization programme; however, after two years of losses the company was liquidated in 1999.

Department of Civil Aviation: POB 629, Maseru 100; tel. 22312499; fax 22310188; e-mail director@civilair.gov.ls; internet www.civilair.gov.ls; Dir KETSO Z. MOEKETSI (acting).

Tourism

Spectacular mountain scenery is the principal tourist attraction, and a new ski resort was opened in 2003. Tourist arrivals totalled 432,966 in 2013, and receipts from tourism amounted to an estimated US $46m. in 2012.

Lesotho Tourism Development Corpn (LTDC): cnr Linare and Parliament Rds, POB 1378, Maseru 100; tel. 22312238; fax 22310189; e-mail ltdc@ltdc.org.ls; internet www.ltdc.org.ls; f. 2000; successor to the Lesotho Tourist Board; Chair. MAMORUTI MALIE.

Defence

Military service is voluntary. As assessed at November 2014, the Lesotho Defence Force (LDF, formerly the Royal Lesotho Defence Force) comprised an estimated 2,000 men, including an air wing of 110 men. The creation of a new commando force unit, the first professional unit in the LDF, was announced in October 2001, as part of ongoing efforts to restructure the armed forces.

Defence Expenditure: Budgeted at M535m. for 2014.

Commander of the Lesotho Defence Force: Lt-Gen. TLALI KAMOLI.

Education

All primary education is available free of charge, and is provided mainly by the three main Christian missions (Lesotho Evangelical, Roman Catholic and Anglican), under the direction of the Ministry of Education and Training. Education at primary schools is officially compulsory for seven years between six and 13 years of age. Secondary education, beginning at the age of 13, lasts for up to five years, comprising a first cycle of three years and a second of two years. According to UNESCO estimates, in 2012 total enrolment at primary schools included 82% of children in the appropriate age-group (80% of boys; 83% of girls); in that year enrolment at secondary schools included 33% of children in the relevant age-group (26% of boys; 41% of girls). Some 8,500 students were enrolled at the National University of Lesotho, at Roma, in 2005/06. Proposed expenditure on education in 2008 represented 23.7% of total government spending. In January 2006 17 new schools, constructed with the assistance of the Government of Japan, were opened; they were expected to accommodate some 14,000 pupils.

LIBERIA

Introductory Survey

LOCATION, CLIMATE, LANGUAGE, RELIGION, FLAG, CAPITAL

The Republic of Liberia lies on the west coast of Africa, with Sierra Leone and Guinea to the north, and Côte d'Ivoire to the east. The climate is tropical, with temperatures ranging from 18°C (65°F) to 49°C (120°F). English is the official language but the 16 major ethnic groups speak their own languages and dialects. Liberia is officially a Christian state, although some Liberians hold traditional beliefs. There are about 670,000 Muslims. The national flag (proportions 10 by 19) has 11 horizontal stripes, alternately of red and white, with a dark blue square canton, containing a five-pointed white star, in the upper hoist. The capital is Monrovia.

CONTEMPORARY POLITICAL HISTORY

Historical Context

Founded by liberated black slaves from the southern USA, Liberia became an independent republic in 1847. The leader of the True Whig Party (TWP), William Tubman, who had been President of Liberia since 1944, died in July 1971 and was succeeded by his Vice-President, William R. Tolbert, who was re-elected in October 1975.

In April 1980 Tolbert was assassinated in a military coup, led by Master Sgt (later Commander-in-Chief) Samuel Doe, who assumed power as Chairman of the newly established People's Redemption Council (PRC), suspending the Constitution and proscribing all political parties. The new regime attracted international criticism for its summary execution of 13 former senior government officials who had been accused of corruption and mismanagement. In July 1981 all civilian ministers received commissions, thus installing total military rule.

A draft Constitution was approved by 78.3% of registered voters in a national referendum in July 1984. In the same month Doe dissolved the PRC and appointed a 58-member Interim National Assembly. Also in July, the ban on political organizations was repealed, prior to presidential and legislative elections. In August Doe established the National Democratic Party of Liberia (NDPL) and formally announced his candidature for the presidency. By early 1985 a total of 11 political associations had been formed; however, two influential parties, the Liberian People's Party (LPP) and the United People's Party (UPP), were proscribed, and apart from the NDPL only three parties—the Liberian Action Party (LAP), the Liberia Unification Party (LUP) and the Unity Party (UP)—were eventually permitted to participate in the elections in October. Doe won the presidential election, receiving 50.9% of the votes. At the concurrent elections to the bicameral National Assembly, the NDPL won 22 of the 26 seats in the Senate and 51 of the 64 seats in the House of Representatives. On 6 January 1986 Doe was inaugurated as President.

Domestic Political Affairs

In December 1989 an armed insurrection by rebel forces began in the north-eastern border region of Nimba County. In early 1990 several hundred deaths ensued in fighting between the Liberian army (the Armed Forces of Liberia—AFL) and the rebels, who claimed to be members of a hitherto unknown opposition group, the National Patriotic Front of Liberia (NPFL), led by a former government official, Charles Taylor. The fighting swiftly degenerated into a war between Doe's ethnic group, the Krahn, and the local Gio and Mano tribes. Taylor's authority as self-proclaimed President of his own interim administration, known as the National Patriotic Reconstruction Assembly, was challenged by a faction of the NPFL, led by Prince Yormie Johnson, which rapidly secured control of parts of Monrovia in July. In the subsequent conflict both government and rebel forces were responsible for numerous atrocities against civilians. The Economic Community of West African States (ECOWAS, see p. 258) repeatedly failed to negotiate a ceasefire, and in late August it dispatched a military force to restore peace in the region. Doe and Johnson accepted this Monitoring Group (ECOMOG), but its initial occupation of the port area of Monrovia encountered armed opposition by Taylor's forces.

On 30 August 1990 exiled representatives of Liberia's principal political parties and other influential groups met at a conference convened by ECOWAS in the Gambian capital, Banjul, where they elected Dr Amos Sawyer, the leader of the LPP, as President of an Interim Government of National Unity (IGNU). Doe was taken prisoner by Johnson's rebel Independent National Patriotic Front of Liberia (INPFL) on 9 September, and was killed on the following day. In early October ECOMOG began an offensive aimed at establishing a neutral zone in Monrovia separating the three warring factions, and it rapidly gained control of central Monrovia. On 22 November Sawyer was inaugurated as Interim President, under the auspices of ECOWAS, in Monrovia. By January 1991 all rebel forces had withdrawn from Monrovia, and in that month Sawyer nominated ministers to the IGNU. Legislative power was vested in a 28-member Interim National Assembly, which represented the principal political factions, including the INPFL; however, the NPFL refused to participate. On 19 April a national conference re-elected Sawyer as Interim President and appointed a member of the INPFL, Peter Naigow (a former minister in Doe's administration), as Vice-President. In June Sawyer nominated a new Council of Ministers, which was subsequently approved by the Interim National Assembly. In August, however, the INPFL representatives, including Naigow, withdrew from the IGNU.

In April 1991, after several incursions by members of the NPFL into Sierra Leone, Sierra Leonean forces entered Liberian territory and launched retaliatory attacks. It was claimed that NPFL forces were supporting a Sierra Leonean resistance movement, the Revolutionary United Front (RUF), in hostilities against government forces of that country. In September members of a newly emerged rebel movement, comprising former supporters of Doe, the United Liberation Movement of Liberia for Democracy (ULIMO), began attacks from Sierra Leone against NPFL forces in north-western Liberia.

At the end of October 1991 a summit meeting between Sawyer and Taylor, which took place in Yamoussoukro, Côte d'Ivoire, resulted in a peace agreement whereby the troops of all warring factions were to be disarmed and restricted to camps, while the NPFL was to relinquish the territory under its control to ECOMOG. In January 1992 an Interim Election Commission and Supreme Court were established, in accordance with the peace accord.

In August 1992 ULIMO launched a renewed offensive in western Liberia, gaining control of Bomi and Grand Cape Mount counties. In October the NPFL claimed that Nigerian aircraft under ECOMOG command had bombed its bases at Kakata and Harbel (the site of the Robertsfield International Airport and the country's principal rubber plantation), and at Buchanan. The NPFL subsequently seized a number of strategic areas on the outskirts of Monrovia. ECOMOG forces (who were supported by members of the AFL and militia loyal to the IGNU) began retaliatory attacks against NPFL positions around the capital. In October ECOMOG units succeeded in capturing the INPFL base at Caldwell, near Monrovia, and forcing Johnson to surrender. (The INPFL was subsequently disbanded.) In November the UN Security Council adopted a resolution imposing a mandatory embargo on the supply of armaments to Liberia, and authorized the UN Secretary-General to send a special representative to the country. In March 1993 ULIMO accepted an invitation from Sawyer to join the IGNU; ULIMO forces in Monrovia were subsequently disarmed. Following a major offensive, ECOMOG had by April regained control of the areas seized by the NPFL, including its bases of Harbel and Buchanan.

Installation of transitional institutions

In July 1993 a conference, attended by the factions involved in the hostilities, was convened (under the auspices of the UN and ECOWAS) in Geneva, Switzerland. Following several days of negotiations, the IGNU, the NPFL and ULIMO agreed to a ceasefire (to be monitored by UN observers and a reconstituted peacekeeping force), and to the establishment of a transitional administration. The peace accord was formally signed in Cotonou, Benin, on 25 July. Under its terms, the IGNU was to be replaced by the Liberian National Transitional Government (LNTG), with a five-member transitional Council of State and a 35-member Transitional Legislative Assembly (which were to comprise representatives of the IGNU, the NPFL and ULIMO), pending elections.

The ceasefire came into effect at the end of July 1993. In August the Council of State was constituted, and Dr Bismark Kuyon, a member of the IGNU, was elected by its members as Chairman. In September the UN Security Council approved the establishment of a UN Observer Mission in Liberia (UNOMIL), initially comprising some 300 military observers, which was to co-operate with ECOMOG and the Organization of African Unity (now the African Union, see p. 188) in monitoring the transitional process; UNOMIL received an initial seven-month mandate (which was subsequently renewed). In October the Transitional Legislative Assembly was established. Sawyer dismissed Kuyon (who had reportedly dissociated himself from the IGNU's refusal to relinquish power prior to disarmament) and appointed Philip Banks, hitherto Minister of Justice, in his place.

Meanwhile, an armed faction styling itself the Liberia Peace Council (LPC), reportedly comprising members of the Krahn ethnic group from Grand Gedeh County, joined by a number of disaffected AFL troops, emerged in September 1993 and entered into conflict with the NPFL in south-eastern Liberia. In December fighting between ULIMO and a newly formed movement, the Lofa Defence Force (LDF), was also reported in Lofa County.

In February 1994 the Council of State elected David Kpomakpor, a representative of the IGNU, as its Chairman. In early March units belonging to UNOMIL and the reinforced ECOMOG force were deployed, and the disarmament of all factions commenced. On 7 March the Council of State was inaugurated. However, the disarmament process was subsequently impeded by an increase in rebel activity, which included fighting between members of the Krahn and Mandingo ethnic groups within ULIMO, particularly in the region of Tubmanburg (in Bomi County, where the movement was officially based).

In May 1994 a 19-member Cabinet was installed, comprising seven representatives of the NPFL, seven of ULIMO and five of the former IGNU. In July, however, a faction known as ULIMO—K (led by Alhaji G. V. Kromah) launched an offensive to recapture Tubmanburg, which was under the control of Maj.-Gen. Roosevelt Johnson's forces (ULIMO—J). On 12 September Taylor, Kromah and the Chief of Staff of the AFL, Lt-Gen. Hezekiah Bowen, meeting in Akosombo, Ghana, signed a peace accord providing for the cessation of hostilities and for the establishment of a reconstituted Council of State, in which four of the five members were to be nominated, respectively, by the three factions and a civilian Liberian National Conference (LNC—which had been convened in Monrovia at the end of August). Meanwhile, following clashes between dissident members of the NPFL and troops loyal to Taylor, the dissidents' Central Revolutionary Council (CRC) announced that Taylor had been deposed and replaced by the Minister of Labour in the LNTG, Thomas Woewiyu, who indicated that he was not prepared to accept the Akosombo agreement. In September the CRC, apparently in alliance with elements of the AFL, ULIMO, the LPC and the LDF, took control of Taylor's base at Gbarnga (in central Bong County); Taylor was reported to have fled to Côte d'Ivoire.

In December 1994 a ceasefire entered into force and reaffirmed the terms of the Akosombo agreement, including provisions for the establishment of demilitarized zones throughout Liberia and for the installation of a reconstituted Council of State, to comprise a single representative of each of the NPFL, ULIMO, the 'Coalition Forces' (a loose alliance comprising the CRC, the LPC, the LDF and elements of the AFL), and the LNC, with a fifth member elected jointly by the NPFL and ULIMO from traditional rulers.

Regional peace initiatives continue

On 19 August 1995 the armed factions (the NPFL, ULIMO—K, the LPC, the CRC, the LDF, ULIMO—J and the AFL) finally signed a compromise agreement providing for the installation of a reconstituted Council of State, which was to remain in power for one year. An academic with no factional affiliations, Prof. Wilton Sankawulo, was to assume the office of Chairman, while the other seats were to be allocated to Taylor, Kromah, George Boley, Oscar Quiah, and Chief Tamba Taylor, who had been nominated by ULIMO and the NPFL. Later that month a ceasefire entered into force, in compliance with the terms of

the peace accord. The Council of State was formally installed on 1 September, and was to remain in place pending elections, scheduled for August 1996. The Council of State subsequently appointed a transitional Council of Ministers.

Deployment of ECOMOG forces commenced, in December 1995. Following continued clashes between the ULIMO factions, however, ULIMO—J attacked ECOMOG troops near Tubmanburg. ECOMOG suspended deployment of its forces, and launched a counter-offensive in an attempt to restore order.

In February 1996 ULIMO—J officials stated that Johnson had been replaced as leader of the movement in the interests of the peace process. In March the Council of State announced his removal from the Council of Ministers. In subsequent clashes between the two factions of ULIMO—J, forces loyal to Johnson allegedly killed a supporter of the new leadership, prompting the Council of State to order that he be arrested on charges of murder. Johnson, however, refused to surrender to the authorities, and became effectively besieged in his private residence in Monrovia. In April government forces, led by Charles Taylor, engaged in hostilities with Johnson's supporters, in an effort to force him to surrender. The principal factions represented in the transitional authorities thus became involved in the conflict: elements of the LPC and AFL (which were predominantly Krahn) supported Johnson's forces, while the NPFL and ULIMO—K opposed them. Fighting rapidly intensified in central Monrovia and some of Johnson's supporters launched attacks in the residential area of Mamba Point (where embassies and offices of humanitarian organizations were situated), seizing a number of civilians as hostages. Later in April a further ceasefire agreement was negotiated under the aegis of the US Government, the UN and ECOWAS, allowing the deployment of ECOMOG troops throughout Monrovia, while most of the remaining hostages were released by Johnson's supporters. In May, during the absence of Johnson (who had left the country under US protection, to attend a planned ECOWAS summit meeting), the NPFL launched a further attack against the Barclay Training Centre, prompting large numbers of civilians to flee to Monrovia Freeport.

In August 1996, at an ECOWAS conference in Abuja, Nigeria, the principal faction leaders (apart from Johnson, who remained abroad) signed a further peace agreement, whereby a reconstituted Council of State was to be installed by the end of that month, with a former senator, Ruth Perry, replacing Sankawulo as Chairman; Taylor and Boley were to remain members of the new administration. Under a revised schedule, elections were to take place at the end of May 1997, and power was to be transferred to an elected government by mid-June, following the dissolution of the armed factions by the end of January of that year. Perry was inaugurated as Chairman of the Council of State in early September 1996; Johnson was again allocated a ministerial portfolio in a subsequent reorganization of the Cabinet. Following the expiry of the deadline for the completion of the disarmament process, which had been extended to early February 1997, ECOMOG announced that about 91% of the rebel forces had relinquished their armaments.

In January 1997 Taylor announced that the NPFL had been officially dissolved, in accordance with the peace agreement; the movement was subsequently reconstituted as a political organization, the National Patriotic Party (NPP). In the same month Kromah declared that ULIMO—K had also ceased to exist as a military organization, and was to be reconstituted as the All Liberian Coalition Party (ALCOP). In March Taylor, Kromah and Boley resigned from the Council of State, in compliance with the peace agreement, to allow their candidacy in the forthcoming elections. From March a number of West African countries began to dispatch additional contingents to reinforce ECOMOG (which was to be increased in size to about 16,000 personnel prior to the elections), with the USA providing logistical and financial assistance.

Charles Taylor elected President

By mid-1997 a total of 13 presidential candidates had emerged, amongst them Ellen Johnson Sirleaf (a former minister in the Tolbert administration and subsequently a World Bank official, who was to contest the election on behalf of the UP). Following a postponement, the elections finally proceeded on 19 July. The elections commission announced on 23 July that Taylor had been elected President, with 75.3% of votes cast; Johnson Sirleaf (who had been widely expected to be Taylor's strongest opponent) received only 9.6% of the votes. In the concurrent elections to the bicameral legislature (at which seats were allocated on a proportionate basis), the NPP secured 49 seats in the 64-member

House of Representatives and 21 seats in the 26-member Senate, the UP won seven seats in the House of Representatives and three in the Senate, while ALCOP obtained three seats in the House of Representatives and two in the Senate. International observers declared the conduct of the elections to have been 'free and fair'. Taylor's overwhelming victory was generally ascribed to the widely held perception that he was the candidate most likely to achieve long-term stability in the country.

Taylor was inaugurated as President on 2 August 1997, and subsequently nominated a 19-member Cabinet, which was approved by the Senate. The new Government retained several members of the previous transitional administration, including Johnson and Woewiyu. A nine-member National Security Council, comprising several government ministers, the Chief of Staff of the Armed Forces and the Commander of ECOMOG, was also established.

At an ECOWAS summit meeting, convened in Abuja, at the end of August 1997, it was agreed that ECOMOG was to be reconstituted and would henceforth assist in the process of national reconstruction, including the restructuring of the armed and security forces, and the maintenance of security. Following the military coup in Sierra Leone in May, ECOMOG was additionally authorized to enforce international sanctions against the new junta led by Maj. Johnny Paul Koroma. The mandate of UNOMIL (which had been progressively reduced in size) officially ended at the end of September. In October, however, Taylor announced that he opposed the use of military force to oust the Koroma regime, and that ECOMOG would no longer be permitted to launch offensives against Sierra Leone from Liberian territory. In December Taylor appointed Kromah (who had taken up residence in Guinea following his electoral defeat in July) to the post of Chairman of a National Commission on Reconciliation. After the seizure of the Sierra Leonean capital, Freetown, by Nigerian-led ECOMOG troops in February 1998, Taylor protested that the arrest by ECOMOG of about 25 senior members of Sierra Leone's ousted junta at James Spriggs Payne Airport was an infringement of Liberian territory. The Liberian Government recalled its ambassador in Nigeria for consultations, and subsequently submitted a formal complaint to ECOWAS.

In March 1998 violent clashes erupted in Monrovia between the security forces and Johnson's supporters; Johnson subsequently claimed that members of Taylor's special security forces had attacked his private residence. ECOMOG troops were deployed to prevent further violence, and, in an attempt to ease tension in the capital, Johnson was removed from the Cabinet and appointed ambassador to India. In the same month Kromah, who had expressed concern regarding his own safety, was removed from his position as Chairman of the National Commission on Reconciliation. In September security forces attempted to arrest Johnson (who had not yet assumed his ambassadorial post), pursuing him to the US embassy compound, where he and a number of his supporters had taken refuge. The Government subsequently announced that Johnson, Kromah and 21 of their associates had been charged with treason, following an abortive coup attempt, and demanded that US embassy officials relinquish Johnson to Liberian authority. After discussions with the Liberian authorities, however, US officials transported Johnson to Sierra Leone. In response to an incursion by Liberian security forces into the US embassy compound during the fighting, the US Government deployed a naval vessel near the Liberian coast. The Liberian Government subsequently issued a formal apology to the USA and announced that an investigation would be conducted into the incident. In October 32 people (several, including Johnson, *in absentia*) were formally charged with treason; their trial commenced in November.

Regional instability

In December 1998 the Government closed Liberia's border with Sierra Leone, in response to the escalation in civil conflict in the neighbouring country, and pledged support for the administration of President Ahmed Kabbah. In January 1999 it was announced that most of the remaining ECOMOG troops in Liberia were to be redeployed to Sierra Leone, following a major offensive by RUF forces against Freetown. A small number of ECOMOG forces remained in Liberia to provide military assistance to the armed forces. In April 13 of the defendants on trial for treason were convicted and sentenced to 10 years' imprisonment.

In August 1999 members of a rebel movement reported to comprise former members of ULIMO—K, known as the Joint Forces for the Liberation of Liberia (JFLL), attacked principal towns in Lofa County from Guinea. Taylor declared a temporary state of emergency in Lofa County and ordered the closure of the border with Guinea (which was reopened in February 2000). In July 2000 rebel forces again launched an offensive from Guinean territory against Voinjama. Another hitherto unknown movement, Liberians United for Reconciliation and Democracy (LURD), believed to be a grouping of former members of the armed factions (particularly ULIMO—K), claimed responsibility for the attacks. In August Johnson Sirleaf and a further 14 prominent opposition leaders (many of whom were abroad) were charged with alleged involvement with the LURD dissidents.

In February 2001 the authorities announced that the Commander of the RUF, Sam Bockarie, had left Liberia, and that the rebels' liaison office had been closed. Nevertheless, in March the UN Security Council renewed the embargo on the supply of armaments to Liberia and voted in favour of a 12-month ban on diamond exports from Liberia and restrictions on the foreign travel of senior government and military officials; these latter measures were deferred for a period of two months to allow the Government time to comply with demands that it expel RUF members from Liberia and end financial and military aid to the rebels. (In October 2000 the US Government had announced the imposition of diplomatic sanctions against Taylor, his relatives and close associates, prohibiting them from entering the USA until Liberia withdrew support for the RUF.) In May 2001, following Taylor's failure to comply with UN demands, the embargo on exports of diamonds from Liberia, together with the travel restrictions on senior government and military officials, entered into effect. In October a UN commission issued a report recommending the extension of the existing sanctions against Liberia; the report also stated that the Liberian Government continued to use revenue generated by the timber industry and maritime activities to finance illicit trade in armaments with the RUF, and proposed the imposition of additional sanctions on timber exports.

By early 2002 LURD forces had gained considerable territory from government troops, and continued to advance southwards towards Monrovia. In response, on 8 February Taylor declared a national state of emergency. At the beginning of March the leader of LURD, Sekou Damate Conneh, announced that his forces aimed to depose Taylor and install a transitional administration in Monrovia. Later that month representatives of LURD failed to attend negotiations between the Liberian authorities and opposition, which were held in Abuja, under the aegis of ECOWAS, and fighting continued, particularly at Liberia's northern border with Guinea.

On 6 May 2002 the UN Security Council adopted a resolution extending the armaments and diamond embargoes, and the travel ban, for a further 12 months. Also in May the Liberian legislature extended for a further six months the national state of emergency, after LURD forces gained further territory, seizing control of Gbarnga, in Bong County. In September Taylor ended the national state of emergency and the ban on political demonstrations, claiming that government forces had regained control of much of the territory captured by LURD.

During early 2003 hostilities frequently crossed into the territory of Côte d'Ivoire, and reports emerged that Ivorian rebel groups, notably the Mouvement pour la Justice et la Paix (MJP) and the Mouvement Populaire Ivoirien du Grand Ouest (MPIGO), had become allied with LURD. By March LURD had advanced to only 20 km from Monrovia, causing large numbers of civilians to take refuge in the capital. Simultaneous heavy fighting for control of Gbarnga was reported; LURD forces had recaptured the town by April. Meanwhile, a new rebel faction, the Movement for Democracy in Liberia (MODEL), attacked and secured Zwedru in Grand Gedeh County. MODEL was believed to comprise former members of the AFL and Doe loyalists, who were mainly based in Côte d'Ivoire (and reportedly supported by the Ivorian Government). On 6 May the UN Security Council renewed the existing embargoes in force against Liberia for a further year, and imposed an additional ban on timber exports (which entered into effect in early July). Also in early May the Liberian authorities announced that Bockarie (who had been indicted by the Special Court established in Sierra Leone to try suspects of war crimes committed during the conflict in the country) had been killed in Liberia during an attempt to arrest him. Subsequently, however, officials at the Special Court claimed that Bockarie and his immediate family had been captured and murdered by Liberian security forces to prevent him from testifying against prominent regional leaders.

Removal of Taylor

Following pressure from the international community, in March 2003 LURD finally agreed to enter into dialogue with Taylor. Peace discussions commenced in Accra, Ghana, on 4 June, but were disrupted by the announcement of Taylor's indictment for war crimes by the Special Court, in connection with his alleged long-standing involvement with the RUF. On the following day Taylor returned to Monrovia, while LURD forces launched a major attack on Monrovia from the movement's base in Tubmanburg, and rapidly reached the capital's western outskirts. LURD's political leadership issued an ultimatum demanding Taylor's resignation, and French military forces commenced the evacuation of foreign nationals. Following the arrival of a MODEL delegation, the peace discussions in Ghana resumed on 9 June. On 17 June a ceasefire agreement was signed by the LURD and MODEL leaders, and by the Minister of Defence, Daniel Chea. Immediately beforehand, government troops recaptured Greenville, forcing LURD to withdraw to positions some 35 km from Monrovia.

Shortly after the ceasefire agreement was signed in Accra, however, Taylor declared that he would remain in office at least until the end of his presidential term in January 2004, and rejected the Special Court indictment against him. Serious breaches of the ceasefire were reported, and on 26 June 2003, after the resumption of heavy fighting between government and rebel forces in and around Monrovia, in which about 300 civilians were killed, US President George W. Bush urged Taylor to resign. At the end of June the UN Secretary-General recommended to the Security Council that a multinational peacekeeping force be deployed in Liberia in response to the critical humanitarian situation, and urged US military intervention. On 6 July Taylor announced that he had accepted, in principle, an offer of asylum from the Nigerian Head of State, Olusegun Obasanjo, but stipulated that he would not leave the country until a peacekeeping operation was installed. Following continued appeals from Liberian civilians for foreign intervention to prevent a humanitarian disaster, a US mission of military observers was dispatched to Liberia. Later in July, after the rebel offensive to oust Taylor had reached the centre of the capital, the US embassy compound (in which some 10,000 Liberian civilians had taken refuge) was repeatedly bombarded. Some 100 US marines were flown in to defend the building, while US naval vessels were stationed off the Liberian coast. Meanwhile, discussions resumed between the government, LURD and MODEL delegations in Accra.

In July 2003 a summit meeting of ECOWAS Heads of State, which was convened in the Senegalese capital, Dakar, agreed to dispatch an initial 1,300 Nigerian peacekeeping troops to Liberia. On 1 August the UN Security Council officially authorized the establishment of a multinational force with a maximum strength of 3,250 troops, to be known as the ECOWAS Mission in Liberia (ECOMIL), which was to restore security to allow the distribution of emergency humanitarian assistance, and prepare for the deployment of a longer-term UN stabilization force. On 11 August, following continued pressure from West African governments and the international community, Taylor relinquished power to the Vice-President, Moses Zeh Blah, before leaving Liberia for exile in the town of Calabar, in south-eastern Nigeria. Blah was inaugurated as interim Head of State, pending the installation of a government of national unity. Taylor's departure fulfilled the main demand of the rebel leadership, who ceded control of Monrovia Freeport to ECOMIL, and a further 200 US military personnel arrived in Liberia to support the peace operation. On 18 August delegates of the incumbent Government, rebel factions, political opposition and civil organizations, under the aegis of the UN, reached a comprehensive peace agreement, which provided for the establishment of a transitional power-sharing government and legislature, to comprise representatives of the participating groupings. Under the accord, Blah was to transfer power to the new administration on 14 October, all armed militia were to be disbanded, and democratic elections were to be conducted by October 2005. On 21 August 2003 the delegations elected Gyude Bryant, a prominent church figure and leader of the LAP, as Chairman of the transitional administration. By the end of August a UN Joint Monitoring Committee had been dispatched to Monrovia, and ECOMIL troops (then numbering 1,500) were taking control of rebel-held territory.

The National Transitional Government

On 19 September 2003 the UN Security Council formally established the UN Mission in Liberia (UNMIL, see p. 88), which was granted an initial one-year mandate (which was subsequently renewed) to support the transitional authorities and the implementation of the August peace agreement. Its deployment in the country (replacing ECOMIL) commenced on 1 October. On 14 October, under the terms of the peace agreement, Bryant was officially inaugurated as Chairman of the two-year power-sharing administration, the National Transitional Government, while the leader of the UPP, Wesley Johnson, became Vice-Chairman. At the same time a 76-member unicameral legislature, the National Transitional Legislative Assembly (NTLA), comprising representatives of the groupings signatory to the August agreement and 15 deputies nominated by the counties, was installed. A prominent member of LURD, George Dweh, was subsequently elected Speaker of the new Assembly. Later in October LURD and MODEL (which were each allocated five ministries in the National Transitional Government) submitted ministerial nominees for approval by the legislature. Of the former Taylor loyalists, Chea retained the post of Minister of Defence, while LURD representatives were awarded the portfolios of justice and finance, and the leader of MODEL, Thomas Nimely Yaya, became Minister of Foreign Affairs. In early December an international arrest notice was issued against Taylor (who remained in Nigeria) for suspected war crimes. Later that month the UN Security Council adopted a resolution maintaining the embargoes on imports of armaments and on exports of timber and diamonds for a minimum of one year

In March 2004, after the remaining ministerial portfolios were finally designated, Bryant inaugurated the National Transitional Government. Following a further struggle for leadership within LURD, its national executive council announced the removal of Sekou Conneh and his replacement by Chayee Doe (a brother of the former President). In September the International Criminal Court (ICC, see p. 336) announced that Liberia had ratified the signatory treaty, thereby allowing the Court jurisdiction to prosecute crimes committed during the civil conflict. A disarmament process organized by UNMIL, under which a total of some 96,000 former combatants had relinquished armaments, officially ended on 31 October, with a ceremony at which the three former armed factions were also officially dissolved (although operations continued after that date). In December the UN Security Council renewed the sanctions in force on armaments, timber and travel for a further year, while the embargo on the export of diamonds was extended for six months (and again extended in mid-2005).

The 2005 elections

Although the adoption of electoral reform legislation was delayed until December 2004, in February 2005 the National Elections Commission (NEC) announced that the presidential and legislative elections would be conducted on 11 October, as scheduled. New prospective presidential candidates notably included George Manneh Weah, a Liberian national and an international association footballer. At the first round of presidential voting on 11 October, which was contested by a total of 22 candidates, Weah secured 28.3% of votes cast, while Johnson Sirleaf won 19.8% of votes and Charles Brumskine of the Liberty Party (LP) 13.9% of votes. At the elections to the 64-member lower House of Representatives Weah's party, the Congress for Democratic Change (CDC), won 15 seats, the LP nine seats, an alliance known as the Coalition for the Transformation of Liberia (COTOL) eight seats and the UP eight seats. At the elections to the 30-member Senate the COTOL secured seven seats, while the CDC, the UP and the LP each received three seats. Some 74.9% of the registered electorate voted in the presidential ballot and 76.5% in the legislative elections. A second presidential round was conducted on 8 November: Johnson Sirleaf defeated Weah, securing 59.4% of votes cast (with 61.0% of the electorate participating). On 23 November, despite claims of electoral malpractice, the NEC officially declared that Johnson Sirleaf had won the presidential election. Violent demonstrations by Weah's supporters in Monrovia resulted in clashes with security forces and the arrest of some 40 protesters. In mid-December, following international pressure, however, Weah agreed to suspend his legal challenge to Johnson Sirleaf's election at the Supreme Court, and subsequently announced that he would abandon his claim to the presidency in the interests of national reconciliation. Later that month the UN Security Council again extended the sanctions on armaments and travel for a further year and those on diamonds and timber for six months. (UN sanctions on the export of timber were finally lifted in September 2006, and those on diamond exports in April 2007.)

Johnson Sirleaf was inaugurated as President on 16 January 2006, thereby becoming the first woman to be elected Head of State in Africa. The two legislative chambers were officially installed on the same day. In February Johnson Sirleaf established a seven-member Truth and Reconciliation Commission (TRC), which was to investigate human rights abuses perpetrated during the civil conflict. In March, shortly after President Obasanjo declared that Nigeria would agree to Taylor's extradition, following an official request from Johnson Sirleaf, Taylor fled from his residence in Calabar. He was apprehended two days later in Borno State, near the border with Cameroon, and dispatched to Liberia, from where he was immediately extradited by UNMIL peacekeepers to the Special Court. In early April Taylor pleaded 'not guilty' to all charges at the Special Court. Tribunal officials subsequently requested that his trial be transferred to the ICC at The Hague, Netherlands, (while remaining under the jurisdiction of the Special Court), in the interests of regional stability. The Dutch authorities acceded to that request on the condition that any sentence handed down to Taylor was served in another country. The United Kingdom subsequently agreed to host Taylor should he be imprisoned, and, following the unanimous approval of the UN Security Council, on 20 June Taylor was transferred to The Hague, where his trial officially commenced in June 2007.

In January 2009 Charles 'Chuckie' Taylor, Jr, son of the former President, was sentenced to 97 years' imprisonment, after being found guilty of charges relating to torture and executions committed while he was head of a security unit during the civil conflict. In April Bryant, former parliamentary Speaker and head of the Liberia Petroleum Refining Corporation (LPRC) Edwin Snowe, and three others who had been accused of embezzling funds from the LPRC during Bryant's chairmanship of the National Transitional Government were acquitted of all charges of corruption while holding public office.

On 1 July 2009 the TRC submitted its final report recommending the establishment of an Extraordinary Criminal Tribunal for Liberia, and the prosecution or investigation of a number of individuals, corporations and institutions for human rights violations. The Commission also recommended that some 50 people who had associated with or financed the warring factions should be barred from public office for a period of 30 years; they included Johnson Sirleaf, following her admission to the Commission in February that she had supported Taylor's NPFL after its insurrection in 1989, and had donated US $10,000 to the movement. The proposed ban against Johnson Sirleaf prompted domestic and international consternation, and speculation that it had been instigated in view of the forthcoming 2011 elections. (Nevertheless, Johnson Sirleaf subsequently declared her intention to seek re-election in 2011.) The National Assembly was required to adopt a resolution on the TRC's report to allow its enactment; in August 2009 the legislature announced that it would consult with the public for about one year before deciding whether or not to implement the Commission's recommendations. In December the UN Security Council suspended for a trial period of one year the armaments embargo imposed on the Liberian Government, in view of the progress made in national reconstruction, although the embargo was at the same time extended to all non-governmental entities and individuals operating in Liberia; the freeze on the assets of former associates of Taylor and the travel embargo were extended for a further year. (The suspension of the armaments embargo for the Government was subsequently renewed on a yearly basis, while the sanctions on members of the former regime remained in force.)

In December 2009 the General Auditing Commission concluded that Minister of Information, Culture and Tourism Bropleh, who had been suspended from office pending investigations, had embezzled some US $358,000 and recommended his prosecution. (Cletus Sieh was subsequently appointed to replace Bropleh.) In February 2010 George Boley was arrested in the USA on grounds of lack of proper documentation. Later that month the Minister of Internal Affairs, Ambulai Johnson, resigned from his post, owing to his alleged mismanagement of the Social Development Fund; he was replaced by Harrison Kahnweah.

The 2011 elections

In July 2010 the National Assembly adopted legislation creating nine additional parliamentary seats to be distributed among the six most populated counties, thereby increasing the total number of seats in the House of Representatives to 73 (with effect from the next elections). At the end of August the National Assembly approved four constitutional amendments, including a provision that the two-round system used in legislative elections would be replaced by a single-round, first-past-the-post system. The NEC announced in September that the amendments were to be submitted for endorsement at a pre-election national referendum, which was scheduled for 23 August 2011. At a party convention in October 2010, Johnson Sirleaf was nominated as the presidential candidate of the UP (which had previously merged with the LUP and LAP, under the chairmanship of former presidential candidate Varney Sherman); the incumbent Vice-President, Joseph Nyumah Boakai, was confirmed as the party's vice-presidential candidate. Former rebel leader Prince Yormie Johnson had also announced that he intended to contest the forthcoming presidential election. In November Johnson Sirleaf reorganized her Government. In January 2011 the Supreme Court, ruling on a challenge brought by one of those prohibited from holding public office by the TRC report of July 2009, declared that the TRC's recommendation was an unconstitutional violation of the rights of those individuals banned (including Johnson Sirleaf). Only an estimated 34.2% of the electorate participated in the national referendum on 23 August 2011, when all four constitutional amendments failed to secure the requisite approval of two-thirds of votes cast.

At the legislative elections, which were conducted on 11 October 2011, the UP won the highest number of seats in the expanded, 73-member House of Representatives, taking 24, while the CDC retained only 11 seats. The UP also secured the highest representation in the Senate, holding nine seats in total, after receiving four seats in the partial elections to the chamber. In the first round of the concurrent presidential election, Johnson Sirleaf won 43.9% of votes cast, and long-standing politician Winston Tubman, representing the CDC, 32.7%; Prince Yormie Johnson, the candidate of the National Union for Democratic Progress, took only 11.6% of votes. The CDC subsequently protested that NEC officials had perpetrated malpractice on behalf of the UP, prompting the head of the Commission to resign. A number of violent incidents were reported during the ensuing unrest, including an arson attack against the UP party headquarters in mid-October and the killing of two supporters of Tubman when security forces opened fire on a gathering in early November. Shortly before the second presidential round took place, Tubman announced the withdrawal of his candidacy and urged an opposition boycott of the poll, in protest at the alleged fraud. In the event, only an estimated 38.6% of the electorate participated in the second round on 8 November: Johnson Sirleaf was re-elected with some 90.7% of votes cast (Tubman, nevertheless, receiving the remaining 9.3% of the votes). In December Johnson Sirleaf removed the Minister of Information, Culture and Tourism, Cletus Sieh, reportedly owing to the release of information regarding protests in Monrovia by students. Tubman finally conceded the legitimacy of Johnson Sirleaf's election to the presidency in January 2012. After her inauguration on 16 January, Johnson Sirleaf formed a new Government, which notably included Augustine Ngafuan (formerly Minister of Finance) as Minister of Foreign Affairs and Amara Konneh (hitherto Minister of Planning and Economic Affairs) as Minister of Finance. In early March the CDC announced the expulsion of Tubman from the party, accusing him of corruption, and the reinstatement of Weah as party leader; Tubman subsequently declared that he was to retire from politics.

Conviction of Charles Taylor

Meanwhile, Taylor's trial at the Special Court reached completion in March 2011, despite frequent boycotts of proceedings by Taylor and his defence counsel. On 26 April 2012 Taylor was found guilty of aiding and abetting the commission of war crimes, but was acquitted of the charges of directing crimes to be carried out. On 30 May he was sentenced to 50 years' imprisonment (which he was to serve in the United Kingdom). An appeal by Taylor against his conviction was dismissed on 26 September 2013 by the Special Court, which upheld the sentence. Despite a request that he serve his prison sentence in Rwanda, rather than the United Kingdom, Taylor was transferred to a British prison in October.

In July 2012 the UN Security Council announced that it had ended the travel bans and asset freezes imposed on 17 Liberian citizens. In a report issued in September, however, the UN Secretary-General criticized the failure of the Liberian authorities to control illegal trade in diamonds in accordance with the

Kimberley Process Certification Scheme (which had been established under a UN resolution in 2003). Later in September the UN Security Council adopted a resolution that (while again authorizing the extension of UNMIL's mandate for a further year) provided for a staged reduction of 4,200 in its military strength, to about 3,750 personnel by mid-2015. Meanwhile, in August 2012 Johnson Sirleaf suspended from office 46 government officials, including one of her sons (who had held the post of Deputy Governor of the Central Bank), for failing to declare their assets to an Anti-Corruption Commission. In October the head of a government Peace and Reconciliation Commission, Leymah Gbowee, resigned, after denouncing perceived corruption and nepotism in Johnson Sirleaf's administration.

In March 2013 President Johnson Sirleaf announced a reorganization of the Cabinet in which new ministers of labour, transport, and commerce and industry were appointed. Further changes to the Government were effected in May. In August a son of Johnson Sirleaf resigned from his posts as senior presidential adviser and Chairman of the National Oil Co, although it was officially denied that his decision was related to the accusations of nepotism in her administration. In the same month a prominent newspaper that had frequently criticized the Government, *Frontline Africa*, was ordered to close and its editor, Rodney Sieh, was placed in custody, after a Supreme Court ruling that the paper pay US $1.6m. for libelling a former agriculture minister. In January 2014 the Supreme Court suspended the Minister of Justice, Christiana Tah, from her post for a period of six months, after she refused to authorize the imprisonment of Sieh. President Johnson Sirleaf appointed several new deputy ministers and heads of state corporations in January, and in the following month nominated a new Chief and Deputy Chief of Staff of the AFL (which had hitherto been headed by a Nigerian officer). In response to further suspected financial mismanagement, in February Johnson Sirleaf imposed a freeze on the accounts of the Liberia Telecommunications Authority, and suspended a lease agreement between the Authority and a Chinese company.

Recent developments: Ebola epidemic

Following an outbreak of the Ebola Virus Disease (EVD) in Guinea in March 2014, the first cases were confirmed in Liberia by the end of that month. In August (by which time the number of deaths from EVD had reached 576 in Liberia) the Government announced a state of emergency; a blockade imposed by security forces on the West Point suburb of Monrovia as part of quarantine measures precipitated violent protests by residents. Later that month President Johnson Sirleaf dismissed 10 government officials who had failed to comply with an order to return to Liberia. Tah tendered her resignation as Minister of Justice in October, complaining that she had been prevented from conducting investigations into fraud allegations against the country's National Security Agency, which was headed by the President's son, Fombah Sirleaf. In December Benedict Sannoh was appointed as the new Minister of Justice. Meanwhile, President Johnson Sirleaf ended the state of emergency in the country on 13 November, following the authorities' success in containing the EVD outbreak. Shortly afterwards, she replaced the Minister of Health as part of a government reorganization, appointing George Werner, hitherto head of the civil service, to the post.

Partial elections to the Senate, which were due in October 2014, were delayed owing to the Ebola epidemic, and finally took place on 20 December. The UP was the most successful party, securing four of the 15 contested seats. Notably, Weah (of the CDC) was overwhelmingly elected in Montserrado County. An official voter turnout of only 25.2% was recorded, the low attendance being partly attributed to concerns surrounding EVD.

By February 2015 the number of new EVD cases in Liberia had declined considerably (to only 11 in the first half of that month); Johnson Sirleaf announced that Liberia's borders would be reopened. Johnson Sirleaf and her Guinean and Sierra Leonean counterparts, meeting in the Guinean capital, Conakry, on 15 February, declared a common strategy with the intention of eradicating the disease by April. According to the World Health Organization, at late February the number of deaths in Liberia attributed to EVD totalled 4,057, with 9,265 suspected and confirmed cases. Schools were also reopened after a closure of six months, although attendance was reported to be poor. In view of the stabilization in the country, the UN Security Council expected to proceed with the planned reduction in UNMIL personnel (who at the end of January numbered 5,819) to 3,750 by July.

In April 2015 Johnson Sirleaf made further changes to the Cabinet, reassigning Werner to the education portfolio, while Dr Bernice Dahn became Minister of Health (subject to confirmation by the Senate).

Foreign Affairs

Following the election of Ellen Johnson Sirleaf as President in November 2005, Liberia's relations with its neighbouring states improved significantly. Johnson Sirleaf chairs the Mano River Union (initially comprising Liberia, Guinea and Sierra Leone), which was reactivated in 2004 and joined by Côte d'Ivoire in 2008. A non-aggression pact was signed with Sierra Leone when the country's President, Ernest Bai Koroma, visited Liberia in September 2007. During the political crisis that followed the 2010 presidential election in Côte d'Ivoire, reports emerged that President Laurent Gbagbo (prior to his arrest in April 2011) had recruited Liberian mercenaries to abduct opponents and carry out extrajudicial executions. Cross-border raids on western Côte d'Ivoire, which were believed to involve Liberian mercenaries together with Ivorian armed elements loyal to Gbagbo operating from Liberia, became larger in scale during 2012. In June the Liberian Government closed the border with Côte d'Ivoire and dispatched troops to the area, in response to an attack near the Ivorian town of Tai, in which seven members of the UN Operation in Côte d'Ivoire were killed. Four Liberian mercenaries were subsequently arrested on suspicion of perpetrating the attack, while a number of Ivorian nationals were also held in detention in Liberia. In October Johnson Sirleaf, meeting President Alassane Ouattara in Abidjan, Côte d'Ivoire, announced the organization of a joint security operation along the border.

The election of Johnson Sirleaf (a former World Bank official) was widely welcomed by the international community, and also resulted in a dramatic improvement in Liberia's relations with the USA and other major aid donors. US President George W. Bush made an official visit to Liberia in February 2008, the first by a US President in 30 years. In October 2003 the National Transitional Government signed an agreement for the resumption of diplomatic relations with the People's Republic of China (thereby ending links with Taiwan); the Chinese Government subsequently provided substantial funding for reconstruction projects in the country. Bilateral relations with Russia were restored in March 2010. Johnson Sirleaf, together with a Liberian peace activist, Leymah Gbowee, jointly received the Nobel Peace Prize in 2011. Johnson Sirleaf and US Secretary of State Hillary Clinton signed an agreement on a US-Liberia Partnership Dialogue in Washington, DC, USA, in January 2013; the inaugural session was held in May. In October the embassy of the United Kingdom, which had been closed since the onset of the civil conflict, was reopened in Monrovia. Following the regional outbreak of Ebola Virus Disease in March 2014 (see *Domestic Political Affairs*), from October the US Administration stationed military personnel in Monrovia to provide logistical support and training for health care workers, and to construct treatment facilities. In December, when the US legislature allocated US $5,480m. to combat Ebola internationally, Johnson Sirleaf acknowledged the US assistance in suppressing the epidemic. In February 2015 it was announced that the US mission in Liberia, which numbered 2,174 military personnel early that year, was to be withdrawn, earlier than expected, although 100 troops were to remain in the country to monitor the Ebola disease.

CONSTITUTION AND GOVERNMENT

Under the Constitution of January 1986, legislative power is vested in the bicameral National Assembly, comprising the 73-member House of Representatives and the 30-member Senate. Members of the House of Representatives are elected by legislative constituency for a term of six years, while each county elects two members of the Senate (one for a term of nine years and one for six years). Executive power is vested in the President, who is elected to office for a six-year term (renewable only once), and who appoints the Government (subject to the approval of the Senate). Following a peace agreement in August 2003, a democratically elected administration was installed in January 2006 (replacing the power-sharing National Transitional Government). The country comprises 15 counties, which are divided into 64 districts.

REGIONAL AND INTERNATIONAL CO-OPERATION

Liberia is a member of the Economic Community of West African States (ECOWAS, see p. 258) and the Mano River Union (see

p. 448), both of which aim to promote closer economic co-operation in the region. Liberia is also a member of the African Union (see p. 188)

Liberia was a founder member of the UN on its establishment in 1945, and has observer status at the World Trade Organization (WTO, see p. 431).

ECONOMIC AFFAIRS

In 2013, according to the World Bank, Liberia's gross national income (GNI), measured at average 2011–13 prices, was US $1,744m., equivalent to $410 per head (or $790 per head on an international purchasing-power parity basis). During 2004–13, it was estimated, the population increased at an average annual rate of 3.4%, while gross domestic product (GDP) per head declined by an average of 7.6% per year. Overall GDP increased at an average annual rate of 11.2%, in real terms, in 2004–13; real GDP increased by 11.3% in 2013.

Agriculture and forestry contributed an estimated 70.1% of GDP in 2013, according to UN estimates. An estimated 26.7% of the formal labour force were, according to official figures, employed in the sector in 2010; FAO estimated that the sector engaged 59.1% of the labour force in mid-2015. The principal cash crops are rubber (which accounted for an estimated 22.2% of export earnings in 2013), cocoa beans and coffee. The principal food crops are cassava, rice, bananas, plantains, sweet potatoes and yams. According to UN estimates, agricultural GDP increased at an average annual rate of 9.2% in 2004–13; the GDP of the agricultural sector increased by 8.0% in 2013.

Industry (including mining, manufacturing, construction and power) contributed 11.3% of GDP in 2013, according to UN estimates. The sector employed an estimated 4.8% of the formal labour force in 2010, according to official figures. Industrial GDP, according to UN estimates, increased at an average annual rate of 12.3% in 2004–13; the GDP of the industrial sector increased by 7.1% in 2013.

The mining and utilities sector contributed an estimated 2.9% of GDP in 2013, according to UN estimates. The mining sector engaged an estimated 1.2% of the formal labour force in 2010, according to official figures. Gold and diamonds are mined, and Liberia possesses significant amounts of barytes and kyanite. The production and export of mineral products were severely disrupted from 1990, as a result of the civil conflict. In January 2005 the Government prohibited diamond-mining in order to support the enforcement of UN sanctions on the export of diamonds (imposed in 2001). However, mineral exports recommenced in 2007 and, in that year, foreign sales of gold accounted for 2.7% of total export revenue; diamonds contributed 1.3%. In 2013 these commodities contributed 4.0% and 3.1% of total exports, respectively. According to UN estimates, the GDP of the mining and utilities sector increased at an average annual rate of 26.4% in 2004–13; the GDP of the sector increased by 6.5% in 2013.

Manufacturing provided an estimated 5.7% of GDP in 2013, according to UN estimates. The sector engaged an estimated 0.9% of the formal labour force in 2010, according to official figures. Manufacturing GDP, according to UN estimates, increased at an average annual rate of 11.3% in 2004–13; the GDP of the manufacturing sector increased by 7.6% in 2013.

Construction provided an estimated 2.6% of GDP in 2013, according to UN estimates. The sector engaged an estimated 2.7% of the formal labour force in 2010, according to official figures. Construction GDP increased at an average annual rate of 6.9% in 2004–13, according to UN estimates; the GDP of the construction sector increased by 6.8% in 2013.

Energy is derived from the consumption of fossil fuels (62.2%) and from hydroelectric power (37.8%). Liberia is dependent on imports of petroleum, which comprised an estimated 22.8% of the value of total imports in 2013.

The services sector contributed 18.6% of GDP in 2013, according to UN estimates. The sector employed an estimated 68.5% of the formal labour force in 2010, according to official figures. According to UN estimates, the GDP of the services sector increased at an average annual rate of 10.4% in 2004–13; the GDP of the sector increased by 7.8% in 2013.

Liberia's large open-registry ('flag of convenience') merchant shipping fleet has become an increasingly significant source of foreign exchange. In 2013 revenue from Liberia's maritime programme accounted for an estimated 3.5% of total revenue.

In 2013, according to IMF figures, Liberia recorded an estimated visible merchandise trade deficit of US $395.2m., and there was a deficit of $535.8m. on the current account of the balance of payments. In 2011 the principal source of imports (41.7%) was the Republic of Korea. The People's Republic of China and Japan were other major providers of imports. The principal market for exports in 2012 was Poland (36.6%); the other major purchasers were Germany and the USA. The principal exports in 2013 were iron ore, rubber and gold. The principal imports in that year were machinery and transport equipment, petroleum, food and live animals, basic manufactures, and beverages and tobacco.

Liberia's overall budgetary deficit was projected to be US $77.1m. in 2013/14, according to IMF figures. Liberia's general government gross debt was L $492m. in 2012, equivalent to 28.1% of GDP. The country's external debt totalled US $487m. at the end of 2012, of which US $208m. was public and publicly guaranteed debt. In 2011 the cost of servicing long-term public and publicly guaranteed debt and repayments to the IMF was equivalent to 0.2% of the value of exports of goods, services and income (excluding workers' remittances). The annual rate of inflation averaged 10.8% in 2004–13; consumer prices increased by 7.7% in 2013, according to the African Development Bank (AfDB). In 2006 unemployment was estimated at about 85.0% of the labour force; this figure, however, refers only to the small formal sector rather than to the economy as a whole.

The installation of a government headed by President Ellen Johnson Sirleaf, a former World Bank economist, in January 2006 marked a turning point in Liberia's economy, which had been ravaged by civil conflict. UN sanctions on the export of timber were lifted in September and those on diamond exports in April 2007; shortly afterwards Liberia joined the Extractive Industries Transparency Initiative. In December the AfDB cancelled US $255.2m. of Liberia's debt, and in March 2008 the country cleared its long-standing overdue obligations with the IMF; the Fund fully restored Liberia's rights and designated it eligible for debt relief under the initiative for heavily indebted poor countries (HIPC). In June 2010 the IMF and World Bank, having determined that Liberia had made the required progress to reach completion point under the HIPC initiative, approved $4,600m. of debt relief, thereby reducing the country's external debt by more than 90%. Foreign investment in the country rose significantly from 2011, with the approval of new concessions in the iron ore and palm oil sectors, and the acquisition by US corporation Chevron of a 70% interest in three offshore exploration areas. In June iron ore exports were resumed after a suspension of about 20 years, following funding by international steel and mining company ArcelorMittal under a 2005 agreement. However, the Government of Johnson Sirleaf was subject to continued criticism for corruption. In November 2012 the IMF approved a three-year Extended Credit Facility arrangement for Liberia, totalling about $78.9m., to finance continued poverty reduction efforts. An outbreak of Ebola Virus Disease which began in March 2014 (see *Domestic Political Affairs*) produced a severe downturn in the economy, in addition to a humanitarian crisis: the growth rate, which had exceeded 11% in 2013, fell to only 0.3% in 2014 (according to official estimates), while inflation accelerated to 9.9% as the disease affected farming and food production. The country's fiscal balance deteriorated as a result of a sharp fall in export and tax revenues. The IMF announced in September that Liberia would receive emergency funding of $49m. to support efforts to combat the disease. In February 2015 the IMF approved the extension of debt relief totalling $100m. for Liberia, Sierra Leone and Guinea, under a newly established Catastrophe Containment and Relief Trust. By that time the number of new Ebola cases in Liberia had decreased significantly. However, recovery in 2015 was expected to be hampered by a sharp fall in the international prices of rubber and iron ore.

PUBLIC HOLIDAYS

2016: 1 January (New Year's Day), 11 February (Armed Forces Day), 9 March (Decoration Day), 15 March (J. J. Roberts' Birthday), 8 April (Fast and Prayer Day), 14 May (National Unification Day), 26 July (Independence Day), 24 August (Flag Day), 3 November (Thanksgiving Day), 29 November (President Tubman's Birthday), 25 December (Christmas Day).

Statistical Survey

Sources (unless otherwise stated): Liberia Institute of Statistics and Geo-Information Services, POB 629, Tubman Blvd, Sinkor, Monrovia; internet www.tlcafrica.com/lisgis/lisgis.htm; Central Bank of Liberia, POB 2048, cnr of Warren and Carey Sts, Monrovia; tel. 6225685 (mobile); fax 6226114 (mobile); internet www.cbl.org.lr.

Area and Population

AREA, POPULATION AND DENSITY

Area (sq km)	97,754*
Population (census results)	
1 February 1984	2,101,628
21 March 2008	
Males	1,739,945
Females	1,736,663
Total	3,476,608
Population (UN estimates at mid-year)†	
2013	4,294,078
2014	4,396,871
2015	4,503,439
Density (per sq km) at mid-2015	46.1

* 37,743 sq miles.
† Source: UN, *World Population Prospects: The 2012 Revision.*

POPULATION BY AGE AND SEX
(UN estimates at mid-2015)

	Males	Females	Total
0–14 years	972,223	932,989	1,905,212
15–64 years	1,234,927	1,227,681	2,462,608
65 years and over	62,645	72,974	135,619
Total	2,269,795	2,233,644	4,503,439

Source: UN, *World Population Prospects: The 2012 Revision.*

COUNTIES
(population at 2008 census)

Bomi	84,119	Margibi	209,923
Bong	333,481	Maryland . . .	135,938
Gbarpolu . . .	83,388	Montserrado . .	1,118,241
Grand Bassa . . .	221,693	Nimba	462,026
Grand Cape Mount .	127,076	Rivercess . . .	71,509
Grand Gedeh . . .	125,258	River Gee . . .	66,789
Grand Kru . . .	57,913	Sinoe	102,391
Lofa	276,863	**Total**	3,476,608

PRINCIPAL TOWNS
(2003)

Monrovia (capital) .	550,200	Harbel	17,700
Zwedru	35,300	Tubmanburg . . .	16,700
Buchanan . . .	27,300	Gbarnga . . .	14,200
Yekepa . . .	22,900	Greenville . . .	13,500
Harper	20,000	Ganta . . .	11,200
Bensonville . . .	19,600		

Source: Stefan Helders, *World Gazetteer.*

Mid-2014 (incl. suburbs, UN estimate): Monrovia 1,223,880 (Source: UN, *World Urbanization Prospects: The 2014 Revision*).

BIRTHS AND DEATHS
(annual averages, UN estimates)

	2000–05	2005–10	2010–15
Birth rate (per 1,000)	41.6	38.6	35.7
Death rate (per 1,000)	13.9	10.3	9.0

Source: UN, *World Population Prospects: The 2012 Revision.*

Life expectancy (years at birth): 60.2 (males 59.3; females 61.2) in 2012 (Source: World Bank, World Development Indicators database).

EMPLOYMENT
(formal sector only)

	2008	2009	2010*
Agriculture and forestry . . .	22,616	34,882	38,615
Mining	1,421	1,907	1,691
Manufacturing	2,215	2,075	1,367
Construction	390	1,659	3,856
Wholesale and retail trade . .	10,028	10,998	7,536
Transport and communications .	4,984	5,563	9,423
Banking and insurance . . .	2,189	4,044	6,426
Business services	6,231	9,467	10,179
Social and community services .	9,213	20,160	28,020
Government	47,681	34,000	37,532
Total	106,968	124,755	144,647

* Estimates.

Total employed in informal sector: 487,000 in 2008; 569,790 in 2009; 672,352 (estimate) in 2010.

Mid-2015 ('000 persons, estimates): Agriculture, etc. 985; Total labour force 1,668 (Source: FAO).

Health and Welfare

KEY INDICATORS

Total fertility rate (children per woman, 2012)	4.9
Under-5 mortality rate (per 1,000 live births, 2012) . . .	75
HIV/AIDS (% of persons aged 15–49, 2013)	1.1
Physicians (per 1,000 head, 2008)	0.01
Hospital beds (per 1,000 head, 2010)	0.8
Health expenditure (2011): US $ per head (PPP)	92
Health expenditure (2011): % of GDP	15.6
Health expenditure (2011): public (% of total)	19.1
Access to water (% of persons, 2012)	75
Access to sanitation (% of persons, 2012)	17
Total carbon dioxide emissions ('000 metric tons, 2010) . .	799.4
Carbon dioxide emissions per head (metric tons, 2010) . .	0.2
Human Development Index (2013): ranking	175
Human Development Index (2013): value	0.412

For sources and definitions, see explanatory note on p. vi.

Agriculture

PRINCIPAL CROPS
('000 metric tons)

	2011	2012	2013
Rice, paddy	298*	291†	238†
Cassava (Manioc)*	515	500	520
Taro (Cocoyam)*	27	28	28
Yams*	21	22	22
Sweet potatoes*	22	23	23
Sugar cane*	265	265	265
Oil palm fruit*	174	176	176
Bananas*	125	127	132
Plantains*	47	47	48
Natural rubber*	63	63	63

* FAO estimate(s).
† Unofficial figure.

Aggregate production ('000 metric tons, may include official, semi-official or estimated data): Total cereals 298 in 2011, 291 in 2012, 238 in 2013; Total roots and tubers 585 in 2011, 572 in 2012, 592 in 2013; Total vegetables (incl. melons) 109 in 2011, 112 in 2012, 116 in 2013; Total fruits (excl. melons) 191 in 2011, 194 in 2012, 200 in 2013.

Source: FAO.

LIVESTOCK
('000 head, year ending September, FAO estimates)

	2011	2012	2013
Cattle	40	40	42
Pigs	288	290	292
Sheep	268	270	275
Goats	340	342	345
Chickens	7,100	7,300	7,600
Ducks	320	320	320

Source: FAO.

LIVESTOCK PRODUCTS
(metric tons, FAO estimates)

	2010	2011	2012
Pig meat	9,020	9,720	9,800
Chicken meat	10,880	11,440	11,600
Game meat	7,500	8,000	8,000
Cows' milk	819	839	845
Hen eggs	5,200	5,375	5,500

2013: Figures assumed to be unchanged from 2012 (FAO estimates).

Source: FAO.

Forestry

ROUNDWOOD REMOVALS
('000 cubic metres, excluding bark)

	2011	2012	2013*
Sawlogs, veneer logs and logs for sleepers	304	338	338
Other industrial wood*	180	180	180
Fuel wood*	7,254	7,508	7,771
Total	7,738	8,026	8,289

* FAO estimates.

Source: FAO.

SAWNWOOD PRODUCTION
('000 cubic metres, including railway sleepers)

	2006	2007	2008
Total (all broadleaved)	60	60	80

2009–13: Figure assumed to unchanged from 2008 (FAO estimate).

Source: FAO.

Fishing

(metric tons, live weight of capture)

	2007	2008	2009*
Freshwater fishes	1,743	763	2,200
African sicklefish	150	185	180
Barracudas	356	126	130
Bobo croaker	201	260	260
Cassava croaker	381	229	220
Clupeoids	n.a.	1	1
Hammerhead sharks	332	n.a.	100
Marlins, sailfishes, etc.	459	180	180
Sardinellas	1,599	626	630
Sharks, rays, skates, etc.	504	108	100
Snappers	243	251	250
Total catch (incl. others)	14,488	7,890	9,500

* FAO estimates.

2010–12: Figures assumed to be unchanged from 2009 (FAO estimates).

Source: FAO.

Mining

	2011	2012	2013
Diamonds ('000 carats)	42	42	44
Gold (kilograms)	448	641	600

Note: In addition to the commodities listed, Liberia produced significant quantities of a variety of industrial minerals and construction materials (clays, gypsum, sand and gravel, and stone), but insufficient information was available to make reliable estimates of output levels.

Source: US Geological Survey.

Industry

SELECTED PRODUCTS
(litres unless otherwise indicated)

	2011	2012	2013*
Beverages	30,503,151	28,099,740	29,239,260
Cement (metric tons)	80,594	121,592	181,829
Paint	295,179	354,005	212,226
Candles (kilograms)	442,575	299,229	163,682
Bleach	694,593	681,160	816,800
Rubbing alcohol	221,184	198,620	227,901
Mattresses (number)	142,000	108,667	100,704
Treated (finished) water (million gallons)	930.2	1,752.2	1,809.8

* Estimates.

Electric energy (million kWh): 353 in 2008–11 (Source: UN Industrial Commodity Statistics Database).

Finance

CURRENCY AND EXCHANGE RATES
Monetary Units
  100 cents = 1 Liberian dollar (L $).

Sterling, Dollar and Euro Equivalents (31 December 2014)
  £1 sterling = L $128.766;
  US $1 = L $82.500;
  €1 = L $100.163;
  L $1,000 = £7.77 = US $12.12 = €9.98.

Average Exchange Rate (L $ per US $)
  2012   73.5148
  2013   77.5200
  2014   83.8925

Note: The aforementioned data are based on market-determined rates of exchange. Prior to January 1998 the exchange rate was a fixed parity with the US dollar (L $1 = US $1).

BUDGET
(US $ million)

Revenue*	2011/12	2012/13†	2013/14‡
Tax revenue	357.0	369.5	378.3
Taxes on income, profits and capital gains	145.4	156.8	158.0
Taxes on goods and services	53.7	67.0	67.7
Taxes on international trade and transactions	149.0	140.8	147.8
Other taxes	8.9	4.8	4.8
Non-tax revenue	73.7	139.9	92.6
Total	430.6	509.4	470.9

Expenditure§	2011/12	2012/13†	2013/14‡
Current expenditure	437.6	493.0	427.0
Wages and salaries . . .	181.4	211.3	200.0
Other goods and services . .	113.9	161.5	129.0
Subsidies and transfers . .	137.5	114.0	90.0
Interest on debt	4.9	6.2	8.0
Capital expenditure	76.4	91.0	201.5
Total	514.0	584.0	628.5

* Excluding grants received (US $ million): 28.3 in 2011/12; 45.7 in 2012/13 (budget estimate); 80.5 in 2013/14 (budget projection).
† Budget estimates.
‡ Budget projections.
§ Includes net lending.

Source: IMF, *Liberia: Third Review Under the Extended Credit Facility Arrangement and Request for Waiver of Nonobservance of Performance Criterion and Modification of Performance Criteria-Staff Report; and Press Release* (July 2014).

INTERNATIONAL RESERVES
(US $ million at 31 December)

	2011	2012	2013
IMF special drawing rights . .	223.56	242.01	266.73
Reserve position in IMF . . .	0.05	0.05	0.05
Foreign exchange	289.72	257.50	226.32
Total	513.33	499.56	493.10

Source: IMF, *International Financial Statistics*.

MONEY SUPPLY
(L $ million at 31 December)

	2011	2012	2013
Currency outside banks* . . .	6,704.3	1,708.5	8,271.7
Demand deposits at commercial banks	23,364.7	22,841.4	31,533.2
Total money (incl. others) . .	31,295.3	24,886.5	39,972.2

* Figures refer only to amounts of Liberian coin in circulation. US notes and coin also circulate, but the amount of these in private holdings is unknown. The amount of Liberian coin in circulation is small in comparison to US currency.

Source: IMF, *International Financial Statistics*.

COST OF LIVING
(Consumer Price Index; base: May 1998 = 100)

	2003	2004	2005
Food	140.9	153.8	167.0
Fuel and light	154.4	217.6	342.1
Clothing	121.2	128.7	137.3
Rent	131.8	156.1	180.9
All items (incl. others) . . .	157.0	169.3	187.6

Source: IMF, *Liberia: Selected Issues and Statistical Appendix* (May 2006).

All items (Consumer Price Index; base 2005 = 100): 179.2 in 2011; 191.5 in 2012; 206.3 in 2013 (Source: African Development Bank).

NATIONAL ACCOUNTS
Expenditure on the Gross Domestic Product
(US $ million at current prices)

	2011	2012	2013
Government final consumption expenditure	235	268	292
Private final consumption expenditure	1,923	2,016	2,358
Gross capital formation . . .	388	440	499
Total domestic expenditure .	2,546	2,724	3,149
Exports of goods and services . .	424	561	513
Less Imports of goods and services	1,429	1,552	1,715
GDP in purchasers' values .	1,540	1,734	1,946
GDP at constant 2005 prices .	1,162	1,257	1,359

Gross Domestic Product by Economic Activity
(US $ million at current prices)

	2011	2012	2013
Agriculture	1,000	1,125	1,263
Mining and utilities	43	48	53
Manufacturing	82	92	103
Construction	38	42	47
Trade, restaurants and hotels .	71	79	89
Transport, storage and communications	78	87	98
Other service activities . . .	117	132	148
Sub-total	1,429	1,605	1,801
Indirect taxes (net)*	111	129	145
GDP in market prices . . .	1,540	1,734	1,946

* Figures obtained as a residual.

Source: UN Statistics Division, National Accounts Main Aggregates Database.

BALANCE OF PAYMENTS
(US $ million)

	2011	2012	2013
Exports of goods	645.7	507.2	624.3
Imports of goods	−2,068.4	−1,011.0	−1,019.6
Balance on goods	−1,422.8	−503.8	−395.2
Exports of services	604.1	178.9	203.1
Imports of services	−1,242.8	−940.7	−942.2
Balance on goods and services	−2,061.5	−1,265.7	−1,134.3
Primary income received . . .	102.1	23.5	22.5
Primary income paid	−14.1	−365.4	−400.3
Balance on goods, services and primary income	−1,973.5	−1,607.5	−1,512.1
Secondary income (net) . . .	1,020.4	1,127.6	976.3
Current balance	−953.0	−479.9	−535.8
Capital account (net)	—	37.4	32.5
Direct investment liabilities . .	1,312.7	646.6	700.3
Other investment assets . . .	−626.5	32.4	−13.4
Other investment liabilities . .	−2.3	117.3	107.4
Net errors and omissions . . .	−21.8	−322.5	−272.0
Reserves and related items .	−291.0	31.2	19.1

Source: IMF, *International Financial Statistics*.

External Trade

PRINCIPAL COMMODITIES
(US $ million)

Imports c.i.f.	2011	2012	2013*
Food and live animals	306.1	195.3	183.9
Rice	121.8	68.7	88.3
Beverages and tobacco . . .	20.4	21.5	100.8
Mineral fuels and lubricants . .	62.0	62.0	46.9
Petroleum	216.9	256.9	275.6
Chemicals and related products .	35.4	48.0	79.2
Basic manufactures	94.1	115.4	154.7
Machinery and transport equipment	250.9	310.9	300.8
Miscellaneous manufactured articles	41.5	28.8	28.3
Total (incl. others)	1,044.2	1,076.4	1,210.9

Exports f.o.b.	2011	2012	2013*
Rubber	226.1	176.8	120.5
Cocoa beans and coffee . . .	14.4	6.6	9.9
Diamonds	17.6	12.4	17.0
Gold	14.9	26.3	22.0
Iron ore	22.2	117.1	312.2
Total (incl. others)	358.1	444.4	543.7

* Preliminary data.

SELECTED TRADING PARTNERS
(US $ million)

Imports c.i.f.	2009	2010	2011
China, People's Republic . . .	88.6	190.8	292.8
Germany	4.7	6.2	26.0
Japan	70.0	84.9	26.0
Korea, Republic	230.0	234.4	435.7
Singapore	77.4	125.2	n.a.
Total (incl. others)	563.0	719.0	1,044.0

Exports f.o.b.	2009	2010	2011
Germany	40.7	8.9	124.1
India	3.1	4.2	43.5
Malaysia	3.7	2.9	39.4
Poland	36.7	53.0	282.8
USA	8.9	43.7	51.4
Total (incl. others)	160.0	200.0	774.0

2012: *Imports:* Japan 26.0; Germany 6.6; Total (incl. others) 1,123.0. *Exports:* Germany 131.6; India 47.1; Malaysia 42.5; Poland 303.4; USA 55.3; Total (incl. others) 829.0.

2013: *Imports:* Total 1,211.0. *Exports:* Total 544.0.

Source: African Development Bank.

Transport

ROAD TRAFFIC
(motor vehicles in use at 31 December)

	2007
Passenger cars	7,428
Buses and coaches	554
Lorries and vans	2,772
Motorcycles and mopeds	333

Source: IRF, *World Road Statistics*.

SHIPPING
Flag Registered Fleet
(at 31 December)

	2012	2013	2014
Number of vessels	3,818	3,825	3,800
Displacement ('000 grt) . . .	130,379.1	131,376.7	131,576.3

Source: Lloyd's List Intelligence (www.lloydslistintelligence.com).

Communications Media

	2011	2012	2013
Mobile cellular telephones ('000 subscribers)	2,029.9	2,393.6	2,555.4

2011: Main telephone lines in use (incl. fixed wireless) 3,200; Broadband subscribers 63.

Source: International Telecommunication Union.

Education
(2013)

	Institutions	Teachers	Students Males	Females	Total
Pre-primary . .	2,544	6,276	148,241	140,298	288,539
Primary . . .	n.a.	n.a.	197,521	176,201	373,722
Secondary . .	776	7,197	70,598	53,466	124,064

Source: Ministry of Education, Monrovia.

Pupil-teacher ratio (primary education, UNESCO estimate): 26.8 in 2010/11 (Source: UNESCO Institute for Statistics).

Adult literacy rate (UNESCO estimates): 60.8% (males 64.8%; females 56.8%) in 2010 (Source: UNESCO Institute for Statistics).

Directory

The Government
HEAD OF STATE

President: ELLEN JOHNSON SIRLEAF (inaugurated 16 January 2006; re-elected 8 November 2011).

Vice-President: JOSEPH NYUMAH BOAKAI.

THE CABINET
(May 2015)

Minister of Agriculture: Dr FLORENCE CHENOWETH.

Minister of Commerce and Industry: AXEL ADDY.

Minister of Defence: BROWNIE SAMUKAI.

Minister of Education: GEORGE WERNER.

Minister of Finance and Development Planning: AMARA M. KONNEH.

Minister of Foreign Affairs: AUGUSTINE NGAFUAN.

Minister of Gender, Children and Social Protection: JULIA DUNCAN-CASSELL.

Minister of Health: Dr BERNICE DAHN.

Minister of Information, Culture and Tourism: LEWIS G. BROWN, II.

Minister of Internal Affairs: MORRIS DUKULY.

Minister of Justice: (vacant).

Minister of Labour: NETO ZARZAR LIGHE.

Minister of Lands, Mines and Energy: ROOSEVELT JAYJAY.

Minister of National Security: VICTOR HELB.

Minister of Posts and Telecommunications: FREDERICK NORKEH.

Minister of Public Works: WILLIAM GYUDE MOORE.

Minister of Transport: ANGELA BUSH.

Minister of Youth and Sports: LENN EUGENE NAGBE.

Minister of State without Portfolio: SYLVESTER GRIGSBY.

MINISTRIES

Office of the President: Executive Mansion, POB 10-9001, Capitol Hill, 1000 Monrovia 10; e-mail gmoore@emansion.gov.lr; internet www.emansion.gov.lr.

Ministry of Agriculture: 19th St, Sinkor, POB 10-9010, 1000 Monrovia 10; tel. 226399; internet www.moaliberia.org.

Ministry of Commerce and Industry: Ashmun St, POB 10-9014, 1000 Monrovia 10; tel. 226283; internet www.moci.gov.lr.

Ministry of Defence: Benson St, POB 10-9007, 1000 Monrovia 10; tel. 226077; internet www.mod.gov.lr.

Ministry of Education: E. G. N. King Plaza, Broad St, POB 10-1545, 1000 Monrovia 10; tel. and fax 226216; internet www.moe.gov.lr.

Ministry of Finance and Development Planning: Broad St, POB 10-9013, 1000 Monrovia 10; tel. 47510680 (mobile); internet www.mfdp.gov.lr.

Ministry of Foreign Affairs: Mamba Point, POB 10-9002, 1000 Monrovia 10; tel. 226763; internet www.mofa.gov.lr.

Ministry of Gender, Children and Social Protection: UN Dr. and Gurley St, Monrovia; e-mail info@mogd.gov.lr; internet mogdliberia.com.

Ministry of Health and Social Welfare: Sinkor, POB 10-9004, 1000 Monrovia 10; tel. 226317; e-mail info@mohsw.gov.lr; internet www.mohsw.gov.lr.

Ministry of Information, Culture and Tourism: Capitol Hill, POB 10-9021, 1000 Monrovia 10; tel. and fax 226269; internet www.micatliberia.com.

Ministry of Internal Affairs: cnr Warren and Benson Sts, POB 10-9008, 1000 Monrovia 10; tel. 226346; e-mail tiahnagbe@mia.gov.lr; internet www.mia.gov.lr.

Ministry of Justice: Ashmun St, POB 10-9006, 1000 Monrovia 10; tel. 227872; internet www.moj.gov.lr.

Ministry of Labour: Mechlin St, POB 10-9040, 1000 Monrovia 10; tel. 226291; internet www.mol.gov.lr.

Ministry of Lands, Mines and Energy: Capitol Hill, POB 10-9024, 1000 Monrovia 10; tel. 226281; internet www.molme.gov.lr.

Ministry of National Security: Monrovia.

Ministry of Posts and Telecommunications: cnr Carey and McDonald Sts, 1000 Monrovia 10; tel. 886552947 (mobile); e-mail internationalbureaulr@yahoo.com; internet www.mopt.gov.lr.

Ministry of Public Works: Lynch St, POB 10-9011, 1000 Monrovia 10; tel. 227972; internet www.mopw.gov.lr.

Ministry of Transport: 1000 Monrovia 10; internet www.mopt.gov.lr.

Ministry of Youth and Sports: Monrovia; internet www.moys.gov.lr.

President

Presidential Election, First Round, 11 October 2011

Candidate	Votes	% of votes
Ellen Johnson Sirleaf (Unity Party) . .	530,020	43.93
Winston A. Tubman (Congress for Democratic Change)	394,370	32.68
Prince Yormie Johnson (National Union for Democratic Progress)	139,786	11.58
Charles Walker Brumskine (Liberty Party)	65,800	5.45
Others	76,666	6.35
Total	**1,206,642**	**100.00**

Presidential Election, Second Round, 8 November 2011

Candidate	Votes	% of votes
Ellen Johnson Sirleaf (Unity Party) . .	607,618	90.71
Winston A. Tubman (Congress for Democratic Change)	62,207	9.29
Total	**669,825**	**100.00**

Legislature

HOUSE OF REPRESENTATIVES

House of Representatives: Capitol Bldg, Monrovia; internet legislature.gov.lr/house.

Speaker: ALEX JANEKAI TYLER.

General Election, 11 October 2011

Party	Seats
Unity Party	24
Congress for Democratic Change	11
Independents	9
Liberty Party	7
National Union for Democratic Progress . . .	6
National Democratic Coalition	5
Alliance for Peace and Democracy	3
National Patriotic Party	3
Movement for Progressive Change	2
Liberia Destiny Party	1
Liberia Transformation Party	1
National Reformation Party	1
Total	**73**

SENATE

Senate: Capitol Bldg, Monrovia; internet legislature.gov.lr/senate.

President: JOSEPH NYUMAH BOAKAI.

General Election, 11 October 2011

Party	Seats
Unity Party	9
Independents	6
National Patriotic Party	4
Congress for Democratic Change	3
Alliance for Peace and Democracy	2
Liberty Party	2
Liberia Destiny Party	1
Liberia Transformation Party	1
National Democratic Coalition	1
National Union for Democratic Progress . . .	1
Total	**30**

Elections for 15 seats in the Senate were held on 20 December 2014. Of these, the Unity Party won four seats, independents won three, the Congress for Democratic Change and the Liberty Party both won two seats and the Alternative National Congress, the National Democratic Coalition, the National Patriotic Party and the People's Unification Party each won one seat.

Election Commission

National Elections Commission: Tubman Blvd, 16th St, Sinkor, Monrovia; e-mail jkennedy@necliberia.org; internet www.necliberia.org; independent; Chair. JEROME G. KORKOYA.

Political Organizations

Some 24 political parties were listed by the National Elections Commission at mid-2015. The most significant of these parties are listed below:

Alliance for Peace and Democracy (APD): Benson St, Monrovia; tel. 6918196 (mobile); e-mail karwease@go.metrostate.edu; internet www.members.tripod.com/tipoteh12/index.html; f. 2005; Chair. MARCUS S. G. DAHN.

Citizens Unification Party (CUP): Monrovia; f. 2011; Chair. MOMOLU FREEMAN.

Congress for Democratic Change (CDC): Tubman Blvd, POB 2799, Monrovia; tel. 6513469 (mobile); internet www.cdcliberia.org; f. 2004; Leader GEORGE MANNEH WEAH; Chair. GEORGE SOLO.

Free Democratic Party (FDP): Center St, Monrovia; tel. 6582291 (mobile); Leader DAVID M. FARHAT; Chair. S. CIAPHA GBOLLIE.

Grassroots Democratic Party of Liberia (GDPL): Monrovia; Chair. GLADYS BEYAN.

Liberia Destiny Party (LDP): Congo Town Back Rd, Monrovia; tel. 6511531 (mobile); f. 2005; Chair. BOIMAH TAYLOR; Sec.-Gen. BORBOR B. KROMAH.

Liberia National Union (LINU): 16th St, Sinkor, Monrovia; tel. 77059282 (mobile); Chair. AARON S. M. WESSEH.

Liberia Transformation Party (LTP): Monrovia; f. 1984; Leader KENNEDY GBLEYAH SANDY; Chair. JULIUS SUKU.

Liberty Party (LP): Old Rd, Sinkor Opposite Haywood Mission, POB 1340, Monrovia; tel. 6547921 (mobile); f. 2005; Chair. J. FONATI KOFFA.

Movement for Progressive Change (MPC): Fiama, 21st St, Sinkor, Monrovia; Leader SIMEON FREEMAN.

Nation Democratic Party of Liberia (NDPL): Capitol By-Pass, Monrovia; f. 1997 from the fmr armed faction the Liberia Peace Council; Chair. D. NYANDEH SIEH, Sr.

National Patriotic Party (NPP): Sinkor, Tubman Bldg, Monrovia; tel. 6515312 (mobile); f. 1997 from the fmr armed faction the National Patriotic Front of Liberia; Leader ROLAND CHRIS YARKPAH MASSAQUOI; Chair. THEOPHILUS C. GOULD.

National Reformation Party (NRP): Duala Market, Monrovia; tel. 6511531 (mobile); Chair. Rev. MAXIMILLIAN T. W. DIABE.

National Union for Democratic Progress (NUDP): VP Rd, Old Rd, Monrovia; tel. 6645421 (mobile); Chair. GBAWOU KOWOU.

National Democratic Coalition: Monrovia; a coalition of opposition parties formed in 2011; Leader DEW MAYSON.

People's Unification Party: Monrovia; Chair. HENRY W. YALLAH.

Progressive Democratic Party (PRODEM): McDonald St, Monrovia; tel. 6521091 (mobile); f. early 2005 by mems of fmr rebel movement, Liberians United for Reconciliation and Democracy (emerged 1999); Chair. GARBLA WILLIAMS.

Unity Party (UP): 86 Broad St, Monrovia; tel. 6512528 (mobile); e-mail info@theunityparty.org; f. 1984; Leader ELLEN JOHNSON SIRLEAF; Chair. HARRY VARNEY GBOTO-NAMBI SHERMAN.

Diplomatic Representation

EMBASSIES IN LIBERIA

Algeria: Capitol By-Pass, POB 2032, Monrovia; tel. 224311; Chargé d'affaires a.i. MUHAMMAD AZZEDINE AZZOUZ.

Cameroon: 18th St and Payne Ave, Sinkor, POB 414, Monrovia; tel. 261374; Ambassador BENG'YELA AUGUSTINE GANG.

China, People's Republic: Tubman Blvd, Congo Town, POB 5970, Monrovia; tel. 228024; fax 226740; e-mail Chinaemb_lr@mfa.gov.cn; internet lr.china-embassy.org; Ambassador ZHANG YUE.

Congo, Democratic Republic: Spriggs Payne Airport, Sinkor, POB 1038, Monrovia; tel. 261326; Ambassador (vacant).

Côte d'Ivoire: Tubman Blvd, Sinkor, POB 126, Monrovia; tel. 261123; Ambassador SORO KAPÉLÉTIEN.

Egypt: Coconut Plantation, Randall St, Mamba Point, POB 462, Monrovia; tel. 226226; fax 226122; Ambassador SAMEH LOTFI.

France: German Compound, Congo Town, Monrovia; tel. 6579373 (mobile); e-mail ambafrance.liberia@yahoo.fr; Ambassador JOËL GODEAU.

Germany: Tubman Blvd, Monrovia; tel. 886438365 (mobile); e-mail info@monrovia.diplo.de; Ambassador RALPH TIMMERMANN.

Ghana: cnr 11th St and Gardiner Ave, Sinkor, POB 471, Monrovia; tel. 261477; Ambassador KODJO ASIMENG WADEE.

Guinea: POB 461, Monrovia; e-mail dore10032@yahoo.com; Ambassador ABDOULAYE DORÉ.

Holy See: Capitol Hill, Monrovia; e-mail nuntiusliberia@gmail.com; Apostolic Nuncio MIROSŁAW ADAMCZYK.

Lebanon: 12th St, Monrovia; tel. 262537; Ambassador MANSOUR ABDALLAH.

Libya: 14th St, Sinkor, Monrovia; Ambassador MUHAMMAD UMARAT-TABI.

Morocco: Tubman Blvd, Congo Town, Monrovia; tel. 262767; Ambassador MOHAMED LASFAR.

Nigeria: Tubman Blvd, Congo Town, POB 366, Monrovia; tel. 6823638 (mobile); fax 226135; e-mail nigerianmonrovia@yahoo.com; Ambassador CHIGOZIE OBI-NNADOZIE.

Qatar: Mamba Point Hotel, 15th St, Tubman Blvd, Monrovia; tel. 555533333 (mobile); e-mail monrovia@mofa.gov.qa; Ambassador MOHAMMAD ISMAIL AL-EMADI.

Sierra Leone: Tubman Blvd, POB 575, Monrovia; tel. 261301; Ambassador BRIMA ACHA KAMARA.

South Africa: Sophie Rd, House No 5, Congo Town, Monrovia; Ambassador MASILO ESAU MEBETA.

Sweden: LCL Compound, 12th St, Sinkor, Oceanfront, Monrovia; tel. 7701738 (mobile); e-mail ambassaden.monrovia@gov.se; internet www.swedenabroad.com/monrovia; Ambassador SOFIA STRAND.

United Kingdom: Leone Compound, 12th St, Beach-side, Sinkor, Monrovia; tel. 77530320 (mobile); e-mail monrovia.generalenquiries@fco.gov.uk; internet www.gov.uk/government/world/liberia; Ambassador DAVID BELGROVE (designate).

USA: POB 98, 502 Benson St, Monrovia; tel. 776777000 (mobile); fax 77010370 (mobile); e-mail ConsularMonrovia@state.gov; internet monrovia.usembassy.gov; Ambassador DEBORAH R. MALAC.

Judicial System

The five-member Supreme Court was established in January 1992 to adjudicate in electoral disputes.

Supreme Court: Temple of Justice, Capitol Hill, Monrovia; internet judiciary.gov.lr; consists of a Chief Justice and four Associate Justices; Chief Justice FRANCIS S. KORKPOR, Sr.

Religion

Liberia is officially a Christian state, although complete religious freedom is guaranteed. Christianity and Islam are the two main religions. There are numerous religious sects, and many Liberians hold traditional beliefs.

CHRISTIANITY

Liberian Council of Churches: 15th St, Sinkor, POB 10-2191, 1000 Monrovia; tel. 886234674 (mobile); e-mail liberiancouncil@yahoo.com; internet www.liberiancouncilofchurches.org; f. 1982; 13 mems, 11 assoc. mems, 4 fraternal mems; Pres. Rt Rev. JONATHAN BAU-BAU BONAPARTE HART.

The Anglican Communion

The diocese of Liberia forms part of the Church of the Province of West Africa, incorporating the local Episcopal Church. Anglicanism was established in Liberia in 1836, and the diocese of Liberia was admitted into full membership of the Province in 1982. The Primate and Metropolitan of the Province is the Bishop of The Gambia.

Bishop of Liberia: Rt Rev. JONATHAN BAU-BAU BONAPARTE HART, POB 10-0277, 1000 Monrovia 10; tel. 224760; fax 227519; e-mail bishop@liberia.net.

The Roman Catholic Church

Liberia comprises the archdiocese of Monrovia and the dioceses of Cape Palmas and Gbarnga. An estimated 9% of the total population are Roman Catholics.

Catholic Bishops' Conference of Liberia: POB 10-2078, 1000 Monrovia 10; tel. 227245; fax 226175; f. 1998; Pres. Rt Rev. LEWIS ZEIGLER (Archbishop of Monrovia).

Archbishop of Monrovia: Most Rev. LEWIS ZEIGLER, Archbishop's Office, POB 10-2078, 1000 Monrovia 10; tel. 6519766 (mobile); fax 77003719 (mobile); e-mail apostolic_adm@yahoo.com.

Other Christian Churches

Assemblies of God in Liberia: POB 1297, Monrovia; f. 1908; 14,578 adherents, 287 churches; Gen. Supt JIMMY KUOH.

Lutheran Church in Liberia (LCL): POB 10-1046, 13th St, Payne Ave, Sinkor, 1000 Monrovia 10; tel. 886213894 (mobile); e-mail lutheranchurchinliberia@yahoo.com; f. 1947 as Evangelical Lutheran Church, reorg. in 1965 under indigenous leadership as LCL; Pres. Bishop D. JENSEN SEYENKULO; 71,196 mems (2010).

Providence Baptist Church: cnr Broad and Center Sts, Monrovia; tel. 77534172 (mobile); e-mail admin@providencebc.net; internet www.providencebc.net; f. 1821; 2,500 adherents, 300 congregations, 6 ministers, 8 schools; Senior Pastor Rev. Dr SAMUEL BROOMFIELD REEVES, Jr.

Liberia Baptist Missionary and Educational Convention, Inc: Baptist House, 98 Tubman Blvd, Sinkor, POB 390, Monrovia; tel. 222661; internet lbmec.org; f. 1880; 72,000 adherents, 270 churches (2007), Pres. Rev. OLU Q. MENJAY; Gen. Sec. JOHN D. KARMO.

United Methodist Church in Liberia: cnr 12th St and Tubman Blvd, POB 1010, 1000 Monrovia 10; tel. 223343; e-mail bishop.jinnis@liberiaumc.org; internet liberiaunitedmethodistchurch.org; f. 1833; c. 168,300 adherents, 600 congregations, 700 ministers, 394 lay pastors; Resident Bishop Rev. Dr JOHN G. INNIS.

Other active denominations include the National Baptist Mission, the Pentecostal Church, the Presbyterian Church in Liberia, the Prayer Band and the Church of the Lord Aladura.

ISLAM

The total community numbers about 670,000.

National Muslim Council of Liberia: POB 417, Monrovia; Leader Shaykh KAFUMBA KONNEH.

The Press

NEWSPAPERS

Daily Observer: POB 1858, Monrovia; tel. 6513788 (mobile); e-mail editor@liberianobserver.com; internet www.liberianobserver.com; f. 1981; independent; daily; Dir KENNETH Y. BEST.

Heritage: cnr Broad and Nelson Sts, Monrovia; e-mail info@heritagenet.net; internet www.news.heritageliberia.net; Man. Editor MOHAMMED M. KANNEH.

Informer: Monrovia; tel. 886519515 (mobile); e-mail editoratinformer@yahoo.com; f. 2003; Editor-in-Chief KAIHENNEH SENGBEH.

The Inquirer: POB 3600, Monrovia; tel. 880547763 (mobile); e-mail info@theinquirer.com.lr; internet www.theinquirer.com.lr; daily; Man. Editor PHILIP WESSEH.

National Chronicle: Carey St, POB 20-1598, Monrovia; tel. 886543189 (mobile); e-mail info@nationalchronicleliberia.com; internet www.nationalchronicleliberia.com; Editor EDWARD MORTEE.

New Dawn: 147 Crown Hill, Broad St, Monrovia; tel. 886484201 (mobile); e-mail mail@thenewdawnliberia.com; internet www.thenewdawnliberia.com; f. 2010; CEO OTHELLO B. GARBLAH.

New Republic: Monrovia; tel. 6568024 (mobile); e-mail etogba2005us@yahoo.com; Publr ALPHONSO TOWEH; Editor-in-Chief ELLIS TOGBA.

News: ACDB Bldg, POB 10-3137, Carey Warren St, Monrovia; tel. 227820; independent; weekly; Chair. WILSON TARPEH; Editor-in-Chief JEROME DALIEH.

PERIODICALS

Business Liberia: Monrovia; f. 2009; publ. by Baker Pearson Communications, Inc; Editor-in-Chief SEANAN DENIZOT.

Liberia Orbit: Voinjama; e-mail orbit@tekmail.com; internet www.liberiaorbit.org; national current affairs; Editor LLOYD SCOTT.

Liberia Travel & Life: Monrovia; tel. 6111542 (mobile); e-mail editorial@liberiatravellifemagazine.com; 4 a year; publ. by Baker Pearson Communications, Inc; Editor-in-Chief HESTA BAKER PEARSON.

New Democrat: Clay St, Central Town, Monrovia; tel. 5548626 (mobile); fax 77249415 (mobile); e-mail newdemnews@yahoo.com; internet www.newdemocrat.info; national news and current affairs; Editor TOM KAMARA.

The People Magazine: Bank of Liberia Bldg, Suite 214, Carey and Warren Sts, POB 3501, Monrovia; tel. 222743; f. 1985; monthly; Editor and Publr CHARLES A. SNETTER.

PRESS ORGANIZATIONS

Liberia Institute of Journalism: Kashour Bldg, 2nd Floor, cnr Broad and Johnson Sts, POB 2314, Monrovia; tel. 227327; Dir VINICIUS HODGES.

Liberia Media Center: LMC Box 1153, 1st St, Sinkor, Jallah Town, Monrovia; tel. 6400206 (mobile); e-mail info@lmcliberia.com; internet lmc.org.lr; f. 2005; Chair. PETER QUAQUA.

Press Union of Liberia: Benson St, POB 20-4209, Monrovia; tel. and fax 227105; internet www.pul.org.lr; f. 1985; Pres. K. ABDULLAI KAMARA.

NEWS AGENCY

Liberian News Agency (LINA): Ministry of Information Bldg, POB 9021, Capitol Hill, Monrovia; tel. 886315022 (mobile); e-mail LINA@liberianewsagency.org; internet www.liberianewsagency.org; Dir-Gen. JAY NAGBE SLOH.

Broadcasting and Communications

TELECOMMUNICATIONS

Cellcom: Haile Selassie Ave, Capitol By-Pass, Monrovia; tel. 77777008 (mobile); fax 77000101 (mobile); e-mail info@cellcomgsm.com; internet www.lr.cellcomgsm.com; mobile cellular telephone provider; CEO JOHN VASIKARAN; 976,038 subscribers (2012).

Comium: Comium Bldg, Congo Town, Monrovia; tel. 5600600 (mobile); fax 5600611 (mobile); e-mail info@comium.com.lr; internet www.comium.com.lr; mobile cellular telephone provider; CEO MICHAEL CARROLL; 137,848 subscribers (2010).

LiberCell: Monrovia; e-mail info@awli.net; f. 2004; mobile cellular telephone provider; Chair. AZZAM SBAITY; CEO BACHAR SAGHIR; 25,705 subscribers (2012).

Libtelco: 18th St and Tubman Blvd, Sinkor, Monrovia; tel. 25551000 (mobile); fax 25551099 (mobile); e-mail info@libtelco.com.lr; internet www.libtelco.com.lr; f. 1973 as the Liberia Telecommunications Corporation; Chair. Dr FREDERICK NORKEH; Man. Dir SEBASTIAN MUAH; 9,618 prepaid subscribers (2013).

Lonestar Cell MTN: LBDI Bldg, Congo Town, Monrovia; tel. 6500000 (mobile); fax 6501101 (mobile); internet www.lonestarcell.com; f. 2001; mobile cellular telephone provider; subsidiary of Mobile Telephone Networks (Pty) Ltd, South Africa; CEO TEBOGO MOGAPI; 1,290,830 subscribers (2012).

Regulatory Authority

Liberia Telecommunications Authority: 12th St, Sinkor, Tubman Blvd, Monrovia; tel. 27302012 (mobile); e-mail info@lta.gov.lr; internet www.lta.gov.lr; f. 2007; Chair. ANGELIQUE WEEKS.

BROADCASTING

Radio

Liberia Communications Network: Congo Town 1000, Monrovia; govt-operated; broadcasts information, education and entertainment 24 hours daily in English, French and several African languages; short-wave service.

Liberia Rural Communications Network: POB 10-02176, 1000 Monrovia 10; tel. 271368; f. 1981; govt-operated; rural devt and entertainment programmes; Dir J. RUFUS KAINE (acting).

Radio Truth FM: Monrovia.

Radio Veritas: POB 3569, Monrovia; tel. 4712834 (mobile); e-mail radioveritas@hotmail.com; internet radioveritas.org; f. 1981; Catholic; independent; nationwide shortwave broadcasts; Dirs Fr ANTHONY BOWAH, LEDGERHOOD RENNIE.

Star Radio: 12 Broad St, Snapper Hill, Monrovia; tel. 77104411 (mobile); e-mail star@liberia.net; internet www.starradio.org.lr; independent news and information station; f. July 1997 by Fondation Hirondelle, Switzerland, with funds from the US Agency for International Development; broadcasts in English, French and 14 African languages; Man. JAMES K. MORLU.

Television

Liberia Broadcasting System: POB 594, Monrovia; tel. 224984; govt-owned; Chair. CLETUS SIEH; Dir-Gen. LEDGERHOOD RENNIE.

Finance

(cap. = capital; res = reserves; dep. = deposits; m. = million; brs = branch; amounts in Liberian dollars, unless otherwise indicated)

BANKING

At the end of 2013 there were nine commercial banks in Liberia.

Central Bank

Central Bank of Liberia: cnr Warren and Carey Sts, POB 2048, 1000 Monrovia; tel. 6225685 (mobile); fax 6226114 (mobile); e-mail webmaster@cbl.org.lr; internet www.cbl.org.lr; f. 1974 as National Bank of Liberia; name changed March 1999; bank of issue; cap. 7,598.5m., res 3,817.4m., dep. 9,226.7m. (Dec. 2009); Gov. JOSEPH MILLS JONES.

Other Banks

AccessBank Liberia Ltd: Johnson St, Monrovia; tel. 77006688 (mobile); f. 2008; CEO MARY CLARE ODONG.

Ecobank Liberia Ltd: Ashmun and Randall Sts, POB 4825, Monrovia; tel. 880512039 (mobile); fax 227029; e-mail ecobanklr@ecobank.com; internet www.ecobank.com; commenced operations Aug. 1999; cap. 689.2m., res 1,608.1m., dep. 19,364.8m. (Dec. 2013); Chair. CLAVENDA BRIGHT-PARKER; Man. Dir KOLA ADELEKE.

First International Bank (Liberia) Ltd: Luke Bldg, Broad St, Monrovia; tel. 886552153 (mobile); e-mail info@fib-lib.com; internet www.fib-lib.com; f. April 2005; Chair. MATILDA PARKER (acting); Man. Dir/CEO WOLE SODIPE.

Global Bank Liberia Ltd (GBLL): cnr 5th St and Tubman Blvd, Sinkor, POB 2053, Monrovia; tel. 6425760 (mobile); e-mail mail@globalbankliberia.com; internet www.globalbanklr.com; f. 2005; Italian-owned; Pres. Dr RICCARDO SEMBIANTE; 6 brs.

Guaranty Trust Bank (Liberia) Ltd (GTBLL): 13th St, Tubman Blvd, POB 0382, Monrovia; tel. 776498652 (mobile); internet www.gtbanklr.com; f. 2007; Chair. OPRAL MASON BENSON; CEO DAN OROGUN.

International Bank (Liberia) Ltd: 64 Broad St, POB 10292, 1000 Monrovia; tel. 886511823 (mobile); e-mail customercare@ibliberia.com; internet www.ibliberia.com; f. 1948 as International Trust Co of Liberia; name changed April 2000; 75.5% owned by Liberian Financial Holdings; 19.1% Trust Bank Ltd (The Gambia); cap. US $12.3m., res −$1.0m., dep. $76.6m. (Dec. 2013); Chair. ESTRADA BERNARD; CEO HENRY SAAMOI; 3 brs.

Liberian Bank for Development and Investment (LBDI): 9th St, Sinkor, POB 547, Monrovia; tel. 227140; fax 226359; e-mail lbdi@lbdi.net; internet www.lbdi.net; f. 1961; 18.7% govt-owned; cap. and res US $12.5m., total assets $26.8m. (Dec. 2001); Chair. AMARA KONNEH; Pres. JOHN B. S. DAVIES, III; 13 brs.

United Bank for Africa Liberia Ltd: cnr Broad and Nelson Sts, POB 4523, Monrovia; tel. 77113330 (mobile); e-mail ubaliberia@ubagroup.com; internet www.ubagroup.com/ubaliberia; f. 2006; CEO CHIOMA MANG.

Banking Association

Liberia Bankers' Association: POB 292, Monrovia; mems include commercial and devt banks; Pres. JOHN B. S. DAVIES, Jr.

INSURANCE

American National Underwriters, Inc: Carter Bldg, 39 Broad St, POB 180, Monrovia; tel. 114921; general; Gen. Man. S. B. MENSAH.

Insurance Co of Africa: 2nd Floor, International Bank Building, 64 Broad St, Monrovia; tel. 6513281 (mobile); internet icaliberia.com; f. 1969; life and general; Pres. SAMUEL OWAREE MINTAH.

National Insurance Corpn of Liberia (NICOL): LBDI Bldg Complex, POB 1528, Sinkor, Monrovia; tel. 262429; f. 1983; state-owned; sole insurer for Govt and parastatal bodies; also provides insurance for the Liberian-registered merchant shipping fleet; Man. Dir MIATTA EDITH SHERMAN.

United Security Insurance Agencies Inc: Randall St, POB 2071, Monrovia; life, personal accident and medical; Dir EPHRAIM O. OKORO.

Trade and Industry

GOVERNMENT AGENCIES

General Services Agency (GSA): Old USTC Compound, UN Dr., POB 10-9027, Monrovia; tel. 6901333 (mobile); e-mail info@gsa.gov.lr; internet www.gsa.gov.lr; Dir-Gen. MARY BROH.

DEVELOPMENT ORGANIZATIONS

Forestry Development Authority: POB 10-3010, Kappa House, Eli Saleby Compound, Monrovia; tel. 224940; fax 226000; e-mail info@fda.gov.lr; internet www.fda.gov.lr; f. 1976; responsible for forest management and conservation; Chair. MARY LAURENE BROWN; Man. Dir HARRISON S. KARNWEA, Sr.

Liberia Industrial Free Zone Authority (LIFZA): One Free Zone, Monrovia; tel. 533671; e-mail mskromah@lifza.com; f. 1975; 98 mems; Man. Dir MOHAMMED S. KROMAH.

National Investment Commission (NIC): Airfield New Rd, Chesseman Ave, Sinkor, POB 9043, Monrovia; tel. 7873001 (mobile); e-mail info@nic.gov.lr; internet www.nic.gov.lr; f. 1979; autonomous body negotiating investment incentives agreements on behalf of Govt, promotes agro-based and industrial devt; Chair. ETMONIA DAVID TARPEH; Exec. Dir CIATA BISHOP.

CHAMBER OF COMMERCE

Liberia Chamber of Commerce: Queen's Ave, Capitol Hill, POB 92, Monrovia; tel. 77857805 (mobile); e-mail info@lcc.org.lr; internet www.lcc.org.lr; f. 1951; Pres. MONIE RALPH CAPTAN; Sec.-Gen. MASSA R. LANSANAH.

INDUSTRIAL AND TRADE ASSOCIATIONS

Liberian Produce Marketing Corpn: POB 662, Monrovia; tel. 222447; f. 1961; govt-owned; exports Liberian produce, provides industrial facilities for processing of agricultural products and participates in agricultural devt programmes; Man. Dir NYAH MARTEIN.

EMPLOYERS' ASSOCIATION

National Enterprises Corpn: POB 518, Monrovia; tel. 261370; importer, wholesaler and distributor of foodstuffs, and wire and metal products for local industries; Pres. EMMANUEL SHAW, Sr.

UTILITIES

Liberia Electricity Corpn (LEC): Waterside, UN Dr., POB 10-165, Monrovia; tel. 777444156 (mobile); e-mail info@lecliberia.com; internet www.lecliberia.com; f. 1973; Chair. BENEDICT SANNOH; CEO GREGORY J. SYLVESTRE.

National Oil Co of Liberia (NOCAL): Episcopal Church Plaza, 3rd and 4th Floors, Ashmun and Randall Sts, 1000 Monrovia; tel. 77023859 (mobile); e-mail info@nocal.com.lr; internet www.nocal.com.lr; f. 2000; Chair. SEWARD M. COOPER; Pres. and CEO RANDOLPH A. K. W. McCLAIN.

Water

Liberia Water and Sewer Corpn: King Sao Bosso St, POB 1079, Monrovia; e-mail info@lwsclr.com; internet www.lwsclr.com; Chair. KIMMIE L. WEEKS; Man. Dir CHARLES B. ALLEN, Jr.

TRADE UNION

Liberian Labor Congress: J. B. McGill Labor Center, Gardnersville Freeway, POB 415, Monrovia; f. 2008 following merger of Liberian Federation of Labor Unions and Congress of National Trade Unions; Pres. ELITHA T. MANNING, Jr; Sec.-Gen. MARCUS S. BLAMAH.

Transport

RAILWAYS

Bong Mine Railway: POB 538, Monrovia; tel. 225222; fax 225770; f. 1958; Gen. Man. HANS-GEORG SCHNEIDER.

ROADS

In 2011 the road network in Liberia totalled an estimated 10,664 km, of which about 574 km were paved. The main trunk road is the Monrovia–Sanniquellie motor road, extending north-east from the capital to the border with Guinea, near Ganta, and eastward through the hinterland to the border with Côte d'Ivoire. Trunk roads run through Tapita, in Nimba County, to Grand Gedeh County and from Monrovia to Buchanan. A bridge over the Mano river connects with the Sierra Leone road network, while a main road links Monrovia and Freetown (Sierra Leone). In 2003 the Liberian authorities announced plans for the extensive rehabilitation of the road network (which had been extensively damaged during the civil conflicts of 1989–96 and 1999–2003), including a highway linking Monrovia with Harper, which was to be funded by the People's Republic of China.

National Transit Authority (NTA): Monrovia; internet nta.com.lr; f. 2008; govt-owned bus operator in 7 counties; Chair. RUTH CEASAR; Man.-Dir KARMO D. VILLE.

SHIPPING

At 31 December 2014 Liberia's open-registry fleet comprised 3,800 vessels, with a total displacement of 131.6m. grt. The fleet was the second largest in the world (after Panama) in terms of gross tonnage in that year.

Liberia Maritime Authority (LiMA): Tubman Blvd, Sinkor, Monrovia; tel. and fax 77206108 (mobile); internet maritimeliberia.com; Chair. THERESA LEIGH-SHERMAN; Commissioner and CEO BINYAH C. KESSELLY.

National Port Authority: Freeport of Monrovia, Bushrod Island, Monrovia; tel. 6402906 (mobile); fax 77861997 (mobile); e-mail natportliberia@yahoo.com; internet www.nationalport authorityliberia.org; f. 1967; administers Monrovia Freeport and the ports of Buchanan, Greenville and Harper; Chair. HENRIQUE TOKPAH; Man. Dir MATILDA PARKER (suspended in April 2015).

CIVIL AVIATION

Liberia's principal airports are Robertsfield International Airport, at Harbel, 56 km east of Monrovia, and James Spriggs Payne Airport, at Monrovia.

Liberia Airport Authority (LAA): Monrovia; Chair. (vacant); Acting Man. Dir ROSE STRYKER.

Liberia Civil Aviation Authority: Monrovia; internet www.liberiacaa.com; Dir-Gen. RICHELIEU A. WILLIAMS.

Tourism

Liberia's natural assets, especially its beaches and the Sapo National Park and other areas of primary tropical rainforest, have the potential to support both a beach-based and an eco-tourism industry. However, no such industry has ever been developed in Liberia and tourism has been entirely in abeyance since 1990 because of the prolonged period of civil conflict that followed from that time. The development of the country's tourist potential is limited by high levels of violent crime and a tourism infrastructure that remains meagre or absent.

Defence

As assessed at November 2014, the total strength of the Liberian armed forces was 2,050 (army of 2,000 and coast guard 50). The UN Mission in Liberia (UNMIL) was established in 2003 and at January 2015 had a total strength of 5,819 uniformed personnel, of whom 4,299 were troops. UNMIL has a mandate to remain in the country until the end of September 2015.

Defence Expenditure: Budgeted at US $24m. in 2014.

Chief of Staff of the Armed Forces of Liberia: Brig.-Gen. DANIEL DEE ZIANKHAN.

Education

Education is provided by a mixture of government, private, church and mosque schools. The civil conflicts of 1989–96 and 1999–2003 devastated the education system as buildings and equipment were damaged and looted, and teachers, parents and children became refugees or internally displaced. However, by September 2005 3,817 of the country's 4,500 schools were reported to be functioning again. Education in Liberia is officially compulsory for 10 years, between six and 16 years of age. Primary education begins theoretically at six years of age and lasts for six years (grades 1–6). Secondary education, beginning theoretically at 12 years of age, lasts for a further six years, and is divided into two three-year cycles, known in Liberia as 'junior high school' (grades 7–9) and 'senior high school' (grades 10-12). Pre-primary education is undertaken from the age of five or younger and is important for those students whose mother language is not English, since English is the language of instruction throughout the school system. School attendance is not enforced; according to UNESCO estimates, in 2011 enrolment at primary schools included

41% of pupils in the relevant age-group (42% boys; 40% girls), while enrolment at secondary schools was equivalent to 45% (50% boys; 41% girls). Although the Constitution includes the aspiration to provide universal free education, and fees in public primary schools have been officially abolished, school attendance is discouraged by the poor quality of education offered, by the remaining school fees, by charges and by the cost of uniforms and travel. The higher education sector consists of the University of Liberia in Monrovia, Cuttington University College in Bong County, the Booker Washington Institute in Kakata, Margibi County, and the William V. S. Tubman College in Maryland County. According to UNESCO, a total of 44,107 students were enrolled in tertiary education in 1999/2000.

LIBYA

Introductory Survey

LOCATION, CLIMATE, LANGUAGE, RELIGION, FLAG, CAPITAL

Libya extends along the Mediterranean coast of North Africa. Its neighbours are Tunisia and Algeria to the west, Niger and Chad to the south, Egypt to the east, and Sudan to the south-east. The climate is very hot and dry. Most of the country is part of the Sahara, an arid desert, but the coastal regions are cooler. Average temperatures range from 13°C (55°F) to 38°C (100°F), but a maximum of 57.3°C (135°F) has been recorded in the interior. Arabic is the official language, although English and Italian are also used in trade. Almost all of the population are Sunni Muslims. The national flag (proportions 2 by 3) has three horizontal stripes, of red, black and green; the black stripe is equal in area to the two other stripes together and has, in its centre, a white crescent and a five-pointed white star. During the rule of Muammar al-Qaddafi, most government departments and the legislature were relocated from Tarabulus (Tripoli) to Surt (Sirte). Following Qaddafi's removal from power in 2011 by forces loyal to the opposition National Transitional Council, Tripoli was redesignated as the capital. However, in 2014 the newly elected House of Representatives was moved to the eastern city of Tobruk, owing to conflict between forces loyal to the internationally recognized Government and militia affiliated to the unofficial General National Congress in Tripoli. The internationally recognized Government was subsequently moved to al-Bayda.

CONTEMPORARY POLITICAL HISTORY

Historical Context

Libya, formerly an Italian colony and occupied by British and French troops in 1942, attained independence as the United Kingdom of Libya in 1951. Muhammad Idris al-Sanusi, Amir of Cyrenaica, became King Idris of Libya. British and US forces maintained bases in Libya in return for economic assistance; however, the discovery of petroleum reserves in 1959 greatly increased the country's potential for financial autonomy.

King Idris was deposed in September 1969, in a bloodless revolution led by a group of nationalist army officers. A Revolutionary Command Council (RCC) was established, with Col Muammar al-Qaddafi as Chairman, and a Libyan Arab Republic was proclaimed. British and US military personnel withdrew from Libya in 1970, and in 1971 British oil interests in Libya were nationalized.

The Arab Socialist Union (ASU) was established in June 1971 as the country's sole political party. People's Congresses and Popular Committees were formed, and an undertaking was made to administer Libya in accordance with Islamic principles. The General National Congress of the ASU held its first session in January 1976; it was subsequently restyled the General People's Congress (GPC).

In March 1977 the GPC endorsed constitutional changes, recommended by Qaddafi, whereby the official name of the country was changed to the Socialist People's Libyan Arab Jamahiriya. Power was vested in the people through the GPC and its constituent parts. The RCC was dissolved, and a General Secretariat of the GPC was established (with Qaddafi as Secretary until March 1979). The GPC elected Qaddafi as Revolutionary Leader of the new state, while the Council of Ministers was replaced by a General People's Committee.

The creation in 1984 of the post of Secretary for External Security and of an office, attached to the Secretariat for Foreign Liaison, to 'combat international terrorism', combined with repressive measures to curb dissident activity, reflected Qaddafi's increasing sensitivity to the growth of opposition groups—principally the National Front for the Salvation of Libya (NFSL), which he accused foreign governments of fostering. In 1986 the country was renamed the Great Socialist People's Libyan Arab Jamahiriya.

Domestic Political Affairs

From 1988 Qaddafi initiated a series of liberalizing economic and political reforms. He encouraged the reopening of private businesses, and declared an amnesty for all prisoners, other than those convicted of violent crimes or of conspiring with foreign powers. Libyan citizens were guaranteed freedom to travel abroad. The GPC created a People's Court and People's Prosecution Bureau to replace the revolutionary courts, and approved a charter of human rights. In August Qaddafi announced that the army was to be replaced by a force of 'Jamahiri Guards', which would be supervised by 'people's defence committees'. In September it was decided to relocate all but two of the GPC secretariats, mostly to the town of Sirte, 400 km east of Tripoli, and in January 1989 Qaddafi announced that all state institutions, including the intelligence service and official Libyan news agency, were to be abolished.

Western media reported in October 1993 that elements loyal to Qaddafi had suppressed an attempted military coup, and that Libya's second-in-command, Maj. Abd al-Salam Jalloud, was among many placed under house arrest. Qaddafi denied the reports, but the appointment of known loyalists to senior positions in the General People's Committee was announced in January 1994. The Secretariat for Arab Unity was abolished in December 1998, in accordance with Qaddafi's recently stated intention to forge closer relations with African rather than Arab countries (see *Foreign Affairs*).

A radical decentralization of the Government was announced in March 2000, whereby almost all of the People's Committees were dissolved and their responsibilities devolved mainly to the local level: only 'sovereign' areas were to remain under the control of the General People's Committee. Al-Ujayli Abd al-Salam Burayni replaced Muhammad Abdullah Bait al-Mal as Secretary for Finance in October, when a further restructuring of the General People's Committee occurred; it had been reported in July that Bait al-Mal, along with the President of the Central Bank of Libya and a further 22 senior Libyan bankers, had been implicated in allegations of financial impropriety. In November 2001 it was announced that more than 40 government and bank officials had been sentenced to varying terms of imprisonment for corruption and embezzlement; reportedly among those convicted was Burayni, who received a one-year prison sentence for negligence.

In June 2003 Qaddafi appointed Shukri Muhammad Ghanem as Secretary of the General People's Committee, in place of Mubarak Abdallah al-Shamikh. Meanwhile, the Secretariat for African Unity was merged with the Secretariat for Foreign Liaison and International Co-operation; Abd al-Rahman Muhammad Shalgam assumed responsibility for both portfolios. Further reorganizations of the Government in March 2004 and March 2006 resulted in the creation of several new secretariats. In the latter month Dr al-Baghdadi Ali al-Mahmoudi became Secretary of the General People's Committee, after Ghanem was appointed Chairman of the National Oil Corporation (NOC).

In June 2006 the US-based organization Human Rights Watch pressed the Libyan Government to allow a full, independent investigation into the deaths of hundreds of inmates at Abu Salim prison in Tripoli in 1996; the alleged massacre was reported to have been caused by security officers opening fire on prisoners protesting against poor living conditions. In September 2006 Human Rights Watch released a report in which it claimed that the Libyan Government routinely subjected refugees and asylum-seekers to violence, arrest without due cause and forcible deportation.

An official source in Tripoli announced in November 2006 that Qaddafi's second son, Seif al-Islam, was to leave Libya to take up employment with an international economic institution. His departure was widely perceived to have been orchestrated by the Government in reaction to his outspoken criticism of the regime during a speech in Sirte in August. In a televised address in August 2007, Seif al-Islam urged the drafting of a new constitution or 'social contract' that would establish, *inter alia*, an independent central bank and a free media and judiciary. He also criticized the Libyan political system for its lack of a freely elected legislature, its refusal to allow the creation of political parties and its ongoing intolerance of political dissent, and called for political power to be more widely distributed, beyond the GPC and the General People's Committee.

In November 2007 an audio tape purporting to be from Dr Ayman al-Zawahiri, the deputy leader of the militant Islamist organization al-Qa'ida, was released; it included a message from Abu Laith al-Libi, the leader of al-Qa'ida in Afghanistan, who identified himself on the tape as also being a member of the Libyan Islamic Fighting Group (LIFG). Al-Libi declared that the LIFG had pledged allegiance to al-Qa'ida. Al-Zawahiri's own message urged the overthrow of the Libyan, Algerian, Moroccan and Tunisian Governments, and criticized Qaddafi for surrendering Libya's nuclear weapons materials to 'crusader masters'. (Libya had abandoned its programmes to produce weapons of mass destruction in December 2003, having reportedly come close to building a nuclear bomb—see *Foreign Affairs*.)

Qaddafi effected a reorganization of the General Secretariat of the GPC and of the General People's Committee in March 2008. Muftah Muhammad Kaiba was appointed as Secretary of the GPC. At the same time Qaddafi announced that he intended to abolish the majority of secretariats within the General People's Committee by the end of that year, in an effort to eliminate corruption and maladministration. Through a Wealth Distribution Programme (WDP), oil wealth would be redistributed by transferring the secretariats' powers to the people to enable them to manage their own affairs, requiring privatization of many sectors of Libyan society; only the secretariats for defence, internal security and foreign affairs would be retained, along with those responsible for strategic infrastructural projects, such as the Great Man-made River Project (see *Economic Affairs*). However, the reforms were subsequently postponed.

In November 2008, meanwhile, there were protests by members of the Tebu tribe in the southern town of Kufra against what they claimed was discrimination practised by the Qaddafi Government against indigenous peoples (including a restriction of access to health and education services). Dozens of people were reported to have been killed in violent confrontations between the Libyan security forces and Tebu tribesmen.

At a meeting of the GPC held in Sirte at the beginning of March 2009, it was announced that the country's Basic People's Congresses had voted to defer implementation of the WDP. At the Sirte meeting Qaddafi implemented a significant reorganization of the General People's Committee. One notable change was the appointment of Musa Kusa, hitherto head of Libya's foreign intelligence service, to replace Shalgam as Secretary for Foreign Liaison and International Co-operation. Meanwhile, al-Shamikh was appointed as Secretary of the GPC, replacing Kaiba. The changes fell far short of the large-scale dismantling of secretariats that Qaddafi had previously outlined.

Increasing prominence of Seif al-Islam Qaddafi

In March 2009 it was announced that, following two years of talks between the Libyan Human Rights Association—chaired by Seif al-Islam Qaddafi—and the LIFG, 170 imprisoned members of the latter group were to be released; it was also revealed that 136 LIFG prisoners had already been freed, having completed a rehabilitation programme. In July the LIFG leadership announced that it was renouncing armed violence and reversed the 2007 decision to align the group with al-Qa'ida. In September 2009 six imprisoned members of the LIFG ruling council published a new 'code' for *jihad*, which denounced the ideologies of al-Qa'ida. More than 100 LIFG members and other Islamist militants were released from prison in late 2009 and 2010.

Meanwhile, in October 2009 it was announced that Seif al-Islam was to be appointed as co-ordinator of social and popular committees—the second most powerful position in the Libyan leadership. The decision was widely interpreted as the formal approval by the Libyan authorities of Qaddafi's son as his designated successor. In January 2010 Qaddafi effected a reorganization of the General Secretariat of the GPC, most notably appointing Muhammad Aboulghasem al-Zwai as Secretary, in place of al-Shamikh. The number of portfolios in the General People's Committee was also reduced from 12 to seven, as part of the ongoing programme of administrative reform.

In December 2009 Seif al-Islam's Human Rights Association published a report detailing the widespread use of torture, wrongful imprisonment and other human rights abuses in Libya, and criticizing the state's dominance of the media. Later that month a report by Human Rights Watch highlighted limited progress in areas such as freedom of expression and freedom of association, and described systemic human rights abuses. Nevertheless, Libya was elected to the UN Human Rights Council in May 2010. In June the human rights organization

Amnesty International condemned the execution in Libya of 18 people from Chad, Egypt and Nigeria, following their conviction on charges of murder; it alleged that the defendants had not been granted a fair trial. Amnesty International also published details concerning a wide array of rights violations that had allegedly been perpetrated by the Libyan Government, including indefinite detentions without trial, the use of torture to extract confessions from prisoners, the disappearance of numerous dissidents, and inhumane treatment of refugees and migrant workers. Meanwhile, the Government ordered the closure of the office in Tripoli of the UN High Commissioner for Refugees (UNHCR), citing the fact that Libya was not a signatory to the 1951 convention on refugees and had not signed any co-operation agreement with UNHCR.

Anti-Qaddafi protests and NATO-led intervention

In mid-January 2011 crowds gathered in several Libyan cities, including Benghazi and Bani Walid, to protest against corruption and protracted delays in the transfer of government-subsidized residential buildings to their owners; protesters seized control of hundreds of vacant residential units in the two cities. Having earlier announced the elimination of all taxes on food products, in late January the Government declared the establishment of a US $24,000m. investment fund, the aim of which was to provide affordable housing for lower-income families.

At the end of January 2011 a Libyan political writer and dissident, Jamal al-Hajji, posted an article on the internet urging Libyans to stage demonstrations 'in support of greater freedoms', seemingly inspired by recent events in Tunisia and Egypt that ultimately led to the removal of those countries' ruling regimes in early 2011. Al-Hajji was arrested at the beginning of February. Protesters gathered outside the police headquarters in Benghazi on 15 February, following the arrest of Fathi Terbil, another prominent critic of the Government and a lawyer who had been campaigning for the release of hundreds of people detained in Abu Salim prison owing to their alleged involvement with militant Islamist groups, including the LIFG. Police officers used violence to disperse the protesters, resulting in more than 40 people being injured. On 16 February Terbil was released, but the protests spread to several other Libyan cities, including al-Bayda and al-Quba, with protesters demanding the resignation of Qaddafi and the Government. Six people were reported to have been killed as the authorities attempted to break up the protests. On the same day the Government announced the release from prison of 110 LIFG members.

In response to a 'day of revolt' staged by opposition forces on 17 February 2011, when protests took place in Tripoli for the first time, the Government was reported to have hired hundreds of mercenaries from several African countries, notably Chad, to increase the ranks of the Libyan army. The Libyan air force deployed fighter jets and helicopters to launch air strikes against demonstrators; on 21 February two senior air force pilots flew to Malta, where they requested political asylum. Violent clashes continued between protesters and the authorities, and by early March some sources, including the Libyan League for Human Rights, estimated that some 6,000 people had been killed as a result of the unrest. By this time much of eastern Libya was reported to be under opposition control, including Benghazi and Tobruk, while rebel forces also controlled a number of cities in the central and northern provinces, including the port towns of Mersa Brega and Ras Lanuf; significant numbers of police and army officers in the region defected to the opposition. Many of Libya's foreign diplomats, including its ambassador in Washington, DC, USA, had renounced Qaddafi and urged the international community to take action to stop the violence. Several prominent government officials had also resigned, including Secretary for Justice Mustafa Muhammad Abd al-Jalil and Secretary for Public Security Gen. Abd al-Fattah Yunis al-Abaidi.

Seif al-Islam Qaddafi gave a televised address on 20 February 2011, in which he blamed the ongoing unrest on 'foreign agents', primarily the Israeli Government. Muammar al-Qaddafi appeared on state television on 23 February, accusing foreign powers (specifically the US and British Governments) of destabilizing Libya and attributing the unrest to the abuse of hallucinogenic drugs. Seif al-Islam's reputation as a reformist within the Qaddafi regime was undermined when video footage materialized on 28 February that purported to show him inciting a crowd of pro-Government supporters to commit violence against the opposition forces, and promising to provide those loyal to his father with weapons.

On 26 February 2011 the opposition forces proclaimed the Transitional National Council of the Libyan Republic (subsequently renamed the National Transitional Council—NTC), which was to constitute the 'political face of the revolution', and affirmed its resolve to draft a new national constitution providing for a free and democratically governed Libya. Following its inaugural meeting, convened on 5 March, the Council declared itself to be the sole representative of the country and urged the international community to act to protect Libyan citizens without recourse to direct military action on Libyan soil. A spokesperson for the Council subsequently clarified that UN-mandated air strikes would not be considered as foreign intervention. Former Secretary for Justice Abd al-Jalil was appointed Chairman of the NTC on 9 March.

Meanwhile, on 21 February 2011 Libya's deputy ambassador to the UN, Ibrahim Dabbashi, urged the Security Council to address the Libyan Government's violent response to the protests, and stated that he could no longer support the Qaddafi regime, which, he argued, was responsible for 'genocide'. Dabbashi's comments prompted the first UN Security Council meeting on the issue of the uprisings in the Middle East and North Africa since the beginning of Tunisia's revolution. On 26 February the Security Council unanimously adopted Resolution 1970, which imposed sanctions including, *inter alia*, the referral of the situation in Libya to the Chief Prosecutor of the International Criminal Court (ICC), the institution of an embargo upon the sale and transport of arms to Libya, and the imposition of a travel ban and an asset freeze on senior members of Qaddafi's regime and on his family. At the beginning of March the UN General Assembly voted to suspend Libya's membership of the Human Rights Council in response to the Government's 'gross and systematic violations' of human rights.

In late February 2011 US Secretary of State Hillary Clinton pledged her country's assistance, including aid, to those elements within Libya seeking to remove Qaddafi from power, and demanded that Qaddafi step down. On 1 March British Prime Minister David Cameron suggested that the United Kingdom might be prepared to supply the Libyan rebels with weapons, and that the North Atlantic Treaty Organization (NATO, see p. 367) should impose an air exclusion zone over Libya. Protesters in Benghazi responded by unveiling banners denouncing foreign intervention, and Cameron's stance encountered considerable opposition from France and Russia, while the USA initially distanced itself from the proposals.

On 17 March 2011 the UN Security Council approved Resolution 1973, which, among other measures, prohibited all flights in Libyan airspace, authorized member states to take 'all necessary measures ... to protect civilians and civilian populated areas under threat of attack' by forces loyal to Qaddafi, 'while excluding a foreign occupation force of any form on any part of Libyan territory', and demanded an immediate ceasefire by Libyan government forces. Despite the announcement by Libyan officials the following day of a ceasefire, Qaddafi's forces continued to use violence to counter opposition groups that had taken control of Mersa Brega, Misurata, Ras Lanuf and Zawia. Air strikes by Allied forces against strategic locations across Libya, including in Tripoli, commenced on 19 March, while on 22 March NATO warships began to enforce an arms embargo imposed against Qaddafi's forces. Two days later NATO members determined to enforce the UN-sanctioned air exclusion zone over Libya, alongside a military operation to prevent further attacks on civilians and civilian-populated areas, undertaken by a multinational coalition under British, French and US command. On 27 March NATO members agreed to assume full command of operations.

Meanwhile, on 23 March 2011 the NTC announced the formation of an Executive Board, which was to serve as Libya's interim executive branch of government; Mahmoud Jibril was appointed as Chairman. The NTC was henceforth to act as the national legislative body, pending the formation of a new permanent government.

At the end of March 2011 British officials revealed that Secretary for Foreign Liaison and International Co-operation Musa Kusa had fled to the United Kingdom. In late 2011 allegations emerged within the British media that, while serving as head of Libya's foreign intelligence service during 1994–2009, Kusa had been involved in the torture of Libyan political detainees, as well as the 1996 massacre at Abu Salim prison. The claims were adamantly denied by Kusa, along with allegations of involvement in or knowledge of the 1988 Lockerbie bombing and the killing in 1984 of British police officer Yvonne Fletcher (see

Foreign Affairs). Following the rescindment by the European Union (EU, see p. 271) of sanctions against him, Kusa relocated to Qatar in April 2011.

Despite being targeted by NATO air strikes, Qaddafi's forces continued to bombard opposition-held areas with heavy artillery, and in early April 2011 Libya's rebel groups were forced to abandon control of towns in the central coastal area, including Mersa Brega and Ras Lanuf. On 10 April an African Union (AU, see p. 188) delegation led by South African President Jacob Zuma arrived in Tripoli to present a proposal for a settlement of the conflict, which included, *inter alia*, an immediate ceasefire and negotiations between regime and opposition representatives over a gradual transition to political reform. Qaddafi indicated his approval in principle, but the plan was rejected by opposition figures, who demanded Qaddafi's ouster as a prerequisite for talks.

At the end of April 2011 one of Qaddafi's sons, Seif al-Arab, and three of his grandchildren were reportedly killed in a NATO air strike on the Libyan leader's compound in central Tripoli. Following the attack, large crowds of pro-Qaddafi demonstrators surrounded the residences of diplomats representing NATO member states; the British embassy was reported to have been set alight and others ransacked, prompting the British Government to order the expulsion of Libya's head of mission in the United Kingdom. On 17 May foreign media and the NTC reported that the Chairman of the NOC, Shukri Muhammad Ghanem, had defected from the Government and fled to Tunisia; speaking from the Italian capital, Rome, on 1 June, Ghanem confirmed his defection. He died in the Austrian capital, Vienna, at the end of April 2012.

Assisted by an intensification of NATO air strikes against government targets, opposition forces made significant military gains during May–June 2011. By July the vast majority of supply lines to government forces in Tripoli had been severed, with fuel supplies running particularly low, after the rebels had cut the supply of oil to the refinery at Zawia.

Meanwhile, on 27 June 2011 the ICC issued an arrest warrant against Qaddafi in respect of crimes against humanity committed during the early weeks of the popular uprising, on the basis of evidence provided by the Office of the Chief Prosecutor which apparently showed that the Libyan leader had directly authorized the use of force against civilians. Arrest warrants were also issued against Seif al-Islam and Libya's head of intelligence, Abdullah al-Sanoussi, both of whom were also alleged to have been responsible for the killing and persecution of civilians. However, the Libyan Government dismissed the warrants, insisting that it did not recognize the legitimacy of the ICC. Following a meeting in Istanbul, Turkey, in mid-July of the Libya Contact Group—formed in late March and comprising 15 Western and Arab diplomats, including US Secretary of State Clinton, British Secretary of State for Foreign and Commonwealth Affairs William Hague, and Qatari Prime Minister and Minister of Foreign Affairs Sheikh Hamad bin Jasim bin Jaber Al Thani—the Group officially recognized the NTC as the sole legitimate authority in Libya. Al-Sanoussi was arrested by the Mauritanian authorities at Nouakchott airport in March 2012; in September he was extradited to Libya, where he was promised a fair trial by the judicial authorities. However, the ICC also sought trial proceedings against al-Sanoussi for alleged 'crimes against humanity' during the uprising in Benghazi in 2011, while France also sought his extradition owing to his alleged involvement in the bombing of a passenger airline over Niger in September 1989 (see *Foreign Affairs*); al-Sanoussi had been convicted by the French authorities *in absentia* in 1999 and handed a term of life imprisonment.

Opposition forces seize control of Tripoli; the killing of Qaddafi

Concerns about the stability and integrity of the NTC were prompted by the killing on 28 June 2011 in unexplained circumstances of the head of the opposition armed forces, former Secretary for Public Security Gen. Abd al-Fattah Yunis al-Abaidi, together with two aides. Yunis had been summoned to appear before an inquiry by the NTC, following allegations that he had been engaged in secret meetings with representatives of Qaddafi, but, according to the NTC, was attacked en route to the meeting by pro-Qaddafi elements seeking to foment division among the opposition. NTC Chairman Abd al-Jalil later announced that the assailant had been captured. However, some observers alleged that the Council had assassinated Yunis amid doubts over his loyalty. In early August the NTC dismissed its Executive Board, citing its inadequate response to Yunis's killing.

With the Government's ability to mount military operations being increasingly undermined by NATO air strikes, by mid-August 2011 opposition forces had made further advances on all fronts, having taken, *inter alia*, Zawia, Zlitan (about 160 km east of Tripoli) and Gharyan (a large town in the Nafusa mountainous area). On the evening of 20 August rebel forces entered Tripoli, clashing with government troops and prompting Qaddafi to appeal for his supporters to help defend the city. Seif al-Islam and Hannibal Qaddafi were apprehended by the opposition forces on 21 August, but subsequently evaded their captors. By 22 August the rebels claimed to have seized control of about 90% of the city, and the following day attacked the Bab al-Aziziya military compound in Tripoli, which had served as Qaddafi's primary base but from which the Libyan leader and his family had already fled; the forces defending the complex surrendered, signalling the effective end of Qaddafi's rule.

The NTC subsequently assumed de facto control of Libya, replacing constitutional decrees issued under his rule with an interim Constitutional Declaration, under the terms of which an interim government was to be installed within 30 days and elections for a 210-member legislature held within 240 days; a new constitution was to be formulated and submitted to a national referendum within 60 days of the legislature's inauguration. Islamic law (*Shari'a*) was to be the principal source of legislation, although Abd al-Jalil sought to convince Western governments of the NTC's commitment to moderate Islam. Tripoli was designated as the capital, and the NTC relocated its operations to the city. On 16 September 2011 the UN General Assembly approved a motion to accept the credentials of diplomatic representatives appointed by the NTC, thereby effectively recognizing the Council as the legitimate governing authority in Libya. On the same day the UN Security Council adopted a resolution establishing the UN Support Mission in Libya (UNSMIL), which was to be charged with assisting the transitional authorities in their post-conflict reconstruction efforts. The Security Council also voted to ease sanctions imposed by Resolution 1973, exempting the NOC from the suspension of assets and similarly easing measures against a number of other key state entities, including the central bank and the Libyan Investment Authority. On 3 October the NTC announced the appointment of an interim administration, with Jibril as Prime Minister. Jibril announced that he would resign from Government following the ultimate defeat of Qaddafi.

A number of mass graves were discovered in and around Tripoli and other towns, including a grave unearthed in Tripoli in mid-September 2011 that was reported to contain the remains of more than 1,270 people, who were widely believed to have been among those killed during the 1996 massacre at Abu Salim prison. In a statement released in October 2011 the International Committee of the Red Cross, which had deployed forensic experts to Libya, at the request of the NTC, to assist in exhuming and identifying the human remains, noted that corpses continued to be discovered on a regular basis at mass graves, hospitals and other sites across Libya.

Fierce fighting occurred between forces loyal to the NTC and pro-Qaddafi forces in Sirte and Bani Walid (the final two remaining strongholds of Qaddafi loyalists) in September–October 2011; thousands of civilians were displaced by the violence. NTC forces finally asserted control of Bani Walid on 18 October, and two days later the last vestiges of support for Qaddafi in Sirte were defeated. Reports emerged that Qaddafi himself had been captured, after the convoy in which he was attempting to flee the city was targeted by a NATO air strike. The NTC confirmed later on 20 October that Qaddafi had died while in the custody of the rebels, initially suggesting that he had been killed in cross-fire following his capture. However, the emergence of video footage depicting Qaddafi injured and being taunted by his captors, and of subsequent footage depicting his corpse, displaying additional bullet wounds, being assaulted and dragged through the streets of Sirte by rebel fighters, prompted speculation that the former leader may have been summarily executed by his captors. Qaddafi's fifth son, Mutassim, was killed in Sirte on the same day. It was alleged that he too had been executed by rebels. Under considerable pressure from foreign governments and human rights groups, on 24 October, one day after Abd al-Jalil had formally proclaimed the liberation of Libya from Qaddafi's rule, the NTC agreed to conduct a full investigation into the circumstances surrounding Qaddafi's death.

Following the death of Qaddafi, Jibril adhered to his pledge by resigning from the interim Government on 23 October 2011. Dr Abd al-Rahim al-Keib, a university professor, was elected as the new interim Prime Minister at the end of the month. On 31 October, despite appeals from the NTC to extend the NATO mission to the end of the year, the UN mandate for military action and the air exclusion zone were ended. Abd al-Jalil was confirmed as interim President on 22 November, and al-Keib's interim Cabinet was formally inaugurated two days later.

On 19 November 2011 Seif al-Islam Qaddafi was captured, together with several aides, near the desert town of Obari in south-western Libya; he had apparently been en route to the Libya–Niger border at the time of his arrest. Seif al-Islam was transported to Zintan, where he remained in detention as of early 2015, amid ongoing wrangling between the Libyan Government and the ICC, as well as with the local authorities in Zintan, over the location of his forthcoming trial. The former insisted that he be tried in Libya, and offered assurances that he would be granted a fair trial, while the latter maintained that, in accordance with the arrest warrant issued against Seif al-Islam in June 2011, he should be transferred to face trial in The Hague, Netherlands.

Despite initial jubilation over the removal of Qaddafi, in mid-December 2011 thousands of protesters gathered in Tripoli and Benghazi to appeal for greater openness and transparency from the interim Government, as well as the removal from the new administration of those who had served in government under Qaddafi. The UN estimated in early 2012 that more than 8,500 prisoners, mostly pro-Qaddafi loyalists, were being held by militia groups, often in unofficial detention centres. Both Amnesty International and Human Rights Watch alleged that some of the armed militias, as well as officially recognized security forces, were engaged in the use of torture against prisoners. On 21 January hundreds of protesters stormed and looted the NTC's headquarters in Benghazi, voicing anger in particular over the Council's perceived lack of public consultation on new electoral laws in advance of forthcoming legislative elections. The following day the NTC Vice-Chairman, Abd al-Hafiz Ghoga, resigned, after he had become a focal point for public anger and amid allegations that he had switched allegiance to the NTC only as the latter gained the ascendancy. Interim President Abd al-Jalil, who claimed that 'hidden hands' were driving the protesters, insisted that the NTC would not step down, warning that such action would lead to civil war.

On 23 January 2012 local tribal fighters loyal to Qaddafi, angered by the NTC's perceived unwillingness to co-operate with them, seized control of Bani Walid, with four fighters loyal to the NTC and eight civilians reported to have been killed. On 25 January the interim Government conceded to the restive town's demands, recognizing a new tribal-based local council, in place of the NTC-appointed council, as the legitimate authority of Bani Walid. Nevertheless, in mid-October pro-Government militias undertook a large-scale military campaign in the town which they claimed was to prevent a further uprising by pro-Qaddafi tribal fighters and to arrest known fugitives; by late October more than 22 people had died. Meanwhile, in mid-February 2012 at least 100 people were estimated to have died in fighting between ethnic Arab and African tribes in Kufra.

The interim Government adopted new electoral laws in February 2012, providing for a parallel voting system, with 120 constituency seats (to be contested by independent candidates) and 80 list seats (to be contested by party lists). In April the NTC approved further legislation, which prohibited the establishment of political organizations formed on the basis of 'religion, ethnicity or tribe', citing the desire to preserve national unity. The legislation was criticized by opposition groups, particularly the Muslim Brotherhood, which had earlier formed the Justice and Construction Party (JCP) to contest the elections to a national assembly. Also in April the NTC announced that Seif al-Islam Qaddafi would be tried in Libya, although the ICC had formally requested that he be transferred to its auspices for trial in The Hague. A spokesman for the NTC stated that the trial would be completed before assembly elections in June. However, later in April 2012 the ICC rejected an appeal by Libya against the request for Seif al-Islam's transfer. In May 2014 the ICC Appeals Chamber issued a final ruling, declaring that the Libyan authorities should transfer Qaddafi's second son to the ICC immediately so that he could be tried on charges of crimes against humanity. Meanwhile, in late June 2012 Dr al-Baghdadi Ali al-Mahmoudi, the former Secretary of the General People's Committee, was extradited to Libya from Tunisia, where he had sought refuge in September 2011. Trial proceedings against al-Mahmoudi, who was charged with involvement in the 'unjust killing' of pro-democracy protesters and with providing some US $25m. in funds to pro-Qaddafi forces during the civil conflict, began in December 2012 and were ongoing in May 2015.

Elections to the General National Congress and formation of a new Government

At elections to the General National Congress (GNC) held on 7 July 2012, the liberal and predominantly secular National Forces Alliance (NFA) of former interim premier Mahmoud Jibril—established in February—won 39 of the 80 seats reserved for political parties. The JCP secured 17 seats and the liberal National Front Party, recently formed as the successor party to the NFSL, won three seats. With an additional 120 seats being reserved for independent candidates, Libya differed from neighbouring 'Arab Spring' countries, Tunisia and Egypt, since Islamists did not constitute a majority in the new assembly. International observers commended the conduct of the elections, despite some instances of violence and protests by those in the east of the country who demanded greater political autonomy. On 8 August, almost one year after the end of Qaddafi's rule, the NTC was formally dissolved at a ceremony in Tripoli and its powers transferred to the GNC. On the following day a moderate Islamist, Muhammad Yousuf Magariaf of the National Front Party, defeated an independent liberal and former diplomat, Ali Zidan, in the vote to elect the President of the GNC; Magariaf thus replaced Abd al-Jalil as Libya's de facto head of state.

Throughout 2012 the Government sought to contain the high levels of inter-tribal and political violence across Libya. After clashes had taken place between supporters of federalism and their pro-NTC opponents in Benghazi in March, in July a group of federalist protesters set fire to election materials at the election commission headquarters. In June 2012 the mountainous area of western Libya, including Zintan, was officially declared a 'military zone' owing to the fierce fighting that was occurring between pro- and anti-Qaddafi tribes. In late August a series of violent attacks perpetrated by Sunni Islamist militants resulted in the destruction of holy shrines belonging to the Sufi branch of Islam in Misurata, Zlitan and Tripoli; two car bombs also exploded in the capital. In November Farraj al-Dursi, the chief of police in Benghazi and a former official of the Qaddafi regime, was shot dead outside his home by unknown assailants. At least 10 other security officials were reported to have been assassinated in Benghazi during 2012.

Meanwhile, on 11 September 2012 the US ambassador, J. Christopher Stevens, and three other US staff members were killed when protests targeting the US consulate in Benghazi escalated into attacks by armed assailants. The following day Mustafa Abushagur, the Deputy Prime Minister in the outgoing interim Government, was elected as Prime Minister at a second round of voting by the GNC; Abushagur narrowly defeated former interim premier Jibril, who had won the first round of voting. However, having twice failed to gain the approval of assembly members for his proposed list of ministers during the first week of October, Abushagur was dismissed as premier-designate on 7 October.

Ali Zidan was elected as Prime Minister-designate by the GNC on 14 October 2012, defeating Muhammad al-Hirari, the Minister of Local Government in the outgoing cabinet. On 31 October a new Cabinet was approved by the legislature; it was reported to be more representative of Libya's various political factions and regions than the two line-ups proposed by Abushagur, and comprised principally liberal and moderate Islamist ministers. On 14 November 20 ministers, including Zidan, were sworn in to office by the GNC President, Magariaf. The previous day four of the original nominees—including Minister of the Interior Ashour Shuwail—had been deemed unfit to take office by the country's Transparency and Integrity Commission (TIC), owing to alleged links with Qaddafi. A further two nominees remained under investigation by the Commission—including the Minister of Foreign Affairs, Ali Suleiman Aujali—while another had withdrawn his candidacy earlier that month for separate reasons. Muhammad al-Barghati was appointed as the Minister of Defence. On 25 November the Minister of International Co-operation, Muhammad Abd al Aziz, assumed additional responsibility for the foreign affairs portfolio on an interim basis. The First Deputy Prime Minister, Sadiq Abd al-Karim Abd al-Rahman, was also named as the temporary Minister of the Interior. However, after the TIC, on 4 December, cleared Shuwail of wrongdoing, he was appointed to the post on 11 December.

Aujali was also found not guilty by the TIC on 27 November 2012, but he reportedly decided in late December not to take up the post for personal reasons. Abd al-Aziz was thus formally named as the Minister of Foreign Affairs on 7 January 2013. On 9 April the GNC finally agreed that the 60-member committee required to draft a new, permanent constitution would be elected at a national election. However, no formal schedule for this process was announced.

Constitutional committee elected amid a deteriorating security situation

By mid-2013 serious concerns were being raised about the apparent breakdown of law and order in many parts of Libya, notably the southern and eastern regions. Radical Sunni Islamist groups continued to wage violence against Sufi and Christian targets, and to exert pressure on the Government to impose *Shari'a* law across the country. Meanwhile, in the oil-producing eastern regions, insurgent groups which had assisted in the ousting of Qaddafi and which now demanded greater political autonomy and a larger share of oil revenues were commencing strikes, protests and takeovers of vital oil export terminals. Moreover, long-standing feuds between Libya's various tribes and ethnic groups were increasingly coming to the fore, while rebel militias were blamed for the assassinations of several leading government and security officials, in some cases owing to their links to the former Qaddafi regime. On 7 May the Minister of Defence, Muhammad Mahmoud al-Barghati, resigned in protest against a siege of government ministries in Tripoli by armed militants who were seeking to force through a so-called political isolation law. This legislation, which was adopted by the GNC on 5 May, barred those who had served in senior government posts during Qaddafi's rule from holding offices of state. Despite the adoption of the political isolation law, the gunmen continued to lay siege to government buildings in the capital. However, al-Barghati subsequently withdrew his resignation, having been asked to remain in his post by Prime Minister Zidan. On 26 May Muhammad Khalifa al-Sheikh was sworn in as the new Minister of the Interior, after Shuwail had resigned for 'personal reasons' five days previously.

On 28 May 2013 Magariaf, who had sought to comply with the recently approved legislation, resigned as President of the GNC. Nuri Ali Abu Sahmain was elected to replace him on 25 June, thereby becoming Libya's de facto head of state. Abu Sahmain, an independent deputy and member of the Amazigh (Berber) minority whose candidacy was endorsed by the JCP, had secured the support of 96 of the GNC's 200 deputies at the second round of voting. On 27 June Minister of Defence al-Barghati was dismissed from his post, after an intensification of violence between rival militias in two districts of Tripoli, as a result of which 10 people died and at least 100 were injured. Zidan, who blamed insurgents loyal to Qaddafi for the unrest, announced that a commission of inquiry would be formed to investigate the events. Al-Barghati was succeeded by Abdallah al-Thani on 5 August. On the same day Maj.-Gen. Abd al-Salam Jadallah al-Obeidi was named as the Chief of Staff of Armed Forces, in succession to Maj.-Gen. Yousef al-Mangoush, who had left his post in early June following serious violence between rival armed groups in Benghazi, which had resulted in 31 people being killed and around 100 injured. Meanwhile, on 3 August the Deputy Prime Minister, Awad al-Barasi, tendered his resignation, citing his failure to carry out his duties effectively owing to the insufficient powers granted to him. On 18 August the recently appointed Minister of the Interior, al-Sheikh, also resigned; Sadiq Abd al-Karim Abd al-Rahman was named as his temporary replacement.

On 19 September 2013 trial proceedings commenced at a special court in Tripoli against 38 senior members of the former regime who were accused of having perpetrated war crimes during the conflict that resulted in Qaddafi's overthrow. The defendants, who included Seif al-Islam—attending the hearings remotely from his prison in Zintan—as well as Libya's former intelligence chief, Abdullah al-Sanoussi, and former Secretary of the General People's Committee, al-Baghdadi al-Mahmoudi, were charged with a number of offences including incitement to violence and rape, kidnapping, torture and using mercenaries to attack protesters. It was reported on 6 March 2014 that Qaddafi's third son, Saadi, had been extradited to Libya from Niger, to which country he had fled following the uprising against his father's rule in 2011. He was accused of having perpetrated a number of crimes during the Qaddafi era and of having shot protesters who were seeking to topple the former leader. Trial proceedings against Saadi al-Qaddafi began in April 2014.

Meanwhile, there was considerable public alarm when Prime Minister Zidan was abducted by members of a militia at a hotel in Tripoli on 10 October 2013 and held for several hours before reportedly being freed by a rival militia. The kidnapping was believed to have been carried out in revenge for the recent capture by US forces of a suspected al-Qa'ida militant in the capital. The first suicide bomb attack since the ouster of Qaddafi occurred in Benghazi on 22 December 2013, when some 13 people (mostly security officials) died in an explosion at a military checkpoint on the outskirts of the city. Islamist militants linked to al-Qa'ida were believed to have carried out the attack. Some analysts suspected the involvement of Ansar al-Sharia, with which Libyan security forces had been engaged in heavy clashes in November. Ansar al-Sharia had previously denied any involvement in other attacks on official targets, including that on the US consulate in Benghazi in September 2012. In a further sign of Libya's deteriorating security situation, in January 2014 the Deputy Minister of Industry, Hassan al-Droui, was shot dead by unknown gunmen in his hometown of Sirte.

On 7 February 2014 the GNC's mandate officially expired; however, GNC President Abu Sahmain stated that the interim parliament needed to extend its term to allow the constitutional committee time to draft a new Libyan constitution. The announcement led to widespread demonstrations by protesters who demanded that fresh elections be called immediately. The election of the 60-member constitutional committee took place on 20 February; voter turnout was recorded at only 45%. The GNC had originally hoped that the committee would begin drafting a new constitution from March and complete its task by July. However, the process was delayed owing to a boycott of the election by Berbers, who claimed to be under-represented and feared an erosion of their rights in the new document; two seats reserved for Berber candidates thus remained vacant. A further 10 seats failed to be filled owing to continuing unrest which prevented voting from taking place in certain areas and, subsequently, a re-run for these seats from being held. In early March Nouri al-Abbar, the head of Libya's Higher Election Commission, admitted that elections for a permanent legislature would not be able to take place for a minimum of five to 10 months. The first session of the currently 48-member constitutional committee was convened in the eastern city of al-Bayda in April.

Zidan was removed from the premiership on 11 March 2014, following a vote of no confidence by the GNC; the vote had been brought by the Islamist parliamentary faction led by the JCP. Abdallah al-Thani, the Minister of Defence, was appointed to replace Zidan on an interim basis. The GNC's action against Zidan was prompted by the national authorities' apparent failure to prevent the export of crude petroleum by federalist rebels that had been in de facto control of four ports in the east of the country—Hariga, Ras Lanuf, Sidra, and Zueitina—since mid-2013. Despite an official naval blockade, an oil tanker registered under the flag of the Democratic People's Republic of Korea (North Korea) had left Sidra port before being apprehended by US naval forces in international waters and returned to Libyan government control. On 19 March 2014 the UN Security Council approved Resolution 1970, which imposed sanctions on those vessels engaged in the illegal export of crude oil from Libya. On 12 March it was reported that Zidan had fled abroad, in contravention of a travel ban imposed on the former premier; it was claimed that he had sought refuge in Germany, where he holds joint nationality. The Libyan authorities sought to question Zidan about the alleged embezzlement of public funds during his time in office.

In late March 2014 the interim Government urged the international community, in particular the UN, to provide assistance in Libya's 'war on terror'. On 17 March a car bomb exploded close to a military academy in Benghazi, killing at least eight newly graduated soldiers; radical Islamists were believed to be behind the attack. Meanwhile, the authorities threatened renewed military action against the federalists besieging the eastern ports in order to bring an end to the siege. The Ministry of Justice announced that a deal had finally been agreed between the two sides on 7 April, allowing the ports of Hariga and Zueitina to be transferred to government control and reopened; control of the other two ports was transferred shortly afterwards. It was reported that, in exchange for relinquishing control, the Government would pay compensation to the federalist rebels, drop charges against them and halt plans for a further military assault.

Recent developments: elections to the House of Representatives and the subsequent political and security crisis

The GNC adopted a new election law on 30 March 2014, according to which the Tripoli-based GNC would be replaced by an elected House of Representatives, which was expected to be located in Benghazi. The system whereby 80 seats were allocated to party lists under a system of proportional representation was to be abandoned, while 30 of the legislature's 200 seats were to be reserved for women. In early April it was reported that the Cabinet had asked that it be granted wider powers by the GNC and that its mandate be extended (the interim Government's mandate being renewable on a two-weekly basis). A government spokesman denied that the al-Thani Cabinet had resigned; however, on 8 April the GNC charged the interim Prime Minister with forming a new administration. During early April anti-Government demonstrations had intensified, with protesters calling for the immediate resignation of the GNC and for presidential and legislative elections to be held. During a day of 'civil disobedience' on 6 April, which included a general strike in Benghazi, the protesters accused the GNC of having failed to provide security.

On 13 April 2014 al-Thani unexpectedly announced that he would not take up the premiership on a permanent basis, citing an apparent attack on his family home in Tripoli by unknown assailants. The GNC failed to elect a candidate at the first round of voting, held on 29 April, and the second round was delayed as the result of an invasion of the parliament by armed militants. When the vote was finally held on 4 May, the legislature elected Ahmad Maitig to the role of Prime Minister-designate. However, later that day, following complaints by a number of deputies, the First Deputy President of the GNC, Ezzedine al-Amawi, declared the vote to be null and void, claiming that the voting procedure had been illegal. Despite this intervention, the President of the GNC, Abu Sahmain, issued a decree on 5 May confirming Maitig's appointment as premier. A new Government under Maitig was sworn in on 26 May; al-Arif Saleh al-Khoja was named as the Minister of the Interior and Milud Ahmad Khalifa Hamid as the Minister of Finance, while the defence and foreign affairs portfolios remained temporarily vacant. Al-Thani refused to hand over power to Maitig, stating that he was awaiting a ruling by the Supreme Court on whether the latter's election had been invalid. The Court declared on 9 June that Maitig's election had indeed been unconstitutional, prompting his swift resignation from office.

Meanwhile, in mid-May 2014 Gen. Khalifa Haftar—a senior Libyan army officer who had lived in exile in the USA from the 1990s before returning as a rebel commander during the 2011 uprising against Qaddafi's rule—began a military campaign in Benghazi and the surrounding area that was termed 'Operation Dignity'. The declared aim of the offensive in eastern Libya, which included air strikes against suspected targets, was to defeat the radical Islamist militias, including Ansar al-Sharia, that were becoming increasingly powerful in that city. On 18 May 2014 Haftar's so-called Libyan National Army and its allies entered the GNC building in Tripoli, where they arrested Islamist deputies and accused the GNC of failing to act in order to prevent radical Islamists from gaining a foothold in many areas of the country. Haftar demanded that the GNC, which he claimed was an illegitimate body, immediately hand over power to the recently elected constitutional committee. Fierce fighting ensued during subsequent weeks between Gen. Haftar's forces and the pro-Islamist militias, ultimately resulting in Libya's newly elected interim parliament being convened in Tobruk rather than Benghazi in August. The violence continued unabated in March 2015, by which time Haftar's militia had allied itself with the regular Libyan army (see below).

Elections to the new House of Representatives were held on 25 June 2014, with the results confirmed by the High National Elections Commission on 22 July. However, turnout was low (at an estimated 45%), and some 12 seats remained unallocated after the vote, owing to boycotts and the closure of polling stations following concerns over security. Although all 200 seats were reserved for individual candidates, many of those contesting the elections were believed to be affiliated to political organizations. Islamists fared poorly at the polls. At the formal inauguration of the interim legislature in Tobruk on 4 August, Ageela Issa Salah Gwaider was elected as the chamber's President, thereby becoming the de facto head of state. A number of the newly elected deputies refused to attend the ceremony, either citing fears for their safety or asserting that it should have taken place in Tripoli. Moreover, Islamist groups refused to recognize the new House of Representatives, instead continuing their support for the outgoing GNC.

Following the inauguration of the House of Representatives in Tobruk, the former GNC, which was predominantly composed of Islamists in the so-called Libya Dawn coalition, held a unilateral session in Tripoli on 25 August 2014. At this session its members elected a pro-Islamist politician, Omar al-Hassi, as a rival Prime Minister to al-Thani. Three days after this announcement, on 28 August, Abdallah al-Thani's Cabinet resigned. On 1 September al-Thani was re-elected as Prime Minister on a permanent basis by the recently convened parliament. Although on 17 September legislators rejected his first list of ministerial candidates, on 22 September a new 13-member Cabinet was approved by the interim parliament; the Government was sworn into office on 28 September. Omar al-Sunki was named as the Minister of the Interior, Kamal al-Hassi as the Minister of Finance, and Muhammad al-Dairi as the Minister of Foreign Affairs and of International Co-operation. The posts of Minister of Defence and Minister of Oil were not allocated; responsibility for those areas was reportedly to be transferred to the Chief of Staff of Armed Forces and to the NOC, respectively. However, it was announced on 23 October that Brig.-Gen. Masoud Erhuma had been appointed as Minister of Defence.

Meanwhile, on 2 September 2014—the day after al-Thani's official appointment in Tobruk—al-Hassi announced the formation of what he termed a 'salvation government', which was duly sworn in by the GNC four days later. At the end of August 2014 it was reported that militias allied with the Libya Dawn coalition had seized control in many districts of Tripoli, including Tripoli International Airport (which was largely destroyed in the fighting—see *Foreign Affairs*). Gen. Haftar's air force was reported to have received assistance from fighter planes of the United Arab Emirates in its strikes against Libya Dawn positions in the capital.

The dispute between the House of Representatives in Tobruk and the GNC in Tripoli continued during late 2014. Moreover, the Government could not meet its objective of transferring the permanent base of the House of Representatives from Tobruk to Benghazi as a result of the escalating conflict between Islamist militia groups and their opponents in the latter city. As the international community became increasingly concerned about the growing political and security crisis across Libya, on 29 September UN negotiators initiated a political dialogue aimed at ending the fighting between forces loyal to the new legislature and those Libya Dawn militias supporting the GNC. However, the UN-sponsored process had not yielded significant results by April 2015, despite the declaration of a partial ceasefire on 18 January between the regular Libyan army and the alliance of militias based in Tripoli, following discussions held in Geneva, Switzerland. By the second week of October 2014 hundreds of Libyans had died as a result of the fighting between rival militias, more than 250,000 people had been forced to leave their homes (at least 100,000 of these since mid-September, according to UNHCR), and there had been widespread damage to official buildings, residential properties, power stations and other vital infrastructure. At the start of November the official Government announced that its forces, now acting jointly with Gen. Haftar's soldiers to defeat the Islamist threat, had made progress in its efforts to recapture districts of Benghazi that had been taken by Ansar al-Sharia and other Islamist groups in July. At least 250 people were killed in the city as the result of the fighting during a two-week period from mid-October. On 6 November the Supreme Court ruled that the procedure under which the House of Representatives had been established was illegal, and ordered the chamber's dissolution. In December the Libyan army initiated a new military offensive aimed at removing pro-Libya Dawn soldiers from Derna and parts of western Libya.

By early 2015 it was apparent that militants pledging allegiance to Islamic State (formerly Islamic State in Iraq and the Levant—ISIL), a jihadist group that controlled territory in northern Syria and Iraq, had gained a significant foothold in parts of Libya. Islamic State extremists had effectively entered Libya's civil conflict in October 2014, when they seized control of the eastern port city of Derna. Fighting was subsequently reported between Islamic State militants and members of rival militias allied with Libya Dawn. On 27 January 2015 Islamist militants exploded a car bomb close to the Corinthia Hotel in central Tripoli (a location which was popular with foreign diplomats and business executives), while at least two gunmen opened fire inside the hotel building, killing nine people (including a US and a French citizen); Islamic State claimed to have carried out the attack. The group was also held responsible for three suicide car bombs that exploded in the eastern town of al-Quba on 20 February, resulting in the deaths of 42 people (including five Egyptian nationals). The attack was believed to have been carried out in retaliation for the Egyptian air strikes which had been launched against Islamic State targets in eastern Libya (see *Foreign Affairs*). Pledging to continue his campaign to rid Libya of such violent extremist groups, on 2 March Gen. Haftar was promoted to the rank of Lt-Gen. and formally appointed to the new post of Commander-in-Chief of the Armed Forces. Meanwhile, in February 2015 the House of Representatives voted to suspend the so-called political isolation law adopted by the GNC in May 2013, meaning that henceforth those government officials who had held senior positions under Qaddafi would be permitted to assume official state duties.

Foreign Affairs

Relations with the USA and the United Kingdom

US President Ronald Reagan (1981–89) severed all economic and commercial relations with Libya in January 1986, accusing the Government of sponsoring international terrorism. In March Libyan forces fired missiles at US fighter aircraft, which were challenging Libya's attempts to enforce recognition of the whole of the Gulf of Sirte as its territorial waters. In retaliatory attacks in April, US military aircraft bombed military installations, airports and official buildings, as well as alleged terrorist training camps and communication centres, in Tripoli and Benghazi; a reported 101 people, including many civilians, died in the raids. The US Administration claimed in justification to have irrefutable proof of Libyan involvement in terrorist attacks and plots against US targets in Europe and the Middle East.

In November 1991 the US and British Governments announced that they would seek to extradite two employees of Libyan Arab Airlines, Abd al-Baset Ali Muhammad al-Megrahi (a former head of security) and Al-Amin Khalifa Fhimah, alleged to have been responsible for an explosion that destroyed a Pan American World Airways (Pan Am) passenger aircraft over Lockerbie, Scotland, in December 1988, resulting in the deaths of 270 people. The Libyan Government denied any involvement in the bombing, and recommended that the allegations be investigated by a neutral body. In January 1992 the UN Security Council adopted a resolution (No. 731) demanding Libya's compliance with requests for the extradition of its two nationals and its co-operation with a French inquiry into the bombing over Niger, in September 1989, of a Union de Transports Aériens (UTA) passenger airline, in which all 171 passengers and crew had been killed. Libya's offer to try on its own territory the two men accused of the Lockerbie bombing was rejected by the USA, the United Kingdom and France. On 31 March 1992 the UN Security Council adopted a resolution (No. 748) providing for the imposition of economic sanctions against Libya if it refused to comply with Resolution 731, and to commit itself to a renunciation of international terrorism, by 15 April. Sanctions, including the severance of international air links, the prohibition of trade in arms and the reduction of Libya's diplomatic representation abroad, were duly imposed on the specified date.

In June 1992 Libya's GPC announced its decision to allow the two Lockerbie suspects to be tried abroad, provided that the proceedings were 'fair and just'. In November 1993 the UN Security Council adopted a resolution (No. 883) providing for the strengthening of the economic sanctions in force against Libya in the event of the country's failure fully to comply with Resolutions 731 and 748 by 1 December. The sanctions, which were duly applied, included: the closure of all Libyan Arab Airlines' offices abroad; a ban on the sale of equipment and services for the civil aviation sector; the sequestration of all Libyan financial resources overseas; and a ban on the sale to Libya of specified items for use in the petroleum and gas industries. In February 1994 US President Bill Clinton recommended that an embargo be imposed on Libya's sales of petroleum if the country continued to defy the international community. In mid-1996, having failed to persuade the UN to agree even tighter sanctions, the US Congress approved unilateral 'secondary' sanctions against Libya (and Iran). The Iran-Libya Sanctions Act (ILSA) sought to penalize companies operating in US markets that were investing more than US $40m. (later amended to $20m.) in Libya's oil and gas industries.

In July 1997 the League of Arab States (the Arab League, see p. 359) formally proposed that the two Libyan suspects in the Lockerbie case be tried by Scottish judges under Scottish law in a neutral country. In September the members of the League urged a relaxation of the air embargo on Libya and voted to defy UN sanctions by permitting aircraft carrying Qaddafi, and other flights for religious or humanitarian purposes, to land on their territory. In August 1998 the United Kingdom and the USA proposed that the trial of the two suspects be held in the Netherlands under Scottish law and presided over by Scottish judges. The UN Security Council adopted a resolution (No. 1192) welcoming the initiative and providing for the suspension of sanctions upon the arrival in the Netherlands of the two suspects.

In a bid to break the impasse arising from Qaddafi's demand that the trial of the Lockerbie suspects include a panel of international judges, envoys from Saudi Arabia and South Africa were dispatched to Libya in January 1999 to negotiate with the Libyan leader. In February they reportedly reached an understanding whereby UN observers would be allowed to monitor the two Libyan suspects during the trial, to ensure that they were not questioned by US and British agents, and afterwards, if they were convicted and imprisoned in Scotland. The diplomatic initiative culminated in March with a visit by President Nelson Mandela of South Africa to Libya, following which, on 6 April, the two Libyans arrived for trial in the Netherlands. They were transferred to Camp Zeist, a former US airbase near Utrecht, designated Scottish territory for the purposes of the trial, where they were formally arrested and charged with murder, conspiracy to murder and contravention of the 1982 Aviation Security Act. The UN Security Council immediately voted to suspend sanctions against Libya indefinitely, although they were not to be permanently revoked until Libya had complied with other conditions stipulated in Resolution 1192 (including the payment of compensation to the families of victims of the Lockerbie bombing). The USA refused to remove the 'secondary' sanctions against Libya, but subsequently announced that it would permit the sale of food and medical items to Libya on a 'case-by-case' basis. Talks between the US and Libyan ambassadors to the UN in June 1999 represented the first official contact between the two countries in 18 years.

The trial of al-Megrahi and Fhimah commenced on 3 May 2000; both pleaded not guilty to all three charges brought against them, and defence lawyers accused a number of organizations, including militant Palestinian resistance groups, of perpetrating the bombing. In January 2001 prosecution lawyers unexpectedly announced that they would no longer pursue charges of conspiracy to murder and contravention of the 1982 Aviation Security Act. On 31 January 2001 the judges announced that they had unanimously found al-Megrahi guilty of the murder of 270 people and sentenced him to life imprisonment, with the recommendation that he serve a minimum of 20 years. The judges accepted that al-Megrahi was a member of the Libyan intelligence services, and, while acknowledging uncertainties in the case, they concluded that the evidence against him left them with no reasonable doubt as to his guilt. Fhimah, however, was unanimously acquitted, owing to a lack of proof. Despite mounting pressure from Arab League states, the British Government asserted that sanctions against Libya would not be permanently revoked until Libya accepted responsibility for the bombing and paid 'substantial' compensation. The newly inaugurated US President, George W. Bush, supported this stance, and in July 2001 the ILSA was extended for a further five-year term.

Meanwhile, demands for further investigation into the bombing, and Qaddafi's role in it, were rejected by senior Scottish legal officials, who stated that there was insufficient evidence to justify any further proceedings against those alleged to have abetted al-Megrahi. Lawyers for al-Megrahi subsequently lodged an appeal against his conviction; the hearing, before five Scottish judges, began at Camp Zeist in January 2002. Al-Megrahi's lawyers based their case on what they termed new 'strong circumstantial evidence', which raised the possibility that the bomb had been placed on the aircraft in London, United Kingdom, and not in Malta, as the trial judges had concluded. In February Seif al-Islam Qaddafi indicated that Libya would pay compensation to the families of those killed in the Lockerbie bombing, regardless of the outcome of the appeal. In March the appeal was unanimously rejected, and al-Megrahi was transferred to a prison in Scotland to begin his sentence.

In July 1999 Libya and the United Kingdom reached agreement on the full restoration of diplomatic relations, after Qaddafi issued a statement in which he accepted Libya's 'general responsibility' for the death of Yvonne Fletcher, a British policewoman who was shot outside the Libyan People's Bureau in London in 1984, and agreed to co-operate with the investigation into the killing. The payment by Libya, in November 1999, of compensation to the victim's family facilitated the reopening of the British embassy in Tripoli in the following month, and in March 2001 Libya appointed an ambassador to the United Kingdom for the first time in 17 years.

In April 2003 it was confirmed that, following negotiations in London between senior British, US and Libyan representatives, Libya had agreed to accept civil responsibility for the actions of its officials in the Lockerbie case and would pay US $10m. in compensation to the families of the victims. Payment was to be a three-stage process: $4m. would be paid to each family on the permanent lifting of UN sanctions; a further $4m. would follow upon the removal of unilateral US sanctions; and a final payment of $2m. would be made when Libya was removed from the list of countries that the USA deemed to support international terrorism. However, Libya would pay only an additional $1m. to each family if the USA did not complete the second and third stages.

After further negotiations, on 16 August 2003 Libya delivered a letter to the President of the UN Security Council stating, *inter alia*, that it: accepted 'responsibility for the actions of its officials' in the Lockerbie bombing; agreed to pay compensation to the families of the victims; pledged co-operation in any further Lockerbie inquiry; and agreed to continue its co-operation in the US-led 'war on terror'. Following the transfer of US $2,700m. in compensation to the International Bank of Settlements, on 12 September 13 of the 15 members of the UN Security Council approved a British-drafted resolution lifting the sanctions imposed against Libya; France (which had demanded a similar amount of compensation for families of victims of the UTA bombing in 1989) and the USA abstained from the vote. Later that month Libya announced its intention to commence dialogue with the USA aimed at normalizing bilateral relations. Nevertheless, the US Administration continued to insist that unilateral sanctions would remain in place until the Libyan Government addressed ongoing US concerns such as the infringement of human rights and pursuit of weapons of mass destruction.

In October 2003 an official of the US Department of State accused Libya of having increased its efforts to purchase components for biological and chemical weapons since the lifting of UN sanctions the previous month, and warned that Libya would be added to the group of countries described by President Bush as forming an 'axis of evil'—comprising Iran, Iraq and North Korea. In mid-December, however, the British Prime Minister, Tony Blair, unexpectedly announced that Libya had agreed to disclose and dismantle its programme to develop weapons of mass destruction and long-range ballistic missiles. The statement was the culmination of nine months of clandestine negotiations between Qaddafi and British and US diplomats, during which the Libyan authorities had reportedly shown evidence of a 'well advanced' nuclear weapons programme, as well as the existence of large quantities of chemical weapons and bombs designed to carry poisonous gas. Libya also agreed to adhere to the Chemical Weapons Convention and to sign an additional protocol allowing the International Atomic Energy Agency (IAEA) to carry out random inspections of its facilities. Upon visiting a number of sites in Tripoli in late December, the Director-General of the IAEA, Dr Muhammad el-Baradei, insisted that Libya's weapons development projects had only been in the initial stages of development. In January 2004 the US Department of State confirmed that British and US intelligence agents had, in October 2003, intercepted a shipment of centrifuges capable of developing weapons-grade uranium destined for Tripoli. Also in January 2004 it was announced that Libya had ratified the IAEA's Comprehensive Nuclear Test Ban Treaty. It was agreed that US and British officials would be responsible for destroying and removing Libya's nuclear material and that the IAEA would verify that the dismantling process was complete.

In February 2004 it was confirmed that a US diplomat had been stationed in that country's interests section of the Belgian embassy in Tripoli, providing the USA with its first permanent diplomatic presence in Libya for 25 years. Also in February the Libyan Secretary for Foreign Liaison and International Co-operation, Abd al-Rahman Muhammad Shalgam, visited London for talks with his British counterpart and Prime Minister Blair; this represented the first meeting between cabinet-level ministers of the two countries in more than 20 years. In late February the USA lifted the restrictions on its citizens travelling to Libya. In March Libya signed an additional IAEA protocol allowing the agency to carry out random inspections of its nuclear facilities; moreover, Libya commenced the destruction of its supplies of chemical weapons and transported all of its remaining nuclear weapons-related equipment to the USA. Later that month the Organisation for the Prohibition of Chemical Weapons verified that Libya's declaration of its chemical weapons inventory, submitted to the UN in early March, had been accurate.

In late March 2004 William Burns, the US Assistant Secretary of the Bureau of Near Eastern Affairs, became the highest-ranking US official to visit Libya in more than 30 years. In April the USA announced that it would remove the restrictions that prevented US petroleum companies and banks from conducting commercial activities in Libya. It was revealed in June that Libya had resumed exports of petroleum to the USA. At the end of the month formal diplomatic relations were re-established between the two countries when a US liaison office was opened in Tripoli. In September President Bush lifted all travel restrictions for charter and commercial flights between Libya and the USA. He also announced that the US $1,300m. of Libyan assets held in the USA or in US banks abroad would be unfrozen. In December, with the USA's unilateral sanctions having been lifted, Libya paid the second instalment of its compensation to the families of those killed in the Lockerbie bombing. In February 2005 the US authorities lifted all restrictions on Libyan diplomats travelling within the USA. In May 2006 the US liaison office in Tripoli was formally upgraded to an embassy, while in June Libya was removed from the US Department of State's list of countries deemed to support international terrorism. However, tensions arose in that month when Libyan lawyers in the USA insisted that, as a result of the expiration in December 2004 of an agreement concerning the transfer of the final portion of compensation for families of the Lockerbie victims, the Libyan Government was no longer obligated to pay the final $2m. promised to each family. Nevertheless, in July 2006 the USA lifted all air transport sanctions against Libya.

Libya signed a memorandum of understanding with the British Government in October 2005, allowing for the deportation from the United Kingdom of Libyans suspected of involvement in terrorist activities. In May 2007 the British oil company BP announced that it was to return to Libya, more than three decades after its expulsion from the country when Qaddafi had nationalized its assets in 1971; BP was granted onshore and offshore exploratory rights in a deal worth an estimated US $900m.

In August 2006 Libyan and US representatives, meeting in Tripoli, signed a joint agreement on the full and final settlement of mutual claims by victims or their relatives in respect of bombings involving the two countries, and the following month Condoleezza Rice became the first US Secretary of State to visit Libya since 1953. In October 2008 Libya paid US $1,500m. into an agreed compensation fund for the relatives of US victims of bombings covered by the agreement. In December 2008 Gene A. Cretz was sworn in as the first US ambassador to Libya since 1972, and in January 2009 Ali Aujali assumed the role of Libyan ambassador to the USA, following the upgrading of Libya's liaison office in Washington, DC, to a full embassy in May 2006. Qaddafi visited the USA for the first time in September to address the UN General Assembly in New York.

In August 2009 the Scottish Cabinet Secretary for Justice, Kenny MacAskill, announced that al-Megrahi was to be freed on compassionate grounds, after discussions between the British and Libyan authorities over al-Megrahi's declining health (he had been diagnosed with terminal cancer in September 2008). The decision provoked outrage from many of the families of the US victims of the Lockerbie bombing and official condemnation by the US authorities. Although the British Government insisted that al-Megrahi's release had been decided by the Scottish devolved administration, a leaked US diplomatic cable published in late 2010 by the WikiLeaks organization indicated that the decision had enjoyed the full support of the British Government, which had reportedly been warned by Qaddafi of possible action against British commercial and diplomatic interests in Libya. Al-Megrahi died in Tripoli in May 2012.

Meanwhile, a trade and investment agreement signed between the USA and Libya in May 2010 provided for the establishment of a bilateral trade and investment council; the USA also agreed to offer assistance in Libya's bid to accede to the World Trade Organization (WTO, see p. 431). However, the apparent amelioration in bilateral relations was severely undermined by the Qaddafi regime's response to the popular protests in Libya in early 2011, which prompted condemnation from the Administration of US President Barack Obama. (For US and British responses to the Libyan Government's handling of the protests and the subsequent installation of the National Transitional Council, see *Domestic Political Affairs*.) The USA accepted the NTC as the 'legitimate governing authority' of Libya in July 2011. In September the US embassy in Tripoli, which had been closed in February, along with many other foreign embassies, was reopened and Cretz returned to his post.

In late September 2011 Scottish prosecutors submitted a formal request to the interim Libyan Government requesting its assistance in uncovering new evidence pertaining to the 1988 Lockerbie bombing. A number of senior government officials who had defected from the Qaddafi regime during mid-2011 had claimed that the bombing had been carried out on the direct orders of the former Libyan leader. Both the US and British Governments praised the new Libyan authorities for having staged the country's first free election for more than four decades in July 2012. Diplomatic relations between the USA and Libya have continued to grow despite the deaths of Cretz's successor, ambassador J. Christopher Stevens, and three other consular officials in Benghazi in September of that year. Deborah K. Jones replaced Stevens as the USA's ambassador to Libya in June 2013. In August the US Government was reported to have charged a number of suspected Libyan militants in connection with the attack in Benghazi. In December the two countries signed a Trade and Investment Framework Agreement, according to which a US-Libya Council on Trade and Investment was to be established. Following a pledge by the Obama Administration in 2013 to provide training to between 5,000 and 8,000 Libyan armed forces, in March 2014 a contingent of US troops arrived in Libya to prepare for a programme of formal military training (due to begin in Bulgaria later that year). EU member states also offered to provide training to new Libyan national army recruits, and the first contingent of former rebel fighters received six months of training in the United Kingdom from June 2014. In April of that year William Burns, the US Deputy Secretary of State, had expressed concern at the serious risk being posed to Libya's political and economic stability as a result of the recent dramatic rise in Islamist extremism. Ahmed Abu Khattala, the prime suspect in the attack on the US consulate in Benghazi in 2012, was captured by US special forces in June 2014, and was expected to be tried by a US civilian court.

In January 2013 the United Kingdom, Germany and other EU countries sought to persuade their citizens to relocate from Benghazi, amid concerns for their safety as a result of the increasing prevalence of armed militias in the city. As the security situation deteriorated further from mid-2014, a large number of embassies in Tripoli were temporarily closed, including the British embassy in August; foreign citizens were urged to leave Libya. In February 2015 the Italian embassy, which by that time was the only European embassy to continue functioning in Tripoli, also decided to return its diplomatic staff to Rome. Meanwhile, the EU announced in July 2014 that it was to provide €2.4m. to assist sections of the Libyan population who were deemed to be 'at risk'; these included a growing number of internally displaced persons—estimated by the United Kingdom-based human rights organization Lawyers for Justice in Libya to have risen to around 400,000 by early 2015.

Regional relations

In 1998 Qaddafi announced his intention to ally Libya more closely with African rather than Arab countries. In October he changed the name of Libya's mission to the Arab League from 'permanent' to 'resident', and in September 1999, on the 30th anniversary of his seizure of power, Qaddafi hosted an extraordinary summit meeting of the Organization of African Unity (OAU) in Sirte, at which he presented his vision of a United States of Africa. The 'Sirte Declaration', a final document adopted by the 43 attending heads of state and government, called for the strengthening of the OAU, the establishment of a pan-African parliament, African monetary union and an African court of justice. The OAU's member states overwhelmingly endorsed the formation of the African Union (AU, see p. 188) in 2001, and in July 2002 Qaddafi travelled to Durban, South Africa, for the 38th and final summit of the OAU, at which the new AU was formally created.

Following a dispute at the Arab League summit held in March 2003, it was alleged in June 2004 that Qaddafi had ordered the assassination of Crown Prince Abdullah of Saudi Arabia, the kingdom's de facto leader. (Libya also reportedly accused Saudi Arabia of financing Libyan opposition groups that had attempted to assassinate Qaddafi.) Libyan officials denied these allegations; however, in December 2004 Saudi Arabia recalled its ambassador from Tripoli and dismissed the Libyan ambassador in the Saudi capital, Riyadh.

In May 2006 Sudanese President Omar Hassan Ahmad al-Bashir expressed gratitude to Qaddafi for the latter's role in finding a resolution to the crisis in Darfur, Sudan, and proposed the establishment of a tripartite committee, comprising representatives of the Libyan and Sudanese Governments and the Sudan Liberation Movement, to oversee the implementation of a peace agreement signed between the two latter parties on 5 May. In July 2007 Libya hosted an international conference on Darfur, co-chaired by the AU and the UN.

In June 2006 ministers responsible for foreign affairs from Algeria, Libya, Mauritania, Morocco and Tunisia convened in Tripoli to discuss efforts to revive the five-nation Union du Maghreb Arabe (UMA—Union of the Arab Maghreb, see p. 450), which had been founded in February 1989 but had remained dormant for more than a decade, predominantly owing to Algerian–Moroccan disagreements concerning Western Sahara. This will to relaunch the UMA was restated in April 2008 during celebrations held in Morocco to mark the 50th anniversary of the summit at which the idea of a union of Arab Maghreb states had initially been proposed.

In March 2007 Qaddafi announced his decision to boycott the Arab League summit meeting in Riyadh, insisting that Libya was an African nation and had 'turned its back to Arabs'. Later that year Qaddafi embarked upon a tour of West Africa, culminating in his attendance in July at an AU summit meeting in the Ghanaian capital, Accra, which focused predominantly on proposals to establish a pan-African government. The majority of those present rejected Qaddafi's appeal for the immediate creation of a 'United States of Africa', and in February 2008 he threatened to sever Libyan ties with Africa, pledging to transfer Libya's African investments to alternative destinations in Arab and European countries if his vision for African unity continued to be ignored. In February 2009 Qaddafi was, none the less, appointed to the chairmanship of the AU and immediately revived his efforts to promote the concept of a 'United States of Africa'. However, the Libyan leader's attempts to be re-elected to the chairmanship in January 2010 were unsuccessful.

In November 2010 Libya and Tunisia agreed to lift all administrative and financial restrictions on the movement of goods and people between their respective countries, in a development that was hailed as an important step towards the achievement of greater Maghreb unity. The two countries also agreed to double the value of bilateral investment, to US $2,000m., and discussed the creation of a free economic zone. In April 2013 the Libyan and Tunisian Governments agreed to establish a joint committee which would supervise the export of Libyan oil to Tunisia, following the conclusion of a bilateral accord in May 2012. In March 2014 Libya closed its principal border crossing with Tunisia, Ras Jedir, for almost a month in an attempt to prevent the smuggling into Tunisia of cheap Libyan oil.

The Arab League suspended Libya's membership of that body in mid-February 2011, citing its disapproval of the Libyan Government's response to the popular protests that commenced earlier that month. During the conflict, both Qatar and the United Arab Emirates contributed aircraft to the NATO coalition, and the former was also reported to have provided the Libyan rebels with significant amounts of financial aid, military training and weapons. Following the ousting of Qaddafi in August, the Arab League formally recognized the NTC as the legitimate representative of the Libyan people and voted to restore the country's membership later that month.

Having at first appeared reluctant to criticize Qaddafi's violent handling of the protesters, in late February 2011 the Chairman of the AU Commission condemned the Libyan Government's 'disproportionate use of force' against civilians, and demanded 'an immediate end of the repression and violence'. A proposal intended to secure an end to the conflict between the Government and the rebel forces presented by the AU in April secured the approval in principle of Qaddafi but was rejected by the NTC, which insisted on the removal from power of Qaddafi. In July the AU declared that its members would not co-operate with the arrest warrants issued by the ICC against Qaddafi, Seif al-Islam and the head of the Libyan intelligence service, contending that the existence of the warrants 'seriously complicates the efforts aimed at finding a negotiated political solution to the crisis'. Following the removal from power of the Qaddafi regime, the AU recognized the NTC as the de facto Libyan Government in mid-September, and stated that it was ready to assist the NTC in its

efforts to rebuild the country and form a new, inclusive government.

A meeting held in Tripoli between representatives from Libya, Egypt and Sudan in May 2013 resulted in a pledge by the three Governments to co-operate more closely in order to develop their joint border regions, create free trade zones, link their electricity grids and improve transport networks between their countries. In mid-2014 the Sudanese Government agreed to join those countries that were already providing military training to Libya's new armed forces.

Violence being perpetrated by radical Islamists in Libya had a profound effect on many neighbouring states during 2014 and the early part of 2015, leading to serious concerns about the possible repercussions for their long-term security. Several African and Arab diplomats in Tripoli were attacked, threatened or kidnapped by Islamist militants. In early February the bodies of seven Coptic Christians from Egypt were discovered on a beach to the east of Benghazi; the men had apparently been executed by members of Ansar al-Sharia, which was reportedly seeking to expel all remaining Christians from the city. In mid-February Islamic State released a video which appeared to show the beheading of 21 Egyptian Copts by its militants on a beach close to Tripoli; the men had been taken hostage by the jihadist group in Sirte in December 2014. The Egyptian Government responded to the murders by authorizing air strikes against Islamic State targets in Derna, in eastern Libya.

Other external relations

Relations with the EU, and particularly with France, generally improved following talks in early 1996 between Libyan and EU representatives in Belgium. In July Qaddafi granted the French authorities investigating the 1989 bombing of the UTA passenger aircraft unprecedented access to Libyan evidence. This resulted in February 1998 in a judge's decision to try *in absentia* six Libyans suspected of involvement in the attack, and in March 1999 a French court sentenced the six suspects to life imprisonment. The French authorities issued international arrest warrants for the Libyans, and threatened to intensify sanctions against Libya if it did not impose the verdicts on the accused. In July Libya began payment of some US $31m. in compensation to the families of those killed in the bomb attack. In September 2003, following an intervention by the French President, Jacques Chirac, the Libyan Government and the families of the UTA bombing reached partial agreement on the payment of additional compensation to the victims' relatives, and in January 2004 Libya agreed to pay them an additional $170m.; the payment was to be made in four equal instalments, resulting in the families of each victim receiving an additional $1m. In December 2005 the Libyan Government was ordered by a French court to pay an additional $4m. in compensation to families of victims of the 1989 bombing not included in the previous agreement.

Relations between the French and Libyan Governments improved in 2005, after France expressed its interest in assisting the development of civil nuclear technology in Libya. In March 2006 a deal on co-operation regarding the development of nuclear energy in Libya was signed by representatives of the two countries during a visit to Tripoli by the Director of France's Commissariat à l'Energie Atomique. Meanwhile, in April 2004 Qaddafi, who was visiting Europe for the first time in 15 years, met with several senior EU politicians in Brussels, Belgium, and addressed the European Commission. The ending of economic sanctions and an arms embargo imposed on Libya by the European Economic Community (now EU) in 1986 was ratified by EU ministers in October 2004. In December 2007 Qaddafi made an official visit to the French capital at the invitation of President Nicolas Sarkozy—the first such invitation from a Western country since Libya had abandoned its nuclear weapons programme in 2003. The visit provoked strong censure from both French and Libyan opposition politicians, as well as international human rights groups, owing to Libya's questionable human rights record. Commercial agreements worth an estimated €10,000m. were signed between the two countries.

Franco-Libyan relations were, however, once more strained in 2008 when Qaddafi refused to attend the inauguration of President Sarkozy's project to create a Union for the Mediterranean, believing this to undermine the role of the AU and to represent France's reassertion of colonial dominance over former North African colonies. During a state visit to Libya in July 2010, Qaddafi and Sarkozy signed a memorandum of understanding intended to boost nuclear energy co-operation, providing for French access to Libya's uranium resources and the eventual construction of a nuclear desalination plant to provide drinking water to the Libyan population. However, following the onset of conflict in Libya in early 2011, the French Government imposed measures against Qaddafi and certain of his officials, and in early March France became the first state officially to recognize the opposition Transitional National Council as the 'legitimate representative of the Libyan people'.

In April 1998, meanwhile, Libya resolved to allow the German authorities to question four Libyans suspected of carrying out a bomb attack on a nightclub in Berlin in 1986. Following a lengthy trial, in November 2001 a court in Berlin sentenced four people, including a Libyan national, to between 12 and 14 years' imprisonment for their involvement in the attack. Although Qaddafi's personal complicity in the incident could not be proven, the presiding judge stated that there was sufficient evidence to ascertain that the bombing had been carried out by members of the Libyan secret service and employees of the Libyan People's Bureau in the former East Germany. In August 2003 the Qaddafi International Charity and Development Foundation, headed by Seif al-Islam, offered to compensate the relatives of the three victims of the Berlin bomb attack. The Libyan authorities signed a deal with their German counterparts in September 2004 agreeing to pay US \$35m. to compensate some 160 non-US citizens injured in the attack.

In July 1998 Italy formally apologized for its colonial rule of Libya. Following the suspension of international sanctions in April 1999, Italy's Prime Minister, Massimo D'Alema, travelled to Libya in December, thus becoming the first EU premier to visit the country since 1992. In December 2000 officials from the two countries signed accords regarding political consultation, visas and the removal of landmines during talks in Rome. In August 2004 Prime Minister Silvio Berlusconi exerted pressure on Qaddafi to place stricter border controls on the country's northern coastline, following an influx of illegal immigrants into the Italian island of Lampedusa from Libya. In October, following a sudden increase in the number of illegal immigrants arriving from North Africa, the Italian Government began a mass expulsion of illegal immigrants to Libya. Also in that month Qaddafi agreed to revoke a ban that prohibited some 20,000 Italian settlers who had been expelled from Libya in 1970 (following Qaddafi's rise to power) from visiting the country.

During a meeting with Qaddafi in Benghazi in August 2008, Berlusconi issued an apology for the 'damage inflicted on Libya by Italy during the colonial era'. The two heads of state also signed a treaty of 'friendship, partnership and co-operation' (which was ratified in Sirte in February 2009), committing Italy to annual payments of US \$200m. to Libya, over a period of 25 years, via investment and infrastructure projects. For its part, Libya agreed to co-operate more fully in efforts to combat illegal immigration, principally through the establishment of joint marine patrols of the Libyan coastline.

Relations between Libya and Italy, France and Germany, together with most other European countries, were severely compromised in early 2011 as a result of the Libyan Government's response to the widespread popular protests in the country. Italian Prime Minister Mario Monti pledged that Italy would continue to release to the control of the Libyan interim administration assets of the former regime held in Italy. The Italian army started to provide military training to some 2,000 Libyan soldiers in April 2014, and the two Governments pursued close co-operation in an attempt to control the flow of refugees from North Africa to Europe.

Meanwhile, Libya came under heavy criticism from EU and US officials in May 2004, after five Bulgarian nurses and a Palestinian doctor were sentenced to death for deliberately infecting more than 400 children at a Benghazi hospital in 1999 with blood containing the HIV virus. The trials were denounced by international human rights associations as being unfair, and the nurses stated that their confessions had been extracted through torture. The Bulgarian Government refused Libya's demand for compensation for the families affected by the case, stating that any payment would constitute an admission of the medical workers' guilt. Following an appeal, in December 2005 the sentences of the six medical workers were overturned by the Supreme Court, and a retrial began in May 2006. Notwithstanding data arising from genetic analysis that strongly suggested that the children had been infected with HIV prior to the defendants' arrival in Libya in 1998, the original verdict was upheld in December 2006 and the six death sentences were reinstated. A further appeal was rejected in July 2007. A few days later, however, the High Judicial Court commuted the medical workers' death sentences to terms of life imprisonment,

following the successful brokerage of a compensation deal, according to which the victims' families would receive a reported US \$1m. for each child infected. After protracted negotiations, Libya finally acquiesced to a request by the Bulgarian Government that the medical workers be allowed to complete their sentences in Bulgaria, and the six were duly released from Libyan custody on 24 July. Upon their return to Bulgaria, they were immediately pardoned by that country's President. In April 2013 a court in the Netherlands, where the Palestinian doctor now resided, ordered the Libyan Government to pay him \$1m. in compensation for the time he had wrongly spent in prison.

Formal negotiations on an EU-Libya Framework Agreement were inaugurated in November 2008. The agreement, intended to encompass economic, political, social and cultural co-operation, was also designed to achieve greater consensus regarding the issue of illegal immigration to EU countries via Libya. During a second round of negotiations held in Tripoli in February 2009, Libya was offered some €20m. in assistance to address illegal migration. Negotiations on the Framework Agreement and ongoing co-operation contracts between the EU and Libya were suspended on 22 February 2011, and on 28 February the EU imposed an arms embargo on Libya in line with the UN Security Council resolution adopted two days earlier that implemented similar sanctions; the EU also prohibited trade with Libya in any equipment that might be used for internal repression and imposed a visa ban and an asset freeze on Qaddafi and other senior officials. After the liberation of Libya from Qaddafi's rule was formally declared in October, in mid-November the EU High Representative for Foreign Affairs and Security Policy, Catherine Ashton, presided over the opening of a new EU delegation office in the *de jure* capital, Tripoli, and met with NTC Chairman Mustafa Muhammad Abd al-Jalil. Following the conclusion of Ashton's visit, the EU indicated that it was ready to resume negotiations on the Framework Agreement, and pledged, in addition to humanitarian aid, up to €30m. towards the NTC's efforts to stabilize the country. During 2012–14 the EU continued to provide financial and technical assistance to the new Libyan authorities in their efforts to improve border security, tackle the threat posed by militant Islamist groups and further develop Libya's political framework.

During a visit to Libya in April 2008 by the Russian President, Vladimir Putin, several agreements were signed on co-operation in energy, military and infrastructure projects. Putin agreed to cancel Libyan debts amounting to some US \$4,500m. In January 2010 the two countries concluded an agreement worth more than \$2,000m. for Libya to purchase more than 20 Russian fighter jets. In February 2011 Russia voted in support of UN Security Council Resolution 1970, implementing an arms embargo and other sanctions against the Libyan authorities owing to its use of force in response to the popular protests, and referring the actions of the regime to the ICC. However, the Russian Government, which remained opposed to any military action against Qaddafi, abstained from the UN Security Council vote in March on Resolution 1973, which authorized the use of force against Libyan government forces in order to protect civilians. Following Qaddafi's ouster, Russia and Libya have continued to pursue military co-operation projects. The Russian Government openly supported the appointment of Abdallah al-Thani as Prime Minister in March 2014.

Increasingly cordial relations with the People's Republic of China have been evident since the latter years of Qaddafi's rule, fuelled by Chinese interest in Libya's oil resources and Libya's continued adherence to the 'one-China' policy (see the chapter on the People's Republic of China). Like Russia, China voted in support of UN Security Council Resolution 1970 in February 2011, but abstained from the vote on Resolution 1973 in March. In late March both countries appealed for an immediate cease-fire, amid concerns about reports of a growing number of civilian casualties arising from NATO air strikes against Libyan government forces. Nevertheless, in September the Chinese Government formally recognized the NTC as the sole legitimate governing authority in Libya, while expressing its hope that existing bilateral treaties and contracts would continue to be implemented. Controversy had been provoked earlier that month by the discovery in Tripoli of documents which revealed that three Chinese state-owned companies had offered to sell heavy weapons valued at around US \$200m. to the Qaddafi regime during its final weeks. However, a spokesperson for the Chinese Ministry of Foreign Affairs claimed that this had been without the knowledge of the Government and that no contracts had been signed.

CONSTITUTION AND GOVERNMENT

Following the overthrow of King Idris I in 1969, a Constitutional Proclamation was issued by the Revolutionary Command Council (see *Contemporary Political History*). In 1977 a further document, the Declaration on the Establishment of the Authority of the People, was approved by the General People's Congress (GPC). Under the system set out in this document, power was vested in the people through People's Congresses, Popular Committees, Trade Unions, and Vocational Syndicates, and with the GPC and its General Secretariat. The head of state was the Revolutionary Leader, elected by the GPC, and executive power was exercised by the General People's Committee. Following the installation of the opposition National Transitional Council (NTC) as the de facto administration in August 2011, all constitutional documents promulgated under Qaddafi's rule were suspended and an interim Constitutional Declaration was issued in its place.

Elections to a 200-member legislature, the General National Congress (GNC), took place in July 2012. Of the total number of seats, 80 were allocated to candidates representing political parties elected on the basis of proportional representation, while the remaining 120 seats were reserved for independents. However, in June 2014 a new legislature, the 200-seat House of Representatives, was elected. All 200 seats in the new chamber were reserved for individual candidates; however, it was thought that many of those contesting the elections were affiliated to political organizations. The new chamber, which replaced the GNC, was inaugurated in August. In November the Supreme Court ruled that the procedure under which the House of Representatives had been created was illegal, and ordered that chamber's immediate dissolution. At May 2015 both the House of Representatives and the GNC remained in operation, the latter under the direction of pro-Islamist groups, although only the House of Representatives retained international recognition (see *Contemporary Political History*).

The President of the legislature assumes the role of head of state. Executive power lies with the Cabinet, led by a Prime Minister. The Cabinet takes office after being approved by a vote of the legislature, to which it is responsible. In April 2013 the GNC declared that the committee charged with drafting a new Libyan constitution would be elected at a national ballot. The election of the 60-member constitutional committee took place on 20 February 2014; however, the start of its work was subsequently delayed.

REGIONAL AND INTERNATIONAL CO-OPERATION

Libya is a member of the African Union (AU, see p. 188), the League of Arab States (the Arab League, see p. 359), the Organization of Arab Petroleum Exporting Countries (OAPEC, see p. 398) and the Union du Maghreb Arabe (UMA—Union of the Arab Maghreb, see p. 450). The Community of Sahel-Saharan States (CEN-SAD, see p. 446) has its headquarters in Tripoli.

Libya joined the UN in September 1990. The country also participates in the Organization of the Petroleum Exporting Countries (OPEC, see p. 406). In 2004 the World Trade Organization (WTO, see p. 431) agreed to commence accession negotiations with Libya. However, as of early 2015 the working party established to examine the application had yet to convene.

ECONOMIC AFFAIRS

In 2009, according to estimates by the World Bank, Libya's gross national income (GNI), measured at average 2007–09 prices, was US $77,140m., equivalent to $12,320 per head (or $16,740 on an international purchasing-power parity basis). During 2004–13, it was estimated, the population increased at an average annual rate of 1.3%, while gross domestic product (GDP) per head decreased, in real terms, by an estimated average of 2.2% per year, according to the IMF. According to IMF estimates, overall GDP decreased, in real terms, at an average annual rate of 1.1% in 2004–13. Libya's GDP was estimated to have contracted by around 62.1% in 2011, owing to a virtual halt in oil production following the outbreak of conflict and political unrest at the beginning of that year. GDP rebounded by 104.5% in 2012 due to the almost complete resumption of oil production, and the increase in construction and infrastructure activity. However, a further GDP contraction, of some 13.6%, was estimated by the IMF in 2013, as a blockade of oil facilities drastically reduced output.

According to UN estimates, agriculture (including forestry and fishing) contributed 2.2% of GDP in 2013. The sector engaged 2.2% of the total labour force in mid-2015, according to FAO estimates. The principal subsistence crops are wheat and barley; other crops include potatoes, watermelons, tomatoes, onions, dates, olives and citrus fruits. An aim of the Great Manmade River Project (GMR), in progress since 1984, is to reclaim some 130,000 ha of arable land; more than 70% of water to be delivered by the GMR is intended for agricultural use. The main agricultural activity is animal husbandry, with sheep and goats being the principal livestock. During 2006–11, according to preliminary official data, agricultural GDP decreased at an average annual rate of 19.6%; the sector's GDP decreased by 0.9% in 2010 and by 69.0% in 2011.

In 2013, according to UN estimates, industry (including mining, manufacturing, construction and power) contributed 63.2% of GDP. Industry engaged 13.1% of the employed labour force in 2009. Preliminary official data indicated that the GDP of the industrial sector decreased at an average annual rate of 23.0% in 2006–11; industrial GDP declined by 72.1% in 2011, compared with an increase of 4.0% in 2010.

Mining (including utilities) contributed 53.4% of GDP in 2013. The mining sector engaged just 2.8% of the employed labour force in 2009. Libya's economy is overwhelmingly reliant on its petroleum and natural gas resources. Hydrocarbons contributed an estimated 94.5% of total government revenue in 2013. At the end of 2013 proven recoverable reserves of petroleum were estimated at 48,472m. barrels, the largest proven reserves in Africa. The production of oil increased to 1.51m. b/d at the end of 2012, but fell to 0.99m. b/d in 2013. As a member of the Organization of the Petroleum Exporting Countries (OPEC, see p. 406), Libya is subject to production quotas agreed by the Organization's Conference. Libya's natural gas reserves are extensive (estimated at 1,549,000m. cu m at the end of 2013). Libya also has reserves of iron ore, salt, limestone, clay, sulphur and gypsum. According to preliminary official figures, the GDP of the mining sector decreased, in real terms, at an average annual rate of 23.0% in 2006–11; mining GDP expanded by 4.0% in 2010, but contracted by 72.0% in 2011.

Manufacturing, according to UN estimates, contributed 4.1% of GDP in 2013. The manufacturing sector engaged 4.4% of the employed labour force in 2009. The principal manufacturing activity is petroleum refining. Other important activities include the production of iron, steel and cement, chemicals-manufacturing, and the processing of agricultural products. Preliminary official figures indicated that the GDP of the manufacturing sector decreased at an average annual rate of 23.9% during 2006–11; the sector's GDP increased by 1.2% in 2010, but declined by 77.0% in 2011.

Construction contributed 5.7% of GDP in 2013, according to UN estimates. The sector engaged only 2.5% of the employed labour force in 2009. Preliminary official figures indicated that the GDP of the construction sector decreased at an average annual rate of 20.0% during 2006–11; the sector's GDP increased by 5.8% in 2010, but decreased by 79.0% in 2011.

Energy is derived principally from natural gas, which contributed 56.3% of total electricity output in 2011, and petroleum (43.7%). Libya is a net exporter of fuels. Many power stations were damaged during the 2011 conflict, although substantial repairs to the electricity infrastructure had been carried out by the end of 2012. Nevertheless, amid rising annual demand for electricity (estimated at some 7%), infrequent power shortages were still occurring in 2012–13. The situation was exacerbated in 2013 by industrial action on the part of oil industry workers to protest against the allocation of Libya's oil revenues among the various regions, as well as by militant attacks targeting oil installations. In July 2014 rebel forces seeking regional autonomy from the central Government ended an 11-month blockade of four vital ports used to transport oil in eastern Libya. The sector continued to be profoundly affected by political uncertainty and ongoing violence in early 2015.

Services contributed 34.7% of GDP in 2013, according to UN estimates. The services sector engaged 81.6% of the employed labour force in 2009. Efforts to reform the financial sector, hitherto highly state-controlled, have notably included the sale, in 2007–08, of minority stakes in two banks to foreign interests. A stock exchange was established in 2007. The Government has invested heavily in recent years to expand and rehabilitate Libya's tourism infrastructure. Visitor arrivals neared 1m. in 2004. During 2006–11, according to preliminary official data, the GDP of the services sector decreased at an average annual rate of 5.8%; services GDP increased by 5.4% in 2010, but decreased by 41.9% in 2011.

In 2013 Libya recorded a visible merchandise trade surplus of US $11,968m., and there was a deficit of $108m. on the current account of the balance of payments. In 2012 the principal source of imports was the People's Republic of China (which provided 12.8% of total imports); Turkey, Italy, Egypt, Tunisia, the Republic of Korea (South Korea), Germany, France (including Monaco) and the USA were also important suppliers. The principal market for exports in 2012 was Italy (23.3%); Germany, China, France and Spain were also significant purchasers. The petroleum sector is overwhelmingly Libya's principal generator of exports revenue: mineral fuels and related materials accounted for some 97.1% of the value of merchandise exports in 2010. The principal imports in that year were machinery and transport equipment, basic manufactures, food and live animals, miscellaneous products, and chemicals.

According to official sources, an overall budgetary deficit of LD 10,520m. was recorded in 2013. According to the Central Bank of Libya, the annual rate of inflation averaged 5.5% in 2004–13; consumer prices increased by an estimated 2.6% in 2013. According to the Ministry of Labour and Retraining, around 15% of the labour force were unemployed in 2013. However, unofficial sources claimed that the unemployment rate was in fact closer to 30%, with a significantly high proportion of young Libyans being out of work.

With the ending of international sanctions in 2003–04, Libya rapidly became a major centre for hydrocarbons exploration, and output of both oil and natural gas expanded strongly. Furthermore, since large areas of Libyan territory remained unexplored, it was believed that reserves (already the largest in Africa) could be significantly higher than estimated. However, oil output and exports were severely disrupted by the conflict between the Government of Muammar al-Qaddafi and opposition forces in 2011; output declined from an average of 1.66m. b/d at the end of 2010 to just 48,000 b/d one year later. Moreover, much of Libya's foreign assets were blocked following the renewed imposition in March 2011 of sanctions by the UN, the USA and the European Union. As a result of the assets freeze, together with the effects of NATO air strikes in and around Tripoli, fuel shortages increased and commodity prices rose sharply. Although the easing of sanctions during late 2011 alleviated economic conditions and improved living standards, many foreign investors were reluctant to return to Libya until the political and security climate had become more stable. In April 2013 the Government announced the launch of a project intended to develop those regions where oil and gas were produced, in an effort to create jobs and stimulate the much-needed diversification away from hydrocarbons. However, the blockade of oil terminals at four ports in eastern Libya from mid-2013 to mid-2014 resulted in another dramatic fall in oil production, with a recorded average figure of 250,000 b/d at the end of 2013. In October 2014 oil production stood at around 840,000 b/d, still only 50% of the figure prior to 2011. Output had declined again, to some 350,000 b/d, by the end of 2014, as oil facilities were forced to close amid the escalating conflict between pro-Islamist forces and those of Libya's internationally recognized Government. This decline had a severe effect on the country's fiscal balance, with a budget deficit of US $18,600m. being recorded for 2014. The IMF forecast a further negative growth rate—of around 19.8%—for 2014. In early 2015 many economic analysts repeated their assessment that Libya was close to financial collapse, as the country was still riven by political divisions and factional fighting. A large number of important oilfields were under the control of militias opposed to the internationally recognized al-Thani Cabinet, and there was an escalation in the violence being perpetrated by radical Islamist groups.

PUBLIC HOLIDAYS

2016: 17 February (Revolution Day), 1 May (May Day), 4 May* (Leilat al-Meiraj, Ascension of Muhammad), 6 July* (Id al-Fitr, end of Ramadan), 12 September* (Id al-Adha, Feast of the Sacrifice), 2 October* (Muharram, Islamic New Year), 11 October* (Ashoura), 23 October (Liberation Day), 11 December* (Mouloud, Birth of Muhammad), 24 December (Independence Day).

* These holidays are dependent on the Islamic lunar calendar and may vary by one or two days from the dates given.

Statistical Survey

Sources (unless otherwise stated): National Corporation for Information and Documentation; Census and Statistical Dept, Sharia Damascus 40, 2nd Floor, Tripoli; tel. (21) 3331731; Central Bank of Libya, POB 1103, Sharia al-Malik Seoud, Tripoli; tel. (21) 3333591; fax (21) 4441488; e-mail info@cbl.gov.ly; internet www.cbl.gov.ly.

Area and Population

AREA, POPULATION AND DENSITY

Area (sq km)	1,676,198*
Population (census results)†	
August 1995	4,404,986
August 2006	
Males	2,610,639
Females	2,687,513
Total	5,298,152
Population (UN estimates at mid-year)	
2013	6,201,523
2014	6,253,448
2015	6,317,080
Density (per sq km) at mid-2015	3.8

* 647,184 sq miles.

† Excluding non-Libyans: 409,326 in 1995 and 359,540 in 2006.

Sources: National Authority for Information and Authentication; UN, *World Population Prospects: The 2012 Revision.*

POPULATION BY AGE AND SEX
(UN estimates at mid-2015)

	Males	Females	Total
0–14 years	949,260	905,811	1,855,071
15–64 years	2,033,188	2,113,831	4,147,019
65 years and over	145,162	169,828	314,990
Total	3,127,610	3,189,470	6,317,080

Source: UN, *World Population Prospects: The 2012 Revision.*

POPULATION BY REGION
(population at 2006 census)

	Area (sq km)	Population	Density (per sq km)
Al-Butnan	84,996	150,353	1.8
Banghazi (Benghazi) . .	11,372	622,148	54.7
Darnah (Darna)	31,511	155,402	4.9
Ghat	68,482	21,329	0.3
Al-Jabal al-Akhdar . . .	11,429	192,689	16.9
Al-Jabal al-Gharbi . . .	76,717	288,944	3.8
Al-Jifarah	2,666	422,999	158.7
Al-Jufrah	139,038	46,899	0.3
Al-Kufrah	433,611	42,769	0.1
Al-Marqab	6,796	410,187	60.4
Al-Marj	13,515	175,455	13.0
Marzuq	356,308	72,513	0.2
Misratah (Misurata) . .	29,172	511,628	17.5

—*continued*	Area (sq km)	Population	Density (per sq km)
Nalut	67,191	87,772	1.3
Al-Nuqat al-Khams . . .	6,089	269,553	44.3
Sabha	17,066	119,038	7.0
Surt (Sirte)	86,399	131,786	1.5
Tarabulus (Tripoli) . . .	835	997,065	1,194.1
Wadi al-Hayat	31,485	70,711	2.2
Wadi al-Shati	90,244	73,443	0.8
Al-Wahah	108,523	164,718	1.5
Al-Zawiyah (Zawia) . . .	2,753	270,751	98.3
Total	1,676,198	5,298,152	3.2

Source: National Authority for Information and Authentication.

PRINCIPAL TOWNS
(population at 2006 census)

Tarabulus (Tripoli, the capital) . .	997,065	Al-Nuquat al-Khams . . .	269,553
Banghazi (Benghazi) . .	622,148	Al-Jabal al-Akhdar .	192,689
Misratah (Misurata)	511,628	Al-Marj	175,455
Al-Jifarah . . .	422,999	Al-Wahah . . .	164,718
Al-Marqab . . .	410,187	Darnah (Darna) . .	155,402
Al-Jabal al-Gharbi .	288,944	Al-Butnan . . .	150,353
Al-Zawiyah (Zawia).	270,751	Surt (Sirte) . . .	131,786

Source: National Authority for Information and Authentication.

Mid-2014 (incl. suburbs, UN estimate): Tarabulus (Tripoli) 1,126,010 (Source: UN, *World Urbanization Prospects: The 2014 Revision*).

BIRTHS, MARRIAGES AND DEATHS

	Registered live births		Registered marriages		Registered deaths	
	Number	Rate (per 1,000)	Number	Rate (per 1,000)	Number	Rate (per 1,000)
2004 . .	119,633	23.5	39,105	7.6	15,765	3.1
2005 . .	120,999	23.3	43,979	8.4	16,425	3.2
2006 . .	124,541	23.2	47,219	8.8	17,975	3.4
2007 . .	128,337	23.7	59,583	11.0	20,045	3.7
2008 . .	132,826	24.1	65,326	11.9	21,481	3.9

Source: National Authority for Information and Authentication.

Life expectancy (years at birth): 75.2 (males 73.3; females 77.1) in 2012 (Source: World Bank, World Development Indicators database).

EMPLOYMENT
('000 persons)

	2007	2008	2009
Agriculture, forestry and fishing .	40.8	74.0	77.7
Mining and quarrying . . .	30.5	35.7	41.5
Manufacturing	66.2	65.6	65.2
Electricity, gas and water . . .	37.1	44.2	50.3
Construction	34.7	34.9	36.3
Trade, restaurants and hotels .	84.2	93.4	109.6
Transport and communications .	65.8	66.0	66.0
Financing, insurance and real estate	40.7	48.2	57.1
Public administration . . .	401.6	397.9	408.2
Education	462.4	456.4	459.7
Health services	79.6	77.0	75.4
Other services	32.8	32.8	30.6
Total	1,376.3	1,426.2	1,477.8

Mid-2015 ('000, estimates): Agriculture, etc. 51; Total labour force 2,276 (Source: FAO).

Health and Welfare

KEY INDICATORS

Total fertility rate (children per woman, 2012) . . .	2.4
Under-5 mortality rate (per 1,000 live births, 2012) . .	15
HIV/AIDS (% of persons aged 15–49, 2003)	0.3
Physicians (per 1,000 head, 2009)	1.9
Hospital beds (per 1,000 head, 2009)	3.7
Health expenditure (2011): US $ per head (PPP) . . .	181
Health expenditure (2011): % of GDP	3.9
Health expenditure (2011): public (% of total) . . .	77.3
Access to water (% of persons, 2002)	72
Access to sanitation (% of persons, 2012)	97
Total carbon dioxide emissions ('000 metric tons, 2010) . .	59,035.0
Carbon dioxide emissions per head (metric tons, 2010) . .	9.8
Human Development Index (2013): ranking	55
Human Development Index (2013): value	0.784

For sources and definitions, see explanatory note on p. vi.

Agriculture

PRINCIPAL CROPS
('000 metric tons)

	2011	2012	2013
Wheat*	166	200	200
Barley	98*	98†	97*
Potatoes	352*	291†	295†
Broad beans, horse beans, dry†	1.0	2.0	2.0
Almonds, with shell† . .	30	32	29
Groundnuts, with shell* .	17	17	17
Olives†	139	135	138
Tomatoes†	223	225	221
Pumpkins, squash and gourds†	34	34	34
Cucumbers and gherkins† .	15	16	16
Chillies and peppers, green†	24	25	26
Onions and shallots, green† .	54	55	54
Onions, dry†	206	208	211
Peas, green†	6	6	6
Carrots and turnips† . .	30	33	31
Watermelons†	243	250	245
Cantaloupes and other melons	26*	28†	29†
Oranges†	48	50	50
Tangerines, mandarins, etc.†	11	12	12
Lemons and limes† . . .	18	19	19
Apples†	20	21	17
Apricots†	24	26	26
Peaches and nectarines† .	13	14	13
Plums and sloes† . . .	51	53	55
Grapes	35*	33*	33†
Figs†	10	10	10
Dates†	166	170	174

* Unofficial figure(s).
† FAO estimate(s).

Aggregate production ('000 metric tons, may include official, semi-official or estimated data): Total cereals 275 in 2011, 307 in 2012, 306 in 2013; Total roots and tubers 352 in 2011, 291 in 2012, 295 in 2013; Total vegetables (incl. melons) 979 in 2011, 1,000 in 2012, 994 in 2013; Total fruits (excl. melons) 403 in 2011, 412 in 2012, 416 in 2013.

Source: FAO.

LIVESTOCK
('000 head, year ending September, FAO estimates)

	2011	2012	2013
Horses	46	46	46
Asses	29	29	29
Cattle	197	198	199
Camels	57	57	58
Sheep	7,100	7,150	7,200
Goats	2,600	2,550	2,600
Poultry	34,000	34,500	34,850

Source: FAO.

LIVESTOCK PRODUCTS
('000 metric tons, FAO estimates)

	2011	2012	2013
Cattle meat	8	8	8
Sheep meat	31	32	32
Goat meat	13	13	13
Chicken meat	124	124	125
Cows' milk	143	145	250
Sheep's milk	62	65	60
Goats' milk	19	20	17
Hen eggs	63	64	60
Wool, greasy	9	10	10

Source: FAO.

Forestry

ROUNDWOOD REMOVALS
('000 cubic metres, excl. bark, FAO estimates)

	2011	2012	2013
Sawlogs, veneer logs and logs for sleepers*	63	63	63
Other industrial wood	53	53	53
Fuel wood	964	975	987
Total	1,080	1,091	1,103

* Annual output assumed to be unchanged since 1978.

Source: FAO.

SAWNWOOD PRODUCTION
('000 cubic metres, incl. railway sleepers, FAO estimates)

	2011	2012	2013
Total (all broadleaved)	31	31	31

Note: Annual output assumed to be unchanged from 1978.

Source: FAO.

Fishing

(metric tons, live weight, FAO estimates)

	2010	2011	2012
Capture	50,000	30,000	35,000
Groupers	950	570	660
Common pandora	6,950	4,200	4,850
Bogue	2,180	1,300	1,500
Surmullet	6,000	3,600	4,150
Jack and horse mackerels	2,720	1,650	1,900
Sardinellas	9,200	5,400	6,250
Dogfish sharks	7,300	4,400	5,100
Aquaculture	240	240	240
Total catch (incl. others)	50,240	30,240	35,240

Source: FAO.

Mining

('000 metric tons unless otherwise indicated, estimates)

	2010	2011	2012
Salt	40	20	30
Gypsum (crude)	250	125	150

Source: US Geological Survey.

Crude petroleum (million barrels): 178.6 in 2011; 530.7 in 2012; 362.6 in 2013.

Natural gas (incl. flared, '000 million cu ft): n.a. in 2011; 827.5 in 2012; 713.4 in 2013.

Industry

SELECTED PRODUCTS
('000 metric tons)

	2011	2012	2013
Jet fuels (incl. kerosene)	784	932	1,154
Motor spirit (petrol)	569	615	640
Naphthas (raw)	649	1,348	1,533
Gas-diesel (distillate fuel) oil	1,522	2,251	2,775
Residual fuel oils	2,242	3,123	4,259

Cement (hydraulic, '000 metric tons, estimates): 7,000 in 2010; 3,500 in 2011; 4,000 in 2012 (Source: US Geological Survey).

Electric energy (million kWh): 30,426 in 2009; 31,613 in 2010; 27,614 in 2011 (Source: UN Industrial Commodity Statistics Database).

Finance

CURRENCY AND EXCHANGE RATES

Monetary Units:
1,000 dirhams = 1 Libyan dinar (LD).

Sterling, Dollar and Euro Equivalents (31 October 2014):
£1 sterling = 2.0805 dinars;
US $1 = 1.3000 dinars;
€1 = 1.6281 dinars;
100 Libyan dinars = £48.06 = $76.92 = €61.42.

Average Exchange Rate (Libyan dinar per US $):
2011   1.2242
2012   1.2617
2013   1.2716

BUDGET
(LD million)

Revenue	2011	2012*	2013*
Hydrocarbon budget allocation	15,830	66,932	51,776
Non-hydrocarbon	983	3,199	2,988
Non-hydrocarbon tax revenue	699	867	993
Taxes on income and profits	461	618	851
Taxes on international trade	238	249	142
Non-hydrocarbon non-tax revenue	285	2,333	1,995
Total	16,813	70,131	54,764

Expenditure	2011	2012*	2013*
Current	21,995	48,442	52,008
Administrative expenditure	17,580	36,733	42,599
Subsidies and other current transfers	4,414	11,709	9,409
Capital	—	5,500	13,277
Budget fund	1,372	—	—
Total	23,367	53,942	65,284

* Preliminary figures.

INTERNATIONAL RESERVES
(US $ million at 31 December)

	2011	2012	2013
Gold (national valuation)	158	158	158
IMF special drawing rights	2,471	2,480	2,499
Reserve position in IMF	454	455	456
Foreign exchange	101,872	117,984	112,243
Total	104,955	121,077	115,355

Source: IMF, *International Financial Statistics*.

MONEY SUPPLY
(LD million at 31 December)

	2011	2012	2013
Currency outside banks . .	14,840.1	13,397.0	13,419.9
Demand deposits at commercial banks	35,435.3	41,950.7	47,153.7
Total money (incl. others) . .	50,275.4	56,833.7	62,222.7

Source: IMF, *International Financial Statistics*.

COST OF LIVING
(Consumer Price Index; base: 2003 = 100)

	2011	2012	2013
Food, beverages and tobacco . .	178.5	171.8	178.2
Clothing and shoes	120.8	141.1	151.4
Housing	122.6	149.6	156.8
All items (incl. others) . . .	150.4	159.6	163.7

NATIONAL ACCOUNTS
(LD million at current prices)

Expenditure on the Gross Domestic Product

	2011	2012	2013
Government final consumption expenditure	19,990.4	27,252.3	24,076.2
Private final consumption expenditure	22,890.1	40,691.0	32,834.5
Gross capital formation . . .	10,367.1	40,252.7	29,840.8
Total domestic expenditure .	53,247.6	108,196.0	89,751.6
Exports of goods and services .	18,073.3	64,230.1	48,605.6
Less Imports of goods and services	21,635.8	51,556.8	40,499.9
GDP in purchasers' values .	49,685.0	120,869.3	94,857.3
GDP at constant 2005 prices .	30,659.7	62,693.9	52,528.7

Source: UN National Accounts Main Aggregates Database.

Gross Domestic Product by Economic Activity

	2010	2011†	2012†
Agriculture, forestry and fishing .	2,543.6	844.3	928.7
Mining and quarrying (incl. hydrocarbons)	60,969.8	22,332.2	76,932.3
Manufacturing	5,809.5	978.0	3,776.2
Electricity, gas and water . .	1,420.5	561.2	1,434.7
Construction	8,066.8	1,391.7	1,530.8
Trade, restaurants and hotels .	4,607.5	2,923.1	4,875.3
Transport, storage and communications	4,432.1	3,317.7	3,553.3
Financial intermediation . . .	1,262.0	745.9	1,066.7
Real estate, renting and business activities	6,636.4	4,546.7	5,819.8
Education and health, etc.* . .	316.5	126.9	253.2
Government, defence and mandatory social insurance .	7,128.8	12,319.3	17,406.0
Other services	98.2	33.7	98.1
Sub-total	103,291.6	50,120.9	117,675.0
Less Financial intermediation services indirectly measured .	753.4	436.0	—
Total	102,538.2	49,684.9	117,675.0

* Private sector only.
† Preliminary figures.

2013 (LD million at current prices): Agriculture, forestry and fishing 2,053.2; Mining and utilities 51,009.2; Manufacturing 3,883.7; Construction 5,423.5; Retail trade and hotel and restaurants 4,742.7; Transport, storage and communication 5,141.6; Other services 23,212.5; *Sub-total* 95,466.4; Net of taxes on products −609.1 (figure obtained as residual); *GDP in purchasers' values* 94,857.3 (Source: UN National Accounts Main Aggregates Database).

BALANCE OF PAYMENTS
(US $ million)

	2011	2012	2013
Exports of goods	19,060	61,026	46,018
Imports of goods	−11,200	−25,590	−34,050
Balance on goods	7,860	35,436	11,968
Exports of services	40	152	180
Imports of services	−4,386	−6,996	−8,472
Balance on goods and services	3,514	28,592	3,677
Primary income received . .	1,210	2,392	2,275
Primary income paid . . .	−1,154	−4,324	−2,808
Balance on goods, services and primary income	3,569	26,661	3,144
Secondary income received . .	304	—	—
Secondary income paid . . .	−681	−2,824	−3,252
Current balance	3,192	23,836	−108
Direct investment assets . . .	−131	−2,509	−882
Portfolio investment assets . .	−324	−540	−1,698
Other investment assets . .	−2,389	−4,501	−1,676
Other investment liabilities . .	471	−341	146
Net errors and omissions . . .	2,550	−2,538	−2,695
Reserves and related items .	3,369	13,408	−6,912

Source: IMF, *International Financial Statistics*.

External Trade

PRINCIPAL COMMODITIES
(LD million)

Imports c.i.f.	2009	2010
Food and live animals	1,663.9	2,320.4
Beverages and tobacco	72.8	101.0
Animal and vegetable oils and fats	72.2	82.1
Crude materials (inedible) except fuels . . .	299.6	604.8
Mineral fuels and related materials	151.5	236.1
Chemical materials	1,056.6	1,287.4
Basic manufactures	3,229.7	4,818.8
Machinery and transport equipment . . .	7,968.9	11,031.6
Miscellaneous products	1,540.8	1,894.1
Total	16,060.6	22,376.3

Exports f.o.b.*	2009	2010
Food and live animals	1.4	0.9
Crude materials (inedible) except fuel . . .	1.2	0.8
Mineral fuels and related products	33,353.3	44,854.1
Chemicals and related products	562.2	989.0
Basic manufactures	151.9	351.4
Total (incl. others)	34,070.9	46,196.3

* Including re-exports.

Total imports: 8,628.0 in 2011; 20,520.0 in 2012.

Total exports: 17,484.0 in 2011; 51,829.0 in 2012.

PRINCIPAL TRADING PARTNERS
(LD million)

Imports c.i.f.	2011	2012
Brazil	112	465
China, People's Republic	795	2,631
Egypt	611	1,574
France (incl. Monaco)	441	759
Germany	432	938
Italy	762	1,665
Korea, Republic	199	1,184
Spain	159	485
Tunisia	1,208	1,347
Turkey	822	2,353
United Kingdom	131	267
USA	316	603
Total (incl. others)	8,628	20,520

Exports (incl. re-exports) f.o.b.	2011	2012
Australia	200	1,156
Austria	369	739
China, People's Republic	1,869	5,789
France (incl. Monaco)	2,491	5,011
Germany	2,502	6,416
Greece	387	1,979
India	333	1,211
Italy	3,991	12,059
Netherlands	481	1,835
Portugal	17	468
Spain	911	3,917
Switzerland	131	1,288
Tunisia	845	924
United Kingdom	604	2,436
USA	606	2,322
Total (incl. others)	17,484	51,829

Transport

ROAD TRAFFIC
(motor vehicles in use at 31 December)

	2007
Passenger cars	1,388,165
Buses and coaches	91,327
Vans and lorries	310,511
Motorcycles and mopeds	36,531

Source: IRF, *World Road Statistics*.

SHIPPING
Flag Registered Fleet
(at 31 December)

	2012	2013	2014
Number of vessels	81	85	87
Total displacement ('000 grt)	1,020.5	1,028.5	1,028.9

Source: Lloyd's List Intelligence (www.lloydslistintelligence.com).

CIVIL AVIATION
(traffic on scheduled services)

	2010	2011
Kilometres flown (million)	55	43
Passengers carried ('000)	2,431	1,896
Passenger-km (million)	4,035	3,084
Total ton-km (million)	493	391

Source: UN, *Statistical Yearbook*.

Passengers carried ('000): 1,398 in 2012; 2,508 in 2013 (Source: World Bank, World Development Indicators database).

Tourism

VISITOR ARRIVALS*

Country of origin	2002	2003	2004
Algeria	70,416	71,657	73,459
Egypt	354,189	429,220	441,230
Morocco	19,076	19,120	20,803
Tunisia	329,145	346,331	366,871
Total (incl. others)	857,952	957,896	999,343

* Including same-day visitors (excursionists).

Tourism receipts (US $ million, excl. passenger transport): 50 in 2009; 60 in 2010.

Source: World Tourism Organization.

Communications Media

	2011	2012	2013
Telephones ('000 main lines in use)	1,000.0	814.0	789.0
Mobile cellular telephones ('000 subscribers)	10,000.0	9,587.0	10,235.3
Broadband subscribers ('000)	70.0	67.3	64.7

Source: International Telecommunication Union.

Education

(2005/06 unless otherwise indicated)

	Teachers	Students
Pre-primary	2,486	22,246
Primary	148,476	755,338
Secondary	152,338	732,614
Tertiary*	15,711	375,028

* 2002/03.

Source: UNESCO Institute for Statistics.

Institutions: Primary and preparatory: general 2,733 (1993/94); Primary and preparatory; vocational 168 (1995/96); Secondary: vocational 312 (1995/96); Universities 13 (1995/96).

Adult literacy rate (UNESCO estimates): 89.9% (males 96.1%; females 83.7%) in 2012 (Source: UNESCO Institute for Statistics).

Directory

The Government

CABINET
(May 2015)

Prime Minister: ABDALLAH AL-THANI.

First Deputy Prime Minister: AL-MAHDI HASSAN MUSTAFA AL-LABAD.

Second Deputy Prime Minister: ABD AL-SALAM AL-BADRI.

Third Deputy Prime Minister: ABD AL-RAHMAN AL-TAHER.

Minister of Justice: AL-MABROUK GHRAIRA UMRAN.

Minister of the Interior: OMAR AL-SUNKI.

Minister of Defence: Brig.-Gen. MASOUD ERHUMA.

Minister of Foreign Affairs and of International Co-operation: MUHAMMAD AL-DAIRI.

Minister of Finance: KAMAL AL-HASSI.

Minister of Health: REDA AL-MENSHAWI.

Minister of Education and Higher Education: FATHI AL-MAJBRI.

Minister of Local Government: MUHAMMAD AL-FAROOQ ABD AL-SALAM.

Minister of Social Affairs: MASSOUD AHMAD BELQASEM SAWA.

Minister of the Economy and Industry: MUNEER ALI ASSR.

MINISTRIES

The internationally recognized Government of Abdallah al-Thani is based in the city of al-Bayda, in eastern Libya, while the ministries' headquarters in Tripoli are under the de facto control of the pro-Islamist 'Government of National Salvation', led by Omar al-Hassi.

Legislature

Elections to a new, 200-seat House of Representatives were held on 25 June 2014, the results of which were confirmed by the High National Elections Commission on 22 July. Some 12 seats remained unallocated, owing to boycotts and the closure of polling stations following concerns over security. All 200 seats were reserved for individual candidates; however, it was thought that many of those contesting the elections were affiliated to political organizations. The new chamber, which replaced the General National Congress, was inaugurated on 4 August in Tobruk. The House of Representatives was due to have its permanent base in Benghazi; however, owing to the intensification of conflict between Islamist militia groups and their opponents in that city, it remained unclear when the new legislature would be able to begin its operations there. On 6 November the Supreme Court ruled that the procedure under which the House of Representatives had been created was illegal, and ordered the chamber's dissolution. The ruling was issued amid an ongoing dispute between the Tobruk-based House of Representatives and the General National Congress, which remained in de facto operation in Tripoli under the direction of pro-Islamist groups.

House of Representatives: Tobruk.

President: AGEELA ISSA SALAH GWAIDER.

Political Organizations

In June 1971 the Arab Socialist Union (ASU) was established as the country's sole authorized political party. The General National Congress of the ASU held its first session in January 1976 and later became the General People's Congress. Following the ouster of Muammar al-Qaddafi, a number of new political organizations were formed, the most prominent among which have been listed below:

Central National Current: f. 2012.

Justice and Construction Party (JCP): Tripoli; tel. (21) 7154443; fax (21) 7154447; e-mail info@ab.ly; internet www.ab.ly; f. 2012; Leader MUHAMMAD SAWAN.

National Forces Alliance (NFA): Tripoli; tel. (21) 4782593; e-mail info@nff.ly; f. 2012; comprises 58 political parties; Leader MAHMOUD JIBRIL; Sec.-Gen. SALAHEDDIN AL-BISHARI.

National Front Party: Tripoli; e-mail tripoli@jabha.ly; internet www.jabha.ly; f. 2012; offshoot of National Front for the Salvation of Libya; Leader MUHAMMAD ALI ABDALLAH.

Union for Homeland: Tripoli; tel. (21) 4445315; fax (21) 4443805; e-mail info@ufh.ly; f. 2012; Leader ABDURRAHMAN SEWEHLI.

Wadi Al-Hayat Gathering: f. 2012.

Diplomatic Representation

In mid-2014 several countries, including Canada, France, Germany, Greece, the United Kingdom and the USA, closed their respective embassies in Libya, citing concerns regarding the safety of diplomatic staff. The closures followed the escalation of conflict between the respective forces of the internationally recognized Government in Tobruk and the pro-Islamist 'Government of National Salvation' based in Tripoli, as well as an increase in the activities of Islamist militant groups (*see Contemporary Political History*).

EMBASSIES IN LIBYA

Afghanistan: POB 4245, Sharia Mozhar al-Aftes, Tripoli; tel. (21) 4841441; fax (21) 4841443; e-mail tripoli@afghanistan.mfa.net; Ambassador (vacant).

Argentina: POB 932, Gargaresh, Madina Syahia, Tripoli; tel. (21) 4771107; fax (21) 4782105; e-mail elbia@mrecic.gov.ar; Chargé d'affaires a.i. MAURICIO NINE.

Austria: POB 3207, Sharia Khalid ibn al-Walid, Garden City, Tripoli; tel. (21) 4443379; fax (21) 4440838; e-mail tripolis-ob@bmeia.gv.at; internet www.bmeia.gv.at/tripolis; Ambassador Dr RONALD STURM.

Bangladesh: POB 5086, Hi Damasq, Tripoli; tel. (21) 4911198; fax (21) 4906616; e-mail bdtripoli@yahoo.com; Ambassador Maj.-Gen. SHAHIDUL HAQUE.

Belarus: POB 1530, Tripoli; tel. (21) 3612555; fax (21) 3614298; e-mail libya@mfa.gov.by; internet libya.mfa.gov.by; Ambassador ALYAKSANDR DEREVIASHKO.

Benin: POB 6676, Sharia Ghout al-Shaal, Tripoli; tel. (21) 4837663; fax (21) 834569; Ambassador LAFIA CHABI.

Bosnia and Herzegovina: POB 6946, Sharia Abd al-Melik bin Kutn, Tripoli; tel. (21) 4774327; fax (21) 4770652; Ambassador IBRAHIM EFENDIĆ.

Brazil: POB 2270, Sharia Ben Ashour, Tripoli; tel. (21) 3614894; fax (21) 3614895; e-mail brcastripoli@ittnet.net; Ambassador AFONSO CARBONAR.

Bulgaria: POB 2945, Sharia Madinet el-Hadeek-Muhammad Farid, Dahra, Tripoli; tel. (21) 3346630; fax (21) 3346633; e-mail embassy.tripoli@mfa.bg; internet www.mfa.bg/embassies/libya; Chargé d'affaires VESELIN PAVLOV.

Burkina Faso: POB 81902, Route de Gargaresh, Tripoli; tel. (21) 4771221; fax (21) 4778037; e-mail ambafasolibye@yahoo.fr; Ambassador YOUSSOUF SANGARE.

Burundi: POB 2817, Sharia Ras Hassan, Tripoli; tel. (21) 608848; Ambassador RAPHAËL BITARIHO.

Canada: POB 93392, al-Fateh Tower Post Office, Tripoli; tel. (21) 3351633; fax (21) 3351630; e-mail trpli@international.gc.ca; internet www.canadainternational.gc.ca/libya-libye; Ambassador DENIS THIBAULT.

Chad: POB 1078, Sharia Muhammad Mussadeq 25, Tripoli; tel. (21) 4443955; Ambassador DAOUSSA DÉBY.

China, People's Republic: POB 5329, Sharia Menstir, Andalus, Gargaresh, Tripoli; tel. (21) 4832914; fax (21) 4831877; e-mail chinaemb_ly@mfa.gov.cn; internet ly.china-embassy.org; Ambassador LI ZHIGUO.

Croatia: Great al-Fatah Towers, Tower 2, 12th Floor, Rm 125, Tripoli; tel. (21) 3351097; fax (21) 3351486; e-mail tripoli@mvep.hr; Ambassador PETAR LJUBIČIĆ.

Cyprus: POB 3284, Wassayat Ebderi, Fashloum, Tripoli; tel. (21) 3622610; fax (21) 3622613; e-mail cyprusembassylibya@gmail.com; Ambassador PERICLES D. STIVAROS.

Czech Republic: POB 1097, Sharia Rewaifaa bin Thabet, Ben Ashour, Tripoli; tel. (21) 3615436; fax (21) 3615437; e-mail tripoli@embassy.mzv.cz; internet www.mzv.cz/tripoli; Ambassador JAN VYČÍTAL.

Egypt: Sharia Omar el-Mokhtar, Tripoli; tel. and fax (21) 3339876; e-mail eg.emb_tripoli@mfa.gov.eg; Ambassador MUHAMMAD ABU BAKR.

Equatorial Guinea: Tripoli.

Eritrea: POB 91279, Tripoli; tel. (21) 4773568; fax (21) 4780152; Ambassador ABDALLA MUSSA.

France: POB 312, Sharia Ben Khafaja, Hay Andalus, Tripoli; tel. (21) 4770452; fax (21) 4770450; e-mail tripoli-amba@diplomatie.gouv.fr; internet www.ambafrance-ly.org; Ambassador ANTOINE SIVAN.

Germany: Palm City, Jansour, Tripoli; tel. (21) 4423930; fax (21) 4844564; e-mail info@tripolis.diplo.de; internet www.tripolis.diplo.de; Ambassador CHRISTIAN MUCH.

Ghana: POB 4169, Andalus 21A, nr Funduk Shati Gargaresh, Tripoli; tel. (21) 4772534; fax (21) 4773557; e-mail ghaemb@all-computers.com; Ambassador KODJO HODARI-OKAE.

Greece: POB 5147, Sharia Jalal Bayar 18, Tripoli; tel. (21) 3338563; fax (21) 4441907; e-mail gremb.tri@mfa.gr; internet www.mfa.gr/tripoli; Ambassador KYRIAKOS AMOIRIDIS.

Guinea: POB 10657, Hay Andalus, Tripoli; tel. (21) 4772793; fax (21) 4773441; e-mail magatte@lttnet.net; Ambassador ABDUL AZIZ SOUMAH.

Hungary: POB 4010, Sharia Talha Ben Abdullah, Tripoli; tel. (21) 3618218; fax (21) 3618220; e-mail tpi.missions@mfa.gov.hu; internet www.mfa.gov.hu/kulkepviselet/LY; Ambassador Dr BÉLA MARTON.

India: POB 3150, Fashloom Area, Nafleen Area, Tripoli; tel. (21) 3409288; fax (21) 3409281; e-mail info@indianembassy.ly; internet indianembassy.ly; Ambassador AZAR A. H. KHAN.

Indonesia: POB 5921, Tripoli; tel. (21) 4842067; fax (21) 4842069; e-mail tripoli.kbri@deplu.go.id; internet tripoli.kemlu.go.id; Ambassador ANWAR RAUDIN.

Iran: POB 6185, Tripoli; tel. (21) 3609552; fax (21) 3611674; e-mail iran_em_tripoli@hotmail.com; Ambassador HOSSEIN AKBARI.

Italy: POB 912, Sharia Vahran 1, Tripoli; tel. (21) 3334131; fax (21) 3331673; e-mail ambasciata.tripoli@esteri.it; internet www.ambtripoli.esteri.it; Ambassador GIUSEPPE BUCCINO GRIMALDI.

Japan: POB 3265, Sharia Jamal al-Din al-Waeli, Hay Andalus, Tripoli; tel. (21) 4781041; fax (21) 4781044; internet www.ly.emb-japan.go.jp; Ambassador TAKASHI ASHIKI.

Korea, Democratic People's Republic: Tripoli; Ambassador KIM TONG JE.

Korea, Republic: POB 4781, Abounawas Area, Sharia Gargaresh, Tripoli; tel. (21) 4831322; fax (21) 4831324; e-mail libya@mofa.go.kr; internet lby.mofa.go.kr; Ambassador JONG-KOOK LEE.

Kuwait: POB 2225, Beit al-Mal Beach, Tripoli; tel. (21) 4440281; fax (21) 607053; Ambassador MUBARAK ABDULLAH AL-ADWANI.

Lebanon: POB 927, Malek Ben Auss, Al Noflyeen St, Tripoli; tel. (21) 3615744; fax (21) 3611740; e-mail emblebanon_ly@hotmail.com; Ambassador MUHAMMAD SKEINE.

Lesotho: POB 5771, Hay Andalus, Tripoli; tel. (21) 4840900; fax (21) 4840901; e-mail lesotho-tripoli@foreign.gov.ls; Ambassador MALE-FETSANE MOHAFA.

Madagascar: POB 652, al-Maidan Zajeir, Tripoli; tel. (21) 3408257; fax (21) 3408256; e-mail ambamtri@yahoo.fr; Ambassador DIEU-DONNÉ MARIE MICHEL RAZAFINDER SIMANIE.

Mali: POB 2008, Sharia Jaraba Saniet Zarrouk, Tripoli; tel. (21) 4444924; Ambassador AMADOU TORÉ.

Mauritania: Sharia Aïssa el-Wakwak, Tripoli; tel. (21) 4443223; Ambassador (vacant).

Morocco: Sharia Ouahchi Ben Harb, Ave Ben Achour, Tripoli; tel. (21) 3617809; fax (21) 3614752; e-mail sifmatripo@hotmail.com; Ambassador MUHAMMAD BELAICH.

Niger: POB 2251, Fachloun Area, Tripoli; tel. (21) 4443104; Ambassador AMADOU TIDJANI ALI.

Nigeria: POB 4417, Sharia Bashir al-Ibrahim, Tripoli; tel. (21) 4443038; e-mail ambassador@nigeriantripoli.org; internet www.nigeriantripoli.org; Ambassador ISA MUHAMMAD (recalled in March 2010).

Oman: Tripoli; tel. (21) 4772879; fax (21) 4773849; e-mail tripoli@mofa.gov.om; Ambassador Dr QASIM BIN MUHAMMAD BIN SALEM AL-SALEHI.

Pakistan: POB 2169, Sharia al-Jamei, Abu Zaid Dorda Area, Tripoli; tel. (21) 3610937; fax (21) 3600412; e-mail pareptripoli@gmail.com; internet www.mofa.gov.pk/libya; Ambassador Lt. Gen. JAVED ZIA.

Philippines: POB 12508, Km 7, Sharia Gargaresh, Abu Nawas, Hay Andalus, Tripoli; tel. (21) 4833966; fax (21) 4836158; e-mail tripoli.pe@dfa.gov.ph; Chargé d'affaires ADELIO ANGELITO CRUZ.

Poland: POB 519, Sharia Ben Ashour 61, Tripoli; tel. (21) 3608569; fax (21) 3615199; e-mail trypolis.amb.sekretariat@msz.gov.pl; internet trypolis.msz.gov.pl; Ambassador PIOTR T. CIEĆWIERZ.

Portugal: Zaid Bem Thabet, Sharia Ben Ashour, Tripoli; tel. (21) 3621352; fax (21) 3621351; Ambassador RUI NOGUEIRA LOPES ALEIXO.

Qatar: POB 6312, Libay, Tripoli; tel. (21) 4832431; fax (21) 4836660; e-mail tripoli@mofa.gov.qa; Ambassador Sheikh MUHAMMAD BIN NASSER BIN JASSIM AL THANI.

Romania: POB 5085, Sharia Ali bin Talib, Ben Ashour, Tripoli; tel. (21) 3615295; fax (21) 3607597; e-mail tripoli@mae.ro; Ambassador NICOLAE MARIN.

Russian Federation: POB 4792, Sharia Mustapha Kamel, Tripoli; tel. (21) 3330545; fax (21) 4446673; e-mail embr@mail.ru; Ambassador IVAN MOLOTKOV.

Rwanda: POB 6677, Villa Ibrahim Musbah Missalati, Andalus, Tripoli; tel. (21) 72864; fax (21) 70317; Chargé d'affaires CHRISTOPHE HABIMANA.

Senegal: POB 6392, el-Arabia Gotchalle 246/5, Gargaresh, Tripoli; tel. (21) 4836090; fax (21) 4838955; e-mail ambassene.tripoli@stcc.presidence.sn; Chargé d'affaires a.i. DIAME SARR.

Serbia: POB 1087, Abdalla Ben Salam St, Ben Ashour Area, Tripoli; tel. (21) 3623205; fax (21) 3623207; e-mail serbianembassy_tripoli@yahoo.com; internet www.tripoli.mfa.gov.rs; Ambassador OLIVER POTEZICA.

Sierra Leone: Tripoli; Ambassador Al-Haji ABUBAKARR JALLOH.

Slovakia: POB 5721, Km 3, Gargaresh, Hay Andalus, Tripoli; tel. (21) 4781388; fax (21) 4781387; e-mail slovembtrp@slovembtrp.com; Ambassador (vacant).

Spain: POB 23302, Sharia el-Amir Abd al-Kader al-Jazairi 36, Tripoli; tel. (21) 3620051; fax (21) 3620061; e-mail emb.tripoli@maec.es; internet www.maec.es/embajadas/tripoli; Ambassador JOSÉ ANTONIO BORDALLO HUIDOBRO.

Sudan: POB 1076, Sharia Gargaresh, Tripoli; tel. (21) 4775387; fax (21) 4774781; e-mail sudtripoli@hotmail.com; Ambassador Haj MAJED SUWAR.

Switzerland: POB 439, Sharia el-Moussawer Ben Maghzamah, off Sharia Ben Ashour, Tripoli; tel. (21) 3614118; fax (21) 3614238; e-mail tri.vertretung@eda.admin.ch; internet www.eda.admin.ch/tripoli; Ambassador MICHEL GOTTRET.

Syria: POB 4219, Sharia Muhammad Rashid Reda 4, Tripoli (Relations Office); tel. (21) 3331783; fax (21) 3339030; Ambassador HILAL AL-ATRASH.

Togo: POB 3420, Sharia Khaled ibn al-Walid, Tripoli; tel. (21) 4449565; fax (21) 3332423.

Tunisia: POB 613, Sharia el-Bashir Ibrahimi, Medinat el-Hadaik, Tripoli; tel. (21) 3331051; fax (21) 4447600; Ambassador RIDHA BOUKADI.

Turkey: POB 947, Sharia Zaviya Dahmani, Tripoli; tel. (21) 3401140; fax (21) 3401146; e-mail embassy.tripoli@mfa.gov.tr; internet tripoli.emb.mfa.gov.tr; Ambassador AHMET YAKICI.

Uganda: POB 80215, Ben Achour, Sharia Jaraba, Tripoli; tel. (21) 3603083; fax (21) 3634471; e-mail info@ugembassylibya.org; internet www.ugembassylibya.org; Ambassador MOSES KIWA SEBUNYA.

Ukraine: POB 4544, Sharia Dhil, Ben Ashour, Tripoli; tel. (21) 3608665; fax (21) 3608666; e-mail emb_ly@mfa.gov.ua; internet www.mfa.gov.ua/libya; Ambassador MYKOLA NAHORNYI.

United Kingdom: 24th Floor, Tripoli Towers (formerly Bourj al-Fateh), Tripoli; tel. (21) 3351084; fax (21) 3403648; e-mail tripoli.press@fco.gov.uk; internet ukinlibya.fco.gov.uk; Ambassador MICHAEL ARON.

USA: Sidi Slim Area, Sharia Wali al-Ahed, Tripoli; tel. (91) 2203239; e-mail tripolipao@state.gov; internet libya.usembassy.gov; Ambassador DEBORAH K. JONES.

Venezuela: POB 2584, Sharia Ben Ashour, Jamaa al-Sagaa Bridge, Tripoli; tel. (21) 3600408; fax (21) 3600407; e-mail embavenezlibia@hotmail.com; Ambassador AFIF TAJELDINE.

Viet Nam: POB 587, Sharia Gargaresh, Tripoli; tel. (21) 4901456; fax (21) 4901499; e-mail dsqvnlib@gmail.com; internet www.vietnamembassy-libya.org; Ambassador DAO DUY TIEN.

Yemen: POB 4839, Sharia Ubei Ben Ka'ab 36, Tripoli; tel. (21) 607472; Ambassador AHMAD ABDULLAH AL-MAJIDI.

Judicial System

The judicial system under the rule of Muammar al-Qaddafi was composed, in order of seniority, of the Supreme Court, Courts of Appeal, and Courts of First Instance and Summary Courts.

Supreme Court: The judgments of the Supreme Court are final. It is composed of the President and several Justices. Its judgments are issued by circuits of at least three Justices (the quorum is three). The Court hears appeals from the Courts of Appeal in civil, penal, administrative and civil status matters; Chief Justice KAMAL DHAN.

Courts of Appeal: These courts settle appeals from Courts of First Instance; the quorum is three Justices. Each court of appeal has a court of assize.

Courts of First Instance and Summary Courts: These courts are first-stage courts in the Jamahiriya, and the cases heard in them are heard by one judge. Appeals against summary judgments are heard by the appellate court attached to the court of first instance, the quorum of which is three judges.

Attorney-General: ABD AL-QADIR JUMAA RADWANI.

Religion

ISLAM

The vast majority of Libyan Arabs follow Sunni Muslim rites.

Grand Mufti of Libya: Sheikh SADEQ AL-GHARIANI.

CHRISTIANITY

The Roman Catholic Church

Libya comprises three Apostolic Vicariates and one Apostolic Prefecture.

Apostolic Vicariate of Benghazi: POB 248, Benghazi; tel. and fax (61) 9081599; e-mail apostvicar@yahoo.com; Vicar Apostolic Mgr SYLVESTER CARMEL MAGRO (Titular Bishop of Salde).

Apostolic Vicariate of Tripoli: POB 365, Dahra, Tripoli; tel. (21) 3331863; fax (21) 3334696; e-mail bishoptripolibya@hotmail.com; internet www.catholicinlibya.com; Vicar Apostolic Mgr GIOVANNI INNOCENZO MARTINELLI (Titular Bishop of Tabuda).

The Anglican Communion

Within the Episcopal Church in Jerusalem and the Middle East, Libya forms part of the diocese of Egypt (q.v.).

Other Christian Churches

The Coptic Orthodox Church is represented in Libya.

The Press

Under the rule of Muammar al-Qaddafi, most newspapers and periodicals were published either by the Jamahiriya News Agency (JANA), by government secretariats, by the Press Service or by trade unions.

DAILIES

Al-Fajr al-Jadid (The New Dawn): POB 91291, Press Bldg, Sharia al-Jamahiriya, Tripoli; tel. (21) 3606393; fax (21) 3605728; e-mail info@alfajraljadeed.com; f. 1969; also publishes bi-monthly English version; Editor AOUN ABDULLAH MADI.

Al-Jamahiriya: POB 4814, Tripoli; tel. (21) 3605731; e-mail info@aljamahiria.com; f. 1980; Arabic; political.

Al-Shams: POB 82331, Al-Sahafa Bldg, Sharia al-Jamhouria, Tripoli; tel. (21) 4442524; fax (21) 609315; e-mail info@alshames.com; Editor MUHAMMAD M. IBRAHIM.

Az-Zahf al-Akhdar (The Green March): POB 14273, Al-Sahafa Bldg, Sharia al-Jamhouria, Tripoli; tel. (21) 4776890; fax (21) 4772502; e-mail info@azzahfalakhder.com; f. 1980; Editor-in-Chief HAMID ABU SALIM.

PERIODICALS

Al-Amal (Hope): POB 4845, Tripoli; e-mail info@alamalmag.com; internet www.alamalmag.com; monthly; social, for children; publ. by the Press Service.

Al-Daawa al-Islamia (Islamic Call): POB 2682, Sharia Sawani, Km 5, Tripoli; tel. (21) 4800294; fax (21) 4800293; f. 1980; weekly (Wed.); Arabic, English, French; cultural; publ. by the World Islamic Call Society; Eds MUHAMMAD IMHEMED AL-BALOUSHI, ABDULAHI MUHAMMAD ABD AL-JALEEL.

Economic Bulletin: POB 2303, Tripoli; tel. (21) 3337106; monthly; publ. by JANA.

Al-Jarida al-Rasmiya (The Official Newspaper): Tripoli; irregular; official state gazette.

Libyan Arab Republic Gazette: Tripoli; weekly; English.

Risalat al-Jihad (Holy War Letter): POB 2682, Tripoli; tel. (21) 3331021; f. 1983; monthly; Arabic, English, French; publ. by the World Islamic Call Society.

Scientific Bulletin: POB 2303, Tripoli; tel. (21) 3337106; monthly.

Al-Thaqafa al-Arabiya (Arab Culture): POB 4587, Tripoli; f. 1973; weekly; cultural; circ. 25,000.

The Tripoli Post: 32, 2nd Floor, Tripoli Tower, Tripoli; tel. and fax (21) 3351740; e-mail editor@tripolipost.com; internet www.tripolipost.com; f. 1999; weekly; English; privately owned; Editor-in-Chief Dr SAID LASWAD.

Al-Usbu al-Thaqafi (The Cultural Week): POB 4845, Tripoli; weekly.

Al-Watan al-Arabi al-Kabir (The Greater Arab Homeland): Tripoli; f. 1987.

Publishers

Al-Dar al-Arabia Lilkitab (Maison Arabe du Livre): POB 3185, Tripoli; tel. (21) 4447287; f. 1973 by Libya and Tunisia.

Al-Dar al-Hikma Publishing House: Tripoli; tel. (21) 3606571; fax (21) 3606610; e-mail info@elgabooks.com.

Al-Fatah University, General Administration of Libraries, Printing and Publications: POB 13543, Tripoli; tel. (21) 4628034; fax (21) 4625045; e-mail m.alfituri@hotmail.com; f. 1955; academic books.

General Co for Publishing, Advertising and Distribution: POB 921, Sirte (Surt); tel. (54) 63170; fax (54) 62100; general, educational and academic books in Arabic and other languages; makes and distributes advertisements throughout Libya.

Ghouma Publishing: POB 80092, Tripoli; tel. (21) 3630864; e-mail ghoumapub@hotmail.com; f. 1993; book publishing, distribution and art production; Gen. Man. MUSTAFA FETOURI.

Broadcasting and Communications

TELECOMMUNICATIONS

General Telecommunications Authority (GTA): POB 866, Sharia Zawia, Tripoli; e-mail info@gta.ly; internet www.gta.ly; f. 2006; supervisory body.

General Directorate of Posts and Telecommunications: POB 81686, Tripoli; tel. (21) 3604101; fax (21) 3604102; Dir-Gen. ABU ZAID JUMA AL-MANSURI.

General Post and Telecommunications Co (GPTC): POB 886, Sharia Zawia, Tripoli; tel. (21) 3617945; fax (21) 3619011; internet www.gptc.ly; f. 1984; operates and develops the postal and telecommunications networks; subsidiaries include Libyana Mobile Phone Co and Al-Madar Al-Jadeed (mobile cellular telecommunications

operators), and Libya Telecom and Technology (internet service provider); Chair. (vacant).

Libyana Mobile Phone Co: POB 90071, Tripoli; tel. (21) 3406555; internet www.libyana.ly; f. 2004.

Al-Madar Al-Jadeed: Tripoli; internet www.almadar.ly; f. 1997; mobile telecommunications network operator; 1.2m. subscribers; Chief Exec. Dr ABDULLA ABOUDA.

BROADCASTING

Radio

Great Socialist People's Libyan Arab Jamahiriya Broadcasting Corporation: POB 80237, Tripoli; tel. (21) 3402107; fax (21) 3403468; e-mail info@en.ljbc.net; internet www.ljbc.net; f. 1968; broadcasts in Arabic; additional satellite channel broadcast for 18 hours a day from 1982; Sec.-Gen. ABDULLAH MANSOUR.

Voice of Africa: POB 4677, Sharia al-Fateh, Tripoli; tel. (21) 4449209; fax (21) 4449875; f. 1973 as Voice of the Greater Arab Homeland; adopted current name in 1998; broadcasts in Arabic, French, English, Swahili and Hausa; Dir-Gen. ABDULLAH AL-MEGRI.

Television

People's Revolution Broadcasting TV: POB 80237, Tripoli; tel. (21) 3402107; fax (21) 3403468; e-mail info@en.ljbc.net; internet www.ljbc.net; f. 1957; broadcasts in Arabic; additional satellite channels broadcast for limited hours in English; Dir ABDULLAH MANSOUR.

Finance

(cap. = capital; res = reserves; dep. = deposits; m. = million; br(s) = branch(es); amounts in Libyan dinars, unless otherwise stated)

BANKING

The Libyan banking sector, hitherto highly state-controlled, was undergoing restructure in the late 2000s. Minority stakes in two state-owned commercial banks were sold to foreign banking interests in 2007–08. It was announced in early 2010 that the Central Bank of Libya (CBL) was to grant two licences to foreign banks for the creation of joint venture banking operations with Libyan investors. However, in August the CBL announced that it had decided to grant just one licence, to UniCredit (Italy); bids from two other European banks and three from the Gulf region were rejected.

Central Bank

Central Bank of Libya (CBL): POB 1103, Sharia al-Malik Seoud, Tripoli; tel. (21) 3333591; fax (21) 4441488; e-mail info@cbl.gov.ly; internet www.cbl.gov.ly; f. 1955 as Nat. Bank of Libya; name changed to Bank of Libya 1963, to Cen. Bank of Libya 1977; state-owned; bank of issue and central bank carrying govt accounts and operating exchange control; commercial operations transferred to Nat. Commercial Bank 1970; cap. 500m., res 909m., dep. 108,079m. (Dec. 2009); Gov. and Chair. SADDEK EL-KABER.

Other Banks

Alwafa Bank: POB 84212, Sharia Alfallah, Tripoli; tel. (21) 4815123; fax (21) 4801247; e-mail info@alwafabank.com; internet www.alwafabank.com; f. 2003; private bank; Chair. and Gen. Man. HADI M. GITELI.

Jumhouria Bank: POB 685, Sharia Omar el-Mokhtar, Tripoli; tel. and fax (21) 4442541; e-mail info@jbank.ly; internet www.jbank.ly; f. 1969 as successor to Barclays Bank Int. in Libya; originally known as Masraf al-Gumhouria; name changed as above 2000; merger with Umma Bank SAL completed mid-2008; cap. 1,000m., res 68m., dep. 25,041m. (Dec. 2011); Chair. MOSBAH MUHAMMAD EL-AKKARI; Gen. Man. AHMED OMAR RAJAB MUHAMMAD; 122 brs.

Libyan Foreign Bank: POB 2542, Tower 2, Dat al-Imad Complex, Tripoli; tel. (21) 3350161; fax (21) 3350164; e-mail info@lfbank.ly; internet www.lafbank.com; f. 1972 as Libyan Arab Foreign Bank; present name adopted 2005; 'offshore' bank wholly owned by Cen. Bank of Libya; cap. US $3,000m., res $738m., dep. $15,622m. (Dec. 2012); Chair. Dr AHMED A. HODANA; Gen. Man. MUHAMMAD M. BEN YOUSUF.

National Commercial Bank SAL: POB 543, Aruba Ave, al-Baida; tel. (21) 3610306; fax (21) 3612267; e-mail ncbly@lttnet.net; internet www.ncb.ly; f. 1970 to take over commercial banking division of Cen. Bank (then Bank of Libya) and brs of Aruba Bank and Istiklal Bank; wholly owned by Cen. Bank; cap. 100m., res 4,685m., dep. 6,317m. (Dec. 2008); Chair. ABD AL-WAHAB MUKHTAR; Gen. Man. SULEIMAN AZZABI; 63 brs.

Sahara Bank SPI: POB 70, Sharia 1 September, Tripoli; tel. (21) 3340663; fax (21) 4443836; e-mail sahbankgm1@lttnet.net; internet saharabank.com.ly; f. 1964 to take over br. of Banco di Sicilia; the Govt sold a 19% stake to BNP Paribas (France) in July 2007; cap. and res 208.2m., total assets 1,951.8m. (March 2003); Chair. and Gen. Man. Dr ABD AL-LATIF ABD AL-HAFIZ EL-KIB; CEO CLAUDE RUFIN; 48 brs.

Wahda Bank: POB 452, Sharia Gamal Abd al-Nasser, Benghazi; tel. (61) 2224256; fax (21) 2224122; e-mail wahda@wahdabank.com; internet www.wahdabank.com; f. 1970 to take over Bank of North Africa, Commercial Bank SAL, Nahda Arabia Bank, Société Africaine de Banque SAL, and Kafila al-Ahly Bank; 19% stake acquired by Arab Bank PLC (Jordan) in February 2008; remainder owned by Cen. Bank of Libya; cap. 432m., res 20m., dep. 6,375m. (Dec. 2010); Chair. YOUNIS EHSHAD; 76 brs.

STOCK EXCHANGE

Libyan Stock Market: Sharia Omar el-Mokhtar, Tripoli; tel. (21) 3365026; fax (61) 9091097; e-mail info@lsm.gov.ly; internet www.lsm.ly; f. 2007; Sec. SULIMAN SALEM AL-SHOHOMIY.

INSURANCE

Libya Insurance Co: POB 80087, Aman Bldg, Sharia al-Taha, Tripoli; tel. (21) 4441499; fax (21) 4444176; e-mail infolt@libtamin.com; internet www.libtamin.com; f. 1964; merged with Al-Mukhtar Insurance Co in 1981; all classes of insurance; Man. ALI AMAR AL-RAGAYEE.

Trade and Industry

There are state trade and industrial organizations responsible for the running of industries at all levels, which supervise production, distribution and sales. There are also central bodies responsible for the power generation industry, agriculture, land reclamation and transport.

GOVERNMENT AGENCIES

Council for Oil and Gas Affairs: f. 2006; holds ultimate responsibility for all matters involving oil, gas and their by-products; Chair. AL-MABROOK BUSEIF.

Great Man-made River Water Utilization Authority (GMRA): POB 7217, Benghazi; tel. (61) 2230392; fax (61) 2230393; e-mail info@gmrwua.com; internet www.gmrwua.com; supervises construction of pipeline carrying water to the Libyan coast from beneath the Sahara desert, to provide irrigation for agricultural projects; Sec. for the Great Man-made River Project ABD AL-MAJID AL-AOUD.

Libyan Investment Authority (LIA): Tripoli; e-mail info@lia.ly; internet www.lia.ly; f. 2006, operations commenced 2007; sovereign wealth fund managing state-allocated assets, including Oil Reserve Fund; Chair. Dr ABD AL-HAFID MAHMOUD ZLITNI.

National Economic Development Board (NEDB): Tripoli; internet www.nedb.ly; f. 2007; charged with the drafting and execution of reform campaigns, and the facilitation of decision-making and action on critical economic issues.

DEVELOPMENT ORGANIZATIONS

Arab Organization for Agricultural Development: POB 12898, Zohra, Tripoli; tel. and fax (21) 3619275; e-mail arabagri@lycos.com; internet www.aoad.org; responsible for agricultural devt projects.

General National Organization for Industrialization: Sharia San'a, Tripoli; tel. (21) 3334995; f. 1970; public org. responsible for the devt of industry.

Kufra and Sarir Authority: Council of Agricultural Development, Benghazi; f. 1972 to develop the Kufra oasis and Sarir area in south-eastern Libya.

CHAMBERS OF COMMERCE

Benghazi Chamber of Commerce, Trade, Industry and Agriculture: POB 208 and 1286, Benghazi; tel. (61) 3372319; fax (61) 3380761; f. 1956; Pres. Dr BADIA; Gen. Man. Dr TAREK TARBAGHIA; 150,000 mems.

Tripoli Chamber of Commerce and Industry: POB 2321, Sharia Najed 6–8, Tripoli; tel. (21) 3336855; fax (21) 3332655; f. 1952; Chair. MUHAMMAD KANOON; Dir-Gen. ABD AL-MONEM H. BURAWI; 30,000 mems.

UTILITIES
Electricity

General Electricity Company of Libya (GECOL): POB 668, Tripoli; tel. (21) 4445068; fax (21) 4447023; e-mail gecol@gecol.net;

internet www.gecol.ly; Sec. of Management Cttee Eng. ABU AL-GHASSIM ONEAS.

STATE HYDROCARBONS COMPANIES

Until 1986 petroleum affairs in Libya were dealt with primarily by the Secretariat of the General People's Committee for Petroleum. This body was abolished in March 1986, and sole responsibility for the administration of the petroleum industry passed to the national companies that were already in existence. The Secretariat of the General People's Committee for Petroleum was re-established in March 1989 and incorporated into the new Secretariat for the General People's Committee for Energy in October 1992. This was dissolved in March 2000, and responsibility for local oil policy was transferred to the National Oil Corporation, under the supervision of the General People's Committee. From 1973 the Libyan Government entered into participation agreements with some of the foreign oil companies (concession holders), and nationalized others. It concluded 85%:15% production-sharing agreements with various oil companies.

National Oil Corporation (NOC): POB 2655, Sharia Bashier Sadawi, Tripoli; tel. (21) 3337141; fax (21) 3331390; e-mail info@noclibya.com; internet en.noclibya.com.ly; f. 1970 to: undertake jt ventures with foreign cos; build and operate refineries, storage tanks, petrochemical facilities, pipelines and tankers; take part in arranging specifications for local and imported petroleum products; participate in general planning of oil installations in Libya; market crude and refined petroleum and petrochemical products; and establish and operate oil terminals; Chair. and Dir-Gen. AL-MABROOK BUSEIF.

Arabian Gulf Oil Co (AGOCO): POB 263, Benghazi; tel. (61) 28931; fax (21) 49031; wholly owned subsidiary of the NOC; Chair. AHMAD MAJBRI.

Oilinvest International NV: Tripoli; f. 1988; wholly owned subsidiary of the NOC; Libya's foreign oil investment arm; Chair. and Gen. Man. AHMAD ABD AL-KARIM AHMAD.

Agip North Africa and Middle East Ltd—Libyan Branch: POB 346, Tripoli; tel. and fax (21) 3335135; Sec. of People's Cttee OMAR AL-SWEIFI.

Azzawiya Oil Refining Co (ARC): POB 6451, Tripoli; tel. (23) 610539; fax (23) 610543; e-mail infoazzawiya@azzawiyaoil.com; internet www.azzawiyaoil.com; f. 1976; Gen. Man. AL-MOAMARE A. SWEDAN.

Brega Oil Marketing Co: POB 402, Sharia Bashir al-Saidawi, Tripoli; tel. (21) 4440830; f. 1971; Chair. Dr DOKALI B. AL-MEGHARIEF.

International Oil Investments Co: Tripoli; f. 1988, with initial capital of US $500m. to acquire 'downstream' facilities abroad; Chair. MUHAMMAD AL-JAWAD.

National Drilling and Workover Co: POB 1454, 208 Sharia Omar Mukhtar, Tripoli; tel. (21) 3332411; f. 1986; Chair. IBRAHIM BAHI.

Ras Lanouf Oil and Gas Processing Co (RASCO): POB 1971, Ras Lanuf, Benghazi; tel. (21) 3605177; fax (21) 607924; f. 1978; Chair. ABULKASIM M. A. ZWARY.

Sirte Oil Co: POB 385, Marsa el-Brega, Tripoli; tel. (21) 607261; fax (21) 601487; internet www.soc.com.ly; f. 1955 as Esso Standard Libya, taken over by Sirte Oil Co 1982; absorbed Nat. Petrochemicals Co in Oct. 1990; exploration, production of crude petroleum, gas and petrochemicals, liquefaction of natural gas; Chair. ABD AL-BASET TAHER AL-REFAE.

Umm al-Jawaby Petroleum Co: POB 693, Tripoli; Chair. and Gen. Man. MUHAMMAD TENTTOUSH.

Waha Oil Co: POB 395, Tripoli; tel. (21) 3331116; fax (21) 3337169; e-mail infowaha@wahaoil.com; internet www.wahaoil.net; Chair. Dr BASHEER MUHAMMAD ELASHAHAB.

Zueitina Oil Co (ZOC): POB 2134, Tripoli; tel. (21) 3338011; fax (21) 3339109; e-mail info@zueitina-ly.com; f. 1986; Chair. of Management Cttee BASHIR BAZAZI.

TRADE UNION

General Federation of Producers' Trade Unions: POB 734, Sharia Istanbul 2, Tripoli; tel. (21) 4446011; f. 1952; affiliated to ITUC; Sec.-Gen. BASHIR IHWIJ; 17 trade unions with 700,000 mems.

Transport
RAILWAYS

There are, at present, no railways in Libya. In 1998, however, the Government invited bids for the construction of a 3,170-km railway, comprising one branch, 2,178 km in length, running from north to south, and another, 992 km in length, running from east to west along the north coast. The railway may eventually be linked to other North African rail networks. Russian Railways OAO was awarded the contract to build a 554-km section of the network between Sirte and Benghazi in April 2008; construction work commenced in August. In 2008–09 a Chinese company was awarded contracts for a further three sections.

Railway Executive Board: POB 41758, Alkhoms, Tripoli; tel. and fax (21) 4801401; e-mail info@libyanrailways.com; oversees the planning and construction of railways; Sec. SAEED RASHID.

ROADS

The most important road is the 1,822-km national coast road from the Tunisian to the Egyptian border, passing through Tripoli and Benghazi. It has a second link between Barce and Lamluda, 141 km in length. Another national road runs from a point on the coastal road 120 km south of Misurata through Sabha to Ghat near the Algerian border (total length 1,250 km). There is a branch 247 km long running from Vaddan to Sirte. A 690-km road, connecting Tripoli and Sabha, and another 626 km long, from Ajdabiya in the north to Kufra in the south-east, were opened in 1983. The Tripoli–Ghat section (941 km) of the third, 1,352-km national road was opened in September 1984. There is a road crossing the desert from Sabha to the frontiers of Chad and Niger. As part of a wide-ranging agreement signed by Libya and Italy in August 2008, the latter agreed to fund construction of a new coastal motorway between the Tunisian and Egyptian borders. Construction work on the project commenced in mid-2009. In addition to the national highways, the west of Libya has about 1,200 km of paved and macadamized roads and the east about 500 km. All the towns and villages of Libya, including the desert oases, are accessible by motor vehicle. In 2001 Libya had an estimated total road network of 83,200 km, of which 57,200 km was paved.

SHIPPING

The principal ports are Tripoli, Benghazi, Mersa Brega, Misurata and al-Sider. Zueitina, Ras Lanuf, Mersa Hariga, Mersa Brega and al-Sider are mainly oil ports. A pipeline connects the Zelten oilfields with Mersa Brega. Another pipeline joins the Sarir oilfield with Mersa Hariga, and the port of Tobruk, and a pipeline from the Sarir field to Zueitina was opened in 1968. A port is being developed at Darnah, and plans were under way for the expansion of the port of Sirte. Libya also has the use of Tunisian port facilities at Sand Gabès, to alleviate congestion at Tripoli. At 31 December 2014 Libya's flag registered fleet consisted of 87 vessels, with a combined displacement of 1.03m. grt, of which 13 were fish carriers, two were gas tankers and three were general cargo ships.

Principal Shipping Companies

General National Maritime Transport Co (GNMTC): POB 80173, el-Shaab Terminal, Tripoli; tel. and fax (21) 4843330; e-mail info@gnmtc.com; internet www.gnmtc.com; f. 1975 to handle all projects dealing with maritime trade; state-owned; Chair. Capt. ALI BELHAG AHMED.

Libya Shipping Agency: POB 4288, Abu Seta area, nr Abokmisha Mosque, Tripoli; tel. (21) 3402528; fax (21) 3403496; e-mail info@libyashipping.com; internet www.libyashipping.com; provides chartering, land transportation and customs clearance services; Gen. Man. IMAD FELLAH.

CIVIL AVIATION

There are four international airports: Tripoli International Airport, situated at Ben Gashir, 34 km (21 miles) from Tripoli; Benina Airport 19 km (12 miles) from Benghazi; Sabha Airport; and Misurata Airport. There are a further 10 regional airports. A US $800m. programme to improve the airport infrastructure and air traffic control network was approved in mid-2001. In the mid-2000s plans were announced for the upgrade and expansion of Tripoli International Airport, which were to include the construction of two new terminals, following which the airport's annual passenger capacity was expected to increase to some 20m., compared with 3m. in 2007. Work on the project commenced in September 2007 and was scheduled for completion by 2011. However, progress was halted owing to the outbreak of conflict in February of that year. In April 2012 the National Transitional Council formally regained control of Tripoli International Airport.

Civil Aviation Authority: Tripoli International Airport, Tripoli; tel. (21) 3605318; fax (21) 3605322; e-mail info@caa.ly; internet www.caa.ly; f. 1954; Dir-Gen. Capt. NASEREDDIN SHAEBELAIN.

Afriqiyah Airways: 1st Floor, Waha Bldg, Sharia Omar al-Mokhtar, Tripoli; tel. (21) 3614026; fax (21) 3341181; e-mail customerservice@afriqiyah.aero; internet www.afriqiyah.aero; f. 2001; state-owned; flights to 29 destinations in Africa, Asia, Europe and the Middle East; Chair. ABD AL-HAKIM FARES; CEO ABUBAKER AL-FORTIA.

Buraq Air: Tripoli International Airport, Tripoli; e-mail lias@buraqair.com; internet www.buraqair.com; f. 2001; first privately owned Libyan airline; scheduled international passenger and cargo flights to Egypt, Morocco, Syria and Turkey; domestic flights from Tripoli, Benghazi and Sabha; Chair. and Man. Dir Capt. MUHAMMAD A. BUBEIDA.

Libyan Airlines: POB 2555, Ben Fernas Bldg, Sharia Haiti, Tripoli; tel. (21) 3614102; fax (21) 3614815; e-mail i.alwani@ln.aero; internet www.libyanairlines.aero; f. 1964 as Kingdom of Libya Airlines; reorg. in 1975 as Libyan Arab Airline; present name adopted 2006; passenger and cargo services from Tripoli, Benghazi and Sabha to destinations in Europe, North Africa, the Middle East and Asia; domestic services throughout Libya; CEO Capt. KHALED TAYNAZ.

Tourism

The principal attractions for visitors to Libya are Tripoli, with its beaches and annual International Fair, the ancient Roman towns of Sabratha, Leptis Magna and Cyrene, and historic oases. There were 999,343 visitor arrivals in 2004; in 2010 receipts from tourism totalled US $60m., excluding passenger transport.

General Board of Fairs: POB 891, Sharia Omar Mukhtar, Tripoli; tel. (21) 3365115; fax (21) 4448385; e-mail info@gbf.com.ly; internet www.libyafairs.com; Head of Fairs GAMAL N. A. AL-AMOUSHI.

General Board of Tourism and Traditional Industries: POB 82063, Tripoli; tel. (21) 3334673; fax (21) 4445336; e-mail info@libyan-tourism.net; Chair. MUHAMMAD SEALNA.

Defence

The Libyan National Army was founded in 2011 by the National Transitional Council after the overthrow of Muammar al-Qaddafi's regime. A restructuring process continued in 2015.

Chief of Staff of Armed Forces: Lt-Gen. KHALIFA BELKACEM HAFTAR.

Chief of Staff of Ground Forces: Brig.-Gen. YOUSUF ABU HAJAR.

Chief of Staff of Air Force: Col ALI MUHAMMAD AL-ABID ABU DIYA.

Chief of Staff of Naval Force: Cdre HASSAN ALI BUSHNAK.

Estimated Defence Expenditure (2013): LD 6,000m.

Military Service: selective conscription; 1–2 years.

Total Armed Forces (as assessed at November 2013): 7,000.

Education

Education is officially compulsory for nine years between six and 15 years of age. Primary education begins at the age of six and lasts for nine years. Secondary education, beginning at 15 years of age, lasts for a further three or four years. In 2005/06 some 755,338 students were enrolled in primary education. At the secondary level there were 732,614 students in the same year. The teaching of French was abolished in Libyan schools in 1983. Libya also has institutes for agricultural, technical and vocational training, of which there were 84 in 2004.

In 1958 the University of Libya opened in Benghazi with Faculties of Arts and Commerce, followed the next year by the Faculty of Science, near Tripoli. Faculties of Law, Agriculture, Engineering, Teacher Training, and Arabic Language and Islamic Studies have since been added to the University. In 1973 the University was divided into two parts, to form the Universities of Tripoli and Benghazi, later renamed Al-Fatah and Ghar Younis universities. The Faculty of Education at Al-Fatah University became Sabha University in 1983. There is a University of Technology (Bright Star) at Mersa Brega and the Al-Arab Medical University at Benghazi. In 1995 the number of public universities had reached 13. In 2002/03 some 375,028 students were enrolled in tertiary education. The Government's budget for 2012 allocated LD 4,600m. (equivalent to 6.7% of total spending) to the Ministry of Education.

LIECHTENSTEIN

Introductory Survey

LOCATION, CLIMATE, LANGUAGE, RELIGION, FLAG, CAPITAL

The Principality of Liechtenstein is in central Europe. The country lies on the east bank of the Upper Rhine river, bordered by Switzerland to the west and south, and by Austria to the north and east. Liechtenstein has an Alpine climate, with mild winters. The annual average temperature is about 10.5°C, while average rainfall per year is 996 mm. The official language is German, of which a dialect—Alemannish—is spoken. Almost all of the inhabitants profess Christianity, and about 79% are adherents of the Roman Catholic Church. The national flag (proportions 3 by 5) consists of two equal horizontal stripes, of royal blue and red, with a golden princely crown, outlined in black, in the upper hoist. The capital is Vaduz.

CONTEMPORARY POLITICAL HISTORY

Historical Context

Liechtenstein has effectively been an independent state since 1719, except while under French domination briefly in the early 19th century. It joined the German Confederation in 1815, but failed to realign itself with other German states upon the dissolution of the Confederation in 1866. In 1919 Switzerland assumed responsibility for Liechtenstein's diplomatic representation, replacing Austria. In 1920 a postal union with Switzerland was agreed, and in 1924 a treaty was concluded with Switzerland whereby Liechtenstein was incorporated in a joint customs union. Franz Josef II became Reigning Prince in 1938 and was succeeded by his son Prince Hans-Adam II in 1989.

Domestic Political Affairs

After 42 years as the dominant party in government, the Fortschrittliche Bürgerpartei (FBP—Progressive Citizens' Party) was defeated by the centre-right Vaterlandische Union (VU—Patriotic Union) at a general election to the Landtag (parliament) in February 1970. Four years later the FBP regained its majority. At the general election in February 1978 the VU, led by Hans Brunhart, won a majority of seats. After protracted negotiations, Brunhart replaced the FBP's Dr Walter Kieber as Prime Minister in April. At the general election in February 1982 the distribution of seats remained unchanged. Following a referendum in July 1984, women were granted the right to vote on a national basis. However, women remained banned from voting on communal affairs in three of Liechtenstein's 11 communes until 1986. (An amendment to the Constitution, declaring equality between men and women, took effect in 1992.) In August 1984 Prince Franz Josef transferred sovereign power to his son, Hereditary (Crown) Prince Hans-Adam, although he remained titular Head of State until his death in November 1989, when he was succeeded by his son (as Hans-Adam II).

The composition of the Landtag remained unchanged following a general election in February 1986, when women voted for the first time in a national poll. In January 1989 the Landtag was dissolved by Prince Hans-Adam, following a dispute between the VU and the FBP regarding the construction of a new museum to accommodate the princely art collection. At the subsequent general election, which took place in March, the number of seats in the Landtag was increased from 15 to 25; the VU retained its majority.

In October 1992 almost 2,000 people demonstrated in Vaduz to protest against a threat by Prince Hans-Adam that he would dissolve the Landtag if deputies did not submit to his wish to hold a proposed referendum to endorse Liechtenstein's entry to the nascent European Economic Area (EEA) shortly in advance of a similar vote in Switzerland. The Prince—a staunch supporter of membership of the EEA—believed that the outcome of the Swiss poll might be prejudicial to that of the Liechtenstein vote, and that, in the event of voters' rejecting EEA membership at an early referendum, Liechtenstein might still be able to join other members of the European Free Trade Association (EFTA, of which Liechtenstein became a full member in 1991, see p. 446) in applying for admission to the European Community (EC, now European Union—EU, see p. 271). A compromise was reached,

whereby the referendum was scheduled to take place shortly after the Swiss vote, while the Government agreed to promote a vote in favour of the EEA and to explore the possibility of applying to the EC should EEA membership be rejected. (The authorities subsequently decided that admission to the EU would not be beneficial to the Principality.) At the referendum in December, although Switzerland's voters had rejected accession to the EEA, Liechtenstein's membership was approved by 55.8% of those who voted (around 87% of the electorate); consequently, the two countries' joint customs union was renegotiated. Liechtenstein joined the EEA in May 1995.

At the general election in February 1993 the VU lost its majority. Negotiations resulted in the formation of a new coalition between the FBP and the VU, and Markus Büchel of the FBP became Prime Minister. In September, however, following a unanimous vote in the Landtag expressing no confidence in his leadership, Büchel was dismissed from his post, and Prince Hans-Adam dissolved the legislature. At a fresh general election, held in October, the VU regained its majority. The VU formed a new coalition with the FBP, with Mario Frick of the VU as Prime Minister.

In March 1996 the Landtag adopted a unanimous motion of loyalty to the hereditary monarchy, after Prince Hans-Adam offered to resign in response to continued tension between him and the legislature. At the next general election, which took place in February 1997, the VU retained its majority and Frick remained Prime Minister. In April the FBP withdrew from the ruling coalition, leaving a single party (the VU) to govern alone for the first time since 1938. The constitutional role of the Reigning Prince came under renewed scrutiny in 1997, when, against the wishes of the Landtag, Prince Hans-Adam refused to reappoint Dr Herbert Wille, a senior judge who had advocated that constitutional issues should be decided by the Supreme Court rather than the monarch. Wille subsequently presented a formal complaint to the European Court of Human Rights, which ruled, in November 1999, that Prince Hans-Adam had restricted Wille's right to free speech.

In December 1999 Prince Hans-Adam requested an Austrian prosecutor, Kurt Spitzer, to investigate allegations in the German press based on an unpublished report of April 1999 by the German secret service that international criminals were using financial institutions in Liechtenstein to launder the proceeds of organized crime. As a result, five people were arrested in May 2000; all five were later released without charge. In his final report, which was published in August, Spitzer concluded that Liechtenstein was no more culpable of money-laundering than any other country in Europe. He blamed the current problems on the Principality's inefficient banking system and the poor application of existing legislation designed to combat economic crimes. In June the Financial Action Task Force on Money Laundering (FATF), a commission of the Organisation for Economic Co-operation and Development (OECD, see p. 377), included Liechtenstein on a list of countries considered uncooperative in international attempts to combat money-laundering. In July, in an effort to improve the country's international reputation, the Government approved the establishment of a new financial investigative unit within the police force and measures to accelerate legal assistance to foreign countries in money-laundering investigations. Furthermore, legislation was promulgated in December requiring financial institutions to maintain more stringent controls over accounts and transactions, including the abolition of anonymous accounts. Liechtenstein was removed from the FATF's list of unco-operative countries in 2001, and, in October of that year, a new financial surveillance unit was established, tasked with enforcing new regulations requiring banks and lawyers to be able to verify the identity of their clients. However, in April 2002 Liechtenstein was among seven jurisdictions identified by OECD as 'unco-operative tax havens' lacking financial transparency, under its initiative to abolish 'harmful tax practices'. Liechtenstein remained one of three countries so designated until May 2009.

At the general election in February 2001 the VU lost its parliamentary majority, securing 11 of the 25 seats in the

Landtag, while the FBP took 13 seats and the social democratic, environmentalist party, the Freie Liste (FL—Free List) one. The VU administration's popularity had been adversely affected by an unresolved dispute with Prince Hans-Adam over his demands for constitutional changes, notably with regard to judicial appointments (the Prince advocated that judges be nominated by the monarch rather than by parliamentary deputies). A new Government comprising solely the FBP, under the leadership of Otmar Hasler, took office in April. In December the Prince threatened to abdicate and take up residence in Austria if his proposed constitutional reforms were not enacted.

The issue of constitutional reform was finally resolved by a national referendum, held in March 2003, in which 64.3% of those who voted (87.7% of the electorate) were in favour of granting the Reigning Prince new powers. Accordingly, the Prince gained the right to dismiss a government even if it retained parliamentary confidence, to appoint an interim administration pending elections, to preside over a panel to select judges, and to veto laws by not signing them within a six-month period. Conversely, the constitutional amendments also divested the Prince of his right to rule by emergency decree for an unlimited period (such a measure was now limited to a maximum of six months) and to nominate government officials. In addition, citizens could now force a referendum on any subject (including the future of the monarchy) by collecting a minimum of 1,500 signatures. A cross-party group which included former premier Frick presented a compromise proposal, which suggested that a princely veto could be overruled by a referendum and sought to limit the Prince's use of emergency legislation to times of war; this proposal received the support of only 16.5% of the voters. The overwhelming support for the Prince's proposed changes was partially attributed to widespread fear that, if fulfilled, his threat of self-imposed exile as a symbolic monarch would cause economic decline and social upheaval (the royal family owns and operates the LGT Bank, the Principality's largest bank and asset management fund). On 15 August 2004 Prince Hans-Adam transferred sovereign power to his son, Hereditary Prince Alois, while remaining titular Head of State.

At the general election in March 2005 the FBP failed to retain an absolute majority, winning 12 of the 25 seats. The VU secured 10 seats, while the FL increased its representation to three seats. The FBP and the VU formed a coalition Government, with Hasler retaining the premiership and Dr Klaus Tschütscher of the VU as Deputy Prime Minister.

In August 2005 a conservative group, the Volksinitiative für das Leben (People's Initiative For Life), submitted 1,889 signatures to the Government in support of its demands for a national referendum to be held on constitutional revisions. The group wished to amend Article 14 of the Constitution so that the highest responsibility of the state would be 'to protect human life from conception until natural death' and also aimed to insert a reference to the state's responsibility to protect human dignity. The initiative was intended to address the potential legalization of abortion and, indirectly, the issues of euthanasia, genetic technology and stem cell research. Having failed to secure sufficient support in the Landtag, the proposals were to be subject to a national referendum. The FBP and the VU jointly drafted a counterproposal to make the protection of life and human dignity a right for Liechtenstein citizens rather than a duty of the state. A further amendment was added explicitly prohibiting the death penalty (which had already been abolished by a revision of the criminal code in 1985). Following its approval by the Landtag in September, the counterproposal was presented to the referendum concurrently with the 'For Life' initiative. At the referendum, held in November, the initiative, which opponents claimed would prevent abortion, birth control and assisted suicide, was rejected by 80.9% of the votes cast, while the counterproposal was adopted, with the support of 79.4% of voters.

At the general election in February 2009, which attracted a turnout of 84.6%, the VU won an absolute majority, securing 13 seats and replacing the FBP as the largest party in the Landtag. The FBP won 11 seats, while the FL's representation declined to just one. Despite the VU's absolute majority, the VU and FBP formed another coalition Government, headed by Tschütscher. The new Prime Minister undertook further to improve the reputation of Liechtenstein's financial system by increasing co-operation with other countries in the fight against tax evasion (see *Foreign Affairs*).

In September 2011 a narrow majority of participants in a referendum rejected the decriminalization of early abortion (a few days prior to the poll Prince Alois had indicated that he would

veto any relaxation of the abortion ban). Although the Prince's threat angered a proportion of the population (believing that it rendered the referendum meaningless), in a further referendum, held on 1 July 2012, 76.1% of those who voted rejected a proposal put forward by pro-democracy campaigners to curb the political power of the Prince by divesting him of his power of veto over decisions reached in national referendums.

The general election of 1 and 3 February 2013 was contested by four groups, rather than the usual three. The new contender was an organization entitled Die Unabhängigen (DU—The Independents), which was established by the parliamentary deputy Harry Quaderer, who left the VU in February 2011. In the poll, which attracted a turnout of 79.8%, the VU lost its majority in the Landtag, securing only eight seats, while the FBP won 10, the DU four and the FL three. The VU's heavy losses were largely attributed to the unpopularity of the outgoing administration's proposed economic austerity measures. A new Government comprising the FBP and the VU was formed in March 2013, led by the FBP's Adrian Hasler, the former chief of the Liechtenstein National Police. Thomas Zwiefelhofer of the VU was appointed Deputy Prime Minister.

In early 2013 a report by Swiss asset manager Swisscanto identified major difficulties in the Liechtenstein public-sector pension fund, amounting to a financial shortfall of 300m. Swiss francs (€250m.). Following a legal investigation, it was confirmed that senior officials were responsible for the financial situation of the pension fund, but that there was insufficient evidence to take action against individuals. In September Parliament approved legislation providing for the creation of a new pension fund for public-sector employees, which was to take the form of an independent foundation. A referendum on options relating to public-sector pensions was held on 15 June 2014; the new scheme entered into effect on 1 July.

Foreign Affairs

In 1950 Liechtenstein became a party to the Statute of the International Court of Justice (ICJ, see p. 25), in 1973 it joined the Organization for Security and Co-operation in Europe (see p. 385) and in 1978 it was admitted to the Council of Europe (see p. 250). Liechtenstein became a full member of the UN in 1990 (hitherto the country had been a member of some UN specialized agencies). In 1991 Liechtenstein attained full membership of the European Free Trade Association (EFTA, see p. 446). Liechtenstein participates in the European Economic Area (EEA), which since 1994 has incorporated Liechtenstein (together with Iceland and Norway) into the internal market of the European Union (EU, see p. 271).

In February 2008, following a meeting of EU ministers responsible for justice and home affairs in Brussels, Belgium, Liechtenstein became an associate member of the EU's Schengen area (which binds signatories to the abolition of border controls) and the Dublin Convention on Asylum (relating to common formal arrangements on asylum). Although the Landtag ratified the agreement in June, the EU process of ratification was not completed until December 2011.

Following the Second World War, Liechtenstein's relations with Czechoslovakia (from 1993 the Czech Republic and Slovakia) were strained. This stemmed from the expulsion of ethnic Germans from Czechoslovakia and the confiscation of their land (without compensation) after the war, under the controversial Beneš Decrees. The Liechtenstein princely family lost a large part of its estates during this time. Liechtenstein, which was a sovereign, neutral state throughout both the First and Second World Wars, claimed that it was unfairly grouped together with Germany under the terms of the Decrees. Czechoslovakia, however, considered the Liechtenstein princely family to have been collaborators with the Nazi regime in Germany during the Second World War, and that its action was thus legitimate. As a result of the dispute, Czechoslovakia refused to recognize Liechtenstein as a sovereign state. In October 2003 Prince Hans-Adam blocked the entry of the Czech Republic and Slovakia (along with that of the eight other EU accession states) into the EEA; the 10 countries were due to become members of the EU on 1 May 2004 and would, under normal circumstances, have automatically joined the EEA. Their accession to the EEA was delayed until November 2003, when Liechtenstein agreed to sign the EEA enlargement treaty. Liechtenstein reiterated its demand that the Czech Republic and Slovakia acknowledge that the Principality was a sovereign, neutral state through both World Wars. To do so, however, would expose these two countries to the possibility of legal action being brought against them by Liechtenstein for the illegal seizure of land. None the less, Liechtenstein established diplomatic relations with the Czech Republic in September 2009, although the two countries stressed that any resolution of the dispute over the confiscated property would be subject to separate negotiations. In December diplomatic relations with Slovakia were also established. A joint commission of historians was set up in 2010 to investigate the background to the property dispute between Liechtenstein and the Czech Republic; its report was endorsed by the ministers for foreign affairs of both countries in January 2014.

Liechtenstein also sought damages from Germany for assets that it claimed Germany had improperly awarded to Czechoslovakia after the Second World War as reparations. The German position was that the assets were seized by Czechoslovakia and that Germany was not responsible. In February 2005, however, the ICJ ruled that it was not competent to make a decision on the claim as it pre-dated the 1980 agreement between Liechtenstein and Germany that disputes between them should be settled by the ICJ.

Liechtenstein's banking secrecy laws were subject to increased international scrutiny in 2008, following the revelation that the German Federal Intelligence Service had paid some €4m. to a former employee of Liechtenstein's LGT Bank for access to records detailing accounts held by German nationals. It appeared that members of Germany's business élite had avoided tax by channelling up to €4,000m. into secret foundations established by banks in Liechtenstein. The German Government demanded greater financial transparency in Liechtenstein, as well as greater co-operation regarding tax evasion. Several other countries (including the USA and the United Kingdom) subsequently began investigations into allegations of tax evasion through secret bank accounts held in Liechtenstein. In response to growing international criticism, Prince Alois announced in August that the country would in future endeavour to co-operate more fully on tax matters, but that this should not be at the expense of the country's 'culture of privacy'. A bilateral agreement was reached with the USA in December, whereby Liechtenstein would co-operate with investigations into suspected tax evasion, while Liechtenstein banks would benefit from increased access to US financial markets. Further negotiations between Liechtenstein and the USA were completed in late 2013 and an agreement on the implementation of the Foreign Account Tax Compliance Act (FATCA) was signed in May 2014, under the terms of which financial institutions were to be obliged to forward to US authorities information on accounts held by individuals taxable in the USA; legislation on the implementation of the FATCA agreement was passed by the Landtag in December. In the month before the April 2009 meeting of the Group of 20 major industrialized and systemically important emerging market nations (G20, see p. 451), Liechtenstein agreed to amend its secrecy laws to allow for greater transparency and to comply with rules on the sharing of bank data set by OECD to combat tax evasion. Consequently, in May OECD removed Liechtenstein from its list of 'unco-operative tax havens', and in November it recognized Liechtenstein as a jurisdiction that had implemented international co-operation standards in tax matters. Liechtenstein undertook at the end of 2014 to be an 'early adopter' of the OECD standard for automatic exchange of financial account information in tax matters. The first exchange of account holder information was to take place by the end of September 2017. By November 2014 Liechtenstein had concluded agreements providing for the exchange of tax information with 35 countries and jurisdictions. In February 2015 it was announced that Liechtenstein had concluded negotiations with Switzerland on a double tax agreement, which was expected to be signed in mid-2015 and to be applied from January 2017. (The new agreement was to replace a less comprehensive 1995 agreement currently in force.)

In June 2014, following a request initially submitted in 2000 which had resulted in a lengthy legal dispute, some €167m. in funds, misappropriated by Nigeria's former military President Sani Abacha and deposited in bank accounts in Liechtenstein, were returned to the Nigerian state.

CONSTITUTION AND GOVERNMENT

Under the Constitution of 1921 (as amended in 1969, 1984, 2003 and 2005), the monarchy is hereditary in the male line. The Reigning Prince, who is constitutionally responsible for foreign affairs, exercises legislative power jointly with the Landtag (parliament). The Landtag comprises 25 members, who are elected by universal adult suffrage for a term of four years (subject to dissolution), on the basis of proportional representation. The country is divided into the two election districts of Oberland (Upper Country) and Unterland (Lower Country),

which elect 15 and 10 members of the Landtag, respectively. A five-member collegial Government is nominated by the Landtag and appointed by the Reigning Prince for a term of four years. Under constitutional changes approved by referendum in 2003, the Reigning Prince is empowered to dismiss governments (even if they retain parliamentary confidence), appoint an interim administration pending an election, approve judicial nominees, veto laws and invoke emergency legislation. According to another constitutional amendment introduced following the 2003 plebiscite, citizens can force a referendum on any subject, including the future of the monarchy, by collecting 1,500 signatures. On 15 August 2004 the sovereign rights pertaining to the Reigning Prince were transferred to the Hereditary (Crown) Prince, who was to exercise them as the representative of the Reigning Prince, who remained head of state.

REGIONAL AND INTERNATIONAL CO-OPERATION

Liechtenstein has important links with neighbouring Switzerland: the two countries are joined in a customs union, and Switzerland is responsible for Liechtenstein's diplomatic interests in countries where Liechtenstein is not directly represented. Liechtenstein is a member of the European Free Trade Association (EFTA, see p. 446) and participates in the European Economic Area (EEA), which incorporates Liechtenstein (together with Iceland and Norway) into the internal market of the European Union (EU, see p. 271). Liechtenstein became an associate member of the EU's Schengen Agreement on border controls in 2008, and its accession to full membership was completed in December 2011. It is also a member of the Council of Europe (see p. 250) and the Organization for Security and Co-operation in Europe (OSCE, see p. 385).

Liechtenstein joined the UN in 1990 and the World Trade Organization (WTO, see p. 431) in 1995.

ECONOMIC AFFAIRS

In 2009, according to estimates by the World Bank, Liechtenstein's gross national income (GNI), measured at average 2007–09 prices, was US $4,903m., equivalent to $136,770 per head (although as 50% of the workforce was domiciled abroad in 2009, this figure is not comparable with those for other countries). During 2004–13 the population increased at an average annual rate of 0.8%, while Liechtenstein's gross domestic product (GDP) per head increased, in real terms, by an average of 2.6% per year during 2004–09. Overall GDP increased, in real terms, at an average annual rate of 3.4% in 2004–09; GDP declined by 1.2% in 2009.

According to the UN, in 2013 the agricultural sector (together with forestry and fishing) accounted for just 0.7% of GDP. Within the agricultural sector the emphasis is on cattle-breeding, dairy farming and market gardening. The principal crops are maize and potatoes. In addition, wine is produced, and forestry is a significant activity. In 2013 0.8% of those employed in Liechtenstein worked in agriculture (including forestry).

In 2013, according to the UN, industry (including production of goods) contributed some 25.7% of GDP. Around 39.3% of those employed in Liechtenstein worked in industrial activity (including mining and quarrying, processing industries, energy and water supply, and construction) in that year.

According to the UN, in 2013 the manufacturing sector accounted for 18.7% of GDP. In that year 31.9% of those employed in Liechtenstein worked in the manufacturing sector. The principal branches of manufacturing are mechanical engineering, electrical machinery, vehicle components and dental instruments.

In 2013, according to the UN, the construction sector accounted for 5.1% of GDP. In that year 7.3% of those employed in Liechtenstein worked in the construction sector.

In 2013 more than 90% of energy requirements were imported from other countries. In that year electricity supplied 29.8% of energy requirements, natural gas 21.1%, fuel oil 14.0%, diesel 11.8% and motor fuel (petrol) 11.5%.

According to the UN, in 2013 73.6% of GDP was generated by the services sector. In that year the sector engaged 59.9% of those employed in Liechtenstein. Financial services are of great importance. Numerous foreign corporations, holding companies and foundations (estimated to number about 75,000) have nominal offices in Liechtenstein, benefiting from the Principality's stable political situation, tradition of bank secrecy (although stricter banking legislation has been introduced in recent years, partly to increase the transparency of the sector) and low fiscal charges. Following the Principality's accession to the European

Economic Area (EEA) in 1995, the registration of foreign banks was permitted. New legislation governing insurance companies was approved in 1996, and during the late 1990s the insurance sector expanded rapidly. The building and hotel trades and other service industries (including tourism) are also highly developed.

With a very limited domestic market, Liechtenstein's industry is export-orientated. In 2013 total exports (excluding Switzerland) amounted to 3,361.7m. Swiss francs, while imports (excluding Switzerland) totalled 1,884.2m. Swiss francs. Switzerland is the principal trading partner. In 2008 Switzerland, which operates a customs union with Liechtenstein, purchased 10.1% of total exports of members of the Liechtenstein Chamber of Commerce and Industry, and the EEA accounted for 48.8%. In 2013 Germany supplied 39.0% of total imports and received 23.6% of total exports. Austria and the People's Republic of China were another major import markets, while other major export markets included the USA, Austria and France. In 2013 principal imports included specialized machinery and electrical products, metals and metal products, chemical products, mineral products, furniture and related products, and vehicles and transport equipment. Principal exports in that year included machinery and electrical products, metals and metal products, vehicles and transport equipment, chemical products, mineral products, and food and animal products.

In 2013, according to official figures, Liechtenstein recorded a visible merchandise trade surplus of 1,477.5m. Swiss francs (excluding Switzerland), while there was a fiscal deficit of 65.0m. Swiss francs. The average annual rate of inflation was 0.4% during 2005–14; consumer prices decreased by 0.1% in 2014. Traditionally, the unemployment rate has been negligible (0.1% of the active labour force, or some 20 persons, in 1990); however, it rose during the 1990s and the 2000s, and stood at 1.3% in 2013. More than one-third of Liechtenstein's population are resident foreigners, many of whom provide the labour for industry, while in 2013 19,140 workers crossed the borders (52.8% of workers in Liechtenstein), mainly from Austria and Switzerland each day, to work in the Principality.

During the first decade of the 21st century Liechtenstein's reputation as a financial centre and secretive tax haven was challenged by foreign governments aiming to combat money-laundering and tax evasion. The widespread recession that affected most developed countries in 2008–09 increased governments' determination to recover the revenues that were due to them. During 2008–14 Liechtenstein concluded bilateral agreements on the exchange of tax information with more than 30 countries and jurisdictions, including the USA and the UK. Liechtenstein's recognition by OECD in November 2009 as a jurisdiction that had implemented international co-operation standards in tax matters was widely viewed as an important development in Liechtenstein's standing as a business location.

Reforms aimed at simplifying the country's own tax system and making it more transparent, while simultaneously increasing its compatibility with EU law came into effect on 1 January 2011. The measures included a uniform corporate tax rate and the abolition of capital gains, inheritance and gift taxes. It was hoped that the reforms, as well as providing additional Government revenue, would also enhance the attractiveness of Liechtenstein for investors and encourage sustainable growth. In mid-2010 the Government revised legislation concerning the financial markets, so as to ensure that Liechtenstein's practices would be consistent with international standards. Amendments to Liechtenstein's Banking Act were approved by the Landtag in late 2014 and the legislation entered into force in February 2015. In response to the impact of the ongoing debt crisis in the eurozone and the country's increasing fiscal deficit, the Government introduced a five-year austerity plan in 2010, including reductions in expenditure on social welfare and health care, and a lowering of state subsidies to the pension system. There were signs of modest recovery in 2010–11, with GDP returning to positive growth—of 8.8% in 2010 and 1.9% in 2011. However, in 2012 another contraction in GDP, of 1.2%, prompted the Government to propose the expansion of the austerity programme. Public opposition to further economic stringency was believed to have contributed to the defeat of Dr Klaus Tschütscher's Government in the general election of February 2013. However, with a record budgetary deficit forecast for 2013, in March of that year Prince Alois urged the new Government to reduce public spending and to aim for a balanced budget as soon as possible. Among the measures subsequently implemented was a 30% reduction in government transfers to municipalities in 2014. The discovery in 2013 of a substantial shortfall in the public-sector pension fund, necessitating the establishment of a new independent scheme, placed additional strains on the budget. A one-off cash transfer to the state's pension fund was expected to result in a deficit equivalent to 5.7% of GDP in 2014, which was to be financed from the Government's liquid assets. Nevertheless, it was planned that the budget would be balanced in 2015 and would subsequently return to surplus: the Government announced in late 2014 that it expected cumulative budget surpluses of 115m. Swiss francs between 2015 and 2018, along with an increase in state reserves.

PUBLIC HOLIDAYS

2016: 1 January (New Year's Day), 2 January (St Berchtold's Day), 6 January (Epiphany), 2 February (Candlemas), 9 February (Shrove Tuesday), 19 March (St Joseph's Day), 25 March (Good Friday), 28 March (Easter Monday), 1 May (Labour Day), 5 May (Ascension Day), 16 May (Whit Monday), 26 May (Corpus Christi), 15 August (National Holiday and Assumption), 8 September (Nativity of the Virgin Mary), 1 November (All Saints' Day), 8 December (Immaculate Conception), 25 December (Christmas Day), 26 December (St Stephen's Day).

Statistical Survey

Source: Amt für Statistik, Äulestrasse 51, 9490 Vaduz; tel. 2366876; fax 2366936; e-mail info.as@llv.li; internet www.as.llv.li.

AREA AND POPULATION

Area: 160.5 sq km (62.0 sq miles).

Population: (at 31 December 2013) 37,129 (Liechtensteiners 24,610).

Density (at 31 December 2013): 231.3 per sq km.

Population by Age and Sex (at 31 December 2013): *0–14 years:* 5,648 (males 2,930, females 2,718); *15–64 years:* 25,710 (males 12,860, females 12,850); *65 years and over:* 5,771 (males 2,610, females 3,161); *Total* 37,129 (males 18,400, females 18,729).

Municipalities (population at 31 December 2013): Schaan 5,925; Vaduz (capital) 5,372; Triesen 4,989; Balzers 4,594; Eschen 4,295; Mauren 4,141; Triesenberg 2,620; Ruggell 2,092; Gamprin 1,649; Schellenberg 1,032; Planken 420; *Total* 37,129.

Births, Marriages and Deaths (2013): Live births 339 (9.2 per 1,000); Marriages 324 (9.2 per 1,000); Deaths 246 (6.1 per 1,000).

Economically Active Population (2013): Agriculture and forestry 275; Industry and skilled trades 14,248 (Mining and quarrying 51, Manufacturing 11,214, Energy and water supply 339, Construction 2,644); Services 21,701 (Retail, repairs, etc. 2,763, Hotels and restaurants 994, Transport and communications 1,793, Banking and insurance 3,226, Real estate, information, business and support services, etc. 3,656, Legal consultancy and trust management 2,632, Public administration 1,761, Education 1,242, Health and social services 2,181, Other services—incl. activities of extraterritorial organizations—1,453); *Total employed* 36,224; Unemployed 480; *Total labour force* 36,704.

HEALTH AND WELFARE
Key Indicators

Under-5 Mortality Rate (per 1,000 live births, 2004): 5.

Physicians (per 1,000 head, 1997): 1.31 (Source: Statistik des Fürstentums Liechtenstein, *Statistisches Jahrbuch—1998*).

Human Development Index (2013): ranking: 18.

Human Development Index (2013): value: 0.889.

For sources (unless specified) and definitions, see explanatory note on p. vi.

AGRICULTURE, ETC.

Note: Figures are for farms with a minimum of either 1 ha of arable land, 30 acres of specialized cultivation, 10 acres of protected cultivation, 8 sows, 80 porkers (or capacity for 80 porkers) or 300 head of poultry, and where livestock owners are covered by the Tierseuchenfond (insurance against epidemics).

Principal Crops (metric tons, 1987): Wheat 460; Oats 4; Barley 416; Silo-maize 27,880. _2010:_ Potatoes 7,751. _2013_ (FAO estimate): Grapes 195 (Source: partly FAO)

Livestock (2013): Cattle 6,010; Pigs 1,655; Horses 466; Sheep 3,522; Goats 269; Hens 12,811.

Dairy Produce (2013, metric tons): Milk delivered to dairies 133,726; Milk for consumption and pasteurization 631; Milk for processing 2,521; Cream 2,217; Yoghurt 821.

Forestry ('000 cubic metres, 2013, FAO estimates): Roundwood removals (excl. bark) 19.2 (Sawlogs, veneer logs and logs for sleepers 6.4, Fuel wood 4.9; Pulpwood 7.8). Source: FAO.

FINANCE

Currency and Exchange Rates: Swiss currency: 100 Rappen (centimes) = 1 Franken (Swiss franc). _Sterling, Dollar and Euro Equivalents_ (31 December 2014): £1 sterling = 1.544 Franken; US $1 = 0.989 Franken; €1 = 1.201 Franken; 10 Franken = £6.48 = $10.11 = €8.33. For average exchange rate, see chapter on Switzerland.

Budget (million Swiss francs, 2010): _Revenue:_ Current 1,095 (Taxes and duties 750; Revenues from assets 275); Capital 19; Total 1,114. _Expenditure:_ Current 1,053 (Social welfare 231; Finance and taxation 332); Capital 77; Total 1,130. _2012_ (million Swiss francs): Total revenue 1,109 (Current 1,090, Capital 19); Total expenditure 1,220 (Current 1,174, Capital 46).

Cost of Living (Consumer Price Index; base: December 2010 = 100): All items 99.3 in 2012; 99.1 in 2013; 99.0 in 2014.

Gross Domestic Product (million Swiss francs at current prices, official estimates): 5,300.4 in 2010; 5,097.1 in 2011; 5,145.8 in 2012 (provisional).

Expenditure on the Gross Domestic Product (million Swiss francs at current prices, 2013): Government final consumption expenditure 573.9; Private final consumption expenditure 2,790.8; Increase in stocks –45.3; Gross fixed capital formation 1,225.7; _Total domestic expenditure_ 4,545.1; Exports of goods and services 3,776.4; _Less_ Imports of goods and services 3,142.4; Statistical discrepancy 55.2; _GDP in purchasers' values_ 5,234.3 (Source: UN, National Accounts Main Aggregates Database)

Gross Domestic Product by Economic Activity (million Swiss francs at current prices, 2013): Agriculture, forestry and fishing 37.6; Mining and utilities 103.0; Manufacturing 994.3; Construction 271.6; Retail trade and hotel and restaurants 869.9; Transport, storage and communication 433.4; Other services 2,609.5; _Total gross value added_ 5,319.3; Net of taxes on products –85.0 (figure obtained as residual); _GDP in purchasers' values_ 5,234.3 (Source: UN, National Accounts Main Aggregates Database).

EXTERNAL TRADE

Note: Imports and exports to and from Liechtenstein presented at Swiss customs, not including trade with Switzerland and goods traffic via Switzerland.

Principal Commodities ('000 Swiss francs, 2013): _Imports:_ Food, animals and other products of agriculture 71,022; Wood pulp, paper and publishing products 73,798; Raw materials, metals, construction and chemical products 168,850; Mineral products 125,304; Vehicles and transport equipment 117,712; Machinery and electrical products 637,016; Metal manufactures and other finished and semi-finished goods 481,517; Furniture and related products 123,219; Total (incl. others) 1,884,218. _Exports:_ Food, animals and other products of

agriculture 212,836; Raw materials, metals, construction and chemical products 289,937; Mineral products 220,905; Vehicles and transport equipment 478,480; Machinery and electrical products 1,275,514; Metal manufactures and other finished and semi-finished goods 661,849; Total (incl. others) 3,361,737.

Principal Trading Partners ('000 Swiss francs, 2013): _Imports:_ Austria 558,241; China, People's Republic 148,455; France 40,023; Germany 735,078; Italy 75,065; Netherlands 25,242; Poland 32,947; United Kingdom 24,938; USA 66,678; Total (incl. others) 1,884,218. _Exports:_ Austria 326,229; China, People's Republic 174,413; France 305,127; Germany 795,000; Hong Kong 53,825; India 32,242; Italy 126,462; Japan 48,324; Mexico 75,084; Russia 77,183; Singapore 80,434; Spain 52,056; Sweden 55,159; United Arab Emirates 39,408; United Kingdom 87,233; USA 448,727; Total (incl. others) 3,361,737.

TRANSPORT

Road Traffic (registered motor vehicles, 1 July 2014): Passenger cars 28,474; Commercial vehicles 647; Motorcycles 4,154; Total (incl. others) 37,787.

TOURISM

Arrivals by Country of Residence (arrivals at accommodation establishments, 2013): Austria 2,663; France 1,435; Germany 16,287; Italy 2,120; Netherlands 1,471; Switzerland 17,651; United Kingdom 1,931; USA 2,230; Total (incl. others) 60,764. Note: Total includes 1,124 residents of Liechtenstein.

COMMUNICATIONS MEDIA

Telephones (2013): 18,000 main lines in use.

Mobile Cellular Telephones (2013): 36,100 subscribers.

Broadband Subscribers (2013): 12,000.

Source: International Telecommunication Union.

EDUCATION
(2007/08 unless otherwise indicated*)

Kindergarten: 49 classrooms; 79 teachers (males 1, females 78); 711 pupils (males 371, females 340). _2012/13:_ 91 teachers; 698 pupils.

Primary†: 138 classrooms; 262 teachers (males 63, females 199); 2,073 pupils (males 1,035, females 1,038). _2012/13:_ 256 teachers; 1,873 pupils.

High School: 34 classrooms; 101 teachers (males 45, females 56); 412 pupils (males 221, females 191). _2012/13:_ 110 teachers; 384 pupils.

Secondary: 45 classrooms; 127 teachers (males 60, females 67); 732 pupils (males 380, females 352). _2012/13:_ 134 teachers; 721 pupils.

Optional 10th School Year: 5 classrooms; 19 teachers (males 10, females 9); 78 pupils (males 32, females 46). _2012/13:_ 18 teachers; 65 pupils.

Vocational Training: 8 classrooms; 16 teachers (males 8, females 8); 124 pupils (males 84, females 40).

Grammar Schools (2004/05 unless otherwise indicated): 38 classrooms (2001/02); 103 teachers; 744 pupils.

Music (2004/05): 91 teachers; 2,519 pupils.

Higher Education (2004/05)‡: 527 students.

Pupil-teacher Ratio (primary education, UNESCO estimate): 7.8 in 2010/11 (Source: UNESCO Institute for Statistics).

* Excluding private institutions.
† Including pre-school and reception classes.
‡ Those studying in Liechtenstein only (931 students attended institutions abroad).

Directory

The Government

HEAD OF STATE

Reigning Prince: HSH Prince HANS-ADAM II (succeeded 13 November 1989).

On 15 August 2004 Prince Hans-Adam II transferred the execution of his sovereign powers to his son, Hereditary Prince Alois.

GOVERNMENT
(May 2015)

A coalition of the Fortschrittliche Bürgerpartei (FBP—Progressive Citizens' Party) and the Vaterländische Union (VU—Patriotic Union).

Prime Minister and Minister of General Government Affairs and of Finance: ADRIAN HASLER (FBP).

Deputy Prime Minister and Minister of Economic Affairs, of Justice and of Home Affairs: Dr THOMAS ZWIEFELHOFER (VU).

Minister of Infrastructure, of the Environment and of Sport: MARLIES AMANN-MARXER (VU).

Minister of Social Affairs: Dr MAURO PEDRAZZINI (FBP).

Minister of Foreign Affairs, of Education and of Cultural Affairs: Dr AURELIA FRICK (FBP).

Alternate Ministers: GEORG WOHLWEND (FBP), ROLAND MOSER (VU), ANDREA KLEIN (VU), CARMEN ZANGHELLINI-PFEIFFER (FBP), ISABEL DONHAUSER-FRICK (FBP).

GOVERNMENT OFFICES

Regierungsgebäude: Regierungsgebäude, Peter-Kaiser-Pl. 1, Postfach 684, 9490 Vaduz; tel. 2366111; fax 2366022; e-mail office@regierung.li; internet www.regierung.li.

Legislature

LANDTAG

Landtagssekretariat des Fürstentums Liechtenstein: Peter-Kaiser-Pl. 3, Postfach 684, 9490 Vaduz; tel. 2366571; fax 2366580; e-mail info@landtag.li; internet www.landtag.li.

President: ALBERT FRICK.

Vice-President: VIOLANDA LANTER-KOLLER.

General Election, 1 and 3 February 2013

Party	Votes*	% of votes	Seats
Fortschrittliche Bürgerpartei (FBP) .	77,644	40.0	10
Vaterländische Union (VU)	65,118	33.5	8
Die Unabhängigen (DU)†.	29,739	15.3	4
Freie Liste (FL) . . .	21,604	11.1	3
Total	194,105	100.00	25

* Each elector was permitted to vote for as many candidates as there were seats allocated to the respective electoral district (15 in Oberland and 10 in Unterland). The total number of valid ballots cast was 14,471.

† A group of Independent candidates.

Election Commissions

Hauptwahl- oder Hauptabstimmungskommission Oberland: c/o Postfach 684, 9490 Vaduz; independent; Chair. MARTIN NÄGELE.

Hauptwahl- oder Hauptabstimmungskommission Unterland: c/o Postfach 684, 9490 Vaduz; independent; Chair. JÖRG BIEDERMANN.

Political Organizations

Fortschrittliche Bürgerpartei (FBP) (Progressive Citizens' Party): Aeulestr. 56, Postfach 1213, 9490 Vaduz; tel. 2377940; fax 2377949; e-mail anita.frick@fbp.li; internet www.fbp.li; f. 1918; Pres. THOMAS BANZER.

Freie Liste (FL) (Free List): Landstr. 140, 9494 Schaan; tel. 2311731; fax 2311733; e-mail info@freieliste.li; internet www .freieliste.li; f. 1985; social democratic and ecological party; Co-Pres DERYA KESCI, PEPO FRICK.

Die Unabhängigen (DU) (The Independents): Feldkircherstr. 50, POB 154, 9494 Schaan; tel. 2300880; e-mail info@du4.li; internet www.du4.li; f. 2013; group of ind. mems of Landtag; Leader HARRY QUADERER.

Vaterländische Union (VU) (Patriotic Union): Fürst-Franz-Josef-Str. 13, 9490 Vaduz; tel. 2398282; fax 2398289; e-mail vu@vu-online .li; internet www.vu-online.li; f. 1936 by merger of the People's Party (f. 1918) and the Heimatdienst movement; Pres. JAKOB BÜCHEL; Sec.-Gen. JNES RAMPONE-WANGER.

Diplomatic Representation

According to an arrangement concluded in 1919, Switzerland has agreed to represent Liechtenstein's interests in countries where it has diplomatic missions and where Liechtenstein is not represented in its own right. In so doing, Switzerland always acts only on the basis of mandates of a general or specific nature, which it may either refuse or accept, while Liechtenstein is free to enter into direct relations with foreign states or to establish its own additional missions. Liechtenstein has nine diplomatic missions abroad, comprising embassies in Berlin (Germany), Bern (Switzerland), Brussels (Belgium, including a permanent mission to the European Union), Washington, DC (USA) and Vienna (Austria, including permanent missions to the Organization for Security and Co-operation in Europe and the UN), as well as a non-resident ambassador to the Holy See, a permanent representative to the Council of Europe in Strasbourg (France), a permanent mission to the UN in New York (USA) and a permanent mission in Geneva (Switzerland).

Judicial System

The Constitution of Liechtenstein provides for an independent judiciary. Jurisdiction in civil and criminal matters is exercised in the first instance by the Landgericht (County Court), on appeal by the Obergericht (Superior Court) and in the third and last instance by the Oberster Gerichtshof (Supreme Court). Cases involving major crime are heard at the Kriminalgericht (Criminal Court). Public law cases are heard by the Staatsgerichtshof (State Court) and the Verwaltungsgerichtshof (Administrative Court of Appeal).

CIVIL AND CRIMINAL COURTS

Landgericht (County Court): Spaniagasse 1, 9490 Vaduz; tel. 2367159; fax 2366539; internet www.gerichte.li; e-mail benedikt .marxer@lg.llv.li; Court of First Instance; 1 presiding judge, and 13 other judges; Presiding Judge Dr PAUL MEIER.

Kriminalgericht (Criminal Court): 9490 Vaduz; bench of 5 judges; Presiding Judge Lic. Iur. DIETMAR BAUR.

Schöffengericht (Court of Assizes): 9490 Vaduz; for minor misdemeanours; bench of 3 judges; Presiding Judge Dr THOMAS SCHMID.

Jugendgericht (Juvenile Court): 9490 Vaduz; bench of 3 judges; Presiding Judge Lic. Iur. THOMAS SCHMID.

Obergericht (Superior Court): 9490 Vaduz; tel. 2366502; fax 2367182; e-mail rudolf.fehr@lg.llv.li; internet www.gerichte.li; Court of Second Instance; divided into 3 senates, each with bench of 5 judges; Presiding Judge Lic. Iur. RUDOLF FEHR.

Oberster Gerichtshof (Supreme Court): 9490 Vaduz; internet www.gerichte.li; Court of Third Instance; bench of 5 judges; Presiding Judge Dr GERT DELLE-KARTH.

ADMINISTRATIVE COURTS

Verwaltungsgerichtshof (Administrative Court of Appeal): Peter-Kaiser-Pl. 1, Postfach 804, 9490 Vaduz; tel. 2366111; e-mail info@vgh .li; internet www.vgh.li; appeal against decrees and decisions of the Government may be made to this court; 5 members; Presiding Judge Lic. Iur. ANDREAS BATLINER.

Staatsgerichtshof (State Court): Städtle 36, Postfach 729, 9490 Vaduz; tel. 2391090; fax 2391091; e-mail kontakt@stgh.li; internet www.stgh.li; 5 members; exists for the protection of fundamental rights and public law; Presiding Judge Lic. Iur. MARZELL BECK.

Religion

CHRISTIANITY

The Principality comprises a single archdiocese of the Roman Catholic Church, Vaduz, created in 1997, which is directly responsible to the Holy See. At 31 December 2006 there were an estimated 26,800 Roman Catholics (some 78.8% of the population). The few Protestants (7.3%) belong to the parish of Vaduz.

Archdiocese of Vaduz: Fürst-Franz-Josef-Str. 112, 9490 Vaduz; tel. 2332311; fax 2332324; e-mail generalvikariat@erzbistum-vaduz .li; internet www.erzbistum-vaduz.li; f. 1997; Archbishop Most Rev. WOLFGANG HAAS.

The Press

Exclusiv: Aubündt 28, 9490 Vaduz; tel. 2328080; fax 2328081; e-mail info@exclusiv.li; internet www.exclusiv.li; f. 1996; monthly; Publr ALBERT MENNEL.

Liechtensteiner Vaterland: Austr. 81, Postfach 884, 9490 Vaduz; tel. 2361616; fax 2361617; e-mail redaktion@vaterland.li; internet www.vaterland.li; f. 1913; publ. by Vaduzer Medienhaus AG; daily (Mon.–Sat.); organ of the VU; Editor-in-Chief GÜNTHER FRITZ; circ. 10,295.

Liechtensteiner Volksblatt: Im alten Riet 103, 9494 Schaan; tel. 2375151; fax 2375155; e-mail redaktion@volksblatt.li; internet www .volksblatt.li; f. 1878; daily (Mon.–Sat.); organ of the FBP; Editor-in-Chief HEINZ ZÖCHBAUER; circ. 9,000.

Liewo Sonntagszeitung: Austr. 81, 9490 Vaduz; tel. 2361616; fax 2361617; e-mail redaktion@liewo.li; internet www.liewo.li; f. 1993 as *Liechtensteiner Wochenzeitung*; publ. by Vaduzer Medienhaus AG; weekly (Sun.); Editor-in-Chief MICHAEL WINKLER; circ. 32,000.

Wirtschaft Regional: Austr. 81, 9490 Vaduz; tel. 2361616; fax 2361617; e-mail redaktion@wirtschaftregional.li; internet www .wirtschaftregional.li; f. 2001; weekly; publ. by Vaduzer Medienhaus AG; Editor-in-Chief PATRICK STAHL.

Publishers

Alpenland Verlag AG: Feldkircher Str. 13, 9494 Schaan; tel. 2395030; fax 2395031; e-mail office@alpenland-verlag.li; internet www.alpenlandverlag.li; Dir MAX MEINHERZ.

BONAFIDES Verlags-Anstalt: Auring 52, 9490 Vaduz; tel. 2654680; fax 3900594; e-mail bva-fl@adon.li.

van Eck Verlag: Haldenweg 8, 9495 Triesen; tel. 3923000; fax 3922277; e-mail info@vaneckverlag.li; internet www.vaneckverlag .li; f. 1982; art, local interest, juvenile, golf, crime fiction; Man. Dirs FRANK P. VAN ECK, PETER GÖPPEL.

GMG Verlag AG: Landstr. 30, 9494 Schaan; tel. 2381166; fax 2381160; e-mail verlag@gmg.biz; internet www.gmg.biz; f. 1990; Man. Dir ARTHUR GASSNER.

Verlag der Liechtensteinischen Akademischen Gesellschaft (LAG): In der Fina 26, Postfach 829, 9494 Schaan; tel. 2323028; fax 2331449; e-mail info@verlag-lag.li; internet www.verlag-lag.li; f. 1972; Dir NORBERT JANSEN.

Liechtenstein-Verlag AG: Landstr. 30, 9494 Schaan; tel. 2396010; fax 2396019; e-mail books@liechtensteinverlag.com; internet www .liechtensteinverlag.com; f. 1946; belles-lettres, legal and scientific books; agents for international literature; Man. ARTHUR GASSNER.

Sändig Reprint Verlag Wohlwend: Am Schrägen Weg 12, 9490 Vaduz; tel. 2323627; fax 2323649; e-mail saendig@adon.li; internet www.saendig.com; f. 1981; natural sciences, linguistics, freemasonry, fiction, folklore, music, history; Dir CHRISTIAN WOHLWEND.

Topos Verlag AG: Industriestr. 26, 9491 Ruggell; tel. 3771111; fax 3771119; e-mail topos@supra.net; internet www.topos.li; f. 1977; law, politics, literature, social science, periodicals; Dir GRAHAM A. P. SMITH.

Broadcasting and Communications

REGULATORY AUTHORITY

Amt für Kommunikation: Gerberweg 5, Postfach 684, 9490 Vaduz; tel. 2366488; fax 2366489; e-mail info@ak.llv.li; internet www.ak.llv .li; f. 1999; national regulatory authority; Dir KURT BÜHLER.

TELECOMMUNICATIONS

FL1: Postfach 45, Industriestr. 31, 9486 Schaanwald; tel. 7970000, fax 7979009; internet www.fl1.li; f. 2000 as Mobilkom Liechtenstein AG; part of Telecom Liechtenstein since 2014; mobile cellular telephone operator.

Orange Liechtenstein AG: Neugrüt 7, 9496 Balzers; f. 2000; mobile cellular telecommunications services; CEO KASIMIR SCHMID.

Telecom Liechtenstein AG: Schaanerstr. 1, 9490 Vaduz; tel. 2377400; fax 2377499; e-mail telecom@telecom.li; internet www .telecom.li; f. 1999; fixed-line and mobile cellular telecommunications, broadband internet access, digital television; Pres. MARKUS WILLI; CEO MATHIAS MAIERHOFER.

BROADCASTING

Radio Liechtenstein: Dorfstr. 24, 9495 Triesen; tel. 3991313; fax 3991366; e-mail telecom@telecom.li; internet www.radio.li; f. 1995; Pres. MICHAEL BIEDERMAN; Editor-in-Chief MARTIN FROMMELT.

Finance

(cap. = capital; res = reserves; dep. = deposits; m. = million; brs = branches; amounts in Swiss francs)

REGULATORY AUTHORITY

Finanzmarktaufsicht Liechtenstein (FMA) (Financial Market Authority of Liechtenstein): Landstr. 109, Postfach 279, 9490 Vaduz; tel. 2367373; fax 2367374; e-mail info@fma-li.li; internet www.fma-li .li; f. 2005; independent authority under the auspices of the Landtag; supervises and executes legislation related to financial markets; Pres. URS PHILIPP ROTH-CUONY; CEO MARIO GASSNER.

BANKING

At the end of February 2015 there were 16 banks in Liechtenstein.

Bank Alpinum AG: Städtle 17, 9490 Vaduz; tel. 2396211; fax 2396221; e-mail info@bankalpinum.com; internet www .bankalpinum.com; fmrly NewCenturyBank, present name adopted 2006; Chair. WOLFGANG SEEGER; CEO URBAN B. EBERLE.

Bank Frick & Co. AG: Landstr. 14, Postfach 43, 9496 Balzers; tel. 3882121; fax 3882122; e-mail bank@bfc.li; internet www.bfc.li; Chair. MARIO FRICK, Sr; CEO EDI WÖGERER.

Bank Vontobel (Liechtenstein) AG: Pflugstr. 20, Postfach 786, 9490 Vaduz; tel. 2364111; fax 2364112; e-mail postmaster@vontobel .li; internet www.vontobel.li; f. 2000; Chair. Dr URS WIDMER; CEO HERBERT J. SCHEIDT.

Banque Pasche (Liechtenstein) SA: Austr. 61, Postfach 832, 9490 Vaduz; tel. 2393333; fax 2393300; e-mail pasche.liechtenstein@ pasche.li; internet www.pasche.li; fmrly Swissfirst Bank (Liechtenstein) AG; 52.5% owned by Banque Pasche CM-CIC Private Banking (Switzerland); Chair. JEAN-FRANÇOIS KURZ; CEO DANIEL BRÜHWILER.

Centrum Bank AG: Kirchstr. 3, Postfach 1168, 9490 Vaduz; tel. 2383838; fax 2383839; e-mail info@centrumbank.com; internet www .centrumbank.com; f. 1993; subsidiary of Verwaltungs- und Privat-Bank AG since Jan. 2015; cap. 20m., res 10m., dep. 1,878.1m. (Dec. 2012); Chair. Dr PETER MARXER; CEO STEPHAN HÄBERLE.

EFG Bank von Ernst AG: Egertastr. 10, Postfach 112, 9490 Vaduz; tel. 2655353; fax 2655363; e-mail info@bve.li; internet www.bve.li; wholly owned by EFG Bank (Switzerland); present name adopted 2009; cap. 25m., res 2.6m., dep. 189.3m. (Dec. 2012); Chair. JEAN-PIERRE CUONI; CEO ERNST WEDER.

Kaiser Partner Privatbank AG: Herrengasse 23, 9490 Vaduz; tel. 2378000; fax 2378001; e-mail bank@kaiserpartner.com; internet www.kaiserritterpartner.com; f. 1999; present name adopted 2011; cap. 10m., res 39.3m., dep. 338.2m. (Dec. 2012); Exec. Chair. FRITZ KAISER; CEO Dr THOMAS TRAUTH.

LGT Bank Ltd (LGT): Herrengasse 12, Postfach 85, 9490 Vaduz; tel. 2351122; fax 2351522; e-mail info@lgt.com; internet www.lgt .com; f. 1920; present name adopted 1996; cap. 291.2m., res 2,189m., dep. 19,338.9m. (Dec. 2012); Group CEO HSH Prince MAXIMILIAN.

Liechtensteinische Landesbank AG (State Bank): Städtle 44, Postfach 384, 9490 Vaduz; tel. 2368811; fax 2368822; e-mail llb@llb .li; internet www.llb.li; f. 1861; present name adopted 1955; cap. 154m., res –205m., dep. 17,090.1m. (Dec. 2012); Chair., Bd of Dirs Dr HANS-WERNER GASSNER; Chair., Management Bd Dr JOSEF FEHR; 4 brs.

Neue Bank AG: Marktgass 20, Postfach 1533, 9490 Vaduz; tel. 2360808; fax 2329260; e-mail info@neuebankag.li; internet www .neuebankag.li; f. 1992; cap. 40m., res 78.5m., dep. 1,157.7m. (Dec. 2012); Chair. GEORG VOGT.

Raiffeisen Privatbank Liechtenstein AG: Austr. 51, Postfach 1621, 9490 Vaduz; tel. 2370707; fax 2370777; e-mail info@raiffeisen .li; internet www.raiffeisen.li; f. 1998; present name adopted 2011; cap. 20m., res 2.4m., dep. 337.9m (Dec. 2012); Chair. GÜNTHER DAPUNT.

Valartis Bank (Liechtenstein) AG: Schaaner Str. 27, 9487 Gamprin-Bendern; tel. 2655656; fax 2655699; e-mail info@valartis.li; internet www.valartis.li; f. 1998 as Hypo Investment Bank (Liechtenstein); cap. 20m., res 11.9m., dep. 1,036.9m (Dec. 2012); renamed 2009 following takeover by Valartis Group AG; CEO, Management Bd Dr ANDREAS INSAM.

Verwaltungs- und Privat-Bank AG (VP Bank): Aeulestr. 6, 9490 Vaduz; tel. 2356655; fax 2356500; e-mail info@vpbank.com; internet www.vpbank.com; f. 1956; cap. 59.1m., res –66.2m., dep. 1,341.6m. (Dec. 2012); Chair. FREDY VOGT; CEO ALFRED W. MOECKLI; 9 brs.

Volksbank AG: Feldkircher Str. 2, 9494 Schaan; tel. 2390404; fax 2390405; e-mail info@volksbank.li; internet www.volksbank.li; f. 1997; Man. Dir STEFAN WOLF.

Bankers' Association

Liechtensteinischer Bankenverband: Austr. 46, Postfach 254, 9490 Vaduz; tel. 2301323; fax 2301324; e-mail info@bankenverband .li; internet www.bankenverband.li; f. 1969; Pres. ADOLF E. REAL; Dir SIMON TRIBELHORN; 14 mems.

INSURANCE

In February 2015 there were 42 insurance companies in Liechtenstein.

Fortuna Lebens-Versicherungs-AG: Städtle 35, 9490 Vaduz; tel. 2361545; fax 2361546; e-mail fl.service@fortuna.li; internet www .fortuna.li; f. 1996.

Liechtensteinische AHV-IV-FAK: Gerberweg 2, Postfach 84, 9490 Vaduz; tel. 2381616; fax 2381600; e-mail ahv@ahv.li; internet www.ahv.li; state-owned; Chair. PETER WOLFF; Dir WALTER KAUFMANN.

Swiss Life (Liechtenstein) AG: In der Specki 3, 9494 Schaan; tel. 3777000; fax 3777099; e-mail slpp@swisslife.com; internet www .swisslife.li; absorbed CapitalLeben Versicherung AG in 2007; life insurance.

Valorlife Lebensversicherungs-AG: Heiligkreuz 43, 9490 Vaduz; tel. 3992950; fax 3992959; e-mail info@valorlife.com; internet www .valorlife.com; f. 1997; subsidiary of Vaudoise Assurances (Switzerland); Pres. ROLF MEHR; Dir SERGE HEDIGER.

Insurance Association

Liechtensteinischer Versicherungsverband eV (LVV): Austr. 46, Postfach 445, 9490 Vaduz; tel. 2374777; fax 2374778; e-mail office@lvv.li; internet www.lvv.li; f. 1998; Pres. CAROLINE VOIGT-JELENIK; 33 mems.

Trade and Industry

CHAMBER OF COMMERCE

Liechtensteinische Industrie- und Handelskammer (Liechtenstein Chamber of Commerce and Industry): Altenbach 8, 9490 Vaduz; tel. 2375511; fax 2375512; e-mail info@lihk.li; internet www.lihk.li; f. 1947 as Liechtensteinische Industriekammer; renamed as present in 1980; Pres. KLAUS RISCH; Gen. Man. JOSEF BECK; 40 mems.

INDUSTRIAL ASSOCIATION

Vereinigung Bäuerlicher Organisationen im Fürstentum Liechtenstein (VBO) (Agricultural Union): Wegacker 5, Postfach 351, 9493 Mauren; tel. 3759069; fax 3759051; e-mail info@vbo.li; internet www.vbo.li; Pres. MARCUS VOGT.

UTILITIES

Electricity

Liechtenstein imported some 90% of its electricity in 2013, mainly from Switzerland.

Liechtensteinische Kraftwerke (LKW): Im alten Riet 17, 9494 Schaan; tel. 2360111; fax 2360112; e-mail lkw@lkw.li; internet www.lkw.li; f. 1923; Pres. PATRIK OEHRI; CEO GERALD MARXER.

Gas

Liechtensteinische Gasversorgung (LGV): Im Rietacker 4, 9494 Schaan; tel. 2361555; fax 2361566; e-mail lgv@lgv.li; internet www.lgv.li; f. 1985; Chair. Dr PATRICK KRANZ; Dir DIETMAR SARTOR.

Water

Gruppenwasserversorgung Liechtensteiner Oberland (GWO): supplies water to Balzers, Planken, Schaan, Triesen, Triesenberg and Vaduz.

Wasserversorgung Liechtensteiner Unterland e.G. (WLU): Industriestr. 36, 9487 Gamprin-Bendern; tel. 3732555; fax 3735136; e-mail info@wlu.li; internet www.wlu.li; supplies water to Eschen, Gamprin, Mauren, Ruggell, and Schellenberg; Pres. FREDDY KAISER.

TRADE UNIONS

Liechtensteinischer ArbeitnehmerInnenverband (LANV) (Employees' Asscn): Dorfstr. 24, 9495 Triesen; tel. 3993838; fax 3993839; e-mail info@lanv.li; internet www.lanv.li; Pres. SIGI LANGENBAHN; Sec. CHRISTINE SCHÄDLER; 1,200 mems.

Liechtensteinische Ingenieur- und Architektenvereinigung (Engineers' and Architects' Asscn): Postfach 323, 9490 Vaduz; tel. 3751728; fax 3751729; e-mail office@lia.li; internet www.lia.li; f. 1967; Pres. JON RITTER; 176 mems.

Wirtschaftskammer Liechtenstein: Zollstr. 23, 9494 Schaan; tel. 2377788; fax 2377789; e-mail info@wirtschaftskammer.li; internet www.wirtschaftskammer.li; f. 1936; aims to protect the interests of Liechtenstein artisans and tradespeople; Pres. MATT ARNOLD; Gen. Man. JÜRGEN NIGG; 3,000 mems.

Transport

RAILWAYS

Liechtenstein is traversed by some 18.5 km of railway track, which is administered by Austrian Federal Railways. There is a station at Nendeln, as well as two halts at Schaan and Schaanwald. A local 9.5-km service connects Feldkirch in Austria and Buchs in Switzerland via Liechtenstein, and the Arlberg Express (Paris, France, to Vienna, Austria) passes through the Principality.

ROADS

Modern roads connect the capital, Vaduz, with all the towns and villages in the Principality. There are approximately 120 km of state roads and more than 260 km of local community roads, all of which are paved. The Rhine and Samina valleys are connected by a tunnel 740 m long. Public transport is provided by a well-developed network of postal buses.

LIEmobil (Verkehrsbetrieb LIECHTENSTEINmobil): Postpl. 7, Postfach 459, 9494 Schaan; tel. 2379494; fax 2366311; e-mail info@liemobil.li; internet www.liemobil.li; operates 39 buses on 15 routes over 105 km; Man. Dir ULRICH FEISST.

INLAND WATERWAYS

A canal of 26 km, irrigating the Rhine valley, was opened in 1943.

Tourism

Liechtenstein has an Alpine setting in the Upper Rhine area. The principal tourist attractions include a renowned postal museum, a National Museum and the Liechtenstein State Art Collection at Vaduz, as well as the Prince's castle (although this is closed to the public) and two ruined medieval fortresses at Schellenberg. Annually, about two-fifths of foreign tourists visit the winter sports resort at Malbun, in the south-east of the Principality. For summer visitors there are some 400 km of hiking trails and an extensive network of cycling paths. In 2013 the number of foreign guests staying in accommodation establishments was 60,764.

Liechtenstein Tourismus: Postfach 139, Städtle 39, 9490 Vaduz; tel. 2396363; fax 2396301; e-mail info@liechtenstein.li; internet www.tourismus.li.

Defence

Although Liechtensteiners under the age of 60 years are liable to military service in an emergency, there has been no standing army since 1868 and there is only a small police force, with some 80 officers.

Education

Pre-primary education starts at the age of four and continues until the age of six. It is not compulsory and is provided free of charge. Compulsory education begins at six years of age. Basic instruction is given for five years at a primary school (Primarschule) until the age of 11, after which a pupil may transfer to a lower secondary school (Oberschule) or secondary school (Realschule) for four years, with the option of an additional year, or to the grammar school (Liechtensteinisches Gymnasium) for eight years. In 2011/12 enrolment at pre-primary level included 70% of children in the relevant age group, while enrolment at primary level included 92% of the children in the relevant age group. There is limited provision for tertiary education in Liechtenstein: a state-run university, the Universität Liechtenstein, which offers degrees in architecture and business sciences; the Private Universität im Fürstentum Liechtenstein (Private University of the Principality of Liechtenstein), which runs postgraduate-level courses in sciences and jurisprudence; the private Liechtenstein-Institut, a research and academic teaching centre; and the private International Academy of Philosophy. There is also the publicly funded Liechtensteinische Musikschule (Liechtenstein Music School), which offers courses at higher education level. Many Liechtensteiners continue their studies at universities in Austria and Switzerland. Liechtenstein also has an art school, an adult education centre and a school for children with severe learning difficulties. Government expenditure on education totalled 164m. Swiss francs in 2013.

LITHUANIA

Introductory Survey

LOCATION, CLIMATE, LANGUAGE, RELIGION, FLAG, CAPITAL

The Republic of Lithuania is situated on the eastern coast of the Baltic Sea, in north-eastern Europe. It is bounded by Latvia to the north, by Belarus to the south-east, by Poland to the south-west and by the Russian exclave, Kaliningrad Oblast, to the west. Lithuania's maritime position moderates an otherwise continental-type climate. Temperatures range from an average of −4.9°C (23.2°F) in January to a July mean of 17.0°C (62.6°F). Rainfall levels vary considerably from region to region: in the far west the annual average is 700 mm–850 mm (28 ins–33 ins), but in the central plain it is about 600 mm (24 ins). The official language is Lithuanian. The predominant religion is Christianity. Most ethnic Lithuanians are Latin-rite Catholics, but there are small communities of Lutherans and Calvinists and other Protestants. Adherents of Russian Orthodoxy are almost exclusively ethnic Slavs, while most Tatars have retained an adherence to Islam. The national flag (proportions 3 by 5) consists of three equal horizontal stripes of yellow (top), green and red (bottom). The capital is Vilnius.

CONTEMPORARY POLITICAL HISTORY

Historical Context

Prior to annexation by the Russian Empire in 1795, Lithuania was united in a Commonwealth with Poland. In 1915, after the outbreak of the First World War, it was occupied by German troops. A 'Lithuanian Conference' was convened in September 1917, which elected a 'Lithuanian Council', headed by Antanas Smetona; it proceeded to declare independence on 16 February 1918. The new state survived a Soviet attempt to create a Lithuanian-Belarusian Soviet republic. Soviet Russia recognized Lithuanian independence in the Treaty of Moscow, signed in July 1920. In October Poland annexed the region of Vilnius, but was forced to recognize the rest of Lithuania as an independent state, with its provisional capital at Kaunas. Lithuania's first Constitution, which declared Lithuania a parliamentary democracy, was adopted in August 1922. In December 1926 Smetona seized power in a military coup, establishing an authoritarian regime that endured until 1940.

According to the 'Secret Protocols' to the Treaty of Non-Aggression (the Molotov-Ribbentrop Pact), signed on 23 August 1939 by the USSR and Germany, Lithuania was to be part of the German sphere of influence. However, the Nazi-Soviet Treaty on Friendship and Existing Borders, agreed in September (following the outbreak of the Second World War), permitted the USSR to take control of Lithuania. In October Lithuania was compelled to agree to the stationing of 20,000 Soviet troops on its territory. In return, the USSR granted the city and region of Vilnius (which Soviet troops had seized in September) to Lithuania. In June 1940 the USSR dispatched a further 100,000 troops to Lithuania and forced the Lithuanian Government to resign. A Soviet-approved People's Government was formed. Elections to a People's Seim (parliament), which only pro-Soviet candidates were permitted to contest, took place in July. The parliament proclaimed the Lithuanian Soviet Socialist Republic on 21 July, and on 3 August it formally became a Union Republic of the USSR. The establishment of Soviet rule was followed by the arrest and imprisonment of many Lithuanian politicians and officials.

Following the Nazi occupation of Lithuania (1941–44), the return of the Soviet Army, in 1944, was not welcomed by most Lithuanians, and anti-Soviet partisan warfare continued until 1952. Some 150,000 people were deported, many to Kazakhstan or to Russian Siberia and the Far East, and leaders and members of the Catholic Church were persecuted and imprisoned. Political parties were disbanded, and political power became the exclusive preserve of the Lietuvos Komunistų Partija (LKP—Communist Party of Lithuania), the local branch of the Kommunisticheskaya Partiya Sovetskogo Soyuza (KPSS—Communist Party of the Soviet Union).

A significant dissident movement was established from the 1960s. With the introduction of the policy of glasnost (openness) by the Soviet leader, Mikhail Gorbachev, in the mid-1980s, a limited discussion of previously censored aspects of Lithuanian history appeared in the press. In February 1988 security forces were deployed to prevent the public celebration of the 70th anniversary of Lithuanian independence. This, together with frustration at the slow pace of reform, led to the establishment in June of the Lithuanian Movement for Reconstruction (Sąjūdis). Sąjūdis organized mass demonstrations to protest against the suppression of national culture and 'russification', and to condemn the signing of the Molotov-Ribbentrop Pact. In accordance with the demands of Sąjūdis, the Lithuanian Supreme Soviet (Supreme Council—legislature) in November recognized Lithuanian as the state language, and traditional Lithuanian state symbols were restored.

Sąjūdis won 36 of the 42 popularly elected Lithuanian seats at elections to the all-Union Congress of People's Deputies in March 1989. On 18 May the LKP-dominated Supreme Soviet approved a declaration of Lithuanian sovereignty, asserting the supremacy of Lithuania's laws over all-Union legislation. Public debate concerning the legitimacy of Soviet rule in Lithuania intensified, and a commission of the Lithuanian Supreme Soviet declared the establishment of Soviet power in 1940 to have been unconstitutional. Despite denunciations of Baltic nationalism by the all-Union authorities, the Lithuanian Supreme Soviet continued to adopt reformist legislation, including the establishment of freedom of religion and the legalization of a multi-party system. In December 1989 the LKP declared itself independent of the KPSS, adopting a new programme and declaring support for multi-party democracy and independent statehood. Meanwhile, Algirdas Brazauskas, the First Secretary of the LKP, was elected Chairman of the Presidium of the Lithuanian Supreme Soviet, defeating three other candidates, including Romualdas Ozolas of Sąjūdis. None the less, Sąjūdis remained the dominant political force in the republic, and its supporters won an overall majority in the elections to the Lithuanian Supreme Soviet in February–March 1990. This new, pro-independence parliament elected Vytautas Landsbergis, the Chairman of Sąjūdis, to replace Brazauskas as its Chairman (de facto President of Lithuania), and on 11 March declared the restoration of Lithuanian independence: Lithuania thus became the first of the Soviet republics to make such a declaration. Kazimiera Danutė Prunskienė, a member of the LKP and hitherto a Deputy Chairman of the Council of Ministers, was appointed Prime Minister.

Domestic Political Affairs

A special session of the all-Union Congress of People's Deputies condemned the Lithuanian declarations as unconstitutional, and Soviet forces occupied LKP buildings in Vilnius. An economic embargo was imposed on Lithuania in April 1990, and remained in force for more than two months, until Lithuania agreed to a six-month moratorium on the independence declaration. However, the Soviet Government soon terminated formal negotiations, which began in August, and in January 1991 Landsbergis revoked the suspension of the declaration of independence. Subsequently, the Soviet authorities dispatched troops to Vilnius, who occupied former KPSS properties that had been nationalized by the Lithuanian Government. Landsbergis mobilized popular support to help to defend the parliament building. In mid-January 13 people were killed and about 500 injured when Soviet troops seized the broadcasting centre in Vilnius. (In August 1999 six former officers of the KPSS-affiliated LKP faction were convicted of complicity in attempts to overthrow the Lithuanian Government in January 1991, and sentenced to between three and 12 years' imprisonment.)

Meanwhile, earlier in January 1991 Prunskienė and her Council of Ministers had resigned after the Supreme Council refused to sanction proposed price increases. Gediminas Vagnorius, a member of the Supreme Council, was appointed Prime Minister. At a referendum on 9 February 90.5% of voters expressed support for the re-establishment of an independent Lithuania and for the withdrawal of the Soviet army from the republic. In common with five other Soviet republics, Lithuania refused to conduct the all-Union referendum on the future of the USSR, which was held in March.

A series of attacks by OMON forces on members of the nascent Lithuanian defence force and on the customs posts on the border with Belarus, combined with the seizure of power in Moscow, the Russian and Soviet capital, by the conservative communist 'State Committee for the State of Emergency' in August 1991, led to fears that there would be a renewed attempt to reimpose Soviet rule in Lithuania. Soviet military vehicles entered Vilnius, and an emergency session of the Supreme Council condemned the putschists and issued a statement supporting the Russian President, Boris Yeltsin. As the coup collapsed, the Lithuanian Government ordered the withdrawal of Soviet forces from the republic and banned the KPSS-affiliated LKP. The Government also began to assume control of the country's borders. The failed coup prompted the recognition of Lithuanian independence by other states, and on 6 September the USSR State Council recognized the independence of Lithuania along with that of Estonia and Latvia. All three countries were admitted to the UN and the Conference on (now Organization for) Security and Co-operation in Europe (OSCE, see p. 385) later in the month.

During the first half of 1992 there was an increasing polarity within the Supreme Council between Sąjūdis deputies and those of the mainly left-wing opposition parties, most prominently the official successor party to the LKP, the Lietuvos Demokratinė Darbo Partija (LDDP—Lithuanian Democratic Labour Party), led by Brazauskas. In April 10 members of the Council of Ministers criticized Vagnorius's 'dictatorial' methods, and two ministers subsequently resigned. Vagnorius tendered his resignation as Prime Minister in May, but remained in the post until July, when the legislature approved a motion of no confidence in his leadership. The Seimas (Parliament—as the Supreme Council had been renamed) appointed Aleksandras Abišala, a close associate of Landsbergis, as Prime Minister; a new Council of Ministers was named shortly afterwards.

In July 1992 the Parliament approved a new electoral law, whereby the legislative elections, scheduled for late 1992, would be held under a mixed system of majority voting (for 71 seats) and proportional representation on the basis of party lists (70 seats). The LDDP emerged as the leading party in the elections to the Parliament, held on 25 October and 15 November, winning 73 of the 141 seats, while an alliance of Sąjūdis and the Citizens' Charter of Lithuania secured only 30 seats. The Lietuvos Krikščionių Demokratų Partija (LKDP—Christian Democratic Party of Lithuania), which was closely aligned with Sąjūdis, won 16 seats. A referendum held concurrently with the first round of the elections approved a new Constitution, which was adopted by the Parliament on 6 November. Pending an election to the new post of President of the Republic, Brazauskas was elected by the Parliament to be its Chairman and acting Head of State. In December Brazauskas appointed Bronislovas Lubys Prime Minister. Lubys formed a new coalition Council of Ministers, including only three representatives of the LDDP.

The presidential election on 14 February 1993 was won by Brazauskas, who won some 60% of the votes cast, defeating his only rival, Stasys Lozoraitis, Lithuania's ambassador to the USA. Brazauskas subsequently resigned from the LDDP. Adolfas Šleževičius succeeded Lubys as Prime Minister in March, and was appointed Chairman of the LDDP in April. In May a new political organization, the conservative Tėvynės Sąjunga (TS—Homeland Union), was formed. Mainly comprising former members of Sąjūdis, and chaired by Landsbergis, the TS rapidly became the principal opposition party.

In December 1995 the operations of Lithuania's two largest commercial banks were suspended on grounds of insolvency. In January 1996 it was revealed that Šleževičius had withdrawn funds from one of these banks, the Lithuanian Joint Stock Innovation Bank (LJIB), only two days before the bank's suspension. Later in the month Romasis Vaitekūnas, who had also withdrawn funds from the LJIB, resigned as Minister of the Interior. Kazys Ratkevičius, the Chairman of the central bank, also resigned. A presidential decree that Šleževičius should leave office was upheld by the Parliament in February, and he was replaced as Prime Minister by Laurynas Mindaugas Stankevičius. Šleževičius also resigned as Chairman of the LDDP, and was succeeded by Česlovas Juršėnas, the Chairman of the Parliament.

A general election took place on 20 October and 10 November 1996. The results confirmed the substantial loss of popular support for the LDDP, which obtained only 12 seats in the Parliament. The TS obtained 70 seats, and the LKDP 16. The right-wing Lietuvos Centro Sąjunga (LCS—Centre Union of Lithuania) won 13 seats and the Lietuvos Socialdemokratų Partija (LSDP—Lithuanian Social Democratic Party) 12. Some 53% of eligible voters participated in the first round, and about 40% in the second. In late November Landsbergis was elected Chairman of the Parliament, and the Parliament approved the appointment of Vagnorius as Prime Minister. Vagnorius's coalition Government was dominated by members of the TS, with three representatives of the LKDP and two of the LCS.

Valdas Adamkus elected as President

The first round of voting in the presidential election held on 21 December 1997 was inconclusive. In a second round on 4 January 1998, Valdas Adamkus (a former environmental protection executive who had been naturalized in the USA) narrowly defeated Artūras Paulauskas (the deputy Prosecutor-General, supported by Lietuvos Liberalų Sąjunga—LLS—the Lithuanian Liberal Union), with 50.4% of the votes. In April Paulauskas announced the formation of a new, centre-left political party, Naujoji sąjunga—Socialliberalai (NS, the New Union—Social Liberals).

Dissent between the President and Prime Minister intensified in April 1999, following Adamkus's criticism of the Government's efforts to combat corruption in the public sector, and at the end of the month Vagnorius announced that he would resign. In May Adamkus invited the Mayor of Vilnius, Rolandas Paksas (of the TS), to form a new government. The new Council of Ministers again comprised representatives of a coalition led by the TS and the LKDP. In October the Council of Ministers endorsed an agreement to sell a stake in the state-owned Mažeikiai Nafta petroleum refinery to a US oil company, despite opposition from Paksas. The decision prompted the resignations of the Ministers of National Economy and of Finance, and, in late October, of Paksas.

At the end of October 1999 Adamkus nominated Andrius Kubilius, the First Deputy Chairman of the Parliament, as Prime Minister. The new Council of Ministers was largely unchanged from the previous administration. After the leader of the LCS, Ozolas, resigned as a Deputy Chairman of the Parliament, the party went into opposition. Having resigned from the TS in the previous month, Paksas was elected Chairman of the LLS in December. Local elections in March 2000 resulted in considerable successes for parties of the left, most notably the NS. A decline in support for the TS was followed by a split in the party, including within the Parliament, thus depriving the TS-LKDP coalition of a majority in the legislature. In May the LSDP and the LDDP, together with two smaller parties, agreed to contest forthcoming legislative elections in alliance, as the A. Brazausko Socialdemokratinė Koalicija (SDK—A. Brazauskas Social Democratic Coalition), after the former President, who had been elected Honorary Chairman.

Some 56.2% of eligible voters participated in legislative elections held on 8 October 2000, at which the TS won only nine seats. Although the SDK obtained the largest representation, with 51 seats, the LLS and the NS (with 34 and 29 seats, respectively) signed a coalition agreement, forming a parliamentary majority with partners including the LCS. The new Council of Ministers, headed by Paksas, was approved in October; Paulauskas was elected Chairman of the Parliament. The LDDP merged with the LSDP in January 2001; the LSDP thereby became the largest single party in the Parliament, and Brazauskas was elected its Chairman.

In June 2001 the six NS members of the Council of Ministers resigned their portfolios, following disagreements with the LLS over privatization and economic reform. Paksas, being unable to form a new coalition, resigned on 20 June. After the NS sought a new alliance with the LSDP, President Adamkus offered the post of Prime Minister to Brazauskas, who was confirmed on 3 July. The LSDP agreed to an informal accord, which granted the NS the same six ministerial positions from which it had withdrawn in June. In September Paksas resigned as Chairman of the LLS, in compliance with intra-party demands; he was replaced by Gentvilas. In December Paksas and 10 other deputies left the parliamentary faction of the LLS, owing, in part, to its failure to nominate Paksas as First Deputy Chairman of the Parliament; they were formally expelled from the party in January 2002, and founded the rightist Liberalų Demokratų Partij (LDP—Liberal Democratic Party) in March, with Paksas as its Chairman.

The results of the first round of voting in the presidential election, held on 22 December 2002, were inconclusive. In a second round, on 5 January 2003, Paksas obtained 54.7% of the votes cast, defeating Adamkus. Paksas was inaugurated as President on 26 February. In March Brazauskas was reappointed as Prime Minister; his Council of Ministers was substantially unchanged. Following the presidential election, Paksas resigned as Chairman of the LDP; Valentinas Mazuronis was elected as his successor. In May Kubilius was elected as Chairman of the TS, in succession to Landsbergis. In the same month the LCS, the LLS and the MKD merged to form the Liberalų Centro Sąjunga (LCS—Liberal and Centre Union), with Artūras Zuokas as Chairman.

The impeachment of President Paksas

In October 2003 a classified report was disclosed, which claimed to provide evidence of links between the presidential adviser on national security, Remigijus Acas, and Yurii Borisov, an ethnic Russian with alleged connections with organized crime groups, who had contributed significant funds to Paksas's presidential election campaign. It was revealed that Paksas had signed a presidential decree permitting Borisov to hold dual citizenship. In December the Parliament approved the conclusion of a special parliamentary commission that the President's conduct had jeopardized national security. On 18 December a parliamentary resolution to initiate impeachment proceedings against Paksas was adopted, and an investigative commission was subsequently established to consider the charges.

On 18 February 2004 the investigative commission endorsed six charges, which were to form the basis for the impeachment of the President: that Paksas represented a threat to national security; that he had failed to protect classified information; that he had attempted illegally to influence the operations of private companies; that he was unable to reconcile his public and private interests; that he had hindered the operations of state institutions; and that he had failed to prevent his advisers from abusing their positions. On the following day the Parliament voted to initiate formal impeachment proceedings and agreed to seek a ruling from the Constitutional Court as to whether the charges constituted a breach of the Constitution. On 31 March the Constitutional Court ruled that the President had severely violated the Constitution by: granting Borisov dual citizenship in exchange for financial support; failing to protect state secrets; and using his presidential office illegally to influence the actions of a company's shareholders. A parliamentary vote on Paksas's impeachment took place on 6 April. Paksas was removed from office, after the necessary three-fifths' majority in the Parliament supported his impeachment. Paulauskas immediately assumed the presidency, in an acting capacity, pending a presidential election, and subsequently suspended his membership of the NS, in compliance with the Constitution. In May the Constitutional Court ruled that legislation recently approved by the Parliament, preventing an impeached head of state from seeking presidential office again, was in accordance with the Constitution, and Paksas was obliged to withdraw his candidacy from the forthcoming presidential election.

The first round of the presidential election, held on 13 June 2004, proved inconclusive. In the second round, held on 27 June, Adamkus was narrowly elected to the presidency, receiving 52.6% of the votes cast, defeating Prunskienė. Meanwhile, Lithuania's first elections to the European Parliament, following the accession of the country to full membership of the European Union (EU, see p. 271) on 1 May, were held concurrently with the first round of presidential voting, with the participation of 46% of the electorate. The recently founded Darbo Partija (DP—Labour Party), headed by a controversial, ethnically Russian business executive, Viktor Uspaskikh, won five of the 13 mandates allocated to Lithuania; the governing LSDP, the LCS and the TS each obtained two seats, while the LDP and the Valstiečių ir Naujosios Demokratijos Partijų Sąjungos (VNDS—Peasants' and New Democracy Union), led by Prunskienė, each won one seat. Adamkus was inaugurated on 12 July, and on the following day the Parliament approved his nomination of Brazauskas as Prime Minister.

Elections to the Parliament, held in two rounds on 10 and 24 October 2004, demonstrated that the DP had further consolidated its support. It became the largest single party in the Parliament, receiving 28.4% of the votes cast on the basis of party lists, and obtaining 39 of the 141 elective seats. A coalition of the LSDP and the NS received 20.7% of the votes cast on the basis of party lists, and 31 seats. The TS obtained 25 seats, and the LCS 18. An LDP-led coalition received 11 seats, while the VNDS obtained 10.

The Parliament approved a coalition Government of the DP, the LSDP, the NS and the VNDS in December 2004. Brazauskas remained Prime Minister, while several prominent members of the LSDP and the NS retained the posts they had held in the outgoing administration. In April 2005 Algirdas Butkevičius resigned as Minister of Finance, after the governing coalition rejected a proposed tax reform programme. He was replaced by Zigmantas Balčytis, hitherto the Minister of Transport, in May. In December the Supreme Court ruled that Paksas was not guilty of divulging confidential state information, while Borisov was granted permission to remain resident in Lithuania.

In April 2006 Paulauskas, the Chairman of the NS, was removed as parliamentary speaker, following a secret ballot in the Parliament, amid accusations that he had been aware of a scandal involving the unauthorized use of official vehicles by government employees. The NS immediately withdrew from the governing coalition. The remaining coalition partners signed a new agreement, and Viktoras Muntianas of the DP was subsequently elected as the new Chairman of the Parliament. At the end of April Paulauskas was re-elected as Chairman of the NS, which in early May declared itself to be in opposition to the Government.

The Government of Gediminas Kirkilas

In May 2006 seven DP deputies renounced their party membership and defected to the newly reconstituted Civil Democracy Party (PDP, formerly the Citizens' Union), citing dissatisfaction with the DP leadership, and in particular Uspaskikh. The ruling coalition's number of seats in the 141-member Parliament was thereby reduced to just 62. Uspaskikh, the subject of ongoing corruption allegations, tendered his resignation as Chairman of the DP later in May. At the end of May the DP withdrew from the ruling coalition, effectively forcing the resignation of the Prime Minister and of the Council of Ministers. Minister of Finance Balčytis was appointed premier in an acting capacity, but in July the Parliament approved the nomination of Gediminas Kirkilas, Vice-Chairman of the LSDP, as Prime Minister. The new Council of Ministers comprised six members of the LSDP, three members of the Lietuvos Valstiečių Liaudininkų Sąjunga (LVLS—Lithuanian Peasant Nationalists' Union, formerly the VNDS), and two members each of the PDP and of the LCS. Balčytis retained the finance portfolio, while Petras Vaitiekūnas of the LVLS was appointed Minister of Foreign Affairs. Kęstutis Dauksys was elected Chairman of the DP in August. Uspaskikh, meanwhile, fled to Russia, where he was detained in September, after a European arrest warrant was issued by the Lithuanian Office of the Prosecutor-General; he was subsequently released without charge.

The rate of participation at the municipal elections held on 25 February 2007 failed to exceed 40% of the electorate. The TS was placed first, with 17.1% of the votes cast, while the LSDP came a close second, with 16.3%; the DP ranked sixth, with 6.4% of the ballot. Uspaskikh and Paksas won seats in Kedainiai and Vilnius, respectively. In March Balčytis resigned as Minister of Finance after his son was acquitted of corrupt practices in his position in a state agency responsible for the distribution of EU funds (although the trial had revealed administrative misconduct on his part); Balčytis was replaced by Rimantas Šadžius, also of the LSDP. In May Prime Minister Kirkilas was elected Chairman of the LSDP, following the resignation of Brazauskas. Uspaskikh returned to Lithuania from Russia in September, and was subsequently placed under house arrest. Having been re-elected Chairman of the DP in November, Uspaskikh was released on bail in April 2008.

In January 2008 an agreement was signed on the expansion of the ruling coalition to include the NS, thereby giving it a majority in the Parliament, with 73 seats. Later that month NS Chairman Paulauskas joined the Government as Minister of the Environment. Česlovas Juršėnas of the LSDP was elected Chairman of the Parliament at the beginning of April, following the resignation of Muntianas in response to media allegations of corruption. Also in April the Minister of Education and Science, Roma Žakaitienė, resigned, following a series of strikes by teachers; she was replaced by Algirdas Monkevičius of the NS. The TS merged with the LKDP in May, to form the Tėvynės Sąjunga-Lietuvos Krikščionys Demokratai (TS-LKD—Homeland Union-Lithuanian Christian Democrats). Also in that month a new political organization, the Tautos Prisikėlimo Partija (TPP—National Revival Party), was established by television presenter Arūnas Valinskas.

The TS-LKD became the largest party in the Parliament following legislative elections, held in two rounds on 12 and

26 October 2008, winning a total of 45 of the 141 seats. In second place, with a total of 25 seats, was the LSDP (which received 11.7% of the votes cast on the basis of party lists), followed by the TPP, with 16 seats, and the Partijos Tvarka ir Teisingumas (TT—Order and Justice Party), with 15. The Lietuvos Respublikos Liberalų Sąjūdis (LRLS—Liberal Movement of the Republic of Lithuania, which had been formed by a splinter group of the LCS in 2006) secured 11 seats, while a DP-led coalition took 10, and the LCS itself won eight. In late October President Adamkus invited the Chairman of the TS-LKD, Andrius Kubilius, to form a government. The poor performance of the parties in the outgoing administration was attributed, in part, to an economic downturn. The rate of participation by the electorate was 48.6% in the first round, and only 32.4% in the second. Uspaskikh was elected to Parliament, but in December the legislature voted to remove his immunity from prosecution, as well as that of two other deputies who were standing trial at the time of their election. Arūnas Valinskas, the leader of the TPP, was elected as Chairman of the Parliament in mid-November.

In late November 2008 the Parliament approved the nomination of Kubilius as Prime Minister, to head a four-party coalition Government controlling 80 seats in the Parliament. The new Council of Ministers, which took office in December, comprised six members of the TS-LKD, three members of the LRLS, two members each of the LCS and of the TPP, and one independent. The TS-LKD assumed responsibility for the economy, finance and national defence portfolios, while Vygaudas Ušackas, hitherto ambassador to the United Kingdom, was appointed Minister of Foreign Affairs. The new Government's introduction of austerity measures in January 2009, in response to the country's economic difficulties, aroused public discontent, and a protest organized that month by trade union leaders in Vilnius was forcibly dispersed by police.

Dalia Grybauskaitė elected as President

Dalia Grybauskaitė, hitherto European Commissioner responsible for Financial Programming and the Budget, was elected as President of Lithuania in a first round of voting on 17 May 2009, receiving 69.1% of the valid votes cast. Her nearest rival among the six other candidates was Algirdas Butkevičius, with 11.8%, who had succeeded Kirkilas as Chairman of the LSDP. A rate of electoral participation of 51.7% was recorded. She took office on 12 July. In the same month Ingrida Simonytė was appointed as Minister of Finance, succeeding Algirdas Gediminas Semeta, who had become Lithuania's representative at the European Commission.

Meanwhile, elections to the European Parliament were conducted on 7 June 2009, with the participation of only 21.0% of the electorate. Of the 12 seats allocated to Lithuania, the TS-LKD won four, the LSDP three and the TT two, while the DP (which had previously held five seats), the Akcja Wyborcza Polaków na Litwie (AWPL—Electoral Action of Poles in Lithuania) and the LRLS each obtained one seat. (Notably, Paksas became a TT member of the European Parliament.)

The Parliament voted to dismiss Valinskas as its Chairman in September 2009 in response to allegations that he had links to an organized crime group. Irena Degutienė, of the TS-LKD, was elected as his successor. The Minister of Foreign Affairs, Vygaudas Ušackas, resigned in January 2010, shortly after the Parliament approved the findings of a parliamentary investigation that had confirmed the existence in Lithuania of two secret detention centres operated by the US Central Intelligence Agency (CIA) in 2002–06. Audronius Ažubalis was subsequently appointed to replace Ušackas.

Administrative reform

In July 2010, as part of a wider programme of administrative reform, 10 governorships and their corresponding county divisions were abolished. Hitherto the highest level of local governance, county-level powers were redistributed to municipal bodies. On 27 February 2011 municipal elections took place, in which the electorate was able to vote for coalitions of independent candidates, as well as for political parties, for the first time.

Meanwhile, in January 2011 the ECHR returned a verdict stating that the decision by the Constitutional Court to impose a 'permanent and irreversible' ban on the appointment of former President Paksas to a position that required an oath of office was in contravention of the principals of the Convention for the Protection of Human Rights and Fundamental Freedoms. Although the ECHR emphasized that it had not assessed the validity of Paksas's 2004 impeachment, Paksas immediately sought to use the ruling as proof that it had been

unconstitutional. (Nevertheless, in September 2012 the Constitutional Court prohibited Paksas from contesting the forthcoming elections.) In March 2011 Dainius Kreivys resigned from his position as Minister of the Economy, owing to claims that he had transferred EU funds to a company that was partly owned by his mother; he was replaced by Rimantas Žylius. In July the NS was merged with the DP. In March 2012 the Minister of the Interior, Raimundas Pailitis, left his post, after his decision to dismiss the directors of the Financial Crime Investigation Service prompted a crisis within the governing coalition. He was replaced by Artūras Melianas in April.

The 2012 legislative elections

Elections to the Parliament were conducted on 14 and 28 October 2012. The parties of the ruling coalition led by the TS-LKD received a total of 36 seats, registering a significant loss in support, while the LSDP's representation increased to 34 seats and that of the DP to 30 seats; the LRLS took 11 seats, the TT 10 and the AWPL nine. An anti-corruption party, Drąsos Kelias (The Way of Courage), won seven seats. One representative of the Lietuvos Valstiečių ir žaliųjų Sąjunga (Lithuanian Peasants' and Greens' Union—formerly the LVLS) was elected, as were two independent deputies. The election results were widely considered to reflect popular discontent with the austerity measures imposed by the Government. At a referendum held concurrently with the first round of the legislative elections, 64.8% of those participating rejected the Government's proposal that a new nuclear power station be constructed at Ignalina to replace a plant closed at the end of 2009 (see *Foreign Affairs*), thereby reversing the result of a referendum conducted in October 2008. A proposal by LSDP Chairman Butkevičius that his party form a ruling coalition with the DP was initially refused by President Grybauskaitė, on the grounds that Uspaskikh and other members of the DP remained under official investigation for tax evasion. On 19 November, however, Grybauskaitė conceded that only the LSDP was able to form a government coalition with a parliamentary majority. Butkevičius was formally appointed Prime Minister on 7 December, and his new Government, comprising members of the LSDP, the DP (these having been selected by the President as technocrats), the TT and the AWPL, secured the approval of the Parliament on 12 December.

In June 2013 Evaldas Gustas of the LSDP was appointed as Minister of the Economy. In July Uspaskikh was sentenced to four years' imprisonment by Vilnius Regional Court, after being convicted in connection with fraudulent DP financial accounts, together with the incumbent DP leader, Vytautas Gapšys (who received a fine), and other senior party officials; Uspaskikh subsequently lodged an appeal against his sentence, and in early October the Chairman of the Parliament, Loreta Graužinienė, succeeded Gapšys as leader of the DP. In November a secret service report stating that Russia planned to disseminate information against Grybauskaitė in an attempt to discredit her was leaked to the media, exacerbating tensions between the coalition government parties, particularly Butkevičius's LSDP, and the President, who issued denials that the presidential office was responsible for the disclosure.

Recent developments: the 2014 presidential election

In December 2013 the LSDP presented Zigmantas Balčytis, a member of the European Parliament, as the party's candidate for the presidential election scheduled to take place in May 2014 (contrary to expectations that Butkevičius would be selected). In April the UN Human Rights Committee, ruling on a further appeal by former President Paksas, stated that the 2004 ban imposed by the Constitutional Court that prevented him from seeking presidential office be annulled, on the grounds that it violated his human rights. Seven presidential candidates secured registration; they included Grybauskaitė, Balčytis and Paulauskas, now of the DP. According to the results of the first round of voting, conducted on 11 May, Grybauskaitė was placed first, with 46.6% of the votes cast. She proceeded to a second round of voting on 25 May, with Balčytis, who had obtained 13.8% in the first round. In the second round of voting Grybauskaitė obtained 59.1% of the votes cast, thereby winning a second term of office. In concurrent elections to the European Parliament on 25 May, the TS-LKD, the LSDP, the LRLS and the TT each won two seats, and the DP, the AWPL and the LVZS each secured one seat.

Grybauskaitė was inaugurated for a second presidential term on 12 July 2014. Her reappointment of Butkevičius to the office of Prime Minister was endorsed by the Parliament on 15 July. A new coalition Government headed by Butkevičius, which was largely unchanged from the previous administration, was approved by President Grybauskaitė on the following day. In August the AWPL Minister of Energy, Jaroslav Neverovič, was removed after he appointed another AWPL member as his deputy, despite objections by Butkevičius. The AWPL was henceforth excluded from the Government, and in September Rokas Masiulis, an independent, became the new Minister of Energy. The Minister of the Interior, Dailis Barakauskas, resigned in October; his resignation followed an investigation into suspected corruption relating to the ministry's public procurement contracts. Barakauskas was replaced in November by a former police commissioner, Saulius Skvernelis.

Meanwhile, further amendments to Lithuania's municipal election law were adopted in July 2014, under which mayors were to be directly elected, rather than, as previously, appointed by political parties. Municipal polls, including the country's first direct mayoral elections, duly took place on 1 March 2015, with a second round on 15 March. The LSDP secured 16 of a total of 60 mayoral posts, while the TS-LKD obtained 11 and the LRLS nine. Remigijus Šimašius of the LRLS was elected Mayor of Vilnius, with 62.7% of the votes cast in the second round, subsequently pledging to improve transparency in the municipality. The LSDP also won an increased number of municipal council seats, securing 359, the TS-LKD taking 253, and the LRLS being third placed, with 217 seats. Meanwhile, in February, in response to heightened security concerns, in particular with regard to relations with Russia (see *Foreign Affairs*), President Grybauskaitė announced plans for the reintroduction of military conscription (suspended since 2008); the proposal secured legislative approval in March. In mid-April the Lithuanian Radio and Television Commission banned broadcasts by the Russian-language TV channel RTR Planeta for a period of three months, owing to claims that the channel's coverage of the situation in Ukraine was inciting conflict.

Minority Ethnic Groups and Citizenship Concerns

Whereas Lithuania's Baltic neighbours, Estonia and Latvia, have large national minorities, ethnic Lithuanians constitute much of the republic's population: in the 2011 census, ethnic Lithuanians represented some 84.1% of the total population, while the two largest minority groups, Poles and Russians, represented 6.6% and 5.8%, respectively. Under citizenship laws adopted in late 1989, all residents of the Republic were eligible to apply for naturalization; by early 1993 more than 90% of the country's non-ethnic Lithuanian residents had been granted citizenship. In an attempt to counter emigration (in particular to the USA), in September 2002 the Parliament approved legislation permitting Lithuanian citizens to hold dual citizenship, thereby facilitating the eventual return of Lithuanian nationals to the country. However, in November 2006 the Constitutional Court ruled that several provisions of this legislation contravened the Constitution, which only allowed dual citizenship to be held in exceptional cases. In July 2008 the Parliament adopted an amended interim law on citizenship, which notably permitted dual citizenship to be held by Lithuanian citizens who had left the country during the occupations of June 1940–March 1990, as well as their children and grandchildren. On 2 December 2010 the Parliament adopted new legislation on citizenship, with amendments and supplements as provided by President Grybauskaitė. In January 2015 Prime Minister Butkevičius announced that a new ethnic minority law, originally proposed by a former party of the governing coalition, the AWPL, would be resubmitted to the Parliament; while the draft legislation was generally intended to strengthen ethnic minority rights, its adoption had previously been obstructed by continued controversy over the proposed use of minority languages in areas with significant minority populations, and of bilingual street signs.

Foreign Affairs

Agreement was reached with Russia in September 1992 on the withdrawal of the estimated 38,000 former Soviet troops remaining in Lithuania, and the final troops left, as scheduled, on 31 August 1993. In November Lithuania and Russia signed several agreements, including an accord on most-favoured nation status in bilateral trade, and another concerning the transportation, via Lithuania, of Russian military equipment and troops from the Russian exclave of Kaliningrad Oblast. In October 1997 President Brazauskas undertook the first official visit to Russia by a Baltic head of state since the disintegration of the former USSR: a state border delimitation treaty was signed, and bilateral co-operation agreements on joint economic zones,

and on the Baltic continental shelf, were also concluded. The border treaty was ratified by the Parliament in October 1999, but was not ratified by Russia until May 2003. Lithuania expressed support for an agreement between the EU and Russia in late 2002, which proposed simplified visa arrangements for Russian citizens traversing Lithuania to reach Kaliningrad. New transit arrangements were implemented in February 2003.

Relations between Lithuania and Russia were strained in June 2008, when the Parliament adopted legislation prohibiting the public display of Soviet and Nazi symbols. In late June several hundred Lithuanian websites were subject to pro-Russian attacks, their content being replaced by the Soviet flag and anti-Lithuanian propaganda. In February 2010, in the highest level bilateral meeting to take place since 2001, Grybauskaitė and Russian premier Vladimir Putin held talks in Helsinki, Finland to discuss co-operation in a number of areas, including energy. In September 2013 the Russian authorities instituted more restrictive border checks on goods lorries from Lithuania, resulting in long delays and losses for Lithuanian cargo carriers; the Russian measures were regarded as being connected with Lithuania's tenure of the rotating EU presidency (see below). In November Russia additionally suspended the import of Lithuanian dairy products. Russia's annexation of the Crimean peninsula in March 2014 (see the chapter on Ukraine) was met with strong concerns in Lithuania. In the same month Russia suspended food imports via the port of Klaipėda. On 24 April the Assembly adopted a resolution demanding the withdrawal of Russian forces (believed to be present, and operating covertly) from Ukraine, and for those troops concentrated in adjacent regions of Russia to be pulled back from the Ukrainian border, while expressing support for the introduction of EU sanctions against Russia. (Russia imposed retaliatory sanctions against EU member states in August, which banned the import of food products from EU member states.) Meanwhile, the Lithuanian and Belarusian Ministers of Defence, meeting in Minsk, Belarus, agreed to continue military bilateral co-operation. Following an increase in intimidatory tactics employed by the Russian military against the territory of the Baltic states (including an incursion by two Russian vessels into Lithuania's maritime zone in April), in September Russian officers detained a Lithuanian shipping vessel in the Barents Sea on the grounds that it had been illegally fishing, subsequently impounding it in the Russian port of Murmansk. The Russian authorities failed to comply with demands from Lithuania and the EU for the immediate release of the vessel, and in October a demand for nearly €2.3m. was issued. The vessel was finally released from Murmansk in February 2015, after a fine of €53,000 was imposed by a local court. Meanwhile, the completion of a project to construct an offshore liquefied natural gas terminal at the port of Klaipėda in October demonstrated Lithuania's diversification from energy dependence on Russia (see *Economic Affairs*).

Lithuania's relations with neighbouring Poland were largely concerned with the status of the Polish minority in Lithuania. In January 1992 Lithuania and Poland signed a 'Declaration on Friendly Relations and Neighbourly Co-operation', which guaranteed the rights of the respective minority ethnic groups and recognized the existing border between the two countries. A full treaty of friendship and co-operation was signed by the respective Heads of State in April 1994. In September 2006 President Adamkus made an official visit to the Polish capital, Warsaw, where he signed a joint declaration with President Lech Kaczyński on a plan to connect the electricity grids of Lithuania and Poland (see *Economic Affairs*); a joint company to manage the project was formed in May 2008. Amid continued conflict in eastern Ukraine, in September 2014 the ministers responsible for defence of Poland, Lithuania and Ukraine signed an agreement in Warsaw establishing a joint military force, the Lithuanian-Polish-Ukrainian Brigade, to participate in peacekeeping operations; it was envisaged that Lithuania would contribute 350 troops to the 4,500-member brigade.

Lithuania enjoys close relations with Estonia and Latvia. Relations between the three states are co-ordinated through the consultative inter-parliamentary Baltic Assembly, the Council of the Baltic Sea States (see p. 249) and the Baltic Council (see p. 459). However, in the mid-1990s Lithuania's relations with Latvia came under strain, as a result of disagreement over the demarcation of the countries' maritime border. In October 1995 the Lithuanian Government protested against Latvia's signature of a preliminary agreement with two foreign petroleum companies to explore oilfields in the disputed waters. The two countries signed an agreement on the Delimitation of the Territorial Sea, Exclusive Economic Zone and Continental Shelf in the Baltic Sea in July 1999. However, protests from the Latvian fishing industry prevented the agreement from being ratified by the Latvian parliament. In December 2000 a protocol was signed for the re-demarcation of the land border between the two countries. Estonia, Latvia and Lithuania established a common Nordic-Baltic energy market in mid-2013, under the European Commission's 2009 Baltic Energy Market Interconnection Plan; the North-Western European power market coupling project, which covered 15 countries including the three Baltic states, and was designed to create an integrated European electricity market, was formally launched in February 2014.

Lithuania pursued close co-operation with, and eventual integration into, the political, economic and defence systems of Western Europe, notably North Atlantic Treaty Organization (NATO, see p. 367) and the EU. In December 1999 a summit meeting of EU Heads of State and Government endorsed proposals to begin accession talks with a number of countries, including Lithuania; formal negotiations commenced in February 2000. As a concession to achieve EU membership, the Government approved a draft national energy strategy in September 1999, which provided for the decommissioning of the first unit of the Ignalina nuclear power plant by 2005. In June 2002 Lithuania agreed to decommission the plant's remaining unit in 2009, in return for a significant contribution from the EU towards the cost of the endeavour. The plant eventually closed in December 2010. In December 2002 Lithuania and nine other countries were formally invited to join the EU on 1 May 2004; at a national referendum, held on 10–11 May 2003, 90.0% of participants voted in favour of membership, and Lithuania duly acceded to the EU as scheduled. On 1 July 2013 Lithuania assumed the rotating Presidency of the Council of the EU for a period of six months. In early June 2014 the European Commission issued a recommendation that Lithuania be admitted to the eurozone, which was approved by the European Parliament and the Council of the European Union in the following month. Lithuania duly adopted the euro on 1 January 2015.

Meanwhile, in November 2002 Lithuania was one of seven countries invited to join NATO; Lithuania became a full member of the Alliance on 29 March 2004. In August 2013 President Grybauskaitė and her Latvian and Estonian counterparts met US President Barack Obama for discussions in Washington, DC. Following Russia's annexation of Ukraine's Crimean peninsula in March 2014 and subsequent escalating conflict in parts of eastern Ukraine (see the chapter on Ukraine), in April a US contingent of 150 troops was stationed in Lithuania to begin training of land forces. Prime Minister Butkevičius visited the USA in October, when he met US Vice-President Joe Biden for discussions on bilateral relations. In January 2015 the Lithuanian Ministry of Defence confirmed that NATO was to establish international command centres in Lithuania and five other Eastern and Central European states, as part of plans to establish an expanded rapid reaction force. Amid continued concerns at a series of Russian military exercises in the Baltic region, it was announced in March that Germany was to dispatch some 500 troops to Lithuania later that year to participate in exercises.

CONSTITUTION AND GOVERNMENT

Under the terms of the Constitution that was approved in a national referendum on 25 October 1992, supreme legislative authority resides with the Seimas (Parliament), which has 141 members, elected by universal adult suffrage for a four-year term (71 deputies are directly elected by majority vote, with 70 being elected from party lists on the basis of proportional representation). The President of the Republic (who is Head of State) is elected by direct popular vote for a period of five years (and a maximum of two consecutive terms). Executive power is vested in the Council of Ministers, headed by the Prime Minister, who is appointed by the President with the approval of the Parliament. Judicial power is exercised by the Constitutional Court, the Supreme Court, the Court of Appeal and district and local courts. Until July 2010 Lithuania was divided into 10 counties. However, in a process of administrative reform, the counties were abolished and their powers were transferred to municipal bodies.

REGIONAL AND INTERNATIONAL CO-OPERATION

Lithuania is a member of the European Bank for Reconstruction and Development (see p. 266), the Council of the Baltic Sea States (see p. 249), of the Baltic Council (see p. 459), of the Council of Europe (see p. 250), and of the Organization for Security and Co-

operation in Europe (see p. 385). In 2004 it acceded to the European Union (see p. 271).

Lithuania joined the UN in 1991, and the World Trade Organization (see p. 431) in 2001. The country is also a member of the North Atlantic Treaty Organization (see p. 367).

ECONOMIC AFFAIRS

In 2013, according to estimates by the World Bank, Lithuania's gross national income (GNI), measured at average 2011–13 prices, was US $44,060m., equivalent to $14,900 per head (or $24,500 per head on an international purchasing-power parity basis). During 2004–13 the population decreased at an average annual rate of 1.5%, while gross domestic product (GDP) per head increased, in real terms, by an average of 4.4% per year. Overall GDP increased, in real terms, by an average of 2.9% annually during 2004–13. Real GDP grew by 3.3%, according to both constant prices and chain-linking methodologies, in 2013.

Agriculture (including hunting, forestry and fishing) contributed 3.8% of GDP, according to preliminary figures, and engaged an estimated 8.4% of the employed population in 2013. The principal crops are wheat, sugar beet, barley, rapeseed and triticale. According to World Bank estimates, agricultural GDP increased, in real terms, at an average annual rate of 1.1% during 2004–10; the GDP of the sector increased by 12.0% in 2012, but decreased by 3.2% in 2013, according to chain-linking methodologies.

Industry (including mining, manufacturing, construction and power) contributed 30.7% of GDP, according to preliminary figures, and engaged an estimated 25.5% of the employed population in 2013. According to World Bank estimates, industrial GDP increased by an average of 1.0% per year during 2004–10; the GDP of the sector decreased by 21.1% in 2009, but increased by 3.3% in 2010.

Mining (including utilities contributed 3.9% of GDP in 2013, according to preliminary figures. Mining and quarrying provided an estimated 0.3% of employment in 2013. Lithuania has significant reserves of peat and materials used in construction (limestone, clay, dolomite, chalk, and sand and gravel), as well as small deposits of petroleum and natural gas. In terms of gross value added, the sector registered growth of 3.0% in 2004, according to official data.

The manufacturing sector contributed 20.2% of GDP, according to preliminary figures, and engaged an estimated 15.4% of the employed labour force in 2013. Based on the value of sales (excluding refined petroleum products), in 2008 the principal branches of manufacturing were food products (particularly dairy products), chemicals (including fertilizers), wood products (particularly furniture), and clothing. According to World Bank estimates, manufacturing GDP increased, in real terms, at an average annual rate of 1.5% during 2004–09. According to chain-linking methodologies, sectoral GDP increased by 4.7% in 2013.

The construction sector contributed 6.5% of GDP, according to preliminary figures, and engaged an estimated 7.7% of the employed labour force in 2013.

In 2011 natural gas accounted for 62.8% of gross electricity production, and hydroelectric sources accounted for 11.3%. Lithuania has substantial petroleum-refining and electricity-generating capacities, which enable it to export refined petroleum products and electricity. Lithuania had been a net exporter of electricity, although in June 2002 formal agreement was reached with the European Union (EU, see p. 271) on the closure of the Ignalina nuclear power plant. The plant's two reactors were decommissioned in 2004 and 2009, in return for substantial financial compensation from the EU. In 2013 imports of mineral fuels accounted for 30.0% of the total value of merchandise imports.

The services sector contributed 65.5% of GDP, according to preliminary figures, and provided an estimated 66.1% of total employment in 2013. The Baltic port of Klaipėda is a significant entrepôt for regional trade. According to World Bank estimates, the GDP of the services sector increased, in real terms, by an average of 2.8% per year in 2004–10; real services GDP decreased by 12.6% in 2009, but increased by 0.7% in 2010.

According to IMF estimates, in 2013 Lithuania recorded a visible merchandise trade deficit of US $1,619.8m., and there was a surplus of $675.3m. on the current account of the balance of payments. In 2013 the principal source of imports was Russia (accounting for 28.1% of the total); other major sources were Germany, Poland, Latvia and the Netherlands. Russia was also the main market for exports in that year (accounting for 19.8% of the total); other principal markets were Latvia, Poland,

Germany, Estonia and Belarus. In 2013 the principal exports were mineral products, machinery and electrical equipment, food and live animals, miscellaneous manufactured articles, chemical products, and manufactured goods. The principal imports were mineral products, machinery and electrical equipment, chemical products, manufactured goods, food and live animals, and miscellaneous manufactured articles.

According to official sources, in 2013 there was a budgetary deficit of 2,993.1m. litai (equivalent to 2.5% of GDP). Lithuania's general government gross debt was 46,948m. litai in 2013, equivalent to 39.3% of GDP. Lithuania's total external debt was US $29,988m. in 2011, of which $12,912m. was public and publicly guaranteed debt. In that year, the cost of servicing long-term public and publicly guaranteed debt and repayments to the IMF was equivalent to 20.1% of the value of exports of goods, services and income (excluding workers' remittances). According to ILO estimates, annual inflation averaged 4.1% in 2004–13. The rate of inflation was 1.0% in 2013. The average rate of unemployment was 11.8% in 2013.

In February 2002 the national currency's fixed rate of exchange was linked to the common European currency, the euro, instead of the US dollar. Lithuania was admitted to the EU's exchange rate mechanism (ERM II) in June 2004, although high rates of inflation and the maintenance of budgetary deficits slightly in excess of the level of 3% of GDP demanded by ERM II delayed Lithuania's adoption of the euro as its currency. As a result of the impact of the international financial crisis, in January 2009 the Government introduced austerity measures, including a 15% reduction in public sector salaries, pension reforms and an increase in value-added tax. In June 2011 the Government enacted legislation providing for a gradual increase, by 2026, of the pension age to 65 years. Although adherence to the austerity measures had proved successful in stabilizing the economy, popular discontent contributed to the

defeat of the Government in legislative elections in October 2012. The new ruling coalition that was established in December subsequently introduced substantial increases in the minimum wage, as well as rises in some excise taxes. Following a significant reduction in the budget deficit by the end of 2013, Lithuania satisfied EU fiscal criteria, and achieved the revised target of 1 January 2015 for admission to the eurozone. Meanwhile, a Lithuania–Poland interconnection, a 1,000-MW electricity link between the Baltic transmission system and the grid of continental Europe, was scheduled for completion by the end of 2015. In accordance with the government priority to reduce dependency on Russian energy supplies, construction of an offshore liquefied natural gas (LNG) terminal at Klaipėda was completed in October, and the facility was to be supplied by Statoil of Norway, under a five-year LNG agreement signed between state enterprise Litgas and Statoil in August. However, Lithuania's export revenue was severely affected by the regional impact of continued conflict in Ukraine during 2014 (see *Foreign Affairs*), which had resulted in the imposition of Western sanctions against Russia in March, and Russia's retaliatory introduction of a ban on the import of foodstuffs from EU states in August. In 2014 GDP growth slowed to an estimated 2.9%, and (despite the benefits to trade of eurozone membership) the growth forecast for 2015 was revised downwards, to 2.3%.

PUBLIC HOLIDAYS

2016: 1 January (New Year's Day), 16 February (National Day), 11 March (Day of the Re-establishment of Independence), 28 March (Easter Monday), 1 May (Labour Day), 24 June (St John's Day), 6 July (Anniversary of the Coronation of Grand Duke Mindaugas), 15 August (Assumption), 1 November (All Saints' Day), 25–26 December (Christmas).

Statistical Survey

Source (unless otherwise indicated): Department of Statistics of the Government of Lithuania (Statistics Lithuania), Gedimino pr. 29, Vilnius 01500; tel. (5) 236-4800; fax (5) 236-4845; e-mail statistika@stat.gov.lt; internet www.stat.gov.lt.

Area and Population

AREA, POPULATION AND DENSITY

Area (sq km)	65,300*
Population (census results)	
6 April 2001	3,483,972
1 March 2011	
Males	1,402,604
Females	1,640,825
Total	3,043,429
Population (official estimates at 1 January)	
2013	2,971,905
2014	2,944,459
2015†	2,921,920
Density (per sq km) at 1 January 2015	44.7

* 25,212 sq miles.
† Provisional figure.

POPULATION BY AGE AND SEX
(official estimates at 1 January 2014)

	Males	Females	Total
0–14 years	220,423	209,665	430,088
15–64 years	953,155	1,017,490	1,970,645
65 years and over	182,417	360,322	542,739
Total	1,355,995	1,587,477	2,943,472

POPULATION BY ETHNIC GROUP
(at 2011 census)

	Number	%
Lithuanian	2,561,314	84.1
Polish	200,317	6.6
Russian	176,913	5.8
Belarusian	36,227	1.2
Others	68,658	2.3
Total	3,043,429	100.0

Note: Classification of ethnic groups reflects national census methodology.

ADMINISTRATIVE DIVISIONS
(official estimates at 1 January 2015, provisional)

County	Area (sq km)	Population	Density (per sq km)
Alytus	5,425	147,853	27.3
Kaunas	8,089	583,058	72.1
Klaipėda	5,209	327,353	62.8
Marijampolė	4,463	151,848	34.0
Panevėžys	7,881	235,479	29.9
Šiauliai	8,540	281,770	33.0
Tauragė	4,411	103,136	23.4
Telšiai	4,350	143,583	33.0
Utena	7,201	140,233	19.5
Vilnius	9,731	807,607	83.0
Total	65,300	2,921,920	44.7

PRINCIPAL TOWNS
(official estimates at 1 January 2015, provisional)

Vilnius (capital)	.	542,664	Šiauliai	104,619
Kaunas		301,296	Panevėžys . . .	95,218
Klaipėda . . .		156,122	Alytus	55,626

BIRTHS, MARRIAGES AND DEATHS

	Registered live births		Registered marriages		Registered deaths	
	Number	Rate (per 1,000)	Number	Rate (per 1,000)	Number	Rate (per 1,000)
2007 . .	30,020	9.3	23,065	7.1	45,624	14.1
2008 . .	31,536	9.9	24,063	7.5	43,832	13.7
2009 . .	32,165	10.2	20,542	6.5	42,032	13.3
2010 . .	30,676	9.9	18,688	6.0	42,120	13.6
2011 . .	30,268	10.0	19,221	6.3	41,037	13.6
2012 . .	30,459	10.2	20,660	6.9	40,938	13.7
2013 . .	30,858	10.4	20,469	6.9	41,511	14.0
2014* . .	31,276	10.6	22,089	7.5	40,210	13.7

* Provisional figures.

Life expectancy (years at birth): 73.9 (males 68.4; females 79.6) in 2012 (Source: World Bank, World Development Indicators database).

IMMIGRATION AND EMIGRATION

	2012	2013	2014*
Immigrants	19,843	22,011	25,853
Emigrants	41,100	38,818	38,471

* Provisional figures.

ECONOMICALLY ACTIVE POPULATION
(annual averages, '000 persons, official estimates)

	2011	2012	2013
Agriculture, hunting, forestry and fishing	106.4	112.2	108.9
Mining and quarrying	2.7	2.4	3.7
Manufacturing	194.9	200.3	199.5
Electricity, gas and water . . .	25.0	27.7	27.5
Construction	85.1	89.6	99.3
Wholesale and retail trade; repair of motor vehicles, motorcycles and personal and household goods	222.5	223.3	227.5
Hotels and restaurants . . .	32.3	32.3	33.4
Transport, storage and communications	117.0	121.9	119.1
Financial intermediation . . .	17.8	18.2	17.7
Real estate, renting and business activities	100.0	102.1	109.5
Public administration and defence; compulsory social security . .	75.6	73.1	79.7
Education	136.2	134.4	125.9
Health and social work . . .	87.4	85.5	84.8
Other community, social and personal service activities . .	48.2	49.9	53.8
Private households with employed persons	1.9	2.6	2.2
Extraterritorial organizations and bodies	0.6	0.3	0.3
Total	1,253.6	1,275.7	1,292.8
Unemployed	28.0	196.8	172.5
Total labour force	1,481.6	1,472.5	1,465.3
Males	735.5	728.2	731.7
Females	746.1	744.3	733.6

Note: Totals may not be equal to the sum of components, owing to rounding.

Health and Welfare

KEY INDICATORS

Total fertility rate (children per woman, 2012) . . .	1.5
Under-5 mortality rate (per 1,000 live births, 2012) . . .	5
HIV/AIDS (% of persons aged 15–49, 2011)	0.1
Physicians (per 1,000 head, 2012)	4.1
Hospital beds (per 1,000 head, 2009)	6.8
Health expenditure (2011): US $ per head (PPP)	1,352
Health expenditure (2011): % of GDP	6.7
Health expenditure (2011): public (% of total)	71.4
Total carbon dioxide emissions ('000 metric tons, 2010) . .	13,560.6
Carbon dioxide emissions per head (metric tons, 2010) . .	4.1
Human Development Index (2013): ranking	35
Human Development Index (2013): value	0.834

For sources and definitions, see explanatory note on p. vi.

Agriculture

PRINCIPAL CROPS
('000 metric tons)

	2011	2012	2013
Wheat	1,869.0	2,998.9	2,862.3
Barley	759.8	741.9	681.8
Rye	85.0	156.6	95.8
Oats	128.5	130.0	162.9
Triticale (wheat-rye hybrid) . .	237.0	434.8	451.1
Potatoes	587.7	572.4	420.3
Sugar beet	877.8	994.5	967.1
Peas, dry	47.5	48.4	54.1
Rapeseed	484.3	632.9	548.7
Cabbages and other brassicas . .	112.9	111.0	78.0
Onions, dry	24.2	27.7	27.2
Carrots and turnips	70.5	67.8	58.7
Apples	49.1	72.5	62.4

Aggregate production ('000 metric tons, may include official, semi-official or estimated data): Total cereals 3,225.6 in 2011, 4,621.9 in 2012, 4,459.3 in 2013; Total roots and tubers 587.7 in 2011, 572.4 in 2012, 420.3 in 2013; Total vegetables (incl. melons) 354.5 in 2011, 340.3 in 2012, 307.8 in 2013; Total fruits (excl. melons) 61.9 in 2011, 87.5 in 2012, 75.9 in 2013.

Source: FAO.

LIVESTOCK
('000 head at 1 January)

	2011	2012	2013
Horses	45	36	30
Cattle	748	752	729
Pigs	929	790	808
Sheep	59	60	83
Goats	16	15	14
Chickens	9,203	8,667	8,820
Turkeys	206	208	206

Source: FAO.

LIVESTOCK PRODUCTS
('000 metric tons)

	2011	2012	2013
Cattle meat	42.0	40.9	37.7
Pig meat	74.9	79.4	87.0
Chicken meat	74.7	79.3	87.5
Cows' milk	1,782.3	1,774.5	1,719.5
Hen eggs	43.8	43.5	42.9
Honey	1.8	1.8	1.8

Source: FAO.

Forestry

ROUNDWOOD REMOVALS
('000 cubic metres, excl. bark)

	2011	2012	2013
Sawlogs, veneer logs and logs for sleepers	3,618	3,396	3,421
Pulpwood	1,728	1,325	1,201
Fuel wood	1,658	2,200	2,431
Total	7,004	6,921	7,053

Source: FAO.

SAWNWOOD PRODUCTION
('000 cubic metres, incl. railway sleepers)

	2011	2012	2013
Coniferous (softwood)	813	710	633
Broadleaved (hardwood)	447	440	487
Total	1,260	1,150	1,120

Source: FAO.

Fishing

(metric tons, live weight)

	2010	2011	2012
Capture	149,851	138,557	66,948
Largehead hairtail	149	401	n.a.
Atlantic redfishes	3,833	2,929	1,498
Jack and horse mackerels	50,850	28,028	22
Sardinellas	16,611	1,177	2,015
European sprat	10,223	9,730	11,245
Chub mackerel	14,137	13,281	5,515
Northern prawn	830	749	475
Aquaculture	3,191*	3,280	3,582
Total catch	153,042*	141,837	70,530

* FAO estimate.
Source: FAO.

Mining

('000 metric tons, unless otherwise indicated)

	2011	2012	2013
Crude petroleum	108	101	86
Dolomite ('000 cubic metres)	1,147	943	1,158
Limestone	1,155	1,329	1,376
Clay ('000 cubic metres)	250	238	240
Peat	362	371	493

Industry

SELECTED PRODUCTS
('000 metric tons, unless otherwise indicated)

	2011	2012	2013
Sausages and smoked meat products	64.4	67.3	72.4
Flour	334.2	341.9	365.5
Refined sugar	134.6	140.8	165.4
Beer ('000 hectolitres)	305.1	284.1	288.6
Wine (hectolitres)	6,123	6,479	5,743
Cotton fabrics (million sq m)	0.2	0.4	0.3
Woollen fabrics (million sq m)	2.3	2.3	2.3
Fabrics of man-made fibres	23.2	15.3	n.a.
Footwear—excl. rubber and plastic ('000 pairs)*	900	900	1,200
Plywood ('000 cubic metres)	56.4	44.0	37.0
Particle board ('000 cubic metres)	647.8	664.4	686.5
Paper and paperboard	144.2	123.5	119.8
Sulphuric acid	766	731	753
Cement*	1,000	1,000	1,000
Cast iron	3.0	3.3	2.9
Television sets ('000)	376.9	209.1	130.0
Refrigerators and freezers ('000)	164.5	196.3	238.9
Bicycles ('000)	327	297	294
Electric energy (million kWh)	3,790	n.a.	n.a.

* Figures are rounded.

Finance

CURRENCY AND EXCHANGE RATES

Monetary Units
100 cents = 1 euro (€).

Sterling and Dollar Equivalents (31 December 2014)
£1 sterling = 1.286 euros;
US $1 = 0.824 euros;
€10 = £7.78 = $12.14.

Average Exchange Rate (euros per US $)
2012   0.7783
2013   0.7532
2014   0.7537

Note: On 1 January 2015 the euro was introduced to Lithuania, replacing the litas (following a transitional two week period during which both currencies circulated concurrently) as the sole legal currency, at a fixed exchange rate of €1 = 3.45280 litai. The majority of financial data given in this survey predate the adoption of the euro, and continue to be presented in terms of litas.

GOVERNMENT FINANCE
(general government transactions, million litai)

Revenue	2011	2012	2013
Taxes	17,162.6	18,319.4	19,296.5
Product and service taxes	12,181.9	12,492.6	13,000.9
Income and profit taxes	4,646.0	5,499.1	5,961.2
Other taxes	334.7	327.7	334.4
Social contributions	12,018.6	12,508.9	13,143.5
Non-tax revenue	2,547.5	2,939.5	3,266.7
Property income	463.8	598.2	357.3
Revenue for the goods and services	1,419.2	1,677.8	1,983.2
Other income	664.5	663.5	926.2
Grants	3,432.8	3,158.2	3,034.1
Total	35,161.5	36,926.0	38,740.8

Expenditure	2011	2012	2013
Compensation of employees . .	10,609.5	10,736.7	11,026.6
Products and services	5,433.9	5,570.7	5,570.2
Consumption of fixed capital . .	3,015.7	3,272.5	3,483.9
Interest	2,040.0	2,400.5	2,285.8
Subsidies	423.2	361.9	303.6
Social benefits	15,542.3	15,677.8	15,621.7
Other current expenditure . .	5,717.2	1,081.1	2,344.3
Capital transfers	790.2	663.1	1,097.8
Total	43,572.0	39,764.3	41,733.9

Source: Ministry of Finance, Vilnius.

INTERNATIONAL RESERVES
(US $ million at 31 December)

	2011	2012	2013
Gold (national valuation) . . .	294.45	311.21	224.71
IMF special drawing rights . .	210.81	211.03	211.45
Reserve position in IMF . . .	0.05	0.05	0.05
Foreign exchange	7,704.51	8,007.09	7,635.78
Total	8,209.82	8,529.38	8,071.99

Source: IMF, *International Financial Statistics*.

MONEY SUPPLY
(million litai at 31 December)

	2011	2012	2013
Currency outside depository corporations	9,681	10,329	10,942
Transferable deposits . . .	21,604	25,567	28,840
Other deposits	18,707	17,506	16,424
Securities other than shares . .	477	491	303
Broad money	50,469	53,893	56,509

Source: IMF, *International Financial Statistics*.

COST OF LIVING
(Consumer Price Index; base: 2000 = 100)

	2011	2012	2013
Food (incl. non-alcoholic beverages)	157.8	162.6	165.4
All items (incl. others) . . .	139.9	144.2	145.7

Source: ILO.

NATIONAL ACCOUNTS
(million litai at current prices)

National Income and Product

	2011	2012	2013*
Compensation of employees . .	42,456.0	44,808.8	47,289.3
Operating surplus and mixed income	40,072.3	43,725.8	45,644.4
Domestic primary incomes .	82,528.3	88,534.6	92,933.7
Consumption of fixed capital . .	14,333.1	15,217.1	16,042.8
Gross domestic product (GDP) at factor cost	96,861.3	103,751.7	108,976.6
Taxes on production and imports .	12,567.5	12,901.9	13,460.2
Less Subsidies	1,538.2	1,627.1	1,742.1
GDP in market prices . . .	107,890.6	115,026.5	120,694.7
Primary incomes received from abroad	3,426.7	3,257.1	2,819.6
Less Primary incomes paid abroad	7,391.4	6,733.7	6,070.5
Gross national income (GNI) .	103,925.8	111,549.9	117,443.8
Less Consumption of fixed capital	14,333.0	15,217.1	16,042.8
Net national income . . .	89,592.8	96,332.8	101,401.0
Current transfers from abroad .	6,350.1	5,164.3	6,780.7
Less Current transfers paid abroad	4,456.1	4,690.0	4,334.4
Net national disposable income	91,486.8	96,807.1	103,847.3

Expenditure on the Gross Domestic Product

	2011	2012	2013*
Final consumption expenditure .	87,068.3	91,962.2	96,100.3
Households	67,230.8	71,769.7	75,521.5
Non-profit institutions serving households	250.2	270.3	281.0
General government	19,587.3	19,922.2	20,297.8
Gross capital formation . . .	23,576.4	22,073.8	23,084.7
Gross fixed capital formation .	19,890.5	19,946.6	21,958.6
Changes in inventories . . .	3,570.2	2,055.0	1,039.4
Acquisitions, less disposals, of valuables	115.7	72.2	86.7
Total domestic expenditure .	110,644.7	114,036.0	119,185.0
Exports of goods and services .	80,985.6	93,985.5	101,470.4
Less Imports of goods and services	83,739.8	92,995.0	99,960.7
GDP in market prices . . .	107,890.6	115,026.5	120,694.7

Gross Domestic Product by Economic Activity

	2011	2012	2013*
Agriculture, hunting, forestry and fishing	3,699.1	4,554.8	4,132.7
Mining and utilities	4,082.1	4,301.1	4,290.2
Manufacturing	19,805.6	21,523.6	22,124.5
Construction	6,264.9	6,167.0	7,102.8
Wholesale and retail trade, transport, hotels and restaurants	30,211.9	33,322.3	35,648.1
Information and communications .	3,023.1	3,137.0	3,347.0
Financial and insurance activities	2,596.9	2,169.6	2,367.0
Real estate	6,056.3	6,366.0	6,674.4
Professional, scientific and technical activities, administrative and support service activities	5,451.4	5,971.1	6,416.7
Public administration, defence, education, human health and social work activities . . .	14,222.1	14,661.1	15,167.5
Arts, entertainment and recreation, repair of household goods and other services . .	1,723.5	1,867.3	2,005.4
Gross value added at basic prices	97,136.9	104,041.1	109,276.2
Taxes on products	12,089.5	12,402.7	12,936.3
Less Subsidies on products . .	1,335.8	1,417.3	1,517.8
GDP in market prices . . .	107,890.6	115,026.5	120,694.7

* Preliminary figures.

BALANCE OF PAYMENTS
(US $ million)

	2011	2012	2013
Exports of goods	27,029.0	28,770.8	31,816.8
Imports of goods	−29,523.5	−30,222.2	−33,436.6
Balance on goods	−2,494.5	−1,451.4	−1,619.8
Exports of services	5,607.3	6,628.1	7,438.0
Imports of services	−3,628.8	−4,775.8	−5,306.3
Balance on goods and services	−516.0	400.9	512.0
Primary income received . . .	924.5	699.7	523.6
Primary income paid . . .	−2,525.8	−2,454.5	−2,296.5
Balance on goods, services and primary income	−2,117.4	−1,353.9	−1,261.0
Secondary income received . .	3,054.2	2,772.2	3,282.5
Secondary income paid . . .	−1,556.0	−1,517.8	−1,346.2
Current balance	−619.1	−99.6	675.3
Capital account (net)	1,052.5	935.7	1,029.2
Direct investment assets . .	−389.9	−274.9	−280.9
Direct investment liabilities . .	1,443.1	574.0	712.4
Portfolio investment assets . .	165.7	−301.7	−753.8
Portfolio investment liabilities .	1,376.2	1,522.0	−1,121.9
Financial derivatives and employee stock options (net)	5.5	6.5	−6.5
Other investment assets . . .	−681.5	124.7	−64.5
Other investment liabilities . .	−535.2	−1,993.0	−779.3
Net errors and omissions . . .	60.8	−375.6	14.3
Reserves and related items .	1,878.1	118.1	−575.6

Source: IMF, *International Financial Statistics*.

External Trade

PRINCIPAL COMMODITIES
(distribution by SITC, million litai)

Imports c.i.f.	2011	2012	2013
Food and live animals . . .	7,341.3	8,567.3	9,639.5
Vegetables and fruit	2,631.1	3,280.0	3,739.9
Crude materials, inedible, except fuels	2,719.9	2,775.4	3,019.7
Mineral fuels, lubricants and related materials	25,977.2	28,271.8	27,121.0
Petroleum, petroleum products and related materials	20,701.4	22,640.9	22,493.5
Gas, natural and manufactured .	3,811.0	4,352.2	3,630.2
Chemicals and related products . . .	10,185.5	11,203.2	11,570.8
Organic chemicals . . .	2,490.4	2,583.1	2,290.7
Manufactured goods . .	9,061.0	9,817.6	10,592.6
Machinery and transport equipment	16,823.7	17,843.2	19,886.9
General industrial machinery and equipment	2,071.8	2,400.5	3,065.5
Electrical machinery, apparatus and appliances	2,202.7	2,565.6	2,879.3
Road vehicles	6,008.0	6,171.1	6,607.9
Miscellaneous manufactured articles	4,887.1	5,201.4	6,113.8
Total (incl. others)	78,812.2	85,902.2	90,489.8

Exports f.o.b.	2011	2012	2013
Food and live animals . .	9,089.5	11,507.3	12,626.2
Vegetables and fruit	2,318.7	2,948.5	3,288.4
Crude materials, inedible, except fuels	3,105.5	3,623.6	3,745.4
Mineral fuels, lubricants and related materials . . .	17,608.3	19,454.6	19,545.9
Petroleum, petroleum products and related materials	16,765.4	18,661.5	18,868.6
Chemicals and related products	9,505.4	10,445.2	10,404.2
Fertilizers	3,355.7	3,410.5	2,764.2
Plastics and articles thereof . .	2,184.8	2,295.7	2,306.7
Manufactured goods . .	6,930.8	7,917.0	8,642.1
Machinery and transport equipment	12,436.9	14,120.1	15,158.8
General industrial machinery and equipment	2,003.9	2,652.6	3,080.0
Road vehicles	4,810.1	4,548.9	4,711.4
Miscellaneous manufactured articles	9,036.9	10,348.4	11,961.3
Furniture and parts thereof . .	3,086.3	3,755.8	4,050.8
Clothing accessories . . .	2,177.8	2,185.5	2,565.1
Miscellaneous manufactured articles	1,998.2	2,304.0	2,663.0
Total (incl. others)	69,576.8	79,577.9	84,747.6

PRINCIPAL TRADING PARTNERS
(million litai)

Imports c.i.f.	2011	2012	2013
Belarus	1,919.7	2,309.2	2,636.2
Belgium	2,496.5	2,492.6	2,971.5
China, People's Republic . . .	1,559.1	1,834.4	1,951.2
Czech Republic	1,001.4	1,225.0	1,422.8
Denmark	1,277.2	1,354.2	1,495.1
Estonia	2,216.1	2,372.9	2,542.4
Finland	1,644.1	1,617.4	1,748.3
France	1,911.5	1,995.5	2,514.5
Germany	7,864.1	8,757.5	9,502.3
Italy	2,727.1	2,788.4	3,733.0
Latvia	5,230.5	5,247.6	5,628.9
Netherlands	3,942.8	4,760.8	4,764.7
Poland	7,151.7	8,450.0	8,631.4
Russia	25,259.8	26,906	25,441.4
Spain	847.6	963.0	1,548.1
Sweden	2,598.7	2,799.4	2,919.8
United Kingdom	1,285.7	1,910.4	2,144.1
USA	917.5	844.9	1,061.9
Total (incl. others)	78,812.2	85,902.2	90,489.8

Exports f.o.b.	2011	2012	2013
Belarus	3,602.8	3,654.8	4,401.2
Belgium	800.6	908.9	1,043.7
Canada	783.0	217.3	192.7
Denmark	1,482.6	1,619.6	1,732.9
Estonia	4,620.0	6,122.3	4,737.6
Finland	931.1	936.3	1,146.5
France	2,880.5	2,492.8	1,981.9
Germany	6,472.0	6,170.6	6,080.6
Italy	1,259.3	1,384.1	1,434.2
Kazakhstan	1,094.5	1,192.6	1,522.0
Latvia	7,118.8	8,569.2	8,438.4
Netherlands	4,266.0	4,619.3	3,721.9
Norway	1,406.1	1,558.1	1,798.6
Poland	4,832.6	4,823.7	6,272.7
Russia	11,532.7	15,036.8	16,811.8
Spain	852.0	584.4	625.8
Sweden	2,494.0	2,578.1	2,780.6
Ukraine	2,305.6	2,852.1	2,924.8
United Kingdom	2,771.1	4,981.6	4,177.9
USA	1,811.4	1,196.6	2,355.7
Total (incl. others)	69,576.8	79,577.9	84,747.6

Transport

RAILWAYS
(traffic)

	2011	2012	2013
Passenger journeys ('000) . . .	4,655.2	4,802.1	4,844.1
Passenger-km (million) . . .	389.1	403.2	391.3
Freight transported ('000 metric tons)	52,329.8	49,377.2	48,028.1
Freight ton-km (million) . . .	15,088	14,171.6	13,343.7

ROAD TRAFFIC
(motor vehicles in use at 31 December)

	2011	2012	2013
Passenger cars	1,713,277	1,753,407	1,808,982
Buses and coaches	13,086	12,649	12,606
Lorries and vans	113,452	113,505	115,367
Motorcycles and mopeds . . .	60,124	64,249	68,152

INLAND WATERWAYS

	2011	2012	2013
Passenger journeys ('000) . . .	1,715.5	1,764.2	1,901.1
Passenger-km (million) . . .	3	3	3
Freight transported ('000 metric tons)	1,037.7	1,049.5	1,076.7
Freight ton-km (million) . . .	4	2	1

SHIPPING

Flag Registered Fleet
(at 31 December)

	2012	2013	2014
Number of vessels	133	132	134
Total displacement ('000 grt) . .	413.0	440.1	444.5

Source: Lloyd's List Intelligence (www.lloydslistintelligence.com).

International Seaborne Freight Traffic
('000 metric tons)

	2011	2012	2013
Goods loaded	28,023	26,564	24,909
Goods unloaded	17,504	17,198	17,476

CIVIL AVIATION
(traffic on scheduled services)

	2011	2012	2013
Passengers carried ('000) . . .	444.6	576.0	444.7
Passenger-km (million) . . .	797	1,070	918
Freight transported ('000 metric tons)	3.5	1.1	1.0
Freight ton-km (million) . . .	3.0	1.0	1.0

Tourism

FOREIGN VISITORS BY COUNTRY OF ORIGIN
(arrivals at accommodation establishments)

	2011	2012	2013
Belarus	92,248	117,037	162,158
Estonia	37,409	39,712	42,086
Finland	36,483	37,545	33,249
France	25,684	26,423	24,645
Germany	128,930	144,975	148,599
Italy	31,490	30,137	28,912
Latvia	66,145	76,431	83,223
Poland	139,632	127,033	127,330
Russia	148,267	214,337	243,599
Sweden	25,303	21,694	23,043
United Kingdom	32,857	37,752	44,167
USA	24,850	25,079	27,805
Total (incl. others)	1,003,843	1,125,338	1,234,919

Receipts from tourism (US $ million, excl. passenger transport): 1,323 in 2011; 1,317 in 2012; 1,467 in 2013 (provisional) (Source: World Tourism Organization).

Communications Media

	2010	2011	2012
Telephones ('000 main lines in use)	753.4	711.9	675.4
Mobile cellular telephones ('000 subscribers)	4,891.0	4,938.0	4,997.3
Internet subscribers ('000) . .	685.2	n.a.	n.a.
Broadband subscribers ('000) . .	590.6	620.9	640.3
Book titles (incl. brochures) . .	3,176	3,278	3,449
Newspapers: number	276	262	252
Newspapers: average circulation (million copies)	188.3	176.2	146.3
Magazines and other periodicals .	561	558	563
Magazines and other periodicals: average circulation (million copies)	59.5	61.7	55.2

2013: Telephones ('000 main lines in use) 624.8; Mobile cellular telephones ('000 subscribers) 4,566.0; Broadband subscribers ('000) 664.1.
Sources: International Telecommunication Union, and Ministry of Education and Science, Vilnius.

Education

(2013/14)

	Institutions	Teachers	Students
General schools	1,208	34,360	357,530
Vocational schools	75	3,633	45,635
Colleges	24	3,409	43,550
Universities	23	9,684	104,923

Pupil-teacher ratio (primary education, UNESCO estimate): 12.4 in 2011/12 (Source: UNESCO Institute for Statistics).

Adult literacy rate (UNESCO estimates): 99.8% (males 99.8%; females 99.8%) in 2011 (Source: UNESCO Institute for Statistics).

Directory

The Government

HEAD OF STATE

President: DALIA GRYBAUSKAITĖ (inaugurated 12 July 2009; re-elected 25 May 2014; inaugurated 12 July 2014).

COUNCIL OF MINISTERS
(May 2015)

A coalition comprising representatives of Lietuvos Socialdemokratų Partija (LSDP—the Lithuanian Social Democratic Party), Darbo Partija (DP—the Labour Party) and Partijos Tvarka ir teisingumas (TT—the Order and Justice Party).

Prime Minister: ALGIRDAS BUTKEVIČIUS (LSDP).

Minister of Agriculture: VIRGINIJA BALTRAITIENĖ (DP).

Minister of Culture: ŠARŪNAS BIRUTIS (DP).

Minister of the Economy: EVALDAS GUSTAS (LSDP).

Minister of Education and Science: DAINIUS PAVALKIS (DP).

Minister of Energy: ROKAS MASIULIS (Independent).

Minister of the Environment: KĘSTUTIS TREČIOKAS (TT).

Minister of Finance: RIMANTAS ŠADŽIUS (LSDP).

Minister of Foreign Affairs: LINAS LINKEVIČIUS (LSDP).

Minister of Health: RIMANTĖ ŠALAŠEVIČIŪTĖ (LSDP).

Minister of the Interior: SAULIUS SKVERNELIS (Independent).

Minister of Justice: JUOZAS BERNATONIS (LSDP).

Minister of National Defence: JUOZAS OLEKAS (LSDP).

Minister of Social Security and Labour: ALGIMANTA PABEDINS-KIENĖ (DP).

Minister of Transport and Communications: RIMANTAS SINKE-VIČIUS (LSDP).

MINISTRIES

Office of the President: S. Daukanto 3, Vilnius 01122; tel. (5) 266-4154; fax (5) 266-4145; e-mail kanceliarija@prezidentas.lt; internet www.president.lt.

Office of the Prime Minister: Gedimino pr. 11, Vilnius 01103; tel. (8) 706-63711; fax (8) 706-63895; e-mail mptarnyba@lrv.lt; internet www.lrv.lt.

Ministry of Agriculture: Gedimino pr. 19, Vilnius 01103; tel. (5) 239-1111; fax (5) 239-1212; e-mail zum@zum.lt; internet www.zum.lt.

Ministry of Culture: J. Basanavičiaus 5, Vilnius 01118; tel. (5) 219-3400; fax (5) 262-3120; e-mail culture@lrkm.lt; internet www.lrkm.lt.

Ministry of the Economy: Gedimino pr. 38, Vasario 16-osios g. 2, Vilnius 01104; tel. (8) 706-64762; fax (8) 706-64845; e-mail kanc@ukmin.lt; internet www.ukmin.lt.

Ministry of Education and Science: A. Volano 2/7, Vilnius 01516; tel. (5) 219-1190; fax (5) 261-2077; e-mail smmin@smm.lt; internet www.smm.lt.

Ministry of Energy: Gedimino pr. 38, Vasario 16-osios g. 2, Vilnius 01104; tel. (8) 706-64715; fax (8) 706-64820; e-mail info@enmin.lt; internet www.enmin.lt.

Ministry of the Environment: A. Jakšto 4/9, Vilnius 01105; tel. (5) 266-3661; fax (5) 266-3663; e-mail info@am.lt; internet www.am.lt.

Ministry of Finance: Lukiškių g. 2, Vilnius 01512; tel. (5) 239-0000; fax (5) 279-1481; e-mail finmin@finmin.lt; internet www.finmin.lt.

Ministry of Foreign Affairs: J. Tumo-Vaižganto g. 2, Vilnius 01511; tel. (5) 236-2444; fax (5) 231-3090; e-mail urm@urm.lt; internet www.urm.lt.

Ministry of Health: Vilniaus g. 33, Vilnius 01506; tel. (5) 268-5110; fax (5) 266-1402; e-mail ministerija@sam.lt; internet www.sam.lt.

Ministry of the Interior: Šventaragio 2, Vilnius 01510; tel. (5) 271-7130; fax (5) 271-8551; e-mail bendrasisd@vrm.lt; internet www.vrm.lt.

Ministry of Justice: Gedimino pr. 30, Vilnius 01104; tel. (5) 266-2981; fax (5) 262-5940; e-mail rastine@tm.lt; internet www.tm.lt.

Ministry of National Defence: Totorių 25/3, Vilnius 01121; tel. (5) 273-5673; fax (5) 264-8517; e-mail pilieciuaptarnavimas@kam.lt; internet www.kam.lt.

Ministry of Social Security and Labour: A. Vivulskio g. 11, Vilnius 03610; tel. (5) 266-4201; fax (5) 266-4209; e-mail post@socmin.lt; internet www.socmin.lt.

Ministry of Transport and Communications: Gedimino pr. 17, Vilnius 01505; tel. (5) 261-2363; fax (5) 212-4335; e-mail sumin@sumin.lt; internet www.sumin.lt.

President

Presidential Election, First Ballot, 11 May 2014

Candidates	Votes	%
Dalia Grybauskaitė	612,485	46.64
Zigmantas Balčytis	181,659	13.83
Artūras Paulauskas	160,139	12.19
Naglis Puteikis	124,333	9.47
Valdemar Tomaševski	109,659	8.35
Artūras Zuokas	69,677	5.31
Bronis Ropė	55,263	4.21
Total	**1,313,215**	**100.00**

Second Ballot, 25 May 2014

Candidates	Votes	%
Dalia Grybauskaitė	700,647	59.05
Zigmantas Balčytis	485,968	40.95
Total	**1,186,615**	**100.00**

Legislature

Parliament
(Seimas)

Gedimino pr. 53, Vilnius 01109; tel. (5) 239-6060; fax (5) 239-6289; e-mail priim@lrs.lt; internet www.lrs.lt.

Chairman: LORETA GRAUŽINIENĖ.

General Election, 14 and 28 October 2012

	Seats		
Parties and blocs	A*	B*	Total
Tėvynės Sąjunga-Lietuvos Krikščionys Demokratai (TS-LKD)	13	23	36
Lietuvos Socialdemokratų Partija (LSDP)	15	19	34
Darbo Partija (DP)	17	13	30
Lietuvos Respublikos liberalų sąjūdis (LRLS)	7	4	11
Partijos Tvarka ir teisingumas (TT)	6	4	10
Akcja Wyborcza Polaków na Litwie (AWPL)	5	4	9
Drąsos Kelias	7	—	7
Lietuvos Valstiečių ir žaliųjų Sąjunga (LVZS)	—	1	1
Independent candidates	—	2	2
Total†	**70**	**71**	**141**

* Of the 141 seats in the Seimas, 70 (A) are awarded according to proportional representation on the basis of party lists, and 71 (B) are elected in single-mandate constituencies.

† Including one further member who remained to be elected from a single-mandate constituency.

Election Commission

Lietuvos Republikos Vyriausioji rinkimų komisija (Central Electoral Committee of the Republic of Lithuania): Gynėjų g. 8, Vilnius 01109; tel. (5) 239-6902; fax (5) 239-6960; e-mail rinkim@vrk.lt; internet www.vrk.lt; Chair. ZENONAS VAIGAUSKAS.

Political Organizations

In March 2013 some 45 political parties were officially registered. The following were among the most significant:

Akcja Wyborcza Polaków na Litwie (AWPL) (Electoral Action of Poles in Lithuania): Pilies g. 16, Vilnius 01123; tel. (5) 233-3103; fax (5) 233-1266; e-mail info@awpl.lt; internet www.awpl.lt; f. 1994; Chair. WALDEMAR TOMASZEWSKI.

Darbo Partija (DP) (Labour Party): Ankštoji 3, Vilnius 01109; tel. (5) 210-7152; fax (5) 210-7153; e-mail info@darbopartija.lt; internet www.darbopartija.lt; f. 2003; absorbed Naujoji sąjunga—Socialliberalai (New Union—Social Liberals) in 2011; Chair. LORETA GRAUŽINIENĖ; 25,227 mems (2014).

Drąsos Kelias (The Way of Courage): Vytauto g. 57-2, Garliava; e-mail drasoskelias.partija@gmail.com; internet drasiauskelias.lt; f. 2012; populist, anti-corruption; Leader JONAS VARKALA; 1,019 mems (Sept. 2012).

Krikščionių partija (Christian Party): Odminių g. 5, Vilnius 01122; tel. and fax (5) 212-6874; e-mail info@krikscioniupartija.lt; internet www.krikscioniupartija.lt; f. 2010 by merger of Christian-Conservative Social Union and Lithuanian Christian Democratic Party; Leader GEDIMINAS VAGNORIUS.

Liberalų Centro Sąjunga (LCS) (Liberal and Centre Union): Vilniaus g. 22/1, Vilnius 01402; tel. (5) 231-3264; fax (5) 261-9363; e-mail info@lics.lt; internet www.lics.lt; f. 2003 by a merger of the Lithuanian Centre Union, Lithuanian Liberal Union and the Modern Christian Democratic Union; Chair. ALGIS ČAPLIKAS; over 5,000 mems.

Lietuvos Lenkų Liaudies Partija/Polska Partia Ludowa (Lithuanian Polish People's Party): Kauno g. 1A, Vilnius 03212; tel. (5) 216-2874; fax (5) 233-5467; e-mail lllp@zebra.lt; internet www.lllp.lt; f. 2002; Chair. ANTONINA POŁTAWIEC.

Lietuvos Respublikos Liberalų Sąjūdis (LRLS) (Liberal Movement of the Republic of Lithuania): Vašingtono aikštė 1, Vilnius 01108; tel. (5) 249-6959; fax (5) 212-1083; e-mail info@liberalai.lt; internet www.liberalai.lt; f. 2006; formed by a splinter group of the LCS; Chair. ELIGIJUS MASIULIS.

Lietuvos rusų sąjunga/Soyuz Russkikh Litvy (Lithuanian Russians' Union): A. Rotundo g. 5, Vilnius 01400; tel. and fax (5) 262-4248; e-mail srl@pochta.ru; internet sojuzrus.lt; f. 1995; Chair. SERGEI DMITRIYEV.

Lietuvos Socialdemokratų Partija (LSDP) (Lithuanian Social Democratic Party): Barboros Radvilaites g. 1, Vilnius 01124; tel. (5) 261-3907; fax (5) 261-5420; e-mail info@lsdp.lt; internet www.lsdp.lt; absorbed the Lithuanian Democratic Labour Party in 2001; Chair. ALGIRDAS BUTKEVIČIUS; 11,000 mems.

Lietuvos Valstiečių ir žaliųjų Sąjunga (LVZS) (Lithuanian Peasants' and Greens' Union): Pamėnkalnio g. 26, Vilnius 01114; tel. (5) 212-0821; fax (5) 212-0822; e-mail info@lvzs.lt; internet www.lvls.lt; f. 2001 by the merger of the New Democracy Party and the Lithuanian Peasants' (Farmers') Party; fmrly Peasants' (Farmers') and New Democratic Party Union (VNDS); name changed to Lithuanian Peasant Nationalists' Union (LVLS) in Feb. 2006; present name adopted Jan. 2012; Chair. RAMŪNAS KARBAUSKIS; 3,500 mems (2012).

Partijos Tvarka ir Teisingumas (TT) (Order and Justice Party): Gedimino pr. 10/1, Vilnius 01103; tel. and fax (5) 269-1618; e-mail tt@tvarka.lt; internet www.tvarka.lt; f. 2002; fmrly Liberalų Demokratų Partija (Liberal Democratic Party); present name adopted 2008; right-wing; Chair. ROLANDAS PAKSAS; 6,500 mems (2007).

Pilietinės Demokratijos Partija (Civil Democracy Party): Kaštonų g. 4, Vilnius 01107; tel. (5) 204-0204; fax (5) 204-0205; e-mail pdpsekretoriatas@gmail.com; internet www.pdp.lt; f. 2006; fmrly Civic Union; Chair. ALGIMANTAS MATULEVIČIUS.

Tautos prisikėlimo partija (TPP) (National Revival Party): Pranciškonų g. 4A/10, Vilnius 01133; tel. (8) 698-09686; fax (5) 240-0493; e-mail tppbustine@inbox.lt; internet www.prisikelimopartija.lt; f. 2008; Leader ARŪNO VALINSKO.

Tėvynės atgimimas ir perspektyva (TAIP) (Homeland Revival and Perspective—YES): Vašingtono aikštė 1, Vilnius 01108; tel. (5) 219-6691; e-mail info@taip.lt; internet www.taip.lt; f. 2011; centre-right; Chair. ARTŪRAS ZUOKAS.

Tėvynės Sąjunga-Lietuvos Krikščionys Demokratai (TS-LKD) (Homeland Union-Lithuanian Christian Democrats): L. Stuokos-Gucevičiaus g. 11, Vilnius 01122; tel. (5) 212-1657; fax (5) 278-4722; e-mail sekretoriatas@tsajunga.lt; internet www.tsajunga.lt; f. 1993 as the conservative Tėvynės Sąjunga (TS—Homeland Union); merged with Lietuvos Krikščionių Demokratų Partija (LKDP—Christian Democratic Party of Lithuania) in May 2008, and name changed as above; Chair. GABRIELIUS LANDSBERGIS; some 18,000 mems.

Diplomatic Representation

EMBASSIES IN LITHUANIA

Armenia: Lenktoji g. 17, Vilnius 08124; tel. (5) 207-5040; fax (5) 207-5042; e-mail armlithuaniaembassy@mfa.am; Ambassador ARA AYVAZYAN.

Austria: Gaono g. 6, Vilnius 01131; tel. (5) 266-0580; fax (5) 279-1363; internet www.bmeia.gv.at/wilna; Ambassador Dr JOHANN SPITZER.

Azerbaijan: Olimpiečių g. 5–7, Vilnius 02051; tel. (5) 219-0042; fax (5) 279-1504; e-mail info@azembassy.lt; Ambassador HASAN MAMMADZADE.

Belarus: Mindaugo g. 13, Vilnius 03225; tel. (5) 266-2200; fax (5) 266-2212; e-mail lithuania.emb@mfa.gov.by; internet lithuania.mfa.gov.by; Ambassador ALEKSANDR M. KOROL.

Belgium: Kalinausko g. 2B, Vilnius 03107; tel. (5) 266-0820; fax (5) 212-6444; e-mail vilnius@diplobel.org; internet www.diplomatie.be/vilnius; Ambassador PETER LESCOUHIER.

Bulgaria: Pylimo 8, Palangos 2, Vilnius 01118; tel. (5) 249-9274; fax (5) 261-9174; e-mail vilnius@bgembassy.lt; internet www.mfa.bg/vilnius; Ambassador MICHAELA TODOROVA.

China, People's Republic: Algirdo g. 36, Vilnius 03218; tel. (5) 216-2862; fax (5) 216-2682; e-mail chinaemb_lt@mfa.gov.cn; internet www.chinaembassy.lt; Ambassador WEI RUIXING.

Czech Republic: Birutės g. 16, Vilnius 08117; tel. (5) 266-1040; fax (5) 266-1066; e-mail vilnius@embassy.mzv.cz; internet www.mzv.cz/vilnius; Ambassador BOHUMIL MAZÁNEK.

Denmark: T. Kosciuškos g. 36, Vilnius 01100; tel. (5) 264-8760; fax (5) 231-2300; e-mail vnoamb@um.dk; internet www.litauen.um.dk; Ambassador JØRGEN MOLDE.

Estonia: A. Mickevičiaus g. 4A, Vilnius 08119; tel. (5) 278-0200; fax (5) 278-0201; e-mail sekretar@estemb.lt; internet www.estemb.lt; Ambassador TOOMAS KUKK.

Finland: Klaipėdos g. 24, Vilnius 03107; tel. (5) 266-8010; fax (5) 212-2441; e-mail sanomat.vil@formin.fi; internet www.finland.lt; Ambassador HARRI MÄKI-REINIKKA.

France: Švarco g. 1, Vilnius 01131; tel. (5) 219-9600; fax (5) 219-9613; e-mail ambafrance.vilnius@diplomatie.gouv.fr; internet www.ambafrance-lt.org; Ambassador PHILIPPE JEANTAUD.

Georgia: Poškos g. 13, Vilnius 08123; tel. (5) 273-6959; fax (5) 272-3623; e-mail embassy@georgia.w3.lt; internet www.lithuania.mfa.gov.ge; Ambassador KHATUNA SALUKVADZE.

Germany: Z. Sierakausko g. 24, Vilnius 03105; tel. (5) 210-6400; fax (5) 210-6446; e-mail info@wilna.diplo.de; internet www.wilna.diplo.de; Ambassador JUTTA SCHMITZ.

Greece: Didžioji 33/Rūdininkų 2, Vilnius 01132; tel. (5) 261-0526; fax (5) 261-0536; e-mail embassy@grembvil.w3.lta; Ambassador MICHAEL-EFSTRATIOS C. DARATZIKIS.

Holy See: Kosciuškos g. 28, Vilnius 01100; tel. (5) 212-3696; fax (5) 212-4228; e-mail nuntiusbalt@aiva.lt; Apostolic Nuncio Most Rev. PEDRO LÓPEZ QUINTANA (Titular Archbishop of Acropolis).

Hungary: Jojailos g. 4, Vilnius 01116; tel. (5) 269-0038; fax (5) 269-0039; e-mail mission.vno@mfa.gov.hu; internet www.mfa.gov.hu/emb/vilnius; Ambassador ZOLTÁN PECZE.

Ireland: Gedimino pr. 1, Vilnius 01103; tel. (5) 262-9460; fax (5) 262-9462; e-mail vilniusembassy@dfa.ie; internet www.embassyofireland.lt; f. 2005; Ambassador DAVID NOONAN.

Italy: Vytauto g. 1, Vilnius 08118; tel. (5) 212-0620; fax (5) 212-0405; e-mail ambasciata.vilnius@esteri.it; internet www.ambvilnius.esteri.it; Ambassador STEFANO TALIANI DE MARCHIO.

Japan: M. K. Čiurlionio g. 82B, Vilnius 03100; tel. (5) 231-0462; fax (5) 231-0461; e-mail info@vn.mofa.go.jp; internet www.lt.emb-japan.go.jp; Ambassador KAZUKO SHIRAISHI.

Kazakhstan: Birutės g. 20A/35, Vilnius 08117; tel. (5) 212-2123; fax (5) 231-3580; e-mail vilnius@mfa.kz; internet kazakhstan.embassy.lt; Ambassador BAURJAN MUHAMEDJANOV.

Latvia: M. K. Čiurlionio g. 76, Vilnius 03100; tel. (5) 213-1260; fax (5) 213-1130; e-mail embassy.lithuania@mfa.gov.lv; internet www.latvia.lt; Ambassador MARTINŠ VIRSIS.

Moldova: Miglos g. 61A, Vilnius 08102; tel. (5) 260-7914; fax (5) 260-7915; e-mail vilnius@mfa.md; internet www.lituania.mfa.gov.md; Ambassador IGOR KLIPII.

Netherlands: Kosciuškos g. 36, Vilnius 01100; tel. (5) 210-4620; fax (5) 210-4629; internet lithuania.nlembassy.org; Ambassador GIJSBERT HENDRIK CHRISTIAAN VAN DER LINGEN.

Norway: Kalinausko g. 24, Vilnius 03107; tel. (5) 261-0000; fax (5) 261-0100; e-mail emb.vilnius@mfa.no; internet www.norvegija.lt; Ambassador DAG MALMER HALVORSEN.

Poland: Smėlio g. 20A, Vilnius 10323; tel. (5) 270-9001; fax (5) 270-9007; e-mail wilno.amb.sekretariat@msz.gov.pl; internet wilno.msz.gov.pl; Ambassador JAROSŁAW CZUBIŃSKI.

Romania: Vivulskio g. 19, Vilnius 03115; tel. (5) 231-0557; fax (5) 231-0652; e-mail ambromania@romania.lt; internet vilnius.mae.ro; Ambassador DAN ADRIAN BĂLĂNESCU.

Russian Federation: Latvių g. 53/54, Vilnius 08113; tel. (5) 272-1763; fax (5) 272-3877; e-mail post@rusemb.lt; internet www.lithuania.mid.ru; Ambassador ALEKSANDR UDALTSOV.

Spain: Algirdo g. 4, Vilnius 03161; tel. (5) 231-3961; fax (5) 231-3962; e-mail emb.vilnius@mae.es; Ambassador EMILIO FERNÁNDEZ-CASTAÑO Y DÍAZ-CANEJA.

Sweden: Didžioji g. 16, Vilnius 01128; tel. (5) 268-5010; fax (5) 268-5030; e-mail ambassaden.vilnius@foreign.ministry.se; internet www.swedenabroad.com/vilnius; Ambassador CECILIA RUTHSTRÖM-RUIN.

Turkey: Didžioji g. 37, Vilnius 01128; tel. (5) 264-9570; fax (5) 212-3277; e-mail embassy.vilnius@mfa.gov.tr; internet vilnius.emb.mfa.gov.tr; Ambassador AYDAN YAMANCAN.

Ukraine: Teatro g. 4, Vilnius 03107; tel. (5) 212-1536; fax (5) 212-0475; e-mail emb_lt@mfa.gov.ua; internet www.mfa.gov.ua/lithuania; Ambassador VALERII ZHOVTENKO.

United Kingdom: Antakalnio g. 2, Vilnius 10308; tel. (5) 246-2900; fax (5) 246-2901; e-mail be-vilnius@britain.lt; internet ukinlithuania.fco.gov.uk; Ambassador DAVID HUNT.

USA: Akmenų g. 6, Vilnius 03106; tel. (5) 266-5300; fax (5) 266-5310; e-mail webemailvilnius@state.gov; internet vilnius.usembassy.gov; Ambassador DEBORAH A. MCCARTHY.

Judicial System

The organs of justice are the Supreme Court, the Court of Appeal, district courts, local courts of administrative areas and a special court—the Commercial Court. The Seimas (Parliament) appoints and dismisses from office the judges of the Supreme Court in response to representations made by the President of the Republic (based upon the recommendation of the chairman of the Supreme Court). Judges of the Court of Appeal are appointed by the President with the approval of the Parliament (on the recommendation of the Minister of Justice), while judges of district and local courts are appointed and dismissed by the President. The Council of Judges submits recommendations to the President of the Republic concerning the appointment of judges, as well as their promotion, transfer or dismissal from office.

The Constitutional Court decides on the constitutionality of acts of the Parliament, as well as of the President and the Government. It consists of nine judges, who are appointed by the Parliament for a single term of nine years; one-third of the Court's members are replaced every three years.

The Office of the Prosecutor-General is an autonomous institution of the judiciary, comprising the Prosecutor-General and local and district prosecutors' offices, which are subordinate to him. The Prosecutor-General and his deputies are appointed for terms of seven years by the President, subject to approval by the Parliament, while the prosecutors are appointed by the Prosecutor-General. The Office of the Prosecutor-General incorporates the Department for Crime Investigation. The State Arbitration decides cases of business litigation. A six-volume Civil Code, in accordance with European Union and international law, came into effect in 2001.

Constitutional Court (Lietuvos Respublikos Konstitucinis Teismas): Gedimino pr. 36, Vilnius 01104; tel. (5) 261-1466; fax (5) 212-7975; e-mail pastas@lrkt.lt; internet www.lrkt.lt; f. 1993; Pres. DAINIUS ŽALIMAS.

Court of Appeal: Gedimino pr. 40/1, Vilnius 01503; tel. (5) 66-3685; fax (5) 66-3060; e-mail apeliacinis@apeliacinis.lt; internet www.apeliacinis.lt; Chair. EGIDIJUS ŽIRONAS.

Supreme Court (Lietuvos Aukščiausiasis Teismas): Gynėjų g. 6, Vilnius 01109; tel. (5) 261-6466; fax (5) 261-6813; e-mail lat@teismas.lt; internet www.lat.lt; Chair. RIMVYDAS NORKUS.

Office of the Prosecutor-General: Rinktinės g. 5A, Vilnius 01515; tel. (5) 266-2305; fax (5) 266-2317; e-mail generaline.prokuratura@prokuraturos.lt; internet www.prokuraturos.lt; Prosecutor-General DARIUS VALYS.

Religion

CHRISTIANITY

The Roman Catholic Church

Catholicism has been the principal religious affiliation in Lithuania since its adoption by the Lithuanian State in 1387. The Catholic Church in Lithuania comprises two archdioceses and five dioceses (all of the Latin rite). There are some 2.4m. adherents in Lithuania.

Lithuanian Bishops' Conference: Skapo 4, Vilnius 01122; tel. (5) 212-5455; fax (5) 212-0972; e-mail lietuvos@yahoo.com; internet lvk.lcn.lt, f. 1965; Pres. Most Rev. GINTARAS GRUŠAS (Metropolitan Archbishop of Vilnius).

Archbishop of Kaunas: Most Rev. SIGITAS TAMKEVIČIUS, Rotušės 14A, Kaunas 44279; tel. (37) 409026; fax (37) 320090; e-mail kurija@kn.lcn.lt; internet www.kaunas.lcn.lt.

Archbishop of Vilnius: Cardinal AUDRYS JUOZAS BAČKIS, Šventaragio 4, Vilnius 01122; tel. (5) 262-7098; fax (5) 212-2807; e-mail curia@vilnensis.lt; internet vilnius.lcn.lt.

Orthodox Churches

Russian Orthodox Church (Moscow Patriarchate)

The first Orthodox communities in Lithuania appeared during the 12th century. While Lithuania formed part of the Russian Empire (1795–1915), Orthodoxy was considered the state religion. There were some 125,000 adherents in 2011.

Lithuanian Orthodox Church (Moscow Patriarchate): Aušros Vartų 10/3, Vilnius 01129; tel. (5) 212-7765; internet www.orthodoxy.lt; Metropolitan of Vilnius and Lithuania CHRYZOSTOM (MARTISHKIN).

Lithuanian Old Believers Pomor Church

The first communities settled in Lithuania in 1679 and the Church was established in 1709. In 2011 there were some 23,000 adherents.

Supreme Council of the Old Believers Pomor Church in Lithuania: Naujininkų g. 20, Vilnius 02109; tel. (5) 269-5271; f. 1925; Chair. GRIGORY BOAROV.

Protestant Churches

Lithuanian Evangelical Lutheran Church

The first parishes were established in 1539–69. The Lithuanian Evangelical Lutheran Church comprises one diocese. In 2011 there were some 18,000 adherents.

Consistory of the Lithuanian Evangelical Lutheran Church (Lietuvos Evangeliku-Liuteronu Bažnycia): Tumo-Vaižganto 50, Tauragė 72263; tel. and fax (446) 61145; e-mail redakcija@liuteronai.lt; internet www.liuteronai.lt; Bishop MINDAUGAS SABUTIS.

Lithuanian Evangelical Reformed Church

The first parishes were established after 1563. In 2011 there were some 7,000 adherents.

Lithuanian Evangelical Reformed Church: POB 661, Vilnius 04008; tel. and fax (5) 245-0656; Pres. of Synodie Collegium POVILAS A. JAŠINSKAS.

ISLAM

Sunni Islam is the religion of the ethnic Tatars of Lithuania. The first Tatar communities settled there in the 14th century. The first mosque in Vilnius was erected in 1558. In 2011 there were some 3,000 adherents.

JUDAISM

The first Jewish communities appeared in Lithuania in the 15th century. In the 15th–17th centuries Vilnius was an important centre of Jewish culture and religion. Before the Second World War approximately 200,000 Jews lived in Lithuania; an estimated 90% were murdered during the German occupation (1941–44). At 1 January 1996 there were five religious communities, with two synagogues (in Vilnius and Kaunas). There were an estimated 1,000 adherents in Lithuania in 2011. There is a small number of Karaites (Karaim), who originate from Crimea, who speak a Turkic language and follow a form of Judaism, resident in Lithuania.

The Press

In 2012 there were 252 newspapers and 563 periodicals published in Lithuania.

The publications listed below are in Lithuanian, except where otherwise indicated.

PRINCIPAL NEWSPAPERS

Kauno diena (Kaunas Daily): Kanto g. 18, Kaunas 44296; tel. (37) 302250; fax (37) 423404; e-mail redakcija@kaunodiena.lt; internet www.kauno.diena.lt; f. 1945; 6 a week; Editor-in-Chief ARUNAS ANDRIUŠKEVIČIUS; circ. 50,000.

Klaipėda: Naujojo Sodo g. 1A, K Centras, Klaipėda 92233; tel. (46) 397750; fax (46) 397700; e-mail redakcija@kl.lt; internet klaipeda.diena.lt; f. 1945; Editor-in-Chief SAULIUS POCIUS.

Kurier Wileński (Vilnius Courier): Birbynių g. 4A, Vilnius 02121; tel. and fax (5) 260-8444; e-mail r.mickiewicz@kurierwilenski.lt; internet www.kurierwilenski.lt; f. 1953; 5 a week; in Polish; Editor-in-Chief ROBERT MICKIEWICZ; circ. 8,000

Lietuvos aidas (Lithuanian Echo): B. Radvilaitės g. 9, Vilnius 01124; tel. (5) 212-4876; e-mail fondas@aidas.lt; internet www .aidas.lt; f. 1917; re-est. 1990; 2 a week; Editor-in-Chief ALGIRDAS PILVELIS; circ. 1,500.

Lietuvos rytas (Lithuanian Morning): Gedimino pr. 12A, Vilnius 01103; tel. (5) 274-3600; fax (5) 274-2000; e-mail news@lrytas.lt; internet www.lrytas.lt; f. 1990; 6 a week, with 3 supplements per week; Editor-in-Chief LIUDAS DAPKUS; circ. 65,000 (Mon.–Fri.), 200,000 (Sat.).

Lietuvos žinios (Lithuanian News): Vykinto g. 14, Vilnius 08117; tel. (5) 249-2152; fax (5) 275-3131; e-mail red@lzinios.lt; internet lzinios.lt; 6 a week; Gen. Dir and Editor-in-Chief RAMŪNAS TERLECKAS.

Respublika (Republic): A. Smetonos g. 2, Vilnius 01115; tel. (5) 212-3112; fax (5) 212-3538; e-mail press@respublika.net; internet www .respublika.lt; f. 1988; 6 a week in Lithuanian, with 5 Russian editions per week; Editor-in-Chief VITAS TOMKUS; circ. 55,000.

Šiaulių kraštas: P. Višinskio g. 26, Šiauliai 77155; tel. (41) 591572; fax (41) 524581; e-mail redakcija@skrastas.lt; internet www .skrastas.lt; f. 1990; 6 a week; Dir and Editor-in-Chief VLADAS VERTELIS.

Vakaro žinios (Evening News): Jogailos g. 11/2-11, Vilnius 01116; tel. and fax (5) 261-6875; e-mail vakarozinios@takas.lt; daily; circ. 70,000.

Vakarų ekspresas (Western Express): M. Mažvydo 3, Klaipėda 92131; tel. (46) 411308; fax (46) 402408; e-mail sekretore@ve.lt; internet www.ve.lt; f. 1990; 6 a week; Editor-in-Chief GINTARAS TOMKUS; circ. 16,000–22,000.

Verslo žinios (Business News): J. Jasinskio 16A, Vilnius 01112; tel. (5) 252-6300; fax (5) 252-6313; e-mail info@vz.lt; internet vz.lt; f. 1994; 5 a week; Editor ROLANDAS BARYSAS; circ. 9,000.

PRINCIPAL PERIODICALS

Artuma (Presence): Rotušės a. 23, Kaunas 44279; tel. and fax (37) 209683; e-mail redakcija@artuma.lt; internet www.artuma.lt; f. 1989 as *Caritas*; name changed as above in 1997; monthly; Catholic family magazine; Editor-in-Chief DARIUS CHMIELIAUSKAS; circ. 12,500.

Kultūros barai (Domains of Culture): Latako g. 3, Vilnius 01125; tel. (5) 262-3861; fax (5) 261-0538; e-mail kulturosbarai@takas.lt; internet www.eurozine.com; f. 1965; monthly; independent cultural magazine; Editor-in-Chief LAIMA KANOPKIENE; circ. 2,200.

Laima: Saltoniškių g. 9, Vilnius 08105; tel. (5) 252-6538; fax (5) 252-6531; e-mail laima@redakcija.lt; internet www.redakcija.lt/ zurnalai/laima; f. 1993; monthly; lifestyle and feature magazine for women; Editor-in-Chief GITANA BUKAUSKIENE; circ. 30,000.

Liaudies kultūra (Ethnic Culture): Barboros Radvilaitės 8, Vilnius 01124; tel. (5) 261-1190; fax (5) 261-2607; e-mail llkc@llkc.lt; internet www.llkc.lt; f. 1988; 6 a year; Gen. Editor DALIA ANTANINA RASTENIENE; circ. 550.

Literatūra ir menas (Literature and Art): Mesiniu 4, Vilnius 01133; tel. (5) 269-1977; fax (5) 212-6556; e-mail lmenas@takas.lt; internet literaturairmenas.lt; f. 1946; weekly; Fridays; publ. by the Lithuanian Writers' Union; Editor-in-Chief KORNELIJUS PLATELIS; circ. 2,000.

Lithuania in the World: J. Basanavičiaus g. 7, Vilnius 01118; tel. (5) 261-4432; fax (5) 212-5560; e-mail info@liw.lt; internet www.liw .lt; f. 1993; 6 a year; in English and Lithuanian; Exec. Editor JOLANTA LAUMENSKAITE; circ. 10,000.

Magazyn Wileński (Vilnius Journal): Laisvės pr. 60, Vilnius 05120; tel. and fax (5) 242-7718; e-mail magazyn@magwil.lt; internet www .magwil.lt; f. 1990; monthly; political, cultural; in Polish; Editor HELENA OSTROWSKA; circ. 5,000.

Mano Namai: Ozo g. 10A, Vilnius 08200; tel. (5) 247-7714; e-mail dalia@manomai.lt; internet www.mano-namai.lt; household, interiors and food; Editor DALIA DAUGIRDIENE.

Metai (Year): K. Sirvydo g. 6, Vilnius 01101; tel. (5) 261-7344; e-mail metai@takas.lt; f. 1991; monthly; journal of the Lithuanian Writers' Union; Editor-in-Chief DANIELIUS MUŠINSKAS; circ. 2,000.

Moteris (Woman): J. Jasinskio 16C, Vilnius 01112; tel. (5) 247-7712; internet www.moteris.lt; f. 1920; monthly; popular, for women; Editor-in-Chief GRAŽINA MICHNEVIČIŪTE; circ. 22,000.

Naujasis Židinys—Aidai (New Hearth—Echoes): Pilies g. 8, Vilnius 01123; tel. (5) 212-0311; fax (5) 212-2363; e-mail naujasis .zidinys@gmail.com; internet www.nzidinys.lt; f. 1991; eight a year; religion, culture, history, politics, humanities and social affairs; Editor-in-Chief NERIJUS ŠEPETYS; circ. 1,000.

Nemunas: Gedimino g. 45, Kaunas 44239; tel. and fax (37) 322244; e-mail redakcija@nemunas.net; internet www.nemunas.net; f. 1967; weekly since 2004; Thursdays; culture and art; journal of the Lithuanian Writers' Union; Editor-in-Chief VIKTORAS RUDŽIANSKAS; circ. 1,500.

Panelė (Young Miss): J. Jasinskio g. 16C, Vilnius 01112; tel. (5) 247-7718; fax (5) 210-2557; e-mail magazine@panele.lt; internet www .panele.lt; f. 1994; monthly; popular, for ages 12–25; Editor-in-Chief JURGA BALTRUKONYTE; circ. 66,000.

Psihologija Tau: Trakų g. 8, Vilnius 01132; tel. (5) 262-6763; fax (5) 262-7671; e-mail redakcija@psichologijatau.lt; internet www .psichologijatau.lt; f. 1991; popular psychology; Editor RŪTA IGNATE.

Septynios meno dienos (7 meno dienos) (Seven Days of Art): Maironio g. 6, Vilnius 01124; tel. (5) 261-3039; e-mail 7md@takas.lt; internet www.7md.lt; f. 1992; weekly; Fridays; media, music, visual arts, theatre, dance and cinema; Editor-in-Chief MONIKA KRIKŠTO-PAITYTE; circ. 1,500.

Tremtinys (Deportee): Laisvės al. 39, Kaunas 44309; tel. (37) 323174; e-mail tremtinys@erdvas.lt; internet www.lpkts.lt/ tremtinys.htm; f. 1988; weekly; publ. of fmr Lithuanian Union of Political Prisoners and Deportees (now part of Homeland Union—Lithuanian Christian Democrats); Editor-in-Chief AUDRONE KAMINS-KIENE; circ. 4,500.

Valstiečių laikraštis (Farmer's Newspaper): Konstitucijos pr. 26, Vilnius 08105; tel. (5) 203-1022; e-mail redakcija@valstietis.lt; internet www.valstietis.lt; f. 1940; 2 a week; Editor-in-Chief MEILE TARAŠKEVIČIENE; circ. 68,000.

Vasario 16 (16 February): J. Gruodžio g. 9/404, Kaunas 44293; tel. (37) 225219; f. 1988; fortnightly; journal of Order and Justice Party; Sec. PRIMAS NOREIKA; circ. 1,600.

NEWS AGENCIES

Baltic News Service (BNS): Jogailos g. 9/1, Vilnius 01116; tel. (5) 205-8501; fax (5) 205-8504; e-mail arturas@bns.lt; internet www.bns .lt; f. 1991; Dir and Editor-in-Chief ARTŪRAS RAČAS.

ELTA Lithuanian News Agency (ELTA Lietuvos Naujienų Agentūra): Gedimino pr. 21/2, Vilnius 01103; tel. (5) 262-8864; fax (5) 261-9507; e-mail zinios@elta.lt; internet www.elta.lt; f. 1920; 18.4% owned by Ziniu Partneriai; 39.5% owned by Respublikos Investicija (both cos controlled by Respublika Gp); Dir GRAZINA RAMANAUSKAITE-TIUMENEVIENE.

Publishers

Aidai: Didžioji g. 34, Vilnius 01128; tel. and fax (5) 212-2363; fax (5) 278-3633; e-mail aidai@aidai.lt; internet www.aidai.lt; culture, literature, social studies, religion and art; Dir JURGITA JANUTENAITE.

Alma littera: Ulonų g. 2, Vilnius 08245; tel. (5) 263-8877; fax (5) 272-8026; e-mail post@almali.lt; internet www.almalittera.lt; f. 1990; fiction, non-fiction, children's books, textbooks; Dir-Gen. IRMANTAS ŠVAŽAS.

Baltos lankos leidykla (White Meadows Publishing House): Gedimino pr. 28, Vilnius 01104; tel. (5) 240-7906; fax (5) 240-7446; e-mail leidykla@baltoslankos.lt; internet www.baltoslankos.lt; f. 1992; literature, humanities, social sciences, fiction and textbooks; Dir KOTRYNA ŽUKAITE.

Eugrimas: Kalvariju 98/42, Vilnius 08211; tel. and fax (5) 273-3955; e-mail info@eugrimas.lt; internet www.eugrimas.lt; f. 1995; academic and professional literature, incl. economics, business, law and politics; Dir EUGENIJA PETRULIENE.

Katalikų pasaulio leidiniai (Editions of the Catholic World): Pylimo 27/14, Vilnius 01309; tel. (5) 212-2422; fax (5) 262-6462; e-mail referente@katalikuleidiniai.lt; internet www .katalikuleidiniai.lt; f. 1990; Dir BIRUTE BARTASŪNAITE.

Leidykla Vaga: Gedimino pr. 50, Vilnius 01110; tel. (5) 249-8121; fax (5) 249-8122; e-mail info@vaga.lt; internet www.vaga.lt; f. 1945 as Lithuanian State Publishing House of Fiction; privatized and restructured in 1994; fiction, non-fiction, art, children's books; Dir VYTAS V. PETROŠIUS.

Lietuvos rašytojų sąjungos leidykla (Lithuanian Writers' Union Publishers): K. Sirvydo 6, Vilnius 01101; tel. and fax (5) 262-8945; e-mail info@rsleidykla.lt; internet www.rsleidykla.lt; f. 1990; fiction, essays, literary heritage, children's books; Dir GIEDRE SORIENE.

Mintis leidykla (Mintis Publishing House): Z. Sierakausko g. 15, Vilnius 03105; tel. (5) 233-2943; e-mail info@mintis.org; internet www.mintis.org; f. 1949; philosophy, politics, history, law, mythology, textbooks, encyclopedias, biographies, fiction; also book distributor, bookshop; Dir LEONARDAS ARMONAS.

Mokslo ir enciklopedijų leidybos centras (Science and Encyclopedia Publishing Centre): L. Asanavičiūtes 23, Vilnius 04315; tel. (5) 245-8526; fax (5) 245-8537; e-mail melc@melc.lt; internet www .melc.lt; f. 1992; fmrly Science and Encyclopedia Publishing Institute; encyclopedias, science and reference books, dictionaries, higher education textbooks, books for the general reader; Dir RIMANTAS KARECKAS.

Presvika: Kauno g. 28, Vilnius 03202; tel. (5) 262-3182; fax (5) 233-3894; e-mail presvika@presvika.lt; internet www.presvika.lt; f. 1996; psychological and educational literature, textbooks, fiction; Dir VIOLETA BILAIŠYTĖ.

Šviesa (Light): Vytauto pr. 23, Kaunas 44352; tel. (37) 409126; fax (37) 342032; e-mail info@sviesa.lt; internet www.sviesa.lt; f. 1945; textbooks and pedagogical literature; Dir JURGITA NACEVIČIENĖ.

Tyto alba: J. Jasinskio g. 10, Vilnius 01112; tel. and fax (5) 249-7595; e-mail info@tytoalba.lt; internet www.tytoalba.lt; f. 1993; contemporary Lithuanian literary fiction and non-fiction, fiction in translation; Dir LOLITA VARANAVIČIENĖ.

Versus Aureus leidykla: Rūdninkų g. 10, Vilnius 01135; tel. and fax (5) 265-2730; e-mail info@versus.lt; internet www.versus.lt; f. 2003; fiction, non-fiction and educational literature; Dir ARTURAS MICKEVIČIUS.

PUBLISHERS' ASSOCIATION

Lietuvos Leidėjų Asociacija (Lithuanian Publishers' Association): Lukiškių g. 5-317, Vilnius 01108; tel. and fax (5) 261-7740; e-mail info@lla.lt; internet www.lla.lt; f. 1989; Dir AIDA VIDA DOBKEVIČIŪTĖ.

Broadcasting and Communications

TELECOMMUNICATIONS

At the end of 2010 there were 51 fixed-line telecommunications service providers and 13 providers of mobile cellular telecommunications active in Lithuania.

BITĖ Lietuva: Žemaitės 15, Vilnius 03504; tel. (6) 560-0656; fax (6) 990-0111; e-mail info@bite.lt; internet www.bite.lt; f. 1995; mobile telecommunications service provider; 0.2m. subscribers (March 2007); CEO FRED HRENCHUK.

Eurocom: Geležinio Vilko g. 18A, Vilnius 08104; tel. (5) 274-4600; fax (5) 274-4612; e-mail eurocom@eurocom.lt; internet www.eurocom.lt; f. 2003; fixed-line and mobile telecommunications, internet service provider; a subsidiary of VP Market; Dir SEDIMINAS JØVAIŠA.

Omnitel: T. Ševčenkos 25, Vilnius 03503; tel. (698) 63333; fax (5) 274-5574; e-mail info@omnitel.net; internet www.omnitel.lt; f. 1991 as Litcom; owned by Telia Sonera (Sweden); telecommunications and internet service provider; Pres. ANTANAS JUOZAS ZABULIS.

Tele2: Sporto 7A, Vilnius 09200; tel. (5) 236-6300; fax (5) 236-6302; e-mail reception.lt@tele2.com; internet www.tele2.lt; f. 1999; owned by Tele2 AB (Sweden); provider of GSM, internet and fixed-line telecommunications services; Chief Exec. PETRAS MASIULIS.

Teo LT AB: Lvovo 25, Vilnius 03501; tel. (5) 262-1511; fax (5) 212-6655; internet www.teo.lt; f. 1992 under the name Lietuvos Telekomas AB; privatized 1998; formerly monopoly provider of telecommunications services; present name adopted 2006; operates public telecommunications network, repairs telecommunications equipment; internet service provider; Chair. ERIK HALLBERG; Gen. Man. ARŪNAS ŠIKŠTA; 3,200 employees.

Regulatory Authority

Communications Regulatory Authority (Ryšių reguliavimo tarnyba): Algirdo 27A, Vilnius 03219; tel. (5) 210-5633; fax (5) 216-1564; e-mail rrt@rrt.lt; internet www.rrt.lt; f. 2001; Dir FELIKSAS DOBROVOLSKIS.

BROADCASTING

Regulatory Authority

Lietuvos radijo ir televizijos komisija (Radio and Television Commission of Lithuania): Šeimyniškių g. 3A, Vilnius 09312; tel. (5) 233-0660; fax (5) 264-7125; e-mail lrtk@rtk.lt; internet www.rtk.lt; f. 1996; licensing and licence compliance; Chair. EDMUNDAS VAITEKŪNAS.

Radio

In 2010, in addition to one publicly owned national radio station, there were 10 private commercial, seven regional and 30 local radio stations.

Lietuvos nacionalinis radijas ir televizija (LRT) (Lithuanian National Radio and Television): S. Konarskio 49, Vilnius 03123; tel. (5) 236-3209; fax (5) 236-3208; e-mail lrt@lrt.lt; internet www.lrt.lt; f. 1926; govt-owned; non-profit public broadcasting co; operates three national radio channels and two national television channels; Chair. of Bd ŽYGINTAS PEČIULIS; Dir-Gen. AUDRIUS SIAURUSEVIČIUS; 650 employees.

Laisvoji banga: Gedimino pr. 50, Vilnius 01110; tel. (5) 2101411; fax (5) 2333121; e-mail info@laisvojibanga.lt; internet www.laisvojibanga.lt; private, commercial; broadcasts news and music; Dir VIDMANTAS VALIUŠAITIS.

M-1: Laisvės pr. 60, Vilnius 05120; tel. (5) 236-0360; fax (5) 236-0366; e-mail m-1@m-1.fm; internet www.m-1.fm; f. 1989; private, commercial; Gen. Man. RŪTA GRUŠNIENĖ.

Pūkas: Šaldytuvų g. 25, Kaunas 45123; tel. (37) 342424; fax (37) 342434; e-mail pukas@pukas.lt; internet www.pukas.lt; f. 1991; private, commercial; operates two radio stations and a television station; Dir KĘSTUTIS PŪKAS.

Radiocentras: Laisvės pr. 60, Vilnius 05120; tel. (5) 212-8706; fax (5) 242-9073; e-mail biuras@rc.lt; internet www.rc.lt; f. 1991; private, commercial; Gen. Man. MINDAUGAS PLESKEVICIUS.

Television

At the end of 2010, in addition to the 28 local and 98 national analogue terrestrial television stations, there were 25 licensed digital terrestrial televisions stations. From October 2012 digital terrestrial television replaced analogue terrestrial television throughout the country.

Lietuvos televizija (LTV): S. Konarskio 49, Vilnius 03123; tel. (5) 236-3100; fax (5) 216-3282; e-mail lrt@lrt.lt; internet www.lrt.lt; f. 1957; subsidiary of LRT (see Radio); programmes in Lithuanian, Russian, Polish, Ukrainian and Belarusian; Dir RIMVYDAS PALECKIS.

Aidas (Echo): Birutės g. 42, Trakai 21117; tel. (650) 57171; fax (528) 55656; e-mail tvaidas@gmail.com; mainly relays German programmes; private, commercial; Dir ČESLOVAS RULEVIČIUS.

Baltijos televizija (BTV): Laisvės pr. 60, Vilnius 05120; tel. (5) 278-0805; fax (5) 278-0804; e-mail info@btv.lt; internet www.btv.lt; f. 1993; broadcasts own programmes and relays German, Polish and US broadcasts; private, commercial; Dir-Gen. LIUTAURAS ELKIMAVIČIUS.

KTV plius: Nemuno g. 79, Panevėžys 37355; tel. (45) 514103; fax (45) 443561; e-mail pictura@kateka.lt; internet www.ktvplius.lt; private, commercial; Pres. ROLANDAS MEILIŪNAS.

LNK TV: Šeškinės g. 20, Vilnius 07156; tel. (5) 243-1058; fax (5) 243-1054; e-mail info@lnk.lt; internet www.lnk.lt; f. 1995; private, commercial; broadcasts TV1; Dir-Gen. ZITA SARAKIENĖ.

PAN-TV: Respublikos g. 19, Panevėžys 35185; tel. (8) 606-86686; e-mail info@pantv.lt; private, commercial; Dir ŠAULIUS BUKELIS.

Raseiniu TV: Vytauto Vilniaus 1A, Raseiniai 60187; tel. (428) 54433; fax (428) 70422; e-mail office@mirkliai.lt; broadcast by VšĮ Raseinių televizijos ir radijo centras; Dir KĘSTUTIS SKAMARAKAS.

Šiaulių TV: Liejyklos g. 10, Šiauliai 78147; tel. and fax (41) 523808; e-mail info@stv.lt; internet www.stv.lt; private; Dir DAIVA PIKTURNIENE.

TV3: Kalvarijų pl. 143, Vilnius 08221; tel. (5) 203-0101; fax (5) 276-4253; e-mail info@tv3.lt; internet www.tv3.lt; f. 1992; broadcasts own programmes (20% of schedule) in Lithuanian and English, and relays international satellite channels; private, commercial; Dir LAURA BLAŽEVIČIŪTĖ.

Finance

(cap. = capital; res = reserves, dep. – deposits; m. = million; brs = branches; amounts in litai)

BANKING

Central Bank

Bank of Lithuania (Lietuvos bankas): Gedimino pr. 6, Vilnius 01103; tel. (5) 268-0029; fax (5) 262-8124; e-mail info@lb.lt; internet www.lb.lt; f. 1922; re-est. 1990; central bank, responsible for supervision of banks, insurance companies, credit unions and other financial institutions; cap. 200.0m., res 794.1m., dep. 4,519.6m. (Dec. 2008); Chair. of Bd VITAS VASILIAUSKAS; 2 brs.

Commercial Banks

Citadele Bankas: K. Kalinausko g. 13, Vilnius 03107; tel. (5) 266-4600; fax (5) 266-4601; e-mail info@citadele.lt; internet www.citadele.lt; f. 1996 as Parex Bankas; renamed in 2010; owned by Citadele banka (Latvia); cap. 148.9m., res 4.8m., dep. 790.8m. (Dec. 2013); Chair. SKIRMANTAS JARECKAS; 6 brs.

DnB Bankas: J. Basanavičiaus g. 26, Vilnius 03601; tel. (5) 239-3444; fax (5) 213-9056; e-mail info@dnb.lt; internet www.dnb.lt; f. 1924; privatized in March 2002; fmrly DnB NORD Bankas; renamed as above in 2011; 100% owned by Bank DnB A/S (Denmark); cap. 656.7m., res 653.0m., dep. 6,422.9m. (Dec. 2013); Chair. of Management Bd, Pres. and CEO BJØRNAR LUND; 78 brs.

Medicinos Bankas: Pamėnkalnio g. 40, Vilnius 01114; tel. (5) 264-4800; fax (5) 264-4801; e-mail info@medbank.lt; internet www.medbank.lt; f. 1992; cap. 68.9m., res 26.2m., dep. 742.9m. (Dec. 2012); Chair. of Management Bd and CEO GINTARAS TREINYS; 7 brs.

SEB Bankas (SEB Bank): Gedimino pr. 12, Vilnius 01103; tel. (5) 268-2800; fax (5) 268-2333; e-mail info@seb.lt; internet www.seb.lt; f. 1990 as Spaudos Bankas; present name adopted 2008; 100% owned by Skandinaviska Enskilda Banken AB (Sweden); cap. 1,034.6m., res 251.8m., dep. 19,715.4m. (Dec. 2012); Pres. and CEO RAIMONDAS KVEDARAS; 46 brs.

Šiaulių Bankas: Tilžės str. 149, Šiauliai 76348; tel. (41) 595607; fax (41) 430774; e-mail info@sb.lt; internet www.sb.lt; f. 1992; cap. 250m., res 36.6m., dep. 4,581.1m. (Dec. 2013); Chair. of Bd VYTAUTAS SINIUS; CEO AUDRIUS ŽIUGŽDA; 74 brs and agencies (2014).

Swedbank: Konstitucijos pr. 20A, Vilnius 03502; tel. (5) 268-4444; fax (5) 258-2700; e-mail info@swedbank.lt; internet www.swedbank.lt; f. 1919; present name adopted 2009; 99.5% owned by Swedbank AB (Sweden); cap. 1,640.1m., res 240.9m., dep. 15,728m. (Dec. 2013); Chair. of Bd ANTANAS DANYS; 77 brs.

Banking Association

Association of Lithuanian Banks (Lietuvos Bankų Asociacija): Konstitucijos pr. 7, Vilnius 09308; tel. (5) 249-6669; fax (5) 249-6139; e-mail info@lba.lt; internet www.lba.lt; f. 1991; Pres. STASYS KROPAS; 10 mems.

STOCK EXCHANGE

NASDAQ OMX Vilnius AB: Lvovo g. 25, Vilnius 09320; tel. (5) 272-3871; fax (5) 272-4894; e-mail vilnius@nasdaq.com; internet www.nasdaqomxbaltic.com; f. 1993; 96.23% owned by the NASDAQ OMX Group (USA); Chair. of Bd ARMINTA SALADŽIENĖ.

INSURANCE
Principal Insurance Companies

Aviva Lietuva: Lvovo g. 25, Vilnius 09320; tel. (5) 269-0169; fax (5) 269-0269; e-mail info@aviva.lt; internet www.aviva.lt; f. 2001 as Commercial Union Lietuva Gyvybės draudimas; present name adopted 2007; owned by Aviva Towarzystwo Ubezpieczeń na Zycie SA, part of the Aviva Group (United Kingdom); Dir-Gen. ASTA GRABINSKĖ.

Ergo Lietuva: Geležinio vilko g. 6A, Vilnius 03507; tel. (5) 268-3000; fax (5) 268-3045; e-mail info@ergo.lt; internet www.ergo.lt; f. 1991; owned by Ergo International AG (Germany); formerly Drauda; name changed as above in 2000; in 2002 merged with Preventa; CEO KĘSTUTIS BAGDONAVIČIUS.

Lietuvos draudimas AB (Lithuanian Insurance): J. Basanavičiaus g. 12, Vilnius 03600; tel. (5) 266-6612; fax (5) 231-4138; e-mail info@ldr.lt; internet www.ld.lt; f. 1921; privatized in 1999; part of RSA group (United Kingdom); principal non-life insurance co in Lithuania; CEO KĘSTUTIS SERPYTIS.

PZU Lietuva: Konstitucijos pr. 7, Vilnius 09308; tel. (5) 279-0007; fax (5) 279-0019; e-mail info@pzu.lt; internet www.pzu.lt; f. 1993; owned by Powszechny Zaklad Ubezpieczen (PZU) SA (Poland); Chair. BOGDAN BENCZAK.

SEB VB Gyvybės Draudimas: Gedimino pr. 12, Vilnius 01103; tel. (5) 268-1528; fax (5) 268-1556; e-mail draudimas@seb.lt; internet www.seb.lt; f. 1999; owned by SEB Vilniaus bankas AB; Dir SONATA G. BUBNELIENĖ.

Swedbank gyvybės draudimas AB (Swedbank Life Insurance): Konstitucijos pr. 20A, Vilnius 09321; tel. (5) 268-4444; fax (5) 258-6732; e-mail info@swedbank.lt; internet www.swedbank.lt; f. 1997; owned by Swedbank AS (Sweden); formerly Lietuvos Draudimo gyvybės draudimas, then Hansa gyvybės draudimas; present name adopted 2009; life; Chair. MINDAUGAS JUSIUS.

Insurance Association

Association of Lithuanian Insurers (LDA) (Lietuvos Draudikų Asociacija): Gedimino pr. 45/11, Vilnius 01109; tel. and fax (5) 231-0381; e-mail asociacija@draudikai.lt; internet www.draudikai.lt; f. 1992; Dir ANDRIUS ROMANOVSKIS; 11 mems.

Supervisory Body

Insurance Supervisory Commission: Ukmergės g. 222, Vilnius 07157; tel. (5) 243-1370; fax (5) 272-3689; e-mail dpk@dpk.lt; internet www.dpk.lt; Chair. MINDAUGAS ŠALČIUS.

Trade and Industry
GOVERNMENT AGENCY

State Property Fund (Valstybės Turto Fondas—VTS): Vilniaus g. 16, Vilnius 01402; tel. (5) 268-4999; fax (5) 268-4997; e-mail info@vtf.lt; internet www.vtf.lt; f. 1995; privatization and management of state-owned and municipal property; Chair. ARNOLDAS BURKOVSKIS; Dir-Gen. JONAS NIAURA.

DEVELOPMENT AGENCY

National Regional Development Agency (Nacionalinė Regionų Plėtros Agentūra): Vilnius g. 88, Šiauliai 76285; tel. (41) 552061; fax (41) 523903; e-mail info@nrda.lt; internet www.nrda.lt; f. 1999 by the Asscn of Lithuanian Chambers of Commerce, Industry and Crafts; Dir AIDA ADEIKIENĖ.

CHAMBERS OF COMMERCE

Association of Lithuanian Chambers of Commerce, Industry and Crafts (Lietuvos prekybos, pramonės ir amatų rūmų asociacija): Vašingtono aikštė, 1–63A, Vilnius 01108; tel. (5) 261-2102; fax (5) 261-2112; e-mail info@chambers.lt; internet www.chambers.lt; f. 1992; mem. of International Chamber of Commerce and of Asscn of European Chambers of Commerce and Industry; Pres. RIMANTAS STANKEVIČIUS.

Kaunas Chamber of Commerce, Industry and Crafts: K. Donelaičio g. 8, POB 2111, Kaunas 44213; tel. (37) 229212; fax (37) 208330; e-mail chamber@chamber.lt; internet www.chamber.lt; f. 1925; re-est. 1991; br. at Marijampolė; Pres. Prof. M. RONDOMANSKAS.

Klaipėda Chamber of Commerce, Industry and Crafts: Danės g. 17, POB 148, Klaipėda 92117; tel. (46) 390861; fax (46) 410626; e-mail klaipeda@chambers.lt; internet www.kcci.lt; Pres. BENEDIKTAS PETRAUSKA; Gen. Dir VIKTORAS KROLIS; 200 mems.

Panevėžys Chamber of Commerce, Industry and Crafts: Respublikos g. 34, Panevėžys 35173; tel. (45) 463687; fax (45) 500309; e-mail panevezys@chambers.lt; internet www.ccic.lt; f. 1991; Pres. SIGITAS GAILIŪNAS; Gen. Dir VISVALDAS MATKEVIČIUS.

Šiauliai Chamber of Commerce, Industry and Crafts: Vilniaus g. 88, Šiauliai 76285; tel. (41) 523224; fax (41) 523903; e-mail siauliai@chambers.lt; internet www.rumai.lt; f. 1993; Dir-Gen. ALFREDAS JONUŠKA.

Vilnius Chamber of Commerce, Industry and Crafts: Algirdo g. 31, Vilnius 03219; tel. (5) 213-5550; fax (5) 213-5542; e-mail vilnius@cci.lt; internet www.cci.lt; f. 1991; Dir-Gen. BORISAS ZAUBIDOVAS; 480 mems.

INDUSTRIAL ASSOCIATION

Lithuanian Confederation of Industrialists (Lietuvos pramonininkų konfederacija—LPK): A. Vienuolio g. 8, Vilnius 01104; tel. (5) 212-5217; fax (5) 212-5209; e-mail info@lpk.lt; internet www.lpk.lt; f. 1989; Pres. ROBERTAS DARGIS.

EMPLOYERS' ORGANIZATION

Lithuanian Business Employers' Confederation (Lietuvos verslo darbdavių konfederacija—LVDK): Algirdo g. 31, Vilnius 03219; tel. (5) 249-8345; fax (5) 249-6448; e-mail info@lvdk.eu; internet www.lvdk.eu; f. 1999; Gen. Dir DANUKAS ARLAUSKAS.

UTILITIES

Energy Agency (Energetikos agentūra): Gedimino pr. 38, Vilnius 01104; tel. (8) 706-64923; fax (8) 706-64876; e-mail eainfo@ena.lt; internet www.ena.lt; f. 1993; state enterprise; attached to the Ministry of Energy; Dir MARIJUS FRANCKEVIČIUS.

Electricity

Lesto: Žvejų g. 14, Vilnius 09310; tel. (5) 277-7524; fax (5) 277-7514; e-mail info@lesto.lt; internet www.lesto.lt; f. 2010 following the reorganization of Rytų Skirstomieji Tinklai and Vakarų Skirstomieji Tinklai; distribution network operator; CEO ARVYDAS TARASEVIČIUS.

Lietuvos Energija AB (Lithuanian Power): Žvejų g. 14, Vilnius 09310; tel. (5) 262-6822; fax (5) 212-6736; e-mail info@lietuvosenergija.lt; internet www.lpc.lt; f. 1995; restructured in 2000; 96.5% owned by LEO LT AB; Chair. of Bd HENRIKAS BERNATAVIČIUS; CEO ALOYZAS KORYZNA.

Gas

Lietuvos Dujos AB (Lithuanian Gas): Aguonų g. 24, Vilnius 03212; tel. (5) 236-0209; fax (5) 236-0200; e-mail ld@lietuvosdujos.lt; internet www.dujos.lt; f. 1995; 17.7% state-owned; 38.9% owned by E.ON Ruhrgas International AG (Germany); 37.1% owned by OAO Gazprom (Russia); natural gas import, sale and distribution; Chair. Dr VALERY GOLUBEV; Gen. Man. VIKTORAS VALENTUKEVIČIUS; 1,900 employees.

TRADE UNIONS

Lithuanian Labour Federation (Lietuvos Darbo Federacija): Vytauto g. 14, Vilnius 03106; tel. and fax (6) 563-4143; e-mail ldforg@ldf.lt; internet www.ldf.lt; f. 1919 as a Christian trade union org.; re-est. 1991; 7,000 mems (2014); Chair. SVAJUNAS ANDRIULIS; Sec.-Gen. JANINA ŠVEDIENĖ.

Lithuanian Trade Union Confederation (Lietuvos profesinių sąjungų konfederacija—LPSK): J. Jasinskio g. 9/213, Vilnius 01111; tel. (5) 249-6921; fax (5) 249-8078; e-mail lpsk@lpsk.lt; internet www.lpsk.lt; f. 2002 by merger of Lithuanian Union of Trade Unions (LPSS) and Lithuanian Trade Union Centre (LPSC); 25 branch trade unions with 60,000 mems; Pres. ARTŪRAS ČERNIAUSKAS.

Transport

RAILWAYS

In 2011 there were 1,767 km of railway track in use in Lithuania, of which 122 km were electrified. Main lines link Vilnius with Minsk (Belarus), Kaliningrad (Russia) and Warsaw (Poland), in the latter case by way of the Belarusian town of Grodno (Horadnia).

Lithuanian Railways (Lietuvos geležinkeliai): Mindaugo g. 12–14, Vilnius 03603; tel. (5) 269-2038; fax (5) 269-2128; e-mail lgkanc@litrail.lt; internet www.litrail.lt; f. 1991; Dir-Gen. STASYS DAILYDKA; 10,334 employees.

ROADS

In 2012 the total length of the road network was estimated at 84,166 km; the motorway network totalled 309 km.

Lithuanian Road Administration (Lietuvos automobilių kelių direkcija—LAKD): J. Basanavičiaus g. 36/2, Vilnius 03109; tel. (5) 232-9600; fax (5) 232-9609; e-mail lakd@lakd.lt; internet www.lakd.lt; Dir-Gen. SKIRMANTAS SKRINSKAS.

SHIPPING

The main port is at Klaipėda. In 2011 there were 452 km of inland navigable waterways. At 31 December 2014 the flag registered fleet comprised 134 vessels, with a total displacement of 444,509 grt.

Port Authority

Klaipėda State Seaport Authority: J. Janonio g. 24, Klaipėda 92251; tel. (46) 499600; fax (46) 499777; e-mail info@port.lt; internet www.portofklaipeda.lt; multi-purpose, deep-water universal port; connects sea, land and rail routes from east and west; Dir-Gen. ARVYDAS VAITKUS.

Ship-owning Company

Lithuanian Shipping Company (AB Lietuvos Jūrų Laivininkystė): Malunininku g. 3, Klaipėda 92264; tel. (46) 393105; fax (46) 393119; e-mail info@ljl.lt; internet www.ljl.lt; f. 1969 as LISCO; partially privatized and renamed as above in June 2001; 56.6% state-owned; transportation of cargo; owns 11 vessels; Gen. Dir RENALDAS VYŠNIAUKAS.

CIVIL AVIATION

There are international airports at Vilnius, Kaunas, Palanga and Šiauliai.

Air Lituanica: Rodūnios kelias 2, Vilnius 02189; tel. (5) 203-4485; fax (5) 203-4493; e-mail fly@airlituanica.com; internet www.airlituanica.com; f. 2013; operates passenger services to major European destinations; CEO GYTIS GUMULIAUSKAS.

Directorate of Civil Aviation (Oro Navigacija): Rodūnios kelias 2, Vilnius 02188; tel. (70) 694502; fax (70) 694522; e-mail info@ans.lt; internet www.ans.lt; Dir-Gen. ALGIMANTAS RAŠČIUS.

Small Planet Airlines: J. Basanavičiaus g. 15, Vilnius 03108; tel. (5) 252-5660; fax (5) 252-5661; e-mail info@smallplanet.aero; internet www.smallplanet.aero; f. 2007 as flyLAL Charters; present name adopted 2010; operates passenger and cargo charter flights; CEO VYTAUTAS KAIKARIS.

Tourism

Tourist attractions in Lithuania include the historic cities of Vilnius, Kaunas, Kėdainiai, Trakai and Klaipėda, coastal resorts, such as Palanga and Kuršių Nerija, and picturesque countryside. Some 1.2m. tourists visited the country in 2013, when tourist receipts (excluding passenger transport) totalled US $1,467m., according to provisional figures.

State Dept of Tourism: Švitrigailos 11M, Vilnius 03228; tel. (5) 210-8796; fax (5) 210-8753; e-mail vtd@tourism.lt; internet www.tourism.lt; Dir NIJOLĖ KLIOKIENĖ.

Defence

As assessed at November 2014, Lithuania's armed forces totalled an estimated 10,950, including an army of 7,500 (including 4,300 active reserves), a navy of 500, an air force of 900, and 2,050 joint troops. There was also a paramilitary force of 11,000 (including a border guard of 4,000) and a total of 6,700 reserves. Lithuania became a full member of the North Atlantic Treaty Organization (NATO) on 29 March 2004. Military service was suspended in 2008, but Parliament voted in favour of its reintroduction in March 2015. Compulsory military service was to last for a period of nine months.

Defence Expenditure: Budgeted at 1,180m. litai in 2014.

Commander-in-Chief of the Armed Forces: Maj.-Gen. JONAS VYTAUTAS ŽUKAS.

Commander of the Land Force: Maj.-Gen. ALMANTAS LEIKA.

Commander of the Air Force: Col AUDRONIS NAVICKAS.

Commander of the Naval Force: Rear-Adm. KĘSTUTIS MACIJAUSKAS.

Education

Education, beginning at six years of age, is free and compulsory until the age of 16. Pre-school education is available for children aged between one and six years. Children spend four years at primary school (Grades 1–4), followed by six years at lower secondary school (basic education, Grades 5–10) and two years at upper secondary school or gymnasium (Grades 10–12). Vocational training is available. From 2003 a standardized tuition fee was introduced for students in higher education, although there were exemptions for the highest achievers. In 2011/12 enrolment in pre-primary education included 76% of children in the relevant age-group, while the comparable rates of enrolment in primary and secondary education were 96% and 98%, respectively. In the 2013/14 academic year 403,165 students were enrolled in 1,283 general and vocational schools. In that year there were 24 colleges and 23 universities; total enrolment in institutions of higher education was 148,473. In 1991 the first independent schools were opened; by 2007/08 there were 26 independent schools, 12 independent colleges and seven independent universities. Lithuanian is the main language of instruction, although in 2007/08 some 4.2% of students at general schools were taught in Russian and 3.4% were taught in Polish. Central government expenditure on education in 2007 amounted to 2,027.1m. litai (9.9% of total expenditure).

LUXEMBOURG

Introductory Survey

LOCATION, CLIMATE, LANGUAGE, RELIGION, FLAG, CAPITAL

The Grand Duchy of Luxembourg is a landlocked country in Western Europe. It is bordered by Belgium to the west and north, by Germany to the east and by France to the south. The climate is temperate, with cool summers and mild winters. The average temperature ranges from 1°C (33°F) in January to 18°C (64°F) in July, while annual rainfall averages 782 mm. Luxembourgish (Lëtzebuergesch), a German-Moselle-Frankish dialect, is the main spoken language and became the third official language—in addition to French and German—in 1984. French is generally used for administrative and legislative purposes, while German is the principal written language of commerce and the press. Almost all of the inhabitants profess Christianity: about 87% are Roman Catholics and a small minority are Protestants. The national flag (proportions 3 by 5) consists of three equal horizontal stripes, of red, white and blue. The capital is the city of Luxembourg.

CONTEMPORARY POLITICAL HISTORY

Historical Context

Luxembourg's independence was affirmed in 1839 under the First Treaty of London, at which time it joined the German Customs Union (Zollverein), to counter French and Belgian influence. However, to prevent war between Prussia and France over the political status of Luxembourg, its independence and neutrality were reaffirmed under the Second Treaty of London in 1867; Luxembourg remained a member of the German Customs Union until 1919. The King of the Netherlands remained as head of state of Luxembourg until 1890, when the Dutch throne passed to his daughter, while he was succeeded as Grand Duke of Luxembourg by Adolphe I, the last Duke of Nassau, in accordance with the Nassau Family Pact, which favoured male heirs.

Luxembourg was invaded and occupied by Germany during the First and Second World Wars. After the Second World War Luxembourg became a founder member of the UN in 1946, the North Atlantic Treaty Organization (NATO, see p. 367) in 1949, and the European Community (later European Union—EU, see p. 271) in 1957. The Belgo-Luxembourg Economic Union has existed since 1922 (following the signing of a treaty in 1921), except during the period of German occupation in 1940–44. In 1948 the Benelux Economic Union (see p. 444) was inaugurated between Belgium, Luxembourg and the Netherlands, becoming effective in 1960, and establishing the three countries as a single customs area in 1970.

Domestic Political Affairs

Pierre Werner, leader of the Chrëschtlech Sozial Vollekspartei (CSV—Christian Social People's Party), became Prime Minister in February 1959 and, during 1959–74, led successive coalition governments in which the CSV was the dominant partner, along with either the Demokratesch Partei (DP—Democratic Party) or the Lëtzebuerger Sozialistesch Arbechterpartei (LSAP—Socialist Workers' Party of Luxembourg). However, following a general election in May 1974, the CSV entered into opposition for the first time since 1919, and a centre-left coalition between the DP and the LSAP was formed under the premiership of the leader of the DP, Gaston Thorn. At the next general election, which took place in June 1979, the CSV increased its representation in the Chambre des Députés (Chamber of Deputies), and Werner formed a coalition Government comprising the CSV and the DP.

At the general election in June 1984 the CSV again secured the largest number of seats in the legislature. A centre-left coalition was formed between the CSV and the LSAP, which had substantially increased its representation, with Jacques Santer of the CSV as Prime Minister. Following elections in June 1989 and June 1994, Santer renewed the CSV-LSAP coalition.

In January 1995 Santer took office as President of the European Commission. He was succeeded as Prime Minister by Jean-Claude Juncker of the CSV, hitherto Minister of the Budget, of Finance and of Labour. The two coalition partners both recorded losses at the general election in June 1999, while the DP and the conservative Aktiounskomitee fir Demokratie a Rentegerechtegkeet (ADR—Action Committee for Democracy and Pensions Justice) increased their representation and the environmentalist party, Déi Gréng (The Greens), retained its five seats in the legislature. Juncker, who remained as Prime Minister, subsequently formed a new centre-right coalition of the CSV and the DP.

In March 1998 Grand Duke Jean conferred broad constitutional powers upon his eldest son and heir, Prince Henri, permitting him to deputize for the Grand Duke in all official capacities. In October 2000, following a reign of 36 years, Grand Duke Jean abdicated and Prince Henri succeeded his father as head of state.

Luxembourg's banking secrecy laws have for many years been a cause of concern. In April 1993 legislation was introduced which permitted the confiscation of deposits in Luxembourg banks accruing from suspected illegal drugs-related activities, and in 1997 the powers of confiscation were extended to include other illegal activities, including arms-smuggling. During that year the country's financial sector came under renewed scrutiny when the Belgian and German authorities both conducted investigations into alleged widespread tax evasion by their citizens and companies based in Luxembourg. Luxembourg was further criticized for refusing, as did Switzerland, to endorse the code of conduct with respect to tax havens drafted by the Organisation for Economic Co-operation and Development (OECD, see p. 377) in April 1998. During 1998 Luxembourg also opposed European Commission proposals for European taxation harmonization, which would oblige Luxembourg to impose tax on non-residents' interest and dividend income, thereby reducing the attraction of Luxembourg as a financial centre. In May 2000, however, Luxembourg endorsed OECD proposals aimed at limiting the use of banking secrecy laws for the purpose of tax evasion. In October the Chamber of Deputies approved a relaxation of such laws to facilitate co-operation with the US authorities in their attempts to halt tax evasion. Luxembourg was exempted for at least six years from a requirement for EU member states to exchange banking information from 2005 under new EU taxation rules concerning overseas investments agreed in 2003 (see *Economic Affairs*).

At the general election held in June 2004 the CSV increased its representation in the legislature to 24 seats. The LSAP secured 14 seats, while the DP took 10, Déi Gréng seven and the ADR five. A new coalition Government comprising the CSV and the LSAP was sworn in the following month, again under the leadership of Juncker. Jean Asselborn of the LSAP was appointed as Deputy Prime Minister and Minister of Foreign Affairs and Immigration.

In April 2006 the ADR adopted a new name, Alternativ Demokratesch Reformpartei (Alternative Democratic Reform Party), in an attempt to broaden its appeal. However, the concurrent redesign of the party's logo to incorporate the colours of the national flag provoked criticism that it was adopting a more right-wing, nationalist stance. Several members of the ADR subsequently resigned from the party, including one of its five deputies, who remained in the legislature as an independent; the ADR consequently lost its status as an official parliamentary group.

In January 2008 two former members of the state security forces were arrested in connection with a bombing campaign which had targeted a number of public buildings in 1984–86. In September 2008 the General Director and the Secretary-General of the police force were dismissed, after the Attorney-General expressed doubts over the credibility of statements made by the two officials regarding the original investigation into the attacks. In January 2012 it was announced that there was sufficient evidence to try the two detainees in connection with the bombings, although both denied any involvement; the trial commenced in February 2013.

In February 2008 Luxembourg became the third EU member state (along with Belgium and the Netherlands) to approve legislation decriminalizing euthanasia and assisted suicide.

However, in December Grand Duke Henri precipitated a constitutional crisis by indicating that he would refuse to ratify the law, citing his religious convictions. Despite his own party's opposition to the bill, Juncker criticized the Grand Duke for disregarding the expressed will of parliament and proposed to amend the Constitution to remove the Grand Duke's powers to veto legislation adopted by the legislature. The amendment received final legislative approval in March 2009, thus, in effect, rendering the monarchy a largely ceremonial role. Meanwhile, the law decriminalizing euthanasia and assisted suicide was promulgated by Grand Duke Henri in March 2009.

At the general election held in June 2009 the CSV increased its representation in the Chamber of Deputies to 26 seats. The LSAP and the DP each lost one seat, taking 13 and nine, respectively, while Déi Gréng's representation was unchanged at seven seats. The ADR won four seats. Juncker renewed the outgoing CSV-LSAP coalition in July; Asselborn remained as Deputy Prime Minister and Minister of Foreign Affairs.

Divisions emerged within the ruling coalition in 2010 over the proposed revision of the wage indexation system, whereby salaries were automatically adjusted according to changes in the cost of living. Fearing that the existing system could lead to a loss of economic competitiveness, the CSV Minister of Finance, Luc Frieden, supported by the LSAP Minister of the Economy and External Trade, Jeannot Krecké, advocated the exclusion of energy, alcohol and tobacco prices from the calculation. However, the proposal was strongly opposed by other members of the LSAP and by the trade unions, and appeared to have been abandoned in September, when it was agreed, none the less, to postpone the next index-linked rise in wages until October 2011, the last having occurred in July 2010. Following the continued failure of trade unions and employers to agree on a reform of the wage indexation system, a further compromise was drawn up by the Government in December 2011 and approved by the Chamber of Deputies in the following month: the next indexation of salaries, which would have been due in March 2012 (owing to high inflation), was deferred until October of that year and a minimum delay of 12 months between adjustments to wages was introduced for the period 2012–14. (The next wage indexation was not expected to take place before mid-2016.)

In February 2012 Krecké resigned as Minister of the Economy and External Trade; although he cited personal reasons as the motivation for his decision, observers noted that he had previously expressed frustration at the slow pace of reform. The LSAP selected Etienne Schneider, hitherto senior adviser at the Ministry of the Economy and External Trade, as Krecké's replacement.

In June 2012 a revision to the laws of succession came into effect, according to which the first-born child of the monarch would henceforth accede to the throne irrespective of gender.

In the wake of the revelation in July 2013 of a scandal involving illegal telephone recordings made by the Service de Renseignement de l'Etat Luxembourgeois (SREL—Luxembourg State Intelligence Service), the LSAP withdrew its support for Prime Minister Juncker—after a parliamentary inquiry found that he had failed adequately to supervise the SREL and inform the Chamber of Deputies of the Service's alleged past misdeeds—and demanded fresh elections. The Prime Minister had also come under persistent criticism for reportedly having focused too much on his EU duties at the expense of domestic concerns. Juncker, while denying any wrongdoing on his part, submitted his resignation on 11 July after more than 18 years in office. An early general election was called for 20 October (the first such in the country since the 1960s). Following the poll, which attracted a turnout of 85%, the CSV's representation in the legislature declined to 23 seats, while the LSAP retained 13 seats, the DP's tally rose to 13 and Déi Gréng secured six. Luxembourg's first liberal administration for decades was appointed in early December in the form of a coalition of the LSAP, the DP and Déi Gréng. The new Government was headed by the mayor of the city of Luxembourg and leader of the DP, Xavier Bettel, while the LSAP's Schneider became Deputy Prime Minister (in addition to being given responsibility for the economy, internal security and defence portfolios).

In June 2014 the Chamber of Deputies approved legislation to permit same-sex marriage and the right to plenary adoption for homosexual couples; the law took effect on 1 January 2015. The Chamber of Deputies announced in October 2014 that a referendum would be held on 7 June 2015 on the following four issues: the lowering of the voting age from 18 years to 16; the right of non-citizens (who had been resident in Luxembourg for at least 10 years) to vote in legislative elections; the state's continuing provision of wages and pensions to Roman Catholic priests and other faith group workers; and the limitation of a government member's term in office to 10 consecutive years.

Foreign Affairs

As a founder member of the European Community (EC, now European Union—EU, see p. 271), of which the city of Luxembourg is one of the main bases, Luxembourg has played a significant role in progress towards European integration since the Second World War. Luxembourg's commitment to such integration was exemplified by its status as one of the original signatories to the Schengen Agreement (named after the town in Luxembourg where the accord was signed by a number of EC member countries in 1990), which binds signatories to the abolition of internal border controls.

In December 2000 the Luxembourg Government played a prominent role in negotiations regarding the Treaty of Nice, which aimed to reform the institutions of the EU in light of its forthcoming enlargements. The terms of the treaty safeguarded Luxembourg's privileged position in the EU: Luxembourg was to continue to have a European Commissioner, to maintain its six seats in the European Parliament and to continue to enjoy a voting weight in the Council of the European Union out of proportion to its size. In July 2001 the Chamber of Deputies ratified the treaty by a large majority. At the same time, Luxembourg continued, much to the frustration of most of its EU partners, to oppose the removal of the Secretariat of the European Parliament from the city of Luxembourg, together with its 1,500 staff, whose continued presence was considered by the Luxembourg Government to be vital to the local economy.

In July 2005 Luxembourg held a national referendum (the first since 1936) on the EU constitutional treaty, which had been approved by the EU in mid-2004. Although there were concerns that the proposed constitution was not wholly advantageous for the smaller member states of the EU, most political parties in Luxembourg supported the treaty, which was approved by some 56.5% of voters in Luxembourg, despite opposition to the document having increased following its rejection by French and Dutch voters at respective referendums in May and June. In December 2007, following a summit meeting in Lisbon, Portugal, EU leaders signed a reform treaty to replace the abandoned constitutional treaty. The so-called Treaty of Lisbon was ratified by the Chamber of Deputies in May 2008 and entered into force in December 2009, following ratification by all of the then 27 EU member states.

As President of the so-called 'Eurogroup' of eurozone finance ministers (a position that he had held since its creation in 2005), Juncker was heavily involved during 2010–12 in negotiations on the provision of assistance to three members of the eurozone in financial difficulties—Greece, Ireland and Portugal—and in wider efforts to safeguard the stability of the eurozone through measures such as the establishment of a temporary European Financial Stability Facility and, subsequently, a permanent European Stability Mechanism (both based in Luxembourg), as well as the introduction of new arrangements designed to increase fiscal discipline. Juncker stood down as Eurogroup President in January 2013; in July 2014 the former Prime Minister was elected as the new President of the European Commission (assuming office in November). Shortly after taking up his new post, however, there were calls from some quarters for Juncker's resignation following allegations that he had engineered large-scale corporate tax avoidance during his tenure of the Luxembourg premiership. Nevertheless, Juncker comfortably survived a motion of no confidence presented to the European Parliament at the end of November.

Meanwhile, in March 2003 the Chamber of Deputies approved the secondment of 10 troops to the NATO-led International Security Assistance Force in Afghanistan (ISAF). Luxembourg's last remaining soldier left Afghanistan in October 2014; the international mission was concluded in December. The Luxembourg Government confirmed that from 2015 it would provide an annual US $5m. to help fund the Afghan security forces. In early 2015 Luxembourg was also contributing to the NATO-led Kosovo Force—KFOR, to EU missions in Mali and the Central African Republic, and to the UN Interim Force in Lebanon (UNIFIL).

In June 2008, at a summit meeting in The Hague, Netherlands, Prime Minister Juncker and his counterparts from Belgium and the Netherlands signed a new Benelux Treaty on political and economic co-operation. The document expanded the scope of the previous treaty, signed in 1958 and due to expire in 2010, to provide for greater co-operation between the three

Governments on justice and home affairs, as well as customs and cross-border trade. In recognition of this broader scope, the official title was changed from the Benelux Economic Union to the Benelux Union. The treaty was ratified by Luxembourg's Chamber of Deputies in May 2009 and entered into force on 1 January 2012, following its ratification by the national legislatures of the other two countries and by the parliaments of Belgium's five federal units.

CONSTITUTION AND GOVERNMENT

The Constitution dates back to 1868, but in 1919 a constituent assembly introduced some important changes, declaring that the sovereign power resided in the nation, that all secret treaties were denounced and that deputies were to be elected by a list system by means of proportional representation, on the basis of universal adult suffrage. Luxembourg is a hereditary and constitutional monarchy. Legislative power is exercised by the unicameral Chambre des Députés (Chamber of Deputies), with 60 members elected by universal adult suffrage for five years (subject to dissolution). Some legislative functions are also entrusted to the advisory Conseil d'Etat (State Council), with 21 members appointed for life by the Grand Duke, but decisions made by this body can be overruled by the legislature.

Executive power is vested in the Grand Duke, but is normally exercised by the Council of Ministers, led by the President of the Government (Prime Minister). The Grand Duke appoints ministers, but they are responsible to the legislature. Luxembourg is divided into three districts (Luxembourg, Diekirch and Grevenmacher), 12 cantons and 106 municipalities.

REGIONAL AND INTERNATIONAL CO-OPERATION

Luxembourg was a founder member of the European Community, now the European Union (EU, see p. 271), and hosts a number of the EU's institutions. It was also a founder member of the Benelux Economic Union (restyled the Benelux Union, see p. 444 in 2008), the Council of Europe (see p. 250) and the Organization for Security and Co-operation in Europe (OSCE, see p. 385).

Luxembourg was a founder member of the UN in 1945. In October 2012, for the first time in the country's history, Luxembourg was elected to hold one of the five non-permanent seats on the UN Security Council during 2013–14. As a contracting party to the General Agreement on Tariffs and Trade, Luxembourg joined the World Trade Organization (WTO, see p. 431) on its establishment in 1995. Luxembourg was also a founder member of the North Atlantic Treaty Organization (NATO, see p. 367) and the Organisation for Economic Co-operation and Development (OECD, see p. 377).

ECONOMIC AFFAIRS

In 2012, according to estimates by the World Bank, Luxembourg's gross national income (GNI), measured at average 2010–12 prices, was US $38,125m., equivalent to $71,810 per head (or $59,750 per head on an international purchasing-power parity basis). During 2004–13, it was estimated, the population increased at an average rate of 1.9% per year, while gross domestic product (GDP) per head remained almost constant with negligible growth during the same period. Overall GDP increased, in real terms, at an average annual rate of 1.9% in 2004–13; in 2012 GDP decreased by 0.2%, but increased by 2.1% in 2013, measured at constant prices, and increased by 2.0% in 2013, according to chain-linking methodologies.

In 2013 agriculture (including forestry and fishing) contributed 0.3% of GDP and 1.1% of the employed labour force were engaged in the agricultural sector. The principal crops are wheat, barley and triticale (a wheat-rye hybrid). Livestock-rearing is also of some importance. Agricultural GDP decreased at an average annual rate of 6.1% in 2004–13; sectoral GDP increased by 17.6% in 2012, but decreased by 6.4% in 2013.

In 2013 industry (including mining, manufacturing, construction and power) provided 12.2% of GDP and engaged 20.1% of the employed labour force. Industrial GDP decreased, in real terms, at an average annual rate of 1.0% in 2004–13; it increased by 0.1% in 2012, but decreased by 6.3% in 2013.

Manufacturing activities contributed 5.2% of GDP and engaged 8.4% of the employed workforce in 2013. Although the country's deposits of iron ore are no longer exploited, the iron and steel industry remains one of the most important sectors of the Luxembourg economy; metal manufactures accounted for 26.7% of total exports in 2013. The Luxembourg steel industry is dominated by ArcelorMittal, which was formed from a merger of

Arcelor and Mittal Steel in 2006. Machinery and other equipment provided 15.4% of total exports in 2013. Other important branches of manufacturing are basic manufactures, and chemicals and related products. The GDP of the manufacturing sector decreased by an average of 3.6% per year in 2004–13. Manufacturing GDP decreased by 6.3% in 2012, and by 0.9% in 2013.

In 2013 construction contributed 5.4% of GDP and engaged 10.5% of the employed labour force. During 2004–13 the sector grew at an average annual rate of 2.4%; sectoral GDP decreased by 10.9% in 2012, but increased by 1.0% in 2013.

In 2012 87.1% of net electricity production was from natural gas, while 3.5% was from hydroelectric installations. Imports of mineral fuels and lubricants comprised 12.1% of the value of total imports in 2012.

In 2013 the services sector contributed 87.5% of GDP and engaged 78.9% of the employed labour force. Favourable laws governing banking secrecy and taxation encouraged the development of Luxembourg as a major international financial centre. Financial services contributed 26.9% of GDP in 2013. In December 2014 there were 148 banks in Luxembourg, most of which were subsidiaries or branches of foreign banks. In accordance with the demands of the European Commission, Luxembourg abolished its preferential tax regime for holding companies from January 2007, although existing companies were permitted to retain their tax benefits until 2010. The replacement regime of 'family private assets management companies', which was aimed at the wealth management sector, was introduced in 2007. Stock exchange activities (notably the Eurobond market and investment portfolio management) are also prominent. Since the mid-1990s Luxembourg has had the largest investment fund sector in Europe: in 2005 investment funds accounted for 8% of GDP. In 2010 there were 96 approved insurance companies in Luxembourg, as well as 244 reinsurance companies. The GDP of the services sector increased, in real terms, at an average annual rate of 2.8% in 2004–13; it decreased by 1.1% in 2012, but rose by 2.9% in 2013.

In 2013, according to IMF figures, Luxembourg recorded a visible merchandise trade deficit of US $8,358m., while there was a surplus of $3,161m. on the current account of the balance of payments. Other members of the European Union (EU, see p. 271) account for much of Luxembourg's foreign trade. In 2013 the principal source of imports (35.1%) was Belgium; other major providers were Germany, France, the USA and the Netherlands. The principal market for exports in that year was Germany (28.2%); other major purchasers were France, Belgium and the Netherlands. The principal exports in 2013 were manufactured goods (particularly metal manufactures), other basic manufactures, machinery, miscellaneous manufactured articles, transport equipment, chemical products, transport equipment and food and live animals. The principal imports were transport equipment, mineral fuels and lubricants, machinery, chemical products, miscellaneous manufactured articles, food and live animals, crude materials, manufactured articles (notably metal manufactures), and other basic manufactures.

In 2013 there was a budgetary deficit of €286.4m., equivalent to 0.6% of GDP. Luxembourg's general government gross debt was €10,511m. in 2013, equivalent to 23.1% of GDP. The annual rate of inflation averaged 2.4% in 2004–13; consumer prices rose by 0.7% in 2014. The rate of unemployment averaged 6.9% in 2013. In 2013 net cross-border commuters from neighbouring states totalled 151,700, constituting 39.4% of the total employed in Luxembourg.

Luxembourg's economy expanded at an average annual rate of more than 5% during 1985–2000, its success based on its development as an international financial centre. The rapid economic expansion of the late 1990s slowed significantly in the early 2000s, but high GDP growth resumed in 2005–07, largely led by the banking and insurance sectors. The banking sector suffered as a result of the global financial crisis from mid-2008, but Luxembourg was otherwise well placed to withstand the downturn, owing to its low levels of public debt and strong public finances. Indeed, despite a temporary deterioration in the fiscal situation following the introduction of stimulus measures, the budget deficit in 2009 was the second lowest in the EU (after Sweden), at 0.9% of GDP, and following a slight widening in 2010, to 1.1%, remained at 0.6%–0.8% of GDP in 2011–13. The Government aimed to return the budget to surplus by 2014. Having contracted by 5.3% in 2009, GDP, measured in constant terms, increased by 2.7% in 2010. More moderate growth of 1.6% was recorded in 2011, mainly owing to the poor performances of exports and the financial sector, which were adversely affected by the sovereign debt crisis in the eurozone. With persistently weak exports and falling output in the steel and construction sectors, GDP contracted by 0.2% in 2012, before returning to positive growth, of 2.1%, in 2013. This recovery was partly owing to the Government's adherence to a policy of fiscal consolidation in 2012–13, including cuts in public expenditure and changes to the pensions system. The unemployment rate remained on a persistently upward trajectory, rising from 5.7% in 2011, to 6.1% in 2012 and further to 6.9% in 2013 (compared with only 2.7% in 2003), while the rate of inflation recorded a gradual decline during 2011–14 (partly as a result of lower petroleum prices) from 3.4% to 0.7%. The future profitability of Luxembourg's financial sector appeared somewhat uncertain, owing to the effects of EU integration, including the harmonization of taxation and regulatory structures, which threatened the banking secrecy and tax advantages that made the country attractive to investors. Under EU rules, Luxembourg had been allowed to retain banking secrecy for a transitional period, levying a withholding tax on non-residents' savings instead, which rose incrementally from 15% in 2005 to 35% from mid-2011. However, under mounting international pressure, Prime Minister Juncker announced in April 2013 that reforms with regard to the automatic exchange of depositors' banking information in line with the EU Savings Directive would be implemented in Luxembourg from January 2015 (thereby replacing the withholding tax system). At the same time, in a move aimed at reassuring the thousands of large multinationals based in Luxembourg, it was stated that the country's secrecy rules for foreign companies would remain unchanged and that the country would continue to benefit from the advantages that exist in its regulatory framework and competitive financial services industry. As greater confidence in sustained recovery in the eurozone led to a rise in domestic demand and services exports, the IMF forecast that annual GDP growth in Luxembourg would reach a moderate level of around 2.0%–2.5% during 2014–19. However, the IMF recommended that in order to sustain steady growth the Government should curtail rapidly increasing public expenditure, and seek to achieve economic diversification beyond the financial sector.

PUBLIC HOLIDAYS

2016: 1 January (New Year's Day), 28 March (Easter Monday), 1 May (Labour Day), 5 May (Ascension Day), 16 May (Whit Monday), 23 June (National Day), 15 August (Assumption), 1 November (All Saints' Day), 25 December (Christmas Day), 26 December (St Stephen's Day).

Statistical Survey

Source (unless otherwise stated): Service Central de la Statistique et des Etudes Economiques (STATEC), Centre Administratif Pierre Werner, 13 rue Erasme, 1468 Luxembourg; tel. 247-84219; fax 46-42-89; e-mail info@statec.etat.lu; internet www.statec.lu.

AREA AND POPULATION

Area: 2,586 sq km (999 sq miles).

Population: 439,539 at census of 15 February 2001; 512,353 (males 254,967, females 257,386) at census of 1 February 2011. *2014* (official estimate at 1 January): 549,680.

Density (at 1 January 2014): 212.6 per sq km.

Population by Age and Sex (official estimates at 1 January 2014): *0–14 years:* 92,554 (males 47,497, females 45,057); *15–64 years:* 379,752 (males 193,641, females 186,111); *65 years and over:* 77,374 (males 33,979, females 43,395); *Total* 549,680 (males 275,117, females 274,563).

Principal Towns (official estimates at 1 January 2014): Luxembourg (capital) 107,247; Esch-sur-Alzette 32,600; Differdange 23,571; Dudelange 19,421; Pétange 17,265.

Births, Marriages and Deaths (2013): Live births 6,115 (birth rate 11.4 per 1,000); Marriages 1,722 (marriage rate 3.2 per 1,000); Deaths 3,822 (death rate 7.1 per 1,000).

Life Expectancy (years at birth): 81.4 (males 79.1; females 83.8) in 2012. Source: World Bank, World Development Indicators database.

Immigration and Emigration (2013): Arrivals 21,098; Departures 10,750.

Employment ('000 persons, 2013): Agriculture, hunting, forestry and fishing 4.1; Mining and quarrying 0.3; Manufacturing 32.2; Electricity, gas and water supply 4.2; Construction 40.6; Wholesale and retail trade, repair of motor vehicles, motorcycles and personal and household goods 50.3; Hotels and restaurants 19.2; Transport, storage and communications 40.2; Financial intermediation 42.8; Real estate, renting and business activities 60.2; Public administration and defence and compulsory social security 22.0; Education 17.8; Health and social work 35.2; Other community, social and personal service activities 11.2; Private households with employed persons 5.3; *Total employed* 385.5.

HEALTH AND WELFARE

Key Indicators

Total Fertility Rate (children per woman, 2012): 1.7.

Under-5 Mortality Rate (per 1,000 live births, 2012): 2.

HIV/AIDS (% of persons aged 15–49, 2011): 0.3.

Physicians (per 1,000 head, 2009): 2.8.

Hospital Beds (per 1,000 head, 2009): 5.6.

Health Expenditure (2011): US $ per head (PPP): 6,020.

Health Expenditure (2011): % of GDP: 6.7.

Health Expenditure (2011): public (% of total): 84.1.

Total Carbon Dioxide Emissions ('000 metric tons, 2010): 10,828.7.

Carbon Dioxide Emissions Per Head (metric tons, 2010): 21.4.

Human Development Index (2013): ranking: 21.

Human Development Index (2013): value: 0.881.

For sources and definitions, see explanatory note on p. vi.

AGRICULTURE, ETC.

Principal Crops ('000 metric tons, 2013): Wheat 91.1; Rye 4.8; Barley 42.5; Oats 5.5; Triticale (wheat-rye hybrid) 25.7; Potatoes 17.5; Rapeseed 15.3; Mushrooms 5.0 (metric tons); Apples 1.9; Grapes 13.4.

Livestock ('000 head, year ending September 2013): Cattle 193.6; Horses 4.7; Pigs 87.5; Sheep 8.6; Chickens 111.3.

Livestock Products (metric tons, 2013): Cattle meat 8,060; Pig meat 11,121; Chicken meat 243; Cow milk 295,855.

Forestry ('000 cubic metres, 2013, FAO estimates): *Roundwood Removals:* 261.4 (Sawlogs, veneer logs and logs for sleepers 132.1, Fuel wood 17.5, Pulpwood 92.5, Other 19.3); *Sawnwood Production* (incl. railway sleepers) 78.3 (coniferous 39.2, broadleaved 39.1).

Source: FAO.

INDUSTRY

Selected Products ('000 metric tons, 2013, unless otherwise indicated): Crude steel 2,090; Rolled steel products 2,377; Wine ('000 hl) 100.9; Beer ('000 hl) 373.7 (2005); Electric energy (million kWh) 3,422 (2012).

FINANCE

Currency and Exchange Rates: 100 cent = 1 euro (€). *Sterling and Dollar Equivalents* (31 December 2014): £1 sterling = 1.286 euros; US $1 = 0.824 euros; €10 = £7.78 = $12.14. *Average Exchange Rate* (euros per US dollar): 0.7783 in 2012; 0.7532 in 2013; 0.7537 in 2014. Note: The national currency was formerly the Luxembourg franc. From the introduction of the euro, with Luxembourg's participation, on 1 January 1999, a fixed exchange rate of €1 = 40.3399 Luxembourg francs was in operation. Euro notes and coins were introduced on 1 January 2002. The euro and local currency circulated alongside each other until 28 February, after which the euro became the sole legal tender.

Central Budget (€ million): *Revenue:* 17,946.4 in 2011; 19,031.8 in 2012; 19,849.8 in 2013. *Expenditure:* 18,075.1 in 2011; 19,059.6 in 2012; 20,136.2 in 2013.

International Reserves (US $ million at 31 December 2013): Gold 86.51; IMF special drawing rights 376.15; Reserve position in IMF

315.43; Foreign exchange 184.84; *Total* 962.93. Source: IMF, *International Financial Statistics*.

Money Supply (incl. shares, depository corporations, national residency criteria, € million at 31 December 2013): Currency issued 2,448 (Banque Centrale du Luxembourg 87,775); Demand deposits 148,490; Other deposits 76,365; Securities other than shares 56,971; Money market fund shares 194,788; Shares and other equity 58,806; Other items (net) −141,751; *Total* 396,118. Source: IMF, *International Financial Statistics*.

Cost of Living (Consumer Price Index; base: 2005 = 100): All items 118.4 in 2012; 120.4 in 2013; 121.2 in 2014.

Expenditure on the Gross Domestic Product (€ million at current prices, 2013): Final consumption expenditure 21,893.7 (Households 13,406.8, Non-profit institutions serving households 660.6, General government 7,826.4); Gross capital formation 7,451.6; *Total domestic expenditure* 29,345.4; Exports of goods and services 92,080.4; *Less* Imports of goods and services 76,137.6; *GDP in market prices* 45,288.1.

Gross Domestic Product by Economic Activity (€ million at current prices, 2013): Agriculture, hunting, forestry and fishing 138.3; Construction 2,185.4; Other industry 2,746.1; Wholesale and retail trade, repair of motor vehicles, motorcycles and personal and household goods, hotels and restaurants and transport and communications 9,084.4; Financial services, real estate, renting and business activities 21,370.8; Other community, social and personal service activities 4,934.6; *Gross value added in basic prices* 40,459.5; Taxes, less subsidies, on products 4,828.6; *GDP in market prices* 45,288.1.

Balance of Payments (US $ million, 2013): Exports of goods 16,978; Imports of goods −25,336; *Balance on goods* −8,358; Exports of services 80,152; Imports of services −48,467; *Balance on goods and services* 23,327; Primary income received 279,476; Primary income paid −299,166; *Balance on goods, services and primary income* 3,638; Secondary income received 7,758; Secondary income paid −8,234; *Current balance* 3,161; Capital account (net) −306; Direct investment assets −366,827; Direct investment liabilities 369,870; Portfolio investment assets −203,136; Portfolio investment liabilities 301,632; Financial derivatives and employee stock options (net) 9,101; Other investment assets −128,012; Other investment liabilities 14,452; Net errors and omissions 145; *Reserves and related items* 80. Source: IMF, *International Financial Statistics*.

EXTERNAL TRADE

Principal Commodities (€ million, 2013): *Imports:* Food and live animals 1,516.2; Beverages and tobacco 480.9; Crude materials (inedible) except fuels 1,488.5; Mineral fuels, lubricants, etc. 2,617.7; Chemicals and related products 1,848.7; Metal manufactures 1,412.6; Other basic manufactures 1,307.2; Machinery and other equipment 2,279.0; Transport equipment 3,370.4; Miscellaneous manufactured articles 1,847.2; Total 18,168.5. *Exports:* Food and live animals 780.2; Crude materials (inedible) except fuels 328.1; Chemicals and related products 959.1; Metal manufactures 2,825.4; Other basic manufactures 1,800.3; Machinery and other equipment 1,634.5; Transport equipment 913.5; Miscellaneous manufactured articles 1,061.8; Total (incl. others) 10,599.0.

Principal Trading Partners (€ million, 2013): *Imports:* Belgium 6,378.8; France 2,249.5; Germany 4,929.3; Italy 403.7; Netherlands 966.1; Switzerland 171.2; United Kingdom 283.3; USA 1,334.0; Total

(incl. others) 18,168.5. *Exports:* Austria 190.6; Belgium 1,414.1; China, People's Republic 164.5; Czech Republic 113.3; France 1,548.6; Germany 2,990.1; Hong Kong 81.9; Italy 371.7; Netherlands 543.5; Poland 243.5; Russia 156.7; Spain 227.1; Sweden 152.8; Switzerland 132.5; Turkey 97.1; United Kingdom 421.0; USA 392.8; Total (incl. others) 10,599.0.

TRANSPORT

Railways (traffic, million, 2013): Passenger-km 385; Freight ton-km (excl. transit traffic) 250.

Road Traffic (motor vehicles in use at 1 January 2014): Cars 362,879; Motorcycles 17,226; Buses and coaches 1,759; Goods vehicles 32,933; Tractors 4,726; Utility vehicles 368; Special vehicles 2,827; Cycles with auxiliary motors 8,527; Total 431,245.

Shipping: *River Traffic* (Port of Mertert, '000 metric tons, 2013): Goods loaded 156, Goods unloaded 530. *Flag Registered Fleet* (at 31 December 2014): Number of vessels 256; Total displacement 3,209,798 grt (Source: Lloyd's List Intelligence—lloydslistintelligence.com).

Civil Aviation (traffic on scheduled services, 2013): Passengers carried 2,197,331; Freight (metric tons) 673,823; Mail (metric tons) 323.

TOURISM

Tourist Arrivals (at accommodation establishments): 934,994 in 2011; 1,020,798 in 2012; 1,044,331 in 2013.

Arrivals by Country (2013): Belgium 189,735; China, People's Republic 35,649; France 126,217; Germany 137,206; Switzerland 21,134; Netherlands 162,583; United Kingdom 64,448; USA 26,655; Total (incl. others) 1,044,331.

Tourism Receipts (US $ million, excl. passenger transport): 4,825 in 2011; 4,615 in 2012; 4,822 in 2013. Source: World Tourism Organization.

COMMUNICATIONS MEDIA

Mobile Cellular Telephones: 788,371 in 2013.

Telephones: 267,600 main lines in use in 2013.

Internet Subscribers ('000, estimate): 168.4 in 2010.

Broadband Subscribers ('000): 177.6 in 2013.

Source: International Telecommunication Union.

EDUCATION

(2012/13 unless otherwise indicated)

Nursery: 1,030 teachers; 10,740 pupils.

Primary: 3,756 teachers; 31,975 pupils.

Secondary and Technical Secondary: 4,148 teachers; 12,958 pupils (secondary), 26,627 pupils (technical secondary).

University-level: 9,890 students, incl. 3,175 studying abroad.

Schools (2004/05): 375 offering a combination of nursery and primary education; 32 secondary (5 private).

Pupil-teacher Ratio (UNESCO estimate): 9.3 in 2009/10 (Source: UNESCO Institute for Statistics).

Directory

The Government

HEAD OF STATE

Grand Duke: HRH Grand Duke HENRI (succeeded to the throne 7 October 2000).

COUNCIL OF MINISTERS
(May 2015)

A coalition of the Demokratesch Partei (DP), the Lëtzebuerger Sozialistesch Arbechterpartei (LSAP) and Déi Gréng.

Prime Minister, and Minister of State, of Communications and Media and of Religious Affairs: XAVIER BETTEL (DP).

Deputy Prime Minister and Minister of the Economy, of Internal Security and of Defence: ETIENNE SCHNEIDER (LSAP).

Minister of Foreign and European Affairs and of Immigration and Asylum: JEAN ASSELBORN (LSAP).

Minister of Justice: FÉLIX BRAZ (Déi Gréng).

Minister of Social Security, of Co-operation and Humanitarian Action and of Sports: ROMAIN SCHNEIDER (LSAP).

Minister of Labour, Employment and Social Economy and Solidarity: NICOLAS SCHMIT (LSAP).

Minister of Sustainable Development and Infrastructure: FRANÇOIS BAUSCH (Déi Gréng).

Minister of Agriculture, Viticulture and Consumer Protection and of Relations with Parliament: FERNAND ETGEN (DP).

Minister of Culture and of Housing: MAGGY NAGEL (DP).

Minister of Finance: PIERRE GRAMEGNA.

Minister of Health and of Equal Opportunities: LYDIA MUTSCH (LSAP).

Minister of the Interior and of the Civil Service and Administrative Reform: DANIEL KERSCH (LSAP).

Minister of Education, Children and Youth, and of Higher Education and Research: CLAUDE MEISCH (DP).

Minister of Family Affairs, Integration and the Greater Region: CORINNE CAHEN (DP).

Minister of the Environment: CAROLE DIESCHBOURG (Déi Gréng).

MINISTRIES

Office of the Prime Minister: 4 rue de la Congrégation, 1352 Luxembourg; tel. 247-82101; fax 46-17-20; e-mail ministere.etat@me
.etat.lu; internet www.gouvernement.lu.

Ministry of Agriculture, Viticulture and Consumer Protection: 1 rue de la Congrégation, 1352 Luxembourg; tel. 247-82478; fax 46-40-27; e-mail info@ma.public.lu; internet www.ma.public.lu.

Ministry of the Civil Service and Administrative Reform: 63 ave de la Liberté, BP 1807, 1931 Luxembourg; tel. 247-83130; fax 26-48-36-21; e-mail info@fonctionpublique.public.lu; internet www
.fonction-publique.public.lu.

Ministry of Culture: 4 blvd Roosevelt, 2450 Luxembourg; tel. 247-86600; fax 26-29-60-38; e-mail info@mc.public.lu; internet www.mc
.public.lu.

Ministry of the Economy: 19–21 blvd Royal, 2449 Luxembourg; tel. 247-82478; fax 46-04-48; e-mail info@eco.public.lu; internet www
.eco.public.lu.

Ministry of Education, Children and Youth: 29 rue Aldringen, 2926 Luxembourg; tel. 247-85100; fax 247-85113; e-mail info@men
.lu; internet www.men.public.lu.

Ministry of Equal Opportunities: 19–21 blvd Royal, 2921 Luxembourg; tel. 247-85814; fax 24-18-86; e-mail info@mega.public.lu; internet www.mega.public.lu.

Ministry of Family Affairs, Integration and the Greater Region: 12–14 ave Emile Reuter, 2919 Luxembourg; tel. 247-86500; fax 247-86570; e-mail info@mfi.public.lu; internet www.mfi
.public.lu.

Ministry of Finance: 3 rue de la Congrégation, 1352 Luxembourg; tel. 247-82600; fax 47-52-41; internet www.mf.public.lu.

Ministry of Foreign and European Affairs: Hôtel St Maximin, 5 rue Notre-Dame, 2240 Luxembourg; tel. 247-82300; fax 22-31-44, e-mail boite.officielle@mae.etat.lu; internet www.mae.lu.

Ministry of Health: Villa Louvigny, allée Marconi, 2120 Luxembourg; tel. 247-85505; e-mail info@ms.public.lu; internet www.ms
.etat.lu.

Ministry of Higher Education and Research: 20 montée de la Pétrusse, 2327 Luxembourg; tel. 247-85206; fax 40-66-98; e-mail guy
.loos@mesr.etat.lu; internet www.mesr.public.lu.

Ministry of Housing: 4 place de l'Europe, 1499 Luxembourg; tel. 247-84819; fax 247-84840; e-mail info@ml.public.lu; internet www
.ml.public.lu.

Ministry of the Interior: 19 rue Beaumont, 1219 Luxembourg; tel. 247-84600; fax 22-11-25; e-mail info@miat.public.lu; internet www
.miat.public.lu.

Ministry of Internal Security: 13 rue Beaumont, 1219 Luxembourg; tel. 247-84659; fax 22-72-76; internet www.gouvernement.lu/
msi.

Ministry of Justice: Centre 13 rue Erasme, 2934 Luxembourg; tel. 247-84537; fax 266-84861; e-mail info@mj.public.lu; internet www
.mj.public.lu.

Ministry of Labour, Employment, and Social Economy and Solidarity: 26 rue Ste Zithe, 2939 Luxembourg; tel. 247-86100; fax 247-86108; e-mail info@mte.public.lu; internet www.mte.public.lu.

Ministry of Social Security: 26 rue Ste Zithe, 2763 Luxembourg; tel. 247-86311; fax 247-86328; e-mail mss@mss.etat.lu; internet www.mss.public.lu.

Ministry of Sports: 66 rue de Trèves, BP 180, 2011 Luxembourg; tel. and fax 247-83400; internet www.sport.public.lu.

Ministry of State: 4 rue de la Congrégation, 1352 Luxembourg; tel. 247-82101; fax 46-17-20; e-mail ministere.etat@me.etat.lu; internet www.etat.lu; (incorporating Ministry of Religious Affairs).

Ministry of Sustainable Development and Infrastructure: Bâtiment Alcide de Gasperi, 4 place de l'Europe, 1499 Luxembourg; tel. 247-82478; fax 46-27-09; e-mail info@developpement
-durable-infrastructures.public.lu; internet www.developpement
-durable-infrastructures.public.lu.

Legislature

CHAMBER OF DEPUTIES

Chambre des Députés: Hôtel de la Chambre des Députés, 19 rue du Marché-aux-Herbes, 1728 Luxembourg; tel. 466-966-1; fax 22-02-301; e-mail info@chd.lu; internet www.chd.lu.

President: MARS DI BARTOLOMEO.

General Election, 20 October 2013

Party	% of votes	Seats
Chrëschtlech Sozial Volkspartei	33.68	23
Lëtzebuerger Sozialistesch Arbechterpartei .	20.28	13
Demokratesch Partei	18.25	13
Déi Gréng	10.13	6
Alternativ Demokratesch Reformpartei . .	6.64	3
Déi Lénk	4.94	2
Piratepartei Lëtzebuerg	2.94	—
Kommunistische Partei Luxemburgs . . .	1.64	—
Partei fir Integral Demokratie	1.50	—
Total	**100.00**	**60**

Advisory Councils

Conseil Economique et Social: Centre Administratif Pierre Werner, 13 rue Erasme, BP 1306, 1013 Luxembourg; tel. 43-58-51; fax 42-27-29; e-mail info@ces.public.lu; internet www.ces.public.lu; f. 1966; consultative body on economics and social affairs; 39 mems; Pres. PASCALE TOUSSING; Sec.-Gen. MARIANNE NATI-STOFFEL.

Conseil d'Etat: 5 rue Sigefroi, 2536 Luxembourg; tel. 47-30-71; fax 46-43-22; e-mail info@conseil-etat.public.lu; internet www
.conseil-etat.public.lu; 21 mems nominated by the sovereign; Pres. VIVIANE ECKER; Sec.-Gen. MARC BESCH.

Political Organizations

Alternativ Demokratesch Reformpartei (ADR) (Alternative Democratic Reform Party): 20 rue de l'Eau, 1449 Luxembourg; tel. 26-20-37 06; fax 26-20-37-36; e-mail adr@chd.lu; internet www.adr
.lu; f. 1987 as Aktiounskomitee 5/6 Pensioun fir jiddfereen (Action Committee 5/6 Pensions for Everyone); name changed to Aktiouns-komitee fir Demokratie a Rentegerechtegkeet (Action Committee for Democracy and Pensions Justice) in 1994; present name adopted 2006; conservative; established to campaign for improved pension rights for private sector employees, but subsequently sought to broaden its concerns; Pres. JEAN SCHOOS.

Chrëschtlech Sozial Volkspartei (CSV) (Christian Social People's Party): 4 rue de l'Eau, BP 826, 2018 Luxembourg; tel. 22-57-31-1; fax 47-27-16; e-mail csv@csv.lu; internet www.csv.lu; f. 1914; advocates political stability, sustained economic expansion, ecological and social progress; 10,300 mems; Pres. MARC SPAUTZ; Sec.-Gen. LAURENT ZEIMET.

Déi Gréng (The Greens): 1 rue de Fort Elisabeth, 1463 Luxembourg; tel. 27-48-27-1; fax 27-48-27-22; e-mail greng@greng.lu; internet www.greng.lu; f. 1983; fmrly Déi Gréng Alternativ (Green Alternative Party); merged with the Gréng Lëscht Ekologesch Initiativ (Green List Ecological Initiative) in 1995; advocates grass-roots democracy, environmental protection, social concern and increased aid to developing countries; Co-Pres FRANÇOISE FOLMER, CHRISTIAN KMIOTEK.

Déi Lénk (The Left): 5 rue Aldringen, BP 817, 2018 Luxembourg; tel. 26-20-20-72; fax 26-20-20-73; e-mail info@lenk.lu; internet www
.dei-lenk.lu; f. 1999; Spokespersons FABIENNE LENTZ, DAVID WAGNER.

Demokratesch Partei (DP) (Democratic Party): 5 rue du St Esprit, 1475 Luxembourg; tel. 22-10-21; fax 22-10-13; e-mail secretariat@dp
.lu; internet www.dp.lu; liberal; Leader XAVIER BETTEL; Gen. Sec. GILLES BAUM.

Kommunistische Partei Luxemburgs/Parti Communiste Luxembourgeois/Kommunistesch Partei Lëtzebuerg (KPL) (Communist Party of Luxembourg): 3 rue Zénon Bernard, BP 403, 4005 Esch-sur-Alzette; tel. 44-60-66-21; fax 44-60-66-66; e-mail kpl@zlv.lu; internet www.kp-l.org; f. 1921; Pres. ALI RUCKERT.

Lëtzebuerger Sozialistesch Arbechterpartei (LSAP) (Socialist Workers' Party of Luxembourg): 68 rue de Gasperich, 1617 Luxembourg; tel. 45-65-73-1; fax 45-65-75; e-mail info@lsap.lu; internet www.lsap.lu; f. 1902; social democratic; 6,000 mems; Pres. CLAUDE HAAGEN; Sec. YVES CRUCHTEN.

Partei fir Integral Demokratie (Party for Full Democracy—PID): BP 31, 9001 Ettelbruck; tel. 88-93-31; fax 26-88-00-72; e-mail contact@pid4you.lu; internet www.pid4you.lu; f. 2013; Leader JEAN COLOMBERA.

Piratepartei Lëtzebuerg (Pirate Party Luxembourg): 1 Sonnestr., 5683 Dalheim; e-mail sven.clement@piratepartei.lu; internet piratepartei.lu; f. 2009; advocates citizens' rights, protection of data, transparency of government; Pres. SVEN CLEMENT.

Diplomatic Representation

EMBASSIES IN LUXEMBOURG

Austria: 3 rue des Bains, 1212 Luxembourg; tel. 47-11-88-1; fax 46-39-74; e-mail luxemburg-ob@bmeia.gv.at; internet www.bmeia.gv.at/luxemburg; Ambassador Dr THOMAS OBERREITER.

Belgium: 4 rue des Girondins, 1626 Luxembourg; tel. 44-27-46-1; fax 45-42-82; e-mail luxembourg@diplobel.fed.be; internet www.diplomatie.be/luxemburg; Ambassador THOMAS ANTOINE.

Cabo Verde: 117 val de Ste Croix, 1371 Luxembourg; tel. 26-48-09-48; fax 26-48-09-49; e-mail ambcvlux@pt.lu; Chargé d'affaires a.i. CLARA DELGADO.

China, People's Republic: 2 rue Van der Meulen, Dommeldange, 2152 Luxembourg; tel. 43-69-91-1; fax 42-24-23; e-mail chianemb_lu@mfa.gov.cn; internet lu.china-embassy.org; Ambassador ZENG XIANQI.

Czech Republic: 2 Rond-Point Robert Schuman, 2525 Luxembourg; tel. 26-47-78; fax 26-47-78-20; e-mail luxembourg@embassy.mzv.cz; internet www.mzv.cz/lucemburk; Ambassador PETR KUBERNÁT.

Finland: 2 rue Heine, 1720 Luxembourg; tel. 49-55-51; fax 49-46-40; e-mail sanomat.lux@formin.fi; internet www.finlande.lu; Ambassador TIMO RANTA.

France: 8B blvd Joseph II, BP 359, 2013 Luxembourg; tel. 45-72-71; fax 45-72-71-227; e-mail ambassade@ambafrance-lu.org; internet www.ambafrance-lu.org; Ambassador GUY YELDA.

Germany: 20–22 ave Emile Reuter, BP 95, 2420 Luxembourg; tel. 45-34-45-1; fax 45-56-04; e-mail info@luxe.diplo.de; internet www.luxemburg.diplo.de; Ambassador CHRISTINE GLÄSER.

Greece: 27 rue Marie-Adélaïde, 2128 Luxembourg; tel. 44-51-93; fax 45-01-64; e-mail gremb.lux@mfa.gr; Ambassador THEODORE GEORGAKELOS.

Ireland: Résidence Christina, 2nd Floor, 28 route d'Arlon, 1140 Luxembourg; tel. 45-06-10-1; fax 45-88-20; e-mail luxembourg@dfa.ie; internet www.embassyofireland.lu; Ambassador PEADAR CARPENTER.

Italy: 5–7 rue Marie-Adélaïde, 2128 Luxembourg; tel. 44-36-44-1; fax 45-55-23; e-mail ambasciata.lussemburgo@esteri.it; internet www.amblussemburgo.esteri.it; Ambassador STEFANO MARIA CACCIAGUERRA RANGHIERI.

Japan: 62 ave de la Faïencerie, BP 92, 2010 Luxembourg; tel. 46-41-51-1; fax 46-41-76; e-mail embjapan@lx.mofa.go.jp; internet www.lu.emb-japan.go.jp; Ambassador ATSUKO NISHIMURA.

Netherlands: 6 rue Ste Zithe, 2763 Luxembourg; tel. 22-75-70; fax 40-30-16; e-mail lux@minbuza.nl; internet www.paysbas.lu; Ambassador PETRUS WOUTERUS KOK.

Poland: 24 rue Guillaume Schneider, 2522 Luxembourg; tel. 26-00-32; fax 26-68-75-74; e-mail luksemburg.amb.sekretariat@msz.gov.pl; internet www.luksemburg.msz.gov.pl; Ambassador BARTOSZ JAŁOWIECKI.

Portugal: 24 rue Guillaume Schneider, 2522 Luxembourg; tel. 46-61-90-1; fax 46-51-69; e-mail luxemburgo@mne.pt; Ambassador CARLOS JOSÉ DE PINHO E MELO PEREIRA MARQUES.

Romania: 41 blvd de la Pétrusse, 2320 Luxembourg; tel. 45-51-51; fax 45-51-63; e-mail ambroum@pt.lu; internet luxemburg.mae.ro; Ambassador ROXANA DANIELA IFTIMIE.

Russian Federation: Château de Beggen, 116 rue Cyprien Merjai, 1719 Luxembourg; tel. 42-23-33; fax 42-23-34; e-mail ambruslu@pt.lu; internet www.ruslux.mid.ru; Ambassador MARK LVOVICH ENTIN.

Spain: 4 blvd Emmanuel Servais, BP 290, 2012 Luxembourg; tel. 46-02-55; fax 46-12-88; e-mail emb.luxemburgo@maec.es; internet www.maec.es/embajadas/luxemburgo; Ambassador CARLOS DE LOJENDIO Y PARDO MANUEL DE VILLENA.

Switzerland: Immeuble Forum Royal, 25A blvd Royal, 3rd Floor, 2449 Luxembourg; tel. 22-74-74-1; fax 22-74-74-20; e-mail lux.vertretung@eda.admin.ch; internet www.eda.admin.ch/luxembourg; Ambassador URS HAMMER.

Turkey: 49 rue Siggy vu Lëtzebuerg, 1933 Luxembourg; tel. 44-32-81; fax 44-32-81-134; e-mail ambassade.luxembourg@mfa.gov.tr; Ambassador LEVENT SAHINKAYA.

United Kingdom: 5 blvd Joseph II, 1840 Luxembourg; tel. 22-98-64; fax 22-98-67; e-mail britemb@internet.lu; internet ukinluxembourg.fco.gov.uk; Ambassador ALICE WALPOLE.

USA: 22 blvd Emmanuel Servais, 2535 Luxembourg; tel. 46-01-23; fax 46-14-01; internet luxembourg.usembassy.gov; Chargé d'affaires a.i. ALISON SHORTER-LAWRENCE.

Judicial System

The lowest courts in Luxembourg are those of the Justices of the Peace, of which there are three, at Luxembourg city, Esch-sur-Alzette and Diekirch. These are competent to deal with civil, commercial and criminal cases of minor importance. Above these are the two District Courts, Luxembourg being divided into the judicial districts of Luxembourg and Diekirch. These are competent to deal with civil, commercial and criminal cases. The Superior Court of Justice includes both a court of appeal, hearing decisions made by District Courts, and the Cour de Cassation. As the judicial system of the Grand Duchy does not employ the jury system, a defendant is acquitted if a minority of the presiding judges find him or her guilty. The highest administrative court is the Comité du Contentieux du Conseil d'Etat. Special tribunals exist to adjudicate upon various matters of social administration such as social insurance. The department of the Procureur Général (Attorney-General) is responsible for the administration of the judiciary and the supervision of judicial police investigations. In July 1996 an amendment to the Constitution introduced a Constitutional Court.

Judges are appointed for life by the Grand Duke, and are not removable except by judicial sentence.

Superior Court of Justice: Cité Judiciaire, Bâtiment CR, 2080 Luxembourg; tel. 47-59-81-1; fax 47-59-81-396; comprises a Court of Appeal and a Court of Cassation; Pres. GEORGES SANTER.

Attorney-General: ROBERT BIEVER.

Religion

CHRISTIANITY

The Roman Catholic Church

For ecclesiastical purposes, Luxembourg comprises a single archdiocese, directly responsible to the Holy See. At 31 December 2006 adherents numbered 393,800 (around 86.5% of the total population).

Archbishop of Luxembourg: Most Rev. JEAN-CLAUDE HOLLERICH, Archevêché, 4 rue Génistre, BP 419, 2014 Luxembourg; tel. 46-20-23; fax 47-53-81; e-mail archeveche@cathol.lu; internet www.cathol.lu.

The Anglican Communion

Within the Church of England, Luxembourg forms part of the diocese of Gibraltar in Europe.

Chaplain: Rev. CHRISTOPHER LYON, 89 rue de Muhlenbach, 2168 Luxembourg; tel. and fax 43-95-93; e-mail chris.lyon@anglican.lu; internet www.anglican.lu; English-speaking church (Anglican Chaplaincy).

Protestant Churches

Protestant Church of Luxembourg: 5 rue de la Congrégation, 1352 Luxembourg; tel. 22-96-70; fax 22-96-70-70; e-mail office@protestant.lu; internet www.protestant.lu; f. 1818 as Protestant Garnison Church, 1868 as multiconfessional community for the Grand Duchy; there are about 1,500 Evangelicals; Pres. Pastor VOLKER STRAUSS.

Protestant Reformed Church of Luxembourg: 11 rue de la Libération, BP 295, 4210 Esch-sur-Alzette; tel. 54-03-45; fax 54-03-46; e-mail eglrefki@pt.lu; internet www.reformiert.lu; f. 1982; 3,500 mems in 4 parishes (2006); Pastor KARL GEORG MARHOFFER.

ISLAM

Centre Culturel Islamique de Luxembourg: 2 route d'Arlon, 8210 Mamer; tel. 31-00-60; fax 26-31-04-26; e-mail info@islam.lu; internet www.islam.lu; f. 1984; Imam HALIL AHMETSPAHIC.

JUDAISM

Chief Rabbi: ALAIN NACACHE, 34 rue Alphouse Munchen, 2172 Luxembourg; tel. 45-23-66; fax 25-04-30.

Consistoire Israélite de Luxembourg (Jewish Community of Luxembourg): 45 ave Monterey, BP 835, 2018 Luxembourg; tel. 45-29-14-20; fax 25-05-30; e-mail info@synagogue.lu; internet www.synagogue.lu; Pres. CLAUDE MARX.

The Press

DAILIES

L'Essentiel: 53 rue Emile Mark, 4620 Differdange; tel. 26-58-66-1; fax 26-58-66-628; e-mail denis.berche@lessentiel.lu; internet www.lessentiel.lu; f. 2007; Mon.–Fri.; French; distributed free of charge; publ. by Edita SA; Editor-in-Chief DENIS BERCHE; circ. 57,666 (2007).

Lëtzebuerger Journal: Résidence de Beauvoir, 51 rue de Strasbourg, BP 2101, 1021 Luxembourg; tel. 49-30-33-1; fax 49-20-65; e-mail journal@journal.lu; internet www.journal.lu; f. 1948; organ of the Democratic Party; Editor-in-Chief CLAUDE KARGER.

Luxemburger Wort: 2 rue Christophe Plantin, 2988 Luxembourg; tel. 49-93-1; fax 49-93-309; e-mail wort@wort.lu; internet www.wort.lu; f. 1848; Editor-in-Chief PAUL LENERT; circ. 70,410 (2012).

Le Quotidien: 44 rue du Canal, 4050 Esch-sur-Alzette; tel. 44-77-77-1; fax 44-77-33-1; e-mail redaction@lequotidien.lu; internet www.lequotidien.lu; f. 2001; French; owned by Editpress and Le Républicain Lorrain; Dir CLAUDE GENGLER; circ. 8,445 (2009).

Tageblatt/Zeitung fir Lëtzebuerg: 44 rue du Canal, 4050 Esch-sur-Alzette; tel. 54-71-31-1; fax 54-71-30; e-mail redaktion@tageblatt.lu; internet www.tageblatt.lu; f. 1913; French and German; Editor-in-Chief DANIÈLE FONCK; circ. 20,046 (2007).

Zeitung vum Lëtzebuerger Vollek: 3 rue Zénon Bernard, 4030 Esch-sur-Alzette; tel. 44-60-66-1; fax 44-60-66-66; e-mail info@zlv.lu; internet www.zlv.lu; f. 1946; organ of the Communist Party; Editor-in-Chief ALI RUCKERT.

PERIODICALS

Aktuell: 60 blvd Kennedy, BP 149, 4002 Esch-sur-Alzette; tel. 54-05-45-1; fax 54-16-20; e-mail ogbl@ogbl.lu; internet www.ogbl.lu; f. 1979; articles in both French and German; monthly; journal of the Luxembourg General Confederation of Labour; Editor-in-Chief JEAN-CLAUDE REDING; circ. 62,000.

Auto Moto: 2 rue Christophe Plantin, 2988 Luxembourg; tel. 49-93-1; monthly; motoring; publ by Saint-Paul Luxembourg SA; circ. 72,345 (2007).

Carrière: BP 2535, 1025 Luxembourg; tel. and fax 85-89-19; e-mail carrieremag@logic.lu; internet www.logic.lu/carriere; f. 1988; women's interest; French and German; Editor MONIQUE MATHIEU; circ. 8,000.

Contacto: 2 rue Christophe Plantin, 2988 Luxembourg; tel. 49-93-1; fax 49-93-386; e-mail contacto@saint-paul.lu; internet www.jornal-contacto.lu; weekly; Portuguese; Editor-in-Chief JOSÉ CORREIA; circ. 22,800.

Echo des entreprises: 7 rue Alcide de Gasperi, BP 1304, 1013 Luxembourg; tel. 43-53-66-1; fax 43-23-28; e-mail echo@fedil.lu; internet www.fedil.lu/echo; f. 1920; 6 a year; industry, commerce; publ. by FEDIL—Business Federation Luxembourg; Dir NICOLAS SOISSON.

Femmes Magazine: 74 rue Ermesinde, 1469 Luxembourg; tel. 26-45-85-86; fax 26-45-84-94; e-mail redaction@femmesmagazine.lu; internet www.femmesmagazine.lu; 11 a year; women's interest; Dirs MARIA PIETRANGELI, PATRICIA SCIOTTI; circ. 20,128 (2007).

D'Handwierk: 2 circuit de la Foire Internationale, BP 1604, 1016 Luxembourg; tel. 42-45-11-1; fax 42-45-25; e-mail info@fda.lu; internet www.fda.lu; monthly; organ of the Fédération des Artisans and the Chambre des Métiers; Editor SANDY MAZEAU.

Horesca: 7 rue Alcide de Gasperi, BP 2524, 1025 Luxembourg; tel. 42-13-55-1; fax 42-13-55-29-9; e-mail horesca@pt.lu; internet www.horesca.lu; monthly; hotel trade, tourism, gastronomy; Editor DAVE GIANNANDREA; circ. 6,000.

Le Jeudi: 1 rue de l'Alzette, 4011 Esch-sur-Alzette; tel. 22-05-50; fax 22-05-44; e-mail redaction@le-jeudi.lu; internet www.lejeudi.lu; f. 1997; weekly; French; Dir DANIÈLE FONCK; circ. 9,965 (2007).

de Konsument: 55 rue des Bruyères, 1274 Howald; tel. 49-60-22-1; fax 49-49-57; e-mail ulc@pt.lu; internet www.ulc.lu; 10 a year; consumer affairs; Man. GUY GOEDERT.

De Lëtzebuerger Bauer: 16 blvd d'Avranches, 2980 Luxembourg; tel. 48-81-61-1; fax 40-03-75; e-mail letzebuerger.bauer@netline.lu; f. 1944; weekly; journal of Luxembourg farming; circ. 7,500.

D'Lëtzebuerger Land: 59 rue Glesener, BP 2083, 1020 Luxembourg; tel. 48-57-57-1; fax 49-63-09; e-mail land@land.lu; internet www.land.lu; f. 1954; weekly (Fri.); political, economic, cultural affairs; Man. Editor ROMAIN HILGERT; circ. 7,500.

Lux-Post: Editions Saphir, 23 rue des Gênets, 1621 Luxembourg; tel. 49-53-63; fax 48-53-70; local news; 4 regional edns; French and German; circ. 135,283 (2007).

Muselzeidung: 30 rue de Trèves, POB 36, 6701 Grevenmacher; tel. 75-87-47; fax 75-84-32; e-mail burton@pt.lu; internet www.muselzeidung.lu; f. 1981; regional magazine; monthly; German; Editor EUGENE BURTON; circ. 46,000.

Revue: 2 rue Dicks, BP 2755, 1027 Luxembourg; tel. 49-81-81-1; fax 48-77-22; e-mail revue@revue.lu; internet www.revue.lu; f. 1945; weekly; illustrated; Dir GASTON ZANGERLÉ; circ. approx. 25,000.

Revue Technique Luxembourgeoise: 7 rue de Gibraltar, 1624 Luxembourg; tel. 26-73-99; fax 45-09-32; e-mail s.reichert@revue-technique.lu; internet www.revue-technique.lu; f. 1908; organ of the Association Luxembourgeoise des Ingénieurs, Architectes et Industriels; quarterly; technology, architecture, engineering, industry, science; Editor-in-Chief MICHEL PETIT.

Sauerzeidung: 30 rue de Trèves, BP 36, 6701 Grevenmacher; tel. 75-87-47; fax 75-84-32; e-mail burton@pt.lu; internet www.muselzeidung.lu; f. 1989; regional newspaper; monthly; German; Publr EUGENE BURTON; circ. 18,000.

Soziale Fortschrett: 11 rue du Commerce, BP 1208, Luxembourg; tel. 49-94-24-1; fax 49-94-24-49; e-mail infocenter@lcgb.lu; internet lcgb.lu; f. 1921; bimonthly; journal of the Confed. of Christian Trade Unions of Luxembourg; Nat. Pres. PATRICK DURY; Man. Editor CHRISTOPHE KNEBELER; circ. 40,000.

Télécran: 2 rue Christophe Plantin, BP 1008, 1010 Luxembourg; tel. 49-93-50-0; fax 49-93-59-0; e-mail telecran@telecran.lu; internet www.telecran.lu; f. 1978; TV and family weekly; illustrated; Editor-in-Chief CLAUDE FRANÇOIS; circ. 36,431 (2007).

Transport: 13 rue du Commerce, BP 2615, 1026 Luxembourg; tel. 22-67-86-1; fax 22-67-09; e-mail syprolux@pt.lu; internet www.fcpt-syprolux.lu; fortnightly; circ. 3,800.

Woxx: 51 ave de la Liberté, 2e étage, BP 684, 2016 Luxembourg; tel. 29-79-99-0; fax 29-79-79; e-mail woxx@woxx.lu; internet www.woxx.lu; f. 1988 as *GréngeSpoun*; weekly; social, ecological, environmental and general issues; Editor LUC CAREGARI; circ. 3,000.

NEWS AGENCY

Agence Europe SA: Val Sainte Croix 7, 1371 Luxembourg; e-mail info@agenceurope.eu; internet www.agenceurope.info; f. 1952.

PRESS ASSOCIATIONS

Association Luxembourgeoise des Editeurs de Journaux: 44 rue du Canal, 4050 Esch-sur-Alzette; tel. 54-71-31-1; fax 53-05-87; e-mail asold@tageblatt.lu; f. 1983; Pres. ALVIN SOLD.

Association Luxembourgeoise des Journalistes: BP 1732, 1017 Luxembourg; tel. and fax 85-88-40; e-mail info@journalist.lu; internet www.journalist.lu; Pres ROGER INFALT.

Publishers

Editions Paul Bauler SA: 3 rue Glesener, 1631 Luxembourg; tel. 48-88-93; fax 40-46-22; e-mail libuf@pt.lu; internet www.libuf.lu; tel. 1996; literature.

Editions Guy Binsfeld: 14 place du Parc, 2313 Luxembourg; tel. 49-68-68-1; fax 40-76-09; e-mail editions@binsfeld.lu; internet www.editionsguybinsfeld.lu; f. 1979; literature, illustrated books, children's; Dir MARC BINSFELD.

Maison Moderne: 10 rue des Gaulois, BP 728, 2017 Luxembourg; tel. 29-66-181; fax 29-66-19; internet www.maisonmoderne.lu; fmrly Editions Mike Koedinger SA; name changed to present 2010; trade and customer magazines, business directories, guidebooks; CEO MIKE KOEDINGER.

Editions Phi: Villa Hadir, 51 rue Emile Mark, 4620 Differdange; tel. 44-44-33-1; fax 44-44-33-55-5; e-mail editions.phi@editpress.lu; internet www.phi.lu; f. 1980; literature, art; owned by Editpress SA; Dir CHRISTINE KREMER.

Editions Schortgen: 108 rue d'Alzette, BP 367, 4004 Esch-sur-Alzette; tel. 54-64-87; fax 53-05-34; e-mail editions@schortgen.lu; internet www.editions-schortgen.lu; art, literature, factual, cuisine, comics; Dir JEAN-PAUL SCHORTGEN.

Editpress Luxembourg SA: 44 rue du Canal, BP 147, 4050 Esch-sur-Alzette; tel. 54-71-31-1; fax 54-71-30; e-mail redaktion@tageblatt.lu; internet www.tageblatt.lu; Dir DANIÈLE FONCK.

Legitech: 10A rue des Mérovingiens, 8070 Bertrange; tel. 26-31-64-1; fax 26-31-64-99; e-mail contact@legitech.lu; internet www.legitech.lu; f. 2006; law and taxation; Dir NICOLAS HENCKES.

Luxemburger Wort: 2 rue Christophe Plantin, 2988 Luxembourg; tel. 49-93-1; fax 49-93-38-6; e-mail wort@wort.lu; internet www.wort.lu; f. 1848; Dir PAUL PECKELS.

PUBLISHERS' ASSOCIATION

Fédération Luxembourgeoise des Editeurs de Livres: 31 blvd Konrad Adenauer, BP 482, 2014 Luxembourg; tel. 43-94-44; fax 43-94-50; f. 1991.

Broadcasting and Communications

TELECOMMUNICATIONS

Cegecom SA: 3 rue Jean Piret, 2350 Luxembourg; tel. 26-49-91; fax 26-49-96-99; e-mail info@cegecom.net; internet www.cegecom.lu; f. 1999; Man. Dirs MICHAEL LEIDINGER, GEORGES MULLER.

Luxembourg Online SA: 14 ave du X Septembre, 2550 Luxembourg; tel. 27-99-00-00; fax 27-99-35-55; e-mail administration@internet.lu; internet www.internet.lu; f. 1995; offers fixed-line and mobile telecommunications and broadband internet access.

Numericable: 283 route d'Arlon, 8011 Strassen; tel. 26-10-23-01; fax 34-93-98; internet www.numericable.lu; fmrly Coditel, name changed 2008; offers digital television, fixed-line telecommunications and broadband internet access; Dir-Gen. CYRIL DUKIC.

Orange SA: 8 rue des Mérovingiens, 8070 Bertrange; fax 27-88-81-00; e-mail clients@orangeluxembourg.lu; internet www.orange.lu; fmrly called VOXmobile; name changed to present in 2009; mobile cellular and fixed-line telecommunications, broadband internet access; owned by Mobistar (Belgium); CEO WERNER DE LAET; 80,678 customers.

POST Luxembourg (POST): 8A ave Monterey, 2020 Luxembourg; tel. 47-65-1; fax 47-51-10; e-mail contact.group@post.lu; internet www.postgroup.lu; f. 2013 following merger of Entreprise des Postes et Télécommunications and LUXGSM SA; post, telecommunications and internet service provider; Pres. SERGE ALLEGREZZA; Man. Dir CLAUDE STRASSER.

Tango: 177 route de Luxembourg, BP 32, 8077 Bertrange; tel. 27-77-71-01; fax 27-77-72-22; e-mail info@tango.lu; internet www.tango.lu; f. 1998; fixed and mobile telephony, as well as broadband internet services; fmrly Tele2Tango; acquired by Belgacom SA (Belgium) in 2008; CEO JEAN-FRANÇOIS WILLAME.

Regulatory Authority

Institut Luxembourgeois de Régulation (ILR): 17 rue du Fossé, 1536 Luxembourg; tel. 28-22-82-28; fax 28-22-82-29; e-mail info@ilr.lu; internet www.ilr.public.lu; Pres. YURIKO BACKES; Dir PAUL SCHUH.

BROADCASTING

Regulatory Authority

Autorité Luxembourgeoise Indépendante de l'Audiovisuel: 19 rue du Fossé, 1536 Luxembourg; tel. 24-78-20-66; e-mail info@alia.lu; Pres. ROMAIN KOHN.

Radio

Eldoradio: 45 blvd Pierre Frieden, 1543 Luxembourg; tel. 40-95-09-1; fax 40-95-09-509; e-mail eldoradio@eldoradio.lu; internet www.eldoradio.lu; popular music station; Dir CHRISTOPHE GOOSSENS.

Radio 100,7: 21A ave J. F. Kennedy, BP 1833, 1855 Luxembourg; tel. 44-00-44-1; fax 44-00-44-98-0; e-mail info@100komma7.lu; internet www.100komma7.lu; f. 1993; non-commercial cultural broadcaster; Pres. FRANÇOISE POOS; Dir JEAN-PAUL HOFFMANN.

Radio Ara: 2 rue de la Boucherie, BP 266, 1247 Luxembourg; tel. 22-22-89; fax 22-22-66; e-mail radioara@pt.lu; internet www.ara.lu; f. 1992; music broadcaster; Man. Dir LISA MCLEAN.

Radio DNR: 2 rue Christophe Plantin, 2339 Luxembourg; tel. 40-70-60-1; fax 40-79-98; e-mail dnr@dnr.lu; internet www.dnr.lu; music broadcaster; Dir LUC WAGNER.

Radio Latina: 2 rue Christophe Plantin, BP 1915, 2988 Luxembourg; tel. 29-95-96-1; fax 40-24-76; e-mail radiolatina@radiolatina.lu; internet www.radiolatina.lu; broadcasts programmes in Portuguese, French, Italian, Spanish and Cabo Verdean Créole; Dir LUC WAGNER.

Radio LRB: 4 rue Saint Benoît zu Peppeng, BP 8, 3201 Bettembourg; tel. 52-44-88-22; fax 52-44-88-33; e-mail info@lrb.lu; internet www.lrb.lu; popular music; Man. POL MERTENS.

RTL Group: 45 blvd Pierre Frieden, 1543 Luxembourg; tel. 24-86-1; fax 24-86-51-39; e-mail oliver.herrgesell@rtlgroup.com; internet www.rtlgroup.com; f. 2000 by merger of CLT-UFA and Pearson TV; 75.1% owned by Bertelsmann AG (Germany), 24.1% by private shareholders; 29 radio stations and 52 television channels (incl. RTL Télé Lëtzebuerg and Den 2. RTL) in 9 countries; Co-CEOs GUILLAUME DE POSCH, ANKE SCHÄFERKORDT.

RTL Radio Lëtzebuerg: 45 blvd Pierre Frieden, 1543 Luxembourg; tel. 42-14-28-00; fax 42-14-22-73-7; e-mail news@rtl.lu; internet www.rtl.lu; f. 1959; broadcasts in Lëtzebuergesch; Station Man. CHRISTOPHE GOOSSENS.

Television

RTL Télé Lëtzebuerg: 45 blvd Pierre Frieden, 1543 Luxembourg; tel. 42-14-28-10; fax 42-14-27-43-1; e-mail online@rtl.lu; internet www.rtl.lu; f. 1969; subsidiary of RTL Group; CEO ALAIN BERWICK; Station Man. STEVE SCHMIT.

Finance

(cap. = capital; res = reserves; dep. = deposits; m. = million;
brs = branches; amounts in euros, unless otherwise indicated)

REGULATORY BODY

Commission de Surveillance du Secteur Financier (CSSF): 110 route d'Arlon, 2991 Luxembourg; tel. 26-25-11; fax 26-25-1-601; e-mail direction@cssf.lu; internet www.cssf.lu; f. 1998; supervision of financial sector; Dir-Gen. JEAN GUILL; Dirs SIMONE DELCOURT, CLAUDE SIMON, ANDRÉE BILLON.

BANKING

In December 2014 there were 148 banks in Luxembourg, most of which were subsidiaries or branches of foreign banks; a selection of the principal banks operating internationally is given below.

Central Bank

Banque Centrale du Luxembourg: 2 blvd Royal, 2983 Luxembourg; tel. 47-74-1; fax 47-74-49-10; e-mail info@bcl.lu; internet www.bcl.lu; f. 1998; represents Luxembourg within the European System of Central Banks (ESCB); cap. 175m., res 0.2m., dep. 15,080.3m. (Dec. 2009); Pres. YVES MERSCH; Exec. Dirs PIERRE BECK, SERGE KOLB.

Principal Banks

ABN AMRO Bank (Luxembourg) SA: 46 ave J. F. Kennedy, 1855 Luxembourg; tel. 26-07-1; fax 26-07-29-99; internet www.abnamroprivatebanking.com/luxembourg; f. 1991 by merger; cap. 162m., res 342.6m., dep. 2,313.5m. (Dec. 2012); Chair. JAN KOOPMAN; Man. Dir TONIKA HIRDMAN.

Banque et Caisse d'Epargne de l'Etat, Luxembourg: 1–2 pl. de Metz, 1930 Luxembourg; tel. 40-15-1; fax 40-15-20-99; e-mail info@bcee.lu; internet www.bcee.lu; f. 1856 as Caisse de l'Epargne de l'Etat du Grand-Duché de Luxembourg; present name adopted 1989; govt-owned; cap. 173.5m., res 824.9m., dep. 34,295.5m. (Dec. 2012); Chair. VICTOR ROD; Pres. and CEO JEAN-CLAUDE FINCK; 75 brs.

Banque Degroof Luxembourg SA: 12 rue Eugène Ruppert, 2453 Luxembourg; tel. 45-35-45-1; fax 25-07-21; e-mail investors.relation@degroof.lu; internet www.degroof.be; f. 1987; cap. 37m., res –3.8m., dep. 1,943.7m. (Sept. 2012); Chair., Supervisory Cttee ALAIN SIAENS; Chair., Management Cttee REGNIER HAEGELSTEEN.

Banque Internationale à Luxembourg SA: 69 route d'Esch, 2953 Luxembourg; tel. 45-90-1; fax 45-90-20-10; e-mail contact@bil.com; internet www.bil.com; f. 1856 as Banque Internationale à Luxembourg; present name adopted 2000; 99.9% owned by Precision Capital and the state of Luxembourg; cap. 141.2m., res 860.7m., dep. 14,706.9m. (Dec. 2012); Chair. PIERRE MARIANI; 40 brs.

Banque LBLux SA: 3 rue Jean Monnet, BP 602, 2180 Luxembourg; tel. 42-43-41; fax 42-43-45-09-9; e-mail bank@lblux.lu; internet www.lblux.lu; f. 1973; present name adopted 2002; owned by BayernLB (Germany); cap. 300m., res 95.2m., dep. 3,566.5m. (Dec. 2012); Chair., Supervisory Bd NILS NIERMANN; Chair., Management Bd ALAIN WEBER.

Banque de Luxembourg SA: 14 blvd Royal, 2449 Luxembourg; tel. 499-24-1; fax 499-24-55-99; internet www.banquedeluxembourg.com; f. 1937; owned by Banque CIC; cap. 104.8m., res 567m., dep. 12,694.7m. (Dec. 2012); Pres. PHILIPPE VIDAL; Man. Dir PIERRE AHLBORN.

Banque Raiffeisen SC: 4 rue Léon Laval, 3372 Leudelange; tel. 24-50-1; fax 22-75-41; e-mail info@raiffeisen.lu; internet www.raiffeisen.lu; f. 1926 as Caisse Centrale Raiffeisen SC; present name adopted 2001; cap. 238.3m., res 220.6m., dep. 5,592m. (Dec. 2012); Chair. ERNEST CRAVATTE; CEO and Gen. Man. GUY HOFFMANN.

Banque J. Safra Sarasin (Luxembourg) SA: 10A blvd Joseph II, 1840 Luxembourg; tel. 45-47-81-1; fax 45-47-81-55-5; e-mail luxembourg@jsafrasarasin.com; internet www.jsafrasarasin.lu; f. 1985; as Banque Safra-Luxembourg SA; name changed to present in 2013; part of J. Safra Sarasin Group (Switzerland); cap. 8.8m., res 140.4m., dep. 2,550.7m. (Dec. 2012); Man. Dir JORGE ALBERTO KININSBERG.

BGL BNP Paribas: 50 ave J. F. Kennedy, 2951 Luxembourg; tel. 42-42-20-00; fax 42-42-20-01; internet www.bgl.lu; f. 1919 as Banque Générale du Luxembourg SA; merged with Fortis Bank Luxembourg SA 2001, restyled Fortis Banque Luxembourg SA in 2005; became part of BNP Paribas and adopted present name in 2009; acquired

BNP Paribas Luxembourg in 2010; cap. 713.1m., res 4,647.1m., dep. 21,247.5m. (Dec. 2013); Chair. GASTON REINESCH; Chairs, Management Bd CARLO THILL, ERIC MARTIN; 39 brs.

BHF-BANK International: 534 rue de Neudorf, 2220 Luxembourg; tel. 45-76-76-1; fax 45-83-24; e-mail direktion@bhf.lu; f. 1972; present name adopted 2005; subsidiary of BHF-Bank AG (Germany); cap. 26m., res 20.6m., dep. 502.9m. (Dec. 2012); Mans THILO SCHIERING, ROLAND STEIES.

Clearstream Banking SA: 42 ave J. F. Kennedy, 1855 Luxembourg; tel. 243-38-081; fax 243-63-80-81; e-mail web@clearstream.com; internet www.clearstream.com; f. 1970 as Cedelbank; present name adopted 2000; private bank; acts as the central bank's securities depository; cap. 57.8m., res 351.1m., dep. 13,127.9m. (Dec. 2012); Chair. RETO FRANCIONI; CEO JEFFREY TESSLER.

Commerzbank International SA (CISAL): 25 rue Edward Steichen, 2540 Luxembourg; tel. 47-60-1; fax 47-60-88-50; e-mail info@commerzbank.lu; internet www.commerzbank.lu; f. 1967; acquired Dresdner Bank Luxembourg SA 2010; cap. 194.8m., res 269.6m., dep. 2,646.8m. (Dec. 2012); Chair. FALK FISCHER.

Crédit Agricole Luxembourg: 39 allée Scheffer, BP 1104, 1011 Luxembourg; tel. 24-67-1; fax 24-67-80-00; e-mail marketing@ca-luxembourg.com; internet www.e-private.com; f. 2005; by merger of Crédit Lyonnais Luxembourg and Crédit Agricole Indosuez Luxembourg; merged with Crédit Agricole Luxembourg Bank in 2008; cap. 465m., res -26.3m., dep. 4,202.2m. (Dec. 2012); Chair. ALAIN MASSIERA; Dir-Gen. JEAN-FRANÇOIS ABADIE.

Crédit Suisse (Luxembourg) SA: 56 Grand-Rue, BP 40, 2010 Luxembourg; tel. 46-00-11-1; fax 46-32-70; internet www.credit-suisse.com; f. 1974; cap. 150m. Swiss francs, res 74.5m. Swiss francs, dep. 5,699.4m. Swiss francs (Dec. 2012); Chair URS ROHNER.

Danske Bank International SA: 13 rue Edward Steichen, BP 173, 2011 Luxembourg; tel. 46-12-75-1; fax 47-30-78; e-mail information@danskebank.lu; internet www.danskebank.lu; f. 1976 as Den Danske Bank International SA; present name adopted 2000; cap. 90.6m., res 34.2m., dep. 1,240.7m. (Dec. 2012); Man. Dir KLAUS MØNSTED PEDERSEN.

DekaBank Deutsche Girozentrale Luxembourg SA: 38 ave J. F. Kennedy, 1855 Luxembourg; tel. 34-09-35; fax 34-09-34-91; e-mail info@deka.lu; internet www.dekabank.lu; f. 1971 as Deutsche Girozentrale International SA; present name adopted 2002, after merger with DekaBank Luxembourg SA; cap. 50m., res 373.8m., dep. 7,418.4m. (Dec. 2012); Chair. OLIVER BEHRENS; Man. Dir RAINER MACH.

Deutsche Bank Luxembourg SA: 2 blvd Konrad Adenauer, 1115 Luxembourg; tel. 42-12-21; fax 42-12-24-49; internet www.db.com/luxembourg; f. 1970 as Deutsche Bank Compagnie Financière Luxembourg; present name adopted 1987; cap. 3,465m., res 1,178.4m., dep. 75,365.3m. (Dec. 2012); Group Co-Chair. Dr ANSHU JAIN, JÜRGEN FITSCHEN.

Deutsche Postbank International SA: PB Finance Centre, 18–20 Parc d'Activités Sydrall, 5365 Munsbach; tel. 34-95-31-1; fax 34-62-06; e-mail deutsche.postbank@postbank.lu; internet www.postbank.de; f. 1993; cap. 600m., res 251.1m., dep. 9,451.1m. (Dec. 2013); Chair. STEFAN JÜTTE.

DZ Privatbank SA: 4 rue Thomas Edison, BP 661, 1445 Strassen; tel. 44-90-31; fax 44-90-32-00-1; e-mail info@dzi.lu; internet www.dzi.lu; f. 1978 as DG Bank Luxembourg SA; name changed as above 2010; 89.7% owned by DZ Bank AG Deutsche Zentral-Genossenschaftsbank; cap. 116.6m., res 511.6m., dep. 10,359.5m. (Dec. 2012); Chair. Dr STEFAN SCHWAB.

Eurobank Private Bank Luxembourg SA: 5 rue Jean Monnet, 2180 Luxembourg; tel. 42-07-24-1; fax 42-07-24-650; e-mail info@eurobankefg.lu; internet www.efgnav.lu; f. 1986; fmrly Eurobank EFG Private Bank Luxembourg SA; present name adopted 2012; subsidiary of EFG Eurobank Ergasias (Greece); cap. 70m., res 29.4m., dep. 5,823.9m. (Dec. 2013); Chair. JEAN PIERRE CUONI; CEO LENA LASCARIS.

HSBC Private Bank (Luxembourg) SA: 16 blvd d'Avranches, BP 733, 2017 Luxembourg; tel. 47-93-31-1; fax 47-93-31-22-6; e-mail hrlu@hsbcpb.com; internet www.hsbcpb.com; f. 1985 as Republic National Bank of New York (Luxembourg) SA; present name adopted 2004; cap. 53m., res 19.2m., dep. 4,119.8m. (Dec. 2012); Chair. and CEO STUART GULLIVER.

ING Luxembourg SA: 52 route d'Esch, 2965 Luxembourg; tel. 44-99-11; fax 44-99-20-60; e-mail luc.verbeken@ing.lu; internet www.ing.lu; f. 1960 as Crédit Européen SA; present name adopted 2003; owned by ING Belgium SA/NV; cap. 83.4m., res 1,337.7m., dep. 10,192.3m. (Dec. 2012); CEO LUC VERBEKEN; 15 brs.

KBL European Private Bankers SA: 43 blvd Royal, 2955 Luxembourg; tel. 47-97-1; fax 47-97-73-91-2; internet www.kbl.lu; f. 1949; fmrly Kredietbank SA Luxembourgeoise; present name adopted 2008; 99% owned by KBC Bank NV (Belgium); cap. 187.2m., res 444.8m., dep. 8,278m. (Dec. 2012); Chair. JACQUES PETERS; 2 brs.

LBBW Luxemburg SA: 10–12 blvd F.D. Roosevelt, BP 84, 2010 Luxembourg; tel. 47-59-21-1; fax 47-59-21-26-9; e-mail info@lbbw.lu; internet www.lbbw.lu; f. 2008, following acquisition of Landesbank Rheinland-Pfalz International by Landesbank Baden-Württemburg (Germany); cap. 615m., res -704.2m., dep. 2,422.1m. (Dec. 2012); Man. Dirs Dr STEFAN GRABOWSKY, ROBY HAAS.

Norddeutsche Landesbank Luxembourg SA: 26 route d'Arlon, 1140 Luxembourg; tel. 45-22-11-1; fax 45-22-11-30-7; e-mail info@nordlb.lu; internet www.nordlb.lu; f. 1972; cap. 205m., res -48m., dep. 12,371.1m. (Dec. 2012); Chair., Management Bd HARRY ROSENBAUM.

Nordea Bank SA: 562 rue de Neudorf, BP 562, 2015 Luxembourg; tel. 43-88-71; fax 43-93-76-11; e-mail nordea@nordea.lu; internet www.nordea.lu; f. 1976 as Privatbanken International (Denmark) SA, Luxembourg; changed name to Unibank SA in 1990, present name adopted 2001; cap. 25m., res 47.9m., dep. 3,938.4m. (Dec. 2012); Chair. BJÖRN WAHLROOS; CEO CHRISTIAN CLAUSEN.

Skandinaviska Enskilda Banken SA: 6A circuit de la Foire Internationale, BP 487, 2014 Luxembourg; tel. 26-23-1; fax 26-23-20-01; e-mail contact@sebprivatebank.com; internet www.sebgroup.lu; f. 1977; present name adopted 2006; cap. 118m., res 47.1m., dep. 3,618.4m. (Dec. 2012); Man. Dir PETER KUBICKI.

Société Européenne de Banque SA: 19–21 blvd du Prince Henri, BP 21, 2010 Luxembourg; tel. 46-14-11; fax 22-37-55; e-mail contact@seb.lu; internet www.seb.lu; f. 1976; cap. 535.1m., res 638.4m., dep. 11,146.4m. (Dec. 2012); subsidiary of Intesa Sanpaolo Holding International SA (Luxembourg); Chair. Prof. ANGELO CALOIA; Man. Dir and CEO MARCO BUS.

Société Générale Bank & Trust: 11 ave Emile Reuter, BP 1271, 2420 Luxembourg; tel. 47-93-11-1; fax 22-88-59; internet www.sgbt.lu; f. 1893; present name adopted 1995; cap. 1,389m., res 244.2m., dep. 33,800.7m. (Dec. 2012); Chair. PATRICK SUET; CEO FRÉDÉRIC GENET.

UBS (Luxembourg) SA: 33A ave J. F. Kennedy, 1855 Luxembourg; tel. 45-12-11; fax 45-12-12-70-0; internet www.ubs.lu; f. 1998 by merger of Swiss Bank Corporation (Luxembourg) SA and Union de Banques Suisses (Luxembourg) SA; cap. 150m. Swiss francs, res 510.1m. Swiss francs, dep. 9,867.1m. Swiss francs (Dec. 2012); Chair. ARTHUR DECURTINS; Group CEO ANDREAS PRZEWLOKA.

UniCredit International Bank (Luxembourg) SA: 8–10 rue Jean Monnet, 2180 Luxembourg; tel. 22-08-42-31-0; fax 46-90-26; e-mail contact@unicreditgroup.lu; internet www.unicreditgroup.eu; fmrly Luxembourg branch of UniCredito Italiano SpA; est. as above 2004; merged with Capitalia Luxembourg SA in 2008; owned by Unicredito Italiano SpA; Group CEO FEDERICO GHIZZONI.

UniCredit Luxembourg SA: 4 rue Alphonse Weicker, 2721 Luxembourg; tel. 42-72-1; fax 42-72-45-00; e-mail contact@hvb.lu; internet www.unicreditbank.lu; f. 1998 by merger of Hypobank International SA and Vereinsbank International SA Luxembourg; fmrly HVB Banque Luxembourg, present name adopted 2009; cap. 238m., res 1,071.5m., dep. 17,612.4m. (Dec. 2012); Pres. and Chair. ANDREAS WÖLFER; CEO ANGELO BRIZI.

Banking Association

Association des Banques et Banquiers Luxembourg (ABBL): 12 rue Erasme, 1468 Luxembourg; tel. 46-36-60-1; fax 46-09-21; e-mail mail@abbl.lu; internet www.abbl.lu; f. 1939; CEO SERGE DE CILLIA.

STOCK EXCHANGE

Société de la Bourse de Luxembourg SA: 35A blvd Joseph II, 1840 Luxembourg; tel. 47-79-36-1; fax 47-32-98; e-mail communication@bourse.lu; internet www.bourse.lu; f. 1928; Chair. FRANK WAGENER; CEO ROBERT SCHARFE.

INSURANCE

In June 2014 there were 324 approved insurance companies and reinsurance companies. A selection of insurance companies is given below:

AME Life Lux SA: 41 rue du Puits Romain, 8070 Bertrange; tel. 47-46-93; fax 47-46-90; e-mail amelife@ame.lu; internet www.amelife.lu; f. 1989; Man. Dir ROMAIN ROSSETTI.

Aon Luxembourg: 534 rue de Neudorf, BP 593, 2220 Luxembourg; tel. 31-71-71; fax 31-71-74; e-mail lambert.schroeder@aon.lu; internet www.aon.com/luxembourg; f. 1994; insurance and reinsurance broker; subsidiary of Aon Corpn (USA); Pres. and CEO GREGORY C. CASE.

AXA Luxembourg: 1 place de l'Etoile, 1479 Luxembourg; tel. 44-24-24-1; fax 45-80-23; e-mail info@axa.lu; internet www.axa.lu; f. 1977; all branches and life; Dir-Gen. MARIE-HÉLÈNE MASSARD; Chair. HENRI DE CASTRIES.

Cardif Lux Vie: 23–25 ave de la Porte Neuve, 2227 Luxembourg; tel. 26-21-41; fax 26-21-49-37-1; e-mail info@cardifluxvie.lu; internet corporate.cardifluxvie.lu; f. 2011 by merger of Cardif Lux International and Fortis Luxembourg Vie; owned by BNP Paribas Cardif, BGL BNP Paribas and Ageas; life and non-life insurance; CEO FABRICE BAGNE.

Groupe Foyer: 12 rue Léon Laval, 2986 Luxembourg; tel. 43-74-37; fax 43-74-32-49-9; internet www.foyer.lu; f. 1922; all branches and life; Pres. HENRI MARX; CEO FRANÇOIS TESCH.

La Luxembourgeoise Société Anonyme d'Assurances SA (LALUX Assurances): 9 rue Jean Fischbach, 3372 Leudelange; tel. 47-61-1; fax 47-61-30-0; e-mail groupell@lalux.lu; internet www .lalux.lu; f. 1989; all branches of non-life; Pres. and Dir-Gen. PIT HENTGEN.

Swiss Life Luxembourg: 25 route d'Arlon, 8009 Strassen; tel. 42-39-59-1; fax 26-43-40; internet www.swisslife.com/luxembourg; f. 1985; part of Swiss Life group.

West of England Shipowners' Mutual Insurance Association (Luxembourg): 33 blvd du Prince Henri, BP 841, 1724 Luxembourg; tel. 47-00-67-1; fax 22-52-53; e-mail thierry.brevet@ westpandi.com; internet www.westpandi.com; f. 1970; marine mutual insurance; Chair. M. T. LOS; Gen. Man. THIERRY BREVET.

Insurance Association

Association des Compagnies d'Assurances (ACA): 12 rue de Mamer, 1468 Luxembourg; tel. 44-21-44-1; fax 44-02-89; e-mail aca@ aca.lu; internet www.aca.lu; f. 1956; Pres. PIT HENTGEN; Chair. MARC HENGEN; 67 mems.

Trade and Industry

GOVERNMENT AGENCY

Société Nationale de Crédit et d'Investissement (SNCI): 7 rue du Saint Esprit, BP 1207, 1475 Luxembourg; tel. 46-19-71-1; fax 46-19-79; e-mail snci@snci.lu; internet www.snci.lu; f. 1978; cap. €375m., res €185m., dep. €741m., assets €1,036m. (Dec. 2007); SNCI finances participations in certain cos, provides loans for investment and research and devt projects, provides export credit; Pres. PATRICK NICKELS; Dir EMMANUEL BAUMANN.

CHAMBER OF COMMERCE

Chambre de Commerce du Grand-Duché de Luxembourg: 7 rue Alcide de Gasperi, 2981 Luxembourg-Kirchberg; tel. 42-39-39-1; fax 43-83-26; e-mail chamcom@cc.lu; internet www.cc.lu; f. 1841; Pres. MICHEL WURTH; 50,000 mems.

INDUSTRIAL AND TRADE ASSOCIATIONS

Centrale Paysanne Luxembourgeoise: 44 rue de la Gare, BP 48, Agrocenter, 7501 Mersch, Luxembourg; tel. 32-64-64; fax 64-64-48-1; e-mail jwillems@cepal.lu; internet www.centralepaysanne.lu; f. 1945; Pres. MARC FISCH; groups all agricultural organizations.

Chambre d'Agriculture (Landwirtschaftskammer): 261 route d'Arlon, BP 81, 8001 Strassen; tel. 31-38-76; fax 31-38-75; e-mail info@lwk.lu; internet www.lwk.lu; Pres. MARCO GAASCH; Sec.-Gen. POL GANTENBEIN.

Confédération Luxembourgeoise du Commerce (CLC): 7 rue Alcide de Gasperi, BP 482, 2014 Luxembourg; tel. 43-94-44; fax 43-94-50; e-mail info@clc.lu; internet www.clc.lu; f. 1909; Pres. FERNAND ERNSTER; Dir THIERRY NOTHUM; 50,000 individual mems and 11,000 mem. cos.

Fédération des Artisans du Grand-Duché de Luxembourg: 2 circuit de la Foire Internationale, BP 1604, 1016 Luxembourg; tel. 42-45-11-1; fax 42-45-25; e-mail info@fda.lu; internet www.fda.lu; f. 1905; Pres. NORBERT GEISEN; Dir ROMAIN SCHMIT; 51 mem. feds.

FEDIL—Business Federation Luxembourg: 7 rue Alcide de Gasperi, BP 1304, 1013 Luxembourg; tel. 43-53-66-1; fax 43-23-28; e-mail fedil@fedil.lu; internet www.fedil.lu; f. 1918; Pres. ROBERT DENNEWALD; Dir NICOLAS SOISSON; c. 450 mems.

UTILITIES

Regulatory Authority

Institut Luxembourgeois de Régulation (ILR): see Broadcasting and Communications.

Electricity and Gas

Enovos International SA: Domaine du Schlassgoard 2, 4327 Esch-sur-Alzette; tel. 27-37-1; fax 27-37-91-00; internet www.enovos.eu/ lu; f. 2009 from merger of Cegedel SA, Soteg SA and Saar Ferngas AG; produces and distributes electricity and gas; fmrly known as Soteg SA; Mems, Exec. Cttee JEAN LUCIUS, ROMAIN BECKER.

Creos Luxembourg SA: 2 rue Thomas Edison, 1445 Strassen; tel. 26-24-1; fax 26-24-51-00; e-mail info@creos.net; internet www .creos-net.lu; f. 1928 as Cegedel SA; renamed in 2009 following merger of Cegedel SA, Soteg SA and Saar Ferngas AG; owns and manages power grids and natural gas pipelines; Chair. MARIO GROTZ.

Enovos Luxembourg: Domaine du Schlassgoard 2, 4327 Esch-sur-Alzette; tel. 27-37-1; fax 27-37-61-11; internet www.enovos.eu/ lu; f. 1928 as Cegedel SA; name changed in 2009 following merger of Cegedel SA, Soteg SA and Saar Ferngas AG; transportation and supply of natural gas and electricity; Chair. MARCO HOFFMANN; Dir-Gen. JEAN LUCIUS.

Société Electrique de l'Our (SEO): 2 rue Pierre d'Aspelt, BP 37, 2010 Luxembourg; tel. 28-27-1; fax 28-27-32-50; e-mail seo@seo.lu; internet www.seo.lu; f. 1951; electricity production and supply; Pres. TOM EISCHEN.

SOTEL Réseau & Cie: 4 rue de Soleuvre, 4321 Esch-sur-Alzette; tel. 55-19-21; fax 57-22-13; f. 2001; distributor of electricity; Man. Dir NICO WIETOR.

SUDGAZ SA: 150 rue Jean-Pierre Michels, BP 383, 4004 Esch-sur-Alzette; tel. 55-66-55-1; fax 57-20-44; e-mail contact@sudgaz.lu; internet www.sudgaz.lu; f. 1899; natural gas sales and distribution co; Pres. JEAN TONNAR.

Water

Responsibility for water supply lies with the municipalities. Many municipalities have formed syndicates to manage water supply, the largest of which is listed below.

Distribution d'Eau des Ardennes (DEA): BP 2, 8701 Useldange; tel. 23-64-24-1; fax 23-63-93-55; e-mail dea@dea.lu; internet www .dea.lu; f. 1929; distribution of drinking water in northern Luxembourg; comprises 36 municipalities; Pres. CHARLES PAULY; Dir PATRICK KOSTER.

TRADE UNIONS

FNCTTFEL—Landesverband der Eisenbahner, Transportarbeiter, Funktionäre und Beamten, Luxemburg (National Union of Luxembourg Railway and Transport Workers and Employees): 63 rue de Bonnevoie, 1260 Luxembourg; tel. 48-70-44-1; fax 48-85-25; e-mail info@landesverband.lu; internet www.landesverband .lu; f. 1909; affiliated to Confédération Générale du Travail (CGT) and International Transport Workers' Federation; Pres. GUY GREIVELDING; 8,000 mems.

Lëtzebuerger Chrëschtleche Gewerkschaftsbond (LCGB) (Confederation of Luxembourg Christian Trade Unions): 11 rue du Commerce, BP 1208 1012 Luxembourg; tel. 49-94-24-1; fax 49-94-24-49; e-mail info@lcgb.lu; internet www.lcgb.lu; f. 1921; Pres. PATRICK DURY; 40,000 mems.

Onofhängege Gewerkschaftsbond Lëtzebuerg/ Confédération Syndicale Indépendante du Luxembourg (OGB-L) (Luxembourg Independent Confederation of Labour): 60 blvd J. F. Kennedy, BP 149, 4002 Esch-sur-Alzette; tel. 54-05-45-1; fax 54-16-20; e-mail ogbl@ogbl.lu; internet www.ogbl.lu; f. 1916; comprises 15 mem. unions; Pres. JEAN-CLAUDE REDING; Sec.-Gen. ANDRÉ ROELTGEN; c. 62,000 mems.

Transport

RAILWAYS

Railways infrastructure is controlled by the state-owned Société Nationale des Chemins de Fer Luxembourgeois (CFL). In 2011 there were 275 km of railway track, of which 262 km were electrified. A high-speed link from Luxembourg to Paris, France, opened in June 2007.

Société Nationale des Chemins de Fer Luxembourgeois (CFL): 9 place de la Gare, BP 1803, 1018 Luxembourg; tel. 49-90-0; fax 49-90-44-70; e-mail info@cfl.lu; internet www.cfl.lu; f. 1946; Pres. JEANNOT WARINGO; Dir-Gen. and CEO ALEX KREMER.

ROADS

At 1 January 2010 there were 2,899 km of roads, of which motorways comprised 152 km. There are six toll-free motorways linking Luxembourg with cities such as Trier in Germany, Thionville in France and Arlon in Belgium.

INLAND WATERWAYS AND SHIPPING

Rhine shipping has direct access to the Luxembourg inland port of Mertert as a result of the canalization of the Moselle river. An offshore shipping register was established in 1991. At 31 December

2014 the flag registered fleet numbered 256 vessels with a combined displacement of 3.2m. grt, of which 16 were gas tankers and 4 were general cargo ships.

Société du Port de Mertert SA: Direction du Port, 6688 Mertert; tel. 74-04-64; fax 74-04-64-30; e-mail info@portmertert.lu; internet www.portmertert.lu; Dir-Gen. JEANNOT POEKER.

CIVIL AVIATION

There is an international airport situated at Findel, north-west of the capital.

Cargolux Airlines International SA: Aéroport de Luxembourg, 2990 Luxembourg; tel. 42-11-1; fax 43-11-37-47; e-mail info@cargolux.com; internet www.cargolux.com; f. 1970; regular international all-freighter services; technological devt; owned by Luxair, a consortium of Luxembourg banks and SAir Logistics (Switzerland); Pres. and CEO DIRK REICH.

Luxair SA (Société Luxembourgeoise de Navigation Aérienne): Aéroport de Luxembourg, 2987 Luxembourg; tel. 24-56-42-42; fax 456-46-05; e-mail callcenter@luxairtours.lu; internet www.luxair.lu; f. 1962; regular services to destinations in Europe and North Africa; Pres. and CEO ADRIEN NEY.

Tourism

Many tourist resorts have developed around the ruins of medieval castles such as Clerf, Esch/Sauer, Vianden and Wiltz. The Benedictine Abbey at Echternach is also much visited. There is a thermal centre at Mondorf-les-Bains, supplied by three mineralized springs. In addition, there are numerous footpaths and hiking trails. The city of Luxembourg, with its many cultural events and historical monuments, is an important centre for congresses. In 2013 there were 1,044,331 tourist arrivals at hotels and other accommodation establishments. Provisional data showed that receipts from tourism totalled US $4,822m. in 2013.

Office National du Tourisme: BP 1001, 1010 Luxembourg; tel. 42-82-82-10; fax 42-82-82-38; e-mail info@visitluxembourg.com; internet www.visitluxembourg.com; f. 1931; 192 mems; Dir ANNE HOFFMANN.

Defence

Luxembourg was a founder member of the North Atlantic Treaty Organization (NATO) in 1949. Compulsory military service was abolished in 1967, but Luxembourg maintains an army of volunteers, totalling 900, and a gendarmerie numbering 610 (as assessed at November 2014). In March 1987 the country became a signatory of the Benelux military convention, together with Belgium and the Netherlands. This aimed at the standardization of training methods and of military equipment in the three countries. In November 2004 Luxembourg committed to contributing troops to one of the 'battlegroups' of the European Union (EU). The EU battlegroups, two of which were to be ready for deployment at any one time, following a rotational schedule, reached full operational capacity from 1 January 2007.

Defence Expenditure: Budget estimated at €189m. for 2013.

Chief of Staff: Gen. ROMAIN MANCINELLI.

Education

Education in Luxembourg is compulsory from the age of four to 16 years. Pre-primary education begins at the age of four years, although an optional pre-primary level for children from the age of three years has been introduced. Luxembourgish is the language of instruction at pre-primary level. Primary education begins at six years of age and lasts for six years. German is the language of instruction in the first year at primary level. French is added to the programme in the second year, and replaces German as the language of instruction at higher secondary level. In 2011/12 the total enrolment in primary education included 92% of children in the relevant age-group, while the total enrolment in secondary education included 86% of children in the relevant age-group. Total enrolment in pre-primary education in 2011/12 included 86% of children in the relevant age-group.

At the age of 12, pupils can choose between secondary school (lycée) and technical education (lycée technique). The first year of secondary school is a general orientation course on comprehensive lines, which is then followed by a choice between two sections: the Classical Section, with an emphasis on Latin, and the Modern Section, which stresses English and other modern languages. The completed secondary course lasts seven years, and leads to the Certificat de Fin d'Etudes Secondaires, which qualifies for university entrance. The technical education course (six to eight years) leads either to a vocational diploma, a technician's diploma (diplôme de technicien) or a technical baccalaureate diploma (bac technique) and is devised in three parts: an orientation and observation course; an intermediate course; and an upper course.

In August 2003 the Government founded the University of Luxembourg through the merger of four major institutions: the Centre Universitaire du Luxembourg (established in 1969); the Institut Supérieur de Technologies (Higher Technological Institute); the Institut Supérieur d'Etudes et de Recherches Pédagogiques (Institute for Higher Studies and Research in Teaching); and the Institut d'Etudes Educatives et Sociales (Institute for Educational and Social Studies).

General government expenditure on national education and vocational training in 2010 was €2,068m., equivalent to 5.1% of gross domestic product.

THE FORMER YUGOSLAV REPUBLIC OF MACEDONIA

Introductory Survey

LOCATION, CLIMATE, LANGUAGE, RELIGION, FLAG, CAPITAL

The former Yugoslav republic of Macedonia (FYRM, or, according to its Constitution, the Republic of Macedonia) is situated in south-eastern Europe. It is bounded by Serbia to the north, Kosovo to the north-west, Albania to the west, Greece to the south and Bulgaria to the east. The republic is predominantly mountainous with a continental climate, although the Vardar (Axiós) river valley, which bisects the country from north-west to south-east, across the centre of the republic and into Greece, has a mild Mediterranean climate with an average summertime temperature of 27°C (80°F). The official language of the republic, under the Constitution of November 1991, is Macedonian, a South Slavic language closely related to Bulgarian, and which is most frequently written in the Cyrillic script. Minority languages, most notably Albanian, are accorded the status of official language in communities where its speakers constitute 20% of the population. Most of the population is nominally Eastern Orthodox Christian. Most of the ethnic Albanians (around one-quarter of the population) are Muslims, as are the majority of the other minority groups. The national flag (proportions 1 by 2) comprises, in the centre of a red field, a yellow disc, with eight yellow rays extending to the edges of the flag. The capital is Skopje.

CONTEMPORARY POLITICAL HISTORY

Historical Context

After the First World War, during which Macedonia was occupied by the Bulgarians and the Central Powers of Austria-Hungary and Germany, Vardar Macedonia, the area now known as the former Yugoslav republic of Macedonia (FYRM), became part of the new Kingdom of Serbs, Croats and Slovenes (formally named Yugoslavia in 1929). In the Second World War, however, the Bulgarian occupation of 1941–44 disillusioned many Yugoslav Macedonians. From 1943 the Partisans of Josip Broz (Tito), the General-Secretary of the Communist Party of Yugoslavia, began to increase their support in the region, and after the war the new Federal People's Republic of Yugoslavia and its communist rulers resolved to include a Macedonian nation as a federal partner. A distinct Macedonian identity was promoted, together with a linguistic policy that encouraged the establishment of a Macedonian literary language distinct from Bulgarian.

The presence of a large ethnic Albanian minority in western Macedonia added to Macedonian insecurities. The proximity of the neighbouring Serbian province of Kosovo, which had a majority ethnic Albanian population, and demands, from the late 1960s, for the creation of an Albanian republic within Yugoslavia, alarmed the Macedonian authorities, which became particularly active against Albanian nationalism from 1981. In 1989 the republican Constitution was amended to allow the introduction of a multi-party system; Macedonia was declared to be a nation state of the ethnic Macedonians, and mention of the Albanian and Turkish minorities was excluded.

Domestic Political Affairs

In November and December 1990 the first multi-party elections to a unicameral Sobranie (Assembly) were held in Macedonia. Following three rounds of voting, the Vnatrešno-Makedonska Revolucionerna Organizacija-Demokratska Partija za Makedonsko Nacionalno Edinstvo (VMRO-DPMNE, Internal Macedonian Revolutionary Organization-Democratic Party for Macedonian National Unity), led by Ljubčo Georgievski, emerged as the single party with the most seats (37) in the 120-member Assembly. The republican branch of the former ruling party, the Sojuz na Komunistite na Makedonija—Partija za Demokratska Preobrazda (SKM-PDP, League of Communists of Macedonia-Party for Democratic Reform), led by Petar Gosev, won 31 seats, and the Partia për Prosperitet Demokratik (PPD—the Party for Democratic Prosperity), together with another

predominantly Albanian party, 25. The republican branch of the federal Savez Reformskih Snaga (SRS—Alliance of Reformist Forces, subsequently the Liberalna Partija na Makedonija—LPM—Liberal Party of Macedonia) won 19 seats. In January 1991 Kiro Gligorov of the SKM-PDP was elected President of the Republic, with Georgievski as Vice-President. The three parties agreed to support a government largely comprising members without political affiliation. In March the Assembly approved a new administration, headed by Nikola Kljušev. The SKM-PDP was renamed the Socijaldemokratski Sojuz na Makedonija (SDSM—Social Democratic Alliance of Macedonia) in April.

The quest for international recognition

On 25 January 1991 the Assembly unanimously adopted a motion declaring the republic a sovereign territory. After June declarations of Croatian and Slovenian 'dissociation' from Yugoslavia, Macedonia, wary of the increasing Serbian domination of the remaining federal institutions, declared its neutrality. On 8 September a referendum (boycotted by the ethnic Albanian population) approved the sovereignty of Macedonia.

Georgievski resigned the vice-presidency in October 1991, and the VMRO-DPMNE announced that it had joined the opposition, stating that the party had been excluded from the decision-making process. On 17 November the Constitution, which declared the sovereignty of the Republic of Macedonia, was endorsed by 96 of the 120 Assembly members, with opposition from the majority of ethnic Albanian deputies. In January 1992 an unofficial referendum conducted among the ethnic Albanian population reportedly resulted in 99.9% of the vote being cast in favour of territorial and political autonomy for the ethnic Albanian population. The complete withdrawal of federal troops from Macedonia in March, in conjunction with the adoption in April of a new Constitution in Yugoslavia, referring only to Serbia and Montenegro, effectively signalled Yugoslav acceptance of Macedonian secession from the federation.

Macedonian affairs were subsequently dominated by efforts to secure wider international recognition. Bulgaria recognized the state of Macedonia (although not the existence of a distinct Macedonian nationality or language) in January 1992, closely followed by Turkey in February, provoking mass protests in Thessaloníki, the capital of the Greek region of Macedonia. The Greek authorities insisted that 'Macedonia' was a geographical term delineating an area that included a large part of northern Greece, and expressed fears that the republic's independence under the name 'Macedonia' might foster claims to future territorial expansion. Greece was instrumental in the formulation of a European Community (EC, now European Union—EU, see p. 271) policy, adopted in early 1992, that the republic should be awarded no formal recognition of independence until stringent constitutional requirements had been fulfilled. In May Gligorov rejected a statement by the EC that it was 'willing to recognize Macedonia as a sovereign and independent state within its existing borders under a name that can be accepted by all concerned'. Negotiations with Greece ended in failure in June. In July, after a motion expressing no confidence in the Government received strong support in the Assembly (and following large demonstrations against its failure to gain international recognition for an independent Macedonia), the Government resigned. The VMRO-DPMNE failed to form a new alliance, and eventually, in September Branko Crvenkovski, the Chairman of the SDSM, was installed as Prime Minister of a coalition Government.

The adoption of a new flag in August 1992 attracted particular opposition from Greece, which objected to the depiction outside Greece of the 'Vergina Star' (regarded as an ancient Greek symbol of Philip of Macedon and Alexander the Great). As a result of a blockade of petroleum deliveries imposed on Macedonia by Greece, reserves at the Skopje petroleum refinery were exhausted by September. In February 1993 Greece agreed to international arbitration over the issue of Macedonia's name, undertaking to abide by its final outcome. On 8 April the republic was admitted to the UN under the temporary name of 'the former Yugoslav republic of Macedonia', pending settlement of the issue of a permanent name by international mediators. However, Greece continued to assert that the use of the Vergina Star and the name 'Macedonia' implied territorial claims on Greek territory, and in October Greece withdrew from UN-sponsored negotiations on the question of a permanent name. In January 1994 Greece requested that the other nations of the EU prevail upon the FYRM (which was, by this time, recognized by all the other EU member states) to make concessions concerning its name, flag and Constitution, and threatened to ban trade with the FYRM. From February (by which time Russia and the USA had formally recognized the FYRM) Greece blocked all non-humanitarian shipments to the FYRM through the port of Thessaloníki, and also road and rail transport links with the FYRM. In April the European Commission initiated legal proceedings against Greece at the Court of Justice of the European Communities. In April 1995 the Court issued a preliminary opinion that the embargo was not in breach of Greece's obligations under the Treaty of Rome. Meanwhile, Greece agreed to resume negotiations in April with the FYRM, under the auspices of the UN; in May the Organization for Security and Co-operation in Europe (OSCE, see p. 385) announced that it was to join the mediation efforts. In September the FYRM Minister of Foreign Affairs and his Greek counterpart signed an interim accord, providing for the mutual recognition of existing frontiers and respect for the sovereignty of each state, and for the free movement of goods and people between the two countries. Greece was to end its trade embargo and veto on the FYRM's entry into international organizations, while the FYRM undertook to abandon its use of the Vergina emblem in any form, and to amend parts of its Constitution that had been regarded by Greece as irredentist; the question of a permanent name for the FYRM was to be the subject of further negotiations. In early October the Assembly approved a new state flag, depicting an eight-rayed sun in place of the Vergina emblem. On 9 October the Assembly ratified the interim accord, which was formally signed by representatives of the FYRM and Greece on 13 October. The border between the two countries was subsequently reopened.

Meanwhile, relations between the FYRM authorities and the minority Albanian population continued to deteriorate. In November 1993 several ethnic Albanians were arrested in the western towns of Gostivar and Tetovo, and in Skopje. The Government announced that a conspiracy to form paramilitary groups, with the eventual aim of establishing an Albanian republic in the west of the FYRM, had been discovered. Further arrests followed, and in June 1994 Mithat Emini, the former General Secretary of the PPD, was sentenced to eight years' imprisonment; nine others received custodial sentences of between five and eight years. (In February 1995 all the sentences were reduced by two years.)

Ethnic Albanian demands and insurgency

The PPD split in February 1994, when a faction led by Xheladin Murati (the Deputy President of the Assembly) and including the party's representatives in the Government and in the legislature, withdrew from the party's congress. The remaining grouping, led by Arben Xhaferi, made more radical demands. The sentencing of Emini and his co-defendants prompted ethnic Albanian deputies to boycott the Assembly in July. Murati resigned from the leadership of his PPD faction (and from his role in the Assembly) later that month, reportedly in protest against the sentences; he was succeeded as party leader by Abdurahman Aliti.

Gligorov, representing the Sojuz za Makedonija (SZM—Alliance for Macedonia, a coalition of the SDSM, the LPM and the Socijalistiska Partija na Makedonija—SPM—Socialist Party of Macedonia), was re-elected President on 16 October 1994, winning 78.4% of the valid votes cast, defeating Georgievski. A first round of voting to the new Assembly took place on the same day. The VMRO-DPMNE, failing to secure any seats, alleged widespread electoral fraud in both elections, and boycotted the second round of legislative voting on 30 October (a third round was necessary in 10 constituencies on 13 November, owing to irregularities in earlier rounds). The final results confirmed that the SZM had won the majority of seats in the Assembly (with the SDSM taking 58 seats, the LPM 29 and the SPM eight). Aliti's wing of the PPD, which had been legally recognized as the successor to the original party, secured 10 seats; allies of Xhaferi had been obliged to stand as independent candidates (Xhaferi was among those to be elected). Gligorov subsequently requested

that Crvenkovski form a new government, and the SDSM-led administration was approved by the Assembly in December.

Ethnic tensions were exacerbated by the opening in February 1995, of an Albanian-language university in Tetovo, when, in ensuing unrest, an ethnic Albanian was killed in clashes with security forces. In July 1996 five of the university's founders, including its rector, received custodial sentences for inciting the riots, prompting further protests. (In May 2000 the Assembly approved legislation granting the university at Tetovo legal status as a private foundation, and in January 2004 further legislation was adopted, transforming it into a state university.)

In October 1995 Gligorov was injured in a car bomb attack in Skopje; he resumed full presidential duties in January 1996. Meanwhile, divisions emerged within the governing alliance, which collapsed in February, prompting the LPM to be excluded from the Government. In September, prior to local elections scheduled for 17 November, the Assembly approved legislation reorganizing the territorial division of the FYRM into 123 municipalities. The SDSM received the greatest number of votes, followed by an opposition coalition led by the VMRO-DPMNE and the PPD. Observers from the Council of Europe (see p. 250) declared that, overall, the elections had been conducted fairly.

A financial scandal emerged in the FYRM in March 1997, involving the embezzlement of funds invested in 'pyramid' savings schemes. In April the Government announced plans to reimburse losses incurred by investors, following the failure of a major savings institution in the south-western town of Bitola, while in May the Governor of the central bank, who was believed to have been involved in the failure of the investment scheme, was replaced. After the VMRO-DPMNE demonstrated in Skopje to demand the resignation of the Government, a reorganized administration was approved by the Assembly at the end of May.

In May 1997 protests were staged in Gostivar against a Constitutional Court ruling prohibiting the use of the Albanian flag in the FYRM. In July the Assembly adopted legislation stipulating that the use of flags representing minority ethnic groups (including Albanians) would only be permitted on national holidays, with the state flag being displayed at the same time. The mayors of Gostivar and Tetovo continued to refuse to comply with the order, and violent clashes, in which three ethnic Albanians were killed, ensued in Gostivar after government officials forcibly removed Albanian flags from municipal buildings. In September the mayor of Gostivar, Rufi Osmani, received a custodial sentence of 13 years (subsequently reduced to seven years), after he was convicted of inciting ethnic tension and rebellion, while the Chairman of the town's municipal council was sentenced to three years' imprisonment for failing to adopt the ruling of the Constitutional Court. In April 1998 the Partia Demokratike Shqiptare (PDSh—Democratic Party of Albanians), which had been formed in the previous year by the amalgamation of Xhaferi's Partia për Prosperitet Demokratik e Shqiptare (Party of Democratic Prosperity of Albanians) and another ethnic Albanian party, withdrew its representatives from all government bodies, in protest against Osmani's imprisonment.

At legislative elections, conducted in two rounds on 18 October and 1 November 1998 a coalition of the VMRO-DPMNE and the newly formed Demokratska Alternativa (DA—Democratic Alternative), secured an absolute majority in the Assembly, with 58 seats, while the SDSM obtained 29 seats, and an alliance of the PPD and the PDSh won 24. Owing to irregularities, a further round of voting took place in two electoral districts, at which one seat was won by the coalition of the VMRO-DPMNE and the DA, and the other by the PPD-PDSh alliance. Later in November Georgievski was nominated as Prime Minister. The PDSh was subsequently invited to join the governing coalition. In early December a new Government, comprising 14 representatives of the VMRO-DPMNE, eight of the DA and five of the PDSh, was formed. In January 1999 the Assembly adopted legislation providing for the release of some 8,000 prisoners, among them Osmani.

Six candidates contested the first round of the presidential election on 31 October 1999. Tito Petkovski, representing the SDSM, secured 33.2% of the votes cast, and Boris Trajkovski, the VMRO-DPMNE candidate, won 20.6%; Vasil Tupurkovski, the DA leader, took 16.0%, and Muharem Nexipi, the PDSh candidate, 14.8%. Petkovski and Trajkovski progressed to a second round, held on 14 November. After the Supreme Court upheld a legal appeal by the SDSM against the results, a further ballot took place in some western regions on 5 December. However, the overall results were almost unchanged: Trajkovski was elected to the presidency, with 52.9% of the votes cast. Trajkovski was formally inaugurated on 15 December. A renewed coalition administration, which contained seven new ministers (including Tupurkovski, the leader of the DA, as a Deputy Prime Minister), was formed on 27 December.

In January 2000 the Government announced that amendments to the Constitution, which would allow higher education to be conducted in the language of minority ethnic groups, would be submitted for approval by the Assembly. In April the Assembly adopted legislation obliging the authorities to return property expropriated under the communist regime. In the same month disaffected members of the VMRO-DPMNE established a breakaway faction, which became known as the VMRO-Vistinska Makedonska Reformska Opcija (VMRO-VMRO, IMRO-True Macedonian Reform Option). In July Georgievski reorganized the Government, reducing the number of ministries from 21 to 14. Local elections took place on 10 and 24 September, amid numerous violent incidents. After a further round of voting took place, as a result of electoral irregularities, it was announced that the parties of the governing coalition had secured 75 of the 123 municipalities. Following prolonged dissent between Georgievski and Tupurkovski, in November the DA withdrew from the coalition Government and from the Assembly. Georgievski subsequently formed a new administration, which, for the first time, included members of the Liberalno-Demokratska Partija (LDP—Liberal Democratic Party).

In early 2001 ethnic Albanian militants, members of the self-styled Ushtria Çlirimtare Kombëtare (UÇK—National Liberation Army), began to infiltrate northern parts of the FYRM from Kosovo, clashing with FYRM security forces. In early March UÇK forces seized the border village of Tanusevci, prompting counter-attacks from government troops. The border with Kosovo was closed after senior government officials visiting the border region were attacked and besieged. Although the authorities regained control of Tanusevci, UÇK forces attempted to occupy Tetovo, precipitating the imposition of curfew regulations in the city. Following an appeal by the Government to the international community for military assistance, the North Atlantic Treaty Organization (NATO, see p. 367) reinforced its military presence at the Kosovo border to inhibit supplies to the UÇK. On 21 March the UN Security Council adopted Resolution 1345, condemning the violence by ethnic Albanian nationalists in the FYRM. Despite reports that the rebels aimed to establish a 'greater Albania' (to include northern and western regions of the FYRM), the UÇK insisted that the conflict had been initiated to put pressure on the FYRM Government to institute constitutional guarantees of equal rights for ethnic Albanians. The prolonged bombardment of rebel positions by government forces resulted in a withdrawal by the UÇK from the Tetovo region. At the end of April eight members of the state security forces were killed in an UÇK attack near the Kosovo border. Their funeral precipitated rioting and attacks by Macedonians on Albanian-owned property in the southern town of Bitola. Government troops subsequently launched an offensive against rebel positions near Kumanovo, after two further members of the armed forces were killed.

Meanwhile, in early April 2001 inter-party discussions regarding the rebels' demands commenced. After signing a Stabilization and Association Agreement with the EU, the Government pledged to initiate political, social and economic reforms by mid-2001. However, the Government continued to oppose principal demands that the Constitution be amended to grant the ethnic Albanian population (hitherto officially categorized as a minority) equal group rights with the Macedonian population, and Albanian the status of a second official language. In early May intensive hostilities resumed in the north of the country. Following EU and NATO mediation, however, it was agreed that the SDSM, the PDSh and the PPD would join a government of national unity. The PPD subsequently demanded that the Government declare a ceasefire in the conflict in the north, as a precondition to its participation in the new administration. After the offensive against the rebels was temporarily suspended, the Assembly approved the Government of national unity (headed by Georgievski) on 13 May. UÇK leaders stated that the rebel movement (which still held several villages) would continue hostilities until the Government agreed to enter into negotiations.

The Ohrid Agreement

On 8 June 2001 Trajkovski announced proposals for a comprehensive peace plan, providing for the proportional representation of ethnic Albanians at all levels of government, the increased

official use of the Albanian language, and a partial amnesty for UÇK combatants. Despite EU support for the plan, the UÇK demanded that the Government end hostilities and enter into negotiations on constitutional reforms, and rebel forces seized the town of Aracinovo, near Skopje. Later in June the Government suspended its offensive against the UÇK. In response, violent protests were staged by Macedonian nationalists at the parliament building in Skopje. On 29 June NATO formally approved an operation to deploy a 3,500-member multinational force in the FYRM to assist in the disarmament of the UÇK, which was to be conditional on the imposition of a lasting ceasefire. On 5 July the Government announced that both sides had signed an official ceasefire agreement. However, in subsequent negotiations on a permanent settlement Georgievski and his nationalist cabinet supporters strongly opposed proposals, detailed by the EU and US special envoys, for the extension of the use of the Albanian language. The ceasefire collapsed after 17 days, when the UÇK launched further attacks on government forces near Tetovo. International diplomatic efforts subsequently intensified, following renewed fears of widespread civil conflict. Further negotiations between government and ethnic Albanian representatives, which commenced at the western town of Ohrid at the end of July, resulted in the resolution of the two main matters of contention (the official use of the Albanian language and the right to proportional representation of ethnic Albanians in the security forces). After the Government announced a unilateral ceasefire, on 13 August the Government and ethnic Albanian leaders at Ohrid signed a framework peace agreement, providing for the amendment of the Constitution to grant greater rights to the ethnic Albanian community. On the following day the UÇK leader, Ali Ahmeti, agreed that the organization would relinquish its armaments to NATO troops. On 22 August the activation order for a NATO mission, Operation Essential Harvest, was released; the 4,500-member force had a mandate to disarm the ethnic Albanian combatants and destroy their weapons within 30 days of its deployment.

In September 2001 parliamentary debate on constitutional reform was delayed by mass nationalist protests against the peace plan. Meanwhile, investigators from the International Criminal Tribunal for the former Yugoslavia (ICTY, see p. 22) at the Hague, Netherlands, had been dispatched to the FYRM to conduct preliminary inquiries into the killing of six ethnic Albanian civilians in the village of Ljuboten in early August; the Minister of Internal Affairs, Ljube Boškoski, was suspected of responsibility for the operation. On 26 September NATO's 30-day disarmament programme was declared to have been successful. On the same day the establishment of a further, reduced NATO mission, Operation Amber Fox, was authorized. The new mission, comprising 700 troops, together with 300 forces already stationed in the FYRM, was deployed, with a three-month renewable mandate to protect EU and OSCE monitors supervising the implementation of the peace agreement. On 27 September Ahmeti announced that the UÇK had been formally dissolved, following the completion of the disarmament process. In October Trajkovski approved plans for the deployment of ethnically mixed security units in regions formerly held by the UÇK.

On 16 November 2001, after extensive debate, the Assembly adopted 15 principal constitutional amendments, including: the revision of the Constitution's preamble to include a reference to members of minority ethnic groups as citizens; the introduction in the Assembly of a 'double majority' system, whereby certain legislation would require the approval of a minority group; the establishment of Albanian as the second official language in districts in which ethnic Albanians accounted for more than 20% of the population; and the right to proportional representation for ethnic Albanians in the Constitutional Court, all areas of government administration and the security forces. Later in November the SDSM and the LDP withdrew from the coalition Government.

In January 2002 the Assembly approved legislation providing for the devolution of greater authority to local government. In the same month a Deputy Prime Minister, Dosta Dimovska, resigned from the Government, following disagreement with Georgievski over issues relating to the deployment of security units in previously UÇK-controlled villages. In February the three principal ethnic Albanian political parties and the former UÇK leadership officially established a co-ordinating council. In March the Assembly adopted legislation granting immunity from prosecution to several thousand former UÇK insurgents (excluding those indictable by the ICTY. The Assembly was dissolved on 18 July, prior to legislative elections, which were scheduled for 15 September and were to be monitored by the OSCE.

In May 2002 Ahmeti established a new political party, the Bashkimi Demokratik për Integrim (BDI—Democratic Union for Integration), which was believed to comprise mainly former UÇK combatants. Later that month two ministers belonging to the VMRO-VMRO resigned from the Government, in protest as what they described as the growing dominance of former UÇK members within the principal ethnic Albanian parties. In the same month the Assembly approved legislation whereby Albanian became an official language. At the end of August ethnic Albanians took hostage five civilians at Gostivar; security forces surrounded an ethnic Albanian base and killed two of the kidnappers. None the less, the elections to the legislature took place peacefully on 15 September, and were declared by OSCE observers to have been conducted democratically. Georgievski's Government was removed from power by a 10-party alliance (led by the SDSM and the LDP), Za Makedonija Zaedno (ZMZ—Together for Macedonia), which secured 60 of the 120 seats in the Assembly. The VMRO-DPMNE won 33 seats and the BDI 16 seats. The ZMZ alliance and the BDI subsequently signed an agreement for the establishment of a coalition Government (which was, however, to exclude former UÇK combatants). The Assembly approved the new administration, comprising members of the SDSM, the LDP and the BDI, and headed by Crvenkovski, on 1 November.

On 14 December 2002 Operation Amber Fox was succeeded by a 450-member mission, Allied Harmony. On 31 March 2003 this contingent was, in turn, replaced by an EU-led mission, Operation Concordia, comprising 350 military personnel from a total of 13 EU member states and 14 non-EU nations. In September, after militants clashed with a security patrol at the border with Kosovo, the authorities dispatched security forces to the region in an operation to suppress dissident activity.

In May 2003 Nikola Gruevski became the new leader of the VMRO-DPMNE. In November Ljupco Jordanovski of the SDSM was elected as the new President of the Assembly, replacing Nikola Poposki, who had been appointed as Deputy Prime Minister and Minister of Finance. In December Operation Concordia was replaced by a 200-member, two-year, EU mission, Operation Proxima, which, in addition to maintaining security and combating organized crime in the country, was to advise the FYRM police forces.

On 26 February 2004 President Trajkovski was killed, together with eight government officials, in a plane crash in Bosnia and Herzegovina. Jordanovski, as speaker of the Assembly, assumed the presidency in an acting capacity. At a presidential election, held on 14 April, Crvenkovski, representing the SDSM, won 42.5% of the votes cast; he progressed to a second round vote against Saško Kedev, a VMRO-DPMNE parliamentary deputy (who had won 34.1%). Two former UÇK commanders, the BDI Secretary-General, Gzim Ostreni, and Zudi Xhelili of the PDSh, also contested the election, obtaining 14.8% and 8.7% of the votes cast, respectively. On 28 April Crvenkovski was elected to the presidency with 62.7% of the vote; he was inaugurated on 12 May.

On 2 June 2004 the Assembly approved the formation of a coalition administration, with Hari Kostov of the SDSM as Prime Minister, and comprising members of that party, the BDI and the LDP. The only new ministerial appointment was that of Siljan Avramovski as Minister of Internal Affairs, replacing Kostov. The Government had, meanwhile, announced plans to redemarcate municipal boundaries, as part of a process of administrative decentralization included in the provisions of the Ohrid Agreement, although there was widespread popular opposition to the proposals. In July, under pressure from the international community, the parties of the governing coalition reached an agreement on the planned redemarcation. The total number of administrative districts was to be reduced from 123 to 84, with the ethnic balance of 26 districts becoming predominantly Albanian. On 26 July a large demonstration was staged in Skopje, in protest against the draft agreement on decentralization, which had been submitted for approval to the Assembly.

On 7 November 2004, following a petition presented by Macedonian nationalist parties, a referendum on the proposed redemarcation of administrative districts was conducted. However, the governing coalition, as well as representatives of the international community, urged a boycott, and voter participation in the referendum was estimated at only 26%, thereby invalidating the results and allowing the reforms to proceed. In

mid-November Kostov resigned as Prime Minister, claiming that the BDI had obstructed the parliamentary approval of reforms essential to attract foreign investment. Later that month Crvenkovski nominated Vlado Buckovski, hitherto Minister of Defence, as Prime Minister. (Buckovski was also elected as Chairman of the SDSM.) On 17 December the Assembly approved a new Government, again comprising members of the SDSM, the LDP and the BDI. In March 2005 the ICTY issued indictments against Boškoski and a former head of security, Johan Tarculovski, in connection with the August 2001 killings in Ljuboten.

The VMRO-DPMNE returns to power

The first round of local government elections, which were to effect the significant devolution of powers to new municipal authorities, took place, with some reported irregularities, on 13 March 2005. A second round of voting in 47 of the 84 municipalities was conducted on 27 March. After upholding claims of irregularities in the first round, the Supreme Court had ordered polls to be repeated in several constituencies, and an OSCE observer mission announced that the second round of the elections in some municipalities again failed to meet OSCE and Council of Europe standards. The PDSh and the PPD, which had urged a boycott of the vote, refused to recognize the results. On 10 April further ballots were conducted in those municipalities in which electoral irregularities had occurred. According to official results, 36 of the mayoral contests were won by the ZMZ coalition, and 15 by the BDI, with the VMRO-DPMNE securing 21 mayoralties. In mid-July, in accordance with the Ohrid Agreement, the Assembly adopted legislation enabling any ethnic minority community to display its flag, together with the state flag, in regions where it constituted at least 50% of the population.

In legislative elections, held on 5 July 2006, the VMRO-DPMNE secured 32.5% of the votes cast, defeating the SDSM, which obtained only 23.3% of the vote. A coalition of the BDI and the PPD secured the majority of ethnic Albanian votes, attracting 12.2% of the total ballot, while Xhaferi's PDSh received 7.2% of the vote. Reported electoral irregularities caused the Supreme Court to demand that elections be repeated in eight constituencies, following which the VMRO-DPMNE's number of seats in the Assembly was increased from 44 to 45. In August Gruevski, the Chairman of the VMRO-DPMNE, was formally appointed as Prime Minister and his Government was approved by the Assembly a few days later. The new coalition administration comprised 10 members of the VMRO-DPMNE, four of the PDSh, three of the Nova Socijaldemokratska Partija (New Social Democratic Party) and one each of the LPM and of the SPM. Ljubiša Georgievski was appointed as President of the Assembly.

In January 2007 the BDI and the PPD announced a boycott of parliamentary proceedings, in protest against their exclusion from Gruevski's Government. In February the Assembly approved a government reorganization, which included the appointment of Imer Aliu (hitherto Minister of the Environment and Physical Planning) as Deputy Prime Minister, responsible for the implementation of the Ohrid Framework Agreement. In April Boškoski and Tarculovski became the first of those accused of war crimes during the 2001 insurgency to stand trial at the ICTY. In May 2007 the PPD announced that its representatives were to resume participation in the Assembly, after reaching an agreement with the VMRO-DPMNE permitting it to join the Government. The BDI also officially ended its boycott of the Assembly (but subsequently withdrew from parliamentary sessions on many occasions). The return of the PPD and the BDI enabled the Assembly to adopt, on 5 June, legislation providing for full co-operation with the ICTY. In December legislation amending the judicial system was approved, as part of the requirements for NATO accession.

In March 2008 the PDSh announced its withdrawal from the Government, in protest against the failure of the VMRO-DPMNE both to recognize the independence of Kosovo from Serbia, which had been proclaimed in the previous month, and to provide increased rights for the use of the Albanian language and flag in the FYRM. Later that month, however, it was reported that the PDSh had retracted its decision, after reaching an agreement with the VMRO-DPMNE on inter-party co-operation to adopt legislation on the use of language. Following the failure of negotiations with Greece on the issue of the country's official name, and Greece's consequent decision to veto NATO membership for the FYRM at a summit meeting of the Alliance held on 2 April, the BDI proposed a motion for the dissolution of the Assembly. The motion received the support of the VMRO-

DPMNE, and was approved on 12 April by the Assembly. Early legislative elections were scheduled for 1 June.

At the elections on 1 June 2008 voting was disrupted in a number of constituencies by outbreaks of violence between rival ethnic Albanian groups, in which at least one person was killed. The OSCE consequently assessed that the conduct of the elections failed to meet international standards. Elections were repeated on 15 June in those districts in which disorder had prevented voting from taking place, and in a small number of constituencies a further round of voting was necessary on 29 June. According to official results, a 19-party coalition, led by the VMRO-DPMNE, known as Za Podobra Makedonika (For a Better Macedonia), secured 48.8% of the votes cast and 63 of the 120 seats in the legislature, thereby becoming the first grouping to obtain an absolute majority in the Assembly. The Sonce Koalicija za Evropa (Sun Coalition for Europe), an eight-party coalition led by the SDSM, was placed second, with 23.7% of the vote, and 27 seats. The BDI received 18 seats (with 12.8%) and the PDSh 11 seats (8.5%). It was subsequently announced that the PPD, which had failed to obtain legislative representation, was to merge with the PDSh. The Assembly approved the formation of a new Government on 26 July, principally comprising members of the VMRO-DPMNE and the BDI. In the same month Boškoski, having been acquitted of all charges at the ICTY, returned to the FYRM. Meanwhile, Tarculovski was sentenced to 12 years' imprisonment for the Ljuboten killings in 2001.

In January 2009 presidential and municipal elections were scheduled for 22 March; it was also announced that the minimum voter turnout required for a valid poll would be reduced from 50% to 40%. Later in January the VMRO-DPMNE selected a university professor and non-party member, Gjorge Ivanov, as its presidential candidate; the SDSM nominated a former minister, Ljubomir Frčkoski. Boškoski also declared his intention to contest the poll as an independent candidate. At the first round of the presidential election, which was contested by seven candidates on 22 March, Ivanov received about 35.1% of the votes cast, while Frčkoski won 20.5%. A second round of voting was scheduled for 5 April, concurrently with run-off ballots for the municipal elections. According to official results, Ivanov was elected to the presidency, with some 63.1% of the votes cast. Voter turnout at the presidential poll was only 42.6% (ethnic Albanian voters staged a boycott). At the two rounds of municipal elections, held concurrently, the coalition led by the VMRO-DPMNE secured 55 mayoralties; the BDI won 14 and SDSM nine. OSCE and Council of Europe observers declared that the organization of the elections met democratic commitments, but recommended further electoral reforms. Ivanov was inaugurated as President on 12 May.

In late May 2009 Crvenkovski was elected as Chairman of the SDSM (a position he had held in 1991–2004). In late June 2009 the Deputy Prime Minister, responsible for European Integration, Ivica Bocevski, tendered his resignation. In early July, following the dismissal of Trajko Slaveski of the VMRO-DPMNE as Minister of Finance and the resignation of two other ministers, the Assembly approved a government reorganization. A law professor, Vasko Naumovski, succeeded Bocevski as Deputy Prime Minister, responsible for European Integration. The incumbent Deputy Prime Minister, responsible for Economic Affairs, Zoran Stavreski, became the new Minister of Finance (while remaining a deputy premier), and was replaced in his former position by a business director, Vladimir Peševski. In early August the Chairman of the PDSh, Menduh Thaçi, announced a parliamentary boycott by party members, on the grounds that some of the provisions of the Ohrid Framework Agreement were not being observed. In September an encyclopedia published by the Macedonian Academy of Arts and Science prompted outrage from Albanian academics and politicians, owing to its portrayal of the Albanian community, including references to ethnic Albanians resident in the territories of the FYRM as 'settlers'. The publication was denounced by the Governments of Albania and Kosovo, while Greece and Bulgaria also objected to its account of Macedonian history. The Academy subsequently suspended distribution of the encyclopedia, and the Academy's editorial board was subsequently replaced and assurances given that the disputed content would be revised. (In May 2013 it was announced that the FYRM and Albania would establish a joint academic council to produce an encyclopedia with an agreed regional history.)

In December 2010 the SDSM, with the support of the main opposition parties, organized a protest demonstration in Skopje,

accusing the Government of economic mismanagement and failing to advance EU integration aspirations. In the same month a parliamentary motion submitted by the SDSM in support of the dissolution of the Assembly was defeated. Later in December the owner of a major independent television channel, A1 TV, Velija Ramkovski, and 16 executives from associated companies were arrested for suspected tax evasion and other corruption offences. In January 2011 employees of A1 TV broadcast news bulletins from street locations outside government offices in Skopje, in protest at the freezing of the station's bank accounts by the authorities, claiming that the corruption investigation was politically motivated. Crvenkovski announced the withdrawal of the SDSM from the Assembly in support of A1 TV; the LDP and other allied parties joined the boycott, which was condemned by the VMRO-DPMNE. In February a court in Skopje ruled in favour of reimposing the freezing of the bank accounts of A1 TV and nine associated companies. Later that month the Chairman of the State Election Commission, a member of the SDSM, tendered his resignation. In March discussions between government and opposition leaders resulted in some progress towards meeting opposition demands for reforms to electoral regulations.

Continuing ethnic tensions

On 30 March 2011 Gruevski announced that the VMRO-DPMNE would propose that early legislative elections be scheduled for June, after Crvenkovski agreed that the SDSM would participate in the poll (although the party's boycott of the Assembly continued). After the Assembly had approved amendments to the electoral code and the appointment of a new Chairman of the State Election Commission (again of the SDSM), a motion dissolving the legislature was unanimously adopted on 14 April. On the following day it was confirmed that elections to the Assembly would take place on 5 June.

At the pre-term parliamentary elections on 5 June 2011, the coalition of parties led by VMRO-DPMNE won 39.0% of the votes cast, obtaining 56 seats in the Assembly (thereby losing its absolute majority). The opposition coalition led by the SDSM strengthened its position, receiving 32.8% of the votes cast and 42 seats; the BDI obtained 10.2% of the vote and 15 seats, and the PDSh 5.9% and eight seats. Under the amendments to electoral legislation approved earlier in the year, the Assembly had been expanded to 123 deputies, with the additional three seats allocated to representatives of FYRM citizens resident abroad. Prior to the establishment of a new administration, Gruevski reached an agreement with BDI leader Ahmeti on certain concessions; in July the new Assembly approved legislative amendments, proposed by the BDI, that allowed languages other than Macedonian to be spoken by ministers and other officials (in addition to legislators) during parliamentary sessions and in local self-government bodies if at least 20% were in favour, extended the law on the use of minority flags, and granted amnesty from prosecution on charges of war crimes to four former UÇK leaders. On 29 July the Assembly approved the formation of a new coalition Government led by the VMRO-DPMNE, again under the premiership of Gruevski and retaining many members of the previous administration. Several representatives of the BDI again received significant portfolios, including Teuta Arifi, who was appointed as Deputy Prime Minister, responsible for European Integration, and Fatmir Besimi, as Minister of Defence (the first time that the post had been held by an ethnic Albanian). At the end of July it was announced that A1 TV had ceased broadcasting, following bankruptcy proceedings.

An incident, in February 2012, in which a police officer had killed two ethnic Albanians in Gostivar over a reported disagreement about parking, precipitated a series of attacks by ethnic Albanian youths against Macedonians in several towns, particularly Skopje and Tetovo, in early March. Some 30 arrests were made in connection with the violence, in which a number of people were injured, while the main Albanian parties appealed for calm. However, further attacks by ethnic Albanians directed at public transport near Kumanovo were reported. Later in March a 'march for peace' rally, organized by a non-governmental organization in Skopje, was attended by some 2,000 protesters, including President Ivanov. In April five Macedonians were found shot and killed at the village of Smilkovci, near Skopje, precipitating a number of protests directed against the ethnic Albanian community in Skopje and other towns. An operation launched by the special police in May resulted in the arrest of 20 ethnic Albanian suspects, many with alleged connections to a radical Islamist group. Later in the month demonstrations by ethnic Albanians, including Islamist elements, were staged in Skopje to demand the release of the detained suspects.

In December 2012 the SDSM boycotted the adoption of the 2013 budget by the Assembly, in protest at what it condemned as excessive government expenditure. SDSM deputies were expelled after disrupting the parliamentary session with violent disturbances, while clashes also occurred outside the parliamentary building. Despite EU and US mediation efforts, the SDSM continued its parliamentary boycott, and urged its followers to stage acts of civil disobedience. In January 2013 the party threatened to increase a campaign of protests that had blockaded roads in central Skopje, after the ruling coalition rejected a number of opposition demands.

In February 2013 several BDI members of government were replaced, following the resignation of officials to contest the local elections; these included Arifi, who was succeeded as Deputy Prime Minister, responsible for European Integration, by Besimi. However, the appointment of a former commander of the UÇK militia, Talat Xhaferi, to replace Besimi as Minister of Defence prompted ethnic Macedonian protests; counter-demonstrations by ethnic Albanians degenerated into violent clashes at the beginning of March, in which some 20 people were injured. Meanwhile, Crvenkovski's announcement that the SDSM would boycott the local elections was followed by the resignation of several prominent members from the party in late February. After further EU mediation, on 1 March it was announced that a resolution to the political impasse had been reached: the SDSM had agreed to end its parliamentary boycott and participate in the local elections, while the Government was to enter into dialogue with the opposition on the scheduling of the next legislative elections and on democratic freedoms in the country. Later in March the Constitutional Court began to consider challenges to a new lustration law (intended to remove former secret police informants of the Communist era from certain professions), which had been adopted in June 2012.

The first round of the local elections took place on 23 March 2013; however, opposition parties immediately complained of alleged violations. A second round of voting was conducted on 7 April. In mid-April the head of the country's Administrative Court resigned, in protest at the Court's annulment of the election of a SDSM candidate in the Skopje municipality of Centar, and of a PDSh candidate in Struga. Polls were repeated in those and a further two constituencies on 22 April, in which the victory of the two opposition candidates was confirmed. Overall, a coalition led by the VMRO-DPMNE had secured control of 58 mayoralties, while the BDI had obtained 14, an alliance led by the SDSM only four and the BDI two. Although the OSCE generally endorsed the conduct of the elections, observers confirmed opposition allegations of voter intimidation and other irregularities.

On 2 June 2013 Zoran Zaev, the mayor of the south-eastern town of Strumica, was elected as the new Chairman of the SDSM, replacing Crvenkovski, who had announced following the local polls that he would not seek re-election to the post. In July Boškoski (who had already received a five-year prison sentence for illegal financing of his party in the 2011 parliamentary elections) was sentenced to a further 12 years' imprisonment, after being convicted by a court in Skopje of involvement in the killing of two members of a criminal network in 2001. Meanwhile, draft media legislation presented by the Government attracted considerable controversy during 2013, particularly owing to the proposed establishment of a new regulatory body that would be empowered to revoke broadcasting licenses and levy penalties on outlets; despite objections from major media organizations, the legislation was adopted by the Assembly, with some amendments, at the end of December.

In February 2014 the Government and opposition parties finally reached agreement on an amended electoral law; the first round of a presidential election was scheduled for 13 April. The BDI opposed Ivanov's candidacy for re-election and urged its supporters to boycott the poll, after the VMRO-DPMNE rejected its demands for the selection of a consensus candidate from the ruling coaltiion. A parliamentary motion by the BDI in favour of further pre-term legislative elections (which were expected to benefit the government parties) was adopted, and the Assembly was dissolved on 5 March; it was announced that the elections would take place on 27 April, to coincide with a possible second presidential round. The presidential election campaign began in late March, by which time Stevo Pendarovski of the SDSM, Iljaz Halimi of the PDSh and Zoran Popovski of the newly established Gragjanska Opciija za Makedonija (GROM—Lightning—

Citizens' Option for Macedonia) had registered to oppose Ivanov. At the first round of the presidential election on 13 April, Ivanov secured 51.7% of votes cast, followed by Pendarovski, with 37.5%; a voter turnout of 48.8% was recorded. A second round of voting between Ivanov and Pendarovski was scheduled, as neither candidate had obtained the support of a majority of the registered electorate, as required by the Constitution. A clash between supporters of the VMRO-DPMNE and the SDSM was reported during the polling in Skopje, and the SDSM subsequently accused the ruling party of electoral malpractice. Although OSCE monitors noted only minor irregularities in the conduct of the elections, they observed significant bias in media coverage favour of the VMRO-DPMNE. Later in April the SDSM filed corruption charges against Gruevski, having released alleged evidence that, before becoming Prime Minister, he had accepted a bribe to facilitate the sale of a bank, Makedonska Banka, which had been privatized in 2004. In the second round of presidential voting, held concurrently with legislative elections on 27 April, Ivanov was re-elected to the presidency, receiving 55.3% of the votes cast, defeating Pendarovski. In the elections to the Assembly, the alliance led by the VMRO-DPMNE increased its representation to 61 seats (one short of an overall majority), with 43.0% of the votes cast, while the alliance led by the SDSM lost support, obtaining 34 seats and 25.3% of the votes cast. The BDI won 13.7% and 19 seats, followed by the PDSh, with 5.9% and seven seats. GROM and Rilindja Demokratike Kombëtare (National Democratic Revival), an ethnic Albanian party led by Rufi Osmani, each won one seat. The SDSM leadership disputed the results of the elections, accusing the ruling VMRO-DPMNE of malpractice.

On 12 May 2014 Ivanov was inaugurated for a second presidential term. Later that month unrest broke out, following the arrest of a young ethnic Albanian suspected of responsibility for the killing of an ethnic Macedonian teenager in a suburb of Skopje. On 19 June Gruevski's new coalition Government, again principally comprising VMRO-DPMNE and BDI members, was approved by the Assembly, despite a boycott of the new legislature by SDSM deputies. Many ministers of the previous administration retained their portfolios, while new appointments included those of VMRO-DPMNE representative Zoran Jolevski as Minister of Defence and Bekim Neziri of the BDI as Minister of the Economy. At the end of that month five ethnic Albanians belonging to an extremist Islamic group (including two who were in detention in Kosovo) were convicted and received sentences of life imprisonment in connection with the killings of five Macedonians in April 2012; a further suspect was acquitted. The verdict prompted protests in a number of towns in early July 2014, which escalated into rioting in Skopje.

Recent developments: state surveillance allegations

On 21 January 2015 the Assembly approved two of several planned constitutional amendments, despite the continued SDSM boycott: these, respectively, permitted the opening an 'international financial zone' in the country, and confirmed the existing definition of marriage as solely constituting the union of a woman and a man. Meanwhile, following increasing antagonism between Gruevski and SDSM leader Zaev, who claimed to be in possession of information highly incriminating to the Government, at the end of January he was formally charged with espionage, after the Prime Minister accused him in a broadcast address of planning a coup attempt. In early February the US embassy issued a statement urging the authorities not to suppress information relating to the case in the media. Shortly afterwards, the SDSM presented allegations that more than 20,000 people, including opposition leaders, NGO activists, journalists, members of the judiciary and other prominent figures, had been subjected to illegal surveillance ordered by Gruevski and the head of secret police, Sašo Mijalkov; recordings of official discussions were released to support the claims, which were strenuously denied by Gruevski. During his first visit to the FYRM later that month EU Commissioner for Enlargement Johannes Hahn expressed concern, and urged an investigation of the opposition claims. Meanwhile, following a boycott and series of protests by students (beginning the previous November), the Government agreed in late February to draft a new higher education law. Zaev continued to release recordings of what were alleged to be highly incriminating conversations between senior government officials, including Minister of Finance Stavreski, who described government economic policies as chaotic, and Minister of Internal Affairs Gordana Jankuloska, who detailed malpractice organized by the authorities in the 2013 local elections. It was announced that European Parliament representatives were to mediate in the escalating dispute.

Foreign Affairs
Regional relations

Both the September 1995 interim agreement with Greece and the November Dayton peace accord (for further details, see Bosnia and Herzegovina) were of great significance for the FYRM, despite the unresolved issue of a permanent name for the country. The FYRM was admitted to the Council of Europe in late September, and to the OSCE in October; in the following month the FYRM joined NATO's 'Partnership for Peace' programme (see p. 371). The agreement with Greece facilitated the establishment of full diplomatic relations with the EU from January 1996, and a declaration on co-operation was signed with the European Free Trade Association (see p. 446) in early April. By the end of 1996 more than 75 countries had recognized the FYRM, with about two-thirds using the country's constitutional name, the Republic of Macedonia.

By 1999 relations with Greece had improved significantly, and the principal border crossing with Greece was reopened in 2000, while work on the construction of a pipeline to transport petroleum from the capital, Skopje, to Thessaloníki, Greece, was completed in 2002. The announcement in 2006 that the international airport near Skopje was to be renamed after Alexander 'the Great' (considered by Greece to be integral to its cultural heritage) provoked renewed tension. Discussions were resumed in 2007, but continued to yield little progress. In October Greece announced that it would veto Macedonian NATO and EU applications should no resolution be reached on the matter. After failing to receive an invitation to join NATO in April 2008 (see *Other external relations*), in November the FYRM submitted a legal challenge against Greece at the International Court of Justice (ICJ, see p. 25), claiming that it had violated the terms of the interim accord of 1995, which stipulated that Greece would not veto the country's accession to international institutions under its provisional name. On 5 December 2011 the ICJ ruled that Greece had contravened the interim accord by vetoing the country's application to join NATO in 2008 and dismissed Greece's counter-claim that the FYRM had previously breached the accord. In July 2012 UN Secretary-General Ban Ki-moon visited Skopje in an effort to revive the dialogue with Greece; Prime Minister Gruevski declared commitment to further dialogue, but urged acceptance of the ICJ ruling. UN-sponsored negotiations continued in New York during 2013, and the UN mediator on the dispute, Matthew Nimetz, visited Skopje and Athens in October. A further round of discussions was conducted in March 2014, but again little progress was reported. The new Greek Government of Alexis Tsipras, which was installed in January 2015, confirmed that it would maintain the strenuous stance of previous administrations in the dispute.

After NATO forces began an intensive aerial bombardment of strategic targets in Yugoslavia in late March 1999 (see Kosovo and Serbia), large numbers of ethnic Albanian refugees fled to the FYRM. Some 14,000 NATO troops were deployed near the border with the Serbian province of Kosovo. By late May some 60,000 refugees had been transported from the FYRM for provisional resettlement abroad, while an estimated 250,000 remained in the country. On 20 June, after the Yugoslav Government accepted a peace plan, NATO announced that the air campaign had officially ended, and the refugees subsequently began to return to Kosovo from the FYRM. Kosovo's declaration of independence, with the support of many EU member states and the USA, on 17 February 2008 was celebrated by ethnic Albanians in Skopje. In October the FYRM announced the extension of diplomatic recognition to Kosovo. The decision prompted an official protest from Serbia. Diplomatic relations with Kosovo were formally established in October 2009, following the ratification of an agreement on the demarcation of the common border by the legislatures of both countries. Following economic co-operation accords reached between the FYRM and Kosovo in early 2011, the Ministers of the Interior of the two states in April signed an agreement establishing joint border patrols. In December the Governments of the FYRM, Montenegro and Albania signed an agreement providing for the abolition of border controls for citizens of their respective states. A memorandum of understanding was signed by the state prosecutors of the FYRM and Kosovo in December 2014 to co-ordinate efforts against organized crime and terrorism. Meanwhile, the FYRM's relations with Serbia also progressively improved: in March 2013 their Governments signed an agreement providing for

improved bilateral relations and co-operation in the EU integration processes of both states. During a visit to Skopje by Serbian Prime Minister Aleksandar Vučić in February 2015, seven co-operation accords, including one on border procedures, were signed.

Other external relations

The Government signed a Stabilization and Association Agreement with the EU in April 2001, which came into effect in April 2004. A formal application for membership of the EU was submitted in March 2004. Following the recommendation of the European Commission, the country was officially declared to have candidate status at an EU summit meeting in Brussels, Belgium, in December 2005. In October 2007 NATO member states adopted a resolution supporting the accession application of the country. The Government expressed confidence that an official invitation would be extended at a NATO summit meeting in Bucharest, Romania, in April 2008; however, in consequence of the unresolved dispute over the country's permanent name, Greece vetoed the application. NATO confirmed that the country had fulfilled other membership prerequisites, and that an invitation would be extended upon the settlement of the matter. In July 2009 the European Commission announced that the country had fulfilled all the requirements for the end of visa restrictions, and in November the abolition of visas for citizens of the FYRM visiting the countries of the Schengen zone was announced, with effect from mid-December. In October the European Commission released a progress report recommending the opening of accession negotiations with the FYRM. However, Greece continued to impose a veto on the beginning of negotiations, and in December EU foreign ministers postponed a decision on establishing a start date for membership negotiations. Despite the continued impasse, in March 2012 the country began a preliminary High-Level Accession Dialogue with the European Commission. At a meeting of the European Council in December, Bulgaria joined Greece in opposing the initiation of negotiations, on the grounds that the FYRM had failed to foster good bilateral relations (following concerns at perceived discrimination against ethnic Bulgarians in the country, and concerns over Bulgaria's willingness to grant citizenship to ethnic Macedonians resident in the FYRM). In January 2013, however, discussions on the signature of a friendship treaty between the two states began. The FYRM assumed the chairmanship of the Central European Free Trade Agreement (see p. 445) for a period of one year at the beginning of 2014. In February the European Parliament adopted a resolution again urging the European Council to approve the start of accession negotiations. However, in December the European Council, for the sixth time, voted not to accept the renewed recommendation of the European Commission that accession negotiations be opened. EU and NATO officials expressed concerns at increased tensions in the country surrounding the political confrontation between the Government and the opposition in early 2015.

CONSTITUTION AND GOVERNMENT

Legislative power in the FYRM is vested in the Sobranie (Assembly), with 120 members, elected for a four-year term by universal adult suffrage (85 in single-seat constituencies and 35 members by proportional representation). The President is directly elected for a five-year term, and appoints a Prime Minister to head the Government. The Ministers are elected by the Assembly. Judicial power is exercised by 27 Courts of First Instance, three Courts of Appeal, the Administrative Court, the Superior Administrative Court, and the Supreme Court. For the purposes of local government, the FYRM is divided into 84 municipalities.

REGIONAL AND INTERNATIONAL CO-OPERATION

The FYRM is a member of the Council of Europe (see p. 250) the Organization for Security and Co-operation in Europe (OSCE, see p. 385) and the Central European Free Trade Agreement (CEFTA, see p. 445).

The FYRM was admitted to the UN in 1993, provisionally as 'the former Yugoslav Republic of Macedonia', pending settlement of the dispute over its name (see *The quest for international recognition*). The country became a member of the World Trade Organization (WTO, see p. 431) in 2003.

ECONOMIC AFFAIRS

In 2013, according to World Bank estimates, the FYRM's gross national income (GNI), measured at average 2011–13 prices, was US $10,106m., equivalent to $4,800 per head (or $11,520 per head on an international purchasing-power parity basis). During 2004–13, it was estimated, the population increased by an average of 0.1% per year, while gross domestic product (GDP) per head increased, in real terms, at an average annual rate of 3.0%. Overall GDP increased, in real terms, at an average annual rate of 3.1% in 2004–13; real GDP decreased by 0.4% in 2012, but increased by 3.1% in 2013.

Agriculture (including hunting, forestry and fishing) contributed a preliminary 11.0% of GDP and engaged 18.7% of the employed labour force in 2013. Dairy farming is significant, and the principal agricultural exports are tobacco, vegetables and fruit. The wine industry is of considerable importance, and the FYRM is also a producer of wheat, maize and barley. During 2004–13 the GDP of the agricultural sector increased at an average annual rate of 1.1%, according to official figures; real agricultural GDP decreased by 6.2% in 2012, but increased by a preliminary 0.4% in 2013.

Industry contributed a preliminary 24.5% of GDP and engaged 30.4% of the employed labour force in 2013. During 2004–13 the GDP of the industrial sector increased, in real terms, at an average annual rate of 3.2%, according to official figures; real industrial GDP increased by 3.3% in 2012 and by a preliminary 11.7% in 2013.

Mining contributed 1.7% of GDP in 2011 and engaged 1.0% of the employed labour force in 2013. The only major mining activity is the production of lignite (brown coal), although there are also deposits of iron, zinc, lead, copper, chromium, manganese, antimony, silver, gold and nickel.

The manufacturing sector contributed an estimated 15.4% of GDP in 2011 and engaged 19.4% of the employed labour force in 2013. The GDP of the manufacturing sector (along with mining and utilities) increased, in real terms, at an average annual rate of 2.3% in 2004–13, according to official figures; real GDP increased by a preliminary 4.9% in 2013.

The construction sector contributed a preliminary 6.6% of GDP and engaged 6.9% of the employed labour force in 2013. The GDP of the sector increased, in real terms, at an average annual rate of 5.9% in 2004–13; real construction GDP increased by 4.8% in 2012 and by a preliminary 32.7% in 2013, according to official estimates.

Energy is derived principally from coal and lignite, which provided 76.9% of the electricity generated in 2011. Hydroelectric sources accounted for 20.8% of production. The first stage of a pipeline from the Bulgarian border to carry natural gas to the FYRM from Russia became operational in 1995. A 214-km pipeline to transport petroleum from the Greek port of Thessaloníki to Skopje was inaugurated in July 2002. Mineral fuels accounted for 16.2% of the value of total imports in 2013.

Services accounted for a preliminary 64.4% of GDP and engaged 50.9% of the employed labour force in 2013. During 2004–13 the GDP of the services sector increased, in real terms, at an average annual rate of 3.7%, according to official figures; services GDP decreased by 0.7% in 2012, but increased by a preliminary 0.4% in 2013.

In 2013 the FYRM recorded a visible merchandise trade deficit of US $2,468.4m., and there was a deficit of $194.1m. on the current account of the balance of payments. In 2013, the principal source of imports was the United Kingdom (accounting for 11.0% of total imports); other major sources were Greece, Germany, Serbia, Italy, the People's Republic of China and Bulgaria. Germany was the principal market for exports in that year (accounting for 35.9% of all exports); other important purchasers were Bulgaria, Italy and Serbia. The main imports in 2013 were basic manufactures, machinery and transport equipment, mineral fuels and lubricants, chemical products, food and live animals, and miscellaneous manufactured articles. The principal exports in that year were basic manufactures, miscellaneous manufactured articles, chemicals and related products,

machinery and transport equipment, food and live animals, inedible crude materials (except fuels), and beverages and tobacco.

The FYRM recorded an overall budgetary deficit of 19,257m. denars in 2013, equivalent to 3.9% of GDP, according to preliminary official figures. General government gross debt was 169.607m. denars in 2013, equivalent to 35.9% of GDP. At the end of 2012 the FYRM's external debt totalled US $6,678m., of which $2,270m. was public and publicly guaranteed debt. In that year the cost of servicing long-term public and publicly guaranteed debt and repayments to the IMF was equivalent to 15.1% of the value of exports of goods, services and income (excluding workers' remittances).The annual rate of inflation averaged 2.4% in 2003–13. Consumer prices increased by 2.8% in 2013. The rate of unemployment was 29.0% in 2013.

Following the entry into force of a Stabilization and Association Agreement with the European Union (EU, see p. 271) in 2004, the European Commission in October 2009 recommended the opening of accession negotiations with the FYRM; however, the unresolved dispute with Greece over the country's constitutional name subsequently prevented endorsement of the recommendation. In early 2011 the FYRM was granted a two-year financial arrangement by the IMF, receiving a €220m. loan. In response to the increasing financial crisis in the euro area, the Government introduced a number of precautionary measures in the banking sector later that year. The country also continued to benefit from the establishment, in the late 2000s, of four 'technological-industrial development zones', which were designed to attract foreign investment. In March 2012 the FYRM began a preliminary dialogue with the EU, which was to reduce the length of any future official negotiations and maintain the course of reforms. In early 2013 the Government estimated that its ongoing 'Skopje 2014' project, an ambitious redevelopment of the capital city that involved the construction of public buildings and monuments in the styles of classical antiquity in the capital, with the aim of stimulating tourism and the construction industry, had cost at least €208m. (far exceeding the €80m. originally projected). Significant infrastructure projects financed by the People's Republic of China included the construction of two new sections of cross-country highways, which began in February 2014; plans to construct a new railway line towards Bulgaria were also initiated. The Government issued a €500m., seven-year Eurobond in July (its third on the international market), the proceeds of which were to finance budget requirements and the repayment of external debt in 2014–15. Growth strengthened slightly to an estimated 3.3% in 2014, although the fiscal deficit, at around 4% of GDP, was slightly higher than expected (following lower government revenue, including from privatizations). The unemployment rate, while remaining the highest in the region, had been gradually reduced. In January 2015 the Constitution was amended to allow the opening of an 'international financial zone' in the country, which would offer tax and other benefits, with the aim of further attracting foreign direct investment and increasing employment.

PUBLIC HOLIDAYS

2016: 1 January (New Year), 6–7 January (Orthodox Christmas), 29 April–2 May (Orthodox Easter), 1 May (Labour Day), 24 May (Day of the Apostles SS Cyril and Methodius), 6 July* (Small Bayram, end of Ramadan), 2 August (National Day), 8 September (Independence Day), 12 September* (Great Bayram, Feast of the Sacrifice), 11 October (Anti-Fascism Day), 23 October (Day of the Macedonian Revolution), 8 December (St Clement of Ohrid Day).

* These holidays are dependent on the Islamic lunar calendar and may vary by one or two days from the dates given.

Statistical Survey

Source (unless otherwise indicated): State Statistical Office of the Republic of Macedonia, 1000 Skopje, Dame Gruev 4; tel. (2) 3295600; fax (2) 3111336; e-mail info@stat.gov.mk; internet www.stat.gov.mk.

Area and Population

AREA, POPULATION AND DENSITY

Area (sq km)	25,713*
Population (census results)†	
20 June 1994	1,945,932
31 October 2002	
Males	1,015,377
Females	1,007,170
Total	2,022,547
Population (official estimates at 31 December)	
2011	2,059,794
2012	2,062,294
2013	2,065,769
Density (per sq km) at 31 December 2013	80.3

* 9,928 sq miles.
† Comprising persons with an official place of residence in the country (including those temporarily abroad for less than a year), persons from other countries who have been granted a residence permit in the FYRM and have been present there for at least a year, and foreigners with refugee status; excluding foreign diplomatic and military personnel.

POPULATION BY AGE AND SEX
(official estimates at 31 December 2013)

	Males	Females	Total
0–14 years	180,104	168,312	348,416
15–64 years	741,382	720,243	1,461,625
65 years and over	113,355	142,373	255,728
Total	1,034,841	1,030,928	2,065,769

POPULATION BY ETHNIC GROUP
(self-declaration at census of 31 October 2002)

	Number	%
Macedonian	1,297,981	64.2
Albanian	509,083	25.2
Turkish	77,959	3.9
Roma (Gypsy)	53,879	2.7
Serb	35,939	1.8
Muslim	17,018	0.8
Vlach	9,695	0.5
Others	20,993	1.0
Total	2,022,547	100.0

Note: Classification of ethnic groups reflects national census methodology.

PRINCIPAL TOWNS
(2004, official estimates)*

Skopje (capital)	515,419	Prilep	76,768
Kumanovo	105,484	Struga	63,376
Bitola	95,385	Ohrid	55,749
Tetovo	86,580	Veles	55,108
Gostivar	81,042	Strumica	54,676

* Population by municipality, except for Skopje, which comprises 10 municipalities.

Source: Ministry of Local Self-Government, Skopje.

Mid-2014 (incl. suburbs, UN estimate): Skopje 501,303 (Source: UN, *World Urbanization Prospects: The 2014 Revision*).

BIRTHS, MARRIAGES AND DEATHS

	Registered live births		Registered marriages		Registered deaths	
	Number	Rate (per 1,000)	Number	Rate (per 1,000)	Number	Rate (per 1,000)
2006	22,786	11.2	14,908	7.3	18,630	9.1
2007	22,688	11.1	15,490	7.6	19,594	9.6
2008	22,945	11.2	14,695	7.2	18,982	9.3
2009	23,684	11.5	14,923	7.3	19,060	9.3
2010	24,296	11.8	14,155	6.9	19,113	9.3
2011	22,770	11.1	14,736	7.2	19,465	9.5
2012	23,568	11.4	13,991	6.8	20,134	9.8
2013	23,138	11.2	13,982	6.8	19,208	9.3

Life expectancy (years at birth): 75.0 (males 72.8; females 77.4) in 2012 (Source: World Bank, World Development Indicators database).

ECONOMICALLY ACTIVE POPULATION
(sample surveys, persons aged 15 years and over)

	2011	2012	2013
Agriculture, hunting, forestry and fishing	120,894	112,623	127,186
Mining and quarrying	5,316	5,636	7,085
Manufacturing	125,206	126,892	131,542
Electricity, gas and water	23,070	20,760	20,678
Construction	39,961	41,024	46,955
Wholesale and retail trade, repair of motor vehicles, motorcycles and articles for personal use and for households	90,892	92,822	91,696
Hotels and restaurants	23,574	23,507	23,986
Transport, storage and communications	39,986	41,642	48,675
Financial intermediation	10,588	9,110	9,274
Real estate, renting and business activities	22,709	27,707	26,055
Public administration and defence, compulsory social security	43,884	43,915	45,066
Education	40,333	42,514	41,467
Health and social work	35,230	36,091	37,912
Other community, social and personal services	21,010	23,887	19,558
Private households with employed persons	1,511	1,344	1,072
Extraterritorial organizations and bodies	920	1,080	631
Total employed	645,085	650,554	678,838
Unemployed	294,963	292,502	277,219
Total labour force	940,048	943,056	956,057
Males	569,987	573,498	573,825
Females	370,061	369,558	382,232

Health and Welfare

KEY INDICATORS

Total fertility rate (children per woman, 2012)	1.4
Under-5 mortality rate (per 1,000 live births, 2012) . . .	7
HIV/AIDS (% of persons aged 15–49, 2013)	<0.1
Physicians (per 1,000 head, 2009)	2.6
Hospital beds (per 1,000 head, 2009)	4.5
Health expenditure (2011): US $ per head (PPP)	784
Health expenditure (2011): % of GDP	6.9
Health expenditure (2011): public (% of total)	63.6
Access to water (% of total population, 2012)	99
Access to sanitation (% of total population, 2012) . . .	91
Total carbon dioxide emissions ('000 metric tons, 2010) . .	10,872.7
Carbon dioxide emissions per head (metric tons, 2010) . .	5.2
Human Development Index (2012): ranking	78
Human Development Index (2012): value	0.740

For sources and definitions, see explanatory note on p. vi.

Agriculture

PRINCIPAL CROPS
('000 metric tons)

	2011	2012	2013
Wheat	256.1	215.0	259.0
Rice, paddy	27.0	24.4	27.9
Barley	129.5	90.4	125.6
Maize	129.3	118.8	135.3
Rye	8.3	7.3	8.9
Potatoes	193.9	170.0	190.9
Sugar beet*	8.0	9.0	9.5
Beans, dry	13.0	11.0	11.4
Olives*	12.0	13.0	13.0
Cabbages and other brassicas .	142.7	128.6	157.4
Tomatoes	165.6	145.8	131.0
Cucumbers and gherkins . . .	49.9	50.1	36.8
Chillies and peppers, green . .	153.8	166.2	152.2
Onions, dry	44.5	43.7	50.8
Beans, green	13.0	11.0	11.4
Watermelons	127.4	127.6	128.4
Apples	124.6	127.2	112.9
Peaches and nectarines . .	9.0	9.0	11.0
Plums and sloes	35.4	35.4	38.9
Grapes	235.1	240.5	292.1
Tobacco, unmanufactured . . .	26.5	27.3	27.9

* FAO estimates.

Aggregate production ('000 metric tons, may include official, semi-official or estimated data): Total cereals 554.9 in 2011, 459.8 in 2012, 561.9 in 2013; Total roots and tubers 193.9 in 2011, 170.0 in 2012, 190.9 in 2013; Total vegetables (incl. melons) 741.1 in 2011, 715.7 in 2012, 711.3 in 2013; Total fruits (excl. melons) 436.2 in 2011, 444.8 in 2012, 488.4 in 2013.

Source: FAO.

LIVESTOCK
('000 head, year ending September)

	2011	2012	2013
Horses	25	22	21
Cattle	265	251	238
Pigs	197	177	167
Sheep	767	732	732
Chickens	1,944	1,776	2,202

Source: FAO.

LIVESTOCK PRODUCTS
('000 metric tons)

	2011	2012	2013
Cattle meat	5.3	5.0	5.5
Sheep meat	6.4	5.6	4.7
Pig meat	8.3	10.6	8.8
Chicken meat	1.6	1.9	1.8
Cows' milk	376.3	349.8	380.7
Sheep's milk	25.8	38.6	34.3
Hen eggs*	16.6	13.3	12.0
Honey	1.1	0.6	0.8
Wool, greasy	1.0	0.9	0.9†

* Unofficial figures.
† FAO estimate.

Source: FAO.

Forestry

ROUNDWOOD REMOVALS
('000 cubic metres, excl. bark)

	2011	2012	2013
Sawlogs, veneer logs and logs for sleepers	98	108	98
Other industrial wood	23	19	16
Fuel wood	476	652	577
Total	597	779	691

Source: FAO.

SAWNWOOD PRODUCTION
('000 cubic metres, incl. railway sleepers)

	2011	2012	2013
Total (all broadleaved) . . .	3	8	4

Source: FAO.

Fishing

(metric tons, live weight)

	2010	2011	2012
Capture	236	268	249
Trouts	50	45	44
Huchen	11	9	7
Aquaculture	1,491	1,368	1,306
Common carp	197	202	194
Other freshwater fishes . . .	56	52	72
Trouts	1,238	1,114	1,040
Total catch	1,727	1,636	1,555

Source: FAO.

Mining

('000 metric tons unless otherwise indicated)

	2010	2011	2012
Lignite	6,583	7,902	7,310
Copper concentrates*†	8	8	10
Lead concentrates*†	38	36	34
Gypsum	143	163	158
Crude steel	292	386	216

* Estimated figure.
† Figures refer to the metal content of concentrates.

Gold (estimates): 450 kg in 2006–08.

Silver: 10,000 kg in 2003.

Source: US Geological Survey.

Industry

SELECTED PRODUCTS

('000 metric tons unless otherwise indicated)

	2009	2010	2011
Flour	77	73	92
Refined sugar	23	38	33
Wine ('000 hl)	1,134	912	1,004
Beer ('000 hl)	636	631	612
Soft drinks ('000 hl)	1,717	1,597	1,248
Cigarettes (million)	5,973	6,751	7,721
Footwear with leather uppers ('000 pairs)	1,343	1,299	1,878
Motor spirit (petrol)	176	161	110
Gas-diesel (distillate fuel) oil	376	364	278
Residual fuel oils	362	260	246
Cement	909	820	981
Ferro-alloys*	60	129	182
Crude steel*	270	292	386
Lead: refined*	38	38	36
Zinc: refined*	35	29	28
Electric energy (million kWh)	6,828	7,260	6,759

* Data from US Geological Survey.

2012: Ferro-alloys 140; Crude steel 216; Lead, refined 34; Zinc, refined 28 (Source: US Geological Survey).

Source (unless otherwise indicated): UN Industrial Commodity Statistics Database.

Finance

CURRENCY AND EXCHANGE RATES

Monetary Units
100 deni = 1 Macedonian denar.

Sterling, Dollar and Euro Equivalents (28 November 2014)
£1 sterling = 77.817 denars;
US $1 = 49.423 denars;
€1 = 61.695 denars;
1,000 denars = £12.85 = $20.23 = €16.21.

Average Exchange Rate (denars per US $)
2011   44.231
2012   47.890
2013   46.395

BUDGET
(million denars)*

Revenue	2012	2013	2014†
Tax revenue	75,619	77,478	85,189
Personal income tax	9,553	10,254	11,194
Profit tax	3,652	4,421	5,005
Value-added tax	38,469	39,835	44,484
Excises	16,596	15,990	16,928
Import duties	4,067	4,255	4,712
Other taxes	3,282	2,723	2,866
Special revenue accounts tax	998	1,075	1,484
Social contributions	40,765	42,438	44,703
Pension insurance	27,524	28,632	30,190
Unemployment contributions	1,746	1,802	1,890
Health insurance	11,495	12,004	12,623
Non-tax revenue	12,626	12,109	14,697
Capital revenue	4,433	3,139	4,177
Foreign donations	3,045	3,451	4,504
Repayment of loans	629	558	800
Total	138,115	140,248	155,554

Expenditure	2012	2013	2014†
Current expenditure	137,083	142,894	154,073
Wages, salaries and allowances	22,714	22,566	23,605
Other purchases of goods and services	14,652	14,877	18,636
Transfers	95,501	100,845	107,431
Pensions	40,893	44,954	48,220
Unemployment benefits	2,239	1,935	1,775
Social benefits	5,604	5,941	6,471
Health care	20,940	21,420	22,217
Interest payments	4,216	4,606	4,401
Capital expenditure	18,757	16,611	21,084
Total	155,840	159,505	175,157

* Figures refer to the consolidated accounts of the general Government, comprising the transactions of the central Government and the operations of extra-budgetary funds.
† Budget figures.

Source: Ministry of Finance, Skopje.

INTERNATIONAL RESERVES
(US $ million at 31 December)

	2011	2012	2013
Gold (national valuation)	345.5	363.3	262.3
IMF special drawing rights	0.8	1.6	4.6
Foreign exchange	2,330.7	2,526.6	2,480.0
Total	2,677.0	2,891.5	2,746.9

Source: IMF, *International Financial Statistics*.

MONEY SUPPLY
(million denars at 31 December)

	2011	2012	2013
Currency outside depository corporations	19,308	20,112	20,706
Transferable deposits	65,859	68,622	73,199
Other deposits	172,212	179,847	188,564
Broad money	257,379	268,581	282,469

Source: IMF, *International Financial Statistics*.

COST OF LIVING
(Consumer Price Index; base: previous year = 100)

	2011	2012	2013
Food (incl. non-alcoholic beverages)	106.2	102.3	103.4
Clothing (incl. footwear)	101.4	105.4	107.0
Housing, fuel and light	105.0	109.2	101.0
All items (incl. others)	103.9	103.3	102.8

NATIONAL ACCOUNTS
(million denars at current prices)

Expenditure on the Gross Domestic Product

	2011	2012	2013*
Government final consumption expenditure	84,188	87,031	88,457
Private final consumption expenditure	345,262	344,852	359,204
Changes in inventories†	25,850	25,583	24,698
Gross fixed capital formation	94,698	109,071	117,382
Acquisitions, less disposal, of valuables	—	350	367
Total domestic expenditure	549,998	566,887	590,108
Exports of goods and services	252,229	211,764	218,736
Less Imports of goods and services	342,438	311,947	309,284
GDP in purchasers' values	459,789	466,703	499,559
GDP in constant 2005 prices	361,714	360,322	370,809

Gross Domestic Product by Economic Activity

	2011	2012	2013*
Agriculture, forestry and fishing	43,895	42,493	48,170
Mining and quarrying	6,915		
Manufacturing	61,918	71,689	78,246
Electricity, gas and water supply	18,215		
Construction	29,924	26,695	28,809
Wholesale and retail trade	61,908		
Hotels and restaurants	5,535	94,317	108,624
Transport and communications	34,863		
Financial services	11,401	13,542	13,828
Real estate and business services‡	46,307	74,714	77,316
Public administration and defence	36,201		
Education	15,396		
Health care and social work	16,058	80,233	81,156
Other community, social and personal services	13,857		
Sub-total	402,392	403,684	436,149
Value added tax	57,737		
Import duties	3,779	63,019	63,410
Less Subsidies on products	4,120		
GDP in purchasers' values	459,789	466,703	499,559

* Preliminary.
† Including statistical discrepancy.
‡ Including imputed rents of owner-occupied dwellings.

BALANCE OF PAYMENTS
(US $ million)

	2011	2012	2013
Exports of goods	3,339.3	2,960.4	3,166.1
Imports of goods	−5,980.3	−5,545.0	−5,634.5
Balance on goods	−2,640.9	−2,584.6	−2,468.4
Exports of services	1,466.6	1,373.7	1,526.2
Imports of services	−974.5	−994.8	−1,059.2
Balance on goods and services	−2,148.8	−2,205.7	−2,001.5
Primary income received	225.0	209.6	200.8
Primary income paid	−412.4	−399.5	−442.3
Balance on goods, services and primary income	−2,336.2	−2,395.7	−2,243.0
Secondary income received	2,142.4	2,166.3	2,146.9
Secondary income paid	−67.6	−71.0	−98.0
Current balance	−261.4	−300.4	−194.1
Capital account (net)	12.0	25.8	23.5
Direct investment assets	−31.7	−185.0	−40.6
Direct investment from liabilities	495.1	282.7	376.5
Portfolio investment assets	−33.5	−9.4	−43.8
Portfolio investment liabilities	−71.8	108.1	−165.0
Other investment assets	−573.0	−107.4	−87.8
Other investment liabilities	585.7	349.4	44.7
Net errors and omissions	11.5	20.9	39.1
Reserves and related items	132.8	184.7	−47.5

Source: IMF, *International Financial Statistics*.

External Trade

PRINCIPAL COMMODITIES
(distribution by SITC, US $ million)

Imports c.i.f.	2011	2012	2013
Food and live animals	672.2	680.7	681.4
Meat and meat preparations	155.3	160.0	169.9
Mineral fuels, lubricants, etc.	1,438.6	1,388.3	1,071.9
Petroleum, petroleum products, etc.	1,056.6	969.2	745.0
Electric energy	228.1	253.2	170.1
Chemicals and related products	827.6	740.0	860.8
Basic manufactures	1,963.2	1,828.3	2,036.6
Iron and steel	437.5	370.0	364.7
Machinery and transport equipment	1,174.9	1,025.6	1,157.5
General industrial machinery	192.0	167.9	198.9
Electrical machinery, apparatus, etc. (excl. telecommunications and sound equipment)	254.1	203.7	262.0
Road vehicles and transport equipment	359.0	277.9	258.6
Miscellaneous manufactured articles	430.8	389.1	424.9
Total (incl. others)	7,027.2	6,510.9	6,599.8

Exports f.o.b.	2011	2012	2013
Food and live animals	373.3	339.2	364.6
Vegetables and fruit	197.1	175.0	193.2
Beverages and tobacco	235.0	237.7	270.0
Beverages	81.5	91.3	87.9
Tobacco and tobacco manufactures	153.5	146.4	182.1
Crude materials (inedible) except fuels	288.5	265.1	278.2
Mineral fuels, lubricants, etc.	390.1	255.6	106.4
Petroleum and petroleum products	333.7	206.8	94.7
Chemicals and related products	747.2	681.1	836.6
Basic manufactures	1,233.4	1,037.6	1,013.1
Textile yarn, fabrics, etc.	60.1	60.0	77.6
Iron and steel	1,011.4	834.2	787.7
Machinery and transport equipment	353.6	397.1	571.1
General industrial machinery	122.9	189.2	285.2
Electrical machinery, apparatus, etc. (excl. telecommunications and sound equipment)	159.0	133.5	199.2
Miscellaneous manufactured articles	836.5	771.9	813.8
Clothing and accessories (excl. footwear)	659.3	598.2	623.9
Total (incl. others)	4,478.3	4,001.9	4,266.9

PRINCIPAL TRADING PARTNERS
(US $ million)

Imports c.i.f.	2011	2012	2013
Austria	133.3	118.9	143.6
Bosnia and Herzegovina	90.1	71.0	63.5
Bulgaria	457.9	407.8	365.7
China, People's Republic	354.9	374.8	379.6
Croatia	133.3	120.8	115.1
Czech Republic	60.5	71.5	90.8
France	125.9	86.6	94.7
Germany	729.7	633.7	693.6
Greece	569.7	803.7	697.8
Italy	427.6	398.5	428.4
Netherlands	69.2	64.5	70.9
Poland	82.2	100.1	101.3
Romania	94.6	120.1	125.8

Imports c.i.f.—*continued*	2011	2012	2013
Russia	684.3	360.4	163.6
Serbia	498.2	481.8	522.3
Slovenia	185.5	150.2	167.4
Spain	63.0	75.3	67.3
Switzerland-Liechtenstein	172.1	147.9	130.2
Turkey	345.4	324.0	314.5
Ukraine	157.6	86.9	92.6
United Kingdom	593.1	560.4	726.8
USA	88.8	82.9	124.1
Total (incl. others)	7,027.2	6,510.9	6,599.8

Exports f.o.b.	2011	2012	2013
Albania	87.3	75.6	78.5
Austria	38.3	49.0	47.1
Belgium	62.5	41.6	66.6
Bosnia and Herzegovina	93.1	84.5	94.7
Bulgaria	308.6	285.4	325.1
China, People's Republic	127.5	158.8	103.9
Croatia	139.6	98.5	100.3
Germany	1,242.5	1,176.5	1,533.6
Greece	218.0	188.0	211.9
Italy	291.1	278.1	275.4
Netherlands	87.5	65.9	67.5
Romania	46.3	52.7	87.1
Serbia	337.5	295.3	269.7
Slovenia	88.2	74.3	59.4
Spain	66.5	46.9	44.7
Turkey	73.4	66.8	71.7
Ukraine	95.8	17.9	22.5
United Kingdom	54.3	62.7	79.8
USA	36.1	56.4	46.0
Total (incl. others)	4,478.3	4,001.9	4,266.9

Transport

RAILWAYS
(traffic)

	2011	2012	2013
Passenger journeys ('000)	1,421	1,013	853
Passenger-km (million)	145	99	80
Freight carried ('000 metric tons)	2,770	2,539	2,283
Freight ton-km (million)	479	423	421

ROAD TRAFFIC
(motor vehicles in use at 31 December)

	2011	2012	2013
Motorcycles	8,373	8,473	8,093
Passenger cars	313,080	301,761	346,798
Buses	2,636	2,719	3,022
Goods vehicles	27,917	26,542	30,167
Tractors, working vehicles and trailers	12,013	11,267	23,557

INLAND WATERS
(lake transport)

	2011	2012	2013
Passengers carried	28,440	17,690	31,660
Passenger-km ('000)	850	899	608

CIVIL AVIATION
(traffic on scheduled services)

	2007	2008	2009
Kilometres flown (million)	3	3	1
Passengers carried ('000)	211	196	87
Passenger-km (million)	253	209	87
Total ton-km (million)	23	18	8

Source: UN, *Statistical Yearbook.*

2010: Passengers carried ('000) 123 (Source: World Bank, World Development Indicators database).

Tourism

TOURISTS BY COUNTRY OF ORIGIN*

	2011	2012	2013
Austria	5,681	6,275	8,376
Albania	13,614	13,412	16,982
Bosnia and Herzegovina	4,959	4,740	4,540
Bulgaria	18,541	19,815	20,914
Croatia	13,885	13,939	12,722
Germany	9,822	11,306	13,065
Greece	45,509	43,976	46,184
Italy	7,140	7,926	7,894
Kosovo	9,829	9,613	11,887
Netherlands	22,219	27,121	25,542
Poland	6,758	7,490	12,980
Serbia	35,692	36,530	38,127
Slovenia	14,063	13,252	13,404
Turkey	39,251	50,406	68,124
United Kingdom	6,139	6,278	6,935
USA	8,082	7,773	9,258
Total (incl. others)	327,471	351,359	399,680

* Figures refer to arrivals from abroad at all accommodation establishments.

Tourism receipts (US $ million, excl. passenger transport): 240 in 2011; 234 in 2012; 270 in 2013 (Source: World Tourism Organization).

Communications Media

	2011	2012	2013
Telephones ('000 main lines in use)	422.1	408.3	399.4
Mobile cellular telephones ('000 subscribers)	2,213.2	2,235.5	2,237.3
Internet subscribers ('000)	260.3	n.a.	n.a.
Broadband subscribers ('000)	259.2	288.4	330.8
Newspapers			
Titles	17	27	22
Circulation (number of copies)	4,614	17,529	16,910
Book production (incl. brochures)			
Titles	910	997	864
Circulation (number of copies)	783	1,098	723
Magazines			
Titles	100	138	87
Circulation ('number of copies)	2,334	4,437	3,135

Source: partly International Telecommunication Union.

Education

(2013/14 unless otherwise indicated)

	Institutions	Teachers	Students
Primary and lower secondary	988	17,219	191,051
Upper secondary	113	7,322	86,418
University level	120	2,251	56,697
Other higher	3	50	1,049

Pupil-teacher ratio (primary education, UNESCO estimate): 15.2 in 2011/12 (Source: UNESCO Institute for Statistics).

Adult literacy rate (UNESCO estimates): 97.5% (males 98.7%; females 96.3%) in 2012 (Source: UNESCO Institute for Statistics).

Directory

The Government

HEAD OF STATE

President of the Republic: Dr GJORGE IVANOV (elected 5 April 2009; inaugurated 12 May; re-elected 27 April 2014; inaugurated 12 May).

COUNCIL OF MINISTERS
(May 2015)

A coalition, principally comprising representatives of Vnatrešno-Makedonska Revolucionerna Organizacija-Demokratska Partija za Makedonsko Nacionalno Edinstvo (VMRO-DPMNE) and the Bashkimi Demokratik për Integrim (BDI).

Prime Minister: NIKOLA GRUEVSKI (VMRO-DPMNE).

Deputy Prime Minister and Minister of Finance: ZORAN STAVRESKI (VMRO-DPMNE).

Deputy Prime Minister, responsible for the implementation of the Ohrid Framework Agreement: MUSA XHAFERI (BDI).

Deputy Prime Minister, responsible for Economic Affairs: VLADIMIR PEŠEVSKI (VMRO-DPMNE).

Deputy Prime Minister, responsible for European Integration: FATMIR BESIMI (BDI).

Minister of Foreign Affairs: NIKOLA POPOSKI (VMRO-DPMNE).

Minister of Defence: ZORAN JOLEVSKI (VMRO-DPMNE).

Minister of Internal Affairs: MITKO ČAVKOV (VMRO-DPMNE).

Minister of Justice: ADNAN JASHARI (BDI).

Minister of Transport and Communications: VLADO MISAJLOVSKI (VMRO-DPMNE).

Minister of the Economy: BEKIM NEZIRI (BDI).

Minister of Agriculture, Forestry and Water Resources: MIHAIL CVETKOV (Socijalistiska Partija na Makedonija).

Minister of Health: NIKOLA TODOROV (VMRO-DPMNE).

Minister of the Information Society and Administration: IVO IVANOVSKI (VMRO-DPMNE).

Minister of Education and Science: ABDILAQIM ADEMI (BDI).

Minister of Local Self-Government: LJIRIM SHABANI (BDI).

Minister of Culture: ELIZABETA KANČESKA MILEVSKA (VMRO-DPMNE).

Minister of Labour and Social Policy: DIME SPASOV (VMRO-DPMNE).

Minister of the Environment and Physical Planning: NURHAN IZAIRI (BDI).

Minister without Portfolio: FURKAN ÇAKO (Makedonya Türk Demokratik Partisi).

Minister without Portfolio: NEŽDET MUSTAFA (Obedinita Partija za Emancipacija).

Minister without Portfolio: VELE SAMAK (VMRO-DPMNE).

Minister without Portfolio: BIL PAVLESKI (Independent).

Minister without Portfolio: XHERI NAUMOF (Independent).

Minister without Portfolio: VISAR FIDA (BDI).

Minister without Portfolio: GORAN MICOVSKI (Independent).

MINISTRIES

Office of the President: 1000 Skopje, Aco Karamanov 33 A; tel. and fax (2) 3253105; e-mail president@president.gov.mk; internet www.president.gov.mk.

Office of the Prime Minister: 1000 Skopje, Ilindenska bb 2; tel. (2) 3118022; fax (2) 3112561; e-mail primeminister@primeminister.gov.mk; internet www.vlada.mk.

Ministry of Agriculture, Forestry and Water Resources: 1000 Skopje, ul. Leninova 2; tel. (2) 3134477; fax (2) 3230429; e-mail info@mzsv.gov.mk; internet www.mzsv.gov.mk.

Ministry of Culture: 1000 Skopje, ul. Gjuro Gjakovik 61; tel. (2) 3240500; fax (2) 3240920; e-mail info@kultura.gov.mk; internet www.kultura.gov.mk.

Ministry of Defence: 1000 Skopje, Orce Nikolov 116; tel. (2) 3282042; fax (2) 3283991; e-mail info@morm.gov.mk; internet www.morm.gov.mk.

Ministry of the Economy: 1000 Skopje, Jurij Gagarin 15; tel. (2) 3093408; fax (2) 3084472; e-mail info@economy.gov.mk; internet www.economy.gov.mk.

Ministry of Education and Science: 1000 Skopje, Mito Hadzivasilev Jasmin bb; tel. (2) 3117896; fax (2) 3118414; e-mail contact@mon.gov.mk; internet www.mon.gov.mk.

Ministry of the Environment and Physical Planning: 1000 Skopje, Goce Delcev, MRTV Bldg; tel. (2) 3251400; fax (2) 3220165; e-mail infoeko@moepp.gov.mk; internet www.moepp.gov.mk.

Ministry of Finance: 1000 Skopje, Mito Hadjivasilev Jasmin bb; tel. (2) 3106159; fax (2) 3106779; e-mail finance@finance.gov.mk; internet www.finance.gov.mk.

Ministry of Foreign Affairs: 1000 Skopje, Filip II Makedonski 7; tel. (2) 3115266; fax (2) 3115790; e-mail mailmnr@mfa.gov.mk; internet www.mfa.gov.mk.

Ministry of Health: 1000 Skopje, ul. 50 Divizija 14; tel. (2) 3112500; fax (2) 3113014; internet www.zdravstvo.gov.mk.

Ministry of the Information Society and Administration: 1000 Skopje, ul. Kiril i Metodij 54; tel. (2) 3200870; fax (2) 3221883; e-mail contact_mis@mis.gov.mk; internet www.mio.gov.mk.

Ministry of Internal Affairs: 1000 Skopje, ul. Dimče Mirčev 9; tel. (2) 3117222; fax (2) 3112468; e-mail kontakt@mvr.gov.mk; internet www.mvr.gov.mk.

Ministry of Justice: 1000 Skopje, Dimitrija Čupovski 9; tel. (2) 3117288; fax (2) 3226975; e-mail cabinet@mjustice.gov.mk; internet www.pravda.gov.mk.

Ministry of Labour and Social Policy: 1000 Skopje, Dame Gruev 14; tel. (2) 3106212; fax (2) 3220408; e-mail mtsp@mtsp.gov.mk; internet www.mtsp.gov.mk.

Ministry of Local Self-Government: 1000 Skopje, ul. Kiril i Metodij 54; tel. 3253921; fax 3253920; e-mail info@mls.gov.mk; internet www.mls.gov.mk.

Ministry of Transport and Communications: 1000 Skopje, ul. Crvena skopska opština 4; tel. (2) 3145497; fax (2) 3126228; e-mail contact@mtc.gov.mk; internet www.mtc.gov.mk.

President

Presidential Election, First Ballot, 13 April 2014

Candidate	Votes	% of votes
Gjorge Ivanov (VMRO-DPMNE) . . .	449,442	51.69
Stevo Pendarovski (SDSM)	326,164	37.51
Iljaz Halimi (PDSh)	38,966	4.48
Zoran Popovski (GROM)	31,368	3.61
Total*	869,547	100.00

* Including 23,607 invalid votes, equivalent to 2.71% of the total.

Second Ballot, 27 April 2014

Candidate	Votes	% of votes
Gjorge Ivanov (VMRO-DPMNE) . . .	534,910	55.28
Stevo Pendarovski (SDSM)	398,077	41.14
Total*	967,694	100.00

* Including 34,707 invalid votes, equivalent to 3.59% of the total.

Legislature

Assembly
(Sobranie)

1000 Skopje, 11 Oktomvri bb; tel. (2) 3112255; fax (2) 3237947; e-mail sobranie@sobranie.mk; internet www.sobranie.mk.

President: TRAJKO VELJANOSKI.

General Election, 27 April 2014

Party	Votes	% of votes	Seats
VMRO-DPMNE*	481,615	42.97	61
SDSM†	283,955	25.34	34
BDI	153,646	13.71	19
PDSh	66,393	5.92	7
GROM	31,610	2.82	1
RDK	17,783	1.59	1
VMRO-NP	16,772	1.50	—
Others	31,316	2.79	—
Total‡	1,139,353	100.00	123

* In coalition with 21 other parties, including the SPM, the Democratic Union, DOM, the MTDP, the DPSM and the OPE.
† In coalition with eight other parties, including the NSDP and the LPM.
‡ Including 37,654 invalid votes, equivalent to 3.36% of the total.

Election Commission

State Election Commission (Drzhavna izborna komisija): 1000 Skopje, ul. Kiril i Metodij 54; tel. (2) 3244744; fax (2) 3244745; e-mail izbori@sec.mk; internet www.sec.mk; Chair. NIKOLA RILKOSKI.

Political Organizations

Bashkimi Demokratik për Integrim/Demokratska Unija za Integracija (BDI) (Democratic Union for Integration): 1200 Tetovo, Rruga 170 No 2, Reçicë e Vogël; tel. (4) 4334398; fax (4) 4334397; e-mail cabinet@bdi.mk; internet www.bdi.org.mk; f. 2002; ethnic Albanian, dominated by fmr mems of rebel National Liberation Army; Chair. ALI AHMETI; Sec.-Gen. ABDILAQIM ADEMI.

Demokracia e Re (DR) (New Democracy): 1000 Skopje, Khristian Todorovski 94A; tel. (2) 2616220; fax (2) 2616217; e-mail info@demokraciaere.org; f. 2008 by fmr mems of the PDSh; Pres. IMER SELMANI.

Demokratska Obnova na Makedonija (DOM) (Democratic Renewal of Macedonia): 1000 Skopje, ul. Nikola Vapcarov 18/1; tel. and fax (2) 5112900; e-mail dommakedonija@yahoo.com; internet www.dom.org.mk; f. 2006; contested 2014 legislative elections as mem. of coalition led by VMRO-DPMNE (q.v.); Leader LILJANA POPOVSKA.

Demokratska Partija Srba u Makedoniji (DPSM) (Democratic Party of Serbs in Macedonia): Skopje, bul. K. Racin 14/9; tel. and fax (2) 3214556; e-mail dpsm@mt.net.mk; internet www.dpsm.info; f. 1992; contested 2014 legislative elections as mem. of coalition led by VMRO-DPMNE (q.v.); Pres. IVAN STOILKOVIĆ.

Gragjanska Opciija za Makedonija (GROM) (Lightning—Citizens' Option for Macedonia): 1000 Skopje, Franklin Ruzvelt 5A; e-mail info@grom.mk; internet www.grom.mk; f. 2013; Pres. STEVCHO JAKIMOVSKI.

Liberalna Partija na Makedonija (LPM) (Liberal Party of Macedonia): 1000 Skopje, ul. Jurij Gagarin 67; tel. and fax (2) 5111833; e-mail info@lp.org.mk; internet www.lp.org.mk; f. 1990; contested 2014 legislative elections as mem. of coalition led by the SDSM; reformist centrist, free-market oriented; Pres. IVON VELIČKOVSKI; Sec.-Gen. Dr GORAN NIKOLOVSKI.

Liberalno-Demokratska Partija (LDP) (Liberal Democratic Party): 1000 Skopje, 11 Oktombri 8; tel. (2) 6091268; e-mail liberaldemocraticparty@gmail.com; internet www.ldp.org.mk; f. 1996; Chair. ANDREJ ZHERNOVISKI.

Makedonya Türk Demokratik Partisi (MTDP) (Democratic Party of Turks in Macedonia): 1000 Skopje, ul. Stiv Naumov 1; tel. and fax (2) 3214053; e-mail info@tdp.org.mk; internet www.tdp.org.mk; contested 2014 legislative elections as mem. of coalition led by VMRO-DPMNE (q.v.); Pres. Dr KENAN HASIPI.

Nova Socijaldemokratska Partija (NSDP) (New Social Democratic Party): 1000 Skopje, ul. Veljko Vlahović 4; tel. (2) 3238775; fax (2) 3290465; e-mail contact@nsdp.org.mk; internet www.nsdp.org.mk; f. 2005; contested 2014 legislative elections as mem. of coalition led by the SDSM; Pres. TITO PETKOVSKI.

Obedinita Partija za Emancipacija (OPE) (United Party for Emancipation): c/o Sobranie, 1000 Skopje, 11 Oktomvri bb; tel. (2) 3112255, ext. 135; e-mail nezdet.mustafa@gs.gov.mk; f. 2002; represents Roma interests; contested 2014 legislative elections as mem. of coalition led by VMRO-DPMNE (q.v.); Leader NEŽDET MUSTAFA.

Partia Demokratike Shqiptare (PDSh) (Democratic Party of Albanians): Tetovo, Sheshi i Qytetit 15/1; tel. and fax (44) 333581; e-mail m.thaci@gurra-pdsh.org; internet www.pdsh.info; f. 1997; officially registered 2002; absorbed the Party for Democratic Prosperity in 2008; Chair. MENDUH THAÇI.

Rilindja Demokratike Kombëtare (RDK) (National Democratic Revival): 1230 Gostivar, Bul. Braqa Gjinoski 110; tel. (7) 8742225; e-mail info@rdk.org.mk; internet www.rdk.org.mk; f. 2011; Chair. Dr RUFI OSMANI.

Socijaldemokratski Sojuz na Makedonija (SDSM) (Social Democratic Alliance of Macedonia): 1000 Skopje, Bihakjka 8; tel. (2) 3293100; fax (2) 3293109; e-mail president@sdsm.org.mk; internet www.sdsm.org.mk; f. 1943; fmrly SKM—PDP, League of Communists of Macedonia—Party of Democratic Reform; Chair. ZORAN ZAEV; Gen. Sec. OLIVER SPASOVSKI.

Socijalistiska Partija na Makedonija (SPM) (Socialist Party of Macedonia): 1000 Skopje, 11 Oktomvri 17; tel. (2) 3228015; fax (2) 3220025; e-mail contact@spm.org.mk; internet www.spm.org.mk; f. 1990; left-wing; contested 2014 legislative elections as mem. of coalition led by VMRO-DPMNE (q.v.); Chair. LJUBISAV IVANOV.

Vnatrešno-Makedonska Revolucionerna Organizacija-Demokratska Partija za Makedonsko Nacionalno Edinstvo (VMRO-DPMNE) (Internal Macedonian Revolutionary Organization-Democratic Party for Macedonian National Unity): 1000 Skopje, Makedonija 17A; tel. (2) 3215550; fax (2) 3215551; e-mail contact@vmro-dpmne.org.mk; internet www.vmro-dpmne.org.mk; nationalist; Pres. NIKOLA GRUEVSKI; Sec.-Gen. KIRIL BOZHINOVSKI.

Vnatrešno-Makedonska Revolucionerna Organizacija-Narodna Partija (VMRO-NP) (Internal Macedonian Revolutionary Organization-People's Party): 1000 Skopje, ul. Nikola Vapcarov br. 2; tel. and fax (2) 6145374; e-mail contact@vmro-np.org.mk; internet www.vmro-np.org.mk; f. 2004 by fmr mems of VMRO-DPMNE (q.v.); Chair. LJUBCHO GEORGIEVSKI.

Diplomatic Representation

EMBASSIES IN THE FORMER YUGOSLAV REPUBLIC OF MACEDONIA

Albania: 1000 Skopje, Slavej Planina 2; tel. (2) 3246726; fax (2) 3246727; e-mail embassy.skopje@mfa.gov.al; internet www.ambasadat.gov.al/republic-of-macedonia; Ambassador PETRIT BUSHATI.

Austria: 1000 Skopje, Mile Popjordanov 8; tel. (2) 3083400; fax (2) 3083150; e-mail skopje-ob@bmeia.gv.at; internet www.aussenministerium.at/skopje; Ambassador Dr THOMAS MICHAEL BAIER.

Bosnia and Herzegovina: 1000 Skopje, Mile Pop-Jordanov 56 B; tel. (2) 3086216; fax (2) 3086221; e-mail emb.bih@neotel.net.mk; internet www.ambasadabih.org.mk; Ambassador ZDRAVKO BEGOVIĆ.

Bulgaria: 1000 Skopje, Zlatko Shnajder 3; tel. (2) 3229444; fax (2) 3246493; e-mail embassy.skopje@mfa.bg; internet www.mfa.bg/embassies/macedonia; Ambassador IVAN PETKOV.

China, People's Republic: 1000 Skopje, 474/20; tel. (2) 3213163; fax (2) 3122500; e-mail chinaembmk@mfa.gov.cn; internet mk.china-embassy.org; Ambassador WEN ZHENSHUN.

Croatia: 1000 Skopje, Bukureška 91; tel. (2) 3248170; fax (2) 3246004; e-mail croemb.skopje@mvpei.hr; internet mk.mvp.hr; Ambassador ZLATKO KRAMARIĆ.

Czech Republic: 1000 Skopje, Salvador Aljende 35; tel. (2) 3109805; fax (2) 3178380; e-mail skopje@embassy.mzv.cz; internet www.mzv.cz/skopje; Ambassador MIROSLAV RAMEŠ.

France: 1000 Skopje, Salvador Aljende 73; tel. (2) 3244300; fax (2) 3244313; e-mail franamba@mt.net.mk; internet www.ambafrance-mk.org; Ambassador LAURENCE AUER.

Germany: 1000 Skopje, Lerinska 59; tel. (2) 3093900; fax (2) 3093899; e-mail info@skop.auswaertiges-amt.de; internet www.skopje.diplo.de; Ambassador Dr CHRISTINE D. ALTHAUSER.

Hungary: 1000 Skopje, Mirka Ginova 27; tel. (2) 3063423; fax (2) 3063070; e-mail mission.skp@mfa.gov.hu; internet www.mfa.gov.hu/emb/skopje; Ambassador Dr JÓZSEF BENCZE.

Iran: 1000 Skopje, Mile Pop Jordanov 12; tel. and fax (2) 3051759; e-mail iriemb@t-home.mk; Ambassador SAIED SADEQH MOHAMMADI.

Italy: 1000 Skopje, Osma Udarna brig. 22; tel. (2) 3236500; fax (2) 3236505; e-mail segreteria.skopje@esteri.it; internet www.ambskopje.esteri.it; Ambassador ERNESTO MASSIMINO BELLELLI.

Kosovo: 1000 Skopje, Samoilova 136; tel. (2) 3290320; fax (2) 3290322; e-mail embassy.macedonia@rks-gov.net; Ambassador YLBER HYSA.

Montenegro: 1000 Skopje, Vasil Stefanovski 7; tel. (2) 3227277; fax (2) 3227254; e-mail macedonia@mfa.gov.me; Ambassador DUŚAN MRDOVIĆ.

Netherlands: 1000 Skopje, Leninova bb 69–71; tel. (2) 3109250; fax (2) 3129309; e-mail sko@minbuza.nl; internet macedonia.nlembassy.org; Chargé d'affaires a.i. JOOP SCHEFFERS.

Poland: 1000 Skopje, Djuro Djaković 50; tel. (2) 3248820; fax (2) 3119744; e-mail skopje.amb.sekretariat@msz.gov.pl; internet www.skopje.msz.gov.pl; Ambassador JACEK MULTANOWSKI.

Qatar: 11000 Skopje, Oktomvriska revolucija 15; tel. and fax (2) 3092370; e-mail macedonia@mofa.gov.qa; Ambassador HASSAN BIN ABDULLAH ZAID AL-MAHMOUD.

Romania: 1000 Skopje, Rajko Zinzifov 42; tel. (2) 3228055; fax (2) 3228036; e-mail romanamb@cabletel.net.mk; internet skopje.mae.ro; Ambassador IUSTINIAN FOCŞA.

Russian Federation: 1000 Skopje, Pirinska 44; tel. (2) 3117160; fax (2) 3117808; e-mail embassy@russia.org.mk; internet www.russia.org.mk; Ambassador OLEG N. SHCHERBAK.

Serbia: 1000 Skopje, Pitu Guli 8; tel. (2) 3129298; fax (2) 3129427; e-mail srbamb@unet.com.mk; internet www.skopje.mfa.gov.rs; Ambassador DUŠANKA DIVJAK-TOMIĆ.

Slovakia: 1000 Skopje, Budimpeštanska 39; tel. (2) 3090360; fax (2) 3090367; e-mail emb.skopje@mzv.sk; internet www.mzv.sk/skopje; Ambassador MARTIN BEZÁK.

Slovenia: 1000 Skopje, Vodnjanska 42; tel. (2) 3103041; fax (2) 3176631; e-mail vsk@gov.si; internet www.skopje.embassy.si; Ambassador BRANKO RAKOVEC.

Spain: 1000 Skopje, 27 Mart 7; tel. (2) 3220717; fax (2) 3215612; e-mail emb.skopje@maec.es; Ambassador RAMÓN ABAROA CARRANZA.

Sweden: 1000 Skopje, Osma Udarna Brigada 2; tel. (2) 3297880; fax (2) 3112065; e-mail ambassaden.skopje@gov.se; internet www.swedenabroad.com/skopje; Ambassador MATS STAFFANSSON.

Switzerland: 1000 Skopje, Maksim Gorki 19; tel. (2) 3103300; fax (2) 3103301; e-mail sko.vertretung@eda.admin.ch; internet www.eda.admin.ch/skopje; Ambassador STEFANO LAZZAROTTO.

Turkey: 1000 Skopje, Slavej Planina bb; tel. (2) 3104710; fax (2) 3117024; e-mail embassy.skopje@mfa.gov.tr; internet skopje.emb.mfa.gov.tr; Ambassador ÖMÜR ŞÖLENDIL.

Ukraine: 1000 Skopje, Albert Svjcer 7–9; tel. and fax (2) 3178120; e-mail emb_mk@mfa.gov.ua; internet macedonia.mfa.gov.ua; Ambassador YURIY O. HONCHARUK.

United Kingdom: 1000 Skopje, Todor Aleksandrov 165; tel. (2) 3299299; fax (2) 3179726; e-mail britishembassyskopje@fco.gov.uk; internet www.gov.uk/government/world/macedonia; Ambassador CHARLES GARRETT.

USA: 1000 Skopje, Samoilova 21; tel. (2) 3102000; fax (2) 3102499; e-mail embskowebm@t-home.mk; internet macedonia.usembassy.gov; Ambassador JESS L. BAILY.

Judicial System

The former Yugoslav republic of Macedonia has 27 Courts of First Instance and three Courts of Appeal. The Republican Judicial Council, which comprises seven members elected by the Sobranie for a term of six years, proposes the election or dismissal of judges to the Sobranie. The Constitutional Court, comprising nine judges elected by the Sobranie with a mandate of nine years, is responsible for the protection of constitutional and legal rights, and ensures that there is no conflict in the exercise of legislative, executive and judicial powers. The Administrative Court, established in 2007, has jurisdiction in numerous administrative matters; a Superior Administrative Court, founded in 2010, serves as a court of second instance in such areas. The Supreme Court is the highest court in the country, and guarantees the equal administration of legislation by all courts.

Constitutional Court (Ustaven Sud na Republika Makedonija): 1000 Skopje, Dimitar Vlahov 19; tel. and fax (2) 3119355; e-mail mail@ustavensud.mk; f. 1964, Pres. ELENA GOSHEVA.

Supreme Court: 1000 Skopje, Krste Misirkova bb; tel. (2) 3136044; fax (2) 3237538; e-mail gordana.stojanova@vsrm.mk; internet www.vsrm.mk; Pres. LIDIJA NEDELKOVA.

Administrative Court: 1000 Skopje, Orce Nikolov; tel. (2) 3203200; fax (2) 3203281; e-mail upravensud@usskopje.mk; internet www.usskopje.mk; f. 2007; Chair. JETMIRE AJDINI-BOŠNJAKU.

Supreme Administrative Court: 1000 Skopje, Nikola Parapunov 31; tel. and fax (2) 3061536; internet www.vusskopje.mk; f. 2010; Chair. ROZALIA KOČKOVSKA.

Office of the Public Prosecutor (Javno Obvinitelstvo na RM): 1000 Skopje, Krste Misirkova bb; tel. (2) 3219850; fax (2) 3219866; e-mail jorm@jorm.org.mk; internet www.jorm.org.mk; Public Prosecutor MARKO ZVRLEVSKI.

Religion

Most ethnic Macedonians are adherents of the Eastern Orthodox Church, and since 1967 there has been an autocephalous Macedonian Orthodox Church. However, the Serbian Orthodox Church (of which the Macedonian Church formed a part) does not recognize the autocephalous church, and nor do other Orthodox Churches. There are some adherents of other Orthodox jurisdictions in the country. Those Macedonian (and Bulgarian) Slavs who converted to Islam during the Ottoman era are known as Pomaks or as ethnic Muslims. The substantial Albanian population is mostly Muslim (mainly Sunni, but there are some adherents of a Dervish sect); there are some Catholic Christians (of both Byzantine and Latin rites) and a small Jewish community.

CHRISTIANITY

Macedonian Orthodox Church: 1000 Skopje, Partizanski Odredi 12, POB 69; tel. (2) 3230697; fax (2) 3230685; internet www.mpc.org.mk; Metropolitan See of Ohrid revived in 1958; autocephaly declared 1967; 1.5m. mems; comprises seven bishoprics in the FYRM and three abroad; Head of Church and Archbishop of Ohrid and Macedonia Metropolitan Archbishop of Skopje STEFAN VELJANOVSKI.

The Roman Catholic Church

The diocese of Skopje, suffragan to the archdiocese of Vrhbosna (based in Sarajevo, Bosnia and Herzegovina), covers most of the former Yugoslav republic of Macedonia. The Bishop is also Apostolic Exarch for Catholics of the Byzantine Rite in the country.

Latin Rite Bishop of Skopje and Apostolic Exarch for the Byzantine Rite Faithful Resident in the former Yugoslav republic of Macedonia: Rt Rev. KIRO STOJANOV, 1000 Skopje, Risto Šiškov 31; tel. and fax (2) 3164123; e-mail katbiskupija@mt.net.mk.

ISLAM

Islamic Community of Macedonia (Bashkësia Fetare Islame e Republikës së Maqedonisë): Skopje, Çairska 52; tel. (2) 3117410; fax (2) 3117883; e-mail bim@bim.org.mk; internet www.bim.org.mk; Leader Haji SULEJMAN REXHEPI.

The Press

In 2012 a total of 27 newspapers and 138 magazines were published in the former Yugoslav republic of Macedonia.

PRINCIPAL DAILY NEWSPAPERS

Dnevnik (Daily): 1000 Skopje, Vasil Gjorgov 16; tel. (2) 3236800; fax (2) 3236801; e-mail dnevnik@dnevnik.com.mk; internet www.dnevnik.com.mk; independent; Editor-in-Chief DARKO JANEVSKI.

Nova Makedonija (New Macedonia): 1000 Skopje, 16-ta Makedonska brigada 18; tel. (2) 5511711; e-mail nm@novamakedonija.com.mk; internet www.novamakedonija.com.mk; f. 1944; morning; in Macedonian; Dir RATKO LAZAREVSKI; Editor-in-Chief ALEKSANDAR DIMKOVSKI; circ. 25,000.

Utrinski Vesnik (Morning Herald): 1000 Skopje, ul. Vasil Gjorgov 16; tel. (2) 3236900; fax (2) 3236901; e-mail contact@utrinski.com.mk; internet www.utrinski.com.mk; Dir Dr SRGJAN KERIM; Editor-in-Chief NINA NINESKA-FIDANOSKA.

Večer (The Evening): 1000 Skopje, ul. Mito Hadjivasilev Jasmin 66; tel. (2) 3219650; fax (2) 3219651; e-mail ivona@vecer.com.mk; internet www.vecer.com.mk; f. 1963; evening; Editor IVONA TALEVSKA; circ. 29,200.

Vest (News): 1000 Skopje, ul. Vasil Gorgov; tel. (2) 3236700; e-mail vest@vest.com.mk; internet www.vest.com.mk; popular; Editor-in-Chief GORAN MIHAILOVSKII.

PERIODICALS

Delo: 1000 Skopje, Mihail Cokov bb; tel. (2) 3133306; fax (2) 3136477; e-mail delo@unet.com.mk; internet www.delo.com.mk; f. 1993; weekly; nationalist; Editor-in-Chief VLADO MOKROV.

Denes (Today): 1000 Skopje, M. H. Jasmin 50; tel. (2) 3110239; fax (2) 3110150; e-mail denes@unet.com.mk; Editor NIK DENES.

Fokus: Skopje, Zheležniča 53; tel. (2) 3111327; fax (2) 3111685; weekly; independent.

Makedonsko Vreme/Macedonian Times: 91000 Skopje, Vasil Gjorgov 39/7; tel. and fax (2) 3121182; e-mail mtimes@unet.com.mk; internet www.unet.com.mk; f. 1994; monthly; politics and current affairs; in Macedonian and English; Editor-in-Chief JOVAN PAVLOVSKI.

Roma Times: Skopje; e-mail mail@dostae.net.mk; f. 2001; 3 a week; circ. 3,000.

Sport Magazine: 1000 Skopje, Mito Hadživasilev Jasmin bb; tel. and fax (2) 3116254; f. 1991; weekly; circ. 6,000.

Trudbenik (Worker): 1000 Skopje, Udarna brigada 12; f. 1945; weekly; organ of Macedonian Trade Unions; Editor SIMO IVANOVSKI.

NEWS AGENCIES

Macedonian Information Agency (Makedonska Informativna Agencija—MIA): 1000 Skopje, Bojmija 2; tel. (2) 2461600; fax (2) 2464048; e-mail mia@mia.mk; internet www.mia.mk; f. 1992; news service in Macedonian, Albanian and English; Exec. Dir LJUPČO JAKIMOSKI.

Macedonian Information Centre (Makedonski Informativen Centar—MIC): 1000 Skopje, Naum Naumovski Borce 73; tel. and fax (2) 3117876; e-mail contact@micnews.com.mk; internet www.micnews.com.mk; f. 1992; English; independent; Man. DRAGAN ANTONOV.

Makfax: 1000 Skopje, 11 Oktomvri 33A; tel. (2) 3227127; fax (2) 3110125; e-mail makfax@makfax.com.mk; internet www.makfax.com.mk; f. 1992; independent; provides daily regional news service; in Macedonian, Albanian and English; Exec. Dir DAVOR PASHOVSKI.

PRESS ASSOCIATION

Journalists' Association of Macedonia: 1000 Skopje, Gradski dzid 13, POB 498; tel. (2) 3298139; fax (2) 3116447; e-mail contact@ znm.org.mk; internet www.znm.org.mk; Pres. NASER SELMANI.

Publishers

Kultura: 1000 Skopje, Sv. Kliment Ohridski 68A; tel. (2) 3111332; fax (2) 3228608; e-mail ipkultura@kultura.com.mk; internet www .kultura.com.mk; f. 1945; history, philosophy, art, poetry, children's literature and fiction; in Macedonian; Dir DIMITAR BAŠEVSKI.

Kulturen Život (Cultural Life) Publishing House: 1000 Skopje, Ruzveltova 6; tel. (2) 3239134; f. 1971; Editor LJUBICA ARSOVSKA.

Makedonska kniga (Macedonian Book) Publishing House: 1000 Skopje, 11 Oktomvri; tel. (2) 3224055; fax (2) 3236951; f. 1947; arts, non-fiction, novels, children's books; Dir SANDE STOJČEVSKI.

Matica Makedonska: 1000 Skopje, Kliment Ohridski 23; tel. (2) 3221138; fax (2) 3229244; f. 1991; Dir RADE SILJAN.

Misla (Thought) Publishing House: 1000 Skopje, Partizanski odredi 1; tel. (2) 3221844; fax (2) 3118439; f. 1966; modern and classic Macedonian and translated literature; Pres. ZLATA BUNTESLEA.

Prosvetno delo (Educational) Publishing House: 1000 Skopje, Dimitrija Čupovski 15; tel. (2) 3117255; fax (2) 3225434; f. 1945; works of domestic writers and textbooks in Macedonian for elementary, professional and high schools; fiction and scientific works; Dir Dr KRSTE ANGELOVSKI.

Tabernakul: 1000 Skopje, Mihail Tsokov bb, POB 251; tel. (2) 3127073; fax (2) 3115329; e-mail contact@tabernakul.com.mk; internet www.tabernakul.com.mk; f. 1989; religion, history, literature, philosophy, popular science; Dir TSVETAN VRAŽIVIRSKI.

Broadcasting and Communications

TELECOMMUNICATIONS

In 2012 there were three main providers of mobile cellular telecommunications services in the former Yugoslav republic of Macedonia and two principal providers of fixed-line telephone services. In 2013 there were 399,400 fixed telephone lines and 2.2m. subscriptions to mobile telecommunications services in the country.

Makedonski Telekom (MT): 1000 Skopje, Orce Nikolov bb; tel. (2) 3100200; fax (2) 3100300; e-mail 122@telekom.mk; internet www .telekom.mk; fmrly Makedonski telekomunikacii; present name adopted 2008; mem. of Deutsche Telekom group (Germany); 34.8% state-owned; CEO ANDREAS MAIERHOFER.

ONE Telecommunications Services: 1000 Skopje, Kuzman Josifovski-Pitu 15; tel. (2) 5411000; e-mail info@one.mk; internet www .one.mk; f. 2003 as Cosmofon; renamed as above after merger with internet services provider on.net in 2009; member of the Telekom Slovenia Group; fixed-line and mobile cellular telecommunications; internet and digital TV services; CEO KLAVDIJ GODNIČ.

T-Mobile Macedonia: 1000 Skopje, Orce Nikolov bb; tel. (2) 3131131; fax (2) 3201267; e-mail kontakt@t-mobile.com.mk; internet www.t-mobile.com.mk; f. 1996 as Mobimak; present name adopted 2006; mobile cellular telecommunications; CEO ZHARKO LUKOVSKI; 1.3m. subscribers (2013).

VIP operator DOOEL Skopje: 1000 Skopje, Vasil Adzilarski bb, 8th Floor; fax (2) 3110077; e-mail kontakt@vipoperator.mk; internet www.vip.mk; f. 2007; subsidiary of MobilKom (Austria); mobile cellular telecommunications services; CEO NIKOLA LJUŠEV.

BROADCASTING

Antenna 5 Radio: 1000 Skopje, Tetovska 35; tel. and fax (2) 3111911; e-mail mail@antenna5.com.mk; internet www.antenna5 .com.mk; f. 1994; 12 transmitters broadcast to 90% of the country; Gen. Man. ZORAN PETROV.

Makedonska Radio-Televizija (MRT): 1000 Skopje, bul. Goce Delčev bb; tel. (2) 5514404; fax (2) 3111821; e-mail mrtsat@mrt.com .mk; internet www.mtv.com.mk; f. 1944 (radio); 1964 (television); fmrly Radiotelevizija Skopje, name changed 1991; three radio channels and three television services; broadcasts in Macedonian, Albanian, Turkish, Serbian, Roma and Vlach; Dirs JANEZ SAJOVIC, BORIS STAVROV; Dir of Radio GRIGORI POPOVSKI; Dir of Television LJUBČO TOZIJA.

SITEL Television: 1000 Skopje, Gradski Stadion bb; tel. (2) 3116566; fax (2) 3229799; e-mail informativna@sitel.com.mk; internet www.sitel.com.mk; f. 1993; owned by SBS Broadcasting Group; Gen. Man. GOVAN IVANOVSKI.

Finance

(cap. = capital; res = reserves; dep. = deposits; m. = million; amounts in new Macedonian denars; brs = branches)

BANKS

At December 2013 the banking system comprised 17 commercial banks and 11 savings houses; 14 of the banks were majority foreign-owned.

National Bank

National Bank of the Republic of Macedonia (Narodna Banka na Republika Makedonija): 1000 Skopje, bul. Kuzman Josifovski Pitu 1; tel. (2) 3108108; fax (2) 3108357; e-mail info@nbrm.mk; internet www.nbrm.mk; f. 1992; central bank and bank of issue; cap. 1,289.7m., res 10,489.7m., dep. 58,924.1m. (Dec. 2008); Gov. DIMITAR BOGOV.

Selected Banks

Alpha Banka a.d. Skopje: 1000 Skopje, ul. Dame Gruev 1; tel. (2) 3251900; fax (2) 3251911; e-mail contact@alphabank.com.mk; internet www.alphabank.com.mk; f. 1993; wholly owned by Alpha Bank AE Athens (Greece); cap. 1,237m., res 792m., dep. 4,946m. (Dec. 2012); Chair. ANDREAS A. GALATOULAS; Gen. Man. MILENA P. PERCHINKOVA; 18 brs.

Halk Banka a.d. Skopje: 1000 Skopje, bul. Mito Hadzivasilev Jasmin bb, POB 421; tel. (2) 3240800; fax (2) 3240801; e-mail halkbank@halkbank.mk; internet www.halkbank.mk; f. 1993; fmrly Izvozna I Kreditna Banka; present name adopted 2012; 98.78% owned by Türkiye Halk Bankası AŞ (Turkey); cap. 2,894.0m., res 459.4m., dep. 12,858.0m. (Dec. 2012); Chief Exec. NECDET PALAKCI; 27 brs.

Komercijalna Banka a.d. Skopje: 1000 Skopje, Orce Nikolov 3; tel. (2) 3168168; fax (2) 3124064; e-mail contact@kb.com.mk; internet www.kb.com.mk; f. 1955; present name adopted 1991; cap. 2,279.1m., res 6,751.3m., dep. 69,409.5m. (Dec. 2012); CEO HARI KOSTOV.

Makedonska Banka za Poddrshka na Razvojot a.d. Skopje (Macedonian Bank for Development Promotion): 1000 Skopje, Dimitrie Chupovski 26; tel. (2) 3115844; fax (2) 3239688; e-mail info@ mbdp.com.mk; internet www.mbdp.com.mk; f. 1998; cap. 1,193.8m., res 765.3m., total assets 12,275.8m. (Dec. 2012); CEO DRAGAN MARTINOVSKI.

NLB Tutunska Banka a.d. Skopje: 1000 Skopje, ul. Majka Tereza 1; tel. (2) 5100601; fax (2) 3105681; e-mail KabinetUO@tb.com.mk; internet www.nlbtb.com.mk; f. 1985; cap. 854.1m., res 3,995.4m., dep. 46,483.1m. (Dec. 2012); Pres. GORGI JANCEVSKI.

Ohridska Banka (Ohrid Bank): 1000 Skopje, Makedonski Prosvetiteli 19; tel. and fax (2) 3167699; e-mail obinfo@ob.com.mk; internet www.ohridskabanka.mk; cap. 1,162.3m., res 224.0m., dep. 20,517.4m. (Dec. 2012); Pres. JITKA PANTUCHKOVA; 5 brs.

Sparkasse Bank Makedonija: 1000 Skopje, Makedonija 9/11; tel. (2) 3200501; fax (2) 3200515; e-mail contact@sparkasse.mk; internet www.sparkasse.mk; f. 1992; present name adopted 2010; 99.5% owned by Steiermärkische Bank und Sparkassen AG (Austria); cap. 1,663.0m., res 861.6m., dep. 10,375.4m. (Dec. 2012); Pres. SAVA DALBOKOV.

Stopanska Banka a.d. Bitola: 7000 Bitola, Dobrivoe Radosavljević 21; tel. (47) 3078520; fax (47) 207541; e-mail stbbt@stbbt.com.mk; internet www.stbbt.com.mk; f. 1948; present name adopted 1995; cap. 1,172.9m., res 1.3m., dep. 5,332.0m. (Dec. 2012); Pres. VLADIMIR EFTIMOSKI.

Stopanska Banka a.d. Skopje: 1000 Skopje, 11 Oktomvri 7; tel. (2) 3295295; fax (2) 3114503; e-mail sbank@stb.com.mk; internet www .stb.com.mk; f. 1944; cap. 3,511.2m., res 831.4m., dep. 63,168.4m. (Dec. 2013); 94.64% owned by National Bank of Greece; CEO DIOMIDIS NIKOLETOPOULOS; 65 brs.

UniBanka—Universalna Investiciona Banka a.d. Skopje (Universal Investment Bank): 1000 Skopje, M. Gorki 6; tel. (2) 3111111; fax (2) 3224162; e-mail info@unibank.com.mk; internet www.unibank.com.mk; f. 1993; present name adopted 2004; cap. 546.0m., res 567.9m., dep. 9,476.2m. (Dec. 2012); Pres. KOSTA MITROVSKI.

STOCK EXCHANGE

Macedonian Stock Exchange (Makedonska Berza a.d. Skopje): 1000 Skopje, Orce Nikolov 75; tel. (2) 3122055; fax (2) 3122069; e-mail mse@mse.org.mk; internet www.mse.com.mk; f. 1995; CEO IVAN STERIEV.

INSURANCE

In 2012 the insurance system in the FYRM comprised 12 insurance companies, 11 insurance brokerage companies and six insurance agencies.

QBE Makedonija: 1000 Skopje, 11 Oktomvri 25; tel. (2) 3115188; fax (2) 3114020; internet www.qbeeurope.com/makedonija; subsidiary of QBE Insurance Group (Australia); stock company for insurance and reinsurance; CEO Frank O'Halloran.

Sava Tabak a.d. Skopje: 1000 Skopje, Zagreb 28a; tel. (2) 5101500; fax (2) 5101502; e-mail contact@sava.com.mk; internet www.sava .com.mk; fmrly Tabak Osiguravanje; 66.67% owned by Sava Re (Slovenia).

Trade and Industry

CHAMBER OF COMMERCE

Economic Chamber of Macedonia (Stopanska Komora na Makedonija): 1000 Skopje, Dimitrija Čupovski 13; tel. (2) 3244000; fax (2) 3244088; e-mail ic@ic.mchamber.org.mk; internet www.mchamber .org.mk; f. 1962; Pres. Branko Azeski.

UTILITIES

Electricity

EVN Macedonia: 1000 Skopje, 11 Oktombri 9; tel. (2) 3205000; fax (2) 3227827; e-mail lenche.karpuzovska@evn.mk; internet www.evn .mk; fmrly Electric Power Co of Macedonia (Elektrostopanstovo na Makedonija); production and distribution of electric power; 90% owned by EVN AG (Austria); Chair. Werner Hengst.

TRADE UNIONS

Federation of Trade Unions of Macedonia: 1000 Skopje; tel. (2) 3231374; fax (2) 3115787; 18 affiliated unions; Pres. Vanco Muratovski.

Transport

RAILWAYS

In 2009 the rail network totalled 699 km, of which 233 km were electrified.

Makedonski Železnici Infrastruktura (MZI) (Macedonian Railways Infrastructure): 1000 Skopje, Jordan Mijalkov 50; tel. (2) 3227903; fax (2) 2462330; e-mail info@mzi.mk; internet www.mzi .mk; railway infrastructure Co; Gen. Dir Irfan Asani.

Makedonski Železnici Transport a.d. Skopje (Macedonian Railways Transport Co): 1000 Skopje, Treta Makedonska Brigada b.b.; tel. (2) 3248701; fax (2) 3248719; e-mail mztransportad@t-home.mk; internet mztransportad.com.mk; f. 2007; operates passenger and cargo services; Gen. Dir Nikola Kostov.

ROADS

In 2012 the FYRM's road network totalled 14,038 km, of which 652 km were main roads while 57.7% of them were paved roads.

CIVIL AVIATION

The FYRM has two international airports, at Ohrid, and the Aleksandar Veliki (Alexander the Great) Airport, near Skopje.

Tourism

Tourist arrivals numbered 399,680 in 2013, when receipts from tourism amounted to US $270m.

Tourist Association of Macedonia: 1000 Skopje, Makedonija 39; tel. (2) 3161348; e-mail tarm@mt.net.mk.

Defence

As assessed at November 2014, national armed forces amounted to 8,000 troops in active service and 4,850 reserves. Paramilitary forces comprised a police force of 7,600, of whom some 5,000 were armed. Conscription was abolished with effect from 2007.

Defence Expenditure: 5,870m. new denars in 2014.

Chief of Staff of the Army: Lt-Gen. Goranco Koteski.

Education

Elementary education is free and compulsory for all children between the ages of seven and 15. Various types of secondary school, beginning at 15 and lasting for four years, are available to those who qualify. In 2009/10 the primary education enrolment ratio included 88% of children in the relevant age-group, while the enrolment ratio in secondary education was equivalent to 82% of children in the relevant age-group. According to the terms of the Constitution, citizens are granted the right to elementary and secondary education in their mother tongue. In 2013/14 some 277,469 students were enrolled in primary and secondary education. There are universities at Skopje, Bitola and Tetovo (the latter of which operates in Albanian). Expenditure on education by the central Government in 2002 was budgeted at 7,591m. new denars (11.4% of total expenditure).

MADAGASCAR

Introductory Survey

LOCATION, CLIMATE, LANGUAGE, RELIGION, FLAG, CAPITAL

The Republic of Madagascar comprises the island of Madagascar, the fourth largest in the world, and several much smaller offshore islands, in the western Indian Ocean, about 500 km (300 miles) east of Mozambique, in southern Africa. The inland climate is temperate; in Antananarivo temperatures are generally between 8°C (48°F) and 27°C (81°F), with cooler, dryer weather between May and October. The coastal region is tropical, with an average daily maximum temperature of 32°C (90°F). The rainy season extends from November to April in the highlands (average annual rainfall is 1,000 mm–1,500 mm) but is more prolonged on the coast, where average annual rainfall can reach 3,500 mm. The official languages are Malagasy and French. Hova and other dialects are also widely spoken. More than 50% of the population follow animist beliefs, while about 41% are Christians and the remainder are Muslims. The national flag (proportions 2 by 3) has a vertical white stripe (one-third of the length) at the hoist and two equal horizontal stripes, of red and green, in the fly. The capital is Antananarivo.

CONTEMPORARY POLITICAL HISTORY

Historical Context

A French possession since 1896, Madagascar became an autonomous state within the French Community in October 1958, as the Malagasy Republic. In May 1959 Philibert Tsiranana, leader of the Parti Social Démocrate (PSD), was elected President. The country achieved full independence on 26 June 1960. Prior to independence France supported the PSD, which was identified with the majority coastal tribes (côtiers), as an alternative to the more nationalistic highland people, the Merina, who were the traditional ruling group on the island.

After 1967 there was growing opposition to the Government's alleged authoritarianism and subservience to French interests. In May 1972, following civil unrest, President Tsiranana transferred full powers to the Army Chief of Staff, Gen. Gabriel Ramanantsoa. In October 1973 pro-Government parties secured a decisive victory in legislative elections. A prolonged crisis followed an attempted military coup in December 1974, and in early February 1975 Ramanantsoa transferred power to Col Richard Ratsimandrava, hitherto Minister of the Interior; however, Ratsimandrava was assassinated shortly afterwards. On 12 February Brig.-Gen. Gilles Andriamahazo assumed power and imposed martial law. All political parties were suspended. In June Andriamahazo was succeeded as Head of State by Lt-Commdr (later Adm.) Didier Ratsiraka, a côtier and a former Minister of Foreign Affairs, who became Chairman of the Conseil Supreme de la Révolution (CSR—Supreme Revolutionary Council).

In a referendum in December 1975 more than 94% of voters approved a new Constitution, which provided for radical administrative and agrarian reforms, and the appointment of Ratsiraka as President of the Republic for a term of seven years. The country's name was changed to the Democratic Republic of Madagascar, and a 'Second Republic' was proclaimed. In March 1976 the Avant-garde de la Révolution Malgache (AREMA—Antoky Ny Revolosiona Malagasy) was founded as the nucleus of the Front National pour la Défense de la Révolution Socialiste Malgache (FNDR), the only political organization permitted by the Constitution. Ratsiraka was re-elected to the presidency in 1982 and 1989.

Domestic Political Affairs

In August 1989 Ratsiraka assented to opposition demands for discussions about the future role and structure of the FNDR. In December the Assemblée Nationale Populaire (People's National Assembly) adopted a constitutional amendment abolishing the requirement for political parties to be members of the FNDR (thereby effectively dissolving the FNDR), despite opposition from the Mouvement pour le Progrès de Madagascar (Mpitolona ho Amin'ny Fandrosoan'ny Madagasikara—MFM) deputies.

In March 1990 the Government formally permitted the resumption of multi-party politics. Numerous new organizations emerged, while other parties that had hitherto operated within the FNDR became official opposition movements. Several pro-Government political associations joined AREMA to form a new coalition, the Mouvement Militant pour le Socialisme Malagasy (MMSM). The principal opposition movements included the Union Nationale pour le Développement et la Démocratie (UNDD) and the MFM. An informal alliance, the Comité des Forces Vives—subsequently known as Forces Vives (FV, Hery Velona)—was formed by 16 opposition factions and other groups.

In June 1991 opposition leaders applied to the Haute Cour Constitutionnelle (HCC—High Constitutional Court) to effect Ratsiraka's removal from office, while the FV organized demonstrations to demand the resignation of the President and the convening of a constitutional conference. The FV formed a 'parallel' administration, which it termed the 'Provisional Government', and in July began a general strike in support of its demands for constitutional reform. The FV appointed Jean Rakotoharison, a retired army general, as President of the 'Provisional Government', and Albert Zafy, the leader of the UNDD, as its Prime Minister. However, Manandafy Rakotonirina, the leader of the MFM, rejected the formation of the 'Provisional Government', and withdrew his party from the FV. Members of the 'Provisional Government' subsequently occupied the premises of six official government ministries. Later in July Ratsiraka ordered the detention of several members of the 'Provisional Government' and imposed a state of emergency in Antananarivo. The FV withdrew from negotiations with the MMSM, in protest against the arrests. In response to increasing public pressure, Ratsiraka dissolved the Council of Ministers and pledged to organize a constitutional referendum before the end of 1991. Members of the 'Provisional Government' were released from custody, and Ratsiraka repealed legislation that authorized the detention of opponents of the Government.

In August 1991 Ratsiraka appointed Guy Razanamasy, the mayor of Antananarivo, as Prime Minister. Later that month Ratsiraka declared Madagascar to be a federation of six states, with himself as President, and claimed to command the support of five provinces where AREMA continued to hold the majority of seats in regional councils. At the end of August Razanamasy formed an interim Government, which did not include any members of the FV or the MFM.

In October 1991 representatives of the Government, the FV, the MFM, church leaders and the armed forces signed an agreement providing for the suspension of the Constitution and the creation of a transitional Government. The CSR and the People's National Assembly were to be replaced by interim bodies. Ratsiraka was to remain as President of the Republic and Razanamasy as Prime Minister. Zafy was designated President of the High State Authority, while Rakotonirina and Pastor Richard Andriamanjato were appointed as joint Presidents of a 131-member National Committee for Economic and Social Regeneration. A new constitution was to be submitted to a national referendum. Zafy subsequently rejected the agreement, on the grounds that Ratsiraka was to retain the nominal post of Commander-in-Chief of the Armed Forces. In November Razanamasy formed a new interim Government, which included three representatives of the MFM and one MMSM member. Zafy agreed to accept the presidency of the High State Authority later that month.

In December 1991 Razanamasy formed a larger Government of national consensus, in which 14 (of 36) portfolios were allocated to Zafy's FV. In January 1992 it was announced that all political factions had now accepted the terms of the October 1991 agreement; the constitutional referendum was scheduled for mid-1992, and local, presidential and legislative elections were to take place by the end of the year. In February the High State Authority for Transition to the Third Republic announced the dissolution of the CSR and the People's National Assembly, in accordance with the agreement.

Establishment of the Third Republic

The draft constitution of the Third Republic, as submitted to the Government in April 1992, provided for a bicameral legislature, comprising a Sénat (Senate) and an Assemblée Nationale (National Assembly). Two-thirds of the members of the Senate were to be selected by an electoral college, with the remaining one-third to be appointed by the President, while the 184-member National Assembly was to be directly elected for a four-year term. The authority of the President was to be reduced, and executive power vested in the Prime Minister, who was to be appointed by the National Assembly.

The new Constitution was approved by 72.2% of votes cast in a national referendum in August 1992. At the presidential election, held in November, Zafy secured 45.1% of votes cast, while Ratsiraka took 29.2%. A second round of voting took place in February 1993, when Zafy won 66.7% of the votes. Zafy's inauguration the following month was accompanied by violent clashes between security forces and federalists in the north. In accordance with the Constitution, Zafy resigned as President of the UNDD at a party congress in May; Emmanuel Rakotovahiny, the Minister of State for Agriculture and Rural Development, was elected as his successor.

Several constituent parties of the FV subsequently presented independent lists of candidates for the forthcoming legislative elections, while the remaining parties in the alliance became known as Forces Vives Rasalama (Hery Velona Rasalama—HVR). The elections, to a reduced, 138-member National Assembly, took place on 16 June 1993; the HVR secured 46 seats, the MFM 15, and a new alliance of pro-Ratsiraka parties 11 seats. The official results indicated that parties supporting Zafy had won 75 seats in the new National Assembly. In August Francisque Ravony was elected Prime Minister and formed a new Council of Ministers. Richard Andriamanjato was elected President of the National Assembly.

In mid-1995 Zafy announced that he was unable to co-operate with Ravony and decreed that a constitutional amendment empowering the President, rather than the National Assembly, to select the Prime Minister be submitted for approval in a national referendum. Ravony indicated that he would resign after the referendum, regardless of the outcome. The referendum proceeded in September, at which the constitutional amendment was approved by 63.6% of votes cast. Ravony duly resigned in October, and Zafy appointed Rakotovahiny as Prime Minister. However, dissension emerged between the parties that supported Zafy over the composition of the new Council of Ministers. In May 1996 a motion of censure against Rakotovahiny's Government was approved by a large majority in the National Assembly. Rakotovahiny submitted his administration's resignation, and Norbert Ratsirahonana, hitherto President of the HCC, was appointed Prime Minister.

Zafy refused to approve the new Government initially proposed by Ratsirahonana, insisting on the inclusion of five UNDD members who had served in the previous Council of Ministers. Ratsirahonana, however, won a vote of confidence in the legislature in July 1996. On 26 July a motion in the National Assembly to remove Zafy from office for numerous contraventions of the Constitution was supported by 99 of the 131 votes cast. The HCC endorsed the President's impeachment in September, upholding the majority of the charges against him; Zafy maintained that his impeachment was illegal, but resigned the same day. Ratsirahonana was appointed interim President by the HCC, pending an election; he formed a new interim Government that represented the majority in the National Assembly and excluded members of the UNDD. Zafy announced his intention to contest the forthcoming election to the presidency, as did Ratsiraka and Ratsirahonana.

Fifteen candidates contested the first round of the presidential election on 3 November 1996; Ratsiraka (with 36.6% of the votes cast) and Zafy (with 23.4%) proceeded to a second round. The head of Libéralisme Economique et Action Démocratique pour la Reconstruction Nationale (LEADER/Fanilo), Herizo Razafimahaleo, obtained 15.1%, and Ratsirahonana 10.1%, of the votes. At the second round, which took place on 29 December, Ratsiraka narrowly won, with 50.7% of the votes cast, although more than 50% of the registered electorate abstained from voting. Ratsiraka was inaugurated as President on 9 February 1997. He appointed Pascal Rakotomavo (a former Minister of Finance) as Prime Minister. Rakotomavo's Government included Razafimahaleo as Deputy Prime Minister, responsible for Foreign Affairs.

In March 1998 extensive revisions to the Constitution, which provided for a 'federal-style' state, composed of six autonomous provinces, and for an increase in the powers of the President, were narrowly endorsed by 51.0% of votes cast at a referendum. Elections to an expanded, 150-member National Assembly took place in May, under a new electoral law. Ratsiraka's party, AREMA, won 63 seats, while the pro-presidential LEADER/Fanilo and the Rassemblement pour le Socialisme et la Démocratie (RPSD) secured 16 and 11 seats, respectively. Ratsirahonana's party, Ny Asa Vita no Ifampitsara (AVI), emerged as the strongest opposition party, with 14 seats, while Zafy's new party, Asa, Faharaminana, Fampandrosoana, Arinda (AFFA), won six seats. In July Tantely Andrianarivo, hitherto Deputy Prime Minister, was appointed as Prime Minister, retaining responsibility for finance and the economy. The new Council of Ministers was dominated by AREMA, with the key portfolios largely unchanged.

The first local government elections since the reintroduction of the three-tier system of local government (provinces, regions and communes), under the amended Constitution of 1998, took place on 14 November 1999. The greatest successes were recorded by nominally independent candidates. Most notably, Marc Ravalomanana, the head of the country's largest agro-industrial processor, Tiko, was elected mayor of Antananarivo.

Disputed presidential election

A presidential election took place on 16 December 2001, contested by six candidates, including Ratsiraka, Zafy, Razafimahaleo and Ravalomanana. According to the official results, Ravalomanana secured 46.2% of the votes cast and Didier Ratsiraka 40.9%, thereby necessitating a second round of voting. However, Ravalomanana's own electoral observers disputed this result, claiming that he had won an outright victory, with 52.2% of the votes, and demanded a public comparison of voting records. The opposition was supported in these demands by international electoral observers. A recount was subsequently conducted, and on 25 January 2002 the HCC endorsed the official results and ruled that a second round of voting should take place within 30 days. Ravalomanana rejected this verdict and appealed for a national strike in protest. A rally of some 500,000 people was staged in Antananarivo, and public sector services were suspended. Strike action continued for several weeks.

On 22 February 2002 Ravalomanana unilaterally declared himself President at a ceremony in Antananarivo attended by 100,000 supporters. The President of the Senate immediately declared Ravalomanana's proclamation to be illegal, and it was widely condemned by the international community. In response, President Ratsiraka declared a three-month 'state of national necessity', according himself broad powers. On 26 February Ravalomanana named Jacques Sylla, a former Minister of Foreign Affairs under Zafy's presidency, as his Prime Minister. Violent clashes erupted between supporters of Ratsiraka and Ravalomanana in Antananarivo, prompting Ratsiraka to decree martial law and appoint a military governor, Gen. Léon-Claude Raveloarison, in the capital. None the less, Ravalomanana proceeded with the formation of his rival Government in early March, while opposition supporters erected barricades against the army and set fire to the military headquarters; 17 of those appointed to Ravalomanana's administration were successfully installed in government offices, accompanied by large crowds of supporters and unopposed by the military. A few days later Gen. Marcel Ranjeva resigned as Minister of the Armed Forces, shortly after Ravalomanana's rival Government had taken control of his offices in Antananarivo. Raveloarison resigned some three weeks after his appointment, having failed to apply martial law and order troops to end protests, on the grounds that this would have incurred deaths.

On 10 April 2002 the Supreme Court ruled that there had been irregularities in the appointment, shortly before the presidential election, of six of the nine judges of the HCC, which had endorsed the official results; one week later the Supreme Court annulled the disputed results and ordered a recount of the votes. On the following day Ratsiraka and Ravalomanana signed a peace accord in Dakar, Senegal, where negotiations had been conducted under the auspices of the Organization of African Unity (OAU—subsequently the African Union, AU, see p. 188), and the UN. Following the completion of the recount, in late April, the HCC ruled that Ravalomanana had secured the presidency, with 51.5% of the votes cast, while Ratsiraka had won 35.9%. Ratsiraka refused to accept the Court's decision. Nevertheless, Ravalomanana was inaugurated as President on 6 May, largely without international recognition, and appointed a new Council of Ministers later that month. Four of the country's six provincial governors, who were loyal to Ratsiraka, subsequently threatened to secede. Heavy fighting ensued, as troops loyal to Ravalomanana conducted a military offensive against areas controlled by Ratsiraka.

Ravalomanana's presidency

In mid-June 2002 Ravalomanana dissolved the Government that he had formed in May, immediately reappointing Sylla as Prime Minister; however, despite nominating six new ministers, he failed to appoint a government of national unity. At the end of June the USA recognized Ravalomanana as the legitimate leader of Madagascar, and endorsement soon followed from France. In early July Ravalomanana's government troops took control of Antsiranana and Toamasina, and Ratsiraka sought exile in France. The new authorities had gained full control of the island by mid-July. Ravalomanana replaced the 30 presidentially appointed members of the Senate, with the approval of the HCC. In August six of the nine members of the HCC were also replaced.

In mid-October 2002 the National Assembly was dissolved in preparation for legislative elections, brought forward from May 2003, in response to pressure from aid donors, in order to finalize the legitimacy of Ravalomanana's mandate. At the elections, which took place on 15 December 2002, Ravalomanana's party, Tiako i Madagasikara (TIM), won 104 of the 160 seats and the pro-Ravalomanana Firaisankinam-Pirenena, an alliance of the AVI and elements of the RPSD, secured a further 22 seats; notably, 23 independent deputies were elected, and the formerly incumbent AREMA party won only three seats. A new Government, appointed in January 2003, included 10 new ministers. In August former President Ratsiraka was sentenced, *in absentia*, to 10 years' hard labour for the embezzlement of public funds and declared unfit for public office.

A presidential election was held on 3 December 2006. According to results released by the HCC on 23 December, Ravalomanana secured 54.8% of votes cast in the first-round ballot. His closest rival was Jean Lahiniriko, who took 11.7% of the votes. The poll was generally accepted by independent observers as free and fair. President Ravalomanana was formally sworn in for a second term in office on 19 January 2007 and the following day he appointed Lt-Gen. Charles Rabemananjara, hitherto Minister of the Interior and Administrative Reform, as Prime Minister. A new Government was established later that month.

At a national referendum conducted on 4 April 2007 75.3% of participants voted in favour of amendments to the Constitution, which included the abolition of autonomous powers for the six provinces. Voter turnout was reported at just 44%. The new Constitution also granted extended powers to the President, including the right to legislate by decree in the event of the declaration of a state of emergency.

President Ravalomanana dissolved the National Assembly on 24 July 2007, claiming that its composition was no longer representative of the recently restructured regional and national administrative order. Elections to the 127-seat legislature (reduced from 160) were held on 23 September, in which the TIM secured 105 seats while independent candidates won 11. However, results in two constituencies were annulled owing to alleged voting irregularities. In October, as part of a governmental reorganization, Cécile Manorohanta was appointed Minister of National Defence. In January 2009 Désiré Rasolofomanana was appointed Minister of Internal Security and Gervais Rakotonirina Minister of the Interior.

The Haute Autorité de la Transition

Relations between President Ravalomanana and the mayor of Antananarivo and leader of the Tanora malaGasy Vonona (TGV), Andry Rajoelina, had become strained in December 2008, when Ravalomanana closed Rajoelina's television station in response to its broadcast of anti-Government programmes and an interview with former President Ratsiraka. Against a background of increasing social discontent in the country, this prompted violent protests by several thousand of Rajoelina's supporters who attacked state-owned television and radio stations and began looting businesses. A political impasse developed, with Rajoelina, speaking at an opposition rally in late January 2009, accusing the President of failing in his duties and insisting that he resign. Violence continued to escalate and large areas of the capital were destroyed by fire, resulting in at least 44 deaths. In early February Rajoelina, who had been gaining popular support, was dismissed from the mayoralty and replaced by Guy Randrianarisoa, resulting in days of further

violent disturbances: some 28 people were killed and more than 200 injured when the security forces fired on demonstrators. Shortly afterwards, the Minister of Defence, Manorohanta, announced her resignation in protest at the actions of the security forces; she was replaced by Vice-Adm. Mamy Ranaivoniarivo. Meanwhile, Rajoelina declared himself President of a Haute Autorité de la Transition (HAT—High Transitional Authority) and named, among others, Monja Roindefo as Prime Minister and Manantsoa Masimana as Minister of the Interior. The parallel administration was not recognized by the international community but received widespread domestic popular support. Nevertheless, the security forces removed a number of Rajoelina's supporters who had attempted to seize four government buildings.

Ravalomanana and Rajoelina held a series of discussions with the aim of finding a resolution to the crisis; however, in February 2009 Rajoelina announced that the talks had failed and urged his supporters to hold daily protests until Ravalomanana agreed to step down. Pressure continued to increase on Ravalomanana and, following a military assault on the presidential residence on 16 March and demands from Rajoelina that the President be arrested, he dissolved the Government and resigned, relinquishing power to a military executive committee led by the most senior figure in the armed forces, Vice-Adm. Hyppolite Ramaroson. Later that day the military transferred executive powers to Rajoelina, despite the terms of the Constitution stipulating that the President should be aged 40 years or above; Rajoelina, at 34 years of age, was too young to fulfil this requirement. Although international organizations refused to acknowledge Rajoelina's authority, and what was perceived as a coup received widespread international condemnation, on 18 March the HCC endorsed Rajoelina's assumption of interim power (he was officially sworn in as President on 21 March), and on 19 March he dissolved the National Assembly and the Senate. Rajoelina announced that elections would be held within two years and that a new constitution would be drafted. Both the AU and the Southern African Development Community (SADC, see p. 420) subsequently suspended Madagascar's membership pending a return to constitutional order.

In late March 2009 Rajoelina appointed a new Government, retaining those ministers named in February; other appointments included Col Noël Rakotonandrasana as Minister of the Armed Forces and Ny Hasina Andriamanjato as Minister of Foreign Affairs. In mid-April Ravalomanana, who had fled to exile in South Africa, named Rakotonirina as his own 'legal' Prime Minister in an attempt to regain his authority and, despite the issuing of a warrant for his arrest, pledged to return to Madagascar. Later in April Rakotonirina was arrested in Antananarivo and charged with threatening the security of the state, illegitimately declaring himself Prime Minister, instigating the destruction of property and the illegal possession of firearms. In early June Ravalomanana was sentenced *in absentia* to four years in prison and fined US $70m.

A summit meeting, mediated by the UN, the AU, SADC and the Organisation Internationale de la Francophonie, was held in Maputo, Mozambique, on 5–9 August 2009. The discussions resulted in agreement between Ravalomanana, Ratsiraka, Zafy and Rajoelina on a Transitional Charter which was to remain in place for a maximum duration of 15 months, pending presidential and legislative elections. The Charter provided for the establishment of a bicameral transitional legislature, and a National Union Government of Transition (NUGT). The Prime Minister of the NUGT was to be selected by consensus and officially appointed by Rajoelina, in his capacity as President of the Transition, and a new constitution was to be drafted.

However, on 5 September 2009 Rajoelina unilaterally, and in contravention of the Maputo accord, named Roindefo as Prime Minister; he subsequently announced the composition of the NUGT. Both decisions were rejected and condemned by the three former Presidents, who declared their determination to implement a power-sharing deal and that they no longer recognized the authority of Rajoelina. Protests in Antananarivo were violently dispersed by the security forces. Negotiations recommenced and the following month Eugène Régis Mangalaza was chosen by consensus as Prime Minister.

In late 2009 Ravalomanana, Ratsiraka and Zafy proceeded with further negotiations in Maputo regarding the composition of a proposed transitional administration; however, Rajoelina stated that he would no longer participate in power-sharing negotiations, and refused permission for aircraft carrying the three men and their delegations to land in Madagascar. On

18 December Mangalaza was dismissed by Rajoelina, who two days later appointed Col (later Gen.) Albert Camille Vital as Prime Minister.

Despite dissatisfaction among international organizations and his domestic political rivals, Rajoelina continued to reject external mediation attempts and any proposals for a power-sharing government, insisting instead on holding legislative elections in March 2010. However, following a request by the AU and subsequent pressure from the UN, which urged continued dialogue on the establishment of a power-sharing government, Rajoelina agreed to postpone the elections, initially until May. In February Andriamanjato, the Deputy Prime Minister, responsible for Foreign Affairs, resigned, citing increasing dissension within the NUGT. Shortly afterwards the AU announced that it would impose sanctions on Madagascar if the resolutions of the Maputo and Addis Ababa power-sharing agreements were not implemented by mid-March. Ramaroson was appointed as Andriamanjato's replacement in late February.

The AU's attempts to persuade Rajoelina to attend further negotiations in Addis Ababa in early March 2010 were unsuccessful, and in mid-March the AU duly imposed sanctions, including the freezing of assets and diplomatic isolation, on 109 individuals, including all members of the NUGT and the HAT. In response, Rajoelina announced that the HAT would seek to charge Ravalomanana with 'corruption, threatening state security and plotting high treason with foreign factions'. Furthermore, Ratsiraka and Zafy would be barred from returning to Madagascar, while members of the three former Presidents' political parties would be prevented from leaving the country and their assets would be frozen.

Vital dismissed Rakotonandrasana from his position as Minister of the Armed Forces in early April 2010, amid rumours of plans to stage a coup. (Some 19 people, including a number of army officers, were subsequently detained by the authorities.) Later in April senior military officials presented Rajoelina with an ultimatum to find a suitable solution to the country's political crisis by the end of the month. Shortly afterwards Rajoelina pledged to appoint a new unity government and indicated his willingness to engage in further talks with Ravalomanana. Discussions between the two, who were also joined by Zafy and Ratsiraka, commenced in late April in Pretoria, South Africa, but ended inconclusively after two days. On 12 May Rajoelina announced that a referendum on constitutional reform would be held on 26 August, prior to presidential and legislative elections. On 25 May Rajoelina formed a new, 32-member Government, which included five members of the military. Meanwhile, on 20 May several people were killed in a confrontation between dissident elements of the gendarmerie (with the support of several hundred anti-Government protesters) and forces loyal to Rajoelina, who accused Ravalomanana of instigating the unrest.

Constitutional referendum

In June 2010 the head of the Commission Electorale Nationale Indépendante pour la Transition (CENIT) announced that the referendum would be postponed, since the draft constitution had not been finalized. On 11 August, following consultations with political parties, the Government signed an agreement rescheduling the constitutional referendum for 17 November, to be followed by legislative elections on 16 March 2011 and the first round of a presidential election on 4 May; under the new accord, Rajoelina would continue to hold office as head of the HAT until the inauguration of the next president, while the HAT was to be reconstituted as a transitional parliament. (However, the political movements of the three former Presidents, Ravalomanana, Ratsiraka and Zafy, which failed to participate in the discussions, denounced what they considered to be the imposition of another unilateral solution.) At the end of August 2010 Ravalomanana was sentenced *in absentia* to life imprisonment for the killing of at least 30 people by his presidential guards in the violence of February 2009. In September 2010 the Government organized a conference of representatives of political parties and civil society, which was to resolve issues related to the implementation of the August agreement; delegates endorsed a proposal that Rajoelina remain as Head of State but appoint a consensus prime minister who was not from his native region, and also supported the replacement of mayors and regional authorities by provisional bodies. On 7 October the HCC approved a decree by Rajoelina establishing a Parlement de la Transition (Transitional Parliament). Accordingly, on 11 October a 256-member lower parliamentary chamber was installed: a gathering of all the political parties and associations that

participated in the drafting of the August agreement, known as l'Espace de Concertation des Partis Politiques (ESCOPOL), was allocated 62 seats, the TIM 52, the TGV 52 and a grouping of parties supporting Rajoelina, the Union des Démocrates et Républicains—Fanovana (UDR—Fanovana) 29. On 12 October a 90-member upper chamber took office; the deputies included 25 representatives of the UDR—Fanovana, 21 of the TIM, 18 of ESCOPOL and 10 of the TGV.

A draft constitution, which included requirements that presidential candidates be at least 35 years of age (rather than the previous minimum of 40 years) and have lived in Madagascar for at least six months prior to the elections, was submitted to the delayed national referendum on 17 November 2010. On the same day some 20 disaffected senior army officers, led by Rakotonandrasana, staged a coup attempt, announcing from a military barracks near Antananarivo that the Government had been overthrown. However, prominent members of the Government and military announced their support for Rajoelina, and on 21 November troops loyal to the HAT stormed the barracks, arresting a number of the officers for threatening state security. Later that month it was announced that a former International Court of Justice judge, Raymond Ranjeva, had also been detained, owing to his alleged connections with the rebels. Two days after the referendum, the CENIT released official results, according to which the new Constitution had been endorsed by about 74.2% of votes cast, with a voter turnout of 52.6% (after the opposition urged a boycott). On 23 November the HCC upheld the results of the referendum, despite opposition complaints of electoral irregularities. The new Constitution of the Fourth Republic of Madagascar entered into effect on 11 December. In January 2011 Ravalomanana submitted a legal complaint to the judicial authorities against the instigators of the effective coup in March 2009.

On 9 March 2011 a new transitional programme proposed by the SADC mediators was signed by eight of the 11 principal political groups, but rejected by the parties of Ravalomanana, Ratsiraka and Zafy, which strenuously opposed the legitimacy conferred on Rajoelina's presidency. Under the new plan, Rajoelina was permitted to remain in office pending elections, and to appoint a consensus Prime Minister proposed by the signatory groups. On the following day the Government of Prime Minister Vital resigned; however, on 16 March Rajoelina reappointed Vital as premier, despite the objections of the three main opposition parties that he failed to meet the consensus criteria of the agreement. On 26 March a new, 32-member administration, termed the Government of National Unity, was established under the transitional programme; nine former government members retained their posts, although members of Ravalomanana's TIM were also included.

Following continued SADC mediation, on 17 September 2011 10 political groups (including those representing Ravalomanana and Zafy) signed a further agreement for a timetable to restore democratic rule: a new government of national unity would be installed by the end of November, while a presidential election was to be organized within one year. (Rajoelina was authorized to remain in office until that time.) Ravalomanana was to be allowed to return to the country under an amnesty for exiles in order to participate in the transitional process. Accordingly, Vital submitted the resignation of his Government on 17 October, and Rajoelina announced the appointment of a former ambassador to the European Union (EU), Jean Omer Beriziky of LEADER/Fanilo, as the new Prime Minister on 28 October. A new Government of National Unity was formed on 21 November; seven ministerial posts were allocated to supporters of Zafy and five to those of Ravalomanana. Later in November Ratsiraka returned to Madagascar at the invitation of Rajoelina, after spending nine years in exile in France.

Delays in the election process

In January 2012, however, an attempt by Ravalomanana to return to Madagascar from South Africa in accordance with the transitional agreement was thwarted, after Rajoelina ordered the closure of all major airports, prompting Ravalomanana's supporters to suspend participation in the transitional institutions. On 21 March 11 people, including Ranjeva and his daughter, were acquitted of complicity in the November 2010 coup attempt, while a senior officer was sentenced to life imprisonment *in absentia* and a further nine defendants received prison terms of between five and seven years. The amnesty law was finally adopted on 12 April 2012, but excluded those who had been found guilty of human rights abuses, notably Ravalomanana. In May police violently suppressed an unauthorized protest in Antananarivo in support of opposition radio station Radio Free FM, which had been staged after the station's director, Lalatiana Rakotondrazafy, and a journalist were detained for broadcasting material critical of Rajoelina. The Government announced in July that an army mutiny had been suppressed, following an operation to regain control of an airport about 10 km from Antananarivo. Radio Free FM was subsequently closed down, owing to alleged intimidation by the armed forces. At the instigation of SADC, discussions between Rajoelina and Ravalomanana, mediated by South African President Jacob Zuma, took place in Seychelles on 25 July; however, the President continued to reject SADC insistence on Ravalomanana's return to Madagascar. At the beginning of August a newly established Commission Electorale Nationale Indépendante pour la Transition (CENIT) finally announced that the first round of a presidential election would be conducted on 8 May 2013, with legislative elections to follow on 3 July. Further discussions between Rajoelina and Ravalomanana were held in August 2012.

Following Zuma's replacement as senior mediator by Tanzanian President Jakaya Kikwete, a further SADC summit meeting, held in early December 2012, resulted in a proposal that neither Rajoelina nor Ravalomanana would contest the forthcoming elections. Ravalomanana subsequently announced his agreement not to participate in the elections. On 20 December the Government declared a state of emergency in Antananarivo, due to an increasing number of armed attacks in the capital. Despite initial reluctance to comply with the SADC recommendations, in January 2013 President Rajoelina, ceding to international pressure, agreed that he would not seek election later that year, but stated that he would contest the next polls in 2018. On 5 February 2013 the CENIT announced that, owing to logistical difficulties, including the organization of voter registration, the first round of the presidential election was to be rescheduled for 24 July, and legislative elections for 25 September. Although the UN endorsed the postponement, Rajoelina criticized the extension of the transitional period.

In early May 2013 the Cour Electorale Spéciale (CES—Special Electoral Court) released a list of 41 candidates who had been approved to contest the presidential poll, among them Rajoelina, despite his earlier confirmation that he would not seek the presidency. Rajoelina maintained that the decision of Ravalomanana's wife, Lalao, to stand in the election had rendered the agreement concluded in January void. SADC subsequently urged Rajoelina, Lalao Ravalomanana and Ratsiraka, who had also featured on the list of approved candidates, to withdraw from the election. The AU Peace and Security Council protested at Rajoelina's candidacy in contravention of the January agreement, while the French Government and the EU suspended funding of the elections, which were once again postponed, until 23 August. On 17 August, in a decision that was widely welcomed, a reconstituted CES prohibited Rajoelina, Lalao Ravalomanana and Ratsiraka from contesting the presidency; donor financing was subsequently restored. The CENIT subsequently set a new date, of 25 October, for the presidential election, with a second round on 20 December when the legislative polls were also scheduled to be held. By the end of August four ministers—including Minister of Foreign Affairs Pierrot Rajaonarivelo and Minister of Finance and Budget Hery Martial Rajaonarimampianina Rakotoarimanana—had resigned their government posts in order to contest the presidency. In September the AU ended the sanctions imposed in 2010 against 109 officials, including Rajoelina, in response to progress in the electoral process.

Presidential and legislative elections

The first round of the presidential election proceeded on 25 October 2013: of the 33 participating candidates, a former Minister of Health, Jean Louis Robinson Richard, received 21.2% of the votes cast, Rajaonarimampianina 15.9% and a former Deputy Prime Minister, Hajo Herivelona Andrianainarivelo, 10.5%. Robinson and Rajaonarimampianina had both formed new political parties, Antoko ny Vahoaka Aloha No Andrianina (AVANA) and Hery Vaovao hoan'i Madagasikara, respectively, in order to contest the election. A second round was contested on 20 December by Rajaonarimampianina, who was supported by Rajoelina, and Robinson, who was the favoured candidate of former President Ravalomanana. According to the official results, Rajaonarimampianina was elected to the presidency with 53.5% of the votes cast. A voter turnout of 61.8% was recorded in the first round and 50.7% in the second. At the concurrent elections to the 151-member National Assembly on 20 December, the party supporting Rajoelina, Miaraka amin'ny

Prezidà Andry Rajoelina (MAPAR), secured 49 seats, while Mouvance Ravalomanana, headed by the former President, took 19, Vondrona politika miara-dia Malagasy Miara-Miainga, led by Andrianainarivelo, 14, and Parti Hiaraka Isika and LEADER/Fanilo five each; a further 31 small parties obtained representation. Some 50.8% of the electorate participated in the legislative polls. The conduct of both elections was endorsed by international observer missions. Although Robinson initially disputed the outcome of the presidential election on grounds of malpractice, it was confirmed by the CES on 17 January 2014, when Robinson conceded defeat. Rajaonarimampianina was inaugurated to the presidency on 25 January; a nearby grenade attack in Antananarivo on the same day resulted in one death and at least 33 injuries. Later that month the AU and SADC announced the restoration of Madagascar's membership. The convening of the new National Assembly on 18 February marked the official end of the transitional period.

Following lengthy negotiations between the two political blocs in the National Assembly, on 11 April 2014 President Rajaonarimampianina appointed as Prime Minister a previously unknown doctor, Laurent Roger Kolo Christophe, who received the support of 12 parliamentary parties. MAPAR, as the party with the largest representation in the National Assembly, disputed the constitutionality of Kolo's appointment. On 19 April the formation of a new, largely technocratic Government was announced. Although two new ministers were MAPAR representatives, it was reported that most party members had refused to join the Government.

Following increasing public discontent at the Government's perceived failure to address severe power shortages, the Minister of Energy, Richard Fihenena, was dismissed in October 2014. A further political crisis was precipitated by the unexpected return of Ravalomanana to Madagascar on 12 October, with the apparent intention of challenging the legitimacy of the incumbent administration. He was immediately placed under house arrest in Antsiranana and a small rally staged by his supporters was dispersed. The AU condemned Ravalomanana's action as potentially destabilizing to the country's ongoing recovery. However, it was announced in November that President Rajaonarimampianina and Ravalomanana would participate in a national reconciliation process. Rajaonarimampianina and former heads of state Ravalomanana (under military escort), Rajoelina, Ratsiraka and Zafy met on 19 December for reconciliation discussions, which were convened under the aegis of the Fiombonan'ny Fiangonana Kristiana eto Madagasikara (FFKM—Christian Council of Churches in Madagascar). These resulted in an agreement by Rajaonarimampianina to release political prisoners; five supporters of Ravalomanana, including a former military adviser, were duly released later that month. On 26 December the Government also announced that Ravalomanana was permitted to serve house arrest at his own residence in Antananarivo. Meanwhile, on 12 December the CENIT presented a draft timetable (subsequently confirmed by the Government), under which delayed local elections would take place on 17 July 2015, following a revision of the electoral register in January.

Recent developments: resignation of the Government

Amid continued electricity outages, in late December 2014 a protester was killed in Toamasina, after an attack against the offices of state power utility JIRAMA was violently suppressed by police, and a further demonstrator died in continued unrest in early January 2015. On 11 January premier Kolo tendered his resignation, together with that of his Government. Two days later, President Rajaonarimampianina appointed a former air force commander, Jean Ravelonarivo, to the office of Prime Minister. Although Rajoelina issued a legal challenge against the appointment, citing procedural irregularities, Ravelonarivo was installed as Prime Minister on 17 January, and a new Government, which included eight new ministers, was appointed later that month. Meanwhile, a further reconciliation meeting between Rajaonarimampianina, Zafy, Ratsiraka, Ravalomana and Rajoelina on 13 January resulted in little progress. A day of national mourning was declared on 28 January, after 68 people were killed in a tropical storm. The HCC in early February upheld President Rajaonarimampianina's appointment of Ravelonarivo. On 19 February Rajoelina, together with Zafy, suspended participation in the reconciliation process, demanding that the new Prime Minister be replaced and that the national reconciliation dialogue be granted a formal legal basis. Nevertheless, in early March the FFKM initiated a second stage of the process, with the organization of regional conferences to collect proposals, and an expanded summit meeting (including the former heads of state) was planned for later that month.

Foreign Affairs

Madagascar's foreign policy is officially non-aligned. Relations with France have been affected by disputes over compensation for nationalized French assets and over the continuing French claim to the Iles Glorieuses, north of Madagascar, and three other islets in the Mozambique Channel. In 1980 the UN voted in favour of restoring all the disputed islets to Madagascar. In early 1986 the Government announced the extension of Madagascar's exclusive economic zone to include the Iles Glorieuses and the three islets. In February 2000 it was agreed that the Iles Glorieuses would be co-administered by France, Madagascar and Mauritius, without prejudice to the question of sovereignty. During the prolonged political crisis in Madagascar from 2009 the French Government expressed support for mediation efforts, and continued to provide emergency assistance to the country. Following continued delays in the election process, in 2013 France also imposed sanctions against members of the regime. After the normalization of relations (see below), President Rajaonarimampianina made an official visit to Paris, France, in September 2014, when he met his French counterpart, François Hollande.

Madagascar's relations with the People's Republic of China were strengthened in January 1999, during a visit by Vice-President Hu Jintao; agreements were signed on the expansion of bilateral economic relations and China's provision of preferential loans to Madagascar. In September 2000 the representative office for Taiwan in Madagascar was closed down, following an official visit by the Malagasy Minister of Foreign Affairs to China. Following the suspension of US and EU donor assistance programmes in Madagascar in response to Andry Rajoelina's assumption of the presidency in March 2009, the transitional Government announced a number of major infrastructure projects that were to be undertaken in collaboration with Chinese companies.

Madagascar's relations with international donor states and institutions were rapidly normalized following democratic elections in late 2013 and the inauguration of President Rajaonarimampianina in January 2014. Rajaonarimampianina subsequently undertook a number of visits abroad, including to the USA in March and Brussels, Belgium, in April, in an effort to secure the restoration of external financial support for his administration.

CONSTITUTION AND GOVERNMENT

On 17 November 2010 the Constitution of the Fourth Republic of Madagascar was approved at a national referendum by some 74% of the participating electorate. The President of the Republic is the Head of State and is elected by direct universal suffrage for a five-year mandate, renewable only once. Candidates for the presidency must be at least 35 years of age and have resided in Madagascar for at least six months prior to the date of the submission of candidacies. The President nominates a Prime Minister from the party or group of parties which secures the largest number of seats in the 151-member Assemblée Nationale (National Assembly). The President also nominates members of the Government, upon the advice of the Prime Minister. Members of the National Assembly are elected by direct universal suffrage for five-year terms. The Constitution also provides for the election of members to the Sénat (Senate), each of whom serves a five-year mandate.

REGIONAL AND INTERNATIONAL CO-OPERATION

Madagascar is a member of the Indian Ocean Commission (see p. 447) and of the Common Market for Eastern and Southern Africa (COMESA, see p. 232). In 2005 Madagascar joined the Southern African Development Community (SADC, see p. 420), although its membership of that organization and of the African Union (see p. 188) was suspended in 2009.

Madagascar became a member of the UN in 1960 and was admitted to the World Trade Organization (WTO, see p. 431) in 1995.

ECONOMIC AFFAIRS

In 2013, according to estimates by the World Bank, Madagascar's gross national income (GNI), measured at average 2011–13 prices, was US $10,163m., equivalent to about $440 per head (or $1,350 per head on an international purchasing-power parity basis). During 2004–13, it was estimated, the population increased at an average annual rate of 2.9%, while gross domestic product (GDP) per head decreased, in real terms, by an average of 0.2% per year. Overall GDP increased, in real terms, at an average annual rate of 2.6% in 2004–13; GDP grew by 2.1% in 2013.

In 2013 the agricultural sector (including forestry and fishing) accounted for an estimated 25.7% of GDP, according to provisional figures from the African Development Bank (AfDB); the sector employed an estimated 75.3% of the economically active population in October–December 2012 and, according to FAO, engaged 67.4% of the total labour force at mid-2015. Rice, the staple food crop, is produced on some 50% of cultivated land. Since 1972, however, imports of rice have been necessary to supplement domestic production. The most important cash crops are spices (which accounted for an estimated 9.0% of total export revenue in 2009, but declined to 5.2% in 2010). Sugar, coconuts, tropical fruits, sweet potatoes and maize are also cultivated. Cattle-farming is important. Sea fishing by coastal fishermen (particularly for crustaceans) is being expanded, while vessels from the European Union (EU) fish for tuna and prawns in Madagascar's exclusive maritime zone, within 200 nautical miles (370 km) of the coast, in return for compensation. According to UN figures, agricultural GDP increased by an average of 1.1% per year in 2004–13; the sector's GDP increased by 1.5% in 2012, but decreased by 6.1% in 2013.

Industry (including mining, manufacturing, construction and power) contributed an estimated 19.1% of Madagascar's GDP in 2013, according to provisional figures from the AfDB, and employed 7.9% of the employed labour force in October–December 2012. According to UN figures, industrial GDP increased at an average annual rate of 5.4% in 2004–13; the sector's GDP grew by 16.4% in 2013.

The mining sector contributed only 0.3% of GDP in 2013, according to provisional AfDB figures. In October–December 2012 the mining sector (together with utilities) engaged 1.3% of the employed labour force. However, Madagascar has sizeable deposits of a wide range of minerals, principally chromite (chromium ore), which, with graphite and mica, is exported, together with small quantities of semi-precious stones. A major project to resume the mining of ilmenite (titanium ore) in south-eastern Madagascar, which would generate some US $550m. over a 30-year period, received approval from the Government in 2001. Construction of the mining facilities and rehabilitation of a deep-sea multi-purpose port at Ehoala, near Fort Dauphin (Tolagnaro), was completed in early 2009. The facility began ilmenite production operations in January, and produced 287,000 metric tons in 2010. Other potential mineral projects included the exploitation of an estimated 100m. tons of bauxite in the south-east of the country, and of nickel and cobalt deposits in Ambatovy, central Madagascar. The presence of significant grades of the platinum group of metals was confirmed, as well as copper and nickel, in 2004. A large nickel-mining project at Ambatovy began production in 2012, with annual output expected eventually to reach 60,000 tons of nickel, 5,600 tons of cobalt and 210,000 tons of ammonium sulphate fertilizer. The multinational project was expected to provide employment for some 6,000 workers. In early 2008 a pilot project in the north-west produced the first petroleum in the country for some 60 years, improving Madagascar's prospects for generating export revenue. According to UN figures, real GDP of the mining sector together with utilities increased by an average of 20.2% per year in 2004–13; the sector's GDP increased by 35.1% in 2012 and by 118.5% in 2013.

According to provisional figures from the AfDB, manufacturing contributed 14.2% of GDP in 2013, and engaged some 5.2% of the employed labour force in October–December 2012. The petroleum refinery at Toamasina, using imported petroleum, provides a significant share of export revenue. Other important branches of manufacturing are textiles and clothing, food products, beverages and chemical products. According to UN figures, manufacturing GDP increased at an average annual rate of 1.9% in 2004–13; the GDP of the sector increased by 2.4% in 2013.

Construction contributed an estimated 3.4% of Madagascar's GDP in 2013, according to provisional AfDB figures; the sector employed 1.4% of the employed labour force in October–December 2012. According to UN figures, real GDP of the construction sector increased by an average of 9.2% per year in 2004–13; the sector's GDP rose by 3.3% in 2013.

Energy generation depends on imports of petroleum (which accounted for an estimated 22.8% of the value of total imports in 2013) to fuel thermal installations. However, hydroelectric resources have also been majorly developed, and accounted for an estimated 56.8% of electricity production in 2013.

The services sector accounted for an estimated 55.2% of GDP in 2013, according to provisional figures from the AfDB, and engaged some 16.9% of the employed labour force in October–December 2012. An information communication technologies business park was under development in Antananarivo as part of an effort to diversify Madagascar's economic growth. In 2010 Madagascar was connected to the Eastern Africa Submarine Cable System, a high bandwidth fibre optic cable that links countries on Africa's eastern coast to the rest of the world, and would enable the transfer of data at speeds 40 times faster than the hitherto available dial-up connection. This was expected to allow the development of service outsourcing activities on the island. According to UN figures, the GDP of the services sector decreased by an average of 2.5% per year in 2004–13; services GDP grew by 1.2% in 2013.

In 2005 Madagascar recorded a visible merchandise trade deficit of US $592m. and there was a deficit of $626m. on the current account of the balance of payments; the trade deficit was estimated to have increased to $890m. in 2007. The principal source of imports in 2013 was the United Arab Emirates (accounting for 20.0% of total imports); other major suppliers were the People's Republic of China, France, India and South Africa. France was the principal market for exports in 2013 (accounting for 25.7% of exports); the USA, China, the Netherlands and Germany were other important purchasers. The principal exports in 2013 were clothing, iron and steel, coffee, tea, cocoa and spices, mineral products, crustaceans, and prepared foodstuffs, beverages, spirits, vinegar and tobacco. The principal imports in that year were mineral products, textiles, machinery and transport equipment, vegetables and vegetable products, and prepared foodstuffs, beverages, spirits, vinegars and tobacco.

According to the official sources, Madagascar's overall budget deficit for 2013 was estimated at 418,000m. ariary. Madagascar's general government gross debt was 8,029.5m. ariary in 2013, equivalent to 34.2% of GDP. Madagascar's external debt totalled US $2,896m. at the end of 2012, of which $2,157m. was public and publicly guaranteed debt. In that year. The cost of servicing long-term public and publicly guaranteed debt and repayments to the IMF was equivalent to 2.1% of the value of exports of goods, services and income (excluding workers' remittances) in 2011. The annual rate of inflation averaged 8.4% in 2005–14; consumer prices increased by 6.1% in 2014. About 1.3% of the labour force was unemployed in October–December 2012.

Economic activity in Madagascar was impeded by political instability during the 2000s, although, with the assistance of the IMF and the World Bank, the country made enough progress to facilitate the restructuring of the significant external debt by international creditors. The economy was severely affected by the suspension of Madagascar's relations with international donor institutions, following the removal of President Marc Ravalomanana in March 2009. In addition to the impact of the political unrest and concomitant sanctions, a continuing financial crisis in Europe adversely affected the country's exports and tourism industry. However, following the completion of the major Amabatovy mining project in the east of the country, it was anticipated that government revenue would benefit in subsequent years from exports of nickel and cobalt. Following protracted delays, democratic presidential and legislative elections were finally conducted in late 2013, and the transitional period officially ended in February 2014. The African Union (see p. 188) and the Southern African Development Community (see p. 420) ended the suspension of Madagascar's membership in January, and the IMF formally restored recognition of the authorities in March. The new President, Hery Martial Rajaonarimampianina Rakotoarimanana, pledged to improve management of Madagascar's resources and to introduce anti-corruption measures. In June the IMF approved a US $47.1m. emergency loan to Madagascar, while the USA reinstated African Growth and Opportunity Act trade status for the country. Growth increased to an estimated 3.0% in 2014. In response to severe tropical storm damage in January 2015, the World Bank extended $400,000 in emergency aid. The Government continued to seek funding for stabilization reforms under the IMF's Extended Credit Facility; following an IMF evaluation mission to Madagascar in February–March, it was announced that the authorities had committed to wide-ranging reforms, including measures to improve tax and customs administration, and the elimination of fuel subsidies, which, together with transfers to loss-making state-owned enterprises, were cited as the main budgetary strains. Meanwhile, severe power shortages, which were widely attributed to the mismanagement of state utility JIRAMA, precipitated increasing social unrest and resulted in the appointment of a new Government in January.

PUBLIC HOLIDAYS

2016: 1 January (New Year), 28 March (Easter Monday), 29 March (Martyr's Day, Commemoration of 1947 Rebellion), 1 May (Labour Day), 5 May (Ascension Day), 15 May (Whitsun), 25 May (Organization of African Unity Day), 26 June (Independence Day), 15 August (Assumption), 1 November (All Saints' Day), 25 December (Christmas).

Statistical Survey

Source (unless otherwise stated): Institut National de la Statistique de Madagascar, BP 485, Anosy Tana, 101 Antananarivo; tel. (20) 2227418; e-mail dridnstat@wanadoo.mg; internet www.instat.mg; Ministry of the Economy and Industry, Bâtiment Commerce, Ambohidahy, 101 Antananarivo: internet www.mepspc.gov.mg.

Area and Population

AREA, POPULATION AND DENSITY

Area (sq km)	587,295*
Population (census results)	
1974–75†	7,603,790
1–19 August 1993	
Males	6,088,116
Females	6,150,798
Total	12,238,914
Population (UN estimates at mid-year)‡	
2013	22,924,850
2014	23,571,962
2015	24,235,390
Density (per sq km) at mid-2015	41.3

* 226,756 sq miles.

† The census took place in three stages: in provincial capitals on 1 December 1974; in Antananarivo and remaining urban areas on 17 February 1975; and in rural areas on 1 June 1975.

‡ Source: UN, *World Population Prospects: The 2012 Revision*.

POPULATION BY AGE AND SEX
(UN estimates at mid-2015)

	Males	Females	Total
0–14 years	5,093,354	5,015,066	10,108,420
15–64 years	6,674,474	6,764,740	13,439,214
65 years and over	314,633	373,123	687,756
Total	**12,082,461**	**12,152,929**	**24,235,390**

Source: UN, *World Population Prospects: The 2012 Revision*.

PRINCIPAL ETHNIC GROUPS
(estimated population, 1974)

Merina (Hova) . .	1,993,000		Sakalava . . .	470,156*
Betsimisaraka . .	1,134,000		Antandroy . .	412,500
Betsileo	920,600		Antaisaka . .	406,468*
Tsimihety . . .	558,100			

* 1972 figure.

PRINCIPAL TOWNS
(population at 1993 census)

Antananarivo			Mahajanga	
(capital)	1,103,304		(Majunga)	106,780
Toamasina	137,782		Toliary (Tuléar)	80,826
(Tamatave)	137,782		Antsiranana (Diégo-.	
Antsirabé	126,062		Suarez)	59,040
Fianarantsoa	109,248			

2001 (estimated population, incl. Renivohitra and Avaradrano): Antananarivo 1,111,392.

Mid-2014 (incl. suburbs, UN estimate): Antananarivo 2,486,590 (Source: UN, *World Urbanization prospects: The 2014 Revision*).

BIRTHS AND DEATHS

	2011	2012	2013
Birth rate (per 1,000)	35.0	33.0	34.7
Death rate (per 1,000)	6.4	6.4	6.8

Source: African Development Bank.

Life expectancy (years at birth): 64.2 (males 62.8; females 65.8) in 2012 (Source: World Bank, World Development Indicators database).

ECONOMICALLY ACTIVE POPULATION
(labour force survey, '000 persons aged 10 years and over, October–December 2012)

	Males	Females	Total
Agriculture, hunting, forestry and fishing	4,175.7	3,683.8	7,859.4
Mining and quarrying	} 77.8	54.6	132.4
Electricity, gas and water			
Manufacturing	199.0	348.6	547.6
Construction	137.9	4.2	142.2
Wholesale and retail trade, transportation, accommodation and food; business and administrative services	517.8	586.4	1,104.3
Public administration, community, social and other services and activities	304.0	352.0	656.0
Total employed	5,412.3	5,029.6	10,441.9
Unemployed	55.4	78.1	133.5
Total labour force	5,467.7	5,107.7	10,575.4

Source: ILO.

Mid-2015 (estimates in '000): Agriculture, etc. 8,588; Total labour force 12,733 (Source: FAO).

Health and Welfare

KEY INDICATORS

Total fertility rate (children per woman, 2012)	4.5
Under-5 mortality rate (per 1,000 live births, 2012)	58
HIV/AIDS (% of persons aged 15–49, 2013)	0.4
Physicians (per 1,000 head, 2007)	0.2
Hospital beds (per 1,000 head, 2010)	0.2
Health expenditure (2011): US $ per head (PPP)	39
Health expenditure (2011): % of GDP	4.1
Health expenditure (2011): public (% of total)	55.9
Access to water (% of persons, 2012)	50
Access to sanitation (% of persons, 2012)	14
Total carbon dioxide emissions ('000 metric tons, 2010)	2,013.2
Carbon dioxide emissions per head (metric tons, 2010)	0.1
Human Development Index (2013): ranking	155
Human Development Index (2013): value	0.498

For sources and definitions, see explanatory note on p. vi.

Agriculture

PRINCIPAL CROPS
('000 metric tons)

	2011	2012	2013
Rice, paddy	4,300	4,551	3,611
Maize	428	448	381*
Potatoes†	225	225	225
Sweet potatoes	1,103	1,110†	1,130†
Cassava (Manioc)	3,490	3,621†	3,115†
Taro (Cocoyam)†	225	232	234
Sugar cane†	3,050	3,270	3,250
Beans, dry†	89	107	116
Groundnuts, in shell*	31	33	33
Coconuts	76*	77*	78†
Oil palm fruit†	21	22	21
Tomatoes†	39	40	39
Bananas†	350	356	355
Oranges†	86	87	87
Guavas, mangoes and mangosteens†	301	310	305
Avocados†	26	26	26
Pineapples†	80	81	80
Cashew apples†	74	75	75
Coffee, green†	67	67	64
Vanilla†	3	3	3
Cinnamon (Canella)†	2	2	3
Cloves†	22	23	23
Sisal†	19	19	19
Tobacco, unmanufactured†	2	2	2

* Unofficial figure(s).
† FAO estimate(s).

Aggregate production ('000 metric tons, may include official, semi-official or estimated data): Total cereals 4,740 in 2011, 5,010 in 2012, 3,998 in 2013; Total roots and tubers 5,043 in 2011, 5,188 in 2012, 4,703 in 2013; Total vegetables (incl. melons) 439 in 2011, 443 in 2012, 440 in 2013; Total fruits (excl. melons) 1,210 in 2011, 1,230 in 2012, 1,221 in 2013.

Source: FAO.

LIVESTOCK
('000 head, year ending September, FAO estimates)

	2011	2012	2013
Cattle	9,956	10,031	10,030
Pigs	1,470	1,502	1,500
Sheep	823	840	839
Goats	1,442	1,473	1,472
Chickens	27,000	27,500	27,000
Ducks	4,300	4,300	4,250
Geese and guinea fowls	3,000	3,000	2,950
Turkeys	2,250	2,250	2,200

Source: FAO.

LIVESTOCK PRODUCTS
('000 metric tons, FAO estimates)

	2011	2012	2013
Cattle meat	165.8	172.1	172.1
Sheep meat	3.2	3.2	3.2
Goat meat	9.8	9.8	9.8
Pig meat	57.4	58.5	58.5
Chicken meat	38.1	38.4	38.4
Duck meat	12.0	12.0	11.8
Goose meat	12.7	12.7	12.6
Turkey meat	9.4	9.4	9.2
Cows' milk	560	570	575
Hen eggs	16.6	17.0	17.0
Other eggs	4.5	4.5	4.5
Honey	4.4	4.5	4.4

Source: FAO.

Forestry

ROUNDWOOD REMOVALS
('000 cubic metres, excl. bark, FAO estimates)

	2011	2012	2013
Sawlogs, veneer logs and logs for sleepers	271	271	271
Pulpwood	10	10	10
Fuel wood	13,100	13,045	13,327
Total	13,381	13,326	13,608

Source: FAO.

SAWNWOOD PRODUCTION
('000 cubic metres, incl. railway sleepers)

	2008	2009*	2010
Coniferous (softwood)	42	42	42*
Broadleaved (hardwood)	50	50	62
Total	92	92	104*

* FAO estimate(s).

2011–13: Production assumed to be unchanged from 2010 (FAO estimates).

Source: FAO.

Fishing

('000 metric tons, live weight)

	2010	2011	2012
Capture*	128.8	116.3	105.0
Cichlids*	20.2	16.5	8.0
Other freshwater fishes	11.2*	10.8	14.7
Narrow-barred Spanish mackerel	3.8	3.8	3.8
Other marine fishes	67.2	59.8*	45.1
Shrimps and prawns	6.5	4.3	9.9
Aquaculture*	6.9	8.8	8.6
Giant tiger prawn	4.0*	5.4	5.0
Total catch*	135.7	125.1	113.5

* FAO estimate(s).

Note: Figures exclude aquatic plants ('000 metric tons, capture only): 0.8 in 2010–12. Also excluded are crocodiles, recorded by number rather than weight, and shells. The number of Nile crocodiles caught was: 2,450 in 2009; n.a. in 2010–12.

Source: FAO.

Mining

(metric tons)

	2010	2011	2012
Chromite*†	134,500	66,700	67,000
Salt (marine)†	75,000	85,000	85,000
Graphite (natural)‡	3,783	3,573	4,100
Mica‡	2,069	3,411	3,500

* Figures refer to gross weight. The estimated chromium content is 27%.
† Estimates.
‡ Figures refer to exports.

Source: US Geological Survey.

Industry

SELECTED PRODUCTS
(metric tons unless otherwise indicated)

	2009	2010	2011
Raw sugar	60,000	80,000	70,000
Cement	370,000	410,000*	410,000*
Electric energy (million kWh)†	1,274	1,360	1,438

* Estimated figure.
† Production by the state-owned utility only, excluding electricity generated by industries for their own use.

2012: Cement 410,000 (estimate).

Sources: US Geological Survey; UN Industrial Commodity Statistics Database.

Finance

CURRENCY AND EXCHANGE RATES

Monetary Units
5 iraimbilanja = 1 ariary.

Sterling, Dollar and Euro Equivalents (31 December 2014)
£1 sterling = 4,052.98 ariary;
US $1 = 2,596.73 ariary;
€1 = 3,152.69 ariary;
10,000 ariary = £2.47 = $3.85 = €3.17.

Average Exchange Rate (ariary per US $)
2012   2,195.0
2013   2,206.9
2014   2,414.8

BUDGET
('000 million ariary, central government operations)

Revenue and grants	2012	2013	2014*
Tax revenue	2,263	2,452	2,983
Taxes on income and profits	513	568	742
Taxes on goods and services	685	690	855
Taxes on international trade and transactions	1,049	1,172	1,365
Non-tax revenue	118	71	62
Grants	263	296	625
Total	2,644	2,818	3,670

Expenditure	2012	2013	2014*
Current expenditure	2,323	2,505	3,071
Wages and salaries	1,167	1,342	1,650
Goods and services	702	861	925
Interest payments	144	124	301
Domestic	106	85	253
Foreign	38	39	49
Other	309	179	195
Capital expenditure	595	730	1,183
Total	2,918	3,236	4,254

* Budget figures.

INTERNATIONAL RESERVES
(excl. gold, US $ million at 31 December)

	2011	2012	2013
IMF special drawing rights	144.5	138.1	128.9
Foreign exchange	1,134.5	1,052.8	776.1
Total	1,279.1	1,190.9	905.0

2014: IMF special drawing rights 102.6.

Source: IMF, *International Financial Statistics*.

MONEY SUPPLY
('000 million ariary at 31 December)

	2011	2012	2013
Currency outside banks . . .	1,477.52	1,516.74	1,607.54
Demand deposits at deposit money banks	1,768.94	1,869.96	1,943.36
Total money	3,246.47	3,386.70	3,550.90

Source: IMF, *International Financial Statistics*.

COST OF LIVING
(Consumer Price Index for Malagasy in Antananarivo; base: 2000 = 100)

	2012	2013	2014
Food	306.6	321.7	339.1
Clothing	227.3	246.4	267.9
Housing, water, electricity, gas and other fuels	368.8	391.2	417.2
All items (incl. others) . . .	306.8	324.7	344.4

NATIONAL ACCOUNTS
('000 million ariary at current prices)

Expenditure on the Gross Domestic Product

	2011	2012*	2013*
Government final consumption expenditure	2,041	2,100	2,042
Private final consumption expenditure	17,588	19,156	20,617
Increase in stocks			
Gross fixed capital formation .	3,528	3,774	3,678
Total domestic expenditure.	23,157	25,030	26,337
Exports of goods and services .	5,358	6,317	6,675
Less Imports of goods and services	8,481	9,573	9,594
GDP in purchasers' values .	20,034	21,774	23,419

Gross Domestic Product by Economic Activity

	2011	2012*	2013*
Agriculture, hunting, forestry and fishing	5,201	5,612	5,684
Mining and quarrying	29	40	62
Manufacturing	2,682	2,908	3,148
Electricity, gas and water . .	222	246	271
Construction	703	718	761
Wholesale and retail trade, restaurants and hotels . . .	2,084	2,247	2,400
Transport and communications .	3,863	4,366	5,172
Finance, insurance, real estate and business services . . .	2,606	2,777	3,039
Public administration and defence	1,305	1,419	1,615
Sub-total	18,695	20,333	22,152
Less Imputed bank service charges	360	432	605
Indirect taxes, less subsidies . .	1,701	1,873	1,871
GDP in purchasers' values .	20,034	21,774	23,419

* Provisional.
Source: African Development Bank.

BALANCE OF PAYMENTS
(US $ million)

	2003	2004	2005
Exports of goods f.o.b.	854	990	834
Imports of goods f.o.b.	−1,111	−1,427	−1,427
Trade balance	−258	−437	−592
Exports of services	322	425	498
Imports of services	−619	−637	−615
Balance on goods and services	−555	−649	−710
Other income received	16	15	24
Other income paid	−94	−89	−104
Balance on goods, services and income	−632	−723	−790
Current transfers received . .	357	245	208
Current transfers paid	−183	−62	−45
Current balance	−458	−541	−626
Capital account (net)	143	182	192
Direct investment from abroad .	13	53	85
Other investment assets . . .	−29	295	11
Other investment liabilities . .	−110	−97	−102
Net errors and omissions . . .	67	−35	91
Overall balance	−374	−143	−349

Source: IMF, *International Financial Statistics*.

External Trade

PRINCIPAL COMMODITIES
(distribution by HS, US $ million)

Imports c.i.f.	2011	2012	2013
Vegetables and vegetable products	181.2	161.7	285.8
Cereals and cereal preparations .	105.5	94.6	205.2
Rice	92.9	85.9	187.6
Animal or vegetable fats and oils, and products thereof .	90.7	57.9	67.6
Prepared foodstuffs; beverages, spirits, vinegars; tobacco and articles thereof .	194.5	149.0	188.4
Sugars and sugar confectionery .	91.7	61.2	74.5
Mineral products	707.8	680.1	894.3
Mineral fuels, oils, distillation products, etc.	663.0	616.0	764.7
Petroleum oils, not crude .	628.7	569.3	697.9
Salt, sulphur, earth, stone, plaster, lime and cement	44.7	63.9	129.3
Chemicals and related products	212.9	224.0	295.6
Medicinal and pharmaceutical products	72.3	83.8	101.2
Plastics, rubber, and articles thereof	117.7	113.5	142.5
Plastics and articles thereof . .	85.1	78.7	100.8
Pulp of wood, paper and paperboard, and articles thereof	87.3	66.4	90.7
Textiles and textile articles .	366.9	328.6	426.1
Wool, yarn and fabric	100.1	87.4	118.6

Imports c.i.f.—*continued*	2011	2012	2013
Woven cotton fabrics	93.2	66.0	81.9
Iron and steel; other base metals and articles of base metal	210.7	154.4	162.9
Articles of iron or steel . . .	98.5	58.4	47.8
Machinery and mechanical appliances; electrical equipment; parts thereof .	420.7	332.8	386.8
Machinery, boilers, etc. . . .	251.7	205.4	259.5
Electrical, electronic equipment .	169.0	127.4	127.3
Vehicles, aircraft, vessels and associated transport equipment	161.2	202.6	182.8
Vehicles other than railway, tramway	135.0	193.5	170.7
Cars (incl. station wagons) . .	56.3	81.6	65.8
Total (incl. others)	2,957.1	2,659.0	3,345.0

Exports f.o.b.	2011	2012	2013
Live animals and animal products	113.8	75.0	112.2
Fish, crustaceans and molluscs and preparations thereof	113.0	73.6	111.1
Crustaceans	101.3	65.6	97.9
Vegetables and vegetable products	277.9	246.4	296.4
Coffee, tea, cocoa, spices . . .	229.4	191.7	221.4
Vanilla	38.9	10.2	76.5
Cloves	172.8	167.7	110.0
Prepared foodstuffs; beverages, spirits, vinegar; tobacco and articles thereof .	100.5	86.0	128.6
Meat, fish and seafood food preparations	45.5	38.6	48.1
Prepared or preserved fish and caviar	43.6	37.7	47.5
Mineral products	214.0	230.7	225.4
Ores, slag and ash	109.7	136.1	118.9
Titanium ores and concentrates.	74.2	72.2	76.1
Niobium, tantalum, vanadium or zirconium ores and concentrates	21.6	44.7	21.6
Mineral fuels, oils, distillation products, etc.	93.9	82.6	90.0
Petroleum oils, not crude . .	93.4	81.0	88.3
Chemicals and related products	44.6	18.7	57.6
Textiles and textile articles .	404.4	347.7	476.4
Articles of apparel and clothing accessories	348.2	302.1	412.3
Jerseys, pullovers, cardigans (knitted or crocheted) . . .	135.9	116.4	134.5
Shawls, scarves, mufflers, mantillas, etc.	45.5	38.2	66.9
Iron and steel; other base metals and articles of base metal	35.0	90.0	439.3
Nickel and articles thereof . .	—	59.4	378.3
Unwrought nickel	—	59.4	378.3
Machinery and mechanical appliances; electrical equipment; parts thereof .	56.5	16.9	28.3
Machinery, boilers, etc. . . .	48.8	12.4	22.1
Vehicles, aircraft, vessels and associated transport equipment	74.2	6.1	45.3
Aircraft, spacecraft, and parts thereof	56.5	1.9	40.8
Aircraft (helicopter, aeroplanes) and spacecraft (satellites) .	56.1	0.4	39.9
Total (incl. others)	1,471.5	1,224.5	1,928.1

Source: Trade Map-Trade Competitiveness Map, International Trade Centre, www.intracen.org/marketanalysis.

PRINCIPAL TRADING PARTNERS
(US $ million)

Imports	2011	2012	2013
Australia	37.1	18.3	16.2
Bahrain	36.9	158.3	70.0
Belgium	31.2	26.8	34.2
Brazil	39.0	24.8	28.0
China, People's Republic . . .	408.5	380.0	487.6
Egypt	44.6	46.8	41.3
France	201.0	160.4	205.8
Germany	90.8	62.7	78.4
India	118.8	129.8	196.4
Indonesia	38.4	34.5	55.4
Italy	43.6	36.1	34.0
Japan	41.0	45.8	48.0
Korea, Republic	31.8	36.2	33.9
Kuwait	31.2	0.2	0.1
Malaysia	69.5	30.4	50.1
Mauritius	99.7	77.3	103.8
Pakistan	103.7	65.4	119.0
Qatar	15.1	29.2	64.7
Singapore	67.7	38.2	26.0
South Africa	170.2	152.2	179.8
Spain	30.1	41.4	59.5
Thailand	53.5	50.5	54.2
Turkey	51.9	58.2	64.0
United Arab Emirates . . .	495.6	389.5	667.8
United Kingdom	31.2	26.0	27.0
USA	100.4	99.1	124.4
Viet Nam	6.1	8.1	38.7
Total (incl. others)	2,957.1	2,659.0	3,345.0

Exports	2011	2012	2013
Belgium	32.2	16.8	73.2
Canada	72.6	69.5	83.7
China, People's Republic . . .	91.5	102.6	133.7
France	529.4	356.9	494.8
Germany	93.0	76.5	100.8
Hong Kong	14.9	14.6	15.6
India	63.0	67.1	47.3
Indonesia	24.4	20.9	6.7
Italy	33.3	38.3	40.5
Japan	10.4	6.1	85.4
Korea, Republic	1.7	17.2	93.1
Mauritius	17.9	17.3	31.1
Netherlands	23.5	27.5	119.1
Singapore	101.2	49.5	35.4
South Africa	34.2	40.0	79.5
Spain	29.3	31.3	41.8
Thailand	17.0	9.8	13.0
United Arab Emirates . . .	16.5	11.2	13.1
United Kingdom	33.1	23.2	34.2
USA	48.1	54.4	146.7
Viet Nam	7.9	15.8	17.6
Total (incl. others)	1,471.5	1,224.5	1,928.1

Source: Trade Map-Trade Competitiveness Map, International Trade Centre, www.intracen.org/marketanalysis.

Transport

ROAD TRAFFIC
(vehicles in use)

	2008	2009
Passenger cars	146,273	141,236
Buses and coaches	280,835	280,835
Lorries and vans	83,788	88,815

Source: IRF, *World Road Statistics*.

SHIPPING

Flag Registered Fleet
(at 31 December)

	2012	2013	2014
Number of vessels	42	43	43
Displacement ('000 grt) . . .	20.3	20.5	20.5

Source: Lloyd's List Intelligence (www.lloydslistintelligence.com).

CIVIL AVIATION
(traffic on scheduled services)

	2010	2011
Kilometres flown (million)	12	11
Passengers carried ('000)	524	548
Passenger-km (million)	1,240	1,095
Total ton-km (million)	135	118

Source: UN, *Statistical Yearbook*.

Passengers carried ('000): 588.2 in 2012; 539.2 in 2013 (Source: World Bank, World Development Indicators database).

Tourism

TOURIST ARRIVALS BY NATIONALITY

	2011	2012	2013
Comoros	4,468	5,969	4,069
Canada and USA	9,193	9,291	5,762
France	114,471	137,578	93,180
Germany	6,504	6,028	3,992
Italy	7,162	8,932	29,841
Mauritius	7,261	8,418	5,498
Réunion	15,360	18,760	17,752
South Africa	7,121	5,967	3,743
United Kingdom	9,213	9,029	4,008
Total (incl. others) . . .	225,055	255,942	196,375

Tourism receipts (US $ million, excl. passenger transport): 308 in 2009; 321 in 2010.

Source: World Tourism Organization.

Communications Media

	2011	2012	2013
Telephones ('000 main lines in use)	236.9	243.0	250.0
Mobile cellular telephones ('000 subscribers)	8,680.8	8,778.6	8,283.6
Internet subscribers ('000) . .	17.7	n.a.	n.a.
Broadband subscribers ('000) . .	6.9	8.7	13.9

Source: International Telecommunication Union.

Education

(2011/12 unless otherwise indicated, UNESCO estimates, public and private schools)

		Pupils ('000)		
	Teachers	Males	Females	Total
Pre-primary (all programmes)* . . .	7,075	81.3	82.4	163.7
Primary (all programmes) .	102,229	2,224.0	2,178.7	4,402.7
Secondary	50,842	718.4	686.7	1,405.1
General	48,866	699.5	677.7	1,377.2
Vocational	1,976	18.9	9.0	27.9
Tertiary	4,439	47.0	43.3	90.3

* 2009/10.

Source: UNESCO Institute for Statistics.

2005/06: 6 universities; 14 private institutes of higher education.

Pupil-teacher ratio (primary education, UNESCO estimate): 43.1 in 2011/12 (Source: UNESCO Institute for Statistics).

Adult literacy rate (UNESCO estimates): 64.5% (males 67.4%; females 61.6%) in 2009 (Source: UNESCO Institute for Statistics).

Directory

The Government

HEAD OF STATE

President: HERY MARTIAL RAJAONARIMAMPIANINA RAKOTOARIMANANA (inaugurated 25 January 2014).

COUNCIL OF MINISTERS
(May 2015)

Prime Minister: Gen. JEAN RAVELONARIVO.

Minister of State, in charge of Presidential Projects, Land Management and Equipment: RIVO RAKOTOVAO.

Minister at the Presidency, in charge of Mining and Petroleum: JOÉLI VALÉRIEN LALAHARISAINA.

Minister of National Defence: Gen. DOMINIQUE JEAN OLIVIER RAKOTOZAFY.

Minister of Foreign Affairs: BÉATRICE ATTALAH.

Minister of Justice, Keeper of the Seals: NOËLINE RAMANANTENASOA.

Minister of Finance and the Budget: FRANÇOIS MARIE MAURICE GERVAIS RAKOTOARIMANANA.

Minister of the Interior and Decentralization: SOLONANDRASANA OLIVIER MAHAFALY.

Minister of Public Security: BLAISE RICHARD RANDIMBISOA.

Minister of the Economy and Planning: Gen. HERILANTO RAVELOHARISON.

Minister of Agriculture: ROLAND RAVATOMANGA.

Minister of Public Health: MAMY LALATIANA ANDRIAMANARIVO.

Minister of National Education: ANDRIANIAINA PAUL RABARY

Minister of Industry and the Development of the Private Sector: NARSON RAFIDIMANANA.

Minister of Trade and Consumer Affairs: HENRY RABESAHALA.

Minister of Public Works: IAROVANA ROLAND RATSIRAKA.

Minister of the Civil Service, Labour and Social Legislation: JEAN DE DIEU MAHARANTE.

Minister of Tourism, Transport and Meteorology: JACQUES ULRICH ANDRIANTIANA.

Minister of Energy and Hydrocarbons: GATIEN HORACE.

Minister of Higher Education and Scientific Research: MARIE MONIQUE RASOAZANANERA.

Minister of Employment, Technical Education and Professional Training: RAMARCEL BENJAMINA RAMANANTSOA.

Minister of the Environment, Ecology, the Sea and Forests: RALAVA BEBOARIMISA.

Minister of Fisheries and Fishing Resources: AHMAD.

Minister of Water, Hygiene and Sanitation: BÉNÉDICTE JOHANITA NDAHIMANANJARA.

Minister of Livestock: ANTHELME RAMPARANY.

Minister of Culture and Handicrafts: BRIGITTE RASAMOELY.

Minister of Posts, Telecommunications and New Technologies: ANDRÉ NEYPATRAIKY RAKOTOMAMONJY.

Minister of Communication and Relations with the Institutions: VONISON ANDRIANJATO RAZAFINDRAMBO.

Minister of Youth and Sport: JEAN ANICET ANDRIAMOSARISOA.

Minister of Population, Social Protection and the Promotion of Women: ONITIANA VOAHARINIAINA RËALY.

Secretary of State at the Ministry of National Defence, responsible for the National Gendarmerie: Gen. DIDIER GÉRARD PAZA.

MINISTRIES

Office of the President: BP 955, 101 Antananarivo; tel. (20) 2254703; fax (20) 2256252; e-mail communication@presidence.gov.mg; internet www.presidence.gov.mg.

Office of the Prime Minister: BP 248, Palais d'Etat Mahazoarivo, 101 Antananarivo; tel. (20) 2264498; fax (20) 2233116; e-mail stp-ca@primature.gov.mg; internet www.primature.gov.mg.

Ministry of Agriculture: BP 301, Anosy, 101 Antananarivo; tel. (20) 2261002; fax (20) 2264308; e-mail info@maep.gov.mg; internet www.agriculture.gov.mg.

Ministry of the Civil Service, Labour and Social Legislation: BP 207, Cité des 67 Hectares, 101 Antananarivo; tel. (20) 2224209; fax (20) 2233856; e-mail ministre@mfptls.gov.mg; internet www.mfptls.gov.mg.

Ministry of Communication and Relations with the Institutions: BP 305, Ampasanimalo, 101 Antananarivo; e-mail communication@mincom.gov.mg.

Ministry of Culture and Handicrafts: 101 Antananarivo; e-mail ministre@mcp.gov.mg; internet www.mcp.gov.mg.

Ministry of the Economy and Planning: Bâtiment Commerce, Ambohidahy, 101 Antananarivo; tel. (20) 2264681; fax (20) 2234530; e-mail sg@mepspc.gov.mg; internet www.economie.gov.mg.

Ministry of Employment, Technical Education and Vocational Training: BP 793, 101 Antananarivo; internet www.metfp.gov.mg.

Ministry of Energy and Hydrocarbons: BP 896, rue Farafaty Ampandrianomby, 101 Antananarivo; tel. and fax (20) 2259556; e-mail memcab@yahoo.fr; internet www.energie.gov.mg.

Ministry of the Environment, Ecology, the Sea and Forests: BP 610, rue Fernand Kasanga, Tsimbazaza, 101 Antananarivo; tel. (20) 2266805; fax (20) 2235410; e-mail dircab@ecologie.gov.mg; internet www.ecologie.gov.mg.

Ministry of Finance and the Budget: BP 61, Antaninarenina, Antananarivo; tel. (20) 2230173; fax (20) 2264680; e-mail mrazanajato@mefb.gov.mg; internet www.mefb.gov.mg.

Ministry of Fisheries and Fishing Resources: 101 Antananarivo; internet www.peche.gov.mg.

Ministry of Foreign Affairs: rue Andriamifidy, Anosy, BP 836, 101 Antananarivo; tel. (20) 2221196; fax (20) 2234484; e-mail contact@mae.gov.mg; internet mae.gov.mg.

Ministry of Higher Education and Scientific Research: 101 Antananarivo; internet www.mesupres.gov.mg.

Ministry of Industry and the Development of the Private Sector: Antananarivo.

Ministry of the Interior and Decentralization: BP 833, Anosy, 101 Antananarivo; tel. (20) 2223084; fax (20) 2235579; internet www.mid.gov.mg.

Ministry of Justice: rue Joel Rakotomalala, BP 231, Faravohitra, 101 Antananarivo; tel. (20) 2237684; fax (20) 2264458; e-mail presse.justice@justice.gov.mg; internet www.justice.gov.mg.

Ministry of Livestock: 101 Antananarivo; internet www.elevage.gov.mg.

Ministry of Mining and Petroleum: rue Farafaty Ampandrianomby, BP 280, 101 Antananarivo; tel. 320311099 (mobile); e-mail contact@mprs.gov.mg; internet www.mines.gov.mg.

Ministry of National Defence: BP 08, Ampahibe, 101 Antananarivo; tel. (20) 2222211; fax (20) 2235420; e-mail mdn@wanadoo.fr; internet www.defense.gov.mg.

Ministry of National Education: BP 247, Anosy, 101 Antananarivo; tel. (20) 2224308; fax (20) 2223897; e-mail mlraharimalala@yahoo.fr; internet www.education.gov.mg.

Ministry of Population, Social Protection and the Promotion of Women: 2 rue Razanakombana, Ambohijatovo, 101 Antananarivo; tel. 330968906 (mobile); e-mail hndev@gmail.com; internet www.population.gov.mg.

Ministry of Posts, Telecommunications and New Technologies: pl. de l'Indépendance, Antaninarenina, 101 Antananarivo; tel. (20) 2222902; fax (20) 2234115; internet www.mtpnt.gov.mg.

Ministry of Presidential Projects, Land Management and Equipment: Antananarivo; internet www.mepate.gov.mg.

Ministry of Public Health: BP 88, Ambohidahy, 101 Antananarivo; tel. (20) 2263121; fax (20) 2264228; e-mail ministre@sante.gov.mg; internet www.sante.gov.mg.

Ministry of Public Security: BP 23 bis, 101 Antananarivo; tel. (20) 2221029; fax (20) 2231861; e-mail policenationale@pn.gov.mg; internet www.policenationale.gov.mg.

Ministry of Public Works: BP 295, 101 Antananarivo; tel. (20) 2228715; fax (20) 2220890; e-mail secreab@mtpm.gov.mg; internet www.mtpm.gov.mg.

Ministry of Tourism, Transport and Meteorology: rue Fernand Kasanga, Tsimbazaza, BP 610, 101 Antananarivo; e-mail info@tourisme.gov.mg; internet www.tourisme.gov.mg.

Ministry of Trade: 101 Antananarivo; internet www.commerce.gov.mg.

Ministry of Water, Hygiene and Sanitation: Antananarivo; e-mail dircab@mineau.gov.mg; internet www.mineau.gov.mg.

Ministry of Youth and Sport: 101 Antananarivo; internet www.mjl.gov.mg.

President

Presidential Election, First Round, 25 October 2013

Candidate	Votes	% of votes
Jean Louis Robinson Richard . . .	949,987	21.16
Hery Martial Rajaonarimampianina Rakotoarimanana	711,534	15.85
Hajo Herivelona Andrianainarivelo .	473,508	10.54
Iarovana Roland Ratsiraka	404,103	9.00
Albert Camille Vital	307,477	6.85
Saraha Georget Rabeharisoa . . .	202,956	4.52
Edgard Marie Noé Razafindravahy . .	195,053	4.34
Pierrot Jocelyn Rajaonarivelo . . .	120,511	2.68
Joseph Martin Randriamampionona . .	104,578	2.33
Benjamin Radavidson Andriamparany .	100,242	2.23
Others	920,598*	20.50
Total	4,490,547†	100.00

* There were 23 other candidates.
† Excluding 335,609 blank or invalid votes.

Presidential Election, Second Round, 20 December 2013

Candidate	Votes	% of votes
Hery Martial Rajaonarimampianina Rakotoarimanana	2,060,124	53.49
Jean Louis Robinson Richard . . .	1,791,336	46.51
Total	3,851,460*	100.00

* Excluding 191,786 blank or invalid votes.

Legislature

National Assembly: Antananarivo; e-mail poste@assemblee-nationale.mg; internet www.assemblee-nationale.mg.

President: JEAN-MAX RAKOTOMAMONJY.

General Election, 20 December 2013

Party	Seats
Miaraka amin'ny Prezidà Andry Rajoelina (MAPAR) .	49
Mouvance Ravalomanana	19
Vondrona politika miara-dia Malagasy Miara-Miainga	14
LEADER/Fanilo	5
Parti Hiaraka Isika	5
Independents	25
Others	30
Total	147*

* The results in four constituencies were annulled.

Election Commission

Commission Electorale Nationale Indépendante pour la Transition (CENIT): Immeuble Microréalisation, 4e étage, 67 ha, 101 Antananarivo; tel. (20) 2225179; fax (20) 2225881; e-mail ceni@ceni-madagascar.mg; internet www.ceni-madagascar.mg; 21 mems; Pres. NDRIANA MAMY RALAIARILIVA.

Political Organizations

In 2013 there were some 208 political organizations registered in Madagascar.

Antoko ny Vahoaka Aloha no Andrianina (AVANA): mem of the Alliance pour la Restauration de la Démocratie (ARD); Leader JEAN-LOUIS ROBINSON.

Comité pour la Réconciliation Nationale (CRN): Villa la Franchise, Lot II-I 160 A, Alarobia, Antananarivo; tel. (20) 2242022; f. 2002 by fmr President Zafy; radical opposition; Leader ALBERT ZAFY.

FAFI-V: f. 2009; Pres. NAIVO NAIVO RAHOLDINA.

Hasin'i Madagasikara: Lot K 7-97 bis IIA Mamory Ivato, BP 682, 101 Antananarivo; tel. 340220665 (mobile); e-mail madahasin@gmail.com; internet hasinimadagasikara.mg; f. 2009; green party; Pres. SARAHA GEORGET RABEHARISOA.

Herim-Bahoaka Mitambatra (HBM) (Union of Popular Forces): formed part of the coalition supporting Marc Ravalomanana prior to the 2006 presidential election; Leader TOVONANAHARY RABETSITONTA.

Hery Vaovao ho an'i Madagasikara (HVM): Antananarivo; Leader HERY MARTIAL RAJAONARIMAMPIANINA RAKOTOARIMANANA.

Hiaraka Isika: Leader CAMILLE VITAL.

Libéralisme Économique et Action Démocratique pour la Reconstruction Nationale (LEADER/Fanilo) (Torch): f. 1993 by Herizo Razafimahaleo; Sec.-Gen. MANASSÉ ESOAVELOMANDROSO.

Malagasy Tonga Saina (MTS): Antananarivo; Pres. ROLAND RATSIRAKA.

Miaraka amin'ny Prezidà Andry Rajoelina (MAPAR): Antananarivo; Leader ANDRY RAJOELINA.

Mouvement pour la Démocratie à Madagascar (MDM): Villa Khannet, Maibahoaka, Ambohidratrimo; tel. (34) 3118672; internet www.mdm-iarivo.mg; Pres. PIERROT RAJAONARIVELO.

Mouvement pour le Progrès de Madagascar (Mpitolona ho Amin'ny Fandrosoan'ny Madagasikara) (MFM): 42 & 44 Cité Ampefiloha Bldg, 101 Antananarivo; tel. (20) 2437560; e-mail contact@mfm-madagascar.com; f. 1972 as Mouvement pour le Pouvoir Prolétarien (MFM); adopted present name in 1990; advocates liberal and market-orientated policies; Leader MANANDAFY RAKOTONIRINA; Sec.-Gen. OLIVIER RAKOTOVAZAHA.

Ny Asa Vita no Ifampitsara (AVI) (People are judged by the work they do): f. 1997 to promote human rights, hard work and devt; Leader NORBERT RATSIRAHONANA.

Parti Socialiste et Démocratique pour l'Union de Madagascar (PSDUM): f. 2006; Pres. JEAN LAHINIRIKO.

Rassemblement pour le Socialisme et la Démocratie (RPSD): f. 1993 by fmr mems of PSD; also known as Renaissance du Parti Social-Démocratique; Jean-Eugène Voninahitsy formed a break away party known as the RPSD Nouveau in 2003; Leader EVARISTE MARSON.

TAMBATRA: Antananarivo; Pres. PETY RAKOTONIAINA.

Tanora malaGasy Vonona (TGV) (Determined Malagasy Youth): Antananarivo; internet www.tgvonona.org; f. 2007; Leader ANDRY RAJOELINA.

Tiako i Madagasikara (TIM) (I Love Madagascar): internet www.tim-madagascar.org; f. 2002; supports former Pres. Ravalomanana; Pres. YVAN RANDRIASANDRATRINIONY.

Vondrona politika miara-dia Malagasy Miara-Miainga (VPM/MMM): Antananarivo; Pres. HAJO ANDRIANAINARIVELO.

Diplomatic Representation

EMBASSIES IN MADAGASCAR

China, People's Republic: Ancien Hôtel Panorama, BP 1658, 101 Antananarivo; tel. (20) 2240129; fax (20) 2240215; e-mail chinaemb_mg@mfa.gov.cn; internet mg.china-embassy.org; Ambassador YANG MIN.

Comoros: Lot IB 50, rue du Dr Théodore Villette, Isoraka, 101 Antananarivo; tel. and fax (20) 2265819; Ambassador CAABI EL-YACHROUTU.

Egypt: Lot MD 378 Ambalatokana Mandrosoa Ivato, BP 4082, 101 Antananarivo; tel. (20) 2245497; fax (20) 2245379; Ambassador MAGID FOAD SALEH FOAD.

France: 3 rue Jean Jaurès, BP 204, 101 Antananarivo; tel. (20) 2239898; fax (20) 2239927; e-mail ambatana@moov.mg; internet www.ambafrance-mada.org; Ambassador FRANÇOIS GOLDBLATT.

Germany: 101 rue du Pasteur Rabeony Hans, BP 516, Ambodirotra, 101 Antananarivo; tel. (20) 2223802; fax (20) 2226627; e-mail info@antananarivo.diplo.de; internet www.antananarivo.diplo.de; Ambassador HARALD GEHRIG.

Holy See: Amboniloha Ivandry, BP 650, 101 Antananarivo; tel. (20) 2242376; fax (20) 2242384; e-mail nuntiusantana@wanadoo.mg; Apostolic Nuncio PAOLO ROCCO GUALTIERI (Titular Archbishop of Sagone).

India: 4 Làlana Emile Rajaonson, Tsaralalana, BP 1787, 101 Antananarivo; tel. (20) 2223334; fax (20) 2233790; e-mail indembmd@blueline.mg; internet www.embassyofindia.mg; Ambassador C. B. THAPLIYAL.

Indonesia: Lot II, J Ter A, Ivandry, 26–28 rue Patrice Lumumba, BP 3969, 101 Antananarivo; tel. (20) 2224915; fax (20) 2332315; e-mail antananarivo.kbri@kemlu.go.id; internet www.kemlu.go.id; Chargé d'affaires e.p. ARTANTO SALMOEN WARGADINATA.

Iran: route Circulaire, Lot II L43 ter, Ankadivato, 101 Antananarivo; tel. (20) 2228639; fax (20) 2222298; Ambassador ABDOL RAHIM HOMATASH.

Japan: 8 rue du Dr Villette, BP 3863, Isoraka, 101 Antananarivo; tel. (20) 2226102; fax (20) 2221769; Ambassador RYUHEI HOSOYA.

Korea, Democratic People's Republic: 101 Antananarivo; tel. (20) 2244442; Ambassador RI YONG HAK.

Libya: Lot IIB, 37A route Circulaire Ampandrana-Ouest, 101 Antananarivo; tel. (20) 2221892; Chargé d'affaires a.i. Dr MOHAMED ALI SHARFEDIN AL-FITURI.

Mauritius: Villa David IV, Manakambahiny, 101 Antananarivo; tel. (20) 2221864; fax (20) 2221939; e-mail memad@moov.mg; Ambassador ERNEST GÉRARD LEMAIRE.

Morocco: Bâtiment D1, Rez-de-chaussée, Ankorondrano, BP 12, 104 Antananarivo; tel. (20) 2221347; fax (20) 2221124; e-mail amar_med@hotmail.com; Ambassador MUHAMMAD AMAR.

Russian Federation: BP 4006, Ivandry-Ambohijatovo, 101 Antananarivo; tel. (20) 2242827; fax (20) 2242642; e-mail ambrusmad@blueline.mg; internet www.madagascar.mid.ru; Ambassador AHKMEDOV STANISLAV ANVAROVICH.

South Africa: Lot IVO 68 bis, rue Ravoninahitriniarivo, Ankorondrano, BP 12101-05, 101 Antananarivo; tel. (20) 2243350; fax (20) 2249514; e-mail antananarivo@foreign.gov.za; Ambassador MOKGETHI SAMUEL MONAISA.

Switzerland: Immeuble ARO, Solombavambahoaka, Frantsay 77, BP 118, 101 Antananarivo; tel. (20) 2262997; fax (20) 2228940; e-mail ant.vertretung@eda.admin.ch; internet www.eda.admin.ch/antananarivo; Ambassador ERIC MAYORAZ.

Turkey: Hotel Carlton, Chambre no. 1410, rue Pierre Stibbe, BP 959, 101 Antananarivo; tel. (20) 2226060; fax (20) 2267609; Ambassador VOLKAN TÜRK VURAL.

United Kingdom: Tour Zital Ankorondrano, 9th Floor, Ravoninahitriniarivo St, 101 Antananarivo; tel. (20).2233053; e-mail beantananarivo@fco.gov.uk; internet www.gov.uk/government/world/madagascar; Ambassador TIMOTHY SPENCER SMART.

USA: Lot 207A, Point Liberty, Andranoro–Antehiroka, BP 5253, 105 Antananarivo; tel. (20) 2348000; fax (20) 2348035; e-mail paoantananarivo@state.gov; internet www.antananarivo.usembassy.gov; Ambassador ROBERT T. YAMATE.

Judicial System

According to the Constitution of the Fourth Republic of Madagascar, endorsed by national referendum on 17 November 2010, justice is administered by the Supreme Court, the High Constitutional Court, the High Court of Justice and any courts of appeal that may be established.

Supreme Court (Cour Suprême): Palais de Justice, Anosy, 101 Antananarivo; 9 mems; Pres. CLÉMENTINE CÉCILE RAJAONERA DELMOTTE; Attorney-General RANARY RAKOTONAVALONA ROBERSON; Chamber Pres YOLANDE RAMANGASOAVINA, FRANÇOIS RAMANANDRAIBE.

High Constitutional Court (Haute Cour Constitutionnelle): BP 835, Ambohidahy, 101 Antananarivo; tel. (20) 2266061; e-mail hcc@hcc.gov.mg; internet www.hcc.gov.mg; interprets the Constitution and rules on constitutional issues; nine mems; Pres. JEAN ERIC RAKOTOARISOA.

High Court of Justice (Haute Cour de Justice): 101 Antananarivo; 9 mems.

Tribunaux de Première Instance: at Antananarivo, Toamasina, Antsiranana, Mahajanga, Fianarantsoa, Toliary, Antsirabé, Ambatondrazaka, Antalaha, Farafangana and Maintirano; for civil, commercial and social matters, and for registration.

Cours Criminelles Ordinaires: tries crimes of common law; attached to the Cour d'Appel in Antananarivo but may sit in any other large town. There are also 31 Cours Criminelles Spéciales dealing with cases concerning cattle.

Tribunaux Spéciaux Economiques: at Antananarivo, Toamasina, Mahajanga, Fianarantsoa, Antsiranana and Toliary; tries crimes specifically relating to economic matters.

Tribunaux Criminels Spéciaux: judges cases of banditry and looting; 31 courts.

Religion

It is estimated that more than 50% of the population follow traditional animist beliefs, some 41% are Christians (about two-thirds of whom are Roman Catholics) and some 7% are Muslims.

CHRISTIANITY

Fiombonan'ny Fiangonana Kristiana eto Madagasikara (FFKM)/Conseil Chrétien des Eglises de Madagascar (Christian Council of Churches in Madagascar): Vohipiraisana, Ambohijatovo-Atsimo, BP 798, 101 Antananarivo; tel. (20) 2623433; e-mail ffkmfoibe@gmail.com; f. 1980; four mems and two assoc. mems; Pres. Pastor SAMOELA JANOA RANDRIANARIVELO; Gen. Sec. Rev. GILBERT RANDRIANIRINA.

Fiombonan'ny Fiangonana Protestanta eto Madagasikara (FFPM)/Fédération des Eglises Protestantes à Madagascar (Federation of the Protestant Churches in Madagascar): VK 3 Vohipiraisana, Ambohijatovo-Atsimo, BP 4226, 101 Antananarivo; tel. (20) 2415888; e-mail edmrazafi@fuller.edu; f. 1958; two mem. churches; Pres Rev. Dr LALA RASENDRAHASINA; Gen. Sec. Dr EDMOND RAZAFIMANANTSOA.

The Anglican Communion

Anglicans are adherents of the Church of the Province of the Indian Ocean, comprising eight dioceses (six in Madagascar, one in Mauritius and one in Seychelles). The Archbishop of the Province is the Bishop of Mauritius. The Church has about 160,000 adherents in Madagascar, including the membership of the Eklesia Episkopaly Malagasy (Malagasy Episcopal Church), founded in 1874.

Bishop of Antananarivo: Rt Rev. SAMOELA JAONA RANARIVELO, Evêché anglican, Lot VK 57 ter, Ambohimanoro, 101 Antananarivo; tel. (20) 2220827; fax (20) 2261331; e-mail eemdanta@yahoo.com.

Bishop of Antsiranana: Rt Rev. Dr OLIVER SIMON, Evêché anglican, 4 rue Grandidier, BP 278, 201 Antsiranana; tel. (20) 8222776; e-mail mgrchungpo@blueline.mg.

Bishop of Fianarantsoa: Rt Rev. GILBERT RATELOSON RAKOTONDRAVELO, Evêché anglican, BP 1418, 531 Fianarantsoa; tel. (20) 7551583.

Bishop of Mahajanga: Rt Rev. JEAN-CLAUDE ANDRIANJAFIMANANA, Evêché anglican, BP 169, 401 Mahajanga; e-mail eemdmaha@dts.mg.

Bishop of Toamasina: Rt Rev. JEAN PAUL SOLO, Evêché anglican, rue James Seth, BP 531, 501 Toamasina; tel. (20) 5332163; fax (20) 5331689.

Bishop of Toliara: Rt Rev. TODD MCGREGOR.

The Roman Catholic Church

Madagascar comprises five archdioceses and 16 dioceses. About 26% of the total population are Roman Catholics.

Bishops' Conference: Conférence Episcopale de Madagascar, 102 bis, rue Cardinal Jerôme Rakotomalala, BP 667, 101 Antananarivo; tel. (20) 2220478; fax (20) 2224854; e-mail ecar@vitelcom.mg; f. 1969; Pres. Most Rev. DÉSIRÉ TSARAHAZANA (Archbishop of Toamasina).

Archbishop of Antananarivo: ODON MARIE ARSÈNE RAZANAKOLONA, Archevêché, Andohalo, BP 3030, 101 Antananarivo; tel. (20) 2220726; fax (20) 2264181; e-mail didih@simicro.org.

Archbishop of Antsiranana: Most Rev. BENJAMIN MARC BALTHASON RAMAROSON, Archevêché, 5 blvd le Myre de Villers, BP 415, 201 Antsiranana; tel. and fax (82) 21605; e-mail archevediego@blueline.mg.

Archbishop of Fianarantsoa: Most Rev. FULGENCE RABEMAHAFALY, Archevêché, pl. Mgr Givelet, BP 1440, Ecar Ambozontany, 301 Fianarantsoa; tel. (20) 7550027; fax (20) 7551436; e-mail ecardiofianar@mel.moov.mg.

Archbishop'ny Toamasina: Most Rev. DÉSIRÉ TSARAHAZANA, 11 rue du Commerce, BP 98, 501 Toamasina; tel. (20) 5332128.

Archbishop of Toliara: Most Rev. FULGENCE RABEONY, Archevêché, Maison Saint Jean, BP 30, 601 Toliara; tel. (20) 9442416; e-mail diocese_tulcar@wanadoo.mg.

Other Christian Churches

Fiangonan'i Jesoa Kristy eto Madagasikara/Eglise de Jésus-Christ à Madagascar (FJKM): Lot 11 B18, Tohatohabato Ranavalona 1, Trano 'Ifanomezantsoa', BP 623, 101 Antananarivo; tel.

(20) 2228237; fax (20) 2227033; e-mail fjkm@wanadoo.mg; internet foibefjkm.mg; f. 1968; Pres. LALA HAJA RASENDRAHASINA; Gen. Sec. Rev. RÉMY RALIBERA; 2m. mems.

Fiangonana Loterana Malagasy (Malagasy Lutheran Church): BP 1741, 19 rue Jules Pochard, 101 Antananarivo; tel. (20) 2422703; e-mail drmodeste@yahoo.fr; internet loterana-malagasy.org; f. 1867; Pres. Rev. Dr ENDOR MODESTE RAKOTO; 3m. mems (2009).

The Press

In 1990 legislation was adopted guaranteeing the freedom of the press and the right of newspapers to be established without prior authorization.

PRINCIPAL DAILIES

Bulletin de l'Agence Nationale d'Information 'TARATRA' (ANTA): 8/10 Làlana Rainizanabololona, Antanimena, BP 194, 101 Antananarivo; tel. (20) 2234308; e-mail administration@taratramada.com; internet www.taratramada.com; f. 1977; Malagasy; Editor-in-Chief HANITRA RABETOKOTANY.

Le Courrier de Madagascar: Antananarivo; internet www.courrierinternational.com; f. 2009; Dir of Publication FRANCK RAMAROSON; circ. 12,000.

L'Express de Madagascar: BP 3893, 101 Antananarivo; tel. (20) 2221934; fax (20) 2262894; e-mail lexpress@malagasy.com; internet www.lexpressmada.com; f. 1995; French and Malagasy; Editor-in-Chief SYLVAIN RANJALAHY; circ. 10,000.

Gazetiko: rue Ravoninahitriniarivo, BP 1414 Ankorondrano, 101 Antananarivo; tel. (20) 2269779; fax (20) 2227351; e-mail gazetiko@midi-madagasikara.mg; internet www.gazetiko.mg; Malagasy; circ. 50,000.

La Gazette de la Grande Ile: Lot II, W 23 L Ankorahotra, route de l'Université, BP 8678, Antananarivo; tel. 340561396 (mobile); e-mail administration@lagazette-dgi.com; internet www.lagazette-dgi.com; French; 24 pages; Pres. LOLA RASOAMAHARO; Editor-in-Chief CHRISTIAN ANDRIANARISOA; circ. 15,000–30,000.

Imongo Vaovao: 11K 4 bis Andravoahangy, BP 7014, 101 Antananarivo; tel. (20) 2233110; f. 1955; Malagasy; Dir ANDRÉ RATSIFEHERA; circ. 15,000.

Madagascar Matin: Antananarivo; Editor-in-Chef LAHINIRIKO DENIS ALEXANDRE; circ. 18,000.

Madagascar Tribune: Immeuble SME, rue Ravoninahitriniarivo, BP 659, Ankorondrano, 101 Antananarivo; tel. (20) 2222635; fax (20) 2222254; e-mail contact@madagascar-tribune.com; internet www.madagascar-tribune.com; f. 1988; independent; French and Malagasy; Editor ANSELME RANDRIAKOTO; circ. 12,000.

Maresaka: Cité Logt. 288, Analamahitsy, 101 Antananarivo; tel. (20) 2431665; f. 1953; independent; Malagasy; Editor R. RABEFANANINA; circ. 5,000.

Midi Madagasikara: Làlana Ravoninahitriniarivo, BP 1414, Ankorondrano, 101 Antananarivo; tel. (20) 2269779; fax (20) 2227351; e-mail contact@midi-madagasikara.mg; internet www.midi-madagasikara.mg; f. 1983; French and Malagasy; Dir-Gen. JULIANA ANDRIAMBELO RAKOTOARIVELO; circ. 21,000 (Mon.–Fri.), 35,000 (Sat.).

Les Nouvelles: 8/10, rue Rainizanabololona, BP 194, 101 Antananarivo; tel. (20) 2235433; fax (20) 2229993; e-mail administration@les-nouvelles.com; internet www.les-nouvelles.com; French and Taratra; f. 2003; Dir-Gen. NAINA ANDRIANTSITOHAINA.

Ny Vaovaontsika: BP 11137, MBS Anosipatrana; tel. (20) 2227717; e-mail nyvaovaontsika@mbs.mg; f. 2004; re-est. as a daily; Malagasy; owned by the Malagasy Broadcasting System; Editor-in-Chief ROLAND ANDRIAMAHENINA; circ. 10,000.

Le Quotidien: BP 11 097, 101 Antananarivo; tel. (20) 2227717; fax (20) 2265447; e-mail lequotidien@mbs.mg; internet www.lequotidien.mg; f. 2003; owned by the Tiko Group plc; French.

La Vérité: Immeuble SODIAT, Mandrosoa Ivato, BP 5068, 105 Antananarivo; tel. (20) 2629521; fax (20) 2244953; e-mail laverite@blueline.com.

PRINCIPAL PERIODICALS

Basy Vava: Lot III E 96, Mahamasina Atsimo, 101 Antananarivo; tel. (20) 2220448; f. 1959; daily; Malagasy; Dir GABRIEL RAMANANJATO; circ. 3,000.

Dans les Médias Demain (DMD): 51 rue Tsiombikibo, BP 1734, Ambatovinaky, 101 Antananarivo; tel. (20) 2241664; fax (20) 2241665; e-mail admin@dmd.mg; f. 1986; independent; economic information and analysis; weekly; Editorial Dir JEAN ERIC RAKOTOARISOA; circ. 4,000.

Gazetinao: Lot IPA 37, BP 1758, Anosimasina, 101 Antananarivo; tel. (20) 1198161; e-mail mitantanasymitarika@yahoo.fr; f. 1976; French and Malagasy; monthly; religion and culture; Editor-in-Chief DAVID ALDEN EINSTEN RAKOTOMAHANINA; circ. 3,000.

L'Hebdo: BP 3893, 101 Antananarivo; tel. (20) 2221934; e-mail courrier@hebdomada.com; f. 2005; French and Malagasy; weekly; Editor-in-Chief NASOLO VALIAVO ANDRIAMIHAJA.

Isika Mianakavy: Ambatomena, 301 Fianarantsoa; f. 1958; Roman Catholic; Malagasy; monthly; Dir J. RANAIVOMANANA; circ. 21,000.

Journal Officiel de la République de Madagascar/Gazetim-Panjakan' Ny Repoblika Malagasy: BP 248, 101 Antananarivo; tel. (20) 2265010; fax (20) 2225319; f. 1883; official announcements; Malagasy and French; weekly; Dir HONORÉE ELIANNE RALALAHARISON; circ. 1,545.

Jureco: BP 6318, Lot IVD 48 bis, rue Razanamaniraka, Behoririka, 101 Antananarivo; tel. (20) 2255271; e-mail jureco@malagasy.com; law and economics; monthly; French; Dir MBOARA ANDRIANARIMANANA.

Lakroan'i Madagasikara/La Croix de Madagascar: BP 7524, CNPC Antanimena, 101 Antananarivo; tel. (20) 2266128; fax (20) 2224854; e-mail lakroa@moov.mg; internet www.lakroa.mg; f. 1927; Roman Catholic; French and Malagasy; weekly; Dir Fr JACQUES MANANTO REHAMA; circ. 15,000.

Ny Mpamangy-FLM: 9 rue Général Gabriel Ramanantsoa Isoraka, 101 Antananarivo; tel. (20) 2228943; f. 1882; monthly; Dir LUCIE NOROSOANOMENJANAHARY; circ. 3,000.

Ny Sakaizan'ny Tanora: BP 538, Antsahaminitra, 101 Antananarivo; tel. (20) 2228943; f. 1878; monthly; Editor-in-Chief ELISABETH RAHELINORO; circ. 5,000.

Revue de l'Océan Indien: Communication et Médias Océan Indien, rue H. Rabesahala, BP 46, Antsakaviro, 101 Antananarivo; tel. (20) 2222536; fax (20) 2234534; e-mail roi@dts.mg; internet www .madatours.com/roi; f. 1980; monthly; French; Dir-Gen. HERY M. A. RANAIVOSOA; circ. 5,000.

Sosialisma Mpiasa: BP 1128, 101 Antananarivo; tel. (20) 2221989; f. 1979; trade union affairs; Malagasy; monthly; Dir PAUL RABEMANANJARA; circ. 5,000.

NEWS AGENCIES

Agence Nationale d'Information 'TARATRA' (ANTA): 7 rue Jean Ralaimongo, Ambohiday, BP 386, 101 Antananarivo; tel. and fax (20) 2236047; e-mail taratra.mtpc@mtpc.gov.mg; f. 1977; Man. Dir JOÉ ANACLET RAKOTOARISON.

Mada: Villa Joëlle, Lot II J 161 R, Ivandry, 101 Antananarivo; tel. (20) 2242428; e-mail courrier@mada.mg; internet www.mada.mg; f. 2003; independent information agency; Dir RICHARD CLAUDE RATOVONARIVO.

Publishers

CITE: rue Samuel Rahamefy Ambatonakanga, BP 74, 101 Antananarivo; tel. (20) 2225386; fax (20) 2233669; e-mail information@cite .mg; internet www.cite.mg; Dir-Gen. HAINGONIRINA RANDRIANARIVONY.

Editions Ambozontany Analamalintsy: Lot IIM 46, BP 7553, 101 Antananarivo; tel. and fax (20) 2243111; e-mail editionsj@moov.mg; f. 1952; religious, educational, historical, cultural and technical textbooks; Dir Fr GUILLAUME DE SAINT PIERRE RAKOTONANDRATONIARIVO.

Editions Mixte: BP 3204, 101 Antananarivo; tel. (20) 2225130; fax (20) 2237616; Dir AINA JEAN RAZAKASOA.

Imprimerie Nouvelle: PK 2, Andranomahery, route de Majunga, BP 4330, 101 Antananarivo; tel. (20) 2221036; fax (20) 2269225; e-mail nouvelle@wanadoo.mg; Dir EUGÈNE RAHARIFIDY.

Imprimerie Takariva: 4 rue Radley, BP 1029, Antanimena, 101 Antananarivo; tel. (20) 2222128; f. 1933; fiction, languages, school textbooks; Man. Dir PAUL RAPATSALAHY.

Madagascar Print and Press Co (MADPRINT): rue Rabesahala, Antsakaviro, BP 953, 101 Antananarivo; tel. (20) 2222536; fax (20) 2234534; f. 1969; literary, technical and historical; Dir GEORGES RANAIVOSOA.

Maison d'Edition Protestante Antso: 19 rue Venance Manifatra, Imarivolanitra, BP 660, 101 Antananarivo; tel. (20) 2220886; fax (20) 2226372; e-mail fjkm@dts.mg; f. 1972; religious, school, social, political and general; Dir HANS ANDRIAMAMPIANINA.

Presse Edition et Diffusion: 51 rue Tsiombikibo Ambatovinaky, 101 Antananarivo; tel. (20) 2256658; e-mail prediff@prediff.mg; internet www.prediff.mg; f. 1995; owns the imprint Editions Jeunes Malgaches; Dir of Publication MARIE MICHÈLE RAZAFINTSALAMA.

Société Malgache d'Edition (SME): BP 659, Ankorondrano, 101 Antananarivo; tel. (20) 2222635; fax (20) 2222254; e-mail tribune@ wanadoo.mg; f. 1943; general fiction, university and secondary textbooks; Man. Dir RAHAGA RAMAHOLIMIHASO.

Société Nouvelle de l'Imprimerie Centrale (SNIC): Route des Hydrocarbures, BP 1414, 101 Antananarivo; tel. (20) 2221118; fax (20) 2234421; e-mail contact@snic.mg; internet www.snic.mg; f. 1961; books, newspapers and magazines; CEO JEREMY RABESAHALA.

Trano Printy Fiangonana Loterana Malagasy (TPFLM): BP 538, 9 rue Général Gabriel Ramanantsoa, 101 Antananarivo; tel. (20) 2224569; fax (20) 2262643; e-mail impluth@yahoo.fr; f. 1877; religious, educational and fiction; Man. JOSEPH RANDRIANARIVELO.

GOVERNMENT PUBLISHING HOUSE

Imprimerie Nationale: BP 38, 101 Antananarivo; tel. (20) 2223675; e-mail dinm@wanadoo.mg; all official publs; Dir JEAN DENIS RANDRIANIRINA.

ASSOCIATION

Association des Editeurs de Madagascar: rue Samuel Rahamefy, 101 Antananarivo; tel. (20) 2225386; e-mail contact@aedim .mg; internet www.aedim.mg; f. 2010; Pres. CLAUDE RABENORO; Sec.-Gen. PATRICK RASOLOFO.

Broadcasting and Communications

REGULATORY AUTHORITY

Office Malagasy d'Etudes et de Régulation des Télécommunications (OMERT): BP 99991, route des Hydrocarbures-Alarobia, 101 Antananarivo; tel. (20) 2242119; fax (20) 2321516; e-mail omert@moov.mg; internet www.omert.org; f. 1997; Gen. Man. AUGUSTIN ANDRIAMANANORO.

TELECOMMUNICATIONS

In 2014 there were four providers of mobile telephone services in the country, one of which, TELMA, also provided fixed-line services.

Airtel Madagascar: Explorer Business Park, Ankorondrano, Antananarivo 101; tel. (33) 1100100; e-mail info.africa@airtel.com; internet africa.airtel.com/madagascar; f. 1997 as Madacom; fmrly Celtel and subsequently Zain Madagascar; name changed as above in 2010; Dir-Gen. HEIKO SCHLITTKE.

blueline: Immeuble Tana, 2000 Ankorondrano, 101 Antananarivo; internet www.blueline.mg; f. 1998; internet and digital television service provider; owned by Gulfsat Madagascar; Dir-Gen. DAMIEN DE LAMBERTERIE.

Madamobil SA: Immeuble ARO Ampefiloha, 3e étage, Porte A32, 101 Antananarivo; tel. (20) 2631886; e-mail contact@life.mg; internet www.life.mg; f. 1997; provides mobile telephone services under the brand name 'Life'; Pres. and Dir PATRICK PERTEGNAZZA.

Orange Madagascar: Antananarivo; internet www.orange.mg; f. 1998; fmrly Antaris, la Société Malgache de Mobiles; name changed as above 2003; mobile telecommunication GSM network provider; market leader; Dir-Gen. MICHEL BARRÉ.

Télécom Malagasy SA (TELMA): BP 763, 101 Antananarivo; tel. (20) 2532705; fax (20) 2253871; e-mail telmacorporate@telma.mg; internet www.telma.mg; 68% owned by Distacom (Hong Kong); owns DTS Wanadoo internet service provider; Chair. DAVID WHITE; Dir-Gen. PATRICK PISAL-HAMIDA.

BROADCASTING

Radio

Le Messager Radio Evangélique: BP 1374, 101 Antananarivo; tel. (20) 2234495; internet mreradio.com; broadcasts in French, English and Malagasy; Dir JOCELYN RANJARISON.

Radio Antsiva: BP 632, Enceinte STEDIC, Village des Jeux, Zone Industrielle Nord, route des Hydrocarbures, 101 Antananarivo; tel. (20) 2254849; e-mail antsiva@freenet.mg; internet www.antsiva.mg; f. 1994; broadcasts in French and Malagasy.

Radio Don Bosco: Maison Don Bosco, BP 60, 105 Ivato; tel. (20) 2244387; fax (20) 2244511; e-mail rdb@radiodonbosco.org; internet www.radiodonbosco.org; f. 1996; Catholic, educational and cultural; Dir LUCA TREGLIA.

Radio Lazan'iarivo (RLI): Lot V A49, Andafiavaratra, 101 Antananarivo; tel. (20) 2229016; fax (20) 2267559; e-mail rli@simicro.mg; broadcasts in French, English and Malagasy; privately owned; specializes in jazz music; Dir IHOBY RABARIJOHN.

Radio MBS (Malagasy Broadcasting System): BP 11137, Anosipatrana, Antananarivo; tel. (20) 2266702; fax (20) 2268941; e-mail marketing@mbs.mg; internet www.mbs.mg; broadcasts by satellite; Man. SARAH RAVALOMANANA.

Radio Nationale Malagasy: BP 442, Anosy, 101 Antananarivo; tel. (20) 2221745; fax (20) 2232715; e-mail rnmdir@dts.mg; internet www .rnm.mg; state-controlled; part of the Office de Radiodiffusion et de Télévision de Madagascar (ORTM); broadcasts in French and Malagasy; Dir LALAO RASOANAIVO.

Radio Viva: Immeuble INJET, Parcelle No. 34, Zone Water Front, Ambodivona, 101 Antananarivo; tel. (20) 2256788; internet www .viva-madagascar.com; Owner ANDRY RAJOELINA.

Television

MA TV: BP 1414 Ankorondrano, 101 Antananarivo; tel. (20) 2220897; fax (20) 2234421; f. 1995; Pres. FREDY ANDRIAMBELO; Dir-Gen. WILLY FREDY ANDRIAMBELO.

MBS Television (Malagasy Broadcasting System): BP 11137, Anosipatrana, Antananarivo; tel. (20) 2266702; fax (20) 2268941; e-mail journaltv@mbs.mg; internet www.mbs.mg; broadcasts in French and Malagasy.

Radio Télévision Analamanga (RTA): Immeuble Fiaro, 101 Antananarivo; tel. (20) 2224503; e-mail rta@rta.mg; internet www .rta.mg; incl. four provincial radio stations; Dir-Gen. SELVEN NAIDU.

Télévision Nationale Malagasy (Televiziona Malagasy—TVM): BP 1202, Anosy, 101 Antananarivo; tel. (20) 2222381; f. 1967; state-controlled; part of the Office de Radiodiffusion et de Télévision de Madagascar (ORTM); broadcasts in French and Malagasy; Dir NIRY RANDRIAMAMPIANINA.

Télévision Viva: Immeuble INJET, Parcelle No. 34, Zone Water Front, Ambodivona, 101 Antananarivo; tel. (20) 2256788; internet www.viva-madagascar.com; Owner ANDRY RAJOELINA.

Finance

(cap. = capital; res = reserves; dep. = deposits; m. = million; brs = branches; amounts in ariary)

BANKING

Central Bank

Banque Centrale de Madagascar: rue de la Révolution Socialiste Malgache, BP 550, 101 Antananarivo; tel. (20) 2221751; fax (20) 2234532; e-mail sbu@bfm.mg; internet www.banque-centrale.mg; f. 1973; bank of issue; cap. 111,000m., res 32,420m., dep. 1,305,852m. (Dec. 2008); Gov. ALAIN HERVÉ RASOLOFONDRAIBE.

Other Banks

Bank of Africa (BOA)—Madagascar: 2 pl. de l'Indépendance, BP 183, 101 Antananarivo; tel. (20) 2239100; fax (20) 2266125; e-mail boa@boa.mg; internet www.boa.mg; f. 1976 as Bankin'ny Tantsaha Mpamokatra; name changed as above 1999; 38.86% owned by Bank of Africa Group (Luxembourg), 10% state-owned; commercial bank, specializes in micro-finance; cap. 45,509.7m., res 71,299.1m., dep. 1,221,365.9m. (Dec. 2013); Pres. ALAIN RASOLOFONDRAIBE; Gen. Man. ABDALLAH IKCHED; 55 brs.

Banque Malgache de l'Océan Indien (BMOI) (Indian Ocean Malagasy Bank): pl. de l'Indépendance, BP 25 bis, Antaninarenina, 101 Antananarivo; tel. (20) 2234609; fax (20) 2234610; e-mail bmoi .st@bnpparibas.com; internet www.bmoinet.net; f. 1989; 75% owned by BNP Paribas SA (France); cap. 6,000m., res 39,800m., dep. 814,800m. (Dec. 2013); Pres. GASTON RAMENASON; Dir ALAIN RIPERT; 8 brs.

Banque SBM Madagascar: rue Andrianary Ratianarivo Antsahavola 1, 101 Antananarivo; tel. (20) 2266607; fax (20) 2266608; e-mail bsbmmtana@sbm.intnet.mu; f. 1998; 79.99% owned by SBM Global Investments Ltd (Mauritius), 20.01% owned by Nedbank Africa Investments Ltd (South Africa); cap. 7,404.1m., res 1,845.6m., dep. 144,994.7m. (Dec. 2010); Chair. CHAITLALL GUNNESS; Gen. Man. KRISHNADUTT RAMBOJUN.

BFV—Société Générale: 14 rue Général Rabehevitra, BP 196, Antananarivo 101; tel. (20) 2220691; fax (20) 2237140; e-mail relation.client@socgen.com; internet www.bfvsg.mg; f. 1977 as Banky Fampandrosoana ny Varotra; changed name in 1998; 70% owned by Société Générale (France), 28.5% state-owned; cap. 14,000.0m., res 77,223.1m., dep. 930,033.2m. (Dec. 2013); Pres. BRUNO MASSEZ; 48 brs.

BNI Madagascar: 74 rue du 26 Juin 1960, BP 174, 101 Antananarivo; tel. (20) 2222800; fax (20) 2233749; e-mail info@bni.mg; internet www.bni.mg; f. 1976 as Bankin 'ny Indostria; 51% owned by IUB Holding (France), 32.58% state-owned; cap. 10,800.0m., res 70,527.2m., dep. 1,079,556.2m. (Dec. 2012); Pres. and Chair. DAMASE ANDRIAMANOHISOA; Man. Dir FRANÇOIS HOFFMAN; 25 brs.

Mauritius Commercial Bank (Madagascar) SA (MCB): 77 rue Solombavambahoaka Frantsay, Antsahavola, BP 197, 101 Antananarivo; tel. (20) 2227262; fax (20) 2228740; e-mail mcb.int@ mcbmadagascar.com; internet www.mcbmadagascar.com; f. 1992 as Union Commercial Bank; name changed as above in 2007; 70% owned by Mauritius Commercial Bank Ltd; cap. 12,000.0m., res 10,187.1m., dep. 196,745.2m. (Dec. 2013); Chair. JEAN FRANÇOIS DESVAUX DE MARIGNY; Gen. Man. MARC MARIE JOSEPH DE BOLLIVIER; 3 brs.

INSURANCE

ARO (Assurances Réassurances Omnibranches): Antsahavola, BP 42, 101 Antananarivo; tel. (20) 2220154; fax (20) 2234464; e-mail antsahavola@aro.mg; internet www.aro.mg; state-owned; Dir-Gen. PATRICK ANDRIAMBAHINY.

ASCOMA Madagascar: 13 rue Patrice Lumumba, BP 673, 101 Antananarivo; tel. (20) 2223162; fax (20) 2222785; e-mail madagascar@ascoma.com; internet www.ascoma.com; f. 1952; Dir MICKAEL GONÇALVES.

Compagnie Malgache d'Assurances et de Réassurances 'Ny Havana': Immeuble 'Ny Havana', Zone des 67 Ha, BP 3881, 101 Antananarivo; tel. (20) 2226760; fax (20) 2224303; e-mail nyhavana@ nyhavana.mg; internet www.nyhavana.mg; f. 1968; state-owned; cap. 7,704m. (2010); Dir-Gen. ROGER EMILE RANAIVOSON.

Mutuelle d'Assurances Malagasy (MAMA): Lot IF, 12 bis Ambalavao-Isotry, BP 185, 101 Antananarivo; tel. (20) 2261882; fax (20) 2261883; e-mail assurancemama@moov.mg; f. 1968; Dir SETH AIMÉ RANDRIANARIJAONA.

Trade and Industry

DEVELOPMENT ORGANIZATIONS

Agence Française de Développement: 23 rue Razanakombana Ambohijatovo, BP 557, Antananarivo; tel. (20) 2220046; fax (20) 2234794; e-mail afdantananarivo@groupe-afd.org; internet www.afd .fr; Dir JEAN-DAVID NAUDET.

Bureau d'Information pour les Entreprises (BIPE): Nouvel Immeuble ARO, Ampefiloha, 101 Antananarivo; tel. (20) 2230512; internet www.bipe.mg; part of the Ministry of the Economy and Industry.

Centre d'Information Technique et Économique de Madagascar (CITE): rue Samuel Ramahefy Ambatonakanga, BP 74, 101 Antananarivo; tel. (20) 2225386; fax (20) 2233669; e-mail cite@cite .mg; internet www.cite.mg; f. 1967; supports and promotes Malagasy businesses; Pres. GÉDÉON RAJAONSON; Dir-Gen. HAINGONIRINA RANDRIANARIVONY.

Economic Development Board of Madagascar (EDBM): ave Gabriel Ramanantsoa, Antaninarenina, 101 Antananarivo; tel. (20) 2268121; fax (20) 2266105; e-mail edbm@edbm.mg; internet www .edbm.gov.mg; f. 2006; service for the facilitation and promotion of investment in Madagascar; advisory service for starting a business, obtaining visas and land acquisition; CEO ERIC RAKOTO ANDRIANTSILAVO.

Office des Mines Nationales et des Industries Stratégiques (OMNIS): 21 Làlana Razanakombana, BP 1 bis, 101 Antananarivo; tel. (20) 2224283; fax (20) 2222985; e-mail secdg@omnis.mg; internet www.omnis.mg; f. 1976; promotes the exploration and exploitation of mining resources, in particular oil resources; Dir-Gen. BONAVENTURE RASOANAIVO.

CHAMBERS OF COMMERCE

Fédération des Chambres de Commerce et d'Industrie de Madagascar (FCCIM): BP 166, 20 rue Henri Razanatseheno, Antaninarenina, 101 Antananarivo; tel. (20) 2221322; fax (20) 2220213; e-mail cciaa@tana-cciaa.org; internet www .cci-madagascar.org; 20 mem. chambers; Pres. CHABANI NOURDINE; Dir-Gen. JOSIELLE RAFIDY.

Chambre de Commerce et d'Industrie d'Antananarivo (CCIA): BP 166, 20 rue Henri Razanatseheno, Antaninarenina, 101 Antananarivo; tel. (20) 2220211; fax (20) 2220211; e-mail communication.tnr@cci.mg; internet www.cci.mg; f. 1993; Pres. JEAN MARTIN RAKOTOZAFY.

EMPLOYERS' ORGANIZATIONS

Groupement des Entreprises de Madagascar (GEM): Kianja MDRM sy Tia Tanindrazana, Ambohijatovo, BP 1338, 101 Antananarivo; tel. (20) 2223841; fax (20) 2221965; e-mail gem@iris.mg; internet www.gem-madagascar.com; f. 1975; 16 nat. syndicates and five regional syndicates comprising 1,000 cos and 59 directly affiliated cos; Pres. JOSÉPHINE NORO ANDRIAMAMONJIARISON; Sec.-Gen. ZINAH RASAMUEL RAVALOSON.

Groupement National des Exportateurs de Vanille de Madagascar (GNEV): BP 21, Antalaha; tel. (13) 20714532; fax (13) 20816017; e-mail rama.anta@sat.blueline.mg; 18 mems; Pres. JEAN GEORGES RANDRIAMIHARISOA.

Malagasy Entrepreneurs' Association (FIV.MPA.MA): II K13 Andravoahangy, Antananarivo; tel. (20) 2269653; e-mail fivmpama@ moov.mg; internet www.fivmpama.mg; comprises 10 trade assocs, representing 200 mems, and 250 direct business mems; Chair. RAMANANTSOA RANDRIAMIFIDIMANANA.

Syndicat des Industries de Madagascar (SIM): Immeuble Holcim, 4e étage, Lot 1 bis, Tsaralalàna; BP 1695, 101 Antananarivo; tel. (20) 2224007; fax (20) 2222518; e-mail syndusmad@moov.mg; internet www.sim.mg; f. 1958; Pres. HERY STÉPHANE RAVELOSON; Exec. Dir CLAUDE RATEFIARISOA; 96 mems (2010).

Syndicat Professionel des Producteurs d'Extraits Aromatiques, Alimentaires et Medicinaux de Madagascar (SYPEAM): 7 rue Rakotoson Toto Radona, Antsahavola, BP 5038, Antananarivo 101; tel. (20) 2235363; e-mail itd.madagascar@moov .mg; f. 1994; Pres. CHARLES RANDRIAMBOLOLONA.

UTILITIES

Electricity and Water

Office de Regulation de l'Electricité (ORE): rue Tsimanindry, Ambatoroka, Antananarivo; tel. (20) 2264813; fax (20) 2264191; e-mail ore@ore.mg; internet www.ore.mg; f. 2004; Pres. AIMÉE ANDRIANASOLO.

Jiro sy Rano Malagasy (JIRAMA): BP 200, 149 rue Rainandriamampandry, Faravohitra, 101 Antananarivo; tel. (20) 2220031; fax (20) 2233806; e-mail dgjirama@jirama.mg; internet www.jirama.mg; f. 1975; controls production and distribution of electricity and water; managed by local manager; Pres. HAJA RESAMPA; Dir-Gen. NESTOR RAZAFINDRORIAKA.

TRADE UNIONS

Cartel National des Organisations Syndicales de Madagascar (CARNOSYMA): BP 1035, 101 Antananarivo.

Confédération des Travailleurs Malagasy Révolutionnaires (FISEMARE): Lot IVN 76-A, Ankadifotsy, BP 1128, Befelatanana-Antananarivo 101; tel. (20) 2221989; fax (20) 2267712; f. 1985; Pres. PAUL RABEMANANJARA.

Confédération des Travailleurs Malgaches (Fivomdronamben'ny Mpiasa Malagasy—FMM): Lot IVM 133 A Antotezanafovoany I, BP 846, 101 Antananarivo; tel. 331121526 (mobile); e-mail rjeannot2002@yahoo.fr; f. 1949; Sec.-Gen. JEANNOT RAMANARIVO; 8,000 mems.

Fédération des Syndicats des Travailleurs de Madagascar (Firaisan'ny Sendika eran'i Madagaskara—FISEMA): Lot III, rue Pasteur Isotry, BP 172, 101 Antananarivo; tel. (33) 1187414; e-mail fisema@gmail.co; internet fisema.org; f. 1956; Sec. Gen. JOSÉ RANDRIANASOLO; 8 affiliated unions representing 60,000 mems.

Sendika Kristianina Malagasy (SEKRIMA) (Christian Confederation of Malagasy Trade Unions): Soarano, route de Mahajanga, BP 1035, 101 Antananarivo; tel. (20) 2223174; f. 1937; Pres. MARIE RAKOTOANOSY; Gen. Sec. JEANNE CLAIRETTE RAZANARIMANANA; 158 affiliated unions representing 40,000 mems.

Union des Syndicats Autonomes de Madagascar (USAM): Lot IIIM 33 BC, Andrefan'Ambohijanahary, BP 1038, 101 Antananarivo; tel. and fax (20) 2227485; e-mail usam@moov.mg; f. 1954; Pres. THÉOPHILE JOËL RUFIN RAZAKARIASY; Sec.-Gen. SAMUEL RABEMANANTSOA; 49 affiliated unions representing 30,000 mems.

Transport

RAILWAYS

In 2012 there were 854 km of railway, including four railway lines, all 1-m gauge track. The northern system, which comprised 673 km of track, links the east coast with Antsirabé, in the interior, via Moramanga and Antananarivo, with a branch line from Moramanga to Lake Alaotra, and was privatized in 2001. The southern system, which comprised 163 km of track, links Manakara, on the east coast, with Fianarantsoa.

Fianarantsoa-Côte Est (FCE): FCE Gare, 301 Fianarantsoa; tel. (34) 5549917; e-mail fce@blueline.mg; internet www .fce-fianarantsoa-madagascar.com; f. 1936; southern network, 163 km; Man. DAUPHIN RAMONJARSOLO.

Madarail: Gare de Soarano, 1 ave de l'Indépendance, BP 1175, 101 Antananarivo; tel. (20) 2234599; fax (20) 2221883; e-mail madarail@ wanadoo.mg; internet www.comazar.com/madarail.htm; f. 2001; operated by VECTURIS (Belgium); 75% owned by Madarail Holding, 25% state-owned; operates the northern network of the Malagasy

railway (673 km); Pres. PATRICK CLAES; Dir (Operations) THÉODORE RASOLONJATOVO; 878 employees.

ROADS

In 2012 there were an estimated 31,640 km of classified roads; about 16.3% of the road network was paved. In 1987 there were 39,500 km of unclassified roads, used only in favourable weather. A road and motorway redevelopment programme, funded by the World Bank (€300m.) and the European Union (EU) (€61m.), began in 2000. In 2002 the EU undertook to disburse US $10m. for the reconstruction of 11 bridges destroyed during the political crisis in that year. In 2003 Japan pledged $28m. to build several bridges and a 15-km bypass. The Government planned to have restored and upgraded 14,000 km of highways and 8,000 km of rural roads to an operational status by 2015. In 2005, according to the IMF, 8,982 km of roads had been maintained or rehabilitated.

INLAND WATERWAYS

The Pangalanes canal runs for 600 km near the east coast from Toamasina to Farafangana. In 1990 432 km of the canal between Toamasina and Mananjary were navigable.

SHIPPING

There are 18 ports, the largest being at Toamasina, which handles about 70% of total traffic, and Mahajanga; several of the smaller ports are prone to silting problems. A new deep-sea port was constructed at Ehoala, near Fort Dauphin, in order to accommodate the activity of an ilmenite-mining development; the first vessel docked at the port in December 2008. At 31 December 2014 the country's flag registered fleet numbered 43 vessels and amounted to 20,547 grt.

CMA—CGM Madagascar: Immeuble Fitaratra Ankorondrano, 3e étage, BP 12042, 101 Antananarivo; tel. (20) 2235949; e-mail tnr .mrajaonarison@cma-cgm.com; internet www.cma-cgm.com; maritime transport; Chair. and CEO ANDRIAMASINJARA RAHERIMANDIMBY.

SCAC-SDV Shipping Madagascar: rue Rabearivelo Antsahavola, BP 514, 102 Antananarivo; tel. (20) 2220631; fax (20) 2247862; operates the harbour in Antananarivo Port.

Société Malgache des Transports Maritimes (SMTM): 6 rue Indira Gandhi, BP 4077, 101 Antananarivo; tel. (20) 2227342; fax (20) 2233327; f. 1963; 59% state-owned; privatization pending; services to Europe; Chair. ALEXIS RAZAFINDRATSIRA; Dir-Gen. JEAN RANJEVA.

Société du Port à Gestion Autonome de Toamasina (SPAT): blvd Ratsimilaho, Ampasimazava Est, Toamasina; e-mail spat@ port-toamasina.com; internet www.port-toamasina.com; Dir-Gen. CHRISTIAN AVELLIN.

CIVIL AVIATION

The Ivato international airport is at Antananarivo, while the airports at Mahajanga, Toamasina and Nosy-Bé can also accommodate large jet aircraft. There are 211 airfields, two-thirds of which are privately owned. In 1996 the Government authorized private French airlines to operate scheduled and charter flights between Madagascar and Western Europe.

Aeromarine: Zone Industrielle FORELLO, Tanjombato, BP 3844, 102 Antananarivo; tel. (20) 2248286; fax (20) 2258026; e-mail aeromarine@blueline.mg; internet www.aeromarine.mg; f. 1991; Dir-Gen. RIAZ BARDAY.

Air Madagascar: 31 ave de l'Indépendance, 101 Antananarivo; tel. (20) 202251000; fax (20) 2233760; e-mail groupe@airmadagascar .com; internet www.airmadagascar.com; f. 1962; internal services to principal towns; external services to the People's Republic of China, the Comoros, Kenya, Mauritius, Mayotte, Réunion, South Africa and Thailand; Dir-Gen. HAJA RAELISON.

Air Transport et Transit Régional (ATTR): tel. (32) 0518811; fax (32) 3205218; e-mail attr.reservation@blueline.mg; internet www .attrmada.com; f. 2006; private; regular local and regional services; services suspended in 2008; Dir-Gen. FRÉDÉRIC RABESAHALA.

Aviation Civile de Madagascar (ACM): 13 rue Fernand Kasanga, BP 4414, 101 Tsimbazaza-Antananarivo; tel. (20) 2222438; fax (20) 2224726; e-mail acm@acm.mg; internet www.acm.mg; f. 2000; Chair. RANTO RABARISOA; Dir-Gen. JAMES ANDRIANALISOA.

Transports et Travaux Aériens de Madagascar (TAM): 17 ave de l'Indépendance, Analakely, Antananarivo; tel. (20) 2222222; fax (20) 2224340; e-mail tamdg@wanadoo.mg; f. 1951; provides airline services; Administrators LALA RAZAFINDRAKOTO, FRANÇOIS DANE.

Tourism

Madagascar's attractions include unspoiled scenery, many unusual varieties of flora and fauna, and the rich cultural diversity of Malagasy life. In 2013 196,375 tourists visited Madagascar, the majority being from France (47.5%). Revenue from tourism totalled US $321m. in 2010.

Direction d'Appui aux Investissements Publiques: BP 610, rue Fernand Kasanga Tsimbazaza, 101 Antananarivo; tel. (20) 2262816; fax (20) 2235410; e-mail mintourdati@wanadoo.mg; internet www .tourisme.gov.mg.

Office National du Tourisme de Madagascar (ONTM): Lot IBG 29c, Antsahavola, 101 Antananarivo; tel. (20) 2266115; fax (20) 2266098; e-mail ontm@moov.mg; internet www .madagascar-tourisme.com; Pres. ERIC KOLLER.

Defence

As assessed at November 2014, Madagascar's total armed forces numbered 13,500 men: army 12,500, navy 500 and air force 500. There was also a paramilitary gendarmerie of 8,100.

Defence Expenditure: Budgeted at 207,000m. ariary for 2015.

Chief of Staff of the Armed Forces: Gen. BÉNI XAVIER RASOLOFONIRINA.

Education

Education is officially compulsory between six and 13 years of age. Madagascar has both public and private schools, although legislation enacted in 1978 envisaged the progressive elimination of private education. Primary education generally begins at the age of six and lasts for five years. Secondary education, beginning at 11 years of age, lasts for a further seven years, comprising a first cycle of four years and a second of three years. A new educational system, comprising 10 years of basic education and two years of secondary education, was intended for gradual introduction from the academic year 2008/09. However, the process of implementation was suspended in March 2009. According to UNESCO estimates, in 2006/07 primary enrolment included 98% of children in the relevant age-group (male 98%; females 99%), while in 2008/09 secondary enrolment included 26% of children in the relevant age-group (males 26%; females 25%). In 2011/12 90,300 students attended institutions providing tertiary education. In 2005/06 there were six universities and 14 private higher education institutes in Madagascar. In 2011 spending on education represented 20.1% of total budgetary expenditure.

MALAWI

Introductory Survey

LOCATION, CLIMATE, LANGUAGE, RELIGION, FLAG, CAPITAL

The Republic of Malawi is a landlocked country in southern central Africa, with Zambia to the west, Mozambique to the south and east, and Tanzania to the north. Lake Malawi forms most of the eastern boundary. The climate is tropical, but much of the country is sufficiently high above sea-level to modify the heat. Temperatures range from 14°C (57°F) to 18°C (64°F) in mountain areas, but can reach 38°C (100°F) in low-lying regions. There is a rainy season between November and April. The official language is English, although Chichewa is being promoted as the basis for a 'Malawi Language'. Chitumbuka, a national language, and Yao are also widely spoken. More than 82% of the population profess Christianity, while a further 13%, largely Asians, are Muslims. Most of the remaining Malawians follow traditional beliefs, although there is also a Hindu minority. The national flag (proportions 2 by 3) has three equal horizontal stripes, of black, red and green, with a rising sun, in red, in the centre of the black stripe. The capital is Lilongwe.

CONTEMPORARY POLITICAL HISTORY

Historical Context

Malawi was formerly the British protectorate of Nyasaland. In 1953 it was linked with two other British dependencies, Northern and Southern Rhodesia (now Zambia and Zimbabwe), to form the Federation of Rhodesia and Nyasaland. The Federation was dissolved in December 1963 and Nyasaland gained independence, as Malawi, on 6 July 1964. The country became a republic and a one-party state, with Dr Hastings Kamuzu Banda, the leader of the Malawi Congress Party (MCP), as its first President, on 6 July 1966. Malawi created a major controversy among African states in 1967 by officially recognizing the Republic of South Africa. In 1971 Banda, named Life President in that year, became the first African head of state to visit South Africa. In 1976, however, Malawi recognized the communist-backed Government in Angola in preference to the South African-supported forces. Malawi did not recognize the 'independence' granted by South Africa to four of its African 'homelands'.

Domestic Political Affairs

Until 1993 all Malawian citizens were obliged to be members of the MCP; no political opposition was tolerated, and only candidates who had been approved by Banda were allowed to contest elections to the National Assembly. Frequent reorganizations of the Cabinet effectively prevented the emergence of any political rival to Banda. However, it was reported in 1983 that a conflict had developed between Dick Matenje, the Minister without Portfolio in the Cabinet and Secretary-General of the MCP, and John Tembo, the Governor of the Reserve Bank of Malawi, concerning the eventual succession to Banda. In May the authorities reported that Matenje and three other senior politicians had died in a road accident; Malawian exiles claimed that the four men had been shot while attempting to flee the country.

Opposition to the Government intensified during 1992 and in September opposition activists formed the Alliance for Democracy (AFORD)—a pressure group operating within Malawi, under the chairmanship of Chakufwa Chihana, a prominent trade union leader—which aimed to campaign for democratic political reform. Another opposition grouping, the United Democratic Front (UDF), was formed in October. In that month Banda conceded that a referendum on the introduction of a multi-party system would take place. However, in November the Government banned AFORD. In the following month Chihana was found guilty of sedition and sentenced to two years' hard labour (reduced to nine months in March 1993).

At the referendum on the introduction of a multi-party system, held on 14 June 1993, 63.2% of those who participated (some 63.5% of the electorate) voted for an end to single-party rule. Banda agreed to the establishment of a National Executive Council to oversee the transition to a multi-party system and the holding of free elections, and of a National Consultative Council to implement the necessary amendments to the Constitution. Both councils were to include members of the Government and the opposition. Banda announced an amnesty for thousands of political exiles, and stated that a general election would be held, on a multi-party basis, within a year. The Constitution was amended to allow the registration of political parties other than the MCP and by August five organizations, including AFORD and the UDF, had been accorded official status.

In September 1993 Banda carried out an extensive cabinet reshuffle, relinquishing the post of Minister of External Affairs, which he had held since 1964. In October 1993 Banda underwent neurological surgery in South Africa. Interim executive power was assumed by a three-member Presidential Council, chaired by the new Secretary-General of the MCP, Gwandaguluwe Chakuamba. In November a further cabinet reorganization relieved Banda of all ministerial responsibilities. Later in November the National Assembly approved a Constitutional Amendment Bill, which, *inter alia*, abolished the institution of life presidency, ended the requirement that election candidates be members of the MCP and repealed the right of the President to nominate members of the legislature exclusively from the MCP.

Having made a rapid and unexpected recovery, Banda resumed full presidential powers in December 1993. Shortly afterwards, in response to increasing pressure from the opposition, the Government amended the Constitution to provide for the appointment of an acting President in the event of the incumbent being incapacitated. In February 1994 the National Assembly approved an increase in the number of elective seats in the legislature from 141 to 177.

On 16 May 1994 the National Assembly adopted a provisional Constitution, which provided for the appointment of a Constitutional Committee and of a human rights commission, and abolished the system of 'traditional' courts. Malawi's first multi-party parliamentary and presidential elections took place on 17 May. In the presidential election the Secretary-General of the UDF, (Elson) Bakili Muluzi (a former government minister and MCP Secretary-General), took 47.3% of the votes cast, defeating Banda (who won 33.6% of the votes). Eight parties contested the legislative elections: of these, the UDF won 85 seats in the National Assembly, the MCP 56 and AFORD 36. The Constitution was introduced for a one-year period on 18 May and was to be subject to further review prior to official ratification one year later.

The Muluzi presidency

President Muluzi and his Vice-President, Justin Malewezi, were inaugurated on 21 May 1994. The new UDF-dominated Government proclaimed an amnesty for the country's remaining political prisoners, and commuted all death sentences to terms of life imprisonment. In August it was announced that Banda, while remaining honorary Life President of the MCP, was to retire from active involvement in politics. Chakuamba, as Vice-President of the party, effectively became the leader of the MCP.

In September 1994 a number of AFORD members were appointed to the Government, including Chihana as Second Vice-President and Minister of Irrigation and Water Development. Meanwhile, the creation of the post of Second Vice-President had necessitated a constitutional amendment, and provoked severe criticism from the MCP. In March 1995 the National Assembly (in the absence of MCP deputies, who boycotted the vote) approved the retention of the second vice-presidency; the Assembly also endorsed recommendations for the establishment—although not before May 1999—of a second chamber of parliament. The Constitution took effect on 18 May 1995.

In June 1994 Muluzi established an independent commission of inquiry to investigate the deaths of Matenje and his associates in May 1983. In January 1995, in accordance with the findings of the commission, Banda was placed under house arrest and Tembo and two former police officers were detained; the four were charged with murder and conspiracy to murder. A former inspector-general of police was charged later in the month. In April Cecilia Kadzamira, Tembo's niece and the former President's 'Official Hostess', was also charged with conspiracy to murder. The case against Kadzamira was abandoned in December, owing to the lack of evidence, and later that month Banda, Tembo and the other defendants were found not guilty of conspiracy to murder and conspiracy to defeat justice. In January 1996 an MCP-owned newspaper printed a statement by Banda in which he admitted that he might unknowingly have been responsible for brutalities perpetrated under his regime and apologized to Malawians for 'pain and suffering' inflicted during his presidency. In November 1997 Banda died in South Africa, where he had been undergoing emergency medical treatment.

Meanwhile, it emerged in mid-1995 that President Muluzi had authorized the payment of some 6.2m. kwacha from the state poverty alleviation account to UDF deputies; there was also evidence of the involvement of government ministers in the smuggling of maize to neighbouring countries. In February 1996 Muluzi announced that an independent Anti-Corruption Bureau (ACB) was to be established to investigate allegations of corruption.

In June 1998 the National Assembly approved legislation providing for the introduction of a single-ballot electoral system to replace the existing multiple-ballot system and for a strengthening of the authority and independence of the Malawi Electoral Commission (MEC). In November legislation was adopted to allow presidential and parliamentary elections to run concurrently (as Muluzi's term was due to end several weeks earlier than that of the National Assembly). In February 1999 the National Assembly adopted a controversial report by the MEC that recommended the creation of a further 72 parliamentary seats, including an additional 42 in the Southern Region, a UDF stronghold. However, in response to widespread opposition to the proposals, the establishment of only 16 of the 72 seats was approved.

Presidential and legislative elections were held on 15 June 1999. Muluzi was re-elected to the presidency, securing 51.4% of the votes cast, while Chakuamba obtained 43.3%. At the elections to the expanded National Assembly the ruling UDF won 94 seats, while the MCP secured 66 seats, AFORD 29 and independent candidates four. In August the UDF regained a parliamentary majority when the four independent deputies decided to ally themselves with the UDF, of which they had previously been members.

Chakuamba, who had maintained a boycott of the new parliament pending the result of his party's challenge to the outcome of the elections, was suspended from the chamber in June 2000. Tembo assumed the leadership of the opposition and appointed his supporters to prominent posts within the MCP. Chakuamba was reinstated in September, and a dispute between the two factions ensued. In October the opposition's petitions against the election results were dismissed by the High Court.

Proposed legislation to change the Constitution to allow Muluzi to seek a third presidential term failed to gain the requisite two-thirds' majority in July 2002. A further attempt to introduce a constitutional amendment also failed in January 2003, when the bill was withdrawn. In March Muluzi declared that he would not seek a third presidential term, and proposed Dr Bingu wa Mutharika, recently appointed Minister of Economic Planning and Development, as his successor, to contest the presidential election scheduled for May 2004.

In May 2003 Tembo and Chakuamba were elected, respectively, as President and Vice-President of the MCP. Tembo was subsequently named as the MCP's candidate to contest the 2004 presidential election. Chakuamba resigned from the MCP and formed the Republican Party (RP). In January 2004 the RP and several other opposition parties announced the formation of the Mgwirizano Coalition to contest the forthcoming presidential election; Chakuamba was elected as the coalition's presidential candidate in February.

Mutharika elected President

At the presidential election held on 20 May 2004 Mutharika, representing the ruling UDF, secured 35.9% of the valid votes cast. Tembo and Chakuamba took 27.1% and 25.7% of the vote, respectively. Cassim Chilumpha, of the UDF, was elected as Vice-President. However, at concurrent elections to the National Assembly the MCP emerged as the largest party, winning 56 of the 193 seats in the legislature, while the UDF secured 49 seats and the Mgwirizano Coalition 25; 39 of the remaining seats were taken by independent candidates, while voting in six constituencies was not conducted owing to irregularities. International observers criticized the conduct of the polls and opposition parties disputed the results. Mutharika was sworn in as

President on 24 May, amid rioting by opposition supporters, and a new Cabinet was appointed in June. Mutharika, in defiance of critics who believed that he would merely serve to act as Muluzi's 'puppet', pledged to take measures to combat corruption and to effect wide-ranging economic reforms. In October former Minister of Finance Friday Jumbe was arrested in connection with illegal sales of maize during 2001–02 while he was General Manager of the Agriculture Development and Marketing Corporation; he was subsequently charged with four counts of corruption. Also in October 2004 it was announced that at least 10 former senior ministers were under investigation by the ACB following the disappearance of more than 10,000m. kwacha during the Muluzi presidency.

In February 2005 Mutharika resigned from the leadership of the UDF—of which Muluzi was Chairman—claiming that the party was opposing his campaign against corruption. Later that month Mutharika announced his intention to form a new political party, the Democratic Progressive Party (DPP), which was formally registered in March. In June the UDF introduced before the National Assembly a motion of impeachment against Mutharika, alleging statutory violations of the Constitution and misuse of public funds.

In October 2005 Muluzi was summoned to appear before the ACB, which was investigating the misappropriation of 1,400m. kwacha in foreign aid during his presidency. It was alleged that much of this money had been diverted to personal bank accounts and had also been used to finance the 2004 presidential campaign. Muluzi was able to obtain an injunction from the High Court, which allowed him to refuse to answer the ACB's questions. In November Vice-President Chilumpha was arrested in connection with the alleged embezzlement of 187m. kwacha during his tenure as Minister of Education. Chilumpha obtained an injunction against criminal proceedings on the grounds that, as the incumbent Vice-President, he was immune from prosecution.

Meanwhile, following an agreement between the UDF and Tembo, in October 2005 the National Assembly voted in favour of instigating proceedings to impeach Mutharika, and he was summoned to face indictment before the legislature later that month. However, the impeachment process was halted by the High Court after concern was expressed over the constitutionality of the process. In December regional leaders brokered talks between Mutharika, Muluzi and Tembo in an attempt to halt the impeachment proceedings; however, they ended without success. The impeachment motion was eventually withdrawn in January 2006.

In February 2006 it was announced that Mutharika had accepted Chilumpha's 'constructive resignation'. In a letter to Chilumpha, the President asserted that Chilumpha had abandoned his duties as Vice-President, leading the Cabinet to conclude that he had resigned. Chilumpha refuted the allegations made against him—*inter alia*, that he had attended only 16 out of 48 cabinet meetings and had left the country without informing Mutharika—and brought the matter before the High Court on the grounds that his dismissal was unconstitutional: as an elected minister he could only be dismissed by Parliament, not by the President. In March the High Court apparently ordered Chilumpha's full restitution; however, the Supreme Court ruled later that month that, although Chilumpha was confirmed in his position as Vice-President, the Government was permitted to divest him of all benefits and entitlements. In April Chilumpha was arrested and charged with treason and conspiring to murder the President. His trial commenced in early 2007, but was subject to numerous delays.

In April 2008 Muluzi was named as the UDF's candidate for the forthcoming presidential election; having previously served two terms in office, opponents objected to his candidacy. However, Muluzi's supporters maintained that the Constitution stipulated only that a President may not serve more than two 'consecutive' terms. In March 2009 the MEC ruled that Muluzi was ineligible to contest the election on the grounds that he had already served as President for the maximum period of two five-year terms. Muluzi appealed against the decision, but in May the Constitutional Court rejected his challenge. He subsequently declared his support for Tembo, who had been selected as the presidential candidate for the newly formed UDF-MCP-New Republican Party electoral alliance.

Meanwhile, reports emerged in May 2008 that eight high-ranking security officials, including former Commander-in-Chief of the Armed Forces Lt-Gen. Joseph Chimbayo, had been arrested following accusations by Mutharika that they had been acting under instruction from Muluzi in an attempt to remove him from office. Muluzi denied the allegations and was later released without charge. In February 2009 Muluzi was again detained on charges of corruption relating to the misappropriation of donor funds during his presidency. His trial commenced in March 2011, but proceedings were repeatedly adjourned.

Mutharika's second term

Mutharika won an overwhelming victory in the presidential election, held on 19 May 2009, with 64.4% of the votes cast, while the DPP retained control of the National Assembly in the concurrent legislative poll. The DPP won 112 of the 192 available seats (voting in one constituency was postponed owing to the death of a candidate), the MCP took only 27 seats and the UDF, the influence of which was predominantly limited to the south of the country, 18 seats. A further 32 seats were secured by independent candidates, many of whom had connections to the DPP. Tembo, who had secured 29.9% of the votes in the presidential election, claimed that there was evidence of electoral fraud; however, the MEC declared the ballot to have been free and fair. In June President Mutharika announced the formation of a new Government, which included a number of new appointments to key roles. Arthur Peter Mutharika, the President's brother, became Minister of Justice and Constitutional Affairs, amid widespread reports that he was being prepared to take over the presidency in 2014. In December 2009 Muluzi stepped down as Chairman of the UDF; he was replaced as party leader on an interim basis by Friday Jumbe, who assumed the position of President of the UDF.

In August 2010 Mutharika effected a cabinet reorganization. The ministers responsible for health, transport, local government and gender were all dismissed, while Peter Mutharika was appointed as Minister of Education, Science and Technology. Furthermore, the President controversially allocated his wife, Callista wa Mutharika, responsibility for maternal, infant and child health, although it was later clarified that she would not be a cabinet member. There was speculation that the Minister of Local Government and Rural Development, Goodall Gondwe, had been replaced because of the repeated postponement of the local elections—last held in 2000 and due since 2005—ostensibly owing to procedural delays and a lack of progress in the implementation of local government reforms. (The local elections were subsequently rescheduled for April 2011.) However, a number of reports in the media claimed that the dismissals had been prompted by a dispute within the DPP over who would become the party's presidential candidate in the 2014 election in place of Mutharika, who was constitutionally prohibited from standing for a third term of office. The President favoured Peter Mutharika and had been manoeuvring against Vice-President Joyce Banda, who was viewed as a potential rival candidate. The dismissed ministers had reportedly criticized the President's efforts to remove Banda from the ruling party.

Amid rising factionalism within the DPP, in September 2010 the party terminated official ties with its youth wing, the allegedly pro-Banda Progressive Democratic Youth Movement, which subsequently denounced the DPP's 'undemocratic endorsement' of Peter Mutharika's candidature. Meanwhile, in a further attempt to marginalize Banda, President Mutharika had transferred some of the Vice-President's responsibilities to his wife. In December the DPP finally expelled Banda, accusing her of involvement in 'anti-party activities' and of 'forming parallel structures in the party and Government'. Despite reported death threats against her, in early 2011 Banda announced the creation of a new political organization, the People's Party (PP), which was officially registered in July.

In January 2011, in a move allegedly orchestrated by Muluzi, the UDF's National Executive Committee elected Dr George Nga Ntafu as party Chairman; however, Jumbe denounced the Committee's action as a 'failed *coup d'état*' and refused to cede control of the leadership of the UDF to Ntafu, effectively splitting the party into two factions. In the following month Jumbe's faction held a separate leadership vote, electing Chilumpha as Chairman and Jumbe as President (the latter being a position not recognized under the UDF's charter). In September, in an attempt to resolve the impasse, both factions agreed to hold another leadership contest. At the election, which was held in October 2012, Atupele Muluzi (the son of the former President) was selected as the new UDF leader. Jumbe established a new party, the Labour Party, in the following month.

In May 2011 the MEC announced that long-delayed local elections would again be postponed, until 2014. On 19 July 2011, in an apparent attempt to intimidate potential demonstrators, the High Court ruled that anti-Government protests scheduled to take place on the following day would be considered illegal, despite the fact that armed DPP activists had been able to stage a rally of their own earlier that day. Nevertheless, on 20–21 July, in the most serious challenge to the authority of the Mutharika administration since the President took office, large-scale demonstrations, orchestrated by civil society organizations, were held throughout the country to protest against the Government's economic policies, shortages of fuel, power and foreign exchange, and the President's increasingly dictatorial tendencies. The violent suppression of the protests by the security forces resulted in the deaths of 19 demonstrators and up to 500 arrests, and attracted domestic and international censure. Discussions, under UN auspices, were held in August between government representatives and protest organizers, although the talks foundered in the following month after the latter suspended their participation due to further violent attacks against their supporters.

Shortly after the demonstrations, Mutharika replaced several senior military officials, including the Commander of the Malawi Defence Force. In September 2011 the President announced the formation of a new Cabinet, after having dissolved the incumbent body the previous month. Most notably, Ken Lipenga was appointed as Minister of Finance and Development Planning, Peter Mutharika became the new Minister of Foreign Affairs and International Co-operation, and Callista wa Mutharika assumed ministerial rank on being given responsibility for combating HIV/AIDS, malnutrition, malaria and tuberculosis. In an apparent violation of the Constitution, President Mutharika refused to name Vice-President Banda, an outspoken critic of the violence employed by the security forces, in his new Cabinet and accused her of colluding with the demonstrators. Also in September, Mutharika commenced legal proceedings at the High Court to determine if Banda had 'constructively' resigned the vice-presidency by assuming the leadership of the opposition PP and failing to attend cabinet meetings. Banda's office had been further weakened in mid-2011 by a 60% reduction in its funding and by the removal of more of its responsibilities.

A number of contentious laws were under review in late 2011, including regulations concerning homosexuality, restrictions on legal challenges against the Government and legislation approved in January that granted the authorities the power to close down newspapers publishing content regarded as being 'contrary to the public interest'. Western donor nations and international organizations had cited these laws and other governance concerns as factors that had led to the suspension or reduction of aid inflows to Malawi during 2011.

Banda assumes power

On 7 April 2012 the death of President Mutharika was officially announced. The President was reported to have died on 5 April after suffering a heart attack in South Africa, where he had been receiving medical attention. In accordance with the country's Constitution, Vice-President Banda was sworn in as Head of State on 7 April and was to serve the remainder of Mutharika's term, which was scheduled to expire in 2014. On 10 April 2012 Banda dismissed the Minister of Information and Civic Education, Patricia Kaliati, and Chief of Police Peter Mukhito. Banda also removed the Governor of the central bank, appointing Charles Chuka to that position. On 26 April Banda announced the formation of a new Government, taking personal responsibility for, *inter alia*, the public service, disaster management and HIV/AIDS. Lipenga was retained as Minister of Finance, one of several government veterans to keep their posts; however, Ephraim Mganda Chiume replaced Peter Mutharika at the foreign affairs ministry, while a number of DPP members who had been dismissed from the party following the disturbances in mid-2011 were awarded posts in the new administration. Most notable among these were Khumbo Kachale, who was named Vice-President and Minister of Health, and Ralph Kasambara who was appointed as Minister of Justice and Attorney-General. Callista wa Mutharika was stripped of her official duties in early May 2012. The new Government pledged to respect human rights, and acted promptly to introduce economic reforms and to normalize relations with the country's major donors. Banda also announced her intention to sell the presidential jet, which Mutharika had controversially purchased at a cost of US $22m. (The aircraft was sold for $15m. in mid-2013.) The change in leadership precipitated mass defections from the DPP and the UDF to the PP, giving Banda's party a majority in the National Assembly.

Banda effected minor cabinet reorganizations in December 2012, July 2013 and January 2014. Anti-Government demonstrations were staged in January 2013 in protest against economic austerity measures and rising inflation. In a further setback for the President, the PP lost its legislative majority in early 2013 due to ongoing political realignments within the National Assembly.

Meanwhile, a commission was established in May 2012 to investigate rumours that Peter Mutharika and his allies had attempted to orchestrate a coup in the immediate aftermath of President Mutharika's death. The commission published its findings in March 2013, and later that month 11 high-ranking members of the late President's administration, including Peter Mutharika and Kaliati, were arrested on treason charges, while a 12th was indicted *in absentia*. It was also confirmed in the commission's report that Mutharika had died on 5 April 2012 in an ambulance en route to hospital in Lilongwe, but that his personal physician had attempted to conceal the death by requesting that an air ambulance evacuate Mutharika to South Africa while his body was connected to medical equipment, thus creating the impression that he was still alive. Gondwe, who was also implicated in conspiring to prevent Banda's accession, resigned from his position as Minister of Economic Planning and Development and was replaced by Ralph Pachalo Jooma. Notwithstanding the charges against him, Peter Mutharika was elected as DPP President in April 2013. Mutharika and his co-accused formally declared their innocence in November.

Paul Mphwiyo, an official within the Ministry of Finance who had been tasked with combating high-level corruption, was shot in September 2013 in an apparent assassination attempt. A major fraud scheme, involving the large-scale misappropriation of public funds, was discovered shortly thereafter. The Government was placed under intense international scrutiny in the wake of the 'Cashgate' scandal, and concerned donors once again suspended financial support. Banda ordered a full investigation and pledged to redouble her anti-corruption efforts, and on 10 October she also took the dramatic step of dismissing the entire Cabinet. The new Government, announced five days later, was largely unchanged from the outgoing administration, but notably included Maxwell Mkwezalamba as Minister of Finance and Fahad Assani as Minister of Justice and Constitutional Affairs, while a portfolio for good governance was also created. Assani's predecessor, Ralph Kasambara, was detained by the police in November after being implicated in the attack on Mphwiyo; he was charged with attempted murder later that month. The results of an independent audit into the 'Cashgate' affair were published in February 2014, revealing that some US $30m. of public funds had been misappropriated during Banda's presidency. The audit report caused widespread outrage and prompted demonstrations in Blantyre. Legal proceedings against those charged with involvement in the fraud scandal (predominantly lower-ranking public servants) had commenced in January, and two of the accused were convicted and imprisoned during the second half of 2014. In November one of the prime suspects in the case, former PP financier Oswald Lutepo, claimed that Banda herself had received illegal payments—an allegation that she vehemently repudiated.

Recent developments: the 2014 elections

Presidential, legislative and local elections were held concurrently on 20 May 2014. The polls were affected by serious logistical problems and outbreaks of violence, however, and voting was extended for a further two days in certain areas. With the early tallies indicating that Banda had lost the presidential contest to the DPP's Peter Mutharika, on 24 May the President, highlighting various alleged irregularities, publicly denounced the elections as fraudulent and declared that the results would be annulled and new polls conducted within 90 days. Banda's announcement precipitated violent demonstrations by DPP activists in Limbe, while MEC Chairman Maxon Mbendela questioned the legality of the President's move, arguing that she had overextended her authority. Later on 24 May, the High Court, responding to appeals from the MEC and the DPP, ruled that Banda's intervention had been unconstitutional and that the vote-tallying process should continue. Although the MEC acknowledged the existence of some electoral irregularities, it claimed that the overall integrity of the polls had not been compromised. Monitors from the Southern African Development Community (SADC) also endorsed the elections. A demonstrator lost his life on 30 May during clashes with the security forces at a gathering in Mangochi, which had been organized by PP and MCP supporters to protest against the polling anomalies and to demand a recount of the votes. Nevertheless, later that day the High Court dismissed a petition for a recount and the MEC promulgated the final election results.

In the presidential poll, Mutharika garnered 36.4% of the votes cast, MCP leader Lazarus Chakwera secured 27.8%, Banda, representing the PP, won 20.2% and UDF President Atupele Muluzi attracted 13.7%. The DPP gained control of 50 seats in the National Assembly, compared with 48 for the MCP, 26 for the PP, 14 for the UDF, and one each for AFORD and Chipani Cha Pfuko; independents won 52 seats. (The ballot for the remaining seat was suspended following the death of a candidate; the DPP subsequently won control of the constituency in a by-election.) Of the 457 local council seats contested, the DPP secured 165, the MCP 131, the PP 65, the UDF 57, independents 35 and smaller parties the remaining four. The rate of participation by the electorate was approximately 70%. Mutharika was sworn in as head of state on 31 May 2014, and a new Cabinet was installed in June. Saulos Klaus Chilima became Vice-President, Gondwe was named as Minister of Finance and Economic Development, Paul Chibingu received the home affairs portfolio, and George Chaponda was appointed as Minister of Foreign Affairs and International Co-operation. Mutharika assumed responsibility for defence, while Atupele Muluzi also joined the Cabinet as the minister responsible for natural resources, energy and mining. Mutharika was afforded immunity from prosecution upon his ascension to the presidency, and the treason charges against him were thus withdrawn on 2 June. (Legal action against his co-defendants was also suspended.)

In April 2015 Mutharika effected a minor reorganization of the Cabinet. Most notably, Atupele Muluzi was appointed Minister of Home Affairs and Internal Security, while Bright Msaka assumed Muluzi's vacated natural resources, energy and mining portfolio.

Foreign Affairs

Regional relations

Relations with Mozambique were frequently strained during the early and mid-1980s by the widely held belief that the Hastings Banda regime was supporting the Resistência Nacional Moçambicana (Renamo—see Mozambique). Following the death of President Samora Machel of Mozambique in an air crash in South Africa in October 1986, the South African Government claimed that documents discovered in the wreckage revealed a plot by Mozambique and Zimbabwe to overthrow the Banda Government. Angry protests from Malawi were answered by denials of the accusations from the Mozambican and Zimbabwean Governments. In December, however, Malawi and Mozambique signed an agreement on defence and security matters, which was believed to include co-operation in eliminating Renamo operations. In July 1988, during an official visit to Malawi, President Joachim Chissano of Mozambique stated that he did not believe Malawi to be supporting Renamo. In December of that year Malawi, Mozambique and the office of the UN High Commissioner for Refugees (UNHCR) signed an agreement to promote the voluntary repatriation of an estimated 650,000 Mozambican refugees who had fled into Malawi during the previous two years. However, by mid-1992 the number of Mozambican refugees in Malawi had reportedly reached 1m. Large numbers of refugees returned to Mozambique in 1993–94, but in May 1995 Malawi demanded the repatriation of the remainder—estimated to total some 39,000—stating that food aid and other assistance to those who failed to leave would be reduced. The programme of the Malawi-Mozambique-UNHCR commission officially ended in November: it was estimated that a total of 1m. refugees had been repatriated.

Malawi and Tanzania held discussions in August 2012 in an attempt to resolve a long-standing disagreement regarding their mutual border in the Lake Malawi region, which was believed to hold significant hydrocarbon reserves. However, Malawi withdrew from the talks in October due to concerns over the production of an official Tanzanian map displaying a revised border, as well as the purported harassment by Tanzania of Malawian fishing vessels operating in the disputed area. Dialogue recommenced in November, but the negotiations soon foundered, prompting both parties to request SADC mediation. Discussions resumed in May 2013 under the auspices of SADC, but little substantive progress towards a resolution had been made by early 2015.

Other external relations

Until early 2008 Malawi was one of a small number of nations that accorded Taiwan recognition as an independent country. In January of that year, however, it was announced that Malawi had withdrawn its support for Taiwan and established diplomatic relations with the People's Republic of China.

The British High Commissioner, Fergus Cochrane-Dyet, was expelled from Malawi in April 2011 owing to his censure of President Mutharika's authoritarian leadership style in a confidential diplomatic cable that had been released by the WikiLeaks organization. In response, the British Government ejected the Malawian High Commissioner from the United Kingdom later that month and suspended aid to Malawi in July, placing the Malawian Government's finances under severe pressure. The UK, along with other Western nations, had become increasingly critical of the Mutharika administration, expressing disapproval of government corruption, restrictions on press freedom and discriminatory laws against homosexuals. The violent suppression of anti-Government protests by the Malawian security forces in July prompted further condemnation from Western powers, and the USA also suspended financial assistance to the country. Although the British High Commissioner was invited to return to Malawi in October, the UK (Malawi's primary source of aid) refused to resume budgetary support due to ongoing concerns over governance and human rights violations. Citing similar considerations, Germany, the European Union, the World Bank and the IMF also withheld funding to Malawi during 2011. In April 2012, however, following Joyce Banda's accession to the presidency, the British Government announced that relations with Malawi would be normalized, and the new High Commissioner commenced his duties in September. Moreover, in mid-2012 Malawi's major bilateral and multilateral development partners confirmed that financial assistance to the country would be restored.

Meanwhile, relations between Malawi and the West deteriorated in October 2011, when Lt-Gen. Omar Hassan Ahmad al-Bashir, the President of Sudan and an alleged war criminal wanted by the International Criminal Court (ICC), attended a regional trade meeting in Lilongwe. Malawi was accused of violating its international obligations, since, as a signatory to the Rome Statute of the ICC, the country had been legally required to arrest al-Bashir and transfer him to ICC custody. Mutharika claimed that, in his capacity as the incumbent President of a non-signatory state, al-Bashir was immune from prosecution. The ICC rejected this argument and in December requested that the UN Security Council investigate the matter, prompting Malawi to threaten to withdraw from the ICC. However, upon Banda's assumption of the presidency, the Malawian Government altered its stance on this matter. Malawi was due to host an African Union (AU) summit meeting in July 2012, and, with the Banda administration eager to repair relations with the international community, it was made clear that al-Bashir's presence would be unacceptable. Although the AU insisted that al-Bashir be permitted to attend, Malawi refused to modify its position, and it was subsequently agreed that the meeting would be relocated to Ethiopia.

CONSTITUTION AND GOVERNMENT

Under the provisions of the Constitution promulgated on 18 May 1995, the Head of State is the President, who is elected by universal adult suffrage, in the context of a multi-party political system, for a term of five years. Executive power is vested in the President, and legislative power in the National Assembly, which has 193 elective seats. Members of the Assembly are elected for five years, by universal adult suffrage, in the context of a multi-party system. Cabinet ministers are appointed by the President. The country is divided into three administrative regions (Northern, Central and Southern), subdivided into 28 districts.

REGIONAL AND INTERNATIONAL CO-OPERATION

Malawi is a member of the African Union (AU, see p. 188), the Southern African Development Community (SADC, see p. 420) and the Common Market for Eastern and Southern Africa (COMESA, see p. 232). Nine members of COMESA, including Malawi, became inaugural members of the COMESA Free Trade Area in October 2000.

Malawi became a member of the UN in 1964 and was admitted to the World Trade Organization (WTO, see p. 431) in 1995. The country also belongs to the International Tobacco Growers' Association (see p. 443).

ECONOMIC AFFAIRS

In 2013, according to estimates by the World Bank, Malawi's gross national income (GNI), measured at average 2011–13 prices, was US $4,419m., equivalent to $270 per head (or $750 per head on an international purchasing-power parity basis). During 2004–13, it was estimated, the population increased at an average annual rate of 3.0%, while gross domestic product (GDP) per head grew, in real terms, by an average of 2.4% per year. Overall GDP increased, in real terms, at an average annual rate of 5.5% in 2004–13; real GDP rose by 5.0% in 2013.

Agriculture (including forestry and fishing) contributed 27.0% of GDP in 2013, according to the World Bank, and engaged an estimated 76.7% of the labour force at mid-2015, according to FAO. The principal cash crops are tobacco (which accounted for 46.6% of total export earnings in 2013), tea and sugar cane. The principal food crops are cassava, maize, potatoes, bananas and plantains. Periods of severe drought and flooding have necessitated imports of basic foods in recent years. During 2004–13, according to the World Bank, agricultural GDP increased at an average annual rate of 3.3%; it declined by 2.8% in 2012, but grew by 5.4% in 2013.

Industry (including manufacturing, mining, construction and power) contributed 18.8% of GDP in 2013, according to the World Bank, and engaged 4.5% of the employed labour force in 1998. During 2004–13 industrial GDP increased by an average of 7.8% per year. Industrial GDP rose by 6.5% in 2013.

Mining and quarrying contributed 1.2% of GDP in 2010, according to the African Development Bank (AfDB), and engaged less than 0.1% of the employed labour force in 1998. Limestone, coal and gemstones are mined, and there are plans to develop deposits of bauxite, high-calcium marble and graphite. There are also reserves of phosphates, uranium, glass sands, asbestos and vermiculite. Environmental and financial concerns have delayed plans to exploit an estimated 30m. metric tons of bauxite deposits at Mount Mulanje. Uranium mining, which commenced at Kayelekera, in northern Malawi, in 2009, was expected to increase the country's export revenue by some 25%. The GDP of the mining sector expanded at an average annual rate of 4.7% in 2010–13, according to official figures; mining GDP grew by 7.6% in 2013.

Manufacturing contributed 10.7% of GDP in 2013, according to the World Bank, and engaged 2.7% of the employed labour force in 1998. During 2004–13 manufacturing GDP increased by an average of 5.9% per year. The GDP of the sector declined by 6.4% in 2012, but grew by 6.2% in 2013, according to the World Bank.

Construction contributed 3.2% of GDP in 2010, according to the AfDB, and engaged 1.6% of the employed labour force in 1998. The GDP of the construction sector increased at an average annual rate of 2.8% in 2010–13, according to official figures; construction GDP rose by 5.5% in 2013.

Production of electrical energy is by hydroelectric (principally) and thermal installations. Some 95% of energy for domestic use is derived from hydroelectric power. In 2000 a hydroelectric power plant, with a generation capacity of 64 MW, was opened at Kapichira. The completion of the Kapichira Hydroelectric Power Phase II Project in January 2014 doubled the capacity of the plant and increased the total generation capacity of Malawi's hydroelectric power plants to 352 MW (against a forecast peak national demand of 350 MW). Meanwhile, in April 2013 an agreement was signed by Malawi and Mozambique to connect Malawi's electricity system to Mozambique's Cahora Bassa hydroelectric power plant, which would increase Malawi's power supply by some 200 MW. Investment in alternative sources of energy, such as solar power, the production of gel fuel from ethanol and coal-mining, was also being encouraged, with the construction of a 300-MW coal-fired plant under consideration. Imports of mineral fuels and lubricants comprised 17.9% of the value of total imports in 2013.

According to the World Bank, the services sector contributed 54.2% of GDP in 2013 and engaged 11.0% of the employed labour force in 1998. The GDP of the services sector increased by an average of 7.5% per year in 2004–13. Services GDP grew by 4.3% in 2013.

According to preliminary figures, Malawi recorded a visible merchandise trade deficit of 239,977.2m. kwacha in 2012, and there was a deficit of 190,031.7m. kwacha on the current account of the balance of payments. In 2013 the principal source of imports was South Africa (providing 21.7% of the total); Mozambique, the People's Republic of China, India and the United Arab Emirates were also notable suppliers. Canada was the principal market for exports (accounting for 11.5% of the total) in that year; other important markets were Belgium, South Africa, the USA, the UK and the People's Republic of China. The principal imports in 2013 were chemicals and related products, mineral products, machinery and mechanical appliances and electrical equipment, iron and steel, other base metals and articles of base metals, vehicles, aircraft, vessels and associated transport equipment, and plastic materials. The principal exports in that year were tobacco, vegetables and vegetable products, ores, slag and ash (mainly uranium or thorium ores and concentrates), and sugars and sugar confectionery.

Programmed figures indicated that in the financial year ending 30 June 2014 Malawi's overall budget deficit was an estimated 66,000m. kwacha. Malawi's general government gross debt was 880,436m. kwacha in 2013, equivalent to 72.9% of GDP. The country's external debt in 2012 totalled US $1,314m., of which $1,023m. was public and publicly guaranteed debt. In 2012 the cost of servicing long-term public and publicly guaranteed debt and repayments to the IMF was equivalent to 2.0% of the value of exports of goods, services and income (excluding workers' remittances). The annual rate of inflation averaged 11.1% in 2004–13, according to ILO figures. Consumer prices increased by an average of 23.8% in 2014, according to official sources. Some 1.4m. people were unemployed in 2007.

Malawi's natural impediments to growth include its landlocked position, the vulnerability of the dominant agricultural sector to drought, and a high rate of population growth. Amid concern regarding the country's susceptibility to the effects of the global financial crisis, in January 2009 the IMF approved a one-year loan of US $77.1m., while in February 2010 the Fund authorized a three-year arrangement under its Extended Credit Facility (ECF), worth $79.4m. However, Malawi's relations with Western donor nations deteriorated in mid-2011, resulting in the withdrawal of vital budgetary support by the UK and the USA. Moreover, the IMF suspended the ECF in June due to the Government's lack of progress in implementing agreed economic reforms. In accordance with the ECF's stipulations, the Government devalued the kwacha by 10% in August, but the IMF declared that this was insufficient and that the exchange rate remained imbalanced, deterring vital investment. The new administration of President Joyce Banda, which took office in April 2012, prioritized the re-establishment of ties with Malawi's traditional international partners. In July the IMF authorized a new three-year ECF arrangement, valued at $156.2m., and additional financial support was provided by the World Bank and the AfDB. British and US funding was also resumed during mid-2012. In May the kwacha was further devalued by around 50% and foreign exchange controls were removed, although a side effect of these measures was a sharp upturn in inflation. Although real GDP rose by just 1.9% in 2012 due to a slowdown in agricultural and manufacturing activity, a recovery in these sectors in 2013 contributed to growth of 5.2% in that year. However, evidence of widespread public sector corruption was uncovered in late 2013, prompting Malawi's development partners to suspend financial assistance once again. The Government introduced austerity measures to offset the impact of this loss of funding and initiated an investigation into the fraud allegations in an effort to reassure its international allies. An increase in agricultural activity supported real GDP growth of 5.7% in 2014, while the inflation rate, which had reached 28.3% in 2013, moderated to 19.6%. However, the economy, particularly the agricultural sector, was negatively affected in early 2015 by severe flooding, which left at least 176 people dead and hundreds of thousands displaced. It consequently seemed unlikely that the IMF's 2015 growth projection of 6.0% would be realized.

PUBLIC HOLIDAYS

2016: 1 January (New Year's Day), 15 January (John Chilembwe Day), 3 March (Martyrs' Day), 25–28 April (Easter), 1 May (Labour Day), 14 May (President Kamuzu Banda's Birthday), 14 June (Freedom Day), 6 July (Republic Day and Id al-Fitr, end of Ramadan*), 13 October (Mothers' Day), 25–26 December (Christmas).

* This holiday is determined by the Islamic lunar calendar and may vary by one or two days from the date given.

Statistical Survey

Sources (unless otherwise indicated): National Statistical Office of Malawi, POB 333, Zomba; tel. 1524377; fax 1525130; e-mail enquiries@statistics.gov.mw; internet www.nsomalawi.mw; Reserve Bank of Malawi, POB 30063, Capital City, Lilongwe 3; tel. 1770600; fax 1772752; e-mail webmaster@rbm.mw; internet www.rbm.mw.

Area and Population

AREA, POPULATION AND DENSITY

Area (sq km)	
Land	94,276
Inland water	24,208
Total	118,484*
Population (census results)	
1–21 September 1998	9,933,868
8–28 June 2008	
Males	6,358,933
Females	6,718,227
Total	13,077,160
Population (official projections at mid-year)	
2013	15,316,860
2014	15,805,239
2015	16,310,431
Density (per sq km) at mid-2015	173.0†

* 45,747 sq miles.
† Land area only.

POPULATION BY AGE AND SEX
(official projections at mid-2015)

	Males	Females	Total
0–14 years	3,787,365	3,772,706	7,560,071
15–64 years	3,991,925	4,251,304	8,243,229
65 years and over	227,425	279,706	507,131
Total	8,006,715	8,303,716	16,310,431

REGIONS
(population projections at mid-2015)

Region	Area (sq km)*	Population ('000)	Density (per sq km)	Regional capital
Southern . .	31,753	7,082.8	223.1	Blantyre
Central . .	35,592	7,065.8	198.5	Lilongwe
Northern . .	26,931	2,161.8	80.3	Mzuzu
Total . . .	94,276	16,310.4	173.0	

* Excluding inland waters, totalling 24,208 sq km.

PRINCIPAL TOWNS
(population at census of June 2008)

Lilongwe (capital) .	674,448	Karonga	40,334
Blantyre . . .	661,256	Kasungu . . .	39,640
Mzuzu . . .	133,968	Mangochi . . .	39,575
Zomba	88,314	Salima	27,852

Mid-2014 (official population projection): Lilongwe 978,780.

BIRTHS AND DEATHS
(annual averages, UN estimates)

	2000–05	2005–10	2010–15
Birth rate (per 1,000)	43.4	41.8	39.9
Death rate (per 1,000)	16.6	13.5	11.5

Source: UN, *World Population Prospects: The 2012 Revision.*

2008 (official estimates): Live births 609,487 (birth rate 46.5 per 1,000); deaths 195,014 (death rate 14.9 per 1,000).

Life expectancy (years at birth): 54.7 (males 54.6; females 54.8) in 2012 (Source: World Bank, World Development Indicators database).

ECONOMICALLY ACTIVE POPULATION
('000, FAO estimates at mid-year)

	2013	2014	2015
Agriculture, etc.	5,375	5,527	5,685
Total labour force (incl. others) .	5,375	7,163	7,412

Source: FAO.

Health and Welfare

KEY INDICATORS

Total fertility rate (children per woman, 2012)	5.5
Under-5 mortality rate (per 1,000 live births, 2012) . . .	71
HIV/AIDS (% of persons aged 15–49, 2013)	10.3
Physicians (per 1,000 head, 2009)	0.02
Hospital beds (per 1,000 head, 2011)	1.3
Health expenditure (2011): US $ per head (PPP)	74
Health expenditure (2011): % of GDP	8.3
Health expenditure (2011): public (% of total)	72.4
Access to water (% of persons, 2012)	85
Access to sanitation (% of persons, 2012)	10
Total carbon dioxide emissions ('000 metric tons, 2010) . .	1,239.4
Carbon dioxide emissions per head (metric tons, 2010) . .	0.1
Human Development Index (2013): ranking	174
Human Development Index (2013): value	0.414

For sources and definitions, see explanatory note on p. vi.

Agriculture

PRINCIPAL CROPS
('000 metric tons)

	2011	2012	2013
Rice, paddy	117.7	111.0	125.2
Maize	3,699.1	3,618.7	3,639.9
Millet	32.9	34.5	39.3
Sorghum	73.3	66.5	86.2
Potatoes	3,613.3	4,152.2	4,536.0
Cassava (Manioc)	4,259.3	4,692.2	4,813.7
Beans, dry	176.8	185.6	189.4
Chickpeas*	75.0	67.0	67.0
Cow peas, dry	31.9	30.7	36.1
Pigeon peas	195.5	237.2	288.0
Groundnuts, with shell . . .	325.2	268.1	380.8

—continued	2011	2012	2013
Cabbages and other brassicas* .	77.0	78.5	82.3
Tomatoes*	39.2	40.5	41.6
Onions, dry*	49.0	51.5	51.7
Guavas, mangoes and			
mangosteens*	112.0	115.0	122.6
Bananas*	357.7	380.0	386.3
Plantains*	351.2	360.0	372.7
Sugar cane*	2,500	2,800	2,900
Coffee, green	4.0	5.7	5.7
Tea*	52.0	53.5	54.0
Tobacco, unmanufactured . . .	174.9	72.6	132.8

* FAO estimate(s).

Aggregate production ('000 metric tons, may include official, semi-official or estimated data): Total cereals 3,925.0 in 2011, 3,832.7 in 2012, 3,892.3 in 2013; Total roots and tubers 7,872.9 in 2011, 8,844.7 in 2012, 9,350.0 in 2013; Total vegetables (incl. melons) 378.8 in 2011, 388.2 in 2012, 396.6 in 2013; Total fruits (excl. melons) 1,053.7 in 2011, 1,089.2 in 2012, 1,115.9 in 2013.

Source: FAO.

LIVESTOCK
('000 head, year ending September)

	2011	2012	2013
Cattle	1,111	1,164	1,242
Pigs	2,161	2,493	2,754
Sheep	229	240	256
Goats	4,443	4,930	4,930
Chickens*	16,500	17,000	17,200

* FAO estimates.

Source: FAO.

LIVESTOCK PRODUCTS
('000 metric tons)

	2011	2012	2013
Cattle meat	34.1	35.7	38.4
Goat meat	27.8	29.8	32.4
Pig meat	44.2	62.0	89.0
Chicken meat*	22.4	22.6	22.8
Cows' milk	50.4	58.6	109.1
Hen eggs*	21.1	21.5	23.0

* FAO estimates.

Source: FAO.

Forestry

ROUNDWOOD REMOVALS
('000 cu m, excluding bark, FAO estimates)

	2011	2012	2013
Sawlogs, veneer logs and logs for			
sleepers	200	200	200
Other industrial wood	1,200	1,200	1,200
Fuel wood	5,466	5,528	5,593
Total	6,866	6,928	6,993

Source: FAO.

SAWNWOOD PRODUCTION
('000 cu m, including railway sleepers, FAO estimates)

	2011	2012	2013
Coniferous (softwood)	30	30	30
Broadleaved (hardwood) . . .	15	15	15
Total	45	45	45

Note: Annual production assumed to be unchanged from 1993.

Source: FAO.

Fishing

('000 metric tons, live weight)

	2010	2011	2012
Capture	98.3	82.4	120.3
Cyprinids	64.1	43.3	87.0
Tilapias	6.9	10.9	6.5
Cichlids	14.3	11.5	9.0
Torpedo-shaped catfishes	1.4	7.3	3.1
Other freshwater fishes	11.5	9.4	14.7
Aquaculture	2.6	2.8	3.2
Total catch	100.9	85.2	123.6

Note: Figures exclude aquatic mammals, recorded by number rather than weight. The number of Nile crocodiles caught was: 3,250 in 2010; 3,600 in 2011; 2,700 in 2012.

Source: FAO.

Mining

('000 metric tons unless otherwise indicated)

	2010	2011	2012
Bituminous coal	65.0	72.3	91.9
Lime	45.9	93.5	95.5
Gemstones (kg)	190,340	215,000	285,000
Stone (crushed for aggregate)	965.6	1,039.2	1,338.6
Limestone	27.1	33.7	41.2

Source: US Geological Survey.

Industry

SELECTED PRODUCTS
('000 metric tons unless otherwise indicated)

	2009	2010	2011
Raw sugar	300.0	278.7	305.0
Cement	232.0	187.5	203.2
Electric energy (million kWh)	1,758.1	2,020.1	1,978.0

Cement ('000 metric tons): 175.0 in 2012 (estimate).

Sources: UN Industrial Commodity Statistics Database; US Geological Survey.

Finance

CURRENCY AND EXCHANGE RATES

Monetary Units
100 tambala = 1 Malawi kwacha (K).

Sterling, Dollar and Euro Equivalents (28 November 2014)
£1 sterling = 784.404 kwacha;
US $1 = 498.193 kwacha;
€1 = 621.894 kwacha;
1,000 Malawi kwacha = £1.27 = $2.01 = €1.61.

Average Exchange Rate (kwacha per US $)
2011   156.515
2012   249.106
2013   364.407

BUDGET
(K '000 million, year ending 30 June)

Revenue*	2011/12	2012/13†	2013/14‡
Tax revenue	188	269	375
Taxes on income and profits	90	129	168
Taxes on goods and services	84	111	162
Taxes on international trade	18	33	47
Non-tax revenue	26	28	54
Total	214	297	428

Expenditure	2011/12	2012/13†	2013/14‡
Wages and salaries	70	97	137
Interest payments	24	33	93
Domestic	22	29	88
Foreign	2	4	5
Goods and services	95	144	156
Other expenditure	57	110	119
Development expenditures	78	104	144
Total	324	489	648

* Excluding grants received (K '000 million): 43 in 2011/12; 176 in 2012/13 (preliminary); 154 in 2013/14 (programmed).
† Preliminary figures.
‡ Programmed figures.

Source: IMF, *Malawi: Third and Fourth Reviews Under the Extended Credit Facility Arrangement, Request for Waivers for Non-observance of Performance Criteria, Extension of the Arrangement, Rephasing of Disbursements, and Modification of Performance Criteria-Staff Report; Staff Supplement; Press Release on the Executive Board Discussion; and Statement by the Executive Director for Malawi* (February 2014).

INTERNATIONAL RESERVES
(US $ million at 31 December)

	2011	2012	2013
Gold (national valuation)	15.68	22.85	22.78
IMF special drawing rights	0.43	0.89	8.72
Reserve position in IMF	3.72	3.75	3.76
Foreign exchange	193.29	218.54	400.63
Total	213.12	246.03	435.89

2014: IMF special drawing rights 9.48; Reserve position in IMF 3.54.

Source: IMF, *International Financial Statistics*.

MONEY SUPPLY
(K million at 31 December)

	2011	2012	2013
Currency outside banks	42,251.0	55,377.5	76,000.1
Demand deposits at commercial banks	99,683.5	97,976.0	121,772.6
Total money	141,934.5	153,353.5	197,772.7

Source: IMF, *International Financial Statistics*.

COST OF LIVING
(Consumer Price Index; base: 2012 = 100)

	2013	2014
Food (incl. non-alcoholic beverages)	123.3	149.4
Clothing (incl. footwear)	124.2	149.0
Rent	141.5	187.2
All items (incl. others)	127.3	157.6

NATIONAL ACCOUNTS
(K million at current prices)

Expenditure on the Gross Domestic Product

	2008	2009	2010
Government final consumption expenditure	92,270	107,993	95,281
Private final consumption expenditure	667,245	816,678	1,021,561
Gross fixed capital formation . .	156,279	144,201	105,304
Changes in inventories . . .	24,897	−30,896	64,559
Total domestic expenditure .	940,691	1,037,976	1,286,705
Exports of goods and services . .	140,932	187,363	183,055
Less Imports of goods and services	333,899	351,357	422,425
GDP in purchasers' values .	747,723	873,982	1,047,336

Gross Domestic Product by Economic Activity

	2008	2009	2010
Agriculture, forestry and fishing .	224,136	265,944	310,167
Mining and quarrying	4,460	7,156	10,528
Manufacturing	87,620	90,708	103,789
Electricity, gas and water . . .	9,749	11,738	13,640
Construction	18,318	24,385	31,393
Wholesale and retail trade, restaurants and hotels . . .	146,651	156,761	181,450
Transport and communications .	40,028	49,608	65,576
Finance, insurance and real estate	79,318	103,875	134,876
Public administration and defence	13,153	13,960	20,058
Other services	69,718	86,345	100,132
GDP at factor cost	693,151	810,479	971,608
Taxes on products	54,572	63,504	75,728
GDP in purchasers' values .	747,723	873,982	1,047,336

Source: African Development Bank.

GDP in constant 2010 prices: 1,069,252 in 2011; 1,091,543 in 2012; 1,157,601 in 2013.

GDP in purchasers' values: 1,150,916.7 in 2011; 1,425,229.5 in 2012; 1,924,110.1 in 2013.

BALANCE OF PAYMENTS
(K million)

	2010	2011	2012
Exports of goods f.o.b.	171,441.0	240,931.4	296,828.4
Imports of goods f.o.b.	−344,286.3	−404,745.3	−536,805.6
Trade balance	−172,845.3	−163,814.0	−239,977.2
Net services	−19,722.1	−21,442.2	−26,669.8
Balance on goods and services	−192,567.4	−185,256.1	−266,647.0
Net other income	−28,610.3	−16,137.3	−18,613.1
Balance on goods, services and income	−221,177.7	−201,393.5	−285,260.0
Net transfers	84,962.9	95,754.3	95,228.3
Current balance	−136,214.8	−105,639.3	−190,031.7
Capital account (net) . . .	90,705.0	98,746.8	90,731.2
Direct investment assets . . .	−6,365.6	−7,756.2	−9,191.1
Direct investment liabilities . .	14,598.7	20,160.9	22,681.0
Portfolio investment assets . .	−15.0	17.8	21.1
Portfolio investment liabilities .	149.0	167.6	188.6
Other investment assets . . .	−5,030.8	−4,511.4	−10,926.9
Other investment liabilities . .	35,467.5	33,090.5	72,981.0
Net errors and omissions . . .	27,086.5	−51,294.6	19,157.2
Overall balance	20,380.4	−17,017.8	−4,389.6

External Trade

PRINCIPAL COMMODITIES
(distribution by HS, US $ million)

Imports c.i.f.	2011	2012	2013
Vegetables and vegetable products	125.2	68.2	140.5
Cereals	85.0	37.5	110.3
Wheat and meslin	82.1	33.6	89.3
Prepared foodstuffs; beverages, spirits, vinegar; tobacco and articles thereof .	124.1	70.5	130.0
Tobacco and tobacco products .	88.4	32.0	89.9
Tobacco unmanufactured and tobacco refuse	83.0	27.1	86.5
Mineral products	348.2	441.6	505.5
Mineral fuels, oils, distillation products, etc.	213.6	341.2	410.4
Petroleum oils, not crude . .	199.1	324.5	387.9
Salt, sulphur, earth, stone, plaster, lime and cement	134.5	100.4	95.1
Chemicals and related products	539.1	684.2	749.7
Pharmaceutical products . . .	179.0	211.2	214.1
Medicament mixtures . . .	129.7	162.4	157.1
Fertilizers	186.2	280.5	341.1
Mineral or chemical fertilizers, nitrogenous	137.1	189.2	209.2
Mixtures of nitrogen, phosphorous or potassium fertilizers	45.7	71.4	117.8
Plastics, rubber, and articles thereof	123.0	142.9	168.5
Plastics and articles thereof . .	88.8	104.5	113.4
Pulp of wood, paper and paperboard, and articles thereof	133.2	104.1	132.0
Printed books, newspapers, pictures, etc.	72.2	47.8	80.6
Unused stamps, cheque forms, banknotes, and bond certificates	61.0	33.1	55.2
Textiles and textile articles .	110.7	94.9	106.9
Iron and steel; other base metals and articles of base metals	142.5	141.2	193.4
Machinery and mechanical appliances; electrical equipment; parts thereof .	323.3	350.8	359.3
Machinery and boilers, etc. . .	195.0	226.1	239.6
Electrical, electronic equipment .	128.2	124.7	119.7
Vehicles, aircraft, vessels and associated transport equipment	162.4	207.7	191.0
Vehicles other than railway, tramway	156.6	203.7	182.9
Cars (incl. station wagons) . .	47.7	84.6	40.5
Optical, medical apparatus, etc.; clocks and watches; musical instruments; parts thereof	125.2	30.6	32.6
Optical, photo, technical, medical, etc. apparatus	124.3	29.9	32.2
Electro-medical apparatus (electro-cardiographs, infra-red, etc.)	112.4	10.8	16.1
Total (incl. others)	2,427.7	2,460.9	2,825.0

Exports f.o.b.	2011	2012	2013
Vegetables and vegetable products	273.0	182.4	231.0
Coffee, tea, cocoa and spices	94.7	79.8	92.2
Tea	86.3	73.6	85.2
Cereals	95.5	2.2	3.9
Maize (corn)	84.9	0.8	1.7
Oil seed, oleagic fruits, grain, seed, fruit, etc.	34.5	45.9	78.5
Groundnuts, not roasted	29.3	38.9	60.7
Prepared foodstuffs; beverages, spirits, vinegar; tobacco and articles thereof	809.9	722.0	684.5
Sugars and sugar confectionery	214.0	43.3	112.3
Tobacco and tobacco products	571.0	662.2	556.4
Tobacco (unmanufactured) and tobacco refuse	569.7	662.2	556.4
Mineral products	126.8	143.2	135.8
Ores, slag and ash	124.5	140.7	134.5
Uranium or thorium ores and concentrates	120.3	140.7	134.5
Textiles and textile articles	69.6	58.4	37.3
Cotton	48.6	49.6	25.9
Cotton, not carded or combed	31.1	37.1	20.3
Total (incl. others)	1,425.3	1,218.0	1,194.4

Source: Trade Map-Trade Competitiveness Map, International Trade Centre, www.intracen.org/marketanalysis.

PRINCIPAL TRADING PARTNERS
(US $ million)

Imports	2011	2012	2013
Argentina	34.7	11.9	9.3
Australia	15.3	10.1	29.8
Botswana	45.2	8.5	8.5
China, People's Republic	224.6	265.6	264.7
Denmark	43.4	37.3	29.2
Germany	31.0	48.1	92.0
Hong Kong	56.1	15.9	14.0
India	279.8	197.0	222.0
Indonesia	23.8	24.6	39.5
Italy	35.5	17.4	28.7
Japan	49.9	60.9	82.9
Kenya	60.3	54.9	40.4
Korea, Republic	21.4	25.6	25.2
Mozambique	45.2	174.6	341.4
Netherlands	60.4	66.6	74.0
Portugal	2.5	66.7	35.5
Saudi Arabia	32.0	55.2	23.3
South Africa	606.0	590.0	612.9
Switzerland	40.6	45.8	56.3
Tanzania	75.2	42.5	47.0
Tunisia	—	32.2	—
United Arab Emirates	113.3	120.3	175.7
United Kingdom	82.2	69.3	72.9
USA	127.8	87.3	74.4
Zambia	110.4	94.8	131.2
Zimbabwe	34.1	30.5	36.6
Total (incl. others)	2,427.7	2,460.9	2,825.0

Exports	2011	2012	2013
Belgium	93.3	91.7	93.6
Canada	125.7	135.2	137.1
China, People's Republic	57.6	59.2	62.2
Côte d'Ivoire	20.0	—	—
Egypt	62.9	60.9	8.3
Germany	46.3	33.7	45.7
India	24.0	25.5	16.3
Kenya	73.7	26.0	32.5
Korea, Republic	22.5	29.7	29.9
Mozambique	45.3	31.5	30.4
Netherlands	25.8	46.8	47.6
Philippines	17.9	12.8	14.9
Poland	20.7	22.3	18.1
Portugal	24.8	30.2	46.5
Russia	30.6	45.1	40.5
South Africa	117.5	86.7	91.3
Spain	53.1	15.6	6.8

Exports—*continued*	2011	2012	2013
Switzerland (incl. Liechtenstein)	18.8	81.5	15.2
Tanzania	29.8	29.8	28.4
Turkey	11.2	6.3	12.6
Ukraine	8.1	10.6	12.3
United Arab Emirates	6.6	14.7	33.0
United Kingdom	109.3	41.0	69.7
USA	76.8	52.1	78.3
Zambia	34.1	23.9	40.2
Zimbabwe	122.3	63.3	48.0
Total (incl. others)	1,425.3	1,218.0	1,194.4

Source: Trade Map-Trade Competitiveness Map, International Trade Centre, www.intracen.org/marketanalysis.

Transport

RAILWAYS
(traffic)

	2010	2011	2012
Passengers carried ('000)	561	271	784
Passenger-km ('000)	35,950	17,360	47,952
Net freight ton-km ('000)	43,990	39,168	35,209

ROAD TRAFFIC
(motor vehicles in use at 31 December)

	2007
Passenger cars	53,300
Lorries and vans	59,800
Buses	6,500
Motorcycles	10,400

Source: IRF, *World Road Statistics*.

SHIPPING

Inland Waterways
(lake transport)

	2010	2011	2012
Passengers carried ('000)	52	57	21
Passenger-km ('000)	4,434	4,047	1,735
Net freight-ton km	2,871	1,367	5,758

CIVIL AVIATION
(traffic on scheduled services)

	2007	2008	2009
Kilometres flown (million)	3	5	5
Passengers carried ('000)	116	160	157
Passenger-km (million)	83	209	200
Total ton-km (million)	8	24	23

Source: UN, *Statistical Yearbook*.

Passengers carried ('000): 87 in 2010; 79 in 2011; 47 in 2012 (Source: World Bank, World Development Indicators database).

Tourism

FOREIGN TOURIST ARRIVALS BY COUNTRY OF RESIDENCE

	2010	2011	2012
Mozambique	159,580	196,629	249,341
North America	44,572	43,778	27,061
Southern Africa*	102,342	115,051	142,540
United Kingdom and Ireland . .	53,897	51,936	52,128
Zambia	80,428	95,766	42,638
Zimbabwe	128,387	131,756	89,802
Total (incl. others)	746,129	767,000	769,722

* Comprising South Africa, Botswana, Lesotho and Swaziland.

Tourism receipts (US $ million, excl. passenger transport): 33 in 2010; 34 in 2011; 34 in 2012.

Source: World Tourism Organization.

Communications Media

	2011	2012	2013
Telephones ('000 main lines in use)	173.5	227.3	33.6
Mobile cellular telephones ('000 subscribers)	3,951.6	4,646.9	5,290.0
Internet subscribers ('000) . .	450.0	n.a.	n.a.
Broadband subscribers ('000) . .	1.1	1.2	2.9

Source: International Telecommunication Union.

Education

(2012 unless otherwise indicated)

	Institutions	Teachers	Students
Primary	5,405	56,534	4,188,677
Secondary	n.a.	11,701	270,064
Tertiary	6*	980	10,473

* 2003 figure.

Pupil-teacher ratio (primary education): 72.0 in 2012.

Adult literacy rate (UNESCO estimates): 61.3% (males 72.1%; females 51.3%) in 2010 (Source: UNESCO Institute for Statistics).

Directory

The Government

HEAD OF STATE

President: Prof. ARTHUR PETER MUTHARIKA (inaugurated 31 May 2014).

Vice-President: SAULOS KLAUS CHILIMA.

CABINET
(May 2015)

President, Minister of Defence and Commander-in-Chief of the Malawi Defence Force and Police Service: Prof. ARTHUR PETER MUTHARIKA

Vice-President and Minister Responsible for Disaster and Relief Management, National Public Events and Chairperson of the Civil Service and Public Service Reform Commission: SAULOS KLAUS CHILIMA.

Minister of Finance, Economic Planning and Development: Dr GOODALL GONDWE.

Minister of Foreign Affairs and International Co-operation: Dr GEORGE CHAPONDA.

Minister of Labour and Manpower Development: HENRY MUSSA.

Minister of Health: Dr JEAN KALILANI.

Minister of Gender, Children, Disability and Social Welfare: PATRICIA ANNE KALIATI.

Minister of Home Affairs and Internal Security: ATUPELE MULUZI.

Minister of Justice and Constitutional Affairs: SAMUEL TEMBENU.

Minister of Information, Tourism and Culture: KONDWANI NANKHUMWA.

Minister of Natural Resources, Energy and Mining: BRIGHT MSAKA.

Minister of Agriculture, Irrigation and Water Development: Dr ALLAN CHIYEMBEKEZA.

Minister of Industry and Trade: JOSEPH MWANAMVEKA.

Minister of Lands, Housing and Urban Development: PAUL CHIBINGU.

Minister of Transport and Public Works: FRANCIS KASAILA.

Minister of Education, Science and Technology: Dr EMMANUEL FABIANO.

Minister of Local Government and Rural Development: TRASIZIO THOM GOWELO.

Minister of Youth and Sports Development: GRACE OBAMA CHIUMIA.

There were also two Deputy Ministers.

MINISTRIES

Office of the President and Cabinet: Private Bag 301, Capital City, Lilongwe 3; tel. 1789311; fax 1788456; internet www.malawi.gov.mw/opc/opc.htm.

Office of the Vice President: POB 30399, Capital City, Lilongwe; tel. 1788444, fax 1788218; e-mail vicepres@malawi.gov.mw.

Ministry of Agriculture, Irrigation and Water Development: POB 30134, Capital City, Lilongwe 3; tel. 1789033; fax 1789218; e-mail agriculture@agriculture.gov.mw; internet www.moafsmw.org.

Ministry of Education, Science and Technology: Capital Hill Circle, Private Bag 328, Capital City, Lilongwe 3; tel. 1789422; fax 1788064; e-mail education@education.gov.mw.

Ministry of Finance, Economic Planning and Development: Capital Hill, POB 30049, Lilongwe 3; tel. 1789355; fax 1789173; e-mail finance@finance.gov.mw; internet www.finance.gov.mw.

Ministry of Foreign Affairs and International Co-operation: POB 30315, Lilongwe 3; tel. 1789323; fax 1788482; e-mail foreign@malawi.net; internet www.foreignaffairs.gov.mw.

Ministry of Gender, Children, Disability and Social Welfare: Gemini House, City Centre, Private Bag 330, Capital City, Lilongwe 3; tel. 1770411; fax 1770826; e-mail gender@malawi.gov.mw; internet www.gender.gov.mw.

Ministry of Health: POB 30377, Capital City, Lilongwe 3; tel. 1789400; fax 1789431; e-mail doccentre@malawi.net.

Ministry of Home Affairs and Internal Security: Private Bag 331, Capital City, Lilongwe 3; tel. 1789177; fax 1789509.

Ministry of Industry and Trade: POB 30366, Capital City, Lilongwe 3; tel. 1770244; fax 1770680; e-mail minci@malawi.net; internet www.trade.gov.mw.

Ministry of Information, Tourism and Culture: Old Malawi Boo Service Bldg, City Centre, Private Bag 326, Capital City, Lilongwe 3; tel. 1773233, fax 1774568; e-mail principal.secretary@information.gov.mw.

Ministry of Justice and Constitutional Affairs: Private Bag 333, Capital City, Lilongwe 3; tel. 1788411; fax 1788332; e-mail justice@justice.gov.mw; internet www.justice.gov.mw; also comprises the Attorney-General's Chambers and the Directorate of Public Prosecutions.

Ministry of Labour and Manpower Development: Capital House, City Centre, Private Bag 344, Lilongwe 3; tel. 1773277; fax 1773805; e-mail labour@malawi.net.

Ministry of Lands, Housing and Urban Development: Lilongwe; internet www.lands.gov.mw.

Ministry of Local Government and Rural Development: POB 30312, Lilongwe 3; tel. 1789388; fax 1788083; e-mail mlgrd@localgovt.mw; internet www.mlgrd.gov.mw.

Ministry of Natural Resources, Energy and Mining: Private Bag 350, Lilongwe 3; tel. 1789488; fax 1788689; internet www.mines.gov.mw.

Ministry of Transport and Public Works: Private Bag 322, Capital City, Lilongwe 3; tel. 1789377; fax 1789328; e-mail c.k.kumangirana@gmail.com; internet www.motpwh.gov.mw.

Ministry of Youth and Sports Development: Lingadzi House, Private Bag 384, Lilongwe 3; tel. 1788758; fax 1788764; e-mail sports@malawi.gov.mw.

President

Presidential Election, 20 May 2014

Candidate	Votes	% of votes
Prof. Arthur Peter Mutharika (DPP)	1,904,399	36.42
Dr Lazarus Chakwera (MCP)	1,455,880	27.84
Dr Joyce Banda (PP)	1,056,236	20.20
Atupele Muluzi (UDF)	717,224	13.72
Others*	94,844	1.81
Total	5,228,583†	100.00

* There were eight other candidates.
† In addition, there were 56,675 spoiled ballots.

Legislature

National Assembly: Parliament Bldg, Private Bag B362, Lilongwe 3; tel. 1773566; fax 1774196; internet www.parliament.gov.mw.

Speaker: RICHARD MSOWOYA.

General Election, 20 May 2014

Party	Seats
Democratic Progressive Party	50
Malawi Congress Party	48
People's Party	26
United Democratic Front	14
Alliance for Democracy	1
Chipani Cha Pfuko	1
Independents	52
Total	192*

* Voting in one constituency did not take place due to the death of a candidate.

Election Commission

Malawi Electoral Commission (MEC): Chisankho House, Private Bag 113, Blantyre; tel. 1822033; fax 1821846; e-mail ceo@mec.org.mw; internet www.mec.org.mw; f. 1998; Chair. MAXON MBENDELA; Chief Elections Officer WILLIE KALONGA.

Political Organizations

At mid-2014 there were some 54 registered political parties in Malawi.

Alliance for Democracy (AFORD): Private Bag 28, Lilongwe; f. 1992; in March 1993 absorbed membership of fmr Malawi Freedom Movement; Chair. ENOCK CHIHANA.

Chipani Cha Pfuko (CCP): POB 30633, Chichiri, Blantyre; tel. 994326296 (mobile); e-mail kaukondekansomba@gmail.com; f. 2012; Pres. DAVIS CHESTER KATSONGA.

Congress of Democrats (CODE): Mzuzu; Pres. RALPH KASAMBARA.

Democratic Progressive Party (DPP): Lilongwe 3; internet dppmw.org; f. 2005 following Bingu wa Mutharika's resignation from the UDF; Pres. Prof. ARTHUR PETER MUTHARIKA.

Malawi Congress Party (MCP): Private Bag 388, Lilongwe 3; tel. 999223228 (mobile); f. 1959; sole legal party 1966–93; Pres. Dr LAZARUS CHAKWERA.

Malawi Democratic Party (MDP): Lilongwe; Pres. (vacant).

Malawi Forum for Unity and Development (MAFUNDE): f. 2002; aims to combat corruption and food shortages; Pres. GEORGE MNESA.

National Rainbow Coalition (NARC): POB 40508, Kanengo, Lilongwe 4; tel. 1774007; f. 2008; Pres. LOVENESS GONDWE.

National Solidarity Movement: Leader NGWAZI KAZUNI KUMWENDA.

New Republican Party (NRP): f. 2005; Pres. ALEXANDER NGULUBE (acting).

People's Party (PP): Lilongwe; f. 2011 by Joyce Banda following her expulsion from the DPP; Pres. JOYCE BANDA; Sec.-Gen. PAUL MAULDI (acting).

People's Progressive Movement (PPM): f. 2003 by fmr mems of the UDF; Pres. MARK KATSONGA; Sec.-Gen. KNOX VARELA.

People's Transformation Party (PETRA): POB 31964, Chichiri, Blantyre 3; tel. 1871577; fax 1871573; e-mail umunthu@sdnp.org.mw; internet www.petra.mw; f. 2002; Pres. KAMUZU CHIBAMBO; Sec.-Gen. DEREK LAKUDZALA.

Republican Party (RP): Lilongwe; Pres. (vacant).

United Democratic Front (UDF): POB 5446, Limbe; internet www.udf.malawi.net; f. 1992; officially merged with the NDA in June 2004 but maintained independent structure; rival faction led by Cassim Chilumpha and Friday Jumbe; Pres. ATUPELE MULUZI; Sec.-Gen. KANDI PADAMBO.

United Independence Party: Blantyre; f. 2014; Leader ABUSA HELEN SINGH.

Diplomatic Representation

EMBASSIES AND HIGH COMMISSIONS IN MALAWI

China, People's Republic: No. 342, Area 43, POB 31799, Lilongwe; tel. 1794751; fax 1794752; e-mail chinaemb_mw@mfa.gov.cn; internet mw.chineseembassy.org/eng; Ambassador ZHANG QINGYANG.

Egypt: 10/247 Tsoka Rd, POB 30451, Lilongwe 3; tel. 1780668; fax 1794660; Ambassador AKRAM MOHSEN HAMDY.

Germany: Convention Dr., POB 30046, Lilongwe 3; tel. 1772555; fax 1770250; e-mail info@lilongwe.diplo.de; internet www.lilongwe.diplo.de; Ambassador Dr PETER WOESTE.

Holy See: c/o Catholic Secretariat of ECM, Chimutu Rd, Area 11, POB 31671, Lilongwe 3; tel. 1772259; fax 1772019; e-mail na.malawi@diplomat.va; Apostolic Nuncio JULIO MURAT.

Ireland: Arwa House, 3rd Floor, Capital City, Lilongwe; tel. 1776405; fax 1776401; e-mail lilongweemdiplomats@dfa.ie; internet www.dfa.ie/irish-embassy/malawi; Ambassador AINE HEARNS.

Japan: Plot No. 14/191, Petroda Glass House, POB 30780, Lilongwe 3; tel. 1770284; fax 1773528; e-mail embmalawi@lw.mofa.go.jp; internet www.mw.emb-japan.go.jp; Ambassador SHUICHIRO NISHIOKA.

Mozambique: Area 40/14A, POB 30579, Lilongwe 3; tel. 1774100; fax 1771342; e-mail embamoc.malawi@minec.gov.mz; High Commissioner MARIA LEOCÁDIA TIVANE MATHE.

Nigeria: Lilongwe; High Commissioner MOHAMMED LAWAN GANA.

South Africa: Kang'ombe House, 3rd Floor, City Centre, POB 30043, Lilongwe 3; tel. 1773722; fax 1772571; e-mail sahc@malawi.net; High Commissioner CASSANDRA MBUYANE-MOKONE.

Tanzania: POB 922, Capital City, Lilongwe 3; tel. 1770150; fax 1770148; e-mail tanzanianhighcomm@tz.lilongwe.mw; High Commissioner PATRICK TSERE.

United Kingdom: British High Commission Bldg, Capital Hill, POB 30042, Lilongwe 3; tel. 1772400; fax 1772657; e-mail bhclilongwe@fco.gov.uk; internet ukinmalawi.fco.gov.uk; High Commissioner MICHAEL NEVIN.

USA: Area 40, Plot No. 18, 16 Jomo Kenyatta Rd, POB 30016, Lilongwe 3; tel. 1773166; fax 1770471; e-mail consularlilong@state.gov; internet lilongwe.usembassy.gov; Ambassador VIRGINIA PALMER.

Zambia: Area 40/2, City Centre, POB 30138, Lilongwe 3; tel. 1772100; fax 1774349; e-mail zambiahighcom@sdnp.org.mw; High Commissioner SALOME MWANANSHIKU.

Zimbabwe: POB 30187, Lilongwe 3; tel. 1774988; fax 1772382; e-mail zimhighcomllw@malawi.net; Ambassador THANDIWE S. DUMBUTSHENA.

Judicial System

The courts administering justice are the Supreme Court of Appeal, High Court and Magistrates' Courts.

The High Court, which has unlimited jurisdiction in civil and criminal matters, consists of the Chief Justice and four puisne judges. Traditional Courts were abolished under the 1994 Constitution. Appeals from the High Court are heard by the Supreme Court of Appeal, in Blantyre.

Supreme Court of Appeal: Blantyre; consists of the Chief Justice and not fewer than 3 other judges.

High Court of Malawi: POB 30244, Chichiri, Blantyre 3; tel. 1670255; fax 1670213; e-mail highcourt@judiciary.mw; internet www.judiciary.mw; Registrar JOSEPH CHIGONA.

Chief Justice: ANDREW NYIRENDA.

Attorney-General: KALEKENI KAPHALE.

Religion

According to the census of 2008, 82.7% of the population profess Christianity. Islam is practised by about 13.0% of the population.

CHRISTIANITY

Malawi Council of Churches (MCC): POB 30068, Capital City, Lilongwe 3; tel. 1783499; fax 1783106; f. 1939; Chair. Rev. ALEX MAULANA; Gen. Sec. Rev. Dr OSBORNE JODA-MBEWE; 24 mem. churches.

The Anglican Communion

Anglicans are adherents of the Church of the Province of Central Africa, covering Botswana, Malawi, Zambia and Zimbabwe. The Church comprises 15 dioceses, including four in Malawi. The current Archbishop of the Province is the Bishop of Northern Zambia. There were about 230,000 adherents in Malawi at mid-2000.

Bishop of Lake Malawi: FRANCIS KAULANDA, POB 30349, Capital City, Lilongwe 3; tel. 1797858; fax 1797548; e-mail anglama@eomw.net.

Bishop of Northern Malawi: Rt Rev. FANUEL EMMANUEL CHIOKO MAGANGANI, POB 120, Mzuzu; tel. 1331486; fax 1333805; e-mail angdiofnm@sdnp.org.mw.

Bishop of Southern Malawi: Rt Rev. ALINAFE KALEMBA, POB 30220, Chichiri, Blantyre 3; tel. 1641218; fax 1641235; e-mail angsoma@sdnp.org.mw; internet www.angsoma.org.mw.

Bishop of Upper Shire: BRIGHTON MALASA, Private Bag 1, Chilema, Zomba; tel. and fax 1539203; e-mail dionorth@zamnet.zm.

Protestant Churches

At mid-2001 there were an estimated 2.1m. Protestants in Malawi.

Baptist Convention of Malawi (BACOMA): Lali Lubani Rd, POB 30212, Chichiri, Blantyre 3; tel. 1671170; e-mail bacoma@sdnp.org.mw; 175,000 adherents, 1,375 churches (2007); Gen. Sec. Rev. FLETCHER KAIYA.

Church of Central Africa Presbyterian (CCAP): Blantyre Synod, POB 413, Blantyre; tel. and fax 1633942; e-mail btsynod@malawi.net; internet www.blantyresynod.org; comprises 3 synods in Malawi (Blantyre, Livingstonia and Nkhoma); Co-ordinator Rev. J.J. MPHATSE; Gen. Sec. DANIEL GUNYA; Exec. Dir ROBSON CHITENGO; more than 1m. adherents in Malawi.

Evangelical Association of Malawi: POB 2120, Blantyre; tel. and fax 999936681 (mobile); Chair. Rev. Dr LAZARUS CHAKWERA; Gen. Sec. FRANCIS MKANDAWIRE.

Evangelical Lutheran Church in Malawi: POB 650, Lutheran Church Centre, Plot 22, Chidzanja Rd, Lilongwe; tel. and fax 1726288; fax 1725910; e-mail elcmwi@elcmw.org; Bishop. Dr JOSEPH P. BVUMBWE; 80,000 mems (2010).

Malawi Assemblies of God (MAOG): off Paul Kagame Rd, Area 32/10, Central Region, POB 1220, Lilongwe; tel. 999664606 (mobile); fax 1762056; e-mail info@malawiassembliesofgod.org; internet www.malawiassembliesofgod.org; Pres. Rev Dr EDWARD CHITSONGA; 639,088 mems in 3,114 churches (2005).

Seventh-day Adventist Church: Robins Rd, Kabula Hill, POB 951, Blantyre; tel. 1820264; fax 1820528; e-mail musda@malawi.net; Pres. FRACKSON KUYAMA; Exec. Sec. BAXTER D. CHILUNGA; 360,000 mems.

The African Methodist Episcopal Church, the Churches of Christ, the Free Methodist Church, the New Apostolic Church and the United Evangelical Church in Malawi are also active. At mid-2000 there were an estimated 2m. adherents professing other forms of Christianity.

The Roman Catholic Church

Malawi comprises two archdioceses and six dioceses. There are some 3.9m. adherents of the Roman Catholic Church (equivalent to approximately 23% of the total population).

Episcopal Conference of Malawi: Catholic Secretariat of Malawi, Chimutu Rd, POB 30384, Capital City, Lilongwe 3; tel. 1782066; fax 1782019; e-mail ecm@malawi.net; internet episcopalconferenceofmalawi.org; f. 1969; Sec.-Gen. Rev. GEORGE BULEYA.

Archbishop of Blantyre: Most Rev. THOMAS MSUSA, Archbishop House, POB 385, Blantyre; tel. and fax 1637905; e-mail archdblantyre@africa-online.net.

Archbishop of Lilongwe: Most Rev. TARCISIUS GERVAZIO ZIYAYE, POB 33, Lilongwe; tel. 1754667; fax 1752767.

ISLAM

Muslim Association of Malawi (MAM): POB 497, Blantyre; tel. 1622060; fax 1623581; f. 1946 as the Nyasaland Muslim Asscn; umbrella body for Muslim orgs; provides secular and Islamic education; Chair. SHEIKH IDRISA MUHAMMAD; Sec.-Gen. Dr SALMIN OMAR IDRUS.

BAHÁ'Í FAITH

National Spiritual Assembly: POB 30922, Lilongwe 3; tel. 1771177; fax 1771713; e-mail bahaimalawi@africa-online.net; f. 1970; mems resident in over 1,200 localities.

The Press

The Daily Times: Scott Rd, Private Bag 39, Blantyre; tel. 1871663; fax 1871233; e-mail dailytimes@bnltimes.com; internet timesmediamw.com; f. 1895; fmrly the *Nyasaland Times*; Mon.–Fri., Sun.; English; publ. by Blantyre Newspapers Ltd (Chayamba Trust); affiliated to the MCP; Editor BRIAN LIGOMEKA; circ. Mon.–Fri. c. 20,000, Sun. c. 40,000 (2006).

The Dispatch: The Dispatch Publications Ltd, POB 30353, Capital City, Lilongwe 3; tel. 1751639; fax 9510120; e-mail thedispatchmw@sdnp.org.mw; Thur. and Sun.; Publr and Man. Editor MARTINES NAMINGHA; circ. Thur. 5,000, Sun. 7,000.

The Enquirer: POB 1745, Blantyre; tel. 1670022; e-mail pillycolette@yahoo.co.uk; English and Nyanja; affiliated to the UDF; Owner LUCIOUS CHIKUNI.

The Lamp: Montfort Media, POB 280, Balaka, Zomba; tel. and fax 1545267; e-mail montfortmedia@gmail.com; f. 1995; fortnightly; Roman Catholic and ecumenical; Editor Fr GAMBA PIERGIORGIO; circ. 5,500.

Malawi Government Gazette: Government Printer, POB 37, Zomba; tel. 1523155; fax 1522301; f. 1894; weekly.

Malawi News: Scott Rd, Private Bag 39, Blantyre; tel. 1871679; fax 1871233; internet timesmediamw.com; f. 1959; weekly; English and Chichewa; publ. by Blantyre Newspapers Ltd (Chayamba Trust); Editor INNOCENT CHITOSI; circ. c. 40,000 (2006).

The Nation: POB 30408, Chichiri, Blantyre 3; tel. 1673611; fax 1674343; e-mail nation@nationmalawi.com; internet www.nationmw.net; f. 1993; daily; publ. by Nation Publs Ltd; weekly edn of *The Weekend Nation* (circ. 30,000); English and Nyanja; Owner ALEKE BANDA; Editor EDWARD CHITSULO; circ. 15,000.

UDF News: POB 3052, Blantyre; tel. 1645314; fax 1645725; e-mail echapusa@yahoo.co.uk; organ of the UDF; fortnightly; English and Nyanja.

Weekly Courier: Lilongwe 3; affiliated to the Democratic Progressive Party; Man. Editor DENIS MZEMBE; circ. c. 3,000 (2006).

There is also an online newspaper, the **Nyasa Times** (internet www.nyasatimes.com).

PERIODICALS

Boma Lathu: POB 494, Blantyre; tel. 1620266; fax 1620039; f. 1973; quarterly; Chichewa; publ. by the Ministry of Information, Tourism and Culture; circ. 100,000.

Business Monthly: POB 906646, Blantyre 9; tel. 16301114; fax 1620039; f. 1995; English; economic, financial and business news; Editor ANTHONY LIVUZA; circ. 10,000.

Fairlane Magazine: POB 1745, Blantyre; tel. 1880205; e-mail fairlane@sndp.org.mw; internet www.fairlanemagazine.com;

f. 2006; 6 a year; lifestyle magazine; English and Chichewa; Man. Dir MARIE FRANCE CHIKUNI.

Kuunika (The Light): POB 17, Nkhoma, Lilongwe; tel. 1722807; e-mail nkhomasynod@globemw.net; f. 1909; monthly; Chichewa; publ. by the Church of Central Africa (Presbyterian) Nkhoma Synod; Presbyterian; Editor Rev. M. C. NKHALAMBAYAUSI; circ. 6,000.

Malawi Medical Journal: College of Medicine and Medical Asscn of Malawi, Private Bag 360, Blantyre 3; tel. and fax 1878254; e-mail mmj@medcol.mw; internet www.mmj.medcol.mw; f. 1980; replaced *Medical Quarterly*; quarterly; Chair. Prof. ERIC BORGSTEIN; Editor-in-Chief Prof. MALCOLM E. MOLYNEUX.

Moni Magazine: POB 5592, Limbe; tel. 1651833; fax 1651171; f. 1964; monthly; Chichewa and English; circ. 40,000.

Moyo Magazine: Health Education Unit, POB 30377, Lilongwe 3; 6 a year; English; publ. by the Ministry of Health; Editor-in-Chief JONATHAN NKHOMA.

Pride: POB 51668, Limbe; tel. 1640569; f. 1999; quarterly; Publr JOHN SAINI.

Together: Montfort Media, POB 280, Balaka, Zomba; tel. 1545267; e-mail together@sdnp.org.mw; f. 1995; quarterly; Roman Catholic and ecumenical, youth; Editor LUIGI GRITTI; circ. 6,000.

Other publications include *Dzukani*, *Inspiration* and *Msilikali*.

NEWS AGENCY

Malawi News Agency (MANA): Ground Floor, Gemini House, Lilongwe; tel. 1771092; fax 1771072; e-mail manaheadqurters@gmail.com; internet www.manaonline.gov.mw; f. 1966; Managing Editor JOHN MCHILIKIZO.

Publishers

Christian Literature Association in Malawi (CLAIM): POB 503, Blantyre; tel. 1620839; f. 1968; Chichewa and English; general and religious; Gen. Man. J. T. MATENJE.

Likuni Press and Publishing House: POB 133, Lilongwe; tel. 1721388; fax 1721141; f. 1949; English and Chichewa; general and religious.

Macmillan Malawi Ltd: Private Bag 140, Kenyatta Dr., Chitawira, Blantyre; tel. 1875773; fax 1875751; e-mail mayeso@macmillanmw.net; Gen. Man. HASTINGS MATEWERE.

Montfort Press and Popular Publications: POB 5592, Limbe; tel. 1651833; fax 1641126; f. 1961; general and religious; Gen. Man. VALES MACHILA.

GOVERNMENT PUBLISHING HOUSE

Government Press: Government Printer, POB 37, Zomba; tel. 1525515; fax 1525175.

Broadcasting and Communications

REGULATORY AUTHORITY

Malawi Communications Regulatory Authority (MACRA): Salmon Amour Rd, Private Bag 261, Blantyre; tel. 1883611; fax 1883890; e-mail info@macra.org.mw; internet www.macra.org.mw; f. 1998; Chair. MARTHA KWATAINE; Dir-Gen. CHARLES NSALIWA.

TELECOMMUNICATIONS

In 2011 dual licences were awarded to all telecommunications operators, permitting them to provide both fixed-line and mobile services. In early 2013 there were two mobile cellular telephone operators, one fixed-line telephone operator and one fixed wireless operator in Malawi.

Access Communications Ltd: Accord Centre, Masauko Chipembere Highway, Limbe, POB 343, Blantyre; tel. 212200200; fax 1871887; e-mail switch@access.mw; internet www.access.mw; f. 2010; fixed wireless.

Airtel Malawi: Mwai House, City Centre, POB 57, Lilongwe; tel. 1774800; fax 1774802; e-mail info.africa@airtel.com; internet africa.airtel.com/malawi; f. 1999; fmrly Zain Malawi, present name adopted in 2010; Man. Dir AMADOU DINA (acting).

Malawi Telecommunications Ltd (MTL): Lamya House, Masauko Chipembere Highway, POB 537, Blantyre; tel. 1846977; fax 1846445; e-mail mtlceo@malawi.net; internet www.mtl.mw; f. 2000 following division of Malawi Posts and Telecommunications Corpn into two separate entities; partially privatized in 2006; 80% owned by Telecom Holdings Ltd, 20% state-owned; fixed-line operator; CEO GAVIN JEFFERY.

Telekom Networks Malawi (TNM): Livingstone Towers, 5th Floor, POB 3039, Blantyre; tel. 888800800 (mobile); fax 1830092; e-mail customercare@tnm.co.mw; internet www.tnm.co.mw; f. 1995; owned by Malawi Telecommunications Ltd; operates mobile cellular telephone network; Chair. Prof. MATTHEWS CHIKAONDA; CEO WILLEM SWART.

BROADCASTING

In early 2011 there were 26 licensed broadcasters in Malawi. In November of that year the Malawi Communications Regulatory Authority awarded licences to four television stations (Galaxy, CAN, ABC and Getway) and four radio stations (Galaxy, Mulakho, Maziko and Usisya).

Radio

Malawi Broadcasting Corpn (MBC): POB 30133, Chichiri, Blantyre 3; tel. 1671222; fax 1671257; e-mail dgmbc@malawi.net; internet www.mbc.mw; f. 1964; merged with Television Malawi in July 2010; state-run; 2 channels: MBC 1 and Radio 2 (MBC 2); programmes in English, Chichewa, Chitonga, Chitumbuka, Kyangonde, Lomwe, Sena and Yao; Chair. EVANS NAMANJA; Dir-Gen. Dr BENSON M. TEMBO (suspended in May 2014).

Private commercial and religious radio stations include:

African Bible College Radio (Radio ABC): POB 1028, Lilongwe; tel. 1761965; fax 1761602; e-mail radioabc@malawi.net; internet africanbiblecolleges.org; f. 1995; regional Christian religious programming; Station Man. MACLEOD MUNTHALI.

Calvary Family Radio: POB 30239, Blantyre 3; tel. 1671627; fax 1671642; e-mail calvaryministries@hotmail.com; operated by the Calvary Family Church; religious community radio station.

Capital Radio 102.5 FM: Umoyo House, 2nd Floor, Victoria Ave, Blantyre; Private Bag 437, Chichiri, Blantyre 3; tel. 1820858; fax 1823382; e-mail stationmanager@capitalradiomalawi.com; internet www.capitalradiomalawi.com; f. 1999; commercial radio station; music, news and entertainment; Man. Dir and Editor-in-Chief ALAUDIN OSMAN.

Channel for All Nations (CAN): POB 1220, Lilongwe; tel. 1761763; fax 1762056; e-mail kawembale@yahoo.com; internet canradiomalawi.com; f. 2004; operated by the Assemblies of God Church; regional Christian religious programming.

Joy FM: Private Bag 17, Limbe, Blantyre; tel. 1638330; fax 1638329; e-mail joyradio@globemalawi.net; commercial radio station; Owner BAKILI MULUZI.

MIJ FM: POB 30165, Chichiri, Blantyre 3; tel. 1675087; fax 1675649; e-mail mij@clcom.net; internet www.mij.mw/aboutradio.html; f. 1996; operated by students of the Malawi Institute of Journalism; community radio station.

Nkhota Kota Community Radio: Private Bag 48, Nkhota Kota; tel. 999628176; internet www.nkhotakotaradio.com; f. 2003 with assistance from UNESCO; focus on social and devt issues; Chair. BLESSINGS MKOLOLA; Man. ALHAJ RAHEED.

Power 101 FM: Raynor Ave, Limbe, POB 761, Blantyre; tel. 1841101; fax 1841387; e-mail fm101@malawi.net; internet www.fm101.mw; f. 1998; commercial radio station; music and entertainment; Dir and Station Man. OSCAR THOMSON.

Radio Islam: Agason Bldg, Milward Rd, PO Box 5400, Limbe; tel. 1841408; fax 1845728; e-mail info@radioislam.org.mw; internet radioislam.org.mw; f. 2001; operated by the Islamic Zakaat Fund; religious programming; Dir MUHAMMAD MUHAMMAD AHMED.

Radio Maria Malawi: POB 408, Mangochi; tel. 1599626; fax 1599691; e-mail radiomaria@africa-online.net; internet www.radiomaria.mw; f. 2003; operated by Asscn of Radio Maria Malawi as part of the World Family of Radio Maria, Italy; Roman Catholic religious programming; Chichewa, Chiyao and English; Gen. Man. JOSEPH KIMU; Dir of Programmes HENRY SAINDI.

Star Radio: Plantation House, 4th Floor, 11 Victoria Ave, Blantyre; tel. and fax 1832787; e-mail info@starradiomw.com; f. 2006; commercial radio station; Station Man. KAJOWOLA PHIRI.

Zodiak Broadcasting Station (ZBS): Private Bag 312, Lilongwe 3; tel. 1762557; fax 1762751; internet www.zodiakmalawi.com; f. 2005; operated by Zodiak Broadcasting Services; programmes in Chichewa and English; Man. Dir GOSPEL KAZAKO.

Television

Calvary Family Television: Blantyre; Christian.

MBC: (see Radio).

Luntha Television: Andiamo Loop, POB 45, Balaka; tel. 1553009; fax 1553492; e-mail info@lunthatv.com; internet www.lunthatv.com; f. 2007; religious broadcaster.

Finance

(cap. = capital; res = reserves; dep. = deposits; m. = million;
br(s). = branch(es); amounts in kwacha)

BANKING

In early 2013 there were 12 banks and two other financial institutions in Malawi.

Central Bank

Reserve Bank of Malawi: Convention Dr., POB 30063, Capital City, Lilongwe 3; tel. 1770600; fax 1772752; e-mail reserve-bank@rbm.mw; internet www.rbm.mw; f. 1965; bank of issue; cap. 19,484m., res 12,191m., dep. 48,715m. (Dec. 2009); Gov. CHARLES CHUKA; br. in Blantyre.

Commercial Banks

Ecobank Malawi Ltd: cnr Victoria Ave and Henderson St, Private Bag 389, Chichiri, Blantyre; tel. 1822099; fax 1820583; e-mail lib@mw.loita.com; internet www.ecobank.com; cap. 146.0m, res 707.3m., dep. 9,834.9m. (Dec. 2012); fmrly Loita Bank Ltd; name changed as above in 2008; Chair. MASAUKO MSUNGAMA; Man. Dir CHARLES ASIEDU; 6 brs.

INDEBank Ltd: INDEBank House, Kaohsiong Rd, Top Mandala, POB 358, Blantyre; tel. 1824855; fax 1824252; e-mail enquiriesho@indebank.com; internet www.indebank.com; f. 1972 as Investment and Devt Bank of Malawi Ltd; cap. 84m, res 1,622.3m., dep. 13,717.9m. (Dec. 2012); 41.38% owned by Trans-Africa Holdings Ltd, 30% owned by Press Trust, 25.67% owned by ADMARC Investments Holding, 2.95% owned by Employee Ownership Scheme; commercial and devt banking; provides loans to statutory corpns and to private enterprises in the agricultural, industrial, tourism, transport and commercial sectors; Chair. ISAAC K. NSAMALA; Man. Dir and CEO WILLIAM CHATSALA; 6 brs.

National Bank of Malawi: 7 Henderson St, POB 945, Blantyre; tel. 1820622; fax 1820321; e-mail chiefexec@natbankmw.com; internet www.natbank.co.mw; f. 1971; 52% owned by Press Corpn Ltd, 25% owned by Old Mutual Group; cap. 467m., res 7,026m., dep. 124,067m. (Dec. 2013); Chair. Dr MATHEWS A. P. CHIKAONDA; CEO GEORGE B. PARTRIDGE; 25 service centres.

NBS Bank Ltd: Ginnery Cnr, Chipembere Highway, off Masajico, POB 32251, Chichiri, Blantyre; tel. 1876222; fax 1875041; e mail nbs@nbsmw.com; internet www.nbsmw.com; f. 2003; 60% owned by NICO, 8% owned by the Nat. Investment Trust; fmrly New Building Society; cap. 363.8m., res 2,866.2m., dep. 47,180.0m. (Dec. 2013); Chair. FELIX L. MLUSU; CEO BERNADETTE MANDOLOMA.

Nedbank (Malawi) Ltd: Development House, cnr Henderson St and Victoria Ave, POB 750, Blantyre; tel. 1620477; fax 1620102; e-mail netbank@nedbank.co.mw; internet www.nedbank.co.mw; f. 1999; fmrly Fincom Bank of Malawi Ltd; 68.8% owned by Nedbank Africa Investments Ltd, 28.4% owned by SBM Nedcor Holdings Ltd; cap. 199,6m., res 819.0m., dep. 8,288.3 (Dec. 2011); Chair. MAZIKO SAUTI PHIRI; Man. Dir RACHEL KAWAWA (acting).

Standard Bank Ltd: Standard Bank Centre, Africa Unity Ave, City Centre, POB 30386, Capital City, Lilongwe 3; tel. 1878823; fax 1878824; e-mail callcentre@standardbank.co.mw; internet www.standardbank.co.mw; f. 1970 as Commercial Bank of Malawi; present name adopted June 2003; 60.18% owned by Stanbic Africa Holdings Ltd, 20.00% owned by Nat. Insurance Co; cap. 213m., res 2,694m., dep. 134,157m. (Dec. 2013); Chair. ALEX CHITSIME; CEO ANDREW MASHANDA; 8 brs.

Development Bank

Opportunity International Bank of Malawi Ltd (OIBM): Opportunity Bank Bldg, POB 1794, Lilongwe; tel. 1758403; fax 1758400; e-mail lilongwe@oibm.mw; f. 2003; 63.7% owned by Opportunity Transformation Investments, USA, 25.3% owned by Opportunity Micro Investments (UK) Ltd, United Kingdom, 11% owned by Trust for Transformation; Chair. FRANCIS PELEKAMOYO.

Discount Houses

CDH Investment Bank: CDH House, 5 Independence Dr., POB 1444, Blantyre; tel. 1821300; fax 1822826; e-mail info@cdh-malawi.com; internet www.cdh-malawi.com; f. 1998; 80% owned by Trans-Africa Holdings; Chair. FRANKLIN KENNEDY; Man. Dir and CEO MISHECK ESAU.

First Discount House Ltd: Umoyo House, 1st Floor, 8 Victoria Ave North, POB 512, Blantyre; tel. 1820219; fax 1823044; e-mail fdh@fdh.co.mw; internet www.fdh.co.mw; f. 2000; 40.16% owned by Kingdom Financial Holdings Ltd, 39.84% owned by Thomson F. Mpinganjira Trust, 20% owned by Old Mutual Life Assurance Co (Malawi) Ltd; Chair. NATHAN MPINGANJIRA; CEO MIKE CHIWALO.

Merchant Banks

First Merchant Bank Ltd: Livingstone Towers, Glyn Jones Rd, Private Bag 122, Blantyre; tel. 1821955; fax 1821978; e-mail fmb.headoffice@fmbmalawi.com; internet www.fmbmalawi.com; f. 1994; 44.9% owned by Zambezi Investments Ltd, 22.5% owned by Simsbury Holdings Ltd, 11.2% owned each by Prime Capital and Credit Ltd, Kenya, and Prime Bank Ltd, Kenya; Chair. RASIKBHAI C. KANTARIA; Man. Dir DHEERAJ DIKSHIT; 7 brs.

Leasing and Finance Co of Malawi Ltd: Livingstone Towers, Glyn Jones Rd, POB 1963, Blantyre; tel. 1820233; fax 1820275; f. 1986; Chair. HITESH ANADKAT; Gen. Man. MBACHAZWA LUNGU.

Savings Bank

Malawi Savings Bank: MSB House, cnr Victoria Ave and Chilembwe Rd, POB 521, Blantyre; tel. 1625111; fax 1621929; e-mail msb@msb.mw; internet www.msb.mw; f. 1994; 99.9% state-owned; Sec.-Treas. P. E. CHILAMBE; Gen. Man. IAN C. BONONGWE.

STOCK EXCHANGE

Malawi Stock Exchange: Old Reserve Bank Bldg, 14 Victoria Ave, Private Bag 270, Blantyre; tel. 1824233; fax 1823636; e-mail mse@mse-mw.com; internet www.mse.co.mw; f. 1996; owned by the Reserve Bank of Malawi; 14 cos listed in 2013; Chair. AUGUSTINE CHITHENGA; CEO SYMON MSEFULA.

INSURANCE

In 2011 the insurance sector comprised 11 insurance companies and one reinsurance company. Of these, seven companies dealt in non-life insurance.

General Alliance Insurance Ltd: Alliance House, Sharp Rd, POB 1811, Blantyre; tel. 1822100; fax 1821088; e-mail info@generalalliancemw.com; internet www.generalalliancemw.com; f. 1996; Chair. RAMESH H. SAVJANI; CEO R. SRINIVASAN.

NICO Holdings Ltd: CHIBISA House, 19 Glyn Jones Rd, POB 501, Blantyre; tel. 1831902; fax 1822364; e-mail info@nicomw.com; internet www.nicomw.com; f. 1970; fmrly National Insurance Co Ltd; transferred to private sector in 1996; incorporates NICO Gen. Insurance Co Ltd, NICO Life Insurance Co Ltd and NICO Technologies Ltd; offices at Blantyre, Lilongwe, Mzuzu and Zomba; agencies countrywide; Chair. ALAUDIN OSMAN; CEO and Man. Dir FELIX L. MLUSU.

Old Mutual Malawi: 30 Glyn Jones Rd, Old Mutual Building, POB 393, Blantyre; tel. 1820677; fax 1822649; e-mail info@oldmutual.co.mw; internet www.oldmutualmalawi.com; f. 1845; subsidiary of Old Mutual PLC, United Kingdom; Chair. JOHANNES GAWAXAB; Man. Dir CHRIS KAPANGA.

REAL Insurance Co of Malawi Ltd: Delamere House, Victoria Ave, POB 442, Blantyre; tel. 1824044; fax 1823862; e-mail blantyre@realinsurance.co.mw; internet www.realinsurance.co.mw; associate of RSA PLC, United Kingdom; Chair. THOMAS O. B. KANYUKA; CEO GRANT MWENECHANYA.

United General Insurance Co Ltd (UGI): Michiru House, Victoria Ave, POB 383, Blantyre; tel. 1821770; fax 1821980; e-mail ugi@ugimalawi.com; internet www.ugimalawi.com; f. 1986 as Pearl Assurance Co Ltd; latterly Property and Gen. Insurance Co Ltd; present name adopted following merger with Fide Insurance Co Ltd in July 1998; 74% owned by ZimRE Holdings, Zimbabwe; Chair. ALBERT NDUNA; Man. Dir IAN K. KUMWENDA.

Vanguard Life Assurance Co (Pvt) Ltd: Mpico House, 2nd Floor, Glyn Jones Rd, POB 1625, Blantyre; tel. 1823326; fax 1823056; e-mail vanguard@vanguardlifemw.com; internet www.vanguardlifemw.com; f. 1999; 90% owned by Fidelity Life Assurance Ltd, Zimbabwe; Chair. S. TEMBO; Man. Dir NOAH MUPFURUTSA.

Trade and Industry

GOVERNMENT AGENCIES

Agricultural Development and Marketing Corpn (ADMARC): POB 5052, Limbe; tel. 1840044; fax 1840486; e-mail admce@admarc.co.mw; internet www.admarc.co.mw; f. 1971; involved in cultivation, processing, marketing and export of grain and other crops; CEO JERRY JANA.

Malawi Housing Corpn: POB 414, Blantyre; tel. 1876822; fax 1872054; e-mail gm@mhcmw.org; internet www.mhcmw.org; f. 1964; 4 regional offices; CEO RODRICK MULONYA; Dep. CEO W. MBEREKA.

Malawi Investment and Trade Centre (MITC): Aquarius House, Private Bag 302, Lilongwe 3; tel. 1770800; fax 1771781; e-mail mitc@mitc.mw; internet www.mitc.mw; f. 2011 following merger of the Malawi Investment Promotion Agency (MIPA) and Malawi Export Promotion Council (MEPC); promotes and facilitates export and investment, and provides technical assistance and training to exporters; CEO CLEMENT KUMBEMBA.

Public Private Partnership Commission: Livingstone Towers, 2nd Floor, Glyn Jones Rd, POB 937, Blantyre; tel. 1823655; fax 1821248; e-mail info@pppc.mw; internet www.pcmalawi.org; f. 1996; fmrly the Privatisation Commission of Malawi; has sole authority to oversee divestiture of govt interests in public enterprises; Chair. ALEX CHITSIME; CEO JIMMY LIPUNGA; 75 privatizations completed by Jan. 2008.

Tobacco Control Commission: POB 40045, Kanengo, Lilongwe 4; tel. 1712777; fax 1712632; e-mail tcclib@tccmw.com; internet www .tccmw.com; f. 1939; regulates tobacco production and marketing; advises Govt on sale and export of tobacco; Chair. MKHOSI JERE; CEO Dr BRUCE MUNTHALI; regional offices in Mzuzu and Limbe.

DEVELOPMENT ORGANIZATIONS

Council for Non-Governmental Organizations in Malawi (CONGOMA): Amina House, Ground Floor, Units 11 12, off Paul Kagame Rd, POB 2264, Lilongwe; tel. 111917800; e-mail congoma@ gmail.com; internet www.congoma.mw; f. 1992; promotes social and economic devt; Chair. VOICE MHONE; Exec. Dir RONALD MTONGA; 380 mem. orgs (2013).

CHAMBER OF COMMERCE

Malawi Confederation of Chambers of Commerce and Industry (MCCCI): Masauko Chipembere Highway, Chichiri Trade Fair Grounds, POB 258, Blantyre; tel. 1871988; fax 1871147; e-mail mccci@mccci.org; internet www.mccci.org; f. 1892; promotes trade and encourages competition in the economy; Chair. MATTHEWS J. CHIKANKHENI; CEO CHANCELLOR L. KAFERAPANJIRA; 400 mems.

INDUSTRIAL AND TRADE ASSOCIATIONS

Coffee Association of Malawi (CAMAL): POB 930, Kidney Cres., Blantyre; tel. 1983737; fax 1333902; e-mail camal@coffeemalawi.org; internet www.coffeemalawi.org; f. 1981; Gen. Man. HARRISON KALUA.

Dwangwa Cane Growers Trust (DCGT): POB 156, Dwangwa; tel. 1295111; fax 1295164; e-mail dcgt@malawi.net; f. 1999; fmrly Smallholder Sugar Authority; CEO WILFRED CHAKANIKA.

National Hawkers and Informal Business Association (NAHIBA): Chichiri Trade Fair, POB 60544, Ndirande, Blantyre; tel. 1945315; fax 1624558; e-mail nazulug@yahoo.com; f. 1995; Exec. Dir EVA JOACHIM.

Tea Association of Malawi Ltd (TAML): Kidney Crescent Rd, POB 930, Blantyre; tel. 1671182; fax 1671427; e-mail taml@malawi .net; internet www.taml.co.mw; f. 1934; Chair. SANGWANI HARA; CEO CLEMENT C. THINDWA; 10 mems.

Tobacco Association of Malawi (TAMA): 13/64 Independence Dr., TAMA House, POB 31360, Lilongwe 3; tel. 1773099; fax 1773493; e-mail tama@tamalawi.com; internet www.tamalawi .com; f. 1929; Pres. RUEBEN JEFRED MAIGWA; Chief Exec. GRAHAM MKUMBA; brs in Mzuzu, Limbe and Chinkhoma; 75,000 mems.

Tobacco Exporters' Association of Malawi Ltd (TEAM): Private Bag 403, Kanengo, Lilongwe 4; tel. 1775839; fax 1774069; f. 1930; Chair. CHARLES A. M. GRAHAM; Gen. Man. H. M. MBALE; 9 mems.

EMPLOYERS' ORGANIZATIONS

Employers' Consultative Association of Malawi (ECAM): Ndola Cres., House No 498A, POB 2134, Blantyre; tel. and fax 1637952; fax 1637950; e-mail ecam@ecammw.com; internet www .ecammw.com; f. 1963; Pres. EMMANUEL BANDA; Exec. Dir BEYANI T. MUNTHALI; 250 mem. asscns and 6 affiliates representing 80,000 employees.

UTILITIES

Electricity

Electricity Supply Corpn of Malawi (ESCOM): ESCOM House, 9 Haile Selassie Rd, POB 2047, Blantyre; tel. and fax 1822000; fax 1822008; e-mail info@escommw.com; internet www.escom.mw; f. 1966; controls electricity generation and distribution; Chair. MORGAN TEMBO; CEO Eng. JOHN KANDULU.

Malawi Energy Regulatory Authority (MERA): Development House, 2nd Floor, City Centre, Private Bag B496, Lilongwe 3; tel. 1775810; fax 1772666; e-mail mera@meramalawi.mw; internet www .meramalawi.mw; f. 2004; regulatory autority; Chair. JOHN D. K. SAKA; CEO RAPHAEL KAMOTO.

Water

Blantyre Water Board: POB 30369, Chichiri, Blantyre 3; tel. 18720000; e-mail bwb@bwb.mw; internet www.bwb.mw; f. 1995;

supplies potable water to Blantyre City and its environs; Chair. W. R. G. MANDOWA; Chief Exec. ANDREW THAWE.

Lilongwe Water Board: Madzi House, off Likuni Rd, POB 96, Lilongwe; tel. 1750366; fax 1752294; e-mail madzi@lwb.mw; internet www.lwb.mw; f. 1947; Chair. HARRY MKANDAWIRE; Gen. Man. GABRIEL M. GONANI.

There are also three regional water boards—Central Region Water Board, Northern Region Water Board, Southern Region Water Board—serving the population in small towns and rural areas.

TRADE UNIONS

Congress of Malawi Trade Unions (COMATU): POB 1443, Lilongwe; tel. 1757255; fax 1770885; Pres. THOMAS L. BANDA; Gen. Sec. PHILLMON E. CHIMBALU.

Malawi Congress of Trade Unions (MCTU): POB 1271, Lilongwe; tel. 1752162; fax 1820716; e-mail mctusecretariat@ mctumw.com; f. 1995 as successor to the Trade Union Congress of Malawi (f. 1964); Pres. CHAULUKA MUWAKE; Sec.-Gen. PONTIUS KALICHERO; 113,000 paid-up mems (2008).

Transport

RAILWAYS

The Central East African Railways Co (fmrly Malawi Railways) operates between Nsanje (near the southern border with Mozambique) and Mchinji (near the border with Zambia) via Blantyre, Salima and Lilongwe, and between Nkaya and Nayuchi on the eastern border with Mozambique, covering a total of 797 km. The Central East African Railways Co and Mozambique State Railways connect Malawi with the Mozambican ports of Beira and Nacala. There is a rail/lake interchange station at Chipoka on Lake Malawi, from where vessels operate services to other lake ports in Malawi. The construction of a 27-km railway line linking Mchinji with Chipata, Zambia, was completed in 2010.

Central East African Railways Co Ltd (CEAR): Station Rd, POB 5144, Limbe; tel. 1640844; fax 1643496; e-mail cear@cearcdn.mw; internet www.cear.mw; f. 1994 as Malawi Railways Ltd; owned by the Sociedade de Desenvolvimento do Corredor de Nacala, a consortium of mining companies of Brazil and Mozambique; freight and passenger service; Man. Dir HENDRYL CHIMWAZA.

ROADS

In 2004 Malawi had a total road network of some 15,500 km, of which 3,600 km was paved. In addition, unclassified community roads total an estimated 10,000 km. All main roads, and most secondary roads, are all-weather roads. Major routes link Lilongwe and Blantyre with Harare (Zimbabwe), Lusaka (Zambia) and Mbeya and Dar es Salaam (Tanzania). A 480-km highway along the western shore of Lake Malawi links the remote Northern Region with the Central and Southern Regions. A project to create a new trade route, or 'Northern Corridor', through Tanzania, involving road construction and improvements in Malawi, was completed in 1992.

Department of Road Traffic: c/o Ministry of Transport and Public Works, Private Bag 257, Capital City, Lilongwe 3; tel. 1756138; fax 1752592; comprises the Roads Authority and the Road Fund Administration.

Roads Authority: Functional Bldg, off Paul Kagame Rd, Private Bag B346, Lilongwe 3; tel. 1753699; fax 1750307; e-mail nra@ nramw.com; internet www.ra.org.mw; f. 2006; established following the division of the National Roads Authority into two separate bodies—the other being the Road Fund Administration; Chair. INKOSI YA MAKOSI M'BELWA; CEO PAUL JOHN KULEMEKA.

United Bus Co: POB 176, Blantyre; tel. 888863912 (mobile); fax 1870038; e-mail ubc@ubcmw.com; internet www.ubcmw.com; f. 2008 by fmr employees of Shire Bus Lines Ltd following its liquidation in 2006; operates local and long-distance bus services between Makata, Blantyre, Malangalanga, Mzimba and Mzuzu and rural areas; services to Harare (Zimbabwe) and Johannesburg (South Africa); Chair. Al-haj Sheik ALIDI LIKONDE.

SHIPPING

There are 23 ports and landing points on Lake Malawi. The four main ports are at Chilumba, Nkhata Bay, Chipoka and Monkey Bay. Ferry services carry around 60,000 passengers annually; the principal cargoes transported are sugar, fertilizer, dried fish and maize. A new landing point at Ngala, near Dwangwa, to carry sugar to Chipoka was inaugurated in 2005. Smaller vessels are registered for other activities, including fishing and tourism. Lake Malawi is at the centre of the Mtwara Development Corridor transport initiative agreed between Zambia, Malawi, Tanzania and Mozambique in December 2004.

Department of Marine Services: c/o Department of Transport and Public Works, Private Bag A-81, Lilongwe; tel. 1751531; fax 1756290; e-mail marinedepartment@malawi.net; responsible for vessel safety and control, ports services, and maritime pollution control; Dir LASTON MAKUZULA.

Malawi Shipping Co (MLS): POB 15, Monkey Bay; tel. and fax 1587221; fax 1587309; e-mail ilala@malawi.net; f. 1994; fmrly Malawi Lake Services Ltd; privatized 2010; conceded to Mota-Engil for 35 years; operates passenger and freight services to Mozambique, and freight services to Tanzania; Gen. Man. JOSE DINIS DA SILVA; 9 vessels, incl. 3 passenger and 4 cargo vessels.

CIVIL AVIATION

Kamuzu (formerly Lilongwe) International Airport was opened in 1982. There is also an international airport at Chileka (Blantyre) and domestic airports at Mzuzu and Karonga in the Northern Region and at the Club Makokola resort near Mangochi.

Department of Civil Aviation: c/o Ministry of Transport and Public Works, Private Bag B311, Lilongwe 3; tel. 1770577; fax 1774986; e-mail aviationhq@malawi.net; Dir L. Z. PHESELE.

Malawian Airlines: Lilongwe; f. 2013 to replace Air Malawi Ltd; 49% owned by Ethiopian Airlines, 51% state-owned; scheduled domestic services; CEO KASSIM GERESU.

Tourism

Fine scenery, beaches on Lake Malawi, big game and an excellent climate form the basis of the country's tourist potential. According to the World Tourism Organization, the number of foreign visitor arrivals was 769,722 in 2012. Receipts from tourism (excluding passenger transport) totalled US $34m. in that year.

Department of Tourism: POB 402, Blantyre; tel. 1620300; fax 1620947; f. 1969; responsible for tourism policy; inspects and licenses tourist facilities, sponsors training of hotel staff and publishes tourist literature; Dir of Tourism Services ISAAC K. MSISKA.

Malawi Tourism Association (MTA): POB 1044, Lilongwe; tel. 1770010; fax 1770131; e-mail mta@malawi.net; internet www .malawi-tourism-association.org.mw; f. 1998; Exec. Dir SAM BOTOMANI.

Defence

As assessed at November 2014, Malawi's defence forces comprised a land army of 5,300, a marine force of 220 and an air force of 200: all form part of the army. There was also a paramilitary police force of 1,500. In 2014 a total of 859 Malawian troops were stationed abroad, of whom 14 were observers.

Defence Expenditure: Budgeted at K17,000m. in 2014.

Commander-in-Chief of the Malawi Defence Force: Prof. ARTHUR PETER MUTHARIKA.

Commander of the Malawi Defence Force: Gen. IGNASIO MAULANA.

Education

Primary education, which is provided free of charge but is not compulsory, begins at six years of age and lasts for eight years. Secondary education, which begins at 14 years of age, lasts for four years, comprising two cycles of two years. According to UNESCO, in 2009 primary enrolment included 97% of children in the relevant age-group (males 94%; females 99%), while secondary enrolment in 2012 included 30% of children in the relevant age-group (males 30%; females 29%). The five constituent colleges of the University of Malawi had a total of 6,454 students in 2008, while 1,428 students were enrolled at Mzuzu University, 358 at the Catholic University and 148 at the University of Livingstonia. A small number of students attend the Marine Training College at Monkey Bay, which was established in 1998. Some students attend institutions in the United Kingdom and the USA. In 2012 there were 10,473 students enrolled at tertiary-level institutions in Malawi. Recurrent expenditure on education in 2008/09 was estimated at 21,413m. kwacha (equivalent to 13.7% of total recurrent expenditure).

MALAYSIA

Introductory Survey

LOCATION, CLIMATE, LANGUAGE, RELIGION, FLAG, CAPITAL

The Federation of Malaysia, situated in South-East Asia, consists of 13 states. Eleven of these are in Peninsular Malaysia, in the southern part of the Kra peninsula (with Thailand to the north and the island of Singapore to the south), and two, Sabah and Sarawak, are on the north coast of the island of Borneo, two-thirds of which comprises the Indonesian territory of Kalimantan. Sarawak also borders Brunei, a coastal enclave in the north-east of the state. The climate is tropical, there is rain in all seasons and temperatures are generally between 22°C (72°F) and 33°C (92°F), with little variation throughout the year. The official language is Bahasa Malaysia, a standardized form of Malay, but English is also widely used. Chinese (Mandarin) and Tamil are the main non-native languages and there are also numerous indigenous tribal languages, the principal one being Iban. Islam is the established religion, practised by about 61% of the population (including virtually all ethnic Malays), while some 20%, including most of the Chinese community, follow Buddhism. The country's Indians are predominantly Hindus. There is a minority of Christians among all races, and traditional beliefs are also practised, particularly in Sabah and Sarawak. Malaysia's national flag (proportions 1 by 2) has 14 horizontal stripes, alternating red and white, with a blue rectangular canton, containing a yellow crescent and a 14-pointed yellow star, in the upper hoist. The national capital is Kuala Lumpur. A new administrative capital, Putrajaya, has been developed south of Kuala Lumpur.

CONTEMPORARY POLITICAL HISTORY

Historical Context

The 11 states of Malaya, under British protection, were united as the Malayan Union in April 1946 and became the Federation of Malaya in February 1948. An armed communist offensive began in 1948, and was not effectively suppressed until the mid-1950s. After 1960 the remainder of the banned Communist Party of Malaya (CPM) took refuge in southern Thailand. Meanwhile, Malaya was granted independence, within the Commonwealth, on 31 August 1957. Malaysia was established on 16 September 1963, through the union of the independent Federation of Malaya (renamed the States of Malaya), the internally self-governing state of Singapore, and the former British colonies of Sarawak and Sabah (North Borneo). Singapore left the federation in August 1965, reducing the number of Malaysia's component states from 14 to 13. The States of Malaya were designated West Malaysia in 1966 and later styled Peninsular Malaysia.

Domestic Political Affairs

In 1970 serious inter-communal rioting, engendered by Malay resentment of the Chinese community's economic dominance and of certain pro-Chinese electoral results, precipitated the resignation of Tunku Abdul Rahman, who had been Prime Minister of Malaya (and subsequently of Malaysia) since independence. The new Prime Minister, Tun Abdul Razak, widened the government coalition, dominated by the United Malays National Organization (UMNO), to create a national front, Barisan Nasional (BN). The BN originally comprised 10 parties, absorbing most of the former opposition parties. In January 1976 the Prime Minister died and was succeeded by Deputy Prime Minister Dato' Hussein bin Onn.

Political stability was subsequently threatened by the resurgence of the communist guerrilla movement, which conducted a series of terrorist attacks in Peninsular Malaysia during 1976–78. However, CPM activity subsequently declined, owing to co-operation between Malaysia and Thailand in military operations along their common border, and in December 1989, following a year of negotiations with the Thai Government, the remaining 1,188 rebels—including recruits from Thailand and Singapore—agreed to terminate all armed activities.

Meanwhile, in October 1977 the expulsion of the Chief Minister (Menteri Besar) of the state of Kelantan from the dominant Parti Islam se Malaysia (PAS—Islamic Party of Malaysia) resulted in violent disturbances in Kelantan and the declaration of a state of emergency by the federal Government. Direct rule was imposed in Kelantan, and the PAS was expelled from the BN coalition in December. In the federal and state elections of July 1978 Hussein consolidated the position of the BN, while the PAS, in opposition, suffered a serious reversal. In 1978, following the federal Government's rejection of proposals for the establishment of a Chinese university, racial and religious tensions resurfaced.

In July 1981 Hussein was succeeded as Prime Minister by Dato' Seri Dr Mahathir Mohamad, Deputy Prime Minister since 1976. Mahathir called a general election in April 1982; the BN coalition won convincingly in all states and increased its overall strength in the House of Representatives.

A new political party, the Parti Bersatu Sabah (PBS—Sabah United Party), won control of the Sabah State Legislative Assembly at an election in April 1985. The legality of the new PBS administration was challenged by Muslim opponents, and in February 1986 the Chief Minister (Ketua Menteri) called a further election. In the May election the PBS won an increased majority of seats in the state legislature, and in June the BN agreed to admit the PBS into the ruling federal coalition, together with the United Sabah National Organization (USNO), which had been expelled in 1984.

In February 1986 Mahathir's leadership of the federal Government and of UMNO was challenged when Deputy Prime Minister Datuk Musa Hitam resigned from the Government, owing to 'irreconcilable differences' with Mahathir. However, Musa retained his position as Deputy President of UMNO. During the following months Musa's supporters became increasingly critical of Mahathir. At an early general election in August, the BN coalition took 148 of the 177 seats in an enlarged House of Representatives: UMNO secured 83 seats, while the Malaysian Chinese Association (MCA) won 17. Of the opposition parties, the Democratic Action Party (DAP) won 24 seats, having gained support from ethnic Chinese voters who were disillusioned with the MCA. In concurrent state elections, the BN retained control of all the State Legislative Assemblies in Peninsular Malaysia. Several ministers who had supported Musa were subsequently demoted or removed from the Government.

In early 1987 there was a serious challenge for the presidency of UMNO from Tengku Razaleigh Hamzah, the Minister of Trade and Industry. None the less, at the UMNO General Assembly in April Mahathir was elected UMNO President for the third time (thereby retaining the position of Prime Minister at the head of the BN coalition), albeit with a greatly reduced majority. The General Assembly also narrowly elected Abdul Ghafar Baba (who had replaced Musa as Deputy Prime Minister in February 1986) as UMNO Deputy President. Mahathir subsequently announced the resignation of Razaleigh from his cabinet post.

Criticism of Mahathir's leadership persisted during 1987, both from within UMNO and from other political parties. At the same time, racial tensions intensified in various parts of the country over Chinese-language education, religion and other issues. In October–November, allegedly to prevent the outbreak of racially motivated riots between Chinese and Malays, 106 people were detained under the provisions of the Internal Security Act (ISA, which allowed detention without trial for up to two years on grounds of national security). Those detained included politicians from all parties (most notably the leader of the DAP, Lim Kit Siang), lawyers, journalists and leaders of pressure groups. Three newspapers were closed by the Government, and political rallies were prohibited. In November the Government introduced legislation to impose stringent penalties on the dissemination by the print media of 'false' news. From December the Minister of Information was empowered to monitor all radio and television broadcasts, and to revoke the licence of any private broadcasting company not conforming with 'Malaysian values'. By April 1989 all the detainees under the ISA had been released (although often under restrictive conditions).

In February 1988 the High Court gave a ruling on a suit filed by dissatisfied members of UMNO, who claimed that, since some of the delegations taking part in the UMNO elections of April 1987 had not been legally registered, the elections should be declared null and void. On account of the irregularities, the Court ruled that UMNO was an 'unlawful society' and that there had been 'no election at all'. Mahathir maintained that the ruling did not affect the legal status of the Government, and the Yang di-Pertuan Agong (head of state), Tunku Mahmood Iskandar, expressed support for the Prime Minister. Later in February 1988 Mahathir announced that UMNO Baru (New UMNO) had been formed and that members of the original party would have to re-register in order to join. Razaleigh and his supporters were excluded from UMNO Baru (hereafter referred to as UMNO).

Tension between the executive and the judiciary was intensified by Parliament's approval in March 1988 of constitutional amendments limiting the power of the judiciary to interpret laws. The Lord President of the Supreme Court, Tun Mohammed Salleh bin Abas, wrote to the Yang di-Pertuan Agong to complain about government attempts to reduce the independence of the judiciary, and was subsequently dismissed from office. In June 1989 the Government introduced a security law removing the right of persons being detained under provisions of the ISA to have recourse to the courts.

In September 1988 Razaleigh and 12 others left the BN to join the opposition in the House of Representatives as independents. Razaleigh's movement established an alliance with the fundamentalist PAS in March 1989, and in May registered as Semangat '46 (Spirit of 1946, a reference to the year of foundation of the original UMNO). The DAP, whose followers were largely urban Chinese, agreed to co-operate with Semangat '46 and the PAS, but refused to join a formal alliance, owing to its opposition to the PAS's proclaimed policy of forming an Islamic state in Malaysia. The opposition parties formed an informal electoral alliance, Gagasan Rakyat (People's Might), to contest the general election held in October 1990. None the less, the BN won 127 of the 180 seats in the enlarged House of Representatives, thus retaining the two-thirds' majority necessary to amend the Constitution. Elections to 11 of the 13 State Legislative Assemblies (excluding Sabah and Sarawak) were held concurrently. The BN obtained a majority of seats in all states except Kelantan, where the Angkatan Perpaduan Ummah (APU—Muslim Unity Movement), another coalition including Semangat '46 and the PAS, won every seat in both the federal and state elections. In November 1990 Mahathir and Abdul Ghafar Baba were unanimously re-elected as President and Deputy President of UMNO. Mahathir appointed Anwar Ibrahim as Minister of Finance and Abdullah Badawi as Minister of Foreign Affairs in February 1991.

In January 1991 Datuk Seri Joseph Pairin Kitingan, the Chief Minister of Sabah and President of the PBS, which had contested the general election with the opposition, was arrested and charged with corruption. It was widely conjectured that his arrest, under the ISA, was politically motivated. In May Jeffrey Kitingan (the brother of the Chief Minister) was also detained under the ISA, accused of plotting Sabah's secession from Malaysia. In March 1993 constitutional amendments were adopted reducing the privileges of the country's nine hereditary rulers (seven of whom are entitled 'Sultan', one 'Raja' and the other 'Yamtuan Besar'), including ending their legal immunity, curtailing their power to pardon the offences of relatives, and allowing parliamentary criticism of their misdeeds. The action was widely suspected to have been instigated by Mahathir owing, in part, to the Sultan of Kelantan's open support for Razaleigh (a prince of Kelantan) in the 1990 general election.

In October 1993 Mahathir was returned unopposed as President of UMNO. In the following month Anwar was elected Deputy President of the party (a particularly significant post as the incumbent was traditionally also accorded the position of Deputy Prime Minister). Anwar was duly appointed Deputy Prime Minister in December.

In April 1993 USNO left the opposition in the Sabah State Legislative Assembly to form a coalition with the ruling PBS. Prior to the announcement, six of the 11 elected representatives of USNO joined UMNO. USNO's defection prompted the federal Government successfully to seek the party's deregistration in August, on the grounds that it had breached its own statutes.

In January 1994 Pairin Kitingan dissolved the Sabah State Legislative Assembly in preparation for an early election. Shortly afterwards Pairin Kitingan was convicted on charges of corruption by the High Court, but fined less than the minimum required to disqualify him from office. Although Pairin Kitingan gained popular sympathy owing both to his perceived

victimization in the corruption case and to his resistance to federal encroachment on Sabahan authority, a faction emerged in the PBS that favoured more harmonious relations with the federal Government. Former members of the deregistered USNO joined the PBS for the election. At the poll in February the PBS won a narrow majority, securing 25 of the 48 elective seats. In March, however, several PBS members defected to the opposition, among them Jeffrey Kitingan, who had been released from detention under the ISA in December 1993. As a result, the PBS was stripped of its majority and Pairin Kitingan was replaced as Chief Minister by Tan Sri Sakaran Dandai, a leader of the Sabah wing of UMNO.

In June 1994 the BN coalition agreed to admit two breakaway parties from the PBS, the Parti Demokratik Sabah (Sabah Democratic Party), led by Datuk Bernard Dompok, and the Parti Bersatu Rakyat Sabah (PBRS—United Sabah People's Party), led by Joseph Kurup. In August Dompok was appointed Minister in the Prime Minister's Department, while Jeffrey Kitingan, who had been cleared of corruption in the High Court in June, became Deputy Minister for Housing and Local Government.

Meanwhile, in May 1994 the House of Representatives approved the 1994 Constitution (Amendment) Act, which further restricted the powers of the monarchy and provided for the restructuring of the judiciary. Hitherto, the Yang di-Pertuan Agong had been competent to withhold assent from and return legislation, within 30 days, to Parliament for further consideration. The amendment required the Yang di-Pertuan Agong to give his assent to a bill within 30 days; if he failed to do so, the bill would, none the less, become law.

In the April 1995 general election the BN won an overwhelming majority, taking 162 of the 192 seats in the enlarged House of Representatives and retaining control of 10 of the 11 State Legislative Assemblies for which voting took place. In Kelantan, which remained the only state under opposition control, a coalition of the PAS and Semangat '46 won a majority of the seats. Despite his election victory, Mahathir's position appeared vulnerable during the divisional elections of UMNO in 1995. The defeat of several Mahathir supporters was widely attributed to the influence of Anwar's associates, and, amid speculation that Anwar might challenge Mahathir for the leadership, in November UMNO's General Assembly adopted an unprecedented resolution to avoid any contest for the two senior party positions in 1996. Mahathir subsequently announced that he would retire in the near future and named Anwar as his successor.

Semangat '46 was formally dissolved in October 1996, and its members were admitted to UMNO. At that month's UMNO General Assembly Mahathir and Anwar were, as anticipated, returned unopposed to their posts. In contrast to the 1993 party elections, in which Anwar's supporters had been particularly successful, a large proportion of Mahathir loyalists were now elected.

Mahathir's response to the regional currency crisis that emerged in 1997, following Thailand's effective devaluation of the baht in July, and his criticism of international investors, was widely perceived to have exacerbated Malaysia's economic position. However, international criticism of Mahathir's outspokenness prompted popular demonstrations of support for the premier within Malaysia and near unanimous support for a vote of confidence in his leadership, which was held in the House of Representatives during November. Meanwhile, political opponents of Anwar attempted to undermine his position through the circulation of a series of letters accusing him of sexual indiscretions.

The first trials of Anwar Ibrahim

Evidence of a growing division between Mahathir and Anwar became apparent at the UMNO annual party congress in June 1998, when Dato' Seri Dr Ahmad Zahid bin Hamidi, the head of the youth wing of UMNO and one of Anwar's supporters, made a speech criticizing what he termed the debilitating impact of corruption in the party. Mahathir responded by publishing a list of hundreds of people and companies who had received privatization contracts in recent years, including close associates of Anwar and members of his family. During the following weeks Mahathir acted to counter the influence of Anwar, promoting allies and dismissing newspaper editors close to Anwar. The resignation in August of the Governor (a close ally of Anwar) and Deputy Governor of the central bank, reportedly owing to a disagreement over policy with Mahathir, indicated the intensification of the rift within the Government. Supporters loyal to the Prime Minister responded to the perceived threat to Mahathir's leadership by circulating a brochure entitled *Fifty Reasons Why*

Anwar Cannot Become Prime Minister, in which Anwar was accused of sexual offences and corruption.

Allegations of Anwar's supposed sexual misconduct increased over the succeeding months, and, following Anwar's refusal to resign, culminated in Mahathir's dismissal of Anwar as Deputy Prime Minister and Minister of Finance on 2 September 1998, on the grounds that he was morally unfit to hold office. On the following day Anwar was expelled from UMNO, and affidavits accusing him of sexual impropriety were filed with the High Court. The allegations were denied by Anwar, who asserted that they constituted part of a senior-level political conspiracy to discredit him. Anwar began a tour of the country, drawing extensive support for his calls for wide-ranging reform of the political system from the many thousands who attended his public appearances. His supporters adopted the slogan '*reformasi*' (reform), which had united the popular forces that ousted President Suharto in Indonesia. In mid-September Anwar's adoptive brother, Sukma Darmawan Samitaat Madja, and a former speech-writer for Anwar were each sentenced to six months' imprisonment after they confessed to illegal homosexual activity with Anwar. The following day, at a meeting attended by at least 40,000 people in Kuala Lumpur, Anwar called directly for Mahathir's resignation, but he was arrested shortly afterwards and detained under the ISA. A further 17 people, including a number of close associates of Anwar, were also detained under the same act. Anwar's arrest provoked popular protests, which erupted into violence when demonstrations involving up to 60,000 people were forcibly dispersed by the security forces.

Following Anwar's arrest, his wife, Wan Azizah Wan Ismail, emerged as the de facto leader of the opposition movement. Despite a restriction order issued against Wan Azizah, demonstrations in protest against Anwar's detention were held throughout September 1998; these became the forum for demands for widespread political reform and for the removal of the restrictions on freedom of speech and assembly imposed under the ISA. At a court hearing in Petaling Jaya, Anwar pleaded not guilty to charges of corruption and sexual impropriety. Allegations made by Anwar, who appeared in court with visible bruising to his face, that he had been severely beaten while in police custody and had subsequently been denied medical attention for a number of days, provoked expressions of extreme concern from foreign governments. Malaysia's Attorney-General publicly admitted in January 1999 that Anwar had been assaulted by the police while in custody.

Anwar's trial on charges of corruption (relating to efforts allegedly made by him in 1997 to obtain through the police written denials that he was guilty of sexual misconduct and sodomy) began in November 1998, and in April 1999 he was found guilty on all charges and sentenced to six years' imprisonment (under Malaysian law, this would be followed by a five-year period of disqualification from political office). Following the verdict, supporters of the former Deputy Prime Minister clashed with security forces outside the court. Violent protests continued for the next three days. Following the trial, three prosecution witnesses who had withdrawn their testimony against Anwar, including his adoptive brother and speech-writer, who claimed that their confessions had been obtained through police coercion, were charged with perjury.

Anwar's second trial, on the charge of illegal homosexual activity, began in June 1999. On the first day of the trial the prosecution amended the wording of its charge, changing (for the second time) the month and year in which the alleged crimes were supposedly committed. The proceedings were beset by numerous delays, including an adjournment in September to allow for medical examination following claims by the defence that Anwar might have been deliberately poisoned while in police custody. (However, the tests detected no clinical signs of any such action.) In April 2000 the Court of Appeal upheld Anwar's conviction on charges of corruption. Moreover, in August the High Court found Anwar guilty of sodomy, sentencing him to a further nine years' imprisonment, thus bringing his term to a total of 15 years. His adoptive brother, Sukma Darmawan, was sentenced to six years' imprisonment for the same offence.

In May 2001 public prosecutors announced that other outstanding charges of corruption and sodomy against Anwar were to be abandoned. In July 2002 Anwar lost his appeal against his corruption conviction, and in April 2003 the appeal against his sodomy conviction was similarly dismissed. A few days previously he had completed his sentence for corruption, the last two years of his six-year sentence having been remitted for good

behaviour. In September 2004 Anwar was released from prison after his appeal against his conviction for sodomy was upheld by the Federal Court, which deemed the evidence against Anwar unreliable. Although he remained disqualified from holding political office until April 2008, owing to his corruption conviction, Anwar announced his intention to resume his campaign for political reform.

Consolidation of power and suppression of dissent

In January 1999, meanwhile, Mahathir effected a major cabinet reorganization, in which Abdullah Badawi was appointed as Deputy Prime Minister and Minister for Home Affairs (a post relinquished by Mahathir). Also in January the UMNO Supreme Council announced its decision to postpone for 18 months elections for senior posts within the party, previously scheduled to be held in June, effectively preventing any potential challenge to Mahathir's leadership from within the party. The BN won a significant victory in the elections to the State Legislative Assembly in Sabah in March, securing 31 of the 48 seats. In April the Parti Keadilan Nasional (PKN—National Justice Party) was launched by Wan Azizah in anticipation of the forthcoming general election; the new party declared that its first act, should it come to power, would be to seek a royal pardon for Anwar.

In November 1999 the Government unexpectedly announced that a general election was to be held at the end of that month. The opposition expressed dissatisfaction at the limited period of time this allowed for campaigning. At the election, a decisive victory was won by the governing BN coalition, which gained 148 of a total of 193 seats in the enlarged House of Representatives, thereby retaining a two-thirds' majority. The opposition coalition, the Barisan Alternatif (Alternative Front), which had been formed by the PAS, the PKN, the DAP and the Parti Rakyat Malaysia (PRM—Malaysian People's Party) in June (and which subsequently selected Anwar as its prime ministerial candidate), won a total of 42 seats, while the opposition PBS, which remained outside the Barisan Alternatif, secured three seats. Despite the BN's victory, UMNO experienced a significant decline in support among Malay voters (mainly in favour of the PAS, which secured 27 seats) and lost 23 seats. The party also performed poorly (again largely at the expense of the PAS) in the assembly elections held simultaneously in 11 Malaysian states. This erosion of confidence in UMNO was widely believed to be a result of the Government's treatment of Anwar and the concomitant decline of public trust in the police and the judicial system. Mahathir announced in December that he intended this (his fifth) term of office to be his last, and for the first time formally identified Abdullah Badawi as his preferred successor. In the same month the Barisan Alternatif nominated Fadzil Nor, President of the PAS, as the new parliamentary leader of the opposition.

At the UMNO party elections in May 2000 Mahathir and Abdullah Badawi were formally elected President and Deputy President of the party, respectively. In June 2001 the Minister of Finance, Daim Zainuddin, resigned, following widespread allegations of his misuse of public funds. Mahathir subsequently assumed responsibility for the finance portfolio.

Meanwhile, government suppression of dissent increased significantly. The deputy leader of the DAP and Anwar's legal representative, Karpal Singh, and the Vice-President of the PKN, Marina Yusoff, were charged under the Sedition Act in January 2000 (although the charges against Karpal were dropped in 2002). In the same month the editor and the printer of the popular PAS newspaper, *Harakah*, were also charged with sedition in connection with an article concerning Anwar's trial. The group editor-in-chief of the *New Straits Times*, Kadir Jasin, was forced to resign in June 2000 over an editorial that questioned UMNO's proposed mode of conduct of forthcoming internal party elections.

The Anwar issue continued to incite public unrest, and in April 2000 a protest to mark the anniversary of Anwar's conviction for corruption was broken up by riot police, with 48 PKN activists being arrested. Public criticism of the Government, and subsequent detentions, became more frequent after Anwar's second conviction, as confidence in Mahathir's leadership continued to decline. Mohamad Ezam Mohamad Noor, Anwar's former political secretary, was arrested in March 2001 for having made allegedly seditious comments, despite already being on trial for releasing a secret report on corruption. A month later he was detained again, along with six other opposition leaders, under the ISA. In August 2002 Ezam Noor was sentenced to a two-year prison term, having been convicted of divulging state secrets;

however, his conviction was overruled by the High Court in April 2004.

In August 2001 Nik Adli Nik Abdul Aziz, son of PAS spiritual leader Datuk Haji Nik Abdul Aziz Nik Mat, was one of 10 men detained under the ISA on suspicion of membership of the Kumpulan Mujahidin Malaysia (KMM), an Islamist fundamentalist group believed to be engaged in a long-term plot to overthrow the Government. The following month the Government announced that Nik Adli was to be detained for two years without trial under the provisions of the ISA. Eight of the nine men arrested with him were also imprisoned.

Meanwhile, in March 2001 Mahathir confirmed that the National Vision Policy (NVP), which had replaced the National Development Plan (NDP) in 2000, was to remain in force until at least 2010. The Prime Minister thus provided for a continuation of the preferential conditions in the fields of education and commerce that had been afforded to the Malay majority by the precursor to the NDP—the New Economic Policy (NEP)—upon its implementation in 1971. (In the event, the NVP was abandoned, and the NEP reinstated, in 2006.)

In September 2001 the opposition was destabilized by the withdrawal of the DAP from the Barisan Alternatif. The party accused the PAS of alienating Chinese voters through its support for an Islamic state. (The PAS subsequently accused the Government of using devious methods to exploit popular fear of Islamist militancy in the aftermath of the September terrorist attacks in the USA.) In the same month the BN won an overwhelming majority in elections to the state legislature in Sarawak. In January 2002 the PBS was formally readmitted to the BN following more than a decade of absence from power.

On 21 November 2001 the Yang di-Pertuan Agong, Sultan Salahuddin Abdul Aziz Shah Al-Haj ibni al-Marhum Sultan Hisamuddin Alam Shah Al-Haj, died at the age of 75. On 13 December the Raja of Perlis, Tuanku Syed Sirajuddin Syed Putra Jamalullail, was sworn in as the new monarch, following his election by secret ballot from among the eight other Malay rulers. The Sultan of Terengganu continued as his deputy.

In June 2002, during a speech to the annual congress of UMNO, Prime Minister Mahathir unexpectedly announced that he intended to resign from the Government with immediate effect. However, he was persuaded to withdraw his resignation shortly afterwards and, following some discussion, it was decided that he would remain in power until October 2003, when he would be succeeded by Abdullah Badawi. Following the death of Fadzil Nor, the President of the PAS, in June 2002, Abdul Hadi Awang assumed the party leadership on an interim basis. In July Abdul Hadi announced the imposition of Islamic law in Terengganu state, of which he was the Chief Minister; however, the Government continued to oppose efforts to enforce the new legal code.

In August 2003 the PKN merged with the smaller PRM, forming the Parti Keadilan Rakyat (PKR—People's Justice Party), in advance of the next general election. The President of the PKN, Wan Azizah, continued as President of the new party. In September it was announced that nine suspected members of the KMM who had been detained under the ISA in August 2001, including Nik Adli Nik Abdul Aziz, would be imprisoned for a further two years. After more than five years of incarceration without charge, Nik Adli was finally released in October 2006.

The Government of Abdullah Badawi

Prime Minister Mahathir Mohamad formally retired in October 2003, after 22 years in power. Abdullah Badawi was then sworn in as Prime Minister, retaining the home affairs portfolio and, in addition, assuming Mahathir's role as Minister of Finance. In November Abdullah was also endorsed as the new Chairman of the BN. In January 2004 Abdullah effected his first cabinet reorganization, nominating Minister of Defence Mohammad Najib Abdul Razak as Deputy Prime Minister.

At an early general election, which took place in March 2004, around eight months ahead of schedule, the BN secured a commanding victory, winning 198 of the 219 seats in the enlarged House of Representatives and taking control of 11 of the 12 contested State Legislative Assemblies, including that of Terengganu, an erstwhile stronghold of the PAS. The PAS retained control of Kelantan only by a narrow margin. The DAP secured 12 seats in the House of Representatives, followed by the PAS, which won seven (compared with 27 at the election of 1999) and the PKR, which retained only one seat, that held by Wan Azizah. Having been sworn in again as head of government, Abdullah Badawi announced a major cabinet reorganization,

although Najib Razak continued as Deputy Prime Minister and Minister of Defence. The Prime Minister launched a National Integrity Plan in April 2004, aimed at reducing corruption and abuse of power. In May the Government allowed journalists to visit a detention centre for those held under the ISA, in an attempt to dispel recent allegations that detainees had been tortured.

Abdullah Badawi's control over UMNO was questioned in September 2004, when three members of his Cabinet failed to secure re-election to the party's Supreme Council at its General Assembly; some observers attributed their defeat to a reaction by party members against the Prime Minister's anti-corruption campaign. None the less, Abdullah and Najib Razak were formally endorsed as the party's President and Deputy President, respectively. UMNO leaders ruled out a return to the party for Anwar, who had been freed from prison earlier in September. In December Anwar launched a nationwide campaign against the ISA. In August 2005 he was awarded RM 4.5m. in damages by the High Court for the false allegations contained within the pamphlet *Fifty Reasons Why Anwar Ibrahim Cannot Become Prime Minister*, published in 1998. In January 2006 Anwar filed a lawsuit against former Prime Minister Mahathir for falsely having depicted him as a homosexual and causing 'irreparable damage' to his reputation. (In September 2005 Mahathir had controversially told reporters that he had dismissed Anwar in 1998 in order to avoid the potential appointment of a homosexual Prime Minister.) However, in July 2007 the High Court dismissed the lawsuit.

In November 2005 Azahari Husin, a notorious Malaysian bomb-maker thought to be responsible for many of the operations of the regional Islamist organization Jemaah Islamiah (JI), was killed in Indonesia during a police operation. In January 2006 another prominent Malaysian Islamist militant, Noordin Mohammad Top, released a message in which he claimed responsibility for the bombings on the Indonesian island of Bali in 2005 and declared himself to be the head of a new South-East Asian Islamist militant organization—Tanzam Qaedat al Jihad (Organization of the Basis of Jihad).

Sultan Tuanku Mizan Zainal Abidin ibni al-Marhum Sultan Mahmud, the Sultan of Terengganu, was sworn in as the country's Yang di-Pertuan Agong on 13 December 2006 and was enthroned on 26 April 2007.

Several scandals involving senior officials emerged in early 2007, including opposition attempts to link Deputy Prime Minister Najib Razak to a murder that his political adviser, Abdul Razak Baginda, was charged with abetting in 2006. Najib denied any connection to the killing or to the victim, Altantuya Shaariibuu, a Mongolian translator. (Abdul Razak was subsequently acquitted of the murder.)

In November 2007 police used force to disperse up to 30,000 demonstrators in Kuala Lumpur who were campaigning for electoral reform. The demonstration, which had been declared illegal, was organized by the Gabungan Pilihanraya Bersih dan Adil (Bersih—the Coalition for Clean and Fair Elections), comprising a number of opposition parties, including the DAP, the PAS and the PKR, and civil society organizations. Bersih's main demands were equal access to the state-controlled media for all parties, a complete revision of the electoral register, the use of indelible ink to prevent multiple voting, and the abolition of postal voting except for diplomats and overseas voters. A second banned demonstration, involving at least 8,000 ethnic Indians, took place outside the British High Commission in Kuala Lumpur later that month, ending in violence, as police clashed with the protesters. The rally was organized by the Hindu Rights Action Force (Hindraf, a coalition of some 30 Hindu non-governmental organizations—NGOs) to highlight perceived discrimination against Indians in Malaysia (who accounted for some 7% of the population) and, more specifically, in support of a lawsuit, filed in the British courts in August, demanding that the British Government pay reparations to the descendants of Indians transported to Malaysia as indentured labourers during the 19th century. In December five Hindraf members were detained under the ISA.

In February 2008 Abdullah Badawi called a general election for 8 March, more than one year earlier than the constitutional deadline. The timing of the election ensured the exclusion of Anwar, whose disqualification from seeking public office was not due to expire until a month later. In the event, the BN sustained heavy losses in the polling for both the enlarged House of Representatives and 12 of the 13 State Legislative Assemblies. (Elections to the Sarawak State Legislative Assembly had been conducted in May 2006, when the BN had won 62 of the 71 seats in the expanded state legislature.) The ruling coalition failed to retain its two-thirds' majority in the House of Representatives, taking only 140 of the 222 seats, and lost control of the Legislative Assemblies of Kedah, Penang, Perak and Selangor. Of the opposition parties, which had pledged not to present candidates against each other, the PKR made the most significant gains in the House of Representatives, winning a total of 31 seats (compared with only one in 2004), while the DAP and the PAS both increased their representation by 16 seats, to 28 seats and 23 seats, respectively. The BN's poor performance was attributed to public discontent with renewed ethnic tensions and rising inflation, as well as concern about crime levels and corruption. Having dismissed demands for his resignation, including from within UMNO, Abdullah reorganized his Cabinet. The Prime Minister retained the finance portfolio, while Najib Razak remained Deputy Prime Minister and Minister of Defence, but most other portfolios were affected by the reallocations. New appointees included Datuk Mohd Zaid bin Ibrahim as a Minister in the Prime Minister's Department. Zaid was charged with reforming the judiciary, the reputation of which had been damaged during the second half of 2007 by allegations of corruption in the appointment process for judges.

In May 2008 Anwar was accused of sodomy by a party aide. Fearing for his safety, Anwar sought temporary refuge at the Turkish embassy in Kuala Lumpur the following month. He was arrested in July, formally charged with sodomy in August and released on bail pending a further hearing. In July, meanwhile, Wan Azizah vacated the seat that she had occupied in the House of Representatives since her husband's conviction in 1999, thus enabling Anwar to stand as a candidate at the ensuing by-election for the seat that he had previously held. Polling took place in August, when Anwar secured an overwhelming victory. As the de facto leader of the opposition, he subsequently gained the support of the PAS.

In October 2008 Abdullah Badawi announced his intention to vacate the presidency of UMNO and to resign as Prime Minister in early 2009, having been placed under increasing pressure to depart, owing to the recent electoral losses suffered by the BN and to his perceived failure effectively to address the issue of corruption. Furthermore, the first parliamentary motion of no confidence against a Malaysian Prime Minister had been drafted in June 2008, only to be withdrawn on a technicality. In September Abdullah had transferred the finance portfolio to Najib Razak, his designated successor, in exchange for that of defence.

Datuk Mohd Zaid bin Ibrahim resigned from his position in the Prime Minister's Department in September 2008, expressing his frustration at the pace of legal reforms and criticizing the authorities' increasing recourse to the ISA to curb dissidence. (Following his resignation, Zaid cautioned against the appointment of Najib Razak as Prime Minister on account of his alleged links to the killing of the Mongolian translator Altantuya Shaariibuu; Zaid was subsequently suspended from UMNO, before joining the PKR in June 2009.)

The editor of online newspaper *Malaysia Today*, Raja Petra Kamaruddin, was arrested under the ISA in September 2008 on the grounds that he had published articles provoking racial tension. Later that month Raja Petra received a two-year detention order on charges of insulting Islam, but this was overruled in November when the High Court found that the Government had acted beyond its legal powers in issuing such an order. Raja Petra also implicated Najib Razak and his wife in the murder of Shaariibuu. In March 2009, after accusing Najib Razak of involvement in the murder of the Mongolian translator, Gobind Singh Deo, a member of the DAP, was banned from Parliament for one year, prompting a walkout by opposition members. Gobind's father, DAP Chairman Karpal Singh, who was also an eminent lawyer and was representing the murdered woman's family, was charged with sedition for allegedly having insulted the Sultan of Perak. Two opposition newspapers, the PAS's *Harakah* and the PKR's *Suara Keadilan*, were banned from publishing for three months by the Government in March 2009, shortly before the appointment of Najib Razak as Prime Minister and the holding of three by-elections in April.

Meanwhile, in February 2009 the BN regained control of Perak state after three PKR members of the State Legislative Assembly defected to the BN. The Sultan of Perak subsequently deposed the Chief Minister, Mohammad Nizar Jamaluddin, appointing a BN member, Datuk Zambry Abdul Kadir, in his place. The formation of a new state Government was strongly contested by the PKR, which argued that the transition was unconstitutional and demanded the holding of fresh state elections. Following a series of protests and parliamentary manoeuvres to obstruct the new Government, PKR legislators were prevented by the police from entering the assembly building. The case was referred to the High Court; however, prior to the Court's ruling, and amid protests and the arrest of dozens of protesters and opposition members, the BN Government forcibly removed the Assembly's Speaker and took control of the state legislature. The next session of the Assembly was then officially opened by the son of the Sultan of Perak. Four days later, in mid-May, the High Court ruled that the opposition was the lawful Government of Perak and that Nizar Jamaluddin was the rightful Chief Minister; on the following day, however, Zambry was reinstated, pending an appeal. In late May the Court of Appeal overruled the High Court's decision and declared that Zambry was in fact the rightful Chief Minister. The Federal Court, Malaysia's highest judicial body, unanimously ruled in February 2010 that the Court of Appeal had been right to rescind the High Court's verdict and reaffirmed Zambry's validity as Chief Minister.

The Government of Najib Razak

Having officially resigned as UMNO President at the party's annual congress in March 2009, Abdullah Badawi formally submitted his resignation as Prime Minister on 2 April; Najib Razak, who had replaced Abdullah as party leader, was inaugurated as Prime Minister on the following day. In a demonstration of support, Mahathir rejoined UMNO. Mahathir had resigned from the party in May 2008, having been outspokenly critical of Abdullah since 2006, insisting that he would not return until Abdullah had resigned. Najib announced the composition of his Cabinet: eight ministers from the outgoing administration were dismissed, while Muhyiddin Yassin, hitherto the Minister of International Trade and Industry, was promoted to the position of Deputy Prime Minister and concurrently awarded the education portfolio.

In his inaugural address, the new Prime Minister, who retained the finance portfolio, pledged to use the ISA more appropriately and to release a group of 13 detainees held under its provisions; Najib also rescinded the suspensions of *Harakah* and *Suara Keadilan*, and pledged to address the problems encountered by minority communities, notably the grievances of Malaysia's ethnic Indians. In May 2009 the 13 detainees were duly released without having been formally charged; among them were members of Hindraf who had been detained since organizing the anti-Government protests of 2007. Furthermore, in June 2009 Najib announced that the Government was to abandon certain aspects of the NEP, which had guided government policy since 1971; non-Malay business people and investors welcomed Najib's proposals, as a result of which, *inter alia*, the majority of public companies would no longer be required to reserve 30% of their shares for ethnic Malays.

In April 2009, despite the seemingly conciliatory tone struck by Najib Razak upon his assumption of the premiership, a new law enhancing the powers of the police to ban demonstrations deemed a threat to public order was approved by the legislature. In July P. Uthayakumar, one of the 13 detainees released in May, registered a new, Indian-based political party: the stated aim of the Human Rights Party (HRP) was politically to empower and liberate Malaysia's ethnic Indians.

The death in July 2009 of Teoh Beng Hock, a journalist and political aide to Ean Yong Hian Wah—a member of the Selangor State Legislative Assembly—caused a public outcry; on the previous day Teoh had been questioned by the Malaysian Anti-Corruption Commission (MACC) in connection with corruption allegations against Ean Yong. The Malaysian authorities claimed that Teoh had committed suicide, while others contended that he had died from injuries sustained during his interrogation. During a mass demonstration in Kuala Lumpur in August, when an estimated 20,000 citizens gathered to protest against the ISA, some protesters took the opportunity to decry the authorities' perceived ill treatment of Teoh, as well as of Anwar. Riot police forcibly dispersed the protesters, and more than 600 people were reported to have been arrested. An inquest into Teoh's death commenced later that month. However, in January 2011 the coroner recorded an open verdict, declaring that there was insufficient evidence to determine how Teoh had died. The verdict was strongly condemned by Teoh's supporters and the political opposition, who contended that evidence had been suppressed during the inquest in order to protect the reputation of the authorities.

In an apparent attempt to appease critics, Najib announced in mid-January 2011 that a Royal Commission of Inquiry was to be held into the MACC's interrogation procedures. Later that month, in response to public criticism of the Commission's apparently limited scope, Najib agreed to widen its remit to include an investigation into the specific circumstances surrounding Teoh's death. The Commission's final report, which was published in July, concluded that Teoh had not been killed by third-party involvement, but had committed suicide following his interrogation by three MACC officers who had employed improper, overly aggressive techniques of questioning. In response, Teoh's family continued to insist that he had been murdered, while a coalition of more than 100 NGOs condemned the document and appealed for the resignations of Najib, the Minister of Home Affairs, the head of the MACC and the Inspector-General of the police force. However, the Government defended the Commission's findings and urged all parties to accept its conclusions. An application seeking a review of the open verdict recorded by the coroner in January was rejected by the High Court in December. However, an appeal against the High Court's ruling was upheld by the Court of Appeal in February 2012, providing for a judicial review of the coroner's verdict. In September 2014 the Court of Appeal rejected the open verdict delivered in January 2011, ruling that there was sufficient evidence to prove that 'a person or persons were responsible for his [Teoh's] death'.

The second trial of Anwar Ibrahim

The second trial of Anwar on sodomy charges, which had commenced in February 2010, was beset by numerous delays and adjournments. Anwar continued to dismiss the allegations against him as a government conspiracy to end his career. The lead defence counsel for Anwar, DAP Chairman Karpal Singh, alleged numerous apparent discrepancies in the prosecution's case and in the testimony of a number of its witnesses, including that of the claimant, Mohd Saiful Bukhari Azlan. Two attempts by Karpal to force the removal of the presiding High Court judge—the first in February 2010 for the judge's alleged lack of objectivity with regard to the case and the second in December following his reported resort to intimidation of the defence during court proceedings—proved unsuccessful, as did appeals (in August 2010 and May 2011) to have the charges against Anwar withdrawn. Meanwhile, in March 2010 the Federal Court ruled that Mahathir's dismissal of Anwar as Deputy Prime Minister and Minister of Finance in September 1998 had been constitutional and valid.

In December 2010 the House of Representatives voted to suspend Anwar for a period of six months, following a parliamentary disciplinary inquiry in response to claims made by Anwar earlier in the year that a government campaign to promote racial unity under the banner of '1Malaysia' had been inspired by the 'One Israel' electoral campaign of the then Israeli Prime Minister, Ehud Barak, in 1999. Anwar was deemed to have misled legislators on the issue, which was a source of considerable embarrassment to the Government. (Muslim-majority Malaysia had no diplomatic relations with Israel and was a staunch proponent of an independent Palestinian state.) Three of Anwar's parliamentary allies, among them Karpal Singh, were also suspended for a six-month period having been cited for contempt, owing to their criticism of the disciplinary action against Anwar.

Meanwhile, the authorities imposed further restrictions on the media during 2010. In July the US-based organization Human Rights Watch appealed to the Government to repeal the 1984 Printing Presses and Publications Act, which effectively granted the Ministry of Home Affairs the right of censorship over all publication content within Malaysia, highlighting the pledge made by the Prime Minister in 2009 to ensure that the media was empowered responsibly to report events without fear of reprisal.

In February 2011 a PKR state legislator, Shuhaimi Shafiei, was charged with sedition after posting a comment on his website in December 2010 that was deemed to be critical of the Sultan of Selangor. Shuhaimi denied any wrongdoing, claiming that he was a victim of political manipulation, as part of a wider effort by the governing coalition to discredit the opposition prior to elections. At elections to the 71-member Sarawak state legislature held in April 2011, the BN's representation declined from 63 to 55 seats, mainly at the expense of gains by the DAP.

The trial of Anwar drew to a close in December 2011, after nearly two years of court proceedings. In early January 2012 the presiding judge announced the High Court's verdict, unexpectedly acquitting Anwar, on the grounds that Saiful's claims remained unsubstantiated since the Court could not be sure

that the DNA evidence against Anwar had not been contaminated. While welcoming the verdict, Anwar's supporters maintained that he should not have been charged in the first place, while some members of the opposition speculated that the whole affair had been orchestrated as a cynical ploy to rebuild public trust in the Najib administration prior to the forthcoming general election. In late January the Government announced its intention to appeal against the High Court's ruling.

The return of the Bersih movement and the repeal of the Internal Security Act

A significant development during the course of 2011 was the return to prominence of the Bersih movement (see *The Government of Abdullah Badawi*), which was now under the chairmanship of Ambiga Sreenevasan, a former President of the Malaysian Bar Council, who declared that Bersih's resumption of activity was a direct consequence of the Government's failure to address the electoral demands made by the movement in November 2007. In advance of a major rally planned for July 2011 by the movement, which had rebranded itself 'Bersih 2.0', the Malaysian authorities were reported to have arrested some 150 Bersih supporters during a police operation designated 'Operation Erase Bersih'. Bersih had initially obtained permission to stage the rally, but this was subsequently withdrawn by the authorities. Nevertheless, the rally went ahead as planned, and was attended by an estimated 10,000–20,000 people. As in 2007, the police resorted to the use of tear gas and water cannons in order to disperse the demonstrators, more than 1,600 of whom were arrested, including Ambiga and the President of the PAS, Abdul Hadi Awang. Although Najib dismissed the rally as representing only a minority of Malaysians, plans for an early election, which many observers had expected to be called in late 2011, were abandoned.

Significant consternation was generated by the Malaysian Government's censorship of an article published in the British periodical *The Economist* in July 2011 regarding the authorities' reportedly over-zealous handling of the Bersih 2.0 rally. Amid mounting criticism, in August Najib conceded that media censorship in Malaysia was no longer effective, with the act of censorship often generating more controversy and ill-feeling than that which was censored, and pledged to review the country's current legislation on media censorship. Najib also announced the creation of a bipartisan panel tasked with reviewing the country's electoral laws. The panel duly recommended a series of reforms, some of which echoed demands made by Bersih 2.0—including the use of indelible ink at polling stations and a review of electoral rolls to remove deceased and duplicate voters—and these were approved by the legislature in December. Although failing to address a number of key opposition demands, including the introduction of longer electoral campaign periods and automatic voter registration, the reforms were none the less widely welcomed as a significant initial step towards ensuring a more fair and free electoral system.

Furthermore, in September 2011 Najib announced that the increasingly vilified ISA, together with three emergency declarations that also provided for detention without charge, were to be repealed. (New security legislation was to be introduced under Article 149 of the Constitution, which would allow for a continuation of detentions without charge in the case of 'preventing subversive activities, organized terrorism and crime to maintain peace and public order'—see below.) Najib also pledged to replace the existing system of annual publishing licences with a system whereby permits, once granted, would not require regular renewal but would be cancelled if regulations were flouted.

Although these reforms—particularly the revocation of the ISA—were widely welcomed, the opposition and other critics of the Government nevertheless questioned the administration's sincere commitment to a sustained process of meaningful democratic reform, claiming that the recently announced measures merely constituted a calculated ploy to bolster popular support ahead of the forthcoming general election (due to be held by the end of June 2013). Furthermore, critics stressed the potentially ominous undertones of Najib's announcement that detentions without charge were still to be allowed in cases pertaining to subversion and terrorism, noting that the terms remained broad and undefined, and contending that the Government had previously, under the provisions of the ISA, fabricated claims of involvement in subversion and terrorism against its political opponents in its efforts to silence dissent. In addition, legislation approved under Article 149 of the Constitution would not be required to uphold the fundamental human liberties enshrined elsewhere in the Constitution—including the rights to life, personal liberty and property, and the freedom of speech, assembly and association. The opposition also pointed to the introduction in November 2011 of new legislation banning street protests as evidence of the insincerity of the Government's claims to be instigating genuine democratic reforms. Meanwhile, in October the Sultan of Kedah, Tuanku Haji Abdul Halim Mu'adzam Shah ibni al-Marhum Badlishah, was appointed as the country's Yang di-Pertuan Agong. The new head of state was duly inaugurated on 13 December 2011, following the expiry of the Sultan of Terengganu's five-year term of office.

Following allegations of her large-scale misuse of public funds, the Minister of Women, Family and Community Development, Dato' Seri Shahrizat Abdul Jalil, resigned from the Cabinet in April 2012 (although she continued in her position as head of the woman's section of UMNO). The opposition once again claimed that the scandal was evidence of systemic corruption within the Government.

The new security legislation intended to replace the ISA, the Security Offences (Special Measures) Act, was adopted by the House of Representatives in April 2012 and came into force in July. The new Act specifically stated that no person could be detained merely for his or her political beliefs and also limited periods of detention without charge to a maximum of 28 days. While welcoming the repeal of the ISA, Anwar asserted that the new Act still contravened human rights principles. Later that month Bersih (which now comprised some 84 NGOs) staged a further rally, 'Bersih 3.0', in the capital in support of its demands for further electoral reform; estimates of the number of participants ranged from 25,000 to more than 100,000. The demonstration turned violent when the police fired tear gas and water cannon at the protesters after barriers were reportedly breached; hundreds of demonstrators were arrested, a number of whom subsequently claimed to have been beaten by the security forces while in detention. The following month Anwar, who had addressed the mass rally at the end of April, was charged with violating laws covering street protests by inciting the demonstrators to break through the barriers.

Recent developments: the 2013 general election

The House of Representatives was dissolved on 3 April 2013, at the request of Prime Minister Najib Razak, and a general election was subsequently scheduled for 5 May. During the election campaign the BN focused on the country's solid economic performance under Najib's premiership, promising to raise living standards further and to attract increased foreign investment, while the opposition alliance Pakatan Rakyat (People's Alliance)—comprising the PKR, the DAP and the PAS, and headed by Anwar Ibrahim—pledged to combat corruption, to improve transparency and to provide free education up to university level.

With analysts predicting a close contest, turnout at the election on 5 May 2013 reached a record high of 84.8% of the electorate. The BN retained its simple majority in the House of Representatives, but recorded its worst ever electoral result, winning 133 of the 222 seats (compared with 140 seats at the 2008 election), and secured less of the popular vote than Pakatan Rakyat. The member parties of Pakatan Rakyat increased their combined representation to 89 seats (from 82), the gain being attributable to the success of the DAP, which secured 38 seats, 10 more than in 2008. The BN performed better at the concurrent elections to 12 of the 13 State Legislative Assemblies (the Sarawak state legislature having been renewed in April 2011—see *The second trial of Anwar Ibrahim*), recovering control of Kedah's state legislature and retaining its majority in eight others. Prime Minister Najib was sworn in on 6 May 2013 to serve a further term of office. New appointments to the Cabinet most notably included Ahmad Zahid bin Hamid as Minister of Home Affairs and Hishammuddin bin Tun Hussein as Minister of Defence (and acting Minister of Transport). On 8 May up to 40,000 opposition supporters protested against the official election results at a demonstration organized by Anwar, who accused the ruling coalition of perpetrating widespread electoral fraud. However, a legal challenge initiated by Pakatan Rakyat against the results proved unsuccessful. Following further protests, PKR Vice-President Tian Chua and several other opposition figures were detained on sedition charges in late May, while PAS Vice-President Husam bin Musa was arrested on similar grounds in June. (Tian Chua received a one-month gaol sentence in January 2014 after being convicted of a minor infraction relating to his participation in the Bersih 3.0 rally in 2012, although he

subsequently appealed against this verdict and was acquitted in November 2014.)

In September 2013 Najib, apparently reneging on his 2009 pledge to revoke some of the discriminatory facets of the NEP, proposed a series of new economic privileges for the ethnic Malay population. Analysts attributed this move to Najib's desire to boost his popularity within the ranks of UMNO prior to the party's leadership election, which was due to be held later that month. In the event, Najib was re-elected as UMNO President in an uncontested poll. In November Abdul Hadi Awang was reappointed President of the PAS, and in the following month Liow Tiong Lai secured the presidency of the MCA. Meanwhile, the Ministry of Home Affairs ordered the suspension of weekly newspaper *The Heat* during December 2013–January 2014, after it published an exposé on government spending. Human Rights Watch drew attention to Malaysia's unsatisfactory rights record in several critical statements released in January. Of particular concern to the group was the approval by the House of Representatives in October 2013 of public security legislation that, like the ISA, provided for indefinite detention without trial in certain circumstances. It also condemned a government crackdown on NGOs and the authorities' continued misuse of the Sedition Act.

On 7 March 2014, just weeks before Anwar was due to contest a local by-election in Selangor, the Court of Appeal controversially annulled the High Court's 2012 judgment acquitting him of sodomy and sentenced him to five years' imprisonment. Anwar's defence team filed an appeal, but the Court's verdict left him ineligible to stand in the by-election. In the event Anwar's wife, Wan Azizah, contested the election to the state assembly in Anwar's place, recording a convincing victory over the UMNO candidate. In July the PKR leadership published a document questioning the integrity of party member and Chief Minister of Selangor Abdul Khalid Ibrahim, and proposed party president Wan Azizah as a candidate to replace him. Following Ibrahim's refusal to stand down as Chief Minister, on 9 August the PKR expelled him from the party; at the request of the Sultan of Selangor, Sultan Sharafuddin Idris Shah, Ibrahim remained as Chief Minister, in the capacity of an independent member of the state assembly. However, on 26 August Ibrahim tendered his resignation as Chief Minister, despite the Sultan requesting that he remain in his post. The PKR then unanimously selected Wan Azizah as their sole candidate for the position of Chief Minister. The Sultan refused to accept her candidacy, reportedly on the grounds that her appointment could prefigure an attempt by Anwar to use the position to depose Razak, and in September the Deputy President of the PKR, Mohamed Azmin Ali, was sworn in as the new Chief Minister of Selangor.

In a further setback for the opposition, in February 2014 DAP Chairman Karpal Singh had been found guilty of sedition by the High Court. Karpal appealed the verdict but died in a road accident in April before the appeal was heard. A number of other opposition politicians, as well as journalists and academics, were arrested on charges of sedition during 2014. In September Anwar himself was charged with sedition in relation to a speech he had made at a political rally in 2011, to mark the launch of a campaign relating to the murder in 2006 of Mongolian translator Altantuya Shaariibuu (see *The Government of Abdullah Badawi*). In November 2014 PKR Vice-President Tian Chua was acquitted of a charge of sedition for suggesting in March 2013 that an intrusion by Filipino militants in Lahad Datu (see *Relations with South-East Asian countries*) was in fact a conspiracy orchestrated by UMNO to divert attention from government unpopularity, and to instil fear in the population. UK-based human rights group Amnesty International demanded that the Government repeal the Sedition Act and condemned the crackdown for creating a 'climate of fear' and undermining the political opposition. However, in November 2014 Prime Minister Najib announced that not only would the Sedition Act be retained but its remit would be extended.

In late June 2014 Prime Minister Najib announced a cabinet reorganization which notably included the appointment of several ethnic Chinese ministers from the MCA, which had recently reversed its earlier decision to decline government posts, claiming that its inclusion in the Cabinet would enable it better to serve the Chinese community. MCA President Liow Tiong Lai was appointed Minister of Transport, replacing acting minister Hishammuddin Hussein. The President of Parti Gerakan Rakyat Malaysia (GERAKAN), Mah Siew Keong, was assigned the position of Minister in the Prime Minister's Department, as was Dr Wee Ka Siong, the Deputy President of the MCA. Three other ethnic Chinese parliamentarians, all from the MCA, were appointed deputy ministers.

In July 2014 a Malaysian Airlines passenger aircraft was shot down over eastern Ukraine, apparently by pro-Russian separatist rebels, with the loss of all 298 passengers and crew. The Government drew commendation for its handling of the crisis—in contrast to its perceived unco-ordinated response to an earlier disaster involving another Malaysian Airlines passenger aircraft, which disappeared over the Indian Ocean in March (see *Other regional relations*). In this later incident the Government procured international co-operation in retrieving passenger remains from Ukraine and, from November, participated in an international investigation into determining responsibility for the crash.

In February 2015 the Federal Court upheld Anwar's conviction by the Court of Appeal in March 2014 on a charge of sodomy; Anwar duly commenced his sentence of five years' imprisonment later that month. The opposition leader accused the judiciary of colluding in a political conspiracy on behalf of the ruling regime, while Human Rights Watch condemned the judgment as a setback for human rights in Malaysia. In mid-March 2015 Anwar's eldest daughter, Nurul Izzah Anwar, a member of the House of Representatives and one of the PKR's Vice-Presidents, was arrested (but released the following day) after criticizing the judiciary over its conviction of her father and questioning its neutrality.

Religious Tensions

The right to religious freedom, as prescribed by the Malaysian Constitution, and the country's multi-faith status were prominent issues during the early 21st century, with ongoing debates about religious conversion laws, the jurisdiction of Islamic and civil courts, and punishments for apostasy. In January 2005, at a nightclub in Kuala Lumpur, about 100 Muslims, including many women, were detained on charges of public indecency and other 'anti-Islamic' crimes. Amid the ensuing public outcry, the legitimacy of these arrests was questioned, as the application of Islamic law in federal territories was restricted to marriage and related matters. The Government subsequently instructed the Federal Territories Islamic Department to abandon the charges. However, similar police operations against nightclubs and hotels continued to be reported, with hundreds of Muslims arrested during 2005–14 for *khalwat*, an offence defined as unmarried men and women meeting 'in close proximity . . . in any secluded place or in a house or room under circumstances which may give rise to suspicion that they were engaged in immoral acts', and which carried a maximum penalty of two years' imprisonment.

In February 2006, meanwhile, the Malaysian Government suspended indefinitely the licence of the *Sarawak Tribune*, in response to the newspaper's decision to reprint controversial cartoons depicting the Prophet Muhammad, which had been published in a Danish newspaper in 2005 and had provoked outrage in the international Muslim community. This was the first time in almost two decades that the licence of a Malaysian publication had been revoked, and the episode renewed concerns about the status of religious freedom and freedom of expression.

During 2007 there were a number of high-profile cases that further provoked religious tension in Malaysia. In May the Federal Court rejected an appeal by a convert from Islam to Christianity to have the word 'Islam' removed from the religion section of her identity card, ruling that Syariah (Islamic law) courts held jurisdiction in this area. Observers noted that the judgment effectively made it impossible to renounce Islam legally, given that apostasy was a criminal offence under Islamic law, and renewed the debate about the constitutionally enshrined right to religious freedom. In August the Government suspended publication of the Tamil-language newspaper *Makkal Osai* for one month, after the newspaper published an image of Jesus Christ apparently smoking a cigarette and drinking alcohol. In December controversy arose over the use of the word 'Allah' by non-Muslims, when a Roman Catholic weekly newspaper, *The Herald*, encountered difficulties in renewing its publishing permit because its Malay-language section employed the word 'Allah' when referring to the Christian God, which the Government argued might confuse Muslims. The newspaper's permit was eventually renewed on the condition that it adhere to a government ban on non-Muslims using the word 'Allah'. *The Herald* filed for a judicial review, insisting that it had used the word 'Allah' to refer to the Christian God for decades and had a constitutional right to do so. In December 2009 the High Court ruled in favour of *The Herald*, reversing the government ban on the use of the word by non-Muslims on the grounds that it was 'unconstitutional'. The ruling resulted in an intensification of Muslim–Christian tensions in Malaysia, provoking a series of violent attacks on churches, mosques and a Sikh temple in early 2010. In October 2013, in a highly contentious decision, the High Court's 2009 judgment was quashed by the Court of Appeal, which declared that the word 'Allah' could be used only by Muslims, although the precise ambit of this new interpretation of the law was unclear. With intercommunal tensions rising, in January 2014 a church in Penang that was allegedly continuing to use the word 'Allah' was attacked with petrol bombs, while hundreds of Bibles that referred to 'Allah' were forcibly confiscated from a Christian organization in Selangor. The Malaysian authorities attracted further international scrutiny in March following the proscription of a popular children's comic, *Ultraman*, which made brief mention of the word 'Allah'. In June the Court of Appeal overturned the 2009 ruling by the High Court that reversed the government prohibition on non-Muslims using the word 'Allah' in a religious context; this judgment was upheld by the Federal Court in January 2015.

Meanwhile, in April 2009, shortly after the inauguration of Najib Razak as Prime Minister, the Government outlawed the religious conversion of children without the prior consent of both parents. The ban followed several controversial cases in which children had been converted to Islam following a divorce, despite vehement objections from the non-Muslim parent. (Such conversions had been aided by rulings issued by Syariah courts.) The Government's decision, in July 2010, to appoint female judges to Syariah courts for the first time was described by Najib as a serious attempt 'to enhance justice in cases involving families and women's rights'.

Following a state visit to the Vatican City by Najib Razak in July 2011, during which he held discussions with Pope Benedict XVI, Malaysia and the Vatican announced the establishment of formal diplomatic relations. The development was widely interpreted as an attempt to reassure Christians in Malaysia, who comprised around 9% of the total population, that the Government was committed to fostering strong ties with the Christian Church. Nevertheless, amid mounting claims by the Muslim community of Christians converting Muslims (a practice that is illegal in many Malaysian states), an intensification of tensions between the two religions in Malaysia was reported in the latter half of 2011 and early 2012, and there were a number of arrests made for alleged incitement of religious hatred.

Foreign Affairs

Malaysia's foreign policy has been dominated by its membership of the Association of Southeast Asian Nations (ASEAN, see p. 210), which was founded in 1967. Prime Minister Mahathir Mohamad was instrumental in bringing Myanmar into ASEAN in 1997 under the Policy of Constructive Engagement. In February 2008 Malaysia ratified the new ASEAN Charter, which had been signed in November 2007 at the 13th summit meeting in Singapore. Malaysia has been involved with Brunei, Viet Nam, the People's Republic of China, the Philippines and Taiwan in disputed sovereignty claims over the Spratly Islands in the South China Sea. In November 2002 the ASEAN member states approved a 'code of conduct' for the islands; the agreement was also sanctioned by China. Proposals to formulate a more legally binding code of conduct were espoused in October 2010, but discussions to this end were not reported to have led to any tangible results by early 2015.

Relations with South-East Asian countries

Relations with Singapore have traditionally been characterized by mistrust since the city-state left the Federation of Malaya in 1965. Resentment grew as Singapore advanced more swiftly than Malaysia in economic terms, creating a certain acrimonious competition between the two countries. Yet, as Malaysia also developed, bilateral relations became more cordial, and co-operation increased. From early 2002, however, tensions arose over the renegotiation of a 1961 agreement (due to expire in 2011) by which Malaysia supplied Singapore with water. Following unsuccessful negotiations in 2002, in February 2003 Prime Minister Mahathir stated that, while Malaysia would cease to supply Singapore with untreated water in 2011, it would continue to supply filtered water, at a reasonable price, for as long as necessary. In January 2005 Malaysia and Singapore appeared to have resolved a dispute over the latter's land reclamation project in the Straits of Johor, which separate the two countries; Malaysia accepted that the reclamation work could proceed, while Singapore agreed to co-operate with Malaysia to ensure navigational safety and environmental protection of the waterway. In 2006, however, relations became strained as a result of Singapore's opposition to Malaysia's construction of a bridge to replace the Johor Straits causeway; building work on the Malaysian side was suspended later that year. Singapore's Prime Minister Lee Hsien Loong visited Malaysia in May 2007 for informal talks with his Malaysian counterpart, Abdullah Badawi. The most significant outcome of the discussions was a decision to form a joint ministerial committee to oversee collaboration on Malaysia's plan to establish an economic development zone in southern Johor, to be known as the Iskandar Development Region.

A long-standing dispute between Malaysia and Singapore over their conflicting claims to the island of Batu Puteh (Pedra Branca) was finally concluded in May 2008 when the International Court of Justice (ICJ, see p. 25)—to which the dispute had been referred as per an agreement signed by the two countries in 2003—ruled in favour of Singapore. In June 2011 a land swap agreement was finalized, under the terms of which Malaysia was to be awarded six parcels of land in exchange for giving up land in Singapore owned by Malayan Railways. Upon the expiry in August 2011 of the 1961 water-sharing agreement, the Singaporean Government transferred ownership of water assets, including water treatment facilities and pump houses, to the Johor state government, and reaffirmed previous claims that Singapore would achieve water self-sufficiency before the scheduled expiry, in August 2061, of the 1962 water-sharing agreement. Following a meeting between Malaysian Prime Minister Najib Razak and Lee Hsien Loong, held in Singapore in February 2013, the two premiers announced plans for the construction of a high-speed rail link between their two countries, with completion anticipated in 2020.

While generally remaining cordial, relations with Indonesia have been periodically adversely affected by the flow of illegal Indonesian immigrants into Malaysia. Following rioting by Indonesian labourers (for which the Indonesian Government issued a formal apology), in January 2001 a temporary ban was imposed on new workers arriving from Indonesia. In November the Malaysian Government announced that it would thenceforth deport 10,000 illegal Indonesian immigrants each month in an attempt to tighten controls on foreign labour in the country. In August 2002 the implementation of new legislation requiring that all illegal immigrants leave Malaysia or risk penalties strained relations with both the Philippines and Indonesia, as the majority of the workers affected were citizens of those countries. In September the Malaysian Government announced a temporary halt to deportations, owing to diplomatic pressure, exacerbated by public protests in Indonesia and the Philippines over the apparently inhumane nature of the expulsions.

At the end of October 2004 a 17-day amnesty began for illegal migrant workers to leave Malaysia voluntarily without penalty. Thousands of Indonesians had fled to Malaysia since the Indonesian authorities had commenced military operations against separatists in the province of Aceh in May 2003. In November 2004 Malaysia agreed to extend the amnesty until the end of the year; the amnesty was subsequently further extended following a request from President Susilo Bambang Yudhoyono of Indonesia. It was reported that around 380,000 of an estimated 1.2m. illegal foreign workers had left Malaysia by the end of January 2005. In February, following talks with President Yudhoyono in Kuala Lumpur, the Prime Minister Abdullah Badawi announced that the amnesty would expire at the end of the month, and in March the forced repatriation of illegal immigrants recommenced. Human rights organizations, including Amnesty International, expressed serious misgivings about the repatriation process, amid allegations of widespread physical abuse of immigrants. In July 2006, according to government estimates, approximately 500,000 illegal immigrants were still living in Malaysia. In October 2007 a temporary ban was imposed on Malaysian employers recruiting new workers from Bangladesh, following a series of cases of ill-treatment of migrants, including the abandonment of several thousand at Kuala Lumpur airport. In January 2008 it was reported that the Malaysian Government aimed to reduce the number of foreign workers in the country from some 2.3m. to 1.5m. by 2015, by introducing stricter regulations on their employment. In early 2009 the Government announced the cancellation of work permits for nearly 100,000 Indonesian and 55,000 Bangladeshi migrant workers, as the Malaysian public increasingly demanded that the local workforce be better protected. The Indonesian Government subsequently imposed a moratorium on sending migrant workers to Malaysia. Following the signing in April 2011 of a memorandum of understanding between the two countries intended better to protect Indonesian migrant workers in Malaysia from abuse by their employers, the Indonesian Government rescinded the moratorium imposed in 2009, with effect from May 2011.

President Yudhoyono issued a formal apology in June 2013 after the Malaysian authorities had been forced to announce a state of emergency in response to a sudden deterioration in air quality in some southern regions resulting from suspected 'slash-and-burn' agricultural practices in Indonesia. Bilateral relations were also negatively affected by Malaysia's continuing campaign of the forcible repatriation of migrant workers. In February 2015 President Joko Widodo of Indonesia made an official visit to Malaysia, where he held bilateral discussions with Prime Minister Najib Razak on border issues, trade and investment and the treatment of Indonesian employees (notably maids) in Malaysia. Later that month the defence ministers of both countries held discussions on ensuring security in the Strait of Melaka.

In May 2002 Malaysia, Indonesia and the Philippines signed an anti-terrorism pact enabling them to exchange intelligence and to launch joint police operations; Thailand and Cambodia acceded to the pact later in the year. In December the ICJ ruled that Malaysia be awarded sovereignty of Sipadan and Ligitan, two small islands off the coast of Borneo, thereby bringing to an end a protracted dispute between Malaysia and Indonesia over conflicting claims to the islands. In July 2004 Malaysia and Indonesia, together with Singapore, commenced co-ordinated patrols of the Strait of Melaka between Malaysia and Indonesia, in an attempt to curb piracy.

Relations with Thailand deteriorated in February 1996, owing to Malaysia's construction of a 27-km wall along the border with Thailand, intended to deter illegal immigration from that country. However, in January 1997 the two countries agreed to co-operate in preventing Bangladeshi migrant workers from entering Malaysia and in expediting the return of illegal Thai workers from Malaysia. However, the Thai Government, as well as those of Indonesia and the Philippines, expressed concern at the arrest and detention of Anwar Ibrahim in September 1998. In January 2004 new Prime Minister Abdullah Badawi visited Thailand for security discussions, following several attacks believed to have been perpetrated by separatists in southern Thailand close to the joint border. The two countries agreed to co-operate in efforts to bring an end to the violence and began joint border patrols. Amid continuing unrest on the Thai side of the border, the Prime Minister of Thailand, Thaksin Shinawatra, visited Malaysia in mid-April for further security talks with Abdullah. In late April Malaysia increased its border security after militants launched a series of attacks on police posts in southern Thailand; the attacks were violently suppressed by the Thai security forces. Security at the border was heightened again in October following renewed clashes in southern Thailand between government troops and Muslim protesters in which 85 people died, many of whom suffocated after being forced into army trucks. Hundreds of Malaysians demonstrated outside the Thai embassy in Kuala Lumpur in protest against the deaths.

A diplomatic dispute arose between the two countries in October 2005, concerning the fate of 131 Muslim villagers who had fled from the violence-stricken province of Narathiwat, in southern Thailand, to neighbouring Malaysia. The Malaysian authorities insisted that they would not sanction the return of the asylum seekers to Thailand unless they received a guarantee of their safety from the Thai authorities. One of the villagers, suspected of involvement in a raid on a Thai military camp in January 2004, was subsequently handed over to the Thai authorities, while the other 130 refugees remained in a Malaysian detention centre in Terengganu. The dispute was finally resolved in February 2006 when the Thai Government indicated that it was prepared to allow the refugees to remain in Malaysia. There was some improvement in bilateral relations from October, when Gen. Surayud Chulanont was appointed as Thai Prime Minister following a coup in which Thaksin was ousted from power. Surayud visited Malaysia later that month, holding talks with Abdullah on the ongoing insurgency in Thailand's southern provinces. In December Abdullah and Surayud officially opened a new bridge across the Golok River, linking Kelantan to Narathiwat, as part of efforts to improve the economy and stability of the border region. In 2013 Malaysia acted as a mediator in peace talks between the Thai Government and one of the Islamist insurgent groups in Thailand, the National Revolution Front. Relations remained cordial following the military coup in Thailand in May 2014; in December Thai Prime Minister Prayut Chan-ocha made an official visit to Malaysia, where he and his Malaysian counterpart, Najib Razak, agreed to increase bilateral trade, and economic development along their mutual border.

Malaysia played an integral role in bringing together the Myanma military junta and opposition leader Aung San Suu Kyi for negotiations in late 2000, although it was believed that financial considerations may have played a significant role, with a promise of direct investment in Myanmar by Malaysia's national petroleum corporation, Petroliam Nasional Bhd (PET-RONAS), in return for progress on the part of the junta. In September 2001 the Myanma leader, Gen. Than Shwe, paid an official visit to Malaysia during which a number of bilateral agreements were signed. In March 2006 the Malaysian Minister of Foreign Affairs, Syed Hamid Albar, was denied access to Suu Kyi on a visit to Myanmar in his role as an ASEAN envoy to assess the country's progress towards political reform. Later that year Albar implied that ASEAN's development was being impeded by the military regime in Myanmar. An improvement in bilateral relations was evident following the staging of legislative elections in Myanmar in November 2010. A Malaysian business delegation to Myanmar in the following month identified numerous new opportunities in the country's rapidly developing oil and gas sector. Following a meeting between the Malaysian Minister of Foreign Affairs and the Myanma Deputy Minister of Foreign Affairs in October 2011, the two countries announced that a joint working committee was to be established to address issues pertaining to immigration and trans-national crime. Bilateral relations were further boosted following a visit to Myanmar by Malaysian Prime Minister Najib Razak in March 2012, during which he held cordial talks with Myanma President Thein Sein. However, in mid-2013 the Malaysian Government expressed serious concern about the brutal intercommunal violence that had recently erupted in Myanmar and that had begun to permeate into the Myanma migrant community within Malaysia. None the less, in early 2015 the Malaysian authorities invited Myanmar to participate as an observer in the Melaka Strait Patrols initiative to combat piracy.

In early February 2013 it was reported that a group of around 200 men from the Philippine island province of Sulu (some of whom were allegedly armed) had landed in Lahad Datu, a remote area of Sabah, and had raised the Philippine flag in the coastal village of Tanduo. The Government of the Philippines denied having sanctioned the actions of the group, which described itself as the 'Royal Security Forces of the Sultanate of Sulu and North Borneo' and which was led by Agbimuddin Kiram, the brother of self-proclaimed Sultan of Sulu Jamalul Kiram III, and urged the men to withdraw at once. The group claimed that Sabah, which had been given to the Sultan of Sulu by the Sultan of Brunei in the 17th century, was still part of Sulu (and, by extension, part of the Philippines). The Malaysian authorities, in turn, maintained that Sabah had, in effect, been sold (rather than simply leased) to the British North Borneo Company by the Sultan of Sulu through a contract drawn up between the two parties in 1878. Following a stand-off between the group and the Malaysian security forces, which had surrounded the village, the situation turned violent at the end of February 2013 when both sides accused the other of opening fire; two police officers and 12 Philippine rebels were reportedly killed in the ensuing shoot-outs. The group demanded that Malaysia recognize it as the rightful owner of Sabah and renegotiate the terms of the 19th-century lease (since Sabah became part of Malaysia in 1963 the latter has paid a token rent to the Sulu Sultanate each year). In early March, as tensions escalated and the death toll rose, the Malaysian authorities dispatched additional troops (including fighter jets) to Sabah, while the Philippine Secretary of Foreign Affairs was sent to Malaysia to attempt to expedite peace negotiations between the rebels and the Malaysian Government. The Malaysian Government rejected the subsequent offer of a ceasefire made by the rebel group, demanding instead its unconditional surrender. By the end of March the Philippine insurgents had been comprehensively defeated by the Malaysian security forces. Approximately 75 people lost their lives during the conflict, and over 100 suspected militants were taken into Malaysian custody. Legal proceedings against 30 people accused of involvement in the Lahad Datu incursion commenced in January 2014 and were still ongoing in early 2015.

Other regional relations

In 1990 a proposal by Mahathir to establish an East Asian Economic Caucus (EAEC), a trade group intended to exclude the USA, met with considerable resistance from the US Government (which continued to promote the US-dominated Asia-Pacific Economic Cooperation forum—APEC, see p. 200) and Australia. In July 1993 ASEAN agreed, despite the continuing reluctance of Japan to participate, that the EAEC should operate as an East Asian interest group within APEC. In November 1999 the third informal summit meeting of the 10 ASEAN countries and the People's Republic of China, Japan and the Republic of Korea (collectively known as 'ASEAN + 3') took place. At the meeting it was agreed to strengthen existing economic co-operation with the distant aim of forming an East Asian bloc with a common market and monetary union. This ambition was brought closer in April 2001 when, at a meeting of the ASEAN + 3 group, plans were agreed for a network of currency 'swap' arrangements to prevent a repetition of the regional financial crisis of 1997. At the annual ASEAN summit meeting held in Laos in November 2004 it was agreed to transform the ASEAN + 3 summit meeting, which was first held in 1997, into the East Asia Summit, with the long-term objective of establishing an East Asian Community. In December 2005 Kuala Lumpur hosted the inaugural East Asia Summit, held during the course of the ASEAN summit meeting. It was agreed that the East Asia Summit should convene annually.

Malaysia's relations with the People's Republic of China have remained extremely cordial, with Malaysia frequently offering public support to China, particularly in response to US criticism, and senior-level reciprocal official visits being undertaken on a regular basis. The importance of bilateral relations was demonstrated in May 2009 when Najib Razak travelled to China in his first official visit to a non-ASEAN country since being inaugurated as Prime Minister the previous month. The implementation in January 2010 of a free trade agreement between ASEAN and China was expected further to deepen Malaysia's growing economic dependence on the People's Republic. In August 2012 Malaysia and China agreed to designate 2014 as 'Malaysia-China Friendship Year' to commemorate the 40th anniversary of the establishment of diplomatic relations, and ties were strengthened further in October 2013 following an official visit to Malaysia by Chinese President Xi Jinping. However, bilateral tensions were evident in March 2014 when a Malaysia Airlines jet carrying, *inter alios*, 153 Chinese passengers disappeared and was presumed lost. Chinese officials criticized what they perceived to be Malaysia's haphazard response to the crisis and demanded greater transparency from the administration of Najib Razak. In May Prime Minister Najib made a state visit to China as part of the celebrations surrounding 'Malaysia-China Friendship Year'.

Malaysia forged closer links with Japan in December 2005 with the signing of a bilateral free trade agreement, which entered into force in July 2006. Under the terms of the accord, the two countries were to eliminate tariffs on all industrial goods and on most agricultural, forestry and fishery products within a 10-year period. In keeping with the spirit of invigorated relations, the Emperor and Empress of Japan paid a state visit to Malaysia in June 2006, and Japanese Prime Minister Shinzo Abe visited Malaysia in August 2007, marking the 50th anniversary of the establishment of diplomatic relations between the two countries. Malaysian Prime Minister Najib Razak made his first official visit to Japan in April 2010, where he met with his Japanese counterpart, Yukio Hatoyama; the two leaders pledged further to strengthen co-operation, including practical measures towards the realization of the concept of an East Asian Community. Bilateral ties were further reinforced following meetings between Prime Ministers Najib and Abe in July and December 2013.

Malaysia's relations with Australia, which were frequently strained under Mahathir—in particular over Malaysian objections to Australia's leadership of the UN-mandated peacekeeping mission in East Timor (now Timor-Leste), with Mahathir claiming that an ASEAN-led mission would be more appropriate—appeared to improve following the succession of Abdullah Badawi to the Malaysian premiership in October 2003. In June 2004, during a visit to Malaysia by the Australian Minister for Foreign Affairs, agreement was reached to hold formal annual talks between the two countries' foreign ministers and separate regular consultations between senior security officials. In April 2005 Abdullah made the first state visit to Australia by a Malaysian premier in more than 20 years. Formal negotiations on a bilateral free trade agreement commenced in the same month. However, relations foundered in February 2010 when more than 50 Australian legislators lodged a formal protest against the second sodomy trial of Anwar Ibrahim, which had commenced earlier in the month (see *Domestic Political Affairs*).

In October 2011, owing to staunch opposition from within the Australian legislature and a High Court ruling on its unconstitutionality, the Australian Government was forced to abandon a proposed amendment to its Migration Act that would have provided for the transfer by the Australian authorities of seaborne asylum seekers to detention centres in Malaysia, where their refugee claims would be processed. An agreement on the issue had been signed between the Malaysian and Australian Governments in July. However, members of the Australian opposition had voiced strong concerns over the human rights record of Malaysia, which is not a party to the 1951 UN Convention relating to the Status of Refugees, and noted the country's poor reputation for the treatment of refugees and immigrant workers. After lengthy negotiations, a free trade agreement between Malaysia and Australia was signed in March 2012 and entered into force on 1 January 2013. The agreement constituted Malaysia's fifth bilateral free trade agreement, following those signed with Japan in December 2005, Pakistan in November 2007, New Zealand in October 2009 and Chile in November 2010.

Other external relations

In June 1997 the inauguration took place of a group that aimed to foster economic co-operation among Muslim developing countries—the Developing-Eight (D-8)—comprising Malaysia, Bangladesh, Egypt, Indonesia, Iran, Nigeria, Pakistan and Turkey. Malaysia continued to express its close relationship with Arab countries through its denouncement of US and British air strikes against Iraq in February 2001, while demanding the removal of UN sanctions. It was hoped that a D-8 agreement on preferential tariffs signed in May 2006 would further strengthen economic relations between the group's members.

During Mahathir's premiership, Malaysia's desire to foster closer ties with other Muslim countries was, on occasion, the source of friction in its relations with the USA. Malaysian-US ties were strained by the involvement of PETRONAS in a consortium that signed an agreement in September 1997 to invest in Iran, in contravention of US sanctions against that country, and deteriorated further in October following Mahathir's suggestion that the economic crisis in South-East Asia was due to hostile Jewish currency speculation aimed at preventing progress among Muslim nations. Bilateral relations were further strained in 1998 following US condemnation of the detention and treatment of former Deputy Prime Minister Anwar Ibrahim and expressions of support by the Administration of US President Bill Clinton for the political reform movement in Malaysia.

However, in September 2001 relations with the USA were considerably strengthened when Mahathir acted quickly to condemn the terrorist attacks on the US mainland. However, Mahathir refused to lend his Government's support to the US-led retaliatory attacks on Afghanistan that had begun earlier that month, voicing concern at the large numbers of civilian casualties resulting from the raids. In November 2002 Malaysia and the USA co-established the Southeast Asia Regional Centre for Counter-Terrorism; based in Kuala Lumpur, the Centre officially opened in July 2003. While Prime Minister Mahathir made clear his opposition to the US-led campaign to remove the regime of Saddam Hussain in Iraq in 2003, relations with the USA remained generally stable, owing largely to the Malaysian Government's ongoing operation against suspected domestic terrorists, which was in line with the global anti-terrorism campaign being pursued by the Administration of George W. Bush.

In 2006 Malaysia and the USA began negotiations on the establishment of a free trade agreement, which drew opposition from several quarters in Malaysia, including farmers and trade unions fearful of the potential impact of US competition on local livelihoods, as well as from US politicians who disapproved of Malaysia's gas agreement with Iran. Negotiations proved problematic and were suspended on several occasions, and the US focus appeared to shift to the establishment of a regional Asia-Pacific trade pact (the proposed Trans-Pacific Partnership). Bilateral relations were improved by a visit to Washington, DC, in April 2010 by Prime Minister Najib Razak. During separate visits to Malaysia in November, US Secretary of State Hillary Clinton and Secretary of Defence Robert Gates spoke highly of the US-Malaysian relationship, commending the performance of the Malaysian Government and praising the South-East Asian country as a vital regional and global influence. The absence of comment by either US official on the allegations that

the criminal charges against Anwar Ibrahim were politically motivated, together with Clinton's refusal to meet with Anwar during her visit, prompted some observers to suggest that the US Administration was compromising its position on human rights in order to preserve cordial relations with the UMNO-led coalition Government, and was a reflection of US efforts to counter China's increasing regional prominence. Nevertheless, the US Administration expressed concern over the Malaysian authorities' handling of the 'Bersih 2.0' rally in July 2011 (see *Domestic Political Affairs*), stating that the US Administration would continue to monitor closely the human rights situation in the country. Malaysia's relations with the USA, Australia and Singapore were strained in November 2013 when leaked US intelligence reports revealed that those countries had apparently been involved in a US-administered regional spying operation which had utilized, *inter alia*, diplomatic premises in Malaysia. US President Barack Obama held discussions with Najib Razak in Kuala Lumpur in April 2014, when the two leaders agreed to upgrade relations between their respective countries to a 'comprehensive partnership' and to enhance co-operation in security, the economy, education and science.

In October 2014 Malaysia was elected to a non-permanent seat on the UN Security Council for a two-year term, effective from 1 January 2015.

CONSTITUTION AND GOVERNMENT

Malaysia is a federation of 13 states. The capital, Kuala Lumpur, is a separate Federal Territory, as is the island of Labuan and the newly developed administrative capital of Putrajaya. The head of state, or Supreme Head of Malaysia, is a monarch (Yang di-Pertuan Agong), elected for a five-year term (with a deputy head of state) by and from the hereditary rulers of nine of the states. The monarch acts on the advice of Parliament and the Cabinet. Parliament consists of the Dewan Negara (Senate) and the Dewan Rakyat (House of Representatives). The Senate has 70 members, including 44 appointed by the head of state, four of whom are from the Federal Territories, and 26 elected members, two chosen by each of the 13 State Legislative Assemblies. The House of Representatives consists of 222 members, elected for five years by universal adult suffrage: 165 from Peninsular Malaysia (including 11 from Kuala Lumpur and one from Putrajaya), 31 from Sarawak and 26 from Sabah (including one from Labuan). The head of state appoints the Prime Minister and, on the latter's recommendation, other ministers. The Cabinet is responsible to Parliament. The country is divided into 149 local authorities, comprising 12 city councils, 39 municipal councils, and 98 district councils.

REGIONAL AND INTERNATIONAL CO-OPERATION

Malaysia is a member of the Association of Southeast Asian Nations (ASEAN, see p. 210), the Asia-Pacific Economic Cooperation (APEC, see p. 200) forum, the Asian Development Bank (ADB, see p. 206), the UN's Economic and Social Commission for Asia and the Pacific (ESCAP, see p. 30), and the Colombo Plan (see p. 445), which promotes economic and social development in Asia and the Pacific.

Malaysia became a member of the UN in 1957. As a contracting party to the General Agreement on Tariffs and Trade (GATT), Malaysia joined the World Trade Organization (WTO, see p. 431) upon its establishment in 1995. Malaysia participates in the Organization of Islamic Cooperation (OIC, see p. 401) and the Developing Eight (D-8, see p. 446) group of Muslim states. The country is a member of the Non-aligned Movement (see p. 462) and of the International Labour Organization (ILO, see p. 139). Malaysia also participates in the Five-Power Defence Arrangements with Australia, New Zealand, Singapore and the UK.

ECONOMIC AFFAIRS

In 2013, according to estimates by the World Bank, Malaysia's gross national income (GNI), measured at average 2011–13 prices, was US \$309,047m., equivalent to \$10,400 per head (or \$22,460 per head on an international purchasing-power parity basis). During 2004–13, it was estimated, the population increased at an average annual rate of 1.8%, while gross domestic product (GDP) per head increased, in real terms, by an average of 3.0% per year. According to the Central Bank of Malaysia (CBM), overall GDP increased, in real terms, at an average annual rate of 4.7% in 2005–13; real GDP grew by 4.7% in 2013.

In 2013 agriculture (including forestry and fishing) contributed 9.4% of GDP and engaged 12.7% of the employed labour force. Malaysia is one of the world's leading producers of palm oil, exports of which contributed 5.8% of the value of total merchandise exports in 2013. Other important crops include rice, rubber, coconuts, pineapples, bananas and cocoa. During 2005–13, according to the CBM, agricultural GDP increased, in real terms, at an average annual rate of 2.8%; sectoral growth was 2.5% in 2013.

Industry (including mining, manufacturing, construction and utilities) contributed 41.0% of GDP and engaged 27.9% of the employed labour force in 2012. During 2005–13, according to the CBM, industrial GDP increased, in real terms, at an average annual rate of 2.2%; growth of 2.5% was recorded in 2013.

In 2013 mining contributed 10.1% of GDP, but engaged only 0.7% of the employed labour force. At the end of 2013 estimated proven gas reserves stood at 1,091,445m. cu m, and petroleum reserves at 3,668m. barrels. Petroleum production in 2013 averaged 656,683 barrels per day, sufficient to maintain production at that year's level for more than 15 years. In 2013 exports of liquefied natural gas accounted for 8.3% of total export revenue, while crude petroleum and condensates provided 4.4% of export earnings. Malaysia is one of the world's leading producers of tin. Bauxite, iron, gold and coal are also mined. The GDP of the mining sector decreased at an average annual rate of 1.5% in 2005–13, according to the CBM; mining GDP grew by 0.7% in 2013.

Manufacturing (the largest export sector) contributed 24.2% of GDP and engaged 17.5% of the employed labour force in 2013. The most important branches of manufacturing include electrical machinery and appliances, food products, metals and metal products, non-electrical machinery, transport equipment, rubber and plastic products, chemical products, wood products and furniture. According to the CBM, during 2005–13 manufacturing GDP increased, in real terms, at an average annual rate of 3.2%; manufacturing GDP rose by 3.5% in 2013.

In 2013 construction contributed 4.2% of GDP and engaged 9.4% of the employed labour force. According to the CBM, during 2005–13 construction GDP increased, in real terms, at an average annual rate of 7.9%; the sector expanded by 18.6% in 2012 and by a further 10.9% in 2013.

Energy is derived principally from Malaysia's own reserves of hydrocarbons. The country's dependence on petroleum as a source of electric energy declined from 55.9% in 1990 to 7.7% in 2011. The share contributed by natural gas to electricity output stood at 44.7% in 2011, while coal accounted for 40.7%. Production of electricity reached 131,632m. kWh in 2013. Imports of fuel accounted for 14.4% of total import costs in 2012.

In 2013 services contributed 49.6% of GDP and engaged 59.3% of the employed labour force. Tourism makes a major contribution to the economy. Revenue from this source reached an estimated US $21,026m. in 2013, in which year tourist arrivals rose to a record 25.7m. In 2013 the financial sub-sector contributed 7.4% of GDP. The GDP of the services sector increased by an average of 7.1% per year in 2005–13, according to CBM data; sectoral growth was 6.0% in 2013.

In 2013 Malaysia recorded a visible merchandise trade surplus of RM 108,230m. and a surplus of RM 39,907m. on the current account of the balance of payments. In 2013 the principal source of imports was the People's Republic of China (accounting for 16.4% of the total). Other important suppliers included Singapore, Japan, the USA, Thailand and Taiwan. The principal markets for exports in that year were Singapore and China (accounting for 13.9% and 13.5%, respectively); other significant purchasers were Japan, the USA and Thailand. The principal imports in 2013 were intermediate goods (notably parts and accessories of capital goods, and miscellaneous processed industrial supplies), as well as capital goods and consumption goods. The principal exports were electrical machinery and parts (particularly semiconductors and electronic components), liquefied natural gas, chemicals and palm oil.

In 2013 an overall budget deficit of RM 38,584m. was recorded, equivalent to 3.9% of GDP. Malaysia's general government gross debt was RM 569,415m. in 2013, equivalent to 57.7% of GDP. According to the Asian Development Bank (ADB), at the end of 2013 Malaysia's external debt totalled US $96,932m. The cost of debt servicing in that year was equivalent to 10.3% of the value of exports of goods and services. The annual rate of inflation averaged 2.6% in 2005–14; consumer prices increased by 2.1% in 2013. The rate of unemployment was 3.1% of the total labour force in 2013.

The Malaysian economy recovered strongly from the global recession of 2008–09, following a series of fiscal stimulus measures. The economy expanded more rapidly than anticipated in 2010, driven by rising commodity prices and high private consumption levels. Net foreign direct investment in Malaysia increased from RM 35,186m. in 2010 to a record RM 45,987m. in 2011, before declining to RM 30,162m. in 2012 and then rallying to RM 36,542m. in 2013. GDP growth slowed to 5.1% in 2011, partly as a result of weakening external demand, but recovered to 5.6% in 2012. In part owing to the Government's fiscal stimulus measures, the fiscal deficit widened to 6.7% of GDP in 2009 (from 3.1% in 2007), before moderating to 5.4% in 2010; by 2014 it was estimated to have narrowed to 3.6% of GDP. While continuing efforts to counter inflation, the Government also implemented a number of measures intended to protect consumer spending, including an increase in fuel subsidies, rises in public sector wages and pensions and the postponement of the planned implementation of a goods-and-services tax. Legislation introducing, for the first time, a minimum wage entered into force on 1 January 2013. Buoyed by the large number of development projects being carried out under the Government's Economic Transformation Programme (launched in 2010) and by the rising demand for new housing, the construction sector performed particularly strongly in 2012. Among the projects under way was the country's largest ever infrastructure project—the construction of a mass rapid transit rail system in Kuala Lumpur at a cost of an estimated US $11,500m. According to the CBM, the economy grew by 4.7% in 2013. The Government announced a number of fiscal consolidation measures in late 2013, including a reduction in fuel and electricity subsidies, and the imposition (from 2015) of a new consumption tax. The lower fuel subsidies contributed to a 2.1% increase in the consumer price index in that year; the rate of inflation rose further to 3.2% in 2014. The ADB estimated GDP growth of 5.7% in 2014. Upon presenting its budget for 2015 in October 2014, the Government forecast GDP growth of 5.7% for 2015. It also announced that construction of the 1,663-km Pan Borneo Highway would proceed but did not specify a start date. The project was forecast to cost some RM 27,000m, an increase from the original estimate of RM 22,000m. proffered in 2010. However, following a significant decrease in the price of oil in late 2014, which was expected to result in a considerable reduction in tax revenue, in January 2015 the Government lowered its projection for GDP growth in that year to 5.0%. It also declared its aim to lower the fiscal deficit to 3.2% of GDP in 2015 and, to this end, announced a cut in operational expenditure, including the suspension for one year of the national service programme and a review of grants to government agencies. However, at the same time, the Government emphasized that planned large infrastructure projects, including a high-speed rail link to Singapore and the Pan-Borneo Highway, would go ahead as scheduled.

PUBLIC HOLIDAYS

Each state has its own public holidays, and the following federal holidays are also observed:

2016: 8–9 February† (Chinese New Year), 1 May (Labour Day), 21 May (Vesak Day), 4 June (Official Birthday of HM the Yang di-Pertuan Agong), 6–7 July* (Hari Raya Puasa, end of Ramadan), 31 August (National Independence Day), 13 September* (Hari Raya Haji, Feast of the Sacrifice), 16 September (Malaysia Day), 3 October* (Muharram, Islamic New Year), 31 October‡ (Deepavali), 12 December* (Mouloud, Prophet Muhammad's Birthday), 25 December (Christmas Day).

*These holidays are dependent on the Islamic lunar calendar and may vary by one or two days from the dates given.

† The first two days of the first moon of the lunar calendar.

‡ Except Labuan and Sarawak.

Statistical Survey

Sources (unless otherwise stated): Department of Statistics, Blok C6, Parcel C, Pusat Pentadbiran Kerajaan Persekutuan, 62514 Putrajaya; tel. (3) 88857000; fax (3) 88889248; e-mail jpbkkp@stats.gov.my; internet www.statistics.gov.my; Bank Negara Malaysia (Central Bank of Malaysia), Jalan Dato' Onn, POB 10922, 50929 Kuala Lumpur; tel. (3) 21741717; fax (3) 21741515; e-mail bnmtelelink@bnm.gov.my; internet www.bnm.gov.my; Departments of Statistics, Kuching and Kota Kinabalu.
Note: Unless otherwise indicated, statistics refer to all states of Malaysia.

Area and Population

AREA, POPULATION AND DENSITY

Area (sq km)	
Peninsular Malaysia	131,554
Sabah (incl. Labuan)	74,286
Sarawak	124,450
Total	330,290*
Population (census results)†	
5–20 July 2000	23,274,690
6 July 2010	
Males	14,562,638
Females	13,771,497
Total	28,334,135
Population (official projections at mid-year)	
2013	29,714,700
2014	30,097,000
2015	30,485,000
Density (per sq km) at mid-2015	92.3

* 127,526 sq miles.
† Including adjustment for underenumeration; enumerated totals were 22,198,276 in 2000 and 27,565,821 in 2010.

POPULATION BY AGE AND SEX
('000, official projections at mid-2015)

	Males	Females	Total
0–14 years	3,969.3	3,764.1	7,733.4
15–64 years	10,828.6	10,143.3	20,972.0
65 years and over	855.9	924.0	1,779.8
Total	**15,653.8**	**14,831.4**	**30,485.2**

Note: Totals may not be equal to the sum of components, owing to rounding.

POPULATION BY ETHNIC GROUP
('000, official projections at mid-2013)

	Peninsular Malaysia	Sabah*	Sarawak	Total
Malays and other indigenous groups .	14,492.9	2,211.3	1,841.8	18,546.0
Chinese	5,648.7	315.6	595.1	6,559.4
Indians	1,957.9	11.8	7.7	1,977.4
Others	135.2	109.5	8.0	252.7
Non-Malaysians . .	1,383.1	873.2	122.8	2,379.1
Total	**23,617.9**	**3,521.4**	**2,575.5**	**29,714.7**

* Including the Federal Territory of Labuan.

Mid-2015: Malays and other indigenous groups 19,152.0; Chinese 6,642.0; Indians 2,012.6; Others 267.4; Non-Malaysians 2,411.4; *Total* 30,485.2.

Note: Classification of ethnicity reflects national methodology. Totals may not be equal to the sum of components, owing to rounding.

ADMINISTRATIVE DIVISIONS
(official population estimates, 2014)

	Area (sq km)	Population ('000)	Density (per sq km)	Capital
States				
Johor (Johore) . .	19,016	3,532.8	186	Johor Bahru
Kedah	9,425	2,057.7	218	Alor Star
Kelantan . . .	15,105	1,707.0	113	Kota Bharu
Melaka (Malacca) .	1,652	860.5	521	Melaka
Negeri Sembilan (Negri Sembilan) .	6,657	1,081.6	162	Seremban
Pahang	35,965	1,584.5	44	Kuantan
Perak	21,022	2,459.9	117	Ipoh
Perlis	795	244.0	307	Kangar
Pulau Pinang (Penang) . . .	1,031	1,662.8	1,613	George Town
Sabah	73,902	3,540.3	48	Kota Kinabalu
Sarawak . .	124,450	2,633.1	21	Kuching
Selangor . . .	7,930	5,866.4	740	Shah Alam
Terengganu (Trengganu) .	12,956	1,123.8	87	Kuala Terengganu
Federal Territories .				
Kuala Lumpur . .	243	1,732.5	7,130	—
Labuan	92	92.5	1,005	—
Putrajaya . . .	49	82.2	1,678	—
Total	**330,290**	**30,261.7**	**92**	

PRINCIPAL TOWNS
(population of local authority areas at 2010 census)

Kuala Lumpur (capital)	1,588,750	Selayang	542,409
Seberang Perai . .	818,197	Shah Alam	541,306
Kajang	795,522	Johor Bahru Tengah .	529,074
Klang	744,062	Johor Bahru . . .	497,067
Subang Jaya . . .	708,296	Melaka Bandaraya Bersejarah . . .	484,885
Pulau Pinang . . .	708,127	Ampang Jaya . .	468,961
Ipoh	657,892	Kota Kinabalu . .	452,058
Petaling Jaya . .	613,977	Kuantan	427,515

BIRTHS AND DEATHS*

	Registered live births		Registered deaths	
	Number	Rate (per 1,000)	Number	Rate (per 1,000)
2005	469,200	18.5	113,700	4.5
2006	465,100	18.1	115,100	4.5
2007	472,000	18.1	118,200	4.5
2008	487,300	18.4	124,900	4.7
2009	496,300	18.5	130,100	4.8
2010	491,200	17.2	131,000	4.6
2011	511,600	17.6	135,500	4.7
2012†	508,800	17.2	136,800	4.6

* Numbers are rounded to nearest 100.
† Preliminary.

Life expectancy (years at birth, official estimates, 2012): Males 72.3; females 77.2.

ECONOMICALLY ACTIVE POPULATION*
(sample surveys, ISIC major divisions, '000 persons aged 15 to 64 years)

	2011	2012	2013
Agriculture, hunting, forestry and fishing	1,410.0	1,601.7	1,682.1
Mining and quarrying	76.0	80.6	87.1
Manufacturing	2,222.3	2,227.9	2,214.8
Electricity, gas and water	122.4	142.5	143.9
Construction	1,133.6	1,163.7	1,244.1
Wholesale and retail trade; repair of motor vehicles, motorcycles and personal and household goods	1,999.5	2,116.0	2,220.2
Hotels and restaurants	942.2	957.0	1,016.1
Transport, storage and communications	812.8	833.2	812.9
Financial intermediation	317.6	322.9	319.2
Real estate, renting and business activities	839.1	907.7	938.6
Public administration and defence; compulsory social security	749.0	697.6	764.2
Education	785.0	786.2	817.4
Health and social work	382.5	414.8	489.9
Other community, social and personal service activities	267.9	274.6	270.0
Private households with employed persons	222.5	194.6	187.3
Extraterritorial organizations and bodies	2.1	2.1	2.2
Total employed	12,284.4	12,723.2	13,210.0
Unemployed	391.4	396.3	424.6
Total labour force	12,675.8	13,119.6	13,634.6

* Excluding members of the armed forces.

Health and Welfare

KEY INDICATORS

Total fertility rate (children per woman, 2012)	2.0
Under-5 mortality rate (per 1,000 live births, 2012)	9
HIV/AIDS (% of persons aged 15–49, 2013)	0.4
Physicians (per 1,000 head, 2010)	1.2
Hospital beds (per 1,000 head, 2010)	1.8
Health expenditure (2011): US $ per head (PPP)	619
Health expenditure (2011): % of GDP	3.8
Health expenditure (2011): public (% of total)	55.2
Access to sanitation (% of persons, 2012)	96
Total carbon dioxide emissions ('000 metric tons, 2010)	216,804.0
Carbon dioxide emissions per head (metric tons, 2010)	7.7
Human Development Index (2013): ranking	62
Human Development Index (2013): value	0.773

For sources and definitions, see explanatory note on p. vi.

Agriculture

PRINCIPAL CROPS
('000 metric tons)

	2011	2012	2013
Rice, paddy	2,576	2,750	2,627
Maize	60	84	88
Sweet potatoes	27	56	59
Cassava (Manioc)	33	41	82
Sugar cane	194	146	214
Coconuts	563	625	647
Oil palm fruit	94,558	93,925	95,728
Cabbages	179	95	95
Tomatoes	137	130	130
Cucumbers and gherkins	67	93	94
Watermelons	221	238	227

—continued	2011	2012	2013
Bananas	306	289	290
Pineapples	309	314	316
Papayas	44	36	36
Coffee, green	15	10	17
Cocoa beans	5	4	3
Pepper	26	26	27
Natural rubber	996	923	826

Aggregate production ('000 metric tons, may include official, semi-official or estimated data): Total cereals 2,636 in 2011, 2,683 in 2012, 2,715 in 2013; Total oilcrops 21,203 in 2011, 21,085 in 2012, 21,590 in 2013; Total vegetables (incl. melons) 1,314 in 2011, 1,281 in 2012, 1,239 in 2013; Total fruits (excl. melons) 960 in 2011, 941 in 2012, 939 in 2013.

Source: FAO.

LIVESTOCK
('000 head, year ending September)

	2011	2012	2013
Cattle	768	743	752
Buffaloes	123	119	118
Goats	476	486	482
Sheep	126	132	130
Pigs	1,801	1,831	1,817
Chickens	232,870	251,158	268,243
Ducks*	48,900	50,000	51,000

* FAO estimates.

Source: FAO.

LIVESTOCK PRODUCTS
('000 metric tons)

	2011	2012	2013
Cattle meat*	25.9	26.3	26.8
Buffalo meat*	4.0	4.0	4.0
Pig meat	231.0	233.2	231.4*
Chicken meat	1,174.3	1,209.6	1,245.8
Duck meat*	112.6	114.0	114.0
Cows' milk	70.8	75.0	79.4
Buffaloes' milk*	9.5	8.9	9.0
Hen eggs	621.5	642.6	664.4
Other poultry eggs*	14.0	14.0	14.0

* FAO estimate(s).

Source: FAO.

Forestry

ROUNDWOOD REMOVALS
('000 cubic metres, excl. bark)

	2011	2012	2013*
Sawlogs, veneer logs and logs for sleepers	15,994	15,892	14,713
Pulpwood*	703	703	703
Other industrial roundwood	1,235	3,036	3,166
Fuel wood*	2,760	2,711	2,664
Total*	20,692	22,342	21,246

* FAO estimates.

Source: FAO.

SAWNWOOD PRODUCTION
('000 cubic metres, incl. railway sleepers)

	2011*	2012	2013†
Total (all broadleaved)	4,011	4,003	4,003

* Unofficial figure.
† FAO estimate.

Source: FAO.

Fishing

('000 metric tons, live weight)

	2010	2011	2012
Capture	1,433.4	1,378.8	1,477.3
Indian scad	82.8	76.8	102.8
Bigeye scad	52.1	50.8	52.8
Indian mackerels	186.2	183.6	187.2
Other marine fishes	899.5	861.0	897.6
Natantian decapods	63.2	72.9	74.2
Squids	50.1	51.4	58.7
Aquaculture*	373.4	287.3	283.8
Torpedo-shaped catfishes . .	63.2	46.8	46.5
Whiteleg shrimp*	68.1	59.4	48.0
Blood cockle	78.0	57.5	38.9
Total catch*	1,806.8	1,666.1	1,761.1

* FAO estimates.

Note: Figures exclude crocodiles, recorded by number rather than by weight. The number of estuarine crocodiles caught was: 861 in 2010; 436 in 2011; 1,407 in 2012. Also excluded are shells and corals. Catches of turban shells (metric tons, FAO estimates) were: 80 in 2010–12. Catches of hard corals (metric tons, FAO estimates) were: 4,000 in 2010–12.

Source: FAO.

Mining

PRODUCTION
(metric tons unless otherwise indicated)

	2011	2012	2013
Tin-in-concentrates	3,343	3,157	n.a.
Bauxite	182,931	121,873	208,770
Iron ore*	8,077,879	10,886,022	12,133,556
Kaolin	405,717	424,622	263,339
Gold (kg)	4,219	4,625	3,823
Hard coal	2,915,788	2,941,620	2,907,463
Ilmenite*†	28,782	22,275	16,043
Crude petroleum ('000 barrels) .	212,794	218,706	214,696
Natural gas (net production, million cu ft)	2,547,555	2,544,305	2,647,898
Zirconium*‡	1,685	442	n.a.

* Figures refer to the gross weight of ores and concentrates.
† Concentrate from amang retreatment plants.
‡ Source: US Geological Survey.

Industry

SELECTED PRODUCTS
('000 metric tons unless otherwise indicated)

	2011	2012	2013
Canned fish, frozen shrimps/ prawns	38.9	43.7	47.5
Coconut oil (crude)	11,134	14,805	16,195
Refined sugar	1,688.6	1,594.7	1,733.1
Soft drinks ('000 litres) . . .	3,357.3	3,809.5	4,005.3
Cigarettes (metric tons) . .	23,604	26,099	22,272
Woven cotton fabrics (million metres)	276.7	392.8	275.7
Veneer sheets ('000 cu metres) .	912.4	871.6	883.1
Plywood ('000 cu metres) . .	3,797.0	3,658.3	3,651.6
Kerosene and jet fuel . . .	3,559.7	3,504.5	3,269.6
Liquefied petroleum gas . .	3,036.3	2,803.6	2,534.1
Inner tubes and tyres ('000) .	30,263	34,063	28,541
Rubber gloves (million pairs) .	30,897.8	31,754.0	34,628
Earthen brick and cement roofing tiles (million) . . .	739.7	874.6	639.4
Cement	21,198	21,726	21,457

—*continued*	2011	2012	2013
Iron and steel bars and rods .	2,562.3	2,817.4	3,162.8
Television receivers ('000) . .	13,966.5	13,054.4	17,072.4
Radio receivers ('000) . . .	47,889	28,365	18,954
Semiconductors (million) . .	16,281	19,765	19,281
Electronic transistors (million) .	34,189	36,119	35,362
Integrated circuits (million) .	33,380	39,391	35,686
Passenger motor cars ('000)* .	455.6	480.3	534.9
Commercial vehicles ('000)* .	65.7	81.8	90.4
Motorcycles and scooters ('000) .	486.9	533.5	498.4
Electric energy (million kWh) .	118,788	124,917	131,632†

* Vehicles assembled from imported parts.
† Provisional.

Tin (smelter production of primary metal, metric tons): 38,737 in 2010; 40,267 in 2011; 37,792 in 2012 (Source: US Geological Survey).

Finance

CURRENCY AND EXCHANGE RATES

Monetary Units
100 sen = 1 ringgit Malaysia (RM—also formerly Malaysian dollar).

Sterling, US Dollar and Euro Equivalents (31 December 2014)
£1 sterling = RM 5.4550;
US $1 = RM 3.4950;
€1 = RM 4.2433;
RM 100 = £18.33 = US $28.61 = €23.57.

Average Exchange Rate (ringgit Malaysia per US $)
2012   3.089
2013   3.151
2014   3.273

FEDERAL BUDGET
(RM million)

Revenue	2011	2012	2013*
Tax revenue	134,885	151,643†	155,952
Taxes on income and profits .	102,242	116,937	120,523
Companies (excl. petroleum) .	46,888	51,288	58,175
Individuals	20,203	22,977	23,055
Petroleum	27,748	33,934	29,753
Export duties	2,081	1,968	1,930
Import duties	2,026	2,282	2,524
Excises on goods	11,517	12,187	12,193
Sales tax	8,577	9,496	10,068
Service tax	4,982	5,583	5,944
Others	3,460	3,190	2,770
Other revenue	50,534	56,270	57,418
Total	185,419	207,913	213,370

Expenditure	2011	2012	2013*
Emoluments	50,148	60,016	61,002
Pensions and gratuities . . .	13,565	14,079	14,842
Debt service charges	17,716	19,537	20,776
Supplies and services	28,949	31,963	33,860
Subsidies	36,256	44,081	43,349
Grants and transfers to state governments	32,157	32,625	34,795
Other expenditure	3,803	3,236	2,647
Total	182,594	205,537	211,270

* Preliminary.

2014 (RM million, estimates): *Revenue:* Tax revenue 171,970 (Taxes on income and profits 133,148, Export duties 2,105, Import duties 2,502, Excises on goods 13,442, Sales tax 10,986, Service tax 6,810, Others 2,977); Other revenue 52,124; Total 224,094. *Expenditure:* Defence and security 26,393; Social services 81,036; Economic services 20,539; General administration 16,982; Other expenditure 72,701; Total 217,651 (Source: Ministry of Finance, Putrajaya).

FEDERAL DEVELOPMENT EXPENDITURE
(RM million)

	2011	2012	2013*
Defence and security	4,569	4,409	4,649
Social services	12,607	12,399	10,884
Education	7,735	7,550	6,438
Health	2,207	1,864	1,738
Housing	762	524	852
Economic services	28,156	28,936	24,646
Agriculture and rural development	1,128	1,906	2,692
Public utilities	6,013	5,519	3,332
Trade and industry	8,364	5,043	6,244
Transport	10,140	10,065	8,152
General administration . . .	1,085	1,187	2,032
Sub-total	46,416	46,932	42,210
Less Loan recoveries	1,082	2,606	1,526
Total	45,334	44,326	40,683

* Preliminary.

2014 (RM million, estimates): Defence and security 3,969; Social services 10,577 (Education 4,895; Health 1,707; Housing 1,047); Economic services 28,843 (Agriculture and rural development 3,105; Public utilities 3,440; Trade and industry 5,830; Transport 8,672); General administration 1,110; *Sub-total* 44,500; *Less* Loan recoveries 949; *Total* 43,551 (Source: Ministry of Finance, Putrajaya).

INTERNATIONAL RESERVES
(US $ million at 31 December)

	2012	2013	2014
Gold (national valuation) . . .	1,940	1,410	1,365
IMF special drawing rights . .	1,976	1,981	1,864
Reserve position in IMF . . .	867	972	942
Foreign exchange	134,940	130,492	111,814
Total	139,723	134,854	115,985

Source: IMF, *International Financial Statistics.*

MONEY SUPPLY
(RM million at 31 December)

	2010	2011	2012
Currency outside depository corporations	47,685	53,488	56,798
Transferable deposits . . .	192,100	219,439	249,609
Other deposits	798,978	919,560	996,366
Securities other than shares . .	26,183	28,058	25,885
Broad money	1,064,945	1,220,545	1,328,658

Source: IMF, *International Financial Statistics.*

COST OF LIVING
(Consumer Price Index; base 2010 = 100)

	2012	2013	2014
Food and non-alcoholic beverages .	107.6	111.5	115.2
Clothing and footwear	99.2	98.6	98.4
Rent and other housing costs, heating and lighting	103.4	105.2	108.8
All items (incl. others) . . .	104.9	107.1	110.5

NATIONAL ACCOUNTS
(RM million at current prices)

Expenditure on the Gross Domestic Product

	2011	2012	2013
Government final consumption expenditure	115,515	127,473	133,704
Private final consumption expenditure	418,767	461,295	504,045
Changes in inventories . . .	8,350	2,639	−7,566
Gross fixed capital formation . .	197,415	241,562	265,013
Total domestic expenditure .	740,047	832,969	895,196
Exports of goods and services . .	810,221	803,042	805,962

—*continued*	2011	2012	2013
Less Imports of goods and services	664,928	694,063	714,425
GDP in purchasers' values .	885,339	941,949	986,733
GDP at constant 2005 prices .	711,760	751,934	787,611

Gross Domestic Product by Economic Activity

	2011	2012	2013
Agriculture, forestry and fishing .	104,302	94,589	91,819
Mining and quarrying	92,406	97,431	99,007
Manufacturing	215,125	228,221	235,988
Electricity, gas and water . . .	20,382	22,040	23,467
Construction	29,648	36,571	41,280
Trade	120,351	128,348	138,797
Restaurants and hotels . . .	23,494	25,435	27,747
Transport and storage . . .	28,343	30,160	31,984
Communications	27,158	29,790	32,720
Finance and insurance . . .	64,447	70,403	72,673
Real estate and business services .	43,102	46,936	51,057
Government services	68,192	80,038	84,916
Other services	39,676	41,800	44,515
Sub-total	876,627	931,762	975,970
Import duties	8,711	10,186	10,763
GDP in purchasers' values .	885,339	941,949	986,733

BALANCE OF PAYMENTS
(RM million)

	2011	2012	2013
Exports of goods f.o.b.	699,591	686,047	679,123
Imports of goods f.o.b.	−548,026	−560,857	−570,892
Trade balance	151,565	125,190	108,230
Exports of services	110,630	116,995	126,839
Imports of services	−116,902	−133,206	−143,532
Balance on goods and services	145,293	108,979	91,537
Other income received . . .	52,491	42,262	47,468
Other income paid	−74,297	−78,312	−81,594
Balance on goods, services and income	123,487	72,929	57,411
Current transfers received . .	4,683	6,661	7,584
Current transfers paid	−25,744	−25,130	−25,087
Current balance	102,426	54,460	39,907
Capital account (net)	−133	241	−21
Direct investment (net) . . .	−9,337	24,415	−5,451
Portfolio investment (net) . . .	26,139	63,859	−3,041
Financial derivatives (net) . .	−76	972	−253
Other investment (net) . . .	6,539	−63,431	−7,062
Net errors and omissions . .	−30,876	−27,814	−9,431
Overall balance	94,682	3,873	14,649

External Trade

PRINCIPAL COMMODITIES
(RM million)

Imports c.i.f.	2011	2012	2013
Capital goods*	80,348	96,098	98,202
Intermediate goods	376,428	363,714	379,455
Miscellaneous industrial supplies, processed . . .	133,774	135,527	144,840
Parts and accessories of capital goods (excl. transportation equipment)	143,451	126,694	131,615
Consumption goods	39,529	43,746	47,584
Total (incl. others)†	573,626	606,677	648,695

Exports f.o.b.	2011	2012	2013
Palm oil	60,310	53,067	41,737
Crude petroleum and condensates	32,452	31,951	31,643
Liquefied natural gas	52,049	55,129	59,567
Semiconductors	107,090	101,789	111,442
Electronic components	75,069	77,000	75,396
Consumer electrical products . .	22,866	18,714	18,225
Industrial and commercial electrical products	24,508	25,480	24,114
Electrical industrial machinery and equipment	27,659	29,204	30,874
Chemicals and chemical products .	47,767	47,318	51,901
Metal manufactures	31,011	29,475	34,926
Total (incl. others)	697,862	702,641	719,992

* Figures net of re-exports.
† Including re-exports.

PRINCIPAL TRADING PARTNERS
(RM million)

Imports c.i.f.	2011	2012	2013
Australia	12,810	14,609	16,492
China, People's Republic . . .	75,706	91,864	106,265
France	9,513	13,025	13,463
Germany	21,976	23,213	22,912
Hong Kong	13,601	13,321	10,485
India	10,191	11,803	16,346
Indonesia	35,113	31,095	27,944
Japan	65,362	62,374	56,360
Korea, Republic	23,271	24,671	30,653
Philippines	4,781	4,801	4,743
Singapore	73,699	80,476	80,249
Taiwan	27,133	25,222	31,530
Thailand	34,480	35,677	38,633
United Kingdom	6,141	6,831	7,316
USA	55,405	49,089	50,682
Viet Nam	10,348	16,096	19,016
Total (incl. others)	573,626	606,677	648,695

Exports f.o.b.	2011	2012	2013
Australia	25,683	29,097	29,225
China, People's Republic . . .	91,551	88,793	97,043
France	8,066	5,461	5,466
Germany	18,456	16,020	16,512
Hong Kong	31,253	30,069	31,251
India	28,154	29,325	25,735
Indonesia	20,841	27,609	33,110
Japan	81,368	83,401	79,197
Korea, Republic	26,252	25,368	26,199
Netherlands	19,281	18,558	20,716
Philippines	10,945	10,472	9,342
Singapore	88,191	95,553	100,257
Taiwan	23,228	21,829	21,741
Thailand	35,742	37,633	39,923
United Kingdom	7,157	6,807	6,848
USA	57,653	60,791	58,055
Viet Nam	11,710	11,807	13,330
Total (incl. others)	697,862	702,641	719,992

Transport

RAILWAYS
(traffic)

	2011	2012	2013*
Passengers carried ('000) . . .	4,279	3,655	3,393
Passenger-km (million) . . .	1,428	1,218	1,099
Freight ('000 metric tons) . . .	6,096	6,142	13,322
Freight ton-km (million) . . .	1,536	1,565	1,762

* Preliminary.

ROAD TRAFFIC
(registered motor vehicles at 31 December)

	2009	2010	2012*
Passenger cars	8,601,808	9,217,881	10,467,014
Buses and coaches	66,581	69,149	73,536
Lorries and vans	936,222	966,177	1,032,004
Motorcycles and mopeds . . .	8,940,230	9,441,907	10,589,818

* Data for 2011 were not available.
Source: IRF, *World Road Statistics*.

SHIPPING
Flag Registered Fleet
(at 31 December)

	2012	2013	2014
Number of vessels	2,168	2,266	2,323
Total displacement ('000 grt) . .	9,481.7	9,156.5	9,382.9

Source: Lloyd's List Intelligence (www.lloydslistintelligence.com).

Seaborne Freight Traffic*
(Peninsular Malaysia, international and coastwise, '000 metric tons)

	2011	2012	2013
Goods loaded	125,472	128,508	132,528
Goods unloaded	153,048	152,484	157,704

* Including transshipments.
Source: UN, *Monthly Bulletin of Statistics*.

CIVIL AVIATION
(traffic on scheduled services)

	2010	2011
Kilometres flown (million)	395	439
Passengers carried ('000)	34,239	38,219
Passenger-km (million)	65,972	73,979
Total ton-km (million)	8,784	9,082

Source: UN, *Statistical Yearbook*.

Passengers carried ('000): 39,165 in 2012; 46,318 in 2013 (Source: World Bank, World Development Indicators database).

Tourism

TOURIST ARRIVALS BY COUNTRY OF RESIDENCE*

	2011	2012	2013
Australia	558,411	507,948	526,342
Brunei	1,239,404	1,258,070	1,238,871
China, People's Republic (incl. Hong Kong and Macao) . . .	1,250,536	1,558,785	1,791,423
India	693,056	691,271	650,989
Indonesia	2,134,381	2,382,606	2,548,021
Japan	386,974	470,008	513,076
Korea, Republic	263,428	283,977	274,622
Philippines	362,101	508,744	557,147
Singapore	13,372,647	13,014,268	13,178,774
Taiwan	233,783	242,519	286,266
Thailand	1,442,048	1,263,024	1,156,452
United Kingdom	403,940	402,207	413,472
Total (incl. others)	24,714,324	25,032,708	25,715,460

* Including Singapore residents crossing the frontier by road through the Johor Causeway.

Source: Malaysia Tourism Promotion Board.

Tourism receipts (US $ million, excl. passenger transport): 19,649 in 2011; 20,251 in 2012; 21,026 in 2013 (Source: World Tourism Organization).

Communications Media

	2011	2012	2013
Telephones ('000 main lines in use)	4,523	4,589	4,536
Mobile cellular telephones ('000 subscribers)	36,661	41,325	42,996
Broadband subscribers ('000) .	2,137.6	2,459.9	2,443.1

Source: International Telecommunication Union.

Education

(at 31 January 2014 unless otherwise specified)

	Institutions	Teachers	Students
Pre-primary	5,943	8,586	194,225
Primary	7,751	240,385	2,698,883
Secondary	2,366	180,469	2,234,621
Regular	1,964	157,581	
Special model	11	1,037	2,049,146
Sports	4	280	
Arts	3	148	
Fully residential . . .	68	4,090	38,642
Technical and vocational .	89	7,801	41,736
Religious	57	3,680	38,975
Special	5	308	789
Government-aided religious schools (GARS)	164	5,528	64,508
Tertiary:*			
Universities	20	n.a.	521,793
Teacher training institutes .	27	3,572	42,342
Polytechnics	30	7,306	91,906
Community colleges . . .	69	2,648	22,031

* Data at 30 June 2013.

Source: Ministry of Education, Putrajaya.

Pupil-teacher ratio (primary education, UNESCO estimate): 12.5 in 2010/11 (Source: UNESCO Institute for Statistics).

Adult literacy rate (UNESCO estimates): 93.1% (males 95.4%; females 90.7%) in 2010 (Source: UNESCO Institute for Statistics).

Directory

The Government

SUPREME HEAD OF STATE

HM Yang di-Pertuan Agong: HRH Sultan Tuanku Haji ABDUL HALIM MU'ADZAM SHAH IBNI AL-MARHUM Sultan BADLISHAH (Sultan of Kedah) (took office 13 December 2011).

Deputy Supreme Head of State

Timbalan Yang di-Pertuan Agong: HRH Sultan MUHAMMAD V (Sultan of Kelantan).

CABINET
(May 2015)

The Government is formed by the Barisan Nasional (National Front), which includes the United Malays National Organization (UMNO), the Parti Bersatu Rakyat Sabah (PBRS), the Parti Pesaka Bumiputera Bersatu (PBB), the Parti Rakyat Sarawak (PRS), the Sarawak United People's Party (SUPP), the United Kadazan People's Organization (UPKO), the Malaysian Indian Congress (MIC), Parti Gerakan Rakyat Malaysia (GERAKAN), the Malaysian Chinese Association (MCA) and four other parties.

Prime Minister and Minister of Finance I: Dato' Sri MOHD NAJIB BIN Tun Haji ABDUL RAZAK (UMNO).

Deputy Prime Minister and Minister of Education I: Tan Sri Dato' Haji MUHYIDDIN BIN MOHD YASSIN (UMNO).

Ministers in the Prime Minister's Department: Dato' Seri JAMIL KHIR BIN BAHAROM (UMNO), Dato' Sri ABDUL WAHID BIN OMAR, Dato' Sri IDRIS JALA, Tan Sri Datuk Seri PANGLIMA JOSEPH KURUP (PBRS), Dato' Seri SHAHIDAN BIN KASSIM (UMNO), Puan Hajah NANCY BINTI SHUKRI (PBB), Datuk JOSEPH ENTULU ANAK BELAUN (PRS), Datuk PAUL LOW SENG KUAN, Dato' SIEW KEONG MAH (GERAKAN), Datuk WEE KA SIONG (MCA).

Minister of Finance II: Dato' Seri Haji AHMAD HUSNI BIN MOHAMAD HANADZLAH (UMNO).

Minister of Education II: Dato' Seri IDRIS BIN JUSOH (UMNO).

Minister of Transport: Datuk Seri LIOW TIONG LAI (MCA).

Minister of Defence: Dato' Seri HISHAMMUDDIN BIN Tun HUSSEIN (UMNO).

Minister of Home Affairs: Dato' Seri Dr AHMAD ZAHID BIN HAMID (UMNO).

Minister of Works: Datuk FADILLAH YUSOF (PBB).

Minister of International Trade and Industry: Dato' Sri MUSTAPA BIN MOHAMED (UMNO).

Minister of Foreign Affairs: Dato' Sri ANIFAH BIN Haji AMAN (UMNO).

Minister of Domestic Trade, Co-operatives and Consumerism: Dato' Haji HASAN BIN MALEK (UMNO).

Minister of Communications and Multimedia: Y. B. Dato' Seri AHMAD SHABERY BIN CHEEK (UMNO).

Minister of Human Resources: Y. B. Dato' RICHARD RIOT ANAK JAEM (SUPP).

Minister of Rural and Regional Development: Dato' Seri Haji MOHD SHAFIE BIN Haji APDAL (UMNO).

Minister of Urban Well-being, Housing and Local Government: Dato' Haji ABDUL RAHMAN BIN DAHLAN (UMNO).

Minister of Youth and Sports: Tuan KHAIRY JAMALUDDIN BIN ABU BAKAR (UMNO).

Minister of Health: Datuk Seri Dr S. SUBRAMANIAM (MIC).

Minister of Federal Territories: Datuk Seri TENGKU ADNAN BIN TENGKU MANSOR (UMNO).

Minister of Plantation Industries and Commodities: Dato' Sri DOUGLAS UGGAH EMBAS (PBB).

Minister of Energy, Green Technology and Water: Datuk Seri Dr MAXIMUS JOHNITY ONGKILI (PBS).

Minister of Agriculture and Agro-based Industry: Dato' Sri ISMAIL SABRI BIN YAAKOB (UMNO).

Minister of Tourism and Culture: Dato' Seri MOHAMED NAZRI BIN ABDUL AZIZ (UMNO).

Minister of Science, Technology and Innovation: Dr EWON EBIN (UPKO).

Minister of Natural Resources and the Environment: Datuk Seri G. PALANIVEL (MIC).

Minister of Women, Family and Community Development: Datuk Hajah ROHANI BINTI Haji ABDUL KARIM (PBB).

MINISTRIES

Prime Minister's Office (Jabatan Perdana Menteri): Federal Government Administration Center, Blok B8, Kompleks Jabatan Perdana Menteri, Pusat Pentadbiran Kerajaan Persekutuan, 62502 Putrajaya; tel. (3) 80008000; fax (3) 80003904; e-mail fuad@pmo.gov.my; internet www.pmo.gov.my.

Ministry of Agriculture and Agro-based Industry: Aras 17, Wisma Tani, 28 Persiaran Perdana, Presint 4, Pusat Pentadbiran Kerajaan Persekutuan, 62624 Putrajaya; tel. (3) 88701000; fax (3) 88886020; e-mail pro@moa.gov.my; internet www.moa.gov.my.

Ministry of Communications and Multimedia (Kementerian Penerangan Komunikasi Dan Kebudayaan): Tingkat 5, Wisma TV, Angkasapuri, Bukit Putra, 50610 Kuala Lumpur; tel. (3) 22825333; fax (3) 22848115; e-mail azmi@kpkk.gov.my; internet www.kpkk.gov .my.

Ministry of Defence (Kementerian Pertahanan): Wisma Pertahanan, Jalan Padang Tembak, 50634 Kuala Lumpur; tel. (3) 26921333; fax (3) 26914163; e-mail portal@mod.gov.my; internet www.mod.gov .my.

Ministry of Domestic Trade, Co-operatives and Consumerism (Kementerian Perdagangan Dalam Negeri, Koperasi Dan Kepengunaan): Aras 13, 13 Persianan Perdana, Presint 2, Pusat Pentadbiran Kerajaan Persekutuan, 62623 Putrajaya; tel. (3) 88825500; fax (3) 88825762; e-mail hasan@kpdnkk.gov.my; internet www.kpdnkk .gov.my.

Ministry of Education (Kementerian Pendidikan): Aras 4, Blok Barat, Bangunan Perdana Putra, Pusat Pentadbiran Kerajaan Persekutuan, 62502 Putrajaya; tel. (3) 20987788; fax (3) 20923763; e-mail muhyiddin@moe.gov.my; internet www.moe.gov.my.

Ministry of Energy, Green Technology and Water (Kementerian Tenaga, Teknologi Hijau dan Air): Aras 6, Blok E4–5, Kompleks E, Pusat Pentadbiran Kerajaan Persekutuan, 62668 Putrajaya; tel. (3) 80008000; fax (3) 88893712; e-mail webmaster@kettha.gov.my; internet www.kettha.gov.my.

Ministry of Federal Territories (Kementerian Wilayah Persekutuan): Aras G–4, Blok 2, Menara Seri Wilayah, Presint 2, 62100 Putrajaya; tel. (3) 88897888; fax (3) 88880375; e-mail zainor@kwp .gov.my; internet www.kwpkb.gov.my.

Ministry of Finance (Kementerian Kewangan): Kompleks Kementerian Kewangan, 5 Persiaran Perdana, Presint 2, Pusat Pentadbiran Kerajaan Persekutuan, 62592 Putrajaya; tel. (3) 88823000; fax (3) 88823893; e-mail shafei@treasury.gov.my; internet www .treasury.gov.my.

Ministry of Foreign Affairs (Kementerian Luar Negeri): Aras 3, Wisma Putra, Pusat Pentadbiran Kerajaan Persekutuan, Presint 2, 62602 Putrajaya; tel. (3) 88874000; fax (3) 88891717; e-mail anifah@ kln.gov.my; internet www.kln.gov.my.

Ministry of Health (Kementerian Kesihatan): Aras 13, Blok E1, E6–7 & E10, Kompleks E, Pusat Pentadbiran Kerajaan Persekutuan, 62590 Putrajaya; tel. (3) 88833888; fax (3) 26985964; e-mail s .subra@moh.gov.my; internet www.moh.gov.my.

Ministry of Home Affairs (Kementerian Hal Ehwal Dalam Negeri): Aras 12, Blok D1–2, Kompleks D, Pusat Pentadbiran Kerajaan Persekutuan, 62546 Putrajaya; tel. (3) 88868000; fax (3) 88891613; e-mail webmaster@moha.gov.my; internet www.moha .gov.my.

Ministry of Human Resources (Kementerian Sumber Manusia): Tingkat 6–9, Blok D3, Parcel D, Pusat Pentadbiran Kerajaan Persekutuan, 62530 Putrajaya; tel. (3) 88865000; fax (3) 88892381; e-mail richardriot@mohr.gov.my; internet www.mohr.gov.my.

Ministry of International Trade and Industry (Kementerian Perdagangan Antarabangsa dan Industri): Tingkat 15, Blok 10, Kompleks Pejabat Kerajaan, Jalan Duta, 50622 Kuala Lumpur; tel. (3) 62033022; fax (3) 62012337; e-mail mustapa@miti.gov.my; internet www.miti.gov.my.

Ministry of Natural Resources and the Environment (Kementerian Sumber Asli dan Alam Sekitar): Aras 17, Wisma Sumber Asli, 25 Persiaran Perdana, Presint 4, Pusat Pentadbiran Kerajaan Persekutuan, 62574 Putrajaya; tel. (3) 88861111; fax (3) 88892672; e-mail palanivel@nre.gov.my; internet www.nre.gov.my.

Ministry of Plantation Industries and Commodities (Kementerian Perusahaan Perladangan dan Komoditi): Aras 6–13, 15 Persiaran Perdana, Presint 2, Pusat Pentadbiran Kerajaan Persekutuan, 62654 Putrajaya; tel. (3) 88803300; fax (3) 88803441; e-mail uggah@mpic.gov.my; internet www.kppk.gov.my.

Ministry of Rural and Regional Development (Kementerian Kemajuan Luar Bandar dan Wilayah): Aras 32, 47 Persiaran Perdana, Presint 4, 62100 Putrajaya; tel. (3) 88912014; fax (3) 88882026; e-mail shafieapdal@rurallink.gov.my; internet www .rurallink.gov.my.

Ministry of Science, Technology and Innovation: Aras 1–7, Blok C4–5, Parcel C, Pusat Pentadbiran Kerajaan Persekutuan, 62662 Putrajaya; tel. (3) 88858000; fax (3) 88889070; e-mail info@ mosti.gov.my; internet www.mosti.gov.my.

Ministry of Tourism and Culture (Kementerian Pelancongan dan Kebudayaan): Aras 18, No. 2, Menara 1, Jalan P5/6, Precinct 5, 62200 Putrajaya; tel. (3) 80008000; fax (3) 88917181; e-mail info@ motac.gov.my; internet www.motac.gov.my.

Ministry of Transport (Kementerian Pengangkutan): Aras 4–7, Blok D5, Parcel D, Pusat Pentadbiran Kerajaan Persekutuan, 62616 Putrajaya; tel. (3) 88808000; fax (3) 88891569; e-mail aduan@mot .gov.my; internet www.mot.gov.my.

Ministry of Urban Well-being, Housing and Local Government (Kementerian Kesejahteraan Bandar, Perumahan dan Kerajaan Tempatan): Aras 2–38, 51 Persiaran Perdana, Presint 4, 62100 Putrajaya; tel. (3) 80008000; fax (3) 88913182; e-mail am_mpkt@ kpkt.gov.my; internet www.kpkt.gov.my.

Ministry of Women, Family and Community Development (Kementerian Pembangunan Wanita, Keluarga dan Masyarakat): No. 55, Persiaran Perdana, Presint 4, 62100 Putrajaya; tel. (3) 80008000; fax (3) 83232000; e-mail info@kpwkm.gov.my; internet www.kpwkm.gov.my.

Ministry of Works (Kementerian Kerja Raya): Tingkat 6, Blok B, Kompleks Kerja Raya, Jalan Sultan Salahuddin, 50580 Kuala Lumpur; tel. (3) 27111100; fax (3) 27111590; e-mail fadillah@kkr .gov.my; internet www.kkr.gov.my.

Ministry of Youth and Sports (Kementerian Belia dan Sukan): Aras 17, Menara KBS, 27 Persiaran Perdana, Presint 4, Pusat Pentadbiran Kerajaan Persekutuan, 62570 Putrajaya; tel. (3) 88713333; fax (3) 88888770; e-mail kj@kbs.gov.my; internet www .kbs.gov.my.

Legislature

PARLIAMENT

Senate
(Dewan Negara)

The Senate has 70 members, of whom 26 are elected. Each State Legislative Assembly elects two members. The Supreme Head of State appoints the remaining 44 members, including four from the three Federal Territories.

President: Tan Sri ABU ZAHAR Dato' NIKA UJANG.

House of Representatives
(Dewan Rakyat)

The House of Representatives has a total of 222 members: 165 from Peninsular Malaysia (including 11 from Kuala Lumpur and one from the Federal Territory of Putrajaya), 31 from Sarawak and 26 from Sabah (including one from the Federal Territory of Labuan).

Speaker: Tan Sri PANDIKAR AMIN MULIA.

Deputy Speakers: Datuk RONALD KIANDEE, Datuk ISMAIL MOHAMED SAID.

General Election, 5 May 2013

Party	Seats
Barisan Nasional	133
United Malays National Organization	88
Parti Pesaka Bumiputera Bersatu	13
Parti Rakyat Sarawak	7
Malaysian Chinese Association	7
Malaysian Indian Congress	4
Parti Bersatu Sabah	4
Sarawak Progressive Democratic Party	4
United Kadazan People's Organization	3
Parti Gerakan Rakyat Malaysia	1
Parti Bersatu Rakyat Sabah	1
Sarawak United People's Party	1
Pakatan Rakyat	89
Democratic Action Party	38
Parti Keadilan Rakyat	30
Parti Islam se Malaysia	21
Total	**222**

The States

JOHOR
(Capital: Johor Bahru)

Sultan: HRH Tuanku IBRAHIM ISMAIL IBNI AL-MARHUM Sultan ISKANDER.

Menteri Besar: Datuk Seri MOHAMMED KHALED NORDIN.

State Legislative Assembly: Tingkat 1, Bangunan Dato' Jaafar Muhammad, Kota Iskandar, 79503 Nusajaya, Johor Darul Ta'zim; tel. (7) 2666070; fax (7) 2908077; e-mail sukpengurusan@johor.gov .my; internet www.johor.gov.my; 56 seats: Barisan Nasional 38; Pakatan Rakyat 18; elected May 2013.

KEDAH
(Capital: Alor Star)

Council of Regency: appointed by the Sultan of Kedah to fulfil his duties during his tenure as the Yang di-Pertuan Agong; four mems; Chair. Tan Sri Tuanku SALLEHUDDIN IBNI AL-MARHUM Sultan BADLISHAH.

Sultan: HRH Tuanku Haji ABDUL HALIM MU'ADZAM SHAH IBNI AL-MARHUM Sultan BADLISHAH.

Menteri Besar: Dato' Paduka MUKHRIZ BIN TUN Dr MAHATHIR.

State Legislative Assembly: Wisma Darul Aman, Alor Setar, 05150 Kedah; e-mail suk@kedah.gov.my; internet www.kedah.gov.my; 36 seats: Barisan Nasional 21; Pakatan Rakyat 15; elected May 2013.

KELANTAN
(Capital: Kota Bharu)

Sultan: HRH Sultan MUHAMMAD V PETRA.

Menteri Besar: Datok AHMAD YAAKOB.

State Legislative Assembly: Kompleks Kota Darulnaim, 15503 Kota Bharu, Kelantan; tel. (9) 7481957; fax (9) 7443203; e-mail portal@kelantan.gov.my; internet www.kelantan.gov.my; 45 seats: Pakatan Rakyat 33; Barisan Nasional 12; elected May 2013.

MELAKA (MALACCA)
(Capital: Melaka)

Yang di-Pertua Negeri: Tan Sri KHALIL YAAKOB.

Ketua Menteri: Datuk Wira Ir IDRIS HARON.

State Legislative Assembly: Kompleks Seri Negeri, Hang Tuah Jaya, 75450 Ayer Keroh, Melaka; tel. (6) 3333333; fax (6) 2328620; internet www.melaka.gov.my; 28 seats: Barisan Nasional 21; Pakatan Rakyat 7; elected May 2013.

NEGERI SEMBILAN
(Capital: Seremban)

Yang di-Pertuan Besar: Tuanku MUKHRIZ IBNI AL-MARHUM Tuanku MUNAWIR.

Menteri Besar: Dato' Seri Haji MOHAMAD BIN Haji HASAN.

State Legislative Assembly: Tingkat 3, Blok B, Wisma Negeri, Jalan Dato' Abdul Malek, 70503 Seremban, Negeri Sembilan; internet www.ns.gov.my; 36 seats: Barisan Nasional 22; Pakatan Rakyat 14; elected May 2013.

PAHANG
(Capital: Kuantan)

Sultan: HRH Haji AHMAD SHAH AL-MUSTA'IN BILLAH IBNI AL-MARHUM Sultan ABU BAKAR RI'AYATUDDIN AL-MU'ADZAM SHAH.

Menteri Besar: Dato' Sri Diraja Haji ADNAN BIN Haji YAAKOB.

State Legislative Assembly: Pejabat Setiausaha Kerajaan, Negeri Pahang, Wisma Sri Pahang, 25503 Kuantan, Pahang Darul Makmur; tel. (9) 5126600; fax (9) 5157448; e-mail webmast@pahang.gov.my; internet www.pahang.gov.my; 42 seats: Barisan Nasional 30; Pakatan Rakyat 12; elected May 2013.

PERAK
(Capital: Ipoh)

Sultan: HRH Sultan Tuanku NAZRIN MUIZZUDDIN SHAH IBNI AL-MARHUM Sultan AZLAN MUHIBBUDDIN SHAH AL-MAGHFURLAH.

Menteri Besar: Dato' Seri Dr ZAMBRY ABDUL KADIR.

State Legislative Assembly: Pejabat Setiausaha Kerajaan Negeri Perak, Bangunan Perak Darul Ridzuan, Bahagian Majlis, Jalan Panglima Bukit Gantang Wahab, 30000 Ipoh; tel. (5) 2095000; fax (5) 2555026; e-mail webadmin@perak.gov.my; internet www.perak.gov.my; 59 seats: Barisan Nasional 31; Pakatan Rakyat 28; elected May 2013.

PERLIS
(Capital: Kangar)

Raja: HM Tuanku SYED SIRAJUDDIN IBNI AL-MARHUM SYED PUTRA JAMALULLAIL.

Menteri Besar: AZLAN MAN.

State Legislative Assembly: Tingkat 4, Kompleks Dewan Undangan Negeri Perlis, 01990 Kangar, Perlis; tel. (4) 9738800; fax (4) 9775863; e-mail sukpls@perlis.gov.my; internet www.perlis.gov.my; 15 seats: Barisan Nasional 13; Pakatan Rakyat 2; elected May 2013.

PULAU PINANG (PENANG)
(Capital: George Town)

Yang di-Pertua Negeri: HE Tun Dato' Seri Dr ABDUL RAHMAN BIN Haji ABBAS.

Ketua Menteri: LIM GUAN ENG.

State Legislative Assembly: Dewan Undangan Negeri Pulau Pinang, Lebuh Light, 10200 Georgetown, Pulau Pinang; tel. (4) 2611955; fax (4) 2636008; internet dun.penang.gov.my; 40 seats: Pakatan Rakyat 30; Barisan Nasional 10; elected May 2013.

SABAH
(Capital: Kota Kinabalu)

Yang di-Pertua Negeri: HE Tun Datuk Seri Haji JUHAR Haji MAHIRUDDIN.

Ketua Menteri: Datuk Seri MUSA Haji AMAN.

State Legislative Assembly: Dewan Undangan Negeri Sabah, Aras 4, Bangunan Dewan Undangan Negeri Sabah, Peti Surat 11247, 88813 Kota Kinabalu; tel. (88) 427533; fax (88) 427333; e-mail pejduns@sabah.gov.my; internet www.sabah.gov.my; 60 seats: Barisan Nasional 48; Pakatan Rakyat 11; Independent 1; elected May 2013.

SARAWAK
(Capital: Kuching)

Yang di-Pertua Negeri: Pehin Sri Haji ABDUL TAIB MAHMUD.

Ketua Menteri (Chief Minister): Tan Sri ADENAN SATEM.

State Legislative Assembly: Bangunan Dewan Undangan Negeri, Petra Jaya, 93502 Kuching, Sarawak; tel. (82) 441955; fax (82) 440628; e-mail supiantt@sarawak.gov.my; internet www.dun.sarawak.gov.my; f. 1867; 71 seats: Barisan Nasional 55; Pakatan Rakyat 15; Independent 1; elected April 2011.

SELANGOR
(Capital: Shah Alam)

Sultan: Tuanku IDRIS SHARAFUDDIN ALHAJ SHAH.

Menteri Besar: Dato' MOHAMED AZMIN ALI.

State Legislative Assembly: Tingkat 2, Bangunan Sultan Salahuddin Abdul Aziz Shah, 40503 Shah Alam, Selangor Darul Ehsan; e-mail webadmin@selangor.gov.my; internet www.selangor.gov.my; 56 seats: Pakatan Rakyat 44; Barisan Nasional 12; elected May 2013.

TERENGGANU
(Capital: Kuala Terengganu)

Sultan: HRH Tuanku MUHAMMAD ISMAIL Sultan MIZAN ZAINAL ABIDIN.

Menteri Besar: Datuk AHMAD RAZIF ABDUL RAHMAN.

State Legislative Assembly: Wisma Darul Iman, 20503 Kuala Terengganu; tel. (9) 6231957; e-mail webmaster@terengganu.gov.my; internet www.terengganu.gov.my; 32 seats: Barisan Nasional 17; Pakatan Rakyat 15; elected May 2013.

Election Commission

Suruhanjaya Pilihan Raya (SPR): Aras 4–5, Blok C7, Parcel C, Pusat Pentadbiran Kerajaan Persekutuan, 62690 Putrajaya; tel. (3) 88856500; fax (3) 88889117; e-mail spr@spr.gov.my; internet www.spr.gov.my; f. 1957; Chair. Tan Sri Dato' Seri ABD AL-AZIZ BIN MUHAMMAD YUSOF.

Political Organizations

Barisan Nasional (BN) (National Front): Suites 1–2, Tingkat 8, Menara Dato' Onn, Pusat Dagangan Dunia Putra, Jalan Tun Ismail, 50480 Kuala Lumpur; tel. (3) 40451071; fax (3) 40451075; internet www.barisannasional.org.my; f. 1973; the governing multiracial coalition of 13 parties; Chair. Dato' Sri MOHD NAJIB BIN Tun Haji ABDUL RAZAK; Sec.-Gen. Datuk Sri Tengku ADNAN Tengku MANSOR; comprises:

Liberal Democratic Party: Tingkat 2, B10–3 and B11–3, Kepayan Perdana Office Lot, off Jalan Lintas Kepayan, 88200 Kota Kinabalu, Sabah; tel. (88) 413286; fax (88) 413289; internet ldp.org.my; f. 1989; Chinese-dominated; Pres. Datuk TEO CHEE KANG; Sec.-Gen. YONG WUI CHUNG.

Malaysian Chinese Association (MCA): Wisma MCA, Tingkat 8, 163 Jalan Ampang, POB 10626, 50450 Kuala Lumpur; tel. (3) 22033888; fax (3) 21619772; e-mail info@mca.org.my; internet www.mca.org.my; f. 1949; 900,000 mems; Pres. Datuk Seri LIOW TIONG LAI; Sec.-Gen. Dato' Seri ONG KA CHUAN.

Malaysian Indian Congress (MIC): Menara Manickavasagam, Tingkat 6, 1 Jalan Rahmat, 50350 Kuala Lumpur; tel. (3) 40424377; fax (3) 40427236; e-mail michq@mic.org.my; internet www.mic.org.my; f. 1946; 401,000 mems (1992); Pres. Datuk G. PALANIVEL; Sec.-Gen. A. PRAKASH RAO.

Parti Bersatu Rakyat Sabah (PBRS) (United Sabah People's Party): POB 20148, Luyang, Kota Kinabalu, 88761 Sabah; tel. (88) 263282; fax (88) 269282; f. 1994; breakaway faction of the PBS; mostly Christian Kadazans; Leader Datuk JOSEPH KURUP.

Parti Bersatu Sabah (PBS) (Sabah United Party): Blok M, Lot 4, Tingkat 2–3, Donggongon New Township, 89500 Penampang, Sabah; tel. (88) 702111; fax (88) 718067; internet www .pbs-sabah.org; f. 1985; left the BN in 1990; rejoined in Jan. 2002; multiracial party; Pres. Datuk Seri JOSEPH PAIRIN KITINGAN; Sec.-Gen. Datuk JOHNNY MOSITUN.

Parti Gerakan Rakyat Malaysia (GERAKAN) (Malaysian People's Movement): Tingkat 5, Menara PGRM, 8 Jalan Pudu Ulu, Cheras, 56100 Kuala Lumpur; tel. (3) 92876868; fax (3) 92878866; e-mail gerakan@gerakan.org.my; internet www .gerakan.org.my; f. 1968; 300,000 mems; Pres. Dato' MAH SIEW KEONG; Sec.-Gen. LIANG TECK MENG.

Parti Pesaka Bumiputera Bersatu (PBB) (United Traditional Bumiputra Party): Lot 401, Jalan Bako, POB 1053, 93722 Kuching, Sarawak; tel. (82) 448299; fax (82) 448294; internet www .pesakabumiputerabersatu.org; f. 1983; Pres. Tan Sri Datuk Patinggi Amar Haji ABDUL TAIB MAHMUD; Dep. Pres. Datuk ALFRED JABU AK NUMPANG.

Parti Progresif Penduduk Malaysia (PPP) (People's Progressive Party): 74 Jalan Rotan, Kampung Attap, 50460 Kuala Lumpur; tel. (3) 22738199; fax (3) 22736199; e-mail kvs@ppp.org.my; internet www.ppp.org.my; f. 1953; est. as Perak Progressive Party; joined the BN in 1972; Pres. Datuk Seri M. KAYVEAS.

Parti Rakyat Sarawak (PRS) (Sarawak People's Party): Lot 9162, Tingkat 1–3, Jalan Pending KTLD, 93450 Kuching, Sarawak; tel. (82) 488331; fax (82) 481332; f. 2003; reported to be considering merger with the SPDP; Pres. Datuk Sri Dr JAMES MASING; Sec.-Gen. Datuk WILFRED NISSOM.

Sarawak Progressive Democratic Party (SPDP): Lot 158–160, Seksyen 20, KTLD 9F/9G/9H, Jalan Badruddin, 93400 Kuching, Serawak; tel. and fax (82) 232805; internet spdp .barisannasional.org.my; f. 2003; est. by breakaway faction of Sarawak Nat. Party; reported to be considering merger with the PRS; Pres. Datuk WILLIAM MAWAN ANAK IKOM; Sec.-Gen. NELSON BALANG RINING.

Sarawak United People's Party (SUPP): 7 Jalan Tan Sri Ong Kee Hui, POB 454, 93710 Kuching, Sarawak; tel. (82) 246999; fax (82) 256510; e-mail supphq@yahoo.com; internet www.supp.org .my; f. 1959; Sarawak Chinese minority party; Pres. Datuk Dr SIM KUI HIAN; Sec.-Gen. Dato' SEBASTIAN TING CHIEW YEW.

United Kadazan People's Organization (UPKO) (United Pasokmomogun Kadazandusun Murut Organization): Penampang Lot 9 & 10, New World Commercial Centre, Tingkat 2–3, Peti Surat 420, 89507 Penampang, Sabah; tel. (88) 718182; fax (88) 718180; e-mail upkohq@gmail.com; internet upko.org; f. 1994; est. as Parti Demokratik Sabah (PDS—Sabah Democratic Party) after collapse of PBS Govt by fmr PBS leaders; represents mostly Kadazandusun, Rungus and Murut communities; Pres. Tan Sri BERNARD GILUK DOMPOK; Sec.-Gen. Datuk DONALD P. MOJUNTIN.

United Malays National Organization (Pertubuhan Kebangsaan Melayu Bersatu—UMNO Baru) (New UMNO): Menara Dato' Onn, 38th Floor, Jalan Tun Ismail, 50480 Kuala Lumpur; tel. (3) 40429511; fax (3) 40412358; e-mail email@umno.net.my; internet www.umno-online.com; f. 1988; replaced the original UMNO (f. 1946), which had been declared an illegal org., owing to the participation of unregistered brs in party elections in April 1987; Supreme Council of 45 mems; 2.5m. mems; Pres. Dato' Sri MOHD NAJIB BIN Tun Haji ABDUL RAZAK; Sec.-Gen. Datuk Seri Tengku ADNAN Tengku MANSOR.

Barisan Jama'ah Islamiah Sa-Malaysia (Berjasa) (Pan-Malaysian Islamic Front): Lot 27, Jalan Besar, 17000 Pasir Mas, Kelantan; e-mail info@berjasa.org; f. 1977; pro-Islamic; 50,000 mems; Pres. Ustaz Haji MOHAMMED YUSSOF BIN HARON.

Bersatu Rakyat Jelata Sabah (Berjaya) (Sabah People's Union): Natikar Bldg, 1st Floor, POB 2130, Kota Kinabalu, Sabah; f. 1975; 400,000 mems; Pres. Haji MOHAMMED NOOR MANSOOR.

Human Rights Party (HRP): 6 Jalan Abdullah, off Jalan Bangsar, 59000 Kuala Lumpur; tel. (3) 22825241; fax (3) 22825245; e-mail info@humanrightspartymalaysia.com; internet www .humanrightspartymalaysia.com; f. 2009; Sec.-Gen. P. UTHAYAKUMAR.

Kongres Indian Muslim Malaysia (KIMMA): 77–1, Medan Sri Bunus, 50100 Kuala Lumpur; tel. (3) 26973967; fax (3) 26970013; e-mail ibupejabatkimma@yahoo.com; internet www.kimma.my; f. 1977; aims to unite Malaysian Indian Muslims politically; 280,000 mems; Pres. Datuk SYED IBRAHIM KADER.

Malaysia Makkal Sakti Party (MMSP): Shah Alam, Selangor; f. 2009; est. by fmr mems of the Hindu Rights Action Force; represents ethnic Indians in Malaysia; Founder R. S. THANENTHIRAN; Pres. KANNAN RAMASAMY.

Pakatan Rakyat (People's Alliance): internet www.pakatanrakyat .my; f. 2008; est. following the legislative election; opposition alliance of the PKR, the DAP and PAS.

> **Democratic Action Party (DAP):** 24 Jalan 20/9, 46300 Petaling Jaya, Selangor; tel. (3) 79578022; fax (3) 79575718; e-mail dap@ dapmalaysia.org; internet www.dapmalaysia.org; f. 1966; main opposition party; advocates multiracial society based on democratic socialism; 12,000 mems; Chair. TAN KOK WAI (acting); Sec.-Gen. LIM GUAN ENG.

> **Parti Islam se Malaysia (PAS)** (Islamic Party of Malaysia): 318A Jalan Raja Laut, 50350 Kuala Lumpur; tel. (3) 26927400; fax (3) 26938399; e-mail editor@parti-pas.org; internet www.pas.org.my; f. 1951; seeks to establish an Islamic state; 700,000 mems; Pres. Dato' Seri ABDUL HADI AWANG; Sec.-Gen. Dato' Haji MUSTAFA ALI.

> **Parti Keadilan Rakyat (PKR)** (People's Justice Party): A1-09, 1 Merchant Sq., 1 Jalan Tropicana Selatan, 47410 Petaling Jaya; tel. (3) 78850530; fax (3) 78850531; e-mail ibupejabat@keadilanrakyat .org; internet www.keadilanrakyat.org; f. 2003; est. following merger of Parti Keadilan Nasional and Parti Rakyat Malaysia; comprises supporters of Anwar Ibrahim; Pres. Datin Seri Dr WAN AZIZAH WAN ISMAIL; Vice-Pres N. SURENDRAN, NURUL IZZAH ANWAR; Sec.-Gen. SAIFUDDIN NASUTION ISMAIL.

Parti Kesejahteraan Insan Tanah Air (KITA) (Malaysian People's Welfare Party): B-2-19, Merchant Sq., Jalan Tropicana Selatan 1, PJU 3, 47410 Petaling Jaya, Selangor; tel. (3) 78850023; fax (3) 78850027; e-mail info@partikita.com; internet www.partikita.com; f. 1995; fmrly Angkatan Keadilan Insan Malaysia (AKIM); relaunched as above in 2010; Pres. Datuk ZAMIL IBRAHIM.

Sarawak National Party (SNAP): 304–305 Bangunan Mei Jun, 1 Jalan Rubber, POB 2960, 93758 Kuching, Sarawak; tel. (82) 254244; fax (82) 253562; internet sarawak-national-party.blogspot.com; f. 1961; deregistered Nov. 2002, but deregistration deferred indefinitely in April 2003 following appeal; Pres. EDWIN DUNDANG BUGAK; Sec.-Gen. EDMUND STANLEY JUGOL.

Sabah Progressive Party (SAPP) (Parti Maju Sabah): Lot 23, Tingkat 2, Bornion Centre, 88300 Kota Kinabalu, Sabah; tel. (88) 242107; fax (88) 249188; e-mail sappkk@streamyx.com; internet www.sapp.org.my; f. 1994; non-racial; Pres. Datuk YONG TECK LEE; Sec.-Gen. Datuk RICHARD YONG WE KONG.

Setia (Sabah People's United Democratic Party): Sabah; f. 1994.

Diplomatic Representation

EMBASSIES AND HIGH COMMISSIONS IN MALAYSIA

Afghanistan: Wisma Chinese Chamber, 2nd Floor, 258 Jalan Ampang, 50450 Kuala Lumpur; tel. (3) 42569400; fax (3) 42566400; Ambassador Dr JAMRAD JAMSHED.

Algeria: 5 Jalan Mesra, off Jalan Damai, 55000 Kuala Lumpur; tel. (3) 21488159; fax (3) 21488154; e-mail dz@algerianembassy.org.my; internet www.algerianembassy.org.my; Ambassador NASREDDINE RIMOUCHE.

Argentina: Suite 16-03, 16th Floor, Menara Keck Seng, 203 Jalan Bukit Bintang, 55100 Kuala Lumpur; tel. (3) 21441451; fax (3) 21441428; e-mail emsia@mrecic.gov.ar; internet www.emsia .mrecic.gov.ar; Ambassador MARÍA ISABEL RENDON.

Australia: 6 Jalan Yap Kwan Seng, 50450 Kuala Lumpur; tel. (3) 21465555; fax (3) 21415773; e-mail public-affairs-klpr@dfat.gov.au; internet www.malaysia.embassy.gov.au; High Commissioner ROD SMITH.

Austria: Suite 10.01-02, Tingkat 10, Wisma Goldhill 67, Jalan Raja Chulan, 50200 Kuala Lumpur; tel. (3) 20570020; fax (3) 23817168; e-mail kuala-lumpur-ob@bmeia.gv.at; internet www.bmeia.gv.at/ kualalumpur; Ambassador CHRISTOPHE CESKA.

Azerbaijan: Lot 589, Jalan 6 Taman Ampang Utama, 68000 Ampang, Selangor Darul Ehsan; tel. (3) 42526800; fax (3) 42571800; e-mail kualalumpur@mission.mfa.gov.az; internet www .azembassy.com.my; Ambassador QALEY ALLAHVERDIYEV.

Bangladesh: 114 Jalan U Thant, 55000 Kuala Lumpur; tel. (3) 21487940; fax (3) 21413381; e-mail mission.kualalumpur@mofa.gov .bd; internet www.bangladesh-highcomkl.com; High Commissioner MD SHAHIDUL ISLAM.

Belgium: Suite 10-02, 10th Floor, Menara Tan & Tan, 207 Jalan Tun Razak, 50400 Kuala Lumpur; tel. (3) 21620025; fax (3) 21620023; e-mail kualalumpur@diplobel.fed.be; internet www.diplomatie.be/ kualalumpur; Ambassador DANIEL DARGENT.

Bosnia and Herzegovina: JKR 854, Jalan Bellamy, 50460 Kuala Lumpur; tel. (3) 21440353; fax (3) 21426025; e-mail embbhkl@mfa.gov.ba; Ambassador TARIK BUKVIĆ.

Brazil: Suite 20-01, 20th Floor, Menara Tan & Tan, 207 Jalan Tun Razak, 50400 Kuala Lumpur; tel. (3) 21711420; fax (3) 21711427; e-mail embassy@brazilembassy.org.my; internet www.brazilembassy.org.my; Ambassador (vacant).

Brunei: Suite 19-01, 19th Floor, Menara Tan & Tan, 207 Jalan Tun Razak, 50400 Kuala Lumpur; tel. (3) 21612800; fax (3) 21631302; e-mail kualalumpur.malaysia@mfa.gov.bn; High Commissioner Dato' Paduka Haji ALAIHUDDIN BIN Dato' Seri Utama Haji AWG MOHAMAD TAHA.

Cambodia: 46 Jalan U Thant, 55000 Kuala Lumpur; tel. (3) 42571150; fax (3) 42571157; e-mail camemb.mys@mfa.gov.kh; internet embassyofcambodia-malaysia.org; Ambassador HRH Samdech Preah ANOCH NORODOM ARUNRASMY.

Canada: Menara Tan & Tan, 17th Floor, 207 Jalan Tun Razak, 50400 Kuala Lumpur; tel. (3) 27183333; fax (3) 27183399; e-mail klmpr@international.gc.ca; internet www.canadainternational.gc.ca/malaysia-malaisie; High Commissioner JUDITH ST GEORGE.

Chile: West Block, 8th Floor, Wisma Selangor Dredging, 142C Jalan Ampang, Peti Surat 27, 50450 Kuala Lumpur; tel. (3) 21616203; fax (3) 21622219; e-mail eochile@embassyofchile.org.my; internet chileabroad.gov.cl/malasia; Ambassador CHRISTIAN REHREN.

China, People's Republic: 229 Jalan Ampang, 50450 Kuala Lumpur; tel. (3) 21428495; fax (3) 21414552; e-mail cn@tm.net.my; internet my.china-embassy.org/eng; Ambassador HUANG HUIKANG.

Colombia: UOA Centre, Tingkat 28, 19 Jalan Pinang, 50450 Kuala Lumpur; tel. (3) 21645488; fax (3) 21645487; e-mail ekualalumpur@cancilleria.gov.co; internet www.ecolombia.com.my; Chargé d'affaires VICTOR HUGO ECHEVERRI JARAMILLO.

Croatia: 21-7, Binjai 8, Lorong Binjai, 50450 Kuala Lumpur; tel. (3) 21815037; fax (3) 21815067; e-mail croemb.kuala-lumpur@mvpei.hr; Chargé d'affaires BRANKO ZEBIC.

Cuba: 18 Jalan Kent 2, off Jalan Maktab, 54000 Kuala Lumpur; tel. (3) 26911066; fax (3) 26911141; e-mail admin@cubemb.com.my; internet www.cubaemb.com.my; Ambassador RUBÉN PÉREZ VALDÉS.

Czech Republic: Suite B, 42nd Floor, Vista Tower, The Intermark, 182 Jalan Tun Razak, 50400 Kuala Lumpur; tel. (3) 21427185; fax (3) 21412727; e-mail kualalumpur@embassy.mzv.cz; internet www.mzv.cz/kualalumpur; Ambassador RUDOLF HYKL.

Denmark: Sunway Tower, 22nd Floor, 86 Jalan Ampang, 50450 Kuala Lumpur; tel. (3) 20322001; fax (3) 20322015; e-mail kulamb@um.dk; internet www.malaysia.um.dk; Ambassador NICOLAI RUGE.

Ecuador: West Block, 10th Floor, Wisma Selangor Dredging, 142C Jalan Ampang, 50450 Kuala Lumpur; tel. (3) 21635078; fax (3) 21635096; e-mail embecua@po.jaring.my; Ambassador LOURDES PUMA PUMA.

Egypt: 12 Jalan Rhu, off Jalan Ampang, 55000 Kuala Lumpur; tel. (3) 42568184; fax (3) 42573515; e-mail embassy.kualalumpur@mfa.gov.eg; internet www.mfa.gov.eg/english/embassies/egyptian_embassy_malaysia/pages/default.aspx; Ambassador SALAH MOHI ELDIN ELWASSIMY.

Fiji: Menara Chan, Tingkat 2, 138 Jalan Ampang, 50450 Kuala Lumpur; tel. (3) 42576617; fax (3) 42576626; e-mail fijihckl@gmail.com; High Commissioner Ratu MELI BAINIMARAMA.

Finland: Wisma Chinese Chamber, 5th Floor, 258 Jalan Ampang, 50450 Kuala Lumpur; tel. (3) 42577746; fax (3) 42577793; e-mail sanomat.kul@formin.fi; internet www.finland.org.my; Ambassador MATTI PULLINEN.

France: 192–196 Jalan Ampang, 50450 Kuala Lumpur; tel. (3) 20535500; fax (3) 20535502; e-mail ambassade.kuala-lumpur-amba@diplomatie.gouv.fr; internet www.ambafrance-my.org; Ambassador CHRISTOPHE PENOT.

Gambia: 10th Floor, Wisma Selangor Dredging, 50450 Kuala Lumpur; tel. (3) 6259649; fax (3) 21813725; e-mail gambiaembassymalaysia@mofa.gov.gm; Ambassador FATOU MAS JOBE-NJIE.

Germany: Menara Tan & Tan, 26th Floor, 207 Jalan Tun Razak, 50400 Kuala Lumpur; tel. (3) 21709666; fax (3) 21619800; e-mail info@kuala-lumpur.diplo.de; internet www.kuala-lumpur.diplo.de; Ambassador HOLGER WILFRIED MICHAEL.

Ghana: 14 Ampang Hilir, off Jalan Ampang, 55000 Kuala Lumpur; tel. (3) 42526995; fax (3) 42578698; e-mail ghcomkl@tm.net.my; High Commissioner BENJAMIN CLEMENT EGHAN.

Guinea: 5 Jalan Kedondong, off Jalan Ampang Hilir, 55000 Kuala Lumpur; tel. (3) 42576500; fax (3) 42511500; e-mail mwcnakry@sotelgui.net.gn; Ambassador Dr ALPHA DIALLO.

Holy See: c/o Ritz-Carlton Residence, Suite 3321, 168 Jalan Imbi, 55100 Kuala Lumpur; tel. (3) 27829052; fax (3) 27829053; e-mail apostolic@nunciature.my; Apostolic Nuncio JOSEPH SALVADOR MARINO (Titular Archbishop of Natchitoches).

India: Menara 1 Mont Kiara, 28th Floor, 1 Jalan Mont Kiara, 50480 Kuala Lumpur; tel. (3) 62052350; fax (3) 61431173; e-mail dhc@indianhighcommission.com.my; internet www.indianhighcommission.com.my; High Commissioner T. S. TIRUMURTI.

Indonesia: 233 Jalan Tun Razak, POB 10889, 50400 Kuala Lumpur; tel. (3) 21164000; fax (3) 21423878; e-mail info@kbrikualalumpur.org; internet www.kbrikualalumpur.org; Ambassador Marshal (retd) HERMAN PRAYINTO.

Iran: 1 Lorong U Thant Satu, off Jalan U Thant, 55000 Kuala Lumpur; tel. (3) 42514824; fax (3) 42521563; e-mail ir_emb@tm.net.my; internet www.iranembassy.com.my; Ambassador (vacant).

Iraq: 2 Jalan Langgak Golf, off Jalan Tun Razak, 55000 Kuala Lumpur; tel. (3) 21480555; fax (3) 21414331; e-mail quaemb@iraqmofamail.net; Ambassador BASSIM KHATTAB AL TOMA.

Ireland: Ireland House, The Amp Walk, 218 Jalan Ampang, POB 10372, 50450 Kuala Lumpur; tel. (3) 21612963; fax (3) 21613427; internet www.embassyofireland.my; Ambassador DECLAN KELLY.

Italy: 99 Jalan U Thant, 55000 Kuala Lumpur; tel. (3) 42565122; fax (3) 42573199; e-mail ambasciata.kualalumpur@esteri.it; internet www.ambkualalumpur.esteri.it; Ambassador MARIO SAMMARTINO.

Japan: 11 Pesiaran Stonor, off Jalan Tun Razak, 50450 Kuala Lumpur; tel. (3) 21772600; fax (3) 21672314; e-mail jis@kl.mofa.go.jp; internet www.my.emb-japan.go.jp; Ambassador MAKIO MIYAGAWA.

Jordan: 2 Jalan Kedondong, off Jalan Ampang Hilir, 55000 Kuala Lumpur; tel. (3) 42521268; fax (3) 42528610; e-mail jorembkl@streamyx.com; internet www.jordanembassy.org.my; Ambassador MAHER LUKASHA.

Kazakhstan: 115 Jalan Ampang Hilir, 55000 Kuala Lumpur; tel. (3) 42522999; fax (3) 42523999; e-mail kuala-lumpur@kazembassy.org.my; internet www.kazembassy.org.my; Ambassador DANIYAR SAREKENOV.

Kenya: 8 Jalan Taman U Thant, 55000 Kuala Lumpur; tel. (3) 21461163; fax (3) 21451087; e-mail admin@kenyahighcom.org.my; internet www.kenyahighcom.org.my; High Commissioner SAMORI AN'GWA OKWIYA.

Korea, Democratic People's Republic: 7 Jalan Batai, Damansara Heights, 59100 Kuala Lumpur; tel. (3) 42569913; fax (3) 42560033; e-mail dprkorea@streamyx.com; Ambassador JANG YONG CHOL.

Korea, Republic: Lot 9 and 11, Jalan Nipah, off Jalan Ampang, 55000 Kuala Lumpur; tel. (3) 42512336; fax (3) 42521425; e-mail korem-my@mofat.go.kr; internet mys.mofat.go.kr/eng/index.jsp; Ambassador CHO BYUNJAE.

Kuwait: 229 Jalan Tun Razak, 50400 Kuala Lumpur; tel. (3) 21410033; fax (3) 21456121; e-mail kuwait@streamyx.com; Ambassador SAAD ABDULLAH SALEH AL-AEOUSI.

Kyrgyzstan: Wisma Sin Heap Lee, 10th Floor, 346 Jalan Tun Razak, 50400 Kuala Lumpur; tel. (3) 21632010; fax (3) 21632024; e-mail info@kgembassymy.com; internet www.kgembassymy.com; Ambassador KYLYCHBEK SULTANOV.

Laos: 7 Jalan Mesra, off Jalan Damai, 55000 Kuala Lumpur; tel. (3) 21487059; fax (3) 21450080; e-mail embassylao-kualalumpur@hotmail.com; Ambassador KHAMPHAN ANLAVAN.

Lebanon: 56 Jalan Ampang Hilir, 55000 Kuala Lumpur; tel. (3) 42516690; fax (3) 42603426; e-mail lebanon@streamyx.com; Ambassador ALI HUSSAIN DAHER.

Libya: 6 Jalan Madge, off Jalan U Thant, 55000 Kuala Lumpur; tel. (3) 21411293; fax (3) 21413549; e-mail ipbkl@yahoo.com; Ambassador Dr ANWAR ABUBAKER ELFEITORI.

Maldives: Suite 07-01, Menara See Hoy Chan, 374 Jalan Tun Razak, 50400 Kuala Lumpur; tel. (3) 21637244; fax (3) 21647244; e-mail mail@maldives.org.my; internet www.maldives.org.my; High Commissioner MOHAMED FAYAZ.

Mauritius: West Block, 17th Floor, Wisma Selangor Dredging, Jalan Ampang, 50450 Kuala Lumpur; tel. (3) 21636301; fax (3) 21636294; e-mail maurhckl@streamyx.com; Chargé d'affaires a.i. VIKASH NEETHALIA.

Mexico: Suite 22-05, 22nd Floor, Menara Tan & Tan, 207 Jalan Tun Razak, 50400 Kuala Lumpur; tel. (3) 21646362; fax (3) 21640964; e-mail embamex@po.jaring.my; internet www.embamex.sre.gob.mx/malasia; Ambassador CARLOS ISAURO FELIX CORONA.

Morocco: Unit 9, 3rd Floor, East Block, Wisma Selangor Dredging, 142B Jalan Ampang, 50450 Kuala Lumpur; tel. (3) 21610701; fax (3) 21623081; e-mail moremb@streamyx.com; internet www.moroccoembassy.org.my; Ambassador AHMED FAUOZI.

Myanmar: 8C Jalan Ampang Hilir, 55000 Kuala Lumpur; tel. (3) 42516355; fax (3) 42513855; e-mail mekl@tm.net.my; Ambassador ZAW MYINT.

Namibia: Suite 15-01, Tingkat 15, Menara HLA, 3 Jalan Kia Peng, 50450 Kuala Lumpur; tel. (3) 21433593; e-mail namhckl@streamyx.com; internet www.namibiahighcommission.com.my; High Commissioner GEBHARD BENJAMIN KANDANGA.

Nepal: Suite 13A-01, 13th Floor, Wisma MCA, 163 Jalan Ampang, 50450 Kuala Lumpur; tel. (3) 21645934; fax (3) 21648659; e-mail info@nepalembassy.com.my; internet www.nepalembassy.com.my; Ambassador Dr NIRANJAN MAN SINGH BASNYAT.

Netherlands: The Amp Walk, 7th Floor, South Block, 218 Jalan Ampang, POB 10543, 50450 Kuala Lumpur; tel. (3) 21686200; fax (3) 21686240; e-mail kll@minbuza.nl; internet malaysia.nlembassy.org; Ambassador HARRY MOLENAAR.

New Zealand: Menara IMC, 21st Floor, 8 Jalan Sultan Ismail, 50250 Kuala Lumpur; tel. (3) 20782533; fax (3) 20780387; e-mail nzhckl@streamyx.com; internet www.nzembassy.com/malaysia; High Commissioner JOHN SUBRITZKY (designate).

Nigeria: 85 Jalan Ampang Hilir, 55000 Kuala Lumpur; tel. (3) 42517843; fax (3) 42524302; e-mail info@nigeria.org.my; internet www.nigeria.org.my; High Commissioner JANET BESSONG ODEKA (acting).

Norway: Suite CD, 53rd Floor, Vista Tower, The Intermark, Jalan Tun Razak, 50400 Kuala Lumpur; tel. (3) 21710000; fax (3) 21710001; e-mail emb.kualalumpur@mfa.no; internet www.norway.org.my; Ambassador HANS OLA URSTAD.

Oman: 109 Jalan U Thant, 55000 Kuala Lumpur; tel. (3) 42577378; fax (3) 42571400; e-mail omanemb@po.jaring.my; internet om-cao.com; Ambassador JANAB FAKHRI MOHAMED AL-SAYYID.

Pakistan: 132 Jalan Ampang, 50450 Kuala Lumpur; tel. (3) 21618877; fax (3) 21645958; e-mail pahickl@gmail.com; High Commissioner HASSAN RAZA.

Papua New Guinea: 11 Lingkungan U Thant, off Jalan U Thant, 55000 Kuala Lumpur; tel. (3) 42575405; fax (3) 42576203; e-mail kundukl@pnghicomkl.my; High Commissioner VEALI VAGI.

Peru: Wisma Selangor Dredging, 6th Floor, South Block, 142A Jalan Ampang, 50450 Kuala Lumpur; tel. (3) 21633034; fax (3) 21633039; e-mail embperu@streamyx.com; Ambassador MARCO VINICIO BALAREZO LIZARZABURU.

Philippines: 1 Changkat Kia Peng, 50450 Kuala Lumpur; tel. (3) 21484233; fax (3) 21483576; e-mail consular@philembassykl.org.my; internet www.philembassykl.org.my; Ambassador JOSÉ EDUARDO E. MALAYA, III.

Poland: No. 10, Lorong Damai 9 off Jalan Damai 55000 Kuala Lumpur; tel. (3) 21610780; fax (3) 21649924; e-mail kualalumpur.amb.sekretariat@msz.gov.pl; internet www.kualalumpur.msz.gov.pl; Ambassador (vacant).

Qatar: 113 Jalan Ampang Hilir, POB 13118, 55000 Kuala Lumpur; tel. (3) 42565552; fax (3) 42565553; e-mail kualalumpur@mofa.gov.qa; Ambassador ESSA BIN MOHAMMED AL MANNAI.

Romania: 114 Jalan Damai, off Jalan Ampang, 55000 Kuala Lumpur; tel. (3) 21423172; fax (3) 21448713; e-mail roembdhm@streamyx.com; internet kualalumpur.mae.ro; Ambassador CONSTANTIN VOLODEA NISTOR.

Russian Federation: 263 Jalan Ampang, 50450 Kuala Lumpur; tel. (3) 42567252; fax (3) 42576091; e-mail rusembmalaysia@yandex.ru; internet www.malaysia.mid.ru; Ambassador VALERY YERMOLOV.

Saudi Arabia: Wisma Chinese Chamber, Tingkat 4, 258 Jalan Ampang, 50450 Kuala Lumpur; tel. (3) 42579433; fax (3) 42578751; e-mail saembssy@tm.net.my; Ambassador FAHAD A. AL-RASHID.

Senegal: 9 Lorong U Thant, off Jalan U Thant, 55000 Kuala Lumpur; tel. (3) 42567343; fax (3) 42563205; e-mail senamb_mal@yahoo.fr; Ambassador MAME BABA CISSÉ.

Singapore: Level 15, West Wing, The Icon, 1 Jalan 1/68F, Jalan Tun Razak, 50400 Kuala Lumpur; tel. (3) 21616277; fax (3) 21616343; e-mail singhc_kul@sgmfa.gov.sg; internet www.mfa.gov.sg/kl; High Commissioner VANU GOPALA MENON.

Slovakia: 11 Jalan U Thant, 55000 Kuala Lumpur; tel. (3) 21150016; fax (3) 21150018; e-mail emb.kualalumpur@mzv.sk; internet www.mzv.sk/kualalumpur; Ambassador MILOŠ BUDAY.

Solomon Islands: Kuala Lumpur; High Commissioner VICTOR NGELE.

Somalia: 55A, 57A, Jalan SS6/12, Kelana Jaya, 47301 Petaling Jaya, Selangor; tel. (3) 78031051; fax (3) 78054616; e-mail info@somaliembassy.com.my; internet www.somaliembassy.com.my; Ambassador NUR FARAH HIRSI.

South Africa: Menara HLA, Suite 22-01, 3 Jalan Kia Peng, 50450 Kuala Lumpur; tel. (3) 21702400; fax (3) 21688591; e-mail sahcadm@streamyx.com; internet www.sahighcomkl.com.my; High Commissioner SAMKELISIWE ISABEL MHLANGA.

Spain: Suite E-12-02, 12th Floor, East Wing, 1 Jalan 1/68F, off Jalan Tun Razak, 50400 Kuala Lumpur; tel. (3) 21620261; fax (3) 21640261; e-mail emb.kualalumpur@maec.es; internet www.exteriores.gob.es/embajadas/kualalumpur/es/Paginas/inicio.aspx; Ambassador CARLOS DOMÍNGUEZ.

Sri Lanka: 12 Jalan Keranji Dua, off Jalan Kedondong, Ampang Hilir, 55000 Kuala Lumpur; tel. (3) 42568987; fax (3) 42532497; e-mail hc.srilanka@unifi.my; internet www.slhc.com.my; High Commissioner IBRAHIM ANSAR.

Sudan: 2A Persiaran Ampang, off Jalan Ru, 55000 Kuala Lumpur; tel. (3) 42569104; fax (3) 42568107; e-mail sudani@sudanembassy-kl.org.my; internet www.sudanembassy-kl.org.my/v/index.php?id=486; Ambassador KHALID ABDELGADIR SHUKRI.

Swaziland: Suite 22-03 & 22-03A, Menara Citibank, 165 Jalan Ampang, 50450 Kuala Lumpur; tel. (3) 21632511; fax (3) 21633326; e-mail info@swazilandkualalumpur.org; internet www.swazilandkualalumpur.org; High Commissioner ZANALE MDLULI.

Sweden: POB 10239, 50708 Kuala Lumpur; tel. (3) 22030200; fax (3) 22030201; e-mail ambassaden.kuala-lumpur@gov.se; internet www.swedenabroad.com/kualalumpur; Ambassador BENGT G. CARLSSON.

Switzerland: 16 Persiaran Madge, 55000 Kuala Lumpur; tel. (3) 21480622; fax (3) 21480935; e-mail kua.vertretung@eda.admin.ch; internet www.eda.admin.ch/kualalumpur; Ambassador Dr ROLF LENZ.

Syria: 93 Jalan U Thant, 55000 Kuala Lumpur; tel. (3) 42516364; fax (3) 42516363; e-mail enquiry@syrianembassy.com.my; internet www.syrianembassy.com.my; Chargé d'affaires a.i. Dr MHD TAWFIQ ABOU GHALON.

Thailand: 206 Jalan Ampang, 50450 Kuala Lumpur; tel. (3) 21488222; fax (3) 21486527; e-mail thaikula@mfa.go.th; internet www.thaiembassy.org/kualalumpur; Ambassador KRIT KRAICHITTI.

Timor-Leste: 62 Jalan Ampang Hilir, 55000 Kuala Lumpur; tel. (3) 42562046; fax (3) 42562016; e-mail embaixada_tl_kl@yahoo.com; Ambassador JOSÉ ANTÓNIO AMORIM DIAS.

Turkey: 118 Jalan U Thant, 55000 Kuala Lumpur; tel. (3) 42572225; fax (3) 42572227; e-mail embassy.kualalumpur@mfa.gov.tr; internet www.kualalumpur.be.mfa.gov.tr; Ambassador BAŞAK TÜRKOĞLU.

Turkmenistan: 14th Floor, Wisma Sin Heap Lee, 346 Jalan Tun Razak, 50400 Kuala Lumpur; tel. (3) 21610421; fax (3) 21610423; e-mail tkmembmalaysia@gmail.com; internet www.embassyturkmenistan.org; Ambassador YAZGULY MAMMADOV.

Ukraine: Suite 22-02, 22nd Floor, Menara Tan & Tan, 207 Jalan Tun Razak, 50400 Kuala Lumpur; tel. (3) 21669552; fax (3) 21664371; e-mail emb_my@mfa.gov.ua; internet www.mfa.gov.ua/malaysia; Ambassador IHOR V. HUMENNYI.

United Arab Emirates: 1 Gerbang Ampang Hilir, off Persiaran Ampang Hilir, 55000 Kuala Lumpur; tel. (3) 42535221; fax (3) 42535220; e-mail uaemal@tm.net.my; Ambassador ABDULLAH MATAR AL MAZROUEI.

United Kingdom: 27th Floor, Menara Binjai 2 Jalan Binjai, 50450 Kuala Lumpur; tel. (3) 21702200; fax (3) 21702370; e-mail political.kualalumpur@fco.gov.uk; internet ukinmalaysia.fco.gov.uk; High Commissioner VICTORIA TREADELL.

USA: 376 Jalan Tun Razak, POB 10035, 50400 Kuala Lumpur; tel. (3) 21685000; fax (3) 21485801; e-mail klconsular@state.gov; internet malaysia.usembassy.gov; Ambassador JOSEPH Y. YUN.

Uruguay: UBN Tower, 6th Floor, 10 Jalan P. Ramlee, 50250 Kuala Lumpur; tel. (3) 20313669; fax (3) 20315669; e-mail urukuala@streamyx.com; Ambassador GERARDO PRATO.

Uzbekistan: Wisma Chinese Chamber, 2nd Floor, 258 Jalan Ampang, 50450 Kuala Lumpur; tel. (3) 42532406; fax (3) 42535406; e-mail uzbekemb@streamyx.com; internet www.malaysia.mfa.uz; Ambassador MURAD ASKAROV.

Venezuela: Suite 20-05, 20th Floor, Menara Tan & Tan, 207 Jalan Tun Razak, 50400 Kuala Lumpur; tel. (3) 21633444; fax (3) 21636819; e-mail info@venezuela.org.my; internet www.venezuela.org.my; Ambassador MANUEL ANTONIO GUZMÁN HERNÁNDEZ.

Viet Nam: 4 Jalan Persiaran Stonor, 50450 Kuala Lumpur; tel. (3) 21484036; fax (3) 21483270; e-mail daisevn@putra.net.my; internet www.mofa.gov.vn/vnemb.my; Ambassador PHAM CAO PHONG.

Yemen: 7 Jalan Kedondong, off Jalan Ampang Hilir, 55000 Kuala Lumpur; tel. (3) 42511793; fax (3) 42511794; e-mail secretary@yemenembassykl.com; internet yemenembassykl.com; Chargé d'affaires MOHAMMED MOTAHAR AL-ASHABI.

Zambia: Suite C, Menara MBF, 5th Floor, Jalan Sultan Ismail, 50250 Kuala Lumpur; tel. (3) 21453512; fax (3) 21453619; e-mail info@zhckl.com.my; internet www.zhckl.com.my; High Commissioner MARTHA MAZIMBA (acting).

Zimbabwe: 124 Jalan Sembilan, Taman Ampang Utama, 68000 Ampang, Selangor Darul Ehsan; tel. (3) 42516779; fax (3) 42517252; e-mail zhck@tm.net.my; Ambassador CUTHBERT ZHAKATA.

Judicial System

Federal Court: Palace of Justice, Presint 3, 62506 Putrajaya; tel. (3) 88803502; fax (3) 88803507; e-mail cj@kehakiman.gov.my; internet www.kehakiman.gov.my; has jurisdiction in any dispute between states or between the Federation and any state, as well as special jurisdiction as to the interpretation of the Constitution; headed by the Chief Justice; the other members of the Federal Court are the President of the Court of Appeal, the two Chief Judges of the High Courts and the Federal Court Judges; Chief Justice Tan Sri ARIFIN BIN ZAKARIA.

Court of Appeal: tel. (3) 88803566; fax (3) 88803595; e-mail mdraus@kehakiman.gov.my; f. 1994 as an intermediary court between the Federal Court and the High Court; Pres. Tan Sri Dato' Seri MOHD RAUS BIN SHARIF.

High Court (Peninsular Malaysia): tel. (3) 88803552; fax (3) 88803556; e-mail cjm@kehakiman.gov.my; has original, appellate and revisional jurisdiction as the federal law provides; Chief Judge Tan Sri Dato' Seri ZULKEFLI BIN AHMAD MAKINUDIN.

High Court (Sabah and Serawak): High Court, Jalan Gersik, 93050 Sarawak; e-mail cjss@kehakiman.gov.my; has original, appellate and revisional jurisdiction as the federal law provides; Chief Judge Tan Sri Datuk Seri RICHARD MALANJUM.

Attorney-General's Chambers: 45 Persiaran Perdana, Presint 4, 62100 Putrajaya; tel. (3) 88722000; fax (3) 88905670; e-mail amsyari@agc.gov.my; internet www.agc.gov.my; Attorney-General Tan Sri ABDUL GANI PATAIL.

Below the Federal Court, the Court of Appeal and the High Courts are the Sessions Courts, which are situated in the principal urban and rural centres. The criminal jurisdiction of the Sessions Courts covers the less serious indictable offences, excluding those that carry the death penalty. Civil jurisdiction of a Sessions Court is up to RM 250,000. The Sessions Judges are appointed by the Yang di-Pertuan Agong. The Magistrates' Courts are also found in the main urban and rural centres and have both civil and criminal jurisdiction, although of a more restricted nature than that of the Sessions Courts. The Magistrates consist of officers from the Judicial and Legal Service of the Federation. They are appointed by the State Authority in which they officiate on the recommendation of the Chief Judge.

There are also Syariah (*Shari'a*) courts for rulings under Islamic law. In July 1996 the Cabinet announced that the Syariah courts were to be restructured with the appointment of a Syariah Chief Judge and four Court of Appeal justices, whose rulings would set precedents for the whole country.

Religion

Islam is the established religion. While freedom of religious practice is enshrined in the Constitution, Malaysia's parallel Islamic judicial system holds great sway over the Muslim majority on religious issues. Almost all ethnic Malays are Muslims, representing 61.3% of the total population in 2010. In that year 19.8% of the population followed Buddhism, 9.2% Christianity and 6.3% Hinduism.

Malaysian Consultative Council of Buddhism, Christianity, Hinduism, Sikhism and Taoism (MCCBCHST): Buddhist Maha Vihara, 123 Jalan Berhala, Brickfields, 50470 Kuala Lumpur; tel. (3) 22739304; fax (3) 22739307; e-mail mccbchst@yahoo.com; f. 1981; a non-Muslim group; Pres. Rev. Dr THOMAS PHILIPS.

ISLAM

Istitut Kefahaman Islam Malaysia (IKIM) (Institute of Islamic Understanding Malaysia): 2 Langgak Tunku, off Jalan Duta, 50480 Kuala Lumpur; tel. (3) 62046200; fax (3) 62014189; e-mail info@ikim.gov.my; internet www.ikim.gov.my; Chair. TUN ABDULLAH BIN AHMAD BADAWI.

Jabatan Kemajuan Islam Malaysia (JAKIM) (Department of Islamic Development Malaysia): Aras 4–9, Blok D7, Pusat Pentadbiran Kerajaan Persekutuan, 62519 Putrajaya; tel. (3) 88864000; fax (3) 88892039; e-mail webmaster@islam.gov.my; internet www.islam.gov.my; Dir-Gen. Haji OTHMAN BIN MUSTAPHA.

BUDDHISM

Malaysian Buddhist Association (MBA): MBA Bldg, 182 Jalan Burmah, 10050 Pinang; tel. (4) 2262690; fax (4) 2263024; e-mail mba.hq@malaysianbuddhistassociation.org; internet www.malaysianbuddhistassociation.org; f. 1959; the national body for Chinese and English-speaking monks, nuns and temples from the Mahayana, Theravada and Vajrayana tradition; nine state brs and 25 other brs nationwide; Pres. Ven. SECK JIT HENG.

Buddhist Missionary Society Malaysia (BMSM): 123 Jalan Berhala, off Jalan Tun Sambanthan, 50470 Kuala Lumpur; tel. (3) 22730150; fax (3) 22733835; e-mail bmsm.malaysia@gmail.com; internet www.bmsm.org.my; f. 1962; Pres. LOH PAI LING.

Buddhist Tzu-Chi Merit Society (Malaysia): 316 Jalan Macalister, 10450 Pulau Pinang; tel. (4) 2281013; fax (2) 2261013; e-mail info@tzuchi.org.my; internet www.tzuchi.org.my.

Malaysian Fo Kuang Buddhist Association: 2 Jalan SS3/33, Taman University, 47300 Petaling Jaya, Selangor; tel. (3) 78776512; fax (3) 78776511; e-mail myfoguang@yahoo.com.

Sasana Abhiwurdhi Wardhana Society: 123 Jalan Berhala, off Jalan Tun Sambanthan, 50490 Kuala Lumpur; f. 1894; the national body for Sri Lankan Buddhists belonging to the Theravada tradition.

Young Buddhist Association of Malaysia (YBAM): 9 Jalan SS25/24, Taman Mayang, 47301 Petaling Jaya, Selangor; tel. (3) 78049154; fax (3) 78049021; e-mail ybam@streamyx.com; internet www.ybam.org.my; f. 1970; 270 mems; Pres. Dr ONG SEE YEW.

CHRISTIANITY

Majlis Gereja-Gereja Malaysia (Council of Churches of Malaysia): 10 Jalan 11/9, 46200 Petaling Jaya, Selangor; tel. (3) 75967092; fax (3) 79560353; e-mail cchurchm@streamyx.org; internet www.ccmalaysia.org; f. 1947; 18 mem. churches; 10 assoc. mems; Pres. Rev. Dr THOMAS PHILIPS (Mar Thoma Syrian Church); Gen. Sec. Rev. Dr HERMEN SHASTRI.

The Anglican Communion

Malaysia comprises three Anglican dioceses, within the Church of the Province of South East Asia.

Primate: Most Rev. Dr JOHN CHEW (Bishop of Singapore).

Bishop of Kuching: Rt Rev. BOLLY ANAK LAPOK, The House of the Epiphany, POB 347, 93704 Kuching, Sarawak; tel. (82) 240187; fax (82) 426488; e-mail bishopk@streamyx.com; has jurisdiction over Sarawak, Brunei and part of Indonesian Kalimantan (Borneo).

Bishop of Sabah: Most Rev. ALBERT VUN CHEONG FUI, Rumah Bishop, Jalan Tangki, POB 10811, 88809 Kota Kinabalu, Sabah; tel. (88) 245846; fax (88) 245942; e-mail dosabah@streamyx.com.

Bishop of West Malaysia: Rt. Rev. NG MOON HING, Bishop's House, 16 Jalan Pudu Lama, 50200 Kuala Lumpur; tel. (3) 20313213; fax (3) 20312728; e-mail anglican@streamyx.com; internet www.anglicanwestmalaysia.org.my.

The Baptist Church

Malaysia Baptist Convention: 2 Jalan Dispensary 2/38, 46000 Petaling Jaya, Selangor; tel. (3) 77823564; fax (3) 77833603; e-mail mbcpj@tm.net.my; internet www.mbc.org.my; Chair. Rev. BERNARD ANG; Gen. Sec. Rev. KOE CHOON HUAN.

The Methodist Church

Methodist Church in Malaysia: 69 Jalan 5/31, 46000 Petaling Jaya, Selangor; tel. (3) 79541811; fax (3) 79541788; e-mail info@methodistchurch.org.my; internet www.methodistchurch.org.my; f. 1885; 164,400 mems; Head Rev. Dr HWA YUNG.

The Presbyterian Church

Presbyterian Church in Malaysia: 7 Jalan Sungai Buaya, Batu 3 1/2, off Jalan Klang Lama, 58100 Kuala Lumpur; tel. (3) 79847361; fax (3) 79809037; e-mail presbych@gmail.com; internet www.gpm.org.my; Moderator Rev. CHUA HUA PENG.

The Roman Catholic Church

Malaysia comprises three archdioceses and six dioceses. At 31 December 2007 approximately 3.0% of the population were adherents.

Catholic Bishops' Conference of Malaysia, Singapore and Brunei: Majodi Centre, 2101 Jalan Masai, Johor; tel. (7) 3871121; fax (7) 3872498; e-mail mpakiam@pd.jaring.my; Pres. Most Rev. MURPHY NICHOLAS XAVIER PAKIAM (Archbishop of Kuala Lumpur).

Archbishop of Kota Kinabalu: Most Rev. JOHN LEE HIONG FUN-YIT HAW, Archbishop's House, POB 10289, 88803, Kota Kinabalu, Sabah; tel. (88) 712297; fax (88) 711954; internet www.kkdiocese.net.

Archbishop of Kuala Lumpur: Most Rev. MURPHY NICHOLAS XAVIER PAKIAM, Archbishop's House, 528 Jalan Bukit Nanas, 50250 Kuala Lumpur; tel. (3) 20788828; fax (3) 20313815; e-mail mpakiam@pd.jaring.my; internet www.archway.org.my.

Archbishop of Kuching: Most Rev. JOHN HA TIONG HOCK, Archbishop's Office, 118 Jalan Tun Abang Haji Openg, POB 940, 93000 Kuching, Sarawak; tel. (82) 242634; fax (82) 425724; e-mail abcofku@pd.jaring.my.

BAHÁ'Í FAITH

Spiritual Assembly of the Bahá'ís of Malaysia: 12 Desa Business Centre, 1–2/F, Jalan 2/109E, Taman Desa, Jalan Klang Lama, 58100

Kuala Lumpur; tel. (3) 79819059; fax (3) 79802058; e-mail nsa-sec@bahai.org.my; internet www.bahai.org.my; f. 1964; mems resident in 800 localities.

The Press

PENINSULAR MALAYSIA DAILIES

English Language

Business Times: Balai Berita 31, Jalan Riong, 59100 Kuala Lumpur; tel. (3) 22822628; fax (3) 22825424; e-mail support@nstp.com.my; internet www.btimes.com.my; f. 1976; morning; Editor SHAHRIMAN JOHARI; circ. 15,000.

The Edge: 1 Menara KLK, Level 3, Jalan PJU 7/6, Mutiara Damansara, 47810 Petaling Jaya, Selangor; tel. (3) 77218000; fax (3) 77218010; e-mail info@bizedge.com; internet www.theedgedaily.com; f. 1996; weekly, with daily internet edition; business and investment news; Publr HO KAY TAT; Editor AZAM ARIS; circ. 20,338.

Malay Mail: Lot 2A, Jalan 13/2, 46200 Petaling Jaya, Selangor; tel. (3) 74951288; fax (3) 74951229; e-mail mmnews@mmail.com.my; internet www.mmail.com.my; f. 1896; afternoon; Man. Editor JOAN LAU; circ. 75,000.

Malaysiakini: 48 Jalan Kemuja, Bangsar Utama, 59000 Kuala Lumpur; tel. (3) 22835567; fax (3) 22892579; e-mail enquiries@malaysiakini.com; internet www.malaysiakini.com; f. 1999; Malaysia's first online newspaper; English and Malay; Editor FATHI ARIS OMAR.

New Straits Times: Balai Berita 31, Jalan Riong, 59100 Kuala Lumpur; tel. (3) 22823322; fax (3) 22821434; e-mail news@nstp.com.my; internet www.nst.com.my; f. 1845; morning; Group Editor-in-Chief Dato' SYED NADZRI SYED HARUN; circ. 74,823.

The Star: 15 Jalan 16/11, 46350 Petaling Jaya, POB 12474, Selangor Darul Ehsan; tel. (3) 79671388; fax (3) 79550439; e-mail msd@thestar.com.my; internet www.thestar.com.my; f. 1971; morning; Group Chief Editor Datuk WONG CHUN WAI; circ. 302,658.

The Sun: Sun Media Corpn Sdn Bhd, 4th Floor, Lot 6, Jalan 51/217, Section 51, 46050 Petaling Jaya, Selangor Darul Ehsan; tel. (3) 77846688; fax (3) 77835871; e-mail info@thesundaily.com; internet www.thesundaily.com; f. 1993; free tabloid newspaper in print and online formats; Man. Dir CHAN KIEN SING; Man. Editor FREDDIE NG; circ. 304,000.

Chinese Language

Chung Kuo Pao (China Press): 80 Jalan Riong, off Jalan Bangsar, 59100 Kuala Lumpur; tel. (3) 22896363; fax (3) 22827125; e-mail enews@chinapress.com.my; internet www.chinapress.com.my; f. 1946; Editor POON CHAU HUAY; Gen. Man. NG BENG LYE; circ. 161,794.

Guang Ming Daily: 19 Jalan Semangat, 46200 Petaling Jaya, Selangor; tel. (3) 79658888; fax (3) 79658477; e-mail gmkl@mail.guangming.com.my; internet www.guangming.com.my; Editor-in-Chief YE NING; circ. 94,287.

Kwong Wah Yit Poh: 19 Jalan Presgrave, 11300 Pinang; tel. (4) 2612312; fax (4) 2628540; e-mail editor@kwongwah.com.my; internet www.kwongwah.com.my; f. 1910; morning; Chief Editor HU JINCHANG; circ. 100,000.

Nanyang Siang Pau (Malaysia): 1st Floor, 1 Jalan SS7/2, 47301 Petaling Jaya, Selangor; tel. (3) 78726888; fax (3) 78726800; e-mail editor@nanyang.com.my; internet www.nanyang.com.my; f. 1923; morning and evening; Editor-in-Chief CHONG CHOONG NAM; circ. 180,000 (daily), 220,000 (Sunday).

Sin Chew Jit Poh (Malaysia): 19 Jalan Semangat, POB 367, Jalan Sultan, 46200 Petaling Jaya, Selangor; tel. (3) 79658888; fax (3) 79556881; e-mail editorial@sinchew.com.my; internet www.sinchew-i.com; f. 1929; morning; Group Editor-in-chief SIEW NYOKE CHOW; circ. 440,002 (daily), 230,000 (Sunday).

Malay Language

Berita Harian: Balai Berita, 31 Jalan Riong, 59100 Kuala Lumpur; tel. (3) 22822323; fax (3) 20567081; e-mail bhnews@bharian.com.my; internet www.bharian.com.my; f. 1957; morning; Group Editor Datuk MIOR KAMARUL SHAHID; circ. 166,400.

Mingguan Perdana: 48 Jalan Siput Akek, Taman Billion, Kuala Lumpur; tel. (3) 619133; Group Chief Editor KHALID JAFRI.

Utusan Malaysia: 46M Jalan Lima, off Jalan Chan Sow Lin, 55200 Kuala Lumpur; tel. (3) 92217055; fax (3) 92227876; e-mail corpcomm@utusan.com.my; internet www.utusan.com.my; Editor ABDUL AZIZ ISHAK; circ. 171,582.

Watan: 23-1 Jalan 9A/55A, Taman Setiawangsa, 54200 Kuala Lumpur; tel. (3) 4523040; fax (3) 4523043; circ. 80,000.

Tamil Language

Makkal Osai: 11B Jalan Murai Dua, Batu Kompleks, off Jalan Ipoh, 52000 Kuala Lumpur; tel. (3) 62512251; fax (3) 62535981; f. 1990; est. as a Sunday newspaper after *Tamil Osai* ceased publication; publ. daily since Dec. 2005; Gen. Man. S. M. PERIASAMY; circ. 52,000 (daily), 95,000 (Sunday).

Malaysia Nanban: 544-3 Batu Complex, off Jalan Ipoh, Batu 3 1/4, 51200 Kuala Lumpur; e-mail news@nanban.com.my; internet www.nanban2u.com; tel. (3) 62515981; fax (3) 62591617; circ. 45,000; Editor M. MALAYANDY.

Tamil Nesan: 23, Jalan SBC 5, Taman Sri Batu Caves, 68100 Batu Caves, Selangor Darul Ehsaan; tel. (3) 61841818; fax (3) 61871818; e-mail mytamilnesan@yahoo.com; internet www.tamilnesan.com.my; f. 1924; morning; Editor-in-Chief PADMANATHAN; circ. 35,000 (daily), 60,000 (Sunday).

SUNDAY NEWSPAPERS

English Language

New Sunday Times: Balai Berita 31, Jalan Riong, 59100 Kuala Lumpur; tel. (3) 2822328; fax (3) 2824482; e-mail news@nstp.com.my; f. 1931; morning; Group Editor Datuk HISHAMUDDIN AUN; circ. 191,562.

Sunday Mail: Balai Berita 31, Jalan Riong, 59100 Kuala Lumpur; tel. (3) 2822328; fax (3) 2824482; e-mail smail@nstp.com.my; f. 1896; morning; Editor JOACHIM S. P. NG; circ. 75,641.

Sunday Star: 13 Jalan 13/6, 46200 Petaling Jaya, POB 12474, Selangor Darul Ehsan; tel. (3) 7581188; fax (3) 7551280; f. 1971; Editor DAVID YEOH; circ. 232,790.

Malay Language

Berita Minggu: Balai Berita 31, Jalan Riong, 59100 Kuala Lumpur; tel. (3) 22822323; fax (3) 20567082; e-mail bhnews@bharian.com.my; f. 1957; morning; Group Editor Datuk MIOR KAMARUL SHAHID; circ. 421,127.

Metro Ahad: Balai Berita 31, Jalan Riong, 59100 Kuala Lumpur; tel. (3) 22822328; fax (3) 22821482; e-mail yaacob@hmetro.com.my; internet www.hmetro.com.my; f. 1995; morning; Editor YAACOB ABDUL RAHIM; circ. 136,974.

Mingguan Malaysia: 11A The Right Angle, Jalan 14/22, 46100 Petaling Jaya; tel. (3) 7563355; fax (3) 7577755; f. 1964; Editor MOHD HASSAN MOHD NOOR; circ. 543,232.

PENINSULAR MALAYSIA PERIODICALS

English Language

Her World: Lot 7, Jalan Bersatu 13/4, Section 13, 46200 Petaling Jaya, Selangor Darul Ehsan; tel. (3) 79527000; fax (3) 79600148; e-mail herworld@bluinc.com.my; internet www.herworld.com.my; monthly; Editor ALICE CHEE LAN NEO; circ. 35,000.

The Herald: Archdiocesan Pastoral Centre, 5 Jalan Robertson, 50150 Kuala Lumpur; tel. (3) 20268290; fax (3) 20268293; e-mail editor@herald.com.my; internet www.heraldmalaysia.com; weekly; Catholic; Publr Most Rev. JULIAN LEOW; Editor Fr LAWRENCE ANDREW; circ. 16,000.

Malaysia Warta Kerajaan Seri Paduka Baginda (HM Government Gazette): Percetakan Nasional Malaysia Berhad, Jalan Chan Sow Lin, 50554 Kuala Lumpur; tel. (3) 92212022; fax (3) 92220690; e-mail pnmb@po.jaring.my; fortnightly.

Malaysian Agricultural Journal: Ministry of Agriculture and Agro-based Industry, Publications Unit, Wisma Tani, Jalan Sultan Salahuddin, 50624 Kuala Lumpur; tel. (3) 2982011; fax (3) 2913758; f. 1901; 2 a year.

Malaysian Forester: Forestry Department Headquarters, Jalan Sultan Salahuddin, 50660 Kuala Lumpur; tel. (3) 26988244; fax (3) 26925657; e-mail skthai@forestry.gov.my; f. 1931; quarterly; Editor THAI SEE KIAM.

The Planter: Wisma ISP, 29 & 31–33 Jalan Taman U Thant, POB 10262, 50708 Kuala Lumpur; tel. (3) 21425561; fax (3) 21426898; e-mail isphq@tm.net.my; internet www.isp.org.my; f. 1919; publ. by Isp Management (M); monthly; Editor AZIZAN ABDULLAH; circ. 4,500.

The Rocket: 24 Jalan 20/9, 46300 Petaling Jaya, Selangor; tel. (3) 79578022; fax (3) 79575718; e-mail rocket@dapmalaysia.org; internet daprocket.com; monthly; official newsletter of Democratic Action Party; also published in Chinese and Malay; Editor TONY PUA.

Young Generation: 11A The Right Angle, Jalan 14/22, 46100 Petaling Jaya, Selangor; tel. (3) 7563355; fax (3) 7577755; monthly; circ. 50,000.

Chinese Language

Mister Weekly: 2A Jalan 19/1, 46300 Petaling Jaya, Selangor; tel. (3) 7562400; fax (3) 7553826; f. 1976; weekly; Editor WONG AH TAI; circ. 25,000.

Mun Sang Poh: 472 Jalan Pasir Puteh, 31650 Ipoh; tel. (5) 3212919; fax (5) 3214006; fortnightly; circ. 77,958.

New Life Post: 80M Jalan SS21/39, Damansara Utama, 47400 Petaling Jaya, Selangor; tel. (3) 7571833; fax (3) 7181809; f. 1972; bi-weekly; Editor LOW BENG CHEE; circ. 231,000.

New Tide Magazine: Nanyang Siang Pau Bldg, 2nd Floor, Jalan 7/2, 47301 Petaling Jaya, Selangor; tel. (3) 76202118; fax (3) 76202131; e-mail newtidemag@hotmail.com; f. 1974; monthly; Editor NELLIE OOI; circ. 39,000.

Malay Language

Dewan Masyarakat: Dewan Bahasa dan Pustaka, Jalan Wisma Putra, POB 10803, 50926 Kuala Lumpur; tel. (3) 2481011; fax (3) 2484211; f. 1963; monthly; current affairs; Editor ZULKIFLI SALLEH; circ. 48,500.

Dewan Pelajar: Dewan Bahasa dan Pustaka, Jalan Wisma Putra, POB 10803, 50926 Kuala Lumpur; tel. (3) 2481011; fax (3) 2484211; f. 1967; monthly; children's; Editor ZALEHA HASHIM; circ. 100,000.

Dewan Siswa: POB 10803, 50926 Kuala Lumpur; tel. (3) 2481011; fax (3) 2484208; monthly; circ. 140,000.

Gila-Gila: 38-1, Jalan Bangsar Utama Satu, Bangsar Utama, 59000 Kuala Lumpur; tel. (3) 22824970; fax (3) 22824967; fortnightly; circ. 70,000.

Harakah: 5 Jalan, 65C, off Jalan Pahang Barat, Pekeliling Business Center, 53000 Kuala Lumpur; tel. (3) 40212009; fax (3) 40212037; e-mail harakahenglish@yahoo.com; internet www.harakahdaily .net; two a week; f. 1980; media organ of the PAS; Group Editor-in-Chief TAUFEK YAHYA.

Jelita: Berita Publishing Sdn Bhd, 16–20 Jalan 4/109E, Desa Business Park, Taman Desa, off Jalan Klang Lama, 58100 Kuala Lumpur; tel. (3) 76208111; fax (3) 76208026; e-mail jelita@ beritapub.com.my; internet www.beritapublishing.com.my; monthly; fashion and beauty magazine; Editor SARIMAH HUSIN; circ. 133,727.

Mangga: 11A The Right Angle, Jalan 14/22, 46100 Petaling Jaya, Selangor; tel. (3) 7563355; fax (3) 7577755; monthly; circ. 56,609.

Mastika: Utusan Karya Sdn Bhd, Lot 6, Jalan 1/1U, Seksyen 10, 43650 Bandar Baru Bangi, Selangor Darul Ehsan; tel. (3) 89262999; fax (3) 89259277; f. 1941; monthly; illustrated magazine; Editor SAHIDAN JAAFAR; circ. 350,000.

Utusan Radio dan TV: 11A The Right Angle, Jalan 14/22, 46100 Petaling Jaya, Selangor; tel. (3) 7563355; fax (3) 7577755; fortnightly; Editor NORSHAII TAMBY; circ. 115,000.

Wanita: 11A The Right Angle, Jalan 14/22, 46100 Petaling Jaya, Selangor; tel. (3) 7563355; fax (3) 7577755; monthly; women; Editor NIK RAHIMAH HASSAN; circ. 28,651.

Punjabi Language

Navjiwan Punjabi News: 52 Jalan 8/18, Jalan Toman, 46050 Petaling Jaya, Selangor; tel. (3) 7565725; f. 1950; weekly; Assoc. Editor TARA SINGH; circ. 9,000.

SABAH DAILIES

Api Siang Pau (Kota Kinabalu Commercial Press): 24 Lorong Dewan, POB 170, Kota Kinabalu; f. 1954; morning; Chinese; Editor Datuk LO KWOCK CHUEN; circ. 3,000.

Borneo Post (Nountan Press Sdn Bhd): 1 Jalan Bakau, 1st Floor, off Jalan Gaya, 88999 Kota Kinabalu; tel. (88) 238001; fax (88) 238002; internet www.theborneopost.com; English; Chief Editor JIMMY ADIT; circ. 22,533.

Daily Express: News House, 16 Jalan Pasar Baru, POB 10139, 88801 Kota Kinabalu; tel. (88) 256422; fax (88) 238611; e-mail forum@dailyexpress.com.my; internet www.dailyexpress.com.my; f. 1963; morning; English, Bahasa Malaysia and Kadazan; Editor-in-Chief SARDATHISA JAMES; circ. 28,555.

Hwa Chiaw Jit Pao (Overseas Chinese Daily News): News House, 16 Jalan Pasar Baru, POB 10139, 88801 Kota Kinabalu; tel. (88) 256422; fax (88) 238611; e-mail sph@dailyexpress.com.my; internet www.ocdn.com.my; f. 1936; morning; Chinese; Editor HII YUK SENG; circ. 16,489.

Merdeka Daily News: Lot 56, BDC Estate, Mile 1½ North Road, POB 332, 90703 Sandakan; tel. (89) 214517; fax (89) 275537; e-mail merkk@tm.net.my; f. 1968; morning; Chinese; Editor-in-Chief FUNG KON SHING; circ. 8,000.

New Sabah Times: Jalan Pusat Pembangunan Masyarakat, off Jalan Mat Salleh, 88100 Kota Kinabalu; tel. (88) 230055; fax (88) 231155; e-mail chng.boonheng@newsabahtimes.com.my; internet www.newsabahtimes.com.my; English, Malay and Kadazan; Editor-in-Chief CHENG BOON HENG; circ. 22,525.

Syarikat Sabah Times: Kota Kinabalu; tel. (88) 52217; f. 1952; English, Malay and Kadazan; circ. 25,000.

Tawau Jih Pao: POB 464, 1072 Jalan Kuhara, Tawau; tel. (89) 72576; Chinese; Editor-in-Chief STEPHEN LAI KIM YEAN.

SARAWAK DAILIES

Berita Petang Sarawak: Lot 8322, Lorong 7, Jalan Tun Abdul Razak, 93450 Kuching; POB 1315, 93726 Kuching; tel. (82) 480771; fax (82) 489006; f. 1972; evening; Chinese; Chief Editor HWANG YU CHAI; circ. 12,000.

Borneo Post: 40 Jalan Tuanku Osman, POB 20, 96000 Sibu; tel. (84) 332055; fax (84) 321255; internet www.borneopost.com.my; morning; English; Man. Dir LAU HUI SIONG; Editor NGUOI HOW YIENG; circ. 60,000.

International Times: Lot 2215, Jalan Bengkel, Pending Industrial Estate, POB 1158, 93724 Kuching; tel. (82) 482215; fax (82) 480996; e-mail news@intimes.com; internet www.intimes.com.my; f. 1968; morning; Chinese; Editor LEE FOOK ONN; circ. 24,292.

Malaysia Daily News: 7 Island Rd, POB 237, 96009 Sibu; tel. (84) 330211; tel. (84) 320540; f. 1968; morning; Chinese; Editor WONG SENG KWONG; circ. 22,735.

Sarawak Tribune and Sunday Tribune: Lot 231, Jalan Abell Utara, 93100 Kuching; tel. (82) 424411; fax (82) 415024; e-mail st@ tru.my; internet tribune.my; f. 1945; English; licence suspended in Feb. 2006; reappeared in May 2010 as New Sarawak Tribune; Editor–in-Chief WILLIAM CHAN; circ. 2,960.

See Hua Daily News: 40 Jalan Tuanku Osman, POB 20, 96000 Sibu; tel. (84) 332055; fax (84) 321255; f. 1952; morning; Chinese; Man. Editor LAU HUI SIONG; circ. 80,000.

United Daily News: Lot 88, Block 3, Piasau Industrial Estate, POB 377, 98007 Miri ; tel. (84) 219251; fax (84) 215037; internet www .eunited.com.my; f. 2004 following merger between Chinese Daily News and Miri Daily News; morning; Chinese; Man. Editor CHRISTINE LIU QING; circ. 35,000.

SARAWAK PERIODICALS

Pedoman Rakyat: Malaysian Information Dept, Mosque Rd, 93612 Kuching; tel. (82) 240141; f. 1956; monthly; Malay; Editor SAIT BIN Haji YAMAN; circ. 30,000.

Pemberita: Malaysian Information Services, Mosque Rd, 93612 Kuching; tel. (82) 247231; internet www.penerangan.gov.my; f. 1950; every 2 months; Iban; Editor PHILIP NYARU BUNDAK; circ. 20,000.

Sarawak Gazette: Sarawak Museum, Jalan Tun Abang Haji Openg, 93566 Kuching; tel. (82) 244232; fax (82) 246680; e-mail amireaha@sarawak.gov.my; f. 1870; 2 a year; English; Chief Editor Datu Haji SALLEH SULAIMAN.

Utusan Sarawak: Lot 231, Jalan Nipah, off Jalan Abell Utara, POB 138, 93100 Kuching; tel. (82) 424411; fax (82) 415024; internet www .utusansarawak.com.my; f. 1949; Malay; Editor-in-Chief WILLIAM CHAN; circ. 32,292.

NEWS AGENCY

Bernama (Malaysian National News Agency): Wisma Bernama, 28 Jalan 1/65A, off Jalan Tun Razak, POB 10024, 50400 Kuala Lumpur; tel. (3) 26939933; fax (3) 26913972; e-mail helpdesk@bernama.com; internet www.bernama.com; f. 1968; general and foreign news, economic features and photo services, public relations wire, screen information and data services, stock market online equities service, real-time commodity and monetary information services; daily output in Malay and English; in June 1990 Bernama was given the exclusive right to receive and distribute news in Malaysia; Editor-in-Chief Datuk YONG SOO HEONG.

PRESS ASSOCIATIONS

Magazine Publishers' Association of Malaysia (MPA): 3-3, Jalan 11/48A, Sentul Blvd, 51000 Kuala Lumpur; tel. (3) 40430500; fax (3) 40437648; e-mail jameselva@brandequity .my; internet www.mpamalaysia.org; 16 mems; Chair. M. V. SWAMINATHAN; Sec. JAMES SELVA.

Persatuan Penerbit-Penerbit Akhbar Malaysia (Malaysian Newspaper Publishers' Asscn): Unit 706, Blok B, Phileo Damansara 1, 9 Jalan 16/11, off Jalan Damansara, 46350 Petaling Jaya, Selangor; tel. (3) 76608535; fax (3) 76608532; e-mail mnpa@macomm.com .my; Chair. MOHD NASIR ALI.

Publishers

JOHOR

Penerbitan Pelangi Sdn Bhd: 66 Jalan Pingai, Taman Pelangi, 80400 Johor Bahru; tel. (7) 3316288; fax (7) 3329201; e-mail pelangi@pelangibooks.com; internet www.pelangibooks.com; f. 1979; children's books, guidebooks and reference; Man. Dir SAMUEL SUM KOWN CHEEK.

Perniagaan Jahabersa: 15 Jalan Dataran 3/3, Taman Kempas, Johor Bahru, 81200 Johor; tel. (7) 2351602; fax (7) 2351603; internet www.jahabersa.com.my; f. 1989; Islamist teachings; Man. Dir JAHABAR SATHIK.

KUALA LUMPUR

Arus Intelek Sdn Bhd: Plaza Mont Kiara, Suite E-06-06, Mont Kiara, 50480 Kuala Lumpur; tel. (3) 62011558; fax (3) 62018698; e-mail afusint@streamyx.com; internet www.arusintelek.com; academic; Man. Datin AZIZAH MOKHZANI.

Berita Publishing Sdn Bhd: 16–20 Jalan 4/109E, Desa Business Park, Taman Desa, off Jalan Klang Lama, 58100 Kuala Lumpur; tel. (3) 76208111; fax (3) 76208018; e-mail su@beritapub.com; internet www.beritapublishing.com.my; education, business, fiction, cookery; Chair. A. KADIR JASIN.

Dewan Bahasa dan Pustaka (DBP) (Institute of Language and Literature): Menara DBP, Aras 10, Jalan Dewan Bahasa, 50460 Kuala Lumpur; tel. (3) 21482220; fax (3) 21449614; e-mail khalik@dbp.gov.my; internet www.prpm.dbp.gov.my; f. 1956; textbooks, magazines and general; Dir Haji ABD. KHALIK BIN SULAIMAN.

Jabatan Penerbitan Universiti Malaya (University of Malaya Press): University of Malaya, Lembah Pantai, 50603 Kuala Lumpur; tel. (3) 79574361; fax (3) 79574473; e-mail adamwong@um.edu.my; internet umpress.um.edu.my; f. 1954; general fiction, literature, economics, history, medicine, politics, science, social science, law, Islam, engineering, dictionaries; Dir ADAM WONG ABDULLAH.

Pustaka Antara Sdn Bhd: Lot UG 07 and 09, Upper Ground Floor, Kompleks Wilayah, 2 Jalan Munshi Abdullah, 50100 Kuala Lumpur; tel. (3) 26980044; fax (3) 26917997; e-mail pantara4@streamyx.com; textbooks, children's, languages, fiction; Man. Dir Datin HAPSAH BINTI MUHAMAD NOR.

Utusan Publications and Distributors Sdn Bhd: 1 and 3 Jalan 3/91A, Taman Shamelin Perkasa, Cheras, 56100 Kuala Lumpur; tel. (3) 92856577; fax (3) 92856341; e-mail rose@utusan.com.my; f. 1976; school textbooks, children's, languages, fiction, general; Exec. Dir ROZITA YUSOFF.

NEGERI SEMBILAN

Bharathi Press: 166 Taman AST, POB 74, 70700 Seremban, Negeri Sembilan Darul Khusus; tel. (6) 7622911; f. 1939; Mans M. SUBRAMANIA BHARATHI, BHARATHI THASAN.

PULAU PINANG

Syarikat United Book Sdn Bhd: 187–189 Lebuh Carnarvon, 10100 Pulau Pinang; tel. (4) 2626891; fax (4) 2626892; textbooks, children's, reference, fiction, guidebooks; Man. Dir CHEW SING GUAN.

SELANGOR

Aras Mega (M) Sdn Bhd: 18, Jalan Damai 2, Taman Desa Damai, Sungai Merab, Kajang, 43000 Selangor; tel. (3) 89258975; fax (3) 89258985; e-mail amsb@arasmega.com; internet www.arasmega.com; f. 1987; Dir ABDUL RAHMAN BIN ABDUL KARIM.

Cemerlang Publications Sdn Bhd: 67 Jalan SP 2/2, Taman Serdang Perdana, Seri Kembangan, 43300 Selangor; tel. (3) 89417748; fax (3) 89417750; e-mail info@cemerlang.com.my; internet www.cemerlang.com.my; Dir TEY KOCK JOO.

Golden Books Centre Sdn Bhd: Wisma ILBS, 10 Jalan PJU 8/5G, Perdana Business Centre, Petaling Jaya, 47820 Selangor; tel. (3) 77273890; fax (3) 77273884; internet www.goldenbookscenter.com; f. 1982; textbooks; Dir Dr SYED IBRAHIM.

International Law Book Services: 10 Jalan PJU 8/5G, Perdana Business Centre, Bandar Damansara Perdana, 47820 Petaling Jaya, Selangor Darul Ehsan; tel. (3) 77274121; fax (3) 77273884; e-mail gbc@pc.jaring.my; internet www.malaysialawbooks.com; CEO Dato' Dr Haji SYED IBRAHIM.

Karnadya Solution Sdn Bhd: 12A, Jalan BP 6/6, Bukit Puchong Commercial Centre, Puchong, 47100 Selangor; tel. (3) 80684763; fax (3) 80685814; e-mail info@karnadya.com.my; internet www.karnadya.com.my; f. 2005; Dir FAIZ AL-SHAHAB.

Malaya Press Sdn Bhd: 1 Jalan TSB 10, Taman Perindustrian Sungai Buloh, 47000 Selangor; tel. (3) 61573158; fax (3) 61573957; e-mail tmp@tmpsb.com; internet www.malayapress.com.my; f. 1959; education; Man. Dir LEW YOK LONG.

Marshall Cavendish (M) Sdn Bhd: Lot 46, Subang Hi-Tech Industrial Park, Batu Tiga, 40000 Shah Alam, Selangor; tel. (3) 51913168; fax (3) 51912168; e-mail eastview@my.marshallcavendish.com; internet www.marshallcavendish.com; f. 1957; fmrly Federal Publications Sdn Bhd; computer and children's magazines, dictionaries, education; Dir DANNY ONG KIM SOO.

Minerva Publications (NS) Sdn Bhd: 51 Jalan SG 3/1, Tan Sri Gombak, Batu Caves, 68100 Selangor; tel. (3) 61882876; fax (3) 61883876; e-mail minerva@streamyx.com; f. 1974; general, children's, reference, medical, law; Dir and Chief Editor SUJAUDEEN; Man. Dir THANJUDEEN.

Oxford Fajar Sdn Bhd: 4 Jalan U1/15, Sekseyen U1, Hicom-Glenmarie Industrial Park, 40150 Shah Alam, Selangor; tel. (3) 56294000; fax (3) 56294006; e-mail dcs@oxfordfajar.com.my; internet www.oxfordfajar.com.my; fmrly Penerbit Fajar Bakti Sdn Bhd; school, college and university textbooks, children's, general; Man. Dir LOKE FOOK YOON.

Pearson Education Malaysia Sdn Bhd: Lot 2, Jalan 215, off Jalan Templer, 46050 Petaling Jaya, Selangor; tel. (3) 78012000; fax (3) 77831906; e-mail inquirymy@pearson.com; internet www.pearsoned.com.my; f. 1961; textbooks, mathematics, physics, science, general, educational materials; Dir WONG WEE WOON; Man. WONG MEI MEI.

Pelanduk Publications (M) Sdn Bhd: 12 Jalan SS 13/3E, Subang Jaya Industrial Estate, 47500 Subang Jaya, Selangor; tel. (3) 56386885; fax (3) 56386575; e-mail pelpub@tm.net.my; internet www.pelanduk.com; f. 1984; politics, history, anthropology, religion, education, language, economics, business and management, culture, self-improvement, women's studies, law; Man. JACKSON TAN.

Penerbit Universiti Kebangsaan Malaysia: Universiti Kebangsaan Malaysia, 43600 UKM, Selangor; tel. (3) 89213138; fax (3) 89254575; e-mail penerbit@ukm.my; internet www.ukm.my/penerbit; Head KAMARUDDIN M. SAID.

Sasbadi Sdn Bhd: Lot 12, Jalan Teknologi 3/4, Taman Sains Selangor 1, Kota Damansara, 47810 Petaling Jaya, Selangor; tel. (3) 61451188; fax (3) 61451199; e-mail enquiry@sasbadi.com; internet www.sasbadi.com; f. 1985; Man. Dir LAW KING HUI.

United Publishing House (M) Sdn Bhd: 5078 Lorong 18/64A, Taman Sri Serdang, Seri Kembangan, 43300 Selangor; tel. (3) 89430631; fax (3) 89436909; e-mail info@uph.com.my; internet www.uph.com.my; f. 1973; children's, dictionaries, textbooks; Dir WONG CHEE KHEONG.

GOVERNMENT PUBLISHING HOUSE

Percetakan Nasional Malaysia Bhd (Malaysia National Printing Ltd): Jalan Chan Sow Lin, 50554 Kuala Lumpur; tel. (3) 92366888; fax (3) 92366999; e-mail inquiries@printnasional.com.my; internet www.printnasional.com.my; fmrly the Nat. Printing Dept; incorporated as a co under govt control in Jan. 1993; Man.Dir MAAMOR B. ALIAS.

PUBLISHERS' ASSOCIATION

Malaysian Book Publishers Association: 7-6, Block E2, Jalan PJU, 1/42A, Dataran Prima, 47301 Petaling Jaya, Selangor; tel. (3) 78805840; fax (3) 78805841; e-mail info@mabopa.com.my; internet www.mabopa.com.my; f. 1969; Pres. Dr HUSSAMUDDIN YAACUB; 196 mems.

Broadcasting and Communications

REGULATORY AUTHORITY

Malaysian Communications and Multimedia Commission: 63000 Cyberjaya, Selangor; tel. (3) 86888000; fax (3) 86881000; e-mail ccd@cmc.gov.my; internet www.skmm.gov.my; monitors the regulatory framework for telecommunications and broadcasting industries and on-line activities; Chair. Dato' MOHAMED SHARIL MOHAMED TARMIZI.

TELECOMMUNICATIONS

Celcom (Malaysia) Sdn Bhd: Menara Celcom, 82 Jalan Raja Muda Abdul Aziz, 50300 Kuala Lumpur; tel. (3) 26883939; fax (3) 36308889; internet www.celcom.com.my; f. 1988; private co licensed to operate mobile cellular telephone service; merged with TM Cellular Sdn Bhd in 2003; Chair. Dato' Sri JAMALUDIN IBRAHIM; CEO Dato' Sri MOHAMMED SHAZALLI RAMLY.

DiGi Telecommunications Sdn Bhd: D'House, Lot 10, Jalan Delima 1/1, Subang Hi-Tech Industrial Park, 40000 Shah Alam, Selangor; tel. (3) 57211800; fax (3) 57210238; internet www.digi.com.my; private co licensed to operate mobile telephone service; Chair. SIGVE BREKKE; CEO LARS-AKE NORLING.

Maxis Communications Bhd: Menara Maxis, Aras 18, Kuala Lumpur City Centre, off Jalan Ampang, 50088 Kuala Lumpur; tel.

(3) 23307000; fax (3) 23300008; internet www.maxis.com.my; f. 1995; provides mobile, fixed-line and multimedia services; approx. 11.4m. subscribers in 2009; Chair. Tan Sri Dato' Seri ARSHAD BIN TUN UDA; CEO JOHAN DENNELIND.

Technology Resources Industries Bhd (TRI): Menara TR, 23rd Floor, 161B Jalan Ampang, 50450 Kuala Lumpur; tel. (3) 2619555; fax (3) 2632018; operates mobile cellular telephone service; Chair. and Chief Exec. Tan Sri Dato' TAJUDIN RAMLI.

Telekom Malaysia Bhd: Tingkat 51, North Wing, Menara Telekom, off Jalan Pantai Baru, 50672 Kuala Lumpur; tel. (3) 22401221; fax (3) 22832415; e-mail help@tm.com.my; internet www.tm.com .my; f. 1984; public listed co responsible for operation of basic telecommunications services; 74% govt-owned; 4.22m. fixed lines (95% of total); Chair. Datuk Dr HALIM SHAFIE; Chief Exec. Dato' Sri MOHD ISA ZAMZAMZAIRANT.

Time dotCom Bhd: 14 Jalan Majistret, U1/26 Hicom Glenmarie Industrial Park, 40150 Shah Alam, Selangor; tel. (3) 50326000; fax (3) 50326010; e-mail customerservice@time.com.my; internet www .time.com.my; f. 1996; est. as Time Telecommunications Holdings Bhd; name changed as above in Jan. 2000; state-controlled co licensed to operate trunk network and mobile cellular telephone service; Chair. ABDUL KADIR MOHAMED KASSIM; CEO AFZAL ABDUL RAHIM.

BROADCASTING

Under the Broadcasting Act (approved in December 1987), the Government is empowered to control and monitor all radio and television broadcasting, and to revoke the licence of any private company violating the Act by broadcasting material 'conflicting with Malaysian values'. The time frame for the switch from analogue to digital services, initially envisaged for 2012–15, was delayed until 2015–20.

Radio

Radio Televisyen Malaysia (RTM): Dept of Broadcasting, Tingkat 2, Wisma TV, Angkasapuri, 50614 Kuala Lumpur; tel. (3) 22825333; fax (3) 22827146; e-mail feedback@rtm.gov.my; internet www.rtm.gov.my; f. 1946; broadcasts in Bahasa Malaysia, English, Chinese (Mandarin and other dialects), Kadazan, Murut, Dusun and Bajau; TV-broadcasting commenced in 1963; operates TV1 and TV2; Dir-Gen. NORHYATI ISMAIL.

Radio Televisyen Malaysia—Sabah: Jalan Tuaran, 88614 Kota Kinabalu; tel. (88) 213444; fax (88) 223493; internet www .rtmsabah.gov.my; f. 1955; television introduced 1971; a dept of RTM; broadcasts programmes over two networks in Bahasa Malaysia, English, Chinese (two dialects), Kadazan, Murut, Dusun and Bajau; Dir of Broadcasting JUMAT ENGSON.

Radio Televisyen Malaysia—Sarawak: Broadcasting House, Jabatan Penyiaran Kawasan Sarawak, Jalan P. Ramlee, 93614 Kuching; tel. (82) 248422; fax (82) 241914; e-mail rtmkuc@rtm.gov .my; internet www.rtmsarawak.gov.my; f. 1954; a dept of RTM; broadcasts mainly in Bahasa Malaysia, English, Chinese and Iban; Dir of Broadcasting NORHYATI ISMAIL.

Astro Radio Sdn Bhd: All Asia Broadcast Centre, Technology Park, Lebuhraya Puchong, Simpang Besi, Bukit Jalil, 57000 Kuala Lumpur; tel. (3) 95438888; fax (3) 95433888; e-mail kl_radio@astro.com .my; internet astroradio.com.my; f. 1997; fmrly Airtime Management and Programming Sdn Bhd; operates 10 stations: Era, Hitz, Lite FM, Mix FM, MY FM, Sinar FM, THR Gegar, THR Raaga, Melody FM and X FM; broadcasts in Chinese, English, Malay and Tamil; Exec. Dir Dr JAKE ABDULLAH.

Media Prima Bhd: 3 Persiaran Bandar Utama, 47800 Petaling Jaya, Selangor; tel. (3) 77266333; fax (3) 77261333; e-mail communications@mediaprima.com.my; internet www.mediaprima .com.my; owns and operates three networks: Fly FM, Hot FM and One FM; Chair. Datuk JOHAN JAAFFAR; CEO AHMAD IZHAM OMAR.

Rediffusion Sdn Bhd: Rediffusion House, 17 Jalan Pahang, 53000 Kuala Lumpur; tel. (3) 4424544; fax (3) 4424614; e-mail mail@ rediffusion.org; internet www.rediffusion.info/Malaya; f. 1949; two programmes; 44,720 subscribers in Kuala Lumpur; 11,405 subscribers in Pinang; 6,006 subscribers in Province Wellesley; 20,471 subscribers in Ipoh; Gen. Man. ROSNI B. RAHMAT.

Suara Islam (Voice of Islam): Islamic Affairs Division, Prime Minister's Department, Blok Utama, Tingkat 1–5, Pusat Pentadbiran Kerajaan Persekutuan, 62502 Putrajaya; f. 1995; Asia-Pacific region; broadcasts in English and Bahasa Malaysia on Islam.

Suara Malaysia (Voice of Malaysia): Wisma Radio, Tingkat 3, South Wing, Angkasapuri, 50740 Kuala Lumpur; tel. (3) 22887826; fax (3) 22847594; e-mail suaramalaysia@rtm.gov.my; internet www.vom.com.my; f. 1963; overseas service in Bahasa Malaysia, Arabic, Myanmar (Burmese), English, Bahasa Indonesia, Chinese (Mandarin/Cantonese), Tagalog and Thai; Controller of Overseas Service STEPHEN SIPAUN.

Television

Radio Televisyen Malaysia; see Radio; regional offices in Sabah and Sarawak.

Measat Broadcast Network Systems Sdn Bhd: All Asia Broadcast Centre, Technology Park Malaysia, Lebuhraya Puchong, Simpang Besi, Bukit Jalil, 57000 Kuala Lumpur; tel. (3) 95434129; fax (3) 95437333; e-mail custcare@astro.com.my; internet www.astro.com .my; nationwide subscription service; Malaysia's first satellite, Measat 1, was launched in Jan. 1996; a second satellite was launched in Oct. 1996; Chair. Haji BADRI Haji MASRI.

Media Prima Bhd: see Radio; operates four stations: Metropolitan Television Sdn Bhd (8TV); Sistem Televisyen Malaysia Bhd (TV3); ntv7; and TV9.

Finance

(cap. = capital; auth. = authorized; res = reserves; dep. = deposits; m. = million; brs = branches; amounts in ringgit Malaysia)

BANKING

In November 2013 there were 27 commercial banks, 16 Islamic banks and 12 investments banks in Malaysia. In 2014 more than 50 banks held offshore licences in Labuan.

Central Bank

Bank Negara Malaysia (Central Bank of Malaysia): Jalan Dato' Onn, POB 10922, 50929 Kuala Lumpur; tel. (3) 26988044; fax (3) 26912990; e-mail bnmtelelink@bnm.gov.my; internet www.bnm.gov .my; f. 1959; bank of issue; financial regulatory authority; cap. 100.0m., res 19,614.2m., dep. 288,999.2m. (Dec. 2010); Gov. and Chair. Tan Sri Dato' Sri Dr ZETI AKHTAR AZIZ; 6 brs.

Commercial Banks

Peninsular Malaysia

Affin Bank Bhd: Menara AFFIN, 17th Floor, 80 Jalan Raja Chulan, 50200 Kuala Lumpur; tel. (3) 20559000; fax (3) 20261415; e-mail head.ccd@affinbank.com.my; internet www.affinbank.com.my; f. 1975; est. as Perwira Habib Bank Malaysia Bhd; name changed to Perwira Affin Bank Bhd in 1994; present name adopted upon merger with BSN Commercial Bank (Malaysia) Bhd in 2001; subsidiary of Affin Holdings Bhd; cap. 1,518.3m., res 1,765.2m., dep. 46,072.8m. (Dec. 2012); Chair. Gen. Tan Sri Dato' Seri ISMAIL Haji OMAR; Pres. and CEO Dato' ZULKIFLEE ABBAS BIN ABDUL HAMID; 106 brs.

Alliance Bank Malaysia Bhd: Menara Multi-Purpose, 3rd Floor, Capital Sq., 8 Jalan Munshi Abdullah, 50100 Kuala Lumpur; tel. (3) 26043333; fax (3) 26946200; e-mail info@alliancefg.com; internet www.alliancebank.com.my; f. 1982 as Malaysian French Bank Bhd; name changed to Multi-Purpose Bank Bhd 1996; name changed as above Jan. 2001, following acquisition of six merger partners; cap. 600.5m., res 1,624m., dep. 38,034.2m. (March 2013); Chair. Dato' THOMAS MUN LUNG LEE, Group CEO JOEL KORNREICH; 89 brs.

AmBank Bhd: 22nd Floor, Bangunan AmBank Group, 55 Jalan Raja Chulan, 50200 Kuala Lumpur; tel. (3) 20362633; fax (3) 20321914; e-mail ir@ambankgroup.com; internet www .ambankgroup.com; f. 1969; wholly owned subsidiary of AMMB Holdings Bhd; fmrly Arab-Malaysian Bank Bhd; name changed as above 2002; cap. 820.3m., res 5,479.6m., dep. 62,147.8m. (March 2013); Chair. Tan Sri AZMAN HASHIM; Man. Dir ASHOK RAMAMURTHY; 175 brs.

Bangkok Bank Bhd (Thailand): 105 Jalan Tun H. S. Lee, 50000 Kuala Lumpur; tel. (3) 21737200; fax (3) 21737300; e-mail bbb@ bangkokbank.com; internet www.bangkokbank.com; f. 1958; cap. 400m., res 138.6m., dep. 2,444.7m. (Dec. 2012); Chair. CHATRI SOPHONPANICH; CEO ROBERT LOKE TAN CHENG; 5 brs.

Bank of America Merrill Lynch: Wisma Goldhill, Jalan Raja Chulan, 50200 Kuala Lumpur; tel. (3) 20321133; fax (3) 20319087; internet www.bankofamerica.com/my; cap. 135.8m., res 124.6m., dep. 1,122.1m. (Dec. 2010); Group CEO BRIAN T. MOYNIHAN.

Bank of Nova Scotia Bhd: Menara Boustead, 69 Jalan Raja Chulan, 50200 Kuala Lumpur; tel. (3) 21410766; fax (3) 21412160; e-mail bns.kualalumpur@scotiabank.com; internet www.scotiabank .com.my; f. 1973; cap. 122.3m., res 166.7m., dep. 1,395.3m. (Oct. 2012); Man. Dir RASOOL KHAN.

Bank of Tokyo-Mitsubishi UFJ (Malaysia) Bhd (Japan): Tingkat 9–11, Menara IMC, 8 Jalan Sultan Ismail, 50250 Kuala Lumpur; tel. (3) 20348000; fax (3) 20788871; e-mail customercare@my.mufg .jp; f. 1996; est. following merger of Bank of Tokyo and Mitsubishi Bank; fmrly known as Bank of Tokyo-Mitsubishi; present name adopted following merger with UFJ; cap. 200m., res 204.3m., dep. 6,014.3m. (Dec. 2012); Chair. LEE DANG FOOK; Pres. and CEO HIDEAKI YAMASHITA.

CIMB Bank Bhd: Bangunan CIMB, 10th Floor, Jalan Semantan Damansara Heights, 50490 Kuala Lumpur; tel. (3) 20848888; fax (3) 20848899; internet www.cimbbank.com.my; f. 1999; est. as Bumiputra Commerce Bank Bhd, following merger of Bank Bumiputra Malaysia Bhd with Bank of Commerce Bhd; name changed as above 2006; cap. 3,994.2m., res 10,996.3m., dep. 219,400.8m. (Dec. 2012); Chair. Dato' HAMZAH BAKAR; Group CEO Dato' MOHAMED NAZIR ABDUL RAZAK ALI; 230 brs.

Citibank Bhd (USA): 165 Jalan Ampang, POB 11725, 50450 Kuala Lumpur; tel. (3) 23830000; fax (3) 23836666; e-mail malaysia .customer.service@citi.com; internet www.citibank.com.my; f. 1959; cap. 121.7m., res 495.3m., dep. 31,111m. (Dec. 2010); Country Officer AJAY BANGA; 3 brs.

Deutsche Bank (Malaysia) Bhd (Germany): 18–20 Menara IMC, 8 Jalan Sultan Ismail, 50250 Kuala Lumpur; tel. (3) 20536788; fax (3) 20319822; internet www.db.com/malaysia; f. 1994; cap. 173.5m., res 535.3m., dep. 7,912.4m. (Dec. 2011); Man. Dir RAYMOND YEOH.

Hong Leong Bank Bhd: Wisma Hong Leong, Tingkat 8, 18 Jalan Perak, 50450 Kuala Lumpur; tel. (3) 21648228; fax (3) 21642503; internet www.hlb.com.my; f. 1905; fmrly MUI Bank Bhd; merged with Wah Tat Bank Bhd in 2001; acquired EON Bank Bhd in 2012; cap. 1,580.1m., res 1,901.7m., dep. 125,554.2m. (June 2011); Chair. Tan Sri QUEK LENG CHAN; CEO and Man. Dir TAN KONG KHOON; 329 brs.

HSBC Bank Malaysia Bhd (Hong Kong): 2 Leboh Ampang, POB 10244, 50100 Kuala Lumpur; tel. (3) 20753000; fax (3) 20701146; internet www.hsbc.com.my; f. 1860; fmrly Hongkong Bank Malaysia Bhd; adopted present name in 1999; cap. 114.5m., res 1,671m., dep. 66,055m. (Dec. 2012); Chair. PETER WONG TUNG SHUN; CEO MUKHTAR HUSSAIN.

Malayan Banking Bhd (Maybank): Menara Maybank, 14th Floor, 100 Jalan Tun Perak, 50050 Kuala Lumpur; tel. (3) 20708833; fax (3) 20702611; e-mail publicaffairs@maybank.com .my; internet www.maybank2u.com.my; f. 1960; acquired Pacific Bank Bhd Jan. 2001; merged with PhileoAllied Bank (Malaysia) Bhd March 2001; cap. 7,478m., res 14,492m., dep. 315,280m. (June 2011); Chair. Tan Sri Dato' MEGAT ZAHARUDDIN MEGAT MOHAMED NOR; Pres. and CEO Dato' Sri ABDUL WAHID OMAR; 327 domestic brs, 30 overseas brs.

OCBC Bank (Malaysia) Bhd: Menara OCBC, 18 Jalan Tun Perak, 50050 Kuala Lumpur; tel. (3) 20345034; fax (3) 26984363; internet www.ocbc.com.my; f. 1932; cap. 291.5m., res 1,433.4m., dep. 64,074.7m. (Dec. 2012); Group Chair. Tan Sri Dato' NASRUDDIN BIN BAHARI; CEO JEFFREY CHEW SUN TEONG; 25 brs.

Public Bank Bhd: Menara Public Bank, 146 Jalan Ampang, 50450 Kuala Lumpur; tel. (3) 21638888; fax (3) 21639917; e-mail pbbcosec@ publicbank.com.my; internet www.publicbank.com.my; f. 1965; merged with Hock Hua Bank Bhd March 2001; cap. 3,531.9m., res 4,958.3m., dep. 237,891.6m. (Dec. 2012); Chair. Tan Sri Dato' Dr TEH HONG PIOW; Man. Dir and CEO Tan Sri Dato' Sri TAY AH LEK; 255 domestic brs, 122 overseas brs.

RHB Bank Bhd: Towers Two and Three, RHB Centre, Jalan Tun Razak, 50400 Kuala Lumpur; tel. (3) 92878888; fax (3) 92879000; e-mail md_ceo@rhbbank.com.my; internet www.rhb.com.my; f. 1997; est. by merger between Development & Commercial Bank Bhd and Kwong Yik Bank Bhd; acquired Sime Bank Bhd 1999; merged with Bank Utama (Malaysia) Bhd 2003; cap. 3,318m., res 3,502m., dep. 121,635m. (Dec. 2011); Non-Exec. Chair.) Dato' MOHAMED KHADAR MERICAN; Man. Dir KELLEE KAM CHEE KHIONG; 150 brs.

Royal Bank of Scotland Bhd: Menara Maxis, Level 1, Kuala Lumpur City Centre, 50088 Kuala Lumpur; tel. (3) 21609888; fax (3) 21609993; e-mail my.customer.care@rbs.com; internet www.rbs.my; f. 1888; cap. 203m., res 238.9m., dep. 2,767.9m. (Dec. 2012); Chair. Tan Sri Dato' MOHD GHAZALI SETH; Country Man. Dir ANDREW MARK SILL.

Standard Chartered Bank Malaysia Bhd: Menara Standard Chartered, Level 16, 30 Jalan Sultan Ismail, 50250 Kuala Lumpur; tel. (3) 77118888; fax (3) 78496868; e-mail Malaysia.feedback@sc .com; internet www.standardchartered.com.my; cap. 163m., res 1,120.1m., dep. 43,879.1m. (Dec. 2012); Chair. Tan Sri Dato' MOHD SHERIFF BIN MOHD KASSIM; CEO OSMAN TARIQUE MORAD; over 30 brs.

United Overseas Bank (Malaysia) Bhd: Menara UOB, Tingkat 2, Jalan Raja Laut, 50738 Kuala Lumpur; tel. (3) 26924511; fax (3) 26913110; e-mail uobcustomerservice@uob.com.my; internet www .uob.com.my; f. 1920; merged with Chung Khiaw Bank (Malaysia) Bhd in 1997 and with Overseas Union Bank (Malaysia) Bhd in 2002; cap. 470m., res 907,341m., dep. 69,942.5m. (Dec. 2012); Chair. ABDUL LATIF BIN YAHAYA; CEO WONG KIM CHOONG; Man. Dir BEH SOO HENG MICHAEL; 45 brs.

Merchant Banks

Affin Merchant Bank Bhd: Menara Boustead, 27th Floor, 69 Jalan Raja Chulan, 50200 Kuala Lumpur; tel. (3) 21423700; fax (3) 21423799; e-mail enquiry@affinmerchantbank.com.my; internet www.affininvestmentbank.com.my; f. 1970; est. as Permata Chartered Merchant Bank Bhd; present name adopted 2001; cap. 222.2m., res 323.4m., dep. 4,519.5m. (Dec. 2011); Chair. Tan Sri YAACOB BIN MOHAMED ZAIN; Man. Dir Datin MAIMOONAH HUSSAIN.

Alliance Investment Bank Bhd (AIB): Menara Multi-Purpose, 19th Floor, Capital Sq., 8 Jalan Munshi Abdullah, 50100 Kuala Lumpur; tel. (3) 26927788; fax (3) 26928787; e-mail eallianceshare@ alliancefg.com; internet www.allianceinvestmentbank.com.my; f. 1974; est. as Amanah-Chase Merchant Bank Bhd; name changed to Alliance Merchant Bank Bhd in 2001, following merger with Bumiputra Merchant Bankers Bhd; name changed as above in 2006, following merger with Kuala Lumpur City Securities (KLCS); cap. 365m., res 166m., dep. 1,799m. (March 2011); Chair. Dato' THOMAS MUN LUNG LEE; CEO RAFIDZ RASIDDI.

AmInvestment Bank Bhd: Bangunan AmBank Group, 22nd Floor, 55 Jalan Raja Chulan, 50200 Kuala Lumpur; tel. (3) 20362633; fax (3) 20782842; e-mail customercare@ambankgroup.com; internet www .ambankgroup.com; f. 1975; fmrly Arab-Malaysian Merchant Bank Bhd; later known as AmMerchant Bank Bhd; name changed as above 2006; cap. 200m., res 240.5m. (March 2012); Chair. Tan Sri Dato' AZMAN HASHIM; Man. Dir KOK TUCK CHEONG; 6 brs.

CIMB Investment Bank Bhd: Bangunan CIMB, 10th Floor, Jalan Semantan, Damansara Heights, 50490 Kuala Lumpur; tel. (3) 20848888; fax (3) 20943566; e-mail info@cimb.com.my; internet www.cimbbank.com.my; f. 1974; fmrly Commerce Int. Merchant Bankers Bhd; present name adopted 2006; cap. 100m., res 175.6m., dep. 2,130.2m. (Dec. 2012); Chair. Tan Sri Dato' MOHD NOR YUSOF; Group Man. Dir and CEO Dato' Sri NAZIR RAZAK.

Maybank Investment Bank Bhd: Menara Maybank, 32nd Floor, 100 Jalan Tun Perak, 50050 Kuala Lumpur; tel. (3) 20591888; fax (3) 20784194; e-mail enquiries@maybank-ib.com; internet www .maybank-ib.com; f. 1973; cap. 50.1m., res 242m. (June 2011), dep. 4,095.3m. (June 2009); Chair. Tan Sri Dato' MEGAT ZAHARUDDIN MEGAT MOHAMED NOR; CEO Tengku Dato' ZAFRUL Tengku ABDUL AZIZ; 2 brs.

MIDF Amanah Investment Bank Bhd: Menara MIDF, Level 21, 82 Jalan Raja Chulan, 50200 Kuala Lumpur; tel. (3) 21738888; fax (3) 21738877; e-mail inquiry-feedback@midf.com.my; internet www .midf.com.my; f. 1975; est. as Utama Wardley Bhd; name changed to Utama Merchant Bank Bhd in 1996; present name adopted 2006; cap. 156.5m., res 493.7m., dep. 4,472.1m. (Dec. 2011); Chair. Tan Sri Dato' MAHMOOD BIN TAIB; Group CEO Datuk MOHAMED NAJIB Haji ABDULLAH; 1 br.

RHB Investment Bank Bhd: Tower Three, 13th Floor, RHB Centre, Jalan Tun Razak, 50400 Kuala Lumpur; tel. (3) 92873888; fax (3) 92870888; e-mail publicaffairs@rhb.com.my; internet www .rhb.com.my; f. 1974; fmrly RHB Sakura Merchant Bankers Bhd; present name adopted 2006; cap. 263.6m., res 291m., dep. 4,604m. (Dec. 2011); Chair. Dato' MOHAMED KHADAR MERICAN; Group Man. Dir KELLEE KAM CHEE KHIONG.

Co-operative Bank

Bank Kerjasama Rakyat Malaysia Bhd: Bangunan Bank Rakyat, Jalan Tangsi, Peti Surat 11024, 50732 Kuala Lumpur; tel. (3) 26129600; fax (3) 26129636; internet www.bankrakyat.com.my; f. 1954; 83,095 mems. of which 823 were co-operatives (Dec. 1996); cap. 2,349m., res 3,266m., dep. 59,102m. (Dec. 2011); Chair. Tan Sri Dato' Sri SABBARUDDIN CHIK; Man. Dir Datuk MUSTAFHA A. RAZAK; 141 brs.

Development Banks

Bank Pembangunan Malaysia Bhd: Menara Bank Pembangunan, Bandar Wawasan, 1016 Jalan Sultan Ismail, 50250 Kuala Lumpur; tel. (3) 26113888; fax (3) 26985701; e-mail feedback@ bpmb.com.my; internet www.bankpembangunan.com; f. 1973; govt-owned; fmrly Bank Pembangunana & Infrastruktur Malaysia Bhd; present name adopted upon merger with Bank Industri & Teknologi Malaysia Bhd in 2005; specializes in infrastructure, maritime and high-technology sectors; cap. 3,078.7m., res 2,000m., dep. 7,457.6m. (Dec. 2010); Non-Exec. Chair. Tan Sri Dato' Sri Dr WAN ABDUL AZIZ BIN WAN ABDULLAH; Pres. and Group Man. Dir Dato' ZAFER HASHIM; 15 brs.

Bank Perusahaan Kecil & Sederhana Malaysia Bhd (SME Bank): Menara SME Bank, Jalan Sultan Ismail, Peti Surat 12352, 50774 Kuala Lumpur; tel. (3) 26152020; fax (3) 26928520; e-mail customercare@smebank.com.my; internet www.smebank.com.my; f. 2005; wholly owned subsidiary of Bank Pembangunan Malaysia Bhd; provides both financial and non-financial assistance to SMEs;

cap. 1,350m., res 13m., dep 1,664m. (Dec. 2010); Chair. Dato' GUMURI HUSSAIN; Man. Dir Datuk MOHD RADZIF MOHD YUNUS.

Sabah Development Bank Bhd: SDB Tower, Wisma Tun Fuad Stephens, km 2.4, Jalan Tuaran, POB 12172, 88824 Kota Kinabalu, Sabah; tel. (88) 232177; fax (88) 261852; e-mail info@sabahdevbank .com; internet www.sabahdevbank.com; f. 1977; wholly owned by Sabah State Govt; cap. 430.0m., res −2,207.0m., dep. 1,421.5m. (Dec. 2012); Chair. PETER SIAU WUI KEE; Man. Dir and CEO Datuk PETER LIM SIONG ENG.

Islamic Banks

Affin Islamic Bank Bhd: Menara Affin, 17th Floor, 80 Jalan Raja Chulan, 50200 Kuala Lumpur; tel. (3) 20559000; fax (3) 20261415; e-mail yourvoice@affinbank.com.my; f. 2006; cap. 260m., res 109.1m., dep. 9,676.3m. (Dec. 2011); Man. Dir and CEO KAMARUL ARIFFIN MOHD JAMIL.

AmIslamic Bank Bhd: Bangunan AmBank Group, 22nd Floor, 55 Jalan Raja Chulan, 50200 Kuala Lumpur; tel. (3) 20362633; fax (3) 20321914; e-mail ir@ambankgroup.com; internet www .ambankgroup.com; f. 1994; wholly owned subsidiary of AMMB Holdings Bhd; cap. 500m., res 17,000m., dep. 23,200m. (March 2013); CEO MOHAMED AZMI MAHMOOD.

Bank Islam Malaysia Bhd: Wisma Bank Islam, 11th Floor, Jalan Dungun, Bukit Damansara, 50490 Kuala Lumpur; tel. (3) 20888000; fax (3) 20888033; e-mail contactcenter@bankislam.com.my; internet www.bankislam.com.my; f. 1983; cap. 2,265.4m., res 628,157.0m., dep. 33,411.2m. (June 2012); Chair. Dato' ZAMANI ABDUL GHANI; Man. Dir Dato' Sri ZUKRI SAMAT; 125 brs.

Bank Muamalat Malaysia Bhd: Menara Bumiputra, 5th Floor, 21 Jalan Melaka, 50100 Kuala Lumpur; tel. (3) 26988787; fax (3) 20325997; e-mail webmaster@muamalat.com.my; internet www .muamalat.com.my; f. 1999; cap. 1,000m., res 259.2m., dep. 18,162.9m. (March 2012); Chair. Tan Sri Dato' Dr MOHD MUNIR ABDUL MAJID; CEO Dato' Haji MOHD REDZA SHAH ABDUL WAHID; 40 brs.

OCBC Al-Amin Bank Bhd: Wisma Lee Rubber, 25th Floor, 1 Jelan Melaka, 50100 Kuala Lumpur; tel. (3) 20345034; fax (3) 26984363; subsidiary of OCBC Bank Bhd; cap. 115m., res 292.3m., dep. 6,173.7m. (Dec. 2012); CEO JEFFREY CHEW SUN TEONG.

Public Islamic Bank Bhd: Menara Public Bank, 27th Floor, 146 Jalan Ampang, 50450 Kuala Lumpur; tel. (3) 21766000; fax (3) 21639917; e-mail islamicbkg@publicislamicbank.com.my; internet www.publicislamicbank.com.my; f. 1973; est. as Asian Int. Merchant Bankers Bhd; became Sime Merchant Bankers Bhd 1996; present name adopted 2008; cap. 193.2m., res 1,815.9m., dep. 26,348.1m. (Dec. 2012); Chair. Tan Sri Dato' Sri Dr TEH HONG PIOW; CEO ABU HASSAN ASSARI BIN IBRAHIM.

Regulatory Authority

Labuan Financial Services Authority (Labuan FSA): Main Office Tower, Tingkat 17, Financial Park Labuan, Jalan Merdeka, 87000 Labuan; tel. (87) 591200; fax (87) 428200; e-mail communication@labuanfsa.gov.my; internet www.labuanibfc.com; f. 1996; est. as Labuan Offshore Financial Services Authority (LOFSA); regulatory and supervisory body for the Labuan International Business and Financial Centre; chaired by Gov. of Bank Negara Malaysia; Dir-Gen. AHMAD HIZZAD BAHARUDDIN.

Offshore Banks

AmInternational (L) Ltd: Main Office Tower, Blok 4, Tingkat 12B, Financial Park Labuan, Jalan Merdeka, 87000 Labuan; tel. (87) 413133; fax (87) 425211; e-mail felix-leong@ambankgroup.com.my; internet www.ambankgroup.com; f. 1995; Head of Br. ISKANDAR MOHAMED HAFIDZ.

Bank of East Asia Ltd, Labuan Branch: Main Office Tower, Tingkat 10C, Financial Park Labuan, Jalan Merdeka, 87000 Labuan; tel. (87) 451145; fax (87) 451148; e-mail arraisag@hkbea.com; Gen. Man. ALVIN ARRAIS.

Bank of Nova Scotia, Labuan Branch: Main Office Tower, Tingkat 10-C2, Financial Park Labuan, Jalan Merdeka, 87000 Labuan; tel. (87) 451101; fax (87) 451099; Man. AUDREY YAP.

Bank of Tokyo-Mitsubishi UFJ Ltd, Labuan Branch: Main Office Tower, Tingkat 12A, Financial Park Labuan, Jalan Merdeka, 87000 Labuan; tel. (87) 410487; fax (87) 410476; e-mail jun_minamoto@hd.mufg.jp; Man. JUN MINAMOTO.

Barclays Bank PLC: Main Office Tower, Tingkat 5A, Financial Park Labuan, Jalan Merdeka, 87000 Labuan; tel. (87) 425571; fax (87) 425575; e-mail siawloong.miaw@barcap.com; Man. MIAW SIAW LOONG.

BNP Paribas, Labuan Branch: Main Office Tower, Tingkat 9F, Financial Park Labuan, Jalan Merdeka, 87000 Labuan; tel. (87)

422328; fax (87) 419328; e-mail krishna.chetti@asia.bnpparibas .com; internet www.bnpparibas.com.my; Head KRISHNA CHETTI.

Cathay United Bank, Labuan Branch: Main Office Tower, Tingkat 3C, Financial Park Labuan, Jalan Merdeka, 87000 Labuan; tel. (87) 452168; fax (87) 453678; e-mail pce@cathaybk.com.tw; Gen. Man. PAN CHUNG-EN.

CIMB Bank (L) Ltd: Main Office Tower, Tingkat 14B, Financial Park Labuan, Jalan Merdeka, 87000 Labuan; tel. (87) 410302; fax (87) 410313; e-mail jemima.haziz@cimb.com; Gen. Man. JEMIMA HAZIZ.

Citibank Malaysia (L) Ltd: Main Office Tower, Tingkat 11F, Financial Park Labuan, Jalan Merdeka, 87000 Labuan; tel. (87) 421181; fax (87) 419671; e-mail clara.ac.lim@citi.com; Gen. Man. CLARA LIM AI CHENG.

City Credit Investment Bank Ltd: Main Office Tower, Tingkat 11-D1, Financial Park Labuan, Jalan Merdeka, 87000 Labuan; tel. (87) 582368; fax (87) 582308; e-mail info@ccibl.net; internet www .citycreditinvestmentbank.com; Chair. Tan Sri Dato' HANAFIAH HUSSAIN; CEO Dato' ABDUL RAHMAN ABDULLAH.

Crédit Agricole CIB, Labuan Branch: Main Office Tower, 6E, Tingkat 6, Financial Park Labuan, Jalan Merdeka, 87000 Labuan; tel. (87) 408331; fax (87) 408335; e-mail hoimeng.chew@ca-cib.com; fmrly known as Crédit Agricole Indosuez, Calyon; Gen. Man. HOI MENG CHEW.

Crédit Suisse AG, Labuan Branch: Main Office Tower, Tingkat 10B, Financial Park Labuan, Jalan Merdeka, 87000 Labuan; tel. (87) 425381; fax (87) 425384; e-mail alfred.lee@credit_suisse.com; investment banking; Gen. Man. LEE CHEE MENG.

Deutsche Bank, Labuan Branch: Main Office Tower, Tingkat 9-G2, Financial Park Labuan, Jalan Merdeka, 87000 Labuan; tel. (87) 439811; fax (87) 439866; internet www.db.com/malaysia; Man. Dir RAYMOND YEOH CHENG SEONG.

Development Bank of Singapore (DBS Bank) Ltd, Labuan Branch: Main Office Tower, Tingkat 10A, Financial Park Labuan, Jalan Merdeka, 87000 Labuan; tel. (87) 595500; fax (87) 423376; internet www.dbs.com/my; Gen. Man. JEFFRY LING.

ECM Libra Investment Bank Ltd: Main Office Tower, Tingkat 3-I1, Financial Park Complex, Jalan Merdeka, 87000 Labuan; tel. (87) 408525; fax (87) 408527; e-mail slchan@ecmlibra.com; Man. CHAN SOON LEE.

Hongkong & Shanghai Banking Corporation, Offshore Banking Unit: Main Office Tower, Tingkat 11-B1, Financial Park Labuan, Jalan Merdeka, 87000 Labuan; tel. (87) 419680; fax (87) 417169; e-mail leechoofoo@hsbc.com.my; Man. FOO LEE CHOO.

ING Bank NV: Main Office Tower, Tingkat 8-B2, Financial Park Labuan, Jalan Merdeka, 87000 Labuan; tel. (87) 425733; fax (87) 425734; e-mail milly.tan@asia.ing.com; Gen. Man. MILLY TAN.

J. P. Morgan Chase Bank, Labuan Branch: Main Office Tower, Tingkat 5F, Financial Park Labuan, Jalan Merdeka, 87000 Labuan; tel. (87) 424384; fax (87) 424390; e-mail alex.law@jpmorgan.com; Gen. Man. ALEX LAW WEI HEONG.

Maybank International (L) Ltd: Main Office Tower, Tingkat 16B, Financial Park Labuan, Jalan Merdeka, 87000 Labuan; tel. (87) 414406; fax (87) 414806; e-mail millmit@streamyx.com; CEO JUBELY PA.

Mizuho Corporate Bank Ltd, Labuan Branch: Main Office Tower, Tingkat 9B–C, Financial Park Labuan, Jalan Merdeka, 87000 Labuan; tel. (87) 417766; fax (87) 419766; Gen. Man. KAZUMASA DOMEN.

Natixis: Main Office Tower, Tingkat 9G, Financial Park Labuan, Jalan Merdeka, 87000 Labuan; tel. (87) 582009; fax (87) 583009; e-mail rizal.abdullah@ap.natixis.com; fmrly Natexis Banque Populaires; Gen. Man. RIZAL ABDULLAH.

OSK Investment Bank (Labuan) Ltd: Lot 3B, Tingkat 5, Wisma Lazenda, Jalan Kemajuan, Labuan; tel. (87) 581885; fax (87) 582885; e-mail kokhoe.yeoh@my.oskgroup.com; CEO YEOH KOK HOE.

Oversea-Chinese Banking Corporation Ltd, Labuan Branch: Main Office Tower, Tingkat 8C, Financial Park Labuan, Jalan Merdeka, 87000 Labuan; tel. (87) 423381; fax (87) 423390; Gen. Man. LEONG WAI MUN.

Public Bank (L) Ltd: Bangunan Lucas Kong, 5 Jalan Merdeka, 87007 Labuan; tel. (87) 414201; fax (87) 412388; e-mail pb11@ streamyx.com; Man. ALEXANDER WONG.

RHB Bank (L) Ltd: Main Office Tower, Tingkat 15B, Financial Park Labuan, Jalan Merdeka, 87000 Labuan; tel. (87) 417480; fax (87) 417486; e-mail rhbl@streamyx.com; Gen. Man. TOH AY LENG.

RUSD Investment Bank Inc: Lot 17, Jalan Kemajuan, 87000 Labuan; tel. (87) 452100; fax (87) 453100; e-mail info@rusdbank.com; internet www.rusdbank.com; Chair. Dr SALEH J. MALAIKAH; CEO NASEERUDDIN A. KHAN.

Sumitomo Mitsui Banking Corpn, Labuan Branch: Main Office Tower, Tingkat 12B-C, Financial Park Labuan, Jalan Merdeka, 87000 Labuan; tel. (87) 410955; fax (87) 410959; e-mail naoki_nakano@my.smbc.co.jp; Pres. and CEO HITOSHI SUYAMA; Gen. Man. NAOKI NAKANO.

UBS AG, Labuan Branch: Main Office Tower, Tingkat 4-A1, Financial Park Labuan, Jalan Merdeka, 87000 Labuan; tel. (87) 421743; fax (87) 421746; e-mail zelie.ho@ubs.com; Man. ZELIE HO SWEE LUM.

United Overseas Bank Ltd, Labuan Branch: Main Office Tower, Tingkat 6A, Financial Park Labuan, Jalan Merdeka, 87000 Labuan; tel. (87) 424388; fax (87) 424389; e-mail lai.takkong@uob.com.my; Gen. Man. LOURDES PREMKUMAR SINNAPPAN.

Banking Associations

Association of Banks in Malaysia (ABM): UBN Tower, Tingkat 34, 10 Jalan P. Ramlee, 50250 Kuala Lumpur; tel. (3) 20788041; fax (3) 20788004; e-mail banks@abm.org.my; internet www.abm.org.my; f. 1973; 24 mems; Chair. Dato' Sri ABDUL WAHID OMAR; Exec. Dir CHUAH MEI LIN.

Institute of Bankers Malaysia: Wisma IBI, 5 Jalan Semantan, Damansara Heights, 50490 Kuala Lumpur; tel. (3) 20956833; fax (3) 20958922; e-mail ibbm@ibbm.org.my; internet www.ibbm.org.my; f. 1977; professional and educational body for the banking and finance industry; Chair. Tan Sri Dato' AZMAN HASHIM; Chief Exec. TAY KAY LUAN.

Malayan Commercial Banks' Association: Tingkat 22, Akademi Etiqa, 23 Jalan Melaka, 50100 Kuala Lumpur; tel. (3) 26983991; fax (3) 26942679; internet mcba.my; 21 mems; Exec. Dir Y. Y. LAM.

Persatuan Institusi Perbankan Tanpa Faedah Malaysia (Association of Islamic Banking Institutions Malaysia—AIBIM): Menara Bumiputera, Tingkat 4, 21 Jalan Melaka, 50100 Kuala Lumpur; tel. (3) 20268002; fax (3) 20268012; e-mail admin@aibim.com; internet www.aibim.com; f. 1995; 24 mems; Pres. Dato' MOHAMED REDZA SHAH ABDUL WAHID; Exec. Dir YUSRY YUSOFF.

STOCK EXCHANGE

Bursa Malaysia: Tingkat 10, Exchange Sq., Bukit Kewangan, 50200 Kuala Lumpur; tel. (3) 20347000; fax (3) 20264122; e-mail customerservice@bursamalaysia.com; internet www.bursamalaysia.com; f. 1973; fmrly Kuala Lumpur Stock Exchange (KLSE); present name adopted 2004; merged with Malaysian Exchange of Securities Dealing and Automated Quotation Bhd (MESDAQ) in March 2002; authorized in 1988 the ownership of up to 49% of Malaysian stockbroking cos by foreign interests; 988 listed cos (Jan. 2008); Chair. TUN MOHAMED DZAIDDIN Haji ABDULLAH; CEO Dato' TAJUDDIN ATAN.

Regulatory Authority

Securities Commission (SC): 3 Persiaran Bukit Kiara, Bukit Kiara, 50490 Kuala Lumpur; tel. (3) 62048777; fax (3) 62015078; e-mail cau@seccom.com.my; internet www.sc.com.my; f. 1993; Chair. Datuk RANJIT AJIT SINGH.

INSURANCE

Principal Insurance Companies

ACE Jerneh Insurance Corpn Sdn Bhd: Wisma Jerneh, 12th Floor, 38 Jalan Sultan Ismail, POB 12420, 50788 Kuala Lumpur; tel. (3) 20583000; fax (3) 20583333; e-mail Inquiries.MY@acegroup.com; internet www.acejerneh.com.my; f. 1970; general; Chair. Tan Sri LEO MOGGIE; 23 brs.

Allianz General Insurance Malaysia Bhd: Plaza Sentral, Suite 3A, Level 15, Blok 3A, Jalan Stesen Sentral 5, 50470 Kuala Lumpur; tel. (3) 22641188; fax (3) 22641199; e-mail partner@allianz.com.my; internet www.allianz.com.my/general; f. 2001; Chair. Tan Sri RAZALI ISMAIL; CEO ZAKRI KHIR.

Allianz Life Insurance Malaysia Bhd: Plaza Sentral, Suite 3A, Level 15, Blok 3A, Jalan Stesen Sentral 5, 50470 Kuala Lumpur; tel. (3) 22641188; fax (3) 22641199; e-mail partner@allianz.com.my; internet www.allianz.com.my; fmrly MBA Life Assurance Sdn Bhd; CEO JENS REISCH.

Etiqa Insurance Bhd: Level 12B, Academy Etiqa, 23 Jalan Melaka, 50100 Kuala Lumpur; tel. (3) 26125301; fax (3) 26125068; internet www.etiqa.com.my; life and general; fmrly Malaysia National Insurance Sdn Bhd, name changed as above after merger with Etiqa in 2007; Chair. Dato' MOHAMAD SALLEH Haji HARUN; CEO ZAHARUDIN DAUD.

Great Eastern Life Assurance (Malaysia) Bhd: Menara Great Eastern, 303 Jalan Ampang, 50450 Kuala Lumpur; tel. (3) 42598888; fax (3) 42598000; e-mail wecare@lifeisgreat.com.my; internet www.lifeisgreat.com.my; CEO KOH YAW HUI.

Hong Leong Assurance Sdn Bhd: Petaling Jaya City Development 15A, Menara B, Level 3, Jalan 219, 46100 Selangor; tel. (3) 76501818; fax (3) 76501991; e-mail corpcomm@hla.hongleong.com.my; internet www.hla.com.my; Chair. Tan Sri QUEK LENG CHAN; Man. Dir and CEO LOH GUAT LAN.

ING Insurance Bhd: Menara ING, 84 Jalan Raja Chulan, POB 10846, 50927 Kuala Lumpur; tel. (3) 21617255; fax (3) 27110175; internet www.ing.com.my; f. 1987; fmrly Aetna Universal Insurance Bhd; Chair. Tengku ABDULLAH IBNI AL-MARHUM Sultan ABU BAKAR.

Manulife Insurance (Malaysia) Bhd: Menara Manulife RB, 12th Floor, 6 Jalan Gelenggang, Damansara Heights, 50490 Kuala Lumpur; tel. (3) 20948055; fax (3) 20935487; internet www.manulife.com.my; f. 1963; life and non-life insurance; fmrly British American Life and General Insurance Bhd; name then changed to John Hancock Life Insurance (Malaysia) Bhd; present name adopted 2005, following 2004 merger between John Hancock Financial Services, Inc and Manulife Financial Corpn; Chair. Dato' Dr ZAHA RINA BINTI ZAHARI.

Mayban Assurance Bhd: Mayban Assurance Tower, Level 15, Dataran Maybank, 1 Jalan Maarof, 59000 Kuala Lumpur; tel. (3) 22972888; fax (3) 22972828; e-mail mayassur@tm.net.my; internet www.maybank2u.com.my; Chair. Dato' JOHAN ARIFFIN.

MBf Insurans Sdn Bhd: Plaza MBf, 5th Floor, Jalan Ampang, POB 10345, 50710 Kuala Lumpur; tel. and fax (3) 2613466; Man. MARC HOOI TUCK KOK.

MCIS Insurance Bhd: Wisma MCIS Zurich, Jalan Barat, 46200 Petaling Jaya, Selangor; tel. (3) 79552577; fax (3) 79571562; e-mail info@mcis.my; internet www.mcis.my; f. 1954; fmrly MCIS Zürich Insurance Bhd; CEO KEVIN JONES.

Multi-Purpose Insurans Bhd: Menara Multi-Purpose, 8th Floor, Capital Sq., 8 Jalan Munshi Abdullah, 50100 Kuala Lumpur; tel. (3) 20349888; fax (3) 26945758; e-mail generalenquiries@mpib.com.my; internet www.mpib.com.my; fmrly Kompas Insurans Bhd; Chair. Tan Sri Dato' Dr YAHYA BIN AWANG.

Overseas Assurance Corpn (Malaysia) Bhd: Menara Great Eastern, Level 18, 303 Jalan Ampang, 50450 Kuala Lumpur; tel. (3) 42597888; fax (3) 48132737; e-mail enquiry@oac.com.my; internet www.oac.com.my; Chair. NORMAN IP; CEO NG KOK KHENG.

Progressive Insurance Sdn Bhd: Plaza Berjaya, Menara BGI, 7th, 9th and 10th Floors, 12 Jalan Imbi, 55100 Kuala Lumpur; tel. (3) 21188000; fax (3) 21188101; e-mail progressive@progressiveinsurance.com.my; internet www.progressiveinsurance.com.my; Chair. Datuk DATU HARUN BIN DATU MANSOR; CEO FRANCIS LAL.

RHB Insurance Bhd: Tower 1, 8th Floor, RHB Centre, Jalan Tun Razak, 50400 Kuala Lumpur; tel. (3) 92812731; fax (3) 92812729; e-mail rhbi_general@rhbinsurance.com.my; internet www.rhb.com.my; Chair. ONG SENG PHEOW.

Tune Insurance Malaysia Bhd: 36 Jalan Ampang, 50450 Kuala Lumpur; tel. (3) 20702828; fax (3) 20724150; internet www.tuneinsurance.com; f. 2002; fmrly Oriental Capital Assurance Bhd; CEO DANIEL SU TIENG TECK.

Uni.Asia General Insurance Bhd: Menara Uni.Asia, 10th Floor, 1008 Jalan Sultan Ismail, 50250 Kuala Lumpur; tel. (3) 2938111; fax (3) 26932893; e-mail callcentre@uniasiageneral.com.my; internet www.uniasiageneral.com.my; f. 1931; fmrly South-East Asia Insurance Bhd; Chair. Dato' Hj KAMIL KHALID ARIFF; CEO DAVID TAN SEE DIP.

Trade and Industry

GOVERNMENT AGENCIES

Danamodal Nasional Bhd (Danamodal): Bangunan Sime Bank, 10th Floor, Jalan Sultan Sulaiman, 50000 Kuala Lumpur; tel. (3) 20312255; fax (3) 20310786; e-mail info@danamodal.com.my; f. 1998; est. to recapitalize banks and restructure financial institutions, incl. arranging mergers and consolidations; Chair. Raja Datuk ARSHAD Raja Tun UDA; Man. Dir MARIANUS VONG SHIN TZOI.

Federal Agricultural Marketing Authority (FAMA): Bangunan FAMA Point, Lot 17304, Jalan Persiaran 1, Bandar Baru Selayang, 68100 Batu Caves, Selangor; tel. (3) 61262020; fax (3) 61383650; e-mail fama@fama.gov.my; internet www.fama.gov.my; f. 1965; est. to supervise, co-ordinate and improve marketing of agricultural produce, and to seek and promote new markets and outlets for agricultural produce; Chair. Dato' Paduka Haji BADRUDDIN BIN AMIRULDIN; Dir-Gen. Haji AHMAD B. ISHAK.

Federal Land Development Authority (FELDA): Wisma FELDA, Jalan Perumahan Gurney, 54000 Kuala Lumpur; tel. (3) 26172617; fax (3) 26920087; e-mail upd@felda.net.my; internet www.felda.net.my; f. 1956; govt statutory body formed to develop land into agricultural smallholdings to eradicate rural poverty; involved in rubber, oil palm and sugar-cane cultivation; Chair. Tan Sri MOHD ISA ABDUL SAMAD; Dir-Gen. Dato' AHMAD TARMIZI ALIAS.

Khazanah Nasional: Petronas Twin Towers, Tower 2, Tingkat 33, 50088 Kuala Lumpur; tel. (3) 20340000; fax (3) 20340300; e-mail info@khazanah.com.my; internet www.khazanah.com.my; f. 1994; state-controlled investment co; assumed responsibility for certain assets fmrly under control of the Ministry of Finance; holds 40% of Telekom Malaysia Bhd, 40% of Tenaga Nasional Bhd, 6.6% of HICOM Bhd and 17.8% of Proton; Chair. Dato' Sri MOHD NAJIB BIN Haji ABDUL RAZAK; Man. Dir Tan Sri Dato' AZMAN BIN Haji MOKHTAR.

Malaysia External Trade Development Corpn (MATRADE): Menara MATRADE, Jalan Khidmat Usaha, off Jalan Duta, 50480 Kuala Lumpur; tel. (3) 62077077; fax (3) 62037253; e-mail info@matrade.gov.my; internet www.matrade.gov.my; f. 1993; responsible for external trade devt and promotion; Chair. Dato' MAH SIEW KEONG.

Malaysian Institute of Economic Research: Podium City Point, Level 2, Kompleks Dayabumi, Jalan Sultan Hishamuddin, 50050 Kuala Lumpur; tel. (3) 22725897; fax (3) 22730197; e-mail zakariah@mier.po.my; internet www.mier.org.my; f. 1985; Chair. Tan Sri Dr SULAIMAN MAHBOB; Exec. Dir Dr ZAKARIAH ABDUL RASHID.

Malaysian Palm Oil Board (MPOB): 6 Persiaran Institusi, Bandar Baru Bangi, 43000 Kajang, Selangor; tel. (3) 87694400; fax (3) 89259446; e-mail webmaster@mpob.gov.my; internet www.mpob.gov.my; f. 2000; est. by merger of Palm Oil Registration and Licensing Authority and Palm Oil Research Institute of Malaysia; Chair. Dato' Seri SHAHRIR BIN ABDUL SAMAD.

Malaysian Timber Industry Board (Lembaga Perindustrian Kayu Malaysia): 13–17 Menara PGRM, 8 Jalan Pudu Ulu, 56100 Cheras, Kuala Lumpur; tel. (3) 92822235; fax (3) 92851477; e-mail info@mtib.gov.my; internet www.mtib.gov.my; f. 1973; promotes and regulates the export of timber and timber products from Malaysia; Chair. Datuk WILFRED MADIUS TANGAU; Dir-Gen. Dr JALALUDDIN BIN HARUN.

Muda Agricultural Development Authority (MADA): MADA HQ, Ampang Jajar, 05990 Alor Setar, Kedah; tel. (4) 7728255; fax (4) 7722667; e-mail promada@mada.gov.my; internet www.mada.gov.my; Chair. Dato' Seri MAHDZIR BIN KHALID; Gen. Man. Dato' Haji ABDUL RAHIM BIN SALEH.

National Economic Action Council: NEAC-MTEN, Prime Minister's Office, Menara Usahawan, Blok Utama, Tingkat 5, 18 Persiaran Perdana, Pusat Pentadbiran Kerajaan Persekutuan, 62652 Putrajaya; tel. (3) 88886513; fax (3) 88882902; e-mail feedback@neac.gov.my; internet www.neac.gov.my; Chair. Tan Sri AMIRSHAM AZIZ.

National Information Technology Council (NITC): c/o The Ministry of Science, Technology and Innovation, Aras 1-7, Blok C4–5, Kompleks C, Pusat Pentadbiran Kerajaan Persekutuan, 62662 Putrajaya; tel. (3) 88858000; fax (3) 88884328; internet www.nitc.my; Sec. Datuk Tengku Dr MOHD AZZMAN SHARIFFADEEN.

National Timber Certification Council: C-8-5, Megan Ave II, 12 Jalan Yap Kwan Seng, 50450 Kuala Lumpur; tel. (3) 21612298; fax (3) 21612293; e-mail info@mtcc.com.my; internet www.mtcc.com.my; Chair. Dato' Dr FREEZAILAH CHE YEOM.

Perbadanan Nasional Bhd (PERNAS): Menara Dato' Onn, Level 9B, 45 Jalan Tun Ismail, 50480 Kuala Lumpur; tel. (3) 26986670; fax (3) 26986617; e-mail enquiries@pns.com.my; internet www.pns.com.my; f. 1969; govt-sponsored; promotes trade, banking, property and plantation development, construction, mineral exploration, steel-manufacturing, inland container transportation, mining, insurance, industrial development, engineering services, telecommunication equipment, hotels and shipping; 10 wholly owned subsidiaries, over 60 jointly owned subsidiaries and 18 assoc. cos; Chair. Datuk IDRIS BIN HASHIM; Man. Dir Tuan Syed KAMARULZAMAN BIN Syed ZAINOL KHODKI SHAHABUDIN.

DEVELOPMENT ORGANIZATIONS

Fisheries Development Authority of Malaysia: Plaza Utama Alam Mesra, Kota Kinabalu, Sabah; tel. (3) 26177000; fax (3) 26911931; e-mail info@lkim.gov.my; internet lkim.gov.my; Chair. Dato' Haji JIDIN BIN MOHD SHAFEE; Dir-Gen. Dato' Haji KHAZIN BIN MOHD HAMZAH.

Johor Corpn: Level 2, Persada Johor, Jalan Abdullah Ibrahim, 80000 Johor Bahru; tel. (7) 2232692; fax (7) 2233175; e-mail pdnjohor@jcorp.com.my; internet www.jcorp.com.my; devt agency of the Johor State Govt; Chair. Dato' Haji ABDUL GHANI BIN OTHMAN; Chief Exec. Haji KAMARUZZAMAN BIN ABU KASSIM.

Kumpulan FIMA Bhd (Food Industries of Malaysia): Plaza Damansara, Blok C, Tingkat 4, Suite 4.1, 45 Jalan Medan Setia 1, Bukit Damansara, 50490 Kuala Lumpur; tel. (3) 20921211; fax (3) 20925923; e-mail enquiry@fima.com.my; internet www.fima.com.my; f. 1972; fmrly govt corpn; transferred to private sector in 1991; promotes food and related industry through investment on its own or by co-ventures with local or foreign entrepreneurs; oil palm,

cocoa and fruit plantation developments; manufacturing and packaging, trading, supermarkets and restaurants; Chair. MUHAMMAD RADZI BIN Haji MANSOR; Man. Dir ROSLAN BIN HAMIR; 1,189 employees.

Majlis Amanah Rakyat (MARA) (Trust Council for the People): Bangunan Medan MARA, 25th Floor, Jalan Raja Laut, 50609 Kuala Lumpur; tel. (3) 26915111; fax (3) 26913620; e-mail webmaster@mara.gov.my; internet www.mara.gov.my; f. 1966; est. to promote, stimulate, facilitate and undertake economic and social development, and to participate in industrial and commercial undertakings and jt ventures; Dir-Gen. IBRAHIM BIN AHMAD.

Malaysian Agricultural Research and Development Institute (MARDI): POB 12301, General Post Office, 50774 Kuala Lumpur; tel. (3) 89437111; fax (3) 89483664; e-mail enquiry@mardi.gov.my; internet www.mardi.gov.my; f. 1969; research and development in food and tropical agriculture; Dir-Gen. Datuk Dr ABD. SHUKOR BIN ABD. RAHMAN.

Malaysian Industrial Development Authority (MIDA): Plaza Sentral, Block 4, 5 Jalan Stesen Sentral, 50470 Kuala Lumpur; tel. (3) 22673633; fax (3) 22747970; e-mail investmalaysia@mida.gov.my; internet www.mida.gov.my; f. 1967; Chair. Tan Sri Dr SULAIMAN MAHBOOB; Dir-Gen. Datuk JALILAH BABA.

Malaysian Industrial Development Finance Bhd (MIDF): Level 21, Menara MIDF, 82 Jalan Raja Chulan, 50200 Kuala Lumpur; tel. (3) 21738888; fax (3) 21738877; e-mail inquiry-feedback@midf.com.my; internet www.midf.com.my; f. 1960 by the Govt; banks, insurance cos, industrial financing, advisory services, project development, merchant and commercial banking services; Chair. Tan Sri Dato' MAHMOOD BIN TAIB; Man. Dir Datuk MOHAMED NAJIB Haji ABDULLAH.

Malaysian Pepper Board: Lot 1115, Jalan Utama, 93916 Kuching, Sarawak; tel. (82) 331811; fax (82) 336877; e-mail info@mpb.gov.my; internet www.mpb.gov.my; f. 2007; govt-owned; est. to replace the Pepper Marketing Bd; responsible for the statutory grading of all Sarawak pepper for export, licensing of pepper dealers and exporters, trading and the development and promotion of pepper-grading, storage and processing facilities; Chair. Datuk ALEXANDER NANTA LINGGI; Dir-Gen. GRUNSIN AYOM.

Pinang Development Corpn: 1 Pesiaran Mahsuri, Bandar Bayan Baru, 11909 Bayan Lepas, Pinang; tel. (4) 6340111; fax (4) 6432405; e-mail enquiry@pdc.gov.my; internet www.pdc.gov.my; f. 1969; development agency of the Pinang State Govt; Gen. Man. Dato' ROSLI JAAFAR.

Sarawak Economic Development Corpn: Menara SEDC, 6th–11th Floors, Sarawak Plaza, Jalan Tunku Abdul Rahman, 93100 Kuching; tel. (82) 416777; fax (82) 424330; e-mail ssedc@po.jaring.my; internet www.sedc.com.my; f. 1972; statutory org. responsible for commercial and industrial development in Sarawak either solely or jtly with foreign and local entrepreneurs; responsible for the development of tourism infrastructure; Chair. Datuk Haji TALIB ZULPILIP.

Selangor State Development Corpn (PKNS): Level 2, Menara HPAIC, Laman Seri Business Park, Seksyen 13, 40100 Shah Alam, Selangor; tel. (3) 55201234; fax (3) 55102149; e-mail wazir@pkns.gov.my; internet www.pkns.gov.my; f. 1964; partially govt-owned; Gen. Man. OTHMAN BIN Haji OMAR.

CHAMBERS OF COMMERCE

Associated Chinese Chambers of Commerce and Industry of Malaysia: Wisma Chinese Chamber, 6th Floor, 258 Jalan Ampang, 50450 Kuala Lumpur; tel. (3) 42603090; fax (3) 42603080; e-mail acccim@acccim.org.my; internet www.acccim.org.my; Pres. Datuk LIM KOK CHEONG; Sec.-Gen. Datuk DAVID CHUA.

Malay Chamber of Commerce Malaysia: 29 & 31 Jalan Lawan Pedang, 13/27 Shah Alam, 40100 Selangor; tel. (3) 55199110; fax (3) 55120801; e-mail info@dpmmns.com.my; internet www.dpmms.com.my; f. 1957; fmrly Associated Malay Chambers of Commerce of Malaya; present name adopted 1992; Pres. Tan Sri ROZALI ISMAIL BIN; Sec.-Gen. ZAKI SAID.

Malaysian Associated Indian Chambers of Commerce and Industry: Megan Ave II, Blok B, 9th Floor, Unit 1, 12 Jalan Yap Kwan Seng, 50450 Kuala Lumpur; tel. (3) 21712616; fax (3) 21711195; e-mail info@maicci.org.my; internet www.maicci.org.my; f. 1950; Pres. Datuk K. K ESWARAN; 8 brs.

Malaysian International Chamber of Commerce and Industry (MICCI) (Dewan Perniagaan dan Perindustrian Antarabangsa Malaysia): C-8-8, Plaza Mont' Kiara, 2 Jalan Kiara, 50480 Kuala Lumpur; tel. (3) 62017708; fax (3) 62017705; e-mail micci@micci.com; internet www.micci.com; f. 1837; brs in Pinang, Perak, Johor, Melaka and Sabah; 1,000 corp. mems; Pres. SIMON WHITELAW; Exec. Dir STEWART J. FORBES.

National Chamber of Commerce and Industry of Malaysia: Menara MATRADE, Level 3, West Wing, Jalan Khidmat Usaha, off

Jalan Duta, 50480 Kuala Lumpur; tel. (3) 62049811; fax (3) 62049711; e-mail enquiry@nccim.org.my; internet www.nccim.org .my; f. 1962; Pres. Tuan Syed ALI MOHAMED ALATTAS; Hon. Sec.-Gen. Dato' Syed HUSSEIN AL-HABSHEE.

Sabah Bumiputera Chamber of Commerce (SBCC): Lot 119, 4th Floor, SBCC Bldg, Locked Bag 154, Jalan Gaya, 88999 Kota Kinabalu; tel. (88) 222442; fax (88) 223454; f. 1972; Pres. Datuk Haji AHMAD ALIP LOPE ABDUL AZIZ; Sec.-Gen. JURIL Haji SUDIN.

Sabah United Chinese Chambers of Commerce (SUCCC): POB 12176, 88824 Kota Kinabalu; tel. (88) 225460; fax (88) 218185; e-mail succc01@tm.net.my; internet www.succc.org; f. 1955; Pres. Datuk Seri Panglima SAU WAH GAN.

Sarawak Chamber of Commerce and Industry (SCCI): DUBS Commercial Centre, 2nd Floor, Lot 376, Seksyen 54, Jalan Petanak, 93100 Kuching; tel. (82) 237148; fax (82) 237186; e-mail scci@cdc.net .my; internet www.scci.org.my; f. 1950; Chair. Datuk Abang Haji ABDUL KARIM Tun Abang Haji OPENG.

INDUSTRIAL AND TRADE ASSOCIATIONS

Federation of Malaysian Manufacturers: Wisma FMM, 3 Persiaran Dagang, PJU 9 Bandar Sri Damansara, 52200 Kuala Lumpur; tel. (3) 62867200; fax (3) 62741266; e-mail webmaster@fmm.org.my; internet www.fmm.org.my; f. 1968; offers guidance and advice relating to trade and industry; presents problems and concerns to the Govt; 2,700 mems (Aug. 2014); Pres. Dato' SAW CHOO BOON; CEO Dr YEOH OON.

Federation of Rubber Trade Associations of Malaysia (FRTAM): 4th Floor, 138 Jalan Tun H. S. Lee, 50000 Kuala Lumpur; tel. (3) 20788114; fax (3) 20700640; e-mail rubassoc@streamyx.com; Hon. Sec. TEO SOON HUAT.

Malayan Agricultural Producers' Association: Plaza Ampang City, 16G-L, Jalan Ampang, 50734 Kuala Lumpur; tel. (3) 42573988; fax (3) 42573113; e-mail mapa@myjaring.net; internet www.mapa .net.my; f. 1996; 353 mem. estates and 108 factories/mills; Pres. Tan Sri Dato' Dr MOHD NOOR BIN ISMAIL; Dir MOHAMAD BIN AUDONG.

Malaysian Automotive Association: F-1-47, Blok F, Jalan PJU 1A/3, 2 Taipan Damansara, Parcel 1, Ara Damansara, 47301 Petaling Jaya, Selangor Darul Ehsan; tel. (3) 78439947; fax (3) 78430847; e-mail secretariat@maa.org.my; internet www.maa.org.my; f. 1960 as Fed. of Malaya Motor Traders' Asscn; renamed following merger with Malaysian Motor Vehicle Assemblers' Asscn in 2000; Pres. Datuk AISHAH AHMAD; Sec.-Gen. GOH CHENG MENG.

Malaysian Iron and Steel Industry Federation: 28E–30E, Tingkat 5, Blok 2, Worldwide Business Park, Jalan Tinju 13/50, Seksyen 13, Shah Alam, 40675 Selangor; tel. (3) 55133970; fax (3) 55133891; e-mail enquiry@misif.org.my; internet www.misif.org.my; Pres. CHOW CHONG LONG; 150 mems.

Malaysian Palm Oil Association (MPOA): Bangunan Getah Asli, 12th Floor, 148 Jalan Ampang, 50450 Kuala Lumpur; tel. (3) 27105680; fax (3) 27105679; e-mail mpoa@mpoa.org.my; internet www.mpoa.org.my; f. 1999; est. as result of rationalization of plantation industry; secr. for producers of palm oil; CEO RAVINDRANATH G. MENON.

Malaysian Pineapple Industry Board: Wisma Nanas, 5 Jalan Padi Mahsuri, Bandar Baru UDA, 81200 Johor Bahru; tel. (7) 2361211; fax (7) 2365694; e-mail umum@mpib.gov.my; internet www.mpib.gov.my; Dir-Gen. Haji SAHDAN BIN SALIM.

Malaysian Rubber Board: POB 10150, 50908 Kuala Lumpur; tel. (3) 92062000; fax (3) 21634492; e-mail general@lgm.gov.my; internet www.lgm.gov.my; f. 1998; implements policies and development programmes to ensure the viability of the Malaysian rubber industry; regulates the industry (in particular, the packing, grading, shipping and export of rubber); Dir-Gen. Dr SALMIAH AHMAD.

Malaysian Rubber Products Manufacturers' Association: 1 Jalan USJ 11/1J, Subang Jaya, 47620 Petaling Jaya, Selangor; tel. (3) 56316150; fax (3) 56316152; e-mail mrpma@po.jaring.my; internet www.mrpma.com.my; f. 1952; Pres. Dato' ONG ENG LONG; 144 mems.

Malaysian Timber Certification Council (MTCC): C-8-5, Megan Ave II, 12 Jalan Yap Kwan Seng, 50450 Kuala Lumpur; tel. (3) 21612298; fax (3) 21612293; e-mail info@mtcc.com.my; internet www.mtcc.com.my; f. 1999; operates a voluntary national timber certification scheme to encourage sustainable forest management; Chair. Dato' Dr FREEZAILAH CHE YEOM; CEO CHEW LYE TENG.

Malaysian Wood Industries Association: Menara PGRM, 18th Floor, 8 Jalan Pudu Ulu, Cheras, 55100 Kuala Lumpur; tel. (3) 92821778; fax (3) 92821789; e-mail mwia@mwia.com.my; internet www.mwia.com.my; f. 1957; Pres. Dato' LOW KIAN CHUAN.

National Tobacco Board Malaysia (Ibu Pejabat Lembaga Tembakau Negara): Kubang Kerian, POB 198, 15720 Kota Bharu, Kelantan; tel. (9) 7652212; fax (9) 7655640; e-mail ltnm@ltn.gov .my; internet www.ltn.gov.my; Dir-Gen. TEO HUI BEK.

Northern Malaya Rubber Millers' and Packers' Association: 22 Pitt St, 3rd Floor, Suites 301–303, 10200 Pinang; tel. (4) 620037; f. 1919; 153 mems; Pres. HWANG SING LUE; Hon. Sec. LEE SENG KEOK.

Palm Oil Refiners' Association of Malaysia (PORAM): 801 C/ 802A Blok B, Executive Suites, Kelana Business Centre, 97 Jalan SS7/2, 47301 Kelana Jaya, Selangor; tel. (3) 74920006; fax (3) 74920128; e-mail info@poram.org.my; internet www.poram.org .my; f. 1975; est. to promote the palm oil refining industry; Chair. MOHD ZAIN ISMAIL; CEO MOHD JAAFAR AHMAD; 90 mems.

Rubber Industry Smallholders Development Authority (RISDA): Bangunan RISDA, km 7, Jalan Ampang, Karung Berkunci 11067, 50990 Kuala Lumpur; tel. (3) 42564022; fax (3) 42576726; e-mail webmaster@risda.gov.my; internet www.risda .gov.my; f. 1973; Chair. Dato' Sri WAN MOHAMMAD ZUKI MOHAMMAD; Dir-Gen. Dato'Sri WAN MOHAMMAD ZUKI MOHAMMAD.

Tin Industry Research and Development Board: West Block, 8th Floor, Wisma Selangor Dredging, Jalan Ampang, POB 12560, 50782 Kuala Lumpur; tel. (3) 21616171; fax (3) 21616179; e-mail mcom@mcom.com.my; Chair. MOHAMED AJIB ANUAR; Sec. MUHAMAD NOR MUHAMAD.

EMPLOYERS' ORGANIZATIONS

Malaysian Employers' Federation: 3A06–3A07, Blok A, Pusat Dagangan Phileo Damansara II, 15 Jalan 16/11, off Jalan Damansara, 46350 Petaling Jaya, Selangor; tel. (3) 79557778; fax (3) 79556808; e-mail mef-hq@mef.org.my; internet www.mef.org.my; f. 1959; Pres. Dato' AZMAN SHAH Dato' Seri HARUN; Exec. Dir Datuk Haji SHAMSUDDIN BARDAN; private sector org. incorporating 13 employer orgs and 4,611 individual enterprises, incl.:

Association of Insurance Employers: c/o Royal Insurance (M) Sdn Bhd, Menara Boustead, 5th Floor, 69 Jalan Raja Chulan, 50200 Kuala Lumpur; tel. (3) 2410233; fax (3) 2442762; Pres. NG KIM HOONG.

Commercial Employers' Association of Peninsular Malaysia: c/o The East Asiatic Co (M) Bhd, 1 Jalan 205, 46050 Petaling Jaya, Selangor; tel. (3) 7913322; fax (3) 7913561; Pres. HAMZAH Haji GHULAM.

Malaysian Chamber of Mines: West Block, Wisma Selangor Dredging, 8th Floor, 142C Jalan Ampang, 50450 Kuala Lumpur; tel. (3) 21616171; fax (3) 21616179; e-mail mcom@mcom.com.my; internet www.mcom.com.my; f. 1914; promotes and protects interests of Malaysian mining industry; Pres. MOHAMED AJIB ANUAR; Exec. Dir MUHAMAD NOR MUHAMAD; 100 mems.

Malaysian Textile Manufacturers' Association: C-9-4, Megan Ave 1, 189 Jalan Tun Razak, 50400 Kuala Lumpur; tel. (3) 21621454; fax (3) 21625148; e-mail info@mtma.org.my; internet www.fashion-asia.com; Pres. THIAN POH TAN; CEO ANDREW HONG; 70 mems.

Pan Malaysian Bus Operators' Association: 88 Jalan Sultan Idris Shah, 30300 Ipoh, Perak; tel. (5) 2549421; fax (5) 2550858; Sec. TEOH EWE HUN.

Sabah Employers' Consultative Association: Dewan SECA, No. 4, Block A, 1st Floor, Bandar Ramai-Ramai, 90000 Sandakan, Sabah; tel. and fax (89) 272846; Chair. LING AH HONG.

Stevedore Employers' Association: 5 Pengkalan Weld, POB 288, 10300 Pinang; tel. (4) 2615091; Pres. ABDUL RAHMAN MAIDIN.

UTILITIES

Energy Commission of Malaysia (Suruhanjaya Tenaga): 12 Jalan Tun Hussein, Precinct 2, 62100 Putrajaya; tel. (3) 88708500; fax (3) 88888637; e-mail fauzih@st.gov.my; internet www.st.gov.my; f. 2002; regulatory body supervising electricity and gas supply; CEO Ir AHMAD FAUZI BIN HASAN.

Electricity

Tenaga Nasional Bhd: 129 Jalan Bangsar, POB 11003, 50732 Kuala Lumpur; tel. (3) 2825566; fax (3) 22833686; e-mail webadmin@ tnb.com.my; internet www.tnb.com.my; f. 1990; est. through corporatization and privatization of Nat. Electricity Bd; 53% govt-controlled; generation, transmission and distribution of electricity in Peninsular Malaysia; generating capacity of 7,621 MW (63% of total power generation); also purchases power from 12 licensed independent power producers; Chair. Tan Sri Dato' Amar LEO MOGGIE; Pres. and CEO Dato' Ir AZMAN BIN MOHAMED.

Sabah Electricity Supply Board (SESB): Wisma SESB, Jalan Tunku Abdul Rahman, 88673 Kota Kinabalu; tel. (88) 282500; fax (88) 282314; e-mail webmaster@sesb.com.my; internet www.sesb .com.my; generation, transmission and distribution of electricity in Sabah; Man. Dir Ir Haji ABDUL RAZAK SALLIM.

Syarikat Sesco Bhd (SESCO): POB 149, 93700 Kuching, Sarawak; tel. (82) 441188; fax (82) 444433; e-mail public_enquiry@sesoc .com.my; internet www.sesco.com.my; fmrly Sarawak Electricity

Supply Corpn; generation, transmission and distribution of electricity in Sarawak; Chair. Datuk ABDUL HAMED SEPAWI; CEO TORSTEIN DALE SJOTVEIT.

Gas

Gas Malaysia Sdn Bhd: 5 Jalan Serendah 26/17, Seksyen 26, Peti Surat 7901, 40732 Shah Alam, Selangor Darul Ehsan; tel. (3) 51923000; e-mail ccu@gasmalaysia.com; internet www.gasmalaysia.com; f. 1992; Chair. Tan Sri Datuk Dr HAMZAH BAKAR; CEO MUHAMAD NOOR HAMID.

Water

Under the federal Constitution, water supply is the responsibility of the State Governments. In 1998, owing to water shortages, the National Water Resources Council was established to co-ordinate management of water resources at national level. Malaysia's sewerage system is operated by Indah Water Konsortium, owned by Prime Utilities.

National Water Resources Council: c/o Ministry of Works, Jalan Sultan Salahuddin, 50580 Kuala Lumpur; tel. (3) 2919011; fax (3) 2986612; f. 1998; co-ordinates management of water resources at national level through co-operation with state water boards; chaired by the Prime Minister.

Regulatory Authorities

Johor State Regulatory Body: c/o Pejabat Setiausaha Kerajaan Negeri Johor, Aras 1, Bangunan Sultan Ibrahim, Jalan Bukit Timbalan, 80000 Johor Bahru; tel. (7) 223850; Dir Haji OMAR BIN AWAB.

Kelantan Water Department: Tingkat Bawah, Blok 6, Kota Darul Naim, 15503 Kota Bharu, Kelantan; tel. (9) 7475240; fax (9) 7475220; e-mail jank@kelantan.gov.my; internet www.jank.kelantan.gov.my; Dir Tengku ADLI BIN Tengku ABDULLAH.

Water Supply Authorities

Kedah Public Works Department: Bangunan Sultan Abdul Halim, Jalan Sultan Badlishah, 05582 Alor Setar, Kedah; tel. (4) 7334041; fax (4) 7341616; internet kedah.jkr.gov.my; Dir Ir ROSLAND BIN GHANI.

Kelantan Water Sdn Bhd: Bangunan Perbadanan Menteri Besar Kelantan, Lot 2 & 257, Jalan Kuala Krai, 15050 Kota Bharu, Kelantan; tel. (9) 7437777; fax (9) 7472030; internet www.airkelantan.com.my; Gen. Man. Ir Haji HANAPI MOHD BIN MAHMUD.

Kuching Water Board: Jalan Batu Lintang, 93200 Kuching, Sarawak; tel. (82) 240371; fax (82) 244546; e-mail juliab@kwb.gov.my; internet www.kwb.gov.my; Chair. Dato' Sri AHMAD TARMIZI BIN Haji SULAIMAN; Gen. Man. MOHD SABARI BIN SHAKERAN.

Labuan Public Works Department: Jalan Kg. Jawa, POB 2, 87008 Labuan; tel. (87) 414040; fax (87) 412370; Dir Ir ZULKIFLY BIN MADON.

LAKU Management Sdn Bhd: Menara Soon Hup, 6th Floor, Lot 907, Jalan Merbau, 98000 Miri; tel. (85) 442000; fax (85) 442005; e-mail laku@lakumyy.po.my; internet www.lakumanagement.com.my; f. 1995; serves Miri, Limbang and Bintulu; Chair. HUBERT THIAN CHONG HUI; CEO WONG TIONG KAI.

Melaka Water Corpn: Tingkat Bawah, 1st and 10th–13th Floors, Graha Maju, Jalan Graha Maju, 75300 Melaka; tel. (6) 2821700; fax (6) 2837266; e-mail baharam@pamwtr.gov.my; Dir Ir Haji BAHARAM BIN Haji MOHAMAD.

Negeri Sembilan Water Department: Wisma Negeri, 70990 Seremban; tel. (6) 7610505; fax (6) 7617841; Dir Ir ZULKIFLI IBRAHIM.

Pahang Water Supply Department (Jabatan Bekalan Air Pahang): Kompleks JBA, Bandar Indera Mahkota, 25200 Kuantan, Pahang; tel. (9) 5712222; fax (9) 5712221; e-mail p-jba@pahang.gov.my; internet jba.pahang.gov.my; corporatized in 2012; Dir Datuk Seri MUHAMMAD SAFIAN ISMAIL.

Perak Water Board (Lembaga Air Perak): Jalan St John, Peti Surat 589, 30760 Ipoh, Perak; tel. (5) 2551155; fax (5) 2556397; internet www.lap.com.my; Dir Dato' Ir Dato' Seri Diraja Dr ZAMBRY BIN Haji ABDUL KADIR.

Pinang Water Supply Corpn (Perbadanan Bekalan Air Pulau Pinang Sdn Bhd): Menara KOMTAR, Level 32, Jalan Pinang, 10000 Pinang; tel. (4) 2634200; fax (4) 2613581; e-mail customer@pba.com.my; internet www.pba.com.my; f. 1973; Gen. Man. Ir JASENI BIN MAIDINSA.

Sabah State Water Department (Jabatan Air Negeri Sabah): Wisma MUIS, Blok A, Tingkat 6, Beg Berkunci 210, 88825 Kota Kinabalu; tel. (88) 232364; fax (88) 232396; e-mail jans.hq@sabah.gov.my; internet www.sabah.gov.my/air; Man. MOHAMAD TAHIR BIN MOHAMAD TALIB.

SAJ Holdings Sdn Bhd: Bangunan Ibu Pejabat SAJ Holdings, Jalan Garuda, Larkin, POB 262, 80350 Johor Bahru; tel. (7) 2244040;

fax (7) 2241990; e-mail support@saj.com.my; internet www.saj.com.my; f. 1999; Exec. Chair. Tan Sri HAMDAN MOHAMED.

Sarawak Public Works Department: Wisma Seberkas, Jalan Tun Haji Openg, 93582 Kuching; tel. (82) 203100; fax (82) 429679; internet www.jkr.sarawak.gov.my; Dir Ir ZURAIMI BIN Haji SABKI.

Selangor Water Supply Co (Syarikat Bekalan Air Selangor Sdn Bhd): POB 5001, Jalan Pantai Baru, 59990 Kuala Lumpur; tel. (3) 2826244; fax (3) 22955168; e-mail puspel@syabas.com.my; internet www.syabas.com.my; f. 1972; CEO Dato' RUSLAN BIN HASSAN.

Sibu Water Board: Km 5, Jalan Salim, POB 405, 96007 Sibu, Sarawak; tel. (84) 211001; fax (84) 211543; e-mail swbs@swb.gov.my; internet www.swb.gov.my; Gen. Man. DANIEL WONG PARK ING.

Terengganu Water Department: Wisma Negeri, Tingkat 3, Jalan Pejabat, 20200 Kuala Terengganu; tel. (9) 6222444; fax (9) 6221510; Dir Ir Haji WAN NGAH BIN WAN.

TRADE UNIONS

Malaysian Trades Union Congress (MTUC): Wisma MTUC, 10-5, Jalan USJ 9/5T, 47620 Subang Jaya, Selangor; POB 3073, 46000 Petaling Jaya, Selangor; tel. (3) 80242953; fax (3) 80243225; e-mail mtucgeneral@gmail.com; internet www.mtuc.org.my; f. 1949; 262 affiliated unions, representing approx. 500,000 workers; Pres. MOHD KHALID ATAN; Sec.-Gen. N. GOPALKISHNAM NADESAN.

Transport

RAILWAYS

Peninsular Malaysia

The state-owned Malayan Railways had a total length of 1,665 km in Peninsular Malaysia in 2010. The main railway line follows the west coast and extends 782 km from Singapore, south of Peninsular Malaysia, to Butterworth (opposite Pinang Island) in the north. From Bukit Mertajam, close to Butterworth, the Kedah line runs north to the Thai border at Padang Besar where connection is made with the State Railway of Thailand. The East Coast Line, 526 km long, runs from Gemas to Tumpat (in Kelantan). A 21-km branch line from Pasir Mas (27 km south of Tumpat) connects with the State Railway of Thailand at the border station of Sungei Golok. Branch lines serve railway-operated ports at Port Dickson and Telok Anson as well as Port Klang and Jurong (Singapore). Malaysia's first Light Rail Transit (LRT) system was opened in the Kuala Lumpur area in 1996. A second line began operating within the same system in 1998; a second LRT system, comprising one line, also commenced operations in that year. An express rail link connecting central Kuala Lumpur and the new Kuala Lumpur International Airport (KLIA) opened in 2001. The construction of a mass rapid transport system commenced in Kuala Lumpur in 2012, with completion scheduled for 2016. In February 2013 plans were announced for the construction of a high-speed rail link between Kuala Lumpur and Singapore, which would be due for completion in 2020.

Keretapi Tanah Melayu Bhd (KTMB) (Malayan Railways): KTMB Corporate Headquarters, Jalan Sultan Hishamuddin, 50621 Kuala Lumpur; tel. (3) 22631111; fax (3) 27105706; e-mail callcenter@ktmb.com.my; internet www.ktmb.com.my; f. 1885; incorporated as a co under govt control in 1992; privatized in 1997; managed by the consortium Marak Unggal (Renong, DRB and Bolton); Chair. Dato' Sri MOHD ZIN BIN MOHAMED.

Sabah

Sabah State Railway: Karung Berkunci 2047, 88999 Kota Kinabalu; tel. (88) 254611; fax (88) 236395; e-mail webmaster.jkns@sabah.gov.my; internet www.sabah.gov.my/railway; 134 track-km of 1-m gauge (2008); goods and passenger services from Tanjong Aru to Tenom, serving part of the west coast and the interior; diesel trains are used; Gen. Man. Haji MOHD ZAIN Haji MOHD SAID.

ROADS

Peninsular Malaysia

Peninsular Malaysia's road system is extensive, in contrast to those of Sabah and Sarawak. By 2012 the road network in Malaysia totalled an estimated 180,882 km.

Sabah

Jabatan Kerja Raya Sabah (Sabah Public Works Department): Jalan Sembulan, Locked Bag 2032, 88582 Kota Kinabalu, Sabah; tel. (88) 244333; fax (88) 237234; e-mail jkrweb@sabah.gov.my; internet www.jkr.sabah.gov.my; f. 1881; implements and maintains public infrastructures such as roads, bridges, buildings and sewerage systems throughout Sabah; maintains a road network totalling 15,756.6 km, of which 5,686.5 km are sealed roads; Dir JOHN ANTHONY.

Sarawak

Jabatan Kerja Raya Sarawak (Sarawak Public Works Department): Tingkat 11–18, Wisma Saberkas, Jalan Tun Abang Haji Openg, 93582 Kuching, Sarawak; tel. (82) 203100; fax (82) 251908; e-mail corporatejkr@gmail.com; internet www.jkr.sarawak.gov.my; implements and maintains public infrastructures in Sarawak; road network totalling 10,979 km, of which 3,986 km are sealed roads; Dir Ir ZURAIMI BIN SABKI.

SHIPPING

In 2014 Malaysia's flag registered fleet comprised 2,323 vessels, with a total displacement of 9,382,900 grt, including 179 general cargo ships, 34 gas tankers, 210 tankers and 8 bulk carriers. The ports in Malaysia are classified as federal ports, under the jurisdiction of the federal Ministry of Transport, or state ports, responsible to the state ministries of Sabah and Sarawak.

Peninsular Malaysia

The federal ports in Peninsular Malaysia are Klang (the principal port), Penang, Johor and Kuantan.

Johor Port Authority: 6A1–8A1 Pusat Perdagangan Pasir Gudang, Jalan Bandar, 81700 Pasir Gudang, Johor; tel. (7) 2534000; fax (7) 2517684; e-mail admin@lpj.gov.my; internet www.lpj.gov.my; f. 1976; Gen. Man. MUHAMMAD RAZIF AHMED.

Johor Port Bhd: POB 151, Wisma Kontena, 81707 Pasir Gudang, Johor; tel. (7) 2535888; fax (7) 2510980; e-mail jpb@johorport.com.my; internet www.johorport.com.my; Chair. Datuk MOHD SIDIK BIN SHAIK OSMAN.

Klang Port Authority: POB 202, Jalan Pelabuhan, 42005 Port Klang, Selangor; tel. (3) 31688211; fax (3) 31689177; e-mail onestopagency@pka.gov.my; internet www.pka.gov.my; f. 1963; Gen. Man. Capt. DAVID RAJAN PADMAN.

Kuantan Port Authority: Tanjung Gelang, POB 161, 25720 Kuantan, Pahang; tel. (9) 5858000; fax (9) 5833866; e-mail lpktn@lpktn.gov.my; internet www.lpktn.gov.my; f. 1974; Gen. Man. Dato' KHAIRUL ANUAR BIN ABDUL RAHMAN.

Penang Port Commission: Level 2, Swettenham Pier Cruise Terminal 1A, 10300 Penang; tel. (4) 2633211; fax (4) 2626211; e-mail sppp@penangport.gov.my; internet www.penangport.gov.my; f. 1956; Gen. Man. NOOR ARIF BIN YUSOFF.

Sabah

The main ports, which are administered by the Sabah Ports Authority, are Kota Kinabalu, Sandakan, Tawau, Lahad Datu, Kudat, Semporna and Kunak. Many international shipping lines serve Sabah. Local services are operated by smaller vessels.

Sabah Ports Authority: Bangunan SPA, Jalan Tun Fuad, Tanjung Lipat, Locked Bag 2005, 88617 Kota Kinabalu, Sabah; tel. (88) 538400; fax (88) 223036; e-mail sabahport@tm.net.my; internet www.lpps.sabah.gov.my; f. 1968; Gen. Man. Eng. MAYONG OMAR.

Sarawak

There are four port authorities in Sarawak: Kuching, Rajang, Miri and Bintulu. Kuching, Rajang and Miri are state ports, while Bintulu is a federal port. Kuching port serves the southern region of Sarawak, Rajang port the central region, and Miri port the northern region.

Kuching Port Authority: Jalan Pelabuhan, Pending, POB 530, 93450 Kuching, Sarawak; tel. (82) 482144; fax (82) 481696; e-mail hq@kuport.com.my; internet www.kpa.gov.my; f. 1961; Gen. Man. LIU MOI FONG.

Rajang Port Authority: Jalan Pulau, 96000 Sibu, Sarawak; tel. (84) 319004; fax (84) 318754; e-mail rpa@rajangport.gov.my; internet www.rajangport.gov.my; f. 1970; Gen. Man. HELEN LIM HUI SHYAN.

Principal Shipping Companies

Malaysia Shipping Corpn Sdn Bhd: Office Tower, Plaza Berjaya, Suite 14C, 14th Floor, 12 Jalan Imbi, 55100 Kuala Lumpur; tel. (3) 21418788; fax (3) 21429214; Chair. Y. C. CHANG.

Malaysian International Shipping Corpn Bhd (National Shipping Line of Malaysia): Menara Dayabumi, Level 25, Jalan Sultan Hishamuddin, 50050 Kuala Lumpur; tel. (3) 22738088; fax (3) 22736602; e-mail miscweb@miscbhd.com; internet www.misc.com.my; f. 1968; regular services between South-East Asia, South Asia, Australia, Japan and Europe; also operates chartering, tanker, haulage and warehousing and agency services; majority stake owned by Petroliam Nasional Bhd (PETRONAS); Chair. Dato' MANHARLAL RATILAL; Pres. and CEO Datuk NASARUDIN BIN MOHD IDRIS.

Perbadanan Nasional Shipping Line Bhd (PNSL): Kuala Lumpur; tel. (3) 2932211; fax (3) 2930493; f. 1982; specializes in bulk cargoes; a wholly owned subsidiary of Konsortium Logistik Bhd; Chair. Tunku Dato' SHAHRIMAN BIN Tunku SULAIMAN; Exec. Dep. Chair. Dato' SULAIMAN ABDULLAH.

Persha Shipping Agencies Sdn Bhd: Bangunan Mayban Trust, Penthouse Suite, Jalan Pinang, 10200 Pinang; tel. (4) 2612400; fax (4) 2623122; Man. Dir MOHD NOOR MOHD KAMALUDIN.

Syarikat Perkapalan Kris Sdn Bhd (The Kris Shipping Co Ltd): POB 8428, 46789 Petaling Jaya, Selangor; tel. (3) 7046477; fax (3) 7048007; domestic services; Chair. Dato' Seri Syed NAHAR SHAHABUDIN; Gen. Man. ROHANY TALIB.

Trans-Asia Shipping Corpn Sdn Bhd: Lot 1A, Persiaran Jubli Perak, Jalan 22/1, Seksyen 22, 40300 Shah Alam, Selangor; tel. (3) 51018888; fax (3) 55488288; e-mail kytan@tasco.com.my; internet www.tasco.com.my; f. 1974; Man. Dir LEE CHECK POH.

CIVIL AVIATION

The new Kuala Lumpur International Airport (KLIA), situated in Sepang, Selangor (50 km south of Kuala Lumpur) began operations in 1998, with an initial capacity of 25m.–30m. passengers a year, which was projected to rise to 45m. by 2020. An express rail link between central Kuala Lumpur and KLIA opened in 2001. There are regional airports at Kota Kinabalu, Pinang, Johor Bahru, Kuching and Pulau Langkawi. In addition, there are airports catering for domestic services at Alor Star, Ipoh, Kota Bharu, Kuala Terengganu, Kuantan and Melaka in Peninsular Malaysia, Sibu, Bintulu and Miri in Sarawak, and Sandakan, Tawau, Lahad Datu and Labuan in Sabah. There are also numerous smaller airstrips.

Department of Civil Aviation (Jabatan Penerbangan Awam Malaysia): 27 Persiaran Perdana, Aras 1–4, Blok Podium, 62618 Putrajaya; tel. (3) 88714000; fax (3) 88901640; e-mail webmaster@dca.gov.my; internet www.dca.gov.my; Dir-Gen. Dato' AZHARUDDIN ABDUL RAHMAN.

AirAsia Sdn Bhd: LCC Terminal Jalan KLIA S3, Southern Support Zone, KLIA, 64000 Sepang, Selangor; tel. (3) 86604333; fax (3) 87751100; e-mail tellus@airasia.com; internet www.airasia.com; f. 1993; 85% owned by HICOM; low-cost national carrier with licence to operate domestic, regional and international flights; Chair. ABDUL AZIZ BIN ABU BAKAR; CEO AIREEN OMAR.

Berjaya Air Sdn Bhd: Sultan Abdul Aziz Shah Airport, Lot No. G4, SkyPark Terminal, 47200 Subang, Selangor; tel. (3) 78468228; fax (3) 78427330; e-mail enquiry@berjaya-air.com; internet www.berjaya-air.com; f. 1989; scheduled and charter domestic services; Pres. Tan Sri Dato' Seri VINCENT TAN CHEE YIOUN.

Firefly: Sultan Abdul Aziz Shah Airport, Admin Bldg 1, 3rd Floor, Kompleks A, 47200 Subang, Selangor; e-mail contactus@fireflyz.com.my; internet www.fireflyz.com.my; f. 2007; wholly owned by Malaysia Airlines; low-cost domestic and regional flights; CEO IGNATIUS ONG.

Malaysia Airlines: Bangunan Pentadbiran 1, Tingkat 3, MAS Kompleks A, Sultan Abdul Aziz Shah Airport, 47200 Subang, Selangor; tel. (3) 78404550; fax (3) 78463932; e-mail tanwf@malaysiaairlines.com.my; internet www.malaysiaairlines.com.my; f. 1971; est. as the Malaysian successor to Malaysia Singapore Airlines (MSA); known as Malaysian Airline System (MAS) until Oct. 1987; 114 international routes and 118 domestic routes; Chair. Tan Sri MOHAMED NOR YUSOF; Man. Dir and CEO AHMAD JAUHARI YAHYA.

Malindo Airways Sdn Bhd: N1, Tingkat 4, Main Terminal Bldg, Kuala Lumpur International Airport, 64000 Sepang, Selangor; e-mail info@malindoair.com; internet www.malindoair.com; f. 2013; low-cost domestic services; CEO CHANDRAN RAMAMURTHY.

Transmile Air Services Sdn Bhd: Cargo Kompleks, Sultan Abdul Aziz Shah Airport, 47200 Subang, Selangor; tel. (3) 78849898; fax (3) 78849899; e-mail info@transmile.com; internet www.transmile.com; f. 1993; scheduled and charter regional and domestic services for cargo; Chair. and Man. Dir LIU TAI SHIN.

Tourism

Malaysia has a rapidly growing tourist industry, and tourism is an important source of foreign exchange earnings. In 2013 a record 25.7m. tourists visited Malaysia, while receipts from tourism rose to US $21,026m. Singapore is the main source of visitors, followed by Indonesia and the People's Republic of China (including Hong Kong and Macao).

Malaysia Tourism Promotion Board (Tourism Malaysia): Tingkat 9, No. 2, Tower 1, Jalan P5/6, Precinct 5, 62200 Putrajaya; tel. (3) 88918000; fax (3) 26935884; e-mail webmaster@tourism.gov.my; internet www.tourismmalaysia.gov.my; f. 1972; est. to co-ordinate and promote activities relating to tourism in Malaysia; Chair. Datuk Dr VICTOR WEE; Dir-Gen. Dato' MIRZA MOHAMMAD TAIYAB.

Sabah Tourist Association: POB 12181, 88824 Kota Kinabalu, Sabah; tel. and fax (88) 239089; e-mail secretariat@sta.my; internet www.sta.my; f. 1963; independent promotional org.; Chair. TONNY CHEW.

Sabah Tourism Board: Mail Bag 112, 88993 Kota Kinabalu, Sabah; tel. (88) 212121; fax (88) 212075; e-mail info@sabahtourism .com; internet www.sabahtourism.com; f. 1976; parastatal promotion org.; Chair. Datuk Seri Tengku ZAINAL ADLIN Tengku MAHAMOOD.

Sarawak Tourism Board: Levels 6 and 7, Bangunan Yayasan Sarawak, Jalan Masjid, 93400 Kuching; tel. (82) 423600; fax (82) 416700; e-mail stb@sarawaktourism.com; internet www .sarawaktourism.com; f. 1995; CEO Datuk RASHID KHAN.

Defence

As assessed at November 2014, the total strength of the armed forces was 109,000: army 80,000 (although this was to be reduced to 60,000–70,000), navy 14,000, air force 15,000; military service is voluntary. Paramilitary forces included the Police-General Operations Force of 18,000 and the People's Volunteer Corps of 240,000. Malaysia is a participant in the Five-Power Defence Arrangements with Singapore, Australia, New Zealand and the United Kingdom.

Defence Expenditure: Budgeted at RM 16,100m. in 2014.

Chief of Malaysian Armed Forces: Gen. Tan Sri Dato' Sri MUHAMMAD ZULKIFELI BIN ZIN.

Chief of Army: Gen. Datuk Raja MOHAMED AFFANDI Raja MOHAMED NOOR.

Chief of Navy: Adm. Tan Sri Dato' Sri ABDUL AZIZ BIN Haji JAAFAR.

Chief of Air Force: Gen. Dato' Seri Haji ROSLAN BIN SAAD.

Education

Under the Malaysian education system, free schooling is provided at government-assisted schools for children between the ages of six and 18. There are also private schools, which receive no government financial aid. Education is compulsory for 11 years between the ages of six and 16 years. In 2010 the adult literacy rate was 93.1% (males 95.4%; females 90.7%). The federal Government's expenditure on education was RM 54,589m. in 2012 (21.6% of total spending). Scholarships are awarded at all levels and there are many scholarship-holders studying at universities and other institutes of higher education at home and abroad.

PRIMARY EDUCATION

The national language, Bahasa Malaysia, is the main medium of instruction, although English, Chinese and Tamil are also used. Two-thirds of the total primary school enrolment is in National Schools where Malay is used and the remainder in National-Type Primary Schools where Tamil or Chinese is used. A place in primary school is now assured to every child from the age of six onwards, and parents are free to choose the language of instruction. At January 2014 some 2.70m. students were enrolled in 7,751 primary schools, at which 240,385 teachers were employed. In 2005 the total enrolment at primary level included 97% of all children in the relevant age-group. The primary school course lasts for six years.

SECONDARY EDUCATION

Bahasa Malaysia is the main medium of instruction in secondary schools, while English is taught as a second language and Chinese and Tamil are taught as pupils' own languages. Private Chinese secondary schools are also in operation. Secondary education lasts for seven years, comprising a first cycle of three years and a second of four. At January 2014 there were 2.23m. students enrolled in 2,366 secondary institutions, at which 180,469 teachers were employed. In 2011 the total enrolment at secondary level included 66% of students (67% of males; 66% of females) in the relevant age-group.

HIGHER EDUCATION

At mid-2013 there were 521,793 students enrolled in 146 institutes of tertiary education (including 20 universities). The Government has attempted to encourage foreign universities to establish campuses in Malaysia to improve standards and reduce the cost of sending Malaysian students abroad to study.

THE MALDIVES

Introductory Survey

LOCATION, CLIMATE, LANGUAGE, RELIGION, FLAG, CAPITAL

The Republic of Maldives (commonly referred to as 'the Maldives') is in southern Asia. The country, lying about 675 km (420 miles) south-west of Sri Lanka, consists of 1,192 small coral islands (of which 194 are inhabited), grouped in 26 natural atolls (but divided, for administrative purposes, into 19 atolls and two cities), in the Indian Ocean. The climate is warm and humid. The annual average temperature is 27°C (80°F), with little daily or seasonal variation, while annual rainfall is generally between 2,540 mm and 3,800 mm (100 ins to 150 ins). The national language is Dhivehi (Maldivian), which is related to Sinhala. Islam is the state religion, and most Maldivians are Sunni Muslims. The national flag (proportions 2 by 3) is red, with a green rectangle, containing a white crescent, in the centre. The capital is Malé.

CONTEMPORARY POLITICAL HISTORY

Historical Context

The Maldives, called the Maldive Islands until 1969, formerly had an elected Sultan as head of state. The islands were placed under British protection, with internal self-government, in 1887. They became a republic in January 1953, but the sultanate was restored in February 1954. The Maldives became fully independent, outside the Commonwealth, on 26 July 1965. Following a referendum, the country became a republic again in November 1968, with Amir Ibrahim Nasir, Prime Minister since 1957, as President. A new Constitution, promulgated in 1968, vested considerable powers in the President, including the right to appoint and dismiss the Prime Minister and the Cabinet of Ministers. The Maldives rejoined the Commonwealth in 1982.

Domestic Political Affairs

President Gayoom in power (1978–2009)

In March 1975, following rumours of a coup conspiracy, President Amir Ibrahim Nasir dismissed the Prime Minister, Ahmed Zaki, and the premiership was abolished. Unexpectedly, President Nasir announced that he would not seek re-election at the end of his second term in 1978. To succeed him, the Majlis (legislature) chose Maumoon Abdul Gayoom, Minister of Transport under Nasir, who was approved by referendum in July 1978 and took office in November. President Gayoom announced that his main priority would be the development of the poor rural regions, while in foreign affairs the existing policy of non-alignment would be continued. In 1980 President Gayoom confirmed reports of an attempted coup against the Government and implicated Nasir in the alleged plot. Nasir, who had left the country after his resignation, was to stand trial, in his absence, on this and other charges, including the misappropriation of government funds. In April 1981 Ahmed Naseem, former Deputy Minister of Fisheries and brother-in-law of Nasir, was sentenced to life imprisonment for plotting to overthrow Gayoom. Nasir himself denied any involvement in the coup, and attempts to extradite him from Singapore proved unsuccessful. (In July 1990, however, President Gayoom officially pardoned Nasir *in absentia*, in recognition of the role that he had played in achieving national independence.) Gayoom was re-elected as President by a national referendum in September 1983 and again in September 1988.

Another attempt to depose President Gayoom took place in November 1988, when a seaborne mercenary force comprising around 80 alleged Sri Lankan Tamil separatists (led by a disaffected Maldivian businessman, Abdullah Luthufi) landed in Malé and endeavoured to seize control of key government installations. At the request of Gayoom, the Indian Government dispatched an emergency contingent of 1,600 troops, which quelled the attempted coup. Nineteen people were reported to have been killed in the fighting. In September 1989 the President commuted to life imprisonment the death sentences imposed on 12 Sri Lankans and four Maldivians who had participated in the aborted coup.

In February 1990 President Gayoom announced proposals for a new policy of liberalization and democratic reform, including the devolution of some of his powers among other official bodies. Although discussions on promoting freedom of speech (particularly in the local press) were held in early 1990, with the President's approval, following the emergence of several politically outspoken magazines, including *Sangu* (The Conchshell), all publications not sanctioned by the Government were subsequently banned, and a number of leading writers and publishers were arrested.

In October 1993 Gayoom's re-election as President for a further five years was endorsed by a national referendum, in which he obtained 92.8% of the popular vote. In November 1994 Gayoom again outlined various measures intended to strengthen the political system and to advance the process of democratization. These included the granting of greater responsibilities to the Cabinet of Ministers, the implementation of regulations governing the conduct of civil servants (in order to increase their accountability), the introduction of democratic elections to island development committees and atoll committees, and the establishment of a Judicial Advisory Council to enact reforms to the judicial system.

A revised Constitution was implemented on 1 January 1998. Under the new 156-article charter, a formal, multi-candidate contest was permitted for the legislature's nomination for the presidency; no restriction was placed on the number of terms that a President might serve; for administrative purposes, the number of atolls was increased from 19 to 20; and the Majlis, henceforth known as the People's Majlis, was enlarged from 48 to 50 seats.

In September 1998 five individuals declared their candidacy for the presidency; the People's Majlis, which at that time was charged with nominating and electing by secret ballot a single candidate to be presented to the country in a referendum, unanimously voted for the incumbent President Gayoom. In the referendum, which was held in October, Gayoom was re-elected for a fifth term, obtaining 90.9% of the popular vote. In November 1999 elections for 42 members of the 50-seat People's Majlis were conducted (on a non-partisan basis).

In early 2001 an attempt by 42 prominent Maldivians, including members of the People's Majlis, former cabinet ministers and business executives, to register the newly formed Maldivian Democratic Party (MDP) was blocked by the People's Majlis on the grounds that the existence of political parties would encourage divisions among the public. In July 2002 the human rights group Amnesty International issued a report citing frequent cases of arbitrary detentions, unfair trials and long-term imprisonment and torture of political opponents in the Maldives. Earlier that month three journalists and a Maldivian businessman were sentenced to life imprisonment on charges of defamation and inciting violence after writing articles strongly criticizing the President and the Government.

A state of emergency was declared in Malé and neighbouring islands in September 2003, following the staging of major anti-Government protests in the capital (the first since President Gayoom came to power in 1978). The protests were provoked by the violent suppression by the National Security Service (NSS) of rioting that had broken out at the prison on Maafushi Island (in Kaafu Atoll) near Malé following the death of an inmate, allegedly as a result of brutality on the part of the prison guards; three other detainees were killed and 17 injured as a result of the NSS crackdown. Gayoom appealed for calm and announced an investigation into the deaths of the prisoners. Eleven members of the NSS were arrested for their alleged involvement in the overzealous curbing of the riots, and the Deputy Chief of the NSS and National Police Commissioner, Brig. Adam Zahir, was removed from office (he was reinstated in February 2004, after the inquiry cleared him of any misconduct). In December 2003 a Human Rights Commission was established in Malé.

Meanwhile, Gayoom's re-election as President for a sixth term was ratified at a referendum in October 2003, when he secured 90.3% of the votes cast. On assuming office Gayoom effected a cabinet reorganization, in which the Attorney-General, Dr

Mohamed Munavvar, and the Minister of Planning and National Development, Ibrahim Hussain Zaki, were dismissed, allegedly for supporting reformers attempting to register a political party. In the same month a group of political activists established the MDP in exile in Sri Lanka, amid rising discontent with the Maldives Government.

In May 2004 the election, by universal suffrage, took place of 42 members (from among 121 independent candidates) to a People's Special Majlis, which was assigned the task of drawing up and implementing constitutional amendments. The President appointed an additional eight people to serve on the council, which also included members of the People's Majlis and the Cabinet of Ministers and which convened in July. Gayoom invited members of the public to put forward suggestions for constitutional reform, and the President himself proposed a number of radical reforms.

In August 2004 President Gayoom declared an indefinite state of emergency after an initially peaceful pro-democracy protest in Malé descended into violence when the authorities moved in to disperse those gathered. Four police officers were reportedly stabbed and about 185 people, including former Attorney-General Dr Munavvar and members of the People's Special Majlis, were arrested during the protest. The Government claimed that the demonstration had been a coup attempt, a charge denied by the MDP, whose exiled founding leader, Mohamed Latheef, accused Gayoom's administration of 'ruthlessly suppressing dissent'. In October the state of emergency was revoked, and in December President Gayoom announced that all charges of treason and public order offences against those taken into custody following the August protest were to be suspended.

On 26 December 2004 a tsunami generated by a massive earthquake in the Indian Ocean, off the coast of Indonesia, devastated many of the low-lying Maldive islands. While the death toll was not as high as initially feared, several of the islands were rendered uninhabitable and an estimated 15,000 people were left homeless. The economic consequences of the catastrophe on the Maldives were extensive, owing in large part to the major contribution made by the tourism industry to the economy.

In January 2005 a total of 149 independent candidates contested elections to the People's Majlis. Candidates backed by the MDP reportedly won 18 of the 42 elective seats. However, the Government stated that only 12 opposition candidates had been successful, claiming that the results indicated widespread popular support for its reform policies. In June the People's Majlis unanimously approved a constitutional amendment permitting the registration of political parties in the Maldives, reversing its 2001 decision against the establishment of multi-party democracy. The MDP was subsequently officially registered in the Maldives as a political party, together with several others, including the Dhivehi Rayyithunge Party (DRP—Maldivian People's Party), established by President Gayoom.

In August 2005 a protest took place in Malé demanding the release of all political prisoners. Shortly afterwards the Chairman of the MDP, Mohamed Nasheed, was arrested, prompting several days of unrest in the capital and on various other atolls. Nasheed was subsequently charged with terrorism and attempting to perpetrate anti-Government actions. (Nasheed, a journalist, political activist and erstwhile People's Majlis deputy, had been detained on several occasions since the early 1990s, primarily for writing articles critical of the Gayoom Government and questioning the validity of the elections held during Gayoom's tenure.)

In a significant development towards the further democratization of the Maldives, from June 2006 representatives of the Government and the MDP conducted informal talks at the British High Commission in Colombo, Sri Lanka. The terms of the resulting agreement included the release of a number of opposition detainees and the advancement of constitutional reform, in return for MDP assurances that the party would curb public demonstrations and renounce violent protest. Nasheed was released in September (although the charges against him were not withdrawn until September 2008). In November 2006 more than 100 members of the MDP were arrested in advance of a planned demonstration to demand the swifter implementation of reforms; the rally was cancelled by the MDP amid fears for the welfare of protesters.

Meanwhile, in early 2006 meetings of the People's Special Majlis were obstructed by President Gayoom's refusal to permit the removal of presidential appointees from the body. The MDP condemned the continued presence of unelected representatives in the constitutional amendment process, and in February the party boycotted the opening of the People's Majlis.

In April 2007 the Minister of Higher Education, Employment and Social Security, Abdulla Yameen Abdul Gayoom, the half-brother of the President, resigned, also standing down as a member of the DRP, and subsequently founded a new political party, the People's Alliance (PA), in 2008. In August 2007 Minister of Justice Mohamed Jameel Ahmed, Attorney-General Dr Hassan Saeed and Minister of Foreign Affairs Dr Ahmed Shaheed all resigned, citing impediments and delays to the programme of democratic reforms. A new organization subsequently launched by the three dissidents, the New Maldives Movement, was declared illegal by the Government in January 2008.

Twelve foreign tourists were injured when a bomb exploded in Malé in September 2007. The explosion—the first recorded terrorist attack to take place in the Maldives—was believed to have been perpetrated by Islamist extremists. In December three Maldivian men were each sentenced to 15 years' imprisonment for their part in the incident, which they confessed to having planned as a deliberate attack on the country's vital tourism industry. In November the Government announced strict measures to combat the perceived threat of growing Islamic fundamentalism, including banning foreign Islamic clerics from visiting the islands without explicit permission.

A new Constitution and the presidency of Mohamed Nasheed

At a referendum held in August 2007, some 62% of those who participated voted in favour of retaining the presidential system of government, in preference to adopting a parliamentary system. In June 2008 the People's Special Majlis approved final amendments to the draft Constitution, which was then passed to the Cabinet of Ministers and the President in turn. A new Constitution was ratified by the President in August; major points included the direct election by popular vote of the President (and his nominated Vice-President) and the restriction of presidential terms of office to two (whether consecutive or not); the removal of the gender bar on the presidency; the establishment of a Supreme Court as the highest judicial authority; and the granting to citizens of the right to hold peaceful demonstrations. The People's Special Majlis and Judicial Advisory Council were duly dissolved, while the Speaker of the People's Majlis was replaced by an elected incumbent. By September a total of 12 political parties had registered in the Maldives. In that month the Election Commissioner, who had been assigned the post by President Gayoom, was replaced by a new five-member Elections Commission, which was nominated and appointed by the People's Majlis.

The first multi-party presidential election in the Maldives was held on 8 October 2008. Despite opposition to Gayoom standing for a seventh presidential term, the DRP argued that the new two-term limit did not exclude him from contesting what would be the first election under the new Constitution. Five other candidates contested the presidency, including MDP leader Mohamed Nasheed. Gayoom secured 40.3% of the vote, Nasheed won 24.9%, Hassan Saeed, who was running as an independent candidate, secured 16.7%, while Qasim Ibrahim of the Jumhooree Party (JP—Republican Party) garnered 15.2% of the vote. The reported turnout was 85.5% of the electorate. As no candidate secured more than 50% in the first round of voting, the two leading candidates contested a second round on 28 October, from which Nasheed emerged victorious, with 53.7% of the vote. He was consequently inaugurated—together with the country's first elected Vice-President, Dr Mohamed Waheed Hassan Manik of the Gaumee Itthihaad Party (GIP—National Unity Party)—on 11 November.

The new President appointed a coalition Cabinet of Ministers, comprising members of the MDP, the GIP, the JP, the Social Liberal Party and the Adhaalath Party (AP—Justice Party), and carried out a significant reorganization of the ministries, including the establishment of a Ministry of Islamic Affairs. Despite protests by the DRP at the alleged unconstitutional nature of his action, President Nasheed appointed eight new members of the People's Majlis to replace the eight appointees of former President Gayoom, thus ensuring the Government had a working majority. One of Nasheed's first acts as President was to request the resignation of the National Police Commissioner, Brig. Adam Zahir, who had long been held personally accountable for various human rights abuses on the part of the police, including torture and custodial deaths—see *President Gayoom in power (1978–2009)*. In December 2008 the Minister of Home Affairs, Qasim Ibrahim of the JP, resigned, citing the Government's unwillingness to allocate funds to prison reform (Ibrahim had recently attracted criticism for his heavy-handed response to a strike by employees at a tourist resort). In February 2009 the President's Special Advisor, Dr Hassan Saeed, stood down from his post and formed a new political party entitled the Dhivehi Qaumee Party (DQP—Maldivian National Party).

In February 2009 the People's Majlis passed two electoral bills, paving the way for the holding of the Maldives' first multi-party legislative elections. A total of 77 seats were contested in the elections, which were held on 9 May; the DRP won the highest number of seats (28), while the MDP secured 25 seats. Although independent candidates took 13 seats, the predominance of the leading parties in the voting appeared to illustrate the population's willing adoption of a party political system.

In August 2009 a controversial decentralization bill was presented to the People's Majlis, the main proposal of which was the division of the existing 21 administrative districts into seven provinces—each headed by a provincial state minister (appointed by the President) and a council. The measure was opposed by the DRP and the PA on the grounds that it posed a threat to representative democracy and the unitary state. A revised Decentralization Act, which recognized the creation of the seven provinces (but not as administrative units), retained the existing 21 administrative districts and the atoll and island chiefs, and provided for the election of island, atoll and city councils, was approved by the legislature in April 2010 and ratified by the President in May. (As part of the process of devolution, the Ministry of Atolls Development had already been dissolved by the President and its responsibilities divided between numerous smaller regional offices.) In October the Government issued a finalized list of administrative divisions, including 184 islands, 19 atolls and two designated cities—Malé and Addu City (formerly Addu Atoll). Meanwhile, in April Gayoom was replaced as leader of the DRP by Ahmed Thasmeen Ali.

A political crisis arose on 29 June 2010, when the Cabinet of Ministers resigned en masse following threats by the opposition to introduce a parliamentary vote of no confidence against each minister; however, Nasheed and his Vice-President remained in their posts. The Government claimed that it had become impossible to work effectively with the opposition-controlled People's Majlis and that the constant use of blocking tactics by the opposition had made the country virtually ungovernable. On the same day two leading opposition figures, Abdulla Yameen of the PA and Qasim Ibrahim of the JP, were placed under house arrest on suspicion of conspiring to overthrow the Government. On 7 July, with the rift between the Government and the opposition appearing deadlocked, President Mahinda Rajapaksa of Sri Lanka arrived in the Maldives, at the request of Nasheed, to act as a mediator in talks between the two sides. Despite the reinstatement of the Cabinet of Ministers by Nasheed later that day, and the subsequent release from house arrest of Yameen and Ibrahim, the political impasse persisted, with the opposition refusing to recognize the legitimacy of Nasheed's administration and violent protests being staged in Malé by supporters of both sides. The constitutional crisis escalated in August, when the People's Majlis voted against legitimizing a number of interim state institutions, including the Supreme Court, the Civil Service Commission and the Human Rights Commission, all of which had been granted a two-year transition period following the introduction of the new Constitution in August 2008. In protest against the opposition's continuing intransigence, the Attorney-General, Husnu Suood, resigned. However, a few days later the power struggle over the judiciary was resolved when the People's Majlis unanimously voted to appoint a permanent Supreme Court and Chief Justice (as nominated by the President).

None the less, the deadlock over the official recognition of the Cabinet continued, with the opposition insisting that the ministers be endorsed on an individual basis and Nasheed claiming that the approval procedure should be carried out on a 'ceremonial' and collective basis. In November 2010 the People's Majlis voted not to endorse seven of the cabinet ministers appointed by the President and demanded that they resign immediately. Despite protests by the MDP that the legislature's action was unconstitutional, on 9 December the Supreme Court ruled that the rejected ministers (including Dr Ahmed Ali Sawad, who had been nominated as the new Attorney-General in August) should not remain in office: they all resigned two days later. Nasheed

subsequently carried out an extensive cabinet reorganization, including the appointment of two of the rejected ministers as advisers, and, in defiance of the judicial ruling, reappointed Sawad as Attorney-General on 13 December. In March 2011 the People's Majlis endorsed the appointments of a further four ministers, but again refused to approve the nomination of Sawad. Over the following months the President appointed new candidates to several key, disputed Cabinet posts, including a new Attorney-General and the ministers responsible for finance and treasury, defence and foreign affairs. Meanwhile, in February multi-party local council elections were held in the Maldives for the first time: the MDP performed strongly in the city councils, while the DRP won the majority of seats in the atoll and island councils.

During the first few months of 2011 serious rifts within the DRP became increasingly apparent and the party effectively split into two opposing factions—one led by Gayoom and the other by his successor as party leader, Ahmed Thasmeen Ali. In April Gayoom's faction announced the establishment of the Zaeem ('Honorary Leader')-DRP (Z-DRP), claiming that it enjoyed the backing of the vast majority of the 40,000 DRP members. At the end of April anti-Government protesters staged a series of large demonstrations in Malé, provoked by rising commodity prices, which continued for eight days. The Government rejected allegations by the opposition that the police had used excessive force; however, several hundred protesters were arrested and dozens injured in clashes with riot police during the demonstrations.

In September 2011 Gayoom officially resigned from the DRP and established a new party, the Progressive Party of Maldives (PPM), to replace the breakaway Z-DRP. Later that month, in the wake of a number of disagreements regarding government policy (including the MDP's supposedly un-Islamic stance), the religiously conservative AP withdrew from the governing coalition. In December the Minister of Finance and Treasury, Ahmed Inaz, resigned following allegations by the MDP that he had held covert political meetings with Gayoom's half-brother Abdulla Yameen (who had recently left the PA to join Gayoom's PPM).

In December 2011, following a demonstration in Malé organized by a number of religious organizations and political parties in protest against the Government's allegedly un-Islamic policies, the Ministry of Tourism announced plans to close down all luxury spas and massage parlours in the country, following claims by Islamist groups that such premises were being used for prostitution. However, amid concerns that the country's vital tourism industry would be adversely affected by this measure, the Government reversed its decision with immediate effect in January and requested that the Supreme Court clarify the situation by issuing a ruling on such services (as well as on the sale of alcohol and pork in tourist resorts).

The ousting of President Nasheed

Mistrust between the Government and the judiciary fuelled a growing sense of instability within the Maldives from late 2011. In October the MDP arranged a public demonstration against alleged maladministration within the judiciary; the ruling party claimed that many judges, the majority of whom had been appointed during Gayoom's presidency, were not adequately qualified to carry out their duties and were open to excessive influence from members of the former regime. The MDP demonstration provoked strong criticism and counter-demonstrations by the opposition, which claimed that the ruling party was attempting to stifle the independence of the judiciary. In mid-January 2012 the Government ordered the arrest of the Chief Judge of the Criminal Court, Abdulla Mohamed, for alleged corruption and political bias. On the previous day Justice Abdulla had overturned the arrest of Mohamed Jameel Ahmed, the Deputy Leader of the DQP, who had been detained for alleged defamation of the Government. (In November 2011 the Judicial Service Commission—JSC—which regulates the Maldivian judiciary, had ruled that Justice Abdulla was guilty of political bias; however, the ruling had been suspended owing to a legal challenge.) The arrest of Justice Abdulla was criticized as unconstitutional by a number of high-ranking officials, including Fathimath Dhiyana Saeed, the Secretary-General of the South Asian Association for Regional Cooperation (SAARC) and a former Attorney-General of the Maldives, who subsequently resigned from her SAARC post in protest against the Government's action. (Saeed was replaced in the post by another Maldivian, former senior diplomat Ahmed Saleem.)

Hostility regarding the detention of Justice Abdulla, as well as the continual undermining of the Government's Islamic credentials by some opposition politicians, served to incite a wave of increasingly unruly anti-Government demonstrations in Malé in the latter half of January 2012. Finally, on 7 February, following concerted assaults on MDP facilities in the capital by anti-Government protesters and alleged police mutineers, Nasheed resigned from the presidency and transferred power to Vice-President Mohamed Waheed Hassan Manik. On the following day Nasheed claimed that what had taken place was, in effect, a coup, carried out with the compliance of Waheed—a claim that was vehemently denied by the new President. On the same day several thousand MDP supporters, led by Nasheed, marched through Malé to protest against his ousting. Numerous violent clashes broke out as riot police used tear gas and batons against the demonstrators. Security forces were also dispatched to Addu City, where there were reports of further violent incidents.

Shortly after President Waheed assumed power, Justice Abdulla was released from detention. Waheed pledged to form a government of national unity, to uphold the rule of law and to re-establish stability in advance of the scheduled 2013 presidential election. In the weeks that followed Waheed appointed a new Cabinet of Ministers argely comprising representatives of parties opposed to the MDP and included several staunch supporters of Gayoom; the MDP refused to participate in what it termed an'illegitimate' administration). Notably, Mohamed Jameel Ahmed, whose arrest had played a significant part in events leading to the ousting of Nasheed, was appointed Minister of Home Affairs. In an attempt to resolve the political crisis, UN Assistant Secretary-General Oscar Fernandez-Taranco held talks with both Waheed and Nasheed, the latter of whom demanded the holding of early elections. Nasheed was reportedly disappointed by the official recognition of the new Maldivian Government by the authorities in the USA and India. On 21 February President Waheed established a three-member Commission of National Inquiry (CNI—chaired by former Minister of Defence and National Security Ismail Shafeeu, widely described as a Gayoom loyalist) whose task it was to investigate the events surrounding Nasheed's resignation and to judge whether or not they constituted a coup. The MDP criticized the new body as lacking impartiality. At the beginning of March it was announced that a presidential commission established by Nasheed in 2009 to investigate alleged corruption by the former Gayoom regime had been disbanded. Later that month Nasheed was summoned before the Human Rights Commission for questioning regarding his role in the arrest of Justice Abdulla; Nasheed claimed that the Ministry of Home Affairs had advised him that the judge posed a potential threat to national security.

Following victories for the PPM and the JP in parliamentary by-elections in mid-April 2012, it was reported that 44 of the 77 members of the Majlis now supported the Waheed-led coalition Government, with the PPM described as the largest of the pro-Government parties. None the less, the MDP remained the single largest faction in the parliament, with the support of 32 members. However, internal dissension within the MDP became apparent at the end of April when the party's President, Dr Ibrahim Didi, and Vice-President, Alhan Fahmy, were forced to leave the party on a vote of no confidence; the two subsequently joined the JP. In June Nasheed was selected as the MDP's candidate for the forthcoming presidential election.

In April 2012 the Commonwealth Ministerial Action Group (CMAG) issued a statement expressing serious concerns regarding the legality of the recent transfer of presidential power in the Maldives and reiterated its earlier demands for the presidential election, scheduled for the latter half of 2013, to be brought forward to 2012. Furthermore, CMAG questioned the legitimacy of the CNI and urged the Government to revise its composition to include an independent, foreign co-chairman and an MDP nominee; failure to act on these recommendations would elicit 'stronger measures' from the Commonwealth (the Maldives had been suspended from membership of CMAG and placed on its formal investigative agenda since late February). In accordance with CMAG's stipulations, the Government finally accepted (after some 10 rejections) a nominee of Nasheed for the CNI, Ahmed 'Gahaa' Saeed, in early June, having earlier appointed a retired Singaporean judge to join the panel as its co-chairman. In addition, two representatives, one from the UN and the other from the Commonwealth, were appointed to act as advisers to the CNI.

Against the background of fruitless all-party talks instigated by Waheed, the MDP launched a campaign of anti-Government protests in Malé from early July 2012 demanding early elections.

Violent clashes frequently broke out between the demonstrators and the police, and hundreds of protesters were arrested. In mid-July Nasheed, his former Minister of Defence and National Security, Lt Tholhath Ibrahim Kaleyfaanu, and three senior officers of the Maldives National Defence Force were formally charged in connection with the illegal detention of Justice Abdulla in January. Although the MDP had suspended its street protests and indicated its willingness to rejoin political dialogue in early August, the situation deteriorated at the end of the month when Ahmed 'Gahaa' Saeed resigned from the CNI, citing the body's alleged lack of integrity and purpose. On the following day the CNI published its report, which concluded that Nasheed had not been ousted by a coup but had stood down voluntarily and that the transfer of power had been 'legal and constitutional'; however, the report also noted the existence of serious problems with the rule of law and order in the Maldives, including acts of brutality on the part of the police force. Waheed asserted that the findings upheld the legitimacy of his administration and requested that the CMAG remove the Maldives from its human rights watch-list. Flouting court-ordered travel restrictions that prevented him from leaving the capital pending his trial on charges of abuse of power, Nasheed launched an electoral campaign in the southern atolls, and failed to attend his first court hearing in October. Several days later, however, Nasheed was arrested and, following a court appearance in Malé, was released on bail. In order to avoid being arrested as a result of another refusal on his part to attend court proceedings, Nasheed sought refuge in the Indian High Commission in February 2013 (where he remained for 10 days). Despite Indian requests that Nasheed be allowed freely to campaign for the forthcoming presidential election, scheduled for 7 September, the MDP leader was detained by police officers in early March. Nasheed's legal representatives subsequently challenged the legitimacy of the panel of judges assembled to hear the case against the former President; the trial stalled in the High Court following the suspension by the JSC of the Chief Justice of the High Court, on an apparently unrelated matter, in July. Meanwhile, following a fact-finding visit to the Maldives in February 2013, the UN Special Rapporteur on the Independence of Judges and Lawyers published a report in May in which she noted that the trial of Nasheed raised serious concerns regarding the fairness of judicial proceedings in the Maldives.

The 2013 presidential election and the legislative elections of 2014

In February 2013 former President Gayoom ended mounting speculation when he announced that he would not contest the presidential election, and in March Abdulla Yameen was selected as the presidential candidate of the PPM. Also in March the People's Majlis ratified a Political Parties Bill, which stipulated that parties would require a minimum of 10,000 members to qualify for registration with the Elections Commission. It was reported that 11 political parties, including President Waheed's GIP, were thus threatened with dissolution. However, following a legal challenge, the Supreme Court issued an injunction against the dissolution of the parties.

In May 2013 the DRP formed an electoral coalition with the GIP; President Waheed was to be the coalition's presidential candidate with DRP leader Ahmed Thasmeen Ali as his running mate. The AP and the DQP, having earlier pledged to co-operate with the GIP, subsequently formed an electoral coalition with the JP, for whom Qasim Ibrahim was again the presidential candidate. Mohamed Jameel Ahmed was dismissed as Minister of Home Affairs in May, following the announcement that he had defected to the PPM and was to stand as Yameen's running mate; he was replaced by Aishath Bisam in July. In August the Minister of Foreign Affairs, Abdul Samad Abdulla, died while receiving medical treatment in Singapore; Asim Ahmed was awarded the foreign affairs portfolio on an interim basis. Meanwhile, in July former President Nasheed, with his trial on charges of abuse of power mired in procedural issues, was accepted by the Elections Commission as the MDP's presidential candidate. In August the PPM signed an electoral coalition agreement with the Maldives Development Alliance (MDA), which had been established in June 2012 under the leadership of Ahmed Shiyam Mohamed, a prominent businessman and member of the People's Majlis.

At the first round of the presidential election, held on 7 September 2013, Nasheed won 45.5% of the valid votes, while Abdulla Yameen secured 25.4%, Qasim Ibrahim garnered 24.1% and the incumbent President Waheed took just 5.1%.

As no candidate had secured a majority of the vote, a run-off poll was scheduled for 28 September. However, amid allegations of electoral irregularities, including the apparent inclusion of deceased and underage persons on the electoral register, Ibrahim lodged an appeal with the Supreme Court seeking to annul the results of the first round of voting. On 23 September the Supreme Court indefinitely postponed the second ballot, pending a ruling on Ibrahim's appeal. Two subsequent attempts by the Elections Commission to stage the run-off poll were forcibly obstructed by the police, upon the orders of the Supreme Court. On 7 October the Supreme Court formally annulled the first-round results and scheduled a fresh election for 20 October. The President of the Elections Commission, Fuwad Thowfeek, criticized the ruling, which was passed (by four votes to three) despite the election having been deemed free and fair by local and external observers. Following further disputes concerning voter registration, the poll was again postponed, until 9 November. In the event, Nasheed attracted 46.4% of the valid votes, while Yameen and Ibrahim secured 29.4% and 23.1%, respectively. At the subsequent run-off poll, held on 16 November, Yameen emerged victorious with 50.9% of the valid votes, narrowly defeating Nasheed with 48.1%.

Yameen was inaugurated as President, together with Mohamed Jameel Ahmed as Vice-President, on 17 November 2013. Yameen appointed a coalition Cabinet of Ministers, comprising members of the PPM, the JP, the MDA and the AP. Notable new appointments included those of Umar Naseer (nominated by the JP; Yameen's defeated rival in the PPM primary election in March) as Minister of Home Affairs, and Dunya Maumoon (of the PPM; a niece of Yameen) as Minister of Foreign Affairs. Col (Rtd) Mohamed Nazim and Abdulla Jihad were reappointed Minister of Defence and National Security and Minister of Finance and Treasury, respectively; Nazim and Jihad both joined the PPM in December. Meanwhile, in November Ahmed Thasmeen Ali resigned the DRP leadership, and within days announced that he had joined the MDP, together with the deputy leader of the DRP, Rozeyna Adam, and Thasmeen's wife, DRP legislator Visam Ali. Mohamed 'Colonel' Nasheed was subsequently appointed interim leader of the DRP. A further three DRP legislators defected to the JP in late November, reducing the number of parliamentary seats commanded by the party to just three.

The second ever local council elections in the Maldives were held in January 2014. The governing coalition won the majority of seats in the atoll and island councils, while the MDP won the majority in Malé and Addu city councils. In February the Elections Commission dissolved eight political parties with less than 3,000 registered members, including the PA and the DQP, thereby reducing the number of registered political parties in the Maldives to six. Later that month the Supreme Court contended that the dissolution of the parties contravened the injunction that it had issued against the dissolution of political parties in March 2013 (see above), and summoned the President and Vice-President of the Elections Commission, together with two electoral commissioners, to face trial on the charge of violating a court order. The four members of the Commission were also charged with contempt of court, a charge pertaining to public criticism levelled against the Court's annulment of the first round of the legislative election in September 2013. In early March 2014 the Court handed down a six-month gaol sentence, suspended for three years, to President of the Elections Commission Fuwad Thowfeek. (Recently introduced regulations authorized the Supreme Court to initiate proceedings against any individual or organization, as well as serve as prosecutor and judge.) Thowfeek and the Vice-President of the Commission, Ahmed Fayaz Hassan, were both dismissed from their posts. In June it was reported that, on the advice of the Supreme Court, the Elections Commission had agreed to reinstate the dissolved political parties.

Some 302 candidates contested the legislative election, which, despite the vacancies within the Elections Commission, went ahead as planned on 22 March 2014. Under an arrangement agreed upon by the governing coalition prior to the polls, the PPM contested 49 seats, the JP contested 28 and the MDA contested eight. The opposition MDP fielded candidates in all 85 seats in the newly expanded People's Majlis, while the AP and the DRP contested 13 seats and six seats, respectively. Turnout was recorded at 78.1% of the registered electorate. According to final results released by the Elections Commission, the parties of the governing coalition secured a comfortable majority, collectively accounting for 53 seats, with the PPM winning 33 seats, the

JP taking 15 and the MDA securing five. The MDP won 26 seats and the AP attained one, while the DRP failed to secure representation; the five remaining seats were secured by independents. A small number of complaints, including claims of voter intimidation and bribery, were formally lodged, but the poll was generally deemed to have been free and fair. Three of the five elected independent candidates subsequently joined the PPM; following the defection of an elected MDP candidate to the PPM at the end of March, the ruling coalition thus controlled 57 of the 85 seats in the People's Majlis—a two-thirds' majority. (By mid-July it was reported that, in total, four independent members, three members of the MDP and two members of the JP had joined the PPM since the election. In addition, Minister of Housing and Infrastructure Dr Mohamed Muizzu had left the AP to join the MDA.) At an MDP national council meeting convened at the beginning of April to discuss restructuring and reforms in the wake of the party's poor performance in the polls, 'Reeko' Moosa Manik resigned as party Chairman and urged other party leaders to follow suit, attributing the blame for the MDP's electoral losses to Nasheed's alleged mismanagement of the party campaign. However, at the same meeting Nasheed was appointed interim party President (the post having remained vacant since 2012).

Recent developments: President Yameen in power

Tensions quickly emerged between the PPM and its main coalition partner, the JP. In the early months of the administration the JP expressed dissatisfaction with the number of political appointees allocated to the party, accusing the PPM of failing to honour its pre-election promises. In May 2014 the JP was expelled from the ruling coalition, following a dispute regarding party leader Qasim Ibrahim's candidature for the post of parliamentary speaker, in direct opposition to the PPM candidate. Abdulla Maseeh Mohamed of the PPM narrowly defeated Ibrahim to take the Speaker's post; the MDP's Moosa Manik narrowly won the election for the Deputy Speaker post. In the following weeks the Government began to replace JP political appointees, although two senior JP cabinet members, Minister of Economic Development Mohamed Saeed and Minister of Environment and Energy Thoriq Ibrahim, retained their positions by joining the PPM. In July it was reported that the PPM had achieved a simple majority in the People's Majlis (43 seats) with the defection of three further JP members since the split in the coalition.

Meanwhile, in April 2014 the Majlis ratified a new penal code which reintroduced the death penalty for the offence of intentional murder, as judged by the Supreme Court; the UN human rights office was swift to express its concern at this development. At the same time, doubts continued to be expressed regarding judicial independence. In September the Supreme Court initiated proceedings against the Human Rights Commission in relation to a report submitted to the UN Human Rights Council by the UN Special Rapporteur on the Independence of Judges and Lawyers, which called for reform of the Court. In December the Majlis voted with a two-thirds' majority to amend the 2010 Judicature Act so as to reduce the Supreme Court bench to five judges. Within days, under the amended legislation, the Chief Justice, Ahmed Faiz, and a second Supreme Court judge, Muthasim Adnan, were removed in a process that was criticized for its lack of transparency. The Deputy Speaker of the Majlis, Moosa Manik, was expelled from the MDP for allegedly defying party instructions to attend the vote. Meanwhile, in October 2014 the passage of a bill amending the Audit Act was swiftly followed by the dismissal and replacement of the Auditor-General just three years into a seven-year term.

In September 2014 legislation aiming to create jobs and stimulate investment in outlying atolls through the establishment and regulation of nine special economic zones (SEZs) was passed in the Majlis. Opposition (MDP) representatives had tabled more than 180 amendments in total, all of which were rejected. Critics of the bill claimed that it would concentrate too much economic power in the hands of a 17-member administrative board of government appointees, and that the fiscal incentives on offer (including exemptions from import duty and profit taxes) and the relaxation of regulations on recruitment of foreign workers could damage the tourism sector. In early December the Government's ability to prepare for emergencies was called into question when a fire broke out at the Maldives Water and Sewerage Co, causing extensive damage to the sole desalination facility serving the capital, Malé. In response to government appeals, emergency drinking-water supplies were sent by air and sea by the Indian, Chinese and Sri Lankan authorities. In addition, the Chinese Government donated US \$500,000 to expedite repairs at the desalination plant.

International concern over the political situation in the Maldives continued to mount in early 2015. In late January the human rights organization Amnesty International claimed that the Government had failed to address the vast majority of human rights issues identified in a report published in 2011, highlighting judicial independence, the emergence of vigilante religious groups, and the abduction and disappearance in 2014 of a journalist, Ahmed Rilwan, as issues of immediate concern. Also in January 2015 the Minister of Defence and National Security, Col (Rtd) Mohamed Nazim, was dismissed from the Cabinet, following the alleged discovery of unauthorized lethal weapons at his private residence during an investigation by the police; it was claimed that he was planning a coup against President Yameen. Nazim was replaced by Maj.-Gen. (Rtd) Moosa Ali Jaleel, a former chief of the National Defence Force and the incumbent High Commissioner to Pakistan.

In February 2015 the JP leader, Qasim Ibrahim, and former President Mohamed Nasheed, leader of the MDP, announced that they had signed an agreement to 'defend the constitution', citing the recent dismissals of the Auditor-General and the Supreme Court judges as evidence that President Yameen and the PPM were acting in breach of the Constitution. Earlier that month Minister of Home Affairs Naseer had left the JP, attributing his decision to the party's 'new course'; with other resignations during February, the JP now held 10 seats in the Majlis and the MDP 21, with the PPM and the MDA holding a combined 51 seats. On 22 February, however, days before a planned anti-Government protest, Nasheed was rearrested on terrorism charges in relation to the detention of Justice Abdulla Mohamed in January 2012 (see *The ousting of President Nasheed*; the previous case against Nasheed had been dropped just days earlier). Also charged, but not arrested, were former Minister of Defence and National Security Tholhath Ibrahim Kaleyfaanu, former Chief of the Defence Forces Maj.-Gen. Moosa Ali Jaleel (the incumbent defence minister), Ibrahim Didi, an MDP member of parliament, and Col (Rtd) Mohamed Ziyad. On 13 March 2015 Nasheed, who had been detained in police custody without bail for the duration of his trial, was found guilty of arresting and illegally detaining Justice Abdulla, and sentenced to 13 years in prison. The trial itself was condemned by Amnesty International as 'deeply flawed and politically motivated', while the UN High Commissioner for Human Rights, the EU and the Commonwealth, as well as the governments of the USA, the United Kingdom and India all issued statements expressing concern over the apparent lack of due process at the trial. Among the chief concerns raised by critics were the court's refusal to hear evidence from numerous defence witnesses, the use of judges involved in the trial as witnesses for the prosecution, and the insufficient time and information provided to the defence team in order to prepare for the initial trial and to mount an appeal. Members of the MDP national council called for targeted boycotts against pro-government resorts and businesses, and urged Nasheed's supporters to continue attending mass protests in Malé. Separate trial proceedings against each of the other defendants accused of terrorism charges in the Justice Abdulla case commenced in late February.

In early April 2015 Tholhath Ibrahim Kaleyfaanu was convicted on terrorism charges at the Criminal Court for his alleged role in the Justice Abdulla case; the former minister was sentenced to 10 years in prison. Col (Rtd) Ziyad and Minister of Defence Jaleel were acquitted by the court in the same case; proceedings against Ibrahim Didi had been postponed at the beginning of the month. Meanwhile, court hearings in the case against former minister Col (Rtd) Mohamed Nazim commenced in mid-March; at the end of the month Nazim was convicted of the illegal possession and importing of lethal weapons (one pistol, a small quantity of ammunition and an alleged explosive device) and sentenced to 11 years' imprisonment. Nazim's legal team launched an appeal in mid-April, following which the defendant was permitted to travel to Singapore to receive medical treatment. Meanwhile, at the end of March the PPM-dominated People's Majlis approved legislation that cancelled the political party membership of anyone serving a prison sentence; the measure was described by critics of the Government as a further attempt to marginalize opponents of the administration, and Nasheed in particular.

On 1 May 2015 a major opposition rally was held in Malé to protest against the growing authoritarianism of the Yameen Government, and the incarceration and alleged mistreatment of former President Nasheed. The demonstration, which was attended by up to 10,000 people, according to some estimates, erupted into violent clashes between protesters and the security forces. Police were reported to have used tear gas and pepper spray to disperse the demonstrators, and almost 200 people were arrested, among whom were leading members of the main opposition parties, including Sheik Imran Abdulla, President of the AP (the AP had withdrawn its support from the ruling coalition in March), Ali Waheed, Chairperson of the MDP, and Ameen Ibrahim, Deputy Leader of the JP.

Environmental Concerns

Environmental issues have become increasingly important in Maldivian politics, with around 80% of the islands no more than one metre above sea level and thus extremely vulnerable to climate change. The Maldives stressed its serious concern with regard to the threat posed to low-lying island countries by the predicted rise in sea levels caused by heating of the earth's atmosphere as a result of pollution (the greenhouse effect) when it hosted the 13th conference of the UN's Intergovernmental Panel on Climate Change (IPCC, see p. 66) in 1997. In March 2002 the Maldives, Kiribati and Tuvalu threatened to take legal action against the USA for refusing to sign the Kyoto Protocol to the UN's Framework Convention on Climate Change and thus, so they claimed, threatening the very survival of the low-lying island states. At the World Summit on Sustainable Development held in September in Johannesburg, South Africa, President Gayoom demanded urgent action, including the universal ratification and implementation of the Kyoto Protocol, to protect low-lying islands and prevent a global environmental catastrophe. In July 2008 a meeting of experts and environment ministers from the Maldives and other SAARC member countries finalized a five-year plan of action to combat the adverse effects of climate change in the region.

On assuming the presidency in November 2008, Mohamed Nasheed immediately announced government plans to use some of the revenue from the tourism sector to establish a sovereign wealth fund to finance a long-term plan to purchase land abroad should the relocation of the Maldivian population become necessary owing to rising sea levels. In March 2009 Nasheed announced plans to make the Maldives the world's first 'carbon neutral' state (i.e. a zero net contributor to greenhouse gas emissions) within 10 years through the exclusive use of renewable energy sources such as wind, wave and solar power, and through carbon offsetting. In June 2012, in a speech to the UN Conference on Sustainable Development, in Rio de Janeiro, Brazil, President Mohamed Waheed Hassan Manik announced plans for the conversion of the Maldives' territorial waters into the world's largest marine reserve within five years. In October the Maldives Energy Authority announced the imminent launch of a five-year, US \$138m. renewable energy project, the aim of which was that 10 islands would be powered solely by renewable energy and 30% of the electricity supply of 30 other islands would be converted to renewable energy; the project, which was to be funded by the World Bank, the Asian Development Bank (see p. 206) and a number of foreign banks, was expected to generate around 26 MW of electricity. A report published by the World Bank in June 2013 cautioned that, with the Maldives confronting a projected increase in sea levels of between 100 cm and 115 cm by 2090, new technological solutions and international co-operation would be essential to assist the country to adapt to, and mitigate, the impact of climate change.

Foreign Affairs

Regional relations

Since independence the Maldives have fostered close relations (economic, cultural and military) with India. India is a major supplier of economic aid to the islands and has helped in the development of the Maldives' infrastructure, including telecommunications, aviation and health facilities. In 1976 the two countries (together with Sri Lanka) amicably settled their maritime boundary and in 1981 signed a wide-ranging trade agreement. Relations were further strengthened in November 1988 as a result of India's prompt military intervention in the failed coup attempt in the Maldives. The close military ties between the countries (which regularly conduct joint naval exercises in the Indian Ocean) were reinforced by the establishment of a Defence Attaché's Office at the Maldivian High Commission in New Delhi in 2005. In August 2009 the two countries signed an important bilateral defence pact aimed at fortifying the security of the islands. In November 2011 Prime Minister Manmohan Singh became the first foreign head of state to address the People's Majlis. Following President Mohamed Nasheed's resignation in February 2012, India afforded official recognition to the new administration of Mohamed Waheed Hassan Manik. At the same time, India attempted to help to quell the political unrest in the Maldives by dispatching Foreign Secretary Ranjan Mathai to hold conciliatory talks with various Maldivian politicians, including Nasheed and Waheed. In May President Waheed embarked on his first official visit to India, during which he sought to reassure Singh that his Government would adhere to all existing agreements and business arrangements between the two countries. However, bilateral relations were strained in November when Waheed's Government terminated a US $511m. contract signed in 2010 between Nasheed's Government and an Indian-Malaysian consortium to modernize and operate Ibrahim Nasir International Airport for 25 years. In June 2014 an international arbitration tribunal ruled that the agreement was binding and awarded damages to be paid to the consortium; the contract was subsequently awarded to a Chinese company (see below). In July 2013 the Maldives and India, together with Sri Lanka, signed a tripartite maritime security agreement, which included plans for, *inter alia*, co-operation in anti-piracy efforts, the surveillance of the countries' respective exclusive economic zones, and search-and-rescue operations. The countries announced in December that the security troika was to be expanded to include Mauritius and the Seychelles. In January 2014 the new President of the Maldives, Abdulla Yameen, visited India in his first official overseas engagement. The President met with Indian Prime Minister Manmohan Singh, and both leaders pledged their commitment to boosting co-operation in trade and development, as well as easing bilateral visa restrictions. At the end of May Yameen attended the inauguration ceremony of India's new Prime Minister, Narendra Modi, holding brief discussions with the new premier. In 2009 India and the Maldives reached agreement on the installation of 10 surveillance stations in the Maldives that would be equipped with navigational military radars linked to the Indian coastal command, as part of an Indian-led coastal surveillance radar system in the Indian Ocean region. However, completion of the radar systems in the Maldives were subsequently delayed by disagreements over technical details, and by early 2015 were not yet operational. Moreover, in response to the trial and imprisonment of former President Mohamed Nasheed, Modi cancelled a planned visit to the Maldives as part of a tour of Indian Ocean nations in March 2015.

Relations between the Maldives and Sri Lanka have traditionally been very amicable. The two countries established diplomatic relations in 1965 and have nurtured close co-operation in many fields, including trade, tourism, energy, fisheries and telecommunications. An open visa policy exists between the two countries. In August 2011 the Sri Lankan Government granted a US $10m. import credit to the Maldives, which, in turn, pledged to take measures to remove more customs duties on goods imported from Sri Lanka. During an official visit to Sri Lanka by President Abdulla Yameen in January 2014, three bilateral agreements were signed, including a pact intended to strengthen co-operation in tackling transnational crime. In June Sri Lankan President Mahinda Rajapaksa paid a reciprocal state visit to the Maldives. Talks were held on health co-operation; strengthening co-operation between the Board of Investment of Sri Lanka and the Maldivian Ministry of Economic Development; and maritime search and rescue.

In recent years the People's Republic of China has cultivated strong relations with the Maldives. The two countries signed a defence agreement in the late 1990s, providing for military co-operation and arms supplies, but China's aim of establishing a military base on the Maldives was not achieved. Economic ties between the two nations have become more important over the last decade or so, with the volume of bilateral trade increasing, substantial Chinese business investment in the islands' infrastructure and large numbers of Chinese tourists visiting the Maldives. The number of Chinese visitors to the Maldives increased at an average annual rate of 48% in 2008–12; some 30% of total visitor arrivals to the Maldives in 2013 were from the People's Republic. Meanwhile, in November 2011 China became the first non-SAARC country to open an embassy in Malé. Following an official visit to China by Waheed in September 2012, the Maldivian President confirmed that China had pledged US $500m. in loans to the Maldives. In September 2014 Chinese President Xi Jinping made a landmark state visit to the Maldives during which the two countries pledged to boost co-operation in

economic and security affairs. The Maldivian authorities expressed their willingness to participate in Chinese plans to create a 21st-century maritime 'silk road'—an advanced trade network linking southern China with South-east Asia, India, East Africa and the Mediterranean. Infrastructure projects in the tourism sector were also discussed during the visit; a preliminary contract agreement was signed with a Beijing company for the expansion and upgrading of Malé's Ibrahim Nasir International Airport (previously contracted to an Indian-Malaysian consortium—see above), and China was also to begin viability studies on a project to build a bridge between Hulhumalé and Malé, to enable swifter connections between the capital and the airport.

In June 2013 the US authorities confirmed that discussions with the Maldivian Government concerning a Status of Forces Agreement had taken place, but insisted that the agreement would only cover military co-operation and support and that there were no plans for a permanent US military presence in the Maldives.

CONSTITUTION AND GOVERNMENT

On 7 August 2008 the President ratified a new 301-article Constitution, which replaced the 1998 Constitution and introduced a directly elected presidency and a democratic system of multi-party legislative elections. Legislative authority is vested in the People's Majlis. The People's Majlis consists of 85 members elected from Malé, Addu City and the 19 administrative atolls for five years by universal adult suffrage. Executive power is vested in the President, who is elected directly by the people, with more than 50% of the vote, for a period of five years. The President (who is not permitted to serve for more than two terms) governs with the assistance of an appointed Cabinet of Ministers (including a Vice-President, who is nominated by the President), which is responsible to the People's Majlis. The country has 21 administrative districts (19 atolls, the capital, Malé, and Addu City), which are grouped into seven provinces.

REGIONAL AND INTERNATIONAL CO-OPERATION

The Maldives is a member of the Asian Development Bank (ADB, see p. 206) and a founder member of the South Asian Association for Regional Cooperation (SAARC, see p. 417), which was formally constituted in December 1985. The country is also a member of the Colombo Plan (see p. 445), which seeks to improve regional co-operation, and became a full member of the Commonwealth (see p. 234) in 1985.

Having joined the UN in 1965, the Maldives is a member of the UN Economic and Social Commission for Asia and the Pacific (ESCAP, see p. 30). As a contracting party to the General Agreement on Tariffs and Trade (GATT), the Maldives became a member of the World Trade Organization (WTO, see p. 431) on its establishment in 1995. The country also participates in the Organization of Islamic Cooperation (OIC, see p. 401) and the Alliance of Small Island States (see p. 459).

ECONOMIC AFFAIRS

In 2013, according to estimates by the World Bank, the Maldives' gross national income (GNI), measured at average 2011–13 prices, was US $1,934m., equivalent to $5,600 per head (or $9,890 per head on an international purchasing-power parity basis). During 2004–13, it was estimated, the population increased at an average annual rate of 1.9%, while gross domestic product (GDP) per head grew, in real terms, by an average of 3.2% per year over the same period. Overall GDP increased, in real terms, at an average annual rate of 5.1% in 2004–13; GDP grew by 3.7% in 2013.

Agriculture, mining (mostly for coral and sand) and fishing contributed 3.9% of GDP in 2013; of this, the primary fishing sector alone accounted for 1.8%. According to FAO estimates, about 12.2% of the total labour force were engaged in the agricultural and fishing sector at mid-2015. In 2013 revenue from exports of marine products totalled US $161.3m., thus accounting for 96.9% of total export earnings. Small quantities of various fruits, vegetables and cereals are produced, but virtually all principal staple foods have to be imported. As a result of saltwater intrusion caused by the Indian Ocean tsunami of December 2004, a significant amount of cultivable land was ruined. The dominant agricultural activity (not including fishing) in the Maldives is coconut production. The GDP of the agriculture, mining and fisheries sector decreased, in real terms, at an average annual rate of 0.7% in 2004–13; real agricultural GDP increased by 1.7% in 2013.

Industry (including manufacturing, construction and utilities) contributed 14.5% of GDP in 2013, and employed 25.4% of the working population at the March 2006 census. Industrial GDP increased, in real terms, at an average annual rate of 3.9% in 2004–13; sectoral growth was 1.2% in 2012, but decreased by 1.2% in 2013.

The manufacturing sector contributed 5.7% of GDP in 2013, and employed 18.3% of the working population at the March 2006 census. There are only a small number of 'modern' manufacturing enterprises in the Maldives, including fish-canning, garment-making and soft-drink bottling. Although cottage industries (such as the weaving of coir yarn and boat-building) employ nearly one-quarter of the total labour force, there is little scope for expansion, owing to the limited size of the domestic market. Because of its lack of manufacturing industries, the Maldives has to import most essential consumer and capital goods. From the late 1980s traditional handicrafts, such as lacquer work and shell craft, revived as a result of the expansion of the tourism sector. Manufacturing GDP decreased, in real terms, at an average annual rate of 0.7% in 2004–13; sectoral GDP grew by 4.6% in 2012, but declined by 5.3% in 2013.

Construction contributed 7.5% of GDP in 2013, and employed 5.6% of the working population at the March 2006 census. Construction GDP increased, in real terms, at an average annual rate of 4.6% in 2004–13; the sector decreased by 2.9% in 2013.

Energy is derived principally from petroleum, and imports of mineral fuels and oils comprised 29.0% of the cost of imports in 2013. Owing to a surge in commercial activities and a significant increase in construction projects in Malé, demand for electricity in the capital grew rapidly in the late 1980s and early 1990s. Accordingly, plans were formulated to augment the generating capacity of the power station in Malé and to improve the distribution network. By 2004 a total of 21 inhabited islands had been provided with electricity. In 2006 the ADB supplied a loan of US $8m. to enable the electrification of a further 20 or so islands. In recent years considerable focus has been placed on the development of renewable energy sources in order to reduce the environmental impact of tourism and the islands' reliance on oil imports.

Following the decline of the shipping industry in the 1980s, tourism gained in importance as an economic sector, and by 1989 it had overtaken the fishing industry as the Maldives' largest source of foreign exchange. The tourism sector recovered well and surprisingly swiftly from the effects of the 2004 tsunami, by the end of 2005 all of the resorts affected by the disaster had reopened. Tourism revenue amounted to US $2,031m. in 2013. In 2013 tourist arrivals increased by 17.4% year-on-year to reach a record high of 1,125,202, and arrivals grew by a further 7.1% in 2014 to reach 1,204,857. The GDP of the tourism sector increased, in real terms, at an average annual rate of 3.5% in 2004–13. The services sector as a whole contributed 81.6% of GDP in 2013, and employed 62.7% of the labour force at the March 2006 census. The GDP of the services sector increased, in real terms, at an average of 5.5% per year in 2004–13; sectoral growth was 4.7% in 2013.

In 2013 the Maldives recorded a visible merchandise trade deficit of US $1,372.0m., and there was a deficit of $176.1m. on the current account of the balance of payments. In 2013 the principal sources of imports were the United Arab Emirates and Singapore (accounting for 28.3% and 16.2% of the total, respectively); other major providers were India, Sri Lanka, Malaysia and Thailand. In that year the principal market for exports was Thailand (accounting for 37.1% of the total); other major purchasers were France, Sri Lanka, the United Kingdom, Germany and Italy. The principal exports were marine products (tuna being the largest export commodity). The principal imports were mineral products, food products, wood, metal and cement, transport equipment, and machinery and mechanical appliances.

In the aftermath of the 2004 tsunami the Maldives received a significant amount of international aid, in the form of grants and concessional loans, principally from the UN, the ADB, the World Bank and Japan (which has traditionally been the Maldives' largest aid donor). According to government figures, foreign financing rose by 53.3% in 2011, compared with the previous year, to reach an estimated 2,013.8m. rufiyaa, and by 11.0% in 2012 to total an estimated 2,365.5m. rufiyaa; foreign grants and loans totalled an estimated 1,861.1m. rufiyaa in 2013. In 2014, in terms of central government finance, there was an estimated fiscal deficit of 1,478.5m. rufiyaa. In 2013, according to the ADB, the overall fiscal deficit of the central Government amounted to the equivalent of 4.7% of GDP. The Maldives' total external debt was US $800m. at the end of 2013. In that year the cost of servicing long-term public and publicly guaranteed debt and repayments to the IMF was equivalent to 2.9% of the value of exports of goods, services and income (excluding workers' remittances). According to the International Labour Organization (ILO, see p. 139), during 2004–12 the average annual rate of inflation was 7.3%. Owing to a sharp rise in global commodity prices (notably petroleum and food), consumer prices have increased substantially in recent years, with a rise of 10.9% in 2012; however, inflation moderated significantly in 2013, to average 4.0%, according to ADB figures. According to 2009/10 Household Income and Expenditure Survey, 11.7% of the total labour force was unemployed at that time (compared with around 2% in 2000).

Partly as a result of the global financial crisis, GDP contracted by 3.6% in the Maldives in 2009. According to ADB figures, GDP grew by 7.1% in 2010 and by 6.5% in 2011, fuelled by intensive development in the tourism sector, aided by private sector finance. In January 2011 the UN-designated status of the Maldives was upgraded from that of 'least developed country' to 'middle-income country'; however, the level of external donor assistance remains relatively high, and as early as 2012 the UN's Committee for Development Policy noted that the prevailing political developments were likely to suppress growth over the next few years. The Maldives has a small, open economy which is vulnerable to changes in petroleum prices worldwide, since it lacks mineral resources; its agricultural sector has little scope for expansion; and its physical geography puts it at risk of natural disasters and environmental hazards. Fiscal consolidation and reform, supported by both the ADB and the IMF, have been major priorities in recent years, as the country has sought to address its persistent fiscal deficit (which amounted to 29% of GDP in 2009). Taxation reforms introduced during 2011–13 (including a tourism goods and services tax, a general goods and services tax and a business profit tax) were supported by a new three-year agreement with the IMF, signed in May 2011. Increased taxation revenue from 2011, combined with a curb on expenditure (including the lowering of public sector wages), helped to narrow the fiscal deficit to 4.7% of GDP by 2013. In an effort to further increase revenue, the rate of the tourism goods and services tax was increased from 8% to 12% from November 2014; the introduction of a personal income tax has also been under parliamentary consideration since 2011. In 2012, amid political upheaval and unrest, GDP growth decreased to just 1.3%, according to the ADB. Meanwhile, government debt was beginning to soar, with the IMF estimating a public debt-to-GDP ratio in excess of 75% for 2012. Fiscal responsibility legislation approved by the parliament in April 2013 was to set limits on government borrowing, so that the level of public debt would be brought below 60% of GDP from 2014; however, according to the IMF, reporting in March 2015, debt in 2014 remained around 75% of GDP. According to the IMF, GDP increased at a rate of 4.7% in 2013, bolstered by a robust performance in the tourism sector. GDP growth was projected by the IMF to maintain momentum in 2014 at around 5.0%, mainly as a result of a rapid expansion in tourist arrivals from Asian markets. Falling global oil and food prices during 2014 meant that the current account deficit also declined, to around 8.4% of GDP in that year.

PUBLIC HOLIDAYS

2016: 1 January (New Year's Day), 12 January (Day Maldives Embraced Islam), 1 May (Labour Day), 6 June* (Ramadan begins), 6 July* (Id al-Fitr, end of Ramadan), 26 July (Independence Day), 12 September* (Id al-Adha, Feast of the Sacrifice), 2 October* (Islamic New Year), 3 November (Victory Day), 11 November (Republic Day), 1 December (National Day), 11 December* (Birth of the Prophet Muhammad).

* These holidays are dependent on the Islamic lunar calendar and may vary by one or two days from the dates given.

Statistical Survey

Source (unless otherwise stated): Department of National Planning, Ministry of Finance and Treasury, Ameenee Magu, Malé 20-379; tel. 3349200; fax 3327351; e-mail stat@planning.gov.mv; internet planning.gov.mv.

AREA AND POPULATION

Area: 298 sq km (115 sq miles).

Population: 298,968 at census of 21–28 March 2006; 341,256 (males 173,172, females 168,084) at census of 20–27 September 2014.

Density (at 2014 census): 1,145.2 per sq km.

Population by Age and Sex (official estimates at mid-2014): *0–14 years:* 89,307 (males 45,401, females 43,906); *15–64 years:* 236,149 (males 118,469, females 117,680); *65 years and over:* 16,392 (males 8,705, females 7,687); *Total* 341,848 (males 172,575, females 169,273). Note: Estimates not adjusted to take account of results of 2014 census.

Administrative Divisions (population, 2014 census, preliminary): *Capital City:* Malé 133,019. *Atolls:* North Thiladhunmathi 12,721; South Thiladhunmathi 18,284; North Miladhunmadulu 12,135; South Miladhunmadulu 10,513; North Maalhosmadulu 14,865; South Maalhosmadulu 8,860; Faadhippolhu 7,905; Malé 11,315; North Ari 5,556; South Ari 8,111; Felidhe 1,567; Mulakatholhu 4,703; North Nilandhe 4,044; South Nilandhe 5,356; Kolhumadulu 8,945; Hadhdhunmathi 11,858; North Huvadhu 8,427; South Huvadhu 11,663; Gnaviyani 8,055; Addu 19,712.

Births, Marriages and Deaths (2012): Registered live births 7,431 (birth rate 22.0 per 1,000); Marriages 5,699 (marriage rate 18.5 per 1,000); Registered deaths 1,135 (death rate 3.0 per 1,000).

Life Expectancy (years at birth): 77.6 (males 76.5; females 78.7) in 2012. Source: World Bank, World Development Indicators database.

Economically Active Population (persons aged 12 years and over, 2006 census): Agriculture, hunting and forestry 4,236; Fishing 8,388; Mining and quarrying 339; Manufacturing 19,259; Electricity, gas and water 1,229; Construction 5,930; Wholesale and retail trade and repairs 11,711; Restaurants and hotels 12,090; Transport, storage and communications 7,098; Financing, insurance, real estate and business services 1,738; Public administration and defence 15,949; Education 9,872; Health and social work 4,182; Other community, social and personal service activities 3,248; Extraterritorial organizations and bodies 216; Activities not adequately defined 4,746; *Total employed* 110,231 (males 69,701, females 40,530); Unemployed 18,605; *Total labour force* 128,836. *Mid-2015* (estimates in '000): Agriculture, etc. 22; Total labour force 181 (Source: FAO).

HEALTH AND WELFARE
Key Indicators

Total Fertility Rate (children per woman, 2012): 2.3.

Under-5 Mortality Rate (per 1,000 live births, 2012): 11.

HIV/AIDS (% of persons aged 15–49, 2013): <0.1.

Physicians (per 1,000 head, 2010): 1.41.

Hospital Beds (per 1,000 head, 2009): 4.3.

Health Expenditure (2011): US $ per head (PPP): 707.

Health Expenditure (2011): % of GDP: 8.1.

Health Expenditure (2011): public (% of total): 44.4.

Access to Water (% of persons, 2012): 99.

Access to Sanitation (% of persons, 2012): 99.

Total Carbon Dioxide Emissions ('000 metric tons, 2010): 1,074.4.

Carbon Dioxide Emissions Per Head (metric tons, 2010): 3.3.

Human Development Index (2013): ranking: 103.

Human Development Index (2013): value: 0.698.

For sources and definitions, see explanatory note on p. vi.

AGRICULTURE, ETC.

Principal Crops (production in long-term leased islands*, metric tons, 2007 unless otherwise indicated): Coconuts 94.4; Tender coconuts 116.2; Aubergines 31.7; Cucumbers 48.6; Pumpkins 48.4; Bitter gourds 4.4 (2006); Ridged peppers 63.6; Papayas 631.1; Watermelons 395.7; Bananas 499. *2013:* Bananas 154.0; Coconuts 564.8; Papayas 306.5 (Source: FAO).
* Comprising the atolls of North Thiladhunmathi, South Thiladhunmathi, North Miladhunmadulu, South Ari, Mulakatholhu, North Nilandhe, Kolhumadulu and Hadhdhunmathi.

Sea Fishing ('000 metric tons, 2012): Total catch 120.0 (Skipjack tuna—Oceanic skipjack 53.4; Yellowfin tuna 44.3). Source: FAO.

INDUSTRY

Selected Products (metric tons, 2013): Frozen fish 44,656.0 (Skipjack 23,293.2); Salted or dried fish 1,906.6; Canned fish 2,354.2.

Electric Energy (million kWh): 246.8 in 2010; 264.7 in 2011; 287.2 in 2012.

FINANCE

Currency and Exchange Rates: 100 laari (larees) = 1 rufiyaa (Maldivian rupee). *Sterling, Dollar and Euro Equivalents* (31 December 2014): £1 sterling = 24.036 rufiyaa; US $1 = 15.400 rufiyaa; €1 = 18.697 rufiyaa; 1,000 rufiyaa = £41.60 = $64.94 = €53.48. *Average Exchange Rate* (rufiyaa per US dollar): 15.365 in 2012; 15.367 in 2013, 15.380 in 2014. Note: Since July 2001 the mid-point rate of exchange has been fixed at US $1 = 12.85 rufiyaa.

Budget (central government finance, million rufiyaa, 2010): *Revenue:* Tax revenue 3,695.9 (Import duty 2,091.3); Other current revenue 4,302.9 (Resort lease rents 2,567.4); Capital revenue 1,363.3; Grants 304.2; Total 9,666.3. *Expenditure:* General administration of public services 2,031.1; Defence 561.7; Public order and internal security 1,046.5; Environmental protection 181.1; Education 2,006.3; Health 838.5; Social security and welfare 743.0; Community programmes 1,593.6; Economic services 920.8 (Agriculture and fishing 124.6, Trade and industry 116.0, Electricity, gas and water 104.6, Transport and communications 469.4, Tourism 106.2); Interest on public debt 329.7; Net lending –13.0; Total 10,239.3 (Current 8,216.9, Capital and net lending 2,022.4). *2013* (estimates): Total revenue and grants 11,735.8 (Current revenue 11,419.4, Capital revenue 108.0, Grants 208.3); Total expenditure and net lending 13,393.7 (Current expenditure 11,379.8, Capital expenditure 2,132.2, Net lending –118.2). *2014* (estimates): Total revenue and grants 14,907.2 (Current revenue 14,366.7, Capital revenue 125.9, Grants 414.6); Total expenditure and net lending 16,385.7 (Current expenditure 13,549.7, Capital expenditure 2,938.5, Net lending –102.5). *2015* (budget figures): Total revenue and grants 21,268.9 (Current revenue 19,298.2, Capital revenue 497.7, Grants 1,473.1); Total expenditure and net lending 22,868.1 (Current expenditure 15,782.5, Capital expenditure 7,062.5, Net lending 23.1).

International Reserves (excl. gold, US $ million at 31 December 2013): IMF special drawing rights 10.50; Reserve position in IMF 3.09; Foreign exchange 368.30; *Total* 381.89. Source: IMF, *International Financial Statistics.*

Money Supply (million rufiyaa at 31 December 2013): Currency outside depository corporations 2,801.89; Transferable deposits 16,684.84; Other deposits 4,189.08; *Broad money* 23,675.81. Source: IMF, *International Financial Statistics.*

Cost of Living (Consumer Price Index; base: 2005 = 100): All items 167.2 in 2011; 177.3 in 2012; 182.1 in 2013. Source: IMF, *International Financial Statistics.*

Gross Value Added in Basic Prices (million rufiyaa at current prices, 2013, provisional): Agriculture (excl. fishing) and mining 778.6; Fishing and fisheries 662.8; Manufacturing 2,106.8; Electricity and water supply 497.2; Construction 2,762.2; Wholesale and retail trade 1,620.9; Transport and communications 4,715.5; Finance, real estate and business services 4,477.6; Tourism 10,817.8; Public administration 5,645.0; Education, health and social services 2,866.1; *Sub-total* 36,950.5; Financial intermediation services indirectly measured –1,609.5; *Gross value added in basic prices* 35,341.0.

Balance of Payments (US $ million, 2013): Exports of goods 331.0; Imports of goods. –1,703.0; *Balance on goods* –1,372.0; Exports of services 2,504.1; Imports of services –652.5; *Balance on goods and services* 479.6; Primary income received 5.2; Primary income paid –374.9; *Balance on goods, services and primary income* 109.9; Secondary income received 3.8; Secondary income paid –289.8; *Current balance* –176.1; Capital account (net) 9.8; Direct investment liabilities 360.8; Portfolio investment liabilities –53.3; Other investment assets –88.2; Other investment liabilities –86.6; Net errors and omissions 102.9; *Reserves and related items* 69.2. Source: IMF, *International Financial Statistics.*

EXTERNAL TRADE

Principal Commodities (US $ million, 2013): *Imports c.i.f.:* Food products 378.9 (Vegetables 61.4; Meat, fish and seafood 78.4;

Beverages and confectioneries 74.2); Furniture, fixtures and fittings 64.9); Petroleum products 503.2 (Diesel fuel 297.0; Aviation fuel 134.3); Transport equipment 120.5; Wood, metal and cement 136.4; Machinery and mechanical appliances 89.8; Electrical and electronic equipment 72.7; Total (incl. others) 1,733.4. *Exports f.o.b.:* Marine products 161.3 (Fresh, chilled or frozen tuna 133.3; Canned or pouched fish 16.5); Total (incl. others) 166.5.

Principal Trading Partners (US $ million, 2013): *Imports:* Australia 32.4; China, People's Republic 81.5; France 34.2; Germany 30.0; India 154.0; Malaysia 85.2; Singapore 281.0; Sri Lanka 101.8; Thailand 86.0; United Arab Emirates 491.4; USA 30.2; Total (incl. others) 1,733.4. *Exports:* France 22.5; Germany 10.0; India 2.5; Italy 8.2; Japan 5.1; Sri Lanka 9.5; Taiwan 2.0; Thailand 61.7; United Kingdom 9.1; USA 4.9; Total (incl. others) 166.5.

TRANSPORT

Road Traffic (motor vehicles in use at 31 December 2012): Passenger cars 3,708; Buses and coaches 132; Lorries and vans 4,145; Motorcycles and mopeds 46,672.

Shipping: *Flag Registered Fleet* (at 31 December 2014): Vessels 61; Total displacement 49,006 grt. Source: Lloyd's List Intelligence (www.lloydslistintelligence.com).

Civil Aviation (traffic at Malé International Airport, 2012): *International Flights:* Arrivals 1,165,695; Departures 1,181,635. *Domestic Flights:* Arrivals 398,159; Departures 398,174.

TOURISM

Tourist Arrivals: 931,333 in 2011; 958,027 in 2012; 1,125,202 in 2013.

Foreign Visitors by Country of Nationality (2013): China, People's Republic 331,719; France 54,328; Germany 93,598; India 38,014; Italy 57,854; Japan 39,463; Russia 76,479; Switzerland 34,102; United Kingdom 85,869; Total (incl. others) 1,125,202.

Tourism Receipts (US $ million): 1,868 in 2011; 1,877 in 2012; 2,031 in 2013 (provisional). Source: World Tourism Organization.

COMMUNICATIONS MEDIA

Telephones (main lines in use): 22,557 in 2013.

Mobile Cellular Telephones: 625,161 in 2013.

Internet Subscribers (incl. mobile internet customers): 87,700 in 2012.

Broadband Subscribers: 20,140 in 2013.

Sources: Telecommunications Authority of Maldives, Malé; International Telecommunication Union.

EDUCATION

Schools (2013): 448 (government 205, community 120, private 123). Source: Ministry of Education.

Teachers (2013): Pre-primary 1,164; Primary 3,411; Lower secondary 3,081; Upper secondary 567. Source: Ministry of Education.

Pupils (2013): Pre-primary 22,480 (males 11,364, females 11,116); Primary 39,408 (males 20,337, females 19,071); Lower secondary 19,876 (males 10,249, females 9,627); Upper secondary 4,138 (males 1,826, females 2,312); Special needs 195 (males 113, females 82). Source: Ministry of Education.

Maldives College of Higher Education: Academic staff 138 (2003); Students 4,388 (2007). Source: Maldives College of Higher Education.

Pupil-Teacher Ratio (primary education, UNESCO estimate): 11.4 in 2011/12 (Source: UNESCO Institute for Statistics).

Adult Literacy Rate (UNESCO estimates): 98.4% (males 98.4%; females 98.4%) in 2006 (Source: UNESCO Institute for Statistics).

Directory

The Government

HEAD OF STATE

President: ADDULLA YAMEEN ABDUL GAYOOM (took office 17 November 2013).

CABINET OF MINISTERS
(May 2015)

A coalition of the Progressive Party of Maldives (PPM) and the Maldives Development Alliance (MDA).

Vice-President: MOHAMED JAMEEL AHMED.

Minister of Home Affairs: UMAR NASEER.

Minister of Finance and Treasury: ABDULLA JIHAD.

Minister of Education: AISHATH SHIHAM (PPM).

Minister of Health: AHMED ZUHOOR.

Minister of Foreign Affairs: DUNYA MAUMOON (PPM).

Minister of Defence and National Security: Maj.-Gen. (Rtd) MOOSA ALI JALEEL.

Minister of Fisheries and Agriculture: MOHAMED SHAINEE.

Minister of Tourism: AHMED ADHEEB ABDUL GHAFOOR (PPM).

Minister of Economic Development: MOHAMED SAEED (PPM).

Minister of Housing and Infrastructure: Dr MOHAMED MUIZZU (MDA).

Minister of Youth and Sports: MOHAMED MALEEH JAMAL (PPM).

Minister of Islamic Affairs: Dr AHMED ZIYAD.

Minister of Environment and Energy: THORIQ IBRAHIM (PPM).

Ministers at the President's Office: ABDULLA AMEEN, MOHAMED HUSSAIN SHAREEF.

Attorney-General: Uz MOHAMED ANIL.

MINISTRIES

President's Office: Boduthakurufaanu Magu, Malé 20-113; tel. 3320701; fax 3325500; e-mail info@presidencymaldives.gov.mv; internet www.presidencymaldives.gov.mv.

Ministry of Defence and National Security: Ameer Ahmed Magu, Malé 20-126; tel. 3322601; fax 3325525; e-mail admin@defence.gov.mv; internet www.defence.gov.mv.

Ministry of Economic Development: Boduthakurufaanu Magu, Malé 20-125, tel. 3323668; fax 3323840; e-mail info@trade.gov.mv; internet www.trade.gov.mv.

Ministry of Education: Velaanaage, 8–9 Floors, Ameer Ahmed Magu, Malé 20-096; tel. 3333262; fax 3321201; e-mail admin@moe.gov.mv; internet www.moe.gov.mv.

Ministry of Environment and Energy: Green Bldg, Handhuvaree Hingun, Maafannu, Malé 20-392; tel. 3018300; fax 3018301; e-mail secretariat@environment.gov.mv; internet www.environment.gov.mv.

Ministry of Finance and Treasury: Ameenee Magu, Blk 379, Malé 20-379; tel. 3349200; fax 3324432; e-mail admin@finance.gov.mv; internet www.finance.gov.mv.

Ministry of Fisheries and Agriculture: 7th Floor, Ameer Ahmed Magu, Malé 20-125; tel. 3322625; fax 3326558; e-mail info@fishagri.gov.mv; internet www.fishagri.gov.mv.

Ministry of Foreign Affairs: Henveiru, Blk 77, Boduthakurufaanu Magu, Malé 20-077; tel. 3323400; fax 3323841; e-mail info@foreign.gov.mv; internet www.foreign.gov.mv.

Ministry of Health: Ameenee Magu, Machangolhi, Malé 20-379; tel. 3328887; fax 3328889; e-mail mohf@health.gov.mv; internet www.health.gov.mv.

Ministry of Home Affairs: Velaanaage Bldg, 10th Floor, Ameer Ahmed Magu, Malé 20-096; tel. 3321752; fax 3324739; e-mail info@homeaffairs.gov.mv; internet www.homeaffairs.gov.mv.

Ministry of Housing and Infrastructure: Ameenee Magu, Maafannu, Malé 20-392; tel. 3004300; fax 3004301; e-mail secretariat@housing.gov.mv; internet www.housing.gov.mv.

Ministry of Islamic Affairs: Islamic Centre, Blk 77, Medhuziyaaraimagu, Malé 20-156; tel. 3323623; fax 3315161; e-mail info@islamicaffairs.gov.mv; internet www.islamicaffairs.gov.mv.

Department of Judicial Administration: Theemuge, Aabruzu, Malé 20-208; tel. 3322303; fax 3325447; e-mail admin@judiciary.gov.mv; internet justice.gov.mv.

Ministry of Law and Gender: Malé.

Ministry of Tourism: Velaanaage, 5th Floor, Ameer Ahmed Magu, Malé 20-096; tel. 3323224; fax 3322512; e-mail info@tourism.gov.mv; internet www.tourism.gov.mv.

Ministry of Youth and Sports: Haveeree Hingun, Maafanu, Malé 20-210; tel. 3347300; fax 3327162; e-mail info@youth.gov.mv; internet www.youth.gov.mv.

President

Presidential Election, First Ballot, 9 November 2013

Candidates	Votes	% of votes
Mohamed Nasheed (Maldivian Democratic Party)	96,764	46.4
Abdulla Yameen Abdul Gayoom (Progressive Party of Maldives)	61,278	29.4
Qasim Ibrahim (Jumhooree Party)	48,131	23.1
Invalid or blank votes	2,331	1.1
Total	208,504	100.0

Presidential Election, Second Ballot, 16 November 2013

Candidates	Votes	% of votes
Abdulla Yameen Abdul Gayoom (Progressive Party of Maldives)	111,203	50.9
Mohamed Nasheed (Maldivian Democratic Party)	105,181	48.1
Other (invalid)	2,237	1.0
Total	218,621	100.0

Legislature

PEOPLE'S MAJLIS

The People's Majlis (People's Council) comprises members elected by the people of Malé and each of the 20 atolls (for a five-year term).

People's Majlis: Malé; tel. 3322617; fax 3324104; e-mail admin@majlis.gov.mv; internet www.majlis.gov.mv.

Speaker: Abdulla Maseeh Mohamed.

Election, 22 March 2014

Party	Seats
Progressive Party of Maldives (PPM)*	33
Maldivian Democratic Party (MDP)	26
Jumhooree Party (JP)*	15
Maldives Development Alliance (MDA)*	5
Adhaalath Party (AP)	1
Independents	5
Total	85

* Members of the Progressive Coalition.

Election Commission

Elections Commission of Maldives: Port Complex Bldg, 5th Floor, Hilaalee Magu, Malé; tel. 3322241; fax 3323997; e-mail info@elections.gov.mv; internet www.elections.gov.mv; f. 1998; 5-mem. independent body nominated and appointed by People's Majlis; Pres. Ahmed Sulaiman; Sec.-Gen. Ahmed Ali; Vice-Pres. Amjad Mustafa; Commrs Mohamed Shakeel, Ismail Habeeb Abdul Raheem, Ahmed Akram.

Political Organizations

Adhaalath Party (AP) (Justice Party): Medhuge, 3rd Floor, Medhu Ziyaarai Magu, Malé; tel. and fax 3342671; e-mail admin@adhaalath.org.mv; internet www.adhaalath.org.mv; f. 2005; Islamic; Pres. Sheikh Imran Abdulla.

Dhivehi Rayyithunge Party (DRP) (Maldivian People's Party): Irufa, Faashanaakilege Magu, Galolhu, Malé; tel. 3320456; fax 3344774; e-mail info@drp.mv; internet www.rayyithun.org; f. 2005; in 2011 the founder of the DRP, former President of the Maldives Maumoon Abdul Gayoom, and his supporters split from the party and launched the Progressive Party of Maldives; Interim Leader Mohamed 'Kaanal' Nasheed; Sec.-Gen. Adam Haleem Ibrahim; 22,500 mems (Feb. 2013).

Gaumee Itthihaad (GIP) (National Unity Party): 1st Floor, Jawahiru Vadhee, Orchid Magu, Malé; tel. 3304002; fax 3308036; e-mail info@gip.org.mv; internet gipmaldives.com; f. 2008; Chair. Dr Mohamed Waheed Hassan Manik.

Jumhooree Party (JP) (Republican Party): M. Chan'beyleege, 4th Floor, Malé; tel. 3305546; fax 3306699; e-mail jumhooreepartysg@gmail.com; internet www.jumhooreeparty.org.mv; Leader Qasim Ibrahim; 12,154 mems (2013).

Maldives Development Alliance (MDA): Aroodhage, 6th Floor, Majeedhee Magu, Maafannu, Malé; tel. 7973551; e-mail inquiry.mda@gmail.com; f. 2012; Pres. Ahmed Shiyam Mohamed.

Maldivian Democratic Party (MDP): H. Sharasha, 2nd Floor, Sosun Magu, Malé 20-059; tel. 3340044; fax 3322960; e-mail secretariat@mdp.org.mv; internet www.mdp.org.mv; f. 2001; fmrly based in Colombo, Sri Lanka; official registration in Maldives permitted June 2005; Pres. Mohamed Nasheed; Chair. Ali Waheed; Sec.-Gen. Anas Abdul Sattar; 45,666 mems (2013).

Progressive Party of Maldives (PPM): Medhuziyaaraiyy Magu, Malé 20-127; tel. 3303838; e-mail info@ppm.mv; internet www.ppm.mv; f. 2011; est. by fmr Pres. of the Maldives (1978–2008) and fmr leader of the DRP Maumoon Abdul Gayoom; Pres. Maumoon Abdul Gayoom; Parliamentary Group Leader Ahmed Nihan; 22,793 mems (Feb. 2013).

Diplomatic Representation

EMBASSIES AND HIGH COMMISSIONS IN THE MALDIVES

Bangladesh: M. Kurinbee Lodge, 5th Floor, Izzudheen Magu, Malé; tel. 3315541; fax 3315543; e-mail bdootmal@dhivehinet.net.mv; High Commissioner Rear Adm. Kazi Sarwar Hossain.

China, People's Republic: H. Nookurikeela, Dhunbugas Magu, Malé; tel. 3010640; fax 3010637; e-mail chinaemb_mdv@mfa.gov.cn; internet mv.chineseembassy.org/eng/; Ambassador Wang Fukang.

India: H. Athireege-Aage, Ameeru Ahmed Magu, Malé; tel. 3323015; fax 3324778; e-mail hoc.male@mea.gov.in; internet www.hcimaldives.in; High Commissioner Rajeev Shahare.

Pakistan: G. Helengely, Lily Magu, Malé; tel. 3323005; fax 3321832; e-mail parepmale@hotmail.com; internet mofa.gov.pk/maldives; High Commissioner Syed Sail Abbas.

Sri Lanka: G. Zafna, Lily Magu, Malé; tel. 3322845; fax 3321652; e-mail highcom@dhivehinet.net.mv; internet www.slhcmaldives.com; High Commissioner W. G. N. H. Dias.

Judicial System

The administration of justice is undertaken in accordance with Islamic (*Shari'a*) law. In 1980 the Maldives High Court was established. There are four courts in Malé, and one island court in every inhabited island. The new Constitution, which was enacted in August 2008, provided for the establishment of a Supreme Court to serve as the highest authority for the administration of justice in the nation. In the following month the President appointed five judges to an interim Supreme Court after consultation with the newly established Judicial Service Commission. In August 2010 a permanent Supreme Court was established; a new Chief Justice and six judges were appointed. In December 2014 the People's Majlis approved an amendment to the Judicature Act that reduced the seven-member Supreme Court bench to five judges. The legislation also provided for the division of the High Court into three regional branches.

Supreme Court: M. Theemuge, Orchid Magu, Malé 20-208; tel. 3009990; fax 3008554; e-mail info@supremecourt.gov.mv; internet www.supremecourt.gov.mv; Chief Justice Abdulla Saeed.

High Court of the Maldives: M. Theemuge, Orchid Magu, Malé 20-208; tel. 3325029; fax 3316471; e-mail info@highcourt.gov.mv; internet www.highcourt.gov.mv; Acting Chief Judge Abdulla Hameed.

Office of the Attorney-General: Huravee Bldg, 3rd Floor, Ameer Ahmed Magu, Malé; tel. 3323809; fax 3314109; e-mail it@agoffice.gov.mv; internet agoffice.gov.mv; Attorney-General Uz Mohamed Anil.

Office of the Prosecutor-General: Malé 20-040; tel. 3000655; fax 3000644; e-mail pgoffice@pgoffice.gov.mv; internet www.pgoffice.gov.mv; Prosecutor-General Muhthaz Muhsin.

Religion

Islam is the state religion, and the majority of Maldivians are Sunni Muslims.

In November 2008 a Ministry of Islamic Affairs was established to replace the Supreme Council for Islamic Affairs, which had been founded in 1996 to authorize state policies with regard to Islam and to advise the Government on Islamic affairs.

The Press

DAILIES

Haama Daily: Ma. Night Rose, Dhilbahaaru Magu, POB 20232, Malé; tel. 3340077; fax 3343726; e-mail haama@haamadaily.com; internet www.haamadaily.com; Dhivehi and English; Chair. QASIM IBRAHIM.

Haveeru Daily: Ameenee Magu, POB 20103, Malé; tel. 3325671; fax 3323103; e-mail haveeru@haveeru.com.mv; internet www.haveeru .com.mv; f. 1979; Dhivehi and English; Chair. MOHAMED ZAHIR HUSSAIN; Editor MOOSA LATHEEF; circ. 4,500.

Miadhu News: G. Maple Leaf, Ameenee Magu, Malé; tel. 3320700; fax 3320500; e-mail admin@miadhu.com.mv; internet www.miadhu .com; Chair. MOHAMED NABEEL; Editor ABDUL LATHEEF.

Minivan News: Malé; tel. 3347889; e-mail editorial@minivannews .com; internet www.minivannews.com; f. 2005; English-language online newspaper; Editor DANIEL BOSLEY.

Raajje Daily: Malé; e-mail info@raajje.mv; internet www .raajjedaily.com; f. 2008; independent; predominantly Dhivehi with English section; Editor HASSAN SAEED.

PERIODICALS

Adduvas: Malé; e-mail adduvasnews@gmail.com; f. 2000; weekly; news, entertainment, health issues and social affairs; Editor AISHATH VELEZINEE.

Furadhaana: Dept of Information, Ministry of Tourism, Arts and Culture, Velaanaage, 5th Floor, Ameer Ahmed Magu, Malé 20-096; tel. 3334333; fax 3334334; e-mail print@maldivesinfo.gov.mv; internet www.maldivesinfo.gov.mv; f. 1990; monthly; Dhivehi; Editor IBRAHIM MANIK; circ. 1,000.

Huvaas Magazine: Ameenee Magu, POB 20103, Malé; tel. 3325671; fax 3323103; e-mail huvaas@haveeru.com.mv; internet www.haveeru.com.mv/huvaas; f. 2001; fortnightly; Chair. Dr MOHAMED ZAHIR HUSSAIN.

Jamaathuge Khabaru (Community News): Centre for Continuing Education, Salahudeen Bldg, Malé 20-04; tel. 3328772; fax 3322223; internet www.cce.edu.mv; monthly; Dhivehi; Editor AHMED ZAHIR; circ. 1,500.

NEWS AGENCY

Haveeru News Service (HNS): POB 20103, Malé; tel. 3325671; fax 3323103; e-mail haveeru@haveeru.com.mv; internet www.haveeru .com.mv; f. 1979, Chair. Dr MOHAMED ZAHIR HUSSAIN; Man. Editor AHMED ZAHIR.

PRESS ORGANIZATIONS AND ASSOCIATIONS

Maldives Journalist Association: M. Seeraazee Kanmatheege, Malé 20-026; tel. 7785669 (mobile); e-mail admin@mja.org.mv; internet mja.org.mv; f. 2009; Pres. AHMED ZAHIR.

Maldives Media Council: Reghendhi Hingun, Malé 20-144; tel. 3003995; fax 3003994; e-mail info@mmc.org.mv; internet www.mmc .org.mv; f. 2010; development and supervision of the media sector; 15 elected mems; Chair. MOHAMED ASIF; Pres. (vacant).

Publishers

Corona Press: Feeroaz Magu, Maafannu, Malé; tel. 3310052; fax 3314741.

Loamaafaanu Print: Alkariyya Bldg, Ground Floor, Ameenee Magu, Malé 20-354; tel. 3317209; fax 3313815; e-mail haveeru@ netlink.net.mv.

Novelty Printers and Publishers: M. Vaarey Villa, Izzudhdheen Magu, Malé 20-317; tel. 3318844; fax 3327039; e-mail novelty@ dhivehinet.net.mv; internet www.novelty.com.mv; f. 1965; general and reference books; Man. Dir ASAD ALI.

Ummeedhee Press: M. Aasthaanaa Javaahirumagu, Malé 20-02; tel. 3325110; fax 3326412; e-mail ummpress@dhivehinet.net.mv; f. 1986; printing and publishing; Principal Officers ABDUL SHAKOOR ALI, MOHAMED SHAKOOR.

Broadcasting and Communications

TELECOMMUNICATIONS

According to the Communications Authority of Maldives, in February 2015 there were 681,435 mobile telephone subscriptions and 22,461 fixed telephone lines. At that time there were 194,476 broadband internet subscriptions, 89.3% of which were accessed via mobile services.

Dhivehi Raajjeyge Gulhun Ltd (Dhiraagu): 19 Medhuziyaaraiy Magu, POB 2082, Malé 20-03; tel. 3322802; fax 3322800; e-mail 123@ dhiraagu.com.mv; internet www.dhiraagu.com.mv; f. 1988; jtly owned by the Maldivian Govt (41.8%) and Cable and Wireless PLC (United Kingdom—52%); operates all nat. and int. telecommunications services in the Maldives (incl. internet service—Dhivehinet); Chair. IBRAHIM ATHIF SHAKOOR; CEO ISMAIL WAHEED.

Ooredoo Maldives: 5th Floor, H. Sunleet, Boduthakurufaanu Magu, POB 2196, Malé 20-005; tel. 9611000; fax 9611001; e-mail 929@ooredoo.mv; internet www.ooredoo.mv; f. 2005; fmrly Wataniya Telecom Maldives Pvt Ltd, name changed as above in 2013; owned by Ooredoo Group (Qatar); provides cellular mobile telephone services throughout the Maldives; Chair. SOLAH FAHUD SULTAN; CEO IBRAHIM HALEEL.

Regulatory Authority

Communications Authority of Maldives: Telecom Bldg, Husnuheena Magu, Malé 20-117; tel. 3323344; fax 3320000; e-mail secretariat@cam.gov.mv; internet www.cam.gov.mv; f. 2003; regulatory authority; CEO ILYAS AHMED.

BROADCASTING

Maldives Broadcasting Commission: Ameenee Magu, Galolhu, Malé; tel. 3334333; fax 3334334; e-mail info@broadcom.org.mv; internet www.broadcom.org.mv; f. 2010; regulatory authority; Pres. MOHAMED SHAHEEB.

Maldives Broadcasting Corpn (MBC): Malé; internet www.mbc .mv; f. 2009; manages Television Maldives, Voice of Maldives and Dhivehi FM; state broadcaster; Chair. MOHAMED 'MADULU' WAHEED.

Radio

Capital Radio: H. Gaadhoo, 1st Floor, Boduthakurufaanu Magu, Malé; tel. 3323223; fax 3325707; e-mail studio@capitalradio936.com; internet www.capitalradio936.com; f. 2007; operated by Asna Maldives Pte Ltd; broadcasts BBC news bulletins, music, current affairs and analysis programmes; Man. Dir ISMAIL ABDULLA.

DhiFM 95.2: G.Champaamoon Bldg, 6th Floor, Daizy Magu, Malé; tel. 3345556; fax 3345559; e-mail admin@dhifm.com; internet dhifm .mv; f. 2007; operated by Maldives Media Co Pvt; broadcasts news, music and general interest programmes in Dhivehi and English; operates 24-hour nationwide service; CEO MASOOD HILMY; Editorial Dir MASOOD ALI.

Dhivehi FM 91: Malé; tel. 3000272; internet www.mbc.mv/ dhivehifm; f. 2006; fmrly Raajje FM; operated by MBC.

Radio Atoll: Ma. Eastern Lagoon, POB 20103, Malé 20; tel. 3349696; fax 3319600; e-mail info@radioatoll.com; internet www .radioatoll.com; broadcasts current affairs, entertainment and general interest programmes; Chair. MOHAMED FAZEEL.

Voice of Maldives (VOM) (Dhivehi Raajjeyge Adu): Voice of Maldives Bldg, Maafannu, Malé; tel. 3314515; fax 3317273; e-mail gs@vom.gov.mv; internet www.vom.gov.mv; radio broadcasting began in 1962 under name of Malé Radio; name changed as above in 1980; operates 1 channel for religious broadcasts and another for music and current affairs; home service in Dhivehi and English; from Feb. 2012 under the control of the MBC; Dir-Gen. BADRU NASEER.

Television

DhiTV: Champa Bldg, Daisy Magu, Galolhu, Malé 20-02; tel. 3304555; fax 3307666; e-mail info@dhitv.com.mv; internet www .dhitv.com.mv; f. 2008; operated by Maldives Media Co Pvt; launched a 24-hour news and entertainment channel, DhiFM Plus, in mid-2012; Chief Exec. MIDHATH ADAM.

Rajjee TV: STO Bldg, 5th floor, Boduthakurufaanu Magu, Malé; tel. 3307773; fax 3307775; e-mail info@raajje.mv; internet raajje.mv; f. 2011; news and current affairs; CEO ABDULLA YAMIN RASHEED.

Television Maldives: Buruzu Magu, Malé 20-144; tel. 3342200; fax 3325083; internet www.mbc.mv/tvm; television broadcasting began in 1978; 2 channels: TVM broadcasts for an average of 18 hrs daily and TVM Plus (f. 1994) broadcasts for 10 hrs daily; from Feb. 2012 controlled by the MBC; covers a 40-km radius around Malé.

Villa Television (VTV): ADK Bldg, 1st Floor, M. Fathimath Iliya, Malé; tel. 3303642; fax 3303641; e-mail info@vtv.com.mv; internet vtv.com.mv; f. 2008; operated by the Island Broadcasting Co Pvt. Ltd; Chair. QASIM IBRAHIM.

Finance

(cap. = capital; res = reserves; dep. = deposits; m. = million; brs = branches; amounts in rufiyaas unless otherwise stated)

BANKING

Central Bank

Maldives Monetary Authority (MMA): Boduthakurufaanu Magu, Malé 20-182; tel. 3312343; fax 3323862; e-mail mail@mma.gov.mv; internet www.mma.gov.mv; f. 1981; bank of issue; supervises and regulates commercial bank and foreign exchange dealings, and advises the Govt on banking and monetary matters; cap. 1m., res 5,151m., dep. 20m. (Dec. 2009); Gov. Dr AZEEMA ADAM.

Commercial Banks

Bank of Maldives PLC: 11 Boduthakurufaanu Magu, Malé 20-094; tel. 3330200; fax 3328233; e-mail info@bml.com.mv; internet www.bankofmaldives.com.mv; f. 1982; 75% state-owned; cap. 269m., res 958m., dep. 9,725.6m. (Dec. 2013); Chair. (vacant); CEO and Man. Dir ANDREW HEALY; 25 brs.

Maldives Islamic Bank (MIB): H. Coconut Villa, Ameer Ahmed Magu, Malé 20-030; tel. 3325555; fax 3007885; e-mail info@mib.com.mv; internet www.mib.com.mv; f. 2011; 85% owned by the Islamic Corpn for Development and 15% by the Govt; offers banking services compliant with Islamic *Shari'a*; cap. 165m., res 2.9m., dep. 840.1m. (Dec. 2013); Chair. NAJMUL HASSAN.

DEVELOPMENT FINANCE ORGANIZATION

Housing Development Finance Corpn Plc: 4th Floor, H. Milani, Sosun Magu, Malé; tel. 3334666; fax 3315138; e-mail info@hdfc.com.mv; internet www.hdfc.com.mv; f. 2004 to provide public housing loans; partially privatized in 2008; 49% of shares held by the Govt; Chair. SANJAYA GUPTA; Man. Dir Dr A. D. PRIYANKA BADDEVITHANA.

STOCK EXCHANGE

Maldives Stock Exchange: Gadhamoo Bldg, 3rd Floor, Boduthakurufaanu Magu, Malé; tel. 3307878; fax 3305034; e-mail info@mse.com.mv; internet www.maldivesstockexchange.com.mv; f. 2002; CEO HASSAN MANIK.

Capital Market Development Authority (CMDA): MTCC Tower, 4th Floor, Boduthakurufaanu Magu, Henveyru, Malé 20-057; tel. 3336619; fax 3336624; e-mail mail@cmda.gov.mv; internet www.cmda.gov.mv; f. 2006; regulates and develops the capital market and the pension industry; Chair. ASHRAF ABDUL RAHEEM; CEO AHMED NASEER.

INSURANCE

Allied Insurance Co of the Maldives (Pte) Ltd: 2nd Floor, Fen Bldg, Ameenee Magu, Machchangolhi Malé 20-375; tel. 3341001; fax 3325035; e-mail info@alliedmaldives.net; internet www.alliedmaldives.com; f. 1985; all classes of non-life insurance; operated by State Trading Organization (see Government Agencies); Chair. MOHAMED RASHEED; Man. Dir AHMED AMEEL.

Amana Takaful (Maldives) PLC: 3rd Floor, H. Mialani, Sosun Magu, Malé; tel. 3315262; fax 3340729; e-mail info@takaful.mv; internet www.takaful.mv; f. 2003; subsidiary of Amana Takaful PLC, Sri Lanka; Chair. TYEAB AKBARALLY; Man. Dir and CEO HAREEZ SULAIMAN.

Trade and Industry

GOVERNMENT AGENCIES

Department of National Planning: Ministry of Finance and Treasury, Ameenee Magu, Malé 20-125; tel. 3349200; fax 3327351; e-mail info@stats.gov.mv; internet planning.gov.mv; f. 1978 as the Nat. Planning Agency; designated a govt ministry, 1982–2008; reconfigured as above in 2008; administered by the Ministry of Finance and Treasury; planning and co-ordination of nat. devt; incorporates the Nat. Planning Council.

Invest Maldives: Ministry of Economic Development, Boduthakurufaanu Magu, Malé 20-125; tel. 3323668; fax 3322528; e-mail info@investmaldives.org; internet www.investmaldives.org; govt agency est. to promote, regulate and license foreign investment; Dir-Gen. (vacant).

Privatization and Corporatization Board: Malé; oversees and advises on privatization of state enterprises; comprises 7 mems, appointed by the President; Pres. MOHAMED NIZAR.

State Trading Organization PLC (STO): STO Bldg, Boduthakurufaanu Magu, Maafannu, Malé 20-345; tel. 3344333; fax 3344511; e-mail info@stomaldives.net; internet www.stomaldives.com; f. 1964 as Athirimaafannuge Trading Account, renamed as above in 1976; became a PLC in 2001; state-controlled commercial org.; imports and distributes staple foods, fuels, pharmaceuticals and general consumer items; acts as purchaser for govt requirements; undertakes long-term devt projects; Chair. AHMED NIYAZ; Man. Dir AHMED SHAHEER.

CHAMBER OF COMMERCE

Maldives National Chamber of Commerce and Industry (MNCCI): G. Viyafari Hiya, Ameenee Magu, Malé 20-04; tel. 3326634; fax 3310233; e-mail mncci@dhivehinet.net.mv; internet mncci.org.mv; f. 1994; merged with Maldivian Traders' Asscn in 2000; Pres. HAMID ISMAIL.

INDUSTRIAL ASSOCIATION

Maldives Association of Construction Industry (MACI): Port Complex, Ground Floor, Hilaalee Magu, Malé; tel. 3318660; fax 3318796; e-mail admin@maci.org.mv; internet maci.org.mv; f. 2001; Pres. MOHAMED ALI JANAH.

UTILITIES

Fenaka Corpn Ltd: Malé; tel. and fax 3007555; internet fenaka.com.mv; f. 2012; state-owned; operates and maintains sewerage systems, electricity and water in islands other than Malé; Chair. MOHAMED NADHEEM; Man. Dir MOHAMED NIMAL.

Electricity

Maldives Energy Authority: Ameenee Magu, Maafannu, Malé 20-392; tel. 3019100; fax 3018576; e-mail secretariat@mea.gov.mv; internet www.energy.gov.mv; f. 2006 to replace Maldives Electricity Bureau; regulatory authority; Dir MUAWIYATH SHAREEF.

State Electric Co (STELCO) Ltd: Ameenee Magu, POB 2184, Malé; tel. 3320982; fax 3327036; e-mail admin@stelco.com.mv; internet www.stelco.com.mv; f. 1997 to replace Maldives Electricity Board; state-owned; generation and distribution of electricity; operates 28 power stations; installed capacity 79,200 kW (2012); Chair. MOHAMED AFEEF HUSSAIN; 550 employees (2012).

Gas

Maldive Gas Pvt Ltd: 02-21 STO Trade Centre, Orchid Magu, Malé; tel. 3335614; fax 3335615; e-mail info@maldivegas.com; internet www.maldivegas.com; f. 1999 as a jt venture between State Trading Org. (90%) and Champa Gas and Oil Co (10%); Chair. AHMED SHIFAN; Man. Dir ABDULLA MAUMOON.

Water

Malé Water and Sewerage Co Pvt Ltd: Fen Bldg, 5th Floor, Ameenee Magu, Machangolhi, POB 2148, Malé 20375; tel. 3323209; fax 3324306; e-mail mail@mwsc.com.mv; internet www.mwsc.com.mv; f. 1995; 76% govt-owned; produces c. 8,500 metric tons of fresh, desalinated water daily; provides water and sewerage services to the islands of Malé, Hulhumalé, Kulhudhufushi and Villingili; provides water services to the islands of Maafushi and Thilafushi; Man. Dir IBRAHIM FAZUL RASHEED.

TRADE UNIONS AND WORKERS' ASSOCIATIONS

The 2008 Constitution provides for a minimum wage and grants employees the right to form trade unions and to organize strikes. A number of workers' associations have been established, notably in the tourism and education sectors, although by early 2015 there were still no trade unions in operation.

Tourism Employees' Association of Maldives (TEAM): 2B M. Coral Gardens, Izzudhdheen Magu, Malé; tel. 3338996; fax 3338995; e-mail info@teammaldives.com; internet www.teammaldives.com; f. 2008; works towards reforming labour rights of hotel and resort workers; Gen. Sec. MAUROOF ZAKIR; Pres. AHMED SHIHAM.

Transport

Transport Authority of the Maldives: Huravee Bldg, 2nd Floor, Ameer Ahmed Magu, Malé; tel. 3343433; fax 3343434; e-mail admin@transport.gov.mv; internet www.transport.gov.mv; regulatory and licensing authority for maritime and land transport; Chair. ABDUL RASHEED NAFIZ.

ROADS

The Maldives has a small road network (88 km in 2010), with the majority of surfaced roads concentrated in Malé and Addu City. The state-owned Maldives Road Development Corporation was established in 2010 to foster development of road infrastructure; in the following year the Government announced plans for a major road construction project. In 2013 the Government confirmed plans for 66 km of new roads in 10 islands, under the road construction project.

SHIPPING

Private vessels operate from the Maldives to Sri Lanka and Singapore at frequent intervals, also calling at points in India, Pakistan, Myanmar, Malaysia, Bangladesh, Thailand, Indonesia and the Middle East. Smaller vessels provide services between the islands on an irregular basis. Malé is the only port handling international traffic. Ambitious plans for the construction of up to 60 new harbours and a transshipment port were under development from 2006. In March 2015 the Government signed a memorandum of understanding with Dubai Ports World of the United Arab Emirates on the development of a new container terminal and free trade zone on Thilafushi island. At 31 December 2014 the flag registered fleet comprised 61 vessels, including 27 general cargoes and 4 fishing tankers, with a total displacement of 49,006 grt.

Maldives Ports Limited: Boduthakurufaanu Magu, Maafannu, Malé 20-250; tel. 3329339; fax 3325293; e-mail info@port.com.mv; internet www.port.com.mv; f. 2008; replaced the former Maldives Port Authority (f. 1986); operates Malé Port and serves as the national ports operator; govt-owned; Chair. MOHAMED JUNAID; CEO MAHDI IMAD.

Maldives Transport and Contracting Co Ltd (MTCC): MTCC Tower, 7th Floor, Boduthakurufaanu Magu, POB 263, Malé 20-181; tel. 3326822; fax 3323221; e-mail info@mtcc.com.mv; internet www.mtcc.com.mv; f. 1980; 60% state-owned, 40% privately owned; marine transport, civil and technical contracting, harbour devt, shipping agents for general cargo, passenger liners and oil tankers; Chair. HUSSAIN SALIM MOHAMED; CEO IBRAHIM ABDUL RAZZAQ HALEEM.

The Silver Company (Pvt) Ltd (SILCO): 6th Floor, H. Honey Due, Gan'dhakoalhi Magu, Malé 20-02; tel. 325621; fax 327808; e-mail nabeel@silco.com.mv; f. 1993; shipping, aviation, yacht-handling, cargo-packing and -forwarding, and customs clearance and delivery services; Man. Dir MOHAMED NABEEL.

Villa Shipping and Trading Co (Pvt) Ltd: Villa Bldg, POB 2073, Malé 20-02; tel. 3325195; fax 3325177; e-mail info@villa.com.mv; internet www.villa.mv; f. 1986; operates 5 tourist resorts and owns a trading operation supported by a fleet of 8 cargo vessels and tankers; Man. Dir QASIM IBRAHIM.

CIVIL AVIATION

Malé International Airport, on Hululé Island near Malé, was officially opened in 1981. In 2010 the Government entered a 25-year agreement with an Indian-Malaysian consortium for the development and management of the airport, including the construction of a new terminal. In mid-2011 the airport was renamed Ibrahim Nasir International. In December 2012, however, the Government revoked the operating agreement and took back full control of the airport. In February 2015 the Government announced plans for the construction of a new runway at Ibrahim Nasir International. Facilities at Gan Airport on Addu atoll, Hanimaadhoo Airport on South Thiladhunmathi atoll and Maamigili Airport (or Villa International) on Alifu Dhaalu atoll have also been upgraded to accommodate international services. In addition, there are domestic airports located on Dharavandhoo Island (Baa atoll), Fuvahmulah Island (Gnaviyani atoll), Kaadedhdhoo Island (Gaafu Dhaalu atoll), Kadhdhoo Island (Hadhdhunmathi atoll), Koodoo Island (Gaafu Alifu atoll) and Thimarafushi Island (Thaa atoll).

Maldives Civil Aviation Authority: Velaanaage, 11th Floor, Ameeru Ahmed Magu, Malé 20-096; tel. 3324992; fax 3323039; e-mail civav@aviainfo.gov.mv; internet www.aviainfo.gov.mv; f. 2012; regulatory authority; from mid-2014 under the supervision of the Ministry of Tourism; Chair. IBRAHIM FAIZAL; CEO HUSSAIN JALEEL.

Maldives Airport Co Ltd (MACL): Ibrahim Nasir International Airport, Hululé 22-000; tel. 3315366; fax 7785366; e-mail info@maclnet.net; internet macl.aero; f. 2000; govt-owned; airport management and aviation services; Chair. MOHAMED SAEED; Man. Dir ADIL MOOSA.

Maldivian: 26 Ameer Ahmed Magu, Malé; tel. 3335566; fax 3314806; e-mail info@iasl.aero; internet www.maldivian.aero; f. 2000; 100% govt-owned; operated by Island Aviation Services Ltd; fmrly known as Island Aviation; re-branded as above in August 2008; national carrier of the Maldives; operates domestic services and int. flights to India, Sri Lanka, Bangladesh and the People's Republic of China; Chair. AHMED SHAFEEU; Man. Dir ABDUL HAARIS.

MEGA Maldives Airlines: Ground Floor, H. Sakeena Manzil, Medhu Ziyarah Magu, Malé 20-127; tel. 3006672; fax 3006671; e-mail reservations@megamaldivesair.com; internet megamaldivesair.com; f. 2009; operates domestic services and int.

services to Hong Kong and the People's Republic of China; Chair. and CEO GEORGE WEINMANN; Man. Dir MIFZAL AHMED.

Trans Maldivian Airways (Pvt) Ltd: Ibrahim Nasir International Airport, POB 2079, Malé; tel. 3315201; fax 3315203; e-mail info@transmaldivian.com; internet www.transmaldivian.com; f. 1989 as Hummingbird Island Airways Pvt Ltd; name changed as above in 2000; acquired Maldivian Air Taxi in 2013; operates 44 seaplanes; Man. Dir EDWARD ALSFORD.

Villa Air (FlyMe): 5th Floor, Villa House, Kandidhonmanik Goalhi, Malé, 20–181; tel. 3013000; e-mail info@villa.com.mv; internet www.flyme.mv; f. 1997; owned by Villa Group; developed a private airport on Maamigili island (South Ari atoll); domestic services under the FlyMe brand launched in 2011; Chair. QASIM IBRAHIM; Man. Dir RILUWAN SHAREEF.

Tourism

The tourism industry brings considerable foreign exchange to the Maldives. The islands' attractions include white sandy beaches, excellent diving conditions and impressive coral formations. At the end of 2013 there were 110 island resorts in operation, providing some 23,677 guest beds; a further 2,716 beds were available on live-aboard safari vessels, and 3,556 beds in hotels and guest houses. In 2002 the Maldives attracted 484,680 foreign tourists; by 2014 tourist arrivals had risen to a record total of 1,204,857 (an increase of some 7.1% compared with the previous year). In 2013 receipts from tourism were estimated at about US $2,700m.

Lets Go Maldives Pvt Ltd: Lets Go Tower, 1st Floor, M. Boaddoo, Haveeree Hingun, Malé 20-320; tel. 3347755; fax 3307755; e-mail info@letsgomaldives.com; internet www.letsgomaldives.com; f. 2006; tourism agency incl. port handling and aviation services; Man. Dir MOHAMED RIYAZ.

Maldives Association of Tourism Industry (MATI): Fasmeeru Bldg, 4th Floor, Boduthakurufaanu Magu, POB 2056, Malé; tel. 3326640; fax 3326641; e-mail mati@dhivehinet.net.mv; internet www.matimaldives.com; f. 1982; promotes and develops tourism; Chair. MOHAMED UMAR MANIKU; Sec.-Gen. AHMED NAZEER.

Maldives Marketing and Public Relations Corpn Ltd (MMPRC): Velaanaage, 4th Floor, Ameeru Ahmed Magu, Malé 20-05; tel. 3323228; fax 3323229; e-mail info@visitmaldives.com; internet www.visitmaldives.com; f. 1998 as Maldives Tourism Promotion Board; renamed as above in 2011; Chair. MOHAMED KHALEEL; Man. Dir ABDULLA ZIYATH.

Maldives Tourism Development Corpn Plc (MTDC): 1st Floor, G. Fathuruvehi, Buruzu Magu, Malé 20-123; tel. 3347766; fax 3347733; e-mail info@mtdc.com.mv; internet www.mtdc.com.mv; Chair. IBTHISHAMA AHMED SAEED; Man. Dir AHMED NIYAZ (acting).

Defence

There is no army, navy or air force. A voluntary National Security Service, which was founded in 1892 and renamed the Maldives National Defence Force in 2006, undertakes paramilitary security duties (including coastguard duties) and comprises some 2,000 members. The first female recruits were sworn into the former National Security Service in 1989.

Defence Budget: Totalled 561.7 rufiyaa (4.0% of total expenditure) in 2010.

Commander-in-Chief of the Maldives National Defence Force: Pres. ABDULLA YAMEEN ABDUL GAYOOM.

Chief of Staff of the Maldives National Defence Force: Maj.-Gen. AHMED SHIYAM.

Education

Education is not compulsory. There are three types of formal education: traditional Koranic schools (*Makthab*), Dhivehi-medium primary schools (*Madhrasa*) and English-medium primary and secondary schools. Primary education begins at six years of age and lasts for five years. Secondary education, beginning at the age of 11, lasts for up to seven years, comprising a first cycle of five years and a second of two years. In 2009 enrolment at primary schools included 94% of children in the relevant age-group; in 2007/08 the ratio for secondary enrolment of pupils in the relevant age-group was an estimated 69%. By 2013 there were a total of 448 schools throughout the islands.

Budgetary expenditure on education by the central Government in 2010 was 2,006.3m. rufiyaa, representing 14.2% of total spending.

MALI

Introductory Survey

LOCATION, CLIMATE, LANGUAGE, RELIGION, FLAG, CAPITAL

The Republic of Mali is a landlocked country in West Africa, with Algeria to the north, Mauritania and Senegal to the west, Guinea and Côte d'Ivoire to the south, and Burkina Faso and Niger to the east. The climate is hot throughout the country. The northern region of Mali is part of the Sahara, an arid desert. It is wetter in the south, where the rainy season is from June to October. Temperatures in Bamako are generally between 16°C (61°F) and 39°C (103°F). The official language is French, but a number of other languages, including Bambara, Maasina Fulfulde, Sonrai, Tamashek, Soninke and Dogon, are widely spoken. According to census figures, in 2009 94.8% of the population were Muslims, while 2.4% were Christians and 2.0% followed traditional animist beliefs. The national flag (proportions 2 by 3) has three equal vertical stripes, of green, gold and red. The capital is Bamako.

CONTEMPORARY POLITICAL HISTORY

Historical Context

Mali, as the former French West African colony of Soudan, merged with Senegal in April 1959 to form the Federation of Mali, which became independent on 20 June 1960. Senegal seceded two months later, and the remnant of the Federation was proclaimed the Republic of Mali on 22 September. Mali's first President was Modibo Keïta, the leader of the Union Soudanaise—Rassemblement Démocratique Africain (US—RDA), who pursued authoritarian socialist policies. Keïta was overthrown in November 1968 by a group of junior army officers, who assumed power as the Comité Militaire pour la Libération Nationale. The Constitution was abrogated, and all political activity was banned. Lt (later Gen.) Moussa Traoré became Head of State.

A draft Constitution, providing for the establishment of a one-party state at the end of a five-year transitional period of military rule, was approved by a national referendum in June 1974. Keïta died in custody in 1977, prompting anti-Government demonstrations. The Union Démocratique du Peuple Malien (UDPM), the only political party, was officially constituted in March 1979, and presidential and legislative elections took place in June. Traoré, the sole candidate for the presidency, was elected for a five-year term; a single list of UDPM candidates for the 82-member Assemblée Nationale (National Assembly) was elected for a four-year term. Traoré and the UPDM were re-elected at all subsequent polls.

Domestic Political Affairs

Mali's first cohesive opposition movements began to emerge in 1990, among them the Comité National d'Initiative Démocratique (CNID) and the Alliance pour la Démocratie au Mali (ADEMA). The security forces harshly repressed violent pro-democracy demonstrations in Bamako in March 1991: official figures later revealed that 106 people were killed, and 708 injured, in three days of unrest. On 26 March it was announced that Traoré had been arrested. A military Conseil National de Réconciliation (CNR), led by Lt-Col (later Gen.) Amadou Toumani Touré, the commander of the army's parachute regiment, assumed power, and the Constitution and its institutions were abrogated. The CNR was succeeded by a 25-member Comité de Transition pour le Salut du Peuple (CTSP), chaired by Touré. It was announced that a national conference would be convened, and that the armed forces would relinquish power to democratic institutions in January 1992. Soumana Sacko (who had briefly been Minister of Finance and Trade in 1987) returned to Mali from the Central African Republic to head a transitional, civilian-dominated government.

The transitional regime undertook the reform of Malian political life. Among those arrested in subsequent months were Gen. Sékou Ly, Brig.-Gen. Mamadou Coulibaly (respectively, Minister of the Interior and Basic Development and Minister of Defence at the time of the violently repressed demonstrations in early 1991) and the former army Chief of Staff, Ousmane Coulibaly. In July 1991 an amnesty for most political prisoners detained under Traoré was proclaimed, and provision made for the legalization of political parties. The CNID was registered as the Congrès National d'Initiative Démocratique, and ADEMA adopted the additional title of Parti Pan-Africain pour la Liberté, la Solidarité et la Justice. Pre-independence parties, banned for many years, re-emerged, most notably the US—RDA.

The National Conference, which began in July 1991, adopted a draft Constitution, an electoral code and a charter governing the activities of political parties. In November the period of transition to democratic rule was extended until March 1992. The draft Constitution was submitted to a national referendum on 12 January 1992, when it was endorsed by 99.8% of those who voted (about 43% of the registered electorate).

At elections to the National Assembly, on 23 February and 8 March 1992, ADEMA won 76 of the 129 seats, the CNID nine seats, and the US—RDA eight. The date for the transition to civilian rule was again postponed, and the first round of the presidential election eventually proceeded on 12 April, contested by nine candidates. The leader of ADEMA, Alpha Oumar Konaré, won the largest share of the votes cast (some 45%). He and his nearest rival, Tiéoulé Mamadou Konaté (of the US—RDA), proceeded to a second round, on 26 April, at which Konaré secured 69% of the votes. Overall, only about 20% of the electorate were reported to have voted in both the presidential election and the legislative polls. Konaré was inaugurated as President on 8 June. He appointed Younoussi Touré (hitherto the national director of the Banque Centrale des Etats de l'Afrique de l'Ouest—BCEAO) as Prime Minister. Touré's first Council of Ministers was dominated by members of ADEMA, although a small number of portfolios were allocated to representatives of the US—RDA and of the Parti pour la Démocratie et le Progrès (PDP).

The trial of Traoré and his associates began in November 1992. In February 1993 Traoré, Ly, Mamadou Coulibaly and Ousmane Coulibaly were sentenced to death, having been convicted, inter alia, of premeditated murder at the time of the March 1991 unrest. The Supreme Court rejected appeal proceedings in May 1993; however, Konaré subsequently indicated that no death penalty would be exacted under his presidency. Charges remained against Traoré, his wife and several others in connection with the 'economic crimes' of the former administration.

Touré resigned in April 1993, following violent disturbances in Bamako prompted by the adverse effects of economic austerity measures. The new Prime Minister, Abdoulaye Sekou Sow (hitherto Minister of State, responsible for Defence, and who was not a member of any political party), implemented an extensive reorganization of the Government. The Council of Ministers remained dominated by ADEMA, but also included representatives of other parties, among them the CNID.

A programme of further austerity measures, announced in September 1993, provoked considerable political controversy. Sow resigned in February 1994, and was replaced by Ibrahim Boubacar Keïta, a member of ADEMA's 'radical' wing, which was opposed to Sow's economic policies. The withdrawal from the coalition of the CNID and the Rassemblement pour la Démocratie et le Progrès (RDP) prompted the appointment of a new Government, again dominated by ADEMA; the PDP in turn withdrew.

Following the election of Keïta as President of ADEMA in September 1994, ADEMA's Vice-President, Mohamed Lamine Traoré, and other prominent figures resigned from the party and subsequently formed the Mouvement pour l'Indépendance, la Renaissance et l'Intégration Africaine (MIRIA). In January 1995 a party established by supporters of the UDPM, the Mouvement Patriotique pour le Renouveau (MPR), was granted official status. In October the Parti pour la Renaissance Nationale (PARENA), comprising several leading members of the CNID, who alleged excessive dominance by the party Chairman, Mountaga Tall, was registered. PARENA and ADEMA established a political alliance in February 1996, and PARENA's leaders, Yoro Diakité and Tiébilé Dramé, were appointed to the Government in July.

The 1997 elections

The first round of elections to the enlarged (147-seat) National Assembly was held on 13 April 1997. Since early results indicated that ADEMA was the only party to have won seats outright in this round, the main opposition parties denounced the results as fraudulent and announced their intention to withdraw from the second round. The opposition parties also withdrew their candidates from the forthcoming presidential election. On 24 April the Constitutional Court invalidated the results of the first round of voting, citing irregularities in the conduct of the poll.

Konaré, not wishing to be the sole candidate in the presidential election scheduled to be held on 11 May 1997, appealed to the opposition to participate. In early May the leader of the Parti pour l'Unité, la Démocratie et le Progrès, Mamadou Maribatou Diaby, announced that he was prepared to contest the presidency. According to the final results, Konaré was re-elected to the presidency, securing 95.9% of the votes cast. Members of the radical opposition, which had campaigned for a boycott by voters, stated that the low rate of participation (28.4% of the registered electorate) effectively invalidated Konaré's victory. Violent protests occurred in Bamako in June, as Konaré was sworn in for a second term of office and the first round of the fresh legislative elections (due on 6 July) was postponed by two weeks.

A small number of opposition parties announced their intention to present candidates for the National Assembly, but a grouping known as the Collectif des Partis Politiques de l'Opposition (COPPO), at this time numbering 18 parties, reiterated its refusal to re-enter the electoral process. Violent disturbances, in which two deaths were reported, preceded the first round of voting on 20 July 1997, which was contested by 17 parties (including five 'moderate' opposition parties) and a number of independent candidates. COPPO asserted that the low rate of participation by voters (at about 12% of the registered electorate in Bamako, and 22% outside the capital) would render the new parliament illegitimate. A second round of voting was necessary for eight seats on 3 August. The final results allocated 130 of the 147 seats to ADEMA, eight to PARENA, four to the Convention Démocratique et Sociale (CDS), three to the Union pour la Démocratie et le Développement (UDD) and two to the PDP.

In September 1997 Konaré held a meeting with some 20 opposition leaders, including representatives of COPPO, at which he presented proposals for a broad-based coalition government. A new Council of Ministers, under Keïta, was appointed in mid-September. The new administration included, in addition to members of ADEMA and its allies, representatives of the moderate opposition parties (among them the UDD and PDP). Further measures intended to promote national reconciliation were implemented, and in December Konaré commuted some 21 death sentences, including those imposed on ex-President Traoré and his associates, to terms of life imprisonment.

In October 1998 the trial for 'economic crimes' began in Bamako of former President Traoré, his wife Mariam, her brother, Abraham Douah Cissoko (the former head of customs), a former Minister of Finance and Trade, Tiénan Coulibaly, and the former representative in France of the Banque de Développement du Mali, Moussa Koné. In January 1999 Traoré, his wife and brother-in-law were sentenced to death, having been convicted of 'economic crimes' to the value of some US $350,000. Coulibaly and Koné were acquitted. In September Konaré commuted the death sentences to terms of life imprisonment.

The 2002 elections

In February 2000 Keïta submitted his Government's resignation. An extensively reorganized Council of Ministers, headed by Prime Minister Mandé Sidibé, was subsequently appointed. In July the National Assembly approved legislation providing for state funding of political parties. In addition, the Assembly adopted an extensive revision of the Constitution proposed by Konaré. (However, a planned referendum to endorse the constitutional amendments was subsequently postponed indefinitely.) Also in July COPPO, which now comprised 15 parties and was led by Almamy Sylla of the RDP, announced that it would participate in the electoral process.

Keïta resigned from the leadership of ADEMA in October 2000, following the announcement that his opponents within the party had succeeded in calling an extraordinary congress of the party, to be held in late November. At the congress, several new members were appointed to ADEMA's executive committee, and Dioncounda Traoré was elected as the new Chairman of the

party. In July 2001 a new party led by Keïta, the Rassemblement pour le Mali (RPM), was officially registered.

In January 2002 Soumaïla Cissé was elected as ADEMA's candidate for the forthcoming presidential election. In March Modibo Keïta, hitherto Secretary-General at the presidency, was appointed as Prime Minister, following Sidibé's resignation to contest the presidency as an independent candidate. In early April 16 opposition parties, including the CNID, the RPM and the MPR, formed an electoral alliance, Espoir 2002, agreeing to support a single opposition candidate (generally expected to be Ibrahim Boubacar Keïta, who was to contest the election on behalf of the RPM) in the event of a second round of voting. Meanwhile, an alliance of 23 political parties, including MIRIA, PARENA and the US—RDA, declared their support for the candidacy of Gen. (retd) Amadou Toumani Touré.

At the first round of the presidential election, which was held on 28 April 2002 and was contested by 24 candidates, Touré secured the largest share of the votes cast, with 28.7%, followed by Cissé, with 21.3%, and Keïta, with 21.0%. Touré and Cissé progressed to a second round of voting, held on 12 May. Touré was elected to the presidency, with 65.0% of the votes cast. The electoral process was marred by allegations of fraud and incompetence, which led the Constitutional Court to annul 25% of the votes cast in the first ballot. None the less, international observers described the elections as generally free and fair. Touré was inaugurated as President on 8 June, and subsequently formed an interim Government. The new Prime Minister and Minister of African Integration, Ahmed Mohamed Ag Hamani, who had held various ministerial posts under Traoré, was regarded as a technocrat.

The elections to the National Assembly in July 2002 further demonstrated the lack of any one dominant political grouping in Mali, while the rate of participation in the second round, at 25.7% nationwide, was low. The RPM emerged as the single largest party, with 46 of the 147 seats (although 20 of its seats had been won in local electoral alliances with other parties of the Espoir 2002 grouping), while other parties of Espoir 2002 obtained a further 21 seats, giving a total of 67 to allies of the RPM. ADEMA secured 45 seats, while the pro-ADEMA Alliance pour la République et la Démocratie won an additional six seats, giving a total of 51. The CNID received 13 seats, while parties belonging to an informal alliance supportive of President Touré, the Convergence pour l'Alternance et le Changement (ACC), including PARENA and the US—RDA, won a total of 10 seats. In early September 19 deputies, comprising those of the ACC parties, several independent deputies and other declared supporters of Touré, formed a grouping within the legislature, with the declared intention of forming a stable presidential majority. Later in the month Ibrahim Boubacar Keïta was elected President of the National Assembly.

In October 2002 Touré announced the formation of a Government of National Unity, although many of the principal posts remained unchanged from the previous interim administration. ADEMA increased its representation in the National Assembly to 53 deputies, becoming the largest party grouping, following its victory in eight by-elections on 20 October.

In April 2004 Ag Hamani tendered his resignation as Prime Minister, apparently in response to a request by President Touré. A new administration, headed by Prime Minister Ousmane Issoufi Maïga, hitherto Minister of Equipment and Transport (and not affiliated to any political party), was formed in early May. Later that month ADEMA and the RPM formed an alliance, which, with ADEMA holding 44 seats and the RPM 35, gave the new grouping a majority in the 147-seat National Assembly.

There was considerable speculation regarding potential realignments of political organizations ahead of the presidential and legislative elections due in 2007. In November 2005 the RPM announced that it would henceforth oppose the Government, stating that it had been increasingly marginalized within the ruling coalition. In February 2006 the executive committee of ADEMA declared that the party would support the candidacy of Touré at the forthcoming presidential election.

Touré's second term

The presidential election was duly held on 29 April 2007; 36.2% of the registered electorate participated. Touré received 71.2% of the total votes cast, securing a second, and final, five-year term while avoiding a second round of voting. His closest rival was Keïta, who received 19.2% of the votes cast. Although a number of opposition candidates challenged the results, most independent observers believed the election to have been conducted fairly.

The legislative elections took place on 1 and 22 July 2007. According to the official results, ADEMA secured 51 seats, while the Union pour la République et la Démocratie (URD) took 34 seats and the RPM 11. However, an overall voter turnout of only 12% was recorded. In total, parties supporting President Touré won 113 seats in the National Assembly. In September ADEMA leader Dioncounda Traoré was elected President of the legislature.

On 27 September 2007 Prime Minister Maïga tendered his resignation and that of his Government. The following day President Touré named Modibo Sidibé, hitherto Secretary-General of the Presidency, as Maïga's successor. Sidibé announced a new Council of Ministers in early October.

In July 2010 the pro-Government Mouvement Citoyen, launched a new political party, the Parti pour le Développement Economique et la Solidarité (PDES), in a move largely regarded as an attempt to consolidate President Touré's influence ahead of the elections due to be held in 2012. Touré, who had already confirmed that he had no intention of seeking to contest a third term of office, expressed his support for the PDES and its members, several of whom, including its President, Hamed Diane Séméga, were government ministers.

At the end of March 2011 Sidibé resigned the premiership, amid speculation that he intended to contest the presidency in 2012. Cissé Mariam Kaïdama Sidibé, who was not affiliated to any political party, was appointed as Mali's first female Prime Minister on 3 April. Her new Council of Ministers notably included members of the opposition RPM and PARENA and the newly created portfolio of state reform. In preparation for the 2012 elections, in June 2011 the Council of Ministers finally adopted a draft law on the amendments to the Constitution, which was approved in the National Assembly on 2 August. The proposed constitutional reforms, which included the establishment of an upper legislative chamber, were to be submitted to a national referendum on 29 April 2012 (when the first round of the presidential election was also scheduled to take place).

Military coup and transitional Government

On 21 March 2012 disaffected members of the armed forces staged a rebellion in protest at the Government's failure to contain the intensifying uprising in the north of the country (see *Tuareg Insurgency*); after launching attacks in Bamako and seizing the presidential palace, on the following day the rebels announced the deposition of Touré's Government and the installation of a Comité National pour le Redressement de la Démocratie et la Restauration de l'Etat (CNRDR—National Committee for the Restoration of Democracy and the State), headed by Capt. Amadou Sanogo. On 2 April, after the CNRDR failed to comply with demands by the Economic Community of West African States (ECOWAS, see p. 258) that it relinquish power, the organization imposed a number of sanctions against Mali. The USA and the African Union (AU, see p. 188), which had suspended Mali's membership in late March, joined an ECOWAS travel ban on the coup leaders. On 6 April the CNRDR reached an agreement with ECOWAS, under which it was to cede power to a transitional government, while the sanctions in force against the country were to be removed and all participants in the coup were to be granted amnesty. On 8 April both Touré (who had emerged from hiding) and Sanogo formally resigned. In accordance with the agreement, and following a decision by the Constitutional Court, on 12 April Dioncounda Traoré took office as Interim President for a transitional period of 40 days. Later that month a transitional Government, under the premiership of Cheick Modibo Diarra, was formed. Further arrests of supporters of Touré were reported, and Sanogo's forces clashed with troops loyal to Touré in Bamako. Following a summit meeting in Dakar, Senegal, in early May ECOWAS issued a statement urging the transitional authorities to establish a timetable for the organization of elections and the full restoration of constitutional order. It was agreed later in May that Traoré would remain as Interim President for a transitional period of one year, while Sanogo would be accorded the status of a former head of state. However, the extension of Traoré's presidential term angered supporters of the coup, several of whom entered the presidential palace and assaulted him. The attack, which caused Traoré to travel to France for medical treatment (where he remained until July), was widely condemned, although followers of Sanogo continued to demand his installation as Interim President in place of Traoré. In late June the National Assembly voted to extend the mandate of parliamentary deputies until the end of the transitional period. On 12 August Traoré reappointed Diarra as Prime Minister; the formation of a new, interim Council of

Ministers, which included five members nominated by officials of the former CNRDR, was announced on 20 August. The AU ended the suspension of Mali's membership on 24 October, when it also announced that it had approved a transitional programme, including plans for the organization of legislative elections within one year of a return to constitutional order.

Election of President Ibrahim Boubacar Keïta

On 11 December 2012 it was announced that Diarra had resigned as Prime Minister, shortly after being placed under house arrest by troops loyal to Sanogo (a development that was condemned by the UN and the USA, which threatened the reimposition of sanctions). Traoré immediately appointed Diango Cissoko, a long-standing government official and hitherto the state ombudsman, to replace him, and another transitional Government was formed in mid-December. On 11 January 2013, following French military intervention in the north (see *Tuareg Insurgency*), the Malian authorities announced a state of emergency, prohibiting public gatherings, rallies and any other potential threats to public order. It was reported in early February that three people had been killed in a further clash between supporters of Sanogo and troops loyal to Touré. In March a newspaper editor who had published an article critical of Sanogo was arrested, and subsequently charged with incitement to revolt. According to a provisional timetable announced by the Government in late February, a presidential election was to take place on 7 July, with legislative elections to follow on 21 July. The timetable was later amended, with the presidential election scheduled to take place on 28 July. The nationwide state of emergency was ended on 6 July in preparation for the forthcoming presidential election; however, violence continued and later that month four election officials and a deputy mayor were briefly held hostage in the northern town of Tessalit.

The presidential election, which was contested by 27 candidates, duly took place on 28 July 2013. Despite some reported shortcomings, including the incompleteness of the electoral register and the continued displacement of thousands of northern Malians, the ballot took place peacefully, and a relatively high official voter turnout, of 51.5%, was recorded. Former Prime Minister Keïta, representing the RPM, secured 39.8% of the votes cast, while Soumaïla Cissé of the URD, won 19.7%, and Dramane Dembélé, the ADEMA candidate, obtained 9.7%. At a second round of voting, held on 11 August, in which 45.8% of the electorate participated, Keïta defeated Cissé with 77.6% of the votes. Keïta, who pledged to restore peace in Mali, was inaugurated as President on 4 September. On the following day he appointed Oumar Tatam Ly, previously an adviser at the BCEAO, as Prime Minister. The new Government formed by Tatam Ly included for the first time the post of Minister of Reconciliation and the Development of the Northern Regions.

Recent developments: legislative elections and the end of the transitional period

The postponed legislative elections took place on 25 November and 15 December 2013, under the revised transitional timetable: the RPM won 66 seats (securing, together with its allied parties, a significant majority of 115 seats), while the URD received 17 and ADEMA 16. Despite a low voter turnout, of 38.6% in the first round and 37.2% in the second, a European Union (EU, see p. 271) observer mission commended the conduct of the elections. Meanwhile, in late November Sanogo was arrested and charged with involvement in the suspected abduction and killing of army officers loyal to Touré in April 2012 (following the discovery of human remains). Furthermore, in December 2013 the Government announced that it was to charge former President Touré with treason, owing to his failure, as Commander-in-Chief of the armed forces, to prevent the seizure of national territory by insurgents. In March 2014 the National Assembly inaugurated a new High Court of Justice, which was to consider the case of treason against Touré.

Disenchanted with Keïta's perceived reluctance to implement government and economic reforms, Tatam Ly tendered his resignation, and that of his cabinet, on 5 April 2014. Moussa Mara, the Minister of Town Planning and Housing, was appointed as his replacement, and a new Government was installed on 11 April. A number of ministers who had served in the Tatam Ly administration were reappointed. The most notable change was the designation of Abdoulaye Diop as Minister of Foreign Affairs, African Integration and International Co-operation.

In the wake of an unsuccessful and much criticized military operation to reassert government control over the northern town of Kidal in mid-May 2014 (see *Tuareg Insurgency*), allegations emerged on 5 June that a coup plot had been thwarted in Bamako. Several army officers were detained by the authorities and questioned in connection with the alleged putsch.

An outbreak of the deadly Ebola Virus Disease (EVD) was reported in Mali in late 2014. The recent impact of the virus in the neighbouring countries of Guinea, Liberia and Sierra Leone had been devastating, leaving thousands of people dead and requiring a major international intervention in order to bring the situation under control. The Malian outbreak, however, was quickly contained, and in January 2015 the country was proclaimed to be free of EVD. A total of six people lost their lives after contracting the virus.

President Keïta, dissatisfied with Mara's performance as Prime Minister, forced him to resign on 8 January 2015. Later that day former Prime Minister Modibo Keïta reassumed the premiership. A new Council of Ministers was appointed on 11 January. Tiéman Hubert Coulibaly was named as the new Minister of Defence and War Veterans, while Mamadou Igor Diarra received the economy and finance portfolio. Dembélé, ADEMA's presidential candidate in the 2013 poll, joined the cabinet as Minister of Town Planning and Housing. The Government announced in March 2015 that local and regional polls, originally scheduled to take place in April, would be delayed owing to logistical and security concerns.

Tuareg Insurgency

In the first half of the 1990s a rebellion in the north of Mali began with the return to West Africa of large numbers of Tuareg nomads, who had migrated to Algeria and Libya. A peace accord, signed in January 1991 in Tamanrasset, Algeria, by representatives of the Traoré Government and delegates from two Tuareg groups, the Mouvement Populaire de l'Azawad (MPA) and the Front Islamique-Arabe de l'Azawad (FIAA), failed to provide a lasting solution to the conflict. Following the overthrow of the Traoré regime, the transitional authorities affirmed commitment to the Tamanrasset accord. However, unrest continued, while thousands of Tuaregs, Moors and Bella (the descendants of the Tuaregs' black slaves) fled to neighbouring countries.

In February 1992, following negotiations between representatives of the Malian Government and of the Mouvements et Fronts Unifiés de l'Azawad (MFUA), comprising the MPA, the FIAA and the Armée Révolutionnaire de l'Azawad (ARLA), with Algerian mediation, a truce entered into force. After further discussions, the Malian authorities and the MFUA signed a draft 'National Pact' in April. In May 1994 the Malian authorities and Tuareg leaders reached agreement regarding the integration of former rebels into the Malian army and of Tuaregs into civilian sectors. However, the success of the agreement was undermined by an intensification of violence in northern Mali. Meanwhile, a Songhaï-dominated black resistance movement, the Mouvement Patriotique Malien Ganda Koy ('Masters of the Land'), emerged.

Further discussions involving Tuareg groups, Ganda Koy and representatives of local communities resulted in the signing, in April 1995, of a co-operation agreement. In June the FIAA announced an end to its armed struggle, and expressed its willingness to join national reconciliation efforts. A programme for the encampment of former rebels, in preparation for their eventual integration into the national army or civilian structures, began in November and ended in February 1996, by which time some 3,000 MFUA fighters and Ganda Koy militiamen had registered and surrendered their weapons. The MFUA and Ganda Koy subsequently issued a joint statement proclaiming the 'irreversible dissolution' of their respective movements. In September 1997 the graduation of MFUA and Ganda Koy contingents in the gendarmerie was reported as marking the integration of all fighters within the national armed and security forces. None the less, the Government expressed concern at the continued proliferation of weapons, as well as the inadequacy of military and administrative structures in the north.

Tensions arose again in May 2006 when Tuareg rebels launched an attack on the town of Kidal and seized three army bases. Military reinforcements were deployed to the region, while the rebel group withdrew to an area close to the Niger border, and demanded negotiations with the Government over the conditions in which the Tuaregs had been forced to live since their integration into the armed forces. Following Algerian-mediated discussions between the Government and the Tuareg group, in July a peace deal was signed in Algiers, Algeria, which included provisions for an investment programme for the region. A further reconciliation agreement was signed in February 2007. After several reported attacks on military personnel by Tuareg rebels in August, the main Tuareg group insisted that it was

continuing to uphold the reconciliation agreement; however, a splinter group announced that it had formed an alliance with Tuareg insurgents in Niger.

In April 2008 a new accord, brokered by Libyan authorities, was signed by the Malian Government and a Tuareg rebel group led by Ibrahim Bahanga, styled the Alliance Tuareg Nord-Mali pour le Changement (ATNMC). However, fighting subsequently intensified. Meeting in Algiers in July, the Government and the leaders of a group believed to be allied to the ATNMC, the Alliance Démocratique du 23 Mai pour le Changement (ADC), reached an agreement on peace and security, and in September the rebels released 44 government soldiers who had been held hostage. Despite the establishment in November of the first joint special unit comprising former rebels and Malian soldiers in accordance with the reconciliation agreement, further unrest was reported in the following month. The Malian military claimed in February 2009 that it had taken the last of the ATNMC positions, and that Bahanga—with a number of followers—had crossed the border into Algeria; Bahanga later sought refuge in Libya. (In August 2011 it was reported that Bahanga had been killed in northern Mali.)

It was reported in late 2011 that many Tuareg combatants returning to Mali from Libya (where they had fought in support of forces loyal to the regime of Col Muammar al-Qaddafi) had joined the Mouvement National pour la Libération de l'Azawad (MNLA), a new rebel group which demanded independence for Mali's northern region. In early 2012 government forces attempted to suppress onslaughts by MNLA forces against the northern towns of Menaka, Aguelhoc and Tessalit. In February, however, the MNLA advanced into southern and western Mali, attacking the towns of Lere and Niafounké. Despite a continued land and air counter-offensive by the Government, in early March it was reported that the MNLA rebels had occupied Tessalit, following a lengthy siege. Later that month the MNLA, which was joined by a newly emerged Islamist movement, Ansar Dine, led by Iyad Ag Agaly, benefited from the disorder resulting from a military coup (see *Domestic Political Affairs*) to advance its insurgency; by the beginning of April the insurgents had gained control of most of northern Mali, including Tombouctou. On 6 April the MNLA declared Azawad (comprising the regions of Gao, Kidal, Tombouctou and part of Mopti district) to be an independent state, prompting statements of condemnation from the AU and ECOWAS. Meanwhile, in early April members of a jihadist organization affiliated to Al-Qa'ida in the Islamic Maghreb (AQIM), the Mouvement Unité pour le Jihad en Afrique de l'Ouest (MUJAO), abducted seven diplomats from the Algerian consulate in the town of Gao.

In May 2012 it was announced that the MNLA and Ansar Dine had agreed to merge and to establish the 'Islamic Republic of Azawad'. However, following increasing divisions between the insurgents, it was reported that the MNLA had withdrawn from the accord, and the ensuing clashes between the two movements during June resulted in the expulsion of MNLA forces from the captured regions. Ansar Dine, together with MUJAO, established its authority in several northern towns in the following months, including Tombouctou, where it began to impose *Shari'a* law and to destroy Sufi Islamic shrines. Meanwhile, MNLA and Ansar Dine leaders declared their willingness to engage in negotiations with ECOWAS, which demanded, however, that Ansar Dine's links with AQIM be severed prior to talks. In July the International Criminal Court, based in The Hague, Netherlands, announced that, at the request of the Malian Government, it was to initiate a preliminary inquiry into reported atrocities committed by armed groups in northern Mali. Three of the abducted Algerian diplomats were released in July; however, following the Algerian authorities' rejection of demands for the release of prisoners, in September MUJAO released a statement declaring that it had executed one of their remaining hostages, the Algerian Vice-Consul. Meanwhile, Ansar Dine continued a territorial advance, securing control of the central town of Douentza in September.

The first direct discussions between government officials and MNLA and Ansar Dine leaders took place in the capital of Burkina Faso, Ouagadougou, on 4 December 2012, with Burkinabè mediation; both insurgent movements issued commitments to suspend hostilities. After urgent requests from ECOWAS, however, on 20 December the UN Security Council approved a resolution authorizing the deployment of an African-led International Support Mission to Mali (AFISMA) to assist the Malian armed forces in combating the insurgency. In response to an appeal by President Traoré, following Ansar Dine's capture of the central town of Konna and continuing advance towards Bamako, on 9 January 2013 the French Government began a military intervention (code-named 'Operation Serval') of some 4,000 French ground troops, together with military fighter jets, in Mali. Deployment of the first contingents of the UN-endorsed AFISMA began on 17 January. At an AU summit meeting in the Ethiopian capital, Addis Ababa, later in January, African leaders welcomed the French military action and approved funds of US \$50m. for AFISMA. In the same month a Tuareg faction broke away from Ansar Dine to form the Mouvement Islamique de l'Azawad, which rejected associations with AQIM. The supported French forces had regained control of Gao, Tombouctou and Kidal by the end of January, and Tessalit by early February. MUJAO staged retaliatory attacks, including suicide bombings at Tessalit, also targeting MNLA members, in response to that movement's co-operation with government and French forces. In late March French-supported government forces repelled an Ansar Dine offensive against Tombouctou. At the end of that month UN Secretary-General Ban Ki-Moon recommended to the UN Security Council that AFISMA (then numbering about 6,300 forces under the command of ECOWAS) be reconstituted as a UN peacekeeping mission with a maximum strength of 11,200 troops and 1,440 police officers, prior to a staged withdrawal of French forces. The French withdrawal commenced in early April; however, following concerns expressed by the Malian authorities, the French Government agreed that a permanent force of 1,000 French troops would remain in the country to support the UN mission. Also in April, after three Chadian soldiers deployed as part of AFISMA were killed in a suicide attack in Kidal, the Chadian Government announced that it would withdraw its 2,000-member contingent from Mali. Later that month the UN Security Council approved the establishment of the United Nations Multidimensional Integrated Stabilization Mission in Mali (MINUSMA), which was to succeed AFISMA on 1 July.

Suicide bomb attacks against army units took place in the region of Gao during May 2013, while Tuareg leaders announced the creation of a new group, the High Council for the Unity of Azawad (HCUA), which sought dialogue with the authorities. In early June government forces gained control of territory from the MNLA and advanced towards Kidal. Following EU- and UN-mediated discussions between the Government and the MNLA and the HCUA in Ouagadougou, on 18 June a preliminary peace agreement was signed, providing for an immediate ceasefire, the disarmament of armed groups in the Kidal region, and the facilitation of elections. The deployment of MINUSMA, which had an authorized strength of 12,640 military and police personnel, formally began on 1 July, as scheduled (at March 2015 the contingent numbered 10,320 personnel). The MNLA withdrew from the peace process in late September 2013, but, after the release of a number of Tuareg prisoners by the Malian authorities in accordance with the June agreement, announced, together with the HCUA, that it was to resume participation in negotiations. Meanwhile, Malian and French troops, supported by MINUSMA, staged further counter-insurgent operations in Gao, Tombouctou and Kidal. In October seven members of MINUSMA were killed in the first suicide attack against the mission near Tessalit. In December two MINUSMA soldiers were killed in another car bomb attack, in Kidal.

A controversial visit to the still contested town of Kidal on 17 May 2014 by Moussa Mara, the recently appointed Prime Minister, prompted anti-Government demonstrations by separatist protesters, which rapidly degenerated into violence. The government compound in the town came under rebel assault, and over 30 civil servants were seized. Although these hostages were soon freed, further violence erupted on 21 May when military reinforcements launched an unsuccessful attack on the town. With AU mediation, government representatives and separatist groups (including the MNLA and the HCUA) concluded a ceasefire agreement on 23 May, and the fighting was brought to a halt. Approximately 50 government troops were killed during the hostilities, and Kidal and the surrounding settlements were effectively left under separatist control. Mara was strongly criticized by opposition parties for what was widely regarded as an embarrassing defeat for the military and for the Government. Soumeylou Boubèye Maïga resigned as Minister of Defence and War Veterans in late May; he was replaced by Ba N'Dao.

A one-year extension of MINUSMA's mandate was approved by the UN Security Council in June 2014. In the following month Malian and French officials finalized a new defence pact, updating an earlier accord dating from 1985. France formally ended 'Operation Serval' in July 2014. It was replaced by a more expansive security mission, 'Operation Barkhane', focused on stabilizing the broader Sahara-Sahel region. The number of French troops in Mali was to be reduced to 1,000.

There was a reported upsurge in militant violence from mid-2014. A suicide bomber murdered four members of MINUSMA in Aguelhoc in June, while a French legionnaire was killed in another suicide attack in Gao in the following month. In August two MINUSMA soldiers died in Tombouctou after militants detonated a car bomb, and a further 10 UN peacekeepers were killed by roadside explosive devices in Kidal in September. MUJAO ambushed and killed nine MINUSMA troops in Gao in October, and another peacekeeper was murdered in Kidal later that month. Four government soldiers lost their lives in November after explosive devices were detonated in Gao. In response to the upturn in violence, MINUSMA announced in November that a rapid reaction force would be deployed in Mali to combat the northern insurgency. An increase in MINUSMA troop numbers was also mooted. In spite of this more assertive stance by MINUSMA, and notwithstanding the success of a major French operation in Kidal in November that had left 24 militants dead, insurgent action continued unabated, with a series of attacks reported in central and northern Mali in January 2015 which resulted in the deaths of at least 15 government and MINUSMA troops. Additional MINUSMA peacekeepers began to be deployed during that month; it was reported that approximately 40 peacekeepers had been killed in Mali by early 2015. Members of al-Mourabitoune, a militant Islamist organization, murdered at least four people in March during a raid on a Bamako restaurant popular with foreigners. The group asserted that the attack had been perpetrated in retaliation for the death of its leader, Ahmed al-Tilemsi, who had been assassinated by French troops in December 2014.

Meanwhile, in June 2014 Algerian mediation efforts yielded the Algiers Declaration, in which the MNLA, the HCUA and the Mouvement Arabe de l'Azawad (MAA) urged the Government to enter into peace negotiations with the separatist movement. Indirect discussions between the central authorities, the MNLA, the HCUA, the MAA and several smaller separatist factions were held in the Algerian capital in the following month, which resulted in agreement being reached on the structure of future peace talks. In addition, the separatists released the soldiers whom they had taken captive during the battle for Kidal in May, while the Government agreed to free a number of imprisoned rebels. Formal negotiations commenced in Algiers in September. A ceasefire agreement was finalized in February 2015, and in March a final peace accord, which would grant the north some degree of autonomy through the creation of regional councils and the transfer of certain competencies, was initialled by the Government and by some of the smaller separatist organizations. However, the MNLA, the HCUA and the MAA continued to express reservations and, in spite of growing international pressure, declined to accede to the agreement. Efforts to resolve the impasse were ongoing in late April.

Foreign Affairs

President Konaré sought to emphasize the role of Mali in ECOWAS, and in November 2000 a 120-member ECOWAS parliament, which was to promote regional co-operation, was inaugurated in Bamako. Mali has forged close relations with Libya, and was a founder member of the Community of Sahel-Saharan States (see p. 446), established in Tripoli, Libya, in 1997.

The presence of large numbers of refugees from the conflict in northern Mali dominated Mali's relations with its neighbours during the 1990s, and even after the completion of the process of repatriation in mid-1998 the north of the country remained vulnerable to cross-border banditry. In February 1999 Mali and Algeria agreed to revive their joint border committee to promote development and stability in the region. At a meeting in Dakar in August, the Malian, Mauritanian and Senegalese ministers responsible for the interior agreed to establish an operational unit drawn from the police forces of the three countries to enforce security in the border area. Bilateral relations between Mali and Mauritania were further strengthened by a military co-operation agreement regarding border security signed in January 2005.

In March 2004 Mali announced that it was to increase anti-terrorism co-operation with the authorities in Algeria, Chad and Niger, following the abduction of a number of foreign nationals in the region. In February 2009 AQIM, which largely operated in southern Algeria and northern Mali, claimed responsibility for the kidnapping of four European tourists the previous month and of two diplomats in December 2008. The diplomats and two of the tourists were released in April 2009, and in June Malian forces, supported by Algerian troops and aircraft, launched an attack on an AQIM base in northern Mali. Of the two remaining hostages, one was reported to have been killed in late May while the other was released in July. In response to the kidnapping of the four European citizens and the seizure in Mauritania (and subsequent transfer to Mali) of three Spanish and two Italian tourists later that year, in January 2010 Mali and Mauritania announced plans to strengthen security co-operation. In the following month, however, relations with neighbouring countries became strained after Mali released four Islamist militants, detained in April 2009 on weapons charges, in exchange for the freeing of a French citizen taken hostage in November. Both Algeria and Mauritania subsequently withdrew their ambassadors from Bamako, claiming that Mali's decision to release the terrorists was an infringement of the agreement on security co-operation reached at the September regional summit. One of the Spanish hostages was set free in March 2010, followed by the other two in August; it was reported that the Spanish Government had paid a ransom to secure their release, although the Spanish authorities denied such claims. The two Italian hostages were released in April. Meanwhile, in March ministers responsible for foreign affairs from seven Saharan states, including Mali, Mauritania and Algeria, meeting in Algiers, agreed to co-ordinate their operations against AQIM. In November 2011 two French nationals were abducted in the central town of Hombori, while a German tourist was killed and a further three foreign nationals were kidnapped in the northern city of Tombouctou. AQIM subsequently issued a statement claiming responsibility for the kidnapping of the five tourists and denouncing the Malian Government's military co-operation with France. In March 2013 AQIM announced that one of the French citizens had been killed in retaliation for the French Government's military intervention in northern Mali. AQIM claimed responsibility on the same grounds for the abduction and killing of two French journalists in Kidal in November. In April 2014 French special forces liberated five charity workers who were being held captive near Tombouctou by MUJAO militants. Approximately 10 rebels lost their lives during the French raid. Later that month, in an apparent act of retaliation, MUJAO murdered a French hostage who had been seized by the group in 2012. Ostensibly following negotiations with certain militant factions, two Algerian officials who had been taken hostage by MUJAO in 2012 were released in August 2014. A prisoner exchange deal organized by the Malian Government led to the release of a French captive by AQIM in December.

The large-scale conflict in northern Mali during 2012 precipitated the internal displacement of an estimated 204,000 Malians, while more than 200,000 fled to Mauritania, Niger and Burkina Faso, according to the office of the UN High Commissioner for Refugees. Following French military intervention in January 2013 (see *Tuareg Insurgency*), the USA provided logistical assistance and the United Kingdom announced that it would dispatch military personnel to assist in the training and reorganization of Mali's armed forces. In late January the EU declared that it would contribute €50m. to finance a UN-endorsed force, while an international donors conference pledged US $455.5m. The French President, François Hollande, visited Tombouctou in early February, and later that month France officially resumed the release of development aid, which had been suspended following the March 2012 coup. Also in February 2013 the EU Training Mission in Mali, to comprise about 500 personnel, was formally established.

CONSTITUTION AND GOVERNMENT

The Constitution of the Third Republic, which was approved in a national referendum on 12 January 1992, provides for the separation of the powers of the executive, legislative and judicial organs of state. Executive power is vested in the President of the Republic, who is elected for five years by universal suffrage. The President appoints a Prime Minister, who, in turn, appoints a Council of Ministers. Legislative power is vested in the 147-seat unicameral Assemblée Nationale (National Assembly), elected for five years by universal suffrage. Elections take place in the context of a multi-party political system.

Mali has eight administrative regions, each presided over by a governor, and a district government in Bamako. The regions are subdivided into 49 *cercles* and 703 *communes* (municipalities).

REGIONAL AND INTERNATIONAL CO-OPERATION

Mali is a member of the African Union (AU, see p. 188), the Economic Community of West African States (ECOWAS, see p. 258), the West African organs of the Franc Zone (see p. 327), the African Groundnut Council, the Niger Basin Authority (see p. 448) and the Organisation pour la Mise en Valeur du Fleuve Sénégal (OMVS, see p. 447).

Mali became a member of the UN in 1960 and was admitted to the World Trade Organization (WTO, see p. 431) in 1995.

ECONOMIC AFFAIRS

In 2013, according to estimates by the World Bank, Mali's gross national income (GNI), measured at average 2011–13 prices, was US $10,224m., equivalent to $670 per head (or $1,540 on an international purchasing-power parity basis). During 2004–13, it was estimated, the population increased at an average annual rate of 3.2%, while gross domestic product (GDP) per head grew, in real terms, by an average of 1.1% per year. According to the World Bank, overall GDP increased, in real terms, at an average annual rate of 4.3% in 2004–13; real GDP contracted by 0.4% in 2012, but grew by 2.2% in 2013.

Agriculture (including livestock-rearing, forestry and fishing) contributed 38.9% of GDP in 2013, according to provisional African Development Bank (AfDB) figures. According to FAO, some 71.5% of the labour force were estimated to be employed in the sector at mid-2015. Mali is among Africa's foremost producers and exporters of cotton (exports of which contributed an estimated 14.9% of the value of total exports in 2012). According to the IMF, cotton production increased from 202,397 metric tons in 2008 to 236,000 tons in 2009. Sheanuts (karité nuts), groundnuts, vegetables and mangoes are also cultivated for export. A government project introduced in 2006 to support diversification in the agricultural sector has had considerable success, resulting, for example, in a 135% increase in the value of mango exports between 2005 and 2009. The principal subsistence crops are rice, maize, millet and sorghum. Cereal imports remain necessary in most years. The livestock-rearing and fishing sectors make an important contribution to the domestic food supply and (in the case of the former) to export revenue, providing 4.4% of total exports in 2012, according to the International Trade Centre, although both are highly vulnerable to drought. According to the World Bank, agricultural GDP increased by an average of 6.2% per year in 2004–12. Sectoral GDP grew by 8.6% in 2012, but declined by 5.8% in 2013, according to the AfDB.

Industry (including mining, manufacturing, construction and power) contributed 22.6% of GDP in 2013, according to provisional AfDB figures. The sector engaged 6.0% of the employed labour force in 2009. According to the World Bank, industrial GDP increased at an average annual rate of 4.1% in 2004–12; it grew by 25.6% in 2011, but contracted by 2.9% in 2012.

Mining contributed 7.8% of GDP in 2013, according to provisional AfDB figures. The sector engaged 0.7% of the employed labour force in 2009. The importance of the sector has increased with the successful exploitation of the country's gold reserves: exports of gold contributed an estimated 65.5% of the value of total exports in 2012. Output of gold rose significantly in the latter half of the 1990s, as new mining facilities commenced operations, and by 2001 Mali had become the third largest gold producer in Africa. Gold production declined by an estimated 16.5% in 2010, according to the IMF, owing to a delay in the opening of a new mine. According to the US Geological Survey, gold production decreased by 1.7% in 2011, but grew by 12.3% in 2012. Two new open-pit mines, at Yalea and Loulo, operated by Randgold Resources (of South Africa), commenced operations in 2005; underground development began at the Loulo-Gounkoto gold-mine complex in 2010 and produced a record 639,219 oz of gold in 2014 (a 10% increase on production in 2013). Salt, diamonds, marble and phosphate rock are also mined. The future exploitation of deposits of iron ore and uranium is envisaged. According to the IMF, the GDP of the mining sector increased at an average annual rate of 46.8% in 1996–2002; according to the AfDB, mining GDP grew by 9.5% in 2012 and by 1.4% in 2013.

The manufacturing sector contributed 7.1% of GDP in 2013, according to provisional AfDB figures. The sector engaged 3.5% of the employed labour force in 2009. The main area of activity is agro-industrial (chiefly the processing of cotton, sugar and rice). Brewing and tobacco industries are also represented, and some construction materials are produced for the domestic market. According to the World Bank, manufacturing GDP increased at an average annual rate of 2.1% in 2004–07. According to provisional AfDB figures, the GDP of the sector rose by 5.2% in 2013.

According to provisional AfDB data, construction contributed 5.3% of GDP in 2013, and engaged 1.6% of the employed labour force in 2009. The GDP of the construction sector declined by an estimated 25.0% in 2012, but grew by 15.0% in 2013.

An agreement on energy supply was reached with Algeria in 1998. From 2001 Mali began to receive power supplies from the Manantali hydroelectric project, in the Kayes region (which was constructed and operated under the auspices of the Organisation pour la Mise en Valeur du Fleuve Sénégal—OMVS), and there were also plans to link the Malian network with those of Côte d'Ivoire, Burkina Faso and Ghana. Imports of petroleum, petroleum products and related materials comprised an estimated 28.7% of the value of merchandise imports in 2012.

The services sector contributed 38.5% of GDP in 2013, according to the AfDB. It engaged 22.6% of the employed labour force in 2009. According to the World Bank, the GDP of the services sector increased at an average annual rate of 6.0% in 2004–12. Services GDP grew by 0.1% in 2011, but declined by 7.8% in 2012.

According to IMF figures, in 2011 Mali recorded a visible merchandise trade deficit of US $332.8m. and there was a deficit of $656.5m. on the current account of the balance of payments. In 2012 the principal sources of imports were Senegal (which supplied 25.1% of total imports), France, the People's Republic of China and Benin. The largest market for exports in that year was South Africa, which accounted for 51.8% of total exports, followed by China, Switzerland-Liechtenstein and Malaysia. The principal exports in 2012 were gold and cotton, while the principal imports were petroleum, petroleum products and related materials, machinery and transport equipment, chemicals and related products, iron and steel, vegetable and vegetable products, and prepared foodstuffs.

In 2013, according to IMF estimates, Mali recorded an overall budget deficit of 156,200m. francs CFA. Mali's general government gross debt was 1,722,830m. francs CFA in 2013, equivalent to 32.1% of GDP. Mali's total external debt was US $3,073m. at the end of 2012, of which $2,797m. was public and publicly guaranteed debt. In 2011, the cost of servicing long-term public and publicly guaranteed debt and repayments to the IMF was equivalent to 2.4% of the value of exports of goods, services and income (excluding workers' remittances). The annual rate of inflation averaged 2.0% in 2008–14. Consumer prices decreased by 0.5% in 2013, but increased by 0.9% in 2013. An estimated 8.8% of the labour force were unemployed in 2004.

Mali's economic development has been hindered by its vulnerability to drought and dependence on imports. In response to the military coup on 21 March 2012 (see *Domestic Political Affairs*), the USA, the European Union (EU, see p. 271) and donor organizations suspended aid to Mali. On 6 April an agreement was reached with the Economic Community of West African States (ECOWAS, see p. 258), under which power was ceded to a new Government for a transitional period, in exchange for the removal of the sanctions that had been imposed against Mali. Meanwhile, an insurrection by Tuareg and Islamist groups (see *Tuareg Insurgency*), which had occupied the north of the country by the end of 2012, intensified a humanitarian crisis in the region. Although military intervention by French and ECOWAS-led forces restored government control in early 2013, hostilities persisted in the north. Following the cancellation of a previous credit arrangement, the IMF agreed to extend an US $18.4m. emergency loan to Mali in January, and other development assistance was resumed. At a conference in May, the EU and other donors pledged some €3,300m., which was conditional on significant progress in governance, the restoration of state services, the organization of elections and the adoption of measures to combat corruption. Despite the continued instability, presidential and legislative elections took place successfully later that year under the transitional programme (see *Domestic Political Affairs*). In December the IMF approved a new Extended Credit Facility (ECF) arrangement of $46.2m. Although the manufacturing and service sectors recovered strongly in 2013, owing to a general improvement in the security situation and the resumption of donor support, the agricultural sector contracted following a poor harvest. Despite this, the World Bank reported that real GDP grew by 2.2% in that year, compared with a contraction of 0.4% in 2012. In May 2014 the IMF expressed concern about Mali's recent acquisition, at enormous expense, of a presidential jet and withheld a $6m. funding tranche that had been due to be released under the ECF. Nevertheless, the Fund authorized the disbursement of $11.7m. of ECF funds in December after the Malian authorities had undertaken remedial measures and reaffirmed their commitment to fiscal prudence. The economy, buoyed by higher cotton output as a result of government initiatives to encourage activity in the sector, expanded by an estimated 7.2% in 2014. Further robust growth, of 5.0%, was forecast for 2015.

PUBLIC HOLIDAYS

2016: 1 January (New Year's Day), 11 January* (Baptism of the Prophet), 20 January (Armed Forces Day), 26 March (Commemoration of the overthrow of Moussa Traoré), 28 March (Easter Monday), 1 May (Labour Day), 25 May (Africa Day, anniversary of the OAU's foundation), 6 July* (Korité, end of Ramadan), 12 September* (Tabaski, Feast of the Sacrifice), 22 September (Independence Day), 11 December* (Mouloud, Birth of the Prophet), 25 December (Christmas Day).

* These holidays are determined by the Islamic lunar calendar and may vary by one or two days from the dates given.

Statistical Survey

Source (unless otherwise stated): Institut National de la Statistique, Bureau Central du Recensement, BP 12, Bamako; tel. 2021–5285; fax 2022-7145; e-mail cnpe.mali@afribonemali.net; internet www.instat.gov.ml.

Area and Population

AREA, POPULATION AND DENSITY

Area (sq km)	1,240,192*
Population (census results)	
17 April 1998†	9,790,492
1 April 2009	
Males	7,204,990
Females	7,323,672
Total	14,528,662
Population (UN estimates at mid-year)‡	
2013	15,301,650
2014	15,768,229
2015	16,258,587
Density (per sq km) at mid-2015	13.1

* 478,841 sq miles.
† Figures are provisional and refer to the *de jure* population.
‡ Source: UN, *World Population Prospects: The 2012 Revision.*

POPULATION BY AGE AND SEX
(UN estimates at mid-2015)

	Males	Females	Total
0–14 years	3,940,007	3,790,180	7,730,187
15–64 years	4,066,199	4,026,123	8,092,322
65 years and over	191,983	244,095	436,078
Total	8,198,189	8,060,398	16,258,587

Source: UN, *World Population Prospects: The 2012 Revision.*

ADMINISTRATIVE DIVISIONS
(population at 2009 census)

District			Koulikoro . . .	2,422,108
Bamako	1,810,366		Mopti . . .	2,036,209
Regions			Ségou	2,338,349
Gao	542,304		Sikasso . . .	2,643,179
Kayes	1,993,615		Tombouctou . .	674,793
Kidal	67,739		**Total**	14,528,662

PRINCIPAL TOWNS*
(population at 2009 census)

Bamako (capital) .	1,810,366	Ségou	133,501
Sikasso	226,618	Mopti	120,786
Kayes	149,129	Gao	86,353
Koutiala . . .	141,444	Kati	84,500

* With the exception of Bamako, figures refer to the population of communes (municipalities).

Mid-2015 (incl. suburbs, UN estimate): Bamako 2,515,000 (Source: UN, *World Urbanization Prospects: The 2014 Revision*).

BIRTHS AND DEATHS
(annual averages, UN estimates)

	2000–05	2005–10	2010–15
Birth rate (per 1,000) . . .	48.2	48.0	47.3
Death rate (per 1,000) . . .	16.7	14.9	13.2

Source: UN, *World Population Prospects: The 2012 Revision*.

Life expectancy (years at birth): 54.6 (males 54.7; females 54.5) in 2012 (Source: World Bank, World Development Indicators database).

EMPLOYMENT
('000 persons, 2009 census)

	Males	Females	Total
Agriculture, hunting and forestry .	2,264.2	1,239.0	3,503.2
Fishing	60.4	25.1	85.5
Mining	29.9	8.9	38.7
Manufacturing	133.5	55.5	189.0
Electricity, gas and water . . .	11.4	0.5	12.0
Construction	86.7	2.6	89.3
Wholesale and retail trade; repair of motor vehicles, motorcycles and personal household goods .	310.7	176.4	487.1
Hotels and restaurants . .	4.3	4.2	8.5
Transport, storage and communications	137.5	21.2	158.7
Financial intermediation . .	3.8	2.8	6.6
Real estate	41.7	7.9	49.6
Public administration . . .	52.3	16.6	68.8
Education	169.8	87.6	257.3
Health and social work . . .	14.1	13.4	27.6
Other social services . . .	59.3	114.3	173.6
Sub-total	3,379.6	1,776.0	5,155.5
Activities not adequately defined .	174.8	139.9	314.7
Total employed	3,554.1	1,915.9	5,470.1

Mid-2015 (estimates in '000)· Agriculture, etc. 3,144; Total labour force 4,395 (Source: FAO).

Health and Welfare

KEY INDICATORS

Total fertility rate (children per woman, 2012)	6.9
Under-5 mortality rate (per 1,000 live births, 2012) . . .	128
HIV/AIDS (% of persons aged 15–49, 2013)	0.9
Physicians (per 1,000 head, 2010)	0.08
Hospital beds (per 1,000 head, 2010)	0.10
Health expenditure (2011): US $ per head (PPP)	85
Health expenditure (2011): % of GDP	6.8
Health expenditure (2011): public (% of total)	43.8
Access to water (% of persons, 2012)	67
Access to sanitation (% of persons, 2012)	22
Total carbon dioxide emissions ('000 metric tons, 2010) . .	623.4
Carbon dioxide emissions per head (metric tons, 2010) . .	<0.1
Human Development Index (2013): ranking	176
Human Development Index (2013): value	0.407

For sources and definitions, see explanatory note on p. vi.

Agriculture

PRINCIPAL CROPS
('000 metric tons)

	2011	2012	2013
Rice, paddy	1,741.5	1,914.9	2,211.9
Maize	1,298.2	1,713.7	1,502.7
Millet	1,462.1	1,772.3	1,152.3
Sorghum	1,191.0	1,212.4	819.6
Fonio	51.0	21.0	22.1
Sweet potatoes*	280.0	265.0	250.0
Cassava (Manioc)* . . .	45.9	40.0	38.0
Yams*	92.0	80.0	78.0
Sugar cane*	360.0	370.0	357.0
Groundnuts, with shell† . . .	224.0	230.0	220.0
Karité nuts (Sheanuts)* . . .	208.0	210.0	195.0
Cottonseed†	299.0	300.0	330.0
Tomatoes*	41.5	42.0	46.7
Onions, dry*	42.0	44.0	43.6
Guavas, mangoes and mangosteens*	50.0	51.0	52.7
Cotton (lint)*	120.0	143.0	126.8

* FAO estimates.
† Unofficial figures.

Aggregate production ('000 metric tons, may include official, semi-official or estimated data): Total cereals 5,777.9 in 2011, 6,674.6 in 2012, 5,736.3 in 2013; Total pulses 168.9 in 2011, 210.4 in 2012, 282.7 in 2013; Total roots and tubers 504.4 in 2011, 475.0 in 2012, 453.0 in 2013; Total vegetables (incl. melons) 876.1 in 2011, 906.4 in 2012, 863.9 in 2013; Total fruits (excl. melons) 432.3 in 2011, 442.8 in 2012, 438.2 in 2013.

Source: FAO.

LIVESTOCK
('000 head, year ending September)

	2011	2012	2013
Cattle	9,438	9,721	10,013
Sheep	12,459	13,081	13,736
Goats	17,349	18,216	19,127
Pigs	76	77	78
Horses	498	507	518
Asses	900	920	940
Camels	941	960	979
Chickens	36,711	35,096	36,850

Source: FAO.

LIVESTOCK PRODUCTS
('000 metric tons)

	2011	2012	2013
Cattle meat*	149.5	169.0	169.0
Sheep meat*	52.7	50.0	51.5
Goat meat*	72.4	75.6	77.8
Chicken meat*	41.2	42.0	44.1
Game meat*	23.7	24.5	24.5
Pig meat*	2.7	2.7	2.7
Cows' milk*	307.1	406.8	259.9
Sheep's milk*	173.4	159.0	157.5
Goats' milk	702.6	715.0	720.0*
Camels' milk	298.8	138.7	242.9

* FAO estimate(s).

Source: FAO.

Forestry

ROUNDWOOD REMOVALS
('000 cubic metres, excl. bark, FAO estimates)

	2011	2012	2013
Sawlogs, veneer logs and logs for sleepers	56	56	60
Other industrial wood	409	417	429
Fuel wood	5,385	5,445	5,505
Total	**5,850**	**5,918**	**5,994**

Source: FAO.

SAWNWOOD PRODUCTION
('000 cubic metres, incl. railway sleepers, FAO estimates)

	2011	2012	2013
Total (all broadleaved)	13*	16	13

* Unofficial figure.

Source: FAO.

Fishing

('000 metric tons, live weight, FAO estimates)

	2010	2011	2012
Capture	100.0	108.1	71.2
Nile tilapia	30.0	32.4	21.3
Elephantsnout fishes	7.0	7.6	5.0
Characins	5.0	5.4	3.6
Black catfishes	4.0	4.3	2.9
North African catfish	25.0	27.0	17.8
Nile perch	6.0	6.5	4.3
Other freshwater fishes	18.9	20.4	13.5
Aquaculture	2.1	2.1	1.0
Total catch	**102.1**	**110.2**	**72.2**

Source: FAO.

Mining

(metric tons unless otherwise indicated)

	2010	2011	2012
Gold (kg)	36,360	35,728	40,132
Salt*	6,000	6,000	n.a.
Semi-precious stones*	10,000	10,000	n.a.

* Estimated figures.

Source: US Geological Survey.

Industry

SELECTED PRODUCTS
('000 metric tons unless otherwise indicated)

	2009	2010	2011
Raw sugar	35	35	35
Cigarettes (million)	975.9	n.a.	n.a.
Electric energy (million kWh)	1,575	1,702	1,702

2007: Fish (dried, salted or in brine), smoked fish and edible fish meal 8.8.

Source: mainly UN Industrial Commodity Statistics Database.

Finance

CURRENCY AND EXCHANGE RATES

Monetary Units
100 centimes = 1 franc de la Communauté Financière Africaine (CFA).

Sterling, Dollar and Euro Equivalents (31 December 2014)
£1 sterling = 843.273 francs CFA;
US $1 = 540.283 francs CFA;
€1 = 655.957 francs CFA;
10,000 francs CFA = £11.86 = $18.51 = €15.24.

Average Exchange Rate (francs CFA per US $)
2012   510.52
2013   494.04
2014   494.41

Note: An exchange rate of 1 French franc = 50 francs CFA, established in 1948, remained in force until January 1994, when the CFA franc was devalued by 50%, with the exchange rate adjusted to 1 French franc = 100 francs CFA. This relationship to French currency remained in effect with the introduction of the euro on 1 January 1999. From that date, accordingly, a fixed exchange rate of €1 = 655.957 francs CFA has been in operation.

BUDGET
('000 million francs CFA)*

Revenue†	2011	2012‡	2013‡
Budgetary revenue	763.0	813.3	842.7
Tax revenue	730.1	758.7	804.5
Non-tax revenue	32.9	54.7	38.2
Special funds and annexed budgets	96.1	99.5	108.5
Total	**859.1**	**912.8**	**951.2**

Expenditure§	2011	2012‡	2013‡
Budgetary expenditure	1,165.4	889.9	1,205.0
Current expenditure	717.3	719.4	800.5
Wages and salaries	265.1	291.1	290.8
Interest payments (scheduled)	35.4	32.9	32.4
Other current expenditure	416.9	395.4	477.3
Capital expenditure	448.1	170.5	404.5
Externally financed	253.9	32.1	175.9
Special funds and annexed budgets	96.1	99.5	108.5
Total	**1,261.5**	**989.4**	**1,313.5**

* Figures represent a consolidation of the central government budget, special funds and annexed budgets.
† Excluding grants received ('000 million francs CFA): 193.9 in 2011; 13.0 in 2012 (estimate); 199.9 in 2013 (estimate).
‡ Estimates.
§ Excluding net lending ('000 million francs CFA): –3.2 in 2011; –2.8 in 2012 (estimate); –6.2 in 2013 (estimate).

2014 (programmed figures): *Revenue:* Budgetary revenue 964.2 (Tax revenue 923.7, Non-tax revenue 40.5); Special funds and annexed budgets 99.5; Total revenue 1,063.7 (excl. grants 317.7). *Expenditure:* Budgetary expenditure 1,558.8 (Current expenditure 874.7, Capital expenditure 684.1); Special funds and annexed budgets 99.5; Total expenditure 1,658.3 (excl. net lending –4.6).

Source: IMF, *Mali: First and Second Reviews Under the Extended Credit Facility Arrangement, Request for Waiver of Performance Criteria, and Request for Modification of Performance Criteria-Staff Report; Press Release; and Statement by the Executive Director for Mali* (December 2014).

INTERNATIONAL RESERVES
(excl. gold, US $ million at 31 December)

	2011	2012	2013
IMF special drawing rights	112.7	112.8	113.0
Reserve position in IMF	15.4	15.4	15.4
Foreign exchange	1,250.6	1,213.2	1,177.3
Total	**1,378.6**	**1,341.4**	**1,305.7**

2014: IMF special drawing rights 106.3; Reserve position in IMF 14.5.

Source: IMF, *International Financial Statistics*.

MONEY SUPPLY
('000 million francs CFA at 31 December)

	2011	2012	2013
Currency outside banks . . .	415.4	514.3	510.0
Demand deposits	677.2	769.5	808.0
Total money (incl. others) . .	1,092.9	1,284.2	1,318.4

Source: IMF, *International Financial Statistics*.

COST OF LIVING
(Consumer Price Index for Bamako: base: 2008 = 100)

	2012	2013	2014
Food and non-alcoholic beverages .	121.8	117.8	117.5
Clothing and footwear	106.2	105.8	108.0
Housing, water, electricity, gas and other fuels	103.7	107.7	111.0
All items (incl. others) . . .	112.3	111.7	112.7

NATIONAL ACCOUNTS
(million francs CFA at current prices)

Expenditure on the Gross Domestic Product

	2011	2012*	2013†
Government final consumption expenditure	859	808	950
Private final consumption expenditure	3,097	3,317	3,604
Changes in inventories . . .	44	298	−138
Gross fixed capital formation .	1,114	849	1,151
Total domestic expenditure .	5,114	5,272	5,567
Exports of goods and services .	1,254	1,517	1,485
Less Imports of goods and services	1,345	1,497	1,627
GDP in purchasers' values .	5,024	5,291	5,425

Gross Domestic Product by Economic Activity

	2011	2012*	2013†
Agriculture, hunting, forestry and fishing	1,773	2,016	1,908
Mining and quarrying . . .	351	422	385
Manufacturing	287	333	348
Electricity, gas and water . .	100	101	116
Construction	263	217	260
Wholesale and retail trade, restaurants and hotels . . .	713	771	837
Transport and communications .	268	280	306
Finance, insurance, real estate and other business services . . .	350	254	295
Public administration and defence	427	411	451
Sub-total	4,532	4,805	4,906
Less Imputed bank service charges	23	24	25
Indirect taxes, less subsidies . .	515	510	545
GDP in purchasers' values .	5,024	5,291	5,425

* Preliminary figures.
† Provisional figures.

Source: African Development Bank.

BALANCE OF PAYMENTS
(US $ million)

	2009	2010	2011
Exports of goods f.o.b.	1,772.2	2,052.6	2,389.8
Imports of goods f.o.b.	−1,982.3	−2,717.2	−2,722.6
Trade balance	−210.1	−664.6	−332.8
Exports of services	355.8	383.7	410.9
Imports of services	−829.6	−1,027.6	−1,128.4
Balance on goods and services	−683.9	−1,308.5	−1,050.3
Other income received	81.6	71.7	58.4
Other income paid	−539.0	−490.7	−520.2
Balance on goods, services and income	−1,141.2	−1,727.5	−1,512.1
Current transfers received . .	648.3	700.8	986.4
Current transfers paid	−162.0	−163.3	−130.7

—continued	2009	2010	2011
Current balance	−654.9	−1,189.9	−656.5
Capital account (net) . . .	384.1	229.6	361.8
Direct investment assets . . .	646.6	371.6	−4.4
Direct investment liabilities . .	102.8	26.9	556.1
Portfolio investment assets . .	−60.3	−462.2	−7.7
Portfolio investment liabilities .	21.3	7.2	62.6
Financial derivatives assets . .	−1.6	−3.9	—
Other investment assets . . .	−370.7	304.9	−468.1
Other investment liabilities . .	554.3	507.9	221.2
Net errors and omissions . . .	−175.3	31.1	−60.7
Reserves and related items .	446.3	−177.0	4.4

Source: IMF, *International Financial Statistics*.

External Trade

PRINCIPAL COMMODITIES
(distribution by HS, US $ million)

Imports c.i.f.	2010	2011	2012
Vegetables and vegetable products	189.7	163.1	209.7
Cereals and cereal preparations .	113.7	105.7	154.1
Prepared foodstuffs; beverages, spirits, vinegar; tobacco and articles thereof .	249.3	214.9	192.3
Mineral products	1,428.6	1,204.0	1,191.4
Mineral fuels, lubricants, etc. .	1,221.0	982.2	993.7
Petroleum oils, not crude . .	1,201.2	961.1	963.3
Salt, sulphur, earth, stone, plaster, lime and cement	207.5	221.8	197.7
Cements, portland and hydraulic	185.3	201.2	176.2
Chemicals and related products	627.3	375.0	466.0
Medicinal and pharmaceutical products	337.6	101.0	145.4
Medicament mixtures . . .	309.5	97.2	141.5
Fertilizers	113.1	157.8	172.6
Plastics, rubber, and articles thereof	221.4	124.2	130.1
Iron and steel, other base metals and articles of base metal	404.8	249.0	225.1
Iron and steel	160.6	113.8	93.3
Articles of iron or steel . . .	168.3	99.2	100.5
Machinery and mechanical appliances; electrical equipment; parts thereof .	804.4	468.3	549.6
Machinery, boilers, etc . . .	508.1	278.9	313.3
Electrical, electronic equipment .	296.4	189.4	236.3
Vehicles, aircraft, vessels and associated transport equipment	331.3	282.4	225.0
Road vehicles	317.7	280.3	222.2
Total (incl. others)	4,703.5	3,351.5	3,462.7

Exports f.o.b.	2010	2011	2012
Live animals and animal products	72.8	77.1	118.4
Live animals	70.8	74.4	114.6
Live bovine animals	48.6	54.8	84.2
Chemicals and related products	37.9	167.8	170.4
Fertilizers	30.2	155.2	160.1
Mixtures of nitrogen, phosphorous or potassium fertilizers	30.0	113.7	119.0
Textiles and textile articles	172.0	209.2	390.4
Cotton	170.3	207.1	388.3
Cotton, not carded or combed	27.9	149.3	13.2
Cotton, carded or combed	139.4	55.6	372.2
Pearls, precious or semi-precious stones, precious metals, and articles thereof	1,578.9	1,691.7	1,717.9
Gold	1,578.7	1,691.1	1,709.3
Total (incl. others)	1,996.3	2,374.5	2,610.4

Source: Trade Map-Trade Competitiveness Map, International Trade Centre, www.intracen.org/marketanalysis.

PRINCIPAL TRADING PARTNERS
(US $ million)

Imports c.i.f.	2010	2011	2012
Australia	51.4	49.3	53.9
Belgium	69.9	48.6	48.4
Benin	467.7	253.9	172.3
Brazil	67.0	76.5	57.7
China, People's Republic	467.4	359.2	367.3
Côte d'Ivoire	371.0	270.0	288.1
France (incl. Monaco)	630.3	344.4	374.2
Germany	111.1	116.3	74.6
Ghana	74.2	107.4	100.2
India	67.7	68.8	91.8
Italy	49.2	30.1	40.6
Japan	121.6	60.1	41.0
Morocco	28.1	38.6	23.7
Netherlands	110.8	24.8	22.5
Niger	—	—	104.7
Russia	49.7	55.4	62.5
Senegal	638.8	716.7	867.9
South Africa	298.0	156.0	106.3
Spain	32.2	35.1	43.3
Togo	105.4	35.7	18.0
Turkey	21.8	35.6	30.0
Ukraine	72.8	64.8	32.5
USA	421.3	83.1	95.2
Total (incl. others)	4,703.5	3,351.5	3,462.7

Exports f.o.b.	2010	2011	2012
Burkina Faso	43.1	99.3	92.9
China, People's Republic	40.8	86.1	203.0
Côte d'Ivoire	39.9	80.6	113.4
France (incl. Monaco)	22.7	34.8	51.9
Indonesia	12.0	39.6	8.5
Italy	120.0	6.3	15.1
Malaysia	24.1	16.5	129.3
Pakistan	20.5	6.5	—
Russia	—	29.0	21.7
Saudi Arabia	—	—	33.9
Senegal	87.8	106.0	65.6
South Africa	1,139.2	1,349.3	1,351.8
Switzerland-Liechtenstein	241.6	279.2	303.6
USA	63.1	5.4	8.0
Total (incl. others)	1,996.3	2,374.5	2,610.4

Source: Trade Map-Trade Competitiveness Map, International Trade Centre, www.intracen.org/marketanalysis.

Transport

ROAD TRAFFIC
(motor vehicles in use at 31 December)

	2009
Passenger cars	107,194
Vans and lorries	49,074
Motorcycles and mopeds	24,700

Source: IRF, *World Road Statistics*.

CIVIL AVIATION

	2011	2012	2013
Passengers carried ('000)	364	182	33

Source: World Bank, World Development Indicators database.

Tourism

FOREIGN VISITORS BY NATIONALITY*

	2009	2010	2011
Austria	660	1,906	1,648
Belgium, Luxembourg and the Netherlands	6,642	6,306	6,397
Canada	10,091	6,147	5,644
France	38,261	42,883	30,207
Germany	5,380	4,937	5,428
Italy	5,307	6,878	5,955
Japan	1,307	2,668	3,148
Middle Eastern states	2,946	2,948	3,910
Scandinavian states	1,791	1,875	2,316
Spain	4,388	5,514	4,811
Switzerland	2,723	2,520	2,815
United Kingdom	4,173	4,422	3,595
USA	16,901	17,545	15,182
West African states	27,408	29,872	33,983
Total (incl. others)	160,012	169,305	159,782

* Arrivals at hotels and similar establishments.

Total tourists arrivals: 101,335 in 2012.

Receipts from tourism (US $ million, excl. passenger transport): 283 in 2010; 267 in 2011.

Source: World Tourism Organization.

Communications Media

	2011	2012	2013
Telephones ('000 main lines in use)	104.7	112.0	114.6
Mobile cellular telephones ('000 subscribers)	10,821.9	14,612.8	19,749.4
Internet subscribers ('000) . .	36.5	n.a.	n.a.
Broadband subscribers ('000) . .	2.4	3.2	2.9

Source: International Telecommunication Union.

Education

(2011/12 unless otherwise indicated)

		Students ('000)		
	Institutions*	Teachers	Males	Females	Total
Pre-primary .	212	1,618†	35.5†	35.7†	71.2†
Primary . .	2,871	43,629†	1,142.6	971.3	2,113.9
Secondary . .	n.a.	33,220†	566.9	396.2	963.1
Tertiary . . .	n.a.	1,856	69.2	28.1	97.3

* 1998/99 figures.
† 2010/11 figure.

2005/06: *Pre-primary:* 412 institutions; 1,510 teachers; 51,071 students; *Primary and Secondary (lower):* 8,079 institutions; 39,109 teachers; 1,990,765 students (1,137,787 males, 852,978 females); *Secondary (higher):* 121 institutions; 1,904 teachers; 47,279 students (31,724 males, 15,555 females—estimates); *Secondary (technical and vocational):* 119 institutions; 41,137 students; *Secondary (teacher-training):* 10,467 students (Source: Office of the Secretary-General of the Government, Bamako).

Source: mainly UNESCO Institute for Statistics.

Pupil-teacher ratio (primary education, UNESCO estimate): 48.5 in 2010/11 (Source: UNESCO Institute for Statistics).

Adult literacy rate (UNESCO estimates): 33.4% (males 43.1%; females 24.6%) in 2011 (Source: UNESCO Institute for Statistics).

Directory

The Government

HEAD OF STATE

President: IBRAHIM BOUBACAR KEÏTA (inaugurated 4 September 2013).

COUNCIL OF MINISTERS
(May 2015)

Prime Minister: MODIBO KEÏTA.

Minister of Rural Development: Dr BOCARY TRÉTA.

Minister of Solidarity, Humanitarian Action and the Reconstruction of the Northern Regions: HAMADOU KONATÉ.

Minister of State Property and Land Affairs: MOHAMED ALY BATHILY.

Minister of National Reconstruction: ZAHABI OULD SIDI MOHAMED.

Minister of Defence and War Veterans: TIÉMAN HUBERT COULIBALY.

Minister of Foreign Affairs, African Integration and International Co-operation: ABDOULAYE DIOP.

Ministry of Territorial Administration and Decentralization: ABDOULAYE IDRISSA MAÏGA.

Minister of the Economy and Finance: MAMADOU IGOR DIARRA.

Minister of Health and Public Hygiene: OUSMANE KONÉ.

Minister of the Digital Economy, Information and Communication, Government Spokesperson: CHOGUEL KOKALA MAÏGA.

Minister Security and Civil Protection: Gen. SADA SAMAKÉ.

Minister of Justice and Human Rights, Keeper of the Seals: MAHAMADOU DIARRA.

Minister of Employment, Youth and Civic Construction: MAHAMANE BABY.

Minister of Higher Education and Scientific Research: MOUNTAGA TALL.

Minister of National Education: KÉNÉKOUO 'BARTHÉLÉMY' TOGO.

Minister of Malians Abroad: Dr ABDRAHAMANE SYLLA.

Minister of Equipment, Transport and Improving Access to Isolated Regions: MAMADOU HACHIM KOUMARÉ.

Minister of Town Planning and Housing: DRAMANE DEMBÉLÉ.

Minister of Labour, the Civil Service and State Reform, in charge of Relations with the Institutions: DIARRA RAKY TALLA.

Minister of Trade and Industry: ABDEL KARIM KONATÉ.

Minister of Land Management and Population: CHEICKNA SEYDI AHAMADI DIAWARA.

Minister of Energy and Water: MAMADOU FRANKALY KÉÏTA.

Minister of Mining: BOUBOU CISSÉ.

Minister of the Promotion of Investment and the Private Sector: MAMADOU GAOUSSOU DIARRA.

Minister of Culture, Handicrafts and Tourism: N'DIAYE RAMATOULAYE DIALLO.

Minister of the Environment, Sanitation and Sustainable Development: MOHAMED AG ERLAF.

Minister of the Promotion of Women, Children and the Family: SANGARÉ OUMOU BAH.

Minister of Religious Affairs and Cults: THIERNO AMADOU OMAR HASS DIALLO.

Minister of Sport: HOUSSEINI AMION GUINDO.

MINISTRIES

Office of the President: BP 10, Koulouba, Bamako; tel. 2070-2000; internet www.koulouba.ml.

Office of the Prime Minister: Quartier du Fleuve, BP 790, Bamako; tel. 2022-4310; fax 2023 9595; e-mail ecrireaupm@primature.gov.ml; internet www.primature.gov.ml.

Office of the Secretary-General of the Government: BP 14, Koulouba, Bamako; tel. 2022-2552; fax 2022-7050; e-mail sgg@sgg.gov.ml; internet www.sgg.gov.ml.

Ministry of Culture, Handicrafts and Tourism: Cité Administrative, Bâtiment N°05, BP E4075, Bamako; tel. 2029-6450; fax 4490-0344; e-mail malibiennale@yahoo.fr; internet www.culture.gouv.ml; internet www.artisanat-tourisme.gouv.ml.

Ministry of Defence and War Veterans: route de Koulouba, BP 2083, Bamako; tel. 2022-5021; fax 2023-2318.

Ministry of the Digital Economy, Information and Communication: ave de l'Yser, Quartier du Fleuve, BP 116, Bamako; tel. and fax 2079-1643; internet www.communication.gouv.ml.

Ministry of the Economy and Finance: BP 234, Bamako; tel. 2222-5858; fax 2222-0192; e-mail sg@finances.gov.ml; internet www.finances.gouv.ml.

Ministry of Employment, Youth and Civic Construction: Bamako; tel. 76338261 (mobile); internet www.mefp.gov.ml.

Ministry of Energy and Water: Bamako; internet www.energie.gouv.ml.

Ministry of the Environment, Sanitation and Sustainable Development: Bamako; internet www.cnvironnement.gov.ml.

Ministry of Equipment, Transport and Improving Access to Isolated Regions: Bamako; tel. 2022-3937; internet www.met.gov.ml.

Ministry of Foreign Affairs, African Integration and International Co-operation: Koulouba, Bamako; tel. 2022-8314; fax 2022-5226; internet www.diplomatie.gouv.ml.

Ministry of Health and Public Hygiene: BP 232, Koulouba, Bamako; tel. 2023-4266; fax 2023-0203; e-mail info@sante.gov.ml; internet www.sante.gov.ml.

Ministry of Higher Education and Scientific Research: BP E5466, Bamako; tel. 2001-55900; fax 2022-2126; e-mail contact .mesrs@gmail.com; internet enseignementsup.gouv.ml.

Ministry of Justice and Human Rights: Quartier du Fleuve, BP 97, Bamako; tel. 2022-2642; fax 2023-0063; e-mail ucprodej@afribone .net.ml; internet www.justice.gouv.ml.

Ministry of Labour, the Civil Service and State Reform: Quartier Administratif, route de Koulouba, BP 80, Bamako; tel. 2022-3431; fax 2023-6741; internet www.fonctionpublique.gouv.ml.

Ministry of Malians Abroad: Cité du Niger, route de l'Hotel Mandé, Bamako; tel. 2021-8148; fax 2021-2505; e-mail maliensdelexterieur@yahoo.fr; internet www.maliens-exterieur .gouv.ml.

Ministry of Mining: BP 238, Bamako; tel. 2022-4184; fax 2022-2160; e-mail infos@mines.gouv.ml; internet www.mines.gouv.ml.

Ministry of National Education: Bamako.

Ministry of National Reconstruction: Bamako.

Ministry of Land Management and Population: face Direction de la RCFM, BP 78, Bamako; tel. 2022-4212; fax 2023-0247.

Ministry of the Promotion of Investment and the Private Sector: Bamako.

Ministry of the Promotion of Women, Children and the Family: porte G9, rue 109, Badalabougou, BP 2688, Bamako; tel. 2022-6659; fax 2023-6660; e-mail mpfef@cefib.com; internet www.mpfef .gov.ml.

Ministry of Religious Affairs and Cults: Bamako.

Ministry of Rural Development: Bamako.

Ministry of Security and Civil Protection: BP E 4771, Bamako; tel. 2022-0082.

Ministry of Solidarity, Humanitarian Action and the Reconstruction of the Northern Regions: Bamako; tel. 2023-2301.

Ministry of Sport: Bamako; internet www.sports.gouv.ml.

Ministry of State Property and Land Affairs: Bamako.

Ministry of Territorial Administration and Decentralization: Bamako.

Ministry of Town Planning and Housing: Bamako.

Ministry of Trade and Industry: BP 234, Koulouba, Bamako; tel. 2022-5156; fax 2022-0192; internet www.miic.gouv.ml.

President

Presidential Election, First Round, 28 July 2013

Candidate	Votes	% of votes
Ibrahim Boubacar Keïta (RPM) . . .	1,175,769	39.79
Soumaïla Cissé (URD)	582,127	19.70
Dramane Dembélé (ADEMA) . . .	286,929	9.71
Modibo Sidibé (FARE)	146,839	4.97
Housseini 'Poulo' Guindo (CODEM) . .	140,345	4.75
Others*	623,255	21.09
Total	**2,955,264†**	**100.00**

* There were 22 other candidates.
† In addition, there were 389,989 invalid or cancelled votes.

Presidential Election, Second Round, 11 August 2013

Candidate	Votes	% of votes
Ibrahim Boubacar Keïta (RPM) . . .	2,355,394	77.62
Soumaïla Cissé (URD)	679,069	22.38
Total	**3,034,463***	**100.00**

* In addition, there were 88,664 invalid votes.

Legislature

National Assembly: BP 284, Bamako; tel. 2021-5724; fax 2021-0374; e-mail assemblee.n@gmail.com; internet assemblee-nationale .ml.

President: ISSAKA SIDIBÉ.

General Election, 25 November and 15 December 2013

Party	Seats
Rassemblement pour le Mali	66
Union pour la République et la Démocratie	17
Alliance pour la Démocratie au Mali—Parti Pan-Africain pour la Liberté, la Solidarité et la Justice	16
Forces Alternatives pour le Renouveau et l'Emergence .	6
Convergence pour le Développement du Mali	5
Parti de la Solidarité Africaine pour la Démocratie et l'Indépendance	5
Congrès National d'Initiative Démocratique—Faso Yiriwa Ton	4
Alliance pour la Solidarité au Mali-Convergence des Forces Patriotiques	3
Mouvement Patriotique pour le Renouveau	3
Parti pour le Développement Economique et la Solidarité	3
Parti pour la Renaissance Nationale	3
Alliance pour la Démocratie et le Progrès	2
Convention Démocratique et Sociale	2
Mouvement pour l'Indépendance, la Renaissance et l'Intégration Africaine	2
Union Malienne du Rassemblement Démocratique Africain Faso Jigi	2
Alliance pour la République	1
Union pour la Démocratie et le Développement . . .	1
Parti pour la Restauration des Valeurs du Mali . . .	1
Yelema	1
Independents	4
Total	**147**

Election Commission

Commission Electorale Nationale Indépendante (CENI): Bamako; Pres. MAMADOU DIAMOUTANI.

Advisory Councils

Economic, Social and Cultural Council: BP E 15, Koulouba, Bamako; tel. 2022-4368; fax 2022-8452; e-mail cesc@cefib.com; f. 1987; Pres. JEAMILLE BITTAR.

High Council of Communities: Bamako; compulsorily advises the Govt on issues relating to local and regional devt; comprises national councillors, elected indirectly for a term of five years; Pres. OUMAROU AG MOHAMED IBRAHIM HAÏDARA.

Political Organizations

At the end of 2012 there were some 138 political parties registered with the Ministry of Territorial Administration, Decentralization and Land Management.

Alliance pour la Démocratie au Mali—Parti Pan-Africain pour la Liberté, la Solidarité et la Justice (ADEMA): rue Fankélé, porte 145, BP 1791, Bamako-Coura; tel. 2022-0368; internet www.adema-pasj.org; f. 1990 as Alliance pour la Démocratie au Mali; Pres. DIONCOUNDA TRAORÉ; Sec.-Gen. MARIMATIA DIARRA.

Alliance pour la Démocratie et le Progrès: Bamako.

Alliance pour la Solidarité au Mali-Convergence des Forces Patriotiques: Bamako; Pres. SOUMEYLOU BOUBÈYE MAÏGA.

Ansar Dine: f. 2012; Islamist; seeks to impose *Shari'a* law in Mali; Pres. IYAD AG AGALY.

Bloc des Alternances pour le Renouveau, l'Intégration et la Coopération Africaine (BARICA): Faladié Sema, ave de l'OUA, Bamako; Pres. MAMADOU SINAYOKO.

Congrès National d'Initiative Démocratique—Faso Yiriwa Ton (CNID): rue 931, route de Sotuba, BP 2572, Bamako; tel. 77117777 (mobile); fax 2023-1861; e-mail mc_tall@hotmail.com; internet www.cnidmali.net; f. 1991; Chair. Me MOUNTAGA TALL; Sec.-Gen. Dr AMADOU SY.

Convention Démocratique et Sociale (CDS): Quinzambougou, rue 535, porte 112, Bamako; tel. 2029-2625; f. 1996; Chair. MAMADOU BAKARY SANGARÉ.

Convention Parti du Peuple (COPP): Hippodrome, rue 234, angle rue 287, porte 1345, BP 9012, Bamako; fax 2021-3591; e-mail lawyergakou@datatech.toolnet.org; f. 1996; Pres. Me MAMADOU GACKOU.

Convergence pour le Développement du Mali: Bamako; Pres. HOUSSÉINOU AMION GUINDO.

Forces Alternatives pour le Renouveau et l'Emergence: Bamako; Leader MODIBO SIDIBÉ.

Mouvement pour l'Indépendance, la Renaissance et l'Intégration Africaine (MIRIA): Dravéla, Bolibana, rue 417, porte 66, Bamako; tel. 2029-2981; fax 2029-2979; e-mail miria12002@yahoo.fr; f. 1994 following split in ADEMA; Pres. MAMADOU KASSA TRAORÉ.

Mouvement Islamique de l'Azawad (MIA): f. 2013 following breakaway from Ansar Dine; Tuareg; Sec.-Gen. ALGABAS AG INTALLA.

Mouvement National de Libération de l'Azawad (MNLA): internet www.mnlamov.net; f. 2011; Tuareg movement seeking independence for the Azawad region; Gen. Sec. BILAL AG ACHERIF.

Mouvement Patriotique pour le Renouveau (MPR): Quinzambougou, BP E 1108, Bamako; tel. 2021-5546; fax 2021-5543; f. 1995; Pres. Dr CHOGUEL KOKALA MAÏGA.

Mouvement Unité pour le Jihad en Afrique de l'Ouest (MUJAO): f. 2011; seeks to launch a *jihad* across West Africa; Leader SULTAN OULD BADI.

Parti Citoyen pour le Renouveau (PCR): Niaréla II, rue 428, porte 592, Bamako; tel. 66720988 (mobile); internet pcrmali.net; f. 2005; Pres. OUSMANE BEN FANA TRAORÉ.

Parti pour la Démocratie et le Progrès/Parti Socialiste (PDP/PS): Korofina sud, rue 96, porte 437, Bamako; tel. 2024-1675; fax 2020-2314; f. 1991; Leader FRANÇOIS KABORÉ.

Parti pour le Développement Economique et la Solidarité (PDES): Hamdallaye, ACI 2000, rue 320, porte 200, Bamako; f. 2010; Pres. HAMED DIANE SÉMÉGA.

Parti pour l'Indépendance, la Démocratie et la Solidarité (PIDS): Hippodrome, rue 250, porte 1183, BP E 1515, Bamako; tel. 2077-4575; f. 2001; Pres. DABA DIAWARA.

Parti pour la Renaissance Nationale (PARENA): rue Soundiata, porte 1397, BP E 2235, Ouolofobougou, Bamako; tel. 2023-4954; fax 2022-2908; e-mail info@parena.org.ml; f. 1995 following split in CNID; Pres. TIÉBILÉ DRAMÉ; Sec.-Gen. DJIGUIBA KEÏTA.

Parti pour la Restauration des Valeurs du Mali: Bamako; Pres. MAMADOU OUMAR SIDIBÉ.

Parti de la Solidarité Africaine pour la Démocratie et l'Indépendance (SADI): Djélibougou, rue 246, porte 559, BP 3140, Bamako; tel. 2024-1004; internet www.partisadi.net; f. 2002; Leader CHEICK OUMAR SISSOKO.

Parti pour la Solidarité et le Progrès (PSP): rue 552, porte 255, Quinzambougou, Bamako; tel. 2021-9960; f. 1945; Pres. OUMAR HAMMADOUN DICKO.

Rassemblement pour la Démocratie et le Progrès (RDP): Niarela, rue 485, porte 11, BP 2110, Bamako; tel. 2021-3092; fax 2024-6795; f. 1991; Pres. BISSI SANGARÉ.

Rassemblement pour le Mali (RPM): Hippodrome, rue 232, porte 130, BP 9057, Bamako; tel. 2021-1433; fax 2021-1336; e-mail siegerpmbko@yahoo.fr; internet www.rpm.org.ml; f. 2001; Pres. IBRAHIM BOUBACAR KEÏTA; Sec.-Gen. Dr BOCARY TRETA.

Union pour la Démocratie et le Développement (UDD): ave OUA, porte 3626, Sogoniko, BP 2969, Bamako; tel. 2020-3971; f. 1991; Leader Me HASSANE BARRY.

Union des Forces Démocratiques pour le Progrès—Sama-ton (UFDP): Quartier Mali, BP E 37, Bamako; tel. 2023-1766; f. 1991; Sec.-Gen. Col YOUSSOUF TRAORÉ.

Union Malienne du Rassemblement Démocratique Africain Faso Jigi (UM-RDA FASO JIGI): Hippodrome, rue RDA, porte 41, BP E 1413, Bamako; tel. and fax 2021-4522; f. 2010; Leader BOCAR MOUSSA DIARRA.

Union pour la République et la Démocratie (URD): Badalabougou, rue 105, porte 483, Bamako; tel. 2021-8642; e-mail contact@urd-mali.net; internet www.urd-mali.net; f. 2003; Pres. YOUNOUSSI TOURÉ; Sec.-Gen. LASSANA KONÉ.

Yelema: Hamdallaye, BP E 2546, Bamako; tel. 75444534 (mobile); e-mail yelema@yelema.net; internet www.yelema.net; Sec.-Gen. ASSETOU SANGARE ROBICHAUD.

Diplomatic Representation

EMBASSIES IN MALI

Algeria: ave de l'OUA, Daoudabougou, BP 02, Bamako; tel. 2020-1883; fax 2022-9374; e-mail ambasabmko@gmail.com; Ambassador NOUREDDINE AYADI.

Brazil: rue 113, porte 62, Badalabougou-ouest, Bamako; tel. 2022-9817; fax 2022-9906; e-mail brasembbamako@mre.gov.br; Ambassador JEORGE JOSÉ FRANTZ RAMOS.

Burkina Faso: Hamdallaye ACI 2000, Commune III, BP 9022, Bamako; tel. 2023-3171; fax 2021-9266; e-mail ambafaso@experco .net; internet www.ambaburkinafaso-mali.org.ml; Ambassador Prof. KODIO LOUGUÉ.

Canada: route de Koulikoro, Immeuble Séméga, Hippodrome, BP 198, Bamako; tel. 2021-2236; fax 2021-4362; e-mail bmako@international.gc.ca; internet www.canadainternational.gc.ca/mali; Ambassador LOUIS DE LORIMIER.

China, People's Republic: route de Koulikoro, Hippodrome, BP 112, Bamako; tel. 2021-3597; fax 2022-3443; e-mail chinaemb_ml@mfa.gov.cn; internet ml.china-embassy.org/fra; Ambassador LU HUIYING.

Côte d'Ivoire: square Patrice Lumumba, Immeuble CNAR, 3e étage, BP E 3644, Bamako; tel. 2022-0389; fax 2022-1376; Ambassador SAMUEL OUATTARA.

Cuba: porte 31, rue 328, Niarela, Bamako; tel. 2021-0289; fax 2021-0293; e-mail emcuba.mali@orangemali.net; internet www .cubadiplomatica.cu/mali; Ambassador CARLOS GUTIERREZ CORRALES.

Denmark: Lots 94-95, Cité du Niger II, BP E 1733, Bamako; tel. 2070-5300; fax 2070-5329; e-mail bkoamb@um.dk; internet mali.um .dk; Ambassador ANDERS GARLY ANDERSEN.

Egypt: Badalabougou-est, BP 44, Bamako; tel. 2022-3565; fax 2022-0891; e-mail mostafa@datatech.net.ml; Ambassador HAMED AHMED CHOUKRY HAMED.

France: Square Patrice Lumumba, BP 17, Bamako; tel. 4497-5757; fax 2022-3136; e-mail ambassade@france-mali.org.ml; internet www .ambafrance-ml.org; Ambassador GILLES HUBERSON.

Germany: Badalabougou-est, rue 14, porte 330, BP 100, Bamako; tel. 2070-0770; fax 2022-9650; e-mail allemagne@orangemali.net; internet www.bamako.diplo.de; Ambassador GÜNTER OVERFELD.

Ghana: ACI 2000 Hamdallaye, rue 408, porte 130, BP 3161, Bamako; tel. 2029-6083; fax 2029-6084; e-mail chancery@ghanaembassy-mali.org; internet www.ghanaembassymali.org; Ambassador MAHMUD KHALID.

Guinea: Immeuble Saybou Maïga, Quartier du Fleuve, BP 118, Bamako; tel. 2022-3007; fax 2021-0806; Ambassador KABINET CONDÉ.

India: 101 ave de l'OUA, Badalabougou-est, BP 8008, Bamako; tel. 2023-5420; fax 2023-5417; e-mail hoc.bamako@mea.gov.in; internet www.amb-inde-bamako.org; f. 2009; Chargé d'affaires a.i. NIKHILESH MOHAN DHIRAR.

Iran: ave al-Quds, Hippodrome, BP 2136, Bamako; tel. 2021-7638; fax 2021-0731; Ambassador SHARIF MOHAMMADI ABOLMOHSEN.

Japan: rue 43 porte 407, Cité du Niger, BP E 4227, Bamako; tel. 2070-0150; fax 2021-7785; internet www.ml.emb-japan.go.jp; Ambassador MASAHIRO KAWADA.

Korea, Democratic People's Republic: Bamako; Ambassador KIM JUN GAP.

Libya: Badalabougou-ouest, face Palais de la Culture, BP 1670, Bamako; tel. 2022-3496; fax 2022-6697; Ambassador Dr ALI MUHAMMAD AL-MAGOURI.

Mauritania: route de Koulikoro, Hippodrome, BP 135, Bamako; tel. 2021-4815; fax 2022-4908; e-mail ambarimbko@yahoo.fr; Ambassador MOHAMED OULD MEKHALLE.

Morocco: Badalabougou-est, rue 25, porte 80, BP 2013, Bamako; tel. 2022-2123; fax 2022-7787; e-mail sifamali@afribone.net.ml; Ambassador HASSAN NACIRI.

Netherlands: rue 437, BP 2220, Hippodrome, Bamako; tel. 2021-9572; fax 2021-3617; e-mail bam@minbuza.nl; internet www.mfa.nl; Ambassador MAARTEN BROUWER.

Nigeria: Badalabougou-est, BP 57, Bamako; tel. 2021-5328; fax 2022-3974; e-mail ngrbko@malinet.ml; Ambassador ILIYA ALI DUNIYA NUHU.

Russian Federation: BP 300, Niarela, Bamako; tel. 2021-5592; fax 2021-9926; e-mail ambrusse_mali@orangemali.net; Ambassador ALEXEY G. DOULIAN.

Saudi Arabia: BP 81, Bamako; tel. 2021-7000; fax 2021-5064; e-mail mlemb@mofa.gov.sa; internet embassies.mofa.gov.sa/sites/mali; Ambassador NAHID BIN ABD AL-RAHMAN AL-HARBI.

Senegal: porte 341, rue 287, angle ave Nelson Mandela, BP 42, Bamako; tel. 2021-0859; fax 2016-9268; Ambassador (vacant).

South Africa: bât. Diarra, Hamdallaye ACI 2000, BP 2015, Bamako; tel. 2029-2925; fax 2029-2926; e-mail bamako@foreign .gov.za; Ambassador RANTOBENG WILLIAM MOKOU.

Spain: Batîment Fondation de l'Enfance, 2ème étage, rue 260, Handallaye ACI 2000, BP 3230, Bamako; tel. 2023-6527; fax 2023-6524; e-mail emb.bamako@maec.es; Ambassador Dr JOSÉ MARÍA MATRES MANSO.

Sweden: Immeuble UATT, 2ème étage, Quatier du Fleuve, Bamako; tel. 2070-7000; fax 2070-7010; e-mail ambassaden.bamako@gov.se; internet www.swedenabroad.com/bamako; Ambassador EVA EMNÉUS.

Tunisia: Hamdallaye ACI 2000, rue 329, porte 53, Bamako; tel. 2023-1754; fax 2023-5665; e-mail chancellerie@ambatun-mali.org .ml; Ambassador TAREK BEN SALEM.

Turkey: Cité du Niger, M-105/112, Niarela, Bamako; tel. 77700007 (mobile); e-mail ambassade.bamako@mfa.gov.tr; internet bamako .be.mfa.gov.tr; Ambassador HIKMET RENAN ŞEKEROĞLU.

USA: ACI 2000, rue 243, porte 297, Bamako; tel. 2070-2300; fax 2070-2479; e-mail webmaster@usa.org.ml; internet mali.usembassy.gov; Chargé d'affaires ANDREW YOUNG.

Venezuela: Badalabougou Ouest, rue 50, prés du Palais de la Culture, BP E34690, Bamako; tel. 2023-2531; fax 2023-2534; e-mail ambavenemali@orangemali.net; Ambassador JOHNY ERREDDY BALZA ARISMENDI.

Judicial System

The 1992 Constitution guarantees the independence of the judiciary.

High Court of Justice: Bamako; competent to try the President of the Republic and government ministers for high treason and for crimes committed in the course of their duties, and their accomplices in any case where state security is threatened; mems designated by the mems of the Assemblée Nationale, and renewed annually; Pres. ABDERHAMANE NIANG.

Supreme Court: BP 7, Bamako; tel. 2022-2406; e-mail csupreme@ afribone.net.ml; internet www.cs.insti.ml; f. 1969; comprises judicial, administrative and auditing sections; judicial section comprises five chambers, administrative section comprises two chambers, auditing section comprises three chambers; Pres. NOUHOUM TAPILY; Sec.-Gen. MAMA SININTA.

Constitutional Court: Hamdallaye ACI 2000, Commune IV, BP E 213, Bamako; tel. 2022-5609; fax 2023-4241; e-mail tawatybouba@ yahoo.fr; internet www.cc.insti.ml; f. 1994; Pres. MANASSA DANIOKO.

There are three Courts of Appeal, seven Magistrates' Courts and also courts for labour disputes.

Religion

According to the 2009 census, 94.8% of the population were Muslims, while 2.4% were Christians and 2.0% followed traditional animist beliefs.

ISLAM

Association Malienne pour l'Unité et le Progrès de l'Islam (AMUPI): Bamako; state-endorsed Islamic governing body.

Chief Mosque: pl. de la République, Bagadadji, Bamako; tel. 2021-2190.

Haut Conseil Islamique: Bamako; f. 2002; responsible for management of relations between the Muslim communities and the State; Pres. MAHMOUD DICKO.

CHRISTIANITY

The Roman Catholic Church

Mali comprises one archdiocese and five dioceses. Approximately 2% of the total population practises Roman Catholicism.

Bishops' Conference: Conférence Episcopale du Mali, Archevêché, BP 298, Bamako; tel. 2222-5499; fax 2222-5214; e-mail cemali@ afribone.net.ml; internet eglisemali.org; f. 1973; Pres. Most Rev. JEAN-BAPTISTE TIAMA (Bishop of Sikasso).

Archbishop of Bamako: JEAN ZERBO, Archevêché, BP 298, Bamako; tel. 2222-5842; fax 2222-7850; e-mail mgrjeanzerbo@ afribonemali.net.

Other Christian Churches

There are several Protestant mission centres, mainly administered by US societies.

BAHÁ'Í FAITH

National Spiritual Assembly: BP 1657, Bamako; e-mail ntirandaz@aol.com.

The Press

The 1992 Constitution guarantees the freedom of the press.

DAILY NEWSPAPERS

Les Echos: Hamdallaye, ave Cheick Zayed, porte 2694, BP 2043, Bamako; tel. 2029-6289; fax 2026-7639; e-mail lesechos@jamana.org;

internet www.lesechos.ml; f. 1989; daily; publ. by Jamana cultural co-operative; circ. 30,000; Dir ALEXIS KALAMBRY; Editor-in-Chief ABOUBACAR SALIPH DIARRA.

L'Essor: square Patrice Lumumba, BP 141, Bamako; tel. 2022-3683; fax 2022-4774; e-mail info@essor.gov.ml; internet www.essor.ml; f. 1949; daily; pro-Govt newspaper; Editor BAKARY COULIBALY; circ. 3,500.

Info Matin: 56 rue 350, Bamako Coura, BP E 4020, Bamako; tel. 7541-4141; fax 2023-8227; e-mail redaction@info-matin.com; internet www.info-matin.com; independent.

Le Républicain: 116 rue 400, Dravéla-Bolibana, BP 1484, Bamako; tel. 2029-0900; fax 2029-0933; internet lerepublicain-mali.com; f. 1992; independent; Dir BOUKARY DAOU.

PERIODICALS

26 Mars: Badalabougou-Sema Gesco, Lot S13, BP MA 174, Bamako; tel. 2029-0459; f. 1998; weekly; independent; Dir BOUBACAR SANGARÉ.

L'Aurore: Niarela 298, rue 438, BP 3150, Bamako; tel. and fax 2021-6922; e-mail aurore@timbagga.com.ml; f. 1990; 2 a week; independent; Dir KARAMOKO N'DIAYE.

Le Canard Déchaîné: Immeuble Koumara, bloc 104, Centre Commercial, Bamako; tel. 76212686 (mobile); fax 2022-8686; e-mail maison.presse@afribone.net.ml; weekly; satirical; Dir OUMAR BABI; circ. 3,000 (2006).

Le Carrefour: ave Cheick Zayed, Hamdallaye, Bamako; tel. 2023-9808; e-mail journalcarrefour@yahoo.fr; f. 1997; Dir MAHAMANE IMRANE COULIBALY.

Le Continent: AA 16, Banankabougou, BP E 4338, Bamako; tel. and fax 2029-5739; e-mail le_continent@yahoo.fr; f. 2000; weekly; Dir IBRAHIMA TRAORÉ.

Le Courrier: 230 ave Cheick Zayed, Lafiabougou Marché, BP 1258, Bamako; tel. and fax 2029-1862; e-mail journalcourrier@webmails .com; f. 1996; weekly; Dir SADOU A. YATTARA; also *Le Courrier Magazine*, monthly.

L'Indépendant: Immeuble ABK, Hamdallaye ACI, BP E 1040, Bamako; tel. and fax 2023-2727; e-mail independant@cefib.com; 2 a week; Dir El Hadj SAOUTI LABASS HAÏDARA.

L'Inspecteur: Immeuble Nimagala, bloc 262, BP E 4534, Bamako; tel. 66724711 (mobile); e-mail inspecteurmali@yahoo.fr; f. 1992; weekly; Dir ALY DIARRA.

Jamana—Revue Culturelle Malienne: BP 2043, Bamako; BP E 1040; e-mail infos@jamana.org; f. 1983; quarterly; organ of Jamana cultural co-operative.

Journal Officiel de la République du Mali: Koulouba, BP 14, Bamako; tel. 2022-5986; fax 2022-7050; official gazette.

Kabaaru: Village Kibaru, Bozola, BP 24, Bamako; f. 1983; state-owned; monthly; Fulbé (Peul) language; rural interest; Editor BARRY BELCO MOUSSA; circ. 3,000.

Kibaru: Village Kibaru, Bozola, BP 1463, Bamako; f. 1972; monthly; state-owned; Bambara and three other languages; rural interest; Editor NIANZÉ SAMAKÉ; circ. 5,000.

Liberté: Immeuble Sanago, Hamdallaye Marché, BP E 24, Bamako; tel. 2028-1898; e-mail ladji.guindo@cefib.com; f. 1999; weekly; Dir ABDOULAYE LADJI GUINDO.

Le Malien: rue 497, porte 277, Badialan III, BP E 1558, Bamako; tel. 2023-5729; fax 2029-1339; e-mail lemalien2000@yahoo.fr; f. 1993; weekly; Dir SIDI KEITA.

Match: 97 rue 498, Lafiabougou, BP E 3776, Bamako; tel. 2029-1882; e-mail bcissouma@yahoo.fr; f. 1997; 2 a month; sports; Dir BABA CISSOUMA.

Musow: BP E 449, Bamako; tel. 2028-0000; fax 2028-0001; e-mail musow@musow.com; internet www.musow.com; women's interest.

Nyéléni Magazine: Niarela 298, rue 348, BP 13150, Bamako; tel. 2029-2401; f. 1991; monthly; women's interest; Dir MAÏMOUNA TRAORÉ.

L'Observateur: Galérie Djigué, rue du 18 juin, BP E 1002, Bamako; tel. and fax 2023-0689; e-mail belcotamboura@hotmail.com; f. 1992; 2 a week; Dir BELCO TAMBOURA.

Le Reflet: Immeuble Kanadjigui, route de Koulikoro, Boulkassoumbougou, BP E 1688, Bamako; tel. 2024-3952; fax 2023-2308; e-mail lereflet@afribone.malinet.ml; weekly; fmrly *Le Carcan*; present name adopted Jan. 2001; Dir ABDOUL KARIM DRAMÉ.

Royal Sports: BP 98, Sikasso; tel. 66724988 (mobile); weekly; also *Tatou Sports*, publ. monthly; Pres. and Dir-Gen. ALY TOURÉ.

Le Scorpion: 230 ave Cheick Zayed, Lafiabougou Marché, BP 1258, Bamako; tel. and fax 2029-1862; f. 1991; weekly; Dir MAHAMANE HAMÈYE CISSÉ.

Le Tambour: rue 497, porte 295, Badialan III, BP E 289, Bamako; tel. and fax 2022-7568; e-mail tambourj@yahoo.fr; f. 1994; 2 a week; Dir YÉRO DIALLO.

NEWS AGENCY

Agence Malienne de Presse et de Publicité (AMAP): Square Patrice Lumumba, BP 141, Bamako; tel. 2022-3683; fax 2022-4774; e-mail amap@afribone.net.ml; internet www.amap.ml; f. 1977; Dir SOULEYMANE DRABO.

PRESS ASSOCIATIONS

Association des Editeurs de la Presse Privée (ASSEP): BP E 1002, Bamako; tel. 66713133 (mobile); e-mail belcotamboura@hotmail.com; Pres. BIRAMA FALL.

Association des Journalistes Professionels des Médias Privés du Mali (AJPM): BP E 2456, Bamako; tel. 2022-1915; fax 2023-5478; Pres. MOMADOU FOFANA.

Association des Professionnelles Africaines de la Communication (APAC MALI): porte 474, rue 428, BP E 731, Bamako; tel. 2021-2912; Pres. MARIÉTOU KONATÉ.

Union Nationale des Journalistes Maliens (UNAJOM): BP 1300, Bamako; tel. 2022-1915; fax 2023-5478; e-mail ibrafam@yahoo.fr; Pres. IBRAHIM FAMAKAN COULIBALY.

Publishers

EDIM SA: ave Kassé Keïta, BP 21, Bamako; tel. 2022-4041; fax 2029-3001; e-mail edim@afribone.net.ml; f. 1972 as Editions Imprimeries du Mali; general fiction and non-fiction, textbooks; Chair. and Man. Dir ALOU TOMOTA.

Editions Donniya: Cité du Niger, BP 1273, Bamako; tel. 2021-4646; fax 2021-9031; internet www.editionsdonniya.com; f. 1996; general fiction, history, reference and children's books in French and Bambara.

Le Figuier: 151 rue 56, Semal, BP 2605, Bamako; tel. and fax 2023-3211; e-mail lefiguier@afribone.net.ml; f. 1997; fiction and non-fiction.

Editions Jamana: ave Cheick Zaycd, BP 2043, Bamako; tel. 2029-6289; fax 2029-7639; e-mail infos@jamana.org; internet www.jamana.org; f. 1988; literary fiction, poetry, reference; Dir-Gen. HAMIDOU KONATÉ.

Editions Teriya: BP 1677, Bamako; tel. 2024 1142; theatre, literary fiction; Dir GAOUSSOU DIAWARA.

Broadcasting and Communications

TELECOMMUNICATIONS

At the end of 2011 there were two telecommunications companies in Mali, both of which provided mobile and fixed line telephone services. In January 2012 a third licence to provide mobile telephone services was awarded to a consortium of Planor and Monaco Telecom. In 2013 there were 114,600 fixed-line telephones in use and 19.8m. subscribers to mobile cellular telephone services.

Orange Mali SA: Immeuble Orange Mali, Hamdallaye, ACI-2000, BP E 3991, Bamako; tel. 4499-9903; fax 4499-9001; e-mail orange@orangemali.com; internet www.orangemali.com; f. 2003 as Ikatel; repackaged under brand name Orange in 2007; fixed-line and mobile cellular telecommunications; jtly owned by France Télécom and Société Nationale des Télécommunications du Sénégal; Dir-Gen. JEAN-LUC BOHÉ; 1,097 fixed lines and 4.7m. subscribers to mobile cellular telecommunications services (2010).

Société des Télécommunications du Mali—Malitel (SOTELMA): Quartier du Fleuve, près de la BCEAO, BP 740, Bamako; tel. 2021-5280; fax 2021-3022; e-mail segal@sotelma.ml; internet www.sotelma.ml; f. 1990; 51% owned by Itissalat al-Maghrib—Maroc Télécom (Morocco), 20% state-owned; operates fixed-line telephone services, also mobile and cellular telecommunications under the brand name Malitel in Bamako, Kayes, Mopti, Ségou and Sikasso; 79,051 fixed lines and 2.69m. subscribers to mobile cellular telecommunications services (2010); Dir-Gen. NOR-EDDINE BOUMZEBRA.

Regulatory Authority

Autorité Malienne de Régulation des Télécommunications/TIC et des Postes (AMRTP): Hamdallaye ACI 2000, rue 390, porte 1849, BP 2206, Bamako; tel. 2023-1490; fax 2023-1494; e-mail crtmali@crt.ml; internet www.crt-mali.org; f. 1999; Dir Dr CHOGUEL K. MAÏGA.

BROADCASTING

Regulatory Authority

Conseil Supérieur de la Communication: BP 1856, Bamako; tel. 2023-2101; fax 2023-2102; f. 1992; Pres. TOGOLA MARIE JACQUELINE NANA.

Radio

In 2010 there were an estimated 400 community, commercial and religious radio stations broadcasting in Mali. Signals from Radio France International, the Voice of America, Radio Chine Internationale, the British Broadcasting Corporation (BBC) and Deutsche Welle are also received.

Office de Radiodiffusion-Télévision Malienne (ORTM): 287 rue de la Marne, BP 171, Bamako; tel. 2021-2019; fax 2021-4205; e-mail ortm@ortm.ml; internet www.ortm-mali.tv; Dir-Gen. BALLY IDRISSA SISSOKO; Dir of Radio SEYDOU BABA TRAORÉ.

> **Radio Mali–Chaîne Nationale:** BP 171, Bamako; tel. 2021-2019; fax 2021-4205; e-mail ortm@spider.toolnet.org; f. 1957; state-owned; radio programmes in French, Bambara, Peul, Sarakolé, Tamashek, Sonrai, Moorish, Wolof, English.

> **Chaîne 2:** Bamako; f. 1993; radio broadcasts to Bamako.

Radio Balanzan: BP 419, Ségou; tel. 2132-0288; commercial.

Radio Bamakan: Marché de Médine, BP E 100, Bamako; tel. and fax 2021-2760; e-mail radio.bamakan@ifrance.com; internet bamakan.net; f. 1991; community station; 104 hours of FM broadcasts weekly; Man. MODIBO DIALLO.

Radio Foko de Ségou Jamana: BP 2043, Bamako; tel. 2132-0048; fax 2022-7639; e-mail radiofoko@cefib.com.

Radio Guintan: Magnambougou, BP 2546, Bamako; tel. 2020-0938; f. 1994; community radio station; Dir RAMATA DIA.

Radio Jamana: BP 2043, Bamako; tel. 2029-6289; fax 2029-7639; e-mail radio@jamana.org; internet www.jamana.org.

Radio Kayira: Djélibougou Doumanzana, BP 3140, Bamako; tel. 2024-8782; fax 2022-7568; internet www.kayira.org; f. 1992; community station; Dir OUMAR MARIKO.

Radio Klédu: Cité du Niger, BP 2322, Bamako; tel. 2021-0018; e-mail rkledudirect@cefib.com; internet www.kleducommunication.com; f. 1992; commercial; Dir-Gen. JACQUES DEZ.

Radio La Bonne Nouvelle (96.6 FM): BP 298, Bamako; tel. 2073-5049; f. 2013; Roman Catholic; Dir JANINE TRAORÉ.

Radio Liberté: BP 5015, Bamako; tel. 2023-0581; f. 1991; commercial station broadcasting 24 hours daily; Dir ALMANY TOURÉ.

Radio Patriote: Korofina-Sud, BP E 1406, Bamako; tel. 2024-2292; f. 1995; commercial station; Dir MOUSSA KEÏTA.

Radio Rurale de Kayes: Plateau, BP 94, Kayes; tel. 2158-0081; e-mail rrk@afribone.net.ml; internet www.radioruraledekayes.net; f. 1988; community stations established by the Agence de Coopération Culturelle et Technique (ACTT); transmitters in Niono, Kadiolo, Bandiagara and Kidal; Dir FILY KEÏTA.

Radio Tabalé: Bamako-Coura, BP 697, Bamako; tel. and fax 2022-7870; internet www.radiotabale.org; f. 1992; independent public-service station; broadcasting 57 hours weekly; Dir TIÉMOKO KONÉ.

Radio Wassoulou: BP 24, Yanfolila; tel. 2165-1097; internet wassoulou.radio.org.ml; commercial.

La Voix du Coran et du Hadit: Grande Mosquée, BP 2531, Bamako; tel. 2021-6344; f. 1993; Islamic station broadcasting on FM in Bamako; Dir El Hadj MAHMOUD DICKO.

Television

Office de Radiodiffusion-Télévision Malienne (ORTM): see Radio; a second channel, Télévision Malienne 2, was launched on 31 December 2011; Dir of Television BALLY IDRISSA SISSOKO.

Multicanal SA: Quinzambougou, BP E 1506, Bamako; tel. 2020-2929; e-mail sandrine@multi-canal.com; internet www.multi-canal.com; private subscription broadcaster; relays international broadcasts; Pres. ISMAÏLA SIDIBÉ; Dir-Gen. MOHAMED KEITA.

Finance

(cap. = capital; res = reserves; dep. = deposits; m. = million; br(s). = branch(es); amounts in francs CFA)

BANKING

Central Bank

Banque Centrale des Etats de l'Afrique de l'Ouest (BCEAO): blvd du 22 octobre 1946, BP 206, Bamako; tel. 2022-2541; fax 2022-4786; internet www.bceao.int; f. 1962; HQ in Dakar, Senegal; bank of issue for the mem. states of Union Economique et Monétaire Ouest-Africaine (UEMOA, comprising Benin, Burkina Faso, Côte d'Ivoire,

Guinea-Bissau, Mali, Niger, Senegal and Togo); cap. 134,120m., res 1,474,195m., dep. 2,124,051m. (Dec. 2009); Gov. KONÉ TIÉMOKO MEYLIET; Dir in Mali KONZO TRAORÉ; brs at Mopti and Sikasso.

Commercial Banks

Bank of Africa—Mali (BOA—MALI): 418 ave de la Marné, Bozola, BP 2249, Bamako; tel. 2070-0500; fax 2070-0560; e-mail information@boamali.net; internet www.boamali.com; f. 1983; 50.22% owned by BOA Group; cap. 7,200.0m., res 7,884.2m., dep. 286,727.0m. (Dec. 2013); Pres. PAUL DERREUMAUX; Dir-Gen. MAMADOU IGOR DIARRA; 23 brs.

Banque Commerciale du Sahel (BCS-SA): ave Bozola 127, BP 2372, Bamako; tel. 2021-0535; fax 2021-1660; e-mail dg@bcss.mali .com; f. 1980; fmrly Banque Arabe Libyo-Malienne pour le Commerce Extérieur et le Développement; 96.61% owned by Libyan-Arab Foreign Bank; Pres. MARIMANTIA DIARRA; Dir-Gen. IBRAHIM ABOUJAFAR SWEAI; 1 br.

Banque de l'Habitat du Mali (BHM): ACI 2000, ave Kwamé N'Krumah, BP 2614, Bamako; tel. 2022-9190; fax 2023-9288; e-mail bhm@bhm-sa.com; internet www.bhm-sa.com; f. 1990; present name adopted 1996; 25.8% owned by Institut National de Prévoyance Social; Pres. and Dir-Gen. MODIBO CISSÉ; 5 brs.

Banque Internationale pour le Commerce et l'Industrie au Mali (BICI–Mali): blvd du 22 octobre 1946, Quartier du Fleuve, BP 72, Bamako; tel. 2070-0700; fax 2023-3373; e-mail bicim-dg@africa .bnpparibas.com; internet www.bicim.ml; f. 1998; 85% owned by BNP Paribas BDDI Participations (France); Pres. and Dir-Gen. PIERRE BEREGOVOY; 8 brs.

Banque Internationale pour le Mali (BIM): blvd de l'Indépendance, BP 15, Bamako; tel. 2022-5066; fax 2022-4566; e-mail bim@ bim.com.ml; internet www.bim.com.ml; f. 1980; present name adopted 1995; 51% owned by Attijariwafa Bank Group (Morocco), 10.5% state-owned; cap. 5,003m., res 9,301m., dep. 167,672m. (Dec. 2009); Pres. BOUBKER JAI; Dir-Gen. ABDELAHAD KETTANI; 14 brs.

Ecobank Mali: Immeuble Amadou Sow, pl. de la Nation, Quartier du Fleuve, BP E 1272, Bamako; tel. 2070-0600; fax 2023-3305; e-mail ecobankml@ecobank.com; internet www.ecobank.com; f. 1998; 49.5% owned by Ecobank Transnational Inc, 17.8% by Ecobank Bénin, 14.9% by Ecobank Togo, 9.9% by Ecobank Burkina; cap. 8,932.2m., res 7,928.9m., dep. 242,111.5m. (Dec. 2013); Pres. SAMBA DIALLO; Dir-Gen. COUMBA SIDIBÉ TOURÉ; 2 brs.

Orabank Mali: Immeuble INVESTIM, ave de la route du Farako, BP 1625, Bamako; tel. 2022-2214; internet www.orabank.net; fmrly Banque Régionale de Solidarité Mali (BRS-Mali); name changed as above in 2014; owned by Oragroup SA (Togo); Dir-Gen. ABDOUL YOUNOUSSI.

Development Banks

Banque de Développement du Mali (BDM-SA): ave Modibo Keita, Quartier du Fleuve, BP 94, Bamako; tel. 2022-2050; fax 2022-5085; e-mail info@bdm-sa.com; internet www.bdm-sa.com; f. 1968; absorbed Banque Malienne de Crédit et de Dépôts in 2001; 27.38% owned by Banque Marocaine du Commerce Extérieur (Morocco), 19.58% state-owned, 15.96% by BCEAO, 15.96% by Banque Ouest-Africaine de Développement; cap. 10,000m., res 16,097.0m., dep. 383,090.0m. (Dec. 2013); Pres. and Dir-Gen. ABDOULAYE DAFFÉ; 14 brs.

Banque Malienne de Solidarité (BMS): Immeuble Diogo Aoua, ACI 2000, BP 1280, Bamako; tel. and fax 2023-5034; fax 2023-5043; e-mail bms-sa@bms-sa.com; internet bms-sa.org; f. 2002; Pres. and Dir-Gen. BABALI BAH; 1 br.

Banque Nationale de Développement Agricole—Mali (BNDA—Mali): Immeuble BNDA, blvd du Mali, ACI 2000, BP 2424, Bamako; tel. 2029-6464; fax 2029-2575; e-mail bnda@ bndamali.com; internet www.bndamali.com; f. 1981; 36.5% state-owned, 22.8% owned by Agence Française de Développement (France), 21.4% owned by Deutsche Entwicklungsgesellschaft (Germany), 19.4% owned by BCEAO; cap. 14,361m., res 9,181.0m., dep. 193,950.6m. (Dec. 2012); Chair., Pres. and Gen. Man. MOUSSA ALASSAME DIALLO; 32 brs.

Financial Institutions

Fonds de Garantie Hypothécaire du Mali: Immeuble ABK, rue 382 porte 128, Hamdallaye, ACI 2000, BP E 5205, Bamako; tel. 2229-2380; fax 2029-2383; e-mail fghm@fghm-sa.com; internet www .fghm-sa.com; f. 2000; home finance; Dir-Gen. BABA DAO.

Société Malienne de Financement (SOMAFI) (Alios Finance Mali): Immeuble Air Afrique, blvd du 22 octobre 1946, BP E 3643, Bamako; tel. 2022-1866; fax 2022-1869; e-mail mali@alios-finance .com; internet www.alios-finance.com; f. 1997; Man. Dir ERIC LECLÈRE.

Banking Association

Association Professionnelle des Banques et Etablissements Financiers (APBEF): Sébénicoro, Bamako; Pres. MOUSSA ALLASSANE DIALLO.

STOCK EXCHANGE

Bourse Régionale des Valeurs Mobilières (BRVM): Chambre de Commerce et de l'Industrie du Mali, pl. de la Liberté, BP E 1398, Bamako; tel. 2023-2354; fax 2023-2359; e-mail abocoum@brvm.org; internet www.brvm.org; f. 1998; nat. branch of BRVM (regional stock exchange based in Abidjan, Côte d'Ivoire, serving the mem. states of UEMOA); Man. AMADOU DJÉRI BOCOUM.

INSURANCE

Allianz Mali: ave de la Nation, BP E4447, Bamako; tel. 2022-4165; fax 2023-0034; e-mail allianz.mali@allianz-ml.com; internet www .allianz-africa.com/mali/index.php; Dir-Gen. OLIVIER PICARD.

Assurances Lafia: Immeuble Assurances Lafia SA, Hamdallaye ACI 2000, ave du Mali, BP 1542, Bamako; tel. 2029-0940; fax 2029-5223; e-mail info@assurancelafia.com; internet www.assurancelafia .com; f. 1983; Dir-Gen. AMINATA DEMBÉLÉ CISSÉ; 17 brs.

Caisse Nationale d'Assurance et de Réassurance du Mali (CNAR): square Patrice Lumumba, BP 568, Bamako; tel. 2021-3117; fax 2021-2369; f. 1969; state-owned; Dir-Gen. LÉOPOLD KEITA; 10 brs.

Compagnie d'Assurance et de Réassurance Sabu Nyuman: rue 350, porte 129, Bamako-Coura, BP 1822, Bamako; tel. 2022-6029; fax 2022-5750; e-mail assur.sn@malinet.ml; f. 1984; Pres. MOMADOU SANOGO; Dir-Gen. YAYA DIARRA.

Gras Savoye Mali: Immeuble SOGEFIH, 3e etage, Quartier du Fleuve, ave Moussa Travele, BP E 5691, Bamako; tel. 2022-6469; fax 2022-6470; e-mail grassavoyemali@ml.grassavoye.com; affiliated to Gras Savoye (France); Man. FAYEZ SAMB.

Nouvelle Alliance d'Assurance (NALLIAS): BP E4666, Bamako; tel. 2022-2244; fax 2022-9422; e-mail contact@nalliasmali.com; f. 2007; Dir-Gen. OUMAR N'DOYE.

Nouvelle Société Interafricaine d'Assurance (NSIA Mali): Immeuble du Patronat, derrière le Gouvernorat, ACI 2000, Bamako; tel. 2023-2440; fax 2023-2441; f. 2009; Dir-Gen. GEORGES ALAIN N'GORAN; also (NSIA Vie Mali); Dir-Gen. KODJO SALAMI WOROU.

Saham Mali SA: ave Modibo Keita, BP E 154, Bamako; tel. 2022-5775; fax 2023-2423; internet www.sahamassurance.ml; f. 1990; fmrly Colina Mali SA; present name adopted 2014; Dir-Gen. MARCUS K. LABAN.

Société Nouvelle d'Assurance—Vie (SONA—VIE): Immeuble Sonavie, ACI 2000, BP E 2217, Bamako; tel. 2029-5400; fax 2029-5501; internet www.sonavie.com; f. 1996; Dir-Gen. MAMADOU TOURÉ.

SUNU Assurances IARD Mali: Immeuble Fily Keïta, Hamdallaye ACI 2000, BPE 1861, Bamako; tel. 2022-0802; e-mail mali.iard@ sunu-group.com; internet www.sunu-group.com; Dir-Gen. DANIEL DIALLO.

Trade and Industry

GOVERNMENT AGENCIES

Agence Nationale pour l'Emploi (ANPE): BP 211, Bamako; tel. 2022-3187; fax 2023-2624; e-mail anpe@anpe-mali.org; internet www.anpe-mali.org; f. 2001; Dir-Gen. Prof. MAKAN MOUSSA SISSOKO.

Agence pour la Promotion des Investissements au Mali (API-Mali): Quartier du Fleuve, BP 1980, Bamako; tel. 2022-9525; fax 2022-9527; e-mail contact@apimali.gov.ml; internet www.apimali .gov.ml; f. 2005; CEO MODIBO KEITA.

Autorité pour la Promotion de la Recherche Petrolière (AUREP): Médina Coura, rue 28, porte 189, BP E 4306, Bamako; tel. 2021-2948; fax 2021-2882; e-mail diawara.baba@aurep.org; internet www.aurep.org; f. 2003; Dir-Gen. BABA DIAWARA.

Direction Nationale des Affaires Economiques (DNAE): BP 210, Bamako; tel. 2022-2314; fax 2022-2256; involved in economic and social affairs.

Direction Nationale des Travaux Publics (DNTP): ave de la Liberté, BP 1758, Bamako; tel. and fax 2022-2902; administers public works.

Guichet Unique–Direction Nationale des Industries: rue Titi Niare, Quinzambougou, BP 96, Bamako; tel. and fax 2022-3166.

Office National des Produits Pétroliers (ONAP): Quartier du Fleuve, rue 315, porte 141, BP 2070, Bamako; tel. 2022-2827; fax 2022-4483; e-mail onapmali@afribone.net.ml; Dir-Gen. TAPA NOUGA NADIO.

Office du Niger: BP 106, Ségou; tel. 2132-0292; fax 2132-0143; e-mail on@office-du-niger.org.ml; internet www.office-du-niger.org.ml; f. 1932; taken over from the French authorities in 1958; restructured in mid-1990s; cap. 7,139m. francs CFA; principally involved in cultivation of food crops, particularly rice; the Office du Niger zone is the western region of the Central Niger Delta; Pres. and Dir-Gen. AMADOU BOYE COULIBALY.

Office des Produits Agricoles du Mali (OPAM): BP 132, Bamako; tel. 2022-3755; fax 2021-0406; e-mail opam@cefib.com; f. 1965; state-owned; manages National (Cereals) Security Stock, administers food aid, responsible for sales of cereals and distribution to deficit areas; cap. 5,800m. francs CFA; Pres. and Dir-Gen. BAKARY DIALLO.

DEVELOPMENT ORGANIZATIONS

Agence pour le Développement du Nord-Mali (ADN): Gao; f. 2005 to replace l'Autorité pour le Développement Intégré du Nord-Mali; govt agency with financial autonomy; promotes devt of regions of Tombouctou, Gao and Kidal; br. in Bamako.

Agence Française de Développement (AFD): Quinzambougou, route de Sotuba, BP 32, Bamako; tel. 2021-2842; fax 2021-8646; e-mail afdbamako@groupe-afd.org; internet www.afd.fr; Country Dir HERVÉ BOUGAULT.

Office de Développement Intégré du Mali-Ouest (ODIMO): pl. Patrice Lumumba, Bamako; tel. 2022-5759; f. 1991 to succeed Office de Développement Intégré des Productions Arachidières et Céréalières; devt of diversified forms of agricultural production; Man. Dir ZANA SANOGO.

Service de Coopération et d'Action Culturelle: square Patrice Lumumba, BP 84, Bamako; tel. 2021-8338; fax 2021-8339; e-mail scac.bamako-amba@diplomatie.gouv.fr; administers bilateral aid from France; Dir DAVID SADOULET.

CHAMBERS OF COMMERCE

Chambre de Commerce et d'Industrie du Mali (CCIM): pl. de la Liberté, BP 46, Bamako; tel. 2022-5036; fax 2022-2120; e-mail ccim@cimali.org; internet www.ccimmali.org; f. 1906; Pres. JEAMILLE BITTAR; Sec.-Gen. DABA TRAORÉ.

Chambre des Mines du Mali (CMM): BP 1707, Bamako; fax 2022-0492; e-mail tambourabelco@gmail.com; internet www.chambredesminesdumali.org; f. 2004; Pres. ABDOULAYE PONA; Sec.-Gen. SÉKOU DIORO DICKO.

EMPLOYERS' ASSOCIATIONS

Association Malienne des Exportateurs de Légumes et Fruits (AMELEF): BP 1291, Bamako; tel. 7608-9048; fax 2029-2836; e-mail csp_mdbn_amelef@yaffa.fr; f. 1984; Pres. BAKARY YAFFA; Sec.-Gen. BIRAMA TRAORÉ.

Association Malienne des Exportateurs de Ressources Animales (AMERA): Bamako; tel. 2022-5683; f. 1985; Pres. AMBARKÉ YERMANGORE; Admin. Sec. ALI HACKO.

Conseil National du Patronat du Mali (CNPM): Immeuble du Patronat, Hamdallaye, ACI 2000, derrière le Gouvernorat du District, route de Sotuba, BP 2445, Bamako; tel. 2021-6311; fax 2021-9077; e-mail cnpm@cnpmali.org; internet www.cnpmali.org; f. 1980 as Fédération Nationale des Employeurs du Mali; Pres. MAMADOU SIDIBÉ; 39 professional groups and 5 regional employers' associations.

UTILITIES

Commission de Régulation de l'Electricité et l'Eau: Bamako; f. 2000; Pres. MOCTAR TOURÉ.

Electricity

Agence Malienne pour le Développement de l'Energie Domestique et l'Electrification Rurale (AMADER): colline de Badalabougou, BP E 715, Bamako; tel. 2023-8567; fax 2023-8239; e-mail itoure@amadermali.net; internet www.amadermali.org; f. 2003; Pres. and Dir-Gen. ISMAËL O. TOURÉ.

Energie du Mali (EdM): square Patrice Lumumba, BP 69, Bamako; tel. 2022-3020; fax 2022-8430; e-mail sekou.edm@cefib.com; internet www.edm-sa.com.ml; f. 1960; 66% state-owned, 34% owned by Industrial Promotion Services (West-Africa); planning, construction and operation of power-sector facilities; cap. 7,880m. francs CFA; Pres. OUSMANE ISSOUFI MAÏGA; Dir-Gen. SÉKOU ALPHA DJITÈYE.

Société de Gestion de l'Energie de Manantali (SOGEM): Parcelle 2501, ACI 2000, BP E 4015, Bamako; tel. 2023-3286; fax 2023-8350; generates and distributes electricity from the Manantali hydroelectric project, under the auspices of the Organisation pour la Mise en Valeur du Fleuve Sénégal; Dir-Gen. SALOUM CISSÉ.

Gas

Air Liquide Maligaz: route de Sotuba, BP 5, Bamako; tel. 2022-2394; internet www.ml.airliquide.com; gas distribution.

There are four other gas distributors in Mali: Sodigaz, Fasogaz, Sigaz and Total.

Water

Société Malienne de Gestion de l'Eau Potable (SOMAGEP): rue 41, Djicoroni, Troukabougou, BP E 708, Bamako; tel. 20-70-41-00; fax 20-22-55-80; e-mail somagep@somagep.ml; internet www.somagep.ml; f. 2010; responsible for the operation of public drinking water supplies; Pres. BOUBACAR KANE.

Société Malienne de Patrimoine de l'Eau Potable (SOMAPEP): Quartier Faso Kanu, Bamako; tel. 2022-0026; fax 2022-0200; internet www.somapep.org; f. 2010; responsible for the management and development of infrastructure for supplying drinking water; CEO ADAMA DIARRA TIÉMOKO.

TRADE UNION FEDERATION

Union Nationale des Travailleurs du Mali (UNTM): Bourse du Travail, blvd de l'Indépendance, BP 169, Bamako; tel. 2022-3699; fax 2023-5945; f. 1963; 13 nat. and 8 regional unions, and 52 local orgs; Sec.-Gen. SIAKA DIAKITÉ.

There are, in addition, several non-affiliated trade unions.

Transport

RAILWAYS

Mali's only railway runs from Koulikoro, via Bamako, to the Senegal border. The line continues to Dakar, Senegal, a total distance of 1,286 km, of which 729 km are in Mali. The track is in very poor condition, and is frequently closed during the rainy season. In 1995 the Governments of Mali and Senegal agreed to establish a joint company to operate the Bamako–Dakar line, and the line passed fully into private ownership in 2003. Plans exist for the construction of a new rail line linking Bamako with Kouroussa and Kankan, in Guinea.

Transrail SA: Immeuble la Roseraie, 310 ave de la liberté, BP 4150, Bamako; tel. 2022-5967; fax 2022-5433; e-mail ericpeiffer@transrailsa.com; f. 2003 on transfer to private management of fmr Régie du Chemin de Fer du Mali; jt venture of Canac (Canada) and Getma (France); Dir-Gen. ERIC PEIFFER.

ROADS

The Malian road network in 2009 comprised 22,474 km, of which about 5,529 km were paved. A bituminized road between Bamako and Abidjan (Côte d'Ivoire) provides Mali's main economic link to the coast; construction of a road linking Bamako and Dakar (Senegal) is to be financed by the European Development Fund. The African Development Bank also awarded a US $31.66m. loan to fund the Kankan–Kouremale–Bamako road between Mali and Guinea. In addition, there are plans to build a road across the Sahara to link Mali with Algeria.

Agence Nationale de la Sécurité Routière: ACI 2000, rue 425, Porte 294, BP 231, Bamako; tel. 2029-3238; f. 2009; road safety; Dir-Gen. ASSA SYLLA.

Autorité Routière du Mali: rue 320, porte 153, Hamdallaye ACI 2000, 03 BP 12, Bamako; tel. 2029-1125; fax 2029-1108; e-mail infos@arfer-mali.net; internet www.arfer-mali.net; f. 2001; Dir-Gen. MORY KANTÉ.

INLAND WATERWAYS

The River Niger is navigable in parts of its course through Mali (1,693 km) during the rainy season from July to late December. The River Senegal was, until the early 1990s, navigable from Kayes to Saint-Louis (Senegal) only between August and November, but its navigability improved following the inauguration, in 1992, of the Manantali dam, and the completion of works to deepen the riverbed.

Compagnie Malienne de Navigation (COMANAV): BP 10, Koulikoro; tel. 2026-2094; fax 2026-2009; f. 1968; 100% state-owned; river transport; Pres. and Dir-Gen. DEMBÉLÉ GOUNDO DIALLO.

Conseil Malien des Chargeurs (CMC): Dar-salam, BP E 4031, Bamako; tel. 2023-0486; fax 2023-0489; e-mail contact@cmchargeurs.com; internet www.cmchargeurs.com; f. 1999; Pres. OUSMANE BABALAYE DAOU.

CIVIL AVIATION

The principal airport is at Bamako-Senou. The other major airports are at Bourem, Gao, Goundam, Kayes, Kita, Mopti, Nioro, Ségou, Tessalit and Tombouctou. There are about 40 small airfields. Mali's airports are being modernized with external financial assistance. In 2005 the Malian Government announced the creation of a new national airline, Air Mali, in partnership with the Aga Khan Fund for Economic Development and Industrial Promotion Services.

Aéroports du Mali: Bamako; internet www.aeroportsdumali.com; f. 1970; responsible for commercial exploitation, maintenance and development of airports; Pres. and Dir-Gen. AYA THIAM DIALLO.

Agence Nationale de l'Aviation Civile (ANAC): route de l'Aéroport de Bamako, Sénou, BP 227, Bamako; tel. 2020-5524; fax 2020-6175; e-mail anacmali@hotmail.com; internet www.anac-mali.org; f. 2005 to replace Direction Nationale de l'Aéronautique Civile (f. 1990); Pres. TOURÉ ALIMATA TRAORÉ; Dir-Gen. ISSA SALEY MAÏGA.

Air Mali: Immeuble Tomota, ave Cheick Zayed, BP E 2286, Bamako; tel. 2022-2424; fax 2022-7111; e-mail dc.cam@cam-mali.org; internet www.air-mali.com; f. 2005; 51% owned by Fonds Aga Khan pour le Développement Economique (AKAFED), 20% state-owned; domestic and international flights; Dir-Gen. ABDERRAHMANE BERTHÉ.

Tourism

Mali's rich cultural heritage is promoted as a tourist attraction. In 2012 101,335 tourists visited Mali, while receipts from tourism totalled US $267m. in 2011. However, insecurity in Mali and in the wider Sahel region has had a negative impact on tourism in the first half of the 2010s. The destruction of Sufi Islamic shrines in Tombouctou by Islamist militants was likely to result in fewer visitors to that city, while the well publicized kidnappings (and killings) of foreign tourists was expected further to reduce visitor numbers.

Ministry of Handicrafts and Tourism: see section on The Government.

Office Malien du Tourisme et de l'Hôtellerie (OMATHO): Centre Commercial, rue Mohamed V, BP 191, Bamako; tel. 2022-5673; fax 2022-5541; e-mail info@officetourismemali.com; internet officetourismemali.com; f. 1995; Dir-Gen. SISSOKO SIRIMAHA HABIBATOU.

Defence

As assessed at November 2014, the active Malian army, which was undergoing a process of reformation, numbered some 4,000 men.

Paramilitary forces numbered 7,800. Military service is by selective conscription and lasts for two years. Following the escalation of an Islamist insurgency during 2012, in January 2013 some 4,000 French ground troops, together with military fighter jets, undertook an intervention mission in northern Mali. The UN Security Council had in December 2012 authorized the deployment of an African-led International Support Mission to Mali (AFISMA) to assist the Malian armed forces in combating the insurgency. In April 2013 the Security Council approved a resolution providing for the reconstitution of AFISMA (then numbering about 6,300 forces under the command of ECOWAS) into the United Nations Multidimensional Integrated Stabilization Mission in Mali (MINUSMA), to comprise 11,200 military personnel and 1,440 police officers, with a 12-month mandate effective from 1 July. At March 2015, MINUSMA's total (military and police) strength stood at 10,320.

Defence Expenditure: Budgeted at 202,000m. francs CFA in 2015.

Chief of Staff of the Armed Forces: Gen. MAHAMANE TOURÉ.

Chief of Staff of the Air Force: Col SOULEYMANE BAMBA.

Chief of Staff of the Land Army: Col MAMADOU ADAMA DIALLO.

Chief of Staff of the National Guard: Col BROULAYE KONÉ.

Education

Education is provided free of charge and is officially compulsory for nine years between seven and 16 years of age. Basic education, which includes six years of primary education, begins at the age of seven and lasts for nine years. Secondary education, from 16 years of age, lasts for a further three years. The rate of school enrolment in Mali is among the lowest in the world. According to UNESCO, in 2012 primary enrolment included 69% of children in the appropriate age-group (males 73%; females 64%), while in 2011 secondary enrolment included only 34% of those in the appropriate age-group (males 40%; females 28%). Tertiary education facilities include the national university, developed in the mid-1990s. In 2011/12 there were some 97,300 students enrolled in tertiary education. Hitherto many students have received higher education abroad, mainly in France and Senegal. In 2010 spending on education represented 16.4% of total budgetary expenditure.

MALTA

Introductory Survey

LOCATION, CLIMATE, LANGUAGE, RELIGION, FLAG, CAPITAL

The Republic of Malta is in southern Europe. The country comprises an archipelago in the central Mediterranean Sea, consisting of the inhabited islands of Malta, Gozo and Comino, and the uninhabited islets of Cominotto, Filfla and St Paul's. The main island, Malta, lies 93 km (58 miles) south of the Italian island of Sicily and 288 km (179 miles) east of the Tunisian coast, the nearest point on the North African mainland. The climate is warm, with average temperatures of 22.6°C (72.7°F) in summer and 13.7°C (56.6°F) in winter. Average annual rainfall is 578 mm (22.8 in). Maltese and English are the official languages, although Italian is also widely spoken. About 94% of the inhabitants are Christians adhering to the Roman Catholic Church, the country's established religion. The national flag (proportions 2 by 3) consists of two equal vertical stripes, white at the hoist and red at the fly, with a representation of the George Cross, edged with red, in the upper hoist. The capital is Valletta, on the island of Malta.

CONTEMPORARY POLITICAL HISTORY

Historical Context

Malta, which had been a Crown Colony of the United Kingdom since 1814, became an independent sovereign state, within the Commonwealth, on 21 September 1964. The Government, led by Dr Giorgio Borg-Olivier of the Partit Nazzjonalista (PN—Nationalist Party), negotiated defence and financial aid agreements, effective over a 10-year period, with the UK.

In June 1971 the Malta Labour Party (MLP), led by Dom Mintoff, assumed power after winning a general election. Pursuing a policy of non-alignment, the MLP Government concluded co-operation agreements with Italy, Libya, Tunisia, the USSR, several East European countries, the USA, the People's Republic of China and others, and abrogated the 1964 Mutual Defence and Assistance Agreement with the UK. This agreement was replaced in 1972 by a new, seven-year agreement, under which Malta was to receive substantially increased rental payments for the use of military facilities by the UK and other members of the North Atlantic Treaty Organization (NATO, see p. 367). British troops were finally withdrawn in March 1979.

Domestic Political Affairs

Malta declared itself a republic on 13 December 1974. The MLP retained power at a general election held in September 1976 and, again, in December 1981, when it secured a majority of three seats in the 65-seat House of Representatives, although obtaining only 49.1% of the votes cast. The PN, which had received 50.9% of the votes cast, contested the result, refused to take its seats in the legislature and organized a campaign of civil disobedience. In March 1983 the PN terminated its legislative boycott, but immediately withdrew again, in protest against a government resolution to loosen ties with the European Community (EC, now the European Union—EU, see p. 271).

In June 1983 the House of Representatives approved controversial legislation, under which about 75% of church property was to be expropriated to provide finance for a programme of universal free education and the abolition of fee-paying church schools. Opponents of the measure denounced it as unconstitutional and a violation of religious liberty, and in September 1984 the courts disallowed the legislation.

Mintoff retired in December 1984 and was replaced as Prime Minister by the new leader of the MLP, Dr Carmelo Mifsud Bonnici. In April 1985 the Government concluded a compromise agreement with the Roman Catholic Church, providing for the phased introduction of free education in church secondary schools, and guaranteeing the autonomy of church schools. However, in July 1988 the introduction of new licensing procedures for church schools prompted demands by the Roman Catholic Church that the state should reduce its supervisory powers over church education.

At a general election held in May 1987 the PN obtained 50.9% of the votes cast, but won only 31 seats in the House of Representatives, while the MLP, with 48.9% of the votes cast, secured the remaining 34 seats. However, in accordance with a constitutional amendment that had been adopted in January (see Constitution and Government), the PN—having received more than 50% of the votes—was allocated four additional seats, giving it a majority of one in the legislature, thereby ending the MLP's 16-year tenure in office. The leader of the PN, Dr Eddie Fenech Adami, became Prime Minister. The PN secured an increased majority of three seats over the MLP at a general election held in February 1992. This result was widely interpreted as an endorsement of the PN's pro-EC policies.

Application for EU membership

On becoming Prime Minister in May 1987, Fenech Adami declared that the Government, while upholding Malta's policy of non-alignment, would seek closer relations with the USA and other Western countries, and would apply for full membership of the EC. A formal application for EC membership was submitted by the Government in July 1990. In June 1993 the European Commission recommended that, subject to the Government of Malta's satisfying the Commission's requirements for regulatory reforms in financial services, competition and consumer protection, favourable consideration should be given to the country's future accession to the EU (as the EC had become in 1992).

Domestic opposition to Maltese accession to the EU had been led by the MLP, on the grounds that EU agricultural policies would increase the cost of living, and that integration into the Union would conflict with Malta's traditional neutrality in foreign relations. In September 1996 the PN Government, seeking to confirm its mandate to pursue the goal of EU membership, called a general election for the following month. Although the PN contested the poll on its record of economic success, the Government's introduction of value-added tax (VAT), as a precondition of Malta's admission to the EU, had proved unpopular with the electorate, and its proposed abolition by the MLP (which would concurrently disqualify Malta from EU membership) was widely regarded as the decisive factor in the election. With a participation rate of 97.1% of the electorate, the MLP won 50.7% of the votes cast, compared with 47.8% for the PN. The MLP obtained 31 seats in the House of Representatives, while the PN received 34. In accordance with the Constitution, the subsequent allocation of an additional four seats to the MLP gave the party a one-seat majority in the legislature. Dr Alfred Sant, the leader of the MLP, formed a Government with the declared intention of replacing the existing association agreement, signed in 1970, with new arrangements providing for an eventual free trade zone between Malta and the EU.

In February 1997 the Government announced the initiation of a 'national discussion' of proposals to legalize divorce. However, the imposition of tax increases and levies on public utilities substantially diminished the Government's popularity. Sant called a general election for September 1998, three years earlier than constitutionally required, at which the PN, led by Fenech Adami, obtained a five-seat majority. Fenech Adami subsequently reactivated Malta's application for full membership of the EU. Accession negotiations recommenced in February 2000 and were formally concluded in December 2002. Malta had obtained 77 exemptions in the discussions, aimed largely at protecting its industrial and agricultural sectors, but also including cultural issues, such as the right to maintain the ban on divorce. At a non-binding referendum held in March 2003 to determine whether the country would join the EU, 53.6% of valid votes cast were in favour of membership.

In accordance with the Constitution, Fenech Adami called a general election for 12 April 2003 to confirm the referendum result, four days before the proposed signing of the EU accession treaty by Malta. At the election the PN won an absolute majority of 35 seats with 51.8% of the votes, while the MLP secured 30 seats. Fenech Adami was sworn in as Prime Minister on 14 April and signed the EU accession treaty in Athens, Greece, two days later. The House of Representatives ratified the treaty in July by 34 votes to 25 (six members boycotted the vote). Malta became a full member of the EU on 1 May 2004.

Developments following EU accession

After the MLP's defeat at the 2003 general election, the party leadership decided to accept the majority public opinion in favour of accession to the EU and work within the reality of EU membership. This decision proved divisive, and was resisted by a faction of the MLP led by Mifsud Bonnici. However, delegates at a subsequent party conference agreed that the MLP would not withdraw Malta from the EU if the party came to power.

In February 2004 Fenech Adami announced his intention to retire as leader of the PN and as Prime Minister. At a party conference later that month the Deputy Prime Minister and Minister for Social Policy, Dr Lawrence Gonzi, was elected as the PN's new leader. Gonzi assumed the premiership in March, also taking responsibility for the finance portfolio, and appointed his former rival for the party leadership, John Dalli, as Minister for Foreign Affairs. Later in March Fenech Adami was elected President by the House of Representatives, following his nomination by Gonzi. His appointment was controversial, as party leaders had not traditionally stood for the post, and it was strongly opposed by the MLP. In July 2004 Dalli resigned as Minister for Foreign Affairs, claiming that he was unable to continue amid attacks from 'different sides', which was thought to be a reference to criticism from within the PN. There were also allegations, which Dalli denied, of his involvement in irregularities regarding a large shipping deal and the handling of ministry travel expenses.

In March 2008 Malta held its first general election since joining the EU; a turnout of 93.3% was reported. The PN, which based its electoral campaign on its economic achievements, secured 49.3% of the votes cast, while the MLP won 48.8% but secured the majority of parliamentary seats. The PN, which although not having won an absolute majority of the votes had none the less won a relative majority, was thus assigned four additional seats to ensure that it had a parliamentary majority. Following the announcement of the results, Sant resigned as MLP leader. In Prime Minister Gonzi's new Cabinet Dr Tonio Borg remained as Deputy Prime Minister but was allocated the foreign affairs portfolio in place of justice and home affairs, while the former parliamentary secretaries, Dr Tonio Fenech and Mifsud Bonnici, were appointed Minister for Finance, the Economy and Investment and Minister for Justice and Home Affairs, respectively. Dalli was reappointed to the Cabinet as Minister for Social Policy.

Following his election in June 2008 as the new leader of the MLP, Dr Joseph Muscat indicated his intention to rejuvenate the party's image and to reform its internal structures. At a special party conference held in November, delegates approved a programme of reforms, most notably including changing the party's official title to Partit Laburista (PL).

In April 2009 Dr George Abela of the PL was unanimously elected President by the House of Representatives, having been nominated by Gonzi, in accordance with an agreement reached by the two main parties earlier that year. It was the first time that a Prime Minister had proposed a member of an opposing party for the presidency.

Following the accession of Dalli to Malta's seat on the European Commission in February 2010, erstwhile parliamentary secretary Joe Cassar assumed much of the former minister's portfolio in his new cabinet role as Minister for Health, the Elderly and Community Care, while the Minister for Education and Culture, Dolores Cristina, was given additional responsibility for family affairs.

In July 2010 a private member's bill proposing the legalization of divorce in Malta (a long-standing point of controversy) was introduced in the House of Representatives by a member of the PN, apparently without the prior knowledge of the party leadership. Support for an amended version of the bill, which was presented in December, was expressed by some members of both the main parties, but opposition appeared to be more prevalent among members of the PN. A motion proposing a referendum on the issue received parliamentary approval in March 2011 after Gonzi, although expressing his personal opposition to divorce, allowed the PN deputies a free vote. The non-binding referendum took place in May and posed the question of whether a divorce should be permitted after four years of marital separation (provided that adequate maintenance was guaranteed and the welfare of any children safeguarded); of the 72% of the electorate who participated, 53.2% voted in favour of the legalization of divorce. The appropriate legislation was accordingly adopted by the House of Representatives in July, and entered into force in October.

In November 2011, after the introduction of widely criticized changes to the national bus system, the opposition proposed a motion of no confidence in the Minister for Infrastructure, Transport and Communications, Austin Gatt. A member of the ruling PN, Franco Debono (who had criticized the Government on various issues, in particular its failure to reform the judicial system), abstained from voting, and the Government therefore only escaped defeat when the Speaker of the House of Representatives used his casting vote in its favour.

In January 2012 Gonzi effected several cabinet changes, including the division of the Ministry of Justice and Home Affairs into two (an action that Debono had repeatedly demanded): Mifsud Bonnici, formerly responsible for the joint portfolio, became Minister for Home Affairs, Local Government and Parliamentary Affairs, while Chris Said, hitherto a parliamentary secretary, became Minister of Justice, Public Dialogue and the Family. Later in January the opposition proposed a new motion of no confidence, this time against the whole Government, citing a long list of alleged shortcomings; Debono again abstained, and once more the Government was saved from defeat only by the Speaker's casting vote. The PL leader, Muscat, urged Gonzi to resolve national uncertainty by holding an early general election.

In February 2012 Gonzi addressed the crisis within the PN by instigating an election to the party leadership; no other candidate was presented, and he was re-elected with 96.5% of the party delegates' votes.

At the end of May 2012 Mifsud Bonnici resigned as Minister for Home Affairs, Local Government and Parliamentary Affairs after losing a legislative motion of no confidence presented by the opposition by 34 votes to 35 (in this instance Debono unexpectedly voted in favour of the motion); Gonzi assumed responsibility for the vacated portfolio. The following week the Government survived a parliamentary motion of confidence (by 35 votes to 34) tabled by the Prime Minister; Debono voted in support of the Government, while demanding the implementation of a number of political and democratic reforms (including a law to regulate political party financing).

In October 2012 former cabinet minister Dalli resigned from his post as EU Commissioner for Health and Consumer Policy in the wake of allegations made by the EU anti-fraud agency that a Maltese entrepreneur had attempted to extract payments from a Swedish oral tobacco (snus) company by pledging to use his contacts with the commissioner to bring about changes to EU tobacco legislation. The Deputy Prime Minister and Minister for Foreign Affairs, Tonio Borg, replaced Dalli in the EU Commission in November; the foreign affairs portfolio in the Maltese Cabinet was assigned to Dr Francis Zammit Dimech.

Recent developments: the fall of the PN Government

Gonzi's Government collapsed in December 2012 (thus bringing to an end some 15 years of PN rule) following the loss of its majority, by 34 votes to 35, in a parliamentary vote on the 2013 budget. The Government's fall was precipitated by Debono's decision to vote against the Government for a variety of reasons, including his opposition to a recent government ruling to transfer management of the country's national bus service to a German operator.

At the general election held on 9 March 2013, which attracted a turnout of some 93%, the PL obtained an absolute majority, of 39 seats (with 54.8% of the votes). The PN secured 26 seats (which was increased to 30—in accordance with electoral reform introduced in 2007—when the party was awarded four at-large seats to adjust for its share of the first-preference votes), with 43.3% of the votes. The environmentalist Alternattiva Demokratika took 1.8% of the votes but won no seats. PL leader Muscat subsequently assumed the premiership and appointed a large, 22-member Cabinet, including Louis Grech as Deputy Prime Minister and Minister for European Affairs and Implementation of the Electoral Manifesto, Dr George Vella as Minister for Foreign Affairs and Dr Emmanuel Mallia as Minister for Home Affairs and National Security. In May Simon Busuttil was elected as the new leader of the PN following Gonzi's resignation in the wake of his party's defeat. Gonzi also relinquished his parliamentary seat, in July.

In January 2014 the European Commission held talks with the Maltese Government regarding the introduction of a controversial scheme, the Individual Investor Programme, by the Maltese authorities to sell Maltese passports (thereby entitling the holder to EU citizenship) to wealthy foreigners—at a cost of at least €1.15m. each, in the form of investment in Malta—without stipulating that they first reside in the country. At the end of January, in response to the concerns of the EU and the PL (which opposed the programme), the Government amended the scheme by requiring that applicants live in the country for at least one year in order to qualify.

In early April 2014 Marie-Louise Coleiro Preca of the PL, hitherto Minister for the Family and Social Solidarity, was elected unanimously by the House of Representatives as Malta's new President. She took office on 4 April. One of Coleiro Preca's first acts in the presidency was to sign a bill legalizing civil unions and adoptions by same-sex partners. In an attempt to improve the accountability of political parties and increase transparency in the political process, in July the Government presented Parliament with draft legislation (originally drawn up by PN legislator Debono in 2012) regarding the regulation of the formation, functioning and financing of political parties. Following allegations of his involvement in a police cover-up regarding a shooting incident, Mallia was forced to resign as Minister for Home Affairs and National Security in December 2014; he was replaced by Carmelo Abela.

Immigration Issues

Following its accession to the EU in 2004, illegal immigration became an increasing problem for Malta, partly owing to its proximity to North Africa. According to the Office of the UN High Commissioner for Refugees (UNHCR, see p. 68), of all EU states Malta received the second largest number of asylum seekers per 1,000 inhabitants in 2005 (after Cyprus). Given Malta's high population density the European Commission supported the Government's request in July 2005 that a proportion of the migrants arriving there be transferred to other EU states. The House of Representatives adopted amendments to refugee legislation in October aimed at facilitating the repatriation of failed asylum seekers. In December a first group of migrants granted refugee status was transferred to the Netherlands. In February 2006 immigrants housed in detention centres across Malta organized protests, claiming that they were poorly fed and kept in insanitary conditions. Malta had previously been criticized by UNHCR over its alleged ill-treatment of asylum seekers.

In July 2006 the EU announced its intention to deploy a police force to patrol the borders of member countries experiencing problems with illegal immigration; the force would include a maritime patrol in the Mediterranean Sea between Malta and North Africa. During 2006–07 there were several incidents in which the Maltese authorities refused to take responsibility for migrants arriving by sea from Africa, usually having set off from Libya. In June 2007 the European Commission accused the Maltese Government of failing to meet its internationally recognized obligation to save lives at sea. The Government insisted, however, that Malta could not accept responsibility for all illegal immigrants rescued in the Mediterranean; it proposed the creation of a system of shared responsibility for rescued migrants between EU member states on a quota basis. From 2008 Malta received financial assistance from the EU's European Refugee Fund (ERF) to help manage the influx of asylum seekers; the ERF was subsequently replaced by the Asylum, Migration and Integration Fund, which was to cover the period 2014–20.

In March 2009 Malta and Libya signed a memorandum of understanding on search and rescue, in order to enhance co-operation between the two countries. In the same month the Maltese Government offered to deploy Maltese military personnel to assist in planned joint patrols of Libyan waters by Italian and Libyan forces, which were intended to curtail the illegal transportation of migrants across the Mediterranean; these patrols commenced in May. Meanwhile, in February Malta, together with Cyprus, Greece and Italy, submitted proposals to the European Commission aimed at strengthening co-operation between member states on immigration and asylum policy, including the establishment of a European Asylum Support Office (EASO). The proposals were adopted at an EU summit in June, and the EASO was formally established in Valletta in 2010. In March of that year Malta disputed new EU rules which stipulated that migrants intercepted by naval patrols in the Mediterranean should be landed in the country whose personnel were leading the patrol in question: the Maltese Government argued that, since Maltese officers led many such patrols, Malta would be obliged to receive a larger number of migrants than would otherwise have been the case. In February 2011, following the popular uprisings in Tunisia and Egypt, and escalating civil unrest in Libya, Malta was among six Mediterranean EU states to request the establishment by the EU of a

'burden-sharing mechanism' and an emergency fund, in anticipation of an increased influx of asylum seekers, particularly from Libya. In September Malta appealed to the new Libyan administration to adhere to international conventions on immigration and the prevention of people-trafficking. In March 2012 the European Commission urged Malta to improve the facilities provided for the reception of migrants and agreed to provide extra funding for this purpose.

Following the arrival of more than 400 migrants (many of whom were from Eritrea) in Malta in July 2013 it was reported that the Maltese authorities were planning to return the asylum seekers to Libya. These alleged plans were thwarted by an emergency intervention on the part of the European Court of Human Rights (ECHR), which had in 2012 declared such 'push back' action illegal.

Other Foreign Affairs

In November 2005 Malta hosted the Commonwealth Heads of Government Meeting. The British Prime Minister, Tony Blair, attended the meeting and later held talks with Gonzi; this was the first visit to Malta by a British Prime Minister in some 60 years.

In July 2005 Malta extended its maritime jurisdiction and established exclusive fisheries zones in response to similar measures being adopted by Libya and Tunisia. In early 2006 Malta and Libya discussed reviving their 1984 friendship and co-operation agreement (a proposal discussed again by the two sides in October 2010) and agreed to consider a number of options with regard to petroleum, not limited to exploration; in March 2008 Libya warned a Canadian petroleum company not to begin operations in an area of the seabed that Malta had licensed the company to explore, but which was claimed by Libya. The disputed delineation of areas of the continental shelf apportioned to Malta and Libya respectively was still under discussion in February 2011, when Prime Minister Gonzi paid a visit to Libya. In February 2006, meanwhile, Malta and Tunisia signed an agreement on joint petroleum exploration and exploitation in zones of the continental shelf located between the two countries. In January 2011 Malta made a formal protest to Italy, after the Italian Government offered licences for petroleum exploration in a contested area of the continental shelf.

The widespread popular unrest that broke out in North Africa and the Middle East during early 2011 was a source of grave concern to Malta, not only because of the expected increase in the number of migrants seeking asylum (see *Immigration Issues*), but also because of the feared impact of regional instability on Malta's economy, with investment and tourism expected to be particularly adversely affected. In February Malta accepted requests from several countries to provide a transit point for many of the thousands of expatriate workers who were being evacuated from Libya by air and sea. NATO aircraft supervising the 'no-fly' zone imposed by the UN over Libya were allowed to land in Malta when necessary. In August Malta recognized the National Transitional Council as Libya's rightful Government, and subsequently agreed to provide a logistical base for humanitarian aid to Libya. Following the death in October of the deposed ruler, Col Muammar al-Qaddafi, at the hands of the rebels, Gonzi and other Maltese ministers visited Libya in November, holding discussions with the new administration on migration, fishing rights and the continental shelf, and undertaking to restore strong links between the two countries through trade and investment.

CONSTITUTION AND GOVERNMENT

Under the 1974 Constitution, legislative power is held by the unicameral House of Representatives, whose 69 members are elected by universal adult suffrage for five years (subject to dissolution) on the basis of proportional representation. The Constitution was amended in 1987 to ensure that a party that received more than 50% of the total votes cast in a general election would obtain a majority of seats in the legislature (by the allocation—if necessary—of additional seats to that party). Another constitutional amendment, adopted in 1996, extended this provision to cases in which a party won the larger number of votes but failed to obtain an absolute majority of votes cast, providing only two parties won seats in Parliament. According to a further amendment introduced in 2007, it was established that the winning margin in a general election was to be reflected in the margin of seats obtained. The President is the constitutional Head of State, elected for a five-year term by the House of Representatives, and executive power is exercised by the Cabinet. The President appoints the Prime Minister and, on the latter's recommendation, other Ministers. The Cabinet is responsible to the House of Representatives.

REGIONAL AND INTERNATIONAL CO-OPERATION

Malta is a member of the European Union (EU, see p. 271) and uses the single currency, the euro. It is also a member of the Council of Europe (see p. 250) and the Organization for Security and Co-operation in Europe (OSCE, see p. 385) and of the Commonwealth (see p. 234).

Malta joined the UN following independence in 1964. As a contracting party to the General Agreement on Tariffs and Trade, Malta joined the World Trade Organization (WTO, see p. 431) on its establishment in 1995. Malta participates in the 'Partnership for Peace' programme of the North Atlantic Treaty Organization (NATO, see p. 367).

ECONOMIC AFFAIRS

In 2013, according to estimates by the World Bank, Malta's gross national income (GNI), measured at average 2011–13 prices, was US $8,882m., equivalent to $20,980 per head (or $28,030 per head on an international purchasing-power parity basis). During 2004–13, it was estimated, the population increased at an average annual rate of 0.6%, while gross domestic product (GDP) per head increased, in real terms, at an average annual rate of 1.7%. According to the World Bank, overall GDP increased, in real terms, at an average annual rate of 2.3% in 2004–13; GDP rose by 2.9% in 2013.

Agriculture (including hunting, forestry and fishing) contributed 1.6% of GDP in 2013, and engaged 1.3% of the working population in March 2014. The principal export crop is potatoes. Tomatoes and other vegetables, cereals (principally wheat and barley) and fruit are also cultivated. Livestock and livestock products are also important, and efforts are being made to develop the fishing industry. During 2004–13, according to the UN, agricultural GDP decreased at an average annual rate of 1.5%. Agricultural GDP increased by 6.7% in 2013.

Industry (including mining, manufacturing, construction and power) provided 17.0% of GDP in 2013, and engaged 20.3% of the employed labour force in March 2014. During 2004–13, according to the UN, industrial GDP decreased at an average annual rate of 1.9%; industrial GDP decreased by 6.8% in 2013.

Mining and quarrying (together with utilities) contributed 1.7% of GDP in 2013, and engaged 2.0% of the employed labour force in March 2014. The principal activities are stone- and sand-quarrying. There are reserves of petroleum in Maltese offshore waters, and petroleum and gas exploration is under way. During 2004–13, according to the UN, real GDP of the mining sector (together with utilities) decreased at an average annual rate of 1.3%; sectoral GDP decreased by 5.4% in 2012, but increased by 4.4% in 2013.

Manufacturing contributed 11.2% of GDP in 2013, and engaged 12.7% of the working population in March 2014. Based on the gross value of output, the principal branches of manufacturing, excluding ship-repairing, in 2007 were electrical and optical equipment (accounting for around 27.3% of the total), chemicals, chemical products and man-made fibres (15.3%), and food products and beverages (13.7%). During 2004–13, according to the UN, manufacturing GDP decreased at an average annual rate of 0.9%. Manufacturing GDP decreased by 0.6% in 2012 and by a further 8.9% in 2013.

Construction contributed 4.1% of GDP in 2013, and engaged 5.6% of the employed labour force in March 2014. During 2004–13, according to the UN, construction GDP decreased at an average annual rate of 4.3%; sectoral GDP decreased by 3.4% in 2013.

Energy is derived principally from imports of crude petroleum and coal. Imports of mineral fuels comprised 45.5% of the value of total imports in 2012. In November 2011 the Government announced that the EU had agreed to allocate funds for a proposed gas pipeline linking Malta to the mainland European gas supply network via Sicily; at early 2015, however, the project still remained under discussion. In December 2013 construction work began on a 95-km underwater power cable between Malta and Sicily to link the former to the mainland electricity grid; the interconnector project, which was expected to be operational by June 2015, aimed to reduce Malta's dependence on its ageing principal power station.

Services provided 81.5% of GDP in 2013, and engaged 78.3% of the employed labour force in March 2014. Tourism is a major source of foreign exchange earnings. In 2012 Malta received 1,444,192 foreign visitors and revenue from the tourism sector

amounted to US $1,345m. In March 2014 6.2% of the employed labour force were engaged in employment in the hotels and restaurants sub-sector. The GDP of the services sector increased at an average annual rate of 3.6% in 2004–13, according to the UN; services GDP increased by 3.0% in 2013.

In 2013 Malta recorded a visible merchandise trade deficit of US $1,484.3m., while there was a surplus of $84.9m. on the current account of the balance of payments. In 2013, according to provisional figures, the principal source of imports (accounting for 24.6% of the total value) was Italy (including San Marino); other major suppliers were Germany, the United Kingdom and the Russian Federation. Germany was the principal market for exports (taking 8.9% of the total value); other significant purchasers were Singapore, France and Libya. The principal domestic exports in 2013 were mineral fuels, accounting for 41.6% of the total, followed by machinery and transport equipment, manufactured goods and chemicals. The principal imports were mineral fuels, accounting for 39.6% of the total, followed by machinery and transport equipment, chemicals, food and live animals, manufactured goods and semi-manufactures.

In 2013 Malta recorded an estimated central budget deficit of €263.2m., and a general government deficit of €203.0m., equivalent to 2.8% of GDP. Malta's general government gross debt was €5,243m. in 2013, equivalent to 72.1% of GDP. According to the International Labour Organization (ILO), the annual rate of inflation averaged 2.4% in 2004–13; consumer prices increased by 1.4% in 2013. In March 2014 the unemployment rate averaged 4.5%.

Following the closure, in 1979, of the British military base and naval docks, on which Malta's economy had been largely dependent, successive governments pursued a policy of restructuring and diversification. The domestic market is limited, owing to the small population. There are few natural resources, and almost all raw materials have to be imported. Malta's development has therefore been based on the promotion of the island as an international financial centre and on manufacturing for export (notably in non-traditional fields, such as electronics, information technology and pharmaceuticals), together with the continuing development of tourism. From 2004 Malta's membership of the EU entailed a commitment on the part of the Government to reduce Malta's fiscal deficit to below 3.0% of GDP in order to comply with the convergence criteria for participation in Economic and Monetary Union (EMU). Through the implementation of strict monetary policies, institutional reform and a privatization programme, Malta reduced its fiscal deficit from more than 10% of GDP in 2003 to 2.2% in 2007. Malta adopted the euro as its currency in January 2008.

Although Malta was affected by the global economic downturn of 2008–09, its banking sector remained relatively unharmed by the financial crisis. However, export revenue and tourism declined sharply and GDP contracted by 2.6% in 2009 (compared with positive growth of 4.4% in 2008). The fiscal deficit increased to 4.5% of GDP in 2008, but narrowed to 3.8% in 2009 and 3.6% in 2010, primarily as a result of increased revenue from taxation. Manufacturing output and tourism both recovered in 2010, although investment, particularly in the construction industry, remained at a comparatively low level. According to the IMF, Malta's GDP expanded by 2.9% in 2010 and by 1.7% in 2011, but growth decelerated to 1.0% in 2012, largely owing to subdued domestic demand and continuing economic weakness within the eurozone. In 2011 the fiscal deficit, at 2.7% of GDP, was below the stipulated EU limit of 3%, but it increased to 3.3% in 2012 as a result of overspending and lower-than-expected revenues. In March 2012 Malta was among the 25 EU member states that signed the Treaty on Stability, Co-ordination and Governance, which placed a legal obligation on signatories to balance their budgets (defined as budget deficits not exceeding 3% of GDP). Strong exports—aided by successful export diversification, particularly within high value-added areas—helped to produce a surplus on the current account of the balance of payments in both 2012 and 2013. The World Bank estimated Malta's public debt to be equivalent to 71.6% of GDP at the end of 2012—higher than the 60% stipulated in the EU's Stability and Growth Pact—and urged the Government to reduce this figure (although it compared favourably with the eurozone average of some 90%); however, the level of public debt rose to 72.1% of GDP in 2013. The high level of debt was partly caused by Malta's contributions over the preceding few years to EU emergency assistance to heavily-indebted eurozone countries. During 2012–14 the annual budgets continued to focus on fiscal consolidation, including reductions in expenditure, the provision of incentives to encourage further investment and job creation, and the safeguarding of social welfare. According to the World Bank, real GDP increased by 2.9% in 2013 (one of the highest levels of growth recorded in the eurozone in that year) as levels of private consumption and investment slowly rose in response to growing confidence. In the same year, buoyed by higher-than-predicted revenue, the Government achieved its target of lowering the fiscal deficit to 2.7% of GDP. In 2014, aided by its relatively diversified economy and stable banking sector, Malta's economic outlook appeared considerably robust, albeit largely dependent on favourable external circumstances and a reining in of the rapid growth in current expenditure—including through prudent wage settlements, pension reform and further curbing public sector employment. The unemployment rate fell from 6.8% in April 2014 to 5.7% in May, which was almost half the size of the EU average (of 10.3%) and was the lowest level recorded in Malta since Eurostat included the country in its unemployment statistics in January 2000. In November 2014 the Ministry of Finance forecast that real GDP would expand by 3.0% in 2014 and by 3.5% in 2015, and that over the same period the fiscal deficit would decrease from 2.1% to 1.6% of GDP.

PUBLIC HOLIDAYS

2016: 1 January (New Year's Day), 10 February (St Paul's Shipwreck), 19 March (St Joseph), 25 March (Good Friday), 31 March (Freedom Day), 1 May (St Joseph the Worker), 7 June (Memorial of the 1919 Riot), 29 June (St Peter and St Paul), 15 August (Assumption), 8 September (Our Lady of Victories), 21 September (Independence Day), 8 December (Immaculate Conception), 13 December (Republic Day), 25 December (Christmas Day).

Statistical Survey

Source (unless otherwise stated): National Statistics Office, Lascaris, Valletta VLT 1921; tel. 21223221; fax 21249841; e-mail nso@magnet.mt; internet www.nso.gov.mt.

AREA AND POPULATION

Area: 316 sq km (122 sq miles).

Population *(de jure* population): 404,962 at census of 27 November 2005; 417,432 (males 207,625, females 209,807) at census of 21 November 2011. *2013* (official estimate at 31 December): 425,384.

Density (at 31 December 2013): 1,346.2 per sq km.

Population by Age and Sex (official estimates at 31 December 2013): *0–14:* 61,212 (males 31,442, females 29,770); *15–64:* 288,148 (males 147,350, females 140,798); *65 and over:* 76,024 (males 33,632, females 42,392); *Total* 425,384 (males 212,424, females 212,960).

Principal Towns (at 31 December 2012): Birkirkara 21,740; Mosta 19,757; San Pawl Il-Bahar 16,873; Qormi 16,313; Żabbar 14,902; Sliema 13,915; Naxxar 12,995; San Gwann 12,307; Żebbuġ 11,633; Valletta (capital) 5,721.

Births, Marriages and Deaths (2013): Registered live births 4,127 (birth rate 9.7 per 1,000), Marriages 2,578 (marriage rate 6.1 per 1,000); Registered deaths 3,236 (death rate 7.6 per 1,000).

Life Expectancy (years at birth, official estimates): 81.9 (males 79.6; females 84.0) in 2013.

Migration (2004, unless otherwise indicated): Emigrants 70 (all to United Kingdom); Returning emigrants 459; Non-Maltese nationals settling in the islands 533 (in 2002). *2010:* Total emigrants 1,863; Total immigrants 1,200.

Economically Active Population (persons in full-time employment, labour force survey, March 2014): Agriculture and hunting 1,543; Fishing 527; Mining and quarrying 309; Manufacturing 20,349; Electricity, gas and water supply 2,910; Construction 9,072; Wholesale and retail trade and repair of motor vehicles, motorcycles and personal and household goods 23,811; Hotels and restaurants 9,921; Transport, storage and communications 14,710; Financial intermediation 7,503; Real estate, renting and business activities 19,599; Public administration and defence and compulsory social security 13,893; Education 15,289; Health and social work 13,600; Other community, social and personal service activities 7,587; Private households with employed persons 7; Extraterritorial organizations and bodies 208; *Total employed* 160,838 (males 103,086, females 57,752); Registered unemployed 7,644; *Total labour force* 168,482. Note: Figures exclude apprentices, trainees and students engaged in holiday work.

HEALTH AND WELFARE

Key Indicators

Total Fertility Rate (children per woman, 2012): 1.4.

Under-5 Mortality Rate (per 1,000 live births, 2012): 7.

HIV/AIDS (% of persons aged 15–49, 2011): 0.1.

Physicians (per 1,000 head, 2012): 3.5.

Hospital Beds (per 1,000 head, 2010): 4.5.

Health Expenditure (2011): US $ per head (PPP): 2,444.

Health Expenditure (2011): % of GDP: 8.7.

Health Expenditure (2011): public (% of total): 63.9.

Total Carbon Dioxide Emissions ('000 metric tons, 2010): 2,588.9.

Carbon Dioxide Emissions Per Head (metric tons, 2010): 6.2.

Human Development Index (2013): ranking: 39.

Human Development Index (2013): value: 0.829.

For sources and definitions, see explanatory note on p. vi.

AGRICULTURE, ETC.

Principal Crops ('000 metric tons, 2013): Wheat 15.0*; Barley 21.0*; Potatoes 12.6; Cabbages and other brassicas 4.4; Tomatoes 12.3; Cauliflowers and broccoli 0.7; Pumpkins, squash and gourds 1.5; Onions, dry 7.4; Garlic 0.7; Broad beans, dry 0.7*; Melons 3.5; Citrus fruit 1.8*; Grapes 4.3.
* FAO estimate.

Livestock ('000 head, year ending September 2013): Cattle 15.2; Pigs 49.5; Sheep 10.9; Goats 4.6; Chickens 1,000*; Horses 1.1*.
* FAO estimate.

Livestock Products ('000 metric tons, 2013): Cattle meat 1.1; Pig meat 5.9; Rabbit meat 1.7*; Chicken meat 4.1; Cows' milk 41.0; Sheep's milk 1.6; Hen eggs 5.1.
* FAO estimate.

Fishing (metric tons, live weight, 2012): Capture 2,201 (Atlantic bluefin tuna 137; Common dolphinfish 181; Swordfish 503); Aquaculture 4,066* (European sea bass 126; Gilthead sea bream 2,604); *Total catch* 6,267*.
* FAO estimate.

Source: FAO.

INDUSTRY

Production ('000 metric tons, 2001, unless otherwise indicated): Limestone flux and calcareous stones 2,000 (Limestone only); Cigarettes (1992, million) 1,475; Washing powders and detergents 9.7; Quicklime (1992, incl. other types of lime) 5; Tankers, launched (1996, number, completions) 5; Other seagoing merchant vessels launched (number, 2002) 1 (5 grt); Electricity (2011, million kWh, by public utilities) 2,194 (Source: UN, *Industrial Commodity Statistics Yearbook* and Database).

FINANCE

Currency and Exchange Rates: 100 cent = 1 euro (€). *Sterling and Dollar Equivalents* (31 December 2014): £1 sterling = 1.286 euros; US $1 = 0.824 euros; €10 = £7.79 = $12.14. *Average Exchange Rate* (euros per US dollar): 0.7783 in 2012; 0.7532 in 2013; 0.7537 in 2014. Note: The national currency was formerly the Maltese lira (LM; plural liri). Malta adopted the euro on 1 January 2008 at a fixed exchange rate of €1 = LM 0.429300. The euro and local currency circulated alongside each other until 31 January, after which the euro became the sole legal tender.

Budget (€ million, central government transactions, 2013): *Revenue:* Income tax 967.6; Customs and excise 178.4; Value-added tax 587.2; Social security 645.3; Grants 173.7; Other revenue 439.9; Total 2,992.1. *Expenditure:* Recurrent expenditure 2,632.6 (Education

182.8, Social security 814.5, Others 1,635.4); Interest payments 227.9; Capital expenditure 394.7; Total 3,255.3.

International Reserves (US $ million at 31 December 2013): Gold (national valuation) 12.0; IMF special drawing rights 137.8; Reserve position in IMF 79.5; Foreign exchange 367.6; Total 596.9. Source: IMF, *International Financial Statistics.*

Money Supply (incl. shares, depository corporations, national residence criteria, € million at 31 December 2013): Currency issued 858 (Central Bank of Malta 896); Demand deposits 5,770; Other deposits 5,440; Securities other than shares 350; Money market fund shares 215; Shares and other equity 8,089; Other items (net) –522; *Total* 20,202. Source: IMF, *International Financial Statistics.*

Cost of Living (Consumer Price Index; base: 2010 = 100): All items 102.7 in 2011; 105.2 in 2012; 106.7 in 2013. Source: IMF, *International Financial Statistics.*

Gross Domestic Product (€ million at constant 2000 prices): 5,005.1 in 2011; 5,037.5 in 2012; 5,156.1 in 2013.

National Income and Product (€ million at current prices, 2013): Compensation of employees 3,224.2; Gross operating surplus and mixed income 3,062.4; *Gross domestic product at factor cost* 6,286.6; Taxes on production and imports 989.6; *Less* Subsidies 89.7; *GDP in purchasers' values* 7,186.4.

Expenditure on Gross Domestic Product (€ million at current prices, 2013): Final consumption expenditure 5,682.6 (General government 1,492.2, Households 4,087.8, Non-profit institutes serving households 102.6); Gross capital formation 1,099.2 (Gross fixed capital formation 1,042.1, Changes in inventories 36.5, Acquisitions, less disposals, of valuables 20.6); *Total domestic expenditure* 6,781.8; Exports of goods and services 6,615.0; *Less* Imports of goods and services 6,210.3; *GDP in purchasers' values* 7,186.4.

Gross Domestic Product by Economic Activity (€ million at current prices, 2013): Agriculture, hunting, forestry and fishing 99.5; Mining and quarrying and utilities 104.4; Manufacturing 699.5; Construction 257.5; Trade, transport, accommodation and food services 1,307.2; Information and communication 411.7; Financial intermediation 506.3; Real estate, renting and business activities 1,053.9; Public administration and defence, compulsory social security, education, health and social work 1,227.3; Other community, social and personal services 593.6; *Gross value added at basic prices* 6,260.7; Indirect taxes 959.0; *Less* Subsidies 33.2; *GDP in purchasers' values* 7,186.4. Note: Financial services indirectly measured assumed to be distributed at origin.

Balance of Payments (US $ million, 2013): Exports of goods 3,771.6; Imports of goods –5,255.8; *Balance on goods* –1,484.3; Exports of services 5,165.9; Imports of services –3,100.7; *Balance on goods and services* 580.9; Primary income received 2,207.1; Primary income paid –2,795.6; *Balance on goods, services and primary income* –7.5; Secondary income received 1,238.2; Secondary income paid –1,145.8; *Current balance* 84.9; Capital account (net) 172.8; Direct investment assets –267.5; Direct investment liabilities –1,868.5; Portfolio investment assets –3,030.0; Portfolio investment liabilities 80.7; Financial derivatives and employee stock options (net) –103.2; Other investment assets 1,566.1; Other investment liabilities 3,473.2; Net errors and omissions –164.7; *Reserves and related items* –56.3. Source: IMF, *International Financial Statistics.*

EXTERNAL TRADE

Principal Commodities (€ million, 2013, provisional): *Imports:* Food and live animals 482.8; Beverages and tobacco 74.1; Animal and vegetable oils and fats 8.5; Crude materials (inedible) except fuels 23.2; Mineral fuels, lubricants, etc. 2,218.4; Chemicals 432.8; Manufactured goods 386.0; Semi-manufactures 304.4; Machinery and transport equipment 1,650.0; Miscellaneous transactions 20.9; Total 5,601.0. *Exports:* Food and live animals 213.8; Beverages and tobacco 35.1; Crude materials (inedible) except fuels 15.3; Mineral fuels, lubricants, etc. 1,600.7; Chemicals 353.3; Manufactured goods

396.8; Semi-manufactures 115.9; Machinery and transport equipment 1,110.7; Miscellaneous transactions 3.2; Total 3,844.8.

Principal Trading Partners (€ million, 2013, provisional): *Imports:* European Union 3,208.3 (United Kingdom 300.5); Other Europe 820.9; Africa 256.4; Americas 294.0; Asia 827.3; Australasia 18.0; South America and Caribbean 92.9; Total 5,601.0 (incl. ships' and aircraft stores and bunkers 83.2). *Exports:* European Union 1,215.1 (United Kingdom 107.4); Other Europe 289.3; Africa 617.3; Americas 211.4; Asia 1,060.7; Australasia 9.8; South America and Caribbean 13.0; Total 3,844.8 (incl. ships' and aircraft stores and bunkers 427.9).

TRANSPORT

Road Traffic (motor vehicles in use, December 2014): Private cars 257,451; Commercial vehicles 47,281; Motorcycles 18,088; Others 11,709; *Total* 334,529.

Shipping: *Flag Registered Fleet* (31 December 2014): Vessels 2,220; Total displacement 57,391,155 grt (Source: Lloyd's List Intelligence—www.lloydslistintelligence.com). *International Freight Traffic* ('000 metric tons, 2007): Goods loaded 410.2; Goods unloaded 1,669.2.

Civil Aviation (traffic on scheduled services, 2011): Kilometres flown (million) 22; Passengers carried ('000) 1,674; Passenger-km (million) 2,537; Total ton-km (million) 231 (Source: UN, *Statistical Yearbook*). *2013:* Passengers carried ('000) 1,603 (Source: World Bank, World Development Indicators database).

TOURISM

Tourist Arrivals (based on departures by air and sea): 1,338,841 in 2010; 1,415,019 in 2011; 1,444,192 in 2012.

Arrivals by Country of Origin (based on departures by air and sea, 2012): France 107,767; Germany 137,322; Italy 202,007; Libya 17,408; Netherlands 39,241; United Kingdom 440,701; Total (incl. others) 1,444,192.

Tourism Receipts (US $ million): 1,132 in 2010; 1,234 in 2011; 1,345 in 2012.

COMMUNICATIONS MEDIA

Telephones (main lines, 2013): 231,331 in use.

Mobile Cellular Telephones (2013): 556,652 subscribers.

Internet Subscribers (2011): 129,300.

Broadband Subscribers (2013): 140,550.

Source: International Telecommunication Union.

EDUCATION

Pre-primary (2011/12 unless otherwise stated): 131 schools (1999/2000); 720 teachers; 9,127 students. Source: UNESCO.

Primary (2011/12 unless otherwise stated): 126 schools (1999/2000); 2,058 teachers; 23,567 students. Source: UNESCO.

Secondary (2010/11 unless otherwise stated): *General:* 75 schools (1999/2000); 3,821 teachers (2009/10); 30,191 students. *Vocational:* 23 schools (1999/2000); 217 teachers (2009/10); 4,927 students. *Junior College* (1995/96): 1 school; 1,800 students. Source: UNESCO, partly *Statistical Yearbook.*

Universities, etc. (2011/12 unless otherwise indicated): 1,386 teachers (2010/11); 12,203 students. Source: UNESCO.

Pupil-teacher Ratio (primary education, UNESCO estimate): 11.5 in 2011/12. Source: UNESCO Institute for Statistics.

Adult Literacy Rate (UNESCO estimates): 92.4% (males 91.2%; females 93.5%) in 2005. Source: UNESCO Institute for Statistics.

Directory

The Government

HEAD OF STATE

President: Marie-Louise Coleiro Preca (took office 4 April 2014).

THE CABINET
(May 2015)

The Government is formed by the Partit Laburista (Labour Party).

Prime Minister: Dr Joseph Muscat.

Deputy Prime Minister and Minister for European Affairs and Implementation of the Electoral Manifesto: Louis Grech.

Minister for Foreign Affairs: Dr George Vella.

Minister for Education and Employment: Evarist Bartolo.

Minister for Sustainable Development, the Environment and Climate Change: Leo Brincat.

Minister for Transport and Infrastructure: Joe Mizzi.

Minister for Gozo: Dr ANTON REFALO.

Minister for Social Dialogue, Consumer Affairs and Civil Liberties: Dr HELENA DALLI.

Minister for the Economy, Investment and Small Business: Dr CHRISTIAN CARDONA.

Minister for Home Affairs and National Security: CARMELO ABELA.

Minister for Finance: Prof. EDWARD SCICLUNA.

Minister for Energy and Health: Dr KONRAD MIZZI.

Minister for the Family and Social Solidarity: Dr MICHAEL FARRUGIA.

Minister for Justice, Culture and Local Government: Dr OWEN BONNICI.

Minister for Tourism: EDWARD ZAMMIT LEWIS.

PARLIAMENTARY SECRETARIES (ATTACHED TO MINISTRIES)

Parliamentary Secretary for Planning and Simplification of Administrative Processes in the Office of the Prime Minister: Dr MICHAEL FALZON.

Parliamentary Secretary for the European Union (EU) Presidency 2017 and EU Funds in the Ministry for European Affairs and Implementation of the Electoral Manifesto: Dr IAN BORG.

Parliamentary Secretary for Research, Innovation, Youth and Sport in the Ministry for Education and Employment: CHRIS AGIUS.

Parliamentary Secretary for Agriculture, Fisheries and Animal Rights in the Ministry for Sustainable Development, the Environment and Climate Change: RODERICK GALDES.

Parliamentary Secretary for Competitiveness and Economic Growth in the Ministry for the Economy, Investment and Small Business: Dr JOSÉ HERRERA.

Parliamentary Secretary for Health in the Ministry for Energy and Health: Dr CHRIS FEARNE.

Parliamentary Secretary for Rights of Persons with Disability and Active Ageing in the Ministry for the Family and Social Solidarity: Dr JUSTYNE CARUANA.

Parliamentary Secretary for Local Government in the Ministry for Justice, Culture and Local Government: Dr STEFAN BUONTEMPO.

MINISTRIES

Office of the President: The Palace, Valletta VLT 1190; tel. 21221221; fax 21241241; internet www.president.gov.mt.

Office of the Prime Minister: Auberge de Castille, Valletta VLT 2000; e-mail joseph.muscat@gov.mt.

Ministry for the Economy, Investment and Small Business: Palazzo Zondadori, 197–198 Merchants St, Valletta; tel. 21226808; e-mail christian.cardona@gov.mt; internet economy.gov.mt.

Ministry for Education and Employment: Great Siege Rd, Floriana VLT 2000; tel. 25689000; fax 25903216; e-mail evarist .bartolo@gov.mt; internet education.gov.mt.

Ministry for Energy and Health: Auberge de Castille, Valletta VLT 2000; tel. 22292500; e-mail customercare.mecw@gov.mt; internet energy.gov.mt.

Ministry for European Affairs and Implementation of the Electoral Manifesto: Auberge d'Aragon, Valletta; tel. 22957306; e-mail louis.grech@gov.mt.

Ministry for the Family and Social Solidarity: 310 Republic St, Valletta VLT 1110; tel. 25903123; e-mail marie-louise.coleiro@gov .mt; internet mfss.gov.mt.

Ministry for Finance: 30 Maison Demandols, South St, Valletta VLT 1102; tel. 25998259; fax 25998429; e-mail info.mfin@gov.mt; internet mfin.gov.mt.

Ministry for Foreign Affairs: Palazzo Parisio, Merchants St, Valletta VLT 1171; tel. 21242191; fax 21236604; e-mail info.mfa@ gov.mt; internet foreignaffairs.gov.mt.

Ministry for Gozo: St Francis Sq., Victoria VCT 1335, Gozo; tel. 22156400; fax 21559360; e-mail gozo@gov.mt; internet mgoz.gov.mt.

Ministry for Home Affairs and National Security: 201 Strait St, Valletta VLT 2000; tel. 25689000; fax 25689350; e-mail customercare .mhas@gov.mt; internet homeaffairs.gov.mt.

Ministry for Justice, Culture and Local Government: 30 Old Treasury St, Valletta VLT 2000; internet mjcl.gov.mt.

Ministry for Social Dialogue, Consumer Affairs and Civil Liberties: Barriera Wharf, Valletta VLT 2000; tel. 20908311; e-mail socialdialogue@gov.mt; internet socialdialogue.gov.mt.

Ministry for Sustainable Development, the Environment and Climate Change: Casa Leone, St Venera; e-mail leo.brincat@gov .mt; internet environment.gov.mt.

Ministry for Tourism: Auberge d'Italie, Merchants St, Valletta VLT 2000; tel. 22915023; fax 22915039; e-mail tourism@gov.mt; internet tourism.gov.mt.

Ministry for Transport and Infrastructure: Francesco Buonamici St, Floriana FRN 1700; tel. 22922200; e-mail joe.mizzi@gov.mt; internet mti.gov.mt.

Legislature

House of Representatives

The Palace, Valletta VLT 1115; tel. 25596000; fax 25596400; e-mail parliament@gov.mt; internet www.parliament.gov.mt.

Speaker: ANĠLU FARRUGIA.

General Election, 9 March 2013

Party	Votes	% of votes	Seats
Partit Laburista (Labour Party)	167,533	54.83	39
Partit Nazzjonalista (Nationalist Party) . . .	132,426	43.34	30
Alternattiva Demokratika (Green Party)	5,506	1.80	—
Others	91	0.03	—
Total	305,556	100.00	69

Election Commission

Electoral Commission: Electoral Office, Evans Bldg, St Elmo Pl., Valletta VLT 2000; tel. 21221994; fax 21236380; e-mail electoral .office@gov.mt; internet www.electoral.gov.mt; independent; Chair. and Chief Electoral Commr JOSEPH CHURCH; Sec. JOE CALLEJA.

Political Organizations

Alternattiva Demokratika (AD) (The Green Party): POB 38, Marsa MTP 1001; tel. 99894962; e-mail info@alternattiva.org.mt; internet www.alternattiva.org.mt; f. 1989; emphasizes social and environmental issues; Chair. ARNOLD CASSOLA; Sec.-Gen. RALPH CASSAR.

Partit Laburista (PL) (Labour Party): National Labour Centre, Mile End Rd, Hamrun HMR 1717; tel. 21249900; e-mail info@ partitlaburista.org; internet www.partitlaburista.org; f. 1921, fmrly known as the Malta Labour Party; adopted current name in 2008; democratic socialist; Leader Dr JOSEPH MUSCAT; Pres. DANIEL MICALLEF.

Partit Nazzjonalista (PN) (Nationalist Party): Herbert Ganado St, Pietà PTA 1541; tel. 21243641; fax 21243640; e-mail admin@pn.org .mt; internet www.pn.org.mt; f. 1880; Christian democratic; Leader SIMON BUSUTTIL; Sec.-Gen. CHRIS SAID.

Diplomatic Representation

EMBASSIES AND HIGH COMMISSIONS IN MALTA

Australia: Villa Ferentina, Ta'Xbiex Terrace, Ta'Xbiex XBX 1034; tel. 21338201; fax 21344059; e-mail aushicom@onvol.net; internet www.malta.embassy.gov.au; High Commr JANE LAMBERT.

Austria: Whitehall Mansions, 3rd Floor, Ta'Xbiex Seafront, Ta'Xbiex XBX 1026; tel. 23279000; fax 21317430; e-mail valletta-ob@bmeia.gv.at; internet www.aussenministerium.at/ botschaft/valletta.html; Ambassador Dr PETRA MARIA SCHNEEBAUER.

Belgium: Europa Centre, 8–9 John Lopez St, Floriana FLN 1400; tel. 21228214; fax 21243246; e-mail valletta@diplobel.fed.be; internet www.diplomatie.be/valletta; Ambassador VINCENT MERTENS DE WILMARS.

China, People's Republic: Karmnu Court, Lapsi St, St Julian's STJ 1264; tel. 23798804; fax 21344730; e-mail chinaemb_mt@mfa .gov.cn; internet mt.chineseembassy.org; Ambassador CAI JINBIAO.

Egypt: Villa Mon Rêve, 10 Sir Temi Zammit St, Ta'Xbiex XBX 1013; tel. 21314158; fax 21319230; e-mail embegmlt@onvol.net; Ambassador Dr MAGDA SAFWAT ABD AL-HAMID BARAKA.

France: 130 Melita St, POB 408, Valletta VLT 1123; tel. 22480600; fax 22480626; e-mail contact@ambafrance-mt.org; internet www.ambafrance-mt.org; Ambassador BÉATRICE LE FRAPER DU HELLEN.

Germany: 'Il-Piazzetta', Entrance B, 1st Floor, Tower Rd, Sliema SLM 1605; POB 48, Marsa MRS 1000; tel. 22604000; fax 22604115; e-mail info@valletta.diplo.de; internet www.valletta.diplo.de; Ambassador KLAUS-PETER BRANDES.

Greece: 6 Ir-Rampa, Ta'Xbiex XBX 1035; tel. 27320888; fax 21320788; e-mail gremb.val@mfa.gr; internet www.mfa.gr/valletta; Ambassador THEODOROS DASKAROLIS.

Holy See: Apostolic Nunciature, 20/22 Pietru Caxaru St, Tal-Virtù, Rabat RBT 2604; tel. 21453422; fax 21453423; e-mail nuntius@onvol.net; Apostolic Nuncio (vacant).

Ireland: Whitehall Mansions, Ta'Xbiex Seafront, Ta'Xbiex XBX 1026; tel. 21334744; fax 21334755; e-mail vallettaembassy@dfa.ie; internet www.embassyofireland.org.mt; Ambassador PÁDRAIG MAC COSCAIR.

Italy: 5 Vilhena St, Floriana FRN 1040; tel. 21233157; fax 21239217; e-mail ambasciata.lavalletta@esteri.it; internet www.amblavalletta.esteri.it; Ambassador GIOVANNI UMBERTO DE VITO.

Kuwait: Triq l-Imdina, Balzan, BZN 9033; tel. 27559977; fax 27881155; e-mail info@kuwaitembassy-malta.com; Ambassador FAISAL AL-MUSAILEEM.

Libya: 40 Abate Rigord St, Ta'Xbiex; tel. 21315715; fax 21488588; e-mail info@libyanembassymalta.com; Chargé d'affaires ALAMIN AL-HABIB.

Netherlands: Whitehall Mansions, 3rd Floor, Ta'Xbiex Seafront, Ta'Xbiex XBX 1026; tel. 21313980; fax 21313990; e-mail val@minbuza.nl; internet malta.nlembassy.org; Ambassador Dr RITA DULCI RAHMAN.

Russian Federation: Ariel House, 25 Anthony Schembri St, Kappara, San Gwann SGN 4239; tel. 21371905; fax 21372131; e-mail rusemb@onvol.net; internet www.malta.mid.ru; Ambassador VLADIMIR MALYGIN.

Spain: Whitehall Mansions, Ta'Xbiex Seafront, Ta'Xbiex XBX 1026; tel. 21317365; fax 21317362; e-mail emb.valletta@maec.es; Ambassador Dr JOSÉ MARIA PONS IRAZAZÁBAL.

Tunisia: Valletta Rd, Attard ATD 9052; tel. 21417070; fax 21413414; e-mail at.lavalette@maltanet.net; internet www.atunisie-mt.org; Ambassador ZOHRA LADGHAM.

Turkey: 35 Sir Luigi Preziosi Sq., Floriana FRN 1154; tel. 21223424; fax 21224308; e-mail embassy.valletta@mfa.gov.tr; Ambassador AYŞE SEZGIN.

United Kingdom: Whitehall Mansions, Ta'Xbiex Seafront, Ta'Xbiex XBX 1026; tel. 23230000; fax 23232216; e-mail bhcvalletta@fco.gov.uk; internet www.gov.uk/government/world/malta; High Commr ROB LUKE.

USA: Ta' Qali National Park, Ta' Qali, ATD 4000; tel. 25614000; fax 25614183; e-mail usembmalta@state.gov; internet malta.usembassy.gov; Ambassador GINA ABERCROMBIE-WINSTANLEY.

Judicial System

The legal system consists of enactments of the Parliament of Malta, and those of the British Parliament not repealed or replaced by enactments of the Maltese legislature. Maltese Civil Law derives largely from Roman Law, while British Law has significantly influenced Maltese public law.

The Constitutional Court, composed of three judges, is appellate in cases involving alleged violations of human rights, the interpretation of the Constitution and the invalidity of laws. It has jurisdiction to decide questions as to membership of the House of Representatives and any reference made to it relating to voting for election of members of the House of Representatives.

The Court of Appeal is composed of three judges, when it hears appeals from the judgments of the Civil Court, and of one judge, when it hears appeals from the Court of Magistrates in its civil jurisdiction. An appeal also lies to the Court of Appeal from the decisions of a number of administrative tribunals, mostly on points of law.

The Court of Criminal Appeal consists of three judges and hears appeals from persons convicted by the Criminal Court. This court, when formed of one judge, hears appeals from judgments delivered by the Court of Magistrates in its criminal jurisdiction.

The Criminal Court is formed by one judge, who sits with a jury of nine persons to try, on indictment, offences exceeding the competence of the Court of Magistrates. This court may, in certain exceptional cases, sit without a jury.

The Civil Court is divided into three sections. The First Hall takes cognisance of all causes of a civil and a commercial nature, exceeding the jurisdiction of the Courts of Magistrates. The Voluntary Jurisdiction Section is assigned all matters of a civil nature, such as authority to proceed the tutorship of minors, adoption, the interdiction and incapacitation of persons, the opening of successions and the confirmation of testamentary executors. The Family Section is assigned matters of a civil nature regulated by titles I, II and IV of the First Book of the Civil Code; the Maintenance Orders (Facilities for Enforcement) Ordinance; the Maintenance Ordinance (Reciprocal Enforcement) Act; the Marriage Act and the Child Abduction and Child Custody Act. One judge presides in all three sections.

The Magistrates' Court, which is composed of one magistrate, exercises both a civil and a criminal jurisdiction. The Court of Magistrates, in civil matters, has an inferior jurisdiction of first instance, limited to claims exceeding €3,494.06 (LM 1,500) but not exceeding €11,646.87 (LM 5,000). In criminal matters, the court has a two-fold jurisdiction: as a court of criminal judicature for the trial of offences which fall within its jurisdiction, and as a court of inquiry in respect of offences which fall within the jurisdiction of a higher tribunal.

The Court of Magistrates for Gozo, in civil matters, has a two-fold jurisdiction—an inferior jurisdiction comparable to that exercised by its counterpart court in Malta, and a superior jurisdiction, both civil and commercial, in respect of causes which in Malta are cognizable by the First Hall of the Civil Court. Within the limits of its territorial jurisdiction, this court has also the powers of a court of voluntary jurisdiction.

The Small Claims Tribunal is presided over by an adjudicator who decides cases on principles of equity, according to law. The Juvenile Court consists of a Magistrate, as Chairman, and two members.

Chief Justice and President of the Court of Appeal and the Constitutional Court: Dr SILVIO CAMILLERI.

Attorney-General: Dr PETER GRECH.

Religion

CHRISTIANITY

The Roman Catholic Church

Malta comprises one archdiocese and one diocese. The Constitution enshrines Roman Catholicism as the state religion. Adherents comprise an estimated 94% of the population.

Bishops' Conference: Conferenza Episcopale Maltese, POB 90, Marsa MRS 1000; tel. 25906135; fax 21223307; e-mail info@episcopalconference.org.mt; internet www.maltadiocese.org; f. 1971; Pres. MARIO GRECH; Sec. Fr JOE MAGRO.

Archbishop of Malta: CHARLES JUDE SCICLUNA, Archbishop's Curia, St Calcedonius Sq., Floriana FRN 1535; POB 29, Valletta; tel. 21235350; fax 21223307; e-mail info@maltadiocese.org.mt.

Bishop of Gozo: Rt Rev. MARIO GRECH, Bishop's Chancery, POB 1, Republic St, Victoria VCT 1000, Gozo; tel. 21556661; fax 21551278; e-mail info@gozodiocese.org; internet gozodiocese.org.

The Anglican Communion

Malta forms part of the Diocese in Europe.

Church of England: Pro-Cathedral of St Paul, Independence Sq., Valletta VLT 1535; tel. 21225714; e-mail anglican@onvol.net; internet www.anglicanmalta.org; Senior Chaplain and Chancellor of the Pro-Cathedral Rev. Canon SIMON GODFREY.

Other Christian Churches

In 2004 there were approximately 680 Jehovah's Witnesses and 148 members of the Church of Jesus Christ of Latter-day Saints (Mormons). The Bible Baptist Church had 30 members and the Fellowship of Evangelical Churches had about 100 affiliates.

OTHER RELIGIONS

There is one Muslim mosque and a Muslim primary school. There are an estimated 3,000 Muslims in the country. There is one Jewish congregation. Zen Buddhism and the Bahá'í Faith have about 30 members each.

The Press

DAILY NEWSPAPERS

The Malta Independent: Standard House, Birkirkara Hill, St Julian's STJ 1149; tel. 21345888; fax 21344860; e-mail tmid@independent.com.mt; internet www.independent.com.mt; English; Editor MICHAEL CARABOTT.

L-orizzont (The Horizon): Union Print Co, A-41 Industrial Estate, Valletta Rd, Marsa MRS 3000; tel. 25900200; fax 21247870; e-mail info@unionprint.com.mt; internet www.orizzont.com.mt; f. 1962; Maltese; organ of the General Workers' Union; Editor JOSEF CARUANA; circ. 20,000 (2008).

The Times: Allied Newspapers Ltd, Strickland House, 341 St Paul St, Valletta VLT 1211; tel. 25594112; fax 25594116; e-mail daily@ timesofmalta.com; internet www.timesofmalta.com; f. 1935; English; Editor RAY BUGEJA.

OTHER NEWSPAPERS

Business Today: Vjal ir-Rihan, San Ġwann SGN 07; tel. 21382741; fax 21385075; internet www.businesstoday.com.mt; Wed.; Man. Editor SAVIOUR BALZAN.

Il-Gensillum (The People Today): Media Centre, National Rd, Blata il-Bajda HMR 1640; tel. 25699119; fax 25699123; e-mail gens@ mediacentre.org.mt; internet www.il-gensillum.com; f. 2004 to succeed *Il-Gens* (The People); Maltese; Roman Catholic; Editor Rev. JOHN AVELLINO; circ. 13,000 (2008).

Illum (Today): MediaToday Co Ltd, Vjal ir-Rihan, San Ġwann SGN 9016; tel. 21382741; fax 21385075; e-mail illum@mediatoday.com .mt; internet www.illum.com.mt; weekly; Maltese; Editor SAVIOUR BALZAN.

KullÄ§add: Centru Nazzjonali Laburista, Mile End Rd, Ä¦amrun HMR 1717; tel. 20901410; fax 21238252; e-mail felix@kullhadd.com; internet www.kullhadd.com; f. 1993; organ of Partit Laburista; Maltese.

The Malta Business Weekly: Standard House, Birkirkara Hill, St Julian's STJ 1149; tel. 21345888; fax 21344860; e-mail csultana@ independent.com.mt; internet www.independent.com.mt; f. 1994; English; Editor CHRISTOPHER SULTANA.

The Malta Independent on Sunday: Standard House, Birkirkara Hill, St Julian's STJ 1149; tel. 21345888; fax 21344884; e-mail tmis@ independent.com.mt; internet www.independent.com.mt; f. 1992; owned by Standard Publications Ltd; English; Editor DAVID LINDSAY.

MaltaToday: MediaToday Co Ltd, Vjal ir-Rihan, San Ġwann SGN 9016; tel. 21382741; fax 21385075; e-mail maltatoday@mediatoday .com.mt; internet www.maltatoday.com.mt; f. 1998; Wed. and Sun.; English; Man. Editor SAVIOUR BALZAN.

Il-Mument (The Moment): Herbert Ganado St, POB 37, Pietà PTA 1450; tel. 25965333; fax 25965525; e-mail mument@media.link.com .mt; f. 1972; Maltese; affiliated to Partit Nazzjonalista; Editor RODERICK AGIUS (acting).

The Sunday Times: Allied Newspapers Ltd, Strickland House, 341 St Paul St, Valletta VLT 1211; tel. 25594500; fax 25594510; e-mail sunday@timesofmalta.com; internet www.timesofmalta.com; f. 1922; English; Editor STEVE MALLIA; circ. 40,000 (2008).

It-Torċa (The Torch): Union Press, A 41, Marsa Industrial Estate, Marsa MRS 3000; tel. 259000200; fax 21247870; e-mail info@ unionprint.com.mt; internet www.torca.com.mt; f. 1944; Maltese; organ of the General Workers' Union; Editor ALEKS FARRUGIA.

SELECTED PERIODICALS

Commercial Courier: Malta Chamber of Commerce, Enterprise and Industry, Exchange Bldgs, Republic St, Valletta VLT 1117; tel. 21233873; fax 21245223; e-mail info@maltachamber.org.mt; internet www.maltachamber.org.mt; bi-monthly; Editor KEVIN J. BORG.

Malta Government Gazette: Department of Information, 3 Castille Pl., Valletta VLT 2000; tel. 22001700; fax 22001775; e-mail info .doi@gov.mt; internet www.doi.gov.mt; f. 1813; 2 a week; official notices; Maltese and English.

The Retailer: Association of General Retailers and Traders, Exchange Bldgs, Republic St, Valletta VLT 1117; tel. 21232881; fax 21232883; internet www.grtu.eu; monthly; publ. by Malta Chamber of Small and Medium-sized Enterprises; Editor VINCENT FARRUGIA.

The Teacher: Teachers' Institute, 213 Republic St, Valletta VLT 1118; tel. 21237815; fax 21244074; e-mail info@mut.org.mt; internet www.mut.org.mt; f. 1919; 2 a year; journal of the Malta Union of Teachers; Editor FRANKLIN BARBARA.

Xpress: Alternattiva Demokratika, POB 38, Marsa MTP 1001; e-mail info@alternattiva.org.mt; monthly; publ. of the Alternattiva Demokratika—The Green Party; Maltese; Editor (vacant).

Publishers

Malta University Publishing: Robert Mifsud Bonnici St, Lija LIA 1404; tel. and fax 21234121; e-mail info@maltauniversitybooks.com; internet www.maltauniversitybooks.com; f. 1995; owned by University of Malta; Maltese folklore, history, law, bibliography and language; also publishes in languages other than Maltese; Administrator REGINALD BARTOLO.

Merlin: 42 Mountbatten St, Blata l-Bajda HMR 1574; tel. 21246472; e-mail info@merlinpublishers.com; internet www.merlinpublishers .com; f. 1964; children's books, fiction.

Midsea Books Ltd: Carmelites St, Sta Venera SVR 1724; tel. 21497046; fax 21496904; internet www.midseabooks.com; f. 1974; imprints Klabb Kotba Maltin (f. 1969) and Heritage Books (f. 1999); history, art, language, heritage, children's books, reference.

Broadcasting and Communications

TELECOMMUNICATIONS

GO PLC: Spencer Hill, POB 40, Marsa MRS 1001; tel. 21210210; fax 25945895; e-mail info@go.com.mt; internet www.go.com.mt; f. 1975; fmrly Maltacom PLC; restyled 2007; mobile cellular and fixed-line telecommunications, broadband internet access, digital television services; 60% owned by TECOM Investments and the Dubai Investment Group, both mems of Dubai Holding; Chair. DEEPAK PADMANABHAN; CEO YIANNOS MICHAELIDES.

Melita PLC: Gasan Centre, Mriehel Bypass, Mriehel BKR 3000; tel. 27788500; fax 22745050; e-mail info@melitaplc.com; internet www .melita.com; f. 1992; offers mobile and fixed-line telecommunications services, and broadband internet access; also digital television services; CEO ANDREI MARC TORRIANI.

Vodafone Malta: Skyparks Business Centre, Malta Int. Airport, Luqa LQA 4000; tel. 99999247; fax 92111369; e-mail 247.mt@ vodafone.com; internet www.vodafone.com.mt; mobile telecommunications and broadband internet services; CEO AMANDA NELSON.

Regulatory Authority

Malta Communications Authority (MCA): Pinto Wharf, Valletta Waterfront, Floriana FRN 1913; tel. 21336840; fax 21336846; e-mail info@mca.org.mt; internet www.mca.org.mt; f. 2001; national agency responsible for regulating electronic communications, postal services and electronic commerce; Chair. EDWARD WOODS.

BROADCASTING

Regulatory Authority

Broadcasting Authority, Malta: 7 Mile End Rd, Ä¦amrun HMR 1719; tel. 21247908; fax 21240855; e-mail info.ba@ba-malta.org; internet www.ba-malta.org; f. 1961; statutory body responsible for the supervision and regulation of radio and television broadcasting; Chair. ANTHONY J. TABONE; CEO PIERRE CASSAR.

Radio and Television

Digital terrestrial television was introduced on 1 February 2011.

Bay Radio: Eden Pl., St George's Bay, St Julian's STJ 3310; tel. 23710100; fax 23710125; e-mail info@bay.com.mt; internet www.bay .com.mt; Station Man. KEVIN DeCESARE.

Calypso Radio 101.8 FM: Calypso Media Communications, 28 New St in Valletta Rd, Luqa; tel. 21578022; fax 21578026; e-mail info@ calypsoradio.com; internet www.calypsoradio.com; Station Man. FRANK CAMILLERI.

Campus FM: Old Humanities Bldg, University of Malta, Tal-Qroqq, Msida; tel. 21333313; fax 21314485; e-mail campusfm@um.edu.mt; internet maltauniversitybroadcasting.com; Station Man. Rev. JOSEPH BORG.

Media.link Communications Co Ltd: Dar Centrali, Herbert Ganado St, Pietà PTA 1450; tel. 21243641; e-mail info@media.link .com.mt; internet medialinkmalta.blogspot.co.uk.

Net TV: Dar Centrali, Herbert Ganado St, Pietà PTA 1450; tel. 21243641; fax 21226645; internet www.nettv.com.mt; f. 1998.

Radio 101: Independence Point, Herbert Ganado St, Pietà PTA 1450; tel. 21241164; fax 21564111; e-mail news@media.link.com .mt; internet www.radio101.com.mt.

ONE Productions Ltd: A28B, Industrial Estate, Marsa MRS 3000; tel. 25682568; fax 25682309; e-mail info@one.com.mt; internet www .one.com.mt; f. 1999; owned by Partit Laburista; Exec. Chair. JASON MICALLEF.

One Television: A28B Industrial Estate, Marsa MRS 3000; tel. 25682800; fax 25682409; e-mail ruth.vella@one.com.mt; broadcasts 126 hours weekly; Dir of Television RUTH VELLA MICALLEF.

One Radio: A28B, Industrial Estate, Marsa MRS 3000; tel. 25682600; fax 21231472; e-mail ray.azzopardi@one.com.mt; broadcasts 24 hours daily; Senior Man. CLINT BAJADA.

Public Broadcasting Services Ltd (PBS): 75 St Luke's Rd, Gwardamangia PTA 1025; tel. 22913100; e-mail info@pbs.com.mt; internet www.tvm.com.mt; f. 1991; govt-owned; operates national radio and television services: Radju Malta, Radju Parlament, Ten Sixty Six, Magic 91.7 and Television Malta; Chair. TONIO PORTUGHESE; CEO ANTON ATTARD.

Radju Marija: Kunvent Patrijiet Dumnikani, Misrah San Duminku, Rabat RBT 2521; tel. 21453105; fax 21453103; e-mail info.mal@radiomaria.org; internet www.radjumarija.org; f. 1995; Pres. Dr JOSEPH MICALLEF.

RTK Radio: Media Centre, National Rd, Blata il-Bajda HMR 1640; tel. 25699400; fax 25699147; e-mail kwright@rtk.com.mt; internet rtk.com.mt; f. 1992; radio station of the Catholic Church of Malta; Chair. Fr JOHN AVELLINO; Station Man. KARL WRIGHT.

Smash TV and Radio: Smash Bldgs, Triq ix-Xewk, Rahal Gdid; tel. 21667777; fax 21697830; e-mail tv@smashmalta.com; internet www .smash.com.mt; f. 1994; Man. Dir JOSEPH BALDACCHINO.

TVM2: 75 St Luke's Rd, Gwardamangia PTA 1025; tel. 21225051; fax 21244601; internet www.tvm.com.mt/tv/tvm2; f. 1996 as Education 22; name changed to present 2012; educational and cultural television channel.

XFM 100.2 FM: 111 Annunciation St, St Venera SVR 1021; tel. 21230228; e-mail info@xfm.com.mt; internet www.xfm.com.mt; f. 2003; programmes in Maltese and English; music; Station Man. DAVID AZZOPARDI.

Finance

(cap. = capital; res = reserves; dep. = deposits; m. = million; brs = branches; amounts in euros, unless otherwise indicated)

REGULATORY AUTHORITY

Malta Financial Services Authority: Notabile Rd, Attard BKR 3000; tel. 21441155; fax 21441189; e-mail communications@mfsa .com.mt; internet www.mfsa.com.mt; f. 2002; regulates activities of the financial services sector, including credit institutions, insurance business, investment services, pensions and trust management, recognized investment exchanges; houses Malta's Companies Registry; Chair. Prof. JOSEPH V. BANNISTER; Dir-Gen. MARIANNE SCICLUNA.

BANKING

Central Bank

Central Bank of Malta: Pjazza Kastilja, Valletta VLT 1060; tel. 25500000; fax 25502500; e-mail info@centralbankmalta.org; internet www.centralbankmalta.org; f. 1968; govt-owned; cap. 20m., res 246.5m., dep. 1,105.6m. (Dec. 2010); Gov. Prof. JOSEF BONNICI.

Commercial Banks

APS Bank Ltd: APS Centre, Tower St, Birkirkara BKR 4012; tel. 21226644; fax 25603001; e-mail headoffice@apsbank.com.mt; internet www.apsbank.com.mt; f. 1910; cap. 42.8m., res 11.7m., dep. 813.1m. (Dec. 2012); Chair. EMMANUEL P. DELIA; CEO EDWARD CACHIA; 6 brs.

Banif Bank (Malta) PLC: Level 2, 203 Rue D'Argens, Gzira GZR 1368; tel. 22601000; fax 21312000; e-mail customercare@banif.com .mt; internet www.banif.com.mt; f. 2008; owned by Grupo Banif (Portugal); cap. 32.5m., res 0.04m., dep. 444.8m. (Dec. 2012); Chair. JOSEPH SAMMUT; CEO JOAQUIM SILVA PINTO; 5 brs.

Bank of Valletta PLC: BOV Centre, Cannon Rd. St Venera SVR 9030; tel. 22751537; fax 22753700; e-mail customercare@bov.com; internet www.bov.com; f. 1974; merged with Valletta Investment Bank Ltd in Oct. 2000; cap. 300m., res 25.6m., dep. 6,255.7m. (Sept. 2013); Chair. JOHN CASSAR WHITE; CEO CHARLES BORG; 46 brs.

HSBC Bank Malta PLC: 233 Republic St, Valletta VLT 1116; tel. 23802380; fax 23804923; e-mail infomalta@hsbc.com; internet www .hsbc.com.mt; f. 1975 as Mid-Med Bank; 70.03% owned by HSBC Europe BV; cap. 87.6m., res 35.1m., dep. 4,559.7m. (Dec. 2013); CEO MARK WATKINSON; 43 brs.

Lombard Bank Malta PLC: 67 Republic St, Valletta VLT 1117; tel. 25581100; fax 25581150; e-mail mail@lombardmalta.com; internet www.lombardmalta.com; f. 1969; cap. 9m., res 22.2m., dep. 465.4m. (Dec. 2012); Chair. MICHAEL C. BONELLO; Dir and CEO JOSEPH SAID; 7 brs.

Mediterranean Bank plc: 10 St Barbara Bastion, Valletta VLT 1961; tel. 25574400; e-mail info@medbank.com.mt; internet medbank.com.mt; f. 2004; its subsidiary, Mediterranean Corporate Bank Ltd, took over operations of Volksbank Malta Ltd in 2014; Chair. FRANCIS J. VASSALLO; CEO MARK A. WATSON; 7 brs.

Principal Offshore Bank

FIMBank PLC: Mercury Tower, The Exchange Financial & Business Centre, Elia Zammit St, St Julian's STJ 3155; tel. 21322100; fax 21322122; e-mail info@fimbank.com; internet www.fimbank.com; f. 1994 as First International Merchant Bank PLC; cap. US $71.5m., res $14.6m., dep. $938.7m. (Dec. 2012); Chair. Dr JOHN C. GRECH; CEO SIMON LAY (acting).

Bankers' Association

Malta Bankers' Association: 48/2 Birkirkara Rd, Attard ATD 1210; tel. 21412210; fax 21424580; e-mail info@maltabankers.org; internet www.maltabankers.org; f. 1962; Chair. MARK WATKINSON; Sec.-Gen. JAMES BONELLO; 27 mem. banks.

STOCK EXCHANGE

Malta Stock Exchange: Garrison Chapel, Castille Pl., Valletta VLT 1063; tel. 21244051; fax 25696316; e-mail borza@borzamalta .com.mt; internet www.borzamalta.com.mt; f. 1992; Chair. Dr ARTHUR GALEA SALOMONE; Chief Exec. EILEEN V. MUSCAT.

INSURANCE

Mediterranean Insurance Brokers (Malta) Ltd: 53 MIB House, Abate Rigord St, Ta'Xbiex XBX 1122; tel. 23433234; fax 21341599; e-mail info@mib.com.mt; internet www.mib.com.mt; f. 1976; Chair. ROB VAN OIJEN; Man. Dir FIONA BORG.

Middlesea Insurance PLC: Middle Sea House, Floriana FRN 1442; tel. 21246262; fax 21248195; internet www.middlesea.com; f. 1981; Chair. MARTIN GALEA; Pres. and CEO ALFREDO MUÑOZ PEREZ.

Numerous foreign insurance companies, principally British, Canadian and Italian, are represented in Malta by local agents.

Insurance Association

Malta Insurance Association: 43A/4, St Paul's Bldgs, West St, Valletta VLT 1532; tel. 21232640; fax 21248388; e-mail mia@ maltainsurance.org; internet www.maltainsurance.org; Dir-Gen. ADRIAN J. GALEA; 18 mem. cos (2013).

Trade and Industry

GOVERNMENT AGENCIES

Malta Enterprise: Gwardamangia Hill, Pietà MEC 0001; tel. 25420000; fax 25423401; e-mail info@maltaenterprise.com; internet www.maltaenterprise.com; f. 2004; Chair. Dr MARIO VELLA.

Malta Investment Management Co Ltd (MIMCOL): Clock Tower, Level 1, Tigné Point Sliema TP 01; tel. 21497970; fax 21499568; e-mail info@mgis.com.mt; internet mimcol.com.mt; f. 1988; manages govt investments in domestic commercial enterprises and encourages their transfer to private sector ownership; Chair. JOHN IVAN FALZON; CEO VINCENT MIFSUD.

DEVELOPMENT ORGANIZATION

FinanceMalta: Garrison Chapel, Castille Pl., Valletta VLT 1063; tel. 21224525; fax 21449212; e-mail contact@financemalta.org; internet www.financemalta.org; public-private initiative to promote international investment in Malta; Chair. KENNETH FARRUGIA.

EMPLOYERS' ORGANIZATIONS

The Malta Chamber of Commerce, Enterprise and Industry: Exchange Bldgs, Republic St, Valletta VLT 1117; tel. 21233873; fax 21245223; e-mail info@maltachamber.org.mt; internet www .maltachamber.org.mt; f. 2009 by merger of Malta Chamber of Commerce and Enterprise with Malta Federation of Industry; Pres. ANTON BORG; 1,200 mems.

Malta Employers' Association: 35/1 South St, Valletta VLT 1100; tel. 21222992; fax 21230227; e-mail admin@maltaemployers.com; internet www.maltaemployers.com; f. 1965; Pres. ARTHUR MUSCAT; Dir-Gen. JOSEPH FARRUGIA.

UTILITIES

Malta Resources Authority: Millennia, 2nd Floor, Aldo Moro Rd, Marsa MRS 9065; tel. 22955000; fax 22955200; e-mail enquiry@mra .org.mt; internet www.mra.org.mt; set up by the Maltese Parliament through the Malta Resources Authority Act of 2000; regulates water and energy utilities; Chair. JAMES CAMENZULI; CEO ANTHONY RIZZO.

Electricity and Gas

Easygas (Malta) Ltd: Valletta Rd, Luqa Malta; tel. 21821557; e-mail info@easygas.com; licensed supplier of LPG gas.

Enemalta Corporation: Triq Belt il-Ħażna, Marsa MRS 1571; tel. 21223601; fax 21246637; e-mail info.emc@enemalta.com.mt; internet www.enemalta.com.mt; f. 1977; state-owned energy corpn responsible for generating and distributing electricity and storing liquefied petroleum gas for the distributors; Exec. Chair. FREDERICK AZZOPARDI.

Liquigas Malta Limited: Kalafrana, B'Buga BBG 3011; tel. 21651661; fax 22486060; e-mail info@liquigasmalta.com; internet www.liquigasmalta.com; jt venture of Liquigas SpA (Italy) and

Multigas Limited (Malta); responsible for providing LPG gas; CEO ROBERTO CAPELLUTO.

Water

Water Services Corporation: Qormi Rd, Luqa LQA 9043; tel. 22445566; fax 22443900; e-mail customercare@wsc.com.mt; internet www.wsc.com.mt; f. 1992; govt corpn responsible for the production and distribution of drinking water and the local sewerage system; Chair. and CEO WILLIAM WAIT.

TRADE UNIONS

Confederation of Malta Trade Unions (CMTU): POB 389, Old Bakery St, Valletta VLT 1456; tel. 99499491; fax 21243961; e-mail cmtu@maltanet.net; internet www.cmtu.org.mt; f. 1958; affiliated to the ITUC and to ETUC; Pres. WILLIAM PORTELLI.

Transport

REGULATORY BODIES

Transport Malta: Sa Maison Rd, Floriana FRN 1612; tel. 21222203; fax 21255740; e-mail info.tm@transport.gov.mt; internet www .transport.gov.mt; regulatory body for transport in Malta; Chair. JAMES PISCOPO.

RAILWAYS

There are no railways in Malta.

ROADS

In 2010 there were 3,096 km of roads, of which about 87.5% were paved. Bus services serve all parts of the main island and most parts of Gozo. In July 2011 a new public transport network of bus services, operated by Arriva Malta, was introduced; however, following a number of operational problems, Arriva ended its operations in Malta in January 2014 and was replaced by Malta Public Transport.

Malta Public Transport: e-mail enquiries@publictransport.com .mt; internet www.publictransport.com.mt; f. 2014; est. to take over from Arriva Malta, which ceased operations in Jan. 2014; bus services in Malta (80 routes) and Gozo (15 routes), including express services.

SHIPPING

Malta's national shipping register is open to ships of all countries. At 31 December 2014 Malta's flag registered fleet comprised 2,220 vessels, with a total displacement of 57.4m. grt, of which 26 were bulk carriers, 59 were gas tankers and 356 were general cargo ships. The island's dry dock facilities are also an important source of revenue.

Bianchi & Co (1916) Ltd: Palazzo Marina, 143 St Christopher St, Valletta VLT 1465; tel. 21232241; fax 21232991; e-mail info@bianchi .com.mt; Man. Dir R. BIANCHI.

Cassar & Cooper Ltd: Valletta Bldgs, 54 South St, POB 311, Valletta VLT 11; tel. 25584000; fax 21237864; e-mail info@ cassar-cooper.com; internet www.cassar-cooper.com; cargo shipping; also ship agency; Dir MICHAEL COOPER.

Gollcher Group: 19 Zachary St, Valletta VLT 1133; tel. 25691100; fax 21234195; e-mail contact@gollcher.com; internet www.gollcher .com; f. 1854; Dir KARL GOLLCHER.

Malta Freeport Terminals Ltd: Freeport Centre, Port of Marsax-lokk, Kalafrana BBG 3011; tel. 21650200; fax 22251900; e-mail marketing@maltafreeport.com.mt; internet www.maltafreeport .com.mt; f. 1988; 2 container terminals; also operates general warehousing facilities; CEO ALEX MONTEBELLO.

Malta Motorways of the Sea Ltd: 21–22 St Barbara Bastion, Valletta VLT 1961; tel. 21251564; fax 21226876; e-mail info@mmos .com.mt; internet www.mmos.com.mt; f. 2005; owned by Grimaldi Group (Italy); operates ro-ro and passenger ferry services between Malta, Italy (including Sicily) and Libya; Man. Dir ERNEST SULLIVAN; Gen. Man. JOSEPH BUGEJA.

Mifsud Brothers Ltd: 14 Lighters Wharf, Grand Harbour Menqa, Marsa MRS 1442; tel. 21232157; fax 21221331; e-mail info@mbl.com .mt; internet www.mbl.com.mt; f. 1860; shipping and travel agents; Man. Dir IVAN MIFSUD.

SMS Shipping: 27 Birkirkara Hill, St Julian's STJ 1143; tel. 25770000; e-mail info@sms.com.mt; internet www.sms.com.mt; ship and forwarding agency; also ship supplies and bunkering; subsidiary of SMS Group Ltd; Chair. NEVILLE MIFSUD.

Sullivan Shipping Agencies Ltd: Exchange Bldgs, Republic St, Valletta VLT 1117; tel. 22296000; fax 21233417; e-mail info@

sullivanshipping.com.mt; internet www.sullivanshipping.com.mt; f. 1888; owned by Sullivan Consolidated Group; Chair. and CEO JOHN E. SULLIVAN.

Thomas Smith & Co Ltd: 12 St Christopher St, Valletta VLT 1468; tel. 22058058; fax 22058299; e-mail info@tcsmith.com; internet www .tcsmith.com; f. 1848; Man. Dir JOE GERADA.

Valletta Waterfront: 45–46 Pinto Wharf, Floriana FRN 1913; tel. 25673000; fax 25673206; e-mail info@vallettacruiseport.com; internet www.vallettawaterfront.com; f. 2001; undertakes cruise and ferry terminal operations; Chair. JOSEPH ZAMMIT TABONA.

Virtu Ferries Ltd: Ta'Xbiex Terrace, Ta'Xbiex XBX 1034; tel. 23491000; fax 21314533; e-mail admin@virtuferries.com; internet www.virtuferries.com; f. 1988; Malta–Sicily (Italy) express passenger ferry service.

CIVIL AVIATION

Malta International Airport is situated at Gudja (8 km from Valletta).

Air Malta PLC: Skyparks Business Centre, Level 2, Malta Int. Airport, Luqa LQA 9020; tel. 21662211; e-mail customercare .airmalta@airmalta.com; internet www.airmalta.com; f. 1973; national airline with a 96.4% state shareholding; scheduled passenger and cargo services to mainland Europe, the UK, North Africa and the Middle East; charter services to the UK and mainland Europe; Chair. LOUIS FARRUGIA; CEO LOUIS GIORDIMAINA.

Tourism

Malta offers climatic, scenic and historical attractions, including fine beaches. Tourism forms a major sector of Malta's economy, generating provisional receipts of US $1,345m. in 2012. Tourist arrivals totalled 1,444,192 in 2012.

Malta Tourism Authority (MTA): Auberge d'Italie, Merchants St, Valletta VLT 1170; tel. 22915000; fax 22915394; e-mail info@ visitmalta.com; internet www.mta.com.mt; Chair. Dr GAVIN GULIA; CEO PAUL BUGEJA.

Defence

As assessed at November 2014, the armed forces of Malta comprised a regular army of 1,950. There was also a reserve of 180. Military service is voluntary.

Defence Expenditure: estimated at €45m. in 2014.

Commander of the Armed Forces: Brig. JEFFREY CURMI.

Education

The Ministry for Education and Employment is responsible for providing all levels of education. From the age of two years and nine months until the age of four years, children study in kindergarten centres, although it is not compulsory. Provision is free in all government schools and church schools. Education is free and compulsory between the ages of five and 16 years. In 2011/12 enrolment at pre-primary level included 74% of children in the relevant age-group. Primary education begins at five years of age and lasts for six years. In 2011/12 enrolment at primary level included 81% of children in the relevant age-group. Secondary education, beginning at 11 years of age, lasts for a maximum of seven years, but this period is extended in the case of technology and vocational courses. Enrolment at secondary level in 2011/12 included 79% of children in the relevant age-group. After completing five years of secondary-level education, students with the necessary qualifications may opt to follow a higher academic, technical or vocational course. The junior college, administrated by the University of Malta, is attended by students aged between 16 and 18 years. It prepares students specifically for a university course by providing them with a Matriculation Certificate after successful completion of a two-year course. About 30% of the student population attend schools administered by the Roman Catholic Church, from kindergarten to higher secondary level. The Government subsidizes the provision of free education for students in church schools. Higher education is available at the University of Malta. There are also a number of technical institutes, specialist schools and an extended skills training scheme for trade school graduates. There were 12,203 students enrolled in higher education in 2011/12. The Government also provides adult education courses. General government expenditure on education amounted to €442.4m. in 2013.

THE MARSHALL ISLANDS

Introductory Survey

LOCATION, CLIMATE, LANGUAGE, RELIGION, FLAG, CAPITAL

The Republic of the Marshall Islands consists of two groups of islands, the Ratak ('sunrise') and Ralik ('sunset') chains, comprising 29 atolls (some 1,225 islets) and five islands, and covering about 180 sq km (70 sq miles) of land. The territory lies within the area of the Pacific Ocean known as Micronesia (which also includes Kiribati, Tuvalu and other territories). The islands lie about 3,200 km (2,000 miles) south-west of Hawaii and about 2,100 km (1,300 miles) south-east of Guam. Rainfall decreases from south to north, with January, February and March being the driest months, although seasonal variations in rainfall and temperature are generally small. The native population comprises various ethno-linguistic groups, but English is widely understood. The principal religion is Christianity. The national flag (proportions 100 by 190) is dark blue, with a representation of a white star (with 20 short and four long rays) in the upper hoist; superimposed across the field are two progressively wider stripes (orange above white), running from near the lower hoist corner to near the upper fly corner. The capital is the Delap-Uliga-Darrit Municipality, on Majuro Atoll.

CONTEMPORARY POLITICAL HISTORY

Historical Context

The first European contact with the Marshall and Caroline Islands was by Spanish expeditions in the 16th century, including those led by Alvaro de Saavedra and Fernão de Magalhães (Ferdinand Magellan), the Portuguese navigator. The islands received their name from the British explorer, John Marshall, who visited them at the end of the 18th century. Spanish sovereignty over the Marshall Islands was recognized in 1886 by the Papal Bull of Pope Leo XIII, which also gave Germany trading rights there (German trading companies had been active in the islands from the 1850s). In 1899 Germany bought from Spain the Caroline Islands and the Northern Mariana Islands (except Guam, which had been ceded to the USA after the Spanish–American War of 1898). In 1914, at the beginning of the First World War, Japan occupied the islands, and received a mandate for their administration from the League of Nations in 1920. After the capture of the islands by US military forces in 1944 and 1945, most of the Japanese settlers were repatriated, and in 1947 the UN established the Trust Territory of the Pacific Islands (comprising the Caroline Islands, the Marshall Islands and the Northern Mariana Islands), to allow the USA to administer the region. The territory was governed by the US Navy from 1947 until 1951, when control passed to a civil administration—although the Northern Mariana Islands remained under military control until 1962.

From 1965 onwards there were increasing demands for local autonomy. In that year the Congress of Micronesia was formed; in 1967 a commission was established to examine the future political status of the islands. In 1970 it declared Micronesians' rights to sovereignty over their own lands, to self-determination, to their own constitution and to revoke any form of free association with the USA. In 1977, after eight years of negotiations, US President Jimmy Carter announced that his Administration intended to adopt measures to terminate the trusteeship agreement by 1981.

On 9 January 1978 the Marianas District achieved separate status as the Commonwealth of the Northern Mariana Islands (q.v.), but remained legally a part of the trusteeship until 1986. The Marshall Islands District drafted its own Constitution, which came into effect on 1 May 1979, and the four districts of Yap, Truk (now Chuuk), Ponape (now Pohnpei) and Kosrae ratified a new Constitution, to become the Federated States of Micronesia (q.v.), on 10 May 1979. In the Palau District a referendum in July 1979 approved a proposed local Constitution, which took effect on 1 January 1981, when the district became the Republic of Palau (q.v.).

The USA signed a Compact of Free Association with the Republic of Palau in August 1982, and reached agreement with the Marshall Islands and the Federated States of Micronesia in October. The trusteeship of the Pacific territory was due to end after the principle and terms of Compacts of Free Association had been approved by the respective peoples and legislatures of the new countries, by the US Congress and by the UN Security Council. Under the Compacts, the four countries (including the Northern Mariana Islands) would be independent of each other and would each manage their respective internal and foreign affairs, while the USA would be responsible for defence and security. Moreover, Marshallese citizens were granted the right to live and work in the USA. The final draft of the Compact of Free Association with the USA was signed by the Marshall Islands in June 1983 and approved by plebiscite in September. Under the terms of the Compact, which took effect on 21 October 1986, the USA was to retain its military bases in the Marshall Islands for at least 15 years and, over the same period, was to provide annual aid of US $30m. The UN Security Council finally ratified the termination of the trusteeship agreement in December 1990.

Domestic Political Affairs

The Marshall Islands' atolls of Bikini and Enewetak were used by the USA for experiments with nuclear weapons: Bikini in 1946–58 and Enewetak in 1948–58. The native inhabitants of Enewetak were evacuated before tests began, and were allowed to return to the atoll in 1980, after much of the contaminated area had supposedly been rendered safe. The inhabitants of Bikini Atoll campaigned for similar treatment, and in 1985 the US Administration agreed to decontaminate Bikini Atoll over a period of 10–15 years. In 1985 the entire population of Rongelap Atoll, which had been engulfed by radioactive fallout from the tests at Bikini in 1954, was forced to resettle on Mejato Atoll, after surveys suggested that levels of radiation at Rongelap remained dangerous. In April 2001, following the adoption by the USA of a new standard of radioactivity considered to be acceptable, some six times lower than the previous level, the Tribunal announced that Ailuk Atoll was to be evacuated and environmental studies conducted.

Under the terms of the Compact, the US Government consented to establish a US $150m. Nuclear Claims Fund to settle claims against the USA resulting from nuclear testing in the Marshall Islands during the 1940s and 1950s. Accordingly, the Marshall Islands Nuclear Claims Tribunal was established in 1988, with jurisdiction to 'render final determination upon all claims past, present and future, of the Government, citizens and nationals of the Marshall Islands' in respect of the nuclear testing programme. A compensation programme was implemented in 1991 for personal injuries deemed to have resulted from the testing programme. The Tribunal initially identified 25 diseases for which credible evidence demonstrated a significant statistical relationship between exposure to radiation and subsequent development of a disease; in response to the findings of later studies, by 2003 the Tribunal's list had been extended to include 11 further conditions. By the end of 2003 compensation awards totalling $83m. had been made to, or on behalf of, 1,865 individuals who had contracted one or more of these conditions. Additionally, an award of some $578m. had been ordered by the Tribunal in May 2000 in respect of a class action brought by the people of Enewetak for loss of and damage to property; and an award of $563m. had been ordered in March 2002 in settlement of a class action brought by the peoples of Bikini Atoll; settlements of similar class actions by the peoples of Rongelap and Utrik Atolls were being finalized, while a new class action had been submitted by the people of Ailuk Atoll. However, only $45.8m. had been made available for actual payment of awards decided by the Tribunal; furthermore, less than $6m. remained of the original value of the Fund. In view of the inadequacy of the Fund to meet the compensation awards made by the Tribunal, in September 2000 the Marshall Islands Government formally petitioned the US Congress for a renegotiation of the settlement agreed under the Compact; the basis of the petition, which sought additional compensation amounting to some $3,000m., was an article of the agreement providing for what were termed 'Changed Circumstances'. In August 2004 the Tribunal declared a deadline for islanders' compensation claims of the end of that month (subsequently extended to 31 December), owing to a severe shortage of funds.

In January 2005, following the publication of a report by the US Department of State's Bureau of East Asian and Pacific Affairs, the Administration of US President George W. Bush recommended that Congress reject the Marshall Islands' request for additional compensation payments, citing a lack of a scientific or legal basis for the request. The Bush Administration's rejection of the appeal was reiterated at a congressional hearing in May. At a Small Islands Summit meeting held in October in the Papua New Guinean capital of Port Moresby, the Marshall Islands' delegation reiterated its demand for a further US $3,000m. in compensation from the US Government. In April 2006 it was announced that the people of Bikini were suing the US Government in the Court of Federal Claims for $560.7m. as compensation or damages: the original award of $563.0m. minus the actual payment of $2.3m. The Marshall Islands Government expressed its support for the action. In April 2007 the Marshall Islands Nuclear Claims Tribunal ruled that claimants of Rongelap should receive $1,000m. in compensation; at the same time, however, the funds available to the Tribunal had decreased to just $1m. In August the Court of Federal Claims dismissed the lawsuit submitted by the people of Bikini Atoll against the US Government on the basis that it had been submitted after the expiry of a six-year statute of limitations for the filing of such claims. The dismissal was upheld by the US Court of Appeals in February 2009 and by the US Supreme Court in April 2010. Meanwhile, in March 2009, following confirmation by France that further consideration was to be given to compensation claims by those affected by its nuclear tests, the Marshall Islands renewed its request for additional compensation from the US Government. An amended version of a US Senate bill first proposed in September 2007, which had sought additional compensation for inhabitants of Bikini, Enewetak, Rongelap and Utrik, was introduced to the upper congressional chamber in February 2011. However, the bill failed to progress past the committee stage.

In January 1994, meanwhile, several senior members of the Marshall Islands' legislature, the Nitijela, demanded that the US authorities release detailed information on the effects of its nuclear-testing programme in the islands. In July documentation released by the US Department of Energy gave conclusive evidence that Marshall Islanders had been deliberately exposed to high levels of radiation in order that its effects on their health could be studied by US medical researchers. Further evidence emerged during 1995 that the USA had withheld the medical records of islanders involved in radiation experiments (which included tritium and chromium-51 injections and genetic and bone-marrow transplant experiments).

Despite the publication of a study conducted by US scientists (in 1992) into contamination levels on Bikini Atoll, which suggested that radiation levels there remained dangerous, in February 1997 a group of Bikini Islanders returned for the first time since 1946 to assist in the rehabilitation of the atoll for resettlement. The operation was to involve the removal of radioactive topsoil (although the matter of its disposal presented a serious problem) and the saturation of the remaining soil with potassium, which was believed to inhibit the absorption of radioactive material by root crops. A report published by the International Atomic Energy Agency in 1998 found that Bikini Atoll remained unsafe for habitation, owing to continuing dangerous levels of radiation. In early 1999 the Nuclear Claims Tribunal demanded the adoption of US Environmental Protection Agency standards in the rehabilitation of contaminated islands, claiming that Marshall Islanders deserved to receive the same treatment as US citizens would in similar circumstances. The US Department of Energy, however, expressed strong resistance to the demand. In February 2001 a report published by an eminent Japanese scientist stated that radiation levels on Rongelap Island, according to research conducted in 1999, had now declined to such a level that human habitation of the island was again possible. Although the USA funded a clean-up and rehabilitation programme on the island, including the construction of new housing and infrastructure, few islanders had returned to Rongelap by 2012 and concerns remained over the actual safety of resettlement. In September 2012, following a fact-finding mission to the Marshall Islands earlier that year, UN Special Rapporteur Călin Georgescu presented a report on the islands' nuclear legacy to the UN Human Rights Council. The document highlighted the health complications and indefinite displacement that the islanders continued to suffer and demanded that the USA provide additional compensation to those islanders affected by the testing and declassify secret documentation on the testing programme. Marshall Islands President Christopher Loeak reiterated the report's proposals in his address to the UN General Assembly later that month.

Another atoll in the Marshall Islands, Kwajalein, has been used since 1947 as a target for the testing of missiles fired from California, USA. The Compact of Free Association as ratified in 1986 committed the US Government to provide an estimated US $170m. in rent over a period of 30 years for land used as the site of a missile-tracking station, and a further $80m. for development projects. The inhabitants of Kwajalein Atoll were concentrated on the small island of Ebeye, adjacent to the US base on Kwajalein Island, before a new programme of weapons-testing began in 1961. Consequent overcrowding reportedly led to numerous social problems on Ebeye. In 1989 the Marshall Islands Government agreed that the USA could lease a further four islands in the atoll, for five years, for the purpose of military tests. A further lease agreement was signed in 1995 for the use of Biken Island (in Aur Atoll) and Wake Island in the missile-testing programme. In January 2003 it was announced that the Marshall Islands Government and the USA had reached agreement on new terms extending the lease of the Kwajalein site, previously scheduled to end in 2016, until 2066 (with the USA retaining the right to extend the lease by a further 20 years). The renegotiated terms envisaged that payments for use of the site would be increased from $13.5m. annually to $16.9m. (including continued provision of $1.9m. annually in social funding for the residents of Ebeye), with a further increase, to more than $19.9m. per year, to enter into effect from 2014. However, Kwajalein landowners asserted that the new arrangement was invalid, since they had not consented to its terms, as constitutionally required, and refused to accept the extension beyond 2016. The dispute appeared finally to have been resolved in May 2011, when the landowners agreed to accept the terms negotiated in 2003 and an agreement was signed.

Meanwhile, following the legislative elections of November 1995, the Marshall Islands President, Iroijlaplap (Paramount Chief) Amata Kabua, who had held the post since its creation in 1979, was re-elected for a fifth term. Upon his death in December 1996, he was replaced by Iroijlaplap Imata Kabua, a cousin, in January 1997.

In 1996 the Nitijela approved legislation allowing for the introduction of gambling in the islands, in order to provide an additional source of revenue. However, following a vociferous campaign against the legislation by local church leaders, in April 1998 the Nitijela voted to repeal the law legalizing gambling: several influential politicians known to have major gambling interests (including Imata Kabua) were disqualified from voting. A second bill containing further measures to ensure the prohibition of all gambling activity in the islands was narrowly approved. Three ministers who had supported the anti-gambling legislation were dismissed in a cabinet reorganization in August. In the following month one of the dismissed ministers proposed a motion of no confidence in Kabua. The President and his supporters boycotted subsequent sessions of the Nitijela, thereby rendering the legislature inquorate and effectively precluding the vote; the motion of no confidence in Kabua was eventually defeated by a margin of one vote in October.

The administrations of President Note (1999–2007)

At the legislative elections of November 1999 the opposition United Democratic Party (UDP) secured a convincing victory over the incumbent administration, winning 18 of the 33 seats in the Nitijela. The former Speaker of the Nitijela, Kessai Note, was elected President in January 2000 (the islands' first non-traditional leader to assume the post). The UDP Chairman, Litokwa Tomeing, became the new Speaker of the legislature. Note subsequently appointed a 10-member Cabinet, and in May established an anti-corruption task force.

In November 2000 it was reported that finance officials had discovered that Imata Kabua had used funds granted to the Marshall Islands under the terms of the Compact of Free Association to pay off a personal loan, although the former President denied any wrongdoing. In January 2001 Kabua and former ministers in his Government presented a motion of no confidence against President Note to the Nitijela, citing a number of alleged failings by the Note Government (although it was suggested that the vote had been intended to delay the publication of a report into mismanagement and corruption on the part of the former Government). The vote was defeated by a margin of 19 to 14.

In September 2000 the Nitijela approved legislation to ensure the closer regulation of the banking and financial sector. In May of that year the Group of Seven industrialized nations (G7) had expressed its view that the Marshall Islands had become a significant centre for the laundering of money generated by international criminal activity, and in June the Marshall Islands was one of more than 30 countries and territories criticized by the Organisation for Economic Co-operation and Development (OECD, see p. 377) for the provision of inappropriate offshore financial establishments; the Marshall Islands remained on the OECD list of unco-operative tax havens until 2007. In October 2002, meanwhile, following a commendation from the IMF on a series of new measures to combat fraud, including specific legislation and the establishment of a Domestic Financial Intelligence Unit, the Financial Action Task Force on Money Laundering (see p. 451) removed the Marshall Islands from its list of countries judged to be unhelpful in the combating of international financial crime. Following the signature of a 12th bilateral tax information exchange agreement, in October 2010, the Marshall Islands was considered by OECD to have substantially implemented the internationally agreed tax standard.

Negotiations began between the USA and the Marshall Islands in July 2001 to renew the provisions of the Compact of Free Association ratified in 1986, which was due to expire at the end of September 2001. A two-year extension was permitted while negotiations were under way, during which time annual assistance to the Marshall Islands was to increase by some US $5.5m. An agreement was originally scheduled for early 2002 in order to allow adequate time for the US Congress to review it and to approve the requisite legislation (by 1 October 2003), but the procedure was postponed until early May 2002 after the Marshall Islands Government submitted a proposal seeking financing of more than $1,000m. over 15 years. The Government had also objected to being allocated 25%–30% less in US grant assistance per caput than that apportioned to the Federated States of Micronesia since the year 2000. In a further attempt to increase the national income, the Government sought to raise significantly the level of taxes levied on the Kwajalein base. In November 2002 the USA and the Marshall Islands announced a programme of direct funding of $822m., to be disbursed over 20 years, in addition to the expansion of many US government services in the islands. It was envisaged that the Marshall Islands would receive some $30.5m. a year; furthermore, a trust fund would be established, to which the USA would contribute $7m. annually in order to provide a means of income after the termination of direct US assistance in 2023 (by the end of 2014 the assets of this fund totalled an estimated $234.6m.). The amended Compact of Free Association was signed by the Marshall Islands and the USA in May 2003. Under the new Compact, Marshall Islanders would for the first time require passports in order to enter the USA. They would, however, retain the right to enter the USA to live, work and study, and would no longer be required to obtain work authorization documentation before taking up employment in the USA. Other than the issue of the Kwajalein lease, a principal obstacle to the negotiation of Compact amendments had been that of immigration: the USA, increasingly preoccupied by issues of homeland security, had been notably concerned to prevent future sales of Marshallese passports (although this controversial programme had officially been suspended in 1997). Final terms, including the restoration of some rights of access to US health care and education programmes, were approved by the US Congress in November 2003, and ratified by President George W. Bush in December.

At legislative elections held in November 2003 the UDP won 20 seats in the 33-member Nitijela. The opposition grouping Aelon Kein Ad (Our Islands), which had campaigned against the terms of the renewed Compact and which received particularly strong support from Marshall Islanders resident in the USA, secured 10 seats. Note was re-elected for a second presidential term in a vote held in the Nitijela in January 2004, defeating Justin deBrum, the candidate of Aelon Kein Ad, by 20 votes to nine.

The administration of President Tomeing (2007–09)

At the legislative elections of November 2007 the level of participation was relatively low, at approximately 50%. Neither the incumbent UDP nor the opposition Aelon Kein Ad succeeded in securing the requisite majority of 17 or more seats; both parties contested the results, amid claims of vote-counting irregularities. While the UDP claimed that it should remain in power, Aelon Kein Ad—which had gained former Speaker and UDP leader Litokwa Tomeing as a member prior to the elections—

maintained that, with the support of independent candidates, its United People's Party coalition would be able to defeat the UDP. Recounts in two constituencies and negotiations between the parties and independent candidates followed. The United People's Party coalition prevailed in January 2008, when the Nitijela elected Tomeing as the country's President by 18 votes (to 15 for the incumbent President Note), and Jurelang Zedkaia as Speaker by the same margin. Tomeing's new Cabinet included Christopher Loeak as Minister in Assistance to the President and Tony deBrum as Minister of Foreign Affairs.

A commission of inquiry charged with examining the organizational failures of the 2007 elections published its findings in August 2008; the electoral failures were attributed to former Minister of Internal Affairs Rien Morris and to the Public Service Commission. It was concluded that Morris had unconstitutionally interfered in the election process by appointing Carl Alik as the Chief Electoral Officer against the wishes of the Public Service Commission. The commission of inquiry made numerous recommendations, including the establishment of an election commission of five independent members, who would be responsible for the appointment of the Chief Electoral Officer.

Tony deBrum was dismissed as Minister of Foreign Affairs in February 2009, following his public criticism of President Tomeing's administration. DeBrum had been particularly critical of the President's perceived failure to provide sufficient support to landowners in their attempts to secure an increase in the rents payable to them by the USA for the use of the military base at Kwajalein Atoll (see above). John Silk was subsequently appointed as deBrum's replacement.

In April 2009 the United People's Party coalition presented a motion of no confidence against President Tomeing, which was defeated by 18 ballots to 14, after UDP legislators voted in Tomeing's favour. Following the defeat of the motion, President Tomeing announced a cabinet reorganization in which several ministers were dismissed, including Loeak, who was replaced as Minister in Assistance to the President by Ruben Zackhras. All of the incoming ministers were members of the opposition UDP. (A previous no-confidence motion tabled against Tomeing in October 2008 had been withdrawn owing to insufficient support.)

President Tomeing was ousted from power when a third motion of no confidence was submitted against him in October 2009. In the first successful vote of no confidence in the history of the Marshall Islands, the motion was carried by 17 ballots to 15. A few days later an election was conducted by the Nitijela to appoint Tomeing's replacement; Jurelang Zedkaia, hitherto Speaker of the Nitijela, emerged victorious, defeating former President Note by 17 votes to 15.

The Zedkaia administration (2009–11)

Zedkaia was sworn in as President in November 2009, pledging to put an end to the factionalism that had characterized the Nitijela since the 2007 elections. With the exception of the Minister of Justice, David Kramer, who resigned and was replaced by Brenson Wase, Zedkaia retained all the members of his predecessor's Cabinet. Alvin Jacklick was elected as the new Speaker of the Nitijela.

In late 2010 allegations emerged of widespread government fraud, with two criminal cases filed against the Ministry of Finance and the Ministry of Health in December. On the opening day of the new parliamentary session in January 2011, President Zedkaia pledged to ensure that those persons found to have been complicit in any wrongdoing would be prosecuted 'to the fullest extent of the law'. By June 12 people were reported to have been charged with theft of US federal funding intended for the Ministries of Education, of Finance and of Health, and police investigations were reported to have uncovered evidence of fraud and theft within government departments dating back as far as 2006.

The Minister of Transportation and Communications, Kenneth Kedi, became the first serving cabinet minister to be charged with a criminal offence in the Marshall Islands' history when he was charged, in June 2011, with 10 criminal counts, including theft and misconduct in public office, in connection with the ongoing investigations into government fraud. When Kedi presented a plea of no contest on three counts, the Attorney-General's office withdrew the remaining seven charges against the minister. Despite being sentenced in July to a 30-day suspended prison term and being ordered to pay a fine of US $1,000, Kedi retained his cabinet post. The Marshall Islands amended its criminal code in order to strengthen its provisions on bribery and other corruption offences in September, and acceded to the UN Convention against Corruption in November.

Recent developments: legislative elections of 2011

In advance of the legislative elections scheduled to be held in November 2011, a new political party, Kien Eo Am (Your Government), was formed by a number of cabinet ministers and senators associated with the incumbent administration of President Zedkaia. At the elections, held on 21 November, 96 candidates vied for the 33 seats in the Nitijela, many standing as independents. Aelon Kein Ad, several members of the UDP and a number of independents subsequently formed a parliamentary majority controlling 20 seats. The new Nitijela was sworn in on 3 January 2012, electing former cabinet minister and traditional chief Christopher Loeak (of Aelon Kein Ad) as President and Donald F. Capelle as Speaker. Loeak, who defeated the incumbent Zedkaia by 21 votes to 11, with one senator casting a vote for Kessai Note (although he had not been officially nominated), was formally inaugurated in mid-January, together with his new Cabinet. Veteran politicians Tony deBrum and Phillip Muller were appointed Minister in Assistance to the President and Minister of Foreign Affairs, respectively; Hilda Heine was allocated the education portfolio, the only woman to be appointed to the Cabinet.

In March 2012 it was reported that a controversial bill to eliminate postal voting from outside the islands had been delayed in response to staunch opposition on the part of overseas Marshall Islanders (who number around 15,000).

The inclusion of the Marshall Islands on the US Department of State's human-trafficking 'Tier 2 Watch List', with the Department's *Trafficking in Persons* annual report published in July 2013, prompted considerable anger within the Republic. The Marshall Islands was again included on the watch list released in July 2014; the 2014 report noted an ongoing government investigation into enforced prostitution in the Marshall Islands, but stated that the Government had made 'limited efforts' to prevent trafficking in the past year and observed that a national plan of action on human-trafficking drafted in August 2013, as well as proposals to establish a national task force on human-trafficking, still awaited approval by the legislature. In March 2015 a government-commissioned report was presented at the UN headquarters in New York, USA, which included the finding that nearly seven in 10 of all women in the Marshall Islands had experienced physical or sexual violence.

The Government comfortably survived a vote of no confidence in November 2013; the opposition had submitted the motion owing to concerns over, *inter alia*, the administration's handling of a minor diplomatic dispute with Taiwan. Another motion of no confidence was registered by the opposition in March 2014 in response to the controversial (and possibly unconstitutional) selection by the Minister of Foreign Affairs, Phillip Muller, of Maj.-Gen. Jamil al-Sayyid, the erstwhile Chief of General Security in Lebanon, as the Marshall Islands' official representative to UNESCO. Al-Sayyid's nomination had been revoked in February, following the publication of an article in the French newspaper *Le Figaro*, which claimed that al-Sayyid would be afforded immunity from prosecution by the appointment, in connection with his alleged involvement in the assassination of Lebanese Prime Minister Rafiq Hariri in 2005, which was being investigated by a UN-backed tribunal. Loeak announced his second cabinet reorganization in a week the day before the motion of no confidence, notably moving Muller to the health portfolio and placing Tony deBrum, the former Minister in Assistance to the President, in charge of foreign affairs. The motion was subsequently defeated by 17 votes to 13. In March 2014 Dennis Momotaro, who had abstained from the no-confidence vote (which counts as a vote in favour in the final count), resigned as Minister of Finance and was replaced by Jack Ading.

In April 2014 the Government filed an unprecedented lawsuit with a US federal court, accusing the USA of violating the Treaty on the Non-Proliferation of Nuclear Weapons, which commits participants to work towards the abolition of nuclear weapons, and seeking a court order requiring the USA to commence negotiations on nuclear disarmament within one year. The Government also filed a similar suit at the International Court of Justice against all nine of the world's nuclear-armed nations. In February 2015 a US federal judge dismissed the lawsuit against the Obama Administration, stating that compelling the USA to negotiate on disarmament would not redress any harm caused to the Marshall Islands by the nuclear tests at Bikini and Enewetak Atolls in 1946–58, and noting that the judiciary did not have the authority to direct the executive branch of government on negotiations with foreign states. The Marshall Islands Government filed an appeal against the dismissal in April 2015.

Meanwhile, in February 2015 the High Court ruled that naturalized citizens had a constitutional right to seek election to the Nitijela, on the grounds that there was no constitutional support for criteria previously introduced by the legislature requiring that electoral candidates have at least one parent of Marshallese descent and traditional land rights through ancestral lineage. The case had been brought before the Court by Jack Niedenthal, whose petition to stand as a candidate in the legislative elections due to be held by November 2015 had been rejected by the Chief Electoral Officer in November 2014, on account of Niedenthal's status as a naturalized citizen.

Environmental Concerns

In his opening address to mark the new parliamentary session in January 2011, President Jurelang Zedkaia identified climate change as 'the single most serious threat' to the Marshall Islands. In February 2013, in an address to the UN Security Council, the Minister in Assistance to the President, Tony deBrum, argued that climate change posed a threat to international security and stressed that the very survival of the Marshall Islands was at stake if global warming were allowed to progress unchecked. (In 2002 the Intergovernmental Panel on Climate Change had projected that global sea level rises as a result of the greenhouse effect—heating of the earth's atmosphere—during the 21st century would submerge over 80% of Majuro Atoll.) In his speech, deBrum noted that climate change was making drinking water scarce, adversely affecting food production and prompting migration to other Pacific islands, as well as to Australia and the USA.

A severe drought in the northern Marshall Islands led President Christopher Loeak to declare a state of emergency in April 2013 and a state of disaster in May; the USA also proclaimed a state of disaster in the region in June. The depletion of potable water resources in the northern atolls resulted in the spread of disease and the temporary displacement of some populations, while widespread crop failure was also reported. Emergency assistance from the Government's bilateral and multilateral development partners (with the USA alone providing US $5.1m. in drought assistance in 2013), notably including the installation of water purification systems, helped to alleviate the crisis. However, another state of emergency was announced in March 2014 after high tides flooded Majuro and adjacent atolls. Minister of Foreign Affairs Phillip Muller attributed the 2013 drought and the March 2014 floods to climate change. Further severe flooding in Majuro, as well as several of the outer islands, in October 2014 and again in January 2015 caused significant damage to property.

The Marshall Islands hosted the 44th annual summit meeting of the Pacific Islands Forum in early September 2013. The summit's main theme was climate change, and member states agreed to lower their greenhouse gas emissions in an effort to encourage larger nations to follow suit—a pledge formalized in the Majuro Declaration for Climate Leadership. President Loeak, in an address to the UN General Assembly in late September, again emphasized the need for concerted global action to address climate change, while UN Secretary-General Ban Ki Moon declared his support for the Majuro Declaration.

Regional Affairs

In February 2010 the leaders of eight western Pacific island states—the Marshall Islands, together with Kiribati, Micronesia, Nauru, Palau, Papua New Guinea, Solomon Islands and Tuvalu—convened in Koror, Palau, for the first Presidential Summit of the Parties to the Nauru Agreement (PNA), a multilateral organization established in 1982 with the aim of protecting the western Pacific region's tuna industry and improving the quality of its tuna fisheries through sustainable management and innovation. (About 25%–30% of the global tuna catch is estimated to be caught in the waters of the eight PNA members.) At the Summit, the member states signed the 'Koror Declaration', which provided for the implementation of a ban on tuna-fishing in an area of the Pacific Ocean. In April the PNA Office was officially opened in Majuro, Marshall Islands. In October the PNA voted substantially to expand the area in which tuna-fishing was prohibited, to encompass some 4.5m. sq km, and to implement further restrictions on tuna-fishing in the wider region, including enhanced observer monitoring of licensed fishing vessels, with effect from 1 January 2011; it was hoped that the new measures would facilitate a 30% targeted reduction in the total tuna catch in the region compared with 2010. At the seventh annual meeting of the PNA fisheries ministers, held in Alotau, Papua New Guinea, in May 2012, the ministers agreed to implement more stringent measures to minimize the impact of fishing on bycatch species (notably whale sharks). At the ninth annual PNA meeting, held in Majuro in June 2014, President Christopher Loeak noted a significant upsurge in tuna revenues since 2010, a trend that he attributed to solidarity among the PNA member states.

The Marshall Islands established full diplomatic relations with Taiwan in November 1998. The action was immediately condemned by the People's Republic of China, which in December severed all diplomatic relations with the islands. In August 2004 the Chinese Vice-Minister of Foreign Affairs, Zhou Wenzhong, expressed his country's willingness to restore normal relations, if the Marshall Islands withdrew its diplomatic recognition of Taiwan. In the following month it was announced that Taiwan was to contribute more than US $40m. over a 20-year period to the Marshall Islands trust fund established in May. In June 2006 a delegation of Marshall Islands parliamentary representatives visited the mainland Chinese capital of Beijing, at the invitation of the National People's Congress, causing consternation among some government officials over the effect on the Marshall Islands' relations with Taiwan. The leader of the delegation insisted that the Marshall Islands was simply responding to an invitation, while the Ministry of Foreign Affairs reaffirmed the country's commitment to Taiwan. In January 2008 the newly elected President, Litokwa Tomeing, who had previously expressed support for alignment with China, nevertheless confirmed that strong links with Taiwan would continue, and reinforced this position during a visit by the Taiwanese Vice-President, Annette Lu, at the end of the month. The Minister of Foreign Affairs, Tony deBrum, and President Tomeing visited Taiwan in February and March, respectively.

Relations with Taiwan were further strengthened in March 2010, when Taiwanese President Ma Ying-jeou visited the Marshall Islands during a week-long tour of South Pacific allies. In late June–early July of that year Jurelang Zedkaia made his first official visit to Taiwan since assuming the presidency in November 2009. During his six-day visit Zedkaia met with President Ma, whereupon the two leaders pledged further to enhance bilateral co-operation in a number of areas, including the fisheries industry, education, and arts and culture. President Ma also expressed his gratitude to the Marshall Islands for advocating more meaningful Taiwanese participation within the international community. Tensions emerged, however, following the suspension in January 2011 of Taiwanese funding (which accounted for almost 8% of total annual budgetary spending in the Marshall Islands), pending the submission by the Marshall Islands Government—as demanded by the Taiwanese authorities—of a progress report detailing the results generated by previous funds. The overdue payment was released by Taiwan in March. In March 2013 President Christopher Loeak made his first official visit to Taiwan since assuming the presidency in January 2012; during his visit, Loeak met with President Ma and both sides called for continued expansion of co-operation to enhance bilateral relations. Further discussions were held between the two leaders during a second state visit to Taiwan by Loeak in November 2014.

The Marshall Islands Government has consistently supported Japan at the International Whaling Commission (IWC), voting in favour of commercial whaling, and also in the country's attempt to secure a permanent seat on the UN Security Council. By 2008 Japan was reported to be the third largest donor of aid to the Marshall Islands (after the USA and Taiwan). Following a covert investigation conducted by a British newspaper, *The Sunday Times*, it was claimed in June 2010 that the Marshall Islands' vote in favour of commercial whaling, together with those of five other countries, had been secured as a result of Japanese bribery that was purported to include offers of additional aid donations, cash incentives and the funding of delegations' visits to whaling meetings. The Japanese authorities insisted that the issue of whaling played no part in Japan's aid programme. (However, in July 2001 the then head of the Japanese Fisheries Agency, Maseyuku Komatsu, had stated publicly that Japan used overseas aid as a tool with which to secure support for its position on whaling, although this was swiftly denied in a formal government statement.) During President Christopher Loeak's first official visit to Japan, in May 2012, he confirmed that the Marshall Islands would continue to support Japan's whaling programme at the IWC and the Japanese bid to be granted a permanent seat on the UN Security Council. The following month, in the largest single Japanese aid project to the islands to date, Japan agreed to fund the construction of two new inter-island ships (a landing craft and a passenger/cargo vessel) at a cost of $16m. Japan's diplomatic relations with the Marshall Islands were upgraded to ambassadorial level in mid-2013. Japan pledged two separate grants to the Marshall Islands in February and March 2014, both worth $1.95m., to be disbursed on, *inter alia*, the purchase of water desalination units and equipment to improve environmental management.

CONSTITUTION AND GOVERNMENT

The Constitution of the Republic of the Marshall Islands, which took effect on 1 May 1979, provides for a parliamentary form of government, with legislative authority vested in the 33-member Nitijela. The Nitijela (members of which are elected, by popular vote, for a four-year term) elects the President of the Marshall Islands (also a four-year mandate) from among its own members. Under the terms of the Compact of Free Association, the Republic of the Marshall Islands is a sovereign, self-governing state. The first Compact was finalized by the Governments of the Marshall Islands and the USA on 25 June 1983, and was effectively ratified by the US Congress on 14 January 1986. A revised Compact was signed by the two countries on 1 May 2003; it was ratified by the US Congress in November 2003, and signed by US President George W. Bush in December of that year. Amendments to the Compact were signed in May 2004.

Local governmental units are the municipalities and villages. Elected Magistrates and Councils govern the municipalities. Village government is largely traditional.

REGIONAL AND INTERNATIONAL CO-OPERATION

The Marshall Islands is a member of the Pacific Community (see p. 410), the Pacific Islands Forum (see p. 413), the UN's Economic and Social Commission for Asia and the Pacific (ESCAP, see p. 30) and the Asian Development Bank (ADB, see p. 206). The Marshall Islands hosts the secretariat of the Parties to the Nauru Agreement, a multilateral organization charged with protecting the tuna industry in the western Pacific region.

The Marshall Islands became a member of the UN in 1991.

ECONOMIC AFFAIRS

In 2013, according to estimates by the World Bank, the Marshall Islands' gross national income (GNI), measured at average 2011–13 prices, was US $221m., equivalent to $4,200 per head. During 2004–13, it was estimated, the population increased at an average annual rate of 0.1%, while gross domestic product (GDP) per head rose, in real terms, at an average rate of 1.5% per year. According to UN figures, overall GDP increased, in real terms, at an average annual rate of 1.6% in 2004–13. According to the Asian Development Bank (ADB), real GDP grew by 3.0% in 2012/13 and by 0.5% in 2013/14.

Agriculture is mainly on a subsistence level. The sector (including fishing and livestock-rearing) contributed 15.5% of GDP in 2013, according to UN figures. According to FAO estimates, some 6,000 people were employed in the sector (mainly in subsistence fishing) at mid-2015. Fishing engaged about 10% of those employed in the private sector in 2009/10. Fish is by far the largest export commodity, accounting for nearly 90% of exports (excluding re-exports of fuel) in 2011/12, according to the IMF. The fishing sector incorporates a commercial tuna-fishing industry, including a transshipment base on Majuro. A new tuna-processing plant, employing more than 600 local workers and built by a Chinese company, had become fully operational by 2009. In 2009/10 fish exports accounted for 27.2% of the total value of exports of goods (including re-exports), compared with 1.7% in 2004/05. The sale of fishing licences is an important source of revenue, accounting for 5.6% of GDP in 2011/12. The principal crops are coconuts, cassava and sweet potatoes. In 2009/10 exports of coconut oil and copra accounted for 7.4% of the total value of exports of goods (including re-exports). According to UN figures, agricultural GDP increased by an average of 0.6% per year during 2004–13. According to the ADB, sectoral GDP rose by 6.2% in 2012/13 and by 4.2% in 2013/14.

Industrial activities (including mining, manufacturing, construction and utilities) contributed 12.1% of GDP in 2013, according to UN figures, and engaged 18.9% of the employed labour force in 1999. Construction and manufacturing employed 14.8% of private sector wage-earners in 2009/10. The islands have few mineral resources, although there are high-grade phosphate deposits on Ailinglaplap Atoll. According to UN figures, the GDP of the industrial sector increased at an average annual rate of 1.8% during 2004–13. According to the ADB, industrial GDP expanded by 8.4% in 2012/13, but contracted by 5.5% in 2013/14.

Manufacturing activity, which provided 1.9% of GDP in 2013, according to UN figures, consists mainly of the processing of coconuts (to produce copra and coconut oil) and other agricultural products, and of fish (see above). According to the IMF, manufacturing engaged 1.2% of those employed in the private sector in 2009/10. Manufacturing GDP increased by an average of 0.6% per year during 2004–13; the sector's GDP expanded by 21.2% in 2012, but declined by 1.9% in 2013.

The construction sector contributed 5.7% of GDP in 2013, according to UN figures. According to the IMF, the sector engaged 13.7% of the employed population in the private sector in 2009/10. Construction GDP grew at an average annual rate of 2.1% during 2004–13; sectoral GDP decreased by 9.9% in 2012, but increased by 24.6% in 2013.

The islands are heavily reliant on imported diesel fuel for energy supplies. Severe difficulties in financing purchases of fuel led to the declaration of a state of economic emergency in 2008. A rapid energy assessment, funded by the ADB, made numerous recommendations for greater energy efficiency in the islands. The wider use of alternative sources of energy, notably solar power, has been encouraged and developed in recent years.

The services sector (comprising trade, transport, storage, communications and other activities) provided 72.4% of GDP in 2013, according to UN figures, and engaged 59.8% of the employed labour force in 1999. The international shipping registry experienced considerable expansion following political unrest in Panama in 1989, and subsequently continued to expand (largely as a result of the reflagging of US, Japanese and South Korean ships in the islands). The number of vessels registered rose from 853 in December 2005 to 3,190 at the end of 2014. According to the World Tourism Organization, tourism receipts totalled US $3.8m. in 2012, when tourist arrivals reached 4,578. According to UN figures, services GDP increased at an average annual rate of 1.2% during 2004–13. According to the ADB, sectoral GDP increased by 1.8% in 2012/13, but contracted by 0.1% in 2013/14.

In 2011/12 the Marshall Islands recorded a visible merchandise trade deficit of US $66.5m., and there was a deficit of $13.9m. on the current account of the balance of payments. According to the ADB, there was a trade deficit of US$69m. in 2013/14, and a current account deficit equivalent to 9.4% of GDP. The principal domestic exports are fish and coconut products. Re-exports accounted for 65.3% of total exports in 2009/10. The principal imports in 2000 included mineral fuels and lubricants (which accounted for 37.3% of the total value of merchandise imports), food and live animals, and machinery and transport equipment. In 2006 the principal sources of imports were the USA (which provided 45.8% of total imports), Australia and Japan. In 2000 the USA was also the principal export destination (purchasing 57.1% of total exports).

In accordance with the terms stipulated in the Compact of Free Association, financial assistance from the USA contributes a large part of the islands' revenue. Grants and military payments from the USA for use of the missile-testing site on Kwajalein, along with trust fund contributions, constitute the major part of government revenue. In 2011/12 the USA was to provide US $67.1m. in Compact funding to the islands. Considerable support has also been provided by Taiwan since the late 1990s (see *Contemporary Political History*). According to the ADB, a budget surplus equivalent to 3.2% of GDP was recorded in 2013/14. The islands' external debt totalled $97m. in 2013. In that year the cost of debt-servicing was estimated to be the equivalent of 9.1% of revenue from the export of goods and services. Annual inflation in Majuro averaged 4.5% in 2003–10. According to the ADB, consumer prices in Majuro increased by 1.9% in 2012/13 and by 1.3% in 2013/14. The ADB estimated that 30.9% of the workforce were unemployed in 2008. The rate of youth unemployment was estimated at 60% in 2006.

Economic development in the Marshall Islands has been hindered by the country's small size, geographical isolation and susceptibility to natural disasters. In addition, infrastructural deficiencies and poorly performing public enterprises have created considerable budgetary pressures in recent years. The amended Compact of Free Association—which was signed by the Marshall Islands and the USA in 2003 (see *Contemporary Political History*), and which provided for the gradual decrease in grant assistance over a 20-year period—posed a further threat to the islands' fiscal stability; a Compact Trust Fund was expected to provide funding from 2024. The budget for 2015/16 projected a 19.5% increase in total revenue, to an estimated US $146.2m., partly owing to improved tax collection; nevertheless, the implementation of tax reforms is still required to broaden the local tax base, further increase government revenue and compensate for the future reduction in grants. According to the IMF, foreign direct investment declined dramatically from $38.0m. in 2009/10 to $4.8m. in 2010/11 and $3.4m. in 2011/12, before rallying slightly, to $4.1m., in 2012/13. According to the ADB, real GDP grew by 3.2% in 2011/12, fuelled mainly by the resumption of work on the airport and the continuing expansion of the fishing industry. GDP registered growth of a further 3.0% in 2012/13; however, the economy grew by just 0.5% in 2013/14, owing in part to a lack of new infrastructure projects. With new projects scheduled to commence, GDP growth was expected to accelerate to 3.5% in 2014/15, before moderating to 1.5% in 2015/16 as those projects neared completion. According to the ADB, the rate of inflation eased from 1.9% in 2012/13 to 1.3% in 2013/14, reflecting weak demand and low import costs. Inflation was projected to remain stable, at 1.4% in 2014/15 and 1.3% in 2015/16.

PUBLIC HOLIDAYS

2016: 1 January (New Year's Day), 1 March (Nuclear Victims' Remembrance Day), 25 March (Good Friday), 2 May (Constitution Day), 3 July (Fishermen's Day), 2 September (Dri-Jerbal—Labour Day), 23 September (Manit—Culture Day), 17 November (Presidents' Day), 2 December (Gospel Day), 25 December (Christmas Day).

Statistical Survey

Source (unless otherwise indicated): Economic Policy, Planning and Statistics Office (EPPSO), Office of the President, POB 2, Majuro, MH 96960; tel. (625) 3802; fax (625) 3805; e-mail planning@ntamar.net; internet www.spc.int/prism/country/mh/stats.

AREA AND POPULATION

Area: 181.4 sq km (70.0 sq miles) (land only); two island groups, the Ratak Chain (88.1 sq km) and the Ralik Chain (93.3 sq km).

Population: 50,840 at census of 1 June 1999; 53,158 (males 27,243, females 25,915) at census of 4 April 2011. *By Island Group* (2011 census): Ratak Chain 33,892 (Majuro Atoll 27,797); Ralik Chain 19,266 (Kwajalein Atoll 11,408). *Mid-2015* (Secretariat of the Pacific Community estimate): 54,880 (Source: Pacific Regional Information System).

Density (mid-2015, land area only): 302.5 per sq km.

Population by Age and Sex (Secretariat of the Pacific Community estimates at mid-2015): *0–14 years:* 21,862 (males 11,320, females 10,542); *15–64 years:* 31,545 (males 16,042, females 15,503); *65 years and over:* 1,473 (males 753, females 720); *Total* 54,880 (males 28,115, females 26,765) (Source: Pacific Regional Information System).

Principal Towns (population of urban settlements, 1999 census): Ebeye 9,345; Darrit (Djarrot) 7,103; Delap 6,339; Rairok 3,846; Laura 2,256; Uliga 2,044. Note: The country's capital is the combined municipality of Delap-Uliga-Darrit.

Births and Deaths (2006): Registered live births 1,576; Registered deaths 318. Note: Registered live births exclude US military personnel, their dependants and contract employees (Source: UN, *Population and Vital Statistics Report*). *2013* (Secretariat of the Pacific Community estimates): Birth rate 29.6 per 1,000; death rate 4.4 per 1,000 (Source: Pacific Regional Information System).

Life Expectancy (years at birth, WHO estimates): 70 (males 68; females 72) in 2012 (Source: WHO, *World Health Statistics*).

Economically Active Population (persons aged 15 years and over, 1999 census): Agriculture and fishery 2,114; Manufacturing 761; Electricity, gas and water 258; Construction 848; Wholesale and retail trade 788; Transport, storage and communications 763; Finance, insurance, real estate and business services 559;

Community, social and personal services 3,803; *Sub-total* 9,894; Activities not reported 247; *Total employed* 10,141 (males 7,008, females 3,133); Unemployed 4,536 (males 2,671, females 1,865); *Total labour force* 14,677 (males 9,679, females 4,998). *2009/10* (private sector only): Fishing 1,062; Manufacturing 50; Construction 593; Wholesale and retail trade 1,738; Hotels and restaurants 150; Transport, storage and communications 324; Financial intermediation 20; Real estate, renting and business activities 221; Health and social work 47; Other services 126; Total employed 4,331 (Source: IMF, *Republic of the Marshall Islands: Statistical Appendix—* December 2011). *Mid-2015* (estimates): Agriculture, etc. 6,000; Total labour force 27,000 (Source: FAO).

HEALTH AND WELFARE

Key Indicators

Total Fertility Rate (children per woman, 2012): 3.4.

Under-5 Mortality Rate (per 1,000 live births, 2012): 38.

Physicians (per 1,000 head, 2010): 0.4.

Hospital Beds (per 1,000 head, 2010): 2.7.

Health Expenditure (2011): US $ per head (PPP): 414.

Health Expenditure (2011): % of GDP: 16.0.

Health Expenditure (2011): public (% of total): 83.0.

Access to Water (% of persons, 2012): 92.

Access to Sanitation (% of persons, 2012): 76.

Total Carbon Dioxide Emissions ('000 metric tons, 2010): 102.7.

Carbon Dioxide Emissions Per Head (metric tons, 2010): 2.0.

For sources and definitions, see explanatory note on p. vi.

AGRICULTURE, ETC.

Principal Crop ('000 metric tons, 2013, FAO estimate): Coconuts 25.0.

Livestock ('000 head, year ending September 2003): Pigs 12.9; Poultry 86.0.

Fishing ('000 metric tons, live weight, 2012, FAO estimates): Bigeye tuna 5.7; Skipjack tuna 55.4; Yellowfin tuna 11.4; Total catch (incl. others) 75.4.

Source: FAO.

INDUSTRY

Electric Energy (million kWh): 111.2 in 2009; 113.7 in 2010; 113.7 in 2011. Source: UN Industrial Commodity Statistics Database.

FINANCE

Currency and Exchange Rates: United States currency is used: 100 cents = 1 United States dollar (US $). *Sterling and Euro Equivalents* (31 December 2014): £1 sterling = US $1.5608; €1 = US $1.2141; US $100 = £64.07 = €82.37.

Budget (US $ million, year ending 30 September 2013, estimates): *Revenue:* Tax revenue 29.0; Grants 54.1; Other revenue 7.2; Total 90.2. *Expenditure:* Recurrent 89.6 (Wages and salaries 38.9; Goods and services 24.8; Interest 1.4; Subsidies 9.9); Capital 2.0; Total 91.6 (excluding net lending −1.4). Source: IMF, *Republic of the Marshall Islands: Staff Report for the 2013 Article IV Consultation* (February 2014).

Cost of Living (Consumer Price Index for Majuro, base: January–March 2003 = 100): All items 141.6 in 2011; 147.7 in 2012; 147.7 in 2013 (Source: Asian Development Bank).

Gross Domestic Product (US $ million at constant 2004 prices): 145.0 in 2010; 145.9 in 2011; 150.5 in 2012. Source: Asian Development Bank.

Expenditure on the Gross Domestic Product (US $ million at current prices, 2013): Government final consumption expenditure 102.1; Private final consumption expenditure 172.0; Gross capital formation 107.2; *Total domestic expenditure* 381.3; Exports of goods and services 23.5; *Less* Imports of goods and services 216.0; *GDP in purchasers' values* 188.7. Source: UN National Accounts Main Aggregates Database.

Gross Domestic Product by Economic Activity (US $ million at current prices, 2013): Agriculture, hunting, forestry and fishing 28.1; Mining, electricity, gas and water 8.1; Manufacturing 3.5; Construction 10.4; Trade, restaurants and hotels 29.1; Transport, storage and communications 15.0; Other activities 87.4; *Sub-total* 181.6; Net of

indirect taxes 7.1 (obtained as a residual); *GDP in purchasers' values* 188.7. Source: UN National Accounts Main Aggregates Database.

Balance of Payments (US $ million, year ending 30 September 2012): Merchandise exports f.o.b. 59.1; Merchandise imports c.i.f. −125.6; *Trade balance* −66.5; Services (net) −48.1; *Balance on goods and services* −114.6; Other income 41.4; *Balance on goods, services and income* −73.2; Private unrequited transfers (net) 59.3; *Current balance* −13.9. Source: IMF, *Republic of the Marshall Islands: Staff Report for the 2013 Article IV Consultation* (February 2014).

EXTERNAL TRADE

Principal Commodities (US $ million): *Imports* (2000): Food and live animals 5.0; Beverages and tobacco 6.0; Crude materials, inedible, except fuels 2.6; Mineral fuels, lubricants and related materials 20.4; Animal and vegetable oils and fats 2.4; Chemicals 0.1; Basic manufactures 3.0; Machinery and transport equipment 8.2; Miscellaneous manufactured articles 1.4; Goods not classified by kind 5.8; Total 54.7. *Exports* (year ending September 2006): Coconut oil (crude) 2.0; Copra cake 0.1; Total (incl. others) 20.3. Sources: IMF, *Republic of the Marshall Islands: Selected Issues and Statistical Appendix* (June 2008). *2009* (US $ million): Total imports 158.3; Total exports 34.3 (Source: Asian Development Bank).

Principal Trading Partners (US $ million): *Imports* (2006): Australia 5.7; Hong Kong 2.1; Japan 5.5; New Zealand 2.2; USA 31.0; Total (incl. others) 126.6 (Source: Asian Development Bank). *Exports* (2000, estimates): USA 5.2; Total (incl. others) 9.1.

TRANSPORT

Road Traffic (vehicles registered, 2004): Trucks 97; Pick-ups 423; Sedans 1,531; Jeeps 55; Buses 62; Vans 62; Scooters 20; Other motor vehicles 154; *Total* 2,404.

Shipping: *Flag Registered Fleet* (at 31 December 2014): Vessels 3,190; Total displacement ('000 grt) 114,726.5. Source: Lloyd's List Intelligence (www.lloydslistintelligence.com).

Civil Aviation (traffic on scheduled services, 2008): Kilometres flown 1m.; Passengers carried 30,000; Passenger-km 42m.; Total ton-km 4m. (Source: UN, *Statistical Yearbook*). *2009:* Passengers carried 27,692 (Source: World Bank, World Development Indicators database).

TOURISM

Tourist Arrivals: 4,563 in 2010; 4,555 in 2011; 4,578 in 2012.

Arrivals by Country (2012): Australia 192; China, People's Republic 87; Japan 448; Micronesia, Federated States 363; Nauru 511; New Zealand 117; Philippines 187; Taiwan 363; USA 1,102; Total (incl. others) 4,578.

Tourism Receipts (US $ million, excl. passenger transport): 4.0 in 2010; 4.3 in 2011; 3.8 in 2012.

Source: World Tourism Organization.

COMMUNICATIONS MEDIA

Telephones (main lines in use, estimate): 4,400 in 2010.

Mobile Cellular Telephones (subscriptions, estimate): 3,800 in 2010.

Source: International Telecommunication Union.

EDUCATION

Pre-primary (2010/11 unless otherwise indicated): 126 teachers (2002/03); 1,448 pupils enrolled (males 726, females 722).

Primary (2010/11 unless otherwise indicated): 103 schools (1998); 526 teachers (2002/03, estimate); 8,546 pupils enrolled (males 4,446, females 4,100).

Secondary (2008/09 unless otherwise indicated): 16 schools (1998); 387 teachers (2002/03, estimate); 5,229 pupils enrolled (males 2,614, females 2,615).

Higher (2002/03 unless otherwise indicated): 1 college (1994); 49 teachers (estimate); 919 students enrolled (males 400, females 519, estimates).

Pupil-teacher Ratio (primary education, UNESCO estimate): 14.5 in 2002/03. *2010/11* (primary education, Majuro only): 17 (Source: Ministry of Education, Majuro).

Source: mostly UNESCO Institute for Statistics.

Directory

The Government

HEAD OF STATE

President: CHRISTOPHER LOEAK (took office 3 January 2012; inaugurated 17 January 2012).

CABINET
(May 2015)

The Government is composed mainly of members of Aelon Kein Ad and the United Democratic Party.

Minister in Assistance to the President: WILBUR HEINE.

Minister of Foreign Affairs and Trade: TONY DEBRUM.

Minister of Education: HILDA HEINE.

Minister of Finance: JACK ADING.

Minister of Transportation and Communication: THOMAS HEINE.

Minister of Health Services: PHILLIP MULLER.

Minister of Public Works and Acting Minister of Resources and Development: HIROSHI YAMAMURA.

Minister of Internal and Outer Island Affairs: DAVID KABUA.

Minister of Justice: RIEN MORRIS.

MINISTRIES

Office of the President: Govt of the Republic of the Marshall Islands, POB 2, Majuro, MH 96960; tel. (625) 3445; fax (625) 3649; e-mail rmiop.press@gmail.com; internet www.rmi-op.net.

Ministry of Education: POB 3, Majuro, MH 96960; tel. (625) 5261; fax (625) 3861; e-mail rmimoe@rmimoe.net.

Ministry of Finance: POB P, Majuro, MH 96960; tel. (625) 5660; fax (625) 3432.

Ministry of Foreign Affairs: POB 1349, Majuro, MH 96960; tel. (625) 3181; fax (625) 4979; e-mail mofasec@ntamar.net.

Ministry of Health Services: POB 16, Majuro, MH 96960; tel. (625) 5661; fax (625) 3432; e-mail rmimohe@ntamar.net.

Ministry of Internal and Outer Island Affairs: POB 18, Majuro, MH 96960; tel. (625) 3240; fax (625) 5353; e-mail rmihpo@ntamar.net.

Ministry of Justice: c/o Office of the Attorney General, POB 890, Majuro, MH 96960; tel. (625) 3244; fax (625) 5218; e-mail agoffice@ntamar.net.

Ministry of Public Works: POB 1727, Majuro, MH 96960; tel. (625) 3720; fax (625) 3005; e-mail secpw@ntamar.net.

Ministry of Resources and Development: POB 1727, Majuro, MH 96960; tel. (625) 3206; fax (625) 7471; e-mail rndsec@ntamar.net.

Ministry of Transportation and Communication: POB 1079, Majuro, MH 96960; tel. (625) 8869; fax (625) 3486; e-mail rmimotc@ntamar.net.

Legislature

THE NITIJELA

The Nitijela (lower house) consists of 33 elected senators. Following the election held on 21 November 2011, Aelon Kein Ad (Our Islands), several members of the United Democratic Party and a number of independents formed a parliamentary majority controlling some 20 seats.

Speaker: DONALD F. CAPELLE.

THE COUNCIL OF IROIJ

The Council of Iroij is the upper house of the bicameral legislature, comprising 12 tribal chiefs who advise the Presidential Cabinet and review legislation affecting customary law, land tenure or any traditional practice.

Chairman: Iroij KOTAK LOEAK.

Election Commission

Electoral Commission: POB 18, Majuro, MH 96900; e-mail rmielectoral@yahoo.com; Chief Electoral Officer ROBSON YASIWO ALMEN.

Political Organizations

Aelon Kein Ad (Our Islands): Majuro; f. 2002; formed United People's Party coalition following 2007 elections; Chair. CHRISTOPHER LOEAK; Leader MICHAEL KABUA.

Kien Eo Am (Your Government): Majuro; f. 2011; est. by supporters of then President Jurelang Zedkaia; Pres. JURELANG ZEDKAIA; Chair. DAVID KRAMER.

United Democratic Party: Majuro; Chair. RUBEN ZACKHRAS; Pres. KESSAI NOTE.

Diplomatic Representation

EMBASSIES IN THE MARSHALL ISLANDS

Japan: A1 Lojkar Village, POB 300, Majuro, MH 96960; tel. (247) 7463; fax (247) 7493; e-mail royoji@ntamar.net; Ambassador MASAKI SAKAI (resident in Federated States of Micronesia).

Taiwan (Republic of China): A5–6 Lojkar Village, Long Island, POB 1229, Majuro, MH 96960; tel. (247) 4141; fax (247) 4143; e-mail eoroc@ntamar.net; internet www.mofa.gov.tw; Ambassador WINSTON WEN-YI CHEN.

USA: POB 1379, Majuro, MH 96960; tel. (247) 4011; fax (247) 4012; e-mail publicmajuro@state.gov; internet majuro.usembassy.gov; Ambassador THOMAS H. ARMBRUSTER.

Judicial System

The judicial system consists of the Supreme Court and the High Court, which preside over District and Community Courts, and the Traditional Rights Court.

Supreme Court of the Republic of the Marshall Islands: POB 378, Majuro, MH 96960; tel. (625) 3201; fax (625) 3323; e-mail jutrep@ntamar.com; internet www.rmicourts.org; Chief Justice DANIEL N. CADRA.

High Court of the Republic of the Marshall Islands: Majuro; e-mail judrep@ntamar.net; Chief Justice CARL B. INGRAM.

District Court of the Republic of the Marshall Islands: Majuro, MH 96960; tel. (625) 3201; fax (625) 3323; Presiding Judge MILTON ZACKIOS.

Traditional Rights Court of the Marshall Islands: Majuro, MH 96960; customary law only; Chief Judge WALTER K. ELBON.

Religion

The population is predominantly Christian, mainly belonging to the Protestant United Church of Christ. The Roman Catholic Church, Assembly of God, Bukot Nan Jesus, Seventh-day Adventists, the Church of Jesus Christ of Latter-day Saints (Mormons), the Full Gospel and the Bahá'í Faith are also represented.

CHRISTIANITY

The Roman Catholic Church

The Apostolic Prefecture of the Marshall Islands included 5,020 adherents at 31 December 2007.

Prefect Apostolic of the Marshall Islands: Rev. Fr RAYMUNDO SABIO, POB 8, Majuro, MH 96960; tel. (625) 6675; fax (625) 5520; e-mail diocesemarshalls@yahoo.com.

Protestant Churches

The Marshall Islands come under the auspices of the United Church Board for World Ministries (475 Riverside Drive, New York, NY 10115, USA); Sec. for Latin America, Caribbean and Oceania Dr PATRICIA RUMER.

BAHÁ'Í FAITH

National Spiritual Assembly: POB 1017, Majuro, MH 96960; tel. (247) 3512; fax (247) 7180; e-mail nsamarshallislands@yahoo.com; internet www.mh.bahai.org; mems resident in 50 localities; Sec. Dr IRENE J. TAAFAKI.

The Press

Kwajalein Hourglass: POB 23, Kwajalein, MH 96555; tel. (355) 3539; e-mail jbennett@kls.usaka.smdc.army.mil; f. 1954; 2 a week; Man. Editor SHEILA GIDEON; circ. 2,300.

Marshall Islands Gazette: monthly; govt publ.

Marshall Islands Journal: POB 14, Majuro, MH 96960; tel. (625) 8143; fax (625) 3136; e-mail journal@ntamar.net; internet www.marshallislandsjournal.com; f. 1970; weekly; Editor GIFF JOHNSON; circ. 3,700.

Broadcasting and Communications

TELECOMMUNICATIONS

National Telecommunications Authority (NTA): POB 1169, Majuro, MH 96960; tel. (625) 3852; fax (625) 3952; e-mail info@ntamar.net; internet www.ntamar.net; privatized in 1991; sole provider of local and long-distance tel. services and internet communications in the Marshall Islands; Chair. RIEN MORRIS; Pres. and CEO THOMAS KIJINER, Jr.

BROADCASTING

Radio

Marshall Islands Broadcasting Co: POB 19, Majuro, MH 96960; tel. (625) 3250; fax (625) 3505; Chief Information Officer PETER FUCHS.

Radio Marshalls V7AB: POB 3250, Majuro, MH 96960; tel. (625) 8411; fax (625) 5353; govt-owned; commercial; programmes in English and Marshallese; Station Man. ANTARI ELBON.

Other radio stations include Micronesia Heatwave and V7AA.

Television

Marshalls Broadcasting Co Television: POB 19, Majuro, MH 96960; tel. (625) 3413; Chief Information Officer PETER FUCHS.

The US Department of Defense operates the American Forces Radio and Television Service for the Bucholz Army Airfield on Kwajalein Atoll.

Finance

(cap. = capital; dep. = deposits; amounts in US dollars)

BANKING

Bank of Guam (USA): POB C, Majuro, MH 96960; tel. (625) 3322; fax (625) 3444; Group Chair., Pres. and CEO LOURDES A. LEON GUERRERO; Country Man. LISA M. LEON GUERRERO.

Bank of the Marshall Islands: POB J, Majuro, MH 96960; tel. (625) 3636; fax (625) 3661; e-mail bankmar@ntamar.net; internet www.bomi.biz; f. 1982; 40% govt-owned; cap. 2.1m., dep. 41.6m. (Dec. 2012); Chair. GRANT LABAUN; Pres. and Gen. Man. PATRICK CHEN; brs in Majuro, Kwajalein, Ebeye and Santo.

Marshall Islands Development Bank: POB 1048, Majuro, MH 96960; tel. (625) 3230; fax (625) 3309; e-mail rmimidb@ntamar.net; f. 1989; lending suspended in 2003; Man. Dir AMON TIBON.

INSURANCE

Majuro Insurance Company: POB 60, Majuro, MH 96960; tel. (625) 8885; fax (625) 8188; Man. LUCY RUBEN.

Marshalls Insurance Agency: POB 113, Majuro, MH 96960; tel. (625) 3366; fax (625) 3189; Man. TOM LIKOVICH.

Moylan's Insurance Underwriters (Marshall) Inc: POB 727, Majuro, MH 96960; tel. (625) 3220; fax (625) 3361; e-mail marshalls@moylans.net; internet www.moylansinsurance.com; Founder, Chair. and Pres. KURT S. MOYLAN; Br. Man. STEVE PHILLIP.

Trade and Industry

DEVELOPMENT ORGANIZATIONS AND STATE AUTHORITIES

Marshall Islands Development Authority: POB 1185, Majuro, MH 96960; tel. (625) 3417; fax (625) 3158; Gen. Man. DAVID KABUA.

Marshall Islands Environmental Protection Authority (RMIEPA): POB 1322, Majuro, MH 96960; tel. (625) 3035; fax (625) 5202; e-mail rmiepa@ntamar.net; internet www.rmiepa.org; Gen. Man. LOWELL ALIK.

Marshall Islands Marine Resources Authority (MIMRA): POB 860, Majuro, MH 96960; tel. (625) 8262; fax (625) 5447; e-mail kiko@mimra.com; internet www.mimra.com; specializes in farming techniques and research and devt; Exec. Dir GLEN JOSEPH.

Tobolar Copra Processing Authority: POB G, Majuro, MH 96960; tel. (625) 3116; fax (625) 7206; e-mail wpcandilas@ntamar.net; Plant Man. WILFREDO CANDILAS.

CHAMBER OF COMMERCE

Marshall Islands Chamber of Commerce: POB 1226, Majuro, MH 96960; tel. (625) 3177; fax (625) 2500; e-mail commerce@ntamar.net; internet marshallislandschamber.net; fmrly known as Majuro Chamber of Commerce; Pres. BRENDA ALIK MADDISON; Sec. JIM MCLEAN.

UTILITIES

Electricity

Marshalls Energy Company: POB 1439, Majuro, MH 96960; tel. (625) 5886; fax (625) 3397; e-mail meccorp@ntamar.net; internet www.mecrmi.net; Gen. Man. DAVID PAUL.

Kwajalein Atoll Joint Utility Resource (KAJUR): POB 5819, Ebeye Island, Kwajalein, MH 96970; tel. (329) 3799; fax (329) 6722; e-mail meccorp@ntamar.net; internet www.mecrmi.net/KAJUR.htm; Man. ROMEO ALFRED.

Water

Majuro Water and Sewage Services: POB 1751, Majuro, MH 96960; tel. (625) 8934; fax (625) 3837; e-mail mwsco@ntamar.net; internet www.mecrmi.net/MWSC.htm; Man. TERRY MELLAN.

CO-OPERATIVES

These include the Ebeye Co-op, Farmers' Market Co-operative, Kwajalein Employees' Credit Union, Marshall Is Credit Union, Marshall Is Fishermen's Co-operative, and the Marshall Is Handicraft Co-operative.

Transport

ROADS

Tarmac and concrete roads are found in the more important islands. In 2007 there were 2,028 km of roads in the Marshall Islands, including 75 km of expressways. Many islands have stone and coral-surfaced roads and tracks.

SHIPPING

The Marshall Islands operates an offshore shipping register. At the end of 2014 the flag registered fleet comprised 3,190 vessels, with a combined displacement of some 114,726,539 grt, including 125 gas tankers, 960 bulk carriers and 88 general cargo ships.

International Registries Inc: 11495 Commerce Park Drive, Reston, VA 20191-1506, USA; tel. (703) 620-4880; fax (703) 476-8522; e-mail info@register-iri.com; internet www.register-iri.com; Pres. WILLIAM R. GALLAGHER.

The Trust Company of the Marshall Islands Inc: Trust Company Complex, Ajeltake Island, POB 1405, Majuro, MH 96960; tel. (247) 3018; fax (247) 3017; e-mail tcmi@ntamar.net; Pres. ALAN SCHOLLAR.

Marshall Islands Ports Authority (MIPA): POB 109, Majuro; tel. (625) 8269; fax (625) 4269; internet rmipa-aip.org; responsible for seaports and airports; Dir JACK CHONG GUM.

CIVIL AVIATION

The Marshall Islands' main airport is the Amata Kabua International Airport.

Air Marshall Islands (AMI): POB 1319, Majuro, MH 96960; tel. (625) 3731; fax (625) 3730; e-mail amisales@ntamar.net; internet www.airmarshallislands.com; f. 1980; internal services for the Marshall Islands; also charter, air ambulance and maritime surveillance operations; agency for Aloha airlines; CEO and Gen. Man. JEFFERSON BARTON.

Continental Airlines Micronesia: POB 156, Majuro; tel. (625) 3209; fax (625) 3730; e-mail cmimaj@ntamar.net; international flights between Majuro, the Federated States of Micronesia, Guam and Honolulu; also internal services between Majuro and Kwajalein; based in Hagåtña, Guam; Man. LEO SION.

Tourism

The islands' attractions include excellent opportunities for diving, game-fishing and the exploration of sites and relics of Second World War battles. Bikini Atoll was listed by UNESCO as a World Heritage site in 2010. In 2008 the Marshall Islands Visitor Authority implemented a four-year tourism development programme focusing on special interest tourism markets. In the longer term, the Visitor Authority planned to promote the development of small island resorts throughout the country. Tourism receipts totalled US $3.8m. in 2012, in which year there were 4,578 tourist arrivals. The leading sources of visitors include the USA and Japan.

Marshall Islands Visitor Authority: POB 5, Majuro, MH 96960; tel. (625) 6482; fax (625) 6771; e-mail tourism@ntamar.net; internet www.visitmarshallislands.com; f. 1997; Gen. Man. BRENDA ALIK MADDISON.

Defence

Defence is the responsibility of the USA, which maintains a military presence on Kwajalein Atoll. The US Pacific Command is based in Hawaii, USA.

Education

There is a school system, based on that of the USA, operated by the state. However, the development of secondary facilities has been constrained by the limitations of resources. In 2010/11 8,546 pupils were enrolled in primary schools, and in 2008/09 5,229 pupils were enrolled in secondary schools. In 2011 enrolment at primary schools included 100% of children in the relevant age-group, and the comparable ratio for secondary schools in 2006/07 was 63%. The College of the Marshall Islands, which became independent from the College of Micronesia in 1993, is based on Majuro; in 2002/03 there were an estimated 919 students enrolled at the College. The Fisheries and Nautical Center offers vocational courses for islanders seeking employment in the fishing industry or on passenger liners, cargo ships and tankers. In the proposed budget for 2011/12, education was allocated the sum of US $22.2m. (16.9% of total government expenditure).

MAURITANIA

Introductory Survey

LOCATION, CLIMATE, LANGUAGE, RELIGION, FLAG, CAPITAL

The Islamic Republic of Mauritania lies in north-west Africa, with the Atlantic Ocean to the west, Algeria and the disputed territory of Western Sahara (occupied by Morocco) to the north, Mali to the east and south, and Senegal to the south. The climate is hot and dry, particularly in the north, which is mainly desert. Average annual rainfall in the capital in the 1990s was 131 mm (5.1 ins). The 1991 Constitution designates Arabic (which is spoken by the Moorish majority) as the official language, and Arabic, Poular, Wolof and Solinke as the national languages. The black population in the south is largely French-speaking, and French is widely used in commercial and business circles. Islam is the state religion, and the inhabitants are almost all Muslims. The national flag (proportions 2 by 3) comprises a green field, bearing, on the vertical median, a yellow five-pointed star between the upward-pointing horns of a yellow crescent. The capital is Nouakchott.

CONTEMPORARY POLITICAL HISTORY

Historical Context

Mauritania, formerly part of French West Africa, achieved full independence on 28 November 1960 (having become a self-governing member of the French Community two years earlier). Moktar Ould Daddah, leader of the Parti de Regroupement Mauritanien (PRM) and Prime Minister since June 1959, became Head of State, and was elected President in August 1961. All parties subsequently merged with the PRM to form the Parti du Peuple Mauritanien, with Ould Daddah as Secretary-General, and Mauritania became a one-party state in 1964. In 1973 Mauritania joined the League of Arab States (see p. 359), and withdrew from the Franc Zone in the following year.

Under a tripartite agreement of November 1975, Spain ceded Spanish (now Western) Sahara to Mauritania and Morocco, to be apportioned between them. The agreement took effect in February 1976, when Mauritania occupied the southern portion of the territory. Fighting ensued between Moroccan and Mauritanian troops and the guerrilla forces of the Frente Popular para la Liberación de Saguia el-Hamra y Río de Oro (the Polisario Front), which sought independence for Western Sahara. Attacks within Mauritania by Polisario forces proved highly damaging to the economy, and, following the removal of Ould Daddah in a bloodless military coup in July 1978, Mauritania renounced its territorial claims in Western Sahara. A peace treaty was signed with Polisario in August 1979 and Morocco announced its annexation of the entire territory.

Domestic Political Affairs

In December 1984, while the Head of State, Lt-Col Mohamed Khouna Ould Haidalla, was temporarily absent from the country, the Prime Minister and Minister of Defence, Lt-Col (later Col) Maaouiya Ould Sid'Ahmed Taya, assumed the presidency.

At a national referendum on 12 July 1991, a draft Constitution, which accorded extensive powers to the presidency and provided for the introduction of a multi-party political system, was supported by 97.9% of those who voted (85.3% of the registered electorate), according to official reports. Meanwhile, legislation permitting the registration of political parties was promulgated: among the first organizations to be accorded official status was the Parti Républicain Démocratique et Social (PRDS), which was closely linked with Taya.

Taya won 62.7% of the votes cast at a presidential election held in January 1992, while at legislative elections held on 6 and 13 March the PRDS took 67 of the 79 seats in the National Assembly; Taya was inaugurated as President on 18 April.

In January 1996 Taya appointed Cheikh el Avia Ould Mohamed Khouna as Prime Minister, to head a new Council of Ministers. At legislative elections held on 11 and 18 October the PRDS won 71 of the 79 seats in the National Assembly. The Rassemblement pour la Démocratie et l'Unité (RDU), closely allied with the administration, also secured a seat. Action pour Changement (APC), which sought to represent the interests of

Haratin (mainly dark-skinned Moors who had formerly been slaves), was the only opposition party to obtain representation in the Assembly; six independent candidates also secured election.

In February 1997 five prominent opposition parties, including the APC, which was chaired by Messaoud Ould Boulkheir, and the Union des Forces Démocratiques—Ere Nouvelle (UFD—EN), formed a coalition, the Front des Partis de l'Opposition (FPO). At the presidential election held on 12 December, Taya was returned to office with 90.9% of the valid votes cast; his nearest rival, Mohamed Lemine Ch'Bih Ould Cheikh Melainine, won 7.0% of the vote. Opposition parties alleged that there had been widespread electoral fraud and disputed the official rate of voter participation, of 73.8%. Taya subsequently appointed Mohamed Lemine Ould Guig, a university academic, as Prime Minister, and a new Council of Ministers was installed. In November 1998 Khouna was again appointed Prime Minister.

Meanwhile, in March 1998 the UFD—EN divided into two rival factions, led by Ahmed Ould Daddah and Moustapha Ould Bedreddine, respectively. In November the Government banned the pro-Iraqi Baathist National Vanguard Party (Taliaa), a constituent member of the FPO, following its criticism of the Mauritanian Government's decision to establish full diplomatic relations with Israel in the previous month.

From late 2000 the Mauritanian Government experienced increasing pressure from opposition groups, including the UFD—EN, to break off diplomatic relations with Israel. In October several pro-Palestinian demonstrations in Nouakchott and Nouadhibou led to violent anti-Israeli protests. Arrests of members of clandestine Islamist groups and of UFD—EN activists were reported. In late October the Council of Ministers officially dissolved the UFD—EN, on the grounds that the party had incited violence and sought to damage Mauritanian national interests. Ould Daddah refused to recognize the dissolution of the party, and the UFD—EN's partners in the FOP condemned the Government's action as unconstitutional. Meanwhile, the faction of the UFD—EN led by Moustapha Ould Bedreddine, which remained authorized, restyled itself as the Union des Forces du Progrès (UFP).

Legislative and municipal elections were held on 19 and 26 October 2001. The PRDS won 64 of the 81 seats in the enlarged National Assembly, and the RDU and the Union pour la Démocratie et le Progrès (UDP), which were now both allied with the ruling party, each secured three seats. The APC was the most successful of the opposition parties, winning four seats, while the UFP and the newly formed Regroupement des Forces Démocratiques (RFD), which replaced the banned UFD—EN, also each took three seats, and the Front Populaire (FP) secured the remaining seat. In November President Taya reappointed Khouna as Prime Minister, and reorganized the Council of Ministers.

In October 2002 the UFP announced that it was to organize a series of meetings intended to promote a 'national dialogue' between the authorities and the opposition parties. However, later that month seven other opposition parties, including the proscribed Convention pour le Changement, the FP and the RFD, formed a new grouping, the Cadre Unifié de l'Opposition (CUO), which also stated as its purpose the co-ordination of dialogue between the opposition and the Government pertaining to democratic reform; the UFP was, notably, excluded from the CUO. Consequently, the initial meeting was postponed indefinitely, and, expressing discontent at the situation, in mid-November the UFP announced its withdrawal from the National Assembly. As a result of the departure of the three UFP deputies from the Assembly, the reduced group of opposition deputies was dissolved.

In March 2003 US-led military action in Iraq, aimed at ousting the Baathist regime of Saddam Hussain, prompted protests in Mauritania, with widespread demonstrations held to demand that the Government sever diplomatic relations with the two principal nations involved in the conflict, the United Kingdom and the USA (and also with Israel). As opposition to the Government's broadly pro-US stance intensified in early May, police raided the headquarters of a tolerated—although not officially authorized—Baathist party, the Parti de la Renaissance Nationale (PRN—Nouhoudh). Three leaders of the PRN were arrested on unspecified charges; 13 other Baathists were also arrested over the following days. (Ten of those arrested were later charged with attempting to re-establish Taliaa.)

Opposition to Taya

In early May 2003 Taya's appointment of Lembrabott Ould Mohamed Lemine as Minister of Culture and Islamic Affairs was regarded as an attempt to reduce tensions between the Government and Islamic communities. However, at the end of May the publication of a pro-Islamist weekly journal, *Al-Rayah*, was suspended, and nine Baathists were convicted by a Nouakchott court of engaging in illegal political activity.

The tensions that had been escalating throughout the first half of 2003 culminated in an attempted coup on 8 June. Exchanges of fire were reported near the presidential palace and at other strategic locations in Nouakchott. According to official reports, 15 people (including six civilians) died in ensuing clashes between the insurgents and the security forces, including the Chief of Staff of the Armed Forces, Col Mohamed Lamine Ould Ndiayane. Government forces regained control of the city on 9 June. Taya subsequently stated that Islamists had been responsible for the rebellion, although other sources claimed that the attempted coup had been prompted by tribal rivalries. At least 12 alleged rebel leaders were subsequently arrested, while more than 30 detained Islamists, who had been freed during the disorder, were reported to have surrendered to the authorities. In July another suspected coup leader, Lt Didi Ould M'Hamed, who had fled to Senegal, was extradited to Mauritania.

In July 2003 Taya appointed a new Prime Minister: Sghaïr Ould M'Barek, a Haratin, was regarded as a close ally of the President. A new Government was subsequently formed. Further arrests of Islamists were reported throughout the month. In August more than 80 members of the military who had been arrested following the attempted coup were released, although many more remained in detention. Some 41 Islamists had also been released from detention by the end of the month, although others continued to face charges. In September it was announced that some 30 members of the military, including 20 senior officers, were to be tried in connection with the coup attempt.

In October 2003 the Constitutional Council approved the nominations of six candidates, including Taya, Ould Daddah, Ould Boulkheir and former President Ould Haidalla, for the forthcoming presidential election. Ould Haidalla was widely regarded as the most credible challenger to Taya, but only secured 18.7% of the votes cast, and Taya was re-elected with 66.7%. Some 60.8% of the electorate participated in the election. Opposition candidates accused the Government of perpetrating fraud at the election, which international observers had not been permitted to monitor.

The trial of more than 190 soldiers and civilians accused of participation in the attempted coup in June 2003 and in subsequent conspiracies to overthrow the Head of State commenced in November 2004. The defendants included the alleged leaders of the group, Saleh Ould Hnana, Capt. Abderahmane Ould Mini and Mohammed Ould Sheikhna, the latter being one of 19 people tried *in absentia*; the civilians on trial included opposition leaders Ould Haidalla, Ould Daddah and Cheikh Ould Horma. Ould Hnana and Ould Mini pleaded guilty to the charge of conspiring to overthrow President Taya, while the remaining accused military personnel entered pleas of not guilty. In February 2005 Ould Hnana, Ould Mini, Ould Sheikhna and a fourth officer, Capt. Mohammed Ould Salek, were sentenced to life imprisonment with hard labour, while 79 others received lesser jail sentences; Ould Haidalla, Ould Daddah and Ould Horma were among the 111 acquitted.

Some 15 soldiers were killed in an attack in June 2005 by some 150 assailants on a military post at Lemgheity, in north-eastern Mauritania, for which an Algerian radical Islamist militant group, the Groupe Salafiste pour la Prédication et le Combat (GSPC), subsequently claimed responsibility. Later in June it was reported that the existence of a radical Islamist group based in Mauritania with links to the GSPC, the Mauritanian Group for Preaching and Jihad, had been uncovered. (In May 2007 the trial of 25 suspected Islamist militants commenced in Nouakchott; several of the accused were being tried *in absentia*. Some of the defendants were charged in connection with the attack in Lemgheity, while others were accused of having received training from the GSPC—which had restyled itself as the al-Qa'ida in the Islamic Maghreb, AQIM. In June 24 of the defendants were

acquitted owing to lack of evidence, and one defendant, who had escaped from prison in April 2006, was sentenced, *in absentia*, to two years' imprisonment for falsifying identity papers.)

The Conseil Militaire pour la Justice et la Démocratie

On 3 August 2005, while President Taya was absent from Mauritania, a group of army officers seized control of state broadcasting services and the presidential palace in a bloodless coup. A 16-member Conseil Militaire pour la Justice et la Démocratie (CMJD) under the leadership of Col Ely Ould Mohamed Vall, hitherto the Director of National Security, who had been regarded as a close ally of Taya, announced that it had assumed power. The CMJD stated that it would preside over the country for a transitional period of up to two years, at the end of which democratic elections, in which members of the CMJD and the Government would be prohibited from participating, would be held; although the National Assembly elected in 2001 was dissolved, the 1991 Constitution and most of its institutions (including the Constitutional Council and judicial bodies) were to be retained, as supplemented and amended by the charter of the CMJD. Taya was prevented from re-entering the country and was flown initially to Niamey, Niger; he subsequently took up residence in The Gambia.

On 7 August 2005 Vall appointed Sidi Mohamed Ould Boubacar, hitherto ambassador to France, as Prime Minister, a position that he had previously held in 1992–96; a new, civilian, Government was named on 10 August 2005, and Vall announced the intention of holding a constitutional referendum within one year. None of the ministers in the outgoing Government were reappointed, although, notably, Ahmed Ould Sid'Ahmed, who, in his former capacity as Minister of Foreign Affairs and Co-operation, had been largely responsible for Mauritania's rapprochement with Israel in 1999, was reappointed to that position. In the immediate aftermath of the coup, which was initially widely condemned internationally, the African Union (AU, see p. 188) announced the suspension of Mauritania's membership pending democratic elections. However, the overthrow of Taya's regime was reported to have widespread domestic support.

In September 2005 the new administration announced that it was to offer a general amnesty for political prisoners; 32 such detainees, principally from among those imprisoned in February for their role in attempted coups in 2003 and 2004, were among the first to benefit from the amnesty. In November the CMJD issued a timetable for the transition to democratic rule: a constitutional referendum was to be held in June 2006, followed by elections to municipal councils and to the National Assembly in November, elections to the Senate in January 2007 and, finally, a presidential election in March. A National Independent Electoral Commission was inaugurated at the end of November 2005. Meanwhile, the former ruling PRDS, which had changed its name to the Parti Républicain Démocratique et Renouvellement (PRDR), elected Ethmane Ould Cheikh Ebi el Maali, hitherto ambassador to Kuwait, as its new President.

In March 2006 the CMJD approved proposals presented by the transitional Government on constitutional amendments to be put to a national referendum on 25 June. The principal changes envisaged included limiting the presidential term of office to five years, renewable only once; stipulating a maximum age of 75 years for presidential candidates; and prohibiting the President from holding any other official post, particularly the leadership of a political party. In May the European Union (EU, see p. 271) announced the resumption of co-operation with Mauritania, which had been suspended following the coup in August 2005.

The constitutional referendum was held, as scheduled, on 25 June 2006. Observers from the AU and the Arab League declared their satisfaction with the conduct of the poll. According to official results, 96.9% of the valid votes cast were in favour of the amendments to the Constitution and a turnout of 76.5% of the registered electorate was recorded. In late June 10 political parties, including the RFD, the FP and the Alliance Populaire Progressiste (APP), announced the formation of the Coalition des Forces de Changements (CDFC) to contest the forthcoming legislative and local elections.

Democratic elections

At the legislative elections, which were held as scheduled on 19 November and 3 December 2006, the RFD took 15 seats, the UFP eight, the PRDR seven and the APP five, while the Réformistes Centristes and the Parti Mauritanien de l'Union et du Changement—Hatem both secured four seats; 41 seats were taken by independent candidates. Indirect elections to the Senate took place on 21 January and 4 February 2007 at which independent candidates secured 34 of the 56 seats, while representatives of the CDFC took 15.

The presidential election took place over two rounds on 11 and 25 March 2007. At the first round, which was contested by 20 candidates, Sidi Mohamed Ould Cheikh Abdellahi took 24.8% of votes cast, while Ould Daddah won 20.7%, Zeine Ould Zeidane 15.3% and Ould Boulkheir 9.8%. The rate of voter participation was recorded at 70.1%. Abdellahi and Ould Daddah thus proceeded to the second round, at which Abdellahi (a government minister under both Moktar Ould Daddah and Taya) was elected President, having secured 52.9% of the valid votes cast. Some 67.5% of the electorate participated in the second round. Abdellahi was inaugurated on 19 April, assuming executive powers in place of the CMJD, which was disbanded, and on the following day he appointed Zeidane as Prime Minister. Later in April a new Government was installed. The elections were largely deemed to have been fair and democratic and on 10 April Mauritania was readmitted to the AU.

In December 2007 four French tourists were shot dead by a group of gunmen near the town of Aleg, in the south-west of Mauritania, in what was initially believed to be a robbery. However, in January 2008 two Mauritanian men with previous convictions for training with the GSPC and having links to al-Qa'ida, were arrested in Guinea-Bissau in connection with the incident and were handed over to the Mauritanian authorities. In April one of the suspects, Sidi Ould Sidna, escaped from police custody in Nouakchott, although he was later recaptured, and on 10 April the alleged leader of the group, Marouf Ould Haiba, was arrested. In May Ould Sidna and Ould Haiba were charged for their role in the murder of the French tourists. (They were subsequently sentenced to death, along with Mohammed Ould Chabarnou.) In September 12 Mauritanian soldiers who were abducted and later found dead, were believed to have been victims of an attack by al-Qa'ida militants.

Meanwhile, in May 2008 Zeidane was dismissed as Prime Minister and replaced by Yahya Ould Ahmed el Waghef, leader of the Pacte National pour la Démocratie et le Développement (PNDD). A 31-member Council of Ministers was approved by Abdellahi, which included members of the opposition UPF and the Islamist Rassemblement National pour la Réforme et le Développement (known as Tewassoul). However, on 1 July a motion of no confidence was submitted by 39 legislators from the PNDD, and the Government resigned on 3 July. Abdellahi initially threatened to dissolve the legislature, but then accepted the Government's resignation and invited el Waghef to form a new Council of Ministers, which was appointed on 10 July.

Military coup

On 6 August 2008 President Abdellahi announced the dismissal of four senior military officials, including Gen. Mohamed Ould Abdel Aziz, the Presidential Chief of Staff. Later that day Ould Abdel Aziz led a bloodless military coup to overthrow Abdellahi and declared himself President of a new interim executive, the Haut Conseil d'Etat (HCE), which included two other generals—Mohamed Ould Cheik Mohamed Ahmed and Felix Negre—and eight colonels. Prime Minister el Waghef was also removed from office and detained along with Abdellahi, although the former Prime Minister was released later in August, while Abdellahi remained under house arrest until December. There was little opposition to the coup, and 107 of the 146 members of the National Assembly declared their support for the new regime. Ould Abdel Aziz claimed that a presidential election would be held 'as soon as possible'. The HCE issued a constitutional ordinance, which stated that it would exercise the powers of the President as defined by the Constitution, and granted Ould Abdel Aziz executive powers. On 14 August Ould Abdel Aziz named Moulaye Ould Mohamed Laghdaf, hitherto Mauritania's ambassador to Belgium and the EU, as the new Prime Minister, and in early September a new Government was formed which featured a number of ministers from the previous administration. The coup received widespread international condemnation and on 9 August the AU again announced Mauritania's suspension from the organization.

In April 2009 Ould Abdel Aziz resigned his position as head of the HCE, in order to contest the presidential election. He was also elected as Chairman of a new political party, the Union pour la République (UPR), which had been formed in March. A spokesman for the Front National pour la Défense de la Démocratie (FNDD), a coalition of political parties opposed to the coup, denounced the planned election, claiming it was a means of legitimizing military rule; in May the FNDD and RFD held a joint demonstration in Nouakchott, in which several thousand people protested against the proposed election.

Meanwhile, in early February 2009 the AU's Peace and Security Council imposed further sanctions, including travel restrictions and a freezing of funds, on some 60 Mauritanian nationals, including five members of the HCE, seven government ministers and 10 parliamentary deputies, and called on AU member states to contribute to efforts to restore political order in Mauritania. However, the Chairman of the AU Assembly, Libyan Revolutionary Leader Col Muammar al-Qaddafi, endorsed the electoral timetable set by the HCE for the presidential election (which had been rejected by the opposition and numerous international bodies), while visiting Mauritania in March.

The Senegalese Government hosted negotiations between representatives of the HCE, the FNDD and the RFD in May 2009, and early the following month all parties agreed upon a resolution to the ongoing political crisis. This provided for the formal resignation of Ould Cheikh Abdellahi (which took place on 27 June), the formation of a transitional unity government and the postponement of the presidential election until 18 July. Furthermore, el Waghef was to be released from custody. Thus, on 27 June the HCE was restyled as the Conseil Supérieur de la Défense Nationale and it was announced that Ba Mamadou dit M'Baré, the President of the Senate who had replaced Ould Abdel Aziz as President of the HCE in April, would act as interim President until the presidential election. The new Government, which was also installed on 27 June, was headed by Ould Mohamed Laghdaf. In early July the AU removed the sanctions imposed in February and restored Mauritania's membership of the organization.

Ould Abdel Aziz elected President

The presidential election, contested by 10 candidates, was duly held on 18 July 2009, and, according to official figures, Ould Abdel Aziz received 52.6% of the valid votes cast. His closest challenger, Messaoud Ould Boulkheir, representing the FNDD, secured 16.3%, while Ould Daddah—the candidate of the RFD—was placed third, with 13.7%. Some 64.6% of the registered electorate participated in the ballot. Several of Ould Abdel Aziz's challengers alleged that electoral fraud had been perpetrated, and the President of the National Independent Electoral Commission resigned from his position, citing doubts regarding the 'reliability' of the poll. None the less, Ould Abdel Aziz's victory was confirmed later in July by the Constitutional Council, which rejected formal challenges from Ould Boulkheir, Ould Daddah and Col Ely Ould Mohamed Vall (who had contested the election as an independent, receiving 3.8% of the votes). Ould Abdel Aziz was sworn in as President on 5 August. He reappointed Ould Mohamed Laghdaf to the premiership on 11 August and a new Government was installed.

At partial elections to the Senate held on 8 and 15 November 2009, the UPR secured 13 of the 17 seats contested. In December a number of the main opposition parties, including the APP, RFD and the UFP, established a new coalition, the Coordination de l'Opposition Démocratique (COD). A government reorganization was effected in March 2011.

Anti-Government protests

In early 2011 trade unions and a newly formed group of youth activists, Mouvement du 25 Février, organized a series of protests in Nouakchott and other towns over a number of issues, such as rapidly rising food prices, poor working conditions and youth unemployment. In response, the Government announced various measures intended to appease the protesters, including a programme to distribute land to impoverished people in Nouakchott and plans to create jobs and increase food production. However, in April the Mouvement du 25 Février organized a major anti-Government rally in Nouakchott; police forcibly prevented demonstrators from entering a square from which they had been barred, arresting some 22 of them. Sporadic protests continued in May and June. In September the organization of a nationwide population census, which had begun in May, prompted protests, and ensuing clashes with security forces, in the southern city of Kaedi by members of a black movement known as Touche Pas à Ma Nationalité (TPMN); the leaders of the movement expressed concerns (which were dismissed by the authorities) that the census discriminated against their ethnic group and that its implementation would lead to deportations. The violence spread to other major towns, including Nouakchott, resulting in the arrest of some 56 people; one protester was killed in the southern town of Maghama, when security forces violently dispersed the demonstrators. Although

25 members of the TPMN movement were released in October, continued arrests and arbitrary detentions of a number of its activists were reported in subsequent months.

Meanwhile, in June 2011 Tewassoul decided to join the COD, while the APP terminated its membership of the coalition, citing differences with the other constituent parties. In August elections to the National Assembly, which had been due to take place in October, were postponed in response to demands from the COD, which insisted that an agreement between the political parties first be established to ensure the transparency of the polls; the legislative elections, together with delayed municipal elections, were subsequently rescheduled for 31 March 2012. (Partial elections to the Senate, which had also been postponed in April, were to be conducted concurrently.) In accordance with a political agreement that was reached by pro-Government and opposition parties in October 2011, on 6 March 2012 the National Assembly adopted constitutional amendments prohibiting coups and any unconstitutional change of government, increasing penalties for slavery, and strengthening the powers of the legislature. Later that month, however, the COD staged a protest in Nouakchott, following the further postponement of the parliamentary elections, purportedly until May.

In April 2012 Biram Ould Dah Ould Ebeid, the President of an anti-slavery organization, the Initiative pour la Résurgence du Mouvement Abolitionniste en Mauritanie (IRA), prompted a number of protests, when he burned Islamic law texts that he claimed condoned slavery. Ould Abeid, together with a further nine IRA activists, was arrested after the incident, and in late May he and six others were charged with threatening state security; their trial commenced in June. On 13 June the Government established a new National Independent Electoral Commission, which was tasked with organizing the legislative elections. However, the COD rejected its authority and organized an anti-Government demonstration in the capital. In October President Ould Abdel Aziz was slightly injured after a military patrol fired on his unmarked convoy. Despite speculation attributing the shooting to a failed military coup attempt, it was officially announced that the incident had been accidental. Ould Abdel Aziz subsequently received medical treatment in France.

Several minor cabinet changes were effected during the first half of 2013. In June President Ould Abdel Aziz rejected a compromise proposal by the President of the National Assembly, APP leader Messaoud Ould Boulkheir, for the formation of a national unity government. In early August the Government announced that the long-delayed legislative and local elections would take place on 12 October. However, after the COD declared its intention to boycott the polls, it was announced later in August that the elections would be further postponed until 23 November. As part of an extensive government reorganization in September, a former governor, Mohamed Ould Ahmed Salem, was appointed Minister of the Interior and Decentralization, while Ahmed Ould Teguedi, hitherto Mauritania's representative to the UN, became Minister of Foreign Affairs and Co operation. In early October negotiations were conducted between the Government and the COD on preparations for the forthcoming elections; however, the dialogue ended without agreement, after which it was confirmed that 10 of the 11 COD parties, the exception being Tewassoul, would boycott the elections on the grounds that they would not be conducted fairly. In the same month Ould Abdel Aziz restructured the armed forces, with the creation of a separate command for each of the armed services.

The 2013 elections

The first round of elections to the National Assembly, which was contested by 74 parties, duly took place on 23 November 2013; the leader of Tewassoul, Mohamed Jemil Ould Mansour, claimed that voting had been marred by widespread irregularities. After a second round, on 21 December, it was announced that the UPR had won a total of 75 of the 146 contested seats (and its allied parties a further 34), while Tewassoul had received 16; 'moderate' opposition parties Parti El Wiam Démocratique et Social (El Wiam) and the APP took 10 and seven seats, respectively. (In addition to ballots cast by district constituency list, the categories of national list and women's national list had been introduced to increase the proportion of women representatives.) An official voter turnout of 76.4% was recorded. In the local elections the UPR won 161 of the 218 contested municipal councils, while Tewassoul took 18.

In mid-February 2014 a new Government was established, again under the premiership of Ould Mohamed Laghdaf, following the formal resignation of the previous administration; 11 new ministers were appointed, although allocation of the principal portfolios was largely unchanged. During an official visit to Mauritania later in February the UN Special Rapporteur on slavery commended efforts by the Government to eliminate the practice (following an announcement in December 2013 that a special tribunal would be established to prosecute cases of slavery), while urging the complete implementation of legislative measures. In early March 2014 the alleged desecration of a copy of the Koran at a mosque precipitated protests in Nouakchott and other towns; one student was killed in clashes between demonstrators and police.

Recents development: Ould Abdel Aziz wins a second term

On 4 June 2014 a demonstration against the presidential election was attended by several thousand supporters of the opposition. The poll, boycotted by the COD, took place as scheduled on 21 June; just 56.5% of the electorate participated and Ould Abdel Aziz won a convincing victory securing 81.9% of the votes. Of the four other candidates, Biram Ould Abeid, who stood as an independent, came second with 8.7%, while Boydeil Ould Houmeid, the leader of El Wiam, won 4.5%. Both the AU and the Arab League expressed their satisfaction with the manner in which the election had been conducted, although the Arab League expressed concern at the heavy security presence at polling stations. Meanwhile, the opposition claimed a victory on the basis that it had persuaded a significant number of voters not to participate.

Ould Abdel Aziz was sworn in as President on 2 August 2014 and pledged to fight mismanagement and inequality in the country. He also expressed his intention to combat terrorism by strengthening the security forces. On 20 August Ould Mohamed Laghdaf resigned and a new Prime Minister, Yahya Ould Hademine, was appointed. Despite the President's promise of change there were just eight new appointments to the Council of Ministers, most notably that of a black defence minister, Ba Amadou Bathia.

In late August 2014 the authorities banned a public rally by the black Mauritanian Forces de Libération des Africains de Mauritanie (FLAM), a movement suppressed during Taya's presidency in the 1980s, when its leadership was either arrested or forced into exile. The FLAM leader, Samba Thiam, had returned to Mauritania from the USA in 2012 with the intention of transforming the movement into a political party.

As part of a widespread clampdown on anti-slavery activists in the country, on 11 November 2014 Ould Abeid and a number of other IRA activists were arrested during a protest march in Rosso, in the south-west of the country. Their detention was widely condemned by a number of bodies, including the human rights organization, Amnesty International, and the European Parliament. Following the arrests a team from the Office of the UN High Commissioner for Human Rights in Mauritania visited Rosso and subsequently urged the Mauritanian Government to conduct an investigation into the events of 11 November, including the conduct of the security forces. The trial of Ould Abeid and the other arrested activists—charged with inciting violence, disturbing public order, offending members of the authorities, and belonging to an unregistered organization—began in Rosso in late December. In mid-January 2015 Ould Abeid and two others were sentenced to two years' imprisonment while the remaining defendants were acquitted. Also in mid-January President Ould Abdel Aziz announced a government reorganization in which Fatma Vall Mint Soueinae was appointed Minister of Foreign Affairs and Co-operation and Mokhtar Ould Diay became Minister of Finance.

Foreign Affairs

Regional relations

Diplomatic relations with Senegal were resumed in April 1992, and the process of reopening the border began in May. In June 2000 relations between Mauritania and Senegal deteriorated after Mauritania accused the new Senegalese administration of relaunching an irrigation project, which involved the use of joint waters from the Senegal river, in contravention of the Organisation pour la Mise en Valeur du Fleuve Sénégal (see p. 448) project. The dispute escalated when the Mauritanian authorities requested that all of its citizens living in Senegal return home and issued the estimated 100,000 Senegalese nationals living in Mauritania with a 15-day deadline by which to leave the country. In mid-June, following mediation by King Muhammad VI of

Morocco and the Presidents of The Gambia and Mali, the Mauritanian Government announced that the decision to expel Senegalese citizens had been withdrawn and that Mauritanians living in Senegal could remain there. President Abdoulaye Wade of Senegal visited Mauritania later that month and announced that the irrigation project had been abandoned.

In February 1989 Mauritania was a founder member, with Algeria, Libya, Morocco and Tunisia, of the Union of the Arab Maghreb (UMA, see p. 450). Diplomatic relations with Libya, severed in 1995, were none the less restored in 1997. Following the overthrow of Qaddafi's regime in 2011, his brother-in-law and former head of military intelligence, Abdullah Senussi, was arrested at Nouakchott airport in March 2012; the Libyan Government submitted a formal request for Senussi's extradition, which was also sought by France and the International Criminal Court. Although President Ould Abdel Aziz initially insisted that Senussi be tried in Mauritania on charges of illegal entry before being extradited, following diplomatic pressure the Mauritanian Government approved his extradition to Libya in early September. Relations between Mauritania and Morocco, having improved somewhat during the 2000s, subsequently became strained owing to Mauritania's recognition, under President Ould Abdel Aziz, of the Polisario Front, the Algerian-backed movement demanding an end to Moroccan presence in Western Sahara. In mid-2014, however, there were hopes for an improvement in Moroccan-Mauritanian relations when Ould Abdel Aziz sent a letter to King Muhammad VI wishing his country 'continued progress and prosperity'.

Relations with both Libya and Burkina Faso were severely strained in the wake of allegations by the Mauritanian Government that those two countries had provided support to rebel elements in the Mauritanian military, accused of participating in the failed coup of June 2003 and of subsequently conspiring to overthrow President Taya (see *Opposition to Taya*). It was alleged that Ould Hnana and Ould Sheikhna, who were held responsible by the Mauritanian authorities for leading the 2003 coup, had been granted refuge in Burkina Faso, while the Libyan Government was accused of assisting the rebels. Libya and Burkina Faso strenuously denied the accusations. In March 2005 a ministerial commission appointed by the UMA to investigate the Mauritanian allegations against Libya concluded that Qaddafi had 'no connection' to the events in Mauritania.

In response to the kidnapping of four European citizens by AQIM in early 2009, and the seizure in Mauritania (and subsequent transfer to Mali) of three Spanish aid workers and two Italian tourists later that year, in January 2010 Mali and Mauritania announced plans to strengthen security co-operation. The following month, however, bilateral relations became strained after the Malian Government approved the release of four Islamist militia (including one Mauritanian citizen), detained in April 2009 on weapons charges, in exchange for the freeing of a French citizen taken hostage in November. Both Algeria and Mauritania subsequently withdrew their ambassadors from Bamako, claiming that Mali's decision to release the terrorists was an infringement of the agreement on security co-operation reached at the September regional summit. In March 2010 foreign ministers from seven Saharan states meeting in the Algerian capital, Algiers, including Mauritania, Mali and Algeria, agreed that they would commence the sharing of operational information and co-operate in their actions against AQIM in an attempt to 'collectively confront the threat of terrorism'. Meanwhile, in February an alleged Mauritanian terrorist, Oumar Ould Sid'Ahmed, who was believed to have been involved in the seizure of the Spanish and Italian citizens in late 2009, was extradited from Mali to Mauritania; in the following month he and six others were charged with kidnapping offences. In July 2010 Ould Sid'Ahmed was sentenced to 12 years' imprisonment for kidnapping the Spanish aid workers (who were released by AQIM in March and August). In September Mauritania's ambassador to Mali returned to his post. Shortly afterwards Mauritanian military forces, in co-operation with the Malian Government, launched a series of ground and air attacks against suspected AQIM militants in northern Mali. In December AQIM abducted a paramilitary officer from the south-eastern town of Adel Begrou, subsequently offering to release him in exchange for the release of two of its imprisoned members. In July 2012 the Mauritanian authorities freed two Islamists from prison, in exchange for the release by a splinter group of AQIM of three European aid workers who had been kidnapped in Algeria in October 2011 and subsequently held hostage in Mali.

In early 2013 Mauritania hosted further regional discussions focusing on security in Mali. Following a meeting with President Ould Abdel Aziz in Nouakchott in April, the French Minister of Foreign Affairs, Laurent Fabius, announced that the Mauritanian Government had agreed to contribute some 1,800 troops to a UN peacekeeping mission in Mali, which commenced operations in July. According to the office of the UN High Commissioner for Refugees (UNHCR), some 72,000 Malian refugees had fled to Mauritania by August, although the humanitarian situation in Mali subsequently appeared to stabilize. On 30 January 2014 President Ould Abdel Aziz assumed the rotational presidency of the AU for a period of one year.

Other external relations

Widespread controversy was provoked both domestically, and in Arab countries, by the establishment of full diplomatic relations between Mauritania and Israel in October 1999. Following the resumption of the Palestinian uprising in September 2000, the Mauritanian Government came under renewed pressure to suspend diplomatic relations with Israel. A visit by the Mauritanian Minister of Foreign Affairs and Co-operation, Dah Ould Abdi, to Israel in May 2001 provoked further controversy, particularly as a result of an appeal by the Arab League, issued earlier that month, for all member countries to cease political contacts with Israel. A further meeting between President Taya, Ould Abdi and Shimon Peres, his Israeli counterpart, in Nouakchott, in October 2002, provoked further controversy. A visit to Mauritania by the Israeli Deputy Prime Minister and Minister of Foreign Affairs, Silvan Shalom, in May 2005 coincided with the detention of several Islamists, and prompted a number of anti-Israeli protests in Nouakchott. In April 2007 newly elected President Abdellahi appealed for a public debate on the future of Mauritania's diplomatic ties with Israel. The Israeli embassy in Nouakchott was attacked in February 2008 by gunmen who opened fire and injured three people. Nevertheless, relations did not seriously deteriorate until after the military coup of 2008. In January 2009 Mauritania recalled its ambassador from Israel and suspended diplomatic relations in response to the Israeli invasion of the Gaza Strip in December 2008; in March 2009 it was reported that the Israeli embassy in Nouakchott had been closed down and the ambassador ordered to leave the country. The Mauritanian Minister of Foreign Affairs and Co-operation announced the 'complete and definitive' abrogation of diplomatic relations with Israel in March 2010. In December 2013 Mauritania signed an economic and technical co-operation agreement with the People's Republic of China.

CONSTITUTION AND GOVERNMENT

Under the provisions of the Constitution adopted in July 1991 and amended in June 2006 and March 2012, the Head of State is the President, who is elected, by universal adult suffrage, for a term of five years, renewable only once. Legislative power is vested in the National Assembly (Al-Jamiya al-Wataniyah), which is elected by universal suffrage for a period of five years, and in the Senate (Majlis al-Shuyukh), which is elected by municipal leaders for a six-year term, one-third of its membership being renewed every two years. All elections are conducted in the context of a multi-party political system. The President of the Republic appoints the Prime Minister and, on the recommendation of the latter, the members of the Council of Ministers.

For the purpose of local administration, Mauritania is divided into 12 wilayat (regions) and the capital district of Nouakchott, together comprising a total of 53 moughataa (counties), which are themselves subdivided into 216 communes (districts).

REGIONAL AND INTERNATIONAL CO-OPERATION

Mauritania is a member of the African Union (AU, see p. 188), of the Organisation pour la Mise en Valeur du Fleuve Sénégal (see p. 448) and of the Union of the Arab Maghreb (see p. 450). Mauritania withdrew from the Economic Community of West African States (see p. 258), with effect from 31 December 2000, owing to decisions adopted by the organization at its summit in December 1999, including the integration of the armed forces of member states and the removal of internal border controls and tariffs.

Mauritania became a member of the UN in 1961 and was admitted to the World Trade Organization (WTO, see p. 431) in 1995.

ECONOMIC AFFAIRS

In 2013, according to estimates by the World Bank, Mauritania's gross national income (GNI), measured at average 2011–13 prices, was US $4,114m., equivalent to $1,060 per head (or $2,850 on an international purchasing-power parity basis). During 2004–13, it was estimated, the population increased at an average annual rate of 2.7%, while gross domestic product (GDP) per head increased, in real terms, by an average of 3.0% per year. According to the World Bank, overall GDP increased, in real terms, at an average annual rate of 5.8% in 2004–13; GDP increased by 6.7% in 2013.

Agriculture (including forestry and fishing) contributed 15.5% of GDP in 2013. In 2015, according to FAO estimates, about 49.2% of the labour force were employed in the sector. Owing to the unsuitability of much of the land for crop cultivation, output of staple foods (millet, sorghum, rice and pulses) is insufficient for the country's needs. Livestock-rearing is the principal occupation of the rural population. Fishing, which in 2013 provided 17.3% of export earnings, supplies 5%–10% of annual GDP and a sizeable proportion of budgetary revenue, and also makes a significant contribution to domestic food requirements. During 2004–13, according to UN estimates, agricultural GDP increased by an average of 5.0% per year; the sector's GDP increased by 8.7% in 2013.

Industry (including mining, manufacturing, construction and power) provided 41.5% of GDP in 2013, and engaged 9.1% of the economically active population in 2000. During 2004–13, according to UN estimates, industrial GDP increased at an average annual rate of 7.1%; it increased by 8.4% in 2013.

Mining contributed 30.4% of GDP in 2013, and engaged 5.1% of the economically active population in 2000. The principal activity in this sector is the extraction of iron ore, exports of which contributed 47.4% of total merchandise export earnings in 2013. Gypsum, salt, gold and copper are also mined. Other exploitable mineral resources include diamonds, phosphates, sulphur, peat, manganese and uranium. Many international companies were involved in offshore petroleum exploration in Mauritania in the early 2000s, with reserves at the Shafr el Khanjar and Chinguetti fields estimated at 450m.–1,000m. barrels; production commenced at Chinguetti in February 2006. According to UN estimates, the GDP of the mining sector (and utilities) increased by an average of 7.2% per year in 2004–13; the sector's GDP increased by 10.7% in 2013.

The manufacturing sector contributed 4.1% of GDP in 2013, and engaged 1.0% of the economically active population in 2000. Fish-processing is the most important activity. The processing of minerals (including imported petroleum) is also of some significance. According to UN estimates, manufacturing GDP increased at an average annual rate of 2.6% in 2004–13; it increased by 2.1% in 2013.

Construction contributed 7.0% of GDP in 2013, and engaged 2.6% of the economically active population in 2000. According to UN estimates, construction GDP increased at an average annual rate of 6.9% in 2004–13; it increased by 0.2% in 2013.

Mauritania began to utilize electricity generated at hydroelectric installations constructed under the auspices of the Organisation pour la Mise en Valeur du Fleuve Sénégal (OMVS) in late 2002, thus reducing the country's dependence on power generated at thermal stations. In 2013 a 15-MW photovoltaic solar power station was officially inaugurated. Imports of petroleum products comprised 20.1% of the total value of merchandise imports in 2013.

The services sector contributed 43.0% of GDP in 2013, and engaged 38.1% of the economically active population in 2000. According to UN estimates, the combined GDP of the services sector increased at an average rate of 4.4% per year during 2004–13. Services GDP rose by 6.1% in 2013.

According to IMF figures, in 2013 Mauritania recorded a visible merchandise trade deficit of US $392.0m. and there was a deficit of $1,262.0m. on the current account of the balance of payments. In 2013 the principal source of imports (18.9%) was the United Arab Emirates; other major suppliers were France, Belgium and the USA. The principal markets for exports (excluding exports of petroleum, gold and copper) in that year were the People's Republic of China (46.4%) and Italy. The principal exports in 2013 were iron ore, fish and petroleum. The principal imports in that year were various equipment and appliances, petroleum products, food products, construction materials, and road vehicles and parts.

Mauritania recorded an overall budget surplus of UM 58,300m. in 2013. The country's general government gross debt was UM 1,097,450m. in 2013, equivalent to 87.6% of GDP. Total external debt in 2012 was US $3,348m., of which $2,940m. was public and publicly guaranteed debt. In 2012 the cost of servicing long-term public and publicly guaranteed debt and repayments to the IMF was equivalent to 4.9% of the value of exports of goods, services and income (excluding workers' remittances). The annual rate of inflation averaged 6.2% in 2004–13; consumer prices increased by an average of 4.1% in 2013. The overall rate of unemployment in 2000 was 28.9%.

The exploitation, from the mid-2000s, of previously untapped petroleum reserves, principally at offshore locations, had a significant impact on Mauritania's economy, which had hitherto been largely dependent on fishing and on the extraction of iron ore. Following the election of Gen. Mohamed Ould Abdel Aziz to the presidency in July 2009, co-operation with the IMF was reinstated and a three-year Extended Credit Facility (ECF) agreement, totalling US $118.1m. in support of efforts to address corruption and poverty and revive development initiatives, was approved in March 2010. Severe drought affected economic performance in 2011, but GDP growth recovered to 7.6% in 2012, and remained strong, at 6.7%, in 2013. In accordance with IMF recommendations, the Mauritanian authorities had pursued a policy of gradual elimination of subsidies, under which domestic fuel prices were raised to international levels in 2012. In mid-2013 the IMF completed its sixth and final review of the country's economic performance under the ECF-supported programme and approved a tranche equivalent to US $16.9m.; the authorities were strongly commended for their fiscal consolidation and structural reform efforts. Government policy continued to be praised by international institutions; a World Bank report in mid-2014 favoured the recent prioritization of public investment in energy and key infrastructure projects. However, the report also referred to the economy's vulnerabilities related to lack of diversification, volatility of international prices and reliance on foreign inflows. In February 2014 it was announced that EU funding of €195m. would be provided in the areas of food security, rule of law and health care for 2014–20. GDP growth declined slightly in 2014, to 6.4%, and was projected to decline still further to 5.5% in 2015, according to the IMF. This was due to reduced growth in the mining sector and lower private investment and consumption. The economy was also seen to be at risk from decreasing iron ore prices and weak trading activity. In addition, there was concern regarding the effects of the prolonged drought; according to the UN World Food Programme, in early 2015 some 20%–30% of Mauritania's population was suffering from high food insecurity.

PUBLIC HOLIDAYS

2016: 1 January (New Year's Day), 1 May (Labour Day), 4 May* (Leilat al-Meiraj, Ascension of Muhammad), 25 May (African Liberation Day, anniversary of the OAU's foundation), 6 July* (Korité—Id al-Fitr, end of Ramadan), 12 September* (Tabaski—Id al-Adha, Feast of the Sacrifice), 2 October* (Islamic New Year), 28 November (Independence Day), 11 December* (Mouloud, Birth of Muhammad).

* These holidays are determined by the Islamic lunar calendar and may vary by one or two days from the dates given.

Statistical Survey

Source (unless otherwise stated): Office National de la Statistique, BP 240, Nouakchott; tel. 45-25-28-80; fax 45-25-51-70; e-mail webmaster@ons.mr; internet www.ons.mr; Banque Centrale de Mauritanie, Avenue de l'Indépendance, BP 623, Nouakchott; tel. 45-25-22-06; fax 45-25-27-59; e-mail info@bcm.mr; internet www.bcm.mr.

Area and Population

AREA, POPULATION AND DENSITY

Area (sq km)	1,030,700*
Population (census results)†	
1–15 November 2000	2,508,159
25 March–8 April 2013‡	
Males	1,707,463
Females	1,751,527
Total	3,458,990
Population (official projection at mid-year)§	
2014	3,545,620
2015	3,631,775
Density (per sq km) at mid-2015	3.5

* 397,950 sq miles.
† Figures include nomads, totalling 128,163 in 2000 and 71,122 (males 38,006, females 33,116) in 2013.
‡ Preliminary results.
§ Projection not adjusted to take account of preliminary results of 2013 census.

POPULATION BY AGE AND SEX
(official projections at mid-2015)

	Males	Females	Total
0–14 years	720,052	686,758	1,406,810
15–64 years	1,036,483	1,067,105	2,103,588
65 years and over	59,391	61,986	121,377
Total	1,815,926	1,815,849	3,631,775

Note: Projections not adjusted to take account of preliminary results of 2013 census.

REGIONS
(population at 2013 census, preliminary)

Region	Area ('000 sq km)	Population	Density (per sq km)	Chief town
Adrar . . .	215	62,678	0.3	Atâr
Assaba . . .	37	323,761	8.8	Kiffa
Brakna . . .	33	309,867	9.4	Aleg
Dakhlet-Nouadhibou .	22	123,232	5.6	Nouadhibou
Gorgol . . .	14	331,558	23.7	Kaédi
Guidimagha .	10	262,785	26.3	Sélibaby
Hodh Echargui.	183	429,707	2.3	Néma
Hodh el Gharbi.	53	294,165	5.6	Aïoun el Atrous
Inchiri . . .	47	17,457	0.4	Akjoujt
Nouakchott (district) . .	1	899,887	899.9	Nouakchott
Tagant . . .	95	79,103	0.8	Tidjikja
Tiris Zemour .	253	52,820	0.2	Zouerate
Trarza . . .	68	271,970	4.0	Rosso
Total . . .	1,030	3,458,990	3.4	

PRINCIPAL TOWNS
(population at census of 2000*)

Nouakchott (capital)	558,195	Kiffa		32,716
Nouadhibou . .	72,337	Bougadoum . . .		29,045
Rosso	48,922	Atâr		24,021
Boghé	37,531	Boutilimit . . .		22,257
Adel Bagrou . .	36,007	Theiekane . . .		22,041
Kaédi	34,227	Ghabou . . .		21,700
Zouerate . . .	33,929	Mal		20,488

* With the exception of Nouakchott, figures refer to the population of communes (municipalities), and include nomads.

Mid-2014 (incl. suburbs, UN estimate): Nouakchott 945,804 (Source: UN, *World Urbanization Prospects: The 2014 Revision*).

BIRTHS AND DEATHS
(annual averages, UN estimates)

	2000–05	2005–10	2010–15
Birth rate (per 1,000)	37.5	36.0	34.3
Death rate (per 1,000)	9.6	9.2	8.7

Source: UN, *World Population Prospects: The 2012 Revision*.

Life expectancy (years at birth): 61.4 (males 59.9; females 62.9) in 2012 (Source: World Bank, World Development Indicators database).

ECONOMICALLY ACTIVE POPULATION
('000, FAO estimates at mid-year)

	2013	2014	2015
Agriculture, etc.	841	863	886
Total (incl. others)	1,694	1,746	1,800

Source: FAO.

Health and Welfare

KEY INDICATORS

Total fertility rate (children per woman, 2012)	4.7
Under-5 mortality rate (per 1,000 live births, 2012) . . .	84
HIV/AIDS (% of persons aged 15–49, 2012)	0.4
Physicians (per 1,000 head, 2009)	0.13
Hospital beds (per 1,000 head, 2006)	0.40
Health expenditure (2011): US $ per head (PPP)	107
Health expenditure (2011): % of GDP	5.9
Health expenditure (2011): public (% of total)	65.2
Access to water (% of persons, 2012)	50
Access to sanitation (% of persons, 2012)	27
Total carbon dioxide emissions ('000 metric tons, 2010) . .	2,214.9
Carbon dioxide emissions per head (metric tons, 2010) . .	0.6
Human Development Index (2013): ranking	161
Human Development Index (2013): value	0.487

For sources and definitions, see explanatory note on p. vi.

Agriculture

PRINCIPAL CROPS
('000 metric tons)

	2011	2012	2013
Rice, paddy	161.1	243.0*	192.0*
Maize	11.6	19.0*	6.0*
Sorghum	24.6	30.0*	94.0*
Millet	0.5	0.7†	0.7†
Peas, dry†	11.0	7.5	8.5
Cow peas, dry†	10.4	12.0	13.0
Beans, dry†	11.9	12.0	12.4
Dates†	21.4	22.0	18.9

* Unofficial figure.
† FAO estimate(s).

Aggregate production ('000 metric tons, may include official, semi-official or estimated data): Total cereals 202 in 2011, 298 in 2012, 297 in 2013; Total pulses 52 in 2011, 53 in 2012, 56 in 2013; Total roots and tubers 7 in 2011–12, 8 in 2013; Total vegetables (incl. melons) 5 in 2011–13; Total fruits (excl. melons) 24 in 2011, 25 in 2012, 22 in 2013.

Source: FAO.

LIVESTOCK
('000 head, year ending September)

	2011	2012	2013
Cattle	1,747	1,750*	1,850*
Goats*	5,550	5,600	5,650
Sheep*	8,900	9,000	9,100
Asses*	170	170	170
Horses*	20	20	20
Camels*	1,400	1,425	1,500
Chickens*	4,400	4,500	4,600

* FAO estimate(s).

Source: FAO.

LIVESTOCK PRODUCTS
('000 metric tons, FAO estimates)

	2011	2012	2013
Goat meat	15.0	16.5	16.5
Camel meat	23.5	23.5	23.5
Chicken meat	4.5	4.6	4.6
Camel milk	26.3	26.8	27.1
Cows' milk	126.0	126.0	126.0
Sheep's milk	115.5	118.3	118.3
Goats' milk	123.8	124.2	126.0
Hen eggs	5.5	5.6	5.8

Source: FAO.

Forestry

ROUNDWOOD REMOVALS
('000 cubic metres, excl. bark, FAO estimates)

	2011	2012	2013
Sawlogs, veneer logs and logs for sleepers	1	1	1
Other industrial wood	2	2	2
Fuel wood	1,877	1,919	1,962
Total	1,880	1,922	1,965

Source: FAO.

SAWNWOOD PRODUCTION
('000 cubic metres, incl. railway sleepers)

	2005	2006	2007*
Broadleaved (hardwood)	7	14	14
Total	7	14	14

* FAO estimates.

2008–13: Production assumed to be unchanged from 2007 (FAO estimates).

Source: FAO.

Fishing

('000 metric tons, live weight)

	2010	2011	2012
Freshwater fishes*	15.0	15.0	15.0
Sardinellas	147.7	165.0	216.2
European pilchard (sardine) . .	16.7	28.0	11.4
European anchovy	5.0	19.6	24.9
Jack and horse mackerels . . .	33.7	47.2	55.6
Chub mackerel	4.6	16.9	22.6
Octopuses	15.8	16.7	25.2
Total catch (incl. others)* . .	276.2	372.0	437.7

* FAO estimates.

Source: FAO.

Mining

('000 metric tons)

	2010	2011	2012
Gypsum	65.2	72.2	75.0
Iron ore: gross weight	11,534	11,160	11,200
Iron ore: metal content* . . .	7,500	7,250	7,280

* Estimates.

Source: US Geological Survey.

Industry

SELECTED PRODUCTS
('000 metric tons unless otherwise indicated)

	2010	2011	2012
Cement*	552	565	644
Crude steel*†	5	5	5
Electric energy (million kWh) .	527.1	541.5	605.9

* Data from US Geological Survey.
† Estimated production.

2013: Electric energy (million kWh) 662.3.

Finance

CURRENCY AND EXCHANGE RATES

Monetary Units
  5 khoums = 1 ouguiya (UM).

Sterling, Dollar and Euro Equivalents (31 December 2013)
  £1 sterling = 492.154 ouguiyas;
  US $1 = 299.000 ouguiyas;
  €1 = 412.351 ouguiyas;
  1,000 ouguiyas = £2.03 = $3.34 = €2.43.

Average Exchange Rate (ouguiyas per US $)
  2011   281.118
  2012   296.620
  2013   300.682

BUDGET
('000 million ouguiyas)

Revenue*	2011	2012	2013
Tax revenue	183.7	250.5	254.0
Taxes on income and profits . .	54.9	80.5	85.7
Tax on business profits . . .	27.4	41.8	41.3
Tax on wages and salaries . .	19.7	31.0	33.6
Taxes on goods and services . .	100.5	133.5	128.1
Value-added tax	64.8	101.3	102.3
Turnover taxes	30.0	23.7	23.2
Tax on petroleum products . .	2.4	3.0	3.4
Other excises	1.4	4.4	5.7
Taxes on international trade .	22.3	29.1	30.2
Non-tax revenue	109.8	99.1	201.0
Fishing royalties and penalties .	36.9	8.7	60.9
Revenue from public enterprises .	32.7	62.0	49.8
Capital revenue	6.0	4.8	2.1
Other revenue (incl. special accounts)	16.8	4.0	65.3
Petroleum revenue	22.9	21.5	20.0
Total	316.4	371.1	474.9

Expenditure†	2011	2012	2013
Current expenditure . . .	238.9	293.0	272.7
Wages and salaries	89.1	94.7	103.8
Equipment maintenance and supplies	51.3	54.6	61.5
Transfers and subsidies . . .	60.2	105.7	70.5
Interest on public debt . . .	15.0	12.6	17.1
Capital expenditure	75.2	126.2	172.1
Restructuring expenditure . .	—	—	0.1
Total	314.1	419.2	444.9

* Excluding grants received ('000 million ouguiyas): 7.7 in 2011; 7.4 in 2012; 23.8 in 2013.
† Excluding restructuring and net lending ('000 million ouguiyas): 9.9 in 2011; 10.8 in 2012; 0.0 in 2013.

INTERNATIONAL RESERVES
(US $ million at 31 December)

	2010	2011	2012
Gold*	16.1	18.0	19.1
IMF special drawing rights . .	0.1	1.5	3.5
Foreign exchange	271.7	483.2	946.0
Total	287.9	502.7	968.6

* Valued at market-related prices.

Source: IMF, *International Financial Statistics*.

MONEY SUPPLY
(million ouguiyas at 31 December)

	2010	2011	2012
Currency outside banks . . .	91,252	113,723	115,293
Demand deposits at deposit money banks	172,001	222,926	246,525
Total money (incl. others) . .	264,517	338,012	363,488

Source: IMF, *International Financial Statistics*.

COST OF LIVING
(Consumer Price Index; base: April 2002–March 2003 = 100)

	2011	2012	2013
Food (incl. beverages)	201.2	209.9	219.2
Clothing (incl. footwear) . . .	180.0	194.0	204.0
Rent and utilities	164.8	170.3	176.9
All items (incl. others) . . .	179.6	188.5	196.2

NATIONAL ACCOUNTS
('000 million ouguiyas at current prices, provisional)

Expenditure on the Gross Domestic Product

	2011	2012	2013
Government final consumption expenditure	177.2	198.5	212.5
Private final consumption expenditure	708.6	863.5	844.2
Gross capital formation . . .	386.2	525.4	474.6
Total domestic expenditure .	1,272.0	1,587.4	1,531.3
Exports of goods and services . .	858.5	831.0	883.1
Less Imports of goods and services	929.1	1,244.2	1,164.6
GDP in purchasers' values .	1,201.4	1,174.2	1,249.8
GDP in constant 1998 prices .	380.9	407.4	434.8

Gross Domestic Product by Economic Activity

	2011	2012	2013
Agriculture, hunting, forestry and fishing	169.1	168.4	175.7
Mining and quarrying	442.8	345.3	345.6
Manufacturing	37.0	42.4	47.0
Construction	61.0	72.3	79.5
Wholesale and retail trade, restaurants and hotels . . .	110.4	126.7	140.8
Finance, insurance and real estate	112.0	125.4	140.1
Transport and communications .	40.6	47.4	50.8
Public administration and defence	135.2	143.6	157.3
Sub-total	1,108.2	1,071.6	1,136.8
Indirect taxes, less subsidies . .	93.2	102.7	112.9
GDP in purchasers' values	1,201.4	1,174.2	1,249.8

BALANCE OF PAYMENTS
(US $ million)

	2011	2012	2013
Exports of goods f.o.b.	2,775.8	2,641.0	2,652.0
Imports of goods f.o.b.	−2,467.4	−3,170.3	−3,044.0
Trade balance	308.3	−529.3	−392.0
Services (net)	−551.8	−863.1	−814.0
Balance on goods and services	−243.5	−1,392.4	−1,206.0
Other income (net)	−155.6	−190.6	−196.0
Balance on goods, services and income	−399.1	−1,583.0	−1,402.0
Current transfers (net) . . .	151.3	319.8	141.0
Private unrequited transfers (net)	31.4	42.7	57.0
Official transfers	120.0	277.1	84.0
Current balance	−247.7	−1,263.3	−1,262.0
Capital account (net)	0.0	31.6	5.0
Direct investment (net) . . .	588.8	1,381.1	1,126.0
Official medium- and long-term loans	243.1	449.8	216.0
Other capital	−332.6	−109.3	223.0
Net errors and omissions . . .	1.5	−1.2	−292.0
Overall balance	253.1	488.7	16.0

External Trade

PRINCIPAL COMMODITIES
('000 million ouguiyas)

Imports	2011	2012	2013
Food products	92.8	126.5	124.1
Cosmetic chemical products . .	11.8	26.1	29.4
Petroleum products	192.5	234.6	241.2
Construction materials . . .	64.9	67.0	72.5
Road vehicles and parts . . .	48.7	74.0	70.2
Various equipment and appliances	224.8	247.9	577.1
Total (incl. others)	689.7	881.8	1,197.9

Exports	2011	2012	2013
Iron ore	393.1	299.7	382.4
Copper	50.4	92.6	91.4
Fish	121.9	182.7	139.7
Petroleum	30.2	80.4	65.3
Total (incl. others)	691.0	777.8	807.3

PRINCIPAL TRADING PARTNERS
('000 million ouguiyas)

Imports c.i.f.	2011	2012	2013
Australia	13.0	6.8	8.0
Belgium	96.5	137.6	115.3
Brazil	9.8	18.1	15.9
China, People's Republic	36.1	48.6	47.0
France	84.5	98.6	116.8
Germany	18.5	27.1	36.8
Italy	2.4	6.4	12.8
Japan	13.2	19.2	15.9
Malaysia	7.3	9.5	7.0
Morocco	15.1	26.6	26.3
Netherlands	18.8	15.3	12.7
Senegal	15.7	12.9	10.7
Singapore	2.4	3.7	6.8
South Africa	7.0	8.4	7.9
Spain	29.0	48.2	45.3
Switzerland	13.1	7.1	8.4
Thailand	6.2	6.6	n.a.
Turkey	10.6	28.7	22.7
United Arab Emirates	178.4	206.8	226.6
United Kingdom	41.4	5.1	8.8
USA	20.8	43.2	67.9
Total (incl. others)	689.7	881.8	1,197.9

Exports c.i.f.	2011	2012	2013
Belgium	31.2	11.1	0.1
China, People's Republic	255.3	342.6	374.4
France	58.7	36.4	20.8
Germany	42.5	34.8	36.9
Italy	69.2	54.0	47.7
Japan	35.8	69.6	31.6
Russia	7.5	8.5	13.2
Spain	47.3	39.6	20.8
United Kingdom	0.3	1.9	2.4
Total (incl. others)	691.0	777.8	807.3

Transport

ROAD TRAFFIC
(motor vehicles registered)

	2004	2005	2006
Passenger cars	6,033	6,040	6,182
Government vehicles	251	317	369
Specialist vehicles	413	542	504

SHIPPING

Flag Registered Fleet
(at 31 December)

	2012	2013	2014
Number of vessels	70	71	72
Total displacement ('000 grt)	25.8	26.0	26.2

Source: Lloyd's List Intelligence (www.lloydslistintelligence.com).

International Seaborne Freight Traffic
(Port of Nouakchott, '000 metric tons)

	2011	2012	2013
Goods loaded	348	373	387
Goods unloaded	2,506	3,173	3,008

Source: Port Autonome de Nouakchott.

CIVIL AVIATION
(traffic on scheduled services)

	2007	2008	2009
Kilometres flown (million)	1	1	1
Passengers carried ('000)	155	154	142
Passenger-km (million)	68	68	64
Total ton-km (million)	6	7	6

Source: UN, *Statistical Yearbook*.

Passengers carried ('000): 114 in 2010; 118 in 2011; 296 in 2012.

Communications Media

	2011	2012	2013
Telephones ('000 main lines in use)	72.3	65.1	54.0
Mobile cellular telephones ('000 subscribers)	3,314.8	4,023.7	3,988.2
Internet subscribers	6,700	n.a.	n.a.
Broadband subscribers	6,120	6,490	7,532

Source: International Telecommunication Union.

Education

(2012/13 unless otherwise indicated)

	Institutions	Teachers	Students Males	Females	Total
Pre-primary	n.a.	251*	n.a.	n.a.	4,856*
Primary	2,676†	17,293	281,859	287,094	568,953
Secondary	n.a.	6,652	127,751	43,514	171,265
Tertiary	4‡	399§	12,634§	5,244§	17,878§

* 2004/05.
† 1998/99.
‡ 1995/96.
§ 2011/12.

Pupil-teacher ratio (primary education, UNESCO estimate): 40.1 in 2011/12.

Adult literacy rate (UNESCO estimates): 58.6% (males 65.3%; females 52.0%) in 2011.

Sources: mainly UNESCO Institute for Statistics and Ministry of National Education, Nouakchott.

Directory

While no longer an official language, French is still widely used in Mauritania, especially in the commercial sector. Many organizations are therefore listed under their French names, by which they are generally known.

The Government

HEAD OF STATE

President: MOHAMED OULD ABDEL AZIZ (inaugurated 5 August 2009, re-elected 21 June 2014).

COUNCIL OF MINISTERS
(May 2015)

Prime Minister: YAHYA OULD HADEMINE.

Minister of Justice: SIDI OULD ZEIN.

Minister of Foreign Affairs and Co-operation: FATMA VALL MINT SOUEINAE.

Minister of National Defence: BA AMADOU BATHIA.

Minister of the Interior and Decentralization: MOHAMED OULD AHMED SALEM OULD MOHAMED RARÉ.

Minister of Economic Affairs and Development: SIDI OULD TAH.

Minister of Finance: MOKHTAR OULD DIAY.

Minister of Islamic Affairs and Original Education: AHMED OULD EHIL DAOUD.

Minister of Petroleum, Energy and Mines: MOHAMED SALEM OULD BÉCHIR.

Minister of the Civil Service, Labour and the Modernization of the Administration: SEYIDNA ALI OULD MOHAMED KHOUNA.

Minister of Health: AHMEDOU OULD HADEMINE OULD JELVOUNE.

Minister of Fisheries and the Maritime Economy: NANY OULD CHROUGHA.

Minister of Trade, Industry and Tourism: NAHA MINT HAMDI OULD MOUKNASS.

Minister of Housing, Urban Development and Land Settlement: ISMAÏL OULD SADEGH.

Minister of Agriculture: BRAHIM OULD M'BARECK OULD MOHAMED EL MOKTAR.

Minister of Stockbreeding: Dr FATMA HABIB.

Minister of Equipment and Transport: ISSELKOU OULD AHMED IZIDBIH.

Minister of Water Resources and Sanitation: MOHAMED OULD KHOUNA.

Minister of National Education: BA OUSMANE.

Minister of Higher Education and Scientific Research: SIDI OULD SALEM.

Minister of Employment, Vocational Training and Information and Communication Technologies: DIA MOKTAR MALAL.

Minister of Culture and Handicrafts: HINDOU MINT AININA.

Minister of Youth and Sport: COUMBA BA.

Minister of Relations with Parliament and of Civil Society, Government Spokesperson: IZIDBIH OULD MOHAMED MAHMOUD.

Minister of Social Affairs, Childhood and Families: LEMINA MINT KOTOB OULD MOMMA.

Minister of the Environment and Sustainable Development: AMEDI CAMARA.

Minister, Secretary-General of the Government: HAWA TANDIA.

Minister-delegate to the Minister of Foreign Affairs and Co-operation, in charge of Maghreb and African Affairs and of Mauritanians Abroad: KHADIJETOU MBARECK FALL.

MINISTRIES

Office of the President: BP 184, Nouakchott; tel. and fax 45-25-26-36.

Office of the Prime Minister: BP 237, Nouakchott; tel. 45-25-33-37; internet www.primature.gov.mr.

Office of the Secretary-General of the Government: BP 184, Nouakchott.

Ministry of Agriculture: BP 366, Nouakchott; tel. 45-25-15-00; fax 45-25-74-75; internet www.agriculture.gov.mr.

Ministry of the Civil Service, Labour and the Modernization of the Administration: BP 193, Nouakchott; tel. and fax 45-25-84-10; internet www.modernisation.gov.mr.

Ministry of Culture and Handicrafts: BP 223, Nouakchott; tel. 45-25-11-30.

Ministry of Economic Affairs and Development: 303 Ilot C, BP 5150, Nouakchott; tel. 45-25-16-12; fax 45-25-51-10; e-mail nfomaed@mauritania.mr; internet www.economie.gov.mr.

Ministry of Employment, Vocational Training and Information and Communication Technologies: Immeuble du Gouvernement, ave Jemal Abdelnasser, BP 5758, Nouakchott; tel. 45-25-45-59; fax 45-24-37-36; internet www.emploi.gov.mr.

Ministry of the Environment and Sustainable Development: Nouakchott.

Ministry of Equipment and Transport: BP 237, Nouakchott; tel. 45-25-33-37; internet www.transports.gov.mr.

Ministry of Finance: BP 001, Nouakchott; tel. and fax 45-00-01-02; e-mail ministre_finance@mf.mr; internet www.finances.gov.mr.

Ministry of Fisheries and the Maritime Economy: BP 137, Nouakchott; tel. 45-25-46-07; fax 45-25-31-46; e-mail ministre@mpem.mr; internet www.peches.gov.mr.

Ministry of Foreign Affairs and Co-operation: BP 230, Nouakchott; tel. 45-25-26-82; fax 45-25-28-60; e-mail info@maec.gov.mr; internet www.diplomatie-mr.com.

Ministry of Health: BP 177, Nouakchott; tel. 45-25-20-52; fax 45-25-22-68; internet www.sante.gov.mr.

Ministry of Higher Education and Scientific Research: BP 227, Nouakchott; tel. 45-29-71-61; internet www.education.gov.mr.

Ministry of Housing, Urban Development and Land Settlement: Nouakchott.

Ministry of the Interior and Decentralization: BP 195, Nouakchott; tel. 45-25-36-61; fax 45-25-36-40; e-mail paddec@mauritania.mr; internet www.interieur.gov.mr.

Ministry of Islamic Affairs and Original Education: Nouakchott; internet www.affislam.gov.mr.

Ministry of Justice: BP 350, Nouakchott; tel. 45-25-10-83; fax 45-25-70-02; internet www.justice.gov.mr.

Ministry of National Defence: Nouakchott; internet www.defense.gov.mr.

Ministry of National Education: BP 387, Nouakchott; tel. 45-25-12-37; fax 45-25-12-22; internet www.enseignement.gov.mr.

Ministry of Petroleum, Energy and Mines: Nouakchott; tel. 45-25-71-40; internet www.petrole.gov.mr.

Ministry of Relations with Parliament and Civil Society: Nouakchott; internet www.relations-parlement.gov.mr.

Ministry of Social Affairs, Childhood and Families: Nouakchott.

Ministry of Stockbreeding: Nouakchott.

Ministry of Trade, Industry and Tourism: BP 182, Nouakchott; tel. 45-25-35-72; fax 45-25-76-71; internet www.commerce.gov.mr.

Ministry of Water Resources and Sanitation: BP 4913, Nouakchott; tel. 45-25-71-44; fax 45-29-42-87; e-mail saadouebih@yahoo.fr; internet www.hydraulique.gov.mr.

Ministry of Youth and Sport: Nouakchott.

President

Presidential Election, 21 June 2014

Candidate	Votes	% of votes
Mohamed Ould Abdel Aziz	580,062	81.94
Biram Ould Dah Ould Ebeid	61,757	8.72
Ibrahim Moctar Sarr	31,381	4.43
Boydiel Ould Houmeid	31,245	4.41
Lalla Meryem Mint Moulaye Idriss	3,453	0.49
Total	707,898	100.00

Legislature

NATIONAL ASSEMBLY
(Al-Jamiya al-Wataniyah)

National Assembly: ave de l'Indépendance, BP 185, Nouakchott; tel. 45-25-11-30; fax 45-25-70-78; internet www.assembleenationale.mr.

President: MOHAMED OULD BOILIL.

General Election, 23 November and 21 December 2013

Party	Constituency seats	National list seats	Women's national list seats	Total seats
Parti de l'Union pour la République	66	4	5	75
Rassemblement National pour la Réforme et le Développement (Tewassoul)	10	3	3	16
Parti EL WIAM	8	1	1	10
L'Alliance Populaire Progressiste	3	2	2	7
Parti El Karam	4	1	1	6
Union pour la Démocratie et le Progrès	4	1	1	6
Alliance pour la Justice et la Démocratie/ Mouvement pour la Rénovation	2	1	1	4
SURSAUT	2	1	1	4
Parti EL VADILA	1	1	1	3
Parti Ravah	1	1	1	3
Parti Républicain pour la Démocratie et le Renouveau	1	1	1	3
Parti de l'Unité et du Développement	1	1	1	3
El Islah	1	—	—	1
Parti de l'Authenticité Mauritanienne	—	1	—	1
Parti Dignité et Action	1	—	—	1
Parti de la Justice Démocratique	—	—	1	1
Parti du Peuple Démocratique	1	—	—	1
Parti Unioniste Démocratique Socialiste	—	1	—	1
Total	**106**	**20**	**20**	**146**

SENATE

(Majlis al-Shuyukh)

Senate: ave de l'Indépendance, BP 5838, Nouakchott; tel. 45-25-68-77; fax 45-25-73-73; internet www.senat.mr.

First Vice-President: MOHAMED EL HACEN OULD EL HAJ.

The total number of seats in the Senate is 56, with three seats reserved for representatives of the Mauritanian diaspora.

Election Commission

National Independent Electoral Commission: 230 ave Moktar Ould Daddah, BP 4550, Nouakchott; tel. 45-24-15-40; fax 45-24-15-44; e-mail ceni@ceni.mr; internet www.ceni.mr; 15 mems; Pres. ABDALLAHI OULD SOUEID AHMED.

Advisory Council

Economic and Social Council: Nouakchott; Pres. MESSAOUD OULD BOULKHEIR.

Political Organizations

A total of 51 political parties or alliances contested the 2013 legislative elections.

Alliance pour la Justice et la Démocratie/Mouvement pour la Rénovation (AJD/MR): Nouakchott; Leader IBRAHIMA MOCTAR SARR.

Alliance Populaire Progressiste (APP): Nouakchott; internet www.app.mr; f. 1991; mem. of Coalition des Forces de Changements, formed in advance of legislative and local elections in 2006; mem. of Coordination de l'Opposition Démocratique coalition, formed in 2010; Pres. MESSAOUD OULD BOULKHEIR.

Alternative (Al-Badil): Nouakchott; f. 2006; mem. of Coordination de l'Opposition Démocratique coalition, formed in 2010; Leader MOHAMED YEHDHIH OULD MOKTAR EL HASSEN.

Forces de Libération Africaines de Mauritanie—Renovation (FLAM—Renovation): Nouakchott; tel. 22-28-77-40 (mobile); internet www.flam-renovation.org; f. 2006 in split from clandestine, exiled, Forces de Libération Africaines de Mauritanie; represents interests of Afro- (Black) Mauritanians; Leader MAMADOU BOCAR BÂ.

Parti El Wiam Démocratique et Social: Leader BOYDEIL OULD HOUMEID.

Parti pour la Liberté, l'Egalité et la Justice (PLEJ): Nouakchott; internet www.plej.biz; mem. of Coordination de l'Opposition Démocratique coalition, formed in 2010; Pres. MAMADOU ALASSANE BÂ.

Parti Mauritanien pour la Défense de l'Environnement (PMDE—Les Verts): Nouakchott; internet pmde.hautetfort.com; ecologist; Pres. MOHAMED OULD SIDI OULD DELLAHI.

Parti Mauritanien pour Renouvellement et la Concorde: Nouakchott; f. 2001; Leader MOULAY EL-HASSEN OULD JIYID.

Parti Mauritanien de l'Union et du Changement—Hatem: Nouakchott; f. 2005 by leadership of the fmr prohibited Knights of Change militia and reformist elements of the fmr ruling Parti Républicain Démocratique et Social; Pres. SALEH OULD HNANA; Sec.-Gen. ABDERAHMANE OULD MINI.

Parti National pour la Démocratie et le Développement (PNDD): Nouakchott; Leader YAHYA OULD EL WAGHEF.

Parti du Rassemblement du Peuple Mauritanien: Nouakchott; f. 2009 by parliamentary deputies in support of ruling military junta; Leader Dr LOULEID OULD WEDAD.

Parti Républicain pour la Démocratie et le Renouveau (PRDR): ZRB, Tevragh Zeina, Nouakchott; tel. 45-29-18-36; fax 45-29-18-00; e-mail info@prdr.mr; internet www.prdr.mr; f. 2006 to replace Parti Républicain Démocratique et Social, the fmr ruling party, prior to coup of Aug. 2005; Leader SIDI MOHAMED OULD MED VALL DIT GHRINY.

Parti Travailliste Mauritanien: Nouakchott; f. 2001; Leader MOHAMED EL HAFEDH OULD DENNA.

Rassemblement des Forces Démocratiques (RFD): Ilot K, 120, BP 4986, Nouakchott; tel. 45 25 67-46; fax 45-25-65-70; e-mail info@rfd-mauritanie.org; internet www.rfd-mauritanie.org; f. 2001; mem. of Coordination de l'Opposition Démocratique coalition, formed in 2010; Pres. AHMED OULD DADDAH.

Rassemblement National pour la Réforme et le Développement (RNRD) (Tewassoul): f. 2007; Islamist; mem. of Coordination de l'Opposition Démocratique coalition, formed in 2010; Leader MOHAMED JEMIL OULD MANSOUR.

Réformistes Centristes: Nouakchott; f. 2006; moderate Islamist grouping.

Reward (Sawab): Nouakchott; f. 2004; social democratic; Chair. of Central Council MOHAMED MAHMOUD OULD GHOULMA; Pres. ABDESSELAM OULD HORMA.

Union du Centre Démocratique (UCD): Nouakchott; f. 2005 by fmr mems of the Parti Républicain Démocratique et Social, the fmr ruling party; Pres. CHEIKH SID'AHMED OULD BABA.

Union pour la Démocratie et le Progrès (UDP): Ilot V, 70, Tevragh Zeina, BP 816, Nouakchott; tel. 45-25-52-89; fax 45-25-29-95; f. 1993; Pres. NAHA HAMDI MINT.

Union des Forces de la Majorité Présidentielle: Nouakchott; coalition comprising eight political parties supporting Pres. Mohamed Ould Abdel Aziz.

Union des Forces du Progrès (UFP) (Ittihad Quwa al-Taqaddum): Nouakchott; e-mail ufpweb2@yahoo.fr; internet www.ufpweb.org; tel. 45-29-32-66; fax 45-24-35-86; e-mail infos@ufpweb.org; f. 2000; mem. of Coordination de l'Opposition Démocratique coalition, formed in 2010; Pres. MOHAMED OULD MAOULOUD; Sec.-Gen. MOHAMED EL MOUSTAPHA OULD BEDREDDINE.

Union de la Jeunesse Démocratique (UJD): f. 2008; promotes patriotism and moderate Islamic values, opposes extremism; Pres. JEDDOU OULD AHMAD.

Union pour la République (UPR): Nouakchott; f. 2009; Chair. ISSELKOU OULD IZID BIH; Sec.-Gen. OUMAR OULD MAATALLAH.

The clandestine **Forces de Libération Africaines de Mauritanie (FLAM)** was founded in 1983 in Senegal to represent Afro-Mauritanians (; BP 5811, Dakar-Fann, Senegal; tel. +221 822-80-77; e-mail ba_demba@yahoo .fr; internet members .lycos .co .uk/flamnet; Pres. SAMBA THIAM); a faction broke away from this organization and returned to Mauritania in early 2006, forming the Forces de Libération Africaines de Mauritanie—Renovation. A further group based in exile is the **Front Arabo-Africain de Salut contre l'Esclavage, le Racisme et le Tribalisme—FAAS** (e-mail faas@caramail .com; internet membres .lycos .fr/faas).

Diplomatic Representation

EMBASSIES IN MAURITANIA

Algeria: Ilot A, Tevragh Zeina, BP 625, Nouakchott; tel. 45-25-35-69; fax 45-25-47-77; Ambassador ZAHANI ABDEL HAMID.

China, People's Republic: rue 42–133, Tevragh Zeina, BP 257, Nouakchott; tel. 45-25-20-70; fax 45-25-24-62; e-mail chinaemb_mr@mfa.gov.cn; internet mr.china-embassy.org; Ambassador WU DONG.

Congo, Democratic Republic: Tevragh Zeina, BP 5714, Nouakchott; tel. 45-25-46-12; fax 45-25-50-53; e-mail ambardc.rim@caramail.com; Chargé d'affaires a.i. TSHIBASU MFUAD.

Egypt: Villa 468, Tevragh Zeina, BP 176, Nouakchott; tel. 45-25-21-92; fax 45-25-33-84; Ambassador Dr YOUSSOUF AHMED CHARGHAOUI.

France: rue Ahmed Ould Hamed, Tevragh Zeina, BP 231, Nouakchott; tel. 45-29-96-99; fax 45-29-69-38; e-mail ambafrance.nouakchott-amba@diplomatie.gouv.fr; internet www.ambafrance-mr.org; Ambassador JOËL MEYER.

Germany: Rue Mamadou Konaté, Tevragh Zeina, BP 372, Nouakchott; tel. 45-25-17-29; fax 45-25-17-22; e-mail info@nouakchott.diplo.de; internet www.nouakchott.diplo.de; Ambassador BIRGITTA SIEFKER-EBERLE.

Iraq: Tevragh Zeina, Nord Villa 399, Nouakchott; tel. 45-24-32-52; fax 45-24-32-51; e-mail nokemb@iraqmfamail.com; Ambassador AHMED NAEEF RASHID AL-DULAIMI.

Japan: Tevragh Zeina, BP 7810, Nouakchott; tel. 45-25-09-77; fax 45-25-09-76; internet www.mr.emb-japan.go.jp; Ambassador JUN YOSHIDA.

Kuwait: Tevragh Zeina, BP 345, Nouakchott; tel. 45-25-33-05; fax 45-25-41-45; Ambassador ADNAN ABDELLAH AL-AHMED.

Libya: BP 673, Nouakchott; tel. 45-25-52-02; fax 45-25-50-53; Ambassador HASSAN MOHAMED KHALIFA.

Mali: Tevragh Zeina, BP 5371, Nouakchott; tel. 45-25-40-81; fax 45-25-40-83; e-mail ambmali@hotmail.com; Ambassador ETHMANE KONÉ.

Morocco: 569 ave Charles de Gaulle, Tevragh Zeina, BP 621, Nouakchott; tel. 45-25-14-11; fax 45-29-72-80; e-mail sifmanktt@mauritel.mr; Ambassador ABDERRAHMANE BENOMAR.

Nigeria: Ilot P9, BP 367, Nouakchott; tel. 45-25-23-04; fax 45-25-23-14; Ambassador Alhaji BALA MOHAMED SANI.

Qatar: ZRB blvd 449, rue Zaina, Nouakchott; tel. 45-25-23-99; fax 45-25-68-87; e-mail nouakchott@mofa.gov.qa; Ambassador MOHAMMED ABDERRAHMANE AL-KEBISSI.

Russian Federation: rue Abu Bakr, BP 221, Nouakchott; tel. 45-25-19-73; fax 45-25-52-96; e-mail ambruss@opt.mr; Ambassador VLADIMIR BAYBAKOV.

Saudi Arabia: Las Balmas, Zinat, BP 498, Nouakchott; tel. 45-25-44-35; fax 45-25-29-49; e-mail mremb@mofa.gov.sa; internet embassies.mofa.gov.sa/sites/mauritania; Ambassador SAOUD BEN ABDEL AZIZ AL-JABIRI.

Senegal: Villa 500, Tevragh Zeina, BP 2511, Nouakchott; tel. 45-25-72-90; fax 45-25-72-91; Ambassador MAHMOUDOU CHEIKH KANE.

South Africa: Hotel Tfeila, Mezzanine Floor, Salon el-Waha, ave Charles de Gaulle, BP 2006, Nouakchott; tel. 45-24-55-90; fax 45-24-55-91; e-mail nouakchott@foreign.gov.za; Ambassador JOHANNES JACOBUS SPIES.

Spain: BP 232, Nouakchott; tel. 45-25-20-80; fax 45-25-40-88; e-mail emb.nouakchott@mae.es; Ambassador ANTONIO TORRES.

Syria: Tevragh Zeina, BP 288, Nouakchott; tel. 45-25-27-54; fax 45-25-45-00; e-mail amb-syrie@toptechnology.mr; Ambassador SAID EL-BENI.

Tunisia: BP 631, Nouakchott; tel. 45-25-28-71; fax 45-25-18-27; Ambassador MOHAMED BEN AYAD.

Turkey: nr Stade Olympique, Tevragh Zeina, BP 5155 Nouakchott; tel. 45-25-78-00; Ambassador MEHMET BILIR.

United Arab Emirates: Tevragh Zeina Quarter, ZRA 742 bis, Nouakchott; tel. 45-25-10-98; fax 45-25-09-92; e-mail embeau@mauritel.mr; Ambassador MOHAMED ABDALLAHI TIKAWI.

USA: rue Abdallaye, BP 222, Nouakchott; tel. 45-25-26-60; fax 45-25-15-92; e-mail tayebho@state.gov; internet mauritania.usembassy.gov; Ambassador LARRY EDWARD ANDRÉ, Jr.

Yemen: Tevragh Zeina, BP 4689, Nouakchott; tel. 45-25-55-91; fax 45-25-56-39; Ambassador MOHAMED ALI YAHYA SHIBAN.

Judicial System

The Code of Law was promulgated in 1961 and subsequently modified to incorporate Islamic institutions and practices. The President of the Republic guarantees the independence of judicial power and is assisted in this task by the Higher Council of the Magistracy. The main courts comprise a Supreme Court, three Courts of Appeal, 13 Regional Tribunals, 13 Labour Tribunals and 53 Departmental Civil Courts. An Audit Court has jurisdiction in financial matters. The members of the High Court of Justice are elected by the National Assembly and the Senate.

Shari'a (Islamic) law was introduced in February 1980. A special Islamic court was established in March of that year, presided over by a magistrate of Islamic law, assisted by two counsellors and two *ulemas* (Muslim jurists and interpreters of the Koran). A five-member High Council of Islam, appointed by the President, advises upon the conformity of national legislation to religious precepts, at the request of the President. A High Council of Fatwas and Appeals for Reprieve, comprising nine members, renewable every two years, was established in 2012.

Audit Court (Cour des Comptes): ave Jemal Abd'Enassir, BP 592, Nouakchott; tel. 45-25-34-04; fax 45-25-49-64; e-mail ccomptes@cc.gov.mr; internet www.cdcmr.mr; audits all govt institutions; Pres. AHMED SALEM OULD HAMMA KHATTAR.

Constitutional Council: f. 1992; includes 6 mems, 3 nominated by the Head of State and 3 designated by the Presidents of the Senate and National Assembly; Pres. SGHAIR OULD M'BAREK; Sec.-Gen. SY ADAMA.

Courts of Appeal: at Nouakchott, Nouadhibou and Kiffa.

High Council of Fatwas and Appeals for Reprieve (Haut Conseil de la Fatwa et des Recours Gracieux): Nouakchott; f. 2012; comprises 9 members, renewable every 2 years; issues fatwas with respect to interpretations of Islamic law; also has the authority to resolve disputes that are not under any court of law; Pres. MOHAMED EL MOCTAR OULD M'BALLA.

High Council of Islam (al-Majlis al-Islamiya al-A'la'): Nouakchott; f. 1992; Pres. AHMED HACEN OULD CHEIKH MOHAMED HAMED.

High Court of Justice: Nouakchott; f. 1961; comprises an equal number of appointees elected from their membership by the National Assembly and the Senate, following each partial or general renewal of those legislative bodies; competent to try the President of the Republic in case of high treason, and the Prime Minister and members of the Government in case of conspiracy against the State.

Supreme Court: BP 201, Palais de Justice, Nouakchott; tel. and fax 45-25-67-40; internet www.coursupreme.ma; f. 1961; comprises an administrative chamber, two civil and social chambers, a commercial chamber and a criminal chamber; Pres. YAHFDHOU OULD MOHAMED YOUSSEF.

Religion

ISLAM

Islam is the official religion, and the population are almost entirely Muslims of the Malekite rite. The major religious groups are the Tijaniya and the Qadiriya. Chinguetti, in the region of Adrar, is the seventh Holy Place in Islam. A High Council of Islam (Haut Conseil Islamique) supervises the conformity of legislation to Muslim orthodoxy.

Haut Conseil Islamique: BP 5949, Nouakchott; tel. 45-25-19-91; fax 45-25-19-17; Pres. AHMED EL HACEN Ould Cheikh Mohamed Hamed.

CHRISTIANITY

Roman Catholic Church

Mauritania comprises the single diocese of Nouakchott, directly responsible to the Holy See. The Bishop participates in the Bishops' Conference of Senegal, Mauritania, Cabo Verde and Guinea-Bissau, based in Dakar, Senegal. There are an estimated 4,500 adherents, mainly non-nationals, in the country.

Bishop of Nouakchott: Most Rev. MARTIN ALBERT HAPPE, Evêché, BP 5377, Nouakchott; tel. 45-25-04-27; fax 45-25-37-51; e-mail mgrmartinhappe@yahoo.fr.

The Press

Al-Akhbar: ave Charles de Gaulle, BP 5346, Nouakchott; tel. 22-00-03-90; e-mail fr.redaction@alakhbar.info; internet fr.alakhbar.info; f. 2003; weekly; Arabic and French; Dir EL HAÏBA OULD CHEIKH SIDATI; Editor-in-Chief MOHAMED DIOP.

Biladi: Immeuble BMCI, 5e étage, apt 508, BP 1122, Nouakchott; tel. and fax 45-24-02-75; e-mail oneina1@gmail.com; internet www.rmibiladi.com; weekly; French; Dir of Publication MOUSSA OULD HAMED; Editor-in-Chief ABDELVETAH OULD MOHAMED.

Le Calame/Al-Qalam: rue 42–62, Tevragh Zeina, 348 Kennedy ave Ouest, BP 1059, Nouakchott; tel. 45-24-08-29; fax 45-24-08-30; e-mail lecalame@yahoo.fr; internet www.lecalame.info; f. 1993; weekly; Arabic and French; independent; Editors-in-Chief RIYAD OULD AHMED EL-HADI (Arabic edn), AHMED OULD CHEIKH (French edn).

Châab: BP 371, Nouakchott; tel. 45-25-29-40; fax 45-25-55-20; e-mail chaab@ami.mr; internet www.ami.mr; f. 1975; daily; Arabic; also publ. in French *Horizons*; publ. by Agence Mauritanienne de l'Information; Dir of Publication YARBA OULD SGHAÏR.

Challenge: BP 1346, Nouakchott; tel. and fax 45-29-22-46; e-mail challengehebdo@yahoo.fr; internet www.challenge-mr.com; weekly.

Ech-tary: BP 1059, Nouakchott; tel. 45-25-50-65; e-mail info@echtary.net; internet www.echtary.com; fortnightly; Arabic; satirical.

Essirage Hebdo: Nouakchott; tel. 45-29-18-51; e-mail info@essirage.net; internet www.essirage.net; weekly.

L'Essor: BP 5310, Nouakchott; tel. 22-30-21-68 (mobile); fax 45-25-95-95; e-mail sidiel2000@yahoo.fr; monthly; the environment and the economy; Dir SIDI EL-MOCTAR CHEÏGUER; circ. 2,500.

L'Eveil-Hebdo: BP 587, Nouakchott; tel. 46-41-28-76; e-mail symoudou@yahoo.fr; internet www.eveilhebdo.info; f. 1991; weekly; independent; Dir of Publication MAMADOU SY.

Journal Officiel: BP 188, Nouakchott; tel. 45-25-33-37; fax 45-25-34-74; fortnightly.

Maghreb Hebdo: BP 5266, Nouakchott; tel. 45-25-98-10; fax 45-25-98-11; f. 1994; weekly; Dir KHATTRI OULD DIÈ.

Mauritanies1: Nouakchott; e-mail contact@mauritanies1.com; internet www.mauritanies1.com; monthly.

Al-Mourabit: Nouakchott; tel. 45-24-95-35; e-mail brahimbakar@almourabit.mr; internet www.almourabit.mr; weekly; French; Editor-in-Chief BRAHIM OULD BAKAR OULD SNEIBA.

Nouakchott-Info: Immeuble Abbas, Tevragh Zeina, BP 1905, Nouakchott; tel. 45-25-02-71; fax 45-25-54-84; e-mail nouakchottinfo@yahoo.fr; internet www.ani.mr; f. 1995; daily; independent; Arabic and French; Dir of Publication and Editor-in-Chief MOHAMED MAHMOUD ABOÜL MAALY.

Points Chauds Online: Ilot L, près de la garde Nationale (face de Mauritanie couleur), Nouakchott; tel. 46-57-57-02; fax 36-63-15-95; e-mail infopointschauds@gmail.com; internet www.pointschauds.info; f. 2002; Editor-in-Chief MOULAYE NAJIM MOULAYE ZEINE.

Le Quotidien de Nouakchott: BP 1153, Nouakchott; tel. 45-24-53-74; e-mail khalioubi@yahoo.fr; internet www.quotidien-nouakchott.com; French; Editor-in-Chief KHALILOU DIAGANA.

Tahalil Hebdo: BP 5205, Nouakchott; tel. 46-31-92-07; fax 22-31-92-07; e-mail contact@journaltahalil.com; internet www.journaltahalil.com; weekly; French; Editor SALIHI ISSELMOU.

La Tribune: BP 6227, Nouakchott; tel. 46-46-18-82 (mobile); e-mail contact@la-tribune.info; internet www.la-tribune.info; weekly; French; Editor-in-Chief KISSIMA TOCKA DIAGANA.

NEWS AGENCY

Agence Mauritanienne de l'Information (AMI): BP 371, Nouakchott; tel. 45-25-29-40; fax 45-25-45-87; e-mail ami@ami.mr; internet www.ami.mr; fmrly Agence Mauritanienne de Presse; state-controlled; news and information services in Arabic and French; Man. Dir YARBA OULD SGHAÏR.

Publishers

Imprimerie Commerciale et Administrative de Mauritanie: BP 164, Nouakchott; textbooks, educational.

Imprimerie Nationale: BP 618, Nouakchott; tel. 45-25-44-38; fax 45-25-44-37; f. 1978; state-owned; Pres. RACHID OULD SALEH; Man. Dir ISSIMOU MAHJOUB.

GOVERNMENT PUBLISHING HOUSE

Société Nationale d'Impression: BP 618, Nouakchott; Pres. MOUSTAPHA SALECK OULD AHMED BRIHIM.

Broadcasting and Communications

TELECOMMUNICATIONS

In 2012 there were three mobile cellular telephone operators in Mauritania, one of which, Mauritel, also provided fixed-line telephone services. In that year there were some 4m. subscribers to mobile telephone services and 65,100 subscribers to fixed-line services.

Chinguitel: Carrefour Cité SMAR, Nouakchott; tel. 22-00-02-91 (mobile); internet www.chinguitel.mr; provides mobile cellular, fixed-line and internet services; Dir-Gen. ABDERAHMAN MOHAMED AHMED OUSMANE.

Mauritel: 563 ave du Roi Fayçal, BP 7000, Nouakchott; tel. 45-25-76-00; fax 45-25-17-00; e-mail webmaster@mauritel.mr; internet www.mauritel.mr; fmrly Société Mauritanienne des Télécommunications; provides fixed-line and mobile cellular telephone services; 46% state-owned, 51% owned by the Compagnie Mauritanienne de Communication (created by Maroc Télécom), 3% owned by Mauritel employees; Dir-Gen. KAMAL OKBA.

Société Mauritano-Tunisienne de Télécommunications (Mattel): 441 ave Charles de Gaulle, Tevragh Zeina, BP 3668, Nouakchott; tel. 45-29-53-54; fax 45-29-81-03; e-mail mattel@mattel.mr; internet www.mattel.mr; f. 2000; operates mobile cellular communications network; Dir-Gen. MOHAMED ALI ESSAHILI.

Regulatory Authority

Autorité de Régulation: 428 rue 23023 Ksar, BP 4908, Nouakchott; tel. 45-29-12-70; fax 45-29-12-79; e-mail webmaster@are.mr; internet www.are.mr; f. 1999; Pres. MOHAMED YAHYA OULD HORMA.

BROADCASTING

In July 2010 the National Assembly passed legislation allowing the establishment of private broadcasters for the first time in Mauritania, thereby ending almost 50 years of state monopoly. In November 2011 the Haute Autorité de la Presse et de l'Audiovisuel awarded licences to five radio and two television channels: Sahara FM, Radio Cobenni, Mauritanides FM, Radio Tenwir and Radio Nouakchott; Mauri–Vision and Télévision Watanya. A further three licences were issued to television channels in March 2013.

Regulatory Authority

Haute Autorité de la Presse et de l'Audiovisuel (HAPA): ave du Roi Fayçal-Ksar, en face de l'UTM, BP 3192, Nouakchott; tel. 45-24-10-88; fax 45-24-10-51; internet www.hapa.mr; f. 2006; Pres. HAMOUD OULD M'HAMED.

Radio

Radio Mauritanie (RM): ave Gamal Abdel Nasser, BP 200, Nouakchott; tel. and fax 45-25-21-64; e-mail rm@radiomauritanie.com; internet www.radiomauritanie.mr; f. 1958; state-controlled; broadcasts 2 channels; 5 transmitters; radio broadcasts in Arabic, French, Sarakolé, Toucouleur and Wolof; Dir MOHAMED CHEIKH OULD SIDI MOHAMED.

Radio Mauritanie also operates 10 local radio stations. Broadcasts from RFI (FM), Africa N°1 and Radio Monte Carlo Doualiya are also received in the country.

Television

Télévision de Mauritanie (TVM): BP 5522, Nouakchott; tel. 45-25-40-67; fax 45-25-40-69; e-mail dgtvm@tvmsat.mr; internet www.tvm.mr; f. 1982; Dir-Gen. KHIRA MINT CHEIKHANI.

Finance

(cap. = capital; res = reserves; dep. = deposits; m. = million;
br(s).= branch(es); amounts in ouguiyas unless otherwise indicated)

BANKING

Central Bank

Banque Centrale de Mauritanie (BCM): ave de l'Indépendance, BP 623, Nouakchott; tel. 45-25-22-06; fax 45-25-27-59; e-mail info@bcm.mr; internet www.bcm.mr; f. 1973; bank of issue; cap. 200m., res 2,869.7m., dep. 96,225.3m. (2009); Gov. SID'AHMED OULD RAISS; 4 brs.

Commercial Banks

Attijari Bank Mauritanie: 91/92 rue Mamadou Konaté, Nouakchott; tel. 45-29-63-74; fax 45-29-64-40; cap. 3,398m. (Dec. 2010); Dir-Gen. HASSAN OUSTANI.

Banque El Amana (BEA): rue Mamadou Konaté, BP 5559, Nouakchott; tel. 45-25-59-53; fax 45-25-34-95; e-mail info@bea.mr; internet www.bea.mr; f. 1996; 72% privately owned, 27% owned by Société Nationale Industrielle et Minière; cap. 6,000.0m., res 63.6m., dep 23,789.7m. (Dec. 2012); CEO AHMED SALEM BOUNA MOKHTAR; Gen. Man. AHMED SALEM ELY EL KORY.

Banque pour le Commerce et l'Industrie (BCI): ave Gamal Abdel Nasser, BP 5050, Nouakchott; tel. 45-29-28-76; fax 45-29-28-77; e-mail info@bci-banque.com; internet www.bci-banque.com; f. 1999; cap. 4,000m. (Dec. 2010); Pres. and Dir-Gen. ISSELMOU OULD DIDI OULD TAJEDINE; 11 brs.

Banque Mauritanienne pour le Commerce International (BMCI): Immeuble Afarco, ave Gamal Abdel Nasser, BP 622, Nouakchott; tel. 45-25-28-26; fax 45-25-20-45; e-mail info@bmci.mr; internet www.bmci.mr; f. 1974; 95.82% owned by Group Abbas; Pres. and Dir-Gen. MOULAY SIDI OULD HACEN OULD ABASS; 18 brs.

Banque Nationale de Mauritanie (BNM): ave Gamal Abdel Nasser, BP 614, Nouakchott; tel. 45-25-26-02; fax 45-25-33-97; e-mail bnm10@bnm.mr; internet www.bnm.mr; f. 1989; privately owned; Pres. and Dir-Gen. MOHAMED OULD NOUEIGUED; 10 brs.

Chinguitty Bank: 57 ave Gamal Abdel Nasser, BP 626, Nouakchott; tel. 45-25-21-73; fax 45-25-33-82; e-mail chinguittybank@mauritel.mr; internet www.chbank.mr; f. 1972; 51% owned by Libyan Arab Foreign Bank, 49% state-owned; Pres. MOHAMED OULD SADEQ; Gen. Man. SALAH ELDDIN MOHAMED EL-WAKWAK; 2 brs.

Générale de Banque de Mauritanie pour l'Investissement et le Commerce SA (GBM): ave de l'Indépendance, BP 5558, Nouakchott; tel. 45-25-36-36; fax 45-25-46-47; e-mail gbm@gbm.mr.com; f. 1995; 70% privately owned; Pres. and Dir-Gen. MOHAMED HMAYEN OULD BOUAMATOU; 1 br.

Orabank Mauritanie: P54, ave du Général Charles de Gaulle 20, rue 42-060, BP 1268, Nouakchott; tel. and fax 45-29-13-60; e-mail info-mr@orabank.net; internet www.orabank.net; f. 2002 as Bacim-Bank; present name adopted 2012; privately owned; cap. 6,921m. (Sep. 2012); Dir-Gen. AZHAR KHAN; 6 brs.

Société Générale Mauritanie (SGM): ave Charles de Gaulle, BP 5085, Nouakchott; tel. 45-29-70-00; fax 45-24-53-00; internet www.sgm.mr; f. 2005; present name adopted 2007; Pres. and Dir-Gen. CHRISTIAN MÉTAUX; 1 br.

Islamic Banks

Banque al-Wava Mauritanienne Islamique (BAMIS): 758 rue 22–018, ave du Roi Fayçal, BP 650, Nouakchott; tel. 45-25-14-24; fax 45-25-16-21; e-mail bamis@bamis.mr; internet www.bamis.mr; f. 1985; fmrly Banque al-Baraka Mauritanienne Islamique; majority share privately owned; cap. 7,000m., dep. 27,487m. (Dec. 2011); Pres. MOHAMED ABDELLAHI OULD ABDELLAHI; Dir-Gen. MOHAMED ABDELLAHI OULD SIDI; Exec. Dir MOHAMED OULD TAYA; 8 brs.

Mouamalat Assahiha Bank: Nouakchott; f. 2013; cap. US $20,000m. (May 2013).

Nouvelle Banque de Mauritanie (NBM): Nouakchott; Pres. ABDEL BAGHI OULD AHMED BOUHA.

INSURANCE

Assurances Générales de Mauritanie: ave Charles de Gaulle, TZA Ilot A 667, BP 2141, Nouakchott; tel. 45-29-29-00; fax 45-29-29-11; e-mail info@agm.mr; internet agm.mr; Man. MOULAYE ELY BOUAMATOU.

Compagnie Nationale d'Assurance et de Réassurance (NASR): 12 ave Gamal Abdel Nasser, BP 163, Nouakchott; tel. 45-25-26-50; fax 45-25-18-18; e-mail nasr@nasr.mr; internet www.nasr.mr; f. 1994; state-owned; Pres. MOHAMED ABDALLAHI OULD SIDI; Dir-Gen. AHMED OULD SIDI BABA.

DAMANE Assurances SA: BP 5080, Nouakchott; tel. 45-25-25-08; internet www.damane-assurances.com; Dir-Gen. MOHAMED O. AHMEDOU JEIREB.

Mauritanienne d'Assurances et de Réassurances (MAR): Nouakchott; tel. 45-24-12-18; e-mail mar@mar-assur.mr; internet www.mar-assur.mr; f. 2002.

TAAMIN: BP 5164, Nouakchott; tel. 45-29-40-00; fax 45-29-40-02; e-mail info@assurancestaamin.com; internet www.assurancestaamin.com; Pres. and Dir-Gen. MOULAYE EL HASSEN OULD MOCTAR EL HASSEN.

Trade and Industry

GOVERNMENT AGENCIES

Autorité de Régulation des Marchés Publics: Nouakchott; Pres. ABOU MOUSSA DIALLO.

Commission Nationale de Contrôle des Marchés Publics: Nouakchott; Pres. AHMED BABA OULD MOULAYE ZEIN.

Commission de Passation des Marchés Publics du Secteur Rural: Immeuble Mouna, No ZRB 180, 2e étage, ave Moctar Ould Daddah, Carrefour cité SMAR, Nouakchott; tel. 45-24-21-74; internet www.cpmpsr.com; Pres. AHMED SALEM OULD BOUBOUTT.

DEVELOPMENT ORGANIZATIONS

Agence Française de Développement (AFD): rue Mamadou Kouaté prolongée, BP 5211, Nouakchott; tel. 45-25-25-25; fax 45-25-49-10; e-mail afdnouakchott@afd.fr; internet www.afd.fr; Country Dir PATRICK ABBES.

Service de Coopération et d'Action Culturelle: BP 203, Nouakchott; tel. 45-29-95-59; fax 45-29-96-15; e-mail scac.nouakchott-amba@diplomatie.fr; administers bilateral aid from France; Dir SYLVAIN FOURCASSIE.

Société Nationale pour le Développement Rural (SONADER): BP 321, Nouakchott; tel. 45-21-18-00; fax 45-25-32-86; f. 1975; Dir-Gen. MOHAMED OULD AHMAHOULLAH.

CHAMBER OF COMMERCE

Chambre de Commerce, d'Industrie et d'Agriculture de Mauritanie (CCIAM): 303 ave de l'Indépendance, BP 215, Nouakchott; tel. 45-25-22-14; fax 45-25-38-95; e-mail cciam_info@yahoo.fr; internet www.chambredecommerce.mr; f. 1954; Pres. MOHAMEDOU OULD MOHAMED MAHMOUD; Sec.-Gen. ABDEL AZIZ WANE.

EMPLOYERS' ORGANIZATION

Union Nationale du Patronat Mauritanien (UNPM): 824 ave de Roi Fayçal, Ksar, BP 383, Nouakchott; tel. 45-25-33-01; fax 45-25-91-08; e-mail germe@opt.mr; internet www.unpm.mr; f. 1960; professional asscn for all employers active in Mauritania; Pres. AHMED BABA OULD AZIZI OULD EL MAMY; Sec.-Gen. SEYID OULD ABDALLAHI.

UTILITIES

Electricity

Société Mauritanienne d'Electricité (SOMELEC): 47 ave de l'Indépendance, BP 355, Nouakchott; tel. 45-29-66-04; fax 45-25-39-95; internet www.somelec.mr; f. 2001; state-owned; transfer to majority private sector ownership proposed; production and distribution of electricity; Pres. MEMMED OULD AHMED; Dir-Gen. MOHAMED OULD BILAL.

Gas

Société Mauritanienne de Gaz (SOMAGAZ): POB 5089, Nouakchott; tel. 45-24-28-58; fax 45-24-29-70; e-mail somagazinfo@somagaz.com; internet www.somagaz.com; f. 1987; production and distribution of butane gas; Dir-Gen. ABDALLAHI OULD BENANE.

Water

Société Nationale d'Eau (SNDE): 106 ave 42-096, Tevragh Zeina, BP 796, Nouakchott; tel. 45-25-52-73; fax 45-25-19-52; e-mail mfoudail@infotel.mr; f. 2001; Pres. CHEIKH OULD BAHA; Dir-Gen. AGHDHAVNA OULD EYIH.

TRADE UNIONS

Confédération Générale des Travailleurs de Mauritanie (CGTM): BP 6164, Nouakchott; tel. 45-25-60-24; fax 45-25-80-57; e-mail admin@cgtm.org; internet cgtm.org; f. 1992; obtained official recognition in 1994; Sec.-Gen. ABDALLAHI OULD MOHAMED.

Confédération Libre des Travailleurs de Mauritanie (CLTM): BP 6902, Nouakchott; fax 45-25-23-16; f. 1995; Sec.-Gen. SAMORY OULD BÉYE.

Confédération Nationale des Travailleurs de Mauritanie (CNTM): Nouakchott; tel. 45-00-17-01; fax 45-24-35-80; internet www.cntm-rim.org; Sec.-Gen. MOHAMED AHMED OULD SALECK.

Union des Travailleurs de Mauritanie (UTM): Bourse du Travail, BP 630, Nouakchott; f. 1961; Sec.-Gen. ABDERAHMANE OULD BOUBOU; 45,000 mems.

Transport

RAILWAYS

A 704-km railway connects the iron-ore deposits at Zouerate with Nouadhibou; a 40-km extension services the reserves at El Rhein, and a 30-km extension those at M'Haoudat. Motive power is diesel-electric. The Société Nationale Industrielle et Minière (SNIM) operates one of the longest (2.4 km) and heaviest (22,000 metric tons) trains in the world.

SNIM—Direction du Chemin de Fer et du Port: BP 42, Nouadhibou; tel. 45-74-51-74; fax 45-74-53-96; e-mail m.khalifa.beyah@zrt.snim.com; internet www.snim.com; f. 1963; Gen. Man. MOHAMED EL-MOCTAR OULD TALEB.

ROADS

In 2012 there were about 11,790 km of roads and tracks, of which only 3,157 km were paved in 2010. The 1,100-km Trans-Mauritania highway, completed in 1985, links Nouakchott with Néma in the east of the country. The construction of a 470-km highway between Nouakchott and Nouadhibou was completed in 2004. Plans exist for the construction of a 7,400-km highway, l'Autoroute Transmaghrébine, linking Nouakchott with the Libyan port of Tubruq (Tobruk).

Autorité de Régulation des Transports: Nouakchott; Pres. CHEIKH SID'AHMED OULD BABA.

Entreprise Nationale de l'Entretien Routier: Nouakchott; Dir-Gen. MADI OULD TALEB.

INLAND WATERWAYS

The Senegal river is navigable in the wet season by small coastal vessels as far as Kayes (Mali) and by river vessels as far as Kaédi; in the dry season it is navigable as far as Rosso and Boghé, respectively. The major river ports are at Rosso, Kaédi and Gouraye.

SHIPPING

The principal port, at Point-Central, 10 km south of Nouadhibou, is almost wholly occupied with mineral exports. There is also a commercial and fishing port at Nouadhibou. The deep-water Port de l'Amitié at Nouakchott, built and maintained with assistance from the People's Republic of China, was inaugurated in 1986, and has a total annual capacity of about 1.5m. metric tons. In 2014 Mauritania's flag registered fleet consisted of 72 vessels and had a total displacement of some 26,198 grt.

Mauritanienne de Transport Maritime: Nouakchott; tel. 45-25-44-79; fax 45-25-44-76; e-mail mtm@mtm.mr; internet www.mtm .mr; f. 1996; Pres. and Dir-Gen. A. KADER KAMIL.

Port Autonome de Nouadhibou: BP 236, Nouadhibou; tel. and fax 45-74-51-36; e-mail contact@pan.mr; internet www.portndb.com; f. 1973; state-owned; Pres. BAL MOHAMED EL HABIB; Dir-Gen. MOHAMED MAMY ELY OULD DAF.

Port Autonome de Nouakchott (Port de l'Amitié): BP 5103, El Mina, Nouakchott; tel. 45-25-38-59; fax 45-25-16-15; e-mail info@ panpa.mr; internet www.panpa.mr; f. 1986; deep-water port; Dir-Gen. AHMEDOU OULD HAMED.

Shipping Companies

Société d'Acconage et de Manutention en Mauritanie (SAMMA): BP 258, Nouadhibou; tel. 45-74-52-63; fax 45-74-52-37; e-mail didi.samma@snim.com; internet www.samma.mr; f. 1960; freight and handling, shipping agent, forwarding agent, stevedoring; Man. Dir DIDI OULD BIHA.

Société Générale de Consignation et d'Entreprises Maritimes (SOGECO): 1765 rue 22-002, Commune du Ksar, BP 351, Nouakchott; tel. 45-25-22-02; fax 45-25-39-03; e-mail sogeco@sogeco .sa.mr; internet www.sogecosa.com; f. 1973; shipping agent, forwarding, stevedoring; Man. Dir SID'AHMED OULD ABEIDNA.

Société Mauritanienne pour la Pêche et la Navigation (SMPN): BP 40254, Nouakchott; tel. 45-25-36-38; fax 45-25-37-87; e-mail smpn@toptechnology.mr; Dir-Gen. ABDALLAHI OULD ISMAIL.

VOTRA: route de l'Aéroport, BP 454, Nouakchott; tel. 45-25-24-10; fax 45-25-31-41; e-mail info@votra.net; internet www.votra.net; Dir-Gen. MOHAMED MAHMOUD OULD MAYE.

CIVIL AVIATION

There are international airports at Nouakchott, Nouadhibou and Néma, and 23 smaller airstrips.

Agence Nationale de l'Aviation Civile (ANAC): BP 91, Nouakchott; tel. 45-24-40-06; fax 45-25-35-78; e-mail anac@anac.mr; internet www.anac.mr; f. 2004; Gen. Man. ABOUBEKRINE SEDDIGH OULD MOHAMED EL HACEN.

Mauritania Airlines International: Aéroport International de Nouakchott, Ancienne Aérogare, Nouakchott; tel. 45-25-67-47; e-mail resa.tarifs@mauritaniaairlines.mr; internet www .mauritaniaairlines.mr; f. 2010; CEO HASSENA OULD ELY.

Tourism

Mauritania's principal tourist attractions are its historical sites, several of which have been listed by UNESCO under its World Heritage Programme, and its game reserves and national parks. Some 29,000 tourists visited Mauritania in 2007/08, according to government figures. Receipts from tourism in that year totalled an estimated US $39m.

Office National du Tourisme: BP 2884, Nouakchott; tel. 45-29-03-44; fax 45-29-05-28; internet www.tourisme-mauritanie.com; f. 2002; Dir KHADIJÉTOU MINT BOUBOU.

SOMASERT: BP 42, Nouadhibou; tel. 45-74-29-91; fax 45-74-90-43; e-mail somasert@snim.com; internet www.somasertsa.com; f. 1987; subsidiary of SNIM; responsible for promoting tourism, managing hotels and organizing tours; Dir-Gen. SAAD CHEIK SAAD BOUH.

Defence

As assessed at November 2014, the armed forces numbered an estimated 15,850 men: army 15,000, navy about 600, air force 250. Full-time membership of paramilitary forces totalled about 5,000. Military service is by authorized conscription, and lasts for two years.

Defence Expenditure: Estimated at UM 44,500m. in 2013.

Chief of Staff of the Armed Forces: Gen. MOHAMED OULD CHEIKH MOHAMED AHMED.

Chief of Staff of the Army: MOHAMED CHEIKH OULD MOHAMED LEMINE.

Chief of Staff of the Navy: Rear Adm. ISSELKOU CHEIKH EL WELI.

Chief of Staff of the Air Force: Col. MOHAMED MOHAMED SALEM LEHREITANI.

Chief of Staff of the National Gendarmerie: Brig.-Gen. SOULTANE OULD MOHAMED ESSOUAD.

Education

Primary education, which is officially compulsory, begins at six years of age and lasts for six years. In 2012 total enrolment at primary schools included 70% of children in the relevant age-group (67% of boys; 72% of girls), according to UNESCO estimates. Secondary education begins at 12 years of age and lasts for seven years, comprising a first cycle of four years and a second of three years. Total enrolment at public secondary schools in 2006 included only 14% of children in the appropriate age-group (15% of boys; 14% of girls), according to UNESCO estimates. In 2011/12 a total of 17,878 students were enrolled at Mauritania's higher education institutions (including the Université de Nouakchott, which was opened in 1983). In 2010 spending on education represented 15.2% of total budgetary expenditure.

MAURITIUS

Introductory Survey

LOCATION, CLIMATE, LANGUAGE, RELIGION, FLAG, CAPITAL

The Republic of Mauritius lies in the Indian Ocean. The principal island, from which the country takes its name, lies about 800 km (500 miles) east of Madagascar. The other main islands are Rodrigues, the Agalega Islands and the Cargados Carajos Shoals (St Brandon Islands). The climate is maritime sub-tropical and generally humid. The average annual temperature is 23°C (73°F) at sea-level, falling to 19°C (66°F) at an altitude of 600 m (about 2,000 ft). Average annual rainfall varies from 890 mm (35 ins) at sea-level to 5,080 mm (200 ins) on the highest parts. Tropical cyclones, which may be severe, occur between September and May. Most of the population are of Indian descent. The most widely spoken languages in 2011 were Creole (40.5%) and Bhojpuri (19.3%). English is the country's official language, and Creole (derived from French) the lingua franca. The principal religious group are Hindus, who comprise more than 50% of the population. About 30% are Christians and 17% are Muslims. The national flag (proportions 2 by 3) has four equal horizontal stripes, of red, blue, yellow and green. The capital is Port Louis.

CONTEMPORARY POLITICAL HISTORY

Historical Context

The islands of Mauritius and Rodrigues, formerly French possessions, passed into British control in 1810. Subsequent settlement came mainly from East Africa and India, and the European population has remained largely French-speaking.

A ministerial form of government was introduced in 1957. The first elections under universal adult suffrage, held in 1959, were won by the Mauritius Labour Party (MLP), led by Dr (later Sir) Seewoosagur Ramgoolam. Mauritius became independent, within the Commonwealth, on 12 March 1968, with Ramgoolam as Prime Minister.

In November 1965 the United Kingdom transferred the Chagos Archipelago (including the atoll of Diego Garcia), a Mauritian dependency about 2,000 km (1,250 miles) north-east of the main island, to the newly created British Indian Ocean Territory (BIOT). Mauritius has subsequently campaigned for the return of the islands, which have been developed as a major US military base. Mauritius also claims sovereignty of the French-held island of Tromelin, about 550 km (340 miles) to the north-west.

Domestic Political Affairs

During the 1970s political opposition to successive coalition governments formed by Ramgoolam was led by a radical left-wing group, the Mouvement Militant Mauricien (MMM), founded by Paul Bérenger. Although the MMM became the largest single party in the Legislative Assembly following a general election in December 1976, Ramgoolam was able to form a new coalition Government with the support of the Parti Mauricien Social Démocrate (PMSD). However, social unrest and rising unemployment undermined popular support for the Government, and at a general election in June 1982 the MMM, in alliance with the Parti Socialiste Mauricien (PSM), won all 60 contested seats on the main island. Aneerood (later Sir Aneerood) Jugnauth, the leader of the MMM, became Prime Minister, and Bérenger Minister of Finance.

The MMM/PSM coalition collapsed in March 1983, when Bérenger and his supporters resigned, following differences concerning economic policy. Jugnauth formed a new Government and a new party, the Mouvement Socialiste Militant (MSM), which subsequently merged with the PSM. A general election took place in August, at which an electoral alliance of the MSM, the MLP and the PMSD, led by Sir Gaëtan Duval, gained a legislative majority. Jugnauth formed a new coalition Government, in which Duval became Deputy Prime Minister. The MLP, however, withdrew from the coalition in February 1984.

Following a general election in August 1987, the MSM again formed an electoral alliance with the PMSD and the MLP; the three parties obtained 39 of the 62 elective seats. Bérenger, who failed to secure a seat, transferred his functions as leader of the opposition in the Legislative Assembly to Dr Paramhansa Nababsingh (while Bérenger himself replaced Nababsingh as Secretary-General of the MMM). A new coalition, led by Jugnauth, took office in September; however, in August 1988, following a disagreement over employment policies, the PMSD withdrew from the coalition.

In July 1990 the MSM and the MMM agreed to form an alliance to contest the next general election, and to promote constitutional measures allowing Mauritius to become a republic within the Commonwealth. This proposal, however, was jointly opposed by the MLP and the PMSD, prompting Jugnauth to dismiss the MLP leader, Sir Satcam Boolell, from the Government, together with two dissident ministers from the MSM. A further three ministers representing the MLP resigned, leaving only one MLP member in the Government. Boolell subsequently relinquished the leadership of the MLP to Dr Navinchandra Ramgoolam (the son of the late Sir Seewoosagur Ramgoolam). In September Jugnauth formed a new coalition Government.

At a general election, which took place on 15 September, an alliance of the MSM, the MMM and the Mouvement des Travaillistes Démocrates (MTD) won 57 of the 62 directly elected seats, while the MLP/PMSD alliance obtained three seats. The two remaining seats were secured by the Organisation du Peuple Rodriguais (OPR). Four 'additional' seats were subsequently allocated to members of the MLP/PMSD alliance. Jugnauth formed a new government coalition, to which nine representatives of the MMM (including Bérenger, who became Minister of External Affairs) and one representative of the MTD were appointed.

In December 1991 the Legislative Assembly approved the constitutional framework for the country's transition to a republic within the Commonwealth. Following the proclamation of the Republic of Mauritius on 12 March 1992, the Legislative Assembly was redesignated as the National Assembly, and the incumbent Governor-General, Sir Veerasamy Ringadoo, became interim President. Later in March the Government announced its choice of Cassam Uteem, the Minister of Industry and Industrial Technology and a member of the MMM, to assume the presidency in June. Uteem was duly elected President by the National Assembly; Sir Rabindrah Ghurburrun, a member of the MMM, took office as Vice-President.

The removal of Bérenger from the Council of Ministers in August 1993, on the grounds that he had repeatedly criticized government policy, precipitated a serious crisis within the MMM, the political bureau of which decided that the other nine members of the party who held ministerial portfolios should remain in the coalition Government. Led by Nababsingh, the Deputy Prime Minister, and Jean-Claude de l'Estrac, the Minister of Industry and Industrial Technology, supporters of the pro-coalition faction announced in October 1993 that Bérenger had been suspended as Secretary-General of the MMM. Bérenger and his supporters responded by expelling 11 MMM officials from the party, and seeking a legal ban on Nababsingh and de l'Estrac from using the party name. The split in the MMM led in November to a government reorganization, in which the remaining two MMM ministers supporting Bérenger were replaced by members of the party's pro-coalition faction. Nababsingh and the dissident faction of the MMM, having lost Bérenger's legal challenge for the use of the party name, formed a new party, the Renouveau Militant Mauricien (RMM), which formally commenced political activity in June 1994.

During the course of a parliamentary debate in November 1994 Bérenger and de l'Estrac accepted a mutual challenge to resign their seats in the National Assembly and to contest by-elections. In the following month the MSM indicated that it would not oppose RMM candidates in the two polls. In January 1995, however, Jugnauth unsuccessfully sought to undermine the MLP/MMM alliance by offering electoral support to the MLP. The by-elections, held in February, were both won by MLP/MMM candidates, and Bérenger was returned to the National Assembly. Following these results, Jugnauth opened political negotiations with the PMSD, the leader of which, Charles Gaëtan Xavier-Luc Duval (the son of Sir Gaëtan Duval), entered the coalition as Minister of Industry and Industrial Technology and

Minister of Tourism. The post of Attorney-General and Minister of Justice was also allocated to the PMSD, and Sir Gaëtan Duval agreed to act as an economic adviser to the Prime Minister. As a result, however, of widespread opposition within the PMSD to participation in the coalition, Xavier-Luc Duval left the Government in October, and Sir Gaëtan Duval subsequently resumed the leadership of the party.

The 1995 general election

At the general election held in December 1995 the MLP/MMM alliance won a decisive victory: of the 62 elected seats, the MLP secured 35, the MMM 25 and the OPR two. Under constitutional arrangements providing representation for unsuccessful candidates attracting the largest number of votes, Sir Gaëtan Duval re-entered the National Assembly, together with two members of the Mouvement Rodriguais (MR) and one representative of Hizbullah, an Islamist fundamentalist group. Ramgoolam became Prime Minister of the new MLP/MMM coalition, with Bérenger as Deputy Prime Minister with responsibility for foreign and regional relations. Sir Gaëtan Duval died in May 1996 and was succeeded in the National Assembly and as leader of the PMSD by his brother, Hervé Duval, although Xavier-Luc Duval continued to command a significant following within the party.

Serious divisions began to emerge within the coalition Government in late 1996, when differences were reported between Ramgoolam and Bérenger over the allocation of ministerial responsibilities and the perception by the MMM of delays in the implementation of social and economic reforms. Bérenger's criticism of the coalition's performance culminated in June 1997 in his dismissal from the Government and the consequent withdrawal of the MMM from the coalition. Following unsuccessful efforts by Ramgoolam to draw the PMSD into a new administration, an MLP Council of Ministers was formed by Ramgoolam, who additionally assumed Bérenger's former responsibilities for foreign affairs. In June the National Assembly re-elected Uteem to a second five-year term as President.

Following the dissolution of the MLP/MMM alliance, Bérenger sought to assume the leadership of a consolidated political opposition to the Government. In August 1997 two small parties, the Mouvement Militant Socialiste Mauricien (MMSM) and the Rassemblement pour la Réforme (RPR), agreed to support Bérenger in this aim. The alliance was extended to include a breakaway faction of the PMSD, the 'Vrais Bleus', under the leadership of Hervé Duval, who had been replaced as party leader by Xavier-Luc Duval, an opponent of co-operation with the MMM. Meanwhile, Jugnauth entered into negotiations with Bérenger for an electoral alliance, and in December 1998 the MSM and the MMM agreed terms for a joint list of candidates.

The MLP announced in mid-1999 its endorsement of the candidature of Xavier-Luc Duval for a legislative by-election to be held in September. Xavier-Luc Duval, after obtaining the vacant seat, joined the Government as Minister of Industry, Commerce, Corporate Affairs and Financial Services, following an extensive government reorganization completed at the end of the month.

The premiership of Anerood Jugnauth

In August 2000 the MSM/MMM alliance was constituted, on the basis that Jugnauth would lead as Prime Minister for three years in the event of victory, before assuming the more honorary role of President, thus allowing Bérenger to become Prime Minister for the remaining two years. The general election was held on 11 September. The MSM/MMM alliance achieved an overwhelming victory, winning 54 of the 62 directly elected seats in the National Assembly, while the MLP/PMSD alliance gained only six seats and the OPR two seats. As agreed, Sir Anerood Jugnauth became Prime Minister again, while Paul Bérenger was appointed Deputy Prime Minister and Minister of Finance. A new Council of Ministers was appointed one week later.

In January 2002 a commission on constitutional and electoral reform presented its proposals at a series of public forums, before submitting them to the Government for consideration. Recommendations included the introduction of a system of proportional representation in legislative elections and a reinforcement of presidential powers. In mid-February controversial legislation on the prevention of terrorism was finally promulgated by the Chief Justice of the Supreme Court, Ariranga Pillay, acting as interim President, following the resignations of both President Uteem and his successor, Vice-President Angidi Chettiar, over the issue. The legislation had been rejected by opposition parties and proved unpopular with many sections of society for arrogating excessive powers to the authorities and infringing on citizens' rights. On 25 February Karl Offman was elected as President by an extraordinary session of the National Assembly, which was boycotted by opposition deputies. Although formally elected for five years, Offman was to relinquish the presidency to Jugnauth in October 2003; in preparation for this, in April 2003 Jugnauth announced his resignation from the leadership of the MSM, to be succeeded by his son, Pravind.

In August 2003, in preparation for the transfer of governing roles, a constitutional amendment was approved by the National Assembly to increase the powers of the President, giving the incumbent the right to refuse a request from the Prime Minister to dissolve the legislature following a vote of no confidence. As agreed, on 1 October Offman resigned as President and was replaced, in an acting capacity, by the Vice-President, Raouf Bundhun, pending the election by the National Assembly of Sir Anerood Jugnauth as his successor one week later. Jugnauth had resigned as Prime Minister on 30 September and was immediately replaced by Paul Bérenger, who appointed a new Council of Ministers.

In February 2005 the Minister of Public Infrastructure, Land Transport and Shipping, Anil Bachoo, and the Minister of Local Government and Solid Waste Management, Mookhesswur Choonee, resigned from the Government. The two erstwhile ministers formed a new opposition party the following month, the Mouvement Sociale Démocrate (MSD), having also resigned from the MSM alleging poor leadership of that party by Pravind Jugnauth. Bachoo and Choonee reportedly disapproved of an apparent pre-electoral agreement between the parties of the ruling coalition, whereby, should they successfully be re-elected to office, Bérenger would relinquish the premiership in mid-term in favour of Pravind Jugnauth, just as the incumbent President (Pravind Jugnauth's father) had in September 2003. The MSD announced the formation of an electoral alliance with the MLP, known as the Social Alliance, thus creating a credible rival political force to the governing parties for the forthcoming legislative elections.

Navinchandra Ramgoolam becomes Prime Minister

At the elections, which were held on 3 July 2005, the Social Alliance bloc defeated the incumbent coalition, winning 38 of the 62 directly elected mandates. The MSM/MMM alliance took 22 seats while the OPR secured two. The rate of voter participation was 81.5%. Ramgoolam was appointed as Prime Minister and a new 19-member Council of Ministers was sworn into office later that month. Following the elections, the PMSD withdrew from the opposition alliance in which it had participated with the MSM and MMM.

In April 2006 the opposition was further weakened when the MSM/MMM alliance collapsed following increasing tensions between Pravind Jugnauth and Bérenger, and the PMSD announced that it was joining the government coalition. The MSM withdrew its support from Bérenger as official leader of the opposition, and he was succeeded by Nando Bodha, the Secretary-General of the MSM and a close ally of Pravind Jugnauth (who had failed to retain his seat in the legislature in July 2005), since the MSM held 11 seats in the National Assembly to the MMM's 10. Bodha's nomination was rejected by Ashock Jugnauth, a senior member of the MSM (and uncle of Pravind), who resigned from the party and established a new opposition party, the Union Nationale. In August 2007 Chettiar resumed the position of Vice-President, replacing Bundhun. In September Bodha resigned as leader of the opposition and in October Bérenger once again assumed the role.

Ramgoolam reorganized the Government in mid-September 2008. Most notably, Anil Bachoo was reinstated as Minister of Public Infrastructure, Land Transport and Shipping, and Arvin Boolell became Minister of Foreign Affairs, Regional Integration and International Trade. On 19 September the National Assembly unanimously re-elected Anerood Jugnauth as President for a second five-year term, and on the following day legislation was approved that allowed for two ministers to hold the title of Vice-Prime Minister: these positions were awarded to Xavier-Luc Duval and Dr Rama Sithanen, with the former also retaining the tourism portfolio, while Sithanen retained the finance portfolio. (The position of Deputy Prime Minister remained the second most senior post in the Council of Ministers—Ahmed Rashid Beebeejaun was appointed to this office and also assumed responsibility for the renewable energy and public utilities portfolio.)

A total of 65 parties and alliances registered to contest the elections on 5 May 2010, most notably the Alliance de l'Avenir, comprising the MLP, the PMSD and the MSM, and the Alliance du Coeur, formed by the MMM, the Union Nationale and the Mouvement Mauricien Social Démocrate. In the event the Alliance de l'Avenir secured 41 of the 62 directly elected seats and was awarded four additional seats. The Alliance du Coeur took 18 directly elected seats and two additional seats, while the remaining directly elected seats were won by the MR (two) and the Front Solidarité Mauricienne (one). A further additional seat was allocated to the OPR, although the eighth seat remained vacant. The rate of voter participation was reported at some 78%. On 11 May Ramgoolam appointed a new Government, in which he also assumed responsibility for the defence, home affairs and external communications portfolio. Beebeejaun was reappointed Deputy Prime Minister, while Xavier-Luc Duval became Vice-Prime Minister and Minister of Social Integration and Economic Empowerment, and Pravind Jugnauth became Vice-Prime Minister and Minister of Finance and Economic Development. Following the death of Chettiar in September, Monique Ohsan-Bellepeau of the MLP was elected Vice-President by the National Assembly in November (becoming the first woman to hold the vice-presidential office).

Governmental restructure

In early 2011 11 former senior members of the MSM rejoined the party, leaving the Union Nationale weakened. However, later that year divisions within the ruling coalition resulted in a series of governmental changes. In June the MSM's Showkutally Soodhun, hitherto Minister of Industry and Commerce, was relieved of the commerce portfolio; the PMSD's Michaël Yeung assumed responsibility, becoming Minister of Business, Enterprise, Commerce and Consumer Protection. More significantly, in July Minister of Health and Quality of Life Santi Bai (Maya) Hanoomanjee—of the MSM—was arrested amid allegations of corruption in relation to the government purchase of a private medical clinic, MedPoint. Hanoomanjee subsequently resigned from office, along with five other MSM ministers who stood down in protest against her arrest. In August Pravind Jugnauth announced that the MSM had effectively been forced from the ruling coalition and that he would be joining the opposition. At that time, a cabinet reorganization was implemented, whereby Xavier-Luc Duval assumed the position of Vice-Prime Minister and Minister of Finance and Economic Development, and Bachoo, retaining the public infrastructure, national development unit, land transport and shipping portfolios, was promoted to Vice-Prime Minister. In September Jugnauth was arrested for his alleged involvement in the fraudulent acquisition of the private medical clinic in which Hanoomanjee had earlier also been implicated. Jugnauth denied charges of a conflict of interest, claiming he had disclosed his shareholder interests in MedPoint at the earliest opportunity and had withdrawn from the cabinet meeting relating to the acquisition. Hanoomanjee was exonerated of any wrongdoing in April 2013, but legal proceedings against Jugnauth on charges of a conflict of interest commenced in April 2014.

Elections to the Rodrigues Regional Assembly were held in February 2012 at which the OPR secured 11 of the Assembly's 21 seats, while the MR took eight and the Front Patriotique Rodriguais two seats. On 30 March Anerood Jugnauth resigned the presidency and announced his intention to return to party politics. The hitherto Speaker of the National Assembly, Kailash Purryag of the MLP, was elected to the presidency on 20 July following a legislative vote; he was inaugurated on the following day. The role of Speaker was subsequently assumed by Peeroo Razack (also a member of the MLP). Meanwhile, the MSM and the MMM had announced the reformation of their alliance, and in municipal elections held on 9 December the MSM/MMM coalition won 53 of the country's 90 council seats, defeating the MLP and its allies, which obtained 36 seats.

Recent developments: the 2014 legislative elections

In March 2014 the Government published proposals for extensive electoral reform. The resulting controversy led in April to the end of the alliance between the MMM and the MSM, and it was subsequently announced that the MMM intended to contest the next legislative elections in alliance with the MLP. On 6 June PMSD leader Xavier-Luc Duval resigned from his post of Vice-Prime Minister and Minister of Finance and Economic Development; he had favoured a 5% (rather than 10%) vote threshold for qualifying for parliamentary representation and accused the MLP of reneging on a promise to the PMSD that any electoral reforms would be subject to approval by referendum. The withdrawal of the PMSD from its coalition with the MLP left

Ramgoolam's Government severely weakened, raising the prospect of early elections. In July, nevertheless, the Prime Minister secured nearly unanimous parliamentary approval of a so-called 'mini-amendment' to the Constitution, which would allow candidates at the next general election not to declare their community, although they would consequently forgo the possibility of gaining a legislative seat as a 'best loser'. Only one deputy, Cehl Meeah, the leader of the FSM, voted against the measure (which was pending full electoral reform), while the three PMSD deputies abstained from the vote.

The legislative elections on 10 December 2014 were regarded as a vote on the MLP's planned constitutional reform (under which the authorities of the President would be significantly increased). The polls resulted in a decisive victory for Anerood Jugnauth's Alliance Lepep, comprising the MSM, PMSD and the Muvman Liberater (formed by breakaway members of the MMM), which secured a total of 51 seats. The coalition of the MLP and the MMM, known as Alliance de l'Unité et de la Modernité, received only 16 seats. A new Government was formed on 17 December; Anerood Jugnauth obtained the posts of Prime Minister, Minister of Defence, Home Affairs and the National Development Unit, Minister of Rodrigues, while Xavier-Luc Duval became Deputy Prime Minister and Minister of Tourism and External Communications.

Foreign Affairs

In November 2000 the British High Court of Justice ruled that the eviction of several thousand inhabitants of the Chagos Archipelago between 1967 and 1973, to allow the construction of a US military base on the atoll of Diego Garcia, had been unlawful, and overturned a 1971 ordinance preventing the islanders from returning to the Archipelago. (The majority of the displaced islanders had been resettled in Mauritius, which had administered the Chagos Archipelago until its transfer to BIOT in 1965.) Following the ruling, the Mauritian Government declared its right to sovereignty over the islands to be indisputable. In November 2001 exiled Chagos islanders demonstrated outside the British High Commission in Port Louis, in support of their demands for compensation from the British Government. In February 2002 legislation allowing the displaced islanders to apply for British citizenship received royal assent in the United Kingdom.

The Social Alliance Government elected in 2005 continued with efforts to regain sovereignty over the Chagos Archipelago. A group of 102 Chagossians was permitted to visit the Archipelago in March 2006 principally in order to visit the graves of relatives. In May the British High Court of Justice overturned the Orders in Council issued by the British Government under the royal prerogative in June 2004, ruling them to be unlawful, and confirmed the right of the islanders to return to the Archipelago without any conditions. In May 2007 the British Court of Appeal confirmed that the residents of the Chagos Archipelago had been unlawfully removed and upheld the displaced islanders' immediate right to return. In November the House of Lords granted the British Government the right to appeal against the Court of Appeal's decision, on the condition that the Chagossians' costs were met by the British Government. In November 2008 the House of Lords ruled in favour of the British Government, thus denying the Chagossians the right to return, citing as its main reason the fact that the United Kingdom would have been obliged to meet the costs of economic, social and educational advancement of the residents. Having exhausted the appeals process in the United Kingdom, the Chagossians announced that they would take their case to the European Court of Human Rights (ECHR). However, in December 2012 the ECHR also ruled in favour of the United Kingdom, declaring that a compensation package agreed in 1982 had constituted a final settlement of the matter.

In April 2010 the British Government announced that it had designated the Chagos Archipelago a marine protection area (MPA), within which all fishing and other activities were to be prohibited. The conservation area, covering some 544,000 sq km, was to be patrolled by a ship vested with the powers to arrest fleets caught fishing illegally, to impose fines of up to £100,000 and to confiscate boats and fishing equipment. The ban on fishing undermined the Chagossians' resettlement plans as it removed the legal means by which they could sustain their standard of living. In December the Mauritian Government announced that it had taken a case against the United Kingdom to the UN International Tribunal for the Law of the Sea on the grounds that the MPA was not compatible with the UN Convention on the Law of the Sea. Furthermore, the Chagossians also appealed for a judicial review of the decision to create the MPA. In January 2013 the Permanent Court of Arbitration adjudged that it was competent to hear the case, in spite of objections by the United Kingdom.

In early 2015 a preliminary feasibility report commissioned by the British Government confirmed that resettlement of the Chagossians on Diego Garcia was viable. On 18 March the Permanent Court of Arbitration issued a ruling that the United Kingdom had breached its international obligations in creating the MPA in 2010. The Court ruled by a vote of three to two that it did not have jurisdiction to decide on the issue of the United Kingdom's sovereignty over the Chagos Islands. (However, two of the judges added a comment that the United Kingdom had 'showed complete disregard for the territorial integrity of Mauritius'.) The British Government was urged to support the right of the displaced Chagossians to return to the Archipelago.

Prime Minister Ramgoolam (together with his counterparts in India and Canada) boycotted the 2013 Commonwealth Heads of Government Meeting, hosted by Sri Lanka in November, owing to concerns about the Sri Lankan Government's human rights practices. According to Commonwealth protocol, as a result of Ramgoolam's failure to attend, the next summit, which had been due to be hosted by Mauritius in 2015, was relocated to Malta.

CONSTITUTION AND GOVERNMENT

Constitutional amendments, which were approved by the Legislative Assembly (henceforth known as the National Assembly) in December 1991 and came into effect on 12 March 1992, provided for the establishment of a republic. The constitutional Head of State is the President of the Republic, who is elected by a simple majority of the National Assembly for a five-year term of office. Legislative power is vested in the unicameral National Assembly, which comprises the Speaker, 62 members elected by universal adult suffrage for a term of five years, up to eight 'additional' members (unsuccessful candidates who receive the largest number of votes at a legislative election, to whom seats are allocated by the Electoral Supervisory Commission to ensure a balance in representation of the different ethnic groups), and the Attorney-General (if not an elected member). Executive power is vested in the Prime Minister, who is appointed by the President and is the member of the National Assembly best able to command a majority in the Assembly. The President appoints other ministers, on the recommendation of the Prime Minister.

REGIONAL AND INTERNATIONAL CO-OPERATION

Mauritius is a member of the Common Market for Eastern and Southern Africa (COMESA, see p. 232), the Southern African Development Community (SADC, see p. 420) and the Indian Ocean Commission (IOC, see p. 447), which aims to promote regional economic co-operation. Mauritius was among the founder members of the Indian Ocean Rim Association for Regional Co-operation (IOR—ARC, see p. 447) in 1997.

Mauritius became a member of the UN in 1968. As a contracting party to the General Agreement on Tariffs and Trade, Mauritius joined the World Trade Organization (WTO, see p. 431) on its establishment in 1995.

ECONOMIC AFFAIRS

In 2013, according to estimates by the World Bank, Mauritius' gross national income (GNI), measured at average 2011–13 prices, was US $12,050m., equivalent to $9,300 per head (or $17,220 per head on an international purchasing-power parity basis). During 2004–13, it was estimated, the population increased at an average annual rate of 0.6%, while gross domestic product (GDP) per head increased, in real terms, by an average of 3.2% per year. Overall GDP increased, in real terms, at an average annual rate of 3.8% in 2004–13; growth in 2013 was 3.2%.

Agriculture (including hunting, forestry and fishing) contributed 3.1% of GDP in 2014 and engaged 8.4% of the employed labour force in 2013. The principal cash crops are sugar cane (which contributed 0.8% of GDP in 2014), tea and tobacco. Food crops include pumpkins, potatoes and tomatoes, pineapples. Chicken farming is also practised. During 2004–13, according to the World Bank, the GDP of the agricultural sector increased by 1.0%; it decreased by 0.2% in 2012, but increased by 4.7% in 2013.

Industry (including mining, manufacturing, construction and utilities) contributed 23.6% of GDP in 2013 and engaged 29.9% of the employed labour force in 2013. During 2004–13, according to the World Bank, industrial GDP increased, in real terms, at an

average annual rate of 1.8%; it increased by 0.9% in 2012, but decreased by 0.2% in 2013. Mining is negligible, accounting for less than 0.1% of employment in 2011 and 0.3% of GDP in 2014.

Manufacturing contributed 16.6% of GDP in 2014 and engaged 20.1% of the employed labour force in 2013. The principal branches of manufacturing are clothing and food products, mainly sugar. Clothing (excluding footwear) provided 39.6% of export earnings in 2011, according to official provisional figures. Factories in the Export Processing Zone (EPZ) import raw materials to produce goods for the export market. Other important products include fish preparations, textiles, and precious stones. During 2004–13, according to the World Bank, the GDP of the manufacturing sector increased, in real terms, at an average annual rate of 1.5%; manufacturing GDP decreased by 2.7% in 2013.

Construction contributed 4.9% of GDP in 2014 and engaged 8.7% of the employed labour force in 2013.

Electric energy is derived principally from thermal (oil-fired) and hydroelectric power stations. Bagasse (a by-product of sugar cane) is also used as fuel for generating electricity, and in 2011 it accounted for 20.2% of electricity produced. Imports of mineral fuels comprised 21.7% of the value of merchandise imports in 2013.

The services sector contributed an estimated 73.3% of GDP and engaged 61.7% of the employed labour force in 2013. Tourism is the third most important source of revenue, after manufacturing and agriculture. The number of foreign tourist arrivals increased to 993,106 in 2013 from 422,000 in 1995. Gross receipts from tourism were estimated to total Rs 40,557m. in 2013. An offshore banking sector and a stock exchange have operated since 1989. According to the World Bank, the real GDP of the services sector increased at an average annual rate of 5.1% in 2004–13; growth in 2013 was 4.3%.

In 2013 Mauritius recorded a visible merchandise trade deficit of US $2,270.3m., and there was a deficit of $1,180.3m. on the current account of the balance of payments. In 2013 the principal source of imports (24.2%) was India; other major suppliers were the People's Republic of China, France and South Africa. The principal market for exports in that year (16.6%) was the United Kingdom; other significant purchasers were France, the USA, Italy, South Africa, Spain and Madagascar. The principal exports (excluding re-exports) in 2012 were miscellaneous manufactured articles, food and live animals, and basic manufactures. The principal imports in that year were mineral fuels and lubricants (especially refined petroleum products), machinery and transport equipment, food and live animals, basic manufactures, miscellaneous manufactured articles, and chemicals.

In 2014 there was an estimated budgetary deficit of Rs 12,621m. (equivalent to 3.3% of GDP). Mauritius' general government gross debt was Rs 197,290m. in 2013, equivalent to 58.8% of GDP. Mauritius' external debt totalled US $4,459m. at the end of 2012, of which $1,343m. was public and publicly guaranteed debt. In that year the cost of servicing long-term public and publicly guaranteed debt and repayments to the IMF was equivalent to 2.4% of the value of exports of goods, services and income (excluding workers' remittances). The annual rate of inflation, according to ILO, averaged 5.5% in 2004–13. Consumer prices increased by an average of 3.2% in 2014. About 7.6% of the labour force were unemployed in 2013.

The geographical location of Mauritius, as well as a number of incentive measures implemented by the Government, has contributed to its successful establishment as an international financial centre. The island is a significant provider of offshore banking and investment services for a number of South Asian countries (particularly India), as well as for members of SADC. The city of Ebene, south of the capital, Port Louis, has been developed since 2001 as a new information technology centre and connector between African and Asian markets. Mauritius signed an interim Economic Partnership Agreement with the European Union (see p. 271) in 2009, thereby receiving preferential access to European markets. In the same year development began on a Chinese special economic zone, the Jin Fei Trade and Economic Co-operation Zone, near Port Louis; it was envisaged that the project, which was expected to be completed in 2016, would generate export earnings equivalent to US $220m. annually. In August 2010 the Government announced a stimulus programme of Rs 12,000m., which was designed to assist businesses affected by the 2008–09 financial crisis in Europe, develop tourism markets in India and the People's Republic of China, and support the sugar sector. The Mauritian Government secured a tender for the establishment in the country of an IMF African Training Institute for central bankers and finance ministry personnel from sub-Saharan Africa, which was officially opened in Ebene in June 2014 (the first such centre in Africa). In early 2015 negotiations were under way with the World Bank for the adoption of a new 2015–20 Country Partnership Framework for Mauritius, which was to focus on the further development of the information, communications and technology sector, among other areas. Economic co-operation also increased with India, which in March extended a \$500m. concessional line of credit to Mauritius for important infrastructure projects in the water and energy sector, while the two countries agreed to continue negotiations on a revised double tax treaty (since under the existing 1983 treaty Mauritian-based companies were exempt from Indian taxes).

GDP growth remained relatively constant, with a slight rise in 2014, to 3.4%, driven predominantly by the services sector.

PUBLIC HOLIDAYS

2016: 1–2 January (New Year), 23 January (Thaipoosam Cavadee), 1 February (Abolition of Slavery Commemoration), 8 February (Chinese New Year), 8 March (Maha Shivaratree), 12 March (National Day), 8 April (Ougadi), 1 May (Labour Day), 6 July* (Id al-Fitr, end of Ramadan), 15 August (Assumption), 5 September (Ganesh Chathurti), 30 October (Diwali), 1 November (All Saints' Day), 2 November (Arrival of Indentured Labourers), 25 December (Christmas Day).

* This holiday is dependent on the Islamic lunar calendar and may vary by one or two days from the date given.

Statistical Survey

Source (unless otherwise stated): Central Statistics Office, LIC Bldg, President John F. Kennedy St, Port Louis; tel. 212-2316; fax 211-4150; e-mail cso@mail.gov .mu; internet statsmauritius.gov.mu.

Area and Population

AREA, POPULATION AND DENSITY

Area (sq km)	2,040*
Population (census results)	
2 July 2000	1,179,137
3-4 July 2011	
Males	611,022
Females	626,069
Total	1,237,091
Population (official estimates at mid-year)†	
2012	1,255,882
2013	1,258,653
Density (per sq km) at mid-2013	617.0

* 788 sq miles.
† Islands of Mauritius and Rodrigues only.

POPULATION BY AGE AND SEX
(Mauritius and Rodrigues islands only, official estimates at mid-2013)

	Males	Females	Total
0–14 years	132,239	128,029	260,268
15–64 years	445,819	445,156	890,975
65 years and over	44,803	62,607	107,410
Total	622,861	635,792	1,258,653

ISLANDS

		Population	
	Area (sq km)	2000 census	2011 census
Mauritius . . .	1,865	1,143,069	1,196,383
Rodrigues . . .	104	35,779	40,434
Other islands . .	71	289	274
Total	2,040	1,179,137	1,237,091

POPULATION BY DISTRICT
(Mauritius and Rodrigues islands only, '000, official estimates at mid-2013)

Black River . . .	78.8	Port Louis . . .	120.7
Flacq	137.9	Riv du Rempart .	107.7
Grand Port . . .	112.8	Rodrigues . . .	41.3
Moka	82.9	Savanne	68.8
Pamplemousses .	138.6		
Plaine Wilhems .	369.2	**Total**	1,258.7

PRINCIPAL TOWNS
(at 2011 census)

Port Louis (capital) .	118,431	Curepipe . . .	77,466
Vacoas/Phoenix .	104,271	Quatre Bornes . .	71,633
Beau Bassin/Rose Hill	103,098		

BIRTHS, MARRIAGES AND DEATHS*

	Registered live births		Registered marriages		Registered deaths	
	Number	Rate (per 1,000)	Number	Rate (per 1,000)	Number	Rate (per 1,000)
2006	17,605	14.1	11,471	18.3	9,162	7.3
2007	17,034	13.5	11,547	18.3	8,498	6.7
2008	16,372	12.9	11,197	17.7	9,004	7.1
2009	15,344	12.0	10,619	16.7	9,224	7.2
2010	15,005	11.7	10,555	16.5	9,131	7.1
2011	14,701	11.7	10,499	16.8	9,170	7.3
2012	14,494	11.5	10,382	16.5	9,343	7.4
2013	13,688	10.9	9,574	15.2	9,440	7.5

* Figures refer to the islands of Mauritius and Rodrigues only. The data are tabulated by year of registration, rather than by year of occurrence.

Life expectancy (years at birth): 73.6 (males 70.0; females 77.3) in 2012 (Source: World Bank, World Development Indicators database).

ECONOMICALLY ACTIVE POPULATION
('000 persons aged 16 years and over, incl. foreign workers)

	2010	2011	2012*
Agriculture, forestry and fishing .	47.7	47.3	47.4
Sugar cane	15.1	14.7	14.1
Mining and quarrying	2.0	2.0	2.3
Manufacturing	113.6	111.4	111.7
Electricity, gas and water . .	5.5	5.6	5.9
Construction	51.5	52.5	53.1
Wholesale and retail trade, repair of motor vehicles and household goods	98.4	99.5	101.5
Hotels and restaurants . . .	38.8	39.6	40.3
Transport, storage and communications	50.5	50.4	52.3
Financial intermediation . . .	12.2	12.5	13.0

—continued	2010	2011	2012*
Real estate, renting and business activities	37.6	37.7	39.2
Public administration and defence; compulsory social security	40.5	40.2	39.8
Education	31.6	32.1	32.6
Health and social work	19.6	20.2	20.4
Other services	8.6	8.7	9.3
Total employed	558.1	559.7	568.8
Males	358.8	358.2	362.9
Females	199.3	201.5	205.9
Unemployed	45.2	46.1	48.3
Total labour force	603.3	605.8	617.1

* Provisional.

2013 ('000 persons): Agriculture, forestry and fishing 46.4; Industry 164.9 (Manufacturing 110.9; Construction 48.3); Services 340.7 (Wholesale and retail trade 95.2; Hotels and restaurants 39.6; Transportation and storage 32.4); *Total employed* 552.0; Unemployed 45.5; *Total labour force* 597.5 (males 366.9, females 230.6).

Health and Welfare

KEY INDICATORS

Total fertility rate (children per woman, 2012)	1.5
Under-5 mortality rate (per 1,000 live births, 2012)	15
HIV/AIDS (% of persons aged 15–49, 2013)	1.1
Physicians (per 1,000 head, 2004)	1.1
Hospital beds (per 1,000 head, 2011)	3.4
Health expenditure (2011): US $ per head (PPP)	767
Health expenditure (2011): % of GDP	4.9
Health expenditure (2011): public (% of total)	48.2
Access to sanitation (% of persons, 2012)	91
Total carbon dioxide emissions ('000 metric tons, 2010)	4,118.0
Carbon dioxide emissions per head (metric tons, 2010)	3.2
Human Development Index (2013): ranking	63
Human Development Index (2013): value	0.771

For sources and definitions, see explanatory note on p. vi.

Agriculture

PRINCIPAL CROPS
('000 metric tons)

	2011	2012	2013
Potatoes	21.6	20.4	16.4
Sugar cane	4,230.2	3,947.3	3,815.7
Coconuts	1.5	1.6*	1.5†
Cabbages and other brassicas	5.1	4.5	4.7
Lettuce and chicory	0.9	0.9	10.1
Tomatoes	11.4	13.2	11.2
Cauliflowers and broccoli	1.6	1.8	2.2
Pumpkins, squash and gourds	19.2	19.0	19.6
Cucumbers and gherkins	9.6	9.4	8.7
Aubergines (Eggplants)	3.2	3.2	3.4
Onions, dry	5.2	7.1	7.8
Carrots and turnips	5.3	4.5	5.0
Bananas	10.5	10.2	10.2
Pineapples	10.9	14.1	16.0
Tea	1.8	1.6	1.6
Tobacco, unmanufactured	0.3	0.2	0.3†

* Unofficial figure.
† FAO estimate.

Aggregate production ('000 metric tons, may include official, semi-official or estimated data): Total cereals 0.6 in 2011, 1.2 in 2012, 1.3 in 2013; Total roots and tubers 23.3 in 2011, 22.6 in 2012, 18.6 in 2013; Total vegetables (incl. melons) 69.4 in 2011, 71.5 in 2012, 71.4 in 2013; Total fruits (excl. melons) 26.5 in 2011, 29.5 in 2012, 32.0 in 2013.

Source: FAO.

LIVESTOCK
('000 head, year ending September)

	2011	2012	2013
Cattle	6.6	7.3	7.0*
Pigs	23	15	15*
Sheep*	16	17	17
Goats	28	27	27*
Chickens*	14,300	14,600	14,500

* FAO estimate(s).

Source: FAO.

LIVESTOCK PRODUCTS
('000 metric tons)

	2011	2012	2013
Cattle meat	3	2	3*
Chicken meat	47	47	47*
Cows' milk	5	6	5
Hen eggs	11	11	12*

* FAO estimate.

Source: FAO.

Forestry

ROUNDWOOD REMOVALS
('000 cubic metres, excl. bark)

	2011	2012	2013
Sawlogs, veneer logs and logs for sleepers	3	1	1
Other industrial wood	1	1	1
Fuel wood	7	5	3
Total	11	7	5

Source: FAO.

SAWNWOOD PRODUCTION
('000 cubic metres, incl. railway sleepers)

	2011	2012	2013
Coniferous (softwood)	1.8	1.0	1.0
Broadleaved (hardwood)	0.1	1.0	1.0
Total	1.9	2.0	2.0

Source: FAO.

Fishing

(metric tons, live weight)

	2010	2011	2012
Capture	7,226	5,143	6,403
Groupers and seabasses	860	547	201
Snappers and jobfishes	739	336	236
Emperors (Scavengers)	3,032	2,313	1,834
Goatfishes	268	48	96
Spinefeet (Rabbitfishes)	372	121	201
Swordfish	27	60	23
Tuna-like fishes	330	300	8
Octopuses	93	78	632
Aquaculture	568	537	514
Red drum	498	456	432
Total catch	7,794	5,680	6,917

Note: Figures exclude aquatic animals, recorded by number rather than weight. The number of Nile crocodiles captured was: 100 in 2010; n.a. in 2011–12.

Source: FAO.

Industry

SELECTED PRODUCTS
('000 metric tons unless otherwise indicated)

	2010	2011	2012*
Fish	62.8	61.0	57.5
Frozen	2.1	1.6	1.7
Canned	59.8	58.7	55.2
Raw sugar	452.5	435.3	409.2
Molasses	143.5	138.6	125.2
Beer and stout ('000 hectolitres)	367.6	373.7	345.9
Iron bars and steel tubes	32.0	35.0	32.2
Fertilizers	24.3	27.0	27.0
Electric energy (million kWh)	2,689	2,730	2,796

* Estimates.

Finance

CURRENCY AND EXCHANGE RATES

Monetary Units
100 cents = 1 Mauritian rupee.

Sterling, Dollar and Euro Equivalents (31 December 2014)
£1 sterling = 49.52 rupees;
US $1 = 31.52 rupees;
€1 = 38.52 rupees;
1,000 Mauritian rupees = £20.19 = $31.52 = €25.96.

Average Exchange Rate (Mauritian rupees per US $)
2012   30.050
2013   30.701
2014   30.622

BUDGET
(million rupees)

Revenue

	2012	2013*	2014*
Tax revenue	64,953	68,421	73,964
Taxes on income, profits and capital gains	14,634	15,863	17,048
Taxes on property	4,556	4,635	5,142
Domestic taxes on goods and services	43,008	45,176	48,682
Taxes on international trade	1,506	1,522	1,586
Other tax revenue	1,249	1,225	1,506
Non-tax revenue	8,841	10,447	12,306
Social contributions	1,051	1,257	1,320
Grants	2,398	1,637	2,271
Other non-tax revenue	5,392	7,553	8,715
Total	73,794	78,868	86,270

Expense/Outlays

Expense by economic type	2012	2013*	2014*
Expenditure	70,255	79,941	86,710
Wages and salaries	18,684	22,930	25,101
Other purchases of goods and services	6,516	7,699	8,406
Interest payments	10,129	9,830	10,870
Subsidies and other current transfers	17,154	19,126	19,469
Social benefits	15,400	17,540	18,779
Other expense	2,373	2,816	2,485
Contingencies	—	—	1,600
Net acquisition of non-financial assets	9,616	12,726	12,181
Total	79,871	92,667	98,891

Outlays by function of government	2012	2013*	2014*
General public services	20,747	22,845	26,039
Public order and safety	7,368	10,521	11,523
Community and social services	42,627	49,955	51,907
Education	11,111	13,328	14,508
Health	7,753	8,882	9,447
Social security and welfare	17,724	20,355	21,619
Housing and community amenities	2,703	4,984	3,760
Recreational, cultural and religious services	742	868	999
Environmental protection	2,594	1,538	1,574
Economic services	9,129	9,347	7,622
Agriculture, forestry, fishing and hunting	2,069	2,503	2,483
Fuel and energy	99	75	65
Mining, manufacturing and construction	331	402	435
Transportation and communications	5,548	5,175	2,841
Tourism	554	513	516
General economic, commercial and labour affairs	225	314	679
Other economic affairs	75	90	301
Contingencies	—	—	1,800
Total expenditure	79,871	92,667	98,891

* Estimates.
Source: Ministry of Finance and Economic Development, Port Louis.

INTERNATIONAL RESERVES
(US $ million at 31 December)

	2012	2013	2014
Gold (market prices)	209.6	150.8	304.4
IMF special drawing rights	153.6	154.0	144.9
Reserve position in IMF	51.7	58.1	55.7
Foreign exchange	2,631.4	3,128.1	3,414.1
Total	3,046.3	3,491.0	3,919.1

Source: IMF, *International Financial Statistics*.

MONEY SUPPLY
(million rupees at 31 December)

	2011	2012	2013
Currency outside depository corporations	20,307.8	22,169.7	23,316.7
Transferable deposits	69,425.8	74,630.8	80,391.4
Other deposits	227,841.5	246,842.4	258,831.7
Securities other than shares	1,961.8	1,974.3	3,069.0
Broad money	319,536.7	345,617.2	365,608.7

Source: IMF, *International Financial Statistics*.

COST OF LIVING
(Consumer Price Index; base: 2012 = 100)

	2011	2013	2014
All items (incl. others)	96.3	103.5	106.9

NATIONAL ACCOUNTS
(million rupees in current prices)

National Income and Product

	2012	2013	2014
Compensation of employees	116,657	127,645	135,128
Operating surplus			
Consumption of fixed capital }	183,292	192,270	204,926
Gross domestic product (GDP) at factor cost	299,949	319,915	340,054
Taxes on production and imports	44,917	47,415	48,551
Less Subsidies	1,032	1,102	1,324
GDP in purchasers' values	343,834	366,228	387,281
Primary incomes received from abroad			
Less Primary incomes paid abroad }	1,121	429	−3,380
Gross national income	344,955	366,657	383,901
Current transfers from abroad			
Less Current transfers paid abroad }	5,013	3,059	3,804
Gross national disposable income	349,968	369,716	387,705

Expenditure on the Gross Domestic Product

	2012	2013	2014
Private final consumption expenditure	254,468	270,261	286,539
Government final consumption expenditure	45,917	52,748	55,761
Gross fixed capital formation	79,185	77,618	75,026
Increase in stocks	5,976	10,321	4,176
Total domestic expenditure	385,546	410,948	421,502
Exports of goods and services	187,688	198,793	218,829
Less Imports of goods and services	229,399	243,514	253,050
GDP in purchasers' values	343,834	366,228	387,281

Gross Domestic Product by Economic Activity

	2012	2013	2014
Agriculture, hunting, forestry and fishing	10,494	10,405	10,578
Sugar cane	3,696	3,238	2,673
Mining and quarrying	1,000	990	969
Manufacturing	50,537	55,021	56,847
Electricity, gas and water	5,284	5,755	6,370
Construction	19,034	17,680	16,729
Wholesale and retail trade, repair of motor vehicles and personal goods	36,807	39,705	42,915
Hotels and restaurants	21,249	19,697	21,728
Transport, storage and communications	31,275	32,721	34,823
Financial intermediation	31,263	32,799	35,253
Real estate, renting and business activities	38,187	41,684	45,368
Public administration and defence; compulsory social security	17,984	21,283	22,766
Education	13,413	15,428	16,231
Health and social work	11,698	13,768	15,027
Other services	14,392	16,022	17,577
Gross value added in basic prices	302,616	322,958	343,181
Taxes, less subsidies, on products	41,218	43,270	44,100
GDP in market prices	343,834	366,228	387,281

BALANCE OF PAYMENTS
(US $ million)

	2011	2012	2013
Exports of goods	2,565.0	2,649.1	2,868.8
Imports of goods	−4,917.4	−5,104.2	−5,139.0
Balance on goods	−2,352.4	−2,455.7	−2,270.3
Exports of services	3,283.1	3,407.9	3,409.7
Imports of services	−2,492.3	−2,443.4	−2,709.2
Balance on goods and services	−1,561.5	−1,491.1	−1,569.8
Primary income received	1,157.0	1,990.7	1,803.1
Primary income paid	−1,276.1	−1,469.0	−1,504.5
Balance on goods, services and primary income	−1,680.6	−969.5	−1,271.2
Secondary income received	402.8	384.0	285.0
Secondary income paid	−282.5	−242.0	−194.1
Current balance	−1,560.3	−827.5	−1,180.3
Capital account (net)	−1.9	−8.0	−4.0
Direct investment assets	−60,991.7	−21,493.1	−25,070.5
Direct investment liabilities	60,002.9	27,163.2	27,259.6
Portfolio investment assets	3,823.7	−268.1	−454.2
Portfolio investment liabilities	5,429.9	2,233.2	2,329.2
Financial derivatives and employee stock options (net)	675.6	114.4	1,205.7
Other investment assets	3,183.1	−7,286.6	−4,233.6
Other investment liabilities	−10,566.0	931.7	587.0
Net errors and omissions	199.8	−367.7	102.1
Reserves and related items	195.1	191.5	541.0

Source: IMF, *International Financial Statistics*.

External Trade

PRINCIPAL COMMODITIES
(million rupees)

Imports c.i.f.	2011	2012	2013*
Food and live animals	26,974	29,792	31,559
Fish and fish preparations	9,280	10,968	11,866
Crude materials, inedible, except fuel	4,915	3,914	4,158
Mineral fuels, lubricants, etc.	31,945	34,532	35,897
Refined petroleum products	26,977	29,269	31,263
Chemicals	12,110	12,493	12,890
Basic manufactures	27,634	28,425	28,618
Machinery and transport equipment	26,357	32,242	32,560
General industrial machinery, equipment and parts	3,860	4,507	4,416
Telecommunications and sound equipment	3,925	4,781	5,879
Other electrical machinery, apparatus, etc.	4,066	5,720	4,725
Road motor vehicles	7,149	8,658	7,866
Miscellaneous manufactured articles	12,964	14,077	14,453
Total (incl. others)	147,815	160,996	165,661

Exports f.o.b.†	2011	2012	2013*
Food and live animals	20,340	24,125	27,217
Basic manufactures	6,533	6,430	7,339
Chemicals and related products	2,165	2,349	2,430
Machinery and transport equipment	1,437	2,283	3,510
Miscellaneous manufactured articles	29,516	30,028	29,290
Total (incl. others)	62,358	67,371	71,967

* Provisional.

† Excluding stores and bunkers for ships and aircraft (million rupees): 11,228 in 2011; 12,287 in 2012; 16,181 in 2013 (provisional).

PRINCIPAL TRADING PARTNERS
(million rupees)*

Imports c.i.f.	2011	2012	2013
Argentina	2,557	2,218	2,173
Australia	3,860	3,671	4,384
Belgium	1,820	1,329	1,111
China, People's Republic	20,780	25,834	24,313
France	13,158	13,363	13,367
Germany	3,551	3,879	4,112
India	34,666	37,191	40,035
Indonesia	2,968	2,736	2,793
Italy	3,144	3,172	3,604
Japan	3,701	4,086	3,913
Korea, Republic	2,261	2,603	3,161
Malaysia	3,320	4,278	3,903
Netherlands	1,735	1,755	1,227
New Zealand	2,198	2,436	2,186
South Africa	10,457	10,535	10,230
Spain	4,462	5,484	6,551
Switzerland	1,563	1,369	1,389
Thailand	3,186	3,195	3,445
Turkey	1,429	1,303	1,457
United Arab Emirates	1,991	2,879	2,842
United Kingdom	3,403	3,230	3,560
USA	2,633	2,801	2,438
Total (incl. others)	147,815	160,996	165,661

Exports f.o.b.	2011	2012	2013
Belgium	1,441	1,916	2,205
France	8,797	8,720	8,594
Germany	1,382	1,246	1,091
Italy	5,159	4,892	6,446
Japan	400	1,033	789
Madagascar	3,973	4,641	4,510
Netherlands	987	1,244	1,829
Réunion	1,997	2,092	1,923
Seychelles	860	883	939
South Africa	4,982	6,693	6,039
Spain	4,315	4,862	4,194
Switzerland	1,176	927	786
United Kingdom	12,644	12,497	11,976
USA	6,667	6,714	7,253
Total (incl. others)	62,358	67,371	71,967

* Imports by country of origin; exports by country of destination (including re-exports, excluding ships' stores and bunkers).

Transport

ROAD TRAFFIC
(motor vehicles registered at 31 December)

	2011	2012	2013
Private vehicles:			
Cars	185,357	197,849	211,586
Motorcycles and mopeds	165,706	173,508	180,785
Commercial vehicles:			
Buses	2,912	2,957	2,963
Taxis	6,907	6,905	6,915
Lorries and trucks	13,539	13,902	14,061

SHIPPING

Flag Registered Fleet
(at 31 December)

	2012	2013	2014
Number of vessels	116	119	120
Total displacement ('000 grt)	192.4	187.4	184.4

Source: Lloyd's List Intelligence (www.lloydslistintelligence.com).

Seaborne Freight Traffic
('000 metric tons)

	2011	2012	2013*
Goods unloaded	5,386	5,933	5,656
Goods loaded†	1,091	1,142	1,080

* Provisional figures.
† Excluding ships' bunkers.

CIVIL AVIATION
(traffic)

	2011	2012	2013*
Aircraft landings	10,121	10,016	9,001
Freight unloaded (metric tons)	21,707	23,300	17,400
Freight loaded (metric tons)	23,414	23,700	19,900

* Provisional.

Tourism

FOREIGN TOURIST ARRIVALS

Country of residence	2011	2012	2013*
France	282,469	256,929	244,752
Germany	56,331	55,186	60,530
India	53,955	55,197	57,255
Italy	52,747	40,009	60,530
Réunion	113,000	139,169	143,114
South Africa	86,232	89,058	94,208
Switzerland	24,362	26,002	27,756
United Kingdom	88,182	87,648	98,017
Total (incl. others)	964,642	965,441	993,106

* Provisional.

Tourism receipts (gross earnings, million rupees): 42,717 in 2011; 44,378 in 2012; 40,557 in 2013 (provisional).

Communications Media

	2011	2012	2013
Telephones ('000 main lines in use)	374.6	349.1	363.0
Mobile cellular telephones ('000 subscribers)	1,294.1	1,485.8	1,533.6
Fixed internet subscribers ('000)	133.2	149.2	166.8*
Broadband subscribers ('000)	116.8	139.0	156.0
Television sets licensed ('000)	316.4	319.3	321.2*
Daily newspapers	11	11	9*
Non-daily newspapers	57	52	55*

* Provisional.

Source: partly International Telecommunication Union.

Education

(2013)

	Institutions	Teachers	Students*
Pre-primary	978	2,425	31,419
Primary	320	5,512	108,853
Secondary	178	8,830	124,309
Technical and vocational	117	729	10,548

* By enrolment.

Pupil-teacher ratio (primary education, UNESCO estimate): 20.9 in 2011/12 (Source: UNESCO Institute for Statistics).

Adult literacy rate (UNESCO estimates): 89.2% (males 92.0%; females 86.7%) in 2011 (Source: UNESCO Institute for Statistics).

Directory

The Government

HEAD OF STATE

President: KAILASH PURRYAG.
Vice-President: MONIQUE OHSAN-BELLEPEAU.

COUNCIL OF MINISTERS
(May 2015)

Prime Minister, Minister of Defence, Home Affairs and the National Development Unit, Minister of Rodrigues: Sir ANEROOD JUGNAUTH.

Deputy Prime Minister and Minister of Tourism and External Communications: CHARLES GAËTAN XAVIER-LUC DUVAL.

Vice-Prime Minister and Minister of Housing and Lands: SHOWKUTALLY SOODHUN.

Vice-Prime Minister and Minister of Energy and Public Utilities: IVAN COLLENDAVELLO.

Minister of Finance and Economic Development: SEETANAH LUTCHMEENARAIDOO.

Minister of Technology, Communication and Innovation: PRAVIND KUMAR JUGNAUTH.

Minister of Youth and Sports: YOGIDA SAWMYNADEN.

Minister of Public Infrastructure and Land Transport: NANDCOOMAR BODHA.

Minister of Education and Human Resources, Tertiary Education and Scientific Research: LEELA DEVI DOOKUN-LUCHOOMUN.

Minister of Health and Quality of Life: ANIL KUMARSINGH GAYAN.

Minister of Local Government: Dr MOHAMMAD ANWAR HISNOO.

Minister of Social Integration and Economic Empowerment: PRITHVIRAJSING ROOPUN.

Minister of Foreign Affairs, Regional Integration and International Trade: MARIE JOSEPH NOËL ETIENNE GHISLAIN SINTAMBOU.

Attorney-General: RAVI YERRIGADOO.

Minister of Agro-Industry and Food Security: MAHEN KUMAR SEERUTTUN.

Minister of Arts and Culture: SANTARAM BABOO.

Minister of Industry, Commerce and Consumer Protection: ASHIT KUMAR GUNGAH.

Minister of Gender Equality, Child Development and Family Welfare: MARIE-AURORE MARIE-JOYCE PERRAUD.

Minister of Financial Services, Good Governance and Institutional Reforms: SUDARSHAN BHADAIN.

Minister of Business, Enterprise and Co-operatives: SOOMILDUTH BHOLAH.

Minister of Social Security, National Solidarity and Reform Institutions: FAZILA DAUREEAWOO.

Minister of Ocean Economy, Marine Resources, Fisheries, Shipping and the Outer Islands: PREMDUT KOONJOON.

Minister of Environment, the National Emergency Centre and the Beach Authority: JAYESHWUR RAJ DAYAL.

Minister of Civil Service Affairs: MARIE ROLAND ALAIN WONG YEN CHEONG.

Minister of Labour, Industrial Relations, Employment and Training: SOODESH SATKAM CALLICHURN.

MINISTRIES

Office of the President: State House, Le Réduit, Port Louis; tel. 454-3021; fax 464-5370; e-mail president@govmu.org; internet president.govmu.org.

Office of the Vice-President: 30 Farquhar Ave, Quatre Bornes, Port Louis; tel. 427-1024; fax 427-1487; e-mail ovp@govmu.org; internet vice-president.govmu.org.

Office of the Prime Minister: New Treasury Bldg, Intendance St, Port Louis; tel. 207-9595; fax 208-8619; e-mail pmo@govmu.org; internet pmo.govmu.org.

Ministry of Agro-Industry and Food Security: Renganaden Seeneevassen Bldg, 8th and 9th Floor, cnr Jules Koenig and Maillard Sts, Port Louis; tel. 212-0854; fax 212-4427; e-mail moa-headoffice@govmu.org; internet agriculture.govmu.org.

Ministry of Arts and Culture: Renganaden Seeneevassen Bldg, 7th Floor, cnr Pope Hennessy and Maillard Sts, Port Louis; tel. 212-2112; fax 210-0681; e-mail moac@govmu.org; internet culture.govmu.org.

Ministry of Business, Enterprise and Co-operatives: Newton Tower, 6th Floor, Sir William Newton St, Port Louis; tel. 405-3100; fax 213-9176; e-mail mbe@govmu.org; internet enterbusiness.govmu.org.

Ministry of the Civil Service and Administrative Reforms: New Government Centre, 7th Floor, Port Louis; tel. 201-2886; fax 212-9528; e-mail civser@mail.gov.mu; internet civilservice.govmu.org.

Ministry of Education and Human Resources: MITD House, Pont Fer, Phoenix; tel. 601-5200; fax 698-9627; e-mail moeministeroffice@govmu.org; internet ministry-education.govmu.org.

Ministry of Energy and Public Utilities: Air Mauritius Centre, 10th Floor, John F. Kennedy St, Port Louis; tel. 405-6710; fax 208-6497; e-mail mpu@govmu.org; internet publicutilities.govmu.org.

Ministry of the Environment, the National Emergency Centre and the Beach Authority: Ken Lee Tower, cnr Barracks and St Georges Sts, Port Louis; tel. 203-6200; fax 212-8324; e-mail menv@govmu.org; internet environment.govmu.org.

Ministry of Finance and Economic Development: Government House, Ground Floor, Port Louis; tel. 201-1146; fax 211-0096; e-mail contactmofed@govmu.org; internet mof.govmu.org.

Ministry of Fisheries: Albion Fisheries Research Centre, Port Louis; tel. 238-4100; fax 238-4184; e-mail fisheries@govmu.org; internet fisheries.govmu.org.

Ministry of Foreign Affairs, Regional Integration and International Trade: Newton Tower, 9th–11th Floors, Sir William Newton St, Port Louis; tel. 405-2500; fax 208-8087; e-mail mfa@govmu.org; internet foreign.govmu.org.

Ministry of Gender Equality, Child Development and Family Welfare: CSK Bldg, cnr Remy Ollier and Emmanuel Anquetil Sts, Port Louis; tel. 206-3700; fax 240-7717; e-mail mwfwcd@govmu.org; internet gender.govmu.org.

Ministry of Health and Quality of Life: Emmanuel Anquetil Bldg, 5th Floor, Sir Seewoosagur Ramgoolam St, Port Louis; tel. 201-2175; fax 208-7222; e-mail moh@mail.gov.mu; internet health.govmu.org.

Ministry of Housing and Lands: Ebene Tower, Plot 52, Ebène; tel. 401-6808; fax 454-6328; e-mail mhou@govmu.org; internet housing.govmu.org.

Ministry of Industry, Commerce and Consumer Protection: Paille en Queue Court, 8th Floor, Port Louis; tel. 210-7100; fax 211-0855; e-mail mind@govmu.org; internet industry.govmu.org.

Ministry of Information and Communication Technology: Air Mauritius Centre, 9th Floor, John F. Kennedy St, Port Louis; tel. 210-0201; fax 212-1673; e-mail mict@mail.gov.mu; internet mict.gov.mu.

Ministry of Labour, Industrial Relations, Employment and Training: Victoria House, cnr St Louis and Barracks Sts, Port Louis; tel. 207-2600; fax 212-3070; e-mail mol@govmu.org; internet labour.govmu.org.

Ministry of Local Government and Outer Islands: Emmanuel Anquetil Bldg, 3rd Floor, cnr Sir Seewoosagur Ramgoolam and Jules Koenig Sts, Port Louis; tel. 201-2155; fax 208-9729; e-mail mlg@mail.gov.mu; internet localgovernment.govmu.org.

Ministry of Public Infrastructure, the National Development Unit, Land Transport and Shipping: Moorgate House, 9th Floor, Sir William Newton St, Port Louis; tel. 208-0281; fax 208-7149; e-mail mpi@govmu.org; internet publicinfrastructure.govmu.org.

Ministry of Social Integration and Economic Empowerment: Air Mauritius Centre, 12th Floor, John F. Kennedy St, Port Louis; tel. 213-0633; fax 213-0537; e-mail msiep@govmu.org; internet socialintegration.govmu.org.

Ministry of Social Security, National Solidarity and Reform Institutions: Renganaden Seeneevassen Bldg, 13th Floor, cnr Jules Koenig and Maillard Sts, Port Louis; tel. 207-0625; fax 212-8190; e-mail mss@mail.govmu.org; internet socialsecurity.govmu.org.

Ministry of Tertiary Education, Science, Research and Technology: Wing B, 11th Floor, Cyber Tower 1, Cyber City, Ebene; tel. 454-1450; fax 468-1441; e-mail tertiary@govmu.org; internet tertiary.govmu.org.

Ministry of Tourism and Leisure: Air Mauritius Centre, 5th Floor, John F. Kennedy St, Port Louis; tel. 211-7930; fax 208-6776; e-mail mtou@govmu.org; internet tourism.govmu.org.

Ministry of Youth and Sports: Emmanuel Anquetil Bldg, 3rd Floor, Sir Seewoosagur Ramgoolam St, Port Louis; tel. 201-2543; fax 211-2986; e-mail mys@govmu.org; internet youthsport.govmu.org.

Legislature

National Assembly: Port Louis; tel. 201-1414; fax 212-8364; e-mail themace@intnet.mu; internet mauritiusassembly.gov.mu.

Speaker: PEEROO RAZACK.

General Election, 10 December 2014

Party	Seats		
	Directly elected	Additional*	Total
Alliance Lepep†	47	4	51
Alliance de l'Unité et de la Modernité‡	13	3	16
Organisation du Peuple Rodriguais.	2	—	2
Total	62	7	69

* Awarded to those among the unsuccessful candidates who attracted the largest number of votes, in order to ensure that a balance of ethnic groups is represented in the Assembly.

† Alliance comprising the Mouvement Socialiste Militant, the Parti Mauricien Social Démocrate and the Muvman Liberater.

‡ Alliance comprising the Mauritius Labour Party and the Mouvement Militant Mauricien.

Election Commission

Electoral Commissioner's Office (ECO): Max City Bldg, 4th Floor, cnr Louis Pasteur and Remy Ollier Sts, Port Louis; tel. 240-9690; fax 241-9409; e-mail elec@govmu.org; internet electoral.govmu .org; under the aegis of the Prime Minister's Office; Commissioner appointed by the Judicial and Legal Service Commission; Electoral Commissioner MOHAMMAD IRFAN ABDOOL RAHMAN.

Political Organizations

Forum des Citoyens Libres (FCL): Leader GEORGES AH-YAN.

Front Solidarité Mauricienne (FSM): Leader CEHL MEEAH.

Mauritius Labour Party (MLP) (Parti Travailliste): 7 Guy Rozemont Sq., Port Louis; tel. 212-6691; fax 210-0189; e-mail info@ labourparty.mu; internet www.labourparty.mu; f. 1936; Leader Dr NAVINCHANDRA RAMGOOLAM; Pres. PATRICK ASSIRVADEN; Sec.-Gen. KAYLANEE JUGGOO.

Mouvement Mauricien Social Démocrate (MMSD): Morcellement Piat, Forest-Side, POB 1, Port Louis; tel. 670-4000; fax 670-1111; e-mail mmsd@orange.mu; internet www.mmsd.mu; f. 2009; Leader ERIC GUIMBEAU.

Mouvement Militant Mauricien (MMM): 21 Poudrière St, Port Louis; tel. 212-6553; fax 208-9939; internet www.mmm.mu; f. 1969; socialist; Pres. ARIANNE NAVARRE-MARIE; Leader PAUL BÉRENGER; Secs-Gen. STEVEN OBEEGADOO, RAJESH BHAGWAN.

Mouvement Rodriguais (MR): Port Mathurin, Rodrigues; tel. 525-56984; fax 831-2648; e-mail nvmally@intnet.mu; f. 1992; represents the interests of Rodrigues; Leader LOUIS JOSEPH (NICHOLAS) VON-MALLY.

Mouvement Socialiste Militant (MSM): Sun Trust Bldg, 1st Floor, 31 Edith Cavell St, Port Louis; tel. 212-8787; fax 212-9334; e-mail info@msmparty.org; internet www.msmparty.org; f. 1983 by fmr mems of the MMM; Leader Dr PRAVIND KUMAR JUGNAUTH; Pres. SHOWKUTALLY SOODHUN; Sec.-Gen. NANDO BODHA.

Organisation du Peuple Rodriguais (OPR): Mont Lubin, Rodrigues; represents the interests of Rodrigues; f. 1976; Leader LOUIS SERGE CLAIR.

Parti Mauricien Social Démocrate (PMSD): Melville, Grand Gaube; internet www.pmsd.mu; centre-right; Leader CHARLES GAËTAN XAVIER-LUC DUVAL; Sec.-Gen. RAMA VALAYDEN.

Union Nationale (UN) (Mauritian National Union): Port Louis; tel. 208-4254; e-mail ashock.jugnauth@unionnationale.mu; internet unionnationale.mu; f. 2006; Chair. ASHOCK JUGNAUTH.

Some of the blocs and parties that participated in the 2014 elections include **Les Verts Fraternels/The Greens** (Leader SYLVIO MICHEL), **Muvman Liberater** (Leader IVAN COLLENDAVELLOO), the **Parti du Peuple Mauricien (PPM)**, the **Rezistans ek Alternativ** (Secretary ASHOK SUBRON) and **Lalit** (lalitmauritius.com).

Diplomatic Representation

EMBASSIES AND HIGH COMMISSIONS IN MAURITIUS

Australia: Rogers House, 2nd Floor, John F. Kennedy St, POB 541, Port Louis; tel. 202-0160; fax 208-8878; e-mail ahc.portlouis@dfat .gov.au; internet www.mauritius.embassy.gov.au; High Commissioner SUSAN COLES.

Bangladesh: Hennessy Court, 8th Floor, Pope Hennessy St (cnr Suffren Rd), Port Louis; tel. 212-9527; fax 212-9639; e-mail mission .portlouis@yahoo.com; High Commissioner ABDUL MANNAN HOWLADER.

China, People's Republic: Royal Rd, Belle Rose, Rose Hill; tel. 454-9111; fax 464-6012; e-mail chinaemb_mu@mfa.gov.cn; internet www .ambchine.mu; Ambassador LI LI.

Egypt: Sun Trust Bldg, 2nd Floor, Edith Cavell St, Port Louis; tel. 213-1765; fax 213-1768; Chargé d'affaires a.i. OSAMA HELMY RIHAN.

France: 14 St George St, Port Louis; tel. 202-0100; fax 202-0110; e-mail ambafr.port-louis@hotmail.fr; internet www.ambafrance-mu .org; Ambassador LAURENT GARNIER.

India: LIC Centre, 6th Floor, John F. Kennedy St, POB 162, Port Louis; tel. 208-8891; fax 208-6859; e-mail hicom.ss@intnet.mu; internet indiahighcom.intnet.mu; High Commissioner ANUP KUMAR MUDGAL.

Libya: John Kennedy Ave (ex-Residence of Dr Malleck), Port Louis; tel. 686-1801; fax 686-2101; e-mail libyambass@orange.mu; Chargé d'affaires a.i. MUAWIA A. O. ABURAWZSHA.

Madagascar: Guiot Pasceau St, Floreal, POB 3, Port Louis; tel. 686-5015; fax 686-7040; e-mail madmail@intnet.mu; internet www .ambamad.mu; Chargé d'affaires a.i. RICHARD VIA.

Pakistan: 9A Queen Mary Ave, Floreal, Port Louis; tel. 698-8501; fax 698-8405; e-mail pareportlouis@hotmail.com; High Commissioner (vacant).

Russian Federation: Queen Mary Ave, Floreal, POB 10, Port Louis; tel. 696-1545; fax 696-5027; e-mail rusemb.mu@intnet.mu; Ambassador VYACHESLAV NIKIFOROV.

South Africa: BAI Bldg, 4th Floor, 25 Pope Hennessy St, POB 908, Port Louis; tel. 212-6925; fax 212-6936; e-mail sahc@intnet.mu; High Commissioner MADUMANE M. MATABANE.

United Kingdom: Les Cascades Bldg, 7th Floor, Edith Cavell St, POB 1063, Port Louis; tel. 202-9400; fax 202-9408; e-mail bhc@intnet .mu; internet www.gov.uk/government/world/mauritius; High Commissioner JONATHAN DREW.

USA: Rogers House, 4th Floor, John F. Kennedy St, POB 544, Port Louis; tel. 202-4400; fax 208-9534; e-mail usembass@intnet.mu; internet mauritius.usembassy.gov; Ambassador SHARI ENGLISH WOODS VILLAROSA.

Judicial System

The laws of Mauritius are derived both from the French Code Napoléon and from English Law. The Judicial Department consists of the Supreme Court, presided over by the Chief Justice and such number of Puisne Judges as may be prescribed by Parliament (19 at March 2014), who are also Judges of the Court of Criminal Appeal and the Court of Civil Appeal. These courts hear appeals from the Intermediate Court, the Industrial Court and 10 District Courts (including that of Rodrigues). The Industrial Court has special jurisdiction to protect the constitutional rights of the citizen. There is a right of appeal in certain cases from the Supreme Court to the Judicial Committee of the Privy Council in the United Kingdom.

Supreme Court: Jules Koenig St, Port Louis; tel. 212-0275; fax 212-9946; internet supremecourt.intnet.mu.

Chief Justice: KHESHOE PARSAD MATADEEN.

Senior Puisne Judge: MARC FRANCE EDDY BALANCY.

Religion

Hindus are estimated to comprise more than 50% of the population, with Christians accounting for some 30% and Muslims 17%. There is also a small Buddhist community.

CHRISTIANITY

The Anglican Communion

Anglicans in Mauritius are within the Church of the Province of the Indian Ocean, comprising seven dioceses (five in Madagascar, one in Mauritius and one in Seychelles). The Archbishop of the Province is the Bishop of Antananarivo, Madagascar.

Bishop of Mauritius (also Archbishop of the Province of the Indian Ocean): Most Rev. GERALD JAMES (IAN) ERNEST, Bishop's House, Phoenix; tel. 686-5158; fax 697-1096; e-mail dioang@intnet.mu.

The Presbyterian Church of Mauritius

Minister: Pasteur ANDRÉ DE RÉLAND, cnr Farquhar and Royal Rds, Coignet, Rose Hill; tel. 464-5265; fax 395-2068; e-mail embrau@bow.intnet.mu; internet pages.intnet.mu/reformee; f. 1814.

The Roman Catholic Church

Mauritius comprises a single diocese, directly responsible to the Holy See, and an apostolic vicariate on Rodrigues. Some 26% of the total population are Roman Catholics.

Bishop of Port Louis: Rt Rev. MAURICE PIAT, Evêché, 13 Mgr Gonin St, Port Louis; tel. 208-3068; fax 208-6607; e-mail eveche@intnet.mu.

BAHÁ'Í FAITH

National Spiritual Assembly: 40 Volcy Pougnet St, Port Louis; tel. 212-2179; e-mail nsamru@intnet.mu; mems resident in 190 localities.

ISLAM

World Islamic Mission (Mauritius): Shah Noorani Centre, 30 Old Moka Rd, Bell Village, Port Louis; tel. 211-1092; fax 210-9445; e-mail wim@wimmauritius.org; internet www.wimmauritius.org; f. 1975; Gen. Sec. HAMADE AUBDOOLLAH.

The Press

DAILIES

China Times: 24 Emmanuel Anquetil St, POB 325, Port Louis; tel. 240-3067; f. 1953; Chinese; Editor-in-Chief LONG SIONG AH KENG; circ. 3,000.

Chinese Daily News: 32 Remy Ollier St, POB 316, Port Louis; tel. 240-0472; f. 1932; Chinese; Editor-in-Chief WONG YUEN MOY; circ. 5,000.

L'Express: 3 rue des Oursins, Riche-Terre, Baie du Tombeau, POB 247, Port Louis; tel. 206-8200; fax 247-1010; internet www.lexpress.mu; f. 1963; owned by La Sentinelle Ltd; English and French; Dir of Publication ARIANE CAVALOT DE L'ESTRAC; Editor-in-Chief JÉRÔME BOULLE; circ. 35,000.

The Independent Daily: Port Louis; internet theindependent.mu.

Le Matinal: AAPCA House, 6 La Poudrière St, Port Louis; tel. 207-0909; fax 213-4069; e-mail editorial@lematinal.com; internet www.lematinal.com; f. 2003; French and English; owned by AAPCA (Mauritius) Ltd; Editor-in-Chief KIRAN RAMSAHAYE.

Le Mauricien: 8 St George St, POB 7, Port Louis; tel. 208-3251; fax 208-7059; e-mail redaction@lemauricien.com; internet www.lemauricien.com; f. 1907; English and French; Dir of Publication JACQUES RIVET; Editor-in-Chief GAËTAN SÉNÈQUE; circ. 35,000.

Le Quotidien: Pearl House, 4th Floor, 16 Sir Virgile Naz St, Port Louis; tel. 208-2631; fax 211-7479; e-mail quotidien@bow.intnet.mu; f. 1996; English and French; Dirs JACQUES DAVID, PATRICK MICHEL; circ. 30,000.

Le Socialiste: Manilall Bldg, 3rd Floor, Brabant St, Port Louis; tel. 208-8003; fax 211-3890; English and French; Editor-in-Chief VEDI BALLAH; circ. 7,000.

WEEKLIES AND FORTNIGHTLIES

5-Plus Dimanche: 3 rue des Oursins, Baie du Tombeau; tel. 206-8200; fax 247-1010; e-mail prod@5plus.mu; internet www.5plus.mu; f. 1994; English and French; Editor-in-Chief MICHAELLA SEBLIN; circ. 30,000.

Bollywood Massala: Le Défi Bldg, Royal Rd, Port Louis; tel. 211-8131; fax 213-0959; e-mail ledefi.plus@intnet.mu; internet www.defimedia.info.

Business Magazine: 3 Brown-Sequard St, 3rd Floor, Port Louis; tel. 202-2300; fax 211-1926; e-mail businessmag@orange.mu; internet www.businessmag.mu; f. 1992; owned by Business Publications Ltd; English and French; Editor JEAN PAUL AROUFF; circ. 7,500.

Le Défi-Plus: Le Défi Bldg, Royal Rd, Port Louis; tel. 211-8131; fax 213-0959; e-mail ledefi.plus@intnet.mu; internet www.defimedia.info; Saturdays; Dir of Publication ESHAN KHODABUX.

L'Hebdo: Le Défi Bldg, Royal Rd, Port Louis; tel. 211-8131; fax 213-0959; e-mail ledefi.plus@intnet.mu; internet www.defimedia.info.

Impact News: 10 Dr Yves Cantin St, Port Louis; tel. 211-5284; fax 211-7821; e-mail farhadr@wanadoo.mu; English and French; Editor-in-Chief FARHAD RAMJAUN.

Lalit de Klas: 153B Royal Rd, GRNW, Port Louis; tel. 208-2132; e-mail lalitmail@intnet.mu; internet www.lalitmauritius.org; English, French and Mauritian Creole; Editor RADA KISTNASAMY.

Mauritius Times: 23 Bourbon St, Port Louis; tel. and fax 212-1313; e-mail mtimes@intnet.mu; internet www.mauritiustimes.com; f. 1954; English and French; Editor-in-Chief MADHUKAR RAMLALLAH; circ. 15,000.

News on Sunday: Dr Eugen Laurent St, POB 230, Port Louis; tel. 211-5902; fax 211-7302; e-mail newsonsunday@news.intnet.mu; f. 1996; owned by Le Défi Group; weekly; English; Editor NAGUIB LALLMAHOMED; circ. 10,000.

Samedi Plus: Port Louis; Editor-in-Chief DHARMANAND DOOHARIKA.

Star: 38 Labourdonnais St, Port Louis; tel. 212-2736; fax 211-7781; e-mail starpress@intnet.mu; internet www.mauriweb.com/star; English and French; Editor-in-Chief REZA ISSACK.

Turf Magazine: 8 George St, POB 7, Port Louis; tel. 207-8200; fax 208-7059; e-mail bdlm@intnet.mu; internet www.lemauricien.com/turfmag; owned by Le Mauricien Ltd.

La Vie Catholique: 28 Nicolay Rd, Port Louis; tel. 242-0975; fax 242-3114; e-mail viecatho@intnet.mu; internet www.laviecatholique.com; f. 1930; weekly; English, French and Creole; Editor-in-Chief DANIÈLE BABOORAM; circ. 9,500.

Week-End: 8 St George St, POB 7, Port Louis; tel. 207-8200; fax 208-7059; e-mail redaction@lemauricien.com; internet www.lemauricien.com/weekend; f. 1966; owned by Le Mauricien Ltd; French and English; Chief Editor GAËTAN SÉNÈQUE; circ. 80,000.

Week-End Scope: 8 St George St, POB 7, Port Louis; tel. 207-8200; fax 208-7059; e-mail wes@lemauricien.com; internet www.lemauricien.com/wes; f. 1989; owned by Le Mauricien Ltd; English and French; Editor-in-Chief GAËTAN SÉNÈQUE.

OTHER SELECTED PERIODICALS

CCI–INFO: 3 Royal St, Port Louis; tel. 208-3301; fax 208-0076; e-mail mcci@intnet.mu; internet www.mcci.org; English and French; f. 1995; quarterly; publ. of the Mauritius Chamber of Commerce and Industry; Man. FAEEZA IBRAHIMSAH.

Le Message de L'Ahmadiyyat: c/o Ahmadiyya Muslim Asscn, POB 6, Rose Hill; tel. 464-1747; fax 454-2223; e-mail darussalaam@intnet.mu; French; yearly; Editor-in-Chief MOUSSA TAUJOO; circ. 1,000.

Le Progrès Islamique: 51B Solferino St, Rose Hill; tel. 467-1697; fax 467-1696; f. 1948; English and French; monthly; Editor DEVINA SOOKIA.

Publishers

Business Publications Ltd: TN Tower, 2nd Floor, St George St, Port Louis; tel. 211-3048; fax 211-1926; internet www.businessmag.mu; f. 1993; English and French.

Editions de l'Océan Indien: Stanley, Rose Hill; tel. 464-6761; fax 464-3445; e-mail eoibooks@intnet.mu; f. 1977; general, textbooks, dictionaries, literature; English, French and Asian languages; Gen. Man. DEVANAND DEWKURUN.

Editions Le Printemps: 4 Club Rd, Vacoas; tel. 696-1017; fax 686-7302; e-mail elp@bow.intnet.mu; Man. Dir A. I. SULLIMAN.

Editions Vizavi: 3 Nahaboo Solim St, Port Louis; tel. 211-2453; e-mail vizavi@orange.mu; internet www.vizavi.mu; f. 1993; Man. Dir PASCALE SIEW.

Broadcasting and Communications

TELECOMMUNICATIONS

In 2012 there were 349,100 subscribers to fixed-line telephone services and 1.5m. subscribers to mobile cellular telephone services.

Mauritius Telecom Ltd: Telecom Tower, Edith Cavell St, Port Louis; tel. 203-7000; fax 208-1070; e-mail ceo@mauritiustelecom.com.mu; internet www.mauritiustelecom.com; f. 1992; 60% owned by Govt of Mauritius, State Bank of Mauritius and National Pensions Fund, 40% owned by France Télécom through RIMCOM; provides all telecommunications services, including internet and digital mobile cellular services; Chair. MOHAMMED ASRAF ALLY DULULL; CEO SARAT DUTT LALLAH.

Cellplus Mobile Communications Ltd: Telecom Tower, 9th Floor, Edith Cavell St, Port Louis; tel. 208-5057; fax 211-6996; e-mail contact@orange.mu; internet www.orange.mu/mobile; f. 1996; introduced the first GSM cellular network in Mauritius and recently in Rodrigues (Cell-Oh); a wholly owned subsidiary of Mauritius Telecom.

Emtel: 10 Ebene Cyber City, Ebene; tel. 454-5400; fax 454-1010; e-mail emtel@emtelnet.com; internet www.emtel.com; f. 1989; CEO SHYAM ROY.

Outremer Télécom Maurice: Hassamal Bldg, Rémono St, POB 113, Rose Hill; tel. 401-9400; fax 401-9422; e-mail info@outremer-telecom.mu; internet www.outremer-telecom.mu; Man. Dir MICHEL RIGOT.

Regulatory Authority

Information and Communication Technologies Authority (ICTA): The Celicourt, 12th Floor, 6 Sir Celicourt Antelme St, Port Louis; tel. 211-5333; fax 211-9444; e-mail icta@intnet.mu; internet www.icta.mu; f. 2002; regulatory authority; Exec. Dir Dr KRISHNA OOLUN.

BROADCASTING

Independent Broadcasting Authority: The Celicourt, 2nd Floor, 6 Sir Celicourt Antelme St, Port Louis; tel. 213-3890; fax 213-3894; e-mail iba@intnet.mu; internet www.iba.mu; Chair. (vacant); Dir (vacant).

Radio

Mauritius Broadcasting Corpn: 1 Royal Rd, Moka; tel. 402-8000; fax 433-3330; e-mail customercare@mbc.intnet.mu; internet www.mbcradio.tv; f. 1964; parastatal organization operating eight national radio services and nine television channels; Chair. CLAUDE RÉGIS NARAIN; Dir-Gen. VIJAY KUMAR PRITUM PARMESSUR.

Radio One: 3 Brown Sequard St, Port Louis; tel. 211-4555; fax 211-4142; e-mail sales@r1.mu; internet www.r1.mu; f. 2002; owned by Sentinelle media group; news and entertainment; Dir-Gen. NICOLAS ADELSON.

Radio Plus: 4B Labourdonnais St, Port-Louis; tel. 208-6002; fax 212-0047; e-mail radioplus@intnet.mu; internet www.radioplus.mu; f. 2002; Admin. Man. RASHID CASSAM.

Top FM: The Peninsula, Caudan Bldg, 7th Floor, 2A Falcon St, Caudan, Port Louis; tel. 213-2121; fax 213-2222; e-mail topfm@intnet.mu; internet www.topfmradio.com; f. 2003; Chair. BALKRISHNA KAUNHYE.

Radio France International and France Inter are also broadcast to Mauritius.

Television

Independent television stations commenced broadcasting from 2002, as part of the liberalization of the sector.

Mauritius Broadcasting Corpn: see RadioBroadcasts from France 24 and TV5 are received in Mauritius.

Finance

(cap. = capital; res = reserves; dep. = deposits; m. = million; brs = branches; amounts in Mauritian rupees unless otherwise stated)

BANKING

Central Bank

Bank of Mauritius: Sir William Newton St, POB 29, Port Louis; tel. 202-3800; fax 208-9204; e-mail info@bom.mu; internet bom.intnet.mu; f. 1966; bank of issue; cap. 1,000.0m., res 19,158.8m., dep. 27,353.7m. (June 2010); Gov. RAMESWURLALL BASANT ROI.

Principal Commercial Banks

ABC Banking Corpn Ltd: 7 Duke of Edinburgh Ave, Place d'Armes, Port Louis; tel. 206-8000; fax 208-0088; internet www.abcbanking.mu; f. 2010; cap. 356.6m., res 30.6m., dep. 8,258.1m. (June 2014); Chair. PHILIPPE CHAN KIN; CEO Dr DONALD AH-CHUEN.

AfrAsia Bank Ltd: Bowen Square, 10 Dr Ferriere St, Port Louis; tel. 208-5500; fax 213-8850; e-mail afrasia@afrasiabank.com; internet www.afrasiabank.com; f. 2007; cap. 3,147.8m., res -131.5m., dep. 40,533.7m. (June 2014); Chair. ARNAUD LAGESSE; CEO JAMES BENOIT.

Bank of Baroda: 32 Sir William Newton St, POB 553, Port Louis; tel. 208-1504; fax 208-3892; e-mail info@bankofbaroda-mu.com; internet www.bankofbaroda-mu.com; f. 1962; total assets 2,655,000m. (June 2007); Vice-Pres. (Mauritius Operations) K. D. BANSAL; 7 brs.

Bank One Ltd: 16 Sir William Newton St, POB 485, Port Louis; tel. 202-9200; fax 210-4712; e-mail info@firstcitybank-mauritius.com; internet www.bankone.mu; f. 1991 as the Delphis Bank Ltd; merged with Union International Bank in 1997; name changed as above in 2008; 50% owned by Investments & Mortgages Bank Ltd (Kenya), 50% by Ciel Investments Ltd; cap. 731.4m., res 172.3m., dep.

15,162.7m. (Dec. 2013); Chair. KIM FOONG (ROGER) LEUNG SHIN CHEUNG; CEO RAVNEET SINGH CHOWDHURY.

BanyanTree Bank Ltd: 13 Nexteracom I, Cybercity, Ebene; tel. 468-1101; fax 468-1901; e-mail info@banyantreebank.com; internet www.banyantreebank.com; f. 2012; CEO PUTHEN VEETTIL GOPAKUMAR.

Barclays Bank Mauritius Ltd: Barclays House, 68-68A Cybercity, POB 284, Ebene; tel. 404-1000; fax 465-2000; e-mail barclays.mauritius@barclays.com; internet www.barclays.mu; f. 1919; absorbed Banque Nationale de Paris Intercontinentale in 2002; cap. 100.0m., res 616.1m., dep. 6,886.7m. (Dec. 2001); Man. Dir RAVIN DAJEE; 16 brs.

Deutsche Bank Mauritius Ltd: Barkly Wharf East, 4th Floor, Le Caudan Waterfront, POB 615, Port Louis; tel. 202-7878; fax 202-7898; internet www.db.com/mauritius.

Habib Bank Ltd: 30 Louis Pasteur St, Port Louis; tel. 217-7600; fax 216-3829; e-mail habib@intnet.mu; internet www.hbl.com/mauritius; f. 1964; Country Man. SAJID BODHY; 2 brs.

Hongkong and Shanghai Banking Corpn Ltd (HSBC): HSBC Centre, 5th Floor, 18 Cyber City, Ebene; tel. 403-0701; fax 403-8300; e-mail hsbcmauritius@hsbc.co.mu; internet www.hsbc.co.mu; f. 1916; CEO ALASTAIR BRYCE; Man. Dir DEAN LAM.

Investec Bank (Mauritius) Ltd: Dias Pier Bldg, 6th Floor, Le Caudan Waterfront, Port Louis; tel. 207-4000; fax 207-4002; internet www.investec.com; f. 1997; cap. US $56.4m., res $43.0m., dep. $670.3m. (March 2013); Chair. HUGH S. HERMAN; CEO CRAIG C. MCKENZIE.

Mauritius Commercial Bank Ltd: MCB Centre, 9–15 Sir William Newton St, POB 52, Port Louis; tel. 202-5000; fax 208-7054; e-mail mcb@mcb.co.mu; internet www.mcb.mu; f. 1838; cap. 2,379.6m., res 3,396.5m., dep. 176,576.9m. (June 2014); Pres. GERARD J. HARDY; CEO PIERRE-GUY NOEL; 42 brs.

Mauritius Post and Co-operative Bank Ltd: 1 Sir William Newton St, Port Louis; tel. 405-9400; fax 208-7270; e-mail mpcb@mpcb.mu; internet www.mpcb.mu; f. 2003; 44.3% owned by The Mauritius Post Ltd, 35.7% state-owned, 10% owned by the Sugar Investment Trust; cap. 383.9m., res 216.4m., dep. 15,500.3m. (Dec. 2013); CEO PAVADAY THONDRAYEN (acting).

National Commercial Bank Ltd (NCB): 1 Queen St, Place d'Armes, Port Louis; tel. 405-4400; fax 468-1500; f. 2015 to replace Bramer Bank; state-owned; cap. 1,000.7m., res 109.9m., dep. 11,877.2m. (Dec. 2013); Chair. SAID LALLOO; CEO ASHRAF ESMAEL; 20 brs.

P. T. Bank Internasional Indonesia (Mauritius): Barkly Wharf, 5th Floor, Le Caudan Waterfront, Port Louis; tel. 210-6365; fax 210-5458; e-mail biimrt@intnet.mu; internet bii.intnet.mu; f. 1998; CEO SARAH JANE KATE NIRSIMLOO.

SBI Mauritius: SBI Tower Mindspace, 6th and 7th Floors, Bhumi Park, 45 Cyber City, Ebene; tel. 404-4900; fax 454-6890; e-mail info@sbimauritius.com; internet www.sbimauritius.com; f. 1978 as Indian Ocean International Bank Ltd; merged with SBI International in 2008 and renamed as above; cap. US $48.6m., res $69.8m., dep. $660.5m. (March 2014); Chair. R. KARTHIKEYAN; Man. Dir and CEO J. S. HIREMATH; 15 brs.

SBM Bank (Mauritius) Ltd: State Bank Tower, 1 Queen Elizabeth II Ave, POB 152, Port Louis; tel. 202-1111; fax 202-1234; e-mail sbm@sbmgroup.mu; internet www.sbmgroup.mu; f. 1973; fmrly State Bank of Mauritius Ltd, present name adopted 2014; cap. 303.7m., res 2,067.5m., dep. 83,233.9m. (Dec. 2013); Chair. MUNI KRISHNA REDDY; CEO JAIRAJ SONOO; 48 brs.

Standard Chartered Bank (Mauritius) Ltd: Ebene House, 2nd Floor, 33 Cyber City, Ebene; tel. 466-5000; fax 466-5161; e-mail info.scbm@sc.com; internet www.standardchartered.com/mu; wholly owned subsidiary of Standard Chartered Bank PLC; offshore banking unit; cap. US $252.6m., res $43.6m., dep. $1,108.7m. (Dec. 2013); CEO SRIDHAR NAGARAJAN.

Development Bank

Development Bank of Mauritius Ltd: rue La Chaussée, POB 157, Port Louis; tel. 203-3600; fax 208-8498; e-mail dbm@intnet.mu; internet www.dbm.mu; f. 1964; name changed as above in 1991; 85% govt-owned; cap. 225.0m., res 1,715.2m., dep. 3,665.0m. (June 2010); Chair. MUHAMMAD IQBAL MALLAM-HASHAM (acting); Man. Dir ROOKUM AUBEELACK (acting); 6 brs.

Principal Offshore Banks

Banque des Mascareignes Ltd: 1 Cathedral Sq., Level 8, 16 Jules Koenig St, POB 43, Port Louis; tel. and fax 207-8600; fax 210-2300; e-mail serviceclient@bm.mu; internet www.banquedesmascareignes.mu; f. 2004; name changed as above 2005; 100% owned by BPCE-IOM (France); cap. 1,749.0m., res 151.1m., dep. 11,768.4m. (Dec. 2013); Chair. PHILIPPE GARSUAULT; CEO HUY HOANG DANG.

Bank of Baroda, Barclays Bank PLC, AfrAsia Bank Ltd, PT Bank International Indonesia, Investec Bank (Mauritius), Standard Chartered Bank (Mauritius) and HSBC Bank PLC also operate offshore banking units.

Islamic Bank

Century Banking Corpn Ltd: Suite 405, Barkly Wharf, 4th Floor, Le Caudan Waterfront, Port Louis; tel. 213-3400; fax 213-9200; e-mail customercomplaints@cbc.com.mu; internet cbc.com.mu; f. 2010; Officer-in-Charge SHAH NAWAZ PARAOUTY.

Banking Organization

Mauritius Bankers Association Ltd (MBA): Newton Tower, Level 15, Sir William Newton St, Port Louis; tel. 213-2390; fax 213-0968; e-mail mba@mba.mu; internet www.mba.mu; f. 1967; Chair. ALASTAIR J. BRYCE; CEO AISHA C. TIMOL; 21 mems.

STOCK EXCHANGE

Financial Services Commission: FSC House, 54 Cyber City, Ebene; tel. 403-7000; fax 467-7172; e-mail fscmauritius@intnet .mu; internet www.fscmauritius.org; f. 2001; regulatory authority for securities, insurance and global business activities; Chair. RAJESHSHARMA RAMLOLL; Chief Exec. CLAIRETTE AH-HEN.

Stock Exchange of Mauritius Ltd: 1 Cathedral Sq., 4th Floor, 16 Jules Koenig St, Port Louis; tel. 212-9541; fax 208-8409; e-mail stockex@sem.intnet.mu; internet www.stockexchangeofmauritius .com; f. 1989; 12 mems; Chair. P. GOPALLEN MOOROOGEN; CEO SUNIL DUTT BENIMADHU.

INSURANCE

In 2012 there were 20 insurance companies operating in Mauritius.

Anglo-Mauritius Assurance Society Ltd: Swan Group Centre, 10 Intendance St, POB 837, Port Louis; tel. 202-8600; fax 211-5050; e-mail info@anglo.mu; internet www.anglo.mu; f. 1951; Chair. CYRIL MAYER; CEO LOUIS RIVALLAND.

BAI Co (Mauritius) Ltd: BAI Centre, 217 Royal Rd, Curepipe; tel. 602-3000; fax 670-3384; e-mail customerservice@bai.intnet.mu; internet www.bai.mu; f. 1988 as British American Insurance Co (Mauritius) Ltd; renamed as above in 2010; Pres. and CEO OUMESHSINGH SOOKDAWOOR.

Indian Ocean General Assurance Ltd: Max City Bldg, 10th Floor, Remy Ollier St, POB 865, Port Louis; tel. 217-6363; fax 217-2829; e-mail iogaltd@intnet.mu; internet iogaltd.com; f. 1971; total assets 221m. (June 2007); Gen. Man. R. L. MATHUR.

Jubilee Insurance (Mauritius) Ltd: Mezzanine Floor, 1 Cathedral Sq., Pope Hennessy St, Port Louis; tel. 202-2200; fax 212-7970; e-mail info@jubileemauritius.com; internet www.jubileeinsurance .com/ma; f. 1998; CEO AZIM DAWOOD.

Lamco International Insurance Ltd: Lamco Bldg, 12 Barracks St, Port Louis; tel. 212-4494; fax 208-0630; e-mail lamco@intnet.mu; internet www.lamcoinsurance.com; f. 1978; CEO SHAIK MAHOMED LATIFF.

Life Insurance Corpn of India: LIC Centre, John F. Kennedy St, POB 310, Port Louis; tel. 212-5316; fax 208-6392; e-mail licemm@ intnet.mu; f. 1956; Chief Man. BISWAJEET GANGULY.

Mauritian Eagle Insurance Co Ltd: IBL House, 1st Floor, Caudan Waterfront, POB 854, Port Louis; tel. 203-2200; fax 203-2299; e-mail caudan@mauritianeagle.com; internet www .mauritianeagle.com; f. 1973; Chair. NICOLAS MAIGROT; Man. Dir DEREK WONG WAN PO.

Mauritius Union Assurance Co Ltd: 4 Léoville l'Homme St, POB 233, Port Louis; tel. 207-5500; fax 212-2962; e-mail info@ mauritiusunion.com; internet www.mauritiusuniongroup.com; f. 1948; Chair. DOMINIQUE GALEA; Group Man. Dir KRIS LUTCHMENARRAIDOO.

New India Assurance Co Ltd: Bank of Baroda Bldg, 3rd Floor, 15 Sir William Newton St, POB 398, Port Louis; tel. 208-1442; fax 208-2160; e-mail niasurance@intnet.mu; f. 1935; general insurance; Chief Man. S. VAIDESWARAN.

Phoenix Insurance (Mauritius) Co Ltd: 36 Sir William Newton St, POB 852, Port Louis; tel. 208-0056; fax 208-1639; e-mail phoenixins@intnet.mu; internet phoenixins.mu; f. 1977; CEO TILAK FERNANDO (acting).

La Prudence Life Insurance: Le Caudan Waterfront, 2nd Floor, Barkly Wharf, POB 882, Port Louis; tel. 207-2500; fax 207-4198; e-mail prudence@intnet.mu; internet www.laprudence.com; acquired by Mauritius Union in 2010; Man. Dir CLAREL MARIE.

State Insurance Co of Mauritius Ltd (SICOM): SICOM Bldg, Sir Celicourt Antelme St, Port Louis; tel. 203-8400; fax 208-7662; e-mail email@sicom.intnet.mu; internet www.sicomgroup.mu; f. 1975; Man. Dir KARUNA G. BHOOJEDHUR-OBEEGADOO.

Sun Insurance Co Ltd: 2 St George St, Port Louis; tel. 213-4477; fax 208-2052; e-mail suninsco@intnet.mu; f. 1981; Man. Dir A. MUSBALLY.

Swan Insurance Co Ltd: Swan Group Centre, 10 Intendance St, POB 364, Port Louis; tel. 207-3500; fax 208-6898; e-mail swan@ intnet.mu; internet www.swangroup.mu; f. 1955; Chair. CYRIL MAYER; CEO LOUIS RIVALLAND.

Trade and Industry

GOVERNMENT AGENCIES

Agricultural Marketing Board (AMB): Dr Georges Leclézio Ave, Moka; tel. 433-4025; fax 433-4837; e-mail agbd@intnet.mu; internet amb.intnet.mu; f. 1964; operates under the aegis of the Ministry of Agro-industry and Food Security; markets certain locally produced and imported food products (such as potatoes, onions, garlic, spices and seeds); provides storage facilities to importers and exporters; Gen. Man. RODNEY RAMA.

Mauritius Meat Authority: Abattoir Rd, Roche Bois, POB 612, Port Louis; tel. 242-5884; fax 217-1077; e-mail mauritiusmeat@ intnet.mu; f. 1974; licensing authority; controls and regulates sale of meat and meat products; also purchases and imports livestock and markets meat products; Gen. Man. VEERBHANOO BHAGEERUTTY.

Mauritius Cane Industry Authority (MCIA): Ken Lee Bldg, 2nd Floor, Edith Cavell St, Port Louis; tel. 208-7466; fax 208-7470; e-mail cs@mcia.mu; regulatory body for the sugar industry; Chair. S. HANOOMANJEE; Exec. Dir Dr G. RAJPATI.

Mauritius Tea Board: Wooton St, Curepipe Rd, Curepipe; POB 28, Eau Coulée; tel. 675-3497; fax 676-1445; e-mail teaboard@intnet.mu; internet www.gov.mu/portal/site/teaboard; f. 1975; regulates and controls the activities of the tea industry; Chair. V. GONDEEA; Gen. Man. ATMARAMSINGH SEEPERGAUTH.

Mauritius Tobacco Board: Plaine Lauzun, Port Louis; tel. 212-2323; fax 208-6426; e-mail tobacco@intnet.mu; internet tobaccoboard.intnet.mu; Chair. RISHI KUMAR CHOONY; Gen. Man. HEMRAJSINGH RAMAHOTAR.

DEVELOPMENT ORGANIZATIONS

Agence Française de Développement (AFD): Bureau 310, 3e étage, Bâtiment Dias Pier, Le Caudan Waterfront, Port Louis; tel. 213-6400; fax 213-6401; e-mail afdportlouis@afd.fr; internet www .afd.fr; Dir MATTHIEU DISCOUR.

Board of Investment—Mauritius (BOI): 1 Cathedral Sq., 10th Floor, 16 Jules Koenig St, Port Louis; tel. 211-4190; fax 208-2924; e-mail invest@boi.intnet.mu; internet www.investmauritius.com; f. 2001 to promote international investment, business and services; Chair. GÉRARD SANSPEUR; Man. Dir KEN POONOOSAMY.

Enterprise Mauritius: Saint James Court, 7th Floor, Saint Denis St, Port Louis; tel. 212-9760; fax 212-9767; e-mail info@em.intnet .mu; internet sourcemauritius.com; f. 2005 from parts of the Mauritius Industrial Development Authority, the Export Processing Zones Development Authority and the Sub-contracting and Partnership Exchange—Mauritius; operates under the aegis of the Ministry of Industry, Commerce and Consumer Protection; Chair. LOUIS AMÉDÉE DARGA; CEO DEV CHAMROO.

Joint Economic Council (JEC): Plantation House, 3rd Floor, pl. d'Armes, Port Louis; tel. 211-2980; fax 211-3141; e-mail jec@intnet .mu; internet jointeconomiccouncil.mu; f. 1970; the co-ordinating body of the private sector of Mauritius, including the main business orgs of the country; Pres. AHMED PARKAR; Dir RAJ MAKOOND.

Mauritius Freeport Authority (MFA): 1 Cathedral Sq., Level 10, 16 Jules Koenig St, Port Louis; tel. 203-3800; fax 208-2924; e-mail contact@investmauritius.com; internet www.efreeport.com; f. 1990; Sr Dir NITIN PANDEA.

National Productivity and Competitiveness Council (NPCC): The Catalyst Bldg, 3rd Floor, Cyber City, Ebene; tel. 467-7700; fax 467-3838; e-mail natpro@intnet.mu; internet www.npccmauritius .com; f. 2000; represents the Govt, the private sector and trade unions; Chair. KEVIN LEERAJSINGH CHUTTUR; Officer-in-Charge DEV APPALSWAMY.

Small and Medium Enterprises Development Authority (SMEDA): Industrial Zone, Coromandel; tel. 233-0500; fax 233-5545; e-mail smeda@orange.mu; internet www.smeda.mu; f. 2006 following the merger of the Small and Medium Industries Development Organization and the National Handicraft Promotion Agency, subsequently Small Enterprises and Handicraft Development Authority; name changed as above in 2009; provides support to potential and existing SMEs; Man. Dir INDIRA SEEBURN.

State Investment Corpn Ltd (SIC): Air Mauritius Centre, 15th Floor, John F. Kennedy St, Port Louis; tel. 202-8900; fax 208-8948; e-mail contactsic@stateinvestment.com; internet www

.stateinvestment.com; f. 1984; provides support for new investment and transfer of technology, in agriculture, industry and tourism; Chair. RAJ DIREVIUM NAGAYA RINGADOO.

CHAMBERS OF COMMERCE

Chinese Chamber of Commerce: Room 305, Jade Court, Jummah Mosque St, Port Louis; tel. and fax 242-0156; e-mail ccoc1908@intnet .mu; internet www.cccmauritius.org; f. 1908; Pres. LI KWONG KEN KWET CHEONG.

Mauritius Chamber of Commerce and Industry: 3 Royal St, Port Louis; tel. 208-3301; fax 208-0076; e-mail mcci@intnet.mu; internet www.mcci.org; f. 1850; 400 mems; Pres. SÉBASTIEN MAMET; Sec.-Gen. RAJU JADDOO.

INDUSTRIAL ASSOCIATIONS

Association of Mauritian Manufacturers (AMM): c/o The Mauritius Chamber of Commerce and Industry, 3 Royal St, Port Louis; tel. 208-3301; fax 208-0076; e-mail amm@mcci.intnet.mu; internet www .mauritianmanufacturers.mu; f. 1995; Pres. GÉRARD BOULLÉ.

Mauritius Sugar Producers' Association (MSPA): Plantation House, 2nd Floor, Edinburgh Ave, Port Louis; tel. 212-0295; fax 212-5727; e-mail mspa@mspa.intnet.mu; internet www.mspa.mu; f. 1947; Chair. GILBERT ESPITALIER NOËL; Dir JEAN LI YUEN FONG.

EMPLOYERS' ORGANIZATION

Mauritius Employers' Federation: MEF-MCCI Bldg, Cyber City, Ebene; tel. 466-3600; fax 465-8200; e-mail mef@intnet.mu; internet www.mef-online.org; f. 1962; Pres. VINCENT DE LABAUVE D'ARIFAT; Dir PRADEEP DURSUN (acting).

UTILITIES

Electricity

Central Electricity Board: Royal Rd, POB 40, Curepipe; tel. 601-1100; fax 675-7958; e-mail ceb@intnet.mu; internet ceb.intnet.mu; f. 1952; state-operated; Chair. BALRAJ NARROO; Gen. Man. SHIAM KRISHT THANNOO.

Water

Central Water Authority: Royal Rd, St Paul, Phoenix; tel. 601-5000; fax 686-6264; e-mail cwa@intnet.mu; internet cwa.gov.mu; corporate body; scheduled for privatization; f. 1973; Chair. PREM SADDUL; Gen. Man. DEV A. AUKLE.

Waste Water Management Authority: Sir Celicourt Antelme St, Port Louis; tel. 206-3000; fax 211-7007; e-mail wma@intnet.mu; internet wmamauritius.mu; f. 2000; Chair. SULAIMAN HANSROD; Officer-in-Charge JAYLALL BUNGSY.

TRADE UNIONS

Federations

Federation of Civil Service and Other Unions (FCSOU): Jade Court, Rm 308, 3rd Floor, 33 Jummah Mosque St, Port Louis; tel. 216-1977; fax 216-1475; e-mail f.c.s.u@intnet.mu; internet www .fcsou.org; f. 1957; 72 affiliated unions with 30,000 mems (2006); Pres. NARENDRANATH GOPEE; Gen. Sec. VIDIANAND NAUGLOO.

General Workers' Federation: 7 Impasse Ruisseau des Creoles, Port Louis; tel. 213-1771; Pres. SERGE JAUFFRET; Sec.-Gen. DEVIANAND NARRAIN.

Mauritius Labour Congress (MLC): 8 Louis Victor de la Faye St, Port Louis; tel. 212-4343; fax 208-8945; e-mail mlcongress@intnet .mu; f. 1963; Pres. HANIFF PEERUN; Gen. Sec. BHOLANATH JEEWUTH.

Mauritius Trade Union Congress (MTUC): Emmanuel Anquetil Labour Centre, James Smith St, Port Louis; tel. 210-8567; f. 1946; Pres. DEWAN QUEDOU.

Transport

RAILWAYS

There are no operational railways in Mauritius.

ROADS

In 2012 there were 2,170 km of paved roads, of which 86 km were motorways, 1,068 km were other main roads, and 608 km were secondary roads. An urban highway links the motorways approaching Port Louis. A motorway connects Port Louis with Plaisance airport.

National Transport Corpn: Bonne Terre Vacoas; tel. 427-5000; fax 426-5489; e-mail cnt.bus@intnet.mu; internet ntc.intnet.mu; Chair. MAXY SIMONET; Gen. Man. (vacant).

SHIPPING

Mauritius is served by numerous foreign shipping lines. In 1990 Port Louis was established as a free port to expedite the development of Mauritius as an entrepôt centre. At 31 December 2014 Mauritius had a merchant fleet of 120 vessels, with a combined displacement of 184,453 grt.

Mauritius Ports Authority: H. Ramnarain Bldg, Mer Rouge, Port Louis; tel. 206-5400; fax 240-0856; e-mail info@mauport.com; internet www.mauport.com; f. 1976; Chair. MAURICE ALLET; Dir-Gen. SHEKUR SUNTAH.

Ireland Blyth Ltd: IBL House, Caudan, Port Louis; tel. 203-2000; fax 203-2001; e-mail iblinfo@iblgroup.com; internet www.iblgroup .com; Chair. THIERRY LAGESSE; CEO NICOLAS MAIGROT.

Mauritius Freeport Development Co Ltd: Freeport Zone 5, Mer Rouge, Port Louis; tel. 206-2000; fax 206-2025; e-mail info@mfd.mu; internet www.mfd.mu; f. 1997; manages and operates Freeport Zone 5, more than 40,000 sq m of storage facility; facilities include dry warehouses, cold warehouses, processing and transformation units, open storage container parks and a container freight station; Chair. RENÉ LECLÉZIO; CEO DOMINIQUE DE FROBERVILLE.

Mauritius Shipping Corpn Ltd: St James Court, Suite 417/418, St Denis St, Port Louis; tel. 208-5900; fax 210-5176; internet www .mauritiusshipping.mu; f. 1985; state-owned; operates two passenger-cargo vessels between Mauritius, Rodrigues, Réunion and Madagascar; Man. Dir Capt. J. PATRICK RAULT.

CIVIL AVIATION

Sir Seewoosagur Ramgoolam International Airport is at Plaisance, 4 km from Mahébourg. From 2006 air routes with France and the United Kingdom were liberalized, allowing new carriers to operate on the routes.

Civil Aviation Department: Sir Seewoosagur Ramgoolam International Airport, Plaine Magnien; tel. 603-2000; fax 637-3164; e-mail civil-aviation@mail.gov.mu; internet civil-aviation.gov.mu; under the aegis of the Prime Minister's Office (External Communications Division); Dir SARUPANAND KINNOO.

Air Mauritius: Air Mauritius Centre, John F. Kennedy St, POB 441, Port Louis; tel. 207-7070; fax 208-8331; e-mail contact@airmauritius .com; internet www.airmauritius.com; f. 1967; 51% state-owned; services to 18 destinations in Europe, Asia, Australia and Africa; Chair. APPALSAMY THOMAS; CEO ANDRIES NATHANIEL VILJOEN.

Tourism

Tourists are attracted to Mauritius by its scenery and beaches, the pleasant climate and the blend of cultures. Accommodation capacity totalled 11,488 rooms in 2008. The number of visitors increased from 300,670 in 1990 to 965,441 in 2012, when the greatest numbers of visitors were from France (27.1%), Réunion (14.4%) and South Africa (9.2%). Some 993,106 tourists visited Mauritius in 2013, according to provisional figures. Gross revenue from tourism in that year was provisionally estimated at MRs 40,557m. The Government sought to increase the volume of tourists visiting the country by improving the jetty facilities in the port in order to welcome cruise ships and by liberalizing air transit routes.

Mauritius Tourism Promotion Authority: Victoria House, 4th and 5th Floor, St Louis St, Port Louis; tel. 210-1545; fax 212-5142; e-mail mtpa@intnet.mu; internet www.tourism-mauritius.mu; f. 1996; Man. Dir KARL MOOTOOSAMY.

Tourism Authority (TA): Victoria House, 1st and 2nd Floor, St Louis St, Port Louis; tel. 213-1740; fax 213-1738; e-mail contact@ tourismauthority.mu; internet www.tourismauthority.mu; f. 2003; parastatal; responsible for licensing, regulating and supervising the activities of tourist enterprises; Dir NIVEN MUNEESAMY.

Defence

The country has no standing defence forces, although as assessed at November 2014 paramilitary forces were estimated to number 2,500, comprising a special 1,750-strong mobile police unit, to ensure internal security, and a coastguard of 800.

Defence Expenditure: Budgeted at Rs 2,580m. in 2014.

Education

Education is officially compulsory and free of charge for 11 years between the ages of five and 16. Primary education begins at five years of age and lasts for six years. Secondary education, beginning at the age of 11, lasts for up to seven years, comprising a first cycle of five years and a second of two years. At March 2005 up to 77% of pre-primary schools were privately run institutions. Primary and secondary education are available free of charge and became compulsory in 2005. According to UNESCO estimates, in 2012 enrolment at primary schools included 98% of pupils in the relevant age-group (males 98%; females 98%), while the comparable ratio for secondary schools in that year was equivalent to 96% (males 94%; females 98%). The education system provides for instruction in seven Asian languages (71% of primary school children and 30% of secondary school children were studying at least one of these in 2005). The Government exercises indirect control of the large private sector in secondary education (in 2005 only 70 of 188 schools were state administered). A total of 7,221 students were enrolled in technical and vocational education in 2012. Of total expenditure by the central Government in 2012, Rs 11,111m. (13.9%) was for education.

MEXICO

Introductory Survey

LOCATION, CLIMATE, LANGUAGE, RELIGION, FLAG, CAPITAL

The United Mexican States is bordered to the north by the USA, and to the south by Guatemala and Belize. The Gulf of Mexico and the Caribbean Sea lie to the east, and the Pacific Ocean and Gulf of California to the west. The climate varies with altitude. The tropical southern region and the coastal lowlands are hot and wet, with an average annual temperature of 18°C (64°F), while the highlands of the central plateau are temperate. Much of the north and west is arid desert. In Mexico City, which lies at about 2,250 m (nearly 7,400 ft) above sea-level, temperatures are generally between 5°C (42°F) and 25°C (78°F). The principal language is Spanish, spoken by more than 90% of the population, while about 8% speak indigenous languages, of which Náhuatl is the most widely spoken. Almost all of Mexico's inhabitants profess Christianity, and about 83% are adherents of the Roman Catholic Church. The national flag (proportions 4 by 7) has three equal vertical stripes from hoist to fly, of green, white and red, with the state emblem (a brown eagle, holding a snake in its beak, on a green cactus, with a wreath of oak and laurel beneath) in the centre of the white stripe. The capital is Mexico City.

CONTEMPORARY POLITICAL HISTORY

Historical Context

Conquered by Hernán Cortés in the 16th century, Mexico was ruled by Spain until the wars of independence of 1810–21. After the war of 1846, Mexico ceded about one-half of its territory to the USA. Attempts at political and social reform by the anti-clerical Benito Juárez precipitated civil war in 1857–60, and the repudiation of Mexico's external debts by Juárez in 1860 led to war with the United Kingdom, the USA and France. The Austrian Archduke Maximilian, whom France tried to install as Emperor of Mexico, was executed, on the orders of Juárez, in 1867. Order was restored during the dictatorship of Porfirio Díaz, which lasted from 1876 until the Revolution of 1910. The Constitution of 1917 embodied the aims of the Revolution by revising land ownership, drafting a labour code and curtailing the power of the Roman Catholic Church. From 1929–2000 the country was dominated by the Partido Revolucionario Institucional (PRI), for much of that time in an effective one-party system, although a democratic form of election was maintained. However, allegations of widespread electoral malpractice persistently arose in connection with PRI victories.

Domestic Political Affairs

In 1976 the PRI candidate, José López Portillo, was elected President with almost 95% of the votes cast. López Portillo initiated reforms to increase minority party representation in the legislature and to widen democratic participation. The high level of political participation in the presidential election of 1982 was without precedent, with left-wing groups taking part for the first time. Miguel de la Madrid Hurtado of the PRI was successful, and that party also secured a large majority at concurrent elections to the Cámara Federal de Diputados (Federal Chamber of Deputies). The new President embarked on a programme of major economic reform, which included the repayment of Mexico's debts and the imposition of severe financial constraints upon the middle and lower classes, leading to growing disaffection among traditional PRI supporters. However, the party was successful at subsequent elections, securing all seven of the available state governorships and 288 of the 300 directly elective seats in the Chamber of Deputies in 1985.

Opposition to the PRI coalesced in 1987 in the formation of a six-party left-wing alliance, the Partido Mexicano Socialista (PMS), and in the emergence of a dissident faction, the Corriente Democrática (CD), within the ruling party. In 1988 the CD and four left-wing parties (including the PMS coalition) formed an electoral alliance, the Frente Democrático Nacional (FDN), headed by Cuauhtémoc Cárdenas Solórzano. The legitimacy of the PRI victory at elections in July was fiercely challenged by the opposition following reports of widespread electoral fraud. For the first time ever, the opposition secured seats in the Senado (Senate).

The new Congreso de la Unión (Congress) immediately assumed the function of an electoral college, in order to investigate the claims of both sides. In September 1988 the allocation of 200 seats in the Chamber of Deputies by proportional representation afforded the PRI a congressional majority and effective control of the electoral college. Opposition members withdrew from the Chamber in protest at the PRI's obstruction of the investigation, enabling the ruling party to ratify Carlos Salinas de Gortari as the new President. The results, although widely regarded as having been manipulated by the PRI, revealed a considerable erosion in support for the party.

Agreements on rescheduling Mexico's vast foreign debts were reached with the 'Paris Club' of official creditors in 1989, and with some 450 commercial banks in 1990. An economic stability pact was also implemented, with the co-operation of employers' organizations and trade unions, although opposition to the measures led to widespread labour unrest. In October proposed constitutional amendments were approved with the unexpected support of the opposition Partido Acción Nacional (PAN). The Federal Electoral Code was approved by the Chamber of Deputies in July 1991 with support from all represented parties, except the Partido de la Revolución Democrática (PRD), the successor party to the FDN. The legislation contained provisions for the compilation of a new electoral roll, the issue of more detailed identification cards for voters, the modification of the Instituto Federal Electoral (IFE—Federal Electoral Institute), and the creation of a federal electoral tribunal.

At mid-term congressional elections in August 1991 the PRI won almost all of the 300 directly elective seats in the Chamber of Deputies (plus 30 of the 200 seats awarded by proportional representation) and 31 of the 32 contested seats in the Senate. The increase in the level of support for the PRI was largely attributed to the success of the Government's programme of economic reform.

The Zedillo presidency, 1994–2000

In March 1994 Luis Donaldo Colosio, the PRI's presidential candidate, was assassinated. Speculation that Colosio had been the victim of a conspiracy within the PRI establishment increased following the arrest of a number of party members associated with police and intelligence agencies. The PRI subsequently named Ernesto Zedillo Ponce de León, Colosio's campaign manager, as the party's presidential candidate. Zedillo was elected in August, defeating the PAN candidate, Diego Fernández de Cevallos, and the PRD nominee, Cuauhtémoc Cárdenas. The PRI was also successful at the concurrent congressional elections. However, numerous incidents of electoral malpractice were reported.

The report of a special investigation into Colosio's murder concluded that an apparently motiveless assassin, Mario Aburto Martínez, had acted alone. Nevertheless, speculation that Colosio had been the victim of a politically motivated campaign of violence, conducted by a cabal of PRI traditionalists in order to check the advance of the party's reformist wing, intensified following the murder, in September 1994, of the PRI Secretary-General, José Francisco Ruiz Massieu. An additional report in February 1995 by the Attorney-General was highly critical of all previous investigations of the Colosio assassination, concluding that the murder had involved at least two gunmen. In the same month Raúl Salinas de Gortari, brother of former President Salinas, was arrested on charges of complicity in Ruiz Massieu's murder, and in April several new conspirators, including five state Governors, were implicated. In October two men were each sentenced to 18 years' imprisonment for the murder of the PRI Secretary-General. In October 1996 the case against Raúl Salinas was prejudiced further by the discovery of a body buried in the grounds of his house. Raúl Salinas was convicted of murder and, in January 1999, sentenced to 50 years' imprisonment (later reduced to 28 years).

In July 1996 the PRI, the PAN, the PRD and the Partido del Trabajo (PT) reached consensus on reforms that would include introducing a directly elected governor of the Federal District, increasing and regulating public financing for political parties, employing proportional representation in elections to the Senate, granting a right of vote to Mexican citizens resident abroad, and allowing the IFE greater independence. The reforms received congressional approval in the following month. However, in November, PRI traditionalists secured the adoption by the Chamber of Deputies of a series of amendments to the electoral reform bill, allowing for a 476% increase in public funding for political parties, the removal of a criminal or electoral responsibility not to exceed campaign finance limits, the expansion of the Government's access to the media, and restrictions on the right of opposition parties to form coalitions.

The PRI lost its overall majority for the first time at elections to the Chamber of Deputies in July 1997, while the PRD and the PAN made substantial gains. The PRI secured a reduced majority at concurrent elections to the Senate, while the PAN and the PRD increased their representation. An informal congressional alliance between the PAN, the PRD, the Partido Verde Ecologista de México (PVEM) and the PT meant that opposition parties were able to take control of important legislative committees.

The Fox presidency, 2000–06

The PRI's candidate in the presidential election of July 2000 was former Secretary of the Interior, Francisco Labastida Ochoa, while former Governor of Guanajuato state, Vicente Fox Quesada, represented a PAN-PVEM alliance known as the Alianza por el Cambio (AC), and Cárdenas was once again the PRD's nominee (officially he stood for the PRD-dominated Alianza por México—AM). Fox secured the presidency with 43% of the votes cast, thus ending the PRI's 71-year hegemony in Mexican government. In the concurrent elections to the Congress, the AC won the largest number of seats, although the PRI remained the largest grouping in the Senate. Fox stated that his priorities were a reduction in poverty, improved relations with the USA, and peace and reconciliation within Mexico.

Following an investigation into allegations that the state petroleum company, Petróleos Mexicanos (PEMEX), had covertly funded Labastida's presidential election campaign, a former director of PEMEX, Manuel Gómez-Peralta, was detained, and a former PEMEX President, Rogelio Montemayor, was arrested in Houston, Texas, USA, during 2002. Opposition parties demanded the reopening of investigations into allegations that Fox's presidential campaign had received foreign funding, and in 2003 the IFE fined both the PAN and the PVEM for accepting illegal campaign funding.

In 2004 Andrés Manuel López Obrador, the PRD Head of Government of the Federal District and a likely candidate in the 2006 presidential election, became the focus of a scandal. Video evidence appeared to show two of his close associates gambling large amounts at a casino in the USA and accepting money from a prominent Argentine businessman, who was accused of corruption. López Obrador denied any knowledge of either incident and claimed that a malicious campaign was being waged against him. The Chamber of Deputies voted in April 2005 to remove López Obrador's immunity. Later that month some 1.2m. people participated in a demonstration in Mexico City in support of their mayor. In May the new Attorney-General rejected all charges against López Obrador and in July he secured the PRD's presidential nomination.

Discord continued within the PRI during 2005 between the supporters of Elba Esther Gordillo Morales, the party's Secretary-General, and party President Roberto Madrazo Pintado in their respective campaigns to secure the nomination for the presidential election. In January Gordillo and the powerful teachers' union, the Sindicato Nacional de Trabajadores de la Educación (SNTE), of which she was President, launched the Nueva Alianza (NA) in order to consolidate support for her candidacy. In August a third faction, Unidad Democrática, more commonly known as Todos Unidos Contra Madrazo (TUCOM—Everyone United against Madrazo), elected Arturo Montiel, the outgoing Governor of the Estado de México, as its nominee for the PRI's presidential candidacy. However, in October, following allegations of corruption (widely assumed to have been fomented by Madrazo), Montiel withdrew from the contest. In November Madrazo won an overwhelming victory in the primary election.

Meanwhile, in October 2005 the former Secretary of Energy, Felipe Calderón Hinojosa, from the traditional, clericist wing of the PAN, unexpectedly won that party's presidential nomination. In December the PRI and the PVEM announced an alliance, Alianza por México, to contest the 2006 elections. The PRD and two smaller left-wing parties, Convergencia and the PT, also formed an alliance, Por el Bien de Todos (For the Good of Everyone).

The Calderón presidency, 2006–12

At the presidential election of July 2006 the PAN's Calderón secured an extremely narrow margin of victory, of just 0.6%, over López Obrador. López Obrador did not accept the results, alleging electoral irregularities. Results of concurrent elections to the Congress were evenly distributed among the three leading parties.

One of the first major challenges that the new Government faced was the increasing unrest in Oaxaca. In June 2006 some 70,000 teachers, supported by indigenous Indian rights activists and local farmers' co-operatives, had begun industrial action in support of salary increases. President-elect Calderón dispatched 5,000 security personnel supported by armoured trucks and helicopters to retake control of the centre of the city. More than 150 people were subsequently arrested, and many more were injured during violent confrontations. In total, 14 people were killed during the disturbances.

A law to reform the electoral system by reducing the influence of money in elections was approved by all three main parties in the Senate in September 2007. The provisions of the reform, *inter alia*, reduced the amount that a party could spend on an election campaign from 270m. to 40m. new pesos, granted each party a limited amount of publicity in the broadcast media, and prohibited the diffusion of propaganda that denigrated parties or candidates; the latter provision was in response to the negative campaign conducted by opponents of López Obrador prior to the 2006 election.

In March 2008 an election to choose the President of the PRD highlighted the divisions between the faction that supported López Obrador's continued claim to the presidency and refused to deal with what it considered to be an illegitimate Government, and those who favoured a more pragmatic approach. Initially, Alejandro Encinas appeared to have defeated the moderate candidate, Jesús Ortega Martínez; however, both sides alleged electoral irregularities. In November the federal electoral tribunal ruled that Ortega was the winner.

The PAN suffered a major defeat in the July 2009 mid-term elections, securing only 143 seats in the Chamber of Deputies (compared with its previous 206 seats), while the PRI more than doubled its representation (237 seats, compared with its previous 108). The PVEM won 22 seats, which, owing to the party's allegiance to the PRI, gave the PRI an absolute majority. The scale of the PAN's defeat prompted the resignation of the party's President.

The worst drought experienced in Mexico in 71 years led to crop failure and serious hardship in the north of the country during 2011. In January 2012 hundreds of farmers and indigenous Tarahumara Indians marched to Mexico City from Chihuahua state to demand increased assistance from the Government.

Victory for Peña Nieto

During early 2012 the main parties announced their candidates for the forthcoming presidential election. The PRD once again selected Andrés Manuel López Obrador, while the PRI chose former Governor of Mexico state Enrique Peña Nieto as their nominee. After considerable internal disagreement, the PAN finally selected Josefina Vásquez Mota. The PRI's decision to separate from the electoral alliance it had formed with the NA was widely seen as an indication that the party wanted to distance itself from controversial NA and SNTE leader Elba Esther Gordillo Morales. The electoral campaign was dominated by economic issues and the ongoing violence associated with the illegal drugs trade (see *Human Rights and the Illegal Drugs Trade*). Some commentators noted a lack of emphasis on the so-called 'war on drugs' in the PAN candidate's campaign, and suggested that the 60,000 people estimated to have been killed in drugs-related violence during the ruling party's six-year presidential term was likely to be a negative factor for many voters.

At the presidential election on 1 July 2012 Peña Nieto was successful for the PRI, securing some 39.2% of the votes cast, while López Obrador garnered 32.4% for the PRD-led alliance; Vásquez Mota of the ruling PAN secured just 26.1% of the votes. Both the PRD and PAN candidates alleged that the election had not been fair and that irregularities had included illegal levels of campaign spending, bribery and manipulation of media coverage. López Obrador refused to concede defeat, lodging a formal complaint over the allegations and demanding a full recount. The

IFE ordered a partial recount, and on 7 July some 60,000 people marched through Mexico City in support of López Obrador. On 30 August the electoral tribunal announced the dismissal of all legal challenges against the results of the elections. López Obrador, who continued to denounce the elections as fraudulent, urged his supporters to engage in 'peaceful, civil resistance' to the new Government, and in September announced the formation of a new political group, aimed predominantly at young people, the Movimiento de Regeneración Nacional (Morena—National Regeneration Movement). Morena finally received official recognition as a registered political party in July 2014.

Meanwhile, at concurrent congressional elections the PRI won the largest number of seats, with 213 in the Chamber of Deputies and 54 in the Senate, but not sufficient to secure a legislative majority. The PAN secured 114 Chamber and 38 Senate seats, while the PRD garnered 104 and 22 seats, respectively.

Reform programme

At his inauguration on 1 December 2012 President Peña Nieto announced that the priorities of his Government would include securing peace within the country, reducing poverty and inequality, and reforming the education system. As part of his planned crime prevention programme, a new national police force of some 10,000 officers in 15 units was launched in mid-December, with the particular aim of reducing rates of kidnapping and extortion. In a gesture of co-operation, the three main parties signed a 'Pact for Mexico' on the new Government's reform programme, which included 95 commitments focusing on social inclusion, security, economic growth, accountability and democratic governance.

A series of reforms aimed at modernizing the education system and addressing corrupt practices in the sector was approved by the legislature in February 2013. The measures, which prompted demonstrations throughout the year, included the establishment of a new independent body to oversee the profession and the introduction of regular assessments for teachers and schools. Vacant posts would be allocated by open competition, rather than by the powerful SNTE. The changes proved controversial among some members of the profession, owing to fears that they signalled the onset of privatization, although the Government strongly denied this. The day after approval of the reforms Elba Esther Gordillo Morales, the controversial SNTE leader, was arrested on suspicion of embezzling some US $200m. in union funds. Gordillo, who had led the union for some 20 years and had wielded considerable political influence, was alleged to have spent millions of dollars on luxury properties in the USA, a private aeroplane, and cosmetic surgery. These charges were withdrawn in November, but new charges, this time of tax evasion, were instead levelled against Gordillo.

In March 2013, as part of the Pact for Mexico, Peña Nieto announced proposed reforms to the country's telecommunications and broadcasting sectors. As well as liberalization of the sector to allow for foreign participation (of up to 49% in broadcasting and 100% in telecommunications), the plans presented to the Congress included the establishment of a new independent regulatory body and the creation of two new national television channels. The proposals received congressional approval in April and became law in June. Reforms to the financial sector that envisaged a greater degree of transparency in the banking system and aimed to encourage economic growth by penalizing institutions that did not assign sufficient resources to lending, were approved in September. Moreover, a series of electoral reforms that included proposals to allow senators to seek re-election for two consecutive terms and deputies for four terms, as well as stricter regulations governing expenditure in electoral campaigns, fewer rules regarding the formation of coalition governments and the replacement of the electoral authority, the IFE, with an Instituto Nacional Electoral (INE), were approved in December.

Most controversial of all the reforms included in the Pact, however, were those concerning the energy sector. The Government's proposals sought to amend the Constitution, specifically to allow state petroleum body PEMEX to enter into profit-sharing contracts with private companies, claiming that investment from foreign interests would allow the organization to expand its capacity for exploration and production. The proposed changes were strongly opposed by the opposition, which refused to accept the Government's claim that they did not constitute a privatization of the country's petroleum industry, and in December 2013 the PRD announced its withdrawal from the Pact in protest. None the less, the reforms, ending the company's 75-year monopoly of the oil industry, secured congressional approval and were promulgated in late December.

In September 2013 Hurricane Manuel struck the south-west of the country, and in the floods, landslides and storms that followed more than 200 people were killed. The extreme weather was estimated to have affected some 1.2m. people across Mexico and two-thirds of the entire national territory.

Peña Nieto announced his commitment to proceed with the Government's reform programme in early 2014, despite the controversy surrounding the changes made to the energy sector. A major campaign organized by the PRD and Morena included a petition with 4.7m. signatories demanding that the Government's decision to end the monopoly of PEMEX and open the oil sector to private investment be put to a referendum. The Supreme Court ruled against any such vote in October. Opposition to the policies of the Pact, however, together with slow economic growth, a low rate of job creation and continued violence in many parts of the country, led to a marked decline in the President's popularity. Public approval ratings for his presidency, which stood at almost 70% in July 2012, had fallen to less than 50% by mid-2014 and further, to an estimated 39%, by December of that year. In an effort to restore public support for his leadership ahead of the mid-term elections scheduled for 7 June 2015, Peña Nieto announced a major public infrastructure investment programme in late 2014.

In late February 2015 the three main parties in the Chamber of Deputies agreed measures to improve public accountability. The initiative followed several instances of high-ranking officials being accused of corruption in late 2014. In particular, the President's wife, Angélica Rivera, and the Secretary of Finance and Public Credit, Luis Videgaray Caso, were both accused of benefiting from their positions after it emerged that both had bought properties from a government contractor. The legislation was intended to strengthen existing institutions and to create a new court to deal with cases of corruption. The law was approved by the Senate in April.

Recent developments: Iguala scandal

In late September 2014 a minor protest by student teachers in Iguala, Guerrero, became a major scandal when police opened fire on the unarmed demonstrators, killing six and capturing 43 people, whom they allegedly handed over to members of the local Guerreros Unidos gang. A mass grave containing the burned remains of many bodies, discovered in early October, was claimed by officials to be those of the captured students. Alleged inconsistencies in the official account of the affair, however, led to mounting expressions of mistrust by relatives of the victims and widespread criticism of the Government's handling of the tragedy. In late October the Governor of Guerrero and six other senior state officials resigned and shortly afterwards the mayor of Iguala and his wife, who had disappeared following the incident, were arrested in Mexico City. The couple were alleged to have close links to criminal organizations in the state. The Government subsequently claimed that weak municipal institutions, easily corrupted by drugs cartels, were to blame, and announced proposals for major security reforms, including the replacement of all 1,800 municipal police forces with 32 state-level operations and new powers enabling the central Government to dissolve local governments suspected of having been infiltrated by drugs cartels. The affair served to undermine further the President's already declining popularity and prompted large-scale, nationwide protests demanding his resignation. In February 2015 Peña Nieto dismissed the Attorney-General, Jesús Murillo Karam, who had been criticized for his handling of the case. In April the Congress approved legislation increasing congressional powers over measures to combat the forced disappearance of people and introducing minimum sentences for those convicted of the crime.

Human Rights and the Illegal Drugs Trade

Amnesty International published a report in 2003 that accused the Government of inefficiency and negligence in investigating the rape and murder of an estimated 307 women (and the disappearance of a further 500) in Ciudad Juárez over the previous 10 years. In 2004 some 130 government officials were investigated for negligence in the ongoing murder investigations. A further report by Amnesty International in that year alleged that the police and military routinely abused peasants, and that torture was commonly practised by police and in the justice system.

In 2002 the investigation into the 'dirty war' of the late 1970s had resulted in the convictions of Brig.-Gen. Mario Acosta and

Gen. Francisco Quirós on charges of protecting the operations of the Juárez cartel; they also faced charges over the disappearance of 143 activists. In November 2003 the Supreme Court ruled that prosecution for murder could proceed even in cases where no body had been found. The ruling enabled prosecutions to proceed for human rights abuses committed during the dirty war; in February 2004 Miguel Nazar Haro, former director of the covert Dirección General de Seguridad, was arrested in connection with the disappearance of left-wing activist Jesús Piedra Ibarra in 1975. In mid-2004 the Supreme Court made a further ruling that cases concerning disappearance could be brought in connection with the suppression of dissent in the 1970s and 1980s. Meanwhile, a special prosecutor was appointed to investigate the role of, among others, former President Luis Echeverría in the dirty war. In December 2004 President Fox announced a National Plan for Human Rights, aimed at eliminating torture and abuse. A subsequent report commissioned by Fox acknowledged government responsibility in the massacres, torture and disappearances of the 1970s. In 2005 the Supreme Court ruled that the Vienna Convention on genocide (which came into force in 2002) could not be applied retrospectively, and the case against Echeverría was dismissed on the grounds that there was no evidence of genocide. This dismissal, however, was itself overruled on appeal in November 2006, thereby reopening the possibility of a prosecution.

Despite efforts by President Fox to address the problem, drugs-related crime continued to escalate during 2005 as the amount of narcotics crossing the Mexican–US border increased. An internecine war between the Tijuana, Golfo and Sinaloa cartels appeared to be taking place in the north of Mexico. Moreover, more than 180 people were killed in Nuevo Laredo, Tamaulipas, in an apparent ongoing conflict between two drugs cartels. President Calderón announced law enforcement as one of his priorities, and a major offensive was subsequently launched in December 2006 against the drugs cartels in Michoacán state with the deployment of 7,000 troops and federal police officers. A second major operation was launched in Tijuana, Baja California, with some 9,000 troops sent into the states of Sinaloa, Durango and Chihuahua. Meanwhile, Calderón was highly commended by the US authorities for his decision in January 2007 to allow the extradition of 15 drugs-trafficking suspects to the USA. The extraditions (which included the head of the Golfo cartel and senior figures from the Sinaloa and Tijuana cartels) represented a significant change in policy from previous administrations. The arrest of Alfredo Beltrán Leyva, a senior leader of the Sinaloa cartel, however, provoked further battles between rival factions of the Sinaloa-based Arellano Félix cartel. Drugs-related violence escalated in 2008, with a reported 6,837 killings, more than twice the murder toll of the previous year. As previously, the violence was particularly, but not exclusively, concentrated in the states of Baja California, Chihuahua and Sinaloa, with 12 decapitated bodies also discovered in Yucatán in August, and a further dozen found in Chilpancingo, Guerrero, in December.

Confronted by widespread insecurity about the increasing crime rate, Calderón launched a three-year plan to introduce 75 anti-crime measures, including the construction of maximum-security gaols and a national database to track mobile telephone usage. Nevertheless, the Government failed to inspire confidence about the security situation in many Mexicans. In that month more than 200,000 people filled the capital's main square in a demonstration to denounce not only murders, kidnappings and drugs-trafficking, but also alleged police and government complicity and corruption. The arrest of one of the Arellano Félix brothers in October, was followed by the revelation that two senior officials in the government unit for the investigation of organized crime, the Subprocuraduría de Investigación Especializada en Delincuencia Organizada (SIEDO), were in the pay of the Beltrán Leyva cartel. The SIEDO's reputation was damaged further in November when its former head, Noé Ramírez, was accused of having accepted US $450,000 from the Sinaloa cartel in exchange for supplying information about police investigations.

Despite the deployment of some 40,000 troops in the war against the drugs cartels, army incursions into the problem areas had little impact and tended to exacerbate violence. In a renewed campaign 7,000 troops and police were deployed in Ciudad Juárez in early 2009, but persistent fears about the role of corrupt officials continued to hamper progress. In May a judge, 10 mayors and 17 other senior officials from Michoacán state were arrested and charged with drugs-related offences.

Moreover, in July 29 state police officers were arrested in connection with the massacre of 12 federal agents in Michoacán in that month.

Ongoing violence in the country was brought to international attention in early 2010, when 13 people were killed in Acapulco. Some of the decapitated victims' bodies were dumped in scenic areas frequented by tourists. In addition, three people associated with the US consulate in Ciudad Juárez (two of whom were US citizens) were murdered. The security situation continued to deteriorate throughout 2010, amid signs that the violence was spreading to states that had previously been less affected, such as Tamaulipas and Nuevo León. In July the director of a prison in Durango was arrested and accused of allowing prisoners to carry out contract killings at night, using prison weapons and vehicles, for gangs involved in organized crime; the prisoners were alleged to have perpetrated three massacres in the city of Torreón. The murders, in August and September, of four mayors (bringing the total number of mayors killed that year to 10) followed that of the PRI candidate for the governorship of Tamaulipas in June. In August the bodies of 72 migrants from various Central and South American countries were discovered in Tamaulipas; the massacre was attributed to members of the Zetas gang and prompted the resignation of the head of the National Institute of Migration. A leading member of the Zetas gang was arrested in October 2012 on suspicion of ordering the massacre and of organizing the escape of 131 inmates from the Piedras Negras prison in Coahuila, during the same period.

The Government released official statistics on drugs-related killings for the first time in 2011: the number of deaths rose to 12,658 in 2010 from 9,614 in 2009 (and 6,837 in 2008). In January 2013 a national newspaper reported that 12,394 people died in violence related to organized crime in 2012; a slightly higher figure than that for 2011 (12,284). However, in 2013 this figure fell to 8,296.

In January 2011, in response to escalating violence in Nuevo León, particularly around its capital, Monterrey (where more than 120 people had reportedly been killed that month), the Government deployed troops to conduct joint patrols with police officers in the state. In the first week of January 38 people were killed in drugs-related violence in the state of Guerrero shortly before gubernatorial elections. In the same month three mayors were assassinated in Coahuila, Morelos and Oaxaca states. In March the municipal government in Ciudad Juárez, where more than 3,100 people had been killed in the previous year, announced the closure of more than 2,000 of the city's streets. A series of marches held across the country in April 2011 in protest against drugs-related violence coincided with the discovery in San Fernando, Tamaulipas, of several mass graves, containing a total of 145 bodies. The local leader of the Zetas gang was arrested in connection with the murders and was also accused of involvement in the massacre of the 72 migrants whose bodies were found in the same area in 2010. Further mass graves were found in Sinaloa and Durango states in April and were believed to be the result of a struggle between the Zetas and Sinaloa cartels to control territory. A further 20 members of the Zetas gang were arrested that month, together with 16 police officers accused of protecting the criminals. In August 2011 some 80 members of the Zetas gang were arrested following an arson attack on a casino in Monterrey in which 53 people were killed. The Government declared three days of national mourning after the attack, which was thought to have been carried out as part of an extortion operation by the Zetas gang. A marked increase in violence in late 2011 in Veracruz, in the east of the country, resulted from a territorial battle between the Zetas and the Nueva Generación gangs. Further arrests of senior gang members during 2012, including those of the leaders of the Golfo and Acapulco cartels, did not appear to have any immediate impact on the murder rate. The shooting of Heriberto Lazcano, the leader of the Zetas gang, by security forces in October, was undermined when a group of Lazcano's associates stole his body from the mortuary where it had been taken after his death. The capture and arrest of Jonathan Salas, known to be the security chief of Mexico's most notorious drugs-trafficker, Joaquín Guzmán ('El Chapo'), in February 2013 was seen as a considerable success for the new Government of President Peña Nieto, as was the capture of El Chapo himself in February 2014.

In February 2012 a total of 44 inmates were killed and 29 escaped during a riot at a high security prison near Monterrey, Nuevo León. According to reports the prison governor, deputy governor and head of security were all affiliated to the Zetas cartel and the deaths were largely caused by fighting between rival gangs. The incident illustrated the ongoing problem of high-level institutional corruption, which continued to impede efforts to combat drugs-related violent crime. As similar incidents continued during the year, a total of 132 prisoners escaped from a prison near the US border in September, while in December 24 people were killed in a gun battle inside a prison in Durango state during an attempted mass escape. In January 2013 more than 150 police officers suspected of having links with the cartels in northern Mexico were arrested. Furthermore, the detention in late 2013 of 13 federal police officers in Acapulco on suspicion of involvement in seven murders and four kidnappings, provided another example of the problems of institutional corruption.

One of the most visible symptoms of the lack of confidence in the Government's ability to tackle drugs-related crime was the increase in vigilante groups establishing self-styled security and policing operations in the areas of the country most affected by drugs violence. In early 2013 an increasing number of armed vigilante, or so-called 'self-defence' groups, began to emerge. Most notable among these were the groups that appeared in Michoacán state, in response to the activities of the Los Caballeros Templarios (Knights Templar) gang. Violence intensified in July with many killings, including the assassination of the commander of the naval base in Puerto Vallarta, on the state's Pacific coast, and of his bodyguard. The Government responded to the surge in violence by deploying an additional 2,000 soldiers, 2,000 marines and 1,000 police officers to the area. However, the security forces' failure to capture the leaders of the Los Caballeros Templarios cartel led to increased activity by the vigilante groups, who by January 2014 were reported to have taken control of at least 20 municipalities in the state. The groups defied government demands to disarm; meanwhile, cartel members accused them of working on behalf of rival drugs gangs. Faced with increasingly lawless conditions, particularly in the area around Apatzingán, and following an appeal by the state Governor for government intervention, the Secretary of the Interior, Miguel Angel Osorio Chong, announced a range of emergency measures, including US $18.7m. of financial assistance and the deployment of 2,000 more police officers, in an attempt to contain the violence and stabilize the state. Dionicio Loya Plancarte ('El Tío'), one of the leaders of the Los Caballeros Templarios gang, was subsequently captured by police. Furthermore, in February 2015 another Caballeros Templarios leader, Servando ('La Tuta') Gómez, was apprehended. Meanwhile, the leaders of the self-defence groups reportedly signed an agreement to co-operate with government forces. It was estimated that a total of 990 people were killed in gang-related violence in Michoacán in 2013.

The disappearance and assumed killing of 43 student teachers in Guerrero in September 2014 (see *Recent developments*) appeared to provide further evidence of official involvement in organized crime, severely challenging the credibility of President Peña Nieto's leadership and prompting him to announce major reforms to the police service. Government figures released during 2014 stated that 93.8% of all crimes committed in Mexico in 2013 were not investigated.

Zapatista Insurgency

On 1 January 1994 armed Indian groups numbering 1,000–3,000 took control of four municipalities of the southern state of Chiapas. The rebels issued the Declaration of the Lacandona Jungle, identifying themselves as the Ejército Zapatista de Liberación Nacional—EZLN (after Emiliano Zapata, who championed the land rights of Mexican peasants during the 1910–17 Revolution), and detailed a series of demands for economic and social change in the region, culminating in a declaration of war against the Government. A charismatic rebel spokesman, 'subcomandante Marcos' (later tentatively identified as Rafael Sebastián Guillén Vicente, a former professor at the Universidad Autónoma Metropolitana), stated that the insurgency had been timed to coincide with the implementation of the North American Free Trade Agreement (NAFTA), which the rebels considered to be the latest in a series of segregative government initiatives adopted at the expense of indigenous groups. Negotiations between the Zapatistas and government representatives concluded with the publication of a document detailing 34 demands of the EZLN, and the Government's response to them. A preliminary accord was reached following the Government's broad acceptance of many of the rebels' stipulations, including an acceleration of the wide-ranging anti-poverty programme in the region, the incorporation of traditional Indian structures of justice and political organization, and a

commitment from the Government to investigate the impact of NAFTA and recent land reform legislation on Indian communities. Official figures suggested that 100–150 guerrillas, soldiers and civilians had been killed during the conflict, while the Roman Catholic Church estimated that there had been as many as 400 casualties. Tensions continued over the following years and in 1997 several thousand Zapatistas and their sympathizers staged a peaceful demonstration in Mexico City, during which the EZLN inaugurated the Frente Zapatista de Liberación Nacional, a political movement that embodied the Zapatistas' ideology. In December there was widespread disquiet at the killing of 45 Indians in a church in the village of Acteal, in the municipality of Chenalhó, Chiapas. Emilio Chuayffet, the Secretary of the Interior, and Julio César Ruiz Ferro, the Governor of Chiapas, were forced to resign, and Gen. Julio César Santiago Díaz, acting chief of staff of Chiapas state police at the time of the massacre, was subsequently charged with failing to intervene to prevent the bloodshed. Moreover, Jacinto Arias, mayor of Chenalhó at the time of the massacre, was convicted in 1999 on charges of supplying the weapons used in the massacre and sentenced to 35 years' imprisonment. In 2002 a further 18 people (in addition to the 70 previously convicted) were each sentenced to 36 years' imprisonment for their involvement in the deaths as part of a paramilitary group with links to the PRI.

In February 2001 subcomandante Marcos and other Zapatista leaders toured Mexico, culminating in a rally in Mexico City attended by some 150,000 people, in support of indigenous rights legislation. In March, the EZLN announced that formal dialogue with the Government would recommence and Marcos successfully negotiated the dismantling of the remaining three garrisons in Chiapas. In April the Congress approved constitutional amendments that recognized and guaranteed indigenous political, legal, social and economic rights, and prohibited discrimination against Indians based on race and tribal affiliation. However, the legislation fell short of granting indigenous peoples the right to autonomy over land and natural resources; in response, the EZLN suspended all contact with the Government. Following the election of a PRI administration in 2012, thousands of Zapatista protesters staged a series of peaceful demonstrations in the Los Altos area of Chiapas to demand indigenous autonomy and justice for marginalized groups. In January 2014, on the 20th anniversary of the initial uprising, the Government announced its intention to re-establish a dialogue with the EZLN. However, in May Marcos announced his resignation as leader of the EZLN, citing internal changes within the organization.

Foreign Affairs

Relations with the USA

Mexico's foreign policy has been determined largely by relations with the USA. The rapid expansion of petroleum production from the mid-1970s gave Mexico a new independence, empowering it to favour the left-wing regimes in Cuba and Nicaragua, opposed by the USA, during the 1980s. Relations between Mexico and the USA remained tense, largely because of disagreement over the problem of illegal immigration from Mexico into the USA and Mexico's failure to take effective action against the illegal drugs trade. NAFTA, comprising Mexico, the USA and Canada, took effect from 1 January 1994. Among the Agreement's provisions were the gradual reduction of tariffs on 50% of products (some 57% of tariffs on agricultural trade between the USA and Mexico were removed immediately), and the establishment of a North American Development Bank (NADBank) charged with the funding of initiatives for the rehabilitation of the two countries' common border. From January 2003 tariffs on a number of agricultural products were reduced or removed entirely, provoking widespread discontent among Mexico's 25m.-strong rural community. In particular, they pointed to the greater subsidies received by US farmers, and to a poor transport infrastructure that resulted in higher costs. Following the collapse, in September 2003, of the fifth Ministerial Conference of the World Trade Organization (WTO) in Cancún, Mexico joined the group of developing countries led by Brazil that opposed US-European Union (EU, see p. 271) subsidies of agricultural products.

The Fox Government sought to persuade the US Administration of George W. Bush to adopt a more liberal position on Mexican immigrants to the USA. However, progress on immigration policy was suspended following the terrorist attacks in the USA on 11 September 2001, and proposals to tighten security on the US–Mexican border were approved by the US Congress in 2002. In that year the two Presidents announced a 'smart border' partnership agreement, intended to facilitate the legal entry of Mexican people and goods into the USA while, at the same time, securing the frontier against possible acts of terrorism. Mexico's subsequent unilateral withdrawal from the Inter-American Treaty of Reciprocal Assistance (the Rio Treaty), the defence pact linking Mexico to the USA, resulted in a deterioration in relations, as did Fox's opposition to the US-led armed intervention to remove the regime of Saddam Hussein in Iraq. In 2004 US officials began managing the security arrangements for US-bound flights leaving Mexico City's airport.

The Mexican Government expressed strong opposition to the USA's Secure Border Initiative, announced in 2005 and envisaging the construction of triple-barrier security fences, monitored by look-out towers, sensors and cameras, along some 1,130 km of the border in order to deter illegal immigrants. Indigenous groups with territories that straddled the border also expressed concern, while others speculated that, by forcing Mexicans to take more dangerous routes into US territory, there would be an increase in the death rate of migrants. The US Congress approved the measures in 2006.

US–Mexican relations deteriorated somewhat following Calderón's accession to the presidency in 2006, partly as a result not only of the USA's continued uncompromising stance on border security, but also of Mexico's improved relations with Cuba and Venezuela. None the less, in 2007 President Bush promised the Mexican Government some US \$500m. per year (subsequently reduced to \$300m.) under the so-called Mérida Initiative in order to combat drugs-related crime. Bush's successor, President Barack Obama, pledged to increase border security and allocated \$700m. for helicopters and law enforcement equipment. The move reflected concerns that drugs-related violence was increasingly affecting US border towns. Calderón addressed the US Congress during a state visit in May 2010, notably urging legislators to introduce measures to restrict the flow of weapons from the USA to drugs gangs in Mexico.

Revelations in 2011 that the US Bureau of Alcohol, Tobacco, Firearms and Explosives, an agency of the Department of Justice, had allowed thousands of weapons to be smuggled into Mexico from the USA in 2009 and 2010, under an operation apparently intended to monitor the movement of arms from US smugglers to Mexican drugs-traffickers, provoked outrage in Mexico. In January 2012 the US Government admitted that serious mistakes had been made under the operation, which was to be investigated by the US House of Representatives' Oversight Committee.

The fundamental difference of viewpoint between Mexico and the USA regarding the illegal drugs trade was starkly illustrated in late 2011 when Calderón urged the US Government to combat the 'insatiable appetite for drugs' in the USA, which had led to such violence in Mexico. Former President Fox joined the debate by appealing to the US Government to legalize drug use, claiming that the consumption of illegal drugs in the USA was responsible for horrifying violence in his country. In addition, Calderón alleged that violence near the border with the USA was exacerbated by the US policy of deporting rather than prosecuting illegal immigrants. In 2010 some 50% of the estimated 400,000 illegal Mexican immigrants deported from the USA had criminal records, and many of these were believed to join gangs upon their return to Mexico.

In March 2013 the US authorities introduced new control measures, in which unmanned surveillance drones were deployed to patrol much of the border. As a potential result, it was reported in late 2014 that more than 50,000 unaccompanied children had been detained while attempting to cross the border from Mexico to the USA. A possible rapprochement in relations between the two countries was suggested by President Obama's support for the reform programme of the Government of President Enrique Peña Nieto, and his affirmation of the USA and Mexico as equal partners. Of even greater significance, however, was the implementation by the Obama Administration in late 2014 of long-awaited reforms allowing some 3.7m. of the estimated 11m. illegal immigrants in the USA (of whom some 60% were believed to be Mexicans) to apply for US work permits.

Other external relations

During the 1990s Mexico concluded agreements for greater economic co-operation and increased bilateral trade with Colombia, Venezuela, Bolivia, Costa Rica, and the EU. Free trade accords with Nicaragua and Chile came into force in 1998 and 1999, respectively. A trade agreement with Guatemala, Honduras and El Salvador (the Northern Triangle) was concluded in 2000. In March of that year Mexico and the EU signed a free trade agreement. In 2011 Mexico concluded a free trade agreement with Peru which aimed to double bilateral trade between the two countries over the next five years. The agreement was also established with the aim of increasing both countries' participation in a Trans-Pacific Partnership (TPP) between Asia and the Latin American Pacific Rim nations. A free trade agreement between Mexico, Nicaragua, El Salvador, Honduras, Guatemala and Costa Rica, designed to improve the integration and efficiency of production chains between the countries, became operational in 2012. In June 2013 Mexico and the People's Republic of China concluded a series of co-operation agreements focused on defence and the food industries, which aimed to address the increasingly large trade deficit that Mexico had developed with China. In April 2014, following a period of strained diplomatic relations between the two countries, the French President, François Hollande, made an official visit to Mexico during which 42 bilateral co-operation agreements, covering a range of areas including education, health care, sustainable development, energy and aeronautics, were signed.

CONSTITUTION AND GOVERNMENT

The present Mexican Constitution was proclaimed on 5 February 1917. Its provisions regarding religion, education, and the ownership and exploitation of mineral wealth reflect the long revolutionary struggle against the concentration of power in the hands of the Roman Catholic Church and the large landowners, and the struggle that culminated, in the 1930s, in the expropriation of the properties of foreign petroleum companies. It has been amended from time to time.

Mexico is a federal republic comprising 31 states and a Federal District (comprising the capital). Legislative power is vested in the bicameral Congreso de la Unión (Congress), elected by universal adult suffrage. The Senado (Senate) has 128 members (four from each state and the Distrito Federal), serving a six-year term. The Cámara Federal de Diputados (Federal Chamber of Deputies), directly elected for three years, has 500 seats, of which 300 are filled from single-member constituencies. The remaining 200 seats, allocated so as to achieve proportional representation, are filled from parties' lists of candidates. Executive power is held by the President, directly elected for six years at the same time as the Senate. Each state has its own constitution and is administered by a Governor (elected for six years) and an elected Chamber of Deputies. The Federal District is administered by a Head of Government.

REGIONAL AND INTERNATIONAL CO-OPERATION

Mexico is a signatory nation to the North American Free Trade Agreement (NAFTA, see p. 367). The country is a member of the Inter-American Development Bank (IDB, see p. 328), of the Latin American Integration Association (ALADI, see p. 358), and of the Community of Latin American and Caribbean States (see p. 460), which was formally inaugurated in December 2011. In June 2012 the Presidents of Mexico, Chile, Colombia and Peru signed a framework agreement in Antofagasta, Chile, creating a new regional economic bloc, the Pacific Alliance (Alianza del Pacífico, see p. 449). Mexico has observer status at the Southern Common Market (Mercado Común del Sur—MERCOSUR, see p. 426), and in 2004 announced its intention of seeking full membership of the group.

Mexico became a member of the UN in 1945. As a contracting party to the General Agreement on Tariffs and Trade, Mexico joined the World Trade Organization (see p. 431) on its establishment in 1995. Mexico was admitted to the Asia-Pacific Economic Co-operation group (APEC, see p. 200) in 1993, and joined the Organisation for Economic Co-operation and Development (see p. 377) in 1994. The country is a member of the Group of 15 (G15, see p. 447) and of the Group of 20 (G20, see p. 451), as well as the Group of Three (see p. 447) (with Colombia and Venezuela).

ECONOMIC AFFAIRS

In 2013, according to estimates by the World Bank, Mexico's gross national income (GNI), measured at average 2011–13 prices, was US \$1,216,087m., equivalent to \$9,940 per head (or \$16,110 per head on an international purchasing-power parity basis). During 2004–13, it was estimated, the population increased at an average annual rate of 1.3%, while gross domestic product (GDP) per head increased, in real terms, by an average of 1.1% per year. Overall GDP increased, in real terms, at an average annual rate of 2.4% in 2004–13; GDP increased by 1.1% in 2013.

Agriculture (including forestry and fishing) contributed 3.5% of GDP in 2013 and engaged 14.1% of the employed labour force in the third quarter of 2014. The staple food crops are maize, wheat, sorghum, barley, rice, beans and potatoes. The principal cash crops are coffee, cotton, sugar cane, and fruit and vegetables (particularly tomatoes). Livestock-raising and fisheries are also important. During 2004–13 agricultural GDP increased at an average annual rate of 1.0%; agricultural GDP increased by 7.3% in 2012 and only by 0.9% in 2013.

Industry (including mining, manufacturing, construction and power) engaged 24.5% of the employed labour force in the third quarter of 2014 and provided 34.8% of GDP in 2013. During 2004–13 industrial GDP increased by an average of 1.3% per year; industrial GDP increased by 3.6% in 2013.

Mining contributed 7.9% of GDP in 2013, and, together with electricity production and distribution, engaged 0.8% of the employed labour force in the third quarter of 2014. During 2004–13 the GDP of the mining sector decreased by an average of 1.0% per year; mining GDP increased by 0.9% in 2012, but decreased by 0.1% in 2013. Mexico has large reserves of petroleum and natural gas (mineral products accounted for an estimated 14.1% of total export earnings in 2013). Zinc, salt, silver, copper, celestite and fluorite are also major mineral exports. In addition, mercury, bismuth, antimony, cadmium, manganese and phosphates are mined, and there are significant reserves of uranium.

Manufacturing provided 17.8% of GDP in 2013 and engaged 16.0% of the employed labour force in the third quarter of 2014. Manufacturing GDP increased at an average annual rate of 1.8% in 2004–13; the sector's GDP increased by 1.1% in 2013. The *maquila* sector (where materials produced on US territory are processed or assembled on the Mexican side of the border) is an important contributor to the economy. *Maquila* exports were valued at an estimated 111,823.8m. new pesos in 2006, equivalent to 45% of total revenue from manufacturing exports. An estimated 1.4m. people were employed in the *maquila* sector in 2010.

Construction engaged 7.7% of the employed labour force in the third quarter of 2014 and provided 7.5% of GDP in 2013. During 2004–13 construction GDP increased by an average annual rate of 1.8% per year; construction GDP increased by 2.5% in 2012, but decreased by 4.8% in 2013.

In 2012, according to the World Bank, some 52.2% of total output of electricity production was derived from natural gas, 18.8% came from petroleum, 11.5% was generated from coal-powered plants and 10.8% came from hydroelectricity. In 2013, according to Petróleos Mexicanos (PEMEX), oil production was an estimated 2.5m. barrels per day, roughly the same level as the previous year. However, production of natural gas was estimated to have decreased to 6,370m. cu ft per day, a 0.2% decrease on the previous year. In 2013 mineral imports were estimated at 9.0% of total merchandise imports.

The services sector contributed 61.7% of GDP in 2013 and engaged 61.4% of the employed labour force in the third quarter of 2014. The GDP of the sector increased by an average of 3.3% per year in 2004–13; the sector expanded by 2.5% in 2013. Tourism is one of Mexico's principal sources of foreign exchange. In 2013 there were an estimated 24.1m. foreign visitors to Mexico (mostly from the USA and Canada). Revenue from the sector totalled US $13,949m. in the same year.

In 2013 Mexico recorded a visible merchandise trade deficit of an estimated US $736m., and there was a deficit of $22,333m. on the current account of the balance of payments. In 2013 the principal source of imports (49.1%) was the USA, which was also the principal market for exports (78.8%). The People's Republic of China was also an increasingly important trading partner. The principal exports in 2013 were mechanical and electrical appliances, vehicles, aircraft, vessels and associated transport equipment, and mineral products; the principal imports in 2013 were mechanical and electrical appliances, vehicles, aircraft, vessels and associated transport equipment, mineral products, base metals, chemical products, and plastics and rubber articles.

In 2013 there was an estimated budgetary deficit of 394,140m. new pesos, equivalent to 2.4% of GDP. Mexico's general government gross debt was 7,471,030m. new pesos in 2013, equivalent to 46.4% of GDP. Mexico's external debt totalled US $354,897m. at the end of 2012, of which $208,649m. was public and publicly guaranteed debt. In that year, the cost of debt-servicing long-term public and publicly guaranteed debt and repayments to the IMF was equivalent to 17.7% of the value of exports of goods, services and income (excluding workers' remittances). The average annual rate of inflation was 4.1% in 2004–13. Consumer prices increased by an average of 3.8% in 2013, according to the International Labour Organization. An estimated 5.2% of the total labour force were unemployed in the third quarter of 2014. It was estimated that remittances were Mexico's second largest source of foreign income, after petroleum exports. In 2014 remittances from Mexicans abroad totalled $23,645m.

The Mexican economy has been vulnerable to economic repercussions associated with its reliance on oil revenues and its excessive dependence on exports to the USA. It continues to depend heavily on inflows of remittances, although these have declined in recent years, owing to stricter US anti-immigration legislation and high unemployment in the USA. In 2013 the new Government of President Enrique Peña Nieto announced an ambitious National Development Plan for 2013–18, focusing on improved education and increased economic productivity. The Plan also included investment of US $23,100m. in transport infrastructure. The country's aim to become an economic leader in the region was assisted by the elimination of tariffs on traded goods within the Pacific Alliance bloc in 2013. Moreover, Peña Nieto's comprehensive reforms programme, under which major changes to the telecommunications, financial and energy sectors were approved in 2013 and 2014 (see *Reform programme*), was expected to lead to significant increases in foreign investment. In October 2014 the Mexican Petroleum Fund was created to manage revenue generated by reforms to the energy sector, which included the removal of PEMEX's 76-year monopoly of the country's oil industry. The first round of oil and gas exploration licensing was to commence in 2015 and continue until 2018, with the 169 available exploration and production blocs predicted to attract $12,500m. from international investors. Low oil prices on the international markets, however, threatened to undermine the estimated earnings from the sale. In late 2014 the Government also announced a major programme of investment in public infrastructure, including the construction of a new airport near Mexico City, which would quadruple the capacity of the current airport to 120m. passengers. The scheme, believed to be one of the largest infrastructure projects in the world, was expected to cost $9,160m., of which 62% was to be state-funded. However, ongoing violence associated with the illegal drugs trade continued to have a negative impact on both foreign investment and the important tourist industry. GDP growth declined from 4.0% in 2012 to 1.1% in 2013, but rose to an estimated 2.7% in 2014, and was forecast to increase further, to 3.7%, in 2015.

PUBLIC HOLIDAYS

2016: 1 January (New Year's Day), 1 February (Constitution Day), 21 March (Birthday of Benito Juárez), 24 March (Maundy Thursday)*, 25 March (Good Friday)*, 1 May (Labour Day), 5 May (Anniversary of the Battle of Puebla)*, 16 September (Independence Day), 2 November (All Souls' Day)*, 21 November (Anniversary of the Revolution), 12 December (Day of Our Lady of Guadalupe)*, 25 December (Christmas).

* Widely celebrated unofficial holidays.

Statistical Survey

Sources (unless otherwise stated): Instituto Nacional de Estadística, Geografía e Informática (INEGI), Edif. Sede, Avda Patriotismo 711, Torre A, 10°, Col. San Juan Mixcoac, Del. Benito Juárez, 03730 México, DF; tel. (55) 5278-1000 (ext. 1282); fax (55) 5278-1000 (ext. 1523); e-mail comunicacionsocial@inegi.org.mx; internet www.inegi.org.mx; Banco de México, Avda 5 de Mayo 1, Col. Centro, Del. Cuauhtémoc, 06059 México, DF; tel. (55) 5237-2000; fax (55) 5237-2370; internet www.banxico.org.mx.

Area and Population

AREA, POPULATION AND DENSITY

Area (sq km)	
Continental	1,959,248
Islands	5,127
Total	1,964,375*
Population (census and by-census results)	
29 October 2005	103,263,388
12 June 2010	
Males	54,855,231
Females	57,481,307
Total	112,336,538
Population (official estimates at mid-year)†	
2013	118,395,054
2014	119,713,203
2015	121,005,815
Density (per sq km) at mid-2015	61.6

* 758,449 sq miles.
† Source: Consejo Nacional de Población (CONAPO), México, DF.

POPULATION BY AGE AND SEX
('000, official estimates at mid-2015)

	Males	Females	Total
0–14 years	17,094.9	16,351.8	33,446.7
15–64 years	38,173.5	41,129.3	79,302.8
65 years and over	3,778.4	4,477.9	8,256.3
Total	59,046.8	61,959.0	121,005.8

Note: Totals may not be equal to the sum of components, owing to rounding.

Source: Consejo Nacional de Población (CONAPO), México, DF.

ADMINISTRATIVE DIVISIONS
(official estimates at mid-2015)

States	Area (sq km)*	Population†	Density (per sq km)	Capital
Aguascalientes (Ags) . . .	5,623	1,287,660	229.0	Aguascalientes
Baja California (BC) . . .	71,540	3,484,150	48.7	Mexicali
Baja California Sur (BCS) .	73,937	763,929	10.3	La Paz
Campeche (Camp.) . .	57,718	907,878	15.7	Campeche
Chiapas (Chis) .	73,680	5,252,808	71.3	Tuxtla Gutiérrez
Chihuahua (Chih.) . . .	247,490	3,710,129	15.0	Chihuahua
Coahuila (de Zaragoza) (Coah.) . . .	151,447	2,960,681	19.5	Saltillo
Colima (Col.) . .	5,629	723,455	128.5	Colima
Distrito Federal (DF) . . .	1,485	8,854,600	5,962.7	Mexico City
Durango (Dgo) .	123,364	1,764,726	14.3	Victoria de Durango
Guanajuato (Gto).	30,617	5,817,614	190.0	Guanajuato
Guerrero (Gro) .	63,618	3,568,139	56.1	Chilpancingo de los Bravos
Hidalgo (Hgo) .	20,855	2,878,369	138.0	Pachuca de Soto
Jalisco (Jal.) . .	78,624	7,931,267	100.9	Guadalajara
México (Méx.) .	22,332	16,870,388	755.4	Toluca de Lerdo
Michoacán (de Ocampo) (Mich.) . . .	58,672	4,596,499	78.3	Morelia
Morelos (Mor.) .	4,894	1,920,350	392.4	Cuernavaca
Nayarit (Nay.) .	27,861	1,223,797	43.9	Tepic
Nuevo León (NL).	64,206	5,085,848	79.2	Monterrey
Oaxaca (Oax.) .	93,348	4,012,295	43.0	Oaxaca de Juárez

States— continued	Area (sq km)*	Population†	Density (per sq km)	Capital
Puebla (Pue.) .	34,246	6,193,836	180.9	Heroica Puebla de Zaragoza
Querétaro (de Arteaga) (Qro) .	11,659	2,004,472	171.9	Querétaro
Quintana Roo (Q.Roo) . .	42,544	1,574,824	37.0	Ciudad Chetumal
San Luis Potosí (SLP) . . .	61,165	2,753,478	45.0	San Luis Potosí
Sinaloa (Sin.) .	57,334	2,984,571	52.1	Culiacán Rosales
Sonora (Son.) .	179,527	2,932,821	16.3	Hermosillo
Tabasco (Tab.) .	24,747	2,383,900	96.3	Villahermosa
Tamaulipas (Tamps) . .	80,155	3,543,366	44.2	Ciudad Victoria
Tlaxcala (Tlax.) .	3,988	1,278,308	320.5	Tlaxcala de Xicohténcatl
Veracruz-Llave (Ver.) . . .	71,856	8,046,828	112.0	Jalapa Enríquez
Yucatán (Yuc.) .	39,675	2,118,762	53.4	Mérida
Zacatecas (Zac.) .	75,412	1,576,068	20.9	Zacatecas
Total . . .	1,959,248	121,005,815	61.8	—

* Excluding islands.
† Source: Consejo Nacional de Población (CONAPO), México, DF.

PRINCIPAL TOWNS
(population at census of June 2010)

Ciudad de México (Mexico City, capital) . . .	8,851,080		Tlalnepantla de Baz (Tlalnepantla) .	664,225
Ecatepec de Morelos (Ecatepec) .	1,656,107		Benito Juárez (Cancún) . . .	661,176
Tijuana	1,559,683		Torreón . . .	639,629
Heroica Puebla de Zaragoza (Puebla)	1,539,819		Santa María Chimalhuacán (Chimalhuacán) .	614,453
Guadalajara . .	1,495,189		Reynosa	608,891
León	1,436,480		Tlaquepaque . .	608,114
Ciudad Juárez . .	1,332,131		Victoria de Durango (Durango) .	582,267
Zapopan	1,243,756		Tuxtla Gutiérrez .	553,374
Monterrey . . .	1,135,550		Veracruz Llave (Veracruz) .	552,156
Nezahualcóyotl . .	1,110,565		Irapuato . . .	529,440
Mexicali	936,826		Tultitlán . . .	524,074
Culiacán Rosales (Culiacán) . .	858,638		Cuautitlán Izcalli .	511,675
Naucalpan de Juárez (Naucalpan) .	833,779		Atizapán de Zaragoza . . .	489,937
Mérida	830,732		Matamoros . . .	489,193
Toluca de Lerdo (Toluca) . . .	819,561		Tonalá	478,689
Chihuahua . . .	819,543		Iztapaluca . . .	467,361
Querétaro . . .	801,940		Ensenada . . .	466,814
Aguascalientes . .	797,010		Jalapa Enríquez (Xalapa) . . .	457,928
Acapulco de Juárez (Acapulco) . .	789,971		San Nicolás de los Garzas . .	443,273
Hermosillo . . .	784,342		Mazatlán . . .	438,434
San Luis Potosí . .	772,604		Nuevo Laredo . .	384,033
Morelia	729,279		Cuernavaca . . .	365,168
Saltillo	725,123		Valle de Chalco (Xico)	357,645
Guadalupe . . .	678,006			

Mid-2014 (incl. suburbs, UN estimate): Ciudad de México (Mexico City, capital) 20,843,500 (Source: UN, *World Urbanization Prospects: The 2014 Revision*).

BIRTHS, MARRIAGES AND DEATHS

	Registered live births		Registered marriages		Registered deaths	
	Number	Rate (per 1,000)	Number	Rate (per 1,000)	Number	Rate (per 1,000)
2005	2,567,906	19.3	595,713	5.7	495,240	4.8
2006	2,505,939	19.0	586,978	5.6	494,471	4.8
2007	2,655,083	18.6	595,209	5.6	514,420	4.9
2008	2,636,110	18.3	589,352	5.5	539,530	4.9
2009	2,577,214	18.0	558,913	5.2	564,673	4.9
2010	2,643,908	17.8	568,632	5.2	592,018	5.0
2011	2,586,287	n.a.	570,954	4.9	590,693	n.a.
2012	2,498,880	n.a.	585,434	5.0	602,354	n.a.

2013 (official projections): Crude birth rate 19.0 per 1,000; Crude death rate 5.7 per 1,000.

2014 (official projections): Crude birth rate 18.7 per 1,000; Crude death rate 5.7 per 1,000.

Life expectancy (years at birth): 77.1 (males 74.8; females 79.6) in 2012 (Source: World Bank, World Development Indicators database).

ECONOMICALLY ACTIVE POPULATION
(sample surveys, '000 persons aged 14 years and over, July-September)

	2012	2013	2014
Agriculture, hunting, forestry and fishing	6,825.5	6,860.3	6,977.1
Mining, quarrying and electricity	449.7	448.2	395.8
Manufacturing	7,535.7	7,819.0	7,928.5
Construction	3,692.8	3,609.8	3,788.0
Trade	9,882.8	9,748.3	9,702.1
Hotels and restaurants	3,380.2	3,409.3	3,367.1
Transport and communications	2,316.7	2,354.0	2,385.5
Finance and business services	3,478.0	3,368.6	3,414.2
Social services	4,014.8	4,013.7	3,997.0
Other services	5,307.7	5,288.2	5,172.2
Public sector	2,369.1	2,381.7	2,298.9
Sub-total	49,253.0	49,301.1	49,426.4
Activities not adequately defined	328.1	275.6	276.0
Total employed	49,581.0	49,576.7	49,702.5
Unemployed	2,668.5	2,732.6	2,746.2
Total labour force	52,249.6	52,309.3	52,448.7
Males	32,284.9	32,262.6	32,737.0
Females	19,964.7	20,046.7	19,711.7

Health and Welfare

KEY INDICATORS

Total fertility rate (children per woman, 2012)	2.2
Under-5 mortality rate (per 1,000 live births, 2012)	16
HIV/AIDS (% of persons aged 15–49, 2013)	0.2
Physicians (per 1,000 head, 2011)	2.1
Hospital beds (per 1,000 head, 2009)	1.6
Health expenditure (2011): US $ per head (PPP)	1,004
Health expenditure (2011): % of GDP	6.0
Health expenditure (2011): public (% of total)	50.3
Access to water (% of persons, 2012)	95
Access to sanitation (% of persons, 2012)	85
Total carbon dioxide emissions ('000 metric tons, 2010)	443,674.0
Carbon dioxide emissions per head (metric tons, 2010)	3.8
Human Development Index (2013): ranking	71
Human Development Index (2013): value	0.756

For sources and definitions, see explanatory note on p. vi.

Agriculture

PRINCIPAL CROPS
('000 metric tons)

	2011	2012	2013
Wheat	3,628	3,274	3,357
Rice, paddy	173	179	180
Barley	487	1,032	594
Maize	17,635	22,069	22,664
Oats	51	84	91
Sorghum	6,429	6,970	6,308
Potatoes	1,433	1,802	1,630
Sugar cane	49,735	50,946	61,182
Beans, dry	568	1,081	1,295
Chick peas	72	272	210
Soybeans (Soya beans)	205	248	239
Groundnuts, with shell	80	115	100
Coconuts*	1,139	1,092	1,064
Safflower seed	131	257	92
Cabbages	239	224	202
Lettuce and chicory	370	335	381
Tomatoes	2,436	3,434	3,283
Cauliflower and broccoli	428	397	481
Pumpkins, squash and gourds	525	565	545
Cucumbers and gherkins	545*	641	637
Chillies and peppers, green	2,132	2,380	2,294
Onions, dry	1,399	1,239	1,270
Carrots and turnips	405	337	348
Bananas	2,139	2,204	2,128
Oranges	4,080	3,668	4,410
Tangerines, mandarins, clementines and satsumas	406	450	494
Lemons and limes	2,148	2,071	2,139
Grapefruit and pomelos	397	415	425
Apples	631	375	859
Peaches and nectarines	167	163	161
Strawberries	229	360	379
Grapes	281	375	350
Watermelons	1,002	1,034	953
Cantaloupes and other melons	564	575	562
Guavas, mangoes and mangosteens	1,827	1,761	1,902
Avocados	1,264	1,316	1,468
Pineapples	743	760	772
Papayas	634	713	765
Coffee, green	237	246	232
Cocoa beans*	83	83	82
Tobacco, unmanufactured	10	15	15

* FAO estimate(s).

Aggregate production ('000 metric tons, may include official, semi-official or estimated data): Total cereals 28,409.5 in 2011, 33,615.0 in 2012, 33,210.3 in 2013; Total fruits (excl. melons) 16,231.4 in 2011, 15,959.3 in 2012, 17,553.0 in 2013; Total vegetables (incl. melons) 12,160.8 in 2011, 13,474.5 in 2012, 13,238.2 in 2013.

Source: FAO.

LIVESTOCK
('000 head, year ending September)

	2011	2012	2013*
Horses*	6,355	6,356	6,356
Asses*	3,260	3,280	3,280
Mules*	3,280	3,285	3,285
Cattle	32,936	31,925	32,000
Pigs	15,547	15,858	16,038
Sheep	8,219	8,406	8,477
Goats	9,004	8,743	8,700
Chickens	510,133	516,711	528,000
Ducks*	8,350	8,350	8,360
Turkeys	4,078	4,016	4,015

* FAO estimates.

Source: FAO.

LIVESTOCK PRODUCTS
('000 metric tons)

	2011	2012	2013
Cattle meat	1,804	1,821	1,807
Sheep meat	57	58	58
Goat meat	44	41	40
Pig meat	1,202	1,239	1,284
Horse meat*	83	83	84
Chicken meat	2,765	2,792	2,808
Cows' milk	10,724	10,881	10,966
Goats' milk	162	156	152
Hen eggs	2,459	2,318	2,516
Honey	58	59	57

* FAO estimates.

Source: FAO.

Forestry

ROUNDWOOD REMOVALS
('000 cubic metres, excl. bark)

	2011	2012	2013*
Sawlogs, veneer logs and logs for sleepers	4,133	3,812*	3,812
Pulpwood	417	805	805
Other industrial wood	330	330*	330
Fuel wood*	38,834	38,840	38,845
Total	43,714	43,787	43,792

* FAO estimate(s).

Source: FAO.

SAWNWOOD PRODUCTION
('000 cubic metres, incl. railway sleepers)

	2011	2012	2013
Coniferous (softwood)	2,068	1,892	2,009
Broadleaved (hardwood)	276	457	485
Total	2,344	2,349	2,494

Source: FAO.

Fishing

('000 metric tons, live weight)

	2010	2011	2012
Capture	1,526.5	1,566.1	1,575.4
Tilapias	62.4	64.9	55.8
California pilchard (sardine)	630.2	592.9	264.5
Yellowfin tuna	101.5	102.4	97.8
American cupped oyster	46.7	42.9	42.5
Jumbo flying squid	42.9	34.8	23.2
Aquaculture	126.2	137.1	143.7
Whiteleg shrimp	104.6	109.8	100.3
Total catch	1,652.7	1,703.2	1,719.1

Note: Figures exclude aquatic plants ('000 metric tons, capture only): 1.7 in 2010; 5.6 in 2011; 6.1 in 2012. Also excluded are aquatic mammals and crocodiles (recorded by number rather than by weight), shells and corals. The number of Morelet's crocodiles caught was: n.a. in 2010; 184 in 2011; 679 in 2012. The catch of marine shells and corals (metric tons) was: 648 in 2010; 523 in 2011; 444 in 2012.

Source: FAO.

Mining

(metric tons unless otherwise indicated)

	2011	2012	2013
Antimony*	5	—	—
Barytes	134,727	139,997	106,166
Bismuth*	935	800	—
Cadmium*	1,485	1,482	1,315
Celestite	40,669	46,190	67,778
Coal	13,718,159	13,656,051	12,242,412
Coke	2,121,866	2,166,046	2,033,684
Copper*	402,430	439,531	409,172
Crude petroleum ('000 barrels per day)†	2,553	2,548	2,522
Diatomite	84,231	84,537	8,756,485
Dolomite	2,785,314	2,111,114	7,995,337
Feldspar	382,497	380,441	150,717
Fluorite	1,206,907	1,237,091	1,210,477
Gas (million cu ft per day)†	6,594	6,385	6,370
Gold (kg)*	84,118	96,650	97,967
Graphite	7,348	7,520	6,520
Gypsum	3,838,348	4,692,510	4,657,572
Iron*	7,763,048	8,047,183	7,362,499
Kaolin	120,003	163,148	340,887
Lead*	182,202	210,382	182,915
Manganese*	170,935	188,294	202,177
Molybdenum*	10,787	11,366	11,340
Salt	8,769,140	8,730,247	9,461,320
Silica	2,542,143	3,592,813	2,703,161
Silver*	4,150,347	4,496,393	4,450,987
Sulphur	959,488	1,010,875	940,048
Wollastonite	47,523	55,204	52,690
Zinc*	447,948	500,125	388,228

* Figures for metallic minerals refer to metal content of ores.
† Source: Petróleos Mexicanos, México, DF.

Industry

SELECTED PRODUCTS
('000 metric tons unless otherwise indicated)

	2009	2010	2011
Wheat flour	2,919	3,054	3,211
Maize (corn) flour	2,304	2,272	2,416
Raw sugar	4,470	4,185	4,557
Beer ('000 hl)	82,236	79,916	84,708
Soft drinks ('000 hl)	172,930	173,392	193,151
Cigarettes (million units)	45,059	44,090	31,274
Cotton yarn (other than sewing thread)	71	82	50
Tyres ('000 units)*	13,540	16,429	18,995
Cement	40,902	39,065	40,552
Non-electric, cooking or heating appliances—household ('000 units)	3,179	3,373	3,151
Refrigerators—household ('000 units)	3,900	4,927	4,883
Passenger cars ('000 units)	1,033	1,464	1,774
Electric energy (million kWh)	261,018	270,968	295,837

* Tyres for road motor vehicles.

Washing machines—household ('000 units): 675 in 2008.

Lorries, buses, tractors, etc. ('000 units): 438 in 2008.

Source: UN Industrial Commodity Statistics Database.

Finance

CURRENCY AND EXCHANGE RATES

Monetary Units
100 centavos = 1 Mexican nuevo peso.

Sterling, Dollar and Euro Equivalents (31 December 2014)
£1 sterling = 22.972 nuevos pesos;
US $1 = 14.718 nuevos pesos;
€1 = 17.869 nuevos pesos;
1,000 Mexican nuevos pesos = £43.53 = $67.94 = €55.96.

Average Exchange Rate (nuevos pesos per US $)
2012   13.169
2013   12.772
2014   13.292

Note: Figures are given in terms of the nuevo (new) peso, introduced on 1 January 1993 and equivalent to 1,000 former pesos.

BUDGET*
(million new pesos)

Revenue	2011	2012	2013
Taxation	1,294,054.1	1,314,439.6	1,561,751.6
Income taxes	720,445.3	758,912.4	905,298.6
Value-added tax	537,142.5	579,987.5	556,793.9
Excise tax	−76,433.5	−130,131.4	−7,423.8
Import duties	26,881.2	27,906.1	29,260.0
Other revenue	1,026,187.6	1,138,094.2	1,141,823.6
Total revenue	2,320,241.7	2,452,533.8	2,703,575.2

Expenditure	2011	2012	2013
Programmable expenditure . .	1,948,209.1	2,095,706.0	2,279,146.2
Current expenditure . . .	400,215.6	429,106.6	407,835.3
Wages and salaries . . .	229,627.3	251,204.7	253,997.8
Acquisitions	21,196.4	20,295.5	18,438.6
Other current expenditure .	149,391.9	157,606.4	135,398.9
Capital expenditure	163,268.7	138,394.1	207,155.7
Transfers	1,384,724.8	1,528,205.3	1,664,155.2
Non-programmable expenditure .	737,446.6	772,028.0	818,569.3
Interest and fees	240,537.6	256,943.5	270,298.5
Revenue sharing	477,256.2	494,264.5	532,455.5
Total expenditure	2,685,655.7	2,867,734.0	3,097,715.5

* Figures refer to the consolidated accounts of the central Government, including government agencies and the national social security system. The budgets of state and local governments are excluded.

INTERNATIONAL RESERVES
(excl. gold, US $ million at 31 December)

	2011	2012	2013
IMF special drawing rights . .	4,084	4,134	4,111
Reserve position in the Fund . .	2,422	2,806	2,708
Foreign exchange	137,485	153,473	168,613
Total	143,991	160,413	175,432

Source: IMF, *International Financial Statistics*.

MONEY SUPPLY
(million new pesos at 31 December)

	2011	2012	2013
Currency outside depository corporations	665,520	733,450	792,260
Transferable deposits	1,452,298	1,560,182	1,734,497
Other deposits	2,372,420	2,655,909	2,832,151
Securities other than shares . .	11,791	6,732	7,724
Broad money	4,502,029	4,956,274	5,366,632

Source: IMF, *International Financial Statistics*.

COST OF LIVING
(Consumer Price Index; base: 2000 = 100)

	2010	2011	2012
Food, beverages and tobacco . .	174.0	183.0	196.9
All items (incl. others) . . .	157.9	163.3	170.0

Source: ILO.

All items (Consumer Price Index; base: 15–29 December 2010 = 100): 105.2 in 2012; 109.2 in 2013.

NATIONAL ACCOUNTS
('000 million new pesos at current prices)

Expenditure on the Gross Domestic Product

	2011	2012	2013
Government final consumption expenditure	1,683.8	1,839.1	1,936.3
Private final consumption expenditure	9,642.5	10,501.6	11,086.3
Increase in stocks	75.5	117.2	85.8
Gross fixed capital formation . .	3,163.3	3,493.7	3,383.0
Total domestic expenditure .	14,565.1	15,951.6	16,491.4
Exports of goods and services .	4,549.0	5,100.6	5,115.3
Less Imports of goods and services	4,730.5	5,276.2	5,226.9
Statistical discrepancy . . .	166.4	−161.0	−275.5
GDP in purchasers' values .	14,550.0	15,615.0	16,104.4
GDP at constant 2008 prices .	12,774.2	13,283.1	13,425.2

Gross Domestic Product by Economic Activity

	2011	2012	2013
Agriculture, forestry and fishing .	470.8	532.5	540.3
Mining and quarrying	1,298.1	1,321.6	1,220.0
Manufacturing	2,393.8	2,701.5	2,754.8
Construction	1,152.5	1,231.1	1,165.3
Electricity, gas and water . .	256.6	251.1	258.0
Trade	2,172.9	2,356.3	2,513.9
Restaurants and hotels . . .	297.9	323.7	341.0
Transport, storage and communications	1,208.7	1,295.6	1,353.7
Finance, insurance, real estate and business services	2,978.8	3,152.8	3,289.0
Public administration	578.3	631.3	661.8
Community, social and personal services	376.3	403.0	424.5
Education	567.7	623.6	663.4
Other activities	291.6	308.9	322.7
Gross value added in basic prices	14,043.9	15,133.0	15,508.5
Net taxes on products	506.1	482.0	595.9
GDP in market prices . . .	14,550.0	15,615.0	16,104.4

BALANCE OF PAYMENTS
(US $ million)

	2011	2012	2013
Exports of goods	349,946	371,378	380,903
Imports of goods	−351,209	−371,151	−381,638
Balance on goods	−1,263	227	−736
Exports of services	15,582	16,146	19,586
Imports of services	−30,375	−30,708	−31,817
Balance on goods and services .	−16,056	−14,335	−12,967
Primary income received . . .	10,569	13,154	10,806
Primary income paid	−29,786	−36,144	−41,986
Balance on goods, services and primary income	−35,274	−37,325	−44,147
Secondary income received . .	23,139	22,768	21,942
Secondary income paid . . .	−178	−209	−128

—continued	2011	2012	2013
Current balance	−12,314	−14,767	−22,333
Direct investment assets . . .	−12,636	−22,470	−9,968
Direct investment liabilities . .	23,009	17,224	35,188
Portfolio investment assets . .	6,049	−8,611	−1,617
Portfolio investment liabilities .	40,622	81,349	50,360
Financial derivatives and employee stock options (net)	−725	117	−477
Other investment assets . . .	−3,674	−6,274	−27,239
Other investment liabilities . .	−2,461	−10,314	12,535
Net errors and omissions . . .	−9,648	−18,738	−18,672
Reserves and related items .	28,222	17,517	17,778

Source: IMF, *International Financial Statistics.*

External Trade

PRINCIPAL COMMODITIES
(distribution by HS, US $ million)

Imports f.o.b.	2011	2012	2013
Vegetables and vegetable products	11,097.1	11,610.2	10,292.5
Mineral products	36,660.2	34,959.9	34,266.8
Mineral fuels and products . .	34,266.8	33,342.6	32,909.5
Petroleum oils other than crude.	7,872.4	27,229.5	25,329.9
Chemicals and related products	27,325.4	28,761.0	29,348.2
Organic chemicals	9,594.6	9,797.1	10,030.6
Plastics, rubber, and articles thereof	24,050.1	26,156.0	27,093.8
Plastics and articles thereof . .	18,486.5	19,835.8	20,809.7
Iron and steel; other base metals and articles thereof .	29,417.1	32,217.7	30,544.3
Machinery and mechanical appliances; electrical equipment; parts and accessories . . .	129,688.1	138,365.9	146,146.6
Mechanical appliances, boilers, parts	53,836.2	60,758.3	62,450.0
Machinery and electrical equipment	75,851.9	77,607.6	83,696.7
Electrical apparatus for line telephony or line telegraphy .	15,971.8	17,186.3	17,975.6
Insulated electric conductors .	8,021.1	8,851.7	10,161.1
Vehicles, aircraft, vessels and associated transport equipment	30,102.2	34,222.0	34,894.6
Road vehicles and parts . . .	28,571.0	32,427.0	33,393.8
Parts and accessories of vehicles	16,801.3	19,046.0	20,521.9
Optical, photographic, measuring, precision and medical apparatus; clocks and watches; musical instruments	11,630.8	12,207.7	12,864.8
Optical and medical instruments .	11,174.5	11,744.2	12,406.5
Total (incl. others)	350,842.9	370,751.6	381,210.2

Exports f.o.b.	2011	2012	2013
Prepared foodstuffs; beverages, spirits, vinegar; tobacco and articles thereof .	9,519.9	9,390.5	10,642.3
Mineral products	59,799.3	57,154.0	53,534.7
Mineral fuels and products . .	55,701.0	52,164.4	48,691.4
Crude oils	49,380.6	46,852.4	42,723.2
Chemicals and related products	10,268.9	11,379.7	11,413.3
Plastics, rubber, and articles thereof	8,780.0	9,939.1	10,513.8
Pearls, precious stones and metals and articles thereof .	13,313.8	13,217.4	9,817.1
Iron and steel; other base metals and articles thereof .	16,831.8	16,577.0	16,791.8
Machinery and mechanical appliances; electrical equipment; parts and accessories	118,955.4	128,649.0	131,789.1
Mechanical appliances, boilers, parts	48,310.7	53,774.5	53,952.5
Machines for processing data .	16,501.6	18,438.7	17,401.3
Machinery and electrical equipment	70,644.8	74,874.5	77,836.5
Electrical apparatus for line telephony or line telegraphy .	15,971.8	17,186.3	17,975.6
Televisions	18,789.7	17,767.6	16,688.9
Vehicles, aircraft, vessels and associated transport equipment	65,063.1	73,099.6	80,740.0
Road vehicles and parts . . .	62,900.8	70,272.8	77,193.0
Automobiles for tourism . .	26,844.1	29,169.3	32,389.4
Goods vehicles	12,466.3	14,800.0	17,560.5
Parts and accessories of vehicles	16,801.3	19,046.0	20,521.9
Optical, photographic, measuring, precision and medical apparatus; clocks and watches; musical instruments	11,077.8	11,921.9	13,004.3
Optical and medical instruments .	10,882.3	11,731.7	12,807.9
Total (incl. others)	349,433.4	370,769.9	380,026.6

Note: The *maquila* sector is responsible for a large percentage of both merchandise imports and exports, but official figures on the value of the sector were last published in 2006, when imports were valued at US $86,527.3m. (equivalent to some 34% of total imports) and exports were valued at $111,823.8m. (almost 45% of total exports).

PRINCIPAL TRADING PARTNERS*
(US $ million)

Imports c.i.f.	2011	2012	2013
Brazil	4,561.9	4,494.5	4,420.6
Canada	9,645.5	9,889.9	9,847.0
China, People's Republic . . .	52,248.0	56,936.1	61,321.4
France	3,359.6	3,466.7	3,685.9
Germany	12,862.6	13,507.8	13,461.0
Italy	4,982.7	5,462.4	5,620.8
Japan	16,493.5	17,655.2	17,076.1
Korea, Republic	13,690.4	13,350.1	13,507.4
Malaysia	5,609.9	4,735.6	5,379.0
Spain	3,843.2	4,081.1	4,311.1
Taiwan	5,769.9	6,183.0	6,689.0
Thailand	3,088.8	3,805.7	4,322.0
USA	174,356.0	185,109.8	187,261.9
Total (incl. others)	350,842.9	370,751.6	381,210.2

Exports f.o.b.	2011	2012	2013
Brazil	4,891.2	5,657.5	5,386.4
Canada	10,694.6	10,937.6	10,452.7
China, People's Republic . . .	5,964.2	5,720.7	6,470.0
Colombia	5,632.6	5,592.3	4,735.2
Germany	4,343.0	4,494.6	3,797.2
Spain	4,904.8	7,075.1	7,137.6
USA	274,426.5	287,842.2	299,439.5
Total (incl. others)	349,433.4	370,769.9	380,026.6

* Imports by country of origin; exports by country of destination.

Transport

RAILWAYS
(traffic)

	2010	2011	2012
Passengers carried ('000)* . .	40,399	41,922	43,830
Passenger-km (million) . . .	843	891	970
Freight carried ('000 tons) . .	104,564	108,433	111,607
Freight ton-km (million) . . .	78,770	79,728	79,353

* Including passengers carried on Linea 1 of the Ferrocarril Suburbano de la Zona Metropolitana del Valle de México.

Source: Dirección General de Planeación, Secretaría de Comunicaciones y Transportes.

ROAD TRAFFIC
('000 vehicles in use at 31 December)

	2009	2010	2012*
Passenger cars	20,524	21,640	23,645
Lorries and vans	8,843	9,183	9,430
Buses and coaches	337	359	,342
Motorcycles and mopeds . . .	1,201	1,157	1,590

* Data for 2011 were not available.

Source: IRF, *World Road Statistics*.

SHIPPING

Flag Registered Fleet
(at 31 December)

	2012	2013	2014
Number of vessels	628	673	723
Total displacement ('000 grt) . .	1,650.7	1,804.0	2,031.2

Source: Lloyd's List Intelligence (www.lloydslistintelligence.com).

Seaborne Shipping
(domestic and international freight traffic, '000 metric tons)

	2011	2012	2013
Goods loaded	164,067	160,575	169,816
Goods unloaded	118,836	122,887	118,880

Source: Coordinación General de Puertos y Marina Mercante.

CIVIL AVIATION
(traffic on scheduled services)

	2011	2012	2013
Passengers carried ('000) . . .	50,764	55,153	60,007
Freight carried ('000 tons) . .	562	559	582

Source: Dirección General de Planeación, Secretaría de Comunicaciones y Transportes.

Tourism

VISITOR ARRIVALS BY COUNTRY OF ORIGIN
(including cross-border visitors)

	2011	2012	2013
Argentina	200,687	251,221	257,820
Brazil	196,266	248,899	267,507
Canada	1,563,146	1,571,543	1,599,425
Chile	76,379	88,148	94,647
Colombia	125,882	163,725	262,653
Costa Rica	44,415	59,361	62,507
France	186,778	202,855	199,866
Germany	165,133	172,841	187,141
Guatemala	44,422	59,091	66,894
Italy	150,690	156,532	154,325
Japan	72,339	85,687	97,226
Korea, Republic	40,303	47,615	59,249
Netherlands	67,821	63,159	57,700
Spain	279,530	278,812	282,255
United Kingdom	330,071	363,142	414,039
USA	18,554,616	18,658,170	18,939,750
Venezuela	88,804	129,331	164,968
Total (incl. others)	23,403,263	23,402,545	24,150,514

Tourism receipts (excluding excursionists, US $ million): 11,869 in 2011; 12,739 in 2012; 13,949 in 2013.

Source: World Tourism Organization.

Communications Media

	2011	2012	2013
Telephones ('000 main lines in use)	19,731.4	20,587.8	20,590.4
Mobile cellular telephones ('000 subscribers)	94,583.2	100,727.2	105,005.7
Internet subscribers ('000)* . .	11,992.1	n.a.	n.a.
Broadband subscribers ('000) . .	11,868.4	12,717.1	13,626.6

* Preliminary.

Source: International Telecommunication Union.

Education

(2011/12)

	Institutions	Teachers	Students ('000)
Pre-primary	91,253	224,146	4,705.5
Primary	99,378	573,849	14,909.4
Secondary (incl. technical) . .	36,563	388,769	6,167.4
Intermediate: professional/ technical	1,369	27,660	383.5
Intermediate: Baccalaureate . .	14,058	258,314	3,950.1
Higher	6,114	326,022	3,027.4

Pupil-teacher ratio (primary education, UNESCO estimate): 28.0 in 2011/12 (Source: UNESCO Institute for Statistics).

Adult literacy rate (UNESCO estimates): 94.2% (males 95.4%; females 93.2%) in 2012 (Source: UNESCO Institute for Statistics).

Directory

The Government

HEAD OF STATE

President: ENRIQUE PEÑA NIETO (took office 1 December 2012).

CABINET
(May 2015)

The Government is formed by the Partido Revolucionario Institucional (PRI).

Secretary of the Interior: MIGUEL ANGEL OSORIO CHONG.

Secretary of Foreign Affairs: JOSÉ ANTONIO MEADE KURIBREÑA.

Secretary of Finance and Public Credit: LUIS VIDEGARAY CASO.

Secretary of National Defence: Gen. SALVADOR CIENFUEGOS ZEPEDA.

Secretary of the Navy: Adm. VIDAL FRANCISCO SOBERÓN SANZ.

Secretary of the Economy: ILDEFONSO GUAJARDO VILLARREAL.

Secretary of Social Development: ROSARIO ROBLES BERLANGA.

Secretary of Communications and Transport: GERARDO RUIZ ESPARZA.

Secretary of Labour and Social Welfare: ALFONSO NAVARRETE PRIDA.

Secretary of the Environment and Natural Resources: JUAN JOSÉ GUERRA ABUD.

Secretary of Energy: PEDRO JOAQUÍN COLDWELL.

Secretary of Agriculture, Livestock, Rural Development, Fisheries and Food: ENRIQUE MARTÍNEZ Y MARTÍNEZ.

Secretary of Public Education: EMILIO CHUAYFFET CHEMOR.

Secretary of Health: MERCEDES JUAN LÓPEZ.

Secretary of Tourism: CLAUDIA RUIZ MASSIEU SALINAS.

Secretary of Territorial, Urban and Agrarian Development: JESÚS MURILLO KARAM.

Secretary of Public Function: VIRGILIO ANDRADE MARTÍNEZ.

Attorney-General: ARELY GÓMEZ GONZÁLEZ.

Legal Counsel to the President: HUMBERTO CASTILLEJOS CERVANTES.

Chief of Staff in the Office of the President: AURELIO NUÑO MAYER.

SECRETARIATS OF STATE

Office of the President: Los Pinos, Col. San Miguel Chapultepec, 11850 México, DF; tel. (55) 5093-5300; fax (55) 5277-2376; e-mail enrique.penanieto@presidencia.gob.mx; internet www.presidencia.gob.mx.

Secretariat of State for Agriculture, Livestock, Rural Development, Fisheries and Food: Avda Municipio Libre 377, Col. Santa Cruz Atoyac, Del. Benito Juárez, 03310 México, DF; tel. (55) 3871-1000; fax (55) 9183-1018; e-mail contacto@sagarpa.gob.mx; internet www.sagarpa.gob.mx.

Secretariat of State for Communications and Transport: Avda Xola, esq. con Ejercito Central, Col. Narvarte, Del. Benito Juárez, 03020 México, DF; tel. (55) 5723-9300; fax (55) 5530-0093; e-mail webmaster@sct.gob.mx; internet www.sct.gob.mx.

Secretariat of State for the Economy: Alfonso Reyes 30, Col. Hipódromo Condesa, Del. Cuauhtémoc, 06140 México, DF; tel. (55) 5729-9100; fax (55) 5729-9320; e-mail primercontacto@economia.gob.mx; internet www.economia.gob.mx.

Secretariat of State for Energy: Insurgentes Sur 890, 17°, Col. del Valle, Del. Benito Juárez, 03100 México, DF; tel. (55) 5000-6000; fax (55) 5000-6222; e-mail calidad@energia.gob.mx; internet www.energia.gob.mx.

Secretariat of State for the Environment and Natural Resources: Blvd Adolfo Ruíz Cortines 4209, Col. Jardines en la Montaña, Del. Tlalpan, 14210 México, DF; tel. (55) 5490-0900; fax (55) 5628-0643; e-mail contactodgeia@semarnat.gob.mx; internet www.semarnat.gob.mx.

Secretariat of State for Finance and Public Credit: Palacio Nacional, Plaza de la Constitución, Col. Centro, Del. Cuauhtémoc, 06000 México, DF; tel. (55) 9158-2000; fax (55) 9158-1142; e-mail secretario@hacienda.gob.mx; internet www.hacienda.gob.mx.

Secretariat of State for Foreign Affairs: Plaza Juárez 20, Col. Centro, Del. Cuauhtémoc, 06010 México, DF; tel. (55) 3686-5100; fax (55) 3686-5582; e-mail atencionciudadanasre@sre.gob.mx; internet www.sre.gob.mx.

Secretariat of State for Health: Lieja 7, 1°, Col. Juárez, Del. Cuauhtémoc, 06600 México, DF; tel. (55) 5286-2383; fax (55) 5553-7917; e-mail portalesweb@salud.gob.mx; internet www.salud.gob.mx.

Secretariat of State for the Interior: Abraham González 48, Col. Juárez, Del. Cuauhtémoc, 06600 México, DF; tel. (55) 5728-7400; fax (55) 5728-7300; e-mail contacto@segob.gob.mx; internet www.gobernacion.gob.mx; includes the Commission of Public Security.

Secretariat of State for Labour and Social Welfare: Periférico Sur 4271, Col. Fuentes del Pedregal, Del. Tlalpan, 14149 México, DF; tel. (55) 3000-2100; fax (55) 5645-5594; e-mail webmaster1@stps.gob.mx; internet www.stps.gob.mx.

Secretariat of State for National Defence: Blvd Manuel Avila Camacho, esq. Avda Industria Militar, 3°, Col. Lomas de Sotelo, Del. Miguel Hidalgo, 11640 México, DF; tel. (55) 2122-8800; fax (55) 5395-2935; e-mail ggalvang@mail.sedena.gob.mx; internet www.sedena.gob.mx.

Secretariat of State for the Navy: Eje 2 oriente, Tramo Heroica, Escuela Naval Militar 861, Col. Los Cipreses, Del. Coyoacán, 04830 México, DF; tel. (55) 5624-6500; e-mail srio@semar.gob.mx; internet www.semar.gob.mx.

Secretariat of State for Public Education: Argentina 28, Col. Centro Histórico, Del. Cuauhtémoc, 06029 México, DF; tel. (55) 3601-1000; fax (55) 5329-6873; e-mail educa@sep.gob.mx; internet www.sep.gob.mx.

Secretariat of State for Public Function: Insurgentes Sur 1735, 10°, Col. Guadalupe Inn, Del. Alvaro Obregón, 01020 México, DF; tel. (55) 2000-3000; e-mail contactociudadano@funcionpublica.gob.mx; internet www.funcionpublica.gob.mx.

Secretariat of State for Social Development: Avda Paseo de la Reforma 116, Col. Juárez, Del. Cuauhtémoc, 06600 México, DF; tel. (55) 5328-5000; e-mail demandasocial@sedesol.gob.mx; internet www.sedesol.gob.mx.

Secretariat of State for Territorial, Urban and Agrarian Development: Avda Heroica Escuela Naval Militar 669, Col. Presidentes Ejidales, 2 Sección, Del. Coyoacán, 04470 México, DF; tel. (55) 5624-0000; fax (55) 5695-6368; e-mail uenlace@sra.gob.mx; internet www.sedatu.gob.mx.

Secretariat of State for Tourism: Avda Presidente Masaryk 172, Col. Bosques de Chapultepec, Del. Miguel Hidalgo, 11580 México, DF; tel. (55) 3002-6300; fax (55) 1036-0789; e-mail atencion@sectur.gob.mx; internet www.sectur.gob.mx.

Office of the Attorney-General: Avda Paseo de la Reforma 211–213, Col. Cuauhtémoc, Del. Cuauhtémoc, 06500 México, DF; tel. (55) 5346-0000; fax (55) 5346-0908; e-mail ofproc@pgr.gob.mx; internet www.pgr.gob.mx.

President and Legislature

PRESIDENT

Election, 1 July 2012

Candidate	Number of valid votes	% of valid votes
Enrique Peña Nieto (PRI-PVEM) . . .	19,226,784	39.19
Andrés Manuel López Obrador (Movimiento Progresista*)	15,896,999	32.40
Josefina Eugenia Vázquez Mota (PAN) .	12,786,647	26.06
Gabriel Ricardo Quadri de la Torre (NA) .	1,150,662	2.35
Total valid votes†	49,061,092	100.00

* An alliance of the PRD, the PT and Movimiento Ciudadano.
† In addition, there were 1,241,154 invalid votes and 20,907 votes for unregistered candidates.

CONGRESS OF THE UNION
(Congreso de la Unión)

Senate
(Senado)

Senate: Avda Paseo de la Reforma 135, esq. Insurgentes Centro, Col. Tabacalera, Del. Cuauhtémoc, 06030 México, DF; tel. (55) 5130-2200; internet www.senado.gob.mx.

President: ERNESTO JAVIER CORDERO ARROYO (PAN).

Election, 1 July 2012

Party	Seats
Partido Revolucionario Institucional (PRI) . .	54
Partido Acción Nacional (PAN)	38
Partido de la Revolución Democrática (PRD) . .	22
Partido Verde Ecologista de México (PVEM) . . .	7
Partido del Trabajo (PT)	5
Nueva Alianza (NA)	1
Movimiento Ciudadano (MC)	1
Total	**128**

Federal Chamber of Deputies
(Cámara Federal de Diputados)

Federal Chamber of Deputies: Avda Congreso de la Unión 66, Col. El Parque, Del. Venustiano Carranza, 15969 México, DF; tel. (55) 5628-1300; internet www.diputados.gob.mx.

President: FRANCISCO AGUSTÍN ARROYO VIEYRA (PRI).

Election, 1 July 2012

Party	Seats
Partido Revolucionario Institucional (PRI) . .	213
Partido Acción Nacional (PAN)	114
Partido de la Revolución Democrática (PRD) . .	104
Partido Verde Ecologista de México (PVEM) . .	28
Movimiento Ciudadano (MC)	16
Partido del Trabajo (PT)	15
Nueva Alianza (NA)	10
Total	**500**

State Governors
(May 2015)

Aguascalientes: CARLOS LOZANO DE LA TORRE (PRI).

Baja California: FRANCISCO VEGA DE LA MADRID (PAN).

Baja California Sur: MARCOS COVARRUBIAS VILLASEÑOR (PAN).

Campeche: FERNANDO EUTIMIO ORTEGA BERNÉS (PRI).

Chiapas: MANUEL VELASCO COELLO (PVEM).

Chihuahua: CÉSAR HORATIO DUARTE JÁQUEZ (PRI).

Coahuila (de Zaragoza): RUBÉN IGNACIO MOREIRA VALDÉZ (PRI).

Colima: MARIO ANGUIANO MORENO (PRI).

Durango: JORGE HERRERA CALDERA (PRI).

Guanajuato: MIGUEL MÁRQUEZ MÁRQUEZ (PAN).

Guerrero: ROGELIO ORTEGA MARTÍNEZ (acting).

Hidalgo: JOSÉ FRANCISCO OLVERA RUIZ (PRI).

Jalisco: JORGE ARISTÓTELES SANDOVAL DÍAZ (PRI).

México: ERUVIEL AVILA VILLEGAS (PRI).

Michoacán (de Ocampo): SALVADOR JARA GUERRERO (Ind.).

Morelos: GRACO LUIS RAMÍREZ GARRIDO ABREU (PRD).

Nayarit: ROBERTO SANDOVAL CASTAÑEDA (PRI).

Nuevo León: RODRIGO MEDINA DE LA CRUZ (PRI).

Oaxaca: GABINO CUÉ MONTEAGUDO (MC).

Puebla: RAFAEL MORENO VALLE ROSAS (PAN).

Querétaro (de Arteaga): JOSÉ CALZADA ROVIROSA (PRI).

Quintana Roo: ROBERTO BORGE ANGULO (PRI).

San Luis Potosí: FERNANDO TORANZO FERNÁNDEZ (PRI).

Sinaloa: MARIO LÓPEZ VALDEZ (PAN).

Sonora: GUILLERMO PADRÉS ELÍAS (PAN).

Tabasco: ARTURO NÚÑEZ JIMÉNEZ (PRD).

Tamaulipas: EGIDIO TORRE CANTÚ (PRI).

Tlaxcala: MARIANO GONZÁLEZ ZARUR (PRI).

Veracruz-Llave: JAVIER DUARTE DE OCHOA (PRI).

Yucatán: ROLANDO RODRIGO ZAPATA BELLO (PRI).

Zacatecas: MIGUEL ALEJANDRO ALONSO REYES (PRI).

Head of Government of the Federal District: MIGUEL ANGEL MANCERA ESPINOSA (PRD).

Election Commission

Instituto Nacional Electoral (INE): Viaducto Tlalpan 100, Col. Arenal Tepepan, Del. Tlalpan, 14610 México, DF; e-mail info@ine .mx; internet www.ine.mx; f. 1990 as Instituto Federal Electoral, reconstituted as above in 2014; independent; Pres. LORENZO CÓRDOVA VIANELLO.

Political Organizations

Movimiento Ciudadano (MC): Louisiana 113, esq. Nueva York, Col. Nápoles, Del. Benito Juárez, 03810 México, DF; tel. (55) 1167-6767; e-mail gestionsocial@convergencia.org.mx; internet www .movimientociudadano.org.mx; f. 1999 as Convergencia por la Democracia; changed name to Convergencia in 2002; restructured and adopted present name in 2011; contested the 2012 elections as part of the Movimiento Progresista; Co-ordinator DANTE ALFONSO DELGADO RANNAURO; Sec. MARÍA ELENA ORANTES LÓPEZ.

Movimiento Regeneración Nacional (Morena): San Luis Potosí 64, esq. Córdoba, Col. Roma, Del. Cuauhtémoc, 06700 México, DF; tel. (55) 4212-4758; internet www.amlo.org.mx; f. 2012, officially registered 2014; created by dissidents from the Partido de la Revolución Democrática (PRD); left-wing; Leader ANDRÉS MANUEL LÓPEZ OBRADOR.

Nueva Alianza (NA): Durango 199, Col. Roma, Del. Cuauhtémoc, 06700 México, DF; tel. (55) 3685-8485; fax (55) 3685-8455; e-mail monica.arriola@nueva-alianza.org.mx; internet www .nueva-alianza.org.mx; f. 2005 by dissident faction of the PRI; includes mems of the Sindicato Nacional de Trabajadores de la Educación and supporters of Elba Esther Gordillo Morales; Pres. LUIS CASTRO OBREGÓN; Sec.-Gen. LUIS ALFREDO VALLES MENDOZA.

Partido Acción Nacional (PAN): Avda Coyoacán 1546, Col. del Valle, Del. Benito Juárez, 03100 México, DF; tel. (55) 5200-4000; e-mail correo@cen.pan.org.mx; internet www.pan.org.mx; f. 1939; democratic party; 150,000 mems; Pres. GUSTAVO ENRIQUE MADERO MUÑOZ; Sec.-Gen. RICARDO ANAYA CORTÉS.

Partido Popular Socialista (PPS): Avda Alvaro Obregón 185, Col. Roma, Del. Cuauhtémoc, 06797 México, DF; tel. (55) 5208-5063; fax (55) 2454-6593; e-mail info@ppsm.org.mx; internet www.ppsm.org .mx; f. 1948 as Partido Popular; Marxist-Leninist; Sec.-Gen. CUAUHTÉMOC AMEZCUA DROMUNDO.

Partido de la Revolución Democrática (PRD): Avda Benjamín Franklin 84, Col. Escandón, Del. Miguel Hidalgo, 11800 México, DF; tel. (55) 1085-8000; fax (55) 1085-8144; e-mail comunicacion@prd.org .mx; internet www.prd.org.mx; f. 1989; centre-left; contested the 2012 elections as part of the Movimiento Progresista; Pres. CARLOS NAVARRETE; Sec.-Gen. HÉCTOR BAUTISTA.

Partido Revolucionario Institucional (PRI): Edif. 2, Insurgentes Norte 59, Col. Buenavista, Del. Cuauhtémoc, 06359 México, DF; tel. (55) 5729-9600; internet www.pri.org.mx; f. 1929 as the Partido Nacional Revolucionario; regarded as the natural successor to the victorious parties of the revolutionary period; broadly based and centrist; Pres. Dr CÉSAR CAMACHO QUIROZ; Sec.-Gen. IVONNE ORTEGA PACHECO.

Partido del Trabajo (PT): Avda Cuauhtémoc 47, Col. Roma Norte, Del. Miguel Hidalgo, 06700 México, DF; tel. and fax (55) 5525-2727; internet www.partidodeltrabajo.org.mx; f. 1990; labour party; contested the 2012 elections as part of the Movimiento Progresista; Leader ALBERTO ANAYA GUTIÉRREZ.

Partido Verde Ecologista de México (PVEM): Loma Bonita 18, Col. Lomas Altas, Del. Miguel Hidalgo, 11950 México, DF; tel. and fax (55) 5257-0188; internet www.partidoverde.org.mx; f. 1987; Spokesman ARTURO ESCOBAR Y VEGA.

The following parties are not officially registered but continue to be politically active:

Fuerza Ciudadana: Rochester 94, Col. Nápoles, 03810 México, DF; tel. (55) 5534-4628; e-mail info@fuerzaciudadana.org.mx; internet www.fuerzaciudadana.org.mx; f. 2002; citizens' asscn; Pres. JORGE ALCOCER VILLANUEVA; Sec. ALBERTO CONSEJO VARGAS.

Partido Democrático Popular Revolucionario: internet pdpr-epr.blogspot.in; f. 1996; political grouping representing the causes of 14 armed peasant orgs.

Partido Socialdemócrata (PSD): Tejocotes 164, Col. Tlacoquemécatl del Valle, Del. Benito Juárez, 03200 México, DF; tel. (55) 5488-1520; fax (55) 5488-1598; internet psdmexico.blogspot.in; f. 2005 as Partido Alternativa Socialdemócrata y Campesina; adopted current name 2008; progressive and peasants' rights; lost political registration following 2009 mid-term elections; Pres. JORGE CARLOS DÍAZ CUERVO.

Illegal organizations active in Mexico include the following:

Ejército Revolucionario Popular Insurgente (ERPI): internet www.enlace-erpi.org; f. 1996; left-wing guerrilla group active in Guerrero, Morelos and Oaxaca; Leader ANTONIO.

Ejército Zapatista de Liberación Nacional (EZLN): e-mail laotra@ezln.org.mx; internet www.ezln.org.mx; f. 1993; left-wing guerrilla group active in the Chiapas region; Leader Subcomandante MOISÉS.

Diplomatic Representation

EMBASSIES IN MEXICO

Algeria: Sierra Madre 540, Col. Lomas de Chapultepec, Del. Miguel Hidalgo, 11000 México, DF; tel. (55) 5520-6950; fax (55) 5540-7579; e-mail embajadadeargelia@yahoo.com.mx; Ambassador RABAH HADID.

Angola: Gaspar de Zúñiga 226, Col. Lomas de Chapultepec, Sección Virreyes, Del. Miguel Hidalgo, 11000 México, DF; tel. (55) 5540-5982; fax (55) 5540-5928; e-mail info@embangolamex.org; Ambassador LEOVIGILDO DA COSTA E SILVA.

Argentina: Avda Palmas 1670, Col. Lomas de Chapultepec, Del. Miguel Hidalgo, 11000 México, DF; tel. (55) 5520-9430; fax (55) 5540-5011; e-mail embajadaargentina@prodigy.net.mx; internet www.embajadaargentina.mx; Ambassador PATRICIA VACA NARVAJA.

Armenia: Avda Alpes 325, Col. Lomas de Chapultepec, Del. Miguel Hidalgo, 11000 México, DF; tel. (52) 6381-5089; e-mail armmexicoembassy@mfa.am; Ambassador GRIGOR HOVHANNISYAN.

Australia: Rubén Darío 55, Col. Polanco, Del. Miguel Hidalgo, 11580 México, DF; tel. (55) 1101-2200; fax (55) 1101-2201; e-mail embaustmex@yahoo.com.mx; internet www.mexico.embassy.gov.au; Ambassador TIM GEORGE.

Austria: Sierra Tarahumara 420, Col. Lomas de Chapultepec, Del. Miguel Hidalgo, 11000 México, DF; tel. (55) 5251-0806; fax (55) 5245-0198; e-mail mexiko-ob@bmaa.gv.at; internet www.embajadadeaustria.com.mx; Ambassador EVA HAGER.

Azerbaijan: Avda Virreyes 1015, Col. Lomas de Chapultepec, Del. Miguel Hidalgo, 11000 México, DF; tel. (55) 5540-4109; fax (55) 5540-1366; e-mail oficina@azembassy.mx; internet www.azembassy.mx; Ambassador ILGAR MUKHTAROV.

Belgium: Alfredo Musset 41, Col. Polanco, Del. Miguel Hidalgo, 11550 México, DF; tel. (55) 5280-0758; fax (55) 5280-0208; e-mail mexico@diplobel.org; internet www.diplomatie.be/mexico; Ambassador HANS CHRISTIAN KINT.

Belize: Bernardo de Gálvez 215, Col. Lomas de Chapultepec, Del. Miguel Hidalgo, 11000 México, DF; tel. (55) 5520-1274; fax (55) 5520-6089; e-mail embelize@prodigy.net.mx; Ambassador OLIVER DEL CID.

Bolivia: Goethe 104, Col. Anzures, Del. Miguel Hidalgo, 11590 México, DF; tel. and fax (55) 5255-3620; e-mail embajada@embol.org.mx; internet www.embol.org.mx; Ambassador MARCOS DOMIC RUÍZ.

Brazil: Lope de Armendáriz 130, Col. Lomas Virreyes, Del. Miguel Hidalgo, 11000 México, DF; tel. (55) 5201-4531; fax (55) 5520-6480; e-mail brasemb.mexico@itamaraty.gov.br; internet mexico.itamaraty.gov.br; Ambassador MARCOS LEAL RAPOSO LOPES.

Bulgaria: Paseo de la Reforma 1990, Col. Lomas de Chapultepec, Del. Miguel Hidalgo, 11000 México, DF; tel. (55) 5596-3295; fax (55) 5596-3283; e-mail Embassy.Mexico@mfa.bg; internet www.mfa.bg/embassies/mexico; Ambassador HRISTO GEORGIEV GUDJEV.

Canada: Schiller 529, Col. Polanco, Del. Miguel Hidalgo, 11560 México, DF; tel. (55) 5724-7900; fax (55) 5724-7980; e-mail mxico@international.gc.ca; internet www.canadainternational.gc.ca/mexico-mexique; Ambassador PIERRE ALARIE (designate).

Chile: Andrés Bello 10, 18°, Col. Polanco, Del. Miguel Hidalgo, 11560 México, DF; tel. (55) 5280-9681; fax (55) 5280-9703; e-mail echilmex@prodigy.net.mx; internet chileabroad.gov.cl/mexico; Ambassador RICARDO NUÑEZ MUÑOZ.

China, People's Republic: Avda San Jerónimo 217B, Del. Alvaro Obregón, 01090 México, DF; tel. (55) 5616-0609; fax (55) 5616-5849; e-mail chinaemb_mx_admin@mfa.gov.cn; internet www.embajadachina.org.mx; Ambassador QIU XIAOQI.

Colombia: Paseo de la Reforma 379, 1° y 5°–6°, Col. Cuauhtémoc, Del. Cuauhtémoc, 06500 México, DF; tel. (55) 5525-0277; fax (55) 5208-2876; e-mail emexico@cancilleria.gov.co; internet mexico.embajada.gov.co; Ambassador JOSÉ GABRIEL ORTIZ ROBLEDO.

Costa Rica: Río Po 113, Col. Cuauhtémoc, Del. Cuauhtémoc, 06500 México, DF; tel. (55) 5525-7764; fax (55) 5511-9240; e-mail embajada@embajada.decostaricaenmexico.org; internet www.embajada.decostaricaenmexico.org; Ambassador MARÍA EUGENIA VENEGAS RENAULD.

Côte d'Ivoire: Tennyson 67, Col. Polanco, Del. Miguel Hidalgo, 11560 México, DF; tel. (55) 5280-8573; fax (55) 5282-2954; e-mail ambacimex@cotedivoiremx.org; internet cotedivoiremx.org; Ambassador OBOU MARCELLIN ABIE.

Cuba: Presidente Masaryk 554, Col. Polanco, Del. Miguel Hidalgo, 11560 México, DF; tel. (55) 5280-8039; fax (55) 5280-0839; e-mail embajada@embacuba.com.mx; internet www.cubadiplomatica.cu/mexico; Ambassador DAGOBERTO RODRÍGUEZ BARRERA.

Cyprus: Sierra Gorda 370, Col. Lomas de Chapultepec, Del. Miguel Hidalgo, 11000 México, DF; tel. (55) 5202-7600; fax (55) 5520-2693; e-mail limassol@prodigy.net.mx; internet www.mfa.gov.cy/embassymexico; Ambassador EVAGORAS VRYONIDES.

Czech Republic: Cuvier 22, esq. Kepler, Col. Nueva Anzures, Del. Miguel Hidalgo, 11590 México, DF; tel. (55) 5531-2777; fax (55) 5531-1837; e-mail mexico@embassy.mzv.cz; internet www.mzv.cz/mexico; Chargé d'affaires a.i. IRENA VALKYOVA.

Denmark: Tres Picos 43, Col. Chapultepec Morales, Del. Miguel Hidalgo, 11580 México, DF; tel. (55) 5255-3405; fax (55) 5545-5797; e-mail mexamb@um.dk; internet www.ambmexicocity.um.dk; Ambassador HENRIK BRAMSEN HAHN.

Dominican Republic: Prado Sur 755 (entre Monte Blanco y Monte Everest), Col. Lomas de Chapultepec, Del. Miguel Hidalgo, 11000 México, DF; tel. (55) 5540-3841; fax (55) 5520-0779; e-mail embajada@embadom.org.mx; internet www.embadom.org.mx; Ambassador FERNANDO ANTONIO PÉREZ MEMÉN.

Ecuador: Tennyson 217, Col. Polanco, Del. Miguel Hidalgo, 11560 México, DF; tel. (55) 5545-3141; fax (55) 5254-2442; e-mail mecuamex@prodigy.net.mx; Ambassador PATRICIO ALFONSO LÓPEZ ARAUJO.

Egypt: Alejandro Dumas 131, Col. Polanco, Del. Miguel Hidalgo, 11560 México, DF; tel. (55) 5281-0823; fax (55) 5282-1294; e-mail embassy.mexicocity@mfa.gov.eg; internet www.mfa.gov.eg/Mexico_Emb; Ambassador YASSER MOHAMED AHMED SHABAN.

El Salvador: Temístocles 88, Col. Polanco, Del. Miguel Hidalgo, 11560 México, DF; tel. (55) 5281-5725; fax (55) 5280-0657; e-mail embesmex@webtelmex.net.mx; Ambassador CARLOS ANTONIO ASCENCIO GIRÓN.

Finland: Monte Pelvoux 111, 4°, Col. Lomas de Chapultepec, Del. Miguel Hidalgo, 11000 México, DF; tel. (55) 5540-6036; fax (55) 5540-0114; e-mail finmex@prodigy.net.mx; internet www.finlandia.org.mx; Ambassador ANNE LAMMILA.

France: Campos Elíseos 339, Col. Polanco, Del. Miguel Hidalgo, 11560 México, DF; tel. (55) 9171-9700; fax (55) 9171-9893; e-mail prensa@ambafrance-mx.org; internet www.ambafrance-mx.org; Ambassador MARYSE BOSSIÈRE.

Georgia: Blvd de Los Virreyes 610, Col. Lomas de Virreyes, Del. Miguel Hidalgo, CP 11000 México, DF; tel. (55) 5520-0118; fax (55) 5520-0897; e-mail mexico.emb@mfa.gov.ge; Ambassador MALKHAZ MIKELADZE.

Germany: Horacio 1506, Col. Los Morales, Del. Miguel Hidalgo, 11530 México, DF; tel. (55) 5283-2200; fax (55) 5281-2588; e-mail info@mexi.diplo.de; internet www.mexiko.diplo.de; Ambassador VIKTOR ELBLING.

Greece: Monte Ararat 615, Col. Lomas de Chapultepec, Del. Miguel Hidalgo, 11010 México, DF; tel. (55) 5520-2070; fax (55) 5520-0948; e-mail grem.mex@mfa.gr; Ambassador POLYXENI STEFANIDOU.

Guatemala: Explanada 1025, Col. Lomas de Chapultepec, Del. Miguel Hidalgo, 11000 México, DF; tel. (55) 5540-7520; fax (55) 5202-1142; e-mail embaguatemx@minex.gob.gt; Ambassador FERNANDO ANDRADE DÍAZ-DURÁN.

Haiti: Sierra Vertientes 840, Col. Lomas de Chapultepec, Del. Miguel Hidalgo, 11000 México, DF; tel. (55) 5557-2065; fax (55) 5395-1654; e-mail ambadh@mail.internet.com.mx; Ambassador MARIE JOSEPH GUY LAMOTHE.

Holy See: Juan Pablo II 118, Col. Guadalupe Inn, Del. Alvaro Obregón, 01020 México, DF; tel. (55) 5663-3999; fax (55) 5663-5308; Apostolic Nuncio Most Rev. CHRISTOPHE PIERRE (Titular Archbishop of Gunela).

Honduras: Alfonso Reyes 220, Col. Condesa, Del. Cuauhtémoc, 06170 México, DF; tel. (55) 5211-5747; fax (55) 5211-5425; e-mail emhonmex@prodigy.net.mx; Ambassador JOSÉ MARIANO CASTILLO MERCADO.

Hungary: Paseo de las Palmas 2005, Col. Lomas de Chapultepec, Del. Miguel Hidalgo, 11000 México, DF; tel. (55) 5596-0523; fax (55) 5596-2378; internet www.mfa.gov.hu/kulkepviselet/MX/hu; Chargé d'affaires a.i. TIBOR ISTVAN KUN.

India: Musset 325, Col. Polanco, Del. Miguel Hidalgo, 11550 México, DF; tel. (55) 5531-1050; fax (55) 5254-2349; e-mail indembmx@prodigy.net.mx; internet www.indembassy.org; Ambassador SUJAN R. CHINOY.

Indonesia: Julio Verne 27, Col. Polanco, Del. Miguel Hidalgo, 11560 México, DF; tel. (55) 5280-6363; fax (55) 5280-7062; e-mail kbrimex@prodigy.net.mx; internet mexicocity.kemlu.go.id; Ambassador HAMDANI DJAFAR.

Iran: Paseo de la Reforma 2350, Col. Lomas Altas, Del. Miguel Hidalgo, 11950 México, DF; tel. (55) 9172-2691; fax (55) 9172-2694; e-mail iranembmex@hotmail.com; internet mexicocity.mfa.ir; Ambassador JALAL KALANTARI.

Iraq: Paseo de la Reforma 1875, Col. Lomas de Chapultepec, Del. Miguel Hidalgo, 11000 México, DF; tel. (55) 5596-0933; fax (55) 5596-0254; e-mail mxcemb@iraqfamail.com; Ambassador ALI YASSIN MOHAMMED.

Ireland: Cerrada Blvd Manuel Avila Camacho 76, 3°, Col. Lomas de Chapultepec, Del. Miguel Hidalgo, 11000 México, DF; tel. (55) 5520-5803; fax (55) 5520-5892; e-mail emexicoembassy@dfa.ie; internet www.irishembassy.com.mx; Ambassador SONJA HYLAND.

Israel: Sierra Madre 215, Col. Lomas de Chapultepec, Del. Miguel Hidalgo, 11000 México, DF; tel. (55) 5201-1500; fax (55) 5201-1555; e-mail ambassadorsec@mexico.mfa.gov.il; internet mexico-city.mfa.gov.il; Ambassador RODICA RADIAN-GORDON.

Italy: Paseo de las Palmas 1994, Col. Lomas de Chapultepec, Del. Miguel Hidalgo, 11000 México, DF; tel. (55) 5596-3655; fax (55) 5596-2472; e-mail segreteria.messico@esteri.it; internet www.ambcittadelmessico.esteri.it; Ambassador ALESSANDRO BUSACCA.

Jamaica: Avda Paseo de las Palmas 1340, Col. Lomas de Chapultepec, 11000 México, DF; tel. (55) 5250-6804; fax (55) 5250-6160; e-mail embajadadejamaica@prodigy.net.mx; Ambassador SANDRA GRANT GRIFFITHS.

Japan: Paseo de la Reforma 395, Apdo 5-101, Col. Cuauhtémoc, Del. Cuauhtémoc, 06500 México, DF; tel. (55) 5211-0028; fax (55) 5207-7743; e-mail embjapmx@mail.internet.com.mx; internet www.mx.emb-japan.go.jp; Ambassador SHUICHIRO MEGATA.

Korea, Democratic People's Republic: Calle Halley 12, Col. Anzures, Del. Miguel Hidalgo, 11590 México, DF; tel. (55) 5250-0263; fax (55) 5545-8775; e-mail dpkoreaemb@prodigy.net.mx; Ambassador AN KUN SONG.

Korea, Republic: Lope de Armendáriz 110, Col. Lomas Virreyes, Del. Miguel Hidalgo, 11000 México, DF; tel. (55) 5202-9866; fax (55) 5540-7446; e-mail embcoreamx@mofat.go.kr; internet mex.mofat.go.kr; Ambassador HONG SEONG-HOA.

Kuwait: Paseo de los Tamarindos 98, Col. Bosques de las Lomas, Del. Cuajimalpa, 05120 México, DF; tel. (55) 9177-8400; fax (55) 9177-8412; e-mail embajadakuwaitmx@gmail.com; Ambassador SAMEEH ESSA JOHAR HAYAT.

Lebanon: Julio Verne 8, Col. Polanco, Del. Miguel Hidalgo, 11560 México, DF; tel. (55) 5280-5614; fax (55) 5280-8870; e-mail embalibano@embajadadelibano.org.mx; internet www.embajadadelibano.org.mx; Ambassador HICHAM HAMDAN.

Libya: Horacio 1003, Col. Polanco, Del. Miguel Hidalgo, 11550 México, DF; tel. (55) 5545-5725; fax (55) 5545-5677; e-mail libia.mexico@yahoo.com; Ambassador MUFTAH ALTAYAR.

Malaysia: Sierra Nevada 435, Col. Lomas de Chapultepec, Del. Miguel Hidalgo, 11000 México, DF; tel. (55) 5282-5166; fax (55) 5282-4910; e-mail mwmexico@prodigy.net.mx; Ambassador Dato' JAMAIYAH MOHAMED YUSOF.

Morocco: Paseo de las Palmas 2020, Col. Lomas de Chapultepec, Del. Miguel Hidalgo, 11000 México, DF; tel. (55) 5245-1786; fax (55) 5245-1791; e-mail sifamex@infosel.net.mx; internet www.marruecos.org.mx; Ambassador ABDERRAHMAN LEIBEK.

Netherlands: Edif. Calakmul, 7°, Avda Vasco de Quiroga 3000, Col. Santa Fe, Del. Alvaro Obregón, 01210 México, DF; tel. (55) 1105-6550; fax (55) 5258-8138; e-mail mex-info@minbuza.nl; internet mexico.nlembajada.org; Ambassador COENRAAD HENDRIK ADOLPH HOGEWONING.

New Zealand: Edif. Corporativo Polanco, 4°, Jaime Balmes 8, Col. Los Morales Polanco, Del. Miguel Hidalgo, 11510 México, DF; tel. (55) 5283-9460; fax (55) 5283-9480; e-mail kiwimexico@prodigy.net.mx; internet www.nzembassy.com/mexico; Ambassador CLARE KELLY.

Nicaragua: Fernando Alencastre 136, Col. Lomas de Chapultepec, Del. Miguel Hidalgo, 11000 México, DF; tel. (55) 5540-5625; fax (55) 5520-2270; e-mail embanic@prodigy.net.mx; Ambassador TAMARA HAWKINS DE BRENES.

Nigeria: Diego Fernández de Córdova 125, Col. Lomas Virreyes, Del. Miguel Hidalgo, 11000 México, DF; tel. (55) 5245-1487; fax (55) 5245-0105; e-mail nigembmx@att.net.mx; internet www.embassyofnigeria.com.mx; Ambassador ZHIRI JAMES GANA.

Norway: Avda de los Virreyes 1460, Col. Lomas Virreyes, Del. Miguel Hidalgo, 11000 México, DF; tel. (55) 5540-3486; fax (55) 5202-3019; e-mail emb.mexico@mfa.no; internet www.noruega.org.mx; Ambassador MERETHE NERGAARD.

Pakistan: Hegel 512, Col. Chapultepec Morales, Del. Miguel Hidalgo, 11570 México, DF; tel. (55) 5203-3636; fax (55) 5203-9907; e-mail parepmex@hotmail.com; Ambassador AITZAZ AHMED.

Panama: Sócrates 339, Col. Polanco, Del. Miguel Hidalgo, 11560 México, DF; tel. (55) 5280-7857; fax (55) 5280-7586; e-mail informes@embpanamamexico.com; Ambassador MANUEL RICARDO PÉREZ.

Paraguay: Homero 415, 1°, esq. Hegel, Col. Polanco, Del. Miguel Hidalgo, 11570 México, DF; tel. (55) 5545-0405; fax (55) 5531-9905; e-mail embapar@prodigy.net.mx; Ambassador VÍCTOR CUEVAS NÚÑEZ.

Peru: Paseo de la Reforma 2601, Col. Lomas Reforma, Del. Miguel Hidalgo, 11000 México, DF; tel. (55) 1105-2270; fax (55) 1105-2279; e-mail embaperu@prodigy.net.mx; Ambassador JAVIER EDUARDO LEÓN OLAVARRÍA.

Philippines: Río Rhin 56, Cuauhtémoc, Del. Cuauhtémoc, 06500 México, DF; tel. (55) 5202-8456; fax (55) 5202-8403; e-mail mexico.pi@dfa.gov.ph; Ambassador CATALINO REINANTE DILEM, Jr.

Poland: Cracovia 40, Col. San Angel, Del. Alvaro Obregón, 01000 México, DF; tel. (55) 5481-2050; fax (55) 5616-7314; e-mail embajadadepolonia@prodigy.net.mx; internet www.meksyk.polemb.net; Ambassador BEATA WOJNA.

Portugal: Avda Alpes 1370, Lomas de Chapultepec, Del. Miguel Hidalgo, 11000 México, DF; tel. (55) 5520-7897; fax (55) 5520-4688; e-mail embpomex@gmail.com; internet embpomex.wordpress.com; Ambassador JOÃO JOSÉ GOMES CAETANO DA SILVA.

Romania: Sófocles 311, Col. Polanco, Del. Miguel Hidalgo, 11560 México, DF; tel. (55) 5280-0197; fax (55) 5280-0343; e-mail secretariat@rumania.org.mx; internet mexico.mae.ro; Ambassador ANA VOICU.

Russian Federation: José Vasconcelos 204, Col. Hipódromo Condesa, Del. Cuauhtémoc, 06140 México, DF; tel. (55) 5273-1305; fax (55) 5273-1545; e-mail embrumex@yandex.ru; internet www.embrumex.org; Ambassador EDUARD MALAYÁN.

Saudi Arabia: Paseo de las Palmas 2075, Col. Lomas de Chapultepec, Del. Miguel Hidalgo, 11000 México, DF; tel. (55) 5596-0173; fax (55) 5020-3160; e-mail saudiemb@prodigy.net.mx; Ambassador HUSSEIN MOHAMMAD ABDULFATAH AL-ASSIRI.

Serbia: Montañas Rocallosas Oeste 515, Col. Lomas de Chapultepec, Del. Miguel Hidalgo, 11000 México, DF; tel. (55) 5520-0524; fax (55) 5520-9927; e-mail embajadaserbia@alestra.net.mx; Ambassador GORAN MESIĆ.

Slovakia: Julio Verne 35, Col. Polanco, Del. Miguel Hidalgo, 11560 México, DF; tel. (55) 5280-6669; fax (55) 5280-6294; e-mail emb.mexico@mzv.sk; internet www.mzv.sk/mexico; Ambassador JAROSLAV BLAŠKO.

South Africa: Edif. Forum, 9°, Andrés Bello 10, Col. Polanco, Del. Miguel Hidalgo, 11560 México, DF; tel. (55) 1100-4970; fax (55) 5282-9259; e-mail safrica@prodigy.net.mx; Ambassador SANDILE NOGXINA.

Spain: Galileo 114, esq. Horacio, Col. Polanco, Del. Miguel Hidalgo, 11550 México, DF; tel. (55) 5282-2271; fax (55) 5282-1520; e-mail emb.mexico@maec.es; internet www.maec.es/embajadas/mexico; Ambassador LUIS FERNÁNDEZ CID DE LAS ALAS PUMARIÑO.

Sweden: Paseo de las Palmas 1375, Col. Lomas de Chapultepec, Del. Miguel Hidalgo, 11000 México, DF; tel. (55) 9178-5010; fax (55) 5540-3253; e-mail suecia@prodigy.net.mx; internet www.suecia.com.mx; Ambassador JÖRGEN HANS PERSSON.

Switzerland: Paseo de las Palmas 405, 11°, Torre Óptima, Col. Lomas de Chapultepec, Del. Miguel Hidalgo, 11000 México, DF; tel. (55) 9178-4370; fax (55) 5520-8685; e-mail vertretung@mex.rep.admin.ch; internet www.eda.admin.ch/mexico; Chargé d'affaires a.i. MIRKO GIULIETTI KNOBLAUCH.

Thailand: Paseo de las Palmas 1610, Col. Lomas de Chapultepec, Del. Miguel Hidalgo, 11000 México, DF; tel. (55) 5540-4551; fax (55) 5540-4817; e-mail thaimex@prodigy.net.mx; internet www.thaiembmexico.co.nr; Ambassador CHIRACHAI PUNKRASIN.

Turkey: Monte Líbano 885, Col. Lomas de Chapultepec, Del. Miguel Hidalgo, 11000 México, DF; tel. (55) 5282-4277; fax (55) 5282-4894; e-mail embajada.mexico@mfa.gov.tr; internet mexico.emb.mfa.gov.tr; Ambassador OGUZ DEMIRALP.

Ukraine: Paseo de la Reforma 730, Col. Lomas de Chapultepec, Del. Miguel Hidalgo, 11000 México, DF; tel. (55) 5282-4085; fax (55) 5282-4768; e-mail emb_mx@mfa.gov.ua; internet www.mfa.gov.ua/mexico; Ambassador RUSLAN SPIRIN.

United Arab Emirates: Paseo de La Reforma 505, Col. Lomas de Chapultepec, Del. Miguel Hidalgo, 11000 México, DF; tel. (55) 5207-0025; fax (55) 5282-4387; e-mail mexico@mofa.gov.ae; Ambassador SAEED RASHAD OBAID SAIF ALZAABI.

United Kingdom: Río Lerma 71, Col. Cuauhtémoc, Del. Cuauhtémoc, 06500 México, DF; tel. (55) 1670-3204; fax (55) 5242-8517; e-mail ukinmex@att.net.mx; internet www.embajadabritanica.com.mx; Ambassador DUNCAN TAYLOR.

USA: Paseo de la Reforma 305, Del. Cuauhtémoc, 06500 México, DF; tel. (55) 5080-2000; fax (55) 5080-2005; internet mexico.usembassy.gov; Ambassador EARL ANTHONY WAYNE.

Uruguay: Hegel 149, 1°, Col. Chapultepec Morales, Del. Miguel Hidalgo, 11560 México, DF; tel. (55) 5531-0880; fax (55) 5545-3342; e-mail uruguaymex@prodigy.net.mx; Ambassador JORGE ALBERTO FERNÁNDEZ.

Venezuela: Schiller 326, Col. Chapultepec Morales, Del. Miguel Hidalgo, 11570 México, DF; tel. (55) 5203-4233; fax (55) 5254-1457; e-mail venezmex@prodigy.net.mx; Ambassador HUGO JOSÉ GARCÍA HERNÁNDEZ.

Viet Nam: Sierra Ventana 255, Col. Lomas de Chapultepec, Del. Miguel Hidalgo, 11000 México, DF; tel. (55) 5540-1632; fax (55) 5540-1612; e-mail vietnam.mx@mofa.gov.vn; internet www.vietnamembassy-mexico.org/vi; Ambassador TUNG LE THANH.

Judicial System

The judicial system is divided into federal and local. The federal judicial system has both ordinary and constitutional jurisdiction, and judicial power is exercised by the Supreme Court of Justice, the Electoral Court, Collegiate and Unitary Circuit Courts and District Courts. The Supreme Court comprises two separate chambers: Civil and Criminal Affairs, and Administrative and Labour Affairs. The Federal Judicature Council is responsible for the administration, surveillance and discipline of the federal judiciary, except for the Supreme Court.

Mexico is divided into 29 judicial circuits. The Circuit Courts may be collegiate, when dealing with the *derecho de amparo* (protection of constitutional rights of an individual), or unitary, when dealing with appeal cases. The Collegiate Circuit Courts comprise three magistrates with residence in 38 cities around the country. The Unitary Circuit Courts comprise one magistrate with residence mostly in the same cities.

Suprema Corte de Justicia de la Nación: Pino Suárez 2, Col. Centro, Del. Cuauhtémoc, 06065 México, DF; tel. (55) 4113-1000; fax (55) 4195-0913; e-mail scjn_presidencia@scjn.gob.mx; internet www.scjn.gob.mx; Pres. and Chief Justice LUIS MARÍA AGUILAR MORALES.

President of the First Chamber—Civil and Criminal Affairs: ALFREDO GUTIÉRREZ ORTIZ MENA.

President of the Second Chamber—Administrative and Labour Affairs: ALBERTO PÉREZ DAYÁN.

Tribunal Electoral del Poder Judicial de la Federación (TEPJF): Carlota Amero 5000, Col. Culhuacán, Del. Coyoacán, 04480 México, DF; tel. (55) 5728-2300; fax (55) 5728-2400; e-mail contactoweb@te.gob.mx; internet www.te.gob.mx; Pres. JOSE ALEJANDRO LUNA RAMOS.

Attorney-General: ARELY GÓMEZ GONZÁLEZ.

Religion

CHRISTIANITY

The Roman Catholic Church

The prevailing religion is Roman Catholicism, but the Church, disestablished in 1857, was for many years, under the Constitution of 1917, subject to state control. For ecclesiastical purposes, Mexico comprises 18 archdioceses, 70 dioceses, five territorial prelatures and two eparchies (both directly subject to the Holy See). According to the 2010 census, some 83% of the population are Roman Catholics.

Bishops' Conference: Conferencia del Episcopado Mexicano (CEM), Edif. S. S. Juan Pablo II, Prolongación Ministerios 26, Col. Tepeyac Insurgentes, Apdo 118-055, 07020 México, DF; tel. (55) 5781-8462; fax (55) 5577-5489; e-mail comunicacion@cem.org.mx; internet www.cem.org.mx; Pres. JOSÉ FRANCISCO ROBLES ORTEGA (Archbishop of Guadalajara).

Archbishop of Acapulco: CARLOS GARFIAS MERLOS, Arzobispado, Quebrada 16, Apdo 201, Centro, 39300 Acapulco, Gro; tel. and fax (744) 482-0763; e-mail parroquiasoledadacapulco@hotmail.com; internet arquiaca.org.

Archbishop of Antequera, Oaxaca: JOSÉ LUIS CHÁVEZ BOTELLO, Leona Vicario 109, Plazuela del Carme Alto, Col. Centro, 68000 Oaxaca, Oax.; tel. (951) 516-4822; fax (951) 514-1348; e-mail comunica@arquioax.org; internet arquioax.org.

Archbishop of Chihuahua: CONSTANCIO MIRANDA WECKMANN, Arzobispado, Avda Cuauhtémoc 1828, Apdo 7, Col. Cuauhtémoc, 31020 Chihuahua, Chih.; tel. (614) 410-3202; fax (614) 410-5621; e-mail arzobispado@arquidiocesischihuahua.com.mx; internet arquidiocesischihuahua.com.mx.

Archbishop of Durango: JOSÉ ANTONIO FERNÁNDEZ HURTADO, Arzobispado, Avda 20 de Noviembre 306, Poniente Centro, Apdo 116, 34000 Durango, Dgo; tel. (618) 811-4242; fax (618) 812-8881; e-mail prensaarquidiocesisdgo@gmail.com; internet arquidiocesisdgo.org.

Archbishop of Guadalajara: Cardinal JOSÉ FRANCISCO ROBLES ORTEGA, Arzobispado, Alfredo R. Plascencia 995, Apdo 61-33, Col. Chapultepec, 44620 Guadalajara, Jal.; tel. (33) 3614-5504; fax (33) 3658-2300; e-mail arzgdl@arquidiocesisgdl.org; internet www.arquidiocesisgdl.org.

Archbishop of Hermosillo: JOSÉ ULISES MACÍAS SALCEDO, Arzobispado, Calle Dr Paliza y Ocampo, Ala Sur de la Catedral, Col. Centenario, 83260 Hermosillo, Son.; tel. (662) 213-2138; fax (662) 213-1327; e-mail arzohmo2@gmail.com; internet arquidiocesishermosillo.org.

Archbishop of Jalapa: HIPÓLITO REYES LARIOS, Arzobispado, Avda Manuel Avila Camacho 73, Apdo 359, Col. Centro, 91000 Jalapa, Ver.; tel. (228) 812-0579; fax (228) 817-5578; e-mail contacto@arquidiocesisdexalapa.com; internet www.arquidiocesisdexalapa.com.

Archbishop of León: JOSÉ GUADALUPE MARTÍN RÁBAGO, Arzobispado, Pedro Moreno 312, Apdo 108, 37000 León, Gto; tel. (477) 713-2527; fax (477) 713-1286; e-mail episcopo@arquidiocesisdeleon.org; internet arquideleon.org.

Archbishop of Mexico City: Cardinal NORBERTO RIVERA CARRERA, Curia del Arzobispado de México, Durango 90, 5°, Col. Roma, Apdo 24433, 06700 México, DF; tel. (55) 5208-3200; fax (55) 5208-5350; e-mail arzobisp@arquidiocesismexico.org.mx; internet www.arquidiocesismexico.org.mx.

Archbishop of Monterrey: Cardinal ROGELIO CABRERA LÓPEZ, Zuazua 1100 Sur con Ocampo Centro, Apdo 7, 64000 Monterrey, NL; tel. (81) 1158-2450; fax (81) 1158-2488; e-mail cancilleria@arquidiocesismty.org; internet www.arquidiocesismty.org.

Archbishop of Morelia: Cardinal ALBERTO SUÁREZ INDA, Arzobispado, Costado Catedral, Frente Avda Madero, Apdo 17, 58000 Morelia, Mich.; tel. (443) 313-2493; fax (443) 312-0919; e-mail asuarezi@cem.org.mx; internet arquidiocesismorelia.mx.

Archbishop of Puebla de los Angeles: VÍCTOR SÁNCHEZ ESPINOSA, Avda 16 de Septiembre 901, Col. Centro Histórico, 72000 Puebla, Pue.; tel. (222) 232-4591; fax (222) 246-2277; e-mail redessociales@arquidiocesisdepuebla.mx; internet www.arquidiocesisdepuebla.mx.

Archbishop of San Luis Potosí: JESÚS CARLOS CABRERO ROMERO, Arzobispado, Francisco Madero 300, Apdo 1, Col. Centro, 78000 San Luis Potosí, SLP; tel. (444) 812-4555; fax (444) 812-7979; e-mail arquinet@iglesiapotosina.org; internet www.iglesiapotosina.org.

Archbishop of Tijuana: RAFAEL ROMO MUÑOZ, Arzobispado, Calle Décima y Avda Ocampo 8525, Apdo 226, 22000 Tijuana, BC; tel. (664) 684-8411; fax (664) 684-7683; e-mail obispado@iglesiatijuana.org; internet www.iglesiatijuana.org.

Archbishop of Tlalnepantla: CARLOS AGUIAR RETES, Arzobispado, Avda Juárez 42, Apdo 268, Col. Centro, 54000 Tlalnepantla, Méx.; tel. (55) 5565-3944; fax (55) 5565-2751; e-mail presidente@celam.org; internet www.tierradeenmedio.org.mx.

Archbishop of Tulancingo: DOMINGO DÍAZ MARTÍNEZ, Arzobispado, Plaza de la Constitución, Apdo 14, 43600 Tulancingo, Hgo; tel. (775) 753-1010; e-mail sgamitra@netpac.net.mx; internet arquidiocesisdetulancingo.org.

Archbishop of Tuxtla Gutiérrez: FABIO MARTÍNEZ CASTILLA, Uruguay 500A, Col. El Retiro, Apdo 365, 29040 Tuxtla Gutiérrez, Chis; tel. (961) 604-0644; fax (961) 614-3297; e-mail aguileracruz@yahoo.com.mx; internet www.arquidiocesisdetuxtla.org.mx.

Archbishop of Yucatán: EMILIO CARLOS BERLIE BELAUNZARÁN, Arzobispado, Calle 58 501, Col. Centro, 97000 Mérida, Yuc.; tel. (999) 924-7777; fax (999) 923-7983; e-mail aryu@prodigy.net.mx; internet www.arquidiocesisdeyucatan.com.mx.

The Anglican Communion

Mexico is divided into five dioceses, which form the Province of the Anglican Church in Mexico, established in 1995.

Bishop of Cuernavaca: JAMES OTTLEY, Minerva 1, Col. Delicias, 62431 Cuernavaca, Mor.; tel. and fax (777) 315-2870; e-mail diocesisdecuernavaca@hotmail.com.

Bishop of Mexico City and Primate of the Anglican Church in Mexico: CARLOS TOUCHÉ PORTER, La Otra Banda 40, Avda San Jerónimo 117, Col. San Ángel, 01000 México, DF; tel. and fax (55) 5616-2205; e-mail diomex@axtel.net; internet www.iglesiaanglicanademexico.org.

Bishop of Northern Mexico: FRANCISCO MANUEL MORENO, Acatlán 102 Oueste, Col. Mitras Centro, 64460 Monterrey, NL; tel. (81) 8333-0922; fax (81) 8348-7362; e-mail diocesisdelnorte@prodigy.net.mx.

Bishop of South-Eastern Mexico: BENITO JUÁREZ MARTÍNEZ, Avda de las Américas 73, Col. Aguacatl, 91130 Jalapa, Ver.; tel. and fax (228) 814-6951; e-mail diocesisdelsureste@prodigy.net.mx

Bishop of Western Mexico: LINO RODRÍGUEZ-AMARO, Francisco Javier Gamboa 255, Col. Barrera, 45150 Guadalajara, Jal.; tel. (33) 3615-5070; fax (33) 3615-4413; e-mail iamoccidente@prodigy.net.mx.

Other Christian Churches

According to the 2010 census, some 7% of the population are Pente-costal or Evangelical Christians.

Church of Jesus Christ of Latter-Day Saints (Mormons): Mexico City Temple, Avda 510, No 90, Col. San Juan de Aragón, 07950 México, DF; tel. (55) 5003-3734; internet www.lds.org; 314,932 mems (2010).

Iglesia Evangélica Luterana de México: Mina 5808 Poniente, Nuevo Laredo, Tamaulipas; Pres. ENCARNACIÓN ESTRADA; 3,000 mems (2010).

Iglesia Luterana Mexicana: POB 1-1034, 44101 Guadalajara, Jal.; tel. (33) 3639-7253; e-mail dtrejocoria@gmail.com; f. 1951; Pres. DANIEL TREJO CORIA; 1,500 mems.

Iglesia Metodista de México, Asociación Religiosa: Miravelle 209, Col. Albert, 03570 México, DF; tel. (55) 5539-3674; e-mail prenapro@iglesia-metodista.org.mx; internet www.iglesia-metodista.org.mx; f. 1873; 55,000 mems; Pres. Rev. RAÚL GARCÍA DE OCHOA; 700 congregations, 25,370 mems (2010); comprises six episcopal areas.

National Baptist Convention of Mexico: Tlalpan 1025A, Col. Américas Unidas, 03610 México, DF; tel. (55) 5539-7720; fax (55) 5539-2302; e-mail comunicacion@cnbm.org.mx; internet www.cnbm.org.mx; f. 1903; Pres. Rev. JOSÉ TRINIDAD BONILLA MORALES; 252,874 mems (2010).

Testigos de Jehová (Jehovah's Witnesses): Avda Jardín 10, Fraccionamiento El Tejocote, 56239 Texcoco, Méx.; tel. (55) 5133-3000; 1.6m. mems (2010).

BAHÁ'Í FAITH

National Spiritual Assembly of the Bahá'ís of Mexico: Emerson 421, Col. Bosque de Chapultpec, 11580 México, DF; tel. (55) 5545-2155; fax (55) 5255-5972; e-mail secretariado@bahai.mx; internet www.bahai.mx; f. 1959; Sec.-Gen. DARYOUSH YALDAEI; mems resident in 1,069 localities.

JUDAISM

According to the 2010 census, the Jewish community numbers 67,476 (less than 1% of the population).

Comité Central de la Comunidad Judía de México: Cofre de Perote 115, Lomas Barrilaco, 11010 México, DF; tel. (55) 5520-9393; fax (55) 5540-3050; e-mail comitecentral@prodigy.net.mx; internet www.tribuna.org.mx; f. 1938; Pres. RAFAEL ZAGA.

The Press

DAILY NEWSPAPERS

México, DF

La Afición: Ignacio Mariscal 23, Apdo 64 bis, Col. Tabacalera, 06030 México, DF; tel. (55) 5140-4900; fax (55) 5546-5852; internet laaficion.milenio.com; f. 1930; sport; Pres. FRANCISCO A. GONZÁLEZ; Exec. Editor CARLOS MARÍN; circ. 85,000.

La Crónica de Hoy: Londres 38, Col. Juárez, 06600 México, DF; tel. and fax (52) 1084-5800; e-mail cronica@cronica.com.mx; internet www.cronica.com.mx; Pres. JORGE KAHWAGI GASTINE; Editorial Dir FRANCISCO BAEZ RODRÍGUEZ.

Diario de México: Chimalpopoca 38, Col. Obrera, Del. Cuauhtémoc, 06800 México, DF; tel. (55) 5442-6526; fax (55) 5442-6520; e-mail info@diariodemexico.com.mx; internet www.diariodemexico.com.mx; f. 1949; morning; Dir-Gen. FEDERICO BRACAMONTES BAZ; Editorial Dir DANIELA NUÑO; circ. 76,000.

Diario Oficial de la Federación: Río Amazonas 62, Col. Cuauhtémoc, 06500 México, DF; tel. (55) 5093-3200; e-mail dof@segob.gob.mx; internet www.dof.gob.mx; f. 1867; govt gazette; Dir-Gen. ALEJANDRO LÓPEZ GONZÁLEZ.

El Economista: Avda Coyoacán 515, Col. del Valle, 03100 México, DF; tel. (55) 5237-0766; fax (55) 5687-3821; e-mail internet@eleconomista.com.mx; internet eleconomista.com.mx; f. 1988; financial; Pres. JORGE NACER GOBERA; Editor-in-Chief LUIS MIGUEL GONZÁLEZ; circ. 37,448.

Esto: Guillermo Prieto 7, 1°, Col. San Rafael, Del. Cuauhtémoc, 06470 México, DF; tel. and fax (55) 5566-1511; fax (55) 5591-0866; e-mail salvador@esto.com.mx; internet www.oem.com.mx/esto; f. 1941; publ. by Organización Editorial Mexicana; morning; sport; Dir SALVADOR AGUILERA GONZÁLEZ; Editor-in-Chief CARLOS GABINO CU UC; circ. 400,000, Mon. 450,000.

Excélsior: Bucareli 1, Apdo 120 bis, Col. Centro, 06600 México, DF; tel. (55) 5128-3000; fax (55) 5566-0223; e-mail foro@excelsior.com.mx; internet www.excelsior.com.mx; f. 1917; morning; ind; Pres. OLEGARIO VÁZQUEZ RAÑA; Editorial Dir PASCAL BELTRÁN DEL RÍO; circ. 200,000.

El Financiero: Lago Bolsena 176, Col. Anáhuac (Pensil), entre Lago Peypus y Lago Onega, 11320 México, DF; tel. (55) 5227-7600; fax (55) 5254-6427; e-mail contacto@elfinanciero.com.mx; internet www.elfinanciero.com.mx; f. 1981; financial; Dir-Gen. MARÍA DEL PILAR ESTANDÍA GONZÁLEZ LUNA; Editor-Gen. ENRIQUE QUINTANA; circ. 119,000.

La Jornada: Avda Cuauhtémoc 1236, Col. Santa Cruz Atoyac, Del. Benito Juárez, 03310 México, DF; tel. (55) 9183-0300; internet www.jornada.unam.mx; f. 1984; morning; Dir-Gen. CARMEN LIRA SAADE; Gen. Man. JORGE MARTÍNEZ JIMÉNEZ; circ. 86,275.

Milenio Diario: México, DF; tel. (55) 5140-4900; internet www.milenio.com; publishes Mexico City and regional edns, and a weekly news magazine, *Milenio Semanal*; Pres. FRANCISCO A. GONZÁLEZ; Dir-Gen. FRANCISCO D. GONZÁLEZ A.

Ovaciones: Lago Zirahuén 279, 20°, Col. Anáhuac, 11320 México, DF; tel. (55) 5328-0700; fax (55) 5260-2219; e-mail bjonofre@ova.com.mx; internet www.ovaciones.com; f. 1947; morning and evening editions; Pres. and Dir-Gen. MAURICIO VÁZQUEZ RAMOS; circ. 130,000; evening circ. 100,000.

La Prensa: Basilio Vadillo 40, Col. Tabacalera, 06030 México, DF; tel. (55) 5228-9977; fax (55) 5521-8209; e-mail oemenlinea@oem.com.mx; internet www.oem.com.mx/laprensa; f. 1928; publ. by Organización Editorial Mexicana; morning; Dir-Gen. MAURICIO ORTEGA CAMBEROS; Editor-in-Chief JESÚS SÁNCHEZ RAMÍREZ; circ. 270,000.

Reforma: Avda México Coyoacán 40, Col. Santa Cruz Atoyac, 03310 México, DF; tel. (55) 5628-7100; fax (55) 5628-7188; internet www.reforma.com; f. 1993; morning; Pres. and Dir-Gen. ALEJANDRO JUNCO DE LA VEGA ELIZONDO; Editorial Dir LÁZARO RÍOS; circ. 94,000.

El Sol de México: Guillermo Prieto 7, 20°, Col. San Rafael, 06470 México, DF; tel. (55) 5566-1511; fax (55) 5535-5560; e-mail enlinea@elsoldemexico.com.mx; internet www.oem.com.mx/elsoldemexico; f. 1965; publ. by Organización Editorial Mexicana; morning and midday; Dir-Gen. RUBÉN PÉREZ GARCÍA; circ. 76,000.

El Universal: Bucareli 8, Apdo 909, Col. Centro, Del. Cuauhtémoc, 06040 México, DF; tel. (55) 5709-1313; fax (55) 5510-1269; e-mail rdirgral@eluniversal.com.mx; internet www.eluniversal.com.mx; f. 1916; morning; ind; centre-left; Pres. JUAN FRANCISCO EALY ORTIZ; Editorial Dir ROBERTO ROCK; circ. 165,629, Sun. 181,615.

Unomásuno: Gabino Barreda 86, Col. San Rafael, México, DF; tel. (55) 1055-5500; fax (55) 5598-8821; e-mail cduran@servidor.unam.mx; internet www.unomasuno.com.mx; f. 1977; morning; left-wing; Pres. NAIM LIBIEN KAUI; circ. 40,000.

PROVINCIAL DAILY NEWSPAPERS

Baja California

El Sol de Tijuana: Rufino Tamayo 4, Zona del Río, 22320 Tijuana, BC; tel. (664) 634-3232; fax (664) 634-2234; e-mail jesparza@elsoldetijuana.com.mx; internet www.oem.com.mx/elsoldetijuana; f. 1989; publ. by Organización Editorial Mexicana; morning; Dir-Gen. ENRIQUE SÁNCHEZ DÍAZ; Editor-in-Chief JOSUÉ SANTIAGO EVES ZAMARRIPA; circ. 50,000.

La Voz de la Frontera: Avda Francisco I. Madero 1545, Col. Nueva, Apdo 946, 21100 Mexicali, BC; tel. (686) 533-4545; fax (686) 552-4243; e-mail ramondiaz@lavozdelafrontera.com.mx; internet www.oem.com.mx/lavozdelafrontera; f. 1964; morning; publ. by Organización Editorial Mexicana; Dir-Gen. FRANCISCO EDGARDO LEAL CORRALES; Dir JUAN GREGORIO AVILÉS TARÍN; circ. 65,000.

Chihuahua

El Diario: Publicaciones Paso del Norte, Avda Paseo Triunfo de la República 3505, Zona Pronaf, 32310 Ciudad Juárez, Chih.; tel. (656) 629-6900; e-mail rgallegos@redaccion.diario.com.mx; internet www.diario.com.mx; f. 1976; Pres. OSVALDO RODRÍGUEZ BORUNDA; Editor ROCÍO GALLEGOS.

El Heraldo de Chihuahua: Avda Universidad 2507, Apdo 1515, 31240 Chihuahua, Chih.; tel. (614) 432-3800; fax (614) 413-9339; e-mail heraldo@elheraldodechihuahua.com.mx; internet www.oem.com.mx/elheraldodechihuahua; f. 1927; publ. by Organización Editorial Mexicana; morning; Dir Dr JAVIER H. CONTRERAS OROZCO; Editor ROBERTO ALVARADO GATES; circ. 27,520, Sun. 31,223.

El Mexicano: Ramón Corona y Galeana 301, 32000 Ciudad Juárez, Chih.; e-mail publicidad@periodicoelmexicano.com.mx; internet www.oem.com.mx/elmexicano; f. 1959; publ. by Organización Editorial Mexicana; morning; Dir RAFAEL NAVARRO BARRÓN; Editor-in-Chief JAIME SALVADOR NÚÑEZ ANGEL; circ. 80,000.

Coahuila

El Siglo de Torreón: Avda Matamoros 1056 Poniente, Col. Centro, 27000 Torreón, Coah.; tel. (871) 759-1200; e-mail cartas@elsiglodetorreon.com.mx; internet www.elsiglodetorreon.com.mx; f. 1922; morning; Editor JAVIER GARZA RAMOS; circ. 38,611, Sun. 38,526.

Vanguardia: Blvd Venustiano Carranza 1918, esq. con Chiapas, República Oriente, 25280 Saltillo, Coah.; tel. (844) 450-1000; e-mail hola@vanguardia.com.mx; internet www.vanguardia.com.mx; Editorial Dir Armando Castilla Galindo.

Colima

Diario de Colima: Avda 20 de Noviembre 580, 28060 Colima, Col.; tel. (312) 312-5688; internet www.diariodecolima.com; f. 1953; Dir-Gen. Héctor Sánchez de la Madrid; Editorial Dir Glenda Libier Madrigal Trujillo.

Guanajuato

Correo de Guanajuato: Carreterra Guanajuato–Juventino Rosas Km 9.5, Col. Carbonera, Apdo 32, 36250 Guanajuato, Gto; tel. (477) 733-1253; fax (477) 733-0057; e-mail correo@correo-gto.com.mx; internet www.periodicocorreo.com.mx; Dir-Gen. Pablo Villanueva Martínez; Editorial Dir Martha Celia Camacho Ledesma.

El Sol de Salamanca: Faja de Oro 800, 36700 Salamanca, Gto; tel. (464) 647-0144; e-mail publicidad@elsoldesalamanca.com.mx; internet www.oem.com.mx/elsoldesalamanca; publ. by Organización Editorial Mexicana; Dir-Gen. Alejandro Herrera Sánchez; Editor-in-Chief Jorge Caudillo Elías.

Guerrero

Novedades de Acapulco: Avda Costera Miguel Alemán 258, Fraccionamiento Hornos, 39355 Acapulco, Gro; tel. (744) 485-1155; e-mail informa@aca-novenet.com.mx; internet www .novedadesacapulco.mx; f. 1969; daily; Editorial Dir Mario Bustos García.

Jalisco

El Informador: Independencia 300, Apdo 3 bis, 44100 Guadalajara, Jal.; tel. (33) 3678-7700; e-mail sistemas@informador.com.mx; internet www.informador.com.mx; f. 1917; morning; Editor Carlos Alvarez del Castillo; circ. 50,000.

El Occidental: Calzada Independencia Sur 324, Apdo 1-699, 44100 Guadalajara, Jal.; tel. (33) 3613-0690; fax (33) 3613-6796; e-mail publicidad@eloccidental.com.mx; internet www.oem.com.mx/eloccidental; f. 1942; publ. by Organización Editorial Mexicana; morning; Dir Javier Valle Chávez; Editor Anselmo Eduardo Vázquez M.; circ. 49,400.

México

ABC: Avda Hidalgo Oriente 1337, Centro Comercial, Col. Ferrocarriles Nacionales, 50070 Toluca, Méx.; tel. (722) 217-9800; fax (722) 217-8402; e-mail redaccion@abctoluca.com.mx; internet www.miled .com; f. 1984; morning; Pres. and Editor Miled Libien Kaui; circ. 65,000.

El Heraldo de Toluca: Salvador Díaz Mirón 700, Col. Sánchez Colín, 50150 Toluca, Méx.; tel. (722) 217-4913; fax (722) 212-3542; e-mail redaccion@heraldotoluca.com.mx; internet www .heraldotoluca.com.mx; f. 1955; morning; Editor Jorge Mena García; circ. 90,000.

Portal–Diario de Toluca: Sebastián Lerdo de Tejada Poniente 864, esq. Agustín Millán, Col. Electricistas Locales, 50040 Toluca, Méx.; tel. (722) 214-5477; fax (722) 214-5463; e-mail portal@portaldigital .com.mx; internet diarioportal.com.mx; f. 1980; morning; Dir-Gen. Esteban Rivera Rivera; Editorial Dir Felipe González López; circ. 22,200.

El Sol de Toluca: Santos Degollado 105, Apdo 54, Col. Centro, 50050 Toluca, Méx.; tel. (722) 214-7077; fax (722) 215-2564; e-mail publicidad@elsoldetoluca.com.mx; internet www.oem.com.mx/elsoldetoluca; f. 1947; publ. by Organización Editorial Mexicana; morning; Dir Alejandra Cordero Casas; Editor-in-Chief Rodrigo Miranda Torres; circ. 42,000.

Michoacán

La Voz de Michoacán: Blvd del Periodismo 1270, Col. Arriaga Rivera, Apdo 121, 58190 Morelia, Mich.; tel. (443) 327-5600; fax (443) 327-3728; e-mail redaccilavoz@voznet.com.mx; internet www .vozdemichoacan.com.mx; f. 1948; morning; Dir-Gen. Miguel Medina Robles; circ. 50,000.

Morelos

El Diario de Morelos: Avda Morelos Sur 132, Col. Las Palmas, 62050 Cuernavaca, Mor.; tel. (777) 362-0220; fax (777) 362-0225; e-mail redaccion@diariodemorelos.com; internet www .diariodemorelos.com; f. 1978; morning; Propr Grupo BRACA de Comunicación; Pres. Miguel Angel Bracamontes Baz; Editor-in-Chief Miriam Estrada Dorantes; circ. 35,000.

Nayarit

Meridiano de Nayarit: Independencia 335, Fracc. Las Aves, Tepic, Nay.; tel. (311) 210-3211; e-mail ventas@meridiano.com.mx; internet meridiano.nnc.mx; f. 1942; morning; Dir Emmanuel Nuñez García; circ. 60,000.

Nuevo León

ABC: Platón Sánchez Sur 411, 64000 Monterrey, NL; tel. (81) 8344-2510; fax (81) 8344-2666; e-mail ventas@periodicoabc.mx; internet www.periodicoabc.mx; f. 1985; morning; Dir-Gen. Gonzalo Estrado Torres; Editorial Dir Reynaldo Márquez; circ. 40,000, Sun. 45,000.

El Norte: Washington 629 Oeste, Apdo 186, 64000 Monterrey, NL; tel. (81) 8150-8100; fax (81) 8343-2476; internet www.elnorte.com; f. 1938; morning; Man. Dir Alejandro Junco de la Vega; Editorial Dir Martha Alicia Treviño; circ. 133,872, Sun. 154,951.

El Porvenir: Galeana Sur 344, entre Washington y 5 de Mayo, Col. Centro, Apdo 218, 64000 Monterrey, NL; tel. (81) 8345-4080; fax (81) 8345-7795; e-mail editorial.elporvenir@prodigy.net.mx; internet www.elporvenir.com.mx; f. 1919; morning; Dir-Gen. José Gerardo Cantú Escalante; Editorial Dir José Manuel Rodríguez Arroyo; circ. 75,000.

Oaxaca

El Imparcial: Armenta y López 312, Apdo 322, 68000 Oaxaca, Oax.; tel. (951) 516-2812; fax (951) 514-7020; e-mail subdireccion@imparcialenlinea.com; internet www.imparcialenlinea.com; f. 1951; morning; Dir-Gen. Benjamín Fernández Pichardo; circ. 17,000, Sun. 20,000.

Puebla

La Opinión: 3 Oriente 1207, Barrio del Analco, 238 Puebla, Pue.; tel. (222) 246-4358; fax (222) 232-7772; e-mail director@opinion.com.mx; internet www.opinion.com.mx; f. 1924; morning; Dir-Gen. Oscar López Morales; Editor-in-Chief Hugo Sánchez Izquierdo; circ. 40,000.

El Sol de Puebla: Avda 3 Oriente 201, Col. Centro, 72000 Puebla, Pue.; tel. (222) 514-3300; fax (222) 246-0869; e-mail elsoldepuebla@elsoldepuebla.com.mx; internet www.oem.com.mx/elsoldepuebla; f. 1944; publ. by Organización Editorial Mexicana; morning; Dir Serafín Salazar Arellano; Editor Ramón Domínguez Sánchez; circ. 67,000.

San Luis Potosí

El Heraldo: Villerías 305, 78000 San Luis Potosí, SLP; tel. (444) 812-3312; fax (444) 812-2081; e-mail redaccion@elheraldoslp.com.mx; internet www.elheraldoslp.com.mx; f. 1954; morning; Dir-Gen. Alejandro Villasana Mena; Editor Aurelio Ventura Florencio; circ. 60,620.

Pulso: Galeana 485, Centro Histórico, 78000 San Luis Potosí, SLP; tel. (444) 812-7575; fax (444) 812-3525; internet www.pulsoslp.com .mx; f. 1988; morning; Dir-Gen. Pablo Valladares García; circ. 60,000.

El Sol de San Luis: Avda Universidad 565, Apdo 342, 78000 San Luis Potosí, SLP; tel. and fax (444) 812-4412; internet www.oem.com .mx/elsoldesanluis; f. 1952; publ. by Organización Editorial Mexicana; morning; Dir José Angel Martínez Limón; Editor-in-Chief Rafael Ruiz Rangel; circ. 60,000.

Sinaloa

El Debate de Culiacán: Madero 556 Poniente, 80000 Culiacán, Sin.; tel. (667) 716-6353; fax (667) 715-7131; e-mail andrea.miranda@debate.com.mx; internet www.debate.com.mx; f. 1972; morning; Dir Rosario I. Oropeza; Editor Andrea Miranda; circ. 23,603, Sun. 23,838.

Noroeste Culiacán: Grupo Periódicos Noroeste, Angel Flores 282 Oeste, Apdo 90, 80000 Culiacán, Sin.; tel. (667) 759-8100; fax (667) 712-8006; e-mail direccion@noroeste.com.mx; internet www .noroeste.com.mx; f. 1973; morning; Dir-Gen. Adrián López Ortiz; Editor Guillermina García Nevares; circ. 35,000.

El Sol de Sinaloa: Blvd Gabriel Leyva Lozano y Corona 320, Apdo 412, 80000 Culiacán, Sin.; tel. (667) 713-1621; fax (667) 713-1800; e-mail publicidad@elsoldesinaloa.com.mx; internet www .elsoldesinaloa.com.mx; f. 1956; publ. by Organización Editorial Mexicana; morning; Dir Javier López López; Editor-in-Chief Arnoldo Ortega Molina; circ. 30,000.

Sonora

Expreso: Blvd Abelardo L. Rodríguez 16, Col. San Benito, 83190 Hermosillo, Son.; tel. (662) 108-3000; fax (662) 108-3006; e-mail romandia@expreso.com.mx; internet www.expreso.com.mx; f. 2005;

Dir-Gen. LUIS FELIPE ROMANDÍA CACHO; Editor CONRADO QUEZADA RODRÍGUEZ; circ. 17,000, Sun. 18,000.

El Imparcial: Sufragio Efectivo y Mina 71, Col. Centro, Apdo 66, 83000 Hermosillo, Son.; tel. (662) 259-4700; fax (662) 217-4483; e-mail lector@elimparcial.com; internet www.elimparcial.com; f. 1937; morning; Pres. and Dir-Gen. JUAN F. HEALY; Editor LOURDES LUGO; circ. 32,083, Sun. 32,444.

Tabasco

Tabasco Hoy: Avda de los Ríos 206, Col. Tabasco 2000, 86035 Villahermosa, Tab.; tel. (993) 316-2135; internet www.tabascohoy .com.mx; f. 1987; morning; Dir-Gen. MIGUEL CANTÓN ZETINA; Editorial Dir HÉCTOR TAPIA MARTÍNEZ DE ESCOBAR; circ. 50,000.

Tamaulipas

El Bravo: Morelos y Primera 129, Apdo 483, 87300 Matamoros, Tamps; tel. (871) 816-0100; fax (871) 816-2007; e-mail ventas@ elbravo.com.mx; internet www.elbravo.com.mx; f. 1951; morning; Dir-Gen. JOSÉ CARRETERO BALBOA; Editorial Dir JESÚS CRUZ MEDRANO; circ. 60,000.

El Diario de Nuevo Laredo: González 2409, Apdo 101, 88000 Nuevo Laredo, Tamps; tel. (867) 712-8444; fax (867) 712-8221; e-mail publicidad@diario.net; internet www.diario.net; f. 1948; morning; Dir-Gen. RUPERTO VILLARREAL MONTEMAYOR; Editor MARCO GUILLERMO VILLARREAL MARROQUÍN; circ. 68,130, Sun. 73,495.

El Mañana de Nuevo Laredo: Juárez y Perú, Col. Juárez, Nuevo Laredo, Tamps; tel. (867) 711-9900; fax (867) 715-0405; e-mail daniel .rosas@elmanana.com.mx; internet www.elmanana.com.mx; f. 1932; morning; Pres. RAMÓN CANTÚ DEÁNDAR; Editor NINFA CANTÚ DEÁNDAR; circ. 16,473, Sun. 20,957.

El Mañana de Reynosa: Calle Matías Canales 504, Apdo 14, Col. Ribereña, 88620 Ciudad Reynosa, Tamps; tel. (899) 921-9950; fax (899) 924-9348; internet www.elmanana.com; f. 1949; morning; Dir JAVIER RAMÍREZ NAVA; Editor ERASMO SALINAS PÉREZ; circ. 52,000.

Prensa de Reynosa: Calle Matamoros y González Ortega, Zona Centro, 88500 Reynosa, Tamps; tel. (899) 922-0299; fax (899) 922-2412; e-mail prensa_88500@yahoo.com; internet laprensa.mx; f. 1963; morning; Dir-Gen. and Editor FÉLIX GARZA ELIZONDO; circ. 60,000.

El Sol de Tampico: Altamira 311 Poniente, Apdo 434, 89000 Tampico, Tamps; tel. (833) 212-1067; fax (833) 212-6821; e-mail publicidad@elsoldetampico.com.mx; internet www.oem.com.mx/ elsoldetampico; f. 1950; publ. by Organización Editorial Mexicana; morning; Dir-Gen. AGUSTÍN F. JIMÉNEZ HERNÁNDEZ; Editor-in-Chief MARIO ALBERTO FERNÁNDEZ AVALOS; circ. 77,000.

Veracruz

Diario del Istmo: Avda Hidalgo 1115, Col. Centro, 96400 Coatzacoalcos, Ver.; tel. (921) 211-8000; e-mail info@istmo.com.mx; internet www.diariodelistmo.com; f. 1979; morning; Dir-Gen. HÉCTOR ROBLES BARAJAS; Editor MIGUEL EDUARDO JIMÉNEZ; circ. 64,600.

El Dictamen: Avda Arista 285, esq. 16 de Septiembre, Fracc. Faros, 91709 Veracruz, Ver.; tel. (229) 931-1745; fax (229) 931-5804; e-mail owar@eldictamen.org; internet www.eldictamen.mx; f. 1898; morning; Pres. BERTHA ROSALIA MALPICA DE AHUED; circ. 25,000, Sun. 28,000.

La Opinión: Poza Rica de Hidalgo, Ver.; e-mail publicidad@ laopinion.com.mx; internet www.laopinion.com.mx; Dir RAÚL GIBB.

Yucatán

Por Esto!: Calle 60, No 576 entre 73 y 71, 97000 Mérida, Yuc.; tel. (999) 24-7613; fax (999) 28-6514; e-mail redaccion@poresto.net; internet www.poresto.net; f. 1991; morning; Dir-Gen. MARIO RENATO MENÉNDEZ RODRÍGUEZ; circ. 26,985, Sun. 28,727.

Zacatecas

Imagen: Calzada Revolución 24, Col. Tierra y Libertad, 98615 Guadalupe, Zac.; tel. and fax (492) 923-8898; e-mail buzon@ imagenzac.com.mx; internet www.imagenzac.com.mx; Dir-Gen. LUIS ENRIQUE MERCADO SÁNCHEZ; Editorial Dir MARÍA DEL CARMEN SALAZAR.

SELECTED WEEKLY NEWSPAPERS

El Heraldo del Bajío: Hermanos Aldama 222, Apdo 299, Zona Centro, 37000 León, Gto; tel. (477) 719-8800; e-mail heraldo@ el-heraldo-bajio.com; internet heraldodelbajio.com; f. 1957; Pres. and Dir-Gen. LEÓN MAURICIO BERCÚN LÓPEZ; circ. 85,000.

Zeta: Avda las Américas 4633, Fraccionamiento El Paraíso, La Mesa, 22440 Tijuana, BC; tel. (664) 681-6913; fax (664) 621-0065; e-mail asistente@zetatijuana.com; internet www.zetatijuana.com; f. 1980; news magazine; Editor ROSARIO MOSSO CASTRO.

SELECTED PERIODICALS

Boletín Industrial: Luis Khune 55-B, Col. Las Águilas, 01710 México, DF; tel. (55) 5337-2200; fax (55) 5337-2222; e-mail ventas@ boletinindustrial.com; internet www.boletinindustrial.com; f. 1983; publ. by Editorial Nova SA de CV; monthly; Pres. and Editor HUMBERTO VALADÉS DÍAZ; circ. 37,100.

Casas y Gente: Tapachula 31, Col. Roma, 06700 México, DF; tel. (55) 5286-7794; fax (55) 5211-7112; e-mail informac@casasgente.com; internet www.casasgente.com; 10 a year; interior design; Dir-Gen. ANNE SÁNCHEZ OSORIO; Editor DONATELLA LOCKHART.

Contenido: Darwin 101, Col. Anzures, 11590 México, DF; tel. (55) 5531-3162; fax (55) 5545-7478; e-mail contenido@contenido.com.mx; internet www.contenido.com.mx; f. 1963; monthly; popular appeal; Editor-in-Chief JOSÉ ANTONIO OLVERA; circ. 124,190.

Cosmopolitan México: Vasco de Quiroga 2000, Col. Santa Fe, Del. Alvaro Obregón, 01210 México, DF; tel. (55) 5261-2600; fax (55) 5261-2704; internet www.cosmoenespanol.com; f. 1973; fortnightly; women's magazine; Publr KATY GARCÍA LAU; Editor ANA VICTORIA TACHÉ BATRES; circ. 300,000.

Expansión: Avda Constituyentes 956, Col. Lomas Altas, 11950 México, DF; tel. and fax (55) 9177-4100; e-mail adortega@ expansion.com.mx; internet www.expansion.com.mx; fortnightly; business and financial; Editor ADOLFO ORTEGA; circ. 54,000.

Fama: Avda Eugenio Garza Sada 2245 Sur, Col. Roma, Apdo 3128, 64700 Monterrey, NL; tel. (81) 8359-2525; internet www.famaweb .com; fortnightly; show business; Pres. JESÚS D. GONZÁLEZ; Dir-Gen. RAÚL MARTÍNEZ GONZÁLEZ; circ. 350,000.

Forbes (Mexico): Montes Urales 754, Reforma Lomas, 11000 México, DF; tel. (55) 5520-0044; e-mail contacto@forbes.com.mx; internet www.forbes.com.mx; Editor VIRIDIANA MENDOZA ESCAMILLA.

Fortuna: Avda Río Churubusco 590, Col. del Carmen, Del. Coyoacán, 04100 México, DF; tel. (55) 5554-9194; e-mail info@ revistafortuna.com.mx; internet www.revistafortuna.com.mx; business; monthly; Dir CLAUDIA VILLEGAS.

Gaceta Médica de México: Academia Nacional de Medicina, Unidad de Congresos del Centro Médico Nacional Siglo XXI, Bloque B, Avda Cuauhtémoc 330, Col. Doctores, 06725 México, DF; tel. (55) 5578-2044; fax (55) 5578-4271; e-mail medigraphic@medigraphic .com; internet www.medigraphic.com; f. 1864; every 2 months; journal of the Academia Nacional de Medicina de México; Editor ALFREDO ULLOA AGUIRRE; circ. 20,000.

Kena Mensual: Río Balsas 101, Col. Cuauhtémoc, 06500 México, DF; tel. (55) 5442-9600; e-mail ginaum@grupoarmonia.com.mx; internet kena.com; f. 1977; fortnightly; women's interest; Editor GINA URETA; circ. 80,000.

Manufactura: Avda Chapultepec 230, esq. Córdoba, Col. Roma Norte, Del. Cuauhtémoc, México, DF; tel. (55) 9177-4369; e-mail mramo@expansion.com.mx; internet www.manufactura.mx; f. 1994; monthly; industrial; Editor-Gen. MILDRED RAMO; circ. 30,000.

Marie Claire: Editorial Televisa, SA de CV, Avda Vasco de Quiroga 2000, Edif. E, 3°, Col. Santa Fe, 01210 México, DF; tel. (55) 5261-2706; fax (55) 5261-2733; e-mail gagrantb@televisa.com.mx; internet www.marieclaire.com.mx; f. 1990; monthly; women's interest; Editor ARIADNE GRANT; circ. 145,000.

Men's Health: Avda Vasco de Quiroga 2000, Col. Santa Fe, Del. Alvaro Obregón, 01210 México, DF; tel. (55) 5265-0990; fax (55) 5261-2733; internet www.menshealthlatam.com; f. 1994; monthly; health; Editor JUAN ANTONIO SEMPERE; circ. 130,000.

Muy Interesante: Vasco de Quiroga 2000, Col. Santa Fe, Del. Alvaro Obregón, 01210 México, DF; tel. (55) 5261-2600; fax (55) 5261-2707; e-mail muyinteresante@televisa.com.mx; internet www .muyinteresante.com.mx; f. 1984; monthly; publ. by Editorial Televisa; scientific devt; Dir FRANCISCO VILLASEÑOR; circ. 250,000.

Negocios y Bancos: Insurgentes Sur 1442, Apdo 2, Col. Actpan, Del. Benito Juárez, 03230 México, DF; tel. (55) 5524-0871; fax (55) 5512-9411; e-mail negociosybancos@yahoo.com.mx; internet www .revistanegociosybancos.com; f. 1951; fortnightly; business, economics; Dir SALVADOR MÁRQUEZ SANDÍN; circ. 10,000.

Nexos: Mazatlán 119, Col. Condesa, Del. Cuauhtémoc, 06140 México, DF; tel. (55) 5241-2510; fax (55) 5241-6930; e-mail bortigoza@ nexos.com.mx; internet www.nexos.com.mx; f. 1978; current affairs; monthly; Dir HÉCTOR AGUILAR CAMÍN.

Proceso: Fresas 13, Col. del Valle, 03100 México, DF; tel. (55) 5636-2028; e-mail buzon@proceso.com.mx; internet www.proceso.com.mx; f. 1976; weekly; news analysis; Dir RAFAEL RODRÍGUEZ CASTAÑEDA; circ. 98,784.

Quién: Avda Constituyentes 956, Col. Lomas Altas, CP 11950, México, DF; tel. (55) 9177-4342; e-mail quien.com@expansion.com .mx; internet www.quien.com; fortnightly; celebrity news, TV, radio, films; Publr ADRIÁN VILLALBA; Editor LUIS NEREO BUENO.

La Revista Peninsular: Calle 35, 489 x 52 y 54, Zona Centro, Mérida, Yuc.; tel. and fax (999) 926-3014; e-mail direccion@larevista

.com.mx; internet www.larevista.com.mx; f. 1988; weekly; news and politics; Dir-Gen. RODRIGO MENÉNDEZ CÁMARA; Editor HUMBERTO ACEVEDO MANZANILLA.

Selecciones del Reader's Digest: Avda Lomas de Sotelo 1102, Col. Loma Hermosa, Del. Miguel Hidalgo, 11200 México, DF; tel. (55) 5351-2500; fax (55) 5395-6691; e-mail servicio.clientes@rd.com; internet mx.selecciones.com; f. 1940; monthly; Editor AUDÓN CORIA; circ. 611,660.

Siempre: Vallarta 20, Col. Tabacalera, 06030 México, DF; tel. and fax (55) 5566-9355; e-mail suscripciones@siempre.com.mx; internet www.siempre.com.mx; f. 1953; weekly; left of centre; Dir BEATRIZ PAGÉS REBOLLAR DE NIETO; Editor ENRIQUE MONTES GARCÍA; circ. 100,000.

Tiempo Libre: Holbein 75 bis, Col. Nochebuena Mixcoac, Del. Benito Juárez, 03720 México, DF; tel. (55) 5611-2884; fax (55) 5611-3982; e-mail buzon@tiempolibre.com.mx; internet www .tiempolibre.com.mx; f. 1980; weekly; entertainment guide; Dir JUAN ALBERTO BECERRA; Editor ALICIA LABRA GÓMEZ; circ. 95,000.

Tú: Vasco de Quiroga 2000, Col. Santa Fe, Del. Alvaro Obregón, 01210 México, DF; tel. (55) 5261-2600; fax (55) 5261-2730; e-mail tu@ editorial.televisa.com.mx; internet www.tuenlinea.com; f. 1980; monthly; teenage; Editor MARÍA ANTONIETA SALAMANCA; circ. 250,000.

TV y Novelas: Vasco de Quiroga 2000, Col. Santa Fe, Del. Alvaro Obregón, 01210 México, DF; tel. (55) 5261-2600; fax (55) 5261-2704; internet www.tvynovelas.com; f. 1982; weekly; television guide and short stories; Editor ARMANDO GALLEGOS; circ. 460,000.

Vanidades: Vasco de Quiroga 2000, Col. Santa Fe, Del. Alvaro Obregón, 01210 México, DF; tel. (55) 5261-2600; fax (55) 5261-2704; e-mail vanidades@editorialtelevisa.com; internet www.vanidades .com; f. 1961; fortnightly; women's magazine; Dir JAQUELINE BLANCO; circ. 290,000.

Vogue (México): Condé Nast México, Montes Urales 415, 4°, Col. Lomas de Chapultepec, 11000 México, DF; tel. (55) 5062-3736; fax (55) 5540-5639; e-mail vogue.contacto@condenast.com.mx; internet www.vogue.mx; f. 1999; monthly; women's fashion; Editorial Dir KELLY TALAMAS; circ. 208,180.

ASSOCIATIONS

Federación de Asociaciones de Periodistas Mexicanos (Fapermex): Humboldt 5, Col. Centro, 06030 México, DF; tel. (55) 5510-2679; e-mail boletin@fapermex.mx; internet www.fapermex .com.mx; Pres. TEODORO RAÚL RENTERÍA VILLA; Sec.-Gen. CONSUELO EGUÍA TONELLA; 88 mem. asscns; c. 9,000 mems.

Federación Latinoamericana de Periodistas (FELAP): Nuevo Leon 144, 1°, Col. Hipódromo Condesa, 06170 México, DF; tel. (55) 5286-6055; fax (55) 5286-6085; e-mail webmaster@felap.org; internet www.felap.org; f. 1976; Pres. JUAN CARLOS CAMAÑO; Sec.-Gen. NELSON DEL CASTILLO.

Fraternidad de Reporteros de México, AC (FREMAC): Avda Juárez 88, Col. Centro, Del. Cuauhtémoc, México, DF; e-mail fraternidadreporteros3000@gmail.com; internet fraternidad reporteros3000.blogspot.com; f. 1995; Pres. RAÚL CORREA ENGUILO; Sec.-Gen. JUAN BAUTISTA AGUILAR.

NEWS AGENCIES

Agencia de Información Integral Periodística (AIIP): Tabasco 263, Col. Roma, Del. Cuauhtémoc, 06700 México, DF; tel. and fax (55) 5514-7389; e-mail aiipmx@aiip.com.mx; internet www.aiip.com.mx; f. 1987; Dir-Gen. MIGUEL HERRERA LÓPEZ.

Agencia Mexicana de Información (AMI): Avda Cuauhtémoc 16, Col. Doctores, 06720 México, DF; tel. (55) 5761-9933; e-mail info@ red-ami.com; internet www.ami.com.mx; f. 1971; Dir-Gen. JOSÉ LUIS BECERRA LÓPEZ; Gen. Man. EVA VÁZQUEZ LÓPEZ.

Notimex, SA de CV: Morena 110, 3°, Col. del Valle, 03100 México, DF; tel. (55) 5420-1163; fax (55) 5420-1188; e-mail ventas@notimex .com.mx; internet www.notimex.com.mx; f. 1968; services to press, radio and television in Mexico and throughout the world; Dir-Gen. HÉCTOR VILLARREAL.

Publishers

Alfaomega Grupo Editor, SA de CV: Pitágoras 1139, Col. Del Valle, Del. Benito Juárez, 03100 México, DF; tel. (55) 5575-5022; fax (55) 5575-2420; e-mail atencionalcliente@alfaomega.com.mx; internet www.alfaomega.com.mx; engineering, management, technology and computing; Dir ALBERTO UMAÑA CARRIZOSA.

Artes de México y del Mundo, SA de CV: Córdoba 69, Col. Roma, 06700 México, DF; tel. (55) 5525-5905; fax (55) 5525-5925; e-mail artesdemexico@artesdemexico.com; internet www.artesdemexico

.com; f. 1988; art, design, poetry; Dir-Gen. ALBERTO RUY SÁNCHEZ LACY.

Cengage Learning Editores, SA de CV: Avda Santa Fe 505, 12°, Col. Cruz Manca, Del. Cuajimalpa, 05349 México, DF; tel. (55) 1500-6000; fax (55) 1500-6019; e-mail clientes.ca@cengage.com; internet www.cengage.com.mx; educational; Country Man. PEDRO TURBAY GARRIDO.

Cidcli, SC (Centro de Información y Desarrollo de la Comunicación y la Literatura Infantiles): Avda México 145-601, Col. Coyoacán, 04100 México, DF; tel. (55) 5659-7524; fax (55) 5659-3186; e-mail marissa@ cidcli.com.mx; internet www.cidcli.com.mx; f. 1980; children's literature; Dir PATRICIA VAN RHIJN ARMIDA.

Círculo Editorial Azteca, SA: Calle de la Luna 225–227, Col. Guerrero, 06300 México, DF; tel. (55) 5526-1157; fax (55) 5526-2557; e-mail info@circuloeditorialazteca.com.mx; internet www .circuloeditorialazteca.com.mx; f. 1956; part of Grupo Salinas; religion, literature and technical; Man. Dir JOSEFINA LARRAGOITI.

Ediciones B México, SA de CV: Bradley 52, Anzures, Del. Miguel Hidalgo, 11590 México, DF; tel. (55) 1101-0660; fax (55) 5254-0569; e-mail info@edicionesb.com; internet www.edicionesb.com.mx; general fiction; Dir CARLOS GRAEF SÁNCHEZ.

Ediciones Era, SA de CV: Calle del Trabajo 31, Col. La Fama, Tlalpan, 14269 México, DF; tel. (55) 5528-1221; fax (55) 5606-2904; e-mail info@edicionesera.com.mx; internet www.edicionesera.com .mx; f. 1960; general and social science, art and literature; Gen. Man. NIEVES ESPRESATE XIRAU.

Ediciones Larousse, SA de CV: Londres 247, Col. Juárez, Del. Cuauhtémoc, 06600 México, DF; tel. (55) 1102-1300; fax (55) 5208-6225; e-mail larousse@larousse.com.mx; internet www.larousse.com .mx; f. 1965; Dir-Gen. GERARDO GUILLERMO GUERRERO IBARRA.

Editorial Avante, SA de CV: Luis G. Obregón 9, 1°, Apdo 45-796, Col. Centro, 06020 México, DF; tel. (55) 5510-8804; fax (55) 5521-5245; e-mail didactips@editorialavante.com.mx; internet www .editorialavante.com.mx; f. 1948; educational, drama, linguistics; Man. Dir Lic. MARIO ALBERTO HINOJOSA SÁENZ.

Editorial Everest Mexicana, SA: Calzada Ermita Iztapalapa 1681, Col. Barrio San Miguel del Iztapalapa, Apdo 55-570, 09360 México, DF; tel. (55) 5685-3704; fax (55) 5685-3433; e-mail editcvem@prodigy.net.mx; f. 1980; general textbooks; Dir JOSÉ LUIS HUIDOBRO LEÓN.

Editorial Gustavo Gili de México, SA: Valle de Bravo 21, Naucalpan, 53050 Méx.; tel. (55) 5560-6011; fax (55) 5360-1453; e-mail info@ggili.com.mx; internet www.ggili.com.mx; f. 1902 in Spain; architecture, design, fashion, art and photography; Dir CARLOS LERMA.

Editorial Herder: Tehuantepec 50, esq. con Ures, Col. Roma Sur, Del. Cuauhtémoc, 06760 México, DF; tel. (55) 5523-0105; fax (55) 5669-2387; e-mail herder@herder.com.mx; internet www.herder .com.mx; social sciences; Dir JAN-CORNELIUS SCHULZ SAWADE.

Editorial Iztaccíhuatl, SA de CV: Miguel E. Schultz, No 21 y 25, Col. San Rafael, 06470 México, DF; tel. (55) 5705-0938; fax (55) 5535-2321; e-mail iztagerencia@editorializtaccihuatl.com.mx; internet www.editorializtaccihuatl.com.mx; Dir NORA MARÍA VIEYRA SICILIA.

Editorial Jus, SA de CV: Donceles 66, Centro Histórico, México, DF; tel. (55) 9150-1400; fax (55) 5529-0951; e-mail aramos@jus.com .mx; internet www.jus.com.mx; f. 1938; history of Mexico, law, philosophy, economics, religion; Dir FELIPE GARRIDO.

Editorial Lectorum, SA de CV: Calle Centeno 79A, Col. Granjas Esmeralda, México, DF; tel. (55) 5581-3202; fax (55) 5646-6892; e-mail direccion@lectorum.com.mx; internet www.lectorum.com .mx; humanities, literature and sciences; Dir-Gen. PORFIRIO LIZARRAGA.

Editorial Limusa, SA de CV: Balderas 95, 1°, Col. Centro, Del. Cuauhtémoc, 06040 México, DF; tel. (55) 5130-0700; fax (55) 5510-9415; e-mail limusa@noriegaeditores.com; internet www.noriega .com.mx; f. 1962; part of Grupo Noriega Editores; science, technical, textbooks; Dir-Gen. CARLOS BERNARDO NORIEGA ARIAS.

Editorial Orión: Calle Sierra Mojada 325, Lomas de Chapultepec, 11000 México, DF; tel. (55) 5520-0224; f. 1942; archaeology, philosophy, psychology, literature, fiction; Man. Dir SILVIA HERNÁNDEZ BALTAZAR.

Editorial Planeta Mexicana, SA de CV: Avda Presidente Masarik 111, 2°, Col. Chapultepec Morales, Del. Miguel Hidalgo, 11570 México, DF; tel. (55) 3000-6200; fax (55) 3000-6257; e-mail rrodriguez@planeta.com.mx; internet www.editorialplaneta.com .mx; general literature, non-fiction; part of Grupo Planeta (Spain); Grupo Planeta incorporates Destino, Editorial Diana, Editorial Joaquín Mortiz, Emecé, Espasa Calpe, Lunwerg Editores, Martínez Roca, Seix Barral, Temas de Hoy and Timun Mas; Man. Dir JOSÉ CALAFELL.

Editorial Porrúa Hnos, SA: Argentina 15, 5°, Col. Centro, 06020 México, DF; tel. (55) 5704-7500; fax (55) 5704-7502; e-mail editorial@

porrua.com; internet www.porrua.com; f. 1944; general literature; Dir José Antonio Pérez-Porrúa Suárez.

Editorial Progreso, SA de CV: Sabino 275, Col. Santa María la Ribera, Del. Cuauhtémoc, 06400 México, DF; tel. (55) 1946-0620; fax (55) 1946-0649; e-mail dirgeneral@editorialprogreso.com.mx; internet www.editorialprogreso.com.mx; f. 1899; educational; Dir Joaquín Flores Segura.

Editorial Serpentina, SA de CV: Santa Margarita 430, Col. Del Valle, 03100 México, DF; tel. (55) 5559-8338; fax (55) 5575-8362; e-mail editorial@editorialserpentina.com; internet www.editorialserpentina.com; f. 2004; cultural, adolescent and children's literature; Dir Alejandra Canales Ucha.

Editorial Trillas, SA: Avda Río Churubusco 385 Pte, Col. Xoco, Apdo 10534, 03330 México, DF; tel. (55) 5688-4233; fax (55) 5604-1364; e-mail fernando@etrillas.com.mx; internet www.etrillas.com.mx; f. 1954; science, technical, textbooks, children's books; Man. Dir Fernando Trillas Salazar.

Fernández Editores, SA de CV: Eje 1 Pte México-Coyoacán 321, Col. Xoco, 03330 México, DF; tel. (55) 5090-7700; fax (55) 5688-9173; e-mail sfernandez@feduca.com.mx; internet www.fernandezeditores.com.mx; f. 1943; children's literature, textbooks, educational toys; Man. Dir Sofía Fernández Peña.

Fondo de Cultura Económica: Carretera Picacho-Ajusco 227, Col. Bosques del Pedregal, Tlalpan, 14200 México, DF; tel. (55) 5227-4672; fax (55) 5227-4659; e-mail director.general@fondodeculturaeconomica.com; internet www.fondodecultura economica.com; f. 1934; economics, history, philosophy, children's books, science, politics, psychology, sociology, literature; state-owned; CEO Joaquín Díez-Canedo.

Grupo Editorial Patria, SA de CV: Renacimiento 180, Col. San Juan Tlihuaca, Del. Azcapotzalco, 02400 México, DF; tel. (55) 5354-9100; fax (55) 5354-9109; e-mail info@editorialpatria.com.mx; internet www.editorialpatria.com.mx; f. 1933; fiction, general trade, children's books; Pres. Carlos Frigolet Lerma.

McGraw-Hill Interamericana de México, SA de CV: Torre A, 17°, Paseo de la Reforma 1015, Col. Santa Fe, 01376 México, DF; tel. (55) 1500-5000; fax (55) 1500-5159; e-mail adriana_velazquez@mcgraw-hill.com; internet www.mcgraw-hill.com.mx; education, business, science; Man. Dir Andrés Rodríguez.

Medios Publicitarios Mexicanos, SA de CV: Eugenia 811, Eje 5 Sur, Col. del Valle, 03100 México, DF; tel. (55) 5523-3342; fax (55) 5523-3379; e-mail editorial@mpm.com.mx; internet www.mpm.com.mx; f. 1958; advertising media rates and data; Gen. Man. Fernando Villamil Ávila.

Ocean Sur Editorial México, SA de CV: 2a Cerrada de Corola 17, Col. El Reloj, Del. Coyoacán, 04640 México, DF; tel. (55) 5421-4165; fax (55) 5553-5512; e-mail mexico@oceansur.com; internet www.oceansur.com; Ibero-American cultural literature; Dir Miguel Ángel Águilar.

Pearson Educación de México, SA de CV: Atlacomulco 500, 4°, Industrial Atoto, Naucalpan de Juárez, 53519 Méx.; tel. (55) 5387-0700; fax (55) 5358-0808; e-mail alma.vallejo@pearsoned.com; internet www.pearsoneducacion.net; f. 1984; educational books under the imprints Addison-Wesley, Prentice Hall, Allyn & Bacon, Longman and Scott Foresman; Pres. Steve Marban; Dir Jaime Andrés Eduardo Valenzuela Solar.

Penguin Random House Group Editorial, SA de CV: Miguel de Cervantes Saavedra 301, 1°, Col. Granada, 11520, México, DF; tel. (55) 3067-8400; e-mail www.megustaleermex@penguin randomhouse.com; internet www.megustaleer.com.mx; f. 1954 as Mondadori, present name adopted 2013 following merger between Bertelsmann and Pearson; general fiction, history, sciences, philosophy, children's books; CEO Roberto Banchik.

Petra Ediciones, SA de CV: Calle El Carmen 268, Col. Camino Real, 45040 México, DF; tel. (55) 3629-0832; fax (55) 3629-3376; e-mail petra@petraediciones.com; internet www.petraediciones.com; art, literature, photography and theatre; Dir María Esperanza Espinosa Barragán.

Reverté Ediciones, SA de CV: Río Pánuco 141a, Col. Cuauhtémoc, 06500 México, DF; tel. (55) 5533-5658; fax (55) 5514-6799; e-mail reverte@reverte.com.mx; internet www.reverte.com; f. 1955; science, technical, architecture; Man. Ramón Reverté Mascó.

Siglo XXI Editores, SA de CV: Avda Cerro del Agua 248, Col. Romero de Terreros, Del. Coyoacán, 04310 México, DF; tel. (55) 5658-7999; fax (55) 5658-7588; e-mail informes@sigloxxieditores.com.mx; internet www.sigloxxieditores.com.mx; f. 1966; art, economics, education, history, social sciences, literature, philology and linguistics, philosophy and political science; Dir-Gen. Dr Jaime Labastida Ochoa; Gen. Man. José María Castro Mussot.

Universidad Nacional Autónoma de México: Dirección General de Publicaciones y Fomento Editorial, Avda del Imán 5, Ciudad Universitaria, 04510 México, DF; tel. (55) 5622-6572; e-mail corbolgg@libros.unam.mx; internet www.unam.mx; f. 1935; publications in all fields; Dir-Gen. Julia Tagüeña Parga.

ASSOCIATIONS

Cámara Nacional de la Industria Editorial Mexicana: Holanda 13, Col. San Diego Churubusco, Del. Coyoacán, 04120 México, DF; tel. (55) 5688-2011; fax (55) 5604-3147; e-mail contacto@caniem.com; internet www.caniem.com; f. 1964; Pres. Víctorico Albores Santiago; Dir-Gen. Carlos M. Espino Gaytán.

Centro Mexicano de Protección y Fomento de los Derechos de Autor, SGC: Avda Cuauhtémoc 1486, Despacho 601a, Col. Santa Cruz Atoyac, Del. Benito Juárez, 03310 México, DF; tel. (55) 5601-3528; fax (55) 5604-9856; e-mail info@cempro.com.mx; internet www.cempro.com.mx; f. 1998; manages intellectual property rights of authors and publrs; Pres. Julio Sanz; Dir-Gen. Valeria Leilani Sánchez Aguiñaga.

Broadcasting and Communications

TELECOMMUNICATIONS

Legislation allowing for the reform of the telecommunication sector was approved by the Congress in July 2014.

Alestra: Optima II, Paseo de las Palmas 275, 8°, Col. Lomas de Chapultepec, 11000 México, DF; tel. (55) 8503-5000; internet www.alestra.com.mx; 49% owned by AT&T; Chair. Armando Garza Sada; Dir-Gen. Rolando Zubirán Shetler.

América Móvil, SA de CV: Edif. Telcel 2, Lago Alberto 366, Col. Anáhuac, 11320 México, DF; tel. (55) 2581-4449; fax (55) 2581-3948; e-mail daniela.lacuna@americamovil.com; internet www.americamovil.com; f. 2000 as a spin off from Telmex; subsidiaries operate mobile telephone services in 18 countries in the Americas; Chair. Patrick Slim Domit; CEO Daniel Hajj Aboumrad.

> **Telcel:** tel. (55) 2581-3333; internet www.telcel.com; f. 1978, present name adopted 1989; subsidiary of above, providing mobile services in Mexico; COO Patricia Raquel Hevia Coto.

> **Teléfonos de México, SA de CV (Telmex):** Parque Vía 190, Col. Cuauhtémoc, 06599 México, DF; tel. (55) 5222-1212; fax (55) 5545-5500; e-mail ri@telmex.com; internet www.telmex.com.mx; majority-owned by América Móvil since 2010; Pres. Carlos Slim Domit; Dir-Gen. Héctor Slim Seade.

AT&T México: Montes Urales 470, Col. Lomas de Chapultepec, 11000 México, DF; internet www.att.com; Pres. (México) Jeffrey McElfresh.

Axtel: Blvd Díaz Ordáz Km 3.33, Zona Industrial, 66215 San Pedro Garza García, NL; tel. (81) 8114-0000; e-mail contacto@axtel.com.mx; internet www.axtel.com.mx; f. 1993; fixed-line operator; Chair. and CEO Tomás Milmo Santos.

Comunicaciones Nextel de México, SA de CV: Paseo de los Tamarindos 90, 29°, Col. Bosques de las Lomas, Del. Cuajimalpa, CP 05120, México, DF; tel. (55) 1018-4000; internet www.nextel.com.mx; f. 1998; fourth largest mobile telephone operator in Mexico; planned purchase by AT&T from NII Holdings, Inc (USA) in 2015; Pres. Salvador Alvarez.

Iusacell, SA de CV: Montes Urales No 460, Col. Lomas de Chapultepec, Del. Miguel Hidalgo, 11000 México, DF; tel. (55) 5109-4400; e-mail ateclientes@iusacell.com.mx; internet www.iusacell.com.mx; f. 1992; operates third largest mobile cellular telephone network in Mexico; 74% owned by Móvil Access, planned purchase by AT&T in 2015; Pres. Ricardo Benjamín Salinas Pliego.

Maxcom Telecomunicaciones, SAB de CV: Guillermo González Camarena 2000, Col. Centro Ciudad Santa Fe, Del. Álvaro Obregón, 01210 México, DF; tel. (55) 5147-1111; internet www.maxcom.com; f. 1996; fixed-line operator; Chair. and Exec. Pres. Jacques Gilksberg; CEO Salvador Alvarez.

Telecomunicaciones de México (TELECOMM): Torre Central de Telecomunicaciones, Eje Central Lázaro Cárdenas 567, 11°, Ala Norte, Col. Narvarte, Del. Benito Juárez, 03020 México, DF; tel. (55) 5090-1166; fax (55) 1035-2408; e-mail muycerca@telecomm.net.mx; internet www.telecomm.net.mx; govt-owned; Dir-Gen. Jorge A. Juraidini Rumilla.

Telefónica México (Movistar México): Prolongación Paseo de la Reforma 1200, Lote B-2, Col. Santa Fe, Col. Cruz Manca, Del. Cuajimalpa de Morelos, 05348 México, DF; tel. (55) 1616-5000; e-mail francisco.caballero@telefonica.com; internet www.telefonica.com.mx; f. 1924 (in Spain); owned by Telefónica, SA (Spain); fixed line, mobile and broadband services; operates telephone service Telefónica Móviles México (Movistar), call centre co Atento, and research and devt co Telefónica I+D; Pres. Francisco Gil Díaz.

Unefon: Periférico Sur 4119, Col. Fuentes del Pedregal, 14141 México, DF; tel. (55) 8582-5000; e-mail ainfante@unefon.com.mx;

internet www.unefon.com.mx; mobile operator; Pres. RICARDO SALINAS.

Regulatory Authorities

Dirección General de Política de Telecomunicaciones y de Radiodifusión: Centro Nacional SCT, Cuerpo C, 1°, Avda Xola y Universidad s/n, Col. Narvarte, Del. Benito Juárez, 03020 México, DF; tel. (55) 5723-9369; fax (55) 5723-9300; e-mail adelacru@sct.gob .mx; internet dgpt.sct.gob.mx; part of Secretariat of State for Communications and Transport; Dir-Gen. ANDRÉS DE LA CRUZ VIELMA.

Instituto Federal de Telecomunicaciones (IFT): Insurgentes Sur 1143, Col. Noche Buena, Del. Benito Juárez, 03720 México, DF; tel. and fax (55) 5015-4000; e-mail quejas@ift.org.mx; internet www .ift.org.mx; fmrly Comisión Federal de Telecomunicaciones—COFE-TEL; reformed and renamed as above in 2013; Pres. GABRIEL OSWALDO CONTRERAS SALDIVAR; Dirs-Gen. LUIS FERNANDO PELAEZ ESPINOSA, LUIS ALDO SÁNCHEZ ORTEGA.

BROADCASTING

Radio

ABC Radio (XEABC): Basilio Badillo 29, Col. Tabacalera, Del. Cuauhtémoc, 06030 México, DF; tel. (55) 3640-5210; fax (55) 3640-5277; e-mail rita@abcradio.com.mx; internet www.abcradio.com.mx; Pres. JAVIER MEDINA; Gen. Man. JOSÉ ANTONIO MARTÍNEZ RAMÍREZ.

Corporación Mexicana de Radiodifusión (CMR): Calle Tetitla 23, esq. Calle Coapa, Col. Toriello Guerra, Del. Tlalpan, 14050 México, DF; tel. (55) 5424-6380; fax (55) 5666-5422; e-mail comentarios@cmr.com.mx; internet www.cmr.com.mx; f. 1962; Pres. ENRIQUE BERNAL SERVÍN; Dir-Gen. OSCAR BELTRÁN MARTÍNEZ DE CASTRO.

Firme, SA (Funcionamiento Íntegro de Radiodifusoras Mexicanas Enlazadas, SA): Ejército Nacional 552, Col. Polanco Reforma, 11550 México, DF; tel. (55) 5250-7788; fax (55) 5250-7906; e-mail radiodifusion@firmesa.com.mx; internet www.firmesa.com.mx; f. 1972; Dir-Gen. LUIS IGNACIO SANTIBÁÑEZ FLORES.

Grupo Acir, SA: Monte Pirineos 770, Col. Lomas de Chapultepec, Del. Miguel Hidalgo, 11000 México, DF; tel. (55) 5201-1700; fax (55) 5201-1771; e-mail servicio@grupoacir.com.mx; internet www .grupoacir.com.mx; f. 1965; comprises 140 stations; Exec. Pres. FRANCISCO IBARRA LÓPEZ.

Grupo Imagen Radio: Mariano Escobedo 700, Col. Anzures, 11590 México, DF; tel. (55) 5089-9000; fax (55) 5089-9139; e-mail rfml@ imagen.com.mx; internet www.imagen.com.mx; Dir-Gen. ERNESTO RIVERA AGUILAR.

Grupo Radio Capital: Montes Urales 425, Col. Lomas de Chapultepec, 1000 México, DF; tel. (55) 3099-3000; fax (55) 5202-2370; e-mail hckaram@gmail.com; internet gruporadiocapital.com.mx; f. 1968; operates 12 radio stations; Dir-Gen. LUIS MACCISE URIBE.

Grupo Radio Centro, SA de CV: Constituyentes 1154, Col. Lomas Atlas, Del. Miguel Hidalgo, 11950 México, DF; tel. (55) 5728-4800; fax (55) 5728-4900; e-mail rcentro@grc.com.mx; internet radiocentro .com.mx; f. 1965; comprises 100 radio stations; Pres. FRANCISCO AGUIRRE GÓMEZ; Dir-Gen. CARLOS AGUIRRE GÓMEZ

Grupo Radio Digital del Sureste: Avda Chapultepec 473, 7°, Col. Juárez, Del. Cuauhtémoc, 06600 México, DF; tel. (55) 5211-1734; fax (55) 5211-7534; e-mail info@gruporadiodigital.com.mx; internet www.gruporadiodigital.com.mx; f. 1946; operates 8 radio stations in 4 provinces; Dir-Gen. SIMÓN VALANCI BUZALI.

Grupo Siete Comunicación: Montecito 38, 31°, Of. 33, Col. Nápoles, Del. Benito Juárez, 03810 México, DF; tel. (55) 9000-0787; fax (55) 9000-0747; e-mail info@gruposiete.com.mx; internet www.gruposiete.com.mx; f. 1997; Pres. Lic. FRANCISCO JAVIER SÁNCHEZ CAMPUZANO; Dir-Gen. PEDRO MOGOYÁN SOLANO.

Instituto Mexicano de la Radio (IMER): Mayorazgo 83, 2°, Col. Xoco, Del. Benito Juárez, 03330 México, DF; tel. (55) 5628-1704; fax (55) 5628-1738; e-mail general@imer.com.mx; internet www.imer .com.mx; f. 1983; Dir-Gen. CARLOS LARA SUMANO.

MVS Radio: Copérnico 183, Col. Anzures, 11590 México, DF; tel. (55) 5263-2156; fax (55) 5263-2189; e-mail eahumada@mvs.com; internet www.mvsradio.com; f. 1968; operates 4 stations, EXA FM, La Mejor FM, FM Globo and Noticias MVS; Pres. JOAQUÍN VARGAS.

Núcleo Radio Mil (NRM): Prolongación Paseo de la Reforma 115, Col. Paseo de las Lomas, Santa Fe, 01330 México, DF; tel. (55) 5258-1200; e-mail radiomil@nrm.com.mx; internet www.nrm.com.mx; f. 1942; comprises 7 radio stations; Pres. and Dir-Gen. EDILBERTO HUESCA PERROTÍN.

Radio Cadena Nacional, SA (RCN): Lago Victoria 78, Col. Granada, 11520 México, DF; tel. (55) 5250-0324; fax (55) 2624-0052; e-mail rcnmex@prodigy.net.mx; internet www.rcn.com.mx; f. 1948; Pres. SERGIO FAJARDO ORTIZ; Gen. Man. GUADALUPE CAMPUZANO.

Radio Educación: Angel Urraza 622, Col. del Valle, 03100 México, DF; tel. (55) 4155-1050; e-mail direccion@radioeducacion.edu.mx; internet www.radioeducacion.edu.mx; f. 1968; Dir-Gen. CARLOS ANTONIO TENORIO MUÑOZ COTA.

Radio Fórmula, SA: Privada de Horacio 10, Col. Polanco, 11560 México, DF; tel. (55) 5282-1016; e-mail jcoello@grupoformula.com .mx; internet www.radioformula.com.mx; f. 1968 as Radio Distrito Federal; Pres. ROGERIO AZCÁRRAGA MADERO.

Radio Universidad Nacional Autónoma de México: Adolfo Prieto 133, Col. del Valle, Del. Benito Juárez, 03100 México, DF; tel. (55) 5536-8989; fax (55) 5687-3989; e-mail contacto@radiounam .unam.mx; internet www.radiounam.unam.mx; Dir-Gen. FERNANDO CHAMIZO GUERRERO.

Radiodifusoras Asociadas, SA de CV (RASA): Durango 341, 2°, Col. Roma, 06700 México, DF; tel. (55) 5286-1222; fax (55) 5211-6159; e-mail rasa@rasa.com.mx; internet www.rasa.com.mx; f. 1956; Exec. Pres. JOSÉ LARIS RODRÍGUEZ; Dir-Gen. SARA LARIS RODRÍGUEZ.

Radiópolis, SA de CV: Tlalpan 3000, Col. Espartaco, Del. Coyoacán, 04870 México, DF; tel. (55) 5327-2000; fax (55) 5679-9710; e-mail rrodriguezg@televisa.com.mx; owned by Televisa, SA de CV and Grupo Prisa; owns 5 radio stations; affiliated to Radiorama, SA de CV (q.v.) in 2004; Dir-Gen. RAÚL RODRÍGUEZ GONZÁLEZ.

Radiorama, SA de CV: Reforma 2620, 2°, Col. Lomas Altas, Del. Miguel Hidalgo, 11950 México, DF; tel. (55) 1105-0000; fax (55) 1105-0002; e-mail grupo@radiorama.com.mx; internet www.radiorama .com.mx; Pres. JAVIER PÉREZ DE ANDA.

Sociedad Mexicana de Radio, SA de CV (SOMER): Paseo de la Reforma 115, 4°, Col. Lomas, Santa Fe, 01330 México, DF; tel. (55) 9177-6660; fax (55) 9177-6677; e-mail somer@somer.com.mx; internet www.somer.com.mx; Dir-Gen. HUMBERTO HUESCA BUSTAMENTE.

El Universal Radio: Bucareli 8, Col. Centro, Del. Cuauhtémoc, 06040 México, DF; tel. (55) 5709-1313; e-mail radio@eluniversal.com .mx; internet www.eluniversalradio.com.mx; Man. ROGELIO ARIAS DÍAZ DE LEÓN.

Television

Canal 22: Edif. Pedro Infante, Atletas 2, Col. Country Club, Del. Coyoacán, 04220 México, DF; tel. (55) 2122-9680; fax (55) 5549-1647; e-mail correo@canal22.org.mx; internet www.canal22.org.mx; f. 1993; part of Consejo Nacional para la Cultura y las Artes of the Govt; Dir-Gen. RAÚL CREMOUX.

MVS (Multivisión): Blvd Manuel Ávila Camacho 147, Col. Chapultepec Morales, 11510 México, DF; tel. (55) 5283-4300; fax (55) 5283-4314; e-mail jvargas@mvs.com; internet www.mvs.com; subscriber-funded; Pres. JOAQUÍN VARGAS GUAJARDO; Vice-Pres. ERNESTO VARGAS.

Once TV: Carpio 475, Col. Casco de Santo Tomás, 11340 México, DF; tel. (55) 5166-4000; fax (55) 5396-8001; e-mail info@oncetvmexico.ipn .mx; internet www.oncetv.ipn.mx; f. 1959; Dir-Gen. MARÍA ENRIQUETA CABRERA CUARÓN.

Televisa, SA de CV: Edif. Televicentro, 8°, Avda Chapultepec 28, Col. Doctores, 06724 México, DF; tel. (55) 5709-3333; fax (55) 5709-3021; e-mail imagencorporativa2@televisa.com.mx; internet www .televisa.com; f. 1973; commercial; 406 affiliated stations; Chair. and CEO EMILIO AZCÁRRAGA JEAN.

Televisión Azteca, SA de CV: Anillo Periférico Sur 4121, Col. Fuentes del Pedregal, 14141 México, DF; tel. (55) 5447-8844; fax (55) 5645-4258; e-mail contacto@tvazteca.com; internet www.tvazteca .com; f. 1992; assumed responsibility for fmr state-owned channels 7 and 13; Pres. RICARDO B. SALINAS PLIEGO; Dir-Gen. MARIO SAN ROMÁN.

Regulatory Authority

Dirección General de Radio, Televisión y Cinematografía (RTC): Roma 41, Col. Juaréz, Del. Cuauhtémoc, 06600 México, DF; tel. (55) 5140-8000; fax (55) 5530-4315; e-mail buzonrtc@segob .gob.mx; internet www.rtc.gob.mx; f. 1977; Dir-Gen. JOSÉ IGNACIO JUÁREZ SÁNCHEZ.

Association

Cámara Nacional de la Industria de Radio y Televisión (CIRT): Avda Horacio 1013, Col. Polanco Reforma, Del. Miguel Hidalgo, 11550 México, DF; tel. (55) 5726-9909; fax (55) 5545-6767; e-mail cirt@cirt.com.mx; internet www.cirt.com.mx; f. 1942; Pres. TRISTÁN CANALES NAJJAR; Dir-Gen. MIGUEL OROZCO GÓMEZ.

Finance

(cap. = capital; res = reserves; dep. = deposits; m. = million;
brs = branches; amounts in new pesos)

BANKING

Supervisory Authority

Comisión Nacional Bancaria y de Valores (CNBV) (National Banking and Securities Commission): Avda Insurgentes Sur 1971, Torre Norte, Sur y III, Col. Guadalupe Inn, Del. Alvaro Obregón, 01020 México, DF; tel. and fax (55) 1454-6000; e-mail info@cnbv.gob .mx; internet www.cnbv.gob.mx; f. 1924; govt commission controlling all credit institutions in Mexico; Pres. JAIME GONZÁLEZ AGUADÉ.

Central Bank

Banco de México (BANXICO): Avda 5 de Mayo 2, Col. Centro, Del. Cuauhtémoc, 06059 México, DF; tel. (55) 5237-2000; fax (55) 5237-2070; e-mail comsoc@banxico.org.mx; internet www.banxico.org.mx; f. 1925; currency issuing authority; autonomous since April 1994; cap. 7.1m., res –66,040m., dep. 878,727m. (Dec. 2009); Gov. AGUSTÍN GUILLERMO CARSTENS CARSTENS; 6 brs.

Commercial Banks

Banco del Bajío, SA: Avda Manuel J. Clouthier 508, Col. Jardines del Campestre, 37128 León, Gto; tel. (477) 710-4649; fax (477) 710-4693; e-mail internacional@bancobajio.com.mx; internet www.bb .com.mx; f. 1994; cap. 2,513.1m., res 7,788.1m., dep. 69,231.1m. (Dec. 2013); Pres. SALVADOR OÑATE ASCENCIO.

Banco Nacional de México, SA (Banamex): Avda Isabel la Católica 44, 06089 México, DF; tel. (55) 5225-5882; fax (55) 5920-7323; e-mail prensa@banamex.com; internet www.banamex.com; f. 1884; transferred to private ownership in 1991; merged with Citibank, SA in 2001; cap. 35,397m., res 87,469m., dep. 516,258m. (Dec. 2013); Chair. MANUEL MEDINA MORA; 1,260 brs.

Banco Santander (Mexico), SA: Mod 401, 4°, Prolongación Paseo de la Reforma 500, Col. Lomas de Santa Fe, Del. Alvaro Obregon, 01219 México, DF; tel. (55) 5261-1543; fax (55) 5261-5549; internet www.santander.com.mx; f. 1864 as Banco Serfin; acquired by Banco Santander Central Hispano (Spain) in Dec. 2000; adopted current name 2008; cap. 11,348m., res 33,715m., dep. 362,470m. (Dec. 2012); Exec. Pres. and Dir-Gen. MARCOS MARTÍNEZ GAVICA; 554 brs.

BANORTE, SA (Grupo Financiero BANORTE): Avda Revolución 3000, Col. Primavera, 64830 Monterrey, NL; tel. (81) 8319-7200; fax (81) 8319-5216; internet www.banorte.com; f. 1899; merged with Banco Regional del Norte in 1985; cap. 15,577m., res 17,933m., dep. 440,145m. (Dec. 2013); Pres. GUILLERMO ORTIZ MARTÍNEZ; CEO ALEJANDRO VALENZUELA DEL RÍO; 1146 brs.

BBVA Bancomer, SA: Centro Bancomer, Avda Universidad 1200, Col. Xoco, 03339 México, DF; tel. (55) 5621-3434; fax (55) 5621-3230; internet www.bancomer.com.mx; f. 2000 by merger of Bancomer (f. 1864) and Mexican operations of Banco Bilbao Vizcaya Argentaria (Spain); privatized in 2002; cap. 9,799m., res 83,466m., dep. 614,634m. (Dec. 2012); Pres. IGNACIO DESCHAMPS GONZÁLEZ; 1,658 brs.

HSBC México: Paseo de la Reforma 347, Col. Cuauhtémoc, Del. Cuauhtémoc, 06500 México, DF; tel. (55) 5721-2222; fax (55) 5721-2393; e-mail contacto@hsbc.com.mx; internet www.hsbc.com.mx; f. 1941; bought by HSBC (United Kingdom) in 2002; name changed from Banco Internacional, SA (BITAL) in 2004; cap. 5,261m., res 33,729m., dep. 291,629m. (Dec. 2012); Chair. LUIS JAVIER PEÑA KEGEL; 1,400 brs.

Scotiabank Inverlat, SA (Canada): Blvd Miguel Avila Camacho 1, 5°, Col. Lomas de Chapultepec, Del. Miguel Hidalgo, 11009 México, DF; tel. (55) 5728-1000; fax (55) 5229-2019; internet www .scotiabankinverlat.com; f. 1977 as Multibanco Comermex, SA; changed name to Banco Inverlat, SA in 1995; 55% holding acquired by Scotiabank Group (Canada) and adopted current name 2001; cap. 7,451m., res 3,871m., dep. 147,133m. (Dec. 2013); Pres. NICOLE REICH DE POLIGNAC; 476 brs.

Development Banks

Banco Nacional de Comercio Exterior, SNC (BANCOMEXT): Periférico Sur 4333, Col. Jardines en la Montaña, Del. Tlalpan, 14210 México, DF; tel. (55) 5449-9100; fax (55) 5652-9408; e-mail bancomext@bancomext.gob.mx; internet www.bancomext.com; f. 1937; cap. 14,959m., res 2,601m., dep. 46,757m. (Dec. 2012); CEO MARIO LABORÍN GÓMEZ; 6 brs.

Banco Nacional del Ejército, Fuerza Aérea y Armada, SNC (BANJERCITO): Avda Industria Militar 1055, 1°, Col. Lomas de Sotelo, Del. Miguel Hidalgo, 11200 México, DF; tel. and fax (55) 5626-0500; e-mail info@banjercito.com.mx; internet www.banjercito.com .mx; f. 1947; cap. 4,853m., res 2,748m., dep. 22,096m. (Dec. 2013); Pres. ERNESTO JOSÉ CORDERO ARROYO.

Banco Nacional de Obras y Servicios Públicos, SNC (BANOBRAS): Avda Javier Barros Sierra 515, Col. Lomas de Santa Fe, Del. Álvaro Obregón, 01219 México, DF; tel. (55) 5270-1200; fax (55) 5270-1564; internet www.banobras.gob.mx; f. 1933; govt-owned; cap. 11,765m., res 3,350m., dep. 245,896m. (Dec. 2009); Dir-Gen. GEORGINA KESSEL MARTÍNEZ.

Compartamos, SAB de CV: Insurgentes Sur 552, Col. Escandón, 11800 México, DF; tel. (55) 5276-7250; fax (55) 5276-7299; e-mail contacto@compartamos.com; internet www.compartamos.com; f. 1990; Dir-Gen. ALVARO RODRÍGUEZ ARREGUI.

Financiera Rural: Agrarismo 227, Col. Escandón, Del. Miguel Hidalgo, CP 11800, México, DF; tel. (55) 5230-1600; internet www .financierarural.gob.mx; f. 2004; state-run devt bank, concerned with agricultural, forestry and fishing sectors; Dir-Gen. JUAN CARLOS CORTÉS.

Nacional Financiera, SNC (NAFIN): Avda Insurgentes Sur 1971, Torre IV, 13°, Col. Guadalupe Inn, 01020 México, DF; tel. (55) 5325-6700; fax (55) 5325-6000; e-mail info@nafin.gob.mx; internet www .nafin.com; f. 1934; cap. 8,805m., res 12,723m., dep. 101,857m. (Dec. 2012); CEO HÉCTOR ALEJANDRO DOMENE; 32 brs.

BANKERS' ASSOCIATION

Asociación de Bancos de México: 16 de Setiembre 27, 3°, Col. Centro Histórico, 06000 México, DF; tel. (55) 5722-4300; internet www.abm.org.mx; f. 1928; Pres. JAVIER ARRIGUNAGA CAMPO; 52 mems.

STOCK EXCHANGE

Bolsa Mexicana de Valores, SA de CV: Paseo de la Reforma 255, Col. Cuauhtémoc, 06500 México, DF; tel. (55) 5726-6000; fax (55) 5726-6836; e-mail cinforma@bmv.com.mx; internet www.bmv.com .mx; f. 1894; Pres. and CEO JAIME RUIZ SACRISTÁN.

INSURANCE

Supervisory Authority

Comisión Nacional de Seguros y Fianzas: Avda Insurgentes Sur 1971, Torre I Sur, 2°, Col. Guadalupe Inn, Del. Álvaro Obregón, CP 01020, México, DF; tel. (55) 5724-7489; e-mail cdiaz@cnsf.gob.mx; internet www.cnsf.gob.mx; Pres. MANUEL SERGIO AGUILERA VERDUZCO.

Principal Companies

ACE Seguros: Bosques de Alisos, 47A, 1°, Col. Bosques de las Lomas, Del. Cuajimalpa, 05120 México, DF; tel. (55) 5258-5800; fax (55) 5258-5899; e-mail info@acelatinamerica.com; internet www .acelatinamerica.com/ACELatinAmericaRoot/Mexico; f. 1990; fmrly Seguros Cigna; Pres. ROBERTO FLORES.

Aseguradora Cuauhtémoc, SA: Manuel Avila Camacho 164, 11570 México, DF; tel. (55) 5250-9800; fax (55) 5540-3204; f. 1944; general; Exec. Pres. JUAN B. RIVEROLL; Dir-Gen. JAVIER COMPEÁN AMEZCUA.

Aseguradora Interacciones: Paseo de la Reforma 383, México, DF; tel. (55) 5326-8600; e-mail on-line@interacciones.com; internet www.interacciones.com; f. 1966; general; 43% owned by Commercial Union (United Kingdom); Dir-Gen. CARLOS GONZÁLEZ.

BBVA Bancomer Seguros: Centro Bancomer, Avda Universidad 1200, Col. Xoco, 03339 México, DF; e-mail servicioaclientes@ segurosbancomer.com.mx; internet www.segurosbancomer.com.mx; Dir-Gen. JUAN PABLO ÁVILA PALAFOX.

Grupo Nacional Provincial, SAB: Avda Cerro de las Torres 395, Col. Campestre Churubusco, Del. Coyoacán, 04200 México, DF; tel. (55) 5227-9000; internet www.gnp.com.mx; f. 1936; mem. of Grupo BAL; general; Chair. ALBERTO BAILLÈRES; CEO ALEJANDRO BAILLÈRES.

MetLife: Blvd Manuel Avila Camacho 32, SKY 14–20 y PH, Col. Lomas de Chapultepec, Del. Miguel Hidalgo, 11000 México, DF; tel. (55) 5328-9000; e-mail contacto@metlife.com.mx; internet www .metlife.com.mx; f. 1931 as Aseguradora Hidalgo, acquired by MetLife Inc in 2002; life; CEO SOFÍA BELMAR.

Quálitas, Cía de Seguros: José María Castorena 426, Col. San José de los Cedros, Cuajimalpa, CP 05200, México, DF; e-mail qualitas@ qualitas.com.mx; internet www.qualitas.com.mx; Pres. JOAQUÍN BROCKMAN LOZANO.

Royal & SunAlliance Mexico: Blvd Adolfo López Mateos 2448, Col. Altavista, 01060 México, DF; tel. (55) 5723-7999; fax (55) 5723-7941; e-mail direccion.general@mx.rsagroup.com; internet www .royalsun.com.mx; f. 1941; acquired Seguros BBV-Probursa in 2001; general, except life; Chair. JOHN NAPIER.

Seguros Azteca, SA: Insurgentes Sur 3579, Tlalpan La Joya, 14000 México, DF; tel. (55) 1720-9854; e-mail infoseguros@segurosazteca

.com.mx; internet www.segurosazteca.com.mx; f. 1933, renamed as above in 2003; general, incl. life; Dir-Gen. ALFREDO HONSBERG.

Seguros Banamex, SA: Venustiano Carranza 63, Col. Centro Histórico, Del. Cuauhtémoc, 06000 México, DF; tel. (55) 1226-8100; e-mail sbainternet@banamex.com; internet www .segurosbanamex.com; f. 1994; life, accident and health; Dir-Gen. DANIEL GARDUÑO GUTIÉRREZ.

Seguros Banorte Generali: Presidente Mazaryk 8, Col. Bosques de Chapultepec, Del. Miguel Hidalgo, CP 11588, México DF; tel. (55) 5141-1414; e-mail privacidad.sbg@banorte.com; internet www .segurosbanorte.com.mx; Dir-Gen. FERNANDO SOLÍS SOBERÓN.

Seguros Monterrey New York Life: Presidente Mazaryk 8, Bosques de Chapultepec, Del. Miguel Hidalgo, México, DF; tel. (55) 5326-9000; fax (55) 5536-9610; e-mail clientes@ monterrey-newyorklife.com.mx; internet www.monterrey -newyorklife.com.mx; f. 1940 as Monterrey Cía de Seguros; acquired by New York Life in 2000; casualty, life, etc.; Dir-Gen. MARIO VELA BERRONDO.

Skandia Vida: Bosque de Ciruelos 162, 1°, Col. Bosques de las Lomas, 11700, México, DF; tel. (55) 5093-0220; e-mail servicio@ skandia.com.mx; internet www.skandia.com.mx; CEO JULIO MÉNDEZ.

Insurance Association

Asociación Mexicana de Instituciones de Seguros, AC (AMIS): Francisco I Madero 21, Col. Tlacopac, San Angel, 01040 México, DF; tel. (55) 5480-0646; fax (55) 5662-8036; e-mail amis@ mail.internet.com.mx; internet www.amis.com.mx; f. 1946; all insurance cos operating in Mexico are mems; Chair. SOFÍA BELMAR BERUMEN; Pres. MARIO VELA BERRONDO.

Trade and Industry

GOVERNMENT AGENCIES

Comisión Federal de Protección Contra Riesgos Sanitarios (COFEPRIS): Monterrey 33, esq. Oaxaca, Col. Roma, Del. Cuauhtémoc, 06700 México, DF; tel. (55) 5080-5200; fax (55) 5207-5521; e-mail mdiosdado@salud.gob.mx; internet www.cofepris.gob.mx; f. 2003; pharmaceutical regulatory authority; Commr MIKEL ARRIOLA.

Comisión Nacional Forestal (CONAFOR): Carretera a Nogales s/n, esq. Periférico Poniente 5360, 5°, San Juan de Ocotán, 45019 Zapopan, Jal.; tel. (33) 3777-7000; fax (33) 3777-7012; e-mail conafor@conafor.gob.mx; internet www.conafor.gob.mx; f. 2001; Dir-Gen. JUAN MANUEL TORRES ROJO.

Comisión Nacional de Hidrocarburos (CNH): Sur 1228, Col. Tlacoquemecatl del Valle, Del Benito Juárez, CP 03200, México, DF; tel. (55) 3626-6086; internet www.cnh.gob.mx; f. 2009; oversees the hydrocarbons sector; Pres. JUAN CARLOS ZEPEDA MOLINA.

Comisión Nacional de Inversiones Extranjeras (CNIE): Dirección General de Inversión Extranjera, Insurgentes Sur 1940, 8°, Col. Florida, 01030 México, DF; tel. (55) 5229-6163; fax (55) 5229-6507; e-mail gcanales@economia.gob.mx; f. 1973; govt commission to co-ordinate foreign investment; Pres. ILDEFONSO GUAJARDO VILLARREAL (Secretary of the Economy).

Comisión Nacional de los Salarios Mínimos (CNSM): Avda Cuauhtémoc 14, 2°, Col. Doctores, Del. Cuauhtémoc, 06720 México 7, DF; tel. (55) 5998-3800; fax (55) 5578-5775; e-mail cnsm1@conasami .gob.mx; internet www.conasami.gob.mx; f. 1962, in accordance with Section VI of Article 123 of the Constitution; national commission on minimum salaries; Man. Dir MIGUEL GONZÁLEZ RAMÍREZ.

Instituto Nacional de Investigaciones Nucleares (ININ): Centro Nuclear de México, Carretera México–Toluca Km 36.5, La Marquesa, 52750 Ocoyoacac, Méx.; tel. (55) 5329-7200; fax (55) 5329-7296; e-mail hernan.rico@inin.gob.mx; internet www.inin .gob.mx; f. 1979 to plan research and devt of nuclear science and technology; 2 nuclear reactors, each with a generating capacity of 654 MW; Dir-Gen. LYDIA CONCEPCIÓN GUTIÉRREZ.

Instituto Nacional de Pesca (INAPESCA) (National Fishery Institute): Pitágoras 1320, Col. Santa Cruz Atoyac, Del. Benito Juárez, 03310 México, DF; tel. (55) 3871-9517; fax (55) 5604-9169; e-mail gerardo.garcia@inapesca.sagarpa.gob.mx; internet www .inapesca.gob.mx; f. 1962; Dir-in-Chief RAÚL ADÁN ROMO TRUJILLO.

Procuraduría Federal del Consumidor (Profeco): Avda José Vasconcelos 208, Col. Condesa, Del. Cuauhtémoc, 06140 México, DF; tel. (55) 5625-6700; internet www.profeco.gob.mx; f. 1975; consumer protection; Procurator LORENA MARTÍNEZ RODRÍGUEZ.

Servicio Geológico Mexicano (SGM): Blvd Felipe Angeles, Carretera México–Pachuca, Km 93.50-4, Col. Venta Prieta, 42080 Pachuca de Soto, Hgo; tel. (771) 711-4266; fax (771) 711-4204; e-mail gintproc@sgm.gob.mx; internet www.sgm.gob.mx; f. 1957;

govt agency for the devt of mineral resources; Dir-Gen. RAÚL CRUZ RÍOS.

DEVELOPMENT ORGANIZATIONS

Centro de Investigación para el Desarollo, AC (CIDAC) (Centre of Research for Development): Jaime Balmes 11, Edif. D, 2°, Col. Los Morales Polanco, 11510 México, DF; tel. (55) 5985-1010; fax (55) 5985-1030; e-mail info@cidac.org.mx; internet www.cidac .org; f. 1984; researches economic and political devt; Pres. LUIS RUBIO; Dir-Gen. VERÓNICA BAZ.

Comisión Nacional de las Zonas Aridas (CONAZA): Blvd Vito Alessio Robles 2556, Col. Nazario S. Ortiz Garza, 25100 Saltillo, Coah.; tel. and fax (844) 450-5200; e-mail contacto@conaza.gob.mx; internet www.conaza.gob.mx; f. 1970; commission to co-ordinate the devt and use of arid areas; Dir-Gen. JOSÉ ABRAHAM IZAGUIRRE.

Fideicomiso de Fomento Mineiro (FIFOMI): Puente de Tecamachalco 26, 2°, Col. Lomas de Chapultepec, Del. Miguel Hidalgo, 11000 México, DF; tel. (55) 5249-9500; e-mail pguerra@fifomi.gob .mx; internet www.fifomi.gob.mx; trust for the devt of the mineral industries; Dir-Gen. ARMANDO PÉREZ GEA.

Fideicomisos Instituídos en Relación con la Agricultura (FIRA): Km 8, Antigua Carretera Pátzcuaro 8555, 58341 Morelia, Mich.; tel. (443) 322-2399; fax (443) 327-6338; e-mail webmaster@ correo.fira.gob.mx; internet www.fira.gob.mx; a group of devt funds to aid agricultural financing, under the Banco de México, comprising Fondo de Garantía y Fomento para la Agricultura, Ganadería y Avicultura (FOGAGA); Fondo Especial para Financiamientos Agropecuarios (FEFA); Fondo Especial de Asistencia Técnica y Garantía para Créditos Agropecuarios (FEGA); Fondo de Garantía y Fomento para las Actividades Pesqueras (FOPESCA); Dir RAFAEL GAMBOA GONZÁLEZ.

Fondo de Operación y Financiamiento Bancario a la Vivienda (FOVI): Ejército Nacional 180, Col. Anzures, 11590 México, DF; tel. (55) 5263-4500; fax (55) 5263-4541; e-mail jmartinez@fovi.gob.mx; internet www.fovi.gob.mx; f. 1963 to promote the construction of low-cost housing through savings and credit schemes; devt fund under the Banco de México; Dir-Gen. MANUEL ZEPEDA PAYERAS.

Instituto Mexicano del Petróleo (IMP): Eje Central Lázaro Cárdenas 152, Col. San Bartolo Atepehuacan, Del. Gustavo A. Madero, 07730 México, DF; tel. (55) 9175-6000; fax (55) 9175-8000; e-mail gdgarcia@imp.mx; internet www.imp.mx; f. 1965 to foster devt of the petroleum, chemical and petrochemical industries; Dir-Gen. VINICIO SURO PEREZ.

CHAMBERS OF COMMERCE

American Chamber of Commerce of Mexico (Amcham): Blas Pascal 205, 3°, Col. Los Morales, 11510 México, DF; tel. (55) 5141-3800; fax (55) 5141-3835; e-mail amchammx@amcham.org.mx; internet www.amcham.com.mx; f. 1917; brs in Guadalajara and Monterrey; Pres. ERNESTO M. HERNÁNDEZ.

Cámara de Comercio, Servicios y Turismo Ciudad de México (CANACO) (Chamber of Commerce, Services and Tourism of Mexico City): Paseo de la Reforma 42, 3°, Col. Centro, Apdo 32005, Del. Cuauhtémoc, 06048 México, DF; tel. (55) 3685-2269; fax (55) 5592-2279; e-mail sos@ccmexico.com.mx; internet www .camaradecomerciodemexico.com.mx; f. 1874; 50,000 mems; Pres. RICARDO NAVARRO BENÍTEZ.

Cámara Nacional de la Industria de Transformación (CANA-CINTRA): Avda San Antonio 256, Col. Ampliación Nápoles, Del. Benito Juárez, 06849 México, DF; tel. (55) 5482-3000; fax (55) 5598-8044; e-mail informes@canacintra.org.mx; internet www.canacintra .org.mx; represents majority of smaller manufacturing businesses; Pres. RODRIGO ALPÍZAR VALLEJO.

Confederación de Cámaras Nacionales de Comercio, Servicios y Turismo (CONCANACO-SERVYTUR) (Confederation of National Chambers of Commerce, Services and Tourism): Balderas 144, 3°, Col. Centro, 06070 México, DF; tel. (55) 5722-9300; e-mail comentarios@concanacored.com; internet www.concanaco.com.mx; f. 1917; Pres. ENRIQUE SOLANA SENTÍES; comprises 283 regional chambers.

CHAMBERS OF INDUSTRY

Central Confederation

Confederación de Cámaras Industriales de los Estados Unidos Mexicanos (CONCAMIN) (Confed. of Industrial Chambers): Manuel María Contreras 133, 4°, Col. Cuauhtémoc, Del. Cuauhtémoc, 06500 México, DF; tel. (55) 5140-7800; fax (55) 5140-7831; e-mail webmaster@concamin.org.mx; internet www.concamin.org .mx; f. 1918; represents and promotes the activities of the entire industrial sector; Pres. FRANCISCO JAVIER FUNTANET MANGE; 108 mem. orgs.

INDUSTRIAL AND TRADE ASSOCIATIONS

Asociación Nacional de Importadores y Exportadores de la República Mexicana (ANIERM) (National Association of Importers and Exporters): Monterrey 130, Col. Roma, Del. Cuauhtémoc, 06700 México, DF; tel. (55) 5584-9522; fax (55) 5584-5317; e-mail anierm@anierm.org.mx; internet www.anierm.org.mx; f. 1944; Pres. LUIS ROBERTO ABREU.

Asociación Nacional de la Industria Química (ANIQ): Angel Urraza 505, Col. del Valle, 03100 México, DF; tel. (55) 5230-5100; internet www.aniq.org.mx; f. 1959; chemicals asscn; Dir-Gen. MIGUEL BENEDETTO; c. 200 mem. cos.

Comisión Nacional de Seguridad Nuclear y Salvaguardias (CNSNS): Dr José María Barragán 779, Col. Narvarte, Del. Benito Juárez, 03020 México, DF; tel. (55) 5095-3200; fax (55) 5095-3295; e-mail je@cnsns.gob.mx; internet www.cnsns.gob.mx; f. 1979; nuclear regulatory authority; Dir-Gen. JUAN EIBENSCHUTZ HARTMAN.

Consejo Empresarial Mexicano de Comercio Exterior, Inversión y Tecnología (COMCE): Lancaster 15, 2° y 3°, Col. Juárez, 06600 México, DF; tel. (52) 5231-7100; fax (55) 5321-7109; e-mail direccion@comce.org.mx; internet www.comce.org.mx; f. 1999 to promote international trade; Pres. VALENTÍN DIEZ MORODO; Dir-Gen. LORENZO YSASI MARTÍNEZ.

Consejo Mexicano de Asuntos Internacionales (COMEXI): Of. 502, Torre Magnum, Sierra Mojada 620, Col. Lomas de Chapultepec, 11000 México, DF; tel. (55) 5202-3776; e-mail info@consejomexicano.org; internet www.consejomexicano.org; Pres. JAIME ZABLUDOVSKY; Dir-Gen. CLAUDIA CALVIN.

Consejo Nacional de la Industria Maquiladora y Manufacturera de Exportación (INDEX): Ejército Nacional 418, 12°, Of. 1204, Col. Chapultepec Morales, Del. Miguel Hidalgo, 11570 México, DF; tel. (55) 2282-9900; fax (55) 2282-9902; e-mail dirgral@index.org.mx; internet www.index.org.mx; f. 1973; Pres. EMILIO CADENA; Sec. FEDERICO SERRANO.

Instituto Nacional de Investigaciones Forestales, Agrícolas y Pecuarias (INIFAP) (National Research Institute for Forestry, Agriculture and Livestock): Avda Progreso No 5, Col. Barrio de Santa Catarina, Del. Coyoacán, 04010 México, DF; tel. (55) 3871-8700; fax (55) 3626-8639; e-mail contacto@inifap.gob.mx; internet www.inifap.gob.mx; f. 1985; forestry conservation and management; plant and animal genetics and management; Dir-Gen. PEDRO BRAJCICH GALLEGOS.

EMPLOYERS' ORGANIZATION

Consejo Coordinador Empresarial (CCE): Lancaster 15, Col. Juárez, 06600 México, DF; tel. (55) 5229-1100; fax (55) 5592-3857; e-mail sistemas@cce.org.mx; internet www.cce.org.mx; f. 1976; co-ordinating body of private sector; Pres. GERARDO GUTIÉRREZ CANDIANI; Dir-Gen. LUIS MIGUEL PANDO LEYVA.

STATE HYDROCARBONS COMPANY

Petróleos Mexicanos (PEMEX): Avda Marina Nacional 329, Col. Petróleos Mexicanos, 11311 México, DF; tel. (55) 1944-2500; fax (55) 5531-6354; e-mail petroleosmexicanos@pemex.com; internet www.pemex.com; f. 1938; govt agency for the exploitation of Mexico's petroleum and natural gas resources; Dir-Gen. EMILIO LOZOYA AUSTIN; 131,000 employees.

UTILITIES

Regulatory Authorities

Comisión Nacional del Agua (CONAGUA): Avda Insurgentes Sur 2416, Col. Copilco el Bajo, Del. Coyoacán, 04340 México, DF; tel. (55) 5174-4000; fax (55) 5550-6721; e-mail direccion@cna.gob.mx; internet www.cna.gob.mx; commission to administer national water resources; Dir-Gen. (vacant).

Comisión Reguladora de Energía (CRE): Avda Horacio 1750, Col. Los Morales Polanco, Del. Miguel Hidalgo, 11510 México, DF; tel. (55) 5283-1515; e-mail calidad@cre.gob.mx; internet www.cre.gob.mx; f. 1994; commission to control energy policy and planning; Pres. FRANCISCO XAVIER SALAZAR DIEZ DE SOLLANO; Exec. Sec. LUIS ALONSO GONZÁLEZ DE ALBA.

Secretariat of State for Energy: see section on The Government (Secretariats of State).

Electricity

Comisión Federal de Electricidad (CFE): Avda Reforma 64, Col. Juárez México, México, DF; tel. (55) 5229-4400; fax (55) 5553-5321; e-mail servicioalcliente@cfe.gob.mx; internet www.cfe.gob.mx; state-owned power utility; Dir-Gen. ENRIQUE OCHOA REZA.

Gas

Gas Natural México (GNM): Jaime Blames 8-703, Col. Los Morales Polanco, 11510 México, DF; e-mail sugerencias@gnm.com.mx; internet www.gasnaturalmexico.com.mx; f. 1994 in Mexico; distributes natural gas in the states of Tamaulipas, Aguascalientes, Coahuila, San Luis Potosí, Guanajuato, Nuevo León and México and in the Distrito Federal; subsidiary of Gas Natural (Spain); Chair. SALVADOR GABARRÓ SERRA.

Petróleos Mexicanos (PEMEX): see State Hydrocarbons Company; distributes natural gas.

TRADE UNIONS

Confederación Regional Obrera Mexicana (CROM) (Regional Confederation of Mexican Workers): Aldama 75, Col. Buenavista, Cuauhtémoc 06350, México, DF; tel. (55) 5566-4426; e-mail revista.crom@gmail.com; internet www.crom.mx; f. 1918; Sec.-Gen. RODOLFO G. GONZÁLEZ GUZMÁN; 120,000 mems, 900 affiliated syndicates.

Confederación Revolucionaria de Obreros y Campesinos de México (CROC) (Revolutionary Confederation of Workers and Farmers): Hamburgo 250, Col. Juárez, Del. Cuauhtémoc, 06600 México, DF; tel. (55) 5254-0316; e-mail crocmodel@hotmail.com; internet www.croc.org.mx; f. 1952; Sec.-Gen. ISIAS GONZÁLEZ CUEVAS; 4.5m. mems in 32 state federations and 17 national unions.

Confederación de Trabajadores de México (CTM) (Confederation of Mexican Workers): Vallarta 8, Col. Tabacalera, Del. Cuauhtémoc, 06030 México, DF; tel. (55) 5141-1730; e-mail ctmorganizacion@prodigy.net.mx; internet ctmorganizacion.org.mx; f. 1936; admitted to ICFTU; Sec.-Gen. HUMBERTO OJEDA; 5.5m. mems.

Congreso del Trabajo (CT): Avda Ricardo Flores Magón 44, Col. Guerrero, 06300 México 37, DF; tel. (55) 5583-3817; internet www.congresodeltrabajo.org.mx; f. 1966; trade union congress comprising trade union federations, confederations, etc.; Pres. ANTONINO BAXZI MATA.

Federación Nacional de Sindicatos Independientes (National Federation of Independent Trade Unions): Isaac Garza 311 Oeste, 64000 Monterrey, NL; tel. (81) 8125-6200; e-mail fnsi@prodigy.net.mx; internet www.fnsi.com.mx; f. 1936; Sec.-Gen. JACINTO PADILLA VALDEZ; 230,000 mems.

Federación de Sindicatos de Trabajadores al Servicio del Estado (FSTSE) (Federation of Unions of Government Workers): Gómez Farías 40, Col. San Rafael, 06470 México, DF; tel. (33) 5128-1600; e-mail contacto@fstse.com; internet www.fstse.com; f. 1938; Sec.-Gen. JOEL AYALA ALMEIDA; 2.5m. mems; 80 unions.

A number of major unions are non-affiliated, including:

Federación Democrática de Sindicatos de Servidores Públicos (Fedessp) (Democratic Federation of Public Servants): Vicente Guerrero 221-1, Col. Miguel Alemán Oaxaca, 68120 México, DF; tel. (55) 5546-2755; e-mail ser60gluz@hotmail.com; internet www.fedessp.org; f. 2005; Nat. Sec. JUAN MANUEL ESPINOZA ZAVALA.

Sindicato Nacional de Trabajadores de la Educación (SNTE) (Education Workers): Venezuela 44, Col. Centro, México, DF; tel. (55) 5704-7000; fax (55) 5702-6303; e-mail info@snte.org.mx; internet www.snte.org.mx; f. 1943; Pres. JUAN DIAZ DE LA TORRE; 1.4m. mems.

The major agricultural unions are:

Confederación Nacional Campesina (CNC) (National Peasant Confederation): Mariano Azuela 121, Col. Santa María de la Ribera, México, DF; tel. (55) 5547-8042; internet www.cnc.org.mx; Pres. GERARDO SÁNCHEZ GARCÍA.

Confederación Nacional de Organizaciones Ganaderas (National Confederation of Stockbreeding Organizations): Calzada Mariano Escobedo 714, Col. Anzures, México, DF; tel. (55) 5254-3210; e-mail teresa.hernandez@cnog.com.mx; internet www.cnog.com.mx; Pres. OSWALDO CHÁZARO MONTALVO; 300,000 mems.

Transport

Secretariat of State for Communications and Transport: see section on The Government (Secretariats of State).

Caminos y Puentes Federales (CAPUFE): Calzada de los Reyes 24, Col. Tetela del Monte, 62130 Cuernavaca, Mor.; tel. (55) 5200-2000; e-mail contacto@capufe.gob.mx; internet www.capufe.gob.mx; Dir-Gen. BENITO NEME SASTRÉ.

RAILWAYS

In 2010 there were 26,717 km of main line track. A 300-km railway link across the isthmus of Tehuantepec connects the Caribbean port of Coatzacoalcos with the Pacific port of Salina Cruz. In 2013 the federal Government announced a project, at a cost of an estimated

US $18,000m., to build a cross-country railway line linking major Mayan historical sites.

Ferrocarril Mexicano, SA de CV (Ferromex): Bosque de Ciruelos 99, Col. Bosques de las Lomas, 11700 México, DF; tel. (55) 5246-3700; e-mail info@ferromex.com.mx; internet www.ferromex.com.mx; 50-year concession awarded to Grupo Ferroviario Mexicano, SA, (GFM) commencing in 1998; owned by Grupo México, SA de CV; 8,500 km of track and Mexico's largest rail fleet; links from Mexico City to Guadalajara, Hermosillo, Monterrey, Chihuahua and Pacific ports; Exec. Pres. ALFREDO CASAR PÉREZ; Dir-Gen. ROGELIO VÉLEZ LÓPEZ DE LA CERDA.

Ferrocarril del Sureste (Ferrosur): Bosque de Ciruelos 180, 1°, Col. Bosques de las Lomas, 11700 México, DF; tel. (55) 5387-6500; e-mail magarcia@ferrosur.com.mx; internet www.ferrosur.com.mx; 50-year concession awarded to Grupo Tribasa in 1998; 66.7% sold to Empresas Frisco, SA de CV, in 1999, owned by Grupos Carso, SA de CV; Man. MIGUEL ANGEL GARCÍA MORALES.

Kansas City Southern de México (KCSM): Avda Manuel L. Barragán 4850, Col. Hidalgo, 64420 Monterrey, NL; tel. (81) 8305-7800; fax (81) 8305-7766; e-mail werdman@kcsouthern.com; internet www.kcsouthern.com; fmrly Ferrocarril del Noreste; 4,242 km of line, linking Mexico City with the ports of Lázaro Cárdenas, Veracruz, Tampico/Altamira and north-east Mexico; Chair. ROBERT J. DRUTEN; Pres. and CEO DAVID L. STARLING.

Servicio de Transportes Eléctricos del Distrito Federal (STE): Avda Municipio Libre 402, 3°, Col. San Andrés Tetepilco, Del. Iztapalapa, 09440 México, DF; tel. (55) 5539-2800; fax (55) 5672-4758; e-mail sugiere@ste.df.gob.mx; internet www.ste.df.gob.mx; suburban tram route with 17 stops upgraded to light rail standard to act as a feeder to the metro; also operates bus and trolleybus networks; Pres. MIGUEL ANGEL MANCERA ESPINOSA (Head of Govt of the Distrito Federal); Dir-Gen. RUBÉN EDUARDO VENADERO MEDINILLA.

Sistema de Transporte Colectivo (Metro) (STC): Delicias 67, 06070 México, DF; tel. (55) 5709-1133; fax (55) 5512-3601; internet www.metro.df.gob.mx; f. 1967; the first stage of a combined underground and surface railway system in Mexico City was opened in 1969; 12 lines, covering 226 km, were operating in 2014, a further 5 lines planned by 2017; the system is wholly state-owned and the fares are partially subsidized; Dir-Gen. JOEL ÓRTEGA CUEVAS.

ROADS

Road transport accounts for about 98% of all public passenger traffic and for about 80% of freight traffic. Mexico's terrain is difficult for overland travel. In 2010 there were 371,936 km of roads, of which 36.4% were paved. Long-distance buses form one of the principal methods of transport in Mexico, and there are some 600 lines operating services throughout the country. In 2010 the Inter-American Development Bank (IDB) approved an amount of US $2.6m. for the Pacific Corridor project (Corredor Pacífico), a highway system connecting Mexico with Panama.

Dirección General de Autotransporte Federal: Calzada de las Bombas 411, Col. Los Girasoles, Del. Coyoacán, 04920 México, DF; tel. (55) 5011-9202; e-mail elizalde@sct.gob.mx; internet dgaf.sct.gob.mx; Dir Dr FEDERICO DOMINGUEZ ZULOAGA.

Metrobús: Avda Cuauhtémoc 16, 5°, Col. Doctores, CP 06720, México, DF; tel. (55) 5761-6858; e-mail oip@metrobus.df.gob.mx; internet www.metrobus.df.gob.mx; bus transport system in Federal District; Dir-Gen. GUILLERMO CALDERÓN AGUILERA.

SHIPPING

Mexico has 140 seaports, 29 river docks and a further 29 lake shelters. More than 85% of Mexico's foreign trade is conducted through maritime transport. At the end of 2014 the flag registered fleet comprised 723 vessels, totalling 2,031,213 grt. The Government operates the facilities of seaports.

Coordinación General de Puertos y Marina Mercante (CGPMM): Avda Nuevo León 210, Col. Hipódromo, 06100 México, DF; tel. (55) 5723-9300; fax (55) 5265-3108; e-mail egarciai@sct.gob.mx; internet cgpmm.sct.gob.mx; Co-ordinator ALEJANDRO CHACÓN DOMÍNGUEZ; Dir-Gen. de Puertos ALEJANDRO HERNÁNDEZ CERVANTES; Dir-Gen. de Marina Mercante MARCO ANTONIO VINAZA MARTÍNEZ.

Port of Acapulco: Administración Portuaria Integral Acapulco, Avda Costera Miguel Alemán s/n, Malecón Fiscal s/n, Col. Centro, CP 39300 Acapulco, Gro; tel. (744) 434-1710; fax (744) 483-1648; e-mail contact@apiacapulcoport.com; internet www.apiacapulcoport.com; f. 1996; Dir-Gen. OCTAVIO GONZÁLEZ FLORES; Harbour Master Capt. ALEJANDRO MARCHENA.

Port of Coatzacoalcos: Administración Portuaria Integral de Coatzacoalcos, SA de CV, Interior Recinto Portuario s/n, Col. Centro, 96400 Coatzacoalcos, Ver.; tel. (921) 211-0270; fax (921) 211-0272; e-mail dirgral@puertocoatzacoalcos.com.mx; internet www.puertocoatzacoalcos.com.mx; Dir-Gen. OVIDIO NOVAL NICOLAU; Harbour Master Capt. GASPAR CIME ESCOBEDO.

Port of Dos Bocas: Administración Portuaria Integral de Dos Bocas, SA de CV, Carretera Federal Puerto Ceiba–Paraíso 414, Col. Quintín Arzuz, 86600 Paraíso, Tab.; tel. (933) 333-2744; fax (933) 337-0480; e-mail ventanilla@puertodosbocas.com.mx; internet www.puertodosbocas.com; Dir-Gen. MIGUEL ANGEL SERVÍN HERNÁNDEZ; Harbour Master Capt. EDUARDO TIBERIO DE LARREA FOURZAN.

Port of Manzanillo: Administración Portuaria Integral de Manzanillo, SA de CV, Avda Teniente Azueta 9, Col. Burócrata, 28250 Manzanillo, Col.; tel. and fax (314) 331-1400; e-mail gcomercial@puertomanzanillo.com.mx; internet www.puertomanzanillo.com.mx; Dir-Gen. FLOR DE MARÍA CAÑAVERAL PEDRERO; Harbour Master Capt. JORGE ARTURO CASTAÑEDA USCANGA.

Port of Tampico: Administración Portuaria Integral de Tampico, SA de CV, Edif. API de Tampico, Zona Centro, 89000 Tampico, Tamps; tel. (833) 241-1400; fax (833) 212-5744; e-mail contacto@puertodetampico.com.mx; internet www.puertodetampico.com.mx; Gen. Dir TEODORO CANTÚ CANTÚ; Harbour Master Capt. MANUEL ACEITUNO RODRÍGUEZ.

Port of Veracruz: Administración Portuaria Integral de Veracruz, SA de CV, Avda Marina Mercante 210, 7°, Col. Centro, 91700 Veracruz, Ver.; tel. (229) 932-2170; fax (229) 932-3040; e-mail mespinosa@puertodeveracruz.com; internet www.puertodeveracruz.com.mx; privatized in 1994; Dir-Gen. JUAN IGNACIO FERNÁNDEZ CARBAJAL; Harbour Master Capt. ENRIQUE CASARRUBIAS GARCÍA.

Transportación Marítima Mexicana, SA de CV (TMM): Avda de la Cúspide 4755, Col. Parque del Pedregal, Del. Tlalpan, 14010 México, DF; tel. (55) 5629-8866; fax (55) 5629-8899; e-mail grupotmm@tmm.com.mx; internet www.tmm.com.mx; f. 1955; cargo services to Europe, the Mediterranean, Scandinavia, the USA, South and Central America, the Caribbean and the Far East; Pres. JOSÉ F. SERRANO SEGOVIA; Sec. IGNACIO RODRÍGUEZ PULLEN.

CIVIL AVIATION

There were 62 international airports in Mexico in 2012. Of these, México, Cancún, Guadalajara, Monterrey and Tijuana registered the highest number of operations. In September 2014 the Government announced plans to construct a new airport in the capital, at a cost of US $9,160m.

Aeropuertos y Servicios Auxiliares (ASA): Edif. B, Avda 602 161, Col. San Juan de Aragón, Del. Venustiano Carranza, 15620 México, DF; tel. (55) 5133-1000; fax (55) 5133-2985; e-mail quejasydenuncias@asa.gob.mx; internet www.asa.gob.mx; f. 1965; oversees airport management and devt; Dir-Gen. ALFONSO SARABIA DE LA GARZA.

Dirección General de Aeronáutica Civil (DGAC): Avda Providencia No 807, 6°, Col. Del Valle, 03100 México, DF; tel. (55) 5523-6642; fax (55) 5523-7207; e-mail hgonzalw@sct.gob.mx; internet dgac.sct.gob.mx; subdivision of Secretariat of State for Communications and Transport; regulates civil aviation; Dir-Gen. GILBERTO LÓPEZ MEYER.

Aeromar, Transportes Aeromar: Hotel María Isabel Sheraton, Paseo de la Reforma 325, Local 10, México, DF; tel. (55) 5514-2248; e-mail web.aeromar@aeromar.com.mx; internet www.aeromar.com.mx; f. 1987; scheduled domestic passenger and cargo services; Pres. FERNANDO FLORES.

Aeroméxico Cargo: Avda Texcoco s/n, esq. Avda Tahel, Col. Peñón de los Baños, 15520 México, DF; tel. (55) 5133-0203; internet www.aeromexicocargo.com.mx; owned by state holding co Consorcio Aeroméxico, SA; cargo airline; Dir-Gen. RAFAEL FIGUEROA.

Aerovías de México (Aeroméxico): Paseo de la Reforma 445, 3°, Torre B, Col. Cuauhtémoc, 06500 México, DF; tel. (55) 5133-4000; fax (55) 5133-4619; internet www.aeromexico.com; f. 1934 as Aeronaves de México, nationalized 1959; sold by state holding co Consorcio Aeroméxico, SA to private investors in 2007; services between most principal cities of Mexico and the USA, Chile, Brazil, Peru, France and Spain; Pres. EDUARDO TRICIO HARO; Dir-Gen. ANDRÉS CONESA LABASTIDA.

Aviacsa: Aeropuerto Internacional, Zona C, Hangar 1, Col. Aviación General, 15520 México, DF; tel. (55) 5716-9005; fax (55) 5758-3823; internet www.aviacsa.com; f. 1990; operates internal flights, and flights to the USA; Dir-Gen. ANDRÉS FABRE.

Interjet (ABC Aerolíneas, SA de CV): Prado Sur 230, 1°, Col. Lomas de Chapultepec, Mexico City, DF; tel. (55) 9178-5500; fax (55) 9178-5513; e-mail atencionaclientes@interjet.com.mx; internet www.interjet.com.mx; f. 2005; budget airline operating internal flights; Pres. MIGUEL ALEMÁN MAGNANI.

Magnicharters (Grupo Aereo Monterrey SA de CV): Calle Donato Guerra No 9, Col. Juárez, México, DF; tel. (55) 5141-1351; internet magnicharters.com.mx; f. 1994; domestic charter flights; Dep. Dir-Gen. Capt. JORGE BADIA.

VivaAerobus: Aeropuerto de Monterrey, Terminal C, Zona de Carga, Carretera Miguel Alemán Km 24, Apodaca, 66600 Nuevo León; tel. (81) 8215-0150; e-mail publicidad@vivaaerobus.com;

internet www.vivaaerobus.com; f. 2006; low-cost domestic airline; Dir-Gen JUAN CARLOS ZUAZUA COSÍO.

Volaris: Aeropuerto Internacional de la Ciudad de Toluca, 50500 Toluca, Méx.; tel. (55) 1102-8000; e-mail comentarios@volaris.com .mx; internet www.volaris.com.mx; f. 2006; operated by Vuela Compañía de Aviación; budget airline operating internal flights; Chair. ALFONSO GONZÁLEZ MIGOYA; Dir-Gen. ENRIQUE BELTRANENA.

Tourism

Tourism remains one of Mexico's principal sources of foreign exchange. Mexico received 24.1m. foreign visitors in 2013, and receipts from tourism in that year were US $13,949m. More than 90% of visitors come from the USA and Canada. The relics of the Mayan and Aztec civilizations and of Spanish Colonial Mexico are of historic and artistic interest. Zihuatanejo, on the Pacific coast, and Cancún, on the Caribbean, have been developed as tourist resorts.

Secretariat of State for Tourism: see section on The Government (Secretariats of State).

Asociación Mexicana de Agencias de Viajes (AMAV): Guanajuato 128, Col. Roma, Del. Cuauhtémoc, 06700 México, DF; tel. (55) 5584-9300; fax (55) 5584-9933; e-mail contacto@amavnacional.com; internet www.ofertasdeviajesmexico.com; f. 1945; asscn of travel agencies; Pres. JORGE HERNÁNDEZ DELGADO; Exec. Vice-Pres. JOSÉ LUIS MONTERO HERNÁNDEZ.

Fondo Nacional de Fomento al Turismo (FONATUR): Tecoyotitla 100, Col. Florida, 01030 México, DF; tel. (55) 5090-4200; fax (55) 5090-4469; e-mail fonatur-dg@fonatur.gob.mx; internet www .fonatur.gob.mx; f. 1956 to finance and promote the devt of tourism; Dir-Gen. ENRIQUE CARRILLO LAVAT.

Defence

As assessed at November 2014, Mexico's regular armed forces numbered 266,550: army 204,950, navy 53,600 (including naval air force, 1,250; marines, 21,500) and air force 8,000. There were also 87,350 reserves. Paramilitary forces numbered 62,900, comprising a federal preventive police force of 41,000, a federal ministerial police force of 4,500 and a rural defence militia numbering 17,400. Military service, on a part-time basis, is by lottery and lasts for one year.

Defence Budget: 98,300m. new pesos in 2014.

Chief of Staff of National Defence: Brig.-Gen. ROBLE ARTURO GRANADOS GALLARDO.

Superintendent and Comptroller of the Army and Air Force: Gen. GILBERTO HERNÁNDEZ ANDREU.

Commander of the Air Force: Gen. CARLOS ANTONIO RODRÍGUEZ MUNGUÍA.

Chief of Staff of the Navy: Vice-Adm. JOAQUÍN ZETINA ANGULO.

Education

State education in Mexico is free and compulsory at primary and secondary level. Primary education lasts for six years between the ages of six and 11. Secondary education lasts for up to six years. In 2011 enrolment at primary schools included 96% of pupils in the relevant age-group, while in 2011 enrolment at secondary schools included 67% of pupils in the relevant age-group. In 2011/12 there were 91,253 nursery schools and 99,378 primary schools. There were 36,563 secondary schools in the same year, attended by 6.2m. pupils. In spite of the existence of more than 80 indigenous languages in Mexico, there were few bilingual secondary schools. In 2011/12 there were an estimated 6,114 institutes of higher education, attended by some 3.0m. students. The 2013 federal budget allocated a preliminary 578,978m. new pesos to education, equivalent to 17.4% of total recurrent expenditure.

THE FEDERATED STATES OF MICRONESIA

Introductory Survey

LOCATION, CLIMATE, LANGUAGE, RELIGION, FLAG, CAPITAL

The Federated States of Micronesia forms (with Palau, q.v.) the archipelago of the Caroline Islands, about 800 km east of the Philippines. The Federated States of Micronesia comprises 607 islands and includes (from west to east) the states of Yap, Chuuk (formerly Truk), Pohnpei (formerly Ponape) and Kosrae. The islands are subject to heavy rainfall, although precipitation decreases from east to west. January, February and March are the driest months; however, seasonal variations in rainfall and temperature are generally small. The annual average temperature is 27°C (81°F). The native population consists of various ethno-linguistic groups, but English is widely understood. The principal religion is Christianity, much of the population being Roman Catholic. The national flag (proportions 10 by 19) consists of four five-pointed white stars, arranged as a circle, situated centrally on a light blue field. The capital is Palikir, on Pohnpei.

CONTEMPORARY POLITICAL HISTORY

Historical Context

The Federated States of Micronesia was formerly part of the US-administered Trust Territory of the Pacific Islands (for history up to 1965, see the Marshall Islands).

From 1965 there were increasing demands for local autonomy within the Trust Territory of the Pacific Islands. In that year the Congress of Micronesia was formed, and in 1967 a commission was established to examine the future political status of the islands. In 1970 the commission declared Micronesians' rights to sovereignty over their own lands, to self-determination, to devise their own constitution and to revoke any form of free association with the USA. In May 1977, after eight years of negotiations, US President Jimmy Carter announced that his administration intended to adopt measures to terminate the trusteeship agreement by 1981. Until 1979 the four districts of Yap, Truk (Chuuk since 1990), Ponape (Pohnpei since 1984) and Kosrae were governed by a local Administrator, appointed by the President of the USA. However, on 10 May 1979 the four districts ratified a new Constitution to become the Federated States of Micronesia. The Constitution was promulgated in 1980.

The USA signed a Compact of Free Association with the Republic of Palau in August 1982, and reached agreement with the Marshall Islands and the Federated States of Micronesia in October. The trusteeship of the Pacific territory was due to end after the principle and terms of Compacts of Free Association had been approved by the respective peoples and legislatures of the new countries, by the US Congress and by the UN Security Council. Under the Compacts, the four countries (including the Northern Mariana Islands) would be independent of each other and would individually manage their respective internal and foreign affairs, while the USA would remain responsible for defence and security. The Federated States of Micronesia approved its Compact by plebiscite in June 1983, and the agreement was ratified by the islands' Congress in September.

US administration of the Federated States of Micronesia was formally ended in November 1986, and the UN Security Council ratified the termination of the trusteeship agreement in December 1990. Ponape was renamed Pohnpei in November 1984, when its Constitution came into effect, and Truk was renamed Chuuk in January 1990, when its new Constitution was proposed (being later adopted).

Domestic Political Affairs

The incumbent President (since 1987), John Haglelgam, was replaced by Bailey Olter, a former Vice-President, in May 1991. At congressional elections in March 1995 Olter was re-elected to the Pohnpei senator-at-large seat (each of the four Micronesian states choosing a senator-at-large to serve a four-year term), and in May was re-elected to the presidency unopposed. In July 1996 Vice-President Jacob Nena became acting President when Olter suffered a stroke, and in May 1997 was sworn in as President of the country.

Congressional elections took place in March 1997 for the 10 senators elected on a two-yearly basis, at which all of the incumbents were returned to office. A referendum held concurrently on a proposed constitutional amendment (which envisaged increasing the allocation of national revenue to the state legislatures from 50% to 80% of the total budget) was approved in Chuuk and Yap, but rejected in Pohnpei and Kosrae.

At the congressional elections held in March 1999, President Nena was re-elected to the Kosrae senator-at-large seat and Vice-President Leo Falcam to the Pohnpei senator-at-large seat. In May Congress elected Falcam as President and the Chuuk senator-at-large, Redley Killion, as Vice-President.

A first round of renegotiations of the Compact of Free Association (certain terms of which were due to expire in 2001) was completed in late 1999. The USA and the Federated States of Micronesia pledged to maintain defence and security relations, and the USA agreed to continue to provide economic aid to the islands. In July 2001 the USA expressed concern that the US $2,600m. that it had given to Micronesia and the Marshall Islands since 1986 had been mismanaged. Upon the expiry on 3 November 2001 of the Compact's funding terms for Micronesia, funding was continued at the Compact's 15-year average level while negotiations proceeded. Following a proposal by the USA in April 2002 to extend economic assistance for a period of 20 years, a new draft funding structure was agreed, and US budget projections for 2004 granted Micronesian citizens access to private health care resources in the USA as part of the Federated States' continued entitlement to US federal programmes. On 1 May 2003 the amended Compact of Free Association, which envisaged direct annual grants from the USA to Micronesia of $76.2m. from 2004, in addition to a further $16m. paid annually into a trust fund for the islands, was signed by the two sides. From 2007 direct grants were to decrease by some $800,000, with this amount being transferred to the trust fund. (The total amount to be paid prior to the expected termination of US assistance in 2023 amounted, in 2004 terms, to some $1,760m.) Furthermore, the Micronesian Government also undertook to provide frequent, strictly monitored audit information on all US funding in order to ensure greater accountability. In October 2003 final agreement was reached on some outstanding security and immigration issues, and representatives of both Governments signed a document of implementation in June 2004.

Nevertheless, there remained widespread concern in the Federated States of Micronesia that the new Compact represented a substantial overall reduction in annual income over the long term. Moreover, the formula for the distribution of Compact funds to each of Micronesia's states and the removal of certain US subsidies remained the subject of considerable controversy. In August 2008 these concerns were renewed when the US Department of the Interior partly suspended Compact funding for the state of Chuuk, citing financial management problems.

Meanwhile, in September 2002 a referendum was held on a number of proposed amendments to the Constitution, including provision for the direct election of presidential candidates, the extension of the right of islanders to hold dual citizenship and changes to the distribution formula for Compact of Free Association funds. The proposals were rejected, having failed to receive the constitutionally required three-quarters' majority of votes.

At the congressional elections of March 2003 President Leo Falcam unexpectedly failed to achieve re-election as senator-at-large for Pohnpei. In May Congress appointed the senator-at-large for Yap, Joseph J. Urusemal, to the presidency. The elections were the subject of some controversy, as it appeared that elected officials had disbursed a portion of the 2002 US funding for Micronesia in order to enhance their electoral prospects. Perceptions of official accountability continued to deteriorate in 2003; in November three serving congressmen were indicted for their role in an alleged fraud involving some US $1.2m. in public funds. In January 2004 members of Congress attempted to introduce legislation effectively absolving public officials from corruption allegations relating to Compact of Free Association funds. The proposals aroused widespread public hostility, and several representatives of state legislatures threatened to secede from the federation unless the proposed bill were withdrawn.

At congressional elections held in March 2005 all but one of the four incumbent senators-at-large were re-elected, and eight of the 10 incumbent senators with two-year mandates were re-elected. (Results from Chuuk were annulled, owing to alleged voting irregularities, and in April a new round of voting was held in the state.) A referendum conducted concurrently with the April poll proposed a number of constitutional amendments, including the question of whether each state should recognize and uphold the laws and judicial rulings of other states, and whether to allow dual citizenship. The proposals received support from a majority of voters, although less than the required three-quarters' majority and were therefore rejected.

At congressional elections held in March 2007 the incumbent senators-at-large for Kosrae, Pohnpei and Yap were re-elected, while Immanuel Mori defeated Vice-President Redley Killion to become senator-at-large for Chuuk. In May, in a congressional vote, Mori was elected President, while Alik L. Alik of Kosrae succeeded Killion as Vice-President. 'Special' congressional elections were conducted in July to fill the seats vacated by Mori and Alik. In a protracted confirmation process, members of Mori's Government were individually nominated and sworn in during the latter half of 2007 and early 2008. A Department of Education was also created.

In April 2007 a Memorandum of Understanding (MOU) was signed between Congress and the state legislatures of Chuuk and Kosrae, allowing Congress to assume disbursement, accounting and reporting responsibilities for all US federal programme grants on behalf of the two states. The MOU was intended to assist the two states in fiscal management and structural issues. In December 2011 Congress announced the termination of the arrangement within six months, deeming the two state legislatures now capable of administering their own federal grants.

Meanwhile, in March 2008 Roosevelt D. Kansou, a senator from Chuuk, was convicted of conspiracy and was consequently removed from his seat in Congress. Tesime Kofot was elected to succeed Kansou in a special ballot in May.

In March 2009 congressional elections were conducted for the 10 senators elected on a two-yearly basis; three incumbents were returned unopposed. At an election to determine the Governor of Chuuk incumbent Wesley Simina was re-elected in a run-off poll in April. In October Peter M. Christian was elected as senator-at-large for Pohnpei, following the death in June of the incumbent, Resio S. Moses.

Alongside gubernatorial and municipal elections held in Yap in November 2010, at which the incumbent Governor Sebastian Anefal was re-elected, a referendum on a proposed amendment to the state Constitution was held. The proposal, granting the state legislature the power to put the question of whether Yap should review its political status to a popular vote, was approved by a sizeable majority. Gubernatorial and municipal elections also took place in Kosrae in November; Lyndon Jackson was elected Governor of the state following a run-off poll in January 2011.

Recent developments

At elections for all 14 seats in Congress in March 2011, President Mori, Vice-President Alik and six other incumbent senators retained their seats. In May Mori and Alik were re-elected to a further four-year term by the newly installed Congress. Special congressional elections were subsequently conducted to fill the seats vacated by Mori and Alik. Mori was replaced as Chuuk's senator-at-large by Wesley Simina, who was in turn replaced as Governor of Chuuk by Johnson Elimo. At a joint inauguration ceremony for the new national Government and Congress in August, President Mori identified climate change, education, health, infrastructural development and private sector development as priority areas of concern for his administration, and also pledged to increase national revenue and foreign investment levels.

In July 2011 Kurt Campbell, the US Assistant Secretary of State for East Asian and Pacific Affairs, announced that the existing visa-free provision whereby citizens of Micronesia, the Marshall Islands and Palau could travel to the USA to live, work or study without restriction was currently under review, owing to mounting objections from US government officials regarding the cost of the provision of health, education and social services to such visitors. In October senator-at-large Peter Christian introduced a resolution to Congress urging the termination of the Compact of Free Association with the USA by 2018 at the latest, in response to the perceived hardening in the stance of the US Administration of President Barack Obama in its relations with the Federated States of Micronesia. In the resolution, Christian accused the US Government of regarding the Compact as an 'act of charity' rather than as a treaty providing for a mutually beneficial relationship between two sovereign states.

At gubernatorial and municipal elections in Pohnpei in November 2011, John Ehsa was re-elected as Governor. In March 2013 elections were conducted for 10 of the 14 seats in Congress; nine of the incumbent senators were re-elected (three of whom were unopposed). At an election to determine the Governor of Chuuk the incumbent Johnson Elimo was re-elected to his post following a run-off poll in April.

In an effort to assist the many Micronesians who decide to migrate to the USA and to enable their successful integration into US society, the Migrant Resource Center was opened in Pohnpei in April 2013. The centre was to offer training and education on a wide range of subjects, including applying for employment in the USA, entering into housing rental agreements, understanding driving regulations, and gaining access to medical and legal services in the country.

In November 2014 government representatives met to discuss issues related to the ending in 2023 of US assistance under the Compact of Free Association. This was the third meeting of the so-called 2023 Planning Committee which had been created in March 2012. Delegates identified the promotion of greater private sector involvement in the economy as a priority for the islands' future financial independence.

Elections for all 14 seats in Congress were held on 3 March 2015. A referendum question on the subject of possible independence for Chuuk state was removed from the ballot papers shortly before the elections in Chuuk, apparently to allow for greater public consultation on the issue. Advocates of independence expressed the hope that Chuuk would be able to negotiate its own agreement with the USA, to come into effect when the Compact expired in 2023.

Environmental Concerns and Human Development

Periodic extreme weather formations have caused loss of life and severe damage to crops, property and infrastructure in Micronesia. The most recent 'super typhoon' to strike the islands, in March 2015, resulted in at least five fatalities, left more than 6,700 people in Chuuk state homeless, and caused major damage to housing, infrastructure and crops. The President declared a state of emergency in Chuuk and Yap states and requested that Congress provide US $4.8m. for immediate relief assistance. In addition, in mid-April the Government appealed to the US Administration to declare Micronesia a federal disaster area, which would enable the release of federal Compact funding.

In 2000 marine biologists issued a warning regarding the erosion of the islands' coastlines, caused by the destruction of the coral reefs by pollution, over-fishing and rising sea temperatures. Concerns about environmental pollution subsequently increased, following reports of damage caused by former US and Japanese military equipment submerged in Micronesian waters.

Micronesia has been a prominent campaigner on the issue of climate change, the effects of which are particularly serious for low-lying island nations. In 2003 President Joseph Urusemal urged the UN General Assembly to work towards combating climate change. At a US congressional hearing in March 2008, the Federated States of Micronesia's Permanent Representative to the UN, Masao Nakayama, argued that climate change was directly affecting Micronesia and enjoined the USA to take action to alleviate the problem. In the following year President Immanuel Mori addressed world leaders at the European Development Days conference in Stockholm, Sweden, declaring that Micronesia's water supplies, agricultural productivity and very existence were threatened by climate change. He appealed to developed nations to establish an Adaptation Fund to assist poorer nations in their efforts to mitigate and adapt to the effects of climate change.

At a conference held in Geneva, Switzerland, in June 2010 of Parties to the Montreal Protocol on Substances that Deplete the Ozone Layer the head of the Micronesian delegation emphasized the importance of taking 'urgent action' more effectively to control the release into the atmosphere of hydrofluorocarbons (HFCs—substances introduced to replace the use of ozone-depleting gases, some of which are believed nevertheless to contribute to climate change). At the annual UN Climate Change Conference held in Cancún, Mexico, in November–December 2010, Micronesia resubmitted a proposal that it had made in the previous year urging governments to take immediate action on the 50% of global warming thought to be caused by gases other than carbon dioxide, including methane and some HFCs.

In December 2009 Micronesia, with the support of the environmental action group Greenpeace, launched an unprecedented transboundary legal challenge against plans by the Czech Republic to expand a coal-fired power station, claiming that the potential environmental damage from what would be one of Europe's largest such stations could threaten the survival of the islands. None the less, in 2014 it was reported that the expansion of the power plant was under way. The islands earned international praise for legislation approved by their Government in December 2013—the Climate Change Act—which made the inclusion of climate adaptation measures a compulsory element in all public policy decisions.

The *Human Development Report 2010*, published by the UN Development Programme (UNDP) in November of that year, included the Federated States of Micronesia in its Human Development Index for the first time. Micronesia was ranked 103rd out of 169 countries, its overall score falling below both the regional and global average. Micronesia fared similarly poorly in subsequent UNDP reports, ranking 124th out of 187 countries in the *Human Development Report 2014*.

In its *2011 Trafficking in Persons Report*, published in June of that year, the US Department of State downgraded the Federated States of Micronesia to its list of countries of particular concern with regard to human trafficking ('Tier Three'). The report noted that, while there was a lack of official data available, the forcing into prostitution of Micronesian women lured to the USA and its territories with promises of well-paid employment was a prevalent problem, as was the prostitution of women and children to crew members on fishing vessels within Micronesia's territorial waters. The report's allegation that Micronesia was not making significant efforts to eliminate human trafficking, and the possibility of a withdrawal of US funding over the issue, led Micronesian legislators to adopt a resolution in November to introduce measures to address the problem. Consequently, in the following year Micronesia was reinstated on the list of 'Tier Two' countries. Subsequent additional efforts to eliminate trafficking led to a further improvement in the islands' ranking in the 2014 report.

In January 2014 a state of emergency was declared by the Governor of Pohnpei after a large Chinese fishing vessel ran aground on the Pohnpei reef in December 2013. The vessel, which was known to contain substantial quantities of oil, gas and chemicals, represented a serious environmental threat to Micronesia, which sought international assistance to arrange for its safe removal.

Statistical information released by the World Health Organization in late 2014 indicated that Micronesia had one of the highest rates of diabetes in the world, with more than 30% of the adult population suffering from the disease.

Regional Affairs

In February 2003 Pohnpei hosted the first summit of Micronesian leaders (the Micronesian Chief Executives' Summit—MCES) and regular such meetings have been held since to discuss co-operation among the states of Micronesia, Palau, the Northern Mariana Islands, the Marshall Islands and Guam in a wide range of areas. At the MCES held in Pohnpei in July 2011, a resolution was signed on the development of a strategic framework to implement a marine-based conservation programme that would establish the world's first regional shark sanctuary in the territorial waters of the Micronesian islands; the resolution also provided for the imposition of a ban on the possession of and trade in shark fins within the sanctuary area. A complete ban on shark fishing in Micronesian waters, which had been partially introduced in 2012, was signed into law by President Mori in early 2015. In August 2012 the first Micronesian Regional Women's Summit was held, in Koror, Palau. At the 20th MCES, held in Yap in July 2014, discussions included potential co-operation between member states in the areas of tourism development, telecommunications and health, particularly the health implications of climate change, such as the increase in mosquito-borne diseases.

Relations between the Federated States of Micronesia and the People's Republic of China have become increasingly close during the early 21st century. In July 2006 the Chinese Minister of Foreign Affairs, Li Zhaoxing, became the most senior Chinese official ever to visit Micronesia, and in September residences built by the Chinese for senior Micronesian officials (including the President and Chief Justice) were presented to the Government. Bilateral relations were further bolstered by the opening of a Micronesian embassy in the Chinese capital of Beijing in 2007 and the appointment therein of a resident ambassador in 2010. A bilateral economic and technical co-operation agreement was signed between Micronesia and China in February 2011, under the terms of which China was to provide US $1.5m. in development aid to the Micronesian Government. In October a proposal was mooted by a private Chinese company, Exhibit and Travel Group (ETG), to construct a major tourism resort in Yap; the plans included the construction of between eight and 10 hotel complexes, providing a total of some 20,000 hotel rooms, as well as convention and entertainment centres, casinos and other leisure facilities. In January 2012 the state government of Yap and the ETG signed an MOU regarding the development of the state's tourism industry and infrastructure. President Immanuel Mori met his Chinese counterpart, Xi Jinping, in Fiji in November 2014 at a meeting between the Chinese head of state and those of the eight Pacific island nations with which China maintains diplomatic relations.

In the early years of the 21st century, Japan was the second largest donor to the Federated States of Micronesia, behind only the USA. Diplomatic relations, established in 1988, were further enhanced in 2008 when the Japanese embassy in Kolonia, Pohnpei, welcomed its first resident ambassador. During an official visit to Japan in 2010, President Mori expressed gratitude for Japanese economic co-operation and assistance in Micronesia, while Japanese Prime Minister Naoto Kan thanked Micronesia for its support of Japan's bid to secure a permanent seat on the UN Security Council. In late 2013 it was announced that Japanese funding of some US $11.7m. would enable the purchase of a new ship to enhance essential transportation services between the islands in Micronesia. In the previous year financial assistance from the Japanese Government had facilitated the extension of the runway at Pohnpei airport. Mori travelled to Japan in November 2014 where he conducted discussions with President Shinzo Abe and sought to promote further Japanese private sector investment in Micronesia.

President Mori's policy of pursuing economic diplomacy with a wide range of international partners continued in 2013–14, when diplomatic relations were established with Montenegro, Uruguay, Lithuania, Mongolia and the Cook Islands. At October 2014 Micronesia enjoyed diplomatic relations with a total of 73 countries.

In August 2014 representatives from the Federated States of Micronesia and the USA signed a maritime boundary treaty clarifying the delimitation of waters between Guam and the Caroline Islands, which had previously overlapped.

CONSTITUTION AND GOVERNMENT

On 10 May 1979 the locally drafted Constitution of the Federated States of Micronesia, incorporating the four states of Kosrae, Yap, Ponape (later Pohnpei) and Truk (later Chuuk), became effective. The federal legislature, the Congress, comprises 14 members (senators). The four states each elect one senator-at-large, for a four-year term. The remaining 10 senators are elected for two-year terms: their seats are distributed in proportion to the population of each state. Each of the four states also has its own Constitution, Governor, Lieutenant-Governor and legislature. The federal President and Vice-President are elected by the Congress from among the four senators-at-large; the offices rotate among the four states. (By-elections are then held for the congressional seats to which the President and Vice-President had been elected.) In November 1986 the Compact of Free Association was signed by the Governments of the Federated States of Micronesia and the USA. Some of its terms, due to expire in 2001, were renegotiated in late 1999, and an amended Compact was signed by the Governments of both countries on 1 May 2003. According to the terms of the Compact, the Federated States of Micronesia is a sovereign, self-governing state.

The municipalities and villages constitute the local government units of the islands. The municipalities are governed by elected Magistrates and Councils. Village government is largely traditional.

REGIONAL AND INTERNATIONAL CO-OPERATION

The Federated States of Micronesia is a member of the Pacific Community (see p. 410), the Pacific Islands Forum (see p. 413), the UN's Economic and Social Commission for Asia and the Pacific (ESCAP, see p. 30) and the Asian Development Bank (ADB, see p. 206). The Federated States of Micronesia hosts the Western and Central Pacific Fisheries Commission, a multilateral agency established in 2004 to manage migratory fish stocks in the region.

The Federated States of Micronesia became a member of the UN in 1991.

ECONOMIC AFFAIRS

In 2013, according to estimates by the World Bank, gross national income (GNI) in the Federated States of Micronesia, measured at average 2011–13 prices, was US $355m., equivalent to $3,430 per head (or $3,840 per head on an international purchasing-power parity basis). During 2004–13, it was estimated, the population decreased at an average annual rate of 0.3%, while gross domestic product (GDP) per head increased, in real terms, by an average of 0.8% per year. Overall GDP increased, in real terms, at an average annual rate of 0.4% during 2004–13. According to the Asian Development Bank (ADB), real GDP contracted by 4.0% in 2012/13 and 3.4% in 2013/14.

The agricultural sector (including forestry and fishing) contributed 27.9% of GDP in 2013, according to UN estimates. According to FAO, the sector engaged about 21.2% of the total labour force at mid-2015. Agriculture is mainly on a subsistence level, although its importance is diminishing. The principal crops are coconuts, cassava, sweet potatoes, bananas and betel nuts. White peppercorns are produced on Pohnpei. In the year to September 2011 fishing access fees, mainly from Japanese fleets, totalled US $18.8m. (some 27.8% of total consolidated general government revenue). Exports of fish are a major source of revenue. The islands' tuna-processing facilities were upgraded in 2009/10, funded with Chinese assistance. According to UN figures, agricultural GDP increased, in real terms, at an average annual rate of 1.7% during 2004–13. According to the ADB, sectoral GDP contracted by 6.2% in 2012/13, but grew by 2.3% in 2013/14.

Industry (including mining, manufacturing, utilities and construction) provided 8.7% of GDP in 2013, according to UN estimates. There is little manufacturing, other than the production of buttons using trochus shells, and the mining sector is negligible. Industrial GDP increased, in real terms, at an average annual rate of 2.9% during 2004–13. According to the ADB, the sector's GDP contracted by 19.6% in 2012/13 and by 40.9% in 2013/14.

Manufacturing contributed just 0.5% of GDP in 2013. Manufacturing GDP decreased, in real terms, at an average annual rate of 12.9% during 2004–13; the sector's GDP decreased by 12.8% in 2012, but increased by 10.2% in 2013.

Construction contributed 6.7% of GDP in 2013. The sector's GDP increased, in real terms, at an average annual rate of 9.5% during 2004–13; construction GDP decreased by 4.1% in 2012 and further by 1.3% in 2013.

The islands are heavily dependent on imported fuels. Purchases of petroleum products accounted for an estimated 26.3% of the value of total imports in the year to September 2012. In 2009 a new bio-gas project was initiated in Pohnpei, the first of four schemes financed by the Chinese province of Zhejiang.

The services sector provided 63.3% of GDP in 2013. A total of 14,788 people were employed in services in 2006/07, equivalent to some 90% of total employment in the formal sector. Tourism is an important industry, with receipts for 2010 totalling some US $25m. The number of tourist arrivals increased from 38,263 in 2012 to 42,109 in 2013. Remittances from overseas emigrants are a significant source of income support. The GDP of the services sector decreased, in real terms, at an average annual rate of 0.3% during 2004–13. According to the ADB, the sector's GDP decreased by 0.8% in 2012/13 and by 1.8% in 2013/14.

According to the ADB, in 2013/14 there was a visible merchandise trade deficit of US $108m., with a surplus equivalent to 14.2% of GDP on the current account of the balance of payments (compared with a deficit equivalent to 10.1% the previous year).

The principal sources of imports in 2012 were the USA (which supplied 38.4% of the total), Guam, Japan and the Philippines. Guam was the principal market for exports in 2007, purchasing 22.5% of the total, followed by the USA. The principal imports in 2012 were mineral products, prepared foodstuffs, beverages and tobacco, machinery, mechanical appliances and electrical equipment, vegetable products, animal and animal products, and base metals and articles thereof. Fish is the major export commodity; marine products accounted for 89.4% of total exports in 2012. Other exports in that year included betel nuts and kava.

A budget surplus equivalent to 11.1% of GDP was recorded in 2013/14. The Federated States of Micronesia relies heavily on financial assistance, particularly from the USA, with funding made available under the Compact of Free Association (see *Contemporary Political History*). Bilateral grants have been provided by Japan, a major donor, and the People's Republic of China. At the end of 2013, according to the ADB, the islands' total external debt stood at $87m. In that year the cost of debt-servicing was equivalent to 6.7% of the value of exports of goods and services. The annual rate of inflation averaged 4.8% in 2004–13. According to ADB figures, consumer prices increased by an annual average of 0.7% in 2013/14. Some 16.2% of the labour force were unemployed in 2010.

The islands' economic development has been limited by a number of factors, including their remote location and the high rate of emigration. It was hoped that the Federated States of Micronesia would be in a position to achieve financial self-sufficiency by 2023, upon the scheduled expiry of the Compact of Free Association (see *Contemporary Political History*). Meanwhile, the trust fund established to support the Micronesian economy in the longer term remained vulnerable to the volatility of international financial markets. The islands received a total of US $69.5m. in Compact funds in 2012/13 (compared with $83.1m. in the previous year), in addition to a supplementary education grant of $38.5m. Aside from the Compact, the islands' main source of income is the sale of fishing licences and remittances from workers overseas. More than one-half of those in paid employment in Micronesia work for the Government, and the development of a larger private sector has been identified as a necessary step towards economic sustainability. According to the ADB, Micronesia's GDP contracted by 4.0% in 2012/13, and by a further 3.4% in 2013/14; the downturn was partly owing to a decline in construction activity and to a large decrease, in 2013/14, in US Compact capital grants. In 2013/14 the budget recorded a surplus equivalent to 11.1% of GDP (up from 2.9% in 2012/13), largely owing to a one-off windfall in revenue from corporate income tax and an increase in income from the sale of fishing rights. Telecommunications, particularly broadband capacity, on the islands were expected to benefit significantly from a project to lay an underwater cable between Palau and Yap. The project, which was announced in mid-2013, was to be funded by some $40m. from the World Bank. A Country Partnership Strategy with the World Bank for 2014–17 was announced in mid-2014. Its first goal was the improvement of the islands' electricity supply and the increased use of renewable energy, towards which $14.4m. was allocated. Other priorities included the promotion of measures to encourage private sector investment. The World Bank's most recent Ease of Doing Business survey, published in October 2014, ranked Micronesia 145th out of 189 countries, citing particularly discouraging factors for potential investors, such as the absence of taxation or licensing incentives, the perceived widespread misuse and misappropriation of government funds, and the fact that resolution of commercial disputes, especially regarding land ownership, can be lengthy. According to the ADB, Micronesia's GDP was forecast to return to positive growth, of 2.3%, in 2014/15, partly as a result of the resumption of upgrade work at Chuuk international airport. The predicted economic recovery was expected to lead to a rise in inflation to around 2.4% in 2014/15.

PUBLIC HOLIDAYS

2016: 1 January (New Year's Day), 25 March (Good Friday), 31 March (Micronesian Culture and Traditions Day), 10 May (Constitution Day), 24 October (United Nations Day), 3 November (Independence Day), 11 November (Veterans of Foreign Wars Day), 25 December (Christmas Day).

Statistical Survey

Source (unless otherwise indicated): Statistics Unit, Office of Statistics, Budget and Economic Management, Overseas Development Assistance and Compact Management (SBOC), POB PS-12, Palikir, Pohnpei, FM 96941; tel. 320-2820; fax 320-5854; e-mail fsmstat@sboc.fm; internet www.sboc.fm/index.php.

AREA AND POPULATION

Area: 700.8 sq km (270.6 sq miles): Chuuk (Truk, 294 islands) 127.4 sq km; Kosrae (5 islands) 109.6 sq km; Pohnpei (Ponape, 163 islands) 345.2 sq km; Yap (145 islands) 118.6 sq km.

Population: 107,008 at census of 1 April 2000; 102,843 (males 52,193, females 50,650) at census of 4 April 2010. *By State* (2010): Chuuk 48,654; Kosrae 6,616; Pohnpei 36,196; Yap 11,377. *2015* (UN estimate at mid-year): 104,460 (Source: UN, *World Population Prospects: The 2012 Revision*).

Density (at mid-2015): 149.1 per sq km.

Population by Age and Sex (UN estimates at mid-2015): *0–14 years:* 35,588 (males 18,423, females 17,165); *15–64 years:* 64,321 (males 33,025, females 31,296); *65 years and over:* 4,551 (males 2,062, females 2,489); *Total* 104,460 (males 53,510, females 50,950). Source: UN, *World Population Prospects: The 2012 Revision*.

Principal Towns (population of municipalities at 2010 census): Weno (Moen) 13,856; Palikir (capital) 6,647; Nett 6,639; Kitti 6,470; Kolonia 6,074. Source: Thomas Brinkhoff, *City Population* (internet: www.citypopulation.de).

Births and Deaths (2003, official estimates): Registered live births 2,568 (birth rate 23.9 per 1,000); Deaths 442 (death rate 4.1 per 1,000). *2006:* Registered live births 2,147. *2010–15* (annual averages, UN estimates): Birth rate 23.6 per 1,000; Death rate 6.2 per 1,000 (Source: UN, *World Population Prospects: The 2012 Revision*).

Life Expectancy (years at birth): 68.9 (males 68.0; females 69.8) in 2012. Source: World Bank, World Development Indicators database.

Economically Active Population (persons aged 15 years and over, 2010 census): Total employed (incl. others) 31,789 (males 18,647, females 13,142); Unemployed 6,130 (males 3,429, females 2,701); *Total labour force* 37,919 (males 22,076, females 15,843). *2000 census:* Agriculture, forestry and fishing 15,216; Total employed 29,175. *Mid-2015* (estimates in '000): Agriculture, etc. 11; Total labour force 52 (Source: FAO).

HEALTH AND WELFARE

Key Indicators

Total Fertility Rate (children per woman, 2012): 3.3.

Under-5 Mortality Rate (per 1,000 live births, 2012): 39.

Physicians (per 1,000 head, 2009): 0.2.

Hospital Beds (per 1,000 head, 2009): 3.2.

Health Expenditure (2011): US $ per head (PPP): 506.

Health Expenditure (2011): % of GDP: 13.7.

Health Expenditure (2011): public (% of total): 91.0.

Access to Water (% of persons, 2012): 89.

Access to Sanitation (% of persons, 2012): 57.

Total Carbon Dioxide Emissions ('000 metric tons, 2010): 102.7.

Carbon Dioxide Emissions Per Head (metric tons, 2010): 1.0.

Human Development Index (2013): ranking: 124.

Human Development Index (2013): value: 0.630.

For sources and definitions, see explanatory note on p. vi.

AGRICULTURE, ETC.

Principal Crops ('000 metric tons, 2013, FAO estimates): Coconuts 57; Cassava 10; Sweet potatoes 3; Vegetables 3; Bananas 2.

Livestock ('000 head, year ending September 2013, FAO estimates): Pigs 33; Cattle 14; Goats 4; Chickens 190.

Livestock Products (metric tons, 2013, FAO estimates): Cattle meat 258; Pig meat 876; Chicken meat 140; Hen eggs 207.

Fishing ('000 metric tons, live weight, 2012): Skipjack tuna 27.0; Yellowfin tuna 7.7; Bigeye tuna 2.8; Total catch (incl. others) 45.8 (FAO estimate).

Source: FAO.

FINANCE

Currency and Exchange Rates: United States currency is used: 100 cents = 1 United States dollar (US $). *Sterling and Euro Equivalents* (31 December 2014): £1 sterling = US $1.5608; €1 = US $1.2141; US $100 = £64.07 = €82.37.

Budget (US $ million, 2012): *Revenue:* Current 74.6 (Tax revenue 38.0, Non-tax revenue 36.6); Grants 140.6; Total 215.2. *Expenditure:* Current 144.8; Capital 67.9; Total 212.7. *2013* (estimates): *Revenue:* Current 82.3; Grants 140.9; Total 223.3. *Expenditure:* Current 146.5; Capital 68.6; Total 215.1 (Source: Asian Development Bank). Note: Figures represent a consolidation of the accounts of the national Government and the four state governments.

International Reserves (US $ '000 at 31 December 2013): IMF special drawing rights 9,591; Reserve position in IMF 0; Foreign exchange 74,751; *Total* 84,342. Source: IMF, *International Financial Statistics*.

Money Supply (US $ '000 at 31 December 2013): Demand deposits at banking institutions 33,743. Source: IMF, *International Financial Statistics*.

Cost of Living (Consumer Price Index, base: April–June 2008 = 100): All items 120.1 in 2011; 126.1 in 2012; 128.0 in 2013.

Gross Domestic Product (US $ million at constant 2005 prices): 252.5 in 2011; 252.5 in 2012; 254.2 in 2013. Source: UN National Accounts Main Aggregates Database.

Expenditure on the Gross Domestic Product (US $ million at current prices, 2013): Final consumption expenditure 416.3; Gross fixed capital formation 103.9; Changes in inventories 6.6; *Total domestic expenditure* 526.8; Exports of goods and services 81.3; *Less* Imports of goods and services 275.1; *GDP in purchasers' values* 333.0. Source: UN National Accounts Main Aggregates Database.

Gross Domestic Product by Economic Activity (US $ million at current prices, 2013): Agriculture, hunting, forestry and fishing 86.7; Mining, electricity, gas and water 4.9; Manufacturing 1.4; Construction 20.8; Trade, restaurants and hotels 45.4; Transport, storage and communications 18.6; Other activities 132.5; *Sub-total* 310.4; Net of indirect taxes 22.7 (obtained as a residual); *GDP in purchasers' values* 333.0. Source: UN National Accounts Main Aggregates Database.

Balance of Payments (US $ million, 2012): Exports of goods 53.9; Imports of goods −183.2; *Trade balance* −129.4; Exports of services and income 38.9; Imports of services and income −80.1; *Balance on goods, services and income* −170.6; Current transfers received 161.7; Current transfers paid −30.3; *Current balance* −39.3; Capital account (net) 64.0; Direct investment (net) 1.0; Portfolio investment (net) 0.2; Other investment (net) −34.5; *Overall balance* −8.6. Source: Asian Development Bank.

EXTERNAL TRADE

Principal Commodities (US $ '000, 2012): *Imports c.i.f.:* Animals and animal products 12,490; Vegetable products 13,877; Prepared foodstuffs, beverages and tobacco 30,593; Mineral products 63,451; Chemical products 9,253; Plastic and rubber 7,560; Base metals and articles thereof 10,229; Machinery, mechanical appliances and electrical equipment 14,833; Transportation equipment 8,570; Total (incl. others) 193,645. *Exports f.o.b.:* Agricultural products 4,412 (Betel nuts 3,544; Kava 482); Prepared foodstuffs 308; Marine products 40,255; Total (incl. others) 45,037.

Principal Trading Partners (US $ '000, 2012): *Imports:* Australia 8,820; China, People's Republic 5,540; Guam 53,882; Hong Kong 5,129; Japan 13,380; Korea, Republic 5,204; Philippines 9,611; Singapore 9,355; Taiwan 1,925; Thailand 1,291; USA 74,340; Total (incl. others) 193,645. *Exports:* Guam 3,696; Marshall Islands 414; USA (mainland only) 485; Total (incl. others) 45,037.

TRANSPORT

Shipping: *Flag Registered Fleet* (at 31 December 2014): Vessels 19; Total displacement (grt) 16,787. Source: Lloyd's List Intelligence (www.lloydslistintelligence.com).

TOURISM

Foreign Tourist Arrivals: 35,378 in 2011; 38,263 in 2012; 42,109 in 2013.

Tourist Arrivals by Country or Region of Residence (2013): Australia 1,429; China, People's Republic 4,531; Europe 2,981; Japan 4,570; Pacific Islands 2,584; Philippines 6,486; Other Asia 10,472; USA 7,967; Total (incl. others) 42,109.

Tourism Receipts (US $ million, incl. passenger transport): 22 in 2008; 24 in 2009; 25 in 2010. Source: World Tourism Organization.

COMMUNICATIONS MEDIA

Telephones (main lines in use, 2013): 10,047.

Mobile Cellular Telephones (2013): 31,393 subscribers.

Broadband Subscribers (2013): 2,063.

Source: International Telecommunication Union.

EDUCATION

Primary (2010/11 unless otherwise indicated): 174 schools (1995); 1,113 teachers (2006/07); 22,919 pupils (Sources: partly UN, *Statistical Yearbook for Asia and the Pacific* and UNESCO Institute for Statistics).

Secondary (2010/11 unless otherwise indicated): 24 schools (1995); 829 teachers (2006/07); 7,351 pupils (Sources: partly UN, *Statistical Yearbook for Asia and the Pacific* and UNESCO Institute for Statistics).

Tertiary (2011/12): 2,109 students.

Pupil-teacher Ratio (primary education, UNESCO estimate): 16.6 in 2006/07 (Source: UNESCO Institute for Statistics).

Adult Literacy Rate (population aged 15 years and over, 2010 census): 95.6% (males 94.9%; females 96.5%).

Directory

The Government

HEAD OF STATE

President: PETER M. CHRISTIAN (took office 11 May 2015).
Vice-President: YOSIWO P. GEORGE.

CABINET
(May 2015)

Secretary of the Department of Finance and Administration: KENSLEY IKOSIA.

Secretary of the Department of Foreign Affairs: LORIN S. ROBERT.

Secretary of the Department of Resources and Development: MARION HENRY.

Secretary of the Department of Health and Social Affairs: Dr VITA AKAPITO SKILLING.

Secretary of the Department of Justice: APRIL DAWN SKILLING.

Secretary of the Department of Transportation, Communication and Infrastructure: FRANCIS I. ITIMAI.

Secretary of the Department of Education: Dr RUFINO MAURICIO.

Public Defender: JULIUS JOEY SAPELALUT.

Postmaster-General: GINGER PORTER MIDA.

Director of the Office of Environment and Emergency Management: ANDREW YATILMAN.

Director of the Office of National Archives, Culture and Historic Preservation: AUGUSTINE KOHLER (acting).

Director of the Office of Statistics, Budget and Economic Management, Overseas Development Assistance and Compact Management: EVELYN ADOLPH.

GOVERNMENT OFFICES

Office of the President: POB PS-53, Palikir, Pohnpei, FM 96941; tel. 320-2228; fax 320-2785; e-mail ppetrus@mail.fm; internet www.fsmpio.fm.

Department of Education: POB PS-87, Palikir, Pohnpei, FM 96941; tel. 320-2609; fax 320-5500; internet www.fsmed.fm.

Department of Finance and Administration: POB PS-158, Palikir, Pohnpei, FM 96941; tel. 320-2640; fax 320-5715; e-mail fsmsofa@mail.fm.

Department of Foreign Affairs: POB PS-123, Palikir, Pohnpei, FM 96941; tel. 320-2641; fax 320-2933; e-mail foreignaffairs@mail.fm; internet www.fsmgov.org/ovmis.html.

Department of Health and Social Affairs: POB PS-70, Palikir, Pohnpei, FM 96941; tel. 320-2619; fax 320-2872; e-mail fsmhealth@mail.fm.

Department of Justice: POB PS-105, Palikir, Pohnpei, FM 96941; tel. 320-2644; fax 320-3243; e-mail par.fsm@gmail.com.

Department of Resources and Development: POB PS-12, Palikir, Pohnpei, FM 96941; tel. 320-2646; fax 320-5854; e-mail fsmrd@dea.fm.

Department of Transportation, Communication and Infrastructure: POB PS-2, Palikir, Pohnpei, FM 96941; tel. 320-2865; fax 320-5853; e-mail transcom@mail.fm; internet www.ict.fm.

Office of the Public Defender: POB PS-174, Palikir, Pohnpei, FM 96941; tel. 320-2648; fax 320-5775.

Public Information Office: POB PS-34, Palikir, Pohnpei, FM 96941; tel. 320-2548; fax 320-4356; e-mail fsmpio@mail.fm.

Legislature

CONGRESS OF THE FEDERATED STATES OF MICRONESIA

The Congress comprises 14 members (senators): four senators-at-large (one for each of the four states), who are elected for a four-year term; and 10 senators who serve a two-year term. The most recent election was held on 3 March 2015, when 14 senators were elected. There are no formal political parties.

Speaker: WESLEY W. SIMINA.

STATE LEGISLATURES

Chuuk State Legislature: POB 189, Weno, Chuuk, FM 96942; tel. 330-4284; fax 330-4282; e-mail speakeroffice@yahoo.com; internet www.chuukstatelegislature.fm; Senate of 10 mems and House of Representatives of 28 mems elected for four years; Gov. JOHNSON ELIMO.

Kosrae State Legislature: POB 187, Tofol, Kosrae, FM 96944; tel. 370-3019; fax 370-2177; e-mail Kenkenzmike@kosraelegislature.org; internet kosraestatelegislature.webs.com; unicameral body of 14 mems serving for four years; Gov. LYNDON H. JACKSON.

Pohnpei State Legislature: POB 114, Kolonia, Pohnpei, FM 96941; tel. 320-2753; fax 320-2754; e-mail legislature@mail.fm; internet www.fm/pohnpeileg; 27 representatives elected for four years (terms staggered); Gov. JOHN EHSA.

Yap State Legislature: POB 39, Colonia, Yap, FM 96943; tel. 350-2108; fax 350-4113; internet www.fsmlaw.org/yap; 10 mems, six elected from the Yap Islands proper and four elected from the Outer Islands of Ulithi and Woleai, for a four-year term; Gov. SEBASTIAN L. ANEFAL.

Election Commission

National Election Commission: POB 1685, Kolonia, Pohnpei, FM 96941; tel. 320-4283; fax 320-7805; e-mail ned@mail.fm; Dir ALBERT T. WELLY.

Political Organizations

There are no formal political parties in the Federated States of Micronesia.

Diplomatic Representation

EMBASSIES IN THE FEDERATED STATES OF MICRONESIA

Australia: POB S, Kolonia, Pohnpei, FM 96941; tel. 320-5448; fax 320-5449; e-mail australia@mail.fm; internet www.fsm.embassy.gov.au; Ambassador Dr TERRY BEVEN.

China, People's Republic: POB 1530, Kolonia, Pohnpei, FM 96941; tel. 320-5575; fax 320-5578; e-mail chinaemb_fm@mfa.gov.cn; internet fm.chineseembassy.org/eng; Ambassador LI JIE.

Japan: Pami Bldg, 3rd Floor, POB 1837, Kolonia, Pohnpei, FM 96941; tel. 320-5465; fax 320-5470; internet www.micronesia.emb-japan.go.jp; Ambassador MASAKI SAKAI.

USA: POB 1286, Kolonia, Pohnpei, FM 96941; tel. 320-2187; fax 320-2186; e-mail usembassy@mail.fm; internet kolonia.usembassy.gov; Ambassador DOROTHEA-MARIA ROSEN.

Judicial System

Supreme Court of the Federated States of Micronesia: POB PS-J, Palikir Station, Pohnpei, FM 96941; tel. 320-2357; fax 320-2756; e-mail fsmsupcourt@mail.fm; internet www.fsmsupremecourt.org; Chief Justice READY JOHNNY (acting).

State Courts and Appellate Courts have been established in Yap, Chuuk, Kosrae and Pohnpei.

Religion

The population is predominantly Christian, mainly Roman Catholic. The Assembly of God, Jehovah's Witnesses, Seventh-day Adventists, the Church of Jesus Christ of Latter-day Saints (Mormons), the United Church of Christ, Baptists and the Bahá'í faith are also represented.

CHRISTIANITY

The Roman Catholic Church

The Federated States of Micronesia forms a part of the diocese of the Caroline Islands, suffragan to the archdiocese of Agaña (Guam). The Bishop participates in the Catholic Bishops' Conference of the Pacific, based in Fiji. At 31 December 2007 there were 79,199 adherents in the diocese.

Bishop of the Caroline Islands: Most Rev. AMANDO SAMO, Bishop's House, POB 939, Weno, Chuuk, FM 96942; tel. 330-2399; fax 330-4585; e-mail diocese@mail.fm.

Other Churches

Calvary Baptist Church: Kolonia, Pohnpei, POB 2179, FM 96941; tel. 320-2830; fax 320-3887; e-mail cca_pohnpei@yahoo.com; Pastor ISAMO WELLES.

Liebenzell Mission USA: POB 66, Schooleys Mountain, NJ 07870; tel. 852-3044; e-mail missions@liebenzellusa.org; internet www.liebenzellusa.org; f. 1942; Global Ministries Dir BILL SCHUIT.

Truth Independent Baptist Church: Kolonia, Pohnpei, POB 65, FM 96941; tel. 320-3643; fax 320-6769; Pastor RICARDO P. VERACRUZ.

United Church of Christ in Pohnpei: Kolonia, Pohnpei, POB 864, FM 96941; tel. 320-2271; fax 320-4404; Pres. BERNELL EDWARD.

The Press

Da Rohng: Jano News Service, POB 510, Kolonia, Pohnpei FM 96941; tel. 320-6494; fax 320-4200; e-mail darohng2005@yahoo.com; Editor MARTIN JANO.

Kaselehlie Press: POB 2222, Pohnpei, FM 96941; tel. 320-6547; fax 320-6571; e-mail kpress@mail.fm; internet www.kpress.info; f. 2001; fortnightly; Man. Editor BILL JAYNES.

Micronesian Alliance: POB 543, Tofol, Kosrae, FM 96944; tel. 370 6131; e-mail equatormedia@yahoo.com; fortnightly.

Broadcasting and Communications

TELECOMMUNICATIONS

FSM Telecommunication Corporation: POB 1210, Kolonia, Pohnpei, FM 96941; tel. 320-2740; fax 320-2745; e-mail customerservice@telecom.fm; internet www.telecom.fm; provides domestic, international and internet services; Pres. and CEO JOHN D. SOHL.

BROADCASTING

Radio

Federated States of Micronesia Public Information Office: POB PS-34, Palikir, Pohnpei, FM 96941; tel. 320-2548; fax 320-4356; e-mail fsmpio@mail.fm; internet www.fsmpio.fm/pio.html; govt-operated; 4 regional stations, each broadcasting 18 hours daily; Information Officer PATRICK BLANK.

Station V6AII: POB 1086, Kolonia, Pohnpei, FM 96941; programmes in English and Pohnpeian; Man. WEIDEN MANUEL.

Station V6AI: POB 117, Colonia, Yap, FM 96943; tel. 350-2174; fax 350-4426; programmes in English, Yapese, Ulithian and Satawalese; Man. SEBASTIAN F. TAMAGKEN.

Station V6AJ: POB 147, Tofol, Kosrae, FM 96944; tel. 370-3040; fax 370-3880; e-mail kosraebroadcast@yahoo.com; programmes in English and Kosraean; Man. MCDONALD ITTU.

Station V6AK: Wenn, Chuuk, FM 96942; tel. 330-2596; programmes in Chuukese and English; Man. JOE COMMOR.

WSZA Yap: Dept of Youth and Civic Affairs, POB 30, Colonia, Yap, FM 96943; tel. 350-2174; Media Dir PETER GARAMFEL.

WSZD Pohnpei: POB 1086, Kolonia, Pohnpei, FM 96941; tel. 320-2296; programmes in English and Pohnpeian; Man. FRANCIS ZARRED.

Television

Island Cable TV—Pohnpei: POB 1628, Pohnpei, FM 96941; tel. 320-2671; fax 320-2444; e-mail ictv@mail.fm; f. 1991; Gen. Man. DAVID O. CLIFFE.

TV Station Chuuk (TTTK): Wenn, Chuuk, FM 96942; tel. 330-4475; commercial.

TV Station Pohnpei (KPON): Central Micronesia Communications, POB 460, Kolonia, Pohnpei, FM 96941; f. 1977; commercial; Tech. Dir DAVID CLIFFE.

TV Station Yap (WAAB): Colonia, Yap, FM 96943; tel. 350-2160; fax 350-4113; govt-owned.

Finance

(cap. = capital; dep. = deposits; m. = million; brs = branches)

BANKING

Regulatory Authority

Federated States of Micronesia Banking Board: POB 1887, Kolonia, Pohnpei, FM 96941; tel. 320-2015; fax 320-5433; e-mail fmbb@mail.fm; f. 1980; Chair. ALEXANDER NARRUHN; Commissioner WILSON F. WAGUK.

Banks are also supervised by the US Federal Deposit Insurance Corporation.

Commercial Banks

Bank of the Federated States of Micronesia: POB 98, Kolonia, Pohnpei, FM 96941; tel. 320-2838; fax 320-5359; cap. US $4.6m., dep. US $84.9m. (Dec. 2012); brs in Kosrae, Yap, Pohnpei and Chuuk.

Bank of Guam (USA): POB 367, Kolonia, Pohnpei, FM 96941; tel. 320-2550; fax 320-2562; e-mail bogpohn@mail.fm; internet www.bankofguam.com; Br. Man. CHRISTOPHER CRUZ; brs in Chuuk, Kosrae and Yap.

Yap Credit Union: POB 610, Colonia, Yap; tel. 350-2142.

Development Bank

Federated States of Micronesia Development Bank: POB M, Kolonia, Pohnpei, FM 96941; tel. 320-2840; fax 320-2842; e-mail info@fsmdb.fm; internet www.fsmdb.fm; f. 1979; total assets US $38.2m. (2010); Chair. JOHN SOHL; Pres. ANNA MENDIOLA; 4 brs. Banking services for the rest of the islands are available in Guam, Hawaii and on the US mainland.

INSURANCE

Actouka Executive Insurance: POB 55, Kolonia, Pohnpei, FM 96941; tel. 320-5331; fax 320-2331; e-mail mlamar@mail.fm.

Moylan's Insurance Underwriters: POB 1448, Kolonia, Pohnpei, FM 96941; tel. 320-2118; fax 320-2519; e-mail pohnpei@moylans.net; Pres. and Gen. Man. MELNER ISAAC.

Oceania Insurance Co: POB 1202, Weno, Chuuk, FM 96942; tel. 330-3036; fax 330-3764; e-mail oceanpac@mail.fm; also owns and manages Pacific Basin Insurance; Region Man. ERICSON MARAR.

Yap Insurance Agency: POB 386, Colonia, Yap; tel. 350-2340; fax 350-2341; e-mail tachelioyap@mail.fm.

Trade and Industry

GOVERNMENT AGENCIES

Coconut Development Authority: POB 297, Kolonia, Pohnpei, FM 96941; tel. 320-2892; fax 320-5383; e-mail fsmcda@mail.fm; f. 1981; responsible for all purchasing, processing and exporting of copra and copra by-products in the islands; Gen. Man. NAMIO NANPEI.

FSM National Fisheries Corporation: POB R, Kolonia, Pohnpei, FM 96941; tel. 320-2529; fax 320-2239; e-mail nfcairfreight@mail.fm; internet www.fsmgov.org/nfc; f. 1984; established in 1990, with the Economic Devt Authority and an Australian co, the Caroline Fishing Corpn (3 vessels); promotes fisheries development; Pres. NICK SOLOMON.

National Oceanic Resource Management Authority (NORMA): POB PS-122, Palikir, Pohnpei, FM 96941; tel. 320-2700; fax 320-2383; e-mail info@norma.fm; internet norma.fm; fmrly Micronesian Fisheries Authority; name changed 2002; responsible for conservation, management and development of tuna resources and for issue of fishing licences; Exec. Dir PATRICK MACKENZIE; Deputy Dir EUGENE PANGELINAN.

Office of Compact Management: 253 Palikir Station, Pohnpei, FM 96941; tel. 320-8375; fax 320-8377; Exec. Dir EHPEL ILON.

Pohnpei Economic Development Authority: POB 738, Kolonia, Pohnpei, FM 96941; tel. 320-2298; fax 320-2775; e-mail eda@mail.fm; chaired by the President of the Federated States of Micronesia; Exec. Dir SHELTEN NETH.

CHAMBERS OF COMMERCE

Chuuk Chamber of Commerce: POB 700, Weno, Chuuk, FM 96941; tel. 330-2318; fax 330-2314; e-mail larry.bruton@mail.fm; Pres. WILLIAM STINNETT.

Kosrae Chamber of Commerce: POB 877, Tofol, Kosrae, FM 96944; tel. 370-3483; e-mail info@kosraechamberofcommerce.org; internet www.kosraechamberofcommerce.org; Chair. WITSON PHILLIP.

Pohnpei Chamber of Commerce: POB 405, Kolonia, Pohnpei, FM 96941; tel. 320-2452; fax 320-5277; e-mail amc@mail.fm; Pres. LEON SENDA.

Yap Chamber of Commerce: Colonia, Yap, FM 96943; tel. 350-2298; Pres. PHILLIP RANGANBAY.

UTILITIES

Chuuk Public Works (CPW): POB 248, Weno, Chuuk, FM 96942; tel. 330-2242; fax 320-4815; Chief HERSIN RUBEN.

Kosrae Utility Authority: POB 277, Tofol, Kosrae, FM 96944; tel. 370-3799; fax 370-3798; e-mail info@kosraepower.com; internet kosraepower.com; corporatized in 1994; Gen. Man. FRED N. SKILLING.

Pohnpei Utilities Corporation: POB C, Kolonia, Pohnpei, FM 96941; tel. 320-2374; fax 320-2422; e-mail info@puc.fm; internet www.puc.fm; f. 1992; provides electricity, water and sewerage services; Gen. Man. FELICIANO PERMAN.

Yap State Public Service Corpn (YSPSC): POB 621, Colonia, Yap, FM 96943; tel. 350-2175; fax 350-2331; f. 1996; provides electricity, water and sewerage services; Gen. Man. FAUSTINO R. YANGMOG.

CO-OPERATIVES

Chuuk: Chuuk Co-operative, Faichuk Cacao and Copra Co-operative Asscn, Pis Fishermen's Co-operative, Fefan Women's Co-operative.

Pohnpei: Pohnpei Federation of Co-operative Asscns (POB 100, Pohnpei, FM 96941), Kapingamarangi Copra Producers' Asscn, Kitti Minimum Co-operative Asscn, Kolonia Consumers' and Producers' Co-operative Asscn, Kosrae Island Co-operative Asscn, Metalanim Copra Co-operative Asscn, Mokil Island Co-operative Asscn, Ngatik Island Co-operative Asscn, Nukuoro Island Co-operative Asscn, PICS Co-operative Asscn, Pingelap Consumers' Co-operative Asscn, Pohnpei Fishermen's Co-operative, Pohnpei Handicraft Co-operative, Uh Soumwet Co-operative Asscn.

Yap Co-operative Association Inc: POB 159, Colonia, Yap, FM 96943; tel. 350-2209; fax 350-4114; e-mail yca@mail.fm; internet yapcoop.com; f. 1952; Pres. FAUSTINO YANGMOG; Gen. Man. TONY GANNGIYAN; 1,832 mems.

Transport

ROADS

In 2004 the Federated States of Micronesia had a total road network of 240 km. Tarmac and concrete roads are found on the more important islands. Other islands have stone- and coral-surfaced roads and tracks.

SHIPPING

Pohnpei, Chuuk, Yap and Kosrae have deep-draught harbours for commercial shipping. The ports provide warehousing and transshipment facilities.

Caroline Fisheries Corporation (CFC): POB 7, Kolonia, Pohnpei, FM 96941; tel. 320-3926; fax 320-4733; e-mail cfc@mail.fm; Gen. Man. MILAN KAMBER.

Pacific Shipping Agency: POB 154, Lelu, Kosrae, FM 96944; tel. 370-3956; fax 370-2912; e-mail KosraeAce@mail.fm; f. 1990; Gen. Man. SMITH SIGRAH.

Pohnpei Transfer & Storage, Inc: POB 340, Kolonia, Pohnpei, FM 96941; tel. 320-2552; fax 320-2389; e-mail fsmlinejv@mail.fm; Gen. Man. JOE VITT.

Truk Transportation Company (TRANSCO): POB 99, Weno, Chuuk, FM 96942; tel. 330-2143; fax 330-2726; e-mail transco@mail.fm; f. 1964; Pres. MYRON HASHIGUCHI; Gen. Man. GIDEON BISALEN.

Waab Transportation Company: POB 177, Colonia, Yap, FM 96943; tel. 350-2301; fax 350-4110; e-mail waabtrans@mail.fm; agents for PM & O Lines (USA); Gen. Man. WILLIAM FITZSIMMONS.

CIVIL AVIATION

The Federated States of Micronesia is served by Continental Micronesia, Our Airline (formerly Air Nauru) and Continental Airlines (USA). Pacific Missionary Aviation, based in Pohnpei and Yap, provides domestic air services. There are international airports on Pohnpei, Chuuk, Yap and Kosrae, and airstrips on the outer islands of Onoun and Ta in Chuuk. The extension of the runway at Pohnpei airport, to accommodate larger aircraft, was completed in June 2012.

Tourism

The tourist industry is a significant source of revenue, although it has been hampered by the lack of infrastructure. Visitor attractions include excellent conditions for scuba-diving (notably in Chuuk Lagoon), Second World War battle sites and relics (many underwater), and the ancient ruined city of Nan Madol on Pohnpei. The number of tourist arrivals totalled 42,109 in 2013. Tourism receipts totalled US $25m. in 2010.

Federated States of Micronesia Visitors Board: National Government, PO Box PS-12, Palikir, Pohnpei, FM 96941; tel. 320-5133; fax 320-3251; e-mail fsminfo@visit-fsm.org; internet www.visit-micronesia.fm.

Chuuk Visitors Bureau: POB FQ, Weno, Chuuk, FM 96942; tel. 330-4133; fax 330-4194; e-mail cvb@mail.fm.

Kosrae Visitors Bureau: POB 659, Tofol, Kosrae, FM 96944; tel. 370-2228; fax 370-3000; e-mail kosrae@mail.fm; internet www.kosrae.com; Administrator GRANT ISMAEL.

Pohnpei Department of Tourism and Parks: POB 66, Kolonia, Pohnpei, FM 96941; tel. 320-2421; fax 320-6019; e-mail tourismparks@mail.fm; Deputy Chief BUMIO SILBANUZ.

Pohnpei Visitors Bureau: POB 1949, Kolonia, Pohnpei, FM 96941; tel. 320-4851; fax 320-4868; e-mail pohnpeiVB@mail.fm; internet www.visit-pohnpei.fm.

Yap Visitors Bureau: POB 988, Colonia, Yap, FM 96943; tel. 350-2298; fax 350-7015; e-mail yvb@mail.fm; internet www.visityap.com; Man. VINCENT TAFILELUW; Sec. ABELYNN TAMAN.

Defence

Defence and security are the responsibility of the USA. The US Pacific Command is based in Hawaii, USA.

Education

Primary education, which begins at six years of age and lasts for eight years, is compulsory. Secondary education, beginning at 14 years of age, comprises two cycles, each of two years. The education system is based on the US pattern of eight years' attendance at an elementary school and four years' enrolment at a high school. The Micronesia Maritime and Fisheries Academy, which was opened in Yap in 1990, provides education and training in fisheries technology at secondary and tertiary levels. The College of Micronesia offers two- and three-year programmes leading to a degree qualification. In 2010/11 there were 22,919 pupils enrolled in primary education and 7,351 pupils enrolled in secondary education. In 2011/12 there were 2,109 pupils studying at college level.

MOLDOVA

Introductory Survey

LOCATION, CLIMATE, LANGUAGE, RELIGION, FLAG, CAPITAL

The Republic of Moldova is a small, landlocked country situated in south-eastern Europe. It is bounded to the north, east and south by Ukraine, and to the west by Romania. The climate is favourable for agriculture, with long, warm summers and relatively mild winters. Average temperatures in Chişinău range from 21°C (70°F) in July to −4°C (24°F) in January. The official language was originally described by the 1994 Constitution as Moldovan, but, following a Constitutional Court ruling in December 2013, the name of the official language was to revert to Romanian (to which Moldovan is essentially identical), as stated in the 1991 Declaration of Independence. Most of the inhabitants of Moldova profess Orthodox Christianity. The national flag (proportions 1 by 2) consists of three equal vertical stripes, of light blue, yellow and red; the yellow stripe has at its centre the arms of Moldova (a shield bearing a stylized bull's head in yellow, set between an eight-pointed yellow star, a five-petalled yellow flower, and a yellow crescent, the shield being set on the breast of an eagle, in gold and red, which holds a green olive branch in its dexter talons, a yellow sceptre in its sinister talons, and a yellow cross in its beak). The capital is Chişinău.

CONTEMPORARY POLITICAL HISTORY

Historical Context

The area of the present-day Republic of Moldova corresponds to only part of the medieval principality of Moldova (Moldavia), which emerged as an important regional power in the 15th century. In the 16th century the principality came under Turkish Ottoman (Osmanlı) domination. Following conflict between the Ottoman and Russian Empires, Moldova was divided into two in 1812: Bessarabia, situated between the Prut and Dniester (Dnestr or Nistru) rivers, in the east, which roughly corresponds to the modern Republic of Moldova, was ceded to Russia, while the Ottomans retained control of western Moldova. A Romanian nationalist movement evolved during the 19th century, culminating in the proclamation of a Romanian state in 1877. In June 1918 Bessarabia was proclaimed an independent republic, but in November it voted to become part of Romania. This union was recognized in the Treaty of Paris (1920). The Union of Soviet Socialist Republics (established in 1922) refused to recognize Romania's claims to the territory, and in October 1924 formed a Moldovan Autonomous Soviet Socialist Republic (ASSR) on the eastern side of the Dniester, within the Ukrainian Soviet Socialist Republic (SSR). In June 1940 Romania was forced to cede Bessarabia and northern Bucovina to the USSR, under the terms of the Treaty of Non-Aggression, concluded with Nazi Germany in August 1939. Northern Bucovina, southern Bessarabia and the Kotovsk-Balta region of the Moldovan ASSR were incorporated into the Ukrainian SSR. The remaining parts of the Moldovan ASSR and of Bessarabia were merged to form the Moldovan SSR, which formally joined the USSR on 2 August 1940. Between July 1941 and 1944 the Moldovan SSR was reunited with Romania, forming part of a Transnistria Governorate, with its capital in Odesa (now in Ukraine). However, the Soviet Army reannexed the region in 1944, and the Moldovan SSR was re-established. As part of the Soviet policy to isolate the region from its historical links with Romania: cross-border traffic virtually ceased, the Cyrillic script was imposed on the Romanian language (which was referred to as Moldovan) and Russian and Ukrainian immigration was encouraged. In the 1950s thousands of ethnic Romanians were deported to Central Asia.

Domestic Political Affairs

In May 1989 a number of cultural and political groups, which were denied legal status, allied to form the Frontul Popular din Moldova (FPM—People's Front of Moldova). In June some 70,000 people attended a protest demonstration, organized by the FPM, on the anniversary of the Soviet annexation of Bessarabia in 1940. In August mass demonstrations were convened in the capital, Chişinău, in support of proposals by the Moldovan Supreme Soviet (Supreme Council—legislature) to declare Romanian the official language of the republic. Following protests by members of non-Romanian ethnic groups, the proposals were amended: legislation was enacted providing for Russian to be retained as a 'language of inter-ethnic communication', but the official language was to be Romanian, written in the Latin script. Following disturbances in Chişinău, on the anniversary of the Bolshevik Revolution on 7 November, the First Secretary of the ruling Partidul Comunist al Moldovei (PCM—Communist Party of Moldova), Semion Grossu, was dismissed. He was replaced by Petru Lucinschi.

The increasing influence of the Romanian-speaking population was strongly opposed by other inhabitants of the republic (who, at the 1989 census, comprised some 35% of the total population). In the areas east of the Dniester, Transnistria or Pridnestrovie, where Russians and Ukrainians predominated, the local authorities refused to implement the language law. Opposition to Moldovan nationalism was led by the Yedinstvo (Unity) Movement (dominated by leading PCM members) and the Slav-dominated Obyedinennyi Sovet Trudovykh Kollektivov (OSTK—United Council of Labour Collectives). Both organizations had links with Gagauz Halkı (Gagauz People), the most prominent of the political groups representing the 150,000-strong Gagauz minority (a Turkic, Orthodox Christian people, resident in southern Moldova). In January 1990 a referendum took place in the eastern town of Tiraspol, in which the predominantly Russian-speaking population voted to seek greater autonomy for Transnistria.

No independent political groups were officially allowed to endorse candidates in elections to the Moldovan Supreme Soviet in February 1990. About 80% of the 380 deputies elected were members of the PCM, but many were sympathetic to the aims of the FPM. The new Supreme Soviet convened in April; Mircea Snegur, a PCM member supported by the FPM, was elected its Chairman. The Government resigned in May, after losing a vote of no confidence. A new Council of Ministers, chaired by Mircea Druc revoked the PCM's constitutional right to power. On 23 June the Supreme Soviet adopted a declaration of sovereignty. In September Snegur was elected to the new post of President of the Republic.

The actions of the Romanian legislative majority provoked anxiety among minority ethnic groups. In August 1990 a 'Gagauz SSR' was proclaimed in the southern region around Comrat (Komrat); in September east-bank Slavs proclaimed the establishment of a secessionist 'Transdniestrian SSR' (containing much of Moldova's industry, and three of the republic's largest five cities), with its self-styled capital at Tiraspol. The Moldovan Supreme Soviet immediately annulled both declarations. In October Moldovan nationalists sought to thwart elections to a Gagauz Supreme Soviet, sending 50,000 armed volunteers to the area. Violence was prevented only by the dispatch of Soviet troops to the region. The new Gagauz Supreme Soviet convened in Comrat, electing Stepan Topal its President. Inter-ethnic violence occurred east of the Dniester in November, prior to elections to a Transnistrian Supreme Soviet.

In December 1990 around 800,000 people, attending a 'Grand National Assembly', voted to reject any new union treaty (as was being negotiated by other Soviet republics); in February 1991 the Moldovan Supreme Soviet resolved not to participate in the all-Union referendum on the future of the USSR. Despite the official boycott, in March some 650,000 people (mostly Russians, Ukrainians and Gagauz) did take part, voting almost unanimously for the preservation of the USSR. In May the designation 'Soviet Socialist' was removed from the republic's name and the Supreme Soviet was renamed Parlamentul (Parliament). In the same month, following a vote of no confidence by the legislature, Druc was removed as Prime Minister.

Independence

Following the attempted coup by conservative communists in Moscow in August 1991, the republican leadership immediately announced its support for the Russian President, Boris Yeltsin. On 27 August, after the coup had collapsed, Moldova proclaimed its independence. In September President Snegur ordered the creation of national armed forces and proscribed the PCM.

At the election to the republican presidency on 8 December 1991, Snegur, the sole candidate, received 98.2% of the votes cast. On 21 December Moldova was among the 11 signatories to the Almatı Declaration establishing the Commonwealth of Independent States (CIS, see p. 241). Moldovan affairs during the first half of 1992 were dominated by the armed conflict in Transnistria (see p. 3094) and by the question of possible unification with Romania, as advocated by the ruling FPM, which in February was re-formed as the Frontul Popular Creştin Democrat (FPCD—Christian Democratic Popular Front). However, popular support for unification remained insubstantial. In June the Government announced its resignation. Andrei Sangheli was appointed Prime Minister, and a new Government was formed, led by the Partidul Democrat Agrar din Moldova (PDAM—Agrarian Democratic Party of Moldova), which largely comprised members of the former communist leadership and which declared its commitment to consolidating Moldovan statehood, rejecting union with Romania.

During 1993 the PDAM drafted a new constitution. Multiparty elections to a new 104-member Parliament were held on 27 February 1994. Polling stations were not opened in Transnistria. The PDAM obtained an overall majority, with 56 seats. An alliance led by the Partidul Socialistilor din Moldova (Socialist Party of Moldova), the successor to the PCM, in alliance with Yedinstvo, won 28 seats. Two groups supporting unification with Romania shared the remaining 20 seats. In a referendum held on 6 March, more than 95% of the votes cast (by 75% of the electorate) supported continued independence. A new Council of Ministers led by Sangheli, solely comprising members of the PDAM, was appointed in April. In May the PCM was permitted to re-form; it became the Partidul Comuniştilor din Republica Moldova (PCRM—Party of Communists of the Republic of Moldova).

The new Constitution, adopted by Parliament in July 1994, entered into force in August, providing for a 'special autonomous status' for Transnistria and the Gagauz-majority areas, Gagauzia, within Moldova. The Constitution described the state language as Moldovan, written in the Latin script.

At the presidential election, held on 17 November 1996, Snegur received 39% of the votes cast, with Lucinschi second. In the 'run-off' election held on 1 December Lucinschi was elected President, with 54% of the votes cast. He was inaugurated as President in January 1997; a new Government, announced later that month, was headed by Ion Ciubuc, a non-party economist.

In parliamentary elections, held on 22 March 1998, the most successful party was the PCRM, led by Vladimir Voronin, which won 40 seats, with 30.1% of the votes cast, ahead of Snegur's Convenţia Democrată din Moldova (CDM—Democratic Convention of Moldova), with 26 seats, the Mişcarea pentru o Moldovă Democratică şi Prosperă (MMDP—Movement for a Democratic and Prosperous Moldova), with 24 seats, and the Partidul Forţelor Democratice (PFD—Party of Democratic Forces), with 11 seats. The PDAM failed to obtain representation. The new Government, appointed in May and led by Ciubuc, comprised members of the coalition led within Parliament by Snegur, including members of the MMDP, the CDM and the PFD.

Ciubuc resigned as Prime Minister in February 1999. One day later Snegur resigned as parliamentary leader of the governing coalition, after his nominee for the premiership was rejected. Lucinschi subsequently nominated Ion Sturza, the Deputy Prime Minister and Minister of the Economy and Reforms, as premier. Parliament narrowly approved Sturza's Government in March. Following local elections in May, the country was formally reorganized into nine provinces and two autonomous entities (Gagauzia and Transnistria, although the latter territory remained outside central government control). In November Sturza lost a parliamentary vote of confidence. Following the failure of Voronin and another candidate for the premiership to secure the necessary legislative support, President Lucinschi's nomination of Dumitru Braghiş was approved in December.

In July 2000 Parliament voted in favour of amending the Constitution to permit the legislature to elect the Head of State, and swiftly overturned President Lucinschi's veto of the amendment. Neither of the two candidates in the ensuing presidential election held in December—Voronin, and the Chairman of the Constitutional Court, Pavel Barbalat—obtained the requisite number of votes to secure victory after three rounds of voting. After four party factions boycotted a fourth round of voting on

21 December, Lucinschi dissolved the legislature and scheduled early parliamentary elections.

At the legislative elections, held on 25 February 2001, the PCRM secured 49.9% of the votes cast and 71 seats. The incumbent premier's Braghiş Alliance obtained 19 seats, and the Partidul Popular Creştin Democrat (PPCD—Christian Democratic People's Party, formerly the FPCD) obtained 11 seats. Organization for Security and Co-operation in Europe (OSCE, see p. 385) observers described the elections, in which 70% of the electorate participated, as free and fair. On 4 April Voronin was elected President, securing 71 legislative votes. Three days later Voronin nominated a non-partisan former businessman, Vasile Tarlev, as premier. Demonstrations, led by the PPCD, took place in Chişinău in January 2002, against the proposed introduction of the compulsory teaching of Russian language and history at schools. In February the only two non-PCRM members of the Council of Ministers tendered their resignations. Following further protests, the proposed reforms were retracted and the Minister of Education was dismissed on 26 February. One day later Vasile Draganel resigned as Minister of the Interior. In March the Deputy Chairman of the PPCD, Vlad Cubreacov, who had been involved in organizing the demonstrations (which the Supreme Court had ruled to be illegal), was kidnapped; he was discovered alive in May. At local elections, held on 25 May and 8 June, the PCRM won the majority of seats, followed by the newly formed Alianţa Moldova Noastră (AMN—Our Moldova Alliance). Following the elections, new legislation on administrative reform, approved in January, came into effect, according to which the provinces and autonomous regions were replaced with 33 districts and two municipalities. In July the AMN was formally constituted as a party, with Braghiş, Serafim Urechean (a former Mayor of Chişinău), and Veaceslav Untilă as its co-leaders. New legislation, approved in December, which sought to promote the use of Russian as a 'language of inter-ethnic communication', while retaining Moldovan as an official language, was a further cause of demonstrations.

From April 2004 the Partidul Democrat din Moldova (PDM—Democratic Party of Moldova, as the MMDP had been renamed) and the Partidul Social Liberal (PSL—Social Liberal Party) agreed to co-operate with the AMN, forming the Moldova Democrată (MD—Democratic Moldova) bloc. In the legislative elections, held on 6 March 2005, the PCRM won 46.0% of the votes cast and 56 seats, the MD bloc 28.5% (34 seats) and the PPCD 9.1% (11 seats). Although the PCRM held a majority of legislative seats, it did not hold the quorum of 61 necessary for the election of a president. At the inaugural session of Parliament, the PDM and PSL deputies withdrew from the MD bloc, which renamed itself the AMN faction. On 4 April Voronin was re-elected by 75 of the 101 deputies; the other candidate, Gheorghe Duca, who had also been nominated by the PCRM, received only one vote. Voronin was inaugurated as President on 7 April; on 19 April Parliament approved a new Government, again led by Tarlev and retaining many members of the previous Council of Ministers. In October Mihai Pop was appointed Minister of Finance, in succession to Zinaida Grecianîi, who became First Deputy Prime Minister. In November Braghiş left the AMN, leaving Urechean as the party's sole leader.

In June 2007 local elections were conducted throughout Moldova; voter turnout was recorded at 52.3%. Although the PCRM was the most successful party overall, Chirtoacă of the Partidul Liberal (PL—Liberal Party) was elected Mayor of Chişinău. On 19 March 2008 Tarlev and his Government resigned. Voronin subsequently nominated Grecianîi to the premiership. On 31 March Parliament voted to approve a new Government by 56 votes; Igor Dodon, the Minister of Economy and Trade, succeeded Grecianîi as First Deputy Prime Minister. In October the erstwhile Minister of Internal Affairs, Valentin Mejinschi, became Deputy Prime Minister.

Prolonged constitutional impasse

Elections to Parliament on 5 April 2009 resulted in a majority for the PCRM, which, according to preliminary results, secured about 49.5% of votes cast, while the PL won 13.1%, the Partidul Liberal Democrat din Moldova (PLDM—Liberal Democratic Party of Moldova) obtained 12.4% and the AMN received 9.8%. Despite a positive assessment of the conduct of the elections by the OSCE and other international observers, protests against alleged electoral malpractice began on 6 April. One day later anti-Government demonstrations degenerated into rioting, including attacks on parliamentary and presidential buildings, and some 200 demonstrators were arrested. Voronin accused the Romanian Government of organizing a coup attempt, and immediately undertook diplomatic reprisals (see *Regional relations*). On 12 April the Constitutional Court ordered a recount of the preliminary election results. Human rights groups corroborated claims that demonstrators in custody were subjected to assaults by police, and it was reported that at least three protesters had died following the arrests. Following negotiations with opposition leaders, mediated by the European Union (EU, see p. 271) Special Representative to Moldova, Voronin announced an amnesty for all suspects in detention or under investigation for involvement in the riots, excepting those with criminal records. On 20 April the Central Electoral Commission announced that the recount had not resulted in a significant change to the results of the poll: the PCRM had secured 60 seats in Parliament, while the PL and PLDM had each received 15 seats, and the AMN 11 seats. On 23 April the Constitutional Court endorsed the election results, and Voronin was elected legislative Chairman on 12 May.

Grecianîi and a further candidate nominated by the PCRM, Stanislav Gropa, contested a presidential election within Parliament on 20 May 2009. Although all 60 PCRM deputies supported Grecianîi, this was one vote too few for her election to be constitutionally valid, and the PL, PLDM and AMN deputies all boycotted the poll. A second ballot on 3 June was again inconclusive. On 10 June Parliament approved an acting, largely unchanged, Council of Ministers, headed by Grecianîi. Meanwhile, the PCRM suffered a reverse when a senior party member and former Chairman of Parliament, Marian Lupu, announced his departure from the party. Lupu joined the PDM (which then lacked legislative representation) later in the month, becoming its Chairman. In early June Parliament approved several amendments to the electoral code, reducing the threshold required for a party to secure parliamentary representation from 6% to 5% of the votes cast and reducing the minimum rate of voter participation required to validate elections from 50% of the electorate plus one vote to 33% plus one vote. On 15 June Voronin issued a decree dissolving Parliament, scheduling new elections for 29 July. On 16 June Voronin appointed PPCD Chairman Iurie Roșca as a Deputy Prime Minister.

Although the PCRM lost its majority at the elections to Parliament conducted on 29 July 2009, it remained the largest party in the legislature, securing 44.7% of the votes cast and 48 of the 101 seats. The PLDM increased its share of the votes cast to 16.6%, receiving 18 seats; the PL obtained 14.7% and 15 seats. The PDM increased its support substantially, obtaining 12.5% of the votes cast and 13 seats, while support for the AMN decreased, to 7.4% and seven seats. A turnout of 58.8% was recorded. On 8 August the PLDM, the PL, the PDM and the AMN announced the formation of a 53-member reformist and pro-EU parliamentary coalition, the Alianța pentru Integrare Europeană (AIE—Alliance for European Integration). On 28 August Mihai Ghimpu, the Chairman of the PL, was elected parliamentary Chairman. On 9 September Grecianîi resigned as Prime Minister. Two days later Voronin resigned as President; Ghimpu thus became acting President. On 17 September Ghimpu signed a decree nominating Vladimir Filat, the President of the PLDM, as Prime Minister. On 25 September a new Council of Ministers assumed office, in which seven posts (including that of Prime Minister) were allocated to the PLDM, five to the PL and four to each of the PDM and the AMN. One Deputy Prime Minister was appointed from each of the four coalition parties. Lupu was nominated as the AIE candidate in the forthcoming presidential election.

Two attempts by the new legislature to elect a President, on 10 November and 7 December 2009, failed. The PCRM boycotted voting, and all 53 deputies from the AIE voted in support of Lupu's candidacy, eight too few for the election to be validated. Consequently, in accordance with the constitutional norms, the legislature was to be dissolved, and further elections held. However, constitutional law dictated that a sitting of Parliament could not be dissolved less than one year after the most recent legislative dissolution. In an attempt to resolve this impasse, in December the Constitutional Court requested that the Venice Commission of the Council of Europe provide its legal opinion. In January 2010 a left-wing and pro-Russian faction of the PCRM announced the formation of the Partidul Moldova Unită—Yedinaya Moldova (United Moldova Party), under the leadership of Vladimir Țurcan, a former Minister of Internal Affairs and ambassador to Russia. In March 2010 the Venice Commission stated that the demand that Parliament be dissolved no more than once a year should take precedence over the requirement that parliamentary dissolution take place when the election of a President had proved impossible on two successive occasions. The Commission also recommended that Moldova adopt constitutional reforms in order to prevent any recurrence of the prolonged inability to elect a President. On 16 March the Constitutional Court confirmed that Parliament could be dissolved only after 16 June (one year after its previous dissolution).

Rival political factions subsequently developed alternative proposals for constitutional reform. On 18 June 2010 Parliament approved a number of amendments to the electoral code, which had been proposed by the AIE: the number of deputies required for a quorum was reduced from 52 to 51; the minimum requirement for a party to secure parliamentary representation was reduced from 5% to 4%, and for independent candidates from 3% to 2%; and the minimum required rate of participation in referendums was reduced from 60% to 33% of the electorate. On 7 July Parliament approved the scheduling of a referendum for 5 September on a new constitutional text, including provisions for the direct popular election of the President. Although 87.8% of the votes in the referendum supported the proposals, the rate of participation, at 30.3%, was insufficient for the reforms to be approved. (The PCRM and other opposition parties had urged a boycott of the plebiscite). On 28 September Ghimpu announced the dissolution of Parliament, and scheduled legislative elections.

The legislative elections on 28 November 2010 were contested by 20 political parties. Neither the PCRM nor the combined parties of the AIE (which had contested the election separately) secured the 61 legislative seats required to elect a new President. The PCRM again won the largest share of votes cast, with 39.3% and 42 seats; the PLDM, with 29.4% of votes, substantially increased its representation to 32 seats, the PDM, with 12.7%, obtained 15 seats, and the PL, with 10%, won 12 seats. Some 63.4% of the electorate voted. On 30 December Parliament elected Lupu as its Chairman, and consequently as acting President, with 57 votes. On 14 January 2011 the formation of a new AIE coalition Government, again under the premiership of Filat, was approved. Nevertheless, the ruling coalition's lack of the parliamentary majority required to elect a President or revise the Constitution presented a continued cause of concern. In February the Constitutional Court ruled that, as more than two months had passed since the expiry of the mandate of an elected President, Parliament had the right to decide when a presidential election should be held. In April the PLDM absorbed the AMN.

In September 2011 the Constitutional Court rejected a request by Parliament that a simple majority of deputies be permitted to elect the President. In October Alexandru Tănase was elected Chairman of the Constitutional Court to replace Dumitru Pulbere, who had demanded that Parliament be dissolved if it failed to elect a President by 28 September. In November Grecianîi, Dodon and a further parliamentary deputy defected from the PCRM to the Partidul Social Democrat (PSD—Social Democratic Party, a small party hitherto without parliamentary representation), prompting renewed hopes that the impasse would be resolved; however, the main political parties subsequently failed to agree on a consensus candidate. On 16 December a further attempt by the AIE to elect Lupu as President was unsuccessful, when he secured only 58 of the required 61 votes.

Nicolae Timofti elected President

From January 2012 the PCRM (which had renewed a boycott of parliamentary sessions) organized weekly protests in Chișinău to demand the resignation of the Government and the organization of further legislative elections. The AIE subsequently entered into negotiations with the PSD, and on 12 March the nomination of a single presidential candidate, an independent judge, Nicolae Timofti, was announced. On 16 March Timofti was elected President, with the support of the three PSD deputies, by 62 votes in Parliament. The PCRM contested the legitimacy of Timofti's election, on the grounds that the term of Parliament had been extended beyond the one-year period allowed to elect a President. In June a further three parliamentary deputies left the PCRM faction and became independents; later that month the PCRM ended its parliamentary boycott.

New legislation, supported by the Government, which had been adopted by Parliament in July 2012, prohibiting the use of communist symbols, entered into force on 1 October; the PCRM appealed to the Constitutional Court against the ban on communist symbols, and maintained that it would not comply with the requirement. In December the death of a businessman, Sorin Paciu, after he had been accidentally shot during a hunting party attended by senior members of the judiciary, including the

Prosecutor-General, Valeriu Zubco (a member of the PDM), precipitated considerable political controversy, including allegations that elements in the Government had sought to prevent an investigation into the circumstances of the shooting. Zubco resigned in January 2013, and charges relating to the incident were brought against another member of the hunting party, Andrei Usatov of the PLDM. The affair exacerbated conflict within the constituent parties of the coalition Government, in particular between the PDM (supported by the PL) and Filat's PLDM. In mid-February Filat effected the removal of a senior member of the PDM, Vladimir Plahotniuc, as First Vice-Chairman of Parliament, on grounds of corrupt business practices. The PDM-controlled National Anti-Corruption Centre subsequently initiated corruption investigations against Dorin Recean, the Minister of Internal Affairs, and two other PLDM ministers, prompting Filat to accuse Plahotniuc of orchestrating a campaign of denigration against his party members, while PDM Chairman Lupu issued demands for Filat's resignation. On 5 March Parliament adopted a motion of no confidence, proposed by the PCRM and supported by PDM deputies, effecting the collapse of Filat's administration. The Government formally resigned on 8 March, although Filat remained as acting Prime Minister until 25 April, when he resigned, after the Constitutional Court ruled that the loss of the vote of no confidence meant that he was ineligible to remain premier; he was succeeded, also in an acting capacity, by the erstwhile Deputy Prime Minister and Minister of Foreign Affairs, Iurie Leancă. In April a schism within the PL occurred, as supporters of the reform of the party and of the continuation of the pro-European coalition Government formed a new faction, the Consiliul de Reformare a Partidului Liberal (CRPL—Liberal Party Reform Council). The seven legislative deputies affiliated with the faction were subsequently expelled from the PL.

Following lengthy negotiations between the former AIE constituent parties (with the CRPL taking the place of the PL), on 30 May 2013 Parliament approved a new coalition Government, headed by Leancă, which principally comprised representatives of the PLDM, the PDM and the CRPL, and included many members of the outgoing administration. New ministers included Natalia Gherman (the daughter of former President Snegur and hitherto the chief negotiator with the EU) as Deputy Prime Minister, Minister of Foreign Affairs and European Integration. On the same day Igor Corman of the PDM was elected Chairman of Parliament. In August Anatol Arapu of the PLDM was appointed Minister of Finance, following the resignation from the post of Veaceslav Negruţă, who had been under investigation in connection with an illicit payment to a businessman. (In September Negruţă also announced his resignation from the PLDM.) Meanwhile, in August the CRPL reconstituted itself as the Partidul Liberal Reformator (PLR—Liberal Reformist Party); a former deputy chairman of the PL, Ion Hadârcă, subsequently became its leader.

In October 2013 agreement was reached with the Transnistrian authorities on the establishment of migration control checkpoints at the administrative border with Transnistria, as a prerequisite for the relaxation of EU visa restrictions for Moldovan citizens; Parliament subsequently adopted legislation accordingly. In December the Constitutional Court ruled that the description of Moldova's official language as Moldovan in the 1994 Constitution was invalid, and should be superseded by its prior description as Romanian in the 1991 Declaration of Independence. In February 2014 Vitalie Marinuţa was dismissed as Minister of Defence, following accusations of poor discipline within the military; he was succeeded in April by Valeriu Troenco, also a member of the PLR. An EU Association Agreement (see *Other external relations*) was ratified by Parliament on 2 July, in a vote that was boycotted by the PCRM.

Recent developments: the 2014 legislative elections

In November 2014 the Central Electoral Commission prohibited a populist pro-Russian party, Partidul Politic 'Patria' (Patria—Fatherland Political Party), from contesting forthcoming parliamentary elections, after a leaked audio recording appeared to show its leader, Renato Usatîi, discussing his close associations with the Russian Federal Security Service (FSB). This followed the discovery of large supplies of armaments in police raids against a pro-Russian extremist group with connections to Patria, and the arrest of five of the movement's members. Meanwhile, a meeting between the leaders of the pro-Russian Partidul Socialiştilor din Republica Moldova (PSRM—Party of Socialists of the Republic of Moldova) and Russian President Vladimir Putin in Moscow signalled Russian government

support for the party in the polls (after a deterioration in relations between the Russian authorities and PCRM leader Voronin).

At the elections to Parliament on 30 November 2014 the PSRM was placed first, with 20.5% of the votes cast and 25 seats, while the representation of the PCRM (which had received the support of the PSRM in the previous two polls) was reduced substantially to 17.5% and 21 seats. The PLDM, also suffering a loss in support, received 20.2% of the votes cast and 23 seats, the PDM 15.8% and 19 seats, and the PL 9.7% and 13 seats. Thus, the pro-European parties together retained a reduced majority in Parliament, and the results were welcomed by the EU. Following lengthy inter-party negotiations, however, it was announced on 23 January 2015 that the PLDM and PDM would form a new minority administration, since the PL had refused to join a new governing coalition. On 13 February the government proposed by Leancă, commanding only 42 seats, failed to secure parliamentary approval. On the following day, however, President Timofti appointed a new candidate nominated by the PLDM, Chiril Gaburici, as Prime Minister-designate. After the support of PCRM deputies was secured, a new minority Government of PLDM and PDM members, headed by Gaburici, was approved in Parliament on 18 February. The three deputy premierships were allocated, respectively, to PDM representatives Victor Osipov and Stephane Bride, the latter also receiving the economy portfolio, and Natalia Gherman of the PLDM, who also became Minister of Foreign Affairs and European Integration.

Gagauzia

During the Transnistrian conflict in 1991–92 (see Transnistria, see p. 3094), the situation in Gagauzia (which constitutes several non-contiguous territories in southern Moldova) remained peaceful, although the region continued to demand full statehood. The 1994 Moldovan Constitution provided for a 'special autonomous status' for Gagauzia, and in December of that year Parliament adopted legislation on the status of Gagauzia, providing for broad self-administrative powers and for Gagauz, Moldovan and Russia all to serve as official languages. Legislative power was to be vested in a regional assembly. A directly elected Başkan (Governor) was to hold a quasi-presidential position, and an Executive Committee as the regional government. The law entered into force in February 1995, and in March a local referendum was held to determine which settlements would form part of the region. Elections to the 35-seat Halk Toplusu (Popular Assembly) took place in May–June, while Gheorghe Tabunscic, the First Secretary of the branch of the PCRM in the principal Gagauz city, Comrat, was elected Başkan. Under the new Constitution, the Başkan became a member of the Council of Ministers of Moldova. In May 1999 Gagauzia, like Transnistria, was designated an autonomous entity within Moldova. Elections to the Popular Assembly and to the post of Başkan were held in August—September. Dumitru Croitor was elected Başkan, with 61.5% of the votes cast in a second round of voting. Croitor sought greater powers for Gagauzia, in particular campaigning for greater fiscal autonomy and for the right to restructure local administrative territorial units. In February 2002 the Popular Assembly adopted a vote of no confidence in Croitor, and scheduled a referendum in the hope of securing his dismissal. On 24 February, when the referendum was scheduled to take place, the regional security forces reportedly seized the offices of the regional electoral commission, declaring its mandate to have expired and the plebiscite to be illegal. President Voronin subsequently visited the region and demanded the resignations of both Croitor and the Chairman of the Popular Assembly. Croitor finally resigned in June. In a 'run-off' election held on 11 October, Tabunscic regained the post of Governor. On 25 July 2003 Parliament officially recognized the autonomous status of Gagauzia through an amendment to the national Constitution. Legislative elections were held in the region in November—December, in which the PCRM and independent candidates each won almost one-half of the seats contested. In December 2006 an independent candidate, Mihail Formuzal, was elected Governor at a second round of voting. Elections to the Popular Assembly took place in March 2008, with a voter turnout of 60.5%. A coalition formed by the PCRM with independent candidates commanded the greatest parliamentary representation, with 14 seats, while supporters of Formuzal won eight seats. In July an independent deputy and prominent journalist, Ana Harlamenco, was elected Chairman of the Popular Assembly. On 22 September the Popular Assembly adopted a resolution recognizing the separatist regions of Abkhazia and South

Ossetia as independent from Georgia, following Russian recognition of those territories as independent states, after a brief military conflict in August.

On 12 December 2010, in an election to the post of Governor, Formuzal (with around 37% of the votes cast) defeated Nicolai Duduglo, the Mayor of Comrat (who received 32%), and Irina Vlah of the PCRM, with 31%. The rate of participation was 57%. In a second round of voting on 26 December, Formuzal, with 51.4% of the votes cast, narrowly defeated Dudoglo, with 48.6%. The Court of Appeal in Comrat rejected an appeal by Dudoglo against the results, and monitors from the Council of Europe upheld the conduct of the elections, while noting certain irregularities. In March 2012 the Popular Assembly signed protocols of co-operation with the Supreme Council of Transnistria. The dismissal, in late June, by the Gagauz Executive Committee, of the territory's representative to Transnistria, Ivan Burguji (who was regarded as a close ally of the authorities there), was criticized by the Popular Assembly, which maintained that the decision required its approval. Elections to the Popular Assembly were conducted, in two rounds, on 9 and 23 September. Some 25 independent candidates were elected, together with seven representatives of the PCRM, two of the PLDM and one of the PSRM.

In March 2013 a group of deputies in the Popular Assembly, led by Burguji, commenced impeachment proceedings against Formuzal, on the grounds of alleged abuse of office, including his failure to consult with the Popular Assembly on the appointment of the regional chief of police. (However, removal of the Governor required endorsement by popular referendum.) On 27 November the Popular Assembly voted in favour of conducting a referendum in the territory on Moldova's EU orientation. A court in Comrat declared the referendum to be illegal in January 2014 and the Moldovan Government refused to provide funds for its organization. However, the Popular Assembly dismissed the court ruling as politically motivated and shortly afterwards, on 2 February, the referendum took place in Gagauzia. With a turnout of 70%, some 98.4% of those participating voted in favour of joining the Russian-led Customs Union, and 97.2% opposed EU integration; responding to a further question, 98.9% supported Gagauzia's right to secede from Moldova in the event that the country lost or surrendered its sovereignty. In March Formuzal met senior Russian officials during a visit to Moscow, when it was agreed that, despite Russia's continued embargo on the import of wine from other regions of Moldova, imports from Gagauzia would be permitted. A gubernatorial election was conducted in Gagauzia on 22 March 2015, when Vlah, who was formally a non-partisan candidate (having left the PCRM), but who was regarded as the favoured candidate of the Russian authorities, and enjoyed the support of the PSRM, was elected Başkan, receiving 51.0% of the votes cast, according to provisional figures, defeating a further nine candidates, including Dudoglo, who was placed second, with 19.1%.

Foreign Affairs

Regional relations

Owing to the changing domestic situation, Moldova's membership of the CIS was equivocal until early 1994. In August 1993 Parliament failed by four votes to ratify the Almatı Declaration, largely owing to the influence of deputies favouring unification with Romania. However, in September President Snegur signed a treaty to join the new CIS economic union. Following Moldova's parliamentary elections of February 1994 and the referendum in March, which strongly endorsed continued independence, Parliament reversed its earlier decision, and in April it finally ratified membership of the CIS. In May 2006 the leaders of Georgia, Ukraine, Azerbaijan and Moldova met in Kyiv, to revive the regional GUAM organization, renaming it the Organization for Democracy and Economic Development—GUAM (see p. 463).

The communist Government elected in 2001 initially undertook a policy of rapprochement with Russia, and in December Parliament ratified a treaty on friendship and co-operation, which had been signed by the two countries' Presidents in November. However, relations deteriorated from 2004, largely owing to developments associated with Transnistria. At the beginning of 2006 Russia attempted to increase the price charged to Moldova for supplies of natural gas. In January a compromise agreement was reached; in return for agreeing to relinquish the Transnistrian assets of the joint-venture company MoldovaGaz to the Russian state-controlled gas supplier, Gazprom (which already held a majority stake in the company), Moldova was to be charged a concessionary price for its gas supplies from Russia.

Leading officials of MoldovaGaz and Gazprom signed a five-year agreement, providing for staged increases in the price of gas supplied to Moldova, while the Moldovan Government was to transfer control of its gas distribution system to Gazprom. In March Russia suspended the import of Moldovan wine and other agricultural products, ostensibly owing to hygiene concerns; the embargo on wine imports was finally ended in late 2007.

Moldova's relations with Russia became further strained after the reformist Government of the AIE assumed office in September 2009. In 2011 Gazprom increased the price of gas supplied to Moldova by about 12% (in accordance with the existing agreement). In September 2013 Russia again prohibited the import of Moldovan wine, ostensibly on grounds of quality. A referendum that was conducted in Gagauzia in February 2014 (despite the opposition of the central authorities) expressed almost unanimous support for the territory joining Russia's customs union, in preference to establishing closer relations with the EU. The Government came under increasing pressure following Russia's de facto military seizure and subsequent annexation of the Crimean peninsula in March (see the chapter on Ukraine), which prompted domestic and international concerns that Russia might undertake similar action in Transnistria; Prime Minister Iurie Leancă appealed to the international community to preserve the territorial unity of Moldova. In the context of escalating conflict in eastern Ukraine and the signature of an Association Agreement by the Moldovan authorities with the EU (see *Other external relations*), in July the Russian authorities extended the embargo on Moldovan imports to include most fruit, vegetables and meat. President Putin was reported to have influenced the success of the pro-Russian PSRM in elections in November (see *Recent developments*). In March 2015 President Timofti voiced further protest at the visit of two Russian parliamentary deputies to meet pro-Russian candidate Irina Vlah in advance of the gubernatorial election in Gagauzia later that month (in which Vlah was the victorious candidate), indicating that further such visits would be prohibited.

Relations with Romania were subject to tensions. A basic political treaty, agreed in 1999, was not signed. In February 2000 many Moldovans applied to obtain Romanian citizenship as formal negotiations on Romania's accession to the EU commenced. Romania subsequently introduced measures to simplify the application process, angering the Moldovan authorities, since the Moldovan Constitution prohibited dual citizenship. The situation was resolved later in the year when Moldova approved legislation permitting its citizens to hold dual citizenship with Israel, Romania or Russia. In March 2007 Moldova strongly criticized Romania for granting Romanian citizenship to large numbers of Moldovans, on the grounds that the policy undermined Moldova's statehood. Romania's accession to full EU membership, which took effect in January 2007, resulted in Moldovan citizens being required to possess entry visas to enter that country; in protest against this, the Moldovan authorities reversed a decision to allow Romania to open two new consulates in the country. In December Moldova expelled two Romanian diplomats, who had allegedly supplied funds to opposition newspapers, for activities 'incompatible with their status'.

The civil disturbances that followed Moldovan legislative elections in April 2009, which led the Government to accuse Romania of organizing an attempted coup, prompted the imposition of a number of sanctions against Romania: most notably, the expulsion of the Romanian ambassador; the recall of the Moldovan envoy to Romania; and the immediate introduction of visa requirements for Romanians entering Moldova. The Romanian President, Traian Băsescu, subsequently pledged that the Romanian Government would expedite the process of granting Romanian citizenship to Moldovans, claiming that some 1m. applications had been received. The visa requirements for Romanian citizens wishing to visit Moldova were rescinded in September. On 8 November 2010 Prime Minister Filat and the Romanian Minister of Foreign Affairs signed the bilateral treaty confirming the border between the two states and providing for closer co-operation. Băsescu made an official visit to Chişinău in July 2013, when he affirmed Romania's support for Moldova's EU integration process. In August 2014 a natural gas pipeline linking the Moldovan border town of Ungheni and the Romanian city of Iaşi was inaugurated at a ceremony attended by Leancă and his Romanian counterpart, Viktor Ponta; once fully operational, the pipeline was intended to begin Moldova's integration into the EU gas market and to reduce its dependence on energy imports from Russia.

Other external relations

Moldova became part of the EU's Eastern Partnership programme, which envisaged free trade and visa arrangements with a number of regional states, in May 2009. Negotiations on an EU Association Agreement began in January 2010. In March 2011, following the installation of a new AIE coalition administration, US Vice-President Joe Biden met government leaders in Chişinău (becoming the most senior US official to have visited Moldova). Following negotiations on co-operation with the EU in the area of Common Security and Defence Policy, on 13 December 2012 a Framework Agreement for the participation of Moldova in EU crisis management operations was signed. In the same month the US Senate endorsed a vote by the lower House of Representatives to end longstanding trade restrictions (imposed against the USSR in 1974) on Moldova. Following the conclusion of negotiations in mid-2013, the Association Agreement, which included the implementation of a Deep and Comprehensive Free Trade Area (DCFTA), was initialled at an EU summit meeting in Vilnius, Lithuania, in November. Following Russia's de facto military seizure and annexation of the Ukrainian region of Crimea (see the chapter on Ukraine), in February–March 2014 Moldovan premier Leancă was invited to visit the USA, where, during meetings with senior officials, he urged a strong response with regard to a potential threat from the Russian military bases in Transnistria. Later in March Russian military exercises were staged in Transnistria, while the US Administration pledged a further $10m. towards the strengthening of Moldova's border security. In April the EU ended visa restrictions for Moldovan citizens holding biometric passports and wishing to visit the Schengen Area (of 26 European States with open borders) for no more than 90 days. Signature of the Association Agreement with the EU was brought forward, and took place on 27 June. The Agreement was ratified by the Moldovan legislature on 2 July, and was provisionally implemented, together with the DCFTA, from 1 September.

CONSTITUTION AND GOVERNMENT

Under the Constitution of 1994, as subsequently amended, supreme legislative power is held by the unicameral Parlamentul (Parliament), which is directly elected every four years. Parliament comprises 101 members. The President is Head of State and holds executive power in conjunction with the Council of Ministers, led by the Prime Minister. The President is elected by the legislature for a four-year term. Judicial power is exercised by the Supreme Court of Justice, the Court of Appeal, tribunals and courts of law. Judges sitting in the courts of law and the Supreme Court of Justice are appointed by the President following proposals by the Higher Magistrates' Council. The country is divided into 32 districts (raione), three municipalities (one of which, Tighina—Bendery, was outside government control), one autonomous territorial unit (Gagauzia) and one territorial unit (The Left Bank of the Nistru, or Transnistria, which remained outside government control in mid-2015).

REGIONAL AND INTERNATIONAL CO-OPERATION

Moldova is a member of the Commonwealth of Independent States (CIS, see p. 241), the Council of Europe (see p. 250), the Organization for Security and Co-operation in Europe (OSCE, see p. 385) and the Organization of the Black Sea Economic Cooperation (BSEC, see p. 399).

Moldova joined the UN in 1992 and became a member of the World Trade Organization (WTO, see p. 431) in 2001.

ECONOMIC AFFAIRS

In 2013, according to estimates by the World Bank, Moldova's gross national income (GNI), measured at average 2011–13 prices, was US $8,772m., equivalent to $2,460 per head (or $5,190 per head on an international purchasing-power parity basis). During 2004–13, it was estimated, the population decreased at an average annual rate of 0.1%, while gross domestic product (GDP) per head increased, in real terms, at an average annual rate of 4.4%. Overall GDP increased, in real terms, at an average annual rate of 4.3% in 2004–13; GDP decreased by 0.7% in 2012, but increased by 8.9% in 2013.

As a result of its extremely fertile land and temperate climate, Moldova's economy is dominated by agriculture and related industries. Some 85% of the country's terrain is cultivated. Agriculture (including hunting, forestry and fishing) contributed 14.5% of GDP and engaged 28.8% of the employed labour force in 2013. Principal crops include wine grapes and other fruit, tobacco, vegetables and grain. The wine industry has traditionally occupied a central role in the economy. According to the World Bank, the GDP of the agricultural sector, in real terms, declined by an average annual rate of 0.4% during 2004–13; agricultural GDP decreased, in real terms, by 20.2% in 2012, but increased by 41.0% in 2013.

Industry (including mining, manufacturing, power and construction) contributed 20.7% of GDP and engaged 17.7% of the employed labour force in 2013. In 2004–13, according to the World Bank, industrial GDP decreased at an average rate of 0.5% per year; industrial GDP increased by 0.8% in 2012 and by 7.4% in 2013.

Mining and quarrying contributed 0.5% of GDP in 2013, and employed just 0.3% of the employed labour force in 2008. Moldova has extremely limited mineral resources. Activity is focused primarily on the extraction and processing of industrial minerals such as gypsum, limestone, sand and gravel. Deposits of petroleum and natural gas were discovered in southern Moldova in the early 1990s; total reserves of natural gas have been estimated at 22,000m. cu m.

The manufacturing sector contributed 13.8% of GDP in 2013 and engaged 10.9% of the employed labour force in 2008. The sector is dominated by food-processing, wine and tobacco production, machine-building and metal-working, and light industry. According to the World Bank, manufacturing GDP increased, in real terms, by an annual average of 0.6% in 2004–13. Manufacturing GDP increased by 1.8% in 2012 and by 8.8% in 2013.

Construction contributed 3.9% of GDP and engaged 5.5% of the employed labour force in 2013.

Moldova relies heavily on imported energy—primarily natural gas and petroleum products—from Russia, Romania and Ukraine. In the mid-2000s Moldova announced its intention to diversify its gas suppliers, and to increase domestic energy production substantially; domestic production represented 23.3% of consumption in 2004. A large proportion of natural gas imports supply the Moldoveneasca power station, located in Transnistria, which contributes much of the country's electricity-generating capacity. The growing importance of natural gas to the generation of electricity has been paralleled by the rapid decline, from the mid-1990s, in the importance of coal-fired power sources; whereas in 1995 some 31.5% of electricity generated in Moldova was of coal origin, by 2004 the contribution of coal to electricity generation was negligible. In February 2005 an Azerbaijani company purchased the unfinished Giurgiulesti petroleum terminal in southern Moldova; the terminal commenced operations in September 2007. Natural gas accounted for 93.6% of electricity production in 2011, when hydroelectric power accounted for 6.1%. Mineral products comprised 22.9% of the value of total merchandise imports in 2013.

Services accounted for 64.8% of GDP and engaged 53.5% of the employed labour force in 2013. The GDP of the services sector increased, in real terms, at an annual average rate of 7.0% in 2004–13. Services GDP increased by 5.2% in 2012 and by only 1.5% in 2013.

In 2013 Moldova recorded a visible merchandise trade deficit of US $3,118.8m., while there was a deficit of $452.3m. on the current account of the balance of payments. In 2013 the principal source of imports was Russia (accounting for 14.3% of the value of total imports). Other major suppliers were Romania, Ukraine, the People's Republic of China, Germany, Turkey and Italy. The main market for exports in that year was Russia (accounting for 26.0% of the value of total exports). Other important purchasers were Romania, Italy, Ukraine and Turkey. In 2013 the principal imports were mineral products, machinery and mechanical appliances, chemicals and related products, prepared foodstuffs, beverages and tobacco, textiles and textile articles, base metals, plastics and rubber, and vehicles and associated transport equipment. The main exports in that year were vegetable products, foodstuffs, beverages and tobacco, textiles and textile articles, machinery and mechanical appliances, chemicals and related products, and base metals.

In 2013 the consolidated state budget recorded a deficit of 1,751m. Moldovan lei, equivalent to 1.7% of GDP. Moldova's general government gross debt was 23.915m. Moldovan lei in 2013, equivalent to 23.8% of GDP. At the end of 2012 Moldova's total external debt totalled US $6,135m., of which $942m. was public and publicly guaranteed debt. In that year, the cost of servicing long-term public and publicly guaranteed debt and repayments to the IMF was equivalent to 15.1% of the value of exports of goods, services and income (excluding workers' remittances). According to the International Labour Organization

(ILO), consumer prices increased at an annual average rate of 7.4% during 2005–14. Consumer prices increased by 5.1% in 2014. The average rate of unemployment was 5.1% in 2013.

Although the economy recorded growth from 2000, Moldova remained the poorest country in Europe. In October 2011 Moldova and seven other member states of the Commonwealth of Independent States (CIS, see p. 241) signed a free trade agreement (although its enactment was delayed pending ratification by all signatory states). In December 2012 the US legislature ended longstanding trade restrictions against Moldova. Following the conclusion of negotiations with the European Union (EU, see p. 271) in mid-2013, an Association Agreement, which provided for the implementation of a Deep and Comprehensive Free Trade Area (DCFTA), was initialled at a summit meeting in November. The Russian Government reimposed a ban on the import of Moldovan wine in September 2013; nevertheless, it was confirmed in October that a Russian consortium had been granted a concession to manage Chișinău International Airport for a 49-year period. A three-year IMF credit facility expired in early 2013, after which the Fund conducted post-programme monitoring discussions with the Moldovan authorities. The IMF and World Bank both expressed support for the Government's National Development Strategy 'Moldova 2020' of structural reforms. However, Moldova's economy was severely affected by the regional impact of continued conflict in Ukraine during 2014, and consequent severe recession in Russia. Total remittances to Moldova fell by 31% year-on year in December. The signature of the Association Agreement with the EU, together with the DCFTA, was brought forward to 27 June, and was followed in July by the extension of Russia's embargo on Moldovan wine imports to include most fruit, vegetables and meat. The construction of a natural gas pipeline between Moldova and Romania was completed in August, in accordance with the Moldovan authorities' priority to reduce dependence on Russian energy imports. Following the collapse of the Russian rouble, the leu weakened by 19% against the US dollar in 2014, and, despite efforts by the central bank, which repeatedly raised interest rates and sold nearly 10% of its foreign currency reserves in early 2015, it had fallen in value by a further 25% by late February. After a recovery amounting to nearly 9% growth in 2013, GDP growth in 2014 was estimated at just 2.0%.

PUBLIC HOLIDAYS

2016: 1 January (New Year's Day), 7–8 January (Russian Orthodox Christmas), 8 March (International Women's Day), 1 May (Labour Day), 1–2 May (Orthodox Easter), 9 May (Victory and Commemoration Day and 'Paștele Blajinilor', Parents' Day), 27 August (Independence Day), 31 August ('Limbă Noastră', National Language Day), 24–25 December (Romanian Orthodox Christmas).

Statistical Survey

Principal source (unless otherwise indicated): State Department for Statistics and Sociology, 2028 Chișinău, șos. Hîncești 53D; tel. (22) 73-37-74; fax (22) 22-61-46; e-mail dass@statistica.md; internet www.statistica.md.

Note: Most data from 1993 onwards exclude the Transnistria (Pridnestrovie) region, which remained outside central government control.

Area and Population

AREA, POPULATION AND DENSITY

Area (sq km)	33,800*
Population (census results)†	
12 January 1989	4,335,360
5–12 October 2004	
Males	1,627,689
Females	1,755,643
Total	3,383,332
12–15 May 2014 (preliminary)‡	2,913,281
Population (official estimates at 1 January)‡	
2012	3,559,541
2013	3,559,497
2014	3,557,634
Density (per sq km) at 1 January 2014‡	105.3

* 13,050 sq miles.
† Figures refer to the *de jure* population. The total at the 1989 census was 4,337,592 (males 2,058,160, females 2,279,432).
‡ Excluding Transnistria; official estimates not adjusted to take account of the preliminary results of the 2014 census.

POPULATION BY AGE AND SEX
(official estimates at 1 January 2014)

	Males	Females	Total
0–14 years	293,202	276,040	569,242
15–64 years	1,284,280	1,347,005	2,631,285
65 years and over	134,024	223,083	357,107
Total	1,711,506	1,846,128	3,557,634

POPULATION BY ETHNIC GROUP*
(permanent inhabitants, 2004 census)

	Number	%
Moldovan	2,564,849	75.8
Ukrainian	282,406	8.4
Russian	201,218	5.9
Gagauz	147,500	4.4
Romanian	73,276	2.2
Bulgarian	65,662	1.9
Others and unknown	48,421	1.4
Total	3,383,332	100.0

* According to official declaration of nationality.

Note: Classification of ethnicity reflects national census methodology.

ADMINISTRATIVE DIVISIONS
('000, population at 1 January 2014, official estimates)

Districts (raione)				
Anenii Noi . .	83.4		Nisporeni . . .	66.1
Basarabeasca . .	28.7		Ocnița	54.9
Briceni . . .	73.9		Orhei	125.4
Cahul . . .	124.7		Rezina	51.2
Cantemir . .	62.3		Rîșcani	68.7
Călărași . . .	78.5		Sîngerei	92.6
Căușeni . . .	91.3		Soroca	100.1
Cimișlia . . .	60.8		Strășeni . . .	92.1
Criuleni . . .	73.7		Șoldănești . . .	42.4
Dondușeni . .	43.7		Ștefan Vodă . .	71.0
Drochia . . .	88.5		Taraclia	44.0
Dubăsari . .	35.2		Telenești . . .	73.1
Edineț . . .	81.6		Ungheni . . .	117.4
Fălești . . .	91.9		*Municipalities*	
Florești . . .	88.7		Bălți	149.8
Glodeni . . .	60.4		Chișinău . . .	804.5
			Autonomous	
Hîncești . . .	121.2		*Territory*	
Ialoveni . . .	100.7		Gagauzia . . .	161.9
Leovà	53.2		**Total**	3,557.6

Population of Transnistria, including Bendery (Tighina) (estimated figure obtained as residual from total country population estimates at 1 January 2003): 601,088.

PRINCIPAL TOWNS
(population at census of 5–12 October 2004)

Chişinău (capital) .	589,455	Soroca	28,362
Bălţi	122,669	Orhei	25,641
Cahul	35,488	Comrat . . .	23,327
Ungheni . . .	32,530	Ceadîr-Lunga . .	19,401

Population at 1 January 2014 (official estimates): Chişinău 674,500, Bălţi 144,900, Cahul 39,600, Ungheni 38,400, Soroca 37,500, Orhei 33,600, Comrat 26,000, Ceadîr-Lunga 22,800.

Principal Towns within Transnistria (estimated population at Moldovan census of 1 January 1996): Tiraspol 187,000; Bendery (Tighina, Bender) 128,000; Rybnitsa (Râbniţa) 62,900.

IMMIGRATION AND EMIGRATION

	2011	2012	2013
Immigrants	2,704	3,093	3,349
Emigrants	3,920	3,062	2,585

BIRTHS, MARRIAGES AND DEATHS

	Registered live births		Registered marriages		Registered deaths	
	Number	Rate (per 1,000)	Number	Rate (per 1,000)	Number	Rate (per 1,000)
2006 . .	37,587	10.5	27,128	7.6	43,137	12.0
2007 . .	37,973	10.6	29,213	8.2	43,050	12.0
2008 . .	39,018	10.9	26,666	7.5	41,948	11.8
2009 . .	40,803	11.4	26,781	7.5	42,139	11.8
2010 . .	40,474	11.4	26,483	7.4	43,631	12.2
2011 . .	39,162	11.0	25,889	7.3	39,234	11.0
2012 . .	39,435	11.1	24,262	6.8	39,560	11.1
2013 . .	37,871	10.6	24,449	6.9	38,060	10.7

Life expectancy (years at birth): 71.9 (males 68.1; females 75.6) in 2013.

ECONOMICALLY ACTIVE POPULATION
(labour force survey, '000 persons aged 15 years and over)

	2011	2012	2013
Agriculture, hunting, forestry and fishing	323.0	303.3	337.9
Industry	153.2	150.9	142.4
Construction	66.8	70.2	65.0
Wholesale and retail trade; repair of motor vehicles, motorcycles and personal and household goods; hotels and restaurants .	223.0	209.3	211.4
Transport, storage and communications	67.0	70.5	73.2
Public administration and defence; compulsory social security; education; health and social work	250.2	247.1	235.6
Other community, social and personal service activities . .	90.4	95.5	107.2
Total employed	1,173.5	1,146.8	1,172.8
Unemployed	84.0	67.7	63.1
Total labour force	1,257.5	1,214.5	1,235.8
Males	642.3	618.4	630.8
Females	615.3	596.1	605.0

Health and Welfare

KEY INDICATORS

Total fertility rate (children per woman, 2012)	1.5
Under-5 mortality rate (per 1,000 live births, 2012) . . .	18
HIV/AIDS (% of persons aged 15–49, 2013)	0.6
Physicians (per 1,000 head, 2011)	3.6
Hospital beds (per 1,000 head, 2009)	6.2
Health expenditure (2011): US $ per head (PPP) . . .	436
Health expenditure (2011): % of GDP	11.4
Health expenditure (2011): public (% of total)	45.5
Access to water (% of persons, 2012)	97
Access to sanitation (% of persons, 2012)	87
Total carbon dioxide emissions ('000 metric tons, 2010) . .	4,855.1
Carbon dioxide emissions per head (metric tons, 2010) . .	1.4
Human Development Index (2013): ranking	114
Human Development Index (2013): value	0.663

For sources and definitions, see explanatory note on p. vi.

Agriculture

PRINCIPAL CROPS
('000 metric tons)

	2011	2012	2013
Wheat	794.8	495.2	1,008.6
Barley	194.0	117.9	218.6
Maize	1,468.3	572.4	1,419.2
Potatoes	350.8	182.0	239.5
Sugar beet	588.6	587.0	1,009.0
Beans, dry	17.0	5.5	11.9
Peas, dry	13.3	10.1	9.9
Sunflower seed	427.4	296.2	504.5
Cabbages and other brassicas .	35.1	23.1	29.0
Tomatoes	83.4	48.5	54.3
Cucumbers and gherkins . .	26.0	20.5	23.1
Chillies and peppers, green . .	24.0	14.6	14.4
Aubergines (Eggplants) . .	7.1	4.2	4.5
Onions, dry	58.3	37.2	51.2
Carrots and turnips . . .	14.3	11.3	17.8
Watermelons	81.8	50.9	53.0
Apples	268.8	281.8	307.2
Plums and sloes	35.0	49.3	55.6
Grapes	594.8	505.9	612.7
Tobacco, unmanufactured . . .	5.4	2.9	2.2

Aggregate production ('000 metric tons, may include official, semi-official or estimated data): Total cereals 2,466.4 in 2011, 1,191.7 in 2012, 2,654.3 in 2013; Total vegetables (incl. melons) 447.7 in 2011, 286.7 in 2012, 349.8 in 2013; Total fruits (excl. melons) 959.0 in 2011, 876.7 in 2012, 1,019.0 in 2013.

Source: FAO.

LIVESTOCK
('000 head at 1 January)

	2011	2012	2013
Horses	52.2	43.6	46.4
Cattle	216.0	203.9	191.2
Pigs	478.5	438.6	410.4
Sheep	787.9	709.9	695.1
Goats	117.6	122.5	128.9
Chickens	34,000*	26,520*	26,000†

* Unofficial figure.
† FAO estimate.

Source: FAO.

LIVESTOCK PRODUCTS
('000 metric tons)

	2011	2012	2013
Cattle meat	9.7	9.5	9.7*
Sheep meat	2.1	2.1	2.1*
Pig meat	63.9	64.5	65.5*
Chicken meat	41.3	38.8	39.0*
Cows' milk	525.8	489.6	485.9
Sheep's milk	22.4	18.7	23.0*
Goats' milk	11.9	16.4	18.0*
Hen eggs*	39.3	34.8	34.5
Honey	2.7	2.6	2.5†
Wool, greasy	2.0	1.8	1.9

* Unofficial figure(s).
† FAO estimate.
Source: FAO.

Forestry

ROUNDWOOD REMOVALS
('000 cubic metres, excl. bark)

	2011	2012	2013
Sawlogs, veneer logs and logs for sleepers	26*	33†	30†
Other industrial wood	17	—	—
Fuel wood	309	489	522
Total	352	521	551

* FAO estimate.
† Unofficial figure.
Source: FAO.

SAWNWOOD PRODUCTION
('000 cubic metres, incl. railway sleepers)

	2011*	2012	2013
Coniferous (softwood)	16	11	2
Broadleaved (hardwood)	18	7	1
Total	34	18	3

* FAO estimates.
Source: FAO.

Fishing

(metric tons, live weight)

	2010	2011	2012
Capture	44	50*	50*
Common carp	2	2*	2*
Crucian carp	9	10*	10*
Aquaculture*	8,800	9,300	9,500
Common carp*	2,900	3,200	3,300
Silver carp*	4,500	4,700	4,700
Total catch*	8,844	9,350	9,550

* FAO estimate(s).
Source: FAO.

Mining

('000 metric tons unless otherwise indicated)

	2010	2011	2012
Limestone*	196.9	295.5	264.5
Gypsum*	99.8	100.5	115.1
Sand and gravel	3,109.7	4,098.8	4,262.3
Peat*†	475	475	n.a.

* Source: US Geological Survey.
† Estimated production.
2013: Sand and gravel 5,293.3.

Industry

SELECTED PRODUCTS
('000 metric tons unless otherwise indicated)

	2011	2012	2013
Fruit and vegetable preserves	67.0	77.8	n.a.
Flour	118.2	101.9	113.1
Raw sugar	88.4	83.4	140.3
Wine ('000 hectolitres)	1,250	1,410	1,400
Mineral water ('000 hectolitres)	1,080	1,070	950
Soft drinks ('000 hectolitres)	720	720	640
Footwear ('000 pairs, excl. rubber)	2,849	3,053	2,940
Glasses and bottles (million)	326.3	223.1	272.5
Electric energy (million kWh)	1,016	932	900*

* Rounded figure.

Cement ('000 metric tons, estimates): 1,100 in 2010; 1,400 in 2011; 1,500 in 2012 (Source: US Geological Survey).

Finance

CURRENCY AND EXCHANGE RATES

Monetary Units
100 bani (singular: ban) = 1 Moldovan leu (plural: lei).

Sterling, Dollar and Euro Equivalents (31 December 2014)
£1 sterling = 24.372 lei;
US $1 = 15.615 lei;
€1 = 18.958 lei;
1,000 Moldovan lei = £41.03 = $64.04 = €52.75.

Average Exchange Rate (Moldovan lei per US $)
2012   12.111
2013   12.587
2014   14.036

STATE BUDGET
(million lei)

Revenue	2011	2012	2013
Tax revenue	25,580	28,863	32,173
Taxes on personal incomes	2,341	3,994	4,258
Domestic taxes on goods and services	13,581	14,335	16,461
Taxes on ownership	281	301	314
Taxes on international trade	1,179	1,287	1,417
Social Fund contributions	6,563	7,150	7,756
Health Fund contributions	1,636	1,798	1,967
Non-tax revenue	1,179	1,341	1,352
Other revenue	3,381	3,327	3,375
Total	30,140	33,530	36,900

Expenditure	2011	2012	2013
Economic services	3,616	4,611	5,801
Social and cultural services	22,946	24,625	26,003
Education	6,869	7,397	7,064
Health	4,260	4,750	5,227
Social assistance and security	11,066	11,626	12,692
Recreational and cultural services	751	852	1,020
Defence services	2,156	2,303	2,773
General state services	1,457	1,751	2,084
External trade	229	243	273
State debt service	662	666	493
Other expenditures	1,035	1,174	1,224
Total	32,101	35,374	38,651

INTERNATIONAL RESERVES
(excluding gold, US $ million at 31 December)

	2012	2013	2014
IMF special drawing rights	1.59	6.41	1.19
Reserve position in IMF	0.01	0.01	0.01
Foreign exchange	2,509.45	2,811.35	2,152.60
Total	2,511.05	2,817.77	2,153.80

Source: IMF, *International Financial Statistics*.

MONEY SUPPLY
(million lei at 31 December)

	2012	2013	2014
Currency outside depository corporations	13,240.80	17,550.46	17,500.10
Transferable deposits	10,721.34	13,485.06	14,528.36
Other deposits	25,551.18	31,595.99	34,113.56
Securities other than shares	0.12	—	—
Broad money	49,513.44	62,631.52	66,142.02

Source: IMF, *International Financial Statistics*.

COST OF LIVING
(Consumer Price Index; base: previous year = 100)

	2012	2013	2014
Food and beverages	103.8	106.6	106.5
Other consumer goods	104.2	104.3	105.5
Services	106.2	102.6	102.5
All items (incl. others)	104.6	104.6	105.1

NATIONAL ACCOUNTS
(million lei at current prices, excl. Transnistria)

Expenditure on the Gross Domestic Product

	2011	2012	2013
Final consumption expenditure	96,090.5	103,062.6	113,169.0
Households	78,104.1	83,664.0	92,910.4
General government	16,583.6	17,838.3	18,539.9
Non-profit institutions serving households	1,402.8	1,560.3	1,718.7
Gross capital formation	19,904.0	20,860.9	24,783.3
Gross fixed capital formation. Acquisitions, less disposals, of valuables	19,178.8	20,864.1	23,061.7
Changes in inventories	725.2	−3.2	1,721.6
Total domestic expenditure	115,994.5	123,923.5	137,952.3
Exports of goods and services	37,033.6	38,364.0	43,564.8
Less Imports of goods and services	70,679.4	74,059.8	81,006.6
GDP in market prices	82,348.7	88,227.8	100,510.5

Gross Domestic Product by Economic Activity

	2011	2012	2013
Agriculture, hunting, forestry and fishing	10,095.2	9,896.2	12,383.1
Mining and quarrying	348.8	364.9	460.8
Manufacturing	9,354.7	10,032.5	11,789.4
Electricity, gas and water supply	1,814.8	1,916.4	2,077.6
Construction	2,719.9	3,041.4	3,372.7
Wholesale and retail trade; repair of motor vehicles, motorcycles and personal and household goods	11,119.2	12,110.7	13,712.6
Hotels and restaurants	1,006.5	1,107.0	1,202.9
Transport, storage and communications	9,001.6	9,433.0	10,093.2
Financial intermediation	4,135.6	4,169.0	4,441.7
Real estate, renting and business activities	6,841.9	7,796.7	8,836.4
Public administration and defence; compulsory social security	3,038.4	3,423.3	3,980.7
Education	5,184.0	5,790.4	6,040.5
Health and social work	3,310.7	3,826.8	4,151.0
Other community, social and personal services	2,192.5	2,521.0	2,887.9
Sub-total	70,164.0	75,429.2	85,430.4
Less Financial intermediation services indirectly measured	1,774.5	1,743.1	1,710.9
Gross value added in basic prices	68,389.6	73,686.1	83,719.5
Taxes, less subsidies, on products and imports	13,959.1	14,541.7	16,791.0
GDP in market prices	82,348.7	88,227.8	100,510.5

BALANCE OF PAYMENTS
(US $ million)

	2011	2012	2013
Exports of goods	1,749.4	1,697.3	1,897.7
Imports of goods	−4,716.1	−4,738.8	−5,016.5
Balance on goods	−2,966.7	−3,041.5	−3,118.8
Exports of services	960.0	1,034.1	1,139.3
Imports of services	−831.4	−907.7	−987.4
Balance on goods and services	−2,838.0	−2,915.1	−2,966.9
Primary income received	926.8	1,049.4	1,163.4
Primary income paid	−355.2	−235.1	−302.6
Balance on goods, services and primary income	−2,266.5	−2,100.8	−2,106.1
Secondary income received	1,519.4	1,625.2	1,790.9
Secondary income paid	−104.9	−126.4	−137.0
Current balance	−851.9	−602.0	−452.3
Capital account (net)	−29.5	−36.7	−35.5
Direct investment assets	−33.8	−29.6	−41.6
Direct investment liabilities	301.4	204.9	249.0
Portfolio investment assets	−5.2	7.0	−0.4
Portfolio investment liabilities	5.1	14.4	10.2
Financial derivatives and employee stock options assets	—	−0.2	−0.1
Financial derivatives and employee stock options liabilities	0.2	—	0.2
Other investment assets	90.8	226.2	−118.0
Other investment liabilities	420.9	307.3	506.6
Net errors and omissions	76.2	85.4	68.2
Reserves and related items	−25.8	176.6	186.4

Source: IMF, *International Financial Statistics*.

External Trade

PRINCIPAL COMMODITIES
(distribution by HS, US $ million)

Imports c.i.f.	2011	2012	2013
Vegetables and vegetable products	199.1	204.6	203.5
Prepared foodstuffs; beverages, spirits, vinegars; tobacco and articles thereof	355.8	380.0	403.5
Mineral products	1,179.6	1,217.6	1,256.7
Mineral fuels, mineral oils and related materials	1,165.4	1,198.1	1,235.6
Chemicals and related products	529.7	558.2	627.0
Pharmaceutical products	214.3	220.4	246.7
Plastics, rubber and articles thereof	304.1	304.2	320.6
Plastics	217.9	220.2	238.5
Textiles and textile articles	383.5	384.8	386.9
Iron and steel; other base metals and articles thereof	312.5	284.4	322.1
Machinery and mechanical appliances; electrical equipment; parts thereof	827.8	786.4	839.7
Boilers, machinery and mechanical appliances, and parts thereof	409.6	380.2	397.5
Electrical machinery and equipment and parts thereof; sound recorders and reproducers, television image and sound recorders and reproducers, and parts and accessories thereof	418.2	406.2	442.2
Vehicles, aircraft, vessels and associated transport equipment	332.6	304.8	300.4
Vehicles other than railway or tramway rolling stock, and parts and accessories thereof	323.7	275.1	288.3
Total (incl. others)	5,191.3	5,212.9	5,492.4

Exports f.o.b.	2011	2012	2013
Vegetables and vegetable products	471.0	360.5	507.0
Edible fruit	187.0	202.3	204.0
Cereals	72.0	36.5	120.8
Oil seeds and oleaginous fruits, etc.	181.5	99.9	166.6
Animal or vegetable fats and oils and products thereof	77.5	89.7	44.0
Prepared foodstuffs; beverages, spirits, vinegars; tobacco and articles thereof	330.6	390.9	427.3
Preparations of vegetables or fruits	68.8	60.4	76.0
Beverages, spirits and vinegars	181.3	215.0	252.3
Chemicals and related products	111.6	145.8	167.9
Pharmaceutical products	77.1	94.0	113.1

Exports f.o.b.—*continued*	2011	2012	2013
Textiles and textile articles	354.7	343.4	330.5
Articles of apparel and clothing accessories, knitted	115.5	103.8	112.9
Articles of apparel and clothing accessories, not knitted	157.4	145.8	142.4
Iron and steel; other base metals and articles thereof	112.9	73.4	123.3
Machinery and mechanical appliances; electrical equipment; parts thereof	283.3	278.6	315.9
Boilers, machinery and mechanical appliances, and parts thereof	103.9	77.2	70.6
Electrical machinery and equipment and parts thereof; sound recorders and reproducers, television image and sound recorders and reproducers, and parts and accessories thereof	179.4	201.5	245.4
Miscellaneous manufactured articles	97.8	108.2	118.9
Furniture; bedding, mattresses, mattress supports, cushions and similar stuffed furnishings; lamps and lighting fittings, not elsewhere specified or included; illuminated signs, illuminated nameplates, etc.; prefabricated buildings	87.6	95.1	109.8
Total (incl. others)	2,216.8	2,161.9	2,428.3

PRINCIPAL TRADING PARTNERS
(US $ million)

Imports c.i.f.	2011	2012	2013
Austria	85.4	123.0	128.4
Belarus	194.7	172.2	178.3
Bulgaria	66.7	78.2	83.0
China, People's Republic	399.8	415.7	478.9
Czech Republic	59.7	65.0	69.3
France	87.0	103.7	101.6
Germany	395.8	386.9	395.6
Greece	68.7	50.0	39.3
Hungary	100.0	89.0	100.3
Italy	348.1	327.6	345.0
Poland	134.6	152.1	142.7
Romania	574.2	620.6	722.1
Russia	823.0	816.9	788.0
Turkey	366.9	388.2	381.0
Ukraine	641.1	594.3	659.1
United Kingdom	64.9	58.0	62.5
USA	79.7	79.1	73.6
Total (incl. others)	5,191.3	5,212.9	5,492.4

Exports f.o.b.	2011	2012	2013
Belarus	75.6	80.7	90.3
Bulgaria	33.8	33.8	32.6
Czech Republic	11.3	16.9	25.6
France	24.0	30.2	35.5
Georgia	13.2	18.4	28.0
Germany	106.5	70.2	113.1
Greece	24.0	13.3	25.3
Hungary	23.3	28.7	15.7
Italy	215.1	202.4	185.2
Kazakhstan	45.5	50.3	39.2
New Zealand	5.3	26.7	32.5
Poland	85.9	74.2	85.3
Romania	376.4	356.7	411.0
Russia	625.5	655.0	631.9
Switzerland	8.0	5.1	47.8
Turkey	73.4	56.1	127.1
Ukraine	153.0	122.4	141.4
United Kingdom	101.8	83.9	105.5
USA	24.9	30.0	25.3
Total (incl. others)	2,216.8	2,161.9	2,428.3

Transport

RAILWAYS
(traffic)

	2012	2013	2014
Passenger journeys (million) . .	4.3	4.1	3.8
Passenger-km (million) . . .	347	330	257
Freight transported (million metric tons)	4.2	5.4	5.0
Freight ton-km (million) . . .	960	1,227	1,182

ROAD TRAFFIC
(motor vehicles in use)

	2011	2012	2013
Passenger cars	426,973	456,379	487,418
Buses and minibuses . . .	21,349	21,433	21,344
Lorries and vans	141,696	151,830	154,163
Trailers and semi-trailers . . .	56,482	58,827	60,797

INLAND WATERWAYS
(traffic)

	2012	2013	2014
Passenger journeys ('000) . .	115.7	116.4	141.6
Passenger-km (million) . . .	0.2	0.2	0.3
Freight transported ('000 metric tons)	144.2	162.6	227.2
Freight ton-km (million) . . .	0.5	0.5	0.8

CIVIL AVIATION
(traffic)

	2012	2013	2014
Passengers carried ('000) . . .	673.0	655.0	897.8
Passenger-km (million) . . .	875	822	1,225
Freight transported ('000 metric tons)	1.4	1.2	1.2
Freight ton-km (million) . . .	1.7	1.1	1.0

Tourism

FOREIGN VISITOR ARRIVALS
(incl. excursionists)

Country of origin	2011	2012	2013
Austria	95	269	308
Bulgaria	289	401	246
France	248	155	364
Germany	1,001	1,275	798
Israel	138	163	147
Italy	445	622	593
Japan	258	193	265
Netherlands	219	288	336
Poland	371	505	823
Romania	1,600	1,782	2,307
Russia	1,404	2,204	1,604
Sweden	334	207	276
Turkey	477	819	557
Ukraine	1,189	987	1,042
United Kingdom	350	664	503
USA	558	534	579
Total (incl. others)	10,788	12,797	13,150

Receipts from tourism (US $ million, excl. passenger transport): 195 in 2011; 213 in 2012; 227 in 2013 (Source: World Tourism Organization).

Communications Media

	2011	2012	2013
Telephones ('000 main lines in use)	1,180.0	1,205.8	1,221.5
Mobile cellular telephones ('000 subscribers)	3,587.4	4,080.1	3,696.8
Internet subscribers ('000) . .	355.1	n.a.	n.a.
Broadband subscribers ('000) . .	355.1	417.2	467.1

Source: International Telecommunication Union.

Education

(2013/14)

	Institutions	Teachers	Students
Pre-primary	1,440	12,334	145,296
Primary and Secondary: general	1,374	32,188	353,207
Secondary: vocational . . .	67	2,144	18,248
Higher: colleges	45	2,475	29,251
Higher: universities	32	5,741	97,285

Pupil-teacher ratio (primary education, UNESCO estimate): 15.8 in 2011/12 (Source: UNESCO Institute for Statistics).

Adult literacy rate (UNESCO estimates): 99.1% (males 99.6%; females 98.6%) in 2012 (Source: UNESCO Institute for Statistics).

Directory

The Government

HEAD OF STATE

President: NICOLAE TIMOFTI.

CABINET OF MINISTERS
(May 2015)

A coalition, principally comprising representatives of the Partidul Liberal Democrat din Moldova (PLDM) and the Partidul Democrat din Moldova (PDM).

Prime Minister: CHIRIL GABURICI (PLDM).

Deputy Prime Minister: VICTOR OSIPOV (PDM).

Deputy Prime Minister, Minister of the Economy: STEPHANE BRIDE (PDM).

Deputy Prime Minister, Minister of Foreign Affairs and European Integration: NATALIA GHERMAN (PLDM).

Minister of Finance: ANATOL ARAPU (PLDM).

Minister of Justice: VLADIMIR GROSU (PLDM).

Minister of Internal Affairs: OLEG BALAN (PLDM).

Minister of Defence: VIOREL CIBOTARU (PLDM).

Minister of Regional Development and Construction: VASILE BÂTCA (PDM).

Minister of Agriculture and the Food Industry: ION SULA (PLDM).

Minister of Transport and Road Infrastructure: VASILE BOT-NARI (PDM).

Minister of the Environment: SERGIU PALIHOVICI (PLDM).

Minister of Education: MAIA SANDU (PLDM).

Minister of Culture: MONICA BABUC (PDM).

Minister of Labour, Social Protection and the Family: RUX-ANDA GLAVAN (PDM).

Minister of Health: MIRCEA BUGA (PLDM).

Minister of Youth and Sport: SERGHEI AFANASENCO (PDM).

Minister of Information and Communications Technologies: PAVEL FILIP (PDM).

Note: the President of the Academy of Sciences of Moldova, GHEORGHE DUCA, and the Başkan (Governor) of the Autonomous Territory of Gagauzia, IRINA VLAH are also members of the Cabinet of Ministers.

MINISTRIES

Office of the President: 2073 Chişinău, bd. Ştefan cel Mare şi Sfânt 154; tel. (22) 23-58-01; internet www.prezident.md.

Office of the Council of Ministers: 2033 Chişinău, Piaţa Marii Adunări Naţionale 1; tel. (22) 25-01-01; fax (22) 23-38-72; e-mail petitii@gov.md; internet www.gov.md.

Ministry of Agriculture and the Food Industry: 2004 Chişinău, bd. Ştefan cel Mare şi Sfânt 162; tel. (22) 23-34-27; fax (22) 21-02-04; e-mail adm_maia@moldova.md; internet www.maia.gov.md.

Ministry of Culture: 2033 Chişinău, Piaţa Marii Adunări Naţionale 1; tel. (22) 22-76-20; fax (22) 23-23-88; e-mail office@mc.gov.md; internet www.mc.gov.md.

Ministry of Defence: 2021 Chişinău, şos. Hînceşti 84; tel. (22) 25-22-22; fax (22) 25-24-00; e-mail ministru@army.md; internet www.army.md.

Ministry of the Economy: 2033 Chişinău, Piaţa Marii Adunări Naţionale 1; tel. (22) 23-74-48; fax (22) 23-40-64; e-mail mineconcom@mec.gov.md; internet www.mec.gov.md.

Ministry of Education: 2033 Chişinău, Piaţa Marii Adunări Naţionale 1; tel. (22) 23-33-48; fax (22) 23-35-15; e-mail vice ministra@edu.md; internet www.edu.md.

Ministry of the Environment: 2005 Chişinău, str. Cosmonauţilor 9; tel. (22) 20-45-07; fax (22) 22-68-58; e-mail egreta@mediu.gov.md; internet www.mediu.gov.md.

Ministry of Finance: 2005 Chişinău, str. Cosmonauţilor 7; tel. (22) 22-66-29; fax (22) 24-00-55; e-mail cancelaria@minfin.moldova.md; internet www.minfin.md.

Ministry of Foreign Affairs and European Integration: 2012 Chişinău, str. 31 August 1989 80; tel. (22) 57-82-07; fax (22) 23-23-02; e-mail secdep@mfa.md; internet www.mfa.gov.md.

Ministry of Health: 2009 Chişinău, str. Vasile Alecsandri 2; tel. (22) 72-99-07; fax (22) 73-87-81; e-mail office@ms.gov.md; internet www.ms.md.

Ministry of Information and Communications Technologies: 2012 Chişinău, bd. Ştefan cel Mare şi Sfânt 134; tel. and fax (22) 23-84-76; e-mail mtic@mtic.gov.md; internet www.mtic.gov.md.

Ministry of Internal Affairs: 2012 Chişinău, bd. Ştefan cel Mare şi Sfânt 75; tel. (22) 25-53-46; e-mail mai@mai.md; internet www.mai.md.

Ministry of Justice: 2012 Chişinău, str. 31 August 1989 82; tel. (22) 23-47-95; fax (22) 23-47-97; e-mail secretariat@justice.gov.md; internet www.justice.gov.md.

Ministry of Labour, Social Protection and the Family: 2009 Chişinău, str. Vasile Alecsandri 1; tel. (22) 26-93-01; fax (22) 26-93-10; e-mail secretariat@mmpsf.gov.md; internet www.mpsfc.gov.md.

Ministry of Regional Development and Construction: 2005 Chişinău, str. Cosmonauţilor 9; tel. (22) 20-45-69; fax (22) 22-07-48; e-mail mcdr@mcdr.gov.md; internet www.mcdt.gov.md.

Ministry of Transport and Road Infrastructure: 2004 Chişinău, bd. Ştefan cel Mare şi Sfânt 162; tel. (22) 82-07-12; fax (22) 54-65-64; e-mail secretariat@mtid.gov.md; internet www.mtid.gov.md.

Ministry of Youth and Sport: 2004 Chişinău, bd. Ştefan cel Mare şi Sfânt 162; tel. and fax (22) 82-08-61; e-mail ministru@mts.gov.md; internet www.mts.gov.md.

President

In voting by the members of Parliament on 16 March 2012, the sole candidate in a presidential election, NICOLAE TIMOFTI, an independent, was elected, having received the votes of 62 of the 101 legislative deputies. Timofti assumed office on 23 March.

Legislature

Parliament
(Parlamentul)

2073 Chişinău, bd. Ştefan cel Mare şi Sfânt 105; tel. (22) 26-82-44; fax (22) 23-30-12; e-mail inform@parlament.md; internet www.parlament.md.

Chairman: ANDRIAN CANDU.

General Election, 30 November 2014

Parties and alliances	Votes	%	Seats
PSRM	327,912	20.51	25
PLDM	322,201	20.16	23
PCRM	279,366	17.48	21
PDM	252,489	15.80	19
PL	154,518	9.67	13
Others	262,032	16.39	—
Total	**1,598,518**	**100.00**	**101**

Election Commission

Comisia Electorală Centrală a Republicii Moldova (Central Electoral Commission of the Republic of Moldova): 2012 Chişinău, str. Vasile Alecsandri 119; tel. (22) 25-14-51; fax (22) 23-40-47; e-mail info@cec.md; internet www.cec.md; Pres. Dr IURIE CIOCAN.

Political Organizations

In February 2015 some 43 political parties were registered with the Ministry of Justice, of which the following were among the most important.

Alianţa Verde Ecologist (AVE) (Green Ecological Alliance): 2001 Chişinău, str. Teilor 7/2; tel. (22) 84-48-06; fax (69) 11-48-21; e-mail pve.moldova@gmail.com; internet www.greenparty.md; f. 1992; Pres. ANATOLIE PROHNIŢCHI.

Partidul Comuniştilor din Republica Moldova (PCRM) (Party of Communists of the Republic of Moldova): 2012 Chişinău, str. N. Iorga 11; tel. (22) 23-46-14; fax (22) 23-36-73; e-mail pcrmcc@gmail.com; internet www.pcrm.md; fmrly the Partidul Comunist al Moldovei (Communist Party of Moldova), banned in Aug. 1991; revived under present name April 1994; First Sec. VLADIMIR VORONIN.

Partidul Democrat din Moldova (PDM) (Democratic Party of Moldova): 2001 Chişinău, str. Tighina 32; tel. (22) 27-82-29; fax (22) 27-82-30; e-mail pdm@mtc.md; internet www.pdm.md; f. 1997; centrist; fmrly Movement for a Democratic and Prosperous Moldova, name changed in April 2000; contested 2005 legislative elections as mem. of the Democratic Moldova bloc; merged with Social Liberal Party in Feb. 2008; Chair. MARIAN LUPU.

Partidul Liberal (PL) (Liberal Party): 2012 Chişinău, str. Bucureşti 87A; tel. (22) 23-26-89; fax (22) 22-80-97; e-mail liberal@pl.md; internet www.pl.md; f. 1993; present name adopted 2005; Chair. MIHAI GHIMPU; 12,000 mems.

Partidul Liberal Democrat din Moldova (PLDM) (Liberal Democratic Party of Moldova): 2012 Chişinău, str. Bucureşti 88; tel. (22) 81-51-54; fax (22) 81-51-63; e-mail info@pldm.md; internet www.pldm.md; f. 2007; absorbed Alianţa Moldova Noastră (Our Moldova Alliance) in 2011; Pres. VLADIMIR FILAT.

Partidul Liberal Reformator (PLR) (Liberal Reformist Party): 2009 Chişinău, str. Mihai Eminescu 68; tel. (22) 26-00-09; e-mail comunicare@plr.md; internet plr.md; f. 2013 by fmr mems of Partidul Liberal (q.v.); Pres. ION HADÂRCĂ.

Partidul Mişcarea 'Acţiunea Europeană' (MAE) (European Action Movement Party): 2012 Chişinău, str. Bernardazzi 57; tel. (22) 24-36-56; e-mail office@ae.md; f. 2006; supports closer integration of Moldova with the European Union; Pres. VEACESLAV UNTILĂ.

Partidul Moldova Unită—Yedinaya Moldova (MU) (United Moldova Party): 2069 Chişinău, str. Armenească 84; tel. (22) 26-81-10; fax (22) 74-68-20; e-mail mail@moldovaunita.md; f. 2010; leftist, supportive of closer relations with Russia; Leader VLADIMIR ŢURCAN.

Partidul Naţional Liberal (PNL) (National Liberal Party): 2069 Chişinău, Calea Ieşilor 6; tel. (22) 21-18-18; fax (22) 21-16-77; e-mail contacts@pnl.md; internet www.pnl.md; f. 2007; right-of-centre liberal party; Pres. VITALIA PAVLICENCO.

Partidul Politic 'Patria' (Patria) (Fatherland Political Party): 2004 Chişinău, str. Bucureşti 117; tel. (22) 02-72-00; fax (22) 02-72-01; e-mail secretariat.pnru@gmail.com; internet ru1.md; f. 2014; not permitted to participate in 2014 legislative election; Leader RENATO USATÎI.

Partidul Popular Creştin Democrat (PPCD) (Christian Democratic People's Party): 2009 Chişinău, str. N. Iorga 5; tel. and fax (22) 23-44-80; e-mail echipa@ppcd.md; internet ppcd.md; f. 1989 as the People's Front of Moldova, renamed 1992, and as above 1999; advocates Moldova's entry into the European Union and the North Atlantic Treaty Organization; Chair. VICTOR CIOBANU.

Partidul Social Democrat (PSD) (Social Democratic Party): 2012 Chişinău, str. 31 August, 101/1; tel. and fax (22) 20-10-22; e-mail info@psdm.md; internet www.psdm.md; f. 1990; Pres. VICTOR ŞELIN.

Partidul Socialiştilor din Republica Moldova (PSRM) (Party of Socialists of the Republic of Moldova): 2005 Chişinău, bd. Grigore Vieru 16/29; tel. and fax (22) 22-96-46; e-mail verval@mail.ru; internet socialistii.md; f. 1996; democratic socialist; Pres. IGOR DODON.

Diplomatic Representation

EMBASSIES IN MOLDOVA

Azerbaijan: 2012 Chişinău, str. Kogelnichanu 64; tel. (22) 23-22-77; fax (22) 22-75-58; e-mail chisinau@mission.mfa.gov.az; internet www.azembassy.md; Ambassador NAMIK HASAN ALIYEV.

Belarus: 2009 Chişinău, str. Mateevici 83/1; tel. (22) 60-29-81; fax (22) 23-83-00; e-mail moldova@mfa.gov.by; internet moldova.mfa .gov.by; Ambassador VYACHESLAV A. OSIPENKO.

Bulgaria: 2012 Chişinău, str. Bucureşti 92; tel. (22) 23-79-83; fax (22) 23-79-78; e-mail embassy.chisinau@mfa.bg; internet www.mfa .bg/embassies/moldova; Ambassador GEORGI PANAYOTOV.

China, People's Republic: 2004 Chişinău, str. Mitropolit Dosoftei 124; tel. (22) 21-07-12; fax (22) 29-60-61; e-mail chinaemb@mtc.md; internet chnembassy@126.com; Ambassador TONG MINGTAO.

Czech Republic: 2005 Chişinău, str. Moara Roşie 23; tel. (22) 20-99-42; fax (22) 29-64-37; e-mail chisinau@embassy.mzv.cz; internet www.mzv.cz/chisinau; Ambassador JAROMÍR KVAPIL.

France: 2012 Chişinău, str. V. Pîrcălab 6; tel. (22) 20-04-00; fax (22) 20-04-01; e-mail infos.chisinau-amba@diplomatie.gouv.fr; internet www.ambafrance-md.org; Ambassador GÉRARD GUILLONNEAU.

Germany: 2012 Chişinău, str. Maria Cibotari 35; tel. (22) 20-06-00; fax (22) 23-46-80; e-mail info@chisinau.diplo.de; internet www .chisinau.diplo.de; Ambassador MATTHIAS MEYER.

Hungary: 2004 Chişinău, bd. Ştefan cel Mare şi Sfânt 131; tel. (22) 23-29-34; fax (22) 22-45-13; e-mail mission.kiv@mfa.gov.hu; internet www.mfa.gov.hu/emb/chisinau; Ambassador MÁTYÁS SZILÁGYI.

Israel: 2001 Chişinău, str. Tighina 12; tel. (22) 54-42-84; fax (22) 54-42-80; Ambassador OREN DAVID (resident in Jerusalem, Israel).

Lithuania: 2001 Chişinău, str. I. Valilenco 24/1; tel. (22) 54-31-94; fax (22) 23-42-87; e-mail amb.md@urm.lt; internet md.mfa.lt; Ambassador VIOLETA MOTULAITĖ.

Poland: 2019 Chişinău, str. Grenoble 126 A; tel. (22) 28-59-50; fax (22) 28-90-00; e-mail kiszyniow.amb.sekretariat@msz.gov.pl; internet www.kiszyniow.msz.gov.pl; Ambassador ARTUR MICHALSKI.

Romania: 2001 Chişinău, str. Bucureşti 66/1; tel. (22) 21-18-13; fax (22) 22-81-29; e-mail secretariat@ambasadaromaniei.md; internet chisinau.mae.ro; Ambassador MARIUS LAZURCA.

Russian Federation: 2004 Chişinău, bd. Ştefan cel Mare şi Sfânt 153; tel. (22) 23-49-41; fax (22) 23-51-07; e-mail domino@mtc.md; internet www.moldova.mid.ru; Ambassador FARIT M. MUKHAMETSHIN.

Sweden: 2004 Chişinău, str. Toma Ciorba 12; tel. (22) 26-73-20; fax (22) 26-73-30; e-mail ambassaden.chisinau@gov.se; internet www .swedenabroad.com/chisinau; Ambassador INGRID TERSMAN.

Turkey: 2021 Chişinău, str. Valeriu Cupcea 60; tel. (22) 50-91-09; fax (22) 22-55-28; e-mail embassy.kishinev@mfa.gov.tr; internet www.chisinau.emb.mfa.gov.tr; Ambassador MAHMET SELIM KARTAL.

Ukraine: 2008 Chişinău, bd. Vasile Lupu 17; tel. (22) 58-21-51; fax (22) 58-51-08; e-mail emb_md@mfa.gov.ua; internet www.mfa.gov .ua/moldova; Ambassador SERHIY I. PYROZHKOV.

United Kingdom: 2012 Chişinău, str. N. Iorga 18; tel. (22) 22-59-02; fax (22) 25-18-59; e-mail enquiries.chisinau@fco.gov.uk; internet www.gov.uk/government/world/moldova; Ambassador PHILIP BATSON.

USA: 2009 Chişinău, str. Mateevici 103; tel. (22) 40-83-00; fax (22) 23-30-44; e-mail chisinau-ca@state.gov; internet moldova .usembassy.gov; Ambassador JAMES D. PETTIT.

Judicial System

Supreme Court of Justice of the Republic of Moldova (Curtea Supremă de Justiţie a Republicii Moldova): 2009 Chişinău, str. M. Kogălniceanu 70; tel. (22) 22-15-47; fax (22) 22-52-27; e-mail info@csj .md; internet www.csj.md; comprises penal, economic, and civil and administrative chambers; Pres. MIHAI POALELUNGI.

Constitutional Court of the Republic of Moldova (Curtea Constitutionala a Republicii Moldova): 2004 Chişinău, str. A. Lăpuşneanu 28; tel. (22) 25-37-08; fax (22) 25-37-44; e-mail curtea@constcourt.md; internet www.constcourt.md; f. 1994; Chair. ALEXANDRU TĂNASE.

Prosecutor-General: CORNELIU GURIN, 2005 Chişinău, str. Mitropolit Bănulescu-Bodoni 26; tel. (22) 22-50-75; fax (22) 21-20-32; internet www.procuratura.md.

Religion

The majority of the inhabitants of Moldova profess Christianity, the largest denomination being the Eastern Orthodox Church.

CHRISTIANITY

Eastern Orthodox Church

In December 1992 the Patriarch of Moscow and All Russia issued a decree altering the status of the Eparchy of Chişinău and Moldova to that of a Metropolitan See, which later became known as the Moldovan Orthodox Church (distinct from the Metropolitanate of Moldova and Bucovina of the Romanian Orthodox Church). In 2002 the Government permitted the registration of an Autonomous Metropolitate of Bessarabia. The recognition of the church, an exarchate of the Romanian Orthodox Church, was confirmed by the Supreme Court in late 2004.

Metropolitanate of Bessarabia, Archbishop of Chişinău: 2004 Chişinău, str. 31 August 161; e-mail gbadea2006@yahoo.com; internet www.mitropoliabasarabiei.ro; Metropolitan of Bessarabia PETRU (PĂDURARU).

Moldovan Orthodox Church (Moscow Patriarchate): 2004 Chişinău, str. Bucureşti 119; tel. (22) 23-78-78; e-mail sec@ mitropolia.md; internet www.mitropolia.md; 1,520 parishes (2004); Metropolitan of Chişinău and all-Moldova VLADIMIR (CANTAREAN).

Roman Catholic Church

At 31 December 2007 there were an estimated 20,000 Catholics in the Republic of Moldova.

Bishop of Chişinău: Rt Rev. ANTON COŞA, 2012 Chişinău, str. Mitropolit Dosoftei 85; tel. (22) 22-34-70; fax (22) 22-52-10; e-mail episcopia@starnet.md.

The Press

The publications listed below are in Moldovan/Romanian, except where otherwise indicated.

PRINCIPAL NEWSPAPERS

Argumenty i Fakty v Moldove (Arguments and Facts in Moldova): 2000 Chişinău, str. Armenească 55/101; tel. (22) 27-89-28; fax (22) 54-65-80; e-mail info@aif.md; internet www.aif.md; f. 1978; Moldovan version of *Argumenty i Fakty* (Russia); in Russian; weekly; Chief Editor YEVGENIYA ANOKHINA; circ. 25,000 (2008).

Curierul Economic (The Economic Courier): 2005 Chişinău, str. Bănulescu-Bodoni 61/103; tel. (22) 40-28-33; fax (22) 40-28-37; e-mail relatiipublice@ase.md; f. 1999; weekly; Chief Editor ZINAIDA LUPAŞCU; circ. 4,000 (2008).

Ekonomicheskoye Obozreniye (Economic Review): 2000 Chişinău, str. S. Lazo 40; tel. (22) 88-77-77; fax (22) 88-77-89; e-mail red@logos.press.md; internet logos.press.md; f. 1990; weekly; in Russian; Chief Editor SERGEI MIŞIN; circ. 9,500 (2008).

Flux: 2004 Chişinău, str. N. Iorga 8; tel. (22) 23-50-91; fax (22) 23-74-75; e-mail ap@flux.md; internet www.flux.md; f. 1995; 5 a week; Chief Editor SERGIU PRAPORŞCIC; circ. 35,000 (Fri.), 3,000 (Mon.– Thur.) (2008).

Glasul (The Voice of the Nation): 2001 Chişinău, str. 31 August 15; tel. (22) 54-27-82; fax (22) 54-31-37; e-mail contact@glasul.md; internet glasul.md; f. 2009 as online successor publication of newspaper *Glasul Naţiunii* (Voice of the Nation, founded in 1989 as *Glasul*); 4 a week; culture, arts, literature, sport, politics.

Jurnal de Chişinău (Chişinău Journal): 2012 Chişinău, str. Vlaicu Pârcălab 63/3; tel. (22) 23-83-31; fax (22) 23-42-30; e-mail cotidian@

jurnal.md; internet www.jurnal.md; f. 1999; 3 a week; Chief Editor RODICA MAHU; circ. 26,000 (2008).

Kishinevskii Obozrevatel (Chişinău Correspondent): 2069 Chişinău, str. Calea Ieşilor 10; tel. and fax (22) 21-02-27; e-mail red@ko.md; internet www.ko.md; f. 1993; weekly; in Russian; Chief Editor IRINA ASTAKHOVA.

Kishinevskiye Novosti (Chişinău News): 2012 Chişinău, str. Puşkin 22; tel. and fax (22) 23-39-18; e-mail ss@kn.md; internet www.kn.md; f. 1991; weekly; in Russian; Chief Editor SERGHEI DROBOT; circ. 9,000 (2008).

Kommersant Plus (Businessman Plus): 2012 Chişinău, str. Puşkin 22/601; tel. and fax (22) 23-36-94; e-mail inform@commert.press.md; internet www.km.press.md; weekly; in Russian; politics and economics, incl. coverage of Gagauzia and Transnistria; Editor ROBERT ZAPADINSKII; circ. 11,000 (2008).

Komsomolskaya Pravda v Moldove (Young Communist League Truth in Moldova): 2012 Chişinău, str. Vlaicu Pîrcălab 45; tel. (22) 22-45-12; fax (22) 22-12-74; e-mail kp@kp.md; internet www.kp.md; f. 1996; daily; in Russian; Moldovan edition of *Komsomolskaya Pravda* (Russia); Editor-in-Chief V. N. SUNGORKIN; circ. 9,000 (2008).

Moldavskiye Vedomosti (Moldovan Gazette): 2012 Chişinău, bd. Ştefan cel Mare 182; tel. and fax (22) 23-86-18; e-mail news@vedomosti.md; internet vedomosti.md; f. 1995; three a week; in Russian; Editor-in-Chief YELENA ZAMURA; circ. 7,500 (2010).

Moldova Suverană (Sovereign Moldova): 2012 Chişinău, str. Puşkin 22, 3rd Floor; tel. and fax (22) 23-35-38; e-mail cotidian@moldova-suverana.md; internet www.moldova-suverana.md; f. 2005; daily; state-owned; Editor ION BERLINSKI; circ. 20,000 (per week).

Nezavisimaya Moldova (Independent Moldova): 2012 Chişinău, str. Puşkin 22; tel. (22) 23-36-08; fax (22) 23-31-41; e-mail mail@nm.md; internet www.nm.md; f. 2005; state-owned; daily; in Russian; Chief Editor IURII TIŞCENCO; circ. 92,700 (per month).

Timpul de Dimineața (The Morning Times): 2005 Chişinău, str. Columna 144E; tel. (22) 22-56-70; e-mail secretariat@timpul.md; internet www.timpul.md; f. 2001; daily; Dir and Chief Editor CONSTANTIN TANASE; circ. 46,750 (2008).

Unimedia: 2012 Chişinău, bd. Ştefan cel Mare 180; tel. and fax (22) 23-54-75; tel. (22) 99-93-30; e-mail info@unimedia.md; internet www.unimedia.info; f. 2005; online only.

PRINCIPAL PERIODICALS

Aquarelle: 2012 Chişinău, str. Puşkin 47/1A/3; tel. and fax (22) 22-07-73; e-mail aquarelle@aquarelle.md; internet www.aquarelle.md; f. 2003; in Russian; monthly; general women's interest; Chief Editor ANGELA SÎRBU; circ. 3,500 (2008).

Curierul Ortodox (The Orthodox Courier): 2060 Chişinău, bd. Traian 3, Biserica Sfîntul Dumitru; tel. (22) 77-25-33; e-mail fustei_nicolae@yahoo.com; internet curierulortodox.info; f. 1995; monthly; publ. of Moldovan Orthodox Church (Moscow Patriarchate); Chief Editor NICOLAE FUŞTEI, circ. 1,200 (2008).

Legea şi Viața (The Law and Life): 2012 Chişinău, str. Puşkin 22/512; tel. and fax (22) 23-37-90; e-mail legea_zakon@mail.ru; internet legeazakon.md; f. 1990; monthly; in Moldovan and Russian; Chief Editor LEONTIE ARSENE; circ. 5,000 (2008).

Moldova (Moldova): 2012 Chişinău, str. Puşkin 22/539; tel. (22) 23-31-46; fax (22) 23-74-63; e-mail revistamoldova@list.ru; internet www.revista.md; f. 2004; monthly; in Moldovan, Russian and English; the arts; Editor NICOLAE ROŞCA; circ. 3,000 (2008).

Profit/Banky i Finansy (Profit/Banks and Finance): 2014 Chişinău, str. Kogălniceanu 76; tel. (22) 23-49-30; fax (22) 23-49-33; e-mail office@profit.md; internet www.profit.md; f. 1995; monthly; in Romanian and Russian; economics and finance; Dir ALEXANDER TANAS; total circ. 5,000 (2015).

Puls (Pulse): 2001 Chişinău, str. Dosoftei 118; tel. (22) 83-81-86; fax (22) 29-59-54; e-mail red@puls.md; internet www.puls.md; online only; in Russian; politics and economics; supports closer relations with Russia and Eurasia; Chief Editor DMITRII KAVRUK; circ. 5,000 (2008).

Săptămîna (The Week): 2012 Chişinău, str. 31 August 107; tel. (22) 22-62-51; fax (22) 22-44-61; e-mail saptamin@mdl.net; internet www.saptamina.md; f. 1992; weekly; politics, economics, social and cultural affairs; Chief Editor VIOREL MIHAIL; circ. 12,722 (2008).

NEWS AGENCIES

Infotag News Agency: 2014 Chişinău, str. Kogălniceanu 76; tel. (22) 23-49-31; fax (22) 23-49-33; e-mail office@infotag.md; internet www.infotag.md; f. 1993; Dir ALEXANDRU TANAS.

State Information Agency—Moldpres: 2012 Chişinău, str. Puşkin 22; tel. (22) 23-23-72; fax (22) 23-26-98; e-mail inform@moldpres.md; internet www.moldpres.md; f. 1940 as ATEM, reorganized 1990 and 1994; Dir VALERIU RENITA.

PRESS ASSOCIATIONS

Association of Independent Press (API): 2005 Chişinău, str. Romana 2/2; tel. (22) 22-09-96; fax (22) 20-36-86; e-mail api@api.md; internet www.api.md; f. 1997; Pres. TUDOR IASCENCO; Exec. Dir PETRU MACOVEI.

Independent Journalism Centre (IJC): 2012 Chişinău, str. Şciusev 53; tel. (22) 21-36-52; fax (22) 22-66-81; e-mail editor@ijc.md; internet www.ijc.md; f. 1994; non-governmental org.

Publishers

Editura Cartea Moldovei: 2004 Chişinău, bd. Ştefan cel Mare şi Sfânt 180; tel. and fax (22) 29-59-35; f. 1996; fiction, non-fiction, poetry, art books; Dir RAISA SUVEICĂ.

Editura Lumina (Light): 2004 Chişinău, bd. Ştefan cel Mare şi Sfânt 180; tel. and fax (22) 29-58-64; e-mail luminamd@mail.ru; internet www.edituralumina.md; f. 1966; educational textbooks; Dir ALEXANDRU STIROVICI; Editor-in-Chief ANATOL MALEV.

Editura Ştiinţa (Science): 2028 Chişinău, str. Academiei 3; tel. (22) 73-96-16; fax (22) 73-96-27; e-mail prini@stiinta.asm.md; internet www.stiinta.asm.md; f. 1959; textbooks, encyclopedias, dictionaries, children's books and fiction in various languages; Dir GHEORGHE PRINI.

Technica-Info: 2004 Chişinău, bd. Ştefan cel Mare şi Sfânt 168; tel. (22) 23-78-61; fax (22) 23-85-04; e-mail bostan@utm.md; internet www.utm.md; f. 1993; technology; educational textbooks; Dir of Bd ION BOSTAN.

Univers Pedagogic: 2020 Chişinău, str. Socoleni 16/1, Centrul Ştiinţific; tel. (22) 24-32-79; e-mail univers_ped@yahoo.com; f. 1991; part of Ministry of Education; textbooks, guide books, children's literature; Dir I. SCUTELNICIUC.

Broadcasting and Communications

TELECOMMUNICATIONS

In 2013 there were 1.2m. main telephone lines in use, and 3.7m. subscriptions to mobile cellular telecommunications services.

Moldcell: 2060 Chişinău, str. Belgrad 3; tel. (22) 20-62-06; fax (22) 20-62-07; e-mail moldcell@moldcell.md; internet www.moldcell.md; f. 1999; mobile telecommunications; owned by Fintur Holdings b.v. (Netherlands); Gen. Man. CHIRIL GABURICI.

Moldtelecom: 2001 Chişinău, bd. Ştefan cel Mare şi Sfânt 10; tel. (22) 57-01-01; fax (22) 57-01-11; e-mail office@moldtelecom.md; internet www.moldtelecom.md; f. 1993; telephone communication and internet service provider; scheduled for partial privatization; Gen. Dir VITALIE IURCU.

Orange Moldova: 2071 Chişinău, str. Alba-Iulia 75; tel. (22) 57-50-10; e-mail orange@orange.md; internet www.orange.md; f. 1998 as Voxtel SA; present name adopted 2007; mobile cellular telecommunications; 56.7% owned by France Telecom Mobiles (France), 33.4% by MMT-BIS; Dir-Gen. LIUDMILA CLIMOC.

Sun Communications: 2001 Chişinău, bd. Ştefan cel Mare şi Sfânt 134; tel. (22) 86-00-00; e-mail info@suntv.com; internet www.suncommunications.md; f. 1993; internet and fixed-line telecommunication services.

Unité: 2001 Chişinău, bd. Ştefan cel Mare şi Sfânt 10; tel. (22) 20-02-00; fax (22) 57-07-00; e-mail marketing@unite.md; internet www.unite.md; f. 2007; mobile cellular communications; 100% owned by Moldtelecom (q.v.).

Regulatory Authority

National Regulatory Agency for Electronic Communications and Information Technology (ANRCETI) (Agenţia Naţională pentru Reglementare în Comunicaţii Electronice şi Tehnologia Informatiei): 2012 Chişinău, bd. Ştefan cel Mare şi Sfânt 134; tel. (22) 25-13-17; fax (22) 22-28-85; e-mail office@anrceti.md; internet www.anrceti.md; f. 2000; Dir GRIGORE VARANIŢĂ.

BROADCASTING

Regulatory Authorities

National Radio Frequencies Centre (Centrul National pentru Frecvente Radio): 2021 Chişinău, str. Drumul Viilor 28/2; tel. and fax (22) 73-39-41; e-mail cnfr@cnfr.md; internet www.cnfr.md; f. 1993; responsible for frequency allocations and monitoring, certification of post and communications equipment and services; Gen. Dir TEODOR CICLICCI.

Radio and Television Co-ordinating Council (Consiliul Coordonator al Audiovizualului): 2012 Chişinău, str. Vlaicu Parcalab 46;

tel. (22) 27-73-91; fax (22) 27-74-71; e-mail office@cca.md; internet www.cca.md; f. 1995; state-owned; regulatory and licensing body; Pres. MARIAN POCAZNOI.

Radio

Radio Moldova: 2028 Chişinău, str. Mioriţa 1; tel. and fax (22) 72-33-47; e-mail a.dorogan@yahoo.fr; internet www.trm.md; f. 1930; subsidiary of Teleradio Moldova (q.v.); broadcasts in Romanian, Russian, Ukrainian, Gagauz and Yiddish; Dir-Gen. ALEXANDRU DOROGAN.

Radio Vocea Basarabiei (Radio Voice of Bessarabia): 2012 Chişinău, str. Puşkin 20A; tel. (22) 80-44-23; e-mail voceabasarabiei@yahoo.com; internet www.voceabasarabiei.net; f. 2000; Dir VEACE-SLAV ŢIBULEAC.

Television

Teleradio Moldova: 2028 Chişinău, str. Mioriţa 1; tel. (22) 72-33-80; fax (22) 72-35-37; e-mail trm@trm.md; internet www.trm.md; f. 1958; state-owned; Pres. CONSTANTIN MARIN; Exec. Dir (TV) MIRCEA SURDU.

Finance

(cap. = capital; res = reserves; dep. = deposits; m. = million; brs = branches; amounts in Moldovan lei)

BANKING

The National Bank of Moldova, established in 1991, is independent of the Government (but responsible to Parliament) and has the power to regulate monetary policy and the financial system. At February 2012 there were 14 authorized commercial banks in operation.

Central Bank

National Bank of Moldova (Banca Naţională a Moldovei): 2005 Chişinău, bd. Grigore Vieru 1; tel. (22) 40-90-06; fax (22) 22-05-91; e-mail official@bnm.org; internet www.bnm.org; f. 1991; cap. 288.9m., res –957.7m., dep. 9,899.4m. (Dec. 2008); Gov. DORIN DRĂGUŢANU.

Commercial Banks

Banca de Economii: 2012 Chişinău, str. Columna 115; tel. (22) 21-80-05; fax (22) 21-80-06; e-mail bem@bem.md; internet www.bem.md; f. 1992; cap. 117.3m., res 18.8m., dep. 4,496.8m. (Dec. 2011); 56.1% owned by Ministry of the Economy; Pres. ILAN SHOR; 37 brs.

Banca de Finanţe şi Comerţ (FinComBank SA—Finance and Trade Bank JSC): 2012 Chişinău, str. Puşkin 26; tel. (22) 26-99-00; fax (22) 23-73-08; e-mail fincom@fincombank.com; internet www.fincombank.com; f. 1993; cap. 131.5m., res 155.7m., dep. 1,050.1m. (June 2011); Chair. OLEG VORONIN; 13 brs.

Banca Socială: 2005 Chişinău, str. Bănulescu-Bodoni 61; tel. (22) 22-14-94; fax (22) 22-42-30; e-mail office@socbank.md; internet www.socbank.md; f. 1991; jt-stock commercial bank; cap. 100.0m., res 97.3m., dep. 2,170.3m. (Dec. 2011); Chair. VLADIMIR SUETNOV; Pres. VALENTIN CUNEV; 20 brs.

Energbank: 2012 Chişinău, str. Tighina 23/3; tel. (22) 54-43-87; fax (22) 85-80-80; e-mail office@energbank.com; internet www.energbank.com; f. 1997; cap. 100.0m., res 23.3m., dep. 1,151.0m. (Dec. 2011); Chair. IURII VASILACHI; 68 brs.

EuroCreditBank: 2001 Chişinău, str. Ismail 33; tel. (22) 50-02-00; fax (22) 54-88-27; e-mail telebank@eurocreditbank.md; internet www.telebank.md; f. 1992; jt-stock co; commercial investment bank; cap. 108.0m., res 26.5m., dep. 253.3m. (Dec. 2011); Pres. AURELIU CINCILEI; 3 brs.

Eximbank: 2004 Chişinău, bd. Ştefan cel Mare şi Sfânt 171/1; tel. (22) 11-02-30; fax (22) 60-16-11; e-mail info@eximbank.com; internet www.eximbank.com; f. 1994; cap. 635.0m., res 11.2m., dep. 1,927.7m. (Dec. 2011); Gen. Dir MARCEL CHIRCĂ.

Mobiasbanca: 2012 Chişinău, bd. Ştefan cel Mare şi Sfânt 81A; tel. (22) 25-64-56; fax (22) 54-19-74; e-mail contactell@mobiasbanca.md; internet www.mobiasbanca.md; f. 1990; 67.9% owned by Société Générale (France); acquired Bancoop in 2001; commercial bank; cap. 100.0m., res 162.0m., dep. 1,889.3m. (Dec. 2011); Pres. RIDHA TEKAIA; 11 brs.

Moldova Agroindbank: 2005 Chişinău, str. Cosmonauţilor 9; tel. (22) 26-89-98; fax (22) 22-80-58; e-mail aib@maib.md; internet www.maib.md; f. 1991; jt-stock commercial bank; cap. 207.5m., res 224.3m., dep. 5,853.8m. (Dec. 2011); Chair. of Bd VICTOR MICULEŢ; Chair. SERGHEI CEBOTARI; 45 brs.

Victoriabank: 2004 Chişinău, str. 31 August 1989 141; tel. (22) 57-61-00; fax (22) 23-45-33; e-mail office@victoriabank.md; internet www.victoriabank.md; f. 1990; cap. 250.0m., res 52.9m., dep. 6,802.9m. (Dec. 2011); Pres. NATALIA POLITOV-CANGAS; 103 brs.

STOCK EXCHANGE

Moldovan Stock Exchange (Bursa de Valori a Moldovei SA): 2001 Chişinău, bd. Ştefan cel Mare şi Sfânt 73; tel. (22) 27-75-94; fax (22) 27-73-56; e-mail postmaster@moldse.md; internet www.moldse.md; f. 1994; Chair. SERGIU CEBOTARI.

INSURANCE

In March 2010 there were 24 insurance companies operating in Moldova.

Acord Grup: 2038 Chişinău, str. Decebal 80/1; tel. (22) 26-44-44; fax (22) 53-88-33; e-mail office@acordgrup.md; internet acordgrup.md; f. 2002; Dir VICTOR GAICIUC.

Asito: 2005 Chişinău, str. Bănulescu-Bodoni 57/1; tel. (22) 22-62-12; fax (22) 22-11-79; e-mail asito@asito.md; internet www.asito.md; f. 1991; 48.3% owned by Moldova Investment Group (United Kingdom); fmrly QBE Asito; Gen. Man. EUGEN ŞLOPAC.

Asterra Grup: 2005 Chişinău, O. Goga 26; tel. (22) 21-17-58; fax (22) 21-17-59; internet www.asterra.md; life and non-life; Dir ANATOLII BANTAŞ.

Donaris Group: 2012 Chişinău, str. 31 August 1989, 108/1; tel. (22) 26-57-01; fax (22) 26-57-13; e-mail office@donaris.md; internet www.donaris.md; f. 1998; life and non-life, insurance and reinsurance; Dir DINU GHERASIM.

Garantie: 2005 Chişinău, str. Puşkin 47/1; tel. (22) 27-00-50; fax (22) 27-00-55; e-mail office@garantie.md; internet www.garantie.md; f. 1993; life and non-life; Pres. ALEXEI TOPOROV.

Grawe Carat Asigurări: 2012 Chişinău, str. Alexandru cel Bun 51; tel. (22) 27-93-32; fax (22) 27-93-56; e-mail office@grawe.md; internet www.grawe.md; f. 1972; life and non-life; Dir PETER KASYK.

Moldasig: 2009 Chişinău, str. M. Eminescu 2; tel. (22) 23-81-61; fax (22) 23-83-46; e-mail moldasig@dnt.md; internet www.moldasig.md; f. 2002; 51% owned by Banca de Economii SA, 25% owned by Calea Ferată din Moldova, 24% owned by Poşta Moldovei; Gen. Dir VITALI I. BODYA.

Moldcargo: 2012 Chişinău, str. V. Alecsandri 97; tel. (22) 24-55-67; fax (22) 27-92-93; e-mail office@moldcargo.md; internet www.moldcargo.md; f. 1999; life and non-life; Dir CRISTINA DOLGHI.

Nova Broker: 2009 Chişinău, Al. Puşkin 4; tel. (22) 22-96-49; e-mail novabroker@gmail.com; internet www.novabroker.md; f. 1993; non-life.

Sigur-Asigur: 2009 Chişinău, str. M. Kogălniceanu 73/2; tel. (22) 25-60-00; fax (22) 27-82-62; e-mail sigurasigur@mdl.net; internet www.sigur-asigur.md; f. 2003; life; Dir SERGIU CERTAN.

Victoria Asigurări: 2005 Chişinău, str. Romană 8; tel. (22) 22-83-50; fax (22) 22-83-52; e-mail office@victoria-asigurari.md; internet www.victoria-asigurari.md; life and non-life; Dir-Gen. OCTAVIAN LUNGU.

Regulatory Commission

National Commission for the Financial Market (Comisia Naţională a Pieţei Financiare): 2012 Chişinău, str. Ştefan cel Mare şi Sfânt, 77; tel. (22) 85-94-01; fax (22) 85-95-04; e-mail cnpf@cnpf.md; internet www.cnpf.md; f. 2007; regulates and supervises non-banking financial market; Chair. ARTUR GHERMAN.

Trade and Industry

GOVERNMENT AGENCIES

Moldovan Investment and Export Promotion Organization (MEPO) (Organizaţia de Atragere a Investiţiilor şi Promovare a Exportului din Moldova): 2009 Chişinău, str. Mateevici 65; tel. (22) 27-36-54; fax (22) 22-43-10; e-mail office@miepo.md; internet www.miepo.md; f. 1999; assists enterprises in increasing exports and improving business environment; Exec. Dir DENIS JELIMALAI.

State Department for Privatization (Departamentul Privatizarii al Republicii Moldova): 2012 Chişinău, str. Puşkin 26; tel. and fax (22) 23-43-50; e-mail privatization@dnt.md; f. 1991; Dir-Gen. ALEKSANDR BANNICOV.

CHAMBER OF COMMERCE

Chamber of Commerce and Industry of the Republic of Moldova (Camera de Comerţ şi Industrie a Republicii Moldova): 2004 Chişinău, str. Ştefan cel Mare şi Sfânt 151; tel. (22) 22-15-52; fax (22) 23-44-25; e-mail camera@chamber.md; internet www.chamber.md; f. 1991; 9 brs, 16 sub-brs; Pres. VALERIU LAZAR.

UTILITIES
Regulatory Authority

National Agency for Energy Regulation (ANRE) (Agentia Nationala pentru Reglementare in Energetica): 2012 Chişinău, str. Columna 90; tel. (22) 54-13-84; fax (22) 85-29-00; e-mail anre@anre.md; internet www.anre.md; f. 1997; autonomous public institution; Gen. Dir SERGIU CIORBA.

Electricity

The sector comprises one transmission company, five distribution companies and four power generation plants.

MoldElectrica IS: 2012 Chişinău, str. V. Alecsandri 78; tel. (22) 25-35-48; fax (22) 25-31-42; e-mail cancelar@moldelectrica.md; internet www.moldelectrica.md; f. 2000 to assume the transmission and distribution functions of Moldtranselectro; Dir GENNADII DIMOV.

Red Union Fenosa: 2024 Chişinău, str. A. Doga 4; tel. (24) 43-11-11; fax (22) 43-12-05; e-mail ot24@ufmoldova.com; internet www.ufmoldova.com; privatized in 2000; wholly owned by Unión Eléctrica Fenosa (Spain); distribution co supplying electricity to Chişinău; Pres. RADU SILVIA.

Gas

MoldovaGaz SA: 2005 Chişinău, str. Albişoara 38; tel. (22) 57-80-02; fax (22) 22-00-02; e-mail office@moldovagaz.md; internet www.moldovagaz.md; f. 1999; national gas pipeline and distribution networks; comprises two transmission companies and 18 distribution companies; 50% owned by Gazprom (Russia) (q.v.), 35% owned by Govt of Moldova, and 13% owned by Property Committee of Transnistria; Pres. ALEKSANDR GUSEV.

TRADE UNIONS

Federation of Trade Unions of Building Industry and Building Material Industry (Federaţia Sindicatelor de Construcţii şi Industria Materialelor de Construcţii—SINDICONS): 2012 Chişinău, str. 31 August 129; tel. 23-71-58; fax (22) 23-71-47; e-mail sindicons.md@gmail.com; Chair. VICTOR TALMACI.

National Trade Union Confederation of Moldova (Confederaţia Naţională a Sindicatelor din Moldova): 2012 Chişinău, str. 31 August 129; tel. (22) 26-65-02; fax (22) 23-45-08; e-mail office@cnsm.md; internet www.cnsm.md; f. 2007 by merger of Confederation of Trade Unions of Moldova and the Moldovan Confederation of Free Trade Unions Solidarity; Pres. OLEG BUDZA; 500,000 union mems.

Trade Union of Energy Workers (Uniunea Sindicatelor din Energetică): 2024 Chişinău, str. A. Doga 4; tel. (22) 43-13-40; fax 22) 43-16-64; Chair. VEACESLAV RUFALA.

Transport
RAILWAYS

In 2010 the total length of railway lines in use was around 1,156 km. Railways connect Chişinău with Odesa (Ukraine) and the Romanian cities of Iaşi and Galaţi.

Calea Ferată din Moldova: 2012 Chişinău, str. Vlaicu Pîrcălab 48; tel. (22) 25-44-08; fax (22) 22-13-80; e-mail secr@railway.md; internet www.railway.md; f. 1992; total network 1,075 km; Dir-Gen. VITALIE STRUNA.

ROADS

In 2012 Moldova's network of roads amounted to 12,846 km (86.3% of which was hard-surfaced), including 3,336 km of main roads.

INLAND WATERWAYS

In 2005 the total length of navigable waterways in Moldova was 424 km. The main river ports are located within the separatist territory of Transnistria, at Tighina (Bender) and at Râbniţa.

CIVIL AVIATION

Moldova has four civilian airports, in Chişinău, Tiraspol (Transnistria), Bălţi and Mărculeşti.

Civil Aviation Administration (Administraţia de stat a Aviaţiei Civile): 2026 Chişinău, Aeroportul Chişinău; tel. (22) 52-40-64; fax (22) 52-91-18; e-mail dgasac@caa.md; internet www.caa.md; f. 1993; Dir-Gen. IURIE ZIDU (acting).

Air Moldova (Compania Aeriana Moldova): 2026 Chişinău, bd. Dacia 80/2, Aeroportul Chişinău; tel. (22) 52-55-02; fax (22) 52-60-09; e-mail info@airmoldova.md; internet www.airmoldova.md; f. 1993; wholly state-owned; scheduled and charter passenger and cargo flights to destinations in Europe and the CIS; Gen. Dir IULIAN SCORPAN.

Tourism

There were 13,150 tourist arrivals, including excursionists, in 2013, when receipts from tourism (excluding passenger transport) totalled US $227m.

Department of Tourism Development: 2004 Chişinău, bd. Ştefan cel Mare şi Sfânt 180, bir. 901; tel. (22) 21-07-74; fax (22) 23-26-26; e-mail dept@turism.md; internet www.turism.md.

Defence

As assessed at November 2014, the Moldovan armed forces numbered 5,350, with an army of 3,250, an air force of 800 and a logistic support force of 1,300. In addition, there were 58,000 reserves. Paramilitary forces attached to the Ministry of Internal Affairs numbered 2,400, including 900 riot police. The term of conscription is 12 months.

Under an agreement concluded in late 1994, the former Soviet 14th Army (under Russian jurisdiction) was to have been withdrawn from Transnistria within three years, but in March 1998 it was announced that Russian forces would remain in Transnistria until a political settlement for the region was reached. Despite subsequent agreements providing for a withdrawal, some 1,500 Russian troops (including 355 peacekeeping troops) remained in Transnistria at November 2014. There were also 12 Organization for Security and Co-operation in Europe troops and 10 Ukrainian military observers in Moldova at that time.

In early 1994 Moldova joined the North Atlantic Treaty Organization's 'Partnership for Peace' programme, although the country's Constitution guarantees a neutral status.

Defence Expenditure: Estimated at 403m. lei in 2015.

Chief of General Staff and Commander of the National Army: Brig.-Gen. IGOR GORGAN.

Education

Primary education begins at seven years of age and lasts for four years. Secondary education lasts for a maximum of seven years, comprising a first cycle of five years and a second of two years. In 2011/12 enrolment at primary schools included 88% of children in the relevant age-group, while the comparable figure for secondary schools was 72%. In 2013/14 some 371,455 students were enrolled at Moldova's 1,441 primary and secondary schools, while 126,536 students were enrolled at the 77 higher education institutions. In 2013 general government expenditure on education amounted to 7,064m. lei, (equivalent to 18.3% of total general spending).

MOLDOVAN SECESSIONIST TERRITORY

The self-styled 'Transnistrian Moldovan Republic' (formerly 'Transnistrian Moldovan Soviet Socialist Republic')—Transnistria or Pridnestrovie, and referred to officially as the Left Bank of the Nistru—inhabited by principally ethnic Russians, Ukrainians and Moldovans, was proclaimed in September 1990. After the dissolution of the USSR at the end of 1991, a military conflict with the authorities of the newly independent Republic of Moldova, in which the Transnistrian authorities enjoyed the de facto support of elements of the Russian military based in the territory, ensued. Although a peace agreement was reached in July 1992, the status of Transnistria remained unresolved, and the territory remained beyond the control of the Moldovan authorities. While the separatist authorities have enjoyed de facto support from Russia, the self-proclaimed 'Republic' is not formally recognized by any state.

TRANSNISTRIA

Introductory Survey

LOCATION, CLIMATE, LANGUAGE, RELIGION, FLAG, CAPITAL

Transnistria comprises the eastern region of Moldova, including all territories on the east ('left') bank of the Nistru (Dniester, Dnestr) river, and also certain districts of the city of Tighina (Bender) on the west bank. The eastern boundary of the territory is with Ukraine. The territory has hot summers and cold winters, with moderate rainfall. The average summer temperature is 21°C (70°F) and the winter average is −3°C (27°F), and precipitation averages 495 mm (19 ins) per year. The separatist authorities use a flag (proportions 1 by 2) with horizontal stripes of red, green, and red, with, on the obverse side only, a gold hammer and sickle in the canton, surmounted by the gold outline of a five-pointed red star. The principal city and capital of the self-proclaimed 'Republic' is Tiraspol.

CONTEMPORARY POLITICAL HISTORY

Historical Context

In October 1924 the USSR, which refused to recognize Romania's claims to the territory of Bessarabia (constituting most of the present-day Republic of Moldova, and which had formed part of the Russian Empire until 1917), established a Moldovan Autonomous Soviet Socialist Republic (ASSR) to the east of the Dniester, within and subordinated to the Ukrainian Soviet Socialist Republic (SSR). The town of Balta (now in Ukraine) was the first capital of this ASSR, but in 1929 the administrative centre of the territory became Tiraspol. Following Soviet territorial gains early in the 'Great Patriotic War' (Second World War) the Moldovan ASSR was abolished and its western territories amalgamated with formerly Romanian-controlled lands in Bessarabia and Bukovina to form the Moldovan SSR—a Union Republic in its own right—in 1940, while eastern territories remained part of the Ukrainian SSR. Although the entire territory came under wartime Romanian control in July 1941, when, with neighbouring territories in Ukraine, it formed part of a Governorate of Transnistria, administered from Odesa (now in Ukraine), after its recapture by the USSR in August 1944 the Moldovan SSR was re-established. Subsequently, Russian and Ukrainian immigration was encouraged, and the territories of Transnistria became the industrial heartland of the Moldovan SSR.

Domestic Political Affairs

As the reformist policies favoured by Soviet leader Mikhail Gorbachev took effect in the late 1980s, Romanian nationalism—including demands for reunification with Romania—became increasingly popular in Moldova, despite opposition from the Slavic population. This opposition was a prominent factor behind the proclamation, in September 1990, of Transnistria's secession from Moldova, as the 'Dnestr Moldovan Soviet Socialist Republic'. The separatists were dominated by conservative communist elements largely opposed to the dissolution of the USSR.

Armed conflict broke out in December 1991, as the Transnistrian leadership, opposed to the Moldovan Government's objective of reunification with Romania, launched a campaign to gain control of all the territories on the east bank of the Dniester, with the ultimate aim of unity with Russia. Over six months of military conflict with Moldovan troops ensued. The situation was complicated by the presence (and involvement in support of the east-bank Slavs) of the former Soviet 14th Army, which was still stationed in the region and jurisdiction over which had been transferred to Russia. By June 1992 some 700 people were believed to have been killed in the conflict. On 21 July, however, a peace agreement was finally negotiated by President Mircea Snegur of Moldova and his Russian counterpart, Boris Yeltsin, whereby Transnistria was to be accorded 'special status' within Moldova, the terms of which were to be formulated subsequently. Later in July Russian, Moldovan and Transnistrian peacekeeping troops were deployed in the region to monitor the ceasefire.

De facto separation from Moldova

Transnistria continued to demand full statehood, and in January 1994 the Moldovan Government accepted proposals by the Conference on Security and Co-operation in Europe (CSCE—later OSCE) for greater autonomy for Transnistria. In April Snegur and the Transnistrian leader, Igor Smirnov, pledged their commitment to a peaceful resolution of the conflict. In July, following the adoption of the new Moldovan Constitution, which provided for a 'special autonomous status' for Transnistria, negotiations commenced on the details of the region's future status. Progress was obstructed by the Transnistrian leadership's demands that the 15,000-strong 14th Army remain in the region as a guarantor of security. In October Moldova and Russia reached an agreement on the gradual withdrawal of the 14th Army, whereupon Transnistria's 'special autonomous status' would take effect. A referendum (declared illegal by President Snegur) was held in Transnistria in March 1995, in which 91% of participants voted against the withdrawal of the 14th Army. In December two further referendums were held in Transnistria: 82.7% of the electorate endorsed a new constitution that proclaimed the region's independence, while 89.7% voted for Transnistria to join the Commonwealth of Independent States (CIS, see p. 241) as a sovereign state. In February 1996, however, the CIS rejected admittance for Transnistria.

Smirnov was re-elected as President of Transnistria in December 1996. In May 1997 Smirnov and the new Moldovan President, Petru Lucinschi, meeting in the Russian capital, Moscow, signed a memorandum on the normalization of relations between Moldova and Transnistria, providing for a common state, with Russia and Ukraine acting as guarantors. In March 1998 a further agreement (the Odesa Accords) was signed by Lucinschi, Smirnov, Russian premier Viktor Chernomyrdin and President Leonid Kuchma of Ukraine, which envisaged that Russian troops would remain in Transnistria until a final political settlement was reached, while Moldova's peacekeeping troops were to be gradually reduced in number. In late May 1999 Transnistria was formally designated an autonomous entity.

In June 2000 the 'Transnistrian Supreme Council (Soviet)' was converted to a unicameral legislature, and in July Smirnov introduced a form of presidential rule. Moldova's relations with the Transnistrian authorities deteriorated in September, following the Moldovan Government's introduction of new customs procedures, in accordance with the requirements of the World Trade Organization (WTO, see p. 431), leading to Transnistria alleging that Moldova was attempting to impose an 'economic blockade' on the region. Smirnov was re-elected to a second presidential term in December in a poll that was recognized by neither Moldova nor the international community.

In July 2002 mediators from Russia, Ukraine and the OSCE submitted a new draft agreement (the 'Kyiv agreement'), according to which Moldova would become a federal state. In February 2003 the European Union (EU) and the USA imposed a travel ban on those Transnistrian officials considered to be 'primarily responsible for a lack of co-operation in promoting a political settlement'. In November Russian President Vladimir Putin announced new proposals for a settlement, which envisaged the establishment of an 'asymmetrical federation'; however, the Moldovan President, Vladimir Voronin, withdrew support for the plan later in the month. In mid-2004 controversy arose over the closure by the Transnistrian authorities of Moldovan-language schools teaching a Moldovan syllabus, in the Latin script. The Moldovan Government responded by withdrawing from the OSCE-mediated negotiation process and imposing economic sanctions on Transnistria, which retaliated in kind. The EU and the USA condemned the closure of the schools and added a further 10 Transnistrian officials to the list of those prohibited from travelling to their countries.

In April 2005 President Viktor Yushchenko of Ukraine, during a summit meeting in Chişinău, presented a plan for the resolution of the Transnistrian conflict, under which Transnistria would be awarded special status within Moldova, and would, moreover, be permitted to participate in foreign-policy decisions that were determined to affect its interests. In June the Moldovan Parliament endorsed the Yushchenko Plan, while noting that it made no mention of either the withdrawal of Russian troops or the establishment of border controls along the Transnistrian–Ukrainian border. In July Moldova ended the trade sanctions imposed against Transnistria in the previous year. All five parties to the negotiations on the status of Transnistria agreed in September to invite the EU and the USA to participate in the process as observers; however, subsequent meetings failed to record any substantive progress. Legislative elections (recognized by neither Moldova nor the international community) were held in Transnistria in December, at which the reformist Obnovleniye (Renewal) bloc won the most seats in the region's Supreme Council.

In November 2005 the EU launched a mission to assist in securing the Transnistrian–Ukrainian border. In March 2006, following an agreement reached with Moldova, Ukraine refused to recognize Transnistria's customs regime and agreed henceforth to deal only in goods processed through the Moldovan customs system. In response, the Transnistrian authorities withdrew from the internationally mediated negotiations and introduced legislation banning all foreign-financed non-governmental organizations.

On 17 September 2006 the Transnistrian authorities conducted an internationally unrecognized referendum on the territory's future status, at which some 97% voted for a continuation of de facto independence from Moldova and an objective of eventual unification with Russia, while some 95% voted against the territory being ruled as part of Moldova. On 10 December Smirnov won a presidential election in Transnistria (again unrecognized by the international community), with 82.4% of votes cast. Shortly after the unilateral declaration of independence by Kosovo (hitherto a UN-administered province within Serbia) in February 2008, Transnistria formally requested that the Russian legislature, the UN and other organizations recognize its independence, although in the event no party did so. In April Smirnov and Moldovan President Vladimir Voronin met for the first time since 2001, in Bendery (Tighina), Transnistria.

On 18 March 2009 a meeting between Voronin and Smirnov was convened in Moscow, under the aegis of Russian President Dmitrii Medvedev. The three leaders signed a declaration providing for the conversion of the existing peacekeeping force in Transnistria into an OSCE-supervised operation, and reiterated commitments to return to the '5+2' negotiating format (comprising Moldova, Transnistria, Russia, Ukraine and the OSCE, together with the USA and the EU). However, Voronin subsequently accused the Transnistrian authorities of failing to respect their obligations to continue dialogue and abandoned a planned meeting with Smirnov in Tiraspol later in March. On 8 July Yevgenii Shevchuk announced his resignation as President of the Transnistrian Supreme Council, citing 'deep disagreements' with Smirnov. The deputy leader of the Obnovleniye parliamentary faction, Anatolii Kaminskii, was elected to the post unopposed later in the month. In July 2010 Kaminskii succeeded Shevchuk as the Chairman of the principal party represented in the Obnovleniye bloc, the Respublikanskaya Partiya 'Obnovleniye' (Obnovleniye—Renewal Republican Party).

Internationally unrecognized legislative elections took place in Transnistria on 12 December 2010; it was reported that the Obnovleniye bloc had won 25 of the 43 seats in the Supreme Council, with about 42% of the electorate participating. Following the installation of a new reformist Government in Transnistria in January 2011, an OSCE initiative for the resumption of negotiations on the status of the territory began. In September the Moldovan premier, Vladimir Filat, and Smirnov met, under OSCE auspices, in Bad Reichenhall, Germany, and again in Moscow. At the end of November negotiations under the '5+2' format formally resumed in the Lithuanian capital, Vilnius, with the mediation of Lithuania (which at that time chaired the OSCE).

Yevgenii Shevchuk elected as President

Prior to the election to the Transnistrian presidency due to be held in late 2011, Smirnov was subject to significant pressure from the Russian authorities to withdraw his candidacy, rather than seeking a fifth term of office. Notably, in late October it was announced that criminal proceedings had commenced in Russia against Smirnov's son, Oleg, who was accused of the embezzlement of humanitarian aid funds that Russia had supplied to Transnistria. Smirnov was, nevertheless, among six candidates to contest the first round of

the election on 11 December, but he was only placed third, with 24.7% of the votes cast, behind Shevchuk, who, contesting the election as an independent candidate, secured 38.6% of votes cast, and Kaminskii, with 26.3%. At the run-off poll between the two leading candidates held on 25 December, Shevchuk was overwhelmingly elected President, securing 73.9% of votes cast; Kaminskii received 19.7%, while 4.5% of the votes were against all candidates. Voter turnout of 58.9% in the first round, and 52.5% in the second was reported. While Kaminskii had been the Russian administration's preferred candidate, Shevchuk was widely regarded as a Russian-orientated reformist.

On 10 January 2012 Shevchuk appointed Petr Stepanov, the General Director of the Transnistrian state-controlled gas-import firm, Tiraspoltransgaz-Pridnestroviye, and the hitherto Minister of Industry, as Chairman of the Government; a substantially reorganized administration was formed later in the month. Also in January a young Moldovan was shot dead by a Russian officer at a checkpoint on Transnistria's de facto border with Moldova, causing the Moldovan Government to renew demands for the Russian military mission to be reconstituted on a civilian basis. Following Shevchuk's election, official negotiations under the '5+2' format were convened in Dublin, Ireland, in February; however, these ended without conclusion, after the Russian and Moldovan delegations presented further procedural demands. On 21 March President Medvedev appointed a Deputy Chairman of the Russian Government (and prominent Russian nationalist), Dmitrii Rogozin, to the new post of his Special Representative to Transnistria. (Similar positions were created for the two Georgian secessionist territories of Abkhazia and South Ossetia, both of which, unlike Transnistria, Russia formally recognized as independent states.) At the end of March Shevchuk and Filat, meeting in Tiraspol, signed a protocol for the resumption of full train services across Transnistria. In the same month the Supreme Council of Transnistria signed protocols of co-operation with the legislature of Gagauzia (similar agreements had earlier been signed with the separatist parliaments of Abkhazia and South Ossetia). Further negotiations under the '5+2' format, convened in Vienna, Austria, in April and July, again resulted in little progress, apparently after the Russian government representative objected to new draft provisions establishing equal status for all the '5+2' participants.

On 13 June Kaminskii resigned as Chairman of the Supreme Council; he was succeeded on the same day by one of his former deputy chairmen, Mikhail Burla. Later in the month Burla was also elected to succeed Kaminskii as Chairman of Obnovleniye.

Meanwhile, in April 2012 it was reported that the Russian Minister of Defence had conducted an inspection of Russian troops in Transnistria, prompting an official protest from the Moldovan authorities. Shortly afterwards, during his first visit to Chişinău and Tiraspol in his new capacity, Rogozin announced, *inter alia*, the intention of the Russian Government to rearm and re-equip its troops in Transnistria as part of the modernization of its army. An official statement issued upon the 20th anniversary of the deployment of Russian troops in Transnistria in July indicated that Russia planned to maintain its military presence in the territory indefinitely until the agreement of a permanent settlement (despite Moldova's demands that it be replaced with an international civilian mission); it was also implied that the only resolution acceptable to Russia would be based on the 'federalization' of Moldova. During a press interview at the end of that month, Russian President Vladimir Putin declared his support for Transnistria's self-determination. On 2 August Shevchuk visited Moscow to meet Rogozin; Russia's state flag and Transnistria's flag (depicting the Soviet symbols) were displayed together at a public appearance of the two officials, implying that Russia regarded Transnistria as constituting a state, despite having refused to grant formal recognition of the territory's statehood.

In September 2012 the EU ended its travel restrictions on former Transnistrian government officials, in recognition of progress in negotiations to resolve the conflict (following the resumption of the '5+2' discussions), but stipulated that further developments, including with respect to the rights of Latin-script Moldovan-language schools to operate in the territory, would be closely monitored. Nevertheless, any advance in negotiations was hampered by tensions surrounding Russia's strenuous objections to Moldova's admission to US and EU defence agreements in late 2012. Following proposed EU cross-border initiatives for economic co-operation, in early November the Russian Government offered 3,000m. roubles to fund the establishment of a 'Eurasian economic region' in Transnistria and to strengthen Russia's military presence in the region. Later that month the new Moldovan President, Nicolae Timofti, strongly rejected a proposal by the Russian Government to establish a representative office in Transnistria of the Russian consulate in Chişinău. Discussions under the '5+2' format were convened in Lviv, Ukraine, in February 2013, after which the OSCE announced that negotiation efforts were to continue in Odesa in May. However, a political crisis in Moldova following the collapse of the pro-EU coalition Government in March presented a further obstacle to the peace process. Tensions between the Moldovan and Transnistrian authorities intensified in April, as a consequence of a number of disputes in and around Bendery, the only area on the west bank of the Nistru controlled by the separatist authorities. The town's authorities announced that, henceforth, any Moldovan police officers in the town (which was jointly patrolled by Moldovan and Transnistrian police, in accordance with a 1992 agreement) would not be permitted to wear uniform. In response, the Moldovan authorities announced that they were to establish new checkpoints in the security zone that separated the areas controlled by Transnistria from the territories controlled by the Moldovan Government. Subsequently, the Transnistrian authorities began constructing checkpoints around the village of Varniţa, near Bendery, which remained under Moldovan control. In late April fighting broke out between residents of the village and Transnistrian special forces, after the residents dismantled the checkpoints. Meanwhile, the Transnistrian authorities claimed that the presence of heavily armed guards at two Moldovan prisons in Bendery constituted the creation of a military base in the city, and demanded the withdrawal of the armed personnel from the prisons. In late May President Shevchuk spoke in support of proposals for relocating the Supreme Council from Tiraspol to Bendery; however, shortly afterwards the Supreme Council voted to reject such proposals, instead approving a resolution that the legislature remain in Tiraspol. In June legislation was enacted providing for the extension of the territory of Transnistria to Varniţa and several other villages under Moldovan control, and the introduction of measures to protect the border; the decree was strongly rejected by the Moldovan authorities.

Meanwhile, on 19 June 2013 Shevchuk appointed Tatyana Turanskaya, a former official in the Transnistria tax inspectorate, as Deputy Chairman of the Government, responsible for Regional Development. Shortly afterwards, she was appointed acting Chairman of the Government, while Stepanov was on vacation. On 10 July Shevchuk announced that he accepted Stepanov's resignation, and that he had appointed Turanskaya as his successor; her appointment was endorsed by the Supreme Council on the same day. Several other government changes were implemented later that month: Vitalii Ulitka, the Chairman of the Committee for Prices and Anti-monopoly Affairs, was appointed additionally as a Deputy Chairman of the Government, while Aleksandr Kisnichan, the Plenipotentiary Representative of the President to the Supreme Council, was additionally appointed Minister of Justice. In September Shevchuk met the Moldovan Prime Minister appointed earlier in the year, Iurie Leancă, in Tiraspol, to discuss the proposed reintroduction of a full freight service on the railway line passing through Transnistria. A further minor government reshuffle was implemented in late September. On 2 October Nataliya Nikiforova resigned as Deputy Chairman of the Government, responsible for Social Policy. In early October the Supreme Council voted in support of a constitutional amendment providing for local city and district administrators to be directly elected, instead of appointed, as hitherto. Shevchuk opposed these proposals (despite having made similar pledges during his campaign for the presidency), which would require approval by the legislature in two further votes.

Negotiations under the '5+2' format resumed in Brussels, Belgium, in October 2013. A further round took place in Ukraine in November, when agreement was reached on the establishment of migration control checkpoints at the administrative border with Transnistria (as a prerequisite for the relaxation of EU visa restrictions for Moldovan citizens); work on improving the identification process for the population of Transnistria was to continue. Meanwhile, the planned initialling of an Association Agreement between Moldova and the EU, at a summit meeting to be held in Vilnius, Lithuania, in November, was a source of controversy in Transnistria, owing to concerns that the terms of the agreement would have the effect of reducing Transnistria's external trade. In mid-October Shevchuk visited Moscow, when Rogozin pledged that Russia would provide assistance to the territory to counteract the consequences of the agreement, while noting that the Transnistrian authorities were 'prepared to give a harsh response' to Moldova entering into an Association Agreement with the EU. After the Association Agreement (which was expected to be formally signed in September 2014) was initialled in November 2013, the European Commission stated, in response to criticism by the Russian ambassador to the EU, that the concomitant provisions for a Deep and Comprehensive Free Trade Agreement would also apply to the territory of Transnistria, subject to its implementation by the territorial authorities.

Recent developments: the crisis in Ukraine

In December 2013 Shevchuk submitted a proposal to the Supreme Council that Transnistria's Constitution be amended to allow the introduction of Russian federal legislation in the territory, with Transnistrian legislation to be subordinate to that of the Russian Federation. After the Council approved the motion on 25 December, work commenced on the drafting and adoption of a constitutional amendment, in advance of the undertaking of the numerous amendments of existing legislation that would be required to bring about

the harmonization of Transnistrian legislation with Russian federal norms. In February 2014 the European Parliament adopted a resolution condemning pressure exercised by the Transnistrian authorities against Romanian-language schools and urging the OSCE to continue monitoring activities particularly in that respect. Following Russia's de facto military seizure and annexation of Crimean peninsula from Ukraine in February–March (see the chapter on Ukraine), in early March the Supreme Council proposed that control over Transnistria's air-space be increased as a counter-response to perceived closer co-operation between the Moldovan authorities and the North Atlantic Treaty Organization (NATO, see p. 367). Concern was also expressed internationally that the presence of Russian troops in Transnistria could be used, either to enforce a similar annexation of Transnistria, or be used in support of elements in neighbouring regions of Ukraine (most notably in Odesa) supportive of their entering into union with Russia. Later that month Russia staged military exercises in Transnistria. On 18 March, when a treaty on the accession of Crimea and the City of Sevastopol to the Russian Federation was signed by the respective political leaders, the Transnistrian Supreme Soviet issued a request also to join the Russian Federation; while this request was welcomed by Russian nationalists, including the senior leadership of the Liberalno-demokraticheskaya Partiya Rossii (Liberal Democratic Party of Russia) and the Kommunistechiskaya Partiya Rossiiskoi Federatsii (Communist Party of the Russian Federation), no formal response was forthcoming from the state authorities.

Regional tensions increased following the escalation of the crisis in eastern Ukraine, and Moldova's signature of an EU Association Agreement in June 2014. While Russia responded with the imposition of trade restrictions against Moldova, in early July Rogozin signed several trade and co-operation agreements with Shevchuk in Moscow. Later that month Shevchuk visited Crimea where he met the new Russian-supported leadership and conducted further discussions with Rogozin. At the same time, relations deteriorated between Transnistria and the new Ukrainian Government, which perceived the territory as constituting a threat to Ukrainian security, as evidenced by the existence of links between former senior officials in the Transnistrian authorities and the secessionist 'People's Republics' of Luhansk and Donetsk in eastern Ukraine, as well as the pro-Russian leadership in Crimea and Sevastopol. Notably, Vladimir Antyufeyev, formerly Transnistria's Minister of State Security between 1992 and 2012, was involved in the Crimean uprising and then became Deputy Prime Minister (and acting Chairman) of the self-proclaimed 'Donetsk People's Republic' until his removal in September 2014, while Aleksandr Karaman, Transnistria's Deputy President in 1990–2001, was appointed a deputy premier in Donetsk in September. Consequently, the Ukrainian authorities increased security measures at the border of Ukraine with Transnistria, placing restrictions on the cross-border movements of male Russian citizens of fighting age, and of certain goods vehicles registered in Russia. At the end of July Ukrainian border guards claimed that reconnaissance unmanned aerial vehicles from Transnistria had violated Ukrainian air space on three occasions, while it was reported that the Ukrainian authorities had begun to construct a 450-km ditch along the border with Transnistria, apparently in order to impede a potential invasion by Russian forces stationed in Transnistria. (According to official figures, Russian troops stationed in Transnistria continued to number about 1,900.) During a visit to both Moldova and Transnistria in August, Rogozin issued assurances that Russia would fulfil its obligations to maintain peace in the region. However, the Transnistrian authorities refused to participate in the next round of '5+2' negotiations, which had been scheduled to take place in Vienna in September. In his annual public address in December, Shevchuk warned of possible armed conflict in Transnistria in 2015. The Ukrainian authorities further reinforced the border with Transnistria with the deployment of an additional 1,000 national guard troops in early 2015, while the Russian Ministry of Defence confirmed Ukrainian reports that some 400 Russian special forces were training Transnistrian soldiers in the territory.

By the end of 2014 Transnistria had suffered a severe economic deterioration, following an economic crisis in Russia related to the imposition of sanctions against the country as a result of its annexation of Crimea and presumed involvement in the ensuing conflict in the Donetsk and Luhansk oblasts of eastern Ukraine. In addition to a decline in exports to Russia, subsidies previously extended by the Russian authorities to the territory had fallen sharply, resulting in a sharp reduction in public sector salaries, and in the withdrawal of pension supplements (which had been granted since 2008). Shevchuk expressed his willingness to co-operate with a new Moldovan Government formed in February 2015 in an effort to overcome the economic difficulties affecting both Transnistria and Moldova.

An OSCE-mediated meeting between Moldovan and Transnistrian representatives took place on 12 March 2015. In the same month, as part of a broader government reorganization, Shevchuk appointed Aleksandr Kisnichan, hitherto Minister of Justice, to the newly created post of Deputy Chairman of the Government, responsible for Legal Regulation and Collaboration with the Organs of State Power. In April a new Ministry, of Regional Development, Transport and Communications was formed; one of the incumbent deputy premiers, Vasilii Vlasov, was appointed as its head.

PUBLIC HOLIDAYS

2016: 1–2 January (New Year), 7 January (Christmas—Julian Calendar), 23 February (Defenders of the Fatherland Day), 8 March (International Women's Day), 1–2 May (Days of Solidarity with Workers), 9 May (Republic Day), 2 September (Liberation Day), 7 November (Great October Socialist Revolution), 24 December (Constitution Day), 25 December (Christmas—Gregorian Calendar).

Transnistria: Directory

The Government of the 'Transnistrian Moldovan Republic'

PRESIDENT

President: YEVGENII V. SHEVCHUK.

CABINET OF MINISTERS
(May 2015)

Chairman of the Government: TATYANA M. TURANSKAYA.

First Deputy Chairman of the Government: MAIYA I. PARNAS.

Deputy Chairman of the Government, Chairman of the Committee for Prices and Anti-monopoly Affairs: VITALII P. ULITKA.

Deputy Chairman of the Government, responsible for International Co-operation, Minister of Foreign Affairs: NINA V. SHTANSKI.

Deputy Chairman of the Government, responsible for Regional Development Affairs, Minister of Regional Development, Transport and Communications: VASILII I. VLASOV.

Deputy Chairman of the Government, responsible for Legal Regulation and Collaboration with the Organs of State Power: ALEKSANDR A. KISNICHAN.

Minister of Finance: YELENA G. GIRZHUL.

Minister of Economic Development: ALEVTINA A. SLINCHENKO.

Minister of Health: TATYANA S. SKRYPNIK.

Minister of Education: IRINA F. KAKHANOVSKAYA.

Minister of Justice: OLGA V. ZVARYCH.

Minister of Agriculture and Natural Resources: ANDREI S. KIRSTA.

Minister of Social Protection and Labour: OKSANA V. BULANOVA.

Minister of Defence: Maj.-Gen. ALEKSANDR A. LUKYANENKO.

Minister of Internal Affairs: GENNADII YU. KUZMICHEV.

Note: the Chairmen of the State Administrations of the seven primary territorial subdivisions are also members of the Government.

MINISTRIES

Office of the President: 3300 Tiraspol, ul. Gorkogo 53; tel. (533) 6-27-20; fax (533) 8-05-02; e-mail psp.pmr@mail.ru; internet president .gospmr.ru.

Office of the Chairman of the Government: 3300 Tiraspol, ul. 25 Oktyabrya 45; tel. (533) 6-27-16; e-mail people@gov-pmr.org; internet gov-pmr.org.

Ministry of Agriculture and Natural Resources: 3300 Tiraspol, ul. Yunosti 58/3; tel. (533) 2-67-45; fax (533) 2-78-96; e-mail ecopmr@ mail.ru; internet ecology-pmr.org.

Ministry of Defence: 3300 Tiraspol, per. K. Tsetkina 6A; tel. (533) 9-70-78; internet www.mopmr.idknet.com.

Ministry of Economic Development: 3300 Tiraspol, ul. Sverdlova 57; tel. (533) 9-63-66; fax (533) 9-74-10; e-mail economy.pmr@gmail .com; internet www.mepmr.org.

Ministry of Education: 3300 Tiraspol, ul. Mira 27; tel. (533) 2-22-29; fax (533) 2-34-97; e-mail prosveshenie@minpros.info; internet www.minpros.info.

Ministry of Finance: 3300 Tiraspol, ul. Karla Marksa 187; tel. and fax (533) 7-86-03; e-mail info@minfin-pmr.org; internet www .minfin-pmr.org.

Ministry of Foreign Affairs: 3300 Tiraspol, ul. Sverdlova 45; tel. and fax (533) 7-43-46; e-mail office@mfa-pmr.org; internet www .mfa-pmr.org.

Ministry of Health: 3300 Tiraspol, per. Dnestrovskii 3; tel. (533) 8-05-25; internet www.minzdravpmr.org.

Ministry of Internal Affairs: 3300 Tiraspol, ul. Manoilova 68; tel. (533) 8-15-29; e-mail shtab-mvd-pmr@rambler.ru; internet www .mvdpmr.org.

Ministry of Justice: 3300 Tiraspol, ul. Lenina 26; tel. (533) 8-18-18; fax (533) 8-17-53; e-mail inbox@justice.idknet.com; internet justice .idknet.com.

Ministry of Regional Development, Transport and Communications: 3300 Tiraspol, ul. Sovetskaya 81A; tel. (533) 9-44-15; fax (533) 9-82-00; e-mail energpmr@gmail.com; internet energodep .gospmr.org.

Ministry of Social Protection and Labour: 3300 Tiraspol, ul. 25 Oktyabrya 114; tel. and fax (533) 8-18-44; e-mail contact@ minsoctrud.org; internet www.minsoctrud.org.

President

Presidential Election, First Round, 11 December 2011

Candidates	Votes	% of votes
Yevgenii Shevchuk (Independent)	95,765	38.55
Anatolii Kaminskii (Obnovleniye)	65,330	26.30
Igor Smirnov (Independent)	61,248	24.66
Oleg Khorzhan (Pridnestrovskaya Kommunisticheskaya Partiya)	12,646	5.09
Others	2,744	1.10
Against all candidates	4,667	1.88
Total*	248,386	100.00

* Including 5,986 invalid votes (2.41% of total votes).

Second Round, 25 December 2011

Candidates	Votes	% of votes
Yevgenii Shevchuk (Independent)	165,502	73.88
Anatolii Kaminskii (Obnovleniye)	44,071	19.67
Against all candidates	9,977	4.45
Total*	224,010	100.00

* Including 4,460 invalid votes (1.99% of total votes).

Legislature

Elections were held to the 43-member Supreme Council on 12 December 2010. It was reported that the Renewal bloc had won 25 of the 43 seats in the Supreme Council, and that the majority of the remaining deputies had no formal party allegiance.

Supreme Council

3300 Tiraspol, ul. 25 Oktyabrya 45; tel. (533) 9-44-49; e-mail kav@ vspmr.org; internet vspmr.org.

Chairman: MIKHAIL P. BURLA.

Election Commission

Central Electoral Commission: 3300 Tiraspol, ul. Shevchenko 12; tel. (533) 72022; fax (533) 73136; e-mail izbircom@cikpmr.idknet .com; internet www.cikpmr.idknet.com; Chair. NADEZHDA V. ZABLOTSKAYA.

Political Organizations

The following are among the principal political parties operating in the 'Transnistrian Moldovan Republic'.

Liberalno-demokraticheskaya Partiya Respubliki Pridnestrovye (LDPR-P) (Liberal Democratic Party of the Transnistrian Republic): Tiraspol, ul. 25 Oktyabrya 37A; tel. and fax (533) 9-53-70; e-mail ldprpr@gmail.com; internet ldprpmr.com; f. 2006; affiliated to the Russian nationalist Liberalno-demokraticheskaya partiya Rossii; Leader ROMAN KHUDYAKOV.

Narodno-demokraticheskaya Partiya 'Proryv' (Proryv) (Breakthrough People's Democratic Party): 2069 Tiraspol, per. Naberezhnyi 1A; tel. (533) 5-66-78; e-mail psproriv@gmail.com; internet www.proriv.wordpress.com; f. 2006; Chair. ALEKSANDR GORELOVSKII.

Pridnestrovskaya Kommunisticheskaya Partiya (Transnistrian Communist Party): 2069 Tiraspol, bulv. Gagarina 1 B; tel. and fax (533) 9-77-76; internet www.pkp.ucoz.ru; f. 1991 as successor to the local branch of the Communist Party of the Soviet Union; allied with the Komunistychna Partiya Ukrayiny and the Kommunisticheskaya Partiya Rossiiskoi Federatskii; Chair. OLEG O. KHORZHAN.

Respublikanskaya Partiya 'Obnovleniye' (Obnovleniye) (Renewal Republican Party): 3300 Tiraspol, ul. 25 Oktyabrya 118; tel. (533) 4-57-44; internet www.obnovlenie.info; f. 2000; allied with the de facto ruling party of Russia, Yedinaya Rossiya; Chair. MIKHAIL P. BURLA.

The Press

In January 2012 some 14 principal newspapers were published in Transnistria, and three news agencies were operating.

PRINCIPAL NEWSPAPERS AND PERIODICALS

Chelovek i ego prava (Man and his Rights): Tiraspol; f. 2003; in Russian; published by the Foundation for the Defence of Human Rights and Effective Politics; human rights, social and political; 48 a year; Editor-in-Chief NICOLAE BUCEACCHI.

Dnestrovskaya Pravda/Adevărul Nistrean (Dniestr/Nistru Truth): 3300 Tiraspol, ul. 25 Oktyabrya 101/236–237; tel. (533) 3-46-86; fax (233) 3-46-86; e-mail tiraspol@dn_prav.mldnet.com; internet www.tiraspol.tripod.com; f. 1941; Russian and Moldovan (Cyrillic script) editions; funded by the authorities of the 'Transnistrian Moldovan Republic'; daily; Editors TATYANA RUDENKO (Russian edn), VLADIMIR COVALI (Moldovan edn).

Dobrâi Deni (Good Afternoon): Rybnitsa; independent; pro-opposition; in Romanian.

Gomin (The Echo): Rybnitsa, ul. Kirova 130; tel. (555) 3-08-61; fax (555) 4-26-27; e-mail gomin130@mail.ru; f. 1996; weekly; in Ukrainian; Chief Editor DMITRII CERNEGA; circ. 2,460 (2008).

Novaya Gazeta (New Gazette): Bendery; f. 2000; in Russian; Editor ANDREI SAFONOV.

Obnovleniye (Renewal): 3300 Tiraspol, ul. 9 Yanvarya 192; tel. (533) 7-43-96; fax (533) 5-00-10; e-mail obnovlenie@idknet.com; internet www.obnovlenie.info; f. 2000; monthly; in Russian; politics and economics; circ. 3,000 (2013); Chair. MIHAIL BURLA.

Partner (Partner): 3300 Tiraspol, ul. Lenina 48; tel. (533) 9-64-80; e-mail makireeva@yandex.ru; internet www.tiraspol.ru/partner; f. 2004; monthly; in Russian; publ. by the Chamber of Commerce and Industry of the 'Transnistrian Moldovan Republic'; Chief Editor MARINA KIREYEVA; circ. 999 (2008).

Pridnestrovye (Transnistria): 3300 Tiraspol, ul. Lunacharskogo 13; tel. (533) 9-30-24; fax (533) 7-47-00; e-mail pridnestr@idknet.com; internet www.pridnestrovie-daily.net; f. 1994; owned by the authorities of the 'Transnistrian Moldovan Republic'; in Russian; politics, economics, culture; 5 a week; Editor-in-Chief NATALIYA VOROBIYEVA; circ. 4,241 (2008).

Sovety Naroda (Councils of the People): 3300 Tiraspol, ul. 25 Oktyabrya 45; tel. (533) 8-10-47; e-mail psvs06@mail.ru; internet vspmr.org/?Part=6#menu; f. 2007; organ of the Supreme Council; in Russian; politics, economics, culture; monthly; Chief Editor S. MELNICHENKO; circ. 4,241 (2008).

NEWS AGENCIES

Dniester: Tiraspol; e-mail dniester.post@gmail.com; internet www.dniester.ru; f. 2009; Russian; online only; Man. ROMAN KONOPLEV.

Lenta PMR (Newswire of the 'Transnistrian Moldovan Republic'): Tiraspol; tel. (533) 8-44-46; e-mail tiras.ru@gmail.com; internet www.tiras.ru; Russian; Editor-in-Chief ROMAN KONOPLEV.

Olvia-Press: 3300 Tiraspol, ul. Rozy Lyuksemburga 10; tel. (533) 8-24-97; fax (533) 8-20-04; e-mail olvia@idknet.com; internet www.olvia.idknet.com; f. 1992; Russian; owned by the authorities of the 'Transnistrian Moldovan Republic'; reports political, economic and cultural devts in the region; Editor-in-Chief OLEG A. YELKOV.

PRESS ASSOCIATION

Media Center Transnistria: 3300 Tiraspol, ul. Kuchurganskaya 38; tel. (777) 5-84-81; e-mail smi.pridnestrovie@gmail.com; f. 2009; fmrly the Creative Union of Young Journalists of Transnistria; promoting the independence of mass media and the development of civil society.

Finance

BANKING

Central Bank

Republican Bank of Transnistria (PRB) (Pridnestrovskii Respublikanskii Bank): 3300 Tiraspol, ul. 25 Oktyabya 71; tel. (533) 5-98-70; fax (533) 5-99-07; e-mail info@cbpmr.net; internet www.cbpmr.net; f. 1992; Chair. EDUARD A. KOSOVSKII.

Trade and Industry

CHAMBER OF COMMERCE

Chamber of Commerce and Industry of the 'Transnistrian Moldovan Republic' (Pridnestrovie) (TPP PMR): 3300 Tiraspol, ul. Lenina 48; tel. (533) 9-42-03; fax (533) 9-42-03; e-mail tpp@tiraspol.ru; internet www.tiraspol.ru; f. 1993; non-commercial partnership; brs in Bendery (Tighina), Rybnitsa (Râbniţa) and Dubossari (Dubăsari); Pres. VASILY KOZHAN.

MONACO

Introductory Survey

LOCATION, CLIMATE, LANGUAGE, RELIGION, FLAG

The Principality of Monaco lies in Western Europe. The country is a small enclave in south-eastern France, about 15 km east of Nice. It has a coastline on the Mediterranean Sea but is otherwise surrounded by French territory. The climate is Mediterranean, with warm, dry summers and mild winters. The official language is French, but Monégasque (a mixture of the French Provençal and Italian Ligurian dialects), Italian and English are also spoken. Most of the population profess Christianity, with about 91% belonging to the Roman Catholic Church. The national flag (proportions 4 by 5) has two equal horizontal stripes, of red and white. The state flag (proportions 4 by 5) displays the princely arms of Monaco (a white shield, held by two monks and superimposed on a pavilion of ermine) on a white background.

CONTEMPORARY POLITICAL HISTORY

Historical Context

The Principality of Monaco is a hereditary monarchy, which has been ruled by the Grimaldi dynasty since 1297. It was abolished during the French Revolution but re-established in 1814. In 1861 Monaco became an independent state under the protection of France. The first Constitution, promulgated in January 1911, vested legislative power jointly in the Prince and a 12-member Conseil National (National Council), selected for a term of five years by a panel comprising nine delegates of the municipality and 21 members elected by male adult suffrage. Agreements in 1918 and 1919 between France and Monaco provided that, should the reigning Prince die without leaving a male heir, Monaco would become an autonomous state under French sovereignty. Prince Louis II, the ruler of Monaco from 1922, died in May 1949, and was succeeded by his grandson, Prince Rainier III. A new Constitution, introduced in December 1962, abolished the principle of the divine right of the monarch, enfranchised women and stipulated that the National Council (enlarged to 18 members) was to be elected solely and directly by universal adult suffrage. Executive power was to be exercised, under the authority of the Prince, by the Council of Government, led by a Minister of State appointed by the Prince.

Domestic Political Affairs

During the 20th century there were no political parties as such in Monaco, although candidates were grouped in electoral lists. Supporters of Prince Rainier, grouped in the Union Nationale et Démocratique (UND), dominated at five-yearly elections in 1963–88, on all but two occasions taking all 18 seats on the National Council. A UND list of candidates was not formed for the 1993 general election, although an electoral list headed by Jean-Louis Campora (the President of the Principality's football team, AS Monaco) won 15 seats. At legislative elections in 1998 the UND list, now headed by Campora, secured all 18 seats.

In the first half of 2002 the National Council approved a number of notable constitutional amendments which were partly intended to expedite Monaco's application for full membership of the Council of Europe (see p. 250), which had been submitted in 1998. The age of majority was lowered from 21 to 18 years, and several executive powers of the Prince were transferred to the National Council, which was to be increased to 24 members (of whom eight were to be elected on the basis of a form of proportional representation) following the elections in 2003. Additionally, the law of succession was modified, to permit succession through the female line.

In late 2002 discontent was reported at a proposal, supported by Campora, to sell AS Monaco to a Russian investment company—Fedcominvest—based in the Principality. Following allegations that Fedcominvest was involved in money-laundering, Prince Rainier, who, on behalf of the Principality, retained ultimate control over the club, prohibited the sale. The scandal appeared to be a significant factor in reducing support for Campora's UND at the legislative elections held in February 2003, when the UND secured only three seats on the enlarged National Council; the remaining 21 seats were awarded to the list of the Union pour Monaco (UpM), a coalition comprising mainly members of the Union pour la Principauté (UP) and the Union Nationale pour l'Avenir de Monaco (UNAM) and led by a former member of the UND, Stéphane Valeri.

In April 2004 the Council of Europe ruled that further reforms were required before Monaco could be considered for full membership; among the principal requirements were the extension to Monégasque citizens of eligibility for several senior government positions, including the Minister of State (who, under the terms of a 1930 treaty, was required to be a French civil servant), and improved fiscal regulation. Following the Council of Europe's decision that talks between France and Monaco had demonstrated significant progress towards the eventual reform of the 1930 convention, Monaco was admitted as a full member in October 2004. A treaty on administrative co-operation between France and Monaco was duly signed in November 2005, allowing Monégasque citizens to be appointed to senior government positions, subject to consultation with the French authorities. Agreements on financial regulation and judicial co-operation were signed concurrently.

On 6 April 2005 Prince Rainier died at the age of 81. He was succeeded by his son, Prince Albert II, who had acted as Regent of the Principality since 31 March. Albert II was formally inaugurated as Head of State on 12 July and enthroned as the Ruling Prince on 19 November.

At legislative elections held in February 2008, the UpM retained its 21 seats in the National Council. The remaining three seats were won by the Rassemblement et Enjeux pour Monaco (REM) list.

In January 2010 Valeri, the President of the National Council, replaced Jean-Jacques Campana as Government Councillor for Social Affairs and Health. Valeri was the first President of the National Council to be appointed to the Council of Government, in a move that was widely held to indicate the growing importance of the legislative body under Prince Albert's reign. Jean-François Robillon was subsequently elected to the presidency of the National Council. In March Michel Roger, a French civil servant, replaced Jean-Paul Proust as Minister of State; Prince Albert had declined to exercise his new authority, under the Franco-Monégasque treaty of 2005, to appoint a Monégasque citizen to the post. In the following month divisions within the UpM prompted the withdrawal from the coalition of the UNAM, which held four seats in the legislature.

Two electoral alliances and one political group contested the legislative elections held on 10 February 2013—Horizon Monaco (comprising REM, the UpM and Synergie Monégasque, and headed by Laurent Nouvion) secured 20 seats, Union Monégasque (comprising the Union des Monégasques and the UNAM, and led by Robillon) won three seats, and the remaining seat was taken by Renaissance (a new party established in late 2012 to defend the interests of the employees of the Principality's largest employer, Société des Bains de Mer). The electoral turnout was 74.6%. Nouvion was subsequently elected President of the National Council. Gilles Tonelli succeeded José Badia as Government Councillor for External Relations and Co-operation in February 2015.

Following the revival of land reclamation plans that had been abandoned in 2008 owing to environmental concerns and funding constraints, in March 2013 Prince Albert announced that a six-hectare extension of the Principality's territory into the sea would be developed in the eastern Portier area; the project, which would increase Monaco's land area by around 3%, was scheduled to be completed by 2024, at an estimated cost of €1,000m.

The line of succession to the Monégasque throne was assured in December 2014 following the birth of twins (a boy and a girl) to Prince Albert and Princess Charlene (whom the Prince married in July 2011). Despite being born shortly after his sister, Princess Gabriella, in accordance with the Principality's laws of succession which favour males, Prince Jacques assumed the role of his father's legitimate heir.

Foreign Affairs

Monaco became a member of the UN in 1993, and participates in the work of a number of other international organizations. In October 2002 Monaco and France signed a treaty of friendship and co-operation to replace the Franco-Monégasque Treaty of 1918. Under its terms, France guaranteed Monaco's full sovereignty and territorial integrity and recognized the law of succession as established by the recent constitutional amendments; the possibility that France might assume sovereignty over Monaco in the event of the throne becoming vacant was thus eliminated. In addition, the treaty provided for the establishment of diplomatic-level relations between the two states, while Monaco agreed to conduct its foreign relations in accordance with France's fundamental interests. In 2006 France upgraded the status of its diplomatic representation in Monaco from consular to ambassadorial level in accordance with the 2002 treaty, becoming the first country to operate an embassy in the Principality. Italy also opened an embassy in Monaco later in the year.

Controversy surrounding the use of Monaco's financial sector for the transfer of funds derived from criminal activities intensified in 1998 with the culmination of an investigation into the deposit (in 1995) of US $5.5m. in cash, suspected of originating from the illegal drugs trade, at a bank in Monaco. The affair led to a crisis in relations between France and the Principality, with the French Government overruling Prince Rainier by refusing to extend the mandate of Monaco's Chief Prosecutor, whom it suspected of not conducting a sufficiently thorough investigation of the scandal. Following further criticisms of Monégasque banking practice in a report by the Organisation for Economic Co-operation and Development (OECD, see p. 377) in 2000, the French Government recommended a rapid revision of the bilateral treaties between Monaco and France, proposing that Monégasque institutions be brought into greater conformity with French excise, fiscal and banking regulations. In a list published in April 2002, OECD defined Monaco as an 'unco-operative tax haven'. In December 2004 the European Union (EU, see p. 271) signed an agreement with Monaco on the taxation of savings income. Under the agreement, savings income, in the form of interest payments made in Monaco to residents of the EU, was to be subject to a withholding tax from 1 July 2005. Monaco also agreed to exchange information on request with EU member states in criminal or civil cases of tax fraud or comparable offences. In March 2009 Monaco announced that it would adopt OECD standards on the sharing of fiscal data, and was consequently removed from the OECD list in May. By mid-2014 Monaco had signed a total of 29 tax information exchange agreements with other countries.

In December 2012 the European Commission published a report outlining options for the further integration of three European microstates—Andorra, Monaco and San Marino—into the EU. The report dismissed EU membership for the three states in the near future, but recommended either membership of the European Economic Area (EEA) or the drawing up of one or several Framework Association Agreement(s) (FAA) with the microstates—preferably on a multilateral, rather than an individual, basis. In March 2015 the EU launched negotiations with the three microstates on Association Agreement(s).

In June 2014 the EU's Committee of Experts on the Evaluation of Anti-Money Laundering Measures and the Financing of Terrorism issued a critical report, stating that the authorities in Monaco needed to ensure that money-laundering cases were detected effectively, and were subject to investigation and prosecution.

CONSTITUTION AND GOVERNMENT

Under the Constitution of 17 December 1962, as amended on 2 April 2002, legislative power is vested jointly in the Prince, a hereditary ruler, and the 24-member Conseil National (National Council), which is elected by universal adult suffrage, partly under a system of proportional representation, for a term of five years. The electorate comprises only Monégasque citizens aged 18 years or over. Executive power is exercised, under the authority of the Prince, by the five-member Council of Government, headed by the Minister of State (a Monégasque or French civil servant appointed by the Prince after consultation with the French Government). The Prince represents the Principality in its relations with foreign powers, and signs and ratifies treaties. For the purposes of local administration there is, additionally, a consultative Conseil Communal (Municipal Council),

comprising 15 members elected for a term of four years, headed by a mayor.

REGIONAL AND INTERNATIONAL CO-OPERATION

Monaco is a member of the Council of Europe (see p. 250) and the Organization for Security and Co-operation in Europe (OSCE, see p. 385). By virtue of its customs union and open border with France, it forms part of the customs territory of the European Union (EU, see p. 271) and participates in the EU's Schengen Agreement on border controls; it also uses the euro as its currency. Monaco joined the UN in 1993.

ECONOMIC AFFAIRS

In 2009, according to World Bank estimates, Monaco's gross national income (GNI), measured at average 2007–09 prices, was US $6,479m., equivalent to US $183,150 per head. According to UN estimates, Monaco's gross domestic product (GDP) was $6,559m. in 2013 (equivalent to $173,377 per head). The population increased at an average annual rate of 1.4% during 2004–13. Monaco has the highest population density of all the independent states in the world. According to official figures, GDP increased, in real terms, at an average annual rate of 4.9% during 2005–13. GDP increased by 1.2% in 2012 and by 9.3% in 2013.

There is no agricultural land in Monaco. In 1990 a Belgian enterprise established an offshore fish farm for sea bass and sea bream. In December 2013 there were just six private sector employees working in the primary sector.

Industry contributed 13.9% of GDP, at constant prices, in 2013. The sector engaged 15.8% of those employed in the private sector in December 2013. Industry is mainly light in Monaco. The principal sectors are chemicals, pharmaceuticals and cosmetics (which together accounted for 40.5% of all industrial turnover in 2010), plastics (30.4%), electrical and electronic goods (9.5%), machine goods, and paper and textile production.

Service industries represent the most significant sector of the economy in Monaco, contributing 86.1% of GDP, at constant prices, in 2013, and providing employment to 84.2% of those working in the private sector in December 2013. At the end of 2009 the total value of deposits in Monaco's private banking sector was estimated at €24,970m. Banking and financial activities accounted for 16.7% of GDP in 2013, while wholesale and retail trade accounted for 15.4%.

Tourism is also an important source of income; the hotel and restaurant sector contributed 7.3% of GDP, at constant prices, in 2013, and (together with other associated activities) engaged 12.8% of those employed in the private sector in December 2013. In 2012 a total of 292,027 tourists (excluding excursionists) visited Monaco, representing a decrease of 1.0% compared with 2011. The greatest number of visitors (excluding excursionists) in 2012 were from France (22.1%), Italy (14.9%), the United Kingdom (10.9%) and the USA (9.1%).

Monaco's external trade is included in the figures for France. Excluding trade within the association with France, in 2013 Monaco's principal merchandise imports were consumer goods and semi-finished non-metallic goods. The most significant exports were semi-finished non-metallic goods, consumer goods and processed agricultural manufactures. Excluding France, the most important sources of imports in 2013 were Italy and the UK (23.7% and 12.2% of the total value, respectively), followed by the People's Republic of China, Germany and Switzerland. Italy and Switzerland were the most important markets for exports (excluding France), contributing 12.1% and 12.0% of total export earnings, respectively. Germany and the UK were also important markets for exports.

In 2013 there was a budgetary surplus of €12.1m.; expenditure amounted to €933.0m. Value-added tax (VAT) contributes about one-half of total government revenue.

Monaco is a prosperous state, which attracts wealthy residents through its tax regime; there is no income or inheritance tax and business rates are favourable. Monaco is largely dependent on imports from France, owing to its lack of natural resources. The economy is reliant on migrant workers (many of whom remain resident in France and Italy). Following the establishment of the state's first casino in the 1860s, tourism became the dominant sector in the economy. In particular, the Principality has sought to establish itself as a major centre of the international conference industry. An 18.3% decline in tourist arrivals in 2009 was attributed to recessionary conditions in the countries that provide the majority of Monaco's visitors, and contributed to a sharp 11.5% contraction in GDP that year. Following some recovery in the tourism sector in 2010 and 2011, when arrivals increased by

5.5% and 5.6%, respectively, the number of arrivals decreased again, by 1.0%, in 2012. GDP grew by 2.5% in 2010 and by 6.7% in 2011, owing in part to rises in tax revenues and corporate profits. The rate of growth of GDP decelerated to 1.2% in 2012 before recording an impressive increase of 9.3% in 2013, largely as a result of significant rises in profits in the real estate and construction sectors. In addition to taxes on legal transactions and property, the profits of the hotel, casino and leisure group, Société des Bains de Mer, which is 69.5% state-owned, generally constitute an important source of government income. However, the company recorded a net loss in 2010/11 (its first since 1996/97), prompting it to announce a three-year recovery plan in February 2012, which included an aim to attract more customers from China and the Russian Federation. Partly as a result of cuts in public expenditure on cultural institutions, the budget deficit decreased by 33.7% in 2011, compared with 2010, and in both 2012 and 2013 a small budgetary surplus was recorded. From the 1980s the financial and real estate sectors expanded, as a series of land reclamation projects increased Monaco's area by 20%, thereby helping to satisfy the growing demand for office and residential space. A number of foreign companies and banks are registered in Monaco in order to take advantage of the low rates of taxation on company profits. In March 2009 Monaco announced that it would adopt Organisation for Economic Co-operation and Development (OECD, see p. 377) standards on transparency and information exchange with regards to bank data, in an effort to combat tax evasion. Consequently, in May Monaco was removed from the OECD list of 'unco-operative tax havens'.

PUBLIC HOLIDAYS

2016: 1 January (New Year's Day), 27 January (St Devota's Day), 28 March (Easter Monday), 1 May (Labour Day), 5 May (Ascension Day), 16 May (Whit Monday), 15 August (Assumption), 1 November (All Saints' Day), 19 November (National Day/Fête du Prince), 8 December (Immaculate Conception), 25–26 December (Christmas).

Statistical Survey

Source (unless otherwise stated): Institut Monégasque de la Statistique et des Etudes Economiques, 9 rue du Gabian, MC 98000; tel. 98-98-98-88; fax 98-98-87-59; internet www.imsee.mc.

AREA AND POPULATION

Area: 2.02 sq km.

Population: 32,020 at census of July 2000; 31,109 (males 15,076, females 15,914) at census of June–July 2008. Note: Total includes 119 persons with gender not declared. *2013* (official estimate at 31 December): 36,950.

Density (at 31 December 2013): 18,292.1 per sq km.

Population by Age and Sex (at 2008 census): *0–14 years:* 3,965 (males 2,010, females 1,955); *15–64 years:* 19,063 (males 9,502, females 9,561); *65 years and over:* 7,366 (males 3,276, females 4,090); *Total* 31,109 (males 15,076, females 15,914). Note: Total includes 715 persons of unknown age-group and 119 persons with gender not declared.

Population by Nationality (at 2008 census): French 8,785; Monégasque 6,687; Italian 5,778; Other 9,859.

Districts (population at 2008 census): Monte-Carlo 14,586; La Condamine 11,946; Fontvieille 3,602; Monaco-Ville 975.

Births, Marriages and Deaths (2013 unless otherwise indicated): Live births 992; Marriages 194 (2006); Deaths 567.

Life expectancy (years at birth, official figures): 84.7 (males 82.3; females 87.2) in 2013.

Employment (December 2013): *Private sector:* Total 46,600 (Manufacturing, mining and quarrying 3,087, Construction 4,297, Finance 3,507, Transport and communication 3,117, Wholesale and retail trade 4,887, Public administration, education, health and welfare 3,727, Hotels and restaurants 5,960, Real estate and business activities 1,471, Other community, social and personal service activities 16,548); *Public sector:* Total 4,192; *All sectors:* Total 50,792.

HEALTH AND WELFARE

Key Indicators

Total Fertility Rate (children per woman, 2012): 1.5.

Under-5 Mortality Rate (per 1,000 live births, 2012): 4.

Physicians (per 1,000 head, 2012): 7.17.

Hospital Beds (per 1,000 head, 1995): 19.6.

Health Expenditure (2011): US $ per head (PPP): 5,937.

Health Expenditure (2011): % of GDP: 4.4.

Health Expenditure (2011): public (% of total): 88.6.

For sources and definitions, see explanatory note on p. vi.

FINANCE

Currency and Exchange Rates: French currency: 100 cent = 1 euro (€). *Sterling and Dollar Equivalents* (31 December 2014): £1 sterling = 1.286 euros; US $1 = 0.824 euros; €10 = £7.78 = $12.14. *Average Exchange Rate* (euros per US dollar): 0.7783 in 2012; 0.7532 in 2013; 0.7537 in 2014. Note: The local currency was formerly the French franc, although some Monégasque currency, at par with the French franc, also circulated. From the introduction of the euro, with French participation, on 1 January 1999, a fixed exchange rate of €1 = 6.55957 French francs was in operation. Euro notes and coins were introduced on 1 January 2002. The euro and local currency circulated alongside each other until 17 February, after which the euro became the sole legal tender.

Budget (€ million, 2013): Revenue 945.1; Expenditure 933.0 (Current expenditure 664.3, Capital expenditure 268.8).

Turnover of the Principality (official figures, private sector only, € million, 2013): Industry 1,126.8; Public works and real estate 382.1; Hotel business 615.7; Banking and finance 1,604.0; Wholesale and retail trade 6,801.0; Transport 451.3; Other activities 515.3; *Total* 11,496.2.

Gross Domestic Product (€ million at constant 2010 prices): 4,003 in 2011; 4,387 in 2012; 4,796 in 2013.

National Income and Product (€ million at constant 2005 prices, 2012): Compensation of employees 2,149.7; Gross operating surplus 1,553.2; Taxes, less subsidies, on production 286.4; *Gross domestic product* 3,989.3.

Gross Domestic Product by Economic Activity (€ million at constant 2010 prices, 2013): Industry 669; Finance 799; Transport and communication 423; Wholesale and retail trade 737; Public administration, education, health and welfare 392; Hotels and restaurants 350; Real estate and business activities 403; Other community, social and personal service activities 1,022; *Total* 4,796.

EXTERNAL TRADE

Note: Monaco's imports and exports are included in the figures for France, and separate figures for Monaco's trade with France are not included here.

Principal Commodities (distribution by HS, € million, 2013): *Imports:* Machinery and mechanical appliances; electrical equipment; parts thereof 157.0; Prepared foodstuffs; beverages, spirits, vinegars; tobacco and articles thereof 43.3; Vehicles, aircraft, vessels and associated transport equipment 157.6; Other industrial products 607.7; Total (incl. others) 1,015.4. *Exports:* Live animal and animal products; vegetable and vegetable products 15.3; Prepared foodstuffs; beverages, spirits, vinegars; tobacco and articles thereof 110.4; Machinery and mechanical appliances; electrical equipment; parts thereof 183.0; Vehicles, aircraft, vessels and associated transport equipment 148.7; Other industrial products 544.2; Total (incl. others) 1,037.1.

Principal Trading Partners (€ million, 2013): *Imports:* Austria 6.2; Belgium 44.1; China, People's Republic 70.2; Dominican Republic 6.1; Germany 66.6; Hong Kong 18.1; Indonesia 11.4; Ireland 27.8; Italy 241.0; Netherlands 11.7; Spain 30.6; Switzerland 50.8; Tunisia 29.1; United Kingdom 123.9; USA 34.5; Viet Nam 12.7; Total (incl. others) 1,015.4. *Exports:* Algeria 24.8; Belgium 48.5; Brazil 15.3; China, People's Republic 48.5; Gabon 14.3; Germany 105.2; Italy 126.0; Netherlands 24.3; Portugal 11.9; Spain 47.8; Switzerland 124.8; Tunisia 19.1; United Kingdom 70.0; USA 36.0; Total (incl. others) 1,037.1.

TRANSPORT

Road Traffic (vehicles in use at 31 December 2012): Passenger cars 26,627; Buses and coaches 116; Lorries and vans 4,579; Motorcycles and mopeds 8,584.

Shipping: *Flag Registered Fleet* (at 31 December 2014): Vessels registered 12; Total displacement: 1,994 grt. Source: Lloyd's List Intelligence (www.lloydslistintelligence.com).

TOURISM

Tourist Arrivals (excluding excursionists): 279,166 in 2010; 294,901 in 2011; 292,027 in 2012. Figures refer to arrivals of foreign visitors at hotels and similar establishments.

Tourist Arrivals by Country (2013): Australia 7,796; France 63,934; Germany 14,234; Italy 44,130; Japan 5,474; Russia 18,770; Switzerland 11,791; United Kingdom 98,632; USA 36,543; Total (incl. others) 327,942.

Source: World Tourism Organization.

COMMUNICATIONS MEDIA

Telephones (2013): 46,850 main lines in use.

Mobile Cellular Telephones (2013): 35,464 subscribers.

Internet Subscribers (2011): 15,900.

Broadband Subscribers (2013): 16,896.

Source: mostly International Telecommunication Union.

EDUCATION

(2012/13 unless otherwise indicated)

Pre-primary: 40 teachers (33 public, 7 private) (2004/05); 1,007 pupils (712 public, 295 private).

Elementary: 174 teachers (146 public, 28 private) (2011/2012); 1,903 pupils (1,352 public, 551 private).

Secondary: 337 teachers (308 public, 29 private) (2011/2012); 6,260 pupils (4,427 public, 1,833 private).

Note: Educational establishments in Monaco in 2004/05 comprised the following: three public pre-primary schools; four primary schools (three public, one private), which integrate pre-primary and elementary age-groups; one public elementary school; three public secondary schools, comprising one lower secondary school, one general upper secondary school and one vocational secondary school; and one private school integrating primary and secondary age-groups. There was also one private higher educational establishment, the International University of Monaco, a business school where instruction is conducted in English.

Source: Direction de l'Education Nationale, de la Jeunesse et des Sports.

Directory

The Government

HEAD OF STATE

Ruling Prince: HSH Prince ALBERT II (succeeded 6 April 2005).

COUNCIL OF GOVERNMENT
(May 2015)

Minister of State: MICHEL ROGER.

Government Councillor for Finance and the Economy: JEAN CASTELLINI.

Government Councillor for the Interior: PATRICE CELLARIO.

Government Councillor for Public Works, the Environment and Urban Development: MARIE-PIERRE GRAMAGLIA.

Government Councillor for Social Affairs and Health: STÉPHANE VALERI.

Government Councillor for External Relations and Co-operation: GILLES TONELLI.

MINISTRY OF STATE AND DEPARTMENTS

Ministry of State: place de la Visitation, MC 98000; tel. 98-98-80-00; fax 98-98-82-17; e-mail sgme@gouv.mc; internet www.gouv.mc.

Department of External Relations and Co-operation: Ministère d'Etat, place de la Visitation, BP 522, MC 98000 Cedex; tel. 98-98-89-04; fax 98-98-85-54; e-mail relext@gouv.mc.

Department of Finance and the Economy: Ministère d'Etat, place de la Visitation, MC 98000; tel. 98-98-82-56.

Department of Social Affairs and Health: Ministère d'Etat, place de la Visitation, MC 98000; tel. and fax 98-98-19-19; e-mail afss@gouv.mc.

Department of the Interior: Ministère d'Etat, place de la Visitation, MC 98000; tel. 98-98-84-56; fax 93-50-82-45.

Department of Public Works, the Environment and Urban Development: Ministère d'Etat, place de la Visitation, MC 98000; tel. 98-98-81-92.

Legislature

National Council
(Conseil National)

2 place de la Visitation, MC 98000; tel. 93-30-41-15; fax 93-25-31-90; e-mail vviora@conseil-national.mc; internet www.conseilnational.mc.

President: LAURENT NOUVION.

Vice-President: CHRISTOPHER STEINER.
Election, 10 February 2013

	% of votes	Seats
Horizon Monaco*	50.34	20
Union Monégasque†	38.99	3
Renaissance‡	10.67	1
Total	100.00	24

* Alliance of Rassemblement et Enjeux pour Monaco (REM), Union pour la Principauté (part of the Union pour Monaco—UpM), and Synergie Monégasque.
† Alliance of Union des Monégasques (UDM) and Union Nationale pour l'Avenir de Monaco (UNAM).
‡ Comprising employees of the Société des Bains de Mer (SBM).

Advisory Councils

Conseil d'Etat (Council of State): Palais de Justice, Monte-Carlo; advises on proposed laws or ordinances submitted for its approval by the Ruling Prince or by the Government, or on any other matter; 12 mems, appointed by the Ruling Prince, following the advice of the Minister of State and the Director of Judicial Services; Pres. PHILIPPE NARMINO; Sec. SÉBASTIEN BIANCHERI.

Conseil de la Couronne (Crown Council): Monte-Carlo; f. 1942; advises the Ruling Prince on matters of state, and must be consulted by the Ruling Prince prior to the implementation of certain constitutional matters, including the signature or ratification of treaties, the dissolution of the Conseil national, questions of naturalization or reintegration, the issuing of pardons or amnesties; 7 mems, appointed for renewable terms of 3 years; Pres. and 3 mems are appointed by free choice of the Ruling Prince, the remaining 3 mems are nominated by the Ruling Prince on the recommendation of the Conseil national; all mems must hold Monégasque nationality; Pres. MICHEL-YVES MOUROU; Sec. RICHARD MILANESIO.

Conseil Economique et Social (Economic and Social Council): Centre Administratif, 8 rue Louis-Notari, MC 98000; tel. 97-97-77-91; fax 93-50-05-96; f. 1945; advises on economic matters; 36 mems, appointed for a term of 3 years; 12 mems directly appointed by Govt, 12 appointed by Govt from list prepared by Union des Syndicats de Monaco, 12 appointed by Govt from list prepared by the Fédération Patronale Monégasque; the Ruling Prince appoints the Pres. and two Vice-Pres from among the mems; Pres. ANDRÉ GARINO; Vice-Pres PIERRE-YVES REICHNECKER, HENRI LEIZE.

Political Organizations

There were traditionally no political parties as such in Monaco; however, since 2003 political groupings have begun to establish a more permanent presence.

Rassemblement et Enjeux pour Monaco (REM) (Rally and Issues for Monaco): 1 rue de Vedel, MC 98000; tel. 92-16-20-13; fax 93-25-20-09; e-mail info@rassemblement-enjeux.org; internet www.rassemblement-enjeux.org; coalition comprising members of the Rassemblement pour Monaco and Valeurs et Enjeux; contested the 2013 parliamentary election as part of Horizon Monaco; Pres. ALAIN FICINI.

Synergie Monégasque: 41 ave Hector Otto, MC 98000; e-mail synergie@monaco.mc; internet www.synergie-mc.org; contested the 2013 parliamentary election as part of Horizon Monaco.

Union pour Monaco (UpM) (Union for Monaco): 11 rue du Gabian, MC 98000 Monaco; coalition including members of the Union pour la Principauté; contested the 2013 parliamentary election as part of Horizon Monaco; Pres. STÉPHANE VALERI.

Union des Monégasques (UDM): BP 524, MC 98015 Monaco; tel. 93-25-23-02; e-mail info@unionmonegasque.mc; internet www.unionmonegasque.mc; f. 2011; contested the 2013 parliamentary election as part of Union Monégasque; Leader JEAN-FRANÇOIS ROBILLON.

Union Nationale pour l'Avenir de Monaco (UNAM) (National Union for the Future of Monaco): Monaco; contested the 2013 parliamentary election as part of Union Monégasque; Pres. ÉRIC GUAZZONE.

Diplomatic Representation

In February 2006 France opened an embassy in Monaco, becoming the first country to institute ambassadorial-level diplomatic relations with the Principality. Italy opened an embassy in Monaco later in the year. By December 2013 ambassadors from 96 countries were accredited to Monaco; most were resident in France, Spain or Belgium.

France: Le Roc fleuri, 1 rue du Tenao, BP 45, MC 98006 Cedex; tel. 92-16-54-60; fax 92-16-54-64; e-mail courrier@ambafrance-mc.org; internet www.ambafrance-mc.org; Ambassador HADELIN DE LA TOUR DU PIN.

Italy: L'Annonciade, 17 ave de l'Annonciade, MC 98000; tel. 93-50-22-71; fax 93-50-06-89; e-mail ambasciata.montecarlo@esteri.it; internet www.ambprincipatomonaco.esteri.it; Ambassador GIUSEPPE FOLINO.

Judicial System

The organization of the legal system is similar to that of France. There is one Justice of the Peace, a Tribunal de Première Instance (Tribunal of First Instance), a Cour d'Appel (Court of Appeal), a Cour de Révision (High Court of Appeal), a Tribunal Criminel (Criminal Tribunal) and finally the Tribunal Suprême (Supreme Tribunal), which deals with infringements of the rights and liberties provided by the Constitution, and also with legal actions aiming at the annulment of administrative decisions for abusive exercise of power.

Palais de Justice: 5 rue Col Bellando de Castro, MC 98000; tel. 98-98-88-11; fax 98-98-85-89.

Director of Judicial Services: PHILIPPE NARMINO.

President of the Supreme Tribunal: HUBERT CHARLES.

President of the Court of Revision: ROGER BEAUVOIS.

First President of the Court of Appeal: BRIGITTE GRINDA-GAMBARINI.

President of the Tribunal of First Instance: MARTINE COULET-CASTOLDI.

Attorney-General: JEAN-PIERRE DRÉNO.

Religion

CHRISTIANITY

The Roman Catholic Church

Monaco comprises a single archdiocese, directly responsible to the Holy See. At 31 December 2006 there were an estimated 29,000 adherents in the Principality, representing about 90.6% of the total population.

Archbishop of Monaco: Most Rev. BERNARD BARSI, Archevêché, 1 rue de l'Abbaye, BP 517, MC 98015 Cedex; tel. 93-30-77-86; fax 92-16-39-31; e-mail info@eglise-catholique.mc; internet www.diocese.mc.

The Anglican Communion

Within the Church of England, Monaco forms part of the diocese of Gibraltar in Europe.

Chaplain: Fr WALTER H. RAYMOND, St Paul's Church House, 22 ave de Grande Bretagne, Monte-Carlo, MC 98000; tel. 93-30-71-06; fax 93-30-50-39; e-mail chaplain@stpaulsmonaco.com; internet www.stpaulsmonaco.com.

The Principality also has two Protestant churches and a synagogue.

The Press

La Gazette de Monaco: BP 130, MC 98003 Cedex; tel. 93-25-56-83; fax 97-98-01-41; e-mail rédaction@lagazette.mc; internet www.lagazettedemonaco.com; f. 1926; monthly; regional information; Dir-Gen. NOËL METTEY; Editor-in-Chief NOËLLE BINE-MULLER; circ. 10,000.

Journal de Monaco: Ministère d'Etat, place de la Visitation, BP 522, MC 98015; tel. 98-98-80-00; fax 93-15-82-17; e-mail journaldemonaco@gouv.mc; internet www.gouv.mc/dataweb/journmon.nsf; f. 1858; edited at the Ministry of State; official weekly; contains texts of laws and decrees; Editor ROBERT COLLE.

Monaco Hebdo: 2 rue de la Lüjerneta, MC 98000; tel. 93-50-56-52; fax 93-50-19-22; e-mail monacohebdo@free.fr; internet www.monacohebdo.mc; f. 1995; Man. Editor ROBERTO TESTA.

Monte-Carlo Méditerranée: 46 blvd des Moulins, 98000 Monaco; tel. and fax 93-25-10-00; Editor-in-Chief CAROLE CHABRIER.

French newspapers are widely read, and a special Monaco edition of the daily *Nice-Matin* is published in Nice, France.

NEWS AGENCY

Monte-Carlo Press: Le Beverly Palace, 13 blvd de Belgique, MC 98000; tel. 97-70-74-24; e-mail mcpress@mcpress.mc; internet www.mcpress.mc; f. 1987.

Publishers

Editions Alpen: 9 ave Albert II, Le Copori, MC 98000; tel. 97-77-62-10; e-mail contact@alpen.mc; internet www.alpen.mc; f. 2002; health and well-being.

Editions Victor Gadoury: 57 rue Grimaldi, MC 98000; tel. 93-25-12-96; fax 93-50-13-39; e-mail contact@gadoury.com; internet www.gadoury.com; f. 1973; numismatics; Man. FRANCESCO PASTRONE.

Marsu Productions: 9 ave des Castelans, MC 98000; tel. 92-05-61-11; fax 92-05-76-60; e-mail contact@marsupilami.com; internet www.marsupilami.com; comic strips, children's entertainment.

Editions du Rocher: 28 rue Comte Félix Gastaldi, BP 521, MC 98015; tel. 99-99-67-17; fax 99-99-67-18; internet www.editionsdurocher.fr; f. 1943; fiction, history, sciences; Pres. ERNESTO ROSSI DI MONTELERA; Man. Dirs MARC LARIVÉ, SERGE BÉRARD; Dir-Gen. PATRICK MAHÉ.

Broadcasting and Communications

TELECOMMUNICATIONS

Direction des Commmunications Electroniques: 23 ave Albert II, MC 98000; tel. 98-98-88-00; fax 97-98-56-57; e-mail nic@gouv.mc; internet www.nic.mc; Dir CHRISTOPHE PIERRE.

Monaco Telecom: 9 rue du Gabian Fontvieille, MC 98000 Cedex; tel. 99-66-33-00; fax 99-66-33-33; e-mail communication@monaco-telecom.mc; internet www.monaco-telecom.mc; f. 1997; 55% owned by NJJ Capital, 45% by the Société Nationale de Financement (wholly owned by Govt of Monaco); incorporates the wholly owned subsidiaries Monaco Telecom International, Société Monégasque de Services de Telecoms (SMST), Société Monégasque de Télédistribution (SMT) and Divona; Pres. ETIENNE FRANZI; Dir-Gen. MARTIN PERONNET.

BROADCASTING

Radio

Monte-Carlo Doualiya: 1 ave Henri Dunant, MC 98000; internet www.mc-doualiya.com; fmr subsidiary of RMC, transferred to Radio-France Internationale in 1996; in French and Arabic; Pres. ALAIN DE POUZILHAC; Man. Dir MARIE-CHRISTINE SARAGOSSE.

Radio Monaco: 7 rue du Gabian, MC 98000; tel. 97-70-07-00; e-mail contact@radio-monaco.com; internet www.radio-monaco.com; Dir-Gen. CHRISTOPHE LAURY.

Riviera Radio: 10 quai Antoine 1er, MC 98000; tel. 97-97-94-80; fax 97-97-94-95; e-mail info@rivieraradio.mc; internet www.rivieraradio.mc; owned by Morris Communications Co (USA); broadcasts in English; Man. Dir PAUL KAVANAGH.

Trans World Radio SC: c/o Courtin Global Assistance, BP 349, MC 98007; tel. 97-77-70-04; fax 92-05-92-32; e-mail cdetwiler@twr.org; internet www.twr.org; f. 1955; Evangelical Christian broadcaster; Pres. LAUREN LIBBY.

Television

Monaco switched from analogue to digital broadcasting in 2011.

TMC Monte-Carlo: 6 bis Antoine 1er, MC 98000; tel. 92-16-54-80; fax 92-16-54-81; e-mail contact@tmc.mc; internet www.tmc.tv; f. 1954; Dir-Gen. CAROLINE GOT.

Finance

(cap. = capital, res = reserves, dep. = deposits, m. = million, br(s) = branch(es), amounts in euros)

BANKING

In 2013 a total of 35 banks, including major British, French, Italian and US banks, were represented in the Principality.

Banque de Gestion Edmond de Rothschild: Les Terrasses, 2 ave de Monte-Carlo, BP 317, MC 980060; tel. 93-10-47-47; fax 93-25-75-57; e-mail bger@lcf-rothschild.mc; internet www.edmond-de-rothschild.mc; f. 1986; present name adopted 1993; cap. 12.0m., res 28.9m., dep. 845.5m. (Dec. 2012); Chair. LEONARDO P. A. POGGI; Gen. Man. GIAMPAOLO BERNINI.

Banque J. Safra Sarasin (Monaco): La Belle Epoque, 15–17 bis ave d'Ostende, MC 98000; tel. 93-10-66-55; fax 93-10-66-00; internet www.jsafrasarasin.mc; f. 1994 as Banque du Gothard (Monaco); present name adopted 2013; 100% owned by Banque Jacob Safra (Switzerland); cap. 40.0m., res 6.7m., dep. 1,073.7m. (Dec. 2012); Pres. JOSEPH SAFRA; Gen. Man. YVES BRACCALENTI.

BNP Paribas Wealth Management Monaco: 15–17 ave d'Ostende, MC 98000; tel. 93-15-68-00; fax 93-15-68-01; e-mail wealthmanagement.monaco@bnpparibas.com; internet www.privatebank.bnpparibas.mc; f. 2003 by merger of United European Bank—Monaco and BNP Paribas Private Bank Monaco; acquired Société Monégasque de Banque Privée and Bank Von Ernst (Monaco) 2005; present name adopted 2009; private banking; cap. 13.0m. (April 2007); Dir-Gen. ERIC GEORGES.

Compagnie Monégasque de Banque: 23 ave de la Costa, BP 149, MC 98007; tel. 93-15-77-77; fax 93-25-08-69; e-mail cmb@cmb.mc; internet www.cmb.mc; f. 1976; 100% owned by Mediobanca—Banca di Credito Finanziario SpA (Italy); cap. 111.1m., res 421.4m., dep. 1,418.9m. (Dec. 2012); Chair. ETIENNE FRANZI; Vice-Chair. ALDO CIVASCHI; 2 brs.

Crédit Foncier de Monaco (CFM Monaco): 11 blvd Albert 1er, BP 499, MC 98012 Cedex; tel. 93-10-20-00; fax 93-10-23-50; internet www.cfm.mc; f. 1922; 77.1% owned by Calyon (France); cap. 35.0m., res 87.5m., dep. 3,447m. (Dec. 2012); Chair. YVES BARSALOU; CEO GILLES MARTINENGO.

Crédit Suisse (Monaco): 27 ave de la Costa, BP 155, MC 98003; tel. 93-15-27-27; fax 93-25-27-99; e-mail alain.ucari@credit-suisse.com; f. 1987; cap. 18m., res 1.4m., dep. 2,211.7m. (Dec. 2012); Chair. FRANCO MULLER; Man. ALAIN UCARI.

EFG Bank (Monaco) SAM: Villa Les Aigles, 15 ave d'Ostende, MC 98000; tel. 93-15-11-11; fax 93-15-11-12; e-mail enquiries_mco@efgbank.com; internet www.efggroup.com; f. 1990; merged with Banque Monegasque de Gestion SA in 2007; name changed to current in 2009; owned by EFG Bank (Switzerland); private banking; cap. 26.9m., res 3.2m., dep. 761.8m. (Dec. 2011); Dir-Gen. GEORGE CATSIAPIS.

HSBC Private Bank (Monaco): 17 ave d'Ostende, MC 98000; tel. 93-15-25-25; fax 93-15-25-00; internet www.hsbcprivatebank.com; f. 1997 as Republic National Bank of New York (Monaco) SA; present name adopted 2004; owned by HSBC Private Banking Holdings (Suisse) SA (Switzerland); private banking; cap. 151.0m., res 4.4m., dep. 5,771.2m. (Dec. 2011); Chief Exec. and Dir-Gen. GÉRARD COHEN.

KBL Monaco Private Bankers: 8 ave de Grande Bretagne, BP 262, MC 98005; tel. 92-16-55-55; fax 92-16-55-99; internet www.europeanprivatebankers.com; f. 1996; owned by KBL European Private Bankers SA; cap. 8.5m., res 3.9m., dep. 345m. (Dec. 2011); Chair. PAUL MARIE JACQUES; Man. Dir STEPHEN BARBALACO.

UBS (Monaco) SA: 2 ave de Grande Bretagne, BP 189, MC 98007; tel. 93-15-58-15; fax 93-15-58-00; e-mail frederic.bernard@ubs.com; internet www.ubs.com/monaco; f. 1956; present name adopted 1998;

owned by UBS AG (Switzerland); cap. 9.2m., res 38.1m., dep. 1,191.3m. (Dec. 2009); Chair. AXEL A. WEBER; CEO SERGIO P. ERMOTTI.

INSURANCE

Assurances C. Sassi AXA: Le Suffren, 7 rue Suffren-Reymond, BP 25, MC 98001; tel. 93-30-45-88; fax 93-25-86-07; e-mail agence.sassi@axa.fr; internet www.axa.fr/sassi.monaco; f. 1968; Dir CYRIL SASSI.

The Eric Blair Network: 11 ave St Michael, 98000 Monaco; tel. 93-50-99-66; fax 97-70-72-00; e-mail info@ericblairnet.com; internet www.ericblairnet.com; Chief Exec. ERIC BLAIR.

Gramaglia Assurances: 14 blvd des Moulins, BP 153, MC 98003 Cedex; tel. 92-16-59-00; fax 92-16-59-01; internet www.gramaglia.mc; f. 1948; Dir PHILIPPE VERDIER.

Mourenon et Giannotti: 22 blvd Princesse Charlotte, MC 98000; tel. 97-97-08-88; fax 97-97-08-80; e-mail monacometg@agence.generali.fr; internet mgassurances.com; f. 1975; Dirs JEAN-PHILIPPE MOURENON, JOSÉ GIANNOTTI.

Trade and Industry

GOVERNMENT AGENCIES

Direction de l'Environnement: 3 ave de Fontvieille, MC 98013; tel. 98-98-80-00; fax 92-05-28-91; e-mail environnement@gouv.mc; Dir CHRISTOPHE PRAT.

Direction de l'Expansion Economique: 9 rue du Gabian, MC 98000; tel. 98-98-98-00; fax 92-05-75-20; e-mail expansion@gouv.mc; comprises 3 divisions: Monaco Welcome and Business Office, General Administration and Intellectual Property; Dir SERGE PIERRYVES.

Direction de la Prospective, de l'Urbanisme et de la Mobilité: 23 ave Albert II, BP 609, MC 98000; tel. 98-98-22-99; fax 98-98-88-02; e-mail prospective@gouv.mc; Dir SÉVERINE CANIS-FROIDEFOND.

Direction des Services Fiscaux: 'Le Panorama', 57 rue Grimaldi, BP 475, MC 98000; tel. 98-98-81-21; fax 93-15-81-55; Dir ANTOINE DINKEL.

CHAMBER OF COMMERCE

Jeune Chambre Economique de Monaco: 1 ave des Castelans, MC 98000; tel. 92-05-20-19; fax 92-05-31-29; e-mail jcemonaco@jcemonaco.mc; internet www.jcemonaco.mc; f. 1963; Pres. CÉDRIC CAVASSINO.

EMPLOYERS' ASSOCIATION

Fédération des Entreprises Monégasques (FEDEM): 'Le Coronado', 20 ave de Fontvieille, MC 98000; tel. 92-05-38-92; fax 92-05-20-04; e-mail info@fedem.mc; internet www.fedem.mc; f. 1944 as Fédération Patronale Monégasque; name changed to present 2014; Pres. PHILIPPE ORTELLI; Sec.-Gen. CORINNE BERTANI; 26 mem. orgs, with nearly 1,000 individual mems.

UTILITIES

Electricity and Gas

Société Monégasque de l'Electricité et du Gaz (SMEG): 10 ave de Fontvieille, BP 633, MC 98013 Cedex; tel. 92-05-05-00; fax 92-05-05-92; e-mail smeg@smeg.mc; internet www.smeg.mc; f. 1890; 64% owned by GDF SUEZ (France); 20% owned by the Govt of Monaco; Chair. JÉRÔME TOLOT; Dir-Gen. GUY MAGNAN.

Water

Société Monégasque des Eaux (SME): 5 ave de Fontvieille, MC 98000; tel. 97-98-51-00; fax 92-05-23-83; e-mail sme@sme.mc; internet www.sme.mc; f. 1983; Pres. STÉPHANE GIACCARDI.

TRADE UNION FEDERATION

Union des Syndicats de Monaco (USM): 28 blvd Rainier III, BP 113, MC 98000; tel. 93-30-19-30; fax 93-25-06-73; e-mail usm@usm.mc; internet www.usm.mc; f. 1944; Pres. BETTY TAMBUSCIO; Sec.-Gen. MONIQUE FERRETE; 41 mem. unions.

Transport

RAILWAYS

The 1.7 km of railway track in Monaco, running from France to Monte-Carlo on the Nice–Menton–Ventimiglia railway line is operated by the French state railway, the Société Nationale des Chemins de fer Français (SNCF). As part of the Government's policy of land reclamation, an underground railway station was opened in 1999.

ROADS

In 2010 there were an estimated 77 km of major roads in the Principality.

SHIPPING

The two main ports in Monaco are Port Hercule and Port Fontvieille. The former is a deep-water port, which provides an anchorage for up to 700 vessels. The latter accommodates up to 275 boats with a maximum draught of three metres. At 31 December 2013 the flag registered fleet comprised 12 vessels, totalling 1,994 grt.

Direction des Affaires Maritimes: quai Jean-Charles Rey, BP 468, MC 98012 Cedex; tel. 98-98-22-80; fax 98-98-22-81; Dir ARMELLE ROUDAUT-LAFON.

Société d'Exploitation des Ports de Monaco (SEPM): 6 quai Antoine 1er, BP 453, MC 98011 Cedex; tel. 97-77-30-00; fax 97-77-30-01; e-mail info@ports-monaco.com; internet www.ports-monaco.com; f. 2002; state-owned; responsible for management and devt of the 2 principal ports in Monaco, at La Condamine (Port Hercule) and Fontvieille; Pres. ALECO KEUSSEOGLOU; Gen. Man. GIANBATTISTA BOREA D'OLMO.

Shipping Companies

d'Amico Dry Ltd: 20 blvd de Suisse, MC 98000 Cedex; tel. 93-10-52-70; fax 93-25-41-62; e-mail info@damicoship.com; internet www.damicoship.com; f. 2002; owned by d'Amico Società di Navigazione SpA (Italy); Pres. PAOLO D'AMICO; Group CEO CESARE D'AMICO.

Central Shipping Monaco SAM: Palais de la Scala, 1 ave Henry Dunan, MC 98000; tel. 97-97-96-26; fax 97-97-96-27; internet www.centralshippingmonaco.mc; petroleum and other cargo.

Société Anonyme Monégasque d'Administration Maritime et Aérienne (SAMAMA): Villa Saint Jean, 3 ruelle Saint Jean, MC 98000; tel. 99-99-51-00; fax 99-99-51-09; e-mail general@samama-monaco.com; f. 1975; Dir-Gen. L. DAVIDSON.

CIVIL AVIATION

There is a helicopter shuttle service between the international airport at Nice, France, and Monaco's heliport at Fontvieille.

Héli Air Monaco SAM: Héliport de Monaco, MC 98000; tel. 92-05-00-50; fax 92-05-00-51; e-mail helico@heliairmonaco.com; internet www.heliairmonaco.com; f. 1976; CEO JACQUES CROVETTO.

Tourism

Tourists are attracted to Monaco by the Mediterranean climate, dramatic scenery and numerous entertainment facilities, including a casino. In 2013 there were 327,942 tourist arrivals in Monaco.

Direction du Tourisme et des Congrès: 2A blvd des Moulins, MC 98030 Cedex; tel. 92-16-61-16; fax 92-16-60-00; e-mail dtc@gouv.mc; internet www.visitmonaco.com; Pres. GUILLAUME ROSE.

Société des Bains de Mer (SBM): place du Casino, BP 139, MC 98000; tel. 98-06-25-25; fax 98-06-26-26; e-mail resort@sbm.mc; internet www.montecarlosbm.com; f. 1863; corpn in which the Govt holds a 69.5% interest; controls the entertainment facilities of Monaco, including the casino and numerous hotels, clubs, restaurants and sporting facilities; Chair. and CEO JEAN-LUC BIAMONTI.

Defence

France is responsible for the Principality's defence.

Education

Education follows the French system. Compulsory education lasts for 10 years for children aged six to 16 years. Primary education begins at six years of age and lasts for five years. Secondary education begins at 11 years of age and lasts for seven years. There is one public institution of higher education, the Académie de Musique et de Théâtre Fondation Prince Rainier III de Monaco (founded 1933), and one private higher educational institution, the International University of Monaco (founded 1986), a business school where instruction is conducted in English and where US-style Bachelors, Masters and Doctoral degree courses are offered. In 2010 expenditure on education was equivalent to 6.4% of total government expenditure.

MONGOLIA

Introductory Survey

LOCATION, CLIMATE, LANGUAGE, RELIGION, FLAG, CAPITAL

Mongolia is a landlocked country in central Asia, with the Russian Federation to the north and the People's Republic of China to the south, east and west. The climate is dry, with generally mild summers but very cold winters. Temperatures in Ulan Bator (traditional spelling; Ulaanbaatar in transcription from Mongolian Cyrillic) range between −32°C (−26°F) and 22°C (71°F). The principal language is Khalkha Mongolian. Kazakh is spoken in the province of Bayan-Ölgii. There is no state religion, but Buddhist Lamaism is being encouraged once again. The national flag (proportions 1 by 2) has three equal vertical stripes, of red, blue and red, with the 'soyombo' symbol (a combination of abstract devices) in gold on the red stripe at the hoist. The capital is Ulan Bator (Ulaanbaatar).

CONTEMPORARY POLITICAL HISTORY

Historical Context

Mongolia, the state created by Ghenghis Khan in the 13th century, was conquered by the Manchu invaders of China in two stages: the lands south of the Gobi in 1636 and the territory north of the Gobi in 1691; these were later called Inner and Outer Mongolia respectively. Following the collapse of Manchu rule in 1911, the princes of Outer Mongolia declared the independence of all Mongolia, but the Republic of China retained control of Inner Mongolia. Outer Mongolia gained autonomy, as a feudal Buddhist monarchy, but Russia accepted Chinese suzerainty over Mongolia in 1915. Following the Russian revolution of 1917, China began to re-establish control in Mongolia in 1919. In 1920 Mongol nationalists appealed to the new Soviet regime for assistance, and in March 1921 they met on Soviet territory to found the Mongolian People's Party (renamed the Mongolian People's Revolutionary Party—MPRP—in 1925) and established a Provisional People's Government. After nationalist forces, with Soviet help, drove anti-Bolshevik troops from the Mongolian capital, the People's Government was proclaimed on 11 July 1921. Soviet Russia recognized the People's Government in November of that year. In November 1924, after the death of Bogd Khan (King) Javzandamba Khutagt VIII, the Mongolian People's Republic was proclaimed.

In 1932 an armed uprising was suppressed with Soviet assistance. Following his reorganization of the MPRP and army leadership in 1936–39, power was held by Marshal Khorloo Choibalsan as Chairman of the Council of People's Commissars (Prime Minister) and MPRP leader. The dictatorship of Choibalsan closely followed the model of the regime of Stalin (Iosif Dzhugashvili, 1924–53) in the USSR. Many thousands of victims included eminent politicians, military officers, religious leaders and intellectuals. In 1939 a Japanese invasion from Manchuria was repelled by Soviet and Mongolian forces at Khalkhyn Gol (Nomonhan). In accordance with the Yalta agreement, which also confirmed the status quo in Mongolia, war was declared on Japan in August 1945, four days before the Japanese surrender, and northern China was invaded. In a Mongolian plebiscite in October, it was reported that 100% of the votes were cast in favour of independence, and this was recognized by China in January 1946.

Domestic Political Affairs

Khorloo Choibalsan died in January 1952 and was succeeded as Chairman of the Council of Ministers (as the role of Prime Minister had been redesignated in 1946) by Yumjaa Tsedenbal, who had been the MPRP's First Secretary since 1940. A new Constitution was adopted in July 1960.

Jamsran Sambuu, Chairman of the Presidium of the People's Great Khural (head of state) since July 1954, died in May 1972. He was replaced in June 1974 by Tsedenbal, who remained First Secretary of the MPRP (restyled General Secretary in 1981) but relinquished the post of Chairman of the Council of Ministers to Jambyn Batmönkh. In August 1984 Tsedenbal was removed from the party leadership and from his position as head of state, apparently owing to ill health, and Batmönkh replaced him as General Secretary of the MPRP. In December Batmönkh also became head of state, while Dumaa Sodnom, hitherto a Deputy Chairman of the Council of Ministers and the Chairman of the State Planning Commission, was appointed Chairman of the Council of Ministers.

Emboldened by the collapse of the communist regimes in Poland and the German Democratic Republic, there was a significant increase in public political activity from late 1989. At an MPRP plenum in March 1990 Batmönkh announced the resignation of the entire Political Bureau as well as of the Secretariat of the Central Committee. Gombojav Ochirbat was elected to replace Batmönkh as General Secretary, Tsedenbal was expelled from the party, and a new five-member Political Bureau was formed.

At a session of the People's Great Khural (legislature), held shortly after the MPRP plenum, Punsalmaa Ochirbat, hitherto the Minister of Foreign Economic Relations and Supply, was elected Chairman of the Presidium of the People's Great Khural, replacing Batmönkh, and other senior positions in the Political Bureau were reallocated. Sharav Gungaadorj, a Deputy Chairman and Minister of Agriculture and the Food Industry, replaced Dumaa Sodnom as Chairman of the Council of Ministers. The Khural also adopted amendments to the Constitution, including the deletion of references to the MPRP as the 'guiding force' in Mongolian society, and approved a new electoral law, with early legislative elections scheduled for mid-1990. In late March an estimated 13,000 disenchanted citizens demonstrated in Ulan Bator to demand the dissolution of the Khural. Opposition leaders called for the introduction of a multi-party electoral law. In May the People's Great Khural adopted a law on political parties, which legalized the new 'informal' parties through official registration, and also adopted further amendments to the Constitution, introducing a presidential system with a standing legislature, the State Little Khural, which was to be elected by proportional representation of parties.

At the July 1990 legislative elections and subsequent re-elections, 430 deputies were elected to serve a five-year term: 357 from the MPRP (in some instances unopposed), 16 from the Mongolian Democratic Party (MDP, the political wing of the Mongolian Democratic Union—MDU), 19 shared among the Mongolian Revolutionary Youth League, the Mongolian National Progress Party (MNPP), and the Mongolian Social-Democratic Party (MSDP), and 39 without party affiliation.

In September 1990 the People's Great Khural elected Punsalmaa Ochirbat to be the country's first President, with a five-year term of office; the post of Chairman of the Presidium of the People's Great Khural was abolished. Dash Byambasüren was appointed Prime Minister (equivalent to the former post of Chairman of the Council of Ministers) and began consultations on the formation of a multi-party government. The newly re-styled Cabinet was elected by the State Little Khural in September and October. Under the amended Constitution, the President, Vice-President and ministers were not permitted concurrently to remain deputies of the People's Great Khural; therefore, re-elections of deputies to the legislature were held in November. Büdragchaa Dash-Yondon, the Chairman of the Ulan Bator City Party Committee, was elected Chairman of the MPRP Central Committee in February 1991.

A new Constitution was adopted by the People's Great Khural in January 1992. It provided for a unicameral Mongolian Great Khural, comprising 76 members, to replace the People's Great Khural, following elections to be held in June. (The State Little Khural was abolished.) The country's official name was changed from the Mongolian People's Republic to Mongolia, and the communist gold star was removed from the national flag.

The elections to the Mongolian Great Khural of June 1992 were contested by the MPRP, an alliance of the MDP, the MNPP and the United Party (UP), the MSDP, six other parties and another alliance. Some 95.6% of the electorate participated in the poll. Candidates were elected by a simple majority, provided that they obtained the support of at least 50% of the electorate in their constituency. The MPRP candidates received 57% of the total votes, but won 70 (71 including a pro-MPRP independent) of the

76 seats in 26 constituencies. The remaining seats were taken by the MDP (two, including an independent), the MSDP, MNPP and UP (one each). In the first session of the Mongolian Great Khural, which opened in July, Puntsag Jasrai (who had served as a Deputy Chairman of the Council of Ministers in the late 1980s) was appointed Prime Minister, and his Cabinet was approved. Natsag Bagabandi, a Vice-Chairman of the MPRP Central Committee, was elected Chairman of the Great Khural (Speaker).

In October 1992 the MDP, MNPP, UP and the Mongolian Renewal Party amalgamated to form the Mongolian National Democratic Party (MNDP), with a General Council headed by the MNPP leader, Davaadorj Ganbold, and including MDU leader Sanjaasüren Zorig and other prominent opposition politicians. In the same month the MPRP Central Committee was renamed the MPRP Little Khural, and its membership was increased to 169 (and subsequently to 198). The MPRP Presidium was replaced by a nine-member party Leadership Council, headed by Büdragchaa Dash-Yondon as its General Secretary.

Following the adoption by the Great Khural of a Presidential Election Law in March 1993, direct elections to the presidency were held in June. President Ochirbat, nominated by a coalition of the MNDP and the MSDP, secured a convincing victory, winning 57.8% of the votes cast, compared with 38.7% for the MPRP's candidate, Lodon Tüdev.

In early 1996 the MPRP forced through the Great Khural the passage of amendments that increased the number of constituencies from 26 to 76, making them all single-seat constituencies, while preserving the majority vote system. To be declared elected, a candidate was required to have received a minimum of 25% of the constituency votes. In response, opposition parties formed an electoral coalition, the Democratic Alliance, which enjoyed the support of the Mongolian Green Party and the MDU.

The end of MPRP rule

At the legislative elections in June 1996, a resounding victory was achieved by the opposition Democratic Alliance, which won 50 of the 76 seats in the Great Khural, receiving 46.7% of the total votes cast. The MPRP took only 25 seats (40.6%), while one seat was won by a candidate of the United Heritage Party (UHP—subsequently also known as the Mongolian Traditional United Party). Electoral turnout was 92.2%. At the legislature's inaugural session in July, the leader of the MSDP, Radnaasümberel Gonchigdorj, was elected as Chairman of the Great Khural, while Mendsaikhan Enkhsaikhan, the leader of the Democratic Alliance, was elected as Prime Minister. Following the conclusion of a three-day boycott of the Great Khural by the MPRP over a dispute concerning the allocation of positions in the legislature, the leader of the MNDP, Tsakhia Elbegdorj, was elected Vice-Chairman of the Great Khural, and a new Government was formed at the end of July.

Following the MPRP's election defeat, and amid growing evidence of a rift between supporters of tradition and advocates of the reform process, in July 1996 the MPRP Little Khural elected a new Leadership Council and General Secretary of the party, Nambar Enkhbayar. In February 1997 several prominent dissenting members resigned from the MPRP, and Natsag Bagabandi was elected party Chairman.

At the presidential election in May 1997, Bagabandi secured a convincing victory with 60.8% of the total votes cast. In a severe setback to the democratic movement, the incumbent Ochirbat received only 29.8%, reflecting popular dissatisfaction at the Democratic Alliance's rigorous economic reform policies. Enkhbayar subsequently replaced Bagabandi as Chairman of the MPRP and in August he won a by-election for Bagabandi's former seat in the Great Khural.

In April 1998 the Democratic Alliance decided that, henceforth, the Cabinet was to comprise members of the Great Khural, headed by the leader of the Alliance. Tsakhia Elbegdorj, leader of the MNDP, was thus appointed Prime Minister, and a new Cabinet was formed in May. The Government became embroiled in a dispute over the amalgamation of the state-owned Reconstruction Bank, declared bankrupt after over-extending its credit, with the private Golomt Bank. Amid accusations that Democratic Alliance leaders had obtained loans from the bank shortly before its failure, the MPRP boycotted the Great Khural. The opposition party rejected the Government's reinstatement of the Reconstruction Bank and returned to the Great Khural in late July to pursue a motion of no confidence in the Government, which was carried by 42 votes to 33, with the support of 15 members of the Democratic Alliance.

Following a protracted dispute between the Democratic Alliance and President Bagabandi over candidates for the premiership, the Democratic Alliance finally nominated Bagabandi's candidate, the Mayor of Ulan Bator, Janlav Narantsatsralt, who was appointed Prime Minister in December 1998. In July 1999, however, Narantsatsralt lost a vote of confidence, in which MSDP members of the Great Khural voted with the opposition MPRP, following the emergence of a letter that the premier had written in January to a Russian government official, in which he seemingly acknowledged Russia's right to privatize its share in the Erdenet copper-mining joint venture without reference to Mongolia. Rinchinnyam Amarjargal was elected as the new Prime Minister at the end of July, and all but one of the ministers of Narantsatsralt's Government were reappointed. In November Amarjargal assumed the presidency of the MNDP, replacing Narantsatsralt.

The 1992 Constitution was amended for the first time in December 1999 by a Great Khural decree supported by all three parliamentary parties, which simplified the procedure for the appointment of the Prime Minister and allowed members of the Great Khural to serve as government ministers while retaining their legislative seats. An attempt by the President to veto the decree was defeated by the Great Khural in January 2000, but the Constitutional Court ruled in March that the decree had been illegal. When the Great Khural reconvened in April, members rejected the ruling and refused to discuss it.

As the legislative elections approached, a breakaway grouping of the MNDP re-established the Mongolian Democratic Party, and a faction of the MSDP founded the Mongolian New Social Democratic Party. Sanjaasüren Oyuun (the sister of Sanjaasüren Zorig, former Minister of Infrastructure Development and founder of the MDU, who had been murdered in October 1998) established the Civil Courage Party (CCP—subsequently also known as Citizens' Will). The CCP formed an electoral alliance with the Mongolian Green Party. The MNDP, unable to reconstitute the previously successful Democratic Alliance with the MSDP, formed a new Democratic Alliance with the Mongolian Believers' Democratic Party.

The MPRP's return to power

At the legislative elections held in July 2000, the MPRP won 72 of the 76 seats in the Great Khural, with 50.2% of the votes cast; Prime Minister Rinchinnyam Amarjargal and his entire Cabinet lost their seats. The level of participation was 82.4% of the electorate. The Democratic Alliance won 13.0% of the votes cast, while the Mongolian Democratic New Socialist Party (MDNSP, which had amalgamated with the Mongolian Workers' Party in 1999) received 10.7% of the vote; each of them won one seat, and the remaining seat was taken by an independent candidate. Lkhamsüren Encbish, the MPRP General Secretary, was elected Chairman of the Great Khural, and the MPRP Chairman, Nambar Enkhbayar, was elected Prime Minister.

At a conference in December 2000 five parties—the MNDP, the MSDP, the Mongolian Democratic Party, the Mongolian Believers' Democratic Party and the Democratic Renewal Party—dissolved themselves and formed a new Democratic Party (DP). Damba Dorligjav, a former Minister of Defence and director of the Erdenet copper enterprise, was elected Chairman of the new party, while former premier Narantsatsralt and the former Minister of the Environment, Sonomtseren Mendsaikhan, were elected as Vice-Chairmen.

In mid-December 2000 the Great Khural readopted the decree of December 1999 amending the 1992 Constitution. President Bagabandi finally approved the amendments in May 2001. Meanwhile, in February the 23rd Congress of the MPRP re-elected Prime Minister Enkhbayar as its Chairman, approved the establishment of a new Little Khural of 244 members and enlarged the party Leadership Council from 11 to 15 members. Lkhamsüren Enebish died in September and was succeeded as MPRP General Secretary by Doloonjin Idevkhten and as Chairman of the Great Khural by Sanjbegz Tömör-Ochir, hitherto MPRP Secretary.

At the presidential election of May 2001, the incumbent Bagabandi, the MPRP candidate, was re-elected, securing nearly 58.0% of the votes cast. Radnaasümberel Gonchigdorj of the DP won 36.6% of the vote, while Luvsandamba Dashnyam of the CCP received 3.5%.

The initial results of the legislative elections in June 2004 (compiled as percentages of the total ballot in each constituency) left the political scene in disarray: the MPRP and the Motherland Democracy (MD) coalition, comprising the MDNSP and the DP, won 36 seats and 34 seats, respectively, in the Great Khural, leaving neither with the necessary majority of 39 (one-half of the seats plus one seat). The three independents elected, although all DP members, were discounted. The Republican Party won one seat and two seats remained vacant owing to the results being contested. The rate of participation was 82.2% of registered voters. Amid mutual accusations of bribery and fraud in several constituencies, efforts to form a government became embroiled in disputes at the new General Election Committee (GEC) and the recently established City Administrative Court.

The GEC submitted the results in 74 of the 76 constituencies to President Bagabandi in early July 2004, at the first session of the newly elected Great Khural, which was boycotted by the MPRP. The MD members were not allowed to take the oath. Meeting separately, 70 of the MPRP members elected in 2000 filed a lawsuit against the President on the grounds that he had contravened the Constitution and allowed the Great Khural to meet without a quorum (57 members being present) before the final session of the outgoing Great Khural had taken place. The closing session of the previous legislature was held in late July 2004. Among other decisions, it released the Great Khural's Deputy Chairman, Jamsran Byambadorj (who had lost his parliamentary seat in the recent elections), to take up a vacant seat in the Constitutional Commission and accused the President of acting unconstitutionally in convening the first session of the incoming legislature. All these decisions were vetoed by President Bagabandi as unconstitutional. (Byambadorj was elected a member, then the Chairman, of the Constitutional Commission in January 2005.)

Postponed after another MPRP boycott, the first plenary session of the new Great Khural was held in late July 2004, when 74 members were sworn in. Following several weeks of discussions, at the end of August former Prime Minister Nambar Enkhbayar of the MPRP was appointed Chairman of the Great Khural, and Tsakhia Elbegdorj of the MD coalition became Prime Minister. Although the newly elected members of the Great Khural agreed on the formation, chairmanship and membership of the Khural's standing committees and subcommittees, discussion of the basic principles for the establishment of a coalition government was protracted. The new Cabinet was finally appointed in September. The deputy ministers, one-half nominated by the MD coalition and one-half by the MPRP, were appointed in November and December, respectively.

Coalition government

Radnaasümberel Gonchigdorj assumed the chairmanship of the DP at the end of December 2004 and installed his supporters in other senior party posts. His predecessor, Mendsaikhan Enkhsaikhan, appeared to retain the backing of the DP's National Assembly. Although a court ruled that the leadership change was contrary to the party's regulations, it declined to intervene. Badarch Erdenebat, the Minister of Defence and leader of the MDNSP, then withdrew from the MD coalition, which collapsed. CCP leader Sanjaasüren Oyuun was obliged to relinquish her post of Deputy Chairwoman of the Great Khural in January 2005. Prime Minister Elbegdorj took over the defence portfolio from Erdenebat in February, and a new Minister of Defence, Tserenkhüü Sharavdorj, was appointed in March. The parliamentary group of the erstwhile MD coalition disbanded, and many DP legislators, including Gonchigdorj (but not Enkhsaikhan), joined the Khural's MPRP group to form a parliamentary 'combined group', of which Gonchigdorj was elected Deputy Chairman. Meanwhile, Doloonjin Idevkhten was replaced as General Secretary of the MPRP by Sanjaa Bayar. In February Jügderdemid Gürragchaa (of the MPRP) and in September Zandaakhüü Enkhbold (of the MD) were declared the winners in the two constituencies where the results of the 2004 elections to the Great Khural had been contested. Gürragchaa was duly sworn in, but Enkhbold had already accepted the post of Chairman of the State Property Committee in December 2004.

At the presidential election held in May 2005, Nambar Enkhbayar (of the MPRP) emerged victorious with more than 53% of the votes cast, defeating Bazarsad Jargalsaikhan (of the Republican Party), Badarch Erdenebat (of the Motherland Party, as the MDNSP had recently been renamed) and Mendsaikhan Enkhsaikhan (of the DP). At the MPRP's congress in June, the Mayor of Ulan Bator, Miyeegombo Enkhbold, was chosen to replace Enkhbayar as party Chairman, while the party Leadership Council was enlarged to 21 members. In July the Great Khural elected the Minister of Justice and Home Affairs, Tsend Nyamdorj (of the MPRP), to replace Enkhbayar as its Chairman.

After an attempt by the MPRP to force the Prime Minister to resign, including the expulsion of DP members from the 'combined' MPRP parliamentary group (the 'group of 62'), and shortly before the closing of its spring 2005 session, the Great Khural voted in favour of the formation of a DP parliamentary group, which 25 party members (headed by Gonchigdorj) joined. The by-election in Enkhbayar's former constituency in August was won by the MPRP Chairman, Miyeegombo Enkhbold.

In January 2006 a Motherland Party deputy defected to the MPRP, thereby increasing the parliamentary representation of the latter to 38 seats. Following demands by the MPRP for Prime Minister Elbegdorj's resignation, the 10 MPRP cabinet ministers resigned and the 'grand coalition' Government was voted out of office. Miyeegombo Enkhbold, MPRP Chairman and Mayor of Ulan Bator, was elected Prime Minister. He formed a new 'national solidarity' Government, which included the Motherland and Republican Party leaders Erdenebat and Jargalsaikhan, former DP member Lamjav Gündalai, who had recently established a new party, the Party of the People, and three DP members—Enkhsaikhan, Narantsatsralt and Mishig Sonompil—who were subsequently expelled from the remnant DP, now excluded from the MPRP's new coalition. (Narantsatsralt was killed in a car accident in November 2007.)

Following his appointment in January 2006 to the post of Deputy Prime Minister, Mendsaikhan Enkhsaikhan and his supporters formed a new party, which was named the National New Party at its first congress in May. A by-election held in September, after the death of a legislator in March, was won by the Minister of Education, Culture and Science, Ölziisaikhan Enkhtüvshin (of the MPRP).

Meanwhile, the high levels of corruption in Mongolia had become a major concern among international partners. Furthermore, the political upheaval of early 2006 delayed a decision on amendments to the 1997 Minerals Law, introduced in December 2005, which caused disquiet among foreign investors in Mongolia's mining industry. Amid much public debate about the merits of state control of the country's resources and various protests, the Great Khural finally adopted a new redaction of the 1997 law in July 2006. According to initial reports, mining licences were to be granted only to companies, not to individuals; foreign and domestic investors in mining were to be taxed at the same rate; stability agreements were to be replaced by investment contracts; and local people in proposed mining areas would be granted greater rights with regard to decisions on exploitation licences. Also, the Government would have the right to acquire up to 50% of the resources of deposits discovered with the help of state funds and to control up to 34% of resources obtained from privately funded deposits. Royalties were to be increased from 2.5% to 5.0%, severe penalties were envisaged for serious environmental damage and the size of foreign workforces would be limited to 10%.

A parliamentary motion of no confidence submitted against the Government in October 2006 was defeated. Meanwhile, in preparation for the legislative elections of mid-2008, the Great Khural approved amendments to the electoral law, restoring 26 large multi-candidate constituencies (similar to those prevailing at the time of the 1992 legislative elections) and introducing a quota of 30% for female members.

In early 2007 it emerged that Tsend Nyamdorj, the Chairman of the Great Khural, had re-edited legislation, including the Election Law and the Minerals Law, after the final texts had been approved by the Great Khural. Following a Constitutional Commission ruling that his actions were unconstitutional, Nyamdorj was obliged to resign from his post in June. He was replaced by the Deputy Chairman, Danzan Lündeejantsan.

At the MPRP's 25th Congress in October 2007, delegates voted to remove Miyeegombo Enkhbold from the chairmanship of the party, in favour of General Secretary Sanjaa Bayar. The members of a new 255-member MPRP Little Khural and 21-member Leadership Council were announced later. Former MPRP secretary Yondon Otgonbayar was elected General Secretary and six new secretaries were approved, including Enkhbold and Nyamdorj. For the first time, intra-party political movements and factions were represented by three Leadership Council members; also of note was the inclusion of four women, one of them a Mongolian Kazakh.

An important consequence of these events was Miyeegombo Enkhbold's resignation as Prime Minister in November 2007, thus facilitating Sanjaa Bayar's election to the position later in the month. After signing co-operation agreements with the CCP and the National New Party, Bayar formed a new Cabinet in

December. Among three female appointees was CCP leader Sanjaasüren Oyuun, who assumed the role of Minister of Foreign Affairs.

In preparation for the next elections, in December 2007 the electoral law was amended to dispense with the recently introduced requirement for a 30% quota of female members in the legislature. President Enkhbayar unsuccessfully attempted to veto the Great Khural's revision of the law. The level of participation in the legislative elections held on 29 June 2008 was reported to be 74.3%. Amid allegations of widespread irregularities, with both the MPRP and the DP accused of malpractice, the Chairman of the DP, Tsakhia Elbegdorj, demanded that the votes be recounted. Following the publication of provisional results awarding a narrow parliamentary majority to the MPRP, thousands of demonstrators took to the streets of Ulan Bator to protest against the perceived electoral fraud. Five people were killed in the rioting that ensued, four from gunshot wounds, and hundreds were injured. About 700 demonstrators were reported to have been detained. The headquarters of the MPRP were wrecked by arson, and the GEC building was also attacked. On 1 July a state of emergency was declared, which remained in place for four days.

It was reported in mid-July 2008 that the GEC had allocated 39 seats in the Great Khural to the MPRP, 25 to the DP, one to the CCP and one to an independent candidate. The winners of 10 of the 76 seats were yet to be declared. Nevertheless, the legislature was instructed by President Enkhbayar to convene its first session. The session duly opened but was swiftly abandoned by DP members, who refused to be inaugurated pending the announcement of the final election results. The withdrawal of the DP from the proceedings removed the quorum required for the registration of legislators. Furthermore, the DP demanded an investigation into the conduct of the elections by the Chairman of the GEC. The Great Khural finally convened at the end of August, with the participation of the DP and with 67 legislators in attendance. Damdin Demberel of the MPRP was appointed as the chamber's Chairman.

On 11 September 2008 the Great Khural re-elected Sanjaa Bayar as Prime Minister. Negotiations between the MPRP and the DP, which had encompassed the contentious issue of the development of the country's mineral resources, resulted in an agreement on the formation of a coalition Government, whereby 60% of the ministerial positions were to be allocated to the MPRP and 40% to the DP. Norov Altankhuyag, who in late August had replaced Elbegdorj as Chairman of the DP following the latter's resignation, became First Deputy Prime Minister. Miyeegombo Enkhbold of the MPRP was appointed as Deputy Prime Minister. Sükhbaatar Batbold (also of the MPRP) was allocated responsibility for external relations, formerly the portfolio of foreign affairs, which had been modified to incorporate economic matters. The Ministry of Trade and Industry was abolished and a new Ministry of Mining and Energy was established.

As the GEC continued its investigations into the disputed results in six constituencies, the DP resumed its boycott of the Great Khural. Following the eventual declaration of the outstanding results, the MPRP held a total of 45 seats in the Great Khural and the DP 27; one seat was occupied by a representative of the CCP, one by a member of the Mongolian Green Party and another by an independent parliamentarian.

The presidential election of 2009 and other events

At the presidential election held on 24 May 2009, the incumbent Nambar Enkhbayar of the MPRP was defeated by the DP's candidate, former Prime Minister Tsakhia Elbegdorj, whose campaign had focused on the issues of corruption and the need for a more equitable distribution of the country's mineral wealth. Elbegdorj, whose candidacy was supported by the Mongolian Green Party and the CCP, received 51.2% of the votes cast. The level of voter participation was 73.6% of the registered electorate. Enkhbayar swiftly conceded defeat, and Elbegdorj was inaugurated in June.

In October 2009 Prime Minister Sanjaa Bayar resigned owing to ill health and was replaced by Sükhbaatar Batbold, hitherto the Minister of External Relations. In the following month Gombojav Zandanshatar of the MPRP was allocated the portfolio of foreign affairs and trade, and Chimed Khürelbaatar, also of the MPRP, was appointed to head the Government Affairs Directorate. Batbold replaced Bayar as Chairman of the MPRP in April 2010.

One of Bayar's last official duties, in October 2009, was to attend the signing of a highly significant agreement with representatives of international mining companies for the development of the Oyu Tolgoi copper and gold deposits. The exploitation of these resources, located in the Gobi region and to be developed in collaboration with Ivanhoe Mines of Canada and Rio Tinto of Australia, was expected to transform the Mongolian economy (see *Economic Affairs*). However, considerable discontent was expressed within Mongolia regarding the large share of the deposits given away to foreign interests, with the Mongolian Government retaining only a 34% stake (although this would increase to 50% after 30 years). In April 2010 about 5,000 demonstrators rallied in Ulan Bator to protest against the inequalities in Mongolian society arising from the perceived inequitable distribution of the benefits of the country's substantial mineral wealth.

In November 2010 the delegates attending the MPRP's 26th party congress in Ulan Bator voted to change the name of the party back to the Mongolian People's Party (MPP), as it had been called from its foundation in 1921 until 1925, when, under Soviet influence, the word 'revolutionary' had been added—a word that Prime Minister Batbold claimed had confrontational connotations that were no longer appropriate for the more pragmatic environment of modern-day Mongolia. Also during the congress, Batbold was re-elected as party Chairman. At the first conference of the renamed party, the Leadership Council was enlarged from 21 to 31 members. In January 2011 former President Nambar Enkhbayar was elected as leader of a new Mongolian People's Revolutionary Party formed by those who had rejected the recent change in the party's name.

The CCP and the Mongolian Green Party merged to form the Civil Courage-Green Party (CC-GP) in March 2011. The new party, jointly chaired by Sanjaasüren Oyuun of the CCP and Dangaasüren Enkhbat of the Mongolian Green Party, was finally registered by the Supreme Court in March 2012.

In April 2011 a group of approximately 200 herdsmen gathered in the central square of Ulan Bator to demand the resignation of the Government and the dissolution of the Great Khural, accusing the Mongolian authorities of having become pawns to foreign mining interests. The protesters appealed for a popular referendum to be staged on the question of conducting parliamentary elections without the participation of political parties. In June around 50 protesters set up a makeshift camp in Ulan Bator's central square and fired arrows at the parliamentary building, in protest against the Government's refusal to acquiesce to the demands for a referendum.

Under considerable pressure from the Great Khural, in September 2011 the Mongolian Government announced its intention to renegotiate the terms of the agreement signed with Ivanhoe Mines and Rio Tinto in October 2009 for the development of the Oyu Tolgoi copper and gold deposits, seeking to increase its stake from 34% to 50%. However, following staunch resistance from the Canadian and Australian firms, the Government agreed to maintain the original terms of agreement, with its stake scheduled to increase to 50% only after 30 years. Meanwhile, in October 2010 the Government had announced the establishment of Erdenes Tavan Tolgoi, a state-owned company that would retain 100% ownership of the Tavan Tolgoi coal deposits, with the company authorized to award development contracts only, in an apparent acknowledgement of the increasing public consternation regarding the extent of foreign ownership of Mongolia's mining industry. Furthermore, in mid-2012 the Government gave away 20% of Erdenes Tavan Tolgoi's shares to the Mongolian population.

In December 2011 the Great Khural approved new electoral legislation, which was to take effect from the legislative elections scheduled for June 2012. Voters would be able to vote for an individual candidate in one of 48 single-seat constituencies, and also for a political party, with 28 members to be indirectly elected in the latter vote on the basis of proportional representation. Parties would be required to obtain at least 5% of the total number of votes nationwide in order to secure parliamentary representation. The legislation also reintroduced the quota for female members that had been introduced prior to the 2008 elections (but which then had been repealed in December 2007), although the percentage of seats to be reserved henceforth for women was set at the lower level of 20%.

Political tensions within the Government led to the DP's withdrawal from the coalition in January 2012. Prime Minister Batbold submitted a list of MPP nominees to replace the six outgoing DP ministers, but this was initially rejected by President Elbegdorj on the grounds that legislative arrangements formally to end the coalition had not yet been made. However, after further consultations, Batbold resubmitted his list, and five of the six proposed appointments were approved by the Great Khural in late January, including those of Jadamba Enkhbayar as Minister of Defence and Damdin Khayankhyarvaa as Minister of Finance; the role of Chief Deputy Prime Minister was abolished.

Also in January 2012, the Great Khural ratified the Second Optional Protocol of the International Covenant on Civil and Political Rights, signalling its intention permanently to abolish the death penalty. The development, which was welcomed by human rights groups, followed a two-year moratorium, introduced in January 2010, on the implementation of capital punishment.

Former President Nambar Enkhbayar was detained in April 2012, following a raid on his home by the security forces. The authorities claimed that he had failed to respond to requests to appear for questioning in connection with an investigation into his alleged misuse of public assets while in power. Amnesty International expressed concern about his treatment, while protests were staged by his supporters in Ulan Bator. Following an 11-day hunger strike protesting his innocence, Enkhbayar was released on bail in May.

In May 2012 the Great Khural adopted new legislation limiting, to 49%, the size of foreign investments in the country's 'strategic' industries, including mining, banking and telecommunications, without both government and parliamentary prior approval. However, the law was applicable only to stakes valued at more than US $76m. or to investments by foreign state-owned companies. The Government admitted that the new legislation had been prompted by a recent unsuccessful bid by the Chinese state-owned company Aluminium Corporation of China (CHALCO) to purchase a majority stake in the Mongolian coal company SouthGobi Resources.

The legislative elections of 2012 and the presidential election of 2013

In the run-up to the legislative elections, which were held (under the new electoral system) on 28 June 2012, the main contenders had attempted to win public support by pledging better wealth distribution. The MPP asserted that, if elected, it would establish a national sovereign wealth fund and increase spending in the health and education sectors, while the DP promised to complete a decade-old programme of free allocation of state-owned agricultural land to the populace. In the event, following challenges to the results in some constituencies that ended in the initial results being overturned, the DP won 36 of the 76 seats in the Great Khural, the MPP secured 24 seats, the newly established Justice Coalition, which comprised the MNDP and the Mongolian People's Revolutionary Party of Nambar Enkhbayar (who had himself been barred from contesting the elections by the GEC owing to his impending trial), obtained 11 seats, the CC-GP took two seats and the three remaining seats were won by independent candidates. Electoral turnout was relatively low, at 65.2%. Owing to the legal challenges to the results, the final two legislators were not sworn in until May 2013.

Outgoing Prime Minister Sükhbaatar Batbold, who blamed his party's defeat on the loss of votes to Enkhbayar's breakaway party, resigned as Chairman of the MPP at a party conference in July 2012; he was replaced by former Minister of Education, Culture and Science Ölziisaikhan Enkhtüvshin. In mid-August the Great Khural finally approved the nomination of DP Chairman Norov Altankhuyag as Prime Minister. A coalition Cabinet, comprising members of the DP, the Justice Coalition and the CC-GP, was endorsed by the legislature later that month. Among the notable appointments were those of Dendev Terbishdagva, the Deputy Chairman of the Mongolian People's Revolutionary Party, as Deputy Prime Minister and of Luvsanvandan Bold of the DP as Minister of Foreign Affairs.

In August 2012 Enkhbayar was convicted of corruption and received a seven-year prison sentence (of which three years were commuted), as well as a sizeable fine. In December the Great Khural approved new electoral legislation in advance of the 2013 presidential election; the new law included provisions for voting at Mongolian embassies by Mongolian citizens living abroad.

The Deputy Speaker of the Great Khural, Sangajav Bayartsogt, who had been Minister of Finance in 2008–12, resigned in April 2013, following the emergence of evidence that from 2008 he had owned an offshore company and held a Swiss bank account that he had failed to declare on the disclosure documents required to assume public office. He was replaced by former premier Miyeegombo Enkhbold.

Also in April 2013, the Great Khural revised the legislation regulating foreign investment in Mongolia's 'strategic' industries that had been enacted in May 2012 (see *The presidential election of 2009 and other events*). The amendment stipulated that, henceforth, foreign private companies seeking to acquire more than 49% of the issued shares of a Mongolian company would no longer require the transaction to be approved by the Great Khural; any such investment made by a foreign state-owned enterprise would, however, still require parliamentary approval.

The presidential election of 26 June 2013 was contested by three candidates: the incumbent President Elbegdorj (of the DP), Minister of Health Natsag Udval (of the Mongolian People's Revolutionary Party—the first female presidential candidate in the country's history) and legislator Badmaanyambuu Bat-Erdene (of the MPP). Elbegdorj, who had campaigned on an anti-graft platform, emerged victorious with 50.2% of the votes cast, compared with 42.0% for Bat-Erdene and just 6.5% for Udval. Turnout was recorded at 66.5%.

Following Mongolia's accession to the Organization for Security and Co-operation in Europe (OSCE) in November 2012, the OSCE had deployed an observation mission to monitor the election. In its final report, published in September 2013, the mission concluded that the election had been conducted 'in an environment that respected fundamental freedoms', but identified a number of procedural issues and noted that the secrecy of votes had not always been ensured. The report also stated that restrictive legal provisions had prevented the media from providing sufficient information to the electorate, and voiced concerns about a lack of strict control mechanisms to ensure transparency in the financing of electoral campaigns.

Despite President Elbegdorj having been re-elected at least partly as a result of his anti-corruption credentials, Mongolia was ranked as the second most corrupt country (after Liberia) of the 107 surveyed by Transparency International in its 2013 Global Corruption Barometer, published in July of that year. One of Elbegdorj's first acts upon his inauguration, also in July, was to issue a presidential pardon for Enkhbayar, whose health was reported to have deteriorated during his imprisonment following his conviction on corruption charges. In August 2014 a police investigation was opened into further fraud allegations against Enkhbayar; the claims were reported to pertain to the purchase of the MPRP's premises in Ulan Bator in 2011.

In October 2013 the Great Khural approved new investment legislation replacing, *inter alia*, legislation on the regulation of foreign investment in Mongolia's 'strategic' sectors, as revised in April of that year. The stipulations of the new law, the main aim of which was to reverse the current slowdown in the economy by increasing the inflow of foreign direct investment, included a further easing of the regulatory approval requirements for foreign private companies investing in Mongolia, and the provision of tax and non-tax incentives intended to encourage both foreign and domestic investment in Mongolia. The law also provided for the establishment by the Ministry of Economic Development of a new investment agency to oversee investment activities within Mongolia.

At the 27th congress of the MPP, held in late October 2013, former premier and serving Deputy Speaker of the Great Khural Miyeegombo Enkhbold was elected, for the second time, as the Chairman of the party. In January 2014 the DP introduced draft legislation proposing the dissolution of political parties without any parliamentary seats. Draft legislation that would have prohibited members of the Great Khural from concurrently serving as cabinet ministers was rejected by the Great Khural in April; at that time some 17 of the 19 cabinet ministers were also members of the Khural. In May the resignation of the Minister of Industry and Agriculture, Khaltmaa Battulga, from the Cabinet was approved by the Great Khural; Battulga was replaced by Sharavdorj Tüvdendorj.

Recent developments: the formation of a new coalition government

A decision announced by Prime Minister Altankhuyag in August 2014 to reduce the number of government ministries from 16 to 13, in an attempt to improve administration and reduce public expenditure, proved deeply unpopular and led to the resignation of seven cabinet ministers, including Minister of Foreign Affairs Luvsanvandan Bold, prompting the MPP to appeal for Altankhuyag to stand down. The proposed restructuring received parliamentary approval in October. In the same month the DP and the Mongolian People's Revolutionary Party concluded a controversial electoral partnership deal in advance of the 2016 legislative poll; a number of DP members were outspoken in their criticism of the agreement, which, they contended, would not only result in certain electoral defeat for the DP but also violated the party's procedural rules. Altankhuyag resigned the DP chairmanship in late October 2014, and was replaced by the Speaker of the Great Khural, Zandaakhüü Enkhbold.

Responding to the political turmoil, and citing a marked slowdown in economic growth and foreign investment, as well as widespread allegations of state corruption and cronyism, in early November 2014 the Great Khural voted to remove Altankhuyag from the premiership; 36 of the 66 members who participated in the ballot (including some members of the DP) voted in favour of his dismissal. Chimed Saikhanbileg, a minister in the outgoing Government, was appointed Prime Minister by the Great Khural two weeks later, during a parliamentary session that was boycotted by the MPP on the grounds that Saikhanbileg's membership of Altankhuyag's Cabinet meant that he had been 'instrumental' in the deterioration of the Mongolian economy. Meanwhile, in mid-November, prior to Saikhanbileg's appointment, the budget for 2015 was finally approved by the Great Khural, having previously been rejected twice amid criticism of excessive spending and over-optimistic economic projections.

One of Saikhanbileg's first acts as Prime Minister was to propose the formation of a coalition government, urging all parties to put aside their political differences in order to address the country's economic challenges collectively (see *Economic Affairs*). In early December 2014 it was announced that the MPP, together with the Justice Coalition (the Mongolian People's Revolutionary Party and the MNDP), had agreed to join the DP-led coalition. The new coalition Government swiftly reversed the consolidation of government ministries introduced by Altankhuyag, and Saikhanbileg's 19-member Cabinet was approved in mid-December. Of the 19 ministers, 10 were DP members, six belonged to the MPP and the remaining three were members of the Justice Coalition. Ukhnaa Khürelsükh of the MPP was appointed Deputy Prime Minister, while the DP's Lundeg Purevsuren became Minister of Foreign Affairs.

Foreign Affairs

Following its admission to the UN in 1961, Mongolia was accorded diplomatic recognition by the United Kingdom (in 1963) and other Western European states, as well as by many developing countries. By January 1987, when Mongolia was finally granted diplomatic recognition by the USA, it maintained diplomatic relations with more than 100 states, a number that had risen to 181 by early 2015.

Regional relations

Relations with the People's Republic of China were good until the onset of the Sino–Soviet dispute in the 1960s. However, Sino-Mongolian relations improved significantly from 1986 when the Chinese Vice-Minister of Foreign Affairs visited Ulan Bator, and the two countries signed agreements on consular relations and trade. A new Treaty of Friendship and Co-operation was concluded during a visit to Ulan Bator by Chinese Premier Li Peng in April 1994, and relations were further consolidated by a series of senior-level bilateral visits during the late 1990s and 2000s. In November 2006 Miyeegombo Enkhbold signed a trade and economic co-operation agreement with China, during his first official visit to that country since becoming Prime Minister in January. Further senior-level visits included that of Chinese Premier Wen Jiabao to Mongolia in June 2010 (the first such visit by a Chinese premier in 16 years), during which the two sides signed an intergovernmental border regime agreement (renewing an accord of 1998). The bilateral relationship was upgraded to a strategic partnership in June 2011. However, tensions arose in November when the Dalai Lama made his eighth visit to Mongolia, at the request of local Buddhists. The Chinese Government remained staunchly opposed to any country affording a political platform to the Dalai Lama; however, the Mongolian Government insisted that the visit had been exclusively religious in nature.

During a state visit to Beijing in October 2013, Prime Minister Norov Altankhuyag met with Chinese Premier Li Keqiang, whereupon the two leaders signed a broad-based agreement outlining key areas of co-operation for the medium- and long-term development of the strategic partnership; among the fields identified for greater co-operation were trade, finance, cross-border security, military technology, mineral resource development and transport. In the same month China Shenhua Energy

Company signed a contract with three Mongolian mining companies to buy 1,000m. metric tons of coal over 20 years, in a deal estimated to be worth some US $50,000m.

A comprehensive strategic partnership agreement, providing for enhanced political, diplomatic and economic co-operation, was signed during a visit to Ulan Bator by Chinese President Xi Jinping in August 2014. Some 26 co-operation agreements were concluded during Xi's visit, including a medium-term economic development agreement, which envisaged an increase in bilateral trade to US $10,000m. by 2020, and a transportation accord allowing landlocked Mongolia to transport mineral resources through Chinese territory and to use Chinese seaports for export transportation. The two sides also agreed to conduct a feasibility study into establishing a cross-border economic co-operation zone, while Xi endorsed a proposal made by President Tsakhia Elbegdorj for the holding of formal Mongolian-Chinese-Russian talks to enhance trilateral co-operation (see below).

Diplomatic relations between Mongolia and Japan were established in 1972, and were consolidated by a number of high-level meetings during the 1990s and 2000s. In February 2007 President Nambar Enkhbayar visited Japan and signed a joint agreement with Japanese Prime Minister Shinzo Abe pledging to expand bilateral relations, including plans to utilize mineral resources in Mongolia. The two leaders agreed to co-operate in resolving tensions caused by the Democratic People's Republic of Korea (North Korea) nuclear dispute and to collaborate in Japan's quest to attain a permanent seat on the UN Security Council. Subsequent senior-level visits included that of President Elbegdorj to Japan in November 2010, during which the two countries signed a Mongolia-Japan Joint Declaration aimed at strengthening bilateral relations at a strategic level. A five-year strategic partnership agreement was signed in September 2013, during a visit to the Japanese capital of Tokyo by Prime Minister Altankhuyag. In February 2014, during a visit to Tokyo by Mongolian Minister of Foreign Affairs Luvsanvandan Bold, Japan pledged to provide financial support for the implementation of the strategic partnership programme. A bilateral economic partnership agreement, the first in Mongolia's history, was concluded in February 2015; it was hoped that the accord would significantly boost trade and investment between the two countries, as well as helping Mongolia to connect to global markets. Japan also pledged an additional loan of 36,850m. yen for the construction of a new international airport serving Ulan Bator; construction of the airport, which had commenced in May 2013, was expected to be completed by the end of 2016.

In May 1999 Mongolia received South Korean President Kim Dae-Jung, marking the first such visit by a Korean head of state. Following talks with the Mongolian Minister of Defence, President Kim obtained the Mongolian Government's support for his policy of political engagement with the North Korean regime. In August 2011 South Korean President Lee Myung-Bak and President Elbegdorj agreed to elevate relations to a 'comprehensive partnership', and pledged to expand co-operation in a wide range of fields, including national and regional defence, energy and mining, infrastructural development, transport and health care. Elbegdorj reaffirmed Mongolian support for South Korea's efforts to resolve the North Korean nuclear issue, stressing that a complete and irreversible denuclearization of North Korea was essential to hopes of regional peace and stability. During a visit to South Korea by Mongolian Minister of Foreign Affairs Luvsanvandan Bold in February 2014, a memorandum of understanding providing for the establishment of a bilateral economic forum was signed to promote enhanced economic co-operation and mutual investment, while the South Korean Government pledged to ease visa conditions for medical tourists and students from Mongolia.

Despite its close ties with South Korea, Mongolia has maintained good relations with North Korea in recent years. In July 2007 Mongolia received the President of the Presidium of the North Korean Supreme People's Assembly, Kim Yong Nam, and a bilateral agreement to co-operate in the areas of public health, medical science and marine transport was signed. In February 2013 the Mongolian Ministry of Foreign Affairs issued a statement denouncing a recent North Korean nuclear test and reaffirming Mongolia's support for the denuclearization of the Korean peninsula. In April it was reported that the Mongolian Independent Agency against Corruption was investigating allegations that the recently resigned head of the Mongolian air force, Brig.-Gen. Tojoony Dashdeleg, had arranged in 2011 to sell salvaged engines from about 20 disused fighter aircraft to North Korea; the North Korean authorities claimed to have paid for but not to have received them. President Elbegdorj made a four-day state visit to the North Korean capital, Pyongyang, in October 2013, becoming the first foreign head of state to visit North Korea since Kim Jong Un assumed the leadership in December 2011. A series of agreements intended to boost co-operation in industry, agriculture, sports, culture and tourism were signed during the visit, but Elbegdorj was not granted a meeting with Kim Jong Un himself. In late 2013 the Mongolian Government launched the Ulan Bator Dialogue on Northeast Asia Security, a new mechanism intended to facilitate a peaceful solution to the Korean peninsula impasse, as well as to decrease regional distrust more generally. The inaugural meeting was held in June 2014 and was attended by representatives from Mongolia, North and South Korea, China, Japan, Russia, the USA, the UK, Germany and the Netherlands.

During an official visit to Russia in January 1993, President Punsalmaagiin Ochirbat and the Russian President, Boris Yeltsin, signed a 20-year Mongolian-Russian Treaty of Friendship and Co-operation to replace the defunct Mongolian-Soviet treaty of 1986. The two leaders also issued a joint statement expressing regret at the execution and imprisonment of Mongolian citizens in the USSR during the Stalinist period. In November 2000 the Russian President, Vladimir Putin, made a brief stop in Ulan Bator en route to a conference in Brunei, thus becoming the most senior Russian or Soviet visitor to Mongolia since 1974. Russia affirmed its commitment to guaranteeing Mongolia's security in connection with its nuclear weapons-free status. When Prime Minister Enkhbayar and his Russian counterpart, Mikhail Kasyanov, met in the Russian capital of Moscow in July 2003, a new five-year agreement on the operation of the Erdenet copper enterprise was reached, preserving Mongolia's 51% ownership of stock.

In December 2003 Russia announced that it had received payment in settlement of Mongolia's outstanding debt of 11,400m. transferable roubles that the Russian Government claimed it was owed for Soviet aid granted during 1947–91 (the Mongolian Government referred to this as the 'big debt'); Russia had waived 98% of the total debt and accepted US \$250m. Prime Minister Enkhbayar celebrated a political and diplomatic victory for the MPRP Government, but the full details of the settlement remained unclear. Russian President Dmitrii Medvedev claimed during a visit to Mongolia in August 2009 that certain issues pertaining to the 'big debt' remained unresolved, but the debt was declared fully settled during a visit to Russia by Prime Minister Sükhbaatar Batbold in December 2010. Meanwhile, bilateral relations were further strengthened by several high-level meetings during 2006–11, including a week-long state visit to Russia by President Elbegdorj in May 2011, during which he held discussions with Medvedev on a range of issues, reportedly including proposals for a bilateral free trade agreement as well as measures further to enhance defence co-operation.

Some 14 bilateral accords were signed during a visit to Mongolia by Russian President Putin in early September 2014, including agreements to ease visa requirements and to modernize Mongolia's principal rail link, the Trans-Mongolian Railway, connecting Russia in the north and China in the south via Ulan Bator. Putin also endorsed Elbegdorj's proposal for formal Mongolian-Chinese-Russian discussions to facilitate increased trilateral co-operation. In mid-September Elbegdorj and Putin, together with Chinese President Xi Jinping, met on the sidelines of a meeting of the Shanghai Cooperation Organization in Dushanbe, Tajikistan; transit transportation and infrastructure were among the principal issues identified for enhanced co-operation. The three heads of state proposed reconvening in Ulan Bator every three years and agreed to establish a mechanism for consulations at the level of deputy foreign minister; the first round of such talks was held in Ulan Bator in October.

Other external relations

Following the US military intervention in Iraq in March 2003, members of the Mongolian army's élite battalion were dispatched to Iraq. (The Mongolian deployment remained in Iraq until September 2008.) In July 2004 President Natsag Bagabandi met President George W. Bush in Washington, DC, USA, and signed a Trade and Investment Framework Agreement. In 2005 the USA provided Mongolia with US \$18m. in military assistance, including regular training exchanges and peacekeeping exercises. In November 2005 President Bush made the first visit to Mongolia by an incumbent US President. During a visit to Washington, DC, in October 2007, President Nambar Enkhbayar met with Bush, whereupon the two leaders signed

a Millennium Challenge Compact that committed \$285m. of US aid to Mongolia, the bulk of which was allocated to improving rail transportation, property rights, education and health care.

President Tsakhia Elbegdorj made an official visit to Washington, DC, in June 2011, during which he met with the US President, Barack Obama, and in August the US Vice-President, Joseph Biden, made a state visit to Ulan Bator. During a visit to Mongolia in July 2012, US Secretary of State Hillary Clinton praised Mongolia as a model of democracy and freedom of expression. A bilateral agreement on international trade and investment transparency, intended to create a more open and predictable environment for Mongolian and US firms to do business, was signed in September 2013 and ratified by the Mongolian legislature in December 2014. Military ties were enhanced by the signing of a joint vision statement during a visit to Mongolia by the US Secretary of Defense, Chuck Hagel, in April 2014, under the terms of which the Obama Administration was to provide additional military training and funding to Mongolia.

In October 2014 it was announced that Mongolia was to host the 11th summit of the Asia-Europe Meeting (ASEM) in 2016. It was hoped that the event, which would represent the largest diplomatic meeting ever to be held in Mongolia, would help to boost the country's international profile and attract new foreign investment.

CONSTITUTION AND GOVERNMENT

Supreme legislative power is vested in the 76-member Mongolian Great Khural (Assembly), elected by universal adult suffrage for four years. The Great Khural recognizes the President on his election and appoints the Prime Minister and members of the Cabinet, which is the highest executive body. The President, who is directly elected for a term of four years, is head of state and Commander-in-Chief of the Armed Forces. Under the terms of a revision to the electoral law approved in December 2011, which took effect from the June 2012 elections, voters can vote for an individual candidate in one of 48 single-seat constituencies, and for a political party, with 28 members to be indirectly elected on the basis of proportional representation.

Mongolia is divided into 21 provinces (*aimag*) and one municipality (Ulan Bator), with appointed governors and elected local assemblies. The provinces themselves are divided into 330 rural districts (*sum*).

REGIONAL AND INTERNATIONAL CO-OPERATION

Mongolia is a member of the Asian Development Bank (ADB, see p. 206), of the Association of Southeast Asian Nations (ASEAN) Regional Forum (ARF, see p. 213) and of the UN's Economic and Social Commission for Asia and the Pacific (ESCAP, see p. 30).

Mongolia became a member of the UN in 1961. It was admitted to the World Trade Organization (WTO, see p. 431) in 1997. Mongolia is also a member of the European Bank for Reconstruction and Development (EBRD, see p. 266), and Mongolbank, the country's central bank, has joined the Bank for International Settlements (BIS, see p. 220). In November 2012 the country acceded to the Organization for Security and Co-operation in Europe (OSCE, see p. 385) as a full participating state; Mongolia had been an OSCE Partner for Co-operation since 2004.

ECONOMIC AFFAIRS

In 2013, according to estimates by the World Bank, Mongolia's gross national income (GNI), measured at average 2011–13 prices, was US \$10,706m., equivalent to \$3,770 per head (or \$8,810 per head on an international purchasing-power parity basis). During 2004–13, it was estimated, the population increased at an average annual rate of 1.4%, while gross domestic product (GDP) per head increased, in real terms, at an average of 7.4% per year. Overall GDP increased, in real terms, at an average annual rate of 9.0% in 2004–13. According to the Asian Development Bank (ADB), real GDP increased by 11.6% in 2013 and by 7.8% in 2014.

Agriculture (including forestry and fishing) contributed 16.5% of GDP in 2013 and engaged 29.8% of the employed labour force. Animal herding is the main economic activity and is practised throughout the country. Most livestock is privately owned. A summer drought in 2009 was followed by unusually low winter temperatures, as a result of which a total of 8.2m. livestock (sheep, goats, horses, cattle and camels) were reported to have died by May 2010; more than one-half of these losses were goats. By the end of 2010 livestock numbers had dwindled, to 32.5m., although a substantial recovery in numbers was recorded over the following four years. The principal crops are wheat, potatoes and vegetables. Production of cereals increased from 387,000 metric tons in 2013 to 518,700 tons in 2014. During 2004–13, according to figures from the World Bank, the GDP of the agricultural sector increased, in real terms, at an average annual rate of 6.0%. According to the ADB, agricultural GDP grew by 19.3% in 2013 and by 14.4% in 2014.

Industry (comprising mining, manufacturing, construction and utilities) provided 33.3% of GDP in 2013 and the sector (excluding printing and publishing) engaged 20.6% of the employed labour force. According to the World Bank, during 2004–13 industrial GDP increased, in real terms, at an average rate of 6.5% per year. According to the ADB, the industrial sector's GDP increased by 15.3% in 2013 and by 16.1% in 2014.

Mining contributed 21.1% of GDP in 2013, and employed less than 2% of the workforce in 2012, according to the ADB. Mongolia has significant, largely unexplored, mineral resources and is a leading producer and exporter of copper, gold, molybdenum and fluorspar concentrates. Mining contributed 89.2% of exports in 2012, according to the ADB. The value of exports of copper concentrate increased from US $770.6m. in 2011 to $2,573.6m. in 2014. In addition to the major copper-molybdenum works at Erdenet, a Mongolian-Russian joint venture, the sites of other mineral deposits are being developed in collaboration with various foreign enterprises, notably the Oyu Tolgoi copper and gold deposits. Production of copper concentrate at Oyu Tolgoi commenced in January 2013, with the first commercial shipment, totalling 5,800 metric tons, exported in July. Full operating capacity—450,000 tons of copper and 330,000 oz of gold annually—was expected to be reached by 2020. Meanwhile, gold production (state procurement) declined from some 22,600 kg in 2006 to 5,995 kg in 2012, before increasing to 11,504 kg by 2014. Output of coal declined from 29.2m. tons in 2013 to 24.4m. tons in 2014. Production at the Ukhaa Khudag section of the vast Tavan Tolgoi coalfield commenced in 2009 and reached 9.2m. tons in 2013. Production at the East Tsankhi section of Tavan Tolgoi commenced in July 2011 and was reported at around 5m. tons in 2013. Following protracted delays, extraction at the West Tsankhi block of Tavan Tolgoi finally commenced in July 2013, with the first shipment of coal exported in September. Other mineral resources include tungsten, tin, uranium and lead. Mongolia's production of crude petroleum has grown rapidly, from 366,800 barrels in 2006 to 7.4m. barrels in 2014 (representing a 44.4% increase on output in 2013). According to the ADB, the GDP of the mining sector expanded at an average annual rate of 6.7% in 2004–13; the sector's GDP increased, in real terms, by 20.7% in 2013 and by 24.2% in 2014 (boosted by expanded production at Oyu Tolgoi).

The manufacturing sector accounted for 7.2% of GDP in 2013. Manufacturing industries are based largely on the products of the agricultural and animal husbandry sector. The principal branches of manufacturing include food products, beverages, textiles and garments. Mongolia is one of the world's foremost producers of cashmere, and the country also manufactures garments, leather goods and carpets. According to figures from the World Bank, manufacturing GDP increased at an average annual rate of 4.2% in 2004–13; the sector's GDP grew by 6.8% in 2013.

Construction accounted for just 3.0% of GDP in 2013 and engaged 6.6% of the employed population. According to figures from the ADB, the sector's GDP decreased by an average of 11.7% per year in 2004–13. The sector expanded by an impressive 66.5% in 2013 as a result of monetary and fiscal stimulus.

Energy is derived principally from thermal power stations, fuelled by coal. Most provincial centres have thermal power stations or diesel generators, while minor rural centres generally rely on small diesel generators. In more isolated areas wood, roots, bushes and dried animal dung are used for domestic fuel. There is much potential for the development of renewable energy resources. Production at the country's first wind farm, located at Salkhit, around 70 km from Ulan Bator, commenced in June 2013; the wind farm was expected to provide some 5% of Mongolia's electricity requirements. Mongolia imports from Russia electricity and petroleum products, including liquid petroleum gas. In 2013 the cost of Mongolia's imports of fuels and lubricants accounted for 25.6% of the total cost of merchandise imports.

The services sector contributed 50.3% of GDP in 2013 and engaged 49.6% of the employed labour force. During 2004–13, according to figures from the World Bank, the GDP of the sector

increased, in real terms, by an average of 10.9% annually. Receipts from tourism were estimated to have reached US $233m. in 2012. The number of visitor arrivals reached 475,892 in 2012, before decreasing to 417,815 in 2013 and to 392,844 in 2014, when about 40% of visitors came from the People's Republic of China. According to the ADB, the GDP of the services sector grew by 6.8% in 2013 and by 4.8% in 2014.

According to IMF figures, Mongolia's visible merchandise trade deficit was US $1,306.3m. in 2013 and there was a deficit of $3,192.0m. on the current account of the balance of payments. In 2014 the principal source of imports was China, supplying 33.7% of the total, followed by Russia, the USA, Japan and the Republic of Korea (South Korea). China was also the principal market for exports in that year, purchasing 87.8% of the total. The principal imports in 2013 were machinery and vehicles, followed by fuels and lubricants, basic manufactures, and food and live animals. The leading exports were fuels and lubricants, followed by raw materials, and specifically copper concentrate. Other significant exports included gold.

Official figures indicated a general government budget deficit of 886,277.4m. tögrög in 2014. According to the ADB, the general government deficit in cash terms was equivalent to 4.1% of GDP in that year, compared with a deficit equivalent to 0.9% of GDP in 2013. Mongolia's total external debt was US $15,388m. at the end of 2014. In that year the cost of debt-servicing was equivalent to 43.9% of the value of exports of goods and services. According to figures from the ADB, the annual rate of inflation averaged 8.2% during 2004–13. Consumer prices rose by 9.9% in 2013 and by 12.8% in 2014, according to the ADB. The number of registered unemployed persons decreased from 42,800 at the end of 2013 to 37,000 at the end of 2014. However, the number of unregistered unemployed persons was believed to be far greater. The official rate of unemployment was 7.7% in in the final quarter of 2014.

In the wake of the international financial crisis of 2008–09, which had a serious impact on the Mongolian economy, the Oyu Tolgoi copper and gold deposits (which could potentially generate annual revenue of more than US $8,000m. for the next 40–50 years) and the Tavan Tolgoi coalfield (the largest coking coal deposit in the world) were regarded as key to re-energizing the country's economic fortunes. However, both projects were beleaguered by numerous issues. A dispute with the British-Australian Rio Tinto Group over the financing of a proposed underground expansion project led to Rio Tinto suspending work on an underground expansion at the mine in July 2013, before dismissing 1,700 workers at the project in August. Negotiations to end the impasse—which also included disagreement over the allocation of revenues generated from the mine, and which contributed significantly to a decline in foreign direct investment (FDI) from $4,400m. in 2012 to $1,800m. in 2013—remained ongoing at early 2015. Despite the implementation in November 2013 of new legislation easing restrictions on investors in the strategic sectors of mining, banking and telecommunications, FDI inflows declined further, to just $800m., in 2014. A proposal by the Mongolian Government to exchange state-owned equity in 'strategic mines' for higher royalties, in a further attempt to boost FDI, was rejected by Rio Tinto in February 2015. Meanwhile, operations at the East Tsankhi block of the Tavan Tolgoi coalfield were halted in August 2014 owing to a dispute with the project's Australian contractor, MacMahon Holdings, over claims by MacMahon that it was owed $22m. in overdue payments. Nevertheless, some progress was made in December, when a new tender to develop the East and West Tsankhi blocks of Tavan Tolgoi was secured by a Chinese-Japanese-Mongolian consortium. Development of the national economy has long been obstructed by severe infrastructural deficiencies, including poor transport links. The completion in September 2013 of the construction of a road linking Choir, in Gobi-Sümber province, with Zamyn-Uud, on the Chinese border, in Dornogobi province, was heralded as a crucial development; the new road connected with existing roads in northern Mongolia to create a 'vertical corridor' traversing the full length of the country, connecting to Russia in the north and China in the south. Similarly, it was hoped that an ADB-funded road improvement project in western Mongolia, completion of which was scheduled for 2020, would reduce the isolation of and encourage development in one of the country's most impoverished regions. Other ongoing concerns of the Government included the need to promote economic diversification (to avoid over-reliance on the troubled mining sector) and the persistent levels of poverty (an estimated 27.4% of the population still lived below the poverty line in 2013). During 2013–14 declines in FDI, coal output and global commodity prices contributed to a 40% depreciation of the tögrög, which in turn led to greater inflationary pressures; consumer price inflation steadily increased from a year-on-year rate of 8.3% in July 2013 to 14.9% in July 2014. The central bank increased its policy interest rate from 10.5% to 12.0% in the latter month and to 13.0% in January 2015, by which time inflation had eased to 9.8%. The ADB projected an inflation rate of 8.9% for 2015 as a whole. Despite a strong overall performance by the mining sector, reflecting expanded production at Oyu Tolgoi, GDP growth moderated to 7.8% in 2014, largely owing to the decline in FDI. A further marked deceleration, to 3.0%, was forecast by the ADB for 2015, as lower prices for exports were anticipated. Amid spiralling public debt levels, an amendment to the Fiscal Stability Law providing for a temporary increase in the maximum allowable debt-to-GDP ratio, from 40% to 58.3%, was approved in January 2015. In February the IMF confirmed that it had received a formal request for support from the new Government of Prime Minister Chimed Saikhanbileg and dispatched a team to Mongolia to initiate discussions.

PUBLIC HOLIDAYS

2016: 1 January (New Year), 8–10 February (Tsagaan Sar, lunar new year), 8 March (International Women's Day), 1 June (Children's Day), 11–13 July (Anniversary of the People's Revolution and Naadam, national sports festival), 14 November (Genghis Khan Day), 29 December (National Freedom and Independence Day).

Statistical Survey

Unless otherwise indicated, revised by Alan J. K. Sanders and the editorial staff

Area and Population

AREA, POPULATION AND DENSITY

Area (sq km)	1,564,116*
Population (census results)	
5 January 2000	2,373,493
19 November 2010†	2,754,685
Population (official estimates at 31 December)	
2012	2,867,700
2013	2,930,300
2014	2,995,900
Density (per sq km) at 31 December 2014	1.9

* 603,909 sq miles.

† Including foreign nationals (16,320), stateless persons (108) and Mongolian citizens resident abroad (107,140).

Note: Official population estimates include Mongolian citizens resident abroad.

POPULATION BY AGE AND SEX
('000, official estimates at 31 December 2013)

	Males	Females	Total
0–14 years	288.2	279.8	568.0
15–64 years	1,141.0	1,109.8	2,250.8
65 years and over	46.6	64.9	111.5
Total	1,475.8	1,454.5	2,930.3

Source: Mongolian Statistical Office.

ADMINISTRATIVE DIVISIONS
(official population estimates at 31 December 2013)

Province (Aimag)	Area ('000 sq km)	Estimated population ('000)	Provincial centre
Arkhangai	55.3	85.7	Tsetserleg
Bayankhongor . . .	116.0	78.4	Bayankhongor
Bayan-Ölgii	45.7	92.4	Ölgii
Bulgan	48.7	54.5	Bulgan
Darkhan-Uul	3.3	99.0	Darkhan
Dornod (Eastern) . . .	123.6	71.5	Choibalsan
Dornogobi (East Gobi) . .	109.5	62.5	Sainshand
Dundgobi (Central Gobi) .	74.7	37.4	Mandalgobi
Gobi-Altai	141.4	53.3	Altai
Gobisümber	5.5	14.8	Choir
Khentii	80.3	67.6	Öndörkhaan
Khovd	76.1	79.0	Khovd
Khövsgöl	100.6	118.8	Mörön

Province (Aimag)— *continued*	Area ('000 sq km)	Estimated population ('000)	Provincial centre
Orkhon	0.8	93.9	Erdenet
Ömnögobi (South Gobi) .	165.4	67.1	Dalanzadgad
Övörkhangai	62.9	101.6	Arvaikheer
Selenge	41.2	103.2	Sükhbaatar
Sükhbaatar	82.3	53.1	Baruun Urt
Töv (Central)	74.0	85.9	Zuun mod
Ulan Bator (Ulaanbaatar)*	4.7	1,372.0	(capital city)
Uvs	69.6	74.0	Ulaangom
Zavkhan	82.5	64.6	Uliastai
Total	1,564.1	2,930.3	

* Ulan Bator, including Nalaikh, and Bagakhangai and Baganuur districts beyond the urban boundary, has special status as the capital city.

Note: Totals may not be equal to the sum of components, owing to rounding.

POPULATION BY ETHNIC GROUP
(resident Mongolian citizens at 2010 census)

	Number	%
Khalkh (Khalkha)	2,168,141	82.4
Kazakh (Khasag)	101,526	3.9
Dörvöd (Durbet)	72,403	2.8
Bayad (Bayat)	56,573	2.2
Buryat (Buriat)	45,087	1.7
Zakhchin	32,845	1.2
Dariganga	27,412	1.0
Uriankhai	26,654	1.0
Other ethnic groups	100,476	3.8
Total	2,631,117	100.0

Note: Data exclude foreign nationals (16,320), stateless persons (108) and Mongolian citizens resident abroad (107,140). Classification of ethnicity reflects national census methodology.

PRINCIPAL LOCALITIES
(population at 2010 census unless otherwise indicated)

Ulan Bator (capital)	1,372,000*	Mörön	35,814
Erdenet	84,187	Bayankhongor . .	29,829
Darkhan	74,985	Ölgii	29,454
Choibalsan . . .	38,615	Khovd	29,046

* Official estimate at 31 December 2013.

BIRTHS, MARRIAGES AND DEATHS

	Registered births		Registered marriages*		Registered deaths	
	Number	Rate (per 1,000)	Number	Rate (per 1,000)	Number	Rate (per 1,000)
2007	56,636	21.7	40,965	15.7	16,259	6.2
2008	63,768	24.0	32,982	12.4	15,413	5.8
2009	69,167	25.5	34,071	12.6	16,911	6.2
2010	63,270	22.9	9,349	3.4	18,293	6.6
2011	68,853	25.1	11,869	4.3	19,155	6.9
2012	73,839	26.0	12,822	4.5	17,761	6.3
2013	79,780	28.2	15,785	5.4	16,192	5.7
2014	82,839	28.3	n.a.	n.a.	16,521	5.7

* Persons aged 18 years and over.

Source: Mongolian Statistical Office.

Life expectancy (years at birth): 69.1 (males 65.4; females 75.0) in 2013 (Source: *Mongolian Statistical Yearbook*).

EMPLOYMENT
('000 employees at 31 December)

	2011	2012	2013
Agriculture, forestry and fishing .	342.8	370.0	329.1
Industry*	127.9	126.1	155.0
Construction	52.0	59.2	72.4
Transport and storage	75.8	56.1	65.9
Trade	152.5	131.3	156.0
Public administration . . .	55.6	62.9	65.3
Education	85.5	86.3	89.8
Science, research and development	11.4	11.3	13.6
Health	36.4	37.5	40.4
Total (incl. others)	1,037.7	1,056.4	1,103.6

* Comprising manufacturing (except printing and publishing), mining and quarrying, electricity and water.

Source: *Mongolian Statistical Yearbook*.

Mongolians working abroad ('000 in 2009, official estimates): 182.5 (Kazakhstan 90.0; Republic of Korea 31.0) (Source: Montsame—Mongolian News Agency).

Registered unemployed ('000 at 31 December): 35.8 in 2012; 42.8 in 2013; 37.0 in 2014 (Sources: Mongolian Statistical Office).

Total unemployed ('000 in 2013): 94.7 (Ulan Bator 20.5) (Source: *Mongolian Statistical Yearbook*).

Health and Welfare

KEY INDICATORS

Total fertility rate (children per woman, 2012)	2.4
Under-5 mortality rate (per 1,000 live births, 2012) . . .	28
HIV/AIDS (% of persons aged 15–49, 2013)	<0.1
Physicians (per 1,000 head, 2008)	2.8
Hospital beds (per 1,000 head, 2010)	5.8
Health expenditure (2011): US $ per head (PPP)	288
Health expenditure (2011): % of GDP	6.0
Health expenditure (2011): public (% of total)	63.3
Access to water (% of persons, 2012)	85
Access to sanitation (% of persons, 2012)	56
Total carbon dioxide emissions ('000 metric tons, 2010) . .	11,510.7
Carbon dioxide emissions per head (metric tons, 2010) . .	4.2
Human Development Index (2013): ranking	103
Human Development Index (2013): value	0.698

For sources and definitions, see explanatory note on p. vi.

Agriculture

PRINCIPAL CROPS
(metric tons)

	2012	2013	2014
Cereals*	479,300	387,000	518,700
Potatoes	245,900	191,600	161,400
Other vegetables	98,900	101,800	104,800
Hay	1,175,100	1,169,300	1,178,674

* Mostly wheat (488,2934 metric tons in 2014), but also small quantities of barley and oats.

Note: In addition, fodder crops were grown amounting to 13,784 metric tons in 2012, 14,390 metric tons in 2013 and 16,976 metric tons in 2014.

LIVESTOCK
(at mid-December census)

	2012	2013	2014
Sheep	18,141,400	20,066,400	23,214,800
Goats	17,558,700	19,227,600	22,008,900
Horses	2,330,400	2,619,400	2,995,800
Cattle	2,584,600	2,909,500	3,413,900
Camels	305,800	321,500	349,300
Pigs	40,421	51,864	n.a.
Poultry	469,400	489,300	n.a.

LIVESTOCK PRODUCTS
('000 metric tons unless otherwise indicated)

	2011	2012	2013
Meat	208.0	220.4	249.7
Beef	53.6	59.7	56.5
Mutton and goat meat . . .	124.3	123.6	156.7
Sheep's wool	17.6	19.1	22.1
Cashmere	4.4	5.1	5.6
Hides and skins ('000)	8,793.3	8,767.6	10,895.1
Milk	458.6	511.0	575.2
Eggs (million)	69.4	56.6	58.4

Source: *Mongolian Statistical Yearbook*.

Forestry

ROUNDWOOD REMOVALS
('000 cubic metres)

	2011	2012	2013
Total	698.9	771.6	718.3

Source: *Mongolian Statistical Yearbook*.

SAWNWOOD PRODUCTION
('000 cubic metres, incl. railway sleepers)

	2012	2013	2014
Total	26.5	17.2	22.0

Source: Mongolian Statistical Office.

Fishing

(metric tons, live weight)

	2010	2011	2012
Total catch (freshwater fishes) .	100	80	61

Source: FAO.

Mining

(metric tons unless otherwise indicated)

	2012	2013	2014
Coal ('000 metric tons)	28,561	29,164	24,415
Fluorspar concentrate	641,600	238,100	374,900
Copper concentrate* . . .	347,600	533,300	712,000
Molybdenum concentrate* . .	4,050	3,869	4,254
Zinc concentrate*	119,100	104,100	93,200
Tungsten concentrate* . . .	66.0	—	—
Iron ore	7,561,400	6,011,200	10,260,500
Gold (kilograms)	5,995	8,904	11,504
Crude petroleum (barrels) . .	3,636,000	5,128,900	7,405,300
Salt	569.2	657.6	—

* Figures refer to the gross weight of concentrates. Copper concentrate has an estimated copper content of 35%, while the metal content of molybdenum concentrate is 47% and that of zinc is 50%; the metal content of tungsten concentrate was not indicated.

Source: Mongolian Statistical Office.

Industry

SELECTED PRODUCTS

	2012	2013	2014
Flour ('000 metric tons)	114.9	188.1	n.a.
Bread ('000 metric tons)	25.4	25.0	30.2
Confectionery ('000 metric tons) .	13.9	18.7	18.8
Salt (metric tons)	2,461	2,178	1,852
Sheep's guts ('000 bunches) . . .	941.9	696.1	n.a.
Vodka ('000 litres)	26,894.4	24,852.3	n.a.
Beer ('000 litres)	65,124.6	63,775.3	67,740.7
Soft drinks ('000 litres)	177,172.1	210,705.3	n.a.
Cashmere (combed) (metric tons) .	417.0	521.8	n.a.
Felt ('000 metres)	251.4	178.1	163.1
Wool, scoured ('000 metric tons) .	1.1	0.9	n.a.
Camelhair blankets ('000 metres) .	8.2	14.7	18.5
Knitwear ('000 garments) . . .	795.6	932.9	954.4
Woollen fabric ('000 metres) . . .	314.9	243.0	n.a.
Sheepskin coats ('000)	9.0	16.8	14.2
Leather coats ('000)	13.9	11.0	n.a.
Carpets ('000 sq metres) . . .	915.8	852.9	743.6
Leather footwear ('000)	18.3	26.5	49.3
Felt footwear ('000 pairs) . . .	34.0	20.8	10.7
Lime ('000 metric tons) . . .	68.2	56.7	58.0
Cement ('000 metric tons) . . .	349.4	258.8	411.3
Bricks (million)	44.5	66.5	n.a.
Copper, cathode (metric tons) . .	2,281.7	2,344.2	2,132.0
Copper wire (metric tons) . . .	1,414.5	145.9	228.0
Electric energy (million kWh) . .	4,096.3	4,317.9	4,632.3

Source: Mongolian Statistical Office.

Finance

CURRENCY AND EXCHANGE RATES

Monetary Units
100 möngö = 1 tögrög (tughrik).

Sterling, Dollar and Euro Equivalents (31 December 2014)
£1 sterling = 2,943.0 tögrög;
US $1 = 1,885.6 tögrög;
€1 = 2,289.3 tögrög;
10,000 tögrög = £3.40 = $5.30 = €4.37.

Average Exchange Rate (tögrög per US $)
2012   1,357.58
2013   1,523.93
2014   1,817.94

BUDGET
(general government accounts, million tögrög)

Revenue	2012	2013	2014
Tax revenue	4,179,321.5	5,072,793.3	5,207,860.9
Income tax	871,401.5	1,109,204.9	1,098,338.5
Corporation tax	524,325.9	660,159.0	621,236.8
Personal income tax . . .	347,019.7	449,045.9	477,101.7
Social security contributions .	650,240.2	874,229.2	971,392.1
Property taxes	21,929.9	43,975.4	50,027.5
Taxes on domestic goods and services	1,642,812.7	1,921,190.3	1,864,396.7
Value-added tax	1,296,450.9	1,435,091.6	1,370,803.4
Excise taxes	312,384.2	449,410.3	454,390.3
Income of special purpose .	33,977.5	36,688.4	39,203.0
Taxes on foreign trade . . .	327,369.8	381,427.0	355,328.9
Customs duties	327,174.6	381,238.3	355,137.3
Other taxes	665,567.4	742,766.6	868,377.2
Non-tax revenue	648,691.3	863,879.6	895,574.2
Revenues from budget entities .	183,595.2	n.a.	n.a.
Grants and transfers	24,681.7	—	118,200.0
Stabilization fund	94,656.5	46,858.6	−78,286.2
Capital revenue	10,426.4	3,393.7	1,743.2
Total	4,957,777.2	5,986,925.2	6,145,092.0

Expenditure	2012	2013	2014
Current expenditure . . .	4,404,111.6	4,552,606.6	5,226,595.1
Goods and services . . .	2,052,438.6	2,391,174.1	2,597,621.8
Wages and salaries . .	1,197,164.8	1,401,530.8	1,566,920.7
Interest payments . . .	125,913.4	270,442.1	500,350.6
Subsidies and transfers . .	2,225,759.6	1,890,990.3	2,128,622.8
Capital expenditure . . .	1,525,357.6	1,490,741.7	1,739,895.8
Foreign financed	97,496.2	254,123.4	233,440.7
Lending (net)	64,331.4	121,337.0	64,878.5
Total	5,993,800.5	6,164,685.3	7,031,369.4

Source: Mongolian Statistical Office.

INTERNATIONAL RESERVES
(US $ million at 31 December)

	2012	2013	2014
Gold (national valuation) . . .	195.32	152.01	111.81
IMF special drawing rights . .	67.79	66.55	62.20
Reserve position in IMF . . .	0.21	0.21	0.20
Foreign exchange	3,862.30	2,029.05	1,477.96
Total	4,125.62	2,247.82	1,652.16

Source: IMF, *International Financial Statistics*.

MONEY SUPPLY
(million tögrög at 31 December)

	2012	2013	2014
Currency outside depository corporations	603,884	582,147	499,258
Transferable deposits	2,090,631	2,485,408	2,756,510
Other deposits	4,787,388	6,189,692	7,191,523
Securities other than shares . .	135,369	203,706	188,531
Broad money	7,617,272	9,460,953	10,235,822

Source: IMF, *International Financial Statistics*.

COST OF LIVING
(Consumer Price Index at December; base: December 2010 = 100)

	2011	2012	2013
Foods	108.6	127.6	144.5
Clothing and footwear	112.4	130.5	153.5
Rent and utilities	112.7	125.1	134.9
All items (incl. others) . . .	108.9	124.2	139.7

Source: *Mongolian Statistical Yearbook*.

All items (Consumer Price Index; base: December 2010 = 100): 109.5 in 2011; 125.9 in 2012; 137.5 in 2013 (Source: IMF, *International Financial Statistics*).

NATIONAL ACCOUNTS

Expenditure on the Gross Domestic Product
('000 million tögrög at current prices)

	2011	2012	2013
Government final consumption expenditure	1,444.2	1,974.9	1,978.6
Private final consumption expenditure	5,509.4	7,392.8	9,466.8
Increase in stocks	1,458.1	1,601.9	3,028.2
Gross fixed capital formation	5,472.7	7,358.0	7,750.7
Total domestic expenditure	13,884.4	18,327.6	22,224.3
Exports of goods and services	6,912.3	7,084.6	7,922.3
Less Imports of goods and services	9,628.5	10,824.2	11,763.5
Statistical discrepancy*	−80.4	−575.1	−833.0
GDP in purchasers' values	11,087.7	14,012.9	17,550.2
GDP at constant 2005 prices	4,891.8	5,498.5	6,144.2

* Referring to the difference between the sum of the expenditure components and official estimates of GDP, compiled from the production approach.

Source: Asian Development Bank.

Gross Domestic Product by Economic Activity
(million tögrög at current prices)

	2011	2012	2013
Agriculture, forestry and fishing	1,365,115.0	1,979,273.8	2,531,199.0
Mining and quarrying	2,329,330.6	2,517,014.6	3,242,240.2
Manufacturing	665,537.0	832,380.3	1,102,979.0
Construction	173,272.4	250,853.4	453,561.2
Electricity, gas, etc.	211,955.5	232,242.9	266,116.2
Water supply, sewerage and waste management	39,346.3	44,979.7	49,852.6
Wholesale and retail trade; repair of motor vehicles and motorcycles	1,020,944.4	1,466,556.0	1,905,056.3
Transport and storage	785,475.4	851,130.7	868,188.7
Hotels and restaurants	93,348.5	138,693.2	161,668.5
Information and communications	295,315.0	373,637.6	408,284.9
Finance and insurance	381,098.0	581,055.2	819,287.8
Real estate and renting	768,719.9	956,844.4	1,259,935.4
Professional, scientific and technical	101,074.3	129,933.6	150,228.1
Administrative and support services	128,534.2	192,634.7	245,416.6
Public administration and defence; compulsory social security	366,726.8	572,896.5	669,716.0
Education	441,036.0	650,191.3	767,213.7
Health and social work	181,390.4	273,168.9	325,034.1
Arts, entertainment and recreation	37,609.2	60,434.5	86,300.1
Other service activities	38,798.6	50,532.7	60,790.8
Sub-total	9,424,627.5	12,154,454.0	15,373,069.0
Taxes, less subsidies, on products	1,663,096.2	1,858,444.3	2,177,104.2
GDP in market prices	11,087,723.8	14,012,898.0	17,550,173.3

Source: Mongolian Statistical Office.

BALANCE OF PAYMENTS
(US $ million)

	2011	2012	2013
Exports of goods	4,816.4	4,381.5	4,267.7
Imports of goods	−5,806.6	−5,933.4	−5,574.0
Balance on goods	−990.1	−1,552.0	−1,306.3
Exports of services	621.3	963.4	710.6
Imports of services	−1,784.6	−2,065.0	−2,039.0
Balance on goods and services	−2,153.4	−2,653.6	−2,634.7
Primary income received	43.7	57.2	51.9
Primary income paid	−888.8	−1,005.3	−750.9
Balance on goods, services and primary income	−2,998.5	−3,601.7	−3,333.8
Secondary income received	452.4	501.8	343.9
Secondary income paid	−214.3	−262.4	−202.1

—continued	2011	2012	2013
Current balance	−2,760.4	−3,362.3	−3,192.0
Capital account (net)	113.9	120.4	125.8
Direct investment assets	−94.5	−44.0	−41.5
Direct investment liabilities	4,714.6	4,451.8	2,150.9
Portfolio investment assets	20.9	−33.9	−11.9
Portfolio investment liabilities	56.0	2,359.3	−144.2
Other investment assets	−2,383.8	−2,483.6	−1,460.3
Other investment liabilities	437.1	892.7	830.6
Net errors and omissions	−76.0	−196.1	−124.2
Reserves and related items	27.9	1,704.4	−1,866.8

Source: IMF, *International Financial Statistics*.

External Trade

PRINCIPAL COMMODITIES
(US $ million)

Imports c.i.f.	2011	2012	2013
Food and live animals	351.9	413.6	429.4
Animal and vegetable oils	32.6	28.7	31.4
Raw materials	26.2	29.2	26.4
Fuels and lubricants	1,205.7	1,480.6	1,627.0
Chemicals	320.8	365.1	364.7
Basic manufactures	981.3	1,038.4	1,036.9
Machinery and vehicles	3,262.5	2,876.8	2,385.9
Manufactured articles	320.2	386.4	340.3
Total (incl. others)	6,598.4	6,738.4	6,357.8

Exports f.o.b.	2011	2012	2013
Food and live animals	29.6	15.5	20.4
Raw materials	1,977.4	1,873.7	2,123.9
Copper concentrate	968.6	838.6	949.0
Fuels and lubricants	2,555.1	2,259.4	1,650.0
Machinery and vehicles	23.3	24.3	66.6
Manufactured articles	37.6	28.0	28.8
Gold, unwrought or in semi-manufactured forms	109.8	122.3	309.8
Total (incl. others)	4,817.5	4,384.7	4,269.1

2014 (preliminary): Total imports 5,236.6; Total exports 5,774.6.

Source: Mongolian Statistical Office.

PRINCIPAL TRADING PARTNERS
(US $ million)

Imports c.i.f.	2012	2013	2014*
China, People's Republic	1,861.6	1,822.6	1,768.1
Germany	246.4	252.2	159.0
Japan	501.6	444.2	367.8
Korea, Republic	467.8	507.4	352.5
Russia	1,847.4	1,561.9	1,549.3
USA	535.9	512.7	229.5
Total (incl. others)	6,738.3	6,357.8	5,236.6

Exports f.o.b.	2012	2013	2014*
Canada	117.3	135.5	1,172.4
China, People's Republic	4,059.7	3,706.3	5,073.3
Germany	16.0	18.4	15.0
Korea, Republic	12.3	13.0	13.7
Russia	79.6	61.8	61.7
United Kingdom	11.9	200.7	398.7
Total (incl. others)	4,384.7	4,269.1	5,774.6

* Preliminary.

Source: Mongolian Statistical Office.

Transport

FREIGHT CARRIED
('000 metric tons)

	2012	2013	2014
Rail	20,445.2	21,035.5	20,996.1
Road	32,898.9	28,747.5	37,639.6
Air	4.0	4.1	3.4
Total (incl. other)	53,348.1	49,787.0	58,639.2

Source: Mongolian Statistical Office.

PASSENGERS CARRIED
(million)

	2012	2013	2014
Rail	4.0	3.8	3.3
Road	313.9	304.2	342.0
Air*	0.8	0.8	0.8
Total	318.7	308.8	346.1

* MIAT only.

Source: Mongolian Statistical Office.

RAILWAYS
(traffic)

	2012	2013	2014
Passengers carried ('000)	4,000.0	3,759.7	3,306.3
Freight carried ('000 metric tons)	20,455.2	21,035.5	20,996.1
Freight ton-km (million)	12,142.7	12,076.5	12,416.3

Source: Mongolian Statistical Office.

ROAD TRAFFIC
(motor vehicles in use)

	2012	2013	2014
Passenger cars	228,650	259,309	303,724
Buses and coaches	21,642	20,400	20,650
Lorries, special vehicles and tankers	95,181	105,155	113,303

Source: Mongolian Statistical Office.

SHIPPING
Flag Registered Fleet
(at 31 December)

	2012	2013	2014
Number of vessels	221	145	293
Total displacement ('000 grt)	608	1,337	1,865

Source: Lloyd's List Intelligence (www.lloydslistintelligence.com).

CIVIL AVIATION
(traffic on scheduled services)

	2011	2012	2013
Passengers carried ('000)	574.0	770.1	767.4
International passengers ('000)	379.2	441.8	441.6
Freight carried (tons)	2,106.9	3,122.0	3,122.3

Source: Mongolian Statistical Office.

Tourism

FOREIGN TOURIST ARRIVALS BY NATIONALITY

Country	2012	2013	2014
Australia	7,480	6,765	13,987
China, People's Republic	228,547	178,326	157,561
France	7,553	7,407	7,733
Germany	8,909	9,499	9,551
Japan	17,119	18,178	18,282
Kazakhstan	10,523	11,422	13,562
Korea, Republic	44,360	45,178	45,476
Russia	83,707	74,468	73,055
United Kingdom	6,804	6,391	5,758
USA	15,587	14,701	13,987
Total (incl. others)	475,892	417,815	392,844

Source: Mongolian Statistical Office.

Tourism receipts (US $ million): 213.3 in 2009; 222.4 in 2010; 233.0 in 2012 (Source: Ministry of Environment and Tourism, Ulan Bator).

Communications Media

	2011	2012	2013
Television receivers ('000 in use)	708.1	n.a.	n.a.
Cable television subscribers ('000)	180.1	231.2	277.9
Telephones ('000 main lines in use)	131.8	149.4	210.4
Mobile cellular telephones ('000 subscribers)	2,942.3	3,426.1	4,247.4
Internet users ('000)	457.6	695.6	762.2
Personal computers ('000 in use)	421.9	478.2	505.6
Books (million printers' sheets)	47.5	60.8	55.5
Newspapers (million printers' sheets)	40.8	69.2	55.9

Newspapers (titles): 126 in 2012.

Periodicals (titles): 93 in 2012.

2014: Cable television subscribers ('000) 360.9; Telephones ('000 main lines in use) 226.4; Mobile cellular telephones ('000 subscribers) 3,561.9.

Sources: mainly *Mongolian Statistical Yearbook*.

Education

(2014/15 unless otherwise indicated)

	Institutions	Teachers	Students ('000)
General education schools:			
Primary (grades 1–3)	62		
Incomplete secondary (grades 4–9)	136	27,449	505.8
Complete secondary (grades 10–11)	564		
Vocational schools			
State-owned	52	2,327	42.8
Private	24		
Universities			
State-owned	10*		88.2*
Private	8*	7,528	27.2*
Other higher education			
State-owned	6*		13.7*
Private	71*		44.5*

* 2013/14.

Note: In addition, 700 students were studying abroad through intergovernmental agreements.

Pre-school institutions (2014/15): 1,171 public and private kindergartens attended by 183,000 infants, with 6,158 pre-school teachers.

Source: Mongolian Statistical Office.

Pupil-teacher ratio (primary education, UNESCO estimate): 28.8 in 2011/12 (Source: UNESCO Institute for Statistics).

Adult literacy rate (15 years and over, 2010 census): 98.3% in urban areas, 96.3% in rural areas.

Directory

Note: Addresses of buildings on Sükhbaatar Square (Sükhbaataryn Talbai) have been changed to Genghis Khan Square (Chingisiin Talbai) in keeping with Ulan Bator City Council's instruction of August 2013.

The Government

PRESIDENCY

President and Commander-in-Chief of the Armed Forces: TSAKHIA ELBEGDORJ (elected 24 May 2009; inaugurated 18 June 2009; re-elected 26 June 2013; inaugurated 10 July 2013).

Head of Presidential Secretariat: PUNTSAG TSAGAAN.

NATIONAL SECURITY COUNCIL

The President heads the National Security Council; the Prime Minister and the Chairman of the Mongolian Great Khural are its members.

National Security Council: State Palace, Chingisiin Talbai 1, Ulan Bator; tel. (11) 263959; e-mail info@nsc.gov.mn; internet www.nsc.gov.mn.

Chairman: TSAKHIA ELBEGDORJ.

Members: ZANDAAKHÜÜ ENKHBOLD, CHIMED SAIKHANBILEG.

Secretary: TSAGAANDARI ENKHTÜVSHIN.

CABINET
(May 2015)

The Government is formed by a coalition comprising the Democratic Party (DP), the Mongolian People's Party (MPP) and the Justice Coalition (the Mongolian People's Revolutionary Party—MPRP—and the Mongolian National Democratic Party—MNDP).

Prime Minister: CHIMED SAIKHANBILEG (DP).

Deputy Prime Minister: UKHNAA KHÜRELSÜKH (MPP).

Minister without Portfolio: MENDSAIKHAN ENKHSAIKHAN (Justice/MNDP).

Head, Cabinet Secretariat: SANGAJAV BAYARTSOGT (DP).

General Ministries

Minister of Environment, Green Development and Tourism: DULAMSUREN OYUNKHOROL (MPP).

Minister of Foreign Affairs: LUNDEG PUREVSUREN (DP).

Minister of Finance: JARGALTULGA ERDENEBAT (MPP).

Minister of Justice: DAMBA DORLIGJAV (DP).

Sectoral Ministries

Minister of Construction and Urban Development: DAMDIN TSOGTBAATAR (MPP).

Minister of Defence: TSERENDASHI TSOLMON (Justice/MNDP).

Minister of Education, Culture and Science: LUVSANNYAM GANTÖMÖR (DP).

Minister of Energy: DASHZEVEG ZORIGT (DP).

Minister of Food and Agriculture: RADNAA BURMAA (DP).

Minister of Health and Sport: GHANGUYAG SHIILEGDAMBA (Justice/MPRP).

Minister of Industry: DONDOGDORJ ERDENEBAT (DP).

Minister of Labour: SODNOM CHINZORIG (MPP).

Minister of Mining: RENTSENDOO JIGJID (DP).

Minister of Population Development and Social Welfare: SODNOMZUNDUIN ERDENE (DP).

Minister of Roads and Transport: NAMKHAI TUMURKHUU (MPP).

MINISTRIES AND GOVERNMENT DEPARTMENTS

Prime Minister's Office: State Palace, Chingisiin Talbai 1, Ulan Bator; tel. (11) 321704; fax (11) 328329; internet www.zasag.mn.

Ministry of Construction and Urban Development: Government Bldg 12, Barilgachdyn Talbai 3, Chingeltei District, Ulan Bator; tel. (11) 327716; fax (11) 322904; e-mail info@mcud.gov.mn; internet www.mcud.gov.mn.

Ministry of Defence: Government Bldg 7, Enkhtaivny Örgön Chölöö 51, Bayanzürkh District, Ulan Bator; tel. (51) 263531; fax (11) 458112; e-mail info@mod.gov.mn; internet www.mod.gov.mn.

Ministry of Economic Development: Government Bldg 2, Negdsen Ündestnii Gudamj 5/1, Chingeltei District, Ulan Bator; tel. and fax (51) 264878; fax (51) 263333; e-mail info@med.gov.mn.

Ministry of Education, Culture and Science: Government Bldg 3, Baga Toiruu 44, Sükhbaatar District, Ulan Bator; tel. (51) 265912; fax (11) 323158; e-mail info@mecs.gov.mn; internet www.mecs.gov.mn.

Ministry of Energy: Government Bldg 14, Chingisiin Örgön Chölöö, 3rd Sub-District, Khan-Uul District, Ulan Bator; tel. 62263051; fax 70043479; e-mail info@energy.gov.mn; internet www.energy.gov.mn.

Ministry of Environment, Green Development and Tourism: Government Bldg 2, Negdsen Ündestnii Gudamj 5/2, Chingeltei District, Ulan Bator; tel. (51) 261966; fax (51) 266171; e-mail webmaster@mne.gov.mn; internet www.mne.mn.

Ministry of Finance: Negdsen Ündestnii Gudamj 5/1, Chingeltei District, Ulan Bator; tel. and fax (51) 260247; fax (11) 320247; e-mail support@mof.gov.mn; internet www.mof.gov.mn.

Ministry of Food and Agriculture: Government Bldg 9A, Enkhtaivny Örgön Chölöö 16A, Bayanzürkh District, Ulan Bator; tel. (51) 261516; fax (11) 453121; e-mail ariunbayar@mofa.gov.mn; internet www.mofa.gov.mn.

Ministry of Foreign Affairs: Enkhtaivny Örgön Chölöö 7A, Sükhbaatar District, Ulan Bator; tel. 62262222; fax (11) 322127; e-mail info@mfa.gov.mn; internet www.mfa.gov.mn.

Ministry of Health and Sports: Government Bldg 8, Olimpiin Gudamj 2, Sükhbaatar District, Ulan Bator; tel. (51) 263913; fax (11) 320916; e-mail admin@moh.mn; internet www.moh.mn.

Ministry of Justice: Government Bldg 5, Khudaldaany Gudamj 6/1, Chingeltei District, Ulan Bator; tel. and fax (51) 267533; e-mail foreign@moj.gov.mn; internet en.moj.gov.mn.

Ministry of Labour: Government Bldg 9, Enkhtaivny Örgön Chölöö 16, Bayanzürkh District, Ulan Bator; tel. (51) 262534; fax (51) 261516; e-mail info@mol.gov.mn; internet www.mol.gov.mn.

Ministry of Mining: Government Bldg 2, Negdsen Ündestnii Gudamj 5/2, Chingeltei District, Ulan Bator; tel. (51) 263506; fax (11) 318169; e-mail info@mm.gov.mn; internet www.mm.gov.mn.

Ministry of Population Development and Social Welfare: Negdsen Ündestnii Gudamj 5, Chingeltei District, Ulan Bator; tel. (11) 264791; fax (11) 328634; e-mail mpdsp@mongolnet.mn; internet www.mpdsp.gov.mn.

Ministry of Roads and Transport: Government Bldg 13, Chingisiin Örgön Chölöö, Sükhbaatar District, Ulan Bator; tel. 62263170; fax (11) 312315; e-mail bulganerden@mrt.gov.mn; internet www.mrt.gov.mn.

Cabinet Secretariat: State Palace, Chingisiin Talbai 1, Ulan Bator; tel. and fax (11) 260817; fax (11) 310011; e-mail info@cabinet.gov.mn; internet www.cabinet.gov.mn.

President and Legislature

PRESIDENT

Office of the President: State Palace, Chingisiin Talbai 1, Ulan Bator; fax (11) 311121; internet www.president.mn.

Election, 26 June 2013

Candidate	Votes*	%
Tsakhia Elbegdorj (Democratic Party)	622,794	50.23
Badmaanyambuu Bat-Erdene (Mongolian People's Party)	520,380	41.97
Natsag Udval (Mongolian People's Revolutionary Party)	80,563	6.50

* The total number of votes cast was 1,239,784 (66.49% of registered voters).

MONGOLIAN GREAT KHURAL

Under the fourth Constitution, which came into force in February 1992, the single-chamber Mongolian Great Khural is the state's supreme legislative body. With 76 members elected for a four-year term, the Great Khural must meet for at least 50 working days in every six months. Its Chairman may act as President of Mongolia when the President is indisposed.

The revised Law on Elections to the Mongolian Great Khural, approved in December 2011, introduced an element of proportional representation at the June 2012 general election. While 48 seats were filled in 28 constituencies by a simple majority vote, the remaining 28 seats were allocated proportionately to parties receiving at least 5% of the total ballot.

Mongolian Great Khural: State Palace, Chingisiin Talbai 1, Ulan Bator; tel. (51) 267016; fax (11) 327016; e-mail secretariat@parliament.mn; internet www.parliament.mn.

Speaker (Chairman): ZANDAAKHÜÜ ENKHBOLD.

Deputy Speakers (Vice-Chairmen): RADNAASÜMBEREL GON-CHIGDORJ (DP), LOG TSOG (Justice/MPRP), MIYEEGOMBO ENKHBOLD (MPP).

Secretary-General: BYAMBADORJ BOLDBAATAR.

General Election, 28 June 2012

Party	Seats
Democratic Party (DP)	36
Mongolian People's Party (MPP)	24
Justice Coalition*	11
Civil Courage-Green Party (CC-GP)	2
Independents	3
Total	76†

* Comprising the Mongolian National Democratic Party (MNDP), which won six seats, and the Mongolian People's Revolutionary Party (MPRP), which won five.
† The 48 seats won by direct election in the 26 constituencies were: DP 22, MPP 19, Justice Coalition four and Independents three. The balance made up from party lists increased these totals to DP 32, MPP 28, Justice 11 and CC-GP two. Subsequently, the results in some constituencies were challenged and overturned, and it was only after several court cases that in May 2013 the last of the 76 members were sworn in.

Election Commission

General Election Committee: Government Bldg 11, Sambuugiin Gudamj 11, Ulan Bator; tel. (11) 263383; fax (11) 326975; e-mail gecm@mongol.net; internet www.gec.gov.mn; f. 1992; Chair. CHOIN-ZON SODNOMTSEREN.

Political Organizations

All-Mongol Labour Party: Ulan Bator; f. 2011; Sec.-Gen. BYAMBA-JAV ODSÜREN.

Citizens' Movement Party: Rm 304, National Information and Technology Park, Baga Toiruu 49, Sükhbaatar District, Ulan Bator; tel. (11) 321900; f. 2007; 815 mems; Chair. D. SÜKHJARGALMAA; Dep. Chair. J. ZANAA.

Civil Courage-Green Party (CC-GP): internet www.greenparty.mn; amalgamation of the Civil Courage Party and the Mongolian Green Party was agreed in January 2011 and began in March; registration approved March 2012; Jt Chairs SANJAASÜREN OYUUN, SAMBUU DEMBEREL, DANGAASÜREN ENKHBAT.

Democratic Party (DP): CPOB 578, Sükhbaatar District, Ulan Bator; tel. (11) 320355; fax (11) 323755; e-mail info@demparty.mn; internet www.demparty.mn; f. 2000; est. by amalgamation of the Mongolian National Democratic Party, Mongolian Social-Democratic Party, Mongolian Democratic Party, Mongolian Democratic Renewal Party and the Mongolian Believers' Democratic Party; Mongolian Social-Democratic Party re-est. as independent party in 2004; c. 150,000 mems. (2008); Chair. ZANDAAKHÜÜ ENKHBOLD; Sec.-Gen. LOMBO ERKHEMBAYAR (acting).

Development Programme Party: Rm 2, Poverty Reduction Programme Foundation Bldg, 14th Sub-District, Sükhbaatar District, Ulan Bator; tel. 96019222; f. 2007; Chair. O. ZAYAA.

Freedom Implementer Party: Varyeta Centre, 1st Sub-District, Bayangol District, Ulan Bator (POB 48/117); tel. 88113439; fax (11) 327899; e-mail freedom_ofmn@yahoo.com; 1,600 mems; f. 2006; Chair. SHOOVDOR TÖMÖRSÜKH.

Justice Coalition: Mongolian Great Khural, State Palace, Chingisiin Talbai 1, Ulan Bator; f. 2012; electoral pact of the Mongolian People's Revolutionary Party (MPRP) and the Mongolian National Democratic Party (MNDP); in January 2012 the MPRP and MNDP signed a nine-year agreement on the formation of the MPRP-MNDP Political Association, which published a list of election candidates of the MPRP-MNDP Third Force Coalition for Establishing Justice; Chair. (MPRP) NAMBAR ENKHBAYAR; Chair. (MNDP) MENDSAIKHAN ENKHSAIKHAN.

Mongolian Conservative Party: Ulan Bator; f. 2012; Leader N. DASHDAVAA.

Mongolian Democratic Movement Party: Rm 306, Ikh Surguuliin Gudamj 3/2, 6th Sub-District, Sükhbaatar District, Ulan Bator

(POB 20A/158); tel. 99009093; f. 2008; 850 mems (2008); Chair. TÖGSMAA OYUUNAA.

Mongolian Green Party: Internom Block B, Amaryn Gudamj 2, Sükhbaatar District, Ulan Bator; tel. 314560; e-mail info@greenparty.mn; internet www.greenparty.mn; f. 1990; political wing of Alliance of Greens; majority of mems joined Civil Courage-Green Party in 2011; Chair. O. BUM-YALAGCH; Sec.-Gen. CH. MÖNKHBAYAR.

Mongolian Liberal Party: Ulan Bator Higher School of Intellect, 4th Sub-District, Chingeltei District, Ulan Bator (POB 23/320); tel. 99852957; fax (11) 328198; f. 1999 as Mongolian Civil Democratic New Liberal Party, renamed 2004; ruling body Little Khural of 90 mems with Leadership Council of nine; 1,300 mems (2008); Chair. B. DASHZEVEG.

Mongolian National Democratic Party (MNDP): No. 2 Bldg, Enkhtaivny Örgön Chölöö 12, 1st Sub-District, Sükhbaatar District, Ulan Bator; tel. (11) 260535; fax (11) 312596; f. 2006; registered under above name in Oct. 2011; est. after a split in the leadership of the Democratic Party upon formation of the 'national solidarity' Govt; fmrly National New Democratic Party (previously National New Party); 2,400 mems (2008); Chair. MENDSAIKHAN ENKHSAIKHAN; Sec.-Gen. BAYANJARGAL TSOGTGEREL.

Mongolian People's Party (MPP): Palace of Independence, Ulan Bator; tel. and fax 77444156; e-mail contact@mpp.mn; internet www.mpp.mn; f. 1920; est. as Mongolian People's Party; renamed as Mongolian People's Revolutionary Party (MPRP) in 1925; reorganized in the 1990s; reverted to Mongolian People's Party in Nov. 2010; 200,196 mems (May 2012); ruling body Baga Khural or Conference (310 mems at March 2012), which elects the Leadership (Steering) Council (31 mems, incl. Sec.-Gen. and nine secretaries); Chair. MIYEEGOMBO ENKHBOLD; Sec.-Gen. JAMIYANG MÖNKHBAT.

Mongolian People's Revolutionary Party (MPRP): Ulan Bator; f. 2011; breakaway faction of the Mongolian People's Party; registered in June 2011; 20,000 mems; Chair. NAMBAR ENKHBAYAR; Dep. Chair. DENDEV TERBISHDAGVA; Sec.-Gen. GANKHUYAG SHIILEGDAMBA.

Mongolian Social-Democratic Party (MSDP): Room 12, No. 5 Bldg, 1st Sub-District, Sükhbaatar District, Ulan Bator (CPOB 680); tel. 99114273; fax (11) 323828; f. 1990; merged in Dec. 2000 to form part of Democratic Party; refounded Jan. 2005; c. 3,000 mems (2008); Chair. A. GANBAATAR; Deputy Chair. D. ENKHZAYAA.

Mongolian Traditional United Party (MTUP): Room 3, Mika Hotel, Elchingiin Gudamj, 1st Sub-District, Sükhbaatar District, Ulan Bator (POB 44/5240); tel. (11) 327690; fax (11) 310133; also known as the United Heritage (conservative) Party; f. 1994; est. as an amalgamation of the United Private Owners' Party and the Independence Party; 1,503 mems (2008); ruling body General Political Council; Chair. BATDELGER BATBOLD; Gen. Sec. L. ÖNÖRBAYAR.

Motherland Party: Motherland Party Central Bldg, Jukovyn Örgön Chölöö 7A, Ulan Bator (POB 49/404); tel. 90150268; fax (11) 453178; f. 1998; amalgamated with Mongolian Workers' Party 1999; fmrly Mongolian Democratic New Socialist Party, name changed as above in 2005; reported to be disbanding in 2009; c. 160,000 mems (2008); Chair. BADARCH ERDENEBAT; Sec. I. ERDENEBAATAR.

National Labour Party: Ulan Bator; registration denied by Supreme Court Feb. 2011; Chair. T. ENKHBAYAR; Sec.-Gen. G. BAYARSAIKHAN.

Republican Party (RP): Rm 106, Buyan Holding Co Bldg, 3rd Sub-District, Bayangol District, Ulan Bator; tel. (11) 344844; fax (11) 344843; f. 2004; 50,000 mems (2008); Chair. BAZARSAD JARGALSAI-KHAN; Sec.-Gen. TS. GANKHUYAG.

United Party of Patriots: Ulan Bator; f. 2012; Chair. G. GANBAT; Sec.-Gen. N. MENDBAYAR.

Diplomatic Representation
EMBASSIES IN MONGOLIA

Belarus: Ulan Bator; e-mail mongolia@mfa.gov.by; Ambassador STANISLAV CHEPURNOY.

Bulgaria: Olimpiin Gudamj 8, Ulan Bator (CPOB 702); tel. (11) 322841; fax (11) 324841; e-mail posolstvob@magicnet.mn; Chargé d'affaires IVAN STAMATOFF.

Canada: Central Tower, 6th Floor, Chingis Khaany Talbai, Sükhbaatar District, Ulan Bator (CPOB 1028); tel. (11) 332500; fax (11) 332515; e-mail ulan@international.gc.ca; internet www.canadainternational.gc.ca/mongolia-mongolie; Ambassador EELCO JAGER.

China, People's Republic: Zaluuchuudyn Örgön Chölöö 10, Sükhbaatar District, Ulan Bator (CPOB 672); tel. (11) 320955; fax (11) 311943; internet mn.chineseembassy.org; Ambassador WANG XIAOLONG.

Cuba: Negdsen Ündestnii Gudamj 5, Ulan Bator (CPOB 710); tel. (11) 323778; fax (11) 327709; Ambassador OMAR LAURO MARRERO.

Czech Republic: Olimpiin Gudamj 14, Ulan Bator (CPOB 665); tel. (11) 321886; fax (11) 323791; e-mail ulaanbaatar@embassy.mzv.cz; internet www.mzv.cz/ulaanbaatar; Ambassador IVANA GROLLOVA.

France: Enkhtaivny Örgön Chölöö 3, Chingeltei District, Ulan Bator (CPOB 687); tel. (11) 324519; fax (11) 319176; e-mail ambafrance@magicnet.mn; internet www.ambafrance-mn.org; Ambassador YVES DELAUNAY.

Germany: Negdsen Ündestnii Gudamj 7, Ulan Bator (CPOB 708); tel. (11) 323325; fax (11) 323905; e-mail info@ulan.diplo.de; internet www.ulan-bator.diplo.de; Ambassador GERHARD THIEDEMANN.

India: Zaluuchuudyn Örgön Chölöö 10, Sükhbaatar District, Ulan Bator (CPOB 691); tel. (11) 329522; fax (11) 329532; e-mail indembmongolia@magicnet.mn; internet www.indianembassy.mn; Ambassador SOMNAT GHOSH.

Japan: Olimpiin Gudamj 8, Sükhbaatar District, Ulan Bator (CPOB 1011); tel. (11) 320777; fax (11) 313332; e-mail jpemb@mongol.net; internet www.mn.emb-japan.go.jp; Ambassador TAKENORI SHIMIZU.

Kazakhstan: Zaisangiin Gudamj 31-6, 1st Sub-District, Khan-Uul District, Ulan Bator (CPOB 291); tel. (11) 315408; fax (11) 341707; e-mail kzemby@mbox.mn; Ambassador KALYBEK I. KOBLANDIN.

Korea, Democratic People's Republic: Khuvisgalchdyn Gudamj, Ulan Bator; tel. (11) 326153; fax (11) 330529; Ambassador HONG GYU.

Korea, Republic: Olimpiin Gudamj 10, Ulan Bator (CPOB 1039); tel. (11) 321548; fax (11) 311157; e-mail kormg@mofat.go.kr; internet mng.mofat.go.kr; Ambassador (vacant).

Kuwait: Town House No. 1, Villa Vesta Town, 11th Sub-District, Khan-Uul District, Ulan Bator; tel. 77444441; fax 77444443; e-mail ulaanbaatar@mofa.gov.kw; Ambassador KHALED AL-FADHLI.

Laos: Ikh Toiruu 59, Sükhbaatar District, Ulan Bator (CPOB 1030); tel. (11) 326440; fax (11) 321048; e-mail emblao@magicnet.mn; Ambassador BOUHANG SAYASANAWO.

Russian Federation: Enkhtaivny Gudamj 6-A, Ulan Bator (CPOB 661); tel. (11) 327191; fax (11) 327018; e-mail embassy_ru@mongol.net; internet www.mongolia.mid.ru; Ambassador ISKANDER KUBAROVICH AZIZOV.

San Marino: Diplomatic Bldg 95 1-5, 4th Sub-District, Chingeltei District, Ulan Bator; tel. 70113998; fax 70113997; Ambassador ROBERTO DI SERIO.

Turkey: Enkhtaivny Gudamj 5, Ulan Bator (CPOB 1009); tel. (11) 311200; fax (11) 313992; e-mail embassy.ulaanbaatar@mfa.gov.tr; internet ulaanbaatar.emb.mfa.gov.tr; Ambassador MURAT KARAGÖZ.

United Kingdom: Enkhtaivny Gudamj 30, Ulan Bator 13 (CPOB 703); tel. (11) 458133; fax (11) 458036; e-mail britemb@mongol.net; internet www.gov.uk/government/world/mongolia; Ambassador CATHERINE ARNOLD (designate).

USA: Ikh Toiruu 59/1, Ulan Bator (CPOB 1021); tel. (11) 329095; fax (11) 320776; e-mail UlaanbaatarACS@state.gov; internet mongolia.usembassy.gov; Ambassador PIPER A. W. CAMPBELL.

Viet Nam: Enkh Taivny Örgön Chölöö 47, Ulan Bator (CPOB 670); tel. (11) 458917; fax (11) 458923; e-mail vinaemba@magicnet.mn; internet www.vietnamembassy-mongolia.org; Ambassador PHAN DANG DUONG.

Judicial System

Under the fourth Constitution, judicial independence was protected by the General Council of Courts, which comprised the Chief Justice, Procurator General, Minister of Law and others. Under a presidential decree of May 2013, they were replaced with three judges, nominated by supervisory, appeal and basic level judges' assemblies, and a representative of the Ministry of Law (Chairman). Members of the Supreme Court are nominated by the Council and appointed (or rejected) by the President. The Chief Justice is chosen from among the members of the Supreme Court and approved by the President for a six-year term. Routine civil, criminal and administrative cases are handled by 30 rural district and inter-district courts and eight urban district courts. There are 22 appellate courts at provincial and capital city level. Some legal cases are required by law to be dealt with by the Supreme Court, appellate courts or special courts (military, railway, etc.). The Procurator General and his deputies, who play an investigatory role, are nominated by the President and approved by the Great Khural for six-year terms.

General Council of Courts: Ulan Bator; Chair. NANZADDORJ LÜNDENDORJ; Exec. Sec. N. DAGVA.

Supreme Court: 40 and 50 Myangat-1, Sambuugiin Gudamj, Ulan Bator; tel. (11) 320622; e-mail contact@supremecourt.gov.mn; internet www.supremecourt.mn; Chief Justice TSEVEGMID ZORIG.

State Procurator's Office: Baga Toiruu 15/1, Chingeltei District, Ulan Bator; tel. (11) 264374; internet www.gpo.gov.mn; Procurator General MAGVANNOROV ENKH-AMGALAN.

Religion

During the early years of communist rule Mongolia's traditional Mahayana Buddhism was virtually destroyed. The 1992 Constitution maintains the separation of Church and state. The Law on State-Church Relations (of November 1993) sought to make Buddhism the predominant religion and restricted the dissemination of beliefs other than Buddhism, Islam and shamanism. In the early 1990s some 2,000 lamas (monks) established small communities at the sites of 120 former monasteries, temples and religious schools, some of which were being restored. The Kazakhs of western Mongolia are nominally Sunni Muslims. Mosques, also destroyed in the 1930s or closed subsequently, are only now being rebuilt or reopened. Traces of shamanism from the pre-Buddhist period still survive. In recent years there has been an increase in Christian missionary activity in Mongolia. According to the November 2010 population census, of those aged over 15 years, 53% were Buddhists, 3.0% Muslims, 2.9% shamanic and 2.2% Christians.

BUDDHISM

At the end of 2013 there were 146 Buddhist temples and monasteries in Mongolia, including 43 in Ulan Bator, with 1,484 lamas, including 682 in Ulan Bator, 2,401 employees and 390 students in religious schools. According to the 2010 population census, Mongolia has more than 1,010,100 Buddhist believers.

Living Buddha: The Ninth Javzandamba Khutagt (Ninth Bogd), Jambalnamdolchoijinjaltsan, died on 1 March 2012. The search for his reincarnation in Mongolia is being organized.

Asian Buddhist Conference For Peace: Gandan, Ulan Bator (CPOB 38); tel. and fax (11) 360069; e-mail blgn_abcp@yahoo.com; Sec.-Gen. Dr T. BULGAN.

Gandantegchinlen Monastery: Zanabazaryn Gudamj, Bayangol District, Ulan Bator; tel. (11) 360354; Centre of Mongolian Buddhists; Khamba Lama (Abbot) DEMBEREL CHOIJAMTS.

'Good Merit' Buddhist Society: Ulan Bator; Pres. Lama A. ERDENEBAT.

Karmapa Monastery: Khamba Lama (Abbot) DAVAASAMBUU TAIVANSAIKHAN.

Pethub Buddhist Institute: Ikh Toiruu, Chingeltei District, Ulan Bator (POB 38/105); tel. (11) 321867; fax (11) 320676; e-mail pethubmongolia@magicnet.mn; internet www.pethubmonastery.com; f. 2001 by Ven. Kushok Bakula Rinpoche (Indian Ambassador to Mongolia 1990–2000).

CHRISTIANITY

At the end of 2013 there were 151 Christian congregations in Mongolia, including 109 in Ulan Bator, with 213 priests and ministers, including 152 in Ulan Bator, 637 employees and 140 students attending Christian studies. According to the November 2010 population census, Mongolia has 41,900 Christian believers.

Roman Catholic Church

The Church is represented in Mongolia by a single mission. At June 2012, according to Vatican sources, there were 800 Roman Catholics, a bishop, 21 priests and 49 missionaries in the country. The main place of worship is the Cathedral of St Peter and St Paul in Ulan Bator.

Catholic Mission: 18th Sub-District, Bayanzürkh District, Ulan Bator (CPOB 694); tel. (11) 458825; fax (11) 458027; f. 1992; Apostolic Prefect Bishop WENCESLAO PADILLA.

Protestant Church

Association of Mongolian Protestants: f. 1990; Pastor M. BOLDBAATAR.

Mongolian Evangelical Alliance: Jijig Ür Bldg, 3rd Sub-District, Bayanzürkh District, Ulan Bator; tel. 70152040; e-mail mea@magicnet.mn; internet www.mea.mn; f. 1998; a branch of the World Evangelical Alliance.

Other Christian Churches

Church of Jesus Christ of Latter-Day Saints (Mormon): Khudaldaany Gudamj, Chingeltei District, Ulan Bator; tel. (11) 312761.

Jesus Reigns Assembly: Ulan Bator; Pastor D. NARANMANDAKH.

Russian Orthodox Church: Holy Trinity Church, Jukovyn Gudamj 55, Bayanzürkh District, Ulan Bator; tel. 99256732; fax (11) 454425; e-mail fatheraleksei@hotmail.com; internet www.pravoslavie.mn; opened in 1864, closed in 1927; services recommenced 1997 for Russian community; new Holy Trinity Church consecrated in June 2009; Head Father ALEKSEI TRUBACH.

Seventh-day Adventist Church: 5th Sub-District, Bayangol District, Ulan Bator; tel. (11) 688031; fax (11) 688032.

ISLAM

At the end of 2013 there were 20 Muslim congregations, with 21 clergy, 84 employees and 182 students. A mosque was due to be built in Ulan Bator. It was stated in March 2005 that Mongolia had 32 mosques in Bayan-Ölgii and Khovd provinces and in the towns of Darkhan and Nalaikh. Mongolia has 57,180 Muslim believers, according to the population census of November 2010.

Chief Imam (Ölgii): KH. BATYRBEK.

Imam of Gümyr Shrine (Ölgii): DÖITENG SHERKHAN.

Association of Mongolian Muslim Societies: f. 2009; Exec. Dir M. AZATKHAN.

BAHÁ'Í FAITH

Bahá'í Society: Ulan Bator; tel. (11) 321867; f. 1989; Leader A. ARIUNAA.

SHAMANISM

There are 55,200 believers in shamanism, according to the population census of November 2010.

Darkhad Shamanic Study Centre: Ulan Bator; Leader CH. TSERENBAAVAI.

Tengeriin Süld Shamanic Union: Ulan Bator; Pres. CH. CHINBAT.

The Press

PRINCIPAL NATIONAL NEWSPAPERS

State-owned publications in Mongolia were denationalized with effect from 1 January 1999, although full privatization could not proceed immediately. As of June 2014, Mongolia had 123 newspapers and 98 periodicals. A total of 43 provincial and town newspapers were published 36 times a year, with four appearing 48 times a year.

Ardchilal (Democracy): Democracy Palace, Erkhüügiin Gudamj, 7th Sub-District, Sükhbaatar District, Ulan Bator (POB 20/360); tel. 70110287; fax 70110187; e-mail info@ardchilal.com; internet www.ardchilal.com; f. 1990; 260 a year; Editor-in-Chief TSEND-AYUUSH TSOLMON; circ. 3,000.

Ardyn Erkh (People's Power): Ardyn Erkh Bldg, West of Mongolkino Studio, 5th Sub-District, Bayanzürkh District, Ulan Bator; tel. and fax 99098705; e-mail ardiin_erkh@mongolnet.mn; f. 2005; original title ceased publication in 1999 (see *Ödriin Sonin*, below); subsequently assumed by new publr; 256 a year; Exec. Dir BAYARMAGNAI TEMÜÜLEN; circ. 3,000.

Mongolyn Medee (Mongolian News): Free Press Foundation, Sükhbaatar District, Ulan Bator; tel. and fax 70113551; e-mail mongoliin_medee@yahoo.com; f. 1998; 256 a year; Editor-in-Chief S. GANTOGOO; Sec. B. OYUUNGEREL; circ. 2,900.

Mongolyn Ünen (Mongolian Truth): Mongolyn Ünen Newspaper Bldg, Amaryn Gudamj, Sükhbaatar District, Ulan Bator; tel. (11) 321287; fax (11) 323223; e-mail unen@mongol.net; internet www.unen.imedia.mn; f. 1920; publ. 1925–2010 by MPRP as *Ünen*; organ of the MPP; 256 a year; Editor-in-Chief B. GANBOLD; circ. 8,330.

Montsame Medee (Montsame News): Montsame News Agency, Jigjidjavyn Gudamj 8, Ulan Bator (CPOB 1514); tel. (11) 314511; e-mail localnews@montsame.mn; internet www.montsame.mn; daily news digest primarily for govt depts; 248 a year; Editor B. NOMINCHIMED.

Ödriin Shuudan (Daily Mail): Central Cultural Palace, Amaryn Gudamj, 8th Sub-District, Sükhbaatar District, Ulan Bator; tel. 50001001; fax (11) 330383; e-mail info@udriinshuudan.mn; internet www.dnn.mn; 256 a year; Editor-in-Chief B. OYUUN-ERDENE.

Ödriin Sonin (Daily News): Ödriin Sonin Bldg, Ikh Toiruu, Sükhbaatar District, Ulan Bator; tel. 99193519; fax 70134164; e-mail info@dailynews.mn; internet www.dailynews.mn; f. 1924; restored 1990; fmrly *Ardyn Erkh*, *Ardyn Ündesnii Erkh*, *Ündesnii Erkh* and *Ödriin Toli*; 312 a year; Editor-in-Chief J. MYAGMARSÜREN; circ. 14,200.

Öglöönii Sonin (Morning News): 1st Sub-District, Bayanzürkh District, Ulan Bator (POB 46/411); tel. and fax (11) 450640; e-mail ugluuniisonin@yahoo.com; f. 2006; 214 a year; Editor-in-Chief L. NINJJAMTS; circ. 7,000.

Önöödör (Today): Mongol News Co Bldg, Juulchny Gudamj 40, Chingeltei District, Ulan Bator; tel. 70111096; fax (11) 330798; e-mail today@mongolnews.mn; internet www.unuudur.com; f. 1996; 300 a year; Editor-in-Chief B. NANDINTÜSHIG; circ. 10,000.

Ulaanbaatar Taims (Ulan Bator Times): Lucky Times Bldg, Ard Ayuushiin Örgön Chölöö, 18th Sub-District, Bayangol District, Ulan Bator; tel. 70123989; fax 70123989; e-mail zulaab2000@yahoo.com; internet www.ubtimes.mn; f. 1929; est. as *Ulaanbaatar Khotyn Medee*; renamed *Ulaanbaataryn Medee* in 1955, *Ulaanbaatar* in 1990, and *Ulaanbaatar Taims* in 1999; publ. by Ulan Bator City Govt; 256 a year; Editor-in-Chief ERDENECHIMEG DAGIIMAA; circ. 3,500.

Uls Töriin Toim (Political Review): Central Sports Palace Ext., 8th Sub-District, Sükhbaatar District, Ulan Bator; tel. 99149788; e-mail ulstoriintoim@yahoo.com; 256 a year; Editor-in-Chief A. MÖNKH-BAYASGALAN.

Ündesnii Shuudan (National Post): Zuuny Shuudan Bldg (fmr Ardyn Erkh Bldg), Ikh Toiruu, Sükhbaataryn District, Ulan Bator; tel. (11) 354632; fax (11) 354631; e-mail undesniishuudan@yahoo.com; internet www.undesniishuudan.mn; f. 2007; 264 a year; Editor-in-Chief BAASANJAV GANBOLD; circ. 9,000.

Zuuny Medee (Century's News): Amaryn Gudamj 1, Ulan Bator; tel. 70116004; fax (11) 321279; e-mail zuuniimedee@yahoo.com; internet www.zuuniimedee.imedia.mn; f. 1991; previously titled *Zasgiin Gazryn Medee*; 312 a year; Editor-in-Chief DEMCHIGJAV OTGONBAYAR; circ. 8,000.

OTHER NEWSPAPERS AND PERIODICALS

Altangadas (Pole Star): Altan Gadas Bldg, Söüliin Gudamj, 2nd Sub-District, Sükhbaatar District, Ulan Bator (CPOB 430); tel. (11) 319411; fax (11) 319414; e-mail info@altangadas.mn; internet www.altangadas.mn; monthly political magazine; Gen. Editor G. SOLONGO.

Arujüldyzdar (Beautiful Stars): Arular Kazakh Women's Association, Ulan Bator; quarterly Kazakh-language magazine; Editor-in-Chief SARAIN AINAGÜL.

Bolson Yavdal (Events): Söüliin Gudamj, Sükhbaatar District, Ulan Bator (POB 36/346); tel. 96664409; e-mail bolsonyavdal@yahoo.com; 36 a year; Editor T. SANGAA.

Business Times: Business Times Bldg, 1st Sub-District, Khan-Uul District, Ulan Bator; tel. and fax (11) 325374; internet www.businesstimes.mn; 48 a year; Editor BATSÜKH SARANTUYAA.

Ekh Orny Manaa (Guard of the Motherland): Main Directorate of Border Defence, Ulan Bator; internet bpo.gov.mn; 36 a year.

Erüül Mend (Health): Super Zuun Co, Ulan Bator (POB 20/412); tel. 99192239; fax (11) 321278; e-mail dr_jargal_d@yahoo.com; publ. by Ministry of Health; monthly; Editor D. JARGALSAIKHAN; circ. 5,600.

Gan Zam (Steel Road): Railway Printing House, Magsarjavyn Gudamj 2, Bayangol District, Ulan Bator (POB 35/88); tel. (21) 244560; internet www.railcom.mn/ganzam; f. 1959; weekly; Editor LKHÜNDEV SENGEE.

Khani (Spouse): National Agricultural Co-operative Members' Association Bldg 12, Khiimor Khotkhon, Bayanzürkh District, Ulan Bator (POB 49/600); tel. (11) 460698; fax (11) 458550; e-mail khani_sonin@yahoo.com; women and family issues; 24 a year; Editor-in-Chief DEMBEREL BATSÜKH; circ. 64,920.

Khödölmör (Labour): Chingisiin Talbai 9, Ulan Bator; tel. (11) 323026; f. 1928; publ. by Confederation of Mongolian Trade Unions; 48 a year; Editor-in-Chief TSOODOL KHULAN; circ. 64,920.

Khökh Tolbo (Blue Spot): Mon-Azi Co Bldg 54, 4th Sub-District, Chingeltei District, Ulan Bator (POB 24/306); tel. (11) 313405; fax (11) 312794; 36 a year; Publr BAT ERDENEBAATAR; Editor-in-Chief E. ENKHTSOLMON; circ. 3,500.

Khümüün Bichig (People and Script): Montsame News Agency, Jigjidjavyn Gudamj 8, Ulan Bator (CPOB 1514); tel. (11) 329486; fax (11) 327857; e-mail khumuun@montsame.mn; current affairs in Mongolian classical script; 36 a year; Editor B. ELBEGZAYAA; circ. 15,000.

Khümüüs (People): Khümüüs Bldg, 1st Sub-District, Bayanzürkh District, Ulan Bator (POB 46/411); tel. 70168363; fax (11) 450323; internet www.humuus.mn; 48 a year; Editor O. MÖNKH-ERDENE.

Khümüüsiin Amidral (People's Lives): Central Palace of Culture, Ulan Bator (POB 46/411); 48 a year; Editor B. AMGALAN.

Khuuli Züin Medeelel (Legal Information): National Legal Institute, Chingisiin Talbai 7, Chingeltei District, Ulan Bator; tel. and fax (11) 315735; e-mail info@legalinstitute.mn; internet www.legalinstitute.mn; f. 1990; 36 a year.

Mash Nuuts (Top Secret): Mongol Shaazan Bldg, 2nd Sub-District, Sükhbaatar District, Ulan Bator (POB 49/113); tel. and fax (11) 328673; e-mail tsecret@mongolnet.mn; monthly; Editor-in-Chief ONON CHINZORIG.

Mongolian Economy: Ikh Surguuliin Gudamj, 6th Sub-District, Sükhbaatar District, Ulan Bator; tel. and fax 70115476; e-mail info@mongolianeconomy.mn; internet www.mongolianeconomy.mn; f. 2011; fortnightly finance, economic and business magazine; Editor D. BEKHBAYAR.

Mongolian Mining Journal: Art House, Suite 702, Juulchin St 44, Chingeltei District, Ulan Bator; tel. 77222400; fax 77222300; e-mail info@mongolianminingjournal.com; internet www.mongolianminingjournal.com; monthly.

Mongoljin Goo (Mongolian Beauty): Mongolian Women's Federation, Sambuugiin Gudamj 3-11, Ulan Bator (POB 44/717); tel. and fax 70118336; e-mail monwofed@magicnet.mn; internet www.mwf.mn; f. 1990; monthly; Editor J. ERDENECHIMEG; circ. 3,000.

Mongolyn Anagaakh Ukhaan (Mongolian Medicine): Ulan Bator (CPOB 696); tel. (11) 112306; fax (11) 451807; e-mail nymadawa@hotmail.com; publ. by Scientific Society of Mongolian Physicians and Mongolian Academy of Sciences; quarterly; Editor-in-Chief Prof. PAGVAJAV NYAMDAVAA.

Mongolyn Khödöö (Mongolian Countryside): Agricultural University, Zaisan, 11th Sub-District, Khan-Uul District, Ulan Bator; tel. (11) 345211; publ. by Mongolian State University of Agriculture and Academy of Agricultural Sciences; 36 a year; Editor-in-Chief Prof. BEGZ DORJ.

Montsame Toim (Montsame Commentary): Montsame News Agency, Jigjidjavyn Gudamj 8, Ulan Bator; tel. (11) 263692; fax (11) 327857; e-mail info@montsame.mn; f. 2013; monthly political and economic magazine; Editor-in-Chief TSEREN SÜRENJAV.

News Week: News Agency Co, Tod Tower, 4th Sub-District, Chingeltei District, Ulan Bator; tel. 91111064; internet www.news.mn; f. 2013; newsprint and online weekly political and economic review; Pres. BAYARMAGNAI TEMÜÜLEN; circ. 20,000.

Niigmiin Toli (Mirror of Society): Monkord Bldg, 4th Sub-District, Chingeltei District, Ulan Bator; tel. 99049531; e-mail enkhtaivan_987@yahoo.com; 264 a year; Editor-in-Chief SANDAG-DORJ ENKHTUUL.

Notstoi Medee (Important News): Maximus Press Co, Ulan Bator (POB 20/359); tel. 99113322; 36 a year; Editor B. GALSANSÜKH.

Nyam Garig (Sunday): Mongol News Co Bldg, Juulchny Gudamj, Ulan Bator; tel. (11) 330797; fax (11) 330798; e-mail weekend@mongolnews.mn; weekly supplement of *Önöödör*; Editor-in-Chief B. BOLDKHÜÜ.

Sankhüügiin Medee (Financial News): Ulan Bator; 36 a year; Editor L. DONDOG.

Serüüleg (Alarm Clock): Business Plaza, Enkhtaivny Örgön Chölöö, Bayanzürkh District, Ulan Bator (CPOB 1094); tel. 99114341; fax 70151401; e-mail seruuleg1996@yahoo.com; 48 a year; Editor-in-Chief CH. ÖLZIIDELGER; circ. 28,600.

Setgüülch (Journalist): Ulan Bator (POB 46/600); tel. (11) 325388; fax (11) 313912; f. 1982, publ. by Union of Journalists; journalism, politics, literature, art, economy; quarterly; Editor TSEND ENKHBAT.

Shine Yörtönts (New Universe): Empathy Centre, Zaluuchuud Hotel, 6th Sub-District, Sükhbaatar District, Ulan Bator; tel. (11) 313019; fax (11) 321520; e-mail info@empathy.mn; internet www.empathypress.mn; quarterly; popular science magazine; Dir ELCI MEIIMET.

Shinjlekh Ukhaany Akademiin Medee (Academy of Sciences News): Yörönkhii Said Amaryn Gudamj 1, Ulan Bator (POB 20A/34); tel. and fax (11) 262247; e-mail mas@mas.ac.mn; internet www.mas.ac.mn; f. 1961; publ. by Academy of Sciences; quarterly; Editor-in-Chief T. GALBAATAR.

Shuurkhai Zar (Quick Advertisement): Enkhtaivny Örgön Chölöö 62, 4th Sub-District, Sükhbaatar District, Ulan Bator (POB 46A/151); tel. and fax (11) 318787; e-mail shzar@mongol.mn; 102 a year; Editor E. TSEYENKHORLOO.

Soyombo: Ministry of Defence, Ulan Bator; tel. 91177221; f. 1924; est. as *Ardyn Tsereg* (People's Soldier); renamed *Ekh Orny Tölöö* (For the Motherland), then *Ulaan Od* (Red Star); weekly; Dep. Editor-in-Chief Lt-Col G. NYAMDORJ.

Strategiin Sudalgaa (Strategic Studies): Institute of Strategic Studies, National Security Council, Ulan Bator (CPOB 870); tel. (11) 260710; fax (11) 324055; f. 1991; 4 a year; Editor DAMBA GANBAT.

Tavan Tsagarig (Five Rings): Mongol News Co Bldg, Juulchny Gudamj, Chingeltei District, Ulan Bator; tel. (11) 70111095; internet www.mongolnews.mn/tavantsagarig; f. 1995; 100 a year; Editor-in-Chief TSAGAANBAATAR BYAMBAA.

Töriin Medeelel (State Information): Editorial Office, Rm 124, State Palace, Ulan Bator; tel. (11) 329612; fax (11) 322866; e-mail turiin_medeelel@parliament.mn; internet www.parl.gov.mn; f. 1990; presidential and governmental decrees, state laws; 48 a year; circ. 5,000.

Üg (The Word): Bldg 86, Chingeltei District, Ulan Bator; tel. 55152675; fax (11) 329795; e-mail ugsonin@mol.mn; journal of the Mongolian Social-Democratic Party (from 2005); Editor-in-Chief ARYAA GANBAATAR.

Zar Medee (Advertisement News): Arvit 20 Ail, 4th Sub-District, Chingeltei District, Ulan Bator; tel. 70110008; fax 70110009; e-mail zar_sonin@yahoo.com; internet zarsonin.mn; personal and company adverts; 100 a year; Editor D. BAYASGALAN.

FOREIGN LANGUAGE PUBLICATIONS

Inspiring Mongolia: Mongolian National Chamber of Commerce and Industry, Mahatma Gandhi Gudamj, 1st Sub-District, Khan-Uul District, Ulan Bator; tel. (11) 327176; fax (11) 324620; e-mail marketing@mongolchamber.mn; internet www.mongolchamber.mn; magazine in English, publ. twice a year; Editor-in-Chief SAMBUU DEMBEREL.

Menggu Xiaoxi Bao (News of Mongolia): Montsame News Agency, Ulan Bator (CPOB 1514); tel. (11) 320077; e-mail mgxxbao@chinggis.com; f. 1929; weekly; in Chinese; Sec. P. OYUUNTSETSEG.

The Mongol Messenger: Montsame News Agency, Jigjidjavyn Gudamj 8, Ulan Bator (CPOB 1514); tel. (51) 266740; fax (11) 325512; e-mail monmessenger@magicnet.mn; f. 1991; weekly newspaper in English; owned by Montsame national news agency; Editor GIVAANDONDOG PÜREVSAMBUU; circ. 2,000.

Mongolian Magazine: Interpress Publishers, Ulan Bator; f. 2004; English-language monthly illustrated magazine about Mongolian history, culture, nature, life and customs.

Mongolia This Week: Ulan Bator; tel. and fax (11) 318339; e-mail mongoliathisweek@mobinet.mn; weekly in English, online daily; Editor-in-Chief D. NARANTUYAA; English Editor ERIC MUSTAFA.

Mongolia Today: Montsame News Agency, Jigjidjavyn Gudamj 8, Ulan Bator (CPOB 1514); quarterly; in English; Editor-in-Chief G. PÜREVSAMBUU.

Mongoliya Segodnya (Mongolia Today): Undruul Hotel, Rm 5, 5th Sub-District, Bayanzürkh District, Ulan Bator (POB 51/404); tel. 88871402; fax (11) 457968; e-mail ms@mongoliyasegodnya.mn; weekly; in Russian; Editor-in-Chief DÜNGER-YAICHIL SOLONGO.

Mongoru Tsushin (Mongolia News): Montsame News Agency, Jigjidjavyn Gudamj 8, Ulan Bator (CPOB 1514); 48 a year; in Japanese.

Montsame Daily News: Montsame News Agency, Jigjidjavyn Gudamj 8, Ulan Bator (CPOB 1514); tel. (11) 99188684; fax (11) 327857; e-mail paula_jlo@yahoo.com; f. 1921; daily English news digest for embassies, etc.

Novosti Mongolii (News of Mongolia): Montsame News Agency, Jigjidjavyn Gudamj 8, Ulan Bator (CPOB 1514); tel. (11) 310157; fax (11) 327857; e-mail novosty_mongolii@yahoo.co.uk; f. 1942; weekly; in Russian; Editor-in-Chief DÜGERSÜREN ARIUNBOLD.

Solongo (Rainbow): Green House, 6th Sub-District, Sükhbaatar District, Ulan Bator (POB 23/628); tel. 91887376; internet www.solongo.net; f. 1992; monthly; about relations with China; in Mongolian and Chinese; Deputy Editor-in-Chief T. BAYANJARGAL.

The UB Post: Mongol News Co, Juulchny Gudamj, Ulan Bator; tel. 70111095; fax (11) 330798; e-mail ubpost@mongolnews.mn; internet ubpost.mongolnews.mn; f. 1996; 144 a year; in English; Editor-in-Chief G. ÖLZIISAIKHAN; circ. 4,000.

NEWS AGENCIES

Eagle News: Kino Üilderviin Gudamj 78, Enkhtaivny Örgön Chölöö, 5th Sub-District, Bayanzürkh District, Ulan Bator; tel. (11) 463080; e-mail contact@eagle.mn; internet www.eagle.mn.

InfoMongolia: Mongolian Eco Resource Co, Ulan Bator; internet www.infoMongolia.com; specializes in news and information about Mongolia in English.

iPost: Ulan Bator; tel. 88014334; internet www.ipost.mn; news and information website run with *Uls Töriin Toim* newspaper and Shonkhor TV channel; Contact L. BAATARKHÜÜ.

Khurd: ONRT TV Centre, Khuvisgalchdyn Gudamj, Ulan Bator; tel. (11) 321832; fax (11) 328334; e-mail info@khurdagency.mn; internet www.khurdagency.mn; information agency of Mongolian National Public Radio; Dir TS. SÜKHBAATAR.

Mongolyn Medee (Mongolian News): Mongolian National Public Radio and Television, Khuvisgalyn Zam, Ulan Bator; Dir S. BATZAYAA.

Montsame (Mongol Tsakhilgaan Medeenii Agentlag) (Mongolian News Agency): Jigjidjavyn Gudamj 8, Ulan Bator (CPOB 1514); tel. (11) 266904; fax (11) 327857; e-mail info@montsame.mn; internet www.montsame.mn; f. 1921; govt-controlled; Gen. Dir ARIYAA BAATARKHUYAG; Editor-in-Chief TS. SÜRENJAV.

News: News Agency Co, Tod Tower, 4th Sub-District, Chingeltei District, Ulan Bator; tel. 91111064; e-mail info@news.mn; internet www.news.mn; services in Mongolian and English; Pres. BAYARMAGNAI TEMÜÜLEN.

PRESS ASSOCIATIONS

Daily Newspaper Association: c/o Önöödör, Mongol News Co, Juulchny Gudamj, Ulan Bator; f. 2006; Pres. S. GANTOGOO.

Mongolian Newspaper Association: Ulan Bator; Pres. RADNAA KHADBAATAR.

Press Institute: Ikh Toiruu 11B, Sükhbaatar District, Ulan Bator (POB 20/347); tel. and fax 11350002; internet www.pressinst.org .mn; Exec. Dir M. MÖNKHMANDAKH.

Publishers

The ending of the state monopoly has led to the establishment of several small commercial publishers, including Shuvuun Saaral (Ministry of Defence), Mongol Khevlel and Soyombo Co, Mongolpress (Montsame), Erdem (Academy of Sciences), Süülenkhüü children's publishers, Sudaryn Chuulgan, Interpress, Sükhbaatar Co, Öngöt Khevlel, Admon, Odsar, Khee Khas Co, etc.

Admon: Amaryn Gudamj 2, Sükhbaatar District, Ulan Bator (CPOB 92); tel. (11) 329253; fax (11) 327251; e-mail admon@magicnet.mn; Dir R. ENKHBAT.

Irmüün: I Media Group, Baga Toiruu 31B, Sükhbaatar District, Ulan Bator; tel. and fax (11) 318073; e-mail info@irmuun.mn; internet www.irmuun.mn; f. 1999; magazine and multimedia publr.

Mongol Khevlel: Mongol Khevlel Bldg, 8th Sub-District, Sükhbaatar District, Ulan Bator; tel. (11) 323636; fax (11) 329180; e-mail monprint@hotmail.com.

Mongol News Group: Mongol News Group Bldg, Juulchny Gudamj, Ulan Bator; tel. (11) 330797; fax (11) 330798; e-mail mntoday@mobinet.mn; f. 1996; owns newspapers *MN-Önöödör, Tavan Tsagarig, Nyam Garig* and *The UB Post*, TV Channel 25 and ABM Co printers; Pres. B. NANDINTÜSHIG.

Mönkhiin Üseg Group: Teeverchdiin Gudamj 27, Sükhbaatar District, Ulan Bator; tel. (11) 319658; fax 70141316; e-mail info@ munkhiin-useg.mn; internet www.munkhiin-useg.mn; Chair. G. BATMÖNKH.

PUBLISHERS' ASSOCIATIONS

Local Press and Information Association: Ulan Bator; f. 2006; Pres. S. SHARAVDORJ.

Mongolian Book Publishers' Association: Ulan Bator; Exec. Dir S. TSERENDORJ.

Mongolian Free Press Publishers' Association: Ulan Bator (POB 24/306); tel. and fax (11) 313405; Pres. BAT ERDENEBAATAR.

Broadcasting and Communications

TELECOMMUNICATIONS

Digital exchanges have been installed in Ulan Bator, Darkhan, Erdenet, Sükhbaatar, Bulgan and Arvaikheer, while radio relay lines have been digitalized between: Ulan Bator–Darkhan–Sükhbaatar; Ulan Bator–Darkhan–Erdenet; and Dashinchilen–Arvaikheer. Mobile telephone companies operate in Ulan Bator and other central towns, in addition to Arvaikheer, Sainshand and Zamyn-Üüd. At mid-2014 a total of 9,000 km of optical fibre internet links had reached 150 rural district centres.

Bodicom: Ulan Bator; tel. (11) 325144; fax (11) 318486; e-mail bodicom@mongolnet.mn.

Datacom: San Business Centre, 8th Sub-District, Sükhbaatar District, Ulan Bator; tel. (11) 327309; e-mail support@datacom.mn; internet www.datacom.mn; service provider for MagicNet connection to internet; domain registration; Dir DANGAASÜREN ENKHBAT.

G-Mobile: G-Mobile House, 4th Sub-District, Chingeltei District, Ulan Bator; tel. and fax 70113638; e-mail info@g-mobile.mn; internet www.g-mobile.mn; Dir-Gen. D. BASBISH.

Incomnet: Enkhtaivny Örgön Chölöö, Bayanzürkh District, Ulan Bator (CPOB 582); tel. and fax (11) 480808; e-mail info@incomnet .mn; internet www.incomnet.mn; internet service provider, satellite communications; Dir-Gen. A. OYUUNCHIMEG.

MagicNet: Rm 222, Ground Floor, Science and Technology Information Centre, Yörönkii Said Amaryn Gudamj, Ulan Bator; tel. (11) 312061; fax (11) 311496; e-mail info@magicnet.mn; internet www .magicnet.mn; internet service provider.

MCS Electronics: Central Tower, Sükhbaataryn Gudamj, 8th Sub-District, Sükhbaatar District, Ulan Bator; tel. (11) 312424; fax (11) 312699; e-mail erm@mcs.mn; internet www.electronics.mcs.mn.

Medeelel Kholboo: Central Post Office Bldg, West cnr of Chingisiin Talbai and Enkhtaivny Örgön Chölöö, Chingeltei District, Ulan Bator; tel. and fax 70112519; internet www.icnc.mn; installation of digital radio relays and fibre optic cables for communications and internet, television and radio.

Micom: Central Post Office Bldg, West cnr of Chingisiin Talbai and Enkhtaivny Örgön Chölöö, Chingeltei District, Ulan Bator (CPOB 1124); tel. (11) 313229; fax (11) 322473; e-mail info@micom.mng.mn; internet www.micom.mn; Dir CH. NARANTUNGALAG.

MobiCom: MobiCom Corpn Central Bldg, Sambuugiin Gudamj 7-1, 5th Sub-District, Chingeltei District, Ulan Bator; tel. (11) 318115; fax (11) 310411; e-mail feedback@mobicom.mn; internet www.mobicom .mn; mobile telephone service provider; Dir-Gen. R. ARIUNTSOGT; CEO DAVID HOLIDAY.

Moncom: Ulan Bator (POB 51/207); tel. (11) 329409; e-mail ch .enkhmend@hotmail.com; pager services.

Mongolia Telecom: Central Post Office Bldg, Sükhbaataryn Gudamj, west cnr of Chingisiin Talbai and Enkhtaivny Örgön Chölöö, Ulan Bator (CPOB 1166); tel. 70102466; fax (11) 327899; e-mail hr@mtcom.net; internet www.telecommongolia.mn; 54.6% state-owned, 40.0% owned by Korea Telecom; Pres. and CEO OONOI SHAALUU; Exec. Dir O. BATCHULUUN.

MonSat: New Horizon Bldg, Olimpiin Gudamj 6, 1st Sub-District, Sükhbaatar District, Ulan Bator; tel. (11) 323705; fax (11) 312699; e-mail monsat@mcs.mn; internet www.monsat.mcs.mn; satellite communications, mobile telephone and internet services.

Newcom: Naiman Zovkhis Bldg, Söüliin Gudamj 21, Sükhbaatar District, Ulan Bator; tel. (11) 313183; fax (11) 318521; e-mail secretary@newcom.mn; internet www.newcom.mn; Chair. TS. BOLD-BAATAR; Exec. Dir B. ÜNENBAT.

Newtel: TEDY Centre, Sambuugiin Gudamj 18, Chingeltei District, Ulan Bator; tel. 75753333; fax (11) 315434; e-mail marketing@ntc .mn; internet www.newtel.mn; Exec. Dir D. BOLOR.

Orbitnet: Central Tower Bldg, Chingisiin Talbai 2, Sükhbaatar District, Ulan Bator; tel. (11) 323705; fax (11) 312699; e-mail orbitnet@mcs.mn; internet www.orbitnet.mcs.mn; Dir P. SÜKH-BAATAR.

Railcom: Mongolian Railways (MTZ), Teeverchdiin Gudamj, 3rd Sub-District, Bayangol District, Ulan Bator (CPOB 376); tel. (21) 242601; e-mail info@railcom.mn; internet www.railcom.mn; telephone, TV and internet service provider.

Sansar Internet: Enkhtaivny Örgön Chölöö 29, 2nd Sub-District, Chingeltei District, Ulan Bator; tel. (11) 322558; fax (11) 322813; e-mail info@sansarcatv.mn; internet www.sansar.mn.

Skytel: Skytel Plaza Centre, Chingisiin Örgön Chölöö 9, Ulan Bator (CPOB 811); tel. (11) 319191; fax (11) 318487; e-mail skytel_comment@yahoo.com; internet www.skytel.mn; mobile telephone and voice mail service provider; Mongolia-Republic of Korea jt venture; Dir-Gen. D. BOLOR; Marketing Man. G. TÜVSHINTÖGS.

Unitel: Central Tower, Chingisiin Talbai 2, Sükhbaatar District, Ulan Bator; tel. 77778888; fax (11) 330708; e-mail info@unitel.mn; internet www.e-unitel.mn; f. 2005 by MBSB Telecom, Uangel Corpn (Republic of Korea) and Dream Choice Co (Canada); mobile telephone service provider; Dir-Gen. B. BILGÜÜN.

BROADCASTING

A 1,900-km radio relay line from Ulan Bator to Altai and Ölgii provides direct-dialling telephone links as well as television services for western Mongolia. New radio relay lines have been built from Ulan Bator to Choibalsan, and from Ulan Bator to Sükhbaatar and Sainshand. Most of the population is in the zone of television reception, following the inauguration of relays via satellites operated by the International Telecommunications Satellite Organization (INTELSAT). At mid-2014 there were 142 television stations and 72 radio stations. Urban television stations broadcast 123 hours a week and rural television stations 77 hours.

All provincial centres receive two channels of Mongolian national television, and all district centres can receive television. At the beginning of 2005 the first legislative measures were taken to end state control, with the approval of the Law on Public Broadcasting, the provisions of which entered into force on 1 July 2005, creating an independent public service broadcaster to be known as Public Radio and Television. In 2009 Mongolia's first internet television station, Mongol TV, was launched. The launching of a national communications satellite was planned for 2015.

The first stage of television digitalization was completed in July 2014, with 10 relay stations operating in Ulan Bator and 244 in the countryside; set-top boxes were available for 178,000 families. Analogue services were to be phased out from 1 January 2016.

Mongolian National Public Radio and Television (ONRT): Mongolian National Public Radio and Television Central Bldg, Khuvisgalyn Zam 3, Bayangol District, Ulan Bator; tel. (11) 322580; f. 2006; replaced the govt-run Directorate of Radio and Television Affairs; budgetary expenditure on ONRT amounted to 5,428.5m. tögrög in 2011; Chair. of National Council LUVSANG PÜREV-DORJ; Dir-Gen. TSAGAAN OYUNDARI; Editor-in-Chief DEMBEREL ERDENETSETSEG.

Radio

Mongolian National Public Radio (Mongolradio): Mongolian National Public Radio and Television Central Bldg, Khuvisgalyn Zam 3, Bayangol District, Ulan Bator; tel. (11) 310007; fax (11)

328284; f. 1934; operates for 17 hours daily on three long-wave and one medium-wave frequency, and VHF; programmes in Mongolian (two); part of Public Radio and Television; Dir L. TSEREN-OCHIR; Dep. Dir B. BAYARSAIKHAN.

Voice of Mongolia: Ulan Bator (CPOB 365); tel. and fax (11) 322580; e-mail densmaa9@yahoo.com; internet www.vom.mn; f. 1964; external service of Mongolradio; broadcasts in Mongolian, Russian, Chinese, English and Japanese on short wave; Dir ZORIGT DENSMAA.

AE and JAAG Co: Ikh Toiruu, Sükhbaatar District, Ulan Bator (POB 20/126); tel. 99114962; e-mail aejaag@magicnet.mn; f. 1996; broadcasts for 4.5–5 hours daily.

FM 95.1 Khamag Mongol (All Mongolia): N and N centre, 5th Sub-District, Sükhbaatar District, Ulan Bator; tel. and fax 70101983; e-mail hamagmongol@yahoo.com.

FM 96.3 Avtoradio: Ulan Bator Business Development Centre, 4th Sub-District, Chingeltei District, Ulan Bator; tel. and fax 70173333; e-mail mongol_media@yahoo.com.

FM 96.9 Elgen Nutag (Homeland): Narkhan Khotkhon 61, 15th Sub-District, Khan-Uul District, Ulan Bator; tel. 99111511; e-mail elgen.nutag@yahoo.com.

FM 98.1 Formula: Ulan Bator Radio Co, Narny Titem, 5th Sub-District, Chingeltei District, Ulan Bator; tel. 70110981; e-mail UBradio@mail.mn.

FM 98.5 Best: Ulan Bator Development Centre, 4th Sub-District, Chingeltei District, Ulan Bator; tel. (11) 339917; e-mail best_985@yahoo.com.

FM 98.9 Royal Radio: Royal Academy, 4th Sub-District, Bayanzürkh District, Ulan Bator; tel. 70157777; e-mail royalradio989@yahoo.com.

FM 99.3 Ineemseglel (Smile): Central Palace of Culture, Sükhbaatar District, Ulan Bator; tel. 99093713; Dir KH. IKHBAYAR.

FM 99.7 Ikh Mongol (Great Mongolia): Grand Plaza, Enkhtaivny Örgön Chölöö, Bayangol District, Ulan Bator; tel. 70121344; e-mail fm_997@yahoo.com; internet www.hitradio.mn.

FM 100.1 Kiss: Ulan Bator Bank, Chingeltei District, Ulan Bator; tel. (11) 312334; e-mail gcrlees2002@yahoo.com.

FM 100.5 Minii Mongol (My Mongolia): Central Palace of Culture, Sükhbaatar District, Ulan Bator; tel. 99194999.

FM 100.9 Khökh Tenger (Blue Sky Radio): Radio 3, MNPRT Bldg, Khuvisgalchdyn Gudamj, Chingeltei District, Ulan Bator; tel. (11) 310007; fax (11) 323096; broadcasts for 12 hours Mon. to Sat. and shorter hours on Sun; short-wave transmitter on 4,850 kHz; Dir L. AMARZAYAA.

FM 101.7 Ulaanbaatar Radio: Narny Titem, 5th Sub-District, Chingeltei District, Ulan Bator; tel. and fax 70113085; Dir U. BULGAN.

FM 102.1 MGL Radio (Homeland): New World TV Bldg, 9th Sub-District, Sükhbaatar District, Ulan Bator; tel. 77011941; internet www.mglradio.mn.

FM 102.5 Minii Nutag (My Home): Grand Plaza, Enkhtaivny Örgön Chölöö, Bayangol District, Ulan Bator; tel. 70121025; fax 70137388; e-mail fmub102.5@yahoo.com.

FM 103.1: Ulan Bator; BBC World Service Relay.

FM 103.6 Tengerleg (Heavenly): TV9 Bldg, Amaryn Gudamj, Sükhbaatar District, Ulan Bator; tel. 70109859; TV-9's radio station; Dir M. BAYANZUL.

FM 104 Life: Business Plaza, Enkhtaivny Örgön Chölöö, 15th Sub-District, Bayanzürkh District, Ulan Bator; tel. and fax (11) 463782; e-mail life_fm104@yahoo.com.

FM 104.5 Ger Büliin Radio (Family Radio): Bldg 10, 2nd Sub-District, Bayanzürkh District, Ulan Bator; tel. (11) 461045; fax (11) 452987.

FM 105.5 Nandin (Precious): Chugo Co, Grand Plaza, Amaryn Gudamj, 2nd Sub-District, Bayangol District, Ulan Bator; tel. and fax 70114440; e-mail tsatstral997@yahoo.com; internet www.hitradio.mn; Dir B. TÜVSHINTÖGS.

FM 106.6: Democratic Party Bldg, Chingisiin Örgön Chölöö, Ulan Bator; tel. (11) 329353; Voice of America news and information in Mongolian, English lessons and music.

FM 107 New Century: Media Group, Central Palace of Culture, 8th Sub-District, Sükhbaatar District, Ulan Bator; tel. 77160107; internet zuundoloo@yahoo.com.

FM 107.5 Shine Dolgion (New Wave): Namyanjügiin Gudamj 40, Bayanzürkh District, Ulan Bator; tel. and fax (11) 452444; relays of Voice of America broadcasts in English and Russian, entertainment programmes; Dir Ts. ARIUNAA.

There are seven long- and short-wave radio transmitters and 49 FM stations in 23 towns. Some rural districts have set up their own small FM radio stations to broadcast local information.

Television

Aist (Stork) Mongolia TV: Aeroflot Bldg, Söüliin Gudamj, 4th Sub-District, Sükhbaatar District, Ulan Bator; tel. (11) 314530; fax (11) 327578; e-mail info@aisttv.mn.

Mongolian Television Association: Ulan Bator; mems: BTV, Channel 25, Eagle, Education, NTV, SBN, TM, TV5, TV8, TV9 and UBS; Chair. M. ULAMBADRAKH.

Mongolian National Public Television (MNTV): Mongolian National Public Radio and Television Central Bldg, Khuvisgalyn Zam 3, Bayangol District, Ulan Bator (CPOB 365); tel. (11) 327214; fax (11) 328939; e-mail mrtv@magicnet.mn; f. 1967; daily 16-hour transmissions, except Mon; short news bulletins in English Mon., Wed. and Fri; part of Public Radio and Television; Dir D. ENKHTUYAA.

Bolovsrol (Education) TV Channel: Enkhüüd Centre, Border Protection Service, Khilchdyn Gudamj, Ulan Bator; tel. (11) 464336; e-mail info@edutv.mn; internet www.edutv.mn; f. 2005; broadcasts 18 hours a day; Gen. Dir NATSAGDORJ SANJ.

C-1: KhiD Co Bldg, Tömörchnii Gudamj, Chingeltei District, Ulan Bator; tel. and fax (11) 325438; e-mail info@c1.mn; internet www.c1.mn; f. 2006; daily 17-hour transmissions; news link with Reuters; Dir BEN MOYLE.

Channel 25: Mongol News Bldg, Juulchny Gudamj, Chingeltei District, Ulan Bator; tel. 99114962; fax (11) 321959; e-mail info@tv25.mn; internet www.tv25.mn; daily 18-hour transmissions; Gen. Man. AYUUSH AVIRMED.

Eagle TV (Channel 8): Eagle News, Kino Üildveriin Gudamj 78, Enkhtaivny Örgön Chölöö, 5th Sub-District, Bayanzürkh District, Ulan Bator; tel. (11) 463080; internet www.eagle-tv.mn; commenced operations in 1996 with Christian message; broadcasts restarted 2005 after two years off air; now owned by Mongolia Media Corpn, subsidiary of Bodi International; broadcasts 18–19 hours a day.

Ekh Oron (Homeland): MNPRT Bldg, Khuvisgalchdyn Gudamj, 11th Sub-District, Bayangol District, Ulan Bator; tel. and fax 70131080; internet www.ekhorontv.mn; broadcasts 20–21 hours a day.

ETV: E Television, Grand Plaza, Enkhtaivny Örgön Chölöö, 2nd Sub District, Bayangol District, Ulan Bator; tel. 70079999; e-mail info@etv.mn; internet www.etc.mn; broadcasts 20 hours a day.

Khiimori Co: Bldg 3A, No. 2 Combined Clinical General Hospital, Ulan Bator; tel. (11) 458531; fax (11) 458569; f. 1995; cable TV service provider.

National Times News: NTN HD Media Group, Ritz House, Ikh Toiruu 180, Bayanzürkh District, Ulan Bator; tel. (11) 483790; fax (11) 483789; internet www.ntn.mn.

New TV (NTV): Capital House, Chingisiin Örgön Chölöö 14, 2nd Sub-District, Khan-Uul District, Ulan Bator; tel. 77110001; fax 77110002; e-mail marketing@ntv.mn; internet www.ntv.mn; broadcasts 18 hours a day; Dir M. ULAMBADRAKH.

Sansar CATV: Sansar Bldg, Enkhtaivny Örgön Chölöö, 2nd Sub-District, Chingeltei District, Ulan Bator; tel. (11) 313752; fax (11) 313770; e-mail info@sansarcatv.mn; internet www.sansarcatv.mn.

SBN (Supervision Broadcasting Network): Khuvisgalchdyn Gudamj, Bayangol District, Ulan Bator; tel. (11) 301641; fax (11) 301642; e-mail contact@sbn.mn; internet www.sbn.mn; Exec. Dir DOLGOR NAMKHAI.

Supervision Cable TV: Supervision Broadcasting Network Bldg, Khuvisgalchdyn Gudamj, 14th Sub-District, Bayangol District, Ulan Bator; tel. (11) 455082; e-mail service@supervision.mn; internet www.supervision.mn.

TV-5: Sapporo Centre, 1st Sub-District, Songinokhairkhan District; tel. (11) 680327; fax (11) 680326; e-mail mgltv5@yahoo.com; internet www.tv5.mn; daily 18-hour transmissions; Editor-in-Chief E. DAGIIMAA.

TV-7: Ulaanbaatar Palas, Chingünjavyn Gudamj, 6th Sub-District, Bayangol District, Ulan Bator; tel. 99995336; e-mail seven_channel@yahoo.com; internet www.tv7.mn.

TV-9: Media Holding Bldg, Amaryn Gudamj 3, Sükhbaatar District, Ulan Bator; tel. and fax 70110628; e-mail tv9_television@tv9mn; f. 2003; 24-hour broadcaster; Dir Ts. ENKHBAT.

UBS (Ulaanbaatar Broadcasting System): Khuvisgalchdyn Gudamj 3, Bayangol District, Ulan Bator; tel. 70140434; fax (11) 300435; e-mail info@ubs.mn; internet www.ubs.mn; f. 1992; fmrly state-owned; privatized in 2005; broadcasts 19 hours a day; Dir U. BULGAN.

Cable television companies (29 in total) operate in 19 towns. There are local television stations in Ulan Bator (three), Darkhan, Sükhbaatar and Baganuur. Chinese, Kazakh, Russian, German and French television services are among those that can also be received.

Finance

(cap. = capital; res = reserves; dep. = deposits; m. = million; brs = branches; amounts in tögrög, unless otherwise stated)

BANKING

Central Bank

Bank of Mongolia (Mongolbank): Baga Toiruu 3, Sükhbaatar District, Ulan Bator; tel. (11) 320413; fax (11) 311471; e-mail info@mongolbank.mn; internet www.mongolbank.mn; f. 1924; est. as the State Bank of the Mongolian People's Republic; cap. 5,000m., res 103,504m., dep. 2,369,433m. (Dec. 2009); Pres. NAIDANSÜREN ZOLJARGAL; Chief Vice-Pres. BOLD JAVKHLAN.

Other Banks

Capital Bank: Sambuugiin Gudamj 43, Chingeltei District, Ulan Bator; tel. 96115040; fax (11) 310833; e-mail info@capitalbank.mn; internet www.capitalbank.mn; cap. 22,000m., res 352.4m., dep. 154,340.6m. (Dec. 2012); f. 1990; 99% owned by Bishrelt Holding Co; Chair. T. BATBAYAR; CEO AGVAANJAMBA ARIUNBOLD; Dep. CEO A. GERELMAA; 59 brs.

Capitron Bank: Capitron Bank Bldg, Usny Gudamj 4, Sükhbaatar District, Ulan Bator; tel. (11) 315503; fax (11) 328372; e-mail info@capitronbank.mn; internet www.capitronbank.mn; f. 2001; cap. 8,000.5m., res 2,214.4m., dep. 101,321.9m. (Dec. 2012); 49% owned by B. Medree, 46% by P. Mönkh-Saikhan; Chair. D. DAGVADORJ; CEO PÜREVJAV MÖNKH-SAIKHAN.

Chingis Khaan Bank: New Century Plaza, Chingisiin Örgön Chölöö 15, Sükhbaatar District, Ulan Bator (POB 28/418); tel. (11) 318367; fax (11) 318373; e-mail bank@ckbank.mn; internet www.ckbank.mn; f. 2001; est. by Millennium Securities Management Ltd and Coral Sea Holdings Ltd (British Virgin Islands); cap. 39,373m., dep. 62,523m. (Dec. 2012); Chair. SERGEI GROMOV; CEO LÜIMED ARIUNAA.

Credit Bank: Chingisiin Talbai 18, 8th Sub-District, Sükhbaatar District, Ulan Bator; tel. (11) 319038; fax (11) 321897; e-mail info@creditbank.mn; internet www.creditbank.mn; f. 1997; owned by Basic Element Finance Ltd, Cyprus; cap. 8,090m., res 20,594m., dep. 12,363m. (July 2006); Chair. MIKHAIL VOLKOV; CEO OLEG TULIN.

Development Bank: Max Tower, Juulchny Gudamj 4/4, Chingeltei District, Ulan Bator; tel. 70130516; fax 70130602; e-mail info@dbm.mn; internet www.dbm.mn; Chair. B. SHINEBAATAR; CEO N. MÖNKHBAT.

Erel Bank: Erel Bank Bldg, Chingisiin Örgön Chölöö, Khan-Uul District, Ulan Bator; tel. 70122222; fax (11) 343387; e-mail info@erelbank.mn; internet www.erelbank.mn; f. 1997; 100% of shares owned by B. Erdenebat; cap. 1,782,865.8m. (Dec. 2013); Chair. BADARCH ERDENEBAT; CEO DAVAAKHÜÜ TÖMÖRKHÜÜ; 7 brs.

Golomt Bank of Mongolia: Golomt Bank Central Bldg, Chingisiin Talbai 3, Ulan Bator; tel. 70117676; fax (11) 312307; e-mail mail@golomtbank.com; internet www.golomtbank.com; f. 1995; est. by Mongolian-Portuguese IBH Bodi International Co Ltd; owned by Bodi group 84.66%, Swiss-MO Investment AG 10.16%, Trafigura Beheer BV 5.02%; cap. 42,295.6m., res 56,160.5m., dep. 2,187,897.4m. (Dec. 2013); Chair. CH. MÖNKHTSETSEG; CEO G. GANBOLD; 89 brs.

Khan Bank (KhAAN or Agricultural Bank): Söüliin Gudamj 25, Sükhbaatar District, Ulan Bator (POB 14250/192); tel. (11) 332333; fax 70117023; e-mail info@khanbank.com; internet www.khanbank.com; f. 1991; purchased by H and S Securities (Japan) in Feb. 2003; cap. 471,229m. (Dec. 2013); owned by Sawada Holdings (Tokyo) 41.3%, Tavan Bogd Trade (Ulan Bator) 22.96% and HS (Hong Kong) 13.1%; Chair. HIDEO SAWADA; Exec. Dir NORIHIKO KATO; 380 brs.

National Investment Bank: NI Bank Bldg, Usny Gudamj 1, Sükhbaatar District, Ulan Bator; tel. (11) 321995; fax (11) 323999; e-mail info@nibank.mn; internet www.nibank.mn; f. 2006; 55% owned by D. Dagvadorj, 22% by UB Diversified Ltd and 22% by Firebird Funds; f. 2006; cap. 8,431.2m., dep. 41,964.3m. (Dec. 2012); Chair. B. BAYARSAIKHAN; CEO P. DAVAA.

State Bank (Töriin Bank): Baga Toiruu 7/1, 1st Sub-District, Chingeltei District, Ulan Bator (POB 44/314); tel. 18001881; fax (11) 330595; e-mail contact@statebank.mn; internet www.statebank.mn; f. 1999; cap. 28,000m., res 217m., dep. 173,161.4m. (Dec. 2011); fmrly Zoos Bank; name changed as above when nationalized in 2009; took control of insolvent Khadgalamj (Savings) Bank July 2013; Chair. JIGJID GANBAT; Exec. Dir D. BATSAIKHAN; 31 brs.

Trade and Development Bank of Mongolia (Khudaldaa Khögjliin Bank): Cnr of Juulchny Gudamj 7 and Baga Toiruu 12, Chingeltei District, Ulan Bator; tel. (11) 327020; fax 70161988; e-mail info@tdbm.mn; internet www.tdbm.mn; f. 1991; 65% owned by Global Investment and Development Co; carries out Mongolbank's foreign operations; cap. 16,525.2m., res 49,360.6m., dep. 2,311,801.8m. (Dec. 2013); 76% equity bought by Banca Commerciale (Lugano) and

Gerald Metals (Stanford, CT), May 2002; Pres. RANDOLPH KOPPA; CEO BALBAR MEDREE; 49 brs.

Transport and Development Bank (Trans Bank): Juulchny Gudamj 35, 1st Sub-District, Chingeltei District, Ulan Bator; tel. (11) 319590; fax (11) 319591; e-mail info@transbank.mn; internet www.transbank.mn; owned by Russian interests; Chair. D. ENKHTAIVAN; CEO S. BAYANKHANGAI.

Ulaanbaatar City Bank: Sükhbaataryn Gudamj 16, Chingeltei District, Ulan Bator (POB 46/370); tel. (11) 319041; fax (11) 330508; e-mail info@ubcbank.mn; internet www.ubcbank.mn; f. 1998; est. by Capital City with assistance from the Bank of Taipei (Taiwan); cap. 52,340,760m. (Dec. 2013); Chair. D. BATJARGAL; CEO A. ENKHMEND.

XacBank: Yörönkhii Said Amaryn Gudamj, Sükhbaatar District, Ulan Bator (POB 20A/72); tel. (11) 318185; fax (11) 328701; e-mail info@xacbank.mn; internet www.xacbank.org; f. 1999; joined by TenGer Finance Group 2001; cap. 20,353.6m., res 45,520.4m., dep. 571,954.9m. (Dec. 2012); owned by Mercy Corps; Pres. GANIBAL AMARTÜVSHIN; CEO MAGVAN BOLD; 23 brs.

Bankers' Association

Mongolian Bank Association: Vista Office, Chingisiin Örgön Chölöö 17, Sükhbaatar District, Ulan Bator (CPOB 101); tel. and fax (11) 323581; e-mail monba@mba.mn; internet www.mba.mn; f. 2000; Pres. M. BOLD; Exec. Dir B. NAIDALAA.

STOCK EXCHANGES

Under a co-operation agreement with the London Stock Exchange, the Millennium IT system was being installed at the Mongolian Stock Exchange at a cost of some US $14m. to raise operations to international standards. Business was interrupted in July 2012 during installation of the system's T+3 add-on, the purpose of which was to restrict low turnover local buying and selling and prepare the exchange for large-scale international trading. Some 66.1m. shares worth 399,100m. tögrög in 2013.

Mongolian Agricultural Commodity Exchange: GB Plaza, Beejingiin Gudamj 37, 8th Sub-District, Sükhbaatar District, Ulan Bator; tel. and fax 70148779; e-mail info@mce.mn; internet www.mce.mn; f. 2013; state-owned; trades in wool, cashmere, camel hair and oilseed.

Stock Exchange: Chingisiin Talbai 3, Ulan Bator; tel. (11) 313747; fax (11) 325170; e-mail info@mse.mn; internet www.mse.mn; f. 1991; CEO DAVAASÜREN ANGAR.

INSURANCE

Ard Daatgal: Central Tower, Chingisiin Talbai 2, Sukhbaatar District, Ulan Bator; tel. 77200088; fax 77200089; e-mail info@arddaatgal.mn; internet www.arddaatgal.mn; f. 1994; est. with Omni Whittington Guernsey; Chair. J. OYUNGEREL; CEO DAGVABALJIR CHULUUNTSETSEG.

Bodi Daatgal: Bodi Tower, Jigjidjavyn Gudamj, Chingeltei District, Ulan Bator; tel. (11) 323444; fax (11) 326535; e-mail bodi@bodiinsurance.mn; internet www.bodiinsurance.mn; Dir L. BOLDKHUYAG.

Ganzam Insurance: Mongolian Railways (MTZ), Zamchdyn Gudamj, Bayangol District, Ulan Bator; tel. and fax (11) 242635; fax (11) 242634.

MIG Daatgal: MIG Bldg, Enkhtaivny Örgön Chölöö, 1st Sub-District, Chingeltei District, Ulan Bator (CPOB 200); tel. (11) 330131; fax (11) 330132; e-mail mig@magicnet.mn; internet www.mig.mn; f. 1997; privately owned; CEO JANDAV BAT-ORSHIKH.

Mongol Daatgal: Enkhtaivny Örgön Chölöö 13, Sükhbaatar District, Ulan Bator; tel. (11) 313901; fax (11) 310347; e-mail insurance@mongoldaatgal.mn; internet www.mongoldaatgal.mn; f. 1934; sold Dec. 2003 to consortium formed by Angara-SKB and Chinggis Khan Bank; CEO TÖMÖR-OCHIR BATZUL.

Monre Daatgal: Company Bldg, Baga Toiruu 37B, Sükhbaatar District, Ulan Bator; tel. 70009000; fax 70006000; e-mail info@monre.mn; internet www.monre.mn.

National Life Daatgal: Colorado Business Centre, Amarsanaagiin Gudamj, Bayangol District, Ulan Bator (POB 48/35); tel. 70110784; fax 70110745; e-mail info@nlic.mn; internet www.nlic.mn; Exec. Dir B. BATBAYAR.

Nomin Daatgal: State Department Store, Khudaldaany Gudamj, Chingeltei District, Ulan Bator; tel. (11) 330023; fax (11) 325528; e-mail insurance@nomin.net; internet www.insurance.nomin.net; CEO SANJAA GANCHIMEG.

UB City Daatgal: New Horizons Centre, Olimpiin Gudamj, Sükhbaatar District, Ulan Bator (POB 46/385); tel. 70119827; fax (11) 319826; e-mail info@ubci.mn; internet www.ubci.mn.

Insurers' Association

Mongolian Insurers' Association (MIA): Sükhbaatar District, Ulan Bator, (POB 450); tel. and fax (11) 323750; e-mail daatgal@mia .mn; internet mia.mn; Exec. Dir BATJARGAL JAMSRAN.

Trade and Industry

GOVERNMENT AGENCIES

Capital Investment Directorate (Invest Mongolia Agency): Ministry of Economic Development, Ulan Bator; f. 2013; Dir SEREETER JAVKHLANBAATAR.

Mineral Resources Authority: Government Bldg 12, Barilgachdyn Talbai 3, Chingeltei District, Ulan Bator; tel. (11) 263628; fax (51) 310370; e-mail info@mram.gov.mn; internet mram.gov.mn; f. 1996; subordinate to Ministry of Mining; Chair. D. ÜÜRIINTUYAA.

Nuclear Energy Directorate: Üildverchii Gudamj, 2nd Sub-District, Khan-Uul District, Ulan Bator; tel. 70139019; e-mail info@nea.gov.mn; internet www.nea.gov.mn; f. 2008; subordinate to Prime Minister; Head N. TEGSHBAYAR.

Petroleum Directorate: Ulan Bator; tel. (11) 631208; fax (11) 631467; e-mail info@pam.gov.mn; internet www.pam.gov.mn; f. 2008; subordinate to Minister of Mining; Head G. ÖLZIIBÜREN.

State Property Committee: management body comprising directors representing various govt ministries, the Financial Regulation Committee, state-owned enterprises and law firms; Chair. D. TSOGTBAATAR.

DEVELOPMENT ORGANIZATIONS

Agricultural Equipment, Science and Technology Production Association: Zaisan 53, Khan-Uul District, Ulan Bator; tel. (11) 341155; fax (11) 327099; e-mail agrtechcor@magicnet.mn; f. 1997; devt of farm machinery, including biogas plants; 100% state-owned; Exec. Dir J. TÜMEN.

Business Council of Mongolia: Express Tower, Enkhtaivny Örgön Chölöö, Ulan Bator; tel. and fax (11) 317027; e-mail info@ bcmongolia.org; internet www.bcmongolia.org; f. 2007; promotes international trade and business links, working with companies, govt departments, embassies and non-governmental orgs; Chair. BAYANJARGAL BYAMBASAIKHAN.

Mongolian Business Development Agency: Yörönkhii Said Amaryn Gudamj, Ulan Bator (CPOB 458); tel. (11) 311094; fax (11) 311092; internet www.mbda-mongolia.org; f. 1994; Gen. Man. D. BAYARBAT.

Mongolian Development Research Centre: Rm 50, Baga Toiruu 13, Chingeltei District, Ulan Bator (POB 20A/63); tel. and fax (11) 315686; internet www.mdrc.mn; f. 1998; Chair. TSEDENDAMBA BATBAYAR.

CHAMBERS OF COMMERCE

Mongolian National Chamber of Commerce and Industry: Makhatma Gandiin Gudamj 11, 1st Sub-District, Khan-Uul District, Ulan Bator 38; tel. (11) 327176; fax (11) 324620; e-mail chamber@ mongolchamber.mn; internet www.mongolchamber.mn; f. 1960; IT and e-business devt, human resources development, public relations, SME and national industrial production, export promotion; Chair. SAMBUU DEMBEREL.

Mongolian International and National Arbitration Centre: e-mail gunnjdagva@mongolchamber.mn; Sec.-Gen. CH. GÜNJDAGVA.

INDUSTRIAL AND TRADE ASSOCIATIONS

Mongolian Air Traffic Controllers' Association: National Air Traffic Services, Chinggis Khaan International Airport, Buyant-Ukhaa, Ulan Bator; tel. (11) 282008; fax (11) 282108; e-mail monatca@mcaa.gov.mn.

Mongolian Builders' Association: Block 3, Urt Tsagaan, Chingeltei District, Ulan Bator; tel. 99112636; fax (11) 318685; Pres. MÖNKHBAYAR BATBAATAR.

Mongolian Coal Association: Ulan Bator; tel. and fax (11) 328582; e-mail coalasso@yahoo.com; Exec. Dir TÜVDENG NARAN.

Mongolian Exporters' Association: Macro Centre, Erkhüügiin Gudamj 7/1, Sükhbaatar District, Ulan Bator (POB 20/352); tel. 99119356; fax (11) 354533; e-mail info@exportmongolia.mn; f. 2006; Pres. DAMBA GALSANDORJ.

Mongolian Farmers' and Flour Producers' Association: Agro-Pro Business Centre, 19th Sub-District, Bayangol District, Ulan Bator; tel. (11) 300114; fax (11) 362875; e-mail agropro@magicnet .mn; f. 1997; research and quality inspection services in domestic farming and flour industry; Pres. SHARAV GUNGAADORJ.

Mongolian Forest Industries Association: Teeverchdiin 32, 1st Sub-District, Bayangol District, Ulan Bator (POB 36/51); tel. 91111191; fax (11) 321500; e-mail tsogoots@gmail.com; f. 1996; Chair. TSEDENPUNTSAG TSOGOO.

Mongolian Institute of Internal Auditors: Ulan Bator; tel. (11) 70119107; e-mail miia@bizcon.mn; internet www.bizcon.mn; Pres. L. OTGONBAYAR.

Mongolian Marketing Association: Ulan Bator; tel. 99096400; fax 70113756; e-mail bold_dag@yahoo.com; Pres. B. DAVAASÜREN; Exec. Dir D. BOLD.

Mongolian Meat Association: Taij Group Bldg B303, Zaisangun Gudamj 8, Khan-Uul District, Ulan Bator (POB 322); tel. 99176995; fax (11) 343117; e-mail meat@mobinet.mn; internet www.monmeat .mn; f. 1999; Pres. L. GANPÜREV; Exec. Dir M. LKHACHINBAL.

Mongolian Metallurgists' Association: School of Technology, Darkhan-Uul Province; tel. (37) 24723; Pres. TS. MÖNKHJARGAL.

Mongolian Motor Transporters' United Association: Ulan Bator; f. 1996; est. as Mongolian National Society of Motor Transport Owners, amalgamated 2005 with the Mongoltrans Transporters' Asscn; 39 mem. businesses and orgs incl. the Private Bus Owners' Asscn, Taxi Owners' Asscn and Large & Small Bus Asscn; Pres. GAVAAG BATKHÜÜ.

Mongolian National Mining Association: 501 Geosan Company Bldg, Ikh Surguuliin Gudamj 8, Ulan Bator; tel. (11) 314877; fax (11) 330032; e-mail info@miningmongolia.mn; internet www .miningmongolia.mn; f. 1994; provides legal protection and represents views of mining interests in govt policy and devt of mineral sector; Pres. DAMJIN DAMBA; Exec. Dir NAMGAR ALGAA.

Mongolyn Nüürs: Ulan Bator (CPOB 147); tel. and fax (11) 682570; asscn of Mongolian coal mines; state-owned; Pres. DORJ DONDOV; Exec. Dir TOSHOON SAMBASANCHIR.

Mongolian Oil Shale Association: Ambassador Office Center, Enkhtaivny Örgön Chölöö 15A/5, Sükhbaatar District, Ulan Bator; tel. 70149971; fax 70149972; e-mail da.ganbold@gmail.com; Pres. DAVAADORJ GANBOLD.

EMPLOYERS' ORGANIZATIONS

Employers' and Owners' United Association: Rm 401, 4th Floor, Mongolian Youth Association 'B' Bldg, Ulan Bator; tel. (11) 326513; Exec. Dir B. SEMBEEJAV.

Federation of Professional Business Women of Mongolia: Ulan Bator; tel. and fax (11) 315638; e-mail mbpw@mongolnet.mn; f. 1992; provides education, training, and opportunities for women to achieve economic independence; Pres. OCHIRBAT ZAYAA; 7,000 mems, 14 brs.

Forestry and Timber Production Managers' Association: Ulan Bator; tel. (11) 341310; e-mail info@fmwa.mn; internet fmwa .mn; f. 2010; Head D. BAASANBYAMBA.

Mongolian Employers' Federation: Tavan Bogd Bldg, Chingisiin Talbai 18, Ulan Bator; tel. and fax (11) 325635; fax (11) 325635; e-mail monef@magicnet.mn; internet www.monef.mn; f. 1990; fmrly Private Industry Owners' Association; 8,600 mems; Vice-Pres. KH. GANBAATAR.

Mongolian Management Association: 102 and 202, Bldg B, The Academy of Management, Chingisiin Örgön Chölöö, Khan Uul District, Ulan Bator; tel. (11) 341570; e-mail info@mamo.mn; internet www.mamo.mn; Pres. DAGVADORJ TSERENDORJ.

Private Business Owners' Association: Tsatsral Mon Bldg, 1st Sub-District, Songinokhairkhan District, Ulan Bator; tel. (11) 682905; Pres. T. NYAMDORJ.

UTILITIES

Electricity

Dulaan Tsakhilgaan Stants-IV: 20th Sub-District, Bayangol District, Ulan Bator; tel. (11) 631768; Mongolia's biggest power station; Exec. Dir B. TSEVEEN.

TEKhs: Ulan Bator; high-voltage grid centred on No. 4 power station supplying Ulan Bator and towns of Sükhbaatar, Darkhan and Erdenet to the north, Öndörkhaan (Chingis Khot) to the east, Sainshand (south-east), Arvaikheer (south-west) and Tsetserleg (west); in 2013 the grid was extended by 400 km of 220 kV lines from Mandalgobi to Tavan Tolgoi and Oyuu Tolgoi mines; Chief Engineer TS. JARGALSAIKHAN.

Ulan Bator Power Distribution Network: Chingisiin Örgön Chölöö 45, Khan-Uul District, Ulan Bator; e-mail info@ubedn.mn; internet www.ubedn.mn; Exec. Dir E. TÜVSHINCHULUUN.

Water

Dulaany Süljee: Ulan Bator; tel. (11) 343047; e-mail engineer@dhc .mn; internet www.dhc.mn; supervision of hot water district heating network in Ulan Bator; Exec. Dir R. KHAIDAV.

USUG (Water Management Office): Tokiogiin Gudamj 5, Bayanzürkh District, Ulan Bator; tel. (11) 455055; fax (11) 450120; e-mail usag@magicnet.mn; supervision of water supply network in Ulan Bator; Chair. OSOR ERDENEBAATAR.

IMPORT AND EXPORT ORGANIZATIONS

Agrotekh Impeks: Ulan Bator; tel. 99119840; imports agricultural machinery and implements, seed, fertilizer, veterinary medicines and irrigation equipment.

Khorshoolol Impeks: Tolgoit, Ulan Bator (CPOB 262); tel. (11) 332926; fax (11) 331128; f. 1964; exports skins, hides, wool and furs, handicrafts and finished products; imports equipment and materials for housing, and for clothing and leather goods; Dir L. ÖLZIIBUYAN.

Kompleks Import: Enkhtaivny Örgön Chölöö 7, Ulan Bator; tel. and fax (11) 688948; f. 1963; imports consumer goods, foodstuffs, sets of equipment and turnkey projects; training of Mongolians abroad; state-owned pending planned privatization; cap. 3,500m. tögrög.

Makh Impeks: 4th Sub-District, Songinokhairkhan District, Ulan Bator; tel. (11) 632471; fax (11) 632517; f. 1946; abattoir, meat-processing, canning, meat imports and exports; 51% share privatized in 1999; cap. 7,800m. tögrög; Exec. Dir N. ODGEREL.

Material Impex: Narny Zam Gudamj 16/5, 4th Sub-District, Bayangol District, Ulan Bator; tel. (11) 363806; e-mail bolortuyaa@materialimpex.mn; internet www.materialimpex.com; f. 1957; exports cashmere, wool products, animal skins; imports glass, roofing material, dyes, sanitary ware, metals and metalware, wallpaper, bitumen, wall and floor tiles; partially privatized Feb. 1999, but most shares still state-owned; Gen. Dir B. ZORIG; 126 employees.

Med Impex International: Barilga Mega Store, Sansar Rd, 1st Sub-District, Bayanzürkh District, Ulan Bator; tel. 70120429; e-mail erdenebat_ts@medimpex.mn; internet www.medimpex.mn; importer of medical equipment from Siemens, Draeger, Agilent and others; Dir T. OTGONTUYAA.

Metall Impeks (Metalimpex): Ulan Bator; tel. (11) 325049; Dir D. GANBAT.

Monfa Trade: Monfarma Trade Co, Khudaldaany Gudamj, 4th Sub-District, Chingeltei District, Ulan Bator; tel. and fax (11) 324420; e-mail monfatrade@mongol.net; procurement and distribution of pharmaceuticals.

Mongol Eksport Co Ltd: Government Bldg 7, 8th Fl., Tusgaar Togtnolyn Talbai, Ulan Bator; tel. (11) 327884; exports wool, hair, cashmere, mining products, antlers, skins and hides; Dir-Gen. D. CHIMEDDAMBAA.

Monnis Group: Monnis Tower, Chingisiin Örgön Chölöö 15, Ulan Bator; tel. (11) 311687; fax (11) 323248; e-mail info@monnis.com; internet www.monnis.com; f. 1998; est. as distributor for Nissan Motor Co Ltd; other commercial interests incl. geology, mining, energy, construction, freight-forwarding, foreign trade, communications, banking and aviation; Chair. B. CHULUUNBAATAR; 700 employees, 8 subsidiaries.

Monos Cosmetics: Monos Bldg, Sonsgolongiin Toiruu 25, 20th Sub-District, Songinokhairkhan District, Ulan Bator; tel. and fax (11) 633257; e-mail cosmetics@monos.mn; internet www.monoscosmetics.mn; f. 1990; production, export and import of cosmetics; Chair. and CEO BALDANDORJ ERDENEKHISHIG; Exec. Dir KH. SOLONGO; 90 employees.

Monos Group: Monos Group Bldg, Namiyangugiin Gudamj, 13th Sub-District, Bayanzürkh District, Ulan Bator; tel. (11) 450054; e-mail monostrade@monos.mn; internet www.monos.mn; f. 1990; production, export and import of medicine, medical equipment and health food; Dir-Gen. LUVSAN ERDENECHIMEG; 280 employees.

Petrovis: Petrovis Co Bldg, Yörönkhii Said Amaryn Gudamj 7 and Baga Toiruu 51, Sükhbaatar District, Ulan Bator; tel. (11) 327051; fax (11) 320426; e-mail marketing@petrovis.mn; internet www.petrovis.mn; oil products importer and distributor; in Feb. 2004 acquired the 80% state-owned shares in the country's biggest distributor NIK (Neft Import Kontsern) for US $8.5m; Chair. J. OYUUNGEREL; Exec. Dir M. KHALIUNBAT.

Tekhnik Import: Ulan Bator; tel. (11) 685190; imports machinery, instruments and spare parts for light, food, wood, building, power and mining industries, road-building and communications; state-owned; Dir-Gen. D. GANTSETSEG.

Tüshig Trade Co Ltd: Enkhtaivny Örgön Chölöö, Ulan Bator (POB 44/481); tel. (11) 323206; fax (11) 314052; exports sheep and camel wool, and cashmere goods; imports machinery for small enterprises, foodstuffs and consumer goods; Dir-Gen. D. GANBAATAR.

Unigas: Midtown Centre, Enkhtaivny Gudamj 15/2, Ulan Bator; tel. (11) 75758869; fax (11) 314018; e-mail info@unigas.mn; internet www.unigas.mn; LPG distributing company; Dir-Gen. D. BAASANTSOGT.

CO-OPERATIVES

Central Association of Consumer Co-operatives: Ulan Bator; tel. and fax (11) 329025; f. 1990; wholesale and retail trade; exports animal raw materials; imports foodstuffs and consumer goods; Chair. G. MYANGANBAYAR.

Mongolian Association of Production Co-operatives: Urt Tsagaan, Khudaldaany Gudamj 12, Chingeltei District, Ulan Bator; tel. (11) 310956; e-mail cumic@mol.mn.

Mongolian Association of Savings and Credit Co-operatives: Bldg 2, State Property Committee, Chingeltei District, Ulan Bator; tel. (11) 313665; Pres. SH. GOOKHÜÜ.

Mongolian Co-operatives Development Centre: Ulan Bator; Dir DANZAN RADNAARAGCHAA.

National Association of Mongolian Agricultural Co-operatives: Enkhtaivny Örgön Chölöö 18A/1, Bayanzürkh District, Ulan Bator; fax (11) 458899; e-mail info@namac.coop; internet www.namac.coop; f. 1992; Pres. SUMIYABAZAR DOLGORSUREN.

National United Association of Mongolian Co-operatives: Ulan Bator; Dir N. ENKHBOLD.

Union of Mongolian Production and Services Co-operatives: Bldg 16, 2nd 40,000, 3rd Sub-District, Chingeltei District, Ulan Bator (POB 46/470); tel. (11) 327583; fax (11) 328446; e-mail umpscoop@hotmail.com; f. 1990; Pres. SAMDAN ENKHTUYAA.

TRADE UNIONS

Confederation of Mongolian Trade Unions: Chingisiin Talbai 9, Chingeltei District, Ulan Bator; tel. 70111598; fax (11) 322128; e-mail info@cmtu.mn; internet www.cmtu.mn; brs throughout the country; Pres. KHAYANKHYARVAA AMGALANBAATAR; Sec.-Gen. GORCHINSÜREN ADIYAA.

Transport

Mongol Trans: Mongol Trans Bldg, Ajilchdyn Gudamj, 3rd Sub-District, Khan-Uul District, Ulan Bator; tel. 70018812; fax (11) 682125; e-mail mte@mongoltrans.mn; internet www.mongoltrans.mn.

Tuushin Co Ltd: Tuushin Bldg, Yörönkhii Said Amaryn Gudamj 2, Sükhbaatar District, Ulan Bator; tel. (11) 312092; fax (11) 325510; e-mail info@tuushin.mn; internet www.tuushin.mn; f. 1990; international freight forwarders; transport and forwarding policy and services, warehousing, customs agent; tourism; offices in Beijing, Moscow and Prague; Dir-Gen. N. ZORIGT.

RAILWAYS

Mongolyn Tömör Zam (Mongolian Railways): Finance Center, 9th Floor, Jigjidjavyn Gudamj 8, Ulan Bator; tel. (11) 336611; fax (11) 336644; e-mail info@mtz.mn; internet www.mtz.mn; f. 2008; state-owned limited co, est. by Erdenes Mongol and Russian Railways (50% each) to modernize Ulan Bator Railway; CEO PÜREVDORJ BAT-ERDENE.

Ulan Bator Railway (UBR): Söüliin Gudamj 42, Bayangol District, Ulan Bator (CPOB 376); tel. and fax (21) 244410; fax (21) 243044; internet www.ubtz.mn; f. 1949; jt-stock co (equal shares) with Russia; Dir G. SEREENENDORJ; Chairs V. N. MOROZOV (Russia), YO. MANLAIBAYAR (Mongolia).

External Lines: from the Russian frontier at Naushki/Sükhbaatar (connecting with the Trans-Siberian Railway) to Ulan Bator and on to the Chinese frontier at Zamyn-Üüd/Erenhot, connecting with Beijing (total length 1,110 km).

Branches: from Darkhan to Sharyn Gol coalfield (length 63 km); branch from Salkhit near Darkhan, westwards to Erdenet (Erdenetiin-ovoo open-cast copper mine) in Orkhon Province (164 km); from Bagakhangai to Baganuur coalmine, south-east of Ulan Bator (96 km); from Khar Airag to Bor-Öndör fluorspar mines (60 km); from Sainshand to Züünbayan oilfield (63 km).

Eastern Railway, linking Mongolia with the Trans-Siberian and Chita via Borzya: from the Russian frontier at Solovyevsk to Choibalsan (238 km), with branch from Chingis Dalan to Mardai uranium mine near Dashbalbar (110 km), possibly inactive. The development of an Ereentsav border rail crossing in north-eastern Dornod Province (for Solovyevsk in Russia) was under discussion.

In 2013 the total length of track, including stations and passing loops, was 1,815 km. In October 2014 the Great Khural approved plans to build broad-gauge (1,520 mm) lines from Arts Suuri to Erdenet, from Tavan Tolgoi to Sainshand, Baruun-Ürt, Khööt and Choibalsan and from Khööt to Nömrög, and standard-gauge (1,435 mm) lines from Tavan Tolgoi to Gashuunsukhait and Khööt to Bichigt (on the border with China).

Ulan Bator Railway launched a railbus service between Ulan Bator's suburban stations in 2014.

IFFC (International Freight Forwarder Co, Ulan Bator Railway): Ulaanbaatar Railway, Söüliin Gudamj 42, Bayangol District, Ulan Bator (CPOB 376); tel. (21) 244846; fax (11) 311342; e-mail info@iffc .mn; internet www.iffc.mn; international freight-forwarding; Dir DASHDAMBA AMARBAYASGALAN.

ROADS

Mongolia divides its road system into state-grade and country-grade roads. State-grade roads (of which there were 12,722 km in 2012) run from Ulan Bator to provincial centres and from provincial centres to the border. Country-grade roads account for the remaining roads, but they are mostly rough cross-country tracks. The length of 'improved roads' reached 7,633 km in 2011, of which 4,063 km were hard-surfaced. To mark the millennium, the Government announced its decision to construct a new east–west road, linking the Chinese and Russian border regions via Ulan Bator. Hard-top roads between Bayankhongor and Ulan Bator, and between Choir and Sainshand were completed in September 2013. A total of 1,557 km of hard-top roads were completed in 2013. It was planned to build 2,200 km of roads in 2014 to link the provincial centres of Mörön, Uliastai, Altai, Choibalsan, Dalanzadgad and Baruun-Urt with Ulan Bator. A new north–south highway, running from Altanbulag on the border with Russia via Ulan Bator to Zamyn-Üüd on the border with China, was to be built during 2014–17.

SHIPPING

In 2014 Mongolia's flag registered fleet comprised 293 vessels, with a total displacement of 1,864,772 grt, including 101 general cargo ships, 90 tankers and 10 bulk carriers.

Maritime Administration: Ulan Bator; state-owned co, operating until 2010 with Singapore-based Maritime Chain as its agent; head of rail and sea transport policy department, Ministry of Roads and Transport; Dir Yo. MANLAIBAYAR.

CIVIL AVIATION

Civil aviation in Mongolia, including the provision of air traffic control and airport management, is the responsibility of the Main Directorate of Civil Aviation, which provides air traffic and airport management services. It also supervises the Mongolian national airline (MIAT) and smaller operators such as Khangarid and Tongeriin Ulaach, which operate local flights. Aeroflot (Russia) and Air China operate flights to Ulan Bator (Chinggis Khaan International Airport). Mongolia has 14 airfields with surfaced runways, and 31 with dirt strips.

In early 2013 Khanbumbat airport at Oyu Tolgoi copper mine was opened, with a runway suitable for C-130 and Boeing 737 aircraft.

Construction of a new international airport for Ulan Bator, with a 3,600 m runway, commenced in 2013 at Khöshigiin Khöndii, south of the capital; it will have a 37-km motorway link. Due for completion in 2016, the airport will have twice the capacity of Chinggis Khaan (Buyant-Ukhaa) airport, where high ground to the south limits the use of the single runway to take-offs and landings to and from the north.

Main Directorate of Civil Aviation: Chinggis Khaan International Airport, Buyant-Ukhaa, Ulan Bator; tel. (11) 282051; fax (11) 282102; e-mail jargalmaa.b@mcaa.gov.mn; internet www.mcaa .gov.mn; Dir-Gen. T. LKHAGVASÜREN; Chief Dep. S. ENKH-AMGALAN.

A-Jet Aviation: Olimpiin Gudamj, 1st Sub-District, Sükhbaatar District, Ulan Bator (POB 46/202); tel. (11) 318480; fax (11) 319780; e-mail aviation@ajet.mn; internet www.ajetaviation.mn; f. 2000; fmrly Central Mongolia Airways; Mi-8 and EC-145 helicopter services for tourists, aerial surveys and photography; Exec. Dir NYAMBAR LKHAMJAV; Man. B. TSOGOO.

Aero Mongolia Co Ltd: Chinggis Khaan International Airport, Buyant-Ukhaa, Ulan Bator (POB 34/105); tel. (11) 330373; fax (11) 330374; e-mail marketing@aeromongolia.mn; internet www .aeromongolia.mn; f. 2001; began operations in 2003; operates scheduled international flights to Irkutsk (Russia) and Hohhot (China), and scheduled internal flights to five provincial centres and Juulchin's South Gobi tourist camp; twice-weekly flights to the Republic of Korea; Dir E. AMARSAIKHAN.

Air Cargo Express: 17th Sub-District, Bayangol District, Ulan Bator; tel. 91915482; e-mail aircargoexpress@magicnet.mn; one Airbus A300-600F aircraft for export cargo flights to the USA and Europe and import cargo flights from the People's Republic of China and the Republic of Korea.

Blue Sky Aviation: Door 2, Apt S-61, Enkhtaivny Örgön Chölöö, 1st Sub-District, Sükhbaatar District, Ulan Bator (CPOB 932); tel. (11) 312085; fax (11) 322857; e-mail bsa@maf.org; internet www .blueskyaviation.mn; jt venture of Mission Aviation Fellowship and Exodus International; operates charter flights and medical

emergency services; f. 1999; Dir TOM MASON; Operations Man. BATSUUR BAYARJIN.

Eznis (Easiness) Airways: Naiman Zovkhis Bldg, Söüliin Gudamj, Sükhbaatar District, Ulan Bator; tel. (11) 333311; fax (11) 331514; e-mail feedback@eznis.com; internet www.eznisairways.com; f. 2006; suspended operations in May 2014; CEO SÜKHBAATAR MÖNKHSÜKH.

Khünnü (Hunnu) Airlines: Narny Zam 15, Sükhbaatar District, Ulan Bator; tel. 70112179; fax (11) 328025; e-mail info@hunnuair .com; internet www.hunnuair.com; f. 2011; fmrly Mongolian Airlines Group, renamed as above in 2013; flights to Mörön, Khovd, Choibalsan, Dalanzadgad, Gobi-Altai, Zavkhan and Bayankhongor; seasonal operator of Airbus A-319 aircraft to Tokyo and Hong Kong, and Fokker 50 aircraft on internal routes; CEO B. BAYAR.

MIAT Cargo: MIAT Bldg, Chinggis Khaan International Airport, Buyant-Ukhaa, Khan-Uul District, Ulan Bator; tel. 70049956; fax 70049645; e-mail ground_ops@miat.com.

Mongolian Civil Air Transport (MIAT): MIAT Bldg, Chinggis Khaan International Airport, Buyant-Ukhaa, Khan-Uul District, Ulan Bator; tel. (11) 333999; fax (11) 379919; e-mail marketing@miat .com; internet www.miat.com; f. 1956; national carrier; operates two Boeing 767-300ER and two Boeing 737-800 aircraft; scheduled services to Moscow, Beijing, Seoul, Osaka, Berlin and Tokyo; internal flights to Mörön and Khovd resumed in July 2009; Chair. D. MAKHBAL; Exec. Dir GUNGAAG JARGALSAIKHAN.

Tengeriin Ulaach Shine (Sky Horse New): Chinggis Khaan International Airport, Buyant-Ukhaa, Khan-Uul District, Ulan Bator (POB 34/17); tel. (11) 285073; fax (11) 379765; e-mail skyhorsenew@ mbox.mn; internal L410 transport for tourists and business passengers; Exec. Dir U. GALBADRAKH.

Thomas Air LLC: Tushig Centre, Söüliin Gudamj 23, 4th Sub-District, Sükhbaatar District, Ulan Bator; tel. 96111459; fax 75851460; e-mail info@thomasair.mn; internet www.thomasair .mn; leasing of Air Tractor AT-602, Pilatus Porter PC6, Maule M-7, aircraft for agricultural and environmental protection work; cargo charters, medical evacuation, crop-dusting, surveys, tourism, flying school; CEO KHULDORJ BÜREN-ERDENE.

Tourism

The country's main attractions are its scenery, wildlife and historical relics. A foreign tourist service bureau was established in 1954, but the tourism sector remained undeveloped. At March 2008 there were 248 tour operators, 326 hotels (with 8,000 beds) and 30 tourist camps (with 6,400 beds). Of the 30 or more hotels in Ulan Bator, all but four are relatively small, and in the peak summer season there is a shortage of rooms. The outlying tourist centres (Terelj, South Gobi, Öndör-Dov and Khujirt) have basic facilities. Tourist arrivals totalled 417,815 in 2013, but declined to 392,844 in 2014; Chinese and Russian tourists remained the most numerous. Tourism revenue reached US $233m. in 2012.

Mongolian National Tourism Centre: Central Sports Palace, Baga Toiruu 55, Ulan Bator; tel. (11) 330675; fax (11) 330778; e-mail marketing@mongoliatourism.gov.mn; internet www.mongolia tourism.gov.mn; Dir O. TSOODOL.

Tourism Information Centre: UB Bank Bldg, Chingisiin Talbai 11, Ulan Bator; tel. 70108687.

Defence

As assessed at November 2014, Mongolia's defence forces numbered 10,000, comprising an army of 8,900 (of whom 3,300 were thought to be conscripts), 800 air defence personnel and 300 construction troops. There was a paramilitary force of about 7,200, comprising 1,200 internal security troops, now disbanded and part of the police, and 6,000 border guards under the Ministry of Law. Army reserves numbered an estimated 137,000. Military service is for 12 months (for males aged 18–25 years), but only about 30% of conscripts are found fit for service. In early 2014 President Tsakhia Elbegdorj initiated the 'Student-Soldier Programme'. Under this programme, in order to supplement the annual call-up of 18-year-olds, students of universities and higher schools were to receive, on a voluntary basis, a week of 'general military training' (two credits) followed by three weeks of 'special military training' (12 credits). A military training centre was to be built for 500–1,000 students.

Each year the capital city and the provinces are allocated a maximum number of local young men of call-up age permitted to purchase exemption from military service. The total number of men who did so rose from 659 in 2013 to 714 in 2014, when the charge per person was set at 4.4m. tögrög (around US $2,600). This charge was equivalent to the estimated average annual cost of a soldier's food, clothing, accommodation, medical services, training, pay, weapons, ammunition and fuel. Financial inducements are offered for regular service soldiers, particularly for those serving in the best-trained and equipped 'élite' battalions, some of whom have served with coalition forces in Iraq and as part of UN peacekeeping operations elsewhere. In 2012 troops from the Main Directorate for Emergency Relief were sent abroad for the first time, to serve as peacekeepers in the UN Mission in South Sudan (UNMISS).

Mongolia has restarted annual military exercises with the Russian army, during which its Soviet-made equipment is serviced and updated. The Mongolian-Russian 'Selenge-2014' tactical exercises were held at Mönkhöt training base near Bayantümen for a fortnight in August 2014. The Russian Far Eastern Military District sent by train 500 men and 100 pieces of equipment, including Akatsiya 152mm self-propelled artillery, Grad systems and Shilka AA guns. For the first time Russian Mi-24 helicopters took part. The exercises were supervised by the CO of General Purpose Troops, Brig.-Gen. Sükhbat and the CoS 36th Army Maj.-Gen. Sharagov. By the beginning of 2012 Mongolia's ground forces had in military service the following (all Soviet-manufactured) equipment: 370 T-54/55 tanks, 310 BMP-1 infantry combat vehicles, 120 BRDM-2 reconnaissance vehicles, 150 BTR-60 armoured transporters, 130 Grad rocket launchers, and 150 D-30 and ML-20 artillery guns. In 2012 Russia reportedly additionally supplied Mongolia with up to 50 T-72A tanks, 40 BTR-70M armoured transporters and a number of Ural vehicles. There were also several reports that the Irkut works would be supplying YaK-130 jet trainers.

Defence Expenditure: Budgeted at 190,000m. tögrög for 2014.

Chief of Staff of the Mongolian Armed Forces: Lt-Gen. TSER-ENDEJID BYAMBAJAV.

Deputy Chief of Staff, Commander General Purpose Troops: Brig.-Gen. RADNAABAZAR SÜKHBAT.

Deputy Chief of Staff, Director of Peacekeeping: Brig.-Gen. BYAMBAASÜREN BAYARMAGNAI.

Commander of Air Defence Troops: Col N. BATKHÜREL.

Education

General education is state-administered. Eleven-year education is compulsory, and 12-year education is being introduced. In the 2014/15 school year there were an estimated 505,800 pupils receiving general education in 762 schools, the teaching staff of which totalled 27,449. The 52 state and 24 private vocational schools, with a total of 42,800 students in 2014/15, train personnel for the service industries, including electricians, drivers and machine operators.

The Mongolian State University has three faculties (biology; chemistry; geography and geology) and nine schools (including foreign languages, mathematics, computer science, law, economics and social sciences). The School of Foreign Service provides diplomatic training. There were 88,200 students enrolled in state universities, and 27,200 enrolled in private universities and colleges in 2013/14.

In 2013/14 there were six state-owned and 71 private institutes of other higher education; 13,700 students were enrolled at the state institutes and 44,500 at the private institutes of higher education, excluding those studying in Russia, Germany, Turkey, the USA and elsewhere. The student enrolment abroad was estimated at 9,550 in 2009/10.

In July 2010 the Government approved a project for reform of higher education during 2010–12, which included structural change such as the consolidation of some colleges and institutes (e.g. the merger of Ulaanbaatar University and the Higher School of Trade and Industry with the Mongolian State University) and an improved admissions policy in order to raise teaching and research standards to international levels.

In general education schools, the first steps were taken to introduce a Cambridge assessment-type curriculum. The news agency Montsame reported in August 2012 that some 70% of private universities and colleges had undergone certification since the process began in May and about 10% were expected to fail and close.

The state budget allocation to the Ministry of Education and Science for 2014 was projected at 1,096,472m. tögrög, equivalent to 15% of total planned budgetary expenditure.

MONTENEGRO

Introductory Survey

LOCATION, CLIMATE, LANGUAGE, RELIGION, FLAG, CAPITAL

Montenegro is situated in the central Balkan peninsula, in south-eastern Europe. Montenegro has frontiers with Bosnia and Herzegovina to the west and north-west, Serbia to the north, Kosovo to the east, and Albania to the south-east, and a short frontier with Croatia in the south-west. There is a western coastline along the Adriatic Sea (part of the Mediterranean). Montenegro has a rugged mountainous terrain, being dominated by the Black Mountains (Crna Gora), from which the country takes its name. The climate is Mediterranean near the coast, and continental inland. Mountainous areas have a colder climate with heavy snowfall in winter. Average temperatures range from between −7°C (19.4°F) and 23°C (73.4°F) inland, and between 11°C (51.8°F) and 28°C (84.2°F) on the coast. Montenegro's mountainous regions receive some of the highest amounts of rainfall in Europe. The 2007 Constitution describes the principal language as Montenegrin, with the Cyrillic and Latin alphabets of equal status. Serbian, Bosnian, and Croatian (all of which, in common with Montenegrin, were formerly described as variants of Serbo-Croat) and Albanian are also in official use. The principal religion is Orthodox Christianity, and there are significant Roman Catholic and Muslim communities. The national flag (proportions 1 by 2) is red, with a golden coat of arms depicting a double-headed eagle. Cetinje is described in the Constitution as the historical capital of Montenegro, while Podgorica is the capital.

CONTEMPORARY POLITICAL HISTORY

Historical Context

After the Second World War, Montenegro became one of the six constituent republics of the federal Yugoslavia established by the Communist Party of Yugoslavia (later the League of Communists of Yugoslavia) under Josip Broz (Tito). Montenegro generally supported the Serbian reassertion of dominance within Yugoslavia after the death of Tito in the 1980s. Institutionally, this was helped by the installation of a new party leadership in the republic, following demonstrations during 1988 in favour of the Serbian leader, Slobodan Milošević. Subsequent reforms reconstituted the Skupština Crne Gore (Assembly of Montenegro) as a unicameral body of 125 members and replaced Montenegro's collective presidency with a directly elected state President. The elections, in December 1990, represented a victory for the ruling Savez Komunista Crne Gore (League of Communists of Montenegro), later renamed the Demokratska Partija Socijalista Crne Gore (DPS—Democratic Party of Socialists of Montenegro), which secured 83 seats in the new legislature, while its presidential candidate, Momir Bulatović, became President. In February 1991 Bulatović invited Milo Đukanović, also of the DPS, to head the republican Government, while Svetozar Marović became the Speaker of the Assembly.

The onset of armed conflict in Yugoslavia prompted Montenegro to adopt a pragmatic response to the disintegration of the Socialist Federal Republic of Yugoslavia. Although Montenegro adopted a declaration of state sovereignty on 18 October 1991 and a new Constitution in November, its continued commitment to the federation with Serbia was confirmed in a referendum in March 1992. The two republics announced a new federal Constitution, creating the Federal Republic of Yugoslavia (FRY), which came into effect on 27 April. A new Montenegrin Constitution was introduced on 12 October and in early 1993 Bulatović was re-elected Montenegrin President, while Đukanović remained premier. Meanwhile, another Montenegrin, Radoje Kontić, became the Yugoslav Prime Minister.

Relations between Montenegro and Serbia deteriorated from the mid-1990s, particularly in response to the attempts of Serbian leader Slobodan Milošević to disassemble Montenegro's separate defence and foreign policy structures. However, the principal division in Montenegrin politics was between the republican presidency and premiership. Đukanović, in early 1997, publicly declared Milošević unfit to hold public office,

and resisted the demands of Bulatović that he dismiss all anti-Milošević ministers in the Montenegrin Government. The ruling DPS (which again won the Montenegrin legislative elections in November 1996) subsequently split into two factions, as a result of Bulatović's support for Milošević (who became the Yugoslav President in July 1997). Bulatović and Đukanović, who by then led separate factions within the DPS, became the leading candidates in the Montenegrin presidential election of October. Đukanović won the second round of voting, with 50.8% of the votes cast.

Đukanović was inaugurated as the President of Montenegro in January 1998, amid violent protests from supporters of Bulatović. A compromise agreement on early legislative elections in May was reached, pending which a transitional Government, led by the Đukanović faction of the DPS, was formed in February. Bulatović's faction refused to participate and renamed itself the Socijalistička Narodna Partija Crne Gore (SNP—Socialist People's Party of Montenegro). In the elections, held in May, the DPS won an outright majority, and a coalition Government, led by Filip Vujanović, was formed in July. Bulatović, who was appointed as Yugoslav Prime Minister in May, proceeded to purge many Montenegrin officials from federal institutions. Montenegro refused to acknowledge the administration of Bulatović, and suspended all links with his Government in August.

Relations with Serbia continued to deteriorate during 1999. Continued military action by Serbian forces against the ethnic Albanian population in the Serbian province of Kosovo led to the aerial bombardment of Yugoslavia by forces of the North Atlantic Treaty Organization (NATO, see p. 367) in March–June, during which Montenegro suffered damage. Montenegro refused to recognize the state of war declared by the Yugoslav Government in March, and Đukanović subsequently refused to place Montenegrin security forces under federal military command, as ordered by President Milošević.

In the aftermath of the conflict in Kosovo, the Yugoslav federation became increasingly unstable. The Government of Montenegro proposed the replacement of the federal system with an association of two states, threatening a referendum on full independence if Milošević did not agree, and in October 1999 the Assembly enacted a citizenship law. Attempting to separate itself from the isolated Serbian economy, in November Montenegro replaced the depreciating Yugoslav dinar with the German Deutsche Mark as its official currency (the federal Constitutional Court declared the measure illegal in January 2000, to little effect). Serbia responded by imposing a full economic embargo against Montenegro in March. Fears of Serbian military action (demonstrated by the federal army's seizure of control over Montenegro's main airport in December 1999) further escalated tensions.

Following elections in September 2000, Milošević was ousted as Yugoslav President in October, and Bulatović subsequently resigned as premier. Đukanović began to advocate full independence for Montenegro, urging a referendum on the issue. At the ensuing legislative elections, held on 22 April 2001, the DPS-led coalition won 36 of the 77 seats, the SNP-led alliance 33 and the pro-independence Liberalni Savez Crne Gore (LSCG—Liberal Alliance of Montenegro) six. Vujanović was reappointed as premier. Meanwhile, negotiations about a new form of association with Serbia were ongoing, which, from November, were mediated by the European Union (EU, see p. 271). The federal Yugoslav leadership and that of both republics signed a framework agreement on confederation on 14 March 2002, providing for a shared presidency and legislature, which would be responsible for foreign and defence policies, and for separate republican economic and other state structures. Crucially, Montenegro had the right to schedule a referendum on independence after three years. Later in March the LSCG resigned from the Government in protest at the agreement. The Assembly approved the accord on 9 April; however, unable to form a new coalition administration, Vujanović dissolved the legislature in July and scheduled further elections.

On 20 October 2002 the DPS-led, pro-independence ruling coalition, the Demokratska Lista za Evropsku Crnu Goru

(Democratic List for a European Montenegro), won 39 of the 75 seats in the republican legislature. Zajedno za Promjene (Together for Changes), which had opposed a looser union with Serbia and was led by the SNP (under a new leadership), retained 30 seats. Vujanović was elected Speaker of the Assembly on 5 November, and became acting President of Montenegro 20 days later, when Đukanović resigned from that post. A dispute over the allocation of ministerial portfolios with the DPS's ally, the Socijaldemokratska Partija Crne Gore (SDP—Social Democratic Party of Montenegro), delayed the formalization of a governing coalition, and the Assembly approved the new Government, headed by Đukanović as Prime Minister, on 8 January 2003. Meanwhile, both the SNP and the LSCG boycotted the presidential election, held on 22 December 2002, which was consequently won by Vujanović, with 83.7% of the votes cast, but with those votes amounting to less than the one-half of the total electorate legally required to validate the result. Vujanović won 82.0% of votes in the repeated poll held on 9 February 2003, but this poll, too, was declared invalid, as only 47% of the electorate voted, prompting the Assembly to abolish the regulation on minimum participation. Vujanović was duly elected President on 11 May, with 62.9% of the votes cast (and about 48% of the electorate participating). Following his election, Vujanović pledged to schedule a referendum on independence for Montenegro after a period of three years.

Domestic Political Affairs

Meanwhile, on 29 January 2003 the Montenegrin Assembly approved the new arrangements for confederation with Serbia. On 4 February the Federal Assembly formally adopted a Constitutional Charter, thereby transforming Yugoslavia into the State Union of Serbia and Montenegro. A new Assembly, President (former Montenegrin parliamentary Speaker and DPS leader Marović) and Prime Minister of the State Union were elected in late February and March. In July the Assembly adopted a new Montenegrin flag and anthem.

After it was agreed that the EU should set the conditions for and supervise the conduct of any referendum on Montenegrin independence, in February 2006, amid much controversy, the EU announced that a proposal of Montenegrin independence would require the approval of 55% of those voting (with a minimum rate of participation of 50% of the registered electorate), in order to secure international recognition. Legislation providing for a referendum to be held on 21 May was duly enacted on 1 March. In April the Government formally presented to the Serbian Government a guarantee of equal status for Serbian citizens within Montenegro in the event of independence.

After independence

Two days after the referendum of 21 May 2006, the electoral authorities declared Montenegro to have voted in favour of independence. With a participation rate of over 86%, some 55.5% of the votes cast at the referendum were in favour of independence, thereby narrowly fulfilling the EU criteria. The Assembly duly declared Montenegro independent on 3 June. Serbia, which declared itself to be the successor state to the State Union of Serbia and Montenegro on 5 June, officially recognized Montenegro's independence in mid-June and established diplomatic relations one week later. Montenegro was admitted to the Organization for Security and Co-operation in Europe (see p. 385) on 22 June and to the UN on 28 June. A new Ministry of Defence formally assumed responsibility for all military units of the State Union on Montenegrin territory, while in July agreement was reached on the division of the financial rights and obligations of the former State Union (of which Montenegro was to receive 5.9% of the convertible currency and gold reserves).

The ruling coalition of the DPS and the SDP won outright legislative elections held on 10 September 2006, securing 41 of the 81 seats in an expanded Assembly. The SNP-led alliance only obtained 11 seats (eight for the SNP itself), being displaced as the largest opposition grouping by the Serbian List, led by Andrija Mandić of the Srpska Narodna Stranka Crne Gore (SNS—Serb People's Party of Montenegro), which took 12 seats. A new, pro-European party, the Pokret za Promjene (PzP—Movement for Changes), also obtained 11 seats. The Liberalna Partija Crne Gore (Liberal Party of Montenegro—the successor organization to the LSCG), in alliance with the Bošnjačka Stranka (Bosniak Party), secured three seats. In October 2006 Đukanović announced that he would not seek to continue his premiership, as he wished to develop his business interests. (He had been accused of involvement with organized crime, and was under investigation by the Italian authorities, mainly in connection with large-scale illicit tobacco trade in the Balkans.) The appointment of a new Government, headed by the hitherto Minister of Justice, Željko Šturanović, was approved by the Assembly on 10 November.

After acrimonious debate, a new Constitution was approved by 55 of the 76 deputies present in the Assembly on 19 October 2007, narrowly achieving the requisite two-thirds' majority of the vote; the Constitution was officially promulgated on 22 October. While the new Constitution met EU standards, it was denounced by Serb parties in Montenegro, which particularly objected to the description of the main official language as Montenegrin.

On 31 January 2008 Šturanović resigned as Prime Minister, on grounds of ill health. On 29 February the appointment of Đukanović as premier and of his Government (which remained unchanged from the previous administration) was narrowly approved, with 41 votes cast, in the Assembly. (Although the Italian investigation into organized crime allegations continued, Đukanović's immunity from prosecution was restored by his return to office.)

Vujanović was re-elected to the presidency on 6 April 2008, with 51.9% of the votes cast, thereby further consolidating the strength of the DPS. Mandić was placed second, with 19.6% of the vote, while the reformist leader of the PzP, Nebojša Medojević, was third, with 16.7%. The rate of voter participation was estimated at about 69%. Vujanović was inaugurated for a second term on 21 May.

In January 2009 the governing coalition submitted a proposal to the Assembly that legislative elections, due to take place in 2010, be brought forward to that March in order to provide the administration with a stronger mandate to fulfil Montenegro's commitments in the EU integration process. On 26 January the Assembly voted in favour of its dissolution to allow early elections, which were duly scheduled for 29 March. Later in January Mandić merged his SNS with the People's Socialist Party to form a new party, Nova Srpska Demokratija (NOVA—New Serbian Democracy).

At the elections to the Assembly on 29 March 2009, Đukanović's Koalicija za Evropsku Crnu Goru (Coalition for a European Montenegro) secured a decisive victory, with 51.9% of the votes cast and 48 seats in the chamber, while the SNP won 16.8% of the vote and 16 seats, NOVA 9.2% of the vote and eight seats, and the PzP 6.0% of the votes and five seats. A participation rate of 66.2% was recorded. The EU praised the democratic organization of the poll, but urged the Government to reform electoral legislation. Following endorsement of Đukanović's premiership, a new Government was approved in the Assembly in early June; the six new ministers included Marović as a Deputy Prime Minister. At local elections on 23 May 2010, the DPS won a majority in seven of the contested 14 municipal councils, and formed a coalition in five others, including in Podgorica.

In October 2010 the mandate of the Governor of the Central Bank, Ljubiša Krgović, was ended, after he criticized the provision of state assistance for the loss-making Prva Banka, in which the brother of Prime Minister Đukanović held a majority share; the Assembly approved Vujanović's nomination of Radoje Žugić (hitherto Director of the Pension and Disability Insurance Fund) to replace Krgović. On 21 December Đukanović tendered his resignation as premier (but was to remain DPS Chairman); Deputy Prime Minister and Minister of Finance Igor Lukšić was nominated by the DPS as his successor. On the same day Marović also resigned his government post, following the initiation of an investigation into the illegal construction of a tourist complex in Budva. Later in December the Mayor of Budva municipality, Rajko Kuljaca, his deputy Dragan Marović (the brother of former Svetozar Marović) and eight other officials were arrested and subsequently charged with abuse of office in connection with the investigation. (In June 2012 Kuljaca and the nine other defendants were sentenced to five years' imprisonment.) On 29 December 2010 the Assembly endorsed the nomination of Lukšić and the establishment of a new Government (comprising the same coalition parties as previously) under his premiership. Milorad Katnić replaced Lukšić as Minister of Finance in the new administration. In September 2011, following protracted negotiations between Lukšić and opposition leaders, the Assembly adopted a new electoral law and amendments to education legislation providing for equality between the Serbian and Montenegrin languages (both of which had been previously considered to be broadly similar dialects of the Serbo-Croat language, or of Serbian) in schools, in accordance with EU criteria for the opening of accession negotiations. In March

2012 an assault against a journalist, Olivera Lakić, working for the daily newspaper *Vijesti*, who had previously been threatened after reporting on the illegal labelling of tobacco products, was condemned by the OSCE, amid increased concerns over media freedom in Montenegro. In July Lakić's assailant was sentenced to nine months' imprisonment.

At the elections to the Assembly held on 14 October 2012, the Koalicija za Evropsku Crnu Goru, again led by Đukanović, secured the most substantial representation, with 46.3% of the votes cast and 39 seats (this none the less representing a loss of support compared with the 2009 elections). An alliance formed by the PzP and NOVA, the Demokratski Front (DF—Democratic Front), obtained 23.2% of the vote and 20 seats, the SNP 11.2% and nine seats, and Pozitivna Crna Gora (PCG—Positive Montenegro) 8.4% and seven seats. A participation rate of 70.6% was recorded, and OSCE observers endorsed the conduct of the elections. Local elections were held in the municipalities of Budva, Nikšić and Kotor, which resulted in an opposition coalition securing control of the Nikšić municipal council. In early November Đukanović negotiated an agreement with the minority parties represented in the Assembly that enabled him to command a parliamentary majority, and was designated Prime Minister by Vujanović. On 4 December the Assembly approved Đukanović's return to the premiership and the formation of his coalition Government; the new administration included four Deputy Prime Ministers, among them Lukšić, who also received the foreign affairs and European integration portfolio.

Recent developments: the 2013 presidential election

In January 2013 a presidential election was officially scheduled for 7 April; Vujanović declared his intention to seek a further term in office, although the SDP opposed his candidacy on the grounds that he had already served two terms (including during the period prior to independence). Following the failure of the opposition parties in Nikšić to agree on the formation of a municipal administration, a poll was repeated there on 7 March, which was won by the DPS. Meanwhile, the leader of the DF, Miodrag Lekić, was registered as the consensus opposition candidate in the forthcoming presidential election.

Vujanović and Lekić both claimed victory shortly after the presidential election was conducted on 7 April 2013. According to the official results that were subsequently released, Vujanović was narrowly re-elected, with 51.2% of the votes cast. Although the Election Commission rejected all complaints of irregularities submitted by Lekić, the DF continued to accuse the authorities of malpractice. Vujanović was inaugurated for a further term of office on 20 May.

In August 2013 critics of Đukanović launched an online campaign demanding his arrest, accusing him of human rights violations and corruption. Later that month the authorities announced an investigation into allegations by a former police officer of the existence of a clandestine police unit that intimidated and harassed public opponents of Đukanović. In October a 'gay pride' rally in Podgorica was disrupted by counter-demonstrators who clashed with police, resulting in some 60 people being injured. (Violence had occurred in response to a similar but smaller rally in Budva in July.) In November a prominent Montenegrin activist on lesbian, gay, bisexual, and transgender concerns was granted political asylum in Canada, on the grounds that the Montenegrin authorities had failed to protect him from repeated assaults and death threats. Attacks on independent journalists continued, meanwhile, and in January 2014 the owners of *Vijesti* appealed to Đukanović to end an alleged campaign against the newspaper, following a bomb attack against its offices the previous month. Also in January the SDP (while remaining in the government coalition) signed an agreement with the opposition PCG to co-operate in local government elections. In February the DF alliance announced a parliamentary boycott, citing the Government's failure to adopt electoral reforms. At partial local elections on 25 May, the DPS received the highest number of votes in 11 of 12 contested municipalities, but only secured majorities in three, necessitating the formation of coalitions in the others. (In early 2015 the establishment of an administration in the Podgorica municipality remained under discussion.)

In February 2015 the Assembly approved legislation under which state intelligence officers with official identification cards would be permitted to access all databases in Montenegro, subject to the approval of the President of the Supreme Court. Human rights groups criticized the new lack of restriction on state surveillance. Prime Minister Đukanović reorganized the Government on 18 March. Among the new appointees was Zoran Pažin, previously Montenegro's representative at the European Court of Human Rights, as the Minister of Justice. In response to concerns at Islamist extremists travelling to the Middle East (notably Syria), on the same day the Assembly adopted legislation introducing penalties of up to 10 years' imprisonment for participation in foreign conflicts.

Foreign Affairs

Regional relations

In March 2008 Prime Minister Đukanović and his Croatian counterpart, meeting in Zagreb, Croatia, declared that the demarcation of the maritime boundary between the two countries around the Prevlaka peninsula (which was regulated by a 2002 interim agreement) would be referred to the International Court of Justice (see p. 25) at The Hague, Netherlands. In October 2008 Montenegro announced official recognition of Kosovo as a sovereign state, following its declaration of independence on 17 February; the decision prompted Serbia to expel the Montenegrin ambassador, while pro-Serbian opposition parties protested in Podgorica to demand the organization of a referendum on the matter. In May 2009 President Vujanović visited the Serbian capital, Belgrade, in an effort to improve bilateral relations; Serbian President Boris Tadić made a reciprocal visit to Montenegro in June. In October Serbia finally accepted the Montenegrin Government's nomination of a new ambassador. In December 2011 the Governments of Montenegro, Albania and the former Yugoslav republic of Macedonia (FYRM) signed an agreement providing for the abolition of border controls for citizens of their respective states. In January 2013 the Serbian President, Tomislav Nikolić, made an official visit to Montenegro. The authorities of Montenegro and Serbia in early 2015 announced further strengthening of co-operation in the areas of criminal investigation, emergency responses and border security.

A dispute erupted with Bosnia and Herzegovina, following the completion of a border demarcation process under an agreement endorsed by the two Governments in November 2014. A resolution was proposed by an opposition deputy in the Bosnian state legislature in January 2015 to demand that the Montenegrin coastal area of Sutorina be ceded to Bosnia and Herzegovina, while a group of Bosnian NGOs also began an initiative to seek international arbitration on the issue. President Vujanović refused to appoint a new ambassador to the Bosnian capital, Sarajevo, in January, as a result of the unresolved dispute.

Other external relations

Following independence in June 2006, Montenegro's admission to international organizations proceeded rapidly. Montenegro was admitted to NATO's 'Partnership for Peace' (see p. 371) programme in December, and officially became a member of the World Bank in the following month, also joining the IMF and the other associated institutions. Montenegro initialled a Stabilization and Association Agreement (SAA) with the EU in March 2007. In May Montenegro was admitted to the Council of Europe (see p. 250). The adoption of a new Constitution that was deemed to be in accordance with EU standards (see *After independence*) allowed the official signature of the SAA at a meeting of EU foreign ministers in October.

At a NATO summit meeting, held in Bucharest, Romania, in April 2008, Montenegro was invited to enter into an intensified dialogue towards membership. (According to a subsequent opinion poll, however, only around one-quarter of Montenegrins supported NATO membership for the country.) In April 2009 the EU Council of Ministers approved consideration of Montenegro's EU membership application (which was officially submitted on 15 December 2008). At the end of November 2009 it was announced that Montenegro had met EU requirements for the abolition of visa requirements, with effect from late December. Also in December Montenegro was granted a NATO Membership Action Plan. The SAA with the EU entered into effect on 1 May 2010, and on 17 December the European Council granted Montenegro EU candidate status. In October 2011 the European Commission recommended that accession negotiations be opened with Montenegro. On 29 April 2012 Montenegro became a full member of the World Trade Organization (WTO, see p. 431). Following approval by EU foreign ministers, accession negotiations with Montenegro were officially opened on 29 June. In January 2014 a draft resolution adopted by the European Parliament on Montenegro's progress towards EU candidacy urged further government efforts in combating corruption and organized crime, and in strengthening the rule of law and the independence of the judiciary. On 25 June the Secretary-General of NATO, Andres Fogh Rasmussen, confirmed that Montenegro would not be invited to join the Alliance in September 2014, but that the country's application would be reconsidered in 2015; reform of the security sector was considered a main condition for membership. A European Parliament resolution adopted in February commended Montenegro's progress in the integration process, while urging, in addition to continued reforms, the resolution of all remaining border disputes with neighbouring states.

CONSTITUTION AND GOVERNMENT

Montenegro became independent of the former State Union of Serbia and Montenegro on 3 June 2006, following a national referendum held on 21 May. The Constitution of Montenegro was adopted by the legislature on 19 October 2007 and was officially promulgated on 22 October. Legislative power is vested in the 81-member Skupština Crne Gore (Assembly of Montenegro), which is directly elected for a period of four years. Executive power is vested in the Government and judicial power in the courts of law. The President is directly elected for a term of five years, and is restricted to two terms in office. Constitutionality and legality are protected by the Constitutional Court. The President nominates the Prime Minister for approval by the Assembly. The Prime Minister proposes the composition of the Government to the Assembly. The Supreme Court is the highest court in Montenegro. For administrative purposes, Montenegro is divided into 21 municipalities.

REGIONAL AND INTERNATIONAL CO-OPERATION

Montenegro is a member of the Organization for Security and Co-operation in Europe (OSCE, see p. 385), the Council of Europe (see p. 250), and the Central European Free Trade Agreement (CEFTA, see p. 445).

Montenegro joined the UN on 28 June 2006.

ECONOMIC AFFAIRS

In 2013, according to estimates by the World Bank, Montenegro's gross national income (GNI), measured at average 2011–13 prices, was US $4,514m., equivalent to $7,260 per head (or $14,600 per head on an international purchasing-power parity basis). During 2004–13, it was estimated, the population increased at an average annual rate of 0.1%, while gross domestic product (GDP) per head increased, in real terms, by an average annual rate of 3.3%. Overall GDP increased, in real terms, at an average annual rate of 3.4% in 2004–13; real GDP decreased by 2.5% in 2012, but increased by 3.5% in 2013.

Agriculture (including hunting, forestry and fishing) contributed 9.8% of GDP and engaged 1.6% of the employed labour force in 2013. The principal crops are potatoes, maize and wheat. The cultivation of fruit (particularly grapes, plums, oranges and tangerines) and vegetables is also important. According to the World Bank, agricultural output increased by an annual average of 3.0% during 2004–13; output decreased by 16.5% in 2012, but increased by 18.5% in 2013.

Industry (including mining, manufacturing, construction and power) contributed 18.8% of GDP and engaged 18.1% of the employed labour force in 2013. According to the World Bank, industrial production increased by an average annual rate of 3.7% during 2004–12; sectoral output decreased by 29.8% in 2012, but increased by 24.6% in 2013.

The mining and quarrying sector contributed 1.3% of GDP and engaged 1.1% of the employed labour force in 2013. The principal minerals extracted are lignite, red bauxite and sea salt. Production in the sector declined by an annual average rate of 2.0% during 2002–06. Output increased by 1.5% in 2011, but decreased by 7.7% in 2012.

The manufacturing sector contributed 5.0% of GDP and engaged 7.5% of the employed labour force in 2013. Production in the sector decreased by an annual average rate of 1.6% during 2004–13, according to the World Bank; output decreased by 18.2% in 2012, but increased by 21.1% in 2013.

The construction sector contributed 5.0% of GDP and engaged 4.9% of the employed labour force in 2013. The real GDP of the sector increased by 15.8% in 2011, but decreased by 11.9% in 2012.

Energy in Montenegro is derived principally from hydroelectric power (which provided about 51.9% of total electricity generated in 2012) and thermoelectric power (48.1%). Imports of mineral fuels accounted for 13.3% of the value of total imports in 2014.

Services contributed 71.4% of GDP and engaged 80.3% of the employed labour force in 2013. According to the World Bank, services GDP increased by an average annual rate of 3.3% during 2004–13; the sector grew by 13.9% in 2012, but declined by 2.8% in 2013.

In 2013 Montenegro recorded a merchandise trade deficit of €994.4m., and there was a deficit of €231.7m. on the current account of the balance of payments. In 2014 the principal source of imports was Serbia (accounting for 26.9% of imports); other major sources were Greece, the People's Republic of China, Bosnia and Herzegovina, Italy, Germany and Croatia. Serbia was also the principal market for exports in that year (taking 23.7% of the total); other important purchasers were Italy, Croatia, and Bosnia and Herzegovina. The principal imports in 2014 were food and live animals, machinery and transport equipment, basic manufactures, miscellaneous manufactured articles, mineral fuels and lubricants, and chemical products. The main exports in that year were basic manufactures, crude materials except fuels, food and live animals, mineral fuels and lubricants, beverages and tobacco, and machinery and transport equipment.

In 2013 the overall budgetary deficit was projected at €18.2m., equivalent to 0.5% of GDP. Montenegro's general government gross debt was €1,935m. in 2013, equivalent to 58.0% of GDP. The total external debt of the country was US $2,833m. in 2012, of which $2,161m. was public and publicly guaranteed debt. In that year, the cost of servicing long-term public and publicly guaranteed debt and repayments to the IMF was equivalent to 13.6% of the value of exports of goods, services and income (excluding workers' remittances). Consumer prices decreased by 1.1% in 2014. The rate of unemployment was 15.8% in 2013.

In November 2006 the EU issued a progress report on Montenegro's first months of independence, which emphasized the need for economic reform to combat a continuing over-reliance on certain sectors of the economy, high unemployment and regulatory obstacles. Agreements on bilateral economic relations were signed with neighbouring and other European countries. High levels of growth followed, based largely on capital growth and massive inflows of foreign direct investment, particularly in the tourism, banking and construction sectors, and a reduction in the rate of unemployment. In October 2007 Montenegro signed a Stabilization and Association Agreement (SAA) with the EU, which entered into effect in May 2010. On 29 April 2012 Montenegro officially joined the World Trade Organization. In accordance with the recommendation of the European Commission, accession negotiations with the EU were opened in June. Meanwhile, a sharp fall in aluminum production in that year, which hampered growth, was attributed to the financial difficulties of the country's principal aluminium company, Kombinat Aluminijuma Podgorica (KAP), in which the state had acquired a stake. In June 2014 the Government finally sold KAP (which had become bankrupt) to a local metal company for €28m., and by late that year operations at the plant had begun to recover and aluminium production to increase. Fiscal adjustment measures undertaken by the authorities during 2013–14 included a freeze in pensions and an increase in the value-added tax rate. However, growth fell in 2014, to an estimated 1.5%, amid a weakening in external demand. A number of enterprises, including the national air carrier, a leading medical institution, and two military companies, were designated for privatization under a draft plan for 2015 presented by the Government in January. The Government also adopted a decree on fostering foreign and domestic investment. In a report issued in February, the IMF urged further reforms of the pension system and cuts in public sector wages, in addition to continued efforts to reduce support to state-owned entities. A resolution adopted by the European Parliament in early 2015 commended Montenegro's progress towards EU candidacy, while also urging further efforts in addressing corruption and implementing other political reforms.

PUBLIC HOLIDAYS

2016: 1–2 January (New Year), 7–8 January (Orthodox Christmas), 29 April–2 May (Orthodox Easter), 1–2 May (Labour Day), 21 May (Independence Day), 13 July (National Day).

Statistical Survey

Source: Statistical Office of Montenegro, 81000 Podgorica, IV Proleterske 2; tel. (20) 241206; fax (20) 241270; e-mail statistika@cg.yu; internet www.monstat.org.

AREA AND POPULATION

Area: 13,812 sq km (5,333 sq miles). *By Municipality* (sq km): Andrijevica 283; Bar 598; Berane 717; Bijelo Polje 924; Budva 122; Cetinje 910; Danilovgrad 501; Herceg Novi 235; Kolašin 897; Kotor 335; Mojkovac 367; Nikšić 2,065; Plav 486; Pljevlja 1,346; Plužine 854; Podgorica 1,441; Rožaje 432; Šavnik 553; Tivat 46; Ulcinj 255; Žabljak 445.

Population: 620,145 at census of 31 October 2003; 620,029 at census of 1 April 2011. *2013* (official estimate at mid-year): 621,207.

Density (at mid-2013): 45.0 per sq km.

Population by Age and Sex (population at 2011 census): *0–14 years:* 118,751 (males 61,766, females 56,985); *15–64 years:* 421,693 (males 210,713, females 210,980); *65 years and over:* 79,585 (males 33,757, females 45,828); *Total* 620,029 (males 306,236, females 313,793).

Population by Municipality (population estimates at mid-2013): Andrijevica 5,019; Bar 42,815; Berane 33,353; Bijelo Polje 45,313; Budva 19,451; Cetinje 16,381; Danilovgrad 18,488; Herceg Novi 30,823; Kolašin 8,061; Kotor 22,627; Mojkovac 8,386; Nikšić 71,843; Plav 12,874; Pljevlja 29,900; Plužine 3,040; Podgorica 190,176; Rožaje 23,083; Šavnik 1,924; Tivat 14,185; Ulcinj 20,019; Žabljak 3,446; *Total* 621,207.

Population by Ethnic Group (self-declaration at 2011 census): Montenegrin 278,865; Serb 178,110; Bosniak 53,605; Albanian 30,439; Muslim 20,537; Croat 6,021. Note: Classification of ethnic groups reflects national census methodology.

Principal Towns (population at 2011 census): Podgorica 150,977; Nikšić 56,970; Pljevlja 19,136; Cetinje 13,918; Bar 13,503; Budva 13,338; Bijelo Polje 12,900; Berane 11,073; Herceg Novi 11,059; Ulcinj 10,707.

Births, Marriages and Deaths (2013): Live births 7,475 (birth rate 12.0 per 1,000); Marriages 3,847 (marriage rate 6.2 per 1,000); Deaths 5,917 (death rate 9.5 per 1,000).

Life Expectancy (years at birth): 74.6 (males 72.4; females 77.0) in 2012 (Source: World Bank, World Development Indicators database).

Economically Active Population (persons aged 15 years and over, annual averages, 2013): Agriculture, hunting, forestry and fishing 2,771; Mining and quarrying 1,874; Manufacturing 12,879; Electricity, gas and water supply 7,804; Construction 8,463; Wholesale and retail trade, repair of motor vehicles, motorcycles, and personal and household goods 37,456; Hotels and restaurants 14,333; Transport, storage and communications 14,822; Financial intermediation 4,467; Real estate, renting and business activities 13,565; Public administration and defence, and compulsory social security 20,541; Education 13,250; Health and social work 11,001; Other community, social and personal service activities 8,248; *Total employed* 171,474; Unemployed 32,190; *Total labour force* 203,664.

HEALTH AND WELFARE
Key Indicators

Total Fertility Rate (children per woman, 2012): 1.7.

Under-5 Mortality Rate (per 1,000 live births, 2012): 6.

Physicians (per 1,000 head, 2011): 2.0.

Hospital Beds (per 1,000 head, 2009): 3.9.

Health Expenditure (2010): US $ per head (PPP): 1,154.

Health Expenditure (2011): % of GDP: 7.2.

Health Expenditure (2011): public (% of total): 58.2.

Access to Water (% of persons, 2012): 98.

Access to Sanitation (% of persons, 2012): 90.

Human Development Index (2013): ranking: 51.

Human Development Index (2013): value: 0.789.

For sources and definitions, see explanatory note on p. vi.

AGRICULTURE, ETC.

Principal Crops (metric tons, 2013, FAO estimates): Wheat 2,300; Maize 9,000; Barley 1,650; Potatoes 135,000; Tobacco 230; Plums 9,000; Olives 2,900; Oranges and tangerines 9,100; Grapes 40,000; Melons (incl. watermelons) n.a. Source: FAO.

Livestock ('000 head, 2013, FAO estimates): Cattle 84.0; Horses 4.0; Pigs 18.0; Sheep 207.0; Poultry 700. Source: FAO.

Livestock Products (metric tons, 2013): Cattle meat 4,600 (FAO estimate); Pig meat 4,000 (FAO estimate); Sheep meat 1,034; Cows' milk ('000 metric tons) 174; Eggs 4,490 (unofficial figure). Source: FAO.

Forestry ('000 cu m, 2013, unless otherwise indicated): *Timber removals:* 481.0 (broadleaved 197.0, coniferous 284.0); *Assortments* (2010 figures): 480.4 (broadleaved 224.8, coniferous 255.6).

Fishing (metric tons, 2013): Total catch 1,579 (marine 741, freshwater 838).

MINING

Selected Products ('000 metric tons, 2013): Lignite 1,692.5; Red bauxite 61.2; Sea salt 10.0.

INDUSTRY

Selected Products ('000 metric tons, 2013, unless otherwise indicated): Wheat flour 96.7; Wines ('000 hl) 93.0; Beer ('000 hl) 400.7; Spruce and fir lumber ('000 cu m) 37.3; Oxygen, nitrogen and acetylene 0.3; Cut marble panels ('000 sq m) 49.3; Steel ingots 19.7; Steel castings 8.0 (2012); Aluminium oxide 58.5 (2009); Aluminium ingots 48.0; Electric energy (kWh) 3,945.0m.

FINANCE

Currency and Exchange Rates: 100 cent = 1 euro (€). *Sterling and Dollar Equivalents* (31 December 2014): £1 sterling = 1.286 euros; US $1 = 0.824 euros; €10 = £7.78 = $12.14. *Average Exchange Rate* (euros per US dollar): 0.7783 in 2012; 0.7532 in 2013; 0.7537 in 2014.

Budget (€ million, 2013, projections): *Revenue:* Total current revenues 1,235.2 (Taxes 755.7, Contributions 398.5, Duties 27.1, Reimbursements 13.2, Other current revenues 33.1, Loan repayments 7.6); Property disbursements 12.0; Grants and loans 340.0; Total revenue 1,587.1. *Expenditure:* Gross wages and salaries 366.1; Other personal income and fringe benefits 12.0; Expenditure for materials and services 90.4; Maintenance 20.4; Interest rates 67.4; Rent 7.9; Subsidies 17.4; Other current expenditure 6.3; Transfers to individuals and institutions 94.3; Social protection transfers 483.0; Capital expenses 74.0; Total loans and loan repayments 2.8; Total reserves 14.1; Payment of debt to residents 112.7; Payment of debt to non-residents 68.8; Payment of liabilities from previous period 60.3; Payment of guarantees 107.2; Total expenditure 1,605.3. Source: Central Bank of Montenegro.

International Reserves (US $ million at 31 December 2013, excl. gold): IMF special drawing rights 40.56; Reserve position in IMF 10.17; Foreign exchange 533.25; *Total* 583.98. Source: IMF, *International Financial Statistics*.

Money Supply (€ million at 31 December 2013): Demand deposits at banking institutions 696.0. Source: IMF, *International Financial Statistics*.

Cost of Living (Consumer Price Index; base: 2013 = 100): All items 94.0 in 2011; 97.8 in 2012, 98.9 in 2014.

Expenditure on the Gross Domestic Product (€ million at current prices, 2013): Government final consumption expenditure 660.2; Private final consumption expenditure 2,712.0; Gross fixed capital formation 638.7; Changes in inventories –8.4; *Total domestic expenditure* 4,002.5; Exports of goods and services 1,390.1; *Less* Imports of goods and services 2,065.5; *GDP in purchasers' values* 3,327.1.

Gross Domestic Product by Economic Activity (€ million at current prices, 2013): Agriculture, hunting, forestry and fishing 266.9; Mining and quarrying 36.1; Manufacturing 137.0; Electricity, gas and water supply 203.9; Construction 136.3; Wholesale and retail trade, repair of motor vehicles, motorcycles, and personal and household goods 388.4; Hotels and restaurants 217.7; Transport, storage and communications 274.1; Financial intermediation 138.4; Real estate, renting and business activities 341.5; Public administration and defence, and compulsory social security 246.5; Education 138.8; Health and social work 128.9; Other community, social and personal service activities 69.4; *Sub-total* 2,723.8; Taxes, less subsidies, on products 603.3; *GDP in purchasers' values* 3,327.1.

Balance of Payments (€ million, 2013): Exports of goods 305.4; Imports of goods –1,299.7; *Trade balance* –994.4; Exports of services 934.5; Imports of services –309.0; *Balance on goods and services*

–368.9; Other income received 158.3; Other income paid –116.0; *Balance on goods, services and income* –326.6; Current transfers received 133.4; Current transfers paid –38.6; *Current balance* –231.7; Capital account (net) 0.5; Direct investments (net) 275.6; Portfolio investments (net) –26.3; Other investments (net) –185.9; Net errors and omissions 188.9; *Overall balance* 21.0. Source: Central Bank of Montenegro.

EXTERNAL TRADE

Principal Commodities (€ million, 2014): *Imports:* Food and live animals 397.7 (Meat and meat preparations 122.5; Cereals 55.6); Beverages and tobacco 63.3; Mineral fuels, lubricants, etc. 236.5 (Petroleum and petroleum products 185.2); Chemical products 181.1 (Medicinal and pharmaceutical products 58.9); Basic manufactures 270.4 (Non-metallic mineral manufactures 75.5; Metal manufactures 61.3); Machinery and transport equipment 338.9 (Electrical equipment 68.8; Road vehicles 97.7); Miscellaneous manufactured articles 239.4 (Articles of apparel and clothing accessories 55.8); Total (incl. others) 1,783.7. *Exports:* Food and live animals 61.8; Beverages and tobacco 41.6 (Beverages 19.5); Crude materials (except fuels) 63.7 (Cork and wood 22.7; Metalliferous ores and metal scrap 33.2); Mineral fuels, lubricants, etc. 51.3; Basic manufactures 82.8 (Iron and steel 4.5; Non-ferrous metals 71.8); Machinery and transport equipment 22.8; Total (incl. others) 338.0.

Principal Trading Partners (€ million, 2014): *Imports:* Albania 32.6; Austria 32.4; Bosnia and Herzegovina 126.7; China, People's Republic 132.7; Croatia 107.6; France 28.3; Germany 114.6; Greece 144.5; Hungary 20.7; Italy 116.0; Macedonia, FYR 26.0; Netherlands 59.6; Poland 16.7; Romania 23.8; Serbia 480.4; Slovenia 56.7; Spain 34.3; Turkey 36.4; Total (incl. others) 1,783.7. *Exports:* Albania 15.2; Austria 1.3; Bosnia and Herzegovina 31.8; Croatia 33.1; Czech Republic 3.1; Germany 5.9; Italy 34.8; Poland 7.6; Russia 4.0; Serbia 80.0; Slovenia 13.3; Turkey 5.8; Total (incl. others) 338.0.

TRANSPORT

Road Transport (2013): 178,662 passenger cars in use.

Railways (traffic, 2013): Passengers carried ('000) 922; Passenger-km ('000) 73,439; Freight carried ('000 metric tons) 1,049; Total ton-km ('000) 104,731.

Shipping: *Flag Registered Fleet* (at 31 December 2014): Vessels 8; Total displacement 96,335 grt (Source: Lloyd's List Intelligence—www.lloydslistintelligence.com). *Freight Traffic* ('000 metric tons, 2013): Goods loaded 597.7; Goods unloaded 669.4.

Civil Aviation (2013): Passenger movements 1,549,277; Freight carried 768 metric tons.

TOURISM

Total Foreign Tourist Arrivals: 1,201,099 in 2011; 1,264,163 in 2012; 1,324,403 in 2013.

Overnight Stays by Nationality (foreign tourists, 2013): Albania 104,310; Bosnia and Herzegovina 631,588; Croatia 102,040; Czech Republic 177,406; France 186,653; Germany 190,827; Italy 124,663; Macedonia, FYR 179,527; Poland 227,413; Russia 2,367,000; Serbia 2,115,867; United Kingdom 122,334; Ukraine 467,782; Total (incl. others) 8,414,215.

COMMUNICATIONS MEDIA

Telephones (main lines in use, 2013): 169,032.

Mobile Cellular Telephones (subscribers, 2013): 993,902.

Broadband Subscribers (2013): 79,441.

EDUCATION

Pre-primary (2013/14): Schools 34; Pupils 16,461; Teaching staff 1,709.

Primary (2013/14 unless otherwise indicated): Schools 432 (2011/12); Pupils 68,133; Teaching staff 4,952.

Secondary (2013/14 unless otherwise indicated): Schools 49 (2011/12); Students 31,258; Teaching staff 2,243 (2008/09).

Higher (incl. faculties, art academies and private institutions, 2008/09, unless otherwise indicated): Schools 38; Students 22,279 (2012/13); Teaching staff 1,405.

Pupil-teacher Ratio (primary education, UNESCO estimate): 7.6 in 2011/12 (Source: UNESCO Institute for Statistics).

Adult Literacy Rate (UNESCO estimates): 98.4% (males 99.4%; females 97.5%) in 2011 (Source: UNESCO Institute for Statistics).

Directory

The Government

HEAD OF STATE

President: Filip Vujanović (elected 11 May 2003, inaugurated 13 June; re-elected 6 April 2008, inaugurated 21 May; re-elected 7 April 2013, inaugurated 20 May).

COUNCIL OF MINISTERS
(May 2015)

The Government comprises members of the Demokratska Partija Socijalista Crne Gore (DPS), the Socijaldemokratska Partija Crne Gore (SDP), the Bošnjačka Stranka (BS) and the Hrvatska Građanska Inicijativa (HGI).

Chairman of the Government: Milo Đukanović (DPS).

Deputy Chairman of the Government, responsible for the Political System and Internal and Foreign Affairs: Duško Marković (BS).

Deputy Chairman of the Government, responsible for Economic Policy and the Financial System, and Minister of the Information Society and Telecommunications: Vujica Lazović (SDP).

Deputy Chairman of the Government, responsible for European Integration, and Minister of Foreign Affairs and European Integration: Igor Lukšić (DPS).

Deputy Chairman of the Government, responsible for Regional Development: Rafet Husović (BS).

General Secretary of the Government: Žarko Šturanović (DPS).

Minister of Justice: Zoran Pažin (DPS).

Minister of Internal Affairs: Raško Konjević (SDP).

Minister of Defence: Milica Pejanović-Đurišić (DPS).

Minister of Finance: Radoje Žugić (Independent).

Minister of Education: Predrag Bošković (DPS).

Minister of Science: Sanja Vlahović (DPS).

Minister of Culture: Pavle Goranović (DPS).

Minister of the Economy: Vladimir Kavarić (DPS).

Minister of Transport and Maritime Affairs: Ivan Brajović (SDP).

Minister of Agriculture and Rural Development: Petar Ivanović (DPS).

Minister of Sustainable Development and Tourism: Branimir Gvozdenović (DPS).

Minister of Health: Budimir Šegrt (DPS).

Minister for Human and Minority Rights: Suad Numanović (DPS).

Minister of Labour and Social Welfare: Zorica Kovačević (DPS).

Minister without Portfolio: Marija Vučinović (HGI).

MINISTRIES

Office of the President: 81000 Podgorica, Sveti Petra Cetinjskog 3; tel. (20) 241410; fax (20) 245849; e-mail filip.vujanovic@predsjednik.me; internet www.predsjednik.me.

Office of the Chairman of the Government: 81000 Podgorica, Karađorđeva bb; tel. (20) 242530; fax (20) 242329; e-mail kabinet@mfa.gov.me; internet www.gov.me.

Ministry of Agriculture and Rural Development: 81000 Podgorica, Rimski trg 46; tel. (20) 482109; fax (20) 482364; e-mail kabinet.mpsv@gov.me; internet www.minpolj.gov.me.

Ministry of Culture: 81250 Cetinje, ul. Njegoševa; tel. (41) 232571; fax (41) 232572; e-mail kabinet.kultura@mku.gov.me; internet www.ministarstvokulture.gov.me.

Ministry of Defence: 81000 Podgorica, ul. Jovana Tomaševića 29; tel. (20) 483561; fax (20) 224702; e-mail kabinet@mod.gov.me; internet www.odbrana.gov.me.

Ministry of the Economy: 81000 Podgorica, Rimski trg 46; tel. (20) 482203; fax (20) 234027; e-mail vesna.besovic@mek.gov.me; internet www.minekon.gov.me.

Ministry of Education: 81000 Podgorica, Vaka Đurovića bb; tel. (20) 410100; fax (20) 410101; e-mail mps@mps.gov.me; internet www .mpin.gov.me.

Ministry of Finance: 81000 Podgorica, Stanka Dragojevića 2; tel. (20) 242835; fax (20) 224450; e-mail mf@mif.gov.me; internet www .mf.gov.me.

Ministry of Foreign Affairs and European Integration: 81000 Podgorica, Stanka Dragojevića 2; tel. (20) 246357; fax (20) 224670; e-mail kabinet@mfa.gov.me; internet www.mip.gov.me.

Ministry of Health: 81000 Podgorica, Rimski trg 46; tel. (20) 482133; fax (7) 8113128; e-mail mzdravlja@gov.me; internet www .mzdravlja.gov.me.

Ministry for Human and Minority Rights: 81000 Podgorica, Rimski trg bb; tel. (20) 482129; fax (20) 234198; e-mail kabinet@mmp .gov.me; internet www.minmanj.gov.me.

Ministry of the Information Society and Telecommunications: 81000 Podgorica, Rimski trg 45; tel. (20) 241412; fax (20) 241790; e-mail kabinet@mid.gov.me; internet www.mid.gov.me.

Ministry of Internal Affairs: 81000 Podgorica, bul. Svetog Petra Cetinjskog 22; tel. (20) 241590; fax (20) 246779; e-mail kabinet@mup .gov.me; internet www.mup.gov.me.

Ministry of Justice: 81000 Podgorica, Vuka Karadžića 3; tel. (20) 407501; fax (20) 407515; e-mail kabinet@mpa.gov.me; internet www .pravda.gov.me.

Ministry of Labour and Social Welfare: 81000 Podgorica, Rimski trg 46; tel. (20) 482148; fax (7) 8113340; e-mail ministar.mrss@mrss .gov.me; internet www.minradiss.gov.me.

Ministry of Science: 81000 Podgorica, Rimski trg 46; tel. (20) 482145; fax (20) 234168; e-mail kabinet@mna.gov.me; internet www .mna.gov.me.

Ministry of Sustainable Development and Tourism: 81000 Podgorica, IV proleterske brigade 19; tel. (20) 446200; fax (20) 446215; e-mail uros.andrijasevic@mrt.gov.me; internet www.mrt .gov.me.

Ministry of Transport and Maritime Affairs: 81000 Podgorica, Rimski trg 46; tel. (20) 234179; fax (20) 234331; e-mail zoran .radonjic@msp.gov.me; internet www.minsaob.gov.me.

President

Presidential Election, 7 April 2013

Candidate	Votes	%
Filip Vujanović (DPS)	161,940	51.21
Miodrag Lekić (Demokratski Front*)	154,290	48.79
Total	316,230	100.00

* Comprising the PzP and NOVA.

Legislature

**Assembly of Montenegro
(Skupština Crne Gore)**

81000 Podgorica, bul. Svetog Petra Cetinjskog 10; tel. (20) 244759; fax (20) 242192; e-mail predsjednik@skupstina.me; internet www .skupstina.me.

Speaker: RANKO KRIVOKAPIĆ.

Election, 14 October 2012

Party	Votes	%	Seats
Koalicija za Evropsku Crnu Goru (Coalition for a European Montenegro)*	165,380	46.33	39
Demokratski Front (Democratic Front)†	82,773	23.19	20
SNP	40,131	11.24	9
Pozitivna Crna Gora	29,881	8.37	7
BS	15,124	4.24	3
Forca za Jedinstvo—Forca për Bashkim (Force for Unity)	5,244	1.47	1
Albanian Coalition‡	3,824	1.07	1
HGI	1,470	0.41	1
Others	13,123	3.68	—
Total	356,950	100.00	81

* Comprising the DPS, the SDP, and the LPCG.
† Comprising NOVA and the PzP.
‡ Comprising the Demokratski Savez u Crnoj Gori (Democratic League of Montenegro), the Partia Demokratike (Democratic Party) and the Albanska Alternativa (Albanian Alternative).

Political Organizations

Bošnjačka Stranka (BS) (Bosniak Party): 84310 Rožaje; tel. (51) 270164; fax (51) 270165; e-mail info@bscg.me; internet www.bscg .me; f. 2006; Pres. RAFET HUSOVIĆ.

Demokratska Partija Socijalista Crne Gore (DPS) (Democratic Party of Socialists of Montenegro): 81000 Podgorica, Jovana Tomaševića bb; tel. (20) 245292; fax (20) 245282; e-mail portparol@dps.me; internet www.dps.me; fmrly League of Communists of Montenegro, present name adopted 1991; contested 2012 legislative elections as mem. of Koalicija za Evropsku Crnu Goru; Chair. MILO ĐUKANOVIĆ.

Demokratska Srpska Stranka Crne Gore (DSS) (Democratic Serbian Party of Montenegro): 81000 Podgorica, Radnička 33; tel. (20) 206120; fax (20) 206121; e-mail dss@cg.yu; internet www.dsscg .com; f. 2003; centre-right; Leader RANKO KADIĆ.

Demokratska Unija Albanaca (DUA) (Democratic Union of Albanians): c/o Skupština Crne Gore, 81000 Podgorica, bul. Svetog Petra Cetinjskog 10; tel. (20) 404565; f. 1993; Leader FERHAT DINOŠA.

Forca e Re Demokratike (FORCA) (New Democratic Power): 85360 Ulcinj, Skenderbeu; tel. (30) 401760; fax (30) 401761; e-mail info@forca.me; internet www.forca.me; f. 2005; principally ethnic Albanian party; Chair. NAZIF CUNGU.

Hrvatska Građanska Inicijativa (HGI) (Croatian Civic Initiative): 85320 Tivat, Luke Tomanovića bb; tel. and fax (32) 660348; e-mail hgicg@t-com.me; internet www.hgi.co.me; f. 2003; joined DPS coalition in 2006; Pres. MARIJA VUČINOVIĆ.

Liberalna Partija Crne Gore (LPCG) (Liberal Party of Montenegro): 81000 Podgorica, Južna tribina Gradskog stadiona, ulaz 5, Ulica 19 Decembra; tel. and fax (20) 220944; e-mail liberalnapartija@t-com .me; internet www.lpcg.me; f. 2004; contested 2012 legislative elections as mem. of Koalicija za Evropsku Crnu Goru; Pres. ANDRIJA POPOVIĆ.

Nova Srpska Demokratija (NOVA) (New Serbian Democracy): 81000 Podgorica, Vojislava Grujića 4; tel. (20) 651903; fax (20) 652147; e-mail centar@nova.org.me; internet www.nova.org.me; f. 2009 by merger of Serb People's Party with People's Socialist Party and other small groups; contested 2012 legislative elections as mem. of the Demokratski Front (Democratic Front) coalition; Pres. ANDRIJA MANDIĆ.

Pokret za Promjene (PzP) (Movement for Changes): 81000 Podgorica, Dalmatinska 130D; tel. and fax (20) 269337; e-mail pzp@ promjene.org; internet www.promjene.org; f. 2002 as non-governmental org.; became political party in 2006; supports European integration; contested 2012 legislative elections as mem. of the Democratic Front coalition; Pres. NEBOJŠA MEDOJEVIĆ.

Pozitivna Crna Gora (Positive Montenegro—PCG): 81000 Podgorica, Crnogorskih serdara bb; tel. and fax (20) 621325; e-mail info@ pozitivnacrnagora.me; internet www.pozitivnacrnagora.me; seek integration of Montenegro into the European Union; f. 2012; Pres. DARKO PAJOVIĆ.

Socijaldemokratska Partija Crne Gore (SDP) (Social Democratic Party of Montenegro): 81000 Podgorica, Jovana Tomaševića bb; tel. (20) 248648; fax (20) 224426; e-mail sdp@sdp.co.me; internet www.sdp.co.me; f. 1990; contested 2012 legislative elections as mem. of Koalicija za Evropsku Crnu Goru; Pres. RANKO KRIVOKAPIĆ.

Socijalistička Narodna Partija Crne Gore (SNP) (Socialist People's Party of Montenegro): 81000 Podgorica, Vaka Đurovića 5; tel. (20) 272421; fax (20) 272420; e-mail snp@t-com.me; internet www .snp.co.me; f. 1997; Pres. SRĐAN MILIĆ.

Diplomatic Representation

Albania: 81000 Podgorica, Stanka Dragojevića 14; tel. (20) 667380; fax (20) 667381; e-mail embassy.potgorica@mfa.gov.al; Ambassador ERNAL FILO.

Austria: 81000 Podgorica, bul. Svetog Petra Cetinjskog 1A; tel. (20) 201135; fax (20) 243544; e-mail podgorica-ob@bmeia.gv.at; Ambassador JOHANN FRÖHLICH.

Bosnia and Herzegovina: 81000 Podgorica, Atinska 58; tel. (20) 618015; fax (20) 618016; e-mail amb.podgorica@mvp.gov.ba; Ambassador ĐORĐE LATINOVIĆ.

Bulgaria: 81000 Podgorica, Vukice Mitrovića 10; tel. (20) 655009; fax (20) 655008; e-mail embassy.podgorica@mfa.bg; internet www .mfa.bg/embassies/montenegro; Ambassador MLADEN CHERVEYAKOV.

China, People's Republic: 81000 Podgorica, Radosava Burića 4A; tel. and fax (20) 609275; e-mail chinaemb_me@hotmail.com; Ambassador CUI ZHIWEI.

Croatia: 81000 Podgorica, Vladimira Ćetkovića 2; tel. (20) 269760; fax (20) 269810; e-mail croemb.podgorica@mvep.hr; Ambassador IVANA PERIĆ.

France: 81000 Podgorica, Atinska 35; tel. (20) 665348; fax (20) 655643; e-mail ambafrance@ambafrance.co.me; internet www .ambafrance-me.org; Ambassador VÉRONIQUE BRUMEAUX.

Germany: 81000 Podgorica, Hercegovačka 10; tel. (20) 441000; fax (20) 667285; internet www.podgorica.diplo.de; Ambassador GUDRUN ELISABETH STEINACKER.

Greece: 81000 Podgorica, Atinska 4C; tel. (20) 655544; fax (20) 655543; e-mail gremb.pod@mfa.gr; Ambassador ILIAS FOTOPOULOS.

Hungary: 81000 Podgorica, Kralja Nikole 104; tel. (20) 602910; fax (20) 625243; e-mail mission.pdg@mfa.gov.hu; internet www.mfa.gov .hu/emb/podgorica; Ambassador KRISZTIÁN PÓSA.

Italy: 81000 Podgorica, Džordža Vašingtona 26; tel. (20) 234661; fax (20) 234663; e-mail segreteria.podgorica@esteri.it; internet www .ambpodgorica.esteri.it; Ambassador VINCENZO DEL MONACO.

Macedonia, former Yugoslav republic: 81000 Podgorica, Hercegovačka 49/3; tel. (20) 667415; fax (20) 667205; e-mail podgorica@mfa .gov.mk; Chargé d'affaires a.i. MILENA KRSTEVA.

Poland: 20000 Podgorica, Kozaračka 79; tel. (20) 608320; fax (20) 658581; e-mail podgorica.amb.sekretariat@msz.gov.pl; internet www.podgorica.polemb.net; Ambassador GRAŻYNA SIKORSKA.

Romania: 81000 Podgorica, Vukice Mitrovića 40; tel. (20) 618040; fax (20) 655081; e-mail ambs.romania.mne@t-com.me; Ambassador FERDINAND NAGY.

Russian Federation: 81000 Podgorica, Veliše Mugoše 1; tel. (20) 272460; fax (20) 272317; e-mail info@ambrus.me; internet www .ambrus.me; Ambassador ANDREI A. NESTERENKO.

Serbia: 81000 Podgorica, Hercegovačka 18; tel. (20) 667305; fax (20) 664301; e-mail embassy.podgorica@mfa.rs; Ambassador ZORAN BINGULAC.

Slovakia: 81000 Podgorica, Crnogorskih Serdara 5; tel. (20) 601440; fax (20) 601456; e-mail emb.podgorica@mzv.sk; internet www.mzv .sk/podgorica; Chargé d'affaires a.i. FRANTIŠEK LIPKA.

Slovenia: 81000 Podgorica, Atinska 41; tel. (20) 618150; fax (20) 655671; e-mail kpg@gov.si; internet podgorica.embassy.si; Ambassador VLADIMIR GASPARIČ.

Turkey: 81000 Podgorica, Radosava Burica bb; tel. (20) 445700; fax (20) 445777; e-mail embassy.podgorica@mfa.gov.tr; internet www .podgorica.be.mfa.gov.tr; Ambassador MEHMET NIYAZI TANILIR.

Ukraine: 81000 Podgorica, ul. Serdara Jola Piletica 15; tel. (20) 227521; fax (20) 227181; e-mail emb_me@mfa.gov.ua; internet www .mfa.gov.ua/montenegro; Chargé d'affaires a.i. VOLODYMYR TSYBULNIK.

United Arab Emirates: 81000 Podgorica, bul. Svetog Petra Cetinjskog 147; tel. (20) 411401; fax (20) 411402; e-mail montenegro@mofa .gov.ae; Ambassador HAFSA ABDULLAH MUHAMMAD SHARIF AL-ULAMA.

United Kingdom: 81000 Podgorica, Ulcinjska 8, Gorica C; tel. (20) 618010; fax (20) 618020; e-mail podgorica@fco.gov.uk; internet www .gov.uk/world/montenegro; Ambassador IAN ROBERT WHITTING.

USA: 81000 Podgorica, Dzona Dzeksona 2; tel. (20) 410500; fax (20) 241358; e-mail podgoricaprot@state.gov; internet podgorica .usembassy.gov; Ambassador MARGARET UYEHARA.

Judicial System

Constitutional Court (Ustavni Sud): 81000 Podgorica, Njegoševa 2; tel. and fax (20) 665410; e-mail ustavni.sud@ustavnisud.me; internet www.ustavnisud.me; comprises a President and five judges; Pres. DESANKA LOPIČIĆ.

Supreme Court (Vrhovni Sud Crne Gore): 81000 Podgorica, Njegoševa 10; tel. (20) 665390; fax (20) 665405; e-mail vrhsud@t-com.me; internet www.sudovi.me; comprises a President and 17 judges; incorporates criminal, civil, commercial and administrative divisions; Pres. VESNA MEDENICA.

Office of the Supreme State Prosecutor (Vrhovni državni tužilac): 81000 Podgorica, Slobode 20; tel. and fax (20) 230624; e-mail vdtcg@tuzilastvo.me; internet www.tuzilastvocg.me; Public Prosecutor IVICA STANKOVIĆ.

Religion

CHRISTIANITY

The Eastern Orthodox Church

Montenegrin Orthodox Church (Crnogorska Pravoslavna Crkva): 81250 Cetinje, Gruda bb; tel. and fax (41) 31310; e-mail crkva@moc-cpc.org; internet www.moc-cpc.org; autocephalous until 1920, when it was dissolved and annexed to the Serbian Orthodox Church; restored 1993; Archbishop of Cetinje and Metropolitan of Montenegro MIHAILO (DEDEIĆ).

Orthodox Metropolitanate of Montenegro and the Littoral—Serbian Orthodox Church (Pravoslavna Mitropolija Crnogorsko Primorska—Srpska Pravoslavna Crkva): 81250 Cetinje; tel. (41) 231273; fax (41) 231273; e-mail mitropolija@t-com.me; internet www.mitropolija.me; Metropolitan of Montenegro and the Littoral AMFILOHIJE (RADOVIĆ).

The Roman Catholic Church

At 31 December 2008 there were an estimated 12,475 adherents in the archdiocese of Bar (which is directly answerable to the Holy See) and an estimated 10,000 adherents in the Diocese of Kotor (which is suffragan to the archdiocese of Split-Makarska, based in Croatia). There is also an Apostolic Exarchate for adherents of the Byzantine Rite in Serbia and Montenegro, based in Belgrade, Serbia.

Archbishop of Bar: Most Rev. ZEF GASHI, 85000 Bar, Popovići 98; tel. (30) 344236; fax (30) 344233.

Bishop of Kotor: Most Rev. ILIJA JANJIĆ, 85330 Kotor, Stari grad 336; tel. (32) 322315; fax (32) 322175.

ISLAM

Almost 20% of the population of Montenegro profess Islam, many being ethnic Slav Muslims (Bosniaks) of the Sandžak region (which was partitioned between Montenegro and Serbia in 1913).

The Press

PRINCIPAL DAILIES

Dan (The Day): 81000 Podgorica, 13 Jula 10; tel. (20) 481520; fax (20) 481522; e-mail dan@t-com.me; internet www.dan.co.me; f. 1999; Chief Editor MLADEN MILUTINOVIĆ.

Pobjeda (Victory): 81000 Podgorica, bul. Revolucije 15, POB 101; tel. (20) 244474; fax (20) 202455; e-mail desk@pobjeda.me; internet www .pobjeda.me; f. 1944; morning; Editor-in-Chief DRAŠKO ĐURANOVIĆ; circ. 5,000 (2014).

Vijesti (The News): 81000 Podgorica, bul. Revolucije 11; tel. (20) 406901; fax (20) 242306; e-mail portal@vijesti.me; internet www .vijesti.me; f. 1997; Editor-in-Chief MIHAILO JOVOVIĆ; CEO ZELJKO IVANOVIĆ.

PERIODICALS

Koha Javore: 81000 Podgorica, bul. Revolucije 9; tel. (20) 247799; fax (20) 247674; e-mail kohajavore@t-com.me; internet www .kohajavore.co.me; weekly; f. 2002; science and culture; in Albanian; Editor-in-Chief ALI SALAJ.

Monitor: 81000 Podgorica, bul. Revolucije 9; tel. (20) 231955; fax (20) 231944; e-mail monitor@t-com.me; internet www.monitor.co .me; f. 1990; weekly; independent; politics, general; Editor-in-Chief ESAD KOČAN.

NEWS AGENCY

Montenegrin News Agency (MINA): Podgorica, ul. Bohinjska 1A; tel. (20) 610100; fax (20) 610271; e-mail mnnews@mnnews.net; internet www.mnnews.net; f. 2002; commercial; Montenegrin, Albanian and English; Exec. Dir JAŠA JOVIĆEVIĆ.

PRESS ASSOCIATION

Asscn of Journalists of Montenegro (UNCG) (Udruženja novinara Crne Gore): 81000 Podgorica; Pres VLATKO VUJOVIĆ.

Publishers

Obod: 81250 Cetinje, Njegoševa 3; tel. (41) 21331; fax (41) 21953; general literature; Dir VASKO JANKOVIĆ.

Pobjeda (Victory) Publishing House: 81000 Podgorica, Južni bul. bb; tel. (20) 44433; f. 1974; poetry, fiction, lexicography and scientific works.

Broadcasting and Communications

TELECOMMUNICATIONS

Despite the liberalization of the sector, the formerly state-owned company, Crnogorski Telekom, continues to dominate the provision of fixed-line telephones, while the rate of subscription to mobile telecommunications services is among the highest in Central and South-Eastern Europe. In 2013 there were 169,032 fixed telephone lines and 993,902 subscriptions to mobile cellular telecommunications services in Montenegro.

Broadband Montenegro (BBM): 81000 Podgorica, Revolucije 66; tel. (20) 247458; fax (20) 247459; e-mail info@bbm.me; internet www.bbm.me.

Crnogorski Telekom: 81000 Podgorica, Moskovska 29; tel. (20) 433433; fax (20) 225752; e-mail office@telekom.me; internet www.telekom.me; 76.53% owned by Magyar Telekom (Hungary); Exec. Dir RÜDIGER J. SCHULZ.

m:tel: 81000 Podgorica, Kralja Nikole 27A; tel. (7) 8100508; e-mail officeinfo@mtel.me; internet www.mtel-cg.com; f. 2007; owned by Telekom Srbija (Serbia) and Ogalar (Netherlands); mobile cellular telecommunications services; Exec. Dir VLADIMIR LUČIĆ.

Telenor Montenegro: 81000 Podgorica, Rimski trg 4; tel. (20) 235000; fax (20) 235035; internet www.telenor.me; f. 1996; fmrly offered services under the brand Promonte; rebranded as above in 2010; 100% owned by Telenor (Norway); mobile cellular telecommunications services; Exec. Dir MICHAEL MALVEBO.

Regulatory Agency

Agency for Electronic Communications and Postal Services (Agencija za elektronske komunikacije i poštansku djelatnost—EKIP): 81000 Podgorica, bul. Džordža Vašingtona bb; tel. (20) 406711; fax (20) 406702; e-mail ekip@ekip.me; internet www.ekip.me; f. 2001 as Agency for Telecommunications; renamed as above in 2008; independent regulatory body; Exec. Dir ZORAN SEKULIĆ.

BROADCASTING

There are 15 public (one national and 14 local) and 34 commercial radio stations operating in Montenegro. In addition to four publicly owned (one national and three local) television stations there are 15 main licensed commercial television stations active in the country.

Regulatory Agency

Agency for Electronic Media of Montenegro (Agencija za Elektronske Medije Crne Gore): 81000 Podgorica, bul. Svetog Petra Cetinjskog 9; tel. (20) 201430; fax (20) 201440; e-mail ard@ardcg.org; internet www.ardcg.org; CEO ABAZ BELI DŽAFIĆ.

Television and Radio

Radiotelevizija Crne Gore (Radio and Television of Montenegro): 81000 Podgorica, Cetinjski put bb; tel. (20) 244497; fax (20) 225497; internet www.rtcg.org; f. 1944 (radio) and 1971 (television); two terrestrial television channels and one satellite channel; two radio channels; Dir-Gen. RADE VOJVODIĆ; Dir of Television RADOJKA RUTOVIĆ; Dir of Radio RADOJICA BULATOVIĆ.

Radio D: 81000 Podgorica, Vasa Raičkovića 18A; tel. (20) 238909; internet www.radioddplus.com; f. 2000; independent; also Radio D Plus; Chief Editor DRAGANA KUKRIĆ.

RTV Corona: 85000 Bar, Jovana Tomaševica, Poslovni centar G-9; tel. and fax (30) 317727; e-mail mcorona@t-com.me; internet www.rtvcorona.com; f. 2000; comprises Radio Corona and TV Corona; information and entertainment; Exec. Dir DRAGAN DESPOTOVIĆ.

TV Vijesti: 81000 Podgorica, Trg Republike bb; tel. (20) 406957; fax (20) 242306; e-mail portal@vijesti.me; internet www.vijesti.me; f. 2007; broadcasts 24 hours a day; information, news, politics, economics, culture, entertainment, sport; Exec. Dir SLAVOLJUB ŠĆEKIC.

Finance

(cap. = capital; res = reserves; dep. = deposits; m. = million; amounts in euros; brs = branches)

BANKING

Central Bank

Central Bank of Montenegro (Centralna Banka Crne Gore—CBCG): 81000 Podgorica, bul. Petra Cetinjskog 6; tel. (20) 480263; fax (20) 403105; e-mail pristup.informacijama@cb-cg.org; internet www.cb-mn.org; f. 2001; cap. 2.5m., res 41.9m., dep. 438.9m. (Dec. 2007); Gov. MILOJICA DAKIĆ.

Selected Banks

At December 2013 some 12 banks were operating in Montenegro, nine of which were foreign-owned.

Crnogorska komercijalna banka a.d. Podgorica (CKB): 81000 Podgorica, Moskovska bb; tel. (20) 404232; fax (20) 235757; e-mail info@ckb.me; internet www.ckb.me; f. 1997; 100% owned by OTP Bank (Hungary); cap. 126.9m., res 0.9m., dep. 554.7m. (Dec. 2012); Pres. JÓZSEF WINDHEIM; 40 brs.

Erste Bank a.d. Podgorica: 81000 Podgorica, ul. Studentska bb; tel. (20) 440440; fax (20) 440432; e-mail info@erstebank.me; internet www.erstebank.me; f. 2002; fmrly Opportunity Bank; present name adopted 2009; subsidiary of Erste Bank der Oesterreichischen Sparkassen AG (Austria); cap. 5.3m., res 3.1m., dep. 211.9m. (Dec. 2012); Chief Exec. ALEKSA LUKIĆ.

NLB Montenegrobanka a.d. Podgorica: 81000 Podgorica, Dragojevića 46; tel. (20) 402146; fax (20) 402250; e-mail info@nlb.me; internet www.nlb.me; f. 1905; fmrly MNB Crnogorska banka—Banque de Montenegro; present name adopted Jan. 2006; 97.4% owned by Nova Ljubljanska Banka d.d. (Slovenia); cap. 39.4m., res 12.7m., dep. 354.9m. (Dec. 2012); Pres. DAVID BENEDEK; CEO ANTON RIBNIKAR.

Prva Banka: 81000 Podgorica, bul. Svetog Petra Cetinjskog 141; tel. (20) 409149; fax (20) 409124; e-mail kabinet@prvabankacg.com; internet www.prvabankacg.com; f. 1901 as Prva Nikšića štedionica; current name adopted in 2007; CEO DARKO RADUNOVIĆ.

STOCK EXCHANGE

Montenegro Stock Exchange (Montenegroberza): 81000 Podgorica, Moskovska 77; tel. and fax (20) 229710; e-mail info@mnse.me; internet www.mnse.me; f. 1993; CEO GOJKO MAKSIMOVIĆ.

INSURANCE

Atlas Life: Podgorica, Stanka Dragojevića 4; tel. (20) 407200; internet www.atlaslife.me; f. 2007; life; Chair. DIJANA ZEČEVIĆ; Exec. Dir DARKO ČABARKAPA.

Delta Generali Osiguranje: Podgorica, Kralja Nikole 27; tel. (20) 444800; fax (20) 444810; e-mail kontakt@deltagenerali.me; internet www.deltagenerali.me; f. 2008; non-life; Exec. Dir DEJAN BAJIĆ.

Grawe Osiguranje a.d. Podgorica (Grawe Insurance): 81000 Podgoric, Ivana Crnojevića 62/1; tel. (20) 210790; fax (20) 210963; e-mail office.podgorica@grawe.at; internet www.grawe.me; f. 2009; life; Exec. Dir MAJA PAVLIČIĆ.

Lovćen Osiguranje a.d. Podgorica (Lovćen Insurance Co Podgorica): 81000 Podgorica, ul. Slobode 13 A; tel. (20) 404400; fax (20) 665281; e-mail lovosig@co.me; internet www.lovcenosiguranje.co.me; majority stake owned by Zavarovalnica Triglav d.d. (Slovenia); insurance and reinsurance; Exec. Dir PURIĆ RADENKO.

Merkur Osiguranje a.d. Podgorica (Merkur Insurance): Podgorica, bul. Džordža Vašingtona br. 2A; tel. (20) 205465; fax (20) 205466; e-mail info@merkurosiguranje.me; internet www.merkurosiguranje.me; f. 2008; life; Exec. Dir MARKO IVANOVIĆ.

Sava Montenegro Osiguranje: 81000 Podgorica, Rimski trg 70, PC 'Kruševac'; tel. and fax (20) 234008; e-mail info@sava.co.me; internet www.sava.co.me; wholly owned by Sava Re (Slovenia); fmrly Montenegro Osiguranje; life and non-life, insurance and reinsurance; Chief Exec. NEBOJŠA ŠĆEKIĆ.

Swiss Osiguranje a.d. Podgorica (Swiss Insurance Co Podgorica): 81000 Podgorica, Novaka Miloševa 6/II; tel. (20) 657300; e-mail sio@t-com.me; internet www.swiss-osiguranje.com/swiss; fmrly Agroosiguranje a.d. Podgorica; life and non-life, insurance and reinsurance; Exec. Dir DRAGAN IVANOVIĆ.

UNIQA Osiguranje: 81000 Podgorica, ul. Svetlane Kane Radević 3; tel. (20) 444704; fax (20) 244340; e-mail info@uniqa.me; internet www.uniqa.co.me; f. 2008; life and non-life; Dir NELA BELEVIĆ.

Regulatory Authority

Agencija za Nadzor Osiguranja Crna Gora (Insurance Supervision Agency of Montenegro): 81000 Podgorica, ul. Moskovska 17A; tel. (20) 513502; fax (20) 513503; e-mail agencija@ano.co.me; internet www.ano.me; f. 2007; Pres. BRANKO VUJOVIĆ.

Trade and Industry

CHAMBER OF COMMERCE

Chamber of Commerce of Montenegro (Privredna Komora Crne Gore): 81000 Podgorica, Novaka Miloševa 29; tel. (20) 230545; fax (20) 230493; e-mail predsjednik@pkcg.org; internet www.pkcg.org; Pres. VELIMIR MIJUSKOVIĆ.

UTILITIES

Electricity

Elektroprivreda Crne Gore a.d. Nikšić (EPCG) (Montenegro Electricity Co): 81400 Nikšić, Vuka Karadžića 2; tel. (40) 204137; fax (40) 214329; e-mail milvujacic@epcg.co.me; internet www.epcg.co.me; production, transmission and distribution of electric power; Exec. Dir ENRICO MALERBA.

Transport

RAILWAYS

The total length of the railway network was 250 km in 2009. The 167-km line between Bar and Vrbnica is electrified.

Željeznica Crne Gore: 81000 Podgorica, trg Goolotočkih žrtava 13; tel. (20) 441100; fax (20) 633957; e-mail milojica.zindovic@zpcg.me; internet www.zcg-prevoz.me; 60.1% state-owned; Chair. of Bd of Dirs DUŠAN RADONJIĆ; Gen. Man. MILOJICA ZINDOVIĆ.

SHIPPING

The principal coastal outlet is the port of Bar, which is linked to the Italian ports of Ancona and Bari by a regular ferry service. At 31 December 2014 Montenegro's flag registered fleet comprised eight vessels, totalling 96,335 grt.

Port of Bar (Luka Bar): 85000 Bar, Luka Bar; tel. (30) 300400; fax (30) 300402; e-mail milijana.simovic@lukabar.me; internet www .lukabar.me; f. 1906; Chair. of Bd Prof. Dr PREDRAG IVANOVIĆ.

CIVIL AVIATION

Montenegro Airlines: 81000 Podgorica, Beogradska 10; tel. (20) 405538; fax (20) 228147; internet www.montenegroairlines.com; f. 1994; operations commenced 1997; direct flights between Podgorica and Tivat (Montenegro), Belgrade and Niš (Serbia), Frankfurt (Germany), Ljubljana (Slovenia), Paris (France), Rome (Italy), Vienna (Austria), and Zurich (Switzerland); Dir ŽIVKO BANJEVIĆ (acting); CEO DALIBORKA PEJOVIĆ.

Tourism

There were 1.3m. foreign tourist arrivals in 2013; in 2011 receipts from tourism amounted to US $777m.

National Tourism Organization of Montenegro: 81000 Podgorica, bul. Svetog Petra Cetinjskog 130; tel. (77) 100001; fax (77) 100009; e-mail info@montenegro.travel; internet www.montenegro .travel; Man. Dir SAŠA RADOVIĆ.

Defence

Following Montenegro's declaration of independence on 3 June 2006, the Montenegrin Government established a Ministry of Defence and revoked compulsory military service. In December Montenegro was admitted to the 'Partnership for Peace' programme of the North Atlantic Treaty Organization (NATO). As assessed at November 2014, Montenegro's total armed forces numbered 2,080, comprising an army of an estimated 1,500, a navy of 350 and an air force of 230. There was, in addition, a paramilitary force of an estimated 10,100, comprising 6,000 Ministry of Internal Affairs personnel and 4,100 members of special police units.

Defence Expenditure: Budgeted at €49m. in 2013.

Chief of Staff: Adm. DRAGAN SAMARDŽIĆ.

Education

Primary education is free and compulsory for all children between the ages of seven and 15 years. A new system of primary education, beginning at the age of six and lasting for nine years, was gradually introduced from 2004/05. Secondary education comprises gymnasia (grammar schools) and art schools that offer four-year programmes, as well as vocational education schools that offer two-, three- or four-year courses. In 2012/13 the primary education enrolment ratio included 98% of children in the relevant age-group, while the enrolment ratio for secondary education was equivalent to 91% of children in the relevant age-group in 2011/12. Higher education is offered at the University of Montenegro, Podgorica, which was established in 1974, and at post-secondary schools. Some 22,279 students were enrolled in higher education in 2012/13.

MOROCCO

Introductory Survey

LOCATION, CLIMATE, LANGUAGE, RELIGION, FLAG, CAPITAL

The Kingdom of Morocco is situated in the extreme north-west of Africa. It has a long coastline on the shores of the Atlantic Ocean and, east of the Strait of Gibraltar, on the Mediterranean Sea, facing southern Spain. Morocco's eastern frontier is with Algeria, while to the south lies the disputed territory of Western Sahara (under Moroccan occupation), which has a lengthy Atlantic coastline and borders Mauritania to the east and south. The Spanish External Territories, Ceuta and Melilla, lie within Moroccan territory on the Mediterranean coast. Morocco's climate is semi-tropical. It is warm and sunny on the coast, while the plains of the interior are intensely hot in summer. Average temperatures are 27°C (81°F) in summer and 7°C (45°F) in winter for Rabat, and 38°C (101°F) and 4°C (40°F), respectively, for Marrakesh. The rainy season in the north is from November to April. The official language is Arabic, but a large minority speak Berber. Spanish is widely spoken in the northern regions, and French in the rest of Morocco. The established religion is Islam, and most of the country's inhabitants are Muslims. There are small minorities of Christians and Jews. The national flag (proportions 2 by 3) is red, with a green pentagram (intersecting lines in the form of a five-pointed star), known as 'Solomon's Seal', in the centre. The capital is Rabat.

CONTEMPORARY POLITICAL HISTORY

Historical Context

In 1912, under the terms of the Treaty of Fez, most of Morocco became a French protectorate, while a smaller Spanish protectorate was instituted in the north and far south of the country. Spain also retained control of Spanish Sahara (now Western Sahara), and Tangier became an international zone in 1923. A nationalist movement developed in Morocco during the 1930s and 1940s, led by the Istiqlal (Independence) grouping, and on 2 March 1956 the French protectorate achieved independence as the Sultanate of Morocco. Sultan Muhammad V, who had reigned since 1927 (although he had been temporarily removed from office by the French authorities between 1953 and 1955), became the first head of state. The northern zone of the Spanish protectorate joined the new state in April 1956, and Tangier's international status was abolished in October. The southern zone of the Spanish protectorate was ceded to Morocco in 1958, but no agreement was reached on the enclaves of Ceuta and Melilla, in the north, the Ifni region in the south, or the Saharan territories to the south of Morocco, which all remained under Spanish control. The Sultan was restyled King of Morocco in August 1957, and became Prime Minister in May 1960. He died in February 1961, and was succeeded by his son, Moulay Hassan, who took the title of Hassan II.

Elections to Morocco's first House of Representatives took place in May 1963, and King Hassan relinquished the post of Prime Minister six months later. In June 1965, however, increasing political fragmentation prompted Hassan to declare a 'state of exception', and to resume full legislative and executive powers. The emergency provisions remained in force until July 1970, when a new Constitution was approved. Elections in the following month resulted in a pro-Government majority in the new Majlis al-Nuab (Chamber of Representatives).

Domestic Political Affairs

In July 1971 an attempted *coup d'état* was suppressed by forces loyal to the King. Among those subsequently arrested were numerous members of the left-wing Union Nationale des Forces Populaires (UNFP), five of whom were sentenced to death. Although a revised Constitution was approved in March 1972 by popular referendum, a general election did not take place until June 1977. Two-thirds of the deputies in the Chamber of Representatives were directly elected, the remainder being elected by local government councils, professional associations and labour organizations. Supporters of the King's policies won a majority of seats in the new legislature. A Government of national unity was formed, including opposition representatives

from Istiqlal and the Mouvement Populaire (MP) in addition to the pro-monarchist independents.

All 14 deputies belonging to the Union Socialiste des Forces Populaires (USFP) withdrew from the Chamber of Representatives in October 1981, when it was announced that the legislative term was to be extended from four to six years. Elections were postponed, and an interim Government of national unity was appointed under Muhammad Karim Lamrani (Prime Minister in 1971–72). The new Government included members of the six main political parties: Istiqlal, the MP, the Parti National Démocrate (PND), the Rassemblement National des Indépendants (RNI), the Union Constitutionnelle (UC) and the USFP. The deferred elections took place in September–October 1984. The USFP made significant gains, but the Chamber of Representatives remained dominated by the centre-right parties. A new Cabinet, appointed in April 1985, included members of the MP, the PND, the RNI and the UC. Lamrani resigned in September 1986, on health grounds, and was replaced by Azzeddine Laraki.

King Hassan announced in March 1992 that the Constitution was to be revised and submitted for approval in a national referendum, in preparation for legislative elections (which had been postponed since 1990, pending settlement of the Western Sahara dispute). The King indicated in July that the elections would take place in November, and that voting would be extended to include Western Sahara—irrespective of the UN's progress in organizing a referendum on the territory's status (see *Western Sahara*). In August the King dissolved the Government, and named Lamrani as Prime Minister in an interim, non-partisan Government. According to official results of the referendum, which proceeded in September, the revised Constitution was endorsed by 99.96% of voters. Under the terms of the new Constitution, the King would retain strong executive powers, including the right to appoint the Prime Minister, but government members would henceforth be nominated by the latter. The Government would be required to reflect the composition of the Chamber of Representatives, and was obliged to submit its legislative programme for the Chamber's approval; new legislation would automatically be promulgated one month after having been endorsed by parliament, regardless of whether royal assent had been received. Provision was also made for the establishment of a constitutional council and of an economic and social council, and guarantees of human rights were enshrined in the Constitution.

Legislative elections eventually took place in June 1993. Parties of the Bloc Démocratique (also called the Koutla Démocratique)—grouping Istiqlal, the USFP, the Parti du Progrès et du Socialisme (PPS), the Organisation de l'Action Démocratique et Populaire (OADP) and the UNFP—won a combined total of 99 of the 222 directly elected seats in the enlarged Chamber. The MP won 33 seats, the RNI 28 and the UC 27. The indirect election (by electoral college) of the remaining 111 members, which followed on 17 September, was less favourable to the Bloc Démocratique, which won only 21 further seats. Of the 333 seats in the Chamber, the USFP now controlled 56, the UC 54, Istiqlal 52, the MP 51 and the RNI 41. Lamrani was reappointed as Prime Minister in November, but in May 1994 King Hassan replaced him with Abdellatif Filali, who retained his post as Minister of State for Foreign Affairs and Co-operation. In July the King appealed to all political parties to participate in a government of national unity, and in October he announced his intention to select a premier from the ranks of the opposition. However, negotiations on the formation of a coalition government failed, apparently owing to the Bloc Démocratique's refusal to join an administration in which Driss Basri (a long-serving government member and close associate of the King) remained as Minister of the Interior and Information, and in January 1995 Hassan instructed Filali to form a new cabinet.

Muhammad Basri, a prominent opposition figure (sentenced to death *in absentia* in 1974) and founder member of both the UNFP and the USFP, returned to Morocco from France in June 1995, after 28 years in exile. It was widely believed that his rehabilitation had been precipitated by the royal amnesty of July

1994 and by the return to Morocco (also from France) in May 1995 of the First Secretary of the USFP, Abderrahmane Youssoufi. Despite King Hassan's assertion that there were no longer any political detainees in Morocco, a report published by the Association Marocaine des Droits Humains (AMDH) in February 1996 claimed that 58 political prisoners (mainly radical Islamists, supporters of independence for Western Sahara and left-wing activists) remained in detention.

In August 1996 the King presented further constitutional amendments, including the creation of an indirectly elected second parliamentary assembly, the Chamber of Advisers (Majlis al-Mustasharin), and the introduction of direct elections for all members of the Chamber of Representatives. Most political parties supported the reforms; however, an appeal by the OADP leadership for a boycott of a planned referendum on the amendments led to a split in the party and the subsequent establishment of the Parti Socialiste Démocratique (PSD). According to official results of the referendum, held in September, the reforms were approved by 99.6% of voters. Legislation regarding the new bicameral parliament was promulgated in August 1997: the Chamber of Representatives was to comprise 325 members, directly elected for a five-year term; the 270 members of the Chamber of Advisers would be indirectly elected, for a nine-year term, by local councils (which would choose 162 members), chambers of commerce (81) and trade unions (27).

At the subsequent elections to the Chamber of Representatives, held in November 1997, the Bloc Démocratique won a combined total of 102 seats (of which the USFP took 57 and Istiqlal 32); the centre-right Entente Nationale took 100 seats (the UC 50 and the MP 40), and centrist parties 97 (including 46 won by the RNI). The Mouvement Populaire Constitutionnel et Démocratique (MPCD), which earlier in the year had formally absorbed members of the Islamist Al Islah wa Attajdid, secured parliamentary representation for the first time, with nine seats. At indirect elections to the Chamber of Advisers, which followed in December, centrist parties won 90 seats (the RNI 42 and the Mouvement Démocratique et Social 33), the Entente Nationale 76 (the UC 28 and the MP 27) and the Bloc Démocratique 44 (Istiqlal 21). In February 1998 the King appointed Youssoufi as Morocco's first Socialist Prime Minister. In October the MPCD was renamed the Parti de la Justice et du Développement—PJD.

The accession of King Muhammad VI

King Hassan died on 23 July 1999, and was succeeded by his elder son, Crown Prince Sidi Muhammad, as King Muhammad VI. Some 8,000 prisoners were freed, and more than 38,000 had their sentences reduced, under the terms of an amnesty decreed by the new King. In August the King ordered the creation within the Conseil Consultatif des Droits de l'Homme (CCDH)—established by King Hassan in April 1990—of an independent commission to determine levels of compensation for families of missing political activists and for those subjected to arbitrary detention. In April 1999 the CCDH had announced that it had been agreed to compensate the families of 112 people who were now officially acknowledged as having 'disappeared' between 1960 and 1990. However, Morocco's independent human rights organizations asserted that the number of missing persons amounted to almost 600. In November 1999 King Muhammad approved the return to Morocco of the family of former opposition activist and UNFP leader Mehdi Ben Barka, who had been abducted and apparently murdered in Paris, France, in 1965.

King Muhammad dismissed the influential Minister of State for the Interior, Driss Basri, in November 1999, apparently in response to the violent suppression of protests in Western Sahara in September. The new Minister of the Interior, Ahmed Midaoui (a former Director of National Security), immediately pledged to work towards the strengthening of democracy and national reconciliation. In April 2000 the Government commenced payments, reportedly totalling 40m. dirhams, in respect of the cases of an initial 40 victims of arbitrary detention, from the fund established the previous year. In September the King appointed Driss Jettou, a former Minister of Finance and Industry, as Minister of the Interior. A royal institute was established in October, charged with preserving the language and culture of the country's Berber population.

In June 2001 the Moroccan authorities granted the French judge leading the inquiry into the disappearance of Mehdi Ben Barka, permission to visit Morocco as part of his investigation. Later that month a former member of the Moroccan special services, Ahmed Boukhari, alleged that Ben Barka had been tortured to death by Morocco's then Minister of the Interior, Gen. Muhammad Oufkir, having been kidnapped in Paris by French police officers working for the Moroccan secret service. Boukhari was subsequently summoned to appear before the French investigation into Ben Barka's disappearance; however, the Moroccan authorities refused to grant him a passport, and in August he was arrested on charges of financial irregularity. Human rights organizations protested that the Moroccan Government was attempting to prevent Boukhari from testifying at the inquiry. In December 2002 Morocco announced that it would co-operate fully with the French investigation, and in January 2003 a French judge travelled to Rabat to interview Boukhari about the disappearance of the former UNFP leader. In October 2007 the French investigating magistrate in the case issued warrants for the arrest of five Moroccan officials suspected of involvement in the case. However, the release of the warrants was deferred, and in October 2009 it was announced that the release was to be suspended to allow the French authorities to obtain more details on the suspects as required by the International Criminal Police Commission (Interpol). The warrants subsequently lapsed, although in August 2012 it was reported that the French magistrate had made a request to the British police for the arrest of one of the officials, Gen. Hosni Benslimane, the head of the Moroccan royal gendarmerie, who was visiting London in his capacity as chief of Morocco's national Olympic committee.

In March 2002 the Government agreed a number of changes to the electoral system, including the introduction of proportional representation and a guarantee that at least 10% of the 325 seats in the lower house would be reserved for women. At the election to the Chamber of Representatives in September, the USFP again won the largest number of seats, although its representation was reduced to 50 seats. The UC, by contrast, fared poorly, retaining just 16 seats. Istiqlal performed strongly, winning 48 seats, as did the PJD, which took 42 seats; the RNI returned 41 members, the MP 27, and the Mouvement National Populaire (MNP) 18. In October King Muhammad appointed Driss Jettou as Prime Minister, and a new Government was announced the following month. The new Cabinet, which included three women, comprised members of the USFP, Istiqlal, the RNI, the MNP, the MP and the PPS, as well as a number of non-affiliated technocrats.

Suicide attacks in Casablanca

In May 2003 some 45 people died and more than 100 others were injured in a series of suicide bomb attacks in central Casablanca, which targeted the Belgian consulate, a Spanish restaurant and a Jewish cultural centre. Among those killed were reported to be 12 suicide bombers. Two further presumed attackers were detained by the security forces, along with some 30 others suspected of involvement in the bombings. The Moroccan authorities believed that the bombers were linked to a small Moroccan-based militant Islamist group, al-Assirat al-Moustaquim (Righteous Path), but that the attacks had been orchestrated by an international terrorist network operating in Europe, possibly al-Qa'ida. In late May the suspected co-ordinator of the attacks, who had been arrested in Fez, died in police custody as a result of ill health. At the end of the month stricter anti-terrorism measures were approved by the legislature, including an increase in the number of offences punishable by the death sentence.

In July 2003 some 10 of 31 alleged members of the radical Islamist group Salafia Jihadia, who had been arrested during police operations against Islamist networks the previous year, were sentenced to death by a court in Casablanca, having been convicted of murder and attempted murder. The remainder of the accused received lengthy prison terms. Later in July it was announced that more than 700 people would be tried in connection with the May bomb attacks; 52 defendants subsequently appeared before Casablanca's criminal court. In August four men, including the two surviving alleged suicide bombers, received death sentences for their part in the violence; 39 others were sentenced to life imprisonment for plotting further attacks in Agadir, Marrakesh and Essaouira. In February 2005 some 10 men were imprisoned for eight years for membership of Salafia Jihadia, and in July two members of Salafia Jihadia were sentenced to death, having been convicted of the murders of five people in Casablanca. In April 2008 nine of the men convicted for their links to the suicide bombings in Casablanca escaped from prison in Kénitra, north of Rabat. It was reported that seven of the fugitives had been rearrested by the Moroccan security forces by January 2009.

Meanwhile, King Muhammad continued to pursue his policies of reform and modernization of Moroccan society, including provision for the teaching of the Berber language in schools. In October 2003 the King announced major revisions to the *mudawana* (family code), which he claimed would promote female equality and protect children's rights. The reforms would raise the legal age of marriage for women from 15 to 18 years, and simplify the procedure for women seeking a divorce from their husband. Although polygamy would not be outlawed under the new legislation, a woman would be able to prevent her husband from taking a second wife, and would also be provided with equal authority and property rights within the marriage. The changes to the *mudawana* were approved by the legislature in January 2004.

In May–June 2006 police arrested more than 500 members of Al-Adl wal-Ihsan (Justice and Charity), an unauthorized but previously tolerated Islamist movement, after unconfirmed reports that it was planning an uprising; most of those detained were quickly released. Al-Adl wal-Ihsan had launched a campaign earlier in 2006 to disseminate information among the general public and recruit new members outside its traditional areas of support such as mosques and universities. In July–August 56 members of the militant Islamist group Ansar al-Mahdi (Followers of the Mahdi) were arrested on suspicion of planning a campaign of violence against the monarchy. Among those detained were several members of the police and armed forces. In January 2008 the leader of Ansar al-Mahdi, Hassan Khattab, was sentenced to 25 years' imprisonment, while 49 other members of the group received prison sentences, having been convicted of various crimes, including plotting to attack government buildings.

In April 2007 suicide bombers targeted the US consulate and a US cultural centre in Casablanca. The attacks coincided with two large explosions in Algiers, Algeria, that were claimed by the al-Qa'ida Organization in the Land of the Islamic Maghreb (AQIM, formerly the Groupe Salafiste pour la Prédication et le Combat—see the chapter on Algeria). Although an online statement purporting to be from al-Qa'ida claimed responsibility for the explosions in Casablanca, Moroccan police insisted that they were the work of a group with no links to external organizations. In October 2008 more than 40 people received prison sentences, ranging from two to 30 years, for their involvement in the bombings.

At the general election of September 2007, Istiqlal secured the largest number of seats in the Chamber of Representatives, winning 52. The PJD took 46 seats, the MP (which had merged with the MNP and the Union Démocratique in 2006) 41, and the RNI 39. The USFP retained only 38 seats, while the UC's representation recovered somewhat, to 27 seats. The rate of participation by voters was a record low of 37% of eligible participants. King Muhammad subsequently appointed Abbas el-Fassi, the leader of Istiqlal and Minister of State in the outgoing administration, as the new Prime Minister, and in October a new Government comprising Istiqlal, the RNI, the USFP and the PPS, along with several independent ministers, took office.

A new political organization, the Parti de l'Authenticité et de la Modernité (PAM), was established in August 2008 by Fouad Ali el-Himma, a former Deputy Minister of the Interior and close ally of King Muhammad. Several existing parties, including the Parti Al Ahd, the Parti de l'Environnement et du Développement and the PND, joined the new grouping; however, differences quickly emerged, and the former leaders of those parties left the PAM to re-form their previous organizations in 2008–09. In May 2009 the PAM announced that it was to withdraw its support from the governing coalition and align itself with the opposition, despite retaining close links to the King. At the municipal elections held in June the PAM supplanted Istiqlal as the major party at local level, winning 21.7% of the total votes cast. In June 2010 Abdelilah Benkirane succeeded Saâdeddine el-Othmani as Secretary-General of the PJD.

In early 2010 King Muhammad announced plans to devolve certain powers from central government to local councils. The programme, under the supervision of a newly created Advisory Committee on Regionalization, aimed to provide regional authorities with greater powers to determine their own development plans; it was ongoing in 2015.

King Muhammad announces constitutional reform

In February 2011 thousands of Moroccans joined street protests in Rabat and a number of other cities to demand improved living conditions, an end to state corruption, and reform of the country's political system—in particular reduced powers for the monarch. Some youths set themselves alight, in imitation of an act of self-immolation by a Tunisian man in December 2010, which had prompted the popular unrest across the Middle East and North Africa that came to be known as the 'Arab spring'. In Morocco the protesters, including left-wing activists, students and Islamists, coalesced in the February 20 Movement for Change, named after the largest pro-reform demonstrations held in around 20 cities on that date.

On 21 February 2011 King Muhammad inaugurated a new Economic and Social Council (Conseil Economique et Social—CES—provision for which had been enshrined in the 1992 Constitution), chaired by a former Minister of the Interior, Chakib Benmoussa. The CES was to formulate a new social chapter and to advise the Government on a wide range of socio-economic issues, including the demands of the labour market. In an address to the nation in March, King Muhammad pledged to implement a review of the Constitution and to introduce other political reforms, notably an independent judiciary, provision for the leader of the party with the largest representation in the Chamber of Representatives to form a government, and implementation of the plan to devolve certain powers to Morocco's regional authorities. A constitutional reform committee was subsequently appointed, and requested to issue its proposals on possible constitutional amendments by June. Proposed reforms would then be subject to approval in a national referendum. None the less, some members of the February 20 Movement began to demand the dismissal of the Cabinet, and complained that King Muhammad retained excessive influence over the committee's work.

Meanwhile, in early March increased powers were granted to the Advisory Council on Human Rights, which was renamed the National Human Rights Council and was to investigate alleged human rights violations. Largely peaceful rallies in support of political, social and economic reforms continued during March and April in cities including Rabat, Casablanca and Marrakesh.

From March 2011 many Islamists held in Moroccan prisons on terrorism-related charges joined hunger strikes in protest against what they deemed to be their unfair detention, leading the Ministry of Justice to initiate a dialogue with representatives of the prisoners in order to address their grievances. In April the King ordered the immediate release of 96 prisoners, many of whom were political detainees—among them Mustapha Moatassim, Secretary-General of the banned Islamist organization al-Badil al-Hadari; the prison terms of a further 94 prisoners were reduced.

In late April 2011 some 17 people were killed (including three Moroccans and eight French nationals) in a bombing at a café in the centre of Marrakesh. AQIM denied responsibility, and the Moroccan authorities stated that they believed the bombing to have been perpetrated by an independent Islamist organization inspired by al-Qa'ida. Trial proceedings against nine Moroccans accused of crimes including committing terrorist acts began in Salé in June. In October one of the defendants was sentenced to death, having been found guilty of carrying out the Marrakesh bombing; a second defendant received a life sentence, while the remaining seven were given prison terms of between two and four years. In March 2012, however, an appeals court converted the second defendant's life sentence to a death sentence, increased the prison terms of six of the remaining seven to between six and 10 years. It was, nevertheless, deemed unlikely that the death sentences would be carried out, since the 'gradual abolition' of the death penalty was one of the changes being implemented under the King's reform programme.

King Muhammad formally announced his proposed changes to the Constitution in June, having received the findings of the reform committee. These included a notable strengthening of the powers of the Prime Minister, who was to replace the King as head of government and who would henceforth appoint the Cabinet and dissolve the legislature. The King would, however, retain the right to chair meetings of an inner 'royal cabinet', and cabinet appointments would still need his approval. Moreover, he would also retain charge of military, security and religious affairs. As amended, the Constitution would provide for, *inter alia*, the appointment as Prime Minister of the leader of the largest party in the Chamber of Representatives; the designation of Berber as an official language of the state; an increase in the rights of women, who would be granted 'civic and social' as well as 'political' equality; and the creation of a Supreme Security Council, as part of efforts to reduce corruption.

At a national referendum on 1 July 2011 the new Constitution—which was to come into effect after the next parliamentary elections—was approved by 98.5% of participating voters. Voter turnout was officially recorded at 73.5%. Although all the main political parties had campaigned in favour of the constitutional changes, the amendments failed to satisfy pro-reform activists, who continued to demand a further easing of the King's still far-reaching powers. Further opposition demonstrations followed the announcement of the outcome of the referendum. Supporters of the monarchy joined large counter-demonstrations.

Morocco's first Islamist-led Government

In August 2011 the Government confirmed that elections to the Chamber of Representatives would be held one year early, on 25 November, in order to allow the new Constitution to take effect. The number of seats in the legislature was to increase from 325 to 395—with 305 seats to be reserved for candidates from local party lists, and the remainder to be allocated to candidates on national lists. Each party would be required to allocate two-thirds of its share of those 90 seats to women and the remaining one-third to men under 40 years of age. In October Al-Adl wal-Ihsan joined other opposition groups in declaring that it would boycott the forthcoming polls. At the elections, the moderate Islamist PJD secured the highest number of seats, winning 107 overall, ahead of Istiqlal, with 60 seats, and the RNI, with 52. The PAM also performed strongly, taking 47 seats. The USFP returned 39 deputies, the MP 32, the UC 23 and the PPS 18. Voter turnout was recorded at 45.4%.

At the end of November 2011, in accordance with the terms of the revised Constitution, Benkirane, as the leader of the largest party in the Chamber of Representatives, was designated as Prime Minister, and in December he reached a coalition agreement with Istiqlal, the MP and the PPS. The new Cabinet was sworn in before the Chamber of Representatives in January 2012. Among the stated key aims of Benkirane's Government, which won a parliamentary vote of confidence at the end of the month, were measures to tackle poverty and corruption, reduce unemployment, particularly high rates of joblessness among young people, and stimulate economic growth. Meanwhile, also in December 2011 Karim Ghellab, of Istiqlal, became President of the Chamber of Representatives.

Social issues continued to dominate the domestic political agenda under the new administration. In May 2012 trade unions organized a mass demonstration in Casablanca to protest against the Government's perceived inaction in implementing substantive reforms, and to demand higher salaries and improved social conditions. The February 20 Movement continued its campaigns, leading a 3,000-strong protest march in Rabat in July. Later that month King Muhammad pledged to continue to pursue the programme of political and social reform, and, in response to the increasing prominence of Salafist activists and clerics, emphasized the moderate identity of Islam in Morocco. In January 2014 the parliament amended a provision of the penal code whereby, in the case of rape of a minor, the perpetrator could evade prosecution by marrying the victim under 'special circumstances'. Women's and human rights groups welcomed the change, but stated that further reforms of the code were needed to protect women against discrimination and violence.

A mass protest took place in Rabat in March 2013, led by trade unionists, human rights activists and members of the February 20 Movement to demand economic and social reforms, and to protest against continuing high rates of unemployment and living costs; some demonstrators demanded the replacement of Prime Minister Benkirane. (Further demonstrations in Rabat in May and July resulted in clashes between protesters and the police.) The Government's announcement, in April, that it was to defer some 15,000m. dirhams in investment spending, in an effort to address the public deficit, drew immediate criticism from its opponents, despite assurances that employment and social measures would not be affected.

Recent developments: a new coalition Government and the growing threat from Islamist militants

In May 2013 Istiqlal announced its withdrawal from the coalition Government, accusing Benkirane of monopolizing decisions in the Cabinet and criticizing his Government for pursuing policies that raised consumer prices. However, following an intervention by King Muhammad, the party revoked its decision. Istiqlal did, however, eventually withdraw from the Government in July. Benkirane subsequently began negotiations with opposition parties in an attempt to form a new coalition and in September the RNI agreed to join a new Government, alongside the PJD, MP and PPS (although five of the six Istiqlal ministers had been temporarily recalled to their posts earlier in the month).

The new Council of Ministers was formally appointed by King Muhammad in October 2013. The RNI received eight portfolios,

including those of foreign affairs, which was allocated to party Chairman Salaheddine Mezouar, and the economy and finance, which was assumed by Muhammad Boussaid. The PJD's representation was reduced, while other key portfolios were allocated to independents.

Opponents of the Government and the monarchy expressed renewed concerns over press freedom in September 2013, following the arrest of Ali Anouzla, the editor of the independent news website *Lakome*. Anouzla was charged with posting a link on his website to an al-Qa'ida video, which was critical of King Muhammad and called for an uprising against the Moroccan authorities. Anouzla was released on bail in October. Online access to *Lakome* within Morocco was subsequently blocked by the Ministry of the Interior. Throughout late 2013 and early 2014 international organizations, including Reporters Without Borders, urged the Government to withdraw the charges against Anouzla; however, in March 2015 his case remained under investigation. In May 2014 he was sentenced on appeal to a one-month suspended sentence for 'defamation and breach of public institutions', in a separate case.

The growing influence of militant Islamism in Moroccan society prompted concerns in 2014. In June the Government issued its Religious Guidance Support Plan, as part of its efforts to curb extremism. Meanwhile, the security forces carried out a number of operations against suspected militant Islamist groups: authorities dismantled an Islamist cell in April and in August troops were reportedly deployed to the border with Algeria to prevent terrorist attacks. The Ministry of the Interior reported in June that it had arrested six members of a recruitment cell for the jihadist group Islamic State (formerly Islamic State in Iraq and the Levant—ISIL), which had recently occupied territory in northern Iraq and Syria; in August–September further arrests were made in several locations across Morocco, while nine were arrested in a joint Moroccan-Spanish operation in Melilla. In September a draft law was announced which made attempting to join armed jihadi groups or attend training camps a criminal offence. Under the terms of the legislation, those found guilty of receiving training would be sentenced to between five and 15 years' imprisonment and fines of up to US $58,000. At the end of October the Government announced a national anti-terrorism plan, which would co-ordinate the activities of the police force, armed forces and auxiliary forces in the area of counter-terrorism. Five people were arrested on suspicion of seeking to join Islamic State in Marrakesh in November, while Islamist militant cells were uncovered in Meknès and el-Hajed, and in al-Hoceima in January 2015; in that month seven people were arrested in Morocco and Spain on charges of recruiting women to join Islamic State. Also in January an Algerian national affiliated to the militant Islamist group Jund al-Khilafa (Soldiers of the Caliphate) suspected of involvement in the abduction and beheading of a French tourist in September 2014 (see the chapter on Algeria) was arrested near Oujda. In November 2014 the Ministry of the Interior had announced the arrest of six men in the region of Berkane, near Oujda, for making a video in which they announced 'the appearance of Jund al-Khilafa' in Morocco. In February 2015 three individuals were arrested for attempting to join Islamic State, in Casablanca and Oujda. Some 2,000 Moroccan citizens were estimated to be fighting alongside Islamist militants in Iraq and Syria in early 2015.

The February 20 Movement for Change held a number of demonstrations in 2014 provoking a robust response from the authorities. In July an activist was sentenced to three years' imprisonment having been convicted of making a false claim of torture, while in August another activist was sentenced to one year in gaol for falsely claiming to have been beaten by police while attending a trade union demonstration in Tangier. Human rights organizations, both domestic and international, expressed concerns over the number of individuals who were thought to be imprisoned for political reasons. According to information published by the Association for the Defence of Human Rights in Morocco, the number had risen significantly during the first half of 2014. In July, on the 15th anniversary of his accession to the throne, King Muhammad granted a pardon to some 13,218 prisoners.

In November 2014 Morocco, which was due to stage the Africa Cup of Nations football tournament in early 2015, announced that it was withdrawing as host due to the risk that supporters and players from West Africa could import into Morocco the Ebola Virus Disease, which had developed into a pandemic on that part of the continent earlier in 2014. Morocco, which had requested that the tournament be postponed until 2016, was subsequently disqualified from the tournament, and in February 2015 the Confederation of African Football fined the Royal Moroccan Football Federation a total of US \$9.0m. for its refusal to host the tournament. Meanwhile, in January the Minister of Youth and Sports, Muhammad Ouzzine, was dismissed from the Government. This followed an incident in which a football stadium in Rabat had been flooded during a match. He was succeeded in an acting capacity by the Minister of Planning and Development, Mohand Laenser.

Western Sahara

Following the cession of the Spanish enclave of Ifni to Morocco in 1969, political opinion in Morocco was united in opposing the continued occupation by Spain of areas considered to be historically parts of Moroccan territory: namely Spanish Sahara and Spanish North Africa (q.v.)—a number of small enclaves on Morocco's Mediterranean coast. A campaign to annex Spanish Sahara, initiated in 1974, received active support from all Moroccan political parties. In October 1975 King Hassan ordered a 'Green March' by more than 300,000 unarmed Moroccans to occupy the territory. The marchers were stopped by the Spanish authorities as soon as they had crossed the border, but in November Spain agreed to cede the territory to Morocco and Mauritania, to be apportioned equally between them. Spain formally relinquished sovereignty of Spanish Sahara in February 1976. Moroccan troops moved into the territory to confront a guerrilla uprising led by the Frente Popular para la Liberación de Saguia el-Hamra y Río de Oro (the Polisario Front), a national liberation movement supported by Algeria and (later) Libya, which aimed to achieve an independent Western Saharan state. Polisario declared the 'Sahrawi Arab Democratic Republic' (SADR) on 27 February, and shortly afterwards established a 'Government-in-exile' in Algeria. In protest, Morocco severed diplomatic relations with Algeria.

Moroccan troops inflicted heavy casualties on the insurgents, but failed to prevent infiltration, harassment and sabotage by Polisario forces. After Mauritania renounced its claim to Saharan territory and signed a peace treaty with the Polisario Front in August 1979, Morocco immediately asserted its claim to the whole of Western Sahara and annexed the region.

In July 1980 the SADR applied to join the Organization of African Unity (OAU, now African Union—AU, see p. 188) as a sovereign state. Although 26 of the 50 members then recognized the Polisario Front as the rightful government of Western Sahara, Morocco insisted that a two-thirds' majority was needed to confer membership. Morocco rejected an OAU proposal for a ceasefire and a referendum on the territory, and heavy fighting resumed in the region in 1981. The SADR was accepted as the OAU's 51st member in early 1982, but a threat by 18 members to leave the organization in protest necessitated a compromise whereby the SADR remained as a member but agreed not to attend meetings. In late 1984 a SADR delegation did attend a summit meeting of the OAU with little opposition from other states, causing Morocco to resign from the organization. Meanwhile, Morocco constructed a 2,500 km defensive wall of sand to surround the territory of Western Sahara.

In October 1985 Morocco announced a unilateral ceasefire in Western Sahara, and invited the UN to supervise a referendum (then scheduled to be held in the territory in the following January). A series of indirect talks between the two sides in 1986–87 failed to make progress, and in January 1988 Polisario forces renewed their offensive against Moroccan positions in Western Sahara. In August, however, it was announced that the Polisario Front and Morocco had provisionally accepted a UN-proposed peace plan, which envisaged the conclusion of a formal ceasefire, a reduction in Moroccan military forces in Western Sahara and the withdrawal of Polisario forces to their bases, to be followed by a referendum on self-determination in Western Sahara. A list of eligible voters was to be based on the Spanish census of 1974. A meeting in Marrakesh in January 1989 between King Hassan and officials of the Polisario Front and the SADR—the first direct contact for 13 years—was followed, in February, by the announcement of a unilateral ceasefire by Polisario. In September, however, Hassan rejected the possibility of official negotiations with the SADR, and Polisario subsequently renewed attacks on Moroccan positions.

UN Security Council Resolution 690, of April 1991, established a peacekeeping force, the UN Mission for the Referendum in Western Sahara (MINURSO, see p. 87), which to implement the 1988 plan for a referendum on self-determination. In June 1991 Polisario agreed to a formal ceasefire, with effect from September, whereupon the MINURSO force, with an initial envisaged strength of 2,000 troops, would deploy in the region. Morocco, for its part, would withdraw one-half of its 130,000 troops from Western Sahara by September. Reports that month suggested that some 30,000 people had entered Western Sahara from Morocco, prompting claims that the Moroccan authorities were attempting to alter the region's demography in advance of the referendum. It was also reported that more than 170,000 Sahrawis who had fled the region since 1976 were being repatriated in order that they might participate in the referendum. By November 1991 only 200 MINURSO personnel had been deployed in Western Sahara, while Morocco had not withdrawn any of its forces from the region. In May 1992 the UN Secretary-General, Dr Boutros Boutros-Ghali, announced that Morocco and Polisario representatives were to begin indirect talks under his auspices. In the same month, however, Morocco appeared to prejudge the result of the proposed referendum by including the population of Western Sahara in the voting lists for its own regional and local elections. In June the SADR Government, which by this time was recognized by 75 countries, appealed to the international community and the UN to condemn alleged Moroccan violations of the ceasefire and to exert pressure for the implementation of the UN peace plan.

In July 1993 the first direct negotiations took place between the Moroccan Government and Polisario, although little progress was achieved. In April 1994 Polisario accepted the UN programme for the registration of voters. However, the work of a UN voter identification commission, which had been due to commence in June, was delayed by the Moroccan Government's objection to the inclusion of OAU observers in the process. In mid-1995 Polisario withdrew from the voter identification process, in protest against the severity of sentences placed upon pro-independence Sahrawi protesters by the Moroccan authorities and against alleged Moroccan violations of the ceasefire. In September the SADR announced the formation of a new 14-member Government, headed by Mahfoud Ali Beïba, and in October the first elected Sahrawi national council was inaugurated at a refugee camp in Tindouf, Algeria. In May 1996 the UN Security Council voted to suspend the registration of voters in Western Sahara until 'convincing proof' was offered by the Moroccan Government and the Sahrawi leadership that they would not further obstruct preparations for the referendum.

In March 1997 the new UN Secretary-General, Kofi Annan, appointed James Baker (a former US Secretary of State) as his Personal Envoy for Western Sahara. By September 1998 a total of 147,350 voters had been identified since the commencement of the process of identification in August 1994, but the issue of disputed tribes remained unresolved. In June 1998, meanwhile, as Morocco intensified its efforts to rejoin the OAU, several member states debated the expulsion from the organization of the SADR; only a minority of OAU member countries continued to recognize its independent status at this time.

During talks with Moroccan and SADR officials in November 1998, the UN warned that it would withdraw from Western Sahara if the two parties failed to show goodwill towards resolving the conflict. Annan presented proposals regarding the disputed tribes, the publication of a list of voters not contested by either party and the repatriation of refugees under the auspices of the UN High Commissioner for Refugees (UNHCR). Although the proposals were accepted by Polisario, the Moroccan authorities expressed reservations. In July 1999 MINURSO published a list of 84,251 people provisionally entitled to vote in the referendum, which was scheduled to be held on 31 July 2000.

In February 1999, meanwhile, the SADR announced the formation of a new Government, led by Bouchraya Hammoudi Bayoune. In September the Polisario Front congress re-elected the President of the SADR, Muhammad Abd al-Aziz, as its Secretary-General. In September King Muhammad established a royal commission to monitor affairs in Western Sahara, and in October, at the King's behest, a Moroccan Government delegation was dispatched to el-Aaiún (Laâyoune), the principal city in Western Sahara, for consultations. Polisario released 191 Moroccan prisoners in November. In January 2000 it was announced that 86,381 of a total of 198,481 people identified in Western Sahara would be eligible to vote in the referendum. However, in February the UN Secretary-General postponed the referendum indefinitely: Annan warned that persistent differences regarding criteria for eligibility to vote meant that the referendum might never take place. By March the number of appeals lodged by those deemed ineligible to vote exceeded 130,000. In October Annan urged Morocco partially to devolve authority in Western

Sahara, stating that if no concessions were granted in this regard, the UN would reactivate referendum plans.

In June 2001 the UN Security Council unanimously approved a compromise resolution (No. 1359), which encouraged Polisario and Morocco to discuss an autonomy plan for Western Sahara without abandoning the postponed referendum. Under the autonomy proposal, formulated by Baker, the inhabitants of Western Sahara would have the right to elect their own legislative and executive bodies; the territory would control most areas of local government for a period of at least five years, during which Morocco would retain control over defence and foreign affairs. A referendum on final status would take place within this five-year period. Representatives of Polisario, Mauritania and Algeria attended talks hosted by Baker in Wyoming, USA, in August; however, Polisario subsequently accused the UN of ceding to Moroccan pressure, and in September Polisario announced its formal rejection of Baker's proposal. King Muhammad visited Western Sahara in October, for the first time since his accession to the throne, and in November granted an amnesty to 56 prisoners there.

Following exploratory negotiations held between Baker and government officials in Mauritania and Algeria, as well as with Abd al-Aziz and King Muhammad, in May 2003 Annan formally released details of a new peace plan for Western Sahara. The so-called Baker Plan II proposed immediate self-government for Western Sahara for a period of four to five years, after which time a referendum would be held in order to give all bona fide residents the opportunity to decide the long-term future of the territory. The UN Security Council approved the proposals in June. Polisario, under strong pressure from Algeria, accepted the plan as a basis for negotiation, but Morocco refused to accept any 'imposed decision' on Western Sahara. In July the Security Council unanimously adopted Resolution 1495, which supported Baker Plan II and urged the parties and states of the region to co-operate fully with the Secretary-General and his Personal Envoy towards its implementation. (Notably, however, following strong opposition from France, the resolution did not demand that Morocco and Polisario comply with the plan.) The resolution also called on Polisario to release without further delay all remaining Moroccan prisoners of war, and for both sides to co-operate with the International Committee of the Red Cross to resolve the fate of persons unaccounted for since the beginning of the conflict. Polisario released more than 600 Moroccan prisoners of war by February 2004.

In April 2004 the UN Security Council unanimously adopted Resolution 1541, which urged the two sides to accept the UN plan to grant Western Sahara immediate self-government. Morocco, however, continued to reject this proposal, maintaining that it could not accept a referendum plan that included independence as an option; instead, it insisted on granting the territory 'autonomy within the framework of Moroccan sovereignty'. In June Baker resigned as Annan's Personal Envoy for Western Sahara and was succeeded by Alvaro de Soto, of Peru, who had hitherto been the Secretary-General's Special Representative for Western Sahara. In September de Soto commenced talks with the Moroccan authorities and Polisario, and a resolution (No. 1570) adopted by the Security Council in October calling for an advancement towards a political solution was welcomed by the Moroccan authorities. In July 2005 Polisario released the remaining 408 Moroccan prisoners of war. In a televised address to mark the 30th anniversary of the Green March, King Muhammad announced his intention to consult with Morocco's political parties on the issue of autonomy for Western Sahara 'within the sovereignty of the kingdom'. However, Polisario immediately rejected the plan, and stated that a referendum was the only viable solution.

During a visit to Western Sahara in March 2006, King Muhammad announced the appointment of a revised Royal Advisory Council for Saharan Affairs (CORCAS—originally established by his father in 1981). The 140 newly appointed members were to assist with the formulation of draft proposals for Sahrawi autonomy. Royal pardons were granted to 216 Sahrawi prisoners, and in April the King ordered the release of all the remaining 48 Sahrawi prisoners held by Morocco.

The 'Moroccan initiative for negotiating an autonomy statute for the Sahara region' was finally presented to the UN Security Council in April 2007. It proposed the granting of extensive legislative, executive and judicial autonomy to the region, with Morocco retaining sovereignty and control of borders, as well as responsibility for national security, and foreign and religious affairs. The plan was rejected by Polisario, which immediately

offered the UN a rival plan for a referendum with three options—full independence, autonomy within Morocco or full integration—including proposals for a special political and economic relationship with Morocco in the event of a vote for independence. At the end of April the Security Council unanimously adopted Resolution 1754, which described Morocco's plan as 'serious and credible', while also noting the Polisario proposal. UN-mediated talks between Morocco and Polisario (attended by representatives of Algeria and Mauritania) took place in June and August in Manhasset, New York, USA; these were followed by two further rounds of negotiations in January and March 2008. While the talks failed to achieve any significant progress, Moroccan officials and Polisario agreed to consider relaxing travel restrictions in the disputed territory. Resolution 1813, adopted by the Security Council in April 2008, emphasized the legitimacy of the Moroccan autonomy proposal.

In April 2009 the Security Council approved Resolution 1871, reiterating the principles of the previous year's resolution. Informal talks took place between representatives of Polisario and the Moroccan Government in Vienna, Austria, in August. However, tensions arose in October when seven Sahrawi human rights activists were arrested in Casablanca and charged with making contact with parties hostile to Morocco after they had visited Sahrawi refugee camps in Tindouf.

Informal discussions between the Moroccan Government and Polisario were held under UN auspices in Armonk, New York, USA, in February 2010, but ended without substantive agreement. UN Security Council Resolution 1920, adopted in April, welcomed progress towards direct negotiations. In May Polisario officials announced that they were suspending contact with MINURSO, because of its failure to implement the referendum on self-determination, and accused the UN mission of supporting Morocco's occupation of Western Sahara. The Moroccan Government, in contrast, expressed its satisfaction that the UN continued to place the focus of bilateral negotiations on Morocco's autonomy proposal. Another round of informal talks (with Algerian and Mauritanian participation) was held in Manhasset in November. Despite a negative assessment of the talks by Polisario representatives, there had reportedly been agreement on the convening of future talks. Meanwhile, there were violent demonstrations in el-Aaiún, after Moroccan security forces forcibly entered a camp close to the city, where a large group of displaced Sahrawis had for several weeks been protesting against social and economic conditions in the territory. According to UN reporting, 11 members of the Moroccan security forces and two Sahrawis (one a minor) were killed. (In February 2013 a military tribunal in Rabat sentenced nine Sahrawi civilians to life imprisonment for their part in the violence.)

A sixth round of UN-sponsored informal talks took place in Valletta, Malta, in March 2011. UN Security Council Resolution 1979, adopted in April, notably emphasized the importance of improving the human rights situation in Western Sahara and the Tindouf camps, and welcomed Morocco's establishment of its National Human Rights Council (see *King Muhammad announces constitutional reform*) with a proposed component concerning Western Sahara. It was reported that further discussions held under UN auspices in June and July 2011 had failed to break the deadlock between Morocco and Polisario. Meanwhile, in June there were reports that a group of young Sahrawis had formed a rival movement to the Polisario Front, to be based in Spain, amid frustration over the failure of the Front to further the negotiations. Abd al-Aziz was re-elected as Secretary-General of the Polisario Front and a new SADR Government was formed in January 2012. In mid-February voting took place in refugee camps in western Algeria and in what Polisario termed 'liberated' territories of Western Sahara for the SADR national council; when the council convened in Tifariti at the end of the month, Khatri Adduh was elected as its speaker for a second term.

A ninth round of informal talks was held in Manhasset in March 2012. The UN Secretary-General's report to the Security Council, published in April, expressed frustration at the perceived obstruction of MINURSO's operations by Morocco. In late April the Security Council adopted Resolution 2044, which, among other remarks, welcomed the commencement of operations by commissions of the Moroccan National Council on Human Rights in el-Aaiún and Dakhla, and anticipated the inauguration—as part of confidence-building measures adopted under UNHCR auspices in Geneva, Switzerland, in January—of the facilitation of family visits by land and advanced communication links.

Progress towards further UN-sponsored talks, planned for June and July 2012, was impeded after the Moroccan Government, in May, withdrew confidence in the Secretary-General's Personal Envoy, Christopher Ross, accusing him of bias. A third meeting of representatives of Morocco, Polisario, Algeria and Mauritania to discuss confidence-building measures was, meanwhile, convened in Geneva in September. Eventually—and following intervention by Ban Ki-Moon—Ross resumed mediation, and, during a visit to the region in October–November, made his first visit to Western Sahara. In early April 2013, in his annual report to the UN Security Council regarding Western Sahara, Ban noted that Ross had secured the continued commitment of the Moroccan Government and Polisario, as well as neighbouring states, to remain engaged in the UN-sponsored effort. However, it had been agreed that, since Morocco and Polisario remained 'strongly attached' to their respective proposals, and had yet to consider possible compromises, to convene further informal talks in the near future would not advance the negotiating process. Ross made a second visit in March–April, with a view to the commencement of bilateral consultations. In mid-April, prior to the annual Security Council vote to extend the MINURSO mission, Morocco cancelled scheduled joint military exercises involving some 1,400 US and 900 Moroccan personnel, following a proposal by the USA to expand the mandate of the peacekeeping force to encompass monitoring and investigation of human rights issues in Western Sahara. Morocco stated that such an extension of MINURSO's remit would represent an attack on its national sovereignty. Resolution 2099, adopted unanimously in late April, included compromise wording which encouraged parties to the conflict to continue their respective efforts to enhance the promotion and protection of human rights in Western Sahara and the refugee camps; and recognized and welcomed steps taken by Morocco to strengthen operations of the National Council on Human Rights in this regard, together with Morocco's ongoing interaction with the UN Human Rights Council. MINURSO'S mandate was extended for a further year, and again in April 2014 when the UN adopted Resolution 2152. In July Kim Bolduc was appointed as Special Representative of the UN Secretary-General and MINURSO Head of Mission.

The Moroccan authorities arrested six Sahrawis in el-Aaiún in May 2013 for participating in pro-independence demonstrations, which descended into violent clashes between protesters and the police. In October Ross visited Rabat and el-Aaiún, where protests were reportedly suppressed by Moroccan security forces. In a measure apparently intended to accommodate the UN, Morocco released four Sahrawis from a prison in el-Aaiún in October; however, violent clashes were reported in the city in November, following a speech by King Muhammad on the anniversary of the Green March, in which he reaffirmed Morocco's sovereignty over Western Sahara. Violent clashes took place in el-Aaiún in June 2014 between Sahrawi demonstrators and the police, during a protest calling for a human rights mechanism within the MINURSO mission. In November the King affirmed that autonomy was the 'maximum' settlement Morocco would offer Polisario, while rejecting any change in the parameters of negotiations, or the possibility of a human rights track in the MINURSO mission. The King urged Algeria to withdraw its support for Polisario, to which the latter responded with a threat to 'return to armed struggle' if Morocco and the international community failed to comply with UN resolutions. In February 2015 Western Saharan activists demanded that Spain desist from deporting a Moroccan human rights activist, who had been sentenced to life in prison *in absentia* by a Moroccan military court in 2013, on charges of killing Moroccan security forces during unrest in el-Aaiún in 2010, amid fears that he would be mistreated in Moroccan custody.

Foreign Affairs

Regional relations

Relations with other North African states, which had been strained by the situation in Western Sahara, improved significantly in the late 1980s. Morocco re-established diplomatic relations with Mauritania in April 1985 (they had been suspended in 1981) and with Algeria in May 1988. In February 1989 North African heads of state, meeting in Marrakesh, signed a treaty establishing the Union du Maghreb Arabe (UMA—Union of the Arab Maghreb, see p. 450). The new body, grouping Morocco, Algeria, Libya, Mauritania and Tunisia, aimed to promote trade by allowing the free movement of goods, services and workers. However, there were political disagreements

particularly concerning Algeria's continued support for the Polisario Front, and over Moroccan condemnation of Iraq's invasion of Kuwait in August 1990. In early 1993 the five UMA members decided that there should be a 'pause' in the development of a closer union; of 15 conventions signed since the inauguration of the UMA, none had been fully applied. However, the organization continued to hold meetings on an annual basis. In December 1995 King Hassan expressed disapproval at Algeria's continued support for the independence of Western Sahara, and demanded that UMA activities be suspended.

During 1999 and 2000 both President Zine al-Abidine Ben Ali of Tunisia and King Muhammad pledged to take measures to reactivate the UMA. A summit meeting of ministers responsible for foreign affairs of the five UMA states proceeded in the Algerian capital in March 2001. However, the meeting quickly broke down following disagreements between Moroccan and Algerian representatives. Libya assumed the chairmanship of the UMA in December 2003, and a summit meeting of the UMA heads of state was scheduled to take place in Tripoli, Libya, in May 2005. However, a statement of renewed support for the Polisario Front by the Algerian President, Abdelaziz Bouteflika, provoked a fresh dispute between Morocco and Algeria days before the meeting was due to begin, and King Muhammad declined to attend. Despite the ongoing failure to convene an official UMA summit, a meeting was held in Tangier in April 2008 to celebrate the 50th anniversary of the first proposal of a union of Arab states in the Maghreb; this was attended by both the Prime Ministers of Morocco and Algeria, along with delegates from the three other UMA member states. The meeting ended amicably, with renewed appeals for regional political and economic co-operation. Ministers responsible for foreign affairs from the UMA member states met again in Tripoli a year later.

The developments arising from the mass protests across the region from the end of 2010 and subsequent changes of government apparently led to the furthering of co-operation between the countries of the Maghreb. Following the ouster of President Ben Ali in January 2011, the new Tunisian Government offered to host a UMA summit meeting in Tunis; and representatives of the five member states attended what was reported as the first meeting for 18 years of the UMA Monitoring Committee of ministers responsible for foreign affairs, which took place in Rabat in February 2012. A meeting of central bank governors and ministers of the UMA countries was held in Nouakchott, Mauritania, in January 2013, attended by the Managing Director of the IMF, Christine Lagarde, at which the establishment was announced of a UMA investment bank to finance, in partnership with the private sector, infrastructural development projects for the region. UMA ministers of the interior met in Rabat in April for discussions on regional security. King Muhammad made an official visit to Tunisia in May 2014, where he held talks with President Moncef Marzouki. They issued a joint communiqué at the end of the visit and reaffirmed their respective attachment to the UMA, and reiterated their determination to work with the other UMA countries to hold a summit meeting in Tunisia before the end of 2014.

Efforts were made to normalize relations between Morocco and Algeria from the late 1990s, although the Western Sahara issue continued to be a particular source of tension, and the border, closed in 1994, remained unopened. Bouteflika was vocal in opposing the UN proposals for Western Sahara in mid-2001, which he claimed unduly favoured Morocco. Morocco asserted that Algerian support for the partition of Western Sahara risked destabilizing the region. During a visit to Algiers by the Moroccan Minister of Foreign Affairs and Co-operation in June 2003, it was agreed to establish three bilateral commissions to consider political, economic and social matters. Following talks in July 2004 between the Moroccan Minister of the Interior and his Algerian counterpart, the two countries signalled their desire to improve diplomatic relations. In May 2005, however, Bouteflika issued a statement renewing Algeria's support for the Polisario Front, and in October allegations by Polisario that Morocco had abandoned African migrants in the Western Saharan desert further increased tensions between the two countries. Prime Minister Driss Jettou accused Algeria of instigating the allegations, and claimed that Algeria had exacerbated the problem by allowing some illegal immigrants to establish camps close to their joint border. In April 2009, at the Tripoli meeting of UMA ministers of foreign affairs, the Moroccan minister declared his country's readiness to renew bilateral relations with Algeria.

During 2011 officials from both countries continued to express their hopes for a swift normalization of relations. Morocco's newly appointed Minister of Foreign Affairs and Co-operation, Saâdeddine el-Othmani, visited Algiers in January 2012 for talks with his Algerian counterpart, Mourad Medelci, and with President Bouteflika. In April it was reported that the new Moroccan Prime Minister, Abdelilah Benkirane, had left the funeral of the first President of independent Algeria, Ahmed Ben Bella, on the instruction of King Muhammad, after discovering that the Polisario leader, Muhammad Abd al-Aziz, was also present. None the less, relations in general continued to improve throughout the year. In April 2013 Morocco's Minister of the Interior, Mohand Laenser, visited Algiers for talks with his counterpart, Dahou Ould Kablia; and, following the Rabat meeting of UMA interior ministers later in the month, Kablia stated that the issue of the two countries' joint border could soon be resolved. However, in July 2013 the Algerian Ministry of Foreign Affairs announced that discussions with Morocco had failed to produce an agreement on reopening the border between the two countries, and criticized Morocco for engaging in a 'distortion campaign' against Algeria, in retaliation for the latter's support for Polisario. In mid-2014 Morocco and Algeria began construction of a barbed-wire fence at the north end of their mutual border, which they announced would eventually run its entire length.

Morocco participated in the international coalition force, led by the North Atlantic Treaty Organisation (NATO, see p. 367), established in March 2011 to protect Libyan civilians from attack by armed forces loyal to Libyan leader Muammar al-Qaddafi. Following the overthrow of Qaddafi in August, and the capture and killing of the Libyan leader by opposition fighters in October, the Moroccan Government offered its support to the National Transitional Council that assumed power in Libya.

From the late 1990s Morocco was actively involved in wider regional integration efforts, as a member of the Community of Sahel-Saharan States (CEN-SAD, see p. 446), and also through bilateral and multilateral free trade arrangements; in May 2001, notably, the Governments of Morocco, Iraq, Jordan and Tunisia agreed, at a meeting in Agadir, to establish a free trade zone.

In September 1994 Morocco became only the second Arab country (after Egypt) to establish direct links with Israel; liaison offices were subsequently opened in Rabat and Tel-Aviv, Israel. In March 1997, however, in condemnation of recent Israeli settlement policy, ministers of foreign affairs of the League of Arab States (the Arab League, see p. 359) recommended a number of sanctions against Israel, including the closure of representative missions. Although in January 2000 Morocco and Israel agreed in principle to upgrade diplomatic relations to ambassadorial level, in October, as the crisis in Israeli–Palestinian relations deepened, Morocco announced that it had closed down Israel's liaison office in Rabat and its own representative office in Tel-Aviv. There was widespread outrage in Morocco in response to the Israeli military offensive in Palestinian-controlled areas of the West Bank from March 2002. Public demonstrations also took place in January 2009 in response to the military campaign launched by Israel against Islamic Resistance Movement (Hamas) targets in the Gaza Strip in December 2008. In October 2010 King Muhammad declined the possibility of holding discussions with the Israeli President, Shimon Peres, who was visiting Morocco to attend a meeting of the World Economic Forum. As Israeli-Palestinian talks within the context of the Middle East peace process remained at an impasse, the King cited his frustration over the Israeli Government's continued refusal to halt its settlement expansion programme.

Morocco's relations with Iran deteriorated abruptly in February 2009, after King Muhammad joined regional and international leaders in condemning a speech by Ali Akbar Nateq Nouri, a senior political figure in Iran, in which he described Bahrain as a former province of Iran; the remark was widely interpreted as an attack on Bahrain's sovereignty. Morocco's chargé d'affaires was recalled from Iran in late February—having apparently been the only diplomat to be summoned by the Iranian authorities to explain their country's response to the incident—and in March Morocco announced the suspension of diplomatic relations. Furthermore, Iran was also accused of interfering in the religious unity of Morocco through its promotion of Shi'a Islam in the mainly Sunni country. In December 2014 Iran and Morocco re-established bilateral relations when they appointed ambassadors to their respective capitals.

In May 2011, amid unprecedented political and social unrest occurring across large parts of the Middle East and North Africa, Morocco was formally, and apparently unexpectedly, invited (with Jordan) to apply to join the Cooperation Council of the Arab States of the Gulf (Gulf Cooperation Council—GCC, see p. 245). In December GCC member states created a development fund, offering both Morocco and Jordan an initial aid payment of US $2,500m. In October 2013 Morocco signed a strategic partnership with the GCC; the two parties created working groups to oversee joint action in trade, investment and education, among other areas.

Other external relations

Morocco signed an association agreement with the European Union (EU, see p. 271) in 1996, which provided for greater political and economic co-operation, financial aid and the eventual establishment of a free trade zone. In October 2008, in recognition of the Government's programme of social and political reforms, Morocco became the first Maghreb country to be accorded 'advanced status' relations with the EU. The new status was expected to enable Morocco to attract more European investment and financial aid, as well as allow Moroccan participation in some EU agencies and committees. In March 2013 the President of the European Commission, José Manuel Barroso, announced in Rabat that negotiations would begin on a comprehensive free trade agreement between the EU and Morocco in April, as well as an agreement on the movement of people between the two jurisdictions.

In 2007 Nicolas Sarkozy, during his election campaign for the French presidency, proposed the establishment of a Mediterranean Union to foster economic and political links between Mediterranean states. The initiative was described by Sarkozy as building on the Barcelona Process launched by Euro-Mediterranean governments in November 1995. The project—by now renamed the Union for the Mediterranean, and encompassing 43 countries, including all 27 EU member states—was formally inaugurated in Paris, France, in July 2008. In April, meanwhile, Morocco and France signed a number of agreements aimed at consolidating bilateral economic and social co-operation. A further 11 co-operation accords were signed in July 2010, including an agreement concerning French assistance to Morocco in nuclear energy. France also pledged €600m. in financial assistance for 2010–12, in support of Morocco's ongoing reform programme. Addressing the Moroccan parliament during a visit to Morocco in April 2013—in the course of which he met with King Muhammad and Prime Minister Benkirane—President François Hollande of France commended what he termed Morocco's 'decisive steps' towards democracy, noting the country's stability and the tolerance guaranteed by the constitutional amendments of 2011. With particular reference to the Islamist-led revolt in northern Mali (q.v.), Hollande emphasized the importance of achieving a resolution of the Western Sahara issue. King Muhammad, for his part, expressed support for the French military intervention in Mali. Bilateral investment accords signed during Hollande's visit were valued at an estimated €300m. Later in the month France supported Morocco in its opposition to US-led efforts at the UN Security Council to extend the MINURSO mandate to including monitoring of human rights issues (see *Western Sahara*). Morocco suspended judicial and legal co-operation agreements with France in early 2014 in protest against an attempt by a French judge to summon Abdellatif Hammouchi, the head of the Moroccan domestic intelligence service, for questioning in connection with allegations of torture made by Moroccan human rights activists. In January 2015 relations improved when the two countries resumed co-operation, although the Moroccan Government denied that it had requested legal immunity for its officials operating in France in future as a precondition. King Muhammad made an official visit to France in February 2015, where he met President Hollande and discussed security co-operation.

Following the approval by the Spanish parliament of statutes of autonomy for the enclaves of Ceuta and Melilla, in February 1995 Morocco intensified its diplomatic campaign to obtain sovereignty over the territories. In January 1998 the two countries established a joint commission to examine security issues, including illegal immigration (to Spain) and drugs-trafficking. The Spanish premier, José María Aznar, visited Morocco in May 2000, and in September, during King Muhammad's first visit to Spain since his accession, two economic co-operation agreements were signed. Nevertheless, relations remained strained owing to lack of progress in negotiations with the EU regarding a new fisheries accord and attacks by Spanish fishermen on lorries carrying Moroccan products through Spanish ports.

In July 2001, in an attempt to limit the increasing number of Moroccans entering Spain illegally, the two countries signed an agreement that would allow as many as 20,000 Moroccans to enter Spain each year in search of employment. In September, however, Spain refuted allegations made by King Muhammad that Spanish criminal associations were responsible for the large increase in numbers of Moroccan economic migrants attempting illegally to cross the Strait of Gibraltar, asserting that collusion between Moroccan police and the smugglers was ongoing. Morocco subsequently recalled its ambassador from Spain. Moroccan–Spanish relations were further strained in July 2002, when a small detachment of Moroccan troops occupied the uninhabited rocky islet of Perejil (called Leila by Morocco), west of the Spanish enclave of Ceuta and close to the Moroccan coastline. Morocco claimed that it was establishing a surveillance post on the island as part of its campaign against illegal emigration and drugs-trafficking. However, Spain insisted that there had been an agreement since 1990 that neither country would occupy Perejil, and, with the support of the EU and NATO, demanded the immediate evacuation of Moroccan troops from the island. Spain's ambassador to Morocco was recalled, and Spanish special forces intervened and forcibly removed Moroccan troops from Perejil. Spanish forces withdrew from the island following US mediation, and talks in Rabat later that month between Morocco and Spain resulted in an agreement to return to the *status quo ante*. In January 2003 King Muhammad temporarily allowed Spanish boats to fish in Moroccan waters, and in the following month the two countries agreed to the return of their respective ambassadors.

In December 2003 Morocco and Spain announced plans to construct a 39-km underwater rail tunnel between the two countries. However, although the feasibility study for the project—the scheduled completion date of which was 2025—was concluded by 2010, no final decision on whether to proceed with the plans had been made by early 2015. Meanwhile, in December 2011 Morocco responded to a decision by the EU not to renew the annual agreement whereby member states paid Morocco for licences to fish in its waters by announcing that EU fishing vessels were no longer permitted to fish off the Moroccan coast. The EU claimed that the current arrangement did not take into consideration the population of Western Sahara, from where most of the fishing took place. In July 2013 a new common fisheries agreement was reached between the EU and Morocco, under the terms of which Morocco would receive €40m. annually in return for allowing boats from 11 EU member states to fish in its waters, including those off Western Sahara. (The agreement was ratified by the Moroccan Government and the EU in December.) In March 2004 a series of bomb attacks on commuter trains in the Spanish capital, Madrid, killed 191 people. A number of Moroccans from the Groupe Islamique Combattant Marocain, who had also been linked with the Casablanca bombings of 2003, were among a group of suspected militant Islamists detained by the Spanish authorities in connection with the attacks, and in December 2004 a Moroccan man, Hassan al-Haski, was charged with having planned the bombings. (Al-Haski was sentenced to 14 years' imprisonment in Spain for his involvement in the Madrid bombings, and, following his extradition to Morocco in 2008, was also convicted of involvement in the Casablanca bombings and sentenced to 10 years' imprisonment.) In May 2004 Morocco and Spain announced plans to establish a joint task force to tackle terrorism and organized crime. However, relations were again strained in mid-2005, after several delegations of Spanish politicians and journalists, seeking to conduct investigations following demonstrations in Western Sahara, were accused by Morocco of supporting Sahrawi independence and were denied permission to enter the disputed territory.

In late 2005 Spain urged Morocco to increase its efforts to prevent illegal border crossings, and later suspended the return of unsuccessful migrants to Morocco, amid claims by human rights organizations that migrants had been taken to the southern Moroccan desert and abandoned by the authorities. At a bilateral summit meeting in March 2007, attended by the Spanish Prime Minister, José Luis Rodríguez Zapatero, the two countries reached an agreement on the prevention of unaccompanied child migrants. Zapatero also welcomed Morocco's plan for autonomy in Western Sahara as a means to the opening of dialogue within the framework of the UN. Morocco temporarily recalled its ambassador to Spain in November, when it was announced that King Juan Carlos of Spain would pay his first royal visit to Ceuta and Melilla. Nevertheless, bilateral relations improved markedly in late 2008, and Prime Ministers Zapatero

and Abbas el-Fassi attended a summit meeting in Madrid in December. Talks at the summit encompassed bilateral relations, immigration, Western Sahara, and economic and security co-operation. A Spanish investment fund of more than €520m. for infrastructure projects in Morocco was subsequently announced. In January 2009 agreements between the two countries on increased co-operation in security and law enforcement were finalized. The first EU-Morocco summit (a product of Morocco's 'advanced status' relations with the EU) was hosted by Spain during its presidency of the EU in March 2010.

There were renewed difficulties between Spain and Morocco in August 2010, after Moroccan demonstrators blockaded the country's border crossing with Melilla to assert their claims of sovereignty over the enclave. The protest followed official complaints by the Moroccan authorities that its citizens who entered the two Spanish enclaves on a daily basis had suffered mistreatment at the hands of the Spanish police. In November, following Spanish criticism of Morocco regarding the deaths of protesters at a camp in Western Sahara, Morocco's Chamber of Representatives voted in favour of referring the status of Ceuta and Melilla to the UN Special Committee on Decolonization. Relations eased somewhat following the attendance of the Spanish Crown Prince at a bilateral economic conference held in Morocco in June 2012. In July, however, it was reported that Morocco had sought clarification of remarks made during a visit to Melilla by the Spanish Minister of Home Affairs suggesting that Spain intended to reinforce its presence in the Chafarinas Islands (administered by Spain as part of Melilla) in order to counter illegal immigration and drugs-trafficking. King Juan Carlos of Spain paid an official visit to Rabat in July 2013, and the Spanish Government declared its intention to become Morocco's largest trading partner, with Spain having already overtaken France as Morocco's principal source of imports in 2012. Within the framework of bilateral accords signed during the visit, King Muhammad granted an amnesty to 48 Spanish nationals held in Moroccan prisons, as requested by King Juan Carlos; controversially, the released prisoners included Daniel Galván Viña, who had been sentenced to 30 years' imprisonment in 2011 for sexual offences against children. Following public protests in Rabat against Galván Viña's pardon, King Muhammad revoked the decision to release him later that month. However, by this time Galván Viña had returned to Spain; a court ruling in November declared that Spanish citizens could not be extradited to Morocco and that Galván Viña was to serve the remainder of his sentence in a Spanish gaol. A Moroccan court sentenced a former Spanish soldier who had served in Melilla to eight years' imprisonment in February 2015, having been convicted of leading a militant Islamist network. Seventeen other members of the group, all believed to be Moroccans, were sentenced to gaol terms of between two and 10 years.

The Moroccan Government was swift to condemn the suicide attacks on the USA in September 2001, for which the al-Qa'ida network was held responsible. In June 2002 the Moroccan authorities announced that they had arrested three Saudi nationals alleged to be members of an Islamist cell linked to al-Qa'ida which was preparing terrorist attacks on US and British warships in the Strait of Gibraltar. Seven Moroccans had also been arrested for allegedly acting as couriers between the suspects in Morocco and al-Qa'ida, which had provided them with funds and logistical support. In February 2003 the three Saudi Arabians were sentenced to 10 years' imprisonment by a court in Casablanca; six of the Moroccans received lesser sentences. Also in February a Moroccan student, Mounir al-Motassadek, who was alleged to have been a member of the cell that had planned and executed the September 2001 attacks, was convicted by a court in Hamburg, Germany, of belonging to a terrorist group and of aiding and abetting the murder of 3,066 people. He was sentenced to 15 years' imprisonment. In March 2004 al-Motassadek's conviction was quashed by the German Federal Criminal Court, and he was released from detention in April. A retrial began in August, and al-Motassadek was acquitted in August 2005 of involvement in the September 2001 attacks; he was nevertheless convicted of belonging to a terrorist organization and sentenced to seven years' imprisonment. In November 2006 the German Federal Court of Justice overturned al-Motassadek's acquittal on charges of accessory to murder, and he was again sentenced to 15 years' imprisonment in January 2007. A final appeal was rejected by the Federal Court of Justice in May.

In June 2004 Morocco became the second Arab country (after Jordan in 2001) to sign a free trade agreement with the USA; the accord was ratified by the Moroccan parliament in January 2005. In recent years the US Administration has praised Morocco for its strong leadership and its efforts against militant Islamist groups. During 2011 US officials also commended the Moroccan Government for the manner in which it responded to the opposition-led pro-democracy protests. Issues of human rights have, none the less, been the cause of some tension, most recently in April 2013, when Morocco opposed US-led efforts at the UN Security Council to include monitoring of human rights within the mandate of MINURSO (see *Western Sahara*). Observers noted that relations had improved after an official visit by King Muhammad to Washington, DC, USA in November, during which he held discussions over security in the Sahel-Sahara region and Morocco's role in suppressing Islamism with US President Barack Obama.

CONSTITUTION AND GOVERNMENT

The 2011 Constitution provides for a modified constitutional monarchy, with a hereditary King as head of state. Legislative power is vested in the Chamber of Representatives (Majlis al-Nuab), with 395 members directly elected, on the basis of universal adult suffrage, for five years, and in the Chamber of Advisers (Majlis al-Mustasharin), with no fewer than 90 and no more than 120 members, three-fifths of whom are elected by electoral colleges of local councils; the remainder are elected by electoral colleges representing chambers of commerce and trade unions. Members of the Chamber of Advisers are elected for a six-year term. Executive power is vested in the King, who must appoint as Prime Minister the leader of the party with the largest representation in the Chamber of Representatives. Upon the Prime Minister's recommendation, the King appoints the other members of the Cabinet. The Government must gain an absolute majority in a vote by the members of the Chamber of Representatives prior to taking office. Both the King and the Prime Minister may dissolve the legislature after consultation.

REGIONAL AND INTERNATIONAL CO-OPERATION

Morocco is a founder member of the Union du Maghreb Arabe (UMA—Union of the Arab Maghreb, see p. 450). The permanent headquarters of the organization are located in Rabat. The country also participates in the League of Arab States (the Arab League, see p. 359) and the Community of Sahel-Saharan States (CEN-SAD, see p. 446).

Morocco became a member of the UN in November 1956, having gained independence in March of that year. As a contracting party to the General Agreement on Trade and Tariffs, Morocco joined the World Trade Organization (WTO, see p. 431) on its establishment in 1995. The country also adheres to the Organization of Islamic Cooperation (OIC, see p. 401).

ECONOMIC AFFAIRS

In 2013, according to estimates by the World Bank, Morocco's gross national income (GNI), measured at average 2011–13 prices, was US $101,815m., equivalent to $3,030 per head (or $7,000 per head on an international purchasing-power parity basis). During 2004–13, it was estimated, the population increased at an average annual rate of 1.1%, while gross domestic product (GDP) per head increased, in real terms, by an average of 3.2% per year. Overall GDP increased, in real terms, at an average annual rate of 4.4% in 2004–13; it increased by 4.4% in 2013.

Agriculture (including forestry and fishing) contributed 16.6% of GDP, according to provisional figures, and engaged 39.4% of the employed labour force in 2013. The principal crops are cereals (mainly wheat and barley), sugar beet and sugar cane, citrus fruit, potatoes, olives, melons and tomatoes. Almost all of Morocco's meat requirements are produced within the country. The sale of licences to foreign fishing fleets is an important source of revenue. According to preliminary figures, seafoods and seafood products accounted for 6.4% of total exports in 2013. According to the World Bank, during 2004–12 agricultural GDP increased at an average annual rate of 2.6%; sectoral GDP increased by 5.1%, in 2011, but declined by 8.2% in 2012.

Industry (including mining, manufacturing, construction and power) provided 28.5% of GDP, according to provisional figures, and the sector (including handicrafts industry and public works) engaged 20.7% of the employed labour force in 2013. According to the World Bank, during 2004–12 industrial GDP increased by an average of 3.7% per year; sectoral GDP grew by 2.1% in 2012.

Mining and quarrying contributed 3.9% of GDP in 2013, according to provisional figures, and engaged only 0.6% of the employed labour force in 2012. The major mineral exports are phosphate rock and its derivatives, which together earned 20.2% of export revenues in 2013, according to preliminary figures. Morocco is the world's largest exporter of phosphate rock. Petroleum exploration activity was revived at the end of the 1990s, and the discovery of major oil and natural gas reserves in the Talsinnt region of eastern Morocco was announced in 2000. Coal, salt, iron ore, barytes, lead, copper, zinc, silver, gold and manganese are mined. Deposits of nickel, cobalt and bauxite have also been discovered. During 1990–2002 mining GDP increased at an average annual rate of 1.3%. According to official estimates, mining GDP increased by 1.8% in 2006.

Manufacturing, together with oil-refining, contributed 15.4% of GDP in 2013, according to provisional figures. The manufacturing sector engaged 10.5% of the employed labour force in 2012. The most important branches, measured by gross value of output, are oil-refining and energy products, food-processing, textiles, and chemicals. According to preliminary figures, manufactured garments accounted for 10.3% of export revenues in 2013. According to the World Bank, during 2004–12 manufacturing GDP increased at an average annual rate of 2.7%; the sector's GDP expanded by 1.7% in 2012.

Construction contributed 6.6% of GDP in 2013, according to provisional figures. The sector engaged 9.3% of the employed labour force in the same year.

In 2011 electric energy was derived principally from coal (47.0%), petroleum (26.4%), natural gas (16.3%) and hydroelectric power stations (7.5%). Facilities for generating wind power have also been developed. In 2009 the Government detailed a US $9,000m. project to develop five solar power plants; the project was due for completion by 2020, and was expected to have a capacity of 2,000 MW, equivalent to some 38% of Morocco's installed energy capacity. Construction of one of the plants, at Ouarzazate, near Marrakesh, was part-financed by the World Bank; the 160-MW first phase was expected to begin electricity production by late 2015. According to preliminary figures, imports of energy and lubricants comprised an estimated 26.9% of the value of total merchandise imports in 2013.

The services sector contributed an estimated 54.9% of GDP, according to provisional figures, and engaged 39.9% of the employed labour force in 2013. The tourism industry is generally a major source of revenue (accounting for some 9% of GDP in 2011), and foreign tourist arrivals totalled some 5.3m. in 2013. According to a 10-year strategy for the tourism industry announced in November 2010, 177,000m. dirhams would be invested in an attempt to raise the number of visitors to 18.6m. per year by 2020. The GDP of the services sector increased by an average of 5.2% per year during 2004–12, and by 6.1% in 2012, according to the World Bank.

In 2013 Morocco recorded a visible merchandise trade deficit of US $21,592m., and there was a deficit of $8,692m. on the current account of the balance of payments. According to preliminary figures, in 2013 the principal source of imports was Spain (which provided 13.5% of merchandise imports); other major suppliers in that year included France, the USA, the People's Republic of China and Italy. France was the principal market for exports (21.4%) in 2013; Spain and Brazil were also important purchasers of Moroccan exports. The principal exports in 2013 were finished consumer products (notably manufactured garments and hosiery), semi-finished products (including phosphoric acid and electronic components), foodstuffs, beverages and tobacco (particularly seafoods and seafood products), finished industrial capital goods, crude mineral products, and energy goods. The principal imports in that year were fuel and energy products (notably crude petroleum), semi-finished products, finished capital goods, finished consumer products, and foodstuffs, beverages and tobacco.

In 2013 Morocco recorded an overall budget deficit of 3,200m. dirhams. The country's general government gross debt was 563,496m. dirhams in 2013, equivalent to 64.6% of GDP. Morocco's total external debt in 2012 was US $33,816m., of which $25,087m. was public and publicly guaranteed debt. In that year, the cost of servicing long-term public and publicly guaranteed debt and repayments to the IMF was equivalent to 11.2% of the value of exports of goods, services and income (excluding workers' remittances). The annual rate of inflation averaged 1.6% in 2006–14; consumer prices increased by an average of 0.4% in 2014. According to official figures, some 9.2% of the labour force was unemployed in 2013.

Morocco has experienced sustained growth since the mid-2000s. However, from 2008 the economy has been affected by unfavourable external conditions, most notably the ongoing difficulties in the eurozone—which affected tourism, export earnings and remittances from abroad—and high prices for commodities. The external current account deficit, which had been in surplus until 2008, reached 8.3% of GDP in 2012, although it had narrowed to 5.8% by 2014, as the value of Moroccan exports increased. The IMF estimated a reduced rate of GDP growth, at 2.9% for 2014, but forecast an increase to 4.4% in 2015. In June 2012 the new Government increased the domestic prices of some subsidized energy products. The fiscal deficit fell to 5.5% of GDP in 2013, from 7.3% in 2012, and to 4.9% in 2014; the Government's objective was to reduce the deficit to 3.0% by 2017. In 2014 the IMF commended the removal of subsidies on all liquid petroleum products, although such measures conflicted with popular pressure on the Government to alleviate deteriorating conditions, including rising living costs. Moreover, the high rate of unemployment remained a particular concern: government figures in early 2014 put the rate of joblessness among 15–24-year-olds at 19%, and urban unemployment at 14%. In April 2013 the Government announced that it was to defer 15,000m. dirhams in planned investment spending, in an effort to reduce the public deficit. In July it announced that it was to invest 4,000m. dirhams in the non-phosphates mining industry, in an attempt to increase annual revenues to 15,000m. dirhams by 2025, and to provide around 15,000 additional jobs.

The Government's 2015 budget, which was approved by parliament in November 2014, provided for a reduction in subsidies from 35,000m. to 23,000m. dirhams in that year. Also in November 2014, parliament approved legislation allowing for the establishment of Islamic banks and the issuance of Islamic debt, while in February 2015 King Muhammad decreed the establishment of the Sharia Committee for Participative Finances, comprising Islamic scholars and financial experts, to regulate the country's Islamic finance industry.

PUBLIC HOLIDAYS

2016: 1 January (New Year), 11 January (Independence Manifesto), 1 May (Labour Day), 6–7 July* (Eid el-Seghir—Id al-Fitr, end of Ramadan), 30 July (Festival of the Throne, anniversary of King Muhammad's accession), 14 August (Oued el-Dahab Day, anniversary of the 1979 annexation), 20 August (The King and People's Revolution), 21 August (Festival of Youth—King Muhammad's Birthday), 12–13 September* (Eid el-Kebir—Id al-Adha, Feast of the Sacrifice), 2 October* (Muharram, Islamic New Year), 6 November (Anniversary of the Green March), 18 November (Independence Day), 11–12 December* (Mouloud, Birth of the Prophet),

* These holidays are dependent on the Islamic lunar calendar and may vary by one or two days from the dates given.

Statistical Survey

Sources (unless otherwise stated): Haut Commissariat au Plan, Direction de la Statistique, rue Muhammad Belhassan el-Ouazzani, BP 178, Rabat 10001; tel. (53) 7773606; fax (53) 7773217; e-mail statguichet@statistic.gov.ma; internet www.hcp.ma; Bank Al-Maghrib, 277 ave Muhammad V, BP 445, Rabat; tel. (53) 7702626; fax (53) 7706667; e-mail webmaster@bkam.ma; internet www.bkam.ma.

Note: Unless otherwise indicated, the data exclude Western (formerly Spanish) Sahara, a disputed territory under Moroccan occupation.

Area and Population

AREA, POPULATION AND DENSITY

Area (sq km)	710,850*
Population (census results)†	
2 September 1994	26,019,280
2 September 2004	
Males	14,640,662
Females	15,039,407
Total	29,680,069
Population (UN estimates at mid-year)‡	
2013	33,008,150
2014	33,492,908
2015	33,955,157
Density (per sq km) at mid-2015	47.8

* 274,461 sq miles. This area includes the disputed territory of Western Sahara, which covers 252,120 sq km (97,344 sq miles).
† Including Western Sahara, with an estimated population of 417,000 at the 2004 census.
‡ Source: UN, *World Population Prospects: The 2012 Revision*.

POPULATION BY AGE AND SEX
(UN estimates at mid-2015)

	Males	Females	Total
0–14 years	4,862,158	4,620,278	9,482,436
15–64 years	11,223,027	11,521,729	22,744,756
65 years and over	736,026	991,939	1,727,965
Total	16,821,211	17,133,946	33,955,157

Source: UN, *World Population Prospects: The 2012 Revision*.

REGIONS
(population at 2004 census)

	Population
Oued el-Dahab Lagouira*	73,067
El-Aaiún Boujdour*	245,562
Guelmim el-Semara†	425,211
Souss Massa-Draa	3,094,985
Gharb Chrarda Beni-Hsen	1,849,776
Chaouia Ouardigha	1,646,051
Marrakech Tensift al-Haou	3,088,338
Oriental	1,908,905
Grand Casablanca	3,615,903
Rabat Salé Zemmour Zaer	2,349,202
Doukkala Abda	1,978,189
Tadla Azilal	1,448,155
Meknès Tafilalet	2,125,608
Fès Boulemane	1,567,846
Taza al-Hoceima Taounate	1,803,051
Tanger Tétouan	2,460,220
Total	29,680,069

* Regions situated in Western Sahara.
† Region partly situated in Western Sahara.

PRINCIPAL TOWNS
(UN estimates at mid-2015)

Casablanca . .	3,514,958	Agadir	590,422
Rabat (capital)*	1,966,802	Tétouan	510,942
Fès (Fez) . .	1,172,112	Oujda	495,099
Marrakech			
(Marrakesh) .	1,133,609	Kénitra†	448,400
Tanger (Tangier) .	981,753	Safi	311,497

* Including Salé and Temara.
† Town situated in Western Sahara.

Source: UN, *World Urbanization Prospects: The 2014 Revision*.

BIRTHS AND DEATHS
(annual averages, UN estimates)

	2000–05	2005–10	2010–15
Birth rate (per 1,000) . . .	20.9	20.1	23.2
Death rate (per 1,000) . . .	6.1	6.3	6.3

Source: UN, *World Population Prospects: The 2012 Revision*.

Life expectancy (years at birth): 70.6 (males 68.9; females 72.5) in 2012 (Source: World Bank, World Development Indicators database).

ECONOMICALLY ACTIVE POPULATION
('000 persons aged 15 years and over)

	2010	2011	2012
Agriculture, hunting, forestry and fishing	4,188.1	4,179.0	4,119.8
Mining and quarrying	41.8	50.2	67.7
Manufacturing	1,182.7	1,148.4	1,102.8
Electricity, gas and water . . .	42.9	37.3	37.9
Construction	1,029.1	1,059.0	1,038.1
Wholesale and retail trade; repairs	1,522.7	1,555.9	1,593.6
Hotels and restaurants . .	248.2	266.8	269.0
Transport, storage and communications	464.6	493.5	470.2
General administration and community services . . .	1,005.1	1,020.4	1,069.7
Financial intermediation, real estate and business services .	665.2	683.9	729.1
Sub-total	10,390.5	10,494.3	10,497.9
Activities not adequately defined .	14.2	15.0	12.7
Total employed	10,404.7	10,509.3	10,510.6
Unemployed	1,037.1	1,028.3	1,038.2
Total labour force	11,441.8	11,537.6	11,548.8

2013 ('000): Agriculture, hunting, forestry and fishing 4,178; Industry (including handicraft) 1,213; Construction and public works 988; Services 4,232; *Sub-total* 10,611; Activities not adequately defined 13; *Total employed* 10,625; Unemployed 1,081; *Total labour force* 11,706.

Health and Welfare

KEY INDICATORS

Total fertility rate (children per woman, 2012)	2.7
Under-5 mortality rate (per 1,000 live births, 2012) . . .	31
HIV/AIDS (% of persons aged 15–49, 2012)	0.1
Physicians (per 1,000 head, 2009)	0.62
Hospital beds (per 1,000 head, 2009)	1.1
Health expenditure (2011): US $ per head (PPP)	321
Health expenditure (2011): % of GDP	6.3
Health expenditure (2011): public (% of total)	33.1
Access to water (% of persons, 2012)	84
Access to sanitation (% of persons, 2012)	75
Total carbon dioxide emissions ('000 metric tons, 2010) . .	50,608.3
Carbon dioxide emissions per head (metric tons, 2010) . .	1.6
Human Development Index (2013): ranking	129
Human Development Index (2013): value	0.617

For sources and definitions, see explanatory note on p. vi.

Agriculture

PRINCIPAL CROPS
('000 metric tons)

	2011	2012	2013
Wheat	6,018	3,878	6,934
Rice, paddy	18	70	38
Barley	2,318	1,201	2,723
Maize	221	90	118
Potatoes	1,721	1,657	1,929
Sugar cane	764	541	620
Sugar beet	3,035	1,627	2,142
Broad beans, dry	171	148	157
Peas, dry	40	29	37
Chick peas	46	33	25
Lentils	45	22	43
Almonds, with shell . . .	96	99	97
Groundnuts, with shell . . .	40	36	39
Olives	1,416	1,316	1,182
Sunflower seeds	48	18	19
Cabbages and other brassicas .	10	11*	10*
Artichokes	43	64	62
Tomatoes	1,218	1,219	1,293
Cauliflowers and broccoli . .	105	61	48
Pumpkins, squash and gourds .	220	257	224
Cucumbers and gherkins . .	51	55	48
Aubergines (Eggplants) . . .	35	50	72
Chillies and peppers, green . .	143	181	180
Onions, dry	861	856	930
Peas, green	160	131	125
String beans	121	134	155
Carrots and turnips	428	707	509
Carobs†	21	21	21
Watermelons	580	575	611
Cantaloupes and other melons .	778	718	700
Figs	115	103	102
Grapes	382	342	436
Dates	103	102	108
Apples	512	486	583
Pears	36	30	39
Quinces	32	46	40
Peaches and nectarines . . .	75	71	78
Plums and sloes	65	75	87
Strawberries	111	140	145
Oranges	850*	962	759
Tangerines, mandarins, clementines and satsumas . .	753	877	664
Apricots	159	122	120
Bananas	277	222	302
Anise, badian, fennel and coriander†	29	30	30

* Unofficial figure.
† FAO estimates.

Aggregate production ('000 metric tons, may include official, semi-official or estimated data): Total cereals 8,689 in 2011, 5,311 in 2012, 9,874 in 2013; Total pulses 340 in 2011, 286 in 2012, 298 in 2013; Total roots and tubers 1,739 in 2011, 1,683 in 2012, 1,955 in 2013; Total vegetables (incl. melons) 5,601 in 2011, 5,634 in 2012, 5,633 in 2013; Total fruits (excl. melons) 3,638 in 2011, 3,775 in 2012, 3,630 in 2013.

Source: FAO.

LIVESTOCK
('000 head, year ending September)

	2011	2012	2013
Cattle	3,038	3,029	3,173
Sheep	18,737	19,006	19,956
Goats	5,991	5,602	6,236
Camels*	55	57	57
Horses	140	138	139
Asses	950	947	944
Mules	465	457	453
Chickens*	175,000	180,000	185,000

* FAO estimates.
Source: FAO.

LIVESTOCK PRODUCTS
('000 metric tons)

	2011	2012	2013
Cattle meat	199	204	254
Sheep meat	143	148	118
Goat meat	24	24	26
Chicken meat	590	560*	602
Cows' milk	2,200	2,500	2,300
Sheep's milk*	38	40	40
Goats' milk*	59	60	62
Hen eggs*	265	272	278
Honey	4	4	5
Wool, greasy*	55	56	56

* FAO estimate(s).

Source: FAO.

Forestry

ROUNDWOOD REMOVALS
('000 cubic metres, excl. bark, FAO estimates)

	2011	2012	2013
Sawlogs, veneer logs and logs for sleepers	113	113	113
Pulpwood	259	259	259
Fuel wood	6,762	6,741	6,720
Total	7,134	7,113	7,092

Source: FAO.

SAWNWOOD PRODUCTION
('000 cubic metres, incl. railway sleepers, FAO estimates)

	2011	2012	2013
Coniferous (softwood)	40	26	43
Broadleaved (hardwood)	40	27	40
Total	80	53	83

Note: Production assumed to be unchanged from 1989.

Source: FAO.

Fishing

('000 metric tons, live weight)

	2010	2011	2012
Capture	1,136.2	958.9	1,171.5
European pilchard (sardine)	771.5	504.0	672.8
Chub mackerel	76.0	121.3	126.6
Jack and horse mackerels	23.2	22.1	22.0
Octopuses	32.0	32.7	18.4
Aquaculture*	1.5	1.4	1.5
Total catch (incl. others)*	1,137.8	960.3	1,173.0

* FAO estimates.

Note: Figures exclude aquatic plants ('000 metric tons, all capture): 7.4 in 2010; 5.8 in 2011; 5.2 in 2012. Also excluded are corals (metric tons, all capture): 7.1 in 2010; 7.4 in 2011; 6.4 in 2012.

Source: FAO.

Mining

('000 metric tons)

	2010	2011	2012
Iron ore*	44.7	78.9	260.7
Copper concentrates*	53.3	43.0	59.0
Lead concentrates*	46.4	43.8	39.1
Manganese ore*	75.6	58.0	90.2
Zinc concentrates*	87.4	90.1	91.6
Phosphate rock†	26,603.0	28,052.0	27,060.0
Fluorspar (acid grade)	89.7	79.2	79.3
Barytes	572.4	769.5	1,021.4
Salt (unrefined)	503.4	720.8	730.0
Bentonite	110.7	97.1	91.2

* Figures refer to the gross weight of ores and concentrates.
† Including production in Western Sahara.

Source: Ministère de l'Energie, des Mines, de l'Eau et de l'Environnement.

Industry

SELECTED PRODUCTS
('000 metric tons unless otherwise indicated)

	2009	2010	2011
Wine*	29	33	34
Olive oil (crude)†	112	147	134
Motor spirit—petrol	313	328	415
Naphthas	335	538	448
Distillate fuel oils	1,385	2,256	2,403
Residual fuel oils	1,492	1,586	2,441
Jet fuel	257	410	553
Petroleum bitumen—asphalt	287	277	315
Liquefied petroleum gas ('000 barrels)	1,241	402	500*
Cement	14,519	14,000	14,000
Electric energy (million kWh)	20,935	22,852	24,364

* Estimated figure(s).
† Unofficial figures.

2012 ('000 metric tons unless otherwise indicated, estimates): Wine 35; Olive oil (crude) 120 (unofficial figure); Liquefied petroleum gas ('000 barrels) 1,000; Cement 14,000.

Sources: FAO, US Geological Survey, UN Industrial Commodity Statistics Database.

Finance

CURRENCY AND EXCHANGE RATES

Monetary Units:
100 centimes (santimat) = 1 Moroccan dirham.

Sterling, Dollar and Euro Equivalents (31 December 2014):
£1 sterling = 14.113 dirhams;
US $1 = 9.024 dirhams;
€1 = 10.978 dirhams;
100 Moroccan dirhams = £7.09 = $11.06 = €9.11.

Average Exchange Rate (dirhams per US $):
2011   8.090
2012   8.628
2013   8.406

GENERAL BUDGET
('000 million dirhams)

Revenue*†	2013‡	2014§	2015§
Tax revenue	199.5	208.5	226.5
Taxes on income and profits	75.1	76.7	85.5
Taxes on property	11.6	14.1	13.4
Taxes on goods and services	99.8	105.1	114.5
Taxes on international trade	8.0	8.1	8.3
Other tax revenues	4.9	4.5	4.8
Non-tax revenue	41.4	36.3	39.3
Total	240.9	244.8	265.8

Expenditure‖	2013‡	2014§	2015§
Wages and salaries	112.4	119.2	124.5
Use of goods and services	59.0	68.5	72.0
Interest	22.5	25.7	26.5
Subsidies	41.6	32.2	23.2
Other expense	13.9	14.8	22.1
Total	249.3	260.4	268.4

* Excluding grants (million dirhams): 6.1 in 2013 (revised figure); 12.3 in 2014 (revised figure); 10.5 in 2015 (budget projection).
† Includes tariffs destined for food subsidies and road fund revenues.
‡ Revised figures.
§ Projections.
‖ Excluding net lending.

Source: IMF, *Morocco: 2013 Article IV Consultation-Staff Report; Press Release; and Statement by the Executive Director for Morocco* (August 2014).

INTERNATIONAL RESERVES
(US $ million at 31 December)

	2011	2012	2013
Gold (national valuation)	1,116	1,179	852
IMF special drawing rights	616	435	378
Reserve position in IMF	108	108	108
Foreign exchange	18,802	15,812	17,918
Total	20,642	17,534	19,256

Source: IMF, *International Financial Statistics*.

MONEY SUPPLY
(million dirhams at 31 December)

	2011	2012	2013
Currency outside depository corporations	158,288	163,641	171,604
Transferable deposits	393,110	410,899	423,899
Other deposits	329,675	339,099	353,366
Securities other than shares	30,480	29,640	29,281
Broad money	911,553	943,278	978,151

Source: IMF, *International Financial Statistics*.

COST OF LIVING
(Consumer Price Index for urban areas; base: 2006 = 100)

	2012	2013	2014
Food and non-alcoholic beverages	119.1	120.6	120.2
Clothing and footwear	108.2	111.6	112.2
Housing, water, electricity, gas and other fuels	105.3	107.1	109.2
All items (incl. others)	110.8	112.9	113.4

NATIONAL ACCOUNTS
(million dirhams at current prices)

Expenditure on the Gross Domestic Product

	2011	2012	2013*
Government final consumption expenditure	146,332	159,118	165,559
Private final consumption expenditure	472,938	495,655	524,395
Change in inventories	42,168	33,006	34,893
Gross fixed capital formation	246,394	258,859	263,272
Total domestic expenditure	907,832	946,638	988,119
Exports of goods and services	285,530	297,170	293,670
Less Imports of goods and services	390,755	416,311	408,998
GDP in purchasers' values	802,607	827,497	872,791

Gross Domestic Product by Economic Activity

	2011	2012	2013*
Agriculture, hunting and forestry	106,342	102,572	124,124
Fishing and aquaculture	8,524	8,003	8,341
Mining and quarrying	41,355	40,343	30,808
Manufacturing	114,338	120,694	123,231
Oil refining and energy products	1,960	1,692	165
Electricity and water	18,962	20,044	21,042
Construction	47,941	50,099	52,833
Commerce	76,977	79,824	81,648
Hotels and restaurants	18,852	19,745	21,838
Transport	28,424	29,158	31,123
Post and communications	22,473	21,329	18,481
Public administration and social security	69,611	74,830	77,937
Other services	186,660	199,397	207,834
Sub-total	742,419	767,730	799,405
Taxes, less subsidies, on imports	60,188	59,767	73,386
GDP in purchasers' values	802,607	827,497	872,791

* Provisional figures.

BALANCE OF PAYMENTS
(US $ million)

	2011	2012	2013
Exports of goods	15,946	16,992	18,262
Imports of goods	−37,333	−38,877	−39,854
Balance on goods	−21,387	−21,885	−21,592
Exports of services	15,899	15,347	14,353
Imports of services	−8,574	−8,136	−7,571
Balance on goods and services	−14,063	−14,675	−14,810
Primary income received	804	616	471
Primary income paid	−2,856	−2,899	−2,243
Balance on goods, services and primary income	−16,115	−16,958	−16,581
Secondary income received	8,071	7,405	8,303
Secondary income paid	−293	−290	−413
Current balance	−8,337	−9,843	−8,692
Direct investment assets	−248	−360	− 445
Direct investment liabilities	2,521	2,842	3,361
Portfolio investment assets	−400	103	178
Portfolio investment liabilities	166	−108	43
Other investment assets	−536	−237	−447
Other investment liabilities	791	−355	365
Net errors and omissions	−370	−410	379
Reserves and related items	−6,413	−8,368	−5,258

Source: IMF, *International Financial Statistics*.

External Trade

PRINCIPAL COMMODITIES
(million dirhams)

Imports c.i.f.	2011	2012	2013*
Foodstuffs, beverages and tobacco	38,810	41,783	35,667
Wheat	11,639	12,067	8,221
Energy and lubricants	90,350	106,619	102,094
Crude petroleum . . .	31,423	37,609	36,326
Refined petroleum products .	50,047	23,368	25,416
Crude products	22,542	22,987	17,803
Semi-finished products . .	76,483	77,113	80,094
Chemical products . . .	11,139	8,127	7,954
Finished capital goods . .	66,313	71,432	78,256
Finished consumer products . .	61,427	65,260	63,789
Pharmaceutical products . .	4,907	4,795	5,030
Textile and cotton fabrics .	7,733	8,021	7,713
Total (incl. others)	357,770	386,949	379,920

Exports f.o.b.	2011	2012	2013*
Foodstuffs, beverages and tobacco	28,644	30,105	33,504
Crustaceans and molluscs . .	5,486	5,831	5,970
Prepared and preserved fish .	4,193	5,702	5,888
Energy and lubricants	4,558	7,429	9,274
Crude mineral products . . .	19,400	18,832	14,883
Phosphates	12,610	12,827	9,097
Semi-finished products . . .	53,960	52,776	44,974
Phosphate derivatives . . .	n.a.	35,568	28,233
Finished industrial capital goods .	26,535	27,459	31,872
Electric wire and cable . . .	16,570	15,219	16,986
Finished consumer products . .	38,090	44,742	47,166
Manufactured garments . .	18,134	19,518	19,017
Hosiery	7,742	8,128	7,253
Total (incl. others)	174,994	184,885	184,685

* Preliminary figures.

PRINCIPAL TRADING PARTNERS
(million dirhams)*

Imports c.i.f.	2011	2012	2013†
Algeria	8,687	9,725	10,799
Belgium-Luxembourg	6,815	6,372	6,971
Brazil	8,412	8,735	6,772
Canada	2,941	3,889	3,549
China, People's Republic . .	23,313	25,599	26,371
France	50,989	48,050	49,123
Germany	16,013	18,493	18,221
India	4,760	4,439	5,289
Italy	18,568	18,973	20,286
Japan	3,363	5,631	2,703
Netherlands	5,893	5,771	6,033
Spain	39,267	50,962	51,451
United Kingdom	7,175	8,481	7,177
USA	28,984	24,703	28,524
Total (incl. others)	357,770	386,949	379,920

Exports f.o.b.	2011	2012	2013†
Algeria	1,899	1,999	1,761
Belgium-Luxembourg	3,501	3,437	4,791
Brazil	9,038	10,890	11,028
China, People's Republic . . .	1,588	2,406	2,871
France	36,844	39,629	39,543
Germany	4,999	5,652	5,021
India	12,164	10,181	6,849
Italy	7,340	6,785	6,977
Netherlands	5,446	5,391	5,499
Spain	31,958	30,383	34,827
United Kingdom	4,889	5,382	4,991
USA	7,950	7,884	7,791
Total (incl. others)	174,994	184,885	184,685

* Imports by country of production; exports by country of last consignment.
† Preliminary figures.

Transport

RAILWAYS
(traffic)*

	2010	2011	2012†
Passengers carried ('000) . . .	30,910	33,879	35,938
Freight ('000 metric tons) . . .	35,669	37,178	37,011

* Figures refer to principal railways only.
† Provisional.

2008: Passenger-km (million) 3,836; Freight ton-km (million) 4,985.

ROAD TRAFFIC
('000 motor vehicles in use at 31 December)

	2011
Passenger cars	2,084.9
Buses and coaches	54.3
Vans and lorries	775.8
Motorcycles and mopeds	33.8

Source: IRF, *World Road Statistics*.

SHIPPING

Flag Registered Fleet
(at 31 December)

	2012	2013	2014
Number of vessels	409	422	423
Total displacement ('000 grt) . .	364.6	351.3	355.8

Source: Lloyd's List Intelligence (www.lloydslistintelligence.com).

International Seaborne Freight Traffic
('000 metric tons)

	2009	2010*	2011*
Goods loaded	20,341	26,123	25,261
Goods unloaded	39,395	43,113	43,779

* Provisional figures.

CIVIL AVIATION
(traffic on scheduled services)

	2010	2011
Kilometres flown (million)	136	135
Passengers carried ('000)	7,144	7,503
Passenger-km (million)	14,366	15,546
Total ton-km (million)	1,475	1,548

Source: UN, *Statistical Yearbook*.

2012 (provisional): Aircraft movements 176,553; Passengers carried ('000) 15,235; Freight carried (metric tons) 51,775.

Tourism

FOREIGN TOURIST ARRIVALS*

Country of nationality	2011	2012	2013
France	1,775,961	1,769,710	1,782,056
Germany	219,576	199,349	237,852
Italy	211,405	196,186	234,912
Spain	693,255	730,882	682,834
United Kingdom	352,141	357,347	403,325
Other European countries . .	255,661	250,455	313,234
Maghreb countries	174,417	219,280	270,227
USA	130,427	140,045	160,033
Total (incl. others)	4,933,883	5,011,729	5,323,333

* Excluding Moroccans resident abroad (4,408,250 in 2011, 4,363,427 in 2012; 4,722,931 in 2013).

Cruise-ship passengers: 319,353 in 2009; 475,915 in 2010; 441,629 in 2011.

Receipts from tourism (US $ million, excl. passenger transport): 7,321 in 2011; 6,697 in 2012; 6,851 in 2013 (Source: World Tourism Organization).

Communications Media

	2011	2012	2013
Telephones ('000 main lines in use)	3,566.1	3,279.1	2,924.9
Mobile cellular telephones ('000 subscribers)	36,553.9	39,016.3	42,423.8
Internet subscribers ('000) . .	591.6	n.a.	n.a.
Broadband subscribers ('000) . .	589.0	681.6	836.1

Source: International Telecommunication Union.

Education

(2013/14 unless otherwise indicated)

	Institutions	Teachers	Pupils/Students		
			Males	Females	Total
Pre-primary . .	24,358	39,824	419,955	326,036	745,991
Primary . .	9,915	157,019	2,111,789	1,918,353	4,030,142
public . . .	7,541	125,496	1,809,449	1,644,819	3,454,268
private . . .	2,374	31,523	302,340	273,534	575,874
Secondary (public and private) . .	4,390	138,861	1,414,145	1,192,094	2,606,239
Tertiary . .	68*	19,598†	235,554‡	210,519‡	505,681§

* 1997/98 figure.
† 2008/09 figure.
‡ 2009/10 figure.
§ 2010/11 figure.

Sources: Ministry of National Education and Vocational Training; Ministry of Higher Education, Scientific Research and Management Training; UNESCO Institute for Statistics.

Pupil-teacher ratio (primary education, UNESCO estimate): 26.0 in 2012/13 (Source: UNESCO Institute for Statistics).

Adult literacy rate (UNESCO estimates): 67.1% (males 76.1%, females 57.6%) in 2011 (Source: UNESCO Institute for Statistics).

Directory

The Government

HEAD OF STATE

Monarch: HM King MUHAMMAD VI (acceded 23 July 1999).

CABINET
(May 2015)

A coalition of the Parti de la Justice et du Développement (PJD), the Rassemblement National des Indépendants (RNI), the Mouvement Populaire (MP), the Parti du Progrès et du Socialisme (PPS) and independents (Ind.).

Prime Minister: ABDELILAH BENKIRANE (PJD).

Minister of State: (vacant).

Minister of the Interior: MUHAMMAD HASSAD (Ind.).

Minister of Foreign Affairs and Co-operation: SALAHEDDINE MEZOUAR (RNI).

Minister of Justice and Liberties: MUSTAFA RAMID (PJD).

Minister of Habous (Religious Endowments) and Islamic Affairs: AHMED TOUFIQ (Ind.).

Secretary-General of the Government: DRISS DAHAK (Ind.).

Minister of the Economy and Finance: MUHAMMAD BOUSSAID (RNI).

Minister of Planning and Development: MOHAND LAENSER (MP).

Minister of Housing and Urban Planning: NABIL BENABDALLAH (PPS).

Minister of Agriculture and Fisheries: AZIZ AKHANNOUCH (Ind.).

Minister of National Education and Vocational Training: RACHID BELMOKHTAR (Ind.).

Minister of Higher Education, Scientific Research and Management Training: LAHCEN DAOUDI (PJD).

Minister of Youth and Sports: (vacant).

Minister of Infrastructure, Transport and Logistics: ABDELAZIZ RABBAH (PJD).

Minister of Health: LAHOUCINE LOUARDI (PPS).

Minister of Communication and Government Spokesperson: MUSTAPHA EL-KHALFI (PJD).

Minister of Energy, Mining, Water and the Environment: ABDELKADER AMARA (PJD).

Minister of Employment and Social Affairs: ABDESSLAM SEDDIKI (PPS).

Minister of Industry, Trade, Investment and the Digital Economy: MOULAY HAFID ELALAMY (Ind.).

Minister of Tourism: LAHCEN HADDAD (MP).

Minister of Solidarity, Women, Family and Social Development: BASSIMA HAKKAOUI (PJD).

Minister of Culture: AHMED AMINE SBIHI (PPS).

Minister of Handicrafts: FATEMA MAROUANE (RNI).

Minister in charge of Relations with Parliament and Civil Society: LAHBIB CHOUBANI (PJD).

Minister-delegate to the Prime Minister, in charge of the Administration of National Defence: ABDELLATIF LOUDIYI (Ind.).

Minister-delegate to the Prime Minister, in charge of Moroccans Resident Abroad and Migration: ANIS BIROU (RNI).

Minister-delegate to the Minister of the Interior: CHARKI DRAISS (Ind.).

Minister-delegate to the Minister of Foreign Affairs and Co-operation: MBARKA BOUAIDA (RNI).

Minister-delegate to the Prime Minister, in charge of General Affairs and Governance: MUHAMMAD EL-OUAFA (Ind.).

Minister-delegate to the Prime Minister, in charge of Civil Service and the Modernization of the Public Sector: MUHAMMAD MOUBDII (MP).

Minister-delegate to the Minister of the Economy and Finance, in charge of the Budget: DRISS EL-AZAMI EL-IDRISSI (PJD).

Minister-delegate to the Minister of Industry, Trade, Investment and the Digital Economy, in charge of Small Business and the Integration of the Informal Economy: MAMOUN BOUHDOUD (PJD).

Minister-delegate to the Minister of Energy, Mining, Water and the Environment, in charge of Water: CHARAFAT AFILAL (PPS).

Minister-delegate to the Minister of Energy, Mining, Water and the Environment, in charge of the Environment: HAKIMA EL-HITI (MP).

Minister-delegate to the Minister of Infrastructure, Transport and Logistics, in charge of Transport: MUHAMMAD NAJIB BOULIF (PJD).

Minister-delegate to the Minister of Higher Education, Scientific Research and Management Training: SOUMIYA BENKHALDOUN (PJD).

Minister-delegate to the Minister of National Education and Vocational Training: ABDELADIM GUERROUJ (MP).

Minister-delegate to the Minister of Industry, Trade, Investment and the Digital Economy, in charge of External Trade: MUHAMMAD ABBOU (RNI).

MINISTRIES

Office of the Prime Minister: Palais Royal, Touarga, Rabat; tel. (53) 7219400; fax (53) 7768656; e-mail courrier@pm.gov.ma; internet www.pm.gov.ma.

Ministry in charge of the Administration of National Defence: Rabat.

Ministry of Agriculture and Fisheries: ave Muhammad V, Quartier Administratif, pl. Abdellah Chefchaouni, BP 607, Rabat; tel. (53) 7665300; fax (53) 7776411; internet www.agriculture.gov.ma.

Ministry of Civil Service and the Modernization of the Public Sector: Quartier Administratif, rue Ahmed Cherkaoui, Agdal, BP 1076, Rabat; tel. (53) 7679930; fax (53) 7778438; e-mail info@mmsp.gov.ma; internet www.mmsp.gov.ma.

Ministry of Communication: ave Allal el-Fassi, Madinat al-Irfane Souissi, 10000 Rabat; tel. (53) 7678112; fax (53) 7680178; e-mail ministre@mincom.gov.ma; internet www.mincom.gov.ma.

Ministry of Culture: 1 rue Ghandi, Rabat; tel. (53) 7209494; fax (53) 7209400; e-mail webmaster@minculture.gov.ma; internet www.minculture.gov.ma.

Ministry of the Economy and Finance: blvd Muhammad V, Quartier Administratif, Chellah, Rabat; tel. (53) 7677501; fax (53) 7677526; e-mail internet@finances.gov.ma; internet www.finances.gov.ma.

Ministry of Employment and Social Affairs: ave Muhammad V, Hassan, BP 5015, Rabat; tel. (53) 7760521; fax (53) 7750192; e-mail communication@emploi.gov.ma; internet www.emploi.gov.ma.

Ministry of Energy, Mining, Water and the Environment: rue Abou Marouane Essaadi, BP 6208, Agdal, Rabat; tel. (53) 7688400; fax (53) 7688863; e-mail dsi@mem.gov.ma; internet www.mem.gov.ma.

Ministry of Foreign Affairs and Co-operation: ave Franklin Roosevelt, Rabat; tel. (53) 7761125; fax (53) 7765508; internet www.diplomatie.ma.

Ministry in charge of General Affairs and Governance: Quartier Administratif, Agdal, BP 412, Rabat; tel. (53) 7687300; fax (53) 7771697; e-mail contact@affaires-generales.gov.ma; internet www.affaires-generales.gov.ma.

Ministry of Habous (Religious Endowments) and Islamic Affairs: al-Mechouar Essaid, Rabat; tel. (53) 7766801; fax (53) 7666037; e-mail infos@islam-maroc.ma; internet www.habous.gov.ma.

Ministry of Handicrafts: Rabat; internet www.artesnet.gov.ma.

Ministry of Health: 335 ave Muhammad V, Rabat; tel. (53) 7761025; fax (53) 7763895; e-mail information@sante.gov.ma; internet www.sante.gov.ma.

Ministry of Higher Education, Scientific Research and Management Training: rue Idriss Al Akbar-Hassan, BP 4500, Rabat; tel. (53) 7217501; fax (53) 7217547; e-mail enssup@enssup.gov.ma; internet www.enssup.gov.ma.

Ministry of Housing, Town Planning and Development: rues al-Jouaze and al-Joumaize, Hay Riad, Secteur 16, 10000 Rabat; tel. (53) 7577000; fax (53) 7577373; e-mail mhuae@mhuae.gov.ma; internet www.mhu.gov.ma.

Ministry of Industry, Trade, Investment and the Digital Economy: 1 ave el-Hassan, Rabat; tel. (53) 7761878; fax (53)

7766265; e-mail ministre@mcinet.gov.ma; internet www.mcinet.gov.ma.

Ministry of Infrastructure, Transport and Logistics: Quartier Administratif, Chellah, Rabat; tel. (53) 7684151; fax (53) 7764825; internet www.mtpnet.gov.ma.

Ministry of the Interior: Quartier Administratif, Chellah, Rabat; tel. (53) 7761868; fax (53) 7762056.

Ministry of Justice and Liberties: pl. Mamounia, Rabat; tel. (53) 7732941; fax (53) 7730772; e-mail kourout@justice.gov.ma; internet www.justice.gov.ma.

Ministry in charge of Moroccans Resident Abroad and Migration: 59 rue Moulouya, Agdal 10000, Rabat; tel. (53) 7776588; fax (53) 7770006; e-mail info@mcmre.gov.ma; internet marocainsdumonde.gov.ma.

Ministry of National Education and Vocational Training: Bab Rouah, Rabat; tel. (53) 7771822; fax (53) 7687255; internet www.men.gov.ma.

Ministry in charge of Relations with Parliament and Civil Society: Nouveau Quartier Administratif, Agdal, Rabat; tel. (53) 7683440; fax (53) 7777719; e-mail contact@mcrpsc.gov.ma; internet www.mcrp.gov.ma.

Ministry of Solidarity, Women, Family and Social Development: 47 ave ibn Sina, Agdal, Rabat; tel. (53) 7684060; fax (53) 7671967; e-mail mdsfs@mdsfs.ma; internet www.social.gov.ma.

Ministry of Tourism: Centre d'Affaires-Aile Sud, Lot 1 C17, ave Ennakhil-Hay Riad, Rabat; tel. (53) 7563729; fax (53) 7716923; e-mail webmaster@tourisme.gov.ma; internet www.tourisme.gov.ma.

Ministry of Youth and Sports: ave ibn Sina, Agdal, Rabat; tel. (53) 7680028; e-mail masterweb@mjs.gov.ma; internet www.mjs.gov.ma.

Legislature

CHAMBER OF REPRESENTATIVES

Chamber of Representatives: POB 431, Rabat; tel. (53) 7679500; fax (53) 7767726; e-mail parlement@parlement.ma; internet www.parlement.ma.

President: RACHID TALBI ALAMI.

General Election, 25 November 2011

	Seats
Parti de la Justice et du Développement (PJD)	107
Istiqlal	60
Rassemblement National des Indépendants (RNI)	52
Parti de l'Authenticité et de la Modernité (PAM)	47
Union Socialiste des Forces Populaires (USFP)	39
Mouvement Populaire (MP)	32
Union Constitutionnelle (UC)	23
Parti du Progrès et du Socialisme (PPS)	18
Parti Travailliste (PT)	4
Mouvement Démocratique et Social (MDS)	2
Parti du Renouveau et de l'Équité (PRE)	2
Parti de l'Environnement et du Développement Durable (PEDDl)	2
Parti Al Ahd Démocratique	2
Others	5
Total	**395***

* Of the total number of seats, 305 seats are reserved for candidates from local party lists, while the remaining 90 seats are allocated to candidates from national lists. Each party must allocate two-thirds of its share of those 90 seats to women and the remaining one-third to men under 40 years of age.

CHAMBER OF ADVISERS

Chamber of Advisers: POB 432, Rabat; tel. (53) 7218304; fax (53) 7733192; e-mail info@conseiller.ma; internet www.conseiller.ma.

President: MUHAMMAD CHEIKH BIADILLAH.

Election, 5 December 1997*

		Seats
Rassemblement National des Indépendants (RNI)	.	42
Mouvement Démocratique et Social (MDS)	. . . .	33
Union Constitutionnelle (UC)	. . . .	28
Mouvement Populaire (MP)	. . . . . .	27
Parti National Démocrate (PND)	. . . . .	21
Istiqlal	. . . .	21
Union Socialiste des Forces Populaires (USFP)	. .	16
Mouvement National Populaire (MNP)	. . . .	15
Parti de l'Action (PA)	. . . .	13
Front des Forces Démocratiques (FFD)	. . . .	12
Parti du Progrès et du Socialisme (PPS)	. . . .	7
Parti Socialiste Démocratique (PSD)	. . . .	4
Parti Démocratique et de l'Indépendance (PDI)	. .	4
Trade unions		
Confédération Démocratique du Travail (CDT)	. .	11
Union Marocaine du Travail (UMT)	. . . .	8
Union Générale des Travailleurs du Maroc (UGTM).		3
Others	. . . .	5
Total	. . . .	**270**

* Of the chamber's 270 members, 162 were elected by local councils, 81 by chambers of commerce and 27 by trade unions. Further elections were held on 15 September 2000, 6 October 2003, 8 September 2006 and 3 October 2009. According to the provisions of the 2011 Constitution, the number of seats in the Chamber was to be reduced to no more than 120.

Political Organizations

Congrès National Ittihadi (CNI): 209 blvd Strasbourg, Résidence C, 2ème étage, Casablanca; tel. and fax (52) 2447664; e-mail onittihadi@caramail.com; f. 2001 by dissident mems of USFP; created Fédération de la Gauche Démocratique with Parti Socialiste Unifié and Parti de l'Avant-garde Démocratique Socialiste in Jan. 2014; Sec.-Gen. ABDESSALAM LAÂZIZ.

Front des Forces Démocratiques (FFD): 13 ave Tariq ibn Ziad, Hassan, Rabat; tel. (53) 7661625; fax (53) 7660621; e-mail forces@menara.ma; internet frontdesforcesdemocratiques.org; f. 1997 after split from PPS.

Istiqlal (Independence): 4 ave Ibn Toumert, Bab el-Had, 50020 Rabat; tel. (53) 7730951; fax (53) 7725417; e-mail p.istiqlal2009@hotmail.com; internet www.partistiqlal.org; f. 1944; aims to raise living standards and to confer equal rights on all; emphasizes the Moroccan claim to Western Sahara; Sec.-Gen. HAMID CHABAT.

Mouvement Démocratique et Social (MDS): 4 ave Imam Malik, route des Zaêrs, Rabat; tel. (57) 7631552; fax (53) 7658253; f. 1996 as Mouvement National Démocratique et Social after split from Mouvement National Populaire; adopted current name in Nov. 1996; Sec.-Gen. MAHMOUD ARCHANE.

Mouvement Populaire (MP): 66 rue Patrice Lumumba, Rabat; tel. (53) 7766431; fax (53) 7767537; e-mail parti_mp@hotmail.fr; internet www.alharaka.ma; f. 1958; merged with the MNP and Union Démocratique in 2006; liberal; Sec.-Gen. MOHAND LAENSER.

Parti de l'Action (PA): 113 ave Allal Ben Abdallah, Rabat; tel. (53) 7206561; f. 1974; advocates democracy and progress; Sec.-Gen. MUHAMMAD EL-IDRISSI.

Parti Al Ahd Démocratique: 14 rue Idriss al-Akbar, rue Tafraout, Hassan, Rabat; tel. (53) 7204816; fax (53) 7204786; e-mail alhakika@iam.net.ma; f. 2002; Chair. NAJIB EL-OUAZZANI.

Parti de l'Authenticité et de la Modernité (PAM): internet www.pam.ma; f. 2008; Founder FOUAD ALI EL-HIMMA; Sec.-Gen. MUSTAPHA BAKKOURI.

Parti de l'Avant-garde Démocratique Socialiste (PADS): 54 ave de la Résistance Océan, Rabat 10000; tel. and fax (53) 7200559; e-mail pads.pads@gmail.com; an offshoot of USFP; legalized in April 1992; created Fédération de la Gauche Démocratique with the Congrès National Ittihadi and the Parti Socialiste Unifié in Jan. 2014; Sec.-Gen. ABDERRAHMAN BENAMEUR.

Parti Démocrate National (PDN): f. May 2009 by fmr members of Parti National Démocrate, following that party's merger into PAM; Sec.-Gen. ABDULLAH KADIRI.

Parti Démocratique et de l'Indépendance (PDI): 9 Lalla Yakout, rue Araar, Apt 11, 2ème étage, blvd d'Anfa, Casablanca; tel. (52) 2200949; fax (52) 2200928; f. 1946; Sec.-Gen. ABDELWAHID MAÂCH.

Parti de l'Environnement et du Développement Durable (PEDD): 25 ave Muhammad Abdou, Agdal, Rabat; tel. and fax (53) 7670620; e-mail info@pedmaroc.ma; internet www.pedmaroc.ma; f. 2002 as Parti de l'Environnement et du Développement;

merged with PAM in 2008; relaunched as above in 2009; environmentalist; Sec.-Gen. Dr AHMAD AL-ALAMI.

Parti des Forces Citoyennes (PFC): 353 blvd Muhammad V, 9ème étage, Casablanca; tel. (52) 2400608; fax (52) 2400613; e-mail citoyennes@iam.net.ma; f. 2001; Sec.-Gen. ABDERRAHIM LAHJOUJI.

Parti de la Justice et du Développement (PJD): ave Abdelwahed Elmorakechi, rue Elyafrani, 4 les Orangers, Rabat; tel. (53) 7208862; fax (53) 7208854; e-mail pjdcontact@gmail.com; internet www.pjd.ma; f. 1967 as Mouvement Populaire Constitutionnel et Démocratique; breakaway party from MP; formally absorbed mems of the Islamic asscn Al Islah wa Attajdid in June 1996; adopted current name in Oct. 1998; Sec.-Gen. ABDELILAH BENKIRANE.

Parti Marocain Libéral (PML): 114 ave Allal Ben Abdellah, 2ème étage, Rabat; tel. (53) 7733670; fax (53) 7733611; e-mail pml@menara.ma; f. 2002; Nat. Co-ordinator MUHAMMAD ZIANE.

Parti du Progrès et du Socialisme (PPS): 29 ave Muhammad VI, Youssoufia, Rabat; tel. (53) 7759464; fax (53) 7759476; e-mail maroc.pps@gmail.com; internet www.ppsmaroc.com; f. 1974; successor to Parti Communiste Marocain (banned in 1952) and Parti de la Libération et du Socialisme (banned in 1969); left-wing; advocates modernization, social progress, nationalization and democracy; 35,000 mems; Sec.-Gen. MUHAMMAD NABIL BENABDELLAH.

Parti de la Réforme et du Développement (PRD): 34 ave Pasteur, Rabat; tel. and fax (53) 7703801; f. 2001 by fmr mems of RNI; Sec.-Gen. MUHAMMAD GOUMANI.

Parti de la Renaissance et de la Vertu: Bouznika; f. 2005; national democratic party based on the principles of Islam; Sec.-Gen. MUHAMMAD KHALIDI.

Parti du Renouveau et de l'Équité (PRE): 16 rue Sebou, Apt 5, Agdal, Rabat; tel. (53) 7777266; fax (53) 7777452; e-mail partipre@yahoo.fr; internet www.pre.ma; f. 2002; Pres. CHAKIR ACHEHBAR.

Parti Socialiste Unifié (PSU): 9 rue d'Agadir, Immeuble Maréchal Ameziane, Casablanca; tel. (52) 2485902; fax (52) 2201852; e-mail psumaroc@yahoo.fr; internet psu.ma; f. 2005 by merger of Parti de la Gauche Socialiste Unifieé and Fidélité à la Démocratie; created Fédération de la Gauche Démocratique with the Congrès National Ittihadi and the Parti de l'Avant-garde Démocratique Socialiste in Jan. 2014; Sec.-Gen. NABILA MOUNIB.

Parti Travailliste (PT): 9 rue Ksar Essouk, Hassan, Rabat; f. 2005; centre-left; announced intention to merge with USFP in 2013; Sec.-Gen. ABDELKRIM BENATIQ.

Rassemblement National des Indépendants (RNI): 6 rue Laos, ave Hassan II, Rabat; tel. (53) 7716168; fax (53) 7563402; internet www.rni.ma; f. 1978 from the pro-Govt independents' group that then formed the majority in the Chamber of Representatives; Pres. SALAHEDDINE MEZOUAR.

Union Constitutionnelle (UC): 158 ave des Forces Armées Royales, Casablanca; tel. (52) 2441144; fax (52) 2441141; e-mail union_constit@menara.ma; f. 1983; 51-mem. Political Bureau; Sec.-Gen. MUHAMMAD ABIED.

Union Marocaine pour la Démocratie (UMD): Rabat; f. 2006; Sec.-Gen. JAMAL MANDRI.

Union Socialiste des Forces Populaires (USFP): 9 ave al-Araâr, Hay Riad, Rabat; tel. (53) 7565511; fax (53) 7565510; e-mail usfp@usfp.ma; internet www.usfp.ma; f. 1959 as Union Nationale des Forces Populaires (UNFP); became USFP in 1974 after UNFP split into 2 separate entities; merged with Parti Socialiste Démocratique in 2005; merged with Parti Travailliste and Parti Socialiste in 2013; democratic socialist and progressive party; 260,000 mems; First Sec. DRISS LACHGAR.

The following movement is not authorized as a political party by the Government, but is generally tolerated:

Al-Adl wal-Ihsan (Justice and Charity): internet www.aljamaa.net; advocates an Islamic state based on *Shari'a* law; rejects violence; Sec.-Gen. MUHAMMAD ABBADI.

The following group is active in the disputed territory of Western Sahara:

Frente Popular para la Liberación de Saguia el-Hamra y Río de Oro (Frente Polisario) (Polisario Front): BP 10, el-Mouradia, Algiers, Algeria; fax (2) 747206; e-mail dgmae@mail.wissal.dz; f. 1973 to gain independence for Western Sahara, first from Spain and then from Morocco and Mauritania; signed peace treaty with Mauritanian Govt in 1979; supported by Algerian Govt; in February 1976 proclaimed the Sahrawi Arab Democratic Republic (SADR); admitted as the 51st mem. of the OAU in Feb. 1982 and currently recognized by more than 75 countries worldwide; its main organs are a 33-mem. Nat. Secretariat, a 101-mem. Sahrawi Nat. Assembly (Parliament) and a 13-mem. Govt; Sec.-Gen. of the Polisario Front and Pres. of the SADR MUHAMMAD ABD AL-AZIZ; Prime Minister of the SADR ABDELKADER TALEB OUMAR.

Diplomatic Representation

EMBASSIES IN MOROCCO

Algeria: Angle ave Muhammad VI, Rue Ghiyata, Soulssi, BP 448, 10001 Rabat; tel. (53) 7661574; fax (53) 7762237; Ambassador AHMED BENYAMINA.

Angola: km 5, 53 Ahmed Rifaï, BP 1318, Souissi, Rabat; tel. (53) 7659239; fax (53) 7653703; e-mail amb.angola@menara.ma; internet www.embaixada-angola-marrocos.org; Ambassador (vacant).

Argentina: 4 ave Mehdi Ben Barka, Souissi, 10000 Rabat; tel. (53) 7755120; fax (53) 7755410; e-mail emarr@mrecic.gov.ar; Ambassador JOSÉ PATRICIO GUTIÉRREZ MAXWELL.

Austria: 2 rue Tiddas, BP 135, 10000 Rabat; tel. (53) 7761698; fax (53) 7765425; e-mail rabat-ob@bmeia.gv.at; internet www.aussenministerium.at/rabat; Ambassador Dr WOLFGANG ANGERHOLZER.

Azerbaijan: rue 3 Abu Hanifa, Aqdal, Rabat; tel. (53) 7671915; fax (53) 7671918; e-mail azembma@menara.ma; Ambassador TAREK ISMAEIL ALIEV.

Bahrain: rue Béni Hassan, km 6.5, route des Zaêrs, Villa 318, POB 1470, Souissi, Rabat; tel. (53) 7633500; fax (53) 7630732; e-mail rabat.mission@mofa.gov.bh; internet www.mofa.gov.bh/rabat; Ambassador KHALID BIN SALMAN BIN JABR AL-MUSALLAM.

Bangladesh: 25 ave Tarek ibn Ziad, BP 1468, Rabat; tel. (53) 7766731; fax (53) 7766729; e-mail bangladoot@menara.ma; internet bangladeshembassy-morocco.webs.com; Ambassador MONIRUL ISLAM.

Belgium: 6 ave de Muhammad el-Fassi, Tour Hassan, Rabat; tel. (53) 7268060; fax (53) 7767003; e-mail rabat@diplobel.fed.be; internet www.diplomatie.be/rabat; Ambassador FRANK CARRUET.

Benin: 30 ave Mehdi Ben Barka, BP 5187, Souissi, 10105 Rabat; tel. (53) 7754158; fax (53) 7754156; e-mail benin@menara.ma; Ambassador NICOLAS AHISSOU CODJO.

Brazil: 10 ave el-Jacaranda, Secteur 2, Hay Riad, 10000 Rabat; tel. (53) 7572730; fax (53) 7714808; e-mail ambassadedubresil@menara.ma; internet rabat.itamaraty.gov.br; Ambassador FREDERICO SALOMÃO DUQUE ESTRADA MEYER.

Bulgaria: 4 ave Ahmed cl-Yazidi, BP 1301, 10000 Rabat; tel. (53) 7765477; fax (53) 7763201; e-mail embassy.rabat@mfa.bg; internet www.mfa.bg/embassies/morocco; Ambassador BORIANA SIMEONOVA.

Burkina Faso: 7 rue al-Bouziri, BP 6484, Agdal, 10101 Rabat; tel. (53) 7675512; fax (53) 7675517; e-mail ambfrba@smirt.net.ma; Ambassador (vacant).

Cameroon: 20 rue du Rif, BP 1790, Souissi, Rabat; tel. (53) 7758818; fax (53) 7750540; e-mail ambacam@iam.net.com; Ambassador MOUHAMADOU YOUSSIFOU.

Canada: 66 ave Mehdi Ben Barka, BP 2040, Souissi, Rabat; tel. (53) 7544949; fax (53) 7544853; e-mail rabat@international.gc.ca; internet www.morocco.gc.ca; Ambassador SANDRA MCCARDELL.

Central African Republic: 65, rue 29 Youssoufia est-ext. de l'etat, BP 770, Agdal, 10000 Rabat; tel. (53) 7658970; fax (53) 7659216; e-mail centreafriquemaghreb1@menara.ma; Ambassador ISMAÏLA NIMAGA.

Chile: 16 rue Prince Sidi Muhammad, Souissi, Rabat; tel. (53) 7636065; fax (53) 7636067; e-mail embachilemarruecos@gmail.com; internet chileabroad.gov.cl/marruecos; Ambassador CARLOS CHARME SILVA.

China, People's Republic: 16 ave Ahmed Balafrej, 10000 Rabat; tel. (53) 7754056; fax (53) 7757519; e-mail chinaemb_ma@mfa.gov.cn; internet ma.china-embassy.org; Ambassador SUN SHUZHONG.

Congo, Democratic Republic: 34 ave de la Victoire, BP 553, 10000 Rabat; tel. (53) 7262280; fax (53) 7207407; e-mail ambardcrabat60@yahoo.fr; Chargé d'affaires a.i. WAWA BAMIALY.

Congo, Republic: 197 ave Général Abdendi Britel, Souissi II, Rabat; tel. (53) 7659966; fax (53) 7659959; Ambassador VALENTIN OLLESSONGO.

Côte d'Ivoire: 21 rue de Tiddas, BP 192, 10001 Rabat; tel. (53) 7763151; fax (53) 7762792; e-mail ambcim@clam.net.ma; Ambassador IDRISSA TRAORE.

Croatia: 73 rue Marnissa, Souissi, Rabat; tel. (53) 7638824; fax (53) 7638827; e-mail vrhrabat@mvep.hr; Ambassador ZVONIMIR FRKA PETEŠIĆ.

Czech Republic: Villa Merzaa, km 4.5, ave Muhammad VI, BP 410, rue Zankat Aït Melloul, Souissi, 10000 Rabat; tel. (53) 7755421; fax (53) 7754393; e-mail rabat@embassy.mzv.cz; internet www.mzv.cz/rabat; Ambassador MICHAELA FROŇKOVÁ.

Denmark: 14 rue Tiddas angle rue Roudana, Quartier Hassan, 10020 Rabat; tel. (53) 7665020; fax (53) 7665021; e-mail rbaamb@um.dk; internet www.rabat.um.dk; Ambassador MICHAEL LUND JEPPESEN.

Dominican Republic: 3 ave Mehdi Ben Barka, Secteur 6, Bloc E, Hay Riad, 10000 Rabat; tel. (53) 7715905; fax (53) 7715957; Ambassador FRANCISCO A. CARABALLO.

Egypt: 31 rue al-Jazair, 10000 Rabat; tel. (53) 7731833; fax (53) 7706821; e-mail embegypt@mtds.com; Ambassador IHAB AHMAD ABD AL-AHAD JAMAL AL-DIN.

Equatorial Guinea: ave President Roosevelt, angle rue d'Agadir 9, Rabat; tel. and fax (53) 7660337; Ambassador MANUEL BIBANG ASECO EYANG.

Finland: 145 rue Soufiane Ben Wahb, BP 590, 10002 Rabat; tel. (53) 7658775; fax (53) 7658904; e-mail sanomat.rab@formin.fi; internet www.finlande.ma; Ambassador CHRISTINA HARTTILA.

France: 1 rue Aguelmane Sidi Ali, BP 577, Agdal, 10190 Rabat; tel. (53) 7689700; fax (53) 7276711; internet www.ambafrance-ma.org; Ambassador CHARLES FRIES.

Gabon: 72 ave Mehdi Ben Barka, BP 10170, Souissi, 10105 Rabat; tel. (53) 7751950; fax (53) 7757550; e-mail chancellerie@ambagabon.ma; internet www.ambagabon.ma; Ambassador ABDOU RAZZAQ GUY KAMBOGO.

The Gambia: 11 rue Cadi Ben Hammadi Senhadji, Souissi, 10000 Rabat; tel. (53) 7638045; fax (53) 7752908; Ambassador ALHAJI EBRIMA N. H. JARJOU.

Germany: 7 Zankat Madnine, BP 235, 10000 Rabat; tel. (53) 7218600; fax (53) 706851; e-mail info@rabat.diplo.de; internet www.rabat.diplo.de; Ambassador VOLKMAR WENZEL.

Ghana: 27 rue Ghomara, La Pinede, Souissi, Rabat; tel. (53) 7757620; fax (53) 7757630; e-mail ghanaemb@menara.ma; Ambassador SAMUEL MBRAYEH QUARTEY.

Greece: km 5.5, ave Muhammad VI, Villa Chems, Souissi, 10000 Rabat; tel. (53) 7638964; fax (53) 7638990; e-mail gremb.rab@mfa.gr; internet www.mfa.gr/missionsabroad/morocco; Ambassador PLATON ALEXIS HADJIMICHALIS.

Guinea: 15 rue Hamzah, Agdal, 10000 Rabat; tel. and fax (53) 7674148; fax (53) 7675070; e-mail ambaguirabat@mae.gov.gn; Ambassador ABOUBACAR KABA.

Holy See: rue Béni M'tir, BP 1303, Souissi, Rabat (Apostolic Nunciature); tel. (53) 7772277; fax (53) 7756213; e-mail nuntius@iam.net.ma; Apostolic Nuncio Most Rev. ANTONIO SOZZO (Titular Archbishop of Concordia).

Hungary: route des Zaêrs, 17 Zankat Aït Melloul, BP 5026, Souissi, Rabat; tel. (53) 7750757; fax (53) 7754123; e-mail mission.rba@kum.hu; internet www.mfa.gov.hu/emb/rabat; Ambassador (vacant).

India: 88, rue Oulad Tidrarine, Souissi, Rabat; tel. (53) 7635801; fax (53) 7634733; e-mail amb.rabat@mea.gov.in; internet www.indianembassyrabat.com; Ambassador KRISHAN KUMAR.

Indonesia: 63 rue Béni Boufrah, km 6, route des Zaêrs, BP 576, 10000 Rabat; tel. (53) 7757860; fax (53) 7757859; e-mail kbrirabat@iam.net.ma; internet www.kemlu.go.id/rabat; Ambassador ENDANG DWI SYARIEF SYAMSURI.

Iran: ave Imam Malik, rue Kadi Muhammad Achour, BP 490, Souissi, 10001 Rabat; tel. (53) 7752167; fax (53) 7659118; e-mail ambassadiran@gmail.com; Ambassador MUHAMMAD TAGHI MOAYED.

Iraq: 39 blvd Mehdi Ben Barka, 10100 Rabat; tel. (53) 7754466; fax (53) 7759749; e-mail rbtemb@iraqmofamail.net; Ambassador HAZEM AHMED MAHMOUD AL-YOUSOFI.

Italy: 2 rue Idriss al-Azhar, BP 111, 10001 Rabat; tel. (53) 7219730; fax (53) 7706882; e-mail ambassade.rabat@esteri.it; internet www.ambrabat.esteri.it; Chargé d'affaires a.i. MARCO ROMITI.

Japan: 39 ave Ahmed Balafrej, Souissi, 10170 Rabat; tel. (53) 7631782; fax (53) 7750078; e-mail amb-japon@fusion.net.ma; internet www.ma.emb-japan.go.jp; Ambassador TSUNEO KUROKAWA.

Jordan: 65 Villa Wafaa Lodgement Militaire, Souissi II, Rabat; tel. (53) 7751125; fax (53) 7758722; e-mail jo.am@iam.net.ma; Ambassador ALI HASSAN EL-KAID.

Korea, Republic: 41 ave Mehdi Ben Barka, Souissi, 10100 Rabat; tel. (53) 7756791; fax (53) 7750189; e-mail morocco@mofat.go.kr; internet mar.mofat.go.kr; Ambassador LEE TAE-HO.

Kuwait: km 4.3, ave Imam Malik, Souissi, Rabat; tel. (53) 7631111; fax (53) 7753591; e-mail alrabat@mofa.gov.kw; Ambassador SHAMLAN ABD AL-AZIZ AL-ROUMI.

Lebanon: 114 ave Abd el-Malek Ben Marouane, Rabat; tel. (53) 7656949; fax (53) 7657195; Ambassador MUSTAPHA HAMDAN.

Liberia: 23 rue Qadi Ben Hamadi Senhaji, Souissi, Rabat; tel. and fax (53) 7638426; e-mail liberanmissioninrabat@yahoo.fr; Chargé d'affaires MORIEBA K. SANOE.

Libya: km 5.5, route de Zaêrs, ave Imam Malik, Souissi, Rabat; tel. (53) 7631871; fax (53) 7631877; Ambassador ABUBAKR ALI SHAKLAWOON.

Malaysia: 17 ave Bir Kacem, Souissi, Rabat; tel. (53) 7658324; fax (53) 7658363; e-mail malrabat@kln.gov.my; internet www.kln.gov.my/perwakilan/rabat; Ambassador JAMAL BIN HASSAN.

Mali: 7 rue Thami Lamdouar, Souissi, Rabat; tel. (53) 7759121; fax (53) 7754742; Ambassador OUSMANE AMADOU.

Mauritania: 6 rue Thami Lamdouar, BP 207, Souissi, 10000 Rabat; tel. (53) 7656678; fax (53) 7656680; e-mail ambarim-rabat@menara.com; internet www.ambarimrabat.ma; Ambassador (vacant).

Mexico: 6 rue Kadi Mohamed Brebri, BP 1789, Souissi, 10100 Rabat; tel. (53) 7631969; fax (53) 7631971; e-mail embamexmar@smirt.net.ma; internet embamex.sre.gob.mx/marruecos; Ambassador ANDRÉS ORDÓÑEZ.

Netherlands: 40 rue de Tunis, BP 329, Hassan, 10001 Rabat; tel. (53) 7219600; fax (53) 7219665; e-mail rab@minbuza.nl; internet www.mfa.nl/rab; Ambassador RON STRIKKER.

Niger: 14 bis, rue Jabal al-Ayachi, Agdal, Rabat; tel. (53) 7674615; fax (53) 7674629; Ambassador OUSSEINI MAMADOU.

Nigeria: 70 ave Omar ibn al-Khattab, BP 347, Agdal, Rabat; tel. (53) 7671857; fax (53) 7672739; e-mail nigerianrabat@menara.ma; internet nigerianrabat.com; Ambassador ABDULLAH MUHAMMAD WALI.

Norway: 6 rue Beni Ritoune, BP 757, Agdal, Souissi, 10106 Rabat; tel. (53) 7664200; fax (53) 7664299; e-mail emb.rabat@mfa.no; internet www.norvege.ma; Ambassador ARE JOSTEIN NORHEIM.

Oman: 21 rue Hamza, Agdal, 10000 Rabat; tel. (53) 7673788; fax (53) 7674567; Ambassador ABDULLAH BIN OBAID AL-HINA'EI.

Pakistan: 37 ave Ahmed Balafrej, Souissi, Rabat; tel. (53) 7631192; fax (53) 7631243; e-mail pareprabat@menara.ma; internet www.mofa.gov.pk/morocco/mission.aspx; Ambassador (vacant).

Peru: 16 rue d'Ifrane, 10000 Rabat; tel. (53) 7723236; fax (53) 7702803; e-mail leprurabat@menara.ma; Ambassador CARLOS MANUEL VELASCO MENDIOLA.

Poland: 23 rue Oqbah, Agdal, BP 425, 10000 Rabat; tel. (53) 7771173; fax (53) 7775320; e-mail rabat.amb.sekretariat@msz.gov.pl; internet rabat.msz.gov.pl; Ambassador WITOLD SPIRYDOWICZ.

Portugal: 5 rue Thami Lamdouar, Souissi, 10100 Rabat; tel. (53) 7756446; fax (53) 7756445; e-mail embaixada@ambportugalrabat.org; internet ambportugalrabat.org; Ambassador MARIA RITA FERRO.

Qatar: 4 ave Tarik ibn Ziad, BP 1220, 10001 Rabat; tel. (53) 7765681; fax (53) 7765774; e-mail rabat@mofa.gov.qa; Ambassador ABDALLAH BIN FALLAH ABDALLAH AL-DAWSSARI.

Romania: 10 rue d'Ouezzane, Hassan, 10000 Rabat; tel. (53) 7724694; fax (53) 7700196; e-mail rabat@mae.ro; internet rabat.mae.ro; Ambassador SIMONA MARIANA IOAN.

Russian Federation: km 4, ave Muhammad VI, Souissi, Rabat; tel. (53) 7753509; fax (53) 7753590; e-mail ambrusmaroc@inbox.ru; internet www.marocco.mid.ru; Ambassador VALERII P. VOROBIEV.

Saudi Arabia: 322 ave Imam Malik, km 3.5, route des Zaêrs, Rabat; tel. (53) 7657454; fax (53) 7639696; e-mail maemb@mofa.gov.sa; Ambassador Dr ABD AL-RAHMAN IBN MUHAMMAD AL-JEDAIE.

Senegal: 17 rue Cadi Ben Hamadi Senhaji, Souissi, BP 365, 10000 Rabat; tel. (53) 7754171; fax (53) 7754149; e-mail ambassene@menara.ma; Ambassador AMADOU SOW.

Serbia: BP 5014, 23 ave Mehdi Ben Barka, Souissi, 10105 Rabat; tel. (53) 7752201; fax (53) 7753258; e-mail sermont@menara.ma; Ambassador SLADJANA PRICA.

South Africa: 34 rue Saâdiens, Rabat; tel. (53) 7689159; fax (53) 7724550; e-mail sudaf@mtds.com; Chargé d'affaires a.i. E. J. JOUBERT.

Spain: 3 rue Aïn Khalouiya, ave Muhammad VI, km 5.3, route des Zaêrs, Souissi, 10000 Rabat; tel. (53) 7633900; fax (53) 7630600; e-mail emb.rabat@maec.es; internet www.exteriores.gob.es/embajadas/rabat; Ambassador JOSÉ DE CARVAJAL SALIDO.

Sudan: 5 ave Ghomara, Souissi, 10000 Rabat; tel. (53) 7752863; fax (53) 7752865; e-mail sudanirab@menara.com; Ambassador SOULEIMAN ABD EL-TAWAB AZZINE.

Sweden: 159 ave Muhammad VI, BP 428, Souissi, 10001 Rabat; tel. (53) 7633210; fax (53) 7758048; e-mail ambassaden.rabat@gov.se; internet www.swedenabroad.com/rabat; Ambassador ANNA HAMMARGREN.

Switzerland: sq. de Berkane, BP 169, 10020 Rabat; tel. (53) 7268030; fax (53) 7268040; e-mail rab.vertretung@eda.admin.ch; internet www.eda.admin.ch/rabat; Ambassador LOUIS BERTRAND.

Syria: km 5.2, route des Zaêrs, BP 5158, Souissi, Rabat; tel. (53) 7757521; fax (53) 7757522; e-mail syriaembassy@menara.ma; Ambassador (vacant).

Thailand: 33 ave Lalla Meriem, Souissi, 10170, Rabat; tel. (53) 7634603; fax (53) 7634607; e-mail thaima@menara.ma; internet www.thaiembassy.org/rabat; Ambassador SUPHORN PHOLMANI.

Tunisia: 6 ave de Fès et 1 rue d'Ifrane, 10000 Rabat; tel. (53) 7730636; fax (53) 7730637; Ambassador CHAFIK HAJJI.

Turkey: 7 ave Abdelkrim Benjelloun, 10010 Rabat; tel. (53) 7661522; fax (53) 7660476; e-mail ambassade.rabat@mfa.gov.tr; internet rabat.emb.mfa.gov.tr; Ambassador ETHEM BARKAN OZ.

Ukraine: 212, rue Mouaouya Ben Houdaig, Cité OLM, Souissi II, 10020 Rabat; tel. (53) 7657840; fax (53) 7754679; e-mail emb_ma@mfa.gov.ua; internet www.mfa.gov.ua/morocco; Ambassador YAROSLAV KOVAL.

United Arab Emirates: 11 ave des Alaouines, 10000 Rabat; tel. (53) 7707070; fax (53) 7724145; e-mail rabat@mofa.gov.ae; internet uae-embassy.ae/embassies/ma; Ambassador AL-ASRI SAID AHMAD AL-DAHIRI.

United Kingdom: 28 ave S. A. R. Sidi Muhammad, BP 45, Souissi, 10105 Rabat; tel. (53) 7633333; fax (53) 7758709; e-mail generalenquiries.rabat@fco.gov.uk; internet www.gov.uk/government/world/morocco; Ambassador CLIVE ALDERTON.

USA: 2 ave de Muhammad el-Fassi, Rabat; tel. (53) 7762265; fax (53) 7765661; e-mail ircrabat@usembassy.ma; internet morocco.usembassy.gov; Ambassador DWIGHT L. BUSH, Sr.

Venezuela: 58 Lot OLM, Villa Yasmine, rue Capitaine Abdeslam el-Moudden el-Alami, Souissi, Rabat; tel. (53) 7650315; fax (53) 7650372; e-mail emvenez@menara.ma; Chargé d'affaires a.i. AHMED ABUSAID.

Yemen: ave Imam Malik, km 6.6, rue Beni Tajit, Quartier des Ambassadeurs, Souissi, Rabat; tel. (53) 7631220; fax (53) 7631267; e-mail yemen@menara.ma; Chargé d'affaires a.i. NAJEEB AHMAD AL-GHARASI.

Judicial System

Supreme Court (Al-Majlis al-Aala): Hay Riad, Ave al-Nakhil, Rabat; tel. (53) 7714931; fax (53) 7715106; e-mail coursupreme@coursupreme.ma; internet www.coursupreme.ma; responsible for the interpretation of the law and regulates the jurisprudence of the courts and tribunals of the Kingdom. The Supreme Court sits at Rabat and is divided into 6 Chambers; First Pres. MUSTAPHA FARÈS.

Courts of Appeal: The 21 courts hear appeals from lower courts and also comprise a criminal division.

Courts of First Instance: The 65 courts pass judgment on offences punishable by up to five years' imprisonment. These courts also pass judgment, without possibility of appeal, in personal and civil cases involving up to 3,000 dirhams.

Communal and District Courts: composed of one judge, who is assisted by a clerk or secretary, and hear only civil and criminal cases.

Administrative Courts: The seven courts pass judgment, subject to appeal before the Supreme Court pending the establishment of administrative appeal courts, on litigation with government departments.

Commercial Courts: The nine courts pass judgment, without the possibility of appeal, on all commercial litigations involving up to 9,000 dirhams. They also pass judgment on claims involving more than 9,000 dirhams, which can be appealed against in the commercial appeal courts.

Permanent Royal Armed Forces' Court: tries offences committed by the armed forces and military officers.

Attorney-General: MUSTAPHA MEDDAH.

Religion

ISLAM

About 99% of Moroccans are Muslims (of whom about 90% are of the Sunni sect), and Islam is the state religion.

CHRISTIANITY

There are about 69,000 Christians, mostly Roman Catholics.

The Roman Catholic Church

Morocco (excluding the disputed territory of Western Sahara) comprises two archdioceses, directly responsible to the Holy See. The Moroccan archbishops participate in the Conférence Episcopale Régionale du Nord de l'Afrique (f. 1985).

Bishops' Conference: Conférence Episcopale Régionale du Nord de l'Afrique, 1 rue Hadj Muhammad Riffaï, BP 258, 10001 Rabat; tel. (53) 7709239; fax (53) 7706282; e-mail secretariatarchev@yahoo.fr; f. 1985; Pres. Most Rev. VINCENT LANDEL (Archbishop of Rabat).

Archbishop of Rabat: Most Rev. VINCENT LANDEL, Archevêché, 1 rue Hadj Muhammad Riffaï, BP 258, 10001 Rabat; tel. (53) 7709239; fax (53) 7706282; e-mail landel@wanadoo.net.ma.

Archbishop of Tangier: Most Rev. SANTIAGO AGRELO MARTÍNEZ, Archevêché, 55 rue Sidi Bouabid, BP 2116, 9000 Tangier; tel. (53) 9932762; fax (53) 9949117; e-mail agrelomar@hotmail.com.

Western Sahara comprises a single Apostolic Prefecture, with an estimated 80 Catholics (2007).

Prefect Apostolic of Western Sahara: Fr ACACIO VALBUENA RODRÍGUEZ, Misión Católica, BP 31, 70001 el-Aaiún; e-mail omisahara@menara.ma.

The Anglican Communion

Within the Church of England, Morocco forms part of the diocese of Gibraltar in Europe. There are Anglican churches in Casablanca and Tangier.

Protestant Church

Evangelical Church: 33 rue d'Azilal, 20000 Casablanca; tel. (52) 2302151; fax (52) 2444768; e-mail eeam@lesblancs.com; f. 1920; established in 8 towns; Pres. Pastor JEAN-LUC BLANC; 1,000 mems.

JUDAISM

It is estimated that there are fewer than 7,000 Jews in Morocco, of whom approximately 5,000 reside in Casablanca, with smaller communities in Rabat and other cities.

Conseil des Communautés Israélites du Maroc: 52 Béni Snassen, Souissi, Rabat; tel. (53) 222861; fax (53) 266953; Pres. SERGE BERDUGO.

The Press

DAILIES

Casablanca

Al-Ahdath al-Maghribia (Moroccan Events): 5 rue Saint-Emilion, Casablanca; tel. (52) 2304611; fax (52) 2442932; e-mail elberini@ahdath.info; internet www.ahdath.info; f. 1998; Arabic; Dir EL-MOKHTAR LARHZIOUI; circ. 30,000 (2013/14).

Assabah (The Morning): Groupe Ecomedia, 70 blvd al-Massira al-Khadra, Casablanca; tel. (52) 2953660; fax (52) 2364358; e-mail assabah@assabah.press.ma; internet www.assabah.press.ma; f. 2000; Arabic; sister publication of *L'Economiste*; Pres. ABDELMOU-NAÏM DILAMI; Dir-Gen. KHALID BELYAZID; circ. 71,935 (2008/09).

Assahra al-Maghribia: 17 rue Othman Ben Affan, Casablanca; tel. (52) 2489120; fax (52) 2203935; e-mail contacter@almaghribia.ma; internet www.almaghribia.ma; f. 1989; Arabic; Dir AHMED NACHATTI.

Aujourd'hui le Maroc: 213 Rond-Point d'Europe, 20490 Casablanca; tel. (52) 2457560; fax (52) 2542009; e-mail contact@aujourdhui.ma; internet www.aujourdhui.ma; f. 2001; French; Dir and Editor SAAD BENMANSOUR; circ. 5,435 (2008/09).

Al-Bayane (The Manifesto): 119 blvd Emile Zola, 8ème étage, BP 13152, Casablanca; tel. (52) 2307882; fax (52) 2308080; internet www.casanet.net.ma/albayane; f. 1971; Arabic and French; organ of the Parti du Progrès et du Socialisme; Dir ALLAL EL-MALEH; Editor AHMED ZAKI; circ. 2,364 (2008/09).

L'Economiste: Groupe Ecomedia, 70 blvd al-Massira al-Khadra, Casablanca; tel. (52) 2953600; fax (52) 2365926; e-mail info@leconomiste.com; internet www.leconomiste.com; f. 1991; French; Pres. ABDELMOUNAÏM DILAMI; Dir-Gen. KHALID BELYAZID; Editor-in-Chief NADIA SALAH; circ. 19,937 (2008/09).

Al-Ittihad al-Ichtiraki (Socialist Unity): 33 rue Amir Abdelkader, BP 2165, Casablanca; tel. (52) 2407385; fax (52) 2619405; e-mail ail@menara.ma; internet www.alittihad.press.ma; Arabic; f. 1983; organ of the Union Socialiste des Forces Populaires; Dir ABD AL-HADI DATE; Editor MUSTAPHA LAÂRAKI; circ. 9,513 (2008).

Libération: 33 rue Amir Abdelkader, BP 2165, Casablanca; tel. (52) 2619400; fax (52) 2620972; e-mail publiberation@gmail.com; internet www.libe.ma; f. 1964; French; organ of the Union Socialiste des Forces Populaires; Dir HABIB EL-MALKI; circ. 2,719 (2008).

Al-Massae (The Evening): 10 ave des Forces Armées Royales, 2ème étage, Casablanca; tel. (52) 2275918; fax (52) 2275597; e-mail contact@almassaepress.ma; f. 2006; Arabic; independent; Dir RACHID NINI; circ. 113,849 (2008/09).

Le Matin du Sahara et du Maghreb: 17 rue Othman Ben Affane, Casablanca; tel. (52) 2489100; fax (52) 2203048; e-mail m.jouahri@lematin.ma; internet www.lematin.ma; f. 1971; French; royalist; Dir-Gen. MUHAMMAD HAITAMI; Editor-in-Chief OMAR DAHBI; circ. 24,816 (2008/09).

Rissalat al-Oumma (The Message of the Nation): 152 ave des Forces Armées Royales, BP 20005, Casablanca; tel. (52) 2901925; fax (52) 2901926; Arabic; weekly edn in French; organ of the Union Constitutionnelle; Dir MUHAMMAD TAMALDOU.

Rabat

Al-Alam (The Flag): ave Hassan II, Lot Vita, BP 141, Rabat; tel. (53) 7294832; fax (53) 7291784; e-mail alalam@alalam.ma; internet www.alalam.ma; f. 1946; Arabic; literary supplement on Sat.; organ of the Istiqlal party; Dir ABD AL-JABBAR SUHEIMAT; Editor-in-Chief HASSAN ABDELKHALEK; circ. 10,274 (2008/09).

Annahar Al Maghribia (The Moroccan Day): 12 pl. des Alaouites, 2ème étage, Rabat; tel. (53) 7737568; fax (53) 7737547; e-mail annahar21@yahoo.fr; internet www.annahar.ma; f. 2002; Arabic; Dir and Editor-in-Chief ABD EL-HAKIM BADI; circ. 6,953 (2008).

Attajdid (Reform): 3 blvd al-Moukawama, BP 9173, Rabat; tel. (53) 7705854; fax (53) 7705852; e-mail attajdid@attajdid.ma; internet www.jadidpresse.com; f. 1999; Arabic; associated with the Parti de la Justice et du Développement; Dir ABDELILAH BENKIRANE; circ. 2,903 (2008/09).

Al-Haraka (Progress): 66 rue Patrice Lumumba, BP 1317, Rabat; tel. (53) 7768667; fax (53) 7767537; e-mail harakamp@menara.ma; internet www.harakamp.ma; Arabic; organ of the Mouvement Populaire; Dir ALI ALAOUI; circ. 1,002 (2008).

L'Opinion: ave Hassan II, Lot Vita, Rabat; tel. (53) 7293002; fax (53) 7293997; e-mail lopinion@lopinion.ma; internet www.lopinion.ma; f. 1962; French; organ of Istiqlal; Dir JAMAL HAJJAM; Editor-in-Chief ALI BENADADA; circ. 18,347 (2008/09).

SELECTED PERIODICALS

Casablanca

actuel: 1 blvd Abdellatif Ben Kaddour, 20050 Casablanca; tel. (52) 2951815; fax (52) 2951814; e-mail courrier@actuel.ma; internet www.actuel.ma; f. 2009; weekly; French; publ. by Logique Presse; Dir and Editor HENRI LOIZEAU.

Al-Ayam (The Days): Espace Paquet, 508 rue Muhammad Smiha, Casablanca; tel. (52) 2442694; fax (52) 2441173; e-mail alayams75@yahoo.fr; internet www.alayam.ma; f. 2001; Arabic; weekly; Editor NOUREDDINE MIFTAH; circ. 22,163 (2008).

CGEM Mag: 23 blvd Muhammad Abdou, Palmiers, 20340 Casablanca; tel. (52) 2997000; fax (52) 2983971; e-mail mustaphamoulay@cgem.ma; internet www.cgem.ma; monthly; French; organ of the Confédération Générale des Entreprises du Maroc; Dir MIRIEM BENSALAH-CHAQROUN; Editor-in-Chief MUSTAPHA MOULAY.

Challenge Hebdo: 58 ave des Forces Armées Royales, Tour des Habous, 13ème étage, Casablanca; tel. (52) 2548150; fax (52) 2318094; e-mail redaction@challengehebdo.com; internet www.challengehebdo.com; weekly; French; business; Dir ADIL LAHLOU; Editor-in-Chief KHALID TRITKI; circ. 8,410 (2008/09).

Construire: 744 rue Boukraa (angle rue Ouled Said), Résidence Hanane Jassim I, Bourgogne, Casablanca; tel. (52) 2273627; fax (52) 2474019; e-mail nlleconstruire@gmail.com; internet www.groupeconstruire-press.com; f. 1940; weekly; French; building and architecture magazine; Dir ABDELKRIM TALAL.

Femmes du Maroc: 18 blvd Massira al-Khadra, Maârif, Casablanca; tel. (52) 2973949; fax (52) 2584595; e-mail courrier@femmesdumaroc.com; internet www.femmesdumaroc.com; monthly; French; lifestyle magazine for women; Dir and Editor-in-Chief ZINEB IBNOUZAHIR LAHLOU; circ. 12,029 (2008/09).

La Gazette du Maroc: ave des Forces Armées Royales, Tour des Habous, 13ème étage, Casablanca; tel. (52) 2548150; fax (52) 2318094; e-mail info@lagazettedumaroc.com; internet www.lagazettedumaroc.com; weekly; French; Dir KAMAL LAHLOU; Editor-in-Chief ABD AL-LATIF EL-AZIZI; circ. 8,969 (2008).

Le Journal Hebdomadaire: 61 ave des Forces Armées Royales, BP 20000, Casablanca; tel. (52) 2546670; fax (52) 2446185; e-mail courrier@lejournal-press.com; internet www.lejournal-press.com; weekly; French; news, politics, economics; Dir ALI AMAR; Editor-in-Chief ABOUBAKR JAMAÏ; circ. 11,895 (2008/09).

Maroc Hebdo International: 4 rue des Flamants, Casablanca; tel. (52) 2238176; fax (52) 2982161; e-mail mhi@maroc-hebdo.press.ma; internet www.maroc-hebdo.com; f. 1991; weekly; French; Editor-in-Chief MUHAMMAD SELHAMI; circ. 10,510 (2008).

Nissae min al-Maghrib (Women of Morocco): Immeuble Zénith I, Lot Attaoufik, route de Nouaceur, Sidi Maârouf, Casablanca; tel. (52) 2973949; fax (52) 2973929; e-mail y.guennoun@akwagroup.com; monthly; Arabic edn of *Femmes du Maroc*; Editor-in-Chief KHADIJA SABIL; circ. 30,703 (2008/09).

La Nouvelle Tribune: 320 blvd Zerktouni, angle rue Bouardel, Casablanca; tel. (52) 2424670; fax (52) 2200031; e-mail courrier@lanouvelletribune.com; internet www.lanouvelletribune.com; f. 1996; weekly (Thur.); French; Dir FAHD YATA; circ. 6,741 (2007).

Parade: Immeuble Zénith I, Lot Attaoufik, route de Nouaceur, Sidi Maârouf, Casablanca; tel. (52) 2973949; fax (52) 2973929; e-mail y .guennoun@akwagroup.com; monthly; French; Editor-in-Chief MARIA DAIF; circ. 4,716 (2006).

Perspectives du Maghreb: 8 blvd Yacoub el Mansour, 31 Maârif, Casablanca; tel. (52) 2257844; fax (52) 2257738; e-mail popmedia@ menara.ma; f. 2005; monthly; French; circ. 6,531 (2007).

La Quinzaine du Maroc: 53 rue el-Bakri, Casablanca; tel. (52) 2440033; fax (52) 2440426; e-mail bastms@editionsmauro.com; internet www.quinzainedumaroc.com; f. 1951; fortnightly; English and French; visitors' guide; Dir HUBERT MAURO.

Le Reporter: 1 Sahat al-Istiqlal, 2ème étage, 20000 Casablanca; tel. (52) 2541103; fax (52) 2541105; e-mail lereporter.ma@gmail.com; internet www.lereporter.ma; f. 1998; weekly; French; Dir BAHIA AMRANI.

TelQuel: 28 ave des Forces Armées Royales, Casablanca; tel. (52) 2250509; fax (52) 2251331; e-mail courrier@telquel.info; internet www.telquel-online.com; f. 2001; weekly; French; Dir AICHA AKALAY; Editor-in-Chief KARIM BOUKHARI; circ. 23,172 (2008/09).

Version Homme: ave des Forces Armées Royales, Tour des Habous, 13ème étage, Casablanca; tel. (52) 2450089; fax (52) 2442213; e-mail redaction@versionhomme.com; internet www.versionhomme.com; monthly; lifestyle magazine for men; Dir ADIL LAHLOU; circ. 6,051 (2008/09).

La Vie éco: 5 blvd Abdallah Ben Yacine, 20300 Casablanca; tel. (52) 2450555; fax (52) 2304542; e-mail vieeco@marocnet.net.ma; internet www.lavieeco.com; f. 1921; weekly; French; economics; Dir FADEL AGOUMI; Editor-in-Chief SAÂD BEN MANSOUR; circ. 16,426 (2008/09).

La Vie Touristique Africaine: 17 rue El Houcine Ben Ali, Casablanca; tel. (52) 2227643; fax (52) 2275319; e-mail contact@ lavietouristique.com; internet lavietouristique.com; fortnightly; French; tourist information; Dir AHMED ZEGHARI.

Al-Watan al-An (The Nation Now): 33 rue Muhammad Bahi, Casablanca; tel. (52) 2251295; fax (52) 2251325; e-mail alwatanpress@menara.ma; weekly; Arabic; news; Editor ABDERRAHIM ARIRI; circ. 5,982 (2008).

Rabat

Al-Alam al-Amazighi: Éditions Amazigh, 5 rue Dakar, BP 477, Rabat; tel. 66-1767073 (mobile); fax (53) 7727283; e-mail lemondeamazigh@hotmail.com; weekly; Berber.

Asdae (Echoes): 30 ave Okba, Rabat; tel. (53) 7773706; e-mail asdae@menara.ma; internet www.asdae.com; weekly; Arabic; Dir and Editor-in-Chief EL-HASSAN ARBAI; circ. 1,415 (2008/09).

Da'ouat al-Haqq (Call of the Truth): al-Michwar al-Said, Rabat; tel. (53) 7766851; e-mail direction_haq@habous.gov.ma; internet www .daouatalhaq.ma; publ. by Ministry of Habous (Religious Endowments) and Islamic Affairs; f. 1957; monthly; Arabic.

Al-Mountakhab (The Team): 42 bis rue de Madagascar, Rabat; tel. (53) 7201774; fax (53) 7201776; e-mail contact@almountakhab.com; internet www.almountakhab.com; f. 1986; fortnightly; Arabic; sport; Dir MUSTAFA BADRI; Editor-in-Chief BADREDDINE IDRISSI; circ. 25,137 (2008/09).

Al-Tadamoun (Solidarity): Apt 1, Immeuble 6, rue Aguensous, ave Hassan II, Les Orangers, BP 1740, Rabat; tel. (53) 7730961; fax (53) 7738851; e-mail amdh1@mtds.com; internet www.amdh.org.ma/ar/ attadamoun; monthly; Arabic; organ of the Association Marocaine des Droits Humains; Dir ABD AL-MAJID SEMLALI EL-HASANI.

Tangier

Achamal 2000: 137 blvd Prince Héritier, 1, Tangier; tel. (53) 9940391; fax (53) 9944216; e-mail ashamal@menara.ma; weekly; Arabic; Editor-in-Chief KHALID MECHBAL; circ. 7,912 (2008/09).

Le Journal de Tanger: 7 bis, rue Omar Ben Abdelaziz, Tangier; tel. (53) 9943008; fax (53) 9945709; e-mail direct@lejournaldetanger .com; internet www.lejournaldetanger.com; f. 1904; weekly; French, English, Spanish and Arabic; Dir ABDELHAK BAKHAT; Editor-in-Chief MUHAMMAD ABOUABDILLAH; circ. 8,776 (2008/09).

NEWS AGENCY

Maghreb Arabe Presse (MAP): 122 ave Allal Ben Abdallah, BP 1049, 10000 Rabat; tel. (53) 7279464; fax (53) 7279465; e-mail mapweb@map.co.ma; internet www.map.ma; f. 1959; Arabic, French, English and Spanish; state-owned; Dir-Gen. KHALIL HACHIMI IDRISSI.

PRESS ASSOCIATIONS

Fédération Marocaine des Editeurs de Journaux (FMEJ): Groupe Ecomedia, 70 blvd al-Massira al-Khadra, Casablanca; tel. (52) 2953600; fax (52) 2365926; f. 2005; Pres. ABDELMOUNAIM DILAMI.

Organisme de Justification de la Diffusion (OJD Maroc): 4 rue des Flamants, Casablanca; tel. (52) 2238176; fax (52) 2981346; e-mail asmaehassani@gmail.com; internet www.ojd.ma; f. 2004; compiles circ. statistics; Pres. AISSAM FATHYA; Dir ASMAE HASSANI.

Publishers

Afrique Orient: 159 bis blvd Yacoub el-Mansour, Casablanca; tel. (52) 2259813; fax (52) 2440080; f. 1983; sociology, philosophy and translations; Dir MUSTAPHA CHAJII.

Belvisi: 17 rue Abbas Ibnou Farnass, BP 8044, Casablanca; tel. (52) 2250973; fax (52) 2986258; f. 1986.

Dar el-Kitab: place de la Mosquée, Quartier des Habous, BP 4018, Casablanca; tel. (52) 2305419; fax (52) 3026630; f. 1948; Arabic and French; philosophy, history, Africana, general and social sciences; state-controlled; Dir BOUTALEB ABDOU ABD AL-HAY; Gen. Man. KHADIJA EL-KASSIMI.

Editions Le Fennec: 89B blvd d'Anfa, 14ème étage, Casablanca; tel. (52) 2209314; fax (52) 2277702; e-mail info@lefennec.com; internet www.lefennec.com; f. 1987; fiction, social sciences; Dir LAYLA B. CHAOUNI.

Editions La Porte: 281 blvd Muhammad V, BP 331, Rabat; tel. (53) 7709958; fax (53) 7706476; e-mail la_porte@meganet.net.ma; law, guides, economics, educational books.

Les Editions Maghrébines: Quartier Industriel, blvd E, N 15, Sin Sebaâ, Casablanca; tel. (52) 2351797; fax (52) 2357892; f. 1962; general non-fiction.

Les Editions Toubkal: Immeuble I. G. A, pl. de la Gare Voyageurs, Bélvèdere, 20300 Casablanca; tel. and fax (52) 22342323; e-mail contact@toubkal.ma; internet www.toubkal.ma; f. 1985; economy, history, social sciences, literature, educational books; Dir MUHAMMAD DIOURI.

Malika Editions: 60 blvd Yacoub el-Mansour, 20100 Casablanca; tel. (52) 2235688; fax (52) 2251651; e-mail edmalika@connectcom.net .ma; internet www.malikaedition.com; art publications.

Tarik Editions: 321 route el-Jadida, 20390 Casablanca; tel. (52) 2259007; fax (52) 2232550; e-mail tarik.edition@gmail.com; internet www.tarikeditions.com; f. 2000; history and social sciences; Dir BICHR BENNANI.

Yomad: 4 rue Melouiya, Apt 7, Agdal, Rabat; tel. (53) 7686430; fax (53) 7686431; e-mail yomadeditions@yahoo.com; internet www .yomadeditions.net; f. 1998; children's literature; Dir NADIA ESSALMI.

GOVERNMENT PUBLISHING HOUSE

Imprimerie Officielle: ave Yacoub el-Mansour, Rabat-Chellah; tel. (53) 7765024; fax (53) 7765179.

Broadcasting and Communications

TELECOMMUNICATIONS

inwi: Lot la Colline II, Sidi Maârouf, 20190 Casablanca; tel. (52) 2900000; e-mail drh.info@inwi.ma; internet www.inwi.ma; f. 2009 as Wana following award of third GSM licence; mobile telephone and internet services launched Feb. 2010; Dir-Gen. FRÉDÉRIC DEBORD.

Itissalat al-Maghrib—Maroc Télécom: ave Annakhil Hay Riad, Rabat; tel. (53) 7719000; fax (53) 7710600; e-mail webmaster@iam .ma; internet www.iam.ma; f. 1998; privatized in 2004; Vivendi SA (France) holds a 53% stake; Chair. ABDESLAM AHIZOUNE.

Méditel: Twin Centre, angle blvd Zerktouni et blvd Massira al-Khadra, Casablanca; e-mail hassan.bouchachia@meditel.ma; internet www.meditel.ma; f. 1999; Caisse de Dépôt et de Gestion (CDG) and FinanceCom hold a 64.4% stake; provides national mobile telecommunications services; Dir-Gen. MICHEL PAULIN; Chair. OTHMAN BENJELLOUN; 11.5m. subscribers (Dec. 2012).

Regulatory Authority

Agence Nationale de Réglementation des Télécommunications (ANRT): Centre d'Affaires, blvd al-Riad, BP 2939, Hay Riad, 10100 Rabat; tel. (53) 7718400; fax (53) 7203862; e-mail com@anrt.ma; internet www.anrt.ma; f. 1998; Dir-Gen. AZDINE EL-MOUNTASSIR BILLAH.

BROADCASTING

Morocco can receive broadcasts from Spanish radio stations, and the main Spanish television channels can also be received in northern Morocco.

Radio

Radio Casablanca: c/o Loukt s.a.r.l, BP 16011, Casa Principal, 20001 Casablanca; e-mail i-rc@maroc.net; internet www.maroc.net/rc; f. 1996; Gen. Man. AMINE ZARY.

Radio Méditerranée Internationale (Médi 1): 3 rue M'sallah, BP 2055, 9000 Tangier; tel. (53) 9936363; fax (53) 9949037; e-mail medi1@medi1.com; internet www.medi1.com; Arabic and French; Man. Dir HASSAN KHIYAR.

Voice of America Radio Station in Tangier: c/o US Consulate-General, chemin des Amoureux, Tangier.

Television

Société Nationale de Radiodiffusion et de Télévision: 1 rue el-Brihi, BP 1042, 10000 Rabat; tel. (53) 7685100; fax (53) 7733733; internet www.snrt.ma; govt station; transmission commenced 1962; 45 hours weekly; French and Arabic; carries commercial advertising; Dir-Gen. and Dir Television FAIÇAL LARAICHI.

SOREAD 2M: Société d'Études et de Réalisations Audiovisuelles, km 7.3, route de Rabat, Aïn-Sebaâ, Casablanca; tel. (52) 2667373; fax (52) 2677856; e-mail portail@tv2m.co.ma; internet www.2m.ma; f. 1988; transmission commenced 1989; public television channel; owned by Moroccan Govt (72%) and by private national foreign concerns; broadcasting in French and Arabic; Man. Dir SAMI EL-JAI.

Finance

(cap. = capital; res = reserves; dep. = deposits; m. = million; br.(s) = branch(es); amounts in dirhams)

BANKING

Central Bank

Bank Al-Maghrib: 277 ave Muhammad V, BP 445, Rabat; tel. (53) 7818181; fax (53) 7567824; e-mail webmaster@bkam.ma; internet www.bkam.ma; f. 1959 as Banque du Maroc; name changed as above in 1987; bank of issue; cap. 500m., res 5,033m., dep. 47,366m. (Dec. 2009); Gov. ABDELLATIF JOUAHRI; Gen. Man. ABDELLATIF FAOUZI; 20 brs.

Other Banks

Attijariwafa Bank: 2 blvd Moulay Youssef, BP 11141, 20000 Casablanca; tel. (52) 2290000; fax (52) 2201125; e-mail contact@attijariwafa.com; internet www.attijariwafabank.com; f. 2004 by merger between Banque Commerciale du Maroc SA and Wafabank; 33.2% owned by Groupe ONA, 14.6% by Grupo Santander (Spain); cap. 2,012m., res 5,453m., dep. 258,825m. (Dec. 2012); Pres. and Dir-Gen. MUHAMMAD EL-KETTANI.

Banque Centrale Populaire (Crédit Populaire du Maroc): 101 blvd Muhammad Zerktouni, BP 10622, 21100 Casablanca; tel. (52) 2202533; fax (52) 2229699; e-mail bcp@banquepopulairemorocco.ma; internet www.cpm.co.ma; f. 1961; 51% state-owned, 49% privately owned; merged with Société Marocaine de Dépot et Crédit in 2003; cap. 16,545m., res 10,079m., dep. 210,949m. (Dec. 2013); Pres. and Man. Dir MUHAMMAD BENCHAÂBOUNE; 530 brs.

Banque Marocaine du Commerce Extérieur SA (BMCE): 140 ave Hassan II, BP 13425, 20000 Casablanca; tel. (52) 2200325; fax (52) 2264965; e-mail communicationfinanciere@bmcebank.co.ma; internet www.bmcebank.ma; f. 1959; transferred to majority private ownership in 1995; cap. 1,794m., res 10,272m., dep. 159,062m. (Dec. 2012); Pres. and Dir-Gen. OTHMAN BENJELLOUN; 310 domestic brs and 3 brs abroad.

Banque Marocaine pour le Commerce et l'Industrie SA (BMCI): 26 pl. des Nations Unies, BP 15573, Casablanca; tel. (52) 22461000; fax (52) 22299406; e-mail adiba.lahbabi@africa.bnpparibas.com; internet www.bmci.ma; f. 1964; 65.05% owned by BNP Paribas (France); cap. 1,281m., res 6,102m., dep. 58,953m. (Dec. 2012); Chair. MOURAD CHERIF; 260 brs.

Citibank-Maghreb: Zénith Millenium, Immeuble 1, Lot Attaoufik, Sidi Maârouf, BP 13362, Casablanca; tel. (52) 2489600; fax (52) 2974197; f. 1967; cap. and res 194.0m., total assets 1,211.0m. (Dec. 2003); Pres. WALTER SIOUFFI; 2 brs.

Crédit Agricole du Maroc SA: 29 rue Abou Faris al-Marini, BP 49, 10000 Rabat; tel. (53) 7208219; fax (53) 7208218; e-mail m_kettani@creditagricole.ma; internet www.creditagricole.ma; f. 1961 as Caisse Nationale de Crédit Agricole; became a limited co and adopted present name in 2003; 78% owned by Ministry of the Economy and Finance; cap. 3,818m., res 1,560m., dep. 58,105m. (Dec. 2012); Chair. TARIQ SIJILMASSI.

Crédit Immobilier et Hôtelier: 187 ave Hassan II, Casablanca; tel. (52) 2479000; fax (52) 2479363; e-mail info-client@cih.co.ma; internet www.cih.co.ma; f. 1920; transferred to majority private

ownership in 1995; cap. 2,660m., res 428,000, dep. 20,452m. (Dec. 2012); Pres. and CEO AHMAD RAHHOU; 91 brs.

Crédit du Maroc SA: 48–58 blvd Muhammad V, BP 13579, 20000 Casablanca; tel. (52) 2477477; fax (52) 2477127; e-mail mohammadine.menjra@ca-cdm.ma; internet www.cdm.co.ma; f. 1963 as Crédit Lyonnais Maroc; name changed as above in 1966; 52.6% owned by Crédit Agricole (France); cap. 2,812m., res 420m., dep. 40,547m. (Dec. 2012); Chair. BALDOMÉRO VALVERDE; 264 domestic brs, 1 br. abroad.

Société Générale Marocaine de Banques SA: 55 blvd Abdelmoumen, BP 13090, 21100 Casablanca; tel. (52) 2424242; fax (52) 2275112; e-mail contact@sgmaroc.com; internet www.sgmaroc.com; f. 1962; cap. 2,050m., res 4,766m., dep. 50,855m. (Dec. 2012); Pres. KHALID CHAMI; 300 brs.

STOCK EXCHANGE

Bourse de Casablanca: angle ave des Forces Armées Royales et rue Muhammad Errachid, Casablanca; tel. (52) 2452626; fax (52) 2452625; e-mail contact@casablanca-bourse.com; internet www.casablanca-bourse.com; f. 1929; Chair. AOMAR YIDAR; CEO K. HAJJI.

INSURANCE

Atlanta Assurances: 181 blvd d'Anfa, BP 13685, 20001 Casablanca; tel. (52) 2957676; fax (52) 2369812; e-mail info@atlanta.ma; internet www.atlanta.ma; f. 1947; cap. 591.6m.; Dir-Gen. MUHAMMAD HASSAN BENSALAH.

AXA Assurance Maroc: 120–122 ave Hassan II, 20000 Casablanca; tel. (52) 2889292; fax (52) 2889189; e-mail communication@axa.ma; internet www.axa.ma; cap. 900m.; Pres. and Dir-Gen. MICHEL HASCOET.

CNIA Saada Assurance: 216 blvd Muhammad Zerktouni, 20000 Casablanca; tel. (52) 2474040; fax (52) 2206081; internet www.cniasaada.ma; f. 2009 by merger of CNIA Assurance and Es-Saada; 53% owned by Groupe Saham; Pres. and Dir-Gen. MOULAY HAFID ELALAMY.

Compagnie d'Assurances et de Réassurances SANAD: 181 blvd d'Anfa, Tours Balzac, Casablanca; tel. (52) 2957878; fax (52) 2360406; e-mail webmaster@sanad.ma; internet www.sanad.ma; f. 1946; cap. 125m.; Chair. MUHAMMAD HASSAN BENSALAH; Dir-Gen. ABDELTIF TAHIRI.

La Marocaine Vie: 37 blvd Moulay Youssef, Casablanca; tel. (52) 2206320; fax (52) 2297307; f. 1978; 83% owned by Société Générale Marocaine de Banques SA; Pres. MARC DUVAL; Gen. Man. KARIM MOULTAKI.

Mutuelle d'Assurances des Transporteurs Unis (MATU): 215 blvd Muhammad Zerktouni, Casablanca; tel. (52) 2954500; fax (52) 2367721; e-mail info@matu.ma; Pres. HADJ OMAR BENNOUNA; Dir-Gen. AHMAD MAZOUZ.

Mutuelle Centrale Marocaine d'Assurances (MCMA): 16 rue Abou Inane, BP 27, Rabat; tel. (53) 7767800; fax (53) 7766440; f. 1968; part of the MAMDA-MCMA group; CEO HICHAM BELMRAH.

RMA Watanya: 83 ave des Forces Armées Royales, 20000 Casablanca; tel. (52) 2312163; fax (52) 2313137; e-mail contact@rmawatanya.com; internet www.rmawatanya.com; f. 2005 by merger of Al-Wataniya and La Royale Marocaine d'Assurances; cap. 1,774m.; Pres. OTHMAN BENJELLOUN.

Société Centrale de Réassurance (SCR): Tour Atlas, pl. Zallaqa, BP 13183, Casablanca; tel. (52) 2460400; fax (52) 2460460; e-mail scr@scrmaroc.com; internet www.scrmaroc.com; f. 1960; cap. 30m.; Chair. AHMAD ZINOUN; Man. Dir MUHAMMAD LARBI NALI.

Société Marocaine d'Assurance à l'Exportation (SMAEX): 24 rue Ali Abderrazak, BP 15953, Casablanca; tel. (52) 2982000; fax (52) 2252070; e-mail smaex@smaex.com; internet www.smaex.com; f. 1988; insurance for exporters in the public and private sectors; assistance for export promotion; Pres. and Dir-Gen. NEZHA LAHRICHI; Asst Dir-Gen. ABDERRAZZAK M'HAIMDAT.

WAFA Assurance: 1–3 blvd Abd al-Moumen, BP 13420, 20001 Casablanca; tel. (52) 2224575; fax (52) 2209103; e-mail webmaster@wafaassurance.com; internet www.attijariwafabank.com; subsidiary of Attijariwafa Bank; Pres. ABDELAZIZ ALAMI; CEO MUHAMMAD EL-KETTANI.

Zurich Assurances Maroc: 166 angle Zerktouni et rue Hafid Ibrahim, 20000 Casablanca; tel. (52) 22499808; fax (52) 22491733; e-mail customerservice@zurich.com; f. 1954; cap. 90m.; all kinds of insurance; Pres. and Dir-Gen. BERTO FISLER.

Insurance Association

Fédération Marocaine des Sociétés d'Assurances et de Réassurances: 154 blvd d'Anfa, Casablanca; tel. (52) 2391850; fax (52) 2391854; e-mail contact@fmsar.ma; internet www.fmsar.org.ma; f. 1958; 15 mem. cos; Pres. MUHAMMAD HASSAN BENSALAH.

Trade and Industry

GOVERNMENT AGENCIES

Agence National pour la Promotion de Petite et Moyenne Entreprise (ANPME): 10 rue Gandhi, BP 211, 10001 Rabat; tel. (53) 7708460; fax (53) 7707695; e-mail info@anpme.ma; internet www.anpme.ma; f. 1973 as the Office pour le Développement Industriel; name changed as above in 2002; state agency to develop industry; Dir-Gen. LATIFA ECHIHABI.

Centre Marocain de Promotion des Exportations (CMPE): 23 rue Ibnou Majed el-Bahar, BP 10937, 20000 Casablanca; tel. (52) 2302210; fax (52) 2301793; e-mail info@marocexport.ma; internet www.cmpe.org.ma; f. 1980; state org. for promotion of exports; Man. Dir SAAD BEN ABDALLAH.

Direction des Entreprises Publiques et de la Privatisation (DEPP): rue Haj Ahmed Cherkaoui, Quartier Administratif, Agdal, Rabat; tel. (53) 7689303; fax (53) 7689347; e-mail talbi@depp.finances.gov.ma; part of the Ministry of the Economy and Finance; in charge of regulation, restructuring and privatization of state enterprises; Dir ABDELAZIZ TALBI.

Office National des Hydrocarbures et des Mines (ONHYM): 5 ave Moulay Hassan, BP 99, 10050 Rabat; tel. (53) 7239898; fax (53) 7709411; e-mail presse@onhym.com; internet www.onhym.com; f. 2003 to succeed Bureau de Recherches et de Participations Minières and Office National de Recherches et d'Exploitations Pétrolières; state agency conducting exploration, valorization and exploitation of hydrocarbons and mineral resources; Dir-Gen. AMINA BENKHADRA.

Société de Gestion des Terres Agricoles (SOGETA): 35 rue Daïet-Erroumi, BP 731, Agdal, Rabat; tel. (53) 7772778; fax (53) 7772765; f. 1973; oversees use of agricultural land; Man. Dir BACHIR SAOUD.

DEVELOPMENT ORGANIZATIONS

Caisse de Dépôt et de Gestion: pl. Moulay el-Hassan, BP 408, 10001 Rabat; tel. (53) 7669000; fax (53) 7763849; e-mail cdg@cdg.ma; internet www.cdg.ma; f. 1959; finances small-scale projects; Dir-Gen. ANASS ALAMI; Sec.-Gen. SAÏD LAFTIT.

Caisse Marocaine des Marchés (Marketing Fund): 101 blvd Abdelmoumen, 4e étage, 20100 Casablanca; tel. (52) 22472683; fax (52) 22472554; e-mail s.benbrahim@cmm.ma; internet www.cmm.ma; f. 1950; cap. 70m. dirhams.

Société de Développement Agricole (SODEA): ave Hadj Ahmed Cherkaoui, BP 6280, Rabat; tel. (53) 7677953; fax (53) 7771514; internet www.sodea.com; f. 1972; state agricultural devt org.; Man. Dir AHMED HAJJAJI.

Société Nationale d'Investissement (SNI): 60 rue d'Alger, BP 38, 20000 Casablanca; tel. (52) 2224102; fax (52) 2484303; f. 1966; transferred to majority private ownership in 1994; cap. 10,900m. dirhams; Pres. and Man. Dir HASSAN OURIAGLI; Sec.-Gen. SAÂD BENDIDI.

CHAMBERS OF COMMERCE

Fédération des Chambres Marocaines de Commerce, d'Industrie et de Services (FCMCIS): 6 rue Erfoud, BP 218, Hassan, Rabat; tel. (53) 7767078; fax (53) 7767896; e-mail fcmcis@menara.ma; internet www.fcmcis.ma; f. 1962; groups the 28 Chambers of Commerce and Industry; Pres. DRISS HOUAT; Dir-Gen. MUHAMMAD LARBI EL-HARRAS.

Chambre de Commerce, d'Industrie et de Services de la Wilaya du Grand Casablanca: 98 blvd Muhammad V, BP 423, Casablanca; tel. (52) 2264327; fax (52) 2268436; e-mail ccisc@ccisc.gov.ma; internet www.ccisc.gov.ma; Pres. HASSAN BERKANI.

Chambre de Commerce, d'Industrie et de Services de la Wilaya de Rabat-Salé: 1 rue Gandhi, BP 131, Rabat; tel. (53) 7706444; fax (53) 7706768; e-mail info@rabat.cci.ma; internet www.ccirabat.ma; Pres. OMAR DERRAJI.

INDUSTRIAL AND TRADE ASSOCIATIONS

Office National Interprofessionnel des Céréales et des Légumineuses (ONICL): 3 ave Moulay Hassan, BP 154, Rabat; tel. (53) 7217300; fax (53) 7709626; e-mail directeur@onicl.org.ma; internet www.onicl.org.ma; f. 1937; Dir-Gen. ABDELLATIF GUEDIRA.

Office National des Pêches: 15 rue Lieutenant Mahroud, BP 16243, 20300 Casablanca; tel. (52) 2242084; fax (52) 2242305; e-mail onp@onp.co.ma; internet www.onp.co.ma; f. 1969; state fishing org.; Man. Dir MAJID KAISSAR EL-GHAIB.

EMPLOYERS' ORGANIZATIONS

Association Marocaine des Exporteurs (ASMEX): 36B blvd Anfa, Casablanca; tel. (52) 2949305; fax (52) 2949473; e-mail asmex@asmex.org; internet www.asmex.org; f. 1982; Pres. HASSAN EL-IDRISI.

Association Marocaine des Industries du Textile et de l'Habillement (AMITH): 92 blvd Moulay Rachid, Casablanca; tel. (52) 2942086; fax (52) 2940587; e-mail amith@amith.org.ma; internet www.textile.ma; f. 1960; 850 mems; textiles, knitwear and ready-made garment mfrs; Pres. MUSTAPHA SAJID; Dir-Gen. MUHAMMAD TAZI.

Association des Producteurs d'Agrumes du Maroc (ASPAM): 283 blvd Zerktouni, Casablanca; tel. (52) 2363946; fax (52) 2364041; e-mail aspam@menara.ma; f. 1958; links Moroccan citrus growers; has its own processing plants; Pres. HASSAN LYOUSSI.

Association Professionnelle des Agents Maritimes, Consignataires de Navires, et Courtiers d'Affrètement du Maroc (APRAM): 219 blvd des Forces Armées Royales, 5ème étage, 20000 Casablanca; tel. (52) 2541112; fax (52) 2541415; e-mail apram@wanadoopro.ma; internet www.apram.ma; f. 1999; 37 mems; Pres. ABDELAZIZ MANTRACH.

Association Professionnelle des Cimentiers (APC): Villa APC, Lot Allaymoune 1, 476 Hay Almatar, Casablanca; tel. (52) 2936660; fax (52) 2904491; e-mail apc@menara.ma; internet www.apc.ma; 4 mems; cement mfrs; Pres. JEAN-MARIE SCHMITZ.

Confédération Générale des Entreprises du Maroc (CGEM): 23 blvd Muhammad Abdou, Quartier Palmiers, 20100 Casablanca; tel. (52) 2997000; fax (52) 2983971; e-mail cgem@cgem.ma; internet www.cgem.ma; 25 affiliated feds; Pres. MUHAMMAD HORANI.

UTILITIES

Electricity and Water

Office National de l'Electricité et de l'Eau Potable: 65 rue Othman Ben Affan, Casablanca 20000; tel. (52) 2668298; fax (52) 2668031; internet www.one.org.ma; f. 2012 by merger of Office National de l'Eau Potable and Office National de l'Electricité; Dir-Gen. ALI FASSI FIHRI.

Gas

Afriquia Gaz: 139 blvd Moulay Ismail, Aïn Sebaâ, 20700 Casablanca; tel. (52) 22639600; fax (52) 22639666; e-mail r.idrissi@akwagroup.com; internet www.afriquiagaz.com; f. 1992; Morocco's leading gas distributor; Pres. ALI WAKRIM; Dir-Gen. TAWFIK HAMOUMI.

TRADE UNIONS

Confédération Démocratique du Travail (CDT): 64 rue al-Mourtada, Quartier Palmier, BP 13576, Casablanca; tel. (52) 2994470; fax (52) 2994473; e-mail cdtmaroc@cdt.ma; internet www.cdtmaroc.net; f. 1978; Sec.-Gen. NOUBIR EL-AMAOUI.

Fédération Démocratique du Travail (FDT): 12 rue Muhammad Diouri, Sidi Belyoute, Casablanca; tel. (52) 2446362; fax (52) 2446365; e-mail bcffdt@gmail.com; internet www.fdtmaroc.com; f. 2003 by fmr mems of CDT associated with USFP; Sec.-Gen. ABD EL-HAMID FATIHI.

Transport

Société Nationale des Transports et de la Logistique (SNTL): rue al-Fadila, Quartier Industriel, BP 114, Chellah, Rabat; tel. (53) 7289300; fax (53) 7797850; e-mail ahachemi@sntl.ma; internet www.sntl.ma; f. 1958; Dir-Gen. OUSSAMA LOUDGHIRI.

RAILWAYS

In 2010 the total length of Moroccan railways was 2,109 route-km. All services are nationalized. Plans for a four-line, 76-km tram system in Casablanca were approved in 2008; line 1, comprising 50 stations on a 29-km route, was inaugurated in December 2012. Meanwhile, a feasibility study into plans for a 39-km railway tunnel under the Strait of Gibraltar linking Morocco and Spain commenced in 2007; however, by mid-2014 the project had yet to receive formal approval. In December 2010 Morocco and France signed an agreement whereby France would provide rolling stock and equipment for the first African high-speed train link; the new line was scheduled to run between Casablanca and Tangier by the end of 2015, and subsequently to be extended to other major Moroccan cities.

Office National des Chemins de Fer (ONCF): 8 bis rue Abderrahmane el-Ghafiki, Rabat-Agdal; tel. (53) 7774747; fax (53) 7774480; e-mail ketary@oncf.ma; internet www.oncf.ma; f. 1963; administers all Morocco's railways; Dir-Gen. MUHAMMAD RABIE KHLIE.

ROADS

In 2011 there were 58,698 km of roads, of which 1,398 km were motorways, 11,364 km were highways, main or national roads, and 10,091 km were secondary or regional roads.

Autoroutes du Maroc (ADM): Hay Riad, Rabat; tel. (53) 7711056; fax (53) 7711059; e-mail naitbrahim.ismail@adm.co.ma; internet www.adm.co.ma; responsible for the construction and upkeep of Morocco's motorway network; Dir-Gen. ANOUAR BENAZZOUZ.

Compagnie de Transports au Maroc (CTM—SA): km 13.5, autoroute Casablanca–Rabat, Casablanca; tel. (52) 2762100; fax (52) 2765428; internet www.ctm.ma; f. 1919; 18 agencies nationwide; privatized in 1993, with 40% of shares reserved for Moroccan citizens; Pres. and Dir-Gen. EZZOUBEIR ERRHAIMINI.

SHIPPING

According to official figures, Morocco's ports handled 96m. metric tons of goods in 2011. The most important ports, in terms of the volume of goods handled, are Casablanca, Jorf Lasfar, Safi and Mohammedia. Tangier is the principal port for passenger services. The first phase of a new container port, Tangier-Med, which had an initial annual capacity of 3.5m. containers, became operational in 2007. Construction work on a second phase began in 2009, which was expected to increase capacity to 8.5m. containers per year on its completion in 2015. At 31 December 2014 Morocco's flag registered fleet consisted of 423 vessels, with a combined displacement of 355,764 grt, of which 305 were fish carriers and six were general cargo ships.

Port Authorities

Agence Nationale des Ports (ANP): 300 lotissement Mandarona, Sidi Maârouf, 20270 Casablanca; tel. (52) 0200700; fax (52) 2786102; internet www.anp.org.ma; f. 2006, following division of Office d'Exploitation des Ports; regulator of port activity; also responsible for development and maintenance of port facilities; Dir-Gen. NADIA LARAKI.

Société d'Exploitation des Ports (Marsa Maroc): 175 blvd Zerktouni, 20100 Casablanca; tel. (52) 2258258; fax (52) 2995217; internet www.sodep.co.ma; f. 2006, following division of Office d'Exploitation des Ports; responsible for management of port terminals and quayside facilities; Pres. MUHAMMAD ABDELJALIL.

Principal Shipping Companies

Agence Med SARL: 3 rue ibn Rochd, 90020 Tangier; tel. (53) 9935875; fax (53) 9932118; e-mail agencemed@mhbland.com; f. 1904; owned by the Bland Group; also at Agadir, Casablanca, Jorf Lasfar, Nador and Safi; Operations Man. CHAFIK ABAROUDI.

Compagnie Chérifienne d'Armement: 5 blvd Abdallah Ben Yacine, 21700 Casablanca, tel. (52) 2309455; fax (52) 2301186, f. 1929; regular services to Europe; Man. Dir MAX KADOCH.

Compagnie Marocaine d'Agences Maritimes (COMARINE): 45 ave des Forces Armées Royales, BP 60, 20000 Casablanca; tel. (52) 2548510; fax (52) 2548570; e-mail comarine@comarine.co.ma.

Compagnie Marocaine de Navigation (COMANAV): 7 blvd de la Résistance, BP 628, Casablanca 20300; tel. (52) 2303012; fax (52) 2302006; e-mail comanav@comanav.co.ma; internet www.comanav.ma; f. 1946 as Cie Franco-Chérifienne de Navigation; name changed as above in 1959; privatization pending; regular services to European, Middle Eastern and West African ports; tramping; Pres. and Dir-Gen. TOUFIQ IDRAIIIMI; Sec.-Gen. MEHDI BELGHITI; 12 agencies.

Intercona: 6 rue Méditérranée, Edifici Coficom, Tangier 90000; tel. (53) 9945907; fax (53) 9945909; e-mail intercona-sa@menara.ma; internet intercona.com; f. 1943; shipping agent; Pres. VICENTE JORRO.

Limadet-ferry: 3 rue ibn Rochd, Tangier; tel. (53) 933639; fax (53) 937173; e-mail headoffice@limadet.com; f. 1966; daily services between Algeciras (Spain) and Tangier; Dir-Gen. RACHID BEN MANSOUR.

Société Marocaine de Navigation Atlas: 81 ave Houmane el-Fatouaki, 21000 Casablanca; tel. (52) 2224190; fax (52) 2200164; e-mail atlas@marbar.co.ma; f. 1976; Chair. HASSAN CHAMI; Man. Dir MUHAMMAD SLAOUI.

Voyages Paquet: 65 ave des Forces Armées Royales, 20000 Casablanca; tel. (52) 2761941; fax (52) 2442108; f. 1970; Pres. MUHAMMAD ELOUALI ELALAMI; Dir-Gen. NAÏMA BAKALI ELOUALI ELALAMI.

CIVIL AVIATION

The main international airports are at Casablanca (King Muhammad V), Rabat, Tangier, Marrakesh, Agadir Inezgane, Fez, Oujda, al-Hocima, el-Aaiún, Ouarzazate, Agadir al-Massira and Nador. The completion of a second runway at King Muhammad V airport was followed by the inauguration, in September 2007, of a second terminal, which increased the airport's annual passenger capacity from 5m. to 11m.

Jet4you: 4 Lot la Colline, Sidi Maârouf, 20270 Casablanca; fax (52) 2584228; internet www.jet4you.com; f. 2006; wholly owned by TUI Travel PLC (United Kingdom); low-cost airline; services to destinations in 5 European countries; CEO JAWAD ZIYAT.

Office National des Aéroports (ONDA): Siège Social Nouasseur, BP 8101, Casablanca; tel. (52) 2539040; fax (52) 2539901; e-mail onda@onda.ma; internet www.onda.ma; f. 1990; Dir-Gen. ZOUHAIR MUHAMMAD EL-AOUFIR.

Royal Air Maroc (RAM): Aéroport de Casablanca-Anfa; tel. (52) 2912000; fax (52) 2912087; e-mail callcenter@royalairmaroc.com; internet www.royalairmaroc.com; f. 1953; 94.4% state-owned; scheduled for partial privatization; domestic flights and services to Western Europe, Scandinavia, the Americas, North and West Africa, the Middle East; Chair. and CEO DRISS BENHIMA.

Tourism

Tourism is Morocco's second main source of convertible currency. The country's tourist attractions include its sunny climate, ancient sites (notably the cities of Fez, Marrakesh, Meknès and Rabat) and spectacular scenery. There are popular holiday resorts on the Atlantic and Mediterranean coasts. In 2013 foreign tourist arrivals totalled 5.3m., compared with 1.6m. in 1996. Tourism receipts, excluding passenger transport, were estimated at US $6,851m. in 2013.

Office National Marocain du Tourisme: angle rue Oued el-Makhazine et rue Zalaga, BP 19, Agdal, Rabat; tel. (53) 7278300; fax (53) 7674015; e-mail contact@onmt.org.ma; internet www.visitmorocco.com; f. 1918; Dir-Gen. ABD EL-RAFFIE ZOUITENE.

Defence

Commander-in-Chief of the Armed Forces: HM King MUHAMMAD VI.

Inspector General of the Royal Moroccan Armed Forces: Lt.-Gen. BOUCHAIB ARROUB.

Inspector General of the Royal Moroccan Air Force: Maj.-Gen. AHMED BOUTALEB.

Inspector General of the Royal Moroccan Navy: Vice Adm. MUHAMMAD LAGHMARI.

Commander of the Royal Moroccan Gendarmerie: Gen. HOSNI BENSLIMANE.

Defence Budget (2014): 31,500m. dirhams.

Military Service: 18 months.

Total Armed Forces (as assessed at November 2014): 195,800 (army 175,000—including some 100,000 conscripts; navy 7,800—including 1,500 marines; air force 13,000). Reserves 150,000.

Paramilitary Forces (as assessed at November 2014): 50,000: royal gendarmerie 20,000; auxiliary force 30,000.

Education

Since independence in 1956, Morocco has tried to resolve a number of educational problems: a youthful and fast-growing population, an urgent need for skilled workers and executives, a great diversity of teaching methods between French, Spanish, Muslim and Moroccan government schools (syllabuses have been standardized since 1967), and, above all, a high degree of adult illiteracy. In recent years increasing attention has been given to education for girls. There are now a number of mixed and girls' schools, notably in urban areas.

In 2013/14 there were an estimated 4,030,142 pupils in primary schools. A decree of November 1963 made education compulsory for children between the ages of seven and 13 years, and this has now been applied in most urban areas; from September 2002 children were to be educated from six years of age. In 2013, according to UNESCO estimates, enrolment at primary level included 98% of the relevant age-group. Instruction is given in Arabic for the first two years and in Arabic and French for the next four years, with English as the first additional language. Teaching in the principal Berber language, Tamazight, began in primary schools in the 2003/04 academic year.

Secondary education, beginning at the age of 13, lasts for up to six years (comprising two cycles of three years), and in 2013/14 provided for an estimated 2,606,239 pupils. In 1988 the secondary school graduation examination, the *baccalauréat*, was replaced by a system of continuous assessment. Secondary enrolment in 2012 was equivalent to 69% of the relevant age-group. Under the 2009 budget, expenditure on education by the central Government was projected at 47,269m. dirhams (21.7% of total spending).

There are eight universities in Morocco, including the Islamic University of al-Quarawiyin at Fez (founded in 859), the Muhammad V University at Rabat (opened in 1957), and an English-language university, inaugurated at Ifrane in 1995. In addition, there are institutes of higher education in business studies, agriculture, mining, law, and statistics and advanced economics. In 2010/11 there were some 505,681 students enrolled in tertiary education.

MOZAMBIQUE

Introductory Survey

LOCATION, CLIMATE, LANGUAGE, RELIGION, FLAG, CAPITAL

The Republic of Mozambique lies on the east coast of Africa, bordered to the north by Tanzania, to the west by Malawi, Zambia and Zimbabwe, and to the south by South Africa and Swaziland. The country has a coastline of about 2,470 km (1,535 miles) on the shores of the Indian Ocean, and is separated from Madagascar, to the east, by the Mozambique Channel. Except in a few upland areas, the climate varies from tropical to subtropical. Rainfall is irregular, but the rainy season is usually from November to March, when average temperatures in Maputo are between 26°C (79°F) and 30°C (86°F). In the cooler dry season, in June and July, the average temperatures are 18°C (64°F) to 20°C (68°F). Portuguese is the official language (spoken by more than 50% of the population), while there are some 39 indigenous languages, the most widely spoken being Makhuwa, Tsonga, Sena and Lomwe. Many of the inhabitants follow traditional beliefs. According to the 2007 census, 56.1% of the population were Christian and 17.9% were Muslim. The national flag (proportions 2 by 3) has three equal horizontal stripes, of green, black and yellow, separated by narrow white stripes. At the hoist is a red triangle containing a five-pointed yellow star, on which are superimposed an open book, a hoe and a rifle. The capital is Maputo (formerly Lourenço Marques).

CONTEMPORARY POLITICAL HISTORY

Historical Context

Mozambique became a Portuguese colony in the 19th century and an overseas province in 1951. Nationalist groups began to form in the 1960s. The Frente de Libertação de Moçambique (Frelimo—Mozambique Liberation Front) was formed in 1962 and launched a military campaign for independence in 1964. After the coup in Portugal in April 1974, negotiations between Frelimo and the new Portuguese Government resulted in a period of rule in Mozambique by a transitional Government, followed by full independence on 25 June 1975. The leader of Frelimo, Samora Machel, became the first President of Mozambique. Between September and December 1977 elections took place to local, district and provincial assemblies and, at national level, to the Assembleia Popular (People's Assembly).

In March 1976 Mozambique closed its border with Rhodesia (now Zimbabwe) and applied economic sanctions against that country. Mozambique was the principal base for Rhodesian nationalist guerrillas, and consequently suffered considerable devastation as a result of offensives launched by Rhodesian government forces against guerrilla camps. The border was reopened in January 1980.

After Zimbabwean independence in April 1980, South Africa adopted Rhodesia's role as supporter of the Mozambican opposition guerrilla group, Resistência Nacional Moçambicana (Renamo), also known as the Movimento Nacional da Resistência de Moçambique. The activities of Renamo subsequently increased, causing persistent disruption to road, rail and petroleum pipeline links from Mozambican ports, which were vital to the economic independence of southern African nations from South Africa. In March 1984 Mozambique and South Africa signed a formal joint non-aggression pact, the Nkomati Accord, whereby each Government undertook to prevent opposition forces on its territory from launching attacks against the other, and a Joint Security Commission was established. The Accord effectively implied that South Africa would withdraw its covert support for Renamo in return for a guarantee by Mozambique that it would prevent any further use of its territory by the then banned African National Congress of South Africa (ANC). However, following an intensification of Renamo activity, in 1985 the Frelimo Government appealed to foreign powers for increased military assistance, and in June it was agreed that Zimbabwe would augment its military presence in Mozambique. A major military offensive against Renamo in July resulted in the capture, in August, of the rebels' national operational command centre. Mozambique subsequently alleged that South Africa had repeatedly violated the Nkomati Accord by providing material support for the rebels. The Joint Security Commission ceased to meet in 1985.

President Machel died in an air crash in South Africa in October 1986. The causes of the incident were unclear, and the Mozambican Ministry of Information declared that it did not exclude the possibility of South African sabotage. (In May 1998 it was announced that South Africa's Truth and Reconciliation Commission—TRC—was to examine evidence relating to the crash. The TRC's final report stated that the evidence was inconclusive, but a number of questions merited further investigation and in early 2006 the South African Government announced that it was to reopen the inquiry into Machel's death.) In November 1986 the Central Committee of Frelimo appointed Joaquim Alberto Chissano, hitherto Minister for Foreign Affairs, as President. At a Frelimo congress in July 1989, the party's exclusively Marxist-Leninist orientation was renounced, and party membership was opened to Mozambicans from all sectors of society.

Meanwhile, in May 1998 Mozambican and South African officials agreed to reactivate the Nkomati Accord and to re-establish the Joint Security Commission; subsequently a joint commission for co-operation and development was established.

Domestic Political Affairs

The introduction, on 30 November 1990, of a new Mozambican Constitution, formally ended Frelimo's single-party rule and committed the State to political pluralism and a free-market economy. The official name of the country was changed from the People's Republic of Mozambique to the Republic of Mozambique. Renamo refused to recognize the new Constitution, declaring that it had been drafted without democratic consultation. The President was henceforth to be elected by direct universal suffrage, and the legislature was renamed the Assembleia da República (Assembly of the Republic). A new law concerning the formation, structure and function of political parties came into effect in February 1991. In accordance with the Constitution, Renamo would not be recognized as a legitimate political party until it had renounced violence completely.

In October 1991 Renamo and the Government signed a protocol agreeing fundamental principles and containing a set of mutual guarantees as a basis for a peace accord. Throughout the discussions (held in Rome, Italy) Renamo continued guerrilla attacks, many of which were launched (despite the Nkomati Accord) from South Africa. Under the terms of the protocol, Renamo effectively recognized the legitimacy of the Government and agreed to enter the multi-party political framework. In return, the Government pledged not to legislate on any of the points under negotiation until a general peace accord had been signed. In November a second protocol was signed by both parties, enabling Renamo to begin functioning as a political party immediately after the signing of a general peace accord.

In March 1992 a third protocol was signed establishing the principles for the country's future electoral system. Under its terms, the elections, to be held under a system of proportional representation, were to be supervised by international observers. An electoral commission was to be established, with one-third of its members to be appointed by Renamo. On 7 August, following three days of discussions in Rome, Chissano and the Renamo leader, Afonso Macacho Marceta Dhlakama, signed a joint declaration committing the two sides to a total ceasefire by 1 October, as part of an Acordo Geral de Paz (AGP—General Peace Agreement). In September Chissano and Dhlakama met in Gaborone, Botswana, to attempt to resolve the deadlocked military and security issues. Chissano offered to establish an independent commission to monitor and guarantee the impartiality of the Serviço de Informação e Segurança do Estado (SISE—State Information and Security Service). In addition, the figure of 30,000 was agreed upon as the number of troops to comprise the joint national defence force.

The AGP was finally signed on 4 October 1992. Under the terms of the agreement, a general ceasefire was to come into force immediately after ratification of the treaty by the legislature. Both the Renamo troops and the government forces were to withdraw to assembly points within seven days of ratification. The new national defence force, the Forças Armadas de Defesa de Moçambique (FADM), would then be created, drawing on equal numbers from each side, with the remaining troops surrendering their weapons to a UN peacekeeping force within six months. A Ceasefire Commission, incorporating representatives from the Government, Renamo and the UN, was to supervise the implementation of the truce regulations. Overall political control of the peace process was to be vested in a Comissão de Supervisão e Controle (CSC—Supervision and Control Commission), comprising representatives of the Government, Renamo and the UN. In addition, Chissano was to appoint a Comissão Nacional de Informação (COMINFO—National Information Commission), with responsibilities including supervision of the SISE. Presidential and legislative elections were to take place, under UN supervision, one year after the signing of the AGP, provided that it had been fully implemented and the demobilization process completed. The AGP was duly ratified by the Assembleia da República and came into force on 15 October. On that day UN observers arrived in Maputo to supervise the first phase of the ceasefire. However, shortly afterwards the Government accused Renamo of systematically violating the accord. Dhlakama subsequently claimed that Renamo's actions had been defensive manoeuvres and, in turn, accused government forces of violating the accord by advancing into Renamo territory.

In November 1992, owing to considerable delays in the formation of the various peace commissions envisaged in the AGP, the timetable for the ceasefire operations was redrafted. In December the UN Security Council finally approved a plan for the establishment of the UN Operation in Mozambique (ONUMOZ), providing for the deployment of some 7,500 troops, police and civilian observers to oversee the process of demobilization and formation of the FADM, and to supervise the forthcoming elections. However, there were continued delays in the deployment of ONUMOZ. In March 1993 the peace process was effectively halted when Renamo withdrew from the CSC and the Ceasefire Commission, protesting that proper provisions had not been made to accommodate its officials. In April Dhlakama announced that his forces would begin to report to assembly points only when Renamo received US $15m. to finance its transition into a political party. Meanwhile, the first UN troops became operational on 1 April.

In June 1993 Renamo rejoined the CSC. The commission subsequently agreed to a formal postponement of the election date to October 1994. A meeting in Maputo of international aid donors, also in June 1993, produced promises of additional support for the peace process, bringing the total pledged by donors to US $520m., including support for the repatriation of 1.5m. refugees from neighbouring countries, the resettlement of 4m.–5m. displaced people and the reintegration of some 80,000 former combatants into civilian life. In November consensus was finally reached on the text of the electoral law, which was promulgated at the end of December. At a meeting of the CSC in mid-November an agreement was signed providing for the confinement of troops, to be concluded by the end of the year.

In February 1994 the UN Security Council announced that, in response to demands made by Renamo, it would be increasing the membership of the UN police corps monitoring the confinement areas from 128 to 1,144. By the end of February only 50% of troops had entered designated assembly points, and none had officially been demobilized. In March, in an effort to expedite the confinement process, the Government announced that it was to commence the unilateral demobilization of its troops. Renamo began the demobilization of its troops shortly afterwards. In April Chissano issued a decree scheduling the presidential and legislative elections for October, and in May the UN Security Council renewed the mandate of ONUMOZ until November.

On 16 August 1994, in accordance with the provisions of the AGP, the government Forças Armadas de Moçambique were formally dissolved and their assets transferred to the FADM, which was inaugurated as the country's official armed forces on the same day. In December the Ceasefire Commission issued its final report, according to which ONUMOZ had registered a combined total of 91,691 government and Renamo troops during the confinement process, of whom 11,579 had enlisted in the FADM (compared with the 30,000 envisaged in the AGP).

Multi-party elections

In August 1994 Renamo formally registered as a political party. In the same month the Partido Liberal e Democrático de Moçambique, the Partido Nacional Democrático and the Partido Nacional de Moçambique formed an electoral coalition, the União Democrática (UD). The presidential and legislative elections took place in October. In the presidential election Chissano secured an outright majority (53.3%) of the votes. His closest rival was Dhlakama, with 33.7%. In the legislative elections Frelimo also secured an overall majority, winning 129 of the 250 seats in the Assembleia da República; Renamo obtained 112 seats, and the UD the remaining nine. In November the UN Security Council extended the mandate of ONUMOZ until the end of January 1995. Chissano was inaugurated as President on 9 December 1994, and the new Government, in which all portfolios were assigned to members of Frelimo, was sworn in on 23 December. By the end of March 1995 only a small unit of ONUMOZ officials remained in the country.

Presidential and legislative elections took place in December 1999. In the presidential contest, Chissano defeated Dhlakama (his sole challenger), taking 52.3% of the valid votes cast. Frelimo secured 133 of the 250 seats in the Assembleia da República; Renamo—União Eleitoral, a Renamo-led coalition of 11 opposition parties, obtained the remaining seats, although Renamo rejected the outcome, claiming that the vote had been fraudulent. In January 2000 Chissano was sworn in for a further five-year presidential term.

In December 2000 Dhlakama and President Chissano held talks in an attempt to resolve the growing tension between their two parties. Dhlakama stated that he was prepared to accept the results of the 1999 elections, while Chissano pledged to consult Renamo about future state appointments. In a second meeting between the two leaders, in January 2001, it was agreed that a number of working groups (including groups on defence and security, constitutional and parliamentary affairs, and the media) would be established in February. At a further meeting, in March, Chissano referred Dhlakama's demand for the appointment of Renamo state governors to the Assembly of the Republic, whose Frelimo representatives were strongly opposed to accommodating Renamo demands. In protest, Dhlakama ceased negotiations in April.

President Chissano announced in May 2001 that he would not stand for re-election on the expiry of his term in 2004. At the long-postponed Renamo congress, held in October 2001, Dhlakama was re-elected party President, while Joaquim Vaz was elected Secretary-General. The holding of a party congress by Renamo for the first time since the end of the civil war, as well as the establishment of a 10-member Political Committee, were regarded as confirmation of the movement's decision to establish itself as a full political party, and to decentralize the party leadership and structure.

In June 2002 Frelimo elected Armando Guebuza as its Secretary-General, and thus also its candidate for the 2004 presidential election. During July Renamo's attempt to establish itself as a legitimate opposition party was threatened after Dhlakama dismissed Vaz as Secretary-General, assuming the position himself, and dissolved the party's Political Committee. Nevertheless, in November the party regained some stability with the appointment of Viana Magalhaes as Secretary-General.

The Conselho Constitucional (CC—Constitutional Council), which was to supervise elections and determine the constitutionality of new legislation, was inaugurated in early November 2003. Municipal elections were held later that month. Despite allegations by Renamo of irregularities, the elections proceeded smoothly, and their conduct was later commended by an observer mission from the European Union (EU, see p. 271), although voter turnout, at 24.2%, was low. Frelimo won a majority in 29 municipalities, while Renamo won a majority in four. Luísa Dias Diogo was appointed as Prime Minister in February 2004 following the resignation of Pascoal Mocumbi.

In November 2004 the Assembleia da República approved changes to the Constitution, which were to take effect on the day following the declaration of the results of the forthcoming presidential and legislative elections. Notably, the President would no longer be afforded immunity from prosecution and a Conselho de Estado (Council of State) was to be created, which would act as an advisory body to the President.

Guebuza elected to the presidency

The presidential and legislative elections took place as scheduled in December 2004. For the first time Mozambicans living abroad were able to vote. Although national and international observers stated that the elections had been generally free and fair, they did express concern at the lack of access that they had been granted to the counting process and about the low rate of voter participation, which was recorded at just 36.3%. Renamo, later joined by other opposition parties, announced that it would not recognize the results owing to alleged irregularities and demanded that the elections be re-run. Official results revealed that Guebuza had won 63.7% of the votes cast at the presidential election, while Dhlakama had taken 31.7%. In the legislative elections, Frelimo secured 160 seats, while Renamo took the remaining 90. Protests lodged by Renamo with the Comissão Nacional de Eleições (CNE—National Elections Commission) and the CC were rejected in January 2005, and Renamo announced that it would accept the election results and participate in the new legislature. Guebuza was sworn in as President on 2 February, and a new Government, again headed by Diogo, was announced the following day. In March Chissano resigned as President of Frelimo and was replaced by Guebuza.

Meanwhile, in February 2005 it was reported that members of Dhlakama's guard, protesting against the non-payment of wages and poor living conditions, had taken five Renamo officials hostage. The following month the Government announced plans to integrate the guards (estimated to number 100–150), who had been maintained by Dhlakama as his personal defence force following the end of the civil war in 1992, into the state security forces; however, such attempts were consistently stalled by Dhlakama. In September 2005 conflict between Frelimo and Renamo supporters led to the deaths of 12 people in Mocímboa da Praia, in Cabo Delgado province, following a disputed by-election earlier in the year.

In November 2005 the Assembly of the Republic adopted legislation providing for the formation of the Council of State. Members of the Council, including Dhlakama, were subsequently appointed by Guebuza and the Assembly of the Republic, and took office in December.

In December 2006 the Assembly of the Republic approved amendments to the electoral legislation. Among the changes were provisions for the restructuring of the CNE, which had been reduced in size to 13 members. Five members were henceforth to be nominated by the Assembly in proportion to the number of seats held by each political party, while the remaining eight members were to be nominated by legally constituted civil society bodies. A 14th member was to be appointed by the Government, but would not have the right to vote. Also approved was a requirement that the electorate re-register every five years and the abolition of the 5% 'barrier clause', whereby only parties that won at least 5% of votes cast had secured representation in the Assembly.

In February 2008 riots broke out in Maputo, as people took to the streets in protest against rising fuel prices and government plans to increase fares on public transport. Some 12 people were killed and hundreds more injured when the police opened fire on the demonstration. The Government subsequently reduced fuel costs for privately operated taxis and minibuses, and cancelled the increase in transport fares.

Frelimo secured a resounding victory in municipal elections in November 2008, winning a majority in 42 of the 43 municipal assemblies, while Renamo retained only one municipality. International observers stated that, despite some minor problems, the elections had been conducted in a transparent and fair manner.

Guebuza's second term

In April 2009 the Assembleia da República adopted electoral legislation under which the presidential, legislative and provincial elections would henceforth be held on the same ballot, and later that month President Guebuza confirmed that the elections would take place concurrently on 28 October. At the presidential election, Guebuza secured an overwhelming victory, taking 75.0% of the valid votes cast. His nearest challenger, Dhlakama, won 16.4%, while Daviz Simango of the newly founded Movimento Democrático de Moçambique (MDM) took 8.6%. Members of the opposition alleged that the vote was compromised by fraudulent activity. The CC acknowledged that certain irregularities had taken place, notably the deliberate invalidation of votes by polling station staff, but that such incidents had not been on a sufficient scale to alter the election results. The CC also confirmed that Guebuza's Frelimo party had increased its majority in the legislature, winning 74.5% of the votes cast and 191 of the 250 seats. Renamo took 17.7% and 51 seats. The MDM was the only other party to gain representation in the Assembly of the Republic, securing eight seats. Frelimo was also declared to have won 704 of the 812 provincial assembly seats, thus consolidating its power at all three levels of government.

Guebuza was inaugurated for a second term as President on 14 January 2010, appointing a new Government five days later. Aires Bonifácio Ali was selected as the new Prime Minister. A Renamo boycott of the legislature, in protest against the conduct

of the 2009 elections, was inconsistently observed by the party's 51 deputies and ended fairly rapidly. Meanwhile, legislation concerning the Assembly decreed that only parties with at least 11 deputies could form an official parliamentary group, meaning that the MDM, with just eight deputies, was not authorized fully to participate in the legislature. However, with Frelimo support this legislation was amended in April 2010, and the MDM was officially designated as the third parliamentary group in the Assembly in May.

Antonio Munguambe, Minister of Transport and Communications in Guebuza's Council of Ministers during 2005–08, was sentenced to 20 years' imprisonment in February 2010 for his involvement in the embezzlement of some US $1.7m. from the state-owned airport management body, Aeroportos de Moçambique. (After launching a successful appeal, in May 2011 Munguambe's sentence was reduced to four years and five months.) Munguambe was the first former or serving government minister to have been imprisoned since the country gained its independence in 1975. In March 2011 Almerino Manhenje was convicted of financial malpractice and abuse of office during his tenure as Minister of the Interior (1995–2005) and received a two-year prison sentence, although he subsequently appealed against this ruling.

Violent demonstrations in protest against rising prices, particularly the cost of bread and other essential foodstuffs, took place in Maputo, Matola, Chimoio and Beira during early September 2010. The Government had implemented an increase in electricity and water rates, while a global decline in wheat production, combined with the country's depreciating currency, had made wheat imports (upon which Mozambique is heavily dependent) less affordable, resulting in higher bread prices. Protesters erected barricades and clashed with police officers, and widespread looting was reported. The police fired tear gas and live ammunition at the demonstrators, causing the deaths of 13 people and more than 600 injuries. Military units were subsequently deployed to reinforce police patrols and dismantle the roadblocks, and more than 400 protesters were arrested. In response to the unrest, the Government announced on 7 September that it would subsidize bread prices, reduce the duties payable on certain imported foodstuffs, lower electricity and water tariffs, and freeze the salaries of senior officials in the Government and public bodies. Although these measures pacified the protesters, they were financially unsustainable and hence only a temporary solution to the long-standing problems of poverty and unemployment.

In December 2010 the Assembly of the Republic approved the establishment of a commission to draft unspecified modifications to the Constitution. Amid suspicions that the Frelimo-dominated commission would propose the removal of presidential term limits, thereby allowing Guebuza to contest a third term in office, Renamo announced in January 2011 that it was boycotting the body. Frelimo officials maintained that the aim of the commission was merely to 'consolidate' the Constitution and rejected claims that it would alter the term-limit clauses. (Guebuza had frequently stated that he would not seek re-election.) The commission was officially inaugurated in October. Frelimo presented its constitutional proposals later that month, which included plans for the establishment of a Constitutional Court (with a broader mandate than the existing CC) and other minor reforms; no mention was made of amending the presidential term limits. Renamo and the MDM denounced Frelimo's proposals as superficial, claiming that they did not warrant the implementation of an expensive and time-consuming constitutional review process. Nevertheless, public consultations on the reforms commenced in February 2013.

In March 2012 two deaths were reported following a violent altercation between the police and armed Dhlakama loyalists at Renamo's headquarters in Nampula. It was suspected that members of Dhlakama's controversial guard had been involved in the incident. Dhlakama and President Guebuza held a meeting in the following month to discuss this matter and other Renamo grievances, and both parties reaffirmed their commitment to maintaining peace within the country. None the less, in October Dhlakama and several hundred of his allies relocated to Gorongosa, Sofala—Renamo's base of operations during the civil war—and began military training exercises in an apparent attempt to intimidate the Government into making concessions. Dhlakama issued a series of demands, including the formation of a transitional administration, the integration of Renamo combatants into the country's security apparatus and a greater opposition presence on the CNE. A government contingent met with Renamo representatives on three occasions in December, but the talks soon foundered. Under legislation adopted during that month, Frelimo, as the largest party in the Assembly of the Republic, was granted the right to designate five appointees to a new CNE (compared with two for Renamo and one for the MDM). Renamo, reiterating earlier threats, declared its intention to boycott and disrupt the upcoming municipal elections (due to take place in November 2013) in protest against the CNE legislation. Some commentators argued that Renamo's frequent ultimatums, boycotts and aggressive posturing were acts of frustration by an organization lacking the necessary popular support to influence policy via normal democratic channels.

Meanwhile, in October 2012 Guebuza appointed Alberto Clementino António Vaquina as Prime Minister and also replaced the heads of the education, tourism, youth, and science ministries. A public probity law came into force in November, requiring public officials to reveal their financial assets and detailing new regulations on potential conflicts of interest. In accordance with the law, a Central Public Ethics Commission was inaugurated in January 2013.

Tensions between Frelimo and Renamo escalated sharply during 2013. In April Renamo militants, apparently provoked by a series of police raids on the party's premises in Muxúnguè, Sofala, stormed a police station in the city, resulting in the deaths of five people. Renamo was also suspected of involvement in an ambush in the region later that month, which left three civilians dead. Talks between the two parties, suspended since December 2012, recommenced in May 2013. Nevertheless, in June Renamo announced its intention to sabotage major road and rail links in Sofala, while the authorities held the opposition group responsible for several armed attacks in the province during that month, targeting both military personnel and civilians, in which an estimated nine people lost their lives. In August another member of the security forces was killed during a raid on a Renamo base in Sofala. The security environment in central and northern Mozambique deteriorated further in October, with a series of violent clashes reported during that month; at least 11 deaths were recorded, and Dhlakama's encampment at Gorongosa was seized by the military. Although it was generally accepted that Renamo lacked the popular approval and offensive capacity to initiate another large-scale conflict, the group's announcement in late October that it was withdrawing from the AGP still generated widespread alarm within the country and without. Mass demonstrations were held in several Mozambican cities at the end of the month in protest against the recent upsurge in violence and kidnappings. None the less, approximately 25 people died in renewed skirmishes and alleged Renamo ambushes between November and January 2014, while internal displacement was becoming a serious problem.

Despite the violent unrest affecting certain parts of the country and a campaign period marred by politically motivated attacks, the municipal elections took place peacefully on 20 November 2013. Frelimo gained control of 49 of the 53 municipalities, and the MDM won majorities in the remaining four (including the major cities of Beira, Nampula and Quelimane); Renamo acted upon its earlier threat to boycott the polls.

Although discussions between Frelimo and Renamo had foundered once again in October 2013, another round of cross-party dialogue commenced in January 2014, and later that month Renamo agreed to participate in the upcoming presidential, legislative and provincial elections, which were due to be held on 15 October. (Filipe Jacinto Nyusi, the Minister of National Defence, was subsequently designated as Frelimo's presidential candidate, while Dhlakama was to represent Renamo once again.) Renamo secured a major concession in February, when legislation increasing the party's representation in an expanded CNE was adopted by the Assembly of the Republic. Although outbreaks of deadly violence continued to be reported during the first half of the year, the ongoing negotiation process precipitated a normalization of the security situation from mid-2014. Dhlakama declared a truce in May, and in August Frelimo and Renamo representatives announced a formal ceasefire and initialled a new peace accord. Under the terms of the agreement, which was signed by Guebuza and Dhlakama in September, Renamo prisoners would be freed, the group's 'residual forces' would be disarmed and integrated into the national security apparatus, and an amnesty would be granted for those involved in the recent hostilities.

Recent developments: the 2014 elections

The presidential, legislative and provincial elections took place as scheduled on 15 October 2014. According to the official results,

Nyusi won the presidential contest with 57.0% of the valid votes cast. Dhlakama performed strongly, garnering a higher-than-expected 36.6% of the votes, while Simango of the MDM received 6.4%. The rate of participation by the electorate was 48.6%. In the legislative poll, Frelimo secured 57.1% of the valid votes and 144 of the 250 seats in the Assembly of the Republic (down from 191 seats in the 2009 election), and thus now lacked the two-thirds' majority that had hitherto allowed the party to alter the Constitution unilaterally. Renamo increased its representation in the legislature, taking 33.2% of the ballot and 89 seats (up from 51 seats in 2009). The remaining 17 seats were won by the MDM, which attracted 8.5% of the votes. Turnout was recorded at 48.5%. Frelimo gained control of 485 of the 811 provincial assembly seats, compared with 294 for Renamo and 32 for the MDM. Frelimo secured majorities in five of the 10 assemblies. Renamo and the MDM both denounced the elections as fraudulent, and the CNE conceded that there had been a number of irregularities. Although regional observers expressed satisfaction with the conduct of the elections, domestic monitors described the polls as 'partly free and fair' and criticized the lack of transparency in the electoral process, while an EU monitoring mission corroborated the reports of electoral irregularities. Renamo initiated a legal challenge, but the CC endorsed the election results in December. Nyusi was sworn in as President on 15 January 2015, and a new Council of Ministers was installed two days later. Carlos Agostinho do Rosário was appointed as Prime Minister, Adriano Afonso Maleiane became Minister of the Economy and Finance, Oldemiro Júlio Marques Balói was given responsibility for foreign affairs and co-operation, and Jaime Basílio Monteiro was named as Minister of the Interior. Dhlakama dismissed the Government as illegitimate and threatened to establish a separate administration in Renamo's electoral strongholds. Renamo deputies, meanwhile, had refused to attend the opening session of the legislature on 12 January. Tensions eased after discussions between Nyusi and Dhlakama on 7 February, and Renamo's legislative boycott was withdrawn shortly thereafter. Guebuza announced his resignation as Frelimo President in late March; Nyusi was elected as his successor.

Foreign Affairs

After independence, Mozambique developed strong international links with the USSR and other countries of the communist bloc, and with neighbouring African states. The country is a member of the Southern African Development Community (SADC, see p. 420), founded in 1979 as the Southern African Development Co-ordination Conference, then with the aim of reducing the region's economic dependence on South Africa, principally by developing trade routes through Mozambique. In December 1996 Mozambique, Malawi, Zambia and Zimbabwe (also SADC members) formally agreed to establish the Beira Development Corridor as a trading route avoiding South Africa's ports. In 1993 full diplomatic relations were established with South Africa. In July 1994 Mozambique and South Africa established a new Joint Defence and Security Commission, replacing the Joint Security Commission originally established in 1984.

During 1995 the activities, principally in the border province of Manica, of a group of mainly Zimbabwean dissidents, known as Chimwenje, came under increasing scrutiny. The group, which was alleged to have links with Renamo, was believed to be preparing for military incursions into Zimbabwe, where it sought the overthrow of President Robert Mugabe. In early 1996 the Chissano Government announced its intention to expel the dissidents from Mozambique. In June, following a series of armed attacks on both sides of the Mozambique–Zimbabwe border, which were believed to have been perpetrated by Chimwenje, the Governments of Mozambique and Zimbabwe agreed to combine and intensify efforts to combat the activities of the dissidents. The group was suppressed in late 1996. During late 2002 and early 2003 Mozambique resettled a number of white Zimbabwean farmers whose land had been appropriated by the Mugabe regime.

Following widespread xenophobic violence in South African townships in May 2008, at least 23 Mozambicans were believed to have been killed and around 40,000 were forced to return to Mozambique. Refugee camps were established on the common border and near Maputo to manage the influx of returnees. Further xenophobic violence erupted in South Africa during March–April 2015, forcing some 2,000 Mozambicans to flee the country. Two Mozambican nationals were killed during the unrest. Meanwhile, in June 2011 Mozambique and South Africa concluded an anti-piracy accord, under the terms of which a

South African patrol vessel was deployed in the Mozambican Channel to bolster Mozambique's efforts to combat the growing problem of piracy in its territorial waters. A further counter-piracy agreement was signed by Mozambique, South Africa and Tanzania in February 2012. In December 2011 Mozambique, Tanzania and the Comoros formally delineated their maritime boundaries.

Relations between Mozambique and landlocked Malawi were strained during late 2010, after the Malawian Government opened a port at Nsanje on the Shire river in October, in an attempt to create a new trade route to the Indian Ocean via the Zambezi river (which passes through Mozambique). The Mozambican authorities seized a barge that was making the inaugural journey to Nsanje, claiming that permission had not been granted for the vessel to travel through Mozambique's waters. Guebuza insisted that a number of technical studies had to be completed before expanded commercial shipping activities on the Zambezi river would be authorized, and Malawi finally conceded to this demand in February 2012. However, commentators suspected that the Mozambican Government's actions were mainly motivated by concerns that the new trade route would be financially detrimental to Mozambique's coastal ports.

CONSTITUTION AND GOVERNMENT

The Constitution of 30 November 1990 (amended in 1996 and 2004) provides for a multi-party political system. Legislative power is vested in the Assembly of the Republic, with 250 members, who are elected for a five-year term. Members are elected by universal, direct adult suffrage in a secret ballot, according to a system of proportional representation. The President of the Republic, who is Head of State, is directly elected for a five-year term; the President holds executive power and governs with the assistance of an appointed Council of Ministers. A Council of State advises the President, who, however, has no obligation to follow its advice. Judicial functions are exercised through the Supreme Court and other courts provided for in the law on the judiciary, which also subordinates them to the Assembly of the Republic. Judges are independent, subject only to the law. Provincial governors, appointed by the President, have overall responsibility for the functions of government within each of the 11 provinces. For the purposes of local government, Mozambique is divided into 53 municipalities.

REGIONAL AND INTERNATIONAL CO-OPERATION

Mozambique is a member of the African Union (see p. 188) and of the Southern African Development Community (SADC, see p. 420).

Mozambique became a member of the UN in 1975 and was admitted to the World Trade Organization (WTO, see p. 431) in 1995. Mozambique was admitted, by special dispensation, as a full member of the Commonwealth (see p. 234) in 1995 and became an observer member of the Organisation Internationale de la Francophonie (see p. 463) in 2006.

ECONOMIC AFFAIRS

In 2013, according to estimates by the World Bank, Mozambique's gross national income (GNI), measured at average 2011–13 prices, was US $15,190m., equivalent to $590 per head (or $1,040 per head on an international purchasing-power parity basis). During 2004–13, it was estimated, the population increased at an average annual rate of 2.6%, while gross domestic product (GDP) per head grew, in real terms, by an average of 4.4% per year. According to official figures, overall GDP increased, in real terms, at an average annual rate of 7.3% in 2004–13; growth in 2013 was 7.3%.

Agriculture (including forestry and fishing) contributed 27.9% of GDP in 2013. At mid-2015 the sector employed an estimated 79.2% of the economically active population, according to FAO. Fishing is a fairly significant export activity: fish, crustaceans and molluscs accounted for 1.0% of total export earnings in 2013. The principal cash crops are cassava, maize, sweet potatoes, bananas and rice. After production of cashews fell sharply in the 1990s, the Government attempted to increase revenue from the crop by promoting production and improving processing facilities. The main subsistence crop is cassava. During 2004–13, according to official figures, agricultural GDP increased by an average of 5.9% per year; growth in 2013 was 3.6%.

Industry (including mining, manufacturing, construction and power) provided 20.6% of GDP in 2013, and employed 5.6% of the economically active population in 1997. During 2004–13, according to official figures, industrial GDP increased at an average

annual rate of 5.7%; the sector grew by 12.8% in 2012 and further by 5.5% in 2013.

Mining contributed 3.5% of GDP in 2013, and employed 0.5% of the economically active population in 1997. Only coal, bauxite, marble, gold and salt are exploited in significant quantities, although gravel and crushed rocks are also mined. In November 2004 the Companhia Vale do Rio Doce (Brazil) was granted a coal-mining concession in Moatize; the mine commenced production in May 2011, with forecast annual production of 11m. metric tons (doubling to 22m. tons from 2014). There are reserves of other minerals, including high-grade iron ore, precious and semi-precious stones, and natural gas. Plans were unveiled in 1994 to exploit natural gas reserves totalling an estimated 55,000m. cu m at Pande, in the province of Inhambane. In 2004 a South African company, SASOL Ltd, was granted a 25-year concession to develop gasfields at Pande and Temane (also in Inhambane province); it was anticipated that the Government would receive revenues of some US $900m. from the project. In early 2004 the construction of a pipeline to transport the gas to South Africa was completed and a gas-processing centre opened in Temane. In 1999 reportedly one of the largest reserves of titanium in the world (estimated at 75m. tons) was discovered in the district of Chibuto, in the province of Gaza; in November 2014, after earlier licences had been revoked, the Government awarded a contract to two Chinese companies to exploit the titanium-bearing heavy sands at Chibuto. Meanwhile, from 2002 the British company Pan African Resources plc undertook a project to investigate the viability of developing a new gold mine in Manica province. Preliminary estimates suggested that gold deposits totalled some 3m. oz. In August 2012 the Manica Gold Project was sold to the Australian company Terranova Minerals (subsequently renamed Auroch Minerals). According to official figures, mining GDP increased at an average annual rate of 17.9% in 2004–13. The mining industry grew by 66.5% in 2012 and further by 15.7% in 2013.

Manufacturing contributed 11.0% of GDP in 2013, and employed 3.0% of the economically active population in 1997. A large aluminium smelter, Mozal, was opened in 2000 and expanded in 2003, with the completion of Mozal II, which more than doubled capacity, to some 580,000 metric tons of aluminium ingots per year. Aluminium production was valued at 19,067,000m. meticais in 2003, equivalent to 16.8% of GDP. Aluminium accounted for 26.5% of total export earnings in 2013. During 2004–13, according to official figures, manufacturing GDP increased at an average annual rate of 2.3%; manufacturing GDP grew by 9.5% in 2012 and further by 2.1% in 2013.

Construction contributed 2.7% of GDP in 2013, and employed 0.8% of the economically active population in 1980, according to census data. According to official figures, construction GDP increased at an average annual rate of 12.2% in 2004–13. Growth in 2013 was 10.0%.

Electrical energy is derived almost exclusively from hydro-electric power, which provided some 99.9% of total electricity production in 2011. Mozambique's important Cahora Bassa hydroelectric plant on the Zambezi river supplies electricity to South Africa and Zimbabwe. By 2004 an extended power supply from Cahora Bassa to Zambézia, Manica and Sofala was in operation. In early 2011 an environmental impact study for the construction of a hydroelectric dam at Mepanda Uncua, some 70 km downstream of Cahora Bassa, was under way. It was envisaged that power from the Mepanda Uncua plant, which would have an initial generating capacity of 1,500 MW (to be expanded to 2,500 MW in a second phase), would also be exported to South Africa. Mozambique currently imports all of its petroleum requirements. Imports of mineral fuels and lubricants comprised 29.4% of the value of total imports in 2013.

The services sector contributed 50.7% of GDP in 2013, and engaged 12.3% of the economically active population in 1997. By the end of the 1990s tourism was the fastest growing sector of the economy. It was hoped that the formal opening, in 2002, of the Great Limpopo Transfrontier Park, comprising South Africa's Kruger National Park, Zimbabwe's Gonarezhou National Park and Mozambique's Limpopo National Park, would attract additional tourists. In 2013 some 1.97m. tourists visited Mozambique, compared with about 711,000 in 2004, and receipts from tourism totalled US $250m. in 2012. The GDP of the services sector increased by an average of 9.3% per year in 2004–13, according to official figures; services GDP grew by 10.2% in 2013.

In 2013 Mozambique recorded a merchandise trade deficit of US $4,356.9m. and there was a deficit of $5,892.3m. on the current account of the balance of payments. In 2013 the principal source of imports was South Africa (providing 32.7% of total imports); other major suppliers were the United Arab Emirates, the People's Republic of China, Singapore and Bahrain. In 2013 the Netherlands was the principal market for exports (receiving 28.6% of the total); South Africa and India were the other significant purchasers. The principal exports in 2013 were mineral products, iron and steel, vehicles, aircraft, vessels and associated transport equipment, and prepared foodstuffs, beverages, spirits, vinegar and tobacco. The main imports in 2013 were mineral fuels and lubricants (particularly petroleum oils), machinery and mechanical appliances, iron and steel and other base metals, optical, photo, technical and medical apparatus, and vehicles, aircraft, vessels and associated transport equipment.

In 2013 there was an overall budgetary deficit of 12,700m. meticais, equivalent to 2.7% of GDP. Mozambique's general government gross debt was 220,520m. meticais in 2013, equivalent to 47.8% of GDP. Total external debt was US $4,788m. in 2012, of which $4,245m. was public and publicly guaranteed debt. In that year, the cost of servicing long-term public and publicly guaranteed debt and repayments to the IMF was equivalent to 1.6% of the value of exports of goods, services and income (excluding workers' remittances). According to the ILO, the average annual rate of inflation was 8.6% in 2004–13; consumer prices increased by an average of 2.5% in 2014. An unemployment rate of 18.7% was recorded in 2004/05.

Mozambique possesses considerable mineral resources, including aluminium, gold, natural gas, petroleum and coal, but is prone to both droughts and flooding. The strength of the extractive sector contributed to economic growth of 7.3% in 2011, with a number of large-scale mining projects commencing operations in that year and investment inflows rising sharply. An upturn in coal production supported a 7.2% increase in real GDP during 2012, according to the IMF. Robust export and investment levels were recorded in that year, and the stability of the

local currency underpinned a marked reduction in the rate of inflation. The economy expanded by 7.3% in 2013, according to official figures, as the mining sector continued to prosper, while consumer price growth remained relatively subdued. However, investor confidence was shaken by the deterioration in the security environment from mid-2013 (see *Domestic Political Affairs*). None the less, the IMF estimated that real GDP grew by 7.5% in 2014, largely driven by increased mining and construction activity. The inflation rate registered a further deceleration in that year. However, the economy, particularly the agricultural sector, was adversely affected in early 2015 by severe flooding, which left at least 159 people dead and thousands more displaced. It consequently appeared unlikely that the IMF's 2015 growth projection of 7.5% would be realized. Meanwhile, during 2011–13 several major natural gas discoveries were announced, leaving Mozambique with some of the largest reserves in Africa. With production expected to begin in 2018 and the broader extractive sector continuing to attract strong interest from foreign investors, Mozambique's medium-term economic outlook appeared positive. The country's substandard infrastructure was a potential obstacle to future growth, but numerous development projects aimed at addressing this problem were under way in 2015.

PUBLIC HOLIDAYS

2016: 1 January (New Year's Day), 3 February (Heroes' Day, anniversary of the assassination of Eduardo Mondlane), 7 April (Day of the Mozambican Woman), 1 May (Workers' Day), 25 June (Independence Day), 7 September (Victory Day—anniversary of the end of the Armed Struggle), 25 September (Anniversary of the launching of the Armed Struggle for National Liberation, and Day of the Armed Forces of Mozambique), 4 October (Peace and National Reconciliation Day), 19 October (Samora Machel Day), 25 December (National Family Day).

Statistical Survey

Source (unless otherwise stated): Instituto Nacional de Estatística, Comissão Nacional do Plano, Av Ahmed Sekou Touré 21, CP 493, Maputo; tel. 21491054; fax 21490384; e-mail webmaster@ine.gov.mz; internet www.ine.gov.mz.

Area and Population

AREA, POPULATION AND DENSITY

Area (sq km)	799,380*
Land	786,380
Inland waters	13,000
Population (census results)	
1 August 1997	15,278,334
1 August 2007	
Males	9,734,678
Females	10,491,618
Total	20,226,296
Population (UN estimates at mid-year)†	
2013	25,833,749
2014	26,472,978
2015	27,121,827
Density (per sq km) at mid-2015	33.9

* 308,641 sq miles.
† Source: UN, *World Population Prospects: The 2012 Revision*.

POPULATION BY AGE AND SEX
(UN estimates at mid-2015)

	Males	Females	Total
0–14 years	6,131,841	6,097,703	12,229,544
15–64 years	6,775,865	7,219,803	13,995,668
65 years and over	380,878	515,737	896,615
Total	13,288,584	13,833,243	27,121,827

Source: UN, *World Population Prospects: The 2012 Revision*.

PROVINCES
(official population estimates at 2013)

Province	Area (sq km)	Population	Density (per sq km)
Cabo Delgado	82,625	1,830,124	22.1
Gaza	75,709	1,367,849	18.1
Inhambane	68,615	1,451,081	21.1
Manica	61,661	1,800,247	29.2
City of Maputo . . .	300	1,209,993	4,033.3
Maputo Province . . .	26,058	1,571,095	60.3
Nampula	81,606	4,767,442	58.4
Niassa	129,056	1,531,958	11.9
Sofala	68,018	1,951,011	28.7
Tete	100,724	2,322,294	23.1
Zambézia	105,008	4,563,018	43.5
Total	799,380	24,366,112	30.5

PRINCIPAL TOWNS
(at 2007 census, preliminary)

Maputo (capital) .	1,099,102		Nacala-Porto . .	207,894
Matola	675,422		Quelimane . . .	192,876
Nampula . . .	477,900		Tete	152,909
Beira	436,240		Xai-Xai	116,343
Chimoio	238,976			

Mid-2014 (incl. suburbs, UN estimate): Maputo 1,173,990 (Source: UN, *World Urbanization Prospects: The 2014 Revision*).

BIRTHS AND DEATHS

	2011	2012	2013
Crude birth rate (per 1,000) . .	41.4	41.1	40.5
Crude death rate (per 1,000) . .	13.5	13.2	12.9

Source: African Development Bank.

Life expectancy (years at birth): 53.1 (males 51.0; females 55.3) in 2013.

ECONOMICALLY ACTIVE POPULATION
('000, FAO estimates at mid-year)

	2013	2014	2015
Agriculture, etc.	9,544	9,788	10,046
Total labour force (incl. others) .	11,968	12,341	12,681

Source: FAO.

Health and Welfare

KEY INDICATORS

Total fertility rate (children per woman, 2012)	5.3
Under-5 mortality rate (per 1,000 live births, 2012) . . .	90
HIV/AIDS (% of persons aged 15–49, 2013)	10.8
Physicians (per 1,000 head, 2012)	0.04
Hospital beds (per 1,000 head, 2011)	0.7
Health expenditure (2011): US $ per head (PPP)	61
Health expenditure (2011): % of GDP	6.4
Health expenditure (2011): public (% of total)	44.0
Access to water (% of persons, 2012)	49
Access to sanitation (% of persons, 2012)	21
Total carbon dioxide emissions ('000 metric tons, 2010) . .	2,882.3
Carbon dioxide emissions per head (metric tons, 2010) . .	0.1
Human Development Index (2013): ranking	178
Human Development Index (2013): value	0.393

For sources and definitions, see explanatory note on p. vi.

Agriculture

PRINCIPAL CROPS
('000 metric tons)

	2011	2012	2013
Rice, paddy	271	147	351*
Maize	2,179	1,177	1,631*
Millet	52	47*	48†
Sorghum	410	239*	188*
Potatoes	190	205	200†
Sweet potatoes†	860	900	890
Cassava (Manioc) . . .	10,093	10,051	10,000†
Cashew nuts, with shell . .	113	65	65†
Groundnuts, with shell . .	96*	113	106*
Coconuts†	266	270	260
Sunflower seed	19	19	18†
Tomatoes	195	250	230†
Bananas	341	470	450†
Oranges	36	46	44†
Grapefruits and pomelos† . .	11	11	11
Guavas, mangoes and mangosteens†	29	31	29
Pineapples†	54	54	53
Papayas†	43	45	43
Tobacco, unmanufactured . .	70	55	56†

* Unofficial figure.
† FAO estimate(s).

Aggregate production ('000 metric tons, may include official, semi-official or estimated data): Total cereals 2,932 in 2011, 1,631 in 2012, 2,239 in 2013; Total roots and tubers 11,152 in 2011, 11,165 in 2012, 11,099 in 2013; Total vegetables (incl. melons) 476 in 2011, 546 in 2012, 501 in 2013; Total fruits (excl. melons) 674 in 2011, 810 in 2012, 784 in 2013.

Source: FAO.

LIVESTOCK
('000 head, year ending September)

	2011*	2012	2013*
Asses*	48	48	48
Cattle	1,400	1,689	1,690
Pigs	1,375	1,688	1,800
Sheep	220	247	250
Goats	4,000	4,334	4,350
Chickens	22,000	18,867	19,000

* FAO estimates.
Source: FAO.

LIVESTOCK PRODUCTS
('000 metric tons)

	2011	2012	2013
Cattle meat*	19	26	26
Goat meat*	20	22	22
Pig meat*	108	122	127
Chicken meat*	28	23	24
Cows' milk*	68	70	70
Goats' milk*	9	9	9
Hen eggs	35*	47	45

* FAO estimate(s).
Source: FAO.

Forestry

ROUNDWOOD REMOVALS
('000 cubic metres, excl. bark, FAO estimates)

	2011	2012	2013
Sawlogs, veneer logs and logs for sleepers	285	336	336
Other industrial wood	1,191	1,191	1,191
Fuel wood	16,724	16,724	16,724
Total	18,200	18,251	18,251

Source: FAO.

SAWNWOOD PRODUCTION
('000 cubic metres, incl. railway sleepers, FAO estimates)

	2011	2012	2013
Coniferous (softwood)	6	6	6
Broadleaved (hardwood) . . .	212	233	233
Total	218	239	239

Source: FAO.

Fishing

(metric tons, live weight)

	2010	2011	2012
Dagaas	13,500	18,330	13,707
Penaeus shrimps	7,313	6,480	5,878
Knife shrimp	1,261	1,288	1,899
Marine fishes	100,870	106,348	131,013
Total catch (incl. others) . . .	163,113*	193,496	213,437

* FAO estimate.

Note: Figures exclude crocodiles, recorded by number rather than by weight. The number of Nile crocodiles caught was: 3,449 in 2010; 17,058 in 2011; 400 in 2012.

Source: FAO.

Mining

('000 metric tons unless otherwise indicated)

	2010	2011	2012*
Bauxite	8.6	10.4	8.4
Coal	38.3	648.2	4,900.0
Gold (kilograms)†	106	111	178
Quartz (metric tons)	707.4	838.7	840.0
Gravel and crushed rock ('000 cubic metres)	824.3	951.1	950.0
Salt (marine)*	120	120	130
Natural gas (million cu m)	3,261	3,438	3,500

* Estimates.
† Figures exclude unreported gold production; total gold output is estimated at 600 kg–900 kg per year.

Source: US Geological Survey.

Industry

SELECTED PRODUCTS
('000 metric tons unless otherwise indicated)

	2005	2006	2007
Wheat flour	204	193	182
Raw sugar	164	172	183
Groundnut oil ('000 metric tons)*	14.0	10.1	7.5
Beer ('000 hl)	1,412	n.a.	n.a.
Soft drinks ('000 hl)	1,149	1,170	1,170
Cigarettes (metric tons)	1,735	2,543	2,571
Footwear (excl. rubber, '000 pairs)	37	37	40
Cement	564	774	771
Electric energy (million kWh)	13,285	14,737	16,076

* FAO estimates.

2008: Raw sugar 250,000 metric tons; Groundnut oil 12,624 metric tons (FAO estimate); Electric energy (million kWh) 15,127.

2009: Raw sugar 252,460 metric tons; Groundnut oil 11,616 metric tons (FAO estimate); Cement 777,000 metric tons; Electric energy (million kWh) 16,963.

2010: Raw sugar 281,730 metric tons; Groundnut oil 20,552 metric tons (FAO estimate); Cement 884,000 metric tons; Electric energy (million kWh) 16,666.

2011: Raw sugar 389,430; Groundnut oil 8,502 metric tons (FAO estimate); Cement 976,000 metric tons; Electric energy (million kWh) 16,830.

2012: Groundnut oil 11,225 metric tons (FAO estimate); Cement 1,184,000 metric tons.

2013: Groundnut oil 8,222 metric tons (FAO estimate).

Sources: FAO; UN Industrial Commodity Statistics Database; US Geological Survey.

Finance

CURRENCY AND EXCHANGE RATES

Monetary Units
100 centavos = 1 metical (plural: meticais).

Sterling, Dollar and Euro Equivalents (31 December 2014)
£1 sterling = 52.44 meticais;
US $1 = 33.60 meticais;
€1 = 40.79 meticais;
1,000 meticais = £19.07 = $29.76 = €24.51.

Average Exchange Rate (meticais per US $)
2012   28.38
2013   30.10
2014   31.35

Note: Between April 1992 and October 2000 the market exchange rate was the rate at which commercial banks purchased from and sold to the public. Since October 2000 it has been the weighted average of buying and selling rates of all transactions of commercial banks and stock exchanges with the public. A devaluation of the metical, with 1 new currency unit becoming equivalent to 1,000 of the former currency, was implemented on 1 July 2006.

BUDGET
('000 million meticais)

Revenue*	2013	2014†	2015†
Taxation	107.6	123.2	128.6
Taxes on income and profits	55.8	57.2	54.0
Domestic taxes on goods and services	38.3	49.4	55.8
Taxes on international trade	10.0	10.8	12.2
Other taxes	3.5	5.7	6.6
Non-tax revenue	19.0	20.8	22.4
Total	126.6	144.0	151.0

Expenditure‡	2013	2014†	2015†
Current expenditure	92.6	126.9	121.4
Compensation of employees	49.5	58.4	63.4
Goods and services	20.4	41.6	27.3
Interest on public debt	4.0	6.1	6.9
Transfer payments	18.8	20.8	23.7
Capital expenditure	61.6	76.1	82.7
Total	154.2	203.0	204.1

* Excluding grants received ('000 million meticais): 24.9 in 2013; 20.9 in 2014 (projection); 21.2 in 2015 (projection).
† Projections.
‡ Excluding net lending ('000 million meticais): 10.0 in 2013; 17.5 in 2014 (projection); 12.8 in 2015 (projection).

Source: IMF, *Republic of Mozambique: Third Review Under the Policy Support Instrument-Staff Report and Press Release* (January 2015).

INTERNATIONAL RESERVES
(US $ million at 31 December)

	2011	2012	2013
IMF special drawing rights	165.05	162.98	160.30
Reserve position in IMF	0.01	0.01	0.01
Foreign exchange	2,303.71	2,607.25	2,982.02
Total	2,468.77	2,770.24	3,142.33

2014: IMF special drawing rights 147.7; Reserve position in IMF 0.04.

Source: IMF, *International Financial Statistics*.

MONEY SUPPLY
('000 million meticais at 31 December)

	2011	2012	2013
Currency outside depository corporations	17,475.6	19,662.7	22,711.3
Transferable deposits	80,102.8	109,534.1	123,309.7
Other deposits	46,223.3	56,816.9	70,404.0
Broad money	143,801.7	186,013.7	216,424.9

Source: IMF, *International Financial Statistics*.

COST OF LIVING
(Consumer Price Index; base: 2000 = 100)

	2009	2010	2011
Food	285.6	329.4	372.8
All items (incl. others)	255.2	287.0	319.2

All items: 327.5 in 2012; 341.5 in 2013; 350.2 in 2014.

Source: ILO.

NATIONAL ACCOUNTS
(million meticais at current prices)

Expenditure on the Gross Domestic Product

	2011	2012	2013
Government final consumption expenditure	75,971	90,943	103,401
Private final consumption expenditure	280,306	302,689	328,264
Change in stocks	3,668	8,538	8,063
Gross fixed capital formation . .	67,081	64,722	73,890
Total domestic expenditure .	427,026	466,893	513,617
Exports of goods and services . .	113,343	119,030	129,575
Less Imports of goods and services	156,761	162,189	177,866
GDP in purchasers' values .	383,608	423,734	465,326
GDP at constant 2009 prices .	338,278	362,211	388,695

Gross Domestic Product by Economic Activity

	2011	2012	2013
Agriculture, livestock and forestry	99,196	104,323	114,401
Fishing	6,523	6,861	7,479
Mining	8,663	13,333	15,405
Manufacturing	43,682	45,577	47,851
Electricity and water . . .	12,402	13,571	15,100
Construction	9,613	11,273	11,570
Wholesale and retail trade; repairs	40,325	42,611	46,021
Restaurants and hotels . . .	10,661	11,202	12,438
Transport and communications .	32,909	36,780	39,842
Financial services	14,392	17,212	22,415
Real estate and business services	27,128	29,591	32,654
Public administration and defence	20,125	22,674	26,163
Education	26,726	32,452	33,158
Health	6,417	7,945	8,396
Other services	3,257	3,363	3,511
Sub-total	362,019	398,766	436,404
Less Financial services indirectly measured . . .	7,104	8,444	11,241
Gross value added in basic prices	354,915	390,322	425,164
Taxes on products . . . . } *Less* Subsidies on products . . }	28,695	33,411	40,162
GDP in market prices . .	383,608	423,734	465,326

BALANCE OF PAYMENTS
(US $ million)

	2011	2012	2013
Exports of goods	3,118.3	3,855.5	4,122.6
Imports of goods	−5,367.6	−7,903.1	−8,479.5
Balance on goods	−2,249.3	−4,047.6	−4,356.9
Exports of services	729.1	1,069.6	1,122.6
Imports of services	−2,164.7	−4,207.4	−3,924.4
Balance on goods and services	−3,684.9	−7,185.4	−7,158.7
Primary income received . . .	179.2	179.7	197.0
Primary income paid	−358.8	−196.1	−249.3
Balance on goods, services and primary income	−3,864.6	−7,201.8	−7,211.0
Secondary income received . .	1,052.9	1,062.2	1,506.0
Secondary income paid . . .	−161.5	−233.0	−187.4
Current balance	−2,973.2	−6,372.6	−5,892.3
Capital account (net)	444.6	456.0	485.7
Direct investment assets . . .	−83.6	−8.9	−522.3
Direct investment liabilities . .	3,645.0	5,635.1	6,697.4
Portfolio investment assets . .	−35.2	21.1	−55.8
Portfolio investment liabilities .	0.2	—	798.4
Other investment assets . . .	−865.0	−302.4	−2,230.6
Other investment liabilities . .	156.0	924.3	1,140.5
Errors and omissions (net) . .	−45.1	24.7	−24.9
Reserves and related items .	243.7	377.4	396.1

Source: IMF, *International Financial Statistics.*

External Trade

PRINCIPAL COMMODITIES
(distribution by HS, US $ million)

Imports c.i.f.	2011	2012	2013
Live animals and animal products	114.0	124.8	175.7
Vegetables and vegetable products	361.5	250.6	468.0
Cereals	308.3	208.9	405.7
Prepared foodstuffs; beverages, spirits, vinegar; tobacco and articles thereof .	174.0	373.1	263.5
Residues, wastes of food industry, animal fodder . . .	14.2	239.5	16.2
Flour of meat, meat offal, fish, crust, etc. unfit for human consumption	1.4	233.8	1.5
Mineral products	1,576.8	1,516.1	3,120.8
Mineral fuels, oils, distillation products, etc.	1,487.8	1,472.9	2,969.5
Petroleum oils, not crude . .	1,097.4	1,135.1	2,063.1
Electrical energy	314.2	306.3	570.3
Chemicals and related products	414.0	324.3	482.4
Iron and steel, other base metals and articles of base metal	1,082.2	1,127.1	1,018.1
Articles of iron or steel . . .	229.4	348.3	197.0
Chain and parts thereof, of iron or steel	2.8	215.2	2.5
Aluminium and articles thereof .	694.9	576.0	517.2
Unwrought aluminium . .	601.4	295.3	488.2
Aluminium bars, rods and profiles	4.2	268.2	6.4
Machinery and mechanical appliances; electrical equipment; parts thereof .	1,112.7	1,165.0	1,440.7
Machinery, boilers, etc. . . .	882.2	879.8	902.6
Self-propelld bulldozers, angledozers, graders, excavators, etc.	205.2	99.5	137.5
Electrical, electronic equipment .	230.5	285.2	538.0
Vehicles, aircraft, vessels and associated transport equipment	724.8	513.3	920.5
Vehicles other than railway, tramway	643.2	488.9	835.5
Trucks and motor vehicles for transport of goods . . .	272.3	241.3	331.7
Optical, medical apparatus, etc.; clocks and watches; musical instruments; parts thereof	40.9	49.5	1,075.9
Optical, photo, technical and medical apparatus . . .	39.9	48.7	1,074.9
Instruments for physical and chemical analysis	2.2	2.1	973.5
Total (incl. others)	6,305.6	6,177.2	10,099.1

Exports f.o.b.	2011	2012	2013
Vegetables and vegetable products	384.8	133.3	144.7
Edible fruit, nuts, peel of citrus fruit, melons	255.5	49.6	55.8
Bananas and plantains, fresh or dried	168.8	23.8	22.1
Prepared foodstuffs; beverages, spirits, vinegar; tobacco and articles thereof .	291.4	403.8	466.7
Sugars and sugar confectionery .	92.6	148.1	190.5
Cane or beet sugar and chemically pure sucrose, in solid form	87.5	146.1	185.7
Tobacco and manufactured tobacco substitutes	179.5	227.9	257.3
Tobacco, unmanufactured . .	178.4	227.9	257.3
Mineral products	772.4	1,204.6	1,509.2
Ores, slag and ash	175.9	238.7	157.9
Titanium ores and concentrates.	122.0	211.5	126.6
Mineral fuels, lubricants, etc. .	586.7	964.9	1,346.5
Coke and semi coke of coal, lignite and peat	20.7	435.2	526.6
Petroleum gases	186.7	248.2	445.4
Electrical energy	297.2	233.4	275.5
Chemicals and related products	9.6	123.5	60.4
Miscellaneous chemical products .	0.1	111.4	52.8
Activated carbon, activated natural mineral products and animal black	—	111.1	52.5
Wood, wood charcoal, cork, and articles thereof . . .	146.1	108.6	50.7
Wood and articles of wood, wood charcoal	146.1	108.6	50.7
Wood sawn or chipped lengthwise	125.2	56.0	30.0
Iron and steel, other base metals and articles of base metal	1,649.9	1,125.4	1,136.2
Aluminium and articles thereof .	1,625.7	1,089.4	1,064.3
Unwrought aluminium . .	276.1	—	—
Aluminium bars, rods and profiles	1,348.7	1,088.6	1,063.2
Vehicles, aircraft, vessels and associated transport equipment	142.8	99.8	278.3
Ships, boats and other floating structures	64.0	81.3	224.3
Optical, medical apparatus, etc.; clocks and watches; musical instruments; parts thereof	7.3	104.8	63.8
Optical, photo, technical and medical apparatus	7.3	104.7	63.7
Total (incl. others)	3,604.1	3,469.9	4,023.7

Source: Trade Map-Trade Competitiveness Map, International Trade Centre, www.intracen.org/marketanalysis.

PRINCIPAL TRADING PARTNERS
(US $ million)

Imports c.i.f.	2011	2012	2013
Australia	104.1	39.7	96.5
Bahamas	21.9	9.8	212.1
Bahrain	108.4	389.5	561.5
Brazil	44.2	283.0	80.8
China, People's Republic . .	373.8	350.2	644.1
France	76.3	24.7	67.6
Germany	34.1	40.2	98.3
India	300.5	200.9	330.1
Japan	185.4	147.2	240.3
Kuwait	169.2	30.0	313.0
Malaysia	63.4	18.8	51.3

Imports c.i.f.—*continued*	2011	2012	2013
Netherlands	676.1	572.9	429.5
Portugal	225.6	304.1	483.3
Singapore	37.1	43.5	629.2
South Africa	2,121.4	1,940.5	3,298.9
Thailand	119.6	80.0	153.2
United Arab Emirates . . .	401.1	454.1	862.2
United Kingdom	222.8	373.4	245.5
USA	292.3	254.0	204.7
Viet Nam	57.2	56.8	120.6
Total (incl. others)	6,305.6	6,177.2	10,099.1

Exports f.o.b.	2011	2012	2013
Belgium	17.6	34.8	48.6
China, People's Republic . .	167.7	637.3	105.0
Germany	75.4	15.7	10.4
Georgia	—	47.4	—
India	87.2	155.1	679.6
Iran	151.7	5.1	—
Italy	51.7	108.0	36.0
Malawi	46.5	26.1	47.9
Malaysia	139.8	4.3	19.3
Netherlands	1,402.1	921.4	1,150.6
Norway	0.1	38.3	3.6
Poland	8.0	50.1	6.5
Portugal	42.7	16.2	104.2
South Africa	584.0	666.8	901.5
Spain	83.4	50.9	74.1
Switzerland	99.8	87.2	79.3
Tanzania	3.2	1.8	68.5
United Kingdom	198.7	177.2	49.0
USA	25.7	61.9	143.6
Zimbabwe	127.3	82.9	74.5
Total (incl. others)	3,604.1	3,469.9	4,023.7

Source: Trade Map-Trade Competitiveness Map, International Trade Centre, www.intracen.org/marketanalysis.

Transport

RAILWAYS
(traffic)

	2011	2012	2013
Passenger-km (million) . . .	248.0	297.0	534.0
Freight ton-km (million) . . .	1,166.0	2,647.0	3,167.0

ROAD TRAFFIC
(motor vehicles in use)

	2011	2012	2013
Light vehicles	270,762	303,707	343,653
Heavy vehicles	92,828	103,564	115,951
Trailers	8,562	10,483	12,944
Tractors	3,800	4,312	4,801
Motorbikes	54,091	61,911	64,987
Total	430,043	483,977	542,336

SHIPPING

Flag Registered Fleet
(at 31 December)

	2012	2013	2014
Number of vessels	75	78	77
Total displacement ('000 grt) . .	35.9	40.8	39.8

Source: Lloyd's List Intelligence (www.lloydslistintelligence.com).

Freight Handled
('000 metric tons)

	2011	2012	2013
Goods loaded and unloaded . .	18,796	25,470	30,119

CIVIL AVIATION
(traffic on scheduled services)

	2007	2008	2009
Kilometres flown (million) . .	8	8	8
Passengers carried ('000) . .	443	463	490
Passenger-km (million) . . .	471	505	552
Total ton-km (million)	48	52	56

Source: UN, *Statistical Yearbook*.

Passengers carried ('000): 576.6 in 2011; 559.6 in 2012; 630.3 in 2013 (Source: World Bank, World Development Indicators database).

Tourism

TOURIST ARRIVALS BY COUNTRY OF RESIDENCE

Country	2011	2012	2013
Malawi	215,374	264,723	236,385
Portugal	67,214	86,504	77,244
South Africa	950,941	971,868	872,017
Swaziland	140,884	64,096	67,007
United Kingdom	70,442	57,322	51,186
USA	36,228	76,603	68,403
Zimbabwe	151,264	198,021	176,823
Total (incl. others)	2,012,640	2,205,853	1,969,716

Tourism receipts (US $ million, excl. passenger transport): 197 in 2010; 231 in 2011; 250 in 2012.

Source: World Tourism Organization.

Communications Media

	2011	2012	2013
Telephones ('000 main lines in use)	88.1	88.1	77.6
Mobile cellular telephones ('000 subscribers)	7,855.3	8,805.0	12,401.3
Internet subscribers ('000) . .	16.3	n.a.	n.a.
Broadband subscribers ('000) . .	21.2	20.5	18.0

Source: International Telecommunication Union.

Education

(2013 unless otherwise indicated)

	Institutions	Teachers	Students
Pre-primary*†	5,689	28,705	1,745,049
Primary‡			
First level	11,457	74,331	4,651,667
Second level	4,587	24,223	782,862
Secondary§			
First level	458	13,387	522,569
Second level	174	4,427	107,381
Technical	94	1,511	31,662
Teacher training‖	18	n.a.	9,314

* Public education only.
† 1997 figures.
‡ Primary education is divided into two cycles of five years followed by two years.
§ Secondary education is divided into two cycles of three years.
‖ 2002 figures.

Source: mainly Ministry of Education.

Pupil-teacher ratio (primary education, UNESCO estimate): 54.8 in 2011/12 (Source: UNESCO Institute for Statistics).

Adult literacy rate (UNESCO estimates): 56.1% (males 70.8%; females 42.8%) in 2010 (Source: UNESCO Institute for Statistics).

Directory

The Government

HEAD OF STATE

President of the Republic and Commander-in-Chief of the Armed Forces: FILIPE JACINTO NYUSI (took office 15 January 2015).

COUNCIL OF MINISTERS
(May 2015)

Prime Minister: CARLOS AGOSTINHO DO ROSÁRIO.

Minister of the Economy and Finance: ADRIANO AFONSO MALEIANE.

Minister of Foreign Affairs and Co-operation: OLDEMIRO JÚLIO MARQUES BALÓI.

Minister of the Interior: JAIME BASÍLIO MONTEIRO.

Minister of National Defence: ATANÁSIO SALVADOR NTUMUKE.

Minister of Agriculture and Food Security: JOSÉ CONDUGUA ANTÓNIO PACHECO.

Minister of State Administration and Public Service: CARMELITA RITA NAMASHULUA.

Minister of Labour, Employment and Social Security: VITÓRIA DIAS DIOGO.

Minister of Presidential Affairs: ADELAIDE ANCHIA AMURANE.

Minister of the Sea, Inland Waters and Fisheries: AGOSTINHO SALVADOR MONDLANE.

Minister of Mineral Resources and Energy: PEDRO CONCEIÇÃO COUTO.

Minister of Justice and Constitutional and Religious Affairs: ABDURREMANE LINO DE ALMEIDA.

Minister of Health: NAZIRA KARIMO VALI ABDULA.

Minister of Youth and Sport: ALBERTO HAWA JANUÁRIO NKUTUMULA.

Minister of Gender, Children and Social Welfare: CIDÁLIA MANUEL CHAÚQUE OLIVEIRA.

Minister of Education and Human Development: LUÍS JORGE MANUEL TEODÓSIO ANTÓNIO FERRÃO.

Minister of Industry and Trade: ERNESTO MAX ELIAS TONELA.

Minister of Transport and Communications: CARLOS ALBERTO FORTES MESQUITA.

Minister of Land, Environment and Rural Development: CELSO ISMAEL CORREIA.

Minister of Culture and Tourism: SILVA ARMANDO DUNDURO.

Minister of Veterans' Affairs: EUSÉBIO LAMBO GUMBIWA.

Minister of Science, Technology and Higher, Technical and Professional Education: JORGE OLÍVIO PENICELA NHAMBIU.

Minister of Public Works, Housing and Water Resources: CARLOS BONETE MARTINHO.

There were also 18 Deputy Ministers.

MINISTRIES

Office of the President: Av. Julius Nyerere 1780, Maputo; tel. 21491121; fax 21492065; e-mail gabimprensa@teldata.mz; internet www.presidencia.gov.mz.

Office of the Prime Minister: Praça da Marinha Popular, Maputo; tel. 21426861; fax 21426881; internet www.portaldogoverno.gov.mz.

Ministry of Agriculture and Food Security: Praça dos Heróis Moçambicanos, CP 1406, Maputo; tel. 21460011; fax 21460055; internet www.minag.gov.mz.

Ministry of Culture and Tourism: Av. 25 de Setembro 1018, CP 4101, Maputo; tel. 21306210; fax 21306212; internet www.mitur.gov .mz.

Ministry of the Economy and Finance: Praça da Marinha Popular, CP 272, Maputo; tel. 21315000; fax 21306261; internet www.mf .gov.mz.

Ministry of Education and Human Development: Av. 24 de Julho 167, CP 34, Maputo; tel. 21492006; fax 21492196; internet www.mec.gov.mz.

Ministry of Foreign Affairs and Co-operation: Av. 10 de Novembro 620–640, Maputo; tel. 21327000; fax 21327020; e-mail minec@minec.gov.mz; internet www.minec.gov.mz.

Ministry of Gender, Children and Social Welfare: Rua de Tchamba 86, CP 516, Maputo; tel. 21490921; fax 21492757; internet www.mmas.gov.mz.

Ministry of Health: Avs Eduardo Mondlane e Salvador Allende 1008, CP 264, Maputo; tel. 21427131; fax 21427133; e-mail mdgedge@dnsdee.misau.gov.mz; internet www.misau.gov.mz.

Ministry of Industry and Trade: Praça 25 de Junho 300, CP 1831, Maputo; tel. 21352600; fax 214262301; e-mail infomic@mic.gov.mz; internet www.mic.gov.mz.

Ministry of the Interior: Av. Olof Palme 46/48, CP 290, Maputo; tel. 21303510; fax 21420084; internet www.mint.gov.mz.

Ministry of Justice and Constitutional and Religious Affairs: Av. Julius Nyerere 33, Maputo; tel. 21491613; fax 21494264; internet www.minjust.gov.mz.

Ministry of Labour, Employment and Social Security: Av. 24 de Julho 2351, CP 281, Maputo; tel. 21428301; fax 21421881; internet www.mitrab.gov.mz.

Ministry of Land, Environment and Rural Development: Rua Kassoende 167, Maputo; tel. 21492403; e-mail jwkacha@virconn .com; internet www.micoa.gov.mz.

Ministry of Mineral Resources and Energy: Av. Fernão de Magalhães 34, 1° andar, CP 294, Maputo; tel. 21314843; fax 320618; e-mail msithole.mirem@tvcabo.co.mz; internet www .mirem.gov.mz.

Ministry of National Defence: Av. Mártires de Mueda 280, CP 3216, Maputo; tel. 21492081; fax 21491619; e-mail mdn@mdn.gov .mz; internet www.mdn.gov.mz.

Ministry of Public Service: Av. Julius Nyerere 3, CP 1225, Maputo; tel. 21485558; fax 21485683; internet www.mfp.gov.mz.

Ministry of Public Works, Housing and Water Resources: Av. Karl Marx 606, CP 268, Maputo; tel. 21430028; fax 21421369; internet www.moph.gov.mz.

Ministry of Science, Technology and Higher, Technical and Professional Education: Av. Patrice Lumumba 770, Maputo; tel. 21352800; fax 21352860; e-mail secretariado@mct.gov.mz; internet www.mct.gov.mz.

Ministry of State Administration: Rua da Rádio Moçambique 112, CP 4116, Maputo; tel. 21426666; fax 21428565; internet www .mae.gov.mz.

Ministry of Transport and Communications: Av. Mártires de Inhaminga 336, CP 276, Maputo; tel. 21430152; fax 21431028; internet www.mtc.gov.mz.

Ministry of Veterans' Affairs: Rua General Pereira d'Eça 35, CP 3697, Maputo; tel. 21490601.

Ministry of Youth and Sport: Av. 25 de Setembro 529, CP 2080, Maputo; tel. 21312172; fax 21300040; e-mail mjd@tvcabo.co.mz; internet www.mjd.gov.mz.

PROVINCIAL GOVERNORS
(May 2015)

Cabo Delgado Province: CELMIRA SILVA.

Gaza Province: STELLA DA GRAÇA PINTO NOVO ZECA.

Inhambane Province: AGOSTINHO ABACAR TRINTA.

Manica Province: ALBERTO RICARDO MONDLANE.

Maputo Province: RAIMUNDO MAICO DIOMBA.

Nampula Province: VICTOR MANUEL BORGES.

Niassa Province: ARLINDO DA COSTA GONÇALO MAZUNGANE CHILUNDO.

Sofala Province: MARIA HELENA TAIPO.

Tete Province: PAOLO AUADE.

Zambézia Province: ABDUL RAZAK NOORMAHOMED.

City of Maputo: IOLANDA MARIA PEDRO CAMPOS CINTURA.

President

Presidential Election, 15 October 2014

Candidate	Votes	% of votes
Filipe Jacinto Nyusi (Frelimo)	2,778,497	57.03
Afonso Macacho Marceta Dhlakama (Renamo)	1,783,382	36.61
Daviz Simango (MDM)	309,925	6.36
Total*	4,871,804	100.00

*Excluding 171,675 invalid votes and 290,186 blank votes.

Legislature

Assembly of the Republic: CP 1516, Maputo; tel. 21400826; fax 21400711; e-mail cdi@sortmoz.com; internet www.parlamento.org .mz.

Chair.: VERÓNICA NATANIEL MACAMO DLHOVO.

General Election, 15 October 2014

Party	Votes	% of votes	Seats
Frelimo	2,575,995	57.14	144
Renamo	1,495,137	33.17	89
MDM	384,538	8.53	17
Others	52,472	1.16	—
Total*	4,508,142	100.00	250

*Excluding 252,535 invalid votes and 458,919 blank votes.

Election Commission

Comissão Nacional de Eleições (CNE): Rua Almeida Ribeiro, Maputo; tel. 21300626; fax 214274360; internet www.stae.org.mz; f. 1997; 13 mems; Pres. ABDUL CARIMO NORDINE SAU.

Political Organizations

Aliança Democrática de Antigos Combatentes para o Desenvolvimento (ADACD): Maputo; f. 2009; coalition comprising the Partido do Progresso do Povo de Moçambique (PPPM), the Partido Socialisa de Moçambique (PSM), the Partido do Congresso Democrático (PACODE) and the Partido da União para a Reconciliação (PUR); Leader JOÃO LIKALAMBA.

Aliança Independente de Moçambique (ALIMO): f. 1998; Leader KHALID HUSSEIN SIDAT.

Coligação União Eleitoral (UE): f. 1999; Co-ordinator MANECA DANIEL.

Partido Ecologista de Moçambique (PEMO): Maputo.

Partido de Unidade Nacional (PUN): TV Sado 9, Maputo; tel. 21419204; Pres. HIPOLITO COUTO.

Frente de Libertação de Moçambique (Frelimo): Rua Pereira do Lago 10, Bairro de Sommerschield, Maputo; tel. 21490181; fax 21490008; e-mail info@frelimo.org.mz; internet www.frelimo.org .mz; f. 1962 by merger of 3 nationalist parties; reorg. 1977 as a 'Marxist-Leninist vanguard movement'; in 1989 abandoned its exclusive Marxist-Leninist orientation; Pres. FILIPE NYUSI; Sec.-Gen. FILIPE CHIMOIO PAÚNDE.

Movimento Democrático de Moçambique (MDM): Av. 25 de Setembro, 1123, Prédio Cardoso, Maputo; tel. 21312041; fax 21426891; e-mail info@mdm.org.mz; internet www.mdm.org.mz; f. 2009; Pres. DAVIZ MBEMPO SIMANGO; Sec.-Gen. LUÍS BOAVIDA MUDIVELA.

Movimento Patriótico para Democracia (MPD): f. 2009; Leader MATIAS DIANHANE BANZE.

Partido Ecologista—Movimento da Terra (ECOLOGISTA—MT): Leader JOÃO PEDRO MASSANGO.

Partido Humanitário de Moçambique (Pahumo): Nampula; f. 2010 by fmr mems of the Frente de Libertação de Moçambique (Frelimo), Resistência Nacional Moçambicana (Renamo) and Partido para a Paz, Democracia e Desenvolvimento (PDD); Pres. CORNÉLIO QUIVELA; Sec.-Gen. JOSÉ HENRIQUE LOPES.

Partido de Liberdade e Desenvolvimento (PLD): f. 2009; Pres. CAETANO SABILE.

Partido Nacional dos Operários e Camponeses (PANAOC): f. 1998; Leader ARMANDO GIL SUEIA.

Partido para a Paz, Democracia e Desenvolvimento (PDD): Av. Amilcar Cabral 570, Maputo; tel. 21486759; fax 21486765; e-mail pdd@tvcabo.co.mz; internet www.pdd.org.mz; f. 2003; liberal; Leader RAÚL MANUEL DOMINGOS.

Partido Popular Democrático (PPD): f. 2004; Leader MARCIANO FIJAMA.

Partido de Reconciliação Democrática Social (PRDS): f. 1998; Leader ARMANDO GIL SUEIA.

Partido de Reconciliação Nacional (PARENA): Maputo; f. 2004; Leader ANDRÉ BALATE.

Partido de Solidariedade e Liberdade (PAZS): f. 2004; Leader CARLOS INÁCIO COELHO.

Partido Trabalhista (PT): f. 1993; Pres. MIGUEL MABOTE; Sec.-Gen. LUÍS MUCHANGA.

Partido os Verdes de Moçambique (PVM): f. 1997; Leader BRUNO SAPEMBA.

Resistência Nacional Moçambicana (Renamo): Av. Julius Nyerere 2541, Maputo; tel. 21493107; internet www.renamo.org .mz; also known as Movimento Nacional da Resistência de Moçambique (MNR); f. 1976; fmr guerrilla group, in conflict with the Govt between 1976 and Oct. 1992; obtained legal status in 1994; Pres. AFONSO MACACHO MARCETA DHLAKAMA; Sec.-Gen. OSSUFO MOMADE.

União Nacional de Moçambique (UNAMO): f. 1987; breakaway faction of Renamo; social democratic; obtained legal status 1992; Pres. CARLOS ALEXANDRE DOS REIS.

União para a Mudança (UM): f. 1993; Leader FRANCISCO MAINDANE MUARIVA.

Diplomatic Representation

EMBASSIES AND HIGH COMMISSIONS IN MOZAMBIQUE

Algeria: Rua de Mukumbura 121–123, CP 1709, Maputo; tel. 21492070; fax 21485067; e-mail ambalgmaputo@tvcabo.co.mz; internet www.ambalgmaputo.org.mz; Ambassador AHMED LAKHDAR TAZIR.

Angola: Av. Kenneth Kaunda 783, CP 2954, Maputo; tel. 21493139; fax 21493930; e-mail embaixada.angola@tvcabo.co.mz; Ambassador ISAÍAS JAIME VILINGA.

Botswana: Quinta Av. Rua 4.517, Costa do Sol, House No. 804/172, Triufo, Maputo; tel. 21451626; fax 21451626; High Commissioner THUSO G. RAMODIMOOSI.

Brazil: Av. Kenneth Kaunda 296, CP 1167, Sommerschield, Maputo; tel. 21484800; fax 21484806; e-mail ebrasil@teledata.mz; internet maputo.itamaraty.gov.br/pt-br; Ambassador LIGIA MARIA SCHERER.

Canada: Av. Kenneth Kaunda 1138, CP 1578, Maputo; tel. 21492623; fax 21492667; e-mail www.canadainternational.gc.ca/mozambique; High Commissioner SHAWN BARBER.

China, People's Republic: Av. Julius Nyerere 3142, CP 4668, Maputo; tel. 21491560; fax 21491196; e-mail chinaemb_mz@mfa.gov .cn; internet mz.chineseembassy.org; Ambassador LI CHUNHUA.

Congo, Democratic Republic: Av. Kenneth Kaunda 127, CP 2407, Maputo; tel. 21497154; fax 21492399; e-mail ambardc@tvcabo.net .mz; Ambassador ANTOINE KOLA MASALA NE BEBY.

Congo, Republic: Av. Kenneth Kaunda 783, CP 4743, Maputo; tel. 21490142; Chargé d'affaires a.i. MONSEGNO BASHA OSHEFWA.

Cuba: Av. Kenneth Kaunda 492, CP 387, Maputo; tel. 21492444; fax 21491905; e-mail embacuba.mozambique@tvcabo.co.mz; internet emba.cubaminrex.cu/mozambique; Ambassador RAFAEL ARÍSTIDES JIMENO LÓPEZ.

Denmark: Av. Julius Nyerere 1162, CP 4588, Maputo; tel. 21480000; fax 21480010; e-mail mpmamb@um.dk; internet mozambique.um.dk; Ambassador MOGENS PEDERSEN.

Egypt: Av. Mao Tse Tung 851, CP 4662, Maputo; tel. 21491118; fax 21491489; e-mail egypt@tvcabo.co.mz; Ambassador FAWZY MOHAMED EL-ASHMAWY.

Finland: Av. Julius Nyerere 1128, CP 1663, Maputo; tel. 21482400; fax 21491662; e-mail sanomat.map@formin.fi; internet www.finland .org.mz; Ambassador SEIJA TORO.

France: Av. Julius Nyerere 2361, CP 4781, Maputo; tel. 21484600; fax 21491727; e-mail ambafrancemz@tvcabo.co.mz; internet www .ambafrance-mz.org; Ambassador SERGE SEGURA.

Germany: Rua Damião de Góis 506, CP 1595, Maputo; tel. 21482700; fax 21492888; e-mail info@maputo.diplo.de; internet www.maputo.diplo.de; Ambassador PHILIPP SCHAUER.

Holy See: Av. Kwame Nkrumah 224, CP 2738, Maputo; tel. 21491144; fax 21492217; e-mail namoz.secret@tvcabo.co.mz; Apostolic Nuncio Most Rev. ANTONIO ARCARI (Titular Archbishop of Caeciri).

India: Av. Kenneth Kaunda 167, CP 4751, Maputo; tel. 21492437; fax 21492364; e-mail hicomind@tvcabo.co.mz; internet www .hicomind-maputo.org; High Commissioner PAVAN KAPOOR.

Ireland: Av. Julius Nyerere 3332, Maputo; tel. 21491440; fax 21493023; e-mail maputoembassy@dfa.ie; Ambassador WILLIAM CARLOS.

Italy: Av. Kenneth Kaunda 387, CP 976, Maputo; tel. 21492229; fax 21490503; e-mail ambasciata.maputo@esteri.it; internet www .ambmaputo.esteri.it; Ambassador ROBERTO VELLANO.

Japan: Av. Julius Nyerere 2832, CP 2494, Maputo; tel. 21499819; fax 21498957; internet www.mz.emb-japan.go.jp; Ambassador EJI HASHIMOTO.

Korea, Democratic People's Republic: Rua da Kaswende 167, Maputo; tel. 21491482; Ambassador PAK KUN GWANG.

Korea, Republic: Av. do Zimbábwe 338, Maputo; tel. 21495625; fax 21495638; e-mail rokembassyinmz@mofa.go.kr; internet mz.mofa.go .kr; Ambassador KANG HEE-YOON.

Malawi: Av. Kenneth Kaunda 75, CP 4148, Maputo; tel. 21492676; fax 21490224; e-mail malawmoz@virconn.com; High Commissioner FRANK VIYAZI.

Mauritius: Rua Dom Carlos 42, Av. do Zimbabwe, Sommerschield, Maputo; tel. 21494624; fax 21494729; e-mail maputo@mail.gov.mu; High Commissioner JEAN HAREL LAMVOHEE.

Netherlands: Av. Kwame Nkrumah 324, CP 1163, Maputo; tel. 21484200; fax 21484248; e-mail map@minbuza.nl; internet www .mozambique.nlambassade.org; Ambassador PASCALLE M. M. GROTENHUIS (designate).

Nigeria: Av. Kenneth Kaunda 821, CP 4693, Maputo; tel. and fax 21490991; internet www.nigeriahighcommission.co.mz; High Commissioner Dr MATILDA KWASHI.

Norway: Av. Julius Nyerere 1162, CP 828, Maputo; tel. 21480100; fax 21480107; e-mail emb.maputo@mfa.no; internet www.norway .org.mz; Ambassador METTE MASST.

Portugal: Av. Julius Nyerere 720, CP 4696, Maputo; tel. 21490316; fax 21491172; e-mail embaixada@embpormaputo.org.mz; Ambassador JOSÉ AUGUSTO DUARTE.

Russian Federation: Av. Vladimir I. Lénine 2445, CP 4666, Maputo; tel. 21417372; fax 21417515; e-mail embrus@tvcabo.co .mz; internet www.mozambique.mid.ru; Ambassador ANDREY V. KEMARSKIY.

South Africa: Av. Eduardo Mondlane 41, CP 1120, Maputo; tel. 21243000; fax 21493029; e-mail SAHCMaputoenquiries@dirco.gov .za; internet www.dirco.gov.za; High Commissioner CHARLES NQAKULA.

Spain: Rua Damião de Góis 347, CP 1331, Maputo; tel. 21492025; fax 21494769; e-mail emb.maputo@maec.es; internet www.exteriores .gob.es/embajadas/maputo; Ambassador SANTIAGO MIRALLES HUETE.

Swaziland: Av. Kwame Nkrumah, CP 4711, Maputo; tel. 21491601; fax 21492117; High Commissioner CHRISTIAN NKAMBULE.

Sweden: Av. Julius Nyerere 1128, CP 338, Maputo; tel. 21480300; fax 21480390; e-mail ambassaden.maputo@gov.se; internet www .swedenabroad.se/maputo; Ambassador IRINA SCHOULGIN NYONI.

Switzerland: Av. Ahmed Sekou Touré 637, CP 135, Maputo; tel. 21315275; fax 21315276; e-mail map.vertretung@eda.admin.ch; internet www.eda.admin.ch/maputo; Ambassador MIRKO MANZONI.

Tanzania: Ujamaa House, Av. dos Mártires da Machava 852, CP 4515, Maputo; tel. 21490110; fax 21494782; e-mail tanzrep-maputo@ tvcabo.co.mz; High Commissioner PASTOR NGAIZA.

Timor-Leste: Av. do Zimbabwe 1586, Maputo; tel. 21493644; fax 21493544; e-mail embrdtl@tvcabo.co.mz; Ambassador MARINA RIBEIRO ALKATIRI.

United Kingdom: Av. Vladimir I. Lénine 310, CP 55, Maputo; tel. 21356000; fax 21356060; e-mail bhcgeneral@gmail.com; internet ukinmozambique.fco.gov.uk/en; High Commissioner JOANNA KUENSSBERG.

USA: Av. Kenneth Kaunda 193, CP 783, Maputo; tel. 21492797; fax 21490114; e-mail maputoirc@state.gov; internet maputo.usembassy .gov; Ambassador DOUGLAS M. GRIFFITHS.

Viet Nam: Av. Francisco Orlando Magumbwe 1026/1048, CP 4501, Maputo; tel. 21497912; fax 21491992; e-mail dsqvnmoz@yahoo.com; internet www.mofa.gov.vn/vnemb.mb; Ambassador NGUYEN VAN TRUNG.

Zambia: Av. Kenneth Kaunda 1286, CP 4655, Maputo; tel. 21492452; fax 21491893; e-mail zhcmap@zebra.uem.mz; High Commissioner JAPHEN MWAKALOMBE.

Zimbabwe: Av. Mártires da Machava 1657, CP 743, Maputo; tel. 21490404; fax 21492237; e-mail zimmaputo@tdm.co.mz; Ambassador AGRIPPAH MUTAMBARA.

Judicial System

The Constitution of November 1990 provides for a Supreme Court and other judicial courts, a Constitutional Council, an Administrative Court, courts-martial, customs courts, maritime courts and labour courts. The Supreme Court consists of professional judges, appointed by the President of the Republic, and judges elected by the Assembly of the Republic. It acts in sections, as a trial court of primary and appellate jurisdiction, and, in plenary session, as a court of final appeal. The Administrative Court controls the legality of administrative acts and supervises public expenditure.

Supreme Court: Av. Vladimir I. Lénine 103, CP 278, Maputo; tel. 1321037; fax 1310674; internet www.ts.gov.mz; Pres. ADELINO MANUEL MUCHANGA.

Constitutional Council: Rua Mateus Sansão Muthemba 493, CP 2372, Maputo; tel. 21487431; fax 21487432; e-mail correiocc@cconstitucional.org.mz; internet www.cconstitucional.org.mz; f. 1990; Pres. HERMENEGILDO GAMITO.

Administrative Court: Praça da Independência, 1117 Maputo; tel. 21345001; fax 21498890; e-mail ta@ta.gov.mz; internet www.ta.gov.mz; Pres. MACHATINE PAULO MARRENGANE MUNGUAMBE.

Attorney-General: BEATRIZ BUCHILI.

Religion

According to the 2007 census, 56.1% of the population were Christian and 17.9% were Muslim. There are, in addition, small Hindu, Jewish and Bahá'í communities.

CHRISTIANITY

There are many Christian organizations registered in Mozambique.

Conselho Cristão de Moçambique (CCM) (Christian Council of Mozambique): Av. Sekou Touré 1063, Maputo; tel. 21322836; fax 21321968; internet ecumenical-services-ccm.webs.com; f. 1948; 22 mem socs; Pres. Rt Rev. ARÃO MATSOLO; Gen. Sec Rev. DINIS MATSOLO.

The Roman Catholic Church

Mozambique comprises three archdioceses and nine dioceses. According to the 2007 census, the number of adherents represented some 28.4% of the total population.

Bishops' Conference: Conferência Episcopal de Moçambique (CEM), Secretariado Geral da CEM, Av. Paulo Samuel Kankhomba 188/RC, CP 286, Maputo; tel. 21490766; fax 21492174; f. 1982; Pres. Most Rev. LÚCIO ANDRICE MUANDULA (Bishop of Xai-Xai).

Archbishop of Beira: Most Rev. CLAUDIO DALLA ZUANNA, Cúria Arquiepiscopal, Rua Correia de Brito 613, CP 544, Beira; tel. 23322313; fax 23327639; e-mail arquidbeira@teledata.mz.

Archbishop of Maputo: Most Rev. FRANCISCO CHIMOIO, Paço Arquiepiscopal, Av. Eduardo Mondlane 1448, CP 258, Maputo; tel. 21326240; fax 21321873.

Archbishop of Nampula: Most Rev. TOMÉ MAKHWELIHA, Paço Arquiepiscopal, CP 84, 70100 Nampula; tel. 26213024; fax 26214194; e-mail arquidiocesenpl@teledata.mz.

The Anglican Communion

Anglicans in Mozambique are adherents of the Anglican Church of Southern Africa (formerly the Church of the Province of Southern Africa). There are two dioceses in Mozambique. The Metropolitan of the Province is the Archbishop of Cape Town, South Africa.

Bishop of Lebombo: Rt Rev. DINIS SALOMÃO SENGULANE, CP 120, Maputo; tel. 21734364; fax 21401093; e-mail bispo_sengulane@virconn.com.

Bishop of Niassa: Rev. MARK VAN KOEVERING, CP 264, Lichinga, Niassa; tel. 27112735; fax 27112336; e-mail bishop.niassa@gmail.com.

Other Churches

Baptist Convention of Mozambique: Av. Maguiguane 386, CP 852, Maputo; tel. 2126852; Pres. Rev. BENTO BARTOLOMEU MATUSSE; 78 churches, 25,000 adherents.

The Church of Jesus Christ of the Latter-Day Saints: Maputo; 9 congregations, 1,975 mems.

Evangelical Lutheran Church in Mozambique: Av. Kim Il Song 520, CP 1488, Sommerschield, Maputo; tel. 212489200; fax 212489201; e-mail mabasso.ielm@tvcabo.co.mz; Sen. Pastor JOSE MABASSO; 12,606 mems (2010).

Free Methodist Church: Pres. Rev. FRANISSE SANDO MUVILE; 214 churches, 21,231 mems.

Igreja Congregational Unida de Moçambique: Rua 4 Bairro 25 de Junho, CP 930, Maputo; tel. 21475820; Pres., Sec. of the Synod A. A. LITSURE.

Igreja Maná: Rua Francisco Orlando Magumbwe 528, Maputo; tel. 21491760; fax 21490896; e-mail adm_mocambique@igrejamana.com; Bishop DOMINGOS COSTA.

Igreja Reformada em Moçambique (IRM) (Reformed Church in Mozambique): CP 3, Vila Ulongue, Anogonia-Tete; f. 1908; Gen. Sec. Rev. SAMUEL M. BESSITALA; 60,000 mems.

Presbyterian Church of Mozambique: Av. Ahmed Sekou Touré 1822, CP 21, Maputo; tel. 21421790; fax 21428623; e-mail ipmoc@zebra.uem.mz; f. 1887; 100,000 adherents; Pres. of Synodal Council Rev. ORIENTE SIBANE.

Seventh-Day Adventist Church: Av. Maguiguana 300, CP 1468, Maputo; tel. and fax 21427200; e-mail victormiconde@teledata.co.mz; 937 churches, 186,724 mems (2004).

Other denominations active in Mozambique include the Church of Christ, the Church of the Nazarene, the Greek Orthodox Church, the United Methodist Church of Mozambique, the Wesleyan Methodist Church, the Zion Christian Church, and Jehovah's Witnesses.

ISLAM

Comunidade Mahometana: Av. Albert Luthuli 291, Maputo; tel. 21425181; fax 21300880; internet www.paginaislamica.8m.com/pg1.htm; Pres. SALEEM AHMED.

Congresso Islâmico de Moçambique (Islamic Congress of Mozambique): represents Sunni Muslims; Chair. ASSANE ISMAEL MAQBUL.

Conselho Islâmico de Moçambique (Islamic Council of Mozambique): Pres. ABDUL CARIMO.

The Press

DAILIES

Correio da Manha: Av. Filipe Samuel Magaia 528, CP 1756, Maputo; tel. 21305322; fax 21305321; e-mail refi@virconn.com; f. 1997; published by Sojornal, Lda; also publishes weekly *Correio Semanal*; Dir REFINALDO CHILENGUE.

Diário de Moçambique: Av. 25 de Setembro 1509, 2° andar, CP 2491, Beira; tel. and fax 23427312; e-mail diariomoc@tdm.co.mz; internet www.diariodemocambique.co.mz; f. 1981; under state management since 1991; Editorial Dir ARTUR RICARDO; Editor FRANCISCO MUIANGA; circ. 5,000 (2003).

Expresso da Tarde: Av. Patrice Lumumba 511, 1° andar, Maputo; tel. 21314912; subscription only; distribution by fax; Dir SALVADOR RAIMUNDO HONWANA.

Mediafax: Av. Amílcar Cabral 1049, CP 73, Maputo; tel. 21301737; fax 21302402; e-mail mediafax@tvcabo.co.mz; f. 1992 by co-operative of independent journalists Mediacoop; news sheet by subscription only, distribution by fax and internet; Editor BENEDITO NGOMANE.

Notícias de Moçambique: Rua Joaquim Lapa 55, CP 327, Maputo; tel. 21420119; fax 21320120; internet www.jornalnoticias.co.mz; f. 1926; morning; f. 1906; under state management since 1991; Pres. ESSELINA MACOME; Dir ROGÉRIO SITOE; circ. 12,793 (2003).

WEEKLIES

Campeão: Av. 24 de Julho 3706, CP 2610, Maputo; tel. and fax 21401810; sports newspaper; Dir RENATO CALDÉIRA; Editor ALEXANDRE ZANDAMELA.

Correio Semanal: Av. Filipe Samuel Magaia 528, CP 1756, Maputo; tel. 21305322; fax 21305312; Dir REFINALDO CHILENGUE.

Desafio: Rua Joe Slovo, 55, Maputo; tel. 21323180; fax 21324902; internet www.desafio.co.mz; Dir ALMIRO SANTOS; Editor BOAVIDA FUNJUA; circ. 3,890 (2003).

Domingo: Rua Joe Slovo 55, CP 327, Maputo; tel. 21431026; fax 21431027; e-mail jornaldomingo@snoticias.co.mz; f. 1981; Sun.; Dir JORGE MATINE; circ. 15,000 (2007).

Fim de Semana: Av. September 25 1123, 1st Floor, Maputo; tel. and fax 21417012; e-mail fimdomes@tvcabo.co.mz; internet www.fimdesemana.co.mz; f. 1997; independent.

Jornal@Verdade: Av. Mártires da Machava 905, Maputo; tel. 843998624; e-mail averdademz@gmail.com; internet www.verdade.co.mz; f. 2008; CEO ERIK CHARAS; Editor-in-Chief EMILDO SAMBO.

Savana: Av. Amílcar Cabral 1049, CP 73, Maputo; tel. 21301737; fax 21302402; e-mail savana@mediacoop.co.mz; internet www.savana

.co.mz; f. 1994; owned by mediacoop, SA; CEO FERNANDO LIMA; Publr KOK NAM; Editor FERNANDO GONÇALVES; circ. 15,000 (2009).

Tempo: Av. Ahmed Sekou Touré 1078, CP 2917, Maputo; tel. 21426191; f. 1970; magazine; under state management since 1991; Dir ROBERTO UAENE; Editor ARLINDO LANGA; circ. 40,000.

Zambeze: Rua José Sidumo, Maputo; tel. 21302019; Dir ANGELO MUNGUAMBE; circ. 2,000 (2003).

PERIODICALS

Agora: Afrisurvey, Lda, Rua General Pereira d'Eça 200, 1° andar, CP 1335, Maputo; tel. 21494147; fax 21494204; internet www.agora .co.mz; f. 2000; monthly; economics, politics, society; Pres. MARIA DE LOURDES TORCATO; Dir JOVITO NUNES; Editor-in-Chief ERCÍLIA SANTOS; circ. 5,000.

Agricultura: Instituto Nacional de Investigação Agronómica, CP 3658, Maputo; tel. 2130091; f. 1982; quarterly; publ. by Centro de Documentação de Agricultura, Silvicultura, Pecuária e Pescas.

Aro: Av. 24 de Julho 1420, CP 4187, Maputo; f. 1995; monthly; Dir POLICARTO TAMELE; Editor BRUNO MACAME, Jr.

Arquivo Histórico: Av. Filipe Samuel Magaia 715, CP 2033, Maputo; tel. 21421177; fax 21423428; f. 1934; Editor JOEL DAS NEVES TEMBE.

Mozambiquefile: c/o AIM, Rua da Radio Moçambique, CP 896, Maputo; tel. 21313225; fax 21313196; e-mail aim@aim.org.mz; internet www.sortmoz.com/aimnews; monthly; Dir GUSTAVO MAVIZ; Editor PAUL FAUVET.

Mozambique Inview: c/o Mediacoop, Av. Amílcar Cabral 1049, CP 73, Maputo; tel. 21430722; fax 21302402; e-mail inview@savana.co .mz; internet www.mediacoop.odline.com; f. 1994; 2 a month; economic bulletin in English; Dir KOK NAM.

Revista Maderazinco: CP 477, Maputo; tel. 823004770; e-mail maderazinco@yahoo.com; internet www.tropical.maderazinco.co .mz; f. 2002; quarterly; literature; Editor ROGÉRIO MANJATE.

Revista Médica de Moçambique: Instituto Nacional de Saúde, Ministério da Saúde e Faculdade de Medicina, Universidade Eduardo Mondlane, CP 264, Maputo; tel. 21420368; fax 21431103; e-mail mdgedge@malarins.uem.mz; f. 1982; 4 a year; medical journal; Editor MARTINHO DGEDGE.

NEWS AGENCY

Agência de Informação de Moçambique (AIM): Rua da Rádio Moçambique, CP 896, Maputo; tel. 21313225; fax 21313196; e-mail aim@aim.org.mz; f. 1975; daily reports in Portuguese and English; Dir GUSTAVO LISSETIANE MAVIE.

Publishers

Arquivo Histórico de Moçambique (AHM): Travessa do Varietá 58, CP 2033, Maputo; tel. 21321178; fax 21423428; internet www .ahm.uem.mz; Dir JOEL DAS NEVES TEMBE.

Central Impressora: c/o Ministério da Saúde, Avs Eduardo Mondlane e Salvador Allende 1008, CP 264, Maputo; tel. 21427131; fax 21427133; owned by the Ministry of Health.

Centro de Estudos Africanos: Universidade Eduardo Mondlane, CP 1993, Maputo; tel. 21490828; fax 21491896; f. 1976; social and political science, regional history, economics; Dir Col SERGIO VIEIRA.

Editora Minerva Central: Rua Consiglieri Pedroso 84, CP 212, Maputo; tel. 2122092; fax 21328816; e-mail geral@minerva.co.mz; internet www.minerva.co.mz; f. 1908; stationers and printers, educational, technical and medical textbooks; Man. Dir J. F. CARVALHO.

Editorial Ndjira, Lda: Av. Ho Chi Minh 85, Maputo; tel. 21300180; fax 21308745; f. 1996.

Empresa Moderna, Lda: Av. 25 de Setembro, CP 473, Maputo; tel. 21424594; f. 1937; fiction, history, textbooks; Man. Dir LOUIS GALLOTI.

Fundo Bibliográfico de Língua Portuguesa: Av. 25 de Setembro 1230, 7° andar, Maputo; tel. 21429531; fax 21429530; e-mail palop@ zebra.uem.mz; f. 1990; state owned; Pres. LOURENÇO ROSÁRIO.

Imprensa Universitária: Universidade Eduardo Mondlane, Praça 19 de Maio, Maputo; internet www.uem.mz/imprensa_universitaris; university press.

Instituto Nacional do Livro e do Disco: Av. 24 de Julho 1921, CP 4030, Maputo; tel. 21434870; govt publishing and purchasing agency; Dir ARMÉNIO CORREIA.

Moçambique Editora: Rua Armando Tivane 1430, Bairro de Polana, Maputo; tel. 21495017; fax 21499071; e-mail info@me.co .mz; internet www.me.co.mz; f. 1996; educational textbooks, dictionaries.

Plural Editores: Av. Patrice Lumumba 765, Maputo; tel. 21360900; fax 21308868; e-mail plural@pluraleditores.co.mz; internet www .pluraleditores.co.mz; f. 2003; educational textbooks; part of the Porto Editora Group.

GOVERNMENT PUBLISHING HOUSE

Imprensa Nacional de Moçambique: Rua da Imprensa, CP 275, Maputo; tel. 21427021; fax 21424858; internet www.imprensanac .gov.mz; part of Ministry of State Administration; Dir VENÂNCIO T. MANJATE.

Broadcasting and Communications

TELECOMMUNICATIONS

The monopoly of Telecomunicações de Moçambique on the provision of fixed-line services was ended in December 2007, although it remained the sole fixed-line operator at mid-2014. There were also three mobile telephone operators at mid-2014.

Moçambique Celular (mCel): Rua Belmiro Obadias Muianga 384, CP 1483, Maputo; tel. 21351100; fax 21351117; internet www.mcel .co.mz; f. 1997 as a subsidiary of TDM; separated from TDM in 2003; mobile cellular telephone provider; Pres. SALVADOR ADRIANO.

Telecomunicações de Moçambique, SARL (TDM): Rua da Sé 2, CP 25, Maputo; tel. 21431921; fax 21431944; e-mail scatdm@tdm.mz; internet www.tdm.mz; f. 1993; Chair. JOAQUIM RIBEIRO PEREIRA DE CARVALHO; Man. Dir MAMUDO IBRAIMO.

Vodacom Moçambique (VM): Time Square Complex, Bloco 3, Av. 25 de Setembro, Maputo; tel. 840900000; fax 840901775; e-mail yumna.bhikha@vm.co.mz; internet www.vm.co.mz; f. 2002; mobile cellular telephone provider; owned by Vodacom Group (South Africa) and local shareholders; Chair. SALIMO ABDULA; Man. Dir JOSÉ DOS SANTOS.

Regulatory Authority

Instituto Nacional das Comunicações de Moçambique (INCM): Av. Eduardo Mondlane 123–127, CP 848, Maputo; tel. 21490131; fax 21494435; e-mail info@incm.gov.mz; internet www .incm.gov.mz; regulates post and telecommunications systems; Pres. ISIDORO PEDRO DA SILVA.

BROADCASTING

Radio

Rádio Encontro: Av. Francisco Manyanga, CP 366, Nampula; tel. 26215588; fax 26215878; e-mail radioencontro@teledata.mz.

Rádio Feba Moçambique: Av. Julius Nyerere 441A, CP 1648, Maputo; tel. 21440002; fax 21440009; e-mail febamoz@org.ue.mz; internet febamoz.go.co.mz.

Rádio Maria: Rua Igreja 156A, Machava Sede, Matola, Maputo; tel. 21750505; fax 21752124; e-mail info.moz@radiomaria.org; internet www.radiomaria.org.mz; f. 1995; evangelical radio broadcasts; Dir Fr JOÃO CARLOS H. NUNES.

Rádio Miramar: Rede de Comunicação, Av. Julius Nyerere 1555, Maputo; tel. 21498440; fax 21486813; e-mail jose.guerra@tvcabo.co .mz; internet www.miramar.co.mz; owned by Rede de Comunicação Miramar; CEO JOSÉ GUERRA.

Rádio Moçambique: Rua da Rádio 2, CP 2000, Maputo; tel. 21431687; fax 21321816; e-mail sepca_mz@yahoo.com.br; internet www.rm.co.mz; f. 1975; programmes in Portuguese, English and vernacular languages; Chair. RICARDO MADAUANE MALATE.

Rádio Terra Verde: Av. Eduardo Mondlane 2623, 5° andar, Maputo; tel. and fax 21302083; fmrly Voz da Renamo; owned by former rebel movement Renamo; transmitters in Maputo and Gorongosa, Sofala province.

Rádio Trans Mundial Moçambique: Av. Eduardo Mondlane 2998, CP 1526, Maputo; tel. 21440003; fax 21440004; e-mail rtransmundial@isl.co.mz.

Television

Rádio Televisão Klint (RTK): Av. Agostinho Neto 946, Maputo; tel. 21422956; fax 21493306; Dir CARLOS KLINT.

RTP África: Rua Pero de Anaia 248, Maputo; tel. (21) 497344; fax (21) 487347; e-mail rtp.a.moc@teledata.mz.

Televisão Miramar: Rua Pereira Lago 221, Maputo; tel. 21486311; fax 21486813; owned by Brazilian religious sect, the Igrega Universal do Reino de Deus (Universal Church of the Kingdom of God).

Televisão de Moçambique, EP (TVM): Av. 25 de Setembro 154, CP 2675, Maputo; tel. 21308117; fax 21308122; e-mail tvm@tvm.co .mz; internet www.tvm.co.mz; f. 1981; Pres. of Administrative Council ARMINDO CHAVANA.

TV Cabo Moçambique: Av. dos Presidentes 68, CP 1750, Maputo; tel. 21480550; fax 21480501; e-mail tvcabo@tvcabo.co.mz; internet www.tvcabo.co.mz; cable television and internet services in Maputo.

Finance

(cap. = capital; res = reserves; dep. = deposits; m. = million; brs = branches; amounts in meticais unless otherwise stated)

BANKING

In 2013 there were 18 banks and eight microbanks in Mozambique.

Central Bank

Banco de Moçambique: Av. 25 de Setembro 1695, CP 423, Maputo; tel. 21354600; fax 21323247; e-mail gpi@bancomoc.mz; internet www.bancomoc.mz; f. 1975; bank of issue; cap. 248.9m., res 845.2m., dep. 43,260.2m. (Dec. 2009); Gov. ERNESTO GOUVEIA GOVE; 4 brs.

National Banks

Banco Mercantil e de Investimento, SARL (BMI): Av. 24 de Julho 3549, Maputo; tel. 21407979; fax 21408887; f. 2001.

Banco Nacional de Investimentos (BNI): Av. Julius Nyerere 3504, Bloco A2, 4668, Maputo; tel. 21498581; fax 21498595; e-mail info@bni.co.mz; internet www.bni.co.mz; f. 2010; 49.5% owned by the Govt of Mozambique, 49.5% owned by the Govt of Portugal, 1% owned by Banco Comercial e de Investimentos, SARL; cap. US $500,000m.; Exec. Dir ADRIANO MALEIANE.

Banco Terra: Av. Samora Machel 341 R/C, CP 69, Maputo; tel. 21359900; fax 21316130; e-mail info@bancoterra.co.mz; internet www.bancoterra.co.mz; f. 2008; provides access to a full range of financial services to the rural and peri-urban population in Mozambique; cap. 1,457.6m., dep. 1,065.1m. (Dec. 2013); 30.7% owned by Rabobank (Netherlands); Pres. H. MERTENS; CEO DOMINIC TERBERG.

Banco Único: Maputo; internet www.bancounico.co.mz; f. 2011; privately owned; total assets US $230m. (2013); Chief Exec. JOÃO FIQUEIREDO; 15 brs.

Barclays Bank Mozambique SA: Av. 25 de Setembro 1184, CP 757, Maputo; tel. 21351700; fax 21323470; e-mail corporatesc@barclays.co.mz; internet www.barclays.co.mz; f. 1995 as Banco Popular de Desenvolvimento (BPD); name changed to Banco Austral SARL in 1998; name changed as above in 2007; 80% owned by Amalgamated Banks of South Africa, 20% owned by União, Sociedade e Participacões, SARL, which represents employees of the bank; cap. 3,316.6m., res 216.6m., dep. 11,024.7m. (Dec. 2013); Chair. LUÍSA DIAS DIOGO; Man. Dir FAISAL MKHIZE; 48 brs and agencies.

BCI (BCI) (Banco Comercial e de Investimentos, SARL): Edif. John Orr's, Av. 25 de Setembro 1465, CP 4745, Maputo; tel. 21353700; fax 21309831; e-mail bci@bci.co.mz; internet www.bci.co.mz; f. 1996; renamed as above following 2003 merger between Banco Comercial e de Investimentos and Banco de Fomento; 51% owned by Caixa Geral de Depósitos (Portugal), 30% Banco Português de Investimento, 18% owned by INSITEC; cap. 3,000.0m., res 1,843.3m., dep. 61,634.6m. (Dec. 2013); Chair. CELSO ISMAEL CORREIA; CEO PAULO ALEXANDRE DUARTE DE SOUSA; 130 brs.

Ecobank Moçambique SA: Av. Vladimir Lénine 210, CP 1106, Maputo; tel. 21313344; fax 21313345; e-mail info@bancoprocredit.co.mz; internet www.ecobank.com; f. 2000 as NovoBanco, subsequently Banco ProCredit; present name adopted 2014; cap. 187.2m., res 24.2m., dep. 1,120.9m. (Dec. 2012); Chair. EVELYNE M. B. F. LEPP; Gen. Man. ADAMA SENE CISSE.

FNB Moçambique: Av. 25 de Setembro 420, 1° andar, sala 8, Maputo; tel. 21356900; fax 21313053; e-mail balcao.sede@fnb.co.mz; internet www.fnb.co.mz; f. 2000; fmrly Banco de Desenvolvimento e de Comércio de Moçambique, name changed as above in 2007.

ICB-Banco Internacional de Comércio, SARL: Av. 25 de Setembro 1915, Maputo; tel. 21311111; fax 21314797; e-mail icbm@icbank-mz.com; internet www.icbank-mz.com; f. 1998; Chair. JOSEPHINE SIVARETNAM; CEO LEE SANG HUAT; 4 brs.

Millennium bim: Av. 25 de Setembro 1800, CP 865, Maputo; tel. 21354496; fax 21354415; e-mail scheman@millenniumbim.co.mz; internet www.millenniumbim.co.mz; f. 1995; name changed from Banco Internacional de Moçambique in 2005; 66.7% owned by Banco Comercial Português, 17.4% by the state; cap. 4,500.0m., res 2,324.9m., dep. 66,046.7m. (Dec. 2013); Pres. MÁRIO FERNANDES DA GRAÇA MACHUNGO; CEO JOÃO FILIPE DE FIGUEIREDO JÚNIOR; 158 brs.

Moza Banco: Av. Kwame Nkrumah 97, CP 1012, Maputo; tel. 21480800; fax 21480801; e-mail info@mozabanco.co.mz; internet www.mozabanco.co.mz; f. 2008; cap. 1,250.0m., res 43.1m., dep.

12,322.1m. (Dec. 2013); Chair. PRAKASH RATILAL; CEO INAETE MERALI.

Standard Bank, SARL (Moçambique): Praça 25 de Junho 1, CP 2086, Maputo; tel. 21352500; fax 21426967; e-mail camal.daude@standardbank.co.mz; internet www.standardbank.co.mz; f. 1966 as Banco Standard Totta de Moçambique; 98.14% owned by Stanbic Africa Holdings, UK; cap. 1,294.0m., res 1,408.2m., dep. 35,118.5m. (Dec. 2012); Man. Dir ANTONIO COUTINHO; 40 brs.

Foreign Banks

BancABC Mozambique: ABC House, Av. Julius Nyerere 999, Polana, CP 1445, Maputo; tel. 21482100; fax 21487474; e-mail abcmoz@africanbankingcorp.com; internet www.bancabc.co.mz; f. 1999; 100% owned by African Banking Corpn Holdings Ltd (Botswana); cap. 323.5m., res 171.9m., dep. 7,957.1m. (Dec. 2013); Chair. BENJAMIM ALFREDO; Man. Dir HÉLDER CHAMBISSE; 2 brs.

Mauritius Commercial Bank (Moçambique) SA: Av. Friedrich Engels 400, Maputo; tel. 21481900; fax 21498675; e-mail contact@mcbmozambique.com; internet www.mcbmozambique.com; f. 1999; name changed as above in June 2007; 81% owned by Mauritius Commercial Bank Group; cap. 125.2m., res 152.0m., dep. 1,475.1m. (Dec. 2013); Chair. PIERRE GUY NOEL; Gen. Man. PETER HIGGINS.

DEVELOPMENT FUND

Fundo de Desenvolvimento Agrário: Rua Joaquim Lapa 192, 2° andar, Maputo; tel. 21302814; fax 21430044; e-mail antonio.andre@ffa.org.mz; f. 2006 to provide credit for small farmers and rural co-operatives; promotes agricultural and rural devt; Sec. ANTÓNIO ANDRÉ.

STOCK EXCHANGE

Bolsa de Valores de Moçambique: Av. 25 de Setembro 1230, Prédio 33, 5° andar, Maputo; tel. 21308826; fax 21310559; e-mail bvm@bvm.co.mz; internet www.bolsadevalores.co.mz; f. 1999; Chair. ANABELA CHAMBUCA.

INSURANCE

In 1991 the Assembly of the Republic approved legislation terminating the state monopoly of insurance and reinsurance activities. In 2005 five insurance companies were operating in Mozambique.

Companhia de Seguros de Moçambique, IMPAR: Rua da Imprensa 625, Prédio 33, Maputo; tel. 21429695; fax 21430640; f. 1992; Pres. INOCÊNCIO A. MATAVEL; Gen. Man. MANUEL BALANCHO.

Empresa Moçambicana de Seguros, EE (EMOSE): Av. 25 de Setembro 1383, CP 1165, Maputo; tel. 21356300; fax 21424526; e-mail comercial@emose.co.mz; internet www.emose.co.mz; f. 1977 as state insurance monopoly; took over business of 24 fmr cos; 80% govt-owned, 20% private; cap. 150m.; Chair. VENÂNCIO MONDLANE.

NICO Moçambique: Av. Kenneth Kaunda 1202, Maputo; tel. 21494208; e-mail info@nicovida.co.mz; internet www.nicovida.co.mz; f. 2012; CEO SIMBA MANUNURE.

Seguradora Internacional de Moçambique: Av. 25 Setembro 1800, Maputo; tel. 21430959; fax 21430241; e-mail simseg@zebra.uem.mz; Pres. MÁRIO FERNANDES DA GRAÇA MACHUNGO.

Trade and Industry

GOVERNMENT AGENCIES

Centro de Promoção de Investimentos (CPI) (Investment Promotion Centre): Rua da Imprensa 332, CP 4635, Maputo; tel. 21313295; fax 21313325; e-mail cpi@cpi.co.mz; internet www.cpi.co.mz; f. 1987; encourages domestic and foreign investment and IT ventures with foreign firms; evaluates and negotiates investment proposals; Dir LOURENÇO SAMBO.

Instituto do Algodão de Moçambique (IAM): Av. Eduardo Mondlane 2221, 1° andar, CP 806, Maputo; tel. 21424264; fax 21430679; e-mail iampab@zebra.uem.mz; internet www.iam.gov.mz; responsible for promotion and devt of the cotton industry; Dir NORBERTO MAHALAMBE.

Instituto do Fomento do Cajú (INCAJU): Maputo; internet incaju.gov.mz; national cashew institute; Dir FILOMENA MAIOPUE.

Instituto Nacional de Açúcar (INA): Rua da Gávea 33, CP 1772, Maputo; tel. 21326550; fax 21427436; e-mail gpsca.ina@tvcabo.co.mz; Chair. ARNALDO RIBEIRO.

Instituto Nacional de Petróleo (INP): Av. Fernão de Magalhães 34, 1°/2° andar, CP 4724, Maputo; tel. 21320935; fax 21320932; e-mail info@inp.gov.mz; internet www.inp.gov.mz; f. 2005; regulates energy sector; Pres. ARSÉNIO MABOTE.

Instituto para a Promoção de Exportações (IPEX): Av. 25 de Setembro 1008, 2° andar, CP 4487, Maputo; tel. 21307257; fax

21307256; e-mail ipex@tvcabo.co.mz; internet www.ipex.gov.mz; f. 1990 to promote and co-ordinate national exports abroad; Pres. Dr JOÃO MACARINGUE.

Unidade Técnica para a Reestruturação de Empresas (UTRE): Rua da Imprensa 256, 7° andar, CP 4350, Maputo; tel. 21426514; fax 21421541; implements restructuring of state enterprises; Dir MOMADE JUMAS.

CHAMBERS OF COMMERCE

Câmara de Comércio de Moçambique (CCM): Rua Mateus Sansão Muthemba 452, CP 1836, Maputo; tel. 21491970; fax 21490428; e-mail ccm@tvcabo.co.mz; internet www.ccmoz.org.mz; f. 1980; Pres. JOÃO AMÉRICO MPFUMO; Sec.-Gen. MANUEL NOTIÇO.

Mozambique-USA Chamber of Commerce: Rua Matheus Sansão Muthemba 452, Maputo; tel. 21492904; fax 21492739; e-mail ccmusa@tvcabo.co.mz; internet www.ccmusa.co.mz; f. 1993; Sec. PETER MUCHIRI.

South Africa-Mozambique Chamber of Commerce (SAMO-ZACC): tel. 768548303; fax 866049050; e-mail info@samozacc.co.za; internet www.samozacc.co.za; f. 2005; Chair. (Mozambique) DAVID ROBBETZE.

TRADE ASSOCIATIONS

Associação das Indústrias do Cajú (AICAJU): Maputo; cashew processing industry asscn; Chair. CARLOS COSTA; 12 mem. cos.

Confederação das Associações Económicas de Moçambique (CTA): Rua de Fernando Ganhão 120, CP 2975, Maputo; tel. 21491914; fax 21493094; internet www.cta.org.mz; Pres. SALIMO ABDULA; Sec. OLGA TIMBA; 58 mem. cos.

STATE INDUSTRIAL ENTERPRISES

Empresa Nacional de Hidrocarbonetos de Moçambique (ENH): Av. Fernão de Magalhães 34, CP 4787, Maputo; tel. 21429456; fax 21421608; controls concessions for petroleum exploration and production; Dir MÁRIO MARQUES.

Petróleos de Moçambique (PETROMOC): Praça dos Trabalhadores 9, CP 417, Maputo; tel. 21427191; fax 21430181; internet www.petromoc.co.mz; f. 1977 to take over the Sonarep oil refinery and its associated distribution co; formerly Empresa Nacional de Petróleos de Moçambique; state directorate for liquid fuels within Mozambique, incl. petroleum products passing through Mozambique to inland countries; CEO JOSÉ NUNO DE OLIVEIRA.

UTILITIES

Electricity

Electricidade de Moçambique (EDM): Av. Agostinho Neto 70, CP 2447, Maputo; tel. 21490636; fax 21491048; e-mail ligacaoexpresso@edm.co.mz; internet www.edm.co.mz; f. 1977; 100% state-owned; production and distribution of electric energy; in 2004 plans were announced to extend the EDM grid to the entire country by 2020, at an estimated cost of US $700m; Pres. MANUEL JOÃO CUAMBE; Dir PASCOAL BACELA; 2,700 employees.

Companhia de Transmissão de Moçambique, SARL (MOTRACO) (Mozambique Transmission Co): Av. 25 de Setembro 420, Prédio JAT, 4° andar, Maputo; tel. 21313427; fax 21313447; e-mail asimao@motraco.co.mz; internet www.motraco.co.mz; f. 1998; jt venture between power utilities of Mozambique, South Africa and Swaziland; electricity distribution; Gen. Man. FRANCIS MASAWI.

Water

Direcção Nacional de Águas: Av. 25 de Setembro 942, 9° andar, CP 1611, Maputo; tel. 21420469; fax 21421403; e-mail watco@zebra.uem.mz; internet www.dnaguas.gov.mz; Dir AMÉRICO MUIANGA.

TRADE UNIONS

Freedom to form trade unions, and the right to strike, are guaranteed under the 1990 Constitution.

Confederação de Sindicatos Livres e Independentes de Moçambique (CONSILMO): Sec.-Gen. JEREMIAS TIMANE.

Organização dos Trabalhadores de Moçambique—Central Sindical (OTM—CS) (Mozambique Workers' Organization—Trade Union Headquarters): Rua Manuel António de Sousa 36, Maputo; tel. 21426786; fax 21421671; internet www.otm.org.mz; f. 1983; 15 affiliated unions with over 94,000 mems; Pres. CARLOS MUCAREIA; Sec.-Gen. ALEXANDRE MUNGUAMBE.

Transport

Improvements to the transport infrastructure since the signing of the General Peace Agreement in 1992 have focused on the development

of 'transport corridors', which include both rail and road links and promote industrial development in their environs. The Beira Corridor, with rail and road links and a petroleum pipeline, runs from Manica, on the Zimbabwean border, to the Mozambican port of Beira, while the Limpopo Corridor joins southern Zimbabwe and Maputo. Both corridors form a vital outlet for the landlocked southern African countries, particularly Zimbabwe. The Maputo Corridor links Ressano Garcia in South Africa to the port at Maputo, and the Nacala Corridor runs from Malawi to the port of Nacala. Two further corridors were planned: the Mtwara Corridor was to link Mozambique, Malawi, Tanzania and Zambia, while the Zambezi Corridor was to link Zambézia province with Malawi.

RAILWAYS

In 2010 the total length of track was 3,116 km, of which 2,072 km were operational. There are both internal routes and rail links between Mozambican ports and South Africa, Swaziland, Zimbabwe and Malawi. During the hostilities many lines and services were disrupted. In the early 2000s work commenced on upgrading the railway system and private companies were granted non-permanent concessions to rehabilitate and operate the railways. In mid-2012 the Government awarded the tender for the construction of a line connecting Moatize with the Malawian railway south of Blantyre; work on the line was expected to be finished within three years. There were also plans for a line to connect Mutarara with Malema. Rehabilitation work on the 670-km Sena railway line linking Beira with Moatize was completed in 2013.

Beira Railway Co: Dondo; f. 2004; 51% owned by Rites & Ircon (India), 49% owned by CFM; rehabilitating and managing Sena and Zimbabwe railway lines.

Portos e Caminhos de Ferro de Moçambique (CFM): Praça dos Trabalhadores, CP 2158, Maputo; tel. 21327173; fax 21427746; e-mail cfmnet@cfmnet.co.mz; internet www.cfmnet.co.mz; fmrly Empresa Nacional dos Portos e Caminhos de Ferro de Moçambique; privatized and restructured in 2002; Chair. ROSÁRIO MUALEIA; comprises 4 separate systems linking Mozambican ports with the country's hinterland, and with other southern African countries, including South Africa, Swaziland, Zimbabwe and Malawi:

  CFM—Centro (CFM—C): Largo dos CFM, CP 236, Beira; tel. 23321000; fax 23329290; lines totalling 994 km linking Beira with Zimbabwe and Malawi, as well as a link to Moatize (undergoing rehabilitation); Exec. Dir JOAQUIM VERÍSSIMO.

  CFM—Norte: Av. do Trabalho, CP 16, Nampula; tel. 26214320; fax 26212034; lines totalling 872 km, including link between port of Nacala with Malawi; management concession awarded to Nacala Corridor Development Co (a consortium 67% owned by South African, Portuguese and US cos) in January 2000; Dir of Railways MANUEL MANICA.

  CFM—Sul: Praça dos Trabalhadores, CP 2158, Maputo; tel. and fax 21430894; lines totalling 1,070 km linking Maputo with South Africa, Swaziland and Zimbabwe, as well as Inhambane–Inharrime and Xai-Xai systems; Exec. Dir JOAQUIM ZUCULE.

  CFM—Zambézia: CP 73, Quelimane; tel. 24212502; fax 24213123; 145-km line linking Quelimane and Mocuba; Dir ORLANDO J. JAIME.

ROADS

In 2012 there were an estimated 30,000 km of roads in Mozambique, of which some 7,000 km were paved.

Administraçao Nacional de Estradas (ANE): Av. de Moçambique 1225, CP 1294, Maputo; tel. 21475157; fax 21475290; internet www.ane.gov.mz; f. 1999 to replace the Direcção Nacional de Estradas e Pontes; implements government road policy through the Direcção de Estradas Nacionais (DEN) and the Direcção de Estradas Regionais (DER); Pres. Eng. LUCIANO DE CASTRO; Dir-Gen. CECÍLIO GRACHANE.

SHIPPING

Mozambique has three main sea ports, at Nacala, Beira and Maputo, while inland shipping on Lake Niassa and the river system remain underdeveloped. At 31 December 2014 Mozambique's flag registered fleet consisted of 77 vessels, totalling 39,772 grt.

Portos e Caminhos de Ferro de Moçambique (CFM-EP): Praça dos Trabalhadores, CP 2159, Maputo; tel. 21427173; fax 21427746; e-mail cfmnet@cfmnet.co.mz; internet www.cfmnet.co.mz; fmrly Empresa Nacional dos Portos e Caminhos de Ferro de Moçambique; privatized and restructured in 2002; Chair. ROSÁRIO MUALEIA; Port Dir CFM-Sul Eng. ANTÓNIO FRANCISCO MANUEL BIÉ; Port Dir CFM-Norte Eng. FRANCO CATUTULA; Port Dir CFM-Centro Dr CÂNDIDO JONE.

Agência Nacional de Frete e Navegação (ANFRENA): Rua Consiglieri Pedroso 396, CP 492, Maputo; tel. 21427064; fax 21427822; Dir FERDINAND WILSON.

Empresa Moçambicana de Cargas, SARL (MOCARGO): Rua Consiglieri Pedroso 430, 1°–4° andares, CP 888, Maputo; tel. 21428318; fax 21302067; e-mail msamaral@mocargo.com; internet www.mocargo.co.mz; f. 1982; shipping, chartering and road transport; Man. Dir MANUEL DE SOUSA AMARAL.

Manica Freight Services, SARL: Praça dos Trabalhadores 51, CP 557, Maputo; tel. 21356500; fax 21431084; e-mail fdimande@manica.co.mz; internet www.manica.co.mz; international shipping agents; Man. Dir AHMAD Y. CHOTHIA.

Maputo Port Development Co, SARL (MPDC): Port Director's Building, Porto de Maputo, CP 2841, Maputo; tel. 21340500; fax 21019908; e-mail info@portmaputo.com; internet www.portmaputo.com; f. 2003; private sector international consortium with concession (awarded 2003) to develop and run port of Maputo until 2033; Chair. ALAN OLIVIER; CEO OSÓRIO LUCAS.

Navique, SARL: Av. Mártires de Inhaminga 125, CP 145, Maputo; tel. 21312705; fax 21426310; e-mail smazoi@navique.co.mz; internet www.navique.com; f. 1985; Chair. J. A. CARVALHO; Man. Dir PEDRO VIRTUOSO.

CIVIL AVIATION

In 2014 there were eight international airports in Mozambique. In 2010 expansion work on Maputo International Airport was completed at an estimated cost of US $75m. to increase annual capacity to 900,000 passengers. In February 2012 Aeroportos de Moçambique announced that it was to invest $500m. over the following three years in the modernization and rehabilitation of the airports at Maputo, Pemba, Nacala-Porto and Tete.

Aeroportos de Moçambique: Av. Acordos de Lusaka 3267, CP 2631, Maputo; tel. 21465375; fax 21465359; internet www.aeroportos.co.mz; under Ministry of Transport and Communications; Chair. MANUEL VETERANO.

Instituto de Aviação Civil de Moçambique (IACM): Maputo; civil aviation institute; Dir ALBERTO MABJAIA.

Linhas Aéreas de Moçambique, SARL (LAM): Aeroporto Internacional de Maputo, CP 2060, Maputo; tel. 21465137; fax 21422936; e-mail jrviegas@lam.co.mz; internet www.lam.co.mz; f. 1980; 80% state-owned; operates domestic services and international services to South Africa, Tanzania, Mayotte, Zimbabwe and Portugal; CEO MARLENE MENDES MANAVE.

Sociedade de Transportes Aéreos/Sociedade de Transporte e Trabalho Aéreo, SARL (STA/TTA): Rua da Tchamba 405, CP 665, Maputo; tel. 21491765; fax 21491763; e-mail sta.tta@sta.co.mz; f. 1991; domestic airline and aircraft charter transport services; acquired Empresa Nacional de Transporte e Trabalho Aéreo in 1997; Chair. JOSÉ CARVALHEIRA; Dir of Operations FERNANDO CARREIRA.

Other airlines operating in Mozambique include Serviço Aéreo Regional, South African Airlines, Moçambique Expresso, SA—Airlink International, Transairways (owned by LAM) and TAP Air Portugal.

Tourism

Tourism, formerly a significant source of foreign exchange, ceased completely following independence, and was resumed on a limited scale in 1980. There were only 1,000 visitors in 1981 (compared with 292,000 in 1972 and 69,000 in 1974). With the successful conduct of multi-party elections in 1994 and the prospect of continued peace, there was considerable scope for development of this sector. By the late 1990s tourism was the fastest growing sector of the Mozambique economy, and a comprehensive tourism development plan was devised, assisted by funding from the European Union. The formal opening of the Great Limpopo Transfrontier Park in 2002, linking territories in Mozambique with South Africa and Zimbabwe, was expected to attract additional tourists. Further national parks were planned. There were 1.97m. foreign tourist arrivals in 2013, and tourism receipts in 2012 totalled an estimated US $250m.

Fundo Nacional do Turismo: Av. 25 de Setembro 1203, CP 4758, Maputo; tel. 21307320; fax 21307324; internet www.futur.org.mz; f. 1993; hotels and tourism; CEO Dr ZACARIAS SUMBANA.

Defence

As assessed at November 2014, total active armed forces were estimated at 11,200 (army 10,000, navy 200, air force 1,000).

Defence Expenditure: Budgeted at an estimated 1,110m. meticais in 2014.

Commander-in-Chief of the Armed Forces: Pres. FILIPE JACINTO NYUSI.

Chief of General Staff: Gen. GRAÇA TOMÁS CHONGO.

Deputy Chief of General Staff: Gen. OLIMPIO CAMBONA.

Education

Primary education is officially compulsory for seven years from the age of six. It is divided into two cycles, of five and two years. Secondary schooling, from 13 years of age, lasts for five years and comprises a first cycle of three years and a second of two years. According to UNESCO estimates, in 2012 86% of children in the relevant age-group were enrolled at primary schools (males 89%; females 84%), while secondary enrolment included only 18% of children in the relevant age group (males 18%; females 17%). There were 31,662 students in technical education in 2013. Two privately owned higher education institutions, the Catholic University and the Higher Polytechnic Institute, were inaugurated in 1996. In 2003 it was announced that education would no longer take place solely in Portuguese, but also in some Mozambican dialects. In the budget for 2015 the education sector was allocated US $1,248m., equivalent to 22.8% of total budgetary spending in that year.

MYANMAR

Introductory Survey

LOCATION, CLIMATE, LANGUAGE, RELIGION, FLAG, CAPITAL

The Republic of the Union of Myanmar (Pyidaungsu Thammada Myanma Naingngandaw—formerly Burma) lies in the north-west region of South-East Asia, between the Tibetan plateau and the Malay peninsula. The country is bordered by Bangladesh and India to the north-west, by the People's Republic of China and Laos to the north-east, and by Thailand to the south-east. The climate is tropical, with an annual average temperature of 27°C (80°F) and monsoon rains from May to October. Average annual rainfall is between 2,500 mm and 5,000 mm in the coastal and mountainous regions of the north and east, but reaches a maximum of only 1,000 mm in the lowlands of the interior. Temperatures in Yangon (Rangoon) are generally between 18°C (65°F) and 36°C (97°F). The official language is Myanmar (Burmese), and there are also a number of tribal languages. About 87% of the population are Buddhists. There are animist, Muslim, Hindu and Christian minorities. The national flag (proportions 2 by 3), which was officially introduced in October 2010, consists of three equal horizontal stripes, of yellow, green and red, with a large, five-pointed white star in the centre. In 2006 the functions of the capital city were transferred from Yangon to the new administrative centre of Nay Pyi Taw.

CONTEMPORARY POLITICAL HISTORY

Historical Context

Burma (now Myanmar) was annexed to British India during the 19th century, and became a separate British dependency, with a limited measure of self-government, in 1937. Japanese forces invaded and occupied the country in 1942, and Japan granted it nominal independence under a government of anti-British nationalists. The Burmese nationalists later turned against Japan and aided Allied forces to reoccupy the country in 1945. They formed a resistance movement, the Anti-Fascist People's Freedom League (AFPFL), led by Gen. Aung San, which became the main political force after the defeat of Japan. Aung San was assassinated in July 1947 and was succeeded by U Nu. On 4 January 1948 the Union of Burma became independent, outside the Commonwealth, with U Nu as the first Prime Minister.

Domestic Political Affairs

During the first decade of independence Burma was a parliamentary democracy, and the Government successfully resisted revolts by communists and other insurgent groups. In 1958 the ruling AFPFL split into two wings—the 'Clean' AFPFL and the 'Stable' AFPFL—and U Nu invited the Army Chief of Staff, Gen. Ne Win, to head a caretaker government. Elections to the Chamber of Deputies in February 1960 gave an overwhelming majority to U Nu, leading the 'Clean' AFPFL (which was renamed the Union Party in March), and he resumed office in April. Despite its popularity, the U Nu administration proved ineffective, and in March 1962 Gen. Ne Win staged a coup to depose U Nu (who was subsequently detained until 1966). The new Revolutionary Council suspended the Constitution and instituted authoritarian control through the government-sponsored Burma Socialist Programme Party (BSPP). All other political parties were outlawed in March 1964.

During the next decade a more centralized system of government was created, in an attempt to win popular support and to nationalize important sectors of the economy. A new Constitution, aiming to transform Burma into a democratic socialist state, was approved in a national referendum in December 1973. The Constitution of the renamed Socialist Republic of the Union of Burma, which came into force in January 1974, confirmed the BSPP as the sole authorized political party, and provided for the establishment of new organs of state. Elections to a legislative People's Assembly took place in January 1974, and in March the Revolutionary Council was dissolved. Ne Win (who, together with other senior army officers, had become a civilian in 1972) was elected President by the newly created State Council. However, Burma's economic problems increased, and in 1974 there were riots over food shortages and social injustices.

Student demonstrations took place in 1976, as social problems mounted. Following an attempted coup by members of the armed forces in July, the BSPP adopted a new economic programme in 1977 in an effort to quell unrest.

An election in January 1978 gave Ne Win a mandate to rule for a further four years, and in March he was re-elected Chairman of the State Council. In May 1980 a general amnesty was declared for political dissidents, including exiles (as a result of which U Nu, who had been living abroad since 1969, returned to Burma). Gen. San Yu, formerly the Army Chief of Staff, was elected Chairman of the State Council in November 1981. In August 1985 Ne Win was re-elected Chairman of the BSPP. Elections for a new People's Assembly were held in November.

In August 1987, owing to the country's increasing economic problems, an unprecedented extraordinary meeting, comprising the BSPP Central Committee, the organs of the State Council and other state bodies, was convened. Ne Win proposed a review of the policies of the past 25 years. In September the withdrawal from circulation of high-denomination banknotes, coupled with rice shortages, provoked student riots (the first civil disturbances since 1976). Owing to continued economic deprivation, further student unrest in Rangoon (now Yangon) in March 1988 culminated in major protests, which were violently suppressed by riot police under the direct command of Sein Lwin, the BSPP Joint General Secretary. The Government's response to further demonstrations in June was again extremely brutal, and many demonstrators were killed. In July vain attempts were made to counter the growing unpopularity of the Government, including the dismissal of the Minister of Home and Religious Affairs and the head of the People's Police Force in Rangoon. (The Prime Minister, also, was subsequently dismissed.) Finally, at an extraordinary meeting of the BSPP Congress, Ne Win resigned as party Chairman and asked the Congress to approve the holding of a national referendum on the issue of a multi-party political system. The Congress rejected the referendum proposal and the resignation of four other senior members of the BSPP, including that of Sein Lwin, but accepted the resignation of San Yu, the BSPP Vice-Chairman.

The subsequent election of Sein Lwin to the chairmanship of the BSPP, and his appointment as Chairman of the State Council and as state President, provoked further student-led riots. In August 1988 martial law was imposed in Rangoon, and thousands of unarmed demonstrators were reportedly massacred by the armed forces throughout the country. Sein Lwin was forced to resign after only 17 days in office. He was replaced by the more moderate Dr Maung Maung, hitherto the Attorney-General, whose response to the continued rioting was conciliatory. Martial law was revoked; Brig.-Gen. Aung Gyi (formerly a close colleague of Ne Win, now an outspoken critic of the regime), who had been detained under Sein Lwin, was released; and permission was given for the formation of the All Burma Students' Union. However, demonstrations persisted, and by September students and Buddhist monks had assumed control of many towns. In that month U Nu requested foreign support for the formation of an 'alternative government'. The emerging opposition leaders, Aung Gyi, Aung San Suu Kyi (daughter of Gen. Aung San) and Gen. (retd) Tin Oo (a former Army Chief of Staff and Minister of Defence), then formed the National United Front for Democracy, which was subsequently renamed the League for Democracy and later the National League for Democracy (NLD).

At an emergency meeting of the BSPP Congress in September 1988 it was decided that free elections would be held within three months and that members of the armed forces, police and civil service could no longer be affiliated to a political party. Now distanced from the BSPP, the armed forces, led by Gen. (later Senior Gen.) Saw Maung, seized power on 18 September, ostensibly to maintain order until multi-party elections could be arranged. A State Law and Order Restoration Council (SLORC) was formed, all state organs (including the People's Assembly, the State Council and the Council of Ministers) were abolished, demonstrations were banned and a night-time curfew was imposed nationwide. Despite these measures, opposition movements demonstrated in favour of an interim civilian government, and it was estimated that more than 1,000 demonstrators were killed in the first few days following the coup. The SLORC announced the formation of a nine-member Government, with Saw Maung as Minister of Defence and of Foreign Affairs and subsequently also Prime Minister. Although ostensibly in retirement, it was widely believed that Ne Win retained a controlling influence over the new leaders. The new Government changed the official name of the country to the Union of Burma (as it had been before 1973). The law maintaining the BSPP as the sole party was abrogated, and new parties were encouraged to register for the forthcoming elections. The BSPP registered as the National Unity Party (NUP). In December 1988, owing to disagreements with Suu Kyi, Aung Gyi was expelled from the NLD after he had founded the Union National Democracy Party. Tin Oo was elected as the new NLD Chairman. U Nu returned to prominence as the leader of a new party, the League for Democracy and Peace (LDP), and also commanded the support of the new Democracy Party.

From October 1988 to January 1989 Suu Kyi campaigned across the nation, and elicited much popular support, despite martial law regulations banning public gatherings of five or more people. In March 1989 there were anti-Government demonstrations in many cities, in protest against the increasing harassment of Suu Kyi and the arrest of many NLD supporters. In July Suu Kyi cancelled a rally to commemorate the anniversary of the assassination of her father, owing to the threat of government violence; two days later, both she and Tin Oo were placed under house arrest.

In May 1989 legislation was ratified providing for multi-party elections to be held on 27 May 1990. In June 1989 the SLORC changed the official name of the country to the Union of Myanmar (Pyidaungsu Myanma Naingngandaw), on the grounds that the previous title conveyed the impression that the population consisted solely of ethnic Burmans. The transliteration to the Roman alphabet of many other place names was changed, to correspond more closely with pronunciation.

In December 1989 Tin Oo of the NLD was sentenced by a military tribunal to three years' imprisonment for his part in the anti-Government uprising in 1988. U Nu was disqualified from contesting the forthcoming general election, owing to his refusal to dissolve the 'alternative government' that he had proclaimed in September 1988. In January 1990 U Nu and other members of the 'alternative government' were placed under house arrest. Later in January Suu Kyi was barred from contesting the election, owing to her 'entitlement to the privileges of a foreigner' (a reference to her marriage to a British citizen) and her alleged involvement with insurgents. Tens of thousands of residents were reported to have been forcibly evicted from densely populated areas in major cities, where anti-Government demonstrations had received much support, and resettled in rural areas during 1989. By February 1990 martial law had been revoked in 18 townships.

In May 1990 93 parties presented a total of 2,296 candidates to contest the general election for the new assembly; there were also 87 independent candidates. The voting was reported to be free and orderly. The NLD received 59.9% of the total votes and won 396 of the 485 contested seats; the NUP obtained 21.2% of the votes, but secured only 10 seats. The NLD demanded the immediate opening of negotiations with the SLORC, and progress towards popular rule. However, the SLORC announced that the election had been intended to provide a Constituent Assembly rather than a legislature. The resulting draft constitution would require endorsement by referendum and subsequent approval by the SLORC. In July the SLORC announced Order 1/90, stating that the SLORC would continue as the de facto Government until a new constitution was drafted. In response, elected members of the NLD urged (independently of their leadership) that an assembly of all elected representatives be convened by September.

In September 1990 the SLORC arrested six members of the NLD, including the acting Chairman, Kyi Maung, and acting Secretary-General, Chit Hlaing, on charges of passing state secrets to unauthorized persons. Kyi Maung was replaced as acting NLD Chairman by Aung Shwe. Influential monks agreed to support the proposed declaration of a provisional government in Mandalay, but the plan was abandoned after government troops surrounded monasteries. The SLORC subsequently ordered the dissolution of all Buddhist organizations involved in anti-Government activities (all except nine sects) and empowered military commanders to impose death sentences on rebellious monks. More than 50 senior members of the NLD were

arrested, and members of all political parties were required to endorse Order 1/90: in acquiescing, the NLD effectively nullified its demand for an immediate transfer of power.

In December 1990 a group of candidates who had been elected to the Constituent Assembly fled to Manerplaw, on the Thai border, and announced a 'parallel government', the National Coalition Government of the Union of Burma (NCGUB), with the support of the Democratic Alliance of Burma (DAB), a broadly based organization uniting ethnic rebel forces with student dissidents and monks. The self-styled Prime Minister of the NCGUB was Sein Win, the leader of the Party for National Democracy (PND) and a cousin of Suu Kyi. The NLD leadership expelled members who had taken part in the formation of the 'parallel government', despite broad support within the NLD. The SLORC subsequently deregistered the PND, the LDP and two other parties and annulled the elected status of the eight members of the NCGUB. In April 1991 Gen. (later Senior Gen. or Field Marshal) Than Shwe, the Vice-Chairman of the SLORC and the Deputy Chief of Staff of the Armed Forces, officially announced that the SLORC would not transfer power to the Constituent Assembly, as the political parties involved were 'subversive' and 'unfit to rule'. In response to continued pressure from the SLORC, the NLD completely reorganized the party's Central Executive Committee, replacing Suu Kyi as General Secretary with the previously unknown U Lwin, and Tin Oo with the former acting Chairman, Aung Shwe.

In July 1991 the SLORC retroactively amended electoral legislation adopted in May 1990, extending the grounds on which representatives of the Constituent Assembly could be disqualified or debarred from contesting future elections to include convictions for breaches of law and order. More than 80 elected representatives had already died, been imprisoned or been forced into exile since the election in May 1990. In September 1991 Ohn Gyaw was appointed Minister of Foreign Affairs in place of Saw Maung, becoming the first civilian in the Cabinet.

In October 1991 Suu Kyi was awarded the Nobel Peace Prize. Sein Win attended the presentation of the award to Suu Kyi's family in Norway in December. In Myanmar, students who staged demonstrations to coincide with the ceremony were dispersed by security forces. It was subsequently announced that Suu Kyi and Tin Oo had been expelled from the NLD.

Three additional members were appointed to the SLORC in January 1992, and the Cabinet was expanded to include seven new ministers, four of whom were civilians. The changes, together with a reorganization of senior ministers in February, were perceived to benefit the Chief of Military Intelligence, Maj.-Gen. (later Lt-Gen.) Khin Nyunt (First Secretary of the SLORC). Khin Nyunt was widely regarded as the most powerful member of the SLORC, owing to Ne Win's continued patronage. However, divisions within the ruling junta, between Khin Nyunt and the more senior officers, were becoming increasingly evident. In March Than Shwe replaced Saw Maung as Minister of Defence, and in April Saw Maung retired as Chairman of the SLORC and Prime Minister for reasons of ill health. Than Shwe was subsequently appointed to both these posts. The SLORC promptly ordered the release of several political prisoners, including U Nu, and announced that Suu Kyi could receive a visit from her family. In June the first meeting took place between members of the SLORC and opposition representatives from the 10 remaining legal parties, in preparation for the holding of a national convention to draft a new constitution.

The National Convention finally assembled in January 1993, but was adjourned several times during the year, owing to the objections of opposition members to SLORC demands for a leading role in government for the armed forces. Towards the end of the year the Chairman of the National Convention's Convening Committee, Aung Toe (the Chief Justice), announced (seemingly without grounds) that a consensus existed in favour of the SLORC's demands, which comprised: the inclusion, in both the lower and upper chambers of a proposed parliament, of military personnel (to be appointed by the Commander-in-Chief of the Armed Forces); the election of the President by an electoral college; the independent self-administration of the armed forces; and the right of the Commander-in-Chief to exercise state power in an emergency (effectively granting legitimate status to a future coup).

In September 1993 an alternative mass movement to the NUP (which had lost credibility through its election defeat in 1990) was formed to establish a civilian front through which the armed forces could exercise control. The Union Solidarity and Development Association (USDA), the aims of which were indistinguishable from those of the SLORC, was not officially registered as a political party, thus enabling civil servants to join the organization, with the incentive of considerable privileges.

The National Convention reassembled in January 1994 and was adjourned in April, having adopted guidelines for three significant chapters of the future Constitution. The changes envisaged Myanmar being renamed the Republic of the Union of Myanmar, comprising seven states (associated with some of the country's minority ethnic groups) and seven regions in central and southern Myanmar (largely representing the areas populated by the ethnic Bamars—Burmans). The Republic would be headed by an executive President, elected by the legislature for five years; proposals for the disqualification of any candidate with a foreign spouse or children would prevent Suu Kyi from entering any future presidential election. Reconvening in September, the Convention again stressed that the central role of the military (as 'permanent representatives of the people') be enshrined in the new Constitution. It was proposed that legislative power be shared between a bicameral Pyidaungsu Hluttaw (Union Assembly) and divisional and state assemblies, all of which were to include representatives of the military. The Pyidaungsu Hluttaw was to be composed of the Pyithu Hluttaw (House of Representatives) and the Amyotha Hluttaw (House of Nationalities): the former would comprise 330 elected deputies and 110 members of the armed forces, and would be elected for five years. The latter would comprise equal numbers of representatives from the proposed seven regions and seven states of the Republic, as well as members of the military, and was to include a maximum of 224 deputies. A general election was scheduled for September 1997 (but never held).

In September 1994, following mediation by a senior Buddhist monk, Suu Kyi was permitted to leave her home to meet Than Shwe and Khin Nyunt. Suu Kyi held a second meeting with senior SLORC members in October and in the following month it was reported that she had met other detained members of the NLD, including Tin Oo. In February 1995 leading members of the SLORC held talks in Yangon with an envoy of the UN Secretary-General. The following month the Government released 31 political prisoners, including Tin Oo and Kyi Maung.

In July 1995 Suu Kyi was unexpectedly granted an unconditional release from house arrest, whereupon she made a conciliatory speech, urging negotiations with the SLORC. Suu Kyi swiftly effected a reconciliation between the early leaders of the NLD with the party's new leadership, which had compromised with the SLORC. Hundreds of supporters gathered daily to hear Suu Kyi speak outside her house in Yangon. Suu Kyi was reinstated as General Secretary of the NLD in October, as part of a reorganization of the party's executive committee; Tin Oo and Kyi Maung were named Vice-Chairmen. Aung Shwe, who had led the 'legal' NLD and represented the party at the National Convention, was retained as party Chairman. Meanwhile, in August Win Htein, Suu Kyi's personal assistant, was arrested and sentenced to seven years' imprisonment (subsequently doubled) for allegedly conspiring with groups in India to destabilize Myanmar.

In November 1995 the National Convention reconvened. The NLD attended the opening session, but later withdrew when the SLORC ignored its requests to expand the Convention to make it truly representative. Denouncing the Convention as illegitimate and undemocratic, the NLD for the first time appealed for international support for its cause. The SLORC, which had already begun to imprison NLD supporters for petty crimes, reacted strongly to the NLD boycott, officially expelling the party from the Convention.

In May 1996 more than 260 members of the NLD (mostly delegates elected to the Constituent Assembly in 1990) were arrested prior to the party's first congress. The majority were detained for the duration of the congress, which only 18 NLD members were able to attend. The congress resolved to draft an alternative constitution. In June the SLORC intensified its action against the NLD with an order banning any organization that held illegal gatherings or obstructed the drafting of the new Constitution by the National Convention; members of a proscribed party could be liable to between five and 20 years' imprisonment. In September police erected roadblocks around Suu Kyi's house, and again detained NLD activists, in order to prevent the holding of another congress. Suu Kyi's telephone line was disconnected, and she was unable to deliver her regular weekend speech for the first time since her release from house arrest. From October the roadblock was set up each week to prevent access to Suu Kyi's speech. The SLORC recommended

talks with NLD officials later that month, but relations quickly deteriorated following an attack on vehicles in which Suu Kyi and other NLD leaders were travelling.

In October 1996 student action in Yangon, in protest against the detention and brutal treatment of fellow students, prompted further repression and numerous arrests (among those detained was Kyi Maung). This was followed in early December by the largest pro-democracy demonstration since 1988, involving more than 2,000 students. The gathering was dispersed peacefully, although some 600 demonstrators were temporarily detained. Smaller student demonstrations continued sporadically until mid-December 1996, when tanks were deployed in Yangon and university establishments were closed indefinitely. At the end of the month some 50 members of the Communist Party of Burma and the NLD were arrested in connection with the protests.

In January 1997 Suu Kyi was allowed to deliver her weekly speech for the first time in three months. However, the SLORC imposed new constraints on media access to Suu Kyi, and barricades remained outside her home. The detention of NLD members increased during 1997, while government propaganda vilifying the opposition was more prolific and Suu Kyi's freedom of movement and association remained restricted. In July, however, Khin Nyunt invited the NLD Chairman, Aung Shwe, to a meeting, which constituted the first senior-level contact between the SLORC and the NLD since the release of Suu Kyi from house arrest in July 1995. The SLORC granted permission for an NLD congress to be held in September 1997.

The State Peace and Development Council

On 15 November 1997 the ruling junta unexpectedly announced the dissolution of the SLORC and its replacement with the State Peace and Development Council (SPDC). The 19-member SPDC comprised exclusively military personnel; the four most senior members of the SLORC retained their positions at the head of the new junta: Than Shwe was appointed Chairman, Gen. Maung Aye (the Commander-in-Chief of the Army) Vice-Chairman, Khin Nyunt First Secretary and Tin Oo (as distinct from Tin Oo of the NLD) Second Secretary. A number of former members of the SLORC were ostensibly promoted to an 'Advisory Group', which was subsequently abolished; five members of this group, who had also held positions in the Cabinet, were placed under house arrest in December, pending investigations into allegations of corruption. The SPDC immediately implemented a reorganization of the Cabinet. The new, 40-member Cabinet included 25 former ministers, but, in contrast to the SLORC (the members of which had virtually all held cabinet portfolios), only one member of the SPDC, Than Shwe, was appointed to serve concurrently as a cabinet minister. In December the SPDC announced another cabinet reorganization and the appointment of a new Chairman (the Minister of Hotels and Tourism, Maj.-Gen. Saw Lwin) and Vice-Chairmen of the National Convention Convening Commission; however, the Convention, which had adjourned in March 1996, remained in recess.

Harassment and persecution of members of the NLD and other opposition movements continued. In March 1998 40 people were arrested on charges of involvement in a conspiracy allegedly led by the exiled All-Burma Students Democratic Front (ABSDF, an armed movement formed in 1988 by students within the DAB, which had officially renounced its armed struggle in 1997) to assassinate leaders of the military junta and perpetrate terrorist attacks on government offices and foreign embassies. The ABSDF, which rejected the allegations, was accused of complicity with the NLD. Six of the accused were sentenced to death in April 1998. However, the SPDC unexpectedly authorized an NLD party congress, attended by 400 delegates, in May to celebrate the eighth anniversary of the general election. In June the NLD demanded that the SPDC reconvene the Pyithu Hluttaw by 21 August, in accordance with the results of the 1990 election. Some 40 elected NLD representatives were detained at the end of June, while the freedom of movement of the other elected party representatives was severely restricted. Suu Kyi attempted to visit NLD members outside Yangon, but was repeatedly obstructed by roadblocks. She was forcibly returned to her home by security personnel after a six-day protest in her car in July, following government refusals to comply with her demands for the release of detained opposition members and the commencement of substantive dialogue with the NLD. In a further incident, in August, Suu Kyi was returned to her home by ambulance after spending 13 days in her car.

Shortly before the NLD's prescribed deadline of 21 August 1998 for convening the Pyithu Hluttaw, the SPDC published an official rejection of the NLD's demands. The NLD responded by declaring its intention unilaterally to convene a 'People's Parliament', which would include elected representatives of all the ethnic minority groups. Large-scale student demonstrations were held in Yangon in support of the NLD's demands; the demonstrators were dispersed by security forces. Arrests of opposition activists increased dramatically, and by early September 193 elected NLD members of the Pyithu Hluttaw and hundreds of party supporters had been detained. In the same month, a 10-member Representative Committee, led by Suu Kyi and Aung Shwe, was established by the NLD to act on behalf of the 'People's Parliament' until a legislature could be convened under the 1990 election law. The Committee asserted that no laws enacted by the military junta over the previous 10 years had legal authority, and additionally demanded the immediate and unconditional release of all political prisoners. Also in September 1998, a number of large pro-Government rallies were held in Yangon. The NLD condemned the alleged use of coercion, intimidation and threats by government military intelligence units to secure the involuntary resignations of vast numbers of NLD members and the closure of a number of regional party offices. Following the death in custody in October of one of its members, the NLD formally denounced the junta's treatment of detained opposition party members in a letter to Than Shwe. In the same month, UN Assistant Secretary-General Alvaro de Soto met with SPDC leaders and also with Suu Kyi during a visit to Myanmar. He reportedly offered large-scale financial and humanitarian aid to the junta in exchange for the initiation of substantive dialogue with the NLD. During October and November about 300 opposition members were released by the Government; however, a further 500 were believed to remain in detention.

In March 1999, despite requests from several foreign governments, the ruling junta refused to grant a visa to Suu Kyi's terminally ill husband, Michael Aris. The junta instead encouraged Suu Kyi to visit Aris in the United Kingdom; however, Suu Kyi declined to leave Myanmar for fear that she would not be allowed to return. Aris died later that month.

In April 1999 the UN adopted a unanimous resolution deploring the escalation in the persecution of the democratic opposition in Myanmar. Nevertheless, the harassment and intimidation continued, and several hundred NLD members were reported to have been forced to resign from the party over the course of the year. In August a series of protests was staged by the opposition to mark the anniversary of the massacre of thousands of pro-democracy demonstrators by the military Government in 1988. In October 1999 the Supreme Court rejected a claim by the NLD that its activities had been 'continuously disrupted, prevented and destroyed' and that hundreds of its members had been illegally detained.

In August 2000 Suu Kyi and 14 NLD colleagues attempted to visit party members in Kunyangon, a town just outside Yangon. The group was stopped by a military roadblock, but refused to return home. A nine-day confrontation finally ended with Suu Kyi and her colleagues being forcibly returned to Yangon. Suu Kyi and eight others were kept under house arrest for the next two weeks. Undeterred, the NLD announced in September that it was to draft a new constitution for the country, an act declared illegal in 1996 and punishable by 20 years' imprisonment. Later in the month another attempt by Suu Kyi to leave Yangon, this time by train to Mandalay, was once more thwarted. The NLD leader was returned home and placed under house arrest yet again, while NLD Vice-Chairman Tin Oo and eight other party workers were taken to a government 'guest house'. Pressure on the NLD increased in October 2000, when a deadline for an eviction order for the party to vacate its headquarters in the capital expired.

Despite the relentless suppression of the opposition, Razali Ismail, the newly appointed UN Secretary-General's Special Envoy to Myanmar, was allowed access to Suu Kyi during a visit in October 2000. A degree of conciliation between the SPDC and the NLD was confirmed in January 2001, when it was announced that the two sides had been holding covert, senior-level talks since the previous October, the first such discussions since 1994. It was reported that Khin Nyunt had met with Suu Kyi several times. At the end of January 2001 the SPDC released Tin Oo and 84 other NLD supporters, who had been detained since Suu Kyi's foiled train journey in September 2000. A few days later a delegation of the European Union (EU, see p. 271) was permitted to meet with Suu Kyi, as was the UN Special Rapporteur on the situation of human rights in Myanmar, Dr Paulo Sérgio Pinheiro, in April 2001.

A bomb explosion in May 2001 reportedly killed 12 people in a market in Mandalay. In the same month it was reported that religious riots in Toungoo, Bago Division, had led to the deaths of 24 Buddhist monks. The disturbances spread to other towns, prompting allegations that the SPDC had instigated the riots in an attempt to divert public attention from political and economic problems.

In February 2001 SPDC Second Secretary Lt-Gen. Tin Oo was killed in a helicopter crash, amid rumours of assassination. In November SPDC Third Secretary Lt-Gen. Win Myint and Deputy Prime Minister Tin Hla were dismissed, and two days later the SPDC announced that five government ministers were to retire, including two other Deputy Prime Ministers. Meanwhile, in mid-2001, as conciliatory discussions continued, the Government ordered the release of a number of NLD members from prison and permitted the reopening of the NLD headquarters in Yangon. In August the release of NLD Chairman Aung Shwe and Vice-Chairman Tin Oo was hailed as an indication of progress. Shortly afterwards Razali Ismail held further talks with Suu Kyi during a visit to Yangon. Ismail revisited the country in November, and expressed satisfaction with the progress that had been made.

In January 2002 it was reported that Suu Kyi had met privately with Gen. Than Shwe for the first time since 1994, raising hopes that the two sides might be close to reaching a breakthrough. In March 2002 the son-in-law and three grandsons of Ne Win were arrested on charges of plotting to overthrow the Government. Four senior military officials, including the Commander-in-Chief of the Air Force and the Chief of Police, were dismissed and questioned in connection with the attempted coup. Ne Win and his daughter were placed under house arrest. Despite suspicions that the coup allegations were linked to internal conflicts within the military, owing to lack of evidence, in September Ne Win's four relatives were convicted of high treason and sentenced to death. In December Ne Win himself died while under house arrest.

In May 2002 Suu Kyi was released from house arrest. The SPDC stated that her release was unconditional and that it would no longer impose any restrictions upon her travel. In November the junta announced the release of 115 prisoners, the largest number to date. In February 2003 it was reported that Suu Kyi wanted existing international economic sanctions to be upheld against the Myanma Government until it began a meaningful dialogue with the opposition. In the same month it was announced that Lt-Gen. Soe Win would assume the still vacant post of Second Secretary of the SPDC. In March Pinheiro restated a UN demand that the junta release all remaining political prisoners, estimated to number 1,200, and enter into serious dialogue with the opposition.

In April 2003 Suu Kyi issued a rare public criticism of the SPDC for refusing to enter into any substantive dialogue with the opposition. In May the political situation deteriorated further when violent confrontations took place in the northern town of Ye-u, between government supporters and opposition members travelling with an entourage conveying Suu Kyi. While the SPDC insisted that the violence had been provoked by the opposition, it was subsequently reported that Suu Kyi's convoy had been ambushed and attacked by pro-Government forces. Around 80 members of the entourage were believed to have been killed. On the following day it was reported that Suu Kyi had been taken into 'protective custody' by the SPDC; meanwhile, the headquarters of the NLD, together with NLD offices across the country, were closed down, and all state universities were shut indefinitely. The junta's detention of Suu Kyi prompted widespread international criticism. At a meeting of ministers of foreign affairs of the Association of Southeast Asian Nations (ASEAN, see p. 210) held in mid-June the organization departed from its traditional policy of non-interference in the affairs of other member states, urging Suu Kyi's release and a peaceful transition to democracy. Later in June, following the failure of its appeal to the SPDC for the release of Suu Kyi, the country's largest aid donor, Japan, suspended all economic aid to Myanmar. In July the Government announced that it had freed 91 of the NLD activists detained after the violence of May and permitted a delegation from the International Committee of the Red Cross (ICRC) to visit Suu Kyi.

In July 2003 it was reported that three cabinet ministers, including Minister of Industry (No. 1) Aung Thaung, had been dismissed. In August a major reorganization of the Government was announced, in which the former First Secretary of the SPDC, Lt-Gen. Khin Nyunt, replaced Senior-Gen. Than Shwe as Prime

Minister. However, Than Shwe remained Chairman of the SPDC and retained the defence portfolio. Lt-Gen. Soe Win became First Secretary and was replaced as Second Secretary by Lt-Gen. Thein Sein.

In September 2003 it was announced that Suu Kyi had returned to her home and was being held under house arrest, having undergone major surgery in hospital. In November five members of the NLD's Central Executive Committee, who had been held in connection with the violence in May, were released. In January 2004 the release of a further 26 members of the NLD was announced; in February NLD Vice-Chairman Tin Oo was placed under house arrest, having been imprisoned since May 2003. Also in January 2004, following a meeting with government officials, representatives from 25 ethnic groups and alliances rejected the proposed 'road map' to democracy outlined by the Prime Minister in August 2003 and reiterated demands for the Government to begin talks with the opposition. In April 2004 the SPDC released the NLD's Chairman, Aung Shwe, and its Secretary, U Lwin, who had both been under house arrest since May 2003, and allowed the party's headquarters to reopen (although the regional offices remained closed).

The National Convention (which had been in recess since 1996) was reconvened in May 2004, despite a boycott by some ethnic minority groups and the NLD. More than 1,000 delegates attended the opening session, which was chaired by SPDC Second Secretary Lt-Gen. Thein Sein. It was stressed that the Convention was to be a continuation of the discussions held between 1993 and 1996, at which a number of constitutional provisions had already been drafted. The Convention was adjourned in July 2004.

In September 2004 the civilian Minister of Foreign Affairs, Win Aung, and his deputy were replaced by senior military officers. Amid reports of a power struggle within the SPDC, Khin Nyunt was removed from the premiership and from his position as Chief of Military Intelligence in October, and was placed under house arrest, apparently owing to his alleged involvement in smuggling by military intelligence staff. Lt-Gen. Soe Win was appointed as Prime Minister, while Lt-Gen. Thein Sein replaced Soe Win as First Secretary of the SPDC. The National Intelligence Bureau was abolished, and many associates of Khin Nyunt were subsequently arrested or dismissed from office.

During November–December 2004 the SPDC ordered the release of more than 14,300 prisoners who, it claimed, had been wrongly imprisoned by the dissolved National Intelligence Bureau. However, according to the opposition, the mass amnesty included only some 54 political prisoners (including the Chairman of the Democracy Party, Thu Wai). In January 2005 speculation about tension within the leadership continued. It was reported in that month that four associates of Khin Nyunt who had been arrested in October 2004 had died in detention, while the closed trials of some 300 others on corruption charges had commenced in a prison in Yangon. The National Convention resumed in February 2005, again without the participation of the NLD and several ethnic minority groups, amid criticism and claims of the Convention's lack of credibility by the EU, the UN and the USA.

In July 2005 Khin Nyunt was convicted on eight charges, including corruption and bribery, and was given a suspended prison sentence of 44 years. In the same month the Government authorized the release of dozens of political prisoners; however, approximately 1,100 dissidents were believed to remain in detention in Myanmar at that time.

In November 2005 the Government announced that it had initiated the first phase of a relocation of the country's administrative capital from Yangon to Pyinmana, a sparsely populated mountainous region about 400 km (nearly 250 miles) to the north of Yangon. According to a government statement, the decision to move to Pyinmana had been made owing to its central location. The new administrative centre was officially named Nay Pyi Taw in March 2006.

Having being refused access to the country for almost two years, Razali Ismail resigned as the UN Secretary-General's Special Envoy to Myanmar in January 2006. Later that month the SPDC adjourned a session of the National Convention, with a view to reconvening towards the end of the year. In April former Minister of Foreign Affairs Win Aung was convicted on corruption and bribery charges, and sentenced to seven years' imprisonment. In the following month the new UN envoy, Ibrahim Gambari, was permitted to enter Myanmar, whereupon he held discussions with Than Shwe and briefly met with Suu Kyi. In September the UN Security Council reviewed the human rights

situation in Myanmar for the first time. Gambari paid a second visit to the country in November and was again allowed to hold a brief meeting with Suu Kyi. In January 2007 a draft resolution urging the Myanma Government to release all political prisoners and end its violation of human rights was submitted to the UN Security Council, sponsored by the USA and the UK. However, the resolution was defeated when the People's Republic of China and the Russian Federation, two of the five permanent members of the Security Council, exercised their right of veto.

Meanwhile, in April 2006 the ABSDF, the Federation of Trade Unions—Burma (FTUB), the NCGUB and the National League for Democracy—Liberated Area (NLD—LA) were denounced as terrorist organizations by the Government, in relation to a series of bomb attacks and attempted bombings in 2000–06. The admission of the foreign press to the proceedings of the reconvened National Convention in October 2006 represented progress to some observers, but the absence of the NLD and the relatively small number of delegates from other political parties did not bode well for democratic reform. In January 2007 it was reported that the SPDC had released 2,831 prisoners in an amnesty to mark Independence Day, although only 30 were political prisoners.

In May 2007 Lt-Gen. Thein Sein, the First Secretary of the SPDC, assumed the role of Prime Minister in an acting capacity, amid conjecture about Lt-Gen. Soe Win's health. During the final session of the National Convention, in July–September, detailed principles for a new Constitution were adopted; a 54-member commission, chaired by Chief Justice Aung Toe, was appointed by the SPDC in October to draft the new charter and commenced work in December without the participation of the opposition.

The protests of September 2007

Substantial increases in fuel prices in August 2007 provoked a series of anti-Government protests in Yangon and other towns. More than 60 demonstrators had been arrested by the end of the month, including leaders of the '88 Generation' students' group who had participated in the 1988 pro-democracy uprising. The protests escalated in September 2007 with the involvement of Buddhist monks. During two days of demonstrations in Pakokku, in central Myanmar, monks held around 20 government officials captive for several hours after the security forces had forcibly dispersed some 300–400 monks, detaining around 10 and injuring several. The All Burma Monks' Alliance (ABMA), a previously unknown group, made a series of demands to the SPDC—an apology for the force used in Pakokku, a reduction in commodity and fuel prices, the release of all political prisoners and those detained for participating in the recent protests, and the initiation of a dialogue with pro-democracy forces—threatening to withdraw all religious services from the authorities if they did not comply by 17 September. The SPDC accused the NLD and 'external groups' of instigating the unrest. Some of the marches were allowed to proceed peacefully, but tear gas was used to disperse a rally of about 1,000 monks and other citizens in the western town of Sittwe. Meanwhile, with the monks' demands unfulfilled, daily marches commenced in Yangon. The ABMA issued a statement describing the military Government as 'the enemy of the people' and pledging to continue protesting until the junta was removed from office. On 22 September Suu Kyi made a brief public appearance when the monks were permitted to pass her residence. On the same day up to 10,000 monks were reported to have marched in Mandalay. On 24 September a mass protest in Yangon was attended by an estimated 50,000–100,000 monks and civilians, including NLD leaders, while demonstrations also took place in more than 20 other towns.

In response, on 26 September 2007 the SPDC imposed a night-time curfew in Yangon and Mandalay, attempted to enforced the ban on gatherings of more than five people and deployed armed troops on the streets. When up to 10,000 monks and other protesters defied government warnings to halt the marches, troops fired live ammunition, reportedly killing five people. Some 200 monks were later reported to have been detained in overnight operations against several monasteries, during which many were allegedly beaten. The Government claimed that 10 people had died in the violence (later raising this figure to 15), but diplomats and witnesses reported that the death toll was much higher, with some estimating that up to 200 had been killed. At an emergency meeting of the UN Security Council, China, Myanmar's closest ally, rejected a US proposal to consider the imposition of sanctions against the Myanma authorities. By the end of the month the uprising had been largely quashed, with many monks in detention. During October the security forces continued to arrest those suspected of involvement in the protests, and reports emerged of ill-treatment and torture in detention centres. In December the UN Special Rapporteur on the situation of human rights in Myanmar, Paulo Sérgio Pinheiro, claimed that at least 31 people had died during the unrest and that 3,000–4,000 people had been arrested in September and October, 500–1,000 of whom were still in detention; according to the security forces, only 80 people, including 21 monks, remained in custody at this time. Meanwhile, the curfew in Yangon and Mandalay was lifted.

UN envoy Gambari visited Myanmar in late September 2007, initially holding discussions with acting Prime Minister Thein Sein and other government ministers, as well as with Suu Kyi; in early October he was finally permitted to meet Than Shwe and Maung Aye. The SPDC agreed to Gambari's recommendation that a government official be appointed to enter into dialogue with Suu Kyi, assigning this role (Minister of Relations with Aung San Suu Kyi) to the Deputy Minister of Labour, Aung Kyi. In mid-October the UN Security Council unanimously adopted a statement deploring the use of violence against peaceful demonstrators in Myanmar, and calling for meaningful dialogue between the Government and Suu Kyi, and the early release of all political prisoners and remaining detainees.

Thein Sein was formally appointed Prime Minister in October 2007, following Soe Win's death earlier that month, and was replaced as First Secretary of the SPDC by Lt-Gen. Thiha Thura Tin Aung Myint Oo. At the same time Aung Kyi was promoted to the position of Minister of Labour, while retaining responsibility for liaising with Suu Kyi. On the following day Aung Kyi and Suu Kyi held their first talks.

In early November 2007 the Myanma Government announced the expulsion of Charles Petrie, the most senior UN official resident in the country. Petrie had recently publicly linked the pro-democracy protests to economic hardship and a 'deteriorating humanitarian situation'. Shortly afterwards Gambari arrived for a further visit, during which he held discussions with Thein Sein and Suu Kyi. Later in the month a second meeting took place between Aung Kyi and Suu Kyi, who was also permitted to meet other members of the NLD for the first time in more than three years. In December the Government announced that it had granted amnesty to 8,585 prisoners since mid-November to mark the conclusion of the National Convention, although it was reported that only 10 were political detainees. Suu Kyi held two further rounds of talks with Aung Kyi in January 2008, and was also permitted to meet NLD colleagues again at the end of the month. In late January the human rights organization Amnesty International claimed that 96 pro-democracy activists had been arrested since November 2007, increasing the total number in detention to 1,850, of whom 700 were accused of participating in the August and September protests.

In February 2008 the SPDC unexpectedly announced that a constitutional referendum would be held in May, followed by multi-party elections in 2010. Chief Justice Aung Toe subsequently confirmed that his commission had completed the draft Constitution. Gambari returned to Myanmar in March 2008, meeting Suu Kyi and several government officials. However, no apparent progress was made during the visit, with the Government rejecting Gambari's proposal that independent observers be allowed to monitor the forthcoming referendum and refusing to consider amending the draft Constitution to allow Suu Kyi to contest elections. Suu Kyi reportedly refused to meet with Gambari during the envoy's visit to Myanmar in August, arousing speculation about her dissatisfaction with the pace of developments. The newly appointed UN Special Rapporteur on the situation of human rights in Myanmar, Tomás Ojea Quintana, also paid a visit in that month.

In May 2008 the devastating Cyclone Nargis struck southern Myanmar. Yangon and four other regions, including the Ayeyarwady (Irrawaddy) Delta, were declared disaster areas. Despite the Government's restrictions on international aid efforts (including refusing entry to foreign aid workers), some provisions supplied by the UN and foreign donors were eventually allowed into the country. By late June the official death toll had risen to more than 84,500. However, the ICRC reckoned that the number of fatalities might be as high as 128,000, while the UN estimated that 2.5m. people had been affected by the cyclone.

Meanwhile, the text of the draft Constitution, which was published in April 2008, included the changing of the country's official name to the 'Republic of the Union of Myanmar'. Also enshrined in the draft was the ultimate establishment of a multi-party democracy. Nevertheless, as proposed in the 1994 sessions of the National Convention, 25% of the seats in the bicameral legislature were to be allocated to representatives of the military nominated by the Commander-in-Chief of the Armed Forces. Furthermore, the Commander-in-Chief of the Armed Forces was also to designate the government ministers responsible for defence, security, home affairs and border affairs, and was to assume executive, legislative and judicial power in the event of a state of emergency being declared, while Suu Kyi's marriage to a foreign citizen would disqualify her from contesting the presidency. Despite the widespread destruction caused by Cyclone Nargis, which prompted the Government to postpone the constitutional referendum in the affected regions, the poll proceeded as scheduled in other areas on 10 May 2008. According to official reports, turnout was high, at 99%, with 92.4% of voters endorsing the new Constitution, thereby completing the ratification process; however, observers remained sceptical.

In September 2008 the junta announced a large-scale amnesty involving as many as 9,000 detainees. Among those released was Win Tin, a senior political activist and founding member of the NLD who had been imprisoned for 19 years; however, in October Ohn Kyaing, another veteran NLD member, was detained. This was followed by the culmination of dozens of trials that had begun in July, with the sentencing of more than 100 activists and dissidents in November. Many defendants received substantial prison terms, some as long as 65 years. Those convicted included senior members of the '88 Generation', the NLD and monks' groups who were accused of involvement in the September 2007 uprising.

In May 2009, shortly before her current term of house arrest was due to expire, Suu Kyi was taken to Insein Prison, following an unauthorized visit to her home by an uninvited US citizen, John Yettaw, who had gained access by swimming across the adjacent lake. She was tried on charges of violating the conditions of her house arrest, and in August was convicted and sentenced to three years' imprisonment with hard labour, although this was commuted to 18 months' house arrest. The verdict was widely criticized by the international community. Yettaw, meanwhile, was sentenced to seven years' imprisonment; however, he was subsequently released and allowed to return to the USA. Suu Kyi's supporters claimed that the Yettaw incident had been exploited by the military junta as a pretext for further prolonging the opposition leader's detention. Opposition leader Tin Oo was finally released from house arrest in February 2010.

The 2010 legislative elections

In March 2010 the junta approved new electoral laws in advance of the forthcoming legislative elections, which, *inter alia*, prohibited anyone with a criminal conviction from belonging to a political party, a rule that was widely interpreted as being intended to force the NLD to expel Suu Kyi from its ranks. The junta formally annulled the NLD's victory in the 1990 general election, stating that the result was invalid since the poll had been conducted under legislation repealed by the newly enacted laws. Divisions emerged within the NLD regarding whether the party should expel Suu Kyi, Tin Oo and other members with criminal convictions in order to be able to contest the elections. Despite some members contending that the NLD's absence from the polling would effectively lead to a one-party political system in which the policies of the military junta would remain unchecked, at the end of March the NLD announced that it would not be registering for the elections, a decision that served severely to compromise the credibility of the poll from the perspective of the international community.

In April 2010 about 20 senior members of the ruling junta, including Prime Minister Thein Sein, resigned from their military positions in what was widely interpreted as a move to circumvent the restriction, to 25% of the total, of the number of legislative seats that were to be allocated to representatives of the military in the imminent elections. Thein Sein applied to register a new political party, the Union Solidarity and Development Party (USDP), of which he assumed the leadership.

In July 2010 it was announced that the USDA, the mass movement formed in September 1993 to establish a civilian front through which the armed forces could exercise control, had disbanded and that its assets had been transferred to the USDP, prompting widespread criticism from critics of the Government, who argued that the assets belonged to the state and that their transfer to the USDP afforded the party an unfair advantage. Also in July 2010 Suu Kyi's former assistant, Win

Htein, was released from prison, having served his sentence of 14 years' imprisonment for conspiracy to destabilize the country.

A date for the elections was finally announced by the junta in August 2010: the first legislative poll in 20 years was to be held on 7 November, one week prior to the scheduled expiry of the detention under house arrest of Suu Kyi. In September the Union Election Commission (UEC—created in March and chaired by a retired army major-general) announced that 37 parties had successfully registered to participate in the elections. Not unexpectedly, the USDP was among those approved, as were the NUP (which had contested the 1990 elections) and the National Democratic Force (a splinter group established in April by a group of 25 former NLD members who did wish to participate in the elections and chaired by Than Nyein); many of the remainder were small, ethnic-based parties contesting a limited number of regional seats. The UEC also announced the formal dissolution of 10 parties, five of which had been dissolved owing to non-registration, including the NLD (the first public confirmation of its suspected dissolution), the Shan Nationalities League for Democracy, which had also performed well in the 1990 elections, and the Union Pa-O National Organization; the remaining five (predominantly ethnic-based) parties were disbanded owing to their alleged non-compliance with regulations governing the registration of candidates. The application of the Kachin State Progressive Party (KSPP) to register for the polls was rejected by the UEC on the grounds that the founding leader of the KSPP, Dr Manam Tu Ja, was a former Vice-President of the Kachin Independence Organization (see *Insurgency and Dissidence*). Also in mid-September the UEC announced the cancellation of voting in about 300 villages across five states that were deemed to be 'troubled', claiming that voting in those areas would not be free or fair; at least 1.5m. people were thus excluded from voting, leading to speculation that the SPDC was endeavouring to disenfranchise Myanmar's ethnic population.

Strict campaigning restrictions governed the official electoral campaign period, which began in late September 2010. Registered parties were each granted 15 minutes of broadcasting time in which to proclaim their electoral platforms on state television and radio (although full scripts were required to be submitted to the UEC for prior approval). In October the SPDC announced the introduction of a new national flag and anthem, and changed the country's official name from the Union of Myanmar to the Republic of the Union of Myanmar, in accordance with the provisions of the 2008 Constitution.

The elections to both chambers of the Pyidaungsu Hluttaw, and to 14 state and regional assemblies, were held, as scheduled, on 7 November 2010. A total of 3,069 candidates from the 37 registered parties contested more than 1,100 seats. There were widespread allegations of voting irregularities committed by supporters of the USDP. The UEC subsequently claimed that voter turnout had totalled 77% of the electorate; however, many independent sources suggested that the actual figure was considerably lower than this, with some claiming a turnout of only 30%. According to official results released by the UEC on 17 November, the USDP secured 259 seats of the 330 contested seats in the 440-member Pyithu Hluttaw; the USDP's closest rival, the Shan Nationalities Democratic Party (SNDP), won just 18, while the NUP received 12, the Rakhine Nationalities Development Party (RNDP) nine and the National Democratic Force eight. Other, mostly ethnic-based, parties collectively accounted for a further 19 seats, with one seat won by an independent; the four remaining seats were unfilled at this time. A similar pattern emerged in the electoral results for the Amyotha Hluttaw, as well as for the seven state and seven regional assemblies. Of the 168 contested seats in the Amyotha Hluttaw, the USDP won 129 seats; the RNDP took seven and the NUP five, while the National Democratic Force, the All Mon Region Democracy Party (AMRDP) and the Chin Progressive Party won four seats each, and the SNDP and the Phalon-Sawaw Democratic Party three seats each. In total, the USDP took 882 of the 1,154 contested seats, while the second-placed NUP won 63. The National Democratic Force was placed joint sixth overall—tied with the AMRDP—with just 16 seats, and Chairman Than Nyein denounced the elections as 'absolutely not free and fair'. Many losing opposition candidates subsequently claimed that the UEC-sanctioned procedures to file a challenge against the results, including a substantial payment for each individual challenge, were designed to confuse and discourage would-be complainants.

On 13 November 2010, two days after her (largely symbolic) final appeal against her detention under house arrest had been rejected, Suu Kyi was finally released, her latest detention order having expired. Thousands of supporters gathered outside the NLD headquarters in Yangon to hear Suu Kyi's first public address since her release. At a press conference, which foreign journalists were allowed to attend, Suu Kyi questioned the legitimacy of the recent elections. The dissolution of the NLD was upheld on appeal by the Supreme Court in January 2011. Meanwhile, in November 2010 new legislation was introduced allowing the Government to draft men and women into the armed forces for a period of two to three years, or for five years during times of national crisis.

In mid-January 2011 Gen. Than Shwe appointed 110 military representatives to the Pyithu Hluttaw, 56 to the Amyotha Hluttaw and 222 to the state and regional assemblies, in accordance with the constitutional quotas. On 31 January the Pyidaungsu Hluttaw convened for the first time, marking the formal completion of the transfer of power from the military junta to an elected parliament under the new Constitution. Legislation announced by state media in November 2010 imposed strict regulations on legislators' conduct during parliamentary sessions: although freedom of speech was to be allowed, words deemed to represent a risk to 'national security and unity' were prohibited while protests in parliament were to be punishable by up to two years' imprisonment; legislators were required to submit parliamentary questions 10 days in advance of a meeting; and media reporting (other than by state media) on parliamentary proceedings was banned. During the first parliamentary session Shwe Mann, formerly Army Chief of Staff, was elected Speaker of the Pyithu Hluttaw, while Khin Aung Myint, a former Minister of Culture, was elected Speaker of the Amyotha Hluttaw.

On 1 February 2011 the Pyidaungsu Hluttaw nominated five legislators for three vice-presidential positions; the three candidates selected would become presidential candidates. Among the five nominees were the outgoing Prime Minister, Thein Sein, and former First Secretary of the SPDC Lt-Gen. Tin Aung Myint Oo; the remaining three nominees were members of ethnic minorities, which was widely interpreted as a conciliatory gesture on the part of the USDP legislators, amid increased tensions in the ethnic border areas in the aftermath of the elections (see *Insurgency and Dissidence*). On 3 February the Pyithu Hluttaw voted for Thein Sein as its presidential candidate, while the Amyotha Hluttaw elected Dr Sai Mauk Kham, a little-known USDP member of the Shan ethnic minority group; Tin Aung Myint Oo, as the vice-presidential nominee of the military representatives in parliament, was automatically approved as the military's presidential candidate. Thein Sein was elected President of Myanmar on 4 February, securing 408 votes; Tin Aung Myint Oo, who won 171 votes, and Sai Mauk Kham, with 75 votes, were confirmed as Vice-Presidents.

Recent developments: reform under President Thein Sein

On 30 March 2011 Thein Sein was inaugurated as the country's President, the first session of the Pyithu Hluttaw was formally concluded, and the SPDC was dissolved, signalling the formal completion of the transfer of power from the military junta and President. Than Shwe was replaced as Commander-in-Chief of the Armed Forces by Gen. Min Aung Hlaing. The 30-member incoming Cabinet was dominated by former military officers who had retired in order to contest the 2010 legislative elections, including about a dozen who had been ministers in the outgoing administration. On 31 March 2011 state media formally announced the creation of an 11-member National Defence and Security Council (NDSC), the establishment of which was provided for under the terms of the 2008 Constitution. Membership of the NDSC comprised the President, the two Vice-Presidents, the Commander-in-Chief and Vice-Commander-in-Chief of the Armed Forces, the Ministers of Defence, of Foreign Affairs, of Home Affairs and of Border Affairs, and the Speakers of the two legislative chambers.

Meanwhile, in February 2011 Than Shwe announced the creation of an eight-member State Supreme Council (SSC), which he himself was to head, appearing to cast doubt on the commitment to genuine democratic reform in Myanmar. Unlike the NDSC, the SSC was not mandated by the 2008 Constitution, and was to be charged with advising the new legislature on all matters of national importance, including defence and national security. The development appeared to answer ongoing speculation as to the future role of Than Shwe, who many observers had expected to be named President; as head of the SSC, Than

Shwe was expected to remain effectively the most powerful figure in the country. Other members of the SSC included former Vice-Chairman of the SPDC Maung Aye and the Speaker of the Pyithu Hluttaw, Shwe Mann.

President Thein Sein signed a general amnesty 'on humanitarian grounds' in May 2011, providing for the release of nearly 15,000 prisoners. However, human rights groups condemned the limited scope of the amnesty, under the terms of which death sentences were commuted to life imprisonment and prison terms were reduced by one year, noting that very few of the country's estimated 2,200 political prisoners were among those being released. Critics contested that the amnesty was merely a ploy calculated to improve the image of the new administration of Thein Sein without making any real civil liberties concessions.

In June 2011 the Government ordered the NLD, which remained an outlawed organization, to desist from all political activities. In early July Suu Kyi made her first trip outside of Yangon since her release from house arrest, visiting the city of Bagan, in Mandalay. The trip, which, although non-political in nature, was widely perceived as a test of the limits on Suu Kyi's freedom, passed off without incident, and later in July Suu Kyi was granted her first formal audience with a member of the new Cabinet, her erstwhile dialogue partner Aung Kyi. Signs of a relaxation in the Government's stance towards Suu Kyi became further evident in August, when she was allowed to make her first political trip outside of Yangon. During her visit to Bago (80 km north of Yangon), hundreds of supporters gathered to listen as Suu Kyi appealed for national unity and many thousands more lined the streets to cheer her passing convoy. Later in the month Suu Kyi made her first visit to Nay Pyi Taw, at the invitation of the Government, in order to attend a government workshop on economic development. During Suu Kyi's visit she also held talks with Thein Sein at the presidential palace—the first time that the two had met in person; in a highly symbolic gesture, the President received her underneath a large portrait of her assassinated father, Gen. Aung San. In a subsequent radio interview, Suu Kyi declared her belief that Thein Sein was sincere in wanting to implement reform, but warned that it remained too early to ascertain how far the reforms would go and to what extent they would affect real change in the lives of the Myanma population.

The Myanma Government's commitment to genuine democratic reform was further called into question in September 2011, following the conviction of a journalist employed by the dissident broadcasting station, the Democratic Voice of Burma (DVB), on the charge of disseminating material online that could threaten the security of the Government. Sithu Zeya, who was already serving an eight-year prison term after photographing the scene of a minor bomb attack in Yangon in April 2010, was sentenced to a further 10 years' imprisonment. According to the DVB, 16 other journalists employed by the station, which remained fiercely critical of the Government, were in detention in Myanmar at mid-2011.

Amid criticism of Sithu Zeya's conviction from human rights groups, legislation providing for greater media freedom and the establishment of a self-regulating Press Council had been drafted by early 2012, although there were subsequent delays in presenting it to the legislature. Nevertheless, increased access to the internet was reported during the latter half of 2011, and journalists did appear to have been afforded greater scope to cover formerly prohibited subjects, including the activities of Suu Kyi. In November legislation allowing the right to protest received parliamentary approval, although permission would need to be requested at least five days in advance of planned demonstrations, which remained banned at government offices, factories and hospitals, and staging a protest without permission would be punishable by one year's imprisonment. Meanwhile, in September the Government announced the creation of a National Human Rights Commission, in a development that was cautiously welcomed by domestic and international rights groups.

A presidential amnesty providing for the release of a further 6,359 prisoners, thought to include around 200 political prisoners, was announced in October 2011. Another presidential amnesty was announced in January 2012, providing for the release of an additional 651 prisoners, including, significantly, Sithu Zeya and others of the country's most prominent political prisoners. Upon his release, Sithu Zeya claimed to have been subjected to physical abuse in prison. He also questioned the intent behind the recent series of reforms implemented by the Thein Sein administration, asserting that the authorities sought only to placate external powers in order to secure foreign investment and an easing of international sanctions.

In its annual report published in January 2012, US-based organization Human Rights Watch acknowledged that the Myanma Government had made 'some significant moves' towards democratization, but stated that the human rights situation in the country had nevertheless remained 'dire' during 2011. Although welcoming the release of a number of political prisoners during the year, the report noted that many more remained in detention, while freedom of expression, association and assembly continued to be 'severely curtailed'. The report also indicated that ethnic violence had escalated, with a number of ceasefires agreed between the Myanma army and ethnic armed groups being broken during the year, and claimed that the army continued to be responsible for indiscriminate attacks and other abuses against civilians in conflict areas, including forced labour, extrajudicial killings, sexual violence and the use of 'human shields'.

Meanwhile, in mid-November 2011 the NLD announced that it was to seek re-registration as a political party with a view to contesting by-elections (subsequently called for 1 April 2012) for 45 seats, including those that had been left vacant by ministerial appointments. The announcement followed the adoption by parliament earlier in the month of a number of amendments to the electoral law, including, crucially, the removal of the clause barring anyone convicted of a crime from membership of a political organization. Parliament also approved legislation permitting, for the first time, the holding of peaceful demonstrations (subject to prior permission being granted by the authorities). The NLD's re-registration application was formally approved in mid-December and in the same month Suu Kyi confirmed her intention to stand as a candidate in the forthcoming by-elections. In January 2012 Suu Kyi was appointed as the NLD's new Chairman, while Tin Oo, hitherto NLD Vice-Chairman, was appointed Chairman of the party's newly formed Patron Committee, which was expected to serve in a primarily advisory capacity.

The NLD won a comprehensive victory in the 45 parliamentary by-elections in April 2012, winning 43 of the 44 seats it contested, including 37 seats in the 440-member lower chamber. International observers approved the conduct of the by-elections, which were regarded by many as a vital test of the Government's commitment to democratic reform, although parliament remained dominated by the military and its allies. Parliament convened with its newly elected members at the end of April, although the NLD deputies, including Suu Kyi, initially refused to take their seats in protest at the wording of the parliamentary oath, which included a commitment to 'safeguard' the Constitution. The NLD had campaigned for constitutional reform, contending that the Constitution, drafted under military rule, was undemocratic since it effectively preserved power for the armed forces. The NLD requested that the wording of the parliamentary oath be altered, substituting 'respect' for 'safeguard'. However, the NLD deputies subsequently agreed to swear the existing parliamentary oath, taking their seats in early May. Tin Aung Myint Oo, who was regarded as an opponent of political reform, submitted his resignation as Vice-President the following day, citing health reasons; he was replaced by the former navy chief Nyan Tun in August.

Meanwhile, having been given a passport in May 2012 for the first time in 24 years, Suu Kyi, in her new de facto role as ambassador for Myanmar, visited a number of countries during the remainder of that year, including Thailand, Switzerland, Ireland, France, Norway (where she accepted the Nobel Peace Prize awarded to her in 1991), the UK, India and the USA. Her willingness to leave Myanmar indicated the confidence that she now appeared to hold in the administration of Thein Sein that she would be permitted to return. In each country that she visited Suu Kyi requested assistance in the furtherance of democratic reform in Myanmar and the genuine empowerment of its people, and warned against complacency and 'reckless optimism'. In her first parliamentary statement, in July, Suu Kyi demanded the introduction of legislation to protect the rights of Myanmar's ethnic minorities, although she did not specifically mention the Muslim Rohingyas in her speech.

A further sign of increasing democratization in Myanmar was the series of street demonstrations conducted in Mandalay and a number of other towns in May 2012 in protest against chronic electricity shortages. The demonstrations were the largest to be held since those organized by the Buddhist monks in 2007. While not acting forcibly to suppress the demonstrations, the authorities warned the protesters to remain within the law and stressed that permission should be sought prior to the staging of any public gatherings. In August 2012 the Government announced the abolition of pre-publication censorship of the media (excluding films), although strict regulations remained in place over what could be included in reports. The following month an interim Press Council was established, headed by a retired senior judge and also including eminent journalists. In December the Government announced that from April 2013 the publication of privately owned newspapers would be permitted for the first time in nearly 50 years.

President Thein Sein carried out a cabinet reorganization in late August/early September 2012; among the notable changes was the appointment of the first female cabinet minister (Dr Daw Myat Ohn Khin, as Minister of Social Welfare, Relief and Resettlement) since 1948 and the replacement of the prominent hardliner, Kyaw Hsan, as Minister of Information by the more moderate Aung Kyi. A few days later the Government appeared further to distance itself from the repressive policies of the past by removing the names of more than 2,000 people from a blacklist drawn up over the preceding decades by the military authorities of those banned from entering or leaving the country on the grounds that they were deemed to pose a security threat. Among those taken off the list (which had consequently been reduced in size to around 4,000 names) were former US Secretary of State Madeleine Albright, the late Philippine President Corazon Aquino, Suu Kyi's two sons, human rights officials and numerous foreign journalists. In a sign of the growing authority of parliament, in early September the Pyithu Hluttaw approved the impeachment of all nine judges of the Constitutional Tribunal (a move that had been approved by the upper house the previous month), following an attempt by the court earlier that year to limit the power of parliamentary committees and commissions. President Thein Sein accepted the subsequent resignations of the judges. Later in September the NCGUB announced its dissolution, on the grounds that the country no longer needed a government-in-exile and in order to promote national reconciliation. A few days before President Thein Sein's scheduled visit to the UN in New York, USA, where he was to seek international support for his programme of reforms, in mid-September the authorities announced the release under a presidential amnesty of more than 500 prisoners, including reportedly more than 50 political detainees. The exact number of political prisoners who remained in custody was still not known (although estimated at 240–300). A further 452 prisoners were released in November, shortly before the historic visit to Myanmar of US President Barack Obama, yet there were no reports of any political detainees being among those set free. On the actual day of Obama's arrival in Myanmar, however, the authorities announced the release of around 40 political prisoners.

In the wake of its overwhelming defeat by the NLD in the by-elections in April 2012, the USDP held its first ever conference in October with the aim of regrouping and drawing up new strategies to prepare for the next general election (due to be held in 2015). Although many had expected the Speaker of the lower house, Shwe Mann, to be assigned the role, Thein Sein was reappointed as Chairman of the governing party. A few days later Thein Sein broke new ground by giving his first news conference in Myanmar. The process of political liberalization continued in January 2013 when the Government abolished a 25-year-old ban on public gatherings of more than five people. Moreover, in February the Government announced plans to establish a committee to review the detention of all remaining political prisoners.

Meanwhile, as the process of liberalization and the easing of restrictive legislation advanced so too did the concepts of political mobilization and public protest. A major grievance that came increasingly to the fore during 2011–12 was public anger over land seizures carried out under military rule. In November 2012 more than 50 demonstrators were reportedly injured when security forces used water cannon and tear gas to break up a sit-in protest (launched earlier that year) against the planned expansion of a huge copper mine in Monywa in the north-west region of Sagaing, which was funded by the Chinese Shandong Wanbao Group. The protesters, who included Buddhist monks, environmentalists and political activists, claimed that local farmers had been forced to accept an agreement in 2010 according to which they were obliged to give up their land in exchange for financial compensation and new housing. In response, the Government asserted that the deal had been voluntary and that only a small minority of farmers had rejected it. Following the

staging of rallies across the country in December 2012 by Buddhist monks in protest against the authorities' crackdown at the mine the previous month, Suu Kyi was appointed to head an official inquiry into the Government's actions and the future of the mine. In February 2013 a report compiled by Myanma lawyers and the US-based Justice Trust claimed that the police had fired military-issue white phosphorous grenades to disperse the protest at the mine in November 2012; these allegations appeared to be corroborated by the fact that many of those injured suffered serious burns. In March 2013 the findings of the investigative commission headed by Suu Kyi confirmed that smoke bombs containing phosphorus had been used against the protesters, but recommended that work on the mine expansion project proceed as planned. However, further clashes between police and protesting farmers who were refusing to surrender their land took place in the following month. In an attempt to assuage public opposition to the expansion of the mine, in July the Myanma authorities agreed new terms with Shandong Wanbao Group, giving the Myanma Government 51% of the venture's revenue (with 30% assigned to the Chinese company and the remaining 19% to the military-owned Union of Myanmar Economic Holdings).

At the NLD's first ever congress, held in Yangon in March 2013, Suu Kyi was unanimously re-elected as the party's leader and the executive committee was enlarged from seven to 15 members. Later that month, in what was viewed as a sign of the growing rapprochement between the opposition and the military, Suu Kyi attended Armed Forces' Day in Nay Pyi Taw for the first time. Also in March the Pyidaungsu Hluttaw agreed to set up a parliamentary joint commission, comprising members of the ruling parties, the opposition and the military, to review the Constitution; among the issues to be covered was reportedly that of the question of greater autonomy for the country's ethnic minorities. In an apparent indication of the Government's willingness further to open up the national political arena to ethnic groups, in October an application made by the senior Kachin leader Dr Manam Tu Ja to register the Kachin State Democracy Party as an official political party, was approved by the UEC. A previous attempt by Tu Ja, in September 2010, to register a Kachin organization as a political party had proved unsuccessful (see *The 2010 legislative elections*). Meanwhile, an amnesty providing for the release of 93 prisoners, reported to include around 56 political prisoners, was announced in April 2013, as was the Government's decision to expand the teaching of ethnic languages in state schools. During his first official visit to the UK, in July, President Thein Sein stated that all political prisoners would be released by the end of the year and that all ongoing trials and investigations connected with the prisoners would be halted. Despite the release of more than 150 such detainees over the next few months and a claim made by the President's Office at the end of December that there were no longer any political prisoners in Myanmar, campaigners believed that some 40 remained incarcerated. Earlier that month it was reported that, as part of the ongoing relaxation of restrictions on the media, the Government had given permission to four international news agencies, including the British Broadcasting Corporation, to establish bureaux in Myanmar. However, given the continuing arrests of journalists and political activists in the first half of 2014, many observers remained sceptical of the Government's professed commitment to democratic reform. The sentencing in September of the high-profile pro-democracy activist Htin Kyaw to at least 11 years' imprisonment on charges of disturbing public order through staging a series of anti-Government protests was widely denounced by rights groups both at home and abroad. Moreover, the publication in May of four bills aimed at restricting interfaith marriage, birth rates and polygamy and imposing stringent regulations on religious conversion prompted accusations by local religious organizations and the UN of discrimination and of attempts by the authorities to stifle religious freedom; the draft legislation was presented to parliament, having been approved by the President, in December. The first of the four bills to be voted on by parliament, concerning population control, was approved in April 2015. Most controversially, the legislation would allow local governments to request a presidential order limiting women in their areas to having one child every three years.

Meanwhile, in an unexpected development, in early January 2014, during a televised address to the nation, President Thein Sein appeared to indicate his support for the implementation of a constitutional amendment to enable Suu Kyi to contest the next presidential election by stating that he did not approve of legislation that barred anyone from standing for the presidency. Yet, despite the President's apparent stance, the proposed constitutional reforms presented by the 109-member parliamentary Constitutional Review Joint Committee (which had been established in July 2013 and included only seven representatives of the NLD) in late January 2014 did not include plans to change either the constitutional clause that made Suu Kyi ineligible to hold the presidency—Article 59(f)—or those that guaranteed the military an entrenched role in politics through its allocation of 25% of the seats in the legislature and its consequent effective right of veto over constitutional amendments (the majority of which required parliamentary approval of at least 75%)—Articles 109 and 436, respectively. However, the proposed changes did include the devolution of certain administrative powers from the central Government to the country's ethnic minorities (with the notable exception of within the armed forces). In February 2014 parliament appointed a Committee for the Implementation of 2008 Constitution Amendment to draft recommendations for constitutional reform no later than six months prior to the holding of legislative and presidential elections scheduled for late 2015. In June 2014 the 31-member Committee, which included 14 representatives of the USDP and seven from the military, but only two representatives of the NLD, voted to retain Article 59(f) in its existing form—banning those with non-Burmese partners or children from contesting the presidency—but proposed amending Article 436 so that changes to most sections of the Constitution would require approval by a parliamentary majority of at least two-thirds rather than the existing three-quarters. A national petition demanding an end to the military's effective power of veto in parliament had been launched by the NLD and the 88 Generation student group in May; by the end of July the NLD claimed to have collected some 5m. signatures. The announcement in October of the release of another 3,000 prisoners (including former military intelligence officers who were reportedly close associates of former Prime Minister Khin Nyunt—who had been released from house arrest in 2012) and the Government's holding of unprecedented round-table talks with the military, ethnic groups and main opposition organizations in the same month, reportedly to discuss the peace process, national reconciliation and political reform, notably took place shortly before US President Obama's second visit to Myanmar (which was hosting the ASEAN summit). In February 2015 Thein Sein approved legislation to permit the holding of a referendum on the proposed constitutional amendments. Six-party talks on the reforms took place in April between Thein Sein, Suu Kyi, the Commander-in-Chief of the Armed Forces, Sr Gen. Min Aung Hlaing, both parliamentary Speakers and a representative of ethnic minorities, legislator Aye Maung. Further discussions were planned.

Insurgency and Dissidence

After Burma gained independence in 1948, various groups conducted armed insurgency campaigns against government forces. The most effective of the ethnic-based insurgency groups was the Karen (Kayin) National Union (KNU), founded in 1948, which led a protracted campaign for the establishment of an independent state for the Karen ethnic group (restyled Kayin in the transliteration changes of 1989), partly through the activities of its military wing, the Karen (Kayin) National Liberation Army (KNLA). The KNU was a member of the National Democratic Front (NDF), an anti-Government organization that at one time comprised 11 ethnic minority groups—including Kachin, Karenni (Kayinni), Mon, Shan, Pa-O, Palaung, Wa, Arakanese (Rakhine) and Lahu parties—formed in 1975 (by five groups, originally) with the aim of making Burma a federal union. By May 1986 the various minority groups in the NDF had agreed to relinquish their individual demands for autonomy, in favour of a unified demand for a federal system of government. At the same time, the Communist Party of Burma (CPB), which had gained control of significant areas in northern Burma, withdrew its demand for a 'one-party' government and entered into an alliance with the NDF. At the second NDF Congress, in June 1987, various leadership changes removed all KNU representatives from senior NDF positions. The new NDF leaders advocated the establishment of autonomous, ethnic-based states within a Burmese union. In November 1988 22 anti-Government groups, led by members of the NDF, formed the Democratic Alliance of Burma (DAB); the KNU leader, Gen. Bo Mya, was elected President.

In April 1989 dissatisfaction with the CPB leadership led to a mutiny by Wa tribespeople, who captured the CPB headquarters, and the party's leaders were forced into exile in the People's

Republic of China. The leaders of the mutiny subsequently accepted SLORC proposals for the erstwhile forces of the CPB army to become government-controlled militia forces in exchange for supplies of rice, financial support and development aid. The former CPB troops agreed to use their main forces against the 25,000-strong rebel separatist Mong Tai Army (formerly the Shan United Army), whose leader, Khun Sa, controlled much of the drug trade in the 'Golden Triangle', the world's major opium-producing area, where the borders of Myanmar, Laos and Thailand meet. The SLORC also approached members of the NDF, and was successful in securing agreements with the Shan State Progressive Party (SSPP), also known as the Shan State Army—North) in September 1989, and with the Pa-O National Organization and the Palaung State Liberation Organization in March and May 1991, respectively. At the third NDF Congress in July, these three movements were expelled, reducing the NDF's membership to eight organizations; Nai Shwe Kyin, the leader of the New Mon State Party (NMSP), was elected as its new President.

Meanwhile, intense fighting between government and rebel forces continued throughout 1989–92. The Kachin Independence Organization (KIO) appeared to have signed a peace agreement with the Government in April 1993, but, owing to its attempts to persuade other members of the DAB to enter discussions with the SLORC, the ceasefire was not announced until October. The agreement was ratified in Yangon in February 1994. The KIO was suspended from the DAB in October 1993 for negotiating separately with the SLORC; however, under Thai pressure, the DAB policy of negotiating as a front was subsequently unofficially abandoned.

In May 1994 the Karenni (Kayinni) National People's Liberation Front concluded a ceasefire agreement with the SLORC, reportedly the 11th insurgent group to do so. This was followed by the declaration of ceasefires by the Kayan New Land Party and the Shan State Nationalities Liberation Organization in July and October, respectively. In December government forces launched a new offensive against the KNU, capturing its headquarters at Manerplaw in January 1995 (and forcing many hundreds of KNU fighters across the border into Thailand). The virtual defeat of the KNU forces was attributed to their reportedly severe lack of ammunition and funds and also to the recent defection from the Christian-led KNU of a mainly Buddhist faction, which established itself as the Democratic Karen (Kayin) Buddhist Army (DKBA). The DKBA, which had accounted for about 10% of the strength of the KNLA, allegedly supported the government forces in their offensive. In February the Myanma army captured the KNU's last stronghold, and in the following month Bo Mya resigned as the Commander-in-Chief of the KNLA (although he remained the leader of the KNU). In March the KNU declared a unilateral ceasefire, with the aim of initiating negotiations with the SLORC. Earlier in the month the Karenni (Kayinni) National Progress Party (KNPP) reportedly became the 14th ethnic insurgent group to abandon its armed struggle against the SLORC. This agreement collapsed in June, however, as government troops entered areas designated in the accord to be under KNPP control. In August 5,000 troops were dispatched to suppress the KNPP rebellion. However, the KNPP continued its armed struggle, with support from the All-Burma Students Democratic Front.

In 1997–98 the DKBA, allegedly supported by government forces, launched a number of attacks on Kayin refugee camps in Thailand, prompting renewed fighting between the KNU and government forces, and leading to the forcible relocation of Kayin away from KNU bases in Myanmar and across the border into Thailand. The Thai armed forces denied collusion with the Myanma troops in the process of forced repatriations of Kayin refugees. In April 1999 the KNU confirmed the deaths of seven members of a group of 13 government officials whom they had abducted in February; the remaining six were said to have been released unharmed. In January 2000 Bo Mya resigned as KNU Chairman owing to ailing health, and was replaced by the former General Secretary of the organization, Saw Ba Thin; Bo Mya assumed the vice-chairmanship. Talks were held between the KNU and the State Peace and Development Council (SPDC) in February–March but proved inconclusive. In late 2000 the Government began to use 'scorched-earth' tactics to deprive the KNU of its support base, displacing up to 30,000 people in eastern Myanmar.

Meanwhile, in December 1993 the SLORC initiated a major offensive against Khun Sa's Mong Tai Army encampments on the Thai border. In May 1994 Khun Sa proclaimed an independent Shan State, of which he declared himself 'President'. In the same month fighting escalated between government forces and the Mong Tai Army near the Thai border, with heavy losses reported on both sides. In March 1995 government forces launched an intensive campaign, lasting several months, against the Mong Tai Army. In August a faction calling itself the Shan State National Army (SSNA) broke away from the Mong Tai Army, accusing Khun Sa of using Shan nationalism as a 'front' for drugs-trafficking. Khun Sa's position was considerably weakened in September, as improving relations between Thailand and Myanmar led to a Thai pledge to close the common border, thus obstructing his supply routes, and ceasefires with neighbouring ethnic groups allowed the Government to deploy troops in hitherto inaccessible areas. Certain ethnic groups, notably the Wa, were also actively engaged in fighting the Mong Tai Army to gain control of the opium trade. In November Khun Sa announced his retirement from all political and military positions, citing his betrayal by the breakaway group. In January 1996 government troops were met with no resistance on entering Homong, and thousands of Khun Sa's former supporters surrendered. Although no formal agreement with the SLORC was announced, it was widely believed that Khun Sa had earlier negotiated a settlement with the authorities since he was not detained and it was officially announced that he would not be extradited to the USA on drugs-trafficking charges. The Mong Tai Army was subsequently transformed into a militia volunteer unit under the command of the armed forces.

Between November 1996 and February 1997 there were reports of clashes between the Shan United Revolutionary Party (a faction of the Mong Tai Army that had not surrendered in January 1996) and government forces. In September 1997 the alliance between three of the major Shan groups who continued their resistance—including the SSNA, remnants of the Mong Tai Army, and the Shan State Peacekeeping Council (SSPC) and its military wing, the Shan State Army (SSA)—was formalized, and the groups joined together in an enlarged SSA. Shan separatist groups launched a further offensive against government troops in November. In May 1999 it was reported that at least 300,000 Shan had been forced from their villages into resettlement camps by government troops. In May 2000 several senior army officers died in an SSA ambush. In the following month more than 60 Shan and hill tribespeople, who had been forcibly relocated and had then attempted to return to their village, were reportedly killed by the Myanma military in a retaliatory attack. In similar incidents in the region in June, as many as 50 other villagers were believed to have been murdered. In 2001 the Government launched several offensives against SSA border camps, causing hundreds more Shan to flee the area.

In January 2000 it was reported that the SPDC was to launch an operation to relocate 50,000 people from opium-growing areas controlled by the United Wa State Army (UWSA—which reached an accommodation with the SLORC in 1989), with the alleged intention of eradicating the production of drugs in the areas by 2005. The relocation programme began to cause ethnic tension in early 2001, as the Shan complained that the Wa tribespeople were occupying land that they had previously owned. It was also claimed that the Wa were still growing opium, in spite of the fact that the scheme had been introduced supposedly to prevent heroin production. By February some 300,000 Shan were reported to have fled to Thailand owing to the Wa influx.

In April 2003 the KNU claimed responsibility for a series of explosions that had destroyed sections of a gas pipeline in Kayin State over the previous two months. Several bombings along the border with Thailand in the following month were also attributed to the KNU. In January 2004 Bo Mya and other KNU officials held talks with government representatives in Yangon, which resulted in the conclusion of an informal ceasefire arrangement between the two sides. However, sporadic fighting continued between government troops and the KNLA. Bo Mya retired as Vice-Chairman of the KNU in December because of ill health; he was replaced by Gen. Tamalabaw. In January 2005 10 government troops were reportedly killed in clashes with the KNU after attacking one of the group's bases near the border with Thailand. Later in that month the KNU demanded a resumption of the peace talks, which had been curtailed at the Government's request in October 2004 following the dismissal of Prime Minister Khin Nyunt. Government offensives in Kayin State in early 2006 were reported to have forced an estimated 15,000 Kayin people to flee from the violence. Bo Mya died in a Thai hospital in December 2006. In February 2007 a relatively small breakaway faction of the KNU led by Htain Maung negotiated a peace

agreement with the Government, but the goals of the KNU itself remained unchanged and its armed campaign continued unabated. Meanwhile, in February 2008 the General Secretary of the KNU, Pado Mahn Sha, was killed by two unidentified gunmen at his home in the Thai border town of Mae Sot; it was speculated that the DKBA was responsible for the assassination. The Chairman of the KNU, Saw Ba Thin, died in May; in October Vice-Chairman Gen. Tamalabaw was appointed as his replacement, while Tamalabaw's daughter, Zipporah Sein, succeeded Mahn Sha as General Secretary.

Following the referendum in 2008 in favour of the new Constitution (see *Domestic Political Affairs*), the SPDC requested that all ethnic minority groups form political parties to enable their participation in the legislative elections scheduled for 2010. However, many were reluctant to do so owing to the reservation of one-quarter of seats in the national and local legislatures for members of the national army. In April 2009 the SPDC demanded that all ethnic ceasefire groups transform into new 'Border Guard Force' (BGF) battalions, each of which was to include a unit of 30 government soldiers and one government officer. Although most of the ceasefire groups initially resisted the order, some—including the DKBA—were gradually coerced into acquiescing. The introduction of the BGFs was widely regarded as an attempt to reduce the risk of ethnic uprisings prior to the 2010 elections. The forthcoming polls were a divisive subject among the ethnic-based groups: some were adamantly opposed to any participation, which, they argued, would lend a false impression of legitimacy to the proceedings, while others contended that a refusal to participate would ensure their total exclusion from the legislative process.

As the elections approached, with the SPDC's rejection of a number of ethnic parties and individual candidates, along with its apparent endeavours to disenfranchise a large number of ethnic voters (see *Domestic Political Affairs*), tensions in the ethnic border areas intensified. In October 2010 the Kachin Independence Army (KIA—the military wing of the KIO, which continued to refuse to become a BGF) was reported to be engaged in a tense stand-off with government troops, following the arrest of three of its members; meanwhile, members of the SSA were reported to have been attacked by government forces in several separate incidents. At the beginning of November six ethnic groups reportedly reached an agreement to join forces in the event of a government attack; a spokesperson for the KIO contested that the ethnic groups had 'no real option but to unite, politically and militarily'. Heavy fighting broke out in Myawaddy on 8 November, immediately following the legislative elections, after a breakaway faction of the DKBA—led by Na Kham Mwe and comprising those opposed to the DKBA leadership's decision to agree to become a BGF—seized control of government buildings in the Kayin town, where they encountered armed opposition from government troops. At least three civilians were killed during the clashes, and an estimated 20,000 Kayin were reported to have fled into neighbouring Thailand to escape the violence. Government troops regained control of Myawaddy a few days later, and issued an ultimatum to the renegade faction, threatening to annihilate it if it did not surrender its weapons and agree to become a BGF by the end of December. However, sporadic fighting continued. In mid-November the DKBA faction and the KNLA agreed to unite in their common pursuit of autonomy.

Intermittent violent clashes in Kayin State and other border areas continued in 2011. Four KIA fighters and 16 government soldiers were reported to have been killed during fierce fighting in Kachin State in June, while thousands of civilians were displaced by the violence, many of them fleeing across the border into China. The Government subsequently accused the KIA of instigating the clashes (which had officially ended the 17-year ceasefire agreement between the KIA and the Myanma authorities), claiming that the rebel troops had ignored an order to withdraw from an area close to the construction site of two Chinese-financed dams in Momauk, the Tarpein dams. Later in June three apparently co-ordinated bomb explosions, in Nay Pyi Taw, Mandalay and Pyin Oo Lwin, were attributed by the authorities to ethnic rebel groups; three people were reported to have been injured in the attacks. Sporadic clashes continued into July, and in August seven people were reported to have been killed when KIA rebels ambushed a vehicle carrying workers from the Tarpein power plant. Meanwhile, in March 2011 the KIO had sent an open letter to the Chinese Government urging it to cancel a hydropower plant and dam project at Myitsone, an area in Kachin State of considerable cultural and ecological significance, and warning that it would not be held responsible if 'civil war' broke out as a result of continued construction. The KIO argued that the Myitsone dam and other Chinese-financed power projects were wreaking severe environmental and social disruption, including the displacement of local communities. (In April 2010 three bombs had been detonated at the Myitsone dam project, killing three people; around 60 people were arrested in Kachin State in May in connection with the explosions.) In an apparent acknowledgement of the concerns expressed by the KIO and many members of the international community, the Myanma Government unexpectedly announced the suspension of the Myitsone project in September 2011 (see *Foreign Affairs*).

In a statement broadcast on national television in August 2011, the Government invited rebel groups to enter into formal dialogue aimed at resolving the ongoing ethnic conflicts. A series of meetings was subsequently held between the Government and the KIO, and in December the Government ordered the military to halt all offensive operations against the KIA; however, intermittent clashes between government troops and KIA rebels continued to be reported in early 2012. Meanwhile, ceasefire agreements were concluded with the SSA and the KNU, in December 2011 and January 2012, respectively. The Government's unconditional release in March of Mahn Nyein Maung, a KNU leader who had been convicted of unlawful association and violating immigration laws and sentenced to 17 years' imprisonment in December 2011, gave new impetus to the peace process. A second round of negotiations with the Government took place in the Kayin State capital of Pa-an in April 2012 and KNU leaders attended a meeting with President Thein Sein in Nay Pyi Taw. A preliminary ceasefire agreement was concluded with the NMSP in February and with the KNPP in March, providing for an end to the fighting, pending discussions on a permanent accord. A further ceasefire agreement was signed with the KNPP in June. Despite the holding of several rounds of peace talks in Myitkyina, the capital of Kachin State, between the KIO and government representatives during 2013–14, the fighting between the two sides persisted.

During 2013–14 there were reports of sporadic fighting in northern Shan State between government troops and the Taaung National Liberation Army (TNLA), which was composed of ethnic Kachin, Shan and Palaung armed groups and which maintained strategic military alliances with the KIA and the SSPP. In February 2015 President Thein Sein declared a state of emergency and martial law in the Kokang Special Region in Shan State after the outbreak of heavy fighting between government troops and an alliance of insurgent groups, including the Myanmar National Democratic Alliance Army (MNDAA), as a result of which more than 130 people were reportedly killed and tens of thousands fled over the border into China. The outbreak of hostilities was allegedly triggered by the return to Myanmar of the leader of the MNDAA, Pheung Kya Shin, after five years of exile in China.

In March 2015, following seven rounds of talks, President Thein Sein witnessed the preliminary signing of a draft nationwide ceasefire agreement between the Government and 16 ethnic armed groups, including the KIO; most of the groups had already concluded bilateral accords with the authorities. The agreement remained subject to approval and formal signature by the Government and the groups' leaders, after which a period of political dialogue was envisaged. Meanwhile, heavy fighting continued in the Kokang Special Region.

The Rohingyas and Inter-communal Unrest

In 1989 the SLORC began resettling Bamar (Burman) Buddhists in the predominantly Muslim areas of Arakan (renamed Rakhine), displacing the local Rohingya Muslims. In April 1991 Rohingya refugees were forced over the border into Bangladesh, as a result of the brutal operations of the Myanma armed forces, including the destruction of villages, widespread killings and pillaging. The Rohingyas had been similarly persecuted in 1976–78, when more than 200,000 of them had sought refuge in Bangladesh. The Rohingyas had finally been repatriated, only to lose their citizenship following the introduction of new nationality legislation in 1982. In November 1991 the SLORC pledged to repatriate genuine Myanma citizens, but claimed that many of the refugees were illegal Bengali immigrants. In April 1992 the Myanma and Bangladeshi Governments signed an agreement providing for the repatriation of those Rohingya refugees in possession of official documentation. However, the repatriation programme was delayed, owing to the continuing flow of refugees to Bangladesh (reaching an estimated 270,000 by the end of June). The first Rohingya refugees were returned to Myanmar in

September, and by May 1995 more than 216,000 refugees had been repatriated.

In April 2000 the International Federation of Human Rights Leagues (Fédération Internationale des Ligues des Droits de l'Homme—FIDH) issued a report condemning the treatment of Rohingya Muslims by the Myanma Government, including forced labour, punitive taxes and extrajudicial killings. The FIDH claimed that the Myanma regime was attempting to force the exodus of Rohingyas from their native Rakhine and criticized the office of the UN High Commissioner for Refugees (UNHCR) for its effective complicity with the regime in designating the more recent refugees as economic migrants. In February 2001 violence between Buddhist and Muslim communities in the state capital, Sittwe, was reported to have resulted in at least 12 deaths, prompting the Government to regulate further the movement of Rohingya and other Muslims in and out of Rakhine.

In December 2009 it was announced that Myanmar had agreed to repatriate about 9,000 Rohingyas living in Bangladeshi camps following a meeting between the two countries' respective foreign ministers. Nevertheless, at mid-2014 more than 32,000 Rohingyas with official refugee status were reported to be living in UNHCR refugee camps in Bangladesh, many of whom appeared to be unwilling to return to Myanmar. In addition, it was estimated that some 200,000 stateless Rohingyas were residing in the impoverished Cox's Bazar area of Bangladesh in squalid unregistered camps.

In a report published in January 2012, the non-governmental organization Arakan Project claimed that although members of Myanmar's new legislature had been able to submit questions during parliamentary sessions on discriminatory policies and restrictions targeting the Rohingya population in Rakhine, replies provided by the Government in August and September 2011 had reaffirmed its commitment to those policies, including the denial of citizenship and marriage rights, and stringent restrictions on movement, justifying their implementation on the grounds of national population growth control and 'illegal migration management'.

Sectarian tension between the Muslim and Buddhist populations in Rakhine heightened from mid-2012, as the number of violent incidents across the state between members of the two communities increased considerably (prompted by the killing, in early June, of 10 Muslim men travelling on a bus in the town of Taungup by a group of Buddhists; it was reported that the victims were mistakenly identified by the mob as having carried out the rape and murder of a Buddhist woman in the town of Ramree in May). President Thein Sein declared a state of emergency and imposed a curfew in Rakhine on 10 June in an attempt to curb the growing unrest. However, within a week the total number of people killed in the violence had reached around 50, tens of thousands (mainly Rohingya Muslims) had been displaced by the fighting and hundreds of Rohingyas were attempting to flee to Bangladesh by boat. Bangladesh's subsequent decision to close its border was criticized by human rights organizations as a violation of international law. Although the communal violence had abated somewhat by mid-July, there were reports of continuing attacks on the Muslim population and their property by both the Buddhist community and—at times—by the security forces themselves. There were also reports of hundreds of arbitrary arrests being carried out by the security forces in Rohingya areas of the state. Having rejected a UN proposal to set up an independent inquiry, in mid-August the Government announced the establishment of a commission, incorporating members from different political and religious groups, which was to identify and then attempt to address the reasons behind the resurgence in sectarian violence in Rakhine. There was another spate of violent clashes between Muslims and Buddhists in Rakhine in late October, leading to at least another 80 deaths, the destruction of hundreds of houses and the displacement of thousands of people into makeshift camps. By the end of the year it was estimated that around 190 people had been killed in the inter-communal violence and some 140,000 had been displaced. In a report released in April 2013, the government commission established in August 2012 proposed doubling the number of security forces in Rakhine and improving their training and equipment. It also recommended that Muslim Rohingyas and Buddhists should continue to be segregated, while acknowledging that this did not represent an appropriate long-term solution, and that Rohingya citizenship claims should be addressed.

In March 2013 it appeared that inter-communal tension had spread elsewhere in Myanmar when clashes erupted between the Muslim and Buddhist communities of the town of Meikhtila in Mandalay Division. Despite the imposition by the Government of a state of emergency in the town and the dispatch of hundreds of riot police to the area, by the end of the month at least 43 people (the majority of whom were Muslims) were reported to have been killed in the violence and more than 12,000 (again, mainly Muslims) forced from their homes. In a worrying development, anti-Muslim violence subsequently broke out in a number of towns further south in the division. As widespread anti-Muslim sentiment appeared to become more entrenched within Myanmar's Buddhist majority, sporadic incidents of sectarian violence were reported across the country throughout the rest of the year and into 2014. According to UN reports, more than 40 Rohingyas were killed in a fresh outbreak of communal violence in Rakhine in January. Critics claimed that the Government was not doing enough effectively to combat the growing problem.

In October 2014 details emerged of a controversial document drawn up by the Government entitled the Rakhine State Action Plan. Included in the document (which referred to the Rohingya Muslims as 'Bengalis' throughout) were proposals to entrench existing discriminatory policies that deprived Rohingyas of Myanma citizenship and to enforce the resettlement by May 2015 of more than 130,000 internally displaced Rohingyas into closed camps prior to their deportation to Bangladesh. The plan was roundly condemned by human rights groups as a blatant attempt further to marginalize the Rohingya population. Earlier in 2014 the Government had prevented the Rohingyas from participating in the national census on the grounds that they were foreigners. In December the UN General Assembly adopted a resolution urging the Myanma authorities to grant full citizenship to the Rohingya minority and to grant them equal access to services. None the less, in February 2015, in the wake of anti-Rohingya protests led by Buddhist monks, President Thein Sein withdrew the temporary voting rights (the so-called 'white papers') that had been granted in 2010 to members of the Rohingya and other minorities who did not hold full citizenship; this meant that those affected would not be permitted to participate in either national referendums or elections.

Foreign Affairs

Following the seizure of power by the military junta under Gen. Ne Win in 1962, Myanmar's foreign relations were characterized by international mistrust and condemnation. As repression by the Myanma military junta increased, in July 1996 opposition leader Aung San Suu Kyi for the first time advocated the imposition of international economic sanctions against the regime. There followed a period of increased economic and diplomatic isolation. After the staging of legislative elections in November 2010, and the transition to an at least nominally democratic, civilian system of governance in early 2011, there were signs of a significant shift in the international community's attitudes towards Myanmar, which appeared increasingly keen to re-engage with both its regional neighbours and those further afield. However, at early 2015 it still remained to be seen whether concessions announced by the Thein Sein administration following its inauguration in March 2011 merely constituted, as some critics alleged, a calculated ploy to expedite the lifting of international sanctions and attract foreign investment, or whether such measures represented a genuine desire to initiate a process of sustained democratic reform and to co-operate fully with the demands of the international community.

Regional relations

The People's Republic of China restored diplomatic relations with Burma in 1978. From 1988, as Burma's international isolation deepened, China assumed an increasingly important role, becoming Myanmar's principal aid donor, supplier of weapons and source of consumer goods. In December 2001 the Chinese President, Jiang Zemin, travelled to Myanmar, becoming the first Chinese head of state to visit the country since 1985. Following successful discussions, the two Governments signed a series of bilateral agreements intended to enhance co-operative ties. Relations were further strengthened over the course of the 2000s through a number of high-level state visits and the signing of numerous additional co-operation agreements.

Ongoing unrest in the Myanma ethnic border areas close to China was a source of tension between the two countries in 2010–15. Some 5,000 Chinese troops were deployed to the border in mid-2010. Following an outbreak of fighting between ethnic Kachin rebels and government troops in June 2011, in part fuelled by Kachin opposition to Chinese-funded dam projects in the northern Myanma state, thousands of civilians fled across the border into China, with some 7,000–10,000 reported to remain there in 2014. (In August 2012 Human Rights Watch alleged that China was flouting international law by forcibly returning Kachin refugees across the border into Myanmar.) In February 2015 heavy fighting between government troops and insurgents in the Kokang Special Region in Shan State prompted tens of thousands of Myanma civilians to flee into China. In March the Chinese Government dispatched fighter jets to patrol its border with Myanmar and lodged a diplomatic protest, following the death of five Chinese nationals in a bomb explosion in the border area. Meanwhile, the decision by the new administration of President Thein Sein in September 2011 to suspend construction of a controversial US $3,600m. Chinese-financed hydroelectric dam for the duration of his tenure (i.e. until at least 2015) was a source of considerable annoyance to the Chinese Government, but was widely welcomed by ethnic and environmentalist groups in Myanmar. Some 90% of the electricity expected to have been generated by the 3,600-MW Myitsone dam was to have been exported to China. Many analysts suggested that the project's suspension was more a response to international than domestic pressures, with the Myanma Government appearing eager to appease Western (and particularly US) concerns over its heavy reliance on China. The proposed creation of a Bangladesh-China-India-Myanmar (BCIM) Economic Corridor, which had been under discussion for more than a decade, moved one step closer to reality in December 2013, following the first working-group meeting of the four involved countries, held in the Chinese city of Kunming; a joint research plan on constructing the corridor, through a network of roads, railways, waterways and airways, was signed by the four participants.

In an attempt to end its isolation, accelerate economic growth and gain protection from Western criticism of its internal affairs, Myanmar applied to join ASEAN and was admitted as a full member of the organization in July 1997. In May 2000 Myanmar hosted a meeting of the economic ministers of the ASEAN member countries. Myanmar enjoyed particularly cordial relations with Indonesia, and the military regime aspired to Indonesia's internationally accepted political system, in which the dominant role of the armed forces was enshrined in the Constitution. In July 2005 it was announced at the ASEAN Ministerial Meeting held in Laos that Myanmar would not assume the chair of ASEAN in 2006 as had been scheduled. Myanmar had recently come under increasing pressure from the international community, and in particular from the other member states of ASEAN, to forgo its turn to assume the rotating chair in order to enable the Myanma Government instead to focus its attention on addressing the country's human rights situation.

In September 2007, in a rare departure from the Association's policy of non-interference in member states' internal affairs, ASEAN foreign ministers, meeting in New York, USA, issued a statement in which they declared that they had expressed their 'revulsion' to their Myanma counterpart over reports that anti-Government protests were being violently suppressed, and had urged the Myanma Government to resume efforts at national reconciliation and to release all political detainees.

Following the holding of legislative elections in Myanmar (and the release from house arrest of Suu Kyi) in November 2010, Viet Nam, in its capacity as ASEAN chair for that year, hailed the polls as 'a significant step forward'. Furthermore, in January 2011 ASEAN urged the USA and other Western nations to remove economic sanctions against Myanmar, stating that the sanctions were impeding the country's development, and appealing for dialogue with Myanmar in order to ensure further progress towards democracy in that country. Following the enactment of domestic reforms by the Myanma Government in the latter half of 2011 (see *Domestic Political Affairs*), at the ASEAN summit meeting held on Bali, Indonesia, in November, the bloc unanimously voted to award Myanmar the chair in 2014. At the summit meeting held in Cambodia in April 2012, ASEAN formally reiterated demands that all sanctions against Myanmar be lifted immediately. Myanmar duly assumed the chair of ASEAN in January 2014, hosting summits in May and November.

Meanwhile, following the release of Suu Kyi from house arrest in July 1995, Japan resumed substantial economic aid to Myanmar, which had been halted in 1988. The international community criticized Japan's decision to resume aid as being premature in the light of Myanmar's failure to end forced labour and other human rights abuses in the country. In November 1999 the

Japanese Prime Minister met with Than Shwe during an ASEAN summit meeting in the Philippine capital, Manila; the meeting was the first between the leader of a major world power and a senior member of the military Government since the junta's suppression of the democratic opposition in 1988. In June 2003, following the junta's reimprisonment of Suu Kyi in May of that year, the Japanese Government once again suspended all economic aid to Myanmar. However, in early 2004 it was announced that Japan was to resume humanitarian aid, having been satisfied that the release of some political prisoners by the SPDC constituted adequate progress towards democracy in the country. In January 2012 the Japanese Ministry of Foreign Affairs commended the Myanma Government for its release of a number of prominent political prisoners and pledged continuing Japanese support for the Thein Sein administration's efforts to 'further advance democratization'. In April, following the by-elections at which 43 NLD candidates were elected to parliament, President Thein Sein paid an official visit to Japan, during which it was announced that Japan would cancel debts owed by Myanmar of more than US $3,700m. and would resume development aid. Agreement was also reached on a plan to establish a special economic zone near Yangon. In March 2013 it was reported that Myanmar was to resume exports of rice to Japan in May, the first such transaction between the two nations since 1968. Relations improved further in May 2013 when Shinzo Abe became the first Japanese Prime Minister to visit Myanmar since 1977. During talks with Thein Sein, Abe announced the cancellation of the remainder of Myanmar's debt with Japan (some $1,740m.) and pledged around $500m. in new loans to finance infrastructure development projects and power station maintenance. In October 2014 it was announced that Japan's three largest banks had secured three of the nine licences on offer for foreign banks to operate in Myanmar.

Relations with Thailand, which had often been strained during the 1990s and early 2000s, deteriorated sharply in mid-2002 when fighting broke out on the bilateral border between government troops, allied with the United Wa State Army, and the Shan State Army (SSA). It was alleged that Thai troops had fired shells into Myanmar, in the belief that the fighting had encroached upon Thai territory. In response, the Myanma Government repeated previous claims that Thailand was providing support to the SSA. The border was closed shortly afterwards, as border incursions continued, but reopened in October. Following the adoption of a policy of 'soft engagement' by the Thai Government, in early 2003 the two countries signed an unprecedented agreement pledging that future military exercises would be conducted at a suitable distance from the border. In December Thailand hosted an international forum, the 'Bangkok Process', at which the Myanma Minister of Foreign Affairs, Win Aung, presented the 'road map' on democratic reform (see *Domestic Political Affairs*) to government representatives from 10 other Asian and European countries. A second 'Friendship Bridge' linking Thailand and Myanmar opened in January 2006.

A decision by the Myanmar junta in July 2010 to close a border crossing at Myawaddy, adjacent to the Thai border town of Mae Sot, was a source of considerable irritation to the Thai Government. The escalation of tensions in Myanmar's ethnic border areas in the immediate aftermath of the November legislative elections (see *Insurgency and Dissidence*) reportedly forced more than 20,000 Myanma nationals to flee into Thailand to escape the violence. Three Thai nationals were injured when mortar and grenade attacks strayed across the Myanma–Thai border during fighting between the Democratic Karen (Kayin) Buddhist Army and Myanma government troops, causing Mae Sot to be evacuated. Thai Prime Minister Abhisit Vejjajiva announced the deployment of additional troops to the area in order to reinforce border security, and offered assurances that Kayin and other Myanma refugees into Thailand would be treated humanely. Between January 2005 and December 2011 more than 70,000 Myanma refugees who had sought refuge in Thailand were resettled in third countries (primarily the USA). According to UNHCR, at early 2015 there were around 72,900 registered and an estimated 51,500 unregistered Myanma refugees resident in nine camps in Thailand. Meanwhile, following a meeting between the Myanma and Thai Ministers of Foreign Affairs in the Myanma border town of Tachilek in December 2010, the Three Pagodas Pass border crossing, a principal 'black market' trade route between Thailand and Myanmar, was reopened after a three-year closure. In January 2011 Myanmar eased border control restrictions between Myawaddy and Mae Sot, allowing the transit of goods via cross-border trading ports to resume; the

border crossing was fully reopened in December. President Thein Sein undertook his first official visit to Thailand in July 2012.

Despite the killing of three Indian soldiers in a clash with Myanma troops on the two countries' border in October 2000, relations between India and Myanmar subsequently improved. Gen. Maung Aye visited India in November, meeting both the country's President and the Prime Minister. In February 2001 India's Minister of External Affairs, Jaswant Singh, visited Myanmar, the first Indian cabinet minister to do so since the SLORC's assumption of power in 1988. While there, Singh officially opened the Tamu–Kalewa highway, a road built by India to increase bilateral trade with Myanmar. In October 2004 the Chairman of the SPDC, Than Shwe, paid the first visit to India by a Myanma head of state in 24 years, agreeing at meetings with the Indian President and Prime Minister to further bilateral co-operation. In March 2006 President Aavul Pakkiri Jainulabidin Abdul Kalam visited Yangon, the first ever state visit to Myanmar by an Indian President. Relations between the two countries were strengthened yet more in 2010–12 by further senior-level official visits and the signature of a series of additional co-operation agreements covering areas such as oil and gas exploration, anti-terrorism measures, defence and bilateral trade and investment. In May 2012 Prime Minister Dr Manmohan Singh became the first Indian premier to visit Myanmar since 1987; during his visit the two countries agreed to establish a joint trade and investment forum. In late 2014 one of the Indian Government's key economic projects was the scheduled completion of a 3,200-km trilateral highway linking India, Myanmar and Thailand by 2018.

In October 2002 the Australian Minister for Foreign Affairs, Alexander Downer, became the most senior Australian politician to visit Myanmar for 20 years. During his stay he met with senior members of the SPDC and with Suu Kyi. In October 2007 the Australian Government imposed financial sanctions on more than 400 Myanma leaders and associates. The Australian Minister for Foreign Affairs, Kevin Rudd, released a statement in October 2010 expressing 'grave reservations' about the validity of the legislative elections due to be held in Myanmar in the following month. Nevertheless, in June–July 2011 Rudd became the first Australian government minister to visit Myanmar since Downer in 2002, meeting with members of the new Myanma Government as well as members of the political opposition, including Suu Kyi. Following the election to parliament of Suu Kyi and other NLD members in April 2012, the Australian Government eased sanctions against Myanmar and announced its intention to normalize trading relations, although an embargo on arms sales remained in place. Following a visit to Myanmar in June, the Australian Minister for Foreign Affairs, Robert Carr, pledged to double aid to Myanmar to almost US $100m. per year by 2015. In March 2013 Thein Sein became the first Myanma head of state to visit Australia since 1974; following his visit, it was announced that Australia, in further recognition of Myanmar's ongoing programme of reforms, was to relax restrictions on defence co-operation (involving military humanitarian aid and peacekeeping) with Myanmar.

Relations with the USA

Following the military junta's refusal to honour the results of the legislative elections in May 1990, and its violent suppression of the opposition, the US Government withdrew its ambassador from Myanmar. In May 1997 the USA imposed trade sanctions in protest at persistent and large-scale repression by the SLORC, prohibiting further investment in Myanmar, although existing US interests in the country remained unaffected. The sanctions were subsequently renewed annually. Following the detention of Suu Kyi in May 2003, in July US President George W. Bush approved the Burmese Freedom and Democracy Act, already adopted by Congress, banning all imports from Myanmar for three years and extending visa sanctions already imposed on SPDC officials. The Act was renewed for a further three years in August 2006. In October 2007 Bush announced the imposition of stricter controls on imports from Myanmar, as well as sanctions affecting the property interests of senior Myanma leaders. In May 2008, furthermore, the US Treasury was ordered to freeze the assets of all state-owned companies in Myanmar.

Following its inauguration in January 2009, the Administration of US President Barack Obama stressed that despite the adoption of a policy of 'pragmatic engagement' with Myanmar, sanctions would remain in place until tangible progress towards democratic change had been achieved in that country. In July Obama renewed the Burmese Freedom and Democracy Act for a further three years, after its approval by the US Congress. In November 2009 Obama attended the ASEAN-US Leaders' Meeting, hosted by Singapore, at which Prime Minister Thein Sein was also present, demonstrating the Obama Administration's stated commitment to re-engaging with Myanmar; previously the USA had boycotted those meetings with ASEAN at which Myanma officials were present. Following Obama's inauguration, the military junta appeared more amenable to requests from US (and other Western) officials to meet with Suu Kyi and vice versa. Nevertheless, the US Administration expressed concern over the electoral legislation enacted by the junta in March 2010, and US economic sanctions against Myanmar were extended for a further year in July. One of the leaked US diplomatic cables published at the end of 2010 by WikiLeaks (an organization publishing leaked private and classified content) revealed that the US Government was deeply concerned by rumours, based on satellite images and other evidence, that Myanmar was developing a covert nuclear weapons programme in remote locations with the assistance of the Democratic People's Republic of Korea (North Korea). Myanmar and North Korea both denied the claims, with the Myanma Government denouncing such allegations as the result of a politically motivated plot orchestrated by 'anti-Government elements' to undermine its efforts to re-engage with the international community. In June 2012, while addressing a security forum in Singapore, the Myanma Minister of Defence, Lt-Gen. Hla Min, asserted that Myanmar had never pursued the development of nuclear weapons and, moreover, had now abandoned research into nuclear power generation, for reasons of cost.

Rejecting appeals by ASEAN for a lifting of sanctions against Myanmar following the staging of legislative elections in November 2010, President Obama announced the renewal of sanctions for a further year in May 2011, and urged the Thein Sein Government more fervently to pursue democratic reforms and to end its 'large-scale oppression' of the political opposition. None the less, in an indication of the US Administration's commitment to enhanced engagement with the Myanma Government, in mid-2011 President Obama appointed a special envoy for Myanmar, Derek Mitchell. Mitchell twice visited Myanmar in the latter half of the year for talks with the Government which were reported to have been constructive. The announcement in mid-November that US Secretary of State Hillary Clinton was to visit Myanmar at the end of the month—the most senior US visit since the military junta seized power in 1962—was widely construed as an acknowledgement of reforms announced by the Thein Sein administration in October, and followed an announcement on the previous day that the opposition NLD was to apply to re-register as a political party, thereby bestowing greater legitimacy on the political process in Myanmar. Some observers suggested that the US Government was keen to foster closer relations with Myanmar also as a means of countering increasing Chinese dominance in the Asia-Pacific region. During her visit, Clinton met with senior government leaders, including President Thein Sein, as well as with Suu Kyi and other NLD leaders, and announced a series of modest measures in recognition of recent progress demonstrated by the Government, including a pledge to support proposals for enhanced co-operation between Myanmar and the World Bank and the IMF. However, she reiterated the need for the Myanma Government to effect further reforms, and urged the Government to sever military ties with North Korea and to resolve the country's ongoing ethnic conflicts (see *Insurgency and Dissidence*).

In February 2012 the Obama Administration announced the easing of one of the sanctions imposed against the Myanma Government in acknowledgement of the latter's progress towards democratic governance. Following the successful conduct of parliamentary by-elections in April, the USA relaxed sanctions further, allowing limited US investment in a number of project areas. It was also announced that an office of the US Agency for International Development would be established in the country and Mitchell, the former special envoy for Myanmar, was subsequently named as the new US ambassador to Myanmar.

Relations between Myanmar and the USA were further strengthened in the latter half of 2012: in July the US Administration announced that US companies were now allowed to 'responsibly do business' in Myanmar (excluding military or financial ventures) and high-profile visits were conducted by the leaders of both countries. During her visit to the USA in September, Suu Kyi met both Obama and Clinton and received the US Congressional Gold Medal that she had been awarded in

2008. The following week President Thein Sein became the first Myanma head of state to visit the USA in 46 years. During his visit, the President addressed the UN General Assembly and was informed by Clinton that the USA would ease its import ban on goods from Myanmar. In a reciprocal visit in November, Obama became the first ever incumbent US President to visit Myanmar, where he held talks with Thein Sein and Suu Kyi. Critics of this symbolic visit claimed that it was premature, given the ongoing ethnic unrest in Rakhine and Kayin State, the continued incarceration of political prisoners and the need for further reform. During his visit, however, Obama made a speech at the University of Yangon in which he demanded an end to communal violence between Muslims and Buddhists. In a further significant development, at the invitation of the USA, Myanmar sent observers to participate in the annual US-led military exercises—'Cobra Gold'—in Thailand, in February 2013 (and again in the following year). In May the US Administration extended targeted sanctions against Myanmar for another year but terminated a visa ban on Myanma government officials and their families which had been in place since 1996. Also in May, during Thein Sein's second visit to the USA, while Obama reiterated his concern over the continuing sectarian unrest it was widely noted that, for the first time, he referred to the country as Myanmar rather than Burma. Targeted US sanctions against Myanmar were extended for another year in May 2014. US President Obama paid a second visit to Myanmar in November to attend the East Asia Summmit (which was convened following the ASEAN leaders' meeting), again holding talks with Thein Sein and Suu Kyi.

Relations with the UN

In June 1999 a resolution condemning Myanmar for its widespread use of forced labour was adopted by the member countries of the UN's International Labour Organization (ILO), and the country was barred from participating in any ILO activities. Following the failure of the ruling junta to carry out ILO recommendations regarding the use of forced labour and the suppression of trade unions in Myanmar, in November 2000 the ILO voted to proceed with sanctions against Myanmar. This was the first time such action had been undertaken in the UN labour body's 81-year history. The ILO subsequently requested its members to review their relations with Myanmar and to adopt sanctions. China, India, Malaysia and Russia voted against the action.

In September 2001 an ILO contingent visited Myanmar to ascertain whether the military junta had honoured its promise to abolish forced labour. In November the ILO issued a report concluding that while some progress had been made, the practice was still endemic in many parts of the country. In March 2002 the ILO agreed to establish a liaison office in Myanmar and, in October, an ILO mission visited the country. However, in June 2009 the ILO denounced the Myanma Government's actions to end forced labour thus far as 'totally inadequate', and insisted that it must amend the new Constitution to include an explicit ban on forced labour. The adoption of new labour legislation in October 2011 granting Myanma workers the right to form trade unions and to strike (with the exception of those working in essential services) was cautiously welcomed by the ILO. In March 2012 the Myanma Government signed a memorandum of understanding with the ILO in which it committed itself to eradicating forced labour by 2015.

Meanwhile, in October 2007 the UN Human Rights Council adopted a resolution deploring the violent repression of peaceful demonstrations in the previous month and urging the release of peaceful protesters and all other political detainees. In November, during his first visit to Myanmar since March 2003, the UN Special Rapporteur on the situation of human rights in Myanmar, Pinheiro, held talks with government ministers and several prominent political prisoners, although he was not permitted to meet Suu Kyi. Following his visit, Pinheiro stated that the Myanma authorities had admitted that 15 people had been killed during the suppression of the anti-Government protests in September 2007 (five more than previously acknowledged), and in the following month he reported that his investigations indicated that at least a further 16 people had died, that 500–1,000 people were still being detained by the authorities (far more than claimed by the Government) and that 74 people were missing. Pinheiro also reported that the ill-treatment of detainees and the poor conditions in which they were being held had resulted in several deaths in custody.

Tomás Ojea Quintana replaced Pinheiro in April 2008. In a report presented to the UN Human Rights Council following his third visit to Myanmar, in February 2010, Ojea Quintana noted 'a pattern of gross and systematic violation of human rights', which, he argued, appeared to be 'the result of a state policy'. In March UN Secretary-General Ban Ki-Moon urged the Myanma Government to create suitable conditions for credible, inclusive elections, which would necessitate the release of political prisoners, including Suu Kyi; he also admitted to frustration at the 'disappointing' progress achieved as a result of UN engagement with the junta, and described the latter's efforts to ensure free and fair elections thus far as 'frustrating'. Shortly after the elections in November, Ibrahim Gambari's replacement as UN Special Envoy to Myanmar, Vijay Nambiar, visited the country, where he met with senior government officials in the outgoing junta, and insisted that they address the widespread concerns about the polls.

An amelioration in relations between the UN and Myanmar became evident following the transfer from military rule to a nominally civilian Government in January 2011. Ojea Quintana was allowed to visit Myanmar in August, his first visit to the country since February 2010, during which he welcomed the Government's 'stated commitments to reform', but urged it to address the long-standing social, economic and development challenges confronting Myanmar. Following a five-day visit in January–February 2012, Ojea Quintana commended the Myanma Government for the 'continuing wave of reforms' since his previous visit, including the establishment of the National Human Rights Commission, but expressed concerns regarding, *inter alia*, the continued detention of a number of political prisoners, and ongoing tensions and conflict with armed ethnic groups in border areas—particularly in Kachin State—noting persistent reports of extrajudicial killings, attacks against civilians, sexual violence, internal displacement, land confiscations, forced labour and the recruitment of child soldiers. In April, at the invitation of President Thein Sein, UN Secretary-General Ban Ki-Moon visited Myanmar, where he met Suu Kyi, as well as the President, and became the first foreigner to address parliament, urging its members to accelerate the pace of reform. In his historic speech to the UN General Assembly in New York in September, Thein Sein asserted that the democratic reforms being carried out in Myanmar were irreversible and paid tribute to Suu Kyi (referring to her, for the first time, as a Nobel laureate). In March 2013 Ojea Quintana expressed his serious concern over the recent spread of inter-communal violence in Myanmar and urged the Government to take steps to counteract this worrying development. In April 2014 the UN adopted a resolution broadening the mandate of the UN Special Rapporteur on the situation of human rights in Myanmar to report on progress in the electoral process and reform in the run-up to the 2015 elections. The following month Ojea Quintana was replaced as UN Special Rapporteur by Yanghee Lee.

Relations with the European Union

From March 1997 the EU withdrew Myanmar's special trading status, in response to concerns over the country's human rights record; two scheduled meetings between the EU and ASEAN, due to take place in late 1997 and early 1999, respectively, were cancelled by the EU, owing to its objection to the representation of Myanmar at the talks. However, an agreement was subsequently reached by the two sides to allow Myanmar to take a 'passive role' in the Joint Co-operation Committee meeting between the EU and ASEAN.

In January 2003 the Myanma Deputy Minister of Foreign Affairs, Khin Maung Win, was permitted to attend an EU-ASEAN summit meeting for the first time since Myanmar's suspension from the meetings in 1997. However, in April 2003 the EU elected to extend its sanctions against the country and to increase the list of SPDC officials subject to visa sanctions and freezing of their assets. These sanctions were subsequently renewed annually. In October 2004 EU foreign ministers implemented an earlier threat to broaden sanctions against Myanmar if the country did not make progress towards democratization in time for an Asia-Europe Meeting of heads of government (ASEM) held in Viet Nam earlier in the month. The ministers agreed to extend the list of Myanma officials subject to visa sanctions and to co-ordinate international bans on investment in the country (although the bans excluded European countries that had already invested in Myanmar).

In November 2007, in response to the violent suppression of anti-Government protests in Myanmar in September, the EU formally increased the number of officials subject to visa sanctions and asset freezing, expanded the scope of an investment ban on state-owned enterprises and imposed a new ban on some

Myanma exports, including timber, metals and gemstones. However, in response to the programme of political reform undertaken by the Myanma Government following the inauguration of President Thein Sein in March 2011, in January 2012 the EU agreed to suspend the bloc's imposition of visa sanctions on senior Myanma officials—including the President, the two Vice-Presidents, the two parliamentary Speakers and members of the Cabinet. In April, following the successful conduct of parliamentary by-elections, the EU opened an embassy-level office in Yangon and announced the suspension of sanctions for a period of one year, allowing trade and investment in Myanmar and ending travel bans on nearly 500 individuals; an embargo on the sale of arms remained in place. In April 2013 the EU decided to make the removal of sanctions permanent, again with the exception of the embargo on arms sales. The first meeting of the EU-Myanmar Task Force took place in Yangon and Nay Pyi Taw in November; the purpose of the high-level Task Force was to provide comprehensive political and economic support to Myanmar during its transition towards the establishment of a fully democratic system.

CONSTITUTION AND GOVERNMENT

A new Constitution was approved in a national referendum in May 2008 and entered into force on 31 January 2011. Multi-party elections, the first for more than 20 years, were held in November 2010; 25% of seats in the bicameral national legislature, which was responsible for choosing the country's President, were reserved for representatives of the military. The new legislature, the Pyidaungsu Hluttaw (Union Assembly), consisted of the 224-member Pyithu Hluttaw (People's Assembly—the lower chamber) and the 440-member Amyotha Hluttaw (House of Nationalities—the upper chamber). Following the inauguration in March 2011 of the new President, the State Peace and Development Council (SPDC), which had been established by the ruling military junta in November 1997, was dissolved. The incoming Cabinet comprised 30 members and was dominated by former military officers, as were the new eight-member State Supreme Council and 11-member National Defence and Security Council, created in February and March 2011, respectively.

REGIONAL AND INTERNATIONAL CO-OPERATION

Myanmar is a member of the Association of Southeast Asian Nations (ASEAN, see p. 210). It is also a member of the Asian Development Bank (ADB, see p. 206), the UN's Economic and Social Commission for Asia and the Pacific (ESCAP, see p. 30) and the Colombo Plan (see p. 445).

Myanmar became a member of the UN in 1948. As a contracting party to the General Agreement on Tariffs and Trade, Myanmar joined the World Trade Organization (WTO, see p. 431) on its establishment in 1995. Myanmar participates in the Non-aligned Movement (see p. 462), and is a member of the International Labour Organization (ILO, see p. 139).

ECONOMIC AFFAIRS

In 1986, according to estimates by the World Bank, Myanmar's gross national income (GNI), measured at average 1984–86 prices, was US $7,450m., equivalent to $200 per head. During 2004–13, it was estimated, the population rose at an average annual rate of 0.7%, while gross domestic product (GDP) per head increased, in real terms, by an average of 7.4% per year. Overall GDP increased at an average annual rate of 8.2% in 2004–13, according to the IMF. The IMF estimated real GDP growth at 8.3% in the financial year ending 31 March 2014.

According to the Asian Development Bank (ADB), agriculture (including forestry and fishing) contributed 30.5% of GDP in 2012/13. The sector engaged an estimated 65.4% of the employed labour force at mid-2015, according to FAO. Rice is the staple crop, and production reached an estimated 28.7m. metric tons in 2013. In 2013/14 pulses and beans accounted for an estimated 6.1% of total exports. Other crops include sugar cane, beans, maize, groundnuts, sesame seed, plantains and rubber. The fishing sector is also important. The total catch reached an estimated 4.5m. metric tons in 2012. Sales of teak and other hardwood provided an estimated 7.7% of total export revenue in 2013/14. Myanmar is currently the world's second largest source of illicit opium (after Afghanistan). According to a survey conducted by the UN Office on Drugs and Crime (UNODC, see p. 80), the area under poppy cultivation expanded by an estimated 13.3% in 2013 to reach 57,800 ha. The potential production of dry opium was thought likely to have increased from 690 tons in 2012 to 870 tons in 2013. According to the ADB, the real GDP of the agricultural sector increased at an average annual rate of 6.0% in 2006/07–10/11. Agricultural GDP increased by 2.0% in 2012/13.

Industry (including mining, manufacturing, construction and utilities) provided 32.1% of GDP in 2012/13, according to the ADB. The industrial sector engaged 22.0% of the employed labour force (excluding activities not adequately defined) in 2005. According to the ADB, between 2006/07 and 2010/11 industrial GDP increased at an average annual rate of 18.5%. The GDP of the industrial sector expanded by 8.0% in 2012/13.

Mining and quarrying contributed 6.1% of GDP in 2012/13, according to the ADB. The sector engaged only 0.7% of the employed labour force in 1997/98. Significant new onshore and offshore discoveries of natural gas and petroleum resulted from exploration and production-sharing agreements with foreign companies, the first of which was signed in 1989. In June 2013 the Government opened bidding for the exploration and development of a further 30 offshore blocks; earlier that year bids had been invited for exploration licences for 18 onshore blocks. Other important minerals that are commercially exploited include tin, copper, coal, lead, jade, gemstones, silver and gold; some of Myanmar's potentially lucrative mineral resources remain largely unexploited. According to ADB data, the GDP of the mining sector increased at an average annual rate of 11.2% between 2006/07 and 2010/11, but decreased by 6.7% in 2012/13.

Manufacturing contributed 19.9% of GDP in 2012/13, according to the ADB, and the sector engaged 9.1% of the employed labour force in 1998. The most important branches are food- and beverage-processing, the production of industrial raw materials (cement, plywood and fertilizers), petroleum refining and textiles. Revenue from garment exports rose from US $695.4m. in 2012/13 to an estimated $884.7m. in 2013/14, equivalent to 7.9% of total exports in the latter year. The real GDP of the manufacturing sector expanded, according to ADB data, at an average annual rate of 19.7% between 2006/07 and 2010/11, and increased by 8.4% in 2012/13.

Construction provided 4.9% of GDP in 2012/13, according to the ADB. The sector engaged only 2.2% of the employed labour force (excluding activities not adequately defined) in 1998. Between 2006/07 and 2010/11, according to ADB figures, construction GDP increased at an average annual rate of 15.4%; the sector's GDP grew by 9.3% in 2012/13.

Energy is derived principally from hydroelectric power, which contributed 70.3% of total electricity production in 2011; natural gas accounted for 21.7% and petroleum 0.4%. The People's Republic of China has provided considerable assistance in the development of hydropower resources. Myanmar's hydropower potential is estimated at around 30,000 MW. Imports of mineral oils accounted for around 16.7% of total imports in 2013/14.

The services sector contributed 37.4% of GDP in 2012/13, according to the ADB, and engaged 25.1% of the employed labour force in 1997/98. Tourism revenue is an increasingly important source of foreign exchange. Revenue from this sector rose nearly fourfold from US $72m. in 2010 to $281m. in 2011. The number of tourist arrivals increased from 900,161 in 2012/13 to 1,131,624 in 2013/14. In 2006/07–10/11, according to ADB data, the GDP of the services sector increased at an average annual rate of 12.1%. Sectoral growth was 12.6% in 2012/13.

In 2013 Myanmar recorded a visible merchandise trade deficit of US $439.9m., and there was a deficit of $1,127.7m. on the current account of the balance of payments. In 2013/14 the principal sources of imports were China (which supplied 29.8% of the total), Singapore, Thailand, Japan, the Republic of Korea and Malaysia. The principal market for exports (38.4%) was Thailand; other significant purchasers were China, India and Singapore. The principal imports in 2013/14 were machinery and transport equipment, refined mineral oils, base metals and manufactures, and electrical machinery and apparatus. The principal exports in that year included gas (which accounted for 29.4% of total export earnings), jade, garments and teak.

An overall budget deficit of 2,886,200m. kyats, equivalent to 4.9% of GDP, was recorded in 2013/14, according to the ADB. Myanmar's general government gross debt was 22,985,450m. kyats in 2012, equivalent to 48.0% of GDP. According to the ADB, the country's outstanding external debt at the end of 2014 totalled US $11,000m.; the cost of servicing external debt in

2013 was equivalent to 2.2% of exports of goods and services. The annual rate of inflation averaged 3.9% in 2001–10. According to official figures, the rate of inflation was 5.7% in 2013/14. The rate of unemployment in 2012 was estimated by the ADB at 4.0% of the labour force.

Progress towards democratic reform by the new Government under President Thein Sein that took office in 2011 led to substantial increases in foreign direct investment (FDI) and tourism revenues as Myanmar began to re-engage with the international community after many years of economic isolation. In the fiscal year ending March 2015 FDI rose to US $8,100m., led by new ventures in energy, manufacturing and telecommunications, a sharp increase from the $4,110m. recorded in 2013/14. Natural gas exports have become an important source of revenue, and in July 2013 China commenced importing gas from Myanmar through a new pipeline linking the two countries (a parallel crude petroleum pipeline was expected to start operating in 2015). Plans for the establishment of special economic zones included the development of a major maritime hub and industrial estate in the southern coastal town of Dawei, and two other zones, in Thilawa near Yangon, and Kyaukphyu on the west coast. The lifting of the majority of international sanctions, as well as having a positive impact on trade and investment, provided renewed access to concessionary finance and aid assistance. In January 2013 the Paris Club of creditor nations agreed to cancel about $6,000m. of Myanmar's debt (some 60% of the total owed), and in May Japan cancelled its remaining Myanma debt. Among economic reforms implemented by the new Government was the introduction in April 2012 of a unified exchange rate, ending the decades-old dual exchange rate (an official rate and a black market rate), with the aim of eliminating the informal currency market. In addition, legislation was introduced in July 2013 giving the Central Bank of Myanmar considerably greater autonomy. In response to the rapid rise in foreign interest in investment, a law approved in November 2012 removed the 50% cap on foreign holdings. There were widespread concerns, however, that economic growth would be severely curtailed by the country's weak infrastructure, limited macroeconomic management capacity and high level of poverty (which stood at some 26% in 2014). According to the IMF, GDP expanded by 8.3% in 2013/14, supported by further investment in the hydrocarbon industries, a buoyant construction sector, as well as increased tourism revenues and foreign remittances, while the rate of inflation rose to an average of 5.7% over that financial year, compared with 2.8% in 2012/13. The ADB estimated GDP growth of 7.7% and inflation of 5.9% in 2014/15. The IMF predicted a favourable economic outlook over the next few years, with GDP continuing to rise and both inflation and the current account deficit largely contained. However, the rapid economic transition posed a number of daunting challenges that required addressing to ensure that growth was sustained and inclusive—these included comprehensive liberalization of the foreign exchange, trade and foreign investment systems; the establishment of modern policy and institutional frameworks to manage and support the budget and financial sector; further expansion of education and health services; the provision of greater access to financial and banking services; and improvements in the collection of reliable statistics to enable effective economic planning and management. In October 2014 the authorities granted preliminary licences to nine foreign banks to operate in Myanmar.

PUBLIC HOLIDAYS

2016: 4 January (Independence Day), 12 February (Union Day), 2 March (Peasants' Day, anniversary of the 1962 coup), 22 March* (Full Moon of Tabaung), 27 March (Armed Forces' Day), 14–16 April* (Maha Thingyan—Water Festival), 17 April* (Myanma New Year), 1 May (Workers' Day), 20 May* (Full Moon of Kason), 18 July* (Full Moon of Waso and beginning of Buddhist Lent), 19 July (Martyrs' Day), 15 October* (Full Moon of Thadingyut and end of Buddhist Lent), 13 November* (Tazaungdaing Festival), 23 November* (National Day), 25 December (Christmas Day).

* A number of holidays depend on lunar sightings.

Statistical Survey

Source (unless otherwise stated): Central Statistical Organization, Ministry of National Planning and Economic Development, Building 32, Nay Pyi Taw; tel. (67) 406325; fax (67) 407265; e-mail cso.stat@mptmail.net.mm; internet www.csostat.gov.mm.

Area and Population

AREA, POPULATION AND DENSITY

Area (sq km)	676,552*
Population (census results)	
31 March 1983	35,307,913
29 March 2014 (provisional)†	
Males	24,821,176
Females	26,598,244
Total	51,419,420
Density (per sq km) at 2014 census	76.0

* 261,218 sq miles.

† Comprising an enumerated population of 50,213,067, plus an estimated population of 1,206,353 for parts of three states where enumeration could not be completed (46,600 in Kachin, 69,753 in Kayin, and 1,090,000 in Rakhine). The total census count for 2014 was significantly less than prevailing official population estimates.

POPULATION BY AGE AND SEX
(UN estimates at mid-2015)

	Males	Females	Total
0–14 years	6,591,002	6,510,236	13,101,238
15–64 years	18,445,303	19,681,025	38,126,328
65 years and over	1,267,562	1,669,134	2,936,696
Total	26,303,867	27,860,395	54,164,262

Source: UN, *World Population Prospects: The 2012 Revision.*

POPULATION BY STATE
(population at 2014 census, provisional)

Ayeyawady . . .	6,175,123		Mon	2,050,282	
Bago	4,863,455		Nay Pyi Taw . .	1,158,367	
Chin	478,690		Rakhine . . .	3,188,963	
Kachin	1,689,654		Sagaing . . .	5,320,299	
Kayah	286,738		Shan	5,815,384	
Kayin	1,572,657		Tanintharyi .	1,406,434	
Magway . . .	3,912,711		Yangon . . .	7,355,075	
Mandalay . . .	6,145,588		**Total** . . .	51,419,420	

Note: Data are comprised of an enumerated population of 50,213,067, plus an estimated population of 1,206,353 for parts of three states where enumeration could not be completed (46,600 in Kachin, 69,753 in Kayin, and 1,090,000 in Rakhine).

PRINCIPAL TOWNS
(population at 2014 census, provisional)

Yangon (Rangoon)* .	5,209,541		Monywa . . .	371,963
Mandalay . . .	1,225,133		Myitkyina . . .	305,347
Nay Pyi Taw				
(capital)* . . .	1,158,367		Magway . . .	288,883
			Mawlamyine	
Bago (Pegu) . .	491,130		(Moulmein) . .	288,120
Hpa-an . . .	421,415		Pathein (Bassein) .	286,684
Taunggyi . . .	380,665			

* In 2006 the functions of the capital city were transferred from Yangon to the new administrative centre of Nay Pyi Taw.

Births and Deaths

BIRTHS AND DEATHS
(annual averages, UN estimates)

	2000–05	2005–10	2010–15
Birth rate (per 1,000)	19.7	18.5	17.3
Death rate (per 1,000)	8.6	8.5	8.5

Source: UN, *World Population Prospects: The 2012 Revision.*

Life expectancy (years at birth): 64.9 (males 62.9; females 67.1) in 2012 (Source: World Bank, World Development Indicators database).

ECONOMICALLY ACTIVE POPULATION
('000, FAO estimates at mid-year)

	2013	2014	2015
Agriculture, etc.	20,929	21,122	21,298
Total labour force (incl. others) .	31,666	32,126	32,566

Source: FAO.

Health and Welfare

KEY INDICATORS

Total fertility rate (children per woman, 2012)	2.0
Under-5 mortality rate (per 1,000 live births, 2012) . . .	52
HIV/AIDS (% of persons aged 15–49, 2013)	0.6
Physicians (per 1,000 head, 2012)	0.6
Hospital beds (per 1,000 head, 2006)	0.6
Health expenditure (2011): US $ per head (PPP)	23
Health expenditure (2011): % of GDP	1.8
Health expenditure (2011): public (% of total)	15.9
Access to water (% of persons, 2012)	86
Access to sanitation (% of persons, 2012)	77
Total carbon dioxide emissions ('000 metric tons, 2010) . .	8,995.2
Carbon dioxide emissions per head (metric tons, 2010) . .	0.2
Human Development Index (2013): ranking	150
Human Development Index (2013): value	0.524

For sources and definitions, see explanatory note on p. vi.

Agriculture

PRINCIPAL CROPS
('000 metric tons)

	2011	2012	2013
Wheat	173	186*	188†
Rice, paddy	29,010	28,080*	28,767*
Maize	1,485	1,500*	1,700*
Millet	180†	185*	185*
Potatoes	565	600†	620†
Sweet potatoes†	48	50	52
Cassava (Manioc) . . .	730	625†	630†
Sugar cane	9,690	9,700†	9,650†
Beans, dry	3,750*	3,650†	3,700†
Peas, dry†	65	66	68
Chick peas	473	500†	490†
Cow peas, dry	173	180†	177†
Pigeon peas	849	820†	800†
Arecanuts†	120	121	120
Soybeans (Soya beans) . .	237	205*	205*
Groundnuts, with shell . .	1,400	1,372*	1,375*

—continued	2011	2012	2013
Coconuts	420*	422*	425†
Sunflower seed	490	350*	360*
Sesame seed	901	870*	890*
Onions, dry	1,143	1,138†	1,141†
Garlic	213	213†	212†
Plantains	955	1,000†	1,000†
Tea	31*	31†	32†
Jute	3	2†	2†
Tobacco, unmanufactured . .	29	29†	29†
Natural rubber	150	150†	148†

* Unofficial figure.
† FAO estimate(s).

Aggregate production ('000 metric tons, may include official, semi-official or estimated data): Total cereals 31,081 in 2011, 30,175 in 2012, 31,068 in 2013; Total roots and tubers 1,342 in 2011, 1,275 in 2012, 1,302 in 2013; Total vegetables (incl. melons) 4,856 in 2011, 4,651 in 2012, 4,753 in 2013; Total fruits (excl. melons) 2,289 in 2011, 2,308 in 2012, 2,308 in 2013.

Source: FAO.

LIVESTOCK
('000 head, year ending September)

	2011	2012*	2013*
Horses*	114	115	116
Cattle	14,088	14,200	14,350
Buffaloes	3,097	3,200	3,250
Pigs	10,497	10,500	10,530
Sheep	854	860	562
Goats	3,852	3,900	3,930
Chickens	176,839	180,000	190,000
Ducks	15,507	16,000	16,100
Geese	1,966	2,000	2,050

* FAO estimates.
Source: FAO.

LIVESTOCK PRODUCTS
('000 metric tons)

	2011	2012*	2013*
Cattle meat	210.0†	215.0	216.0
Buffalo meat	44.0†	45.0	45.9
Goat meat	40.0†	40.0	40.1
Pig meat	619.1	620.0	620.6
Chicken meat	1,079.1	1,080.0	1,082.3
Cows' milk	1,360.0†	1,300.0	1,380.0
Buffaloes' milk	305.6†	307.0	309.0
Goats' milk†	15.0	15.0	15.2
Hen eggs	371.7	380.0	382.0
Other poultry eggs	40.0*	41.0	43.0

* FAO estimate(s).
† Unofficial figure(s).
Source: FAO.

Forestry

ROUNDWOOD REMOVALS
('000 cubic metres, excl. bark)

	2011	2012	2013
Sawlogs, veneer logs and logs for sleepers	3,134	3,349	2,909
Other industrial wood	1,605	1,638	1,638*
Fuel wood*	38,286	38,286	38,286
Total	43,025	43,273	42,833

* FAO estimate(s).
Source: FAO.

SAWNWOOD PRODUCTION
('000 cubic metres, incl. railway sleepers, unofficial figures)

	2004	2005	2006
Coniferous (softwood)	77	61	80
Broadleaved (hardwood) . . .	1,056	1,530	1,530
Total	1,133	1,591	1,610

2007–13: Production assumed to be unchanged from 2006 (unofficial figures).

Source: FAO.

Fishing

('000 metric tons, live weight)

	2010	2011	2012
Capture*	3,063.2	3,333.0	3,579.3
Freshwater fishes	1,002.4	1,163.2	1,246.5
Marine fishes*	2,016.6	2,123.3	2,269.6
Aquaculture	850.7*	816.8	885.2*
Common carp	23.4	22.7	24.7
Roho labeo	546.3	530.8	577.0
Total catch*	3,913.9	4,149.8	4,464.4

* FAO estimate(s).
Source: FAO.

Mining

(metric tons unless otherwise indicated)

	2010	2011	2012
Coal and lignite	217,650	300,000*	300,000*
Crude petroleum ('000 barrels) .	6,806	6,400*	6,500*
Natural gas (million cu m)† . .	12,425	12,500	12,500
Copper ore‡	9,000	9,000	19,000
Lead ore‡*	7,000	8,700	9,800
Zinc ore‡	8,600	9,300	10,000*
Tin concentrates‡	4,000	11,000	10,600*
Gold ore (kilograms)‡§* . . .	100	n.a.	n.a.
Feldspar*§	10,000	10,000	n.a.
Barite (Barytes)	8,975	30,000*	30,000*
Salt (unrefined, excl. brine)* . .	35,000	n.a.	n.a.
Gypsum (crude)	81,051	50,000*	50,000*
Rubies, sapphires and spinel ('000 metric carats)§	3,542	2,990*	3,020*
Jade	38,990	45,000*	45,000*

* Estimated production.
† Marketed production.
‡ Figures refer to the metal content of ores and concentrates (including mixed concentrates).
§ Twelve months beginning 1 April of year stated.

Source: US Geological Survey.

Industry

SELECTED PRODUCTS OF STATE-OWNED ENTERPRISES
('000 metric tons unless otherwise indicated)

	2011/12	2012/13	2013/14
Sugar	0.7	n.a.	2,362
Beer ('000 gallons)	20,895.9	26,138.0	34,087.9
Cigarettes (million)	5,603.9	5,704.7	6,585.3
Cotton fabrics ('000 yards)	10.8	7.4	3.2
Cotton yarn ('000 lbs)	14.3	6.8	2.0
Plywood ('000 sq ft)	230.9	227.9	1,555.8
Fertilizers	165.8	208.6	156.6
Diesel oil ('000 gallons)	51,640	43,586	39,732
Furnace oil ('000 gallons)	12,049	10,820	9,281
Liquefied petroleum gas ('000 gallons)	3,783	4,209	2,879
Motor spirit (petrol, '000 gallons)	131,162	101,220	70,435
Cement	547.2	487.3	476.5
Paper	13.2	4.2	0.6
Soap	11.2	0.7	n.a.
Electric energy (million kWh)	9,711.6	10,964.9	13,048.3

Finance

CURRENCY AND EXCHANGE RATES

Monetary Units
100 pyas = 1 kyat.

Sterling, Dollar and Euro Equivalents (31 December 2014)
£1 sterling = 1,609.965 kyats;
US $1 = 1,031.500 kyats;
€1 = 1,252.344 kyats;
10,000 kyats = £6.21 = $9.69 = €7.99.

Average Exchange Rate (kyats per US $)
2012   640.653
2013   933.570
2014   984.346

Note: In April 2012, in an attempt gradually to unify the disparate official and unofficial exchange rates which had prevailed in the country for decades, the Government initiated a 'managed float' of the kyat on the open market; an initial daily reference exchange rate of US $1 = 818 kyats was published by the central bank on 1 April.

CENTRAL GOVERNMENT BUDGET
(million kyats, year ending 31 March, excl. capital account)

Current revenue and grants	2003/04	2004/05	2005/06
Tax revenue	170,569	297,104	476,945
Taxes on income, profits and capital gains	91,860	138,866	206,676
Domestic taxes on goods and services	74,107	136,626	251,821
General sales, turnover or value-added tax	58,214	112,543	225,121
Taxes on international trade and transactions	4,602	21,613	18,448
Other revenue	213,542	290,190	342,273
Grants	111	171	316
Total	384,222	587,465	819,534

Current expenditure	2003/04	2004/05	2005/06
General public services, incl. public order	114,195	206,848	354,848
Defence	172,633	173,558	197,792
Education	71,665	101,936	68,676
Health	18,808	26,545	21,963
Social security and welfare	7,865	9,933	8,406
Recreational, cultural and religious affairs	4,112	5,863	4,511
Economic affairs and services	194,354	234,513	346,361
Agriculture, etc.	61,056	71,028	93,300
Transportation	119,190	131,839	198,261
Housing and community amenities	7,397	8,622	6,228
Total	591,029	767,818	1,008,785

Source: IMF, *Government Finance Statistics Yearbook*.

2011/12 ('000 million kyats, year ending 31 March): *Revenue:* Current 6,483.0 (Tax revenue 1,719.7, Non-tax revenue 4,763.3); Capital 338.4; Total revenue 6,821.4 (excl. grants 0.2). *Expenditure:* Current 5,560.9; Capital 3,020.7; Total expenditure 8,581.5 (Source: Asian Development Bank).

2012/13 ('000 million kyats, year ending 31 March): *Revenue:* Current 11,487.6 (Tax revenue 1,946.1, Non-tax revenue 9,541.6); Capital 270.3; Total revenue 11,758.0 (excl. grants 25.5). *Expenditure:* Current 8,764.0; Capital 5,409.0; Total expenditure 14,173.0 (Source: Asian Development Bank).

2013/14 ('000 million kyats, year ending 31 March): *Revenue:* Current 13,711.2 (Tax revenue 3,642.0, Non-tax revenue 10,069.2); Capital 259.4; Total revenue 13,970.6 (excl. grants 198.1). *Expenditure:* Current 11,841.9; Capital 5,433.4; Total expenditure 17,275.3 (Source: Asian Development Bank).

INTERNATIONAL RESERVES
(US $ million at 31 December)

	2010	2011	2012
Gold (national valuation)	12.6	12.6	12.6
IMF special drawing rights	2.6	1.0	0.5
Foreign exchange	5,714.3	7,003.0	6,963.5
Total	5,729.5	7,016.6	6,976.6

IMF special drawing rights: 1.7 in 2013; 2.8 in 2014.

Source: IMF, *International Financial Statistics*.

MONEY SUPPLY
('000 million kyats at 31 December)

	2011	2012	2013
Currency outside depository corporations	5,132.60	5,856.76	6,949.18
Transferable deposits	1,556.05	1,778.21	2,636.03
Other deposits	5,542.64	11,323.41	11,920.19
Broad money	12,231.29	18,958.38	21,505.39

Source: IMF, *International Financial Statistics*.

COST OF LIVING
(Consumer Price Index; base: 2006 = 100; year ending 31 March)

	2011/12	2012/13	2013/14
Food (incl. beverages)	157.6	159.3	169.5
Fuel and light	154.1	172.1	188.3
Clothing (incl. footwear)	157.2	162.9	159.4
Rent	268.0	298.3	327.9
All items (incl. others)	163.3	167.9	177.5

NATIONAL ACCOUNTS
(million kyats at current prices, year ending 31 March)

Expenditure on the Gross Domestic Product

	2010/11	2011/12	2012/13
Final consumption expenditure	31,343,453	33,605,530	36,684,537
Increase in stocks	106,059	25,184	361,483
Gross fixed capital formation	9,115,074	13,516,160	15,306,049
Total domestic expenditure	40,564,586	47,146,874	52,352,069
Exports of goods and services	46,150	7,140,425	7,572,517

—continued	2010/11	2011/12	2012/13
Less Imports of goods and services	35,508	7,300,329	7,722,905
Statistical discrepancy . . .	−798,463	−642,732	−474,229
GDP in purchasers' values .	39,776,765	46,344,238	51,727,452
GDP at constant 2010/11 prices	20,792,106	42,004,611	45,209,641

Gross Domestic Product by Economic Activity

	2010/11	2011/12	2012/13
Agriculture, hunting, forestry and fishing .	14,658,961	15,063,106	15,752,894
Mining and quarrying	366,428	2,710,693	3,158,434
Manufacturing	7,900,494	9,132,523	10,301,298
Electricity, gas and water . . .	421,883	481,449	611,061
Construction	1,839,335	2,165,836	2,515,898
Wholesale and retail trade . .	7,971,161	8,929,095	10,010,038
Transport, storage and communications	4,926,584	5,923,921	6,887,326
Finance	37,715	65,318	84,611
Government services	915,720	989,006	1,327,348
Other services	738,484	883,291	1,078,544
GDP in purchasers' values .	39,776,765	46,344,238	51,727,452

Source: Asian Development Bank.

BALANCE OF PAYMENTS
(US $ million)

	2011	2012	2013
Exports of goods	7,699.0	8,220.3	9,022.4
Imports of goods	−7,491.0	−7,628.6	−9,462.2
Balance on goods . . .	208.0	591.7	−439.9
Exports of services	758.5	1,231.3	2,270.9
Imports of services	−1,090.2	−1,459.3	−1,480.9
Balance on goods and services	−123.7	363.7	350.2
Primary income received . . .	200.5	293.3	237.0
Primary income paid . . .	−2,032.5	−2,466.6	−2,529.2
Balance on goods, services and primary income . . .	−1,955.7	−1,809.7	−1,942.1
Secondary income received . .	498.6	664.4	972.4
Secondary income paid . . .	−103.9	−114.3	−158.1
Current balance	−1,561.1	−1,259.6	−1,127.7
Capital account (net)	—	−3.5	6,463.8
Direct investment liabilities . .	2,519.8	1,333.9	2,254.6
Other investment liabilities . .	449.4	981.3	−5,781.2
Net errors and omissions . . .	−137.4	5,864.3	807.2
Reserves and related items .	1,270.7	6,916.3	2,616.7

Source: IMF, *International Financial Statistics*.

External Trade

PRINCIPAL COMMODITIES
(US $ million, year ending 31 March)

Imports c.i.f.	2011/12	2012/13	2013/14
Edible vegetable oil and other hydrogenated oils	394.6	304.0	514.5
Pharmaceutical products . . .	217.9	272.9	253.0
Refined mineral oils	1,926.9	1,591.6	2,300.3
Plastic	312.0	350.7	467.8
Fabric of artificial materials and synthetics	254.0	308.8	405.9
Base metals and manufactures .	946.9	1,025.3	1,542.8
Machinery and transport equipment	1,823.7	2,645.5	4,145.4
Electrical machinery and apparatus	465.8	488.7	708.2
Total (incl. others)	9,035.1	9,068.9	13,759.5

Exports f.o.b.	2011/12	2012/13	2013/14
Rice (incl. broken rice)	267.2	544.1	460.1
Black gram (matpe) bean . . .	471.7	382.8	376.4
Green mung (pedesein) bean . .	202.4	273.7	310.1
Fresh and dried prawns . . .	82.2	94.7	59.7
Fish and fish products	349.4	442.2	311.0
Teak	278.9	327.5	637.5
Other hardwood	271.9	209.8	225.3
Natural gas	3,502.5	3,666.1	3,299.2
Base metals and ores	71.3	92.0	130.1
Garments	497.5	695.4	884.7
Jade	34.2	297.9	1,011.6
Total (incl. others)	9,135.6	8,977.0	11,204.0

PRINCIPAL TRADING PARTNERS
(US $ million, year ending 31 March)

Imports	2011/12	2012/13	2013/14
China, People's Republic . . .	2,786.8	2,719.5	4,105.5
Germany	95.1	144.6	83.2
India	325.4	301.7	493.5
Indonesia	431.8	195.2	438.8
Japan	502.2	1,091.7	1,296.2
Korea, Republic	451.9	343.2	1,218.0
Malaysia	303.4	360.9	839.7
Singapore	2,516.1	2,535.4	2,910.2
Thailand	691.2	696.8	1,377.0
USA	263.6	120.0	79.7
Total (incl. others)	9,035.1	9,068.9	13,759.5

Exports	2011/12	2012/13	2013/14
China, People's Republic . . .	2,214.3	2,238.1	2,910.8
Hong Kong	41.5	12.7	489.1
India	1,046.0	1,018.6	1,143.6
Japan	320.2	406.5	513.3
Korea, Republic	214.8	280.8	352.9
Malaysia	152.0	97.9	108.9
Singapore	542.8	291.4	694.0
Thailand	3,823.8	4,000.6	4,306.3
Total (incl. others)	9,135.6	8,977.0	11,204.0

Transport

RAILWAYS
(traffic, million, year ending 31 March)

	2011/12	2012/13	2013/14
Passenger-miles	3,093	2,366	2,227
Freight ton-miles	722	602	515

ROAD TRAFFIC
(registered motor vehicles at 31 March)

	2012	2013	2014
Passenger cars	267,561	331,468	434,169
Trucks	67,750	74,546	124,597
Buses	19,579	19,812	22,151
Motorcycles	1,955,505	3,219,213	3,595,474
Others	53,352	54,070	61,291
Total	2,363,747	3,699,109	4,237,682

INLAND WATERWAYS
(traffic by state-owned vessels, year ending 31 March)

	2011/12	2012/13	2013/14
Passenger-miles (million) . . .	531	210	146
Freight ton-miles (million) . .	520	332	283

SHIPPING

Flag Registered Fleet
(at 31 December)

	2012	2013	2014
Number of vessels	62	61	66
Displacement ('000 grt) . . .	166.0	160.2	174.2

Source: Lloyd's List Intelligence (www.lloydslistintelligence.com).

International Seaborne Traffic
('000 metric tons)

	2011/12	2012/13	2013/14
Goods loaded	4,267	4,883	5,328
Goods unloaded	8,865	10,244	12,520

CIVIL AVIATION
(traffic on scheduled services)

	2007	2008	2009
Kilometres flown (million) . .	23	23	22
Passengers carried ('000) . . .	1,663	1,638	1,527
Passenger-km (million) . . .	1,609	1,585	1,470
Total ton-km (million)	148	145	134

Source: UN, *Statistical Yearbook*.

Passenger-miles (million): 137.1 in 2011/12; 153.8 in 2012/13; 125.3 in 2013/14.

Freight ton-miles ('000): 144 in 2011/12; 280 in 2012/13; 733 in 2013/14.

Tourism

TOURIST ARRIVALS BY COUNTRY OF NATIONALITY
(year ending 31 March)

	2012	2013	2014
Australia	18,261	24,718	29,175
China, People's Republic . . .	70,805	90,550	125,609
France	30,064	35,462	41,453
Germany	23,063	27,712	32,265
India	16,868	21,042	32,306
Japan	47,690	68,761	83,434
Korea, Republic	34,805	54,934	58,472
Malaysia	30,499	39,758	46,534
Singapore	26,296	39,140	47,692
Taiwan	22,060	30,699	32,664
Thailand	94,342	139,770	198,229
United Kingdom	24,296	33,203	40,921
USA	37,589	53,653	62,631
Total (incl. others)	593,381	900,161	1,131,624

Source: Ministry of Hotels and Tourism, Nay Pyi Taw.

Tourism receipts (US $ million, excl. passenger transport): 72 in 2010; 281 in 2011 (Source: World Tourism Organization).

Communications Media

	2011	2012	2013
Telephones ('000 main lines in use)	523.9	524.2	534.8
Mobile cellular telephones ('000 subscribers)	1,243.6	3,729.6	6,832.4
Internet subscribers ('000) . .	15.3	n.a.	n.a.
Broadband subscribers ('000) . .	18.3	63.9	95.4

Source: International Telecommunication Union.

Education

(2009/10 unless otherwise indicated)

	Institutions*	Teachers	Students
Pre-primary schools . . .	n.a.	9,194	159,270
Primary schools	35,856	181,666	5,125,942
Middle schools	2,058 }	83,703	2,852,447
High schools	858 }		
Vocational schools	86	1,847*	21,343*
Teacher training	17	615*	4,031*
Higher education	45	6,246*	247,348*
Universities	6	2,901*	62,098*

* Data for 1994/95; figure for primary schools excludes 1,152 monastic primary schools with an enrolment of 45,360 in 1994/95.

Tertiary education (2010/11): Teachers 23,238; Students 659,510 (males 280,112, females 379,398).

Source: mainly UNESCO Institute for Statistics.

Pupil-teacher ratio (primary education, UNESCO estimate): 28.2 in 2009/10 (Source: UNESCO Institute for Statistics).

Adult literacy rate (UNESCO estimates): 92.6% (males 95.0%; females 90.5%) in 2012 (Source: UNESCO Institute for Statistics).

Directory

The Government

HEAD OF STATE

President: THEIN SEIN (took office 30 March 2011).
Vice-Presidents: Dr SAI MAUK KHAM, Adm. NYAN TUN.

CABINET
(May 2015)

Ministers of the President's Office: THEIN NYUNT, SOE MAUNG, SOE THEIN, AUNG MIN, HLA TUN, TIN NAING THEIN.
Minister of Defence: Lt-Gen. WAI LWIN.
Minister of Home Affairs: Lt-Gen. KO KO.
Minister of Border Affairs: Lt-Gen. THET NAING WIN.

Minister of Foreign Affairs: WUNNA MAUNG LWIN.
Minister of Information: YE HTUT.
Minister of Culture: AYE MYINT KYU.
Minister of Agriculture and Irrigation: MYINT HLAING.
Minister of Environmental Conservation and Forestry: WIN TUN.
Minister of Finance and Revenue: WIN SHEIN.
Minister of Construction: KYAW LWIN.
Minister of National Planning and Economic Development: Dr KAN ZAW.
Minister of Livestock and Fisheries: OHN MYINT.
Minister of Commerce: WIN MYINT.

Minister of Communications and Information Technology: Gen. MYAT HEIN.

Minister of Labour, Employment and Social Security: AYE MYINT.

Minister of Social Welfare, Relief and Resettlement: Dr DAW MYAT OHN KHIN.

Minister of Mines: Dr MYINT AUNG.

Minister of Co-operatives: KYAW HSAN.

Minister of Transportation: NYAN TUN AUNG.

Minister of Sports: TINT HSAN.

Minister of Industry (No. 1 and No. 2): MAUNG MYINT.

Minister of Rail Transportation: THAN HTAY.

Minister of Energy: Maj.-Gen. ZAYAR AUNG.

Minister of Electric Power: KHIN MAUNG SOE.

Minister of Hotels and Tourism: HTAY AUNG.

Minister of Education: Dr MYA AYE.

Minister of Health: THAN AUNG.

Minister of Religious Affairs: U SOE WIN.

Minister of Science and Technology: Dr KO KO OO.

Minister of Immigration and Manpower: KHIN YI.

MINISTRIES

President's Office: Bldg 18, Nay Pyi Taw; internet www.president-office.gov.mm.

Ministry of Agriculture and Irrigation: Bldg 15, Nay Pyi Taw; tel. (67) 410004; fax (67) 140130; e-mail dg-dap@myanmar.com.mm; internet www.moai.gov.mm.

Ministry of Border Affairs: Bldg 14, Nay Pyi Taw; tel. (67) 409022.

Ministry of Commerce: Bldg 3, Nay Pyi Taw; tel. (67) 408002; fax (67) 408004; e-mail moc@commerce.gov.mm; internet www.commerce.gov.mm.

Ministry of Communications and Information Technology: Bldg 2, Nay Pyi Taw; tel. (67) 407037; e-mail dg.ptd@mptmail.net.mm; internet www.mcpt.gov.mm.

Ministry of Construction: Bldg 11, Nay Pyi Taw; tel. (67) 407073; fax (67) 407181; internet www.construction.gov.mm.

Ministry of Co-operatives: Bldg 16, Nay Pyi Taw; tel. (67) 410033; fax (67) 410036; e-mail mocoop@mptmail.net.mm; internet www.myancoop.gov.mm.

Ministry of Culture: Bldg 35, Nay Pyi Taw; tel. (67) 408023.

Ministry of Defence: Bldg 20, Nay Pyi Taw.

Ministry of Education: Bldg 13, Nay Pyi Taw; tel. (67) 407131; internet www.myanmar-education.edu.mm.

Ministry of Electric Power: Bldg 27 and 38, Nay Pyi Taw; tel. (67) 411083.

Ministry of Energy: Bldg 6, Nay Pyi Taw; tel. (67) 411060; fax (67) 411012; e-mail moe.ho@energy.gov.mm; internet www.energy.gov.mm.

Ministry of Environmental Conservation and Forestry: Bldg 28, Nay Pyi Taw; tel. (67) 405004; e-mail ofpma@mptmail.net.mm; internet www.myanmarteak.gov.mm.

Ministry of Finance and Revenue: Bldg 26, Nay Pyi Taw; tel. (67) 410046; fax (67) 410189; e-mail ho.mofr@mptmail.net.mm; internet www.mofr.gov.mm.

Ministry of Foreign Affairs: Bldg 9, Nay Pyi Taw; tel. (67) 412359; e-mail mofa.aung@mptmail.net.mm; internet www.mofa.gov.mm.

Ministry of Health: Bldg 4, Nay Pyi Taw; tel. (67) 411358; internet www.moh.gov.mm.

Ministry of Home Affairs: Bldg 10, Nay Pyi Taw; tel. (67) 412079.

Ministry of Hotels and Tourism: Bldg 33, Nay Pyi Taw; tel. (67) 406406; fax (67) 406057; e-mail mo.moht@mptmail.net.mm; internet www.myanmartourism.org.

Ministry of Immigration and Manpower: Bldg 23, Nay Pyi Taw; tel. (67) 404026.

Ministry of Industry (No. 1): Bldg 37, Nay Pyi Taw; tel. (67) 408063; fax (67) 408080; e-mail moi1@myanmar.com.mm; internet www.industry1myanmar.com.

Ministry of Industry (No. 2): Bldg 30, Nay Pyi Taw; tel. (67) 405135; e-mail ministryofindustry@gmail.com; internet www.industry2.gov.mm.

Ministry of Information: Bldg 7, Nay Pyi Taw; tel. (67) 412321; e-mail contact@ministryofinformation.gov.mm; internet www.ministryofinformation.gov.mm.

Ministry of Labour, Employment and Social Security: Bldg 51, Nay Pyi Taw; tel. (67) 404339; e-mail mol@mptmail.net.mm; internet www.mol.gov.mm.

Ministry of Livestock and Fisheries: Bldg 36, Nay Pyi Taw; tel. (67) 408045; e-mail molf@livestock-fisheries.gov.mm; internet www.livestock-fisheries.gov.mm.

Ministry of Mines: Bldg 19, Nay Pyi Taw; tel. (67) 409019; fax (67) 409010; internet www.mining.com.mm.

Ministry of National Planning and Economic Development: Bldg 1, Nay Pyi Taw; tel. (67) 407023; fax (67) 407004; e-mail ministry.nped@mptmail.net.mm; internet www.mnped.gov.mm.

Ministry of Rail Transportation: Bldg 29, Nay Pyi Taw; tel. (67) 405034; internet www.mrt.gov.mm.

Ministry of Religious Affairs: Bldg 31, Nay Pyi Taw; tel. (67) 406008; internet www.mora.gov.mm.

Ministry of Science and Technology: Bldg 21, Nay Pyi Taw; tel. (67) 404004; fax (67) 404011; internet www.most.gov.mm.

Ministry of Social Welfare, Relief and Resettlement: Bldg 23, Nay Pyi Taw; tel. (67) 404021; e-mail social-wel-myan@mptmail.net.mm; internet www.myanmar.gov.mm/ministry/MSWRR/index.html.

Ministry of Sports: Bldg 31, Nay Pyi Taw; tel. (67) 406028; e-mail info@myasoc.org; internet www.mosports.gov.mm.

Ministry of Transportation: Bldg 5, Nay Pyi Taw; tel. (67) 411033; fax (67) 411038; e-mail minotran@mptmail.net.mm; internet www.mot.gov.mm.

Legislature

UNION ASSEMBLY

The bicameral legislature, the Pyidaungsu Hluttaw (Union Assembly) comprises the lower chamber of the Pyithu Hluttaw (People's Assembly), which has 440 seats, and the upper chamber of the Amyotha Hluttaw (House of Nationalities), with 224 seats. Under a constitutional provision, 25% of seats in both chambers are reserved for appointed representatives of the armed forces. Elections for 14 state and regional assemblies were held concurrently with the polls for the Pyidaungsu Hluttaw on 7 November 2010.

House of Nationalities
(Amyotha Hluttaw)

The Amyotha Hluttaw comprises 168 civilian representatives (12 from each of the seven states and seven regions) and 56 military representatives, who are appointed by the Commander-in-Chief of the Armed Forces.

Speaker: KHIN AUNG MYINT.

General Election, 7 November 2010

Party	Seats
Union Solidarity and Development Party	129
Rakhine Nationalities Development Party	7
National Unity Party	5
Chin Progressive Party	4
National Democratic Force	4
All Mon Region Democracy Party	3
Phalon-Sawaw Democratic Party	3
Shan Nationalities Democratic Party	3
Chin National Party	2
Wa Democratic Party	1
Others	7
Appointed members*	56
Total	**224**

* Military representatives appointed by the Commander-in-Chief of the Armed Forces.

Note: At by-elections held on 1 April 2012, the National League for Democracy won four seats in the Amyotha Hluttaw, the Shan Nationalities Democratic Party one seat and the Union Solidarity and Development Party (USDP) one seat (a net loss of five seats for the USDP).

People's Assembly
(Pyithu Hluttaw)

Speaker: SHWE MANN.

General Election, 7 November 2010

Party	Seats
Union Solidarity and Development Party	259
Shan Nationalities Democratic Party	18
National Unity Party	12
Rakhine Nationalities Development Party . . .	9
National Democratic Force	8
All Mon Region Democracy Party	3
Pa-O National Organization	3
Chin National Party	2
Chin Progressive Party	2
Phalon-Sawaw Democratic Party	2
Wa Democratic Party	2
Others	10
Appointed members*	110
Total	**440**

* Military representatives appointed by the Commander-in-Chief of the Armed Forces.

Note: At by-elections held on 1 April 2012, the National League for Democracy won 37 seats in the Pyithu Hluttaw.

Election Commission

Union Election Commission (UEC): Nay Pyi Taw; f. 2010; Chair. Lt-Gen. (retd) TIN AYE.

Political Organizations

Registered political parties include:

88 Generation Peace and Open Society (88GPOS): 1039/1040 Thumingala Rd, 16/1 Block, Thingangyun Township, Yangon; tel. (1) 565919; e-mail info@the88generation.org; internet www.the88generation.org; f. 2005; fmrly 88 Generation Students and Youth Organization; Leader MIN KO NAING.

All Mon Region Democracy Party: Lot 7, Holdings Kha 23, 20th St, Myinethaya Ward, Mawlamyine, Mon State; f. 2010; sole party registered for 2010 election representing the Mon ethnic group; advocates democracy and a free-market economy; Chair. NAI NGWE THEIN.

Arakan National Party (ANP): Yangon; f. 2014; formed by the merger of the Rakhine Nationalities Development Party (which was also contributing two mems to the Federal Union Party) and the Arakan (Rakhine) League for Democracy; Leaders AYE THAR AUNG, AYE MAUNG.

Chin National Party: 277 BPI Rd, West Gyogon Ward, Insein Township, Yangon; tel. (1) 646474; e-mail cnpparty@gmail.com; internet www.chinnationalparty.org; f. 2010; Chair. PU ZOZAM; Gen. Sec. SALAI CEU BIK THAWNG.

Democratic Party: 456 Theinphyu Rd, Mingalar Taung Nyunt, Yangon; tel. (1) 386475; e-mail democraticpartymyanmar1@gmail.com; internet democraticmyanmar.com; f. 1988; re-formed 2010; Chair. THU WAI.

Democratic Party for a New Society (DPNS): 4 Thiri Weibar St, Zawana Quarter, Thingangyun Township, Yangon; tel. (9) 31211730; e-mail hq@dpns.org; internet www.dpns.org; f. 1988; 7-mem. cen. exec. cttee; Chair. AUNG MOE ZAW; Gen. Sec. NGWE LIN.

Federal Union Party (FUP): f. 2013; est. by mems of 16 ethnic political parties belonging to the Nationalities Brotherhood Forum to contest the 2015 elections; mems of the 16 political parties who were to contest the election as candidates of the FUP had to resign from their previous party as, under Myanmar's electoral rules, individuals cannot be members of more than one political party; the 16 parties are the Shan Nationalities Democratic Party, the Tai-leng (Red Shan) Nationalities Development Party, the Rakhine Nationalities Development Party, the Phalon-Sawaw Democratic Party, All Mon Region Democracy Party, the Chin National Party, the Kayan National Party, the Inn National Development Party, the Danu Nationalities Democracy Party, the Pa-O National Organization, Taaung (Palaung) National Party, the Asho Chin National Party, the Wa Democratic Party, the Wa National Unity Party, the Ethnic National Development Party and the Mon Democracy Party.

Kachin Democratic Party (KDP): f. 2013; Leader GUMGRAWNG AWNG HKAM.

Kachin State Democracy Party (KSDP): Yuzana Quarter, Myitkyina; f. 2013; Chair. Dr MANAM TU JA.

Kachin State National Congress for Democracy (KNCD): Myitkyina; Leader HKANGDA YAW.

Kaman National Progressive Party: Mya Lay Yone St, Tamwe Township, Yangon; f. 2010; Chair. ZAW WIN; Gen. Sec. TIN HLAING WIN.

Kayin People's Party (KPP): 51 Tawwin Rd, Ward 3, Shwe Pyi Tha, Yangon; f. 2001; Leader SIMON THA; Chair. TUN AUNG MYINT.

Lahu National Development Party: 43 Fourth Lane, Parami Rd, Ward 1, Lashio, Shan State; f. 1988; deregistered 1994; reregistered 2010; Chair. KYA HAR SHE.

Lisu National Development Party (LNDP): Myitkyina; f. 2014.

Mon Democracy Party: Mawlamyine, Mon State; f. 2012; fmrly the Mon National Democratic Front; Chair. NAING NGWE THEIN.

Mro (or) Khami National Solidarity Organization (MKNSO): 202 Sartaik Rd, Pyitawtha Ward, Kyauktaw, Rakhine State; f. 1988; Chair. and Leader SAN THA AUNG.

National Democratic Force: Rm 103, Bldg 3, Dagonlwin Rd, Mittanyunt Ward, Tamway, Yangon; tel. (1) 551654; e-mail info@ndfmyanmar.com; f. 2010; est. by fmr mems of the National League for Democracy; Chair. KHIN MAUNG SWE.

National Democratic Party for Development: Bo Sun Pek Rd, Pabedan Township, Yangon; f. 2010; Chair. MAUNG MAUNG NI.

National League for Democracy (NLD): 97B West Shwegondine Rd, Bahan Township, Yangon; tel. (1) 555156; e-mail info .nldburma@gmail.com; internet www.nldburma.org; f. 1988; est. as Nat. United Front for Democracy; name subsequently changed to League for Democracy; above name adopted 1988; cen. exec. cttee of 20 mems; cen. cttee of 108 mems; Chair. AUNG SAN SUU KYI.

National Political Alliances League: 49 16th St, Lanmadaw Township, Yangon; f. 2010; membership includes breakaway factions from the National League for Democracy; Chair OHN LWIN; Gen Sec TIN WIN.

National Unity Party (NUP): 24 Aung Zeya St, Shwe Taung Gyar Ward 1, Bahan, Yangon; tel. (1) 278180; f. 1962; est. as the Burma Socialist Programme Party; sole legal political party until Sept. 1988, when present name was adopted; 15-mem. cen. exec. cttee and 280-mem. cen. cttee; Chair. THAN TIN.

Pa-O National Organization: 18 West Circular Rd, Zaypaing Ward, Taunggyi, Shan State; internet www.pa-onational.com; signed a ceasefire agreement with the military junta in April 1991; est. by the merger of the Union Pa-O National Organization and the ceasefire group; controls Special Region 6 in southern Shan State; 1,235 mems; Patron AUNG KHAM HTI; Chair. KHUN SAN LWIN; military wing: Pa-O National Army.

Peace and Diversity Party (PDP): 2/2/232 Mahawgani Rd, Htaukkyant, Mingaladon Township, Yangon; tel. 98610719 (mobile); f. 2010; also known as the Difference and Peace Party; Chair. NAY MYO LWIN.

Phalon-Sawaw Democratic Party: Ward 7, Hpa-an Township, Karen State; f. 2010; represents the Karen ethnic group; Chair. KHIN MAUNG MYINT; Gen. Sec. KYI LIN.

Shan Nationalities Democratic Party (SNDP): 9 Thitsar Uyin Housing, Thitsar Rd, Ward 8, South Okkalapa, Yangon; tel. (9) 5018229; f. 2010; also known as the White Tiger Party; Chair. SAI AI PAO.

Shan State Kokang Democratic Party: Laukkaing, Shan State; registered 2012; Chair. ANTONI SU.

Taaung (Palaung) National Party: 110 Bogyoke Aung San Rd, Mingala Ward, Namhsan Township, Shan State; f. 2010; 3,300 mems; Chair AIK MONE; Gen. Sec. MAI OHN KHAING.

Union Democratic Party: 123 U Chit Maung Rd, North-West Saya San Ward, Bahan, Yangon; f. 2010, following a merger between the Public Democracy Party and the Union Democracy Alliance Party; espouses support for democracy, human rights and national reconciliation; Chair. THEIN HTAY; Gen. Sec THEIN THIN AUNG.

Union of Myanmar Federation of National Politics (UMFNP): Bldg F, Rm 301, Pearl Condominium, Kaba Aye Rd, Bahan Township, Yangon; tel. (1) 556554; f. 2010; broadly pro-govt group; Leader AYE LWIN; Gen. Sec. KHIN MAUNG OO.

Union Solidarity and Development Party (USDP): Plot 5, cnr of Yazathingaha Rd and C Rd, Dekkhinathiri Township, Nay Pyi Taw; f. 2010; est. as successor to the Union Solidarity and Development Asscn (USDA—formed in 1993 as civil society group intrinsically linked to the military regime); Chair. SHWE MANN; Gen. Sec. HTAY OO.

Unity and Democracy Party of Kachin State: Myothit Ward, Myitkyina; est. and backed by the military junta; Chair. KHET HTEIN NAN; Sec. PHAU LAR GAM PHAN.

Wa Democratic Party: tel. 4/7 Hsenwi Rd, Ward 8, Lashio, Shan State; f. 2010; Chair. TUN LU.

Wa National Unity Party: Lashio, Shan; fmrly Wa National Development Party; Chair. LOAP PAUNG; Leader SAW PHILIP SAM.

Wunthanu Democratic Party: NanU Lwin Village, Pathein Gyi, Mandalay; f. 2010; fmrly Wunthanu NLD; Leader YE MIN.

In March 2015 representatives of the Myanma Government and 16 ethnic armed groups concluded a draft nationwide ceasefire agreement, which remained subject to formal approval and signature by both sides. The ethnic armed groups were represented by the Nationwide Ceasefire Coordination Team (NCCT), which was established in November 2013, with Nai Hong Sar, the General Secretary of the New Mon State Party as its Chairman, while the government negotiators were styled the Union Peacemaking Work Committee (UPCW).

The following groups are included in the Nationwide Ceasefire Coordination Team:

Arakan Army (AA): e-mail aa.arakanarmy@gmail.com; f. 2010; Commander-in-Chief Brig.-Gen. TWAN MRAT NAING.

Arakan Liberation Party (ALA): Karen State; internet www.arakanalp.com; f. 1968; Leader KHAING RAY KHAING.

Arakan National Council (ANC): POB 64, Mae Ping PO, Chiang Mai 50301, Thailand; e-mail nnl@arakananc.org; f. 2004; Chair. ARIAWANTHA; Gen. Sec. TWAN ZAW.

Chin National Front: Thantlang, Chin State; e-mail chinlandweb@gmail.com; internet www.chinland.org; f. 1988; forces trained by Kachin Independence Army 1989–91; first party congress 1993; carried out an active bombing campaign in 1996–97, mainly in Chin State; joined the Democratic Alliance of Burma (1988), the National Democratic Front (1989) and the Chin National Council (2006); Leader ZING CUNG; military wing: Chin National Army (Leader Col RAL HNIN).

Democratic Karen (Kayin) Benevolent Army: Sonesee Myaing, Myawaddy Township, Karen State; f. 1994, fmrly Democratic Karen Buddhist Army; breakaway group from the Karen (Kayin) National Union; political wing: Klo Htoo Baw Karen (Kayin) Organization (Founder MAHN ROBERT KA ZAN); military wing: Klo Htoo Baw Karen (Kayin) Battalion; a ceasefire agreement with the Govt was effected Nov. 2011; Leader Gen. SAW LAH PWE.

Kachin Independence Organization (KIO): preliminary ceasefire agreement with the Government concluded in May 2013; based in Laiza, Kachin State; f. 1961; (8,000 regular troops in 2012); Chair. LANYAW ZAWNG HRA; military wing: Kachin Independence Army; Leader Lt- Gen. GAM SHAWNG.

Karen (Kayin) National Union (KNU): Law Khee Lar, Karen State; e-mail info@knuhq.org; internet www.knuhq.org; f. 1948; Chair. Gen. MUTU SAY POE; Gen. Sec. PADOH SAW KWE HTOO WIN; military wing: Karen (Kayin) National Liberation Army (KNLA); c. 6,000 troops; Chief of Staff Gen. SAW JOHNNY; preliminary ceasefire agreement with the Government concluded in January 2012.

Karen Peace Council (KNU/KNLA Peace Council): Nawtiyah City, Tokawko, Kawkareik Township, Karen state; e-mail kpcforeign@live.com; internet www.karenpeacecouncil.com; f. 2007; signed a ceasefire agreement with the Govt in Feb. 2012; Chair SAW HTAY MAUNG.

Karenni (Kayinni) National Progressive Party (KNPP): agreement with the State Law and Order Restoration Council (SLORC) signed in March 1995 but subsequently collapsed; resumed fighting in June 1996; ceasefire agreement with the Government concluded in June 2012; Chair. ABEL TWEED; military wing: Karenni (Kayinni) Revolutionary Army; Commander-in-Chief Gen. BEE HTOO.

Lahu Democratic Union: Mong Tong; Leader KHUN SA.

Myanmar National Democratic Alliance Army (MNDAA): agreement with junta reached in March 1989; est. by fmr mems of the CPB; based in Kokang region of northern Shan State; forced into exile by the occupation of its ceasefire zone by govt forces in late 2009; Leader PENG JIASHENG.

New Mon State Party (NMSP): POB 1 Sangkhlaburi, Kanchanaburi 71240, Thailand; e-mail nmsp2006@yahoo.com; internet www.nmsp.info; f. 1958; preliminary ceasefire agreement with the Government concluded in Feb. 2012; Chair. NAI HTAW MON; Gen. Sec. NAI HONG SAR; military wing: Mon National Liberation Army, f. 1971.

Pa-Oh National Liberation Organization (PNLO): internet www.pnlo.org; f. 2009; preliminary ceasefire agreement with the Government concluded in June 2012; Chair. KHUN MYINT TUN.

Palaung State Liberation Front (PSLF): POB 368, Chiang Mai 50000, Thailand; e-mail palaungpslf@gmail.com; f. 1992; est. by mems of Palaung State Liberation Organization opposed to 1991 ceasefire agreement; Chair. AIK BONG; Sec.-Gen. BONE KYAW; military wing: Ta'ang National Liberation Army (TNLA); Commander-in-Chief HOD PLARNG.

Shan State Progress Party (SSPP): Wan Hai, Kehsi Township, northern Shan state; f. 1964; preliminary ceasefire agreement with the Government concluded in January 2012; Leader Lt-Gen. PANG FA; Gen. Sec. KHUN HSAING.

Wa National Organization (WNO): POB 88, Mae Hong Son 58000, Thailand; e-mail wnovaxoffice2010@gmail.com; f. 1982; Chair. Col TA PA LWEH; Gen. Sec. Maj. AIK NYUNT; military wing: Wa National Army (WNA).

Ethnic groups that are not members of the NCCT include:

All-Burma Student Democratic Front (ABSDF): Dagwin; e-mail absdfhq@csloxinfo.com; internet www.absdf8888.org; f. 1988; in 1990 split into two factions, under MOE THI ZUN and NAING AUNG; the two factions reunited in 1993; signed preliminary ceasefire with Govt in Aug. 2013; Chair. THAN KHE; Sec.-Gen. SONNY MAHINDRA.

Communist Party of Burma (CPB): internet www.cp-burma.org; f. 1939; reorg. 1946; operated clandestinely after 1948; participated after 1986 in jt military operations with sections of the NDF; in 1989 internal dissent resulted in the rebellion of about 80% of CPB members, mostly Wa hill tribesmen and Kokang Chinese; the CPB's military efficacy was thus completely destroyed; leadership exiled in the People's Republic of China; Sec.-Gen. KYIN MAUNG.

Kachin Defence Army: agreement with junta reached in Jan. 1991; fmrly the 4th Brigade of the Kachin Independence Army; adopted Border Guard Force (BGF) status in Jan. 2010; Leader MAHTU NAW.

Karenni (Kayinni) National People's Liberation Front: agreement with junta reached in May 1994; transformed into a Border Guard Force (BGF) in Nov. 2009; Leader TUN KYAW.

Kayan National Guard: agreement with junta reached in Feb. 1992; breakaway faction from the KNLP.

Kayan New Land Party (KNLP): agreement with junta reached in July 1994; rejected the junta's Border Guard Force (BGF) proposal; Jt-Sec. Col SAW LWIN.

National Democratic Alliance Army (NDAA) (Mong La): (June 1989); based in eastern Shan State; signed a ceasefire agreement with the Govt. in Sep. 2011; Leader SAI LIN.

Palaung State Liberation Organization: (April 1991); military wing: Palaung State Liberation Army; 7,000–8,000 men.

Shan State Army (SSA): Loi Tai leng, Shan State; formed in 1964, the original SSA was engaged in an armed rebellion against the military regime until the signing of a ceasefire agreement in 1989; elements led by Sao Sai Lek rejected the ceasefire and came to be known as the **Shan State Army—South (SSA—S)**; following the dissolution of the separatist Mong Tai Army (MTA), in 1997 the SSA—S formed an alliance with the Shan State National Army (Leader KARN YORD), the Shan United Revolutionary Army and other MTA remnants; both wings were reunified May 2011; operates five bases close to the Thai–Myanma border; preliminary ceasefire agreement with the Government concluded in December 2011; Chair. Lt-Gen. YAWD SERK; political wing: **Restoration Council of Shan State** (300 mems; cen. cttee of 21 elected mems).

Shan State Nationalities People's Liberation Organization: re-est. 2012; agreement with junta reached in Oct. 1994; Leaders KHUN SEIN SHWE, SOE AUNG LWIN.

United Wa State Army (UWSA): Panghsang, Shan State; f. 1989; signed a ceasefire agreement with the Govt in Sep. 2011; Leader BAO YOU XIANG.

Diplomatic Representation

EMBASSIES IN MYANMAR

Australia: 88 Strand Rd, Yangon; tel. (1) 251810; fax (1) 246159; e-mail austembassy.yangon@dfat.gov.au; internet www.burma.embassy.gov.au; Ambassador NICHOLAS COPPEL.

Bangladesh: 11B Than Lwin Rd, Yangon; tel. (1) 515275; fax (1) 515273; e-mail bdootygn@mptmail.net.mm; internet www.bdembassyyyangon.org; Ambassador MOHAMMAD SUFIUR RAHMAN.

Brazil: 56 Pyay Rd, Yangon; tel. (1) 507225; fax (1) 507483; e-mail administ.yangon@itamaraty.gov.br; internet yangon.itamaraty.gov.br; Ambassador ALCIDES GASTAO ROSTAND PRATES.

Brunei: 17 Kanbawza Ave, Golden Valley, Bahan Township, Yangon; tel. (1) 526985; fax (1) 527165; e-mail yangon.myanmar@mfa.gov.bn; Ambassador Dato' Paduka Haji ABDUR RAHMANI BIN Haji BASIR.

Canada: 9th Floor, Centrepoint Towers, 65 Sule Pagoda Rd, Kyauktada Township, Yangon; Ambassador MARK McDOWELL.

Cambodia: 34 Kaba Aye Pagoda Rd, Bahan Township, Yangon; tel. (1) 549609; fax (1) 541462; e-mail recyangon@myanmar.com.mm; Ambassador SIENG BUNVUTH.

China, People's Republic: 1 Pyidaungsu Yeiktha Rd, Yangon; tel. (1) 221281; fax (1) 227019; e-mail chinaemb_mm@mfa.gov.cn; internet mm.china-embassy.org; Ambassador YANG HOULAN.

Denmark: 7 Pyithu Rd, Mayangon Township, Yangon; tel. (1) 663887; Ambassador PETER LYSHOLT HANSEN.

Egypt: 81 Pyidaungsu Yeiktha Rd, POB 1131, Dagon Township, Yangon; tel. (1) 222886; fax (1) 222865; e-mail embassy.yangon@mofa.gov.eg; internet www.mfa.gov.eg/yangon_emb; Ambassador HANY RIAD MOAWAD.

France: 102 Pyidaungsu Yeiktha Rd, POB 858, Yangon; tel. (1) 212520; fax (1) 212527; e-mail ambafrance.rangoun@diplomatie .gouv.fr; internet www.ambafrance-mm.org; Ambassador THIERRY MATHOU.

Germany: 9 Bogyoke Aung San Museum Rd, POB 12, Yangon; tel. (1) 548951; fax (1) 548899; e-mail info@rangun.diplo.de; internet www.rangun.diplo.de; Ambassador CHRISTIAN-LUDWIG WEBER-LORTSCH.

India: 545–547 Merchant St, POB 751, Kyauktada Township, Yangon; tel. (1) 243972; fax (1) 254086; e-mail indiaembassy@mptmail.net.mm; internet www.indiaembassyyangon.net; Ambassador GAUTAM MUKHOPADHAYA.

Indonesia: 100 Pyidaungsu Yeiktha Rd, POB 1401, Yangon; tel. (1) 254465; fax (1) 254468; e-mail info@kbriyangon.org; internet www .deplu.go.id/yangon; Ambassador ITO SUMARDI.

Israel: 15 Khabaung Rd, Hlaing Township, Yangon; tel. (1) 515115; fax (1) 515116; e-mail info@yangon.mfa.gov.il; internet yangon.mfa .gov.il; Ambassador HAGAY MOSHE BEHAR.

Italy: 3 Inya Myaing Rd, Golden Valley, Bahan Township, Yangon; tel. (1) 527100; fax (1) 514565; e-mail ambyang.mail@esteri.it; internet www.ambyangon.esteri.it; Ambassador PAOLO ANDREA BARTORELLI.

Japan: 100 Natmauk Rd, Bahan Township, Yangon 11021; tel. (1) 549644; fax (1) 549643; e-mail info.cul@yn.mofa.go.jp; internet www .mm.emb-japan.go.jp; Ambassador TATESHI HIGUCHI.

Korea, Republic: 97 University Ave, Bahan Township, POB 1408, Yangon; tel. (1) 527142; fax (1) 513286; e-mail myanmar@mofat.go .kr; internet mmr.mofat.go.kr; Ambassador LEE BAEK-SOON.

Laos: A1 Diplomatic Quarters, Franser Rd, Yangon; tel. (1) 222482; fax (1) 227446; Ambassador LYYING XAYAXANG.

Malaysia: 82 Pyidaungsu Yeiktha Rd, Dagon Township, Yangon; tel. (1) 220249; fax (1) 221840; e-mail malyangon@kln.gov.my; internet www.kln.gov.my/web/mmr_yangon; Ambassador MOHD HANIFF ABD RAHMAN.

Nepal: 16 Natmauk Yeiktha Rd, Tamwe, Yangon; tel. (1) 545880; fax (1) 549803; Ambassador PARAS GHIMIRE.

New Zealand: 43C Inya Myaing Rd, Bahan Township, Yangon; tel. (1) 2306046; fax (1) 2305805; e-mail yangonoffice@mft.net.nz; Ambassador MIKE BURRELL.

Norway: 7 Pyithu Rd, Mayangon Township, Yangon; tel. (1) 669517; e-mail emb.yangon@mfa.no; internet www.myanmar.norway.info; Ambassador ANN OLLESTAD.

Pakistan: A4 Diplomatic Quarters, Pyay Rd, Dagon Township, POB 581, Yangon; tel. (1) 222881; fax (1) 221147; e-mail pakembyangon@gmail.com; internet www.mofa.gov.pk/myanmar; Ambassador EHSAN ULLAH BATTH.

Philippines: 7 Gandamar St, Yankin Township, Yangon; tel. (1) 558149; fax (1) 558154; e-mail p.e.yangon@gmail.com; internet www .philembassy-yangon.com; Ambassador ALEX G. CHUA.

Russian Federation: 38 Sagawa Rd, Dagon Township, Yangon; tel. (1) 241955; fax (1) 241953; e-mail rusinmyan@mptmail.net.mm; internet www.myanmar.mid.ru; Ambassador VASILY BORISOVICH POSPELOV.

Saudi Arabia: 287–289 U Wisara Rd, Sanchaung Township, Yangon; tel. (1) 516952; fax (1) 516951; e-mail biemb@mofa.gov.sa; internet embassies.mofa.gov.sa/sites/myanmar; Ambassador TALAL M. S. ABDULSALAM.

Serbia: 114A Inya Rd, Kamayut Township, POB 943, Yangon; tel. (1) 515282; fax (1) 504274; e-mail serbemb@yangon.net.mn; Ambassador MIODRAG NIKOLIN.

Singapore: 238 Dhamazedi Rd, Bahan Township, Yangon; tel. (1) 559001; fax (1) 559002; e-mail singemb_ygn@sgmfa.gov.sg; internet www.mfa.gov.sg/yangon; Ambassador ROBERT CHUA.

Sri Lanka: 34 Taw Win Rd, POB 1150, Yangon; tel. (1) 222812; fax (1) 221509; e-mail srilankaemb@myanmar.com.mm; internet www .slembyangon.org; Ambassador H. R. PIYASIRI.

Switzerland: 11 Kabaung Lane, Pyay Rd, Hlaing Township, Yangon; tel. (1) 534754; e-mail ygn.vertretung@eda.admin.ch; Ambassador CHRISTOPH BURGENER.

Thailand: 94 Pyay Rd, Dagon Township, Yangon; tel. (1) 222784; fax (1) 221713; e-mail thaiembassyygn@gmail.com; internet www .thaiembassy.org/yangon; Ambassador PISANU SUVANAJATA.

United Kingdom: 80 Strand Rd, Kyauktada Township, POB 638, Yangon; tel. (1) 370865; fax (1) 370866; e-mail BE.Rangoon@fco.gov .uk; internet ukinburma.fco.gov.uk; Ambassador ANDREW PATRICK.

USA: 110 University Ave, Kamayut Township, Yangon; tel. (1) 536509; fax (1) 511069; e-mail consularrangoon@state.gov; internet burma.usembassy.gov; Ambassador DEREK MITCHELL.

Viet Nam: 70–72 Than Lwin Rd, Bahan Township, Yangon; tel. (1) 511305; fax (1) 514897; e-mail vnembmyr@cybertech.net.mm; internet www.vietnamembassy-myanmar.org; Ambassador PHAM THANH DUNG.

Judicial System

The Union Judiciary Law establishing the current judicial system of Myanmar under the 2008 Constitution came into force in October 2010, following which the Supreme Court, the High Courts of the regions and states, the Courts of the self-administered divisions and zones, the District Courts, the Township Courts and other courts were inaugurated.

Supreme Court: Bldg 24, Nay Pyi Taw; tel. (67) 404140; e-mail scunion@mptmail.net.mm; internet www.unionsupremecourt.gov .mm; the highest appellate court; has original jurisdiction enabling it to hear cases in the first instance and revisionary power against a judgment or order delivered by a lower court; comprises seven to 11 sitting justices and a Chief Justice; Chief Justice TUN TUN OO.

Office of the Union Attorney-General: Bldg 25, Nay Pyi Taw; tel. (67) 404054; fax (67) 404106; e-mail ago.h.o@mptmail.net.mm; internet www.oag.gov.mm; Attorney-General Dr TUN SHIN.

Religion

Freedom of religious belief and practice is guaranteed. In 1992 an estimated 87.2% of the population were Buddhists, 5.6% Christians, 3.6% Muslims, 1.0% Hindus and 2.6% animists or adherents of other religions.

BUDDHISM

State Sangha Maha Nayaka Committee: c/o Dept of Promotion and Propagation of the Sasana, Kaba Aye Pagoda Precinct, Mayangone Township, Yangon; tel. (1) 660759.

CHRISTIANITY

Myanmar Naing-ngan Khrityan Athin-dawmyar Kaung-si (Myanmar Council of Churches): 601 Pyay Rd, University PO, Kamayut, Yangon 11041; tel. (1) 537957; fax (1) 296848; e-mail raymond@gmail.com; internet mcc-mm.org; f. 1914; est. as Burma Representative Council of Mission; reconstituted as Burma Council of Churches in 1974; 13 mem. nat. churches, 9 mem. nat. Christian orgs; Pres. Rev. SAW MAR GAY GYI; Gen. Sec. Rt Rev. SMITH N. ZA THAWNG.

The Roman Catholic Church

Myanmar comprises three archdioceses and 11 dioceses. At 31 December 2007 an estimated 1.2% of the total population were adherents.

Catholic Bishops' Conference of Myanmar: 292 Pyay Rd, Sanchaung PO, Yangon 11111; tel. (1) 525868; fax (1) 527198; e-mail secrcbcm@myanmar.com.mm; f. 1982; Pres. Most Rev. PAUL ZINGHTUNG GRAWNG (Archbishop of Mandalay).

Archbishop of Mandalay: Most Rev. PAUL ZINGHTUNG GRAWNG, Archbishop's House, cnr of 82nd and 25th Sts, Mandalay 06011; tel. and fax (2) 33916; e-mail info@mandalayarchdiocese.com; internet www.mandalayarchdiocese.com.

Archbishop of Taunggyi: (vacant), Archbishop's Office, Bayint Naung Rd, Taunggyi 06011; tel. (81) 21689; fax (81) 22164; e-mail ushwe1@gmail.com.

Archbishop of Yangon: Cardinal CHARLES MAUNG BO, Archbishop's House, 289 Theinbyu Rd, Botahtaung PO, Yangon 11161; tel. (1) 246710; fax (1) 379059; e-mail archdygn@myanmar.com.mm.

The Anglican Communion

Anglicans are adherents of the Church of the Province of Myanmar, comprising six dioceses. The Province was formed in February 1970, and contained an estimated 45,000 adherents in 1985.

Archbishop of Myanmar and Bishop of Yangon: Most Rev. STEPHEN THAN MYINT OO, Bishopscourt, 140 Pyidaungsu Yeiktha Rd, Dagon PO, Yangon 11191; tel. (1) 246813; fax (1) 251405; e-mail abcpm@myanmar.com.mm.

Protestant Churches

Lutheran Bethlehem Church: 181–183 Theinbyu St, Mingala Taung Nyunt PO, Yangon 11221; tel. and fax (1) 246585; e-mail jenson-lbc@mail4u.com.mm; Pres. Rev. JENSON RAJAN ANDREWS.

Lutheran Church of Myanmar: 247 Bogkoye St, Kyauktada Township, POB 526, 11182 Yangon; tel. (1) 245626; e-mail lcmyanmar@gmail.com; f. 1995; Pres. Rev. Dr LAL SAWI THANGA.

Mara Evangelical Church: Evangelical Mission, 7/86 Chinpyan Rd, Sittaway, Rakhine State; tel. (1) 645955; e-mail mec1907@gmail.com; f. 1907; 21,573 mems; Gen. Sec. VICTOR VE-U.

Myanmar Baptist Convention: 143 Minye Kyawswa Rd, POB 506, Yangon; tel. (1) 223231; fax (1) 221465; e-mail mbc@mptmail.net.mm; f. 1865; est. as Burma Baptist Missionary Convention; present name adopted 1954; 650,293 mems (2003); Pres. Rev. Dr HONOR NYO; Gen. Sec. Rev. K. D. TU LOM.

Myanmar Lutheran Church: 38D Thar Yar Aye, 1st St, Taung Thu Gone Ward, Insein, Yangon; tel. (1) 642550; e-mail myanmarle@mttmail.net.mm; 2,150 mems; Pres. Rev. ANDREW MANG LONE.

Myanmar Methodist Church: 47 Baho Rd, Thazin Lane, Ah Lone Township 65, Alanpya Pagoda Rd, Dagon, Yangon; Pres. Bishop ZOTHAN MAWIA.

Presbyterian Church of Myanmar: Synod Office, Falam, Chin State; 22,000 mems; Pres. Rev. SUN KANGLO.

Other denominations active in Myanmar include the Lisu Christian Church and the Salvation Army.

The Press

From April 2013 private companies were permitted to publish and circulate daily newspapers, ending a state monopoly on the daily press.

DAILIES

Botahtaung (The Vanguard): 22–30 Strand Rd, Botahtaung PO, POB 539, Yangon; tel. (1) 274310; Myanmar.

The Daily Eleven: 22 South Horse Racing Rd, Tamwe Township, Yangon; internet www.thedailyeleven.com; owned by the Eleven Media Group; f. 2013; Man. Editor Dr THEIN MYINT.

Guardian: 392–396 Merchant St, Botahtaung PO, POB 1522, Yangon; tel. (1) 270150; English.

Kyahmon (The Mirror): 77 52nd St, Dazundaung PO, POB 819, Yangon; tel. (1) 282777; internet www.myanmar.com/newspaper/kyaymon/index.html; Myanmar.

Myanmar Ahlin (New Light of Myanmar): 58 Komin Kochin Rd, Bahan PO, POB 21, Yangon; tel. (1) 544309; internet www.myanmar.com/newspaper/myanmarahlin/index.html; f. 1963; fmrly *Loktha Pyithu Nezin* (*Working People's Daily*); organ of the SPDC; morning; Myanmar; circ. 220,000.

New Light of Myanmar: 22–30 Strand Rd, Yangon; tel. (1) 297028; e-mail webmaster@myanmar.com; internet www.myanmar.com/newspaper/nlm/index.html; f. 1963; fmrly *Working People's Daily*; organ of the SPDC; morning; English; Chief Editor KYAW MIN; circ. 14,000.

The Voice: 458–460, 4th Floor, cnr of 31 St and Manabandula Rd, Pabedan Township, Yangon; tel. (1) 242424; e-mail newsroom@thevoiceweekly.net; internet www.thevoicemyanmar.com; est. as *The Voice Weekly*; launched a daily version in April 2013; Chief Editor KYAW MIN SWE.

Other dailies published in 2014 were *Pyidaungsu* (*The Union*) and *San Taw Chein*.

PERIODICALS

A Hla Thit (New Beauty): 46 90th St, Yangon; tel. (1) 287106; international news.

Dana Business Magazine: 72 8th St, Lanmadaw Township, Yangon; tel. and fax (1) 224010; e-mail dana@mptmail.net.mm; economic; Editor-in-Chief WILLIAM CHEN.

Guardian Magazine: 392–396 Merchant St, Botahtaung PO, POB 1522, Yangon; tel. (1) 296510; f. 1953; nationalized 1964; monthly; English; literary; circ. 11,600.

Kyee Pwar Yay (Prosperity): 296 Bo Sun Pat St, Yangon; tel. (1) 278100; economic; Editor-in-Chief MYAT KHINE.

Myanma Dana (Myanmar's Economy): 210A 36th St, Kyauktada Post Office, Yangon; tel. (1) 284660; economic; Editor-in-Chief THIHA SAW.

Myanmar Times & Business Review: 379–383 Bo Aung Kyaw St, Kyauktada Township, Yangon; tel. (1) 392928; fax (1) 392706; e-mail management@myanmartimes.com.mm; internet www.mmtimes.com; f. 2000; CEO Dr TIN TUN OO.

Myawaddy Journal: Myawaddy Press, 184 32nd St, Yangon; tel. (1) 274655; f. 1989; fortnightly; news; circ. 8,700.

Myawaddy Magazine: Myawaddy Press, 184 32nd St, Yangon; tel. (1) 274655; f. 1952; monthly; literary magazine; circ. 4,200.

Ngwetaryi Magazine: Myawaddy Press, 184 32nd St, Yangon; tel. (1) 274655; f. 1961; monthly; cultural; circ. 3,400.

Shwe Thwe: 529 Merchant St, Yangon; tel. (1) 283611; weekly; bilingual children's journal; publ. by Sarpay Beikman Management Board; circ. 100,000.

Taw Win Journal (Royal Journal): 149 37th St, Yangon; news; Editor-in-Chief SOE THEIN.

Teza: Myawaddy Press, 184 32nd St, Yangon; tel. (1) 274655; f. 1965; monthly; English and Myanmar; pictorial publ. for children; circ. 29,500.

Thwe Thauk Magazine: Myawaddy Press, 184 32nd St, Yangon; f. 1946; monthly; literary.

Ya Nant Thit (New Fragrance): 186 39th St, Yangon; tel. (1) 276799; international news; Editor-in-Chief CHIT WIN MG.

Yangon Times: Yangon Media Group Ltd, 101, 1st Floor, Mahabandoola Condo, Mahabandoola Rd, Pazaungdaung, Yangon; tel. (1) 9010072; fax (1) 9010075; e-mail yangonmediagroup.ltd@gmail.com; internet www.theyangontimes.com; 2 a week; Exec. Dir DAW MYAT MYAT SOE.

NEWS AGENCY

Myanmar News Agency (MNA): 212 Theinbyu Rd, Botahtaung, Yangon; tel. (1) 270893; f. 1963; govt-controlled; Chief Editors ZAW MIN THEIN (domestic section), KYAW MIN (external section).

Publishers

Hanthawaddy Press: 157 Bo Aung Kyaw St, Yangon; f. 1889; textbooks, multilingual dictionaries; Man. Editor ZAW WIN.

Knowledge Publishing House: 130 Bo Gyoke Aung San St, Yegyaw, Yangon; art, education, religion, politics and social sciences.

Kyipwaye Press: 84th St, Letsaigan, Mandalay; tel. (2) 21003; arts, travel, religion, fiction and children's.

Myawaddy Press: 184 32nd St, Yangon; tel. (1) 276889; journals and magazines; CEO THEIN SEIN.

Sarpay Beikman Management Board: 529 Merchant St, Yangon; tel. (1) 283611; f. 1947; encyclopaedias, literature, fine arts and general; also magazines and translations; Chair. AUNG HTAY.

Shumawa Press: 146 West Wing, Bogyoke Aung San Market, Yangon; mechanical engineering.

Shwepyidan: 12A Haiaban, Yegwaw Quarter, Yangon; politics, religion, law.

Smart and Mookerdum: 221 Sule Pagoda Rd, Yangon; arts, cookery, popular science.

Thu Dhama Wadi Press: 55–56 Maung Khine St, POB 419, Yangon; f. 1903; religious; Propr TIN HTOO; Man. PAN MAUNG.

GOVERNMENT PUBLISHING HOUSE

Printing and Publishing Enterprise: 365–367 Bo Aung Kyaw St, Kyauktada Township, Yangon; tel. (1) 294645; f. 1880; est. as Govt Printing Office; Man. Dir AUNG NYEIN.

PUBLISHERS' ASSOCIATION

Myanma Publishers' Union: 146 Bogyoke Market, Yangon.

Broadcasting and Communications

TELECOMMUNICATIONS

In January 2013 the Ministry of Communications and Information Technology announced the planned development of telecommunications services in Myanmar; nationwide licences were granted to Ooredoo and Telenor, and two integrated national mobile licences were to be granted to local operators.

Myanma Posts and Telecommunications (MPT): No. 2 Office Bldg, Special Development Zone, Nay Pyi Taw; tel. (1) 407333; fax (1) 407008; internet www.mpt.net.mm; fmrly the Posts and Telecommunications Corpn; Man. Dir AUNG MAW.

Yatanarpon Teleport: Yatanarpon Cyber City, Mandalay; tel. (2) 5178116; fax (2) 5178004; e-mail helpdesk@teleport.net.mm; internet www.yatanarpon.net.mm; f. 2002; internet and data network services.

Regulatory Authority

Posts and Telecommunications Department: Blk 68, Ayeyar Wun Rd, South Dagon Township, Yangon; tel. (1) 591388; fax (1) 591383; e-mail dg.ptd@mptmail.net.mm; internet www.mcpt.gov.mm/ptd/index.htm; regulatory authority responsible for supervising radio communication, telephone, telegraph and post operations; Dir-Gen. TIN HTWE.

BROADCASTING

Radio

Radio broadcasting is largely state-controlled, although there were eight private radio stations in 2012.

Myanma Radio and Television (MRTV): Tatkone, Nay Pyi Taw; tel. (67) 79212; fax (67) 79205; e-mail mrtv@mptmail.net.mm; internet www.moi.gov.mm/mrtv; govt-owned; fmrly Burma Broadcasting Service; broadcasts in Myanmar, Kachin, Shan, Rakhine, Chin (Falan), Chin (Mindat), Wa, Kokant, Kayin (Sagaw), Kayin (Poe), Mon, Kayah, Cayan, Gaykho, Gaybar and English; Dir-Gen. TINT SWE; Dir of Radio Broadcasting ZEYAR MYO.

Television

Digital television broadcasting began in Myanmar in 2005, with coverage extending to more than one-half of the population by 2010. The removal of analogue service was not envisaged until at least 2025.

Myanma Radio and Television: see Radio; colour television transmission began in 1980.

TV Myawaddy: Hmawbi, Hmawbi Township, Yangon; tel. (1) 620270; f. 1995; military broadcasting station transmitting public information, education and entertainment programmes via satellite.

In 2005 the Democratic Voice of Burma (DVB) began broadcasting Myanmar-language news and educational programmes via satellite from Norway.

Finance

(cap. = capital; res = reserves; dep. = deposits; auth. = authorized; p.u. = paid up; m. = million; br(s) = branch(es); amounts in kyats, unless otherwise stated)

BANKING

Central Bank

Central Bank of Myanmar: Office 55, Nay Pyi Taw; tel. (67) 418243; fax (67) 418152; e-mail director.admin.cbm@mptmail.net .mm; internet www.cbm.gov.mm; f. 1947; est. as People's Bank of the Union of Burma; present name adopted 1990; bank of issue; cap. 350m., dep. 13,545m.; Gov. THAN NYEIN; 37 brs.

State Banks

Myanma Economic Bank (MEB): 26, Myat Pan Thazin Rd, Nay Pyi Taw; tel. (67) 420441; fax (67) 420988; e-mail mebhoadmin@mpt .net.mm; internet www.mebank.com.mm; f. 1975; provides domestic banking network throughout the country; Man. Dir MYAT MAW.

Myanma Foreign Trade Bank: 80–86 Maha Bandoola Garden St, Kyauktada Township, Yangon; tel. (1) 284911; fax (1) 289585; e-mail mftb-hoygn@mptmail-net.mm; f. 1976; handles all foreign exchange and international banking transactions; Chair. and Man. Dir THAN YE; Man. and Sec. HTIN KYAW THEIN.

Myanma Investment and Commercial Bank (MICB): 170–176 Bo Aung Kyaw St, Botahtaung Township, Yangon; tel. (1) 250515; fax (1) 256871; e-mail micb.hoygn@mptmail.net.mm; f. 1989; state-owned; cap. 17,096m., res 2,857m., dep. 278,286m. (March 2012); Chair. and Man. Dir SOE MIN; 1 br.

Private Banks

In 2014 there were 20 private banks operating in Myanmar.

Asia Green Development Bank Ltd (AGD): 168 Thiri Yadanar Market, Nay Pyi Taw; tel. (67) 414622; internet www.agdbank.com; f. 2010; Chair. THAN YI.

Asian Yangon Bank Ltd: 319–321 Maha Bandoola St, Botahtaung Township, Yangon; tel. (1) 245825; fax (1) 245865; f. 1994; est. as Asian Yangon Int. Bank Ltd; name changed as above in 2000; Gen. Man. MYO MYINT.

Ayeyarwady Bank (AYA): 1 Ywama Curve, Ba Yint Naung Rd, Block 2, Hlaing Township, Yangon; tel. (1) 531067; fax (1) 531045; e-mail info@ayabank.com.mm; internet www.ayabank.com; f. 2010; Exec. Chair. ZAW ZAW; Man. Dir THAN ZAW.

Co-operative Bank Ltd: 334–336, cnr of Strand Rd and 23rd St, Latha Township, Yangon; tel. (1) 371848; fax (1) 371851; e-mail contact@cbbankmm.com; internet www.cbbankmm.com; f. 1992; Chair. KHIN MAUNG AYE; Exec. Vice-Chair. KYAW LYNN; 36 brs.

First Private Bank Ltd (FPB): 619–621, cnr of Merchant St and Bo Soon Pat St, Pabedan Township, Yangon; tel. (1) 251750; fax (1) 242320; e-mail fpb.hq@mptmail.net.mm; internet www .fpbbank-myanmar.com; f. 1992; est. as the first publicly subscribed

bank; fmrly Commercial and Devt Bank Ltd; provides loans to private business and small-scale industrial sectors; cap. 5,000m. (March 2008); Chair. Dr SEIN MAUNG; Exec. Dir DAW HLA HLA WIN; 16 brs.

Innwa Bank Ltd: 554–556 Merchant St, cnr of 35th and 36th Sts, Kyauktada Township, Yangon; tel. (1) 254642; fax (1) 254431; f. 1997; Gen. Man. YIN SEIN.

Kanbawza Bank Ltd: 615/1 Pyay Rd, Kamayut Township, Yangon; tel. (1) 538075; fax (1) 538069; e-mail kbzhr@kbzbank.com; internet www.kbzbank.com; f. 1994; Chair. AUNG KO WIN; Sr Man. Dir THAN CHO; 184 brs.

Myanma Citizens Bank Ltd (MCB): 383 Maha Bandoola St, Kyauktada Township, Yangon; tel. (1) 379176; fax (1) 245932; e-mail admin@mcb.com.mm; internet www.mcb.com.mm; f. 1991; partially owned by the Govt; auth. cap. 75,000m., cap. p.u. 17,780m. (31 March 2013); Chair. KYAW HTOO; Man. Dir MYINT WIN; 11 brs.

Myanma Oriental Bank Ltd (MOB): 166–168 Pansodan St, Kyauktada Township, Yangon; tel. (1) 246596; fax (1) 251840; e-mail mobl.ygn@mptmail.net.mm; internet www.mobbankmm .com; f. 1993; Chair. MYA THAN; Man. Dir and CEO WIN MYINT; 9 brs.

Myanmar Industrial Development Bank Ltd: Plot 2, Oktayathiri Quarter, Nay Pyi Taw; f. 1996; cap. US $335m.

Myawaddy Bank Ltd: Plot B-1, near Thiriyadana Super Market, Hotel Zone, Nay Pyi Taw; e-mail mwdbankygn@mtpt400.stems.com; f. 1993; Gen. Mans TUN KYI, WIN HLAING.

Tun Foundation Bank Ltd: 165–167 Bo Aung Kyaw St, Yangon; tel. (1) 240710; e-mail tfbbank@mptmail.net.mm; f. 1997.

Yadanabon Bank Ltd: 58A, 26th St, cnr of 84th and 85th Sts, Aung Myay Thar Zan Township, Mandalay; tel. (2) 23577; f. 1992.

Yangon City Bank Ltd: cnr of Settyon St and Banyerdala St, Mingalar Taung Nyunt Township, Yangon; tel. (1) 289256; fax (1) 289231; f. 1993; auth. cap. 500m.; 100% owned by Yangon City Devt Cttee; Chair. Col MYINT AUNG.

Yoma Bank Ltd: 1 Kungyan St, Mingala Taung Nyunt Township, Yangon; tel. (1) 242138; fax (1) 246548; f. 1993.

Foreign Banks

By May 2013 24 foreign banks had opened representative offices in Yangon. In October 2014 the authorities granted preliminary licences to nine foreign banks to operate in Myanmar.

STOCK EXCHANGE

Myanmar Securities Exchange Centre: 1st Floor, 21–25 Sule Pagoda Rd, Yangon; tel. (1) 283984; f. 1996; jt venture between MEB and Japan's Daiwa Institute of Research; Man. Dir EIJI SUZUKI.

INSURANCE

After a democratically elected Government came to power in March 2011, the insurance sector, formerly monopolized by the state, was liberalized. Myanmar opened its insurance industry to private insurers in 2012, and was expected to open the market to foreign insurers in 2015. In early 2015 16 foreign insurance companies had representative offices in the country.

Ayeyar Myanmar Insurance: 23 Kan Yeik Thar Rd, Lake View Tower, Mingalar Taung Nyunt Township, Yangon; Man. Dir THAN ZAW.

Capital Life Insurance: 285 Bo Aung Kyaw St, Kyauktada Township, Yangon; tel. (1) 374974; fax (1) 374974; e-mail info@ capitallife-insurance.com; internet www.insuranceinmyanmar.com; Dir YAN PAING.

Citizen Business Insurance: 5 Co-op Business Center, Saya San Rd, Yangon; tel. (1) 557640.

First National Insurance: 400–406 Merchant Rd, Botahtaung Township, Yangon; tel. (1) 8610661; fax (1) 8610675; e-mail customerservices@fnipublic.com; internet www.fnipublic.com; Man. Dir YE MIN OO.

Grand Guardian Insurance: Junction Sq Compound, Pyay Rd, Kamayut Township, Yangon; tel. (1) 2305700; fax (1) 2304368; e-mail info@ggipinsurance.com; internet www.ggipinsurance.com; Man. Dir SANDAR HTUN.

IKBZ Insurance Co Ltd: 608 Bo Son Pat Tower, cnr Marchent St and Bo Son Pat St, Yangon; tel. (1) 378842; fax (1) 378840; e-mail info@i-kbz.com; internet www.i-kbz.com; Man. Dir NYO MYINT.

Pillar Of Truth Insurance: 8th Floor, MMB Tower, Upper Pansoedan Rd, Yangon; tel. (1) 383092.

Other privately owned domestic insurance companies that were issued licences in 2012 included Apex Insurance International, Great Future International Insurance, Global Standard Insurance, Green Asia Insurance, Jade King and Queen Service, Mya Wady Insurance, Young Insurance Global Co Ltd, Myintmo Min Insurance and Aung Thitsa Oo Insurance.

In addition, the following foreign insurance companies had representative offices in Myanmar: ACE Insurance, Sompo Japan Insurance, Tokio Marine and Nichido Fire Insurance Co Ltd, Taiyo Life Insurance, Poema Insurance, American International Assurance, Samsung Life Insurance, Great Eastern Life Assurance, Prudential Holdings, Pana Harrison, Manulife Financial Life Insurance, Willis Co, Mitsui Sumitomo Insurance, AIA Insurance and United Overseas Insurance.

Regulatory Authority

Myanma Insurance: 627–635 Merchant St, Yangon; tel. (1) 252373; fax (1) 250275; e-mail myansure@mptmail.net.com; internet www.soft-comm.com/myanma_insurance/index.html; f. 1976; govt-controlled; Man. Dir Col THEIN LWIN; Gen. Man Dr MG MAUNG THEIN.

Trade and Industry

GOVERNMENT AGENCIES

Inspection and Agency Services: 383 Maha Bandoola St, Yangon; tel. (1) 284821; fax (1) 284823; promotes business with foreign cos on behalf of state-owned enterprises; Man. Dir OHN KHIN.

Myanmar Economic Corpn (MEC): 74–76 Shwedagon Pagoda Rd, Dagon Township, Yangon; tel. (1) 254738; (retd) Brig.-Gen. Thura MYINT THIEN.

Myanmar Investment Commission (MIC): Ministry of National Planning and Economic Development, Bldg 32, Nay Pyi Taw; tel. (67) 406334; fax (67) 406333; f. 1994; Chair. MAUNG MAUNG THEIN.

Union of Myanmar Economic Holdings: 72–74 Shwedagon Pagoda Rd, Yangon; tel. (1) 78905; f. 1990; public holding co; auth. cap. 10,000m. kyats; 40% of share capital subscribed by the Ministry of Defence and 60% by members of the armed forces.

CHAMBER OF COMMERCE

Union of Myanmar Federation of Chambers of Commerce and Industry (UMFCCI): 29 Min Ye Kyawswa Rd, Lanmadaw Township, Yangon; tel. (1) 214344; fax (1) 214484; e-mail umfcci@mptmail.net.mm; internet www.umfcci.com.mm; f. 1919; est. as Burmese Chamber of Commerce; present name adopted 1999; Pres. WIN AUNG; Sec.-Gen. Dr MYO THET.

INDUSTRIAL AND TRADE ASSOCIATIONS

Myanmar Aquaculture and Fisheries Association: 74–86 Bo Sun Pat St, Pabedan Township, Yangon; tel. (1) 243150; fax (1) 248177.

Myanmar Computer Industry Association: Myanmar Info-Tech, Main Bldg, Hlaing University Campus, Hlaing Township, Yangon; tel. (1) 652238; e-mail mcia@mail4u.com.mm; internet www.mcia.org.mm; Pres. WAH WAH HTUN.

Myanmar Construction Entrepreneurs' Association: Thanthumar Rd, cnr Thuwunna Rd, Thingankyun Township, Yangon; tel. (1) 579547; fax (1) 575947.

Myanmar Edible Oil Dealers' Association: 81–82 Kantgaw St, Bayint Naung Warehouse, Mayangon Township, Yangon; tel. (1) 680910; Chair. KO KO GYI.

Myanmar Engineers' Association: Bldg 6, Rm 5, MICT Park, Hlaing Township, Yangon; tel. (1) 652294.

Myanmar Fisheries Federation (MFF): cnr Bayint Naung Rd and Say War Sat Yone St, West Gyo Gone, Insein Township, Yangon; tel. (1) 683652; fax (1) 683662; e-mail fish-fed@mff.com.mm; internet www.fishfedmyanmar.com; six mem. asscns; Pres. HTAY MYINT.

Myanmar Garment Manufacturers' Association (MGMA): J V-2 Bldg, between Lanthit St and Wardan St, Seikkan Township, Yangon; tel. (1) 220879; fax (1) 222706; Chair. MYINT SOE.

Myanmar Industries Association: 504–506 Merchant St, Kyauktada Township, Yangon; tel. and fax (1) 241919; f. 1993; Chair. PAW HEIN.

Myanmar Livestock Federation: Livestock Breeding and Veterinary Department Compound, Insein Rd, Insein Township, Yangon; tel. (1) 640820; fax (1) 225955.

Myanmar Rice and Paddy Wholesalers' Association: 504–506 Merchant St, Kyauktada Township, Yangon; tel. (1) 241920.

Myanmar Rice Industry Association: f. 2010; est. to co-ordinate the rice industry, promote private investment and develop the export potential of the sector; provides low-interest loans and improved seeds, fertilizers and technology; 40 exec. mems; Chair. CHIT KHAING.

Myanmar Rice Millers' Association: 69 Theinbyu St, Botahtaung Township, Yangon; tel. (1) 296284; Pres. TIN WIN.

Myanmar Timber Merchants Association: 29 Min Ye Kyaw Swa St, Lanmadaw Township, Yangon; tel. (1) 214838; fax (1) 214840; e-mail mfptma@mptmail.net.mm; internet www.myanmartimberassociation.org; f. 1993; Chair. SEIN LWIN; Sec.-Gen. Dr MYO THET.

Myanmar Women Entrepreneurs' Association: 288–290 Shwedagon Pagoda Rd, Dagon Township, Yangon; tel. (1) 254400; fax (1) 254566; e-mail mwea2008@gmail.com; internet www.mweamm.org; f. 1995; Pres. YI YI MYINT (acting).

UTILITIES

Electricity

Myanma Electric Power Enterprise (MEPE): 197–199 Lower Kyimyindine Rd, Yangon; tel. (1) 410066; fax (1) 440392; e-mail mepe@mptmail.net.mm; Man. Dir KHIN MAUNG ZAW.

Water

Mandalay City Development Committee (Water and Sanitation Dept): cnr of 26th and 72nd Sts, Mandalay; tel. (2) 70431; f. 1992; Head of Water and Sanitation Dept TINT LWIN.

Water Resources Utilization Department (WRUD): Ministry of Agriculture and Irrigation, Office 50, Nay Pyi Taw; tel. (67) 431291; internet wrud.moai.gov.mm; f. 1995; Dir-Gen. KYI HTUT WIN.

Yangon City Development Committee (Water and Sanitation Dept): City Hall, cnr of Maha Bandoola Rd and Sule Pagoda Rd, Kyauktada Township, Yangon; tel. (1) 248112; fax (1) 246016; e-mail priycdc@mptmail.net.mm; internet www.yangoncity.com.mm/ycdc/index.asp; f. 1992; Head of Water and Sanitation Dept ZAW WIN.

CO-OPERATIVES

At 28 February 2015 there were 33,511 co-operative societies.

Central Co-operative Society Ltd: Saya San Plaza, cnr Saya Rd and New University Ave, Bahan Township, Yangon; tel. (1) 557640; fax (1) 553894; e-mail ccscencoop@gmail.com; internet www.ccsmyanmar.com; Chair. KHIN MAUNG AYE.

Co-operative Department: Ministry of Co-operatives, Bldg 16, Nay Pyi Taw; tel. (1) 410339; fax (1) 410024; e-mail coopdeptdg@mptmail.net.mm; internet www.myancoop.gov.mm/co-department.htm; Dir-Gen. AUNG PHYU.

WORKERS' AND PEASANTS' COUNCILS

Peasants' Asiayone (Organization): Yangon; tel. (1) 82819; f. 1977; Chair. Brig.-Gen. THAN NYUNT; Sec. SAN TUN.

Workers' Unity Organization: Central Organizing Committee, 61 Theinbyu St, Yangon; tel. (1) 284043; f. 1968; workers' representative org.; Chair. OHN KYAW; Sec. NYUNT THEIN.

Transport

All railways, domestic air services, passenger and freight road transport services, and inland water facilities are owned and operated by state-controlled enterprises.

RAILWAYS

The railway network comprised 5,726 km of track in 2012, with a further 2,844 km under construction.

Myanma Railways: 361 Theinbyu St, Botahtaung Township, Yangon; tel. (1) 298585; fax (1) 284220; e-mail webmaster@myanmarailways.com; internet www.myanmarailways.com; f. 1877; govt-operated; Man. Dir MIN SWE; Gen. Man. HLA YI.

ROADS

In 2010 the total length of the road network in Myanmar was 34,377 km. The construction of a highway linking Yangon to the Thai border in Kayin State was nearing completion in early 2015.

Road Transportation Department: 375 Bogyoke Aung San St, Yangon; tel. (1) 284426; fax (1) 289716; f. 1963; controls passenger and freight road transport; Man. Dir OHN MYINT.

INLAND WATERWAYS

The principal artery of traffic is the River Ayeyarwady (Irrawaddy), which is navigable as far as Bhamo, about 1,450 km inland, while parts of the Thanlwin and Chindwinn rivers are also navigable.

Inland Water Transport: 50 Pansodan St, Kyauktada Township, Yangon; tel. (1) 380753; fax (1) 380752; e-mail iwt@mpt.net.mm; internet www.iwt.gov.mm; f. 1865; govt-owned; operates cargo and passenger services throughout Myanmar with a fleet of 476 vessels; Man. Dir SOE TINT.

SHIPPING

Yangon is the chief port. Vessels with a displacement of up to 15,000 grt can be accommodated. In December 2014 the Myanma flag registered fleet comprised 66 vessels, with a total displacement of 174,200 grt.

Myanma Port Authority: 10 Pansodan St, POB 1, Yangon; tel. (1) 382722; fax (1) 295134; e-mail mpa@mptmail.net.mm; internet www .myanmaportauthority.com; f. 1880; general port and harbour duties; Man. Dir HTIEN HTAY; Gen. Man. HLAING SOON.

Myanma Five Star Line: 132–136 Theinbyu St, POB 1221, Yangon; tel. (1) 295279; fax (1) 297669; e-mail mfslhq@mptmail.net.mm; internet www.mfsl-shipping.com; f. 1959; cargo services to the Far East and Australia; Man. Dir MAUNG MAUNG NYEIN; Gen. Man. WIN PE; fleet of 26 coastal and ocean-going vessels.

CIVIL AVIATION

Mingaladon Airport, near Yangon, is equipped to international standards. Mandalay International Airport was inaugurated in September 2000, and Nay Pyi Taw International Airport commenced services in 2011. The new Hanthawaddy International Airport under construction in the central Bago region, 80 km north of Yangon, was expected to open in 2018; it was envisaged that it would be the largest airport in the country, handling up to 12m. passenger arrivals annually.

Department of Civil Aviation: Yangon International Airport, Yangon 11021; tel. (1) 533000; fax (1) 533016; e-mail dgdca@dca .gov.mm; internet www.dca.gov.mm; Dir-Gen. TIN NAING TUN.

Air Bagan Ltd: 56 Shwe Taung Gyar St, Bahan Township, Yangon; tel. (1) 514861; fax (1) 515102; e-mail info@airbagan.com.mm; internet www.airbagan.com; f. 2004; domestic services to 17 destinations; Chair. TAY ZA; Man. Dir HTOO THET HTWE.

Air Mandalay: 146 Dhammazedi Rd, Bahan Township, Yangon; tel. (1) 501520; fax (1) 525937; e-mail info@airmandalay.com; internet www.airmandalay.com; f. 1994; jt venture between Air Mandalay Holding, Premier Airlines and Myanmar Airways; operates domestic services and regional services to Thailand and Cambodia; Chair. MAUNG MAUNG OHN; Man. Dir ADAM HTOON.

Golden Myanmar Airlines: Sayar San Plaza, New University Ave Rd, Bahan Township, Yangon; tel. (1) 401484; fax (1) 8604051; internet gmairlines.com; f. 2012; first Myanmar Aviation Public Co; Chair. KHIN MAUNG AYE.

Myanma Airways (UBA): 104 Kanna Rd, Yangon; tel. (1) 246452; fax (1) 371120; e-mail managementoff@myanmaairways.aero; internet myanmaairways.aero; f. 1993; govt-controlled; internal network operates services to 26 airports; Man. Dir NAING S. LWIN.

Myanmar Airways International (MAI): 08-02 Sakura Tower, 339 Bogyoke Aung San Rd, Yangon; tel. (1) 255260; fax (1) 255305; e-mail management@maiair.com; internet www.maiair.com; f. 1993; est. by Myanmar Airways in jt venture with RMT company for international schedule services; operates services to Bangkok, Guangzhou, Hong Kong, Kuala Lumpur, Seoul and Singapore; Man. Dir SI THU.

United Myanmar Air: Summit Parkview Hotel, Yangon; internet www.unitedmyanmar.com; f. 2003; jt venture between Myanmar Airways and Sunshine Strategic Investments Holdings of Hong Kong; international services to Bangkok, Hong Kong, Kuala Lumpur and Singapore; CEO EDWARD TAN.

Yangon Airways: MMB Tower, 5th Floor, 166 Upper Pansodan Rd, Mingalar Taungnyunt Township, Yangon; tel. (1) 383100; fax (1) 383109; e-mail marketing@mmb.com.mm; internet www.yangonair .com; f. 1996; domestic services to 13 destinations; Gen. Man. TIN MAUNG AYE.

Tourism

Yangon, Mandalay, Taunggyi and Pagan possess outstanding palaces, Buddhist temples and shrines. Myanmar hosted the Southeast Asian Games in December 2013. According to the Ministry of Hotels and Tourism, in the year to March 2014 there were 1,131,624 foreign tourist arrivals, compared with 900,161 in 2012/13. Revenue from tourism (including passenger transport) totalled an estimated US $281m. in 2011, according to the World Tourism Organization.

Myanmar Hotels and Tourism Services: 77–91 Sule Pagoda Rd, Yangon 11141; tel. (1) 282013; fax (1) 254417; e-mail mtt.mht@ mptmail.net.mm; govt-controlled; manages all hotels, tourist offices, tourist dept stores and duty-free shops; Man. Dir HLA HTAY.

Myanmar Tourism Promotion Board: Business Centre, 3rd Floor, 223 Signal Pagoda Rd, Yangon; tel. (1) 242828; fax (1) 242800; e-mail mtpb@mptmail.net.mm; internet www .myanmar-tourism.com; Chair. AUNG MYAT KYAW.

Myanmar Travels and Tours: 118–120 Mahabandoola St, Kyauktada Township, Yangon; tel. (1) 371286; fax (1) 254417; e-mail mtt .mht@myanmartravelsandtours.com; internet www.myanmartravelsandtours .com; f. 1964; govt tour operator and travel agent; handles all travel arrangements for groups and individuals; Gen. Man. HTAY AUNG.

Union of Myanmar Travel Association (UMTA): 29 Min Ye Kyawswa Rd, Lanmadaw Township, Yangon; tel. (1) 214941; fax (1) 214945; e-mail UMTA@mptmail.net.mm; internet www.umtanet .org; f. 2002; organizes private travel agencies and tour operators; Chair. MAUNG MAUNG SWE.

Defence

As assessed at November 2014, the total strength of the armed forces was an estimated 406,000 (army 375,000, navy 16,000, air force 15,000). Military service is compulsory for men (between the ages of 18 and 45) and women (between the ages of 18 and 35) for a period of two to three years, or for five years during times of national crisis. Paramilitary forces include a people's police force (72,000 men) and a people's militia (35,000 men). The 11-member National Defence and Security Council was established in March 2011.

Defence Expenditure: Budgeted at US $2,430m. for 2014.

Commander-in-Chief of the Armed Forces: Sr Gen. MIN AUNG HLAING.

Commander-in-Chief of the Army: Vice-Sr Gen. SOE WIN.

Commander-in-Chief of the Navy: Vice-Adm. THURA THET SWE.

Commander-in-Chief of the Air Force: Gen. KHIN AUNG MYINT.

Education

The organization and administration of education is the responsibility of the Ministry of Education. Pre-school education begins at four years of age. Primary education, which is compulsory, lasts for five years between the ages of five and 10. Secondary education, beginning at 10 years of age, comprises a first cycle of four years and a second of two years. In 2010 enrolment at the pre-primary level included 9% of children in the relevant age-group, and in 2007/08 enrolment at primary schools was equivalent to 82% of children in the relevant age-group. In 2010 enrolment in secondary schools included 47% of students in the relevant age-group.

In 2001/02 there were 958 tertiary-level institutions, at which an estimated 587,300 students were enrolled. In 2010/11 some 659,510 students were enrolled in tertiary-level institutions.

In 2013/14 government expenditure on education was forecast at 907,977m. kyats (equivalent to 5.4% of total budgeted spending).

NAMIBIA

Introductory Survey

LOCATION, CLIMATE, LANGUAGE, RELIGION, FLAG, CAPITAL

The Republic of Namibia (formerly known as South West Africa) lies in south-western Africa, with South Africa to the south and south-east, Botswana to the east and Angola to the north. The country has a long coastline on the Atlantic Ocean. The narrow Zambezi Region (formerly known as the Caprivi Strip), between Angola and Botswana in the north-east, extends Namibia to the Zambezi river, giving it a border with Zambia. The climate is generally hot, although coastal areas have relatively mild temperatures. Most of the country is subject to drought and unreliable rainfall. The average annual rainfall varies from about 50 mm (2 in) on the coast to 550 mm (22 in) in the north. The arid Namib Desert stretches along the west coast, while the easternmost area forms part of the Kalahari Desert. The official language is English; however, most of the African ethnic groups have their own languages. At the 2011 census the most widely spoken African languages were Oshiwambo (used in 49% of households), Nama/Damara (11%), Kavango (9%) and Otjiherero (9%). In addition, Afrikaans is spoken (10%) and German is also used. About 90% of the population are Christians. The national flag (proportions 2 by 3) comprises a blue triangle in the upper hoist corner, bearing a yellow sun (a blue-bordered disc, surrounded by 12 triangular rays), separated from a green triangle in the lower fly corner by a white-bordered, broad red stripe. The capital is Windhoek.

CONTEMPORARY POLITICAL HISTORY

Historical Context

South West Africa became a German possession in 1884. The territory excluded the port of Walvis Bay and 12 small offshore islands, previously annexed by the United Kingdom and subsequently incorporated into South Africa. During the First World War South African forces occupied South West Africa in 1914, and in 1915 Germany surrendered the territory. In 1920 the League of Nations entrusted South Africa with a mandate to administer South West Africa. In 1925 South Africa granted a Constitution giving limited self-government to European (white) inhabitants only. No trusteeship agreement was concluded with the UN after the Second World War, and in 1946 the UN refused South Africa's request for permission to annex South West Africa. In 1949 the territory's European voters were granted representation in the South African Parliament. The following year the International Court of Justice (ICJ, see p. 25) issued a ruling that the area should remain under international mandate and that South Africa should submit it to UN control. South Africa refused to comply with this judgment. In October 1966 South Africa's security and apartheid laws were extended to South West Africa, retrospective to 1950.

Opposition within South West Africa to South African rule led to the establishment of two African nationalist organizations, the South West Africa People's Organisation (SWAPO—founded in 1957 as the Ovamboland People's Congress) and the South West African National Union (SWANU—formed in 1959). During 1966 SWAPO's military wing, the People's Liberation Army of Namibia (PLAN), launched an armed struggle for the liberation of the territory. PLAN operated from bases in Angola and Zambia, and was controlled by the external wing of SWAPO (led by Sam Nujoma—the organization's President from 1959). SWAPO also had a legal wing, which was tolerated in South West Africa.

South Africa was consistently criticized at the UN over its extension of apartheid to the territory. The UN General Assembly voted to terminate South Africa's mandate in October 1966, established a UN Council for South West Africa in May 1967, and changed the name of the territory to Namibia in June 1968. In 1971 the ICJ ruled that South Africa's presence was illegal. In 1973 the UN General Assembly recognized SWAPO as 'the authentic representative of the Namibian people', and appointed a UN Commissioner for Namibia to undertake 'executive and administrative tasks'.

A multiracial constitutional conference on the territory's future, organized by the all-white South West Africa Legislative Assembly, was convened in Windhoek in September 1975, attended by representatives of the territory's 11 main ethnic groups. However, neither the UN nor the Organization of African Unity (OAU, now the African Union, AU, see p. 188) recognized this so-called Turnhalle Conference, owing to its ethnic and non-democratic basis. In 1976 and 1977 proposals for procedures whereby Namibia was to achieve independence and formulate a constitution were made by the Turnhalle Conference, but rejected by SWAPO, the UN and the OAU. In September 1977 South Africa appointed an Administrator-General to govern the territory. In November the Turnhalle Conference was dissolved, and the Democratic Turnhalle Alliance (DTA), a coalition of conservative political groups representing the ethnic groups involved in the Turnhalle Conference, was formed.

In early 1978 talks were held between South Africa, SWAPO and a 'contact group' comprising Canada, France, the Federal Republic of Germany, the UK and the USA. In September the contact group's proposals for a Namibian settlement, including the holding of UN-supervised elections, were conditionally accepted by both South Africa and SWAPO and were incorporated in UN Security Council Resolution 435. However, South Africa continued to implement its own internal solution for Namibia with an election for a Constituent Assembly in December. The election was contested by five parties, but boycotted notably by SWAPO. Of the 50 seats in the Assembly, 41 were won by the DTA. In May 1979 South Africa unilaterally established a legislative National Assembly, without executive powers, from the existing Constituent Assembly.

All-party negotiations, held under UN auspices in Geneva, Switzerland, in January 1981, failed in their aim of arranging a ceasefire and eventual UN-supervised elections. Later in 1981 the contact group attempted to secure support for a three-phase independence plan. However, South Africa's insistence (supported by the USA) that any withdrawal of South African forces must be linked to the withdrawal of Cuban troops from Angola was rejected by Angola and the UN. Meanwhile, the Ministerial Council, formed in 1980 and chaired by Dirk Mudge (also Chairman of the DTA), assumed much of the Administrator-General's executive power in September 1981. However, the Ministerial Council was dissolved in January 1983, when, after several months of disagreement with the South African Government regarding the future role of the DTA in the territory, Mudge resigned as Council Chairman. South Africa disbanded the National Assembly and resumed direct rule of Namibia, with Willem van Niekerk as Administrator-General.

The Multi-Party Conference (MPC) was established in November 1983, grouping, initially, seven internal political parties. Boycotted by SWAPO, it appeared to be promoted by South Africa as a means of settling the independence issue outside the framework of Resolution 435, and of reducing SWAPO's dominance in any future post-independence government for Namibia. None the less, South Africa continued to negotiate on the independence issue with SWAPO and Angola. In February 1984 South Africa and Angola agreed to a ceasefire on the Angola–Namibia border, and set up a joint commission to monitor the withdrawal of all South African troops from Angola. Angola undertook to ensure that neither Cuban nor SWAPO forces would move into the areas vacated by the South African troops. Discussions on the independence issue in mid-1984, involving van Niekerk, SWAPO and the MPC, ended inconclusively, as did negotiations in 1984–86 between the South African Government and the US Assistant Secretary of State for African Affairs.

In April 1985 the South African Government accepted a proposal by the MPC for a 'Transitional Government of National Unity' (TGNU) in Namibia. This was formally established in Windhoek in June, although the arrangement was condemned in advance by the contact group and was declared 'null and void' by the UN Secretary-General. The TGNU consisted of an executive Cabinet, drawn from a National Assembly of 62 members who were appointed from among the parties constituting the MPC. Its establishment was accompanied by the proclamation of a 'bill of rights', drafted by the MPC, which prohibited racial discrimination. A Constitutional Council was also established to prepare a constitution for an independent Namibia. The South African Government retained responsibility for foreign affairs, defence and internal security, and all legislation was to be subject to approval by the Administrator-General. Louis Pienaar replaced van Niekerk in this post in July.

During 1987, following the liberalization of labour laws and the legalization of trade unions for black workers in 1986, the trade union movement became increasingly active. In mid-1987 the Constitutional Council published a draft document; however, South Africa indicated that it could not accept the lack of a guarantee of minority rights in the proposal. In March 1988 the Namibian Supreme Court declared the 'AG8' law of 1980 (providing for the election of 'second-tier' legislative assemblies and for the administration of education and health facilities on an ethnic, rather than a geographical, basis) to be in conflict with the 1985 'bill of rights'.

Both Angola and Cuba were reported in January 1988 to have accepted, in principle, the US demand for a complete withdrawal of Cuban troops from Angola, but they reiterated that this would be conditional on the cessation of South African support for the insurgent União Nacional para a Independência Total de Angola (UNITA). In July Angola, Cuba and South Africa reached agreement on 14 'essential principles' for a peaceful settlement, and in August it was agreed that the implementation of Resolution 435 would begin on 1 November. However, it was not until December that Angola, Cuba and South Africa signed a formal treaty designating 1 April 1989 as the implementation date for Resolution 435 and establishing a joint commission to monitor the treaty's implementation. (A further agreement was signed by Angola and Cuba, requiring the evacuation of all Cuban troops from Angola by July 1991.) A Constituent Assembly was to be elected in Namibia on 1 November 1989. South African forces in Namibia were to be confined to their bases, and their numbers reduced to 1,500 by July 1989; all South African troops were to have been withdrawn from Namibia one week after the November election. SWAPO forces were to be confined to bases in Angola in April, before being disarmed and repatriated. A multinational military observer force, the UN Transition Assistance Group (UNTAG), was to monitor the South African withdrawal, and civilian administrators and an international police force were to supervise the election. At the end of February the TGNU was formally disbanded, and on 1 March the National Assembly voted to dissolve itself; until independence the territory was governed by the Administrator-General, in consultation with a Special Representative of the UN Secretary-General, Martti Ahtisaari. Pienaar and Ahtisaari were to be jointly responsible for arranging the November election. In June most racially discriminatory legislation was repealed, and an amnesty was granted to Namibian refugees and exiles: by late September nearly 42,000 people, including Nujoma, had returned to Namibia. Meanwhile, South Africa completed its troop reduction ahead of schedule.

Voting proceeded peacefully on 7–11 November 1989, with the participation of more than 95% of the electorate. SWAPO received 57.3% of all votes cast and won 41 of the Constituent Assembly's 72 seats, while the DTA, with 28.6% of the votes, secured 21 seats. Following the election, South Africa's remaining troops were evacuated from Namibia, while SWAPO's bases in Angola were decommissioned. The SWAPO Government subsequently reached an agreement with South Africa that no legal action would be taken for atrocities committed by either side. The agreement also precluded the establishment of a truth and reconciliation commission.

In February 1990 the Constituent Assembly adopted a draft Constitution, providing for a multi-party democracy based on universal adult suffrage. Later in the month the Constituent Assembly elected Nujoma as Namibia's first President. On 21 March Namibia finally achieved independence; the Constituent Assembly was redesignated the National Assembly, and Nujoma assumed executive power. A Cabinet, headed by the Constituent Assembly Chairman, Hage Geingob (a long-serving SWAPO activist), was also sworn in.

Domestic Political Affairs

Following Namibia's independence, the port of Walvis Bay, its surrounding territory of 1,124 sq km and the 12 offshore Penguin Islands remained under South African jurisdiction. In September 1991 the Namibian and South African Governments agreed to administer the disputed territories jointly, pending a final settlement on sovereignty, and in August 1992 the two countries

announced the forthcoming establishment of a joint administration authority. In August 1993, however, South Africa's multi-party constitutional negotiating committee instructed the Government to prepare legislation for the transfer of sovereignty over Walvis Bay to Namibia. Accordingly, negotiations between Namibia and South Africa resulted in bilateral agreements regarding the future of South African interests in the Walvis Bay area. Namibia formally took control of Walvis Bay and its islands from 1 March 1994.

Namibia's first post-independence presidential and legislative elections in December 1994 resulted in overwhelming victories for Nujoma and SWAPO. Nujoma was elected for a second term as President, securing 76.3% of the votes cast, while SWAPO secured 53 of the elective seats in the National Assembly, with 73.9% of the valid votes cast. The DTA won 15 seats (with 20.8% of the votes), and the United Democratic Front (UDF) two. The remaining two seats were won by the Democratic Coalition of Namibia (an alliance of the National Patriotic Front and the German Union) and the Monitor Action Group (MAG).

At the SWAPO Congress in May 1997 Nujoma was re-elected unopposed as party President. Among the resolutions endorsed by the Congress was a proposal that Nujoma should seek re-election for a third term as national President. It was agreed that the Constitution, which stipulated that a President may serve no more than two consecutive terms, could be exceptionally amended to allow Nujoma to seek a further mandate, since the incumbent had initially been appointed by the Constituent Assembly, and had only once been elected President on a popular mandate. In August 1998 a senior SWAPO official, Ben Ulenga, resigned as Namibia's High Commissioner to the UK, in protest at the proposed arrangement to allow Nujoma to seek a renewed mandate. The exceptional constitutional amendment was approved by the requisite two-thirds' majority in the National Assembly in October and by the National Council in November. Ulenga established a new political party, the Congress of Democrats (CoD).

In August 1998 the DTA's executive announced the suspension of Mishake Muyongo as party President, and dissociated the party from Muyongo's overt support for the secession of the Caprivi Strip—a narrow area of land extending in the north-east, between Angola and Botswana, as far as the Zambezi river (Namibia's border with Zambia). In November it emerged that Muyongo, leading the so-called Caprivi Liberation Movement (CLM), was among more than 100 people who, apparently armed, had crossed into Botswana in October, and who were now seeking asylum in that country. The Namibian Government stated that it had discovered plans for a secessionist rebellion, led by Muyongo and a chief of the Mafwe tribe, Boniface Mamili, in Caprivi. Representatives of the office of the UN High Commissioner for Refugees (UNHCR) subsequently advised the Botswana authorities that the secessionists' fears of persecution, should they be returned to Namibia, were 'plausible'. In subsequent weeks many more people crossed into Botswana, claiming to be fleeing harassment and persecution by the Namibian security forces. During a visit to Botswana in March 1999 Nujoma reached an agreement with President Festus Mogae of that country, whereby the separatist leaders (whose extradition had hitherto been sought by Namibia in order that they could be tried on terrorist charges) would be accorded refugee status, on condition that they be resettled in a third country. Muyongo and Mamili were subsequently granted asylum in Denmark. The agreement also provided for the return to Namibia, under the auspices of UNHCR and without fear of prosecution or persecution, of the estimated 2,500 refugees who had crossed into Botswana since late 1998.

A period of apparent calm in the Caprivi region ended abruptly in early August 1999 with an armed attack by members of an organization styling itself the Caprivi Liberation Army (CLA), who targeted a military base at Mpacha airport and the police headquarters and offices of the Namibian Broadcasting Corporation in the regional capital, Katima Mulilo. At least eight members of the Namibian security forces and five CLA fighters were killed during the attack and its suppression. Nujoma responded by declaring a state of emergency in the region. While there was support within Namibia for the declaration, the CoD, as well as church leaders and human rights organizations, expressed concern at evidence of the ill-treatment of detainees. Visiting Katima Mulilo in late August, Nujoma announced an end to the state of emergency, although army and police reinforcements were to remain in Caprivi. Initially, 12 alleged rebels were remanded on charges of high treason, murder, public violence and illegal possession of firearms; a further 47 suspects were charged with aiding and abetting the rebels. Repatriations of refugees from Botswana were halted following the attack on Katima Mulilo. In September 2001, in response to a request from the Namibian Government, the Gaborone Magistrates' Court in Botswana ordered the extradition of a group of suspected Caprivi separatists who were wanted to stand trial for high treason in connection with the attack on Katima Mulilo. The Namibian Government was also seeking to extradite Muyongo from Denmark to answer similar charges. In October 2003 the trial commenced of 121 Namibians charged with offences related to the attack on Katima Mulilo. In February 2004 the trial judge ruled that 13 of the defendants were 'irregularly before the court', as a result of a process of 'disguised extradition' whereby they had been removed from Zambia and Botswana, and ordered their release. It was reported that the 13 defendants thus acquitted had been immediately rearrested on their release. In August 2007 10 individuals were convicted in relation to the rebellion and sentenced to up to 32 years' imprisonment (although in July 2013 the Supreme Court ordered a retrial), while in February 2013 43 of the accused men were cleared of any wrongdoing. The trial of the remaining defendants was ongoing in early 2015, marking almost 16 years since the suspects had been detained.

Meanwhile, presidential and legislative elections, which were held on 30 November and 1 December 1999, resulted in an overwhelming victory for Nujoma and SWAPO, with Ulenga and the CoD apparently winning support at the expense of the DTA. In the presidential election Nujoma was returned for a third (and final) term of office, with 76.8% of the votes cast, while Ulenga took 10.5% and Katuutire Kaura (Muyongo's successor as President of the DTA) 9.6%. SWAPO won 55 of the elective seats in the National Assembly, with 76.1% of the votes cast (thus ensuring that it retained the two-thirds' majority required to amend the Constitution); the CoD and the DTA each won seven seats (taking, respectively, 9.9% and 9.5% of the total votes cast).

In August 2002 Nujoma reorganized his Cabinet; Theo-Ben Gurirab was appointed Prime Minister, replacing Geingob. Hidipo Hamutenya became Minister of Foreign Affairs, Information and Broadcasting, but was dismissed without explanation in May 2004: many observers regarded the decision as part of a plan by the President to manoeuvre his own choice of successor, the Minister of Lands, Resettlement and Rehabilitation, Hifikepunye Pohamba, into a stronger position. Pohamba was duly selected as SWAPO's presidential candidate later that month.

Pohamba elected President

At national elections held in November 2004 Pohamba was elected President with 76.4% of the votes cast; his nearest rival, Ulenga, secured 7.3%. SWAPO also recorded a decisive victory in the elections to the National Assembly, retaining 55 of the 72 seats with 76.1% of the national vote. The CoD increased its share of the vote but won only five seats. The DTA took four seats, the UDF three and the MAG one seat, while two newly reactivated parties, the National Unity Democratic Organization (NUDO) and the Republican Party (RP), won three seats and one seat, respectively.

Nujoma stood down as President on 21 March 2005, but remained leader of SWAPO. Following his inauguration as President that day, Pohamba announced his Cabinet, which included six new appointees. The former Minister of Higher Education, Training and Employment Creation, Nahas Angula, was appointed as Prime Minister.

Meanwhile, in April 2001 the Government announced that it had allocated N $100m. to acquire land for redistribution on a voluntary basis over a five-year period. At that time approximately 4,000 (mainly white-owned) farms occupied 52% of the total land area, while the Government had acquired only some 6% of the land required for resettlement. In October 2002 the Government announced that it was considering the seizure of white-owned farms for redistribution to the landless black population, and criticized white farmers for taking advantage of the voluntary basis for land redistribution by charging excessively high prices for their land. In March 2004 the Government estimated that it would cost more than US $150m. over a five-year period to redistribute some 9m. ha of land among an estimated 243,000 applicants. The expropriation of the first white-owned commercial farm was carried out in November 2005. Official data indicated that by late 2013 the Government had bought 345 farms (totalling 2.4m. ha) at a cost of N $770m. under the 'willing buyer, willing seller' scheme and resettled just

5,000 people. Budgetary constraints and the rising cost of land had undermined the efficacy of the land redistribution initiative.

In December 2005, meanwhile, the National Assembly approved legislation granting former President Nujoma the title of 'Founding Father'. Pohamba was elected as SWAPO leader in November 2007, following Nujoma's retirement. In the same month a new political party, the Rally for Democracy and Progress (RDP), was registered. Jesaya Nyamu, who was named as acting Chairman of the party, had been Minister of Trade and Industry until 2004 and Hidipo Hamutenya, acting President of the RDP, was formerly Minister of Foreign Affairs.

Pohamba's second term

Presidential and legislative elections were held concurrently in November 2009. In the former poll Pohamba was overwhelmingly re-elected to serve a second presidential term, securing 76.4% of the valid votes cast. Of his 11 challengers, only Hamutenya, representing the RDP, took more than 4% of the vote, winning 11.1%. SWAPO retained its majority in the National Assembly, taking 54 of the 72 seats in the legislative elections, with 75.3% of the national vote. The RDP won eight seats, while the DTA, NUDO and the UDF all secured two seats. Several African observer missions declared the polls to have been transparent, free and fair; however, opposition parties alleged that numerous irregularities had taken place. In March 2010 the Namibian High Court dismissed, owing to 'technical' reasons, a challenge to the results brought by a number of the defeated parties. In response to this ruling, the opposition parties appealed to the Supreme Court, while the RDP, RP and DTA announced a boycott of the National Assembly.

In late March 2010 President Pohamba announced the formation of a new Government, again headed by Prime Minister Angula. In September the Supreme Court overruled the High Court's earlier judgment and declared that the opposition challenge to the 2009 election results was valid, prompting the RDP and the RP to end their six-month boycott of the National Assembly. (The DTA had ended its boycott in June 2010.) However, after hearing their case, in February 2011 the High Court ruled against the opposition parties, concluding that there was insufficient evidence to support their claims of electoral misconduct. Shortly afterwards the opposition grouping announced its intention to appeal once again to the Supreme Court. In October 2012, however, the Supreme Court rejected the opposition's petition, although it did acknowledge that the electoral process had been imperfect.

Meanwhile, leaked documents emerged in mid-2010 relating to the Development Capital Portfolio (DCP), an investment arm of the Government Institutions Pension Fund (GIPF) which had ceased operating in 2002 after suffering huge financial losses due to the collapse of a number of companies to which the GIPF had lent large sums of DCP funds. Among the files was a previously unpublished audit report produced by the country's financial regulator, the Namibia Financial Institutions Supervisory Authority (NAMFISA), which in 2006 had conducted an independent investigation into the DCP's losses. The report described the DCP as being 'deeply flawed' and criticized the weak regulations governing the allocation of DCP funding, while media reports alleged that many of the businessmen awarded DCP loans had close ties with the Government. NAMFISA had recommended an overhaul of the GIPF, including the removal of senior management, and that measures be taken to recover the lost money from the receivers of the loans; however, the report's recipient, Prime Minister Angula, had failed to act on this guidance. The Government was criticized by trade unions and opposition parties for failing to bring to account those responsible for the DCP's losses, which amounted to over N $650m. according to NAMFISA, and there was widespread outrage among the general public. In response, in October 2010 the Government initiated another audit into the DCP's finances and suspended the DCP's successor scheme, the Unlisted Investment Policy. The results of the second audit, presented to the President in February 2011, corroborated the findings from NAMFISA's earlier investigation, and the reform of the GIPF and the introduction of new lending regulations were recommended. Following a protest march in the capital by hundreds of government workers, Pohamba announced that those who had borrowed DCP funds would be pursued for repayment under threat of prosecution, although he appeared reluctant to hold high-ranking GIPF members responsible for the scandal.

After the failure of negotiations on the formation of an opposition electoral alliance, in October 2010 the RDP and the RP announced that they intended to merge in order to present

SWAPO with a more robust challenge in the local and regional elections scheduled for the following month. Nevertheless, the polls, held in late November, resulted in another convincing victory for SWAPO, which secured the overwhelming majority of local and regional council seats. Shortly before the elections the SWAPO-dominated National Assembly had approved controversial legislation granting the President the power to appoint regional governors, who had hitherto been elected by the regional councillors. Opposition parties had strongly criticized the bill, arguing that it would weaken democracy and that it contradicted the Government's declared adherence to decentralization. However, the Government claimed that the new law would enhance national unity and deter potential tribal conflict, while providing governors with a direct channel of communication to the central authorities. In December Pohamba duly appointed the 13 regional governors, all of whom were SWAPO members.

In July 2011 President Pohamba suffered what was described as a mild stroke, raising doubts that he would be able to complete the remainder of his second presidential term, which was due to expire in 2015, and leading to speculation regarding the identity of his successor. The country's Constitution contrasted with SWAPO's own constitution, with the former dictating that the Prime Minister would take over in the event of the President being unable to continue; however, it is the party's prerogative to appoint its Vice-President as the country's next presidential candidate. The ambiguities in the succession process were seemingly resolved in December 2012, when Geingob was re-elected as SWAPO Vice-President and then appointed as Prime Minister; the outgoing premier, Angula, became Minister of Defence.

Pohamba announced a state of emergency in May 2013 in response to acute drought conditions throughout the country. Although the Government implemented a relief operation, the drought had a catastrophic impact upon the agricultural sector and precipitated a deceleration in economic growth in that year. South African President Jacob Zuma, during a visit to Namibia in November, pledged to provide the Namibian authorities with N $100m. in emergency assistance. However, the Government's spending priorities attracted censure in early 2014 when it emerged that the Cabinet had endorsed the construction of a new National Assembly building and new premises for the Prime Minister at an estimated cost of N $640m. and N $610m., respectively. Critics argued that these funds should instead have been directed towards drought relief initiatives and social programmes.

At a party convention in September 2013, McHenry Venaani was selected to succeed Kaura as President of the DTA. Hamutenya, meanwhile, was re-elected as RDP President in November. However, both parties were reportedly beset by factionalism, while the RDP's plans to merge with the RP appeared to have collapsed by March 2014.

Recent developments: the 2014 elections

A constitutional amendment bill was adopted by the National Assembly in August 2014 and by the National Council in the following month, which provided for an increase in the number of seats in the former from 72 to 96 and in the latter from 28 to 42, with effect from the next general election (due in November). The legislation also constitutionalized the presidential appointment of regional governors, created the new position of Vice-President and granted the President the power to designate an additional eight members of the National Assembly with qualified voting rights (as opposed to the six non-voting members hitherto). Opposition parties and civil society organizations criticized the speed with which the bill had been approved, arguing that such an extensive modification of the Constitution merited a comprehensive public consultation and a longer period of legislative debate. Concern was also expressed about the increased scope of the presidential mandate.

As had been widely anticipated, Geingob and SWAPO secured a comfortable victory at the national elections held on 28 November 2014. In the presidential poll, Geingob garnered 86.7% of the votes cast, compared with just 5.0% for Venaani and 3.4% for Hamutenya. SWAPO, with 80.0% of the legislative ballot, gained control of 77 of the 96 elective seats in the enlarged National Assembly, while the DTA won five seats and the RDP three; the remaining 11 seats were distributed among seven smaller parties. The rate of participation by the electorate was 71.9%. Regional monitors endorsed the elections as free and fair.

In early March 2015 Pohamba received the Mo Ibrahim Prize for Achievement in African Leadership, a notable award honouring regional leaders who have demonstrated a strong commitment to upholding democratic values. Geingob was sworn in as President on 21 March, while Nickey Iyambo became Vice-President. A new Cabinet was also installed, with former Minister of Finance Saara Kuugongelwa-Amadhila appointed as Prime Minister. Netumbo Nandi-Ndaitwah was named as Deputy Prime Minister and Minister of International Relations and Co-operation, Calle Schlettwein received the finance portfolio, and Pendukeni Iivula-Ithana was given responsibility for home affairs. Local and regional elections were scheduled to take place later in the year.

Foreign Affairs

Regional relations

Following independence, Namibia became a member of the UN, the Commonwealth, the OAU and the Southern African Development Co-ordination Conference—now the Southern African Development Community (SADC, see p. 420). The Nujoma regime forged close links with post-apartheid South Africa, and in 1997 legislation providing for the cancellation of Namibia's debt (now amounting to N $1,200m.) was formally approved by the South African Parliament. In August 2001 the foreign ministers of Namibia and South Africa held talks regarding their 400-km border; Namibia claimed its southern border extended to the middle of the Orange river, while South Africa claimed that its territory stretched to the northern bank. (When South Africa's borders were reassessed in 1994, following its first democratic elections, the Surveyors-General of both Namibia and South Africa had agreed to place the border in the middle of the river, but the agreement was never signed.) The confusion over the location of the border has led to differences over mineral and fishing rights in the river, as well as grazing rights on its islands. In November 2012 Namibia and South Africa agreed to form a bilateral commission to facilitate greater co-operation between the two countries with respect to economic, diplomatic and security matters.

In March 1993 UNITA alleged that members of the Namibia Defence Force (NDF) had crossed the border into southern Angola to assist Angolan government forces in offensives against UNITA, and subsequently claimed that some 2,000 Cuban troops had landed at Namibia's southern port of Lüderitz, from where they had been transferred to Angola to assist government forces. The Namibian authorities denied any involvement in the Angolan conflict. Namibia subsequently announced that the Government was to contribute 200 NDF troops to the UN peacekeeping mission in Angola.

Following the attack on Katima Mulilo by Caprivi separatists in August 1999, the Namibian Government alleged that UNITA was lending military and logistical support to the CLA. There was considerable speculation that not only was Caprivi an important supply route for UNITA, but also that the Angolan rebel movement was attempting to divert Namibian military resources away from the conflict in the Democratic Republic of the Congo.

Tensions in the region of the Namibia–Angola border escalated from late 1999, after the two countries began joint patrols targeting UNITA, and the Namibian Government authorized the Angolan armed forces to launch attacks against UNITA from Namibian territory. In February 2000 it was announced that Nujoma and President José Eduardo dos Santos of Angola had agreed to implement measures to restore security in the border region; by June more than 50 Namibians had been killed in cross-border raids by the Angolan rebels. Continuing conflict in southern Angola resulted in a large number of refugees entering Namibia (some 6,000 arrived from Angola between November 1999 and August 2000, although increased border security subsequently reduced the flow). In March 2001 President Nujoma ordered a further reinforcement of the Namibian military presence in Caprivi.

In April 2002 the Namibian Government welcomed the signing of a formal ceasefire agreement by the Angolan Government and UNITA. Some stability was restored in the Kavango and Caprivi regions in mid-2002, and in August a number of Angolan refugees were repatriated; the majority of them, estimated at around 20,000, were due to return home in mid-2003, under the auspices of UNHCR. In February 2005 Namibia and Angola reached agreement on a maritime border; negotiations had begun in 1993 but were not formalized until 2003 when a joint commission for delimitation and demarcation was established. In September 2008 Namibia's National Society for Human Rights (NSHR) reported that it had discovered what were believed to be unmarked mass graves near the border with

Angola. The organization claimed that it had 'reasonable cause' to believe the remains it had discovered belonged to victims of the Namibian security forces killed between 1994 and 2003. According to the NSHR, in 1994 the Namibian authorities ordered that all illegal immigrants be cleared from the northern border area, some of whom were accused of being members of UNITA. This allegedly resulted in systematic attacks on local people, who were subject to summary executions and 'forced disappearances': the Namibian Government, however, strongly denied these claims.

In mid-1996 Namibia and Botswana referred a dispute regarding the demarcation of their joint border on the Chobe river (specifically, the issue of the sovereignty of the small, uninhabited island of Kasikili-Sedudu) for adjudication by the ICJ. The Court ruled in December 1999 that the island formed part of the territory of Botswana; the judgment further ruled that nationals of (and vessels flying the flags of) Botswana and Namibia should enjoy equal treatment in the two channels around the island. In January 1998 the two countries' Joint Commission on Defence and Security held an emergency meeting, following allegations by Namibia that troops from Botswana had taken control of a further island in disputed border territory—Situngu Island in the Caprivi Strip. The Joint Commission agreed to expedite the establishment of a Joint Technical Commission for the demarcation of the border. Relations were complicated by the issue of Caprivi secessionism. Situngu is claimed as Mafwe land; furthermore, Namibia's representative in discussions regarding the island, said to be a member of the secessionist movement, was reported to have fled to Angola. In 2003 Botswana and Namibia accepted the demarcation by a joint commission of their joint border along the Kwando, Linyanti and Chobe rivers.

Other external relations

Germany has been a major aid donor to Namibia since independence, and relations are generally close. In September 1995, none the less, during a visit by the German Chancellor, Helmut Kohl, some 300 members of the Herero ethnic group staged a demonstration outside the German embassy in Windhoek to demand compensation for suffering inflicted on the Herero under German rule. The Herero have unsuccessfully filed lawsuits against German companies and the German Government, seeking reparations for the alleged exploitation and eventual extermination of some 65,000 Herero in 1904–07. In January 2004, at a commemoration of the Herero uprising against German rule in 1904, the Government of Germany expressed its regret for the extermination of Herero, but declared itself unwilling to pay compensation to descendants of the victims. During a visit to Namibia in August 2004 the German Minister of Economic Co-operation and Development, Heidemarie Wieczorek-Zeul, apologized to the Herero community for the atrocities carried out during 1904–07. During a visit to Germany in December 2005 President Pohamba rejected an offer of reparations valued at N $160m. Bilateral consultations took place in May 2006 and included a German proposal to invest N $150m., over a 10-year period, in regions inhabited by descendants of populations that had suffered during the colonial occupation. The money would be made available in addition to existing aid commitments, which were reported to amount to some €11m. per year. However, the German Government denied that the additional money was intended as war reparations.

CONSTITUTION AND GOVERNMENT

On 21 March 1990 Namibia became independent, and the Constitution took effect. Executive authority is held by the President, who is the Head of State. According to the Constitution, the President shall be directly elected by universal adult suffrage for a term of five years, and permitted to hold office for a maximum of two terms. (In late 1998 legislation was approved whereby the Constitution was to be exceptionally amended to allow the incumbent President to seek a third term of office.) Legislative power is vested in the National Assembly, comprising 96 members directly elected by universal adult suffrage and as many as eight members nominated by the President; the presidential appointees have qualified voting rights. The National Assembly has a maximum term of five years. An advisory National Council, comprising three representatives from each of the country's 14 Regional Councils, elected for a six-year period, operates as the second chamber of parliament. Each region has its own Governor.

REGIONAL AND INTERNATIONAL CO-OPERATION

Namibia is a member of the African Union (see p. 188), of the Common Market for Eastern and Southern Africa (see p. 232), of the Southern African Development Community (see p. 420), and of the Southern African Customs Union (with Botswana, Lesotho, South Africa and Swaziland); and is also a signatory to the Cotonou Agreement with the European Union.

Namibia became a member of the UN in 1990. As a contracting party to the General Agreement on Tariffs and Trade, Namibia joined the World Trade Organization (WTO, see p. 431) on its establishment in 1995.

ECONOMIC AFFAIRS

In 2013, according to estimates by the World Bank, Namibia's gross national income (GNI), measured at average 2011–13 prices, was US $13,452m., equivalent to US $5,840 per head (or US $9,590 per head on an international purchasing-power parity basis). During 2004–13, it was estimated, the population increased at an average annual rate of 1.6%, while gross domestic product (GDP) per head increased, in real terms, by an average of 2.9% per year. Overall GDP increased, in real terms, at an average annual rate of 4.5% in 2004–13. According to the Bank of Namibia, real GDP increased by 5.1% in 2013.

Agriculture (including hunting, forestry and fishing) contributed 6.1% of GDP in 2013. An estimated 30.0% of the labour force were estimated to be employed in the sector at mid-2015, according to FAO. The principal agricultural activity is beef production; the production of karakul sheepskins is also important. In addition, seal-hunting and ostrich-farming are practised on a commercial basis. The main subsistence crops are root crops, millet and maize, although Namibia remains highly dependent on imports of basic foods, especially in drought years. Plantations of seedless grapes were developed on the banks of the Orange river in the late 1990s, and projected growth in production was expected to increase significantly their contribution to export revenue. In recent years Namibia's traditionally rich fisheries have suffered a reverse, and in February 2006 fishing quotas were further lowered and a five-year moratorium was declared on new fishing rights. Nevertheless, exports of fish and fish products provided 11.5% of total export earnings in 2013. Legislation aimed at developing aquaculture was adopted in 2003 and a number of fish farms were established. Agricultural GDP decreased at an average annual rate of 6.2% in 2007–13; sectoral GDP increased by 8.1% in 2012. The country suffered severe drought conditions in 2013, as a result of which agricultural GDP decreased by a massive 27.5% in that year.

In 2013 industry (including mining, manufacturing, construction and power) contributed 33.0% of GDP and engaged 14.4% of the employed labour force. During 2007–13 industrial GDP increased by an average of 2.1% per year. The GDP of the industry sector grew by 7.8% in 2012 and by 4.8% in 2013.

In 2013 mining and quarrying contributed 13.9% of GDP and engaged 2.0% of the employed labour force. Namibia has rich deposits of many minerals, and is among the world's leading producers of gem diamonds (some 98% of diamonds mined in Namibia are of gem quality). Diamond-mining contributed 65.5% of the sector's GDP in 2013, and diamonds are the principal mineral export, accounting for 21.1% of export earnings in 2013. Total production was 1.7m. carats in 2010, but this declined to an estimated 1.3m. carats in 2011 before increasing again, to 1.6m., in 2012. In 2004 the Israeli company Lev Leviev Diamonds established a diamond-cutting and -polishing factory in Windhoek, the first in Namibia and the largest of its kind in Africa. Copper production, which ceased in 1998, following the liquidation of the Tsumeb Corporation, resumed at the former Tsumeb sites in 2000, but was suspended again in 2008 owing to declining international prices. However, the smelter at Tsumeb, operated by Ongopolo, continued operations, processing imported ore. The Skorpion zinc mine and refinery near Rosh Pinah, opened in 2003 by Anglo American PLC and owned since November 2010 by Vedanta Resources PLC, produces around 150,000 metric tons of zinc per year. Despite health and environmental concerns, a new uranium mine began production at Langer Heinrich in 2007; Namibia was the fifth largest uranium producer in the world in 2013. In addition, lead, gold, salt, fluorspar, marble and semi-precious stones are extracted, and there are also considerable deposits of hydrocarbons, lithium, manganese, tungsten, cadmium and vanadium. Furthermore, Namibia is believed to have substantial reserves of coal, iron ore and platinum. Mining GDP increased at an average annual rate of 0.3% in 2007–13; the sector's GDP increased by 25.1% in 2012 but by only 0.6% in 2013.

Manufacturing contributed 13.0% of GDP and engaged 4.8% of the employed labour force in 2013. The sector has hitherto remained underdeveloped, largely owing to Namibia's economic dependence on South Africa. The principal manufacturing activities are the processing of fish and minerals for export; brewing, meat-processing and the production of chemicals are also significant. Manufacturing GDP increased by an average of 2.4% per year in 2007–13; the sector's GDP decreased by 6.8% in 2012, but increased by 1.9% in 2013.

Construction contributed 4.1% of GDP and engaged 7.0% of the employed labour force in 2013. During 2007–13 construction GDP increased by an average of 8.8% per year. The sector's GDP grew by 8.7% in 2012 and by 29.8% in 2013.

In 2011 some 98.2% of Namibia's electricity production was derived from hydroelectric power, while coal accounted for 1.4% of total production. There is a hydroelectric station at Ruacana, on the Cunene river at the border with Angola, and a second hydroelectric power station was planned at Divundu on the Okavango river. Final agreement was reached on developing the Kudu offshore gas field in early 2006. An 800-MW 'gas-to-power' plant would supply the domestic market and the surplus would be exported to South Africa under an agreement with that country's Electricity Supply Commission. However, the project subsequently suffered repeated delays. Plans for the construction of another, 300-MW gas-fired plant, at Walvis Bay, were also under negotiation in early 2015. Imports of mineral fuels and lubricants accounted for 10.0% of the value of total merchandise imports in 2013. South Africa supplies all of Namibia's petroleum requirements.

In 2013 the services sector contributed 61.0% of GDP and engaged 54.2% of the employed labour force. Tourism is expanding rapidly, and has been the focus of a major privatization initiative. The acquisition of Walvis Bay in 1994, and subsequent establishment there of a free trade zone, was expected to enhance Namibia's status as an entrepôt for regional trade. The GDP of the services sector increased at an average annual rate of 5.8% in 2007–13. Services GDP increased by 3.9% in 2012 and by 8.1% in 2013.

In 2013 Namibia recorded a visible merchandise trade deficit of US $2,002.1m. and there was a deficit of US $683.8m. on the current account of the balance of payments. South Africa was the dominant source of imports in 2013, providing 61.8% of the total, followed by Switzerland. In that year South Africa was also the principal market for Namibian exports (26.7%), followed by Botswana, Switzerland and Angola. The principal exports were pearls, precious stones, precious metals, and articles thereof, vehicles and associated transport equipment, mineral products, live animals and animal products, and iron, steel and base metals. The principal import groups in that year included vehicles and transport equipment (notably road vehicles), mineral products, machinery and mechanical appliances, iron and steel, and base metals, prepared foodstuffs, beverages, spirits and vinegars, and tobacco, chemicals and related products, electrical equipment and parts thereof, and pearls, precious stones, precious metals, and articles thereof.

In the financial year ending 31 March 2015 Namibia recorded an estimated budget deficit of N $7,731.4m. Namibia's general government gross debt was N $26,846m. in 2012, equivalent to 24.4% of GDP. In 1997 South Africa officially cancelled the external public debt inherited by Namibia at independence. Namibia's external debt was estimated at US $716m. in 2003. The annual rate of inflation averaged 6.0% in 2004–14; consumer prices increased by 5.4% in 2014. According to the 2013 labour force survey, some 29.6% of the labour force were unemployed.

Namibia's potential for economic prosperity remains high, given its abundant mineral reserves and well-developed infrastructure, both of which were enhanced in 1994 by the acquisition of sovereignty over Walvis Bay and of important diamond-mining rights. However, tackling poverty and unemployment remain the main challenges for the Government. More than one-quarter of the labour force was unemployed in early 2015, while Namibia's reclassification as an upper middle-income country in 2009 belies the reality of its large income inequality. Moreover, Namibia's economic progress continues to be largely influenced by its dependence on South Africa—the Namibian dollar, introduced in 1993, is at par with the rand. The Government used its expansionary spending policies in early 2012 to encourage domestic demand. However, the IMF, in its largely positive assessment of the Namibian economy in February, noted the country's growing public debt as an area for concern, urging the Government to reduce spending and continue to check the progress of its stimulus programme. According to the IMF, real GDP expanded by 5.0% in 2012, driven by an upturn in diamond and uranium output. Despite a slowdown in the minerals sector and a sharp drought-induced decline in agricultural production, economic growth was 5.1% in 2013, according to the Bank of Namibia. Domestic consumption remained robust and increased activity in the construction and manufacturing sectors was reported. In a further positive development, petroleum was found off the Namibian coast in mid-2013. Although exploitation of this deposit was deemed to be economically unviable, the discovery demonstrated the potential of the area, and oil-prospecting companies consequently intensified their exploration efforts. Meanwhile, the Government maintained its expansionary spending policies in 2014, as expected during an election year, and levels of public debt thus continued to rise. The economy expanded by an estimated 4.3% in 2014 as a result of positive developments in the construction, diamond-mining, manufacturing and retail sectors. The IMF projected that the economy would grow by a further 4.5% in 2015, although the Government forecast an even higher rate of growth, of 5.7%, supported by predicted increases in construction activity and mineral exports. With the mining industry continuing to attract investment, the country's medium-term economic outlook appeared favourable.

PUBLIC HOLIDAYS

2016: 1 January (New Year's Day), 21 March (Independence Day), 25–28 March (Easter), 1 May (Workers' Day), 4 May (Cassinga Day), 5 May (Ascension Day), 25 May (Africa Day, anniversary of the OAU's foundation), 26 August (Heroes' Day), 10 December (Human Rights Day), 25 December (Christmas Day), 26 December (Family Day).

Statistical Survey

Source (unless otherwise indicated): Namibia Statistics Agency, POB 2133, Windhoek; tel. (61) 4313200; fax (61) 4313253; e-mail info@nsa.org.na; internet www.nsa.org.na.

Area and Population

AREA, POPULATION AND DENSITY

Area (sq km)	825,615*
Population (census results)	
28 October 2001	1,830,330
28 August 2011	
Males	1,021,912
Females	1,091,165
Total	2,113,077
Population (official projections at mid-year)	
2013	2,196,086
2014	2,237,894
2015	2,280,716
Density (per sq km) at mid-2015	2.8

* 318,772 sq miles.

POPULATION BY AGE AND SEX
(official projections at mid-2015)

	Males	Females	Total
0–14 years	418,212	411,852	830,064
15–64 years	648,757	698,402	1,347,159
65 years and over	41,307	62,186	103,493
Total	1,108,276	1,172,440	2,280,716

POPULATION BY ETHNIC GROUP
(population, 1988 estimates)

Ovambo	623,000	Caprivian . . .	47,000
Kavango . . .	117,000	Bushmen . . .	36,000
Damara	94,000	Baster	31,000
Herero	94,000	Tswana	7,000
White	80,000	Others	12,000
Nama	60,000	**Total**	1,252,000
Coloured . . .	51,000		

Note: Classification of ethnicity reflects national methodology.

REGIONS
(population at 2011 census)

	Area (sq km)	Population	Density (per sq km)
Caprivi*	14,785	90,596	6.1
Erongo	63,539	150,809	2.4
Hardap	109,781	79,507	0.7
Karas*	161,514	77,421	0.5
Kavango*	48,742	223,352	4.6
Khomas	36,964	342,141	9.3
Kunene	115,260	86,856	0.8
Ohangwena	10,706	245,446	22.9
Omaheke	84,981	71,233	0.8
Omusati	26,551	243,166	9.2
Oshana	8,647	176,674	20.4
Oshikoto	38,685	181,973	4.7
Otjozondjupa	105,460	143,903	1.4
Total	825,615	2,113,077	2.6

* In August 2013 it was announced that henceforth Kavango region would be divided into two new regions to be known as Kavango East and Kavango West. Furthermore, the regions of Caprivi and Karas were to be renamed Zambezi and !Karas (or ||Karas) respectively.

PRINCIPAL TOWNS
(population at 2011 census)

Windhoek . . .	325,858	Rehoboth . . .	28,843
Rundu	63,431	Katima Mulilo . .	28,362
Walvis Bay . .	62,096	Otjiwarongo . .	28,249
Swakopmund . .	44,725	Ondangwa . . .	22,822
Oshakati . . .	36,541	Okahandja . . .	22,639

Mid-2015 (incl. suburbs, UN estimate): Windhoek (capital) 367,987 (Source: UN, *World Urbanization Prospects: The 2014 Revision*).

BIRTHS AND DEATHS
(annual averages, UN estimates)

	2000–05	2005–10	2010–15
Birth rate (per 1,000)	30.4	28.1	26.2
Death rate (per 1,000)	12.1	8.9	7.2

Source: UN, *World Population Prospects: The 2012 Revision*.

Life expectancy (years at birth): 63.9 (males 61.2; females 66.7) in 2012 (Source: World Bank, World Development Indicators database).

ECONOMICALLY ACTIVE POPULATION
(labour force survey, 2013)

	Males	Females	Total
Agriculture, hunting, forestry and fishing	109,398	105,913	215,311
Mining and quarrying	11,433	2,126	13,559
Manufacturing	22,096	10,673	32,769
Electricity, gas and water . . .	3,390	1,353	4,743
Construction	43,972	3,887	47,859
Wholesale and retail trade, repair of motor vehicles, motorcycles and personal and household goods	50,615	54,436	105,051
Restaurants and hotels . . .	9,347	27,420	36,767
Transport, storage and communications	3,184	2,408	5,592
Financial intermediation . . .	4,616	9,992	14,608
Real estate, renting, administrative and business activities	23,125	19,816	42,941
Public administration and defence; compulsory social security . .	19,324	12,619	31,943
Education	14,811	26,987	41,798
Health and social work . . .	4,761	11,819	16,580
Other community, social, cultural and personal services . . .	8,289	9,663	17,952
Private households with employed persons	14,879	42,789	57,668
Extraterritorial organizations and bodies	80	430	510
Sub-total	343,320	342,331	685,651
Not classifiable by economic activity	1,972	2,396	4,368
Total employed	345,292	344,727	690,019
Unemployed	120,212	170,550	290,762
Total labour force	465,504	515,277	980,781

Mid-2015 ('000 persons, FAO estimates): Agriculture, etc. 264; Total labour force 880 (Source: FAO).

Health and Welfare

KEY INDICATORS

Total fertility rate (children per woman, 2012)	3.1
Under-5 mortality rate (per 1,000 live births, 2012) . . .	39
HIV/AIDS (% of persons aged 15–49, 2013)	14.3
Physicians (per 1,000 head, 2007)	0.4
Hospital beds (per 1,000 head, 2009)	2.7
Health expenditure (2011): US $ per head (PPP)	365
Health expenditure (2011): % of GDP	8.6
Health expenditure (2011): public (% of total)	61.3
Access to water (% of persons, 2012)	92
Access to sanitation (% of persons, 2012)	32
Total carbon dioxide emissions ('000 metric tons, 2010) . .	3,175.6
Carbon dioxide emissions per head (metric tons, 2010) . .	1.5
Human Development Index (2013): ranking	127
Human Development Index (2013): value	0.624

For sources and definitions, see explanatory note on p. vi.

Agriculture

PRINCIPAL CROPS
('000 metric tons)

	2011	2012	2013
Wheat*	16.3	14.5	15.0
Maize*	53.8	87.6	40.0
Millet*	42.0	56.0	25.0
Sorghum	4.9†	7.7*	7.0†
Grapes†	22.0	23.0	23.8

* Unofficial figure(s).
† FAO estimate(s).

Aggregate production ('000 metric tons, may include official, semi-official or estimated data): Total cereals 117.0 in 2011, 165.8 in 2012, 87.0 in 2013; Total roots and tubers 357.6 in 2011, 351.5 in 2012, 363.0 in 2013; Total vegetables (incl. melons) 60.5 in 2011, 63.7 in 2012, 66.6 in 2013; Total fruits (excl. melons) 43.8 in 2011, 45.9 in 2012, 46.9 in 2013.

Source: FAO.

LIVESTOCK
('000 head, year ending September, FAO estimates)

	2011	2012	2013
Horses	47	48	48
Asses	140	140	140
Cattle	2,350	2,360	2,370
Sheep	2,850	2,900	2,930
Goats	2,150	2,200	2,235
Pigs	70	72	73
Chickens	5,250	5,300	5,350

Source: FAO.

LIVESTOCK PRODUCTS
('000 metric tons, FAO estimates)

	2011	2012	2013
Cattle meat	34.3	35.8	35.8
Sheep meat	12.3	12.6	13.2
Chicken meat	12.0	12.4	12.5
Cows' milk	115.0	118.0	120.0
Hen eggs	3.4	3.4	3.5
Wool, greasy	1.4	1.5	1.5

Source: FAO.

Fishing

('000 metric tons, live weight)*

	2010	2011	2012
Capture†	379.3	413.9	468.7
Cape hakes (Stokvisse) . . .	146.3	149.8	145.9
Kingklip	5.6	3.1	4.6
Southern African pilchard . .	14.0†	28.7	25.5
Cape horse mackerel			
(Maasbanker)	198.0†	210.2	280.1
Aquaculture	0.5†	0.4	0.4†
Total catch†	379.9	414.4	469.1

* Figures include quantities caught by licensed foreign vessels in Namibian waters and processed in Lüderitz and Walvis Bay. The data exclude aquatic mammals (whales, seals, etc.). The number of South African fur seals caught was: 47,774 in 2010; 45,915 in 2011; 57,880 in 2012. The number of Nile crocodiles caught was: 2 in 2010; 200 in 2011; 801 in 2012.
† FAO estimate(s).

Source: FAO.

Mining

(metric tons unless otherwise indicated)

	2010	2011	2012
Copper ore*	—	3,366	5,304
Lead concentrates*	10,301	9,139	9,000
Zinc concentrates*	53,624	48,950	50,000
Silver ore (kilograms)* . . .	10,000	9,000	9,000
Uranium oxide	4,496	3,258	4,495
Gold ore (kilograms)* . . .	2,675	2,053	2,302
Fluorspar (Fluorite)†	95,002	84,480	67,500‡
Salt (unrefined)	770,636	738,000	725,000
Diamonds ('000 metric carats) .	1,693	1,256	1,629

* Figures refer to the metal content of ores and concentrates.
† Figures (on a wet-weight basis) refer to acid-grade material.
‡ Estimate.

Source: US Geological Survey.

Industry

SELECTED PRODUCTS
(metric tons)

	2010	2011	2012
Unrefined (blister) copper			
(unwrought)*	31,900	43,800	39,800
Electrical energy (million kWh) .	1,488	1,607	n.a.

* Estimates.

Sources: US Geological Survey; UN Industrial Commodity Statistics Database.

Finance

CURRENCY AND EXCHANGE RATES

Monetary Units
100 cents = 1 Namibian dollar (N $).

Sterling, US Dollar and Euro Equivalents (31 December 2014)
£1 sterling = N $18.076;
US $1 = N $11.581;
€1 = N $14.060;
N $100 = £5.53 = US $8.63 = €7.11.

Average Exchange Rate (N $ per US $)
2012   8.2100
2013   9.6551
2014   10.8527

Note: The Namibian dollar was introduced in September 1993, replacing (at par) the South African rand. The rand remained legal tender in Namibia.

CENTRAL GOVERNMENT BUDGET
(N $ million, year ending 31 March)

Revenue*	2012/13	2013/14†	2014/15†
Taxation	35,319.2	37,553.7	49,213.2
Taxes on income and profits	14,536.7	13,924.4	21,182.3
Taxes on property	288.5	243.8	274.1
Domestic taxes on goods and services	6,438.7	8,436.9	9,366.6
Taxes on international trade and transactions	13,795.8	14,726.6	18,116.6
Other taxes	259.6	222.0	273.6
Non-tax revenue	2,650.8	2,395.2	3,252.3
Entrepreneurial and property income	1,740.5	1,754.4	2,455.7
Fines and forfeitures	183.2	80.8	74.9
Administrative fees and charges	722.9	539.7	715.2
Return on capital from lending and equity	4.2	20.3	6.4
Total	37,970.0	39,948.9	52,465.5

Expenditure	2012/13	2013/14†	2014/15†
Current expenditure	30,804.4	38,432.5	48,281.9
Personnel expenditure	13,925.4	17,536.7	21,988.8
Expenditure on goods and other services	5,289.7	6,738.7	8,460.5
Interest payments	1,720.1	2,246.2	2,517.4
Subsidies and other current transfers	9,869.2	11,910.9	15,315.3
Capital expenditure	6,957.4	9,143.9	11,922.1
Capital investment	3,732.2	6205.4	8,893.3
Capital transfers	2,500.8	2,923.2	3,014.7
Total lending and equity participation	724.5	15.4	14.1
Total	38,113.6	47,576.5	60,204.0

* Excluding grants received from abroad (N $ million): 16.8 in 2012/13; 192.6 in 2013/14 (estimate); 7.1 in 2014/15 (estimate).
† Estimates.

Source: Ministry of Finance, Windhoek.

INTERNATIONAL RESERVES
(excluding gold, US $ million at 31 December)

	2011	2012	2013
IMF special drawing rights	8.09	7.86	7.73
Reserve position in IMF	0.12	0.12	0.12
Foreign exchange	1,778.48	1,737.89	1,503.31
Total	1,786.69	1,745.87	1,511.16

Source: IMF, *International Financial Statistics*.

MONEY SUPPLY
(N $ million at 31 December)

	2011	2012	2013
Currency outside depository corporations	1,697.7	1,685.8	2,137.1
Transferable deposits	26,152.8	25,300.9	31,743.1
Other deposits	32,678.7	36,725.0	35,077.7
Broad money	60,529.2	63,711.7	68,957.8

Source: IMF, *International Financial Statistics*.

COST OF LIVING
(Consumer Price Index: December 2012 = 100)

	2011	2012	2013
Food and non-alcoholic beverages	88.5	96.5	102.8
Clothing and footwear	98.0	98.5	102.0
Housing, fuel and power	91.8	97.2	102.2
All items (incl. others)	91.5	97.6	103.1

NATIONAL ACCOUNTS
(N $ million at current prices)

National Income and Product

	2011	2012	2013
Compensation of employees	38,394	45,737	53,265
Operating surplus	34,422	42,200	51,525
Domestic factor incomes	72,815	87,936	104,791
Consumption of fixed capital	9,531	10,380	11,626
Gross domestic product (GDP) at factor cost	82,346	98,317	116,416
Taxes, less subsidies, on production and imports	7,782	8,720	10,192
GDP in purchasers' values	90,128	107,037	126,608
Primary income received from abroad	1,690	1,488	1,888
Less Primary income paid abroad	4,576	4,551	3,079
Gross national income	87,242	103,973	125,418
Less Consumption of fixed capital	9,531	10,380	11,626
National income in market prices	77,711	93,593	113,792
Other current transfers from abroad	8,910	13,839	16,219
Less Other current transfers paid abroad	573	865	1,006
National disposable income	86,048	106,567	129,005

Expenditure on the Gross Domestic Product

	2011	2012	2013
Government final consumption expenditure	20,895	27,498	34,929
Private final consumption expenditure	59,841	68,519	83,570
Change in stocks	−291	1,043	−1,558
Gross fixed capital formation	20,453	27,636	32,525
Total domestic expenditure	100,898	124,696	149,466
Exports of goods and services	41,023	46,390	54,453
Less Imports of goods and services	51,789	64,051	77,314
Statistical discrepancy	−3	1	3
GDP in purchasers' values	90,128	107,037	126,608
GDP in constant 2010 prices	86,827	91,302	95,981

Gross Domestic Product by Economic Activity

	2011	2012	2013
Agriculture and forestry . . .	4,496	5,278	3,590
Fishing	2,921	3,329	3,627
Mining and quarrying	7,832	13,412	16,492
Diamond-mining	4,255	8,148	10,810
Manufacturing	12,303	13,027	15,451
Electricity and water	1,818	2,022	2,406
Construction	3,127	3,554	4,835
Wholesale and retail trade, repairs, etc.	10,305	11,439	14,212
Hotels and restaurants . . .	1,590	1,787	2,068
Transport, storage and communications	4,606	5,011	5,648
Financial intermediation . . .	4,692	5,437	8,166
Real estate and business services .	8,039	8,767	9,385
Public administration and defence	8,769	12,119	15,325
Education	7,403	8,829	10,462
Health	2,923	3,202	3,713
Community, social and personal services	2,626	2,269	2,416
Private households with employed persons	972	1,126	1,110
Sub-total	84,423	100,607	118,907
Less Financial services indirectly measured	1,100	1,315	1,462
GDP at basic prices	83,323	99,292	117,444
Taxes, less subsidies, on products .	6,805	7,745	9,164
GDP in purchasers' values .	90,128	107,037	126,608

Source: Bank of Namibia, Windhoek.

BALANCE OF PAYMENTS
(US $ million)

	2011	2012	2013
Exports of goods	4,406.5	4,368.8	4,614.4
Imports of goods	−5,503.0	−6,523.4	−6,616.5
Balance on goods	−1,096.5	−2,154.6	−2,002.1
Exports of services	741.9	1,075.9	925.8
Imports of services	−782.9	−697.3	−908.5
Balance on goods and services	−1,137.5	−1,776.0	−1,984.8
Primary income received . . .	319.4	299.2	324.1
Primary income paid	−709.8	−849.4	−456.2
Balance on goods, services and primary income	−1,527.9	−2,326.2	−2,117.0
Secondary income received . .	966.2	1,510.1	1,537.6
Secondary income paid . . .	−79.4	−105.5	−104.4
Current balance	−641.1	−921.5	−683.8
Capital account (net)	186.7	148.8	129.2
Direct investment assets . . .	123.6	45.3	−25.7
Direct investment liabilities . .	712.3	616.3	−518.3
Portfolio investment assets . .	−512.1	−709.6	−494.9
Portfolio investment liabilities .	484.2	101.6	12.4
Financial derivatives and employee stock options (net)	5.5	3.9	1.3
Other investment assets . . .	−113.1	289.5	−314.2
Other investment liabilities . .	112.7	−140.8	−514.2
Net errors and omissions . . .	−595.1	−514.6	−160.7
Reserves and related items .	−236.3	−1,081.0	−2,569.0

Source: IMF, *International Financial Statistics*.

External Trade

PRINCIPAL COMMODITIES
(distribution by HS, US $ million)

Imports c.i.f.	2011	2012	2013
Vegetables and vegetable products	191.0	197.3	235.6
Prepared foodstuffs, beverages, spirits and vinegars, tobacco and articles thereof	562.8	603.2	599.3
Mineral products	703.4	1,255.0	1,264.2
Mineral fuels, oils, distillation products, etc.	592.7	861.1	756.9
Petroleum oils, not crude . .	558.0	816.2	715.9
Ores, slag and ash	84.3	354.3	480.7
Copper ores and concentrates .	—	348.4	478.7
Chemicals and related products	622.1	597.7	574.5
Plastics, rubbers, and articles thereof	311.0	237.8	249.6
Plastics and articles thereof . .	224.6	151.5	158.4
Textile and textile articles .	269.4	236.6	240.8
Articles of stone plaster, cement, asbestos, ceramic products and glass products.	233.8	109.0	98.6
Glass and glassware	194.5	62.0	48.5
Pearls, precious or semi-precious stones, precious metals, and articles thereof .	181.0	377.9	418.0
Diamonds, not mounted or set .	172.1	368.8	407.3
Iron and steel, base metals and articles of base metals . .	598.5	596.0	630.3
Articles of iron or steel . . .	283.9	282.5	271.5
Machinery and mechanical appliances; electrical equipment; parts thereof .	1,051.3	1,004.8	1,123.7
Machinery, boilers, etc. . . .	667.4	648.0	724.8
Electrical, electronic equipment .	383.8	356.7	399.0
Vehicles, aircraft, vessels and associated transport equipment	929.2	1,179.3	1,376.5
Vehicles other than railway, tramway	843.8	824.3	846.4
Cars (incl. station wagons) . .	420.2	423.6	379.9
Ships, boats and other floating structures	15.3	298.1	487.0
Total (incl. others)	6,457.3	7,132.0	7,574.5

Exports f.o.b.	2011	2012	2013
Live animals and animal products	1,044.0	962.1	989.7
Meat and edible meat offal . .	188.1	181.5	142.4
Fish, crustaceans, molluscs, aquatic invertebrates . . .	701.1	692.5	730.7
Fish, frozen, whole	396.1	444.0	498.5
Fish fillets and pieces, fresh, chilled or frozen	255.8	197.4	168.4
Prepared food stuff, beverages, spirits and vinegar, tobacco and articles thereof . . .	337.0	349.9	309.8
Beverages, spirits and vinegar .	216.2	240.9	209.9
Mineral products	918.7	1,025.7	1,133.8
Ores, slag and ash	739.7	875.6	968.4
Copper ores and concentrates .	30.0	176.6	215.0
Uranium or thorium ores and concentrates	616.0	613.0	639.1
Pulp of wood, paper and paperboard, and articles thereof	581.2	20.5	26.0
Printed books, newspapers, pictures etc.	571.6	2.8	4.6
Unused stamps, cheque forms, banknotes, bond certificates, etc.	570.8	0.1	—

Exports f.o.b.—*continued*	2011	2012	2013
Pearls, precious or semi-precious stones, precious metals, and articles thereof .	1,406.3	1,468.8	1,431.4
Diamonds, not mounted or set .	1,300.2	1,344.2	1,338.6
Iron and steel, base metals and articles of base metals . .	805.8	531.2	545.5
Copper and articles thereof .	413.2	186.7	199.1
Unrefined copper; copper anodes for electrolytic refining .	341.5	86.4	194.1
Zinc and articles thereof . .	330.2	272.6	274.6
Unwrought zinc	327.4	272.0	274.1
Machinery and mechanical appliances; electrical equipment; parts thereof .	177.1	226.5	283.5
Machinery, boilers, etc. . . .	120.6	170.9	222.9
Vehicles, aircraft, vessels and associated transport equipment .	316.6	366.9	1,245.3
Vehicles other than railway, tramway	188.2	248.2	329.6
Ships, boats and other floating structures	123.2	92.6	893.5
Total (incl. others)	5,900.9	5,377.0	6,337.2

Source: Trade Map-Trade Competitiveness Map, International Trade Centre, www.intracen.org/marketanalysis.

PRINCIPAL TRADING PARTNERS
(US $ million)

Imports c.i.f.	2011	2012	2013
Botswana	30.7	113.3	186.1
China, People's Republic . . .	267.0	287.7	235.2
Denmark	10.4	8.9	122.2
Germany	131.2	140.0	114.5
India	77.5	37.6	52.3
Malawi	74.5	—	—
Marshall Islands	—	—	307.7
Netherlands	23.4	80.8	31.1
South Africa	4,892.6	4,968.6	4,677.9
Switzerland	53.7	426.8	438.8
United Kingdom	229.8	172.9	118.7
USA	52.3	45.1	141.3
Zambia	132.9	110.9	156.5
Total (incl. others)	6,457.3	7,132.0	7,574.5

Exports f.o.b.	2011	2012	2013
Angola	492.0	500.9	466.2
Belgium	327.8	439.2	174.5
Botswana	39.8	364.5	868.6
Canada	280.5	214.2	197.5
China, People's Republic . .	127.1	147.5	143.3
Congo, Democratic Republic . .	92.7	99.8	147.7
Denmark	4.2	12.1	124.5
France	136.1	208.7	230.7
Germany	79.7	90.4	69.4
Italy	187.0	143.8	81.6
Malaysia	3.9	85.0	3.7
Netherlands	159.7	37.0	43.5
South Africa	1,717.8	933.4	1,690.9
Spain	245.9	213.0	211.8
Sweden	58.5	54.0	20.5
Switzerland	76.7	206.9	556.8
Tanzania	1.2	74.1	10.2
United Kingdom	848.8	631.7	135.1
USA	412.0	201.2	215.5
Zambia	34.9	78.4	126.2
Total (incl. others)	5,900.9	5,377.0	6,337.2

Source: Trade Map-Trade Competitiveness Map, International Trade Centre, www.intracen.org/marketanalysis.

Transport

ROAD TRAFFIC
(motor vehicles in use at 31 December)

	2009	2010	2011
Passenger cars	100,460	108,467	118,444
Buses and coaches	3,012	3,452	3,801
Lorries and vans	120,978	131,909	141,980
Motorcycles and mopeds . . .	5,356	5,593	5,682

Source: IRF, *World Road Statistics*.

SHIPPING

Flag Registered Fleet
(at 31 December)

	2012	2013	2014
Number of vessels	122	124	126
Displacement (gross registered tons)	108,203	120,908	127,196

Source: Lloyd's List Intelligence (www.lloydslistintelligence.com).

Seaborne Freight Traffic
('000 freight tons*, year ending 30 August unless otherwise indicated)

	2009/10	2010/11	2011/12
Port of Lüderitz:			
Goods loaded	120.1	177.5	155.6
Goods unloaded	138.7	127.9	127.9
Containers handled (total TEUs)	8,576	3,511	2,724
Port of Walvis Bay:			
Goods loaded	1,239.5	1,372.2	1,455.9
Goods unloaded	2,638.2	2,946.3	3,218.8
Goods transshipped	1,023.5	871.9	1,535.5
Containers handled (total TEUs)	247,743	220,178	334,410

* One freight ton = 40 cu ft (1.133 cu m) of cargo capacity.

Source: Namibian Ports Authority.

CIVIL AVIATION
(traffic on scheduled services)

	2010	2011
Kilometres flown (million)	14	15
Passengers carried ('000)	486	541
Passenger-km (million)	1,428	1,473
Total ton-km (million)	143	148

Source: UN, *Statistical Yearbook*.

Passengers carried ('000): 632 in 2012; 513 in 2013 (Source: World Bank, World Development Indicators database).

Tourism

FOREIGN TOURIST ARRIVALS

Country of origin	2011	2012	2013
Angola	361,480	379,842	426,025
Botswana	28,658	25,273	31,829
Germany	79,721	80,127	79,551
South Africa	272,930	269,393	277,182
United Kingdom	21,584	21,035	23,185
USA	17,946	18,704	19,157
Zambia	42,945	54,020	56,566
Zimbabwe	61,120	80,515	98,792
Total (incl. others)	1,027,230	1,078,935	1,176,041

Tourism receipts (US $ million, excl. passenger transport): 517 in 2011; 485 in 2012; 409 in 2013 (provisional).

Source: World Tourism Organization.

Communications Media

	2011	2012	2013
Telephones ('000 main lines in use)	159.1	171.2	183.5
Mobile cellular telephones ('000 subscribers)	2,240.2	2,435.4	2,538.6
Broadband subscribers ('000) . .	18.5	26.6	29.8

Source: International Telecommunication Union.

Education

(2011/12 unless otherwise indicated)

		Students		
	Teachers	Males	Females	Total
Pre-primary	1,314*	16,414†	16,322†	32,736†
Primary	13,652	211,393	204,061	415,454
Secondary	7,365	86,085	96,860	182,945
Tertiary‡	1,204	8,506	11,201	19,707

* Estimate for 1999/2000.
† 2005/06.
‡ 2007/08.

Source: UNESCO, Institute for Statistics.

Pupil-teacher ratio (primary education, UNESCO estimate): 40.7 in 2011/12 (Source: UNESCO Institute for Statistics).

Adult literacy rate (UNESCO estimates): 88.8% (males 89.0%; females 88.5%) in 2010 (Source: UNESCO Institute for Statistics).

Directory

The Government

HEAD OF STATE

President and Commander-in-Chief of the Defence Force: Dr HAGE GEINGOB (inaugurated 21 March 2015).
Vice-President: Dr NICKEY IYAMBO.

THE CABINET
(May 2015)

President: Dr HAGE GEINGOB.
Vice-President: Dr NICKEY IYAMBO.
Prime Minister: SAARA KUUGONGELWA-AMADHILA.
Deputy Prime Minister and Minister of International Relations and Co-operation: NETUMBO NANDI-NDAITWAH.
Minister of Presidential Affairs: FRANS KAPOFI.
Minister in the Presidency, in charge of the National Planning Commission: TOM ALWEENDO.
Minister of Finance: CALLE SCHLETTWEIN.
Minister of Defence: PENDA YA NDAKOLO.
Minister of Home Affairs and Immigration: PENDUKENI IIVULA-ITHANA.
Minister of Higher Education, Training and Innovation: Dr ITAH MURANGI-KANDJII.
Minister of Education, Arts and Culture: KATRINA HANSE-HIMARWA.
Minister of Industrialization, Trade and SME Development: IMMANUEL NGATJIZEKO.
Minister of Urban and Rural Development: SOPHIA SHANINGWA.
Minister of Poverty Eradication and Social Welfare: Bishop ZEPHANIA KAMEETA.
Minister of Health and Social Services: Dr BERNHARD HAUFIKU.
Minister of Public Enterprises: LEON JOOSTE.
Minister of Works and Transport: ALPHEUS !NARUSEB.
Minister of Safety and Security: CHARLES NAMOLOH.
Minister of Agriculture, Water and Forestry: JOHN MUTORWA.
Minister of Land Reform: UUTONI NUJOMA.
Minister of Information, Communications and Technology: TJEKERO TWEYA.
Minister of Gender Equality and Child Welfare: DOREEN SIOKA.
Minister of Justice: Dr ALBERT KAWANA.
Minister of Labour, Industrial Relations and Employment Creation: ERKKI NGHIMTINA.
Minister of Fisheries and Marine Resources: BERNHARD ESAU.
Minister of Mines and Energy: OBEID KANDJOZE.
Minister of Environment and Tourism: POHAMBA SHIFETA.
Minister of Sport, Youth and National Service: JERRY EKANDJO.
In addition, there were also 29 Deputy Ministers.

MINISTRIES

Office of the President: State House, Robert Mugabe Ave, PMB 13339, Windhoek; tel. (61) 2707111; fax (61) 221780; e-mail angolo@op.gov.na; internet www.op.gov.na.

Office of the Prime Minister: Robert Mugabe Ave, PMB 13338, Windhoek; tel. (61) 2879111; fax (61) 226189; internet www.opm.gov.na.

Ministry of Agriculture, Water and Forestry: Government Office Park, PMB 13184, Windhoek; tel. (61) 2087111; fax (61) 221733; internet www.mawf.gov.na.

Ministry of Defence: PMB 13307, Windhoek; tel. (61) 2049111; fax (61) 232518; e-mail psecretary@mod.gov.na; internet www.mod.gov.na.

Ministry of Education, Arts and Culture: Government Office Park, Luther St, PMB 13186, Windhoek; tel. (61) 2933358; fax (61) 2933368; internet www.moe.gov.na.

Ministry of Environment and Tourism: 2nd Floor, FGI House, Post St Mall, PMB 13346, Windhoek; tel. (61) 2842111; fax (61) 2842216; e-mail kshangula@met.gov.na; internet www.met.gov.na.

Ministry of Finance: Fiscus Bldg, John Meinert St, PMB 13295, Windhoek; tel. (61) 2099111; fax (61) 227702; internet www.mof.gov.na.

Ministry of Fisheries and Marine Resources: Uhland and Goethe Sts, PMB 13355, Windhoek; tel. (61) 2059111; fax (61) 233286; e-mail mfmr@mfmr.gov.na; internet www.mfmr.gov.na.

Ministry of Gender Equality and Child Welfare: Juvenis Bldg, Independence Ave, PMG 13359, Windhoek; tel. (61) 2833111; fax (61) 221304; e-mail genderequality@mgecw.gov.na; internet www.mgecw.gov.na.

Ministry of Health and Social Services: Old State Hospital, Harvey St, PMB 13198, Windhoek; tel. (61) 2032000; fax (61) 227607; e-mail doccentre@mhss.gov.na; internet www.healthnet.org.na.

Ministry of Higher Education, Training and Innovation: Windhoek.

Ministry of Home Affairs and Immigration: Cohen Bldg, Kasino St, PMB 13200, Windhoek; tel. (61) 2922111; fax (61) 2922185; internet www.mha.gov.na.

Ministry of Industrialization, Trade and SME Development: Block B, Brendan Simbwaye Sq., Goethe St, PMB 13340, Windhoek; tel. (61) 2837334; fax (61) 220148; e-mail ingatjizeko@mti.gov.na; internet www.mti.gov.na.

Ministry of Information, Communications and Technology: PMB 13344, Windhoek; tel. (61) 2839111; fax (61) 222343; internet www.mict.gov.na.

Ministry of International Relations and Co-operation: Govt Bldgs, Robert Mugabe Ave, PMB 13347, Windhoek; tel. (61) 2829111; fax (61) 223937; e-mail headquarters@mfa.gov.na; internet www.mfa.gov.na.

Ministry of Justice: Justitia Bldg, Independence Ave, PMB 13248, Windhoek; tel. (61) 2805111; fax (61) 221615.

Ministry of Labour, Industrial Relations and Employment Creation: 32 Mercedes St, Khomasdal, PMB 19005, Windhoek; tel. (61) 2066111; fax (61) 212323; internet www.mol.gov.na.

Ministry of Land Reform: 55 Robert Mugabe Ave, PMB 13343, Windhoek; tel. (61) 2965371; fax (61) 254737; internet www.mlr.gov.na.

Ministry of Mines and Energy: 1st Aviation Rd, PMB 13297, Windhoek; tel. (61) 2848111; fax (61) 238643; e-mail info@mme.gov.na; internet www.mme.gov.na.

Ministry of Poverty Eradication and Social Welfare: Windhoek.

Ministry of Presidential Affairs: Windhoek.

Ministry of Public Enterprises: Windhoek.

Ministry of Safety and Security: Brendan Simbwaye Sq., Goethe St, PMB 13281, Windhoek; tel. (61) 2846111; fax (61) 272487; internet www.mss.gov.na.

Ministry of Sport, Youth and National Service: NDC Bldg, Goethe St, PMB 13391, Windhoek; tel. (61) 270611; fax (61) 2706303; e-mail kkazenambo@mynssc.gov.na; internet www.mynssc.gov.na.

Ministry of Urban and Rural Development: PMB 13289, Windhoek; tel. (61) 2975111; fax (61) 226049.

Ministry of Works and Transport: 6719 Bell St, Snyman Circle, PMB 13341, Windhoek; tel. (61) 2088111; fax (61) 224381; e-mail jngweda@mwtc.gov.na; internet www.mwt.gov.na.

President

Presidential Election, 28 November 2014

Candidate	Votes	% of votes
Hage G. Geingob (SWAPO)	772,528	86.73
McHenry Mike Kanjonokere Venaani (DTA)	44,271	4.97
Hidipo Livius Hamutenya (RDP) . .	30,197	3.39
Asser Ferdinand Mbai (NUDO) . .	16,740	1.88
Henry Ferdinand Mudge (RP) . . .	8,676	0.97
Ignatius Nkotongo Shixwameni (APP) .	7,266	0.82
Others*	11,060	1.24
Total	890,738	100.00

* There were three other candidates.

Legislature

NATIONAL ASSEMBLY

National Assembly: Parliament Bldg, 14c Love St, Private Bag 13323, Windhoek; tel. (61) 2889111; e-mail parliament@parliament.gov.na; internet www.parliament.gov.na.

Speaker: PETER KATJAVIVI.

General Election, 28 November 2014

Party	Votes	% of votes	Seats
SWAPO	715,026	80.01	77
DTA	42,933	4.80	5
RDP	31,372	3.51	3
APP	20,431	2.29	2
UDF	18,945	2.12	2
NUDO	17,942	2.01	2
WRP	13,328	1.49	2
SWANU	6,354	0.71	1
UPM	6,353	0.71	1
RP	6,099	0.68	1
Others	14,860	1.66	—
Total	893,643	100.00	96*

* In addition to the 96 directly elected members, the President of the Republic is empowered to nominate as many as eight members (who enjoy qualified voting rights).

NATIONAL COUNCIL

National Council: Parliament Bldg, 14c Love St, Private Bag 13371, Windhoek; tel. (61) 2028000; internet www.parliament.gov.na.

Chairman: ASSER KUVERI KAPERE.

The second chamber of parliament is the advisory National Council, comprising three representatives from each of the country's 14 Regional Councils, elected for a period of six years.

Election Commission

Electoral Commission of Namibia (ECN): 11 Goethe St, POB 13352, Windhoek; tel. (61) 220337; fax (61) 249348; e-mail mndjarakana@opm.gov.na; internet www.ecn.na; f. 1992; independent; Chair. NOTEMBA TJIPUEJA; Dir of Elections and CEO MOSES K. NDJARAKANA.

Political Organizations

In late 2014 there were 16 registered political parties in Namibia.

All People's Party of Namibia (APP): f. 2008 in Kavango region; splinter group of the CoD, which split in late 2007; Pres. IGNATIUS SHIXWAMENI.

Congress of Democrats (CoD): 8 Storch St, POB 40905, Windhoek; tel. (61) 256954; fax (61) 256980; internet www.cod.org.na; f. 1999 after split from SWAPO; Pres. BEN ULENGA; Nat. Chair. ARNOLD LOSPER; Sec.-Gen. TSUDAO GURIRAB.

Democratic Party of Namibia (DPN): Windhoek; f. 2008; Interim Pres. SALOMON DAWID ISAACKS; Sec.-Gen. ADAM ISAAK.

Democratic Turnhalle Alliance of Namibia (DTA): Rand St, Khomasdal, POB 173, Windhoek; tel. (61) 238530; fax (61) 226494; f. 1977 as a coalition of 11 ethnically based political groupings; reorg. in 1991 to allow dual membership of coalition groupings and the main party; Pres. MCHENRY VENAANI.

Monitor Action Group (MAG): POB 80808, Olympia, Windhoek; tel. (61) 252008; fax (61) 229242; e-mail mag@iway.na; f. 1991 by mems of the National Party of South West Africa alliance; Leader and Chair. J. W. F. (KOSIE) PRETORIUS.

National Democratic Party of Namibia (NDP): Daily Park, POB 2438, Ngweze, Katima Mulilo; f. 2004; Pres. MARTIN LUKATO.

National Unity Democratic Organization (NUDO): Clemence Kapuuo St, Plot 1881, POB 62691, Soweto, Katutura; tel. and fax (61) 211550; e-mail nudoparty@iway.na; internet www.nudoofnamibia.org.na; f. 1964 by the Herero Chiefs' Council; joined the DTA in 1977; broke away from the DTA in 2003; Sec.-Gen. ASSER MBAI.

Rally for Democracy and Progress (RDP): POB 83141, Olympia, Windhoek; tel. (61) 255973; e-mail info@rdp.org.na; internet www.rdp.org.na; f. 2007 by fmr mems of ruling SWAPO party; Pres. HIDIPO HAMUTENYA; Sec.-Gen. JESAYA NYAMU.

Republican Party of Namibia (RP): POB 22605, Windhoek; tel. (61) 244040; fax (61) 244039; e-mail rp@parliament.gov.na; Pres. HENRY FERDINAND MUDGE.

SWAPO Party of Namibia (SWAPO): Hans-Dietrich Genscher St, Plot 2464, Katutura, POB 1071, Windhoek; tel. (61) 238364; fax (61) 232368; internet www.swapoparty.org; f. 1957 as the Ovamboland People's Congress; renamed South West Africa People's Organization in 1960; Acting Pres. HAGE GEINGOB; Vice-Pres. (vacant); Sec.-Gen. PENDUKENI IIVULA-ITHANA.

South West African National Union (SWANU): POB 26529, Katutura, Windhoek; tel. (61) 2882325; fax (88) 637872; e-mail swanu@swanu.org.na; internet www.swanu.org.na; f. 1959 by mems of the Herero Chiefs' Council; formed alliance with the Workers' Revolutionary Party in 1999; Pres. USUTUAIJE MAAMBERUA; Sec.-Gen. Dr TANGENI IIJAMBO.

United Democratic Front of Namibia (UDF): POB 20037, Windhoek; tel. (61) 230683; fax (61) 237175; f. 1989 as a centrist coalition of eight parties; reorg. as a single party in 1999; Nat. Chair. ERIC BIWA; Pres. JUSTUS GAROEB.

United People's Movement (UPM): Rehoboth; internet rehobothbasters.org; f. 2010; Pres. WILLEM BISMARCK; Nat. Chair. JAN VAN WYK.

Workers' Revolutionary Party (WRP): Windhoek; f. 1989; Leader HEWAT BEUKES.

The **Caprivi Liberation Army (CLA)**, f. 1998 as the Caprivi Liberation Movement, seeks secession of the Zambezi Region; conducts military operations from bases in Zambia and Angola; political wing operates from Denmark as the **Caprivi National Union**, led by MISHAKE MUYONGO and BONIFACE MAMILI.

Diplomatic Representation

EMBASSIES AND HIGH COMMISSIONS IN NAMIBIA

Algeria: 96 Gloudina St, Ludwigsdorf, POB 3079, Windhoek; tel. (61) 221507; fax (61) 236376; e-mail Ambalg.w@mweb.com; Ambassador LAHCENE KAID-SLIMANE.

Angola: Angola House, 3 Dr Agostinho Neto St, Ausspannplatz, Private Bag 1220, Windhoek; tel. (61) 227535; fax (61) 221498; e-mail embangola@mweb.com.na; Ambassador MANUEL ALEXANDRE DUARTE RODRIGUES.

Botswana: 101 Nelson Mandela Ave, POB 20359, Windhoek; tel. (61) 221941; fax (61) 236034; internet www.botnam.com.na; High Commissioner GOBOPANG DUKE LEFHOKO.

Brazil: 52 Bismarck St, POB 24166, Windhoek; tel. (61) 237368; fax (61) 233389; e-mail brasemb.windhoek@itamaraty.gov.br; internet windhoek.itamaraty.gov.br/pt-br; Ambassador ANA MARIA SAMPAIO FERNANDES.

China, People's Republic: 13 Wecke St, POB 22777, Windhoek; tel. (61) 372800; fax (61) 225544; e-mail chinaemb_na@mfa.gov.cn; internet na.chineseembassy.org; Ambassador XIN SHUNKANG.

Congo, Democratic Republic: 56 Bismarck St, POB 9064, Windhoek; tel. (61) 256287; fax (61) 256286; Ambassador ANASTAS KABOBA KASONGO WA-KIMBA.

Congo, Republic: 9 Körner St, POB 22970, Windhoek; tel. (61) 257517; fax (61) 240796; e-mail embcongo@iway.na; Ambassador MARIE THÉRÈSE AVÉMEKA.

Cuba: 37 Quenta St, Ludwigsdorf, POB 23866, Windhoek; tel. (61) 227072; fax (61) 231584; e-mail embajada@cubanembassy.net; internet www.cubadiplomatica.cu/namibia; Ambassador GIRALDO MAZOLA.

Egypt: 10 Berg St, POB 11853, Windhoek; tel. (61) 221501; fax (61) 228856; e-mail embassy.windhoek@mfa.gov.eg; internet www.mfa.gov.eg/windhoek_emb; Ambassador MAHMOUD F. ABOU DOUNYA.

Finland: 2 Crohn St (cnr Bahnhof St), POB 3649, Windhoek; tel. (61) 221355; fax (61) 221349; e-mail sanomat.win@formin.fi; internet www.finland.org.na; Ambassador ANNE SALORANTA.

France: 1 Goethe St, POB 20484, Windhoek; tel. (61) 276700; fax (61) 276710; e-mail contact@ambafrance-na.org; internet www.ambafrance-na.org; Ambassador JACQUELINE BASSA-MAZZONI.

Germany: Sanlam Centre, 6th Floor, 154 Independence Ave, POB 231, Windhoek; tel. (61) 273100; fax (61) 222981; e-mail reg1@wind.diplo.de; internet www.windhuk.diplo.de; Ambassador ONNO HÜCKMANN.

Ghana: 5 Nelson Mandela Ave, POB 24165, Windhoek; tel. (61) 221341; fax (61) 221343; e-mail ghanahc@iwwn.com.na; High Commissioner Alhaji ABDUL RAHMAN HARUNA ATTA.

India: 97 Nelson Mandela Ave, POB 1209, Windhoek; tel. (61) 226037; fax (61) 237320; e-mail hicomind@mweb.com.na; internet www.highcommissionofindia.web.na; High Commissioner SATYA PAL MANN.

Indonesia: 103 Nelson Mandela Ave, POB 20691, Windhoek; tel. (61) 2851000; fax (61) 2851231; e-mail kbri@iafrica.com.na; internet www.kemlu.go.id/windhoek; Ambassador AGUSTINUS SUMARTONO.

Iran: 45 Kasteel St, Luxury Hill, POB 23866, Windhoek; tel. (61) 229974; fax (61) 229975; Ambassador KIOMARS FOTOUHI MOQADDAM.

Kenya: Kenya House, 5th Floor, 134 Robert Mugabe Ave, POB 2889, Windhoek; tel. (61) 226836; fax (61) 221409; e-mail kenyanet@mweb.com.na; internet www.khcwindhoek.com; High Commissioner ISAAC NJENGA.

Libya: 8 Conrad Rust St, Ludwigsdorf, POB 124, Windhoek; tel. (61) 234454; fax (61) 234471; Chargé d'affaires a.i. Dr ABDULHAFED JABER.

Malaysia: 63 Joseph Mukwayu Ithana St, Ludwigsdorf, POB 312, Windhoek; tel. (61) 259342; fax (61) 259343; e-mail mwwindhoek@kln.gov.my; internet www.kln.gov.my/perwakilan/windhoek; Chargé d'affaires MUSTAFA HJ MANSUR.

Nigeria: 4 Gen. Murtala Muhammed Ave, Eros Park, POB 23547, Windhoek; tel. (61) 232103; fax (61) 221639; e-mail nhcnam@mweb.com.na; internet www.nhcwindhoek.org; High Commissioner BIODUN NATHANIEL OLORUNFEMI.

Portugal: 4 Karin St, Ludwigsdorf, POB 443, Windhoek; tel. (61) 259791; fax (61) 259792; e-mail ambassaden.windhoek@sida.se; Ambassador HELENA ALEXANDRA ANDRADE FURTADO DE PAIVA.

Russian Federation: 4 Christian St, POB 3826, Windhoek; tel. (61) 228671; fax (61) 229061; e-mail rusemnam@mweb.com.na; internet www.rusemwhk.mid.ru; Ambassador ALEXANDER KHUDIN.

South Africa: RSA House, cnr Jan Jonker St and Nelson Mandela Ave, POB 23100, Windhoek; tel. (61) 2057111; fax (61) 224140; e-mail dibem@foreign.gov.za; internet www.dirco.gov.za/windhoek; High Commissioner YVETTE LILLIAN MAVIVI MYAKAYAKA-MANZINI.

Spain: 58 Bismarck St, POB 21811, Windhoek-West; tel. (61) 223066; fax (61) 227209; e-mail emb.windhoek@mae.es; Ambassador MARÍA DEL CARMEN DÍEZ OREJAS.

Turkey: 14 Cathy St, Ludwigsdorf, POB 090998, Windhoek; tel. (61) 2962929; fax (61) 2962931; e-mail emaral@mfa.gov.tr; Ambassador MURAT AHMET YÖRÜK.

United Kingdom: 116 Robert Mugabe Ave, POB 22202, Windhoek; tel. (61) 274800; fax (61) 228895; e-mail general.windhoek@fco.gov.uk; internet www.ukinnamibia.fco.gov.uk; High Commissioner MARIANNE YOUNG.

USA: 14 Lossen St, PMB 12029, Windhoek; tel. (61) 2958500; fax (61) 2958603; internet windhoek.usembassy.gov; Ambassador THOMAS F. DAUGHTON.

Venezuela: 12 Nelson Mandela Ave, 39 Post St Mall, Private Bag 13353, Windhoek; tel. (61) 227905; fax (61) 227804; e-mail embaven@mweb.com.na; Ambassador JUAN CARLOS BARRIOS HURTADO.

Zambia: 22 Sam Nujoma Dr, cnr Mandume Ndemufayo Ave, POB 22882, Windhoek; tel. (61) 237610; fax (61) 228162; e-mail zahico@iway.na; internet www.zahico.iway.na; High Commissioner WENDY SINKALA.

Zimbabwe: cnr Independence Ave and Grimm St, POB 23056, Windhoek; tel. (61) 228134; fax (61) 226859; e-mail zimbabwe@mweb.com.na; internet www.zimwhk.com; Ambassador ROFINA NDAKAZIVA CHIKAVA.

Judicial System

Judicial power is exercised by the Supreme Court, the High Court, and a number of Magistrate and Lower Courts. The Constitution provides for the appointment of an Ombudsman.

Supreme Court: Private Bag 13398, Windhoek; tel. (61) 279900; fax (61) 224979; e-mail cjudge@iway.na; internet www.ejustice.moj.na; f. 1990; Chief Justice PETER SHIVUTE; Additional Judges SYLVESTER SALUFU MAINGA, JOHANNES DAWID GERHARDUS MARITZ.

High Court: Private Bag 13179, Windhoek; tel. (61) 2921111; fax (61) 221681; e-mail highcourt@superiorcourts.org.na; internet www.ejustice.moj.na; Judge Pres. PETRUS DAMASEB.

Religion

An estimated 90% of the population are Christians.

CHRISTIANITY

Council of Churches in Namibia: 8 Mont Blanc St, POB 41, Windhoek; tel. (61) 374054; fax (61) 62786; e-mail ccn.gensec@mweb.com.na; f. 1978; eight mem. churches; Pres. Bishop AZARIAH KAMBURONA; Gen. Sec. Rev. MARIA KAPERE.

The Anglican Communion

Namibia comprises a single diocese in the Anglican Church of Southern Africa (formerly the Church of the Province of Southern Africa). The Metropolitan of the Province is the Archbishop of Cape Town, South Africa. In 2006 there were an estimated 110,000 Anglicans in the country.

Bishop of Namibia: Rt Rev. NATHANIEL NDAXUMA NAKWATUMBAH, POB 57, Windhoek; tel. (61) 238920; fax (61) 225903; e-mail shirley@mweb.com.na.

Dutch Reformed Church

Dutch Reformed Church in Namibia (Nederduitse Gereformeerde Kerk in Namibië): 46A Schanzen Rd, POB 389, Windhoek; tel. (61) 374350; fax (61) 227287; e-mail clem@ngkn.com.na; internet www.ngkn.com.na; f. 1898; Sec. Rev. CLEM MARAIS; 20,039 mems in 44 congregations (2015).

Evangelical Lutheran

Evangelical Lutheran Church in Namibia (ELCIN): POB 2018, Ondangwa; tel. (65) 240241; fax (65) 240472; e-mail gen.sec@elcin.org.na; internet www.elcin.org.na; f. 1870; became autonomous in 1954; Presiding Bishop Dr SHEKUTAAMBA V. V. NAMBALA; Gen. Sec. Rev. ELIKAIM N. K. SHAANIKA; 703,893 mems (2010).

Evangelical Lutheran Church in the Republic of Namibia (ELCRN) (Rhenish Mission Church): POB 5069, 6 Church St, Ausspanplatz, 9000 Windhoek; tel. (61) 224531; fax (61) 226775; e-mail reg@elcrnam.org; f. 1957; became autonomous in 1972; Pres. Bishop Dr ZEPHANIA KAMEETA; 420,000 mems (2010).

Evangelisch-Lutherische Kirche in Namibia (ELKIN—GELC): POB 233, 12 Fidel Castro St, Windhoek; tel. (61) 224294;

fax (61) 221470; e-mail bishop-office@elcin-gelc.org; internet www .elcin-gelc.org; Pres. Bishop BURGERT BRAND; 4,800 mems (2015).

Methodist

African Methodist Episcopal Church: POB 798, Keetmanshoop; tel. (63) 222347; fax (63) 223026; e-mail erikke5@hotmail.com; bishop resident in Cape Town, South Africa; Rep. Rev. Dr ANDREAS BIWA; c. 8,000 mems in 33 churches.

Methodist Church of Southern Africa: POB 143, Windhoek; tel. (61) 228921; fax (61) 229202; e-mail central@iway.na; internet www .methodist.org.za; Rep. Rev. KEVIN ENDRES.

The Roman Catholic Church

Namibia comprises one archdiocese, one diocese and one apostolic vicariate. Some 18% of the population are Roman Catholics.

Bishops' Conference: Namibian Catholic Bishops' Conference, POB 11525, Windhoek 9000; tel. (61) 224798; fax (61) 228126; e-mail ncbc@windhoek.org.na; f. 1996; Pres. LIBORIUS NDUMBUKUTI NASHENDA (Archbishop of Windhoek).

Archbishop of Windhoek: LIBORIUS NDUMBUKUTI NASHENDA, POB 272, Windhoek 9000; tel. (61) 227595; fax (61) 229836; e-mail rcarch@ iafrica.com.na; internet www.rcchurch.na.

Other Christian Churches

Among other denominations active in Namibia are the Evangelical Reformed Church in Africa, the Presbyterian Church of Southern Africa, Seventh Day Adventists and the United Congregational Church of Southern Africa. At mid-2000 there were an estimated 820,000 Protestants and 192,000 adherents professing other forms of Christianity.

JUDAISM

Windhoek Hebrew Congregation: POB 563, Windhoek; tel. (61) 221990; fax (61) 226444.

BAHÁ'Í FAITH

National Spiritual Assembly: POB 20372, Windhoek; tel. (61) 302663; e-mail bahainamibia@iway.na; Sec. ROSI STEVENSON; mems resident in 215 localities.

The Press

The African Magazine: NCCI, 2 Jenner St, POB 1770, Windhoek; tel. and fax (61) 255018; e-mail info@theafricanmagazin.org; internet www.theafricanmagazin.org.

AgriForum: Agri House, cnr Robert Mugabe Ave and John Meinert St, Private Bag 86641, Eros, Windhoek; tel. (61) 256023; fax (61) 256035; e-mail agriforum@agrinamibia.com.na; internet www .agrinamibia.com.na; f. 1978; monthly; Afrikaans and English; publ. by AgriPublishers; Editor MARIETJIE VAN STADEN; circ. 5,500.

Allgemeine Zeitung: 11 Gen. Murtala Muhammed Ave, POB 86695, Eros, Windhoek; tel. (61) 225822; fax (61) 220225; e-mail azinfo@az.com.na; internet www.az.com.na; f. 1916; publ. by Newsprint Namibia; daily; German; Editor-in-Chief STEFAN FISCHER; circ. 5,000.

Caprivi Vision: NDC Bldg, Plot No. 1127, Lenchwe St, POB 2011, Katima Mulilo; tel. (61) 253162; fax (0) 88614723; e-mail caprivinews@yahoo.com; internet www.caprivivision.com; f. 2002; bi-monthly; Editor RISCO M. LUMAMEZI.

Informanté: POB 11363, Windhoek; tel. (61) 2754363; fax (61) 2754090; e-mail informante1@tqi.na; internet www.informante .web.na; weekly; Editor NGHIDIPO NANGOLO.

Insight Namibia: IMLT Bldg, 70–72 Dr Frans Indongo St, POB 86058, Windhoek; tel. (61) 301438; fax (61) 240385; e-mail editor@ insight.com.na; internet www.insight.com.na; f. 2004; monthly; business and current affairs; Editor FREDERICO LINKS.

Namib Times: 8 Sam Nujoma Ave, POB 706, Walvis Bay; tel. (64) 205854; fax (64) 204813; e-mail newsdesk@namibtimes.net; internet www.namibtimes.net; f. 1958; 2 a week; Afrikaans, English, German and Portuguese; Editor FLORIS STEENKAMP; circ. 4,300.

Namibia Brief: Independence Ave, POB 2123, Windhoek; tel. (61) 251044; fax (61) 237251; e-mail cblatt@iafrica.com.na; 2 a year; English; Editor CATHY BLATT; circ. 7,500.

Namibia Economist: 7 Schuster St, POB 49, Windhoek 9000; tel. (61) 221925; fax (61) 220615; e-mail info@economist.com.na; internet www.economist.com.na; f. 1991; weekly; English; business, finance and economics; Editor DANIEL STEINMANN; circ. 7,000.

Namibiamagazin: Sudetenlandstr. 18, 37085 Goettingen, Germany; tel. and fax (551) 7076781; e-mail redaktion@ namibia-magazin.info; publ. by Klaus Hess Verlag; German; politics,

tourism, culture, economics, and German-Namibian relations; f. 1990; Rep. KLAUS A. HESS.

Namibia Review: Directorate Print Media and Regional Offices, Regular Publications, Turnhalle Bldg, Bahnhof St, PMB 13344, Windhoek; tel. (61) 2839111; fax (61) 224937; e-mail bupe@ webmail.co.za; f. 1992; publ. by the Ministry of Information and Communication Technology; monthly; information on govt policy and developmental issues; Editor ELIZABETH KALAMBO-M'ULE; circ. 5,000.

Namibia Sport: Unit 3, 14 Liliencron St, POB 1246, Windhoek; tel. (61) 224132; fax (61) 224613; e-mail editor@namibiasport.com.na; internet www.namibiasport.com.na; f. 2002; monthly; Editor HELGE SCHUTZ; circ. 2,000.

Namibia Today: 21 Johan Albrecht St, POB 24669, Windhoek; tel. (61) 276730; fax (61) 276381; e-mail editor@namibiatoday.com.na; 2 a week; Afrikaans, English, Otjiherero and Oshiwambo; publ. by SWAPO; Editor ASSER NTINDA; circ. 5,000.

The Namibian: 42 John Meinert St, POB 20783, Windhoek; tel. (61) 279600; fax (61) 279602; e-mail editor@namibian.com.na; internet www.namibian.com.na; f. 1985; daily; English; Editor TANGENI AMUPADHI; circ. 23,000 (Mon.–Thur.), 32,000 (Fri.).

Namibian Sun: 11B Gen. Murtala Muhammad Ave, Eros, POB 86829, Windhoek; tel. (61) 383400; fax (61) 306853; e-mail sun@ namibiansun.com; internet www.namibiansun.com; Mon. to Fri.; English; Editor FESTUS NAKATANA.

NCCI Namibia Business Journal: NCCI Head Office, 2 Jenner St, POB 9355, Windhoek; tel. (61) 228809; fax (61) 228009; publ. by the Namibia Chamber of Commerce and Industry; 6 a year; English; CEO TARAH SHAANIKA; Editor CHARITY MWIYA; circ. 4,000.

New Era: Daniel Tjongarero House, cnr Kerby and W. Kulz Sts, PMB 13364, Windhoek; tel. (61) 273300; fax (61) 220584; e-mail editor@newera.com.na; internet www.newera.com.na; f. 1991; daily; publ. by the Ministry of Information and Communication Technology; English; Chair. MATTHEW GOWASEB; CEO Dr AUDRIN MATHE; circ. 10,000.

Plus Weekly: POB 21506, Windhoek; tel. (61) 233635; fax (61) 230478; e-mail info@namibiaplus.com; publ. by Feddersen Publications; Afrikaans, English and German.

Republikein: 11 Gen. Murtala Muhammed Ave, POB 3436, Eros, Windhoek; tel. (61) 2972000; fax (61) 235674; e-mail republikein@ republikein.com.na; internet www.republikein.com.na; f. 1977; daily; Afrikaans and English; owned by Namibia Media Holdings; Editor DANI BOOYSEN; circ. 21,000.

Sister Namibia: 163 Nelson Mandela Ave, POB 86753, Windhoek; tel. (61) 230618; fax (61) 236371; e-mail director@sisternamibia.org; internet www.sisternamibia.org; f. 1989; 4 a year; publ. by Sister Namibia human rights org.; women's rights and gender equality issues; Dir VIDA DE VOSS; circ. 6,000.

The Southern Times: cnr Dr W. Külz and Kerby Sts, POB 32235, Windhoek; tel. (61) 415800; fax (61) 301095; internet www .southerntimesafrica.com; f. 2004; weekly (Sun.); owned by New Era and Zimpapers, Zimbabwe; printed in Namibia and Zimbabwe; regional; CEO PETER MIETZNER; Editor ITAYI MUSENGEYI.

Space Magazine: Sanlam Centre, 3rd Floor, POB 3717, Windhoek; tel. (61) 225155; e-mail info@spacemagazine.com.na; monthly; English; family life; Publr ESTER SMITH; Editor YANNA SMITH.

Windhoek Observer: 6 Schuster St, POB 2255, Windhoek; tel. (61) 221737; fax (61) 226098; e-mail whkob@africaonline.com.na; f. 1978; weekly; English; Editor KUVEE KANGUEEHI; circ. 14,000.

NEWS AGENCY

Namibia Press Agency (Nampa): cnr Keller and Eugene Marais Sts, POB 26185, Windhoek 9000; tel. (61) 374000; fax (61) 221713; e-mail info@nampa.org; internet www.nampa.org; f. 1991; Chair. RAYMOND REGGIE DIERGAARDT; CEO NGHIDINUA HAMUNIME.

Publishers

ELOC Printing Press: PMB 2013, Oniipa, Ondangwa; tel. (65) 240211; fax (65) 240536; e-mail elocbook@iway.na; internet www .elocbook.iway.na; f. 1901; Exec. Dir JULIUS KAALE.

Gamsberg Macmillan Publishers (Pty) Ltd: 19 Faraday St, POB 22830, Windhoek; tel. (61) 232165; fax (61) 233538; e-mail gmp@ iafrica.com.na; internet www.macmillan-africa.com; imprints incl. New Namibia Books and Out of Africa; Man. Dir HERMAN VAN WYK.

Longman Namibia: Southern Industrial Area, 19 Joule St, POB 6025, Eros, Windhoek; tel. (61) 231214; fax (61) 224019; internet www.longmanafrica.co.za/namibia; Publr LINDA BREDENKAMP.

National Archives of Namibia: 1–9 Eugène Marais St, PMB 13250, Windhoek; tel. (61) 2935211; fax (61) 2935217; e-mail national.archives@moe.gov.na; f. 1939; Chief Archivist WERNER HILLEBRECHT.

Association of Namibian Publishers: POB 40219, Windhoek; tel. (61) 228284; fax (61) 231496; f. 1991; Chair. Dr H. MELBER.

Broadcasting and Communications

REGULATORY AUTHORITY

Communications Regulatory Authority of Namibia (CRAN): Communication House, 56 Robert Mugabe Ave, Windhoek; Private Bag, 13309, Windhoek; tel. (61) 222666; fax (61) 222790; e-mail cran@cran.na; internet www.cran.na; f. 2011; issues broadcasting licences, supervises broadcasting activities and programme content; Chair. LAZARUS JACOBS; CEO (vacant).

TELECOMMUNICATIONS

State-owned Telecom Namibia Ltd (Telecom) has a monopoly on the provision of fixed-line services.

Leo Namibia: POB 40799, Windhoek; tel. 0855550000 (mobile); e-mail info@leo.na; internet www.leo.na; f. 2007; fmrly Cell One, name changed as above in 2009; CEO GERHARD MAY.

Mobile Telecommunications Ltd (MTC): cnr Mosé Tjitendero and Hamutenya Wanahepo Ndadi Sts, Olympia, Windhoek; POB 23051, Windhoek; tel. (61) 2802000; fax (61) 2802124; e-mail feedback@mtc.com.na; internet www.mtc.com.na; f. 1995 as jt venture between Namibia Post and Telecommunications Holdings (NPTH), Telia and Swedfund; 34% owned by Portugal Telecom, 64% by NPTH; Chair. DIRK CONRADIE; Man. Dir MIGUEL GERALDES.

Telecom Namibia Ltd (Telecom): 9 Lüderitz St, POB 297, Windhoek; tel. (61) 2012474; fax (61) 239014; e-mail commpr@telecom.na; internet www.telecom.na; f. 1992; operates fixed-line, fixed wireless and GSM network; state-owned; Chair. CATHERINE M. BEUKES-AMISS; Man. Dir THEO KLEIN (acting).

BROADCASTING

Radio

Namibian Broadcasting Corpn (NBC): Pettenkofer St, Windhoek West, POB 321, Windhoek; tel. (61) 2919111; fax (61) 215767; e-mail aaochamub@nbc.na; internet www.nbc.com.na; f. 1990; runs 10 radio stations, broadcasting daily to 98% of the population in English (24 hours), Afrikaans, German and eight indigenous languages (10 hours); Chair. SVEN THIEME; Dir-Gen. ALBERTUS AOCHAMUB.

Channel 7/Kanaal 7: Ara Straat, Dorado Park, POB 20500, Windhoek; tel. (61) 420050; fax (61) 240190; e-mail channel7@k7.com.na; internet www.k7.com.na; f. 1993; Christian community radio station; English, Afrikaans and Oshiwambo; Man. Dir NEAL VAN DEN BERG.

Katutura Community Radio: Clemence Kapuuo St, POB 70448, KHD, Katutura, Windhoek; tel. (61) 263726; fax (61) 236371; f. 1995 by non-governmental orgs; Dir FREDERICK GOWASEB.

Kudu FM: 158 Jan Jonker St, POB 5369, Windhoek; tel. (61) 247262; fax (61) 247259; e-mail radiokudu@radiokudu.com.na; f. 1998; commercial station affiliated to Omulunga Radio; English, Afrikaans and German.

Ninety Nine FM (Pty) Ltd (99 FM): cnr Alwyn & Perkin Sts, Suiderhof, Windhoek 9000; tel. (61) 383450; fax (61) 230964; e-mail 99@99fm.com.na; internet 99fm.com.na; f. 1994; CEO CHRISNA GREEFF.

Omulunga Radio: POB 40789, Windhoek; tel. (61) 239706; fax (61) 247259; e-mail omulunga@omulunga.com.na; internet www.omulunga.com.na; f. 2002; Ovambo interest station affiliated to Kudu FM; Oshiwambo and English.

Other radio stations include: Kosmos Radio, Radio France International (via relay), Radio 99 and Radio Wave.

Television

Namibian Broadcasting Corpn (NBC): Cullinan St, Northern Industrial, POB 321, Windhoek; tel. (61) 2913111; fax (61) 216209; e-mail aaochamub@nbc.na; internet www.nbc.na; f. 1990; broadcasts television programmes in English to 45% of the population, 18 hours daily; Chair. SVEN THIEME; Dir-Gen. ALBERTUS AOCHAMUB.

One Africa TV: 79 Hosea Kutako Dr., POB 21593, Windhoek; tel. (61) 2891500; fax (61) 259450; internet www.oneafrica.tv; Man. Dir VIVIAN GRAIG.

Trinity Broadcasting Namibia: POB 1587, Swakopmund; tel. (64) 401100; fax (64) 403752; e-mail comments@tbnnamibia.tv; internet www.tbnnamibia.tv; f. 2002; CEO EDNA BOTHA.

Finance

(cap. = capital; res = reserves; dep. = deposits; m. = million; brs = branches; amounts in Namibian dollars)

BANKING

In early 2015 there were five commercial banks in Namibia.

Central Bank

Bank of Namibia: 71 Robert Mugabe Ave, POB 2882, Windhoek; tel. (61) 2835111; fax (61) 2835067; e-mail jerome.mutumba@bon.com.na; internet www.bon.com.na; f. 1990; cap. 40.0m., res 1,662.9m., dep. 10,930.5m. (Dec. 2009); Gov. IPUMBU WENDELINUS SHIIMI; Dep. Gov. EBSON UANGUTA.

Commercial Banks

Bank Windhoek Ltd: Bank Windhoek Bldg, 262 Independence Ave, POB 15, Windhoek; tel. (61) 2991223; fax (61) 223188; e-mail info@bankwindhoek.com.na; internet www.bankwindhoek.com.na; f. 1982; cap. 4.9m., res 2,634.5m., dep. 18,902.1m. (June 2014); Chair. J. C. 'KOOS' BRANDT; Man. Dir CHRISTO DE VRIES; 32 brs.

FIDES Bank Namibia: Windhoek; f. 2010; microfinance institution; Chair. MARIA GAOMAS; CEO KARIN EVERDING.

First National Bank of Namibia Ltd: 209–211 Independence Ave, POB 195, Windhoek; tel. (61) 2992111; fax (61) 2220979; e-mail info@fnbnamibia.com.na; internet www.fnbnamibia.com.na; f. 1987 as First Nat. Bank of Southern Africa Ltd; present name adopted 1990; res 1,269.6m., dep. 22,416.8m. (June 2014); Chair. CLAUS HINRICHSEN; CEO IAN JETZE MILLER LEYENAAR; 28 brs and 12 agencies.

Nedbank Namibia Ltd: 12–20 Dr Frans Indongo St, POB 1, Windhoek; tel. (61) 2959111; fax (61) 2952046; e-mail service@nedbank.com; internet www.nedbank.com.na; f. 1973; fmrly Commercial Bank of Namibia Ltd; subsidiary of Nedbank Group, South Africa; cap. 16.9m., res 142.4m., dep. 8,153.8m. (Dec. 2013); Chair. THEO J. FRANK; Man. Dir LIONEL J. MATTHEWS; 16 brs and 3 agencies.

Standard Bank Namibia Ltd: Standard Bank Centre, cnr Werner List St and Post St Mall, POB 3327, Windhoek; tel. (61) 2942126; fax (61) 2942583; e-mail info@standardbank.com.na; internet www.standardbank.com.na; f. 1915; controlled by Standard Bank Africa; cap. 2.0m., res 567.0m., dep. 16,459.8m. (Dec. 2013); Chair. HERBERT MAIER; Man. Dir MPUMZI PUPUMA; 23 brs.

Agricultural Bank

Agricultural Bank of Namibia (AgriBank): 10 Post St Mall, POB 13208, Windhoek; tel. (61) 2074111; fax (61) 2074289; e-mail info@agribank.com.na; internet www.agribank.com.na; f. 1922; state-owned; total assets 739.1m. (March 2001); Chair. HANS-GUENTHER STIER; CEO LEONARD N. IIPUMBU.

Development Bank

Development Bank of Namibia (DBN): 12 Daniel Munamava St, POB 235, Windhoek; tel. (61) 2908000; fax (61) 2908049; e-mail info@dbn.com.na; internet www.dbn.com.na; f. 2004; Chair. ELIZE ANGULA; CEO MARTIN INKUMBI.

SME Bank: Jan Jonker Rd, Windhoek; internet smebank.com.na; f. 2012; Chair. FRANS KAPOFI; Man. Dir TAWANA MUMVUMA.

REGULATORY AUTHORITY

Namibia Financial Institutions Supervisory Authority (NAMFISA): 154 Independence Ave, Sanlam Centre, 8th Floor, POB 21250, Windhoek; tel. (61) 2905000; fax (61) 2905194; e-mail info@namfisa.com.na; internet www.namfisa.com.na; f. 2001; regulates non-banking financial institutions; Chair. ESTELLE TJIPUKA.

STOCK EXCHANGE

Namibian Stock Exchange (NSX): Robert Mugabe Ave 4, POB 2401, Windhoek; tel. (61) 227647; fax (61) 248531; e-mail info@nsx.com.na; internet www.nsx.com.na; f. 1992; CEO TIAAN BAZUIN; Operations Man. MANDA STEYNBERG.

INSURANCE

Corporate Guarantee and Insurance Co of Namibia Ltd (CGI): Corporate House, 1st Floor, 17 Lüderitz St, POB 416, Windhoek; tel. (61) 259525; fax (61) 255213; e-mail info@corporateguarantee.com; internet www.corporateguarantee.com; f. 1996; wholly owned subsidiary of Nictus Group Ltd since 2001;

Chair. F. R. van Staden; Man. Dir and Principal Officer P. J. de W. Tromp.

Metropolitan Namibia: Metropolitan Pl., 1st Floor, cnr Bülow and Stubel Sts, POB 3785, Windhoek; tel. (61) 2973000; fax (61) 248191; internet www.metropolitan.com.na; f. 1996; subsidiary of Metropolitan Group, South Africa; acquired Channel Life in 2004; Chair. Rairirira Mbetjiha; Man. Dir Jason Nandago.

Namibia National Reinsurance Corpn Ltd (NamibRE): NamibRe Bldg, 1st Floor,No 39, cnr Feld and Lazarett Sts, POB 716, Windhoek; tel. (61) 422800; fax (61) 256904; e-mail administrator@Namibre.com; internet www.namibre.com; f. 2001; 100% state-owned; Man. Dir Anna Nakale-Kawana.

Old Mutual Life Assurance Co (Namibia) Ltd: Mutual Tower, 223 Independence Ave, POB 25548, Windhoek; tel. (61) 2993999; fax (61) 2993813; e-mail infonamibia@oldmutual.com; internet www.oldmutual.com.na; Chair. Peter de Beyer; Man. Dir Johannes Gawaxab.

OUTsurance Insurance Co of Namibia Ltd: Maerua Office Block, 2nd Floor, cnr Jan Jonker St and Robert Mugabe Ave, POB 79, Windhoek; tel. (61) 2997528; fax (61) 2997551; internet www.outsurance.com.na; f. 1990; fmrly Swabou Insurance Co Ltd; acquired by FNB Namibia Holdings Ltd in 2004; short-term insurance.

Sanlam Namibia: 154 Independence Ave, POB 317, Windhoek; tel. (61) 2947418; fax (61) 2947416; e-mail marketing@sanlam.com.na; internet www.sanlam.com.na; f. 1928; subsidiary of Sanlam Ltd, South Africa; merged with Regent Life Namibia, Capricorn Investments and Nam-Mic Financial Services in Dec. 2004; Chair. Koos Brandt; CEO Tertius Stears.

Santam Namibia Ltd: Ausspannplaza Complex, Ausspannplatz, Dr Agostinho Neto Rd, POB 204, Windhoek; tel. (61) 2928000; fax (61) 235225; 60% owned by Santam, South Africa; 33.3% owned by Bank Windhoek Holdings Ltd; acquired Allianz Insurance of Namibia Ltd in 2001; Chair. Machiel Reyneke; Chief Exec. Franco Feris.

Trustco Insurance Ltd: Trustco House, 2 Keller St, POB 11363, Windhoek; tel. (61) 2754000; fax (61) 2754090; internet www.tgi.na; f. 1992; legal, funeral and medical insurance; Chair. Raymond Heathcote; CEO Quinton Zandre van Rooyen.

Trade and Industry

GOVERNMENT AGENCIES

Karakul Board of Namibia—Swakara Fur Producers and Exporters: PMB 13300, Windhoek; tel. (61) 237750; fax (61) 231990; e-mail info@swakara.net; internet www.swakara.net; f. 1982; promotes development of karakul wool and the pelt industry; Chair. Raimar van Hase; Man. Wessel H. Visser.

Meat Board of Namibia: POB 38, Windhoek; tel. (61) 275830; fax (61) 228310; e-mail info@nammic.com.na; internet www.nammic.com.na; f. 1935; facilitates export of livestock, meat and processed meat products; Chair. Poena Potgieter; Gen. Man. Paul Strydom.

Meat Corpn of Namibia (Meatco Namibia): POB 3881, Windhoek; tel. (61) 3216400; fax (61) 3217045; e-mail hoffice@meatco.com.na; internet www.meatco.com.na; f. 1986; processors of meat and meat products at four abattoirs and one tannery; CEO Kobus du Plessis.

Namibian Agronomic Board: 30 David Merero St, POB 5096, Ausspannplatz, Windhoek; tel. (61) 379500; fax (61) 225371; e-mail nabdesk@nammic.com.na; internet www.nab.com.na; f. 1985; Chair. Gernot Eggert; CEO Christof Brock.

National Petroleum Corpn of Namibia (NAMCOR): Petroleum House, 1 Aviation Rd, PMB 13196, Windhoek; tel. (61) 2045000; fax (61) 2045061; e-mail info@namcor.com.na; internet www.namcor.com.na; f. 1965 as Southern Oil Exploration Corpn (South-West Africa) (Pty) Ltd—SWAKOR; present name adopted 1990; state petroleum co; responsible for importing 50% of national oil requirements; Chair. Johannes !Gawaxab; Man. Dir Obeth Kandjoze.

DEVELOPMENT ORGANIZATIONS

Namibia Investment Centre (NIC): Ministry of Trade and Industry, Brendan Simbwaye Sq., Block B, 6th Floor, Goethe St, PMB 13340, Windhoek; tel. (61) 2837335; fax (61) 220278; e-mail nic@mti.gov.na; f. 1990; promotes foreign and domestic investment; Exec. Dir Bernadette Artivor.

Namibia Non-Governmental Organisations' Forum Trust (NANGOF Trust): 24 Mozart St, Windhoek West, POB 70433, Khomasdal, Windhoek; tel. (61) 212503; fax (61) 211306; e-mail info@nangoftrust.org.na; internet www.nangoftrust.org.na; f. 1991 as NANGOF; renamed NANGOF Trust in July 2007; CEO Ivin Lombardt.

National Housing Enterprise: 7 Gen. Murtala Muhammed Ave, Eros, POB 20192, Windhoek; tel. (61) 2927111; fax (61) 222301; internet www.nhe.com.na; f. 1993; replaced Nat. Building and Investment Corpn; provides low-cost housing; manages Housing Trust Fund; 100% state-owned; Chair. Dr Jason Nandago; CEO Vincent Hailulu.

CHAMBERS OF COMMERCE

Chamber of Mines of Namibia (CoM): 3 Schutzen St, POB 2895, Windhoek; tel. (61) 237925; fax (61) 222638; e-mail dmeyer@chamberofmines.org.na; internet www.chamberofmines.org.na; f. 1979; Pres. Werner Duvenhage; Gen. Man. Veston Malango; 105 mems (2013).

Namibia Chamber of Commerce and Industry (NCCI): 2 Jenner St, cnr Simpson and Jenner Sts, POB 9355, Windhoek; tel. (61) 228809; fax (61) 228009; e-mail ncciinfo@ncci.org.na; internet www.ncci.org.na; f. 1990; Chair. M. Namundjebo-Tilahun; CEO Tarah Shaanika; c. 3,000 mems (2008).

EMPLOYERS' ORGANIZATIONS

Construction Industries Federation of Namibia: cnr Stein and Schwabe Sts, POB 1479, Klein Windhoek; tel. (61) 230028; fax (61) 224534; e-mail info@cif.namibia.na; internet www.cifnamibia.com; Pres. Karl Heinz Schulz; Gen. Man. Bärbel Kirchner; 71 contracting mems, 21 small and medium enterprises members, 17 trade mems, 7 affiliated mems.

Namibia Agricultural Union (NAU): PMB 13255, Windhoek; tel. (61) 237838; fax (61) 220193; e-mail nau@agrinamibia.com.na; internet www.agrinamibia.com.na; f. 1947; represents commercial farmers; Pres. Derek Wright; Exec. Man. Sakkie Coetzee.

Namibia National Farmers' Union (NNFU): 4 Axalie Doeseb St, Windhoek West; POB 3117, Windhoek; tel. (61) 271117; fax (61) 271155; e-mail info@nnfu.org.na; internet www.nnfu.org.na; f. 1992; represents communal farmers; Pres. Pintile Davids.

Namibia Professional Hunting Association (NAPHA): 318 Sam Nujoma Dr., Klein Windhoek; POB 11291, Windhoek; tel. (61) 234455; fax (61) 222567; e-mail info@napha.com.na; f. 1974; represents hunting guides and professional hunters; Pres. Kai-Uwe Denker; CEO Melanie Allen; c. 470 mems.

UTILITIES

Electricity

Electricity Control Board: 8 Bismarck St, ECB House, POB 2923, Windhoek; tel. (61) 374300; fax (61) 374304; e-mail info@ecb.org.na; internet www.ecb.org.na; f. 2000; Chair. Jason Nandago; CEO Siseho C. Simasiku.

Namibia Power Corpn (Pty) Ltd (NamPower): NamPower Centre, 15 Luther St, POB 2864, Windhoek; tel. (61) 2054111; fax (61) 232805; e-mail register@nampower.com.na; internet www.nampower.com.na; f. 1964; state-owned; Chair. Maria Nakale; Man. Dir Paulinus Shilamba.

Water

Namibia Water Corporation Ltd (NamWater): 176 Iscor St, Northern Industrial Area, POB 13389, Windhoek; tel. (61) 710000; fax (61) 713000; e-mail shigwedhaj@namwater.com.na; internet www.namwater.com.na; f. 1997; state-owned; CEO Dr Vaino Povanhu Shivute.

TRADE UNIONS

In 2004 there were 27 unions, representing more than 100,000 workers.

Trade Union Federations

National Union of Namibian Workers (NUNW): Mungunda St, Katutura; POB 50034, Windhoek; tel. (61) 215037; fax (61) 215589; f. 1972; affiliated to the SWAPO party; Pres. Connie Pandeni (acting); Sec.-Gen. Job Muniaro (acting); c. 70,000 mems.

Trade Union Congress of Namibia (TUCNA): POB 2111, Windhoek; tel. (61) 246143; fax (61) 212828; f. 2002 following the merger of the Namibia People's Social Movement (f. 1992 as the Namibia Christian Social Trade Unions) and the Namibia Fed. of Trade Unions (f. 1998); Pres. Paulus Hango; Sec.-Gen. Mahongora Kavihuha; c. 45,000 mems (2005).

Transport

RAILWAYS

The main line runs from Nakop, at the border with South Africa, via Keetmanshoop to Windhoek, Kranzberg, Tsumeb, Swakopmund and

Walvis Bay. There are three branch lines, from Windhoek to Gobabis, Otavi to Grootfontein and Keetmanshoop to Lüderitz. The total rail network covers 2,382 route-km. Under phase one of the Northern Railway Line Extension Project, the Kranzberg–Tsumeb line was extended by 248 km to Ondangwa in 2006. Phase two of the project, a further 60-km extension of this line to Oshikango, was officially opened in July 2012, and phase three was to involve the eventual construction of a 58-km international link with Oshakati, Angola. At mid-2015 plans were under way for the construction of a 1,500-km Trans-Kalahari Railway linking Walvis Bay with the Mmamabula coal deposits in Botswana. There were also plans to extend the rehabilitated Mulobezi railway line in Zambia to connect with the Namibian railway system.

TransNamib Holdings Ltd: TransNamib Bldg, cnr Independence Ave and Bahnhof St, PMB 13204, Windhoek; tel. (61) 2982437; fax (61) 2982386; e-mail pubrelation@transnamib.com.na; internet www.transnamib.com.na; f. 1998; state-owned; Chair. Dr PETER OOSTHUIZEN; Acting CEO HIPPY TJIVIKUA.

ROADS

Between 2000 and 2002 the total road network decreased from 66,467 km to 42,237 km, of which 12.8% was paved in 2002. In 2011 there were an estimated 45,645 km of roads, of which 14.5% were paved. A major road link from Walvis Bay to Jwaneng, northern Botswana—the Trans-Kalahari Highway—was completed in 1998, along with the Trans-Caprivi Highway, linking Namibia with northern Botswana, Zambia and Zimbabwe. The Government is also upgrading and expanding the road network in northern Namibia.

Roads Authority: Snyman Circle, Ausspannplatz, Windhoek; tel. (61) 2847000; fax (61) 2847158; e-mail pr@ra.org.na; internet www.ra.org.na; Chair. HILENI KAIFANUA; CEO CONRAD MUTONGA LUTOMBI.

SHIPPING

The ports of Walvis Bay and Lüderitz are linked to the main overseas shipping routes and handle almost one-half of Namibia's external trade. Walvis Bay has a container terminal, built in 1999, and eight berths; it is a hub port for the region, serving landlocked countries such as Botswana, Zambia and Zimbabwe. In 2005 NAMPORT added a N $30m. floating dock to the Walvis Bay facilities with a view to servicing vessels used in the region's expanding petroleum industry. Traditionally a fishing port, a new quay was completed at Lüderitz in 2000, with two berths, in response to growing demand from the offshore diamond industry. At 31 December 2014 Namibia's flag registered fleet comprised 126 vessels, with a combined displacement of 127,196 grt.

African Portland Industrial Holdings (APIH): Huvest Bldg, 1st Floor, AE/Gams Centre, Sam Nujoma Dr., POB 40047, Windhoek; tel. (61) 248744; fax (61) 239485; e-mail jacques@apiholdings.com; f. 1994; 80% owned by Grindrod (South Africa); bulk port terminal operator; Man. Dir ATHOL EMERTON; Sec. JACQUES CONRADIE.

Namibian Ports Authority (NAMPORT): 17 Rikumbi Kandanga Rd, POB 361, Walvis Bay; tel. (64) 2082207; fax (64) 2082320; e-mail jerome@namport.com.na; internet www.namport.com; f. 1994; Chair. JERRY MUADINOHAMBA; Man. Dir GERSON ADOLF BISEY UIRAB.

CIVIL AVIATION

There are international airports at Windhoek (Hosea Kutako) and Walvis Bay (Rooikop), as well more than 20 other, smaller airports and numerous landing strips throughout Namibia.

Directorate of Civil Aviation: POB 12003, Windhoek; tel. (61) 702212; fax (61) 702244; e-mail director@dca.com.na; internet www.dca.com.na; Dir ANGELINE SIMANA PAULO.

Air Namibia: TransNamib Bldg, cnr Independence Ave and Bahnhof St, POB 731, Windhoek; tel. (61) 2996000; fax (61) 2996101; e-mail aarickerts@airnamibia.com.na; internet www.airnamibia.com.na; f. 1946 as South West Air Transport; present name adopted in 1991; state-owned; part-privatization postponed indefinitely in 2003; services to Angola, Botswana, Ghana, South Africa, Zimbabwe, Germany and the UK; Chair. HARALD SCHMIDT; Man. Dir THEOPOLTINA M. NAMASES.

Kalahari Express Airlines (KEA): POB 40179, Windhoek; tel. (61) 245665; fax (61) 245612; f. 1995; domestic and regional flights; Exec. Dir PEINGONDJABI SHIPOH.

Namibia Airports Company (NAC) Limited: 5th Floor, Sanlam Centre Independence Ave, POB 23061, Windhoek; tel. (61) 2955000; fax (61) 2955022; e-mail pr@airports.com.na; internet www.airports.com.na; f. 1998; Chair. NDEUHALA N. KATONYALA; CEO TAMER EL-KALLAWI (acting).

Tourism

Namibia's principal tourist attractions are its game parks and nature reserves, and the development of 'eco-tourism' is being promoted. In 2013 tourist arrivals in Namibia totalled 1,176,041 and, according to provisional figures, tourism receipts (excluding passenger transport) amounted to some US $409m.

Namibia Tourism Board: 1st Floor, Channel Life Towers, 39 Post Street Mall, Private Bag 13244, Windhoek; tel. (61) 2906000; fax (61) 254848; e-mail info@namibiatourism.com.na; internet www.namibiatourism.com.na; Chair. ERICKA AKUENJE; CEO DIGU NAOBEB.

Defence

As assessed at November 2014, the Namibian Defence Force numbered an estimated 9,000 men; there was also a 200-strong navy, operating as part of the Ministry of Fisheries and Marine Resources, and a paramilitary force of 6,000.

Defence Expenditure: Budgeted at N $4,800m. for 2015.

Commander-in-Chief of the Defence Force: Pres. HAGE GEINGOB.

Chief of Staff of the Defence Force: Lt-Gen. JOHN MUTWA.

Commander of the Army: Maj.-Gen. TOMAS NOPOUDYUU HAMUNYELA.

Commander of the Air Force: Air Vice-Marshal MARTIN PINEHAS.

Commander of the Navy: Rear Adm. PETER VILHO.

Education

Education is officially compulsory and free of charge for 10 years between the ages of six and 16 years, or until primary education has been completed (whichever is the sooner). Under the Education Act of 2001, free basic education was extended to grade 12, although it is not compulsory beyond the limits set in the Constitution. Primary education begins at six years of age and lasts for seven years. Secondary education, beginning at the age of 13, lasts for up to five years, comprising a first cycle of three years and a second of two. According to UNESCO estimates, in 2012 enrolment at primary schools included 88% of children in the relevant age-group (males 86%; females 89%), while the comparable ratio for secondary enrolment in 2007 was 51% (males 45%; females 57%). Higher education is provided by the University of Namibia, the Technicon of Namibia, a vocational college and four teacher-training colleges. In 2007/08 some 19,707 students were enrolled in tertiary education. Various schemes for informal adult education are also in operation in an effort to combat illiteracy. In 2009/10 education received an estimated 18.6% of total government expenditure.

NAURU

Introductory Survey

LOCATION, CLIMATE, LANGUAGE, RELIGION, FLAG, CAPITAL

The Republic of Nauru is a small island in the central Pacific Ocean, lying about 40 km (25 miles) south of the Equator and about 4,000 km (2,500 miles) north-east of Sydney, Australia. Its nearest neighbour is Banaba (formerly Ocean Island), in Kiribati, about 300 km (186 miles) to the east. The climate is tropical, with a westerly monsoon season from November to February. Average annual rainfall is about 2,060 mm (80 in), but actual rainfall is extremely variable. Day temperatures vary between 24°C and 34°C (75°–93°F). Of the total resident population in 2011, 94% were indigenous Nauruans. Their language is Nauruan, but English is also widely understood. The majority of Nauruans are Christians, mostly adherents of the Nauruan Protestant Church. The national flag (proportions 1 by 2) is royal blue, divided by a narrow horizontal yellow stripe, with a 12-pointed white star at the lower hoist. The island state has no official capital, but the seat of the legislature and most government offices are in Yaren District.

CONTEMPORARY POLITICAL HISTORY

Historical Context

Nauru, inhabited by a predominantly Polynesian people, organized in 12 clans, was annexed by Germany in 1888. In 1914, shortly after the outbreak of the First World War, the island was captured by Australian forces. It continued to be administered by Australia under a League of Nations mandate (granted in 1920), which also named the United Kingdom and New Zealand as co-trustees. During 1942–45 Nauru was occupied by the Japanese, who deported 1,200 islanders to Truk (now Chuuk), Micronesia, where many died in bombing raids or from starvation. In 1947 the island was placed under UN Trusteeship, with Australia as the administering power on behalf of the Governments of Australia, New Zealand and the UK. The UN Trusteeship Council proposed in 1964 that the indigenous people of Nauru be resettled on Curtis Island, off the Queensland coast. This offer was made in anticipation of the progressive exhaustion of the island's phosphate deposits, and because of the environmental devastation resulting from the mining operations. However, the Nauruans elected to remain on the island. Nauru was accorded a considerable measure of self-government in January 1966, with the establishment of Legislative and Executive Councils, and proceeded to independence on 31 January 1968. Nauru became a full member of the Commonwealth in May 1999, and a member of the UN in September of that year.

Domestic Political Affairs

The Head Chief of Nauru, Hammer DeRoburt, was elected President in May 1968 and re-elected in 1971 and 1973. Dissatisfaction with his increasingly personal rule led to the election of Bernard Dowiyogo (leader of the recently established, informal Nauru Party) to the presidency in 1976. Dowiyogo was re-elected President after a general election in late 1977. However, DeRoburt's supporters adopted tactics of obstruction in Parliament, and in December 1977 Dowiyogo resigned, in response to Parliament's refusal to approve budgetary legislation; he was re-elected shortly afterwards, but was again forced to resign in April 1978, following the defeat of a legislative proposal concerning phosphate royalties. Lagumot Harris, another member of the Nauru Party, succeeded him, but resigned three weeks later when Parliament rejected a finance measure, and DeRoburt was again elected President. He was re-elected in December of that year, in December 1980 and in May and December 1983. In September 1986 DeRoburt resigned, following the defeat of a government budget proposal; he was replaced as President by Kennan Adeang. However, after holding office for only 14 days, Adeang was defeated in a parliamentary vote of no confidence, and DeRoburt subsequently resumed the presidency. Following a general election in December, Adeang was re-elected President (by a narrow margin), but was subsequently ousted by another vote of no confidence; DeRoburt was reinstated as President. The atmosphere of political uncertainty generated by the absence of a clear parliamentary majority led DeRoburt to dissolve Parliament in preparation for a fresh general election in January 1987, following which the incumbent DeRoburt was re-elected to the presidency. In February Adeang announced the establishment of the Democratic Party of Nauru, essentially a revival of the Nauru Party. Eight members of Parliament joined the new party, which declared that its aim was to curtail the extension of presidential powers and to promote democracy. In August 1989 a parliamentary motion of no confidence in DeRoburt (proposed by Adeang) was approved, and Kenas Aroi, a former Minister of Finance, was subsequently elected President. Aroi resigned in December, owing to ill health, and after a general election in the same month Dowiyogo was re-elected President, defeating DeRoburt. At the next presidential election, held shortly after a general election in November 1992, Dowiyogo defeated Buraro Detudamo.

At a general election held in November 1995, when a total of 67 candidates contested the 18 parliamentary seats, all cabinet members were re-elected. A subsequent presidential election resulted in Lagumot Harris's defeat of the incumbent Dowiyogo. The resignation of the Chairman of Air Nauru, in the wake of allegations of misconduct, prompted Parliament to vote on a motion of no confidence in the Government in November 1996. The motion was narrowly approved and Harris was replaced by Dowiyogo as President. Later that month, however, Dowiyogo's new Government was itself defeated in a parliamentary vote of no confidence, and Adeang was elected to the presidency. A further motion of no confidence was passed in December, when Adeang was similarly removed from office. At a subsequent presidential contest Reuben Kun, a former Minister of Finance, defeated Adeang, on the understanding that his administration would organize a general election. An election duly took place in February 1997, at which four new members were elected to Parliament, following an apparent agreement between the supporters of Harris and those of Dowiyogo to end the political manoeuvring that had resulted in several months of instability. At the subsequent election to the presidency Dowiyogo's nominee, Kinza Clodumar, defeated Harris by nine parliamentary votes to eight.

In early 1998 five members of Parliament (including former President Lagumot Harris) were dismissed by Adeang, the Speaker, for refusing to apologize for personal remarks about him that had been published in an opposition newsletter. At the resultant by-elections, held in February, three of the five members were re-elected. A motion expressing no confidence in the President was approved in June, and Dowiyogo was subsequently elected to replace Clodumar. In April 1999 Dowiyogo was himself defeated in a further vote of no confidence; his replacement was Rene Harris, previously Chairman of the Nauru Phosphate Corporation.

Following the legislative elections held in early April 2000, Rene Harris was re-elected President, defeating Dowiyogo by a slim margin. Ludwig Scotty was elected Speaker of Parliament. However, a few days later Scotty and his deputy, Ross Cairn, resigned, stating only that they were unable to continue under the 'current political circumstances'. Harris therefore promptly tendered his resignation and was replaced by Dowiyogo, whereupon Scotty and Cairn were re-elected to their posts in the legislature.

Allegations that Nauru's offshore financial centre was being used extensively by Russian criminal organizations for laundering the proceeds of their illicit activities had led Dowiyogo in March 1999 to order a full review of the banking sector. In early 2000 President Rene Harris announced that Nauru was to suspend its offshore banking services and improve the accountability of existing banks on the island, as part of the Government's efforts to bring Nauru's financial services regulations into compliance with international standards. Dowiyogo made similar commitments following his re-election in April 2000. However, in early 2001 Anthony Audoa, the Minister of Home Affairs, Culture, Health and Women's Affairs, resigned, claiming that Dowiyogo had squandered Nauru's wealth during his various tenures as President and that in promoting the island as a tax haven he had allowed Nauru to be used by Russian criminal gangs to launder their illegal funds. In February 11 members of Nauru's 18-member legislature signed a petition requesting that Dowiyogo attend a special parliamentary session to answer questions relating to the island's alleged role in money-laundering. Russia's central bank claimed that some US $70,000m. of illicit funds had been processed in offshore banks in Nauru (of which there were reportedly more than 400 in early 2001). In March Dowiyogo was ousted from the presidency in a parliamentary vote of no confidence while he was undergoing hospital treatment in Australia. The motion led to Rene Harris regaining the presidency. The Government subsequently approved an Anti-Money Laundering Act in August, but the Paris-based Financial Action Task Force (FATF, see p. 451) found that the new legislation contained several deficiencies and imposed sanctions in December. The Government announced revised anti-money-laundering legislation in the same month.

As a result of continued US pressure, Nauru's Parliament approved a new law in February 2004 to address the continuing problem of money-laundering, along with legislation to close down the country's offshore banks. In October the FATF withdrew countermeasures against the country, and in October 2005, following the implementation of the requisite legislation, Nauru became the last of the Pacific islands to be removed from the FATF list of non-co-operative countries and territories. Furthermore, in December 2003, following the island's commitment to improve transparency and to exchange information on tax matters with other countries, Nauru had been removed from a list of unco-operative tax havens, issued in April 2002 by the Organisation for Economic Co-operation and Development (see p. 377).

In early January 2003, meanwhile, President Rene Harris lost a motion of no confidence, following the defeat of the Government's budget proposals, and was replaced by Bernard Dowiyogo. Nauru's deteriorating financial situation (with Dowiyogo claiming later that month that the island state was on the verge of bankruptcy), in addition to the Government's decision to accept more than 1,000 asylum seekers in return for aid from Australia (see *Processing of Asylum Seekers*), were believed to be major factors in the loss of confidence in Harris. However, Harris applied to the Supreme Court, and on 10 January an injunction was issued against Dowiyogo accepting the presidency, on the grounds that only 11 of the 18 members of Parliament had attended the session when the vote took place, thus rendering it invalid. Despite the injunction, Dowiyogo remained in his post and appointed a new Cabinet. Following several days of political confusion, Harris was reinstated as President on 17 January, after the intervention of Nauru's Chief Justice (based in Melbourne, Australia), but he resigned from the presidency on the following day. In the resultant contest Dowiyogo narrowly defeated Kinza Clodumar to become the new President on 18 January. However, a lack of parliamentary support for Dowiyogo continued to create problems, amid appeals for an early election to resolve the impasse.

In early March 2003 Dowiyogo travelled to Washington, DC, USA, at the request of the US Government, which had threatened to impose harsh economic sanctions on the island and to repossess Air Nauru's only aircraft, if Nauru did not discontinue its offshore banking services. The Administration of George W. Bush was reported to be concerned over the possibility that individuals with links to terrorist organizations might have used the island's financial services to launder their funds. Consequently, Dowiyogo agreed to sign executive orders not to renew any banking licences or to issue any further so-called 'investor passports'. However, shortly after his meeting with the US President, Dowiyogo collapsed and, following emergency heart surgery, died on 9 March. Derog Gioura was appointed acting head of state and on 20 March was elected President by nine parliamentary votes to seven. Legislation providing for the expiry of most offshore banking licences within 30 days (and for the remainder within six months) was approved by Parliament in late March.

Legislative elections took place on 3 May 2003. However, the new Speaker resigned one day after his election, and with no further nominations for the position, Parliament was unable to proceed to a presidential election. The impasse was resolved when a Speaker was finally elected in late May and Ludwig Scotty won the subsequent presidential poll, defeating Kinza Clodumar. However, on 8 August Scotty was ousted from office by a no-confidence motion and was replaced by Rene Harris, who thus became the fourth individual to hold the presidency in 2003. The reasons for Scotty's removal were not clear, although

concerns had been expressed about his plans to close the recently opened embassies in Washington, DC, and in the capital of the People's Republic of China, Beijing (see *Foreign Affairs*).

The resignation of Minister of Justice Godfrey Thoma in February 2004 precipitated a vote of no confidence in the President. A further political crisis arose when the motion received an equal number of votes in favour and against. Moreover, when Parliament was unable to agree on the election of a new Speaker, following the resignation of the incumbent in early April, the resulting impasse meant that Parliament could not be formally convened. The country's deepening financial crisis prompted President Rene Harris to travel to Australia in mid-April to request assistance in averting the island's imminent bankruptcy. On his return to Nauru, Harris was confronted by angry demonstrations by hundreds of government employees (who constituted the majority of paid employees on the island) whose salaries had been unpaid for 12 months. In the same month receivers were appointed to manage the assets of the Nauru Phosphate Royalties Trust (including Nauru's extensive property portfolio in Australia), with the company unable to pay off debts of some $A230m. to US interests. Nauruans working in government-owned buildings in the Australian cities of Melbourne and Sydney were served with eviction notices. Meanwhile, with neither the Government nor the opposition willing to nominate a Speaker from among their respective members (thereby giving the other side a majority in Parliament), the legislature was unable to draw up a budget. In May, however, during another of Harris's overseas trips, the opposition elected one of its members as Speaker and immediately approved legislation making it illegal for a government to operate without a budget. In the following month, and before the Supreme Court had ruled on the matter, Minister of Finance Kinza Clodumar crossed the floor, thus allowing the opposition to approve a motion of no confidence in Harris. Ludwig Scotty was subsequently elected to the presidency. In July Australian Treasury official Peter Depta arrived in Nauru to take up the post of Financial Secretary, effectively assuming control of the island's finances.

Nauru's precarious political situation deteriorated during September 2004, and by the end of the month President Ludwig Scotty had dissolved Parliament and declared a state of emergency. His action had been prompted by the suspension by the Speaker, Russell Kun, of the Minister of Health, Dr Kieren Keke, on the grounds that the latter held dual Nauruan and Australian nationality. Keke's suspension had resulted in the loss of the Government's one-seat majority and a consequent stalemate in Parliament, during which budget legislation could not be approved. Scotty assumed sole responsibility over the government of the country until a general election took place in October. At the election all nine members of Scotty's former Government retained their seats in the legislature, while seven of the nine opposition members of Parliament were not re-elected. President Scotty thereby gained a comfortable parliamentary majority. Within days of its election the new Government approved a budget that included a reduction in public sector salaries and increased import duties. In the following month legislation aimed at discouraging criminals, particularly terrorists, from using the country's financial sector was approved. The sudden death of the Speaker, Vassal Gadoengin, in December 2004 led to the election of Valdon Dowiyogo, a son of the former President, as his replacement in the following month.

Meanwhile, in July 2004 President Scotty held emergency discussions with the Presidents of Kiribati and Tuvalu regarding at least US $2m. in outstanding salary payments owed to the nationals of these two countries employed in Nauru by the Nauru Phosphate Corporation. Nauru's continuing financial crisis led it to appeal for assistance from the Pacific region and the international community. In September the Pacific Islands Forum (see p. 413) offered to help pay the salaries of Nauruan government employees, who had been unpaid for many months (see above).

In January 2005 a parliamentary committee began a review of Nauru's Constitution, motivated by a desire to achieve greater political stability in the country and to improve the accountability of public institutions. In 2006 the committee formed an independent Constitutional Review Commission, which analysed and considered public suggestions, and in mid-2007 a Constitutional Convention met to discuss the Commission's conclusions.

Shortly after the legislative elections of August 2007 Scotty was re-elected as President, defeating Marcus Stephen. Scotty's new Cabinet retained all the ministers of the previous Government. In December, however, Scotty was removed from office in a vote of no confidence, amid allegations of corruption levelled against the Minister of Foreign Affairs and of Finance, David Adeang, and the withdrawal of support of several government members. Marcus Stephen was subsequently elected to replace Scotty.

The new Government's progress was hampered by increasing discord and its lack of a parliamentary majority. In April 2008 David Adeang, now Speaker as well as a member of the opposition, announced the suspension of all nine government members of Parliament. President Stephen subsequently declared a state of emergency and dissolved Parliament. At an early election held later that month, the outgoing Government increased its parliamentary representation to 12 of the 18 legislators. Riddell Akua was elected Speaker and Parliament re-elected Stephen as President; the Cabinet was reinstalled unchanged.

The political impasse of 2010

In February 2010 President Stephen survived a parliamentary vote of no confidence relating to alleged irregularities in the use of overseas loans. In Nauru's first ever referendum, which was conducted at the end of the month, various proposals for constitutional change, including the direct election of the country's President, were rejected by voters; 78% of the electorate participated in the poll.

In early 2010 three government members of Parliament defected to the opposition, amid allegations that Getax, an Australian company which apparently hoped to secure greater control of Nauru's phosphate resources, had attempted to influence the island's politics. Getax had financed a trip to Singapore in January for 11 of the 18 members of the Nauruan Parliament, including the three government supporters who subsequently joined the opposition. These defections, which deprived Stephen's administration of a parliamentary majority, prompted the holding of an early general election on 24 April. In the poll all 18 incumbent members of Parliament were returned to office, thus resulting in no change to the composition of the legislature and again leaving Parliament evenly divided between the two sides (with nine seats each). In mid-May, at its sixth attempt, Parliament chose Godfrey Thoma as Speaker. However, having declared that he would resign if fresh elections were not called within four days, Thoma duly resigned when this condition was not met. Meanwhile, President Stephen indicated that he favoured the amendment of the Constitution to permit the selection of the Speaker from outside Parliament, effectively proposing the addition of a 19th member to the legislature, in order to prevent any recurrence of the impasse that had rendered Parliament unable to function. The Government's candidate for the position of Speaker, Dominic Tabuna, was elected in early June, after reportedly receiving the support of two opposition legislators. However, just three days after taking office, Tabuna resigned in unclear circumstances.

On 11 June 2010, citing the need to approve the budget, President Stephen declared a state of emergency and called fresh elections for 19 June. However, the poll again failed to produce a clear majority for either side: all but one of the 18 incumbent members were returned to office. The sole newcomer, Milton Dube, an independent who won a seat previously held by the opposition, thus held the balance of power. Stephen contended that the results of the second poll indicated a 'rallying' behind his grouping by Nauruans, and urged Dube to lend his support to the interim Government. However, in late June Aloysius Amwano (one of the three opposition members who had withdrawn his support for the Government following the Getax-sponsored trip to Singapore) was elected Speaker; upon taking office, Amwano urged Stephen to resign. The President indicated his willingness to do so, on the condition that a replacement be selected from within his grouping. In early July the interim Government announced that it had secured the support of an opposition member, thereby affording it the majority that it required to form a new Cabinet and elect a President. However, Amwano refused to allow the motion to elect a President to be presented to Parliament, prompting Stephen to issue a presidential order demanding the Speaker's removal from office on the grounds that Amwano was in contravention of his constitutional requirements. In mid-October the Supreme Court ruled that the President had acted within his constitutional rights, following a legal challenge by the opposition to the dismissal of the Speaker and the declaration of a state of emergency.

In late October 2010 it was revealed that, at the request of President Stephen, Australian federal police had begun investigating allegations of bribery by Getax of members of the Nauruan opposition. The police investigation was reportedly terminated in September 2011 owing to a 'lack of jurisdiction'.

Former President Ludwig Scotty accepted his nomination for the post of Speaker, while reaffirming his position as an opposition legislator, and was duly elected in November 2010. Parliament swiftly re-elected Stephen as President, who removed the state of emergency, thereby appearing finally to have resolved the six-month impasse.

Presidential changes of 2011

In October 2011 opposition member David Adeang divulged to Parliament some correspondence between Stephen and a phosphate dealer in Thailand which, so Adeang claimed, proved that Stephen had requested supplementary payments to himself to enable phosphate sales. Stephen pre-empted the subsequent vote of no confidence tabled by Adeang by resigning on 10 November. On the same day Parliament elected former Minister of Commerce, Industry and the Environment Freddy Pitcher as his successor. On 15 November, however, Pitcher was in turn removed from the presidency by a vote of no confidence, once more tabled by Adeang, and was replaced by Sprent Dabwido, a former Minister of Telecommunications, who had defected from the Government to the opposition for the vote against Pitcher. Dabwido subsequently stated that he had backed the vote of no confidence in an attempt to gain opposition support for the passage of previously mooted constitutional reforms (the Parliamentary Amendments Bill, which had been provisionally approved by the legislature in August 2009 pending further amendments) that could avert further political instability and avoid future elections resulting in another hung Parliament. The main proposals of the bill were the election of the Speaker from outside the legislature, the appointment of an Ombudsman, a code of ethics for legislators, and the addition of a 19th member of Parliament. In Dabwido's new Cabinet, Adeang was reinstated to the post of Minister of Finance—a position that he had lost in 2007 following allegations of corruption—and was also allocated the justice and sustainable development portfolios, while the President himself assumed responsibility for several portfolios, including foreign affairs.

Political turmoil and constitutional crisis

On 11 June 2012 President Dabwido unexpectedly dismissed his whole Cabinet, citing his frustration over the legislature's failure to approve the final draft of the Parliamentary Amendments Bill. However, according to some sources, Dabwido ousted the ministers in order to avoid the possibility of a parliamentary no-confidence vote. A new, five-member Cabinet was appointed on the following day. Dr Kieren Keke and former President Marcus Stephen notably returned to office (each being assigned responsibility for several portfolios), while Adeang left the Government.

Following the opposition's unsuccessful introduction of a vote of no confidence in the Government on 7 February 2013, Keke resigned from the Cabinet without any reason being given. In the following week the Government was thrown into further disarray by Dabwido's unexplained dismissal of Stephen and a few days later by the resignation of finance minister Roland Kun. The former portfolios of Keke, Stephen and Kun were divided between the President and his remaining two ministers, Dominic Tabuna and Riddell Akua. Later that month the President appointed two new cabinet members: Aloysius Amwano was allocated the education portfolio and Shadlog Bernicke the health portfolio. None the less, on 1 March, at the request of President Dabwido, the Speaker, Ludwig Scotty, adjourned Parliament indefinitely, citing the continuing unruly behaviour of the legislators. On 9 March Scotty officially announced the dissolution of Parliament and gave notice of the holding of a general election on 6 April. However, following a legal challenge led by Keke, on 15 March the Supreme Court ruled that the adjournment of Parliament had been unconstitutional (since the legislators had not been given the opportunity to debate the measure) and that it was consequently null and void (as was the writ issued for the general election). The Court ordered the Speaker to reconvene Parliament within 28 days. In order to avoid the need to meet this deadline, on 11 April Dabwido withdrew his original request for the dissolution of Parliament, issuing a new notice for its dissolution on 15 April. Two attempts to reconvene Parliament in the following week to discuss the proposed dissolution failed, however, as a boycott by some members resulted in a lack of quorum. The next scheduled sitting of Parliament, on 23 April, was attended by a sufficient number of deputies, but ended swiftly owing to a failure to elect a new Speaker, following Scotty's resignation on 18 April. Although Godfrey Thoma was elected Speaker on 25 April, the political impasse continued into May, as several subsequent sessions of Parliament were again adjourned in the absence of a quorum. The Speaker finally dissolved Parliament on 23 May, and elections were scheduled to take place on 22 June. However, on 27 May the President declared a state of emergency on economic grounds, and the election was brought forward to 8 June.

Recent developments: 2013 elections and state intervention in the judiciary

A record number of 68 candidates contested the legislative elections of 8 June 2013, which were the first elections to a 19-member Parliament—the legislature having been enlarged by one seat in an attempt to avoid the recurrence of the problems associated with a hung Parliament. Ludwig Scotty was subsequently elected as Speaker, and on 11 June former education minister Baron Waqa was elected President, defeating Roland Kun by 13 votes to five. Waqa appointed a six-member Cabinet which included Nauru's second female member of Parliament since independence, Charmaine Scotty, as Minister of Home Affairs, Education and Youth, and Land Management, newcomer Aaron Cook as Minister of Commerce, Industry and Environment, and previous cabinet members David Adeang, Valdon Dowiyogo and Shadlog Bernicke.

In early 2014 Nauru's judicial system underwent a period of intense upheaval. The island's Resident Magistrate and Registrar of the Supreme Court, Peter Law, an Australian citizen, was dismissed and deported from Nauru in January following various accusations levelled against him by the Government, including drunk and disorderly behaviour. Law denied the allegations and claimed that his deportation had been politically motivated, owing to his opposition to the Government's earlier decision to deport two Australian citizens without allowing the two men to challenge the action. Efforts by Chief Justice Geoffrey Eames to intervene by issuing an injunction to prevent Law's deportation were thwarted when the Government cancelled his visa, thereby preventing him from returning to Nauru from Australia. Furthermore, in apparent contravention of Nauruan law, the Government appointed Law's successor (in an acting capacity), Andrew Jacobson, without first consulting Eames. Steven Bliim, Nauru's Solicitor-General, resigned at the end of January in protest at the Government's actions, which were believed by many observers to stem from a desire to curtail criticism of its asylum camps. Both Law and Eames had opposed government proposals to conduct the trials of 16 asylum seekers who had been involved in riots in 2013 within their camp rather than in an open court. The announcement in February that the cost of a journalist visa was to increase from $A200 to $A8,000 lent credence to this view, and home affairs minister Charmaine Scotty subsequently confirmed that the huge rise was intended to control negative news coverage of the camps, which, she argued, impeded their work. In early March the Government appointed a Fijian magistrate, Ropate Cabealawa, to the post of Resident Magistrate and another Fijian lawyer, Graham Leung, to the post of Registrar of the Supreme Court. Later that month Eames submitted his resignation as Chief Justice and harshly criticized the Australian Government for failing to intervene in the situation. The Government of Nauru, meanwhile, announced its intention to introduce a series of reforms to create a more effective and transparent judiciary, including the appointment of more judges to the Supreme Court, a maximum contract period for judges and magistrates, and the permanent separation of the roles of Resident Magistrate and Registrar of the Supreme Court (previously a joint responsibility).

In May 2014 three opposition legislators, including Dr Kieren Keke and Roland Kun, were suspended from Parliament by the Minister of Justice, reportedly for conducting interviews with foreign media organizations, in which they criticized the dismissal of former Resident Magistrate Peter Law and the withdrawal of former Chief Justice Eames' visa. Two more opposition members of Parliament were suspended in June. The subsequent attempts of the suspended legislators to appeal against the Government's actions were rendered problematic through the island's lack of a Chief Justice at that time. In September the Government appointed Joni Madraiwiwi, a former Vice-President of Fiji, as the new Chief Justice, and, in accordance with a pledge made earlier in the year, appointed two additional judges (one Australian and the other Fijian) to the Supreme Court. According to a government statement, the increase in the number of judges in the Supreme Court would remove 'the limitation of only one justice making all decisions'. Also in September Resident Magistrate Cabealawa unexpectedly stood down from his post and was replaced by Emma Garo of Solomon Islands. In December the Supreme Court upheld the suspensions of the five opposition legislators, prompting Kun to condemn the Government as a 'dictatorship'.

Processing of Asylum Seekers

In September 2001 Nauru agreed to accept 310 of 460 predominantly Afghan asylum seekers who were on board a Norwegian freighter, unable to disembark on Christmas Island, in the Indian Ocean, as Australia refused to grant them entry into its territory (see Christmas Island). The Australian Government agreed to fund the processing of the asylum seekers and to pay an undisclosed sum to Nauru, which was to accommodate the asylum seekers in processing camps, initially for three months, while their claims for asylum were assessed. Following the interception of several other boats carrying asylum seekers in Australian waters later the same month, Nauru received a pledge of $A20m. from the Australian Government for agreeing to host 800 asylum seekers. In December Nauru signed an agreement with Australia to accommodate a total of 1,200 at any one time, in return for a further $A10m. of aid. Although the asylum seekers' claims were due to be completed by July 2002, some 700 people remained in the camps at the end of that year. In December the President signed a new agreement with the Australian Government to extend the duration of the camps' operations and to accommodate up to 1,500 asylum seekers.

In mid-2003 the Australian Government was criticized for its detention of some 100 children in the camps on Nauru and for failing to reunite families held in separate camps for extended periods. Concerns about the conditions at the camps and the welfare of the detainees increased during the latter half of 2003, and in December a reported 40 of those held began a hunger strike in order to attract attention to their situation. The Nauruan Government's subsequent appeals for assistance from Australia to care for the hunger strikers, many of whom required hospital treatment, were refused. The hunger strike ended after about a month, and in January 2004 the Australian Government sent a delegation to inspect medical facilities available to asylum seekers on the island. However, the resultant report, which found services for those held in detention to be adequate, was widely regarded as flawed, as it had failed to examine any of the detainees and had been compiled solely by Australian government officials. In June the first group of asylum seekers who had been approved for entry to Australia left the detention centre. By February 2008 all of the detainees had left Nauru, marking the end of Australia's policy of accommodating asylum seekers on the island. In July 2010 President Marcus Stephen expressed Nauru's willingness to reopen the detention centre; however, the new Australian Government of Prime Minister Julia Gillard stated its opposition to any such reopening while Nauru remained a non-signatory to the UN's 1951 Convention relating to the Status of Refugees. In June 2011, following a visit to the island by Australian opposition politician Tony Abbott, who voiced his support for the reopening of the detention centre in preference to an exchange arrangement under negotiation between Australia and Malaysia, President Stephen officially signed the UN Convention.

The sinking of two boats carrying asylum seekers near Christmas Island in two separate incidents in June 2012 (with the subsequent loss of more than 100 lives) and a sharp increase in the number of asylum seekers led to renewed demands by the opposition in Australia for the reopening of the detention centres on Nauru and on Manus Island in Papua New Guinea. Following the recommendations of an expert panel, the Australian Government abruptly reversed its policy and legislation was approved by the Australian Parliament in August to reopen the centres; the first asylum seekers arrived on Nauru in the following month. By February 2013 there were some 450 asylum seekers (mostly from Sri Lanka) in the rudimentary processing camps. As previously, the detainees protested against their poor living conditions and the uncertainty surrounding the length of their detention, and many of them undertook hunger strikes or self-harmed in an attempt to have their concerns addressed. A report published by a monitoring mission of the office of the UN High Commissioner for Refugees (UNHCR) in December 2012 concluded that the camps did not meet international protection standards.

Following weeks of unrest and hunger strikes by refugees protesting at their poor living conditions, and slow progress in processing claims, a riot broke out in July 2013 at one of the camps, involving some 540 asylum seekers who burned down almost all of the camp's buildings, causing around $60m. worth of damage. Some 130 people were charged with criminal offences related to the riot. In August Prime Minister Baron Waqa and his Australian counterpart, Kevin Rudd, signed a memorandum of understanding (MOU) providing Nauru with an additional $A26.6m. to continue with the asylum programme, to rebuild the camp destroyed by the riot and to investigate the feasibility of constructing a third camp on the island. In addition, Nauru agreed to participate in the so-called 'Pacific Solution' policy, which meant that successful asylum seekers would be resettled in Nauru rather than Australia, in line with a similar accord concluded with the Government of Papua New Guinea, involving the permanent accommodation of refugees on Manus Island.

Two further reports published by the UNHCR in November 2013 again condemned conditions at the camps and stated that children and families should not be housed in them. At that time some 700 refugees were being held on Nauru, although in the 14 months since the camps had been reopened only one case had been processed. Apparent restrictions imposed by the Government on Nauru's state media, which prevented it reporting freely on the events surrounding the riot and on subsequent criticism of government policy attracted further controversy in late 2013 (see above). It was reported in April 2014 that the Nauru Government had prevented access to the island by the UN Working Group on Arbitrary Detention, which contended that Australia's transfer of individuals to the camps violated international law. It added that Nauru had breached its international obligations by failing to establish an independent body to investigate alleged torture and human rights abuses in the detention centre, and had breached a deadline in February to establish an independent local body to inspect the centre, a commitment that it was supposed to meet after ratifying the UN Convention against Torture in September 2012. The first asylum seekers to be granted refugee status in Nauru (of whom there were 13) were released into the community in May 2014, having been awarded five-year visas; it was reported that after five years the refugees would be required to seek permanent resettlement in another country. By February 2015 the total number of asylum seekers who had been awarded refugee status in Nauru stood at more than 500, of whom some 400 had been resettled on the island. Australia attracted widespread condemnation in June 2014 when it offered up to $A10,000 to each asylum seeker on Nauru who was willing to return to his or her home country. Moreover, the Australian authorities attracted further opprobrium in August when they covertly transferred some 157 Tamil asylum seekers from the Australian mainland to Nauru, claiming that the asylum seekers had declined to meet with Indian consular officials in Australia. A controversial MOU was signed between Australia and Cambodia in September whereby Cambodia agreed to offer voluntary permanent residency to potentially hundreds of asylum seekers in Nauru in return for Australia giving Cambodia an additional $A35m. in development aid. The agreement was widely condemned by rights groups and by the UN on the grounds that, given Cambodia's relative poverty, lack of humanitarian capacity and its history of human rights abuses, it was completely unsuited to carrying out such a role. However, at early 2015 the future of the MOU appeared in some doubt since very few of the asylum seekers in Nauru (who now totalled nearly 900, including more than 100 children) reportedly appeared to be interested in resettling in Cambodia, despite the Australian Government's insistence that the arrangement was proceeding. In early March tension surrounding the asylum seeker issue heightened when around 200 refugees who had been resettled within the Nauruan community were arrested (on charges of public disorder) while staging a rally denouncing the detention earlier that day of eight other refugees. These eight individuals were reported to have been the organizers of demonstrations held several days previously protesting against the poor living conditions of resettled refugees on the island.

Phosphate-mining Issues

In February 1987 representatives of the British, Australian and New Zealand Governments signed documents effecting the official demise of the British Phosphate Commissioners, who from 1919 until 1970 had overseen the mining of Nauru's phosphate deposits. President DeRoburt subsequently expressed concern about the distribution of the Commissioners' accumulated assets, which were estimated to be worth $A55m. His proposal

that part of this sum be spent on the rehabilitation of areas of the island that had been mined before independence was rejected by the three Governments involved. In 1989 Australia's continued refusal to contribute to the rehabilitation of former phosphate-mining areas prompted Nauru to institute proceedings, claiming compensation from Australia for damage to its environment, at the International Court of Justice in The Hague, Netherlands. However, in August 1993, following negotiations between President Dowiyogo and the Australian Prime Minister, Paul Keating, a Compact of Settlement was signed, under which the Australian Government was to pay Nauru a lump sum of $A57m., followed by $A50m. in instalments over a period of 20 years. New Zealand and the UK subsequently agreed to contribute $A12m. each towards the settlement. In mid-1995 a report commissioned by the Nauruan Government published details of a rehabilitation programme extending over the next 20–25 years and costing $A230m. However, the success of the rehabilitation scheme was dependent on the co-operation of landowners, some of whom were expected to continue to allow areas to be mined for residual ore once phosphate reserves had been exhausted. In mid-1997 Parliament approved the Nauru Rehabilitation Corporation (NRC) Act, providing for the establishment of a corporate body to manage the rehabilitation programme. The NRC held its inaugural meeting in May 1999. The rehabilitation programme (which was to be partly financed by funds from the Compact of Settlement) was expected to transform the mined areas into sites suitable for agriculture, new housing and industrial units, but the project was hampered considerably by delays. Results published in 2004 from a series of test sites on the island indicated that the potential for residual phosphate mining might be greater than had been previously thought (with reported mineable reserves of an estimated 20m. metric tons remaining). A major refurbishment of the island's mining plant was subsequently undertaken, and exports of phosphates resumed in 2006 (see *Economic Affairs*). Intense foreign competition for greater control of Nauru's remaining phosphate resources led to the emergence in 2010 of claims of bribery of local parliamentarians, while in 2011 allegations of corruption related to phosphate sales resulted in the resignation of President Stephen (see *Domestic Political Affairs*).

Foreign Affairs

In 1989 a UN report on the greenhouse effect (the heating of the earth's atmosphere and a resultant rise in sea level) listed Nauru as one of the countries that might disappear beneath the sea in the 21st century, unless drastic action were taken. The Government of Nauru strongly criticized Australia's refusal, at the December 1997 Conference of the Parties to the Framework Convention on Climate Change (see UN Environment Programme, see p. 61), in Kyoto, Japan, to reduce its emissions of pollutant gases known to contribute to the greenhouse effect. However, following a change of government, Australia signed the Kyoto Protocol in December 2007.

Despite such tensions, Nauru maintained generally good relations with Australia, which continued to provide substantial development aid. In August 2009 the two countries signed the Australia-Nauru Partnership for Development. Priority areas included the improvement of the education system and of health facilities in Nauru. In early 2010 the Australian consulate-general in Nauru was upgraded to a full high commission.

In September 2010 the UN opened a bureau on Nauru combining offices of the UN Development Programme, the UN Population Fund and the UN Children's Fund (UNICEF), which was welcomed by President Marcus Stephen as an opportunity to forge closer co-operation with the organization.

In 2011 Nauru began a three-year chairmanship of the Alliance of Small Island States, a position that it aimed to use to encourage awareness of the threat posed to island nations by climate change. Nevertheless, an appeal by President Stephen to the UN Security Council in July of that year, seeking a range of specific actions aimed at preparing for the threat of rising sea levels, failed to gain the Council's approval.

In mid-2002 President Rene Harris announced Nauru's recognition of the People's Republic of China, thus ending 22 years of diplomatic relations with Taiwan. The President promptly accepted US $60m. in aid and $77m. in debt annulment from China. In February 2003 Nauru opened two diplomatic missions, in Washington, DC, and in Beijing. However, suspicions regarding the use of Nauru's facilities (notably its offshore banking sector) by international terrorists were confirmed in the same month when two members of the Islamist al-Qa'ida organization were found to be travelling on Nauruan passports. In March, at the request of the US Government, which had threatened to impose harsh economic sanctions and to repossess Air Nauru's only aircraft if Nauru did not discontinue its offshore banking services, President Bernard Dowiyogo flew to the USA for talks. The Administration of US President George W. Bush was reported to be particularly concerned by the possibility that individuals with links to terrorist organizations might have used the island's financial services in order to launder their funds. In July President Ludwig Scotty announced plans to close the newly opened diplomatic missions, citing economic constraints and his belief that they were not serving their intended purpose. Representatives in China and the USA expressed surprise at the announcement, questioning in particular the President's commitment to ending the lucrative sale of Nauruan passports.

In March 2005 President Scotty made an official visit to mainland China, where he took part in discussions on bilateral aid and economic and technical co-operation. However, in May the Chinese Government revealed that Nauru had severed diplomatic relations with the People's Republic by restoring recognition to Taiwan. In March 2006 it was announced that Taiwan was providing US $3m. in overdue salary payments to some 1,000 former phosphate miners from Kiribati and Tuvalu who had remained stranded on Nauru since the island's financial crisis had resulted in the Government's inability to pay their wages. In the same month Nauru's national carrier recovered its sole aircraft, which had been repossessed in December 2005 owing to unpaid debt, with the help of Taiwanese funding. Following Nauru's re-establishment of diplomatic ties with Taiwan, there was an increase in co-operation between the two countries in a variety of fields, and regular high-level, official visits were undertaken on a reciprocal basis—the most recent being a visit to Taiwan by President Baron Waqa in December 2014.

Nauru attracted considerable controversy in June 2005 when, at a meeting of the International Whaling Commission (IWC) in the Republic of Korea, it voted with Japan to remove the moratorium on commercial whaling introduced in 1986. Japan was accused by some observers of encouraging small, developing countries to join the IWC and of then attempting to influence their voting with financial incentives.

Further international controversy ensued in December 2009 when it was revealed that, in exchange for a commitment of Russian aid reportedly totalling US $50m., Nauru had accorded diplomatic recognition to the secessionist republics of Abkhazia and South Ossetia.

CONSTITUTION AND GOVERNMENT

The Constitution of the Republic of Nauru came into force at independence on 31 January 1968. Legislative power is vested in the unicameral Parliament, with 19 members elected by universal adult suffrage for a term of three years (an increase from the previous 18 members took effect at the 2013 general election). Executive authority is vested in a Cabinet, which consists of the President of the Republic (elected by Parliament) and ministers appointed by him. The Cabinet is collectively responsible to Parliament. For administrative purposes the country is divided into 14 districts, which are themselves grouped into eight electoral constituencies.

REGIONAL AND INTERNATIONAL CO-OPERATION

Nauru is a member of the Pacific Community (see p. 410), of the Pacific Islands Forum (see p. 413) and of the Asian Development Bank (ADB, see p. 206), all of which aim to promote regional development. The country is also a member of the UN's Economic and Social Commission for Asia and the Pacific (ESCAP, see p. 30), having joined the UN in 1999.

ECONOMIC AFFAIRS

In 2013, according to the UN, Nauru's gross domestic product (GDP), measured at current prices, was US $152.9m., equivalent to US $15,211 per head. In 2004–13, it was estimated, GDP increased, in real terms, at an average annual rate of 10.0%, while the population decreased by an average of 0.1% per year. According to the Asian Development Bank (ADB, see p. 206), real GDP expanded by 4.5% in 2012/13 and by 10.0% in 2013/14.

Agricultural activity comprises mainly the small-scale production of tropical fruit, vegetables and livestock, although the production of coffee and copra for export is increasingly significant. According to FAO estimates, agriculture and fishing engaged some 20% of the economically active population at mid-2015. The sector (including hunting and fishing) provided 3.4% of GDP in 2013. Coconuts are the principal crop. Bananas, pineapples and the screw-pine (*Pandanus*) are also cultivated as food crops, while the islanders keep pigs and chickens. Almost all of Nauru's requirements are imported. Increased exploitation of the island's marine resources was envisaged following the approval by Parliament of new fisheries legislation in the late 1990s. However, the sector failed to develop as hoped, and in early 2009 it was reported that a fisheries adviser, funded by Australia, had been engaged. Meanwhile, revenue from fishing licence fees issued to foreign fleets totalled an estimated $A7m. in 2005/06. According to the UN, agricultural GDP increased, in real terms, at an average annual rate of 4.6% during 2004–13. Sectoral GDP increased by 2.1% in 2012 and by 47.0% in 2013.

Industrial activity (mining, manufacturing, construction and utilities) accounted for 52.8% of GDP in 2013. In real terms, according to UN figures, industrial GDP increased at an average annual rate of 45.4% during 2004–13. Sectoral GDP rose by 11.2% in 2013.

Mining and utilities contributed 19.2% of GDP in 2013. Nauru's economy has traditionally been based on the mining of phosphate rock, which constituted four-fifths of the island's surface area. Phosphate extraction was conducted largely by indentured labour, notably by I-Kiribati and Tuvaluan workers. Revenue from phosphate sales was invested in a long-term trust fund, the Nauru Phosphate Royalties Trust (NPRT—see below), and the (now defunct) Nauru Local Government Council. As the depletion of primary (surface) deposits continued, in 2004 an Australian company undertook a survey of the island's potential for secondary phosphate mining. The discovery of substantial new reserves of high-grade phosphate was announced in 2005. In September 2006, following the upgrading of processing facilities, the first major shipment of phosphate for nearly 10 years was exported to India. However, by 2014 primary phosphate reserves were almost completely exhausted, and secondary reserves were expected to last only another 10–20 years. In 2011 Nauru Ocean Resources was granted a contract by the International Seabed Authority to explore for seabed minerals in an area of the northeastern Pacific Ocean reserved for developing states. According to UN figures, the combined GDP of the mining and utilities sectors rose by 11.4% in 2013.

Manufacturing accounted for 33.6% of GDP in 2013, while the construction sector contributed 2.7%. According to UN figures, manufacturing GDP increased, in real terms, by an average of 10.9% per year during 2004–13; sectoral GDP expanded by 3.8% in 2013. During 2004–13, according to UN figures, the GDP of the construction sector increased at an average annual rate of 13.0%; sectoral GDP remained constant in 2012, but increased by 49.8% in 2013.

Energy is derived principally from imported petroleum. Output of electrical energy totalled 23m. kWh in 2011. Electricity supplies remained intermittent for some years until 2009, when the upgrading of the island's generators was completed. In November 2014 Nauru received funding of US $4m. from the ADB and the European Union (see p. 271) to help improve its electricity supply.

The services sector, accounting for 43.8% of Nauru's GDP in 2013, comprises mainly those employed in public service. There is no real tourism sector, and banking services are not readily available. In real terms, the GDP of the services sector decreased at an average annual rate of 6.2% during 2004–13, according to UN figures. The sector's GDP increased by 6.4% in 2012 and by 38.6% in 2013.

According to the ADB, a merchandise trade deficit of US $18.1m. was recorded in 2013. The deficit on the current account of the balance of payments was estimated at 10.3% of GDP in 2006/07. According to the ADB, in 2008 the value of Nauru's exports rose by an estimated 570.7% (owing to strong phosphate sales). Exports increased by 24.3% in 2012, but decreased by 17.1% in 2013, while the cost of imports grew by 27.6% in 2012 and by a further 247.3% in 2013. The principal imports in 2005 were manufactured goods and other manufactured articles (40.4% of total imports), along with machinery and transport equipment, food and live animals. The main exports in 2005 included manufactured goods and crude materials. Phosphate has traditionally been the most important export. The principal export market in 2013 was Nigeria (which purchased 46.5% of the total); the Republic of Korea, Australia, New Zealand and India were also important purchasers. The principal source of Nauru's imports in that year was Australia (providing 92.1% of the total); Singapore and the Republic of Korea were also significant suppliers.

The 2012/13 budget envisaged government expenditure of $A31.6m. (excluding donor-funded development projects). The ADB estimated a budget surplus equivalent to 0.1% of GDP in 2013/14. Under the Australia-Nauru Partnership for Development signed in 2009, aid was to be directed to five priority areas, including infrastructure and services, improvements in the public sector and the promotion of the private sector. Development assistance from Australia was projected at $A27.1m. for 2014/15. Nauru's external debt was estimated by the ADB at US $63m. in 2010. In 2009 the cost of servicing external debt was equivalent to 2.1% of the value of exports of goods and services. The Government's domestic debt was estimated at $A481m. in September 2010. According to the ADB, consumer prices rose by 5.0% in the year to June 2014. According to census figures, the rate of unemployment in 2011 was estimated at 23.0% of the labour force.

After gaining independence in 1968, Nauru benefited from sole control of earnings from phosphate mining, and as a result its income per head was among the highest in the world. However, through a combination of profligate spending and poor investment choices, the assets of the NPRT were estimated to have decreased from a peak value of some $A1,500m. in 1990 to $A300m. in 2003, and in 2004 the portfolio was placed into receivership. (In 2014 the remaining assets of the NPRT were being liquidated and the capital distributed to landowners.) In November 2005 Nauru hosted an international donor meeting, at which it requested support for its National Sustainable Development Strategy (2005–25). The aims of this long-term programme included greater revenue from phosphate production, better use of fisheries resources and the encouragement of local food production. In August 2009 the Pacific Islands Forum agreed that its Pacific Regional Assistance to Nauru initiative, which had commenced in 2004, could be concluded, owing to the economic progress made by Nauru. Despite this, Nauru remained heavily dependent on external support, with budgetary expenditure funded by foreign donors totalling $A33.6m. in 2011/12. Furthermore, the high level of public debt continued to be a major concern. Nevertheless, following a sharp contraction in 2008/09 and stagnation in 2009/10, GDP increased by 3.8% in 2010/11 and by 4.9% in 2011/12, according to the ADB, mainly owing to increased revenue from phosphate exports. The reopening of the processing centre for asylum seekers in September 2012, which had been closed since 2008, meant that the island would once again benefit from the considerable payments made by the Australian authorities; Nauru was expected to receive as much as $A90m. over a five-year period for housing up to 1,500 asylum seekers, following a major expansion of the programme. The recommencement of operations at the centre contributed to GDP growth of 4.5% in 2012/13 and helped to offset declines in phosphate production and exports. In early 2012 the Nauruan Parliament approved the Nauru Trust Fund Bill, which aimed to secure the country's long-term financial autonomy through the replacement of the erstwhile NPRT with a new trust fund, supported by revenue from processing asylum seekers, and from phosphate exports. It was envisaged that the fund, which was to be under the supervision of the ADB, would be established over a 20-year period to allow for the accumulation of contributions from the island's economic partners. The Government allocated $A5m. in its revised 2013/14 budget as an initial contribution to the fund. Despite the political upheaval in 2013 prior to the general election and the judicial crisis in 2014, according to the ADB, robust GDP growth of 10% was recorded in 2013/14, fuelled principally by an increase in construction activities in the detention centre and associated resettlement villages, by greater consumer spending on the part of the recipients of payouts of NPRT assets, and by greater government spending (partly funded by a large increase in visa fees and customs duties generated by the detention centre). In addition, the economy was boosted by a year-on-year increase of 110% in revenue form the sale of fishing licences. The acceleration in growth and resurgence in economic activity arising from the reopening of the centre led to consumer prices increasing by 5.0% in 2013/14, according to the ADB; inflation was forecast to rise further to 8.0% in 2014/15. In May 2014 Nauru applied for membership of the IMF.

PUBLIC HOLIDAYS

2016: 1 January (New Year's Day), 31 January (Independence Day), 25 March (Good Friday), 28 March (Easter), 17 May (Constitution Day), 26 October (Angam Day), 25 December (Christmas Day), 26 December (Boxing Day).

Statistical Survey

Source (unless otherwise indicated): Bureau of Statistics, Ministry of Finance, Government Offices, Yaren District; tel. 444-3142; fax 444-3125; e-mail statistics@naurugov.nr; internet www.spc.int/prism/nauru/.

AREA AND POPULATION

Area: 21.3 sq km (8.2 sq miles).

Population: 8,042 (Nauruan 4,964, Other Pacific Islanders 2,134, Asians 682, Caucasians—mainly Australians and New Zealanders—262) at census of 13 May 1983; 9,919 at census of 17 April 1992; 10,065 at census of 23 September 2002; 10,084 (males 5,105, females 4,979) at census of 30 October 2011.

Density (at 2011 census): 473.4 per sq km.

Population by Age and Sex (Secretariat of the Pacific Community estimates at mid-2015): *0–14 years:* 4,277 (males 2,209, females 2,068); *15–64 years:* 6,374 (males 3,181, females 3,193); *65 years and over:* 186 (males 72, females 114); *Total* 10,837 (males 5,462, females 5,375) (Source: Pacific Regional Information System).

Principal Districts (population at 2011 census, preliminary): Meneng 1,380; Aiwo 1,220; Boe 851; Yaren 747; Buada 739.

Births, Marriages and Deaths (Secretariat of the Pacific Community estimates, 2010, unless otherwise indicated): Registered live births 294 (birth rate 29.8 per 1,000); Marriages (registrations, 1995) 57 (marriage rate 5.3 per 1,000); Registered deaths 88 (death rate 8.9 per 1,000). *2011:* Total births 370; Total deaths 75. *2012:* Total births 319. *2013:* Total births 366.

Life Expectancy (official estimates, years at birth): 59.7 (males 56.8; females 62.7) in 2011.

Economically Active Population (census of 17 April 1992): 2,007 (Elementary occupations 401, Clerks and office workers 355, Craft and related workers 299, Service, shop and market sales workers 250, Professionals 208, Plant, machine operators and assemblers 136, Technicians and associate professionals 115, Legislators, senior officials and managers 18, Agriculture and related workers 2, Not classified 223). *2011 Census:* Total employed 2,883; Unemployed 908; Total labour force 3,791. *Mid-2015* (estimates): Agriculture, etc. 1,000; Total labour force 5,000 (Source: FAO).

HEALTH AND WELFARE

Key Indicators

Total Fertility Rate (children per woman, 2012): 3.0.

Under-5 Mortality Rate (per 1,000 live births, 2012): 37.

Physicians (per 1,000 head, 2010): 0.7.

Hospital Beds (per 1,000 head, 2010): 5.0.

Health Expenditure (2011): US $ per head (PPP): 243.

Health Expenditure (2011): % of GDP: 8.1.

Health Expenditure (2011): public (% of total): 88.0.

For sources and definitions, see explanatory note on p. vi.

AGRICULTURE, ETC.

Principal Crop and Livestock (2013, FAO estimates): Coconuts 2,700 metric tons; Pigs 3,000 head; Chickens 5,000 head.

Livestock Products (metric tons, 2013, FAO estimates): Pig meat 72; Chicken meat 4; Hen eggs 16.

Fishing (metric tons, live weight of capture, 2012): Yellowfin tuna 240; Bigeye tuna 2; Skipjack tuna 30; Total catch (incl. other marine fishes) 493 (FAO estimate).

Source: FAO.

MINING

Phosphate Rock ('000 metric tons, estimates): 84 in 2003; 22 in 2004; 11 in 2005. The phosphoric acid content ('000 metric tons, estimates) was: 26 in 2003; 7 in 2004; 3 in 2005. Source: US Geological Survey.

INDUSTRY

Electric Energy (million kWh): 21 in 2009; 23 in 2010; 23 in 2011. Source: UN Industrial Commodity Statistics Database.

FINANCE

Currency and Exchange Rates: Australian currency: 100 cents = 1 Australian dollar ($A). *Sterling, US Dollar and Euro Equivalents* (31 December 2014): £1 sterling = $A1.9030; US $1 = $A1.2192; €1 = $A1.4802; $A100 = £52.55 = US $82.02 = €67.56. *Average Exchange Rate* (Australian dollars per US $): 0.9658 in 2012; 1.0358 in 2013; 1.1094 in 2014.

Budget ($A '000, year ending 30 June 2007, budget forecasts): *Revenue:* 22,288 (Tax revenue 8,646, Non-tax revenue 13,643); *Expenditure:* 22,226 (Employee expenses 5,890, Operating expenses 8,543, Property expenses 505, Current transfers 2,150, Gross fixed capital formation 4,682, Other 457). *2012:* Total revenue (incl. grants) 31,600; Total expenditure (incl. net lending) 32,500.

Cost of Living (Consumer Price Index; base August 2008 = 100): All items 100.5 in 2012; 98.4 in 2013.

Gross Domestic Product ($A million at constant 2005 prices): 60.9 in 2011; 73.2 in 2012; 92.5 in 2013.

Expenditure on the Gross Domestic Product ($A million in current prices, 2013): Government final consumption expenditure 60.8; Private final consumption expenditure 158.0; Increase in stocks 0.4; Gross fixed capital formation 68.2; *Total domestic expenditure* 287.4; Exports of goods and services 20.8; *Less* Imports of goods and services 149.7; *GDP in purchasers' values* 158.4.

Gross Domestic Product by Economic Activity ($A million in current prices, 2013): Agriculture, hunting and fishing 5.5; Mining and utilities 30.8; Manufacturing 53.8 Construction 4.3; Retail trade and hotel and restaurants 19.8; Transport, storage and communications 14.9; Other services 31.1; *Sub-total* 160.2; Net of indirect taxes −1.8 (obtained as a residual); *GDP in market prices* 158.4.

Source: UN, National Accounts Main Aggregates Database.

EXTERNAL TRADE

Principal Commodities (US $ '000, year ending 30 June 2005): *Imports:* Food and live animals 4,548; Beverages and tobacco 1,891; Crude materials (except food and fuel) 1,741; Mineral fuels and lubricants 1,528; Animal fats and vegetable oils 1,698; Chemical products 3,300; Manufactured goods 11,898; Machinery and transport equipment 5,375; Miscellaneous manufactured articles 1,705; Total (incl. others) 33,683. *Exports:* Food and live animals 293; Crude materials (except food and fuel) 1,489; Chemical products 408; Manufactured goods 2,039; Machinery and transport equipment 616; Miscellaneous manufactured articles 113; Total (incl. others) 4,959.

Principal Trading Partners (US $ million, year ending 31 December 2013): *Imports:* Australia 131.8; Fiji 1.4; Japan 1.2; New Zealand 2.0; Singapore 0.9; USA 0.7; Total (incl. others) 143.1. *Exports:* Australia 16.1; India 4.7; Japan 3.7; Korea, Republic 23.1; New Zealand 15.7; Nigeria 58.1; Total (incl. others) 125.0. Source: Asian Development Bank.

Trade Totals (US $ million, year ending 31 December): *Imports c.i.f.:* 32.3 in 2011; 41.2 in 2012; 143.1 in 2013. *Exports f.o.b.:* 121.2 in 2011; 150.7 in 2012; 125.0 in 2013. Source: Asian Development Bank.

TRANSPORT

Shipping: *Flag Registered Fleet* (at 31 December 2014): Number of vessels 1; Total displacement 948 grt. Source: Lloyd's List Intelligence (www.lloydslistintelligence.com).

Civil Aviation (traffic on scheduled services, 2009): Kilometres flown (million) 4; Passengers carried ('000) 210; Passenger-km (million) 354; Total ton-km (million) 35. Source: UN, *Statistical Yearbook.*

COMMUNICATIONS MEDIA

Telephones (main lines, 2009): 1,900 in use.

Mobile Cellular Telephones (2012): 6,800 subscribers.

Broadband Subscribers (2010): 400.

Source: International Telecommunication Union.

EDUCATION

Pre-primary (2013): 5 schools; 40 teachers; 751 pupils.

Primary (2013): 4 schools; 28 teachers; 1,475 pupils.

Secondary (2013 unless otherwise indicated): 3 schools (2007); 30 teachers; 964 pupils.

Vocational (2003 unless otherwise indicated): 2 schools (2004); 4 teachers; 38 students.

Pupil-teacher Ratio (primary education, UNESCO estimate): 22.4 in 2007/08 (Source: UNESCO Institute for Statistics).

Note: Nauruans studying at secondary and tertiary levels overseas in 2001 numbered 85.

Source: Department of Education, Yaren, Nauru.

Directory

The Government

HEAD OF STATE

President: BARON WAQA (elected 11 June 2013).

CABINET
(May 2015)

President and Minister of Public Service, of Foreign Affairs and Trade, of Climate Change, and of Police and Emergency Services: BARON WAQA.

Minister of Health, of Transport, of Sport and of Fisheries: VALDON DOWIYOGO.

Minister assisting the President, Minister of Finance and Sustainable Development, of Justice, of Eigigu Holdings Corporation, and of Nauru AirCorporation: DAVID ADEANG.

Minister of Education, of Home Affairs, and of Land Management: CHARMAINE SCOTTY.

Minister of Commerce, Industry and Environment, of RONPhos, and of Nauru Rehabilitation Corporation: AARON COOK.

Minister of Nauru Phosphate Royalties Trust, of Telecommunications, and of Nauru Utilities Corporation: SHADLOG BERNICKE.

MINISTRIES

Office of the President: Government Offices, Yaren; tel. 557-3133; fax 444-3776; e-mail andromeda.amram@naurugov.nr.

Ministry of Commerce, Industry and Environment: Government Offices, Yaren; tel. 444-3133; fax 444-3188; e-mail minister .cir@naurugov.nr.

Ministry of Education: Government Offices, Yaren; tel. 444-3130; fax 444-3718; e-mail minister.education@naurugov.nr.

Ministry of Finance and Sustainable Development: Government Offices, Yaren; tel. 557-3133; e-mail minister.finance@ naurugov.nr.

Ministry of Fisheries: Government Offices, Yaren; e-mail minister .fisheries@naurugov.nr.

Ministry of Foreign Affairs and Trade: Government Offices, Yaren; tel. 444-3133; e-mail minister.foreignaffairs@naurugov.nr.

Ministry of Health: Government Offices, Yaren; tel. 444-3133; fax 444-3188; e-mail minister.health@naurugov.nr.

Ministry of Home Affairs: Government Offices, Yaren; fax 444-3891; e-mail minister.homeaffairs@naurugov.nr.

Ministry of Justice: Government Offices, Yaren; tel. 444-3160; fax 444-3108; e-mail minister.justice@naurugov.nr.

Ministry of the Nauru Phosphate Royalties Trust: Government Offices, Yaren; e-mail minister.nprt@naurugov.nr.

Ministry of Police and Emergency Services: Government Offices, Yaren; e-mail minister.police@naurugov.nr.

Ministry of Public Service: Government Offices, Yaren; e-mail minister.publicservice@naurugov.nr.

Ministry of Sport: Government Offices, Yaren; e-mail minister.sport@naurugov.nr.

Ministry of Telecommunications: Government Offices, Yaren; e-mail minister.telecommunications@naurugov.nr.

Ministry of Transport: Government Offices, Yaren; tel. 444-3133; fax 444-3136; e-mail minister.transport@naurugov.nr.

Ministry of Utilities: Government Offices, Yaren; e-mail minister.utilities@naurugov.nr.

Legislature

PARLIAMENT

Following several months of procedural delays in the wake of the dissolution of Parliament on 9 March 2013, legislative elections (at which the number of parliamentary seats was increased from 18 to 19) finally took place on 8 June. Baron Waqa was elected President on 11 June by 13 of the 19 members of Parliament.

Speaker: LUDWIG SCOTTY.

Deputy Speaker: RANIN AKUA.

Political Organizations

Democratic Party of Nauru: c/o Parliament House, Yaren; f. 1987; revival of Nauru Party (f. 1975); Leader KENNAN ADEANG.

Naoero Amo (Nauru First): c/o Parliament House, Yaren; e-mail visionary@naoeroamo.com; f. 2001; Co-Leaders DAVID ADEANG, Dr KIEREN KEKE.

Diplomatic Representation

EMBASSY AND HIGH COMMISSION IN NAURU

Australia: MQ45 & MQ43 NPC OE, Aiwo; tel. 557-3380; fax 557-3382; e-mail george.fraser@dfat.gov.au; internet www.nauru.embassy.gov.au/nuru/home.html; High Commissioner MARTIN QUINN.

Taiwan (Republic of China): Civic Centre, 1st Floor, Aiwo; tel. 557-3333; e-mail nru@mofa.gov.tw; internet www.taiwanembassy.org/nr; Ambassador JOSEPH CHOW.

Judicial System

The Chief Justice presides over the Supreme Court, which exercises original, appellate and advisory jurisdiction. The Resident Magistrate presides over the District Court, and he also acts as Coroner under the Inquests Act 1977. The Supreme Court is a court of record. The Family Court consists of three members, one being the Resident Magistrate as Chairman, and two other members drawn from a panel of Nauruans. The Chief Justice is Chairman of the Public Services Appeals Board and of the Police Appeals Board.

Supreme Court: Yaren; tel. 444-3163; fax 444-3104; Chief Justice Ratu JONI MADRAIWIWI; Judges MOHAMMED SHAFIULLAH KHAN, ELIZABETH HAMILTON-WHITE.

Registrar of the Supreme Court: GRAHAM LEUNG.

Resident Magistrate of the District Court and Chairman of the Family Court: EMMA GARO.

Solicitor-General: (vacant).

Religion

Nauruans are predominantly Christians, adhering either to the Nauruan Congregational Church or to the Roman Catholic Church.

Nauru Congregational Church: Boe District, Nauru; seven congregations.

Roman Catholic Church: POB 224, Nauru; tel. and fax 444-3708; e-mail taewenteangmsc@gmail.com; Nauru forms part of the diocese of Tarawa and Nauru, comprising Kiribati and Nauru. The Bishop resides on Tarawa Atoll, Kiribati.

The Press

Mwinen Ko: Nauru; f. 2010; fortnightly; est. with assistance from AusAID (the Australian Govt's aid agency); Editor SANDRA BILL.

Broadcasting and Communications

TELECOMMUNICATIONS

Digicel Nauru Ltd: Ground Floor, Aiwo Civic Centre, Aiwo; e-mail Nauru_CC_Agents@digicelgroup.com; internet www.digicelnauru.com; f. 2009; a joint venture between Digicel Group and the Nauru Govt; mobile services.

Nauru Telecommunications Service: ICT Centre, Civic Centre Complex, Aiwo, Nauru; tel. 444-3324; fax 444-3111; e-mail director.ict@naurugov.nr.

BROADCASTING

Radio

Nauru Broadcasting Service: Information and Broadcasting Services, Chief Secretary's Department, POB 77, Nauru; tel. 444-3133; fax 444-3153; f. 1968; state-owned and non-commercial; broadcasts in the mornings in English and Nauruan; operates Radio Nauru; Station Man. RIN TSITSI; Man. Dir GARY TURNER.

Television

Nauru Television (NTV): Nauru; tel. 444-3133; fax 444-3153; began operations in June 1991; govt-owned; broadcasts 24 hrs per day on three channels; most of the programmes are supplied by foreign TV companies via satellite or on videotape; a weekly current affairs programme is produced locally; Man. MICHAEL DEKARUBE.

Finance

BANKING

Nauru's only bank, the state-owned Bank of Nauru, ceased operations in 2006, owing to insolvency. A liquidator was appointed in 2011 to finalize its formal closure. In March 2015 the Government announced that Bendigo and Adelaide Bank Ltd of Australia had signed an agreement to establish an agency (to be located at Nauru's Revenue Office) which would provide the island with much-needed banking services.

INSURANCE

Nauru Insurance Corporation: POB 82, Nauru; tel. 444-3346; fax 444-3731; f. 1974; sole licensed insurer and reinsurer in Nauru; Chair. NIMES EKWONA.

Trade and Industry

GOVERNMENT AGENCIES

Nauru Agency Corporation: Civic Centre, 1st Floor, POB 300, Aiwo; tel. 558-7301; e-mail info@nauruoffshore.com; internet www.nauruoffshore.com; f. 1972; management service to assist entrepreneurs in the incorporation of holding and trading corpns and the procurement of trust and insurance licences; CEO R. MOSES.

Nauru Corporation: Civic Centre, Yaren; f. 1925; operated by the Nauru Council; the major retailer in Nauru; Gen. Man. A. EPHRAIM.

Nauru Fisheries and Marine Resources Authority: POB 449, Aiwo; tel. 444-3733; fax 444-3812; e-mail nfmra@cenpac.net.nr; f. 1997; CEO CHARLESTON DEIYE.

Nauru Phosphate Royalties Trust (NPRT): Nauru; statutory corpn; invests phosphate royalties to provide govt revenue; extensive int. interests, incl. hotels and real estate; assets put into receivership in 2004; legislation providing for the establishment of a new Nauru trust fund was adopted in Feb. 2012; Sec. NIRAL FERNANDO.

Nauru Rehabilitation Corporation (NRC): Camp Ibaganiquane, Meneng; tel. and fax 444-3200; e-mail nrcadmin8464@gmail.com; internet www.nrurehab.org.nr; f. 1999; manages and devises programmes for the rehabilitation of those parts of the island damaged by the over-mining of phosphate; CEO REYNOLD DAVID.

UTILITIES

Eigigu Holding Corporation: Civic Centre, Aiwo; tel. 557-8011; public works, water and waste management; also has interests in supermarket retail and television broadcast distribution; Chair. DAVID AINGIMEA.

Nauru Central Utilities (Nauru Utilities Authority): Aiwo; tel. 444-3247; fax 444-3521; e-mail apisake.soakai@naurugov.nr; f. 1968; sole electricity provider; CEO APISAKE SOAKAI.

RONPhos Corporation (Republic of Nauru Phosphate Company): Aiwo; tel. 444-3839; fax 444-2752; f. 1967; est. as Nauru Phosphate Corpn; has operated the phosphate industry and several public services of the Republic of Nauru (including provision of electricity) on behalf of the Nauruan people; present name adopted in 2005 following reorganization; Chair. RIDDELL AKUA; Gen. Man. LESI OLSSON.

Transport

RAILWAYS

There are 5.2 km of 0.9-m gauge railway serving the phosphate workings.

ROADS

A sealed road, 16 km long, circles the island, and another serves Buada District.

SHIPPING

In 1998 finance was secured from the Japanese Government for the construction of a harbour in Anibare District, which was opened in 2000.

Nauru Pacific Line (NPL): Government Bldg, Yaren; tel. 444-3133; f. 1969; operates cargo charter services to ports in Australia, New Zealand, Asia, the Pacific and the west coast of the USA; fleet of seven vessels (five owned and two leased).

CIVIL AVIATION

There is one airport, Nauru International Airport, which is served solely by Nauru Airlines.

Nauru Airlines: Directorate of Civil Aviation, Government Offices, POB 40, Yaren; tel. and fax 557-7000; e-mail info@ourairline.com.au; internet www.ourairline.com.au; f. 1970; established as Air Nauru; known as Our Airline in 2006–14; current name adopted 2014; operates passenger and cargo services to Kiribati, Fiji, Solomon Islands and Australia; Chair. Capt. KEVIN POWER; CEO GEOFFREY BOWMAKER.

Tourism

There is no tourism industry on the island.

Defence

Nauru has no defence forces. Under an informal agreement, Australia is responsible for the defence of the island.

Education

Education is free and compulsory for children between the ages of six and 16. In 2013 the island had five pre-primary schools, with 751 pupils and 40 teachers. In 2013 the island had four primary schools, and in 2007 three secondary schools. In 2013 a total of 1,475 pupils were enrolled in primary education with 28 teachers, and 964 pupils in secondary education with 30 teachers. In addition, there were two vocational training schools in 2004. An extension centre of the University of the South Pacific, based in Suva, Fiji, was opened in Nauru in the late 1980s.

NEPAL

Introductory Survey

LOCATION, CLIMATE, LANGUAGE, RELIGION, FLAG, CAPITAL

The Federal Democratic Republic of Nepal is a landlocked Asian country in the Himalaya mountain range, with India to the east, south and west, and Tibet (the Xizang Autonomous Region), in the People's Republic of China, to the north. The climate varies sharply with altitude, from arctic on the higher peaks of the Himalaya mountains (where the air temperature is permanently below freezing point) to humid subtropical in the central valley of Kathmandu, which is warm and sunny in summer. Temperatures in Kathmandu, which is 1,337 m (4,386 ft) above sea level, are generally between 2°C (35°F) and 30°C (86°F), with an annual average of 11°C (52°F). The rainy season is between June and October. Average annual rainfall varies from about 1,000 mm (40 ins) in western Nepal to about 2,500 mm (100 ins) in the east. The official language is Nepali, which was spoken by 44.6% of the population in 2011. Other languages include Maithir (11.7% in 2011) and Bhojpuri (6.0%). Some 81.3% of the population were Hindus in 2011, with 9.0% Buddhists and 4.4% Muslims. The national flag (proportions 4 by 3) is composed of two crimson pennants, each with a blue border. The upper section contains a white crescent moon (horns upwards and surmounted by a disc with eight rays) and the lower section a white sun in splendour. The capital is Kathmandu.

CONTEMPORARY POLITICAL HISTORY

Historical Context

Although Nepal was an hereditary monarchy, for more than 100 years, until 1951, effective control over the country was wielded by the Rana family, who created the post of hereditary Prime Minister. A popular revolution, led by the Nepali Congress Party (NCP), ousted the Ranas and restored King Tribhuvan to power. A limited constitutional monarchy was established in 1951. During most of the 1950s government was controlled by the monarchy, initially under Tribhuvan and then, after his death in 1955, under his son, Mahendra. In February 1959 King Mahendra promulgated Nepal's first Constitution, providing for a bicameral parliament, including a popularly elected lower house. Elections held later that month resulted in victory for the NCP, led by Bishweshwar Prasad (B. P.) Koirala, who became Prime Minister. However, the King retained a certain degree of power, and persistent differences between the King and the Prime Minister led to a royal coup in December 1960: Nepal's first brief period of democracy was thus brought to an abrupt end. The King dismissed the Council of Ministers and dissolved Parliament. A royal decree of January 1961 banned political parties. King Mahendra accused the Koirala administration of corruption, and in December 1962 he introduced a new Constitution, reasserting absolute royal power and providing for a 'partyless' system of government, based on the Panchayat (village council), with a Prime Minister appointed by the King. In January 1972 King Mahendra died and was succeeded by his son, Birendra. In December 1975 the Government made major changes to the Constitution, which allowed for a widening of the franchise and more frequent elections to the Rashtriya Panchayat (National Assembly), but in no way were the King's powers eroded.

Domestic Political Affairs

B. P. Koirala, the former Prime Minister and an advocate of parliamentary democracy, was acquitted of treason in February 1978. Returning from abroad a year later, he was placed under house arrest in April 1979, but was subsequently released. National unrest grew and, after King Birendra announced in May that there would be a national referendum on whether to restore multi-party democracy, Prime Minister Kirti Nidhi Bista resigned and was succeeded by Surya Bahadur Thapa. In the referendum, held in May 1980, a slim majority (54.8%) of voters supported the Panchayat system with reforms. As a result, the King formed a Constitutional Reforms Commission, and in December he issued a decree under which amendments to the Constitution were made, including the proviso that the

appointment of the Prime Minister by the King would henceforth be on the recommendation of the Rashtriya Panchayat. In accordance with the new provisions, direct legislative elections were held in May 1981, the first of their kind since 1959, although still on a non-party basis. Thapa was re-elected by the Rashtriya Panchayat as Prime Minister in June 1981, and the King installed a new Council of Ministers (on the recommendation of the Prime Minister). An extensive ministerial reorganization took place in October 1982, but this failed to stem increasing official corruption and economic mismanagement. In July 1983, for the first time in the 23-year history of the Panchayat system, the incumbent Prime Minister, Thapa, was ousted, and a new Council of Ministers was formed by a former Chairman of the Rashtriya Panchayat, Lokendra Bahadur Chand, who had successfully introduced a motion expressing no confidence in Thapa.

The Nepali Congress Party and the restoration of democracy

In May 1985 the NCP embarked upon a campaign of civil disobedience, aimed at restoring a multi-party political system and parliamentary rule under a constitutional monarchy. In June a series of bomb explosions, which were attributed to two newly formed anti-monarchist and anti-Government groups and which resulted in fatalities, united an otherwise divided legislature against the terrorists, and forced the predominantly moderate opposition to abandon the campaign of civil disobedience. In August the Rashtriya Panchayat approved a stringent anti-terrorist law, and more than 1,000 people were arrested in connection with the unrest.

In May 1986 about 64% of the electorate voted in a general election, despite a boycott of the polls by the NCP and the pro-China faction of the Communist Party of Nepal (CPN). All the candidates in the election were nominally independents, but it was reported that among the 72 new entrants to the Rashtriya Panchayat were at least 16 members of the Marxist-Leninist faction of the CPN. In June the King nominated 25 additional members of the new Rashtriya Panchayat, and Marich Man Singh Shrestha (previously Chairman of the Rashtriya Panchayat) was elected unopposed by the Assembly as the new Prime Minister.

In late 1989 several political groups dissatisfied with the country's non-party system convened to discuss the formation of a country-wide, peaceful 'movement for the restoration of democracy' to campaign for the replacement of the Panchayat Government by an interim national government, the removal of the ban on political activities, and the introduction of a multi-party system and a constitutional monarchy. The so-called Jana Andolan (People's Movement) was formalized in January 1990 by the NCP and the newly formed United Left Front (ULF—which comprised six factions of the CPN and a labour group). The Government responded to the new movement with a campaign of arrests and censorship; violent demonstrations, strikes and mass arrests ensued. In an effort to end the political unrest, the King dismissed Shrestha's Government on 6 April and nominated a restricted four-member Council of Ministers, under the leadership of the more moderate Chand. The Government initiated talks with the opposition, and on 8 April the King announced that the 30-year ban on political parties was to be ended and that a commission to study constitutional reform was to be established. The Jana Andolan suspended its campaign of demonstrations, but many activists continued to agitate, demanding the removal of the formal structure of the Panchayat system. A week later, the King dismissed the Council of Ministers, announced the dissolution of the Rashtriya Panchayat, and invited the opposition alliance of the NCP and the ULF to form an interim government. On 19 April a new coalition Council of Ministers (including two ministers nominated by the King), under the premiership of the President of the NCP, Krishna Prasad (K. P.) Bhattarai, was sworn in. The new Prime Minister announced that a general election would be held, on a multi-party basis, within a year. The principal task of the interim Government was to prepare a new constitution in accordance with the spirit of multi-party democracy and constitutional monarchy.

In May 1990 the King delegated the legislative powers of the dissolved Rashtriya Panchayat to the new Council of Ministers, empowering it to enact, amend and repeal legislation in order to facilitate the introduction of multi-party democracy. A general amnesty for all political prisoners was announced in May, and in July the death sentence was abolished and the laws restricting freedom of the press and freedom of association were repealed. The draft of the new Constitution, which was published at the end of August, recommended the introduction of a constitutional monarchy; a democratic multi-party system and a bicameral legislature, composed of a 205-member House of Representatives (Pratinidhi Sabha) and a 60-member National Assembly (Rashtriya Sabha); the official guarantee of fundamental rights (including freedom of expression); an independent judiciary; and the placing of the army under the control of a National Defence Council, headed by the Prime Minister. Under the draft Constitution, the King would be allowed to declare a state of emergency on the advice of the Council of Ministers, but such declarations would have to be approved by the House of Representatives within three months. A crucial clause under consideration required the King 'to obey and protect' the Constitution: under the old regime, the King was considered to be above the Constitution. The draft Constitution was approved by the Council of Ministers on 15 October and sent to the King for his endorsement. However, King Birendra amended the draft in a final effort to retain sovereign authority and full emergency powers. This retrograde action provoked violent protests. The Council of Ministers rejected most of the proposed amendments in the royal counter-draft, but agreed to the King's proposal to establish a Council of State (Raj Parishad), with a standing committee headed by a royal appointee; Bhattarai stressed that the committee would not function as a parallel body to the Council of Ministers. He also emphasized that the King would only be permitted to act on judicial, executive and legislative matters on the advice of the Council of Ministers. The new Constitution was officially promulgated on 9 November.

In December 1990 four of the seven constituent members of the ULF broke away from the front, citing their lack of representation in the interim coalition Council of Ministers. In January 1991 two major factions of the CPN (the Marxist and Marxist-Leninist factions) merged to form the CPN (Unified Marxist-Leninist—UML).

The general election was held on 12 May 1991. The NCP contested the election alone rather than aligning itself with its former left-wing Jana Andolan partners. The general election proceeded peacefully and was characterized by a high turnout (65.2% of the electorate). The NCP won a comfortable overall majority, but it was soundly defeated by the UML in the eastern hill districts, in parts of the Terai, and in Kathmandu. The UML established itself as the second largest party in the House of Representatives, followed by the United People's Front (UPF), an amalgam of radical, Maoist groups. The two pro-monarchy parties, the Rashtriya Prajatantra Party (Chand) and the Rashtriya Prajatantra Party (Thapa), led by the former Prime Ministers of those names, managed only four seats between them. Acting Prime Minister Bhattarai lost his seat in the capital, and was replaced in the premiership by Girija Prasad (G. P.) Koirala, the General Secretary of the NCP and brother of the late B. P. Koirala.

By the end of 1991 unity within the ruling NCP was threatened by growing internal dissent among its senior leadership. Under Koirala's premiership the centrist NCP Government shifted to the right. The public image of the monarchy and leading members of the former Panchayat regime were rehabilitated and no charges were brought against senior officials of the former administration for corruption or human rights violations. Replicating the patronage system of the Panchayat regime, the NCP rapidly began to dominate the public administration structure.

The Government came under pressure in April 1992 when a *bandh* (general strike), organized by communist and other opposition parties in Kathmandu in protest against price rises, water shortages and alleged government corruption, resulted in the deaths of at least seven demonstrators following violent clashes with the police. The success of a second general strike, which was held in May and brought Kathmandu to a standstill, demonstrated the continuing strength of the radical left.

In early 1993 the national UML congress abandoned much of the party's Marxist dogma and tacitly acknowledged its commitment to working within a democratic multi-party system.

However, the untimely deaths of the party's General Secretary, Madan Bhandari, and Politburo member Jiv Raj Ashrit in a road accident in May, threw the UML into disarray. The party's rejection of the findings of a government inquiry, which concluded that the deaths had been accidental, provoked nationwide protests in support of demands for an independent inquiry into the so-called Dasdhunga incident. In late May Madhav Kumar (M. K.) Nepal was appointed as the new General Secretary of the UML.

In the mean time, the rehabilitation of officials of the former Panchayat regime continued. In January 1993 the King appointed senior figures of the old administration, including former Prime Ministers Chand and Shrestha, to the 121-member Council of State. In June the right-wing Rashtriya Prajatantra Party (RPP, formed in February 1992, following a merger of the Chand and Thapa factions) held its first national conference in Kathmandu.

The worsening rift within the NCP reached a crisis point in July 1993 when followers of Ganesh Man Singh withdrew their support for Koirala, who thereby lost his parliamentary majority. Consequently, the Prime Minister offered his resignation, prompting the King to dissolve the House of Representatives. Koirala was appointed to serve as interim Prime Minister until the general election, which was brought forward from mid-1996 to 15 November 1994. At the election, which attracted a turnout of 58%, the UML unexpectedly emerged as the single largest party, winning 88 of the 205 seats in the House of Representatives, while the NCP took 85 seats. At the end of the month the UML formed a minority Government under the premiership of its moderate Chairman, Man Mohan Adhikari. Following an attempt to avert a parliamentary motion of no confidence registered by the NCP in June 1995 (by ordering a dissolution of the legislature), the short-lived UML Government was brought down in a further vote of no confidence in September, and swiftly replaced by a coalition Government composed of members of the NCP, RPP and Nepal Sadbhavana Party (NSP), and headed by the NCP's parliamentary leader, Sher Bahadur Deuba.

Political instability and the Maoist insurgency

In March 1996 the Government introduced a number of security measures following a series of violent clashes between a group of Maoist activists and the police in western Nepal—by the end of the year more than 100 people had been killed as a result of the nascent insurgency. The left-wing extremists (many of whom were members of the underground Communist Party of Nepal (Maoist)—CPN (M)—and the UPF) had launched a 'people's revolutionary war' in the hills of Nepal in February, demanding the abolition of the constitutional monarchy and the establishment of a republic.

In January 1997 the UML, already the largest party in the House of Representatives, increased its strength from 87 to 90 deputies, following its success in three by-elections. The NCP-led coalition Government collapsed in March when it lost a vote of confidence in the House of Representatives. Chand was appointed as the new Prime Minister (for the fourth time) at the head of a new coalition Government composed of members of the RPP, the UML, the NSP and the Nepal Workers' and Peasants' Party. However, the new Government proved unstable from the outset, since members of the Thapa faction of the RPP refused to support Prime Minister Chand, and the ideological differences between the communists and the former pro-monarchists appeared insuperable. In May and June the communists replaced the NCP as the country's dominant force in local government, following resounding successes in local elections, which, however, were marred by widespread violence.

In October 1997 the Government lost a vote of no confidence tabled by the NCP. King Birendra appointed Thapa, the President of the RPP, to replace Chand as Prime Minister. Another new coalition Government took office, which comprised members of the RPP and the NSP and was subsequently expanded to include members of the NCP and a number of independents. In February 1998 the Government survived, by a narrow margin, a no-confidence vote introduced by the UML and dissident members of the RPP (including Chand). In January Chand and nine other rebel deputies had been expelled from the RPP, forming a breakaway faction known as the RPP (Chand). In March the UML suffered a serious reverse when about one-half of the party's parliamentary deputies formed a breakaway faction entitled the Communist Party of Nepal (Marxist-Leninist—ML), led by Bam Dev Gautam.

In April 1998 G. P. Koirala (who had succeeded Bhattarai as President of the NCP in May 1996) replaced Thapa as Prime

Minister at the head of an NCP Council of Ministers. In August, in an attempt to strengthen his own precarious administration and to encourage the UML's rivals, the Prime Minister formed an alliance with the ML. Koirala allocated some less important government portfolios to the ML, thus ensuring the Prime Minister of an adequate parliamentary majority. In December, however, the ML withdrew from the coalition Government, alleging that the NCP had failed to implement a number of agreements drawn up between the two parties. Prime Minister Koirala tendered his resignation, but was invited to head an interim administration, which was to hold power until a general election the following year. Members of the NCP, the UML and the NSP, and, for the first time in eight years, a royal nominee, were appointed to the caretaker government. Meanwhile, the 'people's war' waged by the Maoist activists in the hills of west Nepal was gathering momentum.

In May 1999 the NCP won an outright majority in the general election, securing 110 of the 205 seats in the lower house; the UML obtained 68 seats and the RPP (Thapa) took 11 seats, while the ML and the RPP (Chand) both failed to win a single seat. Voting was conducted relatively peacefully, despite threats by Maoist insurgents to disrupt the electoral process. A new Council of Ministers, headed by the veteran NCP leader K. P. Bhattarai and composed solely of NCP members, was appointed at the end of the month.

In November 1999, in an effort to resolve the Maoist insurgency, which, according to government sources, now affected 31 of Nepal's 75 districts and had led to the deaths of more than 1,000 people, Prime Minister Bhattarai offered to grant the guerrillas an amnesty and various rehabilitation measures if they surrendered their arms and entered into negotiations with the Government. In response, the insurgents (who were estimated to number 5,000–6,000 and to have the support of about 8,000 sympathizers) stated that they were not prepared to enter into peace talks until arrest warrants issued against their leaders were withdrawn, official investigations were carried out into alleged extrajudicial killings of suspected militants by the police, and imprisoned activists were released.

G. P. Koirala had initially been supportive of Bhattarai's premiership, but subsequently became vociferous in his criticism of the Government's handling of the Maoist crisis. In February 2000, following mounting pressure caused by a number of internal disagreements, ministerial resignations and the prospect of members of his own party raising votes of no confidence against him, Bhattarai resigned from his post. Following his election as parliamentary leader of the NCP, Koirala was sworn in for a fourth term as Prime Minister, alongside a new Council of Ministers, on 22 March. In May an independent National Human Rights Commission was formed. In its first annual report, published in 2001, the Commission accused both the Maoist insurgents and the security forces of committing serious human rights violations, including murder and torture, during the ongoing conflict.

In April 2000 Prime Minister Koirala activated the National Defence Council, which, according to the Constitution, comprised the Prime Minister, the Minister of Defence and the Commander-in-Chief of the Royal Nepal Army, to resolve the Maoist crisis. In comparison to the inadequately trained and poorly armed police force, which had suffered numerous casualties, the army was much better equipped to deal with the insurgency, and Koirala expressed his wish to mobilize the armed forces in the ongoing fight against militant activity. At the end of August the Maoist crisis worsened: during two Maoist attacks in Dolpa and Lamjung, 24 police officers were killed and 44 were injured. The Royal Nepal Army was criticized for failing to intervene to protect the police from insurgents. It was subsequently decided that the Government would employ the dual approach of using the army, while simultaneously encouraging negotiations, in order to resolve the Maoist crisis. At the end of October the first direct, unofficial negotiations began between the Government and the CPN (M); however, they were short-lived, and the violence resumed in November. By early 2001 Koirala was facing increasing opposition from within and outside his party. Accusations of corruption led to repeated demands for his resignation. In March a number of ministers resigned, while the opposition continued to disrupt parliamentary proceedings; the King responded by proroguing the National Assembly and House of Representatives in April.

The royal family massacre; the Maoist insurgency escalates

On 1 June 2001 King Birendra, Queen Aishwarya and six other members of the royal family were shot dead; the heir to the throne, Crown Prince Dipendra, was gravely wounded. Another family member, Dhirendra Shah, died later in hospital. Initial reports suggested that Prince Dipendra had shot members of his family before shooting himself, following a dispute between himself and his mother regarding his intentions to marry a woman of whom the Queen disapproved. Immediately after the incident Prince Dipendra was pronounced King, and Prince Gyanendra, the brother of the deceased King Birendra, was appointed regent. On 4 June King Dipendra died and was succeeded by Prince Gyanendra. These events caused considerable unrest in Kathmandu, and a curfew was imposed. Following his accession, King Gyanendra established a commission to investigate the royal deaths. The commission, comprising the Chief Justice and the Speaker of the House of Representatives, duly concluded that Dipendra had been responsible for the shootings and that at the time had been under the influence of drugs and alcohol. King Gyanendra bestowed the title of Queen on his wife, Princess Komal; his son, Paras Shah, was declared Crown Prince at the end of October.

In June–July 2001 Maoist leaders, taking advantage of the unrest in Nepal, intensified their activities. In July, under intense pressure over long-standing corruption allegations against him and his failure to curb the Maoist insurgency, Prime Minister Koirala resigned; former premier Sher Bahadur Deuba succeeded Koirala as leader of the NCP and Prime Minister. Immediately after his appointment Prime Minister Deuba persuaded the Maoist leaders to reciprocate his offer of a ceasefire, and peace negotiations commenced in August. However, Maoist insurgents continued to carry out violent acts, prompting tens of thousands of people to take part in demonstrations against the fighting. In October Parliament approved the establishment of a new Armed Police Force. The third round of peace talks, which took place in November, ended in failure, owing to the Maoists' continued demands for the dissolution of the Constitution, the establishment of an interim government, the election of a constituent assembly and, ultimately, a republic. Two days later the leader of the CPN (M), Pushpa Kamal Dahal (better known under his pseudonym, 'Prachanda'—'The Fierce One'), announced the end of the ceasefire. The Maoists established a parallel central government, the 'United People's Revolutionary Government', with parallel local administrations in 40 of the country's 75 districts, and direct rule in 22 districts in western Nepal. Following an escalation in the violence, on 26 November the King declared a state of national emergency. The King termed the Maoists 'terrorists' and promulgated the Terrorist and Disruptive Activities Ordinance 2001, which sanctioned a number of counter-terrorist measures, including the suspension of civil liberties and the imposition of media restrictions.

In February 2002 Maoist insurgents launched their heaviest offensive to date against government outposts; more than 150 people, mainly soldiers and police officers, were killed in the fighting. The army was subsequently instructed to use offensive as well as defensive measures to combat the insurgency. Although the opposition criticized the Government for its handling of the insurgency, it voted for a three-month extension of the state of emergency after the Prime Minister agreed to establish social and economic development programmes in poor rural areas where Maoists were active, and ensured the fair use of the emergency powers.

The violent insurgency escalated in April 2002, and in early May the army launched an intensive attack against Maoist insurgents in Rolpa district, resulting in the deaths of more than 500 guerrillas, according to government sources. A series of counter-attacks and attacks ensued, leading to further hundreds of fatalities. Deuba tabled a parliamentary motion proposing a further extension of the state of emergency, prompting strong opposition from within and outside his party. Growing rifts in the NCP led King Gyanendra unexpectedly to dissolve the House of Representatives on 22 May, on the recommendation of the Prime Minister. A general election was scheduled to take place on 13 November, and the incumbent Government was instructed to rule the country in the interim. Political leaders of all affiliations strongly condemned this decision. On 23 May Deuba was suspended from his party and three days later was expelled from the NCP for three years. In late May King Gyanendra extended the state of emergency by three months.

In the mean time, in February 2002 the UML and its break-away faction, the ML, merged. In June the NCP officially split during a 'general convention' held by the Deuba faction. Eventually, in September the Election Commission recognized the faction led by G. P. Koirala as the official NCP. Several days later Deuba's minority breakaway faction registered as a new political party, the Nepali Congress Party—Democratic (NCP—D). Meanwhile, in April the NSP split into two factions and in July the UPF merged with another communist party, the National People's Front, to form the People's Front Nepal (Janamorcha Nepal).

The state of emergency expired in August 2002 and the Maoists consequently intensified their violent campaign. In October Deuba requested King Gyanendra to postpone the general election (scheduled for November) by one year, citing the deteriorating law and order situation. The King responded by dismissing the Prime Minister and the acting Council of Ministers. He appointed a nine-member interim Government, headed by former premier and monarchist Lokendra Bahadur Chand, and postponed the general election indefinitely. The NCP, UML and legal experts condemned the dismissal of Deuba and his Government and the establishment of a new Council of Ministers as unconstitutional. In December the human rights organization Amnesty International issued a damning report on the human rights situation in Nepal since the collapse of peace talks in November 2001. The army and Armed Police Force were severely criticized for the alleged 'unprecedented levels' of human rights abuses, including torture, arbitrary detention and deaths in custody. In addition, the report accused Maoist insurgents of torturing and killing captives, taking hostages and recruiting children. The report claimed that nearly one-half of the 4,366 people who had died in the conflict since late 2001 were civilians, killed by both security forces and Maoists.

In January 2003 the CPN (M) and the Government announced an immediate ceasefire and agreed to resume peace negotiations after the Government agreed to declassify Maoist activists as terrorists, to withdraw rewards offered for the arrest of Maoist leaders and to cancel international police warrants issued for the guerrilla leaders. Negotiations from February resulted in some progress, with the interim Government agreeing to release several Maoist detainees and to restrict the movement of army troops; however, the third round of negotiations in August ended in impasse over the Maoists' demand for an elected assembly to draft a new constitution. The Maoist leader Prachanda ended the seven-month ceasefire and withdrew from the peace process, while the Government reclassified the insurgents as terrorists.

In the mean time, at the end of May 2003 Prime Minister Chand resigned in response to pressure from leaders of the major political parties. On 4 June the King appointed monarchist and former premier Surya Bahadur Thapa as Prime Minister, rejecting the nomination by the five opposition parties of M. K. Nepal, the General Secretary of the UML. One week later the King appointed a new interim Council of Ministers, which was composed entirely of members of the monarchist RPP. Opposition parties held a large demonstration in Kathmandu, demanding Thapa's resignation, the reinstatement of the legislature and the establishment of an all-party government. On 1 September the Government banned all demonstrations or public gatherings of five or more people in the Kathmandu valley, citing fears of infiltration by Maoist guerrillas. Within days, more than 1,000 pro-democracy protesters, including former premier G. P. Koirala, were arrested for defying the ban and taking part in a demonstration.

The CPN (M) fully resumed its violent campaign in September 2003. In January 2004 the Maoists announced the formation of autonomous people's governments in 10 districts under their control. At the end of the month the CPN (M) stated that it would give priority to development in these areas, and that representatives of the King and the USA (which had proscribed the Maoist party in October 2003 and which was providing the Nepalese army with military assistance for its campaign against the insurgents) were banned from operating in districts under Maoist control. The violence increased, meanwhile, and the Maoists organized a series of disruptive nationwide strikes. The number of people killed in the eight-year 'people's war' had risen sharply to more than 9,130 by March 2004, of whom more than 1,500 had died since the collapse of the ceasefire in August 2003.

In March 2004 the five main opposition parties (including the NCP, hitherto a committed supporter of the constitutional monarchy), announced that a constitutional monarchy had not been successful and that, henceforth, their movement would be directed at achieving the establishment of a republic. In May the Prime Minister tendered his resignation as a result of the continuing political impasse. In June the King appointed Sher Bahadur Deuba as Prime Minister for the third time; two members of the NCP (D) were appointed to a limited Council of Ministers, in which Deuba held the majority of portfolios. The Council was expanded to 31 members in the following month and incorporated ministers from the four-party coalition—comprising the NCP (D), the UML, the RPP and the NSP—that had been formed following the resignation of Prime Minister Thapa.

In November 2004 Prime Minister Deuba set the Maoist rebels a deadline of 13 January 2005 to commence peace talks with the Government; however, Prachanda rejected the proposed deadline. The rejection led to disagreement within the Government over the feasibility of holding elections amid the ongoing insurgency. The Government was destabilized further in November when the founding President of the RPP, former Prime Minister Thapa, announced that he intended to launch a new political party, effectively creating a split once again within the RPP (the Chand and Thapa factions had reunited in 2000).

King Gyanendra imposes direct rule

In February 2005 King Gyanendra abruptly dismissed Prime Minister Deuba and his Government, declared an indefinite state of emergency and announced that, henceforth, he would rule Nepal directly. All communications links into and out of Nepal were severed temporarily, censorship was imposed on the media and former ministers were placed under house arrest. The King claimed that his actions were necessitated by the Prime Minister's failure to halt the Maoist insurgency and to hold legislative elections in the country. In an attempt to prevent protests, the King ordered the detention of large numbers of political activists. Maoist rebels subsequently instigated a two-week blockade of national highways in protest against the King's actions. Shortly after he had assumed supreme power, the King appointed a new, 10-member Council of Ministers, under his chairmanship. King Gyanendra's assumption of power met with an unfavourable international response, with Nepal's key allies, India and the United Kingdom, suspending military aid to the country and several nations recalling their ambassadors from Nepal in protest.

In March 2005 Thapa announced the foundation of his new political party, the Rashtriya Janashakti Party (RJP—National People's Power Party). Meanwhile, the Maoist insurgency intensified, with several clashes taking place between rebels and government troops. The state of emergency was lifted at the end of April, although public meetings and demonstrations continued to be prohibited, and police powers of arrest and detention were extended. In July former Prime Minister Deuba was convicted by the newly established Royal Commission for Corruption Control (RCCC)—a body Deuba refused to recognize—of charges of embezzlement relating to the issuing of a water contract and sentenced to a two-year prison term. (Deuba was released when the RCCC was outlawed in January 2006.)

Meanwhile, in May 2005 an alliance of seven political parties, including the NCP, announced a joint agenda for the restoration of democracy in Nepal, demanding that King Gyanendra end his period of direct rule and that the House of Representatives, which had been dissolved in 2002, be recalled. Moreover, the seven-party alliance subsequently established a dialogue with the CPN (M). In September 2005 the Maoists announced a three-month, unilateral ceasefire, an offer to which the Government responded cautiously. In November the seven-party alliance announced that it had reached a 12-point agreement with the Maoist rebels intended to restore democracy to Nepal. The agreement included a boycott of the February 2006 municipal elections and the election of a constituent assembly, the latter being a long-standing Maoist demand.

In January 2006 the CPN (M) stated that the ceasefire had come to an end, owing to the Government continuing to authorize offensive operations against the rebels. The insurgency subsequently intensified. In the following month the municipal elections were held, taking place in only 36 of the 58 municipal councils owing to an insufficient number of candidates and against the background of a four-day general strike co-ordinated by the Maoists. Turnout reached an estimated 20% of registered voters, according to official figures, although the major opposition parties, which boycotted the polls, claimed that the figure was significantly lower. In March the Maoists instigated an indefinite blockade of Kathmandu in another attempt to force King Gyanendra to end his direct rule.

Reinstatement of Parliament and the Comprehensive Peace Agreement

In April 2006 the opposition alliance called a nationwide general strike. Mass demonstrations followed, in response to which the Government announced the imposition of a 'shoot-on-sight' curfew. As thousands of protesters defied the curfew and violent clashes ensued, King Gyanendra's position appeared increasingly untenable. Following almost three weeks of demonstrations, the King offered to permit the opposition alliance to name a new Prime Minister. However, this offer was rejected and the protests continued. Several days later, in accordance with opposition demands, the King announced that he would reinstate Parliament. The CPN (M), however, vowed to continue its insurgency, accusing the political parties of betraying the 12-point agreement. It did, none the less, agree to observe a three-month ceasefire, which was extended periodically. The opposition alliance subsequently nominated former Prime Minister G. P. Koirala to lead a new Government. The House of Representatives formally convened at the end of April and approved legislation enabling the establishment of a constituent assembly to redraft the country's Constitution.

On 3 May 2006 the Council of Ministers announced a ceasefire with the CPN (M), offering to declassify the group as a terrorist organization in exchange for the holding of peace talks; numerous Maoist prisoners were also released. While the Maoists insisted on the release of all their prisoners, as well as the abolition of the existing Constitution, legislature and monarchy, they attended preliminary discussions with the Government on 26 May. Meanwhile, on 18 May the House of Representatives approved a resolution divesting the King of his role as Commander-in-Chief of the Army, his authority to make military appointments and nominate an heir, and his legal immunity and exemption from taxes. Nepal was officially transformed from a Hindu state into a secular state in an attempt to extricate the concept of a divinely instituted monarchy from the national ideology. The transfer of power away from the monarchy continued in June: the King was no longer able to veto legislation, and he lost the authority to announce government policy.

In June 2006 talks between Koirala and Prachanda led to the announcement that the CPN (M) would be included in a new interim government, which was to oversee elections for a constituent assembly. At Koirala's request, a UN team arrived in Nepal at the end of July to determine weapons management strategies for the Nepalese army and the People's Liberation Army (PLA) of the Maoists. In August it was agreed that the movement of both government and rebel forces would be restricted. In October further negotiations produced a tentative schedule for elections to the constituent assembly. Prachanda reiterated his demand for the declaration of a republic. The Comprehensive Peace Agreement (CPA) that was signed by Koirala and Prachanda on 21 November, provided for the establishment of an interim constitution, assembly and council of ministers by 1 December, and was hailed as the end of a civil war that had claimed the lives of more than 13,000 people. A disarmament agreement soon followed, the terms of which included the complete cessation of hostilities by both sides. The Maoist military forces were to be contained in cantonments and their weapons registered and impounded under UN supervision, while the Nepalese army, which was to remain in barracks, would also have its arms locked away.

With the signing of an Interim Constitution in December 2006, constitutional powers of governance were reassigned from the monarchy to the Prime Minister. The National Assembly and House of Representatives were dissolved with the promulgation of the Interim Constitution in mid-January 2007. In their place, an Interim Parliament was established; this body included members of the original 1999 Parliament as well as appointees selected by the seven-party alliance and the CPN (M). A few days later the Maoists announced the closure of their People's Governments and People's Courts. The UN Mission in Nepal (UNMIN) was established in January 2007, at the request of the seven-party alliance and the CPN (M). UNMIN's main task was to help in overseeing fair and free elections to the constituent assembly and to monitor the proper enactment of the CPA (including the disarmament and integration of the PLA into the regular army).

Meanwhile, in 2007 groups representing the Madhesi people of southern Nepal, which were demanding increased independence for their region and greater representation in government, organized demonstrations and strikes to draw attention to their campaign. The protests were at times violent and clashes with police resulted in several fatalities. Following negotiations between Madhesi groups and the Government, constitutional amendments approved by the Interim Parliament in March provided for proportional representation and a federal style of government, and the revision of constituency boundaries to grant one-half of parliamentary seats to the southern plains, where an estimated 50% of the population resided. Despite these concessions, an element of dissatisfaction remained, with the Madhesi Jana Adhikar Forum Nepal (Madhesi People's Rights Forum Nepal—MPRFN) demanding total autonomy.

In April 2007 an Interim Council of Ministers was approved by the Interim Parliament. G. P. Koirala was reappointed interim Prime Minister, heading an administration that included five members of the CPN (M). The UML was assigned responsibility for foreign affairs and the newly created peace and reconstruction portfolio. In May the Government announced the postponement of elections to the constituent assembly until November, and in July the CPN (M) registered itself as a political party with the Election Commission of Nepal.

Although it had been agreed that the fate of the monarchy lay with the constituent assembly, demands for the declaration of a republic continued to be made. Seven royal palaces were nationalized by the Government in August 2007. In September the NCP and the NCP (D) announced their merger. In the same month the CPN (M) withdrew from the Government, citing the continuing existence of the monarchy and disagreement over the composition of the constituent assembly. A period of intense negotiation ensued, during which the constituent assembly elections were postponed indefinitely and the future of the peace process itself appeared to hang in the balance. However, in December the CPN (M) returned to government after the Interim Parliament approved constitutional amendments ensuring the abolition of the monarchy upon the approval of the constituent assembly. More than one-half of the assembly was to be determined by a system of proportional representation, with the bulk of the remainder to be directly elected, in addition to several appointed deputies; elections were scheduled for April 2008.

Meanwhile, in the latter half of 2007 the security situation deteriorated in the Terai region, where the MPRFN and other Madhesi groups continued to campaign for autonomy. In December a Madhesi cabinet minister and several Madhesi members of the Interim Parliament tendered their resignations, citing the Government's failure to address the ongoing unrest in the Terai. Shortly after these resignations, the Samyukta Loktantrik Madhesi Morcha (SLMM—United Democratic Madhesi Front), an alliance of three political organizations—the MPRFN, the Sadbhavana Party (a breakaway faction of the NSP) and the Terai Madhes Loktantrik Party (Terai Madhes Democratic Party)—was established. In February 2008 blockades orchestrated by the SLMM caused widespread disruption in the south of the country and led to fuel shortages in Kathmandu and elsewhere. Later in the month the Government and the SLMM signed an agreement ending the blockades and allowing for increased autonomy and representation of Madhesis on party lists and in institutions such as the Nepalese army.

The Maoists take power and the monarchy is abolished

At the constituent assembly elections, which were held on 10 April 2008, the CPN (M) won 220 out of a total of 575 elected seats under the mixed electoral system, twice as many as the NCP, which came second with 110 seats. The UML secured 103 seats, putting it in third place and prompting the resignation of the party's General Secretary, M. K. Nepal, while the MPRFN won 52 seats. Although the period leading up to the polls had been marked by bombings and violent clashes, the day of the elections was largely peaceful, with a voter turnout of around 60%. Prachanda declared victory on behalf of the CPN (M) and indicated that he would lead a coalition government. The CPN (M) also urged the King to abdicate voluntarily in advance of the inevitable declaration of a republic. This declaration was duly made following overwhelming approval at the inaugural session of the Constituent Assembly on 28 May, when the monarchy was abolished; King Gyanendra voluntarily vacated the royal palace in Kathmandu in June, opting to move to his summer residence outside the city.

Meanwhile, the CPN (M)'s lack of a parliamentary majority proved to be an obstacle in the formation of a new government, with a lack of consensus between the three major parties over the mandate of the new post of president. In June the interim Prime Minister, G. P. Koirala stated that his resignation would come into effect upon the election of a candidate to the presidency, which, it was decided, would be a largely ceremonial role. In a separate development, the seven-party alliance had reportedly been dissolved. Ram Baran Yadav, who was supported by the NCP, the UML and the MPRFN, was elected President on 21 July after two rounds of voting in the Constituent Assembly, defeating the CPN (M) candidate, Ramraja Prasad Singh. Notably, Yadav, Singh and new Vice-President Paramanada Jha were all Madhesis.

Despite the alliance between the NCP, the UML and the MPRFN in the presidential ballot, in August 2008 Prachanda was elected Prime Minister with the support of the UML and MPRFN in a vote held in the Constituent Assembly, defeating NCP candidate and former premier Sher Bahadur Deuba. Prachanda appointed a new Council of Ministers, comprising members of the CPN (M), the MPRFN, the Sadbhavana Party, the UML, the People's Front Nepal and the Communist Party of Nepal (United) (CPN—U). The NCP remained outside the Government, forming the opposition. On 30 October the Kingdom of Nepal officially became the Federal Democratic Republic of Nepal. A constitutional committee appointed by the Constituent Assembly began drafting the new constitution in December 2008, with a deadline of May 2010 for its promulgation. However, ongoing disputes between the Government and the opposition, and the unresolved issue of the integration of some 19,000 former Maoist fighters into the army—which strained relations between the Government and the military in early 2009—continued to hamper progress in other areas. In January 2009 the CPN (M) was restyled the Unified Communist Party of Nepal (Maoist)—UCPN (M)—following a merger with the CPN (Unity Centre-Masal).

The collapse of the Maoist Government

On 4 May 2009 Nepal was confronted with a serious political crisis following the resignation of Prime Minister Prachanda and the withdrawal of the UCPN (M) from the ruling coalition. This dramatic development resulted from President Yadav's refusal to accept Prachanda's earlier dismissal of the Chief of Army Staff, Lt-Gen. Rukmangad Katuwal, who was allegedly defying government orders to integrate former rebel fighters into the national army (claiming that they were politically indoctrinated) and was actively recruiting new personnel into the army (in contravention of the peace agreement). The UCPN (M) refused to participate in negotiations for the formation of a new coalition government unless the President reversed his decision on the reinstatement of Lt-Gen. Katuwal. On 10 May President Yadav directed the Constituent Assembly to elect a new Prime Minister by a majority vote in an attempt to end the political crisis. On 17 May an alliance of 22 political parties, including the NCP and the UML, filed a claim to form a new coalition government and appealed for a parliamentary vote to elect their candidate, the veteran communist leader M. K. Nepal, as the new prime minister. In response, Prachanda stated that the move to form a new administration that excluded the Maoists was a conspiracy to derail the peace process. None the less, M. K. Nepal was elected to the premiership and was sworn in at the end of May at the head of a new coalition Government.

The Maoists launched a series of widespread anti-Government protests and strikes and threatened to renew their revolutionary insurgency. Their demand for a parliamentary debate on the reinstatement of Lt-Gen. Katuwal (who had since retired) was rejected by Prime Minister Nepal in September 2009. The UCPN (M) responded by continuing to boycott and disrupt the proceedings of the Constituent Assembly, leading a mass rally in the capital in December and organizing a three-day national strike that paralysed the country. The political impasse continued into 2010 and the Maoists intensified their protest campaign, organizing a mass May Day rally in the capital. With the deadline for the introduction of a new constitution (28 May) approaching, the UCPN (M) announced the enforcement of an indefinite general strike. However, the strike was suspended after less than a week to alleviate the hardships being suffered by the Nepalese people and to recommence negotiations with the Government.

On 28 May 2010, following threats by President Yadav to impose emergency or presidential rule if the political impasse were not resolved, the NCP, the UML and the Maoists agreed to extend the tenure of the Constituent Assembly by one year, on the condition that Prime Minister Nepal resigned. Accordingly, M. K. Nepal announced his resignation from the premiership on 30 June; however, he and his Government were to remain in their posts in an acting capacity pending the appointment of a consensus administration by 7 July. When the formation of a new government failed to materialize by this deadline, owing to lack

of agreement between the three main parties, the President declared that the Constituent Assembly would elect a new prime minister by majority vote. This proved an extremely lengthy process: between July and November the Assembly made 16 unsuccessful attempts to elect a new premier. The main candidates in the first seven rounds of voting were Prachanda of the UCPN (M) and Ram Chandra Poudel of the NCP; the UML's candidate, Jhala Nath Khanal, withdrew from the process following his failure to win a majority of votes in the first two rounds of voting in July. On each of the seven occasions that he participated in the poll, Prachanda received more votes than his rival, but failed to achieve the requisite 301-vote majority. The deadlock in the voting process was caused by the persistent abstention of the UML and smaller parliamentary parties (notably the various Madhesi organizations), which claimed that neither candidate was acceptable. The prolonged stalemate led to economic instability (with delays in the implementation of the budget) and widespread public disillusionment with the political parties. The peace process also came to a virtual halt, with thousands of former Maoist militants remaining in UN-monitored holding camps. In September Sushil Koirala was elected as the new President of the NCP, convincingly defeating Deuba, his closest rival. At the end of the month, prior to the eighth attempt by the Constituent Assembly to elect a new prime minister, Prachanda withdrew from the contest following a pact with the UML. With the UCPN (M) now abstaining from the voting process, the sole remaining candidate, Poudel, failed to garner the required majority in the nine further polls that were held in 2010.

In November 2010 the three main parties held a series of crisis talks to discuss the stalled peace process and power-sharing and government formation. To prevent a political vacuum, the Supreme Court ruled in December that no legislators would henceforth be permitted to abstain from voting in the prime ministerial election process. In January 2011, the NCP having withdrawn its candidacy from the scheduled 17th round of prime ministerial elections, President Yadav gave the three main parties a week-long deadline to attempt once again to form a government of national consensus. However, this approach too proved unsuccessful owing to the persistent intransigence of the three parties regarding their respective claims to the leadership of the new government.

On 15 January 2011 UNMIN commenced its withdrawal from Nepal following the decision of the NCP and the UML not to request an extension of the mission's mandate (despite the Maoists' requests to do so). A few days later Prachanda formally handed responsibility for the 19,000 former PLA troops remaining in the holding camps to a special government committee (headed by the Prime Minister), which was to supervise the disarmament, integration and rehabilitation of the ex-militants.

The seven-month political stalemate finally came to an end on 3 February 2011 when the Chairman of the UML, Jhala Nath Khanal, with the support of the UCPN (M) (Prachanda having withdrawn his candidacy at the last minute), was elected Prime Minister by the Constituent Assembly. Khanal won a clear majority, with 368 of the votes cast. A few days after the inauguration of the new Prime Minister it emerged that, prior to Khanal's election, the UCPN (M) and the UML had signed a secret seven-point agreement regarding their future co-operation in government. Of some controversy were allegations that the agreement had included plans to establish a military body of former Maoist combatants that was to be separate from the country's regular army. The NCP, which had decided to stay in opposition in protest against the secret pact between the UML and the Maoists, claimed that the formation of such a body would prove highly detrimental to the peace process. In March, following several weeks of negotiations, Khanal expanded his core three-member UML Council of Ministers to include representatives of the UCPN (M); Krishna Bahadur Mahara was assigned one of the deputy premierships, but Khanal himself retained control of the influential home affairs portfolio. The UML and the Maoists expressed concern at the NCP's refusal to join the Government, claiming that the party's absence would jeopardize the drafting of the constitution (scheduled to be completed by 28 May) and the peace process.

In April 2011 the Council of Ministers was further enlarged to incorporate 12 new UML ministers and state ministers, and in early May, following protracted negotiations with the Maoists, Prime Minister Khanal announced a further expansion of the Government, appointing 12 new UCPN (M) ministers and state ministers. In a major concession to the Maoists, Mahara was accorded the disputed home affairs portfolio, in addition to his existing role as Deputy Prime Minister. The appointment, which effectively gave the UCPN (M) control over Nepal's internal security, was strongly criticized by the opposition and by some members of the UML. The coalition Government was further broadened with the addition of three members of the regional MPRFN—party leader Upendra Yadav was appointed Deputy Prime Minister and Minister of Foreign Affairs—and one representative from both the CPN (U) and the CPN (ML). The allocation of the home affairs portfolio appeared to exacerbate internal schisms within the UCPN (M). Barshaman Pun, a leading Maoist candidate for the home affairs post, resigned as Minister of Peace and Reconstruction; four further Maoist ministerial nominees refused to take their oaths of office during May, as a result of factional disagreements. At the end of May the Government and the main opposition parties signed a five-point agreement that provided for a further three-month extension of the Constituent Assembly, during which the preliminary draft of the new constitution would have to be completed and a functional national unity government formed. Furthermore, Prime Minister Khanal was to resign once consensus had been reached on the composition of a new government.

The Maoists return to power

On 14 August 2011 Prime Minister Khanal tendered his resignation, citing his failure to forge political unity and to make any real progress in the peace process (including the drafting of a new constitution). On 28 August the Constituent Assembly elected Dr Baburam Bhattarai, a Vice-Chairman of the UCPN (M) and former Minister of Finance under Prachanda, as the new Prime Minister. Bhattarai, who was supported by various Madhesi-based parties, won 340 votes, while his only rival, Ram Chandra Poudel of the NCP, received 235 votes. Bhattarai appointed the leader of the MPRFN (Democratic), Bijaya Kumar Gachchhadar, as Deputy Prime Minister and Minister of Home Affairs, but both the NCP and the UML refused to participate in the new Government. Not surprisingly, given the political instability, the deadline of 31 August for drawing up the draft constitution was not met, and on 29 August the Interim Parliament extended the term of the Constituent Assembly by another three months. In early September Prime Minister Bhattarai appointed 12 more ministers to his coalition Government, which now comprised members of the UCPN (M), two factions of the MPRFN, two factions of the Terai Madhes Loktantrik Party and two factions of the Sadbhavana Party. Of especial note was the appointment of Narayan Kaji Shrestha of the UCPN (M) as Deputy Prime Minister and Minister of Foreign Affairs. In October the Prime Minister dismissed Minister of Defence Sarat Singh Bhandari and Minister of Land Reform and Management Prabhu Sah; the former—a senior member of the MPRFN (Democratic)—had made controversial remarks in public regarding the possible future secession of Terai districts from Nepal, while the latter was implicated in a murder case.

Meanwhile, following their party's return to power, in September 2011 the Maoist commanders in the seven largest cantonments around the country commenced their official hand-over of weapons to a special multi-party committee. Despite opposition from a hardline faction within the UCPN (M) led by one of the party's Vice-Chairmen, Mohan Baidya, there was a major breakthrough in the peace process on 1 November when the country's main political parties signed a seven-point agreement, according to which around one-third of the former PLA combatants (some 6,500 men and women) were to be integrated into the regular forces and the remainder were to be offered either a voluntary retirement payment or a rehabilitation package including vocational training. In addition, it was agreed that a truth and reconciliation commission and a missing persons commission would be established, that the Young Communist League—a paramilitary group within the UCPN (M)—would be disbanded, that land captured or confiscated by the PLA would be returned to its original owners, and that a cross-party state restructuring commission would be created to oversee the transition of the country into a federal system.

In the course of November 2011 Prime Minister Bhattarai further expanded his Council of Ministers, bringing the total number of government members to 49 (the largest in Nepal's history). As expected, on 29 November the Interim Parliament extended the term of the Constituent Assembly by another six months; the deadline to complete the draft constitution was now 27 May 2012. In February 2012 a bomb explosion in the centre of Kathmandu killed three people; an obscure militant group called the Unified National Liberation Front claimed responsibility,

citing government corruption and fuel price rises as its main motivation.

In April 2012 all 15 Maoist cantonments, and the arms caches therein, were brought under the direct control of the Nepalese army. Nevertheless, the peace process was still hampered by significant disagreements between the main parties regarding the drafting of the new constitution; notably, over the formation of the proposed federal administrative units. In May, in an effort to expedite progress on the constitution, Prime Minister Bhattarai forged an agreement with the main opposition parties on the establishment of a Government of national unity. The Council of Ministers was duly dissolved and a new cabinet, comprising members of the UCPN (M), the NCP, the UML, the SLMM bloc and a number of smaller parties, was appointed. Bhattarai remained as Prime Minister, while Deputy Prime Ministers Shrestha and Gachchhadhar were reappointed to their posts; Krishna Prasad Sitaula of the NCP and Ishwar Pokharel of the UML were also appointed as Deputy Prime Ministers.

At the same time, the main parties were involved in intensive negotiations on the key outstanding constitutional questions, namely the federal divisions and the constitutional status of the President and the Prime Minister. In May 2012 the parties reportedly agreed that the position of President would be directly elected, while the Prime Minister would be elected by parliament; the extent of the president's powers was not confirmed. The federalism issue, however, remained a major obstacle to the finalization of the constitution, with the UCPN (M) and Madhesi parties advocating provincial demarcation according to ethnicity, but with the NCP and the UML concerned that this approach would be divisive; there was further disagreement over the number of provinces. On 24 May the Supreme Court rejected a proposal by the Government to extend the tenure of the Constituent Assembly by a further three months. The NCP had criticized the proposal and withdrew from the Government on the same day. With limited options within the existing political framework, Bhattarai opted to call fresh constituent assembly elections for 22 November. There was little support for his decision, which other parties in the Government claimed was unconstitutional. The UML and two other parties withdrew from the coalition Government and demanded Bhattarai's resignation. At the end of May, in light of the dissolution of the Constituent Assembly and the consequent expiry of Bhattarai's parliamentary membership, the President gave the Government caretaker status pending the formation of a new administration.

In June 2012 the hardline faction led by Mohan Baidya formally announced its split from the UCPN (M), its primary purpose being to attain the original objectives of the 'people's war', which, it claimed, the UCPN (M) leaders had abandoned. The splinter group assumed the movement's original name, the Communist Party of Nepal (Maoist)—CPN (Maoist). More than a quarter of the UCPN (M)'s central committee was said to have joined the CPN (Maoist).

Formation of a caretaker Government

In July 2012 the failure of the major parties to agree on elections forced the UCPN (M) to postpone the planned November poll. The NCP and the UML continued to demand Bhattarai's resignation and insisted on the formation of a new coalition government consisting of all the main parties as a precondition for their participation in elections. The UCPN (M) urged the NCP and the UML to join the current Government. The Election Commission also maintained that the proposed November elections were unviable, owing to the absence of appropriate constitutional provisions for a second set of constituent assembly elections. In November the Government announced that the elections would take place by mid-May 2013. In January, as the political stalemate continued, violent protests were staged and Prachanda warned that the CPA was under threat if the various parties were unable to come to an agreement. A breakthrough was finally reached in February when the main parties agreed to a postponement of the election date to 21 June and the formation of a non-partisan interim government to oversee the election process. The hardline CPN (Maoist) refused to support the decision and organized a nationwide strike in protest. Nevertheless, a formal agreement involving the main parties was signed in March, declaring the establishment of an 'Interim Election Council', comprising former civil servants and headed by the Chief Justice of the Supreme Court. Bhattarai stood down as Prime Minister and Chief Justice Khil Raj Regmi was sworn in as Chairman of the Interim Election Council and Minister of Defence soon afterwards; as agreed, Regmi subsequently appointed 10 former high-ranking bureaucrats to assume responsibility for all other cabinet portfolios.

In the months following the appointment of the caretaker administration, the CPN (Maoist), with the support of numerous smaller opposition parties, continued to mount protests against the political process; the dissident Maoists demanded the appointment of an all-party coalition government and threatened to disrupt the forthcoming elections should their demands not be met. At the same time, representatives of the UCPN (M), the NCP, the UML and the MPRFN formed a high-level committee (the High-Level Political Mechanism—HLPM) to address the numerous political and constitutional obstacles and to expedite the setting of a date for elections to the new constituent assembly. In June 2013, as widely expected, the interim Government confirmed that the elections would be postponed until 19 November. In September, in an effort to encourage some of the dissident parties to participate in the electoral process, President Yadav endorsed a request by the HLPM to increase the number of members in the new constituent assembly from 491, as originally proposed, to 601 (equal to the number of seats in the previous assembly). The HLPM also agreed that 240 seats in the new constituent assembly should be decided by direct election and 335 seats under a proportional representation (PR) system (with 26 members to be nominated by the cabinet).

Recent developments: the 2013 Constituent Assembly elections

In the weeks leading up to the constituent assembly elections, violent incidents occurred throughout the country as the CPN (Maoist)-led opposition movement orchestrated a series of strikes in protest against the political process (the dissident Maoists demanded that the elections be deferred until April 2014). None the less, the elections were held, as scheduled, on 19 November 2013, with a record turnout of over 75% of the electorate reported. The elections marked a political resurgence for the NCP and the UML, who emerged as the two largest parties, securing a total of 196 seats and 175 seats, respectively. The NCP won 105 of the 240 directly elected seats (with 29.8% of the vote) and 91 of the seats allocated by PR; the UML secured 91 directly elected seats (with 27.6% of the vote) and 84 PR seats. The declining influence of the UCPN (M) resulted in its obtaining only 26 directly elected seats (17.8% of the vote) alongside its 54 PR seats. The royalist RPP won 24 seats in total, becoming the fourth largest party in the legislature. The Madhesi parties also fared poorly: the Madhesi Jana Adhikar Forum (Loktantrik), a splinter group of the MPRFN, won 14 seats, while the MPRFN itself won 10 seats (compared with 52 seats in the previous assembly). Observers surmised that the success of the centrist parties demonstrated that the electorate broadly opposed the federation of Nepal along ethnic or linguistic lines, an objective for which some far left and regionalist parties had campaigned. None the less, neither of the two leading parties had come close to securing an overall majority, and the country was again confronted by the prospect of government based on fragile political compromises. Several bombings were reported in Kathmandu on polling day, injuring at least five people, while other violent incidents including arson and vandalism were reported in the provinces. In western Nepal, a Maoist stronghold, attacks on polling stations and the looting of ballot papers were reported, amid very low voter participation. Police arrested at least 120 people in connection with the election-day incidents.

Prachanda, who lost his own constituency seat but was allocated a seat via PR, called for a suspension of the vote count, claiming that the election had been rigged. However, both domestic and foreign observers, including the EU and former US President Jimmy Carter, stated that the elections were reasonably free and fair, despite incidents of violence. NCP President Sushil Koirala urged the UCPN (M) to participate in the new assembly and to join a consensus government. In a further conciliatory gesture, he offered to allocate the 26 nominated seats in the Assembly to Baidya's CPN (Maoist), which had opposed the elections. However, both the UCPN (M) and the CPN (Maoist) continued to dispute the legitimacy of the election results and demanded an independent inquiry into the conduct of the elections. In late December, the main parties reached agreement on the establishment of a board of inquiry into the allegations of electoral fraud, which encouraged the UCPN (M) eventually to participate in the new legislature.

In early January 2014 the Electoral Commission submitted the final election results to the President, allowing the formation of the Constituent Assembly; the members were sworn in on 21 January. After a delay, during which the UCPN (M) and RPP decided that they would not participate in government, NCP President Sushil Koirala was elected unopposed as Prime Minister by the Constituent Assembly on 10 February, securing 405 votes in favour and 148 against. A new Council of Ministers, comprising 10 members each from the NCP and the UML, was sworn in on 25 February, following protracted negotiations between the two parties. The UML was awarded the key foreign affairs and home affairs portfolios, allocated to, respectively, Mahendra Pandey and Bam Dev Gautam (who was also appointed to the position of Deputy Prime Minister, as was Prakash Man Singh of the NCP). In April Prime Minister Koirala effected a limited expansion of the cabinet, adding two members of the RPP and a member of the CPN (ML). The Constituent Assembly, meanwhile, elected to endorse and continue the work carried out by the previous assembly, and declared its intention to draft a new constitution by January 2015.

In February 2014 K. P. Sharma Oli was elected parliamentary group leader of the UML, defeating Jhala Nath Khanal. In July Oli was elected also as Chairman of the UML, succeeding former Prime Minister M. K. Nepal. In March, in what was viewed as a potentially significant development, the leaders of the UCPN (M) and the CPN (Maoist), Prachanda and Baidya, issued a joint statement demanding that the Government cease arresting their members for alleged transgressions during the civil war and agree to form a working group on issues of mutual concern; both parties also demanded the formation of a truth and reconciliation commission to investigate incidents that took place during the civil war, a previously agreed component of the peace process. The joint statement inevitably provoked speculation that a Maoist reunification was imminent. In the same month the UCPN (M) announced that it was forming an alliance in the Constituent Assembly with several other parties (mainly Madhesi and other ethnic-based parties) committed to an ethnic identity-based federal model of governance, which would ensure representation of the Madhesi and other marginalized groups.

Following the adoption of various amendments proposed by the NCP, UML and UCPN (M), in April 2014 the Constituent Assembly approved a bill concerning the establishment of a Truth and Reconciliation Commission (TRC) and a Commission on Enforced Disappearance (CED), both of which were important conditions of the peace process. The TRC bill, however, attracted criticism from international human rights organizations, including Amnesty International, Human Rights Watch and the International Commission of Jurists, which claimed its provisions violated international human rights norms. The commissions were constituted in February 2015.

The Constituent Assembly's struggle to formulate an inclusive constitution continued during 2014, with participants' substantial differences in approach demanding compromise and consensus on every front. The NCP and UML argued for a more centralized system of governance, with no more than seven provinces, to be divided along geographic and economic lines; and a parliament elected by a simple majority system. The opposition alliance co-ordinated by the UCPN (M) reiterated its support for a federal system based on ethnic identity, with at least 10 provinces; a directly elected executive President; a mixed electoral system, including some proportional representation; and the establishment of a constitutional court with jurisdiction over disputes concerning the Constitution. Even the method of approving the constitution was contested, with the NCP and UML preferring a two-thirds' majority vote in the Constituent Assembly and the opposition alliance threatening to boycott any draft that was not first agreed by broad consensus.

In early January 2015 a 19-party alliance led by the UCPN (M) organized a general strike and a series of mostly peaceful demonstrations, which brought Kathmandu to a halt, in protest against the continued failure to draft the constitution. A few days before the 22 January deadline for the Constituent Assembly to produce a draft of the constitution, with some compromises already reached, violent protests occurred, including inside the Constituent Assembly itself. The deadline was missed, and the Maoists organized further protests, including nationwide rallies in late February and a demonstration in Kathmandu which was attended by some 30,000 people, as President Koirala called for dialogue to be resumed in an effort to resolve the crisis. In March the UCPN (M) ended a six-week boycott of parliamentary committee meetings and returned to negotiations with the ruling coalition, although Prachanda had threatened in the previous month to form a parallel government. Also in March, it was reported that Prachanda and Baidya had begun discussing initiatives for the reunification of the UCPN (M) and the CPN (Maoist), which raised renewed concerns as to the stability of the peace process.

Political concerns, however, were overshadowed by a devastating earthquake with a magnitude of 7.8 on the Richter scale (the most severe to strike the country in 80 years), which struck central Nepal on 25 April 2015. With its epicentre in the central Gorkha district, the earthquake and a series of aftershocks affected at least 30 of Nepal's 75 districts, mainly in western and central regions, causing widespread damage to buildings and infrastructure in the heavily populated Kathmandu Valley as well as in remote mountain villages. By 10 May the death toll was estimated at in excess of 8,000 people, with more than 16,000 people reportedly injured. According to the UN, up to 8m. people had potentially been affected by the disaster. A major international relief effort was quickly launched, although there were severe difficulties in delivering aid to remote mountainous areas that had been rendered inaccessible by the earthquake and resulting avalanches. As well as the major loss of life, extensive damage was reported at some of the country's most important religious and cultural monuments, including the Durbar squares in Kathmandu, Bhaktapur and Lalitpur, which form part of the Kathmandu Valley UNESCO world heritage site. At a special parliamentary session on 7 May, legislators endorsed a cross-party resolution concerning the complete reconstruction of homes, buildings and monuments destroyed by the earthquake. According to the Ministry of Home Affairs, almost 289,000 houses had suffered severe damage and more than 250,000 were partially damaged.

Regional Affairs

In 1978 an earlier Trade and Transit Treaty between Nepal and India was replaced by two new treaties, one concerning bilateral trade between the two countries, the other allowing Nepal to develop trade with other countries via India. Relations with India deteriorated considerably in March 1989, however, when India decided not to renew the treaties, insisting that a common treaty covering both issues be negotiated. Nepal refused, stressing the importance of keeping the treaties separate, on the grounds that trade issues are negotiable, whereas the right of transit is a recognized right of landlocked countries. In response, India closed 13 of the 15 transit points through which most of Nepal's trade was conducted, causing severe shortages of food and fuel. It was widely believed that a major issue aggravating the dispute was Nepal's recent purchase of weapons from the People's Republic of China, which, according to India, violated the Treaty of Peace and Friendship concluded by India and Nepal in 1950. A joint communiqué was signed by the two countries in June 1990, restoring trade relations and reopening the transit points, and assuring mutual consultations on matters of security. A few days earlier, as an apparent gesture of goodwill to India, the Nepalese Government had deferred indefinitely the delivery of the final consignment of Chinese weapons destined for Nepal.

The visit to Kathmandu by the Indian Prime Minister in February 1991 (the first official visit to Nepal by an Indian head of government since 1977) helped to reaffirm the traditionally amicable ties between the two countries. Separate trade and transit treaties were signed during a visit by Prime Minister Koirala to India in December 1991. In February 1996 the Prime Ministers of the two countries formally signed a treaty in New Delhi, India, regarding the shared utilization of the waters of the Mahakali River basin (for irrigation, general consumption and the production of hydroelectric power). The costs and benefits of the project, which involved the construction of a massive hydroelectric power plant, were to be divided between Nepal and India. The Mahakali Treaty was formally endorsed during a visit to Nepal by the Indian Prime Minister in June 1997, and India granted Nepal access to Bangladeshi ports through a new transit facility across Indian territory. Tension between the two countries persisted, however, over border demarcation disputes and, in particular, on the Indian border police's use of territory that Nepal claimed as its own in the far west of the country (namely the strategically situated Kalapani junction between India, Nepal and China).

In 2001 India supplied Nepal with military equipment to assist its neighbour in its campaign against the Maoist insurgency; India also extended offers of financial assistance to the Nepalese authorities. However, from 2003 the Indian Government became increasingly concerned about King Gyanendra's perceived disregard for democracy. India condemned the King's assumption of executive power in February 2005 and suspended military aid to Nepal. It also intensified security along the shared border, owing to increased fears of infiltration by Maoist insurgents and their possible co-operation with rebels operating in India's northeastern states. In July India resumed non-lethal military aid to Nepal. During the Maoists' tenure of power in Nepal in 2008–09 there was growing apprehension among certain sectors of the Indian authorities regarding the Nepalese Maoists' perceived anti-India stance as well as their links with China and with India's own Maoist insurgencies.

In August 2009 the new Prime Minister, M. K. Nepal, made an official visit to India during which the two countries signed a trade treaty and India pledged to assist its neighbour with development projects such as road and rail links (notably the Terai Roads Project, which envisaged the construction of more than 1,450 km of asphalted roads in the Terai region). In January 2011 President Yadav undertook an official visit to India, holding discussions with the Indian Government regarding ongoing attempts to break the political deadlock in Nepal (see *Domestic Political Affairs*); Yadav returned to India for further consultations in December 2012. In October 2011 Nepal's new Maoist Prime Minister, Baburam Bhattarai, signed a Bilateral Investment Promotion and Protection Agreement with India; the agreement was primarily intended to promote Indian investment in Nepal by protecting the rights of foreign investors and providing for compensation to investors in case of losses due to war or civil unrest. In April 2013 Prachanda met with Indian Prime Minister Manmohan Singh in New Delhi, whereupon the Maoist leader gave assurances that the UCPN (M) would not allow anti-Indian activities to be carried out in Nepal, and promoted the concept of trilateral co-operation between Nepal, India and China. In October India resumed the supply of arms to the Nepalese army, citing the successful integration of former Maoist fighters into the army (the CPA of 2006 had prohibited the import of armaments into Nepal). At an intergovernmental conference in December, following the successful conduct of Nepal's constituent assembly elections, officials from both countries discussed plans to boost Indian investment in Nepal, improve transit facilities, control illicit trade and develop hydroelectric facilities in Nepal. In August 2014 the new Indian Prime Minister, Narendra Modi, paid a brief official visit to Nepal (the first visit of its kind in 17 years); Modi expressed support for Nepal's ongoing process of constitutional reform, and announced that India would provide up to US $1,000m. in concessional loans for hydroelectric and other infrastructure projects in Nepal (see *Economic Affairs*). In September the two countries signed a Power Trade Agreement which committed both sides to buy and sell electricity during times of shortage. In 2013/14 India remained Nepal's largest trading partner, accounting for almost 67% of Nepal's total external trade.

China has contributed significantly to the Nepalese economy. The first meeting of a joint committee on economic co-operation took place in 1984. The committee met for a second time (and thenceforth annually) in 1986, when China agreed to increase its imports from Nepal in order to minimize trade imbalances. Relations between Nepal and China improved further during the late 1980s and 1990s, as indicated by reciprocal visits made by high-ranking Nepalese and Chinese officials (notably, a state visit to Nepal by the Chinese President, Jiang Zemin, in 1996). In 2001 Nepal and China signed a co-operation agreement to improve cross-border trade, increase road and aviation links, and promote tourism. China subsequently continued to expand its investments in Nepal, particularly in the areas of hydroelectricity, telecommunications and road construction. In August 2011, during a visit to Kathmandu by a high-ranking Chinese delegation, the two countries signed four agreements on bilateral co-operation worth some NRs 1,000m. In March 2012, shortly after a politically significant visit to the Nepalese capital by Chinese Premier Wen Jiabao, the Nepalese Government signed an agreement with China's Three Gorges Corporation for a US $1,600m. hydroelectricity project, with 75% Chinese investment, constituting at that time the largest foreign investment project in the country to date. Chinese-supported projects launched during 2013 and 2014 included major improvements to the Kathmandu ring-road; a loan agreement for the Nepal Airlines Corporation to procure additional aircraft; and the upgrading of regional airports at Bhairahawa and Pokhara to international status. In December 2014 China announced a fivefold increase in the value of its official aid to Nepal from $24m. in 2014/15 to $128m. in 2015/16; China had already overtaken India as Nepal's leading provider of foreign direct investment in the second half of 2014.

In 1985 it was agreed that Nepal's border with Tibet (the Xizang Autonomous Region) should be opened. Following the outbreak of ethnic violence in Tibet in 1989, however, the border between Nepal and Tibet was closed indefinitely. The Nepalese authorities have been consistent in their commitment to the 'One China' policy and in their efforts to repatriate refugees fleeing from Tibet. In 1993 G. P. Koirala paid an informal visit to Tibet—the first visit to the region by a Nepalese premier since the 1950s. In 1995, however, the Nepalese authorities banned a proposed peace march by Tibetans through Nepalese territory. During a visit to China by the Nepalese Minister of Foreign Affairs in 2000 an agreement was reached to allow Nepal increased use of a new road in Tibet. Greater technological and economic co-operation was also achieved, therefore noticeably increasing bilateral trade. Nepal provoked strong criticism from the UN and Western governments in May 2003, after it helped Chinese officials to deport 18 Tibetan refugees from Kathmandu to Tibet (Nepal's usual policy was to transfer Tibetan refugees to officials of the UN High Commissioner for Refugees—UNHCR). In 2008 a series of demonstrations was held by Tibetan refugees in Kathmandu, as the approach of the Beijing Olympic Games in China drew international attention to the Tibet issue. The Nepalese police force was widely criticized for its suppression of the protests and the arrests of hundreds of activists.

Ties with Bangladesh are also significant, particularly regarding energy co-operation and the utilization of joint water resources. In 1998 the Phulbari Treaty drawn up between India and Bangladesh allowed Nepalese goods access to Bangladesh (and Bangladeshi ports) through a transit route in India across the Siliguri Corridor (the narrow strip of territory linking India's north-eastern states with the rest of the country). In a move that was expected boost agricultural commerce between the two countries, in April 2013 Bangladesh removed import duties on over 100 Nepalese agricultural products. In November 2014 a framework agreement for electricity trade, which aimed to establish an interconnected power grid in the region, was signed by the South Asian Association for Regional Cooperation (SAARC, see p. 417) member states at the Kathmandu summit. In March 2015 it was reported that Nepal and Bangladesh were proposing to establish new power trading organizations to give them greater independence in the growing regional electricity market. Proposals for the establishment of a major hydroelectric power plant, under a Nepalese-Bangladeshi joint-venture agreement, have also been discussed in recent years.

In 1991 thousands of Bhutanese of Nepalese origin began to arrive at refugee camps in eastern Nepal, following the outbreak of political and ethnic unrest in Bhutan. Talks held between Bhutanese and Nepalese government officials in 1993 were inconclusive, with both countries denying responsibility for the refugees: the Nepalese Government refused to consider any solution that did not include the resettlement in Bhutan of all ethnic Nepalese refugees living in the camps; the Bhutanese Government rejected the Nepalese proposal, claiming that the majority of the camp population were not actually Bhutanese, had absconded from Bhutan (thus forfeiting their citizenship) or had departed voluntarily. By early 1996 nearly 100,000 refugees were living in eight camps in the districts of Jhapa and Morang. A breakthrough in the refugee crisis was achieved during negotiations in December 2000, when both countries reached provisional agreement on a formula for verifying the nationality of the refugees, and a Joint Verification Team (JVT) was subsequently established to inspect the camps and classify the inhabitants. After numerous delays, in January 2003 Nepal and Bhutan finally harmonized their positions on the categorization of the refugees into four different groups: Bhutanese nationals who had been forcefully evicted (Category I); Bhutanese nationals who had left Bhutan voluntarily (Category II); non-Bhutanese (Category III); and Bhutanese who had committed criminal acts (Category IV). The two countries later decided that Bhutan would be fully responsible for any Category I persons, while Category II people could apply for either Bhutanese or Nepalese citizenship. However, talks between the two countries were suspended after Bhutanese members of the JVT were attacked in December in the Khudanabari camp by refugees protesting against the terms of the agreement. In October 2006 the US Government offered to resettle as many as 60,000 of the refugees (who by now totalled around 106,000); similar offers followed from Australia, Canada and New Zealand. Despite subsequent reports that the refugees were facing intimidation from political activists who were opposed to the idea of overseas resettlement, the resettlement of refugees in the USA and New Zealand began in late 2007. In April 2011 the Bhutanese Prime Minister, Jigmi Yozer Thinley, in his capacity of SAARC Chairman, visited his Nepalese counterpart, Jhala Nath Khanal, in Kathmandu; the two leaders pledged to resume talks on the refugee issue (stalled since 2003). According to UNHCR, by September 2014 some 92,500 persons claiming Bhutanese refugee status had been resettled in third countries since November 2007: the USA had taken the majority of these (over 75,000), followed by Canada, Australia, New Zealand and various European countries. An estimated 24,000 Bhutanese refugees remained in two camps in eastern Nepal, the majority of whom were reported to have expressed an interest in third country resettlement. Meanwhile, during the inauguration ceremony of India's new Government in May 2014, Prime Minister Sushil Koirala discussed the refugee issue briefly with Bhutanese Prime Minister Tshering Tobgay; however, by mid-2015 substantive bilateral discussions on the issue had yet to recommence.

CONSTITUTION AND GOVERNMENT

In January 2007 the bicameral legislature instituted by the 1990 Constitution was dissolved upon the promulgation of a new Interim Constitution, and a 330-member Interim Parliament was convened by agreement of the seven-party opposition alliance and the Maoist rebels. In accordance with articles stipulated in the Interim Constitution, constitutional powers of governance were reassigned from the monarchy to the acting Prime Minister and the temporary legislature was to facilitate preparations for the democratic election of a constituent assembly. The constituent assembly, with a term of two years, would be responsible for drawing up a new permanent constitution. In December 2007 a parliamentary resolution declaring Nepal a republic received the requisite two-thirds' majority for a constitutional amendment; this decision came into effect at the inaugural session of the 601-seat Constituent Assembly in May 2008. (At this stage, the Interim Parliament was dissolved.) In mid-2008 the Constituent Assembly elected a new President, Vice-President and Prime Minister; the presidency was a largely ceremonial position. Owing to the ongoing political instability, the deadline for the introduction of a new constitution—28 May 2010—was not met, and on that date the tenure of the Constituent Assembly was extended by one year. With the process of drafting a new constitution still incomplete, the tenure of the Constituent Assembly was subsequently extended on several further occasions. When the latest deadline of May 2012 expired, the Constituent Assembly was dissolved. In March 2013 a nonpartisan interim government was established, under the leadership of the Chief Justice of the Supreme Court, in preparation for elections to a new constituent assembly. Delayed elections were held in November, and in January 2014 a new Constituent Assembly was sworn in. The Assembly was charged with drafting a new constitution by 22 January 2015; however, this deadline too was not met.

For the purposes of local administration, Nepal is divided into 14 zones, 75 districts, 3,754 village development committees and 99 municipalities, which are together grouped into five development regions. Each of the districts is headed by a permanent chief district officer, who is responsible for maintaining law and order and for co-ordinating the work of field agencies of the various government ministries.

REGIONAL AND INTERNATIONAL CO-OPERATION

Nepal is a member of the Asian Development Bank (ADB, see p. 206), the South Asian Association for Regional Cooperation (SAARC, see p. 417), the Colombo Plan (see p. 445) and the Bay of Bengal Initiative for Multi-Sectoral Technical and Economic Cooperation (BIMSTEC), all of which seek to encourage regional economic development.

Having joined the UN in 1955, Nepal is a member of the Economic and Social Commission for Asia and the Pacific (ESCAP, see p. 30). Nepal became a member of the World Trade Organization (WTO, see p. 431) in 2004.

ECONOMIC AFFAIRS

In 2013, according to estimates by the World Bank, Nepal's gross national income (GNI), measured at average 2011–13 prices, was US $20,262m., equivalent to $730 per head (or $2,260 per head on an international purchasing-power parity basis). During 2004–13, it was estimated, the population increased at an average annual rate of 1.2%, while gross domestic product (GDP) per head increased, in real terms, by an average of 2.9% per year.

According to official figures, overall GDP increased, in real terms, at an average annual rate of 4.4% in 2004/05–2013/14; real GDP grew by 5.5% in 2013/14.

Agriculture (including forestry and fishing) contributed a preliminary 33.1% of GDP in the fiscal year ending 15 July 2014. The sector was projected to engage an estimated 92.8% of the economically active population at mid-2015, according to FAO figures. The principal crops are rice, sugar cane, potatoes, maize and wheat. During 2004/05–2013/14, agricultural GDP increased by an average of 3.2% per year; the sector grew by only 1.1% in 2012/13 but by a further 4.7% in 2013/14.

Industry (comprising mining, manufacturing, construction and utilities) employed 10.8% of the labour force in 2008, and provided a preliminary 14.7% of GDP in 2013/14, according to official figures. About 60% of Nepal's industrial output derives from traditional cottage industries, and the remainder from modern industries. During 2004/05–2013/14, industrial GDP increased at an average annual rate of 2.9%; industrial production rose by 2.7% in 2013/14.

Mining employed only 0.2% of the labour force in 2008, and contributed a preliminary 0.6% of GDP in 2013/14. During 2004/05–2013/14, mining GDP increased by an average of 3.5% per year. The sector's GDP rose by 3.7% in 2013/14. Mica is mined east of Kathmandu, and there are also small deposits of lignite, copper, talc, limestone, cobalt and iron ore. Geophysical investigations have indicated that the Siwalik range and the Terai belt are potential prospective areas for petroleum.

Manufacturing contributed a preliminary 6.1% of GDP in 2013/14, and employed about 6.6% of the labour force in 2008. Manufacturing GDP increased at an average annual rate of 2.1% in 2004/05–2013/14. Manufacturing production rose by 3.7% in 2012/13 but by only 1.9% in 2013/14. The principal branches of the sector include textiles (particularly carpets and rugs), food products, wearing apparel and tobacco products. Traditional cottage industries include basket-making and the production of cotton fabrics and edible oils.

Construction contributed a preliminary 6.8% of GDP in 2013/14, and employed about 3.1% of the labour force in 2008. Construction GDP increased at an average annual rate of 3.6% in 2004/05–2013/14; it rose by 2.9% in 2013/14.

Energy is derived principally from traditional sources (particularly fuelwood). However, imports of mineral fuel and lubricants (mainly for the transport sector) comprised an estimated 20.8% of the cost of total imports in 2013/14. In addition, Nepal's rivers are exploited for hydroelectric power (HEP) production: the country has a huge potential generating capacity (estimated at 83,000 MW, about one-half of which is considered to be viable), but an installed capacity of only about 600 MW in 2014. The country's generating capacity will be boosted considerably by two major HEP projects at Upper Tamakoshi (with a capacity of 456 MW) and Upper Karnali (900 MW). Construction of the former commenced in 2011, with assistance from the Chinese state-owned Sino Hydro Corporation as well as private Indian contractors, and was scheduled for completion by mid-2016. The Upper Karnali project, to be built by the Indian firm GMR and expected to begin operations in 2021, was approved by the Nepalese Government in September 2014.

The services sector employed 15.3% of the labour force in 2008. The sector contributed a preliminary 50.3% of GDP in 2012/13. The GDP of the services sector increased at an average annual rate of 5.4% in 2004/05–2013/14. Sectoral GDP grew by 6.1% in 2013/14. By the mid-1990s tourism had emerged as Nepal's major source of foreign exchange. However, the Maoist insurgency adversely affected visitor levels in the first half of the 2000s. The cessation of hostilities in 2006—combined with the introduction of additional airline services between Nepal and other Asian countries—led to a significant recovery in the tourism sector. In 2012 tourist arrivals increased by 9.1%, compared with the previous year, to 803,092, before declining slightly in 2013, to 797,616. In the latter year, however, revenue from tourism increased by 23.9% compared with the previous year, to an estimated US $436m.

In 2013 Nepal recorded a visible merchandise trade deficit of US $5,510.6m., while there was a surplus of $1,150.6m. on the current account of the balance of payments. In 2013/14 India was the principal source of imports (supplying 66.7% of the total) and the principal market for exports (65.1%). Other major trading partners were China and the United Arab Emirates for imports, and the USA for exports. In 2013/14 the principal exports were basic manufactures and manufactured goods (particularly woven articles and garments), food and live animals,

miscellaneous manufactured articles, chemicals, and crude materials. The principal imports were mineral fuels and lubricants, basic manufactures, machinery and transport equipment, food and live animals, chemicals, and miscellaneous manufactured articles.

In 2013/14 there was an estimated overall budget deficit of NRs 21,330.1m. Foreign aid plays a vital role in the Nepalese economy. According to the Asian Development Bank, Nepal's total external debt was an estimated US $3,617m. at the end of 2014. In that year the cost of debt-servicing was equivalent to 8.6% of receipts from exports of goods and services. According to figures by the International Labour Organization (ILO), the average annual rate of inflation was 9.0% in 2004–13. According to official figures, consumer prices rose by 9.1% in 2013/14. During the first decade of the 2000s it was estimated that more than 40% of Nepalese workers were underemployed, while urban unemployment, a major problem, particularly among educated youths, stood at around 7%. The national unemployment rate was estimated by the ILO at 2.7% in 2013.

With an inhospitable terrain and high rates of poverty, Nepal is among the least developed countries in the world. Successive administrations since 1991 have pursued a policy of economic liberalization: many state enterprises have been privatized (although there have been delays in the process), and there have been attempts to reduce the fiscal deficit, to restructure the financial sector, and to institute open trade and investment policies. The instability caused by a 10-year civil conflict, the transition from a monarchy to a republic in 2008, and the ensuing political upheaval and general unrest has hindered the country's economic development, and foreign investment has remained negligible by regional standards. None the less, Nepal has enjoyed some success in recent years in tackling poverty: the number of those living below the poverty line (about US $160 a year) was estimated to have decreased to 25% of the population in 2011, although considerable regional disparities persist within the country, with much higher rates of poverty found in the remote hills and mountains of western Nepal. Tourism is a vital sector for driving economic growth, particularly mountaineering (the Himalaya mountains contain many of the world's highest peaks). The number of foreign visitors increased steadily after the end of the civil war, more than doubling between 2006 and 2012. In 2012 the Prime Minister announced an ambitious infrastructure development plan, including hydroelectric power projects, the construction of a second international airport and the projected creation of some 677,000 new jobs, while a UN Development Assistance Framework published in the same year planned for $685m. to be spent on development and international co-operation during 2013–17. Following the successful Constituent Assembly elections in November 2013, Nepal's image as a viable destination for foreign investment was boosted by the introduction of investment reforms, which included support for new businesses and tax exemptions for production-related industries. A deceleration in the rate of growth of remittances (which typically account for around 25% of GDP), together with a widening trade deficit, frequent power outages, a high rate of inflation and falling agricultural production owing to an unfavourable monsoon, all contributed to a decrease in the GDP growth rate from 4.6% in 2011/12 to 3.6% in 2012/13. A recovery in remittances, boosting the services sector, and strong growth in agriculture due to a favourable monsoon, restored growth to 5.5% in 2013/14. However, with a weaker monsoon season expected in 2014/15, GDP growth was projected to moderate to about 4.6% for that year. The devastating earthquake that struck Nepal in late April 2015, causing large-scale loss of life and widespread damage to buildings and infrastructure, was likely to compel a major reassessment of Nepal's economic development plans, as the Government confronted the need to launch an unprecedented programme of relief and reconstruction.

PUBLIC HOLIDAYS

The Nepalese year (Bikram Sambat) 2072 runs from 14 April 2015 to 12 April 2016. The public holidays observed in Nepal vary locally. The dates given below apply to Kathmandu.

2016: 30 January (Martyrs' Day), 9 February* (Sonam Lhosar), 19 February (National Democracy Day), 7 March (Maha Shivaratri), 8 March (International Women's Day), 9 March* (Ghyalpo Lhosar), 22 March (Phagu Purnima/Holi), 13 April (Navabarsha—New Year's Day), 23 (Loktantra Diwas—Democracy Day), 1 May (Labour Day), 21 May (Buddha Purnima/Buddha Jayanti—Lord Buddha's Birthday), 29 May (Republic Day),

6 July (Id al-Fitr—end of Ramadan), 18 August (Janai Purnima/ Raksha Bandhan—Sacred Thread Ceremony), 25 August (Janmashtami—Lord Krishna's Birthday), 12 September (Id al-Adha—Feast of the Sacrifice), 1 October (Ghatasthapana/Navratri), 16 October† (Kojagrat Purnima—End of Dashain), 30 October (Laxmi Puja, first day of Tihar/Diwali—Festival of Lights), 25 December (Christmas Day), 30 December* (Tamu Lhosar).

* Lhosar is a celebration of the Tibetan new year. There are three separate Lhosar festivals, celebrated by Buddhists in different parts of the country and by different ethnic groups.
† Forms part of the extended Dashain holiday, which generally involves up to five days of official holidays.

Note: A number of Hindu, Muslim and Buddhist holidays depend on lunar sightings.

Statistical Survey

Sources (unless otherwise stated): Central Bureau of Statistics, Thapathali, Kathmandu; tel. (1) 4229406; fax (1) 4227720; e-mail info@cbs.gov.np; internet www .cbs.gov.np; Federation of Nepalese Chambers of Commerce and Industry (FNCCI), Pachali Shahid Shukra FNCCI Milan Marg, Teku, POB 269, Kathmandu; tel. (1) 4262061; fax (1) 4261022; e-mail fncci@mos.com.np; internet www.fncci.org.

Area and Population

AREA, POPULATION AND DENSITY

Area (sq km)	147,181*
Population (census results)	
22 June 2001††‡	23,151,423
22 June 2011	
Males	12,849,041
Females	13,645,463
Total	26,494,504
Population (official estimates, year ending 15 July)	
2011/12	26,850,000
2012/13	27,210,000
2013/14§	27,580,000
Density (per sq km) at 2013/14	187.4

* 56,827 sq miles.
† Population is *de jure*.
‡ Includes estimates for certain areas in 12 districts where the census could not be conducted, owing to violence and disruption.
§ Preliminary.

POPULATION BY AGE AND SEX
(at 2011 census)

	Males	Females	Total
0–14 years	4,714,763	4,533,483	9,248,246
15–64 years	7,437,790	8,410,885	15,848,675
65 years and over	696,488	701,095	1,397,583
Total	12,849,041	13,645,463	26,494,504

PRINCIPAL TOWNS
(population at 2011 census)

Kathmandu* . .	1,003,285	Birgunj		139,068
Pokhara . . .	264,991	Butwal		120,982
Lalitpur . . .	226,728	Dharan . . .		119,915
Biratnagar . .	204,949	Mahendranagar .		106,666
Bharatpur . . .	147,777	Dhangadhi . . .		104,047

* Total for urban agglomeration 1,744,240.

Mid-2014 (incl. suburbs, UN estimate): Kathmandu 1,141,730 (Source: UN, *World Urbanization Prospects: The 2014 Revision*).

BIRTHS AND DEATHS
(annual averages, UN estimates)

	2000–05	2005–10	2010–15
Birth rate (per 1,000) . . .	30.8	25.6	21.1
Death rate (per 1,000)	8.2	7.3	6.7

Source: UN, *World Population Prospects: The 2012 Revision*.

2011 (estimates): Birth rate 24.0 per 1,000; Death rate 7.7 per 1,000.

Life expectancy (years at birth): 68.0 (males 66.9; females 69.1) in 2012 (Source: World Bank, World Development Indicators database).

ECONOMICALLY ACTIVE POPULATION
(labour force survey, '000 persons aged 15 years and over, 2008)

	Males	Females	Total
Agriculture, hunting, forestry and fishing	3,429	5,275	8,704
Mining and quarrying	19	8	27
Manufacturing	469	305	773
Electricity, gas and water . .	39	70	109
Construction	326	41	367
Wholesale and retail trade; repair of motor vehicles, motorcycles and personal and household goods	447	245	692
Hotels and restaurants . . .	94	103	197
Transport, storage and communications	191	8	198
Financial intermediation . . .	22	10	32
Real estate, renting and business activities	57	13	71
Public administration and defence; compulsory social security . .	96	13	109
Education	189	96	285
Health and social work . . .	46	31	77
Other community, social and personal services	77	23	99
Private households with employed persons	14	19	33
Extraterritorial organizations and bodies	4	1	5
Total employed	5,519	6,260	11,779
Unemployed	127	126	253
Total labour force	5,646	6,386	12,032

Note: Totals may not be equal to the sum of components, owing to rounding.

Mid-2015 (estimates in '000): Agriculture, etc. 12,008; Total labour force 12,935 (Source: FAO).

Health and Welfare

KEY INDICATORS

Total fertility rate (children per woman, 2012)	2.4
Under-5 mortality rate (per 1,000 live births, 2012) . . .	42
HIV/AIDS (% of persons aged 15–49, 2013)	0.2
Physicians (per 1,000 head, 2004)	0.21
Hospital beds (per 1,000 head, 2006)	5.0
Health expenditure (2011): US $ per head (PPP)	85
Health expenditure (2011): % of GDP	6.1
Health expenditure (2011): public (% of total)	45.3
Access to water (% of persons, 2012)	88
Access to sanitation (% of persons, 2012)	37
Total carbon dioxide emissions ('000 metric tons, 2010) . .	3,755.0
Carbon dioxide emissions per head (metric tons, 2010) . .	0.1
Human Development Index (2013): ranking	145
Human Development Index (2013): value	0.540

For sources and definitions, see explanatory note on p. vi.

Agriculture

PRINCIPAL CROPS
('000 metric tons)

	2011	2012	2013
Wheat	1,746	1,846	1,727
Rice, paddy	4,460	5,072	4,505
Barley	30	35	34
Maize	2,068	2,179	1,999
Millet	303	315	306
Potatoes	2,508	2,584	2,690
Sugar cane	2,718	2,930	2,930
Beans, dry	23	22	21
Pigeon peas	14	14	16
Lentils	207	208	227
Mustard seed	176	145	143
Garlic	41	41	41
Oranges	51	40	35
Apples	43	49	43
Ginger	216	255	235
Jute	14	14	16
Tobacco, unmanufactured	1	3	2

Aggregate production ('000 metric tons, may include official, semi-official or estimated data): Total cereals 8,615 in 2011, 9,458 in 2012, 8,580 in 2013; Total roots and tubers 2,667 in 2011, 2,740 in 2012, 2,845 in 2013; Total vegetables (incl. melons) 3,282 in 2011, 3,377 in 2012, 3,383 in 2013; Total fruits (excl. melons) 1,494 in 2011, 1,935 in 2012, 1,756 in 2013.

Source: FAO.

LIVESTOCK
('000 head, year ending September)

	2011	2012	2013
Cattle	7,226	7,245	7,274
Buffaloes	4,994	5,133	5,242
Pigs	1,108	1,137	1,160
Sheep	805	807	810
Goats	9,186	9,513	9,786
Chickens	39,531	45,171	47,959

Source: FAO.

LIVESTOCK PRODUCTS
('000 metric tons)

	2011	2012	2013
Cattle meat*	51.0	51.4	51.9
Buffalo meat	167.9	172.4	175.1
Sheep meat	2.7	2.7	2.7
Goat meat	52.8	54.0	55.6
Pig meat	17.9	18.3	18.7
Chicken meat	36.1	40.3	42.8
Cows' milk	447.2	468.9	492.4
Buffaloes' milk	1,109.3	1,153.8	1,188.4
Goats' milk*	73.3	73.5	74.0
Hen eggs†	34.5	39.4	43.7

* FAO estimates.
† Unofficial figures.
Source: FAO.

Forestry

ROUNDWOOD REMOVALS
('000 cubic metres, excl. bark, FAO estimates)

	2011	2012	2013
Sawlogs, veneer logs and logs for sleepers	1,260	1,260	1,260
Fuel wood	12,464	12,403	12,344
Total	13,724	13,663	13,604

Source: FAO.

SAWNWOOD PRODUCTION
('000 cubic metres, incl. railway sleepers, unofficial figures)

	2011	2012	2013
Coniferous (softwood)	20	20	20
Broadleaved (hardwood)	610	610	610
Total	630	630	630

Note: Production assumed to be unchanged from 2001.
Source: FAO.

Fishing

('000 metric tons, live weight)

	2010	2011	2012*
Capture	21.5	21.5	21.5
Aquaculture	28.2	31.0	34.5
Common carp	4.2	4.6	5.2
Bighead carp	3.5	3.8	3.6
Silver carp	9.9	10.8	11.5
Total catch	49.7	52.5	56.0

* FAO estimates.
Source: FAO.

Industry

SELECTED PRODUCTS
('000 metric tons unless otherwise indicated, year ending 15 July)

	2010/11	2011/12	2012/13
Cement	84.1	92.5	86.7*
Raw sugar	190.7	200.2	200.2*
Tea	16.3	17.1	17.1*
Noodles	42.8	45.0	46.3*
Cigarettes ('000 million)	13.5	13.9	14.3*
Soap	53.1	55.8	54.7*
Electric energy (million kWh)	3,064.3	3,319.0	3,432.6

* Annual estimate based on data for first eight months.
Vegetable ghee ('000 metric tons): 179.2 in 2005/06; 188.2 in 2006/07; 195.7 in 2007/08.
Paper ('000 metric tons): 29.9 in 2005/06; 31.4 in 2006/07; 32.7 in 2007/08.
Source: Ministry of Finance, Kathmandu.

Finance

CURRENCY AND EXCHANGE RATES

Monetary Units:
100 paisa (pice) = 1 Nepalese rupee (NR).

Sterling, Dollar and Euro Equivalents (31 December 2014):
£1 sterling = NRs 158.296;
US $1 = NRs 101.420;
€1 = NRs 123.134;
1,000 Nepalese rupees = £6.32 = $9.86 = €8.12.

Average Exchange Rate (rupees per US $):
2012   85.197
2013   92.993
2014   99.626

BUDGET
(NRs million, year ending 15 July)*

Revenue†	2012/13	2013/14	2014/15‡
Taxation	259,214.9	312,621.6	374,706.0
Taxes on external trade	56,931.8	69,363.1	80,669.3
Value-added tax	83,418.4	101,526.9	121,730.7
Excise duties	45,852.1	57,164.1	70,297.4
Income and property transfer tax	69,526.9	79,911.4	96,440.8
Other taxes	3,485.8	4,656.1	5,567.8
Non-tax revenue	36,806.2	41,907.8	48,194.0
Interest	527.9	570.5	691.3
Civil administration	11,590.3	13,048.9	15,169.2
Dividend	10,843.7	12,926.5	14,171.1
Rent, royalties and sale of fixed assets	6,236.9	7,033.0	8,187.2
Miscellaneous	7,607.5	8,329.0	9,975.3
Cash balance of previous year, plus irregularities	1,921.2	—	18,535.3
Total	297,942.3	354,529.4	441,435.3

Expenditure by economic type	2012/13	2013/14	2014/15‡
Recurrent expenditure	247,455.5	316,640.1	398,951.2
Compensation of employees	66,046.1	84,260.4	104,912.5
Use of goods and services	23,285.3	29,008.6	63,106.2
Interest payments	13,736.7	17,547.7	23,354.6
Subsidies and grants	106,717.2	143,483.3	148,964.8
Social benefits	37,544.3	42,048.7	58,243.8
Other expenditure	126.0	291.4	369.4
Capital expenditure	54,598.4	63,870.3	116,755.0
Total	302,053.9	380,510.3	515,706.2

Expenditure by sector§	2012/13	2013/14	2014/15‡
General public services	104,534.9	114,764.7	204,878 2
Defence	20,899.2	31,673.8	31,358.6
Public order and safety	37,762.9	43,612.5	34,468.7
Economic affairs	84,118.2	119,471.6	170,198.3
Environmental protection	1,745.2	3,880.6	10,791.4
Housing and community amenities	11,074.2	14,011.4	22,342.4
Health	21,871.7	26,424.4	37,766.5
Recreation, culture and religion	2,411.9	3,838.5	3,981.7
Education	62,429.8	79,356.6	86,034.1
Social protection	11,790.0	12,817.8	16,280.2
Total	358,638.0	449,852.0	618,100.0

*Figures refer to the recurrent and capital budgets of the central Government.
† Excluding grants received (NRs million): 35,229.8 in 2012/13; 47,311.0 in 2013/14; 73,385.9 in 2014/15 (estimate).
‡ Estimates.
§ Including financing (NRs million): 56,584.1 in 2012/13; 69,341.7 in 2013/14; 102,393.8 in 2014/15 (estimate).

Source: Ministry of Finance, Kathmandu.

INTERNATIONAL RESERVES
(US $ million at mid-December)

	2003	2004	2005
Gold*	6.5	6.5	5.4
IMF special drawing rights	0.8	9.7	8.8
Reserve position in IMF	8.6	—	—
Foreign exchange	1,213.1	1,452.5	1,490.2
Total	1,229.0	1,468.7	1,504.4

* Valued at US $42.5 per troy ounce in 2003 and 2004, and at $41.9 in 2005.

IMF special drawing rights (US $ million at mid-December): 78.6 in 2012; 63.4 in 2013; 47.2 in 2014.

Foreign exchange (US $ million at mid-December): 3,541.8 in 2011; 4,227.9 in 2012; 5,230.0 in 2013.

Source: IMF, *International Financial Statistics*.

MONEY SUPPLY
(NRs million at mid-December)*

	2012	2013	2014
Currency outside depository corporations	179,491	219,852	242,418
Transferable deposits	73,846	100,728	110,051
Other deposits	937,402	1,128,050	1,329,975
Broad money	1,190,739	1,448,629	1,682,443

* Excluding Indian currency in circulation.

Source: IMF, *International Financial Statistics*.

COST OF LIVING
(Consumer Price Index, Kathmandu Valley, year ending 15 July; base: 2005/06 = 100)

	2011/12	2012/13	2013/14
Food (incl. beverages)	201.4	223.2	248.6
Clothing and footwear	154.9	173.6	189.1
Housing and utilities	135.6	157.1	164.7
All items (incl. others)	170.6	187.2	204.2

Source: Nepal Rastra Bank, Kathmandu.

NATIONAL ACCOUNTS
(NRs million at current prices, year ending 15 July)

Expenditure on the Gross Domestic Product

	2011/12	2012/13	2013/14*
Final consumption expenditure	1,359,539	1,521,716	1,756,484
Households	1,167,861	1,324,363	1,505,803
Non-profit institutions serving households	27,307	29,161	35,022
General government	164,370	168,192	215,658
Gross capital formation	526,889	624,645	715,057
Gross fixed capital formation	317,185	382,153	446,129
Increase in stocks†	209,704	242,492	268,928
Total domestic expenditure	1,886,428	2,146,361	2,471,541
Exports of goods and services	153,863	181,181	234,192
Less Imports of goods and services	512,948	634,899	777,216
GDP in purchasers' values	1,527,344	1,692,643	1,928,517
GDP at constant 2000/01 prices	670,279	696,101	734,219

* Preliminary figures.
† Including statistical discrepancy.

Gross Domestic Product by Economic Activity

	2011/12	2012/13	2013/14*
Agriculture and forestry	500,465	527,869	583,692
Fishing	5,819	6,646	8,659
Mining and quarrying	8,166	9,616	11,253
Manufacturing	91,164	100,312	108,745
Electricity, gas and water	17,518	20,368	21,726
Construction	98,539	108,979	120,863
Wholesale and retail trade	198,164	228,747	267,510
Restaurants and hotels	25,307	29,886	35,303
Transport, storage and communications	122,354	140,537	156,500
Financial intermediation	58,529	62,183	67,278
Real estate, renting and business	123,213	138,587	150,900
Public administration and defence	30,547	32,236	42,578
Education	81,797	91,736	114,833
Health and social work	20,431	22,327	26,555
Other community and social services	55,461	58,028	73,374
Sub-total	1,437,474	1,578,058	1,789,768
Less Financial intermediation services indirectly measured (FISIM)	49,992	55,205	65,172
GDP at basic prices	1,387,482	1,522,853	1,724,596
Indirect taxes, *less* subsidies	139,862	169,790	203,921
GDP in market prices	1,527,344	1,692,643	1,928,517

* Preliminary figures.

BALANCE OF PAYMENTS
(US $ million)

	2011	2012	2013
Exports of goods	999.0	1,004.3	991.5
Imports of goods	−5,665.1	−5,951.1	−6,502.1
Balance on goods	−4,666.1	−4,946.8	−5,510.6
Exports of services	863.5	924.9	1,182.2
Imports of services	−782.2	−896.3	−978.0
Balance on goods and services	−4,584.8	−4,918.2	−5,306.3
Primary income received	287.7	247.5	326.3
Primary income paid	−140.3	−121.9	−90.2
Balance on goods, services and primary income	−4,437.4	−4,792.7	−5,070.2
Secondary income received	4,778.1	5,447.6	6,275.1
Secondary income paid	−52.1	−78.0	−54.2
Current balance	288.6	576.9	1,150.6
Capital account (net)	189.5	201.6	164.7
Direct investment liabilities	94.0	92.0	73.6
Other investment assets	−300.1	−504.2	−400.5
Other investment liabilities	448.9	294.4	392.2
Net errors and omissions	278.6	56.5	63.8
Reserves and related items	999.7	717.2	1,444.5

Source: IMF, *International Financial Statistics*.

External Trade

PRINCIPAL COMMODITIES
(NRs million, year ending 15 July)

Imports from India

	2011/12	2012/13	2013/14*
Rice	4,267.0	8,455.8	12,379.4
Medicines	10,383.4	13,337.4	15,112.4
Chemicals	4,072.9	2,559.4	2,973.0
Chemical fertilizers	4,506.5	8,485.5	8,025.0
Coal	5,550.4	7,009.9	8,721.3
Cement	3,300.1	9,425.2	9,710.4
Petroleum products	92,255.6	107,138.8	131,331.7
Cold-rolled sheet (in coil)	7,507.9	2,691.9	6,524.6
Hot-rolled sheet (in coil)	5,542.6	5,688.7	11,678.7
Mild steel (MS) billet	19,437.3	22,303.6	24,674.8
Mild steel (MS) wire rod	6,761.0	4,090.0	6,480.3
Transport vehicles and parts	17,051.0	26,297.6	32,963.4
Other machine equipment and parts	8,342.0	12,014.3	15,561.5
Electrical equipment	7,009.8	6,574.0	7,642.7
Agricultural equipment and parts	4,145.8	7,380.3	8,508.1
Total (incl. others)	299,389.6	367,031.2	472,730.6

Imports from Other Countries

	2011/12	2012/13	2013/14*
Crude palm oil	4,210.6	3,390.8	4,133.6
Crude soybean oil	9,962.3	10,627.5	14,778.5
Ready-made garments	1,047.3	5,454.5	6,777.4
Gold	25,770.4	26,113.9	24,794.1
Silver	4,370.9	8,783.1	12,711.2
Polyethylene granules	5,786.7	4,524.6	7,801.7
Electrical equipment	7,311.6	5,795.0	7,468.4
Computer parts	6,150.3	4,543.3	4,774.0
Transport equipment and parts	2,859.3	3,590.7	6,360.6
Other machine equipment and parts	7,197.5	8,131.0	10,875.2
Telecommunications equipment and parts	8,459.0	13,489.4	14,018.7
Total (incl. others)	162,278.1	189,709.1	236,031.2

Exports to India

	2011/12	2012/13	2013/14*
Juice	3,027.1	3,801.6	4,431.5
Catechu (extract of Acacia)	1,002.5	n.a.	n.a.
Cardamom	3,275.5	3,849.6	4,267.2
Polyester yarn	3,657.2	4,742.0	5,153.3
Thread	2,628.2	105.0	180.2
Textiles (cotton, synthetic and others)	5,130.3	5,618.2	5,779.2
Jute goods	4,064.7	4,108.4	4,302.2
Galvanized iron sheet	3,343.4	4,948.4	6,177.0
Other wire	1,809.6	2,728.3	2,070.2
Steel pipes	797.8	n.a.	213.0
Total (incl. others)	49,616.3	51,000.0	59,417.3

Exports to Other Countries

	2011/12	2012/13	2013/14*
Pulses	2,497.0	2,671.4	2,043.9
Animal hides and skins	723.5	1,005.5	1,119.2
Woollen carpet	6,938.0	6,075.0	7,364.7
Ready-made garments	4,006.3	3,083.3	4,222.8
Pashmina goods	3,230.3	1,655.2	2,085.1
Nepalese paper and paper products	587.3	244.2	287.6
Handicraft goods (of metal and wood)	510.1	214.3	379.6
Total (incl. others)	24,644.7	25,917.5	30,875.0

* Provisional.

Source: Nepal Rastra Bank, Kathmandu.

PRINCIPAL TRADING PARTNERS
(NRs million, year ending 15 July, provisional)

Imports	2011/12	2012/13	2013/14
Argentina	6,529.6	8,079.2	7,760.6
China, People's Republic	52,924.9	68,304.9	78,568.2
Germany	2,569.3	3,217.7	6,190.1
India	321,346.4	397,957.9	482,345.3
Indonesia	7,740.5	9,585.6	15,377.9
Japan	4,479.4	4,663.2	4,632.2
Korea, Republic	5,461.0	4,599.5	4,100.9
Malaysia	5,978.2	5,680.4	6,676.5
Saudi Arabia	4,538.4	3,375.3	5,746.6
Singapore	2,646.5	3,335.8	3,841.6
Switzerland	1,914.4	1,625.2	2,368.1
Thailand	8,098.4	9,436.9	9,527.0
Ukraine	3,462.4	3,451.5	3,044.1
United Arab Emirates	32,540.2	37,224.1	40,679.2
United Kingdom	1,899.4	1,628.8	3,904.0
USA	4,885.2	5,207.8	6,326.3
Viet Nam	1,980.5	3,035.5	4,093.4
Total (incl. others)	498,161.1	601,207.5	722,776.8

Exports	2011/12	2012/13	2013/14
Bangladesh	2,578.1	2,730.2	2,140.5
Canada	782.1	643.9	832.5
China, People's Republic	985.7	2,176.7	2,979.9
France	1,062.9	1,053.1	1,333.2
Germany	2,965.9	2,761.3	3,389.1
India	50,933.2	51,788.5	59,458.4
Italy	792.2	785.3	1,002.1
Japan	767.2	962.3	1,049.8
United Kingdom	1,461.9	1,584.2	2,341.8
USA	5,551.9	5,750.1	7,586.4
Total (incl. others)	74,089.1	77,350.7	91,361.0

Source: Trade and Export Promotion Centre (Lalitpur), Ministry of Commerce and Supplies, Kathmandu.

Transport

ROAD TRAFFIC
(vehicles registered)

	2010/11	2011/12	2012/13
Cars, jeeps and vans	8,510	8,711	9,595
Buses and minibuses	2,980	3,255	4,591
Tractors	7,937	8,413	9,795
Other agro-industrial vehicles .	1,969	1,333	3,332
Motorcycles	138,907	145,135	175,381
Total (incl. others)	163,640	170,084	208,483

Source: Department of Transport Management, Kathmandu.

CIVIL AVIATION
(traffic on scheduled services of Royal Nepal Airlines Corporation)

	2007	2008	2009
Kilometres flown (million) . .	11	11	10
Passengers carried ('000) . . .	528	520	484
Passenger-km (million) . . .	947	931	858
Total ton-km (million)	90	88	80

Source: UN, *Statistical Yearbook*.

Passengers carried ('000): 901 in 2011; 777 in 2012; 700 in 2013 (Source: World Bank, World Development Indicators database).

Tourism

FOREIGN TOURIST ARRIVALS

Nationality	2011	2012	2013
Australia	19,824	22,030	22,034
Bangladesh	17,563	16,764	22,410
China, People's Republic . . .	61,917	71,861	113,179
France	26,720	28,805	21,842
Germany	27,472	30,409	22,263
India	149,504	165,815	180,974
Italy	12,621	14,614	9,974
Japan	26,283	28,642	26,694
Korea, Republic	24,488	26,004	19,714
Malaysia	7,381	11,780	18,842
Netherlands	16,836	15,445	10,516
Sri Lanka	59,884	69,476	32,736
Thailand	33,541	36,618	40,969
United Kingdom	39,091	41,294	35,668
USA	42,875	48,985	47,355
Total (incl. others)	736,215	803,092	797,616

Tourism receipts (US $ million, excl. passenger transport): 386 in 2011; 352 in 2012; 436 in 2013 (provisional).

Source: World Tourism Organization.

Communications Media

	2011*	2012	2013
Telephones ('000 main lines in use)	845.5	831.7	851.2
Mobile cellular telephones ('000 subscribers)	13,354.5	16,380.0	19,864.9
Broadband subscribers ('000) . .	94.7	171.1	208.8

* At December.

Internet subscribers ('000 at December): 128.4 in 2010.

Source: International Telecommunication Union.

Education

(2012/13 unless otherwise indicated)

	Teachers	Students ('000)		
		Males	Females	Total
Pre-primary	45,084*	546.4	506.7	1,053.1
Primary	173,714*	2,266.7	2,310.0	4,576.7
Secondary	101,968*	1,528.5	1,560.3	3,088.8
Tertiary	9,932†	225.0‡	160.5‡	385.5‡

* 2011/12.
† 2006/07.
‡ 2010/11.

Source: UNESCO Institute for Statistics.

2013/14: *Institutions:* Primary 34,743; Lower secondary 14,867; Secondary 8,726; Higher secondary 3,596. *Teachers:* Primary 183,922; Lower secondary 51,653; Secondary 38,363; Higher secondary 18,907. *Students:* Primary 4,401,780; Lower secondary 1,828,351; Secondary 896,919; Higher secondary 415,343. Note: Many schools offer education at more than one level. The total number of primary, lower secondary, secondary and higher secondary institutions was 34,782 (Source: Ministry of Education and Sports, Kathmandu).

Pupil-teacher ratio (primary education, UNESCO estimate): 25.6 in 2012/13 (Source: UNESCO Institute for Statistics).

Adult literacy rate (UNESCO estimates): 57.4% (males 71.1%; females 46.7%) in 2011 (Source: UNESCO Institute for Statistics).

Directory

The Government

HEAD OF STATE

President: Dr RAM BARAN YADAV (assumed office 23 July 2008).

Vice-President: PARAMANANDA JHA.

COUNCIL OF MINISTERS
(May 2015)

The Government is formed by the Nepali Congress Party (NCP), the Communist Party of Nepal—Unified Marxist-Leninist (UML), the Rastriya Prajatantra Party (RPP) and the Communist Party of Nepal (Marxist-Leninist) (CPN—ML).

Prime Minister and Minister responsible for Defence, Science, Technology and Environment, Co-operatives, and Poverty Alleviation: SUSHIL KOIRALA (NCP).

Deputy Prime Minister and Minister of Home Affairs: BAM DEV GAUTAM (UML).

Deputy Prime Minister and Minister of Federal Affairs and Local Development: PRAKASH MAN SINGH (NCP).

Minister of Finance: RAM SHARAN MAHAT (NCP).

Minister of Physical Infrastructure and Transportation: BIMALENDRA NIDHI (NCP).

Minister of Law, Justice, Constituent Assembly and Parliamentary Affairs, and of Peace and Reconstruction: NARHARI ACHARYA (NCP).

Minister of Forests and Soil Conservation: MAHESH ACHARYA (NCP).

Minister of Education: CHITRALEKHA YADHAV (NCP).

Minister of Information and Communications: MINENDRA RIJAL (NCP).

Minister of Energy: RADHA KUMARI GYAWALI (UML).

Minister of Irrigation: NARAYAN PRASAD SAUD (NCP).

Minister of Urban Development: NARAYAN KHADKA (NCP).

Minister of Foreign Affairs: MAHENDRA BAHADUR PANDE (UML).

Minister of Health and Population: KHAGRAJ ADHIKARI (UML).

Minister of Culture, Tourism and Civil Aviation: DEEPAK CHANDRA AMATYA (UML).

Minister of General Administration: LAL BABU PANDIT (UML).

Minister of Land Reform and Management: DAL BAHADUR RANA (UML).

Minister of Industry: MAHESH BASNET (UML).

Minister of Agricultural Development: HARI PRASAD PARAJULI (UML).

Minister of Youth and Sports: PURUSHOTTAM PAUDEL (UML).

Minister of Commerce and Supplies: SUNIL BAHADUR THAPA (RPP).

Minister of Women, Children and Social Welfare: NEELAM K. C. KHADKA (CPN—ML).

Minister of State for Labour and Employment: TEK BAHADUR GURUNG (NCP).

Minister of State for Commerce and Supplies: GIRI BAHADUR K. C. (RPP).

MINISTRIES

Office of the Prime Minister and Council of Ministers: Singha Durbar, POB 23312, Kathmandu; tel. (1) 4211000; fax (1) 428570; e-mail info@opmcm.gov.np; internet www.opmcm.gov.np.

Ministry of Agricultural Development: Singha Durbar, Kathmandu; tel. (1) 4211905; fax (1) 4211935; e-mail memoad@moad.gov.np; internet www.moad.gov.np.

Ministry of Commerce and Supplies: Singha Durbar, Kathmandu; tel. (1) 4211631; fax (1) 4211167; e-mail info@mocs.gov.np; internet www.mocs.gov.np.

Ministry of Co-operatives and Poverty Alleviation: Singha Durbar, Kathmandu; tel. (1) 4211860; fax (1) 4211754; internet www.mocpa.gov.np.

Ministry of Culture, Tourism and Civil Aviation: Singha Durbar, Kathmandu; tel. (1) 4211870; fax (1) 4211758; e-mail info@tourism.gov.np; internet www.tourism.gov.np.

Ministry of Defence: Singha Durbar, Kathmandu; tel. (1) 4211289; fax (1) 4211294; e-mail info@mod.gov.np; internet www.mod.gov.np.

Ministry of Education: Singha Durbar, Kathmandu; tel. (1) 4418169; fax (1) 4200375; e-mail infomoe@moe.gov.np; internet www.doe.gov.np.

Ministry of Energy: Singha Durbar, Kathmandu; tel. (1) 4211516; fax (1) 4211510; e-mail info@moen.gov.np; internet www.moen.gov.np.

Ministry of Federal Affairs and Local Development: Singha Durbar, Kathmandu; tel. (1) 4200000; fax (1) 4200318; e-mail ipd@mofald.gov.np; internet www.mofald.gov.np.

Ministry of Finance: Singha Durbar, Kathmandu; tel. (1) 4211461; fax (1) 4211831; e-mail mail@mof.gov.np; internet www.mof.gov.np.

Ministry of Foreign Affairs: Narayanhiti, Kathmandu; tel. (1) 4200182; fax (1) 4200061; e-mail info@mofa.gov.np; internet www.mofa.gov.np.

Ministry of Forests and Soil Conservation: Singha Durbar, Kathmandu; tel. (1) 4211567; fax (1) 4211868; e-mail info@mfsc.gov.np; internet www.mfsc.gov.np.

Ministry of General Administration: Singha Durbar, Kathmandu; tel. (1) 4245367; fax (1) 4242138; e-mail info@moga.gov.np; internet www.moga.gov.np.

Ministry of Health and Population: Singha Durbar Plaza, Ramshah Path, Kathmandu; tel. (1) 4262802; fax (1) 4262896; e-mail info@mohp.gov.np; internet www.mohp.gov.np.

Ministry of Home Affairs: Singha Durbar, Kathmandu; tel. (1) 4211214; fax (1) 4211286; e-mail gunaso@moha.gov.np; internet www.moha.gov.np.

Ministry of Industry: Singha Durbar, Kathmandu; tel. (1) 4211579; fax (1) 4211619; e-mail info@moi.gov.np; internet www.moi.gov.np.

Ministry of Information and Communications: Singha Durbar, Kathmandu; tel. (1) 4211556; fax (1) 4211729; e-mail info@moic.gov.np; internet www.moic.gov.np.

Ministry of Irrigation: Singha Durbar, Kathmandu; tel. (1) 4211426; fax (1) 4200026; e-mail info@moir.gov.np; internet www.moir.gov.np.

Ministry of Labour and Employment: Singha Durbar, Kathmandu; tel. (1) 4211889; fax (1) 4211877; e-mail info@mole.gov.np; internet www.mole.gov.np.

Ministry of Land Reform and Management: Singha Durbar, Kathmandu; tel. (1) 4211666; fax (1) 4211708; e-mail info@molrm .gov.np; internet www.molrm.gov.np.

Ministry of Law, Justice, Constituent Assembly and Parliamentary Affairs: Singha Durbar, Kathmandu; tel. (1) 4211987; fax (1) 4211684; e-mail info@moljpa.gov.np; internet www.moljpa.gov .np.

Ministry of Peace and Reconstruction: Singha Durbar, Kathmandu; tel. (1) 4211550; e-mail info@peace.gov.np; internet www .peace.gov.np.

Ministry of Physical Infrastructure and Transport: Singha Durbar, Kathmandu; tel. (1) 4211782; fax (1) 4211720; e-mail info@ moppw.gov.np; internet www.mopit.gov.np.

Ministry of Science, Technology and Environment: Singha Durbar, Kathmandu; tel. (1) 4211737; fax (1) 4211954; e-mail info@ moste.gov.np; internet www.moste.gov.np.

Ministry of Urban Development: Singha Durbar, Kathmandu; tel. (1) 4211673; fax (1) 4211873; e-mail info@moud.gov.np; internet www.moud.gov.np.

Ministry of Women, Children and Social Welfare: Singha Durbar, Kathmandu; tel. (1) 4200082; fax (1) 4200116; e-mail mail@mowcsw.gov.np; internet www.mowcsw.gov.np.

Ministry of Youth and Sports: Kamalpokhari, Kathmandu; tel. (1) 4200538; fax (1) 4200542; e-mail info@moys.gov.np; internet www .moys.gov.np.

Legislature

CONSTITUENT ASSEMBLY

The Constituent Assembly was first established following elections in April 2008 and was responsible for drafting a new constitution. The Assembly's term of office expired in May 2012. Following lengthy delays, elections to a new Assembly took place on 19 November 2013. The Assembly comprises 601 members, of whom 575 are elected (using a mixed electoral system) and 26 nominated by the Government.

Constituent Assembly of Nepal: Constituent Assembly Secretariat, Singha Durbar, Kathmandu; tel. (1) 4200159; fax (1) 4222923; e-mail nepal.ipu@can.gov.np; internet www.can.gov.np.

Chairman and Speaker: SUBAS CHANDRA NEMBANG.

Vice-Chairman: ONSARI GHARTI MAGAR.

Election, 19 November 2013

Party	Seats*
Nepali Congress Party	196
Communist Party of Nepal (Unified Marxist-Leninist)	175
Unified Communist Party of Nepal (Maoist)	80
Rastriya Prajatantra Party Nepal	24
Madhesi Jana Adhikar Forum Nepal (Loktantrik)	14
Rastriya Prajatantra Party	13
Terai Madhes Loktantrik Party	11
Madhesi Jana Adhikar Forum Nepal	10
Sadbhavana Party	6
Communist Party of Nepal (Marxist-Leninist)	5
Federal Socialist Party	5
Nepal Workers' and Peasants' Party	4
Rastriya Janamorcha	3
Communist Party of Nepal (United)	3
Rashtriya Madhesh Samajwadi Party	3
Terai Madhes Sadbhavana Party	3
Rastriya Janamukti Party	2
Tharuhat Tarai Party Nepal	2
Nepal Pariwar Dal	2
Dalit Janajati Party	2
Akhanda Nepal Party	1
Madhesi Jana Adhikar Forum Nepal (Ganatantrik)	1
Nepali Janata Dal	1
Khambuwan Rashtriya Morcha Nepal	1
Nepa Rastriya Party	1
Jana Jagaran Party Nepal	1
Sanghiya Sadhbhawana Party	1
Madhesh Samata Party Nepal	1
Samajwadi Janata Party	1
Sanghiya Loktantrik Rastriya Manch (Tharuhat)	1
Independents	2
Nominated	26
Total	**601**

*Includes seats determined by proportional representation and 'first-past-the-post' systems.

Election Commission

Election Commission of Nepal: Bahadur Bhawan, Kantipath, Kathmandu; tel. (1) 4228663; fax (1) 4229227; e-mail info@election .gov.np; internet www.election.gov.np; independent; appointed by the Prime Minister, on the recommendation of a Constitutional Council, for a 6-year term; Chief Election Commr NEEL KANTHA UPRETY.

Political Organizations

More than 120 political parties participated in the Constituent Assembly elections of November 2013. Some of the most important parties are listed below.

Communist Party of Nepal (Maoist) (CPN—Maoist): Kathmandu; est. after split in the Unified Communist Party of Nepal (Maoist) in Jun. 2012; 44-mem. cen. cttee; boycotted the 2013 Constituent Assembly elections; Chair. MOHAN BAIDYA.

Communist Party of Nepal (Marxist-Leninist) (CPN—ML): Rudranagar Marga, Ratopul, Kathmandu; tel. (1) 4469033; fax 4469035; e-mail cpnml.cc@gmail.com; internet www.cpnml.org.np; re-formed in 2002 following the reunification of the Communist Party of Nepal (Marxist-Leninist) with the Communist Party of Nepal (Unified Marxist-Leninist); C. P. Mainali, co-founder of the original CPN—ML as a breakaway faction of the CPN (UML) in 1998, had opposed the merger and formed a separate party under the CPN—ML title; Gen. Sec. C. P. MAINALI.

Communist Party of Nepal (Unified Marxist-Leninist) (UML): Madan Nagar, Balkhu, POB 5471, Kathmandu; tel. (1) 4278081; fax (1) 4278084; e-mail uml@ntc.net.np; internet www.cpnuml.org; f. 1991 when two major factions of the Communist Party of Nepal (CPN; f. 1949; banned 1960; legalized 1990)—the Marxist and Marxist-Leninist factions—merged; the Communist Party of Nepal (Marxist-Leninist—ML) seceded in 1998 and rejoined the UML in 2002; the Communist Party of Nepal (Verma) merged with the UML in 2001; Chair. K. P. SHARMA OLI; Gen. Sec. ISHWAR POKHAREL.

Communist Party of Nepal (United): Samyukta Galli, Setopul, Maitidevi, Kathmandu; tel. (1) 4427416; e-mail centraloffice@ncpunited.com; internet www.ncpunited.com; f. 2007 following a split in the Communist Party of Nepal (United Marxist); Chair. CHANDRA DEO JOSHI; Gen. Sec. SUNIL MANANDHAR.

Madhesi Jana Adhikar Forum Nepal (Madhesi People's Rights Forum Nepal, MPRFN): Sanepa, Lalitpur; tel. (1) 5524440; fax (1) 5541278; e-mail mprfnepal@gmail.com; internet www.mprfn.org; f. 2006; Chair. UPENDRA YADAV; Gen. Sec. RAM SAHAYA YADAV; in addition, there are two breakaway factions: the Madhesi Jana Adhikar Forum Nepal—Loktantrik (MPRFN—Democratic), headed by BIJAYA KUMAR GACHCHHADAR; and the Madhesi Jana Adhikar Forum Nepal—Ganatantrik (MPRFN—Republican), headed by JAYA PRAKASH GUPTA.

Nepal Workers' and Peasants' Party: Golmadhi Tole-7, Bhaktapur, Kathmandu; tel. (1) 6610974; fax (1) 6613207; e-mail nwpp@ntc .net.np; Chair. NARAYAN MAN BIJUKCHHEN (Comrade Rohit); Gen. Sec. SUNIL PRAJAPATI.

Nepali Congress Party (NCP): B. P. Smriti Bhavan, B. P. Nagar, Sanepa, Lalitpur; tel. (1) 5555263; fax (1) 5555188; e-mail ncparty@ wlink.com.np; internet www.nepalicongress.org; f. 1947; banned 1960; legalized 1990; Nepali Congress Party—Democratic formed as breakaway faction in 2002, rejoined Sept. 2007; c. 317,000 active mems, 1m. ordinary mems; Pres. SUSHIL KOIRALA; Leader SHER BAHADUR DEUBA; Vice-Pres. RAM CHANDRA POUDEL; Gen. Secs PRAKASH MAN SINGH, KRISHNA PRASAD SITAULA.

Rastriya Janamorcha: Ekta Basti, Kathmandu; tel. (1) 4420226; internet www.rajamo.org; Hindu; pro-royalist; merged with Samyukta Janamorcha Nepal in 2013; Chair. CHITRA BAHADUR K. C.

Rastriya Janamukti Party: Dhobighat Chowk, Ring Rd, POB 5569, Lalitpur; tel. and fax (1) 5527633; e-mail janamukti48@gmail .com; internet www.janamuktiparty.com; f. 1990; Pres. MALBAR SINGH THAPA; Gen. Sec. SURYA RAJBANSI.

Rashtriya Madhesh Samajwadi Party: Gwarko, Lalitpur; tel. 9851036177 (mobile); f. 2012; est. by fmr senior mems of the Madhesi Jana Adhikar Forum Nepal—Loktantrik; Chair. SHARAT SINGH BANDHARI.

Rastriya Prajatantra Party (RPP): Central Office, Charumati, Chabahil Kathmandu; tel. (1) 4471071; fax (1) 4460324; e-mail rppnepal@enet.com.np; internet rppnepal.org; f. 1990; fmrly divided into two factions led by former Prime Ministers Lokendra Bahadur Chand and Surya Bahadur Thapa, respectively; factions reunited in 2013; centre-right, with origins as a monarchist party; Chair. PASHUPATI SHUMSHER J. B. RANA; Leader LOKENDRA BAHADUR CHAND.

Rastriya Prajatantra Party Nepal: Ichchhumati Marga, Baluwatar, Kathmandu; tel. and fax (1) 4430635; internet rppn.org.np;

f. 2008 as splinter group of RPP; monarchist; Chair. KAMAL THAPA; Gen. Sec. CHANDRA BAHADUR GURUNG.

Sadbhavana Party (SP): Kathmandu; Chair. RAJENDRA MAHATO; Gen. Sec. MANISH SUMAN; there is also a breakaway faction entitled the Federal Sadbhavana Party.

Terai Madhes Loktantrik Party (Terai Madhes Democratic Party—TMDP): 657/21 Bhakti Thapa Marg, Bijulibazaar, Kathmandu; tel. (1) 4462398; 9 members of the party separated to form a faction called Terai Madhes Loktantrik Party (Nepal) in Dec. 2010; Pres. MAHANTHA THAKUR.

Unified Communist Party of Nepal (Maoist) (UCPN—M): Central Office, Perishdanda, Koteshwor, Kathmandu; tel. (1) 4602290; fax (1) 4602289; e-mail ucpnminfo69@gmail.com; internet ucpnmaoist.org; f. 1990 as Communist Party of Nepal (Unity Centre), renamed as CPN (Maoist) in 1995; fmr underground political movement, represented in Interim Parliament in 2007; orchestrated 'people's war' in hills of western Nepal (1996–2006); merged with CPN (Unified Marxist-Leninist-Maoist) in Sept. 2007; merged with CPN (Marxist) in Feb. 2008; merged with CPN (Unity Centre-Masal) in Jan. 2009 and name changed as above; 175-mem. cen. cttee; Chair. PUSHPA KAMAL DAHAL ('Prachanda'); Vice-Chair. BABURAM BHATTRAI; Vice-Chair. NARYANKAJI SHRESTHA.

Diplomatic Representation

EMBASSIES IN NEPAL

Australia: Suraj Niwas, Bansbari, POB 879, Kathmandu; tel. (1) 4371678; fax (1) 4371533; internet www.nepal.embassy.gov.au; Ambassador GLENN DARRAN WHITE.

Bangladesh: Bashundhara, Chakrapath, Ward 4, POB 789, Kathmandu; tel. (1) 4390130; fax (1) 4390132; e-mail mission .kathmandu@mofa.gov.bd; internet bangladoot.org.np; Ambassador MASHFEE BINTE SHAMS.

Brazil: 155 Chundevi Marg, Mahargunj, POB 19299, Kathmandu; tel. (1) 4721462; fax (1) 4721464; e-mail marcos.dupart@itamaraty .br; Ambassador MARCOS BORGES D. RIBEIRO.

China, People's Republic: Baluwatar, POB 4234, Kathmandu; tel. (1) 4411740; fax (1) 4414045; e-mail chinaemb_np@mfa.gov.cn; internet np.chineseembassy.org; Ambassador WU CHUNTAI.

Denmark: 761 Neel Saraswati Marg, Lazimpat, POB 6332, Kathmandu; tel. (1) 4413010; fax (1) 4411409; e-mail ktmamb@um.dk; internet www.ambkathmandu.um.dk; Ambassador KIRSTEN ROSENVOLD GEELAN.

Egypt: Naya Bazar Chowk, Saibu Bhaisepati, Lalitpur, POB 792, Kathmandu; tel. (1) 5590544; fax (1) 5592661; e-mail embassy .kathmandu@mfa.gov.eg; internet www.mfa.gov.eg/english/ embassies/Egyptian_Embassy_Nepal; Ambassador BAHER NABIL ABDEL FATTAH HELMY.

Finland: Bishalnagar, POB 2126, Kathmandu; tel. (1) 4416636; fax (1) 4416703; e-mail sanomat.kat@formin.fi; internet www.finland .org.np; Ambassador ASKO JUHANI LUUKKAINEN.

France: 302 Narayan Gopal Rd, Lazimpat, POB 452, Kathmandu; tel. (1) 4412332; fax (1) 4419968; e-mail ambassade@ambafrance-np .org; internet www.ambafrance-np.org; Ambassador MARTINE BASSEREAU.

Germany: 690 Gyaneshwar Marg, POB 226, Kathmandu; tel. (1) 4417200; fax (1) 4416899; e-mail info@kathmandu.diplo.de; internet www.kathmandu.diplo.de; Ambassador MATTHIAS MAYER.

India: 336 Kapurdhara Marg, POB 292, Kathmandu; tel. (1) 4410900; fax (1) 4428279; e-mail hoc.kathmandu@mea.gov.in; internet www.indianembassy.org.np; Ambassador RANJIT RAE.

Israel: Bishramalaya House, Lazimpat St, POB 371, Kathmandu; tel. (1) 4411811; fax (1) 4413920; e-mail info@kathmandu.mfa.gov.il; internet kathmandu.mfa.gov.il; Ambassador YARON MAYER.

Japan: Panipokhari, POB 264, Kathmandu; tel. (1) 4426680; fax (1) 4414101; e-mail inquiry-emb@km.mofa.go.jp; internet www.np .emb-japan.go.jp; Ambassador MASASHI OGAWA.

Korea, Democratic People's Republic: Jhamsikhel, Lalitpur, Kathmandu; tel. (1) 5521855; fax (1) 5525394; e-mail rimnine@ wlink.com.np; Ambassador KIM YONG HAK.

Korea, Republic: Ravibhawan, Kalimati, POB 1058, Kathmandu; tel. (1) 4270172; fax (1) 4272041; e-mail konepemb@gmail.com; internet npl.mofat.go.kr; Ambassador CHOE YONG-JIN.

Malaysia: Blk B, 2nd Floor, Karmachha Sanchaya Kosh Bldg, Pulchowk, POB 24372, Lalitpur, Kathmandu; tel. (1) 5010004; fax (1) 5010492; e-mail malkatmandu@kln.gov.my; internet www.kln .gov.my/perwakilan/kathmandu; Chargé d'affaires a. i. FADLI ADILAH.

Myanmar: 997 Nakhhu Height, Bhaisepati, Lalitpur, POB 2437, Kathmandu; tel. (1) 5592774; fax (1) 5592776; e-mail myanmaremb@

wlink.com.np; internet www.mofa.gov.mm/myanmarmissions/
nepal.html; Ambassador ZAW MYINT.

Norway: Surya Court, Pulchowk, Lalitpur, POB 20765, Kathmandu; tel. (1) 5545307; fax (1) 5545226; e-mail emb.kathmandu@
mfa.no; internet www.norway.org.np; Ambassador KJELL TORMOD
PETTERSEN.

Pakistan: Pushpanjali, Maharajgunj, Chakrapath, POB 202, Kathmandu; tel. (1) 4374024; fax (1) 4374012; e-mail pakembktm@gmail
.com; internet www.mofa.gov.pk/nepal; Ambassador ARSHED SAUD
KHOSA.

Russian Federation: Baluwatar, POB 123, Kathmandu; tel. (1)
4412155; fax (1) 4416571; e-mail ruspos@info.com.np; internet www
.nepal.mid.ru; Ambassador Dr SERGEI V. VELICHKIN.

Saudi Arabia: Sumangal, Maharajgunj, Kathmandu; tel. (1)
4720891; fax (1) 4720837; e-mail kaemb@mofa.gov.sa; internet
embassies.mofa.gov.sa/sites/nepal/en; Ambassador ABDUL NASSER
BIN HUSSAIN AL-HARTHI.

Sri Lanka: Shiva Ashis Niwas, Gairi Marg, Maharajgunj, POB
8802, Kathmandu; tel. (1) 4720623; fax (1) 4720128; e-mail
lankaemb@wlink.com.np; internet www.slembktm.com; Ambassador W. M. SENEVIRATHNA.

Switzerland: Jawalakhel, Ekanta Kuna, SDC-Compound, Lalitpur, POB 113, Kathmandu; tel. (1) 5524927; fax (1) 5525358; e-mail
kat.vertretung@eda.admin.ch; internet www.eda.admin.ch/
kathmandu; Ambassador URS HERREN.

Thailand: 167/4 Ward 3, Maharajgunj-Bansbari Rd, POB 3333,
Kathmandu; tel. (1) 4371410; fax (1) 4371409; e-mail thaiemb@wlink
.com.np; internet www.thaiembnepal.org.np; Ambassador VUTTI
VUTTISANT.

United Kingdom: Lainchaur, POB 106, Kathmandu; tel. (1)
4410583; fax (1) 4411789; e-mail bekathmandu@fco.gov.uk;
internet ukinnepal.fco.gov.uk; Chargé d'affaires a. i. JOHN RANKIN.

USA: Maharajgunj, POB 295, Kathmandu; tel. (1) 4234000; fax (1)
4007272; e-mail usembktm@state.gov; internet nepal.usembassy
.gov; Ambassador PETER W. BODDE.

Judicial System

According to the Interim Constitution, the judicial system has three
tiers: the Supreme Court (which is also a Court of Record), the
Appellate Courts and the District Courts. The Supreme Court consists of a Chief Justice and a maximum of 14 other judges. The Chief
Justice is appointed by the Prime Minister on the recommendation of
the Constitutional Council; other Supreme Court, Appellate Court
and District Court judges are nominated by the Chief Justice on the
recommendation of the Judicial Council. A Constituent Assembly
Court was established in February 2008 to deal with election
matters.

Supreme Court: Ramashah Path, Kathmandu; tel. (1) 4262895;
e-mail info@supremecourt.gov.np; internet www.supremecourt.gov
.np; Chief Justice RAM KUMAR PRASAD SHAH.

Office of the Attorney-General: Ramshah Path, Kathmandu; tel.
(1) 4240210; fax (1) 4262582; e-mail info@attorneygeneral.gov.np;
internet www.attorneygeneral.gov.np; Attorney-General BABU RAM
KUNWAR.

Religion

At the 2011 census, an estimated 81.3% of the population professed
Hinduism, while 9.0% were Buddhists and 4.4% Muslims. The actual
number of Muslims in the country was considered to be much higher,
owing to immigration from Bangladesh. There were an estimated
375,699 Christians (1.4% of the population) in Nepal in 2011.

BUDDHISM

All Nepal Bhikkhu Association: Vishwa Shanti Vihara (World
Peace Temple), 465 Ekadantamarga, Minbhavan, New Baneshwor,
POB 8973 NPC-327, Kathmandu; tel. (1) 4622984; fax (1) 4622250;
e-mail anbanepal@gmail.com; internet www.anba.org.np; f. 1950;
Sec.-Gen. BHIKSHU KONDANYA.

Nepal Buddhist Council: Nahtole, Lalitpur 20; tel. (1) 5534277;
e-mail info@nepalbuddhistcouncil.org.np; internet www
.nepalbuddhistcouncil.org.np; f. 1977; Chair. MAHISWOR RAJ
BAJRACHARYA.

United Trungram Buddhist Foundation: Hattigauda, Bansbari,
POB 3157, Kathmandu; tel. (1) 4370089; fax (1) 4370292; e-mail
info@utbf.org; internet www.utbf.org; Spiritual Dir GYALTRUL
RINPOCHE.

CHRISTIANITY
Protestant Church

Nepal Northern Evangelical Lutheran Church: AT Laxmipur,
POB 3, Babiya Birta, Morang District; tel. 9842045726 (mobile);
e-mail josephsoren@hotmail.com; Pres. Rev. JOSEPH SOREN.

Presbyterian Church of the Kingdom of Nepal: POB 3237,
Kathmandu; tel. and fax (1) 4524450.

The Roman Catholic Church

The Church is represented in Nepal by a single apostolic vicariate. At
31 December 2010 there were an estimated 7,731 adherents in the
country.

Apostolic Vicariate: John Paul II Smriti-Bas, POB 8975, EPC 974,
Kathmandu; tel. (1) 5542802; fax (1) 5521710; e-mail
bishoppaulsimick@gmail.com; f. 1983 as Catholic Mission; Vicar
Apostolic Most Rev. PAUL SIMICK.

The Press

PRINCIPAL DAILIES

The Commoner: Naradevi, POB 203, Kathmandu; tel. (1) 4228236;
f. 1956; English; Publr and Chief Editor GOPAL DASS SHRESTHA; circ.
7,000.

Daily News: Bhimsensthan, POB 171, Kathmandu; tel. (1) 4279147;
e-mail manju_sakya@hotmail.com; f. 1983; Nepali and English;
Chief Editor MANJU RATNA SAKYA; Publr SUBHA LAXMI SAKYA; circ.
20,000.

Gorkhapatra: Dharma Path, POB 23, Kathmandu; tel. (1) 4222921;
fax (1) 4221748; e-mail news.gorkhapatra@gmail.com; internet www
.gorkhapatra.org.np; f. 1901; Nepali; govt-owned; Chair. RAMESH
TOOFAN; Gen. Man. SUSHIL KOIRALA; circ. 75,000.

The Himalayan Times: International Media Network Nepal (Pvt)
Ltd, APCA House, Baidya Khana Rd, Anam Nagar, POB 11651,
Kathmandu; tel. (1) 4770358; fax (1) 4771959; e-mail editorial@
thehimalayantimes.com; internet www.thehimalayantimes.com;
f. 2001; English; Editor AJAYA BHADRA KHANAL.

Kantipur: Kantipur Complex, Subhidhanagar, POB 8559, Kathmandu; tel. (1) 5135000; fax (1) 5135001; e-mail sudheer@kantipur
.com.np; internet www.ekantipur.com; f. 1993; Nepali; Chair. and
Man. Dir KAILASH SIROHIYA; Editor SUDHEER SHARMA; circ. 210,000.

Karobar National Economic Daily: TBI Publications Pvt Ltd, 492
Madhya Marga, Buddhanagar 10, Kathmandu; tel. (1) 4785000; fax
(1) 4785665; e-mail mail@karobardaily.com; internet www
.karobardaily.com; Nepali, with English content available online;
economic and business news; Man. Editor SHISHEER BHATTA.

Kathmandu Post: Kantipur Complex, Subhidhanagar, POB 8559,
Kathmandu; tel. (1) 5135000; fax (1) 5135001; e-mail au@kantipur
.com.np; internet www.kantipuronline.com; f. 1993; English; Editor
AKHILESH UPADHYAY; circ. 40,000.

Nepal Samacharpatra: Kamana Estate, Maru Bhimsensthan,
Kathmandu; tel. (1) 4261179; fax (1) 4218990; e-mail web@
newsofnepal.com; internet newsofnepal.com; f. 1945; Nepali; Editor-
in-Chief PUSHKAR LAL SHRESTHA; circ. 1,000.

Rajdhani: Kupondole, Lalitpur, Kathmandu; tel. (1) 5546300; fax
(1) 5011594; e-mail info@rajdhani.com.np; internet www.rajdhani
.com.np; Editor KAPIL KAFLE; circ. 50,000.

Rising Nepal: Dharma Path, POB 1623, Kathmandu; tel. (1)
4244437; fax (1) 4224381; e-mail trn@gorkhapatra.org.np; internet
www.gorkhapatra.org.np; f. 1965; English; Editor-in-Chief AJAY
RANA; circ. 20,000.

SELECTED PERIODICALS

Arpan: Bhimsensthan, POB 285, Kathmandu; tel. (1) 4244450;
e-mail manju_sakya@hotmail.com; internet www.nepalnews.com/
arpan.php; f. 1964; weekly; Nepali; Publr and Chief Editor MANJU
RATNA SAKYA; circ. 18,000.

Commerce: Bhimsensthan, POB 171, Kathmandu; tel. (1) 4279636;
e-mail manju_sakya@hotmail.com; f. 1971; monthly; English; Publr
and Chief Editor MANJU RATNA SAKYA; Editor SUBHA LAXMI SAKYA;
circ. 12,000.

Himal Southasian: Patan Dhoka, Lalitpur, POB 24393; tel. (1)
5547279; fax (1) 5552141; e-mail info@himalmag.com; internet www
.himalmag.com; f. 1987; monthly; political, business, social and
environmental issues throughout South Asia; Editor-in-Chief KANAK
MANI DIXIT.

Janadharana (People's Opinion): Kathmandu; e-mail
janadharana@gmail.com; weekly; independent; Editor NIMKANT
PANDEY.

Janmabhumi: Janmabhumi Press, Tahachal, Kathmandu; tel. (1) 4280979; fax (1) 4274795; e-mail sirishnp@hotmail.com; f. 1970; weekly; Nepali; Publr and Editor SHIRISH BALLABH PRADHAN.

Madhuparka: Dharmapath, POB 23, Kathmandu; tel. (1) 4222278; f. 1986; monthly; Nepali; literary; Editor OM SHRESTHA; circ. 20,000.

Mulyankan: Kathmandu; monthly, left-wing; Editor JHALAK SUBEDI.

Nepal National Weekly: Kantipur Publications Pvt Ltd, Kantipur Complex, Subhidhanagar, POB 8559, Kathmandu; tel. (1) 5135000; fax (1) 5135025; e-mail prashanta@kantipur.com.np; internet www.ekantipur.com/nepal; f. 2000; weekly; Nepali; Editor PRASHANT ARYAL; circ. 40,000.

Nepali Times: Himalmedia Pvt Ltd, POB 7251, Kathmandu; tel. (1) 5005603; fax (1) 5005518; e-mail editors@nepalitimes.com; internet www.nepalitimes.com; f. 2000; weekly; English; publ. by Himalmedia Pvt Ltd; Publr and Editor KUNDA DIXIT; circ. 15,000.

People's Review: Pipalbot, Dillibazar, POB 3052, Kathmandu; tel. (1) 4417352; fax (1) 4438797; e-mail preview@ntc.net.np; internet www.peoplesreview.com.np; f. 1991; weekly; English; Chief Editor and Publr PUSHPA RAJ PRADHAN; circ. 15,000.

Rastrabani: Kathmandu; tel. (1) 4410339; weekly; Nepali; Chief Editor HARI LAMSAL.

Saptahik Weekly: Kantipur Complex, Subhidhanagar, POB 8559, Kathmandu; tel. (1) 4480100; fax (1) 4466320; e-mail subas@kantipur.com.np; internet www.ekantipur.com/saptahik/; f. 1997; weekly; Nepali; news and entertainment; Editor SUBASH DHAKAL.

Swatantra Manch Weekly: POB 49, Ghattekulo, Kathmandu; tel. (1) 4436374; fax (1) 4435931; e-mail das@ntc.net.np; f. 1985; independent; weekly; Nepali; Publr and Chief Editor VIJOY KUMAR DAS; circ. 40,000.

The Telegraph: Ghattekulo, Laligurans Marg, POB 4063, Kathmandu; tel. (1) 4770370; e-mail tgw@ntc.net.np; internet www.telegraphnepal.com; f. 2007; weekly; English; Chief Editor NARENDRA P. UPADHYAYA.

NEWS AGENCY

Rastriya Samachar Samiti (RSS): Bhadrakali Plaza, POB 220, Kathmandu; tel. (1) 4262912; fax (1) 4262744; e-mail info@rss.com.np; internet www.rss.com.np; f. 1962; state-operated; Chair. KUL CHANDRA WAGLE; Gen. Man. RAM KUMAR KOIRALA.

PRESS ASSOCIATIONS

Federation of Nepalese Journalists (FNJ): Media Village, Tilganga, Kathmandu; tel. (1) 4112763; fax (1) 4112785; e-mail fnjnepal@mail.com.np; internet www.fnjnepal.org; f. 1956; Pres. MAHENDRA BISTA; Gen. Sec. UJIR MAGAR.

Nepal Journalists' Association (NJA): Maitighar, POB 285, Kathmandu; tel. (1) 4262426; e-mail manju_sakya@hotmail.com; internet www.nja.org.np; 5,400 mems; Pres. MANJU RATNA SAKYA; Gen. Sec. NIRMAL KUMAR ARYAL.

Press Council: Sanchargram, Tilganga, POB 3077, Kathmandu; tel. (1) 4112799; fax (1) 4112694; e-mail prescoun_mdf@wlink.com.np; internet www.presscouncilnepal.org; f. 1970; Chair. BORNA BAHADUR KARKI; Sec. LAXMI BILASH KOIRALA.

Publishers

Educational Publishing House: POB 5178, Kathmandu; tel. (1) 4241255; e-mail eph.nepal@gmail.com; f. 1962; educational and technical; Dir JYOTSNA SHRESTHA.

Fine Print: Bishal Nagar Basti, Bishal Nagar, POB 19041, Kathmandu; tel. (1) 4443263; e-mail fineprint@wlink.com.np; internet www.fineprint.com.np; f. 2006; general, non-fiction and fiction; CEO NIRAJ BHARI; Man. Dir AJIT BARAL.

Himal Books: Himal Association, 540 Lazimpat, Narayangopal Sadak, Kathmandu; tel. (1) 4440635; e-mail info@himalbooks.com; internet www.himalbooks.com; f. 1992; subsidiary operation of Himal Association; general interest and academic publications in English and Nepali; Exec. Dir BASANTA THAPA.

Mandala Book Point: Kantipath, POB 528, Kathmandu; tel. (1) 4227711; fax (1) 4255921; e-mail info@mandalabookpoint.com; internet www.mandalabookpoint.com; publishes in a wide range of non-fiction areas, incl. history, politics, religion, languages and reference; also publishes the journal *Studies in Nepali History and Society (SINHAS)*.

Nepal Academy: Kamaladi, Kathmandu; tel. (1) 4221241; fax (1) 4221175; e-mail office@nepalacademy.org.np; internet www.nepalacademy.org.np; f. 1957; fmrly known as Royal Nepal Academy, name changed to present 2007; languages, literature, social sciences, art and philosophy; Chair. GANGA PRASAD UPRETY.

Pilgrims Publishing Nepal (Pvt) Ltd: Thamel, POB 3872, Kathmandu; tel. (1) 4221546; fax (1) 4700943; e-mail pilgrims@wlink.com.np; internet www.pilgrimsbooks.com; f. 1985; Asian studies, religion and travel; offices in Kathmandu and Varanasi (India); also operates Pilgrims Book House book stores in Kathmandu and Patan; Propr KAHANI TIWARI.

Ratna Pustak Bhandar: 71 Ga Bank Marg, POB 98, Kathmandu; tel. (1) 4223026; fax (1) 4248421; e-mail rpb@wlink.com.np; internet ratnabooks.com; f. 1945; textbooks, general, non-fiction and fiction; Propr GOVINDA PRASAD SHRESTHA.

Sajha Prakashan: Pulchowk, Lalitpur, POB 20259, Kathmandu; tel. (1) 5521118; fax (1) 5544236; e-mail sajhap@wlink.com.np; internet www.sajha.org.np; f. 1964; educational, literary and general; Chair. (vacant).

Sunbird Publishers: POB 13363, Kathmandu; tel. (1) 4412799; e-mail sunbirdpublishers@gmail.com; internet www.sunbird.org.np; comprises 2 separate imprints: Ramailo Kitaab for children and Yuwa Pushtak for teenagers.

Vajra Publications: Jyatha, Thamel, POB 21779, Kathmandu; tel. (1) 4220562; e-mail Vajrabooks@hotmail.com; internet www.vajrabookshop.com; publishes books on Nepal and Tibet, covering areas incl. history, religion and anthropology; Man. Dir BIDUR DONGOL.

Tribhuvan University Press: T.U. Press, Kirtipur, Kathmandu; tel. (1) 4331320; e-mail press@tribhuvan-university.edu.np; internet tribhuvan-university.edu.np/t-u-press/; Chief Editor KRISHNA LAL KCHHETRI.

GOVERNMENT PUBLISHING HOUSE

Department of Information: Ministry of Information and Communications, Sanchar Gram, Tilganga, Kathmandu; tel. (1) 4112551; fax (1) 483252; e-mail info@doinepal.gov.np; internet www.doinepal.gov.np.

Broadcasting and Communications

TELECOMMUNICATIONS

According to the Nepal Telecommunications Authority, in January 2015 there were 23.2m. mobile telephone subscribers, representing a mobile penetration rate of 87.6% of the population. At the same time there were 838,900 fixed-line telephone subscribers, and an estimated 10.3m. subscribers to various internet services (giving an internet penetration rate of 38.8%).

Nepal Telecommunications Authority: Bluestar Office Complex, Tripureswor, POB 9754, Kathmandu; tel. (1) 4101030; fax (1) 4101034; e-mail info@nta.gov.np; internet www.nta.gov.np; telecommunications regulatory body; f. 1998; Chair. DIGAMBAR JHA.

Mercantile Communications (Pvt) Ltd: Hiti Pokhari, Durbar Marg, POB 66, Kathmandu; tel. (1) 4445920; fax (1) 4427614; e-mail info@mercantile.com.np; internet www.mos.com.np; f. 1994; internet service provider; CEO SANJIB RAJ BHANDARI.

Ncell (Pvt) Ltd: Krishna Tower, Buddhanagar, New Baneshwor, Kathmandu 10; tel. (980) 5554444; fax (980) 5554442; e-mail info@ncell.com.np; internet www.ncell.com.np; f. 2004; subsidiary of Telia Sonera Group (Sweden); launched Nepal's first privately owned GSM mobile network under Mero Mobile brand in 2005; services rebranded as Ncell in 2010; CEO ERIM TAYLANLAR; 12.1m. subscribers (Jan. 2015).

Nepal Satellite Telecom (Pvt) Ltd (Hello Nepal): Muktishree Tower, New Baneshwor, Kathmandu; tel. (1) 4785602; fax (1) 4785601; e-mail info@nepalsatellite.com.np; internet www.hellonepalgsm.com; f. 2005; awarded licence to provide GSM mobile services in 2008; owned by the Muktishree Group; Chair. MATS SALOMONSSON; 280,917 subscribers (Jan. 2015).

Nepal Telecom (Nepal Doorsanchar Co Ltd): Bhadrakali Plaza, POB 11803, Kathmandu; tel. (1) 4210202; fax (1) 4222424; e-mail rkt@ntc.net.np; internet www.ntc.net.np; f. 1975; operates fixed-line and mobile services; 85% state-owned, 10% owned by Nepalese public, 5% owned by Nepal Telecom employees; Chair. SUNIL BAHADUR MALLA; 11.9m. subscribers (Jan. 2015).

Smart Telecom (Pvt) Ltd (STPL): Ram-Ishwar Bhavan, Kumaripati 20, Lalitpur, POB 8975 Kathmandu; tel. (1) 5008587; fax (1) 5008590; e-mail info@smarttel.com.np; internet www.smarttel.com.np; awarded license to provide rural telecommunications services in 2008; from 2013 licensed to provide nationwide mobile services; 80% owned by Lal Sahu Distribution (Singapore); Chair. SACHIN LAL ACHARYA; CEO ABRAHAM SMITH; 1.3m. subscribers (Jan. 2015).

United Telecom Ltd: Ground Floor, Triveni Complex, Putali Sadak, Kathmandu; tel. (1) 2499092; fax (1) 2499999; e-mail info@utlnepal.com; internet www.utlnepal.com; f. 2003; jt venture between Indian-owned Mahanagar Telephone Nigam Ltd,

Telecommunications Consultants India Ltd, Tata Communications Ltd, and Nepal Ventures Pvt Ltd; Chair. VIMAL WAKHLU; 508,841 subscribers (Dec. 2014).

BROADCASTING

Radio

Radio Nepal: Radio Broadcasting Service, Government of Nepal, Singha Durbar, POB 634, Kathmandu; tel. (1) 4211910; fax (1) 4211952; e-mail rne@wlink.com.np; internet radionepal.gov.np; f. 1951; broadcasts on short-wave, medium-wave and FM frequencies in 20 regional languages, incl. Nepali and English, for 18 hours daily (incl. 2 hours of regional broadcasting in the morning and evening); short-wave station at Khumaltar and medium-wave stations at Bhainsepati, Pokhara, Surkhet, Dipayal, Bardibas and Dharan; FM stations at Kathmandu, Kanchanpur, Rupandhi, Chitwan, Maka-wanpur, Bara, Jumla, Mustang, Ilam, Simikot and Humla; Chair. SUNIL BAHADUR MALLA; Exec. Dir SURESH KUMAR KARKI.

Kantipur FM: Pulchowk Lalitpur EPC 100, 8975, POB 14360, Kathmandu; tel. (1) 5541902; fax (1) 5522731; e-mail kfmmarketing@kantipur.com.np; internet www.radiokantipur.com; f. 1998; broadcasts 24 hrs daily; Man. Dir KAILASH SIROHIYA; Station Man. PRABHAT RIMAL.

Radio Lumbini: Tilottama Municipality, Ward No 6, Manigram, Ruphandehi; tel. (71) 561003; fax (71) 561545; e-mail office@radiolumbini.org; internet www.radiolumbini.org; f. 2000; Chair. KRISHNA PRASAD ARYAL.

Radio Sagarmatha: Bakhundol, Lalitpur, GPOB 6958, Kathmandu; tel. (1) 5528091; fax (1) 5530227; e-mail stationmanager@radiosagarmatha.org; internet radiosagarmatha.org.np; f. 1997; independent; Chair. LAXMAN UPRETI; Station Man. GHAMA RAJ LUITEL.

Television

Nepal Television Corpn: Singha Durbar, POB 3826, Kathmandu; tel. (1) 4220348; fax (1) 4200212; internet www.ntv.org.np; f. 1985; operates NTV and NTV2; programmes in Nepali (50%), English (25%) and Hindi/Urdu (25%); regional station at Kohalpur; Chair. NIR SHAH; Gen. Man. DEEPAK MANI DHITAL (acting).

Avenues TV: 11 Avenues Plaza Tripureshwar, POB 2806, Kathmandu; tel. (1) 4227222; fax (1) 4255177; e-mail atv@avenues.tv; internet www.avenues.tv; f. 2003; news service; Exec. Chair. BHASKAR RAJ RAJKARNIKAR.

Image Channel: Image Complex, POB 5566, Panipokhari, Kathmandu; tel. (1) 4006555; fax (1) 4427262; e-mail ichannel@wlink.com.np; internet www.imagechannels.com; f. 2003; privately owned; Chair. R. K. MANANDHAR.

Kantipur Television Network (KTV): Kantipur Complex, Sub-hidhanagar, POB 7368, Kathmandu; tel. (1) 5135050; fax (1) 5135055; e-mail info@kantipurtv.com; internet www.kantipurtv.com; f. 2003; Chair. HEM RAJ GYAWALI; Man. Dir KAILASH SIROHIYA.

Sagarmatha Television (STV): POB 10537, Rudramati Marg, Dhobikhola, Babarmahal, Kathmandu; tel. (1) 4233071; fax (1) 4233073; e-mail info@sagarmatha.tv; internet www.sagarmatha.tv; f. 2007; news channel; broadcasts in more than 5 dialects; Chair. NIRMAL GURUNG.

Space-Time Network: Minbhavan, New Baneshwor, Kathmandu; tel. (1) 4487228; fax (1) 4492261; e-mail info@spacetimenetwork.com.np; internet www.spacetimenetwork.com.np; f. 1993; satellite transmission services; launched Channel Nepal, the country's first satellite channel, in 2001.

Finance

(auth. = authorized; cap. = capital; dep. = deposits; res = reserves; m. = million; brs = branches; amounts in Nepalese rupees)

BANKING

Central Bank

Nepal Rastra Bank: Central Office, Baluwatar, POB 73, Kathmandu; tel. (1) 4410158; fax (1) 4410159; e-mail fxm@nrb.org.np; internet www.nrb.org.np; f. 1956; bank of issue; 100% state-owned; cap. 3,000m., res 43,930m., dep. 75,703m. (July 2009); Gov. and Chair. Dr CHIRANJIBI NEPAL; 9 brs.

Domestic Commercial Banks

Kumari Bank Ltd: Durbarmarg, POB 21128, Kathmandu; tel. (1) 4221312; fax (1) 4231960; e-mail info@kbl.com.np; internet www.kumaribank.com; f. 2001; auth. cap. 1,603.8m., res 759m., dep. 22,385m. (July 2012); Chair. NOOR PRATAP RANA; CEO UDAYA K. UPADHYAY; 8 brs.

Nepal Bank Ltd: Nepal Bank Bldg, Dharmapath, New Rd, POB 36, Kathmandu; tel. (1) 4222397; fax (1) 4220414; e-mail info@nepalbank.com.np; internet www.nepalbank.com.np; f. 1937; 40% state-owned, 60% owned by Nepalese public; cap. 1,772.8m., res 2,450.5m., dep. 56,052.3m. (July 2012); CEO DEVENDRA PRATAP SHAH; 105 brs.

NIC Asia Bank Ltd: Thapathali Trade Tower, Thapathali, POB 11021, Kathmandu; tel. (1) 5111177; fax (1) 5111180; internet www.nicasiabank.com; f. 2013 following merger of Nepal Industrial and Commercial Bank and Bank of Asia Nepal; privately owned; cap. 2,311.5m., res 2,891.3m., dep. 44,982.9m. (July 2014); Chair. JAGDISH PRASAD AGRAWAL; CEO SASHIN JOSHI; 53 brs (2013).

NMB Bank Ltd: Babarmahal, POB 11543, Kathmandu; tel. (1) 4246160; fax (1) 4246156; e-mail call@nmb.com.np; internet www.nmb.com.np; Chair. PAWAN KUMAR GOLYAN; CEO UPENDRA POUDYAL; 14 brs.

Rastriya Banijya Bank (National Commercial Bank): POB 8368, Singha Durbar Plaza, Kathmandu; tel. (1) 4252595; fax (1) 4252931; e-mail rbb.info@rbb.com.np; internet www.rbb.com.np; f. 1966; 100% state-owned; cap. 8,589m., dep. 91,098m. (July 2013); Chair. NARAHARI DHAKAL; CEO KRISHNA PD. SHARMA; 129 brs, 5 regional offices.

Joint-venture Banks

Bank of Kathmandu Ltd: Kamal Pokhari, POB 9044, Kathmandu; tel. (1) 4414541; fax (1) 4418990; e-mail info@bok.com.np; internet www.bok.com.np; f. 1993; 58% owned by Nepalese public, 42% by local promoters; cap. 1,920.2m., res 1,378.3m., dep. 27,700.9m. (July 2013); Chair. SATYA NARAYAN MANANDHAR; CEO AJAY SHRESTHA; 37 brs.

Everest Bank Ltd (EBL): POB 13384, EBL House, Lazimpath, Kathmandu; tel. (1) 4443377; fax (1) 4443160; e-mail ebl@mos.com.np; internet www.everestbankltd.com; f. 1994; 50% owned by directors, 20% by Punjab National Bank (India) and 30% by the Nepalese public; cap. 1,921.2m., res 2,347.1m., dep. 57,720.4m. (July 2013); Chair. BISHNU KRISHNA SHRESTHA; CEO P. K. MOHAPATRA; 35 brs.

Global Bank Ltd: Adarshanagar, Birgunj 13, POB 45, Parsa; tel. (1) 530337; fax (1) 530338; e-mail info@globalbank.com.np; internet www.globalbanknepal.com; f. 2006; cap. 2,780.8m., res 438.6m., dep. 34,111.4m. (July 2013); Chair. CHANDRA PRASAD DHAKAL; CEO RATNA RAJ BAJRACHARYA.

Himalayan Bank Ltd: Karmachari Sanchaya Kosh Bldg, Tridevi Marg, Thamel, POB 20590, Kathmandu; tel. (1) 4246218; fax (1) 4222800; e-mail hbl@himalayanbank.com; internet www.himalayanbank.com; f. 1993; 20% owned by Habib Bank Ltd (Pakistan); cap. 2,898m., res 2,334.1m., dep. 53,072.3m. (July 2013); Chair. MANOJ BAHADUR SHRESTHA; CEO ASOKE S. J. B. RANA; 12 brs.

Laxmi Bank Ltd: Hattisar, POB 19593, Kathmandu; tel. (1) 4444684; fax (1) 4444640; e-mail info@laxmibank.com; internet www.laxmibank.com; f. 2002; cap. 1,948.1m., res 766.2m., dep. 25,943.5m. (July 2013); Chair. RAJENDRA K. KHETAN; CEO SUDESH KHALING.

Nabil Bank Ltd (Nabil): Nabil House, Kamaladi, POB 3729, Kathmandu; tel. (1) 4429546; fax (1) 4429548; e-mail nabil@nabilbank.com; internet www.nabilbank.com; f. 1984 as Nepal Arab Bank Ltd; name changed as above Jan. 2000; 50% owned by National Bank of Bangladesh, 30% by the Nepalese public and 20% by Nepalese govt financial institutions; cap. 3,046m., res 1,434m., dep. 63,506.1m. (July 2013); Chair. KRISHNA BAHADUR MANANDHAR; CEO ANIL GYAWALI; 48 brs.

Nepal Bangladesh Bank Ltd (NB Bank): Bijuli Bazar, New Baneshwor, POB 9062, Kathmandu; tel. (1) 4783976; fax (1) 4780826; e-mail nbblho@nbbl.com.np; internet www.nbbl.com.np; f. 1994; 50% owned by International Finance Investment and Commerce Bank Ltd (Bangladesh), 20% by Nepalese promoters and 30% public issue; cap. 2,009.4m., res 1,290.5m., dep. 16,952.7m. (July 2012); CEO GYANENDRA PRASAD DHUNGANA; Chair. PUSHPARAJ RAJ KARNIKAR; 19 brs.

Nepal Credit and Commerce Bank Ltd: NB Bldg, Bagh Bazar, Kathmandu; tel. (1) 4246991; fax (1) 4244610; e-mail corporate@nccbank.com.np; internet www.nccbank.com.np; est. as Nepal Bank of Ceylon; reconstituted as above in Sept. 2002 after Bank of Ceylon (Sri Lanka) sold its shares to NB Group (Nepal); cap. 1,470m., res 430m., dep. 16,485.3m. (July 2012); Chair. PRITHIVI RAJ LIGAL; CEO AMRIT CHARAN SHRESTHA; 17 brs.

Nepal Investment Bank Ltd (NIBL): Durbar Marg, POB 3412, Kathmandu; tel. (1) 4228229; fax (1) 4226349; e-mail info@nibl.com.np; internet www.nibl.com.np; f. 1986 as Nepal Indosuez Bank Ltd, name changed as above in June 2002; 50% owned by a consortium of Nepalese investors, 20% by the general public, 15% by Rastriya Banijya Bank and 15% by Rastriya Beema Sansthan; cap. 4,144.8m., res 960.8m., dep. 62,427.6m. (July 2013); Chair. PRITHIVI BAHADUR PANDE; 40 brs.

Nepal SBI Bank Ltd: Corporate Office, Hattisar, POB 6049, Kathmandu; tel. (1) 4435516; fax (1) 4435612; e-mail nsblco@nsbl .com.np; internet www.nepalsbi.com.np; f. 1993; 50% owned by State Bank of India, 30% by Nepalese public, 15% by Employees' Provident Fund (Nepal) and 5% by Agricultural Devt Bank (Nepal); cap. 2,650.2m., res 1,143.7m., dep. 58,920.4m. (July 2013); Chair. HASANA SHARMA; Man. Dir ALOK KUMAR SHARMA.

Standard Chartered Bank Nepal Ltd: Grindlays Bhavan, Naya Baneshwor, POB 3990, Kathmandu; tel. (1) 4246753; fax (1) 4226762; e-mail outserve.nepal@standardchartered.com; internet www.standardchartered.com/np; f. 1986 as Nepal Grindlays Bank; name changed in July 2001; 75% owned by Standard Chartered Bank (United Kingdom) and 25% by the Nepalese public; cap. 2,039m., res 2,546.9m., dep. 39,466.4m. (July 2013); Chair. SUNIL KAUSHAL; CEO JOSEPH SILVANUS; 14 brs.

Development Finance Organizations

Agricultural Development Bank Ltd: Ramshah Path, Kathmandu; tel. (1) 4262885; fax (1) 4262616; e-mail info@adbn.gov.np; internet www.adbl.gov.np; f. 1968; 93.6% state-owned, 2.1% owned by the Nepal Rastra Bank, and 4.3% by co-operatives and private individuals; specialized agricultural credit institution providing credit for agricultural development to co-operatives, individuals and asscns; Chair. GAJA NAND AGRAWAL; CEO TEJ BAHADUR BUDHATHOKI.

Gurkha Development Bank Ltd (GDB): Triveni Complex, Putalisadak, POB 5617, Kathmandu; tel. (1) 4255650; fax (1) 4242829; e-mail info@gdbl.com.np; internet www.gurkhabank.com; Man. Dir AMOD DOMZAN.

Nepal Aawas Finance Ltd: New Baneshwor, POB 5624, Kathmandu; tel. (1) 4780259; fax (1) 4782753; internet www.nepalaawas .com.np; Chair. JITENDRA NATH RIMAL.

Banking Organization

Nepal Bankers' Association (NBA): Central Business Park, Thapathali, Kathmandu; tel. (1) 4101542; fax (1) 4101540; e-mail nepalbankers@mail.com.np; internet www.nepalbankers.com.np; f. 1986; Pres. UPENDRA POUDYAL.

STOCK EXCHANGE

Nepal Stock Exchange Ltd (NEPSE): Singha Durbar Plaza, POB 1550, Kathmandu; tel. (1) 4250755; fax (1) 4262538; e-mail info@ nepalstock.com; internet www.nepalstock.com.np; f. 1976; reorg. 1984; converted in 1993 from Securities Exchange Centre Ltd to Nepal Stock Exchange Ltd; 238 listed cos, 139 scripts; Chair. Dr KRISHNA DEVKOTA; Gen. Man. SITARAM THAPALIYA.

INSURANCE

Alliance Insurance Co Ltd: POB 10811, Tinkune, Kathmandu; tel. (1) 4499220; fax (1) 4499647; e-mail info@allianceinsurance.com .np; internet www.allianceinsurance.com.np; f. 1996; Chair. DEVI PRAKASH BHATTACHAN; CEO SANCHIT BAJRACHARYA (acting).

Everest Insurance Co Ltd: Hattisar, POB 10675, Kathmandu; tel. (1) 4444717; fax (1) 4444366; e-mail info@eic.com.np; internet www .everestinsurance.com; f. 1994; Chair. SURENDRA SILWAL.

Himalayan General Insurance Co Ltd: Babar Mahal, POB 148, Kathmandu; tel. (1) 4231788; fax (1) 4241517; e-mail ktm@hgi.com .np; internet www.hgi.com.np; f. 1993; Chair. RAJ KRISHNA SHRESTHA; CEO MAHENDRA KRISHNA SHRESTHA.

Neco Insurance Ltd: Anamnagar, POB 12271, Kathmandu; tel. (1) 4770415; fax (1) 4770162; e-mail info@necoinsurance.com.np; internet www.necoinsurance.com.np; f. 1994; Chair. RAMESH KUMAR NIRAULA; CEO BISHWO RAM TIMILA (acting).

Nepal Insurance Co Ltd: NIC Bldg, Kulratna Marg, Kamaladi, POB 3623, Kathmandu; tel. (1) 4221353; fax (1) 4225446; e-mail nic@ wlink.com.np; internet www.nepalinsurance.com.np; f. 1947 as Nepal Malchalani Tatha Beema Co; name changed as above in 1991; Chair. Dr DEVRAJ ADHIKARI; Gen. Man. KESHAB DUBADI.

NLG Insurance Co Ltd: Panipokhari, Lazimpat, POB 20600, Kathmandu; tel. (1) 4442646; fax (1) 4416427; e-mail info@nlgi .com.np; internet www.nlg.com.np; 70% owned by National Life Insurance Co Ltd; Chair. KRISHNA PRASAD SHARMA; CEO VIJAYA BAHADUR SHAH.

Premier Insurance Co (Nepal) Ltd: Tripureswor, POB 9183, Kathmandu; tel. (1) 4413543; fax (1) 4413442; e-mail premier@picl .com.np; internet www.premier-insurance.com.np; f. 1994; Chair. RAM LAL SHRESHTHA; Man. Dir SURESH LAL SHRESTHA.

Rastriya Beema Sansthan (National Insurance Corpn): POB 527, Kathmandu; tel. (1) 4262520; fax (1) 4262610; e-mail beema@wlink .com.np; internet www.beema.com.np; f. 1967; Chair. RAJENDRA PRAKASH LOHANI.

Sagarmatha Insurance Co Ltd: Surakshan Bhavan, Bhagawati Marg, Naxal, POB 12211, Kathmandu; tel. (1) 4412367; fax (1) 4412378; e-mail sagarmatha@insurance.wlink.com.np; internet www.sagarmathainsurance.com.np; f. 1996; Chair. RAM KRISHNA MANANDHAR; Exec. Dir KRISHNA BAHADUR BASNYAT.

United Insurance Co (Nepal) Ltd: POB 9075, Trade Tower, Thapathali, Kathmandu; tel. (1) 4246686; fax (1) 5111112; e-mail uic@mail.com.np; internet www.unitedinsurance.com.np; f. 1993; Chair. RAVI BHAKTA SHRESTHA.

Trade and Industry

GOVERNMENT AGENCIES

Investment Board Nepal: Singha Durbar, Kathmandu; tel. (1) 4200269; fax (1) 4200338; e-mail info@investmentboard.gov.np; internet www.investmentboard.gov.np; f. 2011; CEO RADHESH PANT.

National Planning Commission (NPC): Singha Durbar, POB 1284, Kathmandu; tel. (1) 4225879; fax (1) 4226500; e-mail npcs@ npcnepal.gov.np; internet www.npc.gov.np; Sec. SHARADA PRASAD TRITAL.

National Trading Ltd: Teku, POB 128, Kathmandu; tel. (1) 4225799; fax (1) 4225151; e-mail info@nationaltrading.com.np; internet www.nationaltrading.com.np; f. 1962; state trading org.; imports and distributes construction materials and raw materials for industry; also machinery, vehicles and consumer goods; operates bonded warehouse, duty-free shop and related activities; brs in all major towns and one foreign based office in Kolkata, India; Chair. DIRGHARAJ SHRESTHA.

Trade and Export Promotion Centre (TEPC): Na Tole, Pulchowk, Lalitpur, POB 825, Kathmandu; tel. (1) 5525898; fax (1) 5525464; e-mail info@tepc.gov.np; internet www.tepc.gov.np; f. 2006; govt-owned; Chair. MADHAV PRASAD REGMI; Exec. Dir ISHWARI PRASAD GHIMIRE.

DEVELOPMENT ORGANIZATIONS

National Productivity and Economic Development Centre: Balaju Industrial District, POB 1318, Kathmandu; tel. (1) 4350566; fax (1) 4350530; e-mail npo.nepal@gmail.com; functions as secretariat of National Productivity Council; provides services for industrial promotion and productivity improvement through planning research, consultancy, training, seminars and information services; Gen. Man. RAJENDRA BAJRACHARYA.

National Tea and Coffee Development Board (NTCDB): New Baneshwor, POB 9683, Kathmandu; tel. (1) 4495792; fax (1) 4497941; e-mail ntcdboard@wlink.com.np; internet teacoffee.gov .np; f. 1992 to promote and expand the Nepalese tea industry; Exec. Dir RAMAN PRASAD PATHAK.

Nepal Tea Development Corpn Ltd: Triveni Complex, Putali Sadak, Kathmandu; tel. (1) 4224074; fax (1) 4266133; e-mail ntdcktm@gmail.com; internet www.ntdcltd.com.np; f. 1966; privatized in early 2000s; commercial production of tea; Contact SUBHASH C. SHANGHAI.

CHAMBERS OF COMMERCE

Federation of Nepalese Chambers of Commerce and Industry (FNCCI): Pachali Shahid Shukra FNCCI Milan Marg, Teku, POB 269, Kathmandu; tel. (1) 4262061; fax (1) 4261022; e-mail fncci@mos .com.np; internet www.fncci.org; f. 1965; comprises 92 district municipality chambers (DCCIs), 89 commodity asscns, 607 leading industrial and commercial undertakings in both the public and private sector, and 20 bi-national chambers; publishes annual *Nepal and the World: A Statistical Profile*; Pres. PRADEEP JUNG PANDEY; Dir Dr HEMANT KUMAR DABADI.

Birganj Chamber of Commerce and Industries: Hospital Rd, Birta, Birganj; tel. (51) 522290; fax (51) 526049; e-mail bicci@bicci .org.np; internet www.bicci.org.np; f. 1944; 735 mems; Pres. PRADEEP KUMAR KEDIA.

Lalitpur Chamber of Commerce and Industry: Mangal Bazar, Patan Durbar Sq., POB 26, Lalitpur; tel. (1) 5530663; fax (1) 5530661; e-mail lcci@mos.com.np; internet www.lcci.org.np; f. 1967; Pres. AJAR MAN JOSHI; Sec.-Gen. SABIN SHRESTHA.

Nepal Chamber of Commerce: Chamber Bhavan, Kantipath, POB 198, Kathmandu; tel. (1) 4230947; fax (1) 4229998; e-mail chamber@wlink.com.np; internet www.nepalchamber.org; f. 1952; non-profit org. promoting industrial and commercial development; 8,000 regd cos and 1,600 ordinary mems; Pres. SURESH KUMAR BASNET; Sec.-Gen. KAMLESH KUMAR AGRAWAL.

INDUSTRIAL AND TRADE ASSOCIATIONS

Association of Craft Producers: Rhavi Bhavan Mode, POB 3701, Kathmandu; tel. (1) 4275108; fax (1) 4272676; e-mail export@

craftacp.org.np; internet acp.org.np; f. 1984; local non-profit org. providing technical, marketing and management services for craft producers; manufacturer, exporter and retailer of handicraft goods; Exec. Dir MEERA BHATTARAI; Programme Dir REVITA SHRESTHA.

Association of Nepalese Rice, Oil and Pulses Industries: POB 20782, Radha Bhavan, Tripureswor, Kathmandu; tel. (1) 4100115; fax (1) 4437990; e-mail nfma@mcmail.com.np; Pres. CHANDRA KRISHNA KARMACHARYA; Gen. Sec. SATISH KUMAR BOHARA.

Association of Pharmaceutical Producers of Nepal (APPON): 4th Floor, Bagmati Chamber, Teku, Kathmandu; tel. (1) 4100024; fax (1) 4231871; e-mail appoappon123@gmail.com; internet www.appon.org.np; Pres. UMESH LAL SHRESTHA; Sec.-Gen. DEEPAK PRASAD DAHAL.

Cargo Agents' Association of Nepal: Thamel, POB 5355, Kathmandu; tel. (1) 4419019; fax (1) 4419858.

Central Carpet Industries Association of Nepal: POB 2419, Narayanhiti Lazimpat (N), Kathmandu; tel. and fax (1) 4486849; e-mail ccia@enet.com.np; internet www.nepalcarpet.org; Pres. LANK MAN ROKA; Gen. Sec. NYIMA LAMA.

Computer Association of Nepal: POB 4982, 235/39 Maitidevi Marga, Kathmandu; tel. (1) 4432700; fax (1) 4441998; e-mail info@can.org.np; internet www.can.org.np; f. 1992; asscn of the IT Businessmen's Organization; Pres. BINOD DHAKAL.

Confederation of Nepalese Industries: 5th Floor, Trade Tower, Thapathali, Kathmandu; tel. (1) 5111122; fax (1) 5111125; e-mail cni@wlink.com.np; internet www.cnind.org; f. 2000; Pres. NARENDRA KUMAR BASNYAT.

Export Council of Nepal (ECON): Bhagabatisthan, Thamel, POB 13943, Kathmandu; tel. and fax (1) 4441337; fax (1) 4412251; e-mail info@nepalexport.org.np; internet www.nepalexport.org.np; f. 1996; Pres. ARJUN KUMAR BHATTARAI; Sec.-Gen. RESHAM BD. POKHREL.

Federation of Handicraft Associations of Nepal: Upma Marg, Thapathali, POB 784, Kathmandu; tel. (1) 4244231; fax (1) 4222940; e-mail han@wlink.com.np; internet www.nepalhandicraft.org.np; f. 1972; Pres. HEM RATNA SHAKYA.

Federation of Nepal Cottage and Small Industries (FNCSI): Maitighar Height, POB 6530, Kathmandu; tel. (1) 4222751; fax (1) 4215602; e-mail fncsi@ntc.net.np; internet www.fncsi.org; f. 1990; business networks in 74 districts; represents interests and promotes development of nation's micro-, cottage and small industries; 35,000 general mems; Pres. SURESH PRADHAN.

Garment Association of Nepal: Shankhamul Rd, New Baneshwor, POB 21332, Kathmandu; tel. (1) 4780691; fax (1) 4780173; e-mail gan@ntc.net.np; internet www.ganasso.org; Pres. UDAY RAJ PANDEY.

Himalayan Orthodox Tea Producers' Association of Nepal: Bakhundole, Lalitpur; tel. (1) 2041036; e-mail hotpa@mail.com.np; internet www.nepaltea.com.np; f. 1998; non-profit org.; represents and promotes the Himalayan tea sector; Chair. UDAYA CHAPAGAIN.

Leather Footwear and Goods Manufacturers' Association of Nepal: Bag Bazar, POB 19732, Kathmandu; tel. (1) 4219349; e-mail lfgman@ntc.net.np; Pres. HOM NATH UPADHYAYA.

Nepal Foreign Trade Association: Bagmati Chamber, 1st Floor, Milan Marg, Teku, POB 541, Kathmandu; tel. (1) 4223784; fax (1) 4247159; e-mail nfta@mos.com.np; f. 1972; Pres. RAMESH GUPTA; 400 mems.

Nepal Forest Industries Association: Naxal, Nag Pokhari, POB 5623, Kathmandu; tel. (1) 4411865; fax (1) 4413838; e-mail padmasri@ccsl.com.np; Pres. SANJAY GIRI; Sec.-Gen. PRADEEP BANIYA.

Nepal Leather Industries Association: POB 9944, Anamnagar, Kathmandu; tel. (1) 4265248; fax (1) 4228978; e-mail giris@atcnet.com.np; Pres. SANJAY GIRI; Sec.-Gen. RAMESH RAJ POKHAREL.

Nepal Plastic Manufacturers' Association: Kandevsthan, Kupandol, POB 2350, Lalitpur; tel. and fax (1) 5528185; Pres. SHAILENDRA LAL PRADHAN; Sec.-Gen. RAJESWOR LAL JOSHI.

Nepal Trans-Himalayan Border Commerce Association: POB 20801, Mahaboudha, Kathmandu; tel. (1) 4244201; fax (1) 4268417; e-mail nthbta@wlink.com.np; internet nthbca.org.np; promotes trade between Nepal and the People's Republic of China; Pres. DURGA BAHADUR SHRESTHA; Sec. SHYAM PRASAD BAJGAIN.

Silk Association of Nepal: Tripureshwor, Kathmandu; tel. (1) 4254093; e-mail san@nepsilk.wlink.com.np; internet www.nepalsilk.org.np; f. 1992; organizes and promotes sericulture and silk devt activities; Pres. SHANKAR P. PANDEYA.

UTILITIES

Electricity

Nepal Electricity Authority: Durbar Marga, POB 10020, Kathmandu; tel. (1) 4153052; fax (1) 4153067; e-mail info@nea.org.np;

internet www.nea.org.np; f. 1985 following merger; govt-owned; Man. Dir MUKESH RAJ KAFLE.

Butwal Power Co Ltd: 313 Ganga Devi Marga, Buddha Nagar, POB 11728, Kathmandu; tel. (1) 4784026; fax (1) 4780994; e-mail info@bpc.com.np; internet www.bpc.com.np; f. 1966; partially privatized in 2003; principal shareholders: 69.0% owned by Shangri-La Energy Ltd, 9.1% by Govt and 6.1% by Interkraft Nepal AS; 5.9% divided between Nepalese energy orgs and employees; public sector retains 10% ownership; owns and operates Jhimruk and Andhi Khola Hydropower Plants; supplies electricity to the national grid; 326 employees; Chair. PADMA JYOTI.

Chilime Hydropower Co Ltd: Dhumbarahi, Kathmandu; tel. (1) 4370773; fax (1) 4370720; e-mail info@chilime.com.np; internet www.chilime.com.np; 51% owned by Nepal Electricity Authority; Chair. MUKESH RAJ KAFLE.

Department of Electricity Development: 576 Bhakti Thapa Sadak-4, POB 2507, Anamnagar, Kathmandu; tel. (1) 4480326; fax (1) 4480257; e-mail info@doed.gov.np; internet www.doed.gov.np; f. 1993; fmrly Electricity Development Centre; name changed as above 1999; Dir-Gen. DINESH KUMAR GHIMIRE.

Water

Nepal Water Supply Corpn: Tripureshwor Marg, POB 5349, Kathmandu; tel. (1) 4259857; fax (1) 4255516; e-mail nwsc@mos.com.np; internet www.nwsc.gov.np; f. 1990; govt-owned; Chair. PARAMESHOR POKHAREL.

TRADE UNIONS

Nepal Trade Union Congress—Independent (NTUC—I): POB 5507, Kathmandu; tel. (1) 4469954; fax (1) 4469959; e-mail ntuc@wlink.com.np; internet www.ntuci.org.np; f. 1947 as the Nepal Trade Union Congress; 25 affiliated unions; affiliated to ITUC; operates in association with Nepali Congress Party; merged with Democratic Confederation of Nepalese Trade Unions in March 2008 and name changed to the above; Pres. KHILA NATH DAHAL; Gen. Sec. MAHENDRA PRASAD YADAV; 350,000 mems (2013).

General Federation of Nepalese Trade Unions (GEFONT): Man Mohan Labour Bldg, GEFONT Plaza, Putali Sadak, POB 10652, Kathmandu; tel. (1) 4168000; fax (1) 4168012; e-mail dfa@gefont.org; internet www.gefont.org; f. 1989; 19 affiliated unions; Pres. BISHNU RIMAL.

Transport

Department of Transport Management: Minbhawan, Kathmandu; tel. (1) 4474921; fax (1) 4474922; e-mail info@dotm.gov.np; internet www.dotm.gov.np; Dir-Gen. KASHI RAJ DAHAL.

RAILWAYS

A short narrow-gauge line in Janakpur district is the sole railway in operation. However, a feasibility study for a 1,318-km electric rail network was completed in 2010. In addition to a 945-km east–west line, linking the districts of Mechi and Mahakali, the proposed network included a 185-km Kathmandu–Pokhara section and up to six branch lines connecting with the rail network of India.

Nepal Railways Corpn Ltd (NRC): Khajuri, Janakpur; tel. (41) 52082; HQ Jaynagar, India; f. 1937 as Janakpur-Jaynagar Railways; name changed as above June 2004; 53 km open, linking Jaynagar in India with Janakpur and Bijalpura; narrow gauge; Gen. Man. MADAN SINGH MAHAT.

ROADS

In 2010 Nepal had 19,875 km of roads, of which 53.9% had paved surfaces. A 190-km mountain road links the capital, Kathmandu, with the Indian railhead at Raxaul. The Siddhartha Highway, constructed with Indian assistance, connects the Pokhara valley, in mid-west Nepal, with Sonauli, on the Indian border in Uttar Pradesh. The 114-km Arniko Highway connects Kathmandu with Kodari, on the Chinese border. In the early 1990s a 1,030-km East–West Highway (Mahendra Highway) was completed. Another major east–west road project, the Puspalal (or Mid-Hill) Highway Project, was initiated in 2007; the 1,776-km highway, which will connect 23 hilly districts, was reportedly nearing completion in mid-2015.

Roads Board Nepal: Arnico Bldg, Minbhavan, POB 11406, Kathmandu; tel. (1) 4493515; fax (1) 4493542; e-mail info@roadsboardnepal.org; internet www.roadsboardnepal.org; f. 2002; maintenance and devt of the road network; Exec. Dir RAMESH NATH BASTOLA.

CIVIL AVIATION

Tribhuvan International Airport (TIR) is situated about 6 km from Kathmandu. Construction of a new international terminal at TIR commenced in 2013. The main domestic airports are located at Biratnagar, Pokhara, Lumbini (Gautam Buddha) and Nepalgunj. In 2014 there were 32 airports, of various standards, in operation. Work on a project to upgrade Gautam Buddha Airport to international standards commenced in early 2015, while plans for the construction of a regional international airport at Pokhara were also under consideration.

Civil Aviation Authority of Nepal (CAAN): Babar Mahal, Kathmandu; tel. (1) 4262387; fax (1) 4262516; e-mail dgca@caanepal.org.np; internet www.caanepal.org.np; f. 1998; chaired by the Minister of Tourism and Civil Aviation; Dir-Gen. MAHENDRA SINGH RAWAL.

Nepal Airlines Corpn (NAC): NAC Bldg, Kantipath, Kathmandu; tel. (1) 4220757; fax (1) 4225348; e-mail info@nac.com.np; internet nepalairlines.com.np; f. 1958; fmrly Royal Nepal Airlines Corpn; 100% state-owned (scheduled for transfer to private ownership); scheduled services to 19 domestic airfields, international scheduled flights to 5 destinations in the Middle East and the Far East, charter flights; Chair. SHIVA SHARAN NEUPANE; Man. Dir MADAN KHAREL.

Buddha Air: Jawalakhal, Lalitpur, POB 2167, Kathmandu; tel. (1) 5521015; fax (1) 5537726; e-mail buddhaair@buddhaair.com; internet www.buddhaair.com; f. 1997; domestic passenger services; services to Paro, Bhutan, commenced in 2010; services to Varanasi, India, commenced in 2012; Man. Dir BIRENDRA B. BASNET; Chair. SURENDRA B. BASNET.

Sita Air: 9 Sinamangal, POB 9002, Kathmandu; tel. (1) 4110597; fax (1) 4490546; e-mail sapl@wlink.com.np; internet www.sitaair.com.np; f. 2003; Chair. PRITI RANA.

Yeti Airlines: Tilganga, POB 20011, Kathmandu; tel. (1) 4465888; fax (1) 4465115; e-mail yetiair@wlink.com.np; internet www.yetiairlines.com; f. 1998; operates scheduled and chartered domestic flights; Exec. Chair. LHAKPA SONAM SHERPA; Man. Dir ANG TSHERING SHERPA.

Tourism

Major tourist attractions include: Lumbini, the birthplace of Buddha; the lake city of Pokhara; and the Himalaya mountain range, including Mt Everest, the world's highest peak. Since 1989, in an effort to increase tourism, the Government has abolished travel restrictions in remote areas of Nepal that had previously been inaccessible to foreigners. Since 2005 the Government has granted access to numerous additional mountains; in mid-2014 104 new peaks were opened to climbers, raising the total number of accessible mountains to 414. The Maoist insurgency had a detrimental effect on the tourism sector in the early and mid-2000s. The cessation of hostilities in 2006 and the subsequent peace agreement—combined with the introduction of additional airline services between Nepal and other Asian countries—led to a significant recovery in the tourism sector. Tourism arrivals increased from 383,926 in 2006 to 797,616 in 2013; in the latter year, revenue from tourism was estimated at US $436.0m.

Nepal Tourism Board (NTB): Tourist Service Centre, Bhrikuti Mandap, POB 11018, Kathmandu; tel. (1) 4256909; fax (1) 4256910; e-mail info@ntb.org.np; internet www.welcomenepal.com; f. 1998; Chair. SUSHIL GHIMIRE; CEO NANDINI THAPA (acting).

Nepal Association of Tour and Travel Agents (NATTA): Gairidhara Rd, Goma Ganesh, Naxal, POB 362, Kathmandu; tel. (1) 4419409; fax (1) 4418684; e-mail info@natta.org.np; internet www.natta.org.np; f. 1966 to promote and regulate development in the tourism industry; non-governmental org.; more than 550 mems; Pres. D. B. LIMBU; Sec.-Gen. MIHIKA DHAKHWA.

Nepal Mountaineering Association (NMA): Nagpokhari, Naxal, POB 1435, Kathmandu; tel. (1) 4434525; fax (1) 4434578; e-mail office@nepalmountaineering.org; internet www.nepalmountaineering.org; f. 1973; promotes mountaineering and mountain tourism; Pres. ANG TSHERING SHERPA.

Tourist Guide Association of Nepal (TURGAN): Sagar Niwas, POB 5344, Kamaladi, Kathmandu; tel. and fax (1) 4225102; e-mail turgan@wlink.com.np; internet www.tourguidenepal.org.np; Pres. HARE RAM BARAL.

Trekking Agencies' Association of Nepal (TAAN): Maligaun Ganesthan, POB 3612, Kathmandu; tel. (1) 4427473; fax (1) 4419245; e-mail taan@wlink.com.np; internet www.taan.org.np; f. 1979; Pres. RAMESH DHAMALA.

Defence

As assessed at November 2014, Nepal's total armed forces numbered 95,750 men. Paramilitary forces comprised 62,000 men. Military service is voluntary. There was a 15,000-strong Armed Police Force under the Ministry of Home Affairs.

Defence Budget: NRs 305,000m. in 2014.

Chief of the Army Staff: Gen. GAURAV SHAMSHER JUNG BAHADUR RANA.

Education

Primary education, beginning at six years of age and lasting for five years, is officially compulsory and is provided free of charge in government schools. Secondary education, beginning at the age of 11, lasts for a further five years, comprising a first cycle of three years (lower secondary) and a second of two years (secondary). In 2012 enrolment at primary schools included 97% of children in the relevant age-group (boys 98%; girls 97%), while the ratio for secondary enrolment in 2005/06 was equivalent to 43.2% of pupils in the relevant age-group (boys 45.7%; girls 40.5%). Some 8,000 pupils attended the country's 321 primary schools in 1950; by 2012 there were an estimated 34,298 primary schools, with 4.6m. primary pupils. The number of secondary schools rose from two in 1950 to 8,416 in 2012. In 2012 there were an estimated 8.8m. pupils enrolled at secondary schools.

The Tribhuvan University in Kathmandu is the oldest and largest (with 115,608 students in 2001/02) of Nepal's four public universities; there is, in addition, one private university—the Kathmandu University in Banepa.

Proposed expenditure on education by the central Government in the 2013/14 budget was NRs 80,958m. (15.7% of total spending). According to UNESCO, literacy among the adult population of Nepal was only 57.4% in 2011 (males 71.1%; females 46.7%); it was hoped that an adult literacy rate of 70% would be achieved by the conclusion of the 12th Five-Year Plan in 2017.

THE NETHERLANDS

Introductory Survey

LOCATION, CLIMATE, LANGUAGE, RELIGION, FLAG, CAPITAL

The Kingdom of the Netherlands is situated in Western Europe, bordered to the east by Germany and to the south by Belgium. Its northern and western shores face the North Sea. The Caribbean islands of Bonaire, Saba and Sint (St) Eustatius have the status of bijzondere gemeente (special municipalities), while Aruba, Curaçao and Sint (St) Maarten are independent countries within the Kingdom of the Netherlands. The climate is temperate: the average temperature in January is 0°C (32°F), while the average in summer is 21°C (70°F). The official national language is Dutch. There is a Frisian-speaking minority (numbering about 354,000). Since 1996 Frisian has been recognized as an official minority language under the European Charter for Regional or Minority Languages. In 2013 about 25% of the inhabitants were Roman Catholics, about 16% were Protestants and some 5% were Muslims; around 47% did not profess any religion. The national flag (proportions 2 by 3) has three equal horizontal stripes, of red, white and blue. The capital is Amsterdam, but the seat of government is The Hague (Den Haag or 's-Gravenhage).

CONTEMPORARY POLITICAL HISTORY

Historical Context

The Netherlands remained neutral throughout the First World War. During the Second World War the Netherlands was occupied by Germany. Following its liberation in 1945, it became a founder member of the UN. In 1948 the Netherlands formed the Brussels Treaty Organization with Belgium and Luxembourg. The Treaty establishing the Benelux Economic Union (see p. 444) between these three countries was signed in 1958 and came into force in 1960, and a single customs area was established in 1970. The Netherlands was a founder member of the European Community (EC, now European Union—EU, see p. 271). Queen Juliana, who had reigned since 1948, abdicated in favour of her eldest daughter, Beatrix, in April 1980, following the adoption in February of a constitutional amendment that allowed for the accession of the reigning monarch's eldest child, regardless of gender.

Domestic Political Affairs

After the Second World War successive administrations were formed by various coalitions between the several 'confessional' Roman Catholic and Protestant and 'progressive' Socialist and Liberal parties. At a general election held in 1971 left-wing parties made substantial gains. In July 1972 the Government was forced to resign after losing its working majority in the Tweede Kamer (Second Chamber)—or House of Representatives—of the bicameral parliament, the Staten-Generaal (States-General). Another general election took place in November, at which the 'confessional' parties suffered a major reverse, and in May 1973 a new Government was formed by a left-of-centre coalition under the leadership of Dr Joop den Uyl of the Partij van de Arbeid (PvdA—Labour Party).

The coalition collapsed in March 1977; a general election followed in May. Attempts to form a left-of-centre coalition between the PvdA, the Christen Democratisch Appèl (CDA—Christian Democratic Appeal)—an alliance of 'confessional' groupings, which united in 1980 to form a single party—and Democraten '66 were unsuccessful, and in December 1977 Andries van Agt, of the CDA, formed a centre-right coalition Government of the CDA and the right-wing Volkspartij voor Vrijheid en Democratie (VVD—People's Party for Freedom and Democracy). Despite retaining only a narrow majority in the Second Chamber, and several ministerial disagreements, the Government survived its full term in office. A general election was held in May 1981, and a centre-left coalition Government was formed in September, led by van Agt and comprising the CDA, the PvdA and Democraten '66. The Council of Ministers resigned after only five weeks in office, owing to its failure to agree on economic strategy. In November the coalition partners accepted a compromise economic programme, but deep divisions within the Government persisted. The coalition collapsed again in May 1982, when all six PvdA ministers resigned, after which van Agt headed a minority interim Government of the CDA and Democraten '66.

Although the PvdA became the largest party in the Second Chamber (with 47 of 150 deputies) following a general election in September 1982, there was a significant swing to the right. In November a centre-right CDA-VVD coalition was established under the leadership of Ruud Lubbers, who had recently succeeded van Agt as Chairman of the CDA. The CDA-VVD coalition was returned to power at a general election in May 1986, having retained its majority in the Second Chamber. A loss of nine seats by the VVD was offset by a corresponding gain by the CDA, which, with 54 seats, became the party with the largest representation in the Second Chamber. The election did, none the less, produce a shift towards the centrist parties, with the PvdA and Democraten '66 (Democraten 66—D66, as the party was restyled) both gaining seats at the expense of smaller, radical groups. Following the election Wim Kok replaced den Uyl as parliamentary leader of the PvdA. A new CDA-VVD coalition Government was formed in July.

In May 1989 the VVD caused the collapse of the Government by refusing to support Lubbers' proposals for the financing of a 20-year National Environment Policy (NEP), which included a reduction in government spending in sectors such as defence and housing and an increase in taxes on motor fuels. A general election was held in September, at which the CDA again secured 54 seats in the Second Chamber, while the PvdA took 49 seats. The VVD lost five seats. An alliance of left-wing organizations, GroenLinks (Green Left), won six. In October negotiations between the CDA and the PvdA culminated in the formation of a centre-left coalition, again led by Lubbers. The coalition accord envisaged increased welfare provision, to be funded by a reduction in defence expenditure, as well as a programme of job creation and reductions in certain categories of taxation. Kok was appointed Deputy Prime Minister and Minister of Finance. In August 1990 the Government introduced an amended version of the NEP, designated the National Environment Policy Plus (NEPP), which placed strong emphasis on energy conservation and improvements in waste disposal and recycling.

In November 1992 the Second Chamber ratified the Treaty on European Union (which had been signed by EC Heads of Government at Maastricht in December 1991); the Eerste Kamer (First Chamber)—or Senate—approved the Treaty in December.

The CDA performed poorly at the May 1994 general election, winning only 34 seats in the Second Chamber. The PvdA became the party with the largest representation in the Chamber, with 37 seats. The VVD and D66 increased their representation to 31 and 24 seats, respectively. The remaining 24 seats were distributed among eight smaller parties and special issue groups. Negotiations between the PvdA, the VVD and D66 led to the formation in August of a tripartite coalition, with Kok as Prime Minister (after concessions by the PvdA concerning severe reductions in welfare spending).

The PvdA won increased representation at the general election in May 1998, taking 45 seats in the Second Chamber. The VVD secured 38 seats, while the CDA's representation was further reduced, to 29 seats. D66 won only 14 seats, having lost votes to GroenLinks and the Socialistische Partij (SP—Socialist Party). None the less, the PvdA, VVD and D66 agreed to renew their coalition (it was considered that D66 would be useful as an intermediary in conflicts of policy between the two leading partners), and a new Government, again led by Kok, was inaugurated in August.

In May 1999 the Senate rejected the Government's proposal to allow the use of referendums on policy issues, a key demand of D66, after the refusal of a prominent member of the VVD to support the measure. D66 subsequently announced that it could no longer work with the VVD, and withdrew from the ruling coalition, prompting the resignation of the Council of Ministers. However, following a series of talks between the three parties, in June the Government formally withdrew its resignation. In January 2001 the three coalition parties reached a new agreement on the use of referendums. The new proposals were for a judicially non-binding referendum and would not require a change to the Constitution. The temporary referendum law entered into force on 1 January 2002 and expired three years later. Legislation was subsequently adopted to allow a national referendum to be held exceptionally on the proposed EU constitutional treaty in June 2005.

In August 2001 Kok announced that he would not seek re-election for a further term in office at the general election, scheduled for May 2002. He also announced that he would step down as party leader of the PvdA and subsequently endorsed the appointment of Ad Melkert, the parliamentary leader of the party, as his successor. Jaap de Hoop Scheffer, the parliamentary leader of the CDA, resigned in September 2001. He was replaced by Jan Peter Balkenende in the following month.

Report on the Srebrenica massacre; the 2002 election

In April 2002 the entire Council of Ministers resigned following the publication of a report by the Netherlands Institute for War Documentation into the massacre of some 7,000 Bosnian Muslims by Bosnian Serb troops in Srebrenica, Bosnia and Herzegovina, in July 1995. The report blamed the Dutch Government, the Dutch military and the UN for their respective roles in failing to prevent the atrocity and claimed that the 100 lightly armed Dutch peacekeeping troops who had been stationed in the town at the time had been ill-trained and had no clear mandate (see *Foreign Affairs*). The Government remained in office in a caretaker capacity pending the forthcoming general election, which was scheduled to be held in mid-May 2002.

On 6 May 2002 the controversial politician Pim Fortuyn was shot dead in Hilversum, in the central Netherlands, a few days before the general election, in which his newly established party, the populist and anti-immigration Lijst Pim Fortuyn (LPF—Pim Fortuyn List), was expected to secure a substantial proportion of the vote. Fortuyn had formed the movement following his dismissal in January as leader of the Leefbaar Nederland (LN—Livable Netherlands) party for his anti-immigration rhetoric. In April 2003 Volkert van der Graaf, an animal-rights activist who claimed that Fortuyn had presented a threat to vulnerable members of society, was convicted of the murder.

At the general election of May 2002 the CDA won 43 of the 150 seats in the Second Chamber. The LPF took 26 seats, the VVD 24 and the PvdA 23. In the light of their electoral defeats, both the PvdA and the VVD changed their parliamentary leaders, to Jeltje van Nieuwenhoven and Gerrit Zalm, respectively.

Balkenende becomes Prime Minister: 2002–06

Jan Peter Balkenende was inaugurated as Prime Minister on 21 July 2002, at the head of a coalition Government comprising the CDA, the LPF and the VVD. The LPF's new leader, Mat Herben, resigned at the end of July after allegations that he had tried unfairly to influence the selection procedure for the LN's electoral candidates: he was replaced by Harry Wijnschenk. The new Government detailed policies to reform the welfare system and reduce the number of illegal immigrants to the Netherlands, and introduced compulsory instruction for Muslim religious leaders in Dutch values and social conventions. However, following a dispute over the deputy premiership between two LPF ministers, the LPF's coalition partners refused to co-operate further with the party and the Government resigned in October. Balkenende presided over a minority Government, comprising the CDA and the VVD, pending a fresh general election.

At the general election in January 2003 the CDA won 44 seats in the Second Chamber, while the PvdA increased its representation from 23 to 42 seats, under its new leader, Wouter Bos. The VVD received 28 seats, while the LPF, again led by Herben, following the resignation of Wijnschenk in late 2002, secured only eight seats and D66 six. Although the popularity of the right-wing LPF had declined sharply, immigration had become a prominent subject of debate, the VVD echoing Fortuyn's statement that the Netherlands was already 'full'. Disagreements between the CDA and the PvdA over Dutch support for an impending US-led military campaign to remove the regime of Saddam Hussain in Iraq hindered progress on forming a new coalition. In March, in his capacity as Prime Minister of the interim administration, Balkenende announced that while Dutch troops would not directly assist in the campaign, some units of the armed forces and weapons would be made available to help defend Turkey, should the conflict escalate. After the CDA and the PvdA failed to agree on reductions in budgetary expenditure necessary to revive the stagnant economy, in May the CDA negotiated the formation of a centre-right coalition with

the VVD and D66, thereby gaining a majority of six in the 150-seat Second Chamber. The coalition Government, under the renewed premiership of Balkenende, was formally sworn in on 27 May. Two new Deputy Prime Ministers were appointed: Zalm of the VVD, who was also assigned the post of Minister of Finance, and Thom de Graaf of D66, who was also named as Minister of Government Reform and Kingdom Relations.

The Government introduced a number of stringent new policies regarding immigrants and asylum seekers. In January 2004 the Government announced that, in order to prevent the potential destabilization of the employment market, a maximum of 22,000 immigrants from the 10 new EU member states (which were scheduled to join the EU on 1 May) would be permitted to settle in the Netherlands. In February parliament approved a bill authorizing the provision of a repatriation payment and a free flight to their country of origin to failed asylum seekers. The law was condemned by human rights groups, but was welcomed by certain sectors of society that felt threatened by the rising level of unemployment.

In September 2004, in an attempt to reduce the fiscal deficit and prepare for the impact on the economy of an ageing population, the Government announced proposals for an austerity budget for 2005, including reforms to unemployment and disability benefits, reductions in health care expenditure and the elimination of tax benefits for those saving for early retirement. The proposals provoked widespread industrial action and protests. A compromise was reached in November whereby the trade union leaders accepted the proposed disincentive to early retirement and the restriction of eligibility for disability benefits, and agreed to demand only minimal wage increases over the forthcoming year. In March 2005 de Graaf resigned from his ministerial posts after the rejection by parliament of a bill to introduce the direct election of mayors. Alexander Pechtold, the Chairman of D66, replaced him as Minister of Government Reform and Kingdom Relations, while the D66 Minister of Economic Affairs, Laurens Jans Brinkhorst, assumed the additional role of Deputy Prime Minister.

In January 2005, meanwhile, legislation was adopted requiring all citizens and foreigners to carry official identification, in an attempt to improve security after the leader of a militant Islamist organization was convicted of murder, and other members of the group were convicted in connection with threats to kill prominent politicians who were critical of Islam. In October the Minister of Immigration and Integration, Rita Verdonk, announced proposals to prohibit the wearing of traditional Islamic dress, such as face veils, in certain public places. Despite criticism by Muslim and human rights organizations, a motion in support of such measures was narrowly approved by the Second Chamber in December. In March 2006, however, following an investigation into the implications of human rights law on such a ban, the Government failed to reach agreement on the issue, and the proposals were to be reconsidered. In the same month further measures to control immigration were introduced, requiring potential immigrants from the majority of non-EU countries to pass an examination in their country of origin on their knowledge of Dutch culture and language.

In May 2006 the Secretary of State for Education, Culture and Science, Mark Rutte, defeated Verdonk in a contest for the VVD leadership, which had emphasized deep divisions within the party, particularly regarding immigration. During the leadership election campaign, Verdonk had publicly questioned the right to Dutch citizenship of her Somali-born parliamentary colleague, Ayaan Hirsi Ali; in June it was announced that an inquiry had found Hirsi Ali's citizenship claim to be legitimate. A motion of censure in the Second Chamber urging Verdonk's departure from office was defeated. The motion had been supported by D66, the three cabinet members of which subsequently resigned. On 30 June the remaining members of the Government followed suit. A minority interim administration comprising the CDA and the VVD was sworn in on 7 July, with a general election scheduled for November.

The 2006 election and nationalist controversy

At the general election in November 2006 the three largest parties all suffered a reduction in support among the electorate (80.1% of whom voted) compared with the 2003 poll. The CDA emerged as the largest party in the Second Chamber, with 41 of the 150 seats, the PvdA won 33 seats and the VVD 22. The SP achieved the largest electoral gain, winning 25 seats (compared with nine in 2003) and the 'confessional' ChristenUnie (CU—Christian Union) party doubled its representation from three to six seats. The nationalist Partij voor de Vrijheid (PVV—Freedom

Party), which was founded in February 2006 by former VVD parliamentarian Geert Wilders, won nine seats.

Following protracted negotiations, in late February 2007 a centre-left coalition of the CDA, the PvdA and the CU was formed under the renewed premiership of Balkenende. The PvdA leader, Bos, became Deputy Prime Minister and Minister of Finance, and the CU leader, André Rouvoet, Deputy Prime Minister and Minister of Youth and the Family. The appointment of two foreign-born Muslim secretaries of state, both of the PvdA, was criticized by Wilders after it was revealed that, in addition to their Dutch citizenship, they retained their respective Moroccan and Turkish nationalities. The new coalition agreement included a slowing in the reduction of disability payments and a relaxation of restrictions on immigration. In June the Second Chamber approved a government-proposed amnesty for asylum seekers whose applications had been rejected, reversing legislation approved in February 2004 that allowed for their voluntary repatriation.

The limited progress of the Government in implementing its reform programme allowed nationalist groups to dominate the political agenda in late 2007. In October Verdonk resigned her membership of the VVD, following her expulsion from the party's parliamentary group in September for criticizing the leadership. None the less, Verdonk retained her seat in the Second Chamber and a week later she announced the establishment of a new political movement, Trots op Nederland (Proud of the Netherlands), which was formally inaugurated in April 2008. Meanwhile, in March a film that Wilders had produced, which was critical of the Islamic religion, was broadcast on an internet site: the Government accused Wilders of attempting deliberately to cause offence, and in January 2009 the Amsterdam Court of Appeal ordered that Wilders should be prosecuted for 'initiating hatred and discrimination'. The ruling, which took into account not only Wilders' controversial film, but also a letter that had been published in a newspaper in August 2007, in which Wilders described the Koran as 'fascist', reversed an earlier decision by the Dutch prosecution service. Nevertheless, Wilders' PVV enjoyed significant success in elections to the European Parliament in June 2009, securing 17.0% of the votes cast and four seats, second only to the CDA (with 20.1% and five seats). Wilders' trial began in January 2010 in Amsterdam, but was adjourned until later in the year.

Government collapse and the general election of 2010

By late 2008 the Netherlands had begun to suffer the effects of the global financial crisis. In October the Government was obliged to nationalize the Dutch operations of the Belgian-Dutch financial services group, Fortis, and to acquire a minority stake in the country's largest bank, ING. By early 2009 it was clear that the Netherlands had entered a deep recession. Following negotiations between the coalition parties, along with business representatives and trade unions, in March the Government announced fiscal stimulus measures valued at some €6,000m., most notably including a reduction in expenditure on health care, increased spending on public infrastructure projects and an extension of the retirement age to 67 years.

Following long-standing tensions within the governing coalition regarding reductions in government spending, particularly on defence, and the raising of the retirement age, the PvdA withdrew from the coalition in February 2010 after arguing unsuccessfully for an end to Dutch involvement in the conflict in Afghanistan, precipitating the collapse of the Government. The CDA and the CU remained in power in a caretaker capacity pending a general election, scheduled for June; all major policy decisions were consequently placed on hold, and the Council of Ministers was reorganized, with the positions vacated by the PvdA being reassigned to CDA and CU members.

The CDA and the PvdA suffered significant losses at the March 2010 local elections; D66 and the VVD were the main beneficiaries. The PVV achieved its first representation at local level: it won a majority of seats in Almere and became the second largest party in The Hague. Following the PvdA's poor performance, Bos resigned as leader of the party and was replaced by Job Cohen; the SP leader, Agnes Kant, also resigned in March after similarly disappointing results in the local elections, and was replaced by Emile Roemer.

At the general election on 9 June 2010 (which attracted a turnout of 75.4%) the VVD became the largest party in the Second Chamber, with 31 seats, compared with 22 seats at the 2006 general election. The PvdA won 30 seats, a loss of three. The number of seats held by the PVV increased from nine to 24, making Wilders' party the third largest in the Second Chamber.

The CDA secured only 21 seats, down from 41 at the previous election. The SP won 15 seats, compared with 25 previously, while D66 and GroenLinks increased their representation to 10 seats each (from three and seven, respectively), and the CU won five, a loss of one seat. On the day of his party's overwhelming defeat, Balkenende resigned as party leader of the CDA, although he remained as Prime Minister in an interim capacity; the parliamentary leadership of the CDA was assumed by Maxime Verhagen, the interim Minister of Foreign Affairs and of Development Co-operation.

Recent developments: the Governments led by Mark Rutte

Negotiations between the various parties on the formation of a new Government began immediately after the June 2010 election and continued for almost four months. Initially, discussions were held between the VVD, the CDA and the PVV, but many members of the CDA were reluctant to share power with the controversial PVV, whose demands concerning both economic policy and the controls on immigration and Islamic practice met with considerable opposition. Discussions between the VVD and three left-wing parties, the PvdA, D66 and GroenLinks, also failed to reach consensus, particularly on the reductions in government spending proposed by the VVD. Eventually, in October, an agreement was reached whereby the VVD and the CDA would form a minority administration, led by Mark Rutte of the VVD, which would rely on the support of the PVV in the legislature, although no ministerial posts were to be allocated to that party. Together the three parties commanded 76 of the 150 seats in the Second Chamber, a majority of only one. The new administration pledged, *inter alia*, considerably to reduce public spending by 2015, to enlarge the police force, impose new limits on immigration, and ban the wearing of the Islamic face veil in public. Posts in Rutte's Council of Ministers were shared equally between the VVD and the CDA. Notable appointments included Maxime Verhagen, the acting leader of the CDA, as Deputy Prime Minister and Minister of Economic Affairs, Agriculture and Innovation, and Uri Rosenthal (VVD) as Minister of Foreign Affairs, while Jan Kees de Jager (CDA) retained the post of Minister of Finance.

The trial of Geert Wilders on charges of inciting hatred and discrimination, which had been adjourned in January 2010, resumed in October, but at the end of the month a retrial was ordered following allegations that the judges in the case had given the impression of bias against the defendant. In November revelations were published concerning several PVV legislators who, it was reported, had criminal convictions or were under investigation regarding alleged misconduct. Wilders' new trial began in March 2011, and in June he was acquitted; the court ruled that his statements, while offensive, had been permissible within the context of public debate. In early 2012 the PVV provoked fresh controversy by creating a website on which members of the public were invited to make complaints about the behaviour of immigrants from Central and Eastern Europe.

Meanwhile, the VVD performed strongly in provincial elections in March 2011, becoming the largest party in the legislatures of seven provinces (six of which had previously been led by the CDA). During 2011 there was widespread domestic opposition (particularly by the PVV) to the Netherlands' participation in the provision of emergency assistance to Greece as part of the response to the sovereign debt crisis in the eurozone (see *Regional relations*). In October the Dutch legislature was one of the last in the eurozone to approve the expansion of the European Financial Stability Facility (EFSF), under which the Netherlands was obliged to increase the amount of its guarantees to the EFSF from €56,000m. to €98,000m. The PVV opposed the expansion, and the ruling coalition depended on the support of the PvdA, D66 and GroenLinks for the measure to be adopted. In March 2012 the Government was obliged to launch inter-party negotiations on controversial additional reductions in budgetary spending over the next three years, in order to comply with the EU's recently concluded Treaty on Stability, Co-ordination and Governance (the 'fiscal compact'), which imposed legally binding limits on national budget deficits. The reductions were opposed not only by the PVV, which unsuccessfully demanded a national referendum on leaving the eurozone, but also by the PvdA and the SP, which declared that the planned reductions would be too fast and would damage the economy. (In February the leader of the PvdA, Job Cohen, had resigned after accusations that his opposition to the reductions was not forceful enough: he was replaced by Diederik Samsom.) Negotiations on the austerity measures collapsed in April when the PVV refused to support the budget proposals, and Rutte tendered the Government's resignation. It was announced that an early general election would be held in September. Later in April, however, the VVD-CDA coalition, now governing in a caretaker capacity, succeeded in gaining the support of D66, GroenLinks and the CU for the 2013 budget (although it was not to be submitted for parliamentary approval until after the general election). In May the CDA elected Sybrand van Haersma Buma (the party's leader in the legislature) to the vacant party leadership.

At the general election held on 12 September 2012 (which attracted a turnout of 74.6%) the VVD and the PvdA both increased their support in the Second Chamber, winning 41 and 38 of the 150 seats, respectively (compared with 31 and 30 at the 2010 election). The CDA won only 13 seats (compared with 21 previously), and the PVV also lost support, securing 15 seats (against 24). The SP, whose anti-austerity campaign had initially won it a leading place in pre-election opinion polls, retained its 15 seats. After nearly seven weeks of negotiations, in early November 2012 the VVD and the PvdA formed a coalition Government, with Rutte remaining in the post of Prime Minister. Lodewijk Asscher (PvdA) became Deputy Prime Minister with responsibility for social affairs and employment, while Frans Timmermans (PvdA) was appointed Minister of Foreign Affairs, Jeanine Hennis-Plasschaert (VVD) Minister of Defence and Jeroen Dijsselbloem (PvdA) Minister of Finance. The coalition agreement (involving concessions on both sides) envisaged savings amounting to €16,000m. by 2017 in order to balance the budget, including reductions in unemployment benefits and health care benefits, the replacement of student loans by grants, and lower levels of overseas aid.

In December 2012 the Government announced plans to merge three of the country's 12 provinces, namely Noord-Holland, Utrecht and Flevoland, into a single entity—Noordvleugel—by 2015, with the aim of eventually reducing the total number of provinces to either seven or five. Draft legislation on the merger of the first three (by 2016, rather than 2015) was introduced for consultation in June 2013. The Interprovinciaal Overleg (IPO—Association of Provinces) expressed opposition to the plan, despite the Government's claims that the merger would allow greater efficiency in housing provision, development of infrastructure and the management of the countryside. In response to growing widespread opposition, in April 2014 the planned formation of the new province was suspended indefinitely.

In January 2013 Queen Beatrix announced, shortly before her 75th birthday, that she intended to abdicate in April, after 33 years as reigning monarch. Her eldest son, Prince Willem-Alexander, succeeded her on the throne on 30 April.

During March and April 2013 the Government held discussions with trade unions and employers' organizations in an effort to achieve consensus on proposed economic reforms, before submitting budget plans for 2014 to the European Commission. The discussions resulted in a 'social accord', whereby the Government agreed to postpone the implementation of new austerity measures until later in the year, while compromises were reached on reforms to redundancy regulations, unemployment benefit and pensions. In June 2013 it was announced that the current year's budget deficit had fallen below the maximum permitted by the EU (i.e. below an amount equivalent to 3% of gross domestic product—GDP) but that the Government would still need to impose tax increases and reductions in expenditure, together totalling €6,000m., in order to avoid exceeding the limit in the following year. In October D66, the CU and a fundamentalist Christian party, the Staatkundig Gereformeerde Partij (SGP—Political Reformed Party), consented to ensure Senate support for the 2014 budget, after the Government had agreed, among other concessions, to modify proposed cuts in spending on education and child benefit. In December the same three parties agreed to support a controversial reduction in the level of tax-free pensions (adopted by the Second Chamber in June), which would generate some €3,000m. in government revenue.

In October 2013 a PVV member of the legislature was expelled from the party after criticizing its lack of internal democracy and of financial transparency, while in March 2014 two more PVV legislators and the leader of the PVV delegation to the European Parliament left the party, following a meeting at which Wilders encouraged chanting that appeared to threaten residents of Moroccan origin. (Wilders' provocative behaviour led to him being charged in December with inciting racial hatred.) At municipal elections in March the ruling VVD and PvdA both lost support, while the CDA was the most successful party overall

with some 14% of total votes; D66 won a majority of votes in 12 of the 20 largest cities, including Amsterdam, where the PvdA had been the dominant party since the 1940s. At elections to the European Parliament held in May, which attracted a turnout of only 37%, the PVV performed less well than predicted, losing one of its seats to secure just four of the 26 available. The CDA enjoyed the most success, obtaining five seats, while the pro-EU D66 won four. Minister of Foreign Affairs Timmermans resigned from the Government in October to take up a position at the European Commission; he was replaced by his PvdA colleague Bert Koenders. In the wake of the Islamist attacks in Paris in January 2015 (see France), there was a notable surge in support for the PVV, according to popularity polls, and Wilders demanded that the Government take firm action to ensure that such events did not take place in the Netherlands.

In early March 2015 the Minister of Security and Justice, Ivo Opstelten and State Secretary for Security and Justice, Fred Teeven, both of the VVD, resigned after admitting misinforming parliament over a deal that had been made with a drugs trafficker some 15 years earlier and authorized by Teeven, who was then a public prosecutor. The trafficker had been compensated after it could not be proven that money confiscated by the state was obtained illegally. When questioned in parliament in 2014, Opstelten had claimed that the dealer received much less in compensation than was actually the case and that details of the payment were missing.

Dutch Dependencies

The Netherlands East Indies (except West New Guinea, now Papua, which remained under Dutch control until 1963) formally seceded from the Union of the Netherlands, to form the United States of Indonesia in December 1949. In 1975 Suriname became independent, leaving the Netherlands Antilles as the only remaining Dutch dependency. Aruba, formerly part of the Netherlands Antilles, was granted separate status within the Kingdom of the Netherlands in 1986. A commission, established jointly by the Governments of the Netherlands and the Netherlands Antilles, recommended in October 2004 that the islands of Curaçao and St Maarten (in the Netherlands Antilles) should be given autonomous status within the Kingdom of the Netherlands (i.e. have *status aparte*, like that of Aruba), while the three other islands of the dependency, Saba, Bonaire and Sint (St) Eustatius, should be placed under direct rule. In a series of non-binding referendums between 2000 and 2005 a majority of voters in Sint (St) Maarten and Curaçao favoured obtaining *status aparte*, while the electorates of both Bonaire and Saba strongly favoured direct rule. St Eustatius was the only island to favour remaining part of the Netherlands Antilles. None the less, in October 2005 the Dutch Government concluded an outline agreement on constitutional reform with all five islands. Curaçao and St Maarten were to be granted *status aparte*, while Bonaire, Saba and St Eustatius would become koninkrijkseilanden (kingdom islands) with direct ties to the Netherlands. The future status of Bonaire, Saba and St Eustatius was subsequently refined to that of bijzondere gemeente (special municipalities), similar in most ways to other metropolitan Netherlands municipalities, although with separate social security and currency arrangements, for example. However, the populations of the Antillean municipalities would be able to vote in Dutch and European elections (the province of Noord-Holland offered to include the three territories). Following the negotiation of further details, the Dutch Prime Minister, Jan Peter Balkenende, and the Antillean premier, Emily de Jongh-Elhage, signed an agreement confirming the new status of the five islands at a meeting in Curaçao on 15 December 2008. The agreement entered into effect on 10 October 2010.

Foreign Affairs

Regional relations

The Netherlands was a founder member of the North Atlantic Treaty Organization (NATO, see p. 367) in 1949, abandoning its previous policy of neutrality. The treaty establishing the Benelux Economic Union (see p. 444) between the Netherlands, Belgium and Luxembourg was signed in 1958 and came into force in 1960. In June 2008 Balkenende, along with the Prime Ministers of Belgium and Luxembourg, signed a new Benelux Treaty on political and economic co-operation, providing for greater co-operation between the three Governments on justice and home affairs, as well as customs and cross-border trade. In recognition of this, the official title of the organization was to change from the Benelux Economic Union to the Benelux Union.

By May 2011 the treaty had been ratified by the legislatures of the three countries and by the parliaments of the five Belgian federal units; it entered into force on 1 January 2012.

The Netherlands was a founder member of the European Community (EC, now European Union—EU, see p. 271). The EU Treaty establishing a Constitution for Europe was signed by the EU heads of state and of government in October 2004. It required ratification by all of the then 25 EU member countries, either through a referendum or by a vote in the national legislature, before it could come into force. A non-binding referendum on the treaty took place in the Netherlands on 1 June 2005, when 61.6% of those who voted (63% of the electorate) opposed the treaty's ratification. On the following day the Government formally withdrew the proposed legislation. This decisive rejection of the treaty by Dutch voters, and by French voters a few days earlier, prompted several other member countries to postpone indefinitely their own referendums. In June 2007 EU heads of state and of government reached a preliminary agreement for a comprehensive reform treaty. In September Balkenende announced that the new treaty would be submitted to the legislature, thus avoiding the prospect of a further defeat at a national referendum. The Treaty of Lisbon was formally signed by EU leaders on 13 December at a summit meeting in Lisbon, Portugal. The treaty was ratified by parliamentary vote in the Netherlands in July 2008. It came into force on 1 December 2009.

The Netherlands Government supported the creation of the European Financial Stability Facility (EFSF) in 2010, to safeguard the financial stability of the eurozone after the onset of the sovereign debt crisis afflicting some member states, and in July 2011 approved the expansion of the facility, together with a second instalment of emergency assistance for Greece. It supported the German Government in insisting that private creditors should participate in the assistance programme by accepting losses on their loans, and that strict conditions should be attached to emergency assistance for heavily indebted member states, particularly Greece. The Netherlands Government was firmly in favour of the adoption of the Treaty on Stability, Co-ordination and Governance (the 'fiscal compact'), signed in March 2012 by all EU member governments except those of the Czech Republic and the United Kingdom; the treaty made legally binding the previously stipulated limit (an amount equivalent to 3% of GDP) on the budgetary deficits of participating countries. In order to comply with the treaty the Netherlands Government was subsequently obliged (despite domestic opposition) to introduce new restrictions on its own expenditure. During 2012 the Netherlands Government, like that of Germany, opposed the issuing of 'eurobonds' (whereby all eurozone members would guarantee individual states' debts) and the use of EU funds for direct support of banks. With Germany and other member states, the Netherlands successfully urged a reduction in EU budget spending under the Multiannual Financial Framework (MFF) for 2014–20, negotiations for which were concluded in February 2013 and finally approved by the European Parliament in November. In that month the Netherlands (with Denmark, Sweden and the UK) voted against the adoption of the EU's annual budget for 2014, on the grounds that insufficient reductions in expenditure had been made. Meanwhile, in a briefing to the Netherlands legislature in June 2013, the Government expressed the view that 'ever closer union' within the EU was not desirable, and that individual states should retain control of certain areas, including social security benefits, health and safety laws, media regulation and flood risk prevention. As a result of a change in how the gross national incomes of member states were calculated, the Netherlands was obliged to pay a net top-up sum of €642m. in its contribution to the EU budget for 2015.

Other external relations

In January 2003 a parliamentary commission concluded that the state of the Netherlands bore responsibility for the massacre by Bosnian Serbs of some 7,000 Bosnian Muslim men and boys who had taken shelter in or in the vicinity of a UN compound in Potočari, just outside Srebrenica, Bosnia and Herzegovina, in July 1995, but had been ordered to leave by Dutch members of the UN peacekeeping force there. In September 2008 a Netherlands court ruled that the state could not be held responsible for the actions of the peacekeeping force, as they had been operating under a UN mandate. In July 2011, however, a court of appeal ordered the Netherlands Government to pay damages to two of the families whose relatives had been killed: the decision was expected to strengthen the case of thousands of other families who were currently undertaking legal action against the UN and

the Netherlands Government in connection with the massacre. In March 2013 the Netherlands public prosecution department concluded that the officer who had been in charge of the Dutch peacekeeping force should not face charges of facilitating genocide and war crimes. In September the Supreme Court ruled that the state of the Netherlands had been responsible for the deaths of three of the Bosnian Muslims who had been killed at Srebrenica—the three individuals had been employed by the Dutch peacekeeping force. Furthermore, in July 2014 a Dutch court ruled that the state was liable for the deaths of more than 300 other Bosnian Muslims who had been deported from the UN compound at Potočari—the figure fell far short of the total number of those killed since, according to the court, many of those who were killed by the Bosnian Serbs had not actually sought refuge in the compound but rather were sheltering in nearby woods.

Government plans to commit troops to a NATO peacekeeping mission to southern Afghanistan prompted fierce opposition in late 2005. (Some 350 soldiers from the Netherlands were already stationed in the north and east of Afghanistan, while a further 250 were engaged in counter-terrorism operations.) However, following a debate in the Second Chamber, in February 2006 it was announced that 1,200 military personnel were to join the mission in the province of Uruzgan, in central Afghanistan, from August. (Dutch troops had been withdrawn from Iraq in March 2005.) In December 2007 the Second Chamber voted to extend the mandate of Dutch troops in Uruzgan province until December 2010. Despite a NATO request for an extension of the Dutch presence and the collapse of the governing coalition over the issue (see *Domestic Political Affairs*), the Netherlands forces were withdrawn from Afghanistan in July 2010. In January 2011, however, the Government agreed to provide personnel, numbering 545, to train police officers in northern Afghanistan, and this was approved by a small majority in the legislature, after assurances that the mission would be civilian in nature; the mission was concluded in July 2013.

Since 2009 Netherlands naval vessels have been operating off the coast of Somalia as part of efforts by the EU and NATO to combat piracy. In November 2013 it was announced that 368 Netherlands troops were to form part of a UN peacekeeping force in Mali; the first contingent was dispatched in January 2014.

In recent years economic relations with the People's Republic of China have become increasingly important for the Netherlands: since 2003 the Netherlands has been China's second largest trading partner within the EU (after Germany). In November 2013 the Prime Minister, Mark Rutte, visited China, accompanied by a delegation of business representatives, and in March 2014 the Chinese President, Xi Jinping, included a visit to the Netherlands as part of a European tour; during the historic visit—the first by a Chinese head of state—agreements on co-operation in the energy and dairy sectors were concluded by the two countries.

CONSTITUTION AND GOVERNMENT

The Netherlands is a constitutional and hereditary monarchy. Legislative power is held by the bicameral Staten-Generaal (States-General). The Eerste Kamer (First Chamber) or Senaat (Senate) has 75 members and is indirectly elected for four years by members of the 12 Provincial Councils. The Tweede Kamer (Second Chamber) or House of Representatives comprises 150 members and is directly elected by universal adult suffrage for four years (subject to dissolution), on the basis of proportional representation. The head of state has mainly formal prerogatives, and executive power is exercised by the Council of Ministers, which is led by the Prime Minister and is responsible to the States-General. The monarch appoints the Prime Minister and, on the latter's recommendation, other ministers. Each of the 12 provinces is administered by a directly elected Provincial Council, a Provincial Executive and a Sovereign Commissioner, who is appointed by Royal Decree.

REGIONAL AND INTERNATIONAL CO-OPERATION

The Netherlands was a founder member of the European Community, now the European Union (EU, see p. 271), the Benelux Economic Union (see p. 444), the Organization for Security and Co-operation in Europe (OSCE, see p. 385) and the Council of Europe (see p. 250).

The Netherlands was a founder member of the UN in 1945. As a contracting party to the General Agreement on Tariffs and Trade, it joined the World Trade Organization (WTO, see p. 431) on its establishment in 1995. The Netherlands was also a founder member of the North Atlantic Treaty Organization (NATO, see p. 367) and the Organisation for Economic Co-operation and Development (OECD, see p. 377).

ECONOMIC AFFAIRS

In 2013, according to estimates by the World Bank, the Netherlands' gross national income (GNI), measured at average 2011–13 prices, was US $797,211m., equivalent to $47,440 per head (or $43,210 per head on an international purchasing-power parity basis). During 2004–13, it was estimated, the population grew at an average annual rate of 0.4%, while gross domestic product (GDP) per head increased, in real terms, at an average annual rate of 0.5% over the same period. According to official figures, overall GDP increased, in real terms, at an average annual rate of 1.0% in 2004–13; real GDP decreased by 0.7% in 2013.

Agriculture (including hunting, forestry and fishing) contributed an estimated 2.0% of GDP in 2013, and 2.3% of the employed labour force were engaged in the sector in that year. The Netherlands is a net exporter of agricultural products: in 2013 exports of food and live animals provided 12.4% of total export earnings. The principal crops are potatoes, sugar beet, wheat and onions. The main agricultural activity is horticulture; market gardening is highly developed, and the production of cut flowers and bulbs has traditionally been a significant industry, although its contribution to export earnings showed some decline in the early years of the 21st century (partly compensated for by re-exports from other growers to European markets). Livestock farming is also an important activity. According to the Central Bureau of Statistics, during 2004–13 agricultural GDP increased, in real terms, at an average annual rate of 0.8%; the sector's GDP rose by 1.9% in 2013.

Industry (including mining, manufacturing, construction and power) contributed an estimated 22.2% of GDP in 2013 and engaged 15.1% of the employed labour force in that year. According to the Central Bureau of Statistics, industrial GDP increased, in real terms, at an average annual rate of 0.5% in 2004–13; real industrial GDP declined by 0.2% in 2013.

Mining and quarrying provided an estimated 3.6% of GDP in 2013 and engaged 0.1% of the employed labour force in that year. The principal mineral resource is natural gas. Total production in 2013 was an estimated 68,681m. cu m. Reserves of petroleum and salts are also exploited. The GDP of the mining sector declined, in real terms, at an average annual rate of 0.9% in 2004–13; it declined by 0.6% in 2012, but increased by 7.0% in 2013.

Manufacturing contributed an estimated 12.1% of GDP and accounted for 8.9% of the employed labour force in 2013. Several multinational companies are domiciled in the Netherlands, including the electrical firm Philips, the brewer Heineken, and two British-Dutch firms, the food industry company Unilever and the petroleum firm Royal Dutch Shell. According to the Central Bureau of Statistics, manufacturing GDP increased at an average annual rate of 1.0% in 2004–13; it declined by 0.4% in 2013.

The construction sector contributed an estimated 4.6% of GDP in 2013, and engaged 5.5% of the employed labour force in that year. According to the Central Bureau of Statistics, construction GDP decreased at an average annual rate of 0.9% in 2004–13; it decreased by 4.4% in 2013.

In 2012 natural gas provided 54.3% of total electricity production and coal 26.7%. Imports of mineral fuels and lubricants comprised 10.4% of the value of total imports in 2003; by 2013 this figure had increased to 24.7%. In recent years the gradual depletion of the Groningen natural gas field has prompted the exploration of investment possibilities in smaller fields, while successive Governments have sought to promote the utilization of renewable energy resources.

The services sector contributed an estimated 75.8% of GDP and engaged 82.6% of the employed labour force in 2013. Within the sector, financial services, tourism and transport are of considerable importance. The GDP of the services sector increased, in real terms, at an average annual rate of 1.6% in 2004–13; it decreased by 0.5% in 2013.

In 2013 the Netherlands recorded a visible merchandise trade surplus of €66,404m. and there was a surplus of €87,089m. on the current account of the balance of payments. The principal source of imports in 2013 was Germany (contributing 16.4% of the total); other major suppliers were Belgium, the People's Republic of China, the United Kingdom, the USA and the Russian Federation. Germany was also the principal market for exports in that year (accounting for 24.7% of the total); other major purchasers in 2012 were Belgium, the UK and France. The principal exports in 2013 were machinery and transport equipment, mineral fuels and lubricants, chemicals and related products, food and live animals, miscellaneous manufactured articles, and basic manufactures. The principal imports in that year were also machinery and transport equipment, followed by mineral fuels, lubricants, chemicals and related products, miscellaneous manufactured articles, basic manufactures, and food and live animals.

In 2013, according to official estimates, the Netherlands recorded an overall budgetary deficit of €14,629m., equivalent to 2.3% of GDP. The Netherlands' general government gross debt was €441,035m. in 2013, equivalent to 68.6% of GDP. In 2004–13 the annual rate of inflation averaged 1.9%. Consumer prices increased by 2.5% in 2013. The rate of unemployment in 2014 was 8.3%.

The Netherlands' small size and dependence on external trade make it particularly vulnerable to external economic conditions. Decreasing industrial production and increasing labour costs in the 2000s, combined with an ageing population and rising levels of unemployment, led to greater demand for state-funded pensions, health care and welfare benefits. In an attempt to reduce the budget deficit to comply with the limit of 3% of GDP imposed by the EU's Stability and Growth Pact, the Government implemented comprehensive health and social welfare reform, thereby reducing the budget deficit to 0.2% of GDP in 2005; small budget surpluses were recorded in 2006 and 2007. With the onset of the global economic crisis, exports and investment declined sharply in the second half of 2008, while banks suffered severe losses that required significant state intervention. Following the introduction of necessary fiscal stimulus measures, government finances deteriorated substantially, with a budget deficit equivalent to 4.5% of GDP in 2009 and a large increase in the levels of government indebtedness. GDP declined by 3.5% in 2009, but the swift introduction of the stimulus measures limited the negative impact of the global financial crisis on the country, with real GDP growth of 1.7% in 2010 and of 0.9% in 2011. The Government that took office in October 2010 further reduced public expenditure in order to lower the budgetary deficit, which decreased from 5.3% of GDP in 2010 to 4.3% of GDP in 2011. During 2012 and 2013 controversial additional spending cuts and tax increases were enacted in order to comply with the recently adopted EU treaty on fiscal discipline (see *Regional relations*). A contraction in GDP of 1.2% in 2012 reflected reductions in investment, house prices and consumer spending, while the budget deficit narrowed slightly to 4.0% of GDP; inflation rose to 2.5% in that year, largely as a result of high energy prices and an increase in value-added tax. High levels of household debt reduced the level of disposable income, and the constraints imposed by fiscal consolidation contributed to a further decline in GDP, of 0.7% in 2013, although GDP growth of 0.9% in the last quarter of the year suggested a nascent recovery. Unemployment remained above 8% for most of 2013–14, while inflation in 2013, averaging 2.5% for the year as a whole, was more than double the average wage increase. However, largely as a result of a substantial fall in the cost of fuel and energy, the rate of inflation declined to an average of 1.0% in 2014—the lowest rate of increase in consumer prices for more than 25 years. The budget deficit fell below the EU-mandated ceiling, at 2.3% of GDP in 2013 and 2.9% of GDP in 2014, but the Government expressed its determination to maintain austerity policies that would lead to a balanced budget. Modest growth in GDP of an estimated 0.6% was achieved in 2014, and the economy was expected to remain on a gradual upward trajectory in 2015, with GDP projected to expand by a further 0.8% in that year and the budget deficit forecast to decrease to 2.2% of GDP.

PUBLIC HOLIDAYS

2016: 1 January (New Year's Day), 25 March (Good Friday), 28 March (Easter Monday), 27 April (King's Day), 5 May (Ascension Day), 16 May (Whit Monday), 25–26 December (Christmas).

Statistical Survey

Source (unless otherwise stated): Netherlands Central Bureau of Statistics, Henri Faasdreef 312, 2492 JP The Hague; tel. (70) 3373800; fax (70) 3877429; e-mail infoservice@cbs.nl; internet www.cbs.nl.

Area and Population

AREA, POPULATION AND DENSITY

Area (sq km)	
Land	33,718
Inland waters	3,635
Coastal water	4,187
Total	41,540*
Population (census results)†	
1 January 2001‡	15,987,075
1 January 2012‡	
Males	8,282,871
Females	8,447,477
Total	16,730,348
Population (official estimate at 1 January)	
2013	16,779,575
2014	16,829,289
Density (per sq km of land) at 1 January 2014 . . .	499.1§

* 16,039 sq miles.
† Population is *de jure*.
‡ Based on a compilation of continuous accounting and sample surveys.
§ Land area only.

POPULATION BY AGE AND SEX
(official estimates at 1 January 2014)

	Males	Females	Total
0–14 years	1,458,655	1,391,419	2,850,074
15–64 years	5,560,850	5,499,341	11,060,191
65 years and over	1,314,880	1,604,144	2,919,024
Total	**8,334,385**	**8,494,904**	**16,829,289**

PROVINCES
(official population estimates at 1 January 2013)

	Land area (sq km)	Population	Density (per sq km)
Drenthe	2,639	489,918	185.6
Flevoland	1,415	398,441	281.6
Friesland	3,340	646,862	193.7
Gelderland	4,970	2,015,791	405.6
Groningen	2,325	581,705	250.2
Limburg	2,150	1,121,891	521.8
Noord-Brabant	4,914	2,471,011	502.9
Noord-Holland	2,665	2,724,300	1,022.3
Overijssel	3,324	1,139,350	342.8
Utrecht	1,383	1,245,294	900.4
Zeeland	1,784	381,077	213.6
Zuid-Holland	2,808	3,563,935	1,269.2
Total	**33,718**	**16,779,575**	**497.6**

PRINCIPAL TOWNS
(population of municipalities at 1 January 2013)

Amsterdam (capital)*	799,278	Haarlem	153,093
Rotterdam . . .	616,294	Arnhem	149,827
's-Gravenhage/Den			
Haag (The Hague)*	505,856	Amersfoort . . .	149,662
Utrecht	321,916	Zaanstad . . .	149,622
Eindhoven . . .	218,433	Haarlemmermeer .	144,153
		's-Hertogenbosch/Den	
Tilburg	208,527	Bosch	142,817
Groningen . . .	195,418	Zoetermeer . . .	123,092
Almere	195,213	Zwolle	122,562
Breda	178,140	Maastricht . . .	121,819
Nijmegen . . .	166,382	Leiden	119,800
Enschede . . .	158,627	Dordrecht . . .	118,466
Apeldoorn . . .	157,315		

* Amsterdam is the capital, while The Hague is the seat of government.

BIRTHS, MARRIAGES AND DEATHS

	Live births*		Marriages		Deaths*	
	Number	Rate (per 1,000)	Number	Rate (per 1,000)	Number	Rate (per 1,000)
2006 . .	185,057	11.3	72,369	4.4	135,372	8.3
2007 . .	181,336	11.1	72,485	4.4	133,022	8.1
2008 . .	184,634	11.2	75,438	4.6	135,136	8.2
2009 . .	184,915	11.2	73,477	4.4	134,235	8.1
2010 . .	184,397	11.1	75,399	4.5	136,058	8.2
2011 . .	180,060	10.8	71,572	4.3	135,741	8.1
2012 . .	175,959	10.5	70,315	4.2	140,813	8.4
2013 . .	171,341	10.8	64,549	3.8	141,245	8.1

* Including residents outside the country if listed in a Netherlands population register.

Life expectancy (years at birth): 81.1 (males 79.3; females 83.0) in 2012 (Source: World Bank, World Development Indicators database).

IMMIGRATION AND EMIGRATION

	2011	2012	2013
Immigrants	162,962	158,374	164,772
Emigrants	133,194	144,491	145,669

EMPLOYMENT
('000 persons, incl. self-employed, 15 years and over)

	2011	2012*	2013*
Agriculture, hunting, forestry and fishing	201	199	198
Mining and quarrying	8	9	10
Manufacturing	792	783	771
Electricity, gas and water supply .	57	58	58
Construction	522	507	477
Wholesale and retail trade and repair	1,414	1,420	1,405
Hotels and restaurants . . .	355	360	363
Transport, storage and communications	646	648	641
Financial intermediation . . .	261	255	245
Real estate, renting and business activities	1,762	1,747	1,734
Public administration, social security and defence . . .	507	495	488
Education	524	519	512
Health and social work . . .	1,425	1,439	1,427
Other community, social and personal service activities . .	158	158	157
Private households with employed persons	221	216	214
Total employed	**8,854**	**8,812**	**8,700**

* Provisional figures.

Unemployment ('000 persons): 507 in 2012; 656 in 2013; 656 in 2014.

Health and Welfare

KEY INDICATORS

Total fertility rate (children per woman, 2012)	1.8
Under-5 mortality rate (per 1,000 live births, 2012) . . .	4
HIV/AIDS (% of persons aged 15–49, 2011)	0.2
Physicians (per 1,000 head, 2008)	2.9
Hospital beds (per 1,000 head, 2009)	4.7
Health expenditure (2011): US $ per head (PPP) . . .	5,118
Health expenditure (2011): % of GDP	11.9
Health expenditure (2011): public (% of total)	79.5
Total carbon dioxide emissions ('000 metric tons, 2010) . .	182,077.6
Carbon dioxide emissions per head (metric tons, 2010) . .	11.0
Human Development Index (2013): ranking	4
Human Development Index (2013): value	0.915

For sources and definitions, see explanatory note on p. vi.

Agriculture

PRINCIPAL CROPS
('000 metric tons)

	2011	2012	2013
Wheat	1,175	1,302	1,331
Barley	205	206	206
Maize	204	191	247
Rye	6	9	7
Triticale (wheat-rye hybrid) . .	10	12	10
Potatoes	7,333	6,766	6,801
Sugar beet	5,858	5,728	5,727
Cabbages and other brassicas .	249	248	276
Lettuce and chicory	84	93	90
Spinach	34	29	29
Tomatoes	815	805	855
Cauliflowers and broccoli . . .	57	53	51
Cucumbers and gherkins . . .	430	410	400
Aubergines (eggplants) . . .	46	47	48
Chillies and green peppers . .	365	345	325
Onions and shallots, green* . .	37	38	46
Onions, dry	1,541	1,353	1,310
Leeks and other alliaceous vegetables	90	93	106
Beans, green	44	36	34
Peas, green	21	15	18
Carrots and turnips	482	511	555
Mushrooms and truffles . . .	304	307	323
Apples	418	281	314
Pears	336	199	327
Strawberries	47	50	51

* FAO estimates.

Aggregate production ('000 metric tons, may include official, semi-official or estimated data): Total cereals 1,610 in 2011, 1,731 in 2012, 1,811 in 2013; Total roots and tubers 7,333 in 2011, 6,766 in 2012, 6,801 in 2013; Total vegetables (incl. melons) 5,050 in 2011, 4,744 in 2012, 4,820 in 2013; Total fruits (excl. melons) 819 in 2011, 547 in 2012, 710 in 2013.

Source: FAO.

LIVESTOCK
('000 head, year ending September)

	2011	2012	2013
Horses*	136	137	137
Cattle	3,885	3,879	3,999
Chickens	96,919	95,273	97,719
Sheep	1,088	1,043	1,034
Goats	380	397	413
Pigs	12,429	12,234	12,212

* FAO estimates.

Source: FAO.

LIVESTOCK PRODUCTS
('000 metric tons)

	2011	2012	2013
Cattle meat	382	374	374
Sheep meat	13	13	12
Pig meat	1,347	1,332	1,282
Chicken meat	841	889	921
Turkey meat*	58	59	59
Cows' milk	11,642	11,675	12,207
Hen eggs	692	672	703*

* FAO estimate(s).

Source: FAO.

Forestry

ROUNDWOOD REMOVALS
('000 cubic metres, excl. bark)

	2011	2012	2013
Sawlogs, veneer logs and logs for sleepers	326	328	389
Pulpwood	301	318	330
Other industrial wood	62	20	13
Fuel wood	290	290	290
Total	979	955	1,022

Source: FAO.

SAWNWOOD PRODUCTION
('000 cubic metres, incl. railway sleepers)

	2011	2012	2013
Coniferous (softwood)	169	137	159
Broadleaved (hardwood) . . .	69	53	52
Total	238	190	211

Source: FAO.

Fishing

('000 metric tons, live weight)

	2010	2011	2012
Capture*	434.4	370.1	347.3
European plaice	28.3	29.3	32.3
Blue whiting	35.0	4.2	27.2
Atlantic herring	55.8	45.5	85.1
Round sardinella	75.9	44.7	10.2
European pilchard	46.9	52.1	27.0
Atlantic horse mackerel . . .	79.2	76.4	78.8
Atlantic mackerel	24.9	29.8	25.7
Aquaculture*	66.9	43.8	46.1
Blue mussel	56.2	36.7	40.0
Total catch*	501.3	413.9	393.5

* FAO estimates.

Note: Figures exclude aquatic mammals, recorded by number rather than by weight.

Source: FAO.

Mining

	2010	2011	2012
Crude petroleum ('000 barrels) .	7,300	8,121	8,212
Salt ('000 metric tons)* . . .	6,000	6,000	n.a.

* Estimated production.

Source: US Geological Survey.

Natural gas (million cu m, excl. gas flared or recycled): 64,196 in 2011; 63,851 in 2012; 68,681 in 2013 (Source: BP, *Statistical Review of World Energy*).

Industry

SELECTED PRODUCTS
('000 metric tons unless otherwise indicated)

	2009	2010	2011
Mechanical wood pulp* . . .	72	97	34
Newsprint*	273	242	253
Printing and writing paper* . .	653	725	693
Wrapping and packaging paper			
and paperboard*	1,563	1,774	1,681
Synthetic rubber†	n.a.	n.a.	164
Jet fuels	5,526	6,284	7,025
Kerosene	373	288	390
Motor spirit (petrol) . . .	6,971	7,368	n.a.
Naphthas	9,570	7,539	8,215
Gas-diesel (distillate fuel) oil . .	20,384	21,254	20,449
White spirit	39	107	111
Residual fuel (Mazout) oils . .	8,496	9,800	8,481
Lubricating oils	993	916	n.a.
Petroleum bitumen (asphalt) . .	291	183	247
Liquefied petroleum gas . . .	1,403	1,426	1,544
Coke	1,776	2,131	2,007
Coke-oven gas (terajoules) . .	15,421	18,328	18,093
Cement‡§	2,700	2,700	2,700
Pig-iron‖	4,601	5,799	5,943
Crude steel‖	5,194	6,651	6,937
Aluminium (unwrought): primary‡	300	300	300
Refined lead: secondary‡§ . . .	16	17	17
Zinc (unwrought): primary‡ . .	224	254	261
Electricity (million kWh) . . .	113,502	118,140	112,968

* Source: FAO.
† Refers to amounts sold by establishments employing 20 persons or more.
‡ Data from US Geological Survey.
§ Estimates.
‖ Source: World Steel Association (Brussels).

Source: unless otherwise indicated, UN Industrial Commodity Statistics Database.

2012 ('000 metric tons): Mechanical wood pulp 39; Newsprint 255; Printing and writing paper 669; Wrapping and packaging paper and paperboard 1,713; Crude steel 6,866; Pig-iron 5,909; Cement 2,700 (estimate); Aluminium (unwrought—primary) 110 (estimate); Zinc (unwrought—primary) 257 (estimate); Refined lead (secondary) 17 (estimate) (Sources: World Steel Association—Brussels; FAO).

2013 ('000 metric tons, estimates): Mechanical wood pulp 41; Newsprint 250; Printing and writing paper 666; Wrapping and packaging paper and paperboard 1,706; Crude steel 6,713; Pig-iron 5,685 (Source: World Steel Association—Brussels).

Finance

CURRENCY AND EXCHANGE RATES

Monetary Units
100 cent = 1 euro (€).

Sterling and Dollar Equivalents (31 December 2014)
£1 sterling = 1.286 euros;
US $1 = 0.824 euros;
€10 = £7.78 = $12.14.

Average Exchange Rate (euros per US $)
2012   0.7783
2013   0.7532
2014   0.7537

Note: The national currency was formerly the guilder. From the introduction of the euro, with the Netherlands' participation, on 1 January 1999, a fixed exchange rate of €1 = 2.20371 guilders was in operation. Euro notes and coins were introduced on 1 January 2002. The euro and local currency circulated alongside each other until 28 January, after which the euro became the sole legal tender.

GOVERNMENT FINANCE
(general government transactions, non-cash basis, € million)*

Summary of Balances

	2010	2011	2012
Revenue	271,749	273,104	278,149
Less Expense	296,609	295,937	299,608
Net operating balance . . .	−24,860	−22,833	−21,459
Less Net acquisition of non-			
financial assets	4,675	2,778	2,481
Net lending/borrowing . . .	−29,535	−25,611	−23,940

Revenue

	2010	2011	2012
Tax revenue	143,208	139,725	135,339
Taxes on income, profits and			
capital gains	63,581	61,929	58,869
Taxes on goods and services .	71,344	70,400	70,293
Taxes on property	7,674	6,855	6,012
Social contributions . . .	87,225	92,623	99,609
Grants	387	217	210
Other revenue	40,929	40,539	42,991
Total	271,749	273,104	278,149

Expense/Outlays

Expense by economic type†	2010	2011	2012
Compensation of employees . .	59,229	58,893	58,649
Use of goods and services . .	46,869	45,453	45,505
Consumption of fixed capital . .	16,269	16,637	16,957
Interest	11,614	11,936	10,984
Subsidies	9,196	8,596	7,923
Grants	9,465	7,967	8,007
Social benefits	135,167	138,968	143,817
Other expense	8,800	7,487	7,766
Total	296,609	295,937	299,608

Outlays by function of government	2010	2011	2012
General public services . . .	35,001	33,149	32,594
Defence	8,325	8,173	7,531
Public order and safety . . .	12,372	12,109	12,337
Economic affairs	35,495	33,083	31,867
Environment protection . . .	10,422	10,322	10,045
Housing and community amenities	4,378	3,552	3,561
Health	49,108	50,390	53,411
Recreation, culture and religion .	10,761	10,378	10,372
Education	34,272	34,630	34,841
Social protection	101,150	102,929	105,530
Total	301,284	298,715	302,089

* Figures represent a consolidation of the operations of the Government, comprising all central and local government accounts.
† Including net acquisition of non-financial assets.

Source: IMF, *Government Finance Statistics Yearbook*.

2013 (general government transactions, € million, rounded figures, preliminary): *Revenue:* Total 286,159 (Tax revenue 139,060, Social security contributions 97,512, Sales of goods and services 17,235, Other 32,352). *Expenditure:* Total 300,788 (Compensation of employees 59,434, Use of goods and services 41,884, Gross investments in fixed assets 23,276, Social benefits 141,676, Other 34,518).

INTERNATIONAL RESERVES
(US $ million at 31 December)

	2012	2013	2014
Gold (Eurosystem valuation) . .	32,766	23,659	23,985
IMF special drawing rights . .	7,163	7,023	6,621
Reserve position in IMF . . .	4,084	3,881	2,931
Foreign exchange	10,803	11,688	9,755
Total	54,816	46,250	43,292

Source: IMF, *International Financial Statistics*.

MONEY SUPPLY
(incl. shares, depository corporations, national residency criteria, € '000 million at 31 December)

	2011	2012	2013
Currency issued	46.99	48.30	50.66
De Nederlandsche Bank . .	19.71	17.73	16.27
Demand deposits	236.78	249.35	245.06
Other deposits	557.46	569.23	558.45
Securities other than shares . .	553.32	567.06	513.36
Shares and other equity . . .	142.55	153.26	138.20
Other items (net)	−1.96	−9.46	−4.07
Total	1,535.14	1,577.75	1,501.66

Source: IMF, *International Financial Statistics*.

COST OF LIVING
(Consumer Price Index; base: 2000 = 100)

	2009	2010	2011
Food (incl. non-alcoholic beverages)	116.8	116.7	119.3
Electricity, gas and other fuels .	181.9	167.4	177.2
Clothing (incl. footwear) . . .	98.9	98.4	99.4
Rent	125.0	127.7	129.9
All items (incl. others) . . .	120.6	122.1	124.9

2012: Food 106.1; All items (incl. others) 128.0.
2013: Food 108.7; All items (incl. others) 131.2.
Source: ILO.

NATIONAL ACCOUNTS
(€ million at current prices)
National Income and Product

	2011	2012*	2013*
Compensation of employees . .	318,040	323,237	324,389
Net operating surplus/mixed income	156,630	148,721	144,847
Domestic primary incomes .	474,670	471,958	469,236
Consumption of fixed capital . .	107,068	107,668	108,625
Gross domestic product (GDP) at factor cost	581,738	579,626	577,861
Taxes on production and imports .	71,871	70,891	73,918
Less Subsidies	10,680	9,873	8,928
GDP in market prices . . .	642,929	640,644	642,851
Net primary income from the rest of the world	422	7,892	1,380
Gross national income (GNI) .	643,351	648,536	644,231
Less Consumption of fixed capital	107,068	107,668	108,625
Net national income . . .	536,283	540,868	535,606
Net current transfers from the rest of the world	−9,606	−9,586	−13,038
Net national disposable income	526,677	531,282	522,568

Expenditure on the Gross Domestic Product

	2011	2012*	2013*
Government final consumption expenditure	167,158	169,645	169,296
Private final consumption expenditure	288,939	288,629	289,573
Changes in inventories . . .	1,526	2,047	275
Gross fixed capital formation .	130,402	122,099	117,297
Total domestic expenditure .	588,025	582,420	576,441
Exports of goods and services .	497,347	525,559	533,186
Less Imports of goods and services	442,443	467,335	466,776
GDP in purchasers' values .	642,929	640,644	642,851
GDP at constant 2010 prices .	642,018	631,837	627,253

Gross Domestic Product by Economic Activity

	2011	2012*	2013*
Agriculture, hunting, forestry and fishing	9,697	10,323	11,392
Mining and quarrying	18,559	20,327	21,052
Manufacturing	69,979	70,388	70,082
Electricity, gas and water supply .	10,943	10,695	10,624
Construction	30,295	27,694	26,420
Wholesale and retail trade; transport; repair of motor vehicles, motorcycles and personal household goods; hotels and restaurants	113,924	112,668	112,209
Information and communications .	27,889	27,312	26,743
Finance, insurance, real estate and other business activities . .	157,590	155,501	154,817
General government; education; health; social work activities .	125,690	128,950	130,074
Care and other service activities .	15,024	15,059	15,123
GDP at basic prices	579,590	578,917	578,536
Taxes, less subsidies, on imports .	61,454	60,313	62,846
Value-added tax, less imputed bank service charge	1,885	1,414	1,469
GDP in purchasers' values .	642,929	640,644	642,851

* Provisional.

BALANCE OF PAYMENTS
(€ million)

	2011	2012	2013
Exports of goods	544,383	532,971	550,893
Imports of goods	−485,835	−477,469	−484,489
Balance on goods . . .	58,548	55,502	66,404
Exports of services . . .	107,943	105,341	116,833
Imports of services . . .	−94,443	−94,425	−98,236
Balance on goods and services	72,048	66,418	85,001
Primary income received . .	123,485	110,389	109,004
Primary income paid . . .	−104,072	−87,060	−88,284
Balance on goods, services and primary income	91,461	89,747	105,721
Secondary income received . .	14,228	13,526	13,494
Secondary income paid . . .	−30,290	−29,677	−32,126
Current balance	75,399	73,596	87,089
Capital account (net) . . .	−1,377	−12,624	−501
Direct investment assets . .	−40,160	5,162	−41,819
Direct investment liabilities .	21,456	4,736	32,110
Portfolio investment assets . .	−8,484	−66,613	−33,871
Portfolio investment liabilities .	36,115	−1,377	−21,457
Financial derivatives and employee stock options (net)	−9,291	8,813	18,708
Other investment assets . . .	−160,929	65,655	58,010
Other investment liabilities . .	94,069	−74,931	−87,587
Net errors and omissions . . .	−3,533	353	−10,809
Reserves and related items .	3,265	2,767	−128

Source: IMF, *International Financial Statistics*.

External Trade

PRINCIPAL COMMODITIES
(distribution by SITC, € million)

Imports c.i.f.	2011	2012	2013
Food and live animals . . .	32,062	33,623	35,348
Crude materials (inedible) except fuels	15,875	14,920	13,794
Mineral fuels, lubricants, etc. .	80,037	99,604	95,563
Petroleum, petroleum products, etc.	69,589	86,614	82,030
Crude petroleum	32,961	41,944	39,272
Chemicals and related products	46,936	50,323	52,175
Organic chemicals	14,331	14,922	16,158
Medicinal and pharmaceutical products	12,258	13,987	14,518
Basic manufactures . . .	38,287	35,852	35,221
Machinery and transport equipment	103,038	105,147	103,888
Office machines and automatic data-processing equipment . .	26,090	27,562	26,272
Telecommunications and sound equipment	19,239	20,130	20,406
Other electrical machinery, apparatus, etc.	15,857	16,033	16,180
Road vehicles (incl. air-cushion vehicles) and parts (excl. tyres, engines, and electrical parts) .	18,533	17,772	17,518
Miscellaneous manufactured articles	39,412	39,214	40,411
Total (incl. others)	364,922	389,449	386,355

Exports f.o.b.	2011	2012	2013
Food and live animals . . .	48,044	50,047	53,871
Vegetables and fruit	12,323	12,761	13,903
Crude materials (inedible) except fuels	20,841	21,383	19,818
Mineral fuels, lubricants, etc. .	67,812	82,827	85,711
Chemicals and related products	73,462	77,236	74,845
Organic chemicals	19,500	21,304	19,811
Medicinal and pharmaceutical products	18,451	19,390	18,535
Plastics in primary form . . .	12,828	13,160	13,253
Basic manufactures	36,662	35,500	35,207
Machinery and transport equipment	111,812	109,819	109,013
Office machines and automatic data-processing equipment . .	27,350	27,205	26,200
Automatic data-processing machines	11,817	12,089	11,740
Telecommunications and sound equipment	18,592	17,770	17,592
Other electrical machinery, apparatus, etc.	17,672	17,558	16,735
Road vehicles (incl. air-cushion vehicles) and parts (excl. tyres, engines, and electrical parts)	13,772	13,801	13,982
Miscellaneous manufactured articles	36,883	38,291	40,589
Total (incl. others)*	409,358	429,717	433,106

* Including victuals and stores supplied to foreign ships and aircraft.

PRINCIPAL TRADING PARTNERS
(€ million)

Imports c.i.f.	2011	2012	2013
Belgium	36,420	37,701	37,544
Brazil	5,612	5,643	5,810
China, People's Republic . . .	30,874	31,906	31,792
Czech Republic	5,154	5,506	4,743
Denmark	3,303	3,436	4,070
Finland	3,887	3,441	3,452
France	16,785	17,425	17,161
Germany	60,943	61,844	63,492
Ireland	4,604	5,020	5,085
Italy	7,786	7,828	8,067
Japan	10,100	9,931	8,427
Malaysia	5,577	5,744	5,963
Norway	10,343	12,462	13,809
Poland	5,094	5,453	5,522
Russia	16,959	20,332	20,618
Saudi Arabia	3,890	4,666	3,790
Spain	6,564	6,710	6,552
Sweden	6,238	6,758	6,728
United Kingdom	24,505	27,386	27,470
USA	23,541	26,406	26,618
Total (incl. others)	364,922	389,449	386,355

Exports f.o.b.	2011	2012	2013
Austria	5,160	4,927	4,948
Belgium	48,678	48,518	47,831
China, People's Republic	6,696	7,647	7,711
Czech Republic	5,947	5,992	6,015
Denmark	5,176	5,268	5,455
Finland	4,326	4,253	4,136
France	36,245	36,247	35,937
Germany	99,189	106,141	106,928
Italy	19,528	19,582	19,789
Poland	8,411	8,538	9,191
Russia	6,405	7,068	6,828
Spain	12,234	11,847	11,220
Sweden	7,194	7,137	7,564
Switzerland	5,132	5,725	5,615
Turkey	4,749	4,672	4,820
United Kingdom	32,326	34,644	36,535
USA	19,632	20,259	16,895
Total (incl. others)	409,358	429,717	433,106

Transport

RAILWAYS
(traffic)

	1996	1997	1998
Passenger-km (million)	14,131	14,485	14,879
Freight ton-km (million)	3,123	3,406	3,778

Passenger-km (million): 16,808 in 2011; 17,098 in 2012; 17,018 in 2013 (Source: Nederlandse Spoorwegen NV, *Annual Report 2013*).

ROAD TRAFFIC
('000 motor vehicles)

	2012	2013	2014
Passenger cars	7,859	7,916	7,932
Vans and lorries	921	899	880
Buses and coaches	11	10	10
Trailers and semi-trailers	1,085	1,042	1,024
Tractors	71	70	71
Special purpose vehicles	64	63	62
Motorcycles	647	653	654

SHIPPING

Flag Registered Fleet
(at 31 December)

	2012	2013	2014
Number of vessels	2,262	2,334	2,320
Displacement ('000 grt)	8,114.3	8,393.1	8,338.9

Source: Lloyd's List Intelligence (www.lloydslistintelligence.com).

Inland Waterways (traffic): Number of 4,577 (1999); International freight 219.7m. metric tons (1998).

CIVIL AVIATION*
(Netherlands scheduled air services)

	2010	2011
Kilometres flown (million)	451	484
Passengers carried ('000)	26,309	29,214
Passenger-km (million)	81,646	88,964
Total ton-km (million)	14,259	15,126

* Figures include data for airlines based in the territories and dependencies of the Netherlands.

Source: UN, *Statistical Yearbook*.

2012: Passengers carried ('000) 55,653; Freight carried ('000 metric tons) 1,536; Mail (metric tons) 28,375.

2013: Passengers carried ('000) 58,048; Freight carried ('000 metric tons) 1,585; Mail (metric tons) 34,872.

Tourism

FOREIGN TOURIST ARRIVALS
('000)*

Country of origin	2012	2013
Belgium	1,537	1,673
France	666	680
Germany	3,209	3,495
Italy	456	461
Spain	427	395
United Kingdom	1,662	1,680
Total (incl. others)	12,206	12,783

* Arrivals at all accommodation establishments.

Tourism receipts (€ million, excl. passenger transport): 14,661 in 2011; 14,966 in 2012 (provisional); 15,297 in 2013 (provisional).

Communications Media

	2011	2012	2013
Telephones ('000 main lines in use)	7,133	7,182	7,125
Mobile cellular telephones ('000 subscribers)	19,829	19,717	19,060
Broadband subscribers ('000)	6,498	6,654	6,717

Source: International Telecommunication Union.

Education

(2012/13 unless otherwise indicated, provisional)

	Institutions	Students ('000)
Primary	7,039	1,538.0
Secondary	658	961.0
Higher vocational	39*	422.0
University	13*	241.0

* 2011/12.

Directory

The Government

HEAD OF STATE

King of the Netherlands: HM King WILLEM-ALEXANDER (succeeded to the throne 30 April 2013).

COUNCIL OF MINISTERS
(May 2015)

A coalition of the Volkspartij voor Vrijheid en Democratie (VVD—People's Party for Freedom and Democracy) and the Partij van de Arbeid (PvdA—Labour Party).

Prime Minister, Minister of General Affairs: MARK RUTTE (VVD).

Deputy Prime Minister, Minister of Social Affairs and Employment: LODEWIJK ASSCHER (PvdA).

Minister of Foreign Affairs: BERT KOENDERS (PvdA).

Minister of the Interior and Kingdom Relations: RONALD PLASTERK (PvdA).

Minister of Education, Culture and Science: JET BUSSEMAKER (PvdA).

Minister of Finance: JEROEN DIJSSELBLOEM (PvdA).

Minister of Defence: JEANINE HENNIS-PLASSCHAERT (VVD).

Minister of Security and Justice: ARD VAN DER STEUR (VVD).

Minister of Infrastructure and the Environment: MELANIE SCHULTZ VAN HAEGEN (VVD).

Minister of Economic Affairs: HENK KAMP (VVD).

Minister of Health, Welfare and Sport: EDITH SCHIPPERS (VVD).

Minister for Foreign Trade and Development Co-operation: LILIANNE PLOUMEN (PvdA).

Minister for Housing and the Central Government Sector: STEF BLOK (VVD).

State Secretary for Education, Culture and Science: SANDER DEKKER (VVD).

State Secretary for Finance: ERIC WIEBES (VVD).

State Secretary for Infrastructure and the Environment: WILMA MANSVELD (PvdA).

State Secretary for Economic Affairs: SHARON DIJKSMA (PvdA).

State Secretary for Social Affairs and Employment: JETTA KLIJNSMA (PvdA).

State Secretary for Health, Welfare and Sport: MARTIN VAN RIJN (PvdA).

State Secretary for Security and Justice: KLAAS DIJKHOFF (VVD).

MINISTRIES

Office of the Prime Minister, Ministry of General Affairs: Binnenhof 19, POB 20001, 2500 EA The Hague; tel. (70) 3564100; fax (70) 3564683; internet www.rijksoverheid.nl/ministeries/az.

Ministry of Defence: Plein 4, POB 20701, 2500 ES The Hague; tel. (70) 3188188; fax (70) 3187888; e-mail defensievoorlichting@mindef.nl; internet www.rijksoverheid.nl/ministeries/def.

Ministry of Economic Affairs: Bezuidenhoutseweg 30, POB 20401, 2500 EC The Hague; tel. (70) 3796868; internet www.rijksoverheid.nl/ministeries/eleni.

Ministry of Education, Culture and Science: Rijnstraat 50, POB 16375, 2500 BJ The Hague; tel. (70) 4123456; fax (70) 4123450; internet www.rijksoverheid.nl/ministeries/ocw.

Ministry of Finance: Korte Voorhout 7, POB 20201, 2500 EE The Hague; tel. (70) 3428000; fax (70) 3427900; e-mail webmaster@minfin.nl; internet www.rijksoverheid.nl/ministeries/fin.

Ministry of Foreign Affairs: Bezuidenhoutseweg 67, POB 20061, 2500 EB The Hague; tel. (70) 3486486; fax (70) 3484848; internet www.rijksoverheid.nl/ministeries/bz.

Ministry of Health, Welfare and Sport: Rijnstraat 50, POB 20350, 2500 EJ The Hague; tel. (70) 3407911; fax (70) 3407834; internet www.rijksoverheid.nl/ministeries/vws.

Ministry of Infrastructure and the Environment: Plesmanweg 1–6, POB 20901, 2500 EX The Hague; tel. (70) 4560000; fax (70) 4561111; internet www.rijksoverheid.nl/ministeries/ienm.

Ministry of the Interior and Kingdom Relations: Schedeldoekshaven 200, POB 20011, 2500 EA The Hague; tel. (70) 4266426; fax (70) 3639153; internet www.rijksoverheid.nl/ministeries/bzk.

Ministry of Security and Justice: Turfmarkt 147, POB 20301, 2500 EH The Hague; tel. (70) 3707911; fax (70) 3707900; e-mail voorlichting@minjus.nl; internet www.rijksoverheid.nl/ministeries/venj.

Ministry of Social Affairs and Employment: Anna van Hannoverstraat 4, POB 90801, 2509 LV The Hague; tel. (70) 3334444; fax (70) 3334033; internet www.rijksoverheid.nl/ministeries/szw.

Legislature

STATES-GENERAL
(Staten-Generaal)

First Chamber
(Eerste Kamer)

Binnenhof 22, 2513 AA The Hague; POB 20017, 2513 AA The Hague; tel. (70) 3129200; fax (70) 3129390; e-mail postbus@eerstekamer.nl; internet www.eerstekamer.nl.

President: A. BROEKERS-KNOL (VVD).

Election, 23 May 2011

Party	Seats
Volkspartij voor Vrijheid en Democratie (VVD)	16
Partij van de Arbeid (PvdA)	14
Christen Democratisch Appèl (CDA)	11
Partij voor de Vrijheid (PVV)	10
Socialistische Partij (SP)	8
Democraten 66 (D66)	5
GroenLinks (GL)	5
ChristenUnie (CU)	2
50Plus	1
Staatkundig Gereformeerde Partij (SGP)	1
Partij voor de Dieren	1
Independent	1
Total	**75**

Second Chamber
(Tweede Kamer)

Binnenhof 4, 2513 AA The Hague; POB 20018, 2500 EA The Hague; tel. (70) 3182211; internet www.tweedekamer.nl.

President: ANOUCHKA VAN MILTENBURG (VVD).

General Election, 12 September 2012

Party	Votes	%	Seats
Volkspartij voor Vrijheid en Democratie (VVD)	2,504,948	26.58	41
Partij van de Arbeid (PvdA)	2,340,750	24.84	38
Partij voor de Vrijheid (PVV)	950,263	10.08	15
Socialistische Partij (SP)	909,853	9.65	15
Christen Democratisch Appèl (CDA)	801,620	8.51	13
Democraten 66 (D66)	757,091	8.03	12
ChristenUnie (CU)	294,586	3.13	5
GroenLinks (GL)	219,896	2.33	4
Staatkundig Gereformeerde Partij (SGP)	196,780	2.09	3
Partij voor de Dieren	182,162	1.93	2
50Plus	177,631	1.88	2
Others	88,655	0.93	—
Total	**9,424,235**	**100.00**	**150**

Election Commission

Kiesraad (Dutch Electoral Council): Herengracht 21, 2511 EG The Hague; POB 20011, 2500 EG The Hague; tel. (70) 4266266; fax (70) 3450879; e-mail kiesraad@kiesraad.nl; internet www.kiesraad.nl; f. 1917; independent; Chair. Prof. HENK KUMMELING; Sec.-Dir MELLE BAKKER.

Advisory Councils

Raad van State (Council of State): Kneuterdijk 22, POB 20019, 2500 EA The Hague; tel. (70) 4264426; fax (70) 3651380; e-mail voorlichting@raadvanstate.nl; internet www.raadvanstate.nl; comprises a Vice-Pres. and up to 60 mems nominated by the Sovereign, who formally presides over the Council; advises on legislation, constitutional issues, international treaties and all matters of national importance; Vice-Pres. J. PIET HEIN DONNER; Sec. H. H. C. VISSER.

Sociaal-Economische Raad (SER) (Social and Economic Council): Bezuidenhoutseweg 60, POB 90405, 2509 LK The Hague; tel. (70) 3499499; fax (70) 3832535; e-mail m.vander.burg@ser.nl; internet www.ser.nl; f. 1950; tripartite advisory body; advises Govt on social and economic policy; monitors commodity and industrial boards; 33 mems, of whom 11 belong to trade union federations, 11 belong to the employers' organizations, and 11 are independent experts in social and economic affairs appointed by the Crown; Chair. MARIËTTE HAMER; Sec.-Gen. Dr VÉRONIQUE TIMMERHUIS.

Political Organizations

Christen Democratisch Appèl (CDA) (Christian Democratic Appeal): Buitenom 18, POB 30453, 2500 GL The Hague; tel. (70) 3424888; fax (70) 3643417; e-mail cda@cda.nl; internet www.cda.nl; f. 1980 by merger of 3 'confessional' parties; Pres. RUTH PEETOOM; 69,000 mems.

ChristenUnie (CU) (Christian Union): Johan van Oldenbarneveltlaan 46, POB 439, 3800 AK Amersfoort; tel. (33) 4226969; fax (33) 4226968; e-mail info@christenunie.nl; internet www.christenunie.nl; f. 2000 by merger of 2 'evangelical' parties, the Gereformeerd Politiek Verbond and the Reformatorische Politieke Federatie; interdenominational, based on biblical precepts; mem. of European Christian Political Movement; Chair. PIET ADEMA; Parliamentary Leader ARIE SLOB; c. 23,500 mems.

Democraten 66 (D66) (Democrats 66): Hoge Nieuwstraat 30, 2514 EL The Hague; POB 660, 2501 CR The Hague; tel. (70) 3566066; fax (70) 3641917; e-mail info@d66.nl; internet www.d66.nl; f. 1966; Chair. FLEUR GRÄPER VAN KOOLWIJK; Parliamentary Leader ALEXANDER PECHTOLD; 23,500 mems.

Fryske Nasjonale Partij (FNP) (Frisian National Party): Obrechtstrjitte 32, 8916 EN Ljouwert; tel. (58) 2131422; e-mail fnphus@fnp.nl; internet www.fnp.nl; f. 1962; promotes federalism and greater regional autonomy; Leader ANNIGJE TOERING-SCHUURMANS; c. 1,300 mems.

De Groenen (The Greens): POB 1251, 3500 BG Utrecht; tel. (30) 2341545; e-mail info@degroenen.nl; internet www.degroenen.nl; f. 1983; founding mem. of the European Green Party; Pres. OTTO TER HAAR.

GroenLinks (GL) (Green Left): Oudegracht 312, POB 8008, 3503 RA Utrecht; tel. (30) 2399900; fax (30) 2300342; e-mail info@groenlinks.nl; internet www.groenlinks.nl; f. 1990 by merger of Communistische Partij van Nederland, Evangelische Volkspartij, Pacifistisch-Socialistische Partij and Politieke Partij Radikalen; Chair. RIK GRASHOFF; Parliamentary Leader BRAM VAN OJIK; c. 20,000 mems.

Nieuwe Communistische Partij Nederland (NCPN) (New Communist Party of the Netherlands): Haarlemmerweg 177, 1051 LB Amsterdam; tel. (20) 6825019; fax (20) 6828276; e-mail manifest@ziggo.nl; internet www.ncpn.nl; f. 1992; Chair. JOB PRUIJSER.

Nieuwe Midden Partij (NMP) (New Centre Party): POB 2087, 8203 AB Lelijstad; tel. and fax (320) 281412; e-mail info@nmp.nl; internet www.sdnl.nl/nmp.htm; f. 1970; campaigns on economic issues; Leader JOS BRON.

Partij van de Arbeid (PvdA) (Labour Party): Herengracht 54, 1015 BN Amsterdam; tel. (20) 5512155; fax (20) 5512250; e-mail voorzitter@pvda.nl; internet www.pvda.nl; f. 1946 by merger of progressive and liberal organizations; social democratic; Chair. HANS SPEKMAN; Party Leader DIEDERIK SAMSOM; c. 50,000 mems.

Partij voor de Dieren (Party for the Animals): POB 17622, 1001 JM Amsterdam; tel. (20) 5203870; e-mail administratie@partijvoordedieren.nl; internet www.partijvoordedieren.nl; f. 2002; promotes animal rights and animal welfare; Chair. LUUK FOLKERTS.

Partij voor de Vrijheid (PVV) (Freedom Party): POB 20018, 2500 EA The Hague; internet www.pvv.nl; f. 2004 as Groep Wilders; present name adopted 2006; populist, anti-immigration; Leader GEERT WILDERS.

Socialistische Alternatieve Politiek (SAP) (Socialist Political Alternative): Postbus 2096, 3000 CB Rotterdam; tel. (20) 6259272; e-mail redactie@grenzeloos.nl; internet www.grenzeloos.org/sap; f. 1974; Trotskyist.

Socialistische Partij (SP) (Socialist Party): Vijverhofstraat 65, 3032 SC Rotterdam; tel. (10) 2435555; fax (10) 2435566; e-mail onderzoek@sp.nl; internet www.sp.nl; f. 1972; Chair. JAN MARIJNISSEN; Parliamentary Leader EMILE ROEMER; Gen. Sec. HANS VAN HEIJNINGEN; 46,000 mems.

Staatkundig Gereformeerde Partij (SGP) (Political Reformed Party): Dinkel 7, 3068 HB Rotterdam; tel. (82) 7200770; fax (82) 7200784; e-mail voorlichting@sgp.nl; internet www.sgp.nl; f. 1918; Calvinist; female membership banned until 2006; Chair. M. F. VAN LEEUWEN; Parliamentary Leader KEES VAN DER STAAIJ; Gen. Sec. P. A. ZEVENBERGEN; 30,075 mems (2014).

Verenigde Senioren Partij (VSP) (United Senior Citizens' Party): Israëlslaan 37, 3431 AS Nieuwegein; tel. (30) 6300208; fax (30) 6300209; e-mail secretariaat@verenigdeseniorenpartij.nl; Chair. H. J. (HERMAN) TROOST.

Volkspartij voor Vrijheid en Democratie (VVD) (People's Party for Freedom and Democracy): Laan Copes van Cattenburch 52, POB 30836, 2500 GV The Hague; tel. (70) 3613061; fax (70) 3608276; e-mail info@vvd.nl; internet www.vvd.nl; f. 1948; advocates free enterprise, individual freedom and responsibility, but its programme also supports social security and recommends the participation of workers in profits and management; Chair. HENRY KEIZER; Parliamentary Leader HALBE ZIJLSTRA; 38,000 mems.

50Plus: Lange Poten 4, The Hague; e-mail info@50pluspartij.nl; internet 50pluspartij.nl; pursuing pensioners' interests; f. 2009; Chair. JOHN STRUIJLAARD.

Diplomatic Representation

EMBASSIES IN THE NETHERLANDS

Afghanistan: Laan van Meerdervoort 51, POB 10630, 2501 HP The Hague; tel. (70) 4278771; fax (70) 4272540; e-mail info@afghanistanembassy.nl; internet www.afghanistanembassy.nl; Ambassador OBAIDULLAH OBAID.

Albania: Anna Paulownastraat 109B, 2518 BD The Hague; tel. (70) 4272101; fax (70) 4272083; e-mail embalba@xs4all.nl; Ambassador ADIA SAKIQI.

Algeria: Van Stolklaan 1–3, 2585 JS The Hague; tel. (70) 3522954; fax (70) 3061961; e-mail ambalg4@ziggo.nl; internet www.embalgeria.nl; Ambassador NASSIMA BAGHLI.

Argentina: Javastraat 20, 2585 AN The Hague; tel. (70) 3118411; fax (70) 3118410; e-mail epbaj@mrecic.gov.ar; internet www.epbaj.mrecic.gov.ar; Ambassador HÉCTOR HORACIO SALVADOR.

Armenia: Laan van Meerdervoort 90, 2517 AP The Hague; tel. and fax (70) 3311002; fax (70) 3311002; e-mail armembnl@mfa.am; internet netherlands.mfa.am/en; Ambassador DZIUNIK AGHAJANIAN.

Australia: Carnegielaan 4, 2517 KH The Hague; tel. (70) 3108200; fax (70) 3107863; e-mail austemb_thehague@dfat.gov.au; internet www.netherlands.embassy.gov.au; Ambassador NEIL ALLAN MULES.

Austria: Van Alkemadelaan 342, 2597 AS The Hague; tel. (70) 3245470; fax (70) 3282066; e-mail den-huag-ob@bmeia.gv.at; internet www.bmeia.gv.at/denhaag; Ambassador Dr JOHANNES WERNER DRUML.

Azerbaijan: Andries Bickerweg 6, 2517 JP The Hague; tel. (70) 3921939; fax (70) 3469604; e-mail info@azembassy.nl; internet www.azembassy.nl; Ambassador MIR-HAMZA EFENDIYEV.

Bangladesh: Wassenaarseweg 39, 2596 CG The Hague; tel. (70) 3283722; fax (70) 3283524; e-mail mission.hague@mofa.gov.bd; internet www.bangladeshembassy.nl; Ambassador Sheikh MUHAMMED BELAL.

Belarus: Groot Hertoginnelaan 26, 2517 EG The Hague; tel. (70) 3631566; fax (70) 3640555; e-mail netherlands@mfa.gov.by; internet www.netherlands.mfa.gov.by; Ambassador MIKALAI M. BARYSEVICH.

Belgium: J. van Oldenbarneveltlaan 11, 2582 NE The Hague; tel. (70) 3123456; fax (70) 3645579; e-mail thehague@diplobel.fed.be; internet www.diplomatie.be/thehague; Ambassador CHRIS LEO CLARK HOORNAERT.

Bolivia: Nassauplein 2, 2585 EA The Hague; tel. (70) 3616707; fax (70) 3620039; e-mail embolned@embassyofbolivia.nl; Ambassador ENRIQUE EDUARDO RODRÍGUEZ VELTZÉ.

Bosnia and Herzegovina: Bezuidenhoutseweg 223, 2594 AL The Hague; tel. (70) 3588505; fax (70) 3584367; e-mail info@bhembassy.nl; internet www.bhembassy.nl; Ambassador AHMET HALILOVIC.

Brazil: Mauritskade 19, 2514 HD The Hague; tel. (70) 3023959; fax (70) 3023950; e-mail brasil@brazilianembassy.nl; internet haia.itamaraty.gov.br; Ambassador PIRAGIBE DOS SANTOS TARRAGÔ.

Bulgaria: Duinroosweg 9, 2597 KJ The Hague; tel. (70) 3503051; fax (70) 3584688; e-mail embassy.hague@mfa.bg; internet www.mfa.bg/embassies/netherlands; Ambassador NIKOLA KOLEV.

Cameroon: Amaliastraat 14, 2514 JC The Hague; tel. (70) 3469715; fax (70) 3652979; e-mail ambacam-la-haye@planet.nl; internet www.cameroon-embassy.nl; Ambassador ODETTE MELONO.

Canada: Sophialaan 7, POB 30820, 2500 JP The Hague; tel. (70) 3111600; fax (70) 3111620; e-mail info@canada.nl; internet www

.canadainternational.gc.ca/netherlands-pays_bas; Ambassador JAMES LAMBERT.

Chile: Mauritskade 51, 2514 HG The Hague; tel. (70) 3123640; fax (70) 3452109; e-mail echile.holanda@minrel.gov.cl; internet chileabroad.gov.cl/paises-bajos; Ambassador MARÍA TERESA DE JESÚS INFANTE CAFFI.

China, People's Republic: William Lodewijklaan 10, 2517 JT The Hague; tel. (70) 3065091; fax (70) 3551651; e-mail chinaemb_nl@mfa .gov.cn; internet nl.china-embassy.org; Ambassador CHEN XU.

Colombia: Groot Hertoginnelaan 14, 2517 EG The Hague; tel. (70) 3614545; fax (70) 3614636; e-mail elahaya@cancilleria.gov.co; internet paisesbajos.embajada.gov.co; Ambassador JUAN JOSÉ QUINTANA.

Congo, Democratic Republic: Koninginnegracht 60, 2514 AE The Hague; tel. (70) 3659515; fax (70) 3659305; Chargé d'affaires a.i. THOMAS PIERRE NZEZA KONKO.

Costa Rica: Laan Copes van Cattenburch 46, 2585 GB The Hague; tel. (70) 3540780; fax (70) 3584754; e-mail embajada@embacr.nl; internet www.embacr.nl; Ambassador SERGIO GERARDO UGALDE GODÍNEZ.

Côte d'Ivoire: Laan van Meerdervoort 16, 2517 AK The Hague; tel. (70) 3117878; fax (70) 3924017; e-mail embacoti.paysbas@yahoo .com; Ambassador SALLAH BEN ABD EL-KADER HAMZA.

Croatia: Amaliastraat 16, 2514 JC The Hague; tel. (70) 3623638; fax (70) 3927823; e-mail vrhhaag@mvep.hr; internet nl.mvep.hr; Ambassador VESELA MRĐEN KORAĆ.

Cuba: Scheveningseweg 9, 2517 KS The Hague; tel. (70) 3606061; fax (70) 3647586; e-mail embacuba@xs4all.nl; internet www .cubadiplomatica.cu/holanda; Ambassador FERMÍN GABRIEL QUI-ÑONES SÁNCHEZ.

Cyprus: Surinamestraat 15, 2585 GG The Hague; tel. (70) 2172020; fax (70) 3924024; e-mail hagueembassy@mfa.gov.cy; internet www .mfa.gov.cy/embassythehague; Ambassador Dr KYRIACÓS P. KOUROS.

Czech Republic: Paleisstraat 4, 2514 JA The Hague; tel. (70) 3130031; fax (70) 3563349; e-mail hague@embassy.mzv.cz; internet www.mfa.cz/hague; Ambassador JANA REINIŠOVÁ.

Denmark: Koninginnegracht 30, 2514 AB The Hague; tel. (70) 3025959; fax (70) 3025950; e-mail haaamb@um.dk; internet www .ambhaag.um.dk; Ambassador OLE E. MOESBY.

Dominican Republic: Raamweg 21–22, 2596 HL The Hague; tel. (70) 3317553; fax (70) 4049890; e-mail embajadadominicananl@ gmail.com; internet www.embajadadominicana.nl; Ambassador GUILLERMO EDUARDO L. PIÑA CONTRERAS.

Ecuador: Koninginnegracht 84, 2514 AJ The Hague; tel. (70) 3469563; fax (70) 3658910; e-mail info@embassyecuador.eu; internet www.embassyecuador.eu; Ambassador MIGUEL CALAHOR-RANO CAMINO.

Egypt: Badhuisweg 92, 2587 CL The Hague; tel. (70) 3542000; fax (70) 3543304; e-mail info@ambeg.nl; Ambassador TAHER AHMED FARAHAT.

El Salvador: Riouwstraat 137, 2585 HP The Hague; tel. (70) 3249855; fax (70) 3247842; e-mail embajadapaisesbajos@rree.gob .sv; internet embajadaholanda.rree.gob.sv; Ambassador (vacant).

Eritrea: Nassauplein 13, 2585 EB The Hague; tel. (70) 4276812; fax (70) 4277236; e-mail info@emberitrea.nl; Ambassador (vacant).

Estonia: Zeestraat 92, 2518 AD The Hague; tel. (70) 3029050; fax (70) 3029051; e-mail embassy.haag@mfa.ee; internet www.estemb .nl; Ambassador PEEP JAHILO.

Finland: Groot Hertoginnelaan 16, 2517 EG The Hague; tel. (70) 3469754; fax (70) 3107174; e-mail sanomat.haa@formin.fi; internet www.finlande.nl; Ambassador LIISA MARIA TALONPOIKA.

France: Anna Paulownastraat 76, 2518 BJ The Hague; tel. (70) 3125800; fax (70) 3125824; e-mail info@ambafrance-nl.org; internet www.ambafrance-nl.org; Ambassador LAURENT ROGER PIC.

Georgia: Groot Hertoginnelaan 28, 2517 EG The Hague; tel. (70) 3029080; fax (70) 3029081; e-mail thehague.emb@mfa.gov.ge; internet www.netherlands.mfa.gov.ge; Ambassador KONSTANTINE SURGULADZE.

Germany: Groot Hertoginnelaan 18–20, 2517 EG The Hague; tel. (70) 3420600; fax (70) 3651957; e-mail info@den-haag.diplo.de; internet www.niederlande.diplo.de; Ambassador FRANZ JOSEF KREMP.

Ghana: Laan Copes van Cattenburch 70, 2585 GD The Hague; tel. (70) 3384384; fax (70) 3062800; e-mail info@ghanaembassy.nl; internet www.ghanaembassy.nl; Ambassador Dr J. TONY AIDOO.

Greece: Amaliastraat 1, 2514 JC The Hague; tel. (70) 3638700; fax (70) 3563040; e-mail gremb.hag@mfa.gr; internet www .greekembassy.nl; Ambassador TERESA PARASKEVI ANGELATOU.

Guatemala: Javastraat 44, 2585 AP The Hague; tel. (70) 3020253; fax (70) 3602270; e-mail embpaisesbajos@minex.gob.gt; Ambassador GABRIEL EDGARDO AGUILERA PERALTA.

Holy See: Carnegielaan 5, 2517 KH The Hague; tel. (70) 3503363; fax (70) 3521461; e-mail apost.nuntiatuur@inter.nl.net; Apostolic Nuncio Most Rev. ALDO CAVALLI (Titular Archbishop of Vibo).

Hungary: Hogeweg 14, 2585 JD The Hague; tel. (70) 3500404; fax (70) 3521749; e-mail mission.hga@mfa.gov.hu; internet www .hungarianembassy.nl; Ambassador ORSOLYA VERONIKA SZIJJÁRTÓ.

India: Buitenrustweg 2, 2517 KD The Hague; tel. (70) 3469771; fax (70) 3617072; e-mail ambassador@indianembassy.nl; Ambassador RAJESH NANDAN PRASAD.

Indonesia: Tobias Asserlaan 8, 2517 KC The Hague; tel. (70) 3108100; fax (70) 3643331; e-mail bidpen@indonesia.nl; internet www.indonesia.nl; Ambassador (vacant).

Iran: Duinweg 20, 2585 JX The Hague; tel. (70) 3384001; fax (70) 3503224; e-mail info@iranembassy.nl; internet www .iranianembassy.nl; Ambassador ALIREZA JAHANGIRI.

Iraq: Johan de Wittlaan 16, 2517 JR The Hague; tel. (70) 3101260; fax (70) 3101261; e-mail info@embassyofiraq.nl; internet www .embassyofiraq.nl; Ambassador Dr SAAD ABD AL-MAJEED IBRAHIM IBRAHIM.

Ireland: Scheveningseweg 112, 2584 AE The Hague; tel. (70) 3630993; fax (70) 3617604; e-mail thehagueembassy@dfa.ie; internet www.embassyofireland.nl; Ambassador JOHN NEARY.

Israel: Buitenhof 47, 2513 AH The Hague; tel. (70) 3760500; fax (70) 3760555; e-mail info@hague.mfa.gov.il; internet thehague.mfa.gov .il; Ambassador HAIM DIVON.

Italy: Alexanderstraat 12, 2514 JL The Hague; tel. (70) 3021030; fax (70) 3614932; e-mail embitaly.denhaag@esteri.it; internet www .amblaja.esteri.it; Ambassador FRANCESCO AZZARELLO.

Japan: Tobias Asserlaan 2, 2517 KC The Hague; tel. (70) 3469544; fax (70) 3106341; e-mail info@hg.mofa.go.jp; internet www.nl .emb-japan.go.jp; Ambassador MASARU TSUJI.

Jordan: Badhuisweg 79, 2587 CD The Hague; tel. (70) 4167200; fax (70) 4167209; e-mail info@jordanembassy.nl; internet www .jordanembassy.nl; Ambassador AHMAD AL-MUFLEH.

Kazakhstan: Nieuwe Parklaan 69, 2597 LB The Hague; tel. (70) 3634757; fax (70) 3657600; e-mail hague@mfa.kz; internet www .kazembassy.nl; Ambassador MAINURA S. MURZAMADIYEVA.

Kenya: Nieuwe Parklaan 21, 2597 LA The Hague; tel. (70) 3504215; fax (70) 3553594; e-mail info@kenyanembassy-nl.com; Ambassador ROSE MAKENA MUCHIRI.

Korea, Republic: Verlengde Tolweg 8, 2517 JV The Hague; tel. (70) 3586076; fax (70) 3504712; e-mail koreanemb@koreanembassy.nl; internet nld.mofat.go.kr; Ambassador JONG-HYUN CHOE.

Kosovo: Anna Paulownastraat 56A, 2518 BG The Hague; tel. (70) 3020025; fax (70) 3644493; e-mail embassy.netherlands@ks-gov.net; internet www.ambasada-ks.net/nl; Ambassador Dr VJOSA DOBRUNA.

Kuwait: Carnegielaan 9, 2517 KH The Hague; tel. (70) 3123400; fax (70) 3658398; e-mail info@kuwaitembassy.nl; Ambassador HAFEEZ MUHAMMAD SALIM AL-AJMI.

Latvia: Koninginnegracht 27, 2514 AB, The Hague; tel. (70) 3065000; fax (70) 3065009; e-mail embassy.netherlands@mfa.gov .lv; internet www.mfa.gov.lv/netherlands; Ambassador MARIS KLISANS.

Lebanon: Frederikstraat 2, 2514 LK The Hague; tel. (70) 3658906; fax (70) 3620779; e-mail info@lebanonembassy.nl; internet www .lebanonembassy.nl; Chargé d'affaires a.i. ABIR ALI.

Libya: Parkweg 15, 2585 JH The Hague; tel. (70) 355886; fax (70) 3559075; e-mail embassylibia@ziggo.nl; Ambassador BREIK A. B. SWESSI.

Lithuania: Laan van Meerdervoort 20, 2517 AK The Hague; tel. (70) 3855418; fax (70) 3853940; e-mail amb.nl@urm.lt; internet nl.mfa.lt; Ambassador DARIUS JONAS SEMAŠKA.

Luxembourg: Nassaulaan 8, 2514 JS The Hague; tel. (70) 3607516; fax (70) 3462000; e-mail lahaye.amb@mae.etat.lu; internet lahaye .mae.lu; Ambassador PIERRE-LOUIS LORENZ.

Macedonia, former Yugoslav republic: Laan van Meerdervoort 50C, 2517 AM The Hague; tel. (70) 4274464; fax (70) 4274469; e-mail hague@mfa.gov.mk; internet www.missions.gov.mk/hague; Ambassador IGOR POPOV.

Malaysia: Rustenburgweg 2, 2517 KE The Hague; tel. (70) 3506506; fax (70) 3506536; e-mail malaysia@euronet.nl; internet www.kln.gov .my/perwakilan/thehague; Ambassador (vacant).

Malta: Carnegielaan 4–14, 2517 KH The Hague; tel. (70) 3561252; fax (70) 3464796; e-mail maltaembassy.thehague@gov.mt; Ambassador JOSEPH COLE.

Mexico: Nassauplein 28, 2585 EC The Hague; tel. (70) 3602900; fax (70) 3560543; e-mail embamex@embamex-nl.com; internet www .embamex-nl.com; Ambassador EDUARDO IBARROLA-NICOLÍN.

Morocco: Oranjestraat 9, 2514 JB The Hague; tel. (70) 3469617; fax (70) 3562829; e-mail ambamar.lahaye@wanadoo.nl; Ambassador ABD EL-OUAHAB BELLOUKI.

New Zealand: Eisenhowerlaan 77N, 2517 KK The Hague; tel. (70) 3469324; fax (70) 3632983; e-mail hague.info@mfat.govt.nz; internet www.nzembassy.com/netherlands; Ambassador JANET LOWE.

Nicaragua: Eisenhowerlaan 112, 2517 KM The Hague; tel. (70) 3225063; fax (70) 3508331; e-mail info@embanic.nl; Ambassador CARLOS ARGÜELLO GÓMEZ.

Nigeria: Wagenaarweg 5, 2597 LL The Hague; tel. (70) 3501703; fax (70) 3551110; e-mail nigerianthehague@gmail.com; internet www .nigerianembassy.nl; Ambassador Dr NIMOTA NIHINLOLA AKANBI.

Norway: Lange Vijverberg 11, 2513 AC The Hague; tel. (70) 3117611; fax (70) 3659630; e-mail emb.hague@mfa.no; internet www.noorwegen.nl; Ambassador ANNIKEN RAMBERG KRUTNES.

Oman: Nieuwe Parklaan 9, 2597 LA The Hague; tel. (70) 3615800; fax (70) 3605364; e-mail info@embassyofoman.nl; Ambassador SAYYID MUHAMMAD BIN HARIB BIN ABDULLAH AL-SAID.

Pakistan: Amaliastraat 8, 2514 JC The Hague; tel. (70) 3648948; fax (70) 3106047; e-mail parepthehague@mofa.gov.pk; internet www .embassyofpakistan.com; Ambassador MOAZZAM AHMAD KHAN.

Peru: Nassauplein 4, 2585 EA The Hague; tel. (70) 3653500; fax (70) 3651929; e-mail info@embassyofperu.nl; internet www .embassyofperu.nl; Ambassador CARLOS HERRERA RODRÍGUEZ.

Philippines: Laan Copes van Cattenburch 125, 2585 EZ The Hague; tel. (70) 3604820; fax (70) 3560030; e-mail thehague@philembassy .nl; internet www.thehaguepe.dfa.gov.ph; Ambassador JAIME VICTOR BADILLO LEDDA.

Poland: Alexanderstraat 25, 2514 JM The Hague; tel. (70) 7990100; fax (70) 7990137; e-mail haga.amb.sekretariat@msz.gov.pl; internet haga.msz.gov.pl; Ambassador JAN BORKOWSKI.

Portugal: Zeestraat 74, 2518 AD The Hague; tel. (70) 3630217; fax (70) 3615589; e-mail info@portembassy.nl; Ambassador JOSÉ DE BOUZA SERRANO.

Qatar: Borweg 7, 2597 LR The Hague; tel. (70) 4166666; fax (70) 4166660; e-mail hague@mofa.gov.qa; internet www.embassyofqatar .nl; Ambassador KHALID FAHAD AL-KHATER.

Romania: Catsheuvel 55, 2517 KA The Hague; tel. (70) 3223613; fax (70) 3541587; e-mail haga@mae.ro; internet haga.mae.ro; Ambassador IRENY COMAROSCHI.

Russian Federation: Andries Bickerweg 2, 2517 JP The Hague; tel. (70) 3468888; fax (70) 3617960; e-mail ambrusnl@euronet.nl; internet www.netherlands.mid.ru; Ambassador ROMAN KOLODKIN.

Rwanda: Johan van Oldenbarneveltlaan 9B, 2582 NE The Hague; tel. 3926571; fax 4275326; e-mail ambalahaye@gmail.com; internet www.ambalahaye.nl; Ambassador JEAN PIERRE KARABARANGA.

Saudi Arabia: Alexanderstraat 19, 2514 JM The Hague; tel. (70) 3600877; fax (70) 3561452; e-mail amboffice.nl@mofa.gov.sa; internet www.saudiembassy.nl; Ambassador ABD AL-AZIZ ABDULLAH ABD AL-AZIZ ABOHAIMED.

Serbia: Burgemeester van Karnebeeklaan 19, 2585 BA The Hague; tel. (70) 3636800; fax (70) 3602421; e-mail embassy.hague@mfa.rs; internet www.thehague.mfa.gov.rs; Ambassador PETAR VICO.

Slovakia: Parkweg 1, 2585 JG The Hague; tel. (70) 4167777; fax (70) 4167783; e-mail emb.hague@mzv.sk; internet www.mzv.sk/haag; Ambassador JAROSLAV CHLEBO.

Slovenia: Anna Paulownastraat 11, 2518 BA The Hague; tel. (70) 3108690; fax (70) 3626608; e-mail vhg@gov.si; internet www.haag .veleposlanistvo.si; Ambassador ROMAN KIRN.

South Africa: Wassenaarseweg 40, 2596 CJ The Hague; tel. (70) 3924501; fax (70) 3460669; e-mail info@zuidafrika.nl; internet www .zuidafrika.nl; Ambassador VUSI BRUCE KOLOANE.

Spain: Lange Voorhout 50, 2514 EG The Hague; tel. (70) 3024999; fax (70) 3617959; e-mail ambassade.spanje@worldonline.nl; Ambassador FERNANDO ARIAS GONZÁLEZ.

Sri Lanka: Jacob de Graefflaan 2, 2517 JM The Hague; tel. (70) 3655910; fax (70) 3465596; e-mail mission@srilankaembassy.nl; Chargé d'affaires a.i. WATHSALA INDUNIL AMARASINGHE.

Sudan: Koninginnegracht 63–64, 2514 AG The Hague; tel. (70) 3605300; fax (70) 3617975; e-mail info@sudanembassy.nl; Ambassador MOHAMED AL-HASSAN IBRAHIM ALAWAD.

Suriname: Alexander Gogelweg 2, 2517 JH The Hague; tel. (70) 3650844; fax (70) 3617445; e-mail ambassade.suriname@wxs.nl; Chargé d'affaires a.i. CHANTAL RACHIEDA DOEKHIE.

Sweden: Jan Willem Frisolaan 3, 2517 JS The Hague; tel. (70) 4120200; fax (70) 4120211; e-mail ambassaden.haag@gov.se; internet www.swedenabroad.com/thehague; Ambassador HÅKAN EMSGÅRD.

Switzerland: Lange Voorhout 42, POB 30913, 2500 GX The Hague; tel. (70) 3642831; fax (70) 3561238; e-mail hay.vertretung@eda .admin.ch; internet www.eda.admin.ch/denhaag; Ambassador URS BREITER.

Thailand: Laan Copes van Cattenburch 123, 2585 EZ The Hague; tel. (70) 3450766; fax (70) 3451929; e-mail thaiembassy.thehague@ gmail.com; Ambassador ITTIPORN BOONPRACONG.

Tunisia: Gentsestraat 98, 2587 HX The Hague; tel. (70) 3512251; fax (70) 3514323; e-mail at.lahaye@diplomatie.gov.tn; Ambassador MOHAMED KARIM BEN BÉCHER.

Turkey: Jan Evertstraat 15, 2514 BS The Hague; tel. (70) 3023100; fax (70) 3617969; e-mail embassy.thehague@mfa.gov.tr; internet www.lahey.be.mfa.gov.tr; Ambassador SADIK ARSLAN.

Ukraine: Zeestraat 78, 2518 AD The Hague; tel. (70) 3626095; fax (70) 3615565; e-mail embukr@wxs.nl; internet netherlands.mfa.gov .ua; Ambassador OLEKSANDR HORIN.

United Arab Emirates: Eisenhowerlaan 130, 2517 KN The Hague; tel. (70) 3384370; fax (70) 3384373; e-mail info.lahaye@mofa.gov.ae; internet www.uae-embassy.nl; Ambassador ABDULLAH HAMDAN AL-NAQBI.

United Kingdom: Lange Voorhout 10, 2514 ED The Hague; tel. (70) 4270427; e-mail ukinnl@fco.gov.uk; internet www.gov.uk/ government/world/netherlands; Ambassador Sir GEOFFREY ADAMS.

USA: Lange Voorhout 102, 2514 EJ The Hague; tel. (70) 3102209; fax (70) 3102207; e-mail ircthehague@state.gov; internet thehague .usembassy.gov; Ambassador TIMOTHY BROAS.

Uruguay: Mauritskade 33, 2514 HD The Hague; tel. (70) 3609815; fax (70) 3562826; e-mail uruholan@wxs.nl; Ambassador Dr ALVARO MARCELO MOERZINGER PAGANI.

Venezuela: Churchillplein 5, 2517 JW The Hague; tel. (70) 3633805; fax (70) 3656954; e-mail embve.nlhya@gmail.com; internet paisesbajos.embajada.gob.ve; Ambassador HAIFA AISSAMI MADAH.

Viet Nam: Nassauplein 12, 2585 EB The Hague; tel. (70) 3648917; fax (70) 3648656; e-mail vnembassy.nl@mofa.gov.vn; internet www .vietnamembassy.nl; Ambassador NGUYÊN VĂN DOÀN.

Yemen: Scheveningseweg 68, 2517 KX The Hague; tel. (70) 3653936; fax (70) 3563312; e-mail yemenembassy@planet.nl; internet www .yemen-embassy.nl; Ambassador ABDULLA A. AL-SHARIFF AL-SHAMMAM.

Judicial System

Justices and judges must have graduated in law at a Dutch university, and are nominated for life by the Crown. The justices of the Supreme Court are nominated from a list of three compiled by the Second Chamber of the States-General.

SUPREME COURT

De Hoge Raad der Nederlanden: Kazernestraat 52, 2514 CV The Hague; POB 20303, 2500 EH The Hague; tel. (70) 3611311; fax (70) 7530351; e-mail info@hogeraad.nl; internet www.rechtspraak.nl/ organisatie/hoge-raad; for appeals in cassation against decisions of courts of lower jurisdiction; the Supreme Court, as a court of first instance, tries offences committed in their official capacity by members of the States-General and ministers; when dealing with appeals in cassation, the court is composed of five or, in more straightforward cases, of three justices (Raadsheren); Pres. G. J. M. CORSTENS; Procurator-Gen. J. W. FOKKENS; Sec. of the Court J. STORM.

COURTS OF APPEAL

Gerechtshoven: Four courts: Amsterdam, Arnhem-Leeuwarden, 's-Hertogenbosch, and The Hague. A court is composed of three Raadsheren (judges); appeal is from decisions of the District Courts of Justice. Belastingkamers (Fiscal Divisions) of the Courts of Appeal deal with appeals against decisions relating to the enforcement of the fiscal laws (administrative jurisdiction). The court of Arnhem-Leeuwarden has a Pachtkamer (Tenancy Division), composed of three judges and two assessors (a tenant and a landlord), and a Penitentiaire Kamer (Penitentiary Division), composed of three judges and two experts. The Tenancy Division hears appeals from decisions of all Canton Tenancy Divisions. The Penitentiary Division hears appeals against refusals of release on licence, which is usually granted after two-thirds of a prison sentence longer than one year, unless there are special objections from the Minister of Security and Justice. An Ondernemingskamer (Companies Division) is attached to the court at Amsterdam, consisting of three judges and two experts as assessors.

DISTRICT COURTS OF JUSTICE

Arrondissementsrechtbanken: There are 11 district courts for civil and minor penal cases. Each court comprises administrative, civil, criminal and Cantonal courts (which deal with minor civil and criminal offences), and may also include family and juvenile courts, and other special courts. A court is composed of three Rechter (judges); there is no jury; summary jurisdiction in civil cases by the President of the Court; simple penal cases, including economic offences, generally by a single judge (Politierechter). Offences committed by juveniles are (with certain exceptions) tried by a specialized judge (Kinderrechter).

ADMINISTRATIVE COURTS

The administrative courts regulate relations between the authorities and citizens according to the provisions of the General Administrative Law Act. The majority of cases are heard by the Administrative Law Sections of the District Courts, while appeals are heard by the Afdeling Bestuursrechtspraak van de Raad van State (Administrative Law Division of the Council of State), which also acts as the court of sole and last instance in the majority of cases concerning education, the environment and spatial planning. In addition, cases relating to certain areas of administrative law are heard by the following bodies:

Centrale Raad van Beroep (Central Appeals Council): Vrouwe Justitiaplein 1, 3511 EX; POB 16002, 3500 DA Utrecht; tel. (30) 8502100; fax (30) 8502198; e-mail crvb@rechtspraak.nl; internet www.rechtspraak.nl/organisatie/crvb; hears appeals against decisions of the District Courts in matters concerning the public service and social security; Pres. T. G. M. SIMONS.

College van Beroep voor het Bedrijfsleven (Trade and Industry Appeals Tribunal): Prins Clauslaan 60, 2595 AJ The Hague; POB 20021, 2500 EA The Hague; tel. (70) 3813910; fax (70) 3813999; e-mail cbb@rechtspraak.nl; internet www.rechtspraak.nl/organisatie/cbb; hears in first and last instance appeals against decisions enforcing socio-economic and agricultural legislation made by certain bodies, such as regulatory bodies and Chambers of Commerce, and by certain ministers; Pres. R. F. B. VAN ZUTPHEN.

Administration Law Section, Aliens Division, District Court of The Hague: court of sole and last instance in cases involving immigration; brs in Zwolle, 's-Hertogenbosch, Amsterdam and Haarlem. The introduction of a limited right of further appeal is pending.

Tariefcommissie (Tariff Commission): court of sole and last instance for all customs and excise disputes.

Religion

CHRISTIANITY

Raad van Kerken in Nederland (Council of Churches in the Netherlands): Koningin Wilhelminalaan 5, 3818 HN Amersfoort; tel. (33) 4633844; e-mail rvk@raadvankerken.nl; internet www.raadvankerken.nl; f. 1968; 18 mem. churches; Pres. Drs H. J. VAN HOUT; Gen. Sec. Drs K. VAN DER KAMP.

The Roman Catholic Church

The Netherlands comprises one archdiocese and six dioceses. At 31 December 2006 there were an estimated 4,647,300 adherents in the country (28.6% of the population).

Bishops' Conference: Nederlandse Bisschoppenconferentie, Adriaen van Ostadelaan 140, POB 13049, 3507 LA Utrecht; tel. (30) 2326925; fax (30) 2334601; e-mail secrsg@rkk.nl; internet rkkerk.nl; f. 1986; Pres. Cardinal WILLEM JACOBUS EIJK (Archbishop of Utrecht).

Archbishop of Utrecht: Most Rev. WILLEM JACOBUS EIJK, Aartsbisdom, Maliebaan 38–40, 3581 CR Utrecht; tel. (30) 2338030; e-mail secretariaat@aartsbisdom.nl; internet www.aartsbisdom.nl.

Protestant Churches

Christelijke Gereformeerde Kerken in Nederland (Christian Reformed Churches in the Netherlands): POB 334, 3900 AH Veenendaal; Ghandistr. 2, 3902 KD Veenendaal; tel. (318) 582350; e-mail lkb@cgk.nl; internet www.cgk.nl; f. 1834; Relations Dir Rev. J. G. H. VAN DER VINNE; c. 73,400 mems; 180 churches.

Deutsche Evangelische Gemeinde (German Evangelical Church): Bleijenburg 3B, 2511 VC The Hague; tel. (70) 3465727; e-mail deg.haag@tiscali.nl; internet www.evangelische kirche-denhaag.nl; f. 1857; Leaders Pastor JAN MATHIS, Pastor SUSANNE MATHIS-MEURET.

Dutch Mennonites: Algemene Doopsgezinde Sociëteit, Singel 454, 1017 AW Amsterdam; tel. (20) 6230914; fax (20) 6278919; e-mail ads@doopsgezind.nl; internet www.doopsgezind.nl; f. 1811; Pres. OTTO BLEKER; Sec.-Gen. H. W. STENVERS; 9,000 mems; 118 parishes.

Evangelische Broedergemeente (Hernhutters): Zusterpl. 20, 3703 CB Zeist; tel. (30) 6924833; internet www.ebg.nl; f. 1746; Pres. RITA HARRY; 10,000 mems in the Netherlands; 7 parishes.

Hersteld Apostolische Zendingkerk (Restored Apostolic Missionary Church): Hogerbeetsstraat 32, 2242 TR Wassenaar; tel. and fax (318) 438149; e-mail s.de.jong.hazk@hazknederland.org; internet www.hazknederland.org; f. 1863; Pres. Apostle for the Netherlands H. F. RIJNDERS; Sec. J. L. M. STRAETEMANS; 500 mems; 10 parishes.

Protestante Kerk in Nederland (Protestant Church in the Netherlands): POB 8504, 3503 RM Utrecht; tel. (30) 8801880; fax (30) 8801447; e-mail servicedesk@pkn.nl; internet www.pkn.nl; f. 2004; unification of the Nederlandse Hervormde Kerk with the Gereformeerde Kerken in Nederland and the Evangelisch-Lutherse Kerk; 2m. mems, 3,000 parishes in 77 districts; Pres. G. J. KRAMER; Sec.-Gen. Rev. Dr B. PLAISIER.

Remonstrantse Broederschap (Remonstrant Church): Nieuwe Gracht 27A, 3512 LC Utrecht; tel. (30) 2316970; fax (30) 2311055; e-mail info@remonstranten.org; internet www.remonstranten.org; f. 1619; Pres. CEES DE MONCHY; Gen. Sec. TOM MIKKERS; 5,800 mems; 44 parishes.

Unie van Baptistengemeenten in Nederland (Union of Baptist Churches in The Netherlands): Postjesweg 175, 1062 JN Amsterdam; tel. (20) 2103023; e-mail info@baptisten.nl; internet www.baptisten.nl; f. 1881; Pres. JOEKE VAN DER MEI; 12,000 mems.

There are also First Church of Christ, Scientist places of worship in Amsterdam, Haarlem, The Hague and Utrecht.

Other Christian Churches

Anglikaans Kerkgenootschap (Anglican Church): Ary van der Spuyweg 1, 2585 JA The Hague; tel. (70) 3555359; e-mail churchoffice@stjohn-stphilip.org; internet www.stjohn-stphilip.org; f. 1698; Chaplain Rev. ANDREW GREADY.

Katholiek Apostolische Gemeenten (Catholic Apostolic Church): 1E De Riemerstraat 3, 2513 CT The Hague; tel. (70) 3555018; f. 1867; 7 parishes in the Netherlands and 3 in Belgium.

Oud-Katholieke Kerk van Nederland (Old Catholic Church): Koningin Wilhelminalaan 3, 3818 HN Amersfoort; tel. (33) 4620875; e-mail buro@okkn.nl; internet www.okkn.nl; f. 1723 in the Netherlands with Jansenist influence; refuses to accept papal infallibility and other 'new' dogmas of the Roman Catholic Church; in full communion with the Anglican Churches since 1931; Leader and Archbishop of Utrecht Mgr Dr JORIS A. O. L. VERCAMMEN (18 parishes); Bishop of Haarlem Mgr Dr DICK JAN SCHOON (10 parishes); 10,000 mems.

ISLAM

In 2006 there were estimated to be 850,000 Muslims in the Netherlands, representing some 5% of the total population. (Some 4% of the population were Muslims in 2011.)

Contactorgaan Moslims en Overheid (CMO) (Contact Group for Muslims and the Government): Beeklaan 207, 2562 AE The Hague; tel. (70) 3921123; e-mail info@contactorgaanmoslimsenoverheid.nl; internet www.cmoweb.nl; f. 2004; promotes dialogue between Muslim community and the Government; includes 19 Muslim groups; Pres. R. BAL.

JUDAISM

Nederlands Israëlitisch Kerkgenootschap (Organization of Jewish Communities in the Netherlands): Postbus 7967, 1008 AD Amsterdam; tel. (20) 3018484; fax (20) 3018485; e-mail info@nik.nl; internet www.nik.nl; f. 1814; 36 communities with around 5,000 mems; Rabbi RAPHAEL EVERS.

Portugees-Israëlietische Gemeente (Portuguese Synagogue): Mr. Visserplein 3, 1011 RD Amsterdam; tel. (20) 6245351; e-mail info@esnoga.com; internet portugesegemeente.nl; f. 1675; Gen. Sec. MICHELLE GORIN.

BAHÁ'Í FAITH

National Spiritual Assembly (Bahá'í Community of the Netherlands): Riouwstraat 27, 2585 GR The Hague; tel. (70) 3554017; e-mail secretariaat@bahai.nl; internet www.bahai.nl; f. 1962; mems resident in 180 locations.

The Press

PRINCIPAL DAILIES

(All circulation figures as at March 2011, unless otherwise stated)

Alkmaar

Noordhollands Dagblad: Edisonweg 10, POB 2, 1800 AA Alkmaar; tel. (72) 5196196; fax (72) 5124152; e-mail redactiesecretariaat@hollandmediacombinatie.nl; internet www.noordhollandsdagblad

.nl; f. 1799; owned by Telegraaf Media Groep NV; morning; 9 regional edns; Editor PETER HOVESTAD; circ. 135,257.

Amersfoort

AD Amersfoortse Courant: Grote Koppel 8, POB 43, 3800 AA Amersfoort; tel. (33) 4647911; fax (33) 4647334; e-mail ac.redactie@ad.nl; internet www.ad.nl; f. 1887; publ. by AD NieuwsMedia; evening; Editor-in-Chief CHRISTIAAN RUESINK.

Amsterdam

Het Financieele Dagblad (Dutch Financial Daily): FD Mediagroep, Prins Bernhardplein 173, POB 216, 1000 AE Amsterdam; tel. (20) 5928888; fax (20) 5928800; e-mail info@fd.nl; internet www.fd.nl; f. 1796; morning; Mon.–Sat.; Editor JAN BONJER; circ. 62,685.

Metro: Metro Holland BV, Nachtwachtlaan 20, POB 90009, 1006 BA Amsterdam; tel. (20) 5114000; fax (20) 5114090; e-mail info@metronieuws.nl; internet www.metronieuws.nl; f. 2004 in Rotterdam; separate Amsterdam edn since 2005; morning; owned by Metro International SA; Editor ROBERT VAN BRANDWIJK; circ. 480,916.

Het Parool: Jacob Bontiusplaats 9, POB 433, 1000 AK Amsterdam; tel. (20) 5584444; fax (88) 5725095; e-mail redactie@parool.nl; internet www.parool.nl; f. 1940; evening; Editor BARBARA VAN BEUKERING; circ. 85,388.

Sp!ts: POB 2620, 1000 CP Amsterdam; tel. (20) 5853045; fax (20) 5853065; e-mail redactie@spitsnieuws.nl; internet www.spitsnieuws.nl; f. 1998; owned by Telegraaf Media Groep NV; morning; distributed free of charge; Editor JAN-JAAP DE KLOET; circ. 391,178.

De Telegraaf: POB 376, 1000 EB Amsterdam; tel. (88) 8247000; fax (88) 8246968; e-mail redactie@telegraaf.nl; internet www.telegraaf.nl; f. 1893; morning; Editor-in-Chief SJUUL PARADIJS; circ. 550,930.

Trouw (Loyalty): Jacob Bontiusplaats 9, POB 859, 1000 AW Amsterdam; tel. (20) 5629444; fax (88) 5725082; e-mail secretariaat@trouw.nl; internet www.trouw.nl; f. 1943; morning; Editor CEES VAN DER LAAN; circ. 105,440.

De Volkskrant (The People's Journal): Jacob Bontiusplaats 9, 1018 LL Amsterdam; tel. (88) 561555; fax (88) 561561; e-mail redactie@volkskrant.nl; internet www.volkskrant.nl; f. 1919; morning; Editor PHILIPPE REMARQUE; circ. 264,890.

Apeldoorn

Reformatorisch Dagblad: Laan van Westenenk 12, POB 670, 7300 AR Apeldoorn; tel. (55) 5390222; fax (55) 5412288; e-mail redactie@refdag.nl; internet www.refdag.nl; f. 1971; evening; publ. by Erdee Media Groep; Editor-in-Chief WIM B. KRANENDONK; circ. 52,268.

De Stentor: Laan van Westenenk 6, POB 99, 7336 AZ Apeldoorn; tel. (55) 5388388; fax (55) 5388200; e-mail redactiesecretariaat@destentor.nl; internet www.destentor.nl/regio/apeldoorn; f. 2003; evening; publishes 9 regional versions; Editor ALEX ENGBERS; circ. 129,550.

Barneveld

Nederlands Dagblad: Hermesweg 20, POB 111, 3770 AC Barneveld; tel. (342) 411711; fax (342) 411611; e-mail redactie@nd.nl; internet www.nd.nl; f. 1944; morning; Editor-in-Chief SJIRK KUIJPER; circ. 29,505.

Breda

BN/De Stem (The Voice): Spinveld 55, POB 3229, 4800 MB Breda; tel. (76) 5312311; fax (76) 5312355; e-mail redactie@bndestem.nl; internet www.bndestem.nl; f. 1998 by merger of *Brabants Nieuwsblad* and *De Stem*; owned by Koninklijke Wegener NV; morning; Editor JOHAN VAN UFFELEN; circ. 113,073.

Dordrecht

AD De Dordtenaar: POB 54, 3300 AB Dordrecht; tel. (78) 6324711; e-mail dd.redactie@ad.nl; internet www.ad.nl; f. 1946; morning; Group Editor CHRISTIAAN RUESINK.

Eindhoven

Eindhovens Dagblad (ED): Begijnenhof 4–6, POB 534, 5600 AM Eindhoven; tel. (40) 2336336; fax (40) 2436954; e-mail redactie@ed.nl; internet www.ed.nl; owned by Wegener; Editor JOHN VAN DEN OETELAAR; circ. 109,378.

Enschede

De Twentsche Courant Tubantia: Getfertsingel 41, POB 28, 7500 AA Enschede; tel. (53) 4842842; fax (53) 4842200; e-mail enschede@tctubantia.nl; internet www.tctubantia.nl; f. 1844; publ. by Koninklijke Wegener NV; Editor ANDRÉ VIS; circ. 112,599.

's-Gravenhage/Den Haag
(The Hague)

AD Haagsche Courant: Verrijn Stuartlaan, First Floor, Rijswijk, POB 16050, 2500 AA The Hague; tel. (70) 3190911; fax (70) 3954783; e-mail hc.redactie@ad.nl; internet www.ad.nl/denhaag; evening; Group Editor CHRISTIAAN RUESINK.

Nederlandse Staatscourant: Prinses Margrietplantsoen 88, POB 20020, 2500 EA The Hague; tel. (70) 3789639; fax (70) 3855505; internet www.staatscourant.nl; f. 1814; morning; Editor W. M. C. DE JONG; circ. 5,913 (2006).

Groningen

Dagblad van het Noorden: Lübeckweg 2, POB 60, 9700 MC Groningen; tel. (50) 5844444; fax (50) 5844209; e-mail redactie@dvhn.nl; internet www.dvhn.nl; f. 1888; morning; Editor PIETER SIJPERSMA; circ. 130,000 (2012).

Haarlem

Haarlems Dagblad: Stationsplein 86, POB 507, 2003 PA Haarlem; tel. (88) 8241111; e-mail starsredactie@haarlemsdagblad.nl; internet www.haarlemsdagblad.nl; f. 1656; evening; Editors MIKE ACKERMANS, JAN GEERT MAJOOR; combined circ. 39,046.

IJmuider Courant: Kennemerlaan 56, 1972 EP IJmuiden; tel. (255) 561800; fax (255) 561888; e-mail redactie@ijmuidercourant.nl; internet www.ijmuidercourant.nl; daily; Editors MIKE ACKERMANS, JAN GEERT MAJOOR.

's-Hertogenbosch/Den Bosch

Brabants Dagblad: Veemarktkade 8, 5222 AE 's-Hertogenbosch; tel. (73) 6157157; e-mail redactie@bd.nl; internet www.brabantsdagblad.nl; morning; publ. by Wegener NV; Editor TON ROOMS; circ. 115,000.

Hilversum

De Gooi- en Eemlander: Seinstraat 14, 1223 DA Hilversum; tel. (35) 6477000; fax (35) 6477108; e-mail redactie@gooieneemlander.nl; internet www.gooieneemlander.nl; f. 1871; evening; Editors GEERT TEN DAM, JAN-GEERT MAJOOR; circ. 26,549.

Leeuwarden

Leeuwarder Courant: Sixmastraat 15, POB 394, 8901 BD Leeuwarden; tel. (58) 2845406; fax (58) 2845419; e-mail redactie@lc.nl; internet www.lc.nl; f. 1752; evening; Editor HANS SNIJDER; circ. 89,942 (2012).

Leiden

Leidsch Dagblad: 3e Binnenvestgracht 23, POB 54, 2300 AB Leiden; tel. (71) 5356356; fax (71) 5356415; e-mail stadsredactie@leidschdagblad.nl; internet www.leidschdagblad.nl; f. 1860; publ. by HDC Media; morning; Editors MIKE ACKERMANS, JAN-GEERT MAJOOR; circ. 31,923.

Nijmegen

De Gelderlander: Winselingseweg 10, POB 36, 6500 DA Nijmegen; tel. (24) 3650611; fax (24) 3650479; e-mail redactie@gelderlander.nl; internet www.gelderlander.nl; f. 1848; owned by Koninklijke Wegener NV; morning; Editor KEES PIJNAPPELS; circ. 147,771.

Rotterdam

AD: Marten Meesweg 35, POB 8983, 3009 TC Rotterdam; tel. (10) 4066077; e-mail redactie@ad.nl; internet www.ad.nl; f. 1946; fmrly *Algemeen Dagblad*; morning; Group Editor CHRISTIAAN RUESINK; circ. 433,013.

AD Rotterdams Dagblad: Westblaak 180, POB 2999, 3000 CZ Rotterdam; tel. (10) 4004400; e-mail rd.redactie@ad.nl; internet www.ad.nl/rotterdam; f. 1991; evening; Group Editor CHRISTIAAN RUESINK.

NRC Handelsblad: Rokin 65, POB 20673, 1001 NR Amsterdam; tel. (20) 7553000; fax (20) 7553939; e-mail nrc@nrc.nl; internet www.nrc.nl; f. 1970; evening; Editor PETER VANDERMEERSCH; circ. 198,513.

Sittard

Dagblad De Limburger: Mercator 3, POB 5111, 6130 PC Sittard; tel. (46) 4116300; e-mail lezersservice@mgl.nl; internet www.limburger.nl; f. 1845; morning; Editor-in-Chief JOS ADRIAENS; circ. 124,180.

Limburgs Dagblad: Mercator 3, 6135 KW Sittard; tel. (46) 4116000; fax (46) 4116471; e-mail marketing@mgl.nl; internet www.limburger.nl; f. 1918; morning; Editor JOS ADRIAENS; circ. 40,963.

Utrecht

AD Utrechts Nieuwsblad: Vredenburg 24, POB 210, 3500 AE Utrecht; tel. (30) 2360300; e-mail un.brieven@ad.nl; internet www .ad.nl; f. 1993; evening; Group Editor CHRISTIAAN RUESINK.

Vlissingen

Provinciale Zeeuwse Courant: Park Veldzigt 35, POB 91, 4330 AB Middelburg; tel. (118) 434 010; fax (118) 434019; e-mail redactie@ pzc.nl; internet www.pzc.nl; f. 1758; morning; Editor PETER JANSEN; circ. 54,871.

SELECTED WEEKLIES

Adformatie: Heemstedeveste, Poeldijkstraat 4, POB 75462, 1070 AL Amsterdam; tel. (20) 5733644; e-mail redactie@adformatie.nl; internet www.adformatie.nl; advertising, marketing and media; Editor-in-Chief THEO VAN VUGT; circ. 40,000.

Avrobode: 's-Gravelandseweg 52, 1217 ET Hilversum; tel. (35) 6717911; fax (35) 717443; e-mail redactie@avrobode.nl; internet www.avrobode.nl; publ. by Algemene Omroepvereniging; radio and TV guide; Editor REIN VAN ROOIJ; circ. 271,113 (2011).

Boerderij: Hanzestraat 1, POB 4, 7000 BA Doetinchem; tel. (314) 349446; fax (314) 342408; e-mail redactie@boerderij.nl; internet www.boerderij.nl; f. 1915; farming; Editor-in-Chief GEERT HEKKERT; circ. 65,000.

Donald Duck: POB 1680, 2130 JB Hoofddorp; internet www .donaldduck.nl; f. 1952; children's interest; weekly; Publr SUZAN SCHOUTEN HAAGMANS; Editor THOM ROEP; circ. 296,179.

Elsevier: Radarweg 29, POB 152, 1000 AD Amsterdam; tel. (20) 5159944; fax (20) 5159900; e-mail redactie.elsevier@elsevier.nl; internet www.elsevier.nl; f. 1945; current affairs; Chief Editor ARENDO JOUSTRA; circ. 158,303 (2011).

Fashionista: POB 1680, 2130 JB Hoofddorp; tel. (23) 5565117; fax (23) 5565116; e-mail redactie@fashionistamagazine.nl; internet www.fashionistamagazine.nl; teenage girls' interest; Editor MIES DE VRIES; circ. 120,000.

Libelle: POB 1742, 2130 JC Hoofddorp; tel. (88) 5500221; e-mail redactie@libelle.nl; internet www.libelle.nl; f. 1934; women's interest; Editor-in-Chief FRANSKA STUY; circ. 427,110 (2011).

Margriet: POB 1650, 2130 JB Hoofddorp; tel. (88) 5500222; e-mail redactie@margriet.nl; internet www.margriet.nl; f. 1938; women's interest; Editor-in-Chief LEONTINE VAN DEN BOS; circ. 251,230 (2011).

Mikro Gids: POB 10050, 1201 DB Hilversum; tel. (35) 6726880; fax (35) 6726878; internet www.mikrogids.nl; f. 1974; radio and TV guide; Editor-in-Chief HANS SANDERS; circ. 364,261 (2011).

NCRV-Gids: POB 25900, 1202 HW Hilversum; tel. (35) 6726890; internet www.ncrvgids.nl; f. 1966; publ. by Nederlandse Christelijke Radio Vereniging; radio and TV guide; Dir SASKIA DE JONG; Editor MARJOLEINE TEPE; circ. 228,359 (2011).

Nederlands Tijdschrift voor Geneeskunde (Dutch Journal of Medicine): POB 75971, 1070 AZ Amsterdam; tel. (20) 6620150; fax (20) 6735481; e-mail redactie@ntvg.nl; internet www.ntvg.nl; f. 1856; Editor Prof. Dr PETER DE LEEUW; circ. 30,000.

Nieuwe Revu: Capellalaan 65, POB 41006, 2130 MK Hoofddorp; tel. (88) 7518380; e-mail redactie@revu.nl; internet www.revu.nl; f. 1953; general interest; Editor-in-Chief ERIK NOOMEN; circ. 41,140 (2011).

Panorama: Ceylonpoort 5–25, POB 4028, 2037 AA Haarlem; tel. (23) 5304304; fax (23) 5361624; e-mail panorama@smm.nl; internet www.panorama.nl; f. 1913; general interest; Editor FRANS LOMANS; circ. 55,938 (2011).

Privé: POB 1980, 1000 BZ Amsterdam; tel. (20) 5853375; fax (20) 5854225; e-mail redactie@prive.nl; internet www.prive.nl; f. 1977; owned by Telegraaf Media Groep NV; women's interest; Editor EVERT SANTEGOEDS; circ. 167,326 (2011).

Story: Capellalaan 65, POB 1652, 2130 JB Hoofddorp; tel. (23) 5564894; fax (23) 5564911; internet www.story.nl; f. 1974; women's interest; Editor MATTHIEU SLEE; circ. 98,564 (2011).

TeleVizier: POB 580, 1200 AN Hilversum; tel. (35) 6726850; fax (35) 6726878; e-mail redactie@televizier.nl; internet www.televizier.nl; publ. by Algemene Omroepvereniging; radio and TV guide; Editor JEROEN DE GOEIJ; circ. 141,308 (2011).

Tina: Ceylonpoort 5–25, 2037 AA Haarlem; tel. (23) 5304304; fax (23) 5352554; f. 1967; teenage girls' interest; circ. 51,919.

TrosKompas: POB 1431, 1000 BK Amsterdam; tel. (35) 6728798; fax (35) 6728631; e-mail info@troskompas.nl; internet www .troskompas.nl; f. 1966; owned by Hilversumse Media Compagnie; radio and TV guide; Editor EDGER HAMER; circ. 372,286 (2011).

TV Krant: POB 28600, 1202 LR Hilversum; tel. (35) 6728798; fax (35) 6728631; internet www.tvkrant.nl; f. 1990; radio and TV guide; Editor EDGER HAMER; circ. 158,814 (2011).

Vara TV Magazine: Sumatralaan 49, POB 175, 1200 AD Hilversum; tel. (35) 6711445; fax (35) 6711429; e-mail tv.magazine@vara .nl; internet vara.nl; radio and TV guide; Editor RUTGER VERHOEVEN; circ. 500,000.

Veronica: 2a Olympia, POB 22000, 1202 CA Hilversum; tel. (35) 6463333; fax (35) 6463300; e-mail bladredactie@veronicapublishing .nl; internet www.veronicamagazine.nl; f. 1971; radio and TV guide; Editor JOHN LUKKEN; circ. 797,787 (2011).

Viva: POB 1630, 2130 JA Hoofddorp; tel. (23) 5565165; fax (23) 5565200; e-mail redactie@viva.nl; internet www.viva.nl; women's interest; Editor KARIN VAN GILST; circ. 73,003 (2011).

VPRO Gids: POB 11, 1200 JC Hilversum; tel. (35) 6712665; fax (35) 6712552; e-mail gids@vpro.nl; internet www.gids.vpro.nl; radio and TV guide; Editor HUGO BLOM; circ. 1186,564 (2014).

Vrij Nederland: Raamgracht 4, POB 1254, 1000 BG Amsterdam; tel. (20) 5518711; fax (20) 6247476; e-mail redactie@vn.nl; internet www.vn.nl; f. 1940; current affairs; Dir KARIN VAN GILST; Editor FRITS VAN EXTER; circ. 49,752 (2011).

SELECTED PERIODICALS

Art, History and Literature

De Architect: POB 20025, 2501 AG The Hague; tel. (70) 3046777; e-mail redactie@dearchitect.nl; internet www.dearchitect.nl; Dir HARM TILMAN; circ. 4,859 (2010).

Geschiedenis Magazine: Molukkenstraat 200, 1098 TW Amsterdam; tel. (20) 6652759; fax (20) 6657831; e-mail redactie@ geschiedenismagazine.nl; internet www.geschiedenismagazine.nl; f. 1966; 8 a year; history and archaeology; Editor-in-Chief Dr FRANS ANZION; circ. 8,000.

Kunstbeeld: Danzigerkade 9D, 1013 AP Amsterdam; POB 57191, 1040 BB Amsterdam; tel. (20) 5310900; fax (20) 5310971; e-mail redactie@kunstbeeld.nl; internet www.kunstbeeld.nl; monthly; art, sculpture; Editor ANNA VAN LEEUWEN; circ. 6,585 (Jan.–March 2013).

Tableau Fine Arts Magazine: POB 71197, 1008 BD Amsterdam; tel. (20) 6648543; e-mail tableaumedia@kpnplanet.nl; internet www .tableaumagazine.nl; f. 1978; every 2 months; publ. by Tableau Fine Arts Media BV; Editor-in-Chief ANJA FRENKEL; circ. 13,825 (Jan.– March 2013).

Economics and Business

Computable: POB 37109, 1030 BA Haarlem; tel. (23) 2042925; e-mail computable@vnumedia.nl; internet www.computable.nl; Editor JOHANNES VAN BENTUM; circ. 21,049 (Jan.–March 2013).

Elektronica + Embedded Systems: POB 58, 7400 AB Deventer; tel. (570) 504300; fax (570) 504389; e-mail h.vries@mybusinessmedia .nl; internet www.engineersonline.nl; f. 1953; 8 a year; electronics design; Editor HENK DE VRIES; circ. 3,912 (Jan.–March 2013).

Intermediair: Lincolnweg 40, 1033 SN Amsterdam; POB 37040, 1030 AA Amsterdam; tel. (20) 2042000; fax (20) 2042001; e-mail redactie@intermediair.nl; internet www.intermediair.nl; f. 1965; weekly; business recruitment; circ. 240,678.

Management Team: Paul van Vlissingenstr. 10E, 1096 BK Amsterdam; tel. (20) 2620701; e-mail redactie@mt.nl; internet www.mt.nl; f. 1980; 10 a year; management; Editor DOMINIQUE HAIJTEMA; circ. 71,994 (Jan.–March 2013).

PCM (Personal Computer Magazine): Richard Holkade 8, 2033 PZ Haarlem; tel. (23) 5430000; internet www.pcmweb.nl; f. 1982; monthly; computing; Editor-in-Chief XANDER HOOSE; circ. 25,472 (Jan.–March 2013).

Trade Channel: Nieuw Guineastraat 30, 2022 PA Haarlem; tel. (23) 5319022; fax (23) 5317974; e-mail pvroom@tradechannel.com; internet www.tradechannel.com; f. 1945; monthly, 2 edns: *Trade Channel Consumer Goods* and *Trade Channel Industrial & Technical Products*; promotes imports and exports; Editor HENK VAN CAPELLE; circ. 13,286 (consumer edn), 55,000 (technical edn).

Home, Fashion and General

Ariadne at Home: Capellalaan 65, POB 1722, 2130 JC Hoofddorp; tel. (88) 5564435; e-mail redactie@ariadneathome.nl; internet www .ariadneathome.nl; f. 1946; monthly; home decoration; Editor ATY LUITZE; circ. 103,986 (Jan.–March 2013).

Cosmopolitan: Singel 468, 1017 AW Amsterdam; fax (20) 5353600; e-mail cosmopolitan@hearst.nl; internet www.cosmopolitan.nl; f. 1982; monthly; women's interest; Editor ANNE MARIJE DE VRIES LENTSCH; circ. 72,802 (Jan.–March 2013).

Delicious: Capellalaan 65, POB 1632, 2130 JA Hoofddorp; tel. (23) 5565466; fax (23) 5565488; e-mail deliciousmagazine@ sanoma-uitgevers.nl; internet www.deliciousmagazine.nl; f. 1977; monthly; cookery; Editor-in-Chief MAKKIE MULDER; circ. 50,299 (Jan.–March 2013).

HP/De Tijd (The Times): POB 95044, 1090 HA Amsterdam; tel. (20) 5979400; fax (20) 5979490; e-mail redactie@hpdetijd.nl; internet www.hpdetijd.nl; f. 1845 as daily; owned by Audax; changed to weekly in 1974, and to monthly in 2012; progressive; current affairs; Editors-in-Chief DAAN DIJKSMAN, BOUDEWIJN GEELS; circ. 25,605 (Jan.–March 2013).

KIJK: POB 40091, 2130 KZ Hoofddorp; tel. (88) 7518328; e-mail kijk@sanomamedia.nl; internet www.kijkmagazine.nl; science, technology, history and current events; Editor VIVIANNE BENDERMACHER; circ. 40,395 (Jan.–March 2013).

Knipmode: Capellalaan 65, POB 17322130, 2130 JL Hoofddorp; tel. (88) 5565002; e-mail knipmode@sanoma.com; internet www.knipmode.nl; monthly; DIY fashion; Editor-in-Chief PEGGY WEIJERGANG; Publr WOUTER VERKENNIS; circ. 39,413 (Jan.–March 2013).

Nouveau: Capellalaan 65, 2132 JC Hoofddorp; tel. (88) -5565370; e-mail nouveau.nl@sanoma.com; internet www.nouveau.nl; f. 1986; women's interest; Editor-in-Chief BRIGITTE SPEEKMAN; circ. 50,600 (Jan.–March 2013).

Opzij: Danzigerkade 9D, 1013 AP Amsterdam; tel. (88) 7002935; e-mail redactie@opzij.nl; internet www.opzij.nl; f. 1972; monthly; owned by Veen Media; feminist themes; Editor DAPHNE VAN PAASSEN; circ. 45,368 (Jan.–March 2013).

Ouders van Nu: POB 1810, 2130 JE Hoofddorp; tel. (88) 5567208; e-mail redactie@oudersvannu.nl; internet www.oudersvannu.nl; f. 1967; monthly; childcare; Editor H. THOLEN; circ. 49,827 (Jan.–March 2013).

Reader's Digest: POB 23330, 1100 DV Amsterdam; tel. (20) 5678911; fax (20) 6976422; e-mail hetbeste@readersdigest.nl; internet www.readersdigest.nl; f. 1957; monthly; general interest; Country Man. JOOST MARTENS; circ. 63,513 (Jan.–March 2013).

SEN: POB 34080, 3005 GB Rotterdam; fax (102) 092629; e-mail redactie@senmagazine.com; internet www.senmagazine.com; f. 2004; monthly; women's interest; Editor-in-Chief ŞENAY ÖZDEMIR; circ. 20,000.

vtwonen: Capellalaan 65, POB 1692, 2130 JB Hoofddorp; tel. (88) 5564600; e-mail vtwonen.nl@sanoma.com; internet www.vtwonen.nl; f. 1964; monthly; home-owning and decorating; Editor-in-Chief CARLEIN KIEBOOM; circ. 108,910 (Jan.–March 2013).

101 Woonideeën: POB 1702, 2130 JC Hoofddorp; tel. (23) 5564590; e-mail 101woonideeen@sanoma.com; internet www.101woonideeen.nl; f. 1957; monthly; home ideas; Editor ANNET NITERINK; circ. 76,637 (Jan.–March 2013).

Leisure Interests and Sport

Kampeer en Caravankampioen: POB 93200, 2509 BA The Hague; tel. (88) 2692222; e-mail kck@anwb.nl; internet www.anwb .nl/kamperen; f. 1941; monthly; camping and caravanning; publ. by Royal Dutch Touring Club (ANWB); Editor-in-Chief ED LODEWIJKS; circ. 79,354 (Jan.–March 2013).

Kampioen: POB 93200, 2509 BA The Hague; tel. (80) 2692222; fax (70) 3146983; e-mail kampioen@anwb.nl; internet www.kampioen .nl; f. 1885; 10 a year; recreation and tourism; publ. by Royal Dutch Touring Club (ANWB); Editor BERT GORISSEN; circ. 3,422,838 (Jan.–March 2013).

Reizen Magazine: POB 93200, 2509 BA The Hague; tel. (88) 2696670; fax (88) 2697610; e-mail reizen@anwb.nl; internet www .reizen.nl; 10 issues a year; tourism, travel; publ. by Royal Dutch Touring Club (ANWB); Editor-in-Chief MATTHIJS DE WINTER; circ. 55,788 (2013).

Roots: POB 41000, 2130 MK Hoofddorp; tel. (88) 5500155; e-mail info@rootsmagazine.nl; internet www.rootsmagazine.nl; monthly; nature and wildlife; Editor FANNY GLAZENBURG; circ. 21,846 (Jan.–March 2013).

Voetbal International: POB 575, 2800 AN Gouda; e-mail webmaster@vi.nl; internet www.vi.nl; weekly; football; Editors-in-Chief THIJS VAN VEGHEL, TOM VAN HULSEN; circ. 125,655 (Jan.–March 2013).

Waterkampioen: POB 93200, 2509 BA The Hague; tel. (88) 2697049; fax (88) 2697359; e-mail waterkampioen@anwb.nl; f. 1927; monthly; water sports and yachting; publ. by Royal Dutch Touring Club (ANWB); Editor JAN BRIEK; circ. 38,710 (2010).

Scientific and Medical

Huisarts en Wetenschap: Nederlands Huisartsen Genootschap, POB 3231, 3502 GE Utrecht; tel. (30) 2823500; fax (30) 2823501; e-mail redactie@nhg.org; internet www.henw.org; monthly; medical; Editor Dr JUST EEKHOF; circ. 12,735 (Jan.–March 2013).

New Scientist: Danzigerkade 9D, 1013 AP Amsterdam; POB 57191, 1040 BB Amsterdam; e-mail redactie@newscientist.nl; internet www.newscientist.nl; 11 a year; Editor IRENE DE BEL.

NEWS AGENCY

Algemeen Nederlands Persbureau (ANP) (Netherlands News Agency): Verrijn Stuartlaan 7, POB 1, 2501 AA The Hague; tel. (70) 4141414; fax (70) 4140560; e-mail redactie@anp.nl; internet www .anp.nl; f. 1934; official agency of the Netherlands Daily Press Asscn; Man. Dir ERIK VAN GRUIJTHUIJSEN; Editor-in-Chief MARCEL VAN LINGEN.

PRESS ORGANIZATIONS

Buitenlandse Persvereniging in Nederland (Foreign Press Asscn in the Netherlands): Oudezijds Voorburgwal 129, 1012 EP Amsterdam; tel. (20) 4221209; e-mail admin@bpv-fpa.nl; internet www.bpv-fpa.nl; f. 1925; Pres. JAN HENNOP; 120 mems.

Nederlandse Dagbladpers (NDP) (Dutch Asscn of Daily Newspaper Publrs): Hogehilweg 6, POB 12040, 1100 AA Amsterdam-Zuidoost; tel. (20) 4309150; fax (20) 4309199; e-mail info@nuv.nl; internet www.nuv.nl; f. 1908; affiliated to Nederlands Uitgeversverbond; Chair. LOEK HERMANS; Dir GEERT NOORMAN; 31 mems.

De Nederlandse Nieuwsblad Pers (NNP) (Organization of Local News Media in the Netherlands): Hogebrinkerweg 10, 3871 KN Hoevelaken; tel. (33) 4481650; fax (33) 4481652; e-mail nnpnl@nnp .nl; internet www.nnp.nl; f. 1945; asscn of publrs of non-daily local newspapers and other local news media; Sec. J. VAN DER HOEVEN; 60 mems.

Nederlandse Vereniging van Journalisten (Netherlands Association of Journalists): Johannes Vermeerstraat 22, POB 75997, 1070 AZ Amsterdam; tel. (20) 3039700; fax (20) 6624901; e-mail vereniging@nvj.nl; internet www.nvj.nl; f. 1884; publ. *De Journalist* (10 a year); Chair. MARJAN ENZLIN; Gen. Sec. THOMAS BRUNING; 7,300 mems.

Publishers

Uitgeverij Ankh-Hermes BV: Smyrnastraat 5, POB 125, 7400 AC Deventer; tel. (57) 0678900; fax (57) 0624632; e-mail info@ ankh-hermes.nl; internet www.ankh-hermes.nl; f. 1973; health, Eastern and Western religions, astrology, alternative medicine, psychology, esoterics; part of VBK-media since 2011; Publr JOHN VAN SCHAIK.

Ambo Anthos: Herengracht 499, 1017 BR Amsterdam; tel. (20) 5245411; fax (20) 4200422; e-mail info@amboanthos.nl; internet www.amboanthos.nl; literature, cultural history, biographies, history, politics; Dir R. AMMERLAAN.

APA (Academic Publishers Associated): NZ Voorburgwal 286, 1012 RT Amsterdam; tel. (20) 6265544; fax (20) 5285298; e-mail apa@ apa-publishers.com; internet www.apa-publishers.com; f. 1966; subsidiaries: Apantiqua, Holland University Press, Fontes Pers, Oriental Press, Philo Press, van Heusden, Hissink & Co; old, new and reprint edns in the arts, humanities and science; Man. Dir G. VAN HEUSDEN.

De Arbeiderspers–A. W. Bruna Uitgevers BV: Franz Lisztplantsoen 200, POB 40203, 3504 AA Utrecht; tel. (30) 2470411; fax (30) 2410018; e-mail info@apawb.nl; internet www.apawb.nl; f. 1868; A. W. Bruna Uitgevers merged with De Arbeiderspers in 2012 when new name adopted; general fiction and non-fiction; Dir J. A. A. BOEZEMAN.

A. Asher & Co BV: 16 Tuurdijk, 3997 MS Houten; tel. (30) 6011955; fax (30) 6011813; e-mail info@asherbooks.com; internet www .asherbooks.com; f. 1830; natural history; Dirs LAURENS HESSELINK, JULIUS STEINER.

John Benjamins BV: Klaprozenweg 75G, POB 36224, 1020 ME Amsterdam; tel. (20) 6304747; fax (20) 6739773; e-mail customer .services@benjamins.nl; internet www.benjamins.com; f. 1964; linguistics, philology, psychology and art history; antiquarian scholarly periodicals; Man. Dir SELINE BENJAMINS.

Uitgeverij De Bezige Bij BV: Van Miereveldstraat 1, POB 75184, 1070 AD Amsterdam; tel. (20) 3059810; fax (20) 3059824; e-mail info@debezigebij.nl; internet www.debezigebij.nl; f. 1945; Publr MICHIEL GAAF.

Erven J. Bijleveld: Janskerkhof 7, 3512 BK Utrecht, POB 1238, 3500 BE Utrecht; tel. (30) 2310800; fax (30) 2311774; e-mail bijleveld .publishers@wxs.nl; internet www.bijleveldbooks.nl; f. 1865; psychology, sociology, philosophy, religion and history; computer books (as Bijleveld Press); Mans J. B. BOMMELJÉ, L. S. BOMMELJÉ.

Boekencentrum Uitgevers: Goudstraat 50, POB 29, 2700 AA Zoetermeer; tel. (79) 3615481; fax (79) 3615489; e-mail info@ boekencentrum.nl; internet www.boekencentrum.nl; f. 1935; bibles, books and magazines; Dir N. A. DE WAAL.

Bohn Stafleu van Loghum BV: Het Spoor 2, POB 246, 3990 GA Houten; tel. (30) 6383736; fax (30) 6383999; e-mail klachten@bsl.nl; internet www.bsl.nl; mem. of Wolters Kluwer NV holdings group;

social sciences, humanities, medical, dental and nursing; Dir P. J. A. SNAKKERS.

Boom Uitgevers Amsterdam BV: Prinsengracht 747–751, POB 15970, 1001 JX Amsterdam; tel. (20) 6226107; fax (20) 6253327; e-mail info@boomamsterdam.nl; internet www.boomamsterdam.nl; f. 1842; fmrly Boom Pers BV, Meppel; philosophy, educational and social sciences, environment, history; Man. Dir Dr DRIES VAN INGEN.

Brill: Plantijnstraat 2, POB 9000, 2300 PA Leiden; tel. (71) 5353500; fax (71) 5317532; e-mail marketing@brill.com; internet www.brill .com; f. 1683; academic books and periodicals (mainly in English); classics, medieval, renaissance and oriental studies, comparative religion, biology, law; CEO HERMAN PABBRUWE.

CRC Press/Balkema–Taylor & Francis Group (CRC Press/Balkema): Schipholweg 107C, 2316 XC Leiden; POB 11320, 2301 EH Leiden; tel. (71) 5243080; e-mail janjaap.blom@tandf.co.uk; internet www.crcpress.com; f. 1901 as Swets & Zeitlinger Publishers; acquired by Taylor & Francis (UK) in 2003; publr of books on civil engineering, water, geosciences and earth sciences; Sr Publr JANJAAP BLOM.

Uitgeverij De Fontein BV: Herculesplein 96, POB 13288, 3507 LG Utrecht; tel. (88) 7002600; fax (88) 7002999; e-mail info@ uitgeverijdefontein.nl; internet www.defonteinkinderboeken.nl; f. 1981; commercial fiction, non-fiction and children's books; Dir T. AKVELD.

Uitgeverij van Gennep BV: Nieuwezijds Voorburgwal 330, 1012 RW Amsterdam; tel. (20) 6247033; fax (20) 6247035; e-mail info@ vangennep-boeken.nl; internet vangennep-boeken.nl; history, social theory, political science, biographies, literature; Dir CHRIS TEN KATE.

Gottmer Uitgevers Groep: Zijlweg 308, POB 317, 2000 CN Haarlem; tel. (23) 5411190; fax (23) 5274404; e-mail info@gottmer .nl; internet www.gottmer.nl; f. 1937; fiction, non-fiction, children's books, religion, spirituality, travel guides; imprints incl. Altamira, Aramith, Becht, Dominicus and Hollandia; Editorial Dir MELANIE LASANCE.

Uitgeverij Holland BV: Spaarne 110, 2011 CM Haarlem; tel. (23) 5323061; fax (23) 5342908; e-mail info@uitgeverijholland.nl; internet www.uitgeverijholland.nl; f. 1922; literature, reference, science, children's books; Publr J. B. VAN ULZEN.

Uitgeverij Kok: KCC VBK Media, POB 13288, 3507 LG Utrecht; tel. (88) 8002062; e-mail info@kok.nl; internet www.kok.nl; f. 1894; theology, belles-lettres, science, periodicals; mem. of Veen Bosch & Keuning Uitgevers group; 9 subsidiaries; Dir B. A. ENDEDIJK.

Uitgeverij Ten Have: Herculesplein 96, POB 13288, 3507 LG Utrecht; tel. (88) 7002600; fax (88) 7002699; e-mail info@ uitgeverijtenhave.nl; internet www.uitgeverijtenhave.nl; f. 1831; imprint of Uitgeverij Kok; religious; Dir B. A. ENDEDIJK; Editor P. DE BOER.

Uitgeverij Voorhoeve: POB 13288, 3507 LG Utrecht; tel. (35) 5418855; fax (35) 5413174; f. 1876; imprint of Uitgeverij Kok; general non-fiction, children's books; Dir B. A. ENDEDIJK.

Kosmos Uitgevers: Herculespl. 96, POB 13288, 3507 LG Utrecht; tel. (88) 7002600; fax (88) 7002609; e-mail info@kosmosuitgevers.nl; internet www.kosmosuitgevers.nl; f. 1992; mem. of Veen Bosch & Keuning Uitgevers; Dir HILDE VINKEN.

Lemniscaat BV: Vijverlaan 48, POB 4066, 3006 AB Rotterdam; tel. (10) 2062929; fax (10) 4141560; e-mail info@lemniscaat.nl; internet www.lemniscaat.nl; f. 1963; philosophy, psychology, education, development, children's books; Dir J. C. BOELE VAN HENSBROEK.

Uitgeverij Leopold BV: Singel 262, POB 3879, 1001 AR Amsterdam; tel. (20) 5511250; fax (20) 4204699; e-mail info@leopold.nl; internet www.leopold.nl; f. 1923; mem. of Weekbladpers BV; children's books; Dir PAULIEN LOERTS.

Uitgeverij Luitingh-Sijthoff BV: Leidsegracht 105A, POB 289, 1000 AG Amsterdam; tel. (20) 5307340; fax (20) 626251; e-mail info@ lsamsterdam.nl; internet www.luitinghsijthoff.nl; f. 1989, following the merger of Sijthoff (f. 1851) and Luitingh (f. 1947); mem. of Veen Bosch & Keuning Uitgevers publishing group; fiction and popular non-fiction; Man. Dir HANCA LEPPINK.

Malmberg BV: Magistratenlaan 138 POB 233, 5201 AE 's-Hertogenbosch; tel. (73) 6288811; fax (73) 6210512; e-mail malmberg@malmberg.nl; internet www.malmberg.nl; f. 1885; part of SanomaWSOY Group (Finland); educational; Dir J. DRIESSEN.

J. M. Meulenhoff BV: Herengracht 507, 1017 BV Amsterdam; tel. (20) 5353135; fax (20) 5353130; e-mail info@meulenhoff.nl; internet www.meulenhoff.nl; f. 1895; literature, historical, political, social/cultural, art, paperbacks and pocket books; Dir ROB HOGENES.

NDC mediagroep: Sixmastraat 15, POB 394, 8901 PA Leeuwarden; tel. (30) 2845245; e-mail verkoop@ndcmediagroep.nl; internet www .ndcmediagroep.nl; f. 1752; associated with Veen Bosch & Keuning Uitgevers NV (VBK) until 2012; newspapers and magazines; CEO DINA BOONSTRA.

Nienhuis Montessori International BV: Industriepark 14, 7021 AA Zelhem; tel. (314) 627110; fax (314) 627128; e-mail info@nienhuis .nl; internet www.nienhuis.nl; f. 1800; holdings group; publrs and printers specializing in scientific books and periodicals; Dir A. J. NIENHUIS.

Noordhoff Uitgevers: Winschoterdiep 70A, POB 58, 9700 MB Groningen; tel. (50) 5226922; fax (50) 5277599; internet www .noordhoffuitgevers.nl; f. 1836; educational and scientific books, educational software, geographical and historical atlases and maps; Man. Dir Dr A. M. W. HOLL.

Uitgeverij Ploegsma BV: Singel 262, 1016 AC Amsterdam; tel. (20) 5511250; fax (20) 6203509; e-mail info@ploegsma.nl; internet www .ploegsma.nl; subsidiary: Uitgeverij De Brink; Publr MARTINE SCHAAP.

Uitgeverij Prometheus/Bert Bakker: Herengracht 540, POB 1662, 1000 BR Amsterdam; tel. (20) 6241934; fax (20) 6225461; e-mail info@pbo.nl; internet www.uitgeverijprometheus.nl/bb; f. 1893; Dutch and international literature, sociology, history, politics, science; Dir MAI SPIJKERS.

Em. Querido's Uitgeverij BV: Singel 262, 1016 AR Amsterdam; tel. (20) 5511262; fax (20) 6391968; e-mail info@querido.nl; internet www.querido.nl; f. 1915; subsidiary: Uitgeverij Nijgh & van Ditmar; participant in 'Singel 262' holdings group; general fiction, history, children's books, translations from Latin and Greek texts; Dir ARY T. LANGBROEK.

Reed Elsevier NV: Radarweg 29, POB 152, 1000 NX Amsterdam; tel. (20) 5159944; fax (20) 5159900; e-mail redactie.elsevier@elsevier .nl; internet www.elsevier.nl; f. 1979 by merger; subholdings include some 60 subsidiaries in the Netherlands and abroad specializing in reference works, handbooks, weekly magazines, newspapers, trade and technical publs, (postgraduate) scientific books and journals, audiovisual materials, further education study courses, databases; CEO ERIK ENGSTROM.

Elsevier BV Excerpta Medica: Radarweg 29, 1043 NX Amsterdam; tel. (20) 7971400; fax (20) 7971498; e-mail info@ excerptamedica.com; internet www.excerptamedica.com; Pres. EDWARD ROOS.

Editions Rodopi BV: Tijnmuiden 7, 1046 AK Amsterdam; tel. (20) 6114821; fax (20) 4472979; e-mail info@rodopi.nl; internet www .rodopi.nl; f. 1966; Dir Y. L. SCHIPPERS.

SDU Uitgevers: Prinses Beatrixlaan 116, POB 20025, 2500 EA The Hague; tel. (70) 3789911; fax (70) 3854321; e-mail sdu@sdu.nl; internet www.sdu.nl; legal, fiscal, government and industry journals, and books; CEO Dr SANDRA KROON.

Springer: Van Godewijckstraat 30, POB 989, 3311 GX Dordrecht; tel. (78) 6576050; fax (78) 6576467; internet www.springeronline .com; merged with Kluwer Academic Publrs in 2004; publrs of books and journals in the fields of science, technology and medicine, incl., *inter alia*, natural sciences, mathematics, engineering, computer science and psychology; CEO DERK HAANK.

Strengholt United Media: Hofstede 'Oud-Bussem', Flevolaan 41, POB 338, 1400 AH Bussum; tel. (35) 6958430; fax (35) 6958440; e-mail unitedmedia@strengholt.nl; internet www.uitgeverij strengholt.nl; f. 1928; health, biography, music, current affairs, psychology, parapsychology, sports, cookery; Dir T. M. JANSEN.

Uitgeverij De Tijdstroom BV: Janskerkhof 26, POB 775, 3500 AT Utrecht; tel. (30) 2364450; fax (30) 23699354; e-mail info@tijdstroom .nl; internet www.tijdstroom.nl; f. 1921; educational and professional publications on health and welfare, periodicals in these fields; Dir N. F. VAN 'T ZET.

Uitgeverij Unieboek/Het Spectrum: Papiermolen 14–24, POB 97, 3990 DB Houten; tel. (30) 7998300; fax (30) 7998398; e-mail info@ unieboekspectrum.nl; internet www.unieboekspectrum.nl; f. 1890; holding group incorporating 10 publishing houses; general and juvenile literature, popular science, history, art, social, economics, religion, textbooks, etc.

Veen Bosch & Keuning Uitgevers NV (VBK): Herculesplein 94, POB 8049, 3503 RA Utrecht; tel. (88) 7002600; e-mail info@vbku.nl; internet www.vbku.nl; f. 1887; associated with NDC mediagroep (NDC) until 2012; fiction, children's books, travel, cookbooks, poetry; CEO WIET DE BRUIJN.

VNU Business Publications BV: Lincolnweg 40, POB 37040, 1030 AA Amsterdam; tel. (20) 2042000; fax (20) 2042001; e-mail info@bp .vnu.com; internet www.vnubp.nl; trade and fashion, careers, IT, personal computer, management, training.

Wolters Kluwer NV: Zuidpoolsingel 2, POB 1030, 2400 BA, Alphen aan den Rijn; tel. (172) 641400; fax (172) 474889; e-mail info@ wolterskluwer.com; internet www.wolterskluwer.com; f. 1836; operates in legal, tax, accounting, health, risk and compliance, regulatory and financial services; CEO and Chair., Exec. Bd NANCY McKINSTRY.

PUBLISHERS' ASSOCIATIONS

Koninklijke Vereniging van het Boekenvak (KVB) (Royal Asscn for the Book Trade): Hogehilweg 6, POB 12040, 1100 AA Amsterdam; tel. (20) 6240212; fax (20) 6208871; e-mail info@kvb.nl; internet www.kvb.nl; f. 1815; Chair. WOUTER VAN GILS; Dir MARTIJN DAVID; 1,500 mems.

Nederlands Uitgeversverbond (NUV) (Dutch Publrs' Asscn): Hogehilweg 6, POB 12040, 1100 AA Amsterdam Zuidoost; tel. (20) 4309150; fax (20) 4309199; e-mail info@nuv.nl; internet www.nuv.nl; Chair. LOEK HERMANS; Dir G. NOORMAN; 250 mems.

Broadcasting and Communications

TELECOMMUNICATIONS

Koninklijke KPN NV: POB 30000, 2500 The Hague; Maanplein 55, 2516 CK The Hague; POB 30000, 2500 GA The Hague; tel. (70) 3434343; fax (70) 3436568; e-mail webmaster@kpn.com; internet www.kpn.com; privatized 1989; fmrly Koninklijke PTT NV, present name adopted 1998; operates KPN Mobile; acquired Telfort BV in 2005, Enertel NV in 2006 and debitel Nederland BV in 2008; fixed-line operator and internet access provider; Chair. and CEO EELCO BLOK.

Telfort BV: POB 23079, 1100 DN Amsterdam Zuid-Oost; tel. 0800-1771; internet www.telfort.com; f. 1996; mobile cellular telecommunications and internet access; Man. Dir ROBIN CLEMENTS.

Online: POB 16156, 2500 BD The Hague; tel. (20) 5355555; internet www.online.nl; mobile cellular telecommunications and internet access; fmrly Orange Nederland NV; name changed to present in 2008; owned by Deutsche Telekom; CEO DAVID HOLLIDAY.

T-Mobile: Waldorpstr. 60, 2521 CC The Hague; tel. (61) 4095000; internet www.t-mobile.nl; owned by Deutsche Telekom; mobile telephone operator; CEO MARK KLEIN.

UPC Nederland NV: POB 80900, 1005 DA Amsterdam; Kabelweg 51, 1014 BA Amsterdam; tel. (20) 7755000; fax (20) 7756724; e-mail mediarelations@upc.nl; internet www.upc.nl; subsidiary of UPC Broadband; broadband internet, telephone, digital television and radio service provider; Man. Dir ROBERT DUNNE.

Vodafone: Simon Carmiggelstraat 6, POB 2251, 1000 CG Amsterdam; tel. (43) 3555555; e-mail press.nl@vodafone.com; internet www .vodafone.nl; f. 1999; owned by Vodafone Group PLC (UK); CEO ROB SHUTER.

BROADCASTING

Under the Netherlands public broadcasting system the two co-ordinating bodies work with the seven licensed broadcasters to provide a complete range of programmes.

Co-ordinating Bodies

Nederlandse Publieke Omroep (NPO) (Netherlands Public Broadcasting): Bart de Graaffweg 2, 1217 ZL Hilversum; POB 26444, 1202 JJ Hilversum; tel. (35) 6779222; fax (35) 6772649; e-mail npo.communicatie@omroep.nl; internet www.publieke omroep.nl; f. 1969; co-ordination of Dutch national public broadcasting and news, sports and teletext programmes on 6 national public radio and 6 television channels; fmrly Nederlandse Omroep Stichting; Chair. HENK N. HAGOORT.

NTR (Dutch Public Broadcaster for Information, Education and Culture): POB 29000, 1202 MA Hilversum; tel. (35) 6779333; e-mail info@ntr.nl; internet www.ntr.nl; f. 2010 by the merger of national broadcasters Nederlandse Programma Stichting (NPS), Teleac and RVU; Dir PAUL RÖMER.

Broadcasting Associations

AVROTROS: Witte Kruislaan 55, 1217 AM Hilversum; POB 2, 1200 JA Hilversum; tel. (35) 6717715; e-mail info@avro.nl; internet www .avrotros.nl; f. 1923 as Algemene Omroepvereniging AVRO; merged with Televisie en Radio Omroep Stichting (TROS) in 2014 to form AVROTROS; independent; general broadcaster; Chair. ED NIJPELS; Dir ERIC VAN STADE.

Evangelische Omroep (EO): Oude Amersfoortseweg 79, 1213 AC Hilversum; POB 21000, 1202 BA Hilversum; tel. (35) 6474747; fax (35) 6474727; e-mail eo@eo.nl; internet www.eo.nl; f. 1967; Protestant; Chair., Supervisory Bd AD DE BOER; Man. Dir ARJAN LOCK.

Katholieke Radio Omroep (KRO): 's-Gravelandseweg 80, 1217 EW Hilversum; POB 200, 1200 EA Hilversum; tel. (35) 6713911; fax (35) 6713666; e-mail infolijn@kro.nl; internet www.kro.nl; f. 1925; Catholic; 443,000 mems; Pres. Dr MARIANNE VAN DER SLOOT; Man. Dir Dr YVONNE DE HAAN.

Nederlandse Christelijke Radio Vereniging (NCRV): 's-Gravelandseweg 80, 1217 EW Hilversum; POB 25000, 1202 HB Hilversum; tel. (35) 6719911; fax (35) 6719285; e-mail info@ncrv.nl; internet www.ncrv.nl; f. 1924; Protestant; more than 550,000 mems; Chair. Dr JAN BEUMER; Dir COEN ABBENHUIS.

Omroepvereniging VARA: Wim T. Schippersplein 3, 1217 WD Hilversum; POB 175, 1200 AD Hilversum; tel. (35) 6711911; fax (35) 6711333; e-mail vara@vara.nl; internet www.vara.nl; f. 1925; social democratic and progressive; 515,000 mems; Chair. RUUD KOOLE.

Omroepvereniging VPRO: Wim T. Schippersplein 1, 1217 WD Hilversum; POB 11, 1200 JC Hilversum; tel. (35) 6712911; e-mail info@vpro.nl; internet www.vpro.nl; f. 1926; progressive; 339,623 mems; Pres. KICK VAN DER POL; Dir of Radio GERARD WALHOF; Dirs of Television KAREN DE BOK, STAN VAN ENGELEN.

Radio

There are six privately owned national radio stations that are operated on a public service basis, as well as 13 regional stations and about 330 local stations.

Radio 1: internet www.radio1.nl; 24-hour news and sports programming.

Radio 2: 's-Gravelandseweg 80, Postbus 1202, 1217 EW Hilversum; tel. (35) 6775052; fax (35) 6773311; e-mail info@radio2.nl; internet www.radio2.nl; popular music.

3FM: POB 26444, 1202 JJ Hilversum; e-mail redactie@3fm.nl; internet www.3fm.nl; contemporary music.

Radio 4: POB 26444, 1202 JJ Hilversum; e-mail info@radio4.nl; internet www.radio4.nl; popular classical music.

Radio 5: 's-Gravelandseweg 80, Postbus 25350, 1202 HJ Hilversum; tel. (35) 6775052; e-mail info@nporadio5.nl; internet www.radio5.nl; popular music, current affairs and cultural programmes; aimed at people aged over 55 years.

Radio 6: POB 26444, 1202 JJ Hilversum; e-mail redactie@radio6.nl; internet www.radio6.nl; Americana, electronica, folk, jazz and 'world' music.

Television

Television programmes are transmitted on three public channels, each of which is allocated to a different combination of broadcasting associations and other organizations, and on the commercially funded channels operated by RTL Nederland.

RTL Nederland: Barend en Van Dorpweg 2 (Media Park), 1217 WP Hilversum; POB 15016, 1200 TV Hilversum; tel. (35) 6718718; fax (35) 6236892; internet www.rtl.nl; f. 1996 as Holland Media Groep; present name adopted 2004; operates 4 television channels: RTL 4, RTL 5, RTL 7, RTL 8 and 3 digital channels: RTL Crime, RTL Telekids and RTL Lounge; subsidiary of RTL Group (Luxembourg); CEO BERT HABETS.

SBS 6: Plantage Rietlandpark 333, POB 18179, 1001 ZB Amsterdam; tel. (20) 8007000; fax (20) 8007109; e-mail sbs6@ publieksservice.sbs.nl; internet www.sbs6.nl; private broadcaster; Man. PASCAL VAN MEERTEN.

Ziggo: Atoomweg 100, 3542 AB Utrecht; tel. (88) 717 0717; internet www.ziggo.com; f. 2007; subsidiary of Liberty Global PLC; cable television provider; CEO BAPTIEST COOPMANS.

Overseas Broadcasting

BVN TV: POB 222, 1200 JG Hilversum; Bart de Graaffweg 2, 1217 ZL Hilversum; tel. (35) 6724333; fax (35) 6724343; internet www.bvn .tv; f. 1998; by Radio Nederland Wereldomroep, VRT and Nederlandse Publieke Omroep (NPO); daily international transmissions of news and cultural programmes from public service broadcasters in Flanders (Belgium) and the Netherlands; Channel Man. R. VAN BAAREN.

Radio Nederland Wereldomroep (Radio Netherlands Worldwide): Witte Kruislaan 55A, POB 222, 1200 JG Hilversum; tel. (35) 6724211; fax (35) 6724343; e-mail info@rnw.org; internet www.rnw .nl; f. 1947; public service broadcaster; daily transmissions in Arabic, Dutch, English, Indonesian, Papiamento, Portuguese, Sarnami Hindi and Spanish; programme and transcription services for foreign radio and TV stations; Radio Nederland Training Centre (for students from developing countries); Chair. Dr BERNARD BOT; Dir-Gen. ROBERT ZAAL.

Finance

(cap. = capital; res = reserves; dep. = deposits; m. = million;
br(s). = branch(es); amounts in euros)

BANKING

Central Bank

De Nederlandsche Bank NV: Westeinde 1, POB 98, 1000 AB Amsterdam; tel. (20) 5249111; fax (20) 5242500; e-mail info@dnb.nl; internet www.dnb.nl; f. 1815; nationalized 1948; merged with Pensioen- en Verzekeringskamer (Chamber of Insurance and Pensions) in 2004; cap. 500m., res 17,253m., dep. 26,290m. (Dec. 2007); Pres. Prof. KLAAS KNOT; Exec. Dirs HENK BROUWER, Prof. LEX H. HOOGDUIN, JOANNE KELLERMANN.

Principal Commercial Banks

ABN AMRO Bank NV: Gustav Mahlerlaan 10, POB 283, 1082 PP Amsterdam; tel. (20) 6289898; fax (20) 6287740; internet www .abnamro.com; f. 1991 by merger of Algemene Bank Nederland NV and Amsterdam-Rotterdam Bank NV; acquisition by consortium comprising Royal Bank of Scotland PLC (UK), Grupo Santander (Spain) and Fortis agreed in Oct. 2007; Dutch Govt replaced Fortis as stakeholder in Oct. 2008; cap. 940m., res 8,061m., dep. 234,776m. (Dec. 2013); Chair., Management Bd GERRIT ZALM; 915 brs nationally.

Amsterdam Trade Bank NV: Herengracht 469, 1017 BS Amsterdam; tel. (20) 5209429; fax (20) 5209219; e-mail info@atbank.nl; internet www.atbank.nl; f. 1994 as Stolichny Bank International NV; present name adopted 1999; 100% owned by Alfa-Bank (Russia); cap. 117.3m., res 6.5m., dep. 3,377.7m. (Dec. 2012); Chair., Supervisory Bd P. SMIDA; Man. Dirs ALEXEI V. DROVOSSEKOV, J.P.J. KONIJN, ANTON H. DEN HELD.

Bank Nederlandse Gemeenten NV (BNG): Koninginnegracht 2, POB 30305, 2500 GH The Hague; tel. (70) 3750750; fax (70) 3454743; e-mail info@bng.nl; internet www.bng.nl; f. 1914 as NV Gemeentelijke Credietbank; present name adopted 1992; 50% Govt-owned, 50% by provincial and municipal authorities; cap. 139m., res 2,281m., dep. 35,487m. (Dec. 2012); Chair. C. VAN EYKELENBURG.

Dexia Nederland BV: Piet Heinkade 1, POB 808, 1000 AV Amsterdam; tel. (20) 3485000; fax (20) 5571414; e-mail klantenservie@dexiabank.nl; internet www.dexiabank.nl; f. 2001; owned by Dexia banking group; name changed as above in 2010; Chair. B. F. M. KNÜPPE; 1 br.

Friesland Bank NV: Beursplein 1, POB 1, 8900 AA Leeuwarden; tel. (58) 2994499; fax (58) 2994591; e-mail service@frieslandbank.nl; internet www.frieslandbank.nl; f. 1913 as Coöperatieve Zuivel-Bank; present name adopted 1995; cap. 551.6m., dep. 7,077.8m.; total assets 9,481m. (Dec. 2012); Chair. Dr ROBBERT KLAASMAN; Dir A. VLASKAMP; 33 brs.

GE Artesia Bank: Herengracht 539–543, POB 274, 1000 AG Amsterdam; tel. (20) 5204911; fax (20) 6247502; e-mail info@ artesia.nl; internet www.geartesiabank.nl; f. 1863 as the Nederlandsche Credit & Depositobank; became Banque Paribas Nederland in 1984; acquired by GE Commercial Finance (USA) in 2006; cap. 73.7m., res 213.1m., dep. 1,284.9m. (Dec. 2012); CEO STEVEN PRINS; Exec. Bd mems JOHAN BENNING, JOHN-HAROLD EVERY; 2 brs.

ING Bank NV: Amstelveenseweg 500, 1081 KL Amsterdam; tel. (20) 5415411; fax (20) 5415444; e-mail ing@ing.com; internet www.ing .com; f. 1990 by merger of Nationale-Nederlanden and NMB Postbank Groep; Govt acquired an 8.5% stake in Oct. 2008; cap. 525m., res 15,864m., dep. 601,117m. (Dec. 2013); Chair., Supervisory Bd PETER A. F. W. ELVERDING; more than 400 brs.

KAS BANK NV: Nieuwezijds Voorburgwal 225, POB 24001, 1000 DB Amsterdam; tel. (20) 5575911; fax (20) 5576100; e-mail info@ kasbank.com; internet www.kasbank.com; f. 1806 by merger; present name adopted 2002; cap. 15.7m., res 185.1m., dep. 3,117.2m. (Dec. 2013); Chair., Management Bd ALBERT A. RÖELL.

F. van Lanschot Bankiers NV: Hooge Steenweg 29, POB 289, 5200 HC 's-Hertogenbosch; tel. (73) 5483548; fax (73) 5483648; e-mail vanlanschot@vanlanschot.nl; internet www.vanlanschot.nl; f. 1737; merger with CenE Bankiers NV completed 2005; cap. 41m., res 1,507.2m., dep. 11,910.1m. (Dec. 2012); Chair. KARL GUHA; 28 brs.

Mizuho Bank Nederland NV: Apollolaan 171, POB 7075, 1007 JB Amsterdam; tel. (20) 5734343; internet www.mizuhobank.com; f. 2000 by merger of Dai Ichi Kangyo Bank Europe NV and Fuji Bank Nederland NV; name changed in 2013; cap. 141.8m., res 95.6m., dep. 2,108.2m. (Dec. 2011); Chair. TAKASHI TSUKAMOTO; Pres. and CEO YASUHIRO SATO.

NIBC Bank NV: Carnegieplein 4, POB 380, 2501 BH The Hague; tel. (70) 3425625; fax (70) 3459129; e-mail info@nibc.com; internet www .nibc.com; f. 1945 as Herstelbank; present name adopted 2005; cap. 80m., res 293m., dep. 10,283m. (Dec. 2012); Chair., Management Bd and CEO PAULUS DE WILT; 1 br.

Rabobank Nederland (Coöperatieve Centrale Raiffeisen-Boerenleenbank BA): Croeselaan 18, POB 17100, 3500 HG Utrecht; tel. (30) 2160000; fax (30) 2162672; e-mail rabocomm@rn .rabobank.nl; internet www.rabobank.nl; f. 1972 by merger of Coöperatieve Centrale Raiffeisenbank of Utrecht and Coöperatieve Centrale Boerenleenbank of Eindhoven; cap. 8,012m., res 7,697m., dep. 576,644m. (Dec. 2012); Chair., Exec. Bd RINUS MINDERHOUD; 853 brs.

SNS Bank NV: Croeselaan 1, 3503 BJ Utrecht; tel. (30) 2915100; fax (30) 2915300; e-mail info@snsbank.nl; internet www.sns.nl; f. 1971 as Bank der Bondsspaarbanken NV; present name adopted 2002; part of SNS REAAL; cap. 381m., res 1,675m., dep. 49,536m. (Dec. 2012); Group Chair. and CEO S. VAN KEULEN; 256 brs.

Staalbankiers NV: Lange Houtstraat 8, POB 327, 2501 CH The Hague; tel. (70) 3101510; fax (70) 3396515; e-mail info@ staalbankiers.nl; internet www.staalbankiers.nl; f. 1916 as Bankierskantoor Staal & Co NV; present name adopted 2005; mem. of Achmea Groep; cap. 6.5m., res 171.5m., dep. 1,961.5m. (Dec. 2011); Chair. and CEO P. A. DE RUIJTER; Man. Dirs P. J. HUURMAN, D. BECK.

Bankers' Association

Nederlandse Vereniging van Banken (NVB) (Netherlands Bankers' Asscn): Singel 236, POB 3543, 1001 AH Amsterdam; tel. (20) 5502888; fax (20) 6239748; e-mail info@nvb.nl; internet www .nvb.nl; f. 1989; Chair. B. STAAL; Dir HEIN G. M. BLOCKS; 93 mems.

STOCK EXCHANGE

A supervisory authority, the Netherlands Securities Board, commenced activities in 1989.

Euronext Amsterdam: Beursplein 5, POB 19163, 1000 GD Amsterdam; tel. (20) 5504444; fax (20) 5504899; e-mail info@euronext.nl; internet www.euronext.com; subsidiary of NYSE Euronext; Euronext NV was formed by merger of Amsterdam, Paris and Brussels stock exchanges and joined in 2002 by the London futures exchange, LIFFE and the Lisbon stock exchange; merged with New York Stock Exchange in 2007 to form NYSE Euronext; unitary stock and options exchange; Chair. JOOST VAN DER DOES DE WILLEBOIS.

There are also financial futures, grain, citrus fruits and insurance bourses in the Netherlands; a 'spot' market for petroleum operates from Rotterdam.

INSURANCE

Principal Companies

AEGON Nederland: AEGONplein 50, POB 202, 2501 CE The Hague; tel. (70) 3443210; internet www.aegon.nl; f. 1983 by merger; life, accident, health, general and linked activities; Chair. MARCO B. A. KEIM.

ASR: Archimedeslaan 10, POB 2072, 3500 HB Utrecht; tel. (30) 2579111; internet www.asr.nl; f. 2000 by merger of ASR Verzekeringsgroep NV (f. 1720) and AMEV Nederland NV (f. 1883); state-owned; fmrly Fortis ASR Verzekeringsgroep NV; name changed as above in 2008; Chair. JOS BAETEN.

Delta Lloyd Verzekeringen NV: Spaklerweg 4, POB 1000, 1000 BA Amsterdam; tel. (20) 5949111; fax (20) 6937968; internet www .deltalloyd.nl; f. 1807; Chair. NIEK HOEK.

Duinrand Makelaars in Assurantiën: Ruysdaelplein 42, 2282 BJ Rijswijk; tel. (70) 3246788; fax (70) 4150507; e-mail info@duinrand .nl; internet www.duinrand.nl; f. 1990 by merger of Stalpert CV and Fiducia Assurantiën BV in 2009; home, vehicle, non-life; Man. Dir MARCEL DE WIT.

Generali Verzekeringsgroep: Diemerhof 42, 1112 XN Diemen; tel. (20) 6680000; fax (20) 3983000; e-mail uwgenerali@generali.nl; internet www.generali.nl; f. 1870; life and non-life; Gen. Dir FREEK WANSINK.

ING Groep NV: Amstelveenseweg 500, 1081 KL Amsterdam; tel. (20) 5415411; fax (20) 5760950; e-mail nanne.bos@ing.com; internet www.ing.com; f. 1963; Chair., Management Bd RALPH HAMERS.

Nationale-Nederlanden NV: Kantoor Delftse Poort, Weena 505, 3013 AL Rotterdam; tel. (70) 5130303; internet www.nn.nl; f. 1863; subsidiary of ING Groep; CEO R. H. KLIPHUIS.

SNS REAAL: Croeselaan 1, 3521 BJ Utrecht; tel. (30) 2915200; e-mail info@snsreaal.nl; internet www.snsreaal.nl; f. 1997; formed by the merger of SNS group and REAAL group; banking and insurance; life and non-life; Chair. and CEO GERARD VAN OLPHEN.

Regulatory Authority

Autoriteit Financiële Markten (AFM): Vijzelgracht 50, 1017 HS Amsterdam; tel. (20) 7972000; fax (20) 7973800; internet www.afm .nl; Chair. Dr RONALD GERRITSE.

Insurance Association

Verbond van Verzekeraars (Asscn of Insurers): Bordewijklaan 2, POB 93450, 2509 AL The Hague; tel. (70) 3338500; internet www .verzekeraars.nl; f. 1978; Chair. MARCO KEIM; Gen. Man. R. WEURDING.

Trade and Industry

GOVERNMENT AGENCIES

Autoriteit Consument & Markt (ACM) (Authority for Consumers and Markets): Muzenstraat 41, 2511 WB The Hague; POB 16326, 2500 BH The Hague; tel. (70) 7222000; fax (70) 7222355; e-mail info@ acm.nl; internet www.acm.nl; f. 2013; formed by the merger of the Independent Postal and Telecommunications Authority of Netherlands (OPTA), Netherlands Competition Authority (NMA) and the Netherlands Consumers Authority; regulation, competition, consumer protection, market analyses; Chair. CHRIS A. FONTEIJN.

Netherlands Foreign Investment Agency: Prinses Beatrixlaan 2, 2595 AL The Hague; POB 93144, 2509 AC The Hague; tel. (88) 6021142; e-mail info@nfia.nl; internet www.nfia.nl; f. 1978; govt agency; facilitates foreign direct investment.

CHAMBERS OF COMMERCE

There are 12 autonomous Chambers of Commerce and Industry in the Netherlands. The most important are:

Kamer van Koophandel Amsterdam (Chamber of Commerce and Industry for Amsterdam): De Ruyterkade 5, 1013 AA Amsterdam; POB 2852, 1000 CW Amsterdam; tel. (20) 5314000; fax (20) 5314799; internet www.amsterdam.kvk.nl; f. 1811; Pres. PIET VAN VAN STAALDUINEN.

Kamer van Koophandel Rotterdam (Chamber of Commerce for Rotterdam). Blaak 40, 3011 TA Rotterdam; POB 450, 3000 AL Rotterdam; tel. (10) 4027777, fax (10) 4145754; f. 1803; Pres. G. J. H. VAN DER VEGT.

EMPLOYERS' ORGANIZATIONS

De Maatschappij—Nederlandsche Maatschappij voor Nijverheid en Handel (NMNH) (Netherlands Society for Industry and Trade): Jan van Nassaustraat 75, 2596 BP The Hague; tel. (70) 3141940; fax (70) 3247515; e-mail info@de-maatschappij.nl; internet www.de-maatschappij.nl; f. 1777; Pres. LUUC MANNAERTS; more than 3,000 mems.

LTO-Nederland (Netherlands Agricultural Organization): Bezuidenhoutseweg 225, POB 29773, 2502 LT The Hague; tel. (70) 3382700; fax (70) 3382710; e-mail info@lto.nl; internet www.lto.nl; f. 1995; Chair. A. J. MAAT; 50,000 mems.

Nederlands Centrum voor Handelsbevordering (NCH) (Netherlands Council for Trade Promotion): Prinses Beatrixlaan 712, POB 10, 2501 CA The Hague; tel. (70) 3441544; fax (70) 3853531; e-mail info@nchnl.nl; internet www.handelsbevordering.nl; f. 1946 as Centraal Instituut voor Handelsvoorlichting; name changed as above 1975; Man. Dir JAN SIEMONS; 800 mem. cos.

De Nederlandse Tuinbouwraad (NTR) (Netherlands Horticultural Council): POB 1000, 1430 BA Aalsmeer; tel. (297) 395005; e-mail informatie@tuinbouwraad.nl; internet www.tuinbouwraad .nl; f. 1908; Chair. Dr NICO KOOMEN; Sec. GEORGE FRANKE.

NERG (Nederlands Elektronica- en Radiogenootschap): POB 39, 2260 AA Leidschendam; e-mail secretariaat@nerg.nl; internet www .nerg.nl; f. 1920; Chair. Dr A. B. SMOLDERS; Sec. ANNE VAN OTTERLO; c. 400 mems.

Vereniging VNO-NCW (Confederation of Netherlands Industry and Employers): Bezuidenhoutseweg 12, POB 93002, 2509 AA The Hague; tel. (70) 3490349; fax (70) 3490300; internet www.vno-ncw .nl; f. 1997 as merger of Verbond van Nederlandse Ondernemingen (VNO) and Nederlands Christelijk Werkgeversverbond (NCW); represents almost all sectors of the Dutch economy; Pres. HANS DE BOER; mems: 160 asscns representing more than 115,000 enterprises.

UTILITIES

Electricity

ENECO: Marten Meesweg 5, 3068 AV Rotterdam; tel. (10) 888951111; e-mail corporatecommunicatie@eneco.com; internet www.eneco.nl; Chair. J. F. (JEROEN) DE HAAS; 7,000 employees.

E.ON Benelux BV: Capelseweg 400, POB 8642, 3009 AP Rotterdam; tel. (10) 2895711; internet www.eon.nl; f. 2000; replaced Electriciteitsbedrijf Zuid Holland (f. 1941); supplies energy to large-volume customers and distributors; CEO MARKUS BOKELMANN.

Essent: Willemsplein 4, 5211 AK Den Bosch; internet www.essent .nl; f. 1999 by merger of Edon Group and Pnem Mega Group;

electricity generation and supply, also supplier of gas; CEO ERWIN VAN LAETHEM.

Nuon NV: Spaklerweg 20, POB 41920, 1009 DC Amsterdam; tel. (26) 8450271; fax (88) 0983199; internet www.nuon.com; f. 1999; energy and water; Chair., Supervisory Bd ØYSTEIN LØSETH; CEO PETER SMINK.

TenneT BV: Utrechtseweg 310, POB 718, 6800 AS Arnhem; tel. (26) 3731111; fax (26) 3731112; e-mail servicecentre@tennet.org; internet www.tennet.org; f. 1999; independent; Dutch Transmission System operator; manages 220/380-kW national grid and supplies electricity to direct suppliers; Pres. and CEO J. M. (MEL) KROON.

Gas

Full liberalization of the gas market in the Netherlands took effect in July 2004. Although retaining ownership of the main transport network, NV Nederlandse Gasunie passed the legal tasks of the national transmission system operator to a new, state-owned organization, Gas Transport Services BV, founded in July 2004.

ENECO: see Electricity.

Essent: see Electricity.

Gas Transport Services BV: Concourslaan 17, POB 181, 9700 AD Groningen; tel. (50) 5212250; fax (50) 3603036; e-mail customerdesk@gastransport.nl; internet www.gastransportservices .nl; f. 2004; independent; transmission system operator; Dir-Gen. A. J. KRIST.

NV Nederlandse Gasunie: Concourslaan 17, POB 19, 9700 MA Groningen; tel. (50) 5219111; fax (50) 5211999; e-mail communicatie@gasunie.nl; internet www.gasunie.nl; f. 2005; Chair. and CEO HAN FENNEMA.

RWE Obragas NV: Havenweg 1, POB 300, 5700 AH Helmond; tel. (49) 2594831; fax (49) 2594990.

Water

Nuon NV: see Electricity.

Vewin: Bezuidenhoutseweg 12, POB 90611, 2509 LP The Hague; tel. (70) 3490850; fax (70) 3490860; e-mail info@vewin.nl; internet www .vewin.nl; f. 1952; Chair. Dr C. P. VEERMAN; Dir R. M. BERGKAMP.

TRADE UNIONS

Central federations and affiliated unions are mainly organized on a religious, political or economic basis. The most important unions are those of the transport, metal, building and textile industries, the civil service and agriculture.

Central Federations

Christelijk Nationaal Vakverbond in Nederland (CNV) (Christian National Federation of Trade Unions): Tiberdreef 4, POB 2475, 3500 GL Utrecht; tel. (30) 7511001; fax (30) 7511109; e-mail cnvinfo@ cnv.nl; internet www.cnv.nl; f. 1909; affiliated to Int. Trade Union Confed. and European Trade Union Confed; Pres. MAURICE LIMMEN; 350,000 mems; 11 affiliated unions.

Federatie Nederlandse Vakbeweging (FNV) (Netherlands Trade Union Confederation): Naritaweg 10, POB 8456, 1005 AL Amsterdam; tel (20) 5816300; fax (20) 5816319; e-mail info@vc.fnv .nl; internet www.fnv.nl; f. 1975 as confederation of the Netherlands Federation of Trade Unions (f. 1906) and the Netherlands Catholic Trade Union Federation (f. 1909); Pres. TON HEERTS; 17 affiliated unions; 1,367,848 mems (Dec. 2011).

Vakcentrale voor Personeel (VCP) (Federation for Professionals): Bezuidenhoutseweg 60, 2594 AW The Hague; tel. (70) 3499740; e-mail info@vcp.nl; internet www.vcp.nl; f. 1974 as Vakcentrale voor Middengroepen en Hoger Personeel; name changed to present 2014; mem. of the European Trade Union Confederation; Pres. REGINALD VISSER; 66,300 mems.

Principal Unions

Consultative Organization

Stichting van de Arbeid (Labour Foundation): Bezuidenhoutseweg 60, POB 90405, 2509 LK The Hague; tel. (70) 3499577; fax (70) 3499796; e-mail info@stvda.nl; internet www.stvda.nl; f. 1945; central organ of co-operation and consultation between employers and employees; 16 bd mems; Jt Pres J. DE BOER, A. J. M. HEERTS.

Land Reclamation and Development

Without intensive land-protection schemes, nearly the whole of the north and west of the Netherlands (about one-half of the total area of the country) would be inundated by sea water twice a day. A large part of the country (including a section of the former Zuiderzee, now the IJsselmeer) has already been drained.

The Delta Plan, which was adopted in 1958 and provided for the construction of eight dams, a major canal, several locks and a system of dykes, aimed to shorten the southern coastline by 700 km and to protect the estuaries of Zeeland and Southern Holland. The final cost of the delta works project, which had originally been projected at 2,500m. guilders, totalled around 14,000m. guilders, as the result of a complex adaptation to ensure the preservation of the delta's ecological balance.

Transport

RAILWAYS

At the end of 2011 there was a total track network of 3,013 km, of which 2,266 km were electrified. The infrastructure of the Dutch railway network remains wholly under public ownership. Until early 2002 the main railway operator, NS (Nederlandse Spoorwegen), was partially privatized, but, following a sharp deterioration in the quality of service, it was taken back under government control. NS retains a majority of the passenger and freight rolling stock, and station premises, while there is a small number of additional, privately owned network service providers.

NS (Nederlandse Spoorwegen NV—Dutch Rail): POB 2025, 3500 HA Utrecht; Laan van Puntenberg 100, 3511 ER Utrecht; tel. (30) 2359111; fax (30) 2332458; internet www.ns.nl; f. 1937; partially privatized until early 2002, when the Govt reasserted management control; operates passenger services on most railway lines in the Netherlands; Pres. and Man. Dir TIMO HUGES.

Arriva Nederland: Trambaan 3, POB 626, 8440 AP Heerenveen; tel. (51) 36558511; fax (51) 3655808; internet www.arriva.nl; f. 1999; operates 100 trains and 1,000 buses, including cross-border rail services into Germany; Man. Dir ANNE HETTINGA.

DB Schenker Rail Nederland NV: Moreelspark 1, 3511 Utrecht; tel. (30) 2358347; fax (30) 2353666; e-mail jelle.rebbers@dbschenker.com; internet www.rail.dbschenker.nl; fmrly Railion Nederland; international goods transport by rail; Man. Dir Dr AART KLOMPE.

ProRail: POB 2038, 3500 GA Utrecht; Moreelsepark 3, 3511 EP Utrecht; tel. (30) 2357104; fax (30) 2359056; internet www.prorail.nl; f. 2003; manages and maintains railway infrastructure, and controls passenger and freight traffic; independent; Chair. MARION GOUT-VAN SINDEREN.

ROADS

In 2012 there were 2,658 km of motorways, 2,462 km of main roads, 7,802 km of secondary roads and 126,373 km of other roads in the Netherlands.

INLAND WATERWAYS

An extensive network of rivers and canals navigable for ships of 50 metric tons and over, totalling 6,104 km in 2010, has led to the outstanding development of Dutch inland shipping. About one-third of goods transported inside the Netherlands are carried on the canals and waterways. The main commercial waterways have a total length of 2,200 km, and account for about 40% of international freight movements in the country. Dutch inland shipping has access to Germany and France along the Rhine and its branch rivers, and to France and Belgium along the Meuse and Scheldt (including the Rhine-Scheldt link). Ocean traffic reaches Rotterdam via the New Waterway, and the 21-km long North Sea Canal connects Amsterdam to the North Sea.

SHIPPING

The Netherlands is one of the world's leading shipping countries. At the end of 2014 the flag registered fleet comprised 2,320 vessels, with a combined displacement of 8.3m. grt, of which 26 were gas tankers, 218 were fishing vessels and 709 were general cargo ships. The Port of Rotterdam complex, incorporating Europoort (for large oil tankers and bulk carriers), is the main European Union port and one of the busiest in the world.

Principal Companies

Amasus Shipping BV Delfzijl: Zijlvest 22–26, Farmsum, POB 250, 9930 Delfzijl; tel. (596) 649800; fax (596) 649801; e-mail agency@amasus.nl; internet www.amasus.nl; shipowners, managers and operators.

Koninklijke Wagenborg BV: Marktstraat 10, POB 14, 9930 AA Delfzijl; tel. (596) 636911; fax (596) 636250; e-mail info@wagenborg.com; internet www.wagenborg.com; shipowners, managers and operators; Man. Dirs Dr E. VUURSTEEN, Dr G. R. WAGENBORG.

Seatrade Groningen BV: Laan Corpus den Hoorn 200, POB 858, 9700 AW Groningen; tel. (50) 5215300; fax (50) 5215399; e-mail info@seatrade.nl; internet www.seatrade.nl; shipowners, managers and operators; Man. Dir Capt. MARK JANSEN.

Spliethoff's Bevrachtingskantoor BV: POB 409, 1000 AK Amsterdam; Radarweg 36, 1042 AA Amsterdam; tel. (20) 4488400; fax (20) 4488500; e-mail gogracht@spliethoff.com; internet www.spliethoff.com; f. 1921; shipowners, managers and operators.

Stena Line: POB 2, 3150 AA Hoek van Holland; Stationsweg 10, 3151 HS Hoek van Holland; tel. (17) 4389333; fax (17) 4389389; e-mail info.nl@stenaline.com; internet www.stenaline.nl; operates daily (day and night) ferry services for accompanied private cars, commercial freight vehicles and trailers between Hoek van Holland and Harwich (UK); Man. Dir CARL-JOHAN HAGMAN.

Van der Helm–Hudig: Orionweg 6–8, 4782 SC Moerdijk; tel. (10) 2995750; fax (10) 5069126; e-mail info@hudig.nl; internet www.hudig.com; f. 1795; international freight services; Van der Helm Transport Group took over Hudig Freight Services in 2007; Mems, Managing Bd GERARD VAN DER HELM, RICHARD VAN DER HELM, GERARD VAN DER WERFF.

Van Uden Maritime BV: POB 1123, 3000 BC, Rotterdam; Brielselaan 85, 3081 AB Rotterdam; tel. (10) 2973100; fax (10) 4851044; e-mail group@van-uden.nl; internet www.van-uden.nl; f. 1848; agencies in Rotterdam, Amsterdam; liner operators and representatives; international chartering; Man. Dir JASPER BROCADES ZAALBERG.

Vopak: Westerlaan 10, POB 863, 3000 AW Rotterdam; tel. (10) 4002911; fax (10) 4139829; internet www.vopak.com; f. 1999; Chair. EELCO HOEKSTRA.

Vroon BV: Haven Westzijde 21, 4511 AR Breskens; tel. (117) 384910; fax (117) 384218; e-mail info@vroon.nl; internet www.vroon.nl; shipowners, managers and operators; Man. Dir COCO VROON.

Wijnne & Barends' Cargadoors- en Agentuurkantonen BV: POB 123, 9930 AC Delfzijl; Handelskade Oost 5, 9934 AR Delfzijl; tel. (596) 637777; fax (596) 637790; e-mail info@wijnne-barends.nl; internet www.wijnne-barends.nl; f. 1855; became part of Spliethoff Group in 2003; shipowners, managers and operators; cargo services and agents.

Shipping Associations

Koninklijke Vereniging van Nederlandse Reders (KVNR) (Royal Asscn of Netherlands' Shipowners): Bldg Willemswerf, 15th Floor, Boompjes 40, 3011 XB Rotterdam; tel. (10) 4146001; fax (10) 2330081; e-mail info@kvnr.nl; internet www.kvnr.nl; f. 1905; Chair. T. NETELENBOS; Dir MARTIN DORSMAN; 400 mems.

Vereniging Nederlandse Scheepsbouw Industrie (VNSI) (Netherlands Shipbuilding Industry Asscn): Boompjes 40, 3011 XB Rotterdam; tel. (10) 4444333; fax (10) 2130700; e-mail info@scheepsbouw.nl; internet www.vnsi.nl; promotes Dutch shipbuilding on a national basis; Chair. J. J. C. M. VAN DOOREMALEN; 95 mems.

CIVIL AVIATION

The main airport is at Schiphol, near Amsterdam. There are also international airports at Zestienhoven for Rotterdam, Beek for Maastricht, Eelde for Groningen, and at Eindhoven.

KLM (Koninklijke Luchtvaart Maatschappij) NV (Royal Dutch Airlines): POB 7700, 1117 ZL Schiphol; Amsterdamseweg 55, 1182 GP Amstelveen; tel. (20) 6499123; fax (20) 6488069; internet www.klm.com; f. 1919; merged with Air France in 2004 to form holding co Air France–KLM; regular international air services; subsidiaries: KLM Cityhopper, transavia.com; Pres. and CEO PIETER ELBERS.

Martinair Holland NV: Piet Guilonardweg 17, 1117 EE Schiphol; tel. (20) 6011100; fax (20) 6011303; internet www.martinair.nl; f. 1958; part of KLM group; worldwide passenger and cargo services; Man. Dir DIEDERIK PEN.

transavia.com: Piet Guilonardweg 15, POB 7777, 1118 ZM Schiphol Airport; tel. (20) 6046555; internet transavia.com; f. 1965 as Transavia Limburg NV; scheduled and charter services to leisure destinations; subsidiary of KLM; Chair., Supervisory Bd HANS BAKKER; CEO BRAM GRÄBER.

Tourism

The principal tourist attractions in the Netherlands are the cosmopolitan city of Amsterdam (which receives nearly one-half of all tourist visits), the historic towns, the canals, the cultivated fields of spring flowers, the outlying islands, the art galleries and modern architecture. Some 12.8m. foreign tourists stayed in hotels and boarding houses in the Netherlands in 2013. Receipts from tourism (excluding passenger transport) totalled a provisional US $15,297m. in 2013.

NBTC Holland Marketing: Prinses Catharina Amaliastraat 5, POB 63470, 2502 JL The Hague; tel. (70) 3705705; e-mail nbtc@holland.com; internet www.holland.com; f. 1968; Man. Dir Jos VRANKEN.

Royal Dutch Touring Club ANWB: Wassenaarseweg 220, 2596 EC The Hague; tel. (88) 2692999; fax (70) 3146969; e-mail info@anwb.nl; internet www.anwb.nl; f. 1883; CEO GUIDO H. N. L. VAN WOERKOM; 55 brs in Europe; 4m. mems.

Defence

The Netherlands is a member of the North Atlantic Treaty Organization (NATO). Conscription to the armed forces was ended in August 1996, and a gradual reduction in the number of military personnel is ongoing. The total strength of the armed forces, as assessed at November 2013, was 37,400: army 20,850; navy 8,500; air force 8,050. In addition, the Royal Military Constabulary numbered 5,900. Total reserves stood at 3,200 (army 2,700; air force 420; navy 80) and 80 military police. In August 1995 a joint Dutch-German army corps, numbering 28,000 troops, was inaugurated, and in January 1996 the operational units of the Royal Netherlands Navy merged with the Belgian navy under the command of the Admiral of the Benelux. In November 2004 the European Union agreed to create a number of 'battlegroups' (each comprising about 1,500 men), which could be deployed at short notice to carry out peacekeeping activities at crisis points around the world. The battlegroups, two of which were to be ready for deployment at any one time, following a rotational schedule, reached full operational capacity from 1 January 2007.

General Government Defence Expenditure: estimated at €8,000m. in 2015.

Chief of Defence Staff: Gen. TOM MIDDENDORP.

Secretary-General of Defence Staff: ANTONIUS HERMANUS CHRISTOFFEL (TON) ANNINK.

Education

There are two types of school in the Netherlands: public schools, which are maintained by municipalities, and attended by about one-third of all school children; and private schools, which are, for the most part, denominational and are attended by almost two-thirds of the school-going population. Both types of school are fully subsidized by the state. Schools are administered by school boards, responsible to the local authorities or to the private organizations that operate them, thus providing teachers with considerable freedom. The Ministry of Education, Culture and Science, advised by an education council, is responsible for educational legislation and its enforcement.

Full-time education is compulsory in the Netherlands from five to 16 years of age, and part-time education is compulsory for a further two years. Pre-primary education, also known as early childhood education, is offered to educationally disadvantaged children between the ages of two and five years. Almost 99% of children of four years of age attend Basisschool, although it is not compulsory until the age of five years. Primary education lasts for eight years and is followed by various types of secondary education. Secondary education lasts to the age of 18 years, and is provided free of charge. In 2011/12 total enrolment in primary education included 100% of children in the relevant age-group, while total enrolment in secondary education included 89% of children in the relevant age-group. Pre-university schools provide various six-year courses that prepare pupils for university education. General secondary education comprises senior and junior secondary schools, providing five- and four-year courses that prepare pupils for higher vocational institutes and senior secondary vocational education, respectively. In all types there is latitude in the choice of subjects taken. Higher education comprises higher professional education (hoger beroepsonderwijs—HBO) and university education (wetenschappelijk onderwijs—WO). In 2012/13 some 241,000 students were enrolled at the Netherlands' 13 universities, while some 422,000 students were enrolled at institutes of higher vocational education. In addition, students can register with the Open Universiteit Nederland (Open University).

Total government expenditure on education was €34,327m. in 2013.

NETHERLANDS DEPENDENCIES

Ministry of the Interior and Kingdom Relations: Schedeldoekshaven 200, POB 20011, 2500 EA The Hague; tel. (70) 4266426; fax (70) 3639153; internet www.rijksoverheid.nl/ministeries/bzk.
Minister of the Interior and Kingdom Relations: RONALD PLASTERK.

Netherlands Special Municipalities

Following the dissolution of the Netherlands Antilles on 10 October 2010, Bonaire, Saba and Sint (St) Eustatius adopted the status of bijzondere gemeente (special municipalities) within the Kingdom of the Netherlands.

BONAIRE

Introductory Survey

Bonaire lies about 80 km (50 miles) off the coast of Venezuela. The territory, some 288 sq km (111 sq miles), consists of Bonaire and, nestled in its western crescent, the uninhabited islet of Klein Bonaire. Together with Aruba and Curaçao, Bonaire forms the Benedenwindse Eilands or Leeward Islands. The climate is tropical, moderated by the sea, with an average annual temperature of 27.5°C (81°F) and little rainfall. The official languages are Dutch and Papiamento (a mixture of Dutch, Spanish, Portuguese, English, Arawak Indian and several West African dialects), which is the dominant language of the Leeward Islands. Almost all of the inhabitants, which numbered 18,413 at 1 January 2014, profess Christianity, predominantly Roman Catholicism. The population density of the territory was 63.9 per sq km in January 2014. The state flag (proportions 2 by 3) has a large blue triangle in the lower right corner and a smaller yellow triangle in the upper left corner. The triangles are separated by a white strip, inside of which is a black compass and a red six-pointed star (each point represents one of the original six villages of Bonaire). The capital is Kralendijk, on the western coast of the island.

The Leeward Islands, already settled by communities of Arawak Indians, were discovered by the Spanish in 1499 and were seized by the Dutch in the 1630s. After frequent changes in possession, the islands (including Aruba) were finally confirmed as Dutch territory in 1816. Together with the Windward Islands (comprising Sint (St) Eustatius, Saba and Sint (St) Maarten), Bonaire was administered as Curaçao and Dependencies between 1845 and 1948. Slavery was abolished in 1863. In 1954 a Charter gave the federation of six islands full autonomy in domestic affairs, and declared it to be an integral part of the Kingdom of the Netherlands.

From 1954 until 2010 Bonaire was a constituent part of the Netherlands Antilles. Political allegiances were generally divided along island, rather than policy, lines. This led to a series of unstable coalitions governing the federation. By the early 1990s it had become clear that although the metropolitan Dutch Government was unwilling to allow the complete disintegration of the federation, it would consider a less centralized system, or the creation of two federations in the separate island groups.

A referendum on status was conducted on Bonaire in October 1994 (simultaneous plebiscites were also held on St Maarten, St Eustatius and Saba). Some 88% of voters favoured continued federation with the Netherlands.

On 8 October 2004 the Jesurun Commission, established by the Dutch and Antillean Governments and headed by Edsel Jesurun (a former Governor of the Netherlands Antilles), recommended the dissolution of the Netherlands Antilles. The Commission proposed that Bonaire, along with Saba and St Eustatius, should be directly administered by the Dutch Government. In September, in an official referendum, a majority of voters (59%) on Bonaire strongly favoured becoming part of the Netherlands. On 3 December 2005 a preliminary agreement with the Dutch Government that the extant federation be dissolved by 1 July 2007 was duly signed in Curaçao. Under the new structure, Bonaire was to become a koninkrijkseilanden, or kingdom island, with direct ties to the Netherlands, a status equivalent to that of a Dutch province. The future status of Bonaire was subsequently refined to that of a bijzondere gemeente, or special municipality, similar in most ways to other metropolitan Dutch municipalities, although with separate social security and currency arrangements.

An agreement confirming Bonaire's impending accession to special municipality status was signed in The Hague, Netherlands, on 12 October 2006, and included provisions for citizens of the island to participate in Dutch national and local elections and in the election of candidates to the European Parliament. A further transition accord was signed by the Netherlands Antilles central Government, the Island Council of Bonaire, and the Netherlands on 12 February 2007, envisaging Bonaire's complete secession from the federation. Under the terms of this covenant, the Netherlands was to pledge over NA Fl. 1,000m. to facilitate the process of disintegration, with each participating island receiving individual allocations. The metropolitan administration also agreed to write off almost three-quarters of the Antilles' debt.

A meeting was held in Curaçao on 15 December 2008 at which the Dutch Prime Minister, Jan Peter Balkenende, and the Antillean premier, Emily de Jongh-Elhage, signed an agreement confirming the new status of the island. In September 2009, at a meeting of the Dutch State Secretary for the Interior and Kingdom Relations, Ank Bijleveld-Schouten, and representatives of the Netherlands Antilles, it was agreed that the target date for dissolution of the federation would be 10 October 2010.

The Dutch Government postponed the payment of Bonaire's debt in October 2009, after the island's recently formed Executive Council, led by the Partido Demokrátiko Boneriano (PDB), proposed a 'free association' status with the Netherlands, involving greater independence, rather than the planned integration as a municipality. The Dutch Government asserted the island could adopt municipality status, as planned, or assume full self-governance. None the less, the Executive Council proceeded to schedule a referendum on its proposal. Acting on the advice of Bonaire's Lieutenant-Governor, in February 2010 Netherlands Antilles Governor Fritz Goedgedrag cancelled the referendum due to be conducted in March, on the grounds that it contravened international law, as Dutch nationals who had only resided on Bonaire since January 2007 would have been barred from voting. Nevertheless, the referendum was held in December 2010, although the low turnout meant the result was declared invalid. The Unión Patriótiko Boneriano (UPB), which had taken office in September, had urged the electorate to boycott the plebiscite.

On 10 October 2010, following the formal dissolution of the Netherlands Antilles, Bonaire officially became a special municipality of the Netherlands. The US dollar was formally adopted as the island's currency from 1 January 2011, replacing the Netherlands Antilles guilder; the Island Council had opposed the introduction of the euro, the currency of the Netherlands. As part of the Kingdom of the Netherlands, Bonaire became an Overseas Territory in association with the European Union (EU, see p. 271).

At elections to the Island Council on 2 March 2011, the UPB secured four of the nine seats available. The PDB won three seats and the recently formed Movementu Boneiru Liber and Partido Pro Hustisia & Union each won one seat. A coalition government was subsequently formed. Lydia Emerencia was sworn in as the island's new Lieutenant-Governor in March 2012.

Owing to Bonaire's change in administrative status, the island's residents were henceforth entitled to vote in Dutch polls. The islanders' first opportunity to exercise this right came on 12 September 2012, when elections to the Tweede Kamer (Second Chamber—the lower house of the Dutch parliament) were conducted. The Partij van de Arbeid received 23.9% of the valid votes cast in Bonaire, while the Volkspartij voor Vrijheid en Democratie (VVD) garnered 20.9%, the Christen Democratisch Appèl 19.3% and Democraten 66 (D66) 11.5%. The rate of participation by the electorate was just 24.8% (compared with 74.6% nationwide).

Pablo James Kroon was elected as UPB leader in September 2013, replacing Ramonsito Booi. On 26 November the Island Council approved a motion of no confidence in Emerencia, and she submitted her resignation as Lieutenant-Governor three days later. Deputies claimed that Emerencia had, *inter alia*, assumed a unilateral decision-making style and spent too much time travelling abroad on official business. However, some observers suspected that the UPB had orchestrated the no confidence vote in retaliation for the active support that the Lieutenant-Governor had given to various corruption investigations on the island, which had resulted in the prosecution of two senior UPB politicians—Booi and former Executive Council member Burney El Hage. (The Dutch Kingdom Representative in Bonaire, Saba and St Eustatius, Wilbert Stolte, tendered his resignation in September, with effect from 1 May 2014, following accusations that he had misappropriated public funds and that he had intervened in the Bonaire corruption inquiries in an attempt to protect his allies in the UPB.) Emerencia formally stood down on 1 March 2014; she was replaced as Lieutenant-Governor by Edison Rijna. Later that month the Island Council unanimously endorsed a proposal to hold another referendum on Bonaire's constitutional status. The timing and structure of the planned plebiscite were under discussion in early 2015.

Elections to the European Parliament took place in Bonaire on 22 May 2014. The 'ikkiesvooreerlijk.eu' list secured 26.9% of the local ballot, compared with 22.0% for D66 and 15.7% for the VVD. Turnout, however, was just 12.0%.

Island Council elections were held on 18 March 2015. The PDB, UPB and the Movementu di Pueblo Boneriano each won three of the nine council seats, according to preliminary results. Turnout was 78%.

Bonaire's economy is dependent on tourism and petroleum transfers. Approximately 82,000 air passenger arrivals were recorded in 2012, with the majority travelling from the Netherlands and the USA. There was a 5.8% increase in visitor numbers during the first half of 2013 following a sharp rise in tourist arrivals from Latin America. Although no refining takes place on the island, the Bonaire Petroleum Corporation stores oil for transfer from large tankers to smaller ones and is a significant contributor to the economy. Bonaire has reserves of limestone and salt, which are mined; salt production averages 400,000 metric tons per year. There is also a textile factory. Bonaire is a major exporter of aloes. The unemployment rate in 2012 was recorded at 5.8%. In 2014 the annual inflation rate was 1.5%. Gross domestic product totalled US $372m. in 2012.

PUBLIC HOLIDAYS

In addition to the holidays of the metropolitan Netherlands, Bonaire celebrates the following public holidays.

2016: 8 February (Carnival), 1 May (Labour Day), 6 September (Flag Day), 15 December (Kingdom Day).

For statistical information on Bonaire, see the Statistical Survey in Curaçao.

Directory

The Government

HEAD OF STATE

King of the Netherlands: HM King WILLEM-ALEXANDER.

Lieutenant-Governor: EDISON E. RIJNA, Bestuurskantoor, Wilhelminaplein 1, Kralendijk; tel. 717-5330; fax 717-2824; e-mail gezag@bonairelive.com; internet www.bonairegov.an.

ISLAND COUNCIL
(May 2015)

The Government is formed by a coalition of the Movementu di Pueblo Boneriano (MPB), the Unión Patriótiko Boneriano (UPB) and the Partido Demokrátiko Boneriano (PDB).

Island Council: ELVIS TJIN ASJOE (MPB), DAISY COFFIE (MPB), JOSELITO STATIA (MPB), PABLO JAMES KROON (UPB), ESTHER J. BERNABELA (UPB), EDSEL S. WINKLAAR (UPB), CLARK ABRAHAM (PDB), ROBBY BEUKENBOOM (PDB), MARUGIA JANGA (PDB).

Election, 18 March 2015

Party			Seats
Movementu di Pueblo Boneriano (MPB)	.	. .	3
Partido Demokrátiko Boneriano (PDB)	.	. .	3
Unión Patriótiko Boneriano (UBP)	.	. . .	3
Total	. . . .		9

Island Secretary: M. N. GONZALEZ.

Executive Council: EDISON E. RIJNA (Lt-Governor), S. CHIRINO-FELIDA, PABLO JAMES KROON, EDSEL S. WINKLAAR.

MINISTRY

National Office for the Caribbean Netherlands Bonaire (Rijksdienst Caribisch Nederland Bonaire): Kaya International z/n, POB 357, Kralendijk; tel. 715-8303; fax 715-8330; e-mail info@rijksvertegenwoordiger.nl; internet www.rijksdienstcn.com; Kingdom Rep. GILBERT ISABELLA.

Political Organizations

Frakshon Santana: Kralendijk; Leader RAFAEL SANTANA.

Movementu Boneiru Liber (MBL) (Free Bonaire Movement): Passangrahan, Plasa Reina Wilhelmina, Kralendijk; tel. 717-4008; e-mail movementu@gmail.com; f. 2010; Leader BENITO DIRKSZ.

Movementu di Pueblo Boneriano (MPB): Kralendijk; Leader ELVIS TJIN ASJOE.

Partido Demokrátiko Boneriano (PDB) (Bonaire Democratic Party): Kaya America 13A, POB 294, Kralendijk; tel. 717-8903; fax 717-5923; e-mail info@partido-demokrat.org; internet partido-demokrat.org; f. 1954; also known as Democratische Partij—Bonaire (DPB); liberal, promotes self-governance for Bonaire; known as the Aliansa Demokrátika Bonairiana in 2009–10; Leader CLARK ABRAHAM.

Partido Pro Hustisia & Union (PHU): Kralendijk; tel. 796-2650; e-mail m.bijkerk@telbonet.an; internet www.phubonaire.com; f. 2010; Pres. MICHIEL BIJKERK.

Unión Patriótiko Boneriano (UPB) (Patriotic Union of Bonaire): Kaya Sabana 22, Kralendijk; tel. 717-8906; e-mail info@votaupb.com; internet votaupb.com; f. 1969; Christian democratic; Leader PABLO JAMES KROON.

Judicial System

Legal authority is exercised by the Joint Court of Justice of Aruba, Curaçao and St Maarten and of Bonaire, St Eustatius and Saba. Its headquarters are in Curaçao. The Joint Court hears civil, criminal and administrative cases in the first instance and on appeal.

Joint Court of Justice: Plasa Reina Wilhelmina (Fort Oranje), Kralendijk; tel. 717-8172; fax 717-5779; e-mail griffiebonaire@caribjustitia.org; internet www.gemhofvanjustitie.org/vestigingen/bonaire; hears cases in the first instance; Pres. EVERT JAN VAN DER POEL.

Attorney-General: GUUS SCHRAM.

Religion

Almost all of the inhabitants profess Christianity, predominantly Roman Catholicism.

The Press

Arco Bonaire: Kaya Isabel 1, Kralendijk; tel. 717-2427; e-mail info@arcocarib.com; internet www.arcocarib.com; magazine; Editor M. BIJKERK.

Bonaire Reporter: Kaya Gobernador Nicolaas Debrot 200-6, POB 407, Kralendijk; tel. and fax 786-6125; fax 786-6518; e-mail info@bonairenews.com; internet www.bonairereporter.com; English; weekly; Publ. GEORGE DESALVO; Editor-in-Chief LAURA DESALVO.

Broadcasting and Communications

TELECOMMUNICATIONS

Chippie Bonaire: Kaya Caracas 2, Kralendijk; tel. 717-0117; fax 717-0119; e-mail info@uts.an; internet www.chippie.an; mobile telecommunication provider; subsidiary of UTS Group, Curaçao.

Digicel Bonaire: Kaya Grandi 26, Kralendijk; tel. 717-4400; fax 717-4466; e-mail customercare@digicelcuracao.com; internet www.digicelbonaire.com; f. 1999; Chair. DENIS O'BRIEN; CEO (Dutch Caribbean) HANS LUTE.

Telbo NV (Telefonia Bonairiano NV): Kaya Libertador Simon Bolivar 8, Kralendijk; tel. 715-7000; fax 717-5007; e-mail info@telbo.net; internet www.telbo.net; f. 1983; fixed-line and internet services; Gen. Man. GILBERT DE BREE.

BROADCASTING

Radio

Radiodifusión Boneriana NV: Kaya Gobernador Nicolaas Debrot 2, Kralendijk; tel. 717-5947; fax 717-8220; e-mail vozdibonaire@gmail.com; internet www.vozdibonaire.com; f. 1962; operates Alpha FM, Mega FM and Voz di Bonaire; Owner FELICIANO DA SILVA PILOTO.

Trans World Radio (TWR): Kaya Gobernador Nicolaas Debrot 64, Kralendijk; tel. 717-8800; fax 717-8808; e-mail 800am@twr.org; internet www.twr.org; f. 1964; religious, educational and cultural station; programmes to South, Central and North America, and Caribbean, in 5 languages; Pres. LAUREN LIBBY; Station Dir JOSEPH BARKER.

Television
Relay stations provide Bonaire with television programmes from Curaçao.

Finance

BANKING

Regulatory Authority

College Financieel Toezicht (CFT): De Rouvilleweg 39, Willemstad, Curaçao; tel. (9) 461-9081; e-mail info@cft.an; internet www.cft.an; f. 2007; bd of financial supervision; oversees financial administration in Bonaire, Sint Eustatius and Saba; Chair. AGE BAKKER; Rep. of Bonaire, Saba and St Eustatius THEODORE M. PANDT.

Commercial Banks

Girobank, NV: 12 Kaya L.D. Gerharts, Kralendijk; tel. 717-8115; e-mail info@gironet.com; internet www.girobank.net; f. 1965; Pres. and CEO ERIC GARCIA; Man. JOAN SILIE.

Maduro & Curiel's Bank (Bonaire), NV: 1 Kaya L. D. Gerharts, Kralendijk; tel. 715-5520; e-mail info@mcbbonaire.com; internet www.mcbbonaire.com; Man. Dir LEONARD DOMACASSÉ.

Banking Associations

Bonaire Bankers' Association: Maduro & Curiel's Bank (Bonaire) NV, Kaya L. D. Gerharts 1, POB 366, Kralendijk; tel. 717-5520; fax 717-5884; Man. Dir RUDY GOMEZ.

INSURANCE

ENNIA Bonaire: Centrumgebied z/n, POB 349, Kralendijk; tel. 717-8546; fax 717-7546; e-mail mail@ennia.com; internet www.ennia-bonaire.com; f. 1948; part of ENNIA Caribe Holding, NV; Pres. RALPH PALM.

NAGICO Bonaire (National General Insurance Corpn): Kaya Gilberto F. Betico Croes 2, Kralendijk; tel. 717-3022; fax 717-3029; e-mail info.bonaire@nagico.com; internet www.nagico.com; Exec. Dir DETLEF HOOYBOER.

RSA Bonaire: Bonaire District Plaza, Unit 4, Kaya Gobernador Nicolaas Debrot, Kralendijk; tel. 717-8811; fax 717-2112; e-mail info@dc.myguardiangroup.com; internet myguardiangroup.cw; f. 1889; Group Pres. STEVEN MARTINA.

Trade and Industry

CHAMBER OF COMMERCE

Bonaire Chamber of Commerce and Industry: Kaya Grandi 67, POB 52, Kralendijk; tel. 717-5595; fax 717-8995; e-mail office@kvkbonaire.com; internet www.bonairechamber.com; Chair. MARISELLA CROES-ODUBER.

UTILITIES

Contour Global Bonaire: Kaminda Turistiko 1000, Postbus 281, Kralendijk; tel. 699-2802; e-mail caribbean.inquiry@contourglobal.com; internet www.ecopowerbonaire-bv.com; f. 2007 as EcoPower Bonaire BV; sustainable energy producer; acquired by ContourGlobal, LLC (USA) and changed name as above in May 2013; 24-MW integrated wind and diesel power plant; Plant Man. VINCENT KOOIJ.

Water & Energiebedrijf Bonaire (WEB) NV: Kaya Carlos A. Nicolaas 3, POB 381, Kralendijk; tel. 715-8244; fax 717-8756; e-mail

web@webbonaire.com; internet webbonaire.com; f. 1978; Dir ALFREDO KOOLMAN.

TRADE UNIONS

Algemene Federatie van Bonaireaanse Werknemers (AFBW): Kaya Korona 13, Kralendijk; tel. 717-5437; Pres. NILCO ROLLAN.

Federashon Bonaireana di Trabou (FEDEBON): Kaya Krabè 6, POB 324, Nikiboko; tel. and fax 717-8845; e-mail geroldbernabela@bonairelive.com; Pres. GEROLD BERNABELA.

Transport

There are no railways, but Bonaire has a network of all-weather roads.

SHIPPING
There are no ferry services between Bonaire and neighbouring islands; however, there are chartered boats. The port of Kralendijk has piers for dry cargo transfer and cruise vessels. At 31 December 2014 the flag registered fleet comprised one vessel.

Bonaire Port Authority, NV: Fort Oranje, Harbour Office, Kralendijk; tel. 717-8151; fax 717-8797.

Rocargo Services Bonaire, NV: Kaya Industria No. 12, POB 20, Kralendijk; tel. 717-8922; fax 717-8524; e-mail rocargobonaire@rocargo.com; internet www.rocargo.com; f. 1982; ship and liner agency, cargo and freight handlers; Man. MARIELA GOELOE DORTALINA.

CIVIL AVIATION
Bonaire International Airport, NV (Flamingo Airport) at Kralendijk has a runway of 2,880 m (9,449 ft). Bonaire is served by numerous airlines, linking the island with destinations in the Caribbean, Europe, the USA and South America.

Bonaire International Airport, NV (Flamingo Airport): Plasa Medardo SV Thielman 1, Kralendijk; tel. 717-5600; fax 717-5607; e-mail info@flamingoairport.com; internet www.flamingoairport.com; f. 1945; Man. Dir L. A. LAPLACE; CEO MICHAEL NICOLAAS.

Tourism

Bonaire's attractions include scuba-diving and snorkelling facilities, flamingo and donkey sanctuaries, Bonaire National Marine Park, the historic rock paintings of Caquieto Indians and the white, sandy beaches. In 2012 visitor arrivals to the island by air totalled 82,000. In 2010 tourism receipts totalled an estimated US $121m.

Bonaire Hotel and Tourism Association (BONHATA): Kaya Soeur Bartola 15A, POB 358, Kralendijk; tel. 717-5134; fax 717-8534; e-mail info@bonhata.org; internet www.ilovebonaire.com; f. 1980; CEO IRENE DINGJAN.

Tourism Corporation Bonaire (TCB): Kaya Grandi 2, Kralendijk; tel. 717-8322; fax 717-8408; e-mail info@tourismbonaire.com; internet www.tourismbonaire.com; Dir ETHSEL PIETERNELLA.

Defence

The Netherlands is responsible for the defence of Bonaire.

Education

The education system is the same as that of the Netherlands. Dutch is the principal language of instruction, although instruction in Papiamento is also used in primary schools.

SABA

The small, volcanic island of Saba lies in the north-eastern Caribbean Sea, about 27 km (17 miles) north-west of Sint (St) Eustatius. With Sint (St) Maarten, 45 km (28 miles) north of Saba, these three islands comprise the Bovenwindse Eilands, or Windward Islands, although actually in the Leeward group of the Lesser Antilles. Saba is 13 sq km (5 sq miles) in area. The climate is tropical, moderated by the sea, with an average annual temperature of 27.5°C (81°F) and little rainfall. English is the official and principal language, although Dutch is also spoken. Almost all of the inhabitants, of which there were 1,846 in January 2014, profess Christianity, predominantly Roman Catholicism. The population density of the territory was 142 inhabitants per sq km in January 2014. The state flag (proportions 2 by 3) is divided into four triangles, two red at the top, two blue at the

bottom. In the centre of the flag is a white diamond, with a yellow five-pointed star in the centre. The capital is The Bottom.

The Dutch captured Saba, once settled by Carib Indians, in 1640. After frequent changes in possession, the islands were finally confirmed as Dutch territory in 1816, administered by the Dutch West Indian Company. Owing to its difficult terrain, Saba remained sparsely populated. In 1845 Saba was ceded to the Dutch Crown and administered as Curaçao and Dependencies, comprising the Windward Islands and the three territories of the Leeward Islands—Aruba, Bonaire and Curaçao. In 1954 a Charter gave the federation of six islands full autonomy in domestic affairs, and declared the Netherlands Antilles to be an integral part of the Kingdom of the Netherlands.

Despite the 1954 Charter, there were demands for further self-government from elements within the federation for most of the latter half of the 20th century. A referendum on the status issue was held on Saba in October 1994; 91% of voters opted for continued membership of the Antillean federation. Nevertheless, similar plebiscites in the other constituent members of the Netherlands Antilles produced differing results and in October 2004 the Jesurun Commission, established by the Dutch and Antillean Governments and headed by Edsel Jesurun (a former Governor of the Netherlands Antilles), recommended the dissolution of the federation. The Commission proposed that Saba (as well as Bonaire and St Eustatius) should be directly administered by the Dutch Government. In November, in another official referendum, a majority of voters (86%) on Saba again voted in favour of becoming part of the Netherlands. On 3 December 2005 a preliminary agreement with the Dutch Government that the extant federation be dissolved by 1 July 2007 was duly signed in Curaçao. Under the new structure, Saba was to become a koninkrijkseilanden, or kingdom island, with direct ties to the Netherlands, a status equivalent to that of a Dutch province. The future status of Saba was subsequently refined to that of a bijzondere gemeente, or special municipality, similar in most ways to other metropolitan Dutch municipalities, although with separate social security and currency arrangements.

An agreement confirming Saba's impending accession to special municipality status was signed in The Hague, Netherlands, on 12 October 2006, and included provisions for citizens of the island to participate in Dutch national and local elections and in the election of candidates to the European Parliament. A further transition accord was signed by the Netherlands Antilles central Government, the Island Council, and the Netherlands on 12 February 2007, envisaging the island's complete secession from the federation. Under the terms of this covenant, the Netherlands was to pledge over NA Fl. 1,000m. to facilitate the process of disintegration. The metropolitan administration also agreed to write off almost three-quarters of the Antilles' debt. A meeting was held in Curaçao on 15 December 2008 at which the Dutch Prime Minister, Jan Peter Balkenende, and the Antillean premier, Emily de Jongh-Elhage, signed an agreement confirming the new status of the island.

The Antilles Government's announcement in August 2009 that a general election would be held in January 2010, despite plans for the dissolution of the Netherlands Antilles to take place later that year, prompted the Executive Council of Saba to declare its intention to become independent from the Netherlands Antilles. The Island Council argued that the central Government lacked the political will to complete the transition process. However, it was generally agreed that Saba's secession from the federation at this stage would not be legally feasible. In September 2009 it was agreed that the target date for dissolution of the Netherlands Antilles would be 10 October 2010, at which date Saba would become a special municipality of the Netherlands. The US dollar was formally adopted as the island's currency from 1 January 2011, replacing the Netherlands Antilles guilder; the Island Council had opposed the introduction of the euro, the currency of the Netherlands.

Elections to Saba's Island Council were held on 2 March 2011. The Windward Islands People's Movement (WIPM) won four of the five available seats, while the Saba Labour Party (SLP) secured the remaining seat.

Owing to Saba's change in administrative status, the island's residents were henceforth entitled to vote in Dutch polls. The islanders' first opportunity to exercise this right came on 12 September 2012, when elections to the Tweede Kamer (Second Chamber—the lower house of the Dutch parliament) were conducted. Democraten 66 (D66) received 54.5% of the valid votes cast in Saba, while the Partij van de Arbeid garnered 19.8% and the Socialistische Partij (SP) 9.0%. The rate of participation by the electorate was just 28.4%.

Elections to the European Parliament took place in Saba on 22 May 2014. D66 secured 47.8% of the local ballot and the SP obtained 23.0%. Turnout, however, was just 14.2%.

Elections to the Island Council were held on 18 March 2015. The WIPM secured three council seats, while the SLP won two seats.

As Saba is a dormant volcano with rocky shores and only one rocky beach, tourism was slow to develop. However, the island has become known for its eco-tourism opportunities, and tourism has been steadily increasing in recent years, becoming the largest contributor to the economy. The largest number of tourists came from the Netherlands, but the USA and Canada were also significant markets. Approximately 11,000 air passenger arrivals were recorded in 2012, with the majority travelling from the Netherlands and the USA. The Saba University School of Medicine has grown in importance. The institution created about 200 jobs (directly and indirectly) and contributed some US $4.8m. to the economy in 2011. Agriculture remains an important sector, primarily livestock and vegetables, especially potatoes. Saba lace continues to be sold on the island. The unemployment rate in 2012 was recorded at 3.9%. Electricity production in 2013 totalled 9.2m. kWh. In 2013 the inflation rate was 1.2%; inflation rose by 2.0% in 2014. Gross domestic product (GDP) was estimated at $43m. in 2012, with GDP per head totalling $21,900. As a special municipality, Saba must maintain a balanced budget, supervised by the financial supervision authority, the College Financieel Toezicht. Any future economic development of the island depended on, in particular, growth in tourism and the medical school remaining one of the island's economic pillars.

Lieutenant-Governor: JONATHAN JOHNSON, 1 Power St, The Bottom; tel. 416-3311; fax 416-3274; e-mail governor@sabagov.nl; internet www.sabagovernment.com.

Island Council: ROLANDO RICARDO WILSON, CARL BUNCAMPER, EVITON HEYLIGER, ISHMAEL LEVENSTONE, MONIQUE WILSON.

Island Secretary: WIM VAN TWUIJVER.

Executive Council: BRUCE PETER ZAGERS, CHRISTOPHER JOHNSON.

National Office for the Caribbean Netherlands Saba (Rijksdienst Caribisch Nederland Saba): Captain Mathew Levenstone St, Old Antique Inn, The Bottom; tel. 416-3934; e-mail info@rijksdienstcn.com; internet www.rijksdienstcn.com; Kingdom Rep. (resident in Bonaire) GILBERT ISABELLA.

SINT EUSTATIUS

Sint (St) Eustatius (also known as Statia—from the original Spanish name St Anastasia) is a volcanic island, some 21 sq km (8 sq miles) in area, in the north-eastern Caribbean Sea, about 20 km north-east of Saint Christopher (St Kitts) and Nevis. Together with Saba and Sint (St) Maarten, St Eustatius comprises the Bovenwindse Eilands or Windward Islands (although actually in the Leeward group of the Lesser Antilles). The climate is tropical, moderated by the sea, with an average annual temperature of 27.5°C (81°F) and little rainfall. English is the official and principal language, although Dutch is also spoken. There were 4,020 inhabitants of St Eustatius in January 2014, giving a population density of 191.4 people per sq km. Almost all of the inhabitants profess Christianity, predominantly Protestantism. The state flag (proportions 2 by 3) is divided into four five-sided blue squares with red borders. In the centre of the flag is a white diamond, in which an outline of the island appears. At the top of the diamond is a five-pointed gold star. The capital is Oranjestad.

The Dutch settled the Windward Islands, once settled by Carib Indians, in the mid-17th century. St Eustatius came under Dutch control in 1635. After frequent changes in possession, the islands were finally confirmed as Dutch territory in 1816. Together with the Leeward Islands (comprising Aruba, Bonaire and Curaçao), the Windward islands were administered as Curaçao and Dependencies between 1845 and 1948. In the early 18th century St Eustatius prospered as a trading centre and transshipment centre for African slaves. In 1954 a Charter gave the federation of six islands full

autonomy in domestic affairs, and declared it to be an integral part of the Kingdom of the Netherlands.

Political allegiance within the federation was traditionally along island, rather than party lines. These divisions increased following Aruba's secession from the federation in 1986. Demands for further autonomy increased in Curaçao and St Maarten, although the population of St Eustatius remained broadly in favour of maintaining the status quo. In a referendum on status held in October 1994 some 86% of voters opted for continued membership of the Antillean federation. Nevertheless, plebiscites in the other constituent parts of the federation produced differing results, and movements to obtain autonomy in Curaçao and St Maarten increased. In October 2004 the Jesurun Commission, established by the Dutch and Antillean Governments and headed by Edsel Jesurun (a former Governor of the Netherlands Antilles), recommended the dissolution of the federation; support for the continued union had, it was argued, virtually disintegrated on most of the islands. The Commission proposed that Curaçao and St Maarten should become autonomous states within the Netherlands (i.e. have *status aparte*), while Saba, Bonaire and St Eustatius should be directly administered by the Dutch Government. A further referendum on the constitutional futures of St Eustatius took place on 8 April 2005: from a voter turnout of 55%, 76% of the electorate favoured remaining part of the Netherlands Antilles, while 20% voted for closer ties with the Netherlands and 1% preferred to seek complete independence. On 3 December 2005 a preliminary agreement with the Dutch Government that the extant federation be dissolved by 1 July 2007 was duly signed in Curaçao. Under the new structure, St Eustatius was to become a koninkrijkseilanden, or kingdom island, with direct ties to the Netherlands, a status equivalent to that of a Dutch province. The future status of St Eustatius was subsequently refined to that of a bijzondere gemeente, or special municipality, similar in most ways to other metropolitan Dutch municipalities, although with separate social security and currency arrangements.

An agreement confirming St Eustatius's impending accession to special municipality status was signed in The Hague, Netherlands, on 12 October 2006, and included provisions for citizens of the island to participate in Dutch national and local elections and in the election of candidates to the European Parliament. A further transition accord was signed by the Netherlands Antilles central Government, the Island Council of St Eustatius, and the Netherlands on 12 February 2007, envisaging the island's complete secession from the federation. Under the terms of this covenant, the Netherlands was to pledge over NA Fl. 1,000m. to facilitate the process of disintegration, with St Eustatius, Saba and Bonaire receiving individual allocations. The metropolitan administration also agreed to write off almost three-quarters of the Antilles' debt.

On 15 December 2008 the Dutch Prime Minister, Jan Peter Balkenende, and the Antillean premier, Emily de Jongh-Elhage, signed an agreement confirming the new status of the island. In September 2009, at a meeting of the Dutch State Secretary for the Interior and Kingdom Relations, Ank Bijleveld-Schouten, and representatives of the Netherlands Antilles, it was agreed that the target date for dissolution of the federation would be 10 October 2010, when St Eustatius would become a special municipality of the Netherlands. The US dollar was formally adopted as the island's currency from 1 January 2011, replacing the Netherlands Antilles guilder; the Island Council had opposed the introduction of the euro, the currency of the Netherlands.

In elections to the new five-member Island Council held on 2 March 2011, the Democratic Party of St Eustatius (DP) won two seats, while the Progressive Labour Party (PLP), the United People's Coalition (UPC) and the St Eustatius Empowerment Party each won one seat.

Owing to St Eustatius's change in administrative status, the island's residents were henceforth entitled to vote in Dutch polls. The islanders' first opportunity to exercise this right came on 12 September 2012, when elections to the Tweede Kamer (Second Chamber—the lower house of the Dutch parliament) were conducted. The Partij van de Arbeid received 28.2% of the valid votes cast in St Eustatius, while Democraten 66 (D66) garnered 27.9% and the Socialistische Partij 21.8%. The rate of participation by the electorate was just 15.6%.

Executive Council Commissioner Nicolaas Sneek of the DP was forced to stand down from his post in July 2013 after being defeated in a confidence motion in the Island Council. Sneek, who was succeeded by the UPC's Reginald Zaandam, had been accused of nepotism.

Elections to the European Parliament took place in St Eustatius on 22 May 2014. D66 secured 38.5% of the local ballot, compared with 15.4% for the 'ikkiesvooreerlijk.eu' list and 11.5% for GroenLinks. Turnout, however, was just 7.4%.

Another referendum on St Eustatius's constitutional relationship with the Netherlands was staged on 17 December 2014: 65.5% of the valid ballots were cast in favour of the island becoming an autonomous territory within the Kingdom; 32.8% of voters supported the maintenance of the status quo; 1.2% favoured absorption into the Netherlands; and 0.4% voted for independence. However, the participation rate, at 45.4%, was below the 60% threshold that would have made the results legally valid.

In elections to the Island Council on 18 March 2015, the PLP and the DP each won two seats while the UPC won the remaining seat. The new Island Council was sworn in on 26 March.

Lieutenant-Governor: GERALD BERKEL, Govt Bldg, Oranjestad; tel. 318-2552; fax 318-2324; internet www.statiagovernment.com.

Island Council: CLYDE VAN PUTTEN, RICHELLINE LEERDAM, ADELKA SPANNER, NICOLAAS SNEEK, REUBEN MERKMAN.

Island Secretary: MILITZA C. CONNELL-MADURO; tel. 318-3395; fax 318-3394; e-mail sec.islandcouncil@statiagov.com.

Executive Council: GERALD BERKEL (Lt-Governor), MILITZA C. CONNELL-MADURO (Island Sec.), REGINALD C. ZAANDAM, ASTRID MCKENZIE-TATEM.

National Office for the Caribbean Netherlands Sint Eustatius (Rijksdienst Caribisch Nederland Sint-Eustatius): Mazinga Complex A and B, Fort Oranjestraat, POB 26, Oranjestad; tel. 318-3370; e-mail info@rijksvertegenwoordiger.nl; internet www.rijksdienstcn.com; Kingdom Rep. (resident in Bonaire) GILBERT ISABELLA.

Netherlands Autonomous Countries

Under the 1983 Constitution, the Kingdom of the Netherlands comprises territories in Europe (the Netherlands) and in the Caribbean (Aruba, Curaçao and Sint (St) Maarten). The Charter for the Kingdom of the Netherlands, signed by Queen Juliana in 1954, designates these territories as a single realm, ruled by the House of Orange-Nassau. Aruba gained *status aparte* (separate status) within the Kingdom on 1 January 1986. Following further constitutional amendments, on 10 October 2010 Curaçao and St Maarten, formerly part of the Netherlands Antilles, also became independent countries within the Kingdom of the Netherlands.

ARUBA

Introductory Survey

LOCATION, CLIMATE, LANGUAGE, RELIGION, FLAG, CAPITAL

Aruba is one of the group of Benedenwindse Eilands or Leeward Islands, which it forms with Bonaire and Curaçao, and lies in the southern Caribbean Sea, 25 km (16 miles) north of Venezuela and 68 km (42 miles) west of Curaçao. The climate is tropical, with an average annual temperature of 28°C (82°F), but is tempered by north-easterly winds. Rainfall is very low, averaging only about 426 mm (16.8 ins) annually. The official language is Dutch, but the dominant language is Papiamento (a mixture of Dutch, Spanish, English, Arawak Indian and several West African dialects). Spanish and English are also spoken. Most of the inhabitants profess Christianity and belong to the Roman Catholic Church, although a wide variety of other denominations are represented. The national flag (proportions 2 by 3) is blue, with two narrow yellow horizontal stripes in the lower section and a white-bordered four-pointed red star in the upper hoist. The capital is Oranjestad.

CONTEMPORARY POLITICAL HISTORY

Historical Context

The Caribbean island of Aruba was claimed for Spain in 1499, but was first colonized by the Dutch in 1636 and subsequently formed part of the Dutch possessions in the West Indies. Administered from Curaçao after 1845, in 1954 Aruba became a member of the autonomous federation of the Netherlands Antilles. The establishment in 1929 of a large petroleum refinery on the island, at Sint (St) Nicolaas, led to the rapid expansion of the economy and a high standard of living for the islanders. However, many Arubans resented the administrative dominance of Curaçao, and what they regarded as the excessive demands made upon Aruban wealth and resources by the other five islands within the Netherlands Antilles. The island's principal political party, the Movimiento Electoral di Pueblo (MEP), campaigned, from its foundation in 1971 onwards, for Aruban independence and separation from the other islands. In a referendum held in Aruba in 1977 82% of voters supported independence and withdrawal from the Antillean federation. The MEP used its position in the coalition Government of the Netherlands Antilles, formed in 1979, to press for concessions from the other islands towards early independence for Aruba. In 1981 (after the MEP had withdrawn from the Government of the Netherlands Antilles) a provisional agreement regarding Aruba's future was reached between the Dutch and Antillean Governments. Following further discussions, it was agreed in 1983 that Aruba should receive *status aparte* (separate status), within the Kingdom of the Netherlands, from 1 January 1986. The Dutch Government would remain responsible for defence and external relations until independence, while Aruba was to form a co-operative union with the Netherlands Antilles (the Antilles of the Five) in economic and monetary affairs.

Domestic Political Affairs

At local elections in 1983 the MEP increased its representation in the Staten (States, parliament), and the leader of the MEP, Gilberto F. (Betico) Croes, remained as leader of the island Government. Austerity measures introduced in 1984 provoked a series of strikes and demonstrations by civil servants in protest at wage reductions and price rises. The MEP consequently lost popular support and, following parliamentary elections in 1985, was succeeded in government by a coalition of four opposition parties led by the Arubaanse Volkspartij (AVP). Aruba achieved *status aparte*, as planned, on 1 January 1986, and Jan Hendrik Albert (Henny) Eman, leader of the AVP, became its first Prime Minister.

At a general election in January 1989 the MEP came within 28 votes of securing an absolute majority in the parliament. The MEP leader Nelson Oduber formed a Government in coalition with the Partido Patriótico di Aruba (PPA) and the Acción Democrático Nacional (ADN).

The MEP and the AVP each secured nine seats at the January 1993 general election. Despite gaining fewer votes than the AVP, the MEP administration remained in office, renewing the coalition with the ADN and the PPA. In April 1994, however, Oduber announced the Government's resignation, following the withdrawal of the two smaller parties from the coalition. Following a fresh election in July, the AVP formed a coalition with the Organisacion Liberal Arubano (OLA).

In 1994 the Governments of Aruba, the Netherlands and the Netherlands Antilles cancelled plans for Aruba's transition to full independence, due to take place in 1996. The possibility of a transition to full independence at a later date was not excluded, but was not considered a priority, and would, moreover, require the approval of the Aruban people, by referendum, as well as the support of a two-thirds' parliamentary majority.

In September 1997 the States was dissolved after the OLA withdrew from the coalition. A general election was held in December which resulted in a political composition identical to that of the 1993 polls. Following protracted negotiations, the AVP and the OLA renewed their coalition in mid-1998, and a new Council of Ministers, headed by Eman, was appointed.

In June 2001 the governing coalition collapsed, following the withdrawal of the OLA's support for the AVP's plan to privatize the Aruba Tourism Authority. In a general election held in September, the MEP comfortably defeated the incumbent AVP. Oduber was once again appointed Prime Minister and a new single-party Government took office.

At a general election in September 2005 the MEP again won a majority of seats. The victory came in spite of broad public criticism of the Government's unwillingness to defend wage levels from the downward pressure caused by large-scale immigration from South America. Oduber continued as Prime Minister.

The AVP in office

The AVP, led since 2003 by Michiel Eman (the brother of former Prime Minister Henny Eman), defeated the governing MEP in a general election held on 25 September 2009, winning 12 of the 21 parliamentary seats. The MEP obtained eight seats and Partido Democracia Real (PDR) secured the remaining seat. Oduber attributed his party's loss to Dutch interference in Aruba's affairs (see *Foreign Affairs*) and to the recent closure of the petroleum refinery at St Nicolaas (see *Economic Affairs*).

In January 2010 the administration succeeded in resolving a long-running dispute over tax with the refinery owners, the US-based Valero Energy Corporation; the refinery finally resumed operations in January 2011. However, in December Valero revealed that, owing to the challenging global economic climate, the refinery was operating at a loss, and in March 2012 the facility was closed again. Valero held talks with other oil companies to discuss a potential takeover of the refinery, but no firm offers were received. Thus, in September Valero announced its intention to convert the plant into an oil depot, resulting in many job losses.

The AVP was re-elected at a general election conducted on 27 September 2013, gaining control of 13 seats in parliament, compared with seven for the MEP and one for the PDR. The rate of participation by the electorate was recorded at 84%. Eman pledged to continue his efforts to rekindle the island's ailing economy. Elections to the European Parliament were held on 22 May 2014. The Christen Democratisch Appèl won the majority of the local ballot, but turnout was very low.

Recent developments: intra-Kingdom tensions

Eman commenced a hunger strike in July 2014 in protest against the actions of the Dutch authorities, which, owing to concerns about Aruba's precarious fiscal position, had withheld approval of the local administration's 2014 budget and had directed Governor Fredis Refunjol to conduct an investigation into the island's finances. Eman denounced these measures as a violation of Aruban autonomy, but abandoned his hunger strike later that month after Refunjol pledged to expedite his investigation. A modified budget was finally approved in December. Aruba hosted a Kingdom Inter-Parliamentary Consultation in January 2015, which was attended by representatives of the Netherlands, Aruba, Curaçao and Sint Maarten. The delegates agreed to establish a mechanism to help resolve future intra-Kingdom disputes.

Foreign Affairs

Aruba's relations with the Antilles of the Five improved after 1986. Aruba's relations with the 'metropolitan' Netherlands were dominated by Dutch pressure for more control over the large amount of aid that it gave to Aruba, and by the issue of independence, in particular the future arrangements for the island's security: Aruba's strategic position, close to the South American mainland, and the possibility of it being used as a base for drugs-trafficking, were matters of particular concern. In 1990 Aruba adopted the 1988 UN Convention on measures to combat trade in illegal drugs. In 1996, however, the USA included Aruba on its list of major drugs-producing or transit countries. New legislation to facilitate the extradition of suspected drugs-traffickers and money-launderers took effect in the following year and in 1999 US naval and air force patrols began operating from a base in Aruba in an effort to counter the transport of illicit drugs. In 2001 the Caribbean Financial Action Task Force commended the Government on its efforts in combating money-laundering. In the same year the territory was removed from the list of so-called 'uncooperative tax havens' drawn up by the Organisation for Economic Co-operation and Development (OECD, based in Paris, France), after the Government pledged to reform the territory's financial sector. However, in April 2009 Aruba was included in OECD's so-called 'grey list' of territories that had committed to improving financial transparency, but had yet substantially to implement reform. Aruba was removed from the list later that year.

After acquiring *status aparte*, Aruba fostered relations with some of its Caribbean neighbours and with countries in Latin America. This included the development of ties with Venezuela, which had traditionally laid claim to the Dutch Leeward Islands, including Aruba. In 2009 the Dutch Minister of Foreign Affairs refuted allegations by the Venezuelan Government that the US military was being permitted to use airbases on Aruba and Curaçao to launch reconnaissance flights over Venezuelan territory. In 2013 former Venezuelan Vice-President José Vicente Rangel Vale accused the US authorities of planning to stage an attack on Venezuela from these airbases, although the USA asserted that its military activities in Aruba and Curaçao were conducted solely to combating drugs-smuggling. In July 2014 the Aruban authorities, at the USA's behest, detained Venezuela's nominated consul-general to the island, Hugo Carvajal Barrios, a former high-ranking military officer who was suspected of involvement in the illegal drugs trade. The Venezuelan Government protested vociferously and briefly suspended air transport ties with the Dutch Caribbean. Shortly thereafter, the Dutch Ministry of Foreign Affairs concluded that Carvajal's status as incoming consul-general afforded him diplomatic immunity, and he was promptly released from Aruban custody. However, some Aruban and US officials claimed that this judgment had been made under duress: Venezuelan naval assets had been sighted in waters near to Aruba and Curaçao, and Venezuela had reportedly threatened to impose economic sanctions on the Dutch islands and to sever diplomatic relations with the Netherlands. Following the discovery of an alleged coup plot in Venezuela in February 2015, Venezuelan President Nicolás Maduro declared that his nation's air defence zone would henceforth be expanded to encompass the airspace over the Dutch Caribbean islands. Later that month Maduro demanded that Aruba and Curaçao deny future entry to Tucano aircraft (the use of such an aircraft had purportedly been planned in the coup plot).

CONSTITUTION AND GOVERNMENT

Aruba has separate status (*status aparte*) within the Kingdom of the Netherlands. Legislative power is held by the unicameral Staten (parliament) of 21 members, elected by universal adult suffrage for four years (subject to dissolution). Executive power in all domestic affairs is vested in the Council of Ministers (led by the Prime Minister), responsible to parliament. The Governor, appointed by the Dutch Crown for a term of six years, represents the monarch of the Netherlands on Aruba and holds responsibility for external affairs and defence. The Governor is assisted by an advisory council. The Government of Aruba appoints a minister plenipotentiary to represent it in the Government of the Kingdom.

REGIONAL AND INTERNATIONAL CO-OPERATION

Aruba forms a co-operative union with Curaçao and Sint (St) Maarten in monetary and economic affairs, and has observer status with the Caribbean Community and Common Market (CARICOM, see p. 222). As part of the Kingdom of the Netherlands, Aruba is classed as an Overseas Territory in association with the European Union (EU, see p. 271).

ECONOMIC AFFAIRS

In 2013, according to the UN, Aruba's gross national income (GNI) was US $2,433.8m. During 2004–13 the population increased at an average annual rate of 0.5%. According to the central bank, gross domestic product (GDP) per head decreased, in real terms, by an average of 1.1% per year in 2004–13. Overall GDP decreased, in real terms, at an average annual rate of 0.6% in 2004–13. Real GDP decreased by 1.2% in 2012, but increased by 3.9% in 2013.

The agricultural sector engaged 0.6% of the employed labour force in 2010. According to UN estimates, the sector contributed 0.5% of total GDP in 2013. Owing to the poor quality of the soil and the prohibitive cost of desalinated water, the only significant agricultural activity is the cultivation of aloes (used in the manufacture of cosmetics and pharmaceuticals); aloe-based products are exported. Some livestock is raised, and there is a small fishing industry. According to UN estimates, during 2004–13 agricultural GDP increased, in real terms, at an average annual rate of 0.9%; the sector's GDP decreased by 2.2% in 2012, but increased by 4.2% in 2013.

The industrial sector contributed an estimated 15.4% of GDP in 2013, according to UN estimates, and engaged 14.6% of the employed labour force in 2010. The industrial sector, and the island's economy, was based on the refining and transshipment of imported petroleum and petroleum products. The petroleum refinery at St Nicolaas refined 52.9m. barrels of crude petroleum in 2011 before its closure in 2012. Imports of crude petroleum were valued at A Fl. 8,405m. in 2011, before falling to A Fl. 1,353m. in 2012, and to zero in 2013. Exports of refined petroleum were valued at A Fl. 2,055m. in 2012, before decreasing to A Fl. 66m. in 2013 (total exports excluding mineral fuels and free trade zone transactions amounted to just A Fl. 74.7m. in 2013). A petroleum transshipment terminal is still in operation on Aruba, as is a small petrochemicals industry. An advanced-technology coker plant supplies liquefied petroleum gas, largely for export to the USA. There are believed to be exploitable reserves of hydrocarbons within Aruban territory, and Aruba also has reserves of salt. During 2004–13, according to UN estimates, industrial GDP decreased at an average annual rate of 2.9%; the sector's GDP increased by 8.5% in 2012 and by 3.4% in 2013.

Manufacturing contributed an estimated 4.3% of GDP in 2013, according to UN estimates, and engaged 5.0% of the employed labour force in 2010. Light industry is engaged in the production of beverages, building materials, paints and solvents, paper and plastic products, candles, detergents, disinfectants, soaps and aloe-based cosmetics. There is a free zone, and the ports of Oranjestad and Barcadera provide bunkering and repair facilities for ships. According to UN estimates, during 2004–13 manufacturing GDP increased, in real terms, at an average annual rate of 0.3%; the sector's GDP decreased by 2.8% in 2012, but increased by 4.2% in 2013.

The construction sector contributed an estimated 5.3% of GDP in 2013, according to UN estimates, and employed 8.3% of the active workforce in 2010. During 2004–13, according to UN estimates, sectoral GDP decreased at an average annual rate of 2.9%; construction GDP decreased by 6.9% in 2012, but increased by 3.4% in 2013.

Services are Aruba's principal economic activity, employing 84.8% of the active labour force in 2010. According to UN estimates, the sector contributed an estimated 84.2% of GDP in 2013. Aruba's principal source of income is tourism; the sector was estimated directly to provide 26.4% of Aruba's GDP in 2013, according to the World Travel and Tourism Council. The number of stop-over arrivals increased by 4.0% in 2012, to 903,934, and by a further 8.3% in 2013, to 979,256. The number of cruise ship passengers increased in 2012 (to 582,309) and further increased in 2013 (to 688,568). The majority of visitors (56.8% in 2013) were from the USA. Receipts from tourism increased to A Fl. 2,679.7m. in 2013. Financial services are well established in Aruba, particularly the data-processing sector, an important service to US companies in particular. According to UN estimates, during 2004–13 services GDP decreased, in real terms, at an average annual rate of 0.4%; the sector's GDP decreased by 1.5% in 2012, but increased by 4.2% in 2013.

Aruba is obliged to import most of its requirements, particularly machinery and electrical equipment (which accounted for 14.3% of the total value of imports in 2013), foodstuffs and chemical products; in 2013 the island recorded a merchandise trade deficit of US $1,085.5m. There was a deficit on the current account of the balance of payments of US $269.4m. in the same year. In 2013 the principal source of imports, excluding the petroleum sector and the free zone, was the USA (55.4% of the total value); another major source was the Netherlands. The principal export commodity was still refined petroleum. Excluding the petroleum sector and the free zone, the principal export was machinery and electrical equipment, accounting for 14.7% of the total in 2013. The principal market for exports in 2013, again excluding the petroleum sector and the free zone, was also the USA (accounting for 49.5% of the total value of exports), followed by Aruba's fellow members of the Kingdom of the Netherlands.

In 2013 Aruba recorded a budget deficit of A Fl. 295.3m., equivalent to 6.4% of GDP in that year. At the end of 2013 total government debt was A Fl. 3,412.4m. (equivalent to 73.6% of GDP), much of which was owed to the Government of the Netherlands. The average annual rate of inflation was 2.5% in 2004–13; consumer prices fell by 3.8% in 2012, but rose by 0.1% in 2013. Some 7.6% of the labour force were unemployed in 2013.

Aruba used to be considered one of the most prosperous islands in the Caribbean. Concern, however, was expressed that its high public sector wage bill and the generous nature of the island's social welfare system, combined with its ageing population, would threaten the future stability of public finances, already hindered by a narrow taxation base and poor revenue collection. Real GDP grew by an estimated 3.7% in 2011, driven by a recovery in tourist arrivals, increasing domestic consumption, and a strong rise in exports and investment. The reopening of the Valero petroleum refinery also contributed to economic growth. However, production at the facility was suspended again in 2012, leading to a decline in exports and an increase in unemployment. The negative economic repercussions of the closure were partially offset by the strong performance of the tourism industry during that year, but a 1.2% contraction in real GDP was registered in 2012, none the less. According to the Central Bank, an upturn in domestic demand (fuelled by lower utility prices) and an 8.3% rise in stay-over visitor numbers resulted in renewed economic growth of 3.9% in 2013. However, the territory's precarious financial position was a source of serious concern. Although there was a marked recovery in investment levels during 2014 and stay-over tourist arrivals continued to increase, real GDP growth slowed to an estimated 1.6% in that year, owing to a decline in domestic consumption. The implementation of fiscal reforms precipitated a reduction in the deficit, but, in spite of this progress, the public debt stock continued to rise. The Central Bank projected economic growth of 1.5% in 2015, predicated on a further rise in visitor numbers and a resurgence in domestic demand. Meanwhile, an agreement signed by the Government in January 2013 with Spanish company Repsol for offshore oil exploration could, if fruitful, provide a much-needed boost for the economy; preliminary surveying results were reported to be promising.

PUBLIC HOLIDAYS

2016: 1 January (New Year's Day), 25 January (Gilberto F. Croes's Birthday), 8 February (Lenten Carnival), 18 March (National Anthem and Flag Day), 25–28 March (Easter), 27 April (King's Day), 1 May (Labour Day), 5 May (Ascension Day), 25–26 December (Christmas).

Statistical Survey

Sources (unless otherwise stated): Central Bureau of Statistics, Ministry of Finance and Government Organization, Sun Plaza Bldg, 3rd Floor, L. G. Smith Blvd 160, Oranjestad; tel. 5837433; fax 5838057; internet www.cbs.aw; Centrale Bank van Aruba, J. E. Irausquin Blvd 8, POB 18, Oranjestad; tel. 5252100; fax 5252101; e-mail cbaua@setarnet.aw; internet www.cbaruba.org.

AREA AND POPULATION

Area: 180 sq km (69.5 sq miles).

Population: 90,506 at census of 14 October 2000; 101,484 (males 48,241, females 53,243) at census of 29 September 2010. *Mid-2015* (UN estimate): 103,889 Source: UN, *World Population Prospects: The 2012 Revision.*

Density (at mid-2015): 577.2 per sq km.

Population by Age and Sex (UN estimates at mid-2015): *0–14 years:* 19,049 (males 9,701, females 9,348); *15–64 years:* 72,169 (males 34,257, females 37,912); *65 years and over:* 12,671 (males 5,417, females 7,254); *Total* 103,889 (males 49,375, females 54,514). Source: UN, *World Population Prospects: The 2012 Revision.*

Principal Town (population at 2010 census): Oranjestad (capital) 28,294. *Mid-2014* (UN estimate, incl. suburbs): Oranjestad (capital) 29,041 (Source: UN, *World Urbanization Prospects: The 2014 Revision*).

Births, Marriages and Deaths (2013 unless otherwise indicated): Live births 1,154 (birth rate 10.9 per 1,000); Marriages 768 (marriage rate 7.5 per 1,000, 2011); Deaths 560 (death rate 5.3 per 1,000).

Life Expectancy (years at birth): 75.2 (males 72.8; females 77.7) in 2012. Source: World Bank, World Development Indicators database.

Immigration and Emigration (2013): Immigration 3,335; Emigration 2,291.

Economically Active Population (persons aged 14 years and over, 2010 census): Agriculture, hunting and forestry 297; Mining and quarrying 24; Manufacturing 2,334; Electricity, gas and water 529; Construction 3,851; Wholesale and retail trade, repairs 7,523; Hotels and restaurants 9,526; Transport, storage and communications 2,475; Financial intermediation 1,593; Real estate, renting and business activities 4,224; Public administration, defence and social security 4,570; Education 2,078; Health and social work 2,526; Other community, social and personal services 3,492; Private households with employed persons 1,242; Extraterritorial organizations and bodies 14; *Sub-total* 46,299; Activities not adequately defined 227; *Total employed* 46,526; Unemployed 5,519; *Total labour force* 52,045 (males 26,184, females 25,861).

HEALTH AND WELFARE

Total Fertility Rate (children per woman, 2011): 1.8.

Under-5 Mortality Rate (per 1,000 live births, 2010): 16.8.

Physicians (per 1,000 head, 2013): 1.82.

Hospital Beds (per 1,000 head, 2009): 2.8.

Health Expenditure (% of GDP, 2010): 10.0.

Total Carbon Dioxide Emissions ('000 metric tons, 2010): 2,321.2.

Carbon Dioxide Emissions Per Head (metric tons, 2010): 22.8.

Source: partly Pan American Health Organization.

For definitions, see explanatory note on p. vi.

FISHING

Total catch (all capture, metric tons, live weight, 2012): Groupers 10; Snappers and jobfishes 38; Wahoo 45; Other marine fishes 45; Total 138. Source: FAO.

INDUSTRY

Electric Energy (million kWh, 2013): 779.2.

FINANCE

Currency and Exchange Rates: 100 cents = 1 Aruban gulden (guilder) or florin (A Fl.). *Sterling, Dollar and Euro Equivalents* (31 December 2014): £1 sterling = A Fl. 2.794; US $1 = A Fl. 1.790; €1 = A Fl. 2.173; A Fl. 100 = £35.79 = $55.87 = €46.01. Note: the Aruban florin was introduced in January 1986, replacing (at par) the Netherlands Antilles guilder or florin (NA Fl.). Since its introduction, the currency has had a fixed exchange rate of US $1 = A Fl. 1.79.

Budget (A Fl. million, 2013, provisional): *Revenue:* Tax revenue 942.0; Non-tax revenue 195.0; Total 1,137.0. *Expenditure:* Wages 387.6; Wage subsidies 168.2; Goods and services 256.5; Interest payments 164.5; Investments 39.9; Transfer to the General Health Insurance (AZV) 101.5; Total (incl. others) 1,432.3.

International Reserves (US $ million at 31 December 2013): Gold 133.7; Foreign exchange 532.7; *Total* 666.4. Source: IMF, *International Financial Statistics.*

Money Supply (A Fl. million at 31 December 2013): Currency outside banks 213.6; Demand deposits at commercial banks 1,501.0; *Total money* 1,714.6. Source: IMF, *International Financial Statistics.*

Cost of Living (Consumer Price Index; base: December 2006 = 100): All items 119.4 in 2011; 120.1 in 2012; 117.3 in 2013.

Gross Domestic Product (A Fl. million at constant 2000 prices): 3,095 in 2010; 3,211 in 2011; 3,171 in 2012; 3,293 in 2013.

Expenditure on the Gross Domestic Product (A Fl. million at current prices, 2013): Final consumption expenditure 4,244; Gross capital formation 1,062; *Total domestic expenditure* 5,306; Exports of goods and services 3,157; *Less* Imports of goods and services 3,828; *GDP in purchasers' values* 4,634.

Gross Domestic Product by Economic Activity (A Fl. million at current prices, 2013): Agriculture, hunting, forestry and fishing 21; Mining and utilities 255; Manufacturing 192; Construction 236; Wholesale, retail trade, restaurants and hotels 854; Transport, storage and communications 413; Other activities 2,472; *Total gross value added* 4,442; Net taxes on products 192 (figure obtained as a residual); *GDP in purchasers' values* 4,634. Source: UN National Accounts Main Aggregates Database.

Balance of Payments (US $ million, 2013): Exports of goods f.o.b. 278.5; Imports of goods f.o.b. –1,364.1; *Balance on goods* –1,085.5; Exports of services 1,886.4; Imports of services –845.6; *Balance on goods and services* –44.7; Primary income received 34.2; Primary income paid –200.8; *Balance on goods, services and primary income* –211.2; Secondary income received 101.0; Secondary income paid –159.2; *Current balance* –269.4; Capital account (net) 3.0; Direct investment assets –5.1; Direct investment from liabilities 168.8; Portfolio investment assets –7.6; Portfolio investment liabilities 80.3; Financial derivatives and employee stock options (net) 0.4; Other investment assets –4.1; Other investment liabilities –0.9; Net errors and omissions –8.6; *Reserves and related items* –43.1. Source: IMF, *International Financial Statistics.*

EXTERNAL TRADE

Principal Commodities (A Fl. million, 2013): *Imports c.i.f.:* Live animals and animal products 156.2; Food products 243.2; Chemical products 180.2; Base metals and articles thereof 92.8; Machinery and electrical equipment 298.9; Transport equipment 141.0; Total (incl. others) 2,083.5. *Exports f.o.b.:* Live animals and animal products 0.4; Machinery and electrical equipment 11.0; Transport equipment 4.8; Art objects and collectors' items 7.9; Total (incl. others) 74.7. Note: Figures exclude transactions involving mineral fuels and those of the Free Trade Zone of Aruba.

Principal Trading Partners (A Fl. million, 2013): *Imports c.i.f.:* Brazil 27.7; Colombia 36.8; Japan 18.5; Netherlands 251.4; former Netherlands Antilles 44.3; Panama 65.2; USA 1,154.2; Venezuela 25.2; Total (incl. others) 2,083.5. *Exports f.o.b.:* Colombia 2.1; Netherlands 12.0; former Netherlands Antilles 6.7; USA 37.0; Venezuela 1.4; Total (incl. others) 74.7. Note: Figures exclude transactions of the petroleum sector and those of the Free Trade Zone of Aruba.

TRANSPORT

Road Traffic (motor vehicles registered, December 2013): Passenger cars 57,688; Lorries 1,102; Buses 138; Taxis 374; Rental cars 3,570; Government cars 560; Motorcycles 2,048; Total (incl. others) 65,920.

Shipping: *Arrivals* (2011): 2,098 vessels. *Flag Registered Fleet* (31 December 2014): Number of vessels 1; Total displacement 221 grt (Source: Lloyd's List Intelligence—www.lloydslist intelligence.com).

Civil Aviation: *Aircraft Landings:* 19,225 in 2011; 20,542 in 2012; 21,708 in 2013. *Passenger Arrivals:* 980,544 in 2011; 1,020,731 in 2012; 1,093,251 in 2013.

TOURISM

Tourist Arrivals: 1,468,866 (868,973 stop-over visitors, 599,893 cruise ship passengers) in 2011; 1,486,243 (903,934 stop-over visitors, 582,309 cruise ship passengers) in 2012; 1,667,824 (979,256 stop-over visitors, 688,568 cruise ship passengers) in 2013.

Stop-over Visitors by Country of Origin (2013): Netherlands 37,788; USA 556,296; Venezuela 188,020; Total (incl. others) 979,256.

Tourism Receipts (A Fl. million): 2,414.6 in 2011; 2,505.0 in 2012; 2,679.7 in 2013.

COMMUNICATIONS MEDIA

Telephones (2013): 35,000 main lines in use.

Mobile Cellular Telephones (2013): 138,800 subscribers.

Internet Subscribers (2008): 18,400.

Broadband Subscribers (2013): 19,200.

Source: International Telecommunication Union.

EDUCATION

Pre-primary (September 2012): 28 schools (provisional); 2,843 pupils; 150 teachers.

Primary (September 2012): 38 schools (provisional); 9,245 pupils; 513 teachers.

General Secondary (September 2012 unless otherwise indicated): 9 schools (provisional); 7,592 pupils (2009/10); 544 teachers (2009/10).

Technical-Vocational (September 2012, provisional): 1 school; 1,873 pupils; 182 teachers.

Community College (1999/2000): 1 school; 1,187 pupils; 106 teachers.

University (September 2012, provisional): 1 university; 134 students; 12 tutors.

Teacher Training (September 2012, provisional): 1 institution; 150 students; 60 teachers.

Special Education (September 2012): 5 schools; 531 pupils; 77 teachers.

Private, Non-aided (September 2012): 7 schools; 523 pupils; 14 teachers.

International School (2000/01): 1 school; 154 pupils; 25 teachers.

Pupil-teacher Ratio (primary education, UNESCO estimate): 14.8 in 2011/12 (Source: UNESCO Institute for Statistics).

Adult Literacy Rate (UNESCO estimates, 2010): 96.8% (males 96.9%; females 96.7%) (Source: UNESCO Institute for Statistics).

Directory

The Government

HEAD OF STATE

King of the Netherlands: HM King WILLEM-ALEXANDER.

Governor: FREDIS J. REFUNJOL (took office 7 May 2004).

COUNCIL OF MINISTERS
(May 2015)

The Government is formed by the Arubaanse Volkspartij.

Prime Minister and Minister of General Affairs, Science, Innovation and Sustainable Development: MICHIEL GODFRIED EMAN.

Minister of Territorial Development, Infrastructure and Integration: OSLIN BENITO SEVINGER.

Minister of Economic Affairs, Communications, Energy and the Environment: MIKE ERIC DE MEZA.

Minister of Tourism, Transport, Primary Industries and Culture: OTMAR ENRIQUE ODUBER.

Minister of Finance and Government Organization: ANGEL ROALD BERMUDEZ.

Minister of Justice: ARTHUR LAWRENCE DOWERS.

Minister of Education and Family: MICHELLE JANICE HOOYBOER-WINKLAAR.

Minister of Public Health, the Elderly Population and Sports: CARLOS ALEX SCHWENGLE.

Minister of Social Affairs, Youth and Labour: PAULDRICK FRAN-ÇOIS TEODORIC CROES.

Minister Plenipotentiary and Member of the Council of Ministers of the Realm for Aruba in the Netherlands: ALFONSO BOEKHOUDT.

Minister Plenipotentiary of the Realm for Aruba in Washington, DC (USA): JOCELYNE CROES.

Secretary to the Council of Ministers: NICOLE HOEVERTSZ.

MINISTRIES

Office of the Governor: Plaza Henny Eman 3, POB 53, Oranjestad; tel. 5834445; fax 5820730; e-mail info@kabga.aw; internet www .kabga.aw.

Office of the Prime Minister: Government Offices, L. G. Smith Blvd 76, Oranjestad; tel. 5880300; fax 5880024.

Ministry of Economic Affairs, Communications, Energy and the Environment: L. G. Smith Blvd 76, Oranjestad; tel. 5885455; fax 5827526.

Ministry of Education and Family: L. G. Smith Blvd 76, Oranjestad; tel. 5284971; fax 5827531.

Ministry of Finance and Government Organization: Sun Plaza Bldg, 3rd Floor, L. G. Smith Blvd 76, Oranjestad; tel. 5833457; fax 5827538.

Ministry of General Affairs, Science, Innovation and Sustainable Development: L. G. Smith Blvd 76, Oranjestad; tel. 5830001; fax 5827513; e-mail rekenkamer@aruba.gov.aw.

Ministry of Justice: L. G. Smith Blvd 76, Oranjestad; tel. 5830004; fax 5827518.

Ministry of Public Health, the Elderly Population and Sports: L. G. Smith Blvd 76, Oranjestad; tel. 5825751; fax 5827569.

Ministry of Social Affairs, Youth and Labour: L. G. Smith Blvd 76, Oranjestad; tel. 5288998; fax 5285045.

Ministry of Territorial Development, Infrastructure and Integration: L. G. Smith Blvd 76, Oranjestad; tel. 5284945; fax 5827538.

Ministry of Tourism, Transport, Primary Industries and Culture: L. G. Smith Blvd 76, Oranjestad; tel. 5827718; fax 5827556.

Office of the Minister Plenipotentiary for Aruba in the Netherlands: R. J. Schimmelpennincklaan 1, 2517 JN The Hague, Netherlands; tel. (70) 3566200; fax (70) 3451446; e-mail info@arubahuis.nl; internet www.arubahuis.nl.

Office of the Minister Plenipotentiary for Aruba in Washington, DC (USA): 4200 Linnean Ave, NW, Washington, DC 20008, USA; tel. (202) 274-2640; e-mail was-gma@minbuza.nl.

Legislature

STATES
(Staten)

President: MARISOL LOPEZ-TROMP.
General Election, 27 September 2013

Party	Seats
Arubaanse Volkspartij (AVP)	13
Movimiento Electoral di Pueblo (MEP)	7
Partido Democracia Real (PDR)	1
Total	21

Political Organizations

Arubaanse Volkspartij (AVP) (Aruba People's Party): Avda Alo Tromp 56, Oranjestad; tel. 5830911; fax 5837963; internet www.avp.net; f. 1942; advocates Aruba's separate status; Leader MICHIEL GODFRIED EMAN.

Movimiento Electoral di Pueblo (MEP) (People's Electoral Movement): Santa Cruz 74D, Santa Cruz; tel. 5856917; fax 5850768; e-mail info@mep.aw; internet www.mep.aw; f. 1971; socialist; 1,200 mems; Pres. and Leader EVELYN WEVER-CROES.

Partido Democracia Real (PDR) (Real Democracy Party): Oranjestad; tel. 5941900; e-mail andin.bikker@gmail.com; internet www.votapdr.com; f. 2004; Leader ANDIN C. G. BIKKER.

Partido Patriótico di Aruba (PPA) (Patriotic Party of Aruba): Clavelstraat 5, Sint Nicolaas; tel. 5844609; e-mail nisbet@ppa-aruba.org; internet www.ppa-aruba.org; f. 1949; social democratic; opposed to complete independence for Aruba; Leader BENEDICT (BENNY) JOCELYN MONTGOMERY NISBET.

RED Democratico (RED Democratic Network): Belgiestraat 14, Oranjestad; tel. 5820213; e-mail info@red.aw; f. 2003; Leader DIONISIA THERESITA DE CUBA.

Union Patriotico Progresista (UPP): Oranjestad; Leader CANDELARIO A. S. D. WEVER.

Judicial System

Legal authority is exercised by the Joint Court of Justice of Aruba, Curaçao and St Maarten and of Bonaire, St Eustatius and Saba. Its headquarters are in Curaçao. The Joint Court hears civil, criminal and administrative cases in the first instance and on appeal. The Supreme Court of the Netherlands (based in The Hague) is the court of Final Instance for any appeal.

Joint Court of Justice: Wayaca 33E, Oranjestad; tel. 5822294; fax 5821241; internet www.gemhofvanjustitie.org/vestigingen/aruba; hears cases in the first instance.

Attorney-General: ROBERT F. PIETERSZ.

Religion

CHRISTIANITY

The Roman Catholic Church

Roman Catholics form the largest religious community, numbering 76% of the population, according to the 2010 census. Aruba forms part of the diocese of Willemstad (Curaçao), comprising Aruba, Bonaire, Curaçao, St Maarten, St Eustatius and Saba. Willemstad is part of the archdiocese of Port of Spain (Trinidad and Tobago).

Roman Catholic Church (St Fransiscus Church): J. Yrausquin Plein 3, POB 445, Oranjestad; tel. 5821434; fax 5821276; e-mail parokiasanfrancisco@yahoo.com.

The Anglican Communion

Within the Church in the Province of the West Indies, Aruba forms part of the diocese of the North Eastern Caribbean and Aruba. The Bishop is resident in St John's, Antigua and Barbuda. About 0.5% of the population were Anglican, according to the 2010 census.

Anglican Church: Holy Cross, Wm Serne Pretoe 31, Sint Nicolaas; tel. 5845142; fax 5843394; e-mail holycross@setar.boh.aw

Other Christian Churches

According to the 2010 census, 3% of the population were Protestant, 2% Jehovah's Witnesses, 1% Methodist, and 1% Seventh-day Adventist.

Church of Christ: Pastoor Hendrikstraat 107, POB 2206, Sint Nicolaas; tel. 5848172; e-mail lwaymire@setarnet.aw; Minister LARRY WAYMIRE.

Church of Jesus Christ of Latter-Day Saints: Dadelstraat 16, Oranjestad; tel. 5823507.

Dutch Protestant Church: Wilhelminastraat 1, Oranjestad; tel. 5821435; e-mail protestantsegemeente@setarnet.aw.

Evangelical Church of San Nicolas: Jasmijnstraat 7, Sint Nicolaas; tel. 5848973; e-mail norbeth@setarnet.aw; internet www.goodnewsaruba.org; f. 1970; Pastor NORMAN BROWNE.

Faith Revival Center: Rooi Afo 10, Paradera; tel. 5831010; fax 5833070; e-mail frc_aruba@yahoo.com; internet faithrevival.googlepages.com.

Iglesia Evangelica Pentecostal: Asamblea di Dios, Reamurstraat 2, Oranjestad; tel. 5831940.

Jehovah's Witnesses: Guyabastraat 3, Oranjestad; tel. 5828963.

Methodist Church: Bernhardstraat 245, Sint Nicolaas; tel. 5845243; fax 5934810; e-mail relismartinriley@yahoo.com; Supt Rev. RELIS F. MARTIN-RILEY.

New Apostolic Church: Goletstraat 5, Oranjestad; tel. 5833762; Pastor A. DEN HAMER.

Seventh-day Adventist: Pos Chiquito 47A, POB 66, Oranjestad; tel. 5840777; e-mail misionaruba@gmail.com; internet misionaruba.interamerica.org; Pres. MARTIN FORBES.

JUDAISM

According to 2010 census figures, 0.4% of the population was Jewish.

Beth Israel Aruba Synagogue: Adriaan Laclé Blvd 2, POB 655, Oranjestad; tel. 5823272; e-mail rabbi@bethisraelaruba.com; internet www.bethisraelaruba.com; Rabbi DANIEL KRIPPER.

BAHÁ'Í FAITH

Spiritual Assembly: Bucutiweg 19, Oranjestad; tel. 5823104; Contact M. CHRISTIAN.

The Press

DAILIES

Amigoe di Aruba: Bilderdijkstraat 16-2, POB 323, Oranjestad; tel. 5824333; fax 5822368; e-mail arubaredactie@amigoe.com; internet www.amigoe.com; f. 1884; Dutch; Dir SIGRID HAMMELBURG; Editor JEAN MENTENS; circ. 12,000.

Aruba Daily: Engelandstraat 29, POB 577, Oranjestad; tel. 7346150; e-mail news@aruba-daily.com; internet aruba-daily.com; English; Mon.–Sat. morning; Publr RENE VAN NOREL.

Aruba Today: Weststraat 22, Oranjestad; tel. 5827800; fax 5827093; e-mail info@arubatoday.com; internet www.arubatoday.com; English; Editor-in-Chief JULIA C. RENFRO.

Bon Dia Aruba: Weststraat 22, Oranjestad; tel. 5827800; fax 5827044; e-mail noticia@bondia.com; internet www.bondia.com; Papiamento; Dir RICARDO WEVER.

Diario: Engelandstraat 29, POB 577, Oranjestad; tel. 5826747; fax 5828551; e-mail noticia@diario.aw; internet www.diarioaruba.com; f. 1980; Papiamento; morning; Editor and Man. JOSSY M. MANSUR; circ. 15,000.

The Morning News: Caya G. F. (Betico) Croes 111, Oranjestad; tel. 5889517; fax 5889518; e-mail themorningnewsaruba@gmail.com; internet www.themorningnewsaruba.com; f. 2010 by staff of defunct *The News* daily; English; daily.

Publishers

Aruba Experience Publications NV: Miramar Bldg, 3rd Floor, Of. 306, L. G. Smith Blvd 62, Oranjestad; tel. 5887878; fax 5384520; e-mail info@arubaexperience.com; internet www.arubaexperience.com; f. 1985; Gen. Man. SUSAN RUITER.

Caribbean Publishing Co Ltd (CPC): L. G. Smith Blvd 116, Oranjestad; tel. 5820485; fax 5820484; e-mail infoarubayp@globaldirectories.com; internet arubayp.com; subsidiary of Global Directories Ltd, Bermuda.

De Wit and Van Dorp Aruba: Tanki Leendert 103B, Oranjestad; tel. 5823076; fax 5821575; e-mail info@dewitvandorp.com; f. 1948; Gen. Man. LYANNE BEAUJON.

Editorial Charuba: Beatrixstraat 23, Oranjestad; tel. 5943773; fax 5827526; e-mail alivaro@hotmail.com; f. 1982; Pres. ALICE VAN ROMONDT.

ProGraphics Inc: Italiestraat 5, POB 201, Oranjestad; tel. 5824550; fax 5833072; e-mail info@prographicsaruba.com; internet www.prographicsaruba.com; f. 2001; fmrly VAD Printers Inc; Gen. Man. HEIN VAN DER PUTTEN.

Broadcasting and Communications

TELECOMMUNICATIONS

Digicel Aruba: Marisol Bldg, L. G. Smith Blvd 60, POB 662, Oranjestad; tel. 5222222; fax 5222223; e-mail customercarearuba@digicelgroup.com; internet www.digicelaruba.com; f. 2003; owned by an Irish consortium; established a mobile cellular telephone network connecting Aruba with Bonaire and Curaçao in 2006; Chair. DENIS O'BRIEN; CEO (Dutch Caribbean) HANS LUTE; Gen. Man. (Aruba) BOB SPRENGERS.

SETAR (Servicio di Telecomunicacion di Aruba NV): Seroe Blanco z/n, POB 13, Oranjestad; tel. 5251000; fax 5251515; e-mail sysop@setarnet.aw; internet www.setar.aw; f. 1986; Man. Dir ROLAND CROES.

BROADCASTING

Radio

Canal 90 FM Stereo: Van Leeuwenhoekstraat 26, Oranjestad; tel. 5821601; fax 837340; e-mail canal90fm@gmail.com; internet www.canal90fm.aw/index2.htm; Producer M. GRAVENHORST.

Cool FM 98.9: Caya Betico Croes 23, Oranjestad; tel. 5833100; fax 5833101; e-mail publica@coolaruba.com; internet www.coolaruba.com; part of A & K Broadcasting Corpn NV; Dir ALEXANDER PONSON.

Hit 94 FM: Caya Ernesto Petronia 68, Oranjestad; tel. 5820694; fax 5820494; e-mail hit94@setarnet.aw; internet www.hit94fm.com; f. 1993; Dir JOHNNY HABIBE.

Magic 96.5 FM: Caya G. F. (Betico) Croes 164, Oranjestad; tel. 5865353; internet www.magic965.com; Dir ERIN J. CROES.

Power FM 101.7: Piedra Plat 44 C-D, Lok 12, Paradera; tel. 5851017; e-mail info@blizz.aw; internet blizz.aw; Man. RUBEN (SCORPIO) GARCIA.

Radio Carina FM 97.9: Datustraat 10A, Oranjestad; tel. 5821450; fax 5831955; commercial; programmes in Dutch, English, Spanish and Papiamento; Dir-Gen. ALBERT R. DIEFFENTHALER.

Radio Caruso Booy FM: G. M. de Bruynewijk 49, Savaneta; tel. 5847752; fax 5843351; commercial; programmes in Dutch, English, Spanish and Papiamento; Gen. Man. SIRA BOOY.

Radio Victoria: Washington 23A, POB 5291, Oranjestad; tel. and fax 5873444; e-mail radiovictoria@setarnet.aw; internet www.srv931fm.org; f. 1958; religious and cultural FM radio station owned by the Radio Victoria Foundation; programmes in Dutch, English, Spanish, Papiamento, Dutch, Tagalog, Creole and Mandarin; Pres. N. J. F. ARTS.

Voz di Aruba (Voice of Aruba): Van Leeuwenhoekstraat 26, POB 219, Oranjestad; tel. 5823355; commercial; programmes in Dutch, English, Spanish and Papiamento; also operates Canal 90 on FM; Dir A. M. ARENDS, Jr.

Television

ABC Aruba Broadcasting Co NV (ATV): Royal Plaza Suite 223, POB 5040, Oranjestad; tel. 5838150; fax 5838434; e-mail emily@15atv.com; internet www.15atv.com; Rep. EMILY HUDSON.

Telearuba NV: Pos Chiquito 1A, POB 392, Oranjestad; tel. 5851000; e-mail info@telearuba.aw; internet www.telearuba.aw; f. 1963; fmrly operated by Netherlands Antilles Television Co; commercial; owned by SETAR; Gen. Man. M. MARCHENA.

Finance

(cap. = capital; res = reserves; dep. = deposits; m. = million; br(s) = branch(es); amounts in Aruban florins, unless otherwise stated)

BANKING

Central Bank

Centrale Bank van Aruba: J. E. Irausquin Blvd 8, POB 18, Oranjestad; tel. 5252100; fax 5252101; e-mail cbaua@setarnet.aw; internet www.cbaruba.org; f. 1986; cap. 10.0m., res 174.8m., dep. 884.7m. (Dec. 2009); Chair. C. G. MADURO; Pres. JEANETTE R. FIGAROA-SEMELEER.

Commercial Banks

Aruba Bank NV: Camacuri 12, POB 192, Oranjestad; tel. 5277777; fax 5277715; e-mail info@arubabank.com; internet www.arubabank.com; f. 1925; acquired Interbank Aruba NV in 2003; total assets US $1,690m. (Dec. 2012); Chair. B. W. H. GUIS; 5 brs.

Banco di Caribe NV: Vondellaan 31, POB 493, Oranjestad; tel. 5232000; fax 5832422; e-mail management@bancodicaribe.com; internet www.bancodicaribe.com; f. 1987; Gen. Man. and CEO IDEFONS D. SIMON; 1 br.

Caribbean Mercantile Bank NV: Caya G. F. (Betico) Croes 53, POB 28, Oranjestad; tel. 5823118; fax 5824373; e-mail executive_office@cmbnv.com; internet www.cmbnv.com; f. 1963; cap. 4.0m., dep. 1,228.6m. (Dec. 2012); Chair. LIONEL CAPRILES, II; Gen. Man. J. E. WOLTER; 6 brs.

RBC Royal Bank (Aruba) NV: Italiestraat 36, Sasakiweg, Oranjestad; tel. 5233100; fax 58821576; e-mail tt-info@rbc.com; internet www.rbtt.com; f. 2001; fmrly First National Bank of Aruba NV (f. 1985 and acquired by Royal Bank of Trinidad and Tobago Ltd in 1998); name changed as above Mar. 2012; cap. 43.8m., res 17.6m., dep. 997.4m. (Dec. 2012); Chair. PETER J. JULY; 4 brs.

Investment Bank

AIB Bank NV: Wilhelminastraat 34–36, POB 1011, Oranjestad; tel. 5827327; fax 5827461; e-mail info@aib-bank.com; internet www.aib-bank.com; f. 1987 as Aruban Investment Bank; name changed as above in April 2004; total assets 149.0m. (Dec. 2005); Man. Dir FRENDSEL W. GIEL.

Mortgage Bank

Fundacion Cas pa Comunidad Arubano (FCCA): Sabana Blanco 66, Oranjestad; tel. 5223222; fax 5836272; e-mail info@fcca.com; internet www.fcca.com; f. 1979; Man. Dir PETER VAN POPPEL.

INSURANCE

There were seven life insurance companies and 13 non-life insurance companies active in Aruba in 2011.

Pan-American Life Insurance Company of Aruba, NV: Sun Plaza Suite 100, L. G. Smith Blvd 160, Oranjestad; tel. 5821184; fax 5823880; internet www.palig.com; f. 2012; part of Pan-American Life Insurance Group (USA); CEO and Man. Dir (Caribbean) WILLIAM R. SCHULZ, Jr; Gen. Man. VALERY SINOT.

Association

Insurance Association of Aruba (IAA): Sun Plaza 202, Oranjestad; tel. 5825500; fax 5822126; e-mail prakash.gupta@aig.com; Pres. PRAKASH GUPTA; 17 mems.

Trade and Industry

DEVELOPMENT ORGANIZATION

Department of Economic Affairs, Commerce and Industry (Directie Economische Zaken, Handel en Industrie): Sun Plaza Bldg, L. G. Smith Blvd 160, Oranjestad; tel. 5821181; fax 5834494; e-mail deaci@setarnet.aw; internet www.arubaeconomicaffairs.aw; f. 1986; Dir MARIA DIJKHOFF-PITA.

CHAMBERS OF COMMERCE AND INDUSTRY

Aruba Chamber of Commerce and Industry: J. E. Irausquin Blvd 10, POB 140, Oranjestad; tel. 5821566; fax 5883962; e-mail info@arubachamber.com; internet www.arubachamber.com; f. 1930; Pres. DAPHNE AGIUS CESAREO-LEJUEZ; Exec. Dir LEONICIO J. MADURO.

Association of Dutch Caribbean Chambers of Commerce & Industry: J. E. Irausquin Blvd 10, POB 140, Oranjestad; tel. 5821566; fax 5883962; e-mail secretariat@arubachamber.com; f. 2011; asscn of chambers of commerce in Aruba, Bonaire, Curaçao, Saba, Sint Eustatius and Sint Maarten.

TRADE ASSOCIATION

Aruba Trade and Industry Association (ATIA): ATIA Bldg, Pedro Gallegostraat 6, Dakota, POB 562, Oranjestad; tel. 5827593; fax 5833068; e-mail atiaruba@setarnet.aw; internet www.atiaruba.org; f. 1945; Chair. MICHEL HENRIQUEZ; Dir IGMAR REYES; 250 mems.

UTILITIES

Electricity and Water

Utilities Aruba NV: Schelpstraat 12, Oranjestad; tel. 5828277; fax 5828682; e-mail info@utilitiesarubanv.com; internet www.utilitiesarubanv.com; govt-owned holding co; Man. Dir Dr FRANKLIN HOEVERTSZ.

Electriciteit-Maatschappij Aruba (ELMAR) NV: Wilhelminastraat 110, POB 202, Oranjestad; tel. 5237100; fax 5828991; e-mail info@elmar.aw; internet www.elmar.aw; independently managed co, residing under Utilities Aruba NV; electricity distribution; Man. Dir ROBERT HENRIQUEZ; 160 employees.

Water en Energiebedrijf Aruba (WEB) NV: Balashi 76, POB 575, Oranjestad; tel. 5254600; fax 5857681; e-mail info@webaruba.com; internet www.webaruba.com; f. 1991; independently managed co, residing under Utilities Aruba NV; production and distribution of industrial and potable water, and electricity generation; Man. Dir OSLIN J. BOEKHOUDT.

Gas

Aruba Gas Supply Company Ltd (ARUGAS): Barcadera z/n, POB 190, Oranjestad; tel. 5851198; fax 5852187; e-mail sales@arugas.com; internet www.arugas.com; f. 1940; Man. R. P. GEERMAN.

BOC Gases Aruba NV: Balashi z/n, POB 387, Oranjestad; tel. 5852624; fax 5852823; e-mail bocaruba@setarnet.aw; internet www.linde-worldwide.com; owned by Linde Group; Man. Dir J. KENT MASTERS (responsible for Americas, South Pacific and Africa).

TRADE UNION

Federacion di Trahadornan di Aruba (FTA) (Aruban Workers' Federation): Bernhardstraat 23, Sint Nicolaas; tel. 5845448; fax 5845504; e-mail info@fta.aw; internet www.fta.aw; f. 1964; independent; affiliated with the International Trade Union Confed; Pres. JOSÉ RUDOLF (RUDY) GEERMAN; Vice-Pres. HUBERT MARIANO DIRKSZ.

Transport

There are no railways, but Aruba has a network of all-weather roads.

Arubus NV: Sabana Blanco 67, Oranjestad; tel. 5202300; fax 5828633; e-mail marketing@arubus.com; internet www.arubus.com; f. 1979; state-owned; fleet of 48 buses; Man. Dir TEO CROES.

SHIPPING

The island's principal seaport is Oranjestad, whose harbour can accommodate ocean-going vessels. There are also ports at Barcadera and Sint Nicolaas.

Aruba Ports Authority NV: Port Administration Bldg, L. G. Smith Blvd 23, Oranjestad; tel. 5234300; fax 5234343; e-mail info@arubaports.com; internet www.arubaports.com; f. 1981; administration of the ports of Oranjestad and Barcadera; Man. Dir JOSSY FIGUAROA.

Principal Shipping Companies

Aruba Stevedoring Co (ASTEC), NV: Port Administration Bldg, L. G. Smith Blvd 23, Oranjestad; tel. 5822558; fax 5834570; e-mail astec_admin@setarnet.aw; f. 1983; Man. Dir ERNAND MIKE DE L'ISLE.

Global Marine Services NV: De la Sallestraat 71-D, Oranjestad; tel. 5887212; fax 5887210; e-mail info@globalmarineservicesnv.co; internet www.globalmarineservicesnv.com; f. 2004; ship agent, liner shipping services, STS operations and freight services; Man. MARIA WINKEL.

Rocargo Services Aruba, NV: Lago Heightstraat 28, Lago Heights, POB 2527, San Nicolas; tel. 5844900; fax 5844880; e-mail rocargoaruba@rocargo.com; internet www.rocargo.com; f. 1994; shipping and port agents, cargo handling and transportation; Man. JOOP KRAAIJEVELD.

SEL Maduro & Sons (Aruba) Inc: Rockefellerstraat 1, Oranjestad; tel. 55826039; fax 5826136; e-mail vessel_coll@selmaduro.com; internet www.selmaduro.com; ship husbandry and port agent; also provides container services, cargo services, moving services, real estate and travel services; Man. Dir HANS BEAUJON (acting); Man. GRACEO DUNLOCK (Shipping and Container Services).

VR Shipping NV: Executive Bldg, Frankrijkstraat 1, POB 633, Oranjestad; tel. 5821953; fax 5825988; e-mail bronswinkelh@vrshipping.com; internet www.vrshipping.com; f. 1975 as Anthony Veder & Co; name changed as above 2000; Man. HANLEY BRONSWINKEL.

CIVIL AVIATION

The Queen Beatrix International Airport, about 2.5 km from Oranjestad, is served by numerous airlines linking the island with destinations in the Caribbean, Europe, the USA, and Central and South America. The airport underwent a three-stage expansion project in 2014, estimated to cost between US $18m.–$29m.

Aruba Airport Authority NV: Queen Beatrix International Airport, Wayaca z/n, Oranjestad; tel. 5242424; fax 5834229; e-mail p.steinmetz@airportaruba.com; internet www.airportaruba.com; CEO JAMES FAZIO.

Tiara Air: Sabana Blanco 70E, Suite 11, Oranjestad; tel. 5884272; fax 5885002; e-mail sales@tiara-air.com; internet www.tiara-air.com; daily flights to Colombia and Venezuela, scheduled flights to Bonaire, Curaçao; Pres. ALEJANDRO MUYALE.

Tourism

Aruba's white sandy beaches, particularly along the southern coast, are an attraction for foreign visitors, and tourism is a major industry. The number of hotel rooms totalled 7,441 in 2009. In 2013 some 1,667,824 tourists visited Aruba, of whom 979,256 were stop-over visitors and 688,568 were cruise ship passengers. Most stop-over visitors came from the USA (57% in 2013), Venezuela (19%) and the Netherlands (4%). Receipts from tourism totalled A Fl. 2,679.7m. in 2013.

Aruba Cruise Tourism: Royal Plaza Mall, Suite 230, L. G. Smith Blvd 94, POB 5254, Oranjestad; tel. 5833648; fax 5835088; e-mail cruiseinfo@aruba.com; internet cruise.aruba.com; f. 1995 as the Cruise Tourism Authority—Aruba; name changed as above in 2005; non-profit government organization; Gen. Man. GLORIA VEGA.

Aruba Hotel and Tourism Association (AHATA): L. G. Smith Blvd 174, POB 542, Oranjestad; tel. 5822607; fax 5824202; e-mail info@ahata.com; internet www.ahata.com; f. 1965; 101 mems; Chair. EWALD BIEMANS; Pres. and CEO JAMES HEPPLE.

Aruba Tourism Authority (ATA): L. G. Smith Blvd 172, Eagle, Oranjestad; tel. 5823777; fax 5834702; e-mail support@aruba.com; internet www.aruba.com; f. 1953; CEO RONELLA TJIN ASJOE-CROES.

Defence

The Netherlands is responsible for Aruba's defence, and military service is compulsory. The Dutch-appointed Governor is Commander-in-Chief of the armed forces on the island. A Dutch naval contingent is stationed in Curaçao and Aruba.

Education

Kindergarten begins at four years of age. Primary education begins at six years of age and lasts for six years. Secondary education, beginning at the age of 12, lasts for up to six years. In 2010 enrolment at primary schools included 99% of pupils in the relevant age-group, while enrolment at secondary schools in 2011 was 77%. The main language of instruction is Dutch, but Papiamento (using a different spelling system from that of Bonaire and Curaçao) is also used. There is one public university in Aruba. There is also a teacher training college and a number of private institutions. In addition, there is a community college. However, the majority of students continue their studies abroad, generally in the Netherlands. General government spending on education in 2010 was equivalent to 18.3% of total expenditure.

CURAÇAO

Introductory Survey

LOCATION, CLIMATE, LANGUAGE, RELIGION, FLAG, CAPITAL

Curaçao, a constituent part of the Kingdom of the Netherlands, lies about 55 km (34 miles) off the coast of Venezuela in the Caribbean Sea. Together with Aruba and Bonaire, the island forms the Benedenwindse Eilands or Leeward Islands. The climate is tropical, moderated by the sea, with an average annual temperature of 27.5°C (81°F) and little rainfall. The official languages are Dutch and Papiamento (a mixture of Dutch, Spanish, Portuguese, English, Arawak Indian and several West African dialects). Almost all of the inhabitants profess Christianity, predominantly Roman Catholicism. The state flag (proportions 2 by 3) is blue, with a yellow horizontal stripe just below the midline and two white, five-pointed stars in the canton. The capital is Willemstad.

Until October 2010 Curaçao formed part of the Netherlands Antilles, with Bonaire, Sint (St) Maarten, Saba and Sint (St) Eustatius. On 10 October 2010 the Netherlands Antilles was formally dissolved as a federation and Curaçao assumed the new status of an autonomous country within the Kingdom of the Netherlands.

CONTEMPORARY POLITICAL HISTORY

Historical Context

The Leeward Islands, already settled by communities of Arawak Indians, were discovered by the Spanish in 1499 and were seized by the Dutch in the 1630s. Curaçao became prosperous in the late 17th and 18th centuries as an entrepôt for trade in the Caribbean. After frequent changes in possession, the Leeward Islands were finally confirmed as Dutch territory in 1816. The islands (including Aruba and the Windward Islands—comprising St Eustatius, Saba and St Maarten) were administered as Curaçao and Dependencies between 1845 and 1948. Slavery was abolished in 1863, and the islands suffered from an economic decline until the establishment of a petroleum refinery on Curaçao in 1918. During the Second World War Queen Wilhelmina of the Netherlands promised independence, and in 1954 a Charter gave the federation of six islands full autonomy in domestic affairs, and declared it to be an integral part of the Kingdom of the Netherlands.

Domestic Political Affairs

Divisions of political allegiance within the Netherlands Antilles were along island, rather than policy, lines, and Curaçao traditionally dominated administrative affairs. Following Aruba's secession from the federation to assume *status aparte* (separate status) within the Kingdom of the Five, the Antilles of the Five was ruled by a series of unstable coalition Governments. By the early 1990s the metropolitan Government in the Netherlands indicated that it was willing to consider the creation of two federations in separate island groups. A referendum was held on Curaçao in November 1993 regarding its constitutional status; 74% of the electorate voted for a continuance of the island's status as a member of the Antillean federation. The option of *status aparte*, favoured by the Government, received only 18% of the votes cast. As a result, the Government collapsed. A general election took place in February 1994, at which a new, Curaçao-based party, the Partido Antía Restrukturá (PAR), led by Miguel A. Pourier, became the largest single party in the Staten (States, parliament). Pourier assumed the leadership of a broadly based coalition Government.

The PAR lost four of its eight parliamentary seats at a general election in January 1998 and Pourier lacked the support needed to form a new administration. Dissatisfaction with the new Government's attempts to reduce the fiscal deficit led to its collapse in October 1999 and that of the island Government of Curaçao. In the following month former Prime Minister Pourier formed a new broad-based coalition Government. The general election of January 2002 was won by the Curaçao-based Frente Obrero i Liberashon 30 di mei (FOL), led by Anthony Godett. However, the FOL was unable to form a government because of allegations of corruption and mismanagement of party funds. Eventually, in June, a coalition Government under the leadership of the new PAR leader, Etienne Ys, replaced Pourier's caretaker administration.

The Ys Government ruled until April 2003, when the cabinet resigned to allow a fresh governing coalition to be established. Ys was eventually replaced by Mirna Luisa Godett, the sister of Anthony, in August, who formed a FOL-dominated coalition. Godett was forced to resign in April 2004 amid allegations of FOL corruption. The next federal Government was formed by a seven-party coalition, once again led by Ys.

In October 2004 the Jesurun Commission, established by the Dutch and Antillean Governments and headed by Edsel Jesurun (a former Governor of the territory), recommended the dissolution of the Netherlands Antilles; support for the federation had, it was argued, virtually disintegrated on most of the islands. The Commission proposed that Curaçao and St Maarten should become autonomous states within the Netherlands (i.e. have *status aparte*). A further referendum on the constitutional future of Curaçao took place in April 2005: 68% of participants in Curaçao favoured *status aparte*, 23% voted for closer ties with the Netherlands and 5% voted for complete independence. In December 2005 a preliminary agreement with the Dutch Government that the extant federation be dissolved by 1 July 2007 was duly signed in Curaçao. Under the new structure, Curaçao was to become an autonomous member of the Kingdom of the Netherlands.

In November 2006 the Dutch Government granted Curaçao independent governance within the Kingdom of the Netherlands; endorsement of this latter agreement was contingent upon the island ceding authority for the administration of defence, foreign policy and law enforcement matters to the Dutch Government. However, Curaçao's Island Council voted decisively against the accord, averring that further negotiations were required, specifically over the administration of justice (over which they regarded the Dutch Government as having too great an influence). Particular concern had been expressed by the detractors with regard to stipulations for the management of the islands' respective budgets—entailing submission to a joint central bank—and the supervision of their judicial and police departments by the Dutch Government. Representatives of the PAR and conservative Partido Nashonal di Pueblo (PNP), who had voted in favour of the final agreement, left the Island Council in protest at the decision. Their departure left Curaçao without a legitimate government. Furthermore, in January 2007 the Netherlands Government rejected the island's request for a renegotiation of the November accord. Curaçao's abstention jeopardized certain provisions of the agreement that were dependent upon all five islands becoming signatories. The urgency of addressing Curaçao's already burdensome public debt was rendered more acute in light of the fact that the island would no longer benefit from the debt relief awarded by the Netherlands to signatories of the November agreement.

Curaçao was also conspicuously absent from the provisions of a further transition accord signed by the Netherlands Antilles central Government and the other four Island Councils in February 2007, envisaging the islands' complete secession from the federation. Curaçao's exclusion from the restructured Netherlands Antilles precipitated serious concerns for the island's pursuit of autonomy and its future status and relations with the Dutch Government, and, consequently, in July the Curaçao Island Council signed the November accord's 'closing statement', although its late accession to the arrangement precluded the island from the Netherlands Government's debt-restructuring provisions. Opposition-led protests took place in late 2007 in response to the continuing constitutional negotiations. The demonstrators objected to the Dutch Government having the power to intervene in the island's future financial and legal affairs. One week later the Island Council formally ratified the results of the 2005 referendum: at a second demonstration in December opposition parties demanded an end to the negotiations and for the Government to seek to achieve the autonomous status of Curaçao, in accordance with the results of the ballot.

A round table conference was held in Curaçao's capital, Willemstad, on 14–16 December 2008, at which it was established that Curaçao (and St Maarten) would gain autonomy, while the other three islands would become Dutch municipalities. Agreement was reached on the extent of the administrative powers of the Netherlands Government within the two seceding territories. In return for retaining some legal and financial controls over Curaçao and St Maarten, the Netherlands agreed to write off almost three-quarters of the Antilles' debt. The agreement was narrowly endorsed, by 52% of participants, in a referendum in Curaçao on 15 May 2009.

Autonomy

In September 2009 representatives of the Netherlands and the five islands of the Netherlands Antilles agreed that the target date for dissolution of the Netherlands Antilles would be 10 October 2010. Prior to securing autonomy, Curaçao would be required to introduce an appropriate legislative framework and to prepare its public authorities for the additional tasks entailed in administering an independent state.

An election to Curaçao's new designated legislature was held on 27 August 2010. The PAR won eight of the 21 seats, followed by the newly formed Movementu Futuro Korsou (MFK), led by Gerrit Schotte, which gained five seats, and the Pueblo Soberano (PS) with four seats. The Movementu Antia Nobo (MAN) garnered two seats while the FOL and the PNP each secured one seat. The MFK subsequently formed a coalition with the PS and the MAN and on 10 October Schotte was sworn in as Curaçao's first Prime Minister. On the same day Fritz Goedgedrag took office as the autonomous territory's Governor.

The Schotte Government came under scrutiny in October 2011 after the Prime Minister and two fellow MFK ninisters were accused by Central Bank Governor, Emsley Tromp, of corruption. In response, the coalition announced that the international anti-corruption organization Transparency International would conduct an independent investigation into the government of the island. In its report, published in mid-2013, Transparency International urged the island authorities to adopt the UN Convention against Corruption, to strengthen party-financing regulations, and to introduce measures to increase the autonomy and accountability of the civil service. The Government pledged to implement these proposals.

In May 2012 Prime Minister Schotte unexpectedly announced the suspension of the island's intelligence service, the Veiligheidsdienst Curaçao (VDC). He accused VDC agents of plotting a coup against the Government in 2010 and announced that the Netherlands secret service would restructure the agency.

Political instability

Irreconcilable disputes between the constituent parties of the governing coalition led to the collapse of the administration in August 2012. Schotte and the Council of Ministers resigned on 3 August, and an interim Government, headed by Stanley Betrian, was inaugurated on 29 September, with a general election scheduled to take place on 19 October. The Netherlands recognized the interim authorities, although Schotte argued that he was entitled to remain in power until a new government was elected. The PS attracted the most votes in the general election and gained control of five seats in the legislature. The MFK also won five seats, while the PAR (which had been renamed the Partido Alternativo Real in late 2010) and the Partido pa Adelanto i Inovashon Soshal (PAIS) each secured four seats, the MAN two, and the PNP one. Voter turnout was 74.5%. Following lengthy discussions, in mid-December the PS, the PAIS, the PNP and an independent deputy (formerly of the PAR) agreed that, after a transitional period of three–six months, they would form a coalition government. Daniel Hodge was sworn in as transitional Prime Minister on 31 December, and his administration of 'professionals' assumed office on 2 January 2013. Meanwhile, Goedgedrag resigned as Governor in November 2012; he was succeeded, on an interim basis, by Adele van der Pluijm-Vrede.

Hodge announced in March 2013 that his transitional Council of Ministers would resign in preparation for negotiations to form a new coalition government, under the supervision of a Governor-appointed formateur. The new administration, headed by Ivar Asjes of the PS, was finally inaugurated on 7 June. Hodge was elected as PAR leader later that month, but he tendered his resignation in September. (Zita Jesus-Leito was chosen as Hodge's successor in January 2014.) Lucille George-Wout was sworn in as the territory's new Governor in November 2013. Suzy Camelia-Römer was appointed Minister of Traffic, Transport and Urban Planning in March 2015 following the resignation of Earl Balborda, owing to a dispute with the leader of his party, the PNP.

Recent developments

In May 2013 Helmin Wiels, the leader of the PS, was shot dead in Willemstad. A police investigation into this unprecedented act of political violence was immediately launched, and several suspects were arrested. Although one of these suspects, alleged gang member Elvis Kuwas, was convicted of Wiels's murder in August 2014, investigative proceedings were ongoing in early 2015 in an effort to identify the orchestrators of the killing. A number of high-profile public figures had been detained and questioned by the police in mid-2014 in connection with the case: Carlos Monk, a former Minister of Education in the Schotte administration; former Minister of Finance George Jamaloodin; and local businessman Robby dos Santos, Jamaloodin's half-brother.

Schotte's home and offices were raided by the police in December 2013. It subsequently emerged that Schotte was under investigation for his alleged involvement in a money-laundering scheme, and in May 2014 the police detained and interrogated the former premier. Schotte claimed that the investigation was politically motivated. A pre-trial hearing began in March 2015.

Elections to the European Parliament were conducted on 22 May 2014. The Christen Democratisch Appèl won the majority of the local ballot, but turnout was very low.

A dispute between Aruba and Venezuela, relating to the arrest in July 2014 of a Venezuelan diplomat by the Aruban authorities, had ramifications for Curaçao, as the Venezuelan Government responded with countermeasures against all of the Dutch Caribbean islands. Venezuela briefly suspended air transport ties with the Dutch Caribbean and reportedly threatened to impose economic sanctions (including the cancellation of operations at Curaçao's economically important petroleum refinery, which was managed by Venezuela's state-owned oil company Petróleos de Venezuela, SA), while Venezuelan naval assets were sighted in waters near to Curaçao and Aruba. The dispute was resolved later in July after the intervention of the Dutch Ministry of Foreign Affairs. Following the discovery of an alleged coup plot in Venezuela in February 2015, Venezuelan President Nicolás Maduro declared that his nation's air defence zone would henceforth be expanded to encompass the airspace over the Dutch Caribbean islands. Later that month Maduro demanded that Curaçao and Aruba deny future entry to Tucano aircraft (such an aircraft had purportedly been used in the failed coup).

In April 2015 the island's Ombudsman completed an investigation into the Minister Plenipotentiary for Curaçao, Marvelyne Wiels, following accusations of inaccuracies in her curriculum vitae. The report was to be reviewed by the Prime Minister before being made public.

CONSTITUTION AND GOVERNMENT

The Constitution of Curaçao came into effect on 10 October 2010. The Governor of Curaçao, appointed by the Dutch Government for a term of six years, represents the monarch of the Netherlands in the territory. The Governor is assisted by an advisory council. Executive power in internal affairs is invested in the Council of Ministers. The Council of Ministers is responsible to the Staten, the 21-seat parliament, elected by universal adult suffrage.

ECONOMIC AFFAIRS

In 2013 the gross national income (GNI) of Curaçao, measured at current prices, was an estimated US $3,137m., equivalent to some $19,759 per head. Gross domestic product (GDP) was some $3,148m. in 2013 (equivalent to $19,830 per head), according to UN estimates. In 2004–13 the population increased at an average annual rate of 1.6%, while GDP per head increased, in real terms, by an average of 1.4% per year. According to UN estimates, GDP increased, in real terms, at an average annual rate of 3.2% in 2004–13. According to official estimates, real GDP declined by 0.1% in 2012 and by a further 0.8% in 2013.

Agriculture, together with forestry, fishing and mining, contributed an estimated 0.6% of GDP in 2013. The sector employed an average of 0.2% of the working population in the same year. Some 8% of the total land area is cultivated. The chief products are sorghum, divi-divi, groundnuts, beans, fresh vegetables and tropical fruit. A bitter variety of orange is used in the production of Curaçao liqueur. There is also some fishing. According to UN estimates, during 2004–13 agricultural GDP increased, in real terms, at an average annual rate of 1.8%; the sector's GDP declined by 4.4% in 2012, but increased by 1.8% in 2013.

Industry (comprising manufacturing, construction, utilities and mining) contributed an estimated 17.8% of GDP and employed an average of 16.0% of the working population in 2013. According to UN estimates, industrial GDP increased, in real terms, at an average annual rate of 3.9% in 2004–13; real industrial GDP grew by 1.9% in 2012, but declined by 0.8% in 2013.

Curaçao has few significant mineral reserves. The mining and quarrying sector employed only 0.2% of the working population in 2013. The GDP of the mining (along with utilities) sector declined, in real terms, at an average annual rate of 0.4% in 2003–12; it declined by 6.7% in 2011 and by a further 0.2% in 2012, according to UN estimates.

Manufacturing contributed an estimated 8.8% of GDP and employed an average of 6.3% of the working population in 2013; activities include food-processing, production of Curaçao liqueur, and the manufacture of paint, paper, soap and cigarettes. Curaçao's free trade zone is of considerable importance in the economy, but there are very few manufacturing activities. Petroleum refining (using petroleum imported from Venezuela) is the principal industrial activity, with the Isla refinery leased to the Venezuelan state petroleum company, Petróleos de Venezuela (PDVSA). Production capacity at the refinery was about 335,000 barrels per day. An oil spill at the refinery in 2012 caused considerable environmental damage. Petroleum transshipment is also important, and ship repairs at the Curaçao dry dock make a significant contribution to the economy. According to UN estimates, manufacturing GDP increased at an average annual rate of 2.6% in 2004–13; it remained constant in 2012, but declined by 1.8% in 2013.

Construction contributed an estimated 5.4% of GDP in 2013, and employed an average of 7.6% of the working population in the same year. According to UN estimates, construction GDP decreased at an average annual rate of 6.0% in 2004–13; it increased by 2.1% in 2013.

The services sector contributed an estimated 81.6% of GDP and engaged an average of 83.8% of the employed labour force in 2013. Curaçao was a major offshore financial centre. In 2011 the Organisation for Economic Co-operation and Development (based in Paris, France) urged Curaçao to improve financial transparency by accelerating implementation of bilateral agreements on the exchange of information on tax and foreign companies on the island. The financial and business services sector contributed 26.7% of GDP in 2013, and employed an average of 17.6% of the working population. A major industry is tourism, which is the largest employer after the public sector. The number of stop-over tourists to Curaçao as a whole reached 440,063 in 2013. In addition to tourism, Curaçao has sought to establish itself as a centre for regional trade, exploiting its excellent harbours. A free trade zone at the island's airport further enhanced Curaçao's entrepôt status. The GDP of the services sector increased, in real terms, at an average annual rate of 2.8% in 2004–13; it increased by 3.6% in 2013, according to UN estimates.

In 2013 Curaçao recorded a visible merchandise trade deficit (excluding oil products) of NA Fl. 2,170.0m. and there was a deficit of NA Fl. 1,186.3m. on the current account of the balance of payments. Petroleum is the principal commodity for both import and export and, according to unofficial figures compiled from partner countries, accounted for 45.9% of imports and 66.0% of exports in 2009. In 2012 the principal source of imports was the USA (46.4%), the Netherlands and Puerto Rico; the USA was also the principal market for exports (26.0% of the total exports), followed by Bonaire, the Netherlands and Aruba.

In 2013 the central Government recorded a budgetary surplus of NA Fl. 82.5m. At the end of 2008 total domestic debt amounted to NA Fl. 4,998.1m. (70.6% of GDP), while total foreign debt stood at NA Fl. 805.2m. (11.4% of GDP). The average annual rate of inflation was 3.2% in 2004–13; consumer prices increased by an average of 1.3% in 2013. Some 13.0% of the workforce were unemployed in 2013.

Recent years have witnessed a weakening of the economy, leading to high unemployment and increasing rates of emigration. The island was closely linked to Venezuela, which meant it was vulnerable to fluctuations in that country's economy. The important tourism sector withstood the worst of the global economic downturn in 2008–09, focused as it was on the higher-end market. The industry has made significant efforts to diversify arrivals, resulting in marked increases in tourists from North and South America in recent years, although the majority of visitors still come from Europe. According to the Caribbean Tourism Organization, cruise ship and stay-over arrivals rose, respectively, by 41.4% and 4.9% in 2013, and by 6.8% and 2.5% in 2014. The Central Bank reported that real GDP contracted by an estimated 0.5% in 2014, following a decline of 0.8% in 2013. Austerity measures, including an increase in the retirement age and reductions in health care expenditure, were adopted in 2013 in an attempt to stabilize the island's public finances; a rise in property tax was also introduced in April. While these reforms strengthened the Government's fiscal position, they were held to be partly responsible for the recent economic contraction. The Central Bank forecast growth of 0.4% in 2015, supported by the further expansion of the tourism sector, a rise in domestic demand and the construction of a new hospital. The IMF warned, however, that the economy was facing risks related to the island's large current account deficit, weak business environment and inefficient labour market; furthermore, the falling oil price was also likely adversely to affect the economy.

PUBLIC HOLIDAYS

2016: 1 January (New Year's Day), 8 February (Lenten Carnival), 25–28 March (Easter), 27 April (King's Day), 1 May (Labour Day), 5 May (Ascension Day), 2 July (National Flag and Anthem Day), 10 October (Curaçao Day), 25–26 December (Christmas).

Statistical Survey

Note: The Netherlands Antilles was officially dissolved on 10 October 2010. The figures in this Statistical Survey refer to Curaçao only, unless otherwise indicated

Sources (unless otherwise stated): Centraal Bureau voor de Statistiek, Fort Amsterdam, Willemstad, Curaçao; tel. (9) 461-1031; fax (9) 461-1696; internet www.cbs.cw/; Centrale Bank van Curaçao en Sint Maarten, Simon Bolivar Plein 1, Willemstad, Curaçao; tel. (9) 434-5500; fax (9) 461-5004; e-mail info@centralbank.an; internet www.centralbank.cw.

AREA AND POPULATION

Area: 444 sq km (171.4 sq miles).

Population: 150,563 (males 68,848, females 81,715) at census of 26 March 2011; 154,843 (males 70,823, females 84,020) at 1 January 2014.

Density (at 1 January 2014): 348.7 per sq km.

Population by Age and Sex (official estimates at 1 January 2014): *0–14 years:* 29,447 (males 15,120, females 14,327); *15–64 years:* 102,272 (males 46,069, females 56,203); *65 years and over:* 23,124 (males 9,634, females 13,490); *Total* 154,843 (males 70,823, females 84,020).

Principal Town: Willemstad (capital), population (incl. suburbs, UN estimate) 144,730 at mid-2014. Source: UN, *World Urbanization Prospects: The 2014 Revision*.

Births, Marriages and Deaths (2013): Registered live births 1,959 (birth rate 12.7 per 1,000); Registered resident marriages 665 (marriage rate 4.3 per 1,000); Registered deaths 1,250 (death rate 8.1 per 1,000).

Life Expectancy (years at birth, 2013): Males 75.4; females 81.0.

Immigration and Emigration (2013): *Immigration:* Aruba 100; Bonaire 120; China, People's Republic 122; Colombia 211; Dominican Republic 257; India 100; Netherlands 3,384; USA 166; Venezuela 213; Total (incl. others) 5,393. *Emigration:* Aruba 65; Bonaire 136; Netherlands 1,591; Sint Maarten 46; USA 33; Total (incl. others) 2,083.

Economically Active Population (persons aged 15 years and over, 2013): Agriculture, forestry and fishing 139; Mining and quarrying 102; Manufacturing 3,960; Electricity, gas and water 1,236; Construction 4,773; Wholesale and retail trade, repairs 11,994; Hotels and restaurants 6,108; Transport, storage and communications 5,060; Financial intermediation 4,495; Real estate, renting and business activities 6,586; Public administration, defence and social security 4,699; Education 3,520; Health and social work 5,308; Other community, social and personal services 2,814; Private households with employed persons 2,088; Extraterritorial organizations and

bodies 116; *Sub-total* 62,998; Activities not adequately defined 495; *Total employed* 63,493 (males 31,350, females 32,143); Unemployed 9,512; *Total labour force* 73,005.

HEALTH AND WELFARE

(Data refer to Netherlands Antilles)

Total Fertility Rate (children per woman, 2013): 2.2.

Under-5 Mortality Rate (per 1,000 live births, 2010): 13.5.

Physicians (per 1,000 head, 1999): 1.4.

Hospital Beds (per 1,000 head, 2012): 3.4.

Health Expenditure (% of GDP, 2008): 14.0.

Total Carbon Dioxide Emissions ('000 metric tons, 2007): 6,232.5.

Total Carbon Dioxide Emissions Per Head (metric tons, 2007): 32.4.

Source: mostly Pan American Health Organization.

For other sources and definitions, see explanatory note on p. vi.

AGRICULTURE, ETC.

Livestock (Netherlands Antilles, '000 head, year ending September 2012, FAO estimates): Cattle 0.7; Pigs 2.7; Goats 14.0; Sheep 9.4; Chickens 155.

Livestock Products (Netherlands Antilles, metric tons, 2013, FAO estimates): Pig meat 240; Chicken meat 380; Cows' milk 470; Hen eggs 630.

Fishing (all capture, metric tons, live weight, 2012): Atlantic bonito 538; Frigate tuna 238; Skipjack tuna 12,779; Yellowfin tuna 6,792; Bigeye tuna 2,890; Total catch (incl. others) 23,800 (FAO estimate).

Source: FAO.

MINING

(Data refer to Netherlands Antilles)

Production ('000 metric tons, estimate): Salt 500 in 2003–08. Source: US Geological Survey.

INDUSTRY

(Data refer to Netherlands Antilles unless otherwise indicated)

Production ('000 metric tons, 2011, unless otherwise indicated): Jet fuel 629; Kerosene 46 (2004); Residual fuel oils 3,003; Lubricating oils 327 (2007); Petroleum bitumen (asphalt) 1,025; Liquefied petroleum gas, refined 52; Motor spirit (petrol) 1,096; Aviation gasoline 12; Distillate fuel oils (gas-diesel oil) 1,815; Sulphur (recovered) 23 (2008); Electric energy (Curaçao only, million kWh, 2013) 894.1.

FINANCE

Currency and Exchange Rates: 100 cents = 1 Netherlands Antilles gulden (guilder) or florin (NA Fl.). *Sterling, Dollar and Euro Equivalents* (31 December 2014): £1 sterling = NA Fl. 2.794; US $1 = NA Fl. 1.790; €1 = NA Fl. 2.173; NA Fl. 100 = £35.79 = $55.87 = €46.01. *Exchange Rate:* In December 1971 the central bank's mid-point rate was fixed at US $1 = NA Fl. 1.80. In 1989 this was adjusted to $1 = NA Fl. 1.79. In December 2009 it was announced that the US dollar would replace the Netherlands Antilles guilder and florin in Bonaire, St Eustatius and Saba from 1 January 2011, following the dissolution of the previous federation of the Netherlands Antilles in October 2010. In Curaçao and St Maarten, the Netherlands Antilles guilder was expected to be replaced with a newly created Caribbean guilder, but negotiations on the introduction of the new currency appeared to have stalled by 2015.

Central Government Budget (NA Fl. million, 2013): *Revenue:* Tax revenue 1,434.8 (Taxes on income 673.6, Taxes on property 43.1, Taxes on goods and services 551.8, Taxes on international trade and transactions 160.4, Other taxes 5.9); Non-tax revenue 178.8; Total 1,613.6. *Expenditure:* Current expenditure 1,484.6 (Wages and salaries 706.4, Other goods and services 159.3, Interest payments 50.3, Transfers and subsidies 568.6); Capital expenditure (incl. transfers and net lending) 46.5; Total 1,531.1.

International Reserves (Netherlands Antilles, US $ million at 31 December 2009): Gold (national valuation) 356; Foreign exchange 867; Total 1,223. Source: IMF, *International Financial Statistics*.

Money Supply (Curaçao and Sint Maarten, NA Fl. million at 31 December 2013): Currency outside banks 340.6; Demand deposits at commercial banks 3,110.2; Total (incl. others) 3,450.7 (Source: IMF, *Kingdom of the Netherlands—Curaçao and Sint Maarten: 2014 Article IV Consultation-Staff Report; and Press Release* (August 2014)).

Curaçao

Cost of Living (Consumer Price Index; base: October 2006 = 100): All items 117.0 in 2011; 120.7 in 2012; 122.3 in 2013.

Gross Domestic Product (million NA Fl. at current prices, estimates): 5,439.3 in 2011; 5,604.7 in 2012; 5,635.4 in 2013.

Gross Domestic Product by Economic Activity (million NA Fl. at current prices, 2013, estimates): Agriculture, fishing and mining 28.9; Electricity, gas and water 190.2; Manufacturing 455.0; Construction 282.8; Trade 591.9; Hotels and restaurants 212.5; Transport, storage and communications 504.5; Real estate, renting and business activities 383.9; Education 28.8; Health and social welfare 227.3; Other non-financial service activities 183.9; Financial corporations 1,003.4; Government 618.4; Households and non-profit institutions 486.7; *Sub-total* 5,198.1; Net of indirect taxes 437.3; *GDP in purchasers' values* 5,635.4.

Balance of Payments (NA Fl. million, 2013): Exports of goods f.o.b. 1,270.5; Imports of goods f.o.b. –3,440.5; *Trade balance* –2,170.0; Services (net) 1,230.9; *Balance on goods and services* –939.1; Income (net) –75.8; *Balance on goods, services and income* –1,014.9; Current transfers (net) –171.3; *Current balance* –1,186.3; Capital account (net) 46.8; Direct investment (net) 60.1; Portfolio investment (net) 342.3; Other investment (net) 699.8; Net errors and omissions 1.7; *Overall balance* –35.6.

EXTERNAL TRADE

(Note: Although the import and export of petroleum and petroleum products, largely for refinery, transshipment and storage purposes, made a significant contribution to the economy of Curaçao, such transactions are not included in official trade statistics.)

Principal Commodities (NA Fl. million, 2012, excl. petroleum): *Imports c.i.f.:* Food and live animals 486; Beverages and tobacco 116; Chemical products 315; Manufactured goods 335; Machinery and transport equipment 1,002; Miscellaneous articles 404; Total (incl. others) 2,714. *Exports f.o.b.:* Food and live animals 45; Beverages and tobacco 21; Chemical products 32; Manufactured goods 31; Machinery and transport equipment 183; Miscellaneous articles 28; Total (incl. others) 365.

Principal Trading Partners (NA Fl. million, 2012, excl. petroleum): *Imports c.i.f.:* Aruba 28; Brazil 41; China, People's Republic 67; Colombia 59; Japan 38; Korea, Republic 49; Netherlands 442; Panama 104; Puerto Rico 136; Trinidad and Tobago 41; USA 1,260; Venezuela 102; Total (incl. others) 2,714. *Exports f.o.b.:* Aruba 36; Bonaire 82; Botswana 5; Colombia 6; Germany 6; Netherlands 69; Norway 13; Panama 9; Sint Maarten 8; USA 95; Total (incl. others) 365.

TRANSPORT

Road Traffic (motor vehicles registered, excl. government-owned vehicles, 2012): Passenger cars 69,035; Lorries 12,908; Buses 369; Taxis 159; Other cars 404; Motorcycles 1,300.

Shipping: *International Seaborne Freight Traffic* (TEUs moved, 2012): 99,191. *Flag Registered Fleet* (at 31 December 2014): Number of vessels 138; Total displacement 1,350,846 grt (Source: Lloyd's List Intelligence—www.lloydslistintelligence.com).

Civil Aviation (2013 unless otherwise indicated): Aircraft landings 21,684 (Commercial 25,639); Passenger movements 1,757,000 (2012).

TOURISM

Tourist Arrivals: *Stop-overs:* 390,282 (Netherlands 141,536; USA 63,268; Venezuela 61,582) in 2011; 419,810 (Netherlands 138,201; USA 62,262; Venezuela 83,148) in 2012; 440,063 (Netherlands 131,858; USA 61,747; Venezuela 92,123) in 2013. *Cruise ship passengers:* 400,596 in 2011; 436,068 in 2012; 583,994 in 2013.

Tourism Receipts (Netherlands Antilles, NA Fl. million, incl. passenger transport): 1,683.5 in 2002; 1,761.0 in 2003; 1,906.5 in 2004.

COMMUNICATIONS MEDIA

Telephones (December 2012): 71,995 main lines in use.

Mobile Cellular Telephones (December 2012): 204,702 subscribers.

EDUCATION

Students (2013/14 unless otherwise indicated): Primary 17,967; Secondary 11,024; Senior secondary vocational 3,779; University 224 (2013).

Pupil-teacher Ratio (Netherlands Antilles, primary education, UNESCO estimate): 19.8 in 2002/03.

Adult Literacy Rate (Netherlands Antilles, 2011, UNESCO estimates): 96.5% (males 96.6%; females 96.5%).

Source: partly UNESCO Institute for Statistics.

Directory

The Government

HEAD OF STATE

King of the Netherlands: HM King WILLEM-ALEXANDER.

Governor: LUCILLE A. GEORGE-WOUT (sworn in on 4 November 2013).

COUNCIL OF MINISTERS
(May 2015)

The Government is formed by the Pueblo Soberano, the Partido pa Adelanto i Inovashon Soshal and the Partido Nashonal di Pueblo.

Prime Minister and Minister of General Affairs: IVAR ASJES.

Minister of Economic Development: STANLEY PALM.

Minister of Finance: Dr JOSÉ MANUEL R. JARDIM.

Minister of Public Health, Environment and Nature: Dr BERNARD DENZIL WHITEMAN.

Minister of Education, Science, Culture and Sports: IRENE DICK.

Minister of Social Development, Labour and Welfare: RUTHMILDA. D. LARMONIE-CECILIA.

Minister of Justice: NELSON GENARO NAVARRO.

Minister of Traffic, Transport and Urban Planning: SUZY CAMELIA-RÖMER.

Minister of Government Policy, Planning and Public Services: ETIENNE VAN DER HORST.

Minister Plenipotentiary for Curaçao in the Netherlands: MARVELYNE WIELS.

MINISTRIES

Office of the Governor: Fort Amsterdam 2, Willemstad; tel. (9) 461-2148; fax (9) 461-2045; e-mail adjudant@kgcur.org; internet www.gouverneurvancuracao.org.

Office of the Prime Minister: Fort Amsterdam 17, Willemstad; tel. (9) 463-0495; fax (9) 461-7199.

Ministry of Economic Development: Dienst Economische Zaken, Pietermaai 25B, Willemstad; tel. (9) 462-1444; fax (9) 462-7590; e-mail info.meo@gobiernu.cw.

Ministry of Education, Science, Culture and Sports: Scharlooweg 102, Willemstad; tel. (9) 461-5133; fax (9) 461-5320; e-mail info.sae@gobiernu.cw.

Ministry of Finance: Pietermaai 17, Willemstad; tel. (9) 432-8000; fax (9) 461-3339; e-mail directie.financien@gobiernu.cw.

Ministry of General Affairs: Fort Amsterdam 17, Willemstad; tel. (9) 463-0495; e-mail info.gobierno@gobiernu.cw.

Ministry of Government Policy, Planning and Public Services: Breedestraat 39C, Punda, Willemstad; tel. (9) 433-3130; e-mail info.gobiernu@gobiernu.cw.

Ministry of Justice: Wilhelminaplein z/n, Willemstad; tel. (9) 463-0628; fax (9) 461-0598; e-mail Ministerie.Justitie@gobiernu.cw.

Ministry of Public Health, Environment and Nature: Dept of Health, Piscaderaweg 49, Willemstad; tel. (9) 432-5800; fax (9) 738-432-5805; e-mail info.ggd@gobiernu.cw; Dept of Environment and Nature, Straat Rosaweg 124, Willemstad; tel. (9) 736-9012; fax (9) 736-9195; e-mail info.mil@gobiernu.cw.

Ministry of Social Development, Labour and Welfare: Pietermaai Parking & Mall, Willemstad; tel. (9) 434-0300; fax (9) 461-0521; e-mail info.dwi@gobiernu.cw.

Ministry of Traffic, Transport and Urban Planning: Plasa Horacio Hoyer 19, Willemstad; tel. (9) 433-3200; fax (9) 433-3200; tel. info.rop@gobiernu.cw.

Office of the Minister Plenipotentiary for Curaçao in the Netherlands: Kabinet van de Gevolmachtigde Minister van de Curaçao, Badhuisweg 173–175, POB 90706, 2509 LS The Hague, Netherlands; tel. (70) 306-6111; fax (70) 306-6110; internet www.vertegenwoordigingcuracao.nl.

Legislature

STATES
(Staten)

President: MARCOLINO (MIKE) FRANCO (PAIS).
Vice-President: JAIME CORDOBA (PS).
Election, 19 October 2012

Party	Votes	% of votes	Seats
Pueblo Soberano (PS) .	19,716	22.65	5
Movementu Futuro Korsou (MFK) . . .	18,441	21.18	5
Partido Alternativo Real (PAR)*	17,149	19.70	4
Partido pa Adelanto i Inovashon Soshal (PAIS)	15,395	17.68	4
Movementu Antia Nobo (MAN)	8,297	9.53	2
Partido Nashonal di Pueblo (PNP) . . .	5,136	5.89	1
Others	2,924	3.36	—
Total†	87,058	100.00	21

* A PAR deputy, Glenn Sulvaran, subsequently declared he would sit in the States as an Independent, reducing the PAR's parliamentary representation to three.
† In addition, there were 370 invalid/blank votes.

Election Commission

Konseho Supremo Elektoral (KSE): Roodeweg 42, Willemstad; tel. (9) 434-1600; fax (9) 461-8166; e-mail info@kse.cw; internet www .kse.cw; Chair. GEOMALY MARTES.

Political Organizations

Democratische Partij—Curaçao (DP—C) (Democratic Party— Curaçao): Neptunusweg 28, Willemstad; f. 1944; Leader GEORGE HERNANDEZ.

Forsa Kòrsou: F. D. Rooseveltweg 347, Willemstad; tel. (9) 888-3041; fax (9) 888-3504; e-mail forsakorsou@onenet.an; Leader GREGORY DAMOEN.

Frente Obrero i Liberashon 30 di mei (FOL) (Workers' Liberation Front of 30 May): Mayaguanaweg 16, Willemstad; tel. (9) 461-8105; f. 1969; socialist; Leader ANTHONY GODETT.

Movementu Antia Nobo (MAN) (Movement for a New Antilles): Landhuis Morgenster, Willemstad; tel. (9) 468-4781; internet www .new.partidoman.org; f. 1971; socialist; Pres. EUGENE CLEOPA.

Movementu Futuro Korsou (MFK) (Movement for the Future of Curaçao): Salinja Lindbergweg z/n, Willemstad; tel. (9) 461-7766; fax (9) 461-7767; e-mail info@mfk.cw; internet www.mfk.cw; f. 2010; Leader GERRIT F. SCHOTTE.

Partido pa Adelanto i Inovashon Soshal (PAIS): Rozenweg 1, Willemstad; tel. (9) 518-8802; f. 2010; Pres. MARCOLINO (MIKE) FRANCO; Leader ALEX ROSARIA.

Partido Alternativo Real (PAR) (Real Alternative Party): Fokkerweg 26, Unit 3, Willemstad; tel. (9) 465-2566; fax (9) 465-2622; internet www.partido-par.com; f. 1993 as the Partido Antía Restrukturá, renamed as above in 2010; social-Christian ideology; Leader ZITA JESUS-LEITO.

Partido Nashonal di Pueblo (PNP) (National People's Party): Winston Churchillweg 133, Willemstad; tel. (9) 869-6777; fax (9) 869-6688; f. 1958; also known as Nationale Volkspartij; social-Christian party; Leader HUMPHREY DAVELAAR.

Pueblo Soberano (PS) (Sovereign People Party): Willemstad; internet www.pueblosoberano.org; pro-independence; Pres. EDWARD JOSEPH; Sec. GUSTAVO LAUFFER.

Judicial System

Legal authority is exercised by the Joint Court of Justice of Aruba, Curaçao and St Maarten, and of Bonaire, St Eustatius and Saba. The Court hears civil, criminal and administrative cases in the first instance and on appeal. The members of the Joint Court of Justice sit singly as judges in the Courts of First Instance and as a three-member panel in the appeals court. The Supreme Court of the Netherlands (based in The Hague) is the court of Final Instance for any appeal.

Joint Court of Justice: Wilhelminaplein 4, Willemstad; tel. (9) 463-4111; fax (9) 461-8341; e-mail curacao@caribjustitia.org; internet www.gemhofvanjustitie.org; Chief Justice EVERT JAN VAN DER POEL.
Attorney-General: GUUS SCHRAM.

Religion

CHRISTIANITY

Most of the population are Christian. There are also small communities of Jews, Muslims and Bahá'ís.

Curaçaose Raad van Kerken (Curaçao Council of Churches): Periclesstraat 6, Willemstad; tel. (9) 465-3207; fax (9) 461-0733; e-mail ddtic@yahoo.com; f. 1958; six mem. churches; Chair. Rev. PATMORE C. HENRY.

The Roman Catholic Church

Roman Catholics form the largest single group on Curaçao. According to the 2011 census, 73% of the population were Roman Catholic. Curaçao and the other former constituent territories of the Netherlands Antilles, together form the diocese of Willemstad, suffragan to the archdiocese of Port of Spain (Trinidad and Tobago). The Bishop participates in the Antilles Episcopal Conference, currently based in Trinidad and Tobago.

Bishop of Willemstad: Rt Rev. LUIS ANTONIO SECCO, Obispado Pietermaai, Julianaplein 5, Willemstad; tel. (9) 462-5876; fax (9) 462-7437; e-mail bisdomwstad@gmail.com; internet www .willemstaddiocese.org.

Other Christian Churches

The largest of the other churches in Curaçao, according to the 2011 census, were the Pentecostal (7% of the population), Protestant (3%), Seventh-day Adventist (3%), Jehovah's Witnesses (2%) and Evangelist (2%). Other denominations included Methodists, Anglican, Mormons and Baptists.

Iglesia Adventista di Shete Dia—Asosiashon Curaçao & Bonaire: Scalaweg 7, Willemstad; tel. (9) 737-1359; fax (9) 737-8201; e-mail sdaconference@adventcb.org; internet www.adventcb .org.

Iglesia Protestant Uni (United Protestant Church): Fortkerk, Fort Amsterdam, Willemstad; tel. (9) 461-1139; fax (9) 465-7481; e-mail info@vpg-curacao.com; internet www.vpg-curacao.com; f. 1825 by union of Dutch Reformed and Evangelical Lutheran Churches; associated with the World Council of Churches and the Caribbean and North American Council for Mission (CANACOM); Pres. JOHANNES (HANCO) DE LIJSTER; 3 congregations; 11,280 adherents; 3,200 mems.

United Pentecostal Church of Curaçao: Willemstad; internet jrblack.info; Pastor J. R. BLACK.

OTHER RELIGIONS

According to the 2011 census, 0.8% of the population of Curaçao were Hindu, 0.5% were Muslim, and 0.2% were Jewish.

Congregation 'Shaarei Tsedek' Ashkenazi Orthodox Jewish Community: The Herman and Miriam Tauber Jewish Center, 37 Magdalenaweg, Willemstad; tel. (9) 510-5900; e-mail shaareitsedek .shul@gmail.com; internet www.shaareitsedekcuracao.com; 140 mems; Rabbi ARIEL YESHURUN.

Reconstructionist Shephardi Congregation Mikvé Israel-Emanuel: Hanchi di Snoa 29, POB 322, Willemstad; tel. (9) 461-1067; fax (9) 465-4141; e-mail info@snoa.com; internet www.snoa .com; f. 1732 on present site; Rabbi GERALD ZELERMYER; about 150 mems.

The Press

Amigoe: Kaya Fraternan di Skèrpènè z/n, POB 577, Willemstad; tel. (9) 767-2000; fax (9) 767-4084; e-mail directie@amigoe.com; internet www.amigoe.com; f. 1884; Christian; daily; evening; Dutch; Dir ERNEST VOGES; Editor-in-Chief GINO BERNADINA; circ. 12,000.

Antilliaans Dagblad: ABCourant NV, Prof. Kernkampweg z/n, POB 725, Willemstad; tel. (9) 747-2200; e-mail algemeen@ antilliaansdagblad.com; internet www.antilliaansdagblad.com; f. 2003; daily; Dutch; Publr MICHAEL WILLEMSE.

De Curaçaosche Courant: Saliña 147, Willemstad; tel. (9) 461-2766; fax (9) 461-6302; e-mail info@curcourant.com; internet www .curcourant.com; f. 1812; weekly; Dutch; Editor H. C. (PIM) ELISABETH.

Extra: Rector Zwijssenstraat 24, Willemstad; tel. (9) 462-4595; e-mail redactie@extra.an; internet extra.cw; daily; morning; Papiamento; Editor MIKE OEHLERS; circ. 20,000.

Notisia360: Kaya Shon Louis Perret 9, Willemstad; tel. (9) 738-4086; e-mail info@notisia360.com; internet www.notisia360.com; Dutch and Papiamento; Editor-in-Chief ROLAND PERRET GENTIL.

La Prensa: W. I. Compagniestraat 41, Willemstad; tel. (9) 462-3850; f. 1929; daily; evening; Papiamento; Man. R. YRAUSQUIN; Editor SIGFRIED RIGAUD; circ. 10,750.

De Telegraaf (Caribische Editie): ABCourant NV, Prof. Kernkampweg z/n, Willemstad; tel. (9) 747-2200; fax (9) 747-2257; e-mail algemeen@antilliaansdagblad.com; internet www .antilliaansdagblad.com; Caribbean edn of Dutch daily.

Ultimo Noticia: Frederikstraat 100, Willemstad; tel. (9) 462-3446; fax (9) 462-6535; e-mail redakshon@ultimo.cw; daily; morning; Papiamento; Editor CHICHO JONCKHEER.

Vigilante Korsou: Kaya Wilson Papa Godett 24, Pietermaai; tel. (9) 465-3596; fax (9) 465-6571; e-mail redakshon@vigilantekorsou.com; internet www.vigilantekorsou.com; f. 1994; Papiamento.

Publisher

Drukkerij de Stad NV: W. I. Compagniestraat 41, POB 3011, Willemstad; tel. (9) 462-3566; fax (9) 462-2175; e-mail management@ destad.an; internet www.drukkerijdestad.com; f. 1929; Dir KENRICK A. YRAUSQUIN.

Broadcasting and Communications

TELECOMMUNICATIONS

Digicel Curaçao: Biesheuvel 24–25; tel. (9) 736-1056; fax (9) 736-1057; e-mail customercare@digicelcuracao.com; internet www .digicelcuracao.com; f. 1999 as Curaçao Telecom; bought by Digicel (Ireland) in 2005, present name adopted 2006; telephone and internet services; Chair. DENIS O'BRIEN; CEO (Dutch Caribbean) HANS LUTE.

Flow: Kaya Angel J. Leanez 26, Willemstad; tel. (9) 789-3569; f. 2010 following purchase by Columbus Communications Ltd of Curaçao Cable TV; bought by Cable & Wireless (UK) in 2015; Gen. Man. IAIN SERRAO.

United Telecommunication Services, NV (UTS): UTS Headquarters, Rigelweg 2, Willemstad; tel. (9) 777-0101; fax (9) 777-1284; e-mail info@uts.cw; internet www.uts.cw; f. 1999 following merger of Antelecom NV (f. 1908) and SETEL (f. 1979); Antelecom and SETEL still operate under own names; CEO PAUL DE GEUS.

BROADCASTING

Radio

Curom Broadcasting Inc: Roodeweg 64, POB 2169, Willemstad; tel. (9) 462-2020; fax (9) 462-5796; e-mail z86@curom.com; internet www.curom.com; f. 1933; broadcasts in English, Papiamento, Dutch and Spanish; Dir ORLANDO CUALES.

Easy 97.9 FM: Arikokweg 19A, Willemstad; tel. (9) 462-3162; fax (9) 462-8712; e-mail radio@easyfm.com; internet www.easyfm.com; f. 1995; Dir KEVIN CARTHY.

Gold 91.5 FM Curaçao: De Rouvilleweg 7, Ingang Klipstraat, POB 6103, Willemstad; tel. (9) 426-1803; fax (9) 461-9103; e-mail info@ gold915.com; internet www.gold915.com; music station.

Paradise FM: De Rouvilleweg 7, Ingang Klipstraat, POB 6103, Willemstad; tel. (9) 426-1803; fax (9) 461-9103; e-mail studio@ paradisefm.an; internet paradisefm.an; news station.

Radio Caribe: Ledaweg 35, Brievengat, Willemstad; tel. (9) 736-9564; fax (9) 736-9569; f. 1955; commercial station; programmes in Dutch, English, Spanish and Papiamento; Dir-Gen. C. R. HEILLEGGER.

Radio Hoyer NV: Plasa Horacio Hoyer 21, Willemstad; tel. (9) 461-1678; fax (9) 461-6528; e-mail hoyer1@radiohoyer.com; internet www.radiohoyer.com; f. 1954; commercial; two stations: Radio Hoyer I (mainly Papiamento, also Spanish) and II (mainly Dutch, also English) in Curaçao; Man. Dir HELEN HOYER.

Radio Korsou FM: Bataljonweg 7, POB 3250, Willemstad; tel. (9) 737-3012; fax (9) 737-2888; e-mail studio@korsou.com; internet www .korsou.com; f. 1976; 24 hrs a day; programmes in Papiamento and Dutch; Gen. Man. ALAN H. EVERTSZ.

Television

Antilliaanse Televisie Maatschappij NV (TeleCuraçao): Berg Ararat z/n, POB 415, Willemstad; tel. (9) 777-1688; fax (9) 461-4138; e-mail web@telecuracao.com; internet www.telecuracao.com; f. 1960; fmrly operated Tele-Aruba; commercial; owned by United Telecommunication Services; also operates cable service, offering programmes from US satellite television and two Venezuelan channels; CEO PAUL DE GEUS; Gen. Man. HUGO LEW JEN TAI.

Finance

(cap. = capital; res = reserves; dep. = deposits; m. = million; br.(s) = branch(es); amounts in Netherlands Antilles guilders unless otherwise indicated)

BANKING

Regulatory Authority

College Financieel Toezicht (CFT): De Rouvilleweg 39, Willemstad; tel. (9) 461-9081; fax (9) 461-9088; e-mail info@cft.an; internet www.cft.an; f. 2008; board of financial supervision; office on Sint Maarten (q.v.); Chair. AGE BAKKER.

Central Bank

Centrale Bank van Curaçao en Sint Maarten: Simon Bolivar Plein 1, Willemstad; tel. (9) 434-5500; fax (9) 461-5004; e-mail info@ centralbank.cw; internet centralbank.cw; f. 1828 as Curaçaosche Bank, renamed Bank van de Nederlandse Antillen in 1962, present name adopted in 2010; cap. 30.0m., res 610.5m., dep. 2,520.9m. (Dec. 2009); Pres. Dr EMSLEY D. TROMP; br. on St Maarten.

Commercial Banks

Banco di Caribe NV: Schottegatweg Oost 205, POB 3785, Saliña, Willemstad; tel. (9) 432-3000; fax (9) 461-5220; e-mail info@ bancodicaribe.com; internet www.bancodicaribe.com; f. 1973; cap. 20.6m., res 108.1m., dep. 1,371.5m. (Dec. 2013); Chair. R. GIBSON; CEO and Gen. Man. Dir IDEFONS D. SIMON; 5 brs.

CIBC FirstCaribbean International Bank: De Ruyterkade 61, POB 3144, Willemstad; tel. (9) 433-8000; fax (9) 433-8198; e-mail bank.curacao@cibcfcib.com; internet www.cibcfcib.com; f. 1964 as ABN AMRO Bank NV; adopted present name in 2002 following merger of Caribbean operations of CIBC and Barclays Bank PLC; Barclays relinquished its stake in 2006, present name adopted 2011; CEO RIK PARKHILL; Man. Dir (Dutch Caribbean) PIM VAN DER BURG; 1 br.

CITCO Banking Corporation NV: De Ruyterkade 62, POB 707, Willemstad; tel. (9) 732-2322; fax (9) 732-2330; e-mail curacao-bank@ citco.com; internet www.citco.com; f. 1980 as Curaçao Banking Corpn NV; Man. Dir and Gen. Man. JONATHAN LUCKMANN; Man. Dirs RONALD IRAUSQUIN, EUGENE RHUGGENAATH.

Girobank NV: Scharlooweg 35, Willemstad; tel. (9) 433-9999; fax (9) 461-7861; e-mail info@gironet.com; internet www.girobank.net; cap. 46.5m., res 49.2m., dep. 1,236m. (Dec. 2011); Pres. ERIC GARCIA; Man. Dirs STEPHAN CAPELLA, RICHARD RAJACK.

Maduro & Curiel's Bank NV: Plaza Jojo Correa 2–4, POB 305, Willemstad; tel. (9) 466-1100; fax (9) 466-1122; e-mail info@ mcb-bank.com; internet www.mcb-bank.com; f. 1916 as NV Maduro's Bank; merged with Curiel's Bank in 1931; affiliated with Bank of Nova Scotia NV, Toronto, Canada; br. in Bonaire; cap. 51m., res 190.6m., dep. 5,243.7m. (Dec. 2013); Pres. and CEO LIONEL CAPRILES; Man. Dirs RONALD GOMES CASSERES, JOE VAN DONGEN; 15 brs.

Orco Bank NV: Schottegatweg Oost, POB 4928, Landhuis Cerrito, Willemstad; tel. (9) 732 7000; fax (9) 737-6425; e-mail info@orcobank .com; internet www.orcobank.com; f. 1986; cap. 7.8m., res 17.4m., dep. 60m. (Dec. 2011); Man. Dirs M. N. S. SPROCK, M. M. S. BOSKALJON-ROMER; CEO K. R. CANWORD; 3 brs.

Rabobank Curaçao NV: Zeelandia Office Park, Kaya W. F. G. (Jombi), Mensing 14, POB 3876, Willemstad; tel. (9) 465-2011; fax (9) 465-2066; e-mail l.an.curacao.ops@rabobank.com; internet www .rabobank.com; f. 1978; cap. US $53.0m., res $17.8m., dep. $4,535.2m. (Dec. 2003); Chair. R. VAN ZADELHOFF; Gen. Man. T. STEVENS.

RBC Royal Bank NV: Kaya Flamboyan 1, Rooi Catootje, POB 763, Willemstad; tel. (9) 763-8438; fax (9) 737-0620; e-mail tt-info@rbc .com; internet www.rbc.com/caribbean; f. 1997 as Antilles Banking Corpn; name changed to RBTT Bank NV in 2002; name changed as above in 2012; cap. 114.5m., res 139m., dep. 3,553.2m. (Dec. 2010); Pres. and Country Head (Curaçao) ROBERT DA SILVA; 4 brs.

SFT Bank NV: Schottegatweg Oost 44, POB 707, Willemstad, Curaçao; tel. (9) 732-2900; fax (9) 732-2902; e-mail info@sftbank .com; internet www.sftbank.com; f. 1982 as Curaçao Banking Corpn; restructured as CITCO Bank Antilles in 1984; changed name as above in 1995; total assets 453.2m. (Dec. 2011); Man. Dir LEO RIGAUD.

Offshore Banks

Abu Dhabi International Bank NV: Kaya W. F. G. (Jombi), Mensing 36, POB 3141, Willemstad; tel. (9) 461-1299; fax (9) 461-5392; e-mail info@ant-trust.com; internet www.nbad.com; f. 1981; cap. US $20.0m., res $30.0m., dep. $112.2m. (Dec. 2006); Pres. NAGY KOLTA.

DVB Bank America NV: Zeelandia Office Park, Kaya W. F. G. (Jombi) Mensing 14, POB 3107, Willemstad; tel. (9) 431-8700; fax (9) 465-2366; e-mail sandra.sponselee@dvbbank.com; internet www .dvbbank.com; Gen. Man. SANDRA SPONSELEE.

Van Lanschot Bankiers (Curaçao) NV: Schottegatweg Oost 32, POB 4799, Willemstad; tel. (9) 737-1011; fax (9) 737-1086; e-mail info@vanlanschot.com; internet www.vanlanschot.com; f. 1962; wholly owned by F. Van Lanschot Bankiers NV (Netherlands); Man. A. VAN GEEST.

Savings Bank

Curaçaose Postspaarbank (PSB Bank): Schottegatweg Noord 24 Units M-N-O, Willemstad; tel. (9) 432-2000; fax (9) 737-2969; e-mail info@psbbanknv.com; internet www.psbbanknv.com; f. 1905; post office savings bank; Man. Dir GUIVERON WEERT; cap. 21m.; 20 brs.

Banking Associations

Association of International Bankers (IBA): A. M. Chumaceiro Blvd 3, POB 3369, Willemstad; tel. (9) 461-5367; fax (9) 461-5369; e-mail info@ibna.an; internet www.ibna.an; f. 1980; supervisory body for banks operating in Curaçao and Sint Maarten; 32 mems; Pres. ARTHUR ADAMS; Sec. ANTONIO TORRES.

Curaçao Bankers' Association (CBA): Plaza Jojo Correa 2–4, Willemstad; tel. (9) 466-1100; fax (9) 466-1122; e-mail florisela .bentoera@an.rbtt.com; f. 1972; Pres. LIONEL CAPRILES; Sec. FLORISELA BENTOERA.

Curaçao International Financial Services Association (CIFA): Chumaceiro Blvd 3, POB 220, Willemstad; tel. (9) 461-5371; fax (9) 461-5378; e-mail info@cifa-curacao.com; internet www .cifa-curacao.com; f. 1980; represents financial services cos, over 100 mems; Chair. ETIENNE YS.

INSURANCE

ASKA Holding NV (ASKA Levenverzekering NV/ASKA Schadeverzekering NV): Scharlooweg Oost 19, POB 3778, Willemstad; tel. (9) 734-5566; fax (9) 766-5588; e-mail info@askanv.com; internet www.askanv.com; f. 1995; accident and health, motor vehicle, property.

ENNIA Caribe Holding NV: J. B. Gorsiraweg 6, POB 581, Willemstad; tel. (9) 434-3800; fax (9) 434-3873; e-mail mail@ennia.com; internet www.ennia.com; f. 1948 as Nieuw Eerste Nederlandse Insurance Co; changed name as above in 1974; part of the Parman International BV (USA) since 2006; owns Ennia Caribe Schaden NV and Ennia Caribe Zorg NV; Pres. RALPH PALM.

Fatum: Cas Coraweg 2, Roi Katochi, Willemstad; tel. (9) 777-7777; fax (9) 736-3333; e-mail info@dc.myguardiangroup.com; internet myguardiangroup.cw; f. 1904; owned by Guardian Holdings Ltd; bought Royal & Sun Alliance (Antilles) NV in 2012; Pres. and CEO STEVEN MARTINA.

Maduro & Curiel's Insurance Services NV: Lio Capriles Banking Center, Rooi Catootje, POB 305, Willemstad; tel. (9) 466-1855; fax (9) 466-1611; e-mail mcis@mcb-bank.com; internet www .mcb-insurance.com; Man. CHANTIENNE ALCENDOR.

NAA-Citizens Curaçao NV: Salinja 170, Willemstad; tel. (9) 465-7144; fax (9) 461-6269; e-mail rwawoe@citizens-ins.net; internet www.naa-curacao.com; fmrly Netherlands Antilles and Aruba Assurance Company (NA&A) NV; accident and health, motor vehicle, property.

Pan-American Life Insurance Co of Curaçao and Sint Maarten, NV: Pan-American Life Bldg, Schottegatweg Oost 104, Willemstad; tel. (9) 461-3232; fax (9) 461-3240; internet www.palig.com; f. 2012; part of Pan-American Life Insurance Group (USA); CEO and Man. Dir (Caribbean) WILLIAM R. SCHULZ, Jr; Gen. Man. VALERY SINOT.

United Insurance Company Ltd: c/o UNIRISK, Schottegatweg Oost 60, POB 609, Willemstad; tel. (9) 737-4005; fax (9) 737-4006; e-mail info@united.cw; internet www.united.cw.

Trade and Industry

DEVELOPMENT ORGANIZATIONS

Curaçao Industrial and International Trade Development Company NV (CURINDE): Emancipatie Blvd 7, Landhuis Koningsplein; tel. (9) 737-6000; fax (9) 737-1336; e-mail info@ curinde.com; internet www.curinde.com; f. 1980; state-owned; manages the harbour free zone, the airport free zone and the industrial zone; Man. Dir J. JANSEN (acting).

World Trade Center Curaçao (WTCC): POB 6005, Piscadera Bay; tel. (9) 463-6132; fax (9) 463-6573; e-mail ceo@wtccuracao.com; internet www.worldtradecentercuracao.com; CEO CARMELO DE STEFANO.

CHAMBER OF COMMERCE

Curaçao Chamber of Commerce and Industry: Kaya Junior Salas 1, Pietermaai, World Trade Centre Bldg, POB 10, Piscadera Bay; tel. (9) 461-1451; fax (9) 461-5652; e-mail management@ curacao-chamber.cw; internet www.curacao-chamber.cw; f. 1884; Chair. WILLIAM JONCKHEER; Exec. Dir JOHN H. JACOBS.

INDUSTRIAL AND TRADE ASSOCIATION

Curaçao Trade and Industry Association (Vereniging Bedrijfsleven Curaçao—VBC): Kaya Junior Salas 1, POB 49, Willemstad; tel. (9) 461-1410; fax (9) 461-5422; e-mail info@vbcuracao.com; internet www.vbcuracao.com; f. 1944; Pres. BASTIAN KOOYMAN; Exec. Dir JOHAN LIEUW.

STATE HYDROCARBON COMPANY

Refinería di Korsou NV: Ara Hilltop Office Complex, Pletterijweg 1, POB 3627, Willemstad; tel. (9) 461-1050; fax (9) 461-3377; e-mail info@refineriadikorsou.com; internet www.refineriadikorsou.com; f. 1915 by Royal Dutch Shell Co, taken over by Govt and leased to PDVSA of Venezuela in 1985; Man. Dir HERBERT MENSCHE; Pres. OSWALD VAN DER DIJS.

UTILITY

Electricity and Water

Aqualectra Production NV (KAE): Rector Zwijssenstraat 1, POB 2097; tel. (9) 463-2000; fax (9) 463-6685; e-mail info@aqualectra.com; internet www.aqualectra.com; present name adopted in 2001; CEO DARICK JONIS (acting).

TRADE UNIONS

Central General di Trahadonan di Corsow (CGTC) (General Headquarters for Workers of Curaçao): POB 2078, Otrobanda, Willemstad; tel. (9) 737-6097; fax (9) 737-3145; e-mail cgtc.curacao@ gmail.com; f. 1949; Sec.-Gen. ROLAND (NACHO) IGNACIO.

Curaçaosche Federatie van Werknemers (Curaçao Federation of Workers): Schouwburgweg 44, POB 4327, Willemstad; tel. (9) 737-0390; fax (9) 737-1403; e-mail curafed@yahoo.com; f. 1964; Pres. WILFRED SPENCER; Sec.-Gen. GILBERT POULINA; 204 affiliated unions; about 2,000 mems.

Sentral di Sindikatonan di Korsou (SSK) (Central Trade Unions of Curaçao): Schouwburgweg 44, POB 3036, Willemstad; tel. (9) 737-0255; fax (9) 737-5250; e-mail ssk@cura.net; Pres. ALCIDES COVA; 6,000 mems.

Transport

ROADS

There are no railways, but Curaçao has a good system of all-weather roads.

Autobusbedrijf Curaçao NV (ABC): Industrieterrein Buena Vista, Willemstad; tel. (9) 868-4733; fax (9) 868-3026; internet autobusbedrijf.com; f. 1943; bus services.

SHIPPING

Curaçao is an important centre for the refining and transshipment of petroleum. Willemstad is served by the Schottegat harbour. There are a further six ports on the island. A 'mega cruise' facility, with capacity for the largest cruise ships, is on the Otrobanda side of St Anna Bay. Ports at Bullen Bay and Caracas Bay also serve Curaçao. At December 2014 the flag registered fleet comprised 138 vessels, totalling 1,350,846 grt.

Curaçao Ports Authority: Werf de Wilde z/n, POB 689, Willemstad; tel. (9) 434-5999; fax (9) 461-3907; e-mail info@curports.com; internet curports.com; Man. Dir HUMBERTO DE CASTRO.

Principal Shipping Companies

Caribbean Cargo Services NV: Caracasbaaiweg 328, POB 442, Willemstad; tel. (9) 767-2588; fax 747-1155; internet www.ccs.an; Man. Dir LOES VAN DER WOUDE.

Curaçao Drydock Company (CDM): POB 3012; tel. (9) 733-0000; fax (9) 736-5580; f. 1958; state-owned; ship repair yard.

Dammers Ship Agencies Inc: Dammers Bldg, Kaya Flamboyan 11, POB 3018, Willemstad; tel. (9) 737-0600; fax (9) 737-3875; e-mail directorate@dammers-curacao.com; internet www.dammers -curacao.com; f. 1964; fmrly Dammers & van der Heide, Shipping and Trading (Antilles) Inc; Man. Dir MARLON MANUEL.

Gomez Shipping NV: Landhuis Zeelandia z/n, Willemstad; tel. (9) 461-5900; fax (9) 461-3358; e-mail info@gomezshipping.ibm.net; Man. FERNANDO DA COSTA GÓMEZ.

S. E. L. Maduro Shipping: Dokweg 19, Maduro Plaza, POB 3304, Willemstad; tel. (9) 733-1510; fax (9) 733-1538; e-mail maduroship@madurosons.com; internet www.madurosons.com; f. 1837; Man. Dir H. MEIJER.

VR Shipping NV: Scarlet Bldg, Fokkerweg 26, POB 3677, Willemstad; tel. (9) 461-4700; fax (9) 461-2576; e-mail info@vrshipping.com; internet www.vrshipping.com; f. 1975 as Anthony Veder & Co NV; brs in Aruba and Bonaire.

CIVIL AVIATION

Curaçao International Airport is located at Hato, 12 km from Willemstad. In 2014 the airport underwent a US $10m. renovation, including improvements to the runway.

Civil Aviation Authority (CCAA): Seru Mahuma z/n, Willemstad; tel. (9) 839-3319; fax (9) 868-9924; e-mail civilair@gobiernu.cw; Dir Lt-Col (retd) OSCAR DERBY.

Curaçao Airline Association (CAA): Curaçao International Airport, Hato; tel. (9) 839-1111; fax (9) 839-1112; internet curacaoairlinesassociation.org; f. 2003; 42 mems; Pres. GERMAINE RICHIE; Sec. GERHARD GOSELINK.

InselAir: Curaçao International Airport, Hato; tel. (9) 737-0444; e-mail customerrelations@fly-inselair.com; internet www.fly-inselair.com; f. 2006; flights within Caribbean, to Venezuela, Guyana and the USA; CEO ALBERT J. KLUIJVER.

Tourism

Tourism is a major industry on Curaçao. The principal attractions for tourists are the white, sandy beaches, marine wildlife and diving facilities. Stop-over arrivals to Curaçao totalled 440,063 in 2013. The majority of visitors were from the Netherlands (30%) and Venezuela (21%). Tourism receipts totalled US $453m. in 2011.

Curaçao Hospitality and Tourism Association (CHATA): Kaya Junior Salas 01, Willemstad; tel. (9) 465-1005; fax (9) 465-1052; e-mail info@chata.org; internet www.chata.org; f. 1967 as Curaçao Hotel Asscn; Pres. and CEO LIZANNE DINDIAL.

Curaçao Tourist Board: Pietermaai 19, POB 3266, Willemstad; tel. (9) 434-8200; fax (9) 461-5017; e-mail info@curacao.com; internet www.curacao.com; f. 1955; Dir HUGO CLARINDA (acting).

Defence

The Netherlands is responsible for the defence of Curaçao. The Dutch-appointed Governor is Commander-in-Chief of the armed forces on the island. A Dutch naval contingent is stationed in Curaçao and Aruba.

Flag Officer, Caribbean: Cdre HANS LODDER.

Education

Education was made compulsory in 1992. The island's educational facilities are generally of a high standard. The education system is the same as that of the Netherlands. Dutch is the principal language of instruction, although lessons are also taught in Papiamento in primary schools. Primary education begins at six years of age and lasts for six years. Secondary education lasts for a further five years.

SINT MAARTEN

Introductory Survey

Sint (St) Maarten lies in the north-eastern Caribbean Sea, 20 km (12 miles) to the north of Saint-Barthélemy, a French Overseas Collectivity. St Maarten shares a land border with Saint-Martin, the northern half of the island and another Overseas Collectivity of France. St Maarten, as well as Saba (45 km to the south) and Sint (St) Eustatius (56 km south) are known as the Bovenwindse Eilands or Windward Islands (although they actually lie in the Leeward group of the Lesser Antilles). The climate is tropical, moderated by the sea, with an average annual temperature of 27.5°C (81°F) and little rainfall. The official language is English, although Dutch is also spoken. Almost all of the inhabitants profess Christianity, predominantly Protestantism. The state flag (proportions 2 by 3) comprises two equal horizontal stripes, red over blue, with a white triangle at the hoist. In the centre of the triangle is the territory's coat of arms. The capital is Philipsburg.

The Dutch settled the Windward Islands, once inhabited by Carib Indians, in the mid-17th century. The island of St Maarten was divided between the Dutch and the French in 1648, but conflicts over ownership continued for many decades before finally, in 1817, the current partition line between the Dutch and French territories was established. The Dutch part of the island then prospered as a slave-based plantation economy and a major exporter of salt. Together with the Leeward Islands (comprising Aruba, Bonaire and Curaçao), the Windward islands were administered as Curaçao and Dependencies between 1845 and 1948. The territory attracted immigration from Europe, particularly Dutch Protestants but also some French. During the Second World War Queen Wilhelmina of the Netherlands promised independence, and following the end of the war calls for independence became more persistent in St Maarten (as well as in Curaçao—see separate chapter). In 1954 the Dutch Government gave the federation of six islands full autonomy in domestic affairs, and declared it to be an integral part of the Kingdom of the Netherlands.

Political allegiance within the federation was traditionally along island, rather than party lines. These divisions increased following Aruba's secession from the federation in 1986. Calls for further autonomy increased in Curaçao and St Maarten. By the early 1990s it appeared that, while the metropolitan Government was unwilling to allow the complete disintegration of the federation, it was prepared to consider a less centralized system or the creation of two federations in the separate island groups. Nevertheless, in a referendum on the status issue held in St Maarten in October 1994, 60% of the electorate voted to remain within the Antillean federation, while the option of *status aparte* (separate status) received 32% of the vote.

A further referendum on the constitutional future of St Maarten took place on 23 June 2000. Only 4% of participants favoured maintaining the status quo. Some 69% favoured obtaining *status aparte* within the Kingdom of the Netherlands, 14% favoured complete independence and 12% preferred a restructuring of the Antilles of the Five. However, the Dutch Government indicated that it would not support a request by St Maarten to receive *status aparte*. In February 2003 the Dutch Minister of Interior and Kingdom Relations confirmed that the Netherlands would not permit St Maarten to leave the federation.

The Jesurun Commission, established by the Dutch and Antillean Governments and headed by Edsel Jesurun (a former Governor of the territory), on 8 October 2004 recommended the dissolution of the Netherlands Antilles; support for the federation had, it was argued, virtually disintegrated on most of the islands. The Commission proposed that St Maarten (and Curaçao) should become an autonomous state within the Netherlands (i.e. have *status aparte*), while Saba, Bonaire and St Eustatius should be directly administered by the Dutch Government. A preliminary agreement with the Dutch Government was signed in Curaçao on 3 December 2005; the accord set out that the extant federation be dissolved by 1 July 2007 and that St Maarten would become an autonomous member of the Kingdom of the Netherlands.

On 2 November 2006 the Dutch Government granted St Maarten (and Curaçao) independent governance within the Kingdom of the Netherlands, with the exception of matters of defence, foreign policy and law enforcement. The metropolitan administration would assume responsibility for the Netherlands Antilles' substantial collective debt. St Maarten's Island Council acceded to the proposed agreement on 28 November; however, progress towards dissolving the federation was delayed by the Curaçao Island Council's voting against ratification of the accord, citing concern over provisions relating to judicial matters, policing and debt relief (see Curaçao). The Dutch Government refused to countenance renegotiation of the terms of the agreement. Nevertheless, on 12 February 2007, at a meeting in Philipsburg, a further transition accord was signed by the Island Councils of Saba, Bonaire, St Eustatius and St Maarten, and the Netherlands, establishing a target date of 15 December 2008 for the dissolution of the federation.

During 2008 it became increasingly clear that the December deadline for constitutional change would not be met. Negotiations continued, however, and at a round table conference in Willemstad, Curaçao, on 14–16 December 2008, representatives of all five islands of the federation and the Dutch Prime Minister, Jan Peter Balkenende, agreed on the new political structure of the Netherlands Antilles. St Maarten would become self-governing except in matters of defence, foreign policy, justice and finance. In return for retaining some legal and financial controls over St Maarten, the Dutch Government agreed to write off almost three-quarters of the Antilles' debt. Negotiations stalled, however, on other matters, particularly policing and sound financial management. In September 2009 it was agreed that a second proposed dissolution date of January 2010 was unattainable, and that constitutional change would be set for 10 October of that year. Prior to securing autonomy, St Maarten would be required to introduce an appropriate legislative framework and to prepare its public authorities for the additional tasks entailed in administering an independent state.

An election was held on 17 September 2010 to St Maarten's new 15-seat legislature. The National Alliance (NA), comprising the Sint Maarten Patriotic Alliance and the National Progressive Party, gained seven seats, while the United People's Party (UP) won six seats and the Democratic Party (DP) the remaining two seats. The UP and the DP agreed to form a coalition government following the introduction of the new Constitution. The DP's leader, Sarah Wescot-Williams, took office as the autonomous territory's first Prime Minister on 10 October, on the same day that the first meeting of parliament was convened. Eugene Holiday assumed the office of Governor.

The UP and DP coalition administration collapsed at the end of April 2012 after the UP parliamentary leader, Romain Laville, resigned from the party in protest at what he perceived to be a lack of progress with the legislative agenda. He and two other deputies then withdrew their support for the coalition. The Council of Ministers submitted its resignation on 8 May. An agreement on the formation of a new administration was signed by the NA, the DP and three independents (including Laville) on 11 May. The new coalition Government, which was again headed by Wescot-Williams, took office on 21 May. However, in May 2013 several members of the coalition again retracted their support for the administration, precipitating its collapse. The UP and the DP, with the backing of an independent legislator, agreed to form another coalition Government, which was duly inaugurated on 14 June. Wescot-Williams continued to serve as Prime Minister.

Elections to the European Parliament took place on 22 May 2014. Democraten 66 won the majority of the local ballot, although turnout was very low. Meanwhile, during the first half of 2014 St Maarten was granted associate membership of the Association of Caribbean States (see p. 444) and the UN Economic Commission for Latin America and the Caribbean.

At a general election conducted on 29 August 2014, the UP, with 42.5% of the valid votes cast, secured seven of the 15 seats in the legislature. The NA won four seats, while the DP and the United St Maarten Party (US Party) each gained control of two seats. In early September the NA, the DP and the US Party, which combined had a one-seat legislative majority, announced their intention to form a coalition government. However, these plans collapsed later that month when DP deputy Van Hugh Cornelius de Weever withdrew his support and instead endorsed a rival proposal for the establishment of a UP-led administration. With de Weever's support (and, subsequently, that of a former member of the US Party, turned independent), the UP commanded a narrow parliamentary majority, and thus in early October Governor Holiday requested that UP leader Theo Heyliger commence the government formation process. (Shortly thereafter, Wescot-Williams, the DP's other newly elected legislator, also gave her backing to the UP, but in November she retracted this support and de Weever was ejected from the DP.) Further complications emerged in late October, however, as the Dutch authorities demanded that Heyliger and his proposed ministers be subjected to enhanced vetting measures to ensure the integrity of the incoming administration. Heyliger denounced this intervention as 'unconstitutional', but the Dutch Government maintained that it was a prudent step given the concerns raised in several recent reports about alleged corruption in St Maarten. Some observers suggested that the Dutch authorities had intervened in an effort to prevent the island premiership from being assumed by Heyliger, who had been accused of corruption by several mainland politicians. Island legislators responded by approving a motion that rejected the Netherlands' demands, while in early November the outgoing Wescot-Williams administration also adopted a non-co-operative stance, citing the alleged violation of the territory's autonomy. Nevertheless, under increasing pressure, Heyliger declared in mid-November that he would not be seeking the premiership, nor any other cabinet-level position. In early December it was reported in the local media that four prospective members of the proposed UP-led government had failed the vetting process owing to doubts about their integrity. Following the approval of replacement candidate ministers, a new administration, headed by the UP's Marcel Gumbs, finally took office on 19 December. De Weever, now an independent, was appointed as Minister of Public Health, Social Development and Labour.

Aruba hosted a Kingdom Inter-Parliamentary Consultation in January 2015, attended by representatives of the Netherlands, Aruba, Curaçao and St Maarten. The delegates agreed to establish a mechanism to help resolve future intra-Kingdom disputes. Also in January, recently elected UP deputy Silvio Matser received a two-year gaol term after being found guilty of tax fraud. In the previous month another prominent member of the ruling party, former cabinet minister Maria Buncamper-Molanus, had also been charged with tax fraud. In February the Gumbs administration announced a series of measures to promote probity in the public sector, including the formation of an Integrity Chamber. However, the Dutch Government expressed doubts about the independence of this new body and demanded that it be reformed—a move that evoked considerable resentment in St Maarten and further soured bilateral relations.

Tourism is the country's main economic sector. In addition, aggregate is also quarried and consumed primarily by the local construction industry, which contributed 6.7% of gross domestic product (GDP) in 2012. Official data for 2013 indicated that the unemployment rate moderated to 9.2%, from 12.0% 2012, while inflation slowed to 2.5% (down from 4.0% in 2012). According to the Central Bank, real GDP rose by 0.3% in 2011 and by 1.4% in 2012. Supported by increased activity in the tourism, construction and manufacturing sectors, the economy grew by 1.0% in 2013. The Government estimated that real GDP expanded by a further 1.4% in 2014 owing to the continued strength of the tourism industry. Stay-over arrivals rose from 466,955 in 2013 to 499,326 in 2014, while cruise ship visitors increased from 1.8m. to 2.0m. over the same period.

PUBLIC HOLIDAYS

2016: 1 January (New Year's Day), 25 March (Good Friday), 28 March (Easter Monday), 27 April (King's Day), 29 April (Carnival Day—Jouvert Jump Up), 1 May (Labour Day), 5 May (Ascension Day), 25 May (Whit Monday), 1 July (Emancipation Day), 11 November (St Maarten Day), 15 December (Kingdom Day), 25–26 December (Christmas).

Statistical Survey

Note: The Netherlands Antilles was officially dissolved on 10 October 2010. The figures in this Statistical Survey refer to Sint Maarten only, unless otherwise indicated.

Sources (unless otherwise stated): Department of Statistics (STAT), Ministry of Tourism, Economic Affairs, Transport and Telecommunications (TEZVT), Juancho Yrausquin Blvd 6, Units 7/8, Philipsburg; tel. 542-2151; fax 542-9907; internet www.sintmaartengov.org; Centrale Bank van Curaçao en Sint Maarten, Walter Nisbeth Rd 25, Philipsburg; tel. 542-3529; fax 542-4307; e-mail info@centralbank.an; internet www.centralbank.cw.

AREA AND POPULATION

Area: 34 sq km (13.1 sq miles).

Population (resident population at census of 9 April 2011): 33,609 (males 15,868, females 17,741).

Density (at 2011 census): 988.5 per sq km.

Population by Age and Sex (resident population at 2011 census): *0–14 years:* 7,405 (males 3,543, females 3,862); *15–64 years:* 24,275 (males 11,415, females 12,860); *65 years and over:* 1,929 (males 910, females 1,019); *Total* 33,609 (males 15,868, females 17,741).

Births, Marriages and Deaths (2010 unless otherwise indicated): Births 496; Registered marriages 232 (marriage rate 5.7 per 1,000, 2008); Deaths 160.

Life Expectancy (years at birth, 2014): 77.8 (males 75.5; females 80.2). Source Pan American Health Organization.

Immigration and Emigration (2009): *Immigration:* Dominican Republic 160; Guadeloupe 79; Guyana 128; India 84; Netherlands 297; Total (incl. others) 2,170. *Emigration:* Aruba 40; Netherlands 365; USA 10; Total (incl. others) 827. *2010:* Total immigration 859; Total emigration 873.

Economically Active Population (labour force survey at June, persons aged 15 years and over, 2009): Agriculture, fishing and mining 163; Manufacturing 646; Electricity, gas and water 325; Construction 2,307; Wholesale and retail trade, repairs 4,146; Hotels and restaurants 2,729; Transport, storage and communications 2,031; Financial intermediation 692; Real estate, renting and business activities 2,520; Public administration, defence and social security 1,600; Education 723; Health and social work 633; Other community, social and personal services 1,910; Private households with employed persons 648; Extraterritorial organizations and bodies 305; *Total employed* 21,378; Unemployed 2,966; *Total labour force* 24,344 (males 12,545, females 11,799). Source: Netherlands Antilles Central Bureau of Statistics.

FISHING

Fishing (all capture, metric tons, live weight, 2012, FAO estimate): Marine fishes 180; Total catch (incl. others) 181 (Source: FAO).

FINANCE

Currency and Exchange Rates: 100 cents = 1 Netherlands Antilles gulden (guilder) or florin (NA Fl.). *Sterling, Dollar and Euro Equivalents* (31 December 2014): £1 sterling = NA Fl. 2.794; US $1 = NA Fl. 1.790; €1 = NA Fl. 2.173; NA Fl. 100 = £35.79 = $55.87 = €46.01. *Exchange Rate:* In December 1971 the Netherlands Antilles' central bank's mid-point rate was fixed at US $1 = NA Fl. 1.80. In 1989 this was adjusted to $1 = NA Fl. 1.79. In December 2009 it was announced that the US dollar would replace the Netherlands Antilles guilder and florin in Bonaire, St Eustatius and Saba from 1 January 2011, following the dissolution of the previous federation of the Netherlands Antilles in October 2010. In Curaçao and St Maarten, the Netherlands Antilles guilder was expected to be replaced with a newly created Caribbean guilder, but negotiations on the introduction of the new currency appeared to have stalled by 2015.

Budget (NA Fl. million, 2013): *Revenue:* Tax revenue 329.6; (Taxes on income and profits 150.4, Indirect taxes 179.2); Non-tax revenue 92.4; Total 422.0. *Expenditure:* Wages and salaries 183.5; Goods and services 95.1; Subsidies and transfers 85.2; Social security 39.3; Interest payment 10.8; Other expenditures 13.0; Total 426.9.

Cost of Living (Consumer Price Index; base: October 2006 = 100): All items 116.3 in 2011; 121.0 in 2012; 124.0 in 2013.

Gross Domestic Product (million NA Fl. at current prices): 1,597.2 in 2010; 1,667.7 in 2011; 1,760.2 in 2012.

Gross Domestic Product by Economic Activity (million NA Fl. at current prices, 2012): Agriculture, fishing and mining 2.8; Electricity, gas and water 54.1; Manufacturing 28.9; Construction 108.6; Trade, restaurants and hotels 392.8; Transport, storage and communications 201.7; Real estate, renting and business activities 394.4; Health and social welfare 47.1; Other community, social and personal services 73.0; Financial corporations 163.2; Government 151.4; *Sub-total* 1,618.1; Net of indirect taxes 142.2; *GDP in purchasers' values* 1,760.2.

Balance of Payments (NA Fl. million, 2013): Exports of goods f.o.b. 316.2; Imports of goods f.o.b. −1,658.2; *Trade balance* −1,342.0; Services (net) 1,432.1; *Balance on goods and services* 90.1; Income (net) −40.7; *Balance on goods, services and income* 49.4; Current transfers (net) −24.1; *Current balance* 25.3; Capital account (net) 15.4; Direct investment (net) 54.5; Portfolio investment (net) −94.5; Other investment (net) −135.8; Net errors and omissions 122.6; *Overall balance* −12.5.

EXTERNAL TRADE

Principal Commodities (distribution by SITC, NA Fl. million, 2008): *Imports:* Food and live animals 92.4; Beverages and tobacco 38.3; Mineral fuels, lubricants, etc. 165.6; Manufactured goods classified chiefly by material 116.1; Machinery and transport equipment 86.5; Miscellaneous manufactured articles 277.0; Total (incl. others) 813.2. *Exports f.o.b.:* Food and live animals 15.8; Beverages and tobacco 33.3; Manufactured goods classified chiefly by material 7.1; Machinery and transport equipment 9.3; Miscellaneous manufactured articles 46.0; Total (incl. others) 116.1. *Imports* 1,736 in 2011; 1,838 in 2012; 1,904 in 2013 (estimate). *Exports:* 1,842 in 2011; 2,095 in 2012; 2,171 in 2013 (estimate).

TRANSPORT

Road Traffic (motor vehicles registered at 31 December 2008, excl. government-owned vehicles): Passenger cars 17,882; Lorries 2,950; Buses 135; Taxis 249; Rental cars 2,496; Motorcycles and mopeds 828.

Shipping (cruise ship arrivals): 596 in 2011; 622 in 2012; 629 in 2013.

Civil Aviation (Princess Juliana International Airport traffic, 2008, unless otherwise indicated): Commercial landings 62,757; Passenger movements 1,644,323 (2012).

TOURISM

Tourist Arrivals: *Stop-overs:* 424,340 (Canada 33,256; Netherlands 16,607; USA 219,204) in 2011; 456,720 (Canada 40,426; Netherlands 16,414; USA 238,538) in 2012; 466,955 (Canada 46,300; Netherlands 16,019; USA 246,188) in 2013. *Cruise ship passengers:* 1,656,159 in 2011; 1,753,215 in 2012; 1,779,384 in 2013.

COMMUNICATIONS MEDIA

Telephones (2008): 12,779 main lines in use.

Mobile Cellular Telephones (2008): 68,749 subscribers.

EDUCATION

University of Sint Maarten (2006/07): 217 students (males 64, females 153).

Directory

The Government

HEAD OF STATE

King of the Netherlands: HM King WILLEM-ALEXANDER.

Governor: EUGENE HOLIDAY.

COUNCIL OF MINISTERS
(May 2015)

The Government is formed by members of the United People's Party, the Democratic Party and Independents.

Prime Minister, Minister of General Affairs and Acting Minister of Public Housing, Spatial Planning, Environment and Infrastructure: MARCEL F. GUMBS.

Minister of Justice and Acting Minister of Public Health, Social Development and Labour: DENNIS L. RICHARDSON.

Minister of Finance: MARTINUS J. HASSINK.

Minister of Education, Culture, Youth and Sports: RITA A. BOURNE-GUMBS.

Minister of Public Health, Social Development and Labour: VAN HUGH CORNELIUS DE WEEVER.

Minister of Tourism, Economic Affairs, Transport and Telecommunication: CLARET M. CONNOR.

Minister Plenipotentiary of Sint Maarten in the Netherlands: JOSIANE FLEMING-ARTSEN.

MINISTRIES

Office of the Governor: 3 Falcon Dr., Harbour View, Philipsburg; tel. 542-1160; fax 542-1187; e-mail kabinet@kabgsxm.com; internet www.kabgsxm.com.

Office of the Prime Minister: Clem Labega Sq., POB 943, Philipsburg; tel. 542-2233; fax 542-4300; internet www.sintmaartengov.org.

All government offices are located in Philipsburg.

Legislature

STATES
(Staten)

President: LLOYD J. RICHARDSON.

General Election, 29 August 2014

Party	Valid votes	% of valid votes	Seats
United People's Party (UP) . .	6,211	42.67	7
National Alliance (NA) . . .	4,055	27.86	4
Democratic Party (DP) . . .	2,342	16.09	2
United St Maarten Party (US Party)	1,647	11.31	2
One St Maarten People Party (OSPP)	169	1.16	—
Social Reform Party (SRP) . .	132	0.91	—
Total*	14,556	100.00	15

*In addition, there were 80 blank and 191 invalid votes cast.

Political Organizations

Democratic Party (DP) (Democratische Partij): Tamarind Tree Dr. 4, Union Rd, Cole Bay; tel. 543-1166; fax 542-4296; Leader SARAH A. WESCOT-WILLIAMS.

National Alliance (NA): Philipsburg; comprises the Sint Maarten Patriotic Alliance and the National Progressive Party; Leader WILLIAM MARLIN; Deputy Leader SILVERIA JACOBS.

One St Maarten People Party (OSPP): Philipsburg; e-mail onestmaartenpeopleparty@gmail.com; internet www.facebook.com/OSPPSXM; f. 2013; Leader LENNY F. PRIEST.

Social Reform Party (SRP): Philipsburg; f. 2013; Pres. JACINTO MOCK; Vice-Pres. ALEJANDRO ALVAREZ.

United People's Party (UP): Philipsburg; f. 2010; Leader THEO HEYLIGER.

United St Maarten Party (US Party): Philipsburg; e-mail unitedstmaartenparty@gmail.com; internet www.facebook.com/sxmusp; f. 2013; Pres. CECILE NICOLAS; Leader FRANS RICHARDSON.

Judicial System

Legal authority is exercised by the Joint Court of Justice of Aruba, Curaçao and St Maarten and of Bonaire, St Eustatius and Saba. Its headquarters are in Curaçao. The Joint Court hears civil, criminal and administrative cases in the first instance and on appeal. The Supreme Court of the Netherlands (based in The Hague) is the final court of appeal.

Joint Court of Justice: The Courthouse, Front St 58, Philipsburg; tel. 542-3205; fax 542-5451; e-mail sintmaarten@caribjustitia.org; internet www.gemhofvanjustitie.org; Chief Justice LISBETH HOEFDRAAD.

Constitutional Court: Philipsburg; Pres JACOB (BOB) WIT.

Court of First Instance: The Courthouse, Front St 58, Philipsburg; tel. 542-3205; fax 542-5451; Chief Judge KOEN LUIJKS.

Attorney-General: GUUS SCHRAM.

Religion

The majority of Sint (St) Maarten's population profess Christianity (82% at the 2011 census). Roman Catholicism forms the largest single group on St Maarten, with 33% claiming adherence. St Maarten and the other former constituent territories of the former Netherlands Antilles, as well as Aruba, together form the diocese of Willemstad, suffragan to the archdiocese of Port of Spain (Trinidad and Tobago). The Bishop participates in the Antilles Episcopal Conference, currently based in Trinidad and Tobago. Other churches include Pentecostalist (15%), Methodist (10%), Adventist (7%) and Baptist (5%). Within the Anglican Communion (3% of the population), St Maarten forms part of the diocese of the North Eastern Caribbean and Aruba, within the Church in the Province of the West Indies. The Bishop is resident in St John's, Antigua and Barbuda. Some 5% of the population are Hindu.

The Press

Daily Herald: Bush Rd 22, POB 828, Philipsburg; tel. 542-5253; fax 542-5913; e-mail editorial@thedailyherald.com; internet www.thedailyherald.com; daily; English.

Teen Times: Bush Rd 22, POB 828, Philipsburg; tel. 542-5597; e-mail info@teentimes.com; for teenagers by teenagers; sponsored by the *Daily Herald*; English; Editor-in-Chief MICHAEL GRANGER.

Publisher

House of Nehesi Publishers (HNP): POB 460, Philipsburg; tel. 554-7089; e-mail nehesi@sintmaarten.net; internet www.houseofnehesipublish.com; f. 1986; fiction and non-fiction; Pres. JACQUELINE SAMPLE.

Broadcasting and Communications

TELECOMMUNICATIONS

Caribserve (New Technologies Group, NV): Harbor View Corporate Park, Brooks Tower, Suite 5A/B, Philipsburg; tel. 542-4233; fax 542-4229; e-mail info@caribserve.net; internet www.caribserve.net; internet service provider; subsidiary of UTS, NV; Gen. Man. ROY RICHARDSON.

Scarlet, BV: Three Palms Plaza, 60 Welfare Rd, Colebay; tel. 544-5529; fax 544-2336; e-mail info@scarlet-sxm.com; internet www.scarlet-sxm.com; also operates in Aruba, Bonaire and Curaçao.

TelEm Group (St Maarten Telecommunications Group): Soualiga Blvd 5, Philipsburg; tel. 546-0200; e-mail info@telemgroup.an; internet www.telemgroup.an; f. 1975; comprises TelEm (local), TelCell NV (digital mobile), TelNet Communications NV (internet) and SMITCOMS NV (international); Chair. RAFAEL BOASMAN; CEO (vacant).

UTS St Maarten: Codville Webster Rd 2, Philipsburg; tel. 542-0101; fax 542-4922; e-mail info@uts.sx; internet www.sxm.uts.an; CEO GLEN CARTY; Man. CHRISTINA SPROCK.

Regulatory Authority

Bureau Telecommunications and Post St Maarten (BTP): Sparrow Rd 1-D, Harbour View, Philipsburg; tel. 542-4699; e-mail info@sxmregulator.sx; internet www.sxmregulator.sx; f. 2010; Chair. BRENDA BROOKS; CEO PEGGY ANN BRANDON.

BROADCASTING

Radio

Philipsburg Broadcasting: 106 A. T. Illidge Rd, Philipsburg; tel. 543-2200; fax 543-2229; owns and operates Laser 101 FM, Oasis 96.3 FM and Tropixx 105.5 FM; Man. Dir FRANCIS CARTY.

Voice of St Maarten (PJD2 Radio): 187 Back St, POB 366, Philipsburg; tel. 542-2580; fax 542-2356; internet www.pjd2radio.com; f. 1959; also operates PJD3 on FM (24 hrs); commercial; programmes in English; Gen. Man. DONALD R. HUGHES.

Television

Leeward Broadcasting Corporation—Television: POB 375, Philipsburg; tel. 525-3491; transmissions for approx. 10 hours daily.

TV 15 (Sint Maarten Cable TV Channel 15): 4 Johan Vermeer St, POB 515, Madame Estate; tel. 542-4361; e-mail info@sxmtv15.com; internet www.sxmtv15.com; Station Man. DAVEY WOODS.

WTN TV (Channel 10): Obersi Bldg, Sparrow Rd 1B, Harbour View, Philipsburg; tel. 542-2785; e-mail info@wtntv.com; internet www.wtntv.com; f. 2010; subsidiary of Obersi Group of Cos; CEO ALVIN OBERSI; Gen. Man. ROBERTO GIBBS.

Finance

(cap. = capital; res = reserves; dep. = deposits; m. = million; brs = branches)

BANKING

Regulatory Authority

College Financieel Toezicht (CFT): Convent Bldg, 26 Front St, Philipsburg; tel. 543-0331; fax 543-0379; e-mail info@cft.an; internet www.cft.an; f. 2008; board of financial supervision; office on Curaçao (q.v.); Chair. AGE BAKKER; Mem. (St Maarten) RICHARD GIBSON.

Central Bank

Centrale Bank van Curaçao en Sint Maarten: 25 W. J. A. Nisbeth Rd, Pondfill, Philipsburg; tel. 542-3520; fax 542-4307; e-mail info@centralbank.cw; internet centralbank.cw; Br. Man. L. HASSELL.

Commercial Banks

CIBC FirstCaribbean International Bank: 38 Back St, Philipsburg; tel. 542-3511; fax 542-4531; internet www.firstcaribbeanbank.com; f. 2002 following merger of Caribbean operations of Barclays Bank PLC and CIBC; Barclays relinquished its stake to CIBC in 2006, present name adopted in 2011; CEO RIK PARKHILL; Man. Dir (Dutch Caribbean) PIM VAN DER BURG; 2 brs.

Scotiabank St Maarten (Canada): 62 Back St, Philipsburg; tel. 542-2262; fax 542–2435; e-mail bns.stmaarten@scotiabank.com; internet www.scotiabank/ansma/en; f. 1969; Country Man. RAYMOND GREEN; 3 brs.

Windward Islands Bank Ltd: Clem Labega Sq. 7, POB 220, Philipsburg; tel. 546-2942; fax 542-4761; e-mail info@wib-bank.net; internet www.wib-bank.net; affiliated to Maduro & Curiel's Bank NV; f. 1960; cap. and res 53.2m. NA Fl., dep. 662.2m. NA Fl. (Dec. 2006); Chair. LEONEL CAPRILES, III; Man. Dir JAN J. BEAUJON.

Banking Association

St Maarten Bankers' Association: Clem Labega Sq. 7, Philipsburg; tel. 542-2313; fax 542-6355; Pres. J. BEAUJON.

INSURANCE

Pan-American Life Insurance Company of Curaçao and St Maarten, NV: Professional Office Park, Osprey Dr. 4, Bldg 2, Unit 1B, Yuancho Yrausquin Blvd, Philipsburg; tel. 542-3195; fax 542-5001; internet www.palig.com; f. 2012; part of Pan-American Life Insurance Group (USA); CEO and Man. Dir (Caribbean) WILLIAM R. SCHULZ, Jr; Gen. Man. VALERY SINOT.

Trade and Industry

CHAMBER OF COMMERCE

St Maarten Chamber of Commerce and Industry: Cannegieter St 11, POB 454, Philipsburg; tel. 542-3590; fax 542-3512; e-mail info@sxmcoci.org; f. 1979; Pres. TAMARA LEONARD; Exec. Dir (vacant).

INDUSTRIAL AND TRADE ASSOCIATION

St Maarten Hospitality and Trade Association: W. J. A. Nisbeth Rd 33A, POB 486, Philipsburg; tel. 542-0108; fax 542-0107; e-mail info@shta.com; internet www.shta.com; Pres. EMIL LEE; Exec. Dir ROBERT DUIBOURCQ (acting).

UTILITY

GEBE St Maarten: W. J. A. Nisbeth Rd 35, Pondfill, POB 123, Philipsburg; tel. 542-2213; fax 542-4810; e-mail gebesxm@nvgebe.com; internet www.nvgebe.com; f. 1961; generates and distributes electricity via island network; operates island water supply system on St Maarten and St Eustatius; Chair. JULIUS LAMBERT; Dir PAUL MARSHALL (acting).

TRADE UNION

Windward Islands Chamber of Labour Unions (WIFOL): W. J. A. Nisbeth Rd 89, POB 1097, Pondfill, Philipsburg; tel. 542-2797; fax 542-6631; e-mail wifol@sintmaarten.net; comprises 6 unions: Windward Islands Federation of Labour (WIFOL); Windward Islands Civil Servants Union/Private Sector Union (WICSU/PSU); Windward Islands Teachers' Union (WITU); St Maarten Communications Union; Windward Islands Health Care Union Asscn (WIHCUA); and the Asscn of Staff Employees of GEBE; Pres. THEOPHILUS THOMPSON.

Transport

SHIPPING

St Maarten is one of the Caribbean's leading ports for visits by cruise ships. Pier facilities can accommodate up to six cruise ships.

Intermar, SA: 1 Intermar Dr., 2 Groundove Rd, POB 497, Philipsburg; tel. 542-4734; fax 542-5895; e-mail bvdmark@intermar-sxm.com; internet www.intermar-sxm.com; Gen. Man. BOB VAN DER MARK.

SEL Maduro & Sons (WWI) Inc.: 1 Emmaplein Bldg, POB 63, Philipsburg; tel. 542-3407; fax 542-2958; e-mail madops@maduro.org; internet www.maduro-sxm.com; f. 1837; Man. Dir H. L. CHANCE.

St Maarten Ports Authority (SMPA): J. Yrausquin Blvd, POB 146, Philipsburg; tel. 542-2307; fax 542-5048; e-mail comments@portofstmaarten.com; internet www.portofstmaarten.com; f. 1989; Chair. JOSEPH RICHARDSON; Man. Dir MARK MINGO.

CIVIL AVIATION

Princess Juliana International Airport is located 16 km from Philipsburg. A new terminal was completed in 2006, enhancing the airport's annual passenger-handling capacity by 2.5m.

Windward Express Airways: Princess Juliana International Airport; tel. 545-2001; fax 545-2224; e-mail reservations@windwardexpress.com; internet www.windwardexpress.com; f. 2000; domestic and limited Caribbean island charter flights, incl. destinations with restricted access; passenger and cargo flights; Pres. JEAN HALLEY.

Windward Islands Airways International (WIA—Winair) NV: POB 2088, Princess Juliana International Airport; tel. 545-4237; fax 545-2002; e-mail info@fly-winair.com; internet www.fly-winair.com; f. 1961; govt-owned since 1974; scheduled and charter flights throughout north-eastern Caribbean; Man. Dir EDWIN HODGE.

Tourism

The island is famous for its diving and snorkelling locations, and hiking trails to Mount Concordia and to the cliffs of Cupecoy. The annual Heineken Regatta and the St Maarten Carnival also attract visitors. There were 466,955 stop-over arrivals and 1,779,384 cruise ship passengers in 2013, while tourism receipts were estimated at US $719m. in 2011.

St Maarten Tourism Bureau: Krippa Bldg, Unit 10, Juancho Yrausquin Blvd 6, Philipsburg; tel. 542-2337; fax 542-2734; e-mail info@e-stmaarten.com; internet www.vacationstmaarten.com.

Defence

The Netherlands is responsible for the defence of St Maarten. Military service is compulsory. The Governor is Commander-in-Chief of the armed forces in the territory. A Coast Guard Force operates from St Maarten.

Education

Education was made compulsory in 1992. The education system is the same as that of the Netherlands, and is generally of a high standard. English is the official language of instruction. Primary education begins at six years of age and lasts for six years. Secondary education lasts for a further five years.

NEW ZEALAND

Introductory Survey

LOCATION, CLIMATE, LANGUAGE, RELIGION, FLAG, CAPITAL

The Dominion of New Zealand lies in the South Pacific Ocean, about 1,750 km (1,100 miles) south-east of Australia. It consists of North Island (Te Ika-a-Maui) and South Island (Te Waipounamu), separated by the narrow Cook Strait, and several smaller islands, including Stewart Island (or Rakiura) in the south. The climate is temperate and moist, with an average temperature of 12°C (52°F), except in the far north, where higher temperatures are reached. The official languages are English and Maori. At the 2013 census, 11.6% of respondents professed adherence to Roman Catholicism, 10.8% to the Anglican Church and 7.5% to Presbyterianism. The national flag (proportions 1 by 2) is dark blue, with a representation of the United Kingdom flag as a canton in the upper hoist. In the fly are four five-pointed red stars, edged in white, in the form of the Southern Cross constellation. The capital is Wellington, on North Island.

CONTEMPORARY POLITICAL HISTORY

Historical Context

New Zealand is a former British colony. It became a dominion, under the British Crown, in 1907 and achieved full independence by the Statute of Westminster, adopted by the British Parliament in 1931 and accepted by New Zealand in 1947. With Australia and the USA, New Zealand signed the ANZUS Security Treaty (see p. 459) in 1951. In 1962 Western Samoa (now Samoa, q.v.), formerly administered by New Zealand, achieved independence, and in 1965 the Cook Islands attained full internal self-government, but retained many links, including common citizenship, with New Zealand. In October 1974 Niue, one of New Zealand's island territories, obtained similar status 'in free association with New Zealand'. New Zealand retains two Dependent Territories, Ross Dependency and Tokelau (see New Zealand's Dependent Territories).

Domestic Political Affairs

At a general election in November 1975, the New Zealand National Party secured 55 of the 87 seats in the House of Representatives to defeat the incumbent New Zealand Labour Party, which took the remaining 32 seats. The National Party, under Robert (later Sir Robert) Muldoon, who had led the National Party since July 1974, took office at a time of worsening economic recession, following the international energy crisis of 1973–74. The new Government introduced a programme of economic austerity, and in 1976 reduced the annual intake of migrants from 30,000 to 5,000, while conducting a campaign against illegal immigrants.

The National Party retained power at the general election in November 1978, with 50 of the 92 seats in the enlarged House of Representatives, but its share of the vote decreased markedly. Labour won 41 seats, and the Social Credit Party obtained the remaining seat. In the November 1981 election Muldoon's majority was further reduced. The National Party won 47 seats in the House, while Labour, which again received more votes, secured 43 seats and the Social Credit Party (despite obtaining 20.6% of votes cast) only two.

In February 1984 Muldoon's Government antagonized New Zealand's trade unions by effecting legislation to ban 'closed shop' agreements with employers, thus giving employees the right to choose whether or not to join a trade union. Further legislation was used in June to compel striking construction workers to return to work. In the same month, owing to dissent within his own party, Muldoon called an early general election for July. The Labour Party secured 56 of the 95 seats in an enlarged House of Representatives, while the National Party took 37 seats; the Social Credit Party took the remaining two seats. David Lange (the leader of the Labour Party since February 1983) became Prime Minister. James McLay defeated Muldoon in an election for the leadership of the National Party in November 1984, but he was replaced as party leader by his deputy, James (Jim) Bolger, in March 1986.

The Labour Government introduced controversial deregulatory measures to improve the country's economic situation. The initial success of these measures, together with widespread popular support for the Government's anti-nuclear policy (see below), contributed to another victory for the Labour Party in a general election in August 1987. Of the 97 seats in the expanded House of Representatives, the Labour Party secured 58 and the National Party 39.

In 1987 Lange's Government initiated a contentious programme of privatization of state-owned enterprises. In November 1988 policy disagreements prompted Lange to dismiss the minister responsible for the privatization programme, Richard Prebble. Lange was accused by cabinet colleagues of acting without consultation, and in December Roger (later Sir Roger) Douglas, the Minister of Finance, declared that he would not serve another term under Lange. Douglas was dismissed from office, and later that month unsuccessfully challenged Lange for the leadership of the Labour Party. In May 1989 the formation of the NewLabour Party (led by a former president of the Labour Party, Jim Anderton) was announced: the party aimed to appeal to disillusioned Labour supporters. In August Douglas was elected by Labour Members of Parliament (MPs) to a vacant cabinet post, prompting Lange to resign. Shortly afterwards, Geoffrey Palmer, hitherto the deputy leader of the Labour Party, was elected the party's parliamentary leader and Prime Minister.

In January 1990 Palmer effected an extensive government reorganization. The return of Prebble to the Cabinet, in his former post as Minister of State-owned Enterprises, provoked anger within the Labour Party. The Government aroused further hostility by its introduction of a substantial fee for tertiary-level students and by the continued sale of state assets, especially that of the telecommunications company Telecom. In September, less than eight weeks before the next general election, Palmer resigned as Prime Minister. Michael Moore, the Minister of External Relations and Trade (who had also contested the August 1989 leadership election), replaced Palmer as Prime Minister and Labour Party leader. At the general election of October 1990, the National Party took 67 of the 97 seats in the House of Representatives; the Labour Party won 29 seats, while the NewLabour Party retained its sole seat. Jim Bolger, as leader of the National Party, thus became Prime Minister.

A series of controversial economic proposals announced by the new Government shortly after assuming office—including the repeal of legislation on equal pay for women, reductions in welfare expenditure, and a freeze in the levels of old-age pensions—elicited widespread popular discontent. Protest marches took place in April 1991, and groups representing the elderly petitioned—unsuccessfully—the British monarch (through the Governor-General) to dismiss the Government. Two National Party MPs resigned from the party in August, in protest against the proposals, and the Minister of Maori Affairs, Winston Peters, who had openly criticized the Government's economic strategy, was dismissed in October. In November Sir Robert Muldoon announced that he would resign from the legislature in early 1992, in protest against the Government's economic policies.

In December 1991 a coalition was formed by minor parties as a challenge to the two main parties. The grouping, known as the Alliance, consisted of the NewLabour Party, the New Zealand Democratic Party (as the Social Credit Party had been renamed in 1985), the Green Party of Aotearoa—New Zealand and Mana Motuhake. In September 1992 a preliminary referendum on proposed electoral reform was held. The electorate voted overwhelmingly in favour of the replacement of the 'first-past-the-post' system by a form of proportional representation; of the four alternatives offered, the mixed member proportional (MMP) system (similar to that used in Germany) received the greatest support. The new rules were to be implemented at the 1996 election, following a second, binding referendum.

In March 1993 the outspoken Winston Peters resigned from his parliamentary seat in order to stand for re-election as an independent candidate. The by-election in April resulted in an overwhelming victory for Peters, the major political parties having declined to present candidates. In July Peters established a new party, New Zealand First.

At the general election held in November 1993, the National Party, which had campaigned mainly on the Government's record of economic recovery, was narrowly returned to office, securing 50 of the 99 seats in the enlarged House of Representatives. The Labour Party won 45 seats, the Alliance two and New Zealand First two. At a concurrent, second referendum on electoral reform, 54% of voters favoured the adoption of the MMP system.

In October 1994 Peter Dunne, a former cabinet minister, resigned from the Labour Party, following differences over the party's policy on taxation, and declared his intention to remain in the House of Representatives as an independent member. He subsequently established a new party, Future New Zealand. The traditional two-party system was further challenged in early 1995, when support for ACT New Zealand, co-founded by former Minister of Finance Sir Roger Douglas, began to increase rapidly. In June 1995, however, the position of the ruling party was strengthened by the formation of United New Zealand by seven members of the House of Representatives (four National, two Labour and Future New Zealand leader Dunne). The new grouping pledged its support for the Government on issues of confidence. In February 1996, for the first time since the early 1930s, a formal coalition Government was established when the National Party formed an official alliance with United New Zealand. In the ensuing government reorganization, Dunne joined the Cabinet as Minister of Revenue and Internal Affairs. In March 1996 Sir Michael Hardie Boys replaced Dame Catherine Tizard as Governor-General.

At the first general election under the MMP system, held in October 1996, no party achieved an outright majority. The National Party received 34.1% of the votes cast and took 44 of the 120 seats in the expanded House of Representatives, the Labour Party (28.3%) secured 37 seats and New Zealand First (13.1%) garnered 17 seats, while the Alliance won 13 seats, ACT New Zealand eight and United New Zealand one. A notable development was the increase in the number of Maori MPs from six to 15, a figure almost equivalent to the proportion of Maori (the country's aboriginal inhabitants) in the population as a whole. Following protracted negotiations, a coalition Government was formed in December between the National Party and Winston Peters's New Zealand First. Jim Bolger continued as Prime Minister, while Peters was appointed Deputy Prime Minister and Treasurer.

In October 1997 thousands of protesters took to the streets to demand the resignation of the Government, its policies on health and education having attracted particular criticism. Following a leadership challenge from cabinet minister Jenny Shipley, in November the Prime Minister announced his intention to resign. Shipley was thus sworn in as New Zealand's first female Prime Minister in December. In the subsequent government reorganization, most supporters of Bolger retained their portfolios and Peters continued as Deputy Prime Minister and Treasurer.

In August 1998, following an acrimonious dispute regarding the sale of the Government's stake in Wellington airport, Peters was dismissed from the Cabinet, and the coalition Government was dissolved. Rejecting demands for an early general election, Shipley reallocated many cabinet portfolios. Although Minister of Maori Affairs Tau Henare (who in late 1998 founded a new party, Mauri Pacific, having been removed as deputy leader of New Zealand First in July) was the only former New Zealand First minister to retain his cabinet post, three other erstwhile members of the party remained as ministers outside the Cabinet. Despite the defection of Peters to the opposition, Shipley was able to secure the support of eight of the 16 New Zealand First MPs, and in September she secured a vote of confidence in the House of Representatives.

The minority Government's position was further weakened by a series of misfortunes from late 1998, including allegations in early 1999 that the Minister of Tourism, Murray McCully, had acted inappropriately regarding the handling of a major contract for the advertising business of the New Zealand Tourism Board. In February, as the Prime Minister became personally implicated in the affair and as opposition MPs accused her of deliberately misleading the legislature over her association with the head of the advertising agency in question, the Government narrowly survived a motion of no confidence. McCully relinquished the tourism portfolio in April.

The Labour Party's return to power

At the general election of November 1999, the Labour Party, having secured 38.7% of the votes cast, was allocated 49 of the 120 seats in the House of Representatives, while the National Party, with 30.5% of the votes, received 39 seats. The Alliance (which had absorbed the Liberal Party in 1998) was allocated 10 seats and ACT New Zealand nine seats. The Green Party (which was no longer a member of the Alliance) won seven seats, while New Zealand First's representation declined to five seats, and United New Zealand took the one remaining seat. Having previously discounted any co-operation with the Green Party, the Labour Party was obliged to seek the support not only of the Alliance but also of the seven Green MPs. The leader of the Labour Party, Helen Clark (who had served as Deputy Prime Minister in 1989–90), thus became Prime Minister. The minority Government, which incorporated several members of the Alliance, took office in December 1999. Jim Anderton, the leader of the Alliance, was appointed Deputy Prime Minister, Minister of Economic Development and Minister of Industry and Regional Development. One of the new Government's stated priorities was the 'Closing the Gaps' initiative, which aimed to address the socio-economic disparities between the Maori and non-Maori communities, particularly in health, housing, education, income and the incidence of crime. In June 2000 the Minister of Maori Affairs, Dover Samuels, was forced to resign following allegations of sexual misconduct.

In April 2001 Dame Silvia Cartwright (New Zealand's first female High Court Judge) took office as Governor-General. Her appointment created an unprecedented situation in which the five most important public roles in the country (those of Prime Minister, Leader of the Opposition, Attorney-General and Chief Justice, along with that of Governor-General) were all occupied by women.

In October 2001 Shipley resigned as leader of the National Party and was replaced by Bill English, a former Minister of Health. In December Anderton was placed under considerable pressure from left-wing members of the Alliance to withdraw his support for the Government's involvement in the US-led military campaign in Afghanistan. In April 2002, after months of discord, the Alliance split. Anderton and six other members of the party agreed to form a breakaway party, later named the Progressive Coalition, but continued to support the ruling coalition. The seven MPs were expelled from the Alliance later in April. Laila Harré, Minister of Women's Affairs, Youth Affairs and Statistics, succeeded Anderton as leader of the Alliance and confirmed her party's continuing support for the incumbent Government.

Some 77% of registered voters participated in the general election, which took place earlier than planned (partly owing to the disintegration of the Alliance), in July 2002. The Labour Party received 41% of the votes cast, but failed to secure an overall majority in the House of Representatives, winning 52 of the 120 seats. The National Party performed badly, winning only 21% of the votes; its representation declined by 12 seats to 27. New Zealand First secured 13 seats, ACT New Zealand nine, the Green Party nine and UnitedFuture New Zealand (UFNZ, which had been formed in 2000 by the merger of United New Zealand and Future New Zealand) eight. The Progressive Coalition took two seats, while the Alliance failed to secure any parliamentary representation. Clark formed a minority coalition Government with the Progressive Coalition, and also secured the support of UFNZ.

In June 2003 Clark announced that the Government intended to draw up new legislation to ensure that the country's coastline and seabed were owned by the Crown, following a ruling by the Court of Appeal that Maori tribes could pursue their own claims to ownership of the Marlborough Sands foreshore and seabed in South Island. Maori condemned the Government's actions as 'colonialist'. In October the legislature voted overwhelmingly in favour of the Anti-Terrorism Act (an extension of the 2002 Terrorism Suppression Act), which widened the powers of the police force and created various new offences. The Green Party opposed the legislation, claiming that it infringed upon civil liberties. Legislation providing for the replacement of the monarch's Privy Council (based in London, United Kingdom) as New Zealand's court of final appeal by an independent Supreme Court, consisting of five judges headed by the Chief Justice, was approved in October 2003; the new court began functioning in July 2004.

As part of a government reorganization effected in February 2004, Clark created the post of Co-ordinating Minister for Race Relations after opinion polls indicated a decline in support for her administration over its policies towards the Maori. (Earlier in February Clark had promised a review of state assistance for Maori, on the grounds that policies should be based on need and not on any perceived privilege.)

In April 2004 Clark dismissed the Associate Minister of Maori Affairs, Tariana Turia, after Turia stated that she intended to vote against the Government's Foreshore and Seabed Bill, which would ensure that coastal areas were owned by the Crown, on the grounds that the proposed legislation was in contravention of the rights of indigenous Maori. The Prime Minister secured a narrow victory in a vote of no confidence precipitated by Turia's subsequent resignation as a Labour Party MP from the House of Representatives in May. Meanwhile, a two-week *hikoi* (protest march) against the planned legislation arrived outside the Parliament building in Wellington.

In July 2004 Turia, running as a candidate of the newly formed Maori Party, retook her former parliamentary seat in a by-election. In November the controversial Foreshore and Seabed Bill was narrowly approved by the legislature, after the Government secured the support of New Zealand First. (However, the legislation was repealed following the adoption in March 2011 of the Marine and Coastal Area (Takutai Moana) Act 2011—see *Maori Land Rights and the Waitangi Tribunal Process*.) A major government reorganization in February 2005 included the departure of Attorney-General Margaret Wilson from the Cabinet in order to succeed Jonathan Hunt as Speaker of the House of Representatives. Deputy Prime Minister Michael Cullen became the new Attorney-General, while retaining his existing portfolios.

At the general election held in September 2005, the Labour Party secured victory by a narrow margin, winning 41.1% of the votes cast and 50 seats. The National Party won 39.1% of the votes and 48 seats, a significant improvement in comparison with its performance at the 2002 election. The Maori Party secured 2.1% of the vote, winning four of the seven seats reserved for Maoris. As the Labour Party had failed to gain an overall majority, it subsequently entered into a coalition with the Progressive Party (as the Progressive Coalition had been renamed in April 2004), which had won only one seat. With the more informal support of New Zealand First and UFNZ, this brought the total number of legislative seats controlled by the Government, again headed by Clark, to 61. New Zealand First leader Winston Peters was appointed Minister of Foreign Affairs, and Peter Dunne of UFNZ was allocated the revenue portfolio, but with the unusual provision that both would remain outside the Cabinet. The appointment of Peters drew widespread criticism, owing to his anti-immigration views.

In March 2006 David Parker resigned as Attorney-General, having admitted that he had made an error while filing an annual return for a company with which he was involved; however, he retained the cabinet portfolios of energy and transport. Deputy Prime Minister Michael Cullen subsequently became Attorney-General for the second time, holding the post concurrently with the finance and tertiary education portfolios.

In May 2006 Maj.-Gen. Jerry (later Lt-Gen. Sir Jerry) Mateparae, hitherto Chief of the Army, became the first Maori to be appointed Chief of the New Zealand Defence Force. In August Te Arikinui (Dame Te Atairangikaahu, the Maori Queen) died, bringing to an end her 40-year reign, and her son, Tuheitia Paki, took the throne. Also in August Anand (later Sir Anand) Satyanand, a retired judge of Indo-Fijian descent, replaced Dame Silvia Cartwright as Governor-General upon the expiry of her term of office.

In October 2006 the Auditor-General, Kevin Brady, published a report on an investigation into campaign funding during the 2005 legislative elections. Brady found that the Labour Party had improperly spent $NZ768,000 of taxpayers' money on its election campaign; several other parties, including New Zealand First and the Green Party, were similarly implicated in breaches of regulations, albeit for smaller sums. Labour promptly announced that it was to reimburse the funds. Legislation retrospectively validating the relevant election campaign expenditure was swiftly enacted by the House of Representatives, but controversy persisted. In November 2006 the leader of the National Party, Don Brash, tendered his resignation, amid allegations (strenuously denied) of irregular campaign practices on his part prior to the 2005 elections. John Key was subsequently elected unopposed to the leadership of the National Party.

With opinion poll results suggesting an increase in support for the National Party, Prime Minister Clark announced a

ministerial reorganization in October 2007. In August 2008 Winston Peters relinquished the foreign affairs and racing portfolios, following the launch of an investigation by the Serious Fraud Office into allegations of irregular donations to his New Zealand First party. Clark assumed responsibility for the portfolios, pending the outcome of the inquiry. In October the investigation concluded that Peters had not committed any fraud. However, he did not resume his ministerial role, owing to the imminence of the general election.

The National Party-led coalition Government

At the general election held in November 2008, the National Party won 58 seats in the House of Representatives, having received 44.9% of the votes cast. The Labour Party took 43 seats, with 34.0% of the votes, and nine seats were won by the Green Party. Turnout was almost 79.5% of the registered electorate. In the absence of an overall majority for the National Party, John Key took office as the new Prime Minister at the head of an informal coalition administration, having secured the support of members of ACT New Zealand (which had won five seats), the Maori Party (also five seats) and UFNZ (one seat). The Maori Party had won 2.4% of the party list vote (thus entitling it to three seats in the House), but had secured five constituency seats, two of which were awarded as 'overhang' seats under the MMP electoral system, as the party had won more constituency seats than it was entitled to based on its proportion of party list votes; the total number of seats in the legislature thus increased to 122. Bill English of the National Party was appointed as Deputy Prime Minister and Minister of Finance. Other notable appointments to the new Cabinet included New Zealand's first minister of Asian origin, Pansy Wong (also of the National Party), who was given responsibility for the portfolios covering ethnic affairs and women's affairs. Five cabinet posts were assigned to members of the National Party's coalition partners—the so-called 'support party ministers'; of these, Tariana Turia, the co-leader of the Maori Party, was appointed as Minister for the Community and Voluntary Sector. As global financial conditions rapidly deteriorated and New Zealand entered recession, the incoming Government underlined that its immediate priority was to address the country's economic difficulties. Following the electoral defeat of the Labour Party, Clark resigned as party leader, and was replaced by Phil Goff, whose portfolios in the outgoing Government had included that of defence.

In June 2009 the Prime Minister accepted the resignation of John Worth, Minister for Land Information, Archives New Zealand and the National Library, and Associate Minister of Justice, following a series of allegations of inappropriate behaviour and a police investigation into accusations of harassment. Taito Phillip Field, a former Labour cabinet member and New Zealand's first legislator of Pacific island descent, was sentenced to a six-year prison term in October after being found guilty in August of corruption, bribery and perverting the course of justice; he thus became the first senior New Zealand politician to be convicted of such charges. In February 2010 the Minister of Fisheries and of Housing, Phil Heatley, submitted his resignation in response to allegations of irregularities relating to claims for parliamentary expenses. However, he was subsequently exonerated, following an investigation by the Auditor-General, and reinstated in his cabinet position.

Meanwhile, in November 2009 parliamentary approval was narrowly secured for the Government's contentious emissions trading scheme (ETS), intended to encourage the reduction of environmentally harmful greenhouse gas emissions. The opposition Labour Party regarded the ETS as a weaker and more expensive version of a similar initiative that it had proposed in 2008 Nevertheless, the trading scheme entered into effect during the latter half of 2010.

Following the Government's announcement in March 2010 of proposals to replace the divisive Foreshore and Seabed Act (see *Maori Land Rights and the Waitangi Tribunal Process*), in April the Government unexpectedly declared its support for the controversial UN Declaration on the Rights of Indigenous Peoples, thereby officially acknowledging the Maori right to self-determination (within the boundaries of New Zealand law). Labour had refused to support the non-binding Declaration in 2007, owing to fears that it would conflict with the Waitangi Tribunal process and the Constitution by potentially prompting further Maori land claims, while bestowing additional rights upon the Maori but excluding the remainder of the country's population.

In April 2010 the Government launched a new welfare initiative, Whanau Ora ('family wellness'). By providing social services through a single consolidated agency, the programme was primarily intended to redress the consistently low social indicators of Maori, although it was emphasized that the scheme was open to all. Tariana Turia was appointed to head the programme, the portfolio being added to her existing ministerial responsibilities. The Government announced funding for the scheme of $NZ134m. over a four-year period, well short of the $NZ1,000m. initially envisaged.

Some 20,000 demonstrators converged in Auckland in May 2010 (reportedly the largest demonstration in the country for some 20 years) to protest against controversial government plans to initiate mining operations in protected conservation zones.

In November 2010 Pansy Wong resigned as Minister of Ethnic Affairs and of Women's Affairs, following allegations of misuse of a parliamentary travel allowance; she was replaced by Hekia Parata, also of the National Party. Prime Minister Key subsequently announced that the Government was to introduce legislation that would provide for ministerial allowances to be controlled by the independent Remuneration Authority; hitherto, all ministerial entitlements were determined by the Prime Minister and Speaker, with the Remuneration Authority responsible only for setting ministers' base salaries. In December Wong resigned from the House of Representatives; the vacated seat was retained by the National Party in a by-election in March 2011.

Meanwhile, legislation to reform the electoral finance system before the next general election, due in late 2011, was adopted by Parliament in December 2010. The legislation, which, *inter alia*, clarified regulations governing matters such as donations to political parties, replaced the complex, and unpopular, 2007 Electoral Finance Act, which had been repealed in late 2009.

A state of national emergency was declared in Christchurch following an earthquake 10 km south-east of the city in February 2011. The natural disaster claimed the lives of 185 people and caused widespread damage to buildings and infrastructure, the total cost of which was estimated at around $NZ17,000m.; the state of emergency remained in force for nearly 10 weeks. Key effected a minor reorganization of ministerial portfolios, temporarily transferring the responsibilities held by the Leader of the House of Representatives, Gerry Brownlee, (who had been responsible for addressing the issues arising from an earlier earthquake which had struck about 40 km west of Christchurch in September 2010), in order to allow him to focus exclusively on recovery efforts.

The 2011 general election

In February 2011 Prime Minister Key announced that the general election was to be held on 26 November. Concurrently with the election, a non-binding referendum on the issue of the MMP system was to be held, at which voters were to be asked two questions: first, if they favoured the retention of the current system; and, second, which alternative system they preferred from a range of options.

Maori Party legislator Hone Harawira was expelled from the Maori Party's parliamentary caucus in February 2011 owing to his outspoken criticism of the party's support for the National-led Government despite the latter pursuing what he argued was anti-Maori legislation—a reference to the Marine and Coastal Area (Takutai Moana) Bill (see *Maori Land Rights and the Waitangi Tribunal Process*). Harawira resigned from the Maori Party later in the month. In April Harawira announced the formation of a new, left-leaning political party, Mana, and in the following month he resigned from the House of Representatives in order to seek re-election in the Te Tai Tokerau constituency as leader of the new party. Harawira duly secured re-election by a comfortable margin at the ensuing by-election in June.

Meanwhile, in March 2011 Lt-Gen. Sir Jerry Mateparae, who had relinquished the post of Chief of the New Zealand Defence Force in January, was named as the new Governor-General of New Zealand. He was formally inaugurated in August, upon the expiry of Sir Anand Satyanand's term of office.

In April 2011 the Minister of Justice, for State-owned Enterprises and of Commerce, Simon Power, relinquished responsibility for state-owned enterprises, citing his desire to avoid a potential conflict of interest prior to a planned transition into the business sector following the forthcoming general election. The Minister of Health and of State Services, Tony Ryall, was awarded concurrent responsibility for the vacated portfolio. The Ministry of Agriculture and Forestry and the Ministry of Fisheries officially merged in July, although they retained separate identities until the creation of the Ministry for Primary

Industries in April 2012. Meanwhile, an unexpected application by former National Party leader Don Brash for the leadership of ACT New Zealand was ratified by the party's board of trustees at the end of April 2011.

At the general election of November 2011, the National Party—as in 2008—narrowly failed to secure an overall majority, winning 59 seats, having received 47.3% of the vote. The Labour Party's representation continued to decline, to just 34 seats (27.5% of the vote), while the Green Party garnered 14 seats, New Zealand First eight and the Maori Party three (including one 'overhang' seat); ACT New Zealand, Mana and UFNZ each secured one seat. With only one 'overhang' seat awarded, the size of the legislature was thereby reduced from 122 to 121 seats. Turnout was recorded at 74% of the registered electorate. In the concurrent referendum on the voting system, 57.8% of voters favoured the retention of the MMP system. Following negotiations, Key secured the support of all three of the National Party's coalition partners in the outgoing administration (ACT New Zealand, UFNZ and the Maori Party), which was sufficient to form a coalition Government with control of a 64-seat majority in the House of Representatives.

The new Government, again led by Prime Minister Key, who also retained the tourism portfolio, was inaugurated in December 2011. Bill English remained Deputy Prime Minister and Minister of Finance. Gerry Brownlee retained the Canterbury earthquake recovery portfolio and was awarded concurrent responsibility for transport. Other notable appointments included that of Dr Jonathan Coleman, hitherto Minister of Immigration and of Broadcasting, as the new Minister of Defence and of State Services, while ACT New Zealand's sole MP, John Banks, was appointed Minister for Regulatory Reform and for Small Business, and UFNZ leader Peter Dunne retained the revenue portfolio.

Meanwhile, Labour Party leader Phil Goff and deputy leader Annette King tendered their resignations three days after the election; they were replaced, respectively, by David Shearer and Grant Robertson. Don Brash had also resigned as leader of ACT New Zealand, declaring that he accepted full responsibility for the party's worst ever electoral performance; John Banks was elected as his replacement in February 2012.

Recent developments: 2014 re-election of the Key administration

Dr Nick Smith resigned as Minister for Climate Change Issues, for the Environment and of Local Government in March 2012, after it was revealed that he had failed in 2011 to declare a conflict of interest during his previous tenure as Minister for ACC (Accident Compensation Corporation, a government agency that provides insurance for personal injuries). Prime Minister Key redistributed Smith's former portfolios among existing ministers in April 2012. A new Ministry of Business, Innovation and Employment was established in July, from the merger of the functions of several existing ministries and departments. In November Kate Wilkinson resigned as Minister of Labour after a royal commission concluded that her office had failed to prevent a disaster at Pike River coal mine in November 2010 in which 29 people had lost their lives. She initially retained responsibility for several other portfolios, but was removed from the Government in January 2013, when Prime Minister Key announced several further cabinet changes, including the unexpected return of Nick Smith, as Minister of Conservation and of Housing, and the appointment of a number of newcomers to government.

In September 2012 Prime Minister Key was forced to issue a public apology after confirming a few days previously that the New Zealand Government Communications Security Bureau (GCSB) had illegally spied on German internet entrepreneur Kim Dotcom, who had been granted permanent residency by New Zealand in 2010. The unlawful surveillance, which had been uncovered by lawyers representing Dotcom, had been conducted prior to his arrest by the New Zealand police, at the request of US authorities, in January 2012 on racketeering, copyright infringement and money-laundering charges related to his company Megaupload, which allowed users to host and share large files. Megaupload was shut down by the US authorities and Dotcom's assets were frozen, (although Dotcom launched a new file-sharing company in January 2013). Dotcom denied any wrongdoing and pledged to challenge efforts to extradite him to the USA. (His extradition hearing was eventually scheduled to take place in June 2015.)

As a result of the political fallout from the incident, which prompted concern from some quarters about the apparently servile nature of New Zealand's relationship with the USA, an official review into the GCSB was carried out by the Cabinet Secretary, Rebecca Kitteridge. The resultant Kitteridge report was leaked to the media in April 2013, causing considerable embarrassment to the Government. The sensitive report identified 88 cases since 2003 in which GSCB may have acted illegally, and recommended, *inter alia*, the reorganization of the Bureau into a 'simpler, less fragmented' organization. In August 2013 the House of Representatives approved the Government Communications Security Bureau and Related Legislation Amendment Bill, which, in line with Kitteridge's recommendations, clarified the legal parameters and increased external oversight of the GCSB. Critics of the new legislation, including the Green Party, argued that the law represented an affront to freedom of expression and the right to live without surveillance. Meanwhile, in May New Zealand First leader Winston Peters claimed that the Kitteridge report had been leaked by UFNZ leader Peter Dunne, who denied having done so. However, Dunne was forced to resign as Minister for Revenue in June, having refused fully to co-operate with a request for information from an inquiry into the leaking of the report.

In October 2013 the leader of ACT New Zealand, John Banks, tendered his resignation as Minister for Regulatory Reform and for Small Business, following a court ruling that he should stand trial on the charge of filing a false electoral return after the Auckland mayoralty campaign in 2010. Although members of the opposition claimed that, with the leaders of two of the National Party's coalition partners having been forced to step down, the Key administration's position had become untenable, the Government dismissed appeals for an early election.

In March 2014 Key set the date of the next election as 20 September. He also announced on the following day that a referendum would be held within three years to determine whether to change the national flag (potentially excluding the United Kingdom's national flag, the Union Jack). Also in March Dotcom launched a new political party, the Internet Party, to contest the forthcoming general election (scheduled to be held in September) on a platform of internet freedom, faster and cheaper internet services and protection of privacy; the new party was officially registered in May. However, Dotcom himself would be ineligible to stand for election as, under New Zealand law, candidates for political office are required to hold New Zealand citizenship. In June the Internet Party announced an electoral alliance with the Mana Movement; the new alliance was styled Internet MANA. In the same month John Banks (who had been replaced in March as leader of ACT New Zealand by Jamie Whyte) resigned from his parliamentary seat, following his conviction at the High Court for filing a false electoral return. However, in November the Court of Appeal overturned his conviction and a retrial was subsequently scheduled to be held in July 2015.

Meanwhile, at the end of August 2014 the Minister of Justice and for ACC, Judith Collins, tendered her resignation amid allegations that in 2011, during her earlier tenure as Minister of Police, she had attempted to undermine the Director of the Serious Fraud Office, a charge she denied.

At the legislative elections held on 20 September 2014, which attracted a turnout of 77.9%, the National Party was returned to power. However, the party again fell slightly short of obtaining an overall majority in the legislature, winning 47.0% of the vote and 60 of the 121 seats. The Labour Party—losing support for the fourth election in a row—secured 32 seats (25.1%), the Green Party retained its 14 seats (10.7%) and New Zealand First increased its representation to 11 seats (8.7%). The Maori Party won two seats (1.3%), while ACT New Zealand and UFNZ (each with less than 1% of the vote) obtained one seat apiece—that of UFNZ being an 'overhang' seat. The Conservative Party, which took 4.0% of the vote, failed to win representation, as did Internet MANA (1.4%). Having re-entered support agreements with UFNZ, ACT New Zealand and the Māori Party, Key was sworn in for a third successive term as Prime Minister on 8 October at the head of a new National-led coalition Government. There was some reorganization of portfolios, but the key ministers—for finance, foreign affairs and internal affairs—retained their posts, and only one new cabinet member was appointed. A new ministry, covering national security and intelligence, was created; the Prime Minister himself assumed responsibility for the portfolio and announced plans to establish a National Security Committee of Cabinet which would be tasked with overseeing the national intelligence and security sector. Following his

party's poor performance in the elections, the leader of the Labour Party, David Cunliffe (who had replaced David Shearer in September 2013), resigned; in November he was succeeded as Labour leader by Andrew Little

Upon securing re-election, Key confirmed that he would hold a referendum on whether to change the country's national flag, to a new design. Key suggested that he would favour a new flag featuring a silver fern on a black background, as used by New Zealand sporting teams, although at the same time he expressed his support for the British monarch remaining as head of state. In February 2015 the Government announced the formation of a Flag Consideration Panel, the 12 members of which were 'respected New Zealanders' who had been nominated by a cross-party group of MPs. From May the Panel was to lead a public engagement process to select, publicize and discuss potential designs for a new flag, three or four of which would then (together with the current flag) be put to a national referendum in late 2015 in order to choose the most popular. There would be a second national referendum, in April 2016, to decide whether to retain the existing flag or to replace it with the alternative flag that was most preferred by voters in the first referendum. The outcome of the referendums were to be legally binding.

In October 2014 New Zealand was elected as a non-permanent member of the UN Security Council for a term of two years, effective from 1 January 2015.

Maori Land Rights and the Waitangi Tribunal Process

During 1987 there were protests by the Maori concerning their cultural and economic rights and, in particular, their claims to land in accordance with the Treaty of Waitangi, concluded in 1840 by the British Government and Maori leaders, whereby sovereignty had been ceded to the United Kingdom in return for the Maori people's retention of hunting and fishing grounds. In November 1987 a ruling by the Waitangi Tribunal, reconvened in 1975 to consider retrospectively the claims of Maori land rights activists, recommended the restoration of an Auckland harbour headland to the Maori people. By 1994 about 75% of the country was subject to land claims by Maori groups. In December of that year the Government offered the sum of $NZ1,000m., payable over a 10-year period, in full and final settlement of outstanding claims for compensation. However, the condition that all future land claims be renounced was rejected by most Maori groups. In the same month an historic agreement between the Government and the Tainui people of Waikato provided for the return of land confiscated in 1863 and for the deposit over a period of five years of $NZ65m. in a land acquisition trust.

In May 1995 the Prime Minister and the Queen of the Tainui people signed an agreement relating to a full and final settlement, valued at $NZ170m., of land grievances dating back to 1863. However, increasing ethnic tension was demonstrated by the destruction in September 1995 of an old school building by Maori protesters involved in a land dispute and by the burning down in October of an historic church, the 'Maori Cathedral', at Otaki, in an apparent retaliatory arson attack by white extremists. In November, in a highly significant ceremony in Wellington, Queen Elizabeth II gave her personal assent to the legislation ending the Tainui grievances when she signed the Waikato Raupatu Claims Settlement Act: this implemented the $NZ170m. agreement, including the return of 15,780 ha of land, and incorporated an apology from the Crown for the loss of lives and for the confiscation of property. A final settlement payment of $NZ13m. was made to the Tainui tribe in late 2000.

In July 1997 a Maori tribe that had been driven off its land in the 1840s lodged a claim to the site of the Parliament building in Wellington. The Ngati Tama also presented claims to other areas of the capital, while declaring their willingness to negotiate. At a ceremony in Wellington in September, following six years of negotiations, the Government and South Island's Ngai Tahu (one of New Zealand's smallest Maori tribes) reached a final agreement regarding a $NZ170m. settlement. The Government's offer also included the right to name mountains and rivers, often in combination with the English equivalents, and incorporated a full apology from the Crown. In November the historic deed of full and final settlement was signed by the Prime Minister and representatives of the Ngai Tahu. In March 1998 the Ngai Tahu Claims Settlement Bill was duly submitted to the House of Representatives, where it received approval six months later. In July, exercising for the first time its power of compulsory recommendation, the Waitangi Tribunal ordered the Government to return to the Ngati Turangitukua land (now valued at $NZ6.1m.) that had been confiscated from its Maori owners more than 30 years previously to permit the construction of housing for workers engaged on an electric power project in the central North Island.

In March 2001 the Ngati Ruanui became the first Taranaki tribe to conclude a deed of settlement with the Government, amounting to $NZ41m. In early 2003 the Ngati Awa voted in favour of a treaty settlement with the Government, which included an apology from the Crown, the return of 64 ha of land and $NZ42m. In August 2005 Prime Minister Helen Clark announced that all historical Maori land claims under the Treaty of Waitangi would have to be filed by 1 September 2008, in order that they could be settled by 2020 (contemporary claims could be filed beyond this deadline). By 2007 the Waitangi Tribunal had reportedly been able to settle only about 20 claims. On the closing date for registration the Waitangi Tribunal received more than 1,000 new historical grievance claims from Maori communities. In October 2007 the Government instigated a campaign to persuade Maoris living in Australia to return to New Zealand.

In June 2008, in a settlement valued at $NZ418m., the New Zealand Government signed an agreement with seven Maori tribes to transfer ownership of 176,000 ha of Crown forestry land in the central North Island, originally ceded under the Treaty of Waitangi. The Maori tribes, which represented approximately 100,000 people, also stood to receive backdated forest rental payments of $NZ223m., in addition to future annual rental income and carbon credits. In February 2009 the Government awarded $NZ300m. in compensation to eight Maori tribes, comprising more than 12,000 members, in recognition of historic injustices arising from violations of the Treaty of Waitangi and illegal seizures of land. Furthermore, in the first such decision relating to an issue of intellectual property, the Government recognized that the Ka Mate haka, the 'war dance' traditionally performed by the New Zealand rugby team at international games but increasingly being used for commercial exploitation, had been written in the 1820s by Maori chief Te Rauparaha, an ancestor of the Ngati Toa tribe. A $NZ25m. settlement encompassing the greater Wellington region was agreed in July 2009; significantly, the *iwi* (tribe) involved in the agreement issued an unprecedented formal statement of forgiveness to the Crown.

The Ngati Kuia concluded a deed of settlement with the Crown in October 2010, the first such agreement in South Island since 1997; the settlement included an apology from the Crown, the return of culturally sensitive land and $NZ24m. in compensation. The Ngati Porou, New Zealand's second largest *iwi*, comprising about 72,000 members, signed a deed of settlement with the Crown in December 2010, which included the return of approximately 5,900 ha of land and $NZ110m. in compensation. The Ngai Tamanuhiri became the first Turanga *iwi* to conclude a deed of settlement with the Crown, in March 2011, which included the return of culturally sensitive land, together with the payment of $NZ11.1m. in compensation. A deed of settlement was also concluded between the Crown and another of New Zealand's three Turanga *iwi*, the Rongowhakaata, in September, which similarly provided for the return of culturally sensitive land and the payment of compensation, amounting to $NZ22m., as well as a formal apology from the Crown for, *inter alia*, the unjustified use of military force in Turanga, the detention without trial of Rongowhakaata prisoners on the Chatham Islands and the summary executions of prisoners at Ngatapa in 1869. Further deeds of settlement were signed between the Crown and the Ngati Makino, the Ngati Manuhiri and the Ngati Whatua o Kaipara in April, May and September 2011, respectively, each of which provided for the return to the tribes of culturally sensitive land, together with compensation of $NZ11.9m., $NZ9.0m. and $NZ22.1m., respectively. The settlement process continued throughout 2012–14 with the signature of yet more deeds between the Crown and various Maori tribes. Of particular note was the deed of settlement drawn up between the Crown and the Ngai Tuhoe in 2012 which included (for the first time in such a document) a pledge by the Government to transform the 'social circumstances' of the members of the tribe through a Social Services Management Plan.

In December 2012 the High Court ruled against an application by the New Zealand Maori Council filed earlier that year requesting a judicial review of the Government's planned partial divestment of its assets in a number of energy companies; the Council argued that such sales would prejudice any future recognition of Maori rights over the country's water and geothermal resources.

In November 2014 the Waitangi Tribunal published its report on the first stage of its inquiry into the respective understandings of the Maori and Crown of the 1835 Declaration of Independence and the 1840 Treaty of Waitangi. The report claimed that when they signed the Treaty the Maori chiefs did not in doing so agree to cede sovereignty to Britain. It further asserted that Britain entered treaty negotiations with the intention of acquiring sovereignty, but did not explain this to the tribal chiefs, who agreed to share authority over enforcement of law over people and territories. While the Ngapuhi and other northern tribes welcomed the ruling, the Attorney-General Chris Finlayson stated that the findings of the report did not alter the fact that the Crown exercised sovereignty in New Zealand.

Maori fishing rights

In response to Maori grievances over fishing rights, in 1989, in an interim agreement, the Crown transferred 10% of the country's fishing quota, together with $NZ50m. and shareholdings in fishing companies, to the Maori Fisheries Commission, which had been established to resolve the issue of the allocation among Maori of fisheries resources. In 1992 the Treaty of Waitangi (Fisheries Claims) Settlement Act (or so-called Sealord deal) was adopted, marking the full and final settlement of Maori fishing claims under the Treaty. According to the agreement, the *iwi* would receive a 50% share in Sealord products (Sealord being New Zealand's largest fishing company), 20% of all new species brought under the quota management system and a further $NZ18m.

The allocation of fisheries assets among the tribes proved the subject of much litigation. In April 1997, despite having no coastline, urban Maori were outraged at a proposal by the Treaty of Waitangi Fisheries Commission (as the Maori Fisheries Commission had now become) to allocate fishery assets on a tribal basis, rather than according to *iwi* size as the populous northern tribes demanded. The Ngai Tahu and other *iwi*, meanwhile, argued that the length of coastline and traditional fishing grounds should determine the allocation of assets. In early 1998 it was announced that new regulations were to govern the management of 'customary' fishing by *tangata whenua* (people of the land), whereby Maori were permitted to take an unlimited amount of seafood provided that it was not for pecuniary gain.

In mid-1998 the Waitangi Tribunal ruled that urban Maori without blood ties should be accorded similar negotiating rights to those of traditional *iwi*. The historic decision thus acknowledged urban Maori trusts as modern tribes. In August, however, a High Court judge ruled in favour of traditional Maori tribes, effectively declaring that urban Maori groups had no claim to fishery assets. In October 1999, furthermore, the urban Maori claim was rejected by the Court of Appeal. In September 2004 the final version of the Maori Fisheries Act was approved by the House of Representatives. The new legislation transferred control to Maori tribes of some $NZ750m. in fisheries assets; around one-half of these assets was to be allocated directly to the *iwi* and the other half was to be managed centrally, with the creation of the country's largest fishing group, Aotearoa Fisheries Ltd, which would have an interest in approximately one-third of New Zealand's lucrative commercial fishing industry.

In June 2010 Prime Minister John Key announced that the Government, the Maori Party and *iwi* leaders had reached an agreement providing for the repeal of the Foreshore and Seabed Act and its replacement with new legislation that would abrogate Crown ownership of the coastal areas in question and place them in the public domain, thereby also preventing Maori ownership claims, while allowing Maori groups to seek recognition of their customary rights from the Government or by application to the High Court—a right that had been denied to them under the Foreshore and Seabed Act. The Marine and Coastal Area (Takutai Moana) Bill was introduced to Parliament in August, whereupon it encountered significant opposition, including from Maori Party legislator Hone Harawira, who argued that the draft legislation was 'a fraud' since Maori seeking to claim customary rights over foreshore and seabed areas would be required to prove unbroken tenure since 1840 of the areas in question, which, he contended, the vast majority of Maori would be unable to do. Conversely, the Coastal Coalition, an umbrella organization comprising those who believed the foreshore and seabed to be 'the birthright and common heritage of all New Zealanders equally' and should remain under the ownership of the Crown, opposed the bill as a 'massive coastal land grab for the Maori'. An opinion poll conducted in February 2011 indicated that just 11% of Maori approved of the Marine and Coastal Area (Takutai Moana) Bill. Nevertheless, in March the legislation was narrowly approved by the House of Representatives, having been supported by the National Party, the Maori Party and UFNZ. In the previous month Harawira had resigned from the Maori Party (see *Domestic Political Affairs*).

Foreign Affairs

The Labour Government that took office at the end of 1972 adopted a more independent policy than that of its predecessors. It phased out New Zealand's military commitments under the South-East Asia Treaty Organization and established diplomatic relations with the People's Republic of China. New Zealand became committed to the objective of the global elimination of all nuclear weapons, and in November 1996 was a co-sponsor of a UN resolution, overwhelmingly adopted by the General Assembly, to promote the establishment of a nuclear-weapons-free southern hemisphere. In October 2000 New Zealand ratified the Waigani Convention, which banned the export of hazardous and radioactive waste to the Pacific islands.

Regional relations

New Zealand has played an active role in Pacific island affairs. In 1997, in the quest for peace in Papua New Guinea, it participated in a peacekeeping force on the secessionist island of Bougainville. New Zealand hosted discussions between the Papua New Guinea Government and representatives of the secessionist movement, and in January 1998 a permanent ceasefire agreement was signed in Christchurch. New Zealand strongly condemned the coup in Fiji in May 2000. New Zealand led a Commonwealth delegation, together with Australia, to negotiate with the ethnic militias involved in a coup in Solomon Islands in June 2000. A New Zealand naval frigate was dispatched to the islands to serve as a venue for peace talks, and a ceasefire agreement was signed in October. In mid-2003 New Zealand troops joined forces from Australia and several Pacific islands to provide a peacekeeping force in Solomon Islands (the last of the remaining New Zealand troops withdrew from the islands in November 2012). New Zealand, together with Australia, deployed security forces to Tonga in November 2006 to restore stability following violent demonstrations. Tonga established a high commission in Wellington in 2009, but this was closed in September 2011, as part of Tongan government spending cuts.

In December 2006 Prime Minister Helen Clark condemned the military coup in Fiji as an 'outrage'; the Government subsequently imposed defence, travel and development sanctions. Further sanctions were announced in June 2007 after New Zealand's high commissioner to Fiji was expelled because of his alleged interference in the country's internal affairs. In December 2008 the acting high commissioner of New Zealand in Fiji was expelled, in response to which her Fijian counterpart was asked to leave New Zealand. In April 2009 New Zealand was particularly critical of the abrogation of the Fijian Constitution and subsequent developments in Fiji. New Zealand's high commissioner to Fiji was expelled again in November in response to the New Zealand Government's continuing firm stance towards the Fijian regime; a reciprocal expulsion by New Zealand followed soon afterwards. Although senior diplomats returned to the respective missions in early 2010, the exchange was not at ambassadorial level. In January 2012 New Zealand expressed disappointment at the imposition by the Fijian regime of repressive new legislation, which was widely condemned as a setback for hopes of a restoration of democracy in the country. However, following progress made by Fiji towards the drafting of a new constitution and the organization of elections in 2014, in July 2012 New Zealand agreed to restore full diplomatic relations (at ambassadorial level) with Fiji.

Meanwhile, in June 2008 the New Zealand Government released details of its Pacific Development Strategy Plan, which envisaged expenditure of $NZ2,000m. in official development assistance to the Pacific region over an eight-year period. The new initiative aimed to improve health services and education facilities, to strengthen governance, to reduce poverty and to promote economic growth in the Pacific islands. Minister of Foreign Affairs Murray McCully visited Vanuatu and Solomon Islands in June 2011, and Tonga, Samoa, the Cook Islands and Niue in July, to discuss regional issues and priorities for the Pacific Islands Forum, the 42nd summit meeting of which was hosted by New Zealand in Auckland in September.

Although New Zealand's trade with the People's Republic of China assumed increasing significance from the 1990s, relations were strained by the issue of China's nuclear-testing programme. Relations were further tested in September 1996 when the Dalai Lama, the exiled spiritual leader of Tibet, visited New Zealand, where he was welcomed by the Prime Minister. In September 1997, however, the New Zealand Deputy Prime Minister expressed support for China's application to join the World Trade Organization (WTO, see p. 431). In November 1998 New Zealand's decision to accord Taiwanese government officials similar privileges to those granted to representatives of the People's Republic provoked serious concern in China. During a visit to China in July 1999, however, the Prime Minister of New Zealand reaffirmed her country's support for the 'one China' policy. In March 2008 it was reported that China had agreed to grant 'most favoured nation' status to New Zealand as part of a free trade agreement between the two countries, which was signed in the following month. The signature of this accord, the provisions of which were to be phased in gradually over 12 years, represented the first time that China had entered into a comprehensive free trade agreement with a developed country. The value of New Zealand's exports to China have grown significantly since the implementation of the free trade agreement, increasing from US $2,300m. in 2008 to US $8,200m. in 2013, in which year China overtook Australia to become New Zealand's largest export market. In addition, in 2012 China was the largest source of New Zealand's students from overseas and the second largest source of tourist arrivals to New Zealand. Meanwhile, five agreements were signed during a visit to Wellington in September 2011 by Chinese Vice-Premier Hui Liangyu, including a memorandum of understanding (MOU) providing for greater co-operation between New Zealand and the state-run China Development Bank on infrastructural development projects, including in the earthquake-struck Canterbury region. Meanwhile, a Closer Economic Partnership Agreement (CEPA) was signed with Hong Kong in March 2010 and entered into force in January 2011. In July 2013 New Zealand and Taiwan signed a free trade agreement (to be fully enforced by 2025), the first such agreement concluded by Taiwan with a developed country that had established diplomatic relations with the People's Republic. New Zealand referred to Taiwan in the agreement as the 'separate customs territory' rather than as a sovereign state. Responding to the development, the mainland Chinese Government stated that it did not object to trade and other agreements between Taiwan and countries with which China had established diplomatic relations, provided that such agreements did not constitute the establishment of 'official relations'.

Relations with the countries of South-East Asia continued to assume greater significance. In June 2001 President Abdurrahman Wahid of Indonesia undertook an official visit to New Zealand, the first by an Indonesian head of state for 26 years. In July 2005 New Zealand signed the Treaty of Amity and Co-operation of the Association of Southeast Asian Nations (ASEAN, see p. 210). In December New Zealand was represented at the inaugural East Asia Summit meeting, convened in Malaysia and attended by leaders of ASEAN members and various other countries of the Asia-Pacific region. In February 2009 (along with Australia) New Zealand signed a free trade agreement with ASEAN, which entered into force in January 2010. A separate free trade agreement with Malaysia, a significant export market for New Zealand, was signed in October 2009 and entered into force in July 2010; the agreement provided for the elimination of trade tariffs on 99.5% of New Zealand's exports to Malaysia within seven years. Minister of Foreign Affairs McCully visited Indonesia and Malaysia in October 2010; during his visit to the former, the Indonesia-New Zealand Friendship Council was established. Following the devastating impact of Typhoon Haiyan in the Philippines in November 2013, a planned visit to the South-East Asian country by Prime Minister Key was cancelled to allow the Philippine Government to concentrate on relief and recovery efforts. The New Zealand Government pledged aid of $NZ2.15m. and emergency supplies to assist in the relief operation, as well as announcing the launch of a $NZ2.3m. initiative in conjunction with the Philippines Red Cross to support future disaster relief operations.

New Zealand's foreign policy has continued to be influenced by the country's need to diversify its export markets, particularly within Asia; the Republic of Korea (South Korea), for example, has become a significant trading partner—New Zealand's fifth largest in 2014, with total trade valued at an estimated $NZ4,054m.—and in November 2014 a New Zealand-South Korean free trade agreement was concluded. Closer relations with Singapore and Thailand have also been developed; a CEPA was signed between New Zealand and Thailand in 2005. The New Zealand and Thai premiers exchanged reciprocal visits in 2013, with Thai Prime Minister Yingluck Shinawatra visiting Wellington in March and Key visiting Bangkok in November.

Relations with Japan, which was New Zealand's fourth largest trading partner in 2014, have been strained by New Zealand's opposition to the East Asian country's controversial whaling programme. Up until 2014 Japan caught an estimated 1,000 whales each year, which the New Zealand Government, along with many others within the international community, contended was in direct breech of a ban on commercial whaling introduced by the International Whaling Commission (IWC, see p. 438) in 1986, to which Japan is a signatory. The Japanese Government maintained that its whaling activities were for scientific-based research programmes, which is permitted under the IWC agreement. In 2010 New Zealand supported Australia in bringing a case to the International Court of Justice (ICJ) against Japan for whaling in the Antarctic, contending that it constituted commercial whaling. In March 2014 the ICJ delivered a non-binding ruling that Japan should halt its whaling programme in the Antarctic as it had not sufficiently justified that the quotas it set were necessary for the purposes of scientific research. In response, Japan temporarily suspended its Antarctic whaling activities. Later that year, however, the New Zealand Government expressed concern at Japan's stated intention, despite the ICJ ruling, to resume research whaling in 2015 (albeit with reduced quotas).

New Zealand signed the ANZUS Security Treaty with Australia and the USA in 1951. From 1984 New Zealand's relations with both Australia and the USA were severely tested by the issue of the nuclear ban (see *The ANZUS Treaty and other relations with the USA*). In 1982 New Zealand signed an agreement for a 'closer economic relationship' with Australia; trade barriers between the two countries were eliminated in 1990. During her first state visit to New Zealand since acceding to the Australian premiership in June 2010, Prime Minister Julia Gillard met with her New Zealand counterpart, John Key, in Wellington, whereupon the two leaders pledged thenceforth to hold bilateral prime ministerial discussions on an annual basis. Visiting the Australian capital, Canberra, in October 2013, Key became the first foreign leader to meet with incoming Australian Prime Minister Tony Abbott following the latter's election in the previous month.

The ANZUS Treaty and other relations with the USA

In 1984 the Lange Government's pledge to ban from New Zealand's ports all vessels believed to be carrying nuclear weapons, or powered by nuclear energy, placed considerable strain on the country's relations with Australia and the USA, its partners in ANZUS. The ban was duly imposed in February 1985. In July 1986 the US Government announced its intention to devise new, bilateral defence arrangements with Australia, and in August the USA's military obligations to New Zealand under the ANZUS Treaty were formally suspended. In February 1987 the US Government announced its decision not to renew a 1982 MOU, whereby New Zealand was able to purchase military equipment from the USA at favourable prices. The Lange Government subsequently defined a new defence strategy, based on increased self-reliance for the country's military forces. In June 1987 legislation banning nuclear-armed ships was formally enacted by the New Zealand House of Representatives, despite opposition from the National Party. In September 1989 New Zealand agreed the terms for a joint venture with Australia to build as many as 12 naval frigates to patrol the South Pacific. The decision proved to be contentious because of the high costs and because of allegations that the Government was succumbing to political pressure from Australia to return to the ANZUS alliance and abandon its independent anti-nuclear stance. In March 1990 the National Party announced its support for the anti-nuclear policy, a position that it maintained after its election to office in October.

The US Government's decision, in September 1991, to remove nuclear weapons from surface naval vessels and the announcement, in July 1992, that its warships no longer carried tactical nuclear weapons were welcomed by the New Zealand Government, and in February 1994 the USA resumed senior-level contacts with New Zealand, suspended since 1985. After attending the summit meeting of the Asia-Pacific Economic Cooperation (APEC, see p. 200) forum held in Auckland in September 1999, US President Bill Clinton announced the end of the 14-year ban on New Zealand's participation in military exercises with the USA, in preparation for the dispatch of a multinational peacekeeping force to East Timor (now Timor-Leste—q.v.), of which New Zealand troops were to form part.

Following the suicide attacks in the USA of 11 September 2001, in October New Zealand provided troops from the Special Air Service (SAS) for the US-led military campaign against the al-Qa'ida organization, held principally responsible for the attacks, and its Taliban hosts in Afghanistan. However, US policy in the 'war on terror' was a source of concern in New Zealand. In May 2003 Prime Minister Clark warned the USA and the UK that they had set a dangerous precedent by invading Iraq, in order to remove the regime of Saddam Hussain, without the endorsement of a UN resolution. None the less, New Zealand provided humanitarian support for Iraq and assistance in the rehabilitation of the country once the UN had authorized reconstruction efforts following the ousting of Saddam Hussain.

In March 2004 the New Zealand Government, which had already sent members of the New Zealand Defence Force to Afghanistan to assist in reconstruction efforts in the province of Bamian (Bamyan), agreed to send SAS troops back to that country to take part in the search for senior al-Qa'ida leaders. A further SAS deployment in Afghanistan was effected in September 2009, following a US request for additional military assistance; in February 2011 it was announced that the deployment was to be extended for 12 months, effective from April, but with a reduction in the number of personnel, from 70 to 35 troops. The SAS deployment was concluded, as scheduled, at the end of March 2012. Having suffered 10 military fatalities since commencing its mission in Afghanistan a decade earlier, in April 2013 the New Zealand Defence Force withdrew its remaining contingent of around 140 troops from Bamian, some five months earlier than initially scheduled. A small group of non-combat military personnel from New Zealand remained in the Afghan capital of Kabul.

An improvement in relations with the USA was indicated in July 2008 by the visit to New Zealand of Condoleezza Rice, the US Secretary of State and thus the most senior representative of the US Government to visit the country since the late 1990s. Rice's discussions with Prime Minister Clark and with the Minister of Foreign Affairs focused on trade issues, renewing hopes that a free trade agreement between the two countries might be negotiated. In September 2008 the US Government announced that it was to enter into negotiations with New Zealand and the three other member states of the Trans-Pacific Strategic Economic Partnership Agreement (known as P4—a trade liberalization agreement, comprising New Zealand, Singapore, Brunei and Chile, that had entered into effect in 2006), with a view to joining the Trans-Pacific Partnership, a proposed regional regulatory and investment agreement under negotiation, as of early 2015, by the P4 member states and the USA, together with Australia, Canada, Japan, Malaysia, Mexico, Peru and Viet Nam. Meanwhile, in November 2010 US Secretary of State Hillary Clinton visited Wellington, whereupon she and the New Zealand Minister of Foreign Affairs, Murray McCully, signed a strategic co-operation agreement, which effectively formalized the amelioration in bilateral relations and greater engagement between the two countries in recent years. The so-called Wellington Declaration focused on enhancing dialogue and practical co-operation between New Zealand and the USA across a wide range of bilateral, Pacific and international issues, including combating the effects of climate change and the co-ordination of disaster recovery initiatives, and committed the two countries to regular diplomatic, trade and defence discussions. Improved bilateral relations were further cemented in 2011 by visits to Washington, DC, USA, by McCully in May, during which he held discussions with Secretary of State Clinton, and by Prime Minister John Key in July, when he met with President Barack Obama. In June 2012, in Washington, DC, the New Zealand Minister of Defence, Dr Jonathan Coleman, and his US counterpart, Leon Panetta, signed an agreement (the so-called Washington Declaration) to expand defence co-operation between their two countries, including in the areas of maritime security and disaster relief. Following a visit to New Zealand by Panetta in September (the first visit to New Zealand by a US Secretary of Defense since 1986), the USA lifted the ban imposed in 1986 that prevented New Zealand naval ships from docking at its ports. A New Zealand frigate subsequently visited the US naval base in Guam, in May 2013, and in October the two countries announced the resumption of bilateral military co-operation after nearly 30 years, providing for increased co-operation in peacekeeping initiatives, humanitarian assistance and disaster relief in the Asia-Pacific region, as well as joint military training exercises.

Other external relations

In July 1985 the *Rainbow Warrior*, the flagship of the anti-nuclear environmentalist group Greenpeace (which was to have led a flotilla to Mururoa Atoll, in French Polynesia, to protest against France's testing of nuclear weapons in the South Pacific), was blown up and sunk in Auckland Harbour. One member of the crew was killed as a result of the explosion. Two agents of the French secret service were tried for manslaughter in November and sentenced to 10 years' imprisonment. Following requests by the French Government for the release or repatriation of the agents, in July 1986 New Zealand and France reached an agreement whereby the agents were to be transferred to detention on Hao Atoll, in French Polynesia, for three years. The French Government made a formal apology for its part in the sabotage operation, and paid the New Zealand Government $NZ7m. in compensation. By May 1988, however, both the agents had been taken back to France, ostensibly for medical reasons. In May 1990 a UN arbitration panel ruled that France's repatriation of the agents constituted a substantial violation of the 1986 agreement, but it stated that the agents would not be required to return to Hao Atoll. France agreed to pay an initial US $2m. into a joint fund intended to foster close and friendly relations between the two countries. In April 1991 the French Prime Minister, Michel Rocard, visited New Zealand and again apologized for the sinking of the *Rainbow Warrior*, while reiterating that French testing of nuclear weapons in the Pacific was to continue. Relations between the two countries deteriorated in July, following the French Government's announcement that it had conferred an honour for distinguished service on one of the two agents responsible for the sabotage of the *Rainbow Warrior*. In July 2005 an article in a French newspaper confirmed that the sinking of the *Rainbow Warrior* had been authorized by the then French President, François Mitterrand. Meanwhile, France announced the suspension of its nuclear testing in the South Pacific in April 1992.

President Jacques Chirac's announcement in June 1995 that France was to resume its nuclear-testing programme in the South Pacific provoked international condemnation. New Zealand suspended military relations with France, and the New Zealand ambassador to Paris was recalled. In March 1996 (the French tests having been concluded) France, the United Kingdom and the USA finally acceded to the South Pacific Nuclear-Free Zone Treaty (Treaty of Rarotonga—Pacific Islands Forum, see p. 413), thus opening the way to improved relations with New Zealand and other Pacific nations. In October 1997, following an official visit to Paris by the New Zealand Prime Minister, the resumption of normal relations with France was declared, and a number of senior-level bilateral visits took place in subsequent years, including, most recently, a state visit to France by Prime Minister John Key in September 2013, during which he held discussions with French President François Hollande on, *inter alia*, bilateral trade and investment links and co-operation in the Pacific.

As part of her Golden Jubilee tour of the Commonwealth, Queen Elizabeth II visited New Zealand in February 2002. Having previously stated that New Zealand's eventual transition to a republic was inevitable, Prime Minister Helen Clark attracted some criticism for her absence from the country on the day of the Queen's arrival. During a state visit to London in September 2013, Prime Minister John Key met with his British counterpart, David Cameron; the two premiers discussed, among other issues, foreign policy, defence and trade links, including progression towards an eventual bilateral free trade agreement.

Negotiations between New Zealand and India on a bilateral free trade agreement (which would help New Zealand to reduce its dependence on its principal trading partner, China) commenced in Wellington in April 2010, with a 10th round of negotiations being held in New Delhi in February 2015; although both sides noted progress, a number of challenging issues still remained unresolved.

Negotiations on a free trade agreement between New Zealand and the Customs Union of Belarus, Russia and Kazakhstan commenced in February 2011; a ninth round of negotiations was held in Moscow in July 2012, although formal talks appeared to stall thereafter. The impasse appeared more entrenched following the seizure by pro-Russian forces of much of the Crimean peninsula in south-eastern Ukraine in February 2014, and the staging of a referendum in March on the question of whether the people of Crimea wished to secede and become a part of Russia. The New Zealand Government expressed deep concern about the 'unjustified threat' to Ukraine's territorial integrity and stated that it would not recognize the result of the poll. At March 2015, in light of the persistent instability in Crimea, the suspension of

free trade talks between New Zealand and Russia and its custom union partners appeared unlikely to be lifted in the near future.

In July 2014 New Zealand and the European Union (EU) successfully concluded negotiations on the EU-New Zealand Partnership Agreement on Relations and Cooperation, in what was reported to be the first step towards the drawing up of an eventual free trade agreement between the two parties.

CONSTITUTION AND GOVERNMENT

New Zealand has no written Constitution. Executive power is vested in the British monarch, as head of state, and is exercisable by an appointed representative, the Governor-General, who must be guided by the advice of the Executive Council (Cabinet), led by the Prime Minister. Legislative power is vested in the unicameral Parliament; the House of Representatives is elected for three years by universal adult suffrage. A system of mixed member proportional (MMP) representation was introduced in 1996. The legislature comprises 120 seats (70 electorate members, including seven seats reserved for Maori, and 50 being chosen from party lists). However, under the MMP system, the awarding of 'overhang' seats is allowed in the case of a party winning more constituency seats than it would be entitled to based on its proportion of party list votes; as a result, the legislature comprised a total of 121 seats following both the 2011 and the 2014 elections. The Governor-General appoints the Prime Minister and, on the latter's recommendation, other Ministers. The Cabinet is responsible to the House.

REGIONAL AND INTERNATIONAL CO-OPERATION

New Zealand is a member of Asia-Pacific Economic Cooperation (APEC, see p. 200), the Pacific Community (see p. 410), the Pacific Islands Forum (see p. 413) and the Cairns Group (see p. 500). The country is also a member of the Colombo Plan (see p. 445) and of the UN's Economic and Social Commission for Asia and the Pacific (ESCAP, see p. 30).

New Zealand joined the UN in 1945. New Zealand began a two-year term as a non-permanent member of the UN Security Council on 1 January 2015. As a contracting party to the General Agreement on Tariffs and Trade (GATT), the country joined the World Trade Organization (WTO, see p. 431) upon its establishment in 1995. New Zealand is also a member of the Organisation for Economic Co-operation and Development (OECD, see p. 377).

ECONOMIC AFFAIRS

In 2012, according to estimates by the World Bank, New Zealand's gross national income (GNI), measured at average 2010–12 prices, was US $157,614m., equivalent to US $35,550 per head (or US $30,750 per head on an international purchasing-power parity basis). During 2004–13, it was estimated, the population increased at an average annual rate of 1.0%, and gross domestic product (GDP) per head increased, in real terms, by an average of 0.9% per year. According to the UN, overall GDP increased, in real terms, at an average annual rate of 1.8% in 2004–13. According to chain-linking methodologies, GDP increased by 2.4% in the year ending March 2014.

Agriculture (including fishing, forestry and logging) contributed 6.9% of GDP in the year ending March 2014. About 6.0% of the employed labour force were engaged in the sector in 2014. The principal crops are potatoes, wheat, barley and maize. Fruit (particularly kiwi fruit, apples and pears) and vegetables are also cultivated. New Zealand is a major producer of wool, although its significance as a source of export earnings has declined in recent years. Meat and dairy products contributed 11.6% and 28.8% of export earnings, respectively, in 2014. A severe drought on the North Island in early 2013 (described as the worst to occur in some 30 years) led to substantial losses in the agricultural sector. The forestry industry is important, with exports of logs, wood and wood articles totalling $NZ3,672m. in 2014 (equivalent to 7.2% of total export earnings). The fisheries sector is of increasing significance, with exports worth $NZ1,375m. (equivalent to 2.7% of total export earnings) in 2014. According to UN figures, agricultural GDP (including fishing and forestry) increased at an average annual rate of 1.4% in 2004–13. The GDP of the sector declined by 2.7% in the year ending March 2013, but increased by 1.9% in the year ending March 2014, according to chain-linking methodologies.

Industry (including mining, manufacturing, construction and utilities) provided 23.4% of GDP in the year ending March 2012. The sector engaged 20.8% of the employed labour force in 2014. In 2004–13 industrial GDP increased at an average annual rate of 0.8%, according to the UN; industrial GDP, measured at constant prices, grew by 3.7% in 2013.

Mining contributed only 2.1% of GDP in the year ending March 2012; the sector engaged just 0.3% of the employed labour force in 2014. New Zealand has substantial coal reserves; petroleum, natural gas, iron, gold and silica are also exploited. A considerable amount of natural gas is used to produce synthetic petrol. According to the UN, the combined GDP of the mining and utilities sectors increased at an average annual rate of 2.2% in 2004–13. According to chain-linking methodologies, the GDP of the mining sector (excluding utilities) grew by 0.3% in the year ending March 2014.

Manufacturing contributed 12.1% of GDP in the year ending March 2012. The sector engaged 10.7% of the employed labour force in 2014. The principal branches of manufacturing are food products, printing and publishing, wood and paper products, chemicals, metals and metal products, machinery and transport equipment. According to the UN, in 2004–13 manufacturing GDP decreased by an average of 0.8% per year. Manufacturing GDP increased by 2.2% in the year ending March 2014, according to chain-linking methodologies.

Construction contributed 5.8% of GDP in the year ending March 2012. The sector engaged 8.9% of the employed labour force in 2014. According to the UN, the GDP of the construction sector grew at an average annual rate of 3.6% in 2004–13. According to chain-linking methodologies, sectoral GDP increased by 12.0% in 2013/14.

Energy is derived mainly from domestic supplies of hydro-electric power, natural gas and coal. Hydroelectric power supplied 51.5% of total electricity output in 2012 and gas 20.3%. Imports of petroleum and its products comprised 15.3% of the total value of merchandise imports in 2014.

The services sector provided 69.7% of GDP in the year ending March 2012. The sector engaged 73.2% of the employed labour force in 2014. Tourism became the single largest source of foreign exchange in the late 1980s. Visitor arrivals increased from 2.71m. in 2013 to 2.86m. in 2014, while tourism receipts rose from $NZ6,342m in 2012 to $NZ6,672m. in 2013. In 2004–13 the GDP of the services sector increased at an average annual rate of 2.1%, according to the UN.

New Zealand's visible merchandise trade balance moved into surplus in 2009. In 2013 a surplus of US $1,159m. was recorded, although there was a deficit of US $6,090m. on the current account of the balance of payments. In 2014 the principal sources of imports were the People's Republic of China (19.9%), Australia, the USA and Japan. China was also the principal market for exports in that year (purchasing 16.9%), followed by Australia, the USA and Japan. The main exports in 2014 were dairy products, meat, prepared foodstuffs, beverages, spirits, vinegar, and tobacco, logs, wood and wood articles, iron and steel, and other base metals, machinery, mechanical appliances, and electronic equipment. The main imports were machinery, mechanical appliances and electrical equipment, mineral products, vehicles, parts and accessories, chemicals and related products, prepared foodstuffs, beverages, spirits, vinegar and tobacco, and plastic materials.

In the year ending June 2014 there was an estimated budgetary deficit of $NZ2,400m. In December 2012 total overseas debt was estimated by the central bank at $NZ252,553m. (comprising

$NZ200,072m. owed by the corporate sector and $NZ52,481m. of official government debt), equivalent to 120.7% of GDP. New Zealand's general government gross debt was $NZ79,972m. in 2013, equivalent to 36.1% of GDP. Annual inflation averaged 2.4% in 2005–14. Consumer prices increased by 1.2% in 2014. The average rate of unemployment was 5.4% in 2013/14.

In mid-2008, for the first time in nine years, New Zealand entered economic recession. In order to address the repercussions of the global economic crisis, in December 2008 the new Government of Prime Minister John Key announced a financial stimulus programme. By April 2009 the Reserve Bank of New Zealand had lowered the interest rate to a record low level of 2.5%, where it remained until April 2010 when it was raised to 3.0%. In March 2011, however, with the objective of mitigating the economic impact of the Christchurch earthquake in February, the rate was again reduced to 2.5%. Amid greater inflationary pressures, the interest rate was raised four times in 2014 to reach 3.5%, and central bank officials indicated that the rate was likely to increase further in 2015. Year-on-year inflation stood at 0.8% in March 2015 and was forecast to fall lower in that year, although the Treasury forecast that it would reach its target level of 2.0% by 2017. Meanwhile, following two successive years of recession, the economy returned to positive growth, of 1.5%, in the year ending March 2011, and continued to expand over the following three years—by 1.9% in 2011/12, 2.3% in 2012/13 and 2.4% in 2013/14, according to chain-linking methodologies. The rate of unemployment declined from 6.7% in 2011/12 to 6.2% in 2012/13 and further to 5.7% in December 2014. On the down side, however, youth unemployment stood at 14.2% in December 2014. The budget for the year ending June 2015, presented in May 2014, forecast an operating surplus of $NZ372m. (following a deficit of $NZ2,400m. in 2013/14), and the reduction of net government debt to less than 20% of GDP by 2020/21. The budget allocated an additional $NZ400m. for reconstruction activities in Christchurch, taking the Government's share of the redevelopment costs to around $NZ15,400m. It also included measures to extend parental leave and offer free medical consultations. As part of efforts to reduce the public debt, the Government reduced its shareholding in a number of state assets in 2013, notably in Air New Zealand, Mighty River Power and Meridian Energy; a minority stake in a third state energy firm, Genesis Energy, was listed on the stock market in April 2014. The Treasury forecast that the rate of economic expansion would reach 3.5% in 2014/15, with growth driven by further reconstruction activities in the Canterbury region and by domestic demand. The principal threat to continuing economic expansion was the slowing of the Chinese economy.

PUBLIC HOLIDAYS

2016: 1–2 January (New Year), 6 February (Waitangi Day, anniversary of 1840 treaty), 25 March (Good Friday), 28 March (Easter Monday), 27 April (ANZAC Day, anniversary of 1915 landing at Gallipoli), 13 June (Queen's Official Birthday), 24 October (Labour Day), 25 December (Christmas), 26 December (Boxing Day).

In addition to these national holidays, each region celebrates an anniversary day.

Statistical Survey

Source (unless otherwise stated): Statistics New Zealand, Aorangi House, 85 Molesworth St, POB 2922, Wellington 1; tel. (4) 931-4600; fax (4) 931-9135; e-mail info@stats.govt.nz; internet www.stats.govt.nz.

Area and Population

AREA, POPULATION AND DENSITY

Area (sq km)	270,534*
Population (census results)†	
7 March 2006	4,027,947
5 March 2013	
Males	2,064,018
Females	2,178,030
Total	4,242,048
Population (official estimates at mid-year)	
2013	4,442,100
2014‡	4,509,900
Density (per sq km) at mid-2014	16.7

* 104,454 sq miles.
† Figures refer to the population usually resident. The total population (including foreign visitors) was: 4,143,282 in 2006; 4,353,198 in 2013.
‡ Provisional.

POPULATION BY AGE AND SEX
('000, population at mid-2014)

	Males	Females	Total
0–14 years	467.1	444.2	911.3
15–64 years	1,506.6	1,441.6	2,948.2
65 years and over	300.9	349.5	650.4
Total	2,209.6	2,300.3	4,509.9

ADMINISTRATIVE REGIONS
(official population estimates at mid-2014)

	Area (sq km)	Population ('000)	Density (per sq km)
North Island			
Northland	13,296	166.1	12.5
Auckland	5,048	1,527.1	302.5
Waikato	26,170	430.8	16.5
Bay of Plenty	11,428	282.3	24.7
Gisborne	8,355	47.1	5.6
Hawke's Bay Region . .	13,764	159.0	11.6
Taranaki	7,227	114.8	15.9
Manawatu-Wanganui . .	22,687	232.2	10.2
Wellington	8,056	491.5	61.0
Total North Island . . .	116,031	3,450.8	29.7
South Island			
Tasman	14,538	49.1	3.4
Nelson	444	49.3	111.0
Marlborough	12,493	44.8	3.6
West Coast	23,351	32.8	1.4
Canterbury	45,845	574.3	12.5
Otago	31,476	211.7	6.7
Southland	25,392	96.5	3.8
Total South Island . . .	153,540	1,058.5	6.9
Area outside regions . . .	963	0.6	0.6
Total	270,534	4,509.9	16.7

Note: Totals may not be equal to the sum of components, owing to rounding.

PRINCIPAL CENTRES OF POPULATION
(official estimates at mid-2014)

Auckland city . .	471,900	Palmerston North .	84,300
Christchurch . .	362,000	Hastings district .	77,400
Wellington (capital) .	200,100	Rotorua district .	68,500
Hamilton . . .	141,615	Napier	60,100
Dunedin	124,600	Nelson	49,300
Tauranga . . .	121,700		

BIRTHS, MARRIAGES AND DEATHS

	Live births*		Marriages†		Deaths*	
	Number	Rate (per '000)	Number	Rate (per '000)	Number	Rate (per '000)
2006 . .	59,193	14.1	21,423	5.1	28,245	6.8
2007 . .	64,044	15.1	21,494	5.1	28,522	6.7
2008 . .	64,343	15.1	21,948	5.1	29,188	6.8
2009 . .	62,543	14.5	21,628	5.0	28,964	6.7
2010 . .	63,897	14.6	20,940	4.8	28,438	6.5
2011 . .	61,403	13.9	20,231	4.6	30,082	6.8
2012 . .	61,178	13.8	20,521	4.6	30,099	6.8
2013 . .	58,717	13.1	19,237	4.3	29,568	6.6

* Data for births and deaths are tabulated by year of registration rather than by year of occurrence.
† Based on the resident population concept, replacing the previous de facto concept.

Life expectancy (years at birth): 81.2 (males 79.4; females 83.0) in 2012 (Source: World Bank, World Development Indicators database).

IMMIGRATION AND EMIGRATION

	2012	2013	2014
Long-term immigrants* . . .	85,255	93,965	109,317
Long-term emigrants†	86,420	71,497	58,395

* Figures refer to persons intending to remain in New Zealand for 12 months or more, and New Zealand citizens returning after an absence of 12 months or more.
† Figures refer to New Zealand citizens intending to remain abroad for 12 months or more, and overseas migrants departing after a stay of 12 months or more.

ECONOMICALLY ACTIVE POPULATION
(labour force sample survey, April–June, '000 persons aged 15 years and over, excl. armed forces)

	2012	2013	2014
Agriculture, forestry and fishing	147.2	147.1	138.6
Mining and quarrying	6.1	6.5	7.5
Manufacturing	246.5	242.6	246.5
Electricity, gas and water . . .	17.9	16.7	22.3
Construction	171.3	176.1	205.7
Wholesale and retail trade; repair of motor vehicles, motorcycles and personal and household goods; restaurants and hotels .	429.5	432.4	448.8
Transport, storage and communications	154.4	156.2	146.9
Financial intermediation . . .	68.2	69.6	67.8
Real estate, renting and business activities	295.3	297.7	308.5
Public administration and defence; compulsory social security . .	118.0	121.7	132.7
Education and training . . .	201.2	191.3	201.1
Health and social work . . .	227.5	239.6	248.1
Other community, social and personal service activities . .	131.3	130.8	138.1
Sub-total	2,214.4	2,228.3	2,312.6
Activities not adequately defined	6.0	8.2	6.4
Total employed	2,220.4	2,236.5	2,319.0
Unemployed	156.4	148.2	132.0
Total labour force	2,376.8	2,384.7	2,451.0
Males	1,253.5	1,259.9	1,302.4
Females	1,123.2	1,124.8	1,148.6

Health and Welfare

KEY INDICATORS

Total fertility rate (children per woman, 2012)	2.1
Under-5 mortality rate (per 1,000 live births, 2012) . . .	6
HIV/AIDS (% of persons aged 15–49, 2011)	0.1
Physicians (per 1,000 head, 2010)	2.7
Hospital beds (per 1,000 head, 2011)	2.3
Health expenditure (2011): US $ per head (PPP) . . .	3,175
Health expenditure (2011): % of GDP	10.3
Health expenditure (2011): public (% of total) . . .	82.7
Total carbon dioxide emissions ('000 metric tons, 2010) . .	31,550.9
Carbon dioxide emissions per head (metric tons, 2010) . .	7.2
Human Development Index (2013): ranking	7
Human Development Index (2013): value	0.910

For sources and definitions, see explanatory note on p. vi.

Agriculture

PRINCIPAL CROPS

('000 metric tons)

	2011	2012	2013
Wheat	383	489	448
Barley	368	439	416
Maize	210	211	202
Oats	28	18	20
Potatoes*	530	550	560
Peas, dry	32	20	23
Cabbages and other brassicas* .	37	43	42
Lettuce and chicory*	28	34	32
Tomatoes*	63	95	94
Cauliflowers and broccoli* . .	37	39	36
Pumpkins, squash and gourds* .	148	153	147
Onions and shallots, green* . .	228	257	260
Peas, green*	38	38	37
Carrots and turnips*	60	88	86
Maize, green*	61	80	79
Grapes	328	340*	369*
Apples*	445	448	439
Pears*	27	30	28
Kiwi fruit	420†	376†	382*

* FAO estimate(s).
† Unofficial figure.

Aggregate production ('000 metric tons, may include official, semi-official or estimated data): Total cereals 999 in 2011, 1,168 in 2012, 1,098 in 2013; Total roots and tubers 544 in 2011, 566 in 2012, 577 in 2013; Total vegetables (incl. melons) 871 in 2011, 1,005 in 2012, 997 in 2013; Total fruits (excl. melons) 1,332 in 2011, 1,309 in 2012, 1,334 in 2013.

Source: FAO.

LIVESTOCK

('000 head at 30 June)

	2011	2012	2013
Cattle	10,021	10,180	10,182
Sheep	31,132	31,263	30,787
Goats	85	90	80
Pigs	327	314	298
Horses	56	57	57
Chickens	13,800	14,480	14,720*
Ducks†	180	180	180
Geese and guinea fowls† . . .	80	80	82
Turkeys†	76	76	77

* Unofficial figure.
† FAO estimates.
Source: FAO.

LIVESTOCK PRODUCTS

('000 metric tons)

	2011	2012	2013
Cattle meat	622.6	603.0	563.7
Sheep meat	465.3	448.2	450.1
Pig meat	50.2	49.8	39.5
Chicken meat	158.3	169.9	169.1
Game meat	22.9	22.9	23.7
Cows' milk	17,339	19,129	18,883
Hen eggs*	51.1	53.5	54.0
Other poultry eggs*	3.2	3.2	3.2
Honey	9.5	10.4	17.9
Wool, greasy	163.7	165.0*	165.0*

* FAO estimate(s).

Source: FAO.

Forestry

ROUNDWOOD REMOVALS

('000 cubic metres, FAO estimates)

	2011	2012	2013
Sawlogs, veneer logs and logs for sleepers	22,136	23,507	26,266
Pulpwood	3,994	3,908	3,708
Total	26,130	27,415	29,974

Source: FAO.

SAWNWOOD PRODUCTION

('000 cubic metres, year ending 31 March)

Species	2011/12	2012/13	2013/14
Radiata pine	3,760	3,883	3,791
Douglas fir	92	103	110
Rimu and miro	2	2	1
Total (incl. others)	3,886	4,019	3,936

Source: Forestry Statistics Section, Ministry of Agriculture and Forestry, Wellington.

Fishing

('000 metric tons, live weight)

	2010	2011	2012
Capture	436.2	429.8	440.7
Southern blue whiting . . .	38.6	35.0	29.9
Blue grenadier (Hoki)	110.0	118.5	128.0
Oreo dories	2.6	8.7	11.8
Jack and horse mackerels . .	41.0	38.7	42.8
Snoek (Barracouta)	26.4	27.0	28.4
Skipjack tuna	22.2	19.8	16.8
Wellington flying squid . . .	32.6	37.0	35.3
Aquaculture	110.6	117.3	100.2
New Zealand mussel . . .	95.2	101.3	86.4
Total catch	546.8	547.1	540.8

* Excluding catches made by chartered vessels and landed outside New Zealand.

Note: Figures exclude aquatic plants (metric tons, all capture); 408 in 2010; 501 in 2011; 1,241 in 2012. Also excluded are aquatic mammals (recorded by number rather than by weight). The number of whales and dolphins caught was: 22 in 2010; 19 in 2011; 43 in 2012.

Source: FAO.

Mining

('000 metric tons unless otherwise indicated)

	2010	2011	2012
Coal (incl. lignite)	5,330	4,944	4,926
Gold (kg)	13,494	11,761	10,164
Crude petroleum ('000 barrels) .	19,302	16,591	14,149
Gross natural gas (million cu m) .	5,052	4,678	5,188
Liquid petroleum gas ('000 barrels)	1,200	1,200	1,200
Ironsands	2,439	2,357	2,395
Silica sand	113.2	109.3	73.1
Limestone	4,450	3,277	3,136

Source: US Geological Survey.

Industry

SELECTED PRODUCTS
(metric tons unless otherwise indicated)

	2012	2013	2014
Wine (million litres)	194.0	248.4	320.4
Chemical wood pulp*	842,567	799,753	832,325
Mechanical wood pulp* . . .	712,404	694,750	635,725
Newsprint*	296,628	239,400	144,121
Other paper and paperboard* .	562,691	585,504	589,029
Fibre board (cu m)*	717,083	727,203	697,818
Particle board (cu m)* . . .	163,703	156,037	147,454
Veneer (cu m)*	678,874	620,515	646,779
Plywood (cu m)*	355,553	326,250	345,534
Cement ('000 metric tons)† . .	1,200	n.a.	n.a.
Aluminium—unwrought ('000 metric tons):			
primary	326.9	n.a.	n.a.
secondary	n.a.	n.a.	n.a.

* Source: Ministry of Agriculture and Forestry, Wellington.
† Estimates.

Sources (unless otherwise stated): US Geological Survey; New Zealand Wine Online.

2011 ('000 metric tons unless otherwise indicated): Jet fuels 1,048; Motor spirit (petrol) 1,326; Gas-diesel (distillate fuel) oils 1,923; Residual fuel oils 594; Electric energy (million kWh) 44,496 (Source: UN, *Industrial Commodity Statistics Database*).

Finance

CURRENCY AND EXCHANGE RATES

Monetary Units
100 cents = 1 New Zealand dollar ($NZ).

Sterling, US Dollar and Euro Equivalents (31 December 2014)
£1 sterling = $NZ1.994;
US $1 = $NZ1.277;
€1 = $NZ1.551;
$NZ100 = £50.16 = US $78.29 = €64.48.

Average Exchange Rate (New Zealand dollars per US $)
2012   1.2343
2013   1.2194
2014   1.2055

GOVERNMENT FINANCE
(central government operations, $NZ million, year ending 30 June)
Summary of Balances

	2010/11	2011/12	2012/13
Revenue	72,536	72,618	75,838
Less Expense	86,318	75,767	76,393
Net operating balance . . .	−13,782	−3,149	−555
Less Net acquisition of non-financial assets	3,627	2,069	1,685
Net lending/borrowing . . .	−17,409	−5,218	−2,240

Revenue

	2010/11	2011/12	2012/13
Tax revenue	54,862	58,826	62,232
Taxes on income, profits and capital gains	32,795	35,333	38,156
Taxes on goods and services .	20,000	21,317	21,901
Taxes on property	6	4	3
Taxes on international trade and transactions	1,978	2,089	2,124
Other taxes	83	83	47
Sales of goods and services . .	4,493	4,900	4,775
Interest revenue and dividends .	3,737	3,365	3,655
Social contributions	2,745	2,782	2,586
Grants	1,394	1,144	1,396
Other revenue	5,305	1,601	1,194
Total	72,536	72,618	75,838

Expense/Outlays

Expense by economic type*	2010/11	2011/12	2012/13
Compensation of employees . .	18,255	18,881	19,119
Purchase of goods and services .	8,542	8,771	9,117
Consumption of fixed capital . .	2,915	2,674	2,622
Interest	3,659	3,966	4,320
Subsidies and transfers . . .	18,905	7,031	6,317
Grants	1,959	2,045	2,405
Social benefits	32,084	32,399	32,493
Total	86,318	75,767	76,393

* Including net acquisition of non-financial assets.

Outlays by function of government	2010/11	2011/12	2012/13
General public services . . .	21,540	20,264	21,025
Defence	1,641	1,528	1,532
Public order and safety . . .	4,310	4,327	5,176
Economic affairs	5,190	5,102	5,387
Environment protection . . .	593	612	664
Housing and community amenities	876	801	292
Health	14,192	14,844	15,108
Recreation, culture and religion .	878	894	885
Education	14,534	14,827	14,512
Social protection	22,564	12,569	11,813
Total	86,318	75,767	76,393

INTERNATIONAL RESERVES
(excl. gold, US $ million at 31 December)

	2011	2012	2013
IMF special drawing rights . .	1,272	1,258	1,303
Reserve position in IMF . . .	499	547	606
Foreign exchange	15,242	15,779	14,409
Total	17,012	17,584	16,318

Source: IMF, *International Financial Statistics*.

MONEY SUPPLY
($NZ million at 31 December)

	2008	2009	2010
Currency outside banks . .	3,526	3,580	3,720
Demand deposits at banking institutions	31,361	31,316	32,760
Total money	34,888	34,896	36,480

Broad money: 238,446 in 2011; 253,611 in 2012; 268,384 in 213.

Source: IMF, *International Financial Statistics.*

COST OF LIVING
(Consumer Price Index; base: 2000 = 100)

	2012	2013	2014
Food (incl. beverages) . . .	144.8	145.4	146.1
All items (incl. others) . . .	136.6	138.1	139.8

Source: ILO.

NATIONAL ACCOUNTS
($NZ million at current prices, year ending 31 March)

Expenditure on the Gross Domestic Product

	2011/12	2012/13*	2013/14*
Government final consumption expenditure	41,392	41,724	43,428
Private final consumption expenditure	122,110	125,975	130,338
Change in inventories	1,283	598	1,857
Gross fixed capital formation .	42,216	45,910	50,928
Total domestic expenditure .	207,001	214,207	226,551
Exports of goods and services .	64,749	62,762	67,175
Less Imports of goods and services	61,451	61,235	63,227
GDP in market prices . . .	210,300	215,735	230,498

* Provisional figures.

Gross Domestic Product by Economic Activity

	2009/10	2010/11	2011/12
Agriculture	8,653	10,641	10,596
Fishing	1,291	1,366	1,576
Forestry and logging	1,127	1,336	1,147
Mining and quarrying . . .	4,132	4,335	4,002
Manufacturing	22,493	22,440	23,383
Electricity, gas and water . . .	6,163	6,501	6,548
Construction	10,785	10,637	11,100
Wholesale and retail trade . .	17,680	18,533	19,113
Hotels and restaurants . . .	3,993	4,091	4,314
Transport, storage and communications	13,890	14,686	15,686
Financial intermediation (incl. insurance)	11,238	10,237	11,414
Property and business activities .	25,972	27,355	28,600
Ownership of dwellings . . .	10,827	11,731	12,320
Public administration and defence	12,325	12,787	13,289
Education	9,229	9,635	9,923
Health and community services .	11,959	12,340	12,392
Cultural and recreational services	2,878	2,913	3,030
Personal and other services . .	3,945	4,026	4,139
Statistical discrepancy	1	−1	−2
Gross value added at basic prices	178,581	185,589	192,570
Goods and services tax on production	12,415	14,033	15,778
Import duties	1,859	2,008	1,952
GDP in market prices . . .	192,855	201,630	210,300

BALANCE OF PAYMENTS
(US $ million)

	2011	2012	2013
Exports of goods	38,381.6	37,866.5	39,969.5
Imports of goods	−36,151.7	−37,772.4	−38,811.1
Balance on goods	2,230.0	94.1	1,158.5
Exports of services	12,981.7	13,165.8	13,265.2
Imports of services	−11,875.1	−12,148.7	−12,341.1
Balance on goods and services	3,336.6	1,111.2	2,082.5
Primary income received . . .	4,521.9	4,986.2	5,181.4
Primary income paid	−12,499.8	−12,639.3	−12,927.2
Balance on goods, services and primary income	−4,641.4	−6,541.9	−5,663.3
Secondary income received . .	1,040.5	1,029.9	1,029.0
Secondary income paid	−1,220.6	−1,451.4	−1,455.2
Current balance	−4,821.4	−6,963.4	−6,089.5
Capital account (net) . . .	10,116.7	−409.1	−70.9
Direct investment assets . . .	−2,518.1	503.9	−677.2
Direct investment liabilities . .	4,064.0	2,209.1	1,005.3
Portfolio investment assets . .	−1,019.3	−5,071.9	−7,375.1
Portfolio investment liabilities .	4,292.3	9,377.6	4,634.9
Other investment assets . . .	−4,386.2	2,133.9	1,502.2
Other investment liabilities . .	−339.5	−4,439.2	−1,193.0
Net errors and omissions . . .	−4,974.5	3,172.8	7,420.7
Reserves and related items .	413.9	513.8	−842.7

Source: IMF, *International Financial Statistics.*

External Trade

PRINCIPAL COMMODITIES
(distribution by HS, $NZ million)

Imports c.i.f.	2012	2013	2014*
Prepared foodstuffs; beverages, spirits, vinegar; tobacco and articles thereof	3,347	3,405	3,668
Mineral products	8,667	8,486	8,000
Mineral fuels, mineral oils and products of their distillation; bituminous substances; mineral waxes	8,345	8,182	7,688
Chemicals and related products	4,476	4,367	4,362
Plastics, rubber, and articles thereof	2,345	2,396	2,533
Plastic and plastic articles . .	1,741	1,803	1,937
Pulp of wood, paper and paperboard, and articles thereof	1,301	1,265	1,234
Textiles and textile articles .	2,111	2,164	2,220
Iron and steel, other base metals and articles of base metal	2,232	2,216	2,348
Machinery and mechanical appliances; electrical equipment; parts thereof .	9,924	9,861	10,221
Boilers, machinery and mechanical appliances . . .	6,059	6,058	6,389
Electrical machinery and equipment	3,865	3,803	3,832

Imports c.i.f.—*continued*	2012	2013	2014*
Vehicles, aircraft, vessels and associated transport equipment	6,129	7,174	9,309
Vehicles; other than railway or tramway rolling stock, and parts and accessories thereof	5,186	5,831	6,762
Aircraft, spacecraft and parts thereof	722	853	1,908
Optical, medical apparatus, etc.; clocks and watches; musical instruments; parts thereof	1,475	1,430	1,560
Total (incl. others)	47,219	48,360	50,094

Exports f.o.b.	2012	2013	2014*
Live animals and animal products	18,801	20,865	22,853
Dairy produce; birds' eggs; natural honey; edible products of animal origin, not elsewhere specified or included	11,562	13,591	14,733
Meat and edible offal	5,166	5,277	5,935
Vegetables and vegetable products	2,278	2,238	2,518
Fruit, nuts and related products	1,564	1,483	1,774
Prepared foodstuffs; beverages, spirits, vinegar; tobacco and articles thereof	4,250	4,460	4,445
Beverages, spirits and vinegar	1,475	1,492	1,581
Mineral products	2,362	1,888	1,658
Mineral fuels, mineral oils and products of their distillation; bituminous substances; mineral waxes	2,191	1,727	1,584
Chemicals and related products	2,347	2,194	2,361
Wood, wood charcoal, cork, and articles thereof	3,164	3,861	3,674
Logs, wood and wood articles	3,162	3,859	3,672
Iron and steel, other base metals and articles of base metal	3,008	2,045	1,955
Machinery and mechanical appliances; electrical equipment; parts thereof	2,835	2,594	2,534
Boilers, machinery and mechanical appliances; parts thereof	1,716	1,528	1,610
Total (incl. others)†	46,064	48,044	51,243

* Provisional figures.
† Including re-exports.

PRINCIPAL TRADING PARTNERS
($NZ million)

Imports c.i.f.*	2012	2013	2014†
Australia	7,184	6,424	6,244
Brunei	1,202	597	457
Canada	579	568	524
China, People's Republic	7,713	8,260	8,680
France	918	1,224	1,171
Germany	2,098	2,229	2,465
Indonesia	659	871	848
Italy	787	879	929
Japan	3,053	3,087	3,416
Korea, Republic	1,809	1,962	2,295
Kuwait	231	438	491
Malaysia	1,835	2,026	2,332
Oman	1,174	390	29

Imports c.i.f.*—*continued*	2012	2013	2014†
Qatar	525	603	549
Russia	282	574	522
Saudi Arabia	1,027	933	806
Singapore	2,110	2,023	2,061
Taiwan	782	781	766
Thailand	1,509	1,658	1,762
United Arab Emirates	333	1,030	883
United Kingdom	1,261	1,228	1,332
USA	4,386	4,527	5,931
Total (incl. others)	47,219	48,360	51,243

* Excluding specie and gold.
† Provisional figures.

Exports*	2012	2013	2014†
Algeria	424	291	583
Australia	9,908	9,125	8,772
Canada	565	527	581
China, People's Republic	6,859	9,965	9,991
Germany	739	737	665
Hong Kong	869	770	736
India	786	669	622
Indonesia	838	886	931
Japan	3,211	2,829	2,938
Korea, Republic	1,555	1,633	1,759
Malaysia	888	911	987
Netherlands	570	606	847
Philippines	678	754	751
Saudi Arabia	687	546	754
Singapore	845	1,021	1,008
Taiwan	828	883	1,011
Thailand	626	703	790
United Arab Emirates	611	656	917
United Kingdom	1,395	1,397	1,548
USA	4,231	4,071	4,706
Venezuela	459	406	116
Viet Nam	451	481	548
Total (incl. others)	46,064	48,044	50,094

* Including re-exports, but excluding specie and gold.
† Provisional figures.

Transport

RAILWAYS
(traffic, year ending 30 June)

	2010/11	2011/12	2012/13
Freight ('000 metric tons)	15,700	17,455	17,265
Passengers ('000)	11,662	11,636	11,668

Source: New Zealand Railways Corporation.

ROAD TRAFFIC
(vehicles licensed at June)

	2011	2012	2013
Passenger cars	2,344,864	2,358,095	2,379,939
Taxis	7,362	7,157	7,261
Buses and service coaches	19,653	19,794	20,457
Trailers and caravans	465,104	475,127	485,832
Motorcycles and mopeds	64,070	61,626	60,900
Tractors	29,223	29,808	29,863
Trucks	422,452	426,603	437,134
Total (incl. others)	3,392,955	3,419,056	3,463,131

Source: New Zealand Transport Agency.

SHIPPING

Flag Registered Fleet
(at 31 December)

	2012	2013	2014
Number of vessels	150	153	130
Displacement (grt)	237,148	254,441	245,035

Source: Lloyd's List Intelligence (www.lloydslistintelligence.com).

International Seaborne Freight Traffic
('000 metric tons, year ending 30 June)

	2004/05	2005/06	2006/07*
Goods loaded	21,894	21,840	22,986
Goods unloaded	19,164	18,119	18,499

* Provisional.

CIVIL AVIATION
(domestic and international traffic on scheduled services)

	2010	2011
Kilometres flown (million)	188	190
Passengers carried ('000)	13,319	13,771
Passenger-km (million)	23,568	24,653
Total metric ton-km (million)	2,788	3,313

Source: UN, *Statistical Yearbook*.

Passengers carried ('000): 13,937 in 2012; 13,717 in 2013 (Source: World Bank, World Development Indicators database).

Tourism

VISITOR ARRIVALS
('000)

Country of residence	2012	2013	2014
Australia	1,156	1,218	1,248
China, People's Republic . . .	197	229	265
Germany	64	70	79
Japan	72	75	81
Korea, Republic	53	51	55
United Kingdom	190	192	194
USA	178	201	221
Total (incl. others)	2,565	2,718	2,857

Tourism receipts ($NZ million): 6,780 in 2011; 6,342 in 2012; 6,672 in 2013.

Source: Tourism Research Council, Wellington.

Communications Media

	2011	2012	2013
Telephones ('000 main lines in use)	1,880	1,880	1,850
Mobile cellular telephones ('000 subscribers)	4,820	4,922	4,766
Internet subscribers ('000) . .	1,400	n.a.	n.a.
Broadband subscribers ('000) . .	1,140	1,240	1,316

Source: International Telecommunication Union.

Education

(July 2014 unless otherwise indicated)

	Institutions	Teachers (full-time equivalent)	Students
Early childhood services[1] .	5,100	15,608	200,922[2]
Primary schools[3]	1,961	27,398[4,5]	439,494
Composite schools[6] . . .	167	2,682[4,5]	52,378
Secondary schools[7] . . .	366	20,614[4,5]	272,313
Special schools	38	1,216[4,5]	3,073
Polytechnics	20[8]	4,325[4]	143,916[1]
Colleges of education . . .	4[8]	301[9]	62,381[4]
Universities	8[8]	7,784[4]	173,153[1]
Wananga[10]	3[8]	691[4]	38,974[1]
Private training establishments receiving government grants . . .	522[8]	4,177[8]	75,079[1]

[1] 2013 figure.
[2] Includes children on the regular roll of kindergartens, playcentres, the Correspondence School, Te Kohanga Reo, Early Childhood Development Unit funded playgroups, Early Childhood Development Unit funded Pacific islands language groups, education and care centres (including home-based child care).
[3] Primary schools include Full Primary Years 1–8, Contributing Years 1–6, Intermediate Years 7–8.
[4] 2012 figure.
[5] Teachers employed in state schools at 1 April 2012.
[6] Composite schools provide both primary and secondary education (includes area schools and the Correspondence School).
[7] Secondary schools include Years 7–15, Years 9–15.
[8] 2003 figure.
[9] 2006 figure.
[10] Tertiary institutions providing polytechnic and university level programmes specifically for Maori students, with an emphasis on Maori language and culture.

Source: Ministry of Education, Wellington.

Pupil-teacher ratio (primary education, UNESCO estimate): 14.6 in 2010/11 (Source: UNESCO Institute for Statistics).

Directory

The Government

Head of State: HM Queen ELIZABETH II (acceded to the throne 6 February 1952).

Governor-General and Commander-in-Chief: Lt-Gen. Sir JERRY MATEPARAE (assumed office 31 August 2011).

CABINET
(May 2015)

The Government is formed by the National Party, with the support of ACT New Zealand, the Maori Party and UnitedFuture New Zealand.

Prime Minister, Minister for National Security and Intelligence, and Minister of Tourism, also responsible for Ministerial Services: JOHN KEY.

Deputy Prime Minister and Minister of Finance, also responsible for HNZC: BILL ENGLISH.

Minister of Defence and Minister for Canterbury Earthquake Recovery, also responsible for the Earthquake Commission: GERRY BROWNLEE.

Minister for Economic Development, for Regulatory Reform, for Tertiary Education, Skills and Employment, and Minister of Science and Innovation, also responsible for Novopay: STEVEN JOYCE.

Minister of State Services, of Local Government and Minister for Social Housing: PAULA BENNETT.

Minister of Health and Minister for Sport and Recreation: Dr JONATHAN COLEMAN.

Minister of Justice, of Broadcasting, and Minister for Courts and for Communications: AMY ADAMS.

Attorney-General, Minister for Treaty of Waitangi Negotiations, and Minister in Charge of NZ Security Intelligence Service, also responsible for the GCSB: CHRISTOPHER FINLAYSON.

Minister of Transport, and of Energy and Resources: SIMON BRIDGES.

Minister of Education: HEKIA PARATA.

Minister for Social Development: ANNE TOLLEY.

Minister for the Environment, and for Building and Housing: Dr NICK SMITH.

Minister of Foreign Affairs: MURRAY MCCULLY.

Minister for Primary Industries and for Racing: NATHAN GUY.

Minister for Youth, for ACC and Minister of Civil Defence: NIKKI KAYE.

Minister of Trade and Minister for Climate Change Issues: TIM GROSER.

Minister of Immigration and of Police and Minister for Workplace Relations and Safety: MICHAEL WOODHOUSE.

Minister of Revenue and Minister for State Owned Enterprises: TODD MCCLAY.

Minister for Pacific Peoples and for Ethnic Communities, and Minister of Corrections: PESETA SAM LOTU-IIGA.

Minister for Arts, Culture and Heritage, and for Senior Citizens, and Minister of Conservation: MAGGIE BARRY.

MINISTERS OUTSIDE CABINET

Minister of Veterans' Affairs and of Statistics, and Minister for Small Business: CRAIG FOSS.

Minister for the Community and Voluntary Sector, and for Food Safety: JO GOODHEW.

Minister for Disability Issues and Minister of Customs: NICKY WAGNER.

Minister for Land Information and for Women: LOUISE UPSTON.

Minister of Commerce and Consumer Affairs: PAUL GOLDSMITH.

SUPPORT PARTY MINISTERS

Minister for Maori Development and for Whanau Ora: TE URUROA FLAVELL.

Minister of Internal Affairs: PETER DUNNE.

MINISTRIES AND GOVERNMENT DEPARTMENTS

Department of the Prime Minister and Cabinet: Executive Wing, Parliament Bldgs, Wellington 6011; tel. (4) 817-9743; fax (4) 472-3181; e-mail dpmc.information@dpmc.govt.nz; internet www.dpmc.govt.nz.

Ministry of Business, Innovation and Employment: 15 Stout St, POB 1473, Wellington 6011; tel. (4) 917-0199; fax (4) 917-0190; e-mail info@mbie.govt.nz; internet www.mbie.govt.nz.

Ministry of Civil Defence and Emergency Management: 70-84 Lambton Quay, Wellington 6145; tel. (4) 817-8555; fax (4) 817-8554; e-mail emergency.management@dpmc.govt.nz; internet www.civildefence.govt.nz.

Department of Conservation: 18–32 Manners St, Wellington 6011; tel. (4) 471-0726; fax (4) 381-3057; e-mail enquiries@doc.govt.nz; internet www.doc.govt.nz.

Department of Corrections: POB 1206, Wellington 6140; tel. (4) 460-3000; fax (4) 460-3208; e-mail info@corrections.govt.nz; internet www.corrections.govt.nz.

Ministry for Culture and Heritage: ASB House, Level 4, 101 The Terrace, POB 5364, Wellington 6011; tel. (4) 499-4229; fax (4) 499-4490; e-mail info@mch.govt.nz; internet www.mch.govt.nz.

Ministry of Defence: Freyberg House, Level 4, 2–12 Aitken St, POB 12-703, Wellington; tel. (4) 496-0999; fax (4) 496-0859; e-mail info@defence.govt.nz; internet www.defence.govt.nz.

Ministry of Education: 45–47 Pipitea St, Level 3, POB 1666, Thorndon, Wellington 6140; tel. (4) 463-8000; fax (4) 463-8001; e-mail info@minedu.govt.nz; internet www.minedu.govt.nz.

Ministry for the Environment: Environment House, 23 Kate Sheppard Pl., POB 10-362, Thorndon, Wellington 6143; tel. (4) 439-7400; fax (4) 439-7700; e-mail info@mfe.govt.nz; internet www.mfe.govt.nz.

Ministry of Foreign Affairs and Trade: 195 Lambton Quay, Private Bag 18901, Wellington 5045; tel. (4) 439-8000; fax (4) 4392-8505; e-mail enquiries@mfat.govt.nz; internet www.mfat.govt.nz.

Ministry of Health: 20 Aitken St, POB 5013, Wellington 6011; tel. (4) 496-2000; fax (4) 496-2340; e-mail info@health.govt.nz; internet www.health.govt.nz.

Department of Inland Revenue: POB 39010, Wellington Mail Centre, Lower Hutt 5045; tel. (4) 978-0779; e-mail nonres@ird.govt.nz; internet www.ird.govt.nz.

Department of Internal Affairs: 46 Waring Taylor St, POB 805, Wellington 6011; tel. (4) 495-7200; e-mail info@dia.govt.nz; internet www.dia.govt.nz.

Ministry of Justice: Justice Centre, 19 Aitken St, DX 10088, Wellington; tel. (4) 918-8800; fax (4) 918-8820; e-mail info@justice.govt.nz; internet www.justice.govt.nz.

Ministry of Maori Development (Te Puni Kokiri): Te Puni Kokiri House, 143 Lambton Quay, POB 3943, Wellington 6011; tel. (4) 819-6000; fax (4) 819-6299; e-mail info@tpk.govt.nz; internet www.tpk.govt.nz.

Ministry of Pacific Island Affairs: ASB Bldg, Level 2, 101–103 The Terrace, POB 833, Wellington 6011; tel. (4) 473-4493; fax (4) 473-4301; e-mail contact@mpia.govt.nz; internet www.mpia.govt.nz.

Ministry for Primary Industries: Pastoral House, 25 The Terrace, POB 2526, Wellington; tel. (4) 894-0100; fax (4) 894-0720; e-mail info@mpi.govt.nz; internet www.mpi.govt.nz.

Ministry of Social Development: Bowen State Bldg, Bowen St, POB 1556, Wellington 6011; tel. (4) 916-3300; fax (4) 918-0099; e-mail information@msd.govt.nz; internet www.msd.govt.nz.

State Services Commission: Reserve Bank Bldg, Level 10, 2 The Terrace, POB 329, Wellington 6140; tel. (4) 495-6600; fax (4) 495-6686; e-mail commission@ssc.govt.nz; internet www.ssc.govt.nz.

Statistics New Zealand (Tatauranga Aotearoa): Statistics House, The Boulevard, Harbour Quays, POB 2922, Wellington 6140; tel. (4) 931-4600; fax (4) 931-4030; e-mail info@stats.govt.nz; internet www.stats.govt.nz.

Ministry of Tourism: 33 Bowen St, POB 5640, Wellington; tel. (4) 498-7440; fax (4) 498-7445; e-mail info@tourism.govt.nz; internet www.tourism.govt.nz.

Ministry of Transport: SAS House, Level 6, 89 The Terrace, POB 3175, Wellington 6140; tel. (4) 439-9000; fax (4) 439-9001; e-mail info@transport.govt.nz; internet www.transport.govt.nz.

Treasury: Level 5, 1 The Terrace, POB 3724, Wellington 6011; tel. (4) 472-2733; fax (4) 473-0982; e-mail info@treasury.govt.nz; internet www.treasury.govt.nz.

Ministry for Women: Qual IT House, Level 9, 22 The Terrace, POB 10-049, Wellington 6143; tel. (4) 915-7112; fax (4) 916-1604; e-mail info@women.govt.nz; internet www.women.govt.nz.

Ministry of Youth Development: Bowen State Bldg, Level 7, Bowen St, POB 1556, Wellington; tel. (4) 916-3300; fax (4) 918-0091; e-mail mydinfo@myd.govt.nz; internet www.myd.govt.nz.

Legislature

PARLIAMENT

Parliament comprises the Crown and the elected House of Representatives.

House of Representatives

Speaker: DAVID CARTER.

General Election, 20 September 2014

Party	Number of party votes	% of votes	Electorate seats	List seats	Total seats
NZ National Party .	1,131,501	47.04	41	19	60
NZ Labour Party . .	604,534	25.13	27	5	32
Green Party . . .	257,356	10.70	—	14	14
New Zealand First .	208,300	8.66	—	11	11
Maori Party . . .	31,850	1.32	1	1	2
ACT New Zealand .	16,689	0.69	1	—	1
UnitedFuture New Zealand . . .	5,286	0.22	1	—	1
Conservative . . .	95,598	3.97	—	—	—
Internet MANA . .	34,095	1.42	—	—	—
Total (incl. others) .	2,416,481	100.00	71	50	121

Election Commission

Electoral Commission of New Zealand: 34–42 Manners St, POB 3220, Wellington; tel. (4) 474-0670; fax (4) 474-0674; e-mail enquiries@elections.govt.nz; internet www.elections.org.nz; f. 2010; independent Crown entity; assumed responsibilities of Chief Electoral Office and previous Electoral Commission in Oct. 2010; Chair. Sir HUGH WILLIAMS; Chief Electoral Officer ROBERT PEDEN.

Political Organizations

At February 2015 there were 18 registered parties in New Zealand, 15 of which contested the general election in September of that year.

ACT New Zealand: Level 2, 27 Gillies Ave, Newmarket, Auckland 1023; tel. (9) 523-0470; e-mail info@act.org.nz; internet www.act.org.nz; f. 1994; supports free enterprise, tax reform and choice in education and health; Pres. JOHN THOMPSON; Leader DAVID SEYMOUR.

Conservative Party of New Zealand: PO Box 99638, Auckland 1149; tel. (9) 520-2082; e-mail office@conservativeparty.org.nz; internet www.conservativeparty.org.nz; f. 2011; Chair. BRIAN DOBBS; Leader COLIN CRAIG.

Green Party of Aotearoa—New Zealand: Level 2, 17 Garrett St, Te Aro, POB 11-652, Wellington; tel. (4) 801-5102; fax (4) 801-5104; e-mail greenparty@greens.org.nz; internet www.greens.org.nz; f. 1989; fmrly Values Party, f. 1972; Leader METIRIA TUREI.

Internet Party: 46-50 Bloomfield Terrace, Lower Hutt, Wellington 5010; tel. (64) 220914620 (mobile); e-mail hello@internet.org.nz; internet internet.org.nz; f. 2014; founded and funded by Kim Dotcom; contested the 2014 election in alliance with the Mana Movement as Internet MANA; Party Sec. MICHAEL MARSOM (acting); Chief Exec. (vacant).

Mana Movement (MANA): Level 16, Bowen House, 70/84 Lambton Quay, Wellington 6011; tel. (4) 817-6955; fax (4) 499-7269; e-mail info@mana.net.nz; internet www.mana.net.nz; f. 2011; advocates development and equality of income for local people; contested the 2014 election in an alliance with the Internet Party as Internet MANA; Pres. LISA MCNAB; Leader HONE HARAWIRA.

Maori Party: POB 50-271, Porirua; tel. (4) 817-8259; fax (4) 499-7269; e-mail hekeretari2@maoriparty.com; internet www.maoriparty.org; f. 2004; Co-Leaders TE URUROA FLAVELL, MARAMA FOX; Pres. NAIDA GLAVISH.

New Zealand First Party: Albany, North Shore City, POB 301158, Auckland 0752; tel. and fax (9) 422-2370; e-mail nzf.website@parliament.govt.nz; internet nzfirst.org.nz; f. 1993; Leader WINSTON PETERS; Pres. ANNE MARTIN.

New Zealand Labour Party: Fraser House, Level 1, 160–162 Willis St, POB 784, Wellington; tel. (4) 384-7649; fax (4) 384-8060; e-mail office@labourparty.org.nz; internet labour.org.nz; f. 1916; advocates an organized economy guaranteeing an adequate standard of living to every person able and willing to work; Pres. NIGEL HAWORTH; Leader ANDREW LITTLE; Gen. Sec. TIM BARNETT.

New Zealand National Party: 41 Pipitea St, Thorndon, Wellington 6011; tel. (4) 894-7014; fax (4) 894-7031; e-mail hq@national.org.nz; internet www.national.org.nz; f. 1936; centre-right; supports private enterprise and competitive business, together with maximum personal freedom; Pres. PETER GOODFELLOW; Leader JOHN KEY.

UnitedFuture New Zealand (UFNZ): Freepost Parliament, Private Bag 18888, Wellington 6160; tel. (4) 871-9410; e-mail garrod@xtra.co.nz; internet unitedfuturenz@gmail.com; f. 2000 by merger of Future New Zealand (f. 1994 by Peter Dunne, a fmr Labour minister) and United New Zealand (f. 1995 by four mems of Nat. Party, two mems of Labour Party and Dunne); Leader PETER DUNNE; Pres. ROBIN GUNSTON.

Other registered parties are 1Law4All, Alliance, Aotearoa Legalise Cannabis Party, Ban 1080, the Civilian Party, Focus New Zealand, the New Zealand Democratic Party for Social Credit and the NZ Independent Coalition.

Diplomatic Representation

EMBASSIES AND HIGH COMMISSIONS IN NEW ZEALAND

Argentina: Prime Finance Tower, Level 14, 142 Lambton Quay, POB 5430, Wellington; tel. (4) 472-8330; fax (4) 472-8331; e-mail enzel@mrecic.gov.ar; internet www.enzel.mrecic.gov.ar; Ambassador FERNANDO ESCALONA.

Australia: 72–76 Hobson St, Thorndon, POB 4036, Wellington; tel. (4) 473-6411; fax (4) 498-7135; e-mail nzinbox@dfat.gov.au; internet www.australia.org.nz; High Commissioner MICHAEL POTTS.

Brazil: Maritime Tower, Level 13, 10 Customhouse Quay, POB 5432, Wellington 6011; tel. (4) 473-3516; fax (4) 473-3517; e-mail brasemb@brazil.org.nz; internet www.brazil.org.nz; Ambassador EDUARDO GRADILONE.

Canada: 125 The Terrace, Level 11, POB 8047, Wellington; tel. (4) 473-9577; fax (4) 471-2082; e-mail wlgtn@international.gc.ca; internet www.canadainternational.gc.ca/new_zealand-nouvelle _zelande; High Commissioner CAROLINE CHRÉTIEN.

Chile: Pencarrow House, 1 Willeston St, Wellington; tel. (4) 471-6270; fax (4) 472-5324; e-mail echile@embchile.co.nz; internet chileabroad.gov.cl/nueva-zelanda/en; Ambassador ISAURO TORRES.

China, People's Republic: 2–6 Glenmore St, Kelburn, Wellington; tel. (4) 472-1382; fax (4) 474-9622; e-mail administration@chinaembassy.org.nz; internet www.chinaembassy.org.nz; Ambassador WANG LUTONG.

Cuba: 76 Messines Rd, Karori, Wellington; tel. (4) 464-2210; fax (4) 464-2207; e-mail embajada@xtra.co.nz; Ambassador MARÍA DEL CARMEN HERRERA CASEIRO.

Fiji: 31 Pipitea St, Thorndon, POB 3940, Wellington; tel. (4) 473-5401; fax (4) 499-1011; e-mail viti@paradise.net.nz; internet www.fiji.org.nz; Head of Mission MERE TORA (acting).

France: Sovereign House, Levels 12 and 13, 34–42 Manners St, POB 11-343, Wellington 6142; tel. (4) 384-2555; fax (4) 384-2577; e-mail ambassade@ambafrance-nz.org; internet www.ambafrance-nz.org; Ambassador FLORENCE JEANBLANC-RISLER.

Germany: 90–92 Hobson St, POB 1687, Wellington; tel. (4) 473-6063; fax (4) 473-6069; e-mail info@wellington.diplo.de; internet www.wellington.diplo.de; Ambassador Dr ANNE-MARIE SCHLEICH.

Greece: Petherick Tower, Level 11, 38–42 Waring Taylor St, POB 24-066, Wellington; tel. (4) 473-7775; fax (4) 473-7441; e-mail gremb.wel@mfa.gr; internet www.mfa.gr/wellington; Chargé d'affaires a.i. CHARALAMPOS LAFTSIDIS.

Holy See: Apostolic Nunciature, POB 22-004, Wellington 6441; tel. (4) 387-3470; fax (4) 387-8170; e-mail nuntius@ihug.co.nz; Apostolic Nuncio Most Rev. MARTIN KREBS (Titular Archbishop of Taborenta).

India: 180 Molesworth St, POB 4045, Wellington 6015; tel. (4) 473-6390; fax (4) 499-0665; e-mail hicomind@hicomind.org.nz; internet www.hicomind.org.nz; High Commissioner RAVI THAPAR.

Indonesia: 70 Glen Rd, Kelburn, POB 3543, Wellington; tel. (4) 475-8698; fax (4) 475-9374; e-mail wellington.kbri@kemlu.go.id; internet www.kemlu.go.id; Ambassador JOSÉ ANTONIO MORATO TAVARES.

Iran: 151 Te Anau Rd, POB 14733, Wellington; tel. (4) 386-2976; fax (4) 939-8108; e-mail info@iranembassy.org.nz; internet www.wellington.mfa.ir; Ambassador JALALADDIN NAMINI MIYANJI.

Israel: Level 13, Bayley's Bldg, 36 Brandon St, Wellington; tel. (4) 439-9500; fax (4) 439-9555; e-mail info@wellington.mfa.gov.il; internet wellington.mfa.gov.il; Ambassador YOSEF LIVNE.

Italy: 34–38 Grant Rd, Thorndon, POB 463, Wellington; tel. (4) 473-5339; fax (4) 472-7255; e-mail ambasciata.wellington@esteri.it; internet www.ambwellington.esteri.it/ambasciata_wellington; Ambassador CARMELO BARBARELLO.

Japan: The Majestic Centre, Level 18, 100 Willis St, POB 6340, Wellington 6011; tel. (4) 473-1540; fax (4) 471-2951; e-mail enquiry@wl.mofa.go.jp; internet www.nz.emb-japan.go.jp; Ambassador YASUAKI NOGAWA.

Korea, Republic: ASB Bank Tower, Level 11, 2 Hunter St, POB 11-143, Wellington; tel. (4) 473-9073; fax (4) 472-3865; e-mail ea-nz@mofa.go.kr; internet nzl-wellington.mofa.go.kr; Ambassador KIM HAE-YONG.

Malaysia: 10 Washington Ave, Brooklyn, POB 9422, Wellington; tel. (4) 385-2439; fax (4) 385-6973; e-mail mwwelton@xtra.co.nz; internet www.kln.gov.my/web/nzl_wellington; High Commissioner Dato LIM KIM ENG.

Mexico: AMP Chambers, Level 2, 185–187 Featherston St, POB 11-510, Wellington; tel. (4) 472-0555; fax (4) 496-3559; e-mail embassy@embamex.org.nz; internet www.sre.gob.mx/nuevazelandia; Ambassador LEONORA RUEDA.

Netherlands: Co-operative Bank Bldg, 10th Floor, cnr Featherston and Ballance Sts, Wellington 6011; tel. (4) 471-6390; fax (4) 471-2923; e-mail wel@minbuza.nl; internet www.netherlandsembassy.co.nz; Ambassador ROBERT ZAAGMAN.

Pakistan: 182 Onslow Rd, Khandallah, Wellington 6035; tel. (4) 479-0026; fax (4) 479-4315; e-mail pakhcwellington@xtra.co.nz; internet www.pakistanhc.org.nz; High Commissioner ZEHRA H. AKBARI.

Papua New Guinea: Goethe-Institut Bldg, Level 5, 148–150 Cuba St, POB 197, Wellington; tel. (4) 385-2474; fax (4) 385-2477; e-mail exec.assist@pnghc.org.nz; internet pngnz.org/highcom/; High Commissioner Brig.-Gen. FRANCIS AGWI.

Philippines: 50 Hobson St, Thorndon, Wellington 6011; tel. (4) 890-3741; fax (4) 890-3740; e-mail embassy@wellington-pe.co.nz; internet www.philembassy.org.nz; Ambassador Dr VIRGINIA HONRADO BENAVIDEZ.

Poland: City Chambers, Level 9, 142–144 Featherston St, POB 10211, Wellington; tel. (4) 499-7844; fax (4) 499-7846; e-mail wellington.amb.sekretariat@msz.gov.pl; internet www.wellington.mfa.gov.pl; Ambassador ZBIGNIEW GNIATKOWSKI.

Russian Federation: 57 Messines Rd, Karori, Wellington; tel. (4) 476-6113; fax (4) 476-3843; e-mail russia@clear.net.nz; internet www .newzealand.mid.ru; Ambassador VALERY TERESHCHENKO.

Samoa: 1A Wesley Rd, Kelburn, POB 1430, Wellington; tel. (4) 472-0953; fax (4) 471-2479; e-mail info@samoa.org.nz; internet www .samoa.org.nz; High Commissioner LEASI PAPALI'I SCANLAN.

Singapore: 17 Kabul St, Khandallah, POB 13140, Wellington; tel. (4) 470-0850; fax (4) 479-4066; e-mail singhc_wlg@sgmfa.gov.sg; internet www.mfa.gov.sg/wellington; High Commissioner PETER CHAN JER HING.

Solomon Islands: Wakefield House, Level 1, 90 The Terrace, POB 5981, Wellington 6145; tel. (4) 472-2827; fax (4) 472-2811; e-mail info@sihc.org.nz; internet www.sihc.org.nz; High Commissioner JOY KERE.

South Africa: State Insurance Bldg, Level 7, 1 Willis St, POB 25406, Wellington; tel. (4) 815-8484; fax (4) 472-5010; e-mail wellington@ dirco.gov.za; internet www.dirco.gov.za/Wellington/consular services.html; High Commissioner NTOMBIZODWA MSUTHUKAZI LALLIE.

Spain: BNZ Trust House Bldg, Level 11, 50 Manners St, POB 24-150, Wellington 6142; tel. (4) 802-5665; fax (4) 801-7701; e-mail emb .wellington@maec.es; internet www.exteriores.gob.es/Embajadas/ Wellington/es/Paginas/inicio.aspx; Ambassador MANUEL VITURRO DE LA TORRE.

Switzerland: 10 Customhouse Quay, Level 12, POB 25004, Wellington 6011; tel. (4) 472-1593; fax (4) 499-6302; e-mail wel .vertretung@eda.admin.ch; internet www.eda.admin.ch/wellington; Ambassador Dr DAVID VOGELSANGER.

Thailand: 110 Molesworth St, POB 12-247, Wellington; tel. (4) 496-2900; fax (4) 476-8610; e-mail thailand@thaiembassynz.org.nz; internet www.thaiembassy.org/wellington; Ambassador MARIS SANGIAMPONGSA.

Turkey: 15–17 Murphy St, Level 8, POB 12-248, Thorndon, Wellington; tel. (4) 472-1292; fax (4) 472-1277; e-mail embassy .wellington@mfa.gov.tr; Ambassador DAMLA YESIM SAY.

Tuvalu: Wakefield House, Level 2, 90 The Terrace, Wellington; tel. (21) 552–250; e-mail s.laloniu@yahoo.com; Ambassador SAMUELU LALONIU.

United Kingdom: 44 Hill St, POB 1812, Wellington; tel. (4) 924-2888; fax (4) 473-4982; e-mail ppa.mailbox@fco.gov.uk; internet ukinnewzealand.fco.gov.uk; High Commissioner JONATHAN SINCLAIR.

USA: 29 Fitzherbert Terrace, POB 1190, Wellington; tel. (4) 462-6000; fax (4) 499-0490; internet newzealand.usembassy.gov; Ambassador MARK GILBERT.

Viet Nam: Grand Plimmer Tower, Level 21, 2–6 Gilmer Terrace, POB 8042, Wellington; tel. (4) 473-5912; fax (4) 473-5913; e-mail embassyvn@clear.net.nz; internet www.vietnamembassy-new zealand.org; Ambassador NGUYEN VIET DUNG.

Judicial System

The Judicial System of New Zealand comprises a Supreme Court, a Court of Appeal, a High Court and District Courts, all of which have civil and criminal jurisdiction, and the specialist courts, the Employment Court, the Family Court, the Youth Court and the Maori Land Court.

The Ministry of Justice also administers tribunals to hear and resolve disputes over facts of law, including the Employment Tribunal (administered by the Department of Labour), Disputes Tribunal, Complaints Review Tribunal, Residential Tenancies Tribunal, Waitangi Tribunal, Environment Court, Deportation Review Tribunal and Motor Vehicles Disputes Tribunal.

Supreme Court: 85 Lambton Quay, Wellington; tel. (4) 918-8222; fax (4) 914-3560; e-mail supremecourt@justice.govt.nz; internet www.courtsofnz.govt.nz/about/supreme; f. 2004; replaced the Judicial Committee of the Privy Council in the United Kingdom as the final appellate court, following the Supreme Court Act 2003; the right to appeal to the Supreme Court is granted only if the Court is satisfied that the case involves a matter of general or public importance or commercial significance, or in order to correct or prevent a substantial miscarriage of justice; the Chief Justice is the head of the judiciary in New Zealand and is the Head of Bench of the Supreme Court, which consists of 5 other judges; Chief Justice Dame SIAN ELIAS.

Court of Appeal: cnr Molesworth and Aitken Sts, Wellington; tel. (4) 914-3540; fax (4) 914-3570; e-mail courtofappeal@justice.govt.nz; hears appeals from the High Court and from jury trials in the district courts, although it does have some original jurisdiction; its decisions are final, except in cases that may be appealed to the Supreme Court; appeals regarding convictions and sentences handed down by the

High Court or District Trial Courts are by leave only; Pres. ELLEN FRANCE.

High Court: ; the High Court is the superior court for general jurisdiction in New Zealand; it is a single national court which sits in a number of courthouses; judges are permanently located in Wellington, Auckland and Christchurch and go on circuit to other locations as required; it hears appeals from lower courts and tribunals (excluding those that go directly to the Court of Appeal), and reviews administrative actions; Chief High Court Judge HELEN WINKELMANN.

District Courts: internet www.courtsofnz/district; have an extensive criminal and civil law jurisdiction, hearing civil cases, while Justices of the Peace can hear minor criminal and traffic matters; the Family Court, which is a division of the District Courts, has the jurisdiction to deal with dissolution of marriages, adoption, guardianship applications, domestic actions, matrimonial property, child support, care and protection applications regarding children and young persons, and similar matters; there are 145 District Court judges and a Chief District Court Judge; Chief District Court Judge JAN-MARIE DOOGUE.

Attorney-General: the senior Law Officer of the Crown with principal responsibility for the Government's administration of the law and a Minister of the Crown responsible for the Crown Law Office, the Serious Fraud Office and the Parliamentary Counsel Office CHRISTOPHER FINLAYSON.

Religion

CHRISTIANITY

Te Runanga Whakawhanaunga i Nga Hahi o Aotearoa (Maori Council of Churches in New Zealand): Private Bag 11903, Ellerslie, Auckland; tel. (9) 525-4179; fax (9) 525-4346; f. 1982; 4 mem. churches; Administrator TE RUA GRETHA.

The Anglican Communion

The Anglican Church in Aotearoa, New Zealand and Polynesia comprises Te Pihopatanga o Aotearoa and eight dioceses (one of which is Polynesia). According to the 2013 census, the Church had 459,771 adherents (10.8% of the population) in New Zealand.

Primate of the Anglican Church in Aotearoa, New Zealand and Polynesia, and Bishop of Aotearoa: Rt Rev. WILLIAM BROWN TUREI, POB 568, Gisborne 4040; tel. (6) 867-8856; fax (9) 377-6962; e-mail browntmihi@xtra.co.nz.

General Secretary and Treasurer of the Anglican Church in Aotearoa, New Zealand and Polynesia: Rev. MICHAEL HUGHES, POB 87-188, Meadowbank, Auckland 1742; tel. (9) 521-4439; fax (9) 521-4490; e-mail gensec@ang.org.nz; internet www.anglican.org.nz.

The Roman Catholic Church

For ecclesiastical purposes, New Zealand comprises one archdiocese and five dioceses. According to the 2013 census, the Roman Catholic Church had 492,105 adherents (11.6% of the population) in New Zealand.

Bishops' Conference: New Zealand Catholic Bishops' Conference, Catholic Centre, 22–30 Hill St, POB 1937, Wellington 6140; tel. (4) 496-1747; fax (4) 496-1746; e-mail adickinson@nzcbc.org.nz; internet www.catholic.org.nz; f. 1974; Pres. Most Rev. JOHN DEW (Archbishop of Wellington); Sec. Rev. PATRICK DUNN (Bishop of Auckland); Exec. Officer ANNE DICKINSON.

Archbishop of Wellington: Cardinal JOHN ATCHERLEY DEW, Catholic Centre, 22–30 Hill St, POB 1937, Wellington 6140; tel. (4) 496-1766; fax (4) 496-1330; e-mail g.burns@wn.catholic.org.nz; internet www.wn.catholic.org.nz.

Other Christian Churches

According to the 2013 census, there were 330,516 adherents to the Presbyterian, Congregational and Reformed Churches, and 102,879 adherents to the Methodist Church; a further 330,516 people described themselves as Christian without specifying which denomination.

Baptist Churches of New Zealand: 473 Great South Rd, POB 12149, Penrose, Auckland; tel. (9) 526-0333; fax (9) 526-0334; e-mail info@baptist.org.nz; internet www.baptist.org.nz; f. 1882; 21,937 mems; Pres. BRIAN KENNING; Nat. Leader CRAIG VERNALL.

Congregational Union of New Zealand: 8C Kirrie Dr., Te Atatu South, Auckland; tel. (9) 837-2220; fax (9) 620-8291; e-mail cunzsecretary@xtra.co.nz; internet www.congregational.org.nz; f. 1884; 600 mems, 13 churches; Chair. PETER ECCLES; Sec. LUISA FAITAUA.

Lutheran Church of New Zealand: POB 7606, Wellington 6242; tel. (4) 385-2540; e-mail lcnz@clear.net.nz; internet www.lcnz.org.nz; 1,130 mems (2010); Pres. Rev. MARK WHITFIELD.

Methodist Church of New Zealand: Connexional Office, POB 931, Christchurch 8140; tel. (3) 366-6049; fax (3) 358-7146; e-mail info@methodist.org.nz; internet www.methodist.org.nz; 18,548 mems; Gen. Sec. Rev. DAVID BUSH.

Presbyterian Church of Aotearoa New Zealand: Terralink House, Level 1, 275–283 Cuba St, POB 9049, Wellington; tel. (4) 801-6000; fax (4) 801-6001; e-mail info@presbyterian.org.nz; internet www.presbyterian.org.nz; f. 1840; 30,000 mems; Moderator Rev. RAY COSTER; Assembly Convenor Rev. WAYNE MATHESON.

There are several Maori Churches in New Zealand, with a total membership of over 30,000. These include the Ratana Church of New Zealand, Ringatu Church, Church of Te Kooti Rikirangi, Absolute Maori Established Church, Destiny Church and United Maori Mission. The Antiochian Orthodox Church, the Assemblies of God, the Greek Orthodox Church of New Zealand, the Liberal Catholic Church and the Society of Friends (Quakers) are also active.

BAHÁ'Í FAITH

National Spiritual Assembly of the Bahá'ís of New Zealand: POB 21-551, Henderson, Auckland 1231; tel. (9) 837-4866; fax (9) 837-4898; e-mail nationaloffice@bahai.org.nz; internet www.bahai.org.nz; f. 1957; CEO BETH LEW.

The Press

NEWSPAPERS AND PERIODICALS
Principal Dailies

Ashburton Guardian: 161 Burnett St, POB 77, Ashburton; tel. (3) 307-7900; fax (3) 307-7980; e-mail enquiries@theguardian.co.nz; internet www.guardianonline.co.nz; f. 1879; morning; Mon.–Sat.; Gen. Man. DESME DANIELS; Editor COEN LAMMERS, circ. 4,819 (2013).

Bay of Plenty Times: 108 Durham St, Private Bag 12002, Tauranga; tel. (7) 577-7770; fax (7) 578-0047; e-mail editor@bopp.co.nz; internet www.bayofplentytimes.co.nz; f. 1872; evening; Mon.–Sat.; Gen. Man. DAVID MACKENZIE; Editor SCOTT INGLIS; circ. 15,621 (2013).

The Daily Post: 1143 Hinemoa St, POB 1442, Rotorua; tel. (7) 348-6199; fax (7) 348-0220; e-mail editor@dailypost.co.nz; internet www.dailypost.co.nz; f. 1885; evening; Gen. Man. GREG ALEXANDER; Editor KIM GILLESPIE; circ. 8,044 (2013).

The Dominion Post: Level 7, Telecom Central, 42–52 Willis St, POB 3740, Wellington; tel. (4) 474-0000; fax (4) 474-0584; e-mail editor@dompost.co.nz; internet www.dompost.co.nz; f. 2002; est. by merger of the *Evening Post* and *The Dominion*; morning; Mon.–Sat.; Gen. Man. GERARD WATT; Editor BERNADETTE COURTNEY; circ. 213,000 (2014).

Gisborne Herald: 64 Gladstone Rd, POB 1143, Gisborne; tel. (6) 869-0600; fax (6) 869-0643; e-mail info@gisborneherald.co.nz; internet www.gisborneherald.co.nz; f. 1874; evening; Man. Dir MICHAEL MUIR; Editor JEREMY MUIR; circ. 6,662 (2013).

Greymouth Star: Werita St, POB 3, Greymouth; tel. (3) 769-7900; fax (3) 768-6205; internet www.greystar.co.nz; f. 1866; Mon.–Sat. (evening); Gen. Man. JOHN GOULDING; Editor PAUL MADGWICK; circ. 4,254 (2013).

Hawke's Bay Today: 113 Karamu Rd, POB 180, Hastings; tel. (6) 873-0800; fax (6) 873-0812; e-mail editor@hbtoday.co.nz; internet www.hbtoday.co.nz; f. 1999; evening; conservative; Gen. Man. RUSSELL BROUGHTON; Editor ANDREW AUSTIN; circ. 21,013 (2013).

Manuwatu Standard: 57–64 The Square, POB 3, Palmerston North; tel. (6) 356-9009; fax (6) 350-9545; e-mail editor@msl.co.nz; internet www.manawatustandard.co.nz; f. 1880; evening; Editor MICHAEL CUMMINGS; circ. 13,776 (2013).

Marlborough Express: 62–66 Arthur St, POB 242, Blenheim 7274; tel. (3) 520-8900; fax (3) 520-8911; e-mail steve.mason@mex.co.nz; internet www.mex.co.nz; f. 1866; Gen. Man. VANESSA WATSON; Editor STEVE MASON; circ. 7,135 (2014).

Nelson Mail: 15 Bridge St, POB 244, Nelson; tel. (3) 548-7079; fax (3) 546-2802; e-mail mailbox@nelsonmail.co.nz; internet www.stuff.co.nz/nelsonmail; f. 1866; evening; Gen. Man. CRAIG DENNIS; Editor BILL MOORE; circ. 13,065 (2013).

New Zealand Herald: POB 32, Auckland; tel. (9) 379-5050; fax (9) 373-6421; internet www.nzherald.co.nz; f. 1863; morning; CEO MARTIN SIMONS; Editor-in-Chief TIM MURPHY; circ. 147,593 (2013).

The Northern Advocate: 88 Robert St, POB 210, Whangarei; tel. (9) 470-2899; fax (9) 470-2869; e-mail daily@northernadvocate.co.nz; internet www.northernadvocate.co.nz; f. 1875; evening; 6 a week; Gen. Man. ALEX LAWSON; Editor CRAIG COOPER; circ. 11,840 (2013).

The Oamaru Mail: 80 Thames St, POB 343, Oamaru; tel. (3) 434-9970; fax (3) 433-0549; e-mail news@oamarumail.co.nz; internet www.oamarumail.co.nz; f. 1876; Mon.–Fri.; morning; Gen. Man. TONY NIELSEN; Editor SALLY BROOKER; circ. 2,503 (2013).

Otago Daily Times: 52 Stuart St, POB 517, Dunedin; tel. (3) 477-4760; fax (3) 474-7422; e-mail odt.editorial@alliedpress.co.nz; internet www.odt.co.nz; f. 1861; morning; 6 a week; Man. Dir JULIAN C. S. SMITH; Editor MURRAY KIRKNESS; circ. 37,175 (2013).

The Press: 22 Cathedral Sq., Private Bag 4722, Christchurch 8140; tel. (3) 379-0940; fax (3) 364-8492; e-mail letters@press.co.nz; internet www.press.co.nz; f. 1861; morning; Editor JOANNA NORRIS; circ. 70,042 (2013).

Southland Times: 67 Esk St, POB 805, Invercargill 9840; tel. (3) 211-1130; fax (3) 214-9905; e-mail letters@stl.co.nz; internet www.southlandtimes.co.nz; f. 1862; morning; Mon.–Sat.; Commercial Man. GARRY FERRIS; circ. 25,121 (2013).

Taranaki Daily News: 49–65 Currie St, POB 444, New Plymouth; tel. (6) 757-6862; fax (6) 758-4653; e-mail editor@dailynews.co.nz; internet www.stuff.co.nz/dailynews; f. 1857; morning; Sr Commercial Devt Man. ADRIAN SOLE; Editor ROY PILOTT; circ. 20,092 (2013).

Timaru Herald: POB 46, Timaru; tel. (3) 684-4129; fax (3) 688-1042; e-mail editor@timaruherald.co.nz; internet www.timaruherald.co.nz; f. 1864; morning; Commercial Man. NICK SYMISTER; Editor PETER O'NEILL; circ. 11,533 (2013).

Waikato Times: Private Bag 3086, Hamilton; tel. (7) 849-6180; fax (7) 849-9554; e-mail news@waikatotimes.co.nz; internet www.stuff.co.nz/waikatotimes; f. 1872; morning; independent; Gen. Man. GARETH CODD; Editor JONATHAN MACKENZIE; circ. 32,162 (2013).

Wairarapa Times-Age: cnr Perry St and Chapel St, POB 445, Masterton; tel. (6) 378-9999; fax (6) 378-2371; internet www.times-age.co.nz; f. 1938; morning; 6 a week; Gen. Man. ANDREW DENHOLM; Editor HEATHER MCCRACKEN; circ. 5,812 (2013).

Wanganui Chronicle: 100 Guyton St, POB 433, Wanganui; tel. (6) 349-0710; fax (6) 349-0721; e-mail news@wanganuichronicle.co.nz; internet www.wanganuichronicle.co.nz; f. 1856; morning; Gen. Man. ANDY JARDEN; Editor MARK DAWSON; circ. 9,820 (2013).

Weeklies and Other Newspapers

Best Bets: 60 Stanley St, Parnell, Auckland; tel. (9) 520-8208; e-mail alan.caddy@nzracingboard.co.nz; Thur.; horse-racing, trotting and greyhounds; Editor ALAN CADDY; circ. 10,000.

Herald on Sunday: 58 Albert St, POB 32, Auckland; tel. (9) 373-9323; fax (9) 373-9372; internet www.heraldonsunday.co.nz; f. 2004; Editor BRYCE JOHNS; circ. 99,014 (2013).

MG Business: POB 20-034, Bishopdale, Christchurch 8543; tel. (3) 358-3219; fax (3) 358-4490; internet www.mgpublications.co.nz; f. 1876; fmrly Mercantile Gazette; fortnightly; economics, finance, management, stock market, politics; Editor BILL HORSLEY; circ. 16,300.

The National Business Review: POB 1734, Auckland 1140; tel. (9) 307-1629; fax (9) 373-3997; e-mail ngibson@nbr.co.nz; internet www.nbr.co.nz; f. 1970; weekly; Editor-in-Chief NEVIL GIBSON; circ. 6,190 (2013).

New Zealand Gazette: POB 805, Wellington 6140; tel. (4) 462-0313; e-mail gazette@dia.govt.nz; internet www.gazette.govt.nz; official govt publ; f. 1841; weekly; Chief Exec COLIN MACDONALD; circ. 1,000.

New Zealand Truth Weekly: Truth Publications Ltd, POB 9613, Newmarket, Auckland 1149; tel. (9) 909-3660; fax (9) 373-5410; e-mail editor@truth.co.nz; internet www.truth.co.nz; f. 1905; Friday; local news and features, TV and entertainment, sports; owned by Truth Publs Ltd; Editor WAYNE BUTLER; circ. 24,000.

North Shore Times: POB 33-235, Takapuna, Auckland; tel. (9) 489-4189; fax (9) 486-6700; e-mail nsnews@snl.co.nz; f. 1949; 3 a week; Man. MICHELE CHAPMAN; Editor PETER ELEY; circ. 69,834 (2010).

The Star: 12 Venture Place, POB 1467, Christchurch; tel. (3) 379-7100; fax (3) 364-7462; e-mail barry@christchurchstar.co.nz; internet www.starcanterbury.co.nz; f. 1868; fmrly Christchurch Star; 2 a week; Editor BARRY CLARKE; circ. 118,170.

Sunday News: POB 1327, Auckland; tel. (9) 925-9857; fax (9) 358-3003; e-mail letters@sunday-news.co.nz; internet www.sundaynews.co.nz; Editor LEE UMBERS; circ. 33,214 (2013).

Sunday Star-Times: POB 1327, Auckland 1140; tel. (9) 925-9700; fax (9) 309-0258; e-mail letters@star-times.co.nz; internet www.stuff.co.nz/sunday-star-times; f. 1994 by merger; Editor DAVID KEMEYS; circ. 123360 (2013).

Taieri Herald: 92 Gordon Rd, POB 105, Mosgiel; tel. (3) 489-7123; fax (3) 489-7668; e-mail katie.tucholski@stl.co.nz; f. 1962; weekly; morning; Editor DARYL HOLDEN; circ. 13,068 (2011).

Wairarapa News: Media House, 89 Chapel St, POB 902, Masterton; tel. (6) 370-5690; fax (6) 370-5699; e-mail editor@wainews.co.nz; f. 1869, weekly; Editor WALT DICKSON; circ. 21,019 (2010).

Other Periodicals

AA Directions: POB 5, Auckland 1010; tel. (9) 966-8800; fax (9) 966-8975; e-mail editor@aa.co.nz; internet www.aa.co.nz/online; f. 1991; quarterly; official magazine of the New Zealand Automobile Asscn; Editor KATHRYN WEBSTER; circ. 542,242 (2010).

Architecture New Zealand: AGM Publishing Ltd, Private Bag 99915, Newmarket, Auckland; tel. (9) 846-4068; fax (9) 846-8742; e-mail justine.harvey@agm.co.nz; internet www.agm.co.nz; f. 1987; every 2 months; Man. Dir PARUL SHEOPURI; Editor JUSTINE HARVEY; circ. 5,609 (2010).

Australian Women's Weekly (NZ edition): Wellesley St, Private Bag 92-512, Auckland; tel. (9) 308-2945; fax (9) 302-0667; e-mail aww@acpmagazines.co.nz; f. 1987; monthly; Editor FIONA FRASER; circ. 80,032 (2010).

Dairy News: Shortland St, POB 3855, Auckland 1140; tel. (9) 307-0399; fax (9) 307-0122; e-mail sudeshk@ruralnews.co.nz; internet www.ruralnews.co.nz; fortnightly; Editor SUDESH KISSUN; circ. 27,726 (2013).

Fashion Quarterly: ACP Media Centre, Private Bag 92-512, Auckland; tel. (9) 308-2409; fax (9) 302-2878; e-mail fq@acpmagazines.co.nz; f. 1982; 6 a year; Editor FIONA HAWTIN; circ. 24,167 (2011).

Grapevine: Private Bag 92-124, Auckland; tel. (9) 813-4956; fax (9) 813-4957; e-mail info@grapevine.org.nz; internet www.grapevine.org.nz; f. 1981; 4 issues a year; family magazine; Editor MIKE COONEY; circ. 125,000.

Home New Zealand: 100 Beaumont St, Westhaven, Auckland 1141; tel. (9) 308-2700; e-mail homenewzealand@acpmagazines.co.nz; f. 1936; fmrly *NZ Home and Entertaining*; bi-monthly; design, architecture, lifestyle; Editor JEREMY HANSEN; circ. 11,286 (2014).

Info-Link: AGM Publishing Ltd, 409 New North Rd, Kingsland, Auckland; tel. (9) 846-4068; fax (9) 846-8742; e-mail infolink@agm.co.nz; internet www.info-link.co.nz; quarterly; Publr PARUL SHEOPURI; Editor MARK LONGLEY; circ. 19,303 (2008).

Inwood Magazine: POB 17124, Greenlane, Auckland 1546; tel. (9) 269-4531; fax (9) 535-7295; e-mail info@inwoodmag.com; internet www.inwoodmag.com; f. 1993; monthly; forestry; Man. Dir TONY NEILSON; circ. 8,000.

Landfall: Otago University Press, POB 56, Dunedin; tel. (3) 479-8807; fax (3) 479-8385; e-mail rachel.scott@otago.ac.nz; internet www.otago.ac.nz/press/landfall; f. 1947; 2 a year; new fiction, poetry, biographical and critical essays, cultural commentary; Publr RACHEL SCOTT; Editor DAVID EGGLETON; circ. 650.

Mana Magazine: POB 1101, Rotorua; tel. (7) 349-0260; fax (7) 349-0258; e-mail editor@manaonline.co.nz; internet www.manaonline.co.nz; f. 1991; Maori news magazine; Editor DEREK FOX.

New Idea New Zealand: 48 Greys Ave, 4th Floor, Auckland; tel. (9) 979-2726; fax (9) 979-2721; f. 1992; weekly; women's interest; Editor HAYLEY MCLARIN; circ. 50,563 (2010).

New Zealand Dairy Exporter: 8 Weld St, POB 529, Feilding; tel. (6) 323-7104; fax (6) 323-7101; e-mail amelia.grant@nzx.com; internet www.dairymag.co.nz; f. 1925; monthly; Editor GLENYS CHRISTIAN; circ. 7,201 (2010).

New Zealand Gardener: Wellesley St, POB 6341, Auckland 1141; tel. (4) 909-6800; fax (4) 909-6802; e-mail mailbox@nzgardener.co.nz; internet www.nzgardener.co.nz; f. 1944; monthly; Editor LYNDA HALLIAN; circ. 40,954 (2014).

New Zealand Horse and Pony: POB 12965, Penrose, Auckland; tel. (9) 634-1800; fax (9) 634-2948; e-mail rowan.dixon@horse-pony.co.nz; internet www.horse-pony.co.nz; f. 1959; monthly; Editor ROWAN DIXON; circ. 10,033 (2014).

New Zealand Management: Adrenalin, POB 65092, Mairangi Bay, Auckland; tel. (9) 478-4771; fax (9) 478-4779; e-mail editor@management.co.nz; internet www.management.co.nz; f. 1955; monthly; business; Publr CATHY PARKER; circ. 7,997 (2011).

New Zealand Medical Journal: NZMA, POB 156, Wellington; tel. (3) 472-4741; fax (3) 471-0838; e-mail nzmj@nzma.org.nz; internet journal.nzma.org.nz; f. 1887; publ. by New Zealand Medical Asscn; online publ.; articles free to non-subscribers 6 months after publ; 20 a year; Editor Prof. FRANK A. FRIZELLE; circ. 5,000.

New Zealand Science Review: POB 1874, Wellington; tel. (021) 487-284; e-mail editor@scientists.org.nz; internet www.scientists.org.nz; f. 1942; 4 a year; reviews, policy and philosophy of science; Editor Dr ALLEN PETREY.

New Zealand Woman's Day: Wellesley St, Private Bag 92-512, Auckland; tel. (9) 308-2718; fax (9) 357-0978; e-mail wdaynz@acpmagazines.co.nz; weekly; Editor SIDO KITCHIN; circ. 98,171 (2014).

New Zealand Woman's Weekly: Victoria St West, POB 90-119, Auckland 1142; tel. (9) 373-9400; fax (9) 373-9405; e-mail editor@nzww.co.nz; internet www.nzwomansweekly.co.nz; f. 1932; Mon.;

women's issues and general interest; Editor LOUISE WRIGHT; circ. 59,672 (2014).

Next: Level 4, cnr Fanshawe and Beaumont Sts, Westhaven, Private Bag 92-512, Auckland 1036; tel. (9) 308-2775; fax (9) 377-6725; e-mail next@acpmagazines.co.nz; f. 1991; monthly; home and lifestyle; owned by ACP Media; Editor SARAH HENRY; circ. 40,089 (2014).

North & South: Wellesley St, Private Bag 92-512, Auckland; tel. (9) 366-5337; fax (9) 308-9498; e-mail north&south@bauermedia.co.nz; f. 1986; monthly; current affairs and lifestyle; Editor VIRGINIA LARSON; circ. 26,857 (2014).

NZ Catholic: POB 147-000, Ponsonby, Auckland 1034; tel. (9) 360-3067; fax (9) 360-3065; e-mail editor@nzcatholic.org.nz; internet www.nzcatholic.org.nz; f. 1996; fortnightly; Roman Catholic; Man. Editor PETER GRACE; circ. 6,700.

NZ Farmer: POB 3086, Waikato Mail Centre, Hamilton; tel. (7) 849-6180; e-mail nzfarmer@fairfaxmedia.co.nz; internet www.nzfarmer.co.nz; f. 2014; weekly; Editor JON MORGAN; circ. 76,721 (2014).

NZ House and Garden: 317 New North Rd, Eden Terrace, POB 6341, Wellesley St, Auckland; tel. (9) 909-6800; fax (9) 909-6802; e-mail editor@nzhouseandgarden.co.nz; internet www.nzhouseandgarden.co.nz; f. 1994; monthly; Editor SALLY DUGGAN; circ. 48,053 (2014).

NZ Listener: Victoria St West, POB 90-783, Auckland 1142; tel. (9) 373-9400; fax (9) 373-9406; e-mail submissions@listener.co.nz; internet www.listener.co.nz; f. 1939; weekly; current affairs and entertainment; Editor PAMELA STIRLING; Publr and Chief Exec. SARAH SANDLEY; circ. 53,346 (2014).

Otago Southland Farmer: POB 105, Mosgiel; tel. (3) 489-7123; fax (3) 489-7668; e-mail newspapersales@stl.co.nz; f. 1982; fortnightly; Editor MARK HOTTON; circ. 20,589 (2013).

Pacific Wings: POB 57163, Mana, Porirua 5247; tel. (4) 233-8368; e-mail editor@pacificwingsmagazine.com; internet www.pacificwingsmagazine.com; f. 1932; monthly; aviation; Editor and Publr ROB NEIL; circ. 20,000.

PC World: IDG Communications, POB 37966, Parnell, Auckland 1151; tel. (9) 902-2759; fax (9) 909-6989; e-mail elias_plastiras@idg.com.au; internet pcworld.co.nz; f. 1988; monthly; Editor ELIAS PLASTIRAS; circ. 12,120 (2010).

Prodesign: AGM Publishing Ltd, Private Bag 99-915, Newmarket, Auckland; tel. (9) 846-2722; fax (9) 846-8742; e-mail michael.barrett@agm.co.nz; f. 1992; every 2 months; publ. of the Designers' Institute of New Zealand; Editor MICHAEL BARRETT; circ. 5,717 (2010).

PSA Journal: PSA House, 11 Aurora Terrace, POB 3817, Wellington 6140; tel. (4) 495-7633; fax (4) 917-2051; e-mail enquiries@psa.org.nz; internet www.psa.org.nz; f. 1913; 4 a year; journal of the NZ Public Service Asscn; Pres. PAULA SCHOLES; circ. 52,000.

Reader's Digest: POB 90-487, Mail Service Centre, Auckland; e-mail editor@readersdigest.co.nz; internet www.readersdigest.co.nz; f. 1950; monthly; Editor SUE CARNEY; circ. 49,041 (2014).

RSA Review: RNZRSA National Headquarters, POB 27248, Wellington 6030; tel. (6) 384-7994; fax (6) 385-3325; e-mail enquiries@rsa.org.nz; internet www.rsa.org.nz; quarterly; official magazine of the Royal New Zealand Returned and Services' Asscn; Editor BARRY ALLISON; circ. 95,000.

Rural News: POB 3855, Auckland; tel. (9) 307-0399; fax (9) 307-0122; e-mail editor@ruralnews.co.nz; internet www.ruralnews.co.nz; f. 1988; fortnightly; Man. Editor ADAM FRICKER; circ. 81,232 (2014).

Spanz: POB 9049, Wellington; tel. (4) 801-6000; fax (4) 801-6001; e-mail angela@presbyterian.org.nz; internet www.presbyterian.org.nz; f. 1987; bi-monthly; magazine of Presbyterian Church; circ. 21,500.

Time New Zealand: POB 198, Auckland 1015; fax (9) 366-4706; internet www.time.com; weekly; circ. 23,970 (2008).

TV Guide (NZ): 317–319 New North Rd, Eden Terrace, POB 6341, Auckland; tel. (9) 909-6902; fax (9) 909-6912; e-mail julie.eley@fairfaxmedia.co.nz; internet www.stuff.co.nz/entertainment/tv; f. 1986; weekly; Editor JULIE ELEY; circ. 117,299 (2014).

United Nations Association New Zealand: UNANZ, POB 24494, Wellington 6142; tel. (4) 496-9638; e-mail office@unanz.org.nz; internet unanz.org.nz; f. 1946; every 3 months; Pres. Prof. GRAHAM HASSALL.

NEWS AGENCY

South Pacific News Service Ltd (Sopacnews): Lambton Quay, POB 5026, Wellington; tel. and fax (3) 472-8329; e-mail farthing@deepsouth.co.nz; f. 1948; Man. Editor NEALE MCMILLAN.

PRESS COUNCIL

New Zealand Press Council: The Terrace, 79 Boulcott St, POB 10879, Wellington; tel. (4) 473-5220; fax (4) 471-1785; e-mail info@ presscouncil.org.nz; internet www.presscouncil.org.nz; f. 1972; Chair. JOHN HANSEN; Exec. Dir M. E. MAJOR.

PRESS ASSOCIATIONS

Commonwealth Press Union (New Zealand Section): POB 1066, Wellington; tel. (4) 472-6223; fax (4) 471-0987; Sec. LINCOLN GOULD.

Newspaper Publishers' Association of New Zealand (Inc): Newspaper House, 93 Boulcott St, POB 1066, Wellington 6015; tel. (4) 472-6223; fax (4) 471-0987; e-mail npa@npa.co.nz; internet www.npa.co.nz; f. 1898; 31 mems; Pres. MICHAEL MUIR; CEO TIM PANKHURST.

Publishers

Auckland University Press: Private Bag 92019, University of Auckland, Auckland 1142; tel. (9) 373-7528; fax (9) 373-7465; e-mail press@auckland.ac.nz; internet www.press.auckland.ac.nz; f. 1966; scholarly press; Dir SAM ELWORTHY.

Canterbury University Press: University of Canterbury, Private Bag 4800, Christchurch 8140; tel. (3) 364-2914; fax (3) 364-2044; e-mail universitypress@canterbury.ac.nz; internet www.cup .canterbury.ac.nz; f. 1991; academic and general; Publr CATHERINE MONTGOMERY.

The Caxton Press Ltd: 113 Victoria St, POB 36411, Christchurch 8146; tel. (3) 366-8516; fax (3) 365-7840; e-mail bruce@caxton.co.nz; internet www.caxton.co.nz; f. 1935; human and general interest, local and NZ history, tourist publs; Man. Dir BRUCE BASCAND.

Dunmore Publishing Ltd: POB 250-80, Wellington 6146; tel. (4) 472-2705; fax (4) 471-0604; e-mail books@dunmore.co.nz; internet www.dunmore.co.nz; f. 1971; non-fiction, educational; Publr SHARMIAN FIRTH.

Hachette New Zealand Ltd: POB 3255, Shortland St, Auckland 1140; tel. (9) 379-1480; fax (9) 379-1489; e-mail contact@hachette.co .nz; internet www.hachette.co.nz; f. 1971; fmrly Hachette Livre NZ Ltd; Chair. MATT RICHELL.

HarperCollins Publishers (New Zealand) Ltd: POB 1, Shortland St, Auckland 1140; tel. (9) 443-9400; fax (9) 443-9403; e-mail info@harpercollins.co.nz; internet www.harpercollins.co.nz; f. 1888; general and educational; CEO JAMES KELLOW.

Huia Publishers: 39 Pipitea St, Thorndon, Wellington 6011; tel. (4) 473-9262; fax (4) 473-9265; internet www.huia.co.nz; f. 1991; books on Maori history and people, textbooks, translations; Publrs ROBYN BARGH, EBONI WAITERE.

Learning Media Ltd: POB 90712 Victoria St, Auckland 1142; tel. (4) 472-5522; fax (4) 472-6444; e-mail info@learningmedia.co.nz; internet www.learningmedia.co.nz; f. 1947; est. as School Publs; state-owned enterprise; contract publishing, professional devt services, and educational products in a range of media and languages; Chief Exec. DAVID GLOVER.

Legislation Direct: POB 12357, Wellington 6144; tel. (4) 568-0005; fax (4) 568-0003; e-mail Ldorders@legislationdirect.co.nz; internet www.legislationdirect.co.nz; general publishers and leading distributor of government publs; fmrly Govt Printing Office/GP Publications; Sales Dir PHIL DIAMOND.

LexisNexis NZ Ltd: Level 1, 138 The Terrace, POB 472, Wellington 6011; tel. (4) 385-1479; fax (4) 385-1598; internet www.lexisnexis.co .nz; legal; CEO MIKE WALSH.

McGraw-Hill Book Co, New Zealand Ltd: Private Bag 11904, Ellerslie, Auckland 1005; tel. (9) 526-6200; fax (9) 526-6216; e-mail cservice_auckland@mcgraw-hill.com; internet www.mcgraw-hill .com.au; f. 1974; educational; Man. Dir MURRAY ST LEGER.

New Zealand Council for Educational Research: POB 3237, Wellington 6140; tel. (4) 384-7939; fax (4) 384-7933; e-mail sales@ nzcer.org.nz; internet www.nzcer.org.nz; f. 1934; scholarly, research monographs, educational, academic, periodicals; Publishing Man. DAVID ELLIS; Dir ROBYN BAKER.

Otago University Press: POB 56, Dunedin; tel. (3) 479-8807; fax (3) 479-8385; e-mail university.press@otago.ac.nz; internet www.otago .ac.nz/press; f. 1958; publishes titles on New Zealand, the Pacific and Asia, with special emphasis on history, literature, the arts and natural and social sciences; also educational titles and journals; Publr RACHEL SCOTT.

Pearson Education New Zealand Ltd: Private Bag 102-902, North Shore City, Auckland 0745; tel. (9) 442-7400; fax (9) 442-7401; e-mail customer.service@pearsonnz.co.nz; internet www

.pearsoned.co.nz; f. 1968; fmrly Addison Wesley Longman; educational; Dirs ROSEMARY STAGG, P. FIELD.

Penguin Group (NZ) Ltd: Private Bag 102-902, North Shore Mail Centre, Auckland 0745; tel. (9) 442-7400; fax (9) 442-7401; e-mail publishing@penguin.co.nz; internet www.penguin.co.nz; f. 1973; Man. Dir MARGARET THOMPSON.

Wendy Pye Ltd: Sunshine Bookshop, 413 Great South Rd, Ellerslie, Auckland 1051; tel. (9) 525-3575; fax (9) 525-4205; e-mail sales@ sunshine.co.nz; internet www.sunshinebooks.com.au; children's fiction and educational; Man. Dir WENDY PYE.

Random House New Zealand Ltd: Private Bag 102-950, North Shore Mail Centre, Auckland; tel. (9) 444-7197; fax (9) 444-7524; e-mail admin@randomhouse.co.nz; internet www.randomhouse.co .nz; f. 1977; general; Man. Dir KAREN FERNS.

Victoria University Press: POB 600, Wellington 6140; tel. (4) 463-6580; fax (4) 463-6581; e-mail victoria-press@vuw.ac.nz; internet www.victoria.ac.nz/vup; f. 1970; Publr FERGUS BARROWMAN.

PUBLISHERS' ASSOCIATION

Publishers' Association of New Zealand Inc: Private Bag 102-006, North Shore, Auckland 0745; tel. (9) 280-3212; fax (9) 477-5570; e-mail admin@publishers.org.nz; internet www.publishers.org.nz; f. 1977; Dir ANNE DE LAUTOUR.

Broadcasting and Communications

In August 2013 55 telecommunications and broadcasting operators were registered in New Zealand.

TELECOMMUNICATIONS

CallPlus: Level 4, 110 Symonds St, POB 108-109, Auckland; tel. (9) 915-7575; e-mail support@callplus.co.nz; internet www.callplus.co .nz; f. 1996; 100% New Zealand-owned; full-service telecommunications co; Gen. Man. KELVIN HUSSEY.

Compass Communications Ltd: Compass House, Level 2, 162 Grafton Rd, Grafton, POB 2533, Auckland; tel. (9) 965-2200; fax (9) 965-2270; internet www.compass.net.nz; f. 1995; CEO KARIM HUSSONA.

Kordia: Level 3, 162 Victoria St, POB 2495, Auckland; tel. (9) 551-7000; fax (9) 916-6402; internet www.kordiasolutions.com; fmrly known as THL Group; name changed as above 2006; telecommunications, broadcasting and converged solutions; operates in New Zealand and Australia; Chair. DAVID CLARKE; CEO SCOTT BARTLETT.

Orcon Internet Ltd: POB 302362, North Harbour, Auckland 0751; tel. (9) 444-4414; e-mail support@orcon.net.nz; internet www.orcon .net.nz; state-owned; provides mobile and internet services; CEO GREG MCALISTER.

Spark New Zealand: Telecom Place, 167 Victoria St West, Auckland 1010; tel. (4) 801-9000; fax (4) 385-3469; e-mail support@ sparkdigital.co.nz; internet www.spark.co.nz; Chair. MARK VERBIEST; Man. Dir SIMON MOUTTER.

Two Degrees Mobile Ltd: Symonds St, POB 8355, Auckland 1150; tel. 222002000 (mobile); e-mail info@2degreesmobile.co.nz; internet www.2degreesmobile.co.nz; CEO ERIC HERTZ.

Vodafone New Zealand Ltd: 20 Viaduct Harbour Ave, Auckland 1030; tel. (9) 355-2007; fax (9) 962-9300; e-mail lee.maddox@ vodafone.com; internet www.vodafone.co.nz; fmrly Bell South; cellular network; over 2m. subscribers; CEO RUSSELL STANNERS.

Woosh Wireless Ltd: 58 Tay St, Invercargill; tel. (3) 218-6274; fax (3) 218-2767; e-mail support@woosh.com; internet www.woosh.com; f. 1999 as Walker Wireless Ltd; name changed as above 2003; provides internet and telephony services; 75% owned by Craig Wireless Systems Ltd (USA); Chair. ROD INGLIS; Gen. Man. RICHARD FRY.

WorldxChange Communications Ltd: Tower Two, Level 9, 55–65 Shortland St, POB 3296, Auckland; tel. (9) 950-1300; fax (9) 950-1301; e-mail info@wxc.co.nz; internet www.wxc.co.nz; CEO GLENN JOHNSTONE.

Regulatory Authority

Energy and Communications Branch, Ministry of Business, Innovation and Employment: 15 Stout St, POB 1473, Wellington; tel. (4) 472-0030; fax (4) 473-4638; e-mail info@med.govt.nz; internet www.mbie.govt.nz; CEO DAVID SMOL.

BROADCASTING
Radio

Radio New Zealand Ltd: RNZ House, 155 The Terrace, POB 123, Wellington; tel. (4) 474-1999; fax (4) 474-1459; e-mail rnz@radionz.co .nz; internet www.radionz.co.nz; f. 1936; Crown-owned entity, operating non-commercial national networks: Radio New Zealand National and Radio New Zealand Concert; parliamentary broadcasts on AM Network; Radio New Zealand News and Current Affairs; short-wave service, Radio New Zealand International; Chair. RICHARD GRIFFIN; CEO and Editor-in-Chief PAUL THOMPSON.

The Radio Network of New Zealand Ltd: 54 Cook St, Private Bag 92-198, Auckland; tel. (9) 373-0000; fax (9) 367-4802; e-mail reception@radionetwork.co.nz; internet www.radionetwork.co.nz; operates 128 commercial stations, reaching 1.4m. people; CEO JANE HASTINGS.

Association

Radio Broadcasters' Association (NZ) Inc: POB 8049,Symonds St, Auckland; tel. (9) 378-0788; fax (9) 378-8180; e-mail info@rba.co.nz; internet www.rba.co.nz; represents commercial radio industry; Exec. Council Chair. NORM COLLISON; Exec. Dir BILL FRANCIS; 13 mems.

Television

Television New Zealand (TVNZ) Ltd: Television Centre, 100 Victoria St West, POB 3819, Auckland; tel. (9) 916-7000; fax (9) 916-7216; e-mail news@tvnz.co.uk; internet www.tvnz.co.nz; f. 1960; the television service is responsible for the production of programmes for 6 TV networks: TV ONE, TV2, TV ONE plus 1,TV2+1, TVNZ Heartland and TVNZ Kidzone24; networks are commercial all week and transmit in colour; channels broadcast 24 hours a day, 7 days a week, and reach 99.9% of the population; Chair. WAYNE WALDEN; CEO KEVIN KENRICK.

Maori Television: 9–15 Davis Cres., POB 113-017, Newmarket, Auckland; tel. (9) 539-7000; fax (9) 539-7199; e-mail info@maoritelevision.com; internet www.maoritelevision.com; f. 2003; owned by the Crown and Te Putahi Paoho; operates 2 stations; Te Reo station, launched in early 2008, broadcasts Maori-language programmes daily; Maori Television channel broadcasts Maori- and English-language programmes; Chair. GARRY MURIWAI; CEO JIM MATHER.

Private Television

Auckland Independent Television Services Ltd: POB 1629, Auckland.

Sky Network Television Limited: 10 Panorama Rd, Mt Wellington, Auckland; tel. (9) 579-9999; fax (9) 579-0910; internet www.skytv.co.nz; f. 1990; UHF service on 7 channels, satellite service; 829,421 subscribers (June 2011); Chair. PETER MACOURT; CEO JOHN FELLET.

TV3 Network Services Ltd: Symonds St, Private Bag 92-624, Auckland; tel. (9) 928-9000; fax (9) 366-5984; internet www.tv3.co.nz; f. 1989; operated by MediaWorks NZ; CEO PAUL MAHER.

Finance

(cap. = capital; res = reserves; dep. = deposits; m. = million; br.(s) = branch(es); amounts in New Zealand dollars)

BANKING

Central Bank

Reserve Bank of New Zealand (RBNZ): 2 The Terrace, POB 2498, Wellington 6011; tel. (4) 472-2029; fax (4) 473-8554; e-mail rbnz-info@rbnz.govt.nz; internet www.rbnz.govt.nz; f. 1933; cap. 1,600m., res 1,085m., dep. 19,464m. (June 2010); Gov. GRAEME WHEELER; Chair. Dr ROD CARR.

Regulatory Authority

Financial Markets Authority: Level 2, 1 Grey St, Wellington; tel. (4) 472-9830; fax (4) 472-8076; internet www.fma.govt.nz; f. 2011; regulatory body for securities exchanges, financial advisers and brokers, trustees and issuers, and auditors; Chair. SIMON ALLEN; CEO SEAN HUGHES.

Registered Banks

At August 2013 there were 22 registered banks in New Zealand.

ANZ National Bank Ltd: ANZ Tower, Level 14, 215–229 Lambton Quay, Wellington; tel. (4) 470-3142; fax (4) 494-4000; internet www.anz.co.nz; f. 1979; subsidiary of Australia and New Zealand Banking Group Ltd of Melbourne, Australia; fmrly ANZ Banking Group (New Zealand) Ltd; name changed as above 2004 following merger with Nat. Bank of New Zealand Ltd; cap. 6,943m., res 187m., dep. 79,245m. (Sept. 2011); Chair. JOHN JUDGE; CEO and Dir DAVID HISCO; 143 brs and sub-brs.

ASB Bank Ltd: ASB Tower, cnr Albert and Wellesley Sts, Auckland; tel. (9) 306-3000; fax (9) 302-1815; e-mail helpdesk@asbbank.co.nz;

internet www.asbbank.co.nz; f. 1847; est. as Auckland Savings Bank, name changed 1988; cap. 3,048m., res 65m., dep. 55,145m. (June 2013); Chair. G. R. WALKER; Man. Dir BARBARA J. CHAPMAN; 138 brs.

Bank of India (New Zealand) Ltd: 10 Manukau Rd, Epsom, POB 99491, Auckland; tel. (9) 926-5797; fax (9) 526-9719; e-mail boinz.md@bankofindia.co.in; internet www.bankofindia.co.nz; Man. Dir RANJIT JHA.

Bank of New Zealand (BNZ): Level 4, 80 Queen St, Auckland; tel. (4) 931-8209; internet www.bnz.co.nz; f. 1861; owned by Nat. Australia Bank; cap. 2,761m., res 179m., dep. 45,902m. (Sept. 2012); Chair. JOHN WALLER; Man. Dir and CEO ANDREW THORBURN; 179 domestic brs and 1 overseas br.

Citibank NA (USA): Citibank Centre, Level 11, 23 Customs St East, POB 3429, Auckland 1140; tel. (9) 307-1902; fax (9) 308-9928; e-mail citinewzealand@citi.com; internet www.citi.co.nz; Chief Country Officer DEREK SYME; 2 brs.

Deutsche Bank New Zealand: Vero Centre, Level 36, 48 Shortland St, Auckland; tel. (9) 351-1000; fax (9) 351-1001; e-mail deutsche-ausnz.press@db.com; internet www.deutsche-bank.co.nz; f. 1986; fmrly Bankers Trust New Zealand; Chair. Dr JOSEF ACKERMANN.

Hongkong and Shanghai Banking Corporation Ltd (Hong Kong): Level 19, HSBC House, 1 Queen St, Auckland 1010; tel. (9) 918-8688; fax (9) 918-8797; e-mail premier@hsbc.co.nz; internet www.hsbc.co.nz; CEO NOEL GERARD MCNAMARA; 6 brs.

Kiwibank Ltd: Private Bag 39888, Wellington Mail Centre, Lower Hutt 5045; tel. (4) 473-1133; fax (4) 462-7922; internet www.kiwibank.co.nz; f. 2002; 100% New Zealand-owned; savings bank for small depositors; cap. 360m., res 4m., dep. 12,759m. (June 2013); Chair. ROB MORRISON; Chief Exec. PAUL BROCK.

Rabobank (New Zealand): POB 38-396, Wellington Mail Centre, Wellington; tel. (4) 819-2700; fax (4) 819-2706; e-mail wellington.enquiry@rabobank.com; internet www.rabobank.co.nz; f. 1996; full subsidiary of Rabobank Nederland; Chair. JOHN PALMER; CEO BENJAMIN RUSSELL; 30 brs.

TSB Bank Ltd: POB 240, New Plymouth; tel. (6) 872-2265; fax (6) 968-3815; internet www.tsbbank.co.nz; f. 1850; cap. 10m., dep. 4,939.6m. (March 2013); Chair. ELAINE GILL; CEO and Man. Dir KEVIN MURPHY; 24 brs.

Westpac New Zealand: 16 Takutai St, Auckland 1010; tel. (9) 367-3999; e-mail westpacnz@westpac.co.nz; internet www.westpac.co.nz; acquired Trust Bank New Zealand; New Zealand division of Westpac Banking Corpn (Australia); Chair. PETER WILSON; CEO PETER CLARE; 200 brs.

Association

New Zealand Bankers' Association: 80 The Terrace, Level 15, POB 3043, Wellington 6140; tel. (4) 802-3358; fax (4) 473-1698; e-mail nzba@nzba.org.nz; internet www.nzba.org.nz; f. 1891; Chief Exec. KIRK HOPE.

STOCK EXCHANGE

New Zealand Exchange Ltd (NZX): NZX Centre, Level 2, 11 Cable St, POB 2959, Wellington 6140; tel. (4) 472-7599; fax (4) 496-2893; e-mail info@nzx.com; internet www.nzx.com; Chair. ANDREW HARMOS; CEO TIM BENNETT.

INSURANCE

ACE Insurance NZ Ltd: POB 734, Auckland 1140; tel. (9) 377-1459; fax (9) 303-1909; e-mail michael.poole@ace-ina.com; internet www.aceinsurance.co.nz; Pres. GILES WARD.

Atradius: POB 10485, Wellington 6143; tel. (4) 815-8112; fax (4) 473-8469; e-mail info.nz@atradius.com; internet www.atradius.co.nz; f. 1925; fmrly known as Gerling NCM; name changed as above following acquisition by Deutsche Bank and Swiss Re; trade credit insurance services.

AXA New Zealand Ltd: POB 1692, Wellington 6140; tel. (4) 474-4500; fax (4) 161-699; e-mail askus@axa.co.nz; internet www.axa.co.nz; Gen. Man. SID MILLER.

BNZ Life Insurance Ltd: POB 1299, Wellington; tel. (4) 382-2577; fax (4) 474-6883; e-mail emily davies@bnz.co.nz; internet www.bnz.co.nz; Chair. JOHN WALLER; Man. Dir and CEO ANDREW THORBURN.

Farmers' Mutual Group: POB 1943, Palmerston North Central, Palmerston North 4440; tel. (6) 356-9456; fax (6) 356-4603; internet fmg.co.nz; f. 1905; comprises Farmers' Mutual Finance Ltd and other cos; insurance, investment and financial services for the New Zealand rural sector; Chair. GREG GENT.

ING Life (NZ) Ltd: Victoria St West, Private Bag 92131, Auckland 1142; tel. (9) 442-4800; fax (9) 442-4801; e-mail clientserviceslife@onepath.co.nz; internet www.inglife.co.nz; operates ANZ- and The Nat. Bank-branded insurance policies; CEO HELEN TROUP; Man. Dir, Insurance NAOMI BALLANTYNE.

New Zealand Insurance: NZI, Private Bag 92130, Auckland 1142; tel. (9) 969-6000; fax (9) 309-7097; e-mail craig.dowling@iag.co.nz; internet www.nzi.co.nz; owned by Insurance Australia Group New Zealand Ltd; Exec. Gen. Man. TRAVIS ATKINSON.

New Zealand Local Government Insurance Corporation Ltd (Civic Assurance): POB 5521, Wellington 6145; tel. (4) 978-1250; fax (4) 978-1260; e-mail info@civicassurance.co.nz; internet www.civicassurance.co.nz; f. 1960; local govt insurance provider; fire, motor, all risks, accident; Chief Exec. TIM SOLE.

QBE Insurance (International) Ltd: AMP Centre, Level 6, 29 Customs St West, Auckland; tel. (9) 366-9920; fax (9) 366-9930; internet www.qbe.co.nz/insurance.html; f. 1890; Gen. Man. ROSS CHAPMAN.

Sovereign Ltd: Private Bag Sovereign, Auckland Mail Centre 1142; tel. (9) 487-9963; fax (9) 487-8003; e-mail enquire@sovereign.co.nz; internet www.sovereign.co.nz; f. 1989; life insurance and investment; CEO SYMON BREWIS-WESTON.

State Insurance Ltd: POB 3233, Wellington 6140; tel. (9) 969-1150; fax (4) 476-9664; internet www.state.co.nz; f. 1905; mem. NRMA Insurance Group; Gen. Man. CRAIG OLSEN.

Tower Insurance Ltd: Tower Centre, Level 11, 22 Fanshawe St, POB 90347, Auckland; tel. (9) 369-2000; fax (9) 369-2246; e-mail contactus@tower.co.nz; internet www.tower.co.nz; f. 1869; fmrly Nat. Insurance Co of New Zealand; Chair. MICHAEL STIASSNY; CEO and Exec. Dir DAVID HANCOCK.

Associations

Insurance Council of New Zealand: Asteron House, Level 2, 139 The Terrace, POB 474, Wellington; tel. (4) 472-5230; fax (4) 473-3011; e-mail icnz@icnz.org.nz; internet www.icnz.org.nz; f. 1895; Chief Exec. TIM GRAFTON.

Investment Savings and Insurance Association of New Zealand Inc: City Chambers, cnr Johnston and Featherston Sts, POB 1514, Wellington 6140; tel. (4) 473-8730; fax (4) 471-1881; e-mail isi@isi.org.nz; internet www.isi.org.nz; f. 1996 from Life Office Asscn and Investment Funds Asscn; represents cos that act as manager, trustee, issuer, insurer, etc. of managed funds, life insurance and superannuation; Chair. SEAN CARROLL; Chief Exec. PETER NEILSON.

Trade and Industry

GOVERNMENT AGENCY

New Zealand Trade and Enterprise (NZTE): POB 2878, Wellington 6140; tel. (4) 816-8100; fax (4) 816-8101; e-mail info@nzte.govt.nz; internet www.nzte.govt.nz; f. 2003; national govt devt agency, with global network of offices; provides businesses, organizations and investors with access to goods and services; facilitates partnerships with New Zealand businesses and investment opportunities; Chair. ANDREW FERRIER; CEO PETER CHRISP.

CHAMBERS OF COMMERCE

Auckland Regional Chamber of Commerce and Industry: POB 47, Auckland 1140; tel. (9) 309-6100; fax (9) 309-0081; e-mail auckland@chamber.co.nz; internet www.chamber.co.nz; CEO MICHAEL BARNETT; Chair. JOHN LINDSAY.

Canterbury Employers' Chamber of Commerce: 57 Kilmore St, POB 359, Christchurch 8140; tel. (3) 366-5096; fax (3) 379-5454; e-mail info@cecc.org.nz; internet www.cecc.org.nz; f. 1859; formed through merger of Employers' Fed. and Chamber of Commerce; employment and business support services, incl. legal consultancy and international trade advice, business performance and training, networking and advocacy; Chief Exec. PETER TOWNSEND; Pres. PETER DAVIES.

Employers' Chamber of Commerce Central: POB 1087, Wellington 6140; tel. (4) 473-7224; fax (4) 473-4501; e-mail ema@emacentral.org.nz; internet www.eccc.org.nz; f. 1997 as Employers' and Manufacturers' Association (Central Inc); renamed as above following merger with Wellington Regional Chamber of Commerce; CEO KEN HARRIS; 2,200 mems.

Otago Chamber of Commerce Inc: Level 3, 442 Moray Pl., POB 5173, Dunedin 9058; tel. (3) 479-0181; fax (3) 477-0341; e-mail office@otagochamber.co.nz; internet www.otagochamber.co.nz; f. 1861; CEO D. MCGOWAN; Pres. A. COPEMAN.

Wellington Employers' Chamber of Commerce: POB 1590, Wellington 6140; tel. (4) 473-7224; fax (4) 473-4501; e-mail info@wecc.org.nz; internet www.wecc.org.nz; f. 1856; fmrly Wellington Regional Chamber of Commerce; Chief Exec. KEN HARRIS; Pres. RICHARD STONE; 1,000 mems.

INDUSTRIAL AND TRADE ASSOCIATIONS

Employers' and Manufacturers' Association (Northern Inc): 159 Khyber Pass Rd, Grafton, Private Bag 92066, Auckland; tel. (9) 367-0900; fax (9) 367-0902; e-mail ema@ema.co.nz; internet www.ema.co.nz; f. 1886; fmrly Auckland Manufacturers' Asscn; Chief Exec. ALASDAIR THOMPSON; Pres. GRAHAM MOUNTFORT; 5,000 mems.

ENZA: 405 Williams St, POB 279, Hastings; tel. (9) 878-1898; fax (9) 878-1850; e-mail info@enza.co.nz; internet www.enza.co.nz; f. 1956; owned by Turners and Growers Ltd; fmrly New Zealand Apple and Pear Marketing Bd; exports apples, pears and kiwifruit; creates new apple varieties; Man. Dir JEFF WESLEY; Gen. Man. SNOW HARDY.

Federated Farmers of New Zealand (Inc): POB 715, Wellington; tel. (4) 473-7269; fax (4) 473-1081; e-mail receptionwgton@fedfarm.org.nz; internet www.fedfarm.org.nz; f. 1945; Pres. DON NICOLSON; CEO CONOR ENGLISH; 16,000 mems.

Horticulture New Zealand: POB 10232, The Terrace, Wellington 6143; tel. (4) 472-3795; fax (4) 471-2861; e-mail info@hortnz.co.nz; internet www.hortnz.co.nz; est. by merger of New Zealand Fruitgrowers' Fed., New Zealand Berryfruit Fed. and New Zealand Vegetable and Potato Growers' Fed; 7,000 mems; Pres. and Chair. ANDREW FENTON; CEO PETER SILCOCK.

Kiwifruit New Zealand (KNZ): POB 4683, Mt Maunganui South 3149; tel. (7) 572-3685; fax (7) 572-5934; e-mail richard.procter@knz.co.nz; internet www.knz.co.nz; f. 2000; Chair. Sir BRIAN ELWOOD.

Meat and Wool New Zealand: POB 121, Wellington 6140; tel. (4) 473-9150; fax (4) 474-0800; e-mail enquiries@beeflambnz.com; internet www.meatandwoolnz.com; Chair. MIKE PETERSEN; CEO Dr SCOTT CHAMPION.

Meat Industry Association of New Zealand (Inc) (MIA): Wellington Chambers, Level 5, 154 Featherston St, Wellington 6011; tel. (4) 473-6465; fax (4) 473-1731; e-mail info@mia.co.nz; internet www.mia.co.nz; Chair. W. J. (BILL) FALCONER; CEO TIM RITCHE.

National Beekeepers Association of New Zealand (Inc): Adecco House, Level 6, 330 Lambton Quay, POB 10792, Wellington; tel. (6) 471-6254; e-mail secretary@nba.org.nz; internet www.nba.org.nz; f. 1913; 700 mems; Pres. R. LEAHY; Secs L. CRIMP.

New Zealand Animal By-Products Exporters' Association: 11 Longhurst Terrace, POB 12-222, Christchurch; tel. (3) 332-2895; fax (3) 332-2825; 25 mems; Sec. J. L. NAYSMITH.

New Zealand Council of Wool Exporters Inc: POB 2857, Christchurch; tel. (3) 353-1049; fax (3) 374-6925; e-mail cwe@woolexport.net; internet www.woolexport.net; f. 1893; Exec. Man. R. H. F. NICHOLSON; Pres. JOHN DAWSON.

The New Zealand Forest Owners' Association: POB 1208, Wellington 6140; tel. (4) 473-4769; fax (4) 499-8893; e-mail nzfoa@nzfoa.org.nz; internet www.nzfoa.org.nz; f. 1926; Pres. PETER BERG; Chief Exec. DAVID RHODES.

New Zealand Fruit Wine and Cider Makers Inc: POB 912, New Plymouth; tel. and fax (6) 769-9009; e-mail admin@fruitwines.co.nz; internet www.fruitwines.co.nz; f. 1985; 40 mems; represents all non-grape wine, cider, perry and mead makers in New Zealand; Chair. JUSTIN HALL; Exec. Officer CHRISTINE GARNHAM.

New Zealand Manufacturers' and Exporters' Association (MEA): POB 13152, Armagh, Christchurch 8141; tel. (3) 353-2540; fax (3) 353-2549; e-mail cma@cma.org.nz; internet www.mea.org.nz; f. 2007; est. by merger of Canterbury Manufacturers' Asscn and New Zealand Engineers' Fed; CEO JOHN L. WALLEY; Pres. BRIAN WILLOUGHBY.

New Zealand Meat Board: POB 121, Wellington 6140; tel. (4) 473-9150; fax (4) 474-0801; e-mail info@nzmeatboard.org; internet www.nzmeatboard.org; f. 1922; Chair. MIKE PETERSEN; 10 mems.

New Zealand Pork Industry Board (NZ Pork): Level 4, 94 Dixon St, POB 4048, Wellington 6140; tel. (4) 917-4750; fax (4) 385-8522; e-mail info@pork.co.nz; internet www.pork.co.nz; f. 1937; Chair. IAN CARTER; CEO OWEN SYMMANS.

New Zealand Retailers' Association Inc: POB 12086, Wellington 6144; tel. (4) 805-0830; fax (4) 805-0831; e-mail helpline@retail.org.nz; internet www.retail.org.nz; 6,000 direct mems; Pres. TERRY CORNELIUS; CEO MARK JOHNSTON.

New Zealand Timber Industry Federation: POB 308, Wellington; tel. (4) 473-5200; fax (4) 473-6536; e-mail inquiries@nztif.co.nz; internet www.nztif.co.nz; f. 1983; 350 mems; Exec. Dir WAYNE. S. COFFEY.

Registered Master Builders Association of New Zealand (Inc): Level 6, 234 Wakefield St, POB 1796, Wellington; tel. (4) 385-8999; fax (4) 385-8995; e-mail mbinfo@masterbuilder.org.nz; internet www.masterbuilder.org.nz; Chief Exec. WARWICK QUINN.

Seafood New Zealand: POB 297, Manners St, Wellington 6142; tel. (4) 385-4005; fax (4) 385-2727; e-mail info@seafood.org.nz; internet www.seafoodnewzealand.org.nz; fmrly New Zealand Seafood Industry Council; CEO TIM PANKHURST; Chair. GEORGE CLEMENT.

EMPLOYERS' ORGANIZATION

Business New Zealand: Lumley House, Level 6, 3–11 Hunter St, POB 1925, Wellington; tel. (4) 496-6555; fax (4) 496-6550; e-mail admin@businessnz.org.nz; internet www.businessnz.org.nz; f. 2001; Chief Exec. PHIL O'REILLY.

UTILITIES

Energy Efficiency and Conservation Authority (EECA): POB 388, Wellington 6140; tel. (4) 470-2200; fax (4) 499-5330; e-mail info@eeca.govt.nz; internet www.eeca.govt.nz; f. 2000; Chair. THOMAS CAMPBELL; Chief Exec. MIKE UNDERHILL.

Gas and Electricity

Following parliamentary approval of the Electricity Industry Bill in September 2010, the Electricity Authority was established on 1 November to replace the Electricity Commission.

Electricity Authority: ASB Bank Tower, Level 7, 2 Hunter St, POB 10041, Wellington 6143; tel. (4) 460-8860; fax (4) 460-8879; e-mail info@ea.govt.nz; internet www.ea.govt.nz; f. 2010; replaced Electricity Commission; independent regulatory body supervising electricity sector; Chair. Dr BRENT LAYTON; Chief Exec. CARL HANSEN.

Contact Energy Ltd: Harbour City Tower, Level 1, 29 Brandon St, POB 10742, Wellington; tel. (4) 449-4001; fax (4) 499-4003; e-mail help@contact-energy.co.nz; internet www.contactenergy.co.nz; f. 1996; generation of electricity, wholesale and retail of energy; Chair. GRANT KING; CEO DENNIS BARNES.

Genesis Energy Ltd: Private Bag 3131, Hamilton 3240; tel. (9) 838-7863; fax (9) 580-4891; internet www.genesisenergy.co.nz; f. 1999; state-owned; generation and retail of electricity and gas; Chair. Dame JENNY SHIPLEY; Chief Exec. ALBERT BRANTLEY.

The Marketplace Co Ltd (M-CO): NZX Ltd, Level 2, NZX Center, 11 Cable St, POB 2959, Wellington 6140; tel. (4) 473-5240; fax (4) 473-5247; e-mail info@m-co.com; internet www.m-co.co.nz; f. 1993; administers wholesale electricity market; acquired by NZX Ltd in 2009; Chief Exec. CARL HANSEN.

Meridian Energy Ltd: POB 2128, Christchurch; tel. (3) 353-9500; fax (3) 353-9501; e-mail contactus@meridianenergy.co.nz; internet www.meridianenergy.co.nz; state-owned; generation and retail of electricity; Chair. CHRIS MOLLER; Chief Exec. MARK BINNS.

Mighty River Power Ltd: Level 14, 23–29 Albert St, POB 90-399, Auckland; tel. (9) 308-8200; fax (9) 308-8209; e-mail enquiries@mightyriver.co.nz; internet www.mightyriverpower.co.nz; f. 1998; electricity generation and retail; cos include Vector Electricity; Chair. JOAN WITHERS; Chief Exec. DOUG HEFFERMAN.

NGC Holdings Ltd: NGC Bldg, Level 8, 44 The Terrace, Private Bag 39-980, Wellington Mail Centre, Wellington; tel. (4) 462-8700; fax (4) 462-8600; internet www.ngc.co.nz; f. 1992; fmrly Natural Gas Corpn Holdings Ltd; name changed as above 2002; purchase, processing and transport of natural gas; wholesale and retail sales; Chair. MICHAEL STIASSNY; Chief Exec. BRYAN CRAWFORD.

Nova Energy: 52 Commerce St, POB 404, Whakatane 3158; tel. (7) 922-2700; fax (7) 307-0922; e-mail info@novaenergy.co.nz; internet www.novaenergy.co.nz; fmrly Nova Gas Ltd, merged with Bay of Plenty Energy in 2012; generation, purchase and supply of electricity, LPG, natural gas and solar energy; owned by the Todd Corpn; CEO BABU BAHIRATHAN.

Orion New Zealand Ltd: POB 13896, Christchurch 8141; tel. (3) 363-9898; fax (3) 363-9899; e-mail info@oriongroup.co.nz; internet www.oriongroup.co.nz; f. 1998; electricity distribution network; Chair. CRAIG BOYCE; CEO ROB JAMIESON.

Todd Energy Ltd: 95 Customhouse Quay, POB 3141, Wellington; tel. (4) 471-6555; fax (4) 472-2474; e-mail energy@toddenergy.co.nz; internet www.toddenergy.co.nz; CEO PAUL MOORE.

Transpower New Zealand Ltd: Transpower House, Level 7, 96 The Terrace, POB 1021, Wellington; tel. (4) 495-7000; fax (4) 495-7100; internet www.transpower.co.nz; f. 1994; manages national grid; Chair. MARK VERBIEST; Chief Exec. PATRICK STRANGE.

TrustPower Ltd: Private Bag 12-023, Tauranga Mail Centre, Tauranga 3143, Auckland; tel. (7) 574-4754; fax (7) 574-4803; e-mail enquiries@trustpower.co.nz; internet www.trustpower.co.nz; f. 1920 as Tauranga Electric Power Board; independent generator; Chair. Dr BRUCE HARKER; CEO VINCE HAWKSWORTH.

Vector Electricity Ltd: 101 Carlton Gore Rd, Newmarket, Auckland 1023; tel. (9) 978-7788; fax (9) 978-7799; e-mail info@vector.co.nz; internet www.vector.co.nz; owned by Vector Ltd; fmrly Mercury Energy Ltd; operates power networks in Auckland, Manukau and Papakura; distributes natural gas in Auckland; Chair. MICHAEL STIASSNY; Group CEO SIMON MACKENZIE.

Wanganui Gas Ltd: 179 Hill St, POB 32, Wanganui; tel. (6) 349-0909; fax (6) 345-4931; e-mail enquiries@wanganuigas.co.nz; internet www.wanganuigas.co.nz; f. 1879; supplier of gas on North Island; Chair. MATTHEW J DOYLE; Chief Exec. TREVOR GOODWIN.

Water

Waste Management NZ Ltd: 86 Lunn Ave, Mt Wellington, Private Bag 14-919, Panmure, Auckland 1741; tel. (9) 527-1300; fax (9) 570-1417; internet www.wastemanagement.co.nz; f. 1985; waste collection, recovery and disposal; liquid waste collection and processing; recycling; subsidiary of Transpacific Industries Group; Chief Financial Officer KEVIN BUGDEN.

Watercare Services Ltd: Private Bag 92521, Wellesley St, Auckland 1141; tel. (9) 442-2222; fax (9) 970-1461; e-mail info@water.co.nz; internet www.watercare.co.nz; f. 1993; provides water and waste water services in the Auckland area; Chair. ROSS KEENAN; Chief Exec. MARK FORD.

TRADE UNIONS

New Zealand Council of Trade Unions: Education House, West Block, 178 Willis St, POB 6645, Wellington 6141; tel. (4) 385-1334; fax (4) 385-6051; e-mail helenk@nzctu.org.nz; internet www.union.org.nz; f. 1937; present name since 1987; affiliated to ITUC; 40 affiliated unions with more than 350,000 mems; Pres. HELEN KELLY; Sec. PETER CONWAY.

Transport

RAILWAYS

At early 2014 there was more than 4,000 km of railway track in New Zealand and over 3,000 level crossings.

New Zealand Railways Corporation (NZRC—KiwiRail): POB 593, Wellington 6140; tel. 800-801-070; fax (4) 473-1589; e-mail kiwirail@kiwirail.co.nz; internet www.kiwirail.co.nz; f. 2008; state-owned enterprise, est. following Govt's purchase of rail and inter-island ferry operations of Toll NZ Ltd; Chair. JOHN SPENCER; Chief Exec. JIM QUINN.

ROADS

In 2012 there were a total of 94,160 km of maintained roads in New Zealand. There were 10,916 km of national roads and 83,244 km of regional roads.

New Zealand Transport Agency: Victoria Arcade, 50 Victoria St, Private Bag 6995, Wellington 6141; tel. (4) 894-5400; fax (4) 894-6100; e-mail info@nzta.govt.nz; internet www.nzta.govt.nz; f. 2008; formed by merger of Land Transport NZ and Transit NZ; Crown entity charged with contributing to an integrated, safe, responsive and sustainable land transport system; Chair. CHRIS MOLLER; Chief Exec. GEOFF DANGERFIELD.

SHIPPING

There are 13 main seaports, of which the most important are Auckland, Tauranga, Wellington, Lyttleton (the port of Christchurch) and Port Chalmers (Dunedin). At December 2014 the New Zealand flag registered fleet comprised 130 vessels, with a total displacement of 245,035 grt.

Principal Companies

Maersk New Zealand: The CPO, Level 3, 12 Queen St, Auckland; tel. (9) 359-3499; fax (9) 359-3488; e-mail nezcsedir@maersk.com; internet www.maerskline.com; f. 1928; CEO SØREN SKOU.

Matson South Pacific Ltd: 68 Anzac Ave, Auckland; tel. (9) 302-2204; fax (9) 302-0096; e-mail info@matson.co.nz; internet www.reefship.co.nz; f. 2013, fmrly Reef Shipping Ltd, acquired by Matson Inc in 2012; operates services between New Zealand and the Pacific islands; Gen. Man. JASON WARD.

Sofrana Unilines NZ Ltd: 38 Ponsonby Rd, POB 3614, Auckland; tel. (9) 356-1400; fax (9) 356-1429; e-mail info@sofrana.co.nz; internet www.sofrana.co.nz; Chair. DIDIER LEROUX; Man. Dir BENOIT MARCENAC.

Other major shipping companies operating services to New Zealand include Blue Star Line (NZ) Ltd and Columbus Line, which link New Zealand with Australia, the Pacific islands, South-East Asia and the USA.

CIVIL AVIATION

There are long-distance international airports at Auckland and Christchurch. International airports at Dunedin, Queenstown, Rotorua and Wellington provide limited regional connectivity.

Civil Aviation Authority of New Zealand: Asteron Centre, 55 Featherston St, POB 3555, Wellington; tel. (4) 560-9400; fax (4) 569-2024; e-mail info@caa.govt.nz; internet www.caa.govt.nz; Dir of Civil Aviation GRAEME HARRIS.

Principal Airlines

Air Nelson: Private Bag 32, Nelson 7042; tel. (3) 547-8700; fax (3) 547-8788; e-mail airnelsonadmin@airnz.co.nz; internet www.airnelson.co.nz; f. 1979; owned by Air New Zealand, operates along with Mount Cook and Eagle Air as Air New Zealand Link; present name adopted 1986; operates services throughout New Zealand; Gen. Man. GRANT KERR.

Air New Zealand: Private Bag 92007, Auckland 1142; tel. (9) 336-2287; fax (9) 366-2664; e-mail investor@airnz.co.nz; internet www.airnewzealand.co.nz; f. 1942; privatized in 1989, recapitalized by the Govt in 2001; 53% govt-owned; services to and from Australia, the Pacific islands, Asia, Europe and North America, as well as regular daily services to regional New Zealand; Chair. TONY CARTER; CEO CHRISTOPHER LUXON.

Virgin Australia (NZ) Ltd: internet www.virginaustralia.com; f. 2003 as Pacific Blue Airlines; renamed as above in 2011; wholly owned subsidiary of Virgin Australia; services to Australia and the Pacific islands; CEO MARK PITT.

Tourism

New Zealand's principal tourist attractions are its mountains, lakes, forests, volcanoes, hot springs and beaches. The sector makes a substantial contribution to the country's economy. Visitor arrivals increased from 2.72m. in 2013 to 2.86m. in 2014, while tourism receipts rose from $NZ6,342m. in 2012 to $NZ6,672m. in 2013. The majority of visitors are from Australia, the People's Republic of China, the UK and the USA.

Tourism New Zealand: Vodafone House, Level 22, 157 Lambton Quay, POB 95, Wellington; tel. (4) 462-8000; fax (4) 917-5495; e-mail enquiries@tnz.govt.nz; internet www.newzealand.com; f. 1901; responsible for marketing of New Zealand as a tourism destination; offices in Auckland, Wellington and Christchurch; 13 offices overseas; Chair. KERRY PRENDERGAST; Chief Exec. KEVIN BOWLER.

Defence

As assessed at November 2014, the total strength of the regular forces was 8,500: army 4,250, navy 1,900 and air force 2,350. In addition, there were approximately 2,290 regular reserves (army 1,800, navy 300, air force 190) and 1,800 territorial reserves. Military service is voluntary. New Zealand is a participant in the Five-Power Defence Arrangements with Australia, Malaysia, Singapore and the UK.

Defence Expenditure: Budgeted at $NZ3,710m. for 2014.

Chief of Defence Force: Lt-Gen. TIM KEATING.

Chief of Army: Maj.-Gen. ARTHUR DAVID GAWN.

Chief of Navy: Rear-Adm. JACK STEER.

Chief of Air Force: Air Vice-Marshal MICHAEL YARDLEY.

Commander Joint Forces New Zealand: Maj.-Gen. TIM GALL.

Education

Education in New Zealand is free and secular in state schools. It is compulsory for all children aged six to 16 years, although in practice almost 100% start at the age of five years. Budgetary expenditure on education by the central Government in 2012/13 totalled $NZ14,512m., representing 19.0% of total spending.

In July 2013 there were 200,922 children enrolled in early childhood education services, while in July 2014 439,494 pupils were enrolled in primary classes at 1,961 schools. A total of 272,313 pupils attended 366 secondary schools in July 2014. Composite schools, which were attended by 52,378 pupils in July 2014, provide education at both primary and secondary level.

In 2011 enrolment at primary level included 99% of all students in the relevant age-group, while enrolment at secondary institutes included 97% of all students in the relevant age-group.

NEW ZEALAND'S DEPENDENT TERRITORIES

New Zealand's two Dependent Territories are the Ross Dependency, which is situated in Antarctica, and Tokelau, located in the Pacific Ocean.

ROSS DEPENDENCY

The Ross Dependency comprises the sector of Antarctica between 160°E and 150°W (moving eastward) and the islands lying between those degrees of longitude and south of latitude 60°S. It has been administered by New Zealand since 1923 and has a total area of 750,310 sq km (289,700 sq miles), comprising a land area of 413,540 sq km and an ice shelf of 336,770 sq km. The Territory rises to a height of 3,794 m above sea level at the peak of the volcano, Mount Erebus.

Scott Base was established by New Zealand in 1957 on Ross Island, and in the following year the Ross Dependency Research Committee was formed to supervise New Zealand activity on the Territory. In 1968 a new scientific station was set up by New Zealand at Lake Vanda, about 130 km (80 miles) west of Scott Base; owing to environmental concerns, the Vanda Station was closed down in 1995. In addition to Scott Base, there are currently three other stations located in the Territory: the US McMurdo Station, which, like the Scott Base, is permanently occupied; the seasonally occupied US Amundsen-Scott South Pole Station; and the summer-occupied

Italian Zucchelli Station. In 1986 traces of petroleum were discovered in the Territory, more than 600 m below the seabed. The Ross Dependency Research Committee was disbanded in 1995. Legislation approved in the mid-1990s consolidated measures aimed at conserving the region's flora and fauna (which includes 18 species of penguin, six species of seal and several rare species of whale) included in the Antarctic Treaty (see p. 457), and reinforced the Convention for the Conservation of Antarctic Marine Living Resources. Since 1997 New Zealand has conducted exploratory fishing for toothfish in the Ross Sea; the fishing is conducted under strict supervision and quotas. In October 2012 the New Zealand and US Governments presented a joint proposal to the Commission for the Conservation of Antarctic Marine Living Resources (see p. 456) on the establishment of a Marine Protected Area in the Ross Sea. However, the Commission repeatedly failed to reach agreement on the proposal. At the annual meeting in October 2014 the proposal was blocked again by the People's Republic of China and Russia.

TOKELAU

Introductory Survey

LOCATION, CLIMATE, LANGUAGE, RELIGION, FLAG, CAPITAL

Tokelau consists of three atolls (Atafu, Nukunonu and Fakaofo), which lie about 480 km (300 miles) north of Samoa, in the Pacific Ocean. The annual average temperature is 28°C (82°F), July being the coolest month and May the warmest; rainfall is heavy but inconsistent. The principal language is Tokelauan (a Polynesian language), although English is also widely spoken. The population is almost entirely Christian, with 67% adhering to the Congregational Christian Church (a Protestant denomination) and 30% to the Roman Catholic Church. The national flag (proportions 1 by 2) is dark blue, with four five-pointed white stars in the form of the Southern Cross constellation in the upper hoist and a yellow canoe in full sail facing towards the hoist across the bottom. Tokelau has no capital, each atoll having its own administrative centre. However, the seat of government, the Office of the Council for the Ongoing Government of Tokelau (formerly the Council of Faipule), is recognized as 'the capital' and is rotated on a yearly basis among the three atolls.

CONTEMPORARY POLITICAL HISTORY

Historical Context

The Tokelau (formerly Union) Islands became a British protectorate in 1877. At the request of the inhabitants, the United Kingdom annexed the islands in 1916 and included them within the Gilbert and Ellice Islands Colony (now Kiribati and Tuvalu). The British Government transferred administrative control of the islands to New Zealand by legislation enacted in 1925, effective from February 1926. The group was officially designated the Tokelau Islands in 1946, and sovereignty was transferred to New Zealand by legislation of 1948, effective from January 1949. From 1962 until the end of 1971 the High Commissioner for New Zealand in Western Samoa (now Samoa) was also the Administrator of the Tokelau Islands. In November 1974 the administration of the Tokelau Islands was transferred to the Ministry of Foreign Affairs in New Zealand. In 1976 the Tokelau Islands were officially redesignated Tokelau.

Domestic Political Affairs

A programme of constitutional change, agreed in 1992 and formalized in January 1994, provided for a more defined role for Tokelau's political institutions, as well as for their expansion. A process of relocating the Tokelau Public Service (hitherto based in Apia, Western Samoa—now Samoa) to the Territory began in 1994, and by 1995 all government departments, except Transport and Communications and part of the Administration and Finance Department, had been transferred to Tokelauan soil. However, the Tokelau Apia Liaison Office (formerly the Office for Tokelau Affairs) was to remain in Western Samoa, owing to that country's more developed communications facilities.

The development of Tokelau's institutions at a national level prompted renewed interest in the islands' prospects for greater internal autonomy. In a statement to the UN Special Committee on Decolonization in June 1987, Tokelau had expressed a desire to achieve a greater degree of political autonomy, while maintaining its relationship with New Zealand. In June 1994 the General Fono, the Territory's highest advisory body, adopted a National Strategic Plan, which gave details of Tokelau's progression (over the next five to 10 years) towards increased self-determination and, possibly, free association with New Zealand. The executive and administrative powers of the Administrator were formally transferred, in that year, to the General Fono and, when the Fono was not in session, to the Council of Faipule (cabinet). A draft constitution was subsequently drawn up. In May 1996 the New Zealand House of Representatives approved the Tokelau Amendment Bill, granting the General Fono the power to enact legislation, to impose taxes and to declare public holidays, effective from 1 August 1996 (although New Zealand was to retain the right to legislate for Tokelau).

Following electoral reforms introduced in the latter half of the 1990s, delegates were, for the first time, elected to the General Fono for a three-year term in January 1999; they had previously been nominated by each Taupulega (Island Council or Council of Elders). As part of the same reform process, the number of delegates to the General Fono was reduced from 27 to 18. At the elections two of the Territory's Faipule (political leaders) were re-elected, while the third Faipule and all three Pulenuku (Village Mayor) posts were secured by new candidates. At the elections in January 2002 a population-based pattern of representation was adopted by the General Fono.

Meanwhile, mounting fears among islanders that, despite their wishes, New Zealand was seeking to loosen its ties with Tokelau, led the New Zealand Minister of Foreign Affairs to state in April 2000 that his country would not impose independence on the Territory and that any change in its political status would occur only with the consent of Tokelauans. In early 2001 the head of the Tokelau Public Service Commission, Aleki Silau, reiterated the islanders' reluctance to renounce New Zealand citizenship. A report by the UN Special Committee on Decolonization in 2002 listed Tokelau as one of 16 dependent territories that it was seeking to encourage towards independence. However, a UN decolonization mission, which visited the islands in September of that year, was informed that the majority of Tokelauans wanted to remain part of New Zealand and that the Territory was far too dependent on that country to change its status. Meanwhile, under legislation approved in 1999, management of the islands' Public Service was formally transferred to Tokelau in July 2001. In July 2003 responsibility for the islands' budget was transferred to the General Fono.

A number of constitutional changes were instituted in October 2003. The Council of Faipule was renamed the Council for the Ongoing Government of Tokelau, henceforth to comprise the three Faipule and the three Pulenuku (although the ministerial posts were to be shared among the Faipule only). In November New Zealand's Governor-General, Dame Silvia Cartwright, made an official visit to Tokelau to sign the Principles of Partnership agreement. The document was described by New Zealand's Minister of Foreign Affairs, Phil Goff, as a step closer to decolonization for the islands. Goff reiterated that the final decision on Tokelau's future would be made by its inhabitants, although he also confirmed that he expected the islands to adopt a system of self-government in free association with New Zealand, similar to that existing in Niue and the Cook Islands. In March 2004 it was announced that new powers were to be granted to the three atolls' Taupulega, giving them greater control over local affairs. In June the Administrator's powers were formally transferred from the General Fono to the three Taupulega, as part of the Modern House of Tokelau Project.

In August 2004 New Zealand's Prime Minister, Helen Clark, made an official visit to Tokelau (the first such visit in more than 20 years). During the visit Clark expressed her confidence that the islanders would vote in favour of free association with New Zealand when the issue was finally put to a referendum. In November leaders from Tokelau travelled to New Zealand for a series of meetings with Goff, following which certain elements to be included in a treaty of free association with New Zealand were agreed upon. However, contrary to the New Zealand Government's expectations, at a referendum on the issue of the future status of Tokelau held between 11 and 15 February 2006 the requisite two-thirds' majority in favour of the proposed change to free association with New Zealand was not received: 349 votes were cast in favour of greater self-government, while 232 voters wanted Tokelau to remain a Dependent Territory. In June it was announced that the General Fono had agreed to the holding of another referendum on the issue of Tokelau's status.

In October 2006 David Payton replaced Neil Walter as Tokelau's Administrator. The decision to appoint a New Zealand diplomat to the position was interpreted by some observers as a reflection of a lack of confidence in the people of Tokelau and their ability to manage their own affairs. At the second referendum on Tokelau's status, conducted in October 2007, the level of participation was reported to be almost 100%. However, support for self government was again not sufficient to produce the requisite two-thirds' majority, with 246 out of 692 voters rejecting the proposal. At the elections to the General Fono held in January 2008 the number of delegates elected was increased to 20 (from 15 in the 2005 elections) in line with the rise in population.

In February 2005, meanwhile, all three atolls were struck by Cyclone Percy, which caused widespread damage to infrastructure, homes and crops. Nukunonu suffered severe flooding as a result of the storm. In response, the New Zealand Government approved some $NZ500,000 in emergency aid.

Recent developments

On 7 September 2009, in a development regarded as important in advancing the islands' identity, the New Zealand Governor-General, Sir Anand Satyanand, formally presented Tokelau with an official flag, in place of the New Zealand flag used hitherto.

In April 2010 Tokelau declared a whaling sanctuary in its territorial waters. The New Zealand Ministry of Foreign Affairs was not consulted prior to this declaration, despite the fact that the implementation of such a whale sanctuary would require New Zealand's assistance. Nevertheless, the New Zealand Government indicated that it would support Tokelau's bid to implement the ban on whaling. In September 2011 Tokelau announced that its entire exclusive economic zone (comprising some 319,031 sq km) was henceforth to be designated as a shark sanctuary.

Elections to the General Fono were held in January 2011, when 20 delegates were again elected. In February Jonathan Kings replaced John Allen as the islands' Administrator. Allen had replaced David Payton in an acting capacity in 2009.

A state of emergency was declared in early October 2011 in response to a severe shortage of fresh water in Tokelau, which led

to significant pressures on food sources, with livestock and crops both affected, and underscored the need for the Tokelauan authorities to develop more effective water resource management policies. Later in the month the Secretariat of the Pacific Regional Environment Programme (SPREP) disbursed funding to enable Tokelau urgently to address the challenges posed by the ongoing drought. New Zealand, the USA and Samoa also provided assistance, in the form of deliveries of desalinated water, and, following the first substantial rainfall in nearly six months, the state of emergency was rescinded in late October. SPREP also pledged to assist Tokelau in long-term water resource management planning, including increasing water storage capacity and improving water conservation. In September 2013 the New Zealand Government announced a five-year, $NZ5m. initiative intended to assist five Pacific states vulnerable to water shortages, including Tokelau, better to manage their fresh water resources.

Meanwhile, in December 2011 Tokelau, along with Samoa, switched to the western side of the Date Line, in order to facilitate the conduct of business with Australia and New Zealand by being in a similar time zone. It was reported in April 2013 that Tokelau and New Zealand were jointly to formulate a strategic plan to enhance the performance and development of the Tokelauan police force.

In May 2013 it was announced that the Council for the Ongoing Government of Tokelau was to double its number of ministers, to include the three Pulenuku; all ministerial responsibilities had hitherto been shared between the three Faipule. In the same month proposals were mooted for the introduction of a formal reservation for women of a number of seats in the General Fono.

Elections to the General Fono were held on 23 January 2014, when 20 delegates were elected. Three new members were elected to the six-member Council for the Ongoing Government, including Saili Patea Peau, who thus became the first female to be elected to the Council.

Foreign Affairs

New Zealand is responsible for the external relations of Tokelau. Strong links are maintained with Samoa, to the people of which the Tokelauans are closely related. There is considerable co-operation in health and education matters.

In December 1980 New Zealand and the USA signed a treaty whereby a US claim to Tokelau, dating from 1856, was relinquished. At the same time New Zealand abandoned a claim, on behalf of Tokelau, to Swains Island, which had been administered by the USA since 1925 as part of American Samoa. The treaty was ratified in August 1983, although there was some dissent in Tokelau. In March 2007 the Faipule of Fakaofo, Kolouei O'Brien, declared that if the islands achieved greater autonomy then Tokelau would wish to enter immediate negotiations with the USA regarding the return of Swains Island.

In 1989 Tokelau supported efforts by the South Pacific Forum to impose a regional ban on drift-net fishing (which was believed to have resulted in a serious depletion in tuna stocks). In November New Zealand prohibited drift-net fishing within Tokelau's exclusive economic zone (which extends to 200 nautical miles—370 km—from the islands' coastline). Tokelau was one of the 15 signatories of the Convention for the Prohibition of Fishing with Long Drift Nets in the South Pacific, which was drafted by the South Pacific Forum in 1989 and came into force in May 1991. At the annual meeting of the Pacific Islands Forum (formerly the South Pacific Forum) in August 2002, New Zealand endorsed Tokelau's membership of the Forum Fisheries Agency. Tokelau was granted observer status at the Pacific Islands Forum in October 2005; this was upgraded to associate membership in August 2014.

A visit to the islands by the Prime Minister of Tuvalu in mid-1996, for the signing of a mutual co-operation agreement (covering shipping, trade and fisheries), was widely interpreted as an indication of Tokelau's increased autonomy. A further co-operation agreement was concluded in March 2003, following a five-day visit to the islands by the Prime Minister of Samoa. Tokelau's traditional leaders agreed a framework for annual meetings with the Samoan Government to discuss issues of concern and mutual benefit in what was regarded as a sign of the growing relationship between the two parties.

In November 2011 Tokelau was one of eight Pacific states and territories that jointly established the Polynesian Leaders Group (see p. 463), which was broadly viewed as being intended to provide a counterweight to the Melanesian Spearhead Group. The first formal meeting of the Group, which pledged to enhance co-operation among its members across a wide range of fields, including trade and investment, education, climate change and health, was held in the Cook Islands, on the sidelines of the annual Pacific Islands Forum summit, in August 2012.

CONSTITUTION AND GOVERNMENT

Tokelau is administered under the authority of the Tokelau Islands Act 1948, incorporating subsequent amendments and regulations. The administration of Tokelau is the responsibility of the Minister of

Foreign Affairs of New Zealand, who is empowered to appoint an Administrator to the Territory. In practice, most of the Administrator's powers are delegated to the Official Secretary, who heads the Tokelau Apia Liaison Office, as well as to the General Fono and the Council for the Ongoing Government of Tokelau (formerly the Council of Faipule). Each atoll has its own Taupulega (Island Council or Council of Elders), which comprises the heads of family groups together with two elected members, the Faipule and the Pulenuku. The Faipule represents the atoll in its dealings with the administering power and the public service, and presides over the Council and the court. The Pulenuku is responsible for the administration of village affairs. The Faipule and the Pulenuku are democratically elected by universal adult suffrage every three years. Ministerial portfolios are distributed among the three Faipule and three Pulenuku, who together form the six-member Council for the Ongoing Government of Tokelau. The Faipule choose one of their number on a rotational basis to hold the title Ulu-O-Tokelau (Head of Tokelau) for a term of one year. The territorial assembly, the General Fono, is a meeting of 20 delegates, who are elected by universal adult suffrage for a three-year term (including the three Faipule and the three Pulenuku) and who represent the entire Territory. Members of the General Fono elect a Chairman, and hold three or four sessions a year on the atoll of the Ulu-O-Tokelau.

REGIONAL AND INTERNATIONAL CO-OPERATION

Tokelau is a member of the Pacific Community (see p. 410), and, as a Dependent Territory of New Zealand, has been represented by that country in the Pacific Islands Forum (see p. 413) and other international organizations. In October 2005 Tokelau was granted observer status at the Pacific Islands Forum and became an associate member of the body in August 2014. In November 2011 Tokelau was one of eight founding members of the Polynesian Leaders Group (see p. 463).

ECONOMIC AFFAIRS

According to estimates by the UN Development Programme (UNDP), in 1982 Tokelau's gross national product (GNP) was US $1.2m., equivalent to US $760 per head. Gross domestic product (GDP) was estimated at US $1.5m. in 1993. Between the censuses of 2001 and 2011 the population declined at an average rate of 0.9% per year.

Agriculture (including fishing) is, excluding copra production, of a basic subsistence nature. Coconuts (the source of copra) are the only cash crop, for which there is an increasingly limited market. Pulaka, breadfruit, papayas, the screw-pine (*Pandanus*) and bananas are cultivated as food crops. Livestock comprises pigs, ducks and other poultry. Ocean and lagoon fish and shellfish are staple constituents of the islanders' diet. The sale to foreign fleets of fishing licences permitting them to operate in Tokelau's exclusive economic zone (EEZ) provides an important, albeit fluctuating, source of income (see below).

The industrial sector has been constrained by a lack of resources. Manufacturing comprises mainly the production of handicrafts, notably woven items such as mats. However, the opening on Atafu, in 1990, of a factory processing highly priced yellowfin tuna provided another important source of income. The principal markets for the product are New Zealand and Japan.

Energy was traditionally provided by diesel-powered generators, the fuel for which was imported via Samoa at considerable expense. With funding from New Zealand, a major power project to supply all three atolls with a more reliable source of electricity was initiated in 2002. Over the following decade, greater emphasis was placed on the development of renewable forms of energy, particularly solar power. In conjunction with the Governments of New Zealand and France, UNDP and UNESCO, in 2003 Tokelau embarked on a programme aimed at utilizing the Territory's solar energy potential for grid-connected power generation. In October 2012, following the installation of 4,032 solar panels (totalling 1 MW) and 1,344 batteries by the New Zealand company PowerSmart, it was announced that Tokelau had become the world's first territory to have the capacity to meet its energy requirements solely through solar power. It was expected, however, that around 7% of the Territory's energy would continue to be provided by generators (for cloudy days, working by night and for emergencies), which would now be powered by locally produced coconut oil rather than diesel.

The services sector is dominated by village services and public administration. The tourism sector is limited, having remained undeveloped owing to the lack of air services and the difficulty of access. There is just one recognized hotel and one resort, both of which are located on the central atoll of Nukunonu. Fewer than 30 tourists visited the islands in 2001. Following the purchase by a Dutch entrepreneur of the islands' internet domain address '.tk' in 2001, more than 1.6m. names had been registered to the facility by 2007. Although the Government's precise earnings from Dot TK were not disclosed, the services of this joint venture with Teletok, the islands' communications company, were reported to be proving highly lucrative. The establishment of Dot TK was believed to

have increased annual government revenue by about 10%. In 2012 revenue from Dot TK was reported to account for about one-sixth of Tokelau's GDP. Meanwhile, the concomitant upgrading of Tokelau's communications infrastructure, including a broadband connection via satellite, greatly enhanced the islanders' own information technology facilities. In March 2007, however, a leading information technology publication reported that '.tk' was the most insecure web domain in the world. A content-filtering system was subsequently installed, in an attempt to reduce the risks. Furthermore, in March 2008 an international software security company reported that, along with Niue, in per caput terms Tokelau was one of the world's worst offenders with regard to the relaying of unsolicited e-mails.

Imports to the value of $NZ1.7m. were purchased in 2002. The principal imports in that year were food and live animals (accounting for 55.2% of the total cost of imports), mineral fuels (11.6%) and miscellaneous manufactured goods (11.0%).

In 1999/2000 there was a budgetary deficit of $NZ0.9m. Tokelau's budget for 2001/02 was to include at least $NZ4.2m. from New Zealand and an estimated $NZ1.7m. to be obtained from local revenues such as fisheries licensing, duty, taxes, philatelic sales, freight charges and interest earned. Tokelau assumed responsibility for the management of its own budgetary affairs in 2003. Since then most of New Zealand's bilateral assistance has been transferred directly to the Territory's budget, thereby enabling Tokelau to finance its recurrent expenditure on services such as transport, education and health. Local revenue was estimated to have reached about $NZ2m. in 2005. Receipts from EEZ fees rose from $NZ286,000 in 2004 to an estimated $NZ569,000 in 2005. Fees from shipping, radio excises and customs duties provide another source of revenue; local receipts from such duties increased from $NZ372,000 in 2004 to an estimated $NZ388,000 in 2005. The sale of postage stamps and souvenir coins (which are legal tender, although New Zealand currency is in general use) also makes a significant contribution to the Territory's income. Receipts from this source increased from $NZ54,000 in 2004 to an estimated $NZ70,000 in 2005. Some revenue is provided by remittances from Tokelauans working abroad, mainly in New Zealand. Official development assistance from New Zealand decreased from $NZ20.3m. in 2013/14 to $NZ14.0m. in 2014/15, although this was supplemented with special project funding. In addition to its links to New Zealand, Tokelau maintains a bilateral development assistance plan with Australia, focused upon human resource development. In 2014/15 Australia was to provide Tokelau with development assistance totalling an estimated $A1.5m. (up from $A800,000 in 2013/14). Consumer prices rose by 4.4% in 2014.

Tokelau's agricultural development has been constrained by the lack of suitable cultivable soil and by the adverse effects of inclement weather. In February 2005 Cyclone Percy caused serious destruction on the islands, coinciding with 'king tides' that flooded the Territory resulting in widespread damage. Moreover, the Territory's small size, remote location, lack of land-based resources and the population's continuing migration to New Zealand have severely hindered economic development. Following the initiation in 2004 of a plan by the Secretariat of the Pacific Community that focused on community-based activities and included the increased exploitation of the islands' giant clam resources, Tokelau's fisheries revenue increased significantly, reaching some $NZ5m. in 2012/13. Meanwhile, in 2004 the Tokelau International Trust Fund (TITF) was established, with assistance from New Zealand and with the objective of enhancing the Territory's prospects for long-term self-reliance. Since 2004 Australia and the United Kingdom have also contributed to the TITF, along with Tokelau itself. Following New Zealand's contribution of $NZ15m. in November 2008, the assets of the TITF totalled $NZ52m., and by December 2014 this figure had risen to $NZ79.7m. In 2013/14 Australia contributed $A384,000 to the TITF. A National Strategic Plan for 2010–15 (entitled 'Healthy and Active Communities with Opportunities for All') was approved by Tokelau, in partnership with New Zealand, in 2010, although the plan was not implemented until 2011. Areas targeted for development included transport, renewable energy, fisheries, good governance, sustainability, education and health. With Tokelau accessible only by sea (via Apia, Samoa), the maintenance of adequate shipping services remained a major focus. New Zealand's provision of a new ferry, with a capacity of 50 passengers, on lease from July 2012 was a very welcome development; the provision of the ferry constituted part of a $NZ17m. transport package offered by the New Zealand Government. Budgetary support from New Zealand for the 2013/14 financial year totalled $NZ11.7m. An $NZ8m. contract to build a new passenger cargo ship, with a passenger capacity of 60, to service the Tokelau–Apia route was awarded to a Bangladeshi company in December 2013; the new vessel was expected to become operational in 2015. The construction of an airstrip, to encourage tourism, has been intermittently considered. Under the Administrative Assistance scheme (part of the Principles of Partnership agreement—see *Contemporary Political History*), the limited capacity of the Tokelau Public Service is supplemented by the resources of various New Zealand government departments through short-term secondments of staff, training or mentoring. In November 2014 the Tokelau

Government signed a memorandum of understanding with the US-owned fish cannery firm Tri Marine International (which opened a new tuna cannery in American Samoa in early 2015) to co-operate in the management of Tokelau's tuna industry to ensure long-term sustainability.

PUBLIC HOLIDAYS

2016: 1 January (New Year's Day), 6 February (Waitangi Day, anniversary of 1840 treaty), 25 March (Good Friday), 28 March (Easter Monday), 25 April (ANZAC Day, anniversary of 1915 landing at Gallipoli), 13 June (Queen's Official Birthday), 26 October (Labour Day), 25 December (Christmas), 26 December (Boxing Day).

Statistical Survey

Source (unless otherwise indicated): Tokelau National Statistical Office, Tokelau Apia Liaison Office, POB 3298, Apia, Samoa; tel. 20822; fax 21761; e-mail tevakai@lesamoa.net; internet www.tokelaunso.tk.

AREA AND POPULATION

Area: Atafu 3.5 sq km; Nukunonu 4.7 sq km; Fakaofo 4.0 sq km; Total 12.2 sq km (4.7 sq miles).

Population: 1,466 at census of 19 October 2006; 1,411 (males 701, females 710) at census of 18 October 2011 (including 226 persons usually resident but absent on census night). *2013* (official estimates at December): 1,383 (males 683, females 700). *By Atoll* (December 2013): Atafu 447; Nukunonu 400; Fakaofo 489; Samoa 47; Total 1,383.

Density (at December 2013): 113.4 per sq km.

Population by Age and Sex (at December 2013): *0–14 years:* 413 (males 213, females 200); *15–64 years:* 852 (males 413, females 439); *65 years and over:* 118 (males 57, females 61); *Total* 1,383 (males 683, females 700).

Births and Deaths (1996): Birth rate 33.1 per 1,000; Death rate 8.2 per 1,000. *2010* (Secretariat of the Pacific Community estimates): Live births 26 (birth rate 22.1 per 1,000); Registered deaths 9 (death rate 7.6 per 1,000) (Source: Pacific Regional Information System). *2011 Census:* Birth rate 22.5 per 1,000.

Life Expectancy (years at birth, 1996, official estimates): Males 68; Females 70. Source: Ministry of Foreign Affairs and Trade, Wellington.

Economically Active Population (2001 census, persons aged 15 years and over): Construction 78; Retail trade 12; Hotels and restaurants 4; Transport 7; Communications 20; Village services 182; Public administration 59; Education 53; Medical 23; Total 438. *2011 Census:* Total in paid employment 489 (males 287, females 202).

HEALTH AND WELFARE

Key Indicators

Access to Water (% of households, 2012): 93.

Access to Sanitation (% of households, 2012): 97.

For sources and definitions, see explanatory note on p. vi.

AGRICULTURE, ETC.

Principal Crops (metric tons, 2013, FAO estimates): Coconuts 4,300; Roots and tubers 200; Bananas 15.

Livestock (year ending September 2013, FAO estimates): Pigs 1,000; Chickens 5,000.

Livestock Products (metric tons, 2013, FAO estimates): Pig meat 20; Chicken meat 5; Hen eggs 8.

Fishing (metric tons, live weight, 2012): Total catch 248.

Source: FAO.

INDUSTRY

Production (1990, estimate): Electric energy 300,000 kWh.

FINANCE

Currency and Exchange Rates: New Zealand currency is legal tender. Tokelau souvenir coins have also been issued. New Zealand currency: 100 cents = 1 New Zealand dollar ($NZ); *Sterling, US Dollar and Euro Equivalents* (31 December 2014): £1 sterling = $NZ1.9936; US $1 = $NZ1.2773; €1 = $NZ1.5508; $NZ100 = £50.16 =

US $78.29 = €64.48. *Average Exchange Rate* ($NZ per US $): 1.2343 in 2012; 1.2194 in 2013; 1.2055 in 2014.

Budget ($NZ, year ending 30 June 1998): *Revenue:* Local 734,950; New Zealand subsidy 4,600,000; Total 5,334,950. *Expenditure:* Total 5,208,449.

Cost of Living (Consumer Price Index at April–June; base: April–June 2012 = 100): All items 100.5 in 2013; 104.9 in 2014.

Development Assistance from New Zealand ($NZ million, estimates): 20.3 in 2012/13; 20.3 in 2013/14; 14.0 in 2014/15.

EXTERNAL TRADE

Principal Commodities ($NZ, 2002): *Imports:* Food and live animals 923,766; Mineral fuels, lubricants, etc. 194,779; Animal and vegetable oils, fats and waxes 50,012; Chemicals and related products 45,429; Manufactured goods 183,488; Total (incl. others) 1,673,389.

COMMUNICATIONS MEDIA

Telephones (2010): 300 main lines in use.

Source: International Telecommunication Union.

EDUCATION

Schools (1999): 3 (one school for all levels on each atoll).

Teachers (2003): Primary 23; Secondary 17.

Pupils (2011 census): Pre-primary 16; Primary 267; Secondary 236; University 78; Other tertiary 48.

Students Overseas (1999): Secondary 22; Tertiary 20.

Pupil-teacher Ratio (primary education, UNESCO estimate): 5.8 in 2002/03 (Source: UNESCO Institute for Statistics).

Directory

The Government

(May 2015)

Administrator: JONATHAN KINGS (took office in Feb. 2011).

FAIPULE

The title of Ulu-O-Tokelau (Head of Tokelau) is held on a one-year rotational basis by each Faipule in turn. At elections held on 23 January 2014 new Faipule were chosen on Atafu and Nukunonu, while the incumbent Faipule was re-elected on Fakaofo. The Faipule of Nukunonu, Sio Perez, became the Ulu-O-Tokelau in February 2015.

Faipule of Fakaofo: FOUA TOLOA.

Faipule of Nukunonu: SIO PEREZ.

Faipule of Atafu: KURESA NASAU.

PULENUKU

At elections held on 23 January 2014 a new Pulenuku (Village Mayor) was chosen on Fakaofo, while the two incumbent Pulenuku on Atafu and Nukunonu were re-elected.

Pulenuku of Fakaofo: MOSE PELASIO.

Pulenuku of Nukunonu: PANAPA SAKARIA.

Pulenuku of Atafu: FAAFETAI TAUMANU.

GOVERNMENT OFFICES

Council for the Ongoing Government of Tokelau: POB 3298, Apia, Samoa; tel. 20822; fax 21761; e-mail tevakai@lesamoa.net; internet www.tokelau.org.nz; Gen. Man. (vacant).

Tokelau Apia Liaison Office/Ofiha o Fehokotakiga Tokelau Ma Apia: 1st Floor, Samoa National Provident Fund Plaza Bldg, Apia, Samoa; tel. 20822; fax 21761; e-mail maka@lesamoa.net; internet www.tokelau-govt.info; responsible for transport, accounting and consular functions; Gen. Man. JOVILISI SUVEINAKAMA.

The Tokelau Public Service has seven departments, divided among the three atolls, with a supervising administrative official located in each village. Two departments are established on each atoll, while the seventh department, the Council for the Ongoing Government of Tokelau (formerly the Council of Faipule), rotates on a yearly basis in conjunction with the position of Ulu-O-Tokelau. Management of the Tokelau Public Service was formally transferred to Tokelau in July 2001.

Legislature

GENERAL FONO

The General Fono, or territorial assembly, is a meeting of 20 delegates representing the Territory, including the Faipule and Pulenuku; it is the highest advisory body and must be consulted by the administration about all policy affecting the Territory. The General Fono has responsibility for the territorial budget and has the power to enact legislation, impose taxes and declare public holidays. The assembly, which comprises seven members from Atafu, seven from Fakoafa and six from Nukunonu, is elected by universal suffrage. The most recent election took place on 23 January 2014. Members of the General Fono elect a Chairman, and hold between three and four sessions a year on the Ulu-O-Tokelau's atoll.

Chairman: IOSUA ALENI.

Judicial System

Tokelau's legislative and judicial systems are based on the Tokelau Islands Act 1948 and subsequent amendments and regulations. The Act provided for a variety of British regulations to continue in force and, where no other legislation applies, the law of England and Wales in 1840 (the year in which British sovereignty over New Zealand was established) was to be applicable. New Zealand statute law applies in Tokelau only if specifically extended there. In 1986 legislation formalized the transfer of High Court civil and criminal jurisdiction from Niue to New Zealand. Most cases are judged by the Commissioner established on each atoll, who has limited jurisdiction in civil and criminal matters. Commissioners are appointed by the New Zealand Governor-General, after consultation with the elders of the atoll.

Commissioner of Fakaofo: PENEHE TULAFONO.

Commissioner of Nukunonu: IOANE TUMUA.

Commissioner of Atafu: FELETI LOPA.

Religion

On Atafu almost all inhabitants are members of the Congregational Christian Church and on Nukunonu all are Roman Catholic, while both denominations are represented on Fakaofo. Some 67% of the total population adhere to the Congregational Christian Church, and 30% to the Roman Catholic Church.

CHRISTIANITY

Roman Catholic Church

The Church is represented in Tokelau by a Mission, established in 1992. There were an estimated 500 adherents at 31 December 2007.

Superior: Mgr OLIVER P. ARO, Catholic Mission, Nukunonu, Tokelau (via Apia, Samoa); tel. 4160; fax 4236; e-mail dr.tovite@clear.net.n3.

Broadcasting and Communications

Each atoll has a radio station to broadcast shipping and weather reports. Radio-telephone provided the main communications link with other areas until the late 1990s. A new telecommunications system established at a cost of US $2.76m. ($1m. of which was provided by New Zealand) and operating through an earth station, linked to a communications satellite, on each atoll, became operational in 1997. A new weekly radio programme, called Vakai, broadcast by Samoa Broadcasting Service to Tokelau's three atolls, was launched in 2004.

TELECOMMUNICATIONS

Telecommunications Tokelau Corporation (TeleTok): Fenuafala, Fakaofo; tel. 3100; fax 3108; e-mail apvitale@clear.net.nz; f. 1996; govt-owned; telephone and internet services; Gen. Man. AUKUSITINO VITALE.

Finance

There are no banks in operation in Tokelau; however, the Office of Tokelau Affairs provides a facility for deposits and withdrawals, and pays interest on accounts. Commercial and other banking facilities are available in Apia, Samoa.

Trade and Industry

A village co-operative store was established on each atoll in 1977. These stores are operated by village management committees, which work with the public service administration to reduce the costs of imported goods. Most imports are purchased from Samoa, with an increasing amount coming from New Zealand and Fiji. Local industries include copra production, woodwork and plaited craft goods, and the processing of tuna. In October 2012, following the installation of 4,032 solar panels (totalling 1 MW) and 1,344 batteries by the New Zealand company PowerSmart, it was announced that Tokelau had the capacity to meet its energy requirements solely through solar power. It was expected, however, that around 7% of the Territory's energy would continue to be provided by generators, which would be powered by locally produced coconut oil.

Transport

There are no roads or motor vehicles. Unscheduled inter-atoll voyages by sea are forbidden because the risk of missing landfall is too great. Passengers and cargo are transported by vessels that anchor off shore, as there are no harbour facilities. The vessel *Forum Tokelau*, operated by Pacific Forum Line, began a monthly service between Tokelau and Apia, Samoa, in 1997. A New Zealand-funded inter-atoll vessel commenced service in 1991, providing the first regular link between the atolls for 40 years. A new ferry, *PB Matua*, with a passenger capacity of up to 50 persons, commenced services between Apia and Tokelau in July 2012. The provision of the ferry (on lease) by the New Zealand Government was part of a range of transport measures, worth a total of $NZ17m., which also included an investigation into the proposed construction of a small coral airstrip on Nukunonu and the development of safe and effective ship-to-shore operations. A new passenger cargo ship, with a passenger capacity of 60, to service the Tokelau–Apia route was expected to become operational in 2015.

Education

Education is provided free of charge, and attendance is virtually 100%. Kindergarten facilities are available for children from the age of three years, while primary education takes place between the ages of five and 14. The provision of an additional year of schooling, for those aged 15, is rotated among the territory's three schools every five years. In 2003 there were 23 primary school teachers and 17 secondary school teachers. Pupil enrolment recorded by the 2011 census totalled 16 at pre-primary level, 267 at primary level, 236 at secondary level, 78 at university level and 48 in other tertiary education. The New Zealand Department of Education provides advisory services and some educational equipment. The Education Department of Samoa organizes daily radio broadcasts. Scholarships are awarded for secondary and tertiary education, and for vocational training, in New Zealand, Australia and other Pacific countries. Link arrangements exist between Tokelau and the Fiji-based University of the South Pacific, which has an outpost on each atoll that is electronically connected. In 2004 a total of 53 Tokelauans over the age of 15 years were studying overseas under the Tokelau Sponsorship Scheme (34 in Samoa, 12 in New Zealand and seven in Fiji). In 2001 there were some 169 Tokelauan pupils enrolled at the Samoa Secondary School. Australia also provides scholarships.

NEW ZEALAND'S ASSOCIATED STATES

New Zealand's two Associated States are the self-governing Cook Islands and Niue, both of which are situated in the Pacific Ocean.

THE COOK ISLANDS

Introductory Survey

LOCATION, CLIMATE, LANGUAGE, RELIGION, FLAG, CAPITAL

The 13 inhabited and two uninhabited islands of the Cook Islands are located in the southern Pacific Ocean and lie between American Samoa, to the west, and French Polynesia, to the east. The islands extend over about 2m. sq km (more than 750,000 sq miles) of ocean, and form two groups: the Northern Cooks, which are all atolls and include Pukapuka, Rakahanga and Manihiki, and the Southern Cooks, including Aitutaki, Mangaia and Rarotonga, which are all volcanic islands. From December to March the climate is warm and humid, with the possibility of severe storms; from April to November the climate is mild and equable. The average annual rainfall on Rarotonga is 2,012 mm (79 in). The official languages are English and Cook Islands Maori (Rarotongan). The principal religion is Christianity, with 49% of the population adhering to the Congregationalist Cook Islands Christian Church, according to the 2011 census. The islands' flag (proportions 1 by 2) displays 15 five-pointed white stars (representing the islands of the group) on a royal blue field, with the United Kingdom's Union Flag as a canton in the upper hoist. The capital is Avarua, on Rarotonga.

CONTEMPORARY POLITICAL HISTORY

Historical Context

The first Europeans to visit the islands were members of a British expedition, led by Capt. James Cook (after whom the islands are named), in 1773. The Cook Islands was proclaimed a British protectorate in 1888, and a part of New Zealand in 1901.

On 4 August 1965 the Cook Islands became a self-governing Territory in free association with New Zealand. The islanders are New Zealand citizens. Sir Albert Henry, leader of the Cook Islands Party (CIP), was elected Premier in 1965 and re-elected in 1971, 1974 and March 1978. However, in July 1978, following an inquiry into alleged electoral malpractice, the Chief Justice disallowed votes cast in the elections to the Legislative Assembly (later renamed Parliament) by Cook Islands expatriates who had been flown from New Zealand, with their fares paid from public funds. The amended ballot gave a majority to the Democratic Party (DP), and its leader, Dr (later Sir) Thomas Davis, was sworn in as Premier. In August 1979 Sir Albert Henry was convicted of conspiracy to defraud, and was formally stripped of his knighthood.

Domestic Political Affairs

In May 1981 the Cook Islands' Constitution was amended to increase the membership of Parliament from 22 to 24, and to extend the parliamentary term from four to five years. In March 1983 Sir Thomas Davis lost power to the CIP, under Geoffrey (later Sir Geoffrey) Henry, cousin of former Premier Sir Albert Henry. However, with one seat already subject to re-election, Geoffrey Henry's majority of three was reduced by the death of one CIP member of Parliament and the transfer of allegiance to the DP by another. Henry resigned in August, and a general election in November returned the DP to power under Davis. In August 1984 Davis formed a coalition Government with the CIP, with Henry as Deputy Prime Minister. In mid-1985, however, Davis dismissed Henry, who had endorsed an unsuccessful motion expressing no confidence in the Government, and Henry's supporters withdrew from the coalition. Henry's successor as Deputy Prime Minister was Dr (later Sir) Terepai Maoate, one of four CIP members who continued to support the Davis Government, in defiance of the CIP central committee.

Davis was forced to resign as Prime Minister in July 1987, after the approval of a parliamentary motion expressing no confidence in his administration. He was succeeded by Dr Pupuke Robati of the DP. Geoffrey Henry again became Prime Minister following a general election victory for the CIP in January 1989. The defection in mid-1990 of a member of Parliament from the DP to the CIP provided the latter with the minimum two-thirds' majority support necessary to amend the Constitution. In August 1991 a constitutional amendment was approved to increase the number of members of Parliament to 25, and at an election to the newly created seat a CIP candidate won.

At a general election in March 1994 the CIP increased its majority, winning 20 seats in Parliament; the DP secured three seats and the Alliance Party (established in 1992 by Norman George) two. Davis, who failed to win a seat, subsequently resigned as leader of the DP. A referendum held simultaneously to the election revealed that a majority of the electorate favoured retaining the Territory's current name (69.8% of voters) and national anthem (80.2%), while 48.5% favoured the retention of its flag.

In August 1997 Parliament approved the Outer Islands Local Government Act, providing for a new budgetary system to allocate funds for projects in the outer islands and for increased powers for local authorities, with the aim of significantly reducing central government administration of the outer islands. As part of the plan, three new government bodies were elected in April 1998. Meanwhile, in December 1997 the Ministry of Public Works, Survey, Housing, Water Supply and Environment Services was closed down for exceeding its budget. The minister responsible, Tom Marsters, resigned in protest against the closure, which resulted in the loss of more than 100 public servants' jobs, problems with the supply of utilities (particularly water) and the suspension of several development projects.

At the legislative elections of June 1999 the CIP won 11 of the 25 seats in Parliament, the Democratic Alliance Party (DAP, a grouping that included the DP) 10 seats and the New Alliance Party (NAP, formerly the Alliance Party) four seats. Sir Geoffrey Henry of the CIP was reappointed Prime Minister and formed a new Cabinet, following the establishment of a political coalition with the NAP, the leader of which, Norman George, became Deputy Prime Minister. However, three members of the CIP subsequently left the party to form a coalition with the DAP, in protest against the alliance with the NAP, and at the end of July Henry resigned and was replaced by one of the dissident CIP members, Dr Joe Williams. Williams was confirmed as the new Prime Minister by 13 votes to 12 in a parliamentary vote of confidence. Williams' appointment provoked a public protest in Rarotonga, exacerbated by general discontent at the nomination of a Prime Minister whose parliamentary constituency was outside the Cook Islands (having been elected to the seat reserved for non-resident voters). The result in the legislative elections of the contest for the Pukapuka seat, which had been won by former Prime Minister Inatio Akaruru by just one vote, was challenged by the DAP. The Court of Appeal subsequently declared the result invalid, stripping the Government of its one-seat majority. The result of a by-election held in September to decide the Pukapuka seat was again said to be invalid and a further by-election was scheduled. The Government became a minority administration in October when the Prime Minister dismissed Norman George and the Minister of Education, following their defection to the opposition. In November Williams resigned, shortly before a vote of no confidence was to be tabled against him by Dr Terepai Maoate, now the leader of the opposition DAP. Maoate won the vote by 14 votes to 11 and was appointed Prime Minister, forming a new coalition Government with the NAP. He subsequently reappointed Norman George to the post of Deputy Prime Minister.

In early 2000 the islands of Penrhyn, Pukapuka, Rakahanga and Manihiki expressed their desire to become fully devolved and to take sole control over areas such as administration, public expenditure and justice. In response, the Government pledged gradually to phase out the Ministry of Outer Islands Development, as well as the post of Government Representative in the outer islands.

In July 2001 Norman George was again dismissed from the position of Deputy Prime Minister, this time owing to Maoate's belief that George was attempting to undermine him. He was replaced by Dr Robert Woonton. However, Woonton was also highly critical of Maoate's leadership. In late 2001 the rift between the Prime Minister and his Cabinet widened. Woonton announced his resignation, which Maoate refused to accept. This led to a motion of no confidence in the Prime Minister, which he only narrowly survived. In February 2002 Maoate lost a second motion of no confidence, and he was replaced by Woonton. In an extensive ministerial reorganization Sir Geoffrey Henry returned to the Cabinet as Deputy Prime Minister.

In November 2002 Parliament approved a constitutional amendment abolishing the requirement for electoral candidates to reside in the islands for a qualifying period of three months. This action was widely interpreted as a way of retaining the overseas voters' parliamentary seat for the CIP leader, Dr Joe Williams, who lived permanently in New Zealand. In the same month the CIP and the DP formed a coalition Government (the fifth such coalition since the previous election), which left Norman George, who had been recently dismissed from his cabinet position, as the sole opposition member of Parliament. The Government's action prompted a demonstration outside the parliament building by some 150 people, organized by a recently formed organization, the Group for Political Change. The protesters claimed that the virtual absence of an opposition constituted an erosion of democracy and appealed to the Prime Minister to commit to an early general election. However, in January 2003 the CIP was ousted from the coalition. The continued political manoeuvring was widely denounced for creating a climate of instability in the islands. Public dissatisfaction with the situation resulted in the presentation of a petition to the Government in March signed by a significant percentage of the population; the petition demanded, *inter alia*, a reduction in the number of members of Parliament, the introduction of a shorter parliamentary term and the abolition of the overseas seat. In the same month businessman Teariki Heather announced the formation of a new political party, the Cook Islands National. In September legislation was approved providing for the abolition of the overseas seat and for a referendum (to be held concurrently with the next general election) on a proposal to shorten the parliamentary term from five years to four. (An earlier referendum on this issue in 1999 had narrowly failed to receive the support of the two-thirds' majority required to amend the Constitution.) In November 2003 Dr Terepai Maoate, who had been appointed Deputy Prime Minister earlier in the year, and the Minister of Justice, Tangata Vavia, resigned following an unsuccessful attempt by Maoate to propose a motion of no confidence in the Government.

The elections of 2004 and 2006

At a general election in September 2004 the DP won 14 of the 24 seats, the CIP secured nine and an independent candidate took the remaining seat. Prime Minister Robert Woonton regained his seat by only four votes, amid accusations that he had secured the support of some voters through bribery. In the concurrent referendum 82.3% of participating voters favoured the shortening of the parliamentary term from five years to four. The period immediately after the election was characterized by political manoeuvring and the initiation of several legal cases challenging the outcome in a number of constituencies. In November Woonton announced that the DP was to form a coalition government with the CIP. This decision was widely opposed within the DP, and prompted the resignation of the Deputy Prime Minister, Aunty Mau Munokoa. Further controversy was caused by the appointment of Norman George to the position of Speaker. In December, with the DP effectively divided over Woonton's actions, Jim Marurai, of the minority Democratic Tumu Party, was elected Prime Minister and a coalition was formed between his party and the CIP. It was understood that Marurai would serve as Prime Minister for the first two years of the parliamentary term and would then be replaced by Sir Geoffrey Henry of the CIP. However, in August 2005 Henry was dismissed from the coalition Government and replaced by DP leader Dr Terepai Maoate. In September two further CIP cabinet ministers were dismissed and replaced by DP members. Marurai declared that the coalition had been dissolved, claiming that the action followed threats to his leadership.

The islands suffered considerable damage in February and March 2005 when five cyclones struck. The resultant damage to housing, infrastructure and crops was estimated at $NZ25m. In March 2006 Woonton, who had previously been appointed as the islands' High Commissioner to New Zealand, was dismissed from that post, following allegations that he had been involved in an attempt to oust the islands' Government.

In July 2006 a by-election victory for the opposition CIP gave it a parliamentary majority, prompting the Queen's Representative, Sir Frederick Goodwin, to dissolve the legislature and to call an early election. Provisional results of the election, held on 26 September, indicated that the DP had secured 15 of the 24 parliamentary seats and the CIP seven, with one seat being taken by an independent candidate. Henry Puna, who had succeeded Sir Geoffrey Henry as leader of the CIP, failed to retain his seat. A by-election to resolve the tied result in the remaining constituency resulted in victory for the CIP candidate in November. In the following month it was announced that a by-election would also be held in Titikaveka after the eligibility of the winning candidate, Robert Wigmore of the DP, was called into question. Wigmore won the Titikaveka by-election in February 2007, thus taking the final result of the 2006 election to 15 seats for the DP and eight for the CIP, along with one independent. Jim Marurai, who had returned to the DP, thus retained the position of Prime Minister, although Maoate continued as leader of the DP. In August 2007 Wilkie Rasmussen, the cabinet member responsible for foreign affairs, among other portfolios, was elected deputy leader of the DP, having left the CIP prior to the 2006 election.

Recent developments: the elections of 2010 and 2014

Following the dismissal from the Cabinet of Wilkie Rasmussen in July 2009, on the grounds that he had allegedly colluded with members of the opposition in order to establish a new government (claims that were denied by Rasmussen), the foreign affairs portfolio was reassigned to the Deputy Prime Minister, Sir Terepai Maoate. However, in December Prime Minister Jim Marurai dismissed Maoate owing to his role in an abortive deal to purchase a fuel depot, which had lost the Government some $NZ2m. Three DP ministers resigned in protest against Maoate's dismissal. In the subsequent cabinet reorganization in January 2010, Robert Wigmore became Deputy Prime Minister and was also allocated responsibility for foreign affairs. Rasmussen was reappointed to the Cabinet, securing the finance portfolio, among other responsibilities.

In February 2010 the island of Aitutaki was devastated by Cyclone Pat, which damaged up to 90% of the island's housing and disabled communications and electricity lines. Following the declaration of a state of disaster, in March the New Zealand Government pledged $NZ5.5m. in reconstruction aid. The Cook Islands Government was censured for the slow pace of the recovery effort, and, despite demands from the DP and the CIP for Marurai to recall Parliament so that official approval could be given to the New Zealand aid programme, the Prime Minister controversially refused to reconvene the legislature until September, apparently owing to a threat of a motion of no confidence being tabled by the opposition.

Following a lengthy trial on corruption charges dating back to 1999–2002, Norman George was found not guilty in May 2010. George alleged that the charges against him had been politically motivated and accused Maoate of having used his former position as Attorney-General to influence the police investigation.

In an escalating dispute within the DP regarding the dismissal from government of Sir Terepai Maoate in December 2009, all six members of the Cabinet, including Marurai, were expelled from the party in March 2010. However, at a conference held in June, the six were readmitted to the party; Wigmore was elected party Leader in place of Maoate, with Rasmussen returned as his deputy. In September 2010 Maoate was defeated in his bid to secure election as the DP candidate for the Rarotonga seat of Ngatangiia; the former premier subsequently announced that he would be contesting the election as an independent candidate.

Meanwhile, in August 2010 Marurai announced that the next legislative elections were to be held in November, and that a popular referendum on parliamentary reform, comprising a proposal to reduce the number of parliamentary seats, was to take place concurrently. The participation in the elections of some 16 independents (12 more than in the 2006 poll), together with the emergence of, and the fielding of six candidates by, Te Kura O Te Au, represented a significant challenge to the traditional two-party contest between the CIP and the DP. Established earlier in the year, Te Kura O Te Au pledged to pursue political reform that remained 'in tune with spiritual and cultural values'.

However, in the event, the elections held on 17 November 2010 were, as in previous polls, entirely dominated by the two main parties. Not unexpectedly, given the fractious past 12 months experienced by the incumbent DP, the CIP secured a commanding victory, winning 16 of the 24 seats, and thus a two-thirds' majority, while the DP garnered just eight seats. Turnout, at about 78%, was considerably lower than in previous polls. According to the results of the referendum on parliamentary reform, 59.2% of voters cast their ballot in support of the proposal to reduce the number of seats, thus falling short of the two-thirds' majority required to force Parliament to take action.

CIP Leader Henry Puna, who regained the parliamentary seat that he had lost in 2006, was inaugurated as Prime Minister on 1 December 2010. On the following day he announced the composition of his Cabinet, which included Tom Marsters as Deputy Prime Minister. Norman George, who had publicly questioned the competence of Puna shortly after the election, was not included. Ministerial portfolios were assigned to the cabinet ministers a few days later, with Puna taking, *inter alia*, the portfolios of justice and of energy and renewable energy. Puna identified the national economy as the main priority of the new Government. Sir Geoffrey Henry was appointed parliamentary Speaker in February 2011.

Government targets announced in July 2011 envisaged 50% of the Cook Islands' energy needs being met by renewable sources (solar and wind power) by 2015, rising to 100% by 2020. Funding sources for the required renewable energy projects, which were presented as an effort to reduce carbon emissions and thereby to stem the pace of climate change, were to include the People's Republic of China, Japan and the UN Development Programme.

In February 2012, as a result of the ill health of the DP Leader, Robert Wigmore, the party's Deputy Leader, Wilkie Rasmussen, was appointed leader of the opposition. Following Wigmore's death in April, Rasmussen succeeded him as Leader of the DP and was confirmed in this position at a party conference in August. Meanwhile, Sir Geoffrey Henry died in May and was replaced as parliamentary Speaker by the Secretary-General of the Cook Islands Red Cross, Niki Rattle. The appointment of Rattle was criticized by the opposition, which held that, although not stipulated by the Constitution, an elected member of Parliament should have been afforded the position.

Allegations made by a New Zealand-based magazine in February 2013 that the Cook Islands Trading Company, which imports the carbonated beverage Coca-Cola, had secured an arrangement during the mid-1980s under which its import duties had been reduced until 2009 continued to generate considerable controversy in early 2014. The so-called 'Colagate' deal was reported to have cost the Cook Islands millions of dollars in lost revenue, and appeals for the establishment of an anti-corruption agency within the Cook Islands to investigate such cases attracted significant popular support. In March the Cook Islands Public Accounts Committee announced that a formal inquiry into the legality of the arrangement, and the circumstances surrounding it, was to commence in the following month; however, as a result of the holding of an early general election in April, the inquiry was delayed indefinitely.

Meanwhile, in June 2013 Deputy Prime Minister Tom Marsters was appointed to replace Sir Frederick Goodwin as Queen's Representative. Masters subsequently resigned from the Cabinet in July to assume his new role; Teariki Heather was appointed as the new Deputy Prime Minister in December. In August cabinet minister Teina Bishop resigned from government following allegations of corruption and bribery surrounding his management of the marine resources portfolio; the marine resources portfolio was assumed by Puna. Bishop was reinstated in the Cabinet in January 2014, with responsibility for the education and tourism portfolios.

On 17 April 2014 Prime Minister Puna instructed Queen's Representative Marsters to dissolve Parliament in preparation for early legislative elections. Teina Bishop, who was accused by Puna of destabilizing the Government, resigned from the Cabinet on 18 April and subsequently left the CIP to form a new party—the One Cook Islands Movement (OCIM). The DP claimed that the Prime Minister had called early elections to avoid a no-confidence vote in Parliament, an allegation which Puna denied. In the legislative elections, which were held on 9 July, the CIP retained its parliamentary majority by a slim margin, winning 13 of the 24 contested seats, and Puna remained in the premiership. The DP secured eight seats—although Rasmussen lost control of his constituency—and the OCIM won two. The electoral turnout was a reported 73.3%. The reinstated CIP Government was to function in an acting capacity pending the outcome of a number of petitions presented by the opposition regarding the elections. An electoral petition filed by the DP accusing Puna of having allegedly bribed voters in the run-up to the elections was dismissed by the High Court in September. However, later that month following a decision by the High Court to uphold another petition by the DP—this one disputing the result in the Tamarua constituency, the number of seats held by the CIP was reduced from 13 to 12 (removing the overall majority of the ruling party), while the number of seats held by the DP was increased from eight to nine. Furthermore, following a recount in November of the votes posted in the Mitiaro constituency in July (when a tie between the CIP and the DP had been declared), the seat was awarded to the DP, which now controlled 10 seats in Parliament. In December the Court of Appeal ruled that the election of the Minister of Education, Moana Ioane, in the Aitutaki constituency of Vaipae-Tautu was void as he had been shown to have bribed a voter. This decision reduced the CIP to a minority Government with only 11 seats. In mid-March 2015 the defection of the DP member of Parliament Albert Nicholas to the CIP resulted in the parliamentary strength of the ruling party reverting to 12 seats. Later in the month Nicholas was appointed Minister of Internal Affairs in place of Nandi Glassie, who was given responsibility for the justice portfolio. At the by-election for the constituency of Vaipae-Tautu, which took place at the end of March, the CIP's Moana Ioane won the seat, finally giving the governing party a majority with 13 seats.

The Offshore Financial Sector

A reported increase in the number of Russian nationals opening accounts in the Cook Islands led to allegations in early 1999 that the islands' offshore financial centre was being used extensively by criminal organizations for 'laundering' the proceeds of their activities. The claims were vigorously denied by banking officials. However, in June 2000 the naming of the islands by the Paris-based Financial Action Task Force (FATF, see p. 451) as one of a number of countries and territories that had failed to co-operate in regional efforts to combat money-laundering, along with the islands' identification by the Organisation for Economic Co-operation and Development (OECD, see p. 377) as a tax haven that lacked financial transparency, led to increased international pressure on the Government to implement stricter controls over its offshore financial centre. Consequently, legislation was approved in August of that year providing for the creation of the Money Laundering Authority and the introduction of new regulations aimed at reducing criminal activity in the sector. In February 2005 the Cook Islands was finally removed from the FATF list of non-co-operative countries and territories.

In February 2009 the Government introduced legislation into Parliament to abolish offshore banks in the Cook Islands, arguing that the cost of regulating such organizations outweighed any financial benefits that they brought to the country. The Banking Amendment Bill, which provided for the closure of offshore banks operating without the requisite domestic licence, was approved by the islands' Parliament in August 2010. However, in April 2009 OECD had included the Cook Islands on its so-called 'grey list' of countries that, while committed to the internationally agreed tax standard, had yet to implement substantial measures to combat tax evasion. In response, the Government sought to negotiate agreements on tax information exchange with other nations, and in September 2010 the Cook Islands was removed from the 'grey list', having signed the requisite 12th such agreement, with France.

Foreign Affairs

Since becoming a self-governing Territory in 1965, the Cooks Islands has developed a distinct identity in its external relations. Although not a sovereign state, by early 2015 it had established diplomatic relations with more than 40 countries and international organizations, including most recently with the Federated States of Micronesia and Tonga in late 2014—thereby concluding the Cook Islands' formalization of diplomatic relations with all of its fellow member states of the Pacific Islands Forum (see p. 413).

In August 1985 eight members of the South Pacific Forum (subsequently restyled the Pacific Island Forum), including the Cook Islands, signed a treaty on Rarotonga, designating a 'nuclear-free' zone in the South Pacific. The treaty imposed a ban on the manufacture, testing, storage and use of nuclear weapons, and the dumping of nuclear waste, in the region.

In January 1986, following the rift between New Zealand and the USA in respect of the ANZUS (see p. 459) security arrangements, Sir Thomas Davis declared the Cook Islands a neutral party, because he considered that New Zealand (which has control over the Cook Islands' defence and foreign policy) was no longer in a position to defend the islands. The proclamation of neutrality meant that the Cook Islands would not enter into a military relationship with any foreign power, and, in particular, would prohibit visits by US warships. Visits by US naval vessels were allowed to resume by the Government of Geoffrey (later Sir Geoffrey) Henry. In November 2007 the Cook Islands and the USA signed agreements on maritime surveillance and anti-trafficking measures. In August 2012 Hillary Clinton became the first US Secretary of State to visit the Cook Islands when she attended the summit meeting of the Pacific Islands Forum in Rarotonga. Many observers held that the increased involvement of the USA in the Pacific region was an attempt to offset the growing diplomatic and economic influence of the People's Republic of China in that area of the world.

In 1991 the Cook Islands signed a treaty of friendship and co-operation with France, covering economic development, trade and surveillance of the islands' exclusive economic zone (EEZ). The establishment of closer relations with France was widely regarded as an expression of the Cook Islands Government's dissatisfaction with existing arrangements with New Zealand. However, relations deteriorated when the French Government resumed its programme of nuclear weapons testing at Mururoa Atoll, French Polynesia, in September 1995. Henry was fiercely critical of the decision and dispatched a *vaka* (traditional voyaging canoe) with a crew of Cook Islands' traditional warriors to protest near the test site. The tests were concluded in January 1996. Full diplomatic relations with France were established in 2000.

Meanwhile, the islands established diplomatic relations at ambassadorial level with the People's Republic of China in July 1997. In November 1998 Henry made an official visit to China, during which the two countries signed a bilateral trade agreement and each conferred the status of 'most favoured nation' on the other. Henry stated that the move constituted a further attempt by his Government to reduce the islands' dependence on New Zealand. During 2008–09 the Government accepted loans totalling nearly US $40m. from China, much of which was to fund preparations for the 2009 South Pacific Mini Games, which were to be hosted by the Cook Islands in September of that year. The Government's acceptance of the loans resulted in threats of legal action from the local Chamber of Commerce and prompted demands for a public inquiry from the opposition, which claimed that the Cook Islands could not afford to repay such large sums of money. In March 2010 Minister of Finance Wilkie Rasmussen stated that the Government was extremely reluctant to accept a $NZ37.5m. Chinese loan for projects to upgrade the road and water systems in Rarotonga owing to the islands' already high external debt levels. During a visit to China by Teina Bishop, the Minister of Marine Resources, in November 2011, a fishing agreement was signed under the terms of which Chinese vessels would be allowed to conduct exploratory fishing for tuna and swordfish in the Cook Islands' EEZ for a period of three years. The Cook Islands was expected to earn a total of $NZ2.4m. from the agreement. The Cook

Islands and China also signed an agreement providing for Chinese assistance, in the form of funding and labour, for the pearl-farming industry on the islands. In August 2012 a major infrastructure project to improve Rarotonga's water mains system was announced; of the project's total estimated cost of around $NZ60m., the majority was to be funded by a $NZ15m. grant from New Zealand and a $NZ32m. loan from China. The joint undertaking was particularly notable for the fact that it represented the first time that China had entered into partnership with a developed country to deliver an aid and development project. The project was officially launched in February 2014.

In December 2010 the New Zealand Minister of Foreign Affairs, Murray McCully, made an official visit to the Cook Islands, where he met with incoming Prime Minister Henry Puna and his new Cabinet; issues discussed were reported to have included New Zealand's programme of development assistance to the islands, with education, health care and tourism identified as the main priorities for assistance. Further bilateral talks were held in the Cook Islands in early 2011, at which the two Governments agreed to establish regular ministerial-level consultations to advance matters of mutual interest; the first Joint Ministerial Forum was held in the Cook Islands in May. In August 2012 McCully and the New Zealand Prime Minister, John Key, both attended the Pacific Islands Forum summit in Rarotonga. In August 2013 McCully announced the provision of additional funding to the Cook Islands, for the upgrade of sanitation services on the islands. In the following month the New Zealand Government announced a five-year, $NZ5m. initiative intended to assist five Pacific states vulnerable to water shortages, including the Cook Islands, better to manage their fresh water resources. The third Joint Ministerial Forum was held in Aitutaki in February 2014.

In September 2008 the Cook Islands became a member of the International Maritime Organization (IMO) after securing the approval of two-thirds of the organization's members, rendering it eligible for IMO funding and assistance. In April 2009 the Cook Islands Government submitted a claim, via the UN Secretary-General, to the Commission on the Limits of the Continental Shelf to extend its seabed boundaries by over 400,000 sq km. The application, the first such claim to be lodged by a Pacific island nation, was motivated by the Government's desire to gain access to potential reserves of petroleum, gas and manganese. A sub-commission was established, in mid-2011, to examine the application; as of early 2015, it had yet to issue its recommendations.

In November 2011 the Cook Islands was one of eight Pacific states and territories that jointly established the Polynesian Leaders Group (see p. 463), which was widely viewed as being intended to provide a counterweight to the Melanesian Spearhead Group. The first formal meeting of the Group, which pledged to enhance co-operation among its members across a wide range of fields, including trade and investment, education, climate change and health, was held in Rarotonga, on the sidelines of the Pacific Islands Forum summit, in August 2012. During the summit, Prime Minister Henry Puna announced the establishment of a shark sanctuary in the EEZ around the Cook Islands; the sanctuary, which was officially inaugurated in December, was contiguous with a sanctuary set up by French Polynesia in the same month.

CONSTITUTION AND GOVERNMENT

Under the Constitution of 1965, the Cook Islands is an internally self-governing state in free association with New Zealand, which is responsible for the Cook Islands' external affairs and defence (although the Territory has progressively assumed control over much of its foreign policy). Executive authority is vested in the British monarch, who is head of state, and is exercised through her official representative; a representative of the New Zealand Government (redesignated High Commissioner in 1994) resides on Rarotonga. Executive government is carried out by the Cabinet, consisting of the Prime Minister and between five and seven other ministers. The Cabinet is collectively responsible to the Parliament, which is formed of 24 members (decreased from 25 in 2004, following the abolition of the seat for a member chosen by non-resident voters) who are elected by universal adult suffrage every four years (reduced from five years by a referendum in 2004). The House of Ariki, which comprises up to 24 members who are hereditary chiefs, can advise the Government, but has no legislative powers. The Koutu Nui is a similar body, comprising sub-chiefs. Each of the main islands has an elected island council, and a government representative who is appointed by the Prime Minister.

REGIONAL AND INTERNATIONAL CO-OPERATION

The Cook Islands has membership of the Pacific Community (see p. 410) and the Pacific Islands Forum (see p. 413) and is an associate member of the UN Economic and Social Commission for Asia and the Pacific (ESCAP, see p. 30). In 1999 the Cook Islands was granted observer status at the Lomé Conventions with the European Union (subsequently superseded by the Cotonou Agreement, see p. 321). In 2011 the Cook Islands was one of eight founding members of the Polynesian Leaders Group (see p. 463).

ECONOMIC AFFAIRS

In 2013, according to provisional official figures, the Cook Islands' gross domestic product (GDP), measured at current prices, totalled $NZ360.0m., and GDP per head was $NZ19,357. During 2004–13, it was estimated, the population decreased at an average annual rate of 1.0%, and GDP per head decreased, in real terms, by an average of 3.6% per year. Overall GDP decreased, in real terms, at an estimated average annual rate of 0.2% in 2004–13. According to revised official figures, GDP contracted by 1.7% in the year ending 30 June 2013 and by a further 1.2% in 2013/14.

According to provisional official figures, agriculture (including fishing) contributed 6.2% of GDP in 2013. The sector engaged 4.3% of the employed labour force in 2011, according to that year's census. Cash crops include coconuts and tropical fruits such as mangoes, pineapples, bananas and papayas. Cassava, sweet potatoes and vegetables are cultivated as food crops. Pigs and poultry are the main livestock kept. The sale of fishing licences to foreign fleets provides an important source of income. Revenue from the export of fresh and chilled fish reached an estimated $NZ12.1m. in 2013, providing 93.4% of export earnings. Pearl oyster farming is also an important industry. Receipts from pearl exports totalled an estimated $NZ100,000 (equivalent to 1.1% of total export earnings) in 2013. The real GDP of the agricultural sector (including pearl farming) increased by an average of 0.3% per year during 2004–13. According to provisional figures, the sector's GDP increased by 3.2% in 2012 and by a further 14.9% in 2013.

Industry (comprising mining and quarrying, manufacturing, construction and utilities) provided 6.6% of GDP in 2013, according to provisional figures. The sector engaged 11.7% of the employed labour force in 2011. Industrial GDP decreased, in real terms, by an average of 1.9% per year during 2004–13; according to provisional figures, sectoral GDP increased by 10.7% in 2012, but decreased by 26.6% in 2013.

The manufacturing sector engaged 3.4% of the employed labour force in 2011. The manufacturing and mining sectors together accounted for 2.4% of GDP in 2013, according to provisional figures. The real GDP of manufacturing and mining decreased by an average of 3.0% per year during 2004–13. According to provisional figures, the combined GDP of the two sub-sectors declined by 7.9% in 2012 and by a further 2.5% in 2013.

According to provisional figures, construction contributed 2.9% of GDP in 2013; the sector engaged 5.9% of the employed labour force in 2011. The GDP of the construction sector decreased at an average annual rate of 2.0% during 2004–13; according to provisional figures, the sector's GDP increased by 29.7% in 2012, but decreased by 47.2% in 2013.

The islands depend on imports for their energy requirements. According to the Asian Development Bank (ADB), fuel imports were equivalent to 28% of GDP in 2011. Mineral fuels and lubricants accounted for 17.8% of total import costs in 2013. In July 2011 the Government announced targets of 50% of the Cook Islands' energy needs being met by renewable sources (solar and wind power) by 2015, and 100% by 2020. A 6-MW solar power project was approved by the ADB in September 2013; the US $500m. project, to be funded by the Japan Fund for Poverty Reduction, would generate an estimated 8.6 GWh per year, providing a significant boost to a power system that in 2011 generated 33.8 GWh in total.

According to provisional figures, service industries contributed 87.2% of GDP in 2013. The sector engaged 84.0% of the employed labour force in 2011. The GDP of the services sector increased, in real terms, at an average annual rate of 0.1% in 2004–13; according to provisional figures, services GDP increased by 2.7% in 2012, but decreased by 3.3% in 2013. Tourism expanded considerably from the late 1980s, and generated revenue of an estimated US $110m. in 2010. According to provisional figures, visitor arrivals rose slightly from 121,158 in 2013 to 121,458 in 2014. According to provisional figures, the restaurants and hotels sector contributed 18.0% of GDP in 2013. Offshore banking, introduced to the islands in 1982, expanded rapidly, with more than 2,000 international companies registered by 1987. In August 2010, however, legislation to abolish offshore banks operating without a domestic licence was approved by Parliament; the banks concerned were given 12 months in which to cease their operations. According to provisional figures, the financial and business services sector provided 9.4% of GDP in 2013. The sector engaged 5.3% of the employed labour force (including persons occupied in the real estate sector) in 2011. Significant revenue is provided by remittances from emigrants (who outnumber the residents of the islands more than three-fold).

In 2013 the cost of imports amounted to $NZ138.9m. (according to official estimates), while export revenue totalled some $NZ13.0m., resulting in a trade deficit of $NZ125.9m. The principal exports in 2013 were fresh and chilled fish, and pearls. The principal imports in that year were food and live animals, machinery and transport equipment, mineral fuels and lubricants, basic manufactures, miscellaneous manufactured articles, beverages and tobacco, and chemicals. The principal source of imports in 2013 was New Zealand (which supplied 70.2% of the total). Australia was also a significant source of imports. Japan (which purchased 38.6% of the total) was the principal market for exports in that year.

In the financial year ending June 2014 the budget deficit was equivalent to 3.0% of GDP, according to the ADB. Development assistance is provided mainly by New Zealand and Australia. New Zealand contributed a total of $NZ25m. of official development assistance to the Cook Islands during 2013/14, and assistance in 2014/15 was forecast to be $NZ28m. In order to improve the effectiveness of their respective aid packages, New Zealand manages Australia's annual development assistance contribution of $A2m. to the Cook Islands through a delegated co-operation arrangement which was drawn up in 2004. It was estimated by the ADB that at the end of 2013 the islands' external debt stood at US $79m. and that the cost of debt servicing in 2012 was equivalent to 64.6% of the value of exports of goods and services. The annual rate of inflation in Rarotonga averaged 3.6% in 2006–14; according to the ADB, consumer prices increased by 2.6% in 2012/13 and by 1.6% in 2013/14. According to the census of 2011, the unemployment rate was 8.2% of the total labour force.

The National Sustainable Development Plan and the 20-year Infrastructure Master Plan, which were announced in 2007, envisaged substantial capital expenditure. In October 2009, following the deterioration in global economic conditions, an economic recovery programme, which included support for vulnerable families and funding for infrastructural projects, was implemented. The economy has become heavily dependent on tourism, despite concerns that the Cook Islands might be unable to sustain such rapid development in the longer term. The islands' Government continues to subsidize Air New Zealand flights on the route between Los Angeles, USA, and Rarotonga, as well as a weekly direct flight from the Australian city of Sydney, which was introduced in 2011. According to the ADB, visitor arrivals increased by 1.6% in 2013/14, to around 123,000. The Government had earlier set the rather optimistic target of an increase in annual arrivals to 150,000 by 2016. Largely attributable to a decline in capital investments caused by delays in the implementation of development projects, GDP contracted by 1.7% in 2012/13 and by a further 1.2% in 2013/14, according to revised official figures. However, the ADB forecast that GDP would return to positive growth, of 2.1%, in 2014/15 as development projects progressed, before recording a slight contraction in the following year as the projects were completed. Fisheries and pearls typically account for around three-quarters of total export earnings. The sector expanded by 9.8% in 2012, fuelled by a strong performance in the fisheries industry; however, the value of pearl exports continued to decline, although it was hoped that the downward trend might be stemmed by the implementation of Chinese-funded development programmes that aimed to double pearl output by 2015. Inflation eased from the latter half of 2012, in line with declining international commodity prices, falling from 2.6% in 2012/13 to 1.6% in 2013/14. The Government continued to run a budgetary deficit, although it narrowed slightly from the equivalent of 3.8% of GDP in 2012/13 to 3.0% of GDP in 2013/14. However, as a result of the Government's continuing expansionary fiscal policies, the deficit was forecast to increase to 7.3% of GDP in 2014/15. Improved tax revenue collection and lower fuel prices in 2013/14 were offset by a 32.6% increase in total expenditure, compared with 2012/13. Tax collection was boosted by a series of tax reforms introduced in December 2013, including an increase in the rate of value-added tax, from 12.5% to 15.0%, effective from 1 April 2014. In November the Pacific Island Forum Fisheries Agency signed an agreement under which it would receive some US $90m. from the US Government and US tuna industry in exchange for 8,300 fishing days in 2015. The Cook Islands was expected to earn an estimated US $10m. annually from the deal.

PUBLIC HOLIDAYS

2016: 1 January (New Year's Day), 2 January (Second day of New Year), 25 March (Good Friday), 28 March (Easter Monday), 24 April (for ANZAC Day, anniversary of 1915 landing at Gallipoli), 13 June (Queen's Official Birthday), 6 July (Ra o te Ui Ariki—Anniversary of the Establishment of the House of Ariki), 4 August (Constitution Day), 26 October (Cook Islands Gospel Day), 25 December (Christmas), 26 December (Boxing Day).

Statistical Survey

Sources (unless otherwise stated): Cook Islands Statistics Office, Ministry of Finance and Economic Management, POB 41, Rarotonga; tel. 29511; fax 21511; e-mail info@stats.gov.ck; internet www

.stats.gov.ck; Prime Minister's Department, Government of the Cook Islands, Avarua, Rarotonga; tel. 29300; fax 22856.

AREA AND POPULATION

Area: 236.7 sq km (91.4 sq miles).

Population (resident population): 15,324 at census of 1 December 2006; 14,974 (males 7,490, females 7,484) at census of 1 December 2011. *By Island* (2011 census): Rarotonga 10,572; Aitutaki 1,771; Atiu 468; Mangaia 562; Manihiki 238; Mauke 300; Mitiaro 189; Nassau 73; Palmerston (Avarua) 60; Penrhyn (Tongareva) 213; Pukapuka 451; Rakahanga 77; Total 14,974. Note: The enumerated totals, including visitors temporarily resident on census night, were 19,342 in 2006 and 17,794 in 2011. *Mid-2014* (official estimate): 13,500.

Density (at mid-2014): 57.0 per sq km.

Population by Age and Sex (resident population at 2011 census): *0–14 years:* 4,332 (males 2,220, females 2,112); *15–64 years:* 9,300 (males 4,629, females 4,671); *65 years and over:* 1,342 (males 641, females 701); *Total* 14,974 (males 7,490, females 7,484).

Population by Ethnic Group (resident population at 2011 census): Cook Island Maori 12,180; Part Cook Island Maori 1,005; Other 1,789; *Total* 14,974. Note: Classification of ethnicity reflects national census methodology.

Births, Marriages and Deaths (2013): Registered live births 256 (birth rate 18.3 per 1,000); Registered marriages 843 (marriage rate 6.0 per 1,000); Registered deaths 115 (death rate 8.2 per 1,000).

Life Expectancy (years at birth, WHO estimates): 76 (males 73; females 78) in 2012. Source: WHO, *World Health Statistics*.

Economically Active Population (resident population aged 15 years and over, 2011 census): Agriculture, hunting, forestry and fishing 297; Mining and quarrying 70; Manufacturing 270; Electricity, gas and water 66; Construction 409; Trade, restaurants and hotels 2,539; Transport, storage and communications 524; Financing, insurance, real estate and business services 368; Community, social and personal services 2,395; *Total employed* 6,938 (males 3,708, females 3,230); *Unemployed* 616 (males 331, females 285); *Total labour force* 7,554 (males 4,039, females 3,515). *Mid-2015* (estimates): Agriculture, etc. 2,000; Total labour force 9,000. Source: FAO.

HEALTH AND WELFARE

Key Indicators

Total Fertility Rate (children per woman, 2012): 2.4.

Under-5 Mortality Rate (per 1,000 live births, 2012): 11.

Physicians (per 1,000 head, 2009): 2.9.

Hospital Beds (per 1,000 head, 2005): 6.3.

Health Expenditure (2011): US $ per head (PPP): 404.

Health Expenditure (2011): % of GDP: 3.6.

Health Expenditure (2011): public (% of total): 91.0.

Access to Sanitation (% of persons, 2012): 97.

For sources and definitions, see explanatory note on p. vi.

AGRICULTURE, ETC.

Principal Crops (metric tons, 2013, FAO estimates): Cassava 1,030; Sweet potatoes 625; Coconuts 1,850; Tomatoes 191; Watermelons 56; Guavas, mangosteens and mangoes 251; Papayas 427; Bananas 63; Oranges 51. *Aggregate Production* (metric tons, may include official, semi-official or estimated data): Roots and tubers 3,205; Vegetables (incl. melons) 1,749; Fruits (excl. melons) 1,073.

Livestock (head, year ending September 2013, FAO estimates): Cattle 130; Pigs 32,200; Goats 1,010; Poultry 20,000; Horses 305.

Livestock Products (metric tons, 2013, FAO estimates): Hen eggs 36; Pig meat 555; Chicken meat 20.

Forestry ('000 cu m, 2013, FAO estimate): Roundwood removals (excl. bark) 5.

Fishing (metric tons, live weight, 2012): Albacore 2,614; Yellowfin tuna 386; Bigeye tuna 333; Total catch (incl. others) 4,202 (FAO estimate).

Source: FAO.

INDUSTRY

Electric Energy (production, million kWh): 33.6 in 2011; 32.9 in 2012; 32.5 in 2013 (provisional).

FINANCE

Currency and Exchange Rates: New Zealand currency is legal tender. In mid-1995 it was announced that the Cook Islands dollar (formerly the local currency, at par with the New Zealand dollar) was to be withdrawn from circulation. New Zealand currency: 100 cents = 1 New Zealand dollar ($NZ); for details of exchange rates, see Tokelau.

Budget ($NZ '000, year ending 30 June 2011): *Revenue:* Total revenue 102,687 (Tax 84,674, Other current 8,725, Capital 9,288). (Note: Revenue excludes grants of 34,560). *Expenditure:* Total expenditure 121,644 (Current 96,723, Capital 24,921). *2014/15* (budget estimates): Total revenue 186,966; Total expenditure 140,792.

Overseas Aid ($NZ '000): Official development assistance from New Zealand (incl. $A1.5m. annual contributions from Australia, but administered by New Zealand) 42,000 for 2012/13–2014/15. Source: Ministry of Foreign Affairs and Trade, Wellington.

Cost of Living (Consumer Price Index for Rarotonga; base: December 2006 = 100): All items 123.6 in 2012; 125.9 in 2013; 128.5 in 2014.

Gross Domestic Product ($NZ '000 at constant 2006 prices): 276,169 in 2011; 288,326 in 2012; 274,461 in 2013 (provisional).

Gross Domestic Product by Economic Activity ($NZ '000 in current prices, 2013, provisional): Agriculture and fishing 25,536; Mining, quarrying and manufacturing 8,239; Electricity, gas and water 4,981; Construction 10,921; Wholesale and retail trade 97,970; Restaurants and hotels 66,677; Transport and communications 47,018; Finance and business services 34,985; Education and health services 18,947; Public administration 32,162; Other community, social and personal services 7,193; Ownership of dwellings 18,293; *Sub-total* 372,922; *Less* Imputed bank service charge 12,880; *GDP in purchasers' values* 360,041.

EXTERNAL TRADE

Principal Commodities ($NZ '000, 2013): *Imports c.i.f.:* Food and live animals 32,756; Beverages and tobacco 9,520; Mineral fuels, lubricants, etc. 24,743; Chemicals 8,278; Basic manufactures 14,837; Machinery and transport equipment 32,283; Miscellaneous manufactured articles 13,419; Total (incl. others) 138,928. *Exports f.o.b.:* Live fish 19; Fish, fresh or chilled 12,129; Pearls 142; Total (incl. others) 12,984.

Principal Trading Partners ($NZ '000, 2013): *Imports:* Australia 9,303; Fiji 5,181; Japan 1,416; New Zealand 97,458; USA 3,943; Total (incl. others) 138,928. *Exports:* Australia 394; Japan 5,015; New Zealand 274; USA 99; Total (incl. others) 12,984.

TRANSPORT

Road Traffic (new registrations, Rarotonga, 2013): Motorcycles 1,260; Cars and jeeps 323; Vans and pick-ups 137; Trucks and buses 32; Others 14; *Total* 1,766.

Shipping: *Flag Registered Fleet* (at 31 December 2014): Number of vessels 265; Total displacement 1,411,681 grt. Source: Lloyd's List Intelligence (www.lloydslistintelligence.com).

Civil Aviation (2013): *Aircraft Movements:* 891 departures. *Freight Traffic* (metric tons): Goods loaded 109; Goods unloaded 1,243.

TOURISM

Foreign Tourist Arrivals: 122,384 in 2012; 121,158 in 2013 (provisional); 121,458 in 2014 (provisional).

Tourist Arrivals by Country of Residence (2014): Australia 22,033; Canada 1,873; Germany 2,224; New Zealand 79,959; United Kingdom 2,748; USA 4,955; Total (incl. others) 121,458.

Tourism Revenue (US $ million, excl. passenger transport): 103 in 2009; 110 in 2010. Source: World Tourism Organization.

COMMUNICATIONS MEDIA

Telephones (main lines, 2010): 7,200 in use.

Mobile Cellular Telephones (2010): 7,800 subscribers.

Broadband Subscribers (2010): 1,700.

Source: International Telecommunication Union.

EDUCATION

Pre-primary (2014): 25 schools; 33 teachers; 460 pupils.

Primary (2014): 11 schools; 111 teachers; 1,843 pupils.

Secondary (incl. high schools, 2014): 4 schools; 124 teachers; 1,718 pupils.

Higher (2012 unless otherwise indicated): 41 teachers (1980); 275 pupils (Source: Ministry of Education, Rarotonga; UNESCO, *Statistical Yearbook*).

Pupil-teacher Ratio (primary education, UNESCO estimate): 14.8 in 2011/12. Source: UNESCO Institute for Statistics.

Directory

The Government

Queen's Representative: TOM MARSTERS.
New Zealand High Commissioner: NICK HURLEY.

CABINET
(May 2015)

The Government is formed by the Cook Islands Party.

Prime Minister, Minister of Foreign Affairs and Immigration: HENRY PUNA.

Deputy Prime Minister and Minister of Infrastructure and Planning: TEARIKI HEATHER.

Minister of Justice: NANDI GLASSIE.

Minister of Agriculture, Environment, and Business Trade Investment Board: KIRIAU TUREPU.

Minister of Finance: MARK BROWN.

Minister of Internal Affairs, Ombudsman, Youth and Sports, and Punanga Nui: ALBERT NICHOLAS.

Minister of Education, Marine Resources and Tourism: MONA IOANE.

GOVERNMENT OFFICES

Office of the Queen's Representative: Titikaveka, POB 134, Rarotonga; tel. and fax 29311; fax 28311; e-mail queenrep@oyster.net.ck.

Office of the Prime Minister: Government of the Cook Islands, Private Bag, Avarua, Rarotonga; tel. 25494; fax 20856; e-mail coso@pmoffice.gov.ck; internet www.pmoffice.gov.ck.

Office of the Public Service Commissioner: POB 24, Rarotonga; tel. 29421; fax 21321; e-mail opscinfo@cookislands.gov.ck; internet www.psc.gov.ck.

New Zealand High Commission: Philatelic Bureau Bldg, 1st Floor, Takuvaine Rd, Avarua, POB 21, Rarotonga; tel. 22201; fax 21241; e-mail nzhcraro@oyster.net.ck; internet www.nzembassy.com/cook-islands.

Ministries

Ministry of Agriculture: POB 96, Rarotonga; tel. 28711; fax 21881; e-mail support@agriculture.gov.ck; internet www.agriculture.gov.ck.

Ministry of Cultural Development: POB 8, Rarotonga; tel. 20725; fax 23725; e-mail parts@culture.gov.ck; internet www.culture.gov.ck.

Ministry of Education: POB 97, Rarotonga; tel. 29357; fax 28357; e-mail info@education.gov.ck; internet www.education.gov.ck.

Ministry of Finance and Economic Management: POB 120, Rarotonga; tel. 29511; fax 21511; e-mail richard.neves@cookislands.gov.ck; internet www.mfem.gov.ck.

Ministry of Foreign Affairs and Immigration: POB 105, Rarotonga; tel. 29347; fax 21247; e-mail secfa@mfai.gov.ck; internet www.mfai.gov.ck.

Ministry of Health: POB 109, Rarotonga; tel. 29664; fax 23109; e-mail aremaki@health.gov.ck; internet www.health.gov.ck.

Ministry of Infrastructure: POB 102, Rarotonga; tel. 20321; fax 24321; e-mail info@moip.gov.ck; internet www.ici.gov.ck.

Ministry of Internal Affairs: POB 98, Rarotonga; tel. 29370; fax 23608; e-mail intaff@cookislands.gov.ck; internet www.intaff.gov.ck.

Ministry of Justice: POB 111, Rarotonga; tel. 29410; fax 29610; e-mail offices.justice@cookislands.gov.ck; internet www.justice.gov.ck.

Ministry of Marine Resources: POB 85, Rarotonga; tel. 28721; fax 29721; e-mail rara@mmr.gov.ck; internet www.mmr.gov.ck.

Ministry of Transport: POB 61, Rarotonga; tel. 28810; fax 21191; e-mail security@transport.net.ck; internet www.transport.gov.ck.

National Environment Service: POB 371, Rarotonga; tel. 21256; fax 22256; e-mail resources@environment.org.ck; internet www.environment.gov.ck.

Advisory Chambers

House of Ariki: POB 13, Rarotonga; tel. 26500; fax 21260; Pres. TRAVEL TOU ARIKI.

Koutu Nui: POB 13, Rarotonga; tel. 29317; fax 21260; e-mail clerk@parliament.gov.ck; Pres. TURI MATAIAPO MARIA HENDERSON.

Legislature

PARLIAMENT

Parliamentary Service

POB 13, Rarotonga; tel. 26500; fax 21260; e-mail nvaloa@parliament.gov.ck.

Speaker: NIKI RATTLE.

General Election, 9 July 2014

Party	Number of votes	% of votes	Seats
Cook Islands Party (CIP)	3,442	40.84	13*
Democratic Party (DP)	3,863	45.83	9*
One Cook Islands Movement . . .	790	9.37	2
Others†	334	3.97	—
Total	8,429	100.00	24

* When the results of the election were declared in July 2014 the Cook Islands Party (CIP) was awarded 13 seats in the legislature and the Democratic Party (DP) eight seats. However, in September 2014 the High Court upheld a petition by the DP in the Tamarua constituency, bringing the totals to CIP 12 seats and DP nine seats. A recount in November in the Mitiaro constituency (where a draw had been recorded in July) awarded the seat to the DP, bringing its total to 10 seats. In December the Court of Appeal ruled that the election in the Aitutaki constituency of Vaipae-Tautu was void, leaving the CIP with only 11 seats. A defection by a DP member to the CIP in March 2015 brought the totals to CIP 12 seats and DP nine. The CIP won the by-election in Vaipae-Tautu later in March, giving the CIP 13 seats.
† Includes 65 informal/blank votes (0.77% of the total votes).

Political Organizations

Cook Islands Party (CIP): Rarotonga; f. 1965; Pres. RAU NGA; Leader HENRY PUNA.

Democratic Party (DP): POB 73, Rarotonga; tel. 21224; e-mail demo1@oyster.net.ck; f. 1972; Pres. SEAN WILLIS; Leader WILLIAM HEATHER; Gen. Sec. EDDIE DROLLET.

One Cook Islands Movement (OCIM): Rarotonga; f. 2014; Leader TEINA BISHOP; Pres. GEORGE TURIA.

Party Tumu: c/o Parliament, POB 13, Rarotonga; f. 2010; est. as Cook Islands Party Tumu; obliged to change name as above following court ruling; Leader ALBERT NICHOLAS.

Te Kura O Te Au: Rarotonga; f. 2010; based upon People's Movement; advocates reform in accordance with spiritual and cultural values; opposed to Sunday flights to Aitutaki; Leader TIM TEPAKI.

Judicial System

The judiciary comprises the Privy Council, the Court of Appeal and the High Court. The High Court exercises jurisdiction in respect of civil, criminal and land titles cases on all the islands, except for Mangaia, Pukapuka and Mitiaro, where disputes over land titles are settled according to custom. The Court of Appeal hears appeals against decisions of the High Court. The Privy Council, sitting in the United Kingdom, is the final appellate tribunal for the country in civil, criminal and land matters.

High Court: POB 144, Avarua, Rarotonga; tel. 24567; fax 21567; e-mail offices@justice.gov.ck; Chief Justice TOM WESTON.

Attorney-General: HENRY PUNA.

Solicitor-General: KIM SAUNDERS.

President of the Court of Appeal: Sir IAN BARKER.

Religion

CHRISTIANITY

The principal denomination is the Cook Islands (Congregational) Christian Church, to which 49% of the resident population belonged at the 2011 census, while 17% adhered to the Roman Catholic Church and 8% were Seventh-day Adventists.

Religious Advisory Council of the Cook Islands: POB 763, Rarotonga; tel. 23778; fax 21767; e-mail tpere@oyster.net.ck; f. 1972; six mem. churches; Pres. Pastor TUTAI PERE.

The Roman Catholic Church

The Cook Islands form the diocese of Rarotonga, suffragan to the archdiocese of Suva (Fiji). At 31 December 2007 the diocese contained an estimated 2,471 adherents. The Bishop participates in the Catholic Bishops' Conference of the Pacific, based in Suva.

Bishop of Rarotonga: Rev. PAUL DONOGHUE, Catholic Diocese, Avarua, POB 147, Rarotonga; tel. 20817; fax 29817; e-mail sbish@oyster.net.ck.

The Anglican Communion

The Cook Islands are within the diocese of Polynesia, part of the Church of the Province of New Zealand. The Bishop of Polynesia is resident in Fiji.

Protestant Churches

Cook Islands Christian Church: Takamoa, POB 93, Rarotonga; tel. 26452; 11,193 mems (1986); Pres. Rev. TANGIMETUA TANGATA-TUTA; Gen. Sec. WILLIE JOHN.

Seventh-day Adventists: POB 31, Rarotonga; tel. 22851; fax 22852; e-mail umakatu@oyster.net.ck; 732 mems (1998); Pres. UMA KATU.

Other churches active in the islands include the Assembly of God, the Church of Latter-day Saints (Mormons), the Apostolic Church, the Jehovah's Witnesses and the Baptist Church.

BAHÁ'Í FAITH

Administrative Committee of the Bahá'ís of Cook Islands: POB 1, Rarotonga; tel. 20658; e-mail nsacooks@bahai.org.ck; mems resident in 6 localities; Sec. ELLEN RAMER.

The Press

Cook Islands Herald: Tutakimoa, POB 126, Rarotonga; e-mail bestread@ciherald.co.ck; internet www.ciherald.co.ck; weekly; Publr GEORGE PITT; Editor CHARLES L. PITT.

Cook Islands News: POB 15, Rarotonga; tel. 22999; fax 25303; e-mail editor@cookislandsnews.com; internet www.cinews.co.ck; f. 1954; est. by Govt; transferred to private ownership in 1989; 6 a week; mainly English; Editor JOHN WOODS; circ. 2,100.

Cook Islands Star: POB 798, Rarotonga; tel. 29965; e-mail jason@oyster.net.ck; fortnightly; Chief Reporter JASON BROWN.

Broadcasting and Communications

TELECOMMUNICATIONS

Telecom Cook Islands Ltd (TCI): Avarua, POB 106, Rarotonga; tel. 29680; fax 26174; e-mail sales@telecom.co.ck; internet www.telecom.co.ck; 60% of shares acquired by Bluesky Samoa in 2015; CEO ADOLFO MONTENEGRO (acting); Chair. TEMU OKOTAI.

BROADCASTING

Radio

Cook Islands Broadcasting Corpn (CIBC): Avarua, POB 126, Rarotonga; tel. 29460; fax 21907; f. 1989; est. to operate new TV service, and radio service of former Broadcasting and Newspaper Corpn; state-owned; Gen. Man. EMILE KAIRUA.

Radio Cook Islands: tel. 20100; e-mail tunein@radio.co.ck; internet www.radio.co.ck; broadcasts in English and Maori 18 hours daily.

KC Radio: Avarua, POB 521, Rarotonga; tel. 23203; f. 1979; est. as Radio Ikurangi; commercial; operates station ZK1ZD; broadcasts 18 hours daily on FM; Man. Dir and Gen. Man. DAVID SCHMIDT.

Television

Cook Islands Broadcasting Corpn (CIBC): see Radio.

Cook Islands TV (CITV): Parekura, 00682 Avarua, Rarotonga; tel. 29461; fax 21907; e-mail newsteam@citv.co.ck; f. 1989; operated by Elijah Communications; broadcasts nightly, in English and Maori; 10 hours of local programmes per week; remainder provided by Television New Zealand.

Finance

(cap. = capital; dep. = deposits; m. = million; brs = branches)

Financial Supervisory Commission: Avarua, POB 594, Rarotonga; tel. 20798; fax 21798; e-mail Inquire@fsc.gov.ck; internet www.fsc.gov.ck; f. 1981; est. as Cook Islands Monetary Bd; present name adopted 2003; supervises banks and insurance cos; licenses trustee cos; registers international cos, limited liability cos, trusts, financial institutions, etc.; Commr PAUL HECKLES; Chair. RAYMOND NEWNHAM.

Trustee Companies Association (TCA): Rarotonga; controlling body for the offshore financial sector; Sec. LOU COLVEY.

BANKING

Legislation was adopted in 1981 to facilitate the establishment of offshore banking operations.

Development Bank

Bank of the Cook Islands (BCI): Avarua, POB 113, Rarotonga; tel. 29341; fax 29343; e-mail cash@bci.co.ck; internet www.bci.co.ck; f. 2003; est. by merger of Cook Islands Devt Bank and Cook Islands Savings Bank; 100% state-owned; finances devt projects in all areas of the economy and helps islanders to establish small businesses and industries by providing loans and management advisory assistance; Man. Dir TERUATU RINGI; 10 brs throughout the Cook Islands.

Commercial Banks

ANZ Cook Islands: ANZ House, Maire Nui Dr., Avarua, POB 907, Rarotonga; tel. 21750; fax 21760; e-mail murphyp@anz.co.uk; internet www.anz.com/cookislands; Chair. JOHN MORSCHEL; CEO MICHAEL SMITH.

Capital Security Bank Ltd: ANZ House, Avarua, POB 906, Rarotonga; tel. 22505; fax 22506; e-mail info@csb.co.ck; internet www.capitalsecuritybank.com; cap. US $1.2m., dep. US $149m. (Dec. 2010); Man. Dir DAVID STEENS.

Westpac Banking Corpn (Australia): Main Rd, Avarua, POB 42, Rarotonga; tel. 22014; fax 20802; e-mail westpaccookislands@westpac.com.au; internet www.westpac.co.ck; Man. CARMEL BUTLER.

INSURANCE

Cook Islands Insurance: POB 44, Rarotonga.

International General Insurance (Cook Islands) Ltd: Avarua, POB 11, Rarotonga; tel. 20514; fax 20667; e-mail info@internationalgeneral.com; internet www.internationalgeneral.com; f. 1982.

Trade and Industry

GOVERNMENT AGENCIES

Business Trade Investment Board: Private Bag, Avarua, Rarotonga; tel. 24296; fax 24298; e-mail info@btib.gov.ck; internet www.btib.gov.ck; f. 1996; est. as replacement for Devt Investment Council; present name adopted 2009, following a merger between the Development Investment Board (DIB) and Small Business Enterprise Centre (SBEC); promotes, monitors and regulates foreign investment, promotes international trade, advises the private sector and Govt, and provides training in business skills; Chair. GRANT PRIEST; CEO TERRY RANGI.

Cook Islands Investment Corporation: Rarotonga; tel. 29391; fax 29381; e-mail ciic@oyster.net.ck; f. 1998; manages govt assets and shareholding interests; Chair. JULIAN DASHWOOD; CEO TAMARII TUTANGATA.

Cook Islands Public Service Commission: POB 24, Rarotonga; tel. 29421; fax 21321; e-mail epati@psc.gov.ck; internet www.psc.gov.ck; Commr NAVY EPATI; CEO PRISCILLA MARUARIKI.

Cook Islands Trading Corporation (CITC): Private Bag 1, Avarua, Rarotonga; tel. 22000; fax 20857; e-mail directors@citc.co.ck; internet kiaorana.net/citc; f. 1891; principal importer, distributor, wholesaler and retailer of products in the Cook Islands; Exec. Chair. TREVOR CLARKE; Gen. Man. GAYE WHITTA.

CHAMBER OF COMMERCE

Chamber of Commerce: POB 242, Rarotonga; tel. 20925; e-mail chamber@commerce.co.ck; internet www.cookislandschamber.org; f. 1956; represents the private sector in the Cook Islands; Pres. STEVE ANDERSON.

INDUSTRIAL AND TRADE ASSOCIATION

Pearl Guild of the Cook Islands: POB 257, Rarotonga; tel. 21902; fax 21903; e-mail trevon@oyster.net.ck; f. 1994; monitors standards of quality in the pearl industry and develops marketing strategies; Pres. TREVON BERGMAN.

UTILITIES

Electricity

Te Aponga Uira O Tumutevarovaro (TAUOT) (Rarotonga Electricity Authority): POB 112, Rarotonga; tel. 20054; fax 21944; e-mail atimoti@electricity.co.ck; internet www.teaponga.com; Chair. APII TIMOTI.

Water

Water Supply Department: Arorangi, POB 102, Rarotonga; tel. 20034; fax 21134.

TRADE UNIONS

Airport Workers' Association: Rarotonga Int. Airport, POB 90, Rarotonga; tel. 25890; fax 21890; e-mail jessie@airport.gov.ck; f. 1985; Pres. (vacant).

Cook Islands Industrial Union of Waterside Workers: Avarua, Rarotonga.

Cook Islands Workers' Association (CIWA): Avarua, POB 403, Rarotonga; tel. 24422; fax 24423; e-mail ciwa@oyster.net.ck; largest union in the Cook Islands; Pres. ANTHONY TURUA; Gen. Sec. TUAINE MAUNGA; 700 mems (2006).

Transport

ROADS

On Rarotonga a 33-km sealed road encircles the island's coastline. A partly sealed inland road, parallel to the coastal road and known as the Ara Metua, is also suitable for vehicles. Roads on the other islands are mainly unsealed.

SHIPPING

The main ports are on Rarotonga (Avatiu), Penrhyn, Mangaia and Aitutaki. The Cook Islands National Line operates a three-weekly cargo service between the Cook Islands, Tonga, Samoa and American Samoa. The Avatiu Port Development Project to rehabilitate and expand the capacity of the port so that it could accommodate larger vessels was completed in 2013.

Apex Maritime: POB 378, Rarotonga; tel. 27651; fax 21138.

Cook Islands National Line: POB 264, Rarotonga; tel. 20374; fax 20855; 30% govt-owned; operates 3 fleet cargo services between the Cook Islands, Niue, Samoa, Norfolk Island, Tonga and New Zealand; Dirs CHRIS VAILE, GEORGE ELLIS.

Cook Islands Shipping Ltd: Arorangi, POB 2001, Rarotonga; tel. 24905; fax 24906.

Ports Authority: POB 84, Rarotonga and Aitutaki; tel. 21921; fax 21191; e-mail info@ports.co.ck; internet www.ports.co.ck; Gen. Man. NOOROA TOU.

Reef Shipping Ltd: Rarotonga; tel. 25193; fax 25194; e-mail shipping@xcil.co.ck; operates services between New Zealand and the Pacific islands.

Taio Shipping Ltd: POB 2001, Rarotonga; tel. 24905; fax 24906; e-mail taio@oyster.net.ck; f. 1991; inter-island cargo shipping service; Dir TAPI TAIO.

Triad Maritime (1988) Ltd: Rarotonga; fax 20855.

CIVIL AVIATION

An international airport was opened on Rarotonga in 1974. Air Raratonga, the national airline, operates domestic inter-island services and flights to French Polynesia, Niue, Samoa and Tonga. Air New Zealand offers flights to Auckland, Los Angeles and Sydney, Virgin Australia to Auckland and Air Tahiti to Papeete.

Airport Authority, Cook Islands: POB 90, Rarotonga; tel. 25890; fax 21890; e-mail aaci@airport.gov.ck; f. 1986; CEO JOE NGAMATA.

Air Rarotonga: POB 79, Rarotonga; tel. 22888; fax 23288; e-mail admin@airraro.co.ck; internet www.airraro.com; f. 1978; privately owned; operates internal passenger and cargo services and charter services to Niue and French Polynesia; Man. Dir EWAN F. SMITH.

Tourism

Tourism is the most important industry in the Cook Islands. According to provisional figures, in 2014 the number of foreign tourist arrivals reached 121,458, the majority of whom came from New Zealand. Australia is also an important source of tourists. Most of the tourist facilities are to be found on Rarotonga and Aitutaki, but the outer islands also offer attractive scenery. Revenue from tourism was estimated at some US $110m. in 2010.

Cook Islands Tourism Corporation: POB 14, Rarotonga; tel. 29435; fax 21435; e-mail tourism@cookislands.gov.ck; internet www.cookislands.travel; Chair. EWAN F. SMITH; CEO HALOTOA FUA.

Education

Free secular education is compulsory for all children between six and 15 years of age. In 2014 there were 25 pre-primary schools, 11 primary schools and 4 secondary schools (including high schools). In 2014 there were 460 pupils enrolled in pre-primary education, 1,843 in primary education and 1,718 in secondary education. Enrolment at primary schools in 2010 included an estimated 94% of children in the relevant age-group, while the comparable ratio for secondary schools in 2011 was 78% (males 72%; females 84%). Under the New Zealand Training Scheme, the New Zealand Government offers overseas scholarships in New Zealand, Fiji, Papua New Guinea, Australia and Samoa for secondary and tertiary education, career-training and short-term in-service training. There is an extension centre of the University of the South Pacific (based in Fiji) in the Cook Islands. Projected budgetary expenditure on education reached a record $NZ14.0m. in 2014/15 (equivalent to around 13% of total spending).

NIUE

Introductory Survey

LOCATION, CLIMATE, LANGUAGE, RELIGION, FLAG, CAPITAL

Niue is a coral island, located in the Pacific Ocean, about 480 km (300 miles) east of Tonga and 930 km (580 miles) west of the southern Cook Islands. Rainfall occurs predominantly during the hottest months, from December to March, when the average temperature is 27°C (81°F). Average annual rainfall is 7,715 mm (298 in). Niuean, a Polynesian language, and English are spoken. The population is predominantly Christian, with some 63% belonging to the Ekalesia Niue, a Protestant church, in 2001. Niue's flag (proportions 1 by 2) is yellow, bearing, in the upper hoist corner, the United Kingdom's Union Flag with a yellow five-pointed star on each arm of the cross of St George and a slightly larger yellow five-pointed star on a blue disc in the centre of the cross. More than 30% of the population resides in Alofi, which is the capital and administrative centre of Niue.

CONTEMPORARY POLITICAL HISTORY

Historical Context

The first Europeans to discover Niue were members of a British expedition, led by Capt. James Cook, in 1774. Missionaries visited the island throughout the 19th century, and in 1900 Niue was declared a British protectorate. In 1901 Niue was formally annexed to New Zealand as part of the Cook Islands, but in 1904 it was granted a separate administration.

In October 1974 Niue attained 'self-government in free association with New Zealand'. Niueans retain New Zealand citizenship, and the migration of Niueans to New Zealand has been a cause of concern, with many more Niueans living in New Zealand than on Niue. Robert (from 1982, Sir Robert) Rex, who had been the island's political leader since the early 1950s, was Niue's Premier when it became self-governing, and retained the post at three-yearly general elections during 1975–90.

Domestic Political Affairs

In December 1992 Sir Robert Rex died, and Young Vivian, the leader of the Niue People's Action Party (NPAP—Niue's sole political party), who had been serving as acting Premier at the time of Rex's death, was unanimously elected Premier by the Government. Legislative elections took place in February 1993, and in the following month Frank Lui, a former cabinet minister, was elected by the Niue Assembly (Fono Ekepule) as Premier, defeating Vivian by 11 votes to nine. Among Lui's stated objectives were the development of tourism and a continuation of efforts to encourage Niueans resident in New Zealand to return to the island.

In March 1994 Vivian proposed an unsuccessful motion of no confidence in the Government, and a further attempt by the opposition to introduce a similar motion was invalidated in the High Court in October on a procedural matter. However, during the ensuing debate, the Minister of National Planning and Economic Development, Sani Lakatani, resigned in order to join the opposition as its deputy leader, thus leaving the Government with only 10 official supporters in the Niue Assembly. Subsequent opposition demands for the intervention of the Governor-General of New Zealand in dissolving the legislature, in preparation for a fresh general election, were rejected, and, despite Lui's assurance that an early election would take place in order to end the atmosphere of increasing political uncertainty, polls were not held until February 1996. The Premier and his three cabinet ministers were re-elected to their seats, although support among the electorate for candidates of the Niue People's Party (NPP, as the NPAP had been renamed in 1995) and independents appeared fairly equally divided. Lui was re-elected by the Niue Assembly as Premier, defeating Robert Rex, Jr, the son of Niue's first Premier, by 11 votes to nine.

At the general election of March 1999 Lui lost his legislative seat and subsequently retired from politics. The Minister of Finance, Aukuso Pavihi, also failed to be re-elected. The leader of the NPP, Sani Lakatani, was elected Premier by the new Assembly, defeating O'Love Jacobsen by 14 votes to six. Lakatani's stated priority as Premier was to oversee an increase in Niue's population to at least 3,000; he claimed that the sharp decline in the number of residents constituted a threat to the island's self-governing status.

At the general election held in April 2002 all 20 incumbent members were returned to the Niue Assembly. Independent candidate Toke Talagi polled the highest number of votes (445), but overall the NPP was victorious. However, despite having polled the second-highest number of votes (428), Lakatani did not command the general support of his party, and a leadership challenge was mounted by his deputy, Young Vivian. Following several days of lobbying within the NPP, Vivian was chosen as Premier. Vivian announced that the party had the support of 10 elected members, having formed a coalition with several independents associated with Talagi. Lakatani was appointed Deputy Premier later that year.

The NPP was dissolved in July 2003 as a result of ongoing disagreement among its members and the failure of several projects. In September the opposition expressed concern that a significant amount of public money was being used to fund overseas trips by government members. At the time of the statement seven of the Niue Assembly's 20 members (including two cabinet ministers) were absent on engagements overseas.

In January 2004 Cyclone Heta, which was described as the worst in the island's recent history, caused the deaths of two people and the destruction of many buildings, along with the loss of most food crops. In addition, there was extensive damage to Niue's infrastructure, communications and coral reef. Relief supplies were sent from New Zealand as part of an initial aid programme worth some US $3.5m. It was estimated that US $23m. would be needed for a rebuilding programme to be carried out over a five-year period.

The Government conducted a survey in September 2004 to assess the current population of the island. When its findings were made public in October, some observers disputed the figure of 1,550 (which many believed was higher than the reality, in order to attract more favourable levels of economic assistance). A local newspaper conducted a similar survey and estimated a resident population of 1,300. In July 2005 the Premier announced that ongoing efforts to attract Niueans back to the island, notably by promoting the farming and fisheries sectors, were to be increased. The people of Niue were also to be granted better access to health care following an agreement concluded in November between the Niue Ministry for Health and the Counties Manukau District Health Board of New Zealand. The agreement was expected to facilitate the referral of Niuean patients to New Zealand.

In November 2004 Niue's High Commissioner to New Zealand, Hima Takelesi Douglas (hereafter referred to as Hima Takelesi), announced his intention to return to the island to contest the forthcoming general election. His stated motivation was a desire to form a stronger partnership with the 20,000 Niueans resident in New Zealand, in an attempt to ensure that Niue retained its current status and did not become incorporated into New Zealand. At the election, held in April 2005, Hima Takelesi succeeded in securing a seat in the Niue Assembly. Young Vivian was re-elected Premier several days later, defeating O'Love Jacobsen by 17 votes to three.

In February 2007, in an attempt to ease its financial difficulties, the Government announced a 10% decrease in public servants' salaries, along with a reduction in working hours for certain employees and decreases in local grants. In the following month a parliamentary motion of no confidence submitted by the opposition against Premier Vivian, in protest against the Government's alleged financial mismanagement, was defeated. Niue's financial problems were again highlighted in late 2007, when a member of the opposition reported that the island's financial secretary had admitted the Government's bankruptcy.

In June 2008 a general election was held, with 11 of the 20 parliamentary seats being contested. Three new members were elected to the Niue Assembly, including Togia Sioneholo, hitherto Secretary of Justice, who defeated Hima Takelesi. Former Minister of Finance Toke Talagi was subsequently elected Premier by 14 parliamentary votes to five, thereby succeeding the incumbent Young Vivian. Talagi assumed responsibility for numerous ministerial portfolios, including planning, economic development, finance, external affairs and environment. The new Premier declared that his immediate priority was to address the island's economic situation.

In February 2009, after a delay of almost two years, modified legislation providing for the introduction of a new consumption tax, which would be applicable to visitors to the island, was finally approved by the Niue Assembly. Owing to its likely impact on low-income families, the controversial tax had encountered widespread opposition within the Assembly, culminating in the filing of a motion of no confidence in Premier Talagi in early February (which had been defeated by 11 votes to six).

In December 2010 the Cabinet approved, in principle, a proposal mooted by Talagi to construct a casino on Niue in a bid to expand the island's tourism industry. The proposal, if pursued, was expected to require the introduction of legislation to ensure the proper management and operation of the casino. O'Love Jacobsen resigned from the Cabinet in March 2011, following her appointment as High Commissioner to New Zealand.

A general election was held in May 2011, following which Talagi was re-elected as Premier, having secured the support of 12 of the 20 incoming assembly members. The cabinet portfolios were reallocated and a further reorganization in June included the appointment of two assistant ministers. Prior to the poll in May the parliamentary Speaker, Atapana Siakimotu, had announced his retirement after nine years in office; Ahohiva Levi was chosen as his replacement.

In May 2011 it was announced that a judicial code of conduct was being drafted for Niue, by members of the local judiciary in conjunction with a British magistrate serving as a consultant for the Pacific Judicial Development Programme. It was hoped that the code of conduct, which required all judges to remain independent and above influence, would reinforce public confidence in Niue's judiciary and better inform the public of the judiciary's responsibilities.

In November 2011 former Minister of Justice Togia Sioneholo alleged that the appointment in June of two assistant ministers to the Cabinet was in breach of the Constitution, which stated that the Cabinet should comprise four ministers only. Sioneholo argued that the two appointees were assistant ministers in nominal terms only, since they had been awarded responsibility for portfolios hitherto awarded to full ministers, and urged the Niue High Court to intervene. In the following month members of the Niue Assembly voted in favour of significant increases in parliamentary salaries, which were to be funded by interest accrued by the island's trust fund. However, some opposition legislators argued that the funds would be better spent on development projects.

Recent developments: the 2014 general election

In mid-January 2014 a proposal by Premier Talagi for Niue to house asylum seekers on behalf of the Australian Government as part of the latter's offshore processing plans was rejected by the Niue Assembly, by 10 votes to three. Later in January a four-day working week was implemented in most departments of the public sector, with employees continuing to receive the same level of pay. The initiative was introduced in lieu of a promised 20% wage increase for public servants, which Talagi stated the Government was unable to finance; however, teachers were to receive a wage increase, instead of a four-day working week. The measure elicited much controversy, with critics arguing that it would diminish productivity, and questioning the implications for essential services such as the police. In February a motion of no confidence in the Government submitted by opposition legislators was defeated by 12 votes to seven.

Following the general election held on 12 April 2014 Toke Telagi was re-elected as Premier (defeating Stanley Kalauni), having secured the support of 12 of the 20 incoming assembly members. On the same day Togia Pihigia was elected as the new Speaker of the Assembly, replacing the outgoing Ahohiva Levi, who had not been nominated for the post. Talagi appointed three ministers on 29 April, while himself assuming responsibility for the majority of portfolios in the Cabinet.

The Offshore Financial Sector

In late 1999 allegations made by a foreign news agency that Niue was being used by criminal organizations for 'laundering' the proceeds of their illegal activities were strongly denied by Premier Sani Lakatani. However, the naming of the island in a report by the Financial Action Task Force (FATF, see p. 451) in June 2000 as one of a number of countries and territories that had failed to co-operate in regional efforts to combat money-laundering led the Government to suspend the issue of any further offshore banking licences until stricter regulations governing the financial sector had been introduced. In early 2001 the USA imposed sanctions on Niue (including a ban on transactions with US banks), claiming that the island had not implemented all the recommendations of the report. Lakatani appealed directly to US President George W. Bush to end the embargo, which he described as having a devastating effect on Niue's

economy. The Government stressed its commitment to meeting international requirements in its financial sector but claimed that it was experiencing difficulty in doing so, given its limited legal resources. Moreover, the Premier expressed strong disapproval that a nation as powerful as the USA should inflict such hardship on a small, economically vulnerable island, and he urged other Pacific islands targeted by the FATF report to unite in protest against such impositions.

Having failed to meet an FATF deadline in August 2001, in February 2002 Niue pledged to repeal its offshore banking legislation. The FATF announced in April that, in view of the island's commitment to improving the transparency of its tax and regulatory systems, the organization was to remove Niue from its list of non-co-operative territories; the decision was duly implemented in October. The bank-licensing legislation was repealed in June.

Although by 2002 most offshore financial activity had ostensibly ended, the sector once again came under scrutiny in April 2009 when Niue was placed on a 'grey list' of nations compiled by the Organisation for Economic Co-operation and Development (OECD, see p. 377) owing to the island's failure to have concluded the requisite number of tax information exchange agreements (TIEAs). Having previously signed only one such agreement (with New Zealand, in August 2012), Niue's subsequent conclusion of seven further TIEAs resulted in the island being removed from the 'grey list' in 2014. In addition, in October of that year Niue pledged to commence implementing the OECD's new international standard on Automatic Exchange of Information in 2017.

Relations with New Zealand

In March 2000 a Niue-New Zealand joint consultative committee met, for the first time, in Alofi to consider the two sides' future constitutional relationship. Later that year the committee proposed to conduct a survey of islanders' views and to consider all options, from reintegration with New Zealand to full independence. In early 2001 Hima Takelesi was appointed Niue's first High Commissioner to New Zealand. New Zealand remained committed to annual assistance of $NZ6.3m. in the years 2001–03. A total of 20,148 Niueans were recorded as resident in New Zealand at New Zealand's 2001 census, increasing to 22,476 at New Zealand's 2006 census.

In October 2004, the New Zealand Prime Minister, Helen Clark, made an official visit to Niue to celebrate the 30-year anniversary of the island's attainment of self-governing status. She urged expatriate Niueans to return to the island and support efforts to regenerate its infrastructure and economy. She also announced a programme to introduce the Niuean language into the education curriculum from pre-school level onwards by 2006, as part of the Taoga Niue initiative, which aimed to preserve traditional customs and cultural practices on the island. The Halavaka ke he Monuina Arrangement (HkhMA), a bilateral agreement signed during Clark's visit in October 2004 with the goal of facilitating closer co-operation between the various government agencies of Niue and New Zealand, represented a major shift in New Zealand's approach to the management of its relationship with Niue. In addition, Clark confirmed that $NZ6m. was to be made available to rebuild the hospital destroyed by Cyclone Heta. The new hospital, located at Kaimiti, opened in March 2006.

Premier Toke Talagi criticized the New Zealand Government in June 2009 for withholding investment funds pledged as part of the HkhMA, particularly a $NZ2m. tranche that had been allocated for the island's tourism industry. In the following month, during New Zealand Prime Minister John Key's first visit to Niue and amid rising tensions, Key emphasized that the tourism aid would not be dispensed without a more detailed plan of how it was to be spent. In late 2009, however, the New Zealand Government expressed a willingness to finance an expansion of the island's main hotel, Matavai Resort, alongside concurrent reforms to the taxation and property ownership laws in Niue. (A New Zealand-funded refurbishment and expansion project at the hotel was completed in 2013.)

A report published by a New Zealand parliamentary committee in December 2010 included a critical assessment of Niue, contending that 40 years of New Zealand aid to the island had yielded 'almost no return'. The report urged Niue to reduce the size of its parliament, arguing that a 20-member legislature for an electorate comprising just 600 voters was 'an abuse of trust and responsibility', and noted that the island was caught in a 'vicious cycle' in which its economic difficulties were both reflected in, and exacerbated by, its ongoing population decline. The committee concluded that Niue could never be a sustainable economic entity, and proposed that the island be redesignated as a retirement village in which inhabitants would be granted access to the same services as other New Zealand citizens. The proposals received a mixed response, with some arguing that the proposal raised serious questions about the long-term constitutionality of Niue, while others contended that a harmonization of services between New Zealand and Niue would attract expatriate Niueans back to the island, which would provide a stimulus to its economy. For his part, Premier Talagi contested that the island economy was viable and that the most significant impediment to economic growth and development was the New Zealand Government, which, he argued, was frustrating efforts to expand the Niuean tourism sector owing to a reluctance to release funds.

In September 2011 a joint development aid agreement was signed providing for New Zealand funding of $NZ15m., over a three-year period, for tourism-related development projects on Niue. In June 2013 Niue and New Zealand signed an agreement intended to promote co-operation on social services policy and delivery. Under the arrangement, the New Zealand Ministry of Social Development was, *inter alia*, to assist in the development and implementation of a social protection policy in Niue, including a proposed review of the Niuean social welfare system. During a visit to Niue in October, the Governor-General of New Zealand, Sir Jerry Mateparae, commended the Niuean Government's efforts to implement a range of measures intended to bolster the island's economic self-reliance. However, he also stressed the need to arrest the decline in Niue's population and to offer improved opportunities to those remaining on, or seeking to migrate to, the island. In June 2014 Prime Minister Key visited Niue on a tour of the Pacific islands, during which he opened the new terminal of Hanan International Airport and announced that New Zealand would provide Nauru with funds totalling $NZ1.5m. to support tourism, renewable energy and the stability of the island's electricity grid.

Foreign Affairs

Following almost 10 years of consultations, Niue and the USA signed a maritime boundary treaty in May 1997, delineating the precise boundary between the territorial waters of Niue and American Samoa. In October 2003 Niue's Premier issued a statement inviting the residents of Tuvalu (whose continued existence on those islands was increasingly threatened by rising sea levels) to migrate to Niue. The Government of Tuvalu subsequently requested that Niue produce a memorandum of understanding giving formal details of this invitation and of the rights that Tuvaluans would enjoy on Niue. Further discussions between officials from the two Governments took place in 2005. In October 2006 Niue agreed to join the Regional Assistance Mission to Solomon Islands (RAMSI), with the deployment of two Niuean police officers to Solomon Islands. In August 2008 Niue hosted the annual summit meeting of the Pacific Islands Forum (see p. 413), at which the Niue Declaration on Climate Change was endorsed. In May 2009 an FAO conference on Pacific food security, and a meeting of the Pacific Islands Forum Fisheries Agency, were convened in Niue. The island hosted a meeting of the Pacific Island Forum ministers responsible for economic affairs in October 2010 and the Pacific Climate Change Roundtable in March 2011. In November 2011 Niue was one of eight Pacific states and territories that jointly established the Polynesian Leaders Group (see p. 463), which was widely viewed as being intended to provide a counter-weight to the Melanesian Spearhead Group. The first formal meeting of the Group, which pledged to enhance co-operation among its members across a wide range of fields, including trade and investment, education, climate change and health, was held in the Cook Islands, on the sidelines of the annual Pacific Islands Forum summit, in August 2012. In August 2014 Premier Toke Telagi expressed his dissatisfaction with the level of financial support allocated to Niue as a member of the Smaller Island States Unit of the Pacific Islands Forum and threatened to leave the sub-group.

Niue established diplomatic relations with the People's Republic of China in 2007. In February 2011 China was reported to have provided funding for the extension of Niue's airport terminal. Following a meeting with the Chinese ambassador in that month, Premier Toke Talagi welcomed the burgeoning bilateral relationship and expressed his belief that closer co-operation would be forged between the two countries, particularly in the tourism and fisheries sectors. However, in June 2014 Premier Talagi, while acknowledging China's role as a significant aid donor to Niue, asserted that he did not expect China ever to rival New Zealand in the strength of its relations with the island.

Niue established diplomatic relations with Australia in February 2013. Australia's high commissioner to New Zealand is accredited to Niue.

CONSTITUTION AND GOVERNMENT

Under the Niue Constitution Act 1974, the island enjoys self-government in free association with New Zealand. The New Zealand Government remains responsible for the island's defence and external affairs, although in practice Niue may conduct its own external relations. Executive government is carried out by the Premier and three other ministers. Legislation is the responsibility of the Niue Assembly (Fono Ekepule), which has 20 members (14 village representatives and six elected on a common roll), but New Zealand, if called upon to do so by the Assembly, will also legislate for the island. There is a New Zealand representative in Niue, whose status was upgraded to that of High Commissioner in 1993. The Governor-General of New Zealand acts as the sovereign's representative for Niue.

REGIONAL AND INTERNATIONAL CO-OPERATION

Niue is a member of the Pacific Community (see p. 410) and of the Pacific Islands Forum (see p. 413). It is an associate member of the UN's Economic and Social Commission for Asia and the Pacific (ESCAP, see p. 30). In 2000 Niue became a signatory of the Cotonou Agreement (see p. 321) with the European Union (EU). In 2011 Niue was one of eight founding members of the Polynesian Leaders Group (see p. 463).

ECONOMIC AFFAIRS

Niue's gross domestic product (GDP) was estimated at $NZ30.7m. in 2011, and GDP per head was estimated at $NZ16,575 in 2009. The population decreased at an average annual rate of 1.0% in 2001–2011, according to provisional census figures.

Agriculture, forestry and fishing contributed 16.3% of GDP in 2011. According to the census of 2006, the sector engaged 15.9% of the employed labour force. Two-thirds of the land surface is uncultivable, but many households practise subsistence gardening. The principal crops are coconuts, taro, yams, cassava and sweet potatoes. A taro export scheme was successfully introduced in the early 1990s, and production of the crop increased by more than 500% in 1993. Exports of taro, principally to New Zealand, contributed nearly 89% of total export earnings in 2008, being facilitated by a regular shipping service introduced in 2003. Plans to increase the production of vanilla as an export crop were discussed in 2003, but the promising crop was destroyed by the cyclone of early 2004. The reintroduction of vanilla cultivation, as well as that of organic nonu (or noni, a fruit renowned for its medicinal properties), for export was initiated during 2004 as part of the Government's post-cyclone recovery programme. Honey is also produced for export. Pigs, poultry, goats and beef cattle are raised, mainly for local consumption. An island development plan for 2003 included proposals to develop Niue's fishing industry by employing a fleet of used Korean fishing vessels. The construction of a fish-processing factory at Amanau was completed in 2004. It was estimated that the new plant, which was a joint project with the New Zealand shipping company Reef Group, might raise $NZ9m. annually in revenue. Fishing licences to five New Zealand vessels and four Samoan vessels were issued. However, a series of problems resulted in operational difficulties at the plant. Operations were suspended in 2007, and Reef Group went into receivership in November 2012.

Industry (including mining, manufacturing, construction and utilities) contributed only 5.1% of GDP in 2011. In 2006 industry engaged 17.1% of the labour force. The manufacturing sector has been very limited, accounting for a mere 2.4% of GDP in 2011. A noni juice factory opened in 2004. Exploration for deposits of uranium continued on the island in 2006, but in November it was announced that no commercially viable resources had been identified. The extensive damage caused by Cyclone Heta led to much activity in the construction sector from early 2004, as rebuilding programmes commenced.

The island remains dependent upon imported diesel fuel for its energy requirements. In collaboration with the international environmentalist group Greenpeace, in December 2005 Niue confirmed its commitment to the development of wind power, hoping to become one of the first locations in the world to be completely reliant on renewable energy sources. In April 2009 Niue signed a memorandum of understanding on the Pacific Petroleum Project, a regional initiative that aimed to reduce the energy costs of the Pacific islands through collective negotiations for the bulk procurement of petroleum supplies. In October 2012 Premier Talagi announced that a Japanese-funded solar power project was to be constructed on Niue; the solar power grid would initially provide up to 30% of Niue's energy requirements, as well as substantially reducing the island's dependency on fuel imports. The grid commenced operations in February 2014 and was expected to save the Government around $NZ137,000 per year.

The services sector contributed 78.6% of GDP in 2011. In 2006 the sector engaged 66.9% of the labour force. The Government is the most important employer, engaging 512 members of the paid labour force in December 2004, when an estimated 269 people were employed in the private sector. Tourism has begun to make a significant contribution to the economy; foreign tourist arrivals increased from 5,047 in 2012 to 7,047 in 2013. The vast majority of arrivals were from New Zealand. Receipts from tourism amounted to US $2.0m. in 2011. From the 1990s various attempts to secure new sources of revenue in Niue included the leasing of the island's telecommunications facilities to foreign companies for use in specialist telephone services. However, this enterprise (which earned the island an estimated $NZ1.5m. per year) caused considerable controversy when it was revealed that Niue's telephone code had been made available to companies offering personal services considered indecent by the majority of islanders. The sale of Niue's internet domain name '.nu' generated significant revenue but led to further controversy when a report published in 2004 claimed that the island was hosting some 3m. pages of pornographic material via its '.nu' domain. In 2008, furthermore, an international software security company reported that, along with

Tokelau, Niue had become one of the world's worst offenders in per caput terms with regard to the relaying of unsolicited e-mails. Niue's inaugural mobile telephone service was launched in July 2011.

Niue records an annual trade deficit, with imports generally far exceeding exports. The value of Niue's exports totalled only $NZ346,000 in 2011, while the cost of the island's imports reached almost $NZ14.0m. New Zealand is the island's main trading partner, supplying more than 95% of its imports in 2008. The principal exports in 2008 were taro, coconut and vanilla. The principal imports were mineral products (which constituted 38.3% of the total cost of imports), base metals, machinery and prepared foodstuffs.

The budget for 2012/13 projected expenditure of $NZ44.05m. and revenue of $NZ44.06m. Official development assistance from New Zealand was projected to total $NZ13.0m. in 2014/15. Other donors include Australia, the People's Republic of China, Japan, France and various multilateral organizations. With the objective of providing Niue with an independent source of future revenue, in 2006 the Niue International Trust Fund was established, with a total contribution of $NZ10m. from New Zealand and Australia. By 2014 the trust fund's assets stood at around $NZ50m. From 2014 the Government of Niue had access to revenue from the fund (in the form of interest earned from the capital). The annual rate of inflation averaged 4.8% in 2003–13. Consumer prices increased by 2.2% in 2012, but decreased by 1.2% in 2013. According to the 2011 census, the unemployment rate was estimated at 2.7% of the labour force.

Upon taking office in June 2008, Premier Toke Talagi stated that his priority was to be the economy of Niue, with a particular focus on the control of government expenditure and the creation of new sources of revenue. In April 2009 a controversial new consumption tax entered into effect (see *Contemporary Political History*); levied at a rate of 12.5%, the tax on goods and services was expected to make a substantial contribution to government revenue. Talagi's Government identified the tourism sector as a potential source of higher income. However, constraints on development included the lack of business expertise and dearth of professional skills among the islanders. Upon securing re-election in May 2011, Talagi pledged to continue efforts to stabilize Niue's economy and identified fisheries and mining as additional sources of potential revenue. Personal income tax was to be reduced, while the reach of the consumption tax introduced in April 2009 was to be extended. A US $6m. project, funded by aid from New Zealand, to refurbish and expand the Matavai Resort, Niue's main hotel, was completed in 2013. Meanwhile, a new tourist visitor centre opened in September 2011; a new hotel, the Matavai Motel, commenced operations in December 2012; the Chinese Government had provided funds for the expansion of Niue's airport terminal; and plans were being considered for the establishment of a casino, as well as the construction of a new Chinese-financed hotel. From May 2014 Air New Zealand introduced a new weekly mid-week flight, in addition to the one weekly flight on Saturday already offered. However, subsequent expansion of the tourism sector would remain dependent on further improvement of air services to Niue. New Zealand's official development assistance to Niue totalled $NZ14.1m. in 2013/14. The main focus of the aid programme was economic sustainability, principally through development of the tourism sector. The Niue Tourism Authority Board published a strategic plan in July 2014 with the aim of increasing visitor arrivals to 10,000 by 2015. Meanwhile, it was hoped that improvements in the field of information and communications technology—including a project funded by the European Union to replace all electric cables on the island and connect all households to a new fibre optic system, which was completed in January 2015—would bolster economic development and encourage foreign investment in Niue.

PUBLIC HOLIDAYS

2016: 1 January (New Year's Day), 2 January (Commission Day), 6 February (Waitangi Day, anniversary of 1840 treaty), 25 March (Good Friday), 28 March (Easter Monday), 24 April (for ANZAC Day, anniversary of 1915 landing at Gallipoli), 13 June (Queen's Official Birthday), 19 October (Constitution Day celebrations), 28 October (Peniamina's Day), 25 December (Christmas), 26 December (Boxing Day).

Statistical Survey

Source (unless otherwise indicated): Statistics Unit, Economics, Planning, Development Office, Government of Niue, POB 95, Alofi; tel. 4219; fax 4148; e-mail statsniue@mail.gov.nu; internet www.spc .int/prism/country/nu/stats.

AREA AND POPULATION

Area: 261.5 sq km (100.9 sq miles).

Population (census totals are *de facto*, including visitors): 1,625 at census of September 2006 (an estimated 22,473 Niueans lived in New Zealand at the time of the 2006 census); 1,611 at census of 10 September 2011 (the *de jure* total in 2011 was 1,607, comprising 1,460 on-island residents and 147 residents temporarily absent).

Density (at 2011 census): 6.2 per sq km.

Population by Age and Sex (on-island residents at 2011 census): *0–14 years:* 386 (males 183, females 203); *15–64 years:* 893 (males 459, females 434); *65 years and over:* 181 (males 80, females 101); *Total* 1,460 (males 722, females 738).

Population by Ethnic Group (2001 census, declared ethnicity): Niuean 1,399; Caucasian 81; Pacific Islander 182; Niuean/Caucasian 28; Niuean/Pacific Islander 42; Asian 4. Note: Classification of ethnicity reflects national census methodology. *2011:* Niuean 971; Part Niuean 195; Non-Niuean 294.

Principal Villages (on-island resident population at 2011 census): Alofi (capital) 560; Hakupu 127; Avatele 130; Tamakautoga 127; Tuapa 87.

Births, Marriages and Deaths (including Niueans temporarily resident in New Zealand, 2011 unless otherwise indicated): Live births 22; Marriages 12 (2009); Deaths 9.

Life Expectancy (years at birth, WHÒ estimates): 74 (males 72; females 78) in 2012. Source: WHO, *World Health Statistics*.

Immigration and Emigration (2011): Arrivals 7,773; Departures 7,712.

Economically Active Population (persons aged 15 years and over, 2011 census): Agriculture, forestry and fishing 75; Mining, electricity, gas, water and construction 35; Manufacturing 20; Construction 47; Trade, restaurants and hotels 121; Transport, storage and communications 59; Finance, real estate, business activities 33; Education and health 113; Community, social and personal services 153; Other service activities 29; Private households with employed persons 35; *Total employed* 720; Unemployed 20; *Total labour force* 740 (males 413, females 327).

HEALTH AND WELFARE

Key Indicators

Total Fertility Rate (children per woman, 2006): 2.6.

Under-5 Mortality Rate (per 1,000 live births, 2012): 25.

Physicians (per 1,000 head, 2008): 3.0.

Hospital Beds (per 1,000 head, 2006): 5.2.

Health Expenditure (2011): US $ per head (PPP): 3,175.

Health Expenditure (2011): % of GDP: 10.6.

Health Expenditure (2011): public (% of total): 98.9.

For sources and definitions, see explanatory note on p. vi.

AGRICULTURE, ETC.

Principal Crops (metric tons, 2013, FAO estimates): Taro 3,000; Sweet potatoes 250; Yams 155; Coconuts 3,200; Bananas 80; Lemons and limes 88. *Aggregate Production* ('000 metric tons, may include official, semi-official or estimated data): Vegetables (incl. melons) 135; Fruits (excl. melons) 763.

Livestock (year ending September 2013, FAO estimates): Cattle 115; Pigs 2,100; Chickens 15,000.

Livestock Products (metric tons, 2013, FAO estimates): Pig meat 61; Chicken meat 20; Cows' milk 60; Hen eggs 16; Honey 6.

Forestry (cu m, 2013 unless otherwise indicated): Roundwood removals 613; Sawnwood production 201 (1985).

Fishing (metric tons, live weight, 2012): Total catch 7.

Source: FAO.

INDUSTRY

Production (2011, estimate): Electric energy 3 million kWh. Source: UN Industrial Commodity Statistics Database.

FINANCE

Currency and Exchange Rates: 100 cents = 1 New Zealand dollar ($NZ). For details, see Tokelau.

Budget ($NZ '000, year ending 30 June 2006, provisional): Internal revenue 14,206; New Zealand budgetary support 6,953; *Total revenue* 21,159; Recurrent expenditure 21,417; Capital 90; *Total Expenditure* 21,507. *2006/07* ($NZ '000, forecasts): Internal revenue 16,499; New Zealand budgetary support 6,915; Total revenue 23,414; Recurrent expenditure 23,364; Capital projects 50; Total expenditure 23,414. *2012/13* ($NZ '000, forecasts): Total revenue 44,055; Total expenditure 44,052.

Overseas Aid ($NZ '000, 2014/15, provisional): Official development assistance from New Zealand 13,000. Source: Ministry of Foreign Affairs and Trade, Wellington.

Cost of Living (Consumer Price Index; base: July–Sept. 2003 = 100): All items 150.0 in 2011; 153.3 in 2012; 151.4 in 2013.

Gross Domestic Product ($NZ '000 in current prices): 21,468 in 2007; 22,771 in 2008; 25,460 in 2009. *2011* $NZ '000 in current prices, Secretariat of the Pacific Community estimate): Gross domestic product 30,724.1 (Source: Pacific Regional Information System).

Gross Domestic Product by Economic Activity ($NZ '000 in current prices, Secretariat of the Pacific Community estimates, 2011): Agriculture, forestry and fishing 4,807.3; Mining and quarrying 20.2; Manufacturing 704.6; Electricity, gas and water 552.7; Construction 217.2; Trade 3,336.2; Restaurants and hotels 1,588.7; Transport, storage and communications 1,310.9; Financial and business services, real estate, etc. 2,481.1; Public administration 13,400.4; Other community, social and personal services 1,082.0; *Sub-total* 29,501.2; *Less* Imputed bank service charge 351.2; *GDP at factor cost* 29,150.0; Indirect taxes, less subsidies 1,574.1; *GDP in purchasers' values* 30,724.1 Source: Pacific Regional Information System.

EXTERNAL TRADE

Principal Commodities ($NZ '000, 2008): *Imports c.i.f.:* Animals and animal products 679; Prepared foodstuffs 1,250; Mineral products 4,206; Chemical products 321; Plastics and rubber 195; Wood and wood products 403; Base metals and articles thereof 1,176; Machinery, mechanical appliances and electrical equipment 915; Miscellaneous manufactured articles 461; Total (incl. others) 10,968. *Exports f.o.b.:* Taro 24; Coconut 2; Vanilla 1; Total (incl. others) 27. *2009:* Total imports 9,361.

Principal Trading Partners ($NZ '000, 2008): *Imports c.i.f.:* China, People's Republic 113; Japan 296; New Zealand 10,478; Total (incl. others) 10,968. *Exports f.o.b.:* Total 27. *2009:* Total imports 9,361.

TRANSPORT

Road Traffic (2011 census): Passenger cars 399; Motorcycles 80; Vans 184; Trucks 130; Pick-ups 117; Others 16; *Total* 926.

International Shipping: *Flag Registered Fleet* (at 31 December 2014): Vessel 15; Total displacement 52,950 grt. Source: Lloyd's List Intelligence (www.lloydslistintelligence.com).

TOURISM

Foreign Tourist Arrivals: 6,094 in 2011; 5,047 in 2012; 7,047 in 2013.

Tourist Arrivals by Country of Residence (2013): Australia 648; Germany 52; New Zealand 5,489; United Kingdom 105; USA 116; Total (incl. others) 7,047.

Tourism Receipts (US $ million, excl. passenger transport): 2.0 in 2010; 2.0 in 2011.

Source: World Tourism Organization.

COMMUNICATIONS MEDIA

Telephones (2013): 1,000 main lines in use.

Mobile Cellular Telephones (2009): 1,100 units in use.

Source: International Telecommunication Union.

EDUCATION

Pre-primary and Primary (2006): 1 school; 212 pupils (males 104, females 108); 20 teachers (males 3, females 17).

Secondary (2006): 1 school; 191 pupils (males 102, females 89); 31 teachers (males 9, females 22).

Source: Department of Education, Niue.

Pupil-teacher Ratio (primary education, UNESCO estimate): 11.9 in 2004/05. Source: UNESCO Institute for Statistics.

Directory

The Government

New Zealand High Commissioner: ROSS ARDERN.

Secretary to Government: RICHARD HIPA.

CABINET
(May 2015)

Premier, Chairman of the Cabinet and Minister responsible for Finance, Customs and Revenue and Government Assets, Premier's Department (Civil Aviation, Crown Law, External Affairs, Planning, Economic Development and Statistics), Housing, Public Service Commission, Police and National Security, Tourism, and Immigration and Population: TOKE TUFUKIA TALAGI.

Minister of Social Services, Justice, Health and Education: POKOTOA SIPELI.

Minister of Infrastructure, Transport, Communications and Utilities: DALTON TAGELAGI.

Minister of Natural Resources, Agriculture, Forestry, Fisheries, Meteorological Services and Environment: BILLY TALAGI.

GOVERNMENT OFFICES

All ministries are in Alofi.

Office of the New Zealand High Commissioner: Tapeu, POB 78, Alofi; tel. 4022; fax 4173; e-mail sog.hipa@mail.gov.nu.

Office of the Secretary to Government: POB 40, Alofi; tel. 4220; fax 4232; e-mail richard.hipa@mail.gov.nu.

Legislature

ASSEMBLY
(Fono Ekepule)

The Assembly has 20 members (14 village representatives and six members elected on a common roll). The most recent general election was held on 12 April 2014.

Speaker: TOGIA PIHIGIA.

Political Organizations

There have been no active political parties on Niue since the disbanding, in 2003, of the Niue People's Party (f. 1987—Niue's sole political party to date). All politicians on the island are de facto independents.

Judicial System

The Chief Justice of the High Court, which exercises civil and criminal jurisdiction, and the Judge of the Land Court, which is concerned with litigation over land and titles, visit Niue quarterly. In addition, locally appointed lay justices exercise limited criminal and civil jurisdiction. Appeals against High Court judgments are heard in the Court of Appeal of Niue, while appeals against Land Court judgments are heard in the Land Appellate Court. Established in 1992, sessions of the Court of Appeal of Niue are usually held in the New Zealand capital of Wellington. In April 2009, however, for the first time the four New Zealand judges heard various cases, including several land disputes, on Niue itself. The final appellate tribunal in civil, criminal and land matters is the Privy Council, sitting in the United Kingdom.

Chief Justice of the High Court: PATRICK SAVAGE.

Registrar of the High Court: JUSTIN KAMUPALA.

Religion

About 62% of the population belong to the Ekalesia Niue, a Protestant Congregationalist organization, which had 956 adherents at the time of the 2006 census. Within the Roman Catholic Church, which had 138 adherents (equivalent to 9% of the population) in 2006, Niue forms part of the diocese of Tonga. The Church of Jesus Christ of Latter-day Saints (Mormon—which had 127 adherents in 2006), the Seventh-day Adventists and the Jehovah's Witnesses are also represented.

Ekalesia Kerisiano Niue: Head Office, POB 25, Alofi; tel. 4195; fax 4352; e-mail ekalesia.niue@niue.nu; f. 1846; est. by London Missionary Society, became Ekalesia Niue in 1966; Pres. Rev. AIFOLIA POUMALE; Gen. Sec. Rev. NUKANUKA TAUEVIHI.

The Press

Niue Business News: 20 Lautamina Rd, Mutalau 110175; tel. 3317; fax 4010; e-mail sioneholof@gmail.com; f. 2000; owned by Tropical Suppliers; electronic; previously publ. in print as *Niue Economic Review*; CEO FRANK SIONEHOLO.

Niue Star: weekly; f. 1993; Niuean and English; publ. in Alofi until destruction of office by Cyclone Heta in 2004; operations transferred to Auckland, New Zealand; Publr MIKE JACKSON; circ. 800.

Broadcasting and Communications

TELECOMMUNICATIONS

In 2003 Niue became the first location in the world to have a national wireless internet system allowing access from anywhere on the island by means of solar-powered aerials attached to coconut palms. A four-fold expansion of the island's internet capacity was announced in March 2010. In 2014 Niue had the highest level of internet penetration per head of population in the Pacific. A mobile telephone service was introduced in 2011.

Director of Posts and Telecommunications: POB 37, Alofi; tel. 4000; fax 4010.

Internet Niue: Rocket Systems Ltd, Fatalupe, POB 229, Alofi; tel. 4638; fax 4237; internet internetniue.nu; f. 1997; operated by Rocket Systems Ltd and upgraded by PacTel Int; provides free Wi-Fi internet access to the whole island; Dir EMANI FAKAOTIMANAVA-LUI.

Telecom Niue: POB 37, Alofi; tel. 4000; e-mail telecom.callcentre@ mail.gov.nu; internet www.telecomniue.com; Dir RICHARD HIPA.

BROADCASTING

Radio

Broadcasting Corporation of Niue: POB 68, Alofi; tel. 4026; fax 4217; operates radio and TV services; govt-owned; Chair. NEAL MORRISSEY; CEO TREVOR TIAKIA; Gen. Man. PATRICK LINO.

Radio Sunshine: broadcasts in English and Niuean between 6 a.m. and 10 p.m. Mon.–Sat.

Television

Broadcasting Corporation of Niue: see Radio.

Television Niue broadcasts in English and Niuean six days a week from 5 p.m. to 11 p.m.

Finance

DEVELOPMENT BANK

Niue Development Bank: POB 34, Alofi; tel. 4335; fax 4290; e-mail devbank@niue.nu; internet niuedevelopmentbank.nu; f. 1993; govt-owned; began operations July 1994; Chair. MISIATA TASMANIA; Gen. Man. VAINE PASISI.

COMMERCIAL BANK

Kiwibank Ltd: Alofi; replaced the branch of Bank South Pacific in 2013.

Trade and Industry

GOVERNMENT AGENCIES

Business Advisory Service: Alofi; tel. 4228.

Office of Economic Affairs, Planning and Development, Statistics and Trade and Investment: POB 42, Alofi; tel. 4148; e-mail business.epdsu@mail.gov.nu; responsible for planning and financing activities in the agricultural, tourism, industrial sectors, business advisory and trade and investment.

CHAMBER OF COMMERCE

Niue Chamber of Commerce: POB 213, Alofi; tel. 4399; e-mail chamber@niue.nu; Chair. AVI RUBEN; Pres. ROSSALOFA REX.

UTILITIES

Niue Power Corporation: POB 198, Alofi; tel. 4119; fax 4385; e-mail gm.npc@mail.gov.nu; Gen. Man. SPEEDO HETUTU.

TRADE UNION

Niue Public Service Association: Alofi; f. 2006; Pres. FRANK SIONEHOLO.

Transport

ROADS

There are 123 km of all-weather roads and 106 km of access and plantation roads.

SHIPPING

The best anchorage is an open roadstead at Alofi, the largest of Niue's 14 villages. The New Zealand Shipping Corporation operates a monthly service between New Zealand, Nauru and Niue. Fuel supplies are delivered by a tanker (the *Pacific Explorer*) from Fiji. In December 2002 the Government signed an agreement with Reef Shipping Ltd to provide a service to New Zealand every three to four weeks. The Reef Group went into receivership in November 2012, but its primary shipping assets were acquired by US company Matson South Pacific Ltd, which relaunched the service from Niue to New Zealand in January 2013. Legislation providing for the creation of a new registry permitting ships to sail under the Niuean flag was adopted in March 2012; the registry opened later that year, under the management of a Singaporean company.

CIVIL AVIATION

Hanan International Airport has a total sealed runway of 2,350 m, following the completion of a 700 m extension in 1995, with New Zealand assistance. In 2005 Air New Zealand began a weekly service between Auckland and Niue. The frequency of this service was increased to twice weekly from May 2014. Meanwhile, in early 2011 the provision of funding by the People's Republic of China, to finance improvements that included the extension of the airport terminal, was confirmed; the extension was formally opened in June 2014.

Tourism

Niue has a small but significant tourism industry (specializing in holidays based on activities such as diving, rock-climbing, caving and game fishing), which has benefited from an increase in the frequency of flights between the island and New Zealand. The Matavai Resort provides the main tourist facilities; the resort underwent a major refurbishment in 2012. In December 2014 the Niue authorities transferred the management of the resort to the New Zealand Scenic Hotel Group in a bid further to boost tourism on the island.In September 2011 it was announced that over a three-year period New Zealand was to provide a total of $NZ15m. for the purposes of tourism development projects. Tourism receipts (excluding passenger transport) totalled US $2m. in 2011. Most visitors are from New Zealand. Visitor arrivals increased from 5,047 in 2012 to 7,047 in 2013.

Niue Tourism Development Board: Alofi; f. 2010; govt agency; Chair SONYA TALAGI (acting).

Niue Tourism Office: POB 42, Alofi; tel. 4224; fax 4225; e-mail info@niueisland.com; internet www.niueisland.com; Dir of Tourism HAYDEN PORTER.

Education

Education is free and compulsory between six and 16 years of age (the school-leaving age having been raised from 14 in 1998). In 1987 the island's seven village primary schools were closed and a single national primary school was opened at Halamahaga. In 2006 this bilingual (Niuean/English) primary school had 20 teachers and an enrolment of 212 pupils. There was one secondary school, at Paliati, with a teaching staff of 31 and a total enrolment of 191 pupils in 2006. Higher education takes place at the Niue Extension Centre of the University of the South Pacific (based in Fiji), on government training schemes or by correspondence. Some study overseas, in the Pacific region and New Zealand. A private university—St Clements University Higher Education School-Niue—offering online business and information technology courses opened in late 2003.

NICARAGUA

Introductory Survey

LOCATION, CLIMATE, LANGUAGE, RELIGION, FLAG, CAPITAL

The Republic of Nicaragua lies in the Central American isthmus, bounded by the Pacific Ocean to the west and by the Caribbean Sea to the east. Its neighbours are Honduras, to the north, and Costa Rica, to the south. The climate is tropical, with an annual average temperature of 25.5°C (78°F). The rainy season extends from May to October. The national language is Spanish, although English is also spoken on the Caribbean coast. Almost all of the inhabitants profess Christianity, and a majority are Roman Catholics. The national flag (proportions 3 by 5) has three equal horizontal stripes, of blue, white and blue, with the state emblem (a triangle enclosing a dark blue sea from which rise five volcanoes, in green, surmounted by a Phrygian cap from which extend white rays and, at the top, a rainbow, all encircled by the words, in gold capitals, 'República de Nicaragua' and 'América Central') in the centre of the white stripe; the same flag without the state emblem is an alternative version of the civil flag. The capital is Managua.

CONTEMPORARY POLITICAL HISTORY

Historical Context

Nicaragua was under Spanish rule from the 16th century until 1821. It then became part of the Central American Federation until 1838. From 1927 US troops were based in Nicaragua at the request of the Government, which was opposed by a guerrilla group, led by Augusto César Sandino. In 1933, following the establishment of the National Guard (commanded by Gen. Anastasio Somoza García), the US troops left Nicaragua. Sandino was assassinated in 1934, but some of his followers (Sandinistas) continued actively to oppose the new regime. Somoza seized power in a coup in 1935 and took office as President in 1936. Apart from a brief interlude in the late 1940s, Somoza remained as President until September 1956, when he was assassinated. However, the Somoza family continued to dominate Nicaraguan politics until 1979.

Domestic Political Affairs

In 1962 the left-wing Frente Sandinista de Liberación Nacional (FSLN—Sandinista National Liberation Front) was formed with the object of overthrowing the Somozas by revolution. Gen. Anastasio Somoza Debayle, son of the former dictator, became President in 1967, holding office until 1972. The Congreso Nacional (National Congress) was dissolved, and a triumvirate ruled until Gen. Somoza was re-elected President in September 1974. In 1978 the murder of Pedro Joaquín Chamorro Cardenal, the leader of the opposition coalition and the editor of *La Prensa* (the country's only independent newspaper), provoked violent demonstrations against the Government.

In June 1979 the FSLN formed a provisional Junta of National Reconstruction. With the FSLN in command of many towns, President Somoza resigned and left the country. (He was assassinated in Paraguay in 1980.) After the Sandinistas had gained control of the capital, the Junta and its Provisional Governing Council took power in July 1979 as the Government of National Reconstruction. The 1974 Constitution was abrogated, and the bicameral Congress dissolved. A Basic Statute, providing for the creation of an appointed Council of State to act as an interim legislature, was issued. The National Guard was disbanded and replaced by the Ejército Popular Sandinista (Sandinista People's Army). In August the Junta issued a 'Statute on Rights and Guarantees for the Citizens of Nicaragua', providing for basic personal freedoms and restoring freedom of the press and broadcasting. Civil rights were restored in January 1980. In March 1981 Commdr Daniel Ortega Saavedra was appointed Co-ordinator of the Junta and of its new consultative body, the Council of Government.

By 1981 discontent at the postponement of elections and the increasing hegemony of the Sandinistas had led to the creation of counter-revolutionary forces ('Contras'), who were mostly members of the former National Guard and operated from camps in Honduras. Meanwhile, relations between the US and

Nicaraguan Governments had seriously deteriorated, culminating in the suspension of US economic aid. In the same year the US Government donated US \$10m. in support of the Contras, while covert operations by the US Central Intelligence Agency (CIA) attempted to destabilize the Sandinista regime. The Sandinista Government declared a state of emergency in 1982. However, the intensity of attacks by the Fuerzas Democráticas Nicaragüenses, anti-Sandinista guerrillas based in Honduras, increased. A Contra group, the Alianza Revolucionaria Democrática, was also established in Costa Rica, led by Edén Pastora Gómez, a prominent figure in the revolution who had become disillusioned with the Sandinistas.

In 1984 talks commenced between the Nicaraguan and US Governments in order to foster peace negotiations proposed by the Contadora group (Colombia, Mexico, Panama and Venezuela), which was attempting to find solutions to disputes involving Central America. However, although the Sandinistas agreed to sign a peace agreement, the USA rejected the accord on the grounds that the forthcoming Nicaraguan elections would not be fairly conducted. Despite the decision by the US Congress to allocate US \$27m. in non-military aid to the Contras, the Nicaraguan Government agreed to resume negotiations with the USA. Meanwhile, however, the civil conflict escalated, and clashes along Nicaragua's borders with Costa Rica and Honduras became increasingly frequent.

A presidential election and elections to a constituent assembly were held in November 1984. The assembly was to draw up a constitution within two years of taking office. In August the Government had restored the majority of the civil rights that had been previously suspended. Ortega, the FSLN candidate, won the presidential ballot, and his party won a majority of seats in the National Constituent Assembly, which replaced the Council of State.

In 1986 the US Congress approved assistance for the Contras worth US \$100m. Later the same year the US Government disclosed that funds accruing from its clandestine sales of military equipment to Iran had been used to support the Contras.

In January 1987 a new Constitution was promulgated; on the same day, however, civil liberties, guaranteed in the Constitution, were again suspended by the renewal of the five-year-old state of emergency. In February the Governments of Costa Rica, El Salvador, Guatemala and Honduras approved a peace plan for Nicaragua, largely based on earlier Contadora proposals, but placing greater emphasis on democratization, including the ending of the state of emergency. Following some modification, in August the peace plan was signed by the Presidents of the five nations. In accordance with the plan, a four-member National Commission for Reconciliation was created, chaired by Cardinal Miguel Obando y Bravo, the Archbishop of Managua, a leading critic of the Government. In January 1988 the Government ended the state of emergency, and consented to participate directly in negotiations with the Contras, which resulted in March in a 60-day ceasefire (which was later extended until November 1989). The Government agreed to the gradual release of political prisoners and to the participation of the Contras in domestic political dialogue and, eventually, in elections. In August 1988 the US Senate approved the provision of a further US \$27m. in aid for the Contras. As the hope of further military aid diminished, the Contras retreated into Honduras.

In February 1989, at a meeting of the five Central American Presidents in El Salvador, it was agreed that, in return for the dismantling of Contra bases in Honduras, there would be moves towards greater democracy in Nicaragua, including a general election by February 1990. Contra rebels were to be permitted to return to vote, on condition that they relinquished their armed struggle under a proposed demobilization plan. In August 1989 the five Presidents signed an agreement in Tela, Honduras, providing for the voluntary demobilization, repatriation or relocation of the Contra forces within a 90-day period. An International Commission of Support and Verification was established by the UN and the Organization of American States (OAS, see p. 392).

In November 1989 President Ortega declared the ending of the ceasefire with the Contras, on the grounds that the rebels had made insufficient progress in implementing the Tela agreement and disbanding their forces stationed in Honduras. In response, the UN Security Council established the UN Observer Group in Central America (ONUCA) to monitor compliance with the Tela agreement, to prevent cross-border incursions by rebels and to assist in supervising the forthcoming Nicaraguan elections.

Chamorro in power

The general election of February 1990 resulted in an unexpected victory for Violeta Barrios de Chamorro (the widow of Pedro Chamorro), the presidential candidate of the recently formed Unión Nacional Opositora (UNO), comprising 14 opposition parties. After the election, the Sandinista Government decreed an immediate ceasefire. The President-elect pledged to 'depoliticize' the security forces, and urged the Contra rebels to disband and return to civilian life. However, the UNO had not secured a sufficient majority of seats in the Asamblea Nacional (National Assembly) to make amendments to the Constitution. Before the transfer of power on 25 April, a General Amnesty and National Reconciliation Law was adopted: this was designed to pre-empt retaliatory measures against outgoing officials and to quash legal proceedings against those who had committed politically motivated crimes against the State since 1979.

On 19 April 1990 a ceasefire was agreed by the Contras and the Sandinista armed forces. The Contras agreed to surrender their weapons, and to assemble in 'security zones' supervised by UN troops. A transitional agreement between the outgoing Government and the UNO administration provided for a reduction in the strength of the security forces and their subordination to civilian authority. In return for a commitment from the Contras to sign the demobilization accords, the Government agreed to the establishment of a special police force, composed of former Contra rebels, in order to guarantee security within the demobilization zones. Demobilization of the Contra rebels was officially concluded on 27 June, signifying the end of 11 years of civil war in Nicaragua.

On assuming office, the UNO Government attempted to reverse much Sandinista policy. The suspension of the civil service law in May 1990 provoked a public sector strike and Chamorro was forced to concede wage increases of 100%. Following further protests the Government formed a National Agrarian Commission to study problems of land distribution and illegal land seizures. In mid-1991, however, the emergence of groups of re-armed Contra rebels (known as Re-contras) became apparent. They claimed to represent thousands of demobilized Contras in the north of the country who had not received land and aid promised by the resettlement plan.

Despite the phased disarmament of the Re-contras and the Re-compas (groups of re-armed Sandinistas) in early 1992, groups of former combatants began joining forces to form the Revueltos. In May the Government allocated 800 plots of land outside the capital to the Revueltos. However, rebel activity continued. In February 1994 a peace agreement was signed that provided for the demobilization of a prominent Re-contra group, the Frente Norte 3-80, in return for which the rebels were granted an amnesty and the right to be incorporated into the national police force. Nevertheless, violent incidents continued.

In June 1991 the FSLN withdrew its 39 deputies from the National Assembly in protest against the proposal to revoke two laws concerning redistribution of property. The so-called *piñata* laws, that guaranteed the property rights of the thousands of people who had benefited from the land expropriation under the Sandinistas, had been introduced by the FSLN immediately prior to the transfer of power to the Chamorro administration. In August the legislature approved the abrogation of the *piñata* laws, but President Chamorro vetoed parts of the bill that she deemed to be unconstitutional. Disagreement over the property issue had by now led to the alienation of Chamorro of the majority of UNO deputies, and the legislature only narrowly failed to overturn the veto in December. In May 1992 the US Congress suspended aid to Nicaragua, on the grounds that the Government had failed to compensate US citizens for land expropriated under the Sandinista regime. In September Chamorro established a property ombudsman's office and signed an agreement specifying that all unjustly confiscated property would be returned (or the rightful owners compensated).

A serious legislative crisis arose in September 1992, when the President of the National Assembly, Alfredo César, convened the legislature in the absence of the deputies of the FSLN and the Grupo de Centro (dissident UNO deputies who had maintained

their allegiance to the Government), recruiting substitute deputies in order to elect new legislative authorities. In December Chamorro ordered the army to occupy the assembly building and appointed a provisional administration to manage parliamentary affairs pending the election of new legislative authorities. In October 1993 the Alianza Política Opositora (APO—as the UNO had become) and the FSLN signed an agreement providing for the implementation of partial constitutional reforms. The National Assembly reconvened in January 1994, and new legislative authorities were elected. In November some 67 constitutional amendments were approved, which adjusted the balance of authority in favour of the legislature, notably regarding external loans, debt negotiations and international trade agreements, and reduced the presidential and legislative terms, but withdrew the absolute ban on presidential re-election (although consecutive terms remained prohibited). The amendments were deemed illegal by the FSLN leadership, but won the support of FSLN deputies, reflecting the divisions within the party. Following Chamorro's refusal to promulgate the reforms, the National Assembly enacted them. A resolution to the dispute was achieved by the signing of a political accord between the Government and the legislature in June 1995, which included a moderation of amendments intended to reduce presidential authority.

The Alemán and Bolaños administrations

Presidential and legislative elections were held in October 1996. Arnoldo Alemán Lacayo of the Partido Liberal Constitucionalista (PLC), the candidate of the Alianza Liberal, secured the presidency. The Alianza Liberal also won the largest number of seats in the National Assembly, although it failed to gain a majority.

In June 1999 the Government and the FSLN began negotiations on constitutional and electoral reform. The principal amendments adopted included a reduction in the proportion of votes necessary for a President to be elected outright from 45% to 35%, thus increasing the likelihood of an FSLN victory. In return, Alemán, whose administration had been confronted by allegations of corruption, was guaranteed a seat in the National Assembly after leaving office, thus making him virtually immune from prosecution. Other reforms included the restructuring of the judiciary and the electoral authorities.

At presidential and legislative elections in November 2001 former Vice-President and PLC candidate Enrique Bolaños Geyer was elected President, with 56% of votes cast, while Ortega, standing again for the FSLN, secured 42%. The PLC also won a majority of seats in the National Assembly. Bolaños immediately encountered opposition from within his own party over the issue of selecting the President of the National Assembly. In March 2002 the Attorney-General announced that Alemán, who had been elected to the post against Bolaños' wishes, was to face charges of fraud and embezzlement. Bolaños subsequently made several unsuccessful attempts to remove Alemán's congressional immunity, as internal divisions within the PLC meant that he lacked the votes necessary to have the motion approved.

In September 2002 several of Alemán's relatives and former members of his Government were convicted of laundering some US $100m. from state communications, infrastructure, insurance and petroleum enterprises. FSLN members joined the Bolaños faction of the PLC to vote to remove Alemán as President of the legislature. In December the National Assembly approved a motion revoking Alemán's immunity; the former President was immediately put under house arrest.

In October 2002 Bolaños himself became the subject of allegations of fraud. In response to charges filed with the Supreme Court, that he and his Vice-President, José Rizo Castellón, had used an illegal fund controlled by Alemán to finance his 2001 electoral campaign, Bolaños renounced his presidential immunity. In November Bolaños and Rizo were formally charged with embezzling US $4.1m. from public funds. Deepening divisions within the PLC led to the announcement in March 2003 that the pro-Alemán faction of the party was in opposition to the Government, in protest at the Government's alliance with the FSLN. In December Alemán was found guilty of money-laundering, fraud and theft of state funds and was sentenced to 20 years' imprisonment and fined $17m. Owing to ill health, however, he was to serve his prison term under house arrest. In the same month the alliance between the FSLN and the pro-Bolaños PLC members collapsed, following the latter's insistence on Alemán's release.

In March 2004 President Bolaños, Vice-President Rizo and 31 other senior members of the PLC were accused of illegal campaign-financing during the previous presidential election. In October the Comptroller-General requested that Bolaños be removed from power for withholding information regarding the financing of his 2001 election campaign. Supporters of the President claimed that the request was politically motivated, as the office of the Comptroller-General was controlled by the FSLN and the anti-Bolaños faction of the PLC. At the invitation of Bolaños, a delegation arrived from the OAS to investigate the Comptroller-General's findings and Ortega subsequently agreed to withdraw FSLN support for the initiation of impeachment proceedings against the President until after the November municipal elections.

The FSLN won a decisive victory in the local elections of November 2004. The following day a two-thirds' majority in the National Assembly voted in support of constitutional reforms limiting presidential powers. The reforms would notably require the President to seek legislative ratification for key appointments and would enable the Assembly to remove officials deemed to be incompetent. Despite opposition from President Bolaños, who maintained that the reforms were unconstitutional, they were approved by the Assembly in January 2005. Meanwhile, accusations against Bolaños and his associates of illegal campaign-financing persisted. In September 2005 seven Central American heads of state gathered in Managua to demonstrate their support for Bolaños.

Dissent over the proposed constitutional reforms impeded the Government's legislative agenda in 2005, including efforts to gain approval for the proposed Dominican Republic-Central American Free Trade Agreement (CAFTA-DR, comprising Nicaragua, Costa Rica, the Dominican Republic, El Salvador, Guatemala, Honduras and the USA). Following the intervention of the US Assistant Secretary of State, who publicly criticized the PLC-FSLN legislative pact and proposed the implementation of CAFTA-DR without Nicaragua, in October the FSLN withdrew its opposition to the trade agreement, which was swiftly approved by the National Assembly.

The return of Ortega

Presidential and legislative elections took place in November 2006. Ortega, who had sought to distance himself from the more extreme Sandinista policies of the 1980s, was elected to the presidency with 38% of the votes cast. Eduardo Montealegre Rivas of the Alianza Liberal Nicaragüense (ALN), a recently founded party composed primarily of dissident former PLC members opposed to Alemán, secured 28%, while former Vice-President Rizo, a close ally of Alemán, took 27% for the PLC. The FSLN also became the largest party in the National Assembly.

Ortega took office on 10 January 2007, appointing his wife, Rosario Murillo Zambrana, to the newly created cabinet position of Co ordinator of the Communication and Citizenship Council, in which role she was to be responsible for all government publicity. Later that month the President issued a decree more than halving his own salary and substantially lowering those of government ministers and other senior officials. The National Assembly adopted amendments to legislation on the role of the executive, giving the President greater control over the police force and the military and establishing 'Citizen Power Councils'. Amid concerns regarding the potential power of these Councils, which were intended to encourage direct democracy by co-ordinating the work of non-governmental organizations and public institutions, opposition parties insisted that they should not assume any of the functions of government ministries.

Also in January 2007 the legislature approved the further postponement, for one year, of the constitutional amendments limiting presidential powers that had been due to take effect that month. A special commission was charged in February with drafting new constitutional reform. In January 2008 the Supreme Court annulled the law postponing the implementation of the constitutional reforms, although it also declared invalid the majority of the reforms themselves. However, it did not annul the law requiring the President to seek legislative approval of key appointments, with the result that this reform duly entered into force.

The 2008 municipal elections

Events surrounding the municipal elections of November 2008 increased tensions between the FSLN and its opponents. The Government had postponed the elections in the North Atlantic Autonomous Region, owing to the damage caused by Hurricane Felix in 2007. Anti-Government protesters claimed that the FSLN was acting to avoid an electoral defeat in the region, and riots led to two deaths. In June 2008 the Consejo Supremo Electoral (CSE—Supreme Electoral Council), composed of seven magistrates aligned with either the FSLN or the PLC, revoked the legal status of two opposition parties for administrative reasons, provoking criticism that the PLC-FSLN legislative pact continued to pose a threat to multi-party democracy. In the elections in November, the FSLN secured 105 of the 146 contested mayoralties, including that of Managua, while the PLC took 37. However, allegations of widespread fraud undermined the results. The FSLN made significant gains in municipal elections held in the North Atlantic region in January 2009. A report by the non-governmental anti-corruption organization Transparency International alleged that electoral fraud had occurred in at least 40 of the 146 municipalities.

Judicial controversy

The Government continued to attract controversy during 2009, securing the removal of the one-term limit on presidential tenure by means of a ruling by the constitutional panel of the highly politicized Supreme Court. The ruling was deemed illegal on the basis that only the National Assembly could effect constitutional change. A presidential decree issued in January 2010, extending the terms of incumbent electoral and judicial officials, in defiance of a constitutional provision according the National Assembly responsibility for such appointments, prompted the opposition to boycott the legislature. Following the refusal of two FSLN-aligned Supreme Court judges to leave their posts on the expiry of their terms in April, opposition deputies attempted to convene with the aim of overturning Ortega's controversial decree, but were forcibly prevented from doing so by government supporters. The crisis escalated in August, with the replacement of seven PLC-affiliated judges who had refused to participate in court sessions in protest; five of the substitute judges were aligned with the ruling party and two with the opposition. The Supreme Court subsequently upheld both decrees issued by Ortega and in October the National Assembly approved a new version of the Constitution, incorporating the changes.

The re-election of Ortega

Ortega was victorious in the presidential election of 6 November 2011, winning 62.5% of the valid votes cast, followed by former PLC member Fabio Gadea Mantilla, representing an alliance of the Partido Liberal Independiente (PLI), with 31.0%, and Alemán for the PLC, with only 5.9%. The FSLN also performed strongly in the concurrent legislative elections, securing an unexpected two-thirds' majority in the National Assembly, with 62 of the 90 elective seats, while the PLI took 26 seats and the PLC two. Gadea and the outgoing Vice-President, Jaime René Morales Carazo of the FSLN, were both awarded supplementary legislative seats, in accordance with electoral rules. However, Gadea rejected the results, alleging widespread manipulation of the vote by the FSLN. International observers from the OAS and the European Union (EU) also expressed concern about the transparency of the vote, as well as the independence of the CSE. Three opposition supporters and one Sandinista were killed in post-election violence in the north of the country.

Notwithstanding the allegations of fraud, Ortega's overwhelming victory and that of his party was widely attributed to the popularity and success of the Government's poverty reduction and other social programmes (largely funded by Venezuela) and the stability of the economy. Gadea announced that he would not take up the supplementary seat to which he was entitled as second-placed presidential candidate, as he refused to accept defeat. President Ortega was inaugurated for a further term of office on 10 January 2012 in a ceremony boycotted by the main opposition parties.

The confiscation, in February 2012, of land belonging to a Swiss-Nicaraguan investor, and its transferral to the ownership of former Sandinista guerrilla Edén Pastora (who had reconciled with Ortega since unsuccessfully contesting the 2006 presidential election), provoked consternation within the private sector regarding the Government's respect for property rights. In the following month thousands of former Sandinista combatants blocked roads in several northern provinces for more than one week, demanding a range of benefits that they had been promised prior to demobilization in the early 1990s. The Government agreed to address their demands, but there was renewed unrest in mid-2012. Legislation on benefits for veterans, including pension provision, health care, housing assistance and land title rights, was finally approved in January 2013.

In April 2012 the President of the National Assembly, René Núñez Téllez, announced that the long-awaited election by the legislature of 23 senior judicial and electoral officials was to take place. Although the mandates of the incumbents of these posts had expired, they had continued serving in accordance with the decree issued by Ortega in January 2010 (see *Judicial controversy*), when the FSLN notably lacked a legislative majority. It was noted, however, that several officials, including the President of the CSE, Ortega ally Roberto Rivas Reyes, were not among those to be replaced, despite their mandates also having expired.

Reforms to legislation on municipalities, which provided for an increase in the number of councillors from 2,178 to 6,534 and permitted the re-election of local officials, were adopted by the National Assembly in May 2012. Critics accused the Ortega administration of seeking to expand its control at municipal level.

The FSLN consolidated its power at the municipal elections of November 2012, securing control of 134 of the 153 municipalities and 16 of the 17 departmental and regional capitals. In Managua, the FSLN's Daisy Torres was re-elected as mayor with 83% of the votes cast. Civil society groups claimed that fraud had been perpetrated in four municipalities, although the CSE rejected official opposition challenges to the results in four municipalities. Violence marred the period surrounding the elections: a PLC candidate was shot dead in Siuna, in the North Atlantic Autonomous Region, in late October, and three people were killed the day after polling, as clashes broke out in several municipalities between government and opposition supporters.

Constitutional changes

The presence of armed groups, operating most notably in the North Atlantic Autonomous Region and Jinotega areas near the border with Honduras, became a cause for concern in 2013. The Government, which maintained that the groups were criminal gangs with no political motives, had sought to disrupt their activities by implementation of a rural security plan which had led to more than 1,000 arrests. However, in late 2013 ongoing reports of violence, involving the deaths of several civilians, led leaders of the Catholic church in the area to urge the Government to engage in dialogue with the groups.

In November 2013 protesters from opposition parties, human rights groups and the Catholic church demonstrated in Managua against Ortega's proposed changes to the Constitution. The planned amendments included the further relaxation of the rules governing presidential re-election, which would allow Ortega to run for a fourth term (and third consecutive term), measures to concentrate power in the executive and to extend the role of the military. Proposals also included change in the percentage of votes necessary to win the presidency from at least 35% of the valid votes and a five point margin to a more vague 'relative majority', and a move to prohibit deputies from switching parties. Despite vociferous domestic and international opposition (notably from the US authorities, which opined that the changes could be detrimental to Nicaragua's democracy), the reforms received legislative approval in January 2014. The National Assembly also passed legislation allowing for the re-appointment of the head of the armed forces (appointed by the President for a five-year term) and for military officers concurrently to serve in the executive.

At local elections in March 2014 in the North and South Atlantic Autonomous Regions the FSLN further confirmed its dominance, attracting 52% of the vote in the North Atlantic, compared to 21% won by indigenous party Yatama, and 19% by the PLC, and 48% in the South Atlantic, where the PLC won only 19% and Yatama 7%. Yatama alleged electoral fraud, and shortly afterwards ended its alliance with the FSLN in the National Assembly in protest.

n July 2014 the PLC and the PLI announced their decision to merge to form a united opposition grouping in preparation for the elections scheduled for November 2016. The two parties had repeatedly expressed the view that President Ortega had abused his position by appointing FSLN sympathizers to the judiciary and to electoral authorities, and by making constitutional changes that extend his power and favour his continuance in office.

Recent developments: the Gran Canal project

In July 2012 the National Assembly approved a government proposal to create a new state body with responsibility for planning the construction of an inter-oceanic canal. In June 2013 the National Assembly approved legislation granting a Hong Kong company a 50-year concession to build and operate a so-called 'Gran Canal'. The decision prompted protests from opposition and environmental groups, but in December the Supreme Court rejected all appeals lodged against the project, thereby granting it the legal right to proceed.

In late December 2014 the construction of the inter-oceanic Gran Canal officially began. The project, a fenced waterway some 30 m deep and 178 miles long, was the largest infrastructure scheme ever undertaken in the country, and was estimated to cost US \$40,000m. The plans had attracted considerable opposition for the alleged lack of consultation with local communities, the incomplete feasibility studies and the scale of the expected negative impact on wildlife and the ecosystem along the canal's route. A petition with some 60,000 signatories was presented to the Government by former Sandinista leader Henry 'Modesto' Ruiz and a demonstration by more than 5,000 people took place in Managua in mid-December. At the official launch of the works several protesters were injured in violent clashes with the police and foreign journalists reported being intimidated by the authorities. The Government maintained that the canal would bring significant economic benefits to Nicaragua.

Edward Centeno was appointed Minister of Agriculture and Forestry in February 2015 following the departure of Ariel Bucardo, allegedly owing to differences with Rosario Murillo, Ortega's wife and fellow member of the Cabinet. In the previous month Salvador Mansell Castrillo had succeeded Emilio Rappaccioli as Minister of Energy and Mines after the latter was appointed adviser to the President on renewable energy issues.

Foreign Affairs

Relations with the USA

Full military relations between Nicaragua and the USA, suspended since 1980, were re-established in 2001. In 2004 the Government agreed to destroy one-half of its stockpile of surface-to-air missiles. However, dissatisfaction with a lack of progress on the issue prompted the USA to suspend military aid to Nicaragua in 2005. Talks between the two countries concerning the destruction of the missiles took place during 2008, but did not result in agreement. The dispute regarding the results of the 2008 municipal elections strained international relations and led the EU and the USA to suspend budgetary aid to Nicaragua. The 2011 general election also provoked international concern: US Secretary of State Hillary Clinton described the election as a 'setback to democracy', while US-based human rights group Freedom House removed Nicaragua from its list of electoral democracies, owing to alleged irregularities. Further sanctions by the US authorities in 2012 led to the withholding of aid, and the threatened cancellation of a property waiver (under which US support for countries that had not compensated US citizens for confiscated property would be withdrawn) was likely to inflict significant financial damage upon Nicaragua. The US Government again criticized the electoral process in Nicaragua, following the municipal elections of November 2012.

Other regional relations

In 1999, following confrontations with Honduras, Nicaragua initiated proceedings at the International Court of Justice (ICJ, see p. 25) in The Hague, Netherlands, to determine the maritime delimitation in the Gulf of Fonseca. A further dispute prompted Nicaragua to sever commercial ties with, and impose import taxes on, Honduras, in direct contravention of Central American free trade undertakings. Nicaragua lifted the sanctions following mediation by the OAS in 2000, when both countries agreed to observe a maritime exclusion zone in the Caribbean and to reduce troop numbers on their common border. However, following further illegal incursions by both sides, in 2001 Nicaragua submitted documentation to the ICJ contesting the treaty. Nicaragua and Honduras subsequently concluded a confidence-building agreement, which provided for OAS observers to monitor the actions of army and navy forces on both sides of the common border. The ICJ ruled on a revised maritime border approximately mid-way between the two countries in 2007, which was accepted by both parties.

In 1997 relations with Costa Rica became strained when the latter began deporting Nicaraguans who were residing illegally in the country. Further antagonism had developed between the two countries in 1998 when Nicaragua prohibited Costa Rican civil guards from carrying arms while navigating the San Juan river, which forms the border between the two countries. According to a long-standing treaty, the river, which is Nicaraguan territory, was only to be used by Costa Rica for commercial purposes. In 2000 both Governments agreed a procedure that would allow armed Costa Rican police officers to patrol the river, but continued disagreement prompted Costa Rica to refer the matter to the ICJ in 2005. In response, President Bolaños ordered troops patrolling the border area to prohibit the passage of armed Costa Rican police officers, and imposed a 35% tariff on Costa Rican imports. In 2009 the ICJ upheld Nicaragua's right to regulate traffic on the river and ruled that Costa Rican police vessels were not permitted to use it. In early 2011 the ICJ ordered both sides to withdraw personnel from the border, following allegations that Nicaraguan troops had violated Costa Rican territory. Furthermore, later that year Nicaragua initiated new legal proceedings against Costa Rica, claiming that the construction of a road parallel to the southern bank of the San Juan river violated Nicaragua's sovereignty and was causing environmental damage. The ICJ ruled in Costa Rica's favour in December 2013. In February 2013 it was reported that Nicaragua had requested that the ICJ grant it navigational rights on the Colorado river, which is Costa Rican territory, provoking condemnation from the Costa Rican Government. Moreover, in July the Costa Rican authorities accused Nicaragua of offering petroleum exploration concessions in Costa Rican maritime territory. Ortega's remarks in the following month, suggesting that Nicaragua might seek to reclaim the border province of Guanacaste, which had been annexed to Costa Rica in 1824, provoked controversy and the country's ambassador was recalled. In February 2014 Costa Rica submitted a further protest to the ICJ, claiming that the Nicaraguan Government was offering oil exploration concessions that fell within Costa Rican maritime territory. Tensions between the two countries deepened in November when Costa Rica's foreign minister sent a formal note of protest to his Nicaraguan counterpart complaining about works on the Costa Rican side of the river.

In 2001 a dispute with Colombia arose after a Nicaraguan fishing vessel was captured, allegedly in Colombian waters. A request by Nicaragua to the ICJ that its claim over territorial waters in the Caribbean Sea and around the islands of San Andrés and Providencia be recognized was dismissed in 2007. The ICJ issued its final judgment in November 2012, confirming Colombian sovereignty over all seven disputed cays and smaller islands, but awarding Nicaragua control of an estimated 75,000 sq km of territorial waters hitherto considered Colombian. The binding ruling was generally interpreted as a victory for Nicaragua, with the Colombian Government rejecting the new maritime border and ordering its naval forces to remain in the waters, while the Nicaraguan Government announced plans to commence oil explorations in its new waters. The leaders of both countries insisted that the dispute would be resolved peacefully. However, relations deteriorated significantly in 2013 with Nicaragua accusing Colombia of multiple violations of its maritime territory, culminating in November in Nicaragua filing a further case with the ICJ and Colombia recalling its ambassador in Managua.

President Ortega sought to strengthen relations with other left-wing administrations in Latin America. In 2007 he confirmed Nicaragua's participation in the Bolivarian Alliance for the Peoples of our America-People's Trade Treaty (Alianza Bolivariana para los Pueblos de Nuestra América-Tratado de Comercio de los Pueblos—ALBA-TCP, see p. 459), which had been devised by Venezuela as an alternative model to the US-promoted Free Trade Area of the Americas. Furthermore, Ortega signed a number of economic agreements with Venezuela, which pledged substantial financial assistance to Nicaragua, including the construction of a petroleum refinery and the provision of low-interest loans for impoverished Nicaraguans. Under its Petrocaribe initiative, Venezuela was to supply Nicaragua with 10,000 barrels of petroleum per day at preferential rates and 32 electricity generators to alleviate severe energy shortages. In 2010 Ortega announced that ALBA-TCP funds would be used to finance the provision of monthly bonuses of US $25 for some 120,000 (later increased to 147,500) public sector workers; the bonus was raised to $31 per month a year later. Venezuela was reported to have provided Nicaragua with some $1,590m. during 2007–10. Financial co-operation from Venezuela continued to rise in 2011, reaching $609m. (more than 90% of which was related to subsidized petroleum), an increase of 14% from 2010. Following Venezuelan President Hugo Chávez's death in 2013, concerns mounted in Nicaragua regarding the possibility of a future decline in financial assistance from Venezuela, despite

the election of Chávez's favoured successor, Nicolás Maduro; these fears persisted in early 2015.

In 2013 Nicaragua made efforts to strengthen its relations with Russia, which in that year was its second most important financial donor (after Venezuela). Early that year a training centre for anti-drugs-trafficking operations was opened with Russian financial assistance. In May 2014 Nicaragua's finance and trade ministers led a delegation to Russia to attend trade talks, and in that month it was announced that Nicaragua was to host installations for Russia's global satellite navigation system GLONASS. Reports in 2014 that the Russian Government was planning to establish military facilities in Nicaragua led to expressions of concern about Russian influence in the country.

CONSTITUTION AND GOVERNMENT

A new Constitution was promulgated in January 1987. Amendments to the Constitution were approved by the National Assembly in 1995, 2000, 2010 and 2014. Executive power is vested in the President, who is elected by popular vote for a five-year term. The President is assisted by a Vice-President and an appointed Cabinet. Legislative power is held by the National Assembly, elected by universal adult suffrage, under a system of proportional representation, for a five-year term.

REGIONAL AND INTERNATIONAL CO-OPERATION

Nicaragua is a member of the Organization of American States (see p. 392), the Central American Common Market (CACM, see p. 228), the Inter-American Development Bank (see p. 328), the Association of Caribbean States (see p. 444), and of the Community of Latin American and Caribbean States (see p. 460), which was formally inaugurated in December 2011. Implementation of the Dominican Republic-Central American Free Trade Agreement (CAFTA-DR) with the USA, which entailed the gradual elimination of tariffs on most industrial and agricultural products over the following 10 and 20 years, respectively, began in 2006. Nicaragua was a member of the Venezuela-led Bolivarian Alliance for the Peoples of our America-People's Trade Treaty (Alianza Bolivariana para los Pueblos de Nuestra América-Tratado de Comercio de los Pueblos—ALBA-TCP, see p. 459). A free trade agreement between Nicaragua, Costa Rica, El Salvador, Guatemala, Honduras and Mexico was signed in November 2011. In 2012 Nicaragua, with other Central American countries, concluded a free trade agreement with the EU. Nicaragua is a founder member of the UN. As a contracting party to the General Agreement on Tariffs and Trade, Nicaragua joined the World Trade Organization (see p. 431) on its establishment in 1995.

ECONOMIC AFFAIRS

In 2013, according to estimates by the World Bank, Nicaragua's gross national income (GNI), measured at average 2011–13 prices, was US $10,834m., equivalent to $1,780 per head (or $4,440 per head on an international purchasing-power parity basis). During 2004–13 the population increased at an average annual rate of 1.4%, while gross domestic product (GDP) per head grew, in real terms, by an average of 2.2% per year. Nicaragua's GDP increased, in real terms, by an average of 3.6% per year in 2004–13; GDP expanded by an estimated 4.6% in 2013.

Agriculture (including forestry and fishing) contributed an estimated 16.9% of GDP in 2013 and engaged some 31.5% of the employed workforce in 2011. The principal cash crops are coffee (which accounted for 14.6% of export earnings in 2013), sugar cane, groundnuts and beans. Maize, rice and beans are the principal food crops. Meat and meat products accounted for 16.0% of export earnings in 2013. According to the World Bank, agricultural GDP increased at an average annual rate of 3.8% during 2004–12; agricultural GDP increased by 1.0% in 2012.

Industry (including mining, manufacturing, construction and power) provided an estimated 30.9% of GDP in 2013 and engaged 18.5% of the employed labour force in 2011. According to the World Bank, industrial GDP increased by an average of 3.8% per year during 2004–12; the sector expanded by 9.4% in 2012.

Mining contributed an estimated 3.1% of GDP in 2013 and engaged 0.7% of the employed labour force in 2011. Nicaragua has workable deposits of gold, silver, copper, lead, antimony, zinc and iron; its non-metallic minerals include limestone, gypsum, bentonite and marble. In 2013 gold accounted for 18.0% of export earnings. According to official estimates, the GDP of the mining sector increased at an average annual rate of 4.3% in 2003–11; according to official estimates, the sector's GDP increased by an estimated 11.7% in 2011.

Manufacturing contributed some 19.3% of GDP in 2013 and engaged 11.4% of the employed labour force in 2011. The principal branches of manufacturing were food products, beverages and tobacco. The *maquila* (or assembly) sector was important. The principal products were clothing, footwear, aluminium frames and jewellery. Manufacturing GDP increased, according to the World Bank, by an average of 4.0% per year in 2004–12; the sector's GDP grew by 5.0% in 2012.

Construction contributed some 5.8% of GDP in 2013 and engaged 5.9% of the employed labour force in 2011. Construction GDP fell, according to official figures, by an average of 1.3% per year in 2003–11; the sector's GDP decreased by an estimated 13.3% in 2010, but increased by an estimated 21.7% in 2011.

Energy is derived principally from imported petroleum (about 66.0% in 2011), although two hydroelectric plants in the department of Jinotega accounted for some 11.6% of the electrical energy generated in the country in that year. Imports of crude petroleum comprised 9.1% of the total value of imports in 2013. In that year Nicaragua produced an estimated 4,158.6m. kWh of electrical energy.

The services sector contributed an estimated 52.2% of GDP in 2013 and engaged 50.0% of the employed labour force in 2011. The tourism sector has become increasingly significant in recent years; in 2013, according to provisional figures, annual tourism income totalled US $417m., with arrivals put at around 1,230,000, an increase of 4.2% on the previous year's figure. According to the World Bank, the GDP of the services sector increased by an average of 2.0% per year in 2004–12; the sector's GDP increased by 1.0% in 2012.

In 2013 Nicaragua recorded a visible merchandise trade deficit of US $2,279.4m., and there was a deficit of $1,279.5m. on the current account of the balance of payments. In 2013 the principal sources of imports were Venezuela (18.9% of the total) and the USA (15.0%); other major suppliers were Mexico and Nicaragua's partners in the Central American Common Market (CACM—Costa Rica, El Salvador, Guatemala and Honduras, see p. 228). The USA was the principal market for exports (25.2% of the total) in 2013; other notable purchasers were Venezuela, Canada and El Salvador. The principal exports in 2013 were gold, meat, coffee and sugar. The principal imports were intermediate goods, non-durable consumer goods, mineral fuels and lubricants, and capital goods.

In 2013 Nicaragua recorded a central budgetary deficit of 3,057.9m. córdobas, equivalent to 1.1% of GDP. Nicaragua's general government gross debt was 441,035m. córdobas in 2013, equivalent to 68.6% of GDP. At the end of 2012 Nicaragua's total external debt was US $8,858m., of which $3,055m. was public and publicly guaranteed debt. In that year, the cost of servicing long-term public and publicly guaranteed debt and repayments to the IMF was equivalent to 12.3% of the value of exports of goods, services and income (excluding workers' remittances). During 2004–13 the average annual rate of increase in consumer prices was 8.9%, according to the IMF. Consumer prices rose by an annual average of 7.2% in 2013. An estimated 5.9% of the labour force was unemployed in 2012.

A focus on social policies by the administration of Daniel Ortega, which took office in 2007, resulted in a reduction in poverty rates, although in 2014 Nicaragua remained the second poorest country in the western hemisphere. Following criticism of the conduct of the municipal and general elections in 2008 and 2011, respectively (see *Contemporary Political History*), the USA, the European Union and several European countries suspended or halted aid to Nicaragua, although contributions from Venezuela, which have been substantial during Ortega's presidency, continued to rise. Financial assistance from Russia has also become increasingly important, accounting for almost 30% of total assistance in 2013. Remittances from Nicaraguans working abroad, primarily in Costa Rica and the USA, are an important source of revenue, equivalent to 4.7% of GDP in 2013. Remittances reached US $1,135.8m. in 2014. Foreign investors are attracted by Nicaragua's low labour costs and relative security compared with other Central American countries, with the majority of finance directed at the energy and telecommunications sectors and free trade zones. Renewable energy projects are of particular interest to investors, in line with a government aim to increase the proportion of energy generated by renewable sources to 80% by 2017. Nicaragua was named in the 2013 Global Climate Risk Index as one of the three countries already worst affected by climate change. The important coffee industry was believed to be particularly vulnerable, with changing rainfall patterns and the increased prevalence of crop diseases, such as rust, reducing production. In 2013 gold was the most significant source of export revenue, with earnings of the commodity exceeding those of coffee for the first time. Construction of the Gran Canal, which began in late December 2014 with some US $40,000m. of private Chinese finance, was expected to boost economic activity. According to some forecasts, the canal was expected to double Nicaragua's GDP by 2020. However, concerns about the project's impact on local communities and the environment remained (see *Recent developments*). According to official estimates, GDP growth was 4.6% in 2013, rose to 5.0% in 2014 and was forecast to remain at 5.0% in 2015.

PUBLIC HOLIDAYS

2016: 1 January (New Year's Day), 24 March (Maundy Thursday), 25 March (Good Friday), 1 May (Labour Day), 19 July (Liberation Day), 14 September (Battle of San Jacinto), 15 September (Independence Day), 2 November (All Souls' Day, afternoon only), 8 December (Immaculate Conception), 25 December (Christmas Day).

Various local holidays are also observed.

Statistical Survey

Sources (unless otherwise stated): Banco Central de Nicaragua, Carretera Sur, Km 7, Apdos 2252/3, Zona 5, Managua; tel. 265-0500; fax 265-2272; e-mail bcn@cabcn.gob.ni; internet www.bcn.gob.ni; Instituto Nacional de Información de Desarrollo, Los Arcos, Frente Hospital Fonseca, Managua; tel. 266-6178; e-mail webmaster@inide.gob.ni; internet www.inide.gob.ni.

Area and Population

AREA, POPULATION AND DENSITY

Area (sq km)	
Land	120,340
Inland water	10,034
Total	130,373*
Population (census results)	
25 April 1995	4,357,099
28 May–11 June 2005	
Males	2,534,491
Females	2,607,607
Total	5,142,098
Population (official estimates at mid-year)	
2011	5,888,946
2012	6,071,045
2013	6,134,270
Density (per sq km) at mid-2013	51.0†

* 50,337 sq miles.
† Land area only.

POPULATION BY AGE AND SEX
(official estimates at mid-2013)

	Males	Females	Total
0–14 years	1,032,913	992,975	2,025,888
15–64 years	1,867,801	1,961,249	3,829,050
65 years and over	129,276	150,056	279,332
Total	3,029,990	3,104,280	6,134,270

ADMINISTRATIVE DIVISIONS
(land area only, population estimates at mid-2012)

	Area (sq km)	Population	Density (per sq km)	Capital
Departments.				
Chinandega	4,822.4	423,062	87.7	Chinandega
León	5,138.0	404,471	78.7	León
Managua	3,465.1	1,448,271	418.0	Managua
Masaya	610.8	348,254	570.2	Masaya
Carazo	1,081.4	186,898	172.8	Jinotepe
Granada	1,039.7	200,991	193.3	Granada
Rivas	2,161.8	174,589	80.8	Rivas
Estelí	2,229.7	220,703	99.0	Estelí
Madriz	1,708.2	158,020	92.5	Somoto
Nueva Segovia	3,491.3	243,014	69.6	Ocotal
Jinotega	9,222.4	417,372	45.3	Jinotega
Matagalpa	6,803.9	542,419	79.7	Matagalpa
Boaco	4,176.7	174,682	41.8	Boaco
Chontales	6,481.3	182,838	28.2	Juigalpa
Río San Juan	7,540.9	122,666	16.3	San Carlos
Autonomous Regions:				
Atlántico Norte (RAAN)	32,819.7	453,541	13.8	Bilwi
Atlántico Sur (RAAS)	27,546.3	369,254	13.4	Bluefields
Total	120,339.5	6,071,045	50.4	—

PRINCIPAL TOWNS
(population estimates at mid-2012)

Managua (capital)	1,028,808	Chinandega		133,361
León	201,100	Tipitapa		130,627
Masaya	166,588	Granada		123,697
Matagalpa	150,643	Estelí		122,924

Mid-2014 (incl. suburbs, UN estimate): Managua 950,736 (Source: UN, *World Urbanization Prospects: The 2014 Revision*).

BIRTHS, MARRIAGES AND DEATHS
(annual averages, UN estimates)

	2000–05	2005–10	2010–15
Birth rate (per 1,000)	26.3	24.8	22.9
Death rate (per 1,000)	5.0	4.7	4.6

Source: UN, *World Population Prospects: The 2012 Revision.*

2007: Registered live births 128,171; Registered marriages 20,918; Registered deaths 17,288. Note: Registration believed to be incomplete.

Life expectancy (years at birth): 74.5 (males 71.5; females 77.6) in 2012 (Source: World Bank, World Development Indicators database).

ECONOMICALLY ACTIVE POPULATION
('000, population aged 10 years and over)

	2009	2010	2011
Agriculture, forestry and fishing	600.8	834.2	900.1
Mining and quarrying	5.7	10.9	19.7
Manufacturing	274.6	299.2	326.3
Electricity, gas and water	10.9	13.8	13.4
Construction	99.4	103.0	169.3
Trade, restaurants and hotels	485.9	638.9	700.7
Transport and communications	86.6	97.7	104.2
Financial services	82.7	80.8	95.0
Public administration	90.2	—	—
Social and personal services	359.6	513.3	530.2
Total employed	2,096.5	2,591.7	2,858.9
Unemployed	186.2	220.1	180.2
Total labour force	2,282.7	2,811.8	3,039.2

2012: Total employed 2,986.4; Unemployed 187.7; Total labour force 3,174.1.

Health and Welfare

KEY INDICATORS

Total fertility rate (children per woman, 2012)	2.5
Under-5 mortality rate (per 1,000 live births, 2012)	24
HIV/AIDS (% of persons aged 15–49, 2013)	0.2
Physicians (per 1,000 head, 2003)	0.4
Hospital beds (per 1,000 head, 2010)	0.8
Health expenditure (2011): US $ per head (PPP)	292
Health expenditure (2011): % of GDP	7.6
Health expenditure (2011): public (% of total)	54.3
Access to water (% of persons, 2012)	85
Access to sanitation (% of persons, 2012)	52
Total carbon emissions ('000 metric tons, 2010)	4,547.1
Carbon dioxide emissions per head (metric tons, 2010)	0.8
Human Development Index (2013): ranking	132
Human Development Index (2013): value	0.614

For sources and definitions, see explanatory note on p. vi.

Agriculture

PRINCIPAL CROPS
('000 metric tons)

	2011	2012	2013
Rice, paddy*	488.0	440.0	460.0
Maize	523.0*	471.0*	545.9
Sorghum	91.0	58.0*	88.2
Cassava (Manioc)†	75.1	78.0	78.0
Sugar cane	5,431.1	6,718.2	7,026.6
Beans, dry	234.2	233.9	225.6
Groundnuts, in shell	184.3*	200.0*	189.5
Oil palm fruit†	86.7	80.0	100.0
Bananas	39.7	40.9	37.2
Plantains†	64.4	66.0	66.8
Oranges†	95.1	100.0	99.2
Pineapples†	56.8	60.0	60.1
Coffee, green	103.9	86.9	83.9

* Unofficial figure(s).
† FAO estimates.

Aggregate production ('000 metric tons, may include official, semi-official or estimated data): Total cereals 1,102 in 2011, 969 in 2012, 1,094 in 2013; Total roots and tubers 125 in 2011, 1,275 in 2012, 1,221 in 2013; Total vegetables (incl. melons) 63 in 2011, 67 in 2012, 68 in 2013; Total fruits (excl. melons) 272 in 2011, 283 in 2012, 280 in 2013.

Source: FAO.

LIVESTOCK
('000 head, year ending September, FAO estimates)

	2011	2012	2013
Cattle	3,750	3,750	3,740
Pigs	495	495	494
Goats	8	8	7
Horses	268	269	269
Asses	9	9	9
Mules	48	48	48
Poultry	19,800	20,600	21,100

Source: FAO.

LIVESTOCK PRODUCTS
('000 metric tons)

	2011	2012	2013
Cattle meat	128.6	115.9	120.7
Pig meat*	7.9	8.0	8.0
Horse meat*	2.6	2.7	2.7
Chicken meat	99.8	87.5	123.4
Cows' milk	760.0	765.0	768.0
Hen eggs	26.3	27.8	30.7

* FAO estimates.

Source: FAO.

Forestry

ROUNDWOOD REMOVALS
('000 cubic metres, excl. bark, FAO estimates)

	2011	2012	2013
Sawlogs, veneer logs and logs for sleepers	118	118	118
Fuel wood	6,110	6,125	6,141
Total	6,228	6,243	6,259

Source: FAO.

SAWNWOOD PRODUCTION
('000 cubic metres, incl. railway sleepers, FAO estimates)

	2009	2010	2011
Coniferous	12	29	29
Broadleaved	40	77	33
Total	52	106	62

2012–13: Figures assumed to be unchanged from 2011 (FAO estimates).

Source: FAO.

Fishing

('000 metric tons, live weight)

	2010	2011	2012
Capture	38.1	33.6	33.9
Snooks	0.9	0.8	0.7
Snappers	1.3	1.5	1.9
Yellowfin tuna	10.7	8.9	8.2
Skipjack tuna	4.2	3.9	4.0
Common dolphinfish	0.2	0.3	0.5
Caribbean spiny lobsters	3.7	4.0	4.2
Penaeus shrimp	2.6	2.4	1.1
Aquaculture	17.0	15.8	24.4
Whiteleg shrimp	16.6	15.7	24.3
Total catch	55.0	49.3	58.2

Source: FAO.

Mining

	2010	2011	2012
Gold (kg)	4,900	6,395	6,981
Silver (kg)	6,995	7,927	10,207
Gypsum and anhydrite (metric tons)	20,330	29,710	34,890

Source: US Geological Survey.

Industry

SELECTED PRODUCTS
('000 barrels unless otherwise indicated)

	2011	2012*	2013*
Liquid gas	192	101	127
Motor spirit	828	584	830
Kerosene	275	200	225
Diesel	1,657	1,129	1,556
Fuel oil	2,361	1,558	2,004
Bitumen (asphalt)	74	36	52
Electric energy (million kWh)	3,824.2	3,956.0	4,158.6

* Preliminary figures.

Cement ('000 metric tons, estimates): 530 in 2010; 600 in 2011–12 (Source: US Geological Survey).

Finance

CURRENCY AND EXCHANGE RATES

Monetary Units
100 centavos = 1 córdoba.

Sterling, Dollar and Euro Equivalents (31 December 2014)
£1 sterling = 41.515 córdobas;
US $1 = 26.598 córdobas;
€1 = 32.293 córdobas;
1,000 córdobas = £24.09 = $37.60 = €30.97.

Average Exchange Rate (córdobas per US dollar)
2012   23.547
2013   24.723
2014   25.959

Note: In February 1988 a new córdoba, equivalent to 1,000 of the former units, was introduced, and a uniform exchange rate of US $1 = 10 new córdobas was established. Subsequently, the exchange rate was frequently adjusted. A new currency, the córdoba 'oro' ('gold' córdoba), was introduced as a unit of account in May 1990 and began to be circulated in August. The value of the 'gold' córdoba was initially fixed at par with the US dollar, but in March 1991 the exchange rate was revised to $1 = 25,000,000 new córdobas (or 5 'gold' córdobas). On 30 April 1991 the 'gold' córdoba became the sole legal tender. Since January 1993 a 'crawling peg' system of daily official exchange rate adjustments in the value of the córdoba against the US dollar has been pursued by the central bank.

CENTRAL GOVERNMENT BUDGET
(million córdobas)

Revenue and grants	2011	2012*	2013*
Taxation	31,824.6	37,221.7	40,785.0
Income tax	11,143.7	13,107.4	14,520.8
Property tax	191.2	239.1	311.4
Taxes on goods and services	18,945.8	22,035.4	23,989.8
Value-added tax	12,876.0	15,151.5	16,736.0
Excise tax	6,069.9	6,884.0	7,253.7
Other taxes	22.0	23.5	77.3
International trade and transactions taxes	1,521.8	1,816.4	1,885.7
Other revenue	2,720.0	3,500.5	3,248.6
Total	34,544.6	40,722.2	44,033.6

Expenditure	2011	2012*	2013*
Compensation of employees	11,957.1	13,629.7	15,203.8
Goods and services	5,537.6	6,099.2	6,349.5
Interest payments	2,261.9	2,466.3	2,519.6
Domestic	1,552.8	1,686.7	1,564.7
External	709.1	779.5	954.9
Current and capital transfers	10,339.6	11,620.1	12,847.8
Social security contributions	822.0	1,079.5	963.9
Other expenditure	1,904.4	2,871.7	3,091.2
Total	32,822.7	37,766.2	40,975.7

* Preliminary figures.

2013 (consolidated accounts of central government and public sector, million córdobas): *Revenue* Tax revenues 42,796.7; Social contributions 12,805.5; Other revenue 11,808.2; Total 67,410.4 (excl. grants 2,757.6). *Expenditure* Compensation of employees 18,600.8; Goods and services 14,945.2; Interest payments 2,731.3; Current and capital transfers 12,924.5; Social benefits 8,900.3; Other expenditures 3,475.6; Total 61,577.7 (excl. net acquisition of non-financial assets 11,454.1).

INTERNATIONAL RESERVES
(excluding gold, US $ million at 31 December)

	2011	2012	2013
IMF special drawing rights	175.77	163.09	146.86
Foreign exchange	1,716.48	1,724.13	1,846.10
Total	1,892.25	1,887.21	1,992.96

Source: IMF, *International Financial Statistics*.

MONEY SUPPLY
(million córdobas at 31 December)

	2011	2012	2013
Currency outside depository corporations	9,686.4	10,874.4	11,523.1
Transferable deposits	17,622.2	22,001.9	27,819.1
Other deposits	44,754.4	50,279.9	59,047.6
Broad money	72,062.9	83,156.2	98,389.8

Source: IMF, *International Financial Statistics*.

COST OF LIVING
(Consumer Price Index; base: 2006 = 100)

	2011	2012	2013
Food and non-alcoholic beverages	165.0	177.4	194.1
Clothing	141.6	152.6	160.9
Housing, water, electricity, gas and fuel	140.0	145.9	153.2
All items (incl. others)	149.9	159.9	171.4

NATIONAL ACCOUNTS
(million córdobas at current prices)

Expenditure on the Gross Domestic Product

	2011*	2012†	2013†
Final consumption expenditure	204,898.0	229,796.4	253,673.6
Gross capital formation	51,957.0	58,361.2	56,905.0
Total domestic expenditure	256,873.0	288,157.6	310,578.6
Exports of goods and services	88,923.7	107,879.5	112,748.3
Less Imports of goods and services	123,810.1	145,383.8	145,056.8
GDP in purchasers' values	221,968.6	250,653.4	278,270.2
GDP at constant 2006 prices	137,085.8	143,876.3	150,503.7

Gross Domestic Product by Economic Activity

	2011*	2012†	2013†
Agriculture, hunting, forestry and fishing	38,593.0	41,477.1	42,611.5
Mining and quarrying	5,975.4	7,636.9	7,817.5
Manufacturing	37,845.4	40,846.3	48,685.8
Electricity, gas and water	5,640.6	5,785.2	6,564.1
Construction	8,399.0	12,067.7	14,690.1
Wholesale and retail trade	28,238.1	31,646.1	34,973.1
Transport and communications	13,027.0	15,523.5	16,318.0
Finance, insurance and business services	7,582.3	8,603.2	10,287.4
General government services	18,786.6	21,385.2	24,890.9
Other services	37,027.4	41,330.5	45,048.1
Sub-total	201,114.8	226,301.7	251,886.5
Net taxes on products	20,853.8	24,351.6	26,383.6
GDP in purchasers' values	221,968.6	250,653.4	278,270.2

* Preliminary figures.
† Estimates.

BALANCE OF PAYMENTS
(US $ million)

	2011	2012	2013
Exports of goods	3,666.2	4,146.1	4,122.5
Imports of goods	−5,844.0	−6,441.7	−6,401.9
Balance on goods	−2,177.8	−2,295.6	−2,279.4
Exports of services	772.5	861.6	877.2
Imports of services	−840.8	−921.8	−933.0
Balance on goods and services	−2,246.1	−2,355.8	−2,335.2
Primary income received	21.1	24.8	22.5
Primary income paid	−271.1	−326.0	−335.8
Balance on goods, services and primary income	−2,496.1	−2,657.0	−2,648.5
Secondary income (net)	1,229.6	1,309.8	1,369.0

—continued	2011	2012	2013
Current balance	−1,266.5	−1,347.2	−1,279.5
Capital account (net) . . .	248.3	237.8	231.0
Direct investment assets . . .	−6.8	−43.3	−104.1
Direct investment liabilities . .	967.9	804.6	845.1
Portfolio investment assets . .	−207.5	70.4	147.8
Portfolio investment liabilities .	−12.9	−6.4	−2.3
Other investment assets . .	307.1	128.2	−147.7
Other investment liabilities . .	701.3	945.5	701.1
Net errors and omissions . . .	−658.4	−792.2	−279.6
Reserves and related items .	72.6	−2.5	111.7

Source: IMF, *International Financial Statistics*.

External Trade

PRINCIPAL COMMODITIES
(US $ million, preliminary)

Imports c.i.f.	2011	2012	2013
Consumer goods	1,654.8	1,813.1	1,813.4
Non-durable consumer goods .	1,339.3	1,450.2	1,462.2
Durable consumer goods . .	315.5	362.9	351.2
Petroleum, mineral fuels and lubricants	1,256.4	1,286.6	1,186.3
Crude petroleum	615.6	441.8	509.2
Mineral fuels and lubricants .	639.3	844.9	677.1
Intermediate goods	1,337.4	1,522.6	1,520.4
Primary materials and intermediate goods for agriculture and fishing . .	271.9	320.4	312.6
Primary materials and intermediate goods for industry	799.7	887.8	888.7
Construction materials . . .	265.8	314.4	319.1
Capital goods	947.2	1,220.4	1,094.5
For agriculture and fishing . .	64.7	77.8	69.8
For industry	532.1	708.8	577.0
For transport	350.4	433.8	447.7
Miscellaneous	8.0	8.5	9.4
Total	5,203.7	5,851.3	5,624.1

Exports f.o.b.	2011	2012	2013
Cattle on hoof	18.6	18.6	39.2
Fresh fish	16.3	16.8	17.9
Lobster	45.9	43.9	44.5
Shrimp	62.2	67.5	67.8
Coffee	429.3	521.8	349.5
Groundnuts	96.1	132.5	102.9
Beans	30.2	51.8	44.8
Bananas	2.4	2.5	2.3
Tobacco (leaf)	6.3	8.4	4.7
Meat and meat products . .	427.0	451.4	383.8
Refined sugars, etc.	156.3	194.9	176.0
Cheese	81.4	94.7	94.7
Refined petroleum	15.2	49.8	18.7
Wood products	13.3	11.8	13.0
Chemical products	27.9	35.4	33.4
Gold	352.3	422.8	431.6
Porcelain products	8.3	8.2	8.5
Total (incl. others)	2,264.0	2,677.4	2,400.7

PRINCIPAL TRADING PARTNERS
(US $ million, preliminary)

Imports c.i.f.	2011	2012	2013
Costa Rica	438.2	462.4	477.4
Ecuador	10.0	8.2	8.7
El Salvador	234.0	320.6	278.6
Germany	65.0	68.4	73.4
Guatemala	347.8	350.6	359.3
Honduras	169.7	164.2	209.4
Japan	145.0	174.4	146.5
Korea, Republic	90.8	81.7	82.7
Mexico	406.3	443.2	464.6
Russia	67.9	78.9	66.9
Spain	54.7	107.0	81.8
USA	905.4	1,075.8	842.9
Venezuela	1,139.8	1,176.8	1,064.4
Total (incl. others)	5,203.7	5,851.3	5,624.1

Exports f.o.b.	2011	2012	2013
Belgium	34.1	66.0	21.4
Canada	273.4	317.6	313.6
Costa Rica	98.8	115.4	119.3
El Salvador	206.6	245.3	213.4
France	25.9	30.9	47.0
Germany	32.9	29.1	30.1
Guatemala	71.0	76.4	84.4
Honduras	59.4	66.5	79.3
Italy	33.4	35.5	28.7
Japan	23.3	24.4	20.7
Mexico	82.8	70.1	47.7
Puerto Rico	45.3	35.5	27.7
Spain	36.4	32.7	30.6
Taiwan	38.4	10.7	65.5
United Kingdom	38.5	44.6	40.1
USA	648.8	765.3	605.8
Venezuela	302.6	444.0	384.0
Total (incl. others)	2,264.0	2,677.4	2,400.7

Transport

ROAD TRAFFIC
(motor vehicles in use)

	2009	2010	2012*
Passenger cars	101,021	96,021	129,401
Buses and coaches	38,665	36,291	16,939
Lorries and vans	192,544	196,700	193,037
Motorcycles and mopeds . . .	87,247	112,632	169,055

* Data for 2011 were not available.

Source: IRF, *World Road Statistics*.

SHIPPING

Flag Registered fleet
(at 31 December)

	2012	2013	2014
Number of vessels	7	7	8
Total displacement (grt) . . .	3,949	4,427	5,217

Source: Lloyd's List Intelligence (www.lloydslistintelligence.com).

International Seaborne Freight Traffic
('000 metric tons)

	2011	2012*	2013*
Imports	2,781.3	2,883.3	2,751.6
Exports	654.8	772.3	870.0
Total international cargo movements	3,436.1	3,655.6	3,621.6

* Estimates.

CIVIL AVIATION
(traffic at Augusto César Sandino airport)

	2011	2012*	2013*
Passengers carried ('000) . . .	1,116.2	1,197.2	1,206.3
Freight carried (metric tons) . .	21,835	22,885	22,219

* Estimates.

Tourism

TOURIST ARRIVALS BY COUNTRY OF ORIGIN

	2011	2012	2013
Canada	25,676	30,710	33,832
Costa Rica	136,466	160,108	163,758
El Salvador	138,120	152,741	150,963
Guatemala	83,408	92,877	94,957
Honduras	230,965	251,804	273,015
Panama	22,451	24,517	24,676
USA	213,986	240,846	243,039
Total (incl. others)	1,060,031	1,179,581	1,229,410

Tourism receipts (US $ million, excl. passenger transport): 378 in 2011; 422 in 2012; 417 in 2013.

Source: World Tourism Organization.

Communications Media

	2011	2012	2013
Telephones ('000 main lines in use)	287.6	299.1	325.0
Mobile cellular telephones ('000 subscribers)	4,823.5	5,851.7	6,808.9
Broadband subscribers ('000) . .	85.1	101.3	131.7

Source: International Telecommunication Union.

Education

(2009/10 unless otherwise indicated)

	Institutions*	Teachers	Students		
			Males	Females	Total
Pre-primary .	5,980	10,289	109,836	108,226	218,062
Primary . . .	8,251	30,571	475,981	447,764	923,745
Secondary: general . .	1,249	15,089	224,668	240,533	465,201
Tertiary: university level	35	3,630†	47,683‡	51,222‡	98,905‡
Tertiary: other higher . . .	73	210†	1,902‡	2,770‡	4,672‡

* 2002/03 figures.
† 2001/02 figure.
‡ 2003/04 figure.

Sources: UNESCO, *Statistical Yearbook*; Ministry of Education.

Pupil-teacher ratio (primary education, UNESCO estimate): 30.2 in 2009/10 (Source: UNESCO Institute for Statistics).

Adult literacy rate (UNESCO estimates): 80.5% (males 79.7%; females 81.4%) in 2007 (Source: UNESCO Institute for Statistics).

Directory

The Government

HEAD OF STATE

President: José Daniel Ortega Saavedra (elected 5 November 2006; re-elected 6 November 2011).
Vice-President: Moises Omar Halleslevens Acevedo.

CABINET
(May 2015)

The Government is formed by the Frente Sandinista de Liberación Nacional.

Minister of Foreign Affairs: Samuel Santos López.
Minister of the Interior: Ana Isabel Morales Mazún.
Minister of Defence: Dr Martha Ruiz Sevilla.
Minister of Finance and Public Credit: Iván Acosta.
Minister of Development, Industry and Trade: Dr Orlando Solórzano Delgadillo.
Minister of Labour: Alba Luz Torres Briones.
Minister of the Environment and Natural Resources: Juanita Argeñal Sandoval.
Minister of Transport and Infrastructure: Pablo Fernando Martínez Espinoza.
Minister of Agriculture and Forestry: Edward Francisco Centeno Gadea.
Minister of Health: Dr Sonia Castro González.
Minister of Education: Miriam Ráudez.
Minister of the Family, Adolescence and Childhood: Marcia Ramírez Mercado.
Minister of Energy and Mines: Salvador Mansell Castrillo.
Secretary to the Presidency: Paul Oquist.
Co-ordinator of the Communication and Citizenship Council: Rosario Murillo Zambrana.

MINISTRIES

Office of the President: Casa Presidencial, Managua; fax 2266-3102; e-mail daniel@presidencia.gob.ni; internet www.presidencia.gob.ni.

Ministry of Agriculture and Forestry: Km 8½, Carretera a Masaya, Managua; tel. 2276-0512; fax 2276-0204; e-mail ministro@magfor.gob.ni; internet www.magfor.gob.ni.

Ministry of Defence: De los semáforos el Redentor, 4 c. arriba, donde fue la casa 'Ricardo Morales Aviles', Managua; tel. 2222-2201; fax 2222-5439; e-mail prensa.midef@midef.gob.ni; internet www.midef.gob.ni.

Ministry of Development, Industry and Trade: Edif. Central, Km 6, Carretera a Masaya, Apdo 8, frente a camino de oriente, Managua; tel. 2248-9300; fax 2270-095; e-mail acastilb@mific.gob.ni; internet www.mific.gob.ni.

Ministry of Education: Centro Cívico, Módulo K, Planta Alta, Apdo 505, Managua; tel. 2265-0046; fax 2265-0081; e-mail webmaster@mined.gob.ni; internet www.mined.gob.ni.

Ministry of Energy and Mines: Hospital Bautista, 1 c. al oeste, 1 c. al norte, Managua; tel. 2280-9500; fax 2280-9516; e-mail despacho@mem.gob.ni; internet www.mem.gob.ni.

Ministry of the Environment and Natural Resources: Km 12½, Carretera Norte, Apdo 5123, Managua; tel. 2233-1111; fax 2263-1274; e-mail jargenal@marena.gob.ni; internet www.marena.gob.ni.

Ministry of the Family, Adolescence and Childhood: De donde fue ENEL Central, 100 m al sur, Managua; tel. 2278-1620; e-mail mramirez@mifamilia.gob.ni; internet www.mifamilia.gob.ni.

Ministry of Finance and Public Credit: Frente a la Asamblea Nacional, Apdo 2170, Managua; tel. 2222-6530; fax 2222-6430; e-mail webmaster@mhcp.gob.ni; internet www.hacienda.gob.ni.

Ministry of Foreign Affairs: Del Antiguo Cine González, 1 c. al sur, sobre Avda Bolívar, Managua; tel. 2244-8000; fax 2228-5102; e-mail despacho.ministro@cancilleria.gob.ni; internet www.cancilleria.gob.ni.

Ministry of Health: Complejo Nacional de Salud 'Dra Concepción Palacios', costado oeste Colonia Primero de Mayo, Apdo 107, Managua; tel. 2289-7164; e-mail webmaster@minsa.gob.ni; internet www .minsa.gob.ni.

Ministry of the Interior: Edif. Silvio Mayorga, Costado oeste de la DGI Sajonia, Apdo 68, Managua; tel. 2222-7538; fax 2222-2789; e-mail relacionespublicas@migob.gob.ni; internet www.migob.gob .ni.

Ministry of Labour: Estadio Nacional, 400 m al norte, Apdo 487, Managua; tel. 2222-2115; fax 2228-2103; e-mail info@mitrab.gob.ni; internet www.mitrab.gob.ni.

Ministry of Transport and Infrastructure: Frente al Estadio Nacional Denis Martínez, Apdo 26, Managua; tel. 2222-5952; fax 2222-5111; e-mail webmaster@mti.gob.ni; internet www.mti.gob.ni.

President and Legislature

PRESIDENT

Election, 6 November 2011

Candidate	Votes	% of total
José Daniel Ortega Saavedra (FSLN) . .	1,569,287	62.46
Fabio Gadea Mantilla (PLI-UNE) . . .	778,889	31.00
Arnoldo Alemán Lacayo (PLC)	148,507	5.91
Enrique Quiñónez (ALN)	10,003	0.40
Roger Guevara (APRE)	5,898	0.23
Total	**2,512,584**	**100.00**

NATIONAL ASSEMBLY
(Asamblea Nacional)

National Assembly: Complejo Legislativo Carlos Nuñez, Avda Peatonal Gen. Augusto C. Sandino, Apdo 4659, Managua; tel. 2276-8488; e-mail info@asamblea.gob.ni; internet www.asamblea .gob.ni.

President: RENÉ NÚÑEZ TÉLLEZ.

Election, 6 November 2011

Party	Valid votes cast	% of valid votes	Seats
Frente Sandinista de Liberación Nacional (FSLN)	3,178,669	60.75	62
Partido Liberal Independiente (PLI)*	1,646,203	31.45	26
Partido Liberal Constitucionalista (PLC)	340,945	6.51	2
Alianza Liberal Nicaragüense (ALN)	44,528	0.86	—
Alianza por la República (APRE).	22,380	0.43	—
Total	**5,232,725†**	**100.00**	**92‡**

* Supported by the Unidad Nicaragüense por la Esperanza (UNE).
† Each elector had two votes: one for representatives at regional level (for which there were 70 seats) and one for representatives at national level (20 seats). The total number of votes cast at regional level was 2,630,889, while at national level 2,601,836 votes were cast.
‡ Under the Constitution, one seat is reserved for the President of the Republic. Furthermore, another seat is given to the second-placed candidate in the presidential election. Thus, the FSLN's total number of seats increased to 63, while the PLI's representation increased to 27.

Election Commission

Consejo Supremo Electoral (CSE): Iglesia Las Palmas, 1 c. al sur, Apdo 2241, Managua; tel. 2268-7948; e-mail info@cse.gob.ni; internet www.cse.gob.ni; Pres. ROBERTO JOSÉ RIVAS REYES.

Political Organizations

Alianza Liberal Nicaragüense (ALN): del Hotel Mansión Teodolinda, 3c abajo, Managua; e-mail hebertaln@hotmail.com; fmrly Movimiento de Salvación Liberal; adopted current name in 2006; Sec.-Gen. CARLOS GARCÍA.

Alianza por la República (APRE): Busto José Martí, 4 c. arriba, 3 y ½ c. al lago, Managua; tel. 2264-2446; e-mail partido.apre@gmail

.com; f. 2004 by supporters of Pres. Enrique Bolaños Geyer; Pres. CARLOS CANALES.

Partido Social Cristiano Nicaragüense (PSC): Ciudad Jardín, Pizza María, 1 c. al lago, Managua; tel. 2249-3460; e-mail pscnicaragua@hotmail.com; f. 1957; 42,000 mems; Pres. ABEL REYES TÉLLEZ; Sec.-Gen. ANTONIO BENITO GÓMEZ.

Camino Cristiano Nicaragüense (CCN): Costado, 1 c. al sur, 1 c. arriba, Calle 27 de Mayo, Managua; tel. 2254-5411; fax 2254-5405; e-mail info@caminocristianonicaraguense.org; internet www .caminocristianonicaraguense.org; Pres. GUILLERMO ANTONIO OSORNO MOLINA; Sec. OSWALDO BONILLA.

Frente Sandinista de Liberación Nacional (FSLN): Costado oeste Parque El Carmen, Managua; tel. and fax 2266-8173; f. 1960; Gen. Sec. JOSÉ DANIEL ORTEGA SAAVEDRA.

Movimiento Renovador Sandinista (MRS): De los semáforos del Ministerio de Gobernación, ½ c. al norte, Managua; tel. 2250-9461; fax 2278-0268; e-mail info@partidomrs.com; internet www .partidomrs.com; f. 1995; fmr faction of Frente Sandinista de Liberación Nacional (q.v.); contested the 2011 elections in alliance with the Unidad Nicaragüense por la Esperanza (q.v.); Pres. ANA MARGARITA VIJIL.

Movimiento de Unidad Cristiana (MUC): Del Portón del Cementerio Periférico, 1 c. al norte, Avda América 505, Managua; tel. 2249-5672; e-mail paritdomuc@hotmail.com; Pres. Pastor DANIEL ORTEGA REYES.

Partido Indígena Multiétnico (PIM): Residencial Los Robles, de Farmacentro 1 c. al este, 80 varas al sur, Managua; Pres. RAYFIELD HODGSON.

Partido Liberal Constitucionalista (PLC): Semáforos Country Club 100 m al este, Apdo 4569, Managua; tel. 2278-8705; fax 2278-1800; f. 1967; formed an alliance in 2014 with the Partido Liberal Independiente (q.v.) to contest the 2016 elections; Pres. MARÍA HAYDÉE OSUNA; Nat. Sec. MIGUEL ROSALES ORTEGA.

Partido Liberal Independiente (PLI): Ciudad Jardín, H-4, Calle Principal, Managua; tel. 2249-5547; internet partido liberalindependiente.org; f. 1944; formed an alliance with the Partido Liberal Constitucionalista (PLC) in 2014 to contest the 2016 elections; Pres. EDUARDO MONTEALEGRE RIVAS.

Partido Unionista Centroamericano (PUCA): Cine Cabrera, 1 c. al este, 20 m al norte, Managua; f. 1904; legal status suspended in April 2013; Pres. BLANCA ROJAS ECHAVERRY.

Unidad Nicaragüense por la Esperanza (UNE): Managua; f. 2010; contested the 2011 elections in alliance with the Partido Liberal Independiente (q.v.).

Unión Demócrata Cristiana (UDC): De Iglesia Santa Ana, 2 c. abajo, Barrio Santa Ana, Apdo 3089, Managua; tel. 2266-2576; f. 1976 as Partido Popular Social Cristiano; present name adopted in 1993; legal status suspended in 2013; Pres. AGUSTÍN JARQUÍN ANAYA.

Yatama (Yapti Tasba Masraka Nanih Aslatakanka): Of. de Odacan, Busto José Martí, 1 c. al este y ½ c. al norte, Managua; tel. 2228-1494; Atlantic coast Miskito org.; Leader BROOKLYN RIVERA BRYAN.

Diplomatic Representation

EMBASSIES IN NICARAGUA

Argentina: Reparto Las Colinas, Calle Prado Ecuestre 235B (interseción con Calle los Mangos), Apdo 703, Managua; tel. 2255-0062; fax 2276–2654; e-mail enica@mrecic.gov.ar; internet www.enica.mrecic .gov.ar; Ambassador MARCELO FELIPE VALLE FONROUGE.

Brazil: Km 7³⁄₄, Carretera Sur, Quinta los Pinos, Apdo 264, Managua; tel. 2265-0035; fax 2265-2206; e-mail ebrasil@ibw.com.ni; Ambassador LUIZ FELIPE MENDOÇA FILHO.

Chile: Entrada principal los Robles, Semáforos Hotel Milton Princess, 1 c. abajo, 1 c. al sur, Apdo 1289, Managua; tel. 2278-0619; fax 2270-4073; e-mail echileni@amnet.com.ni; internet chileabroad.gov .cl/nicaragua; Ambassador HERNÁN JAVIER ALEJANDRO MENA TABOADA.

Colombia: De la Entrada 1, 1 c. al sur, 1 c. al este, 40m al sur, Casa 53, Santo Domingo, Altos del Mirador, Managua; tel. 2255-1742; fax 2276-1549; e-mail enicaragua@cancilleria.gov.co; internet nicaragua.embajada.gov.co; Ambassador LUZ STELLA JARA PORTILLA.

Costa Rica: Reparto Las Colinas, Calle La Floresta 185, Managua; tel. 2276-0314; fax 2276-6399; e-mail infembcr@cablenet.com.ni; Ambassador JAVIER SANCHO BONILLA.

Cuba: 3a Entrada a Las Colinas, 400 varas arriba, 75 al sur, Managua; tel. 2276-0742; fax 2276-0166; e-mail embacuba@ embacuba.net.ni; internet www.cubadiplomatica.cu/nicaragua; Ambassador EDUARDO MARTÍNEZ BORBONET.

Dominican Republic: Reparto Las Colinas, Prado Ecuestre 100, con Curva de los Gallos, Apdo 614, Managua; tel. 2276-2029; fax 2276-0654; e-mail embdom@cablenet.com.ni; Ambassador Luis José González Sánchez.

Ecuador: Barrio Bolonia, Sede Central Los Pipitos, $1\frac{1}{2}$ c. al oeste, Managua; tel. 2268-1098; fax 2266-8081; e-mail ecuador@ibw.com.ni; Ambassador Aminta del Rosario Buenaño Rugel.

El Salvador: Reparto Las Colinas, Avda del Campo y Pasaje, Los Cerros 142, Apdo 149, Managua; tel. 2276-0712; fax 2276-0711; e-mail embajadanicaragua@rree.gob.sv; internet embajada nicaragua.rree.gob.sv; Ambassador Juan José Figueroa Tenas.

France: Iglesia el Carmen $1\frac{1}{2}$ c. abajo, Apdo 1227, Managua; tel. 2264-8970; fax 2264-8991; e-mail info@ambafrance-ni.org; internet www.ambafrance-ni.org; Ambassador Antoine Joly.

Germany: Bolonia, de la Rotonda El Güegüense, $1\frac{1}{2}$ c. al lago, contiguo a Optica Nicaragüense, Apdo 29, Managua; tel. 2266-3917; fax 2266-7667; e-mail alemania@cablenet.com.ni; internet www.managua.diplo.de; Ambassador Karl-Otto König.

Guatemala: Km $11\frac{1}{2}$, Carretera a Masaya, Apdo E-1, Managua; tel. 2279-9609; fax 2279-9610; e-mail embnic@minex.gob.gt; Ambassador Héctor Darío Gularte Estrada.

Holy See: Apostolic Nunciature, Km 10.8, Carretera Sur, Apdo 506, Managua; tel. 2265-8657; fax 2265-7416; e-mail nuntius@cablenet.com.ni; Apostolic Nuncio Most Rev. Fortunatus Nwachukwu (Titular Archbishop of Aquaviva).

Honduras: Residencial Las Colinas, 2da entrada, Prado Ecuestre 298, Managua; tel. 2276-2406; fax 2276-1998; e-mail hondurasnic@yahoo.com; Chargé d'affaires a.i. Jacqueline Claudett Abudoj Mena.

Iran: De ECAMI 150 mts al oeste, Casa 8-1, Altos de Santo Domingo, Managua; tel. 2276-1010; e-mail embirannic@cablenet.com.ni; Ambassador Morteza Khalaj.

Italy: Residencial Bolonia, Rotonda El Güegüense, 1 c. al norte, $\frac{1}{2}$ c. al oeste, Apdo 2092, Managua 4; tel. 2266-2961; fax 2266-3987; e-mail ambasciata.managua@esteri.it; internet www.ambmanagua.esteri.it; Ambassador Renato Maria Ricci.

Japan: Plaza España, 1 c. abajo y 1 c. al lago, Bolonia, Apdo 1789, Managua; tel. 2266-8668; fax 2266-8566; e-mail embjpnic@ibw.com.ni; internet www.ni.emb-japan.go.jp; Ambassador Masaharu Sato.

Korea, Republic: De la Rotonda El Güegüense 3. al oeste, $\frac{1}{2}$ c. al sur, casa A-45, Apdo LV101, Managua; tel. 2254-8107; fax 2254-8131; e-mail nicaragua@mofat.go.kr; internet nic.mofat.go.kr; Ambassador Doo Sik Kim.

Libya: Bolonia de donde fue la Mansión Teodolinda, 1 c. al sur, Apdo 867, Managua; tel. 2266-8540; fax 2266-8542; e-mail ofilibia@hotmail.com; Chargé d'affaires a.i. Mohamed I. A. Issa.

Luxembourg: Residencial Bolonia del Hospital Militar, 1 c. al lago y 1 $\frac{1}{2}$ abajo, Contiguo al Hotel Maracas Inn, Apdo 969, Managua; tel. 2268-1881; fax 2266-7965; e-mail secretariat.managua@mae.etat.lu; Chargé d'affaires a.i. Thierry René Liippert.

Mexico: Contiguo a Optica Matamoros, Km $4\frac{1}{2}$, Carretera a Masaya, 25 varas Arriba, Altamira, Apdo 834, Managua; tel. 2278-4919; fax 2278-2886; e-mail embamex@turbonett.com.ni; internet embamex.sre.gob.mx/nicaragua; Ambassador Juan Rodrigo Labardini Flores.

Panama: Casa 93, Reparto Mántica, del Cuartel General de Bomberos 1 c. abajo, Apdo 1, Managua; tel. 2277-0501; fax 2278-4083; e-mail embdpma@enitel.com.ni; Ambassador Eddy Rodríguez.

Peru: Del Hospital Militar, 1 c. al norte, 2 c. hacia oeste, casa 325, Apdo 211, Managua; tel. 2266-8678; fax 2266-8679; e-mail embajada@peruennicaragua.com.ni; internet www.peruennicaragua.com.ni; Ambassador Rudecindo Vega Carreazo.

Russian Federation: Reparto Las Colinas, Calle Vista Alegre 214, Apdo 249, Managua; tel. 2276-0374; fax 2276-0179; e-mail rossia@cablenet.com.ni; internet www.nicaragua.mid.ru; Ambassador Nikolay M. Vladimir.

Spain: Avda Central 13, Las Colinas, Apdo 284, Managua; tel. 2276-0966; fax 2276-0937; e-mail emb.managua@maec.es; internet www.maec.es/embajadas/managua; Ambassador Rafael Garranzo García.

Taiwan (Republic of China): Optica Matamoros, 2 c. abajo, $\frac{1}{2}$ c. al lago, Carretera a Masaya, Planes de Altamira, Apdo 4653, Managua; tel. 2277-1333; fax 2267-4025; e-mail nic@mofa.gov.tw; Ambassador Ying-Whei Hsing.

USA: Km $5\frac{1}{2}$, Carretera Sur, Apdo 327, Managua; tel. 2252-7100; fax 2252-7304; e-mail managuaconsulariv@state.gov; internet nicaragua.usembassy.gov; Ambassador Phyllis Marie Powers.

Venezuela: Costado norte de la Iglesia Santo Domingo, Las Sierritas, Casa 27, Apdo 406, Managua; tel. 2272-0267; fax 2272-2265; e-mail embaveznica@cablenet.com.ni; Ambassador José Francisco Arrúe de Pablo.

Judicial System

The Supreme Court deals with both civil and criminal cases, acts as a Court of Cassation, appoints Judges of First Instance, and generally supervises the legal administration of the country.

Corte Suprema de Justicia: Km $7\frac{1}{2}$ Carretera Norte, Managua; tel. 2233-2128; fax 2233-0004; e-mail webmaster@csj.gob.ni; internet www.poderjudicial.gob.ni; Pres. Dr Alba Luz Ramos Vanegas.

Attorney-General: Dr Joaquín Hernán Estrada Santamaría.

Religion

All religions are tolerated. Almost all of Nicaragua's inhabitants profess Christianity, and the majority belong to the Roman Catholic Church. The Moravian Church predominates on the Caribbean coast.

CHRISTIANITY

The Roman Catholic Church

Nicaragua comprises one archdiocese, six dioceses and the Apostolic Vicariate of Bluefields. According to the latest available census figures (2005), some 58% of the population aged five years and above are Roman Catholics.

Bishops' Conference: Conferencia Episcopal de Nicaragua, Ferretería Lang 1 c. al norte, 1 c. al este, Zona 3, Las Piedrecitas, Apdo 2407, Managua; tel. 2266-6292; fax 2266-8069; e-mail cen@tmx.com.ni; internet www.cen-nicaragua.org; f. 1975; statute approved 1987; Pres. Sócrates René Sándigo Jirón (Bishop of Juigalpa).

Archbishop of Managua: Cardinal Leopoldo José Brenes Solórzano, Arzobispado, Apdo C-68, Managua; tel. 2255-1019; fax 2276-0130; e-mail prensa@curiamanagua.org; internet www.curiamanagua.org.

The Anglican Communion

Nicaragua comprises one of the five dioceses of the Iglesia Anglicana de la Región Central de América.

Bishop of Nicaragua: Rt Rev. Sturdie W. Downs, Apdo 1207, Managua; tel. 2222-5174; fax 2222-6701; e-mail episcnic@tmx.com.ni.

Protestant Churches

Some 22% of the population aged five years and above are members of evangelical churches, according to the last census (2005).

Baptist Convention of Nicaragua: Apdo 2593, Managua; e-mail cbnsgeneral@stbnica.org; f. 1917; 135 churches, 20,000 mems (2006); Pres. Rev. Félix Pedro Ruiz Rivera; Sec. Rev. Guadalupe Antonio Gómez Ríos.

The Moravian Church in Nicaragua: Iglesia Morava, Puerto Cabezas; tel. and fax 2792-2222; e-mail gonzalomoravo@gmail.com; 199 churches, 83,000 mems; Leader Rt Rev. John Wilson.

The Nicaraguan Lutheran Church of Faith and Hope: Apdo 151, Managua; tel. 2266-4467; fax 2268-2401; e-mail luterana@iluterana.org; f. 1994; 7,050 mems (2010); Pres. Rev. Victoria Cortez Rodríguez.

The Press

NEWSPAPERS AND PERIODICALS

Bolsa de Noticias: Col. Centroamérica, Grupo L 852, Apdo VF-90, Managua; tel. 2270-0546; fax 2277-4931; e-mail diseno@bolsadenoticias.com.ni; internet www.bolsadenoticias.com.ni; f. 1974; daily; Dir María Elsa Suárez García; Editor-in-Chief María Elena Palacios.

Confidencial: De Pharoahs Casino, 2 c. abajo, 2 c. al sur, Managua; tel. 2277-5134; fax 2270-7017; e-mail info@confidencial.com.ni; internet www.confidencial.com.ni; weekly; political analysis; Dir Carlos F. Chamorro; Editors Iván Olivares, Carlos Salinas Maldonado.

La Gaceta, Diario Oficial: De la Rotonda de Plaza Inter, 1 c. arriba, 2 c. al lago, Managua; tel. 2228-3791; fax 2228-4001; e-mail lagaceta@presidencia.gob.ni; internet www.lagaceta.gob.ni; f. 1912; morning; daily; official; Dir Dr Leopoldo Castrillo.

Hoy: Km $4\frac{1}{2}$, Carretera Norte, Apdo 192, Managua; tel. 2255-6767; fax 2255-6780; e-mail mario.mairena@hoy.com.ni; internet www.hoy.com.ni; Editor Mario Mairena.

La Jornada: Entrada Principal de Villa Progreso, 3 c. al norte, Casa A-350, Managua; tel. 2251-8277; e-mail info@lajornadanet.com; internet www.lajornadanet.com; f. 1986; Dir and Editor Raúl Arévalo Alemán.

Nuevo Diario: Pista P. Joaquín Chamorro, Km 4, Carretera Norte, Apdo 4591, Managua; tel. 2249-0499; fax 2249-0700; e-mail info@elnuevodiario.com.ni; internet www.elnuevodiario.com.ni; f. 1980; morning; daily; independent; Editor-in-Chief ROBERTO COLLADO; circ. 45,000.

El Observador Económico: De Pricesmart, 2 c. al lago, Apdo 2074, Managua; tel. 2266-8708; fax 2266-8711; e-mail info@elobservadoreconomico.com; internet www.elobservadoreconomico.com; Dir-Gen. ALEJANDRO MARTÍNEZ CUENCA.

La Prensa: Km 4½, Carretera Norte, Apdo 192, Managua; tel. 2255-6767; fax 2255-6780; e-mail info@laprensa.com.ni; internet www.laprensa.com.ni; f. 1926; morning; daily; independent; Pres. JAIME CHAMORRO CARDENAL; Editor-in-Chief EDUARDO ENRÍQUEZ; circ. 30,000.

Revista Encuentro: Universidad Centroamericana, Apdo 69, Managua; tel. 2278-3923; fax 2267-0106; e-mail dirinv@ns.uca.edu.ni; internet encuentro.uca.edu.ni; f. 1968; termly; academic publ. of the Universidad Centroamericana; Dir JORGE ALBERTO HUETE PÉREZ; Editor WENDY BELLANGER.

Revista Envío: Edif. Nitlapán, 2°, Campus Universidad Centroamericana, Apdo A-194, Managua; tel. 2278-2557; fax 2278-1402; e-mail info@envio.org.ni; internet www.envio.org.ni; f. 1981; 11 a year; political, economic and social analysis; edns in Spanish, English and Italian; Dir GREGORIO VÁSQUEZ; Editor MARÍA LÓPEZ VIGIL.

Revista Revelaciones: esq. suroeste del Colegio San Francisco, ½ c. al oeste, Estelí; tel. 2713-7578; e-mail info@revistarevelaciones.com; internet revistarevelaciones.com; monthly; Dir GEMA HERNÁNDEZ; Editor BRENDA ESTRADA.

Trinchera de la Noticia: Semáforos de la Tenderi, 1 c. abajo, 10 varas abajo, Ciudad Jardín, Managua; tel. 2240-0114; e-mail info@trinchera.com.ni; internet www.trinchera.com.ni; daily; Dir XAVIER REYES ALBA; Man. EMILIO NÚÑEZ TENORIO.

Visión Sandinista: Costado este, Parque El Carmen, Managua; tel. and fax 2268-1565; e-mail vision@ibw.com.ni; internet www.visionsandinista.com; f. 1997; weekly; official publ. of the Frente Sandinista de Liberación Nacional; Dir MAYRA REYES SANDOVAL.

Association

Unión de Periodistas de Nicaragua (UPN): Apdo 4006, Managua; tel. 2271-2436; e-mail uperiodistasnic@yahoo.com; internet www.aquinicaragua.com/periodistas2.html; Pres. CÁNDIDA DÍAZ.

Publishers

Academia Nicaragüense de la Lengua: Avda del Campo, 42 Las Colinas, Apdo 2711, Managua; fax 2249-5389; e-mail pavsa@munditel.com.ni; internet www.anilengua.com; f. 1928; languages; Dir JORGE EDUARDO ARELLANO SANDINO.

Ediciones Océano, SA: Km 7½, Carretera a Masaya, Contiguo a Nitalsa, Managua; tel. 2276-1372; fax 2276-1443; e-mail edocanic@ibw.com.ni; internet www.oceano.com; Spanish culture and language; Pres. JOSÉ LLUIS MONREAL.

Editora de Arte SA: Etapa 53, Col. Los Robles III, Managua; tel. 278-5856; e-mail editarte@editarte.com.ni; internet www.editarte.com.ni.

Editorial Nueva Nicaragua: Paseo Salvador Allende, Km 3½, Carretera Sur, Apdo 073, Managua; fax 266-6520; f. 1981; Pres. Dr SERGIO RAMÍREZ MERCADO.

Editorial Unión: Altagracia Rest Los Ranchos, 4½ c. al sur, Managua; tel. 2266-0019; travel.

Librería Hispanoamericana (HISPAMER): Costado este de la UCA, Apdo A-221, Managua; tel. 2278-1210; fax 2278-1210; e-mail webmaster@hispamer.com.ni; internet hispamer.com.ni; f. 1991; Man. JESÚS DE SANTIAGO.

UCA Publicaciónes: Avda Universitaria, Rotonda Rubén Darío 150 m al oeste, Apdo 69, Managua; tel. 2278-5951; fax 2278-5951; e-mail comsj@ns.uca.edu.ni; internet www.uca.edu.ni; academic publishing dept of the Universidad Centroamericana; Dir MARIO SÁNCHEZ.

Universidad Nacional Agraria: Km 12½ Carretera Norte, Apdo 453, Managua; tel. 2233-1619; fax 2233-1950; e-mail info@una.edu.ni; internet www.una.edu.ni; sciences.

Broadcasting and Communications

TELECOMMUNICATIONS

Claro: Villafontana, 2°, Apdo 232, Managua; tel. 2277-3057; fax 2270-2128; e-mail cliente@claro.com.ni; internet www.claro.com.ni;

f. 2006 by merger of ALÓ PCS (f. 2002) and Empresa Nicaragüense de Telecomunicaciones (Enitel, f. 1925); subsidiary of América Móvil, SA de CV (Mexico); Chair. PATRICIO SLIM DOMIT; Gen. Man. ROBERTO SANSÓN.

Telefónica Celular de Nicaragua, SA (Movistar Nicaragua—TCN): Edif. Movistar, Km 6½, Carretera a Masaya, Managua; tel. 2277-0731; fax 2268-0389; e-mail gerardo.mena@telefonica.com.ni; internet www.movistar.com.ni; Gen. Man. JUAN MANUEL ARGÜELLO.

Regulatory Body

Instituto Nicaragüense de Telecomunicaciones y Correos (Telcor): Edif. Telcor, Avda Bolívar diagonal a Cancillería, Apdo 2264, Managua; tel. 2222-7350; fax 2222-7554; e-mail mgutierrez@telcor.gob.ni; internet www.telcor.gob.ni; Exec. Pres. ORLANDO CASTILLO.

BROADCASTING

Radio

La Nueva Radio YA: Pista de la Resistencia, Frente a la Universidad Centroamericana, Managua; tel. 2278-8336; fax 2278-8334; e-mail info@nuevaya.com.ni; internet nuevaya.com.ni; f. 1990 as Radio Ya; restyled as above in 1999; operated by Entretenimiento Digital, SA; Dir-Gen. DENNIS SCHWARTZ.

Radio Católica: Altamira D'Este 621, 3°, Apdo 2183, Managua; tel. 2278-0836; fax 2278-2544; e-mail oramos@radiocatolica.org; internet www.radiocatolica.org; f. 1961; controlled by Conferencia Episcopal de Nicaragua; Dir Fr ROLANDO ÁLVAREZ; Gen. Man. ALBERTO CARBALLO MADRIGAL.

Radio Corporación, Gadea y Cía: Avda Ponciano Lombillo, Ciudad Jardín Q-20, Apdo 24242, Managua; tel. 2249-1619; fax 2244-3824; e-mail rc540@radio-corporacion.com; internet www.radio-corporacion.com; f. 1995; Gen. Man. FABIO GADEA MANTILLA; Asst Man. CARLOS GADEA MANTILLA.

Radio Estrella: Sierritas de Santo Domingo, frente al Cementerio, Apdo UNICA 104, Managua; tel. 2276-0241; fax 2276-0062; e-mail radiosm@radioestrelladelmar.com; internet www.radioestrelladelmar.org; f. 1997; Catholic; Dir FRANCISCO VELÁSQUEZ.

Radio Nicaragua: Villa Fontana, Contiguo a Enitel, Apdo 4665, Managua; tel. 2227-2330; fax 2267-1448; e-mail director@radionicaragua.com.ni; internet www.radionicaragua.com.ni; f. 1960; govt station; Dir-Gen. ALBERTO CARBALLO MADRIGAL.

Radio Ondas de Luz: Costado Sur del Hospital Bautista, Apdo 607, Managua; tel. and fax 2249-7058; internet www.miradioondasdeluz.com; f. 1959; religious and cultural station; Pres. GUILLERMO OSORNO MOLINA.

Radio Sandino: Paseo Tiscapa Este, Contiguo al Restaurante Mirador, Apdo 4776, Managua; tel. 2228-1330; fax 2262-4052; internet www.radiosandino.com; f. 1977; station controlled by the Frente Sandinista de Liberación Nacional; Pres. RAFAEL ORTEGA MURILLO; Gen. Man. WILLIAM BURGOS.

Radio Segovia: Ocotal, Nueva Segovia; tel. 2732-2870; fax 2732-2271; e-mail info@radiosegovia.net; internet www.radiosegovia.net; f. 1980; commercial; Dir RÓGER SOLÍS COREA.

Radio Tiempo: Barrio San Judas, Supermercado Pali, 2 c. al sur, Apdo 3337, Managua; tel. 8821-0258; e-mail radionuevotiempofm@yahoo.com; internet www.nuevotiempofm.com; f. 1976; Dir DAVID MURILLO.

Radio Universidad: Avda Card, 3 c. abajo, Apdo 2883, Managua; tel. 2278-4743; fax 2277-5057; internet radiouniversidadnica.com; f. 1984; Dir LUIS LÓPEZ RUIZ.

There are some 50 other radio stations.

Television

Canal 4: Montoya, 1 c. al sur, 2 c. arriba, Managua; tel. 2228-1310; fax 2222-4067; internet www.multinoticiastv4.com.

Canal 15: Lomas de Tiscapa, Frente al Hospital Militar, Managua; tel. 2266-9086; fax 2266-0318; internet www.canal15.com.ni; f. 1995; Dir VERÓNICA CHÁVEZ.

Nicavisión, Canal 12: Bolonia Dual Card, 1 c. abajo, ½ c. al sur, Apdo 2766, Managua; tel. 2266-0691; fax 2266-1424; f. 1993; Dir MARIANO VALLE PETERS.

Televicentro de Nicaragua, SA, Canal 2: Casa del Obrero, 6½ c. al sur, Apdo 688, Managua; tel. 2268-2222; fax 2266-3688; e-mail tvnoticias@canal2.com.ni; internet www.canal2.com.ni; f. 1965; Pres. OCTAVIO SACASA RASKOSKY; Gen. Man. ALEJANDRO SACASA PASOS.

Televisora Nicaragüense, SA (Telenica 8): De la Mansión Teodolinda, 1 c. al sur, ½ c. abajo, Bolonia, Apdo 3611, Managua; tel. 2266-5021; fax 2266-5024; e-mail webmaster@tn8.tv; internet www.tn8.tv; f. 1989; sold to private buyer in 2010; Gen. Man. JOSÉ MOJICA MEJÍA.

TV Red, Canal 11: Hotel Mansión, Teodolinda, 2 c. abajo, Managua; tel. 2222-7788; e-mail veronica.rocha@tvred.com.ni; internet www .tvredcanal11.com.ni; Gen. Man. VERÓNICA ROCHA.

Finance

(cap. = capital; res = reserves; dep. = deposits; m. = million; amounts in córdobas)

BANKING

Supervisory Authority

Superintendencia de Bancos y de Otras Instituciones Financieras: Edif. SIBOIF, Km 7, Carretera Sur, Apdo 788, Managua; tel. 2265-1555; fax 2265-0965; e-mail correo@siboif.gob.ni; internet www .siboif.gob.ni; f. 1991; Supt Dr VICTOR M. URCUYO VIDAURRE.

Central Bank

Banco Central de Nicaragua: Carretera Sur, Km 7, Apdos 2252/3, Zona 5, Managua; tel. 2255-7171; fax 2265-0495; e-mail info@bcn.gob .ni; internet www.bcn.gob.ni; f. 1960; bank of issue and govt fiscal agent; cap. and res 4,941m., dep. 42,721m. (Dec. 2009); Pres. ALBERTO JOSÉ GUEVARA OBREGÓN.

Private Banks

Banco de América Central (BAC): Km 4½, Carretera a Masaya, Managua; tel. 2274-4444; fax 2274-4441; e-mail serviciocliente@bac .com.ni; internet www.bac.net/nicaragua; f. 1991; total assets 10,516m. (1999); Gen. Man. JUAN CARLOS SANSÓN CALDERA; 66 brs.

Banco Citibank de Nicaragua: Plaza España, Rotonda el Güegüense 25 m al oeste, Managua; tel. 2280-9360; fax 2266-8796; e-mail info@bancouno.com.ni; internet www.citi.com.ni; Gen. Man. AMALIA BARRIOS VELÁSQUEZ.

Banco Lafise Bancentro (BANCENTRO): Edif. BANCENTRO, Km 5½ Carretera a Masaya, Managua; tel. 2278-2777; fax 2278-6001; e-mail info@bancolafise.com.ni; internet www.lafise.com; f. 1991; fmrly Banco de Crédito Centroamericano; name changed as above in 2010; cap. 1,344.4m., res 557.9m., dep. 24,826.7m. (Dec. 2012); Pres. ROBERTO JOSÉ ZAMORA LLANES; Gen. Man. CARLOS ALBERTO BRICEÑO RÍOS; 72 brs.

STOCK EXCHANGE

Bolsa de Valores de Nicaragua: Edif. Oscar Pérez Cassar, Centro BANIC, Km 5½, Carretera Masaya, Apdo 121, Managua; tel. 2278-3830; fax 2278-3836; e-mail informacionbvn@bolsanic.com; internet bolsanic.com; f. 1993; Pres. Dr RAÚL A. LACAYO SOLÓRZANO.

INSURANCE

State Company

Instituto Nicaragüense de Seguros y Reaseguros (INISER): Centro Comercial Camino de Oriente, Km 4.5, Carretera a Masaya, Apdo 1147, Managua; tel. 2255-7575; e-mail iniser@iniser.com.ni; internet www.iniser.com.ni; f. 1979 to assume the activities of all the pre-revolution national private insurance cos; Exec. Pres. EDUARDO HALLESLEVENS; Vice-Pres JUAN JOSÉ UBEDA.

Private Companies

ASSA Cía de Seguros, SA: Edif. El Centro, MR-67, Rotonda El Periodista, 400 m al norte, Managua, Nicaragua; tel. 2276-9000; internet www.assanet.com.ni; Pres. Dr LEONEL ARGÜELLO RAMÍREZ; Gen. Man. GIANCARLO BRACCIO.

Mapfre Nicaragua, SA: Edif. Invercasa, 1°, Managua; tel. 2276-8890; fax 2278-6358; e-mail rfong@mapfre.com.ni; internet www .mapfre.com.ni; fmrly Aseguradora Mundial; changed name as above in 2010; Pres. JOSÉ RAMÓN TOMÁS FORÉS; Gen. Man. RYDDER FONG.

Seguros América, SA: Centro Pellas, Km 4½ Carretera a Masaya, Managua; tel. 2274-4200; fax 2274-4202; e-mail info@ segurosamerica.com.ni; internet www.segurosamerica.com.ni; f. 1996; Pres. ADOLFO BENARD; Man. DANILO MANZANARES ENRÍQUEZ.

Seguros Lafise, SA: Centro Financiero Lafise, Km 5½, Carretera a Masaya, Managua; tel. 2278-2777; fax 2278-0888; e-mail seguros@ seguroslafise.com.ni; internet www.seguroslafise.com.ni; fmrly Seguros Centroamericanos (Segurossa); Pres. ROBERTO ZAMORA LLANES; Gen. Man. CLAUDIO TABOADA RODRÍGUEZ.

Trade and Industry

GOVERNMENT AGENCIES

Empresa Nicaragüense de Alimentos Básicos (ENABAS): Salida a Carretera Norte, Apdo 1041, Managua; tel. 2248-1640; e-mail direccion.administrativa@enabas.gob.ni; internet www .enabas.gob.ni; f. 1979; controls trading in basic foodstuffs; Exec. Dir HERMINIO ESCOTO GARCÍA.

Instituto de Desarrollo Rural (IDR) (Institute of Rural Development): B3, Camino de Oriente, Apdo 3593, Managua; tel. 2255-8777; e-mail divulgacion@idr.gob.ni; internet www.idr.gob.ni; f. 1995; Exec. Dir PEDRO HASLAM MENDOZA.

Instituto Nicaragüense de Apoyo a la Pequeña y Mediana Empresa (INPYME): De la Shell Plaza el Sol, 1 c. al sur, 300 m abajo, Apdo 449, Managua; tel. 278-2607; fax 277-0598; e-mail bcantillo@inpyme.gob.ni; internet www.inpyme.gob.ni; supports small and medium-sized enterprises; Exec. Dir MARTHA LORENA BRIONES.

Instituto Nicaragüense de Tecnología Agropecuaria (INTA): Col. Centroamérica, contiguo al Distrito 5, Apdo 1247, Managua; tel. 2278-0471; fax 2278-0373; e-mail oaip@inta.gob.ni; internet www .inta.gob.ni; f. 1993; Dir-Gen. MARÍA MARÍA JOSÉ COREA.

Instituto de la Vivienda Urbana y Rural (INVUR): Km 4½, Carretera Sur, contiguo a INISER, Managua; tel. 2226-6112; e-mail gmartinez@invur.gob.ni; internet www.invur.gob.ni; housing devt; Pres. JUDITH SILVA; CEO JUDITH SILVA.

DEVELOPMENT ORGANIZATIONS

Asociación de Productores y Exportadores de Nicaragua (APEN): Iglesia San Francisco 20 varas arriba, Casa 1280, Bolonia, Managua; tel. 2268-6053; fax 2268-1905; internet www.apen.org.ni; Pres. ENRIQUE ZAMORA LLANES; Sec. JORGE SAMPER BLANCO.

Cámara de Industrias de Nicaragua: Rotonda el Güegüense, Plaza España 300 m al sur, Apdo 1436, Managua; tel. 2266-8847; fax 2266-1891; e-mail cadin@cadin.org.ni; internet www.cadin.org.ni; f. 1964; Pres. RODRIGO CALDERA; Vice-Pres. MARIO AMADOR.

Cámara Nicaragüense de la Construcción (CNC): Bolonia de Aval Card, 2 c. abajo, 50 varas al sur, Managua; tel. 2226-3363; fax 2266-3327; e-mail info@construccion.org.ni; internet www .construccion.org.ni; f. 1961; construction industry; Pres. BENJAMÍN LANZAS SOMARRIBA; Vice-Pres. RODRIGO PEREIRA REYES.

Instituto Nicaragüense de Fomento Municipal (INIFOM): Edif. Central, Carretera a la Refinería, entrada principal residencial Los Arcos, Apdo 3097, Managua; tel. and fax 2266-6050; e-mail eduardo.centeno@inifom.gob.ni; internet www.inifom.gob.ni; Pres. GUIOMAR AMINTA IRÍAS TORRES.

PRONicaragua: Edif. PRONicaragua, Restaurante TipTop, 1 c. al oeste, Km 4½, Carretera a Masaya, Managua; tel. 2270-6400; fax 2277-3299; e-mail info@pronicaragua.org; internet www .pronicaragua.org; f. 2002; investment and export promotion agency; br. in Washington, DC (USA); Exec. Dir JAVIER CHAMORRO RUBIALES.

CHAMBERS OF COMMERCE

Cámara de Comercio Americana de Nicaragua: Plaza España, Rotonda el Güegüense, 400 m al sur, 75 m al este, detrás de American Airlines, Managua; tel. and fax 2266-2758; e-mail avil.ramirez@ amcham.org.ni; internet www.amcham.org.ni; f. 1974; Pres. ALFREDO ANTONIO ARTILES.

Cámara de Comercio de Nicaragua (CACONIC): Rotonda el Güegüense 400 m al sur, 20 m al oeste, Managua; tel. 2268-3505; fax 2268-3600; e-mail comercio@caconic.org.ni; internet www.ccsn.org .ni; f. 1892; 904 mems; Pres. ROSENDO BARANELLO; Exec. Dir EDUARDO FONSECA.

Cámara Oficial Española de Comercio de Nicaragua: Restaurante la Marseilleisa, ½ c. arriba, Los Robles, Apdo 4103, Managua; tel. 2278-9047; fax 2278-9088; e-mail camacoesnic@cablenet.com.ni; internet www.camacoesnic.com.ni; Pres. ALFREDO MARÍN XIMÉNEZ; Dir JUAN JOSÉ COBOS.

EMPLOYERS' ORGANIZATIONS

Asociación de Café Especiales de Nicaragua (ACEN): Oficentro Norte, Km 5, Carretera Panamericana Norte, Managua; tel. 2249-0180; fax 2249-0182; internet www.acen.org.ni; coffee producers and exporters; Exec. Dir EDWIN RUÍZ.

Consejo Superior de la Empresa Privada (COSEP): De Telcor Zacarías Guerra, 1 c. abajo, Apdo 5430, Managua; tel. 2276-3333; fax 2276-1666; e-mail cosep@cablenet.com.ni; internet www.cosep.org .ni; f. 1972; consists of Cámara de Industrias de Nicaragua (CADIN), Unión de Productores Agropecuarios de Nicaragua (UPANIC), Cámara de Comercio, Cámara de la Construcción, Confederación Nacional de Profesionales (CONAPRO), Instituto Nicaragüense de Desarrollo (INDE); mem. of Coordinadora Democrática

Nicaragüense; Pres. Dr José Adán Aguerri Chamorro; Exec. Dir María Germania Carrión Soto.

Instituto Nicaragüense de Desarrollo (INDE): Col. Los Robles, del Hotel Colón 1 c. al sur, 1 c. abajo, mano izquierda, frente a Funeraria Reñazco, Managua; tel. 2252-5800; fax 2270-9866; e-mail inde@inde.org.ni; internet www.inde.org.ni; f. 1963; private business org.; 650 mems; Pres. Sergio Argüello; Vice-Pres. Eduardo Caldera.

Unión Nacional de Agricultores y Ganaderos (UNAG): Km 3½, Carretera Sur, Residencial Las Palmas, Managua; tel. 2250-2033; fax 2266-2135; e-mail unag@unag.org.ni; internet www.unag.org.ni; f. 1981; Pres. Alvaro Fiallos Oyanguren; Sec. Douglas Alemán.

Unión de Productores Agropecuarios de Nicaragua (UPA-NIC): Edif. Jorge Salazar, Reparto Serrano, DGI Central, 1 c. al norte ½ c. al este, Apdo 2351, Managua; tel. 2276-2439; fax 2251-0307; e-mail upanic@ibw.com.ni; internet www.upanic.org.ni; private agriculturalists' asscn; Pres. Michael Edwin Healy Lacayo; Sec. Manuel Alvarez Solórzano.

UTILITIES

Regulatory Bodies

Comisión Nacional de Energía y Minas (CNEM): Hospital Bautista, 1 c. al oeste, 1 c. al norte, Managua; f. 2010; Pres. Salvador Mansell Castrillo (Minister of Energy and Mines).

Instituto Nicaragüense de Acueductos y Alcantarillados (INAA): De la Mansión Teodolinda, 3 c. al sur, Bolonia, Apdo 1084, Managua; tel. 2266-7882; fax 2266-7917; e-mail inaa@inaa.gob.ni; internet www.inaa.gob.ni; f. 1979; water regulator; Exec. Pres. Carlos Schutze Sugrañes.

Instituto Nicaragüense de Energía (INE): Rotonda Centroamérica, 350 m al oeste, Managua; tel. 2277-1475; fax 2228-3104; e-mail mbaltodano@ine.gob.ni; internet www.ine.gob.ni; Pres. José David Castillo Sánchez; Exec. Sec. Mariela del Carmen Cerrato Vásquez.

Electricity

Empresa Nicaragüense de Electricidad (ENEL): Ofs Centrales, Pista Juan Pablo II y Avda Bolívar, Managua; tel. 2277-4159; fax 2267-2683; e-mail relapub@ibw.com.ni; internet www.enel.gob.ni; responsible for planning, organization, management, administration, research and development of energy resources; Pres. Salvador Mansell Castrillo (Minister of Energy and Mines); Sec. Ernesto Martínez Tiffer.

Empresa Nacional de Transmisión Eléctrica, SA (ENA-TREL): De la Rotonda Centroamérica, 700 m al oeste, Villa Fontana, Apdo 283, Managua; tel. 2252-7400; fax 2267-4379; internet www.enatrel.gob.ni; operates the electricity transmission network; Exec. Pres. Salvador Mansell Castrillo.

ORMAT Momotombo Power Co: Momotombo; internet www.ormat.com; f. 1999 on acquisition of 15-year concession to rehabilitate and operate Momotombo power plant; 30 MW capacity geothermal plant; subsidiary of ORMAT International, Inc; CEO Isaac Angel.

Unión Fenosa DISSUR y DISNORTE: Centro Pellas, 7°, Km 4 ½ de la Carretera a Masaya, Managua; tel. 2274-4700; e-mail comunicacion@ni.unionfenosa.com; internet www.disnorte-dissur.com.ni; electricity distribution co; privatized in 2000; distributes some 1,460 GWh (DISSUR 658 GWh, DISNORTE 802 GWh); Country Man. Carlos Hernández.

Water

Empresa Nicaragüense de Acueductos y Alcantarillados Sanitarios (ENACAL): Km 5, Carretera sur 505, Asososca; tel. 2266-7875; e-mail comunicacion@enacal.com.ni; internet www.enacal.com.ni; Exec. Pres. Evert Alemán Lara.

TRADE UNIONS

Central Sandinista de Trabajadores (CST): Iglesia del Carmen, 1 c. al oeste, ½ c. al sur, Managua; tel. 2265-1096; fax 2240-1285; Sec.-Gen. Roberto González Gaitán; 40,000 mems.

Central de Trabajadores de Nicaragua (CTN) (Nicaraguan Workers' Congress): De la Iglesia del Carmen, 1 c. al sur, ½ c. arriba y 75 varas al sur, Managua; tel. 2268-3061; fax 2265-2056; e-mail ctn@alfanumeric.com.ni; f. 1962; mem. of Coordinadora Democrática Nicaragüense; Sec.-Gen. Antonio Huembes Trejos.

Confederación General de Trabajadores Independientes (CGT-i) (Independent General Confederation of Labour): Centro Comercial Nejapa, 1 c. arriba y 3 c. al lago, Managua; tel. 2222-5195; fax 2228-7505; e-mail salasara@yahoo.es; f. 1953; Sec.-Gen. Nilo M. Salazar Aguilar; 4,843 mems (est.) from 6 federations with 40 local unions, and 6 non-federated local unions.

Confederación de Unificación Sindical (CUS) (Confederation of United Trade Unions): Casa Q3, del Colegio la Tenderi 2½ c. arriba, Ciudad Jardín, Managua; tel. 8895-7221; e-mail cusorganizacion@yahoo.com; internet cusnicaragua.org; f. 1972; affiliated to the Inter-American Regional Organization of Workers; mem. of Coordinadora Democrática Nicaragüense; Sec.-Gen. José Espinoza Navas.

Frente Nacional de los Trabajadores (FNT) (National Workers' Front): Residencial Bolonia, de la Optica Nicaragüense, 2 c. arriba, 20 varas al sur, Managua; tel. 2266-3065; fax 2266-7457; e-mail prensa@fnt.org.ni; internet www.fnt.org.ni; f. 1979; affiliated to Frente Sandinista de Liberación Nacional; Sec.-Gen. Dr Gustavo Porras Cortés.

Transport

RAILWAYS

There are no functioning railways in Nicaragua. The state-owned rail operator, Ferrocarril de Nicaragua, ceased operations in 1994, and the only remaining private line closed in 2001.

ROADS

In 2010 there were an estimated 22,111 km of roads, of which 6,018 km were highways and 2,045 km were secondary roads. In 2010 the Inter-American Development Bank approved a US $20m. loan for road improvements. The Pan-American Highway runs for 384 km in Nicaragua and links Managua with the Honduran and Costa Rican frontiers and the Atlantic and Pacific Highways, connecting Managua with the coastal regions.

Fondo de Mantenimiento Vial (FOMAV): Km 3½, Carretera Sur, Managua; tel. 2268-2247; fax 2268-6831; internet www.fomav.gob.ni; devt and maintenance of the national road network; Exec. Dir Karen Deyanira Molina Valle.

SHIPPING

Corinto, Puerto Sandino, San Juan del Sur and Potosí, on the Pacific, and Puerto Cabezas, El Bluff (Bluefields) and El Rama, on the Caribbean, are the principal ports. Corinto deals with about 60% of trade. In addition to sea ports, there are small ports on two inland lakes. Construction of a 270-km inter-oceanic canal across the country, funded by a Chinese consortium, began in late 2014. At 31 December 2014 the flag registered fleet comprised eight vessels, totalling 5,217 grt.

Empresa Portuaria Nacional (EPN): Residencial Bolonia, de la Optica Nicaragüense ½ c. abajo, Managua; tel. 2222-2059; fax 2266-3488; e-mail epn_puertos@epn.com.ni; internet www.epn.com.ni; Pres. Virgilio Silva Mungüia.

CIVIL AVIATION

The principal airport is the Augusto C. Sandino International Airport in Managua. There are some 185 additional airports in Nicaragua.

Empresa Administradora de Aeropuertos Internacionales (EAAI): Km 11, Carretera Norte, POB 5179, Managua; tel. 2233-1624; fax 2263-1072; e-mail czamora@eaai.com.ni; internet www.eaai.com.ni; autonomous govt entity; operates Managua International Airport and 3 national airports: Bluefields, Puerto Cabezas and Corn Island; Gen. Man. Orlando Castillo Guerrero.

La Costeña: Augusto C. Sandino International Airport, Km 11, Carretera Norte, Managua; tel. 2298-5360; fax 2263-1281; e-mail info@lacostena.com.ni; internet www.lacostena.com.ni; Gen. Man. Alfredo Caballero.

Tourism

Nicaragua attracts tourists for its landscapes, the twin volcanoes, Maderas and Concepción, and the lake Cocibolca. Other destinations of interest are the colonial cities of León and Granada, the Corn Islands, and ecological reserves such as the Indio Maíz Biological Reserve. In 2013 tourist arrivals totalled 1.23m. and receipts from tourism US $417m.

Asociación Nicaragüense de Agencias de Viajes y Turismo (ANAVYT): Edif. Policlínica Nicaragüense, Reparto Bolonia, Apdo 1045, Managua; tel. 2266-9742; fax 2266-4474; e-mail aeromund@cablenet.com.ni; f. 1966; Pres. Ana María Rocha C.

Cámara Nacional de Turismo (CANATUR): Edif. de la Camara Española Nicaragüense, Restaurante la Marseillaise, 50 m al este, Managua; tel. 2270-2587; fax 2278-9971; e-mail direccion@canaturnicaragua.org; internet www.canatur-nicaragua.org; f. 1976; Pres. Sylvia de Levy; Exec. Dir Zenayda Laguna.

Instituto Nicaragüense de Turismo (INTUR): Del Hotel Crowne Plaza, 1 c. al sur, 1 c. al oeste, Apdo 5088, Managua; tel. 2254-5191;

fax 2222-6610; e-mail promocion@intur.gob.ni; internet www.intur
.gob.ni; f. 1998; Exec. Pres. MARÍO SALINAS PASOS; Sec.-Gen. ELVIA
ESTRADA ROSALES.

Defence

As assessed at November 2014, Nicaragua's professional armed
forces numbered an estimated 12,000: army 10,000, navy 800 and
air force 1,200. A constitutional amendment in 2014 allowed for the
establishment of military reserves. There is a voluntary military
service which lasts 18–36 months.

Defence Budget: an estimated 2,150m. córdobas in 2014.

Commander-in-Chief of the Army: Gen. JULIO CÉSAR AVILÉS
CASTILLO.

Education

Primary and secondary education in Nicaragua is provided free of
charge. Primary education, which is officially compulsory, begins at
seven years of age and lasts for six years. Secondary education,
beginning at the age of 13, lasts for up to five years, comprising a first
cycle of three years and a second of two years. In 2010 enrolment at
primary schools included 92% of children in the relevant age-group.
Secondary enrolment in that year included 46% of children in the
relevant age-group, according to UNESCO estimates. Some 923,745
pupils attended primary schools and 458,321 students attended
secondary schools in 2009/10. There are nine universities, of which
four are state-run, and many commercial schools. In 2011 budgetary
expenditure on education was projected at US $3.8m, representing
23.0% of total government expenditure.